AMERICAN SALARIES AND WAGES SURVEY

Seventh Edition

Statistical Data Derived
from More Than 200
Government, Business &
News Sources

Helen S. Fisher

GALE®

THOMSON
GALE™

Detroit • New York • San Diego • San Francisco • Cleveland • New Haven, Conn. • Waterville, Maine • London • Munich

THOMSON

GALE

American Salaries and Wages Survey, Seventh Edition

Helen S. Fisher, Editor

Project Editor
Amanda C. Quick

Editorial
Arsen Darnay, Robert Lazich, Susan Turner, Editorial Code and Data, Inc.

Product Design
Cynthia Baldwin

Manufacturing
NeKita McKee

For more information, contact
The Gale Group, Inc.
27500 Drake Rd.
Farmington Hills, MI 48331-3535
Or you can visit our Internet site at
http://www.gale.com

ISBN 0-7876-4023-9
ISSN 1055-7628

Printed in the United States of America
10 9 8 7 6 5 4 3 2 1

AMERICAN SALARIES AND WAGES SURVEY

CONTENTS

INTRODUCTION

American Salaries & Wages Survey (*ASWS*), now in its seventh edition, is a compilation of 933 occupational combinations (2,620 occupations) and their corresponding salaries obtained from 197 federal and state government sources and various trade associations and journals.

Incorporating wage data for the period 1997 through 2003, *ASWS* provides extensive compensation information for industry, economic planners and developers, human resources professionals, employment counselors, job seekers, and job changers. Most of the data shown were collected in the last quarter of 2001 and released, for the first time, early in 2003.

Features of this edition include:

- Data from197 sources.
- More than 88,700 individual entries.
- 933 occupational combinations representing 2,620 occupations.
- More geographical coverage than in the last edition: 479 geographical areas, including national data and 12 regions, 3 territories, 51 states, and 412 cities, of which 344 are reported as 258 metropolitan statistical areas and 68 as independent cities or urbanized counties.
- Occupational outline of contents with numerous cross references
- Geographical outline of contents.
- Updated employment statistics for 2000 and 2010.
- Complete source listings for further research.

Sources

In order to provide a comprehensive data base, wage information was sought at the city level, the county or state region level, the state level, the U.S. region level, and the national level. Most Federal data are from the Occupational Employment Statistics (OES) annual survey. It samples and contacts approximately 400,00 establishments annually and about 1.2 million establishements over a three year period. Data from this program are available for 695 detailed occupations. Other occupations were identified using a variety of soruces.

A number of trade/professional associations conduct annual wage surveys of their members. Typically, these groups survey members of their professional societies to obtain data and report wages across the nation or within U.S. regions. Because the number of uniformly defined entries has significantly increased, fewer *entries* from these sources, and from trade journals, could be included.

Occupational Titles

Federal data—and state data reported through the Federal government—follow the Standard Occupational Classification System (SOC). This system has now been adopted by the Occupational Employment Statistics program of the Bureau of Labor Statistics.

Occupational titles from other sources follow no particular standard. They are reproduced essentially as reported. Therefore it is possible to find both *Registered Nurse* under R and *Nurse Practitioner* under N. The Outline of Contents provides a cross-referenced alphabetical listing of all titles to help the user identify all variants of an occupation. Thus *Nurse* provides references to *Registered Nurse* and vice versa.

Wage Denominations

Wage figures presented in *ASWS* are given in the form provided by the original source—hourly, daily, weekly, monthly, or annual. A wage conversion chart is provided for your convenience in Appendix II. The denomination type is referred to by its first letter in the wage denomination column (H for hourly, W for weekly, etc.). The number of wage calculations varies from source to source; one source may provide only an average wage figure, another may report only a median. Many reports, however, give three or more calculated wage amounts — a mid-level value such as average or median, as well as a low and a high value. In some cases, ranges are provided; when the range is of such magnitude that it will not fit the space provided, abbreviations are used. A value for annual compensation such as 30-37500, for instance, means $30,000 to $37,500 per annum. Occasionally the low and high figures will be replaced by or supplemented with percentile or quartile figures. *ASWS* presents, wherever possible, three points on the wage spectrum: Low, Mid, and High. The ideal entry will show Lowest Wage Paid, Average Wage Paid, and Highest Wage

Paid. But these figures are not always available; therefore, a coding system is used to specify what type of wage amount is being presented. For example,

- **FQ** stands for First Quartile and means that 25% of the workers surveyed earned less than the dollar amount shown.

- **TQ** stands for Third Quartile and means that 75% of the workers surveyed earned less than the dollar amount shown and 25% earned more than the dollar amount shown. All abbreviations of wage types are listed in alphabetical order at the bottom of every page in the data section.

Organization

Outlines of Contents

ASWS includes two outlines of contents providing access to the salaries listed. The Outline of Contents provides the reader with the means to find all listings of an occupation, despite variations in naming conventions. It lists the primary occupational classifications found in the main body of *ASWS,* in alphabetical order. In addition, the outline supplies derivations of those titles and cross-references them to their base forms. For example, the primary occupational title, Architect, can be found in the data section. The Outline of Contents provides several additional titles, including:

Chief Architect
Junior Architect
Landscape Architect
Marine Engineer and Naval Architect
Network Architect
Senior Architect
Systems Architect

The reader is advised to check the Outline of Contents when seeking wage information about a particular occupation in order to locate all available entries. The Geographic Outline is a listing of geographic locations down to the state level and the primary occupations provided for those locations. Metro areas and cities are not listed individually because the same occupations tend to be present at the state and local levels.

Main Body

The main body of *ASWS* is organized alphabetically by primary occupation first, then by secondary occupation and/or industry designation, then by geographic area. Data are presented in an eight-column table. The following is an explanation of these data columns from left to right.

Occupation/Type/Industry Column–

Lists the primary occupational title (e.g., Accountant), the secondary occupational title/type (e.g., Web Design) and/or the industry designation (e.g., Transportation & Utilities or Manufacturing). In cases where both a secondary title and an industry designation are provided, the secondary title precedes the industry.

Location Column–

Specifies the geographical area to which the data refer. The column is organized by size of region in descending order: national data, U.S. regional (e.g., Southwest) data, statewide data, metropolitan statistical area (MSA) and county data, and city data. If the area is smaller than a U.S. state, the location is followed by its two-letter postal code (e.g., MI for Michigan). ***Please note***: Cities appear alphabetically by state, so that California cities will appear ahead of those located in New Jersey, for instance.

Wage Denomination (Per) Column–

Specifies intervals at which the wage amount is paid to the employee. The single-letter codes are translated at the bottom of each page. Wages may be given in hourly, daily, weekly, monthly, or annual denominations. A wage conversion table is provided in Appendix II.

Low, Mid, and High Columns–

The columns list the wage figures for each entry in U.S. dollars. Each amount is followed by an explanatory code. A typical code is AHW, standing for Average Hourly Wage, or AAW, standing for Average Annual Wage. Sometimes references to "quartiles" may be found. The third quartile (TQ) wage, for instance, means that 75% of individuals earned less than the amount shown and 25% earned more.

Source Column–

Alphanumeric codes in this column refer to titles of sources from which data were obtained. A code like AZBLS means that the source is Bureau of Labor Statistics data supplied by the State of Arizona. These codes are explained in Appendix I.

Date Column–

Specifies the dates to which respective entries refer. If a particular source did not report a precise date, an approximate date ("2000") is provided.

Code Listings Block–

An explanation for all wage codes is shown at the bottom of each page. These abbreviations may also be found in the Abbreviations Table, Appendix III.

ASWS has four appendices, some of which have been mentioned above.

Appendix I - Sources

Appendix I lists 197 organizations which contributed data from one or multiple wage surveys or job banks. The appendix is organized alphabetically by source codes.

Appendix II - Wage Conversion Table

Appendix II is a table that translates an hourly wage into its weekly, monthly, and annual equivalents. The reader, however, should note that these equivalencies are only approximate since wages reported in hourly formats may pertain to work weeks of different lengths.

Appendix III - Abbreviations

Appendix III lists and explains the abbreviations used throughout *ASWS.* Source abbreviations, of course, are explained in Appendix I.

Appendix IV - Employment by Occupation, 2000 and 2010

Appendix IV reproduces a portion of the BLS Occupational Matrix, a data base that lists 695 detail occupations and shows total employment in 2000 together with projections to the year 2010. The appendix provides three presentations — alphabetical, by largest employment, and by growth — to help the user gain further insight into wage trends in the United States.

Data Limitations

A number of points should be kept in mind when using *ASWS* for wage information. *ASWS* is a compilation of a large number of sources. Some are scientific surveys, some are job offers, and some are themselves compilations of other sources. No attempt was made to standardize the data from these sources. Therefore, the user should take great care drawing general conclusions. Variations and/or skewed data occur in title derivations, wage calculations, job descriptions, and methodology. Note, however, that data from the government surveys (sources that end in BLS) are largely comparable place to place.

In this edition, occupational titles are generally more uniform and follow Federal naming conventions much more consistently than in the first four editions. Ambiguous titles, however, continue to exist.

The editors have made a limited effort to edit the occupational titles presented. Grammatical forms and punctuation have been made consistent whenever possible. Titles are presented in singular forms (Nurse *vs* Nurses).

It is important to bear in mind that wage variations between different entries with the same occupational title may be due to differences in job responsibilities.

ASWS provides base salary figures only. Unless otherwise specified, supplemental compensation — i.e., fringe benefits, overtime, bonuses, etc. — have not been included.

Wage figures shown are not adjusted in any way to reflect cost of living. Salaries may be significantly higher in major metropolitan areas than in smaller towns because living costs in the "big city" are high.

Acknowledgments

ASWS was initially suggested to Gale by Ms. Flower L. Hund, Central Missouri State University, Warrensburg, Mo. From the start, the editors have attempted to realize, in practice, Ms. Hund's original concepts; to the extent that they have succeeded, the credit is Ms. Hund's; she is, however, in no way responsible for shortcomings in *ASWS*.

The editors would like to thank the many individuals in state government and in associations who helped in the creation of *ASWS* by providing reports, data, clarifications, and permissions.

Comments and Suggestions

Comments on *ASW*S or suggestions for improvement of its usefulness, format, and coverage are always welcome. Although we have made every effort to be as accurate and consistent as possible, errors may be noted by others; we will appreciate having these called to our attention. Please contact:

Editor
American Salaries & Wages Survey
Gale
27500 Drake Road
Farmington Hills, MI 48331-3535
Phone: (248)-699-GALE
BusinessProducts@gale.com

OUTLINE OF CONTENTS

F

G

H

I

J

K

L

M

Q

R

U

V

W

GEOGRAPHICAL OUTLINE OF CONTENTS

Nebraska - continued:

New Jersey - continued:

New Mexico

New York - continued:

North Carolina

North Carolina - continued:

Geographical Outline of Contents

Wyoming - continued:

Puerto Rico

Guam

OCCUPATIONS

Occupation/Type/Industry	Location	Per	Low	Mid	High	Source	Date
Accident Investigator							
Air traffic	United States	Y	21000 ASL		60000 ASH	AEAC	1/99-1/99
Account Executive							
Assistant, Medical Marketing	United States	Y		38500 AW		MM&M	1/01-1/02
Accountant	United States	Y	39052 AE			TIME	1/00-1/01
Web Design	United States	Y		49796 AW		DFMAR	1/01-1/02
Accountant and Auditor	Alabama	Y	24840 FQ	45430 AW	70760 TQ	ALBLS	10/01-12/01
	Birmingham MSA, AL	Y	28210 FQ	50400 AW	78760 TQ	ALBLS	10/01-12/01
	Huntsville MSA, AL	Y	25520 FQ	44930 AW	69450 TQ	ALBLS	10/01-12/01
	Mobile MSA, AL	Y	19620 FQ	35420 AW	53920 TQ	ALBLS	10/01-12/01
	Montgomery MSA, AL	Y	26970 FQ	49530 AW	80750 TQ	ALBLS	10/01-12/01
	Alaska	Y	28140 FQ	49630 AW	72530 TQ	AKBLS	10/01-12/01
	Anchorage MSA, AK	Y	30070 FQ	50020 AW	71770 TQ	AKBLS	10/01-12/01
	Arizona	Y	26670 FQ	45180 AW	67680 TQ	AZBLS	10/01-12/01
	Phoenix-Mesa MSA, AZ	Y	27590 FQ	46790 AW	69000 TQ	AZBLS	10/01-12/01
	Tucson MSA, AZ	Y	24850 FQ	40230 AW	60250 TQ	AZBLS	10/01-12/01
	Arkansas	Y	24160 FQ	45430 AW	72120 TQ	ARBLS	10/01-12/01
	Fayetteville-Springdale-Rogers MSA, AR	Y	17850 FQ	38770 AW	56580 TQ	ARBLS	10/01-12/01
	Fort Smith MSA, AR-OK	Y	23950 FQ	42290 AW	63370 TQ	ARBLS	10/01-12/01
	Little Rock-North Little Rock MSA, AR	Y	25530 FQ	49200 AW	93850 TQ	ARBLS	10/01-12/01
	California	Y	32950 FQ	55840 AW	88220 TQ	CABLS	10/01-12/01
	Bakersfield MSA, CA	Y	30970 FQ	52220 AW	77130 TQ	CABLS	10/01-12/01
	Chico-Paradise MSA, CA	Y	26060 FQ	44220 AW	66530 TQ	CABLS	10/01-12/01
	Fresno MSA, CA	Y	28820 FQ	45790 AW	67500 TQ	CABLS	10/01-12/01
	Los Angeles-Long Beach PMSA, CA	Y	33560 FQ	55620 AW	88120 TQ	CABLS	10/01-12/01
	Merced MSA, CA	Y	31380 FQ	48570 AW	68360 TQ	CABLS	10/01-12/01
	Modesto MSA, CA	Y	30270 FQ	46390 AW	66430 TQ	CABLS	10/01-12/01
	Oakland PMSA, CA	Y	35570 FQ	57560 AW	92780 TQ	CABLS	10/01-12/01
	Orange County PMSA, CA	Y	33660 FQ	55950 AW	83800 TQ	CABLS	10/01-12/01
	Redding MSA, CA	Y	29110 FQ	47520 AW	71540 TQ	CABLS	10/01-12/01
	Riverside-San Bernardino PMSA, CA	Y	30320 FQ	51950 AW	83870 TQ	CABLS	10/01-12/01
	Sacramento PMSA, CA	Y	34020 FQ	54440 AW	82370 TQ	CABLS	10/01-12/01
	Salinas MSA, CA	Y	31180 FQ	52700 AW	82260 TQ	CABLS	10/01-12/01
	San Diego MSA, CA	Y	31550 FQ	50180 AW	74730 TQ	CABLS	10/01-12/01
	San Francisco PMSA, CA	Y	34300 FQ	60610 AW	90470 TQ	CABLS	10/01-12/01
	San Jose PMSA, CA	Y	34740 FQ	60910 AW	93720 TQ	CABLS	10/01-12/01
	San Luis Obispo-Atascadero-Paso Robles MSA, CA	Y	29530 FQ	53380 AW	87050 TQ	CABLS	10/01-12/01
	Santa Barbara-Santa Maria-Lompoc MSA, CA	Y	33290 FQ	55730 AW	86680 TQ	CABLS	10/01-12/01
	Santa Cruz-Watsonville PMSA, CA	Y	34750 FQ	54310 AW	72660 TQ	CABLS	10/01-12/01
	Santa Rosa PMSA, CA	Y	33330 FQ	51970 AW	78120 TQ	CABLS	10/01-12/01
	Stockton-Lodi MSA, CA	Y	33540 FQ	55870 AW	96440 TQ	CABLS	10/01-12/01
	Vallejo-Fairfield-Napa PMSA, CA	Y	37530 FQ	73810 AW	110510 TQ	CABLS	10/01-12/01
	Ventura PMSA, CA	Y	35000 FQ	54070 AW	84010 TQ	CABLS	10/01-12/01
	Visalia-Tulare-Porterville MSA, CA	Y	31460 FQ	49400 AW	74420 TQ	CABLS	10/01-12/01
	Colorado	Y	31250 FQ	53010 AW	85200 TQ	COBLS	10/01-12/01
	Boulder-Longmont PMSA, CO	Y	31440 FQ	47270 AW	66880 TQ	COBLS	10/01-12/01
	Colorado Springs MSA, CO	Y	29820 FQ	46640 AW	69880 TQ	COBLS	10/01-12/01
	Denver PMSA, CO	Y	33060 FQ	56650 AW	89890 TQ	COBLS	10/01-12/01

AAW	Average annual wage	**AOH**	Average offered, high	**ASH**	Average starting, high	**H**	Hourly	**M**	Monthly	**S**	Special: hourly and annual
AE	Average entry wage	**AOL**	Average offered, low	**ASL**	Average starting, low	**HI**	Highest wage paid	**MTC**	Median total compensation	**TQ**	Third quartile wage
AEX	Average experienced wage	**APH**	Average pay, high range	**AW**	Average wage paid	**HR**	High end range	**MW**	Median wage paid	**W**	Weekly
AO	Average offered	**APL**	Average pay, low range	**FQ**	First quartile wage	**LR**	Low end range	**SQ**	Second quartile wage	**Y**	Yearly

Occupation/Type/Industry	Location	Per	Low	Mid	High	Source	Date
Accountant and Auditor	Fort Collins-Loveland MSA, CO	Y	29140 FQ	42530 AW	64800 TQ	COBLS	10/01-12/01
	Greeley PMSA, CO	Y	31120 FQ	48770 AW	70670 TQ	COBLS	10/01-12/01
	Connecticut	Y	35300 FQ	58990 AW	96440 TQ	CTBLS	10/01-12/01
	Bridgeport PMSA, CT	Y	35510 FQ	61170 AW	101380 TQ	CTBLS	10/01-12/01
	Danbury PMSA, CT	Y	36130 FQ	63660 AW	106270 TQ	CTBLS	10/01-12/01
	Hartford MSA, CT	Y	35250 FQ	57490 AW	96710 TQ	CTBLS	10/01-12/01
	New Haven-Meriden PMSA, CT	Y	34450 FQ	58900 AW	102110 TQ	CTBLS	10/01-12/01
	New London-Norwich MSA, CT-RI	Y	29010 FQ	47880 AW	73510 TQ	CTBLS	10/01-12/01
	Stamford-Norwalk PMSA, CT	Y	38790 FQ	63160 AW	91670 TQ	CTBLS	10/01-12/01
	Waterbury PMSA, CT	Y	35950 FQ	58050 AW	90720 TQ	CTBLS	10/01-12/01
	Delaware	Y	30110 FQ	48290 AW	73450 TQ	DEBLS	10/01-12/01
	Wilmington-Newark PMSA, DE-MD	Y	30840 FQ	49650 AW	75320 TQ	DEBLS	10/01-12/01
	District of Columbia	Y	33080 FQ	56680 AW	88230 TQ	DCBLS	10/01-12/01
	Washington PMSA, DC-MD-VA-WV	Y	32230 FQ	55370 AW	86810 TQ	DCBLS	10/01-12/01
	Florida	Y	28330 FQ	49000 AW	78180 TQ	FLBLS	10/01-12/01
	Daytona Beach MSA, FL	Y	27850 FQ	62700 AW		FLBLS	10/01-12/01
	Fort Lauderdale PMSA, FL	Y	27840 FQ	49500 AW	75100 TQ	FLBLS	10/01-12/01
	Fort Myers-Cape Coral MSA, FL	Y	28190 FQ	44290 AW	67270 TQ	FLBLS	10/01-12/01
	Fort Pierce-Port St. Lucie MSA, FL	Y	30680 FQ	51770 AW	81760 TQ	FLBLS	10/01-12/01
	Fort Walton Beach MSA, FL	Y	27380 FQ	44220 AW	67900 TQ	FLBLS	10/01-12/01
	Gainesville MSA, FL	Y	25120 FQ	40680 AW	59310 TQ	FLBLS	10/01-12/01
	Jacksonville MSA, FL	Y	25310 FQ	48770 AW	80040 TQ	FLBLS	10/01-12/01
	Lakeland-Winter Haven MSA, FL	Y	30530 FQ	48170 AW	70870 TQ	FLBLS	10/01-12/01
	Melbourne-Titusville-Palm Bay MSA, FL	Y	29660 FQ	47280 AW	69810 TQ	FLBLS	10/01-12/01
	Miami PMSA, FL	Y	30270 FQ	54490 AW	93000 TQ	FLBLS	10/01-12/01
	Naples MSA, FL	Y	32290 FQ	52560 AW	82730 TQ	FLBLS	10/01-12/01
	Ocala MSA, FL	Y	28610 FQ	47170 AW	72050 TQ	FLBLS	10/01-12/01
	Orlando MSA, FL	Y	29200 FQ	44920 AW	62560 TQ	FLBLS	10/01-12/01
	Pensacola MSA, FL	Y	25780 FQ	41310 AW	66890 TQ	FLBLS	10/01-12/01
	Sarasota-Bradenton MSA, FL	Y	27510 FQ	46740 AW	69060 TQ	FLBLS	10/01-12/01
	Tallahassee MSA, FL	Y	25510 FQ	49350 AW	85480 TQ	FLBLS	10/01-12/01
	Tampa-St. Petersburg-Clearwater MSA, FL	Y	28070 FQ	46620 AW	72150 TQ	FLBLS	10/01-12/01
	West Palm Beach-Boca Raton MSA, FL	Y	32580 FQ	51730 AW	81810 TQ	FLBLS	10/01-12/01
	Georgia	Y	29620 FQ	47210 AW	72510 TQ	GABLS	10/01-12/01
	Atlanta MSA, GA	Y	31790 FQ	49680 AW	77010 TQ	GABLS	10/01-12/01
	Augusta-Aiken MSA, GA-SC	Y	26470 FQ	45920 AW	75010 TQ	GABLS	10/01-12/01
	Columbus MSA, GA-AL	Y	27690 FQ	41920 AW	60410 TQ	GABLS	10/01-12/01
	Macon MSA, GA	Y	24940 FQ	39190 AW	60510 TQ	GABLS	10/01-12/01
	Savannah MSA, GA	Y	25320 FQ	42230 AW	71170 TQ	GABLS	10/01-12/01
	Hawaii	Y	27550 FQ	45350 AW	68080 TQ	HIBLS	10/01-12/01
	Honolulu MSA, HI	Y	27830 FQ	46170 AW	69020 TQ	HIBLS	10/01-12/01
	Idaho	Y	28590 FQ	44270 AW	65160 TQ	IDBLS	10/01-12/01
	Boise City MSA, ID	Y	29990 FQ	43660 AW	60130 TQ	IDBLS	10/01-12/01
	Illinois	Y	28330 FQ	50060 AW	80880 TQ	ILBLS	10/01-12/01
	Champaign-Urbana MSA, IL	Y	23250 FQ	38660 AW	59420 TQ	ILBLS	10/01-12/01
	Chicago PMSA, IL	Y	29860 FQ	52180 AW	87590 TQ	ILBLS	10/01-12/01
	Peoria-Pekin MSA, IL	Y	17390 FQ	41860 AW	66110 TQ	ILBLS	10/01-12/01
	Rockford MSA, IL	Y	23570 FQ	43840 AW	68590 TQ	ILBLS	10/01-12/01
	Springfield MSA, IL	Y	29150 FQ	44170 AW	61740 TQ	ILBLS	10/01-12/01
	Indiana	Y	28380 FQ	46900 AW	71160 TQ	INBLS	10/01-12/01
	Elkhart-Goshen MSA, IN	Y	30570 FQ	47670 AW	82920 TQ	INBLS	10/01-12/01
	Evansville-Henderson MSA, IN-KY	Y	29120 FQ	45600 AW	71030 TQ	INBLS	10/01-12/01
	Fort Wayne MSA, IN	Y	23850 FQ	42450 AW	63880 TQ	INBLS	10/01-12/01
	Gary PMSA, IN	Y	29110 FQ	47570 AW	69980 TQ	INBLS	10/01-12/01
	Indianapolis MSA, IN	Y	29370 FQ	48570 AW	73160 TQ	INBLS	10/01-12/01
	Lafayette MSA, IN	Y	29790 FQ	44370 AW	62130 TQ	INBLS	10/01-12/01
	South Bend MSA, IN	Y	28120 FQ	44290 AW	65480 TQ	INBLS	10/01-12/01
	Iowa	Y	25800 FQ	42440 AW	63360 TQ	IABLS	10/01-12/01
	Cedar Rapids MSA, IA	Y	29670 FQ	48070 AW	70890 TQ	IABLS	10/01-12/01

AAW	Average annual wage	**AOH**	Average offered, high	**ASH**	Average starting, high	**H**	Hourly	**M**	Monthly	**S**	Special: hourly and annual
AE	Average entry wage	**AOL**	Average offered, low	**ASL**	Average starting, low	**HI**	Highest wage paid	**MTC**	Median total compensation	**TQ**	Third quartile wage
AEX	Average experienced wage	**APH**	Average pay, high range	**AW**	Average wage paid	**HR**	High end range	**MW**	Median wage paid	**W**	Weekly
AO	Average offered	**APL**	Average pay, low range	**FQ**	First quartile wage	**LR**	Low end range	**SQ**	Second quartile wage	**Y**	Yearly

Occupation/Type/Industry	Location	Per	Low	Mid	High	Source	Date
Accountant and Auditor	Davenport-Moline-Rock Island MSA, IA-IL	Y	25820 FQ	41240 AW	61880 TQ	IABLS	10/01-12/01
	Des Moines MSA, IA	Y	28640 FQ	44180 AW	63270 TQ	IABLS	10/01-12/01
	Kansas	Y	29360 FQ	49200 AW	80340 TQ	KSBLS	10/01-12/01
	Topeka MSA, KS	Y	29730 FQ	43810 AW	61950 TQ	KSBLS	10/01-12/01
	Wichita MSA, KS	Y	29580 FQ	46910 AW	69950 TQ	KSBLS	10/01-12/01
	Kentucky	Y	24870 FQ	42770 AW	65550 TQ	KYBLS	10/01-12/01
	Lexington MSA, KY	Y	24960 FQ	41450 AW	62370 TQ	KYBLS	10/01-12/01
	Louisville MSA, KY-IN	Y	29700 FQ	46190 AW	68670 TQ	KYBLS	10/01-12/01
	Louisiana	Y	24320 FQ	41710 AW	62780 TQ	LABLS	10/01-12/01
	Baton Rouge MSA, LA	Y	25440 FQ	43560 AW	64560 TQ	LABLS	10/01-12/01
	Houma MSA, LA	Y	23360 FQ	37020 AW	56810 TQ	LABLS	10/01-12/01
	Lafayette MSA, LA	Y	25540 FQ	41230 AW	61240 TQ	LABLS	10/01-12/01
	Lake Charles MSA, LA	Y	21000 FQ	40580 AW	65860 TQ	LABLS	10/01-12/01
	New Orleans MSA, LA	Y	26160 FQ	42720 AW	63060 TQ	LABLS	10/01-12/01
	Shreveport-Bossier City MSA, LA	Y	22060 FQ	41180 AW	63630 TQ	LABLS	10/01-12/01
	Maine	Y	25020 FQ	41850 AW	60160 TQ	MEBLS	10/01-12/01
	Portland MSA, ME	Y	29700 FQ	43150 AW	56680 TQ	MEBLS	10/01-12/01
	Maryland	Y	32150 FQ	53210 AW	75690 TQ	MDBLS	10/01-12/01
	Baltimore PMSA, MD	Y	32500 FQ	52890 AW	70900 TQ	MDBLS	10/01-12/01
	Massachusetts	Y	30750 FQ	51390 AW	73530 TQ	MABLS	10/01-12/01
	Boston PMSA, MA-NH	Y	30960 FQ	52420 AW	74790 TQ	MABLS	10/01-12/01
	Brockton PMSA, MA	Y	31330 FQ	49040 AW	68890 TQ	MABLS	10/01-12/01
	Lawrence PMSA, MA-NH	Y	32540 FQ	49930 AW	70330 TQ	MABLS	10/01-12/01
	Lowell PMSA, MA-NH	Y	33550 FQ	50050 AW	72510 TQ	MABLS	10/01-12/01
	New Bedford PMSA, MA	Y	29210 FQ	47010 AW	69210 TQ	MABLS	10/01-12/01
	Springfield MSA, MA	Y	29270 FQ	45000 AW	64040 TQ	MABLS	10/01-12/01
	Worcester PMSA, MA-CT	Y	31190 FQ	46940 AW	66670 TQ	MABLS	10/01-12/01
	Michigan	Y	30010 FQ	52510 AW	82780 TQ	MIBLS	10/01-12/01
	Ann Arbor PMSA, MI	Y	28060 FQ	50030 AW	75800 TQ	MIBLS	10/01-12/01
	Detroit PMSA, MI	Y	32180 FQ	55530 AW	87850 TQ	MIBLS	10/01-12/01
	Flint PMSA, MI	Y	29100 FQ	49950 AW	76630 TQ	MIBLS	10/01-12/01
	Grand Rapids-Muskegon-Holland MSA, MI	Y	31890 FQ	52510 AW	88150 TQ	MIBLS	10/01-12/01
	Kalamazoo-Battle Creek MSA, MI	Y	30550 FQ	51090 AW	76570 TQ	MIBLS	10/01-12/01
	Lansing-East Lansing MSA, MI	Y	30080 FQ	50760 AW	71060 TQ	MIBLS	10/01-12/01
	Saginaw-Bay City-Midland MSA, MI	Y	27840 FQ	50850 AW	80150 TQ	MIBLS	10/01-12/01
	Minnesota	Y	31830 FQ	50800 AW	74600 TQ	MNBLS	10/01-12/01
	Duluth-Superior MSA, MN-WI	Y	28520 FQ	44460 AW	63550 TQ	MNBLS	10/01-12/01
	Minneapolis-St. Paul MSA, MN-WI	Y	33620 FQ	52930 AW	79070 TQ	MNBLS	10/01-12/01
	St. Cloud MSA, MN	Y	30580 FQ	44600 AW	65330 TQ	MNBLS	10/01-12/01
	Mississippi	Y	24740 FQ	41310 AW	63340 TQ	MSBLS	10/01-12/01
	Biloxi-Gulfport-Pascagoula MSA, MS	Y	24460 FQ	45590 AW	71510 TQ	MSBLS	10/01-12/01
	Jackson MSA, MS	Y	25040 FQ	39310 AW	57370 TQ	MSBLS	10/01-12/01
	Missouri	Y	25460 FQ	44190 AW	69050 TQ	MOBLS	10/01-12/01
	Kansas City MSA, MO-KS	Y	29900 FQ	49300 AW	80900 TQ	MOBLS	10/01-12/01
	St. Louis MSA, MO-IL	Y	24890 FQ	44530 AW	69540 TQ	MOBLS	10/01-12/01
	Springfield MSA, MO	Y	20140 FQ	39200 AW	61500 TQ	MOBLS	10/01-12/01
	Montana	Y	22060 FQ	38940 AW	61380 TQ	MTBLS	10/01-12/01
	Billings MSA, MT	Y	19440 FQ	39980 AW	74090 TQ	MTBLS	10/01-12/01
	Nebraska	Y	26520 FQ	45970 AW	70550 TQ	NEBLS	10/01-12/01
	Lincoln MSA, NE	Y	27290 FQ	43060 AW	63630 TQ	NEBLS	10/01-12/01
	Omaha MSA, NE-IA	Y	26470 FQ	46650 AW	70870 TQ	NEBLS	10/01-12/01
	Nevada	Y	30380 FQ	47560 AW	70740 TQ	NVBLS	10/01-12/01
	Las Vegas MSA, NV-AZ	Y	30350 FQ	46970 AW	69660 TQ	NVBLS	10/01-12/01
	Reno MSA, NV	Y	30120 FQ	48490 AW	74270 TQ	NVBLS	10/01-12/01
	New Hampshire	Y	28310 FQ	43950 AW	62080 TQ	NHBLS	10/01-12/01
	Manchester PMSA, NH	Y	30980 FQ	44670 AW	56490 TQ	NHBLS	10/01-12/01
	Nashua PMSA, NH	Y	29980 FQ	42560 AW	60670 TQ	NHBLS	10/01-12/01
	Portsmouth-Rochester PMSA, NH-ME	Y	29550 FQ	44670 AW	64290 TQ	NHBLS	10/01-12/01
	New Jersey	Y	33590 FQ	57270 AW	86670 TQ	NJBLS	10/01-12/01
	Atlantic-Cape May PMSA, NJ	Y	30220 FQ	47830 AW	70380 TQ	NJBLS	10/01-12/01
	Bergen-Passaic PMSA, NJ	Y	38920 FQ	64370 AW	103980 TQ	NJBLS	10/01-12/01
	Jersey City PMSA, NJ	Y	35930 FQ	56690 AW	84940 TQ	NJBLS	10/01-12/01
	Middlesex-Somerset-Hunterdon PMSA, NJ	Y	35520 FQ	59450 AW	90180 TQ	NJBLS	10/01-12/01

AAW	Average annual wage	AOH	Average offered, high	ASH	Average starting, high	H	Hourly	M	Monthly	S	Special: hourly and annual
AE	Average entry wage	AOL	Average offered, low	ASL	Average starting, low	HI	Highest wage paid	MTC	Median total compensation	TQ	Third quartile wage
AEX	Average experienced wage	APH	Average pay, high range	AW	Average wage paid	HR	High end range	MW	Median wage paid	W	Weekly
AO	Average offered	APL	Average pay, low range	FQ	First quartile wage	LR	Low end range	SQ	Second quartile wage	Y	Yearly

Occupation/Type/Industry	Location	Per	Low	Mid	High	Source	Date
Accountant and Auditor	Monmouth-Ocean PMSA, NJ	Y	30860 FQ	55200 AW	93470 TQ	NJBLS	10/01-12/01
	Newark PMSA, NJ	Y	33100 FQ	55270 AW	82990 TQ	NJBLS	10/01-12/01
	Trenton PMSA, NJ	Y	36020 FQ	58270 AW	85520 TQ	NJBLS	10/01-12/01
	New Mexico	Y	24980 FQ	42080 AW	61910 TQ	NMBLS	10/01-12/01
	Albuquerque MSA, NM	Y	27800 FQ	43530 AW	62610 TQ	NMBLS	10/01-12/01
	Las Cruces MSA, NM	Y	21040 FQ	35730 AW	53020 TQ	NMBLS	10/01-12/01
	New York	Y	32500 FQ	59040 AW	97190 TQ	NYBLS	10/01-12/01
	Albany-Schenectady-Troy MSA, NY	Y	30130 FQ	50100 AW	75370 TQ	NYBLS	10/01-12/01
	Binghamton MSA, NY	Y	28650 FQ	49130 AW	75410 TQ	NYBLS	10/01-12/01
	Buffalo-Niagara Falls MSA, NY	Y	27630 FQ	46360 AW	74040 TQ	NYBLS	10/01-12/01
	Dutchess County PMSA, NY	Y	30630 FQ	50470 AW	77910 TQ	NYBLS	10/01-12/01
	Nassau-Suffolk PMSA, NY	Y	36230 FQ	59570 AW	97370 TQ	NYBLS	10/01-12/01
	New York PMSA, NY	Y	35490 FQ	63200 AW	108360 TQ	NYBLS	10/01-12/01
	Newburgh PMSA, NY-PA	Y	30520 FQ	50750 AW	77910 TQ	NYBLS	10/01-12/01
	Rochester MSA, NY	Y	30280 FQ	50780 AW	83950 TQ	NYBLS	10/01-12/01
	Syracuse MSA, NY	Y	29670 FQ	50030 AW	78430 TQ	NYBLS	10/01-12/01
	Utica-Rome MSA, NY	Y	24920 FQ	41110 AW	67180 TQ	NYBLS	10/01-12/01
	North Carolina	Y	27880 FQ	47400 AW	74560 TQ	NCBLS	10/01-12/01
	Asheville MSA, NC	Y	24450 FQ	45160 AW	72330 TQ	NCBLS	10/01-12/01
	Charlotte-Gastonia-Rock Hill MSA, NC-SC	Y	29910 FQ	48670 AW	71420 TQ	NCBLS	10/01-12/01
	Fayetteville MSA, NC	Y	26580 FQ	47270 AW	79000 TQ	NCBLS	10/01-12/01
	Greensboro-Winston-Salem-High Point MSA, NC	Y	23920 FQ	44190 AW	73580 TQ	NCBLS	10/01-12/01
	Hickory-Morganton-Lenoir MSA, NC	Y	26430 FQ	45090 AW	74630 TQ	NCBLS	10/01-12/01
	Raleigh-Durham-Chapel Hill MSA, NC	Y	30670 FQ	50740 AW	82250 TQ	NCBLS	10/01-12/01
	Wilmington MSA, NC	Y	26920 FQ	43100 AW	63280 TQ	NCBLS	10/01-12/01
	North Dakota	Y	22690 FQ	37810 AW	55990 TQ	NDBLS	10/01-12/01
	Fargo-Moorhead MSA, ND-MN	Y	26290 FQ	41190 AW	59320 TQ	NDBLS	10/01-12/01
	Ohio	Y	28720 FQ	48510 AW	74940 TQ	OHBLS	10/01-12/01
	Akron PMSA, OH	Y	29110 FQ	47520 AW	74300 TQ	OHBLS	10/01-12/01
	Canton-Massillon MSA, OH	Y	28160 FQ	53890 AW	143660 TQ	OHBLS	10/01-12/01
	Cincinnati PMSA, OH-KY-IN	Y	29330 FQ	48180 AW	73920 TQ	OHBLS	10/01-12/01
	Cleveland-Lorain-Elyria PMSA, OH	Y	29800 FQ	50860 AW	85480 TQ	OHBLS	10/01-12/01
	Columbus MSA, OH	Y	29820 FQ	47280 AW	70510 TQ	OHBLS	10/01-12/01
	Dayton-Springfield MSA, OH	Y	28280 FQ	50850 AW	80700 TQ	OHBLS	10/01-12/01
	Hamilton-Middletown PMSA, OH	Y	28220 FQ	46260 AW	68490 TQ	OHBLS	10/01-12/01
	Mansfield MSA, OH	Y	21310 FQ	41000 AW	65260 TQ	OHBLS	10/01-12/01
	Toledo MSA, OH	Y	24030 FQ	44110 AW	65600 TQ	OHBLS	10/01-12/01
	Youngstown-Warren MSA, OH	Y	26940 FQ	49060 AW	75320 TQ	OHBLS	10/01-12/01
	Oklahoma	Y	24680 FQ	40940 AW	62920 TQ	OKBLS	10/01-12/01
	Oklahoma City MSA, OK	Y	24940 FQ	41150 AW	65000 TQ	OKBLS	10/01-12/01
	Tulsa MSA, OK	Y	26150 FQ	43110 AW	64010 TQ	OKBLS	10/01-12/01
	Oregon	Y	30820 FQ	47930 AW	71000 TQ	ORBLS	10/01-12/01
	Eugene-Springfield MSA, OR	Y	30580 FQ	48610 AW	72920 TQ	ORBLS	10/01-12/01
	Medford-Ashland MSA, OR	Y	28660 FQ	43670 AW	65410 TQ	ORBLS	10/01-12/01
	Portland-Vancouver PMSA, OR-WA	Y	31880 FQ	50470 AW	75310 TQ	ORBLS	10/01-12/01
	Salem PMSA, OR	Y	29250 FQ	42280 AW	58880 TQ	ORBLS	10/01-12/01
	Pennsylvania	Y	26730 FQ	46570 AW	72080 TQ	PABLS	10/01-12/01
	Allentown-Bethlehem-Easton MSA, PA	Y	24370 FQ	46190 AW	69240 TQ	PABLS	10/01-12/01
	Erie MSA, PA	Y	24480 FQ	38100 AW	55440 TQ	PABLS	10/01-12/01
	Harrisburg-Lebanon-Carlisle MSA, PA	Y	28050 FQ	46150 AW	70620 TQ	PABLS	10/01-12/01
	Johnstown MSA, PA	Y	19890 FQ	34040 AW	51260 TQ	PABLS	10/01-12/01
	Lancaster MSA, PA	Y	29740 FQ	46390 AW	63600 TQ	PABLS	10/01-12/01
	Philadelphia PMSA, PA-NJ	Y	31470 FQ	52160 AW	81200 TQ	PABLS	10/01-12/01
	Pittsburgh MSA, PA	Y	25000 FQ	42710 AW	68680 TQ	PABLS	10/01-12/01
	Reading MSA, PA	Y	26700 FQ	42890 AW	64900 TQ	PABLS	10/01-12/01
	Scranton-Wilkes-Barre-Hazleton MSA, PA	Y	23640 FQ	36880 AW	56500 TQ	PABLS	10/01-12/01
	York MSA, PA	Y	25390 FQ	42590 AW	62670 TQ	PABLS	10/01-12/01
	Rhode Island	Y	29460 FQ	47420 AW	70710 TQ	RIBLS	10/01-12/01

AAW Average annual wage; **AE** Average entry wage; **AEX** Average experienced wage; **AO** Average offered; **AOH** Average offered, high; **AOL** Average offered, low; **APH** Average pay, high range; **APL** Average pay, low range; **ASH** Average starting, high; **ASL** Average starting, low; **AW** Average wage paid; **FQ** First quartile wage; **H** Hourly; **HI** Highest wage paid; **HR** High end range; **LR** Low end range; **M** Monthly; **MTC** Median total compensation; **MW** Median wage paid; **SQ** Second quartile wage; **S** Special: hourly and annual; **TQ** Third quartile wage; **W** Weekly; **Y** Yearly

Occupation/Type/Industry	Location	Per	Low	Mid	High	Source	Date
Accountant and Auditor	Providence-Fall River-Warwick MSA, RI-MA	Y	29260 FQ	47480 AW	70670 TQ	RIBLS	10/01-12/01
	South Carolina	Y	23970 FQ	40560 AW	63390 TQ	SCBLS	10/01-12/01
	Charleston-North Charleston MSA, SC	Y	23330 FQ	39600 AW	59880 TQ	SCBLS	10/01-12/01
	Columbia MSA, SC	Y	22700 FQ	37290 AW	54180 TQ	SCBLS	10/01-12/01
	Greenville-Spartanburg-Anderson MSA, SC	Y	26470 FQ	41390 AW	64920 TQ	SCBLS	10/01-12/01
	Myrtle Beach MSA, SC	Y	21070 FQ	37300 AW	56300 TQ	SCBLS	10/01-12/01
	South Dakota	Y	28050 FQ	39590 AW	56150 TQ	SDBLS	10/01-12/01
	Sioux Falls MSA, SD	Y	30040 FQ	42300 AW	59740 TQ	SDBLS	10/01-12/01
	Tennessee	Y	26650 FQ	45480 AW	69550 TQ	TNBLS	10/01-12/01
	Chattanooga MSA, TN-GA	Y	23650 FQ	42400 AW	67150 TQ	TNBLS	10/01-12/01
	Clarksville-Hopkinsville MSA, TN-KY	Y	26920 FQ	40420 AW	56560 TQ	TNBLS	10/01-12/01
	Johnson City-Kingsport-Bristol MSA, TN-VA	Y	22380 FQ	39380 AW	57570 TQ	TNBLS	10/01-12/01
	Knoxville MSA, TN	Y	22850 FQ	46610 AW	80880 TQ	TNBLS	10/01-12/01
	Memphis MSA, TN-AR-MS	Y	26490 FQ	45360 AW	70870 TQ	TNBLS	10/01-12/01
	Nashville MSA, TN	Y	30290 FQ	48310 AW	69750 TQ	TNBLS	10/01-12/01
	Texas	Y	29100 FQ	50710 AW	76650 TQ	TXBLS	10/01-12/01
	Amarillo MSA, TX	Y	23310 FQ	38430 AW	61920 TQ	TXBLS	10/01-12/01
	Austin-San Marcos MSA, TX	Y	28600 FQ	47380 AW	72060 TQ	TXBLS	10/01-12/01
	Beaumont-Port Arthur MSA, TX	Y	26000 FQ	43490 AW	68880 TQ	TXBLS	10/01-12/01
	Brazoria PMSA, TX	Y	28610 FQ	56030 AW	90600 TQ	TXBLS	10/01-12/01
	Brownsville-Harlingen-San Benito MSA, TX	Y	25810 FQ	40280 AW	64410 TQ	TXBLS	10/01-12/01
	Corpus Christi MSA, TX	Y	25050 FQ	40890 AW	65210 TQ	TXBLS	10/01-12/01
	Dallas PMSA, TX	Y	31640 FQ	59650 AW	117520 TQ	TXBLS	10/01-12/01
	El Paso MSA, TX	Y	26390 FQ	44220 AW	59330 TQ	TXBLS	10/01-12/01
	Fort Worth-Arlington PMSA, TX	Y	30480 FQ	49650 AW	79030 TQ	TXBLS	10/01-12/01
	Galveston-Texas City PMSA, TX	Y	26200 FQ	43680 AW	66410 TQ	TXBLS	10/01-12/01
	Houston PMSA, TX	Y	31760 FQ	50290 AW	71030 TQ	TXBLS	10/01-12/01
	Killeen-Temple MSA, TX	Y	27670 FQ	41660 AW	65330 TQ	TXBLS	10/01-12/01
	Laredo MSA, TX	Y	27020 FQ	56290 AW	120910 TQ	TXBLS	10/01-12/01
	Longview-Marshall MSA, TX	Y	24610 FQ	46800 AW	80200 TQ	TXBLS	10/01-12/01
	Lubbock MSA, TX	Y	26280 FQ	48960 AW	72860 TQ	TXBLS	10/01-12/01
	McAllen-Edinburg-Mission MSA, TX	Y	22710 FQ	37590 AW	56610 TQ	TXBLS	10/01-12/01
	Odessa-Midland MSA, TX	Y	22940 FQ	48830 AW	99370 TQ	TXBLS	10/01-12/01
	San Antonio MSA, TX	Y	26820 FQ	42470 AW	65130 TQ	TXBLS	10/01-12/01
	Tyler MSA, TX	Y	27960 FQ	46300 AW	71420 TQ	TXBLS	10/01-12/01
	Waco MSA, TX	Y	28690 FQ	43560 AW	63490 TQ	TXBLS	10/01-12/01
	Utah	Y	26580 FQ	43150 AW	65570 TQ	UTBLS	10/01-12/01
	Provo-Orem MSA, UT	Y	24920 FQ	38340 AW	55810 TQ	UTBLS	10/01-12/01
	Salt Lake City-Ogden MSA, UT	Y	28510 FQ	44090 AW	66350 TQ	UTBLS	10/01-12/01
	Vermont	Y	32680 FQ	52950 AW	77840 TQ	VTBLS	10/01-12/01
	Burlington MSA, VT	Y	34450 FQ	56410 AW	77970 TQ	VTBLS	10/01-12/01
	Virginia	Y	29100 FQ	49620 AW	76970 TQ	VABLS	10/01-12/01
	Lynchburg MSA, VA	Y	21450 FQ	43470 AW	69000 TQ	VABLS	10/01-12/01
	Norfolk-Virginia Beach-Newport News MSA, VA-NC	Y	28400 FQ	43910 AW	66930 TQ	VABLS	10/01-12/01
	Richmond-Petersburg MSA, VA	Y	29090 FQ	48210 AW	73610 TQ	VABLS	10/01-12/01
	Roanoke MSA, VA	Y	27330 FQ	41380 AW	58560 TQ	VABLS	10/01-12/01
	Washington	Y	32990 FQ	55540 AW	89710 TQ	WABLS	10/01-12/01
	Bremerton PMSA, WA	Y	29750 FQ	46290 AW	68150 TQ	WABLS	10/01-12/01
	Olympia PMSA, WA	Y	30690 FQ	47280 AW	68800 TQ	WABLS	10/01-12/01
	Richland-Kennewick-Pasco MSA, WA	Y	33160 FQ	51880 AW	75770 TQ	WABLS	10/01-12/01
	Seattle-Bellevue-Everett PMSA, WA	Y	35060 FQ	59220 AW	107760 TQ	WABLS	10/01-12/01
	Spokane MSA, WA	Y	31220 FQ	48010 AW	72030 TQ	WABLS	10/01-12/01
	Tacoma PMSA, WA	Y	31010 FQ	48170 AW	71640 TQ	WABLS	10/01-12/01
	Yakima MSA, WA	Y	31980 FQ	50000 AW	69740 TQ	WABLS	10/01-12/01
	West Virginia	Y	23550 FQ	38810 AW	60060 TQ	WVBLS	10/01-12/01
	Charleston MSA, WV	Y	25530 FQ	41260 AW	66080 TQ	WVBLS	10/01-12/01

AAW Average annual wage; **AE** Average entry wage; **AEX** Average experienced wage; **AO** Average offered; **AOH** Average offered, high; **AOL** Average offered, low; **APH** Average pay, high range; **APL** Average pay, low range; **ASH** Average starting, high; **ASL** Average starting, low; **AW** Average wage paid; **FQ** First quartile wage; **H** Hourly; **HI** Highest wage paid; **HR** High end range; **LR** Low end range; **M** Monthly; **MTC** Median total compensation; **MW** Median wage paid; **SQ** Second quartile wage; **S** Special: hourly and annual; **TQ** Third quartile wage; **W** Weekly; **Y** Yearly

Occupation/Type/Industry	Location	Per	Low	Mid	High	Source	Date
Accountant and Auditor	Huntington-Ashland MSA, WV-KY-OH	Y	24240 FQ	43860 AW	72320 TQ	WVBLS	10/01-12/01
	Wisconsin	Y	27790 FQ	47850 AW	71300 TQ	WIBLS	10/01-12/01
	Appleton-Oshkosh-Neenah MSA, WI	Y	29230 FQ	45950 AW	71200 TQ	WIBLS	10/01-12/01
	Green Bay MSA, WI	Y	29800 FQ	50030 AW	78980 TQ	WIBLS	10/01-12/01
	Madison MSA, WI	Y	32240 FQ	48540 AW	67700 TQ	WIBLS	10/01-12/01
	Milwaukee-Waukesha PMSA, WI	Y	30750 FQ	52730 AW	84130 TQ	WIBLS	10/01-12/01
	Racine PMSA, WI	Y	27190 FQ	43290 AW	62150 TQ	WIBLS	10/01-12/01
	Wyoming	Y	25040 FQ	43940 AW	70110 TQ	WYBLS	10/01-12/01
	Cheyenne MSA, WY	Y	23770 FQ	34750 AW	48220 TQ	WYBLS	10/01-12/01
	Puerto Rico	Y	17680 FQ	29790 AW	44170 TQ	PRBLS	10/01-12/01
	Virgin Islands	Y	26110 FQ	37600 AW	53550 TQ	VIBLS	10/01-12/01
	Guam	Y	20440 FQ	34180 AW	49900 TQ	GUBLS	10/01-12/01
Actor	Arizona	Y	18180 FQ	42630 AW	87260 TQ	AZBLS	10/01-12/01
	Phoenix-Mesa MSA, AZ	Y	19870 FQ	39710 AW	79380 TQ	AZBLS	10/01-12/01
	California	Y	13650 FQ	52050 AW	130130 TQ	CABLS	10/01-12/01
	Los Angeles-Long Beach PMSA, CA	Y	13620 FQ	53070 AW	132750 TQ	CABLS	10/01-12/01
	Orange County PMSA, CA	Y	17030 FQ	41920 AW	71370 TQ	CABLS	10/01-12/01
	Sacramento PMSA, CA	Y	24250 FQ	31560 AW	47930 TQ	CABLS	10/01-12/01
	San Diego MSA, CA	Y	18830 FQ	34360 AW	66440 TQ	CABLS	10/01-12/01
	San Francisco PMSA, CA	Y	21900 FQ	60680 AW	107890 TQ	CABLS	10/01-12/01
	San Jose PMSA, CA	Y	13230 FQ	20780 AW	33830 TQ	CABLS	10/01-12/01
	Santa Barbara-Santa Maria-Lompoc MSA, CA	Y	18190 FQ	46340 AW	111200 TQ	CABLS	10/01-12/01
	Colorado	Y	13030 FQ	42360 AW	71000 TQ	COBLS	10/01-12/01
	Denver PMSA, CO	Y	12980 FQ	43350 AW	71200 TQ	COBLS	10/01-12/01
	Connecticut	Y	14560 FQ	34500 AW	54160 TQ	CTBLS	10/01-12/01
	Washington PMSA, DC-MD-VA-WV	Y	13010 FQ	28670 AW	52610 TQ	DCBLS	10/01-12/01
	Florida	Y	15630 FQ	25840 AW	37160 TQ	FLBLS	10/01-12/01
	Fort Myers-Cape Coral MSA, FL	Y	14920 FQ	24410 AW	35120 TQ	FLBLS	10/01-12/01
	Jacksonville MSA, FL	Y	16420 FQ	24920 AW	36180 TQ	FLBLS	10/01-12/01
	Miami PMSA, FL	Y	17880 FQ	21720 AW	31240 TQ	FLBLS	10/01-12/01
	Sarasota-Bradenton MSA, FL	Y	14460 FQ	23740 AW	39440 TQ	FLBLS	10/01-12/01
	Tampa-St. Petersburg-Clearwater MSA, FL	Y	11740 FQ	16870 AW	23650 TQ	FLBLS	10/01-12/01
	West Palm Beach-Boca Raton MSA, FL	Y	18700 FQ	29620 AW	34890 TQ	FLBLS	10/01-12/01
	Georgia	Y	17790 FQ	22570 AW	29780 TQ	GABLS	10/01-12/01
	Hawaii	Y	11850 FQ	32500 AW	59660 TQ	HIBLS	10/01-12/01
	Honolulu MSA, HI	Y	11690 FQ	28850 AW	92460 TQ	HIBLS	10/01-12/01
	Idaho	Y	11270 FQ	15380 AW	21530 TQ	IDBLS	10/01-12/01
	Illinois	Y	12320 FQ	39200 AW	125510 TQ	ILBLS	10/01-12/01
	Indiana	Y	14310 FQ	21610 AW	31220 TQ	INBLS	10/01-12/01
	Indianapolis MSA, IN	Y	14850 FQ	21690 AW	31490 TQ	INBLS	10/01-12/01
	Kentucky	Y	13670 FQ	28300 AW	46690 TQ	KYBLS	10/01-12/01
	Louisville MSA, KY-IN	Y	15270 FQ	27740 AW	47610 TQ	KYBLS	10/01-12/01
	Louisiana	Y	12180 FQ	21060 AW	35680 TQ	LABLS	10/01-12/01
	Baton Rouge MSA, LA	Y	12220 FQ	26090 AW	58900 TQ	LABLS	10/01-12/01
	Maine	Y	12350 FQ	25190 AW	50740 TQ	MEBLS	10/01-12/01
	Maryland	Y	12220 FQ	22350 AW	36140 TQ	MDBLS	10/01-12/01
	Baltimore PMSA, MD	Y	12430 FQ	22890 AW	39200 TQ	MDBLS	10/01-12/01
	Massachusetts	Y	14030 FQ	25840 AW	38930 TQ	MABLS	10/01-12/01
	Boston PMSA, MA-NH	Y	14030 FQ	28110 AW	40380 TQ	MABLS	10/01-12/01
	Michigan	Y	14240 FQ	24410 AW	49770 TQ	MIBLS	10/01-12/01
	Minnesota	Y	14020 FQ	36140 AW	46380 TQ	MNBLS	10/01-12/01
	Minneapolis-St. Paul MSA, MN-WI	Y	14060 FQ	32350 AW	44540 TQ	MNBLS	10/01-12/01
	Missouri	Y	16440 FQ	30930 AW	47240 TQ	MOBLS	10/01-12/01
	Kansas City MSA, MO-KS	Y	18130 FQ	34680 AW	46820 TQ	MOBLS	10/01-12/01
	Nevada	Y	21250 FQ	41480 AW	61140 TQ	NVBLS	10/01-12/01
	Las Vegas MSA, NV-AZ	Y	24870 FQ	43320 AW	66120 TQ	NVBLS	10/01-12/01
	New Hampshire	Y	12150 FQ	25850 AW	40240 TQ	NHBLS	10/01-12/01
	New Jersey	Y	14800 FQ	36570 AW	64640 TQ	NJBLS	10/01-12/01
	Newark PMSA, NJ	Y	15030 FQ	35560 AW	44270 TQ	NJBLS	10/01-12/01
	New York	Y	11780 FQ	27650 AW	51040 TQ	NYBLS	10/01-12/01
	Nassau-Suffolk PMSA, NY	Y	13850 FQ	42180 AW	90050 TQ	NYBLS	10/01-12/01
	New York PMSA, NY	Y	11770 FQ	27680 AW	51570 TQ	NYBLS	10/01-12/01

AAW	Average annual wage	**AOH**	Average offered, high	**ASH**	Average starting, high	**H**	Hourly	**M**	Monthly	**S**	Special: hourly and annual
AE	Average entry wage	**AOL**	Average offered, low	**ASL**	Average starting, low	**HI**	Highest wage paid	**MTC**	Median total compensation	**TQ**	Third quartile wage
AEX	Average experienced wage	**APH**	Average pay, high range	**AW**	Average wage paid	**HR**	High end range	**MW**	Median wage paid	**W**	Weekly
AO	Average offered	**APL**	Average pay, low range	**FQ**	First quartile wage	**LR**	Low end range	**SQ**	Second quartile wage	**Y**	Yearly

Occupation/Type/Industry	Location	Per	Low	Mid	High	Source	Date
Actor	Ohio	Y	11940 FQ	20930 AW	40210 TQ	OHBLS	10/01-12/01
	Cincinnati PMSA, OH-KY-IN	Y	12380 FQ	25120 AW	43700 TQ	OHBLS	10/01-12/01
	Cleveland-Lorain-Elyria PMSA, OH	Y	12260 FQ	17960 AW	32760 TQ	OHBLS	10/01-12/01
	Dayton-Springfield MSA, OH	Y	16570 FQ	21380 AW	27910 TQ	OHBLS	10/01-12/01
	Oklahoma	Y	12330 FQ	19510 AW	22740 TQ	OKBLS	10/01-12/01
	Oregon	Y	14700 FQ	36230 AW	68610 TQ	ORBLS	10/01-12/01
	Portland-Vancouver PMSA, OR-WA	Y	18120 FQ	27510 AW	42830 TQ	ORBLS	10/01-12/01
	Pennsylvania	Y	13230 FQ	38490 AW	91550 TQ	PABLS	10/01-12/01
	Harrisburg-Lebanon-Carlisle MSA, PA	Y	12140 FQ	23480 AW	43950 TQ	PABLS	10/01-12/01
	Philadelphia PMSA, PA-NJ	Y	13940 FQ	39300 AW	90860 TQ	PABLS	10/01-12/01
	South Carolina	Y	16670 FQ	37380 AW	70340 TQ	SCBLS	10/01-12/01
	Charleston-North Charleston MSA, SC	Y	12650 FQ	18440 AW	21470 TQ	SCBLS	10/01-12/01
	South Dakota	Y	14160 FQ	19540 AW	24080 TQ	SDBLS	10/01-12/01
	Tennessee	Y	17280 FQ	44720 AW	117290 TQ	TNBLS	10/01-12/01
	Texas	Y	11500 FQ	17110 AW	15330 TQ	TXBLS	10/01-12/01
	Austin-San Marcos MSA, TX	Y	16070 FQ	31810 AW	47780 TQ	TXBLS	10/01-12/01
	Dallas PMSA, TX	Y	20870 FQ	75270 AW	124860 TQ	TXBLS	10/01-12/01
	Houston PMSA, TX	Y	17770 FQ	35690 AW	47260 TQ	TXBLS	10/01-12/01
	San Antonio MSA, TX	Y	11470 FQ	12730 AW	14280 TQ	TXBLS	10/01-12/01
	Vermont	Y	15230 FQ	25770 AW	41520 TQ	VTBLS	10/01-12/01
	Virginia	Y	11930 FQ	34740 AW	86060 TQ	VABLS	10/01-12/01
	Norfolk-Virginia Beach-Newport News MSA, VA-NC	Y	12360 FQ	36550 AW	73770 TQ	VABLS	10/01-12/01
	Richmond-Petersburg MSA, VA	Y	11820 FQ	31750 AW	86290 TQ	VABLS	10/01-12/01
	Washington	Y	15120 FQ	44450 AW	92980 TQ	WABLS	10/01-12/01
	Seattle-Bellevue-Everett PMSA, WA	Y	14890 FQ	49100 AW	95340 TQ	WABLS	10/01-12/01
	Milwaukee-Waukesha PMSA, WI	Y	12130 FQ	30460 AW	45290 TQ	WIBLS	10/01-12/01
	Puerto Rico	Y	11980 FQ	14800 AW	21850 TQ	PRBLS	10/01-12/01
Actuary	Alabama	Y	39950 FQ	83910 AW	136780 TQ	ALBLS	10/01-12/01
	Arizona	Y	36080 FQ	64620 AW	111160 TQ	AZBLS	10/01-12/01
	California	Y	41550 FQ	78590 AW	137600 TQ	CABLS	10/01-12/01
	Colorado	Y	41820 FQ	72900 AW	118220 TQ	COBLS	10/01-12/01
	Connecticut	Y	45440 FQ	87170 AW	145220 TQ	CTBLS	10/01-12/01
	District of Columbia	Y	37760 FQ	78050 AW	135550 TQ	DCBLS	10/01-12/01
	Florida	Y	35520 FQ	71480 AW	128100 TQ	FLBLS	10/01-12/01
	Georgia	Y	34410 FQ	67670 AW	121000 TQ	GABLS	10/01-12/01
	Illinois	Y	36870 FQ	69060 AW	120300 TQ	ILBLS	10/01-12/01
	Indiana	Y	42280 FQ	71810 AW	118090 TQ	INBLS	10/01-12/01
	Iowa	Y	36200 FQ	74470 AW	120010 TQ	IABLS	10/01-12/01
	Kansas	Y	43420 FQ	77700 AW	141620 TQ	KSBLS	10/01-12/01
	Kentucky	Y	39620 FQ	64790 AW	95190 TQ	KYBLS	10/01-12/01
	Louisiana	Y	34040 FQ	66670 AW	116790 TQ	LABLS	10/01-12/01
	Maine	Y	43570 FQ	75160 AW	111670 TQ	MEBLS	10/01-12/01
	Maryland	Y	41250 FQ	70850 AW	109600 TQ	MDBLS	10/01-12/01
	Massachusetts	Y	44820 FQ	81810 AW	138340 TQ	MABLS	10/01-12/01
	Michigan	Y	38540 FQ	68870 AW	114580 TQ	MIBLS	10/01-12/01
	Minnesota	Y	46160 FQ	86970 AW		MNBLS	10/01-12/01
	Missouri	Y	45760 FQ	81940 AW		MOBLS	10/01-12/01
	Nebraska	Y	31680 FQ	68250 AW	114510 TQ	NEBLS	10/01-12/01
	Nevada	Y	40350 FQ	69170 AW	109420 TQ	NVBLS	10/01-12/01
	New Hampshire	Y	37040 FQ	66740 AW	140440 TQ	NHBLS	10/01-12/01
	New Jersey	Y	36060 FQ	70350 AW	132000 TQ	NJBLS	10/01-12/01
	New York	Y	39910 FQ	84050 AW		NYBLS	10/01-12/01
	North Carolina	Y	44220 FQ	75580 AW	124250 TQ	NCBLS	10/01-12/01
	North Dakota	Y	35800 FQ	45570 AW	56510 TQ	NDBLS	10/01-12/01
	Ohio	Y	38380 FQ	71420 AW	132700 TQ	OHBLS	10/01-12/01
	Oklahoma	Y	18800 FQ	44110 AW	85550 TQ	OKBLS	10/01-12/01
	Oregon	Y	36100 FQ	59720 AW	91630 TQ	ORBLS	10/01-12/01
	Pennsylvania	Y	41260 FQ	75630 AW	121860 TQ	PABLS	10/01-12/01
	Rhode Island	Y	39970 FQ	59080 AW	85260 TQ	RIBLS	10/01-12/01
	South Carolina	Y	26010 FQ	65450 AW	138070 TQ	SCBLS	10/01-12/01
	Tennessee	Y	40230 FQ	80150 AW		TNBLS	10/01-12/01
	Texas	Y	40950 FQ	74660 AW	131470 TQ	TXBLS	10/01-12/01
	Utah	Y	18890 FQ	53150 AW	95500 TQ	UTBLS	10/01-12/01

AAW Average annual wage **AOH** Average offered, high **ASH** Average starting, high **H** Hourly **M** Monthly **S** Special: hourly and annual
AE Average entry wage **AOL** Average offered, low **ASL** Average starting, low **HI** Highest wage paid **MTC** Median total compensation **TQ** Third quartile wage
AEX Average experienced wage **APH** Average pay, high range **AW** Average wage paid **HR** High end range **MW** Median wage paid **W** Weekly
AO Average offered **APL** Average pay, low range **FQ** First quartile wage **LR** Low end range **SQ** Second quartile wage **Y** Yearly

Occupation/Type/Industry	Location	Per	Low	Mid	High	Source	Date
Actuary	Virginia	Y	39590 FQ	69660 AW	121100 TQ	VABLS	10/01-12/01
	Washington	Y	39840 FQ	67980 AW	122770 TQ	WABLS	10/01-12/01
	Wisconsin	Y	41050 FQ	70990 AW	117180 TQ	WIBLS	10/01-12/01
	Puerto Rico	Y	19980 FQ	35070 AW	56070 TQ	PRBLS	10/01-12/01
Fellow	United States	Y		150000 AW		DMN	1/01-1/02
Administrative Law Judge							
Federal Government	United States	Y		1425000 AW		OPM13	2003
Administrative Law Judge, Adjudicator, and Hearing Officer	United States	Y		61240 MW		OOH7	1999-2000
	Alabama	Y	34520 FQ	49310 AW	69560 TQ	ALBLS	10/01-12/01
	Montgomery MSA, AL	Y	33070 FQ	50510 AW	71350 TQ	ALBLS	10/01-12/01
	Alaska	Y	36780 FQ	56010 AW	80770 TQ	AKBLS	10/01-12/01
	Arizona	Y	34180 FQ	52710 AW	84760 TQ	AZBLS	10/01-12/01
	Phoenix-Mesa MSA, AZ	Y	35630 FQ	52550 AW	77530 TQ	AZBLS	10/01-12/01
	Tucson MSA, AZ	Y	35210 FQ	62300 AW	123520 TQ	AZBLS	10/01-12/01
	Arkansas	Y	23960 FQ	43760 AW	77380 TQ	ARBLS	10/01-12/01
	Little Rock-North Little Rock MSA, AR	Y	24220 FQ	43540 AW	74770 TQ	ARBLS	10/01-12/01
	California	Y	38060 FQ	70810 AW	112000 TQ	CABLS	10/01-12/01
	Fresno MSA, CA	Y	55650 FQ	93340 AW	126040 TQ	CABLS	10/01-12/01
	Los Angeles-Long Beach PMSA, CA	Y	38690 FQ	70180 AW	111580 TQ	CABLS	10/01-12/01
	Oakland PMSA, CA	Y	32930 FQ	52920 AW	90450 TQ	CABLS	10/01-12/01
	Riverside-San Bernardino PMSA, CA	Y	50080 FQ	87100 AW	118050 TQ	CABLS	10/01-12/01
	Sacramento PMSA, CA	Y	38350 FQ	88360 AW	113550 TQ	CABLS	10/01-12/01
	San Diego MSA, CA	Y	36590 FQ	63070 AW	109850 TQ	CABLS	10/01-12/01
	San Francisco PMSA, CA	Y	46580 FQ	78390 AW	115260 TQ	CABLS	10/01-12/01
	San Jose PMSA, CA	Y	53860 FQ	92560 AW	123200 TQ	CABLS	10/01-12/01
	Colorado	Y	37180 FQ	59010 AW	86680 TQ	COBLS	10/01-12/01
	Denver PMSA, CO	Y	36540 FQ	58910 AW	90880 TQ	COBLS	10/01-12/01
	Connecticut	Y	48870 FQ	67710 AW	89250 TQ	CTBLS	10/01-12/01
	Delaware	Y	31570 FQ	50340 AW	82880 TQ	DEBLS	10/01-12/01
	Washington PMSA, DC-MD-VA-WV	Y	36160 FQ	66540 AW	105750 TQ	DCBLS	10/01-12/01
	Florida	Y	33770 FQ	63740 AW	135140 TQ	FLBLS	10/01-12/01
	Jacksonville MSA, FL	Y	38170 FQ	59740 AW	90690 TQ	FLBLS	10/01-12/01
	Orlando MSA, FL	Y	39180 FQ	79830 AW	143010 TQ	FLBLS	10/01-12/01
	Tampa-St. Petersburg-Clearwater MSA, FL	Y	31090 FQ	51730 AW	78720 TQ	FLBLS	10/01-12/01
	Georgia	Y	32010 FQ	51390 AW	78880 TQ	GABLS	10/01-12/01
	Atlanta MSA, GA	Y	31970 FQ	50200 AW	71180 TQ	GABLS	10/01-12/01
	Hawaii	Y	38970 FQ	58500 AW	83230 TQ	HIBLS	10/01-12/01
	Idaho	Y	35370 FQ	45340 AW	64590 TQ	IDBLS	10/01-12/01
	Illinois	Y	33210 FQ	50420 AW	69160 TQ	ILBLS	10/01-12/01
	Chicago PMSA, IL	Y	35270 FQ	52470 AW	73500 TQ	ILBLS	10/01-12/01
	Indiana	Y	25500 FQ	53320 AW	111370 TQ	INBLS	10/01-12/01
	Iowa	Y	34520 FQ	58480 AW	81370 TQ	IABLS	10/01-12/01
	Des Moines MSA, IA	Y	33620 FQ	58960 AW	84910 TQ	IABLS	10/01-12/01
	Kansas	Y	32370 FQ	61770 AW	118640 TQ	KSBLS	10/01-12/01
	Louisville MSA, KY-IN	Y	28960 FQ	45970 AW	69090 TQ	KYBLS	10/01-12/01
	Louisiana	Y	29620 FQ	52220 AW	95420 TQ	LABLS	10/01-12/01
	New Orleans MSA, LA	Y	32080 FQ	53040 AW	93510 TQ	LABLS	10/01-12/01
	Maine	Y	32490 FQ	48190 AW	77990 TQ	MEBLS	10/01-12/01
	Maryland	Y	35080 FQ	45290 AW	56270 TQ	MDBLS	10/01-12/01
	Baltimore PMSA, MD	Y	35200 FQ	44950 AW	56010 TQ	MDBLS	10/01-12/01
	Massachusetts	Y	36760 FQ	57320 AW	89880 TQ	MABLS	10/01-12/01
	Boston PMSA, MA-NH	Y	36510 FQ	56470 AW	86140 TQ	MABLS	10/01-12/01
	Michigan	Y	38710 FQ	67880 AW	97760 TQ	MIBLS	10/01-12/01
	Detroit PMSA, MI	Y	38460 FQ	64770 AW	95950 TQ	MIBLS	10/01-12/01
	Minnesota	Y	30780 FQ	60230 AW	106980 TQ	MNBLS	10/01-12/01
	Minneapolis-St. Paul MSA, MN-WI	Y	30590 FQ	60520 AW	106940 TQ	MNBLS	10/01-12/01
	Mississippi	Y	24360 FQ	47470 AW	82690 TQ	MSBLS	10/01-12/01
	Jackson MSA, MS	Y	30200 FQ	51190 AW	80590 TQ	MSBLS	10/01-12/01
	Missouri	Y	35990 FQ	48260 AW	62850 TQ	MOBLS	10/01-12/01
	Kansas City MSA, MO-KS	Y	36860 FQ	47040 AW	56320 TQ	MOBLS	10/01-12/01
	St. Louis MSA, MO-IL	Y	30270 FQ	51300 AW	82180 TQ	MOBLS	10/01-12/01
	Montana	Y	29810 FQ	45840 AW	64010 TQ	MTBLS	10/01-12/01

AAW Average annual wage **AOH** Average offered, high **ASH** Average starting, high **H** Hourly **M** Monthly **S** Special: hourly and annual
AE Average entry wage **AOL** Average offered, low **ASL** Average starting, low **HI** Highest wage paid **MTC** Median total compensation **TQ** Third quartile wage
AEX Average experienced wage **APH** Average pay, high range **AW** Average wage paid **HR** High end range **MW** Median wage paid **W** Weekly
AO Average offered **APL** Average pay, low range **FQ** First quartile wage **LR** Low end range **SQ** Second quartile wage **Y** Yearly

Occupation/Type/Industry	Location	Per	Low	Mid	High	Source	Date
Administrative Law Judge, Adjudicator, and Hearing Officer	Nebraska	Y	32490 FQ	50980 AW	82260 TQ	NEBLS	10/01-12/01
	Nevada	Y	31710 FQ	49340 AW	80130 TQ	NVBLS	10/01-12/01
	Las Vegas MSA, NV-AZ	Y	30880 FQ	56060 AW	95520 TQ	NVBLS	10/01-12/01
	New Hampshire	Y	29380 FQ	48780 AW	67380 TQ	NHBLS	10/01-12/01
	New Jersey	Y	40610 FQ	71650 AW	120250 TQ	NJBLS	10/01-12/01
	Atlantic-Cape May PMSA, NJ	Y	62840 FQ	73360 AW	91440 TQ	NJBLS	10/01-12/01
	Newark PMSA, NJ	Y	39040 FQ	69090 AW	121470 TQ	NJBLS	10/01-12/01
	New Mexico	Y	29440 FQ	45350 AW	66210 TQ	NMBLS	10/01-12/01
	Albuquerque MSA, NM	Y	29920 FQ	47540 AW	75960 TQ	NMBLS	10/01-12/01
	New York	Y	37770 FQ	63040 AW	89630 TQ	NYBLS	10/01-12/01
	Albany-Schenectady-Troy MSA, NY	Y	54390 FQ	71030 AW	97560 TQ	NYBLS	10/01-12/01
	Buffalo-Niagara Falls MSA, NY	Y	28700 FQ	53690 AW	96660 TQ	NYBLS	10/01-12/01
	Nassau-Suffolk PMSA, NY	Y	58880 FQ	78050 AW	111210 TQ	NYBLS	10/01-12/01
	New York PMSA, NY	Y	39150 FQ	61680 AW	82700 TQ	NYBLS	10/01-12/01
	Syracuse MSA, NY	Y	51550 FQ	76020 AW	128370 TQ	NYBLS	10/01-12/01
	North Carolina	Y	30420 FQ	49330 AW	82120 TQ	NCBLS	10/01-12/01
	Greensboro-Winston-Salem-High Point MSA, NC	Y	32180 FQ	49730 AW	76990 TQ	NCBLS	10/01-12/01
	North Dakota	Y	32510 FQ	52140 AW	84080 TQ	NDBLS	10/01-12/01
	Cincinnati PMSA, OH-KY-IN	Y	26050 FQ	67440 AW	127570 TQ	OHBLS	10/01-12/01
	Cleveland-Lorain-Elyria PMSA, OH	Y	31250 FQ	51300 AW	79970 TQ	OHBLS	10/01-12/01
	Dayton-Springfield MSA, OH	Y	38390 FQ	59810 AW	113990 TQ	OHBLS	10/01-12/01
	Oklahoma	Y	28100 FQ	47150 AW	73110 TQ	OKBLS	10/01-12/01
	Oklahoma City MSA, OK	Y	30900 FQ	52540 AW	95800 TQ	OKBLS	10/01-12/01
	Oregon	Y	30210 FQ	48020 AW	69010 TQ	ORBLS	10/01-12/01
	Portland-Vancouver PMSA, OR-WA	Y	31360 FQ	51430 AW	71480 TQ	ORBLS	10/01-12/01
	Pennsylvania	Y	31230 FQ	53910 AW	84950 TQ	PABLS	10/01-12/01
	Johnstown MSA, PA	Y	52690 FQ	70620 AW	103220 TQ	PABLS	10/01-12/01
	Philadelphia PMSA, PA-NJ	Y	32750 FQ	53220 AW	86320 TQ	PABLS	10/01-12/01
	Pittsburgh MSA, PA	Y	31130 FQ	56650 AW	86380 TQ	PABLS	10/01-12/01
	Rhode Island	Y	33420 FQ	61380 AW	106840 TQ	RIBLS	10/01-12/01
	Providence-Fall River-Warwick MSA, RI-MA	Y	34110 FQ	61070 AW	105320 TQ	RIBLS	10/01-12/01
	South Dakota	Y	29540 FQ	47080 AW	69250 TQ	SDBLS	10/01-12/01
	Tennessee	Y	28240 FQ	54650 AW	120430 TQ	TNBLS	10/01-12/01
	Memphis MSA, TN-AR-MS	Y	26420 FQ	61430 AW	130720 TQ	TNBLS	10/01-12/01
	Nashville MSA, TN	Y	29650 FQ	51170 AW	85710 TQ	TNBLS	10/01-12/01
	Texas	Y	28090 FQ	55050 AW	99660 TQ	TXBLS	10/01-12/01
	Dallas PMSA, TX	Y	38330 FQ	74830 AW	134290 TQ	TXBLS	10/01-12/01
	Fort Worth-Arlington PMSA, TX	Y	27600 FQ	65010 AW	132310 TQ	TXBLS	10/01-12/01
	Houston PMSA, TX	Y	33060 FQ	58410 AW	102760 TQ	TXBLS	10/01-12/01
	San Antonio MSA, TX	Y	31330 FQ	70120 AW	134320 TQ	TXBLS	10/01-12/01
	Utah	Y	27190 FQ	48630 AW	80070 TQ	UTBLS	10/01-12/01
	Salt Lake City-Ogden MSA, UT	Y	28870 FQ	50580 AW	81840 TQ	UTBLS	10/01-12/01
	Virginia	Y	34990 FQ	64570 AW	103510 TQ	VABLS	10/01-12/01
	Norfolk-Virginia Beach-Newport News MSA, VA-NC	Y	29170 FQ	50410 AW	122020 TQ	VABLS	10/01-12/01
	Richmond-Petersburg MSA, VA	Y	31500 FQ	48720 AW	77850 TQ	VABLS	10/01-12/01
	Roanoke MSA, VA	Y	29300 FQ	47820 AW	68880 TQ	VABLS	10/01-12/01
	Washington	Y	31420 FQ	49900 AW	72870 TQ	WABLS	10/01-12/01
	Seattle-Bellevue-Everett PMSA, WA	Y	35720 FQ	54980 AW	81090 TQ	WABLS	10/01-12/01
	Spokane MSA, WA	Y	34480 FQ	60750 AW	108750 TQ	WABLS	10/01-12/01
	West Virginia	Y	29510 FQ	47870 AW	75990 TQ	WVBLS	10/01-12/01
	Huntington-Ashland MSA, WV-KY-OH	Y	32370 FQ	50600 AW	74630 TQ	WVBLS	10/01-12/01
	Wisconsin	Y	30370 FQ	56750 AW	97460 TQ	WIBLS	10/01-12/01
	Milwaukee-Waukesha PMSA, WI	Y	31870 FQ	54070 AW	90490 TQ	WIBLS	10/01-12/01
	Wyoming	Y	18710 FQ	39990 AW	56320 TQ	WYBLS	10/01-12/01
	Puerto Rico	Y	27640 FQ	56000 AW	84250 TQ	PRBLS	10/01-12/01

AAW	Average annual wage	**AOH**	Average offered, high	**ASH**	Average starting, high	**H**	Hourly	**M**	Monthly	**S**	Special: hourly and annual
AE	Average entry wage	**AOL**	Average offered, low	**ASL**	Average starting, low	**HI**	Highest wage paid	**MTC**	Median total compensation	**TQ**	Third quartile wage
AEX	Average experienced wage	**APH**	Average pay, high range	**AW**	Average wage paid	**HR**	High end range	**MW**	Median wage paid	**W**	Weekly
AO	Average offered	**APL**	Average pay, low range	**FQ**	First quartile wage	**LR**	Low end range	**SQ**	Second quartile wage	**Y**	Yearly

Occupation/Type/Industry	Location	Per	Low	Mid	High	Source	Date
Administrative Services Manager	Alabama	Y	20980 FQ	48000 AW	85750 TQ	ALBLS	10/01-12/01
	Birmingham MSA, AL	Y	24310 FQ	51820 AW	91240 TQ	ALBLS	10/01-12/01
	Huntsville MSA, AL	Y	26470 FQ	57790 AW	95660 TQ	ALBLS	10/01-12/01
	Mobile MSA, AL	Y	18880 FQ	43780 AW	73990 TQ	ALBLS	10/01-12/01
	Montgomery MSA, AL	Y	20210 FQ	46530 AW	80610 TQ	ALBLS	10/01-12/01
	Alaska	Y	27200 FQ	48910 AW	75060 TQ	AKBLS	10/01-12/01
	Anchorage MSA, AK	Y	30050 FQ	49230 AW	72870 TQ	AKBLS	10/01-12/01
	Arizona	Y	27400 FQ	55670 AW	89930 TQ	AZBLS	10/01-12/01
	Phoenix-Mesa MSA, AZ	Y	29970 FQ	57910 AW	91760 TQ	AZBLS	10/01-12/01
	Tucson MSA, AZ	Y	23470 FQ	51000 AW	87490 TQ	AZBLS	10/01-12/01
	Arkansas	Y	22790 FQ	47910 AW	78910 TQ	ARBLS	10/01-12/01
	Fayetteville-Springdale-Rogers MSA, AR	Y	22020 FQ	44560 AW	70000 TQ	ARBLS	10/01-12/01
	Fort Smith MSA, AR-OK	Y	23700 FQ	48050 AW	75240 TQ	ARBLS	10/01-12/01
	Little Rock-North Little Rock MSA, AR	Y	26650 FQ	55450 AW	89460 TQ	ARBLS	10/01-12/01
	California	Y	30680 FQ	62270 AW	102650 TQ	CABLS	10/01-12/01
	Bakersfield MSA, CA	Y	26050 FQ	56600 AW	94730 TQ	CABLS	10/01-12/01
	Chico-Paradise MSA, CA	Y	29740 FQ	49760 AW	71500 TQ	CABLS	10/01-12/01
	Fresno MSA, CA	Y	25670 FQ	54450 AW	88230 TQ	CABLS	10/01-12/01
	Los Angeles-Long Beach PMSA, CA	Y	31360 FQ	63430 AW	97780 TQ	CABLS	10/01-12/01
	Merced MSA, CA	Y	30230 FQ	56030 AW	94570 TQ	CABLS	10/01-12/01
	Modesto MSA, CA	Y	22840 FQ	49590 AW	79620 TQ	CABLS	10/01-12/01
	Oakland PMSA, CA	Y	31570 FQ	65220 AW	108470 TQ	CABLS	10/01-12/01
	Orange County PMSA, CA	Y	31280 FQ	63760 AW	109810 TQ	CABLS	10/01-12/01
	Redding MSA, CA	Y	20530 FQ	34960 AW	56080 TQ	CABLS	10/01-12/01
	Riverside-San Bernardino PMSA, CA	Y	25870 FQ	56780 AW	92920 TQ	CABLS	10/01-12/01
	Sacramento PMSA, CA	Y	28530 FQ	60200 AW	97470 TQ	CABLS	10/01-12/01
	Salinas MSA, CA	Y	29340 FQ	54090 AW	88560 TQ	CABLS	10/01-12/01
	San Diego MSA, CA	Y	30210 FQ	58130 AW	97340 TQ	CABLS	10/01-12/01
	San Francisco PMSA, CA	Y	34260 FQ	64230 AW	108080 TQ	CABLS	10/01-12/01
	San Jose PMSA, CA	Y	42820 FQ	74790 AW	117690 TQ	CABLS	10/01-12/01
	San Luis Obispo-Atascadero-Paso Robles MSA, CA	Y	24490 FQ	50420 AW	106400 TQ	CABLS	10/01-12/01
	Santa Barbara-Santa Maria-Lompoc MSA, CA	Y	31360 FQ	57920 AW	91580 TQ	CABLS	10/01-12/01
	Santa Cruz-Watsonville PMSA, CA	Y	29320 FQ	57960 AW	94800 TQ	CABLS	10/01-12/01
	Santa Rosa PMSA, CA	Y	30190 FQ	51100 AW	79960 TQ	CABLS	10/01-12/01
	Stockton-Lodi MSA, CA	Y	30900 FQ	55270 AW	92200 TQ	CABLS	10/01-12/01
	Vallejo-Fairfield-Napa PMSA, CA	Y	29660 FQ	54550 AW	90830 TQ	CABLS	10/01-12/01
	Ventura PMSA, CA	Y	31390 FQ	60000 AW	96920 TQ	CABLS	10/01-12/01
	Visalia-Tulare-Porterville MSA, CA	Y	26810 FQ	59080 AW	95120 TQ	CABLS	10/01-12/01
	Colorado	Y	26110 FQ	57650 AW	96090 TQ	COBLS	10/01-12/01
	Boulder-Longmont PMSA, CO	Y	29040 FQ	61410 AW	108780 TQ	COBLS	10/01-12/01
	Colorado Springs MSA, CO	Y	26640 FQ	55050 AW	91390 TQ	COBLS	10/01-12/01
	Denver PMSA, CO	Y	28000 FQ	61260 AW	102580 TQ	COBLS	10/01-12/01
	Fort Collins-Loveland MSA, CO	Y	27570 FQ	56120 AW	84000 TQ	COBLS	10/01-12/01
	Greeley PMSA, CO	Y	23990 FQ	47950 AW	81080 TQ	COBLS	10/01-12/01
	Connecticut	Y	36970 FQ	69390 AW	112250 TQ	CTBLS	10/01-12/01
	Bridgeport PMSA, CT	Y	27000 FQ	65370 AW	114510 TQ	CTBLS	10/01-12/01
	Danbury PMSA, CT	Y	22920 FQ	58610 AW	98930 TQ	CTBLS	10/01-12/01
	Hartford MSA, CT	Y	46660 FQ	75000 AW	113930 TQ	CTBLS	10/01-12/01
	New Haven-Meriden PMSA, CT	Y	33780 FQ	61500 AW	101870 TQ	CTBLS	10/01-12/01
	New London-Norwich MSA, CT-RI	Y	33830 FQ	65100 AW	110680 TQ	CTBLS	10/01-12/01
	Stamford-Norwalk PMSA, CT	Y	42740 FQ	74930 AW	119940 TQ	CTBLS	10/01-12/01
	Waterbury PMSA, CT	Y	28000 FQ	60330 AW	108040 TQ	CTBLS	10/01-12/01
	Delaware	Y	16790 FQ	54150 AW	99260 TQ	DEBLS	10/01-12/01
	Wilmington-Newark PMSA, DE-MD	Y	16620 FQ	54050 AW	100450 TQ	DEBLS	10/01-12/01
	District of Columbia	Y	30450 FQ	54520 AW	88850 TQ	DCBLS	10/01-12/01
	Washington PMSA, DC-MD-VA-WV	Y	30280 FQ	56780 AW	92630 TQ	DCBLS	10/01-12/01
	Florida	Y	24630 FQ	54430 AW	94320 TQ	FLBLS	10/01-12/01
	Daytona Beach MSA, FL	Y	25160 FQ	47650 AW	74410 TQ	FLBLS	10/01-12/01

AAW	Average annual wage	**AOH**	Average offered, high	**ASH**	Average starting, high	**H**	Hourly	**M**	Monthly	**S**	Special: hourly and annual
AE	Average entry wage	**AOL**	Average offered, low	**ASL**	Average starting, low	**HI**	Highest wage paid	**MTC**	Median total compensation	**TQ**	Third quartile wage
AEX	Average experienced wage	**APH**	Average pay, high range	**AW**	Average wage paid	**HR**	High end range	**MW**	Median wage paid	**W**	Weekly
AO	Average offered	**APL**	Average pay, low range	**FQ**	First quartile wage	**LR**	Low end range	**SQ**	Second quartile wage	**Y**	Yearly

Occupation/Type/Industry	Location	Per	Low	Mid	High	Source	Date
Administrative Services Manager	Fort Lauderdale PMSA, FL	Y	26930 FQ	58400 AW	93850 TQ	FLBLS	10/01-12/01
	Fort Myers-Cape Coral MSA, FL	Y	21570 FQ	45410 AW	87880 TQ	FLBLS	10/01-12/01
	Fort Pierce-Port St. Lucie MSA, FL	Y	19490 FQ	43600 AW	83080 TQ	FLBLS	10/01-12/01
	Fort Walton Beach MSA, FL	Y	24870 FQ	48370 AW	74240 TQ	FLBLS	10/01-12/01
	Gainesville MSA, FL	Y	18450 FQ	46890 AW	91730 TQ	FLBLS	10/01-12/01
	Jacksonville MSA, FL	Y	21950 FQ	55330 AW	93180 TQ	FLBLS	10/01-12/01
	Lakeland-Winter Haven MSA, FL	Y	24320 FQ	49460 AW	81180 TQ	FLBLS	10/01-12/01
	Melbourne-Titusville-Palm Bay MSA, FL	Y	24490 FQ	56060 AW	93180 TQ	FLBLS	10/01-12/01
	Miami PMSA, FL	Y	26120 FQ	59000 AW	106890 TQ	FLBLS	10/01-12/01
	Naples MSA, FL	Y	25700 FQ	48020 AW	80960 TQ	FLBLS	10/01-12/01
	Ocala MSA, FL	Y	21990 FQ	47240 AW	84620 TQ	FLBLS	10/01-12/01
	Orlando MSA, FL	Y	24520 FQ	52910 AW	94270 TQ	FLBLS	10/01-12/01
	Pensacola MSA, FL	Y	20090 FQ	43290 AW	85200 TQ	FLBLS	10/01-12/01
	Sarasota-Bradenton MSA, FL	Y	26500 FQ	52090 AW	88550 TQ	FLBLS	10/01-12/01
	Tallahassee MSA, FL	Y	20940 FQ	72670 AW		FLBLS	10/01-12/01
	Tampa-St. Petersburg-Clearwater MSA, FL	Y	27900 FQ	54190 AW	92530 TQ	FLBLS	10/01-12/01
	West Palm Beach-Boca Raton MSA, FL	Y	28640 FQ	58850 AW	99220 TQ	FLBLS	10/01-12/01
	Georgia	Y	31190 FQ	55380 AW	86940 TQ	GABLS	10/01-12/01
	Atlanta MSA, GA	Y	31950 FQ	56660 AW	87830 TQ	GABLS	10/01-12/01
	Columbus MSA, GA-AL	Y	33080 FQ	58910 AW	90920 TQ	GABLS	10/01-12/01
	Macon MSA, GA	Y	30510 FQ	55950 AW	92660 TQ	GABLS	10/01-12/01
	Savannah MSA, GA	Y	31340 FQ	56590 AW	89490 TQ	GABLS	10/01-12/01
	Hawaii	Y	30350 FQ	51690 AW	81890 TQ	HIBLS	10/01-12/01
	Honolulu MSA, HI	Y	30890 FQ	52630 AW	83860 TQ	HIBLS	10/01-12/01
	Idaho	Y	21360 FQ	45130 AW	72980 TQ	IDBLS	10/01-12/01
	Boise City MSA, ID	Y	24170 FQ	49860 AW	79900 TQ	IDBLS	10/01-12/01
	Illinois	Y	22820 FQ	46610 AW	77050 TQ	ILBLS	10/01-12/01
	Champaign-Urbana MSA, IL	Y	17240 FQ	41700 AW	71740 TQ	ILBLS	10/01-12/01
	Chicago PMSA, IL	Y	25190 FQ	48970 AW	80110 TQ	ILBLS	10/01-12/01
	Peoria-Pekin MSA, IL	Y	18000 FQ	43870 AW	82290 TQ	ILBLS	10/01-12/01
	Rockford MSA, IL	Y	19330 FQ	39220 AW	68170 TQ	ILBLS	10/01-12/01
	Springfield MSA, IL	Y	22470 FQ	45430 AW	73370 TQ	ILBLS	10/01-12/01
	Indiana	Y	24270 FQ	50620 AW	87260 TQ	INBLS	10/01-12/01
	Elkhart-Goshen MSA, IN	Y	23250 FQ	50050 AW	82740 TQ	INBLS	10/01-12/01
	Evansville-Henderson MSA, IN-KY	Y	22230 FQ	48190 AW	83060 TQ	INBLS	10/01-12/01
	Fort Wayne MSA, IN	Y	24000 FQ	56220 AW	103940 TQ	INBLS	10/01-12/01
	Gary PMSA, IN	Y	26470 FQ	49230 AW	85610 TQ	INBLS	10/01-12/01
	Indianapolis MSA, IN	Y	26970 FQ	54810 AW	89860 TQ	INBLS	10/01-12/01
	Lafayette MSA, IN	Y	21660 FQ	47160 AW	75360 TQ	INBLS	10/01-12/01
	South Bend MSA, IN	Y	20880 FQ	44470 AW	71840 TQ	INBLS	10/01-12/01
	Iowa	Y	24540 FQ	52980 AW	88200 TQ	IABLS	10/01-12/01
	Cedar Rapids MSA, IA	Y	31490 FQ	60040 AW	92310 TQ	IABLS	10/01-12/01
	Davenport-Moline-Rock Island MSA, IA-IL	Y	21080 FQ	47130 AW	83570 TQ	IABLS	10/01-12/01
	Des Moines MSA, IA	Y	29780 FQ	58100 AW	95200 TQ	IABLS	10/01-12/01
	Kansas	Y	28550 FQ	51260 AW	84840 TQ	KSBLS	10/01-12/01
	Topeka MSA, KS	Y	30410 FQ	45800 AW	71220 TQ	KSBLS	10/01-12/01
	Wichita MSA, KS	Y	27910 FQ	55000 AW	90650 TQ	KSBLS	10/01-12/01
	Kentucky	Y	23940 FQ	47010 AW	78430 TQ	KYBLS	10/01-12/01
	Lexington MSA, KY	Y	21130 FQ	44280 AW	77110 TQ	KYBLS	10/01-12/01
	Louisville MSA, KY-IN	Y	25570 FQ	47870 AW	78290 TQ	KYBLS	10/01-12/01
	Louisiana	Y	21330 FQ	42490 AW	74250 TQ	LABLS	10/01-12/01
	Baton Rouge MSA, LA	Y	26240 FQ	44200 AW	60210 TQ	LABLS	10/01-12/01
	Houma MSA, LA	Y	20950 FQ	50970 AW	94110 TQ	LABLS	10/01-12/01
	Lafayette MSA, LA	Y	19830 FQ	41700 AW	70640 TQ	LABLS	10/01-12/01
	Lake Charles MSA, LA	Y	20080 FQ	43190 AW	74430 TQ	LABLS	10/01-12/01
	New Orleans MSA, LA	Y	23910 FQ	46450 AW	81900 TQ	LABLS	10/01-12/01
	Shreveport-Bossier City MSA, LA	Y	20860 FQ	41090 AW	70100 TQ	LABLS	10/01-12/01
	Maine	Y	23220 FQ	44070 AW	70180 TQ	MEBLS	10/01-12/01
	Portland MSA, ME	Y	27620 FQ	46970 AW	70400 TQ	MEBLS	10/01-12/01
	Maryland	Y	28640 FQ	47780 AW	80620 TQ	MDBLS	10/01-12/01
	Baltimore PMSA, MD	Y	28530 FQ	42180 AW	67940 TQ	MDBLS	10/01-12/01
	Massachusetts	Y	31780 FQ	59940 AW	95280 TQ	MABLS	10/01-12/01
	Boston PMSA, MA-NH	Y	35370 FQ	63000 AW	102670 TQ	MABLS	10/01-12/01

AAW	Average annual wage	**AOH**	Average offered, high	**ASH**	Average starting, high	**H**	Hourly	**M**	Monthly	**S**	Special: hourly and annual
AE	Average entry wage	**AOL**	Average offered, low	**ASL**	Average starting, low	**HI**	Highest wage paid	**MTC**	Median total compensation	**TQ**	Third quartile wage
AEX	Average experienced wage	**APH**	Average pay, high range	**AW**	Average wage paid	**HR**	High end range	**MW**	Median wage paid	**W**	Weekly
AO	Average offered	**APL**	Average pay, low range	**FQ**	First quartile wage	**LR**	Low end range	**SQ**	Second quartile wage	**Y**	Yearly

Occupation/Type/Industry	Location	Per	Low	Mid	High	Source	Date
Administrative Services Manager	Brockton PMSA, MA	Y	34110 FQ	58630 AW	90550 TQ	MABLS	10/01-12/01
	Lawrence PMSA, MA-NH	Y	30010 FQ	56580 AW	91130 TQ	MABLS	10/01-12/01
	Lowell PMSA, MA-NH	Y	29180 FQ	67160 AW	116720 TQ	MABLS	10/01-12/01
	New Bedford PMSA, MA	Y	25720 FQ	46690 AW	71040 TQ	MABLS	10/01-12/01
	Springfield MSA, MA	Y	25740 FQ	50410 AW	79770 TQ	MABLS	10/01-12/01
	Worcester PMSA, MA-CT	Y	29640 FQ	55890 AW	85400 TQ	MABLS	10/01-12/01
	Michigan	Y	31860 FQ	64730 AW	107310 TQ	MIBLS	10/01-12/01
	Ann Arbor PMSA, MI	Y	26800 FQ	64160 AW	105750 TQ	MIBLS	10/01-12/01
	Detroit PMSA, MI	Y	38740 FQ	69270 AW	113200 TQ	MIBLS	10/01-12/01
	Flint PMSA, MI	Y	22670 FQ	51710 AW	86400 TQ	MIBLS	10/01-12/01
	Grand Rapids-Muskegon-Holland MSA, MI	Y	37790 FQ	69090 AW	111840 TQ	MIBLS	10/01-12/01
	Kalamazoo-Battle Creek MSA, MI	Y	29100 FQ	56360 AW	82820 TQ	MIBLS	10/01-12/01
	Lansing-East Lansing MSA, MI	Y	26910 FQ	55160 AW	96720 TQ	MIBLS	10/01-12/01
	Saginaw-Bay City-Midland MSA, MI	Y	24440 FQ	60550 AW	105450 TQ	MIBLS	10/01-12/01
	Minnesota	Y	38590 FQ	65350 AW	96380 TQ	MNBLS	10/01-12/01
	Duluth-Superior MSA, MN-WI	Y	29630 FQ	55480 AW	83640 TQ	MNBLS	10/01-12/01
	Minneapolis-St. Paul MSA, MN-WI	Y	39840 FQ	66700 AW	98050 TQ	MNBLS	10/01-12/01
	St. Cloud MSA, MN	Y	32380 FQ	60260 AW	93350 TQ	MNBLS	10/01-12/01
	Mississippi	Y	20350 FQ	40550 AW	68570 TQ	MSBLS	10/01-12/01
	Biloxi-Gulfport-Pascagoula MSA, MS	Y	20920 FQ	39220 AW	64130 TQ	MSBLS	10/01-12/01
	Jackson MSA, MS	Y	19590 FQ	43290 AW	74790 TQ	MSBLS	10/01-12/01
	Missouri	Y	20360 FQ	46800 AW	79380 TQ	MOBLS	10/01-12/01
	Kansas City MSA, MO-KS	Y	25490 FQ	53210 AW	88440 TQ	MOBLS	10/01-12/01
	St. Louis MSA, MO-IL	Y	20970 FQ	48410 AW	82820 TQ	MOBLS	10/01-12/01
	Springfield MSA, MO	Y	20630 FQ	43930 AW	73710 TQ	MOBLS	10/01-12/01
	Montana	Y	17980 FQ	35110 AW	58670 TQ	MTBLS	10/01-12/01
	Billings MSA, MT	Y	14060 FQ	29700 AW	49310 TQ	MTBLS	10/01-12/01
	Nebraska	Y	25370 FQ	52440 AW	88560 TQ	NEBLS	10/01-12/01
	Lincoln MSA, NE	Y	30690 FQ	53840 AW	86580 TQ	NEBLS	10/01-12/01
	Omaha MSA, NE-IA	Y	25810 FQ	54220 AW	87920 TQ	NEBLS	10/01-12/01
	Nevada	Y	29820 FQ	56200 AW	91150 TQ	NVBLS	10/01-12/01
	Las Vegas MSA, NV-AZ	Y	29440 FQ	55720 AW	91550 TQ	NVBLS	10/01-12/01
	Reno MSA, NV	Y	28030 FQ	52880 AW	89640 TQ	NVBLS	10/01-12/01
	New Hampshire	Y	24090 FQ	48760 AW	83670 TQ	NHBLS	10/01-12/01
	Manchester PMSA, NH	Y	21220 FQ	43660 AW	72400 TQ	NHBLS	10/01-12/01
	Nashua PMSA, NH	Y	27230 FQ	50970 AW	89220 TQ	NHBLS	10/01-12/01
	Portsmouth-Rochester PMSA, NH-ME	Y	23570 FQ	51290 AW	84860 TQ	NHBLS	10/01-12/01
	New Jersey	Y	45990 FQ	79660 AW	127900 TQ	NJBLS	10/01-12/01
	Atlantic-Cape May PMSA, NJ	Y	44310 FQ	72520 AW	109230 TQ	NJBLS	10/01-12/01
	Bergen-Passaic PMSA, NJ	Y	38280 FQ	79370 AW	140560 TQ	NJBLS	10/01-12/01
	Jersey City PMSA, NJ	Y	52490 FQ	89520 AW	143940 TQ	NJBLS	10/01-12/01
	Middlesex-Somerset-Hunterdon PMSA, NJ	Y	49940 FQ	81400 AW	123470 TQ	NJBLS	10/01-12/01
	Monmouth-Ocean PMSA, NJ	Y	36350 FQ	71890 AW	117390 TQ	NJBLS	10/01-12/01
	Newark PMSA, NJ	Y	47890 FQ	81640 AW	130710 TQ	NJBLS	10/01-12/01
	Trenton PMSA, NJ	Y	50580 FQ	76510 AW	106560 TQ	NJBLS	10/01-12/01
	New Mexico	Y	22580 FQ	47150 AW	77910 TQ	NMBLS	10/01-12/01
	Albuquerque MSA, NM	Y	25690 FQ	53030 AW	90620 TQ	NMBLS	10/01-12/01
	Las Cruces MSA, NM	Y	21020 FQ	42940 AW	70030 TQ	NMBLS	10/01-12/01
	New York	Y	38680 FQ	82540 AW		NYBLS	10/01-12/01
	Albany-Schenectady-Troy MSA, NY	Y	32920 FQ	70470 AW	117460 TQ	NYBLS	10/01-12/01
	Binghamton MSA, NY	Y	36450 FQ	65570 AW	104330 TQ	NYBLS	10/01-12/01
	Buffalo-Niagara Falls MSA, NY	Y	35960 FQ	60220 AW	103660 TQ	NYBLS	10/01-12/01
	Dutchess County PMSA, NY	Y	36220 FQ	73090 AW	131310 TQ	NYBLS	10/01-12/01
	Nassau-Suffolk PMSA, NY	Y	32400 FQ	80590 AW		NYBLS	10/01-12/01
	New York PMSA, NY	Y	44750 FQ	90470 AW		NYBLS	10/01-12/01
	Newburgh PMSA, NY-PA	Y	33960 FQ	68510 AW	122220 TQ	NYBLS	10/01-12/01
	Rochester MSA, NY	Y	33590 FQ	69350 AW	126770 TQ	NYBLS	10/01-12/01
	Syracuse MSA, NY	Y	34790 FQ	69970 AW	124700 TQ	NYBLS	10/01-12/01
	Utica-Rome MSA, NY	Y	36000 FQ	70070 AW	111400 TQ	NYBLS	10/01-12/01
	North Carolina	Y	23660 FQ	51240 AW	91020 TQ	NCBLS	10/01-12/01
	Asheville MSA, NC	Y	23950 FQ	43620 AW	69890 TQ	NCBLS	10/01-12/01
	Charlotte-Gastonia-Rock Hill MSA, NC-SC	Y	26330 FQ	62630 AW		NCBLS	10/01-12/01

AAW	Average annual wage	AOH	Average offered, high	ASH	Average starting, high	H	Hourly	M	Monthly	S	Special: hourly and annual
AE	Average entry wage	AOL	Average offered, low	ASL	Average starting, low	HI	Highest wage paid	MTC	Median total compensation	TQ	Third quartile wage
AEX	Average experienced wage	APH	Average pay, high range	AW	Average wage paid	HR	High end range	MW	Median wage paid	W	Weekly
AO	Average offered	APL	Average pay, low range	FQ	First quartile wage	LR	Low end range	SQ	Second quartile wage	Y	Yearly

Occupation/Type/Industry	Location	Per	Low	Mid	High	Source	Date
Administrative Services Manager	Fayetteville MSA, NC	Y	22350 FQ	41170 AW	66230 TQ	NCBLS	10/01-12/01
	Greensboro-Winston-Salem-High Point MSA, NC	Y	24720 FQ	51710 AW	87920 TQ	NCBLS	10/01-12/01
	Hickory-Morganton-Lenoir MSA, NC	Y	24290 FQ	50120 AW	91380 TQ	NCBLS	10/01-12/01
	Raleigh-Durham-Chapel Hill MSA, NC	Y	25300 FQ	53070 AW	89470 TQ	NCBLS	10/01-12/01
	Wilmington MSA, NC	Y	22160 FQ	47930 AW	78280 TQ	NCBLS	10/01-12/01
	North Dakota	Y	20690 FQ	38560 AW	63320 TQ	NDBLS	10/01-12/01
	Fargo-Moorhead MSA, ND-MN	Y	21200 FQ	41850 AW	68130 TQ	NDBLS	10/01-12/01
	Ohio	Y	24090 FQ	50410 AW	84700 TQ	OHBLS	10/01-12/01
	Akron PMSA, OH	Y	27860 FQ	54520 AW	86610 TQ	OHBLS	10/01-12/01
	Canton-Massillon MSA, OH	Y	19630 FQ	45720 AW	84380 TQ	OHBLS	10/01-12/01
	Cincinnati PMSA, OH-KY-IN	Y	24120 FQ	50500 AW	86350 TQ	OHBLS	10/01-12/01
	Cleveland-Lorain-Elyria PMSA, OH	Y	27150 FQ	52170 AW	85420 TQ	OHBLS	10/01-12/01
	Columbus MSA, OH	Y	26850 FQ	53840 AW	87280 TQ	OHBLS	10/01-12/01
	Dayton-Springfield MSA, OH	Y	27020 FQ	51940 AW	87490 TQ	OHBLS	10/01-12/01
	Hamilton-Middletown PMSA, OH	Y	23000 FQ	45500 AW	78220 TQ	OHBLS	10/01-12/01
	Mansfield MSA, OH	Y	22500 FQ	45500 AW	80730 TQ	OHBLS	10/01-12/01
	Toledo MSA, OH	Y	16430 FQ	47590 AW	85300 TQ	OHBLS	10/01-12/01
	Youngstown-Warren MSA, OH	Y	21160 FQ	49820 AW	83580 TQ	OHBLS	10/01-12/01
	Oklahoma	Y	18990 FQ	39740 AW	68560 TQ	OKBLS	10/01-12/01
	Oklahoma City MSA, OK	Y	19540 FQ	40440 AW	69010 TQ	OKBLS	10/01-12/01
	Tulsa MSA, OK	Y	19400 FQ	41920 AW	74760 TQ	OKBLS	10/01-12/01
	Oregon	Y	34640 FQ	59960 AW	90440 TQ	ORBLS	10/01-12/01
	Eugene-Springfield MSA, OR	Y	31150 FQ	50800 AW	79060 TQ	ORBLS	10/01-12/01
	Medford-Ashland MSA, OR	Y	28490 FQ	53210 AW	82560 TQ	ORBLS	10/01-12/01
	Portland-Vancouver PMSA, OR-WA	Y	40070 FQ	64950 AW	96360 TQ	ORBLS	10/01-12/01
	Salem PMSA, OR	Y	33220 FQ	52540 AW	77840 TQ	ORBLS	10/01-12/01
	Pennsylvania	Y	22570 FQ	52290 AW	92830 TQ	PABLS	10/01-12/01
	Allentown-Bethlehem-Easton MSA, PA	Y	23490 FQ	48480 AW	81610 TQ	PABLS	10/01-12/01
	Erie MSA, PA	Y	14550 FQ	32670 AW	63590 TQ	PABLS	10/01-12/01
	Harrisburg-Lebanon-Carlisle MSA, PA	Y	15370 FQ	49520 AW	86610 TQ	PABLS	10/01-12/01
	Johnstown MSA, PA	Y	22040 FQ	48030 AW	82150 TQ	PABLS	10/01-12/01
	Lancaster MSA, PA	Y	22910 FQ	47270 AW	79950 TQ	PABLS	10/01-12/01
	Philadelphia PMSA, PA-NJ	Y	27940 FQ	59200 AW	100200 TQ	PABLS	10/01-12/01
	Pittsburgh MSA, PA	Y	22870 FQ	55150 AW	126040 TQ	PABLS	10/01-12/01
	Reading MSA, PA	Y	24190 FQ	50460 AW	83380 TQ	PABLS	10/01-12/01
	Scranton-Wilkes-Barre-Hazleton MSA, PA	Y	25760 FQ	51670 AW	84220 TQ	PABLS	10/01-12/01
	York MSA, PA	Y	22300 FQ	40670 AW	70510 TQ	PABLS	10/01-12/01
	Rhode Island	Y	41240 FQ	74330 AW	116720 TQ	RIBLS	10/01-12/01
	Providence-Fall River-Warwick MSA, RI-MA	Y	32370 FQ	66250 AW	109230 TQ	RIBLS	10/01-12/01
	South Carolina	Y	22530 FQ	43760 AW	83690 TQ	SCBLS	10/01-12/01
	Charleston-North Charleston MSA, SC	Y	20630 FQ	35320 AW	58070 TQ	SCBLS	10/01-12/01
	Columbia MSA, SC	Y	23900 FQ	43910 AW	73560 TQ	SCBLS	10/01-12/01
	Greenville-Spartanburg-Anderson MSA, SC	Y	23500 FQ	41300 AW	71080 TQ	SCBLS	10/01-12/01
	Myrtle Beach MSA, SC	Y	19940 FQ	31460 AW	44860 TQ	SCBLS	10/01-12/01
	South Dakota	Y	42360 FQ	60690 AW	85680 TQ	SDBLS	10/01-12/01
	Sioux Falls MSA, SD	Y	45860 FQ	64230 AW	88990 TQ	SDBLS	10/01-12/01
	Tennessee	Y	20490 FQ	42390 AW	68890 TQ	TNBLS	10/01-12/01
	Chattanooga MSA, TN-GA	Y	21530 FQ	40890 AW	66880 TQ	TNBLS	10/01-12/01
	Clarksville-Hopkinsville MSA, TN-KY	Y	19330 FQ	43010 AW	70020 TQ	TNBLS	10/01-12/01
	Johnson City-Kingsport-Bristol MSA, TN-VA	Y	19440 FQ	35400 AW	60530 TQ	TNBLS	10/01-12/01
	Knoxville MSA, TN	Y	19070 FQ	40060 AW	64760 TQ	TNBLS	10/01-12/01
	Memphis MSA, TN-AR-MS	Y	22220 FQ	45330 AW	74650 TQ	TNBLS	10/01-12/01
	Nashville MSA, TN	Y	23180 FQ	45500 AW	69580 TQ	TNBLS	10/01-12/01
	Texas	Y	22630 FQ	51830 AW	89720 TQ	TXBLS	10/01-12/01
	Amarillo MSA, TX	Y	20820 FQ	52810 AW	100750 TQ	TXBLS	10/01-12/01
	Austin-San Marcos MSA, TX	Y	29140 FQ	59460 AW	90110 TQ	TXBLS	10/01-12/01

AAW	Average annual wage	**AOH**	Average offered, high	**ASH**	Average starting, high	**H**	Hourly	**M**	Monthly	**S**	Special: hourly and annual
AE	Average entry wage	**AOL**	Average offered, low	**ASL**	Average starting, low	**HI**	Highest wage paid	**MTC**	Median total compensation	**TQ**	Third quartile wage
AEX	Average experienced wage	**APH**	Average pay, high range	**AW**	Average wage paid	**HR**	High end range	**MW**	Median wage paid	**W**	Weekly
AO	Average offered	**APL**	Average pay, low range	**FQ**	First quartile wage	**LR**	Low end range	**SQ**	Second quartile wage	**Y**	Yearly

Occupation/Type/Industry	Location	Per	Low	Mid	High	Source	Date
Administrative Services Manager	Beaumont-Port Arthur MSA, TX	Y	23660 FQ	55320 AW	91880 TQ	TXBLS	10/01-12/01
	Brazoria PMSA, TX	Y	25670 FQ	54050 AW	84060 TQ	TXBLS	10/01-12/01
	Brownsville-Harlingen-San Benito MSA, TX	Y	16250 FQ	40480 AW	68640 TQ	TXBLS	10/01-12/01
	Corpus Christi MSA, TX	Y	21100 FQ	42620 AW	71200 TQ	TXBLS	10/01-12/01
	Dallas PMSA, TX	Y	24880 FQ	55140 AW	95980 TQ	TXBLS	10/01-12/01
	El Paso MSA, TX	Y	22340 FQ	43710 AW	72590 TQ	TXBLS	10/01-12/01
	Fort Worth-Arlington PMSA, TX	Y	19840 FQ	50110 AW	89920 TQ	TXBLS	10/01-12/01
	Houston PMSA, TX	Y	24300 FQ	52430 AW	91540 TQ	TXBLS	10/01-12/01
	Killeen-Temple MSA, TX	Y	19690 FQ	43550 AW	72730 TQ	TXBLS	10/01-12/01
	Laredo MSA, TX	Y	17970 FQ	42460 AW	79790 TQ	TXBLS	10/01-12/01
	Longview-Marshall MSA, TX	Y	21980 FQ	43190 AW	71510 TQ	TXBLS	10/01-12/01
	Lubbock MSA, TX	Y	19560 FQ	44510 AW	74960 TQ	TXBLS	10/01-12/01
	McAllen-Edinburg-Mission MSA, TX	Y	16930 FQ	45250 AW	81150 TQ	TXBLS	10/01-12/01
	Odessa-Midland MSA, TX	Y	15790 FQ	40010 AW	72830 TQ	TXBLS	10/01-12/01
	San Antonio MSA, TX	Y	22390 FQ	53360 AW	92950 TQ	TXBLS	10/01-12/01
	Tyler MSA, TX	Y	15200 FQ	41100 AW	77130 TQ	TXBLS	10/01-12/01
	Waco MSA, TX	Y	18260 FQ	44430 AW	81170 TQ	TXBLS	10/01-12/01
	Utah	Y	21870 FQ	47310 AW	79870 TQ	UTBLS	10/01-12/01
	Provo-Orem MSA, UT	Y	19650 FQ	39240 AW	61950 TQ	UTBLS	10/01-12/01
	Salt Lake City-Ogden MSA, UT	Y	24700 FQ	48530 AW	76550 TQ	UTBLS	10/01-12/01
	Vermont	Y	26790 FQ	60420 AW	96250 TQ	VTBLS	10/01-12/01
	Burlington MSA, VT	Y	28820 FQ	63790 AW	99010 TQ	VTBLS	10/01-12/01
	Virginia	Y	27450 FQ	55190 AW	93060 TQ	VABLS	10/01-12/01
	Lynchburg MSA, VA	Y	24680 FQ	50430 AW	87730 TQ	VABLS	10/01-12/01
	Norfolk-Virginia Beach-Newport News MSA, VA-NC	Y	24900 FQ	49330 AW	83480 TQ	VABLS	10/01-12/01
	Richmond-Petersburg MSA, VA	Y	26910 FQ	58460 AW	96190 TQ	VABLS	10/01-12/01
	Roanoke MSA, VA	Y	26950 FQ	52560 AW	92020 TQ	VABLS	10/01-12/01
	Washington	Y	40300 FQ	68510 AW	104980 TQ	WABLS	10/01-12/01
	Bremerton PMSA, WA	Y	31190 FQ	60570 AW	90070 TQ	WABLS	10/01-12/01
	Olympia PMSA, WA	Y	39360 FQ	66490 AW	95530 TQ	WABLS	10/01-12/01
	Richland-Kennewick-Pasco MSA, WA	Y	48790 FQ	72630 AW	102270 TQ	WABLS	10/01-12/01
	Seattle-Bellevue-Everett PMSA, WA	Y	41590 FQ	71350 AW	109520 TQ	WABLS	10/01-12/01
	Spokane MSA, WA	Y	38450 FQ	60730 AW	87950 TQ	WABLS	10/01-12/01
	Tacoma PMSA, WA	Y	39230 FQ	68050 AW	97960 TQ	WABLS	10/01-12/01
	Yakima MSA, WA	Y	37510 FQ	67280 AW	101830 TQ	WABLS	10/01-12/01
	West Virginia	Y	21800 FQ	42930 AW	69200 TQ	WVBLS	10/01-12/01
	Charleston MSA, WV	Y	24310 FQ	45360 AW	70840 TQ	WVBLS	10/01-12/01
	Huntington-Ashland MSA, WV-KY-OH	Y	22510 FQ	42250 AW	69200 TQ	WVBLS	10/01-12/01
	Wisconsin	Y	24070 FQ	54120 AW	92010 TQ	WIBLS	10/01-12/01
	Appleton-Oshkosh-Neenah MSA, WI	Y	23400 FQ	61060 AW	121030 TQ	WIBLS	10/01-12/01
	Green Bay MSA, WI	Y	25120 FQ	52980 AW	87150 TQ	WIBLS	10/01-12/01
	Madison MSA, WI	Y	28450 FQ	59810 AW	95860 TQ	WIBLS	10/01-12/01
	Milwaukee-Waukesha PMSA, WI	Y	25460 FQ	55660 AW	94620 TQ	WIBLS	10/01-12/01
	Racine PMSA, WI	Y	21230 FQ	58870 AW	97090 TQ	WIBLS	10/01-12/01
	Wyoming	Y	18300 FQ	41790 AW	69000 TQ	WYBLS	10/01-12/01
	Cheyenne MSA, WY	Y	32420 FQ	52180 AW	69810 TQ	WYBLS	10/01-12/01
	Puerto Rico	Y	25440 FQ	47690 AW	80960 TQ	PRBLS	10/01-12/01
	Virgin Islands	Y	34050 FQ	50600 AW	70610 TQ	VIBLS	10/01-12/01
	Guam	Y	16510 FQ	39230 AW	58260 TQ	GUBLS	10/01-12/01
Administrator and Coordinator Family Planning	United States	Y		49230 AW	52778 MW	CTU	1/01-1/02
Adult Literacy, Remedial Education, and GED Teacher and Instructor	Alabama	Y	17060 FQ	29660 AW	45150 TQ	ALBLS	10/01-12/01
	Alaska	Y	26150 FQ	36650 AW	56180 TQ	AKBLS	10/01-12/01
	Arizona	Y	19020 FQ	30560 AW	47420 TQ	AZBLS	10/01-12/01
	Arkansas	Y	22990 FQ	39640 AW	61920 TQ	ARBLS	10/01-12/01

AAW	Average annual wage	AOH	Average offered, high	ASH	Average starting, high	H	Hourly	M	Monthly	S	Special: hourly and annual
AE	Average entry wage	AOL	Average offered, low	ASL	Average starting, low	HI	Highest wage paid	MTC	Median total compensation	TQ	Third quartile wage
AEX	Average experienced wage	APH	Average pay, high range	AW	Average wage paid	HR	High end range	MW	Median wage paid	W	Weekly
AO	Average offered	APL	Average pay, low range	FQ	First quartile wage	LR	Low end range	SQ	Second quartile wage	Y	Yearly

Occupation/Type/Industry	Location	Per	Low	Mid	High	Source	Date
Adult Literacy, Remedial Education, and GED Teacher and Instructor	California	Y	36460 FQ	69470 AW	106390 TQ	CABLS	10/01-12/01
	Colorado	Y	20050 FQ	29780 AW	45800 TQ	COBLS	10/01-12/01
	Connecticut	Y	29360 FQ	41820 AW	58050 TQ	CTBLS	10/01-12/01
	Delaware	Y	23930 FQ	38730 AW	55980 TQ	DEBLS	10/01-12/01
	District of Columbia	Y	23230 FQ	44960 AW	55990 TQ	DCBLS	10/01-12/01
	Florida	Y	18660 FQ	33600 AW	54320 TQ	FLBLS	10/01-12/01
	Georgia	Y	15190 FQ	31780 AW	53510 TQ	GABLS	10/01-12/01
	Hawaii	Y	29670 FQ	37530 AW	45160 TQ	HIBLS	10/01-12/01
	Illinois	Y	13670 FQ	31160 AW	49860 TQ	ILBLS	10/01-12/01
	Indiana	Y	19630 FQ	28960 AW	38480 TQ	INBLS	10/01-12/01
	Iowa	Y	18910 FQ	34440 AW	54290 TQ	IABLS	10/01-12/01
	Kansas	Y	23180 FQ	39410 AW	94660 TQ	KSBLS	10/01-12/01
	Kentucky	Y	15190 FQ	27750 AW	40240 TQ	KYBLS	10/01-12/01
	Louisiana	Y	13570 FQ	33260 AW	53980 TQ	LABLS	10/01-12/01
	Maine	Y	23850 FQ	35610 AW	50120 TQ	MEBLS	10/01-12/01
	Maryland	Y	23490 FQ	33050 AW	44290 TQ	MDBLS	10/01-12/01
	Massachusetts	Y	22000 FQ	36870 AW	54420 TQ	MABLS	10/01-12/01
	Michigan	Y	27820 FQ	44320 AW	64100 TQ	MIBLS	10/01-12/01
	Minnesota	Y	28460 FQ	40870 AW	57050 TQ	MNBLS	10/01-12/01
	Mississippi	Y	14740 FQ	31730 AW	46220 TQ	MSBLS	10/01-12/01
	Missouri	Y	21810 FQ	33420 AW	43700 TQ	MOBLS	10/01-12/01
	Montana	Y	16580 FQ	31300 AW	54020 TQ	MTBLS	10/01-12/01
	Nebraska	Y	20130 FQ	31700 AW	44730 TQ	NEBLS	10/01-12/01
	Nevada	Y	18800 FQ	32170 AW	47990 TQ	NVBLS	10/01-12/01
	New Hampshire	Y	22230 FQ	32960 AW	44610 TQ	NHBLS	10/01-12/01
	New Jersey	Y	22740 FQ	41540 AW	66270 TQ	NJBLS	10/01-12/01
	New Mexico	Y	20110 FQ	34410 AW	51890 TQ	NMBLS	10/01-12/01
	New York	Y	22490 FQ	40120 AW	71710 TQ	NYBLS	10/01-12/01
	North Carolina	Y	22670 FQ	31650 AW	41560 TQ	NCBLS	10/01-12/01
	North Dakota	Y	21510 FQ	27230 AW	33880 TQ	NDBLS	10/01-12/01
	Ohio	Y	18140 FQ	30950 AW	49430 TQ	OHBLS	10/01-12/01
	Oklahoma	Y	13880 FQ	31840 AW	47480 TQ	OKBLS	10/01-12/01
	Oregon	Y	20190 FQ	42480 AW	72900 TQ	ORBLS	10/01-12/01
	Pennsylvania	Y	19210 FQ	31380 AW	50760 TQ	PABLS	10/01-12/01
	Rhode Island	Y	25060 FQ	42520 AW	58450 TQ	RIBLS	10/01-12/01
	South Carolina	Y	18700 FQ	36490 AW	55070 TQ	SCBLS	10/01-12/01
	South Dakota	Y	16650 FQ	28910 AW	43770 TQ	SDBLS	10/01-12/01
	Tennessee	Y	17090 FQ	28610 AW	43700 TQ	TNBLS	10/01-12/01
	Texas	Y	18390 FQ	33950 AW	49700 TQ	TXBLS	10/01-12/01
	Utah	Y	15730 FQ	29800 AW	46720 TQ	UTBLS	10/01-12/01
	Vermont	Y	24680 FQ	32050 AW	40730 TQ	VTBLS	10/01-12/01
	Virginia	Y	18730 FQ	34710 AW	50220 TQ	VABLS	10/01-12/01
	Washington	Y	23680 FQ	34500 AW	46720 TQ	WABLS	10/01-12/01
	West Virginia	Y	17890 FQ	32720 AW	44770 TQ	WVBLS	10/01-12/01
	Wisconsin	Y	21750 FQ	39500 AW	61070 TQ	WIBLS	10/01-12/01
	Puerto Rico	Y	14620 FQ	22570 AW	30760 TQ	PRBLS	10/01-12/01
Advertising and Promotions Manager	Alabama	Y	22190 FQ	46240 AW	82010 TQ	ALBLS	10/01-12/01
	Birmingham MSA, AL	Y	27260 FQ	53280 AW	88380 TQ	ALBLS	10/01-12/01
	Huntsville MSA, AL	Y	26200 FQ	44860 AW	72110 TQ	ALBLS	10/01-12/01
	Mobile MSA, AL	Y	22520 FQ	46560 AW	86700 TQ	ALBLS	10/01-12/01
	Montgomery MSA, AL	Y	23760 FQ	46630 AW	91980 TQ	ALBLS	10/01-12/01
	Alaska	Y	26590 FQ	48240 AW	76410 TQ	AKBLS	10/01-12/01
	Anchorage MSA, AK	Y	25360 FQ	50240 AW	83670 TQ	AKBLS	10/01-12/01
	Arizona	Y	31070 FQ	58140 AW	89530 TQ	AZBLS	10/01-12/01
	Phoenix-Mesa MSA, AZ	Y	35990 FQ	60620 AW	90090 TQ	AZBLS	10/01-12/01
	Tucson MSA, AZ	Y	27430 FQ	52690 AW	86540 TQ	AZBLS	10/01-12/01
	Arkansas	Y	22850 FQ	50000 AW	87320 TQ	ARBLS	10/01-12/01
	Fayetteville-Springdale-Rogers MSA, AR	Y	17440 FQ	42860 AW	71450 TQ	ARBLS	10/01-12/01
	Little Rock-North Little Rock MSA, AR	Y	28130 FQ	58990 AW	104520 TQ	ARBLS	10/01-12/01
	California	Y	35350 FQ	76980 AW	142720 TQ	CABLS	10/01-12/01
	Bakersfield MSA, CA	Y	26340 FQ	53120 AW	91560 TQ	CABLS	10/01-12/01
	Chico-Paradise MSA, CA	Y	28870 FQ	49580 AW	76140 TQ	CABLS	10/01-12/01
	Fresno MSA, CA	Y	26220 FQ	55110 AW	95360 TQ	CABLS	10/01-12/01
	Los Angeles-Long Beach PMSA, CA	Y	36940 FQ	80610 AW		CABLS	10/01-12/01

AAW Average annual wage; AE Average entry wage; AEX Average experienced wage; AO Average offered; AOH Average offered, high; AOL Average offered, low; APH Average pay, high range; APL Average pay, low range; ASH Average starting, high; ASL Average starting, low; AW Average wage paid; FQ First quartile wage; H Hourly; HI Highest wage paid; HR High end range; LR Low end range; M Monthly; MTC Median total compensation; MW Median wage paid; SQ Second quartile wage; S Special: hourly and annual; TQ Third quartile wage; W Weekly; Y Yearly

Occupation/Type/Industry	Location	Per	Low	Mid	High	Source	Date
Advertising and Promotions Manager	Modesto MSA, CA	Y	25870 FQ	52090 AW	91020 TQ	CABLS	10/01-12/01
	Oakland PMSA, CA	Y	33970 FQ	73650 AW	142100 TQ	CABLS	10/01-12/01
	Orange County PMSA, CA	Y	37660 FQ	73180 AW	118390 TQ	CABLS	10/01-12/01
	Riverside-San Bernardino PMSA, CA	Y	32940 FQ	66930 AW	124290 TQ	CABLS	10/01-12/01
	Sacramento PMSA, CA	Y	28200 FQ	68090 AW	135360 TQ	CABLS	10/01-12/01
	Salinas MSA, CA	Y	33180 FQ	58670 AW	87390 TQ	CABLS	10/01-12/01
	San Diego MSA, CA	Y	29670 FQ	64860 AW	124750 TQ	CABLS	10/01-12/01
	San Francisco PMSA, CA	Y	38100 FQ	77520 AW	136500 TQ	CABLS	10/01-12/01
	San Jose PMSA, CA	Y	58880 FQ	105950 AW		CABLS	10/01-12/01
	San Luis Obispo-Atascadero-Paso Robles MSA, CA	Y	29220 FQ	55830 AW	105100 TQ	CABLS	10/01-12/01
	Santa Barbara-Santa Maria-Lompoc MSA, CA	Y	36760 FQ	71470 AW	122830 TQ	CABLS	10/01-12/01
	Santa Cruz-Watsonville PMSA, CA	Y	34640 FQ	83900 AW		CABLS	10/01-12/01
	Santa Rosa PMSA, CA	Y	32740 FQ	66490 AW	111700 TQ	CABLS	10/01-12/01
	Stockton-Lodi MSA, CA	Y	28730 FQ	61140 AW	124740 TQ	CABLS	10/01-12/01
	Vallejo-Fairfield-Napa PMSA, CA	Y	27740 FQ	62690 AW	128030 TQ	CABLS	10/01-12/01
	Ventura PMSA, CA	Y	31310 FQ	69540 AW	119230 TQ	CABLS	10/01-12/01
	Visalia-Tulare-Porterville MSA, CA	Y	30350 FQ	53290 AW	83730 TQ	CABLS	10/01-12/01
	Colorado	Y	30780 FQ	60510 AW	102680 TQ	COBLS	10/01-12/01
	Boulder-Longmont PMSA, CO	Y	35290 FQ	65680 AW	103650 TQ	COBLS	10/01-12/01
	Colorado Springs MSA, CO	Y	31530 FQ	53320 AW	90060 TQ	COBLS	10/01-12/01
	Denver PMSA, CO	Y	34130 FQ	64790 AW	112810 TQ	COBLS	10/01-12/01
	Fort Collins-Loveland MSA, CO	Y	25320 FQ	57090 AW	108930 TQ	COBLS	10/01-12/01
	Greeley PMSA, CO	Y	25270 FQ	47350 AW	83510 TQ	COBLS	10/01-12/01
	Connecticut	Y	37620 FQ	76430 AW	141070 TQ	CTBLS	10/01-12/01
	Bridgeport PMSA, CT	Y	29200 FQ	66930 AW	121780 TQ	CTBLS	10/01-12/01
	Danbury PMSA, CT	Y	38250 FQ	83200 AW		CTBLS	10/01-12/01
	Hartford MSA, CT	Y	35980 FQ	66480 AW	105990 TQ	CTBLS	10/01-12/01
	New Haven-Meriden PMSA, CT	Y	35680 FQ	73310 AW	121710 TQ	CTBLS	10/01-12/01
	New London-Norwich MSA, CT-RI	Y	37620 FQ	63910 AW	108560 TQ	CTBLS	10/01-12/01
	Stamford-Norwalk PMSA, CT	Y	43910 FQ	88290 AW		CTBLS	10/01-12/01
	Waterbury PMSA, CT	Y	46260 FQ	78260 AW	123400 TQ	CTBLS	10/01-12/01
	Delaware	Y	26200 FQ	68070 AW		DEBLS	10/01-12/01
	Wilmington-Newark PMSA, DE-MD	Y	26940 FQ	71370 AW		DEBLS	10/01-12/01
	District of Columbia	Y	35490 FQ	58550 AW	101750 TQ	DCBLS	10/01-12/01
	Washington PMSA, DC-MD-VA-WV	Y	33650 FQ	63740 AW	110350 TQ	DCBLS	10/01-12/01
	Florida	Y	28200 FQ	60920 AW	108140 TQ	FLBLS	10/01-12/01
	Daytona Beach MSA, FL	Y	22070 FQ	51930 AW	86080 TQ	FLBLS	10/01-12/01
	Fort Lauderdale PMSA, FL	Y	33270 FQ	65480 AW	108100 TQ	FLBLS	10/01-12/01
	Fort Myers-Cape Coral MSA, FL	Y	27050 FQ	53240 AW	85660 TQ	FLBLS	10/01-12/01
	Fort Pierce-Port St. Lucie MSA, FL	Y	33550 FQ	48470 AW	67100 TQ	FLBLS	10/01-12/01
	Fort Walton Beach MSA, FL	Y	31490 FQ	54090 AW	88720 TQ	FLBLS	10/01-12/01
	Gainesville MSA, FL	Y	25100 FQ	59190 AW	118670 TQ	FLBLS	10/01-12/01
	Jacksonville MSA, FL	Y	29380 FQ	69510 AW	133120 TQ	FLBLS	10/01-12/01
	Lakeland-Winter Haven MSA, FL	Y	24530 FQ	43420 AW	73470 TQ	FLBLS	10/01-12/01
	Melbourne-Titusville-Palm Bay MSA, FL	Y	28000 FQ	51700 AW	81850 TQ	FLBLS	10/01-12/01
	Miami PMSA, FL	Y	34960 FQ	68770 AW	110030 TQ	FLBLS	10/01-12/01
	Naples MSA, FL	Y	27830 FQ	68570 AW		FLBLS	10/01-12/01
	Orlando MSA, FL	Y	29540 FQ	59610 AW	101770 TQ	FLBLS	10/01-12/01
	Pensacola MSA, FL	Y	23500 FQ	49590 AW	85200 TQ	FLBLS	10/01-12/01
	Sarasota-Bradenton MSA, FL	Y	25080 FQ	55390 AW	88240 TQ	FLBLS	10/01-12/01
	Tallahassee MSA, FL	Y	36090 FQ	67520 AW	111520 TQ	FLBLS	10/01-12/01
	Tampa-St. Petersburg-Clearwater MSA, FL	Y	24200 FQ	57240 AW	106510 TQ	FLBLS	10/01-12/01
	West Palm Beach-Boca Raton MSA, FL	Y	30790 FQ	66430 AW	113410 TQ	FLBLS	10/01-12/01
	Georgia	Y	33080 FQ	65990 AW	126890 TQ	GABLS	10/01-12/01

AAW	Average annual wage	AOH	Average offered, high	ASH	Average starting, high	H	Hourly	M	Monthly	S	Special: hourly and annual
AE	Average entry wage	AOL	Average offered, low	ASL	Average starting, low	HI	Highest wage paid	MTC	Median total compensation	TQ	Third quartile wage
AEX	Average experienced wage	APH	Average pay, high range	AW	Average wage paid	HR	High end range	MW	Median wage paid	W	Weekly
AO	Average offered	APL	Average pay, low range	FQ	First quartile wage	LR	Low end range	SQ	Second quartile wage	Y	Yearly

Occupation/Type/Industry	Location	Per	Low	Mid	High	Source	Date
Advertising and Promotions Manager	Atlanta MSA, GA	Y	34870 FQ	71280 AW	132800 TQ	GABLS	10/01-12/01
	Augusta-Aiken MSA, GA-SC	Y	30190 FQ	49790 AW	82410 TQ	GABLS	10/01-12/01
	Columbus MSA, GA-AL	Y	30200 FQ	48940 AW	71950 TQ	GABLS	10/01-12/01
	Macon MSA, GA	Y	34030 FQ	54070 AW	73140 TQ	GABLS	10/01-12/01
	Savannah MSA, GA	Y	28440 FQ	43080 AW	63430 TQ	GABLS	10/01-12/01
	Hawaii	Y	31470 FQ	65820 AW	136690 TQ	HIBLS	10/01-12/01
	Honolulu MSA, HI	Y	31470 FQ	67150 AW	144830 TQ	HIBLS	10/01-12/01
	Idaho	Y	24640 FQ	43310 AW	64660 TQ	IDBLS	10/01-12/01
	Boise City MSA, ID	Y	25760 FQ	43490 AW	58690 TQ	IDBLS	10/01-12/01
	Illinois	Y	29580 FQ	63760 AW	115330 TQ	ILBLS	10/01-12/01
	Champaign-Urbana MSA, IL	Y	22450 FQ	50450 AW	81490 TQ	ILBLS	10/01-12/01
	Chicago PMSA, IL	Y	31270 FQ	68130 AW	121860 TQ	ILBLS	10/01-12/01
	Peoria-Pekin MSA, IL	Y	24410 FQ	47080 AW	75770 TQ	ILBLS	10/01-12/01
	Rockford MSA, IL	Y	21450 FQ	46650 AW	84600 TQ	ILBLS	10/01-12/01
	Springfield MSA, IL	Y	23630 FQ	43770 AW	72340 TQ	ILBLS	10/01-12/01
	Indiana	Y	27710 FQ	52270 AW	90260 TQ	INBLS	10/01-12/01
	Elkhart-Goshen MSA, IN	Y	29950 FQ	56920 AW	92410 TQ	INBLS	10/01-12/01
	Evansville-Henderson MSA, IN-KY	Y	24350 FQ	47010 AW	76220 TQ	INBLS	10/01-12/01
	Fort Wayne MSA, IN	Y	26720 FQ	49570 AW	90070 TQ	INBLS	10/01-12/01
	Gary PMSA, IN	Y	26470 FQ	39900 AW	60880 TQ	INBLS	10/01-12/01
	Indianapolis MSA, IN	Y	30490 FQ	58390 AW	103630 TQ	INBLS	10/01-12/01
	South Bend MSA, IN	Y	25810 FQ	52380 AW	86870 TQ	INBLS	10/01-12/01
	Iowa	Y	23840 FQ	47070 AW	78550 TQ	IABLS	10/01-12/01
	Cedar Rapids MSA, IA	Y	21580 FQ	49800 AW	82450 TQ	IABLS	10/01-12/01
	Davenport-Moline-Rock Island MSA, IA-IL	Y	21660 FQ	44480 AW	75880 TQ	IABLS	10/01-12/01
	Des Moines MSA, IA	Y	29200 FQ	47970 AW	83920 TQ	IABLS	10/01-12/01
	Kansas	Y	30420 FQ	54680 AW	86490 TQ	KSBLS	10/01-12/01
	Topeka MSA, KS	Y	33790 FQ	67010 AW	118240 TQ	KSBLS	10/01-12/01
	Wichita MSA, KS	Y	30090 FQ	51090 AW	88060 TQ	KSBLS	10/01-12/01
	Kentucky	Y	25530 FQ	49760 AW	89190 TQ	KYBLS	10/01-12/01
	Lexington MSA, KY	Y	25570 FQ	49010 AW	94800 TQ	KYBLS	10/01-12/01
	Louisville MSA, KY-IN	Y	27380 FQ	49450 AW	82540 TQ	KYBLS	10/01-12/01
	Louisiana	Y	24610 FQ	53090 AW	108640 TQ	LABLS	10/01-12/01
	Baton Rouge MSA, LA	Y	22860 FQ	52530 AW	96920 TQ	LABLS	10/01-12/01
	Lafayette MSA, LA	Y	26320 FQ	48660 AW	69240 TQ	LABLS	10/01-12/01
	Lake Charles MSA, LA	Y	21070 FQ	39600 AW	68440 TQ	LABLS	10/01-12/01
	New Orleans MSA, LA	Y	28730 FQ	56360 AW		LABLS	10/01-12/01
	Shreveport-Bossier City MSA, LA	Y	22850 FQ	45850 AW	70770 TQ	LABLS	10/01-12/01
	Maine	Y	27070 FQ	52040 AW	97690 TQ	MEBLS	10/01-12/01
	Portland MSA, ME	Y	29120 FQ	63810 AW	126750 TQ	MEBLS	10/01-12/01
	Maryland	Y	29470 FQ	60910 AW	114020 TQ	MDBLS	10/01-12/01
	Baltimore PMSA, MD	Y	27910 FQ	60440 AW	113090 TQ	MDBLS	10/01-12/01
	Massachusetts	Y	32940 FQ	67340 AW	122240 TQ	MABLS	10/01-12/01
	Boston PMSA, MA-NH	Y	35720 FQ	69970 AW	124840 TQ	MABLS	10/01-12/01
	Brockton PMSA, MA	Y	25960 FQ	63780 AW		MABLS	10/01-12/01
	Lawrence PMSA, MA-NH	Y	36270 FQ	67450 AW	105320 TQ	MABLS	10/01-12/01
	Lowell PMSA, MA-NH	Y	38060 FQ	79690 AW	140710 TQ	MABLS	10/01-12/01
	New Bedford PMSA, MA	Y	24550 FQ	44500 AW	69500 TQ	MABLS	10/01-12/01
	Springfield MSA, MA	Y	22890 FQ	58690 AW	122940 TQ	MABLS	10/01-12/01
	Worcester PMSA, MA-CT	Y	33880 FQ	56140 AW	90490 TQ	MABLS	10/01-12/01
	Michigan	Y	32180 FQ	73950 AW		MIBLS	10/01-12/01
	Ann Arbor PMSA, MI	Y	28030 FQ	53890 AW	90040 TQ	MIBLS	10/01-12/01
	Detroit PMSA, MI	Y	33450 FQ	83790 AW		MIBLS	10/01-12/01
	Flint PMSA, MI	Y	26630 FQ	52970 AW	85870 TQ	MIBLS	10/01-12/01
	Grand Rapids-Muskegon-Holland MSA, MI	Y	35330 FQ	68280 AW	120700 TQ	MIBLS	10/01-12/01
	Kalamazoo-Battle Creek MSA, MI	Y	31500 FQ	68480 AW	131580 TQ	MIBLS	10/01-12/01
	Lansing-East Lansing MSA, MI	Y	37290 FQ	58610 AW	95270 TQ	MIBLS	10/01-12/01
	Saginaw-Bay City-Midland MSA, MI	Y	39000 FQ	75590 AW	140310 TQ	MIBLS	10/01-12/01
	Minnesota	Y	39080 FQ	76700 AW	140130 TQ	MNBLS	10/01-12/01
	Duluth-Superior MSA, MN-WI	Y	35050 FQ	52660 AW	80900 TQ	MNBLS	10/01-12/01
	Minneapolis-St. Paul MSA, MN-WI	Y	40100 FQ	79290 AW	143120 TQ	MNBLS	10/01-12/01
	Mississippi	Y	22550 FQ	45820 AW	77750 TQ	MSBLS	10/01-12/01
	Biloxi-Gulfport-Pascagoula MSA, MS	Y	21060 FQ	48250 AW	85670 TQ	MSBLS	10/01-12/01

AAW	Average annual wage	**AOH**	Average offered, high	**ASH**	Average starting, high	**H**	Hourly	**M**	Monthly	**S**	Special: hourly and annual
AE	Average entry wage	**AOL**	Average offered, low	**ASL**	Average starting, low	**HI**	Highest wage paid	**MTC**	Median total compensation	**TQ**	Third quartile wage
AEX	Average experienced wage	**APH**	Average pay, high range	**AW**	Average wage paid	**HR**	High end range	**MW**	Median wage paid	**W**	Weekly
AO	Average offered	**APL**	Average pay, low range	**FQ**	First quartile wage	**LR**	Low end range	**SQ**	Second quartile wage	**Y**	Yearly

Occupation/Type/Industry	Location	Per	Low	Mid	High	Source	Date
Advertising and Promotions Manager	Jackson MSA, MS	Y	28810 FQ	46490 AW	73400 TQ	MSBLS	10/01-12/01
	Missouri	Y	27270 FQ	54220 AW	92750 TQ	MOBLS	10/01-12/01
	Kansas City MSA, MO-KS	Y	30130 FQ	56610 AW	91450 TQ	MOBLS	10/01-12/01
	St. Louis MSA, MO-IL	Y	29700 FQ	57100 AW	96160 TQ	MOBLS	10/01-12/01
	Springfield MSA, MO	Y	22040 FQ	43260 AW	68590 TQ	MOBLS	10/01-12/01
	Montana	Y	21630 FQ	41360 AW	70260 TQ	MTBLS	10/01-12/01
	Billings MSA, MT	Y	21430 FQ	34280 AW	55880 TQ	MTBLS	10/01-12/01
	Nebraska	Y	24700 FQ	48850 AW	80420 TQ	NEBLS	10/01-12/01
	Lincoln MSA, NE	Y	25120 FQ	42650 AW	65880 TQ	NEBLS	10/01-12/01
	Omaha MSA, NE-IA	Y	25520 FQ	53310 AW	88520 TQ	NEBLS	10/01-12/01
	Nevada	Y	31930 FQ	57650 AW	94970 TQ	NVBLS	10/01-12/01
	Las Vegas MSA, NV-AZ	Y	31090 FQ	56610 AW	92390 TQ	NVBLS	10/01-12/01
	Reno MSA, NV	Y	30890 FQ	60530 AW	116200 TQ	NVBLS	10/01-12/01
	New Hampshire	Y	25790 FQ	52330 AW	94830 TQ	NHBLS	10/01-12/01
	Manchester PMSA, NH	Y	26450 FQ	59000 AW	107090 TQ	NHBLS	10/01-12/01
	Nashua PMSA, NH	Y	31190 FQ	59600 AW	103940 TQ	NHBLS	10/01-12/01
	Portsmouth-Rochester PMSA, NH-ME	Y	24520 FQ	49390 AW	90240 TQ	NHBLS	10/01-12/01
	New Jersey	Y	39280 FQ	80070 AW	139720 TQ	NJBLS	10/01-12/01
	Atlantic-Cape May PMSA, NJ	Y	30180 FQ	58230 AW	89590 TQ	NJBLS	10/01-12/01
	Bergen-Passaic PMSA, NJ	Y	40400 FQ	82860 AW	144400 TQ	NJBLS	10/01-12/01
	Jersey City PMSA, NJ	Y	37840 FQ	83490 AW		NJBLS	10/01-12/01
	Middlesex-Somerset-Hunterdon PMSA, NJ	Y	39620 FQ	83280 AW	140490 TQ	NJBLS	10/01-12/01
	Monmouth-Ocean PMSA, NJ	Y	38450 FQ	65960 AW	108280 TQ	NJBLS	10/01-12/01
	Newark PMSA, NJ	Y	41740 FQ	81890 AW		NJBLS	10/01-12/01
	Trenton PMSA, NJ	Y	38360 FQ	75530 AW	120260 TQ	NJBLS	10/01-12/01
	New Mexico	Y	25470 FQ	46950 AW	71800 TQ	NMBLS	10/01-12/01
	Albuquerque MSA, NM	Y	29130 FQ	52230 AW	75730 TQ	NMBLS	10/01-12/01
	New York	Y	37660 FQ	91290 AW		NYBLS	10/01-12/01
	Albany-Schenectady-Troy MSA, NY	Y	32080 FQ	65630 AW	128150 TQ	NYBLS	10/01-12/01
	Binghamton MSA, NY	Y	26430 FQ	60350 AW	117300 TQ	NYBLS	10/01-12/01
	Buffalo-Niagara Falls MSA, NY	Y	31380 FQ	58590 AW	96050 TQ	NYBLS	10/01-12/01
	Nassau-Suffolk PMSA, NY	Y	35170 FQ	83440 AW		NYBLS	10/01-12/01
	New York PMSA, NY	Y	44150 FQ	99970 AW		NYBLS	10/01-12/01
	Newburgh PMSA, NY-PA	Y	24030 FQ	52610 AW	79910 TQ	NYBLS	10/01-12/01
	Rochester MSA, NY	Y	31580 FQ	57800 AW	102540 TQ	NYBLS	10/01-12/01
	Syracuse MSA, NY	Y	31350 FQ	54600 AW	102500 TQ	NYBLS	10/01-12/01
	Utica-Rome MSA, NY	Y	34590 FQ	63840 AW	125320 TQ	NYBLS	10/01-12/01
	North Carolina	Y	26230 FQ	58390 AW	108970 TQ	NCBLS	10/01-12/01
	Asheville MSA, NC	Y	26840 FQ	43650 AW	66460 TQ	NCBLS	10/01-12/01
	Charlotte-Gastonia-Rock Hill MSA, NC-SC	Y	30900 FQ	61170 AW	110750 TQ	NCBLS	10/01-12/01
	Fayetteville MSA, NC	Y	24600 FQ	42720 AW	60380 TQ	NCBLS	10/01-12/01
	Greensboro-Winston-Salem-High Point MSA, NC	Y	30170 FQ	65750 AW	121670 TQ	NCBLS	10/01-12/01
	Hickory-Morganton-Lenoir MSA, NC	Y	24540 FQ	48190 AW	103360 TQ	NCBLS	10/01-12/01
	Raleigh-Durham-Chapel Hill MSA, NC	Y	25460 FQ	62860 AW	119310 TQ	NCBLS	10/01-12/01
	Wilmington MSA, NC	Y	22030 FQ	43910 AW	69730 TQ	NCBLS	10/01-12/01
	North Dakota	Y	21190 FQ	39170 AW	62930 TQ	NDBLS	10/01-12/01
	Fargo-Moorhead MSA, ND-MN	Y	22320 FQ	40320 AW	57240 TQ	NDBLS	10/01-12/01
	Ohio	Y	27260 FQ	57780 AW	101270 TQ	OHBLS	10/01-12/01
	Akron PMSA, OH	Y	31750 FQ	63430 AW	99930 TQ	OHBLS	10/01-12/01
	Canton-Massillon MSA, OH	Y	24950 FQ	55820 AW	95990 TQ	OHBLS	10/01-12/01
	Cincinnati PMSA, OH-KY-IN	Y	28340 FQ	60840 AW	107040 TQ	OHBLS	10/01-12/01
	Cleveland-Lorain-Elyria PMSA, OH	Y	30450 FQ	58120 AW	91420 TQ	OHBLS	10/01-12/01
	Columbus MSA, OH	Y	29780 FQ	61150 AW	121540 TQ	OHBLS	10/01-12/01
	Dayton-Springfield MSA, OH	Y	25740 FQ	57940 AW	103870 TQ	OHBLS	10/01-12/01
	Hamilton-Middletown PMSA, OH	Y	28860 FQ	58350 AW	110370 TQ	OHBLS	10/01-12/01
	Toledo MSA, OH	Y	24520 FQ	51560 AW	87850 TQ	OHBLS	10/01-12/01
	Youngstown-Warren MSA, OH	Y	24820 FQ	58010 AW		OHBLS	10/01-12/01
	Oklahoma	Y	23530 FQ	47200 AW	74970 TQ	OKBLS	10/01-12/01
	Oklahoma City MSA, OK	Y	23290 FQ	46670 AW	73700 TQ	OKBLS	10/01-12/01
	Tulsa MSA, OK	Y	28390 FQ	53600 AW	82210 TQ	OKBLS	10/01-12/01

Occupation/Type/Industry	Location	Per	Low	Mid	High	Source	Date
Advertising and Promotions Manager	Oregon	Y	29710 FQ	59920 AW	110090 TQ	ORBLS	10/01-12/01
	Eugene-Springfield MSA, OR	Y	22450 FQ	56520 AW	92850 TQ	ORBLS	10/01-12/01
	Portland-Vancouver PMSA, OR-WA	Y	29890 FQ	63910 AW	115660 TQ	ORBLS	10/01-12/01
	Salem PMSA, OR	Y	30090 FQ	57730 AW	118610 TQ	ORBLS	10/01-12/01
	Pennsylvania	Y	26250 FQ	56050 AW	97200 TQ	PABLS	10/01-12/01
	Allentown-Bethlehem-Easton MSA, PA	Y	31880 FQ	59040 AW	90870 TQ	PABLS	10/01-12/01
	Erie MSA, PA	Y	24110 FQ	46000 AW	84350 TQ	PABLS	10/01-12/01
	Harrisburg-Lebanon-Carlisle MSA, PA	Y	28730 FQ	56000 AW	89760 TQ	PABLS	10/01-12/01
	Lancaster MSA, PA	Y	28620 FQ	59350 AW	120930 TQ	PABLS	10/01-12/01
	Philadelphia PMSA, PA-NJ	Y	27030 FQ	62610 AW	118260 TQ	PABLS	10/01-12/01
	Pittsburgh MSA, PA	Y	27680 FQ	56740 AW	99520 TQ	PABLS	10/01-12/01
	Reading MSA, PA	Y	26500 FQ	55720 AW	96100 TQ	PABLS	10/01-12/01
	Scranton-Wilkes-Barre-Hazleton MSA, PA	Y	24630 FQ	48740 AW	93330 TQ	PABLS	10/01-12/01
	York MSA, PA	Y	28440 FQ	48290 AW	79650 TQ	PABLS	10/01-12/01
	Rhode Island	Y	31560 FQ	63580 AW	112310 TQ	RIBLS	10/01-12/01
	Providence-Fall River-Warwick MSA, RI-MA	Y	30370 FQ	58610 AW	98600 TQ	RIBLS	10/01-12/01
	South Carolina	Y	27060 FQ	53190 AW	91490 TQ	SCBLS	10/01-12/01
	Charleston-North Charleston MSA, SC	Y	27980 FQ	50900 AW	85080 TQ	SCBLS	10/01-12/01
	Columbia MSA, SC	Y	25140 FQ	51550 AW	87560 TQ	SCBLS	10/01-12/01
	Greenville-Spartanburg-Anderson MSA, SC	Y	28990 FQ	52730 AW	92000 TQ	SCBLS	10/01-12/01
	Myrtle Beach MSA, SC	Y	23680 FQ	50290 AW	94420 TQ	SCBLS	10/01-12/01
	South Dakota	Y	39640 FQ	66210 AW	101770 TQ	SDBLS	10/01-12/01
	Tennessee	Y	26290 FQ	59430 AW		TNBLS	10/01-12/01
	Chattanooga MSA, TN-GA	Y	23550 FQ	44390 AW	70510 TQ	TNBLS	10/01-12/01
	Johnson City-Kingsport-Bristol MSA, TN-VA	Y	25610 FQ	38300 AW	56460 TQ	TNBLS	10/01-12/01
	Knoxville MSA, TN	Y	24840 FQ	55200 AW	90900 TQ	TNBLS	10/01-12/01
	Memphis MSA, TN-AR-MS	Y	29860 FQ	73540 AW		TNBLS	10/01-12/01
	Nashville MSA, TN	Y	25760 FQ	55500 AW	104740 TQ	TNBLS	10/01-12/01
	Texas	Y	25260 FQ	58730 AW	111920 TQ	TXBLS	10/01-12/01
	Amarillo MSA, TX	Y	25480 FQ	42440 AW	65040 TQ	TXBLS	10/01-12/01
	Austin-San Marcos MSA, TX	Y	30810 FQ	72080 AW	135860 TQ	TXBLS	10/01-12/01
	Beaumont-Port Arthur MSA, TX	Y	20890 FQ	45320 AW	81690 TQ	TXBLS	10/01-12/01
	Corpus Christi MSA, TX	Y	24820 FQ	51170 AW	111380 TQ	TXBLS	10/01-12/01
	Dallas PMSA, TX	Y	29180 FQ	66310 AW	118550 TQ	TXBLS	10/01-12/01
	El Paso MSA, TX	Y	16640 FQ	42090 AW	79390 TQ	TXBLS	10/01-12/01
	Fort Worth-Arlington PMSA, TX	Y	28040 FQ	58400 AW	111790 TQ	TXBLS	10/01-12/01
	Galveston-Texas City PMSA, TX	Y	23380 FQ	45090 AW	89780 TQ	TXBLS	10/01-12/01
	Houston PMSA, TX	Y	23460 FQ	53690 AW	100670 TQ	TXBLS	10/01-12/01
	Killeen-Temple MSA, TX	Y	25620 FQ	43420 AW	60070 TQ	TXBLS	10/01-12/01
	Longview-Marshall MSA, TX	Y	21220 FQ	44270 AW	84770 TQ	TXBLS	10/01-12/01
	Lubbock MSA, TX	Y	22130 FQ	39900 AW	56760 TQ	TXBLS	10/01-12/01
	McAllen-Edinburg-Mission MSA, TX	Y	25460 FQ	47280 AW	82130 TQ	TXBLS	10/01-12/01
	Odessa-Midland MSA, TX	Y	24730 FQ	36090 AW	62910 TQ	TXBLS	10/01-12/01
	San Antonio MSA, TX	Y	28680 FQ	62030 AW	96910 TQ	TXBLS	10/01-12/01
	Tyler MSA, TX	Y	22620 FQ	46850 AW	108660 TQ	TXBLS	10/01-12/01
	Waco MSA, TX	Y	21570 FQ	38950 AW	59490 TQ	TXBLS	10/01-12/01
	Utah	Y	25110 FQ	48390 AW	85070 TQ	UTBLS	10/01-12/01
	Provo-Orem MSA, UT	Y	17480 FQ	51000 AW	96080 TQ	UTBLS	10/01-12/01
	Salt Lake City-Ogden MSA, UT	Y	27610 FQ	46800 AW	79690 TQ	UTBLS	10/01-12/01
	Vermont	Y	33700 FQ	60010 AW	100050 TQ	VTBLS	10/01-12/01
	Burlington MSA, VT	Y	32550 FQ	65660 AW	116400 TQ	VTBLS	10/01-12/01
	Virginia	Y	29910 FQ	64310 AW	111450 TQ	VABLS	10/01-12/01
	Lynchburg MSA, VA	Y	22560 FQ	54420 AW	100370 TQ	VABLS	10/01-12/01
	Norfolk-Virginia Beach-Newport News MSA, VA-NC	Y	23750 FQ	58590 AW	145010 TQ	VABLS	10/01-12/01
	Richmond-Petersburg MSA, VA	Y	29780 FQ	59510 AW	93900 TQ	VABLS	10/01-12/01

AAW	Average annual wage	**AOH**	Average offered, high	**ASH**	Average starting, high	**H**	Hourly	**M**	Monthly	**S**	Special: hourly and annual
AE	Average entry wage	**AOL**	Average offered, low	**ASL**	Average starting, low	**HI**	Highest wage paid	**MTC**	Median total compensation	**TQ**	Third quartile wage
AEX	Average experienced wage	**APH**	Average pay, high range	**AW**	Average wage paid	**HR**	High end range	**MW**	Median wage paid	**W**	Weekly
AO	Average offered	**APL**	Average pay, low range	**FQ**	First quartile wage	**LR**	Low end range	**SQ**	Second quartile wage	**Y**	Yearly

Occupation/Type/Industry	Location	Per	Low	Mid	High	Source	Date
Advertising and Promotions Manager	Roanoke MSA, VA	Y	31830 FQ	48570 AW	70560 TQ	VABLS	10/01-12/01
	Washington	Y	37180 FQ	73400 AW	127260 TQ	WABLS	10/01-12/01
	Seattle-Bellevue-Everett PMSA, WA	Y	41070 FQ	79430 AW		WABLS	10/01-12/01
	Spokane MSA, WA	Y	38450 FQ	75960 AW		WABLS	10/01-12/01
	Tacoma PMSA, WA	Y	37010 FQ	62450 AW	95460 TQ	WABLS	10/01-12/01
	West Virginia	Y	23540 FQ	44810 AW	71970 TQ	WVBLS	10/01-12/01
	Charleston MSA, WV	Y	24650 FQ	49430 AW	75110 TQ	WVBLS	10/01-12/01
	Huntington-Ashland MSA, WV-KY-OH	Y	25350 FQ	41220 AW	61630 TQ	WVBLS	10/01-12/01
	Wisconsin	Y	24120 FQ	51970 AW	90760 TQ	WIBLS	10/01-12/01
	Appleton-Oshkosh-Neenah MSA, WI	Y	27060 FQ	50410 AW	86800 TQ	WIBLS	10/01-12/01
	Green Bay MSA, WI	Y	23940 FQ	52970 AW	88650 TQ	WIBLS	10/01-12/01
	Madison MSA, WI	Y	27400 FQ	57600 AW	119920 TQ	WIBLS	10/01-12/01
	Milwaukee-Waukesha PMSA, WI	Y	26800 FQ	58350 AW	95500 TQ	WIBLS	10/01-12/01
	Racine PMSA, WI	Y	30350 FQ	57630 AW	97940 TQ	WIBLS	10/01-12/01
	Wyoming	Y	20910 FQ	38130 AW	59070 TQ	WYBLS	10/01-12/01
	Puerto Rico	Y	23130 FQ	38610 AW	74520 TQ	PRBLS	10/01-12/01
	Virgin Islands	Y	26380 FQ	40350 AW	59580 TQ	VIBLS	10/01-12/01
	Guam	Y	20100 FQ	41940 AW	67710 TQ	GUBLS	10/01-12/01
Advertising Sales Agent	Alabama	Y	15200 FQ	37890 AW	66810 TQ	ALBLS	10/01-12/01
	Birmingham MSA, AL	Y	19270 FQ	44640 AW	77110 TQ	ALBLS	10/01-12/01
	Huntsville MSA, AL	Y	15660 FQ	39220 AW	69190 TQ	ALBLS	10/01-12/01
	Mobile MSA, AL	Y	15750 FQ	33780 AW	55650 TQ	ALBLS	10/01-12/01
	Montgomery MSA, AL	Y	18190 FQ	36100 AW	61380 TQ	ALBLS	10/01-12/01
	Alaska	Y	20400 FQ	39960 AW	68920 TQ	AKBLS	10/01-12/01
	Anchorage MSA, AK	Y	20670 FQ	43030 AW	75240 TQ	AKBLS	10/01-12/01
	Arizona	Y	18860 FQ	40420 AW	75050 TQ	AZBLS	10/01-12/01
	Phoenix-Mesa MSA, AZ	Y	18930 FQ	40630 AW	75530 TQ	AZBLS	10/01-12/01
	Tucson MSA, AZ	Y	18630 FQ	46860 AW	87370 TQ	AZBLS	10/01-12/01
	Arkansas	Y	16760 FQ	36630 AW	65210 TQ	ARBLS	10/01-12/01
	Fayetteville-Springdale-Rogers MSA, AR	Y	16930 FQ	32540 AW	52600 TQ	ARBLS	10/01-12/01
	Fort Smith MSA, AR-OK	Y	18370 FQ	38300 AW	67170 TQ	ARBLS	10/01-12/01
	Little Rock-North Little Rock MSA, AR	Y	23780 FQ	42320 AW	71340 TQ	ARBLS	10/01-12/01
	California	Y	23250 FQ	60680 AW	129950 TQ	CABLS	10/01-12/01
	Bakersfield MSA, CA	Y	16970 FQ	43940 AW	112350 TQ	CABLS	10/01-12/01
	Chico-Paradise MSA, CA	Y	17880 FQ	40720 AW	69280 TQ	CABLS	10/01-12/01
	Fresno MSA, CA	Y	16650 FQ	37090 AW	69820 TQ	CABLS	10/01-12/01
	Los Angeles-Long Beach PMSA, CA	Y	24850 FQ	63650 AW	137500 TQ	CABLS	10/01-12/01
	Modesto MSA, CA	Y	21870 FQ	47400 AW	85620 TQ	CABLS	10/01-12/01
	Oakland PMSA, CA	Y	26640 FQ	53420 AW	97460 TQ	CABLS	10/01-12/01
	Orange County PMSA, CA	Y	25020 FQ	54620 AW	95690 TQ	CABLS	10/01-12/01
	Redding MSA, CA	Y	18760 FQ	39180 AW	62500 TQ	CABLS	10/01-12/01
	Riverside-San Bernardino PMSA, CA	Y	16900 FQ	44710 AW	91280 TQ	CABLS	10/01-12/01
	Sacramento PMSA, CA	Y	24240 FQ	52820 AW	93270 TQ	CABLS	10/01-12/01
	Salinas MSA, CA	Y	24100 FQ	49930 AW	103180 TQ	CABLS	10/01-12/01
	San Diego MSA, CA	Y	21500 FQ	56310 AW	106550 TQ	CABLS	10/01-12/01
	San Francisco PMSA, CA	Y	27200 FQ	89120 AW		CABLS	10/01-12/01
	San Jose PMSA, CA	Y	32210 FQ	63500 AW	100620 TQ	CABLS	10/01-12/01
	San Luis Obispo-Atascadero-Paso Robles MSA, CA	Y	21110 FQ	52470 AW	105100 TQ	CABLS	10/01-12/01
	Santa Barbara-Santa Maria-Lompoc MSA, CA	Y	24610 FQ	46280 AW	83280 TQ	CABLS	10/01-12/01
	Santa Cruz-Watsonville PMSA, CA	Y	29820 FQ	66140 AW	112490 TQ	CABLS	10/01-12/01
	Santa Rosa PMSA, CA	Y	23630 FQ	57440 AW	128150 TQ	CABLS	10/01-12/01
	Stockton-Lodi MSA, CA	Y	20170 FQ	40920 AW	70990 TQ	CABLS	10/01-12/01
	Vallejo-Fairfield-Napa PMSA, CA	Y	26270 FQ	46450 AW	62770 TQ	CABLS	10/01-12/01
	Ventura PMSA, CA	Y	23370 FQ	53080 AW	103860 TQ	CABLS	10/01-12/01
	Visalia-Tulare-Porterville MSA, CA	Y	15320 FQ	37810 AW	68140 TQ	CABLS	10/01-12/01
	Colorado	Y	23080 FQ	44330 AW	71610 TQ	COBLS	10/01-12/01
	Boulder-Longmont PMSA, CO	Y	21330 FQ	36020 AW	56310 TQ	COBLS	10/01-12/01

AAW	Average annual wage	**AOH**	Average offered, high	**ASH**	Average starting, high	**H**	Hourly	**M**	Monthly	**S**	Special: hourly and annual
AE	Average entry wage	**AOL**	Average offered, low	**ASL**	Average starting, low	**HI**	Highest wage paid	**MTC**	Median total compensation	**TQ**	Third quartile wage
AEX	Average experienced wage	**APH**	Average pay, high range	**AW**	Average wage paid	**HR**	High end range	**MW**	Median wage paid	**W**	Weekly
AO	Average offered	**APL**	Average pay, low range	**FQ**	First quartile wage	**LR**	Low end range	**SQ**	Second quartile wage	**Y**	Yearly

Occupation/Type/Industry	Location	Per	Low	Mid	High	Source	Date
Advertising Sales Agent	Colorado Springs MSA, CO	Y	22700 FQ	43690 AW	77950 TQ	COBLS	10/01-12/01
	Denver PMSA, CO	Y	27160 FQ	48530 AW	73640 TQ	COBLS	10/01-12/01
	Fort Collins-Loveland MSA, CO	Y	18200 FQ	35870 AW	65620 TQ	COBLS	10/01-12/01
	Greeley PMSA, CO	Y	31790 FQ	52400 AW	90280 TQ	COBLS	10/01-12/01
	Connecticut	Y	23530 FQ	54090 AW	103470 TQ	CTBLS	10/01-12/01
	Bridgeport PMSA, CT	Y	26510 FQ	62460 AW	132730 TQ	CTBLS	10/01-12/01
	Danbury PMSA, CT	Y	24060 FQ	53450 AW		CTBLS	10/01-12/01
	Hartford MSA, CT	Y	20610 FQ	50650 AW	94920 TQ	CTBLS	10/01-12/01
	New Haven-Meriden PMSA, CT	Y	26750 FQ	48100 AW	84800 TQ	CTBLS	10/01-12/01
	New London-Norwich MSA, CT-RI	Y	25670 FQ	40370 AW	60800 TQ	CTBLS	10/01-12/01
	Stamford-Norwalk PMSA, CT	Y	31880 FQ	62550 AW	113950 TQ	CTBLS	10/01-12/01
	Waterbury PMSA, CT	Y	19210 FQ	42850 AW	90130 TQ	CTBLS	10/01-12/01
	Delaware	Y	24730 FQ	41880 AW	73760 TQ	DEBLS	10/01-12/01
	Wilmington-Newark PMSA, DE-MD	Y	26480 FQ	44960 AW	78740 TQ	DEBLS	10/01-12/01
	District of Columbia	Y	19840 FQ	49690 AW	103870 TQ	DCBLS	10/01-12/01
	Washington PMSA, DC-MD-VA-WV	Y	24570 FQ	63670 AW	139700 TQ	DCBLS	10/01-12/01
	Florida	Y	19320 FQ	43320 AW	81900 TQ	FLBLS	10/01-12/01
	Daytona Beach MSA, FL	Y	16650 FQ	38700 AW	68770 TQ	FLBLS	10/01-12/01
	Fort Lauderdale PMSA, FL	Y	18740 FQ	46600 AW	82160 TQ	FLBLS	10/01-12/01
	Fort Myers-Cape Coral MSA, FL	Y	17390 FQ	41010 AW	67060 TQ	FLBLS	10/01-12/01
	Fort Pierce-Port St. Lucie MSA, FL	Y	14880 FQ	24630 AW	44750 TQ	FLBLS	10/01-12/01
	Fort Walton Beach MSA, FL	Y	12130 FQ	29080 AW	55050 TQ	FLBLS	10/01-12/01
	Gainesville MSA, FL	Y	13740 FQ	37480 AW	62020 TQ	FLBLS	10/01-12/01
	Jacksonville MSA, FL	Y	19970 FQ	45260 AW	89310 TQ	FLBLS	10/01-12/01
	Lakeland-Winter Haven MSA, FL	Y	14640 FQ	32270 AW	58520 TQ	FLBLS	10/01-12/01
	Melbourne-Titusville-Palm Bay MSA, FL	Y	19470 FQ	43030 AW	70800 TQ	FLBLS	10/01-12/01
	Miami PMSA, FL	Y	23340 FQ	50790 AW	92170 TQ	FLBLS	10/01-12/01
	Naples MSA, FL	Y	15820 FQ	46680 AW	106550 TQ	FLBLS	10/01-12/01
	Ocala MSA, FL	Y	18380 FQ	32680 AW	53510 TQ	FLBLS	10/01-12/01
	Orlando MSA, FL	Y	14270 FQ	39540 AW	67860 TQ	FLBLS	10/01-12/01
	Pensacola MSA, FL	Y	19900 FQ	31890 AW	44780 TQ	FLBLS	10/01-12/01
	Sarasota-Bradenton MSA, FL	Y	17050 FQ	40620 AW	78730 TQ	FLBLS	10/01-12/01
	Tallahassee MSA, FL	Y	20670 FQ	36540 AW	56020 TQ	FLBLS	10/01-12/01
	Tampa-St. Petersburg-Clearwater MSA, FL	Y	21290 FQ	39290 AW	70210 TQ	FLBLS	10/01-12/01
	West Palm Beach-Boca Raton MSA, FL	Y	20220 FQ	49010 AW	91570 TQ	FLBLS	10/01-12/01
	Georgia	Y	17000 FQ	37770 AW	64480 TQ	GABLS	10/01-12/01
	Atlanta MSA, GA	Y	17580 FQ	39610 AW	67370 TQ	GABLS	10/01-12/01
	Augusta-Aiken MSA, GA-SC	Y	18920 FQ	30930 AW	44230 TQ	GABLS	10/01-12/01
	Columbus MSA, GA-AL	Y	16960 FQ	31020 AW	51870 TQ	GABLS	10/01-12/01
	Macon MSA, GA	Y	18070 FQ	30500 AW	43660 TQ	GABLS	10/01-12/01
	Savannah MSA, GA	Y	18180 FQ	28550 AW	41020 TQ	GABLS	10/01-12/01
	Hawaii	Y	19730 FQ	42870 AW	79300 TQ	HIBLS	10/01-12/01
	Honolulu MSA, HI	Y	21510 FQ	44920 AW	82230 TQ	HIBLS	10/01-12/01
	Idaho	Y	15590 FQ	33530 AW	59140 TQ	IDBLS	10/01-12/01
	Boise City MSA, ID	Y	15530 FQ	32410 AW	60670 TQ	IDBLS	10/01-12/01
	Illinois	Y	17650 FQ	44510 AW	78480 TQ	ILBLS	10/01-12/01
	Champaign-Urbana MSA, IL	Y	17940 FQ	39530 AW	64230 TQ	ILBLS	10/01-12/01
	Chicago PMSA, IL	Y	18180 FQ	47350 AW	85570 TQ	ILBLS	10/01-12/01
	Peoria-Pekin MSA, IL	Y	17580 FQ	32200 AW	46200 TQ	ILBLS	10/01-12/01
	Rockford MSA, IL	Y	18550 FQ	36650 AW	59690 TQ	ILBLS	10/01-12/01
	Springfield MSA, IL	Y	24680 FQ	46900 AW	67190 TQ	ILBLS	10/01-12/01
	Indiana	Y	18980 FQ	38300 AW	69550 TQ	INBLS	10/01-12/01
	Elkhart-Goshen MSA, IN	Y	19460 FQ	37690 AW	63280 TQ	INBLS	10/01-12/01
	Evansville-Henderson MSA, IN-KY	Y	14710 FQ	34440 AW	66810 TQ	INBLS	10/01-12/01
	Fort Wayne MSA, IN	Y	20480 FQ	39440 AW	56520 TQ	INBLS	10/01-12/01
	Gary PMSA, IN	Y	19220 FQ	38140 AW	76800 TQ	INBLS	10/01-12/01
	Indianapolis MSA, IN	Y	20890 FQ	46630 AW	95770 TQ	INBLS	10/01-12/01
	Lafayette MSA, IN	Y	20100 FQ	36890 AW	65640 TQ	INBLS	10/01-12/01
	South Bend MSA, IN	Y	20620 FQ	44320 AW	82710 TQ	INBLS	10/01-12/01
	Iowa	Y	14290 FQ	30620 AW	51020 TQ	IABLS	10/01-12/01

AAW	Average annual wage	**AOH**	Average offered, high	**ASH**	Average starting, high	**H**	Hourly	**M**	Monthly	**S**	Special: hourly and annual
AE	Average entry wage	**AOL**	Average offered, low	**ASL**	Average starting, low	**HI**	Highest wage paid	**MTC**	Median total compensation	**TQ**	Third quartile wage
AEX	Average experienced wage	**APH**	Average pay, high range	**AW**	Average wage paid	**HR**	High end range	**MW**	Median wage paid	**W**	Weekly
AO	Average offered	**APL**	Average pay, low range	**FQ**	First quartile wage	**LR**	Low end range	**SQ**	Second quartile wage	**Y**	Yearly

Occupation/Type/Industry	Location	Per	Low	Mid	High	Source	Date
Advertising Sales Agent	Cedar Rapids MSA, IA	Y	19050 FQ	34730 AW	61550 TQ	IABLS	10/01-12/01
	Davenport-Moline-Rock Island MSA, IA-IL	Y	15930 FQ	30740 AW	52270 TQ	IABLS	10/01-12/01
	Des Moines MSA, IA	Y	22850 FQ	39230 AW	58530 TQ	IABLS	10/01-12/01
	Kansas	Y	17750 FQ	37830 AW	68680 TQ	KSBLS	10/01-12/01
	Topeka MSA, KS	Y	18130 FQ	36720 AW	59340 TQ	KSBLS	10/01-12/01
	Wichita MSA, KS	Y	18050 FQ	44000 AW	80100 TQ	KSBLS	10/01-12/01
	Kentucky	Y	13070 FQ	32120 AW	58030 TQ	KYBLS	10/01-12/01
	Lexington MSA, KY	Y	16740 FQ	39310 AW	75050 TQ	KYBLS	10/01-12/01
	Louisville MSA, KY-IN	Y	19260 FQ	37590 AW	63640 TQ	KYBLS	10/01-12/01
	Louisiana	Y	16260 FQ	35890 AW	63410 TQ	LABLS	10/01-12/01
	Baton Rouge MSA, LA	Y	18620 FQ	42150 AW	72460 TQ	LABLS	10/01-12/01
	Houma MSA, LA	Y	16310 FQ	30210 AW	63300 TQ	LABLS	10/01-12/01
	Lafayette MSA, LA	Y	21090 FQ	37500 AW	63190 TQ	LABLS	10/01-12/01
	Lake Charles MSA, LA	Y	16120 FQ	29370 AW	50790 TQ	LABLS	10/01-12/01
	New Orleans MSA, LA	Y	17330 FQ	40730 AW	71080 TQ	LABLS	10/01-12/01
	Shreveport-Bossier City MSA, LA	Y	15130 FQ	26300 AW	38710 TQ	LABLS	10/01-12/01
	Maine	Y	21360 FQ	39550 AW	64380 TQ	MEBLS	10/01-12/01
	Portland MSA, ME	Y	24990 FQ	44270 AW	69220 TQ	MEBLS	10/01-12/01
	Maryland	Y	23000 FQ	49070 AW	89010 TQ	MDBLS	10/01-12/01
	Baltimore PMSA, MD	Y	19980 FQ	44220 AW	79620 TQ	MDBLS	10/01-12/01
	Massachusetts	Y	20780 FQ	45900 AW	87090 TQ	MABLS	10/01-12/01
	Boston PMSA, MA-NH	Y	20820 FQ	45890 AW	88210 TQ	MABLS	10/01-12/01
	Brockton PMSA, MA	Y	37660 FQ	43330 AW	47490 TQ	MABLS	10/01-12/01
	Lawrence PMSA, MA-NH	Y	15270 FQ	32750 AW	58510 TQ	MABLS	10/01-12/01
	Lowell PMSA, MA-NH	Y	22480 FQ	50290 AW	71570 TQ	MABLS	10/01-12/01
	New Bedford PMSA, MA	Y	23630 FQ	43420 AW	74300 TQ	MABLS	10/01-12/01
	Springfield MSA, MA	Y	16970 FQ	45970 AW	92360 TQ	MABLS	10/01-12/01
	Worcester PMSA, MA-CT	Y	19310 FQ	47490 AW	90860 TQ	MABLS	10/01-12/01
	Michigan	Y	20430 FQ	44310 AW	79520 TQ	MIBLS	10/01-12/01
	Ann Arbor PMSA, MI	Y	18850 FQ	41350 AW	85010 TQ	MIBLS	10/01-12/01
	Detroit PMSA, MI	Y	24110 FQ	48360 AW	85140 TQ	MIBLS	10/01-12/01
	Flint PMSA, MI	Y	16050 FQ	39470 AW	66930 TQ	MIBLS	10/01-12/01
	Grand Rapids-Muskegon-Holland MSA, MI	Y	23130 FQ	47690 AW	82850 TQ	MIBLS	10/01-12/01
	Kalamazoo-Battle Creek MSA, MI	Y	19810 FQ	45000 AW	83240 TQ	MIBLS	10/01-12/01
	Lansing-East Lansing MSA, MI	Y	21020 FQ	47660 AW	87310 TQ	MIBLS	10/01-12/01
	Saginaw-Bay City-Midland MSA, MI	Y	17290 FQ	37370 AW	65690 TQ	MIBLS	10/01-12/01
	Minnesota	Y	19020 FQ	41830 AW	79050 TQ	MNBLS	10/01-12/01
	Duluth-Superior MSA, MN-WI	Y	18090 FQ	34910 AW	54330 TQ	MNBLS	10/01-12/01
	Minneapolis-St. Paul MSA, MN-WI	Y	20590 FQ	46890 AW	88990 TQ	MNBLS	10/01-12/01
	St. Cloud MSA, MN	Y	19070 FQ	34160 AW	65940 TQ	MNBLS	10/01-12/01
	Mississippi	Y	18450 FQ	31320 AW	51730 TQ	MSBLS	10/01-12/01
	Biloxi-Gulfport-Pascagoula MSA, MS	Y	17400 FQ	26460 AW	37450 TQ	MSBLS	10/01-12/01
	Jackson MSA, MS	Y	20280 FQ	38000 AW	70170 TQ	MSBLS	10/01-12/01
	Missouri	Y	15400 FQ	38060 AW	71750 TQ	MOBLS	10/01-12/01
	Kansas City MSA, MO-KS	Y	17770 FQ	39020 AW	70510 TQ	MOBLS	10/01-12/01
	St. Louis MSA, MO-IL	Y	22590 FQ	46590 AW	89850 TQ	MOBLS	10/01-12/01
	Springfield MSA, MO	Y	13210 FQ	31790 AW	56600 TQ	MOBLS	10/01-12/01
	Montana	Y	16590 FQ	30110 AW	47180 TQ	MTBLS	10/01-12/01
	Billings MSA, MT	Y	19590 FQ	41850 AW	70860 TQ	MTBLS	10/01-12/01
	Nebraska	Y	16780 FQ	36400 AW	66530 TQ	NEBLS	10/01-12/01
	Lincoln MSA, NE	Y	14070 FQ	38870 AW	70060 TQ	NEBLS	10/01-12/01
	Omaha MSA, NE-IA	Y	20340 FQ	40870 AW	77980 TQ	NEBLS	10/01-12/01
	Nevada	Y	20470 FQ	47450 AW	95480 TQ	NVBLS	10/01-12/01
	Las Vegas MSA, NV-AZ	Y	23040 FQ	49840 AW	102630 TQ	NVBLS	10/01-12/01
	Reno MSA, NV	Y	18590 FQ	38640 AW	67140 TQ	NVBLS	10/01-12/01
	New Hampshire	Y	18000 FQ	38810 AW	66650 TQ	NHBLS	10/01-12/01
	Manchester PMSA, NH	Y	25570 FQ	50010 AW	69770 TQ	NHBLS	10/01-12/01
	Nashua PMSA, NH	Y	18890 FQ	35250 AW	57390 TQ	NHBLS	10/01-12/01
	Portsmouth-Rochester PMSA, NH-ME	Y	21200 FQ	40550 AW	70570 TQ	NHBLS	10/01-12/01
	New Jersey	Y	24300 FQ	46390 AW	80180 TQ	NJBLS	10/01-12/01
	Atlantic-Cape May PMSA, NJ	Y	24490 FQ	40230 AW	70130 TQ	NJBLS	10/01-12/01
	Bergen-Passaic PMSA, NJ	Y	25550 FQ	53050 AW	107760 TQ	NJBLS	10/01-12/01
	Jersey City PMSA, NJ	Y	20320 FQ	39700 AW	69770 TQ	NJBLS	10/01-12/01

AAW	Average annual wage	**AOH**	Average offered, high	**ASH**	Average starting, high	**H**	Hourly	**M**	Monthly	**S**	Special: hourly and annual
AE	Average entry wage	**AOL**	Average offered, low	**ASL**	Average starting, low	**HI**	Highest wage paid	**MTC**	Median total compensation	**TQ**	Third quartile wage
AEX	Average experienced wage	**APH**	Average pay, high range	**AW**	Average wage paid	**HR**	High end range	**MW**	Median wage paid	**W**	Weekly
AO	Average offered	**APL**	Average pay, low range	**FQ**	First quartile wage	**LR**	Low end range	**SQ**	Second quartile wage	**Y**	Yearly

Occupation/Type/Industry	Location	Per	Low	Mid	High	Source	Date
Advertising Sales Agent	Middlesex-Somerset-Hunterdon PMSA, NJ	Y	23200 FQ	39400 AW	63260 TQ	NJBLS	10/01-12/01
	Monmouth-Ocean PMSA, NJ	Y	22030 FQ	48580 AW	87370 TQ	NJBLS	10/01-12/01
	Newark PMSA, NJ	Y	28420 FQ	48060 AW	81300 TQ	NJBLS	10/01-12/01
	Trenton PMSA, NJ	Y	24910 FQ	46210 AW	76290 TQ	NJBLS	10/01-12/01
	New Mexico	Y	17590 FQ	31730 AW	50130 TQ	NMBLS	10/01-12/01
	Albuquerque MSA, NM	Y	19670 FQ	33690 AW	47570 TQ	NMBLS	10/01-12/01
	Las Cruces MSA, NM	Y	12790 FQ	25490 AW	45010 TQ	NMBLS	10/01-12/01
	New York	Y	24220 FQ	58520 AW	107090 TQ	NYBLS	10/01-12/01
	Albany-Schenectady-Troy MSA, NY	Y	24100 FQ	42660 AW	73830 TQ	NYBLS	10/01-12/01
	Binghamton MSA, NY	Y	17240 FQ	38730 AW	72460 TQ	NYBLS	10/01-12/01
	Buffalo-Niagara Falls MSA, NY	Y	21460 FQ	45550 AW	85620 TQ	NYBLS	10/01-12/01
	Dutchess County PMSA, NY	Y	20070 FQ	46710 AW	89610 TQ	NYBLS	10/01-12/01
	Nassau-Suffolk PMSA, NY	Y	20520 FQ	53120 AW	103670 TQ	NYBLS	10/01-12/01
	New York PMSA, NY	Y	30540 FQ	65480 AW	112390 TQ	NYBLS	10/01-12/01
	Newburgh PMSA, NY-PA	Y	25290 FQ	36040 AW	45200 TQ	NYBLS	10/01-12/01
	Rochester MSA, NY	Y	21260 FQ	47860 AW	86600 TQ	NYBLS	10/01-12/01
	Syracuse MSA, NY	Y	14880 FQ	39900 AW	77920 TQ	NYBLS	10/01-12/01
	Utica-Rome MSA, NY	Y	13060 FQ	33140 AW	63690 TQ	NYBLS	10/01-12/01
	North Carolina	Y	18200 FQ	42520 AW	81540 TQ	NCBLS	10/01-12/01
	Asheville MSA, NC	Y	13690 FQ	37010 AW	79090 TQ	NCBLS	10/01-12/01
	Charlotte-Gastonia-Rock Hill MSA, NC-SC	Y	22320 FQ	55690 AW	105640 TQ	NCBLS	10/01-12/01
	Fayetteville MSA, NC	Y	16200 FQ	35980 AW	72380 TQ	NCBLS	10/01-12/01
	Greensboro-Winston-Salem-High Point MSA, NC	Y	23960 FQ	46320 AW	85670 TQ	NCBLS	10/01-12/01
	Hickory-Morganton-Lenoir MSA, NC	Y	19250 FQ	33350 AW	46810 TQ	NCBLS	10/01-12/01
	Raleigh-Durham-Chapel Hill MSA, NC	Y	18150 FQ	39870 AW	69530 TQ	NCBLS	10/01-12/01
	Wilmington MSA, NC	Y	18500 FQ	36790 AW	57240 TQ	NCBLS	10/01-12/01
	North Dakota	Y	14020 FQ	29990 AW	49020 TQ	NDBLS	10/01-12/01
	Fargo-Moorhead MSA, ND-MN	Y	13700 FQ	30850 AW	51620 TQ	NDBLS	10/01-12/01
	Ohio	Y	19950 FQ	42470 AW	76280 TQ	OHBLS	10/01-12/01
	Akron PMSA, OH	Y	20260 FQ	39810 AW	70600 TQ	OHBLS	10/01-12/01
	Canton-Massillon MSA, OH	Y	22540 FQ	47300 AW	71890 TQ	OHBLS	10/01-12/01
	Cincinnati PMSA, OH-KY-IN	Y	19290 FQ	44560 AW	82400 TQ	OHBLS	10/01-12/01
	Cleveland-Lorain-Elyria PMSA, OH	Y	22520 FQ	46580 AW	83550 TQ	OHBLS	10/01-12/01
	Columbus MSA, OH	Y	23510 FQ	48750 AW	89890 TQ	OHBLS	10/01-12/01
	Dayton-Springfield MSA, OH	Y	18430 FQ	37200 AW	65770 TQ	OHBLS	10/01-12/01
	Hamilton-Middletown PMSA, OH	Y	24490 FQ	43710 AW	74850 TQ	OHBLS	10/01-12/01
	Mansfield MSA, OH	Y	19980 FQ	45240 AW	75850 TQ	OHBLS	10/01-12/01
	Toledo MSA, OH	Y	19150 FQ	37620 AW	62720 TQ	OHBLS	10/01-12/01
	Youngstown-Warren MSA, OH	Y	23210 FQ	43990 AW	79120 TQ	OHBLS	10/01-12/01
	Oklahoma	Y	13600 FQ	32960 AW	57940 TQ	OKBLS	10/01-12/01
	Oklahoma City MSA, OK	Y	14910 FQ	42380 AW	86670 TQ	OKBLS	10/01-12/01
	Tulsa MSA, OK	Y	14000 FQ	31880 AW	55920 TQ	OKBLS	10/01-12/01
	Oregon	Y	18860 FQ	36490 AW	60570 TQ	ORBLS	10/01-12/01
	Eugene-Springfield MSA, OR	Y	16240 FQ	36550 AW	66740 TQ	ORBLS	10/01-12/01
	Medford-Ashland MSA, OR	Y	18900 FQ	42560 AW	68330 TQ	ORBLS	10/01-12/01
	Portland-Vancouver PMSA, OR-WA	Y	21030 FQ	38120 AW	64180 TQ	ORBLS	10/01-12/01
	Salem PMSA, OR	Y	18640 FQ	32810 AW	55370 TQ	ORBLS	10/01-12/01
	Pennsylvania	Y	18540 FQ	41950 AW	79550 TQ	PABLS	10/01-12/01
	Allentown-Bethlehem-Easton MSA, PA	Y	19540 FQ	43900 AW	84470 TQ	PABLS	10/01-12/01
	Erie MSA, PA	Y	16260 FQ	32050 AW	49240 TQ	PABLS	10/01-12/01
	Harrisburg-Lebanon-Carlisle MSA, PA	Y	19810 FQ	37080 AW	63760 TQ	PABLS	10/01-12/01
	Johnstown MSA, PA	Y	16180 FQ	28900 AW	53070 TQ	PABLS	10/01-12/01
	Lancaster MSA, PA	Y	23170 FQ	41660 AW	63290 TQ	PABLS	10/01-12/01
	Philadelphia PMSA, PA-NJ	Y	20440 FQ	48440 AW	87630 TQ	PABLS	10/01-12/01
	Pittsburgh MSA, PA	Y	18510 FQ	42680 AW	83850 TQ	PABLS	10/01-12/01
	Reading MSA, PA	Y	19130 FQ	38920 AW	76340 TQ	PABLS	10/01-12/01
	Scranton-Wilkes-Barre-Hazleton MSA, PA	Y	17040 FQ	36020 AW	66260 TQ	PABLS	10/01-12/01
	York MSA, PA	Y	13960 FQ	32030 AW	61100 TQ	PABLS	10/01-12/01

AAW	Average annual wage	**AOH**	Average offered, high	**ASH**	Average starting, high	**H**	Hourly	**M**	Monthly	**S**	Special: hourly and annual
AE	Average entry wage	**AOL**	Average offered, low	**ASL**	Average starting, low	**HI**	Highest wage paid	**MTC**	Median total compensation	**TQ**	Third quartile wage
AEX	Average experienced wage	**APH**	Average pay, high range	**AW**	Average wage paid	**HR**	High end range	**MW**	Median wage paid	**W**	Weekly
AO	Average offered	**APL**	Average pay, low range	**FQ**	First quartile wage	**LR**	Low end range	**SQ**	Second quartile wage	**Y**	Yearly

Occupation/Type/Industry	Location	Per	Low	Mid	High	Source	Date
Advertising Sales Agent	Rhode Island	Y	19990 FQ	38860 AW	69210 TQ	RIBLS	10/01-12/01
	Providence-Fall River-Warwick MSA, RI-MA	Y	20000 FQ	39120 AW	70410 TQ	RIBLS	10/01-12/01
	South Carolina	Y	15790 FQ	41290 AW	81010 TQ	SCBLS	10/01-12/01
	Charleston-North Charleston MSA, SC	Y	19770 FQ	37790 AW	62350 TQ	SCBLS	10/01-12/01
	Columbia MSA, SC	Y	19780 FQ	47640 AW	106350 TQ	SCBLS	10/01-12/01
	Greenville-Spartanburg-Anderson MSA, SC	Y	16360 FQ	54950 AW	145260 TQ	SCBLS	10/01-12/01
	Myrtle Beach MSA, SC	Y	12060 FQ	27090 AW	44630 TQ	SCBLS	10/01-12/01
	South Dakota	Y	19590 FQ	32370 AW	47720 TQ	SDBLS	10/01-12/01
	Sioux Falls MSA, SD	Y	22070 FQ	38060 AW	59080 TQ	SDBLS	10/01-12/01
	Tennessee	Y	15080 FQ	35860 AW	65550 TQ	TNBLS	10/01-12/01
	Chattanooga MSA, TN-GA	Y	20590 FQ	40310 AW	68640 TQ	TNBLS	10/01-12/01
	Clarksville-Hopkinsville MSA, TN-KY	Y	19170 FQ	30840 AW	45380 TQ	TNBLS	10/01-12/01
	Johnson City-Kingsport-Bristol MSA, TN-VA	Y	14220 FQ	29030 AW	51650 TQ	TNBLS	10/01-12/01
	Knoxville MSA, TN	Y	18280 FQ	41300 AW	71860 TQ	TNBLS	10/01-12/01
	Memphis MSA, TN-AR-MS	Y	13710 FQ	39440 AW	71440 TQ	TNBLS	10/01-12/01
	Nashville MSA, TN	Y	16250 FQ	37200 AW	67370 TQ	TNBLS	10/01-12/01
	Texas	Y	15680 FQ	44400 AW	89870 TQ	TXBLS	10/01-12/01
	Amarillo MSA, TX	Y	16080 FQ	45010 AW	79130 TQ	TXBLS	10/01-12/01
	Austin-San Marcos MSA, TX	Y	18160 FQ	47110 AW	94740 TQ	TXBLS	10/01-12/01
	Beaumont-Port Arthur MSA, TX	Y	13950 FQ	34060 AW	67920 TQ	TXBLS	10/01-12/01
	Brownsville-Harlingen-San Benito MSA, TX	Y	15250 FQ	34620 AW	61200 TQ	TXBLS	10/01-12/01
	Corpus Christi MSA, TX	Y	12190 FQ	31500 AW	66280 TQ	TXBLS	10/01-12/01
	Dallas PMSA, TX	Y	17750 FQ	54500 AW		TXBLS	10/01-12/01
	El Paso MSA, TX	Y	17470 FQ	43860 AW	76130 TQ	TXBLS	10/01-12/01
	Fort Worth-Arlington PMSA, TX	Y	16890 FQ	42120 AW	77760 TQ	TXBLS	10/01-12/01
	Galveston-Texas City PMSA, TX	Y	13130 FQ	27340 AW	49130 TQ	TXBLS	10/01-12/01
	Houston PMSA, TX	Y	17830 FQ	42880 AW	78350 TQ	TXBLS	10/01-12/01
	Killeen-Temple MSA, TX	Y	16330 FQ	41170 AW	88310 TQ	TXBLS	10/01-12/01
	Laredo MSA, TX	Y	14310 FQ	63150 AW		TXBLS	10/01-12/01
	Longview-Marshall MSA, TX	Y	17110 FQ	38490 AW	56560 TQ	TXBLS	10/01-12/01
	Lubbock MSA, TX	Y	22130 FQ	55180 AW	115390 TQ	TXBLS	10/01-12/01
	McAllen-Edinburg-Mission MSA, TX	Y	15360 FQ	32570 AW	72710 TQ	TXBLS	10/01-12/01
	Odessa-Midland MSA, TX	Y	14870 FQ	37760 AW	73370 TQ	TXBLS	10/01-12/01
	San Antonio MSA, TX	Y	17020 FQ	37420 AW	61410 TQ	TXBLS	10/01-12/01
	Tyler MSA, TX	Y	20650 FQ	44100 AW	86100 TQ	TXBLS	10/01-12/01
	Waco MSA, TX	Y	12430 FQ	37640 AW	63830 TQ	TXBLS	10/01-12/01
	Utah	Y	19460 FQ	37380 AW	67120 TQ	UTBLS	10/01-12/01
	Provo-Orem MSA, UT	Y	13500 FQ	29890 AW	43670 TQ	UTBLS	10/01-12/01
	Salt Lake City-Ogden MSA, UT	Y	20520 FQ	40080 AW	76700 TQ	UTBLS	10/01-12/01
	Vermont	Y	19980 FQ	36450 AW	56470 TQ	VTBLS	10/01-12/01
	Burlington MSA, VT	Y	23760 FQ	43070 AW	76400 TQ	VTBLS	10/01-12/01
	Virginia	Y	18610 FQ	54130 AW	133770 TQ	VABLS	10/01-12/01
	Lynchburg MSA, VA	Y	15520 FQ	40960 AW	86070 TQ	VABLS	10/01-12/01
	Norfolk-Virginia Beach-Newport News MSA, VA-NC	Y	16770 FQ	37570 AW	68650 TQ	VABLS	10/01-12/01
	Richmond-Petersburg MSA, VA	Y	20410 FQ	53820 AW	125520 TQ	VABLS	10/01-12/01
	Roanoke MSA, VA	Y	17440 FQ	41580 AW	67730 TQ	VABLS	10/01-12/01
	Washington	Y	20350 FQ	41110 AW	74580 TQ	WABLS	10/01-12/01
	Bremerton PMSA, WA	Y	18620 FQ	37730 AW	63930 TQ	WABLS	10/01-12/01
	Olympia PMSA, WA	Y	16840 FQ	27610 AW	41520 TQ	WABLS	10/01-12/01
	Richland-Kennewick-Pasco MSA, WA	Y	17510 FQ	33360 AW	51070 TQ	WABLS	10/01-12/01
	Seattle-Bellevue-Everett PMSA, WA	Y	21260 FQ	43890 AW	85160 TQ	WABLS	10/01-12/01
	Spokane MSA, WA	Y	20120 FQ	36580 AW	61740 TQ	WABLS	10/01-12/01
	Tacoma PMSA, WA	Y	24140 FQ	41420 AW	66410 TQ	WABLS	10/01-12/01
	Yakima MSA, WA	Y	19690 FQ	39690 AW	71310 TQ	WABLS	10/01-12/01
	West Virginia	Y	14310 FQ	31890 AW	54690 TQ	WVBLS	10/01-12/01
	Charleston MSA, WV	Y	17750 FQ	35300 AW	65670 TQ	WVBLS	10/01-12/01

AAW	Average annual wage	AOH	Average offered, high	ASH	Average starting, high	H	Hourly	M	Monthly	S	Special: hourly and annual
AE	Average entry wage	AOL	Average offered, low	ASL	Average starting, low	HI	Highest wage paid	MTC	Median total compensation	TQ	Third quartile wage
AEX	Average experienced wage	APH	Average pay, high range	AW	Average wage paid	HR	High end range	MW	Median wage paid	W	Weekly
AO	Average offered	APL	Average pay, low range	FQ	First quartile wage	LR	Low end range	SQ	Second quartile wage	Y	Yearly

Occupation/Type/Industry	Location	Per	Low	Mid	High	Source	Date
Advertising Sales Agent	Huntington-Ashland MSA, WV-KY-OH	Y	14520 FQ	31800 AW	55480 TQ	WVBLS	10/01-12/01
	Wisconsin	Y	20360 FQ	42470 AW	77790 TQ	WIBLS	10/01-12/01
	Appleton-Oshkosh-Neenah MSA, WI	Y	21010 FQ	40670 AW	71450 TQ	WIBLS	10/01-12/01
	Green Bay MSA, WI	Y	19780 FQ	37660 AW	69650 TQ	WIBLS	10/01-12/01
	Madison MSA, WI	Y	23500 FQ	44890 AW	74800 TQ	WIBLS	10/01-12/01
	Milwaukee-Waukesha PMSA, WI	Y	24200 FQ	50070 AW	88200 TQ	WIBLS	10/01-12/01
	Racine PMSA, WI	Y	26610 FQ	41840 AW	69940 TQ	WIBLS	10/01-12/01
	Wyoming	Y	15900 FQ	24570 AW	36580 TQ	WYBLS	10/01-12/01
	Puerto Rico	Y	13290 FQ	31560 AW	57740 TQ	PRBLS	10/01-12/01
	Guam	Y	14920 FQ	30750 AW	56030 TQ	GUBLS	10/01-12/01
Aerospace Engineer	Alabama	Y	46960 FQ	70440 AW	93610 TQ	ALBLS	10/01-12/01
	Huntsville MSA, AL	Y	47610 FQ	71260 AW	94430 TQ	ALBLS	10/01-12/01
	Arizona	Y	47890 FQ	70430 AW	102050 TQ	AZBLS	10/01-12/01
	Arkansas	Y	41660 FQ	61400 AW	83670 TQ	ARBLS	10/01-12/01
	California	Y	53570 FQ	74910 AW	102020 TQ	CABLS	10/01-12/01
	Bakersfield MSA, CA	Y	50310 FQ	75230 AW	103860 TQ	CABLS	10/01-12/01
	Los Angeles-Long Beach PMSA, CA	Y	54030 FQ	73480 AW	96580 TQ	CABLS	10/01-12/01
	Oakland PMSA, CA	Y	46800 FQ	76450 AW	112800 TQ	CABLS	10/01-12/01
	Riverside-San Bernardino PMSA, CA	Y	53170 FQ	83270 AW	120970 TQ	CABLS	10/01-12/01
	Sacramento PMSA, CA	Y	50830 FQ	68480 AW	92100 TQ	CABLS	10/01-12/01
	San Diego MSA, CA	Y	55250 FQ	73660 AW	95360 TQ	CABLS	10/01-12/01
	San Jose PMSA, CA	Y	54730 FQ	74490 AW	99500 TQ	CABLS	10/01-12/01
	Ventura PMSA, CA	Y	42970 FQ	81260 AW	115110 TQ	CABLS	10/01-12/01
	Colorado	Y	48270 FQ	68480 AW	94150 TQ	COBLS	10/01-12/01
	Colorado Springs MSA, CO	Y	63320 FQ	83120 AW	109230 TQ	COBLS	10/01-12/01
	Denver PMSA, CO	Y	47980 FQ	67010 AW	90910 TQ	COBLS	10/01-12/01
	Connecticut	Y	51610 FQ	72740 AW	97530 TQ	CTBLS	10/01-12/01
	New Haven-Meriden PMSA, CT	Y	52310 FQ	80100 AW	114770 TQ	CTBLS	10/01-12/01
	District of Columbia	Y	56000 FQ	80480 AW	109350 TQ	DCBLS	10/01-12/01
	Washington PMSA, DC-MD-VA-WV	Y	45800 FQ	72360 AW	105810 TQ	DCBLS	10/01-12/01
	Florida	Y	44030 FQ	67760 AW	105080 TQ	FLBLS	10/01-12/01
	Fort Walton Beach MSA, FL	Y	49000 FQ	66310 AW	87340 TQ	FLBLS	10/01-12/01
	Jacksonville MSA, FL	Y	48380 FQ	62910 AW	80790 TQ	FLBLS	10/01-12/01
	Miami PMSA, FL	Y	39160 FQ	70820 AW	113860 TQ	FLBLS	10/01-12/01
	Orlando MSA, FL	Y	46470 FQ	72900 AW	111390 TQ	FLBLS	10/01-12/01
	Tampa-St. Petersburg-Clearwater MSA, FL	Y	44990 FQ	66480 AW	92080 TQ	FLBLS	10/01-12/01
	West Palm Beach-Boca Raton MSA, FL	Y	46540 FQ	65710 AW	100820 TQ	FLBLS	10/01-12/01
	Georgia	Y	42120 FQ	68460 AW	97720 TQ	GABLS	10/01-12/01
	Atlanta MSA, GA	Y	38550 FQ	66990 AW	97660 TQ	GABLS	10/01-12/01
	Savannah MSA, GA	Y	51720 FQ	71200 AW	93380 TQ	GABLS	10/01-12/01
	Illinois	Y	47430 FQ	55280 AW	71030 TQ	ILBLS	10/01-12/01
	Chicago PMSA, IL	Y	47450 FQ	54630 AW	69010 TQ	ILBLS	10/01-12/01
	Indiana	Y	48860 FQ	60590 AW	82800 TQ	INBLS	10/01-12/01
	Indianapolis MSA, IN	Y	49260 FQ	60320 AW	81440 TQ	INBLS	10/01-12/01
	Kansas	Y	45250 FQ	64720 AW	90090 TQ	KSBLS	10/01-12/01
	Wichita MSA, KS	Y	45340 FQ	64650 AW	89690 TQ	KSBLS	10/01-12/01
	Kentucky	Y	47520 FQ	53960 AW	64050 TQ	KYBLS	10/01-12/01
	Louisiana	Y	49160 FQ	70200 AW	101020 TQ	LABLS	10/01-12/01
	Maryland	Y	49610 FQ	74050 AW	103280 TQ	MDBLS	10/01-12/01
	Baltimore PMSA, MD	Y	46370 FQ	62660 AW	94090 TQ	MDBLS	10/01-12/01
	Massachusetts	Y	49200 FQ	76360 AW	113190 TQ	MABLS	10/01-12/01
	Boston PMSA, MA-NH	Y	53060 FQ	81030 AW	114990 TQ	MABLS	10/01-12/01
	Michigan	Y	44250 FQ	61080 AW	83860 TQ	MIBLS	10/01-12/01
	Detroit PMSA, MI	Y	42030 FQ	60230 AW	86270 TQ	MIBLS	10/01-12/01
	Grand Rapids-Muskegon-Holland MSA, MI	Y	46160 FQ	58680 AW	75190 TQ	MIBLS	10/01-12/01
	Minnesota	Y	39960 FQ	57810 AW	78340 TQ	MNBLS	10/01-12/01
	Minneapolis-St. Paul MSA, MN-WI	Y	40250 FQ	59300 AW	82610 TQ	MNBLS	10/01-12/01
	Mississippi	Y	50080 FQ	75590 AW	108500 TQ	MSBLS	10/01-12/01
	Biloxi-Gulfport-Pascagoula MSA, MS	Y	49990 FQ	75750 AW	108930 TQ	MSBLS	10/01-12/01
	Kansas City MSA, MO-KS	Y	34760 FQ	73820 AW	111330 TQ	MOBLS	10/01-12/01

AAW	Average annual wage	AOH	Average offered, high	ASH	Average starting, high	H	Hourly	M	Monthly	S	Special: hourly and annual
AE	Average entry wage	AOL	Average offered, low	ASL	Average starting, low	HI	Highest wage paid	MTC	Median total compensation	TQ	Third quartile wage
AEX	Average experienced wage	APH	Average pay, high range	AW	Average wage paid	HR	High end range	MW	Median wage paid	W	Weekly
AO	Average offered	APL	Average pay, low range	FQ	First quartile wage	LR	Low end range	SQ	Second quartile wage	Y	Yearly

Occupation/Type/Industry	Location	Per	Low	Mid	High	Source	Date
Aerospace Engineer	New Jersey	Y	49220 FQ	70340 AW	93160 TQ	NJBLS	10/01-12/01
	Monmouth-Ocean PMSA, NJ	Y	51410 FQ	66610 AW	85830 TQ	NJBLS	10/01-12/01
	Newark PMSA, NJ	Y	56750 FQ	73390 AW	91090 TQ	NJBLS	10/01-12/01
	New Mexico	Y	57160 FQ	85420 AW	115250 TQ	NMBLS	10/01-12/01
	Albuquerque MSA, NM	Y	63200 FQ	89650 AW	115200 TQ	NMBLS	10/01-12/01
	Las Cruces MSA, NM	Y	48660 FQ	68430 AW	89820 TQ	NMBLS	10/01-12/01
	New York	Y	51360 FQ	78760 AW	113820 TQ	NYBLS	10/01-12/01
	Buffalo-Niagara Falls MSA, NY	Y	47130 FQ	66270 AW	95230 TQ	NYBLS	10/01-12/01
	Nassau-Suffolk PMSA, NY	Y	59470 FQ	85740 AW	116380 TQ	NYBLS	10/01-12/01
	North Carolina	Y	45100 FQ	62860 AW	84740 TQ	NCBLS	10/01-12/01
	Ohio	Y	53060 FQ	73620 AW	98810 TQ	OHBLS	10/01-12/01
	Cleveland-Lorain-Elyria PMSA, OH	Y	59400 FQ	81250 AW	108230 TQ	OHBLS	10/01-12/01
	Dayton-Springfield MSA, OH	Y	56810 FQ	75400 AW	99570 TQ	OHBLS	10/01-12/01
	Oklahoma	Y	47000 FQ	59530 AW	81300 TQ	OKBLS	10/01-12/01
	Oklahoma City MSA, OK	Y	42060 FQ	61620 AW	81700 TQ	OKBLS	10/01-12/01
	Tulsa MSA, OK	Y	47340 FQ	58550 AW	81400 TQ	OKBLS	10/01-12/01
	Oregon	Y	34130 FQ	72420 AW		ORBLS	10/01-12/01
	South Carolina	Y	47550 FQ	65430 AW	88410 TQ	SCBLS	10/01-12/01
	Greenville-Spartanburg-Anderson MSA, SC	Y	48680 FQ	67730 AW	89470 TQ	SCBLS	10/01-12/01
	Texas	Y	47390 FQ	70170 AW	97530 TQ	TXBLS	10/01-12/01
	Dallas PMSA, TX	Y	48470 FQ	74010 AW	105610 TQ	TXBLS	10/01-12/01
	Fort Worth-Arlington PMSA, TX	Y	44290 FQ	65340 AW	90670 TQ	TXBLS	10/01-12/01
	Houston PMSA, TX	Y	47910 FQ	71030 AW	98610 TQ	TXBLS	10/01-12/01
	San Antonio MSA, TX	Y	48650 FQ	74480 AW	113880 TQ	TXBLS	10/01-12/01
	Waco MSA, TX	Y	51850 FQ	76350 AW	125560 TQ	TXBLS	10/01-12/01
	Utah	Y	42820 FQ	64380 AW	90740 TQ	UTBLS	10/01-12/01
	Salt Lake City-Ogden MSA, UT	Y	42600 FQ	65570 AW	92020 TQ	UTBLS	10/01-12/01
	Virginia	Y	45340 FQ	70790 AW	103730 TQ	VABLS	10/01-12/01
	Norfolk-Virginia Beach-Newport News MSA, VA-NC	Y	51840 FQ	76880 AW	106070 TQ	VABLS	10/01-12/01
	Washington	Y	53950 FQ	75530 AW	99300 TQ	WABLS	10/01-12/01
	Seattle-Bellevue-Everett PMSA, WA	Y	54020 FQ	75590 AW	99400 TQ	WABLS	10/01-12/01
Aerospace Engineering and Operations Technician	Alabama	Y	31940 FQ	48900 AW	72820 TQ	ALBLS	10/01-12/01
	Huntsville MSA, AL	Y	35960 FQ	55470 AW	76180 TQ	ALBLS	10/01-12/01
	Arizona	Y	32160 FQ	55180 AW	77410 TQ	AZBLS	10/01-12/01
	Phoenix-Mesa MSA, AZ	Y	33470 FQ	55880 AW	77890 TQ	AZBLS	10/01-12/01
	California	Y	39400 FQ	55570 AW	74350 TQ	CABLS	10/01-12/01
	Los Angeles-Long Beach PMSA, CA	Y	39620 FQ	57260 AW	77250 TQ	CABLS	10/01-12/01
	San Jose PMSA, CA	Y	43110 FQ	60150 AW	75650 TQ	CABLS	10/01-12/01
	Colorado	Y	36630 FQ	51950 AW	70080 TQ	COBLS	10/01-12/01
	New Haven-Meriden PMSA, CT	Y	33210 FQ	50320 AW	69150 TQ	CTBLS	10/01-12/01
	Washington PMSA, DC-MD-VA-WV	Y	30860 FQ	48310 AW	67730 TQ	DCBLS	10/01-12/01
	Florida	Y	30860 FQ	45030 AW	57720 TQ	FLBLS	10/01-12/01
	Fort Lauderdale PMSA, FL	Y	39800 FQ	46970 AW	57340 TQ	FLBLS	10/01-12/01
	Miami PMSA, FL	Y	38910 FQ	48940 AW	57870 TQ	FLBLS	10/01-12/01
	Orlando MSA, FL	Y	36070 FQ	48040 AW	61760 TQ	FLBLS	10/01-12/01
	Tampa-St. Petersburg-Clearwater MSA, FL	Y	26890 FQ	41520 AW	58250 TQ	FLBLS	10/01-12/01
	Georgia	Y	31890 FQ	43890 AW	58130 TQ	GABLS	10/01-12/01
	Savannah MSA, GA	Y	31430 FQ	40860 AW	46260 TQ	GABLS	10/01-12/01
	Hawaii	Y	35850 FQ	56130 AW	76360 TQ	HIBLS	10/01-12/01
	Honolulu MSA, HI	Y	34810 FQ	56330 AW	80230 TQ	HIBLS	10/01-12/01
	Illinois	Y	39110 FQ	54860 AW	79050 TQ	ILBLS	10/01-12/01
	Chicago PMSA, IL	Y	40010 FQ	54230 AW	81200 TQ	ILBLS	10/01-12/01
	Iowa	Y	23670 FQ	36750 AW	59000 TQ	IABLS	10/01-12/01
	Kentucky	Y	31960 FQ	45870 AW	57400 TQ	KYBLS	10/01-12/01
	Louisiana	Y	24230 FQ	39920 AW	62880 TQ	LABLS	10/01-12/01
	Maryland	Y	31760 FQ	49290 AW	68460 TQ	MDBLS	10/01-12/01
	Massachusetts	Y	37960 FQ	67340 AW		MABLS	10/01-12/01
	Boston PMSA, MA-NH	Y	39080 FQ	71730 AW		MABLS	10/01-12/01

AAW	Average annual wage	**AOH**	Average offered, high	**ASH**	Average starting, high	**H**	Hourly	**M**	Monthly	**S**	Special: hourly and annual
AE	Average entry wage	**AOL**	Average offered, low	**ASL**	Average starting, low	**HI**	Highest wage paid	**MTC**	Median total compensation	**TQ**	Third quartile wage
AEX	Average experienced wage	**APH**	Average pay, high range	**AW**	Average wage paid	**HR**	High end range	**MW**	Median wage paid	**W**	Weekly
AO	Average offered	**APL**	Average pay, low range	**FQ**	First quartile wage	**LR**	Low end range	**SQ**	Second quartile wage	**Y**	Yearly

Occupation/Type/Industry	Location	Per	Low	Mid	High	Source	Date
Aerospace Engineering and Operations Technician	Michigan	Y	24020 FQ	39100 AW	53810 TQ	MIBLS	10/01-12/01
	Detroit PMSA, MI	Y	25430 FQ	37880 AW	46120 TQ	MIBLS	10/01-12/01
	Grand Rapids-Muskegon-Holland MSA, MI	Y	21770 FQ	39860 AW	56270 TQ	MIBLS	10/01-12/01
	Minnesota	Y	33770 FQ	47960 AW	59120 TQ	MNBLS	10/01-12/01
	Minneapolis-St. Paul MSA, MN-WI	Y	38720 FQ	48970 AW	58660 TQ	MNBLS	10/01-12/01
	New Jersey	Y	29370 FQ	45180 AW	59380 TQ	NJBLS	10/01-12/01
	New Mexico	Y	33340 FQ	44610 AW	57500 TQ	NMBLS	10/01-12/01
	New York	Y	36990 FQ	49660 AW	61870 TQ	NYBLS	10/01-12/01
	Buffalo-Niagara Falls MSA, NY	Y	26070 FQ	44190 AW	61020 TQ	NYBLS	10/01-12/01
	North Carolina	Y	26210 FQ	48070 AW	69020 TQ	NCBLS	10/01-12/01
	Ohio	Y	27340 FQ	43020 AW	59450 TQ	OHBLS	10/01-12/01
	Cleveland-Lorain-Elyria PMSA, OH	Y	29210 FQ	44150 AW	77790 TQ	OHBLS	10/01-12/01
	Columbus MSA, OH	Y	26120 FQ	37830 AW	51600 TQ	OHBLS	10/01-12/01
	Oklahoma	Y	24250 FQ	43170 AW	58150 TQ	OKBLS	10/01-12/01
	Oklahoma City MSA, OK	Y	25410 FQ	39250 AW	47840 TQ	OKBLS	10/01-12/01
	Tulsa MSA, OK	Y	23980 FQ	43430 AW	58190 TQ	OKBLS	10/01-12/01
	Pennsylvania	Y	33840 FQ	51050 AW	68840 TQ	PABLS	10/01-12/01
	Harrisburg-Lebanon-Carlisle MSA, PA	Y	41120 FQ	49830 AW	57860 TQ	PABLS	10/01-12/01
	Pittsburgh MSA, PA	Y	31370 FQ	47680 AW	58040 TQ	PABLS	10/01-12/01
	Rhode Island	Y	31570 FQ	37210 AW	45370 TQ	RIBLS	10/01-12/01
	Tennessee	Y	29130 FQ	48010 AW	69690 TQ	TNBLS	10/01-12/01
	Nashville MSA, TN	Y	32690 FQ	51840 AW	72250 TQ	TNBLS	10/01-12/01
	Texas	Y	29270 FQ	46880 AW	67150 TQ	TXBLS	10/01-12/01
	Austin-San Marcos MSA, TX	Y	25270 FQ	38640 AW	49580 TQ	TXBLS	10/01-12/01
	Dallas PMSA, TX	Y	29200 FQ	46320 AW	67750 TQ	TXBLS	10/01-12/01
	Fort Worth-Arlington PMSA, TX	Y	38350 FQ	52930 AW	70020 TQ	TXBLS	10/01-12/01
	Utah	Y	21890 FQ	38670 AW	57800 TQ	UTBLS	10/01-12/01
	Salt Lake City-Ogden MSA, UT	Y	21480 FQ	36720 AW	55840 TQ	UTBLS	10/01-12/01
	Virginia	Y	31070 FQ	49950 AW	80270 TQ	VABLS	10/01-12/01
	Norfolk-Virginia Beach-Newport News MSA, VA-NC	Y	30350 FQ	46260 AW	77470 TQ	VABLS	10/01-12/01
	Washington	Y	41340 FQ	60830 AW	85530 TQ	WABLS	10/01-12/01
	Seattle-Bellevue-Everett PMSA, WA	Y	41590 FQ	60980 AW	85660 TQ	WABLS	10/01-12/01
	Wisconsin	Y	28230 FQ	42890 AW	58540 TQ	WIBLS	10/01-12/01
Agent and Business Manager							
Artists, Performers, and Athletes	California	Y	37260 FQ	89990 AW		CABLS	10/01-12/01
Artists, Performers, and Athletes	Los Angeles-Long Beach PMSA, CA	Y	39730 FQ	91420 AW		CABLS	10/01-12/01
Artists, Performers, and Athletes	San Diego MSA, CA	Y	38320 FQ	69950 AW		CABLS	10/01-12/01
Artists, Performers, and Athletes	San Francisco PMSA, CA	Y	44600 FQ	115610 AW		CABLS	10/01-12/01
Artists, Performers, and Athletes	Boulder-Longmont PMSA, CO	Y	24470 FQ	29330 AW	34440 TQ	COBLS	10/01-12/01
Artists, Performers, and Athletes	District of Columbia	Y	28450 FQ	44070 AW	97080 TQ	DCBLS	10/01-12/01
Artists, Performers, and Athletes	Washington PMSA, DC-MD-VA-WV	Y	33840 FQ	59120 AW	92100 TQ	DCBLS	10/01-12/01
Artists, Performers, and Athletes	Daytona Beach MSA, FL	Y	18810 FQ	24090 AW	31910 TQ	FLBLS	10/01-12/01
Artists, Performers, and Athletes	Miami PMSA, FL	Y	26520 FQ	72390 AW	101440 TQ	FLBLS	10/01-12/01
Artists, Performers, and Athletes	Orlando MSA, FL	Y	18770 FQ	36540 AW	69560 TQ	FLBLS	10/01-12/01
Artists, Performers, and Athletes	Tampa-St. Petersburg-Clearwater MSA, FL	Y	44530 FQ	115910 AW		FLBLS	10/01-12/01
Artists, Performers, and Athletes	Illinois	Y	21550 FQ	45360 AW	70930 TQ	ILBLS	10/01-12/01
Artists, Performers, and Athletes	Chicago PMSA, IL	Y	21110 FQ	44240 AW	72810 TQ	ILBLS	10/01-12/01
Artists, Performers, and Athletes	Indiana	Y	36320 FQ	44890 AW	65110 TQ	INBLS	10/01-12/01
Artists, Performers, and Athletes	Indianapolis MSA, IN	Y	36550 FQ	44610 AW	64630 TQ	INBLS	10/01-12/01
Artists, Performers, and Athletes	Baton Rouge MSA, LA	Y	32130 FQ	85940 AW		LABLS	10/01-12/01
Artists, Performers, and Athletes	Massachusetts	Y	45520 FQ	50920 AW	56550 TQ	MABLS	10/01-12/01
Artists, Performers, and Athletes	Michigan	Y	23460 FQ	43020 AW	69860 TQ	MIBLS	10/01-12/01
Artists, Performers, and Athletes	Detroit PMSA, MI	Y	24260 FQ	43740 AW	70470 TQ	MIBLS	10/01-12/01
Artists, Performers, and Athletes	Missouri	Y	19770 FQ	36300 AW	50440 TQ	MOBLS	10/01-12/01
Artists, Performers, and Athletes	Kansas City MSA, MO-KS	Y	35540 FQ	44310 AW	55180 TQ	MOBLS	10/01-12/01
Artists, Performers, and Athletes	St. Louis MSA, MO-IL	Y	19720 FQ	35050 AW	45610 TQ	MOBLS	10/01-12/01
Artists, Performers, and Athletes	Nevada	Y	28200 FQ	48620 AW	55710 TQ	NVBLS	10/01-12/01

AAW	Average annual wage	**AOH**	Average offered, high	**ASH**	Average starting, high	**H**	Hourly	**M**	Monthly	**S**	Special: hourly and annual
AE	Average entry wage	**AOL**	Average offered, low	**ASL**	Average starting, low	**HI**	Highest wage paid	**MTC**	Median total compensation	**TQ**	Third quartile wage
AEX	Average experienced wage	**APH**	Average pay, high range	**AW**	Average wage paid	**HR**	High end range	**MW**	Median wage paid	**W**	Weekly
AO	Average offered	**APL**	Average pay, low range	**FQ**	First quartile wage	**LR**	Low end range	**SQ**	Second quartile wage	**Y**	Yearly

Occupation/Type/Industry	Location	Per	Low	Mid	High	Source	Date
Agent and Business Manager							
Artists, Performers, and Athletes	Las Vegas MSA, NV-AZ	Y	27690 FQ	44740 AW	55070 TQ	NVBLS	10/01-12/01
Artists, Performers, and Athletes	New Jersey	Y	30490 FQ	68180 AW		NJBLS	10/01-12/01
Artists, Performers, and Athletes	Bergen-Passaic PMSA, NJ	Y	28370 FQ	41510 AW	66370 TQ	NJBLS	10/01-12/01
Artists, Performers, and Athletes	Monmouth-Ocean PMSA, NJ	Y	30940 FQ	63210 AW	104270 TQ	NJBLS	10/01-12/01
Artists, Performers, and Athletes	Newark PMSA, NJ	Y	39780 FQ	88030 AW		NJBLS	10/01-12/01
Artists, Performers, and Athletes	New York	Y	40770 FQ	95610 AW		NYBLS	10/01-12/01
Artists, Performers, and Athletes	New York PMSA, NY	Y	40500 FQ	96410 AW		NYBLS	10/01-12/01
Artists, Performers, and Athletes	Ohio	Y	26490 FQ	44860 AW	66980 TQ	OHBLS	10/01-12/01
Artists, Performers, and Athletes	Oklahoma	Y	22860 FQ	42390 AW	70040 TQ	OKBLS	10/01-12/01
Artists, Performers, and Athletes	Pennsylvania	Y	13090 FQ	40320 AW	59800 TQ	PABLS	10/01-12/01
Artists, Performers, and Athletes	Harrisburg-Lebanon-Carlisle MSA, PA	Y	13260 FQ	26030 AW	47260 TQ	PABLS	10/01-12/01
Artists, Performers, and Athletes	Philadelphia PMSA, PA-NJ	Y	13890 FQ	45680 AW	60760 TQ	PABLS	10/01-12/01
Artists, Performers, and Athletes	South Carolina	Y	20080 FQ	28860 AW	48830 TQ	SCBLS	10/01-12/01
Artists, Performers, and Athletes	Columbia MSA, SC	Y	21060 FQ	32220 AW	57160 TQ	SCBLS	10/01-12/01
Artists, Performers, and Athletes	Tennessee	Y	51750 FQ	67600 AW	87500 TQ	TNBLS	10/01-12/01
Artists, Performers, and Athletes	Memphis MSA, TN-AR-MS	Y	65450 FQ	78160 AW	92020 TQ	TNBLS	10/01-12/01
Artists, Performers, and Athletes	Nashville MSA, TN	Y	52260 FQ	65860 AW	84080 TQ	TNBLS	10/01-12/01
Artists, Performers, and Athletes	Texas	Y	13690 FQ	31270 AW	57230 TQ	TXBLS	10/01-12/01
Artists, Performers, and Athletes	Austin-San Marcos MSA, TX	Y	23070 FQ	28170 AW	40720 TQ	TXBLS	10/01-12/01
Artists, Performers, and Athletes	Dallas PMSA, TX	Y	12280 FQ	31570 AW	65430 TQ	TXBLS	10/01-12/01
Artists, Performers, and Athletes	Fort Worth-Arlington PMSA, TX	Y	22870 FQ	27070 AW	27840 TQ	TXBLS	10/01-12/01
Artists, Performers, and Athletes	Virginia	Y	35790 FQ	59350 AW	92010 TQ	VABLS	10/01-12/01
Artists, Performers, and Athletes	Seattle-Bellevue-Everett PMSA, WA	Y	28680 FQ	32480 AW	34960 TQ	WABLS	10/01-12/01
Artists, Performers, and Athletes	Wisconsin	Y	23780 FQ	40250 AW	69140 TQ	WIBLS	10/01-12/01
Agricultural and Food Science Technician	Alabama	Y	16330 FQ	27940 AW	46560 TQ	ALBLS	10/01-12/01
	Arkansas	Y	17170 FQ	28430 AW	55780 TQ	ARBLS	10/01-12/01
	California	Y	13750 FQ	27240 AW	44370 TQ	CABLS	10/01-12/01
	Colorado	Y	21870 FQ	31780 AW	45200 TQ	COBLS	10/01-12/01
	Connecticut	Y	20140 FQ	38700 AW	56480 TQ	CTBLS	10/01-12/01
	Delaware	Y	19070 FQ	27780 AW	36800 TQ	DEBLS	10/01-12/01
	Florida	Y	18730 FQ	23090 AW	31750 TQ	FLBLS	10/01-12/01
	Georgia	Y	20600 FQ	28990 AW	40130 TQ	GABLS	10/01-12/01
	Hawaii	Y	19650 FQ	27090 AW	37610 TQ	HIBLS	10/01-12/01
	Idaho	Y	16970 FQ	28640 AW	45620 TQ	IDBLS	10/01-12/01
	Illinois	Y	16830 FQ	30490 AW	47640 TQ	ILBLS	10/01-12/01
	Indiana	Y	16090 FQ	31180 AW	50440 TQ	INBLS	10/01-12/01
	Iowa	Y	12560 FQ	28490 AW	51720 TQ	IABLS	10/01-12/01
	Kansas	Y	20140 FQ	31050 AW	48330 TQ	KSBLS	10/01-12/01
	Kentucky	Y	20250 FQ	31790 AW	44520 TQ	KYBLS	10/01-12/01
	Louisiana	Y	16600 FQ	33710 AW	51300 TQ	LABLS	10/01-12/01
	Maryland	Y	24570 FQ	39080 AW	60630 TQ	MDBLS	10/01-12/01
	Massachusetts	Y	24210 FQ	34190 AW	54200 TQ	MABLS	10/01-12/01
	Michigan	Y	19470 FQ	33240 AW	52870 TQ	MIBLS	10/01-12/01
	Minnesota	Y	23300 FQ	31280 AW	43240 TQ	MNBLS	10/01-12/01
	Mississippi	Y	15260 FQ	26720 AW	39930 TQ	MSBLS	10/01-12/01
	Missouri	Y	19210 FQ	35020 AW	56190 TQ	MOBLS	10/01-12/01
	Nebraska	Y	19180 FQ	29610 AW	43070 TQ	NEBLS	10/01-12/01
	New Jersey	Y	20610 FQ	36890 AW	55380 TQ	NJBLS	10/01-12/01
	New York	Y	17170 FQ	28200 AW	39750 TQ	NYBLS	10/01-12/01
	North Carolina	Y	18840 FQ	27980 AW	38890 TQ	NCBLS	10/01-12/01
	North Dakota	Y	14970 FQ	25030 AW	39020 TQ	NDBLS	10/01-12/01
	Ohio	Y	15170 FQ	27380 AW	44150 TQ	OHBLS	10/01-12/01
	Oklahoma	Y	18820 FQ	28830 AW	40610 TQ	OKBLS	10/01-12/01
	Oregon	Y	15880 FQ	26270 AW	40930 TQ	ORBLS	10/01-12/01
	Pennsylvania	Y	19600 FQ	31730 AW	44940 TQ	PABLS	10/01-12/01
	South Carolina	Y	13710 FQ	25420 AW	41890 TQ	SCBLS	10/01-12/01
	Tennessee	Y	15130 FQ	29630 AW	49120 TQ	TNBLS	10/01-12/01
	Texas	Y	17110 FQ	29430 AW	44390 TQ	TXBLS	10/01-12/01
	Utah	Y	14140 FQ	27940 AW	34930 TQ	UTBLS	10/01-12/01
	Vermont	Y	19470 FQ	27550 AW	41010 TQ	VTBLS	10/01-12/01
	Virginia	Y	16250 FQ	26320 AW	37430 TQ	VABLS	10/01-12/01
	Washington	Y	19520 FQ	33420 AW	46240 TQ	WABLS	10/01-12/01
	Wisconsin	Y	17200 FQ	30650 AW	50580 TQ	WIBLS	10/01-12/01
Agricultural and Food Scientist	Alabama	Y	32080 FQ	47930 AW	69260 TQ	ALBLS	10/01-12/01
	Alaska	Y	40180 FQ	62090 AW	86970 TQ	AKBLS	10/01-12/01

AAW	Average annual wage	**AOH**	Average offered, high	**ASH**	Average starting, high	**H**	Hourly	**M**	Monthly	**S**	Special: hourly and annual
AE	Average entry wage	**AOL**	Average offered, low	**ASL**	Average starting, low	**HI**	Highest wage paid	**MTC**	Median total compensation	**TQ**	Third quartile wage
AEX	Average experienced wage	**APH**	Average pay, high range	**AW**	Average wage paid	**HR**	High end range	**MW**	Median wage paid	**W**	Weekly
AO	Average offered	**APL**	Average pay, low range	**FQ**	First quartile wage	**LR**	Low end range	**SQ**	Second quartile wage	**Y**	Yearly

Occupation/Type/Industry	Location	Per	Low	Mid	High	Source	Date
Agricultural and Food Scientist	Arizona	Y	28620 FQ	47960 AW	71300 TQ	AZBLS	10/01-12/01
	Phoenix-Mesa MSA, AZ	Y	29010 FQ	52400 AW	80880 TQ	AZBLS	10/01-12/01
	Arkansas	Y	26930 FQ	49040 AW	77790 TQ	ARBLS	10/01-12/01
	California	Y	29240 FQ	55800 AW	92310 TQ	CABLS	10/01-12/01
	Chico-Paradise MSA, CA	Y	31230 FQ	52360 AW	93040 TQ	CABLS	10/01-12/01
	Fresno MSA, CA	Y	39310 FQ	71030 AW	109530 TQ	CABLS	10/01-12/01
	Los Angeles-Long Beach PMSA, CA	Y	26090 FQ	53900 AW	89060 TQ	CABLS	10/01-12/01
	Modesto MSA, CA	Y	33750 FQ	74140 AW	110360 TQ	CABLS	10/01-12/01
	Oakland PMSA, CA	Y	35170 FQ	58190 AW	81810 TQ	CABLS	10/01-12/01
	Orange County PMSA, CA	Y	21470 FQ	38570 AW	63440 TQ	CABLS	10/01-12/01
	Riverside-San Bernardino PMSA, CA	Y	26570 FQ	52040 AW	82450 TQ	CABLS	10/01-12/01
	Sacramento PMSA, CA	Y	39110 FQ	58560 AW	74870 TQ	CABLS	10/01-12/01
	Salinas MSA, CA	Y	29710 FQ	49510 AW	72750 TQ	CABLS	10/01-12/01
	San Francisco PMSA, CA	Y	26700 FQ	65880 AW	109150 TQ	CABLS	10/01-12/01
	San Jose PMSA, CA	Y	38730 FQ	60200 AW	82410 TQ	CABLS	10/01-12/01
	Santa Rosa PMSA, CA	Y	33070 FQ	40930 AW	51400 TQ	CABLS	10/01-12/01
	Stockton-Lodi MSA, CA	Y	34590 FQ	50660 AW	78330 TQ	CABLS	10/01-12/01
	Vallejo-Fairfield-Napa PMSA, CA	Y	32360 FQ	56920 AW	95670 TQ	CABLS	10/01-12/01
	Visalia-Tulare-Porterville MSA, CA	Y	30310 FQ	53340 AW	97210 TQ	CABLS	10/01-12/01
	Colorado	Y	30100 FQ	50220 AW	74810 TQ	COBLS	10/01-12/01
	Denver PMSA, CO	Y	31010 FQ	49260 AW	71300 TQ	COBLS	10/01-12/01
	Fort Collins-Loveland MSA, CO	Y	38850 FQ	65190 AW	101590 TQ	COBLS	10/01-12/01
	Connecticut	Y	40990 FQ	69160 AW	107400 TQ	CTBLS	10/01-12/01
	New Haven-Meriden PMSA, CT	Y	32240 FQ	71540 AW	111300 TQ	CTBLS	10/01-12/01
	District of Columbia	Y	35270 FQ	70720 AW	106540 TQ	DCBLS	10/01-12/01
	Washington PMSA, DC-MD-VA-WV	Y	36000 FQ	68240 AW	103380 TQ	DCBLS	10/01-12/01
	Florida	Y	26380 FQ	49850 AW	81940 TQ	FLBLS	10/01-12/01
	Gainesville MSA, FL	Y	24750 FQ	48250 AW	83230 TQ	FLBLS	10/01-12/01
	Tampa-St. Petersburg-Clearwater MSA, FL	Y	13080 FQ	39760 AW	66690 TQ	FLBLS	10/01-12/01
	West Palm Beach-Boca Raton MSA, FL	Y	31750 FQ	47980 AW	73350 TQ	FLBLS	10/01-12/01
	Georgia	Y	29280 FQ	49850 AW	75640 TQ	GABLS	10/01-12/01
	Atlanta MSA, GA	Y	25910 FQ	47530 AW	73140 TQ	GABLS	10/01-12/01
	Hawaii	Y	36400 FQ	51620 AW	70810 TQ	HIBLS	10/01-12/01
	Honolulu MSA, HI	Y	36480 FQ	51390 AW	69470 TQ	HIBLS	10/01-12/01
	Idaho	Y	38680 FQ	56370 AW	78990 TQ	IDBLS	10/01-12/01
	Boise City MSA, ID	Y	45490 FQ	59820 AW	81200 TQ	IDBLS	10/01-12/01
	Illinois	Y	25730 FQ	51540 AW	83450 TQ	ILBLS	10/01-12/01
	Champaign-Urbana MSA, IL	Y	24390 FQ	51440 AW	94800 TQ	ILBLS	10/01-12/01
	Chicago PMSA, IL	Y	29570 FQ	53560 AW	84830 TQ	ILBLS	10/01-12/01
	Indiana	Y	29930 FQ	52040 AW	83880 TQ	INBLS	10/01-12/01
	Fort Wayne MSA, IN	Y	26890 FQ	55390 AW	88000 TQ	INBLS	10/01-12/01
	Gary PMSA, IN	Y	31780 FQ	47970 AW	77020 TQ	INBLS	10/01-12/01
	Indianapolis MSA, IN	Y	32020 FQ	59390 AW	87610 TQ	INBLS	10/01-12/01
	Iowa	Y	28150 FQ	53380 AW	90590 TQ	IABLS	10/01-12/01
	Kansas	Y	25460 FQ	40570 AW	57890 TQ	KSBLS	10/01-12/01
	Louisville MSA, KY-IN	Y	31910 FQ	47940 AW	69380 TQ	KYBLS	10/01-12/01
	Louisiana	Y	33860 FQ	53460 AW	75470 TQ	LABLS	10/01-12/01
	Maine	Y	26260 FQ	43760 AW	59700 TQ	MEBLS	10/01-12/01
	Maryland	Y	31540 FQ	58400 AW	93220 TQ	MDBLS	10/01-12/01
	Baltimore PMSA, MD	Y	27640 FQ	48010 AW	69070 TQ	MDBLS	10/01-12/01
	Massachusetts	Y	33630 FQ	60590 AW	87500 TQ	MABLS	10/01-12/01
	Boston PMSA, MA-NH	Y	31610 FQ	56230 AW	83030 TQ	MABLS	10/01-12/01
	Michigan	Y	23250 FQ	64610 AW	109500 TQ	MIBLS	10/01-12/01
	Minnesota	Y	32350 FQ	53950 AW	85420 TQ	MNBLS	10/01-12/01
	Minneapolis-St. Paul MSA, MN-WI	Y	31590 FQ	54900 AW	87690 TQ	MNBLS	10/01-12/01
	Mississippi	Y	30090 FQ	55990 AW	83550 TQ	MSBLS	10/01-12/01
	Missouri	Y	25750 FQ	53260 AW	90700 TQ	MOBLS	10/01-12/01
	Kansas City MSA, MO-KS	Y	32730 FQ	49790 AW	63570 TQ	MOBLS	10/01-12/01
	St. Louis MSA, MO-IL	Y	27640 FQ	51490 AW	75260 TQ	MOBLS	10/01-12/01
	Montana	Y	34140 FQ	50300 AW	68260 TQ	MTBLS	10/01-12/01
	Nebraska	Y	27590 FQ	50560 AW	83860 TQ	NEBLS	10/01-12/01
	Lincoln MSA, NE	Y	37710 FQ	65930 AW	91150 TQ	NEBLS	10/01-12/01

AAW	Average annual wage	**AOH**	Average offered, high	**ASH**	Average starting, high	**H**	Hourly	**M**	Monthly	**S**	Special: hourly and annual
AE	Average entry wage	**AOL**	Average offered, low	**ASL**	Average starting, low	**HI**	Highest wage paid	**MTC**	Median total compensation	**TQ**	Third quartile wage
AEX	Average experienced wage	**APH**	Average pay, high range	**AW**	Average wage paid	**HR**	High end range	**MW**	Median wage paid	**W**	Weekly
AO	Average offered	**APL**	Average pay, low range	**FQ**	First quartile wage	**LR**	Low end range	**SQ**	Second quartile wage	**Y**	Yearly

Occupation/Type/Industry	Location	Per	Low	Mid	High	Source	Date
Agricultural and Food Scientist	Omaha MSA, NE-IA	Y	31020 FQ	49940 AW	77210 TQ	NEBLS	10/01-12/01
	Nevada	Y	35420 FQ	51280 AW	69580 TQ	NVBLS	10/01-12/01
	New Hampshire	Y	37970 FQ	56160 AW	83090 TQ	NHBLS	10/01-12/01
	New Jersey	Y	36580 FQ	68510 AW	106690 TQ	NJBLS	10/01-12/01
	Bergen-Passaic PMSA, NJ	Y	40080 FQ	69070 AW	102980 TQ	NJBLS	10/01-12/01
	Newark PMSA, NJ	Y	31780 FQ	68190 AW	115710 TQ	NJBLS	10/01-12/01
	New Mexico	Y	39540 FQ	54160 AW	73010 TQ	NMBLS	10/01-12/01
	New York	Y	27260 FQ	49880 AW	83530 TQ	NYBLS	10/01-12/01
	New York PMSA, NY	Y	37850 FQ	57010 AW	85100 TQ	NYBLS	10/01-12/01
	Rochester MSA, NY	Y	23070 FQ	42970 AW	56280 TQ	NYBLS	10/01-12/01
	North Carolina	Y	30490 FQ	46250 AW	74600 TQ	NCBLS	10/01-12/01
	Charlotte-Gastonia-Rock Hill MSA, NC-SC	Y	26470 FQ	36240 AW	51350 TQ	NCBLS	10/01-12/01
	Greensboro-Winston-Salem-High Point MSA, NC	Y	30550 FQ	47640 AW	81150 TQ	NCBLS	10/01-12/01
	Raleigh-Durham-Chapel Hill MSA, NC	Y	31970 FQ	46770 AW	71870 TQ	NCBLS	10/01-12/01
	North Dakota	Y	28460 FQ	43550 AW	62690 TQ	NDBLS	10/01-12/01
	Fargo-Moorhead MSA, ND-MN	Y	27090 FQ	39850 AW	68000 TQ	NDBLS	10/01-12/01
	Ohio	Y	26660 FQ	52550 AW	83060 TQ	OHBLS	10/01-12/01
	Cincinnati PMSA, OH-KY-IN	Y	30030 FQ	59930 AW	105420 TQ	OHBLS	10/01-12/01
	Cleveland-Lorain-Elyria PMSA, OH	Y	21570 FQ	43200 AW	65010 TQ	OHBLS	10/01-12/01
	Columbus MSA, OH	Y	40070 FQ	57110 AW	78350 TQ	OHBLS	10/01-12/01
	Oklahoma	Y	31590 FQ	52690 AW	78240 TQ	OKBLS	10/01-12/01
	Oregon	Y	32750 FQ	49570 AW	76850 TQ	ORBLS	10/01-12/01
	Portland-Vancouver PMSA, OR-WA	Y	31730 FQ	51100 AW	83270 TQ	ORBLS	10/01-12/01
	Salem PMSA, OR	Y	31280 FQ	45940 AW	61210 TQ	ORBLS	10/01-12/01
	Pennsylvania	Y	29080 FQ	53690 AW	89190 TQ	PABLS	10/01-12/01
	Pittsburgh MSA, PA	Y	29130 FQ	55670 AW	92940 TQ	PABLS	10/01-12/01
	South Carolina	Y	25750 FQ	49330 AW	78690 TQ	SCBLS	10/01-12/01
	South Dakota	Y	29730 FQ	43300 AW	58450 TQ	SDBLS	10/01-12/01
	Tennessee	Y	30270 FQ	46160 AW	71850 TQ	TNBLS	10/01-12/01
	Memphis MSA, TN-AR-MS	Y	31370 FQ	47180 AW	80490 TQ	TNBLS	10/01-12/01
	Nashville MSA, TN	Y	28460 FQ	42640 AW	61670 TQ	TNBLS	10/01-12/01
	Texas	Y	24840 FQ	46760 AW	71550 TQ	TXBLS	10/01-12/01
	Dallas PMSA, TX	Y	27080 FQ	48840 AW	86760 TQ	TXBLS	10/01-12/01
	San Antonio MSA, TX	Y	26150 FQ	42120 AW	62350 TQ	TXBLS	10/01-12/01
	Utah	Y	24240 FQ	41030 AW	65870 TQ	UTBLS	10/01-12/01
	Salt Lake City-Ogden MSA, UT	Y	26790 FQ	43450 AW	67030 TQ	UTBLS	10/01-12/01
	Vermont	Y	26740 FQ	50110 AW	71800 TQ	VTBLS	10/01-12/01
	Virginia	Y	21540 FQ	49780 AW	81200 TQ	VABLS	10/01-12/01
	Richmond-Petersburg MSA, VA	Y	31390 FQ	59230 AW	86130 TQ	VABLS	10/01-12/01
	Washington	Y	32210 FQ	53570 AW	82100 TQ	WABLS	10/01-12/01
	Richland-Kennewick-Pasco MSA, WA	Y	39150 FQ	54770 AW	71850 TQ	WABLS	10/01-12/01
	Seattle-Bellevue-Everett PMSA, WA	Y	36800 FQ	55990 AW	81810 TQ	WABLS	10/01-12/01
	Yakima MSA, WA	Y	25940 FQ	40050 AW	53880 TQ	WABLS	10/01-12/01
	West Virginia	Y	24370 FQ	55810 AW	85220 TQ	WVBLS	10/01-12/01
	Appleton-Oshkosh-Neenah MSA, WI	Y	24270 FQ	37470 AW	52020 TQ	WIBLS	10/01-12/01
	Green Bay MSA, WI	Y	25740 FQ	56970 AW	90820 TQ	WIBLS	10/01-12/01
	Milwaukee-Waukesha PMSA, WI	Y	27740 FQ	47800 AW	87640 TQ	WIBLS	10/01-12/01
	Wyoming	Y	21360 FQ	40030 AW	59380 TQ	WYBLS	10/01-12/01
	Puerto Rico	Y	21640 FQ	29590 AW	43410 TQ	PRBLS	10/01-12/01
Agricultural Engineer	Alabama	Y	56520 FQ	81840 AW	118240 TQ	ALBLS	10/01-12/01
	Arizona	Y	31760 FQ	49080 AW	79880 TQ	AZBLS	10/01-12/01
	California	Y	37740 FQ	58640 AW	87850 TQ	CABLS	10/01-12/01
	Colorado	Y	40010 FQ	58740 AW	74500 TQ	COBLS	10/01-12/01
	Florida	Y	27790 FQ	47110 AW	70940 TQ	FLBLS	10/01-12/01
	Georgia	Y	31910 FQ	48040 AW	70210 TQ	GABLS	10/01-12/01
	Indiana	Y	31950 FQ	59240 AW	96930 TQ	INBLS	10/01-12/01
	Iowa	Y	23370 FQ	36980 AW	64580 TQ	IABLS	10/01-12/01
	Minnesota	Y	36070 FQ	40160 AW	44000 TQ	MNBLS	10/01-12/01
	Nebraska	Y	33970 FQ	50260 AW	70140 TQ	NEBLS	10/01-12/01
	New Mexico	Y	43270 FQ	68210 AW	100080 TQ	NMBLS	10/01-12/01

AAW Average annual wage **AOH** Average offered, high **ASH** Average starting, high **H** Hourly **M** Monthly **S** Special: hourly and annual
AE Average entry wage **AOL** Average offered, low **ASL** Average starting, low **HI** Highest wage paid **MTC** Median total compensation **TQ** Third quartile wage
AEX Average experienced wage **APH** Average pay, high range **AW** Average wage paid **HR** High end range **MW** Median wage paid **W** Weekly
AO Average offered **APL** Average pay, low range **FQ** First quartile wage **LR** Low end range **SQ** Second quartile wage **Y** Yearly

Occupation/Type/Industry	Location	Per	Low	Mid	High	Source	Date
Agricultural Engineer	Ohio	Y	36920 FQ	54910 AW	80220 TQ	OHBLS	10/01-12/01
	Oklahoma	Y	46080 FQ	60210 AW	83460 TQ	OKBLS	10/01-12/01
	Pennsylvania	Y	33770 FQ	65580 AW	108870 TQ	PABLS	10/01-12/01
	Tennessee	Y	27190 FQ	52880 AW	74220 TQ	TNBLS	10/01-12/01
	Texas	Y	42820 FQ	71310 AW	103200 TQ	TXBLS	10/01-12/01
	Washington	Y	46670 FQ	62760 AW	88720 TQ	WABLS	10/01-12/01
	Wisconsin	Y	42270 FQ	55300 AW	74080 TQ	WIBLS	10/01-12/01
Agricultural Equipment Operator	Alabama	H	5.65 FQ	9.30 AW	17.27 TQ	ALBLS	10/01-12/01
	Arizona	H	5.59 FQ	8.12 AW	13.53 TQ	AZBLS	10/01-12/01
	Arkansas	H	5.67 FQ	8.17 AW	12.44 TQ	ARBLS	10/01-12/01
	California	H	6.57 FQ	9.20 AW	13.30 TQ	CABLS	10/01-12/01
	Colorado	H	6.88 FQ	9.74 AW	14.11 TQ	COBLS	10/01-12/01
	Florida	H	6.09 FQ	8.53 AW	12.52 TQ	FLBLS	10/01-12/01
	Georgia	H	6.48 FQ	7.84 AW	8.87 TQ	GABLS	10/01-12/01
	Hawaii	H	8.83 FQ	10.85 AW	13.63 TQ	HIBLS	10/01-12/01
	Idaho	H	5.86 FQ	8.95 AW	12.82 TQ	IDBLS	10/01-12/01
	Illinois	H	8.36 FQ	11.48 AW	16.19 TQ	ILBLS	10/01-12/01
	Indiana	H	8.71 FQ	11.97 AW	16.59 TQ	INBLS	10/01-12/01
	Iowa	H	7.02 FQ	10.86 AW	16.03 TQ	IABLS	10/01-12/01
	Kansas	H	7.19 FQ	11.64 AW	16.81 TQ	KSBLS	10/01-12/01
	Kentucky	H	7.85 FQ	11.25 AW	15.96 TQ	KYBLS	10/01-12/01
	Louisiana	H	5.66 FQ	7.37 AW	9.72 TQ	LABLS	10/01-12/01
	Maryland	H	10.50 FQ	16.06 AW	23.13 TQ	MDBLS	10/01-12/01
	Michigan	H	8.39 FQ	11.88 AW	15.78 TQ	MIBLS	10/01-12/01
	Minnesota	H	8.52 FQ	11.32 AW	14.61 TQ	MNBLS	10/01-12/01
	Mississippi	H	5.95 FQ	9.68 AW	12.96 TQ	MSBLS	10/01-12/01
	Missouri	H	5.59 FQ	6.98 AW	9.57 TQ	MOBLS	10/01-12/01
	Montana	H	7.72 FQ	10.22 AW	12.85 TQ	MTBLS	10/01-12/01
	Nebraska	H	7.03 FQ	10.45 AW	17.36 TQ	NEBLS	10/01-12/01
	New Jersey	H	7.23 FQ	10.47 AW	16.32 TQ	NJBLS	10/01-12/01
	New Mexico	H	5.75 FQ	8.10 AW	10.71 TQ	NMBLS	10/01-12/01
	New York	H	5.67 FQ	8.80 AW	12.51 TQ	NYBLS	10/01-12/01
	North Carolina	H	6.78 FQ	8.73 AW	12.12 TQ	NCBLS	10/01-12/01
	North Dakota	H	6.80 FQ	9.61 AW	12.94 TQ	NDBLS	10/01-12/01
	Ohio	H	7.31 FQ	10.99 AW	14.72 TQ	OHBLS	10/01-12/01
	Oklahoma	H	6.13 FQ	8.30 AW	11.13 TQ	OKBLS	10/01-12/01
	Oregon	H	6.93 FQ	9.64 AW	13.83 TQ	ORBLS	10/01-12/01
	Pennsylvania	H	6.14 FQ	11.16 AW	16.18 TQ	PABLS	10/01-12/01
	South Carolina	H	6.08 FQ	8.63 AW	13.02 TQ	SCBLS	10/01-12/01
	South Dakota	H	7.94 FQ	10.63 AW	12.98 TQ	SDBLS	10/01-12/01
	Tennessee	H	5.62 FQ	8.54 AW	14.29 TQ	TNBLS	10/01-12/01
	Texas	H	5.55 FQ	6.71 AW	8.51 TQ	TXBLS	10/01-12/01
	Utah	H	7.54 FQ	10.66 AW	16.04 TQ	UTBLS	10/01-12/01
	Vermont	H	8.09 FQ	11.61 AW	16.27 TQ	VTBLS	10/01-12/01
	Washington	H	7.19 FQ	10.34 AW	15.04 TQ	WABLS	10/01-12/01
	Wisconsin	H	7.72 FQ	11.51 AW	16.19 TQ	WIBLS	10/01-12/01
	Puerto Rico	H	5.76 FQ	8.11 AW	12.57 TQ	PRBLS	10/01-12/01
Agricultural Inspector	Alabama	H	7.05 FQ	10.85 AW	19.66 TQ	ALBLS	10/01-12/01
	Arizona	H	7.56 FQ	12.04 AW	18.58 TQ	AZBLS	10/01-12/01
	Arkansas	H	7.19 FQ	11.32 AW	19.10 TQ	ARBLS	10/01-12/01
	California	H	7.73 FQ	12.58 AW	20.73 TQ	CABLS	10/01-12/01
	Colorado	H	11.79 FQ	16.63 AW	22.53 TQ	COBLS	10/01-12/01
	Connecticut	H	15.62 FQ	23.63 AW	32.47 TQ	CTBLS	10/01-12/01
	Florida	H	11.34 FQ	14.70 AW	19.49 TQ	FLBLS	10/01-12/01
	Georgia	H	9.01 FQ	13.65 AW	19.77 TQ	GABLS	10/01-12/01
	Hawaii	H	15.87 FQ	20.64 AW	26.70 TQ	HIBLS	10/01-12/01
	Idaho	H	10.92 FQ	15.19 AW	20.43 TQ	IDBLS	10/01-12/01
	Illinois	H	9.47 FQ	16.25 AW	22.76 TQ	ILBLS	10/01-12/01
	Indiana	H	9.97 FQ	18.07 AW	29.63 TQ	INBLS	10/01-12/01
	Iowa	H	11.70 FQ	15.80 AW	21.94 TQ	IABLS	10/01-12/01
	Kansas	H	10.98 FQ	19.67 AW	38.68 TQ	KSBLS	10/01-12/01
	Kentucky	H	11.47 FQ	17.52 AW	25.82 TQ	KYBLS	10/01-12/01
	Louisiana	H	7.58 FQ	14.15 AW	22.91 TQ	LABLS	10/01-12/01
	Maine	H	9.83 FQ	15.00 AW	20.32 TQ	MEBLS	10/01-12/01
	Massachusetts	H	11.67 FQ	16.21 AW	20.96 TQ	MABLS	10/01-12/01
	Michigan	H	12.08 FQ	20.57 AW	27.21 TQ	MIBLS	10/01-12/01
	Minnesota	H	9.92 FQ	17.44 AW	24.94 TQ	MNBLS	10/01-12/01
	Mississippi	H	8.89 FQ	12.26 AW	17.51 TQ	MSBLS	10/01-12/01
	Missouri	H	9.44 FQ	14.54 AW	23.54 TQ	MOBLS	10/01-12/01
	Nebraska	H	11.20 FQ	17.22 AW	24.27 TQ	NEBLS	10/01-12/01
	New Jersey	H	9.58 FQ	17.25 AW	27.18 TQ	NJBLS	10/01-12/01

AAW	Average annual wage	**AOH**	Average offered, high	**ASH**	Average starting, high	**H**	Hourly	**M**	Monthly	**S**	Special: hourly and annual
AE	Average entry wage	**AOL**	Average offered, low	**ASL**	Average starting, low	**HI**	Highest wage paid	**MTC**	Median total compensation	**TQ**	Third quartile wage
AEX	Average experienced wage	**APH**	Average pay, high range	**AW**	Average wage paid	**HR**	High end range	**MW**	Median wage paid	**W**	Weekly
AO	Average offered	**APL**	Average pay, low range	**FQ**	First quartile wage	**LR**	Low end range	**SQ**	Second quartile wage	**Y**	Yearly

Occupation/Type/Industry	Location	Per	Low	Mid	High	Source	Date
Agricultural Inspector	New Mexico	H	9.04 FQ	12.83 AW	16.90 TQ	NMBLS	10/01-12/01
	New York	H	13.90 FQ	18.08 AW	24.00 TQ	NYBLS	10/01-12/01
	North Carolina	H	9.02 FQ	15.52 AW	22.08 TQ	NCBLS	10/01-12/01
	North Dakota	H	8.95 FQ	15.00 AW	25.97 TQ	NDBLS	10/01-12/01
	Ohio	H	11.80 FQ	17.43 AW	24.04 TQ	OHBLS	10/01-12/01
	Oklahoma	H	7.60 FQ	12.38 AW	17.13 TQ	OKBLS	10/01-12/01
	Oregon	H	9.60 FQ	13.93 AW	22.53 TQ	ORBLS	10/01-12/01
	Pennsylvania	H	6.69 FQ	15.37 AW	22.79 TQ	PABLS	10/01-12/01
	South Carolina	H	7.10 FQ	10.19 AW	15.80 TQ	SCBLS	10/01-12/01
	South Dakota	H	9.53 FQ	14.41 AW	20.85 TQ	SDBLS	10/01-12/01
	Texas	H	7.17 FQ	12.46 AW	21.11 TQ	TXBLS	10/01-12/01
	Utah	H	11.73 FQ	16.19 AW	21.19 TQ	UTBLS	10/01-12/01
	Vermont	H	13.39 FQ	18.98 AW	25.23 TQ	VTBLS	10/01-12/01
	Virginia	H	12.07 FQ	17.07 AW	21.78 TQ	VABLS	10/01-12/01
	Washington	H	10.12 FQ	15.28 AW	21.72 TQ	WABLS	10/01-12/01
	Wisconsin	H	11.12 FQ	16.73 AW	22.82 TQ	WIBLS	10/01-12/01
	Puerto Rico	H	6.89 FQ	8.80 AW	14.27 TQ	PRBLS	10/01-12/01
Agricultural Pilot	United States	Y	20000 ASL		70000 ASH	AEAC	1/99-1/99
Agricultural Sciences Teacher							
Postsecondary	Alabama	Y	30060 FQ	67890 AW	107070 TQ	ALBLS	10/01-12/01
Postsecondary	Arizona	Y	29710 FQ	51460 AW	83240 TQ	AZBLS	10/01-12/01
Postsecondary	California	Y	38680 FQ	69350 AW	103870 TQ	CABLS	10/01-12/01
Postsecondary	Colorado	Y	29480 FQ	51300 AW	87500 TQ	COBLS	10/01-12/01
Postsecondary	Delaware	Y	40530 FQ	73740 AW	107200 TQ	DEBLS	10/01-12/01
Postsecondary	Florida	Y	50470 FQ	75990 AW	111990 TQ	FLBLS	10/01-12/01
Postsecondary	Georgia	Y	25340 FQ	52700 AW	90670 TQ	GABLS	10/01-12/01
Postsecondary	Hawaii	Y	44880 FQ	69500 AW	105730 TQ	HIBLS	10/01-12/01
Postsecondary	Illinois	Y	14560 FQ	46040 AW	84150 TQ	ILBLS	10/01-12/01
Postsecondary	Iowa	Y	40800 FQ	69610 AW	104950 TQ	IABLS	10/01-12/01
Postsecondary	Kansas	Y	34680 FQ	67650 AW	99710 TQ	KSBLS	10/01-12/01
Postsecondary	Kentucky	Y	38810 FQ	66970 AW	99400 TQ	KYBLS	10/01-12/01
Postsecondary	Louisiana	Y	15340 FQ	46360 AW	76990 TQ	LABLS	10/01-12/01
Postsecondary	Maryland	Y	40970 FQ	69400 AW	96880 TQ	MDBLS	10/01-12/01
Postsecondary	Minnesota	Y	43080 FQ	70320 AW	98080 TQ	MNBLS	10/01-12/01
Postsecondary	Mississippi	Y	36970 FQ	58500 AW	84920 TQ	MSBLS	10/01-12/01
Postsecondary	Missouri	Y	31180 FQ	57610 AW	90550 TQ	MOBLS	10/01-12/01
Postsecondary	Nebraska	Y	47960 FQ	76030 AW	110260 TQ	NEBLS	10/01-12/01
Postsecondary	New Mexico	Y	42720 FQ	67520 AW	89880 TQ	NMBLS	10/01-12/01
Postsecondary	North Carolina	Y	33480 FQ	53960 AW	70560 TQ	NCBLS	10/01-12/01
Postsecondary	North Dakota	Y	36250 FQ	60620 AW	85260 TQ	NDBLS	10/01-12/01
Postsecondary	Ohio	Y	31090 FQ	61780 AW	95200 TQ	OHBLS	10/01-12/01
Postsecondary	Oklahoma	Y	31940 FQ	44580 AW	56420 TQ	OKBLS	10/01-12/01
Postsecondary	Oregon	Y	46850 FQ	64550 AW	87380 TQ	ORBLS	10/01-12/01
Postsecondary	Pennsylvania	Y	39870 FQ	70720 AW	106790 TQ	PABLS	10/01-12/01
Postsecondary	South Carolina	Y	32200 FQ	52880 AW	73490 TQ	SCBLS	10/01-12/01
Postsecondary	Tennessee	Y	36420 FQ	62900 AW	92600 TQ	TNBLS	10/01-12/01
Postsecondary	Texas	Y	32480 FQ	58090 AW	88530 TQ	TXBLS	10/01-12/01
Postsecondary	Utah	Y	45610 FQ	67430 AW	93420 TQ	UTBLS	10/01-12/01
Postsecondary	Virginia	Y	45440 FQ	73630 AW	108440 TQ	VABLS	10/01-12/01
Postsecondary	Washington	Y	47220 FQ	69020 AW	98680 TQ	WABLS	10/01-12/01
Postsecondary	Wyoming	Y	36850 FQ	61050 AW	83530 TQ	WYBLS	10/01-12/01
Air Traffic Controller	United States	Y		82520 MW		OOH1	2002
	United States	Y		82520 MW		OOH6	1999-2000
	United States	Y	18000 ASL		130000 ASH	AEAC	1/99-1/99
	Alabama	H	19.63 FQ	30.54 AW	41.43 TQ	ALBLS	10/01-12/01
	Alaska	H	22.23 FQ	33.19 AW	49.24 TQ	AKBLS	10/01-12/01
	Arizona	H	22.80 FQ	37.37 AW	53.01 TQ	AZBLS	10/01-12/01
	Phoenix-Mesa MSA, AZ	H	22.60 FQ	40.78 AW	54.35 TQ	AZBLS	10/01-12/01
	Arkansas	H	18.79 FQ	32.70 AW	45.48 TQ	ARBLS	10/01-12/01
	California	H	27.30 FQ	43.04 AW	60.73 TQ	CABLS	10/01-12/01
	Los Angeles-Long Beach PMSA, CA	H	28.22 FQ	43.61 AW	58.01 TQ	CABLS	10/01-12/01
	Oakland PMSA, CA	H	30.29 FQ	47.71 AW	64.86 TQ	CABLS	10/01-12/01
	Orange County PMSA, CA	H	14.78 FQ	31.23 AW	50.63 TQ	CABLS	10/01-12/01
	Colorado	H	20.99 FQ	41.20 AW	54.36 TQ	COBLS	10/01-12/01
	Denver PMSA, CO	H	27.39 FQ	42.08 AW	55.57 TQ	COBLS	10/01-12/01
	Connecticut	H	16.61 FQ	29.59 AW	45.52 TQ	CTBLS	10/01-12/01
	Washington PMSA, DC-MD-VA-WV	H	31.52 FQ	47.37 AW	63.84 TQ	DCBLS	10/01-12/01
	Florida	H	19.73 FQ	39.60 AW	54.47 TQ	FLBLS	10/01-12/01

AAW	Average annual wage	AOH	Average offered, high	ASH	Average starting, high	H	Hourly	M	Monthly	S	Special: hourly and annual
AE	Average entry wage	AOL	Average offered, low	ASL	Average starting, low	HI	Highest wage paid	MTC	Median total compensation	TQ	Third quartile wage
AEX	Average experienced wage	APH	Average pay, high range	AW	Average wage paid	HR	High end range	MW	Median wage paid	W	Weekly
AO	Average offered	APL	Average pay, low range	FQ	First quartile wage	LR	Low end range	SQ	Second quartile wage	Y	Yearly

Occupation/Type/Industry	Location	Per	Low	Mid	High	Source	Date
Air Traffic Controller	Georgia	H	26.13 FQ	45.22 AW	62.90 TQ	GABLS	10/01-12/01
	Atlanta MSA, GA	H	35.27 FQ	48.95 AW	64.38 TQ	GABLS	10/01-12/01
	Hawaii	H	18.14 FQ	32.64 AW	51.62 TQ	HIBLS	10/01-12/01
	Idaho	H	22.47 FQ	31.80 AW	41.20 TQ	IDBLS	10/01-12/01
	Illinois	H	18.83 FQ	42.88 AW	64.73 TQ	ILBLS	10/01-12/01
	Chicago PMSA, IL	H	19.04 FQ	45.94 AW	65.70 TQ	ILBLS	10/01-12/01
	Indiana	H	26.60 FQ	41.62 AW	56.37 TQ	INBLS	10/01-12/01
	Iowa	H	22.80 FQ	30.30 AW	39.93 TQ	IABLS	10/01-12/01
	Kansas	H	26.17 FQ	41.70 AW	53.91 TQ	KSBLS	10/01-12/01
	Kentucky	H	20.31 FQ	37.19 AW	52.23 TQ	KYBLS	10/01-12/01
	Louisiana	H	18.70 FQ	27.57 AW	39.32 TQ	LABLS	10/01-12/01
	Maryland	H	20.53 FQ	38.00 AW	52.76 TQ	MDBLS	10/01-12/01
	Baltimore PMSA, MD	H	32.33 FQ	42.90 AW	53.76 TQ	MDBLS	10/01-12/01
	Massachusetts	H	20.69 FQ	38.17 AW	53.71 TQ	MABLS	10/01-12/01
	Boston PMSA, MA-NH	H	38.26 FQ	46.82 AW	54.83 TQ	MABLS	10/01-12/01
	Michigan	H	19.24 FQ	33.47 AW	50.68 TQ	MIBLS	10/01-12/01
	Detroit PMSA, MI	H	18.72 FQ	33.82 AW	53.53 TQ	MIBLS	10/01-12/01
	Grand Rapids-Muskegon-Holland MSA, MI	H	22.67 FQ	34.11 AW	42.37 TQ	MIBLS	10/01-12/01
	Minnesota	H	29.03 FQ	44.03 AW	55.12 TQ	MNBLS	10/01-12/01
	Minneapolis-St. Paul MSA, MN-WI	H	29.69 FQ	44.80 AW	55.21 TQ	MNBLS	10/01-12/01
	Mississippi	H	19.20 FQ	27.88 AW	38.51 TQ	MSBLS	10/01-12/01
	Missouri	H	22.77 FQ	37.82 AW	53.19 TQ	MOBLS	10/01-12/01
	Kansas City MSA, MO-KS	H	30.39 FQ	43.96 AW	54.26 TQ	MOBLS	10/01-12/01
	St. Louis MSA, MO-IL	H	22.58 FQ	38.90 AW	53.84 TQ	MOBLS	10/01-12/01
	Montana	H	27.81 FQ	32.15 AW	40.21 TQ	MTBLS	10/01-12/01
	Nebraska	H	23.78 FQ	30.71 AW	40.42 TQ	NEBLS	10/01-12/01
	Nevada	H	29.04 FQ	39.98 AW	52.85 TQ	NVBLS	10/01-12/01
	New Hampshire	H	26.57 FQ	46.46 AW	62.66 TQ	NHBLS	10/01-12/01
	Nashua PMSA, NH	H	40.94 FQ	49.07 AW	63.77 TQ	NHBLS	10/01-12/01
	New Jersey	H	19.83 FQ	34.02 AW	48.59 TQ	NJBLS	10/01-12/01
	New Mexico	H	25.32 FQ	40.06 AW	53.25 TQ	NMBLS	10/01-12/01
	New York	H	27.41 FQ	44.36 AW	63.87 TQ	NYBLS	10/01-12/01
	Albany-Schenectady-Troy MSA, NY	H	20.74 FQ	33.84 AW	42.58 TQ	NYBLS	10/01-12/01
	New York PMSA, NY	H	22.51 FQ	41.36 AW	53.42 TQ	NYBLS	10/01-12/01
	North Carolina	H	22.64 FQ	36.19 AW	51.49 TQ	NCBLS	10/01-12/01
	North Dakota	H	21.99 FQ	28.65 AW	33.98 TQ	NDBLS	10/01-12/01
	Ohio	H	28.34 FQ	42.95 AW	57.30 TQ	OHBLS	10/01-12/01
	Columbus MSA, OH	H	19.37 FQ	38.18 AW	52.53 TQ	OHBLS	10/01-12/01
	Dayton-Springfield MSA, OH	H	20.71 FQ	33.57 AW	44.93 TQ	OHBLS	10/01-12/01
	Oklahoma	H	19.05 FQ	31.92 AW	48.93 TQ	OKBLS	10/01-12/01
	Tulsa MSA, OK	H	33.14 FQ	39.52 AW	50.41 TQ	OKBLS	10/01-12/01
	Oregon	H	18.28 FQ	32.68 AW	49.58 TQ	ORBLS	10/01-12/01
	Portland-Vancouver PMSA, OR-WA	H	16.38 FQ	35.22 AW	51.43 TQ	ORBLS	10/01-12/01
	Pennsylvania	H	28.10 FQ	39.15 AW	53.14 TQ	PABLS	10/01-12/01
	Philadelphia PMSA, PA-NJ	H	26.92 FQ	44.47 AW	55.06 TQ	PABLS	10/01-12/01
	South Carolina	H	21.54 FQ	30.71 AW	40.57 TQ	SCBLS	10/01-12/01
	South Dakota	H	18.82 FQ	25.67 AW	33.29 TQ	SDBLS	10/01-12/01
	Tennessee	H	28.85 FQ	43.15 AW	57.18 TQ	TNBLS	10/01-12/01
	Knoxville MSA, TN	H	29.77 FQ	36.49 AW	42.60 TQ	TNBLS	10/01-12/01
	Texas	H	21.37 FQ	41.05 AW	61.45 TQ	TXBLS	10/01-12/01
	Fort Worth-Arlington PMSA, TX	H	30.47 FQ	46.75 AW	64.21 TQ	TXBLS	10/01-12/01
	Houston PMSA, TX	H	20.18 FQ	41.21 AW	63.39 TQ	TXBLS	10/01-12/01
	Utah	H	28.63 FQ	42.28 AW	53.60 TQ	UTBLS	10/01-12/01
	Salt Lake City-Ogden MSA, UT	H	29.64 FQ	43.19 AW	53.73 TQ	UTBLS	10/01-12/01
	Virginia	H	30.35 FQ	46.43 AW	63.66 TQ	VABLS	10/01-12/01
	Norfolk-Virginia Beach-Newport News MSA, VA-NC	H	19.97 FQ	34.93 AW	49.59 TQ	VABLS	10/01-12/01
	Washington	H	29.00 FQ	42.48 AW	54.05 TQ	WABLS	10/01-12/01
	Seattle-Bellevue-Everett PMSA, WA	H	29.25 FQ	43.51 AW	54.31 TQ	WABLS	10/01-12/01
	West Virginia	H	19.41 FQ	28.91 AW	37.85 TQ	WVBLS	10/01-12/01
	Wisconsin	H	16.43 FQ	27.77 AW	41.76 TQ	WIBLS	10/01-12/01
	Milwaukee-Waukesha PMSA, WI	H	15.78 FQ	27.95 AW	44.82 TQ	WIBLS	10/01-12/01
Federal Government	United States	Y		53313 MW		OOH6	1999-2000

AAW	Average annual wage	**AOH**	Average offered, high	**ASH**	Average starting, high	**H**	Hourly	**M**	Monthly	**S**	Special: hourly and annual
AE	Average entry wage	**AOL**	Average offered, low	**ASL**	Average starting, low	**HI**	Highest wage paid	**MTC**	Median total compensation	**TQ**	Third quartile wage
AEX	Average experienced wage	**APH**	Average pay, high range	**AW**	Average wage paid	**HR**	High end range	**MW**	Median wage paid	**W**	Weekly
AO	Average offered	**APL**	Average pay, low range	**FQ**	First quartile wage	**LR**	Low end range	**SQ**	Second quartile wage	**Y**	Yearly

Occupation/Type/Industry	Location	Per	Low	Mid	High	Source	Date
Aircraft Cargo Handling Supervisor	Alabama	H	8.53 FQ	14.33 AW	22.85 TQ	ALBLS	10/01-12/01
	Alaska	H	10.04 FQ	16.01 AW	22.79 TQ	AKBLS	10/01-12/01
	Anchorage MSA, AK	H	9.75 FQ	15.75 AW	22.74 TQ	AKBLS	10/01-12/01
	Arizona	H	9.55 FQ	16.33 AW	27.26 TQ	AZBLS	10/01-12/01
	Phoenix-Mesa MSA, AZ	H	9.43 FQ	14.98 AW	25.53 TQ	AZBLS	10/01-12/01
	Arkansas	H	6.90 FQ	15.59 AW	31.71 TQ	ARBLS	10/01-12/01
	California	H	11.32 FQ	18.42 AW	27.11 TQ	CABLS	10/01-12/01
	Bakersfield MSA, CA	H	9.73 FQ	16.48 AW	29.24 TQ	CABLS	10/01-12/01
	Los Angeles-Long Beach PMSA, CA	H	11.58 FQ	18.07 AW	26.85 TQ	CABLS	10/01-12/01
	Orange County PMSA, CA	H	9.66 FQ	15.60 AW	25.63 TQ	CABLS	10/01-12/01
	Riverside-San Bernardino PMSA, CA	H	11.08 FQ	18.25 AW	26.72 TQ	CABLS	10/01-12/01
	Sacramento PMSA, CA	H	11.80 FQ	18.15 AW	37.42 TQ	CABLS	10/01-12/01
	San Diego MSA, CA	H	12.03 FQ	18.31 AW	27.78 TQ	CABLS	10/01-12/01
	San Francisco PMSA, CA	H	13.67 FQ	21.35 AW	30.87 TQ	CABLS	10/01-12/01
	Colorado	H	11.72 FQ	19.92 AW	30.46 TQ	COBLS	10/01-12/01
	Denver PMSA, CO	H	11.42 FQ	18.51 AW	25.89 TQ	COBLS	10/01-12/01
	Connecticut	H	11.47 FQ	20.93 AW	31.96 TQ	CTBLS	10/01-12/01
	Hartford MSA, CT	H	11.54 FQ	17.39 AW	21.93 TQ	CTBLS	10/01-12/01
	Washington PMSA, DC-MD-VA-WV	H	13.78 FQ	23.23 AW	33.94 TQ	DCBLS	10/01-12/01
	Florida	H	9.69 FQ	16.12 AW	25.35 TQ	FLBLS	10/01-12/01
	Fort Lauderdale PMSA, FL	H	11.61 FQ	19.49 AW	33.37 TQ	FLBLS	10/01-12/01
	Miami PMSA, FL	H	8.82 FQ	14.00 AW	19.32 TQ	FLBLS	10/01-12/01
	Orlando MSA, FL	H	9.86 FQ	17.13 AW	37.14 TQ	FLBLS	10/01-12/01
	Georgia	H	11.57 FQ	26.51 AW	41.72 TQ	GABLS	10/01-12/01
	Hawaii	H	9.14 FQ	16.96 AW	26.44 TQ	HIBLS	10/01-12/01
	Illinois	H	9.75 FQ	21.55 AW	38.04 TQ	ILBLS	10/01-12/01
	Chicago PMSA, IL	H	9.65 FQ	20.54 AW	34.37 TQ	ILBLS	10/01-12/01
	Indiana	H	10.27 FQ	17.03 AW	27.01 TQ	INBLS	10/01-12/01
	Gary PMSA, IN	H	9.83 FQ	19.76 AW	33.48 TQ	INBLS	10/01-12/01
	Indianapolis MSA, IN	H	11.05 FQ	19.47 AW	27.41 TQ	INBLS	10/01-12/01
	Iowa	H	10.08 FQ	14.92 AW	18.31 TQ	IABLS	10/01-12/01
	Davenport-Moline-Rock Island MSA, IA-IL	H	16.76 FQ	29.92 AW	44.46 TQ	IABLS	10/01-12/01
	Des Moines MSA, IA	H	14.14 FQ	15.72 AW	17.36 TQ	IABLS	10/01-12/01
	Kansas	H	10.42 FQ	19.10 AW	29.36 TQ	KSBLS	10/01-12/01
	Kentucky	H	13.41 FQ	20.77 AW	27.77 TQ	KYBLS	10/01-12/01
	Louisville MSA, KY-IN	H	10.12 FQ	15.64 AW	25.44 TQ	KYBLS	10/01-12/01
	Louisiana	H	11.41 FQ	20.06 AW	33.36 TQ	LABLS	10/01-12/01
	New Orleans MSA, LA	H	14.94 FQ	21.14 AW	33.62 TQ	LABLS	10/01-12/01
	Maryland	H	12.18 FQ	18.53 AW	26.61 TQ	MDBLS	10/01-12/01
	Baltimore PMSA, MD	H	13.54 FQ	18.36 AW	25.60 TQ	MDBLS	10/01-12/01
	Massachusetts	H	11.19 FQ	17.37 AW	27.04 TQ	MABLS	10/01-12/01
	Boston PMSA, MA-NH	H	11.16 FQ	17.11 AW	26.05 TQ	MABLS	10/01-12/01
	Michigan	H	12.13 FQ	19.41 AW	29.79 TQ	MIBLS	10/01-12/01
	Detroit PMSA, MI	H	12.12 FQ	17.83 AW	25.53 TQ	MIBLS	10/01-12/01
	Minnesota	H	10.13 FQ	17.95 AW	27.15 TQ	MNBLS	10/01-12/01
	Minneapolis-St. Paul MSA, MN-WI	H	10.84 FQ	20.08 AW	30.34 TQ	MNBLS	10/01-12/01
	Mississippi	H	7.91 FQ	11.15 AW	13.94 TQ	MSBLS	10/01-12/01
	Missouri	H	9.67 FQ	15.10 AW	21.30 TQ	MOBLS	10/01-12/01
	Kansas City MSA, MO-KS	H	12.21 FQ	18.91 AW	26.73 TQ	MOBLS	10/01-12/01
	St. Louis MSA, MO-IL	H	9.61 FQ	17.26 AW	27.40 TQ	MOBLS	10/01-12/01
	Springfield MSA, MO	H	8.76 FQ	12.64 AW	19.01 TQ	MOBLS	10/01-12/01
	Nebraska	H	6.66 FQ	13.11 AW	17.41 TQ	NEBLS	10/01-12/01
	Nevada	H	11.97 FQ	18.39 AW	27.85 TQ	NVBLS	10/01-12/01
	Las Vegas MSA, NV-AZ	H	11.68 FQ	17.80 AW	27.80 TQ	NVBLS	10/01-12/01
	Reno MSA, NV	H	12.28 FQ	17.82 AW	26.99 TQ	NVBLS	10/01-12/01
	New Jersey	H	10.98 FQ	21.72 AW	33.33 TQ	NJBLS	10/01-12/01
	Bergen-Passaic PMSA, NJ	H	18.68 FQ	24.68 AW	32.86 TQ	NJBLS	10/01-12/01
	Middlesex-Somerset-Hunterdon PMSA, NJ	H	24.25 FQ	29.96 AW	36.97 TQ	NJBLS	10/01-12/01
	Newark PMSA, NJ	H	10.34 FQ	19.31 AW	32.03 TQ	NJBLS	10/01-12/01
	New Mexico	H	8.16 FQ	13.37 AW	24.29 TQ	NMBLS	10/01-12/01
	New York	H	10.19 FQ	19.46 AW	32.42 TQ	NYBLS	10/01-12/01
	Buffalo-Niagara Falls MSA, NY	H	9.37 FQ	21.96 AW	30.66 TQ	NYBLS	10/01-12/01
	Nassau-Suffolk PMSA, NY	H	10.15 FQ	21.89 AW	34.86 TQ	NYBLS	10/01-12/01
	New York PMSA, NY	H	10.03 FQ	18.55 AW	32.28 TQ	NYBLS	10/01-12/01

AAW	Average annual wage	**AOH**	Average offered, high	**ASH**	Average starting, high	**H**	Hourly	**M**	Monthly	**S**	Special: hourly and annual
AE	Average entry wage	**AOL**	Average offered, low	**ASL**	Average starting, low	**HI**	Highest wage paid	**MTC**	Median total compensation	**TQ**	Third quartile wage
AEX	Average experienced wage	**APH**	Average pay, high range	**AW**	Average wage paid	**HR**	High end range	**MW**	Median wage paid	**W**	Weekly
AO	Average offered	**APL**	Average pay, low range	**FQ**	First quartile wage	**LR**	Low end range	**SQ**	Second quartile wage	**Y**	Yearly

Occupation/Type/Industry	Location	Per	Low	Mid	High	Source	Date
Aircraft Cargo Handling Supervisor	North Carolina	H	11.24 FQ	17.46 AW	25.85 TQ	NCBLS	10/01-12/01
	Charlotte-Gastonia-Rock Hill MSA, NC-SC	H	11.84 FQ	16.75 AW	24.64 TQ	NCBLS	10/01-12/01
	Greensboro-Winston-Salem-High Point MSA, NC	H	8.67 FQ	14.69 AW	20.31 TQ	NCBLS	10/01-12/01
	Ohio	H	10.82 FQ	19.69 AW	27.30 TQ	OHBLS	10/01-12/01
	Cincinnati PMSA, OH-KY-IN	H	12.40 FQ	20.75 AW	27.88 TQ	OHBLS	10/01-12/01
	Cleveland-Lorain-Elyria PMSA, OH	H	13.95 FQ	21.78 AW	28.65 TQ	OHBLS	10/01-12/01
	Columbus MSA, OH	H	10.16 FQ	19.68 AW	26.59 TQ	OHBLS	10/01-12/01
	Dayton-Springfield MSA, OH	H	10.65 FQ	14.88 AW	19.85 TQ	OHBLS	10/01-12/01
	Toledo MSA, OH	H	9.79 FQ	19.88 AW	26.99 TQ	OHBLS	10/01-12/01
	Oklahoma	H	10.02 FQ	14.92 AW	19.56 TQ	OKBLS	10/01-12/01
	Oklahoma City MSA, OK	H	9.65 FQ	14.98 AW	22.43 TQ	OKBLS	10/01-12/01
	Oregon	H	9.79 FQ	23.50 AW	40.46 TQ	ORBLS	10/01-12/01
	Portland-Vancouver PMSA, OR-WA	H	9.80 FQ	24.90 AW	41.04 TQ	ORBLS	10/01-12/01
	Pennsylvania	H	15.80 FQ	25.76 AW	39.11 TQ	PABLS	10/01-12/01
	Philadelphia PMSA, PA-NJ	H	14.69 FQ	27.09 AW	42.22 TQ	PABLS	10/01-12/01
	Pittsburgh MSA, PA	H	9.12 FQ	22.33 AW	37.96 TQ	PABLS	10/01-12/01
	South Carolina	H	15.67 FQ	28.47 AW	35.54 TQ	SCBLS	10/01-12/01
	Charleston-North Charleston MSA, SC	H	12.76 FQ	20.05 AW	27.53 TQ	SCBLS	10/01-12/01
	Greenville-Spartanburg-Anderson MSA, SC	H	17.98 FQ	34.77 AW	54.98 TQ	SCBLS	10/01-12/01
	Tennessee	H	8.75 FQ	16.09 AW	26.30 TQ	TNBLS	10/01-12/01
	Nashville MSA, TN	H	11.38 FQ	16.87 AW	25.98 TQ	TNBLS	10/01-12/01
	Texas	H	8.82 FQ	19.46 AW	32.36 TQ	TXBLS	10/01-12/01
	Austin-San Marcos MSA, TX	H	9.22 FQ	15.99 AW	24.48 TQ	TXBLS	10/01-12/01
	Dallas PMSA, TX	H	9.71 FQ	18.78 AW	32.42 TQ	TXBLS	10/01-12/01
	El Paso MSA, TX	H	5.99 FQ	9.65 AW	18.18 TQ	TXBLS	10/01-12/01
	Fort Worth-Arlington PMSA, TX	H	15.53 FQ	28.57 AW	45.66 TQ	TXBLS	10/01-12/01
	Houston PMSA, TX	H	13.65 FQ	25.16 AW	39.49 TQ	TXBLS	10/01-12/01
	Laredo MSA, TX	H	12.76 FQ	19.86 AW	22.68 TQ	TXBLS	10/01-12/01
	San Antonio MSA, TX	H	9.38 FQ	15.08 AW	24.66 TQ	TXBLS	10/01-12/01
	Utah	H	8.09 FQ	17.40 AW	28.43 TQ	UTBLS	10/01-12/01
	Salt Lake City-Ogden MSA, UT	H	8.07 FQ	16.73 AW	29.24 TQ	UTBLS	10/01-12/01
	Virginia	H	13.13 FQ	21.86 AW	33.67 TQ	VABLS	10/01-12/01
	Norfolk-Virginia Beach-Newport News MSA, VA-NC	H	12.25 FQ	21.82 AW	40.94 TQ	VABLS	10/01-12/01
	Washington	H	10.58 FQ	20.91 AW	33.72 TQ	WABLS	10/01-12/01
	Seattle-Bellevue-Everett PMSA, WA	H	11.46 FQ	23.38 AW	34.44 TQ	WABLS	10/01-12/01
	West Virginia	H	8.69 FQ	13.68 AW	21.03 TQ	WVBLS	10/01-12/01
	Wisconsin	H	11.27 FQ	21.00 AW	34.84 TQ	WIBLS	10/01-12/01
	Milwaukee-Waukesha PMSA, WI	H	8.55 FQ	18.72 AW	28.89 TQ	WIBLS	10/01-12/01
	Puerto Rico	H	7.65 FQ	12.33 AW	17.90 TQ	PRBLS	10/01-12/01
Aircraft Mechanic							
Alaska Airlines	United States	H		26.00 AW		USATOD1	2002
American Airlines	United States	H		27.00 AW		USATOD1	2002
Continental Airlines	United States	H		27.00 AW		USATOD1	2002
Delta Airlines	United States	H		30.00 AW		USATOD1	2002
Northwest Airlines	United States	H		34.00 AW		USATOD1	2002
United Airlines	United States	H		26.00 AW		USATOD1	2002
US Airways	United States	H		29.00 AW		USATOD1	2002
Aircraft Mechanic and Service Technician	Alabama	H	11.97 FQ	18.56 AW	27.71 TQ	ALBLS	10/01-12/01
	Huntsville MSA, AL	H	14.09 FQ	23.39 AW	38.42 TQ	ALBLS	10/01-12/01
	Montgomery MSA, AL	H	13.54 FQ	17.66 AW	21.35 TQ	ALBLS	10/01-12/01
	Alaska	H	14.66 FQ	20.73 AW	28.75 TQ	AKBLS	10/01-12/01
	Anchorage MSA, AK	H	14.86 FQ	20.48 AW	28.48 TQ	AKBLS	10/01-12/01
	Arizona	H	13.26 FQ	19.38 AW	26.98 TQ	AZBLS	10/01-12/01
	Phoenix-Mesa MSA, AZ	H	13.68 FQ	19.51 AW	27.20 TQ	AZBLS	10/01-12/01
	Tucson MSA, AZ	H	13.75 FQ	19.43 AW	26.60 TQ	AZBLS	10/01-12/01
	Arkansas	H	10.49 FQ	19.20 AW	28.76 TQ	ARBLS	10/01-12/01

AAW	Average annual wage	AOH	Average offered, high	ASH	Average starting, high	H	Hourly	M	Monthly	S	Special: hourly and annual
AE	Average entry wage	AOL	Average offered, low	ASL	Average starting, low	HI	Highest wage paid	MTC	Median total compensation	TQ	Third quartile wage
AEX	Average experienced wage	APH	Average pay, high range	AW	Average wage paid	HR	High end range	MW	Median wage paid	W	Weekly
AO	Average offered	APL	Average pay, low range	FQ	First quartile wage	LR	Low end range	SQ	Second quartile wage	Y	Yearly

Occupation/Type/Industry	Location	Per	Low	Mid	High	Source	Date
Aircraft Mechanic and Service Technician							
	Fayetteville-Springdale-Rogers MSA, AR	H	13.82 FQ	18.51 AW	25.39 TQ	ARBLS	10/01-12/01
	Fort Smith MSA, AR-OK	H	7.53 FQ	13.21 AW	20.27 TQ	ARBLS	10/01-12/01
	Little Rock-North Little Rock MSA, AR	H	13.44 FQ	21.67 AW	31.90 TQ	ARBLS	10/01-12/01
	California	H	12.09 FQ	20.61 AW	27.68 TQ	CABLS	10/01-12/01
	Bakersfield MSA, CA	H	15.62 FQ	21.65 AW	26.76 TQ	CABLS	10/01-12/01
	Fresno MSA, CA	H	12.18 FQ	18.87 AW	27.85 TQ	CABLS	10/01-12/01
	Los Angeles-Long Beach PMSA, CA	H	12.21 FQ	20.90 AW	28.62 TQ	CABLS	10/01-12/01
	Oakland PMSA, CA	H	16.01 FQ	22.53 AW	27.17 TQ	CABLS	10/01-12/01
	Orange County PMSA, CA	H	11.86 FQ	19.32 AW	28.27 TQ	CABLS	10/01-12/01
	Redding MSA, CA	H	10.72 FQ	16.41 AW	23.02 TQ	CABLS	10/01-12/01
	Riverside-San Bernardino PMSA, CA	H	15.20 FQ	21.15 AW	26.33 TQ	CABLS	10/01-12/01
	Sacramento PMSA, CA	H	11.58 FQ	19.03 AW	23.95 TQ	CABLS	10/01-12/01
	Salinas MSA, CA	H	15.67 FQ	19.78 AW	23.71 TQ	CABLS	10/01-12/01
	San Diego MSA, CA	H	12.86 FQ	20.78 AW	29.09 TQ	CABLS	10/01-12/01
	San Jose PMSA, CA	H	14.42 FQ	23.05 AW	30.03 TQ	CABLS	10/01-12/01
	Santa Rosa PMSA, CA	H	9.10 FQ	19.55 AW	33.78 TQ	CABLS	10/01-12/01
	Stockton-Lodi MSA, CA	H	9.87 FQ	16.22 AW	23.98 TQ	CABLS	10/01-12/01
	Vallejo-Fairfield-Napa PMSA, CA	H	14.34 FQ	21.66 AW	26.71 TQ	CABLS	10/01-12/01
	Ventura PMSA, CA	H	15.14 FQ	19.86 AW	25.45 TQ	CABLS	10/01-12/01
	Visalia-Tulare-Porterville MSA, CA	H	9.44 FQ	13.36 AW	19.49 TQ	CABLS	10/01-12/01
	Colorado Springs MSA, CO	H	15.28 FQ	22.32 AW	32.01 TQ	COBLS	10/01-12/01
	Fort Collins-Loveland MSA, CO	H	9.52 FQ	16.80 AW	26.42 TQ	COBLS	10/01-12/01
	Connecticut	H	12.13 FQ	20.48 AW	28.58 TQ	CTBLS	10/01-12/01
	Bridgeport PMSA, CT	H	15.23 FQ	22.62 AW	29.03 TQ	CTBLS	10/01-12/01
	Danbury PMSA, CT	H	14.67 FQ	18.11 AW	25.62 TQ	CTBLS	10/01-12/01
	Hartford MSA, CT	H	13.76 FQ	21.52 AW	29.21 TQ	CTBLS	10/01-12/01
	New London-Norwich MSA, CT-RI	H	13.75 FQ	18.56 AW	24.30 TQ	CTBLS	10/01-12/01
	Stamford-Norwalk PMSA, CT	H	9.61 FQ	14.89 AW	25.45 TQ	CTBLS	10/01-12/01
	Delaware	H	14.10 FQ	20.03 AW	25.98 TQ	DEBLS	10/01-12/01
	Wilmington-Newark PMSA, DE-MD	H	10.86 FQ	19.56 AW	27.70 TQ	DEBLS	10/01-12/01
	Washington PMSA, DC-MD-VA-WV	H	12.13 FQ	22.24 AW	36.19 TQ	DCBLS	10/01-12/01
	Florida	H	12.23 FQ	19.66 AW	29.80 TQ	FLBLS	10/01-12/01
	Daytona Beach MSA, FL	H	8.63 FQ	14.53 AW	20.87 TQ	FLBLS	10/01-12/01
	Fort Lauderdale PMSA, FL	H	11.66 FQ	19.35 AW	26.88 TQ	FLBLS	10/01-12/01
	Fort Pierce-Port St. Lucie MSA, FL	H	12.19 FQ	17.44 AW	21.72 TQ	FLBLS	10/01-12/01
	Fort Walton Beach MSA, FL	H	14.55 FQ	19.78 AW	26.24 TQ	FLBLS	10/01-12/01
	Jacksonville MSA, FL	H	15.09 FQ	20.78 AW	31.00 TQ	FLBLS	10/01-12/01
	Lakeland-Winter Haven MSA, FL	H	11.67 FQ	16.10 AW	21.41 TQ	FLBLS	10/01-12/01
	Melbourne-Titusville-Palm Bay MSA, FL	H	14.37 FQ	19.23 AW	24.38 TQ	FLBLS	10/01-12/01
	Miami PMSA, FL	H	12.09 FQ	19.39 AW	30.55 TQ	FLBLS	10/01-12/01
	Naples MSA, FL	H	10.79 FQ	18.53 AW	29.45 TQ	FLBLS	10/01-12/01
	Orlando MSA, FL	H	11.58 FQ	18.59 AW	27.05 TQ	FLBLS	10/01-12/01
	Tallahassee MSA, FL	H	11.24 FQ	16.64 AW	20.79 TQ	FLBLS	10/01-12/01
	Tampa-St. Petersburg-Clearwater MSA, FL	H	17.03 FQ	23.96 AW	33.57 TQ	FLBLS	10/01-12/01
	West Palm Beach-Boca Raton MSA, FL	H	11.06 FQ	21.74 AW	33.06 TQ	FLBLS	10/01-12/01
	Georgia	H	14.98 FQ	24.26 AW	33.70 TQ	GABLS	10/01-12/01
	Atlanta MSA, GA	H	16.13 FQ	25.56 AW	34.10 TQ	GABLS	10/01-12/01
	Augusta-Aiken MSA, GA-SC	H	13.01 FQ	21.05 AW	31.05 TQ	GABLS	10/01-12/01
	Columbus MSA, GA-AL	H	9.66 FQ	22.67 AW	32.75 TQ	GABLS	10/01-12/01
	Macon MSA, GA	H	13.89 FQ	17.59 AW	21.12 TQ	GABLS	10/01-12/01
	Savannah MSA, GA	H	14.49 FQ	20.63 AW	27.21 TQ	GABLS	10/01-12/01
	Hawaii	H	14.85 FQ	22.54 AW	31.13 TQ	HIBLS	10/01-12/01
	Honolulu MSA, HI	H	15.92 FQ	23.12 AW	31.66 TQ	HIBLS	10/01-12/01
	Idaho	H	11.70 FQ	17.61 AW	22.72 TQ	IDBLS	10/01-12/01
	Boise City MSA, ID	H	14.71 FQ	19.01 AW	23.54 TQ	IDBLS	10/01-12/01
	Illinois	H	14.54 FQ	21.93 AW	28.11 TQ	ILBLS	10/01-12/01

AAW	Average annual wage	**AOH**	Average offered, high	**ASH**	Average starting, high	**H**	Hourly	**M**	Monthly	**S**	Special: hourly and annual
AE	Average entry wage	**AOL**	Average offered, low	**ASL**	Average starting, low	**HI**	Highest wage paid	**MTC**	Median total compensation	**TQ**	Third quartile wage
AEX	Average experienced wage	**APH**	Average pay, high range	**AW**	Average wage paid	**HR**	High end range	**MW**	Median wage paid	**W**	Weekly
AO	Average offered	**APL**	Average pay, low range	**FQ**	First quartile wage	**LR**	Low end range	**SQ**	Second quartile wage	**Y**	Yearly

Occupation/Type/Industry	Location	Per	Low	Mid	High	Source	Date
Aircraft Mechanic and Service Technician	Chicago PMSA, IL	H	14.85 FQ	22.33 AW	28.23 TQ	ILBLS	10/01-12/01
	Peoria-Pekin MSA, IL	H	16.94 FQ	21.30 AW	26.32 TQ	ILBLS	10/01-12/01
	Springfield MSA, IL	H	12.26 FQ	16.94 AW	23.48 TQ	ILBLS	10/01-12/01
	Elkhart-Goshen MSA, IN	H	14.35 FQ	20.22 AW	26.88 TQ	INBLS	10/01-12/01
	Evansville-Henderson MSA, IN-KY	H	6.04 FQ	14.86 AW	20.35 TQ	INBLS	10/01-12/01
	Fort Wayne MSA, IN	H	14.94 FQ	20.19 AW	26.06 TQ	INBLS	10/01-12/01
	Gary PMSA, IN	H	6.81 FQ	13.28 AW	19.11 TQ	INBLS	10/01-12/01
	Iowa	H	11.94 FQ	18.02 AW	23.98 TQ	IABLS	10/01-12/01
	Des Moines MSA, IA	H	14.47 FQ	19.12 AW	24.95 TQ	IABLS	10/01-12/01
	Kansas	H	14.74 FQ	19.57 AW	25.38 TQ	KSBLS	10/01-12/01
	Topeka MSA, KS	H	15.19 FQ	19.06 AW	22.93 TQ	KSBLS	10/01-12/01
	Wichita MSA, KS	H	15.02 FQ	19.91 AW	25.73 TQ	KSBLS	10/01-12/01
	Kentucky	H	14.41 FQ	20.00 AW	27.72 TQ	KYBLS	10/01-12/01
	Louisville MSA, KY-IN	H	14.34 FQ	18.85 AW	25.66 TQ	KYBLS	10/01-12/01
	Louisiana	H	13.57 FQ	19.86 AW	26.76 TQ	LABLS	10/01-12/01
	Houma MSA, LA	H	14.40 FQ	20.64 AW	26.44 TQ	LABLS	10/01-12/01
	New Orleans MSA, LA	H	12.48 FQ	19.61 AW	26.83 TQ	LABLS	10/01-12/01
	Shreveport-Bossier City MSA, LA	H	13.90 FQ	18.71 AW	23.60 TQ	LABLS	10/01-12/01
	Maine	H	11.07 FQ	15.88 AW	21.28 TQ	MEBLS	10/01-12/01
	Maryland	H	14.02 FQ	25.48 AW	41.22 TQ	MDBLS	10/01-12/01
	Baltimore PMSA, MD	H	14.69 FQ	23.89 AW	35.53 TQ	MDBLS	10/01-12/01
	Massachusetts	H	11.57 FQ	20.82 AW	28.99 TQ	MABLS	10/01-12/01
	Boston PMSA, MA-NH	H	11.47 FQ	21.55 AW	30.33 TQ	MABLS	10/01-12/01
	Springfield MSA, MA	H	14.48 FQ	18.55 AW	23.77 TQ	MABLS	10/01-12/01
	Michigan	H	11.51 FQ	19.03 AW	26.25 TQ	MIBLS	10/01-12/01
	Ann Arbor PMSA, MI	H	12.26 FQ	18.65 AW	25.54 TQ	MIBLS	10/01-12/01
	Detroit PMSA, MI	H	11.44 FQ	19.63 AW	26.54 TQ	MIBLS	10/01-12/01
	Grand Rapids-Muskegon-Holland MSA, MI	H	11.80 FQ	18.65 AW	28.33 TQ	MIBLS	10/01-12/01
	Kalamazoo-Battle Creek MSA, MI	H	11.65 FQ	18.72 AW	25.15 TQ	MIBLS	10/01-12/01
	Lansing-East Lansing MSA, MI	H	13.58 FQ	20.75 AW	26.67 TQ	MIBLS	10/01-12/01
	Saginaw-Bay City-Midland MSA, MI	H	10.54 FQ	15.24 AW	20.09 TQ	MIBLS	10/01-12/01
	Mississippi	H	14.34 FQ	17.95 AW	22.20 TQ	MSBLS	10/01-12/01
	Biloxi-Gulfport-Pascagoula MSA, MS	H	14.38 FQ	19.03 AW	25.18 TQ	MSBLS	10/01-12/01
	Missouri	H	14.28 FQ	20.63 AW	26.83 TQ	MOBLS	10/01-12/01
	Kansas City MSA, MO-KS	H	12.15 FQ	19.43 AW	26.76 TQ	MOBLS	10/01-12/01
	St. Louis MSA, MO-IL	H	15.50 FQ	20.90 AW	26.79 TQ	MOBLS	10/01-12/01
	Springfield MSA, MO	H	10.56 FQ	17.21 AW	21.16 TQ	MOBLS	10/01-12/01
	Montana	H	11.54 FQ	17.42 AW	24.80 TQ	MTBLS	10/01-12/01
	Billings MSA, MT	H	11.38 FQ	16.28 AW	22.28 TQ	MTBLS	10/01-12/01
	Nebraska	H	12.27 FQ	17.98 AW	24.75 TQ	NEBLS	10/01-12/01
	Omaha MSA, NE-IA	H	12.37 FQ	19.29 AW	28.30 TQ	NEBLS	10/01-12/01
	Nevada	H	14.74 FQ	20.34 AW	26.09 TQ	NVBLS	10/01-12/01
	Las Vegas MSA, NV-AZ	H	12.42 FQ	19.68 AW	27.37 TQ	NVBLS	10/01-12/01
	Reno MSA, NV	H	15.36 FQ	20.24 AW	25.83 TQ	NVBLS	10/01-12/01
	New Hampshire	H	14.40 FQ	20.13 AW	27.51 TQ	NHBLS	10/01-12/01
	Manchester PMSA, NH	H	15.05 FQ	23.02 AW	34.56 TQ	NHBLS	10/01-12/01
	Nashua PMSA, NH	H	14.19 FQ	19.92 AW	29.08 TQ	NHBLS	10/01-12/01
	Portsmouth-Rochester PMSA, NH-ME	H	14.83 FQ	19.18 AW	23.65 TQ	NHBLS	10/01-12/01
	New Jersey	H	12.73 FQ	19.96 AW	27.48 TQ	NJBLS	10/01-12/01
	Atlantic-Cape May PMSA, NJ	H	10.76 FQ	17.49 AW	22.01 TQ	NJBLS	10/01-12/01
	Bergen-Passaic PMSA, NJ	H	10.81 FQ	19.20 AW	35.99 TQ	NJBLS	10/01-12/01
	Middlesex-Somerset-Hunterdon PMSA, NJ	H	13.34 FQ	19.13 AW	31.44 TQ	NJBLS	10/01-12/01
	Monmouth-Ocean PMSA, NJ	H	11.65 FQ	16.64 AW	23.16 TQ	NJBLS	10/01-12/01
	Newark PMSA, NJ	H	14.89 FQ	21.37 AW	27.82 TQ	NJBLS	10/01-12/01
	Trenton PMSA, NJ	H	11.36 FQ	20.18 AW	28.68 TQ	NJBLS	10/01-12/01
	New Mexico	H	9.85 FQ	17.45 AW	24.44 TQ	NMBLS	10/01-12/01
	Albuquerque MSA, NM	H	10.70 FQ	19.02 AW	27.44 TQ	NMBLS	10/01-12/01
	New York	H	12.72 FQ	21.01 AW	30.41 TQ	NYBLS	10/01-12/01
	Albany-Schenectady-Troy MSA, NY	H	12.16 FQ	18.09 AW	25.50 TQ	NYBLS	10/01-12/01
	Buffalo-Niagara Falls MSA, NY	H	14.09 FQ	20.20 AW	25.62 TQ	NYBLS	10/01-12/01
	Dutchess County PMSA, NY	H	13.91 FQ	19.93 AW	28.17 TQ	NYBLS	10/01-12/01

AAW	Average annual wage	AOH	Average offered, high	ASH	Average starting, high	H	Hourly	M	Monthly	S	Special: hourly and annual
AE	Average entry wage	AOL	Average offered, low	ASL	Average starting, low	HI	Highest wage paid	MTC	Median total compensation	TQ	Third quartile wage
AEX	Average experienced wage	APH	Average pay, high range	AW	Average wage paid	HR	High end range	MW	Median wage paid	W	Weekly
AO	Average offered	APL	Average pay, low range	FQ	First quartile wage	LR	Low end range	SQ	Second quartile wage	Y	Yearly

Occupation/Type/Industry	Location	Per	Low	Mid	High	Source	Date
Aircraft Mechanic and Service Technician	Nassau-Suffolk PMSA, NY	H	13.08 FQ	20.61 AW	27.56 TQ	NYBLS	10/01-12/01
	New York PMSA, NY	H	12.06 FQ	21.88 AW	32.84 TQ	NYBLS	10/01-12/01
	Newburgh PMSA, NY-PA	H	13.75 FQ	17.94 AW	21.23 TQ	NYBLS	10/01-12/01
	Rochester MSA, NY	H	11.07 FQ	18.22 AW	24.84 TQ	NYBLS	10/01-12/01
	Syracuse MSA, NY	H	17.81 FQ	22.74 AW	30.03 TQ	NYBLS	10/01-12/01
	Utica-Rome MSA, NY	H	14.65 FQ	17.56 AW	21.17 TQ	NYBLS	10/01-12/01
	North Carolina	H	12.50 FQ	20.37 AW	27.11 TQ	NCBLS	10/01-12/01
	Fayetteville MSA, NC	H	17.41 FQ	22.86 AW	31.61 TQ	NCBLS	10/01-12/01
	Greensboro-Winston-Salem-High Point MSA, NC	H	11.30 FQ	16.34 AW	21.28 TQ	NCBLS	10/01-12/01
	Raleigh-Durham-Chapel Hill MSA, NC	H	14.80 FQ	20.27 AW	27.50 TQ	NCBLS	10/01-12/01
	North Dakota	H	11.39 FQ	16.30 AW	21.83 TQ	NDBLS	10/01-12/01
	Fargo-Moorhead MSA, ND-MN	H	11.27 FQ	17.21 AW	24.35 TQ	NDBLS	10/01-12/01
	Ohio	H	10.17 FQ	19.49 AW	28.75 TQ	OHBLS	10/01-12/01
	Akron PMSA, OH	H	10.47 FQ	18.91 AW	26.46 TQ	OHBLS	10/01-12/01
	Cincinnati PMSA, OH-KY-IN	H	10.80 FQ	21.28 AW	35.35 TQ	OHBLS	10/01-12/01
	Cleveland-Lorain-Elyria PMSA, OH	H	8.17 FQ	15.99 AW	23.58 TQ	OHBLS	10/01-12/01
	Columbus MSA, OH	H	12.92 FQ	20.67 AW	28.22 TQ	OHBLS	10/01-12/01
	Dayton-Springfield MSA, OH	H	13.73 FQ	20.11 AW	27.24 TQ	OHBLS	10/01-12/01
	Toledo MSA, OH	H	14.55 FQ	20.66 AW	26.63 TQ	OHBLS	10/01-12/01
	Youngstown-Warren MSA, OH	H	17.05 FQ	21.21 AW	26.16 TQ	OHBLS	10/01-12/01
	Oklahoma	H	11.51 FQ	17.12 AW	22.52 TQ	OKBLS	10/01-12/01
	Oklahoma City MSA, OK	H	11.50 FQ	17.12 AW	21.47 TQ	OKBLS	10/01-12/01
	Tulsa MSA, OK	H	11.52 FQ	17.32 AW	24.62 TQ	OKBLS	10/01-12/01
	Oregon	H	13.47 FQ	18.85 AW	24.94 TQ	ORBLS	10/01-12/01
	Portland-Vancouver PMSA, OR-WA	H	13.76 FQ	18.88 AW	24.78 TQ	ORBLS	10/01-12/01
	Salem PMSA, OR	H	12.01 FQ	20.66 AW	26.72 TQ	ORBLS	10/01-12/01
	Pennsylvania	H	10.24 FQ	20.92 AW	31.15 TQ	PABLS	10/01-12/01
	Harrisburg-Lebanon-Carlisle MSA, PA	H	17.85 FQ	26.02 AW	33.95 TQ	PABLS	10/01-12/01
	Johnstown MSA, PA	H	17.03 FQ	19.30 AW	22.97 TQ	PABLS	10/01-12/01
	Lancaster MSA, PA	H	10.51 FQ	15.72 AW	20.61 TQ	PABLS	10/01-12/01
	Philadelphia PMSA, PA-NJ	H	10.66 FQ	20.65 AW	28.52 TQ	PABLS	10/01-12/01
	Pittsburgh MSA, PA	H	10.55 FQ	18.71 AW	25.18 TQ	PABLS	10/01-12/01
	Rhode Island	H	14.40 FQ	20.82 AW	32.82 TQ	RIBLS	10/01-12/01
	Providence-Fall River-Warwick MSA, RI-MA	H	14.66 FQ	20.73 AW	32.09 TQ	RIBLS	10/01-12/01
	South Carolina	H	11.67 FQ	17.25 AW	22.70 TQ	SCBLS	10/01-12/01
	Charleston-North Charleston MSA, SC	H	14.57 FQ	20.48 AW	27.73 TQ	SCBLS	10/01-12/01
	Columbia MSA, SC	H	13.93 FQ	19.08 AW	27.25 TQ	SCBLS	10/01-12/01
	Greenville-Spartanburg-Anderson MSA, SC	H	11.31 FQ	15.85 AW	20.94 TQ	SCBLS	10/01-12/01
	South Dakota	H	11.51 FQ	17.74 AW	25.50 TQ	SDBLS	10/01-12/01
	Sioux Falls MSA, SD	H	14.93 FQ	19.68 AW	25.80 TQ	SDBLS	10/01-12/01
	Tennessee	H	9.74 FQ	19.05 AW	30.01 TQ	TNBLS	10/01-12/01
	Chattanooga MSA, TN-GA	H	20.52 FQ	31.92 AW	41.75 TQ	TNBLS	10/01-12/01
	Clarksville-Hopkinsville MSA, TN-KY	H	18.04 FQ	24.29 AW	32.08 TQ	TNBLS	10/01-12/01
	Knoxville MSA, TN	H	12.73 FQ	18.89 AW	26.75 TQ	TNBLS	10/01-12/01
	Memphis MSA, TN-AR-MS	H	10.92 FQ	19.49 AW	26.84 TQ	TNBLS	10/01-12/01
	Nashville MSA, TN	H	7.95 FQ	17.43 AW	31.38 TQ	TNBLS	10/01-12/01
	Texas	H	13.89 FQ	20.26 AW	27.96 TQ	TXBLS	10/01-12/01
	Amarillo MSA, TX	H	8.75 FQ	17.09 AW	24.54 TQ	TXBLS	10/01-12/01
	Austin-San Marcos MSA, TX	H	14.03 FQ	21.85 AW	33.26 TQ	TXBLS	10/01-12/01
	Brazoria PMSA, TX	H	6.35 FQ	13.95 AW	17.79 TQ	TXBLS	10/01-12/01
	Brownsville-Harlingen-San Benito MSA, TX	H	5.74 FQ	8.93 AW	14.83 TQ	TXBLS	10/01-12/01
	Corpus Christi MSA, TX	H	14.78 FQ	19.31 AW	24.92 TQ	TXBLS	10/01-12/01
	Dallas PMSA, TX	H	13.65 FQ	20.38 AW	28.75 TQ	TXBLS	10/01-12/01
	El Paso MSA, TX	H	10.23 FQ	20.46 AW	30.36 TQ	TXBLS	10/01-12/01
	Fort Worth-Arlington PMSA, TX	H	14.50 FQ	20.75 AW	28.02 TQ	TXBLS	10/01-12/01
	Galveston-Texas City PMSA, TX	H	14.81 FQ	21.86 AW	27.32 TQ	TXBLS	10/01-12/01
	Houston PMSA, TX	H	14.06 FQ	22.49 AW	28.85 TQ	TXBLS	10/01-12/01
	Killeen-Temple MSA, TX	H	8.14 FQ	15.41 AW	27.88 TQ	TXBLS	10/01-12/01

AAW Average annual wage; AE Average entry wage; AEX Average experienced wage; AO Average offered; AOH Average offered, high; AOL Average offered, low; APH Average pay, high range; APL Average pay, low range; ASH Average starting, high; ASL Average starting, low; AW Average wage paid; FQ First quartile wage; H Hourly; HI Highest wage paid; HR High end range; LR Low end range; M Monthly; MTC Median total compensation; MW Median wage paid; SQ Second quartile wage; S Special: hourly and annual; TQ Third quartile wage; W Weekly; Y Yearly

Occupation/Type/Industry	Location	Per	Low	Mid	High	Source	Date
Aircraft Mechanic and Service Technician	San Antonio MSA, TX	H	14.40 FQ	18.64 AW	24.92 TQ	TXBLS	10/01-12/01
	Utah	H	13.11 FQ	19.73 AW	29.84 TQ	UTBLS	10/01-12/01
	Salt Lake City-Ogden MSA, UT	H	13.20 FQ	19.82 AW	29.94 TQ	UTBLS	10/01-12/01
	Vermont	H	11.26 FQ	17.06 AW	27.70 TQ	VTBLS	10/01-12/01
	Burlington MSA, VT	H	11.69 FQ	17.53 AW	28.50 TQ	VTBLS	10/01-12/01
	Virginia	H	11.91 FQ	19.17 AW	26.93 TQ	VABLS	10/01-12/01
	Norfolk-Virginia Beach-Newport News MSA, VA-NC	H	13.08 FQ	18.44 AW	25.43 TQ	VABLS	10/01-12/01
	Richmond-Petersburg MSA, VA	H	10.38 FQ	18.61 AW	25.91 TQ	VABLS	10/01-12/01
	Roanoke MSA, VA	H	9.71 FQ	17.81 AW	22.85 TQ	VABLS	10/01-12/01
	Washington	H	14.10 FQ	20.44 AW	27.44 TQ	WABLS	10/01-12/01
	Olympia PMSA, WA	H	11.03 FQ	18.62 AW	25.57 TQ	WABLS	10/01-12/01
	Seattle-Bellevue-Everett PMSA, WA	H	14.17 FQ	20.61 AW	27.77 TQ	WABLS	10/01-12/01
	Spokane MSA, WA	H	15.22 FQ	19.35 AW	24.72 TQ	WABLS	10/01-12/01
	Tacoma PMSA, WA	H	15.87 FQ	21.40 AW	26.37 TQ	WABLS	10/01-12/01
	West Virginia	H	12.54 FQ	20.51 AW	31.50 TQ	WVBLS	10/01-12/01
	Charleston MSA, WV	H	17.22 FQ	20.74 AW	27.03 TQ	WVBLS	10/01-12/01
	Wisconsin	H	12.40 FQ	18.61 AW	25.62 TQ	WIBLS	10/01-12/01
	Green Bay MSA, WI	H	9.64 FQ	17.59 AW	30.92 TQ	WIBLS	10/01-12/01
	Madison MSA, WI	H	14.08 FQ	18.48 AW	23.33 TQ	WIBLS	10/01-12/01
	Milwaukee-Waukesha PMSA, WI	H	13.22 FQ	19.30 AW	25.96 TQ	WIBLS	10/01-12/01
	Wyoming	H	11.92 FQ	18.35 AW	26.09 TQ	WYBLS	10/01-12/01
	Cheyenne MSA, WY	H	10.68 FQ	18.20 AW	25.88 TQ	WYBLS	10/01-12/01
	Puerto Rico	H	10.02 FQ	17.44 AW	26.57 TQ	PRBLS	10/01-12/01
	Virgin Islands	H	13.76 FQ	18.60 AW	24.63 TQ	VIBLS	10/01-12/01
Aircraft Structure, Surfaces, Rigging, and Systems Assembler	Alabama	H	9.27 FQ	12.04 AW	15.34 TQ	ALBLS	10/01-12/01
	Arizona	H	14.24 FQ	19.58 AW	25.89 TQ	AZBLS	10/01-12/01
	Arkansas	H	10.96 FQ	13.79 AW	19.75 TQ	ARBLS	10/01-12/01
	California	H	11.27 FQ	21.10 AW	27.29 TQ	CABLS	10/01-12/01
	Colorado	H	11.16 FQ	17.55 AW	25.65 TQ	COBLS	10/01-12/01
	Connecticut	H	11.64 FQ	19.23 AW	26.68 TQ	CTBLS	10/01-12/01
	Florida	H	9.24 FQ	13.27 AW	17.81 TQ	FLBLS	10/01-12/01
	Georgia	H	9.53 FQ	12.56 AW	16.59 TQ	GABLS	10/01-12/01
	Illinois	H	7.14 FQ	10.28 AW	15.99 TQ	ILBLS	10/01-12/01
	Indiana	H	8.30 FQ	13.61 AW	22.25 TQ	INBLS	10/01-12/01
	Kentucky	H	7.01 FQ	12.87 AW	19.55 TQ	KYBLS	10/01-12/01
	Louisiana	H	14.35 FQ	18.92 AW	24.40 TQ	LABLS	10/01-12/01
	Massachusetts	H	9.34 FQ	16.38 AW	22.44 TQ	MABLS	10/01-12/01
	Michigan	H	7.37 FQ	10.05 AW	14.62 TQ	MIBLS	10/01-12/01
	Minnesota	H	7.58 FQ	11.39 AW	16.15 TQ	MNBLS	10/01-12/01
	New York	H	9.20 FQ	13.39 AW	20.33 TQ	NYBLS	10/01-12/01
	North Carolina	H	8.03 FQ	12.51 AW	16.32 TQ	NCBLS	10/01-12/01
	Ohio	H	6.55 FQ	11.88 AW	20.48 TQ	OHBLS	10/01-12/01
	South Carolina	H	10.29 FQ	13.79 AW	17.58 TQ	SCBLS	10/01-12/01
	Tennessee	H	10.24 FQ	17.27 AW	25.04 TQ	TNBLS	10/01-12/01
	Texas	H	12.85 FQ	18.96 AW	26.02 TQ	TXBLS	10/01-12/01
	Virginia	H	6.66 FQ	11.97 AW	21.26 TQ	VABLS	10/01-12/01
	West Virginia	H	9.30 FQ	14.59 AW	21.80 TQ	WVBLS	10/01-12/01
Airfield Operations Specialist	Alaska	H	10.54 FQ	18.21 AW	27.99 TQ	AKBLS	10/01-12/01
	California	H	14.01 FQ	23.32 AW	32.87 TQ	CABLS	10/01-12/01
	Colorado	H	12.18 FQ	17.99 AW	25.55 TQ	COBLS	10/01-12/01
	Connecticut	H	9.24 FQ	18.22 AW	31.50 TQ	CTBLS	10/01-12/01
	Florida	H	8.54 FQ	15.15 AW	21.58 TQ	FLBLS	10/01-12/01
	Georgia	H	13.07 FQ	31.32 AW	53.84 TQ	GABLS	10/01-12/01
	Hawaii	H	8.49 FQ	13.69 AW	19.74 TQ	HIBLS	10/01-12/01
	Illinois	H	8.81 FQ	16.48 AW	27.99 TQ	ILBLS	10/01-12/01
	Indiana	H	12.09 FQ	18.99 AW	31.94 TQ	INBLS	10/01-12/01
	Louisiana	H	7.65 FQ	12.94 AW	18.38 TQ	LABLS	10/01-12/01
	Michigan	H	10.03 FQ	15.17 AW	19.14 TQ	MIBLS	10/01-12/01
	Minnesota	H	11.27 FQ	19.40 AW	25.61 TQ	MNBLS	10/01-12/01
	Montana	H	11.50 FQ	16.45 AW	21.24 TQ	MTBLS	10/01-12/01
	Nebraska	H	5.77 FQ	8.05 AW	11.53 TQ	NEBLS	10/01-12/01
	New Jersey	H	12.81 FQ	19.70 AW	35.43 TQ	NJBLS	10/01-12/01

AAW	Average annual wage	**AOH**	Average offered, high	**ASH**	Average starting, high	**H**	Hourly	**M**	Monthly	**S**	Special: hourly and annual
AE	Average entry wage	**AOL**	Average offered, low	**ASL**	Average starting, low	**HI**	Highest wage paid	**MTC**	Median total compensation	**TQ**	Third quartile wage
AEX	Average experienced wage	**APH**	Average pay, high range	**AW**	Average wage paid	**HR**	High end range	**MW**	Median wage paid	**W**	Weekly
AO	Average offered	**APL**	Average pay, low range	**FQ**	First quartile wage	**LR**	Low end range	**SQ**	Second quartile wage	**Y**	Yearly

Occupation/Type/Industry	Location	Per	Low	Mid	High	Source	Date
Airfield Operations Specialist	New York	H	9.71 FQ	17.88 AW	26.89 TQ	NYBLS	10/01-12/01
	North Carolina	H	10.42 FQ	19.84 AW	37.68 TQ	NCBLS	10/01-12/01
	Ohio	H	8.62 FQ	14.80 AW	23.11 TQ	OHBLS	10/01-12/01
	Oklahoma	H	10.42 FQ	24.59 AW	35.38 TQ	OKBLS	10/01-12/01
	Tennessee	H	7.52 FQ	12.15 AW	16.82 TQ	TNBLS	10/01-12/01
	Texas	H	8.95 FQ	18.57 AW	35.44 TQ	TXBLS	10/01-12/01
	Virginia	H	10.51 FQ	16.22 AW	20.96 TQ	VABLS	10/01-12/01
Airline Pilot, Copilot, and Flight Engineer	Alabama	Y	48780 FQ	64930 AW	88160 TQ	ALBLS	10/01-12/01
	Birmingham MSA, AL	Y	47930 FQ	57720 AW	76040 TQ	ALBLS	10/01-12/01
	Mobile MSA, AL	Y	23530 FQ	53320 AW	85550 TQ	ALBLS	10/01-12/01
	Alaska	Y	34630 FQ	82890 AW		AKBLS	10/01-12/01
	Anchorage MSA, AK	Y	35320 FQ	88840 AW		AKBLS	10/01-12/01
	Tucson MSA, AZ	Y	52770 FQ	72310 AW	90620 TQ	AZBLS	10/01-12/01
	Arkansas	Y	33850 FQ	68390 AW	110300 TQ	ARBLS	10/01-12/01
	Little Rock-North Little Rock MSA, AR	Y	54090 FQ	80970 AW	113030 TQ	ARBLS	10/01-12/01
	Los Angeles-Long Beach PMSA, CA	Y	72200 FQ	116960 AW		CABLS	10/01-12/01
	Orange County PMSA, CA	Y	27390 FQ	55620 AW	87410 TQ	CABLS	10/01-12/01
	Riverside-San Bernardino PMSA, CA	Y	23730 FQ	65340 AW	88840 TQ	CABLS	10/01-12/01
	Sacramento PMSA, CA	Y	46220 FQ	69030 AW	88890 TQ	CABLS	10/01-12/01
	San Diego MSA, CA	Y	38620 FQ	56990 AW	84100 TQ	CABLS	10/01-12/01
	Vallejo-Fairfield-Napa PMSA, CA	Y	44130 FQ	66190 AW	96180 TQ	CABLS	10/01-12/01
	Ventura PMSA, CA	Y	32650 FQ	56470 AW	117950 TQ	CABLS	10/01-12/01
	Colorado Springs MSA, CO	Y	47670 FQ	60120 AW	90450 TQ	COBLS	10/01-12/01
	Connecticut	Y	33040 FQ	79080 AW		CTBLS	10/01-12/01
	Bridgeport PMSA, CT	Y	33000 FQ	57170 AW	78940 TQ	CTBLS	10/01-12/01
	Hartford MSA, CT	Y	33080 FQ	84420 AW		CTBLS	10/01-12/01
	Delaware	Y	60640 FQ	79180 AW	113590 TQ	DEBLS	10/01-12/01
	Wilmington-Newark PMSA, DE-MD	Y	60910 FQ	78550 AW	113340 TQ	DEBLS	10/01-12/01
	Washington PMSA, DC-MD-VA-WV	Y	104550 FQ	136320 AW		DCBLS	10/01-12/01
	Florida	Y	33390 FQ	100350 AW		FLBLS	10/01-12/01
	Fort Lauderdale PMSA, FL	Y	22480 FQ	70810 AW		FLBLS	10/01-12/01
	Fort Walton Beach MSA, FL	Y	51650 FQ	67310 AW	78330 TQ	FLBLS	10/01-12/01
	Jacksonville MSA, FL	Y	24470 FQ	57060 AW	92130 TQ	FLBLS	10/01-12/01
	Miami PMSA, FL	Y	47480 FQ	115320 AW		FLBLS	10/01-12/01
	Orlando MSA, FL	Y	27830 FQ	92370 AW		FLBLS	10/01-12/01
	Pensacola MSA, FL	Y	29830 FQ	44470 AW	72670 TQ	FLBLS	10/01-12/01
	Tampa-St. Petersburg-Clearwater MSA, FL	Y	31930 FQ	45090 AW	67360 TQ	FLBLS	10/01-12/01
	Macon MSA, GA	Y	24180 FQ	92240 AW		GABLS	10/01-12/01
	Savannah MSA, GA	Y	66680 FQ	111280 AW		GABLS	10/01-12/01
	Hawaii	Y	48490 FQ	115970 AW		HIBLS	10/01-12/01
	Honolulu MSA, HI	Y	48900 FQ	116370 AW		HIBLS	10/01-12/01
	Idaho	Y	29730 FQ	52800 AW	84850 TQ	IDBLS	10/01-12/01
	Illinois	Y	38050 FQ	101300 AW		ILBLS	10/01-12/01
	Chicago PMSA, IL	Y	38720 FQ	102550 AW		ILBLS	10/01-12/01
	Indiana	Y	36980 FQ	50720 AW	86330 TQ	INBLS	10/01-12/01
	Fort Wayne MSA, IN	Y	18770 FQ	45480 AW	78690 TQ	INBLS	10/01-12/01
	Indianapolis MSA, IN	Y	39130 FQ	52010 AW	87920 TQ	INBLS	10/01-12/01
	Iowa	Y	32380 FQ	61010 AW	94580 TQ	IABLS	10/01-12/01
	Kansas	Y	32280 FQ	66700 AW	125450 TQ	KSBLS	10/01-12/01
	Wichita MSA, KS	Y	36530 FQ	69520 AW	139450 TQ	KSBLS	10/01-12/01
	Kentucky	Y	40640 FQ	107890 AW		KYBLS	10/01-12/01
	Lexington MSA, KY	Y	28010 FQ	57670 AW	91980 TQ	KYBLS	10/01-12/01
	Louisville MSA, KY-IN	Y	39230 FQ	105860 AW		KYBLS	10/01-12/01
	Louisiana	Y	41590 FQ	66310 AW	90740 TQ	LABLS	10/01-12/01
	Lake Charles MSA, LA	Y	34110 FQ	72600 AW	129760 TQ	LABLS	10/01-12/01
	New Orleans MSA, LA	Y	45470 FQ	66270 AW	86750 TQ	LABLS	10/01-12/01
	Shreveport-Bossier City MSA, LA	Y	45470 FQ	63880 AW	87880 TQ	LABLS	10/01-12/01
	Maine	Y	26250 FQ	48090 AW	77900 TQ	MEBLS	10/01-12/01
	Massachusetts	Y	52880 FQ	109780 AW		MABLS	10/01-12/01
	Boston PMSA, MA-NH	Y	54610 FQ	111920 AW		MABLS	10/01-12/01
	Michigan	Y	24460 FQ	69350 AW		MIBLS	10/01-12/01
	Detroit PMSA, MI	Y	23890 FQ	68590 AW		MIBLS	10/01-12/01

AAW	Average annual wage	**AOH**	Average offered, high	**ASH**	Average starting, high	**H**	Hourly	**M**	Monthly	**S**	Special: hourly and annual
AE	Average entry wage	**AOL**	Average offered, low	**ASL**	Average starting, low	**HI**	Highest wage paid	**MTC**	Median total compensation	**TQ**	Third quartile wage
AEX	Average experienced wage	**APH**	Average pay, high range	**AW**	Average wage paid	**HR**	High end range	**MW**	Median wage paid	**W**	Weekly
AO	Average offered	**APL**	Average pay, low range	**FQ**	First quartile wage	**LR**	Low end range	**SQ**	Second quartile wage	**Y**	Yearly

Occupation/Type/Industry	Location	Per	Low	Mid	High	Source	Date
Airline Pilot, Copilot, and Flight Engineer							
	Grand Rapids-Muskegon-Holland MSA, MI	Y	24910 FQ	52450 AW	86140 TQ	MIBLS	10/01-12/01
	Minnesota	Y	38600 FQ	84710 AW		MNBLS	10/01-12/01
	Minneapolis-St. Paul MSA, MN-WI	Y	47920 FQ	91340 AW		MNBLS	10/01-12/01
	Mississippi	Y	31180 FQ	52200 AW	84570 TQ	MSBLS	10/01-12/01
	Missouri	Y	21980 FQ	53240 AW	86840 TQ	MOBLS	10/01-12/01
	Kansas City MSA, MO-KS	Y	31850 FQ	51770 AW	77870 TQ	MOBLS	10/01-12/01
	St. Louis MSA, MO-IL	Y	20920 FQ	55170 AW	89680 TQ	MOBLS	10/01-12/01
	Montana	Y	32180 FQ	50520 AW	70990 TQ	MTBLS	10/01-12/01
	Nebraska	Y	39950 FQ	72310 AW	116370 TQ	NEBLS	10/01-12/01
	Nevada	Y	26190 FQ	65720 AW		NVBLS	10/01-12/01
	Las Vegas MSA, NV-AZ	Y	25900 FQ	66030 AW		NVBLS	10/01-12/01
	Reno MSA, NV	Y	30470 FQ	64890 AW	107160 TQ	NVBLS	10/01-12/01
	New Hampshire	Y	19200 FQ	55940 AW		NHBLS	10/01-12/01
	Portsmouth-Rochester PMSA, NH-ME	Y	19110 FQ	56160 AW		NHBLS	10/01-12/01
	Atlantic-Cape May PMSA, NJ	Y	29060 FQ	65660 AW	104530 TQ	NJBLS	10/01-12/01
	Bergen-Passaic PMSA, NJ	Y	22050 FQ	64870 AW	113270 TQ	NJBLS	10/01-12/01
	Middlesex-Somerset-Hunterdon PMSA, NJ	Y	24460 FQ	68470 AW	113940 TQ	NJBLS	10/01-12/01
	Trenton PMSA, NJ	Y	22320 FQ	66260 AW	112940 TQ	NJBLS	10/01-12/01
	New Mexico	Y	30050 FQ	57560 AW	89960 TQ	NMBLS	10/01-12/01
	Albuquerque MSA, NM	Y	30860 FQ	63020 AW	93160 TQ	NMBLS	10/01-12/01
	New York	Y	34770 FQ	73700 AW		NYBLS	10/01-12/01
	Albany-Schenectady-Troy MSA, NY	Y	48030 FQ	94520 AW		NYBLS	10/01-12/01
	Buffalo-Niagara Falls MSA, NY	Y	27700 FQ	45510 AW	75050 TQ	NYBLS	10/01-12/01
	Nassau-Suffolk PMSA, NY	Y	27330 FQ	53530 AW	87020 TQ	NYBLS	10/01-12/01
	New York PMSA, NY	Y	35570 FQ	75510 AW		NYBLS	10/01-12/01
	North Carolina	Y	56160 FQ	104480 AW		NCBLS	10/01-12/01
	Greensboro-Winston-Salem-High Point MSA, NC	Y	59370 FQ	91090 AW		NCBLS	10/01-12/01
	North Dakota	Y	23830 FQ	40240 AW	66410 TQ	NDBLS	10/01-12/01
	Cincinnati PMSA, OH-KY-IN	Y	40310 FQ	109690 AW		OHBLS	10/01-12/01
	Toledo MSA, OH	Y	32540 FQ	54240 AW	95690 TQ	OHBLS	10/01-12/01
	Oklahoma	Y	39720 FQ	106570 AW		OKBLS	10/01-12/01
	Oklahoma City MSA, OK	Y	41000 FQ	72040 AW	90740 TQ	OKBLS	10/01-12/01
	Tulsa MSA, OK	Y	39920 FQ	109450 AW		OKBLS	10/01-12/01
	Oregon	Y	20930 FQ	50350 AW	86160 TQ	ORBLS	10/01-12/01
	Portland-Vancouver PMSA, OR-WA	Y	20890 FQ	50230 AW	86290 TQ	ORBLS	10/01-12/01
	South Carolina	Y	28650 FQ	55320 AW	89640 TQ	SCBLS	10/01-12/01
	Greenville-Spartanburg-Anderson MSA, SC	Y	29490 FQ	49520 AW	75440 TQ	SCBLS	10/01-12/01
	South Dakota	Y	26400 FQ	47540 AW	79370 TQ	SDBLS	10/01-12/01
	Tennessee	Y	38940 FQ	90590 AW		TNBLS	10/01-12/01
	Chattanooga MSA, TN-GA	Y	33130 FQ	73050 AW	109160 TQ	TNBLS	10/01-12/01
	Knoxville MSA, TN	Y	22520 FQ	47380 AW	84860 TQ	TNBLS	10/01-12/01
	Nashville MSA, TN	Y	47670 FQ	74340 AW	110280 TQ	TNBLS	10/01-12/01
	Texas	Y	35910 FQ	108470 AW		TXBLS	10/01-12/01
	Corpus Christi MSA, TX	Y	48090 FQ	58020 AW	81240 TQ	TXBLS	10/01-12/01
	Dallas PMSA, TX	Y	27630 FQ	76380 AW	139640 TQ	TXBLS	10/01-12/01
	El Paso MSA, TX	Y	20760 FQ	47500 AW	73500 TQ	TXBLS	10/01-12/01
	San Antonio MSA, TX	Y	28400 FQ	82210 AW	140580 TQ	TXBLS	10/01-12/01
	Virginia	Y	58220 FQ	126940 AW		VABLS	10/01-12/01
	Norfolk-Virginia Beach-Newport News MSA, VA-NC	Y	20500 FQ	42250 AW	73670 TQ	VABLS	10/01-12/01
	Washington	Y	41410 FQ	113450 AW		WABLS	10/01-12/01
	Seattle-Bellevue-Everett PMSA, WA	Y	62530 FQ	124110 AW		WABLS	10/01-12/01
	Spokane MSA, WA	Y	25400 FQ	44110 AW	79970 TQ	WABLS	10/01-12/01
	Tacoma PMSA, WA	Y	38440 FQ	63020 AW	87430 TQ	WABLS	10/01-12/01
	West Virginia	Y	37580 FQ	73620 AW		WVBLS	10/01-12/01
	Wisconsin	Y	25080 FQ	54690 AW	97970 TQ	WIBLS	10/01-12/01
	Milwaukee-Waukesha PMSA, WI	Y	23070 FQ	45710 AW	60710 TQ	WIBLS	10/01-12/01
	Wyoming	Y	27180 FQ	54170 AW	80990 TQ	WYBLS	10/01-12/01
	Cheyenne MSA, WY	Y	35220 FQ	57110 AW	83250 TQ	WYBLS	10/01-12/01

AAW	Average annual wage	**AOH**	Average offered, high	**ASH**	Average starting, high	**H**	Hourly	**M**	Monthly	**S**	Special: hourly and annual
AE	Average entry wage	**AOL**	Average offered, low	**ASL**	Average starting, low	**HI**	Highest wage paid	**MTC**	Median total compensation	**TQ**	Third quartile wage
AEX	Average experienced wage	**APH**	Average pay, high range	**AW**	Average wage paid	**HR**	High end range	**MW**	Median wage paid	**W**	Weekly
AO	Average offered	**APL**	Average pay, low range	**FQ**	First quartile wage	**LR**	Low end range	**SQ**	Second quartile wage	**Y**	Yearly

Occupation/Type/Industry	Location	Per	Low	Mid	High	Source	Date
Airline Pilot, Copilot, and Flight Engineer	Virgin Islands	Y	25370 FQ	41090 AW	61480 TQ	VIBLS	10/01-12/01
Airplane Captain	United States	Y		70000 AW		BCAVIA	1/01-1/01
Airplane Maintenance Technician	United States	Y		50000 AW		BCAVIA	1/01-1/01
Airport Security Screener	United States	Y		37273 AW		USATOD	2001-2001
	United States	H	10.00 AE			NYT1	2000-2000
	Mobile, AL	Y	26639 ASL		38458 ASH	ASR	2002
	Anchorage, AK	Y	29500 ASL		44250 ASH	ASR	2002
	Louisville, KY	Y	26639 ASL		38458 ASH	ASR	2002
	Baltimore, MD	Y	26309 ASL		39463 ASH	ASR	2002
	Grand Rapids, MI	Y	26639 ASL		38458 ASH	ASR	2002
	Spokane, WA	Y	26639 ASL		38458 ASH	ASR	2002
Ambulance Driver and Attendant							
Except Emergency Medical Technician	Alabama	H	5.59 FQ	7.79 AW	12.19 TQ	ALBLS	10/01-12/01
Except Emergency Medical Technician	Arizona	H	5.97 FQ	8.17 AW	11.09 TQ	AZBLS	10/01-12/01
Except Emergency Medical Technician	Phoenix-Mesa MSA, AZ	H	7.20 FQ	9.30 AW	11.87 TQ	AZBLS	10/01-12/01
Except Emergency Medical Technician	Arkansas	H	6.63 FQ	10.70 AW	16.45 TQ	ARBLS	10/01-12/01
Except Emergency Medical Technician	California	H	7.36 FQ	13.67 AW	24.16 TQ	CABLS	10/01-12/01
Except Emergency Medical Technician	Los Angeles-Long Beach PMSA, CA	H	7.54 FQ	13.27 AW	28.61 TQ	CABLS	10/01-12/01
Except Emergency Medical Technician	Oakland PMSA, CA	H	9.80 FQ	15.68 AW	24.79 TQ	CABLS	10/01-12/01
Except Emergency Medical Technician	Orange County PMSA, CA	H	7.13 FQ	10.79 AW	14.32 TQ	CABLS	10/01-12/01
Except Emergency Medical Technician	Riverside-San Bernardino PMSA, CA	H	7.79 FQ	16.31 AW	25.49 TQ	CABLS	10/01-12/01
Except Emergency Medical Technician	San Francisco PMSA, CA	H	8.77 FQ	13.18 AW	16.17 TQ	CABLS	10/01-12/01
Except Emergency Medical Technician	Colorado	H	7.18 FQ	14.38 AW	25.71 TQ	COBLS	10/01-12/01
Except Emergency Medical Technician	Denver PMSA, CO	H	7.38 FQ	17.95 AW	26.81 TQ	COBLS	10/01-12/01
Except Emergency Medical Technician	Hartford MSA, CT	H	7.55 FQ	9.91 AW	13.03 TQ	CTBLS	10/01-12/01
Except Emergency Medical Technician	New London-Norwich MSA, CT-RI	H	8.59 FQ	10.43 AW	13.04 TQ	CTBLS	10/01-12/01
Except Emergency Medical Technician	Delaware	H	7.67 FQ	10.14 AW	11.58 TQ	DEBLS	10/01-12/01
Except Emergency Medical Technician	Wilmington-Newark PMSA, DE-MD	H	7.81 FQ	10.39 AW	14.94 TQ	DEBLS	10/01-12/01
Except Emergency Medical Technician	Washington PMSA, DC-MD-VA-WV	H	6.59 FQ	10.02 AW	13.60 TQ	DCBLS	10/01-12/01
Except Emergency Medical Technician	Florida	H	6.79 FQ	9.25 AW	12.70 TQ	FLBLS	10/01-12/01
Except Emergency Medical Technician	Fort Lauderdale PMSA, FL	H	7.00 FQ	15.10 AW	27.47 TQ	FLBLS	10/01-12/01
Except Emergency Medical Technician	Fort Myers-Cape Coral MSA, FL	H	5.92 FQ	8.78 AW	12.11 TQ	FLBLS	10/01-12/01
Except Emergency Medical Technician	Jacksonville MSA, FL	H	7.22 FQ	9.42 AW	12.63 TQ	FLBLS	10/01-12/01
Except Emergency Medical Technician	Orlando MSA, FL	H	6.21 FQ	7.97 AW	9.11 TQ	FLBLS	10/01-12/01
Except Emergency Medical Technician	Tampa-St. Petersburg-Clearwater MSA, FL	H	6.25 FQ	7.64 AW	8.77 TQ	FLBLS	10/01-12/01
Except Emergency Medical Technician	Georgia	H	5.76 FQ	9.05 AW	15.58 TQ	GABLS	10/01-12/01
Except Emergency Medical Technician	Idaho	H	6.97 FQ	10.97 AW	14.15 TQ	IDBLS	10/01-12/01
Except Emergency Medical Technician	Illinois	H	7.50 FQ	12.10 AW	17.49 TQ	ILBLS	10/01-12/01
Except Emergency Medical Technician	Chicago PMSA, IL	H	8.36 FQ	12.24 AW	16.78 TQ	ILBLS	10/01-12/01
Except Emergency Medical Technician	Indiana	H	6.24 FQ	8.81 AW	12.40 TQ	INBLS	10/01-12/01
Except Emergency Medical Technician	Gary PMSA, IN	H	6.24 FQ	8.33 AW	11.65 TQ	INBLS	10/01-12/01
Except Emergency Medical Technician	Indianapolis MSA, IN	H	6.12 FQ	9.77 AW	13.22 TQ	INBLS	10/01-12/01
Except Emergency Medical Technician	Iowa	H	5.82 FQ	8.24 AW	11.49 TQ	IABLS	10/01-12/01
Except Emergency Medical Technician	Davenport-Moline-Rock Island MSA, IA-IL	H	14.72 FQ	22.28 AW	26.60 TQ	IABLS	10/01-12/01
Except Emergency Medical Technician	Kansas	H	6.19 FQ	10.25 AW	14.97 TQ	KSBLS	10/01-12/01
Except Emergency Medical Technician	Kentucky	H	7.36 FQ	8.70 AW	12.01 TQ	KYBLS	10/01-12/01
Except Emergency Medical Technician	Louisiana	H	5.90 FQ	8.40 AW	11.84 TQ	LABLS	10/01-12/01
Except Emergency Medical Technician	Lafayette MSA, LA	H	6.26 FQ	9.25 AW	12.75 TQ	LABLS	10/01-12/01
Except Emergency Medical Technician	New Orleans MSA, LA	H	5.66 FQ	7.00 AW	8.66 TQ	LABLS	10/01-12/01
Except Emergency Medical Technician	Maine	H	6.04 FQ	8.29 AW	11.87 TQ	MEBLS	10/01-12/01
Except Emergency Medical Technician	Maryland	H	8.33 FQ	10.54 AW	13.54 TQ	MDBLS	10/01-12/01
Except Emergency Medical Technician	Baltimore PMSA, MD	H	8.58 FQ	10.26 AW	13.02 TQ	MDBLS	10/01-12/01
Except Emergency Medical Technician	Massachusetts	H	6.89 FQ	11.12 AW	15.54 TQ	MABLS	10/01-12/01
Except Emergency Medical Technician	Boston PMSA, MA-NH	H	6.79 FQ	11.44 AW	16.25 TQ	MABLS	10/01-12/01
Except Emergency Medical Technician	Michigan	H	6.07 FQ	9.48 AW	15.02 TQ	MIBLS	10/01-12/01
Except Emergency Medical Technician	Detroit PMSA, MI	H	9.01 FQ	14.30 AW	20.36 TQ	MIBLS	10/01-12/01
Except Emergency Medical Technician	Minnesota	H	5.88 FQ	9.90 AW	18.49 TQ	MNBLS	10/01-12/01
Except Emergency Medical Technician	Minneapolis-St. Paul MSA, MN-WI	H	7.04 FQ	10.73 AW	15.33 TQ	MNBLS	10/01-12/01
Except Emergency Medical Technician	Mississippi	H	5.77 FQ	8.12 AW	12.62 TQ	MSBLS	10/01-12/01

AAW Average annual wage; **AE** Average entry wage; **AEX** Average experienced wage; **AO** Average offered; **AOH** Average offered, high; **AOL** Average offered, low; **APH** Average pay, high range; **APL** Average pay, low range; **ASH** Average starting, high; **ASL** Average starting, low; **AW** Average wage paid; **FQ** First quartile wage; **H** Hourly; **HI** Highest wage paid; **HR** High end range; **LR** Low end range; **M** Monthly; **MTC** Median total compensation; **MW** Median wage paid; **SQ** Second quartile wage; **S** Special: hourly and annual; **TQ** Third quartile wage; **W** Weekly; **Y** Yearly

Occupation/Type/Industry	Location	Per	Low	Mid	High	Source	Date
Ambulance Driver and Attendant							
Except Emergency Medical Technician	Missouri	H	6.60 FQ	9.54 AW	13.76 TQ	MOBLS	10/01-12/01
Except Emergency Medical Technician	St. Louis MSA, MO-IL	H	6.97 FQ	10.16 AW	14.21 TQ	MOBLS	10/01-12/01
Except Emergency Medical Technician	Nebraska	H	8.17 FQ	10.24 AW	12.69 TQ	NEBLS	10/01-12/01
Except Emergency Medical Technician	Nevada	H	7.54 FQ	13.01 AW	21.71 TQ	NVBLS	10/01-12/01
Except Emergency Medical Technician	New Hampshire	H	6.59 FQ	9.13 AW	11.51 TQ	NHBLS	10/01-12/01
Except Emergency Medical Technician	New Jersey	H	7.25 FQ	9.54 AW	12.60 TQ	NJBLS	10/01-12/01
Except Emergency Medical Technician	Bergen-Passaic PMSA, NJ	H	8.01 FQ	10.53 AW	13.89 TQ	NJBLS	10/01-12/01
Except Emergency Medical Technician	Monmouth-Ocean PMSA, NJ	H	5.99 FQ	8.09 AW	10.70 TQ	NJBLS	10/01-12/01
Except Emergency Medical Technician	Newark PMSA, NJ	H	7.40 FQ	9.50 AW	12.19 TQ	NJBLS	10/01-12/01
Except Emergency Medical Technician	New Mexico	H	5.87 FQ	8.13 AW	10.68 TQ	NMBLS	10/01-12/01
Except Emergency Medical Technician	Albuquerque MSA, NM	H	6.82 FQ	9.04 AW	10.89 TQ	NMBLS	10/01-12/01
Except Emergency Medical Technician	New York	H	7.02 FQ	10.58 AW	15.92 TQ	NYBLS	10/01-12/01
Except Emergency Medical Technician	Nassau-Suffolk PMSA, NY	H	8.84 FQ	11.47 AW	16.70 TQ	NYBLS	10/01-12/01
Except Emergency Medical Technician	New York PMSA, NY	H	6.23 FQ	9.61 AW	14.00 TQ	NYBLS	10/01-12/01
Except Emergency Medical Technician	Rochester MSA, NY	H	7.23 FQ	10.59 AW	16.63 TQ	NYBLS	10/01-12/01
Except Emergency Medical Technician	Syracuse MSA, NY	H	7.18 FQ	10.37 AW	15.38 TQ	NYBLS	10/01-12/01
Except Emergency Medical Technician	North Carolina	H	6.54 FQ	8.66 AW	11.16 TQ	NCBLS	10/01-12/01
Except Emergency Medical Technician	North Dakota	H	5.68 FQ	7.25 AW	8.79 TQ	NDBLS	10/01-12/01
Except Emergency Medical Technician	Ohio	H	5.97 FQ	9.42 AW	14.89 TQ	OHBLS	10/01-12/01
Except Emergency Medical Technician	Akron PMSA, OH	H	7.50 FQ	11.44 AW	16.22 TQ	OHBLS	10/01-12/01
Except Emergency Medical Technician	Cincinnati PMSA, OH-KY-IN	H	6.98 FQ	9.03 AW	12.76 TQ	OHBLS	10/01-12/01
Except Emergency Medical Technician	Cleveland-Lorain-Elyria PMSA, OH	H	5.66 FQ	9.52 AW	15.57 TQ	OHBLS	10/01-12/01
Except Emergency Medical Technician	Youngstown-Warren MSA, OH	H	7.51 FQ	9.51 AW	11.93 TQ	OHBLS	10/01-12/01
Except Emergency Medical Technician	Oklahoma	H	5.63 FQ	7.21 AW	10.27 TQ	OKBLS	10/01-12/01
Except Emergency Medical Technician	Oregon	H	6.82 FQ	9.10 AW	11.54 TQ	ORBLS	10/01-12/01
Except Emergency Medical Technician	Portland-Vancouver PMSA, OR-WA	H	7.08 FQ	9.61 AW	12.58 TQ	ORBLS	10/01-12/01
Except Emergency Medical Technician	Pennsylvania	H	5.83 FQ	7.93 AW	10.60 TQ	PABLS	10/01-12/01
Except Emergency Medical Technician	Harrisburg-Lebanon-Carlisle MSA, PA	H	5.53 FQ	6.35 AW	6.97 TQ	PABLS	10/01-12/01
Except Emergency Medical Technician	Philadelphia PMSA, PA-NJ	H	6.47 FQ	8.52 AW	10.93 TQ	PABLS	10/01-12/01
Except Emergency Medical Technician	Pittsburgh MSA, PA	H	5.67 FQ	7.30 AW	10.14 TQ	PABLS	10/01-12/01
Except Emergency Medical Technician	Scranton-Wilkes-Barre-Hazleton MSA, PA	H	5.81 FQ	7.38 AW	8.64 TQ	PABLS	10/01-12/01
Except Emergency Medical Technician	Rhode Island	H	10.23 FQ	13.18 AW	17.41 TQ	RIBLS	10/01-12/01
Except Emergency Medical Technician	Providence-Fall River-Warwick MSA, RI-MA	H	7.05 FQ	12.05 AW	16.35 TQ	RIBLS	10/01-12/01
Except Emergency Medical Technician	Greenville-Spartanburg-Anderson MSA, SC	H	5.88 FQ	8.35 AW	11.01 TQ	SCBLS	10/01-12/01
Except Emergency Medical Technician	Tennessee	H	6.75 FQ	9.82 AW	13.97 TQ	TNBLS	10/01-12/01
Except Emergency Medical Technician	Memphis MSA, TN-AR-MS	H	6.35 FQ	10.51 AW	16.12 TQ	TNBLS	10/01-12/01
Except Emergency Medical Technician	Texas	H	6.43 FQ	9.05 AW	11.54 TQ	TXBLS	10/01-12/01
Except Emergency Medical Technician	Austin-San Marcos MSA, TX	H	5.97 FQ	9.03 AW	11.16 TQ	TXBLS	10/01-12/01
Except Emergency Medical Technician	Houston PMSA, TX	H	7.21 FQ	9.66 AW	12.19 TQ	TXBLS	10/01-12/01
Except Emergency Medical Technician	San Antonio MSA, TX	H	7.16 FQ	9.14 AW	12.28 TQ	TXBLS	10/01-12/01
Except Emergency Medical Technician	Waco MSA, TX	H	8.18 FQ	9.67 AW	11.73 TQ	TXBLS	10/01-12/01
Except Emergency Medical Technician	Vermont	H	7.68 FQ	9.12 AW	10.66 TQ	VTBLS	10/01-12/01
Except Emergency Medical Technician	Virginia	H	5.93 FQ	8.70 AW	11.86 TQ	VABLS	10/01-12/01
Except Emergency Medical Technician	Norfolk-Virginia Beach-Newport News MSA, VA-NC	H	5.91 FQ	8.95 AW	12.92 TQ	VABLS	10/01-12/01
Except Emergency Medical Technician	Washington	H	8.90 FQ	11.81 AW	13.33 TQ	WABLS	10/01-12/01
Except Emergency Medical Technician	West Virginia	H	5.53 FQ	6.27 AW	7.26 TQ	WVBLS	10/01-12/01
Except Emergency Medical Technician	Wisconsin	H	5.67 FQ	7.69 AW	10.28 TQ	WIBLS	10/01-12/01
Except Emergency Medical Technician	Milwaukee-Waukesha PMSA, WI	H	6.09 FQ	8.31 AW	10.31 TQ	WIBLS	10/01-12/01
Except Emergency Medical Technician	Wyoming	H	6.03 FQ	10.27 AW	13.58 TQ	WYBLS	10/01-12/01
Except Emergency Medical Technician	Puerto Rico	H	5.57 FQ	6.78 AW	7.04 TQ	PRBLS	10/01-12/01
Amusement and Recreation Attendant	Alabama	H	5.57 FQ	6.92 AW	9.56 TQ	ALBLS	10/01-12/01
	Alaska	H	7.71 FQ	11.99 AW	20.04 TQ	AKBLS	10/01-12/01
	Arizona	H	5.52 FQ	7.38 AW	10.37 TQ	AZBLS	10/01-12/01
	Arkansas	H	5.63 FQ	6.62 AW	8.32 TQ	ARBLS	10/01-12/01
	California	H	6.42 FQ	8.20 AW	11.06 TQ	CABLS	10/01-12/01
	Colorado	H	5.94 FQ	8.35 AW	11.46 TQ	COBLS	10/01-12/01
	Connecticut	H	6.61 FQ	9.48 AW	14.42 TQ	CTBLS	10/01-12/01
	Delaware	H	6.52 FQ	8.12 AW	11.91 TQ	DEBLS	10/01-12/01
	District of Columbia	H	6.69 FQ	10.24 AW	13.91 TQ	DCBLS	10/01-12/01
	Florida	H	5.63 FQ	7.11 AW	9.90 TQ	FLBLS	10/01-12/01

AAW Average annual wage; AE Average entry wage; AEX Average experienced wage; AO Average offered; AOH Average offered, high; AOL Average offered, low; APH Average pay, high range; APL Average pay, low range; ASH Average starting, high; ASL Average starting, low; AW Average wage paid; FQ First quartile wage; H Hourly; HI Highest wage paid; HR High end range; LR Low end range; M Monthly; MTC Median total compensation; MW Median wage paid; SQ Second quartile wage; S Special: hourly and annual; TQ Third quartile wage; W Weekly; Y Yearly

Occupation/Type/Industry	Location	Per	Low	Mid	High	Source	Date
Amusement and Recreation Attendant	Georgia	H	5.73 FQ	7.43 AW	10.06 TQ	GABLS	10/01-12/01
	Hawaii	H	6.18 FQ	9.48 AW	13.72 TQ	HIBLS	10/01-12/01
	Idaho	H	5.63 FQ	7.16 AW	10.01 TQ	IDBLS	10/01-12/01
	Illinois	H	5.64 FQ	7.77 AW	10.52 TQ	ILBLS	10/01-12/01
	Indiana	H	5.64 FQ	7.28 AW	10.16 TQ	INBLS	10/01-12/01
	Iowa	H	5.56 FQ	6.72 AW	8.40 TQ	IABLS	10/01-12/01
	Kansas	H	5.65 FQ	7.70 AW	10.52 TQ	KSBLS	10/01-12/01
	Kentucky	H	5.60 FQ	6.89 AW	8.52 TQ	KYBLS	10/01-12/01
	Louisiana	H	5.50 FQ	6.87 AW	9.22 TQ	LABLS	10/01-12/01
	Maine	H	5.84 FQ	8.34 AW	11.85 TQ	MEBLS	10/01-12/01
	Maryland	H	5.66 FQ	7.46 AW	10.10 TQ	MDBLS	10/01-12/01
	Massachusetts	H	6.94 FQ	8.61 AW	11.00 TQ	MABLS	10/01-12/01
	Michigan	H	5.71 FQ	8.01 AW	10.99 TQ	MIBLS	10/01-12/01
	Minnesota	H	5.78 FQ	8.49 AW	10.89 TQ	MNBLS	10/01-12/01
	Mississippi	H	5.62 FQ	7.47 AW	10.45 TQ	MSBLS	10/01-12/01
	Missouri	H	5.63 FQ	7.32 AW	9.95 TQ	MOBLS	10/01-12/01
	Montana	H	5.69 FQ	6.96 AW	8.59 TQ	MTBLS	10/01-12/01
	Nebraska	H	5.63 FQ	7.51 AW	11.30 TQ	NEBLS	10/01-12/01
	Nevada	H	5.74 FQ	7.35 AW	9.30 TQ	NVBLS	10/01-12/01
	New Hampshire	H	6.10 FQ	8.10 AW	10.53 TQ	NHBLS	10/01-12/01
	New Jersey	H	5.59 FQ	7.59 AW	10.45 TQ	NJBLS	10/01-12/01
	New Mexico	H	5.78 FQ	7.96 AW	10.75 TQ	NMBLS	10/01-12/01
	New York	H	5.71 FQ	8.14 AW	12.08 TQ	NYBLS	10/01-12/01
	North Carolina	H	5.63 FQ	7.36 AW	10.11 TQ	NCBLS	10/01-12/01
	North Dakota	H	5.61 FQ	6.82 AW	8.52 TQ	NDBLS	10/01-12/01
	Oklahoma	H	5.63 FQ	7.22 AW	9.22 TQ	OKBLS	10/01-12/01
	Oregon	H	6.87 FQ	8.29 AW	10.47 TQ	ORBLS	10/01-12/01
	Pennsylvania	H	5.60 FQ	7.06 AW	9.77 TQ	PABLS	10/01-12/01
	Rhode Island	H	6.58 FQ	8.77 AW	13.09 TQ	RIBLS	10/01-12/01
	South Carolina	H	5.66 FQ	7.41 AW	10.61 TQ	SCBLS	10/01-12/01
	South Dakota	H	5.69 FQ	6.98 AW	8.64 TQ	SDBLS	10/01-12/01
	Tennessee	H	5.68 FQ	7.86 AW	12.01 TQ	TNBLS	10/01-12/01
	Texas	H	5.70 FQ	7.36 AW	10.28 TQ	TXBLS	10/01-12/01
	Utah	H	5.56 FQ	6.98 AW	8.69 TQ	UTBLS	10/01-12/01
	Vermont	H	6.59 FQ	8.57 AW	11.82 TQ	VTBLS	10/01-12/01
	Virginia	H	5.60 FQ	7.15 AW	9.34 TQ	VABLS	10/01-12/01
	Washington	H	6.84 FQ	9.02 AW	11.66 TQ	WABLS	10/01-12/01
	West Virginia	H	5.70 FQ	7.38 AW	10.38 TQ	WVBLS	10/01-12/01
	Wisconsin	H	5.69 FQ	7.52 AW	10.02 TQ	WIBLS	10/01-12/01
	Wyoming	H	5.69 FQ	7.94 AW	10.97 TQ	WYBLS	10/01-12/01
	Puerto Rico	H	5.65 FQ	6.67 AW	8.56 TQ	PRBLS	10/01-12/01
	Virgin Islands	H	5.86 FQ	7.42 AW	9.30 TQ	VIBLS	10/01-12/01
	Guam	H	5.54 FQ	6.76 AW	8.90 TQ	GUBLS	10/01-12/01
Anesthesiologist	United States	Y	180000 ASL	240000 AW	300000 ASH	USATOD3	1/01-1/02
	Alabama	Y	106480 FQ	136060 AW		ALBLS	10/01-12/01
	Arkansas	Y	132750 FQ	142150 AW		ARBLS	10/01-12/01
	California	Y	102010 FQ	136750 AW		CABLS	10/01-12/01
	Los Angeles-Long Beach PMSA, CA	Y	78700 FQ	97890 AW		CABLS	10/01-12/01
	Colorado	Y	135910 FQ	141550 AW		COBLS	10/01-12/01
	Connecticut	Y	123350 FQ	135730 AW		CTBLS	10/01-12/01
	Hartford MSA, CT	Y	137710 FQ	137470 AW		CTBLS	10/01-12/01
	District of Columbia	Y	58390 FQ	94370 AW		DCBLS	10/01-12/01
	Washington PMSA, DC-MD-VA-WV	Y	66150 FQ	126450 AW		DCBLS	10/01-12/01
	Florida	Y	30560 FQ	128740 AW		FLBLS	10/01-12/01
	Georgia	Y	60360 FQ	125590 AW		GABLS	10/01-12/01
	Illinois	Y	47360 FQ	110360 AW		ILBLS	10/01-12/01
	Chicago PMSA, IL	Y	39970 FQ	85780 AW		ILBLS	10/01-12/01
	Peoria-Pekin MSA, IL	Y	36690 FQ	101700 AW		ILBLS	10/01-12/01
	Indiana	Y	87690 FQ	126620 AW		INBLS	10/01-12/01
	Indianapolis MSA, IN	Y	85200 FQ	122710 AW		INBLS	10/01-12/01
	Kentucky	Y		143410 AW		KYBLS	10/01-12/01
	Louisville MSA, KY-IN	Y		143130 AW		KYBLS	10/01-12/01
	Louisiana	Y	81370 FQ	114650 AW		LABLS	10/01-12/01
	Houma MSA, LA	Y	94300 FQ	117710 AW		LABLS	10/01-12/01
	Lafayette MSA, LA	Y	93740 FQ	117640 AW		LABLS	10/01-12/01
	Baltimore PMSA, MD	Y	86340 FQ	128940 AW		MDBLS	10/01-12/01
	Massachusetts	Y	117330 FQ	137470 AW		MABLS	10/01-12/01
	Michigan	Y	97460 FQ	129150 AW		MIBLS	10/01-12/01

AAW	Average annual wage	AOH	Average offered, high	ASH	Average starting, high	H	Hourly	M	Monthly	S	Special: hourly and annual
AE	Average entry wage	AOL	Average offered, low	ASL	Average starting, low	HI	Highest wage paid	MTC	Median total compensation	TQ	Third quartile wage
AEX	Average experienced wage	APH	Average pay, high range	AW	Average wage paid	HR	High end range	MW	Median wage paid	W	Weekly
AO	Average offered	APL	Average pay, low range	FQ	First quartile wage	LR	Low end range	SQ	Second quartile wage	Y	Yearly

Occupation/Type/Industry	Location	Per	Low	Mid	High	Source	Date
Anesthesiologist	Detroit PMSA, MI	Y	97640 FQ	126570 AW		MIBLS	10/01-12/01
	Grand Rapids-Muskegon-Holland MSA, MI	Y	89510 FQ	124470 AW		MIBLS	10/01-12/01
	Minnesota	Y	106260 FQ	124690 AW	145440 TQ	MNBLS	10/01-12/01
	Minneapolis-St. Paul MSA, MN-WI	Y	108660 FQ	123750 AW	142640 TQ	MNBLS	10/01-12/01
	Mississippi	Y	94860 FQ	125680 AW		MSBLS	10/01-12/01
	Missouri	Y	97540 FQ	131950 AW		MOBLS	10/01-12/01
	Kansas City MSA, MO-KS	Y		142890 AW		MOBLS	10/01-12/01
	St. Louis MSA, MO-IL	Y	80930 FQ	121410 AW		MOBLS	10/01-12/01
	New Jersey	Y	72990 FQ	127070 AW		NJBLS	10/01-12/01
	New York	Y	135150 FQ	141260 AW		NYBLS	10/01-12/01
	Nassau-Suffolk PMSA, NY	Y	137610 FQ	142330 AW		NYBLS	10/01-12/01
	Rochester MSA, NY	Y	40690 FQ	105520 AW		NYBLS	10/01-12/01
	North Carolina	Y	95360 FQ	123010 AW		NCBLS	10/01-12/01
	Ohio	Y	107330 FQ	136220 AW		OHBLS	10/01-12/01
	Cincinnati PMSA, OH-KY-IN	Y	84860 FQ	125550 AW		OHBLS	10/01-12/01
	Oklahoma	Y	98810 FQ	124150 AW		OKBLS	10/01-12/01
	Tulsa MSA, OK	Y	97600 FQ	114460 AW		OKBLS	10/01-12/01
	Pennsylvania	Y	92410 FQ	126900 AW		PABLS	10/01-12/01
	Harrisburg-Lebanon-Carlisle MSA, PA	Y	84430 FQ	106920 AW	140830 TQ	PABLS	10/01-12/01
	Philadelphia PMSA, PA-NJ	Y	91280 FQ	128620 AW		PABLS	10/01-12/01
	Pittsburgh MSA, PA	Y	25290 FQ	92070 AW	124000 TQ	PABLS	10/01-12/01
	Scranton-Wilkes-Barre-Hazleton MSA, PA	Y	93200 FQ	125090 AW		PABLS	10/01-12/01
	Rhode Island	Y	109520 FQ	138720 AW		RIBLS	10/01-12/01
	Providence-Fall River-Warwick MSA, RI-MA	Y	109520 FQ	138720 AW		RIBLS	10/01-12/01
	South Carolina	Y	54900 FQ	120370 AW		SCBLS	10/01-12/01
	South Dakota	Y	95690 FQ	109100 AW		SDBLS	10/01-12/01
	Tennessee	Y	103490 FQ	134160 AW		TNBLS	10/01-12/01
	Texas	Y	138050 FQ	136780 AW		TXBLS	10/01-12/01
	Virginia	Y		142630 AW		VABLS	10/01-12/01
	Washington	Y	96680 FQ	128840 AW		WABLS	10/01-12/01
	Seattle-Bellevue-Everett PMSA, WA	Y	40720 FQ	102160 AW		WABLS	10/01-12/01
	West Virginia	Y	108650 FQ	136800 AW		WVBLS	10/01-12/01
	Wisconsin	Y	91170 FQ	119970 AW		WIBLS	10/01-12/01
	Milwaukee-Waukesha PMSA, WI	Y	86760 FQ	123420 AW		WIBLS	10/01-12/01
	Puerto Rico	Y	27920 FQ	66770 AW		PRBLS	10/01-12/01
Animal Breeder	Arkansas	H	5.60 FQ	8.27 AW	13.17 TQ	ARBLS	10/01-12/01
	California	H	6.60 FQ	9.18 AW	13.20 TQ	CABLS	10/01-12/01
	Iowa	H	7.39 FQ	10.40 AW	15.52 TQ	IABLS	10/01-12/01
	Kentucky	H	7.57 FQ	12.23 AW	21.25 TQ	KYBLS	10/01-12/01
	Missouri	H	7.57 FQ	11.85 AW	19.22 TQ	MOBLS	10/01-12/01
	Ohio	H	10.30 FQ	14.77 AW	21.36 TQ	OHBLS	10/01-12/01
	Virginia	H	6.66 FQ	10.55 AW	14.07 TQ	VABLS	10/01-12/01
Animal Control Worker	Alabama	Y	14570 FQ	22000 AW	30590 TQ	ALBLS	10/01-12/01
	Alaska	Y	14500 FQ	32680 AW	47870 TQ	AKBLS	10/01-12/01
	Arizona	Y	14740 FQ	24590 AW	33910 TQ	AZBLS	10/01-12/01
	Arkansas	Y	12460 FQ	18420 AW	26360 TQ	ARBLS	10/01-12/01
	California	Y	16040 FQ	27800 AW	39840 TQ	CABLS	10/01-12/01
	Colorado	Y	12580 FQ	24940 AW	39450 TQ	COBLS	10/01-12/01
	Connecticut	Y	18360 FQ	27930 AW	42900 TQ	CTBLS	10/01-12/01
	Florida	Y	18020 FQ	23550 AW	30940 TQ	FLBLS	10/01-12/01
	Georgia	Y	16040 FQ	22250 AW	29310 TQ	GABLS	10/01-12/01
	Idaho	Y	14020 FQ	19870 AW	28870 TQ	IDBLS	10/01-12/01
	Illinois	Y	12520 FQ	23770 AW	38150 TQ	ILBLS	10/01-12/01
	Indiana	Y	13640 FQ	22790 AW	33200 TQ	INBLS	10/01-12/01
	Iowa	Y	13630 FQ	25670 AW	36390 TQ	IABLS	10/01-12/01
	Kansas	Y	14100 FQ	21370 AW	32750 TQ	KSBLS	10/01-12/01
	Kentucky	Y	11530 FQ	16560 AW	23850 TQ	KYBLS	10/01-12/01
	Louisiana	Y	15140 FQ	19520 AW	23660 TQ	LABLS	10/01-12/01
	Maine	Y	13510 FQ	19630 AW	26920 TQ	MEBLS	10/01-12/01
	Maryland	Y	17850 FQ	30690 AW	44350 TQ	MDBLS	10/01-12/01
	Massachusetts	Y	15280 FQ	25930 AW	39920 TQ	MABLS	10/01-12/01
	Michigan	Y	20830 FQ	30890 AW	42470 TQ	MIBLS	10/01-12/01
	Minnesota	Y	15010 FQ	29730 AW	37390 TQ	MNBLS	10/01-12/01
	Mississippi	Y	15560 FQ	21320 AW	27140 TQ	MSBLS	10/01-12/01

AAW	Average annual wage	AOH	Average offered, high	ASH	Average starting, high	H	Hourly	M	Monthly	S	Special: hourly and annual
AE	Average entry wage	AOL	Average offered, low	ASL	Average starting, low	HI	Highest wage paid	MTC	Median total compensation	TQ	Third quartile wage
AEX	Average experienced wage	APH	Average pay, high range	AW	Average wage paid	HR	High end range	MW	Median wage paid	W	Weekly
AO	Average offered	APL	Average pay, low range	FQ	First quartile wage	LR	Low end range	SQ	Second quartile wage	Y	Yearly

Occupation/Type/Industry	Location	Per	Low	Mid	High	Source	Date
Animal Control Worker	Missouri	Y	13920 FQ	23250 AW	34040 TQ	MOBLS	10/01-12/01
	Montana	Y	12600 FQ	23340 AW	34380 TQ	MTBLS	10/01-12/01
	Nebraska	Y	16000 FQ	24520 AW	35070 TQ	NEBLS	10/01-12/01
	Nevada	Y	15560 FQ	33500 AW	52190 TQ	NVBLS	10/01-12/01
	New Hampshire	Y	14430 FQ	21680 AW	33530 TQ	NHBLS	10/01-12/01
	New Jersey	Y	19530 FQ	31610 AW	51840 TQ	NJBLS	10/01-12/01
	New Mexico	Y	16340 FQ	23100 AW	29310 TQ	NMBLS	10/01-12/01
	New York	Y	15760 FQ	25280 AW	37920 TQ	NYBLS	10/01-12/01
	North Carolina	Y	18370 FQ	24810 AW	32380 TQ	NCBLS	10/01-12/01
	North Dakota	Y	23000 FQ	38020 AW	52490 TQ	NDBLS	10/01-12/01
	Ohio	Y	13220 FQ	23300 AW	34910 TQ	OHBLS	10/01-12/01
	Oklahoma	Y	12040 FQ	20700 AW	32940 TQ	OKBLS	10/01-12/01
	Oregon	Y	15650 FQ	32540 AW	43640 TQ	ORBLS	10/01-12/01
	Pennsylvania	Y	12890 FQ	24450 AW	34130 TQ	PABLS	10/01-12/01
	Rhode Island	Y	14680 FQ	25640 AW	37020 TQ	RIBLS	10/01-12/01
	South Carolina	Y	15760 FQ	21330 AW	28640 TQ	SCBLS	10/01-12/01
	Tennessee	Y	13710 FQ	21900 AW	30330 TQ	TNBLS	10/01-12/01
	Texas	Y	16380 FQ	24800 AW	37480 TQ	TXBLS	10/01-12/01
	Utah	Y	15260 FQ	24910 AW	35320 TQ	UTBLS	10/01-12/01
	Virginia	Y	18480 FQ	29090 AW	43500 TQ	VABLS	10/01-12/01
	Washington	Y	18410 FQ	30890 AW	44660 TQ	WABLS	10/01-12/01
	Wisconsin	Y	13180 FQ	32030 AW	69030 TQ	WIBLS	10/01-12/01
	Wyoming	Y	11630 FQ	22110 AW	34060 TQ	WYBLS	10/01-12/01
Animal Trainer	Arizona	H	5.99 FQ	10.91 AW	19.39 TQ	AZBLS	10/01-12/01
	California	H	6.73 FQ	12.26 AW	19.31 TQ	CABLS	10/01-12/01
	Colorado	H	8.95 FQ	12.82 AW	16.71 TQ	COBLS	10/01-12/01
	Connecticut	H	8.53 FQ	15.08 AW	24.86 TQ	CTBLS	10/01-12/01
	Delaware	H	7.16 FQ	10.36 AW	13.91 TQ	DEBLS	10/01-12/01
	Florida	H	6.78 FQ	12.37 AW	19.53 TQ	FLBLS	10/01-12/01
	Georgia	H	6.17 FQ	10.72 AW	17.23 TQ	GABLS	10/01-12/01
	Illinois	H	7.79 FQ	18.14 AW	22.70 TQ	ILBLS	10/01-12/01
	Indiana	H	6.13 FQ	10.95 AW	17.00 TQ	INBLS	10/01-12/01
	Kansas	H	5.89 FQ	9.64 AW	19.79 TQ	KSBLS	10/01-12/01
	Kentucky	H	6.41 FQ	12.64 AW	23.13 TQ	KYBLS	10/01-12/01
	Louisiana	H	5.98 FQ	10.15 AW	16.92 TQ	LABLS	10/01-12/01
	Maryland	H	6.23 FQ	12.46 AW	20.21 TQ	MDBLS	10/01-12/01
	Massachusetts	H	9.23 FQ	14.72 AW	22.31 TQ	MABLS	10/01-12/01
	Michigan	H	7.06 FQ	10.34 AW	16.28 TQ	MIBLS	10/01-12/01
	Minnesota	H	7.17 FQ	12.80 AW	22.06 TQ	MNBLS	10/01-12/01
	Missouri	H	6.20 FQ	14.20 AW	25.94 TQ	MOBLS	10/01-12/01
	Nevada	H	6.36 FQ	14.06 AW	20.93 TQ	NVBLS	10/01-12/01
	New Hampshire	H	5.65 FQ	11.69 AW	18.31 TQ	NHBLS	10/01-12/01
	New Jersey	H	8.22 FQ	13.91 AW	21.28 TQ	NJBLS	10/01-12/01
	New Mexico	H	5.59 FQ	7.71 AW	10.52 TQ	NMBLS	10/01-12/01
	New York	H	6.38 FQ	14.95 AW	23.49 TQ	NYBLS	10/01-12/01
	North Carolina	H	6.18 FQ	11.23 AW	22.56 TQ	NCBLS	10/01-12/01
	Ohio	H	6.14 FQ	10.19 AW	16.21 TQ	OHBLS	10/01-12/01
	Oklahoma	H	5.60 FQ	11.69 AW	20.95 TQ	OKBLS	10/01-12/01
	Oregon	H	6.54 FQ	8.30 AW	12.80 TQ	ORBLS	10/01-12/01
	Pennsylvania	H	6.06 FQ	9.60 AW	15.06 TQ	PABLS	10/01-12/01
	South Carolina	H	6.02 FQ	10.61 AW	18.04 TQ	SCBLS	10/01-12/01
	Tennessee	H	6.09 FQ	12.41 AW	18.27 TQ	TNBLS	10/01-12/01
	Texas	H	7.14 FQ	14.30 AW	20.64 TQ	TXBLS	10/01-12/01
	Virginia	H	6.20 FQ	9.27 AW	15.13 TQ	VABLS	10/01-12/01
	Wisconsin	H	10.29 FQ	14.83 AW	26.38 TQ	WIBLS	10/01-12/01
	Puerto Rico	H	5.64 FQ	8.31 AW	18.55 TQ	PRBLS	10/01-12/01
Announcer	Alabama	Y	11720 FQ	19440 AW	32460 TQ	ALBLS	10/01-12/01
	Alaska	Y	14390 FQ	30540 AW	45280 TQ	AKBLS	10/01-12/01
	Arizona	Y	13560 FQ	34330 AW	59770 TQ	AZBLS	10/01-12/01
	Arkansas	Y	11920 FQ	18900 AW	27700 TQ	ARBLS	10/01-12/01
	California	Y	16140 FQ	31360 AW	57240 TQ	CABLS	10/01-12/01
	Colorado	Y	13290 FQ	31520 AW	52450 TQ	COBLS	10/01-12/01
	Connecticut	Y	15540 FQ	35090 AW	61660 TQ	CTBLS	10/01-12/01
	Delaware	Y	13950 FQ	21200 AW	33880 TQ	DEBLS	10/01-12/01
	District of Columbia	Y	13920 FQ	42030 AW	95240 TQ	DCBLS	10/01-12/01
	Florida	Y	12400 FQ	31180 AW	57410 TQ	FLBLS	10/01-12/01
	Georgia	Y	12710 FQ	22700 AW	34240 TQ	GABLS	10/01-12/01
	Hawaii	Y	12250 FQ	22470 AW	41530 TQ	HIBLS	10/01-12/01
	Idaho	Y	12330 FQ	22290 AW	33940 TQ	IDBLS	10/01-12/01
	Illinois	Y	12180 FQ	29920 AW	62910 TQ	ILBLS	10/01-12/01
	Indiana	Y	12170 FQ	23600 AW	39000 TQ	INBLS	10/01-12/01

AAW Average annual wage; **AE** Average entry wage; **AEX** Average experienced wage; **AO** Average offered; **AOH** Average offered, high; **AOL** Average offered, low; **APH** Average pay, high range; **APL** Average pay, low range; **ASH** Average starting, high; **ASL** Average starting, low; **AW** Average wage paid; **FQ** First quartile wage; **H** Hourly; **HI** Highest wage paid; **HR** High end range; **LR** Low end range; **M** Monthly; **MTC** Median total compensation; **MW** Median wage paid; **SQ** Second quartile wage; **S** Special: hourly and annual; **TQ** Third quartile wage; **W** Weekly; **Y** Yearly

Occupation/Type/Industry	Location	Per	Low	Mid	High	Source	Date
Announcer	Iowa	Y	12040 FQ	20240 AW	32700 TQ	IABLS	10/01-12/01
	Kansas	Y	11970 FQ	21530 AW	31850 TQ	KSBLS	10/01-12/01
	Kentucky	Y	11800 FQ	25480 AW	37800 TQ	KYBLS	10/01-12/01
	Louisiana	Y	12540 FQ	26000 AW	40030 TQ	LABLS	10/01-12/01
	Maine	Y	12290 FQ	25410 AW	42070 TQ	MEBLS	10/01-12/01
	Maryland	Y	14380 FQ	31850 AW	64630 TQ	MDBLS	10/01-12/01
	Massachusetts	Y	15180 FQ	36330 AW	63490 TQ	MABLS	10/01-12/01
	Michigan	Y	13010 FQ	31270 AW	56720 TQ	MIBLS	10/01-12/01
	Minnesota	Y	12860 FQ	23840 AW	35700 TQ	MNBLS	10/01-12/01
	Mississippi	Y	12310 FQ	20320 AW	31170 TQ	MSBLS	10/01-12/01
	Missouri	Y	12350 FQ	24780 AW	42800 TQ	MOBLS	10/01-12/01
	Montana	Y	12170 FQ	20190 AW	31260 TQ	MTBLS	10/01-12/01
	Nebraska	Y	12200 FQ	22530 AW	35900 TQ	NEBLS	10/01-12/01
	Nevada	Y	18530 FQ	34670 AW	58730 TQ	NVBLS	10/01-12/01
	New Hampshire	Y	12940 FQ	23560 AW	35930 TQ	NHBLS	10/01-12/01
	New Jersey	Y	14710 FQ	30340 AW	57390 TQ	NJBLS	10/01-12/01
	New Mexico	Y	11950 FQ	21640 AW	34150 TQ	NMBLS	10/01-12/01
	New York	Y	13240 FQ	34400 AW	89190 TQ	NYBLS	10/01-12/01
	North Carolina	Y	12140 FQ	24000 AW	37090 TQ	NCBLS	10/01-12/01
	North Dakota	Y	11940 FQ	20470 AW	35740 TQ	NDBLS	10/01-12/01
	Ohio	Y	12450 FQ	29450 AW	54930 TQ	OHBLS	10/01-12/01
	Oklahoma	Y	11840 FQ	18910 AW	29130 TQ	OKBLS	10/01-12/01
	Oregon	Y	14510 FQ	26740 AW	42040 TQ	ORBLS	10/01-12/01
	Pennsylvania	Y	12300 FQ	34680 AW	84040 TQ	PABLS	10/01-12/01
	Rhode Island	Y	16760 FQ	38060 AW	105120 TQ	RIBLS	10/01-12/01
	South Carolina	Y	11890 FQ	20410 AW	32230 TQ	SCBLS	10/01-12/01
	South Dakota	Y	12950 FQ	22680 AW	34690 TQ	SDBLS	10/01-12/01
	Tennessee	Y	11760 FQ	20740 AW	35280 TQ	TNBLS	10/01-12/01
	Texas	Y	12250 FQ	24090 AW	40390 TQ	TXBLS	10/01-12/01
	Utah	Y	13200 FQ	36200 AW	75380 TQ	UTBLS	10/01-12/01
	Vermont	Y	13850 FQ	23390 AW	33680 TQ	VTBLS	10/01-12/01
	Virginia	Y	12410 FQ	24140 AW	40560 TQ	VABLS	10/01-12/01
	Washington	Y	14170 FQ	29800 AW	50480 TQ	WABLS	10/01-12/01
	West Virginia	Y	12120 FQ	27270 AW	55500 TQ	WVBLS	10/01-12/01
	Wisconsin	Y	13930 FQ	26020 AW	43150 TQ	WIBLS	10/01-12/01
	Wyoming	Y	12430 FQ	21060 AW	37460 TQ	WYBLS	10/01-12/01
	Puerto Rico	Y	11780 FQ	20510 AW	35970 TQ	PRBLS	10/01-12/01
	Guam	Y	13230 FQ	23010 AW	48190 TQ	GUBLS	10/01-12/01
Anthropologist and Archeologist	Alabama	Y	23270 FQ	33400 AW	58280 TQ	ALBLS	10/01-12/01
	Alaska	Y	25070 FQ	48200 AW	73470 TQ	AKBLS	10/01-12/01
	Arizona	Y	31150 FQ	44590 AW	62380 TQ	AZBLS	10/01-12/01
	Arkansas	Y	21550 FQ	38980 AW	53040 TQ	ARBLS	10/01-12/01
	California	Y	25580 FQ	46880 AW	69480 TQ	CABLS	10/01-12/01
	Colorado	Y	22350 FQ	37220 AW	55830 TQ	COBLS	10/01-12/01
	Florida	Y	22800 FQ	34920 AW	58170 TQ	FLBLS	10/01-12/01
	Georgia	Y	22490 FQ	46740 AW	74020 TQ	GABLS	10/01-12/01
	Hawaii	Y	38600 FQ	54820 AW	76220 TQ	HIBLS	10/01-12/01
	Idaho	Y	36980 FQ	48000 AW	62250 TQ	IDBLS	10/01-12/01
	Illinois	Y	20420 FQ	33440 AW	54050 TQ	ILBLS	10/01-12/01
	Kentucky	Y	21890 FQ	33690 AW	49960 TQ	KYBLS	10/01-12/01
	Louisiana	Y	19170 FQ	34210 AW	65190 TQ	LABLS	10/01-12/01
	Michigan	Y	23510 FQ	37230 AW	55460 TQ	MIBLS	10/01-12/01
	Minnesota	Y	28860 FQ	45460 AW	60970 TQ	MNBLS	10/01-12/01
	Missouri	Y	34420 FQ	49400 AW	71860 TQ	MOBLS	10/01-12/01
	Montana	Y	27370 FQ	44600 AW	64030 TQ	MTBLS	10/01-12/01
	Nevada	Y	32440 FQ	48800 AW	67680 TQ	NVBLS	10/01-12/01
	New Jersey	Y	25630 FQ	39760 AW	61250 TQ	NJBLS	10/01-12/01
	New Mexico	Y	23440 FQ	43620 AW	69060 TQ	NMBLS	10/01-12/01
	New York	Y	22570 FQ	34380 AW	55400 TQ	NYBLS	10/01-12/01
	North Carolina	Y	30320 FQ	43260 AW	58900 TQ	NCBLS	10/01-12/01
	Oregon	Y	30040 FQ	42950 AW	63760 TQ	ORBLS	10/01-12/01
	Pennsylvania	Y	19470 FQ	34550 AW	50080 TQ	PABLS	10/01-12/01
	South Carolina	Y	23080 FQ	33350 AW	51480 TQ	SCBLS	10/01-12/01
	South Dakota	Y	26990 FQ	39070 AW	55150 TQ	SDBLS	10/01-12/01
	Texas	Y	21550 FQ	37740 AW	60700 TQ	TXBLS	10/01-12/01
	Utah	Y	28020 FQ	42950 AW	56430 TQ	UTBLS	10/01-12/01
	Virginia	Y	18860 FQ	32620 AW	51510 TQ	VABLS	10/01-12/01
	Washington	Y	26690 FQ	44190 AW	64480 TQ	WABLS	10/01-12/01
	Wisconsin	Y	21050 FQ	37910 AW	58250 TQ	WIBLS	10/01-12/01
	Wyoming	Y	22450 FQ	35630 AW	53050 TQ	WYBLS	10/01-12/01
	Puerto Rico	Y	20450 FQ	29690 AW	45140 TQ	PRBLS	10/01-12/01

AAW Average annual wage; **AE** Average entry wage; **AEX** Average experienced wage; **AO** Average offered; **AOH** Average offered, high; **AOL** Average offered, low; **APH** Average pay, high range; **APL** Average pay, low range; **ASH** Average starting, high; **ASL** Average starting, low; **AW** Average wage paid; **FQ** First quartile wage; **H** Hourly; **HI** Highest wage paid; **HR** High end range; **LR** Low end range; **M** Monthly; **MTC** Median total compensation; **MW** Median wage paid; **SQ** Second quartile wage; **S** Special: hourly and annual; **TQ** Third quartile wage; **W** Weekly; **Y** Yearly

Occupation/Type/Industry	Location	Per	Low	Mid	High	Source	Date
Anthropology and Archeology Teacher							
Postsecondary	Alabama	Y	24370 FQ	55990 AW	92080 TQ	ALBLS	10/01-12/01
Postsecondary	California	Y	39030 FQ	64900 AW	94330 TQ	CABLS	10/01-12/01
Postsecondary	Colorado	Y	33880 FQ	56630 AW	90050 TQ	COBLS	10/01-12/01
Postsecondary	District of Columbia	Y	38240 FQ	61110 AW	88620 TQ	DCBLS	10/01-12/01
Postsecondary	Florida	Y	39640 FQ	62680 AW	94290 TQ	FLBLS	10/01-12/01
Postsecondary	Georgia	Y	42010 FQ	66450 AW	97550 TQ	GABLS	10/01-12/01
Postsecondary	Hawaii	Y	41310 FQ	62520 AW	90330 TQ	HIBLS	10/01-12/01
Postsecondary	Illinois	Y	22770 FQ	59350 AW	93290 TQ	ILBLS	10/01-12/01
Postsecondary	Indiana	Y	34200 FQ	55590 AW	87370 TQ	INBLS	10/01-12/01
Postsecondary	Kentucky	Y	37510 FQ	52780 AW	69970 TQ	KYBLS	10/01-12/01
Postsecondary	Maryland	Y	29220 FQ	66210 AW	107030 TQ	MDBLS	10/01-12/01
Postsecondary	Massachusetts	Y	28680 FQ	57120 AW	89190 TQ	MABLS	10/01-12/01
Postsecondary	Michigan	Y	38010 FQ	59200 AW	88760 TQ	MIBLS	10/01-12/01
Postsecondary	Minnesota	Y	35340 FQ	51550 AW	68430 TQ	MNBLS	10/01-12/01
Postsecondary	Mississippi	Y	37320 FQ	47070 AW	64840 TQ	MSBLS	10/01-12/01
Postsecondary	Missouri	Y	26630 FQ	59300 AW	92080 TQ	MOBLS	10/01-12/01
Postsecondary	Nevada	Y	29020 FQ	62530 AW	96770 TQ	NVBLS	10/01-12/01
Postsecondary	New Jersey	Y	30420 FQ	67410 AW	98810 TQ	NJBLS	10/01-12/01
Postsecondary	New York	Y	36980 FQ	68230 AW	105320 TQ	NYBLS	10/01-12/01
Postsecondary	North Carolina	Y	37740 FQ	64470 AW	97010 TQ	NCBLS	10/01-12/01
Postsecondary	Ohio	Y	36370 FQ	58830 AW	87590 TQ	OHBLS	10/01-12/01
Postsecondary	Oklahoma	Y	38210 FQ	62600 AW	92040 TQ	OKBLS	10/01-12/01
Postsecondary	Oregon	Y	40380 FQ	63080 AW	90020 TQ	ORBLS	10/01-12/01
Postsecondary	Pennsylvania	Y	39470 FQ	63860 AW	92420 TQ	PABLS	10/01-12/01
Postsecondary	Tennessee	Y	35360 FQ	52800 AW	73290 TQ	TNBLS	10/01-12/01
Postsecondary	Texas	Y	34940 FQ	59310 AW	92340 TQ	TXBLS	10/01-12/01
Postsecondary	Virginia	Y	37730 FQ	63460 AW	94950 TQ	VABLS	10/01-12/01
Postsecondary	Washington	Y	30440 FQ	53320 AW	83310 TQ	WABLS	10/01-12/01
Postsecondary	Wisconsin	Y	22600 FQ	49910 AW	76790 TQ	WIBLS	10/01-12/01
Applications Developer							
Information Technology	United States	Y	58000 AOL			IOMA5	1/01-1/02
Appraiser and Assessor of Real Estate	Alabama	Y	18550 FQ	42080 AW	68520 TQ	ALBLS	10/01-12/01
	Birmingham MSA, AL	Y	17450 FQ	46520 AW	69260 TQ	ALBLS	10/01-12/01
	Huntsville MSA, AL	Y	26550 FQ	50710 AW	69150 TQ	ALBLS	10/01-12/01
	Mobile MSA, AL	Y	24340 FQ	38870 AW	64050 TQ	ALBLS	10/01-12/01
	Montgomery MSA, AL	Y	22400 FQ	43840 AW	65910 TQ	ALBLS	10/01-12/01
	Alaska	Y	36810 FQ	56420 AW	81300 TQ	AKBLS	10/01-12/01
	Anchorage MSA, AK	Y	32520 FQ	54430 AW	83470 TQ	AKBLS	10/01-12/01
	Arizona	Y	21030 FQ	40420 AW	67200 TQ	AZBLS	10/01-12/01
	Phoenix-Mesa MSA, AZ	Y	28120 FQ	49260 AW	71250 TQ	AZBLS	10/01-12/01
	Tucson MSA, AZ	Y	17900 FQ	36800 AW	48670 TQ	AZBLS	10/01-12/01
	Arkansas	Y	16300 FQ	26480 AW	42970 TQ	ARBLS	10/01-12/01
	Fayetteville-Springdale-Rogers MSA, AR	Y	16920 FQ	24120 AW	36290 TQ	ARBLS	10/01-12/01
	Fort Smith MSA, AR-OK	Y	20900 FQ	30970 AW	44050 TQ	ARBLS	10/01-12/01
	Little Rock-North Little Rock MSA, AR	Y	25140 FQ	42560 AW	64470 TQ	ARBLS	10/01-12/01
	California	Y	34430 FQ	55960 AW	85760 TQ	CABLS	10/01-12/01
	Chico-Paradise MSA, CA	Y	38050 FQ	46470 AW	60650 TQ	CABLS	10/01-12/01
	Fresno MSA, CA	Y	33850 FQ	52050 AW	83060 TQ	CABLS	10/01-12/01
	Los Angeles-Long Beach PMSA, CA	Y	38380 FQ	53940 AW	80690 TQ	CABLS	10/01-12/01
	Modesto MSA, CA	Y	23450 FQ	44570 AW	80040 TQ	CABLS	10/01-12/01
	Oakland PMSA, CA	Y	29220 FQ	59470 AW	90870 TQ	CABLS	10/01-12/01
	Orange County PMSA, CA	Y	28300 FQ	57760 AW	89520 TQ	CABLS	10/01-12/01
	Riverside-San Bernardino PMSA, CA	Y	38300 FQ	50630 AW	69950 TQ	CABLS	10/01-12/01
	Sacramento PMSA, CA	Y	39000 FQ	56680 AW	74730 TQ	CABLS	10/01-12/01
	Salinas MSA, CA	Y	52390 FQ	67250 AW	74250 TQ	CABLS	10/01-12/01
	San Diego MSA, CA	Y	36880 FQ	48690 AW	61910 TQ	CABLS	10/01-12/01
	San Francisco PMSA, CA	Y	33990 FQ	63390 AW	107800 TQ	CABLS	10/01-12/01
	San Jose PMSA, CA	Y	34700 FQ	67920 AW	120240 TQ	CABLS	10/01-12/01
	San Luis Obispo-Atascadero-Paso Robles MSA, CA	Y	27230 FQ	60510 AW	74230 TQ	CABLS	10/01-12/01
	Santa Barbara-Santa Maria-Lompoc MSA, CA	Y	38080 FQ	52530 AW	70540 TQ	CABLS	10/01-12/01

AAW Average annual wage	**AOH** Average offered, high	**ASH** Average starting, high	**H** Hourly	**M** Monthly	**S** Special: hourly and annual
AE Average entry wage	**AOL** Average offered, low	**ASL** Average starting, low	**HI** Highest wage paid	**MTC** Median total compensation	**TQ** Third quartile wage
AEX Average experienced wage	**APH** Average pay, high range	**AW** Average wage paid	**HR** High end range	**MW** Median wage paid	**W** Weekly
AO Average offered	**APL** Average pay, low range	**FQ** First quartile wage	**LR** Low end range	**SQ** Second quartile wage	**Y** Yearly

Occupation/Type/Industry	Location	Per	Low	Mid	High	Source	Date
Appraiser and Assessor of Real Estate	Santa Cruz-Watsonville PMSA, CA	Y	38080 FQ	47790 AW	63250 TQ	CABLS	10/01-12/01
	Santa Rosa PMSA, CA	Y	33660 FQ	59380 AW	92510 TQ	CABLS	10/01-12/01
	Ventura PMSA, CA	Y	28570 FQ	46430 AW	65470 TQ	CABLS	10/01-12/01
	Visalia-Tulare-Porterville MSA, CA	Y	38950 FQ	54140 AW	77490 TQ	CABLS	10/01-12/01
	Colorado	Y	24050 FQ	53080 AW	109030 TQ	COBLS	10/01-12/01
	Boulder-Longmont PMSA, CO	Y	34860 FQ	52830 AW	71030 TQ	COBLS	10/01-12/01
	Denver PMSA, CO	Y	23790 FQ	58980 AW	119080 TQ	COBLS	10/01-12/01
	Fort Collins-Loveland MSA, CO	Y	35370 FQ	41960 AW	52140 TQ	COBLS	10/01-12/01
	Connecticut	Y	29490 FQ	46670 AW	63400 TQ	CTBLS	10/01-12/01
	Bridgeport PMSA, CT	Y	23430 FQ	45430 AW	60440 TQ	CTBLS	10/01-12/01
	Danbury PMSA, CT	Y	35360 FQ	49740 AW	59240 TQ	CTBLS	10/01-12/01
	Hartford MSA, CT	Y	31430 FQ	47010 AW	67770 TQ	CTBLS	10/01-12/01
	New Haven-Meriden PMSA, CT	Y	32780 FQ	52360 AW	72570 TQ	CTBLS	10/01-12/01
	New London-Norwich MSA, CT-RI	Y	22730 FQ	40230 AW	56220 TQ	CTBLS	10/01-12/01
	Stamford-Norwalk PMSA, CT	Y	32260 FQ	52480 AW	87180 TQ	CTBLS	10/01-12/01
	Waterbury PMSA, CT	Y	33720 FQ	48350 AW	57670 TQ	CTBLS	10/01-12/01
	Delaware	Y	26190 FQ	57320 AW	112380 TQ	DEBLS	10/01-12/01
	Wilmington-Newark PMSA, DE-MD	Y	28060 FQ	61390 AW	117820 TQ	DEBLS	10/01-12/01
	District of Columbia	Y	34190 FQ	65560 AW	88040 TQ	DCBLS	10/01-12/01
	Washington PMSA, DC-MD-VA-WV	Y	20110 FQ	41280 AW	70440 TQ	DCBLS	10/01-12/01
	Florida	Y	22340 FQ	43590 AW	70270 TQ	FLBLS	10/01-12/01
	Daytona Beach MSA, FL	Y	26760 FQ	45500 AW	69770 TQ	FLBLS	10/01-12/01
	Fort Lauderdale PMSA, FL	Y	31600 FQ	57000 AW	103220 TQ	FLBLS	10/01-12/01
	Fort Myers-Cape Coral MSA, FL	Y	20500 FQ	57300 AW	109690 TQ	FLBLS	10/01-12/01
	Fort Pierce-Port St. Lucie MSA, FL	Y	21000 FQ	49190 AW	124650 TQ	FLBLS	10/01-12/01
	Fort Walton Beach MSA, FL	Y	28290 FQ	34410 AW	43700 TQ	FLBLS	10/01-12/01
	Jacksonville MSA, FL	Y	30290 FQ	45040 AW	64620 TQ	FLBLS	10/01-12/01
	Lakeland-Winter Haven MSA, FL	Y	23820 FQ	28020 AW	28970 TQ	FLBLS	10/01-12/01
	Miami PMSA, FL	Y	30860 FQ	51730 AW	98730 TQ	FLBLS	10/01-12/01
	Orlando MSA, FL	Y	27500 FQ	43010 AW	67820 TQ	FLBLS	10/01-12/01
	Pensacola MSA, FL	Y	19960 FQ	40150 AW	66300 TQ	FLBLS	10/01-12/01
	Tampa-St. Petersburg-Clearwater MSA, FL	Y	22260 FQ	42750 AW	60390 TQ	FLBLS	10/01-12/01
	West Palm Beach-Boca Raton MSA, FL	Y	26550 FQ	40940 AW	59190 TQ	FLBLS	10/01-12/01
	Georgia	Y	22960 FQ	34510 AW	52040 TQ	GABLS	10/01-12/01
	Atlanta MSA, GA	Y	28480 FQ	34880 AW	49760 TQ	GABLS	10/01-12/01
	Augusta-Aiken MSA, GA-SC	Y	24960 FQ	36790 AW	46560 TQ	GABLS	10/01-12/01
	Columbus MSA, GA-AL	Y	21600 FQ	26740 AW	32380 TQ	GABLS	10/01-12/01
	Macon MSA, GA	Y	22920 FQ	41060 AW	58470 TQ	GABLS	10/01-12/01
	Savannah MSA, GA	Y	21210 FQ	39580 AW	68550 TQ	GABLS	10/01-12/01
	Hawaii	Y	31750 FQ	46210 AW	65560 TQ	HIBLS	10/01-12/01
	Honolulu MSA, HI	Y	30280 FQ	46040 AW	66390 TQ	HIBLS	10/01-12/01
	Idaho	Y	23250 FQ	43140 AW	70890 TQ	IDBLS	10/01-12/01
	Boise City MSA, ID	Y	30660 FQ	59880 AW	108560 TQ	IDBLS	10/01-12/01
	Illinois	Y	16940 FQ	38900 AW	60450 TQ	ILBLS	10/01-12/01
	Champaign-Urbana MSA, IL	Y	21860 FQ	42030 AW	69250 TQ	ILBLS	10/01-12/01
	Chicago PMSA, IL	Y	20180 FQ	40820 AW	62990 TQ	ILBLS	10/01-12/01
	Peoria-Pekin MSA, IL	Y	22630 FQ	42080 AW	66170 TQ	ILBLS	10/01-12/01
	Rockford MSA, IL	Y	26010 FQ	42760 AW	56630 TQ	ILBLS	10/01-12/01
	Springfield MSA, IL	Y	22820 FQ	39520 AW	63460 TQ	ILBLS	10/01-12/01
	Indiana	Y	12810 FQ	25370 AW	37930 TQ	INBLS	10/01-12/01
	Evansville-Henderson MSA, IN-KY	Y	13600 FQ	32190 AW	56410 TQ	INBLS	10/01-12/01
	Fort Wayne MSA, IN	Y	12220 FQ	21970 AW	33110 TQ	INBLS	10/01-12/01
	Gary PMSA, IN	Y	15200 FQ	55210 AW		INBLS	10/01-12/01
	Indianapolis MSA, IN	Y	13050 FQ	26600 AW	38670 TQ	INBLS	10/01-12/01
	Lafayette MSA, IN	Y	14310 FQ	26740 AW	50450 TQ	INBLS	10/01-12/01
	South Bend MSA, IN	Y	12590 FQ	22460 AW	34200 TQ	INBLS	10/01-12/01
	Iowa	Y	24130 FQ	37280 AW	45850 TQ	IABLS	10/01-12/01
	Cedar Rapids MSA, IA	Y	31010 FQ	47700 AW	94020 TQ	IABLS	10/01-12/01

AAW	Average annual wage	**AOH**	Average offered, high	**ASH**	Average starting, high	**H**	Hourly	**M**	Monthly	**S**	Special: hourly and annual
AE	Average entry wage	**AOL**	Average offered, low	**ASL**	Average starting, low	**HI**	Highest wage paid	**MTC**	Median total compensation	**TQ**	Third quartile wage
AEX	Average experienced wage	**APH**	Average pay, high range	**AW**	Average wage paid	**HR**	High end range	**MW**	Median wage paid	**W**	Weekly
AO	Average offered	**APL**	Average pay, low range	**FQ**	First quartile wage	**LR**	Low end range	**SQ**	Second quartile wage	**Y**	Yearly

Occupation/Type/Industry	Location	Per	Low	Mid	High	Source	Date
Appraiser and Assessor of Real Estate	Davenport-Moline-Rock Island MSA, IA-IL	Y	16770 FQ	30820 AW	58020 TQ	IABLS	10/01-12/01
	Des Moines MSA, IA	Y	37620 FQ	42510 AW	46730 TQ	IABLS	10/01-12/01
	Kansas	Y	24560 FQ	44330 AW	69640 TQ	KSBLS	10/01-12/01
	Topeka MSA, KS	Y	27540 FQ	45190 AW	67210 TQ	KSBLS	10/01-12/01
	Wichita MSA, KS	Y	29780 FQ	46350 AW	69000 TQ	KSBLS	10/01-12/01
	Kentucky	Y	22250 FQ	48770 AW	83020 TQ	KYBLS	10/01-12/01
	Louisville MSA, KY-IN	Y	19230 FQ	41920 AW	73950 TQ	KYBLS	10/01-12/01
	Louisiana	Y	22530 FQ	30770 AW	43660 TQ	LABLS	10/01-12/01
	Baton Rouge MSA, LA	Y	11120 FQ	15450 AW	30220 TQ	LABLS	10/01-12/01
	Houma MSA, LA	Y	20580 FQ	47510 AW		LABLS	10/01-12/01
	New Orleans MSA, LA	Y	22980 FQ	27750 AW	28010 TQ	LABLS	10/01-12/01
	Maine	Y	22690 FQ	42160 AW	59210 TQ	MEBLS	10/01-12/01
	Portland MSA, ME	Y	26770 FQ	49990 AW	84990 TQ	MEBLS	10/01-12/01
	Maryland	Y	26240 FQ	41760 AW	58510 TQ	MDBLS	10/01-12/01
	Baltimore PMSA, MD	Y	25850 FQ	41090 AW	57640 TQ	MDBLS	10/01-12/01
	Massachusetts	Y	20150 FQ	42340 AW	66520 TQ	MABLS	10/01-12/01
	Boston PMSA, MA-NH	Y	23520 FQ	48820 AW	74360 TQ	MABLS	10/01-12/01
	Brockton PMSA, MA	Y	15000 FQ	50340 AW	72210 TQ	MABLS	10/01-12/01
	Lawrence PMSA, MA-NH	Y	21320 FQ	42110 AW	68640 TQ	MABLS	10/01-12/01
	Lowell PMSA, MA-NH	Y	19670 FQ	34320 AW	49810 TQ	MABLS	10/01-12/01
	Springfield MSA, MA	Y	14900 FQ	38580 AW	61080 TQ	MABLS	10/01-12/01
	Worcester PMSA, MA-CT	Y	15860 FQ	41790 AW	59460 TQ	MABLS	10/01-12/01
	Michigan	Y	18380 FQ	39990 AW	64880 TQ	MIBLS	10/01-12/01
	Ann Arbor PMSA, MI	Y	36470 FQ	49840 AW	70620 TQ	MIBLS	10/01-12/01
	Detroit PMSA, MI	Y	24380 FQ	43160 AW	63970 TQ	MIBLS	10/01-12/01
	Flint PMSA, MI	Y	26550 FQ	38180 AW	50240 TQ	MIBLS	10/01-12/01
	Grand Rapids-Muskegon-Holland MSA, MI	Y	22470 FQ	37580 AW	55270 TQ	MIBLS	10/01-12/01
	Kalamazoo-Battle Creek MSA, MI	Y	31260 FQ	42450 AW	61390 TQ	MIBLS	10/01-12/01
	Lansing-East Lansing MSA, MI	Y	12120 FQ	41010 AW	70430 TQ	MIBLS	10/01-12/01
	Saginaw-Bay City-Midland MSA, MI	Y	21360 FQ	41440 AW	58820 TQ	MIBLS	10/01-12/01
	Minnesota	Y	26760 FQ	50830 AW	82580 TQ	MNBLS	10/01-12/01
	Duluth-Superior MSA, MN-WI	Y	33920 FQ	47950 AW	58750 TQ	MNBLS	10/01-12/01
	Minneapolis-St. Paul MSA, MN-WI	Y	25700 FQ	53060 AW	85890 TQ	MNBLS	10/01-12/01
	Mississippi	Y	19810 FQ	33380 AW	51290 TQ	MSBLS	10/01-12/01
	Jackson MSA, MS	Y	25900 FQ	36420 AW	52210 TQ	MSBLS	10/01-12/01
	Missouri	Y	16650 FQ	35360 AW	59410 TQ	MOBLS	10/01-12/01
	Kansas City MSA, MO-KS	Y	32940 FQ	49740 AW	72230 TQ	MOBLS	10/01-12/01
	St. Louis MSA, MO-IL	Y	20850 FQ	37180 AW	61350 TQ	MOBLS	10/01-12/01
	Montana	Y	20460 FQ	32320 AW	46240 TQ	MTBLS	10/01-12/01
	Nebraska	Y	22070 FQ	42520 AW	75640 TQ	NEBLS	10/01-12/01
	Lincoln MSA, NE	Y	28470 FQ	49430 AW	90770 TQ	NEBLS	10/01-12/01
	Omaha MSA, NE-IA	Y	21740 FQ	45440 AW	91500 TQ	NEBLS	10/01-12/01
	Nevada	Y	30590 FQ	46780 AW	65060 TQ	NVBLS	10/01-12/01
	Las Vegas MSA, NV-AZ	Y	25730 FQ	43990 AW	63810 TQ	NVBLS	10/01-12/01
	New Hampshire	Y	19540 FQ	40250 AW	79070 TQ	NHBLS	10/01-12/01
	Manchester PMSA, NH	Y	28120 FQ	61640 AW	87450 TQ	NHBLS	10/01-12/01
	Portsmouth-Rochester PMSA, NH-ME	Y	28820 FQ	37910 AW	55320 TQ	NHBLS	10/01-12/01
	New Jersey	Y	29980 FQ	49620 AW	74310 TQ	NJBLS	10/01-12/01
	Atlantic-Cape May PMSA, NJ	Y	12200 FQ	30630 AW	46250 TQ	NJBLS	10/01-12/01
	Bergen-Passaic PMSA, NJ	Y	23900 FQ	46320 AW	80470 TQ	NJBLS	10/01-12/01
	Middlesex-Somerset-Hunterdon PMSA, NJ	Y	26880 FQ	45460 AW	65070 TQ	NJBLS	10/01-12/01
	Monmouth-Ocean PMSA, NJ	Y	31480 FQ	55740 AW	79890 TQ	NJBLS	10/01-12/01
	Newark PMSA, NJ	Y	31580 FQ	51030 AW	76690 TQ	NJBLS	10/01-12/01
	Trenton PMSA, NJ	Y	35620 FQ	52890 AW	70210 TQ	NJBLS	10/01-12/01
	New Mexico	Y	16280 FQ	29260 AW	46370 TQ	NMBLS	10/01-12/01
	Albuquerque MSA, NM	Y	16670 FQ	30900 AW	57590 TQ	NMBLS	10/01-12/01
	New York	Y	25240 FQ	45840 AW	68730 TQ	NYBLS	10/01-12/01
	Albany-Schenectady-Troy MSA, NY	Y	25180 FQ	43990 AW	68770 TQ	NYBLS	10/01-12/01
	Binghamton MSA, NY	Y	17320 FQ	33120 AW	45250 TQ	NYBLS	10/01-12/01
	Buffalo-Niagara Falls MSA, NY	Y	28690 FQ	49160 AW	68550 TQ	NYBLS	10/01-12/01
	Dutchess County PMSA, NY	Y	13090 FQ	36770 AW	67010 TQ	NYBLS	10/01-12/01
	Nassau-Suffolk PMSA, NY	Y	29300 FQ	42800 AW	66410 TQ	NYBLS	10/01-12/01

AAW	Average annual wage	**AOH**	Average offered, high	**ASH**	Average starting, high	**H**	Hourly	**M**	Monthly	**S**	Special: hourly and annual
AE	Average entry wage	**AOL**	Average offered, low	**ASL**	Average starting, low	**HI**	Highest wage paid	**MTC**	Median total compensation	**TQ**	Third quartile wage
AEX	Average experienced wage	**APH**	Average pay, high range	**AW**	Average wage paid	**HR**	High end range	**MW**	Median wage paid	**W**	Weekly
AO	Average offered	**APL**	Average pay, low range	**FQ**	First quartile wage	**LR**	Low end range	**SQ**	Second quartile wage	**Y**	Yearly

Occupation/Type/Industry	Location	Per	Low	Mid	High	Source	Date
Appraiser and Assessor of Real Estate	New York PMSA, NY	Y	38020 FQ	63780 AW	99400 TQ	NYBLS	10/01-12/01
	Newburgh PMSA, NY-PA	Y	24400 FQ	43060 AW	66590 TQ	NYBLS	10/01-12/01
	Rochester MSA, NY	Y	28430 FQ	48340 AW	71930 TQ	NYBLS	10/01-12/01
	Syracuse MSA, NY	Y	14860 FQ	42120 AW	59050 TQ	NYBLS	10/01-12/01
	Utica-Rome MSA, NY	Y	21720 FQ	33900 AW	43740 TQ	NYBLS	10/01-12/01
	North Carolina	Y	24690 FQ	41110 AW	64370 TQ	NCBLS	10/01-12/01
	Charlotte-Gastonia-Rock Hill MSA, NC-SC	Y	29200 FQ	45370 AW	70590 TQ	NCBLS	10/01-12/01
	Greensboro-Winston-Salem-High Point MSA, NC	Y	29220 FQ	45160 AW	66840 TQ	NCBLS	10/01-12/01
	Raleigh-Durham-Chapel Hill MSA, NC	Y	29460 FQ	48270 AW	91960 TQ	NCBLS	10/01-12/01
	North Dakota	Y	13740 FQ	32210 AW	54410 TQ	NDBLS	10/01-12/01
	Ohio	Y	26600 FQ	48300 AW	73740 TQ	OHBLS	10/01-12/01
	Akron PMSA, OH	Y	16920 FQ	49400 AW	89280 TQ	OHBLS	10/01-12/01
	Cincinnati PMSA, OH-KY-IN	Y	27080 FQ	52530 AW	83100 TQ	OHBLS	10/01-12/01
	Cleveland-Lorain-Elyria PMSA, OH	Y	29450 FQ	61240 AW	95430 TQ	OHBLS	10/01-12/01
	Columbus MSA, OH	Y	28970 FQ	43830 AW	65300 TQ	OHBLS	10/01-12/01
	Dayton-Springfield MSA, OH	Y	25430 FQ	47840 AW	69850 TQ	OHBLS	10/01-12/01
	Mansfield MSA, OH	Y	20730 FQ	35670 AW	44740 TQ	OHBLS	10/01-12/01
	Toledo MSA, OH	Y	24160 FQ	43890 AW	70050 TQ	OHBLS	10/01-12/01
	Youngstown-Warren MSA, OH	Y	37180 FQ	45150 AW	56130 TQ	OHBLS	10/01-12/01
	Oklahoma	Y	17870 FQ	29040 AW	47020 TQ	OKBLS	10/01-12/01
	Oklahoma City MSA, OK	Y	19350 FQ	29670 AW	46850 TQ	OKBLS	10/01-12/01
	Tulsa MSA, OK	Y	19300 FQ	39050 AW	58010 TQ	OKBLS	10/01-12/01
	Oregon	Y	30550 FQ	51840 AW	69820 TQ	ORBLS	10/01-12/01
	Eugene-Springfield MSA, OR	Y	27930 FQ	47430 AW	67240 TQ	ORBLS	10/01-12/01
	Portland-Vancouver PMSA, OR-WA	Y	36960 FQ	57000 AW	71110 TQ	ORBLS	10/01-12/01
	Pennsylvania	Y	18850 FQ	47910 AW	84670 TQ	PABLS	10/01-12/01
	Allentown-Bethlehem-Easton MSA, PA	Y	26000 FQ	47430 AW	70500 TQ	PABLS	10/01-12/01
	Harrisburg-Lebanon-Carlisle MSA, PA	Y	15080 FQ	43550 AW	83490 TQ	PABLS	10/01-12/01
	Lancaster MSA, PA	Y	16940 FQ	37480 AW	63190 TQ	PABLS	10/01-12/01
	Philadelphia PMSA, PA-NJ	Y	19010 FQ	51260 AW	86120 TQ	PABLS	10/01-12/01
	Pittsburgh MSA, PA	Y	30700 FQ	53900 AW	82910 TQ	PABLS	10/01-12/01
	Scranton-Wilkes-Barre-Hazleton MSA, PA	Y	22890 FQ	28060 AW	38660 TQ	PABLS	10/01-12/01
	York MSA, PA	Y	12040 FQ	20040 AW	39960 TQ	PABLS	10/01-12/01
	Rhode Island	Y	32560 FQ	63050 AW	93670 TQ	RIBLS	10/01-12/01
	Providence-Fall River-Warwick MSA, RI-MA	Y	31700 FQ	61880 AW	93550 TQ	RIBLS	10/01-12/01
	South Carolina	Y	14990 FQ	29080 AW	44250 TQ	SCBLS	10/01-12/01
	Charleston-North Charleston MSA, SC	Y	27920 FQ	31880 AW	35050 TQ	SCBLS	10/01-12/01
	Columbia MSA, SC	Y	18020 FQ	35960 AW	62960 TQ	SCBLS	10/01-12/01
	Greenville-Spartanburg-Anderson MSA, SC	Y	17670 FQ	32950 AW	46970 TQ	SCBLS	10/01-12/01
	South Dakota	Y	20550 FQ	30580 AW	41830 TQ	SDBLS	10/01-12/01
	Sioux Falls MSA, SD	Y	28880 FQ	35190 AW	46070 TQ	SDBLS	10/01-12/01
	Tennessee	Y	19510 FQ	42610 AW	70610 TQ	TNBLS	10/01-12/01
	Chattanooga MSA, TN-GA	Y	13460 FQ	36350 AW	78700 TQ	TNBLS	10/01-12/01
	Johnson City-Kingsport-Bristol MSA, TN-VA	Y	21860 FQ	33570 AW	51900 TQ	TNBLS	10/01-12/01
	Memphis MSA, TN-AR-MS	Y	18160 FQ	40710 AW	75440 TQ	TNBLS	10/01-12/01
	Nashville MSA, TN	Y	25090 FQ	39580 AW	63630 TQ	TNBLS	10/01-12/01
	Texas	Y	19920 FQ	39340 AW	56160 TQ	TXBLS	10/01-12/01
	Austin-San Marcos MSA, TX	Y	32570 FQ	46410 AW	65540 TQ	TXBLS	10/01-12/01
	Beaumont-Port Arthur MSA, TX	Y	25830 FQ	45440 AW	71420 TQ	TXBLS	10/01-12/01
	Corpus Christi MSA, TX	Y	28090 FQ	39910 AW	57170 TQ	TXBLS	10/01-12/01
	Dallas PMSA, TX	Y	30330 FQ	45870 AW	65990 TQ	TXBLS	10/01-12/01
	Fort Worth-Arlington PMSA, TX	Y	22000 FQ	45470 AW	55430 TQ	TXBLS	10/01-12/01
	McAllen-Edinburg-Mission MSA, TX	Y	22480 FQ	29470 AW	35570 TQ	TXBLS	10/01-12/01
	Odessa-Midland MSA, TX	Y	36090 FQ	44630 AW	58330 TQ	TXBLS	10/01-12/01
	San Antonio MSA, TX	Y	28650 FQ	42370 AW	58970 TQ	TXBLS	10/01-12/01
	Utah	Y	13320 FQ	35830 AW	54640 TQ	UTBLS	10/01-12/01

AAW Average annual wage; **AE** Average entry wage; **AEX** Average experienced wage; **AO** Average offered; **AOH** Average offered, high; **AOL** Average offered, low; **APH** Average pay, high range; **APL** Average pay, low range; **ASH** Average starting, high; **ASL** Average starting, low; **AW** Average wage paid; **FQ** First quartile wage; **H** Hourly; **HI** Highest wage paid; **HR** High end range; **LR** Low end range; **M** Monthly; **MTC** Median total compensation; **MW** Median wage paid; **SQ** Second quartile wage; **S** Special: hourly and annual; **TQ** Third quartile wage; **W** Weekly; **Y** Yearly

Occupation/Type/Industry	Location	Per	Low	Mid	High	Source	Date
Appraiser and Assessor of Real Estate	Provo-Orem MSA, UT	Y	24380 FQ	36340 AW	54760 TQ	UTBLS	10/01-12/01
	Salt Lake City-Ogden MSA, UT	Y	12420 FQ	35410 AW	54830 TQ	UTBLS	10/01-12/01
	Vermont	Y	16760 FQ	37430 AW	66020 TQ	VTBLS	10/01-12/01
	Burlington MSA, VT	Y	20690 FQ	48190 AW	80680 TQ	VTBLS	10/01-12/01
	Virginia	Y	21400 FQ	39630 AW	67700 TQ	VABLS	10/01-12/01
	Lynchburg MSA, VA	Y	11780 FQ	29180 AW	69060 TQ	VABLS	10/01-12/01
	Norfolk-Virginia Beach-Newport News MSA, VA-NC	Y	22690 FQ	40620 AW	69560 TQ	VABLS	10/01-12/01
	Richmond-Petersburg MSA, VA	Y	25030 FQ	44150 AW	67510 TQ	VABLS	10/01-12/01
	Roanoke MSA, VA	Y	19350 FQ	35960 AW	54260 TQ	VABLS	10/01-12/01
	Washington	Y	29810 FQ	46750 AW	67630 TQ	WABLS	10/01-12/01
	Bremerton PMSA, WA	Y	38460 FQ	52050 AW	67810 TQ	WABLS	10/01-12/01
	Seattle-Bellevue-Everett PMSA, WA	Y	30490 FQ	45180 AW	60390 TQ	WABLS	10/01-12/01
	Spokane MSA, WA	Y	28510 FQ	50750 AW	83560 TQ	WABLS	10/01-12/01
	Tacoma PMSA, WA	Y	31750 FQ	60560 AW	110540 TQ	WABLS	10/01-12/01
	West Virginia	Y	13500 FQ	26320 AW	48280 TQ	WVBLS	10/01-12/01
	Wisconsin	Y	13740 FQ	40700 AW	65970 TQ	WIBLS	10/01-12/01
	Appleton-Oshkosh-Neenah MSA, WI	Y	26790 FQ	39460 AW	65740 TQ	WIBLS	10/01-12/01
	Green Bay MSA, WI	Y	31740 FQ	44510 AW	61230 TQ	WIBLS	10/01-12/01
	Madison MSA, WI	Y	11920 FQ	27780 AW	50170 TQ	WIBLS	10/01-12/01
	Milwaukee-Waukesha PMSA, WI	Y	32000 FQ	52210 AW	81600 TQ	WIBLS	10/01-12/01
	Racine PMSA, WI	Y	30250 FQ	46440 AW	70820 TQ	WIBLS	10/01-12/01
	Wyoming	Y	19450 FQ	36020 AW	53820 TQ	WYBLS	10/01-12/01
	Cheyenne MSA, WY	Y	20220 FQ	39110 AW	55350 TQ	WYBLS	10/01-12/01
	Puerto Rico	Y	20090 FQ	25280 AW	27840 TQ	PRBLS	10/01-12/01
	Guam	Y	17050 FQ	36030 AW	55890 TQ	GUBLS	10/01-12/01
Arbitrator, Mediator, and Conciliator	United States	Y		43060 MW		OOH7	1999-2000
	Arizona	Y	24090 FQ	48470 AW	75640 TQ	AZBLS	10/01-12/01
	Arkansas	Y	28880 FQ	43480 AW	63150 TQ	ARBLS	10/01-12/01
	California	Y	25870 FQ	52790 AW	77540 TQ	CABLS	10/01-12/01
	Colorado	Y	20610 FQ	33980 AW	49920 TQ	COBLS	10/01-12/01
	District of Columbia	Y	32510 FQ	57650 AW	94920 TQ	DCBLS	10/01-12/01
	Florida	Y	49070 FQ	91380 AW	113990 TQ	FLBLS	10/01-12/01
	Georgia	Y	25060 FQ	44740 AW	59360 TQ	GABLS	10/01-12/01
	Idaho	Y	29610 FQ	52200 AW	85890 TQ	IDBLS	10/01-12/01
	Illinois	Y	13490 FQ	52310 AW	110680 TQ	ILBLS	10/01-12/01
	Indiana	Y	12080 FQ	42090 AW	69510 TQ	INBLS	10/01-12/01
	Iowa	Y	28530 FQ	42050 AW	59700 TQ	IABLS	10/01-12/01
	Kansas	Y	26700 FQ	41110 AW	61070 TQ	KSBLS	10/01-12/01
	Louisiana	Y	13530 FQ	53450 AW	137700 TQ	LABLS	10/01-12/01
	Maryland	Y	26020 FQ	44980 AW	66850 TQ	MDBLS	10/01-12/01
	Massachusetts	Y	31050 FQ	49110 AW	74120 TQ	MABLS	10/01-12/01
	Michigan	Y	29510 FQ	49570 AW	80480 TQ	MIBLS	10/01-12/01
	Minnesota	Y	37760 FQ	60170 AW	85770 TQ	MNBLS	10/01-12/01
	Mississippi	Y	13210 FQ	28750 AW	75630 TQ	MSBLS	10/01-12/01
	Missouri	Y	25420 FQ	44570 AW	70560 TQ	MOBLS	10/01-12/01
	Nevada	Y	36840 FQ	71700 AW		NVBLS	10/01-12/01
	New Jersey	Y	19950 FQ	58840 AW	102620 TQ	NJBLS	10/01-12/01
	New York	Y	40390 FQ	62460 AW	85820 TQ	NYBLS	10/01-12/01
	North Carolina	Y	24100 FQ	46910 AW	70000 TQ	NCBLS	10/01-12/01
	Ohio	Y	21890 FQ	44230 AW	64280 TQ	OHBLS	10/01-12/01
	Pennsylvania	Y	14560 FQ	50470 AW		PABLS	10/01-12/01
	Tennessee	Y	23630 FQ	32760 AW	51440 TQ	TNBLS	10/01-12/01
	Texas	Y	15050 FQ	40310 AW	70690 TQ	TXBLS	10/01-12/01
	Virginia	Y	14650 FQ	33820 AW	52490 TQ	VABLS	10/01-12/01
	Washington	Y	34170 FQ	54150 AW	70010 TQ	WABLS	10/01-12/01
	Wisconsin	Y	13830 FQ	45820 AW	80250 TQ	WIBLS	10/01-12/01
	Puerto Rico	Y	20700 FQ	28560 AW	37230 TQ	PRBLS	10/01-12/01
Architect							
Except Landscape and Naval	Alabama	Y	39850 FQ	61190 AW	91450 TQ	ALBLS	10/01-12/01
Except Landscape and Naval	Birmingham MSA, AL	Y	39730 FQ	59460 AW	97190 TQ	ALBLS	10/01-12/01
Except Landscape and Naval	Huntsville MSA, AL	Y	47560 FQ	59950 AW	70890 TQ	ALBLS	10/01-12/01

AAW	Average annual wage	AOH	Average offered, high	ASH	Average starting, high	H	Hourly	M	Monthly	S	Special: hourly and annual
AE	Average entry wage	AOL	Average offered, low	ASL	Average starting, low	HI	Highest wage paid	MTC	Median total compensation	TQ	Third quartile wage
AEX	Average experienced wage	APH	Average pay, high range	AW	Average wage paid	HR	High end range	MW	Median wage paid	W	Weekly
AO	Average offered	APL	Average pay, low range	FQ	First quartile wage	LR	Low end range	SQ	Second quartile wage	Y	Yearly

Occupation/Type/Industry	Location	Per	Low	Mid	High	Source	Date
Architect							
Except Landscape and Naval	Mobile MSA, AL	Y	40500 FQ	71320 AW	104400 TQ	ALBLS	10/01-12/01
Except Landscape and Naval	Montgomery MSA, AL	Y	44670 FQ	59300 AW	70200 TQ	ALBLS	10/01-12/01
Except Landscape and Naval	Alaska	Y	47610 FQ	68780 AW	89780 TQ	AKBLS	10/01-12/01
Except Landscape and Naval	Anchorage MSA, AK	Y	45890 FQ	66010 AW	88320 TQ	AKBLS	10/01-12/01
Except Landscape and Naval	Arizona	Y	36430 FQ	53910 AW	83540 TQ	AZBLS	10/01-12/01
Except Landscape and Naval	Phoenix-Mesa MSA, AZ	Y	37340 FQ	54630 AW	84710 TQ	AZBLS	10/01-12/01
Except Landscape and Naval	Tucson MSA, AZ	Y	30210 FQ	50600 AW	76150 TQ	AZBLS	10/01-12/01
Except Landscape and Naval	Arkansas	Y	31090 FQ	52440 AW	78870 TQ	ARBLS	10/01-12/01
Except Landscape and Naval	Fayetteville-Springdale-Rogers MSA, AR	Y	29080 FQ	55530 AW	104510 TQ	ARBLS	10/01-12/01
Except Landscape and Naval	Little Rock-North Little Rock MSA, AR	Y	38000 FQ	50470 AW	69570 TQ	ARBLS	10/01-12/01
Except Landscape and Naval	California	Y	38190 FQ	61490 AW	90830 TQ	CABLS	10/01-12/01
Except Landscape and Naval	Bakersfield MSA, CA	Y	32690 FQ	48230 AW	68870 TQ	CABLS	10/01-12/01
Except Landscape and Naval	Fresno MSA, CA	Y	38710 FQ	54190 AW	70930 TQ	CABLS	10/01-12/01
Except Landscape and Naval	Los Angeles-Long Beach PMSA, CA	Y	36230 FQ	64200 AW	95560 TQ	CABLS	10/01-12/01
Except Landscape and Naval	Oakland PMSA, CA	Y	38640 FQ	59310 AW	91490 TQ	CABLS	10/01-12/01
Except Landscape and Naval	Orange County PMSA, CA	Y	36640 FQ	53820 AW	82680 TQ	CABLS	10/01-12/01
Except Landscape and Naval	Redding MSA, CA	Y	36210 FQ	53350 AW	62900 TQ	CABLS	10/01-12/01
Except Landscape and Naval	Riverside-San Bernardino PMSA, CA	Y	31760 FQ	51650 AW	75710 TQ	CABLS	10/01-12/01
Except Landscape and Naval	Sacramento PMSA, CA	Y	40310 FQ	64130 AW	86970 TQ	CABLS	10/01-12/01
Except Landscape and Naval	San Diego MSA, CA	Y	48460 FQ	64260 AW	87920 TQ	CABLS	10/01-12/01
Except Landscape and Naval	San Francisco PMSA, CA	Y	40440 FQ	63280 AW	96280 TQ	CABLS	10/01-12/01
Except Landscape and Naval	San Jose PMSA, CA	Y	56090 FQ	72910 AW	98390 TQ	CABLS	10/01-12/01
Except Landscape and Naval	Santa Barbara-Santa Maria-Lompoc MSA, CA	Y	47450 FQ	64760 AW	86580 TQ	CABLS	10/01-12/01
Except Landscape and Naval	Santa Rosa PMSA, CA	Y	37540 FQ	64080 AW	122780 TQ	CABLS	10/01-12/01
Except Landscape and Naval	Colorado	Y	32950 FQ	55240 AW	83630 TQ	COBLS	10/01-12/01
Except Landscape and Naval	Boulder-Longmont PMSA, CO	Y	35710 FQ	68210 AW	102270 TQ	COBLS	10/01-12/01
Except Landscape and Naval	Colorado Springs MSA, CO	Y	37290 FQ	53950 AW	71420 TQ	COBLS	10/01-12/01
Except Landscape and Naval	Denver PMSA, CO	Y	32590 FQ	52780 AW	76890 TQ	COBLS	10/01-12/01
Except Landscape and Naval	Fort Collins-Loveland MSA, CO	Y	37480 FQ	56890 AW	83320 TQ	COBLS	10/01-12/01
Except Landscape and Naval	Greeley PMSA, CO	Y	38370 FQ	53030 AW	71170 TQ	COBLS	10/01-12/01
Except Landscape and Naval	Connecticut	Y	38170 FQ	64570 AW	104510 TQ	CTBLS	10/01-12/01
Except Landscape and Naval	Bridgeport PMSA, CT	Y	42280 FQ	71770 AW	108800 TQ	CTBLS	10/01-12/01
Except Landscape and Naval	Danbury PMSA, CT	Y	38220 FQ	63250 AW	91930 TQ	CTBLS	10/01-12/01
Except Landscape and Naval	Hartford MSA, CT	Y	35150 FQ	57790 AW	85600 TQ	CTBLS	10/01-12/01
Except Landscape and Naval	New Haven-Meriden PMSA, CT	Y	49470 FQ	64980 AW	93410 TQ	CTBLS	10/01-12/01
Except Landscape and Naval	Stamford-Norwalk PMSA, CT	Y	38550 FQ	69130 AW	123200 TQ	CTBLS	10/01-12/01
Except Landscape and Naval	Delaware	Y	24090 FQ	55150 AW	96570 TQ	DEBLS	10/01-12/01
Except Landscape and Naval	Wilmington-Newark PMSA, DE-MD	Y	45080 FQ	66400 AW	99710 TQ	DEBLS	10/01-12/01
Except Landscape and Naval	District of Columbia	Y	33500 FQ	57510 AW	87740 TQ	DCBLS	10/01-12/01
Except Landscape and Naval	Washington PMSA, DC-MD-VA-WV	Y	33370 FQ	58170 AW	88040 TQ	DCBLS	10/01-12/01
Except Landscape and Naval	Florida	Y	40810 FQ	63310 AW	86680 TQ	FLBLS	10/01-12/01
Except Landscape and Naval	Daytona Beach MSA, FL	Y	39270 FQ	57010 AW	88120 TQ	FLBLS	10/01-12/01
Except Landscape and Naval	Fort Lauderdale PMSA, FL	Y	43730 FQ	62550 AW	81680 TQ	FLBLS	10/01-12/01
Except Landscape and Naval	Fort Myers-Cape Coral MSA, FL	Y	40510 FQ	67840 AW	88140 TQ	FLBLS	10/01-12/01
Except Landscape and Naval	Fort Walton Beach MSA, FL	Y	31600 FQ	46880 AW	63360 TQ	FLBLS	10/01-12/01
Except Landscape and Naval	Gainesville MSA, FL	Y	29570 FQ	36620 AW	49130 TQ	FLBLS	10/01-12/01
Except Landscape and Naval	Jacksonville MSA, FL	Y	37910 FQ	54600 AW	84880 TQ	FLBLS	10/01-12/01
Except Landscape and Naval	Melbourne-Titusville-Palm Bay MSA, FL	Y	37890 FQ	63880 AW	90130 TQ	FLBLS	10/01-12/01
Except Landscape and Naval	Miami PMSA, FL	Y	56950 FQ	66040 AW	83270 TQ	FLBLS	10/01-12/01
Except Landscape and Naval	Naples MSA, FL	Y	28500 FQ	65470 AW	111260 TQ	FLBLS	10/01-12/01
Except Landscape and Naval	Orlando MSA, FL	Y	43210 FQ	63630 AW	91660 TQ	FLBLS	10/01-12/01
Except Landscape and Naval	Pensacola MSA, FL	Y	34450 FQ	66880 AW	87990 TQ	FLBLS	10/01-12/01
Except Landscape and Naval	Tallahassee MSA, FL	Y	25750 FQ	46400 AW	72170 TQ	FLBLS	10/01-12/01
Except Landscape and Naval	Tampa-St. Petersburg-Clearwater MSA, FL	Y	41490 FQ	55620 AW	72360 TQ	FLBLS	10/01-12/01
Except Landscape and Naval	West Palm Beach-Boca Raton MSA, FL	Y	44430 FQ	72050 AW	91800 TQ	FLBLS	10/01-12/01
Except Landscape and Naval	Georgia	Y	35150 FQ	61050 AW	88270 TQ	GABLS	10/01-12/01
Except Landscape and Naval	Atlanta MSA, GA	Y	35690 FQ	61490 AW	88260 TQ	GABLS	10/01-12/01
Except Landscape and Naval	Augusta-Aiken MSA, GA-SC	Y	47290 FQ	59700 AW	75620 TQ	GABLS	10/01-12/01

AAW	Average annual wage	AOH	Average offered, high	ASH	Average starting, high	H	Hourly	M	Monthly	S	Special: hourly and annual
AE	Average entry wage	AOL	Average offered, low	ASL	Average starting, low	HI	Highest wage paid	MTC	Median total compensation	TQ	Third quartile wage
AEX	Average experienced wage	APH	Average pay, high range	AW	Average wage paid	HR	High end range	MW	Median wage paid	W	Weekly
AO	Average offered	APL	Average pay, low range	FQ	First quartile wage	LR	Low end range	SQ	Second quartile wage	Y	Yearly

Occupation/Type/Industry	Location	Per	Low	Mid	High	Source	Date
Architect							
Except Landscape and Naval	Macon MSA, GA	Y	14860 FQ	67400 AW	110840 TQ	GABLS	10/01-12/01
Except Landscape and Naval	Savannah MSA, GA	Y	13530 FQ	54100 AW	89290 TQ	GABLS	10/01-12/01
Except Landscape and Naval	Hawaii	Y	31130 FQ	52370 AW	74450 TQ	HIBLS	10/01-12/01
Except Landscape and Naval	Honolulu MSA, HI	Y	38430 FQ	53150 AW	74750 TQ	HIBLS	10/01-12/01
Except Landscape and Naval	Idaho	Y	36730 FQ	75650 AW	114700 TQ	IDBLS	10/01-12/01
Except Landscape and Naval	Boise City MSA, ID	Y	38110 FQ	50910 AW	72530 TQ	IDBLS	10/01-12/01
Except Landscape and Naval	Illinois	Y	35730 FQ	55700 AW	86270 TQ	ILBLS	10/01-12/01
Except Landscape and Naval	Champaign-Urbana MSA, IL	Y	36240 FQ	63820 AW	97420 TQ	ILBLS	10/01-12/01
Except Landscape and Naval	Chicago PMSA, IL	Y	35650 FQ	54970 AW	85690 TQ	ILBLS	10/01-12/01
Except Landscape and Naval	Rockford MSA, IL	Y	38430 FQ	60960 AW	89880 TQ	ILBLS	10/01-12/01
Except Landscape and Naval	Indiana	Y	33140 FQ	58280 AW	96280 TQ	INBLS	10/01-12/01
Except Landscape and Naval	Evansville-Henderson MSA, IN-KY	Y	45750 FQ	61940 AW	85800 TQ	INBLS	10/01-12/01
Except Landscape and Naval	Fort Wayne MSA, IN	Y	37920 FQ	59990 AW	80570 TQ	INBLS	10/01-12/01
Except Landscape and Naval	Gary PMSA, IN	Y	34550 FQ	73670 AW	136930 TQ	INBLS	10/01-12/01
Except Landscape and Naval	Indianapolis MSA, IN	Y	37350 FQ	57750 AW	87420 TQ	INBLS	10/01-12/01
Except Landscape and Naval	Lafayette MSA, IN	Y	40260 FQ	87410 AW		INBLS	10/01-12/01
Except Landscape and Naval	South Bend MSA, IN	Y	41180 FQ	65150 AW	110240 TQ	INBLS	10/01-12/01
Except Landscape and Naval	Iowa	Y	28420 FQ	49720 AW	80200 TQ	IABLS	10/01-12/01
Except Landscape and Naval	Cedar Rapids MSA, IA	Y	30880 FQ	53740 AW	90530 TQ	IABLS	10/01-12/01
Except Landscape and Naval	Des Moines MSA, IA	Y	31170 FQ	45200 AW	62290 TQ	IABLS	10/01-12/01
Except Landscape and Naval	Kansas	Y	30300 FQ	54380 AW	86600 TQ	KSBLS	10/01-12/01
Except Landscape and Naval	Topeka MSA, KS	Y	32770 FQ	51310 AW	80960 TQ	KSBLS	10/01-12/01
Except Landscape and Naval	Wichita MSA, KS	Y	30490 FQ	55030 AW	88730 TQ	KSBLS	10/01-12/01
Except Landscape and Naval	Kentucky	Y	29730 FQ	59700 AW	112240 TQ	KYBLS	10/01-12/01
Except Landscape and Naval	Lexington MSA, KY	Y	26290 FQ	45580 AW	70430 TQ	KYBLS	10/01-12/01
Except Landscape and Naval	Louisville MSA, KY-IN	Y	40050 FQ	56440 AW	80460 TQ	KYBLS	10/01-12/01
Except Landscape and Naval	Louisiana	Y	31650 FQ	56790 AW	76000 TQ	LABLS	10/01-12/01
Except Landscape and Naval	Baton Rouge MSA, LA	Y	33510 FQ	73330 AW		LABLS	10/01-12/01
Except Landscape and Naval	New Orleans MSA, LA	Y	31790 FQ	45540 AW	62970 TQ	LABLS	10/01-12/01
Except Landscape and Naval	Shreveport-Bossier City MSA, LA	Y	16290 FQ	44340 AW	66940 TQ	LABLS	10/01-12/01
Except Landscape and Naval	Maine	Y	32140 FQ	51130 AW	71940 TQ	MEBLS	10/01-12/01
Except Landscape and Naval	Maryland	Y	31490 FQ	53120 AW	82110 TQ	MDBLS	10/01-12/01
Except Landscape and Naval	Baltimore PMSA, MD	Y	31680 FQ	54860 AW	92860 TQ	MDBLS	10/01-12/01
Except Landscape and Naval	Massachusetts	Y	35530 FQ	63840 AW	90280 TQ	MABLS	10/01-12/01
Except Landscape and Naval	Boston PMSA, MA-NH	Y	35850 FQ	64160 AW	90380 TQ	MABLS	10/01-12/01
Except Landscape and Naval	Michigan	Y	45110 FQ	68010 AW	88200 TQ	MIBLS	10/01-12/01
Except Landscape and Naval	Ann Arbor PMSA, MI	Y	39050 FQ	58530 AW	85260 TQ	MIBLS	10/01-12/01
Except Landscape and Naval	Detroit PMSA, MI	Y	54590 FQ	74260 AW	88920 TQ	MIBLS	10/01-12/01
Except Landscape and Naval	Flint PMSA, MI	Y	42420 FQ	65360 AW	88040 TQ	MIBLS	10/01-12/01
Except Landscape and Naval	Grand Rapids-Muskegon-Holland MSA, MI	Y	40810 FQ	54730 AW	73720 TQ	MIBLS	10/01-12/01
Except Landscape and Naval	Kalamazoo-Battle Creek MSA, MI	Y	34800 FQ	52250 AW	72080 TQ	MIBLS	10/01-12/01
Except Landscape and Naval	Lansing-East Lansing MSA, MI	Y	39250 FQ	59300 AW	80620 TQ	MIBLS	10/01-12/01
Except Landscape and Naval	Saginaw-Bay City-Midland MSA, MI	Y	32530 FQ	57110 AW	75660 TQ	MIBLS	10/01-12/01
Except Landscape and Naval	Minnesota	Y	35610 FQ	57970 AW	86080 TQ	MNBLS	10/01-12/01
Except Landscape and Naval	Minneapolis-St. Paul MSA, MN-WI	Y	36300 FQ	58070 AW	86000 TQ	MNBLS	10/01-12/01
Except Landscape and Naval	St. Cloud MSA, MN	Y	37350 FQ	64810 AW	105530 TQ	MNBLS	10/01-12/01
Except Landscape and Naval	Mississippi	Y	33810 FQ	65340 AW	115190 TQ	MSBLS	10/01-12/01
Except Landscape and Naval	Jackson MSA, MS	Y	30950 FQ	55740 AW	86290 TQ	MSBLS	10/01-12/01
Except Landscape and Naval	Missouri	Y	30220 FQ	51260 AW	82310 TQ	MOBLS	10/01-12/01
Except Landscape and Naval	Kansas City MSA, MO-KS	Y	31940 FQ	55770 AW	85270 TQ	MOBLS	10/01-12/01
Except Landscape and Naval	St. Louis MSA, MO-IL	Y	31060 FQ	51360 AW	81500 TQ	MOBLS	10/01-12/01
Except Landscape and Naval	Springfield MSA, MO	Y	13870 FQ	45770 AW	92040 TQ	MOBLS	10/01-12/01
Except Landscape and Naval	Montana	Y	33070 FQ	56820 AW	107260 TQ	MTBLS	10/01-12/01
Except Landscape and Naval	Nebraska	Y	37460 FQ	63410 AW	95980 TQ	NEBLS	10/01-12/01
Except Landscape and Naval	Lincoln MSA, NE	Y	35130 FQ	55950 AW	85270 TQ	NEBLS	10/01-12/01
Except Landscape and Naval	Omaha MSA, NE-IA	Y	37860 FQ	64920 AW	104480 TQ	NEBLS	10/01-12/01
Except Landscape and Naval	Nevada	Y	40340 FQ	61990 AW	100640 TQ	NVBLS	10/01-12/01
Except Landscape and Naval	Las Vegas MSA, NV-AZ	Y	35840 FQ	66760 AW	112580 TQ	NVBLS	10/01-12/01
Except Landscape and Naval	Reno MSA, NV	Y	38890 FQ	51840 AW	67670 TQ	NVBLS	10/01-12/01
Except Landscape and Naval	New Hampshire	Y	33560 FQ	55100 AW	86140 TQ	NHBLS	10/01-12/01
Except Landscape and Naval	Manchester PMSA, NH	Y	35010 FQ	53780 AW	72950 TQ	NHBLS	10/01-12/01
Except Landscape and Naval	Nashua PMSA, NH	Y	32880 FQ	63740 AW	125700 TQ	NHBLS	10/01-12/01
Except Landscape and Naval	Portsmouth-Rochester PMSA, NH-ME	Y	41680 FQ	57670 AW	81040 TQ	NHBLS	10/01-12/01
Except Landscape and Naval	New Jersey	Y	38270 FQ	63530 AW	102380 TQ	NJBLS	10/01-12/01

AAW	Average annual wage	AOH	Average offered, high	ASH	Average starting, high	H	Hourly	M	Monthly	S	Special: hourly and annual
AE	Average entry wage	AOL	Average offered, low	ASL	Average starting, low	HI	Highest wage paid	MTC	Median total compensation	TQ	Third quartile wage
AEX	Average experienced wage	APH	Average pay, high range	AW	Average wage paid	HR	High end range	MW	Median wage paid	W	Weekly
AO	Average offered	APL	Average pay, low range	FQ	First quartile wage	LR	Low end range	SQ	Second quartile wage	Y	Yearly

Occupation/Type/Industry	Location	Per	Low	Mid	High	Source	Date
Architect							
Except Landscape and Naval	Atlantic-Cape May PMSA, NJ	Y	12620 FQ	46910 AW	82890 TQ	NJBLS	10/01-12/01
Except Landscape and Naval	Bergen-Passaic PMSA, NJ	Y	42150 FQ	70670 AW	105190 TQ	NJBLS	10/01-12/01
Except Landscape and Naval	Jersey City PMSA, NJ	Y	42420 FQ	64300 AW	88990 TQ	NJBLS	10/01-12/01
Except Landscape and Naval	Middlesex-Somerset-Hunterdon PMSA, NJ	Y	45790 FQ	66890 AW		NJBLS	10/01-12/01
Except Landscape and Naval	Monmouth-Ocean PMSA, NJ	Y	41690 FQ	65080 AW	92410 TQ	NJBLS	10/01-12/01
Except Landscape and Naval	Newark PMSA, NJ	Y	34940 FQ	59570 AW	103090 TQ	NJBLS	10/01-12/01
Except Landscape and Naval	Trenton PMSA, NJ	Y	46040 FQ	61650 AW	88070 TQ	NJBLS	10/01-12/01
Except Landscape and Naval	New Mexico	Y	27740 FQ	45840 AW	67810 TQ	NMBLS	10/01-12/01
Except Landscape and Naval	Albuquerque MSA, NM	Y	27470 FQ	45260 AW	66210 TQ	NMBLS	10/01-12/01
Except Landscape and Naval	New York	Y	38190 FQ	63640 AW	93720 TQ	NYBLS	10/01-12/01
Except Landscape and Naval	Albany-Schenectady-Troy MSA, NY	Y	36920 FQ	61140 AW	88980 TQ	NYBLS	10/01-12/01
Except Landscape and Naval	Buffalo-Niagara Falls MSA, NY	Y	30500 FQ	57180 AW	93330 TQ	NYBLS	10/01-12/01
Except Landscape and Naval	Dutchess County PMSA, NY	Y	41040 FQ	65670 AW	96980 TQ	NYBLS	10/01-12/01
Except Landscape and Naval	Nassau-Suffolk PMSA, NY	Y	38500 FQ	58990 AW	88360 TQ	NYBLS	10/01-12/01
Except Landscape and Naval	New York PMSA, NY	Y	38690 FQ	65950 AW	97810 TQ	NYBLS	10/01-12/01
Except Landscape and Naval	Rochester MSA, NY	Y	35980 FQ	56540 AW	85730 TQ	NYBLS	10/01-12/01
Except Landscape and Naval	Syracuse MSA, NY	Y	36410 FQ	49920 AW	69670 TQ	NYBLS	10/01-12/01
Except Landscape and Naval	Utica-Rome MSA, NY	Y	20880 FQ	37720 AW	65210 TQ	NYBLS	10/01-12/01
Except Landscape and Naval	North Carolina	Y	31840 FQ	52240 AW	81220 TQ	NCBLS	10/01-12/01
Except Landscape and Naval	Asheville MSA, NC	Y	32500 FQ	43330 AW	57380 TQ	NCBLS	10/01-12/01
Except Landscape and Naval	Charlotte-Gastonia-Rock Hill MSA, NC-SC	Y	37410 FQ	59450 AW	100950 TQ	NCBLS	10/01-12/01
Except Landscape and Naval	Fayetteville MSA, NC	Y	27590 FQ	48950 AW	78360 TQ	NCBLS	10/01-12/01
Except Landscape and Naval	Greensboro-Winston-Salem-High Point MSA, NC	Y	41880 FQ	70880 AW	128460 TQ	NCBLS	10/01-12/01
Except Landscape and Naval	Raleigh-Durham-Chapel Hill MSA, NC	Y	30100 FQ	43540 AW	57670 TQ	NCBLS	10/01-12/01
Except Landscape and Naval	Wilmington MSA, NC	Y	31660 FQ	44360 AW	60820 TQ	NCBLS	10/01-12/01
Except Landscape and Naval	North Dakota	Y	30490 FQ	53700 AW	87420 TQ	NDBLS	10/01-12/01
Except Landscape and Naval	Fargo-Moorhead MSA, ND-MN	Y	34620 FQ	55530 AW	86080 TQ	NDBLS	10/01-12/01
Except Landscape and Naval	Ohio	Y	34230 FQ	56350 AW	81460 TQ	OHBLS	10/01-12/01
Except Landscape and Naval	Akron PMSA, OH	Y	38680 FQ	53230 AW	68640 TQ	OHBLS	10/01-12/01
Except Landscape and Naval	Canton-Massillon MSA, OH	Y	40930 FQ	66660 AW	90070 TQ	OHBLS	10/01-12/01
Except Landscape and Naval	Cincinnati PMSA, OH-KY-IN	Y	32820 FQ	62940 AW	108210 TQ	OHBLS	10/01-12/01
Except Landscape and Naval	Cleveland-Lorain-Elyria PMSA, OH	Y	39010 FQ	61280 AW	81570 TQ	OHBLS	10/01-12/01
Except Landscape and Naval	Columbus MSA, OH	Y	30400 FQ	53880 AW	84360 TQ	OHBLS	10/01-12/01
Except Landscape and Naval	Dayton-Springfield MSA, OH	Y	33910 FQ	55750 AW	85120 TQ	OHBLS	10/01-12/01
Except Landscape and Naval	Youngstown-Warren MSA, OH	Y	36680 FQ	52970 AW	79140 TQ	OHBLS	10/01-12/01
Except Landscape and Naval	Oklahoma	Y	46580 FQ	57600 AW	76660 TQ	OKBLS	10/01-12/01
Except Landscape and Naval	Oklahoma City MSA, OK	Y	43610 FQ	60940 AW	87540 TQ	OKBLS	10/01-12/01
Except Landscape and Naval	Tulsa MSA, OK	Y	47260 FQ	55870 AW	72120 TQ	OKBLS	10/01-12/01
Except Landscape and Naval	Oregon	Y	33470 FQ	56210 AW	86460 TQ	ORBLS	10/01-12/01
Except Landscape and Naval	Eugene-Springfield MSA, OR	Y	32430 FQ	50870 AW	71790 TQ	ORBLS	10/01-12/01
Except Landscape and Naval	Portland-Vancouver PMSA, OR-WA	Y	34010 FQ	57060 AW	88920 TQ	ORBLS	10/01-12/01
Except Landscape and Naval	Pennsylvania	Y	35620 FQ	56210 AW	83980 TQ	PABLS	10/01-12/01
Except Landscape and Naval	Allentown-Bethlehem-Easton MSA, PA	Y	29870 FQ	56350 AW	88920 TQ	PABLS	10/01-12/01
Except Landscape and Naval	Harrisburg-Lebanon-Carlisle MSA, PA	Y	45530 FQ	59500 AW	81160 TQ	PABLS	10/01-12/01
Except Landscape and Naval	Lancaster MSA, PA	Y	35940 FQ	54210 AW	82880 TQ	PABLS	10/01-12/01
Except Landscape and Naval	Philadelphia PMSA, PA-NJ	Y	38160 FQ	57300 AW	84890 TQ	PABLS	10/01-12/01
Except Landscape and Naval	Pittsburgh MSA, PA	Y	32950 FQ	52660 AW	79170 TQ	PABLS	10/01-12/01
Except Landscape and Naval	Reading MSA, PA	Y	25230 FQ	48530 AW	76580 TQ	PABLS	10/01-12/01
Except Landscape and Naval	Scranton-Wilkes-Barre-Hazleton MSA, PA	Y	43550 FQ	55770 AW	73890 TQ	PABLS	10/01-12/01
Except Landscape and Naval	York MSA, PA	Y	35540 FQ	56400 AW	83950 TQ	PABLS	10/01-12/01
Except Landscape and Naval	Rhode Island	Y	40020 FQ	66160 AW	99400 TQ	RIBLS	10/01-12/01
Except Landscape and Naval	Providence-Fall River-Warwick MSA, RI-MA	Y	36350 FQ	62980 AW	93110 TQ	RIBLS	10/01-12/01
Except Landscape and Naval	South Carolina	Y	31240 FQ	63150 AW	125550 TQ	SCBLS	10/01-12/01
Except Landscape and Naval	Charleston-North Charleston MSA, SC	Y	28830 FQ	49390 AW	72860 TQ	SCBLS	10/01-12/01
Except Landscape and Naval	Columbia MSA, SC	Y	30870 FQ	52800 AW	73800 TQ	SCBLS	10/01-12/01
Except Landscape and Naval	Greenville-Spartanburg-Anderson MSA, SC	Y	39510 FQ	57050 AW	87980 TQ	SCBLS	10/01-12/01

AAW Average annual wage **AE** Average entry wage **AEX** Average experienced wage **AO** Average offered **AOH** Average offered, high **AOL** Average offered, low **APH** Average pay, high range **APL** Average pay, low range **ASH** Average starting, high **ASL** Average starting, low **AW** Average wage paid **FQ** First quartile wage **H** Hourly **HI** Highest wage paid **HR** High end range **LR** Low end range **M** Monthly **MTC** Median total compensation **MW** Median wage paid **SQ** Second quartile wage **S** Special: hourly and annual **TQ** Third quartile wage **W** Weekly **Y** Yearly

Occupation/Type/Industry	Location	Per	Low	Mid	High	Source	Date
Architect							
Except Landscape and Naval	South Dakota	Y	33530 FQ	50440 AW	69440 TQ	SDBLS	10/01-12/01
Except Landscape and Naval	Tennessee	Y	32370 FQ	69110 AW		TNBLS	10/01-12/01
Except Landscape and Naval	Knoxville MSA, TN	Y	22650 FQ	54570 AW	111990 TQ	TNBLS	10/01-12/01
Except Landscape and Naval	Memphis MSA, TN-AR-MS	Y	33640 FQ	51750 AW	71880 TQ	TNBLS	10/01-12/01
Except Landscape and Naval	Nashville MSA, TN	Y	31440 FQ	50060 AW	79530 TQ	TNBLS	10/01-12/01
Except Landscape and Naval	Texas	Y	33250 FQ	54830 AW	84220 TQ	TXBLS	10/01-12/01
Except Landscape and Naval	Austin-San Marcos MSA, TX	Y	38210 FQ	50040 AW	57420 TQ	TXBLS	10/01-12/01
Except Landscape and Naval	Dallas PMSA, TX	Y	32750 FQ	56180 AW	88220 TQ	TXBLS	10/01-12/01
Except Landscape and Naval	El Paso MSA, TX	Y	35180 FQ	52570 AW	90010 TQ	TXBLS	10/01-12/01
Except Landscape and Naval	Fort Worth-Arlington PMSA, TX	Y	36220 FQ	53810 AW	72190 TQ	TXBLS	10/01-12/01
Except Landscape and Naval	Galveston-Texas City PMSA, TX	Y	30140 FQ	49880 AW	71100 TQ	TXBLS	10/01-12/01
Except Landscape and Naval	Houston PMSA, TX	Y	37490 FQ	58370 AW	88250 TQ	TXBLS	10/01-12/01
Except Landscape and Naval	Lubbock MSA, TX	Y	16630 FQ	39200 AW	57210 TQ	TXBLS	10/01-12/01
Except Landscape and Naval	San Antonio MSA, TX	Y	36860 FQ	53540 AW	77590 TQ	TXBLS	10/01-12/01
Except Landscape and Naval	Utah	Y	32390 FQ	53110 AW	70610 TQ	UTBLS	10/01-12/01
Except Landscape and Naval	Salt Lake City-Ogden MSA, UT	Y	30690 FQ	51860 AW	70660 TQ	UTBLS	10/01-12/01
Except Landscape and Naval	Vermont	Y	44350 FQ	67260 AW	90330 TQ	VTBLS	10/01-12/01
Except Landscape and Naval	Burlington MSA, VT	Y	41900 FQ	60030 AW	87170 TQ	VTBLS	10/01-12/01
Except Landscape and Naval	Virginia	Y	38480 FQ	61840 AW	90090 TQ	VABLS	10/01-12/01
Except Landscape and Naval	Norfolk-Virginia Beach-Newport News MSA, VA-NC	Y	37480 FQ	59290 AW	82290 TQ	VABLS	10/01-12/01
Except Landscape and Naval	Richmond-Petersburg MSA, VA	Y	38400 FQ	55080 AW	70940 TQ	VABLS	10/01-12/01
Except Landscape and Naval	Roanoke MSA, VA	Y	32250 FQ	85250 AW	143430 TQ	VABLS	10/01-12/01
Except Landscape and Naval	Washington	Y	37880 FQ	55850 AW	78470 TQ	WABLS	10/01-12/01
Except Landscape and Naval	Bremerton PMSA, WA	Y	33170 FQ	65690 AW		WABLS	10/01-12/01
Except Landscape and Naval	Olympia PMSA, WA	Y	41350 FQ	56430 AW	70280 TQ	WABLS	10/01-12/01
Except Landscape and Naval	Richland-Kennewick-Pasco MSA, WA	Y	40350 FQ	58900 AW	84100 TQ	WABLS	10/01-12/01
Except Landscape and Naval	Seattle-Bellevue-Everett PMSA, WA	Y	37960 FQ	55530 AW	79380 TQ	WABLS	10/01-12/01
Except Landscape and Naval	Spokane MSA, WA	Y	36700 FQ	57770 AW	84710 TQ	WABLS	10/01-12/01
Except Landscape and Naval	Yakima MSA, WA	Y	31540 FQ	43050 AW	60080 TQ	WABLS	10/01-12/01
Except Landscape and Naval	West Virginia	Y	27780 FQ	53460 AW	83970 TQ	WVBLS	10/01-12/01
Except Landscape and Naval	Charleston MSA, WV	Y	40850 FQ	68230 AW	95800 TQ	WVBLS	10/01-12/01
Except Landscape and Naval	Wisconsin	Y	30370 FQ	56580 AW	87740 TQ	WIBLS	10/01-12/01
Except Landscape and Naval	Appleton-Oshkosh-Neenah MSA, WI	Y	29380 FQ	48680 AW	79030 TQ	WIBLS	10/01-12/01
Except Landscape and Naval	Green Bay MSA, WI	Y	31660 FQ	53950 AW	80930 TQ	WIBLS	10/01-12/01
Except Landscape and Naval	Madison MSA, WI	Y	32740 FQ	55400 AW	83780 TQ	WIBLS	10/01-12/01
Except Landscape and Naval	Milwaukee-Waukesha PMSA, WI	Y	30010 FQ	61470 AW	140790 TQ	WIBLS	10/01-12/01
Except Landscape and Naval	Puerto Rico	Y	30460 FQ	66240 AW		PRBLS	10/01-12/01
Except Landscape and Naval	Virgin Islands	Y	32530 FQ	51990 AW	102610 TQ	VIBLS	10/01-12/01
Except Landscape and Naval	Guam	Y	30180 FQ	60810 AW	95590 TQ	GUBLS	10/01-12/01
Web Design	United States	Y		75952 AW		DFMAR	1/01-1/02
Architectural and Civil Drafter	Alabama	Y	20810 FQ	34410 AW	48090 TQ	ALBLS	10/01-12/01
	Birmingham MSA, AL	Y	21180 FQ	34750 AW	48120 TQ	ALBLS	10/01-12/01
	Huntsville MSA, AL	Y	23280 FQ	35790 AW	45530 TQ	ALBLS	10/01-12/01
	Mobile MSA, AL	Y	24220 FQ	35460 AW	44690 TQ	ALBLS	10/01-12/01
	Montgomery MSA, AL	Y	18620 FQ	32770 AW	47430 TQ	ALBLS	10/01-12/01
	Alaska	Y	29480 FQ	42160 AW	56880 TQ	AKBLS	10/01-12/01
	Anchorage MSA, AK	Y	29070 FQ	41690 AW	57560 TQ	AKBLS	10/01-12/01
	Arizona	Y	25020 FQ	39040 AW	55180 TQ	AZBLS	10/01-12/01
	Phoenix-Mesa MSA, AZ	Y	26380 FQ	40160 AW	55620 TQ	AZBLS	10/01-12/01
	Tucson MSA, AZ	Y	20500 FQ	34170 AW	48790 TQ	AZBLS	10/01-12/01
	Arkansas	Y	21940 FQ	32990 AW	46280 TQ	ARBLS	10/01-12/01
	Fort Smith MSA, AR-OK	Y	21570 FQ	28590 AW	36510 TQ	ARBLS	10/01-12/01
	Little Rock-North Little Rock MSA, AR	Y	26130 FQ	35960 AW	49660 TQ	ARBLS	10/01-12/01
	California	Y	25960 FQ	44910 AW	65890 TQ	CABLS	10/01-12/01
	Bakersfield MSA, CA	Y	15270 FQ	32790 AW	53070 TQ	CABLS	10/01-12/01
	Fresno MSA, CA	Y	22300 FQ	35710 AW	48200 TQ	CABLS	10/01-12/01
	Los Angeles-Long Beach PMSA, CA	Y	35160 FQ	50520 AW	69950 TQ	CABLS	10/01-12/01
	Modesto MSA, CA	Y	21900 FQ	41240 AW	69750 TQ	CABLS	10/01-12/01
	Oakland PMSA, CA	Y	16090 FQ	41140 AW	61550 TQ	CABLS	10/01-12/01

AAW	Average annual wage	AOH	Average offered, high	ASH	Average starting, high	H	Hourly	M	Monthly	S	Special: hourly and annual
AE	Average entry wage	AOL	Average offered, low	ASL	Average starting, low	HI	Highest wage paid	MTC	Median total compensation	TQ	Third quartile wage
AEX	Average experienced wage	APH	Average pay, high range	AW	Average wage paid	HR	High end range	MW	Median wage paid	W	Weekly
AO	Average offered	APL	Average pay, low range	FQ	First quartile wage	LR	Low end range	SQ	Second quartile wage	Y	Yearly

Occupation/Type/Industry	Location	Per	Low	Mid	High	Source	Date
Architectural and Civil Drafter	Orange County PMSA, CA	Y	26770 FQ	47360 AW	65950 TQ	CABLS	10/01-12/01
	Redding MSA, CA	Y	27830 FQ	38670 AW	57890 TQ	CABLS	10/01-12/01
	Riverside-San Bernardino PMSA, CA	Y	23270 FQ	40770 AW	61040 TQ	CABLS	10/01-12/01
	Sacramento PMSA, CA	Y	29650 FQ	45200 AW	61220 TQ	CABLS	10/01-12/01
	Salinas MSA, CA	Y	33060 FQ	46990 AW	58010 TQ	CABLS	10/01-12/01
	San Diego MSA, CA	Y	26770 FQ	39800 AW	56700 TQ	CABLS	10/01-12/01
	San Francisco PMSA, CA	Y	35880 FQ	55330 AW	80290 TQ	CABLS	10/01-12/01
	San Jose PMSA, CA	Y	25670 FQ	39720 AW	53450 TQ	CABLS	10/01-12/01
	San Luis Obispo-Atascadero-Paso Robles MSA, CA	Y	23610 FQ	29690 AW	40020 TQ	CABLS	10/01-12/01
	Santa Barbara-Santa Maria-Lompoc MSA, CA	Y	26950 FQ	35670 AW	50190 TQ	CABLS	10/01-12/01
	Santa Rosa PMSA, CA	Y	28860 FQ	44280 AW	60910 TQ	CABLS	10/01-12/01
	Stockton-Lodi MSA, CA	Y	20960 FQ	39340 AW	61390 TQ	CABLS	10/01-12/01
	Vallejo-Fairfield-Napa PMSA, CA	Y	27480 FQ	47530 AW	82430 TQ	CABLS	10/01-12/01
	Ventura PMSA, CA	Y	34290 FQ	50160 AW	70460 TQ	CABLS	10/01-12/01
	Visalia-Tulare-Porterville MSA, CA	Y	22710 FQ	31740 AW	44220 TQ	CABLS	10/01-12/01
	Colorado	Y	25430 FQ	37740 AW	50120 TQ	COBLS	10/01-12/01
	Boulder-Longmont PMSA, CO	Y	28660 FQ	39300 AW	51100 TQ	COBLS	10/01-12/01
	Colorado Springs MSA, CO	Y	26110 FQ	35140 AW	45870 TQ	COBLS	10/01-12/01
	Denver PMSA, CO	Y	26040 FQ	38690 AW	52830 TQ	COBLS	10/01-12/01
	Fort Collins-Loveland MSA, CO	Y	24630 FQ	36000 AW	53070 TQ	COBLS	10/01-12/01
	Connecticut	Y	25940 FQ	42770 AW	64050 TQ	CTBLS	10/01-12/01
	Bridgeport PMSA, CT	Y	27460 FQ	39850 AW	52050 TQ	CTBLS	10/01-12/01
	Hartford MSA, CT	Y	26170 FQ	40720 AW	55790 TQ	CTBLS	10/01-12/01
	New Haven-Meriden PMSA, CT	Y	24540 FQ	36470 AW	53180 TQ	CTBLS	10/01-12/01
	New London-Norwich MSA, CT-RI	Y	30890 FQ	41380 AW	56130 TQ	CTBLS	10/01-12/01
	Stamford-Norwalk PMSA, CT	Y	30300 FQ	53780 AW	73090 TQ	CTBLS	10/01-12/01
	Delaware	Y	21840 FQ	41670 AW	66200 TQ	DEBLS	10/01-12/01
	Wilmington-Newark PMSA, DE-MD	Y	21860 FQ	43280 AW	67840 TQ	DEBLS	10/01-12/01
	District of Columbia	Y	24580 FQ	33630 AW	43040 TQ	DCBLS	10/01-12/01
	Washington PMSA, DC-MD-VA-WV	Y	26030 FQ	38060 AW	52260 TQ	DCBLS	10/01-12/01
	Florida	Y	24730 FQ	37050 AW	50270 TQ	FLBLS	10/01-12/01
	Daytona Beach MSA, FL	Y	23130 FQ	36250 AW	51300 TQ	FLBLS	10/01-12/01
	Fort Lauderdale PMSA, FL	Y	26670 FQ	39810 AW	54150 TQ	FLBLS	10/01-12/01
	Fort Myers-Cape Coral MSA, FL	Y	23800 FQ	35250 AW	45900 TQ	FLBLS	10/01-12/01
	Fort Pierce-Port St. Lucie MSA, FL	Y	19970 FQ	31490 AW	49270 TQ	FLBLS	10/01-12/01
	Fort Walton Beach MSA, FL	Y	23060 FQ	27190 AW	34950 TQ	FLBLS	10/01-12/01
	Gainesville MSA, FL	Y	21160 FQ	28920 AW	37710 TQ	FLBLS	10/01-12/01
	Jacksonville MSA, FL	Y	20860 FQ	30720 AW	43770 TQ	FLBLS	10/01-12/01
	Lakeland-Winter Haven MSA, FL	Y	24550 FQ	35780 AW	50440 TQ	FLBLS	10/01-12/01
	Melbourne-Titusville-Palm Bay MSA, FL	Y	23600 FQ	33290 AW	44480 TQ	FLBLS	10/01-12/01
	Miami PMSA, FL	Y	32670 FQ	40520 AW	50870 TQ	FLBLS	10/01-12/01
	Naples MSA, FL	Y	25430 FQ	37340 AW	48240 TQ	FLBLS	10/01-12/01
	Ocala MSA, FL	Y	20870 FQ	30690 AW	43510 TQ	FLBLS	10/01-12/01
	Orlando MSA, FL	Y	25960 FQ	42390 AW	57200 TQ	FLBLS	10/01-12/01
	Pensacola MSA, FL	Y	20610 FQ	27410 AW	34280 TQ	FLBLS	10/01-12/01
	Sarasota-Bradenton MSA, FL	Y	27340 FQ	36090 AW	50550 TQ	FLBLS	10/01-12/01
	Tallahassee MSA, FL	Y	21230 FQ	32330 AW	45040 TQ	FLBLS	10/01-12/01
	Tampa-St. Petersburg-Clearwater MSA, FL	Y	24910 FQ	35840 AW	47220 TQ	FLBLS	10/01-12/01
	West Palm Beach-Boca Raton MSA, FL	Y	29680 FQ	37530 AW	45290 TQ	FLBLS	10/01-12/01
	Georgia	Y	24360 FQ	37440 AW	54790 TQ	GABLS	10/01-12/01
	Atlanta MSA, GA	Y	25390 FQ	38140 AW	53160 TQ	GABLS	10/01-12/01
	Augusta-Aiken MSA, GA-SC	Y	24140 FQ	41200 AW	66960 TQ	GABLS	10/01-12/01
	Columbus MSA, GA-AL	Y	15240 FQ	28800 AW	43390 TQ	GABLS	10/01-12/01
	Hawaii	Y	19040 FQ	34000 AW	48750 TQ	HIBLS	10/01-12/01
	Honolulu MSA, HI	Y	18470 FQ	33890 AW	49320 TQ	HIBLS	10/01-12/01
	Idaho	Y	22000 FQ	34310 AW	49570 TQ	IDBLS	10/01-12/01

AAW	Average annual wage	**AOH**	Average offered, high	**ASH**	Average starting, high	**H**	Hourly	**M**	Monthly	**S**	Special: hourly and annual
AE	Average entry wage	**AOL**	Average offered, low	**ASL**	Average starting, low	**HI**	Highest wage paid	**MTC**	Median total compensation	**TQ**	Third quartile wage
AEX	Average experienced wage	**APH**	Average pay, high range	**AW**	Average wage paid	**HR**	High end range	**MW**	Median wage paid	**W**	Weekly
AO	Average offered	**APL**	Average pay, low range	**FQ**	First quartile wage	**LR**	Low end range	**SQ**	Second quartile wage	**Y**	Yearly

Occupation/Type/Industry	Location	Per	Low	Mid	High	Source	Date
Architectural and Civil Drafter	Boise City MSA, ID	Y	20580 FQ	35170 AW	56460 TQ	IDBLS	10/01-12/01
	Illinois	Y	23180 FQ	33290 AW	49140 TQ	ILBLS	10/01-12/01
	Champaign-Urbana MSA, IL	Y	28080 FQ	35100 AW	43450 TQ	ILBLS	10/01-12/01
	Chicago PMSA, IL	Y	23650 FQ	32450 AW	46190 TQ	ILBLS	10/01-12/01
	Peoria-Pekin MSA, IL	Y	27750 FQ	35110 AW	46890 TQ	ILBLS	10/01-12/01
	Rockford MSA, IL	Y	30460 FQ	42440 AW	63040 TQ	ILBLS	10/01-12/01
	Indiana	Y	23000 FQ	34530 AW	51100 TQ	INBLS	10/01-12/01
	Elkhart-Goshen MSA, IN	Y	24850 FQ	31780 AW	36560 TQ	INBLS	10/01-12/01
	Evansville-Henderson MSA, IN-KY	Y	22670 FQ	34540 AW	55350 TQ	INBLS	10/01-12/01
	Fort Wayne MSA, IN	Y	24620 FQ	34700 AW	44550 TQ	INBLS	10/01-12/01
	Gary PMSA, IN	Y	24590 FQ	38400 AW	53870 TQ	INBLS	10/01-12/01
	Indianapolis MSA, IN	Y	24660 FQ	36790 AW	54020 TQ	INBLS	10/01-12/01
	South Bend MSA, IN	Y	22630 FQ	38730 AW	57040 TQ	INBLS	10/01-12/01
	Iowa	Y	21580 FQ	34690 AW	49270 TQ	IABLS	10/01-12/01
	Cedar Rapids MSA, IA	Y	19690 FQ	31350 AW	49880 TQ	IABLS	10/01-12/01
	Davenport-Moline-Rock Island MSA, IA-IL	Y	20180 FQ	27990 AW	37680 TQ	IABLS	10/01-12/01
	Des Moines MSA, IA	Y	25870 FQ	35780 AW	45490 TQ	IABLS	10/01-12/01
	Kansas	Y	23240 FQ	36210 AW	52780 TQ	KSBLS	10/01-12/01
	Topeka MSA, KS	Y	18100 FQ	29970 AW	43360 TQ	KSBLS	10/01-12/01
	Wichita MSA, KS	Y	22420 FQ	33890 AW	44810 TQ	KSBLS	10/01-12/01
	Kentucky	Y	20150 FQ	33120 AW	49320 TQ	KYBLS	10/01-12/01
	Lexington MSA, KY	Y	22710 FQ	32700 AW	47950 TQ	KYBLS	10/01-12/01
	Louisville MSA, KY-IN	Y	22910 FQ	36980 AW	58130 TQ	KYBLS	10/01-12/01
	Louisiana	Y	20930 FQ	35320 AW	54040 TQ	LABLS	10/01-12/01
	Baton Rouge MSA, LA	Y	20320 FQ	34340 AW	55880 TQ	LABLS	10/01-12/01
	Houma MSA, LA	Y	19690 FQ	27730 AW	37480 TQ	LABLS	10/01-12/01
	Lafayette MSA, LA	Y	17080 FQ	30140 AW	43260 TQ	LABLS	10/01-12/01
	Lake Charles MSA, LA	Y	19670 FQ	35900 AW	60610 TQ	LABLS	10/01-12/01
	New Orleans MSA, LA	Y	27680 FQ	40480 AW	56460 TQ	LABLS	10/01-12/01
	Shreveport-Bossier City MSA, LA	Y	19900 FQ	29450 AW	39510 TQ	LABLS	10/01-12/01
	Maine	Y	24820 FQ	33220 AW	43330 TQ	MEBLS	10/01-12/01
	Portland MSA, ME	Y	28190 FQ	34190 AW	43970 TQ	MEBLS	10/01-12/01
	Maryland	Y	27250 FQ	39940 AW	53990 TQ	MDBLS	10/01-12/01
	Baltimore PMSA, MD	Y	25940 FQ	39030 AW	54090 TQ	MDBLS	10/01-12/01
	Massachusetts	Y	29810 FQ	42720 AW	59670 TQ	MABLS	10/01-12/01
	Boston PMSA, MA-NH	Y	30050 FQ	43260 AW	61090 TQ	MABLS	10/01-12/01
	Brockton PMSA, MA	Y	30680 FQ	41930 AW	55850 TQ	MABLS	10/01-12/01
	Lawrence PMSA, MA-NH	Y	21330 FQ	38350 AW	57180 TQ	MABLS	10/01-12/01
	Lowell PMSA, MA-NH	Y	30400 FQ	41970 AW	60480 TQ	MABLS	10/01-12/01
	Springfield MSA, MA	Y	32310 FQ	42160 AW	53270 TQ	MABLS	10/01-12/01
	Worcester PMSA, MA-CT	Y	27200 FQ	39770 AW	55160 TQ	MABLS	10/01-12/01
	Michigan	Y	27200 FQ	39090 AW	48860 TQ	MIBLS	10/01-12/01
	Ann Arbor PMSA, MI	Y	24430 FQ	36990 AW	50080 TQ	MIBLS	10/01-12/01
	Detroit PMSA, MI	Y	32020 FQ	39880 AW	45870 TQ	MIBLS	10/01-12/01
	Flint PMSA, MI	Y	26780 FQ	41430 AW	54690 TQ	MIBLS	10/01-12/01
	Grand Rapids-Muskegon-Holland MSA, MI	Y	26340 FQ	37090 AW	51750 TQ	MIBLS	10/01-12/01
	Lansing-East Lansing MSA, MI	Y	22190 FQ	35320 AW	50310 TQ	MIBLS	10/01-12/01
	Saginaw-Bay City-Midland MSA, MI	Y	21530 FQ	34220 AW	50310 TQ	MIBLS	10/01-12/01
	Minnesota	Y	26630 FQ	38010 AW	50560 TQ	MNBLS	10/01-12/01
	Duluth-Superior MSA, MN-WI	Y	20440 FQ	32920 AW	48700 TQ	MNBLS	10/01-12/01
	Minneapolis-St. Paul MSA, MN-WI	Y	28540 FQ	39510 AW	53680 TQ	MNBLS	10/01-12/01
	St. Cloud MSA, MN	Y	21170 FQ	31890 AW	44060 TQ	MNBLS	10/01-12/01
	Mississippi	Y	20640 FQ	38190 AW	56600 TQ	MSBLS	10/01-12/01
	Biloxi-Gulfport-Pascagoula MSA, MS	Y	19110 FQ	38080 AW	60300 TQ	MSBLS	10/01-12/01
	Jackson MSA, MS	Y	30450 FQ	44110 AW	56940 TQ	MSBLS	10/01-12/01
	Missouri	Y	23550 FQ	35570 AW	50450 TQ	MOBLS	10/01-12/01
	Kansas City MSA, MO-KS	Y	24230 FQ	35430 AW	50890 TQ	MOBLS	10/01-12/01
	St. Louis MSA, MO-IL	Y	24620 FQ	38170 AW	52890 TQ	MOBLS	10/01-12/01
	Springfield MSA, MO	Y	19230 FQ	33330 AW	49310 TQ	MOBLS	10/01-12/01
	Montana	Y	22230 FQ	32900 AW	48830 TQ	MTBLS	10/01-12/01
	Billings MSA, MT	Y	23730 FQ	33450 AW	53100 TQ	MTBLS	10/01-12/01
	Nebraska	Y	22730 FQ	33190 AW	44140 TQ	NEBLS	10/01-12/01
	Lincoln MSA, NE	Y	20520 FQ	30920 AW	42610 TQ	NEBLS	10/01-12/01
	Omaha MSA, NE-IA	Y	24450 FQ	34200 AW	44550 TQ	NEBLS	10/01-12/01
	Nevada	Y	29990 FQ	39760 AW	53660 TQ	NVBLS	10/01-12/01

AAW	Average annual wage	**AOH**	Average offered, high	**ASH**	Average starting, high	**H**	Hourly	**M**	Monthly	**S**	Special: hourly and annual
AE	Average entry wage	**AOL**	Average offered, low	**ASL**	Average starting, low	**HI**	Highest wage paid	**MTC**	Median total compensation	**TQ**	Third quartile wage
AEX	Average experienced wage	**APH**	Average pay, high range	**AW**	Average wage paid	**HR**	High end range	**MW**	Median wage paid	**W**	Weekly
AO	Average offered	**APL**	Average pay, low range	**FQ**	First quartile wage	**LR**	Low end range	**SQ**	Second quartile wage	**Y**	Yearly

Occupation/Type/Industry	Location	Per	Low	Mid	High	Source	Date
Architectural and Civil Drafter	Las Vegas MSA, NV-AZ	Y	28860 FQ	42210 AW	57480 TQ	NVBLS	10/01-12/01
	Reno MSA, NV	Y	31160 FQ	40970 AW	53370 TQ	NVBLS	10/01-12/01
	New Hampshire	Y	27420 FQ	35680 AW	49420 TQ	NHBLS	10/01-12/01
	Manchester PMSA, NH	Y	23660 FQ	33660 AW	47020 TQ	NHBLS	10/01-12/01
	Nashua PMSA, NH	Y	26740 FQ	36560 AW	52750 TQ	NHBLS	10/01-12/01
	Portsmouth-Rochester PMSA, NH-ME	Y	28960 FQ	37290 AW	46730 TQ	NHBLS	10/01-12/01
	New Jersey	Y	29840 FQ	43810 AW	66180 TQ	NJBLS	10/01-12/01
	Atlantic-Cape May PMSA, NJ	Y	25950 FQ	41110 AW	63280 TQ	NJBLS	10/01-12/01
	Bergen-Passaic PMSA, NJ	Y	29180 FQ	46330 AW	76250 TQ	NJBLS	10/01-12/01
	Jersey City PMSA, NJ	Y	29740 FQ	43720 AW	61160 TQ	NJBLS	10/01-12/01
	Middlesex-Somerset-Hunterdon PMSA, NJ	Y	29900 FQ	47510 AW	74230 TQ	NJBLS	10/01-12/01
	Monmouth-Ocean PMSA, NJ	Y	32970 FQ	42510 AW	60340 TQ	NJBLS	10/01-12/01
	Newark PMSA, NJ	Y	30930 FQ	41080 AW	54430 TQ	NJBLS	10/01-12/01
	Trenton PMSA, NJ	Y	29400 FQ	47420 AW	75510 TQ	NJBLS	10/01-12/01
	New Mexico	Y	22310 FQ	32020 AW	42480 TQ	NMBLS	10/01-12/01
	Albuquerque MSA, NM	Y	23030 FQ	31860 AW	41820 TQ	NMBLS	10/01-12/01
	New York	Y	29550 FQ	41660 AW	57720 TQ	NYBLS	10/01-12/01
	Albany-Schenectady-Troy MSA, NY	Y	24260 FQ	34330 AW	43900 TQ	NYBLS	10/01-12/01
	Binghamton MSA, NY	Y	17520 FQ	33040 AW	44780 TQ	NYBLS	10/01-12/01
	Buffalo-Niagara Falls MSA, NY	Y	25060 FQ	36400 AW	53700 TQ	NYBLS	10/01-12/01
	Dutchess County PMSA, NY	Y	29840 FQ	38940 AW	65350 TQ	NYBLS	10/01-12/01
	Nassau-Suffolk PMSA, NY	Y	38520 FQ	45400 AW	55300 TQ	NYBLS	10/01-12/01
	New York PMSA, NY	Y	30380 FQ	42900 AW	64300 TQ	NYBLS	10/01-12/01
	Rochester MSA, NY	Y	29640 FQ	38650 AW	49670 TQ	NYBLS	10/01-12/01
	Syracuse MSA, NY	Y	24900 FQ	35730 AW	48550 TQ	NYBLS	10/01-12/01
	Utica-Rome MSA, NY	Y	20960 FQ	34720 AW	49040 TQ	NYBLS	10/01-12/01
	North Carolina	Y	23380 FQ	36620 AW	51570 TQ	NCBLS	10/01-12/01
	Asheville MSA, NC	Y	25230 FQ	35190 AW	45300 TQ	NCBLS	10/01-12/01
	Charlotte-Gastonia-Rock Hill MSA, NC-SC	Y	28260 FQ	39490 AW	57220 TQ	NCBLS	10/01-12/01
	Fayetteville MSA, NC	Y	23320 FQ	33570 AW	42900 TQ	NCBLS	10/01-12/01
	Greensboro-Winston-Salem-High Point MSA, NC	Y	21290 FQ	34550 AW	44010 TQ	NCBLS	10/01-12/01
	Raleigh-Durham-Chapel Hill MSA, NC	Y	26800 FQ	39100 AW	53140 TQ	NCBLS	10/01-12/01
	Wilmington MSA, NC	Y	19240 FQ	29200 AW	46800 TQ	NCBLS	10/01-12/01
	North Dakota	Y	21020 FQ	28900 AW	36750 TQ	NDBLS	10/01-12/01
	Fargo-Moorhead MSA, ND-MN	Y	21070 FQ	28670 AW	36930 TQ	NDBLS	10/01-12/01
	Ohio	Y	23240 FQ	35210 AW	48570 TQ	OHBLS	10/01-12/01
	Akron PMSA, OH	Y	19670 FQ	31510 AW	45350 TQ	OHBLS	10/01-12/01
	Canton-Massillon MSA, OH	Y	17530 FQ	31550 AW	45450 TQ	OHBLS	10/01-12/01
	Cincinnati PMSA, OH-KY-IN	Y	21890 FQ	36760 AW	51960 TQ	OHBLS	10/01-12/01
	Cleveland-Lorain-Elyria PMSA, OH	Y	29950 FQ	35730 AW	45280 TQ	OHBLS	10/01-12/01
	Columbus MSA, OH	Y	24650 FQ	35010 AW	46300 TQ	OHBLS	10/01-12/01
	Dayton-Springfield MSA, OH	Y	26410 FQ	40510 AW	55750 TQ	OHBLS	10/01-12/01
	Hamilton-Middletown PMSA, OH	Y	21090 FQ	36390 AW	54950 TQ	OHBLS	10/01-12/01
	Toledo MSA, OH	Y	21220 FQ	35230 AW	50650 TQ	OHBLS	10/01-12/01
	Youngstown-Warren MSA, OH	Y	25390 FQ	38560 AW	56480 TQ	OHBLS	10/01-12/01
	Oklahoma	Y	23550 FQ	36880 AW	55220 TQ	OKBLS	10/01-12/01
	Oklahoma City MSA, OK	Y	23210 FQ	35240 AW	50970 TQ	OKBLS	10/01-12/01
	Tulsa MSA, OK	Y	29360 FQ	41150 AW	60250 TQ	OKBLS	10/01-12/01
	Oregon	Y	26300 FQ	37380 AW	52060 TQ	ORBLS	10/01-12/01
	Eugene-Springfield MSA, OR	Y	24390 FQ	35510 AW	56370 TQ	ORBLS	10/01-12/01
	Medford-Ashland MSA, OR	Y	24590 FQ	31460 AW	39670 TQ	ORBLS	10/01-12/01
	Portland-Vancouver PMSA, OR-WA	Y	29490 FQ	39580 AW	53120 TQ	ORBLS	10/01-12/01
	Salem PMSA, OR	Y	25310 FQ	36550 AW	48600 TQ	ORBLS	10/01-12/01
	Pennsylvania	Y	23460 FQ	35980 AW	51010 TQ	PABLS	10/01-12/01
	Allentown-Bethlehem-Easton MSA, PA	Y	24480 FQ	35630 AW	51760 TQ	PABLS	10/01-12/01
	Erie MSA, PA	Y	23130 FQ	32320 AW	42680 TQ	PABLS	10/01-12/01
	Harrisburg-Lebanon-Carlisle MSA, PA	Y	25370 FQ	35970 AW	49240 TQ	PABLS	10/01-12/01
	Johnstown MSA, PA	Y	19700 FQ	29030 AW	42190 TQ	PABLS	10/01-12/01
	Lancaster MSA, PA	Y	24940 FQ	36230 AW	50200 TQ	PABLS	10/01-12/01

AAW Average annual wage **AE** Average entry wage **AEX** Average experienced wage **AO** Average offered **AOH** Average offered, high **AOL** Average offered, low **APH** Average pay, high range **APL** Average pay, low range **ASH** Average starting, high **ASL** Average starting, low **AW** Average wage paid **FQ** First quartile wage **H** Hourly **HI** Highest wage paid **HR** High end range **LR** Low end range **M** Monthly **MTC** Median total compensation **MW** Median wage paid **SQ** Second quartile wage **S** Special: hourly and annual **TQ** Third quartile wage **W** Weekly **Y** Yearly

Occupation/Type/Industry	Location	Per	Low	Mid	High	Source	Date
Architectural and Civil Drafter	Philadelphia PMSA, PA-NJ	Y	26850 FQ	37390 AW	48650 TQ	PABLS	10/01-12/01
	Pittsburgh MSA, PA	Y	22100 FQ	39690 AW	63190 TQ	PABLS	10/01-12/01
	Reading MSA, PA	Y	23790 FQ	32160 AW	45270 TQ	PABLS	10/01-12/01
	Scranton-Wilkes-Barre-Hazleton MSA, PA	Y	20330 FQ	31900 AW	44840 TQ	PABLS	10/01-12/01
	York MSA, PA	Y	24740 FQ	34350 AW	44360 TQ	PABLS	10/01-12/01
	Rhode Island	Y	31660 FQ	50270 AW	71500 TQ	RIBLS	10/01-12/01
	Providence-Fall River-Warwick MSA, RI-MA	Y	26590 FQ	47880 AW	72180 TQ	RIBLS	10/01-12/01
	South Carolina	Y	24820 FQ	37410 AW	59040 TQ	SCBLS	10/01-12/01
	Charleston-North Charleston MSA, SC	Y	20790 FQ	32320 AW	45600 TQ	SCBLS	10/01-12/01
	Columbia MSA, SC	Y	25350 FQ	39790 AW	58170 TQ	SCBLS	10/01-12/01
	Greenville-Spartanburg-Anderson MSA, SC	Y	25560 FQ	35980 AW	57000 TQ	SCBLS	10/01-12/01
	Myrtle Beach MSA, SC	Y	23550 FQ	33780 AW	52690 TQ	SCBLS	10/01-12/01
	South Dakota	Y	20620 FQ	28960 AW	37050 TQ	SDBLS	10/01-12/01
	Sioux Falls MSA, SD	Y	20530 FQ	29490 AW	39860 TQ	SDBLS	10/01-12/01
	Tennessee	Y	22590 FQ	39840 AW	59830 TQ	TNBLS	10/01-12/01
	Chattanooga MSA, TN-GA	Y	27620 FQ	45280 AW	63610 TQ	TNBLS	10/01-12/01
	Clarksville-Hopkinsville MSA, TN-KY	Y	20770 FQ	31590 AW	45310 TQ	TNBLS	10/01-12/01
	Johnson City-Kingsport-Bristol MSA, TN-VA	Y	24260 FQ	35970 AW	52490 TQ	TNBLS	10/01-12/01
	Knoxville MSA, TN	Y	20130 FQ	34700 AW	55100 TQ	TNBLS	10/01-12/01
	Memphis MSA, TN-AR-MS	Y	23210 FQ	41370 AW	67550 TQ	TNBLS	10/01-12/01
	Nashville MSA, TN	Y	21410 FQ	38280 AW	55470 TQ	TNBLS	10/01-12/01
	Texas	Y	23900 FQ	41010 AW	63020 TQ	TXBLS	10/01-12/01
	Austin-San Marcos MSA, TX	Y	18780 FQ	33350 AW	46290 TQ	TXBLS	10/01-12/01
	Beaumont-Port Arthur MSA, TX	Y	21680 FQ	33480 AW	48320 TQ	TXBLS	10/01-12/01
	Brazoria PMSA, TX	Y	29290 FQ	42910 AW	66010 TQ	TXBLS	10/01-12/01
	Brownsville-Harlingen-San Benito MSA, TX	Y	19570 FQ	27150 AW	37410 TQ	TXBLS	10/01-12/01
	Corpus Christi MSA, TX	Y	20250 FQ	31910 AW	42400 TQ	TXBLS	10/01-12/01
	Dallas PMSA, TX	Y	26400 FQ	40160 AW	57750 TQ	TXBLS	10/01-12/01
	El Paso MSA, TX	Y	21160 FQ	35000 AW	48040 TQ	TXBLS	10/01-12/01
	Fort Worth-Arlington PMSA, TX	Y	18370 FQ	36920 AW	52420 TQ	TXBLS	10/01-12/01
	Houston PMSA, TX	Y	28650 FQ	50670 AW	85350 TQ	TXBLS	10/01-12/01
	Longview-Marshall MSA, TX	Y	25160 FQ	35510 AW	50730 TQ	TXBLS	10/01-12/01
	Lubbock MSA, TX	Y	17680 FQ	27060 AW	37800 TQ	TXBLS	10/01-12/01
	McAllen-Edinburg-Mission MSA, TX	Y	14190 FQ	22580 AW	31710 TQ	TXBLS	10/01-12/01
	Odessa-Midland MSA, TX	Y	20190 FQ	38510 AW	66250 TQ	TXBLS	10/01-12/01
	San Antonio MSA, TX	Y	23030 FQ	34050 AW	44710 TQ	TXBLS	10/01-12/01
	Waco MSA, TX	Y	20940 FQ	28710 AW	37000 TQ	TXBLS	10/01-12/01
	Utah	Y	20730 FQ	33440 AW	49160 TQ	UTBLS	10/01-12/01
	Provo-Orem MSA, UT	Y	22880 FQ	33190 AW	48260 TQ	UTBLS	10/01-12/01
	Salt Lake City-Ogden MSA, UT	Y	23390 FQ	34790 AW	50940 TQ	UTBLS	10/01-12/01
	Vermont	Y	25320 FQ	40470 AW	53860 TQ	VTBLS	10/01-12/01
	Burlington MSA, VT	Y	23880 FQ	35050 AW	47510 TQ	VTBLS	10/01-12/01
	Virginia	Y	23100 FQ	34790 AW	48240 TQ	VABLS	10/01-12/01
	Lynchburg MSA, VA	Y	19940 FQ	32230 AW	46400 TQ	VABLS	10/01-12/01
	Norfolk-Virginia Beach-Newport News MSA, VA-NC	Y	24260 FQ	36410 AW	47200 TQ	VABLS	10/01-12/01
	Richmond-Petersburg MSA, VA	Y	25860 FQ	38660 AW	54010 TQ	VABLS	10/01-12/01
	Roanoke MSA, VA	Y	23220 FQ	31580 AW	42000 TQ	VABLS	10/01-12/01
	Washington	Y	24870 FQ	39700 AW	58850 TQ	WABLS	10/01-12/01
	Olympia PMSA, WA	Y	24530 FQ	36210 AW	46870 TQ	WABLS	10/01-12/01
	Richland-Kennewick-Pasco MSA, WA	Y	30610 FQ	43030 AW	59370 TQ	WABLS	10/01-12/01
	Seattle-Bellevue-Everett PMSA, WA	Y	24330 FQ	39490 AW	61090 TQ	WABLS	10/01-12/01
	Spokane MSA, WA	Y	25120 FQ	33600 AW	43390 TQ	WABLS	10/01-12/01
	Tacoma PMSA, WA	Y	30700 FQ	41230 AW	54220 TQ	WABLS	10/01-12/01
	West Virginia	Y	21100 FQ	32000 AW	46250 TQ	WVBLS	10/01-12/01
	Charleston MSA, WV	Y	21690 FQ	31720 AW	44190 TQ	WVBLS	10/01-12/01

AAW Average annual wage **AOH** Average offered, high **ASH** Average starting, high **H** Hourly **M** Monthly **S** Special: hourly and annual
AE Average entry wage **AOL** Average offered, low **ASL** Average starting, low **HI** Highest wage paid **MTC** Median total compensation **TQ** Third quartile wage
AEX Average experienced wage **APH** Average pay, high range **AW** Average wage paid **HR** High end range **MW** Median wage paid **W** Weekly
AO Average offered **APL** Average pay, low range **FQ** First quartile wage **LR** Low end range **SQ** Second quartile wage **Y** Yearly

Occupation/Type/Industry	Location	Per	Low	Mid	High	Source	Date
Architectural and Civil Drafter	Huntington-Ashland MSA, WV-KY-OH	Y	24550 FQ	32120 AW	41170 TQ	WVBLS	10/01-12/01
	Wisconsin	Y	25240 FQ	38280 AW	54750 TQ	WIBLS	10/01-12/01
	Appleton-Oshkosh-Neenah MSA, WI	Y	25810 FQ	35720 AW	50460 TQ	WIBLS	10/01-12/01
	Green Bay MSA, WI	Y	29610 FQ	37110 AW	44450 TQ	WIBLS	10/01-12/01
	Madison MSA, WI	Y	27740 FQ	36500 AW	44260 TQ	WIBLS	10/01-12/01
	Milwaukee-Waukesha PMSA, WI	Y	25920 FQ	43230 AW	67750 TQ	WIBLS	10/01-12/01
	Wyoming	Y	19910 FQ	29340 AW	38620 TQ	WYBLS	10/01-12/01
	Puerto Rico	Y	12980 FQ	22980 AW	34970 TQ	PRBLS	10/01-12/01
	Guam	Y	21410 FQ	31690 AW	47120 TQ	GUBLS	10/01-12/01
Architectural Intern							
Web Design	United States	Y		35230 AW		DFMAR	1/01-1/02
Architecture Teacher							
Postsecondary	Alabama	Y	34350 FQ	56640 AW	75960 TQ	ALBLS	10/01-12/01
Postsecondary	California	Y	24140 FQ	53000 AW	82070 TQ	CABLS	10/01-12/01
Postsecondary	San Francisco PMSA, CA	Y	33140 FQ	49830 AW	72460 TQ	CABLS	10/01-12/01
Postsecondary	Washington PMSA, DC-MD-VA-WV	Y	27260 FQ	63010 AW	103300 TQ	DCBLS	10/01-12/01
Postsecondary	Florida	Y	42610 FQ	66260 AW	105520 TQ	FLBLS	10/01-12/01
Postsecondary	Gainesville MSA, FL	Y	41910 FQ	64890 AW	102640 TQ	FLBLS	10/01-12/01
Postsecondary	Miami PMSA, FL	Y	39310 FQ	61990 AW	102500 TQ	FLBLS	10/01-12/01
Postsecondary	Tallahassee MSA, FL	Y	45580 FQ	69180 AW	111760 TQ	FLBLS	10/01-12/01
Postsecondary	Tampa-St. Petersburg-Clearwater MSA, FL	Y	49010 FQ	70090 AW	101170 TQ	FLBLS	10/01-12/01
Postsecondary	Idaho	Y	36210 FQ	48170 AW	64870 TQ	IDBLS	10/01-12/01
Postsecondary	Illinois	Y	15630 FQ	53060 AW	92490 TQ	ILBLS	10/01-12/01
Postsecondary	Chicago PMSA, IL	Y	16030 FQ	53780 AW	92540 TQ	ILBLS	10/01-12/01
Postsecondary	Indiana	Y	31950 FQ	57630 AW	89070 TQ	INBLS	10/01-12/01
Postsecondary	Kansas	Y	37730 FQ	58150 AW	84290 TQ	KSBLS	10/01-12/01
Postsecondary	Kentucky	Y	36860 FQ	60160 AW	92110 TQ	KYBLS	10/01-12/01
Postsecondary	Louisiana	Y	33490 FQ	54630 AW	71410 TQ	LABLS	10/01-12/01
Postsecondary	Maryland	Y	40720 FQ	66230 AW	102060 TQ	MDBLS	10/01-12/01
Postsecondary	Baltimore PMSA, MD	Y	40400 FQ	55730 AW	80060 TQ	MDBLS	10/01-12/01
Postsecondary	Massachusetts	Y	36540 FQ	54720 AW	75700 TQ	MABLS	10/01-12/01
Postsecondary	Boston PMSA, MA-NH	Y	35630 FQ	54700 AW	77760 TQ	MABLS	10/01-12/01
Postsecondary	Michigan	Y	35440 FQ	57320 AW	84810 TQ	MIBLS	10/01-12/01
Postsecondary	Detroit PMSA, MI	Y	34780 FQ	54310 AW	78850 TQ	MIBLS	10/01-12/01
Postsecondary	Minnesota	Y	36980 FQ	54430 AW	71840 TQ	MNBLS	10/01-12/01
Postsecondary	Minneapolis-St. Paul MSA, MN-WI	Y	36290 FQ	54440 AW	72010 TQ	MNBLS	10/01-12/01
Postsecondary	Mississippi	Y	36880 FQ	50740 AW	67890 TQ	MSBLS	10/01-12/01
Postsecondary	Missouri	Y	34680 FQ	56240 AW	89710 TQ	MOBLS	10/01-12/01
Postsecondary	St. Louis MSA, MO-IL	Y	31120 FQ	56760 AW	91150 TQ	MOBLS	10/01-12/01
Postsecondary	Nebraska	Y	47390 FQ	70680 AW	88990 TQ	NEBLS	10/01-12/01
Postsecondary	New Jersey	Y	39770 FQ	62020 AW	97300 TQ	NJBLS	10/01-12/01
Postsecondary	New York	Y	41780 FQ	83900 AW		NYBLS	10/01-12/01
Postsecondary	North Carolina	Y	30660 FQ	50930 AW	76760 TQ	NCBLS	10/01-12/01
Postsecondary	Raleigh-Durham-Chapel Hill MSA, NC	Y	29120 FQ	54310 AW	83300 TQ	NCBLS	10/01-12/01
Postsecondary	Ohio	Y	32300 FQ	52970 AW	83280 TQ	OHBLS	10/01-12/01
Postsecondary	Oregon	Y	45850 FQ	63690 AW	89570 TQ	ORBLS	10/01-12/01
Postsecondary	Pennsylvania	Y	27670 FQ	60990 AW	114150 TQ	PABLS	10/01-12/01
Postsecondary	Philadelphia PMSA, PA-NJ	Y	32090 FQ	58430 AW	92340 TQ	PABLS	10/01-12/01
Postsecondary	Rhode Island	Y	48250 FQ	65880 AW	90310 TQ	RIBLS	10/01-12/01
Postsecondary	South Carolina	Y	33920 FQ	53600 AW	79730 TQ	SCBLS	10/01-12/01
Postsecondary	Tennessee	Y	40290 FQ	59650 AW	74060 TQ	TNBLS	10/01-12/01
Postsecondary	Texas	Y	27310 FQ	52500 AW	81690 TQ	TXBLS	10/01-12/01
Postsecondary	Houston PMSA, TX	Y	26090 FQ	52850 AW	82520 TQ	TXBLS	10/01-12/01
Postsecondary	Virginia	Y	26520 FQ	56910 AW	88420 TQ	VABLS	10/01-12/01
Postsecondary	Washington	Y	29860 FQ	58370 AW	95020 TQ	WABLS	10/01-12/01
Postsecondary	Seattle-Bellevue-Everett PMSA, WA	Y	23140 FQ	55280 AW	94420 TQ	WABLS	10/01-12/01
Postsecondary	Wisconsin	Y	27760 FQ	52340 AW	72330 TQ	WIBLS	10/01-12/01
Postsecondary	Puerto Rico	Y	28340 FQ	41740 AW	70060 TQ	PRBLS	10/01-12/01
Archivist, Curator, and Museum Technician	Alabama	Y	18740 FQ	34620 AW	52960 TQ	ALBLS	10/01-12/01
	Birmingham MSA, AL	Y	25100 FQ	40010 AW	55850 TQ	ALBLS	10/01-12/01

AAW Average annual wage · AE Average entry wage · AEX Average experienced wage · AO Average offered · AOH Average offered, high · AOL Average offered, low · APH Average pay, high range · APL Average pay, low range · ASH Average starting, high · ASL Average starting, low · AW Average wage paid · FQ First quartile wage · H Hourly · HI Highest wage paid · HR High end range · LR Low end range · M Monthly · MTC Median total compensation · MW Median wage paid · SQ Second quartile wage · S Special: hourly and annual · TQ Third quartile wage · W Weekly · Y Yearly

Occupation/Type/Industry	Location	Per	Low	Mid	High	Source	Date
Archivist, Curator, and Museum Technician	Montgomery MSA, AL	Y	23920 FQ	35370 AW	52270 TQ	ALBLS	10/01-12/01
	Alaska	Y	19970 FQ	38890 AW	57700 TQ	AKBLS	10/01-12/01
	Anchorage MSA, AK	Y	19980 FQ	33820 AW	53470 TQ	AKBLS	10/01-12/01
	Arizona	Y	22410 FQ	44610 AW	74870 TQ	AZBLS	10/01-12/01
	Tucson MSA, AZ	Y	20780 FQ	35720 AW	55390 TQ	AZBLS	10/01-12/01
	Arkansas	Y	12690 FQ	26650 AW	43210 TQ	ARBLS	10/01-12/01
	California	Y	25030 FQ	48260 AW	77550 TQ	CABLS	10/01-12/01
	Los Angeles-Long Beach PMSA, CA	Y	32420 FQ	57070 AW	87600 TQ	CABLS	10/01-12/01
	Oakland PMSA, CA	Y	27910 FQ	41060 AW	57750 TQ	CABLS	10/01-12/01
	Orange County PMSA, CA	Y	19640 FQ	39220 AW	66100 TQ	CABLS	10/01-12/01
	Riverside-San Bernardino PMSA, CA	Y	20280 FQ	43660 AW	65440 TQ	CABLS	10/01-12/01
	Sacramento PMSA, CA	Y	33790 FQ	50860 AW	77340 TQ	CABLS	10/01-12/01
	Salinas MSA, CA	Y	20880 FQ	41730 AW	69270 TQ	CABLS	10/01-12/01
	San Diego MSA, CA	Y	22630 FQ	43030 AW	74580 TQ	CABLS	10/01-12/01
	San Francisco PMSA, CA	Y	24830 FQ	45200 AW	76810 TQ	CABLS	10/01-12/01
	San Jose PMSA, CA	Y	26510 FQ	45730 AW	67570 TQ	CABLS	10/01-12/01
	Santa Barbara-Santa Maria-Lompoc MSA, CA	Y	28350 FQ	41720 AW	66440 TQ	CABLS	10/01-12/01
	Ventura PMSA, CA	Y	21410 FQ	36970 AW	63650 TQ	CABLS	10/01-12/01
	Visalia-Tulare-Porterville MSA, CA	Y	23390 FQ	45470 AW	69790 TQ	CABLS	10/01-12/01
	Colorado	Y	19700 FQ	39830 AW	71610 TQ	COBLS	10/01-12/01
	Colorado Springs MSA, CO	Y	24330 FQ	44220 AW	60650 TQ	COBLS	10/01-12/01
	Denver PMSA, CO	Y	20520 FQ	42310 AW	79950 TQ	COBLS	10/01-12/01
	Fort Collins-Loveland MSA, CO	Y	14890 FQ	30390 AW	50470 TQ	COBLS	10/01-12/01
	Connecticut	Y	21400 FQ	39020 AW	60280 TQ	CTBLS	10/01-12/01
	Hartford MSA, CT	Y	21290 FQ	40010 AW	70950 TQ	CTBLS	10/01-12/01
	New Haven-Meriden PMSA, CT	Y	20620 FQ	40430 AW	58590 TQ	CTBLS	10/01-12/01
	New London-Norwich MSA, CT-RI	Y	27070 FQ	41130 AW	62970 TQ	CTBLS	10/01-12/01
	District of Columbia	Y	28470 FQ	50970 AW	76800 TQ	DCBLS	10/01-12/01
	Washington PMSA, DC-MD-VA-WV	Y	22590 FQ	46300 AW	71260 TQ	DCBLS	10/01-12/01
	Florida	Y	20990 FQ	41560 AW	71800 TQ	FLBLS	10/01-12/01
	Fort Lauderdale PMSA, FL	Y	22700 FQ	41850 AW	69490 TQ	FLBLS	10/01-12/01
	Gainesville MSA, FL	Y	24130 FQ	43870 AW	89450 TQ	FLBLS	10/01-12/01
	Jacksonville MSA, FL	Y	17210 FQ	27320 AW	42820 TQ	FLBLS	10/01-12/01
	Miami PMSA, FL	Y	25930 FQ	47410 AW	88950 TQ	FLBLS	10/01-12/01
	Orlando MSA, FL	Y	24060 FQ	42660 AW	72650 TQ	FLBLS	10/01-12/01
	Tallahassee MSA, FL	Y	22770 FQ	47030 AW	77280 TQ	FLBLS	10/01-12/01
	Tampa-St. Petersburg-Clearwater MSA, FL	Y	17060 FQ	37230 AW	67730 TQ	FLBLS	10/01-12/01
	West Palm Beach-Boca Raton MSA, FL	Y	26800 FQ	53590 AW	131010 TQ	FLBLS	10/01-12/01
	Georgia	Y	16300 FQ	33740 AW	55940 TQ	GABLS	10/01-12/01
	Atlanta MSA, GA	Y	20290 FQ	37220 AW	60990 TQ	GABLS	10/01-12/01
	Hawaii	Y	24030 FQ	36750 AW	55840 TQ	HIBLS	10/01-12/01
	Honolulu MSA, HI	Y	23980 FQ	37520 AW	59940 TQ	HIBLS	10/01-12/01
	Idaho	Y	20160 FQ	31290 AW	45380 TQ	IDBLS	10/01-12/01
	Illinois	Y	19260 FQ	39620 AW	69600 TQ	ILBLS	10/01-12/01
	Chicago PMSA, IL	Y	20970 FQ	41440 AW	72950 TQ	ILBLS	10/01-12/01
	Indiana	Y	16390 FQ	33240 AW	57620 TQ	INBLS	10/01-12/01
	Fort Wayne MSA, IN	Y	15870 FQ	28070 AW	42370 TQ	INBLS	10/01-12/01
	Indianapolis MSA, IN	Y	24610 FQ	42660 AW	66990 TQ	INBLS	10/01-12/01
	Lafayette MSA, IN	Y	15740 FQ	27320 AW	42420 TQ	INBLS	10/01-12/01
	South Bend MSA, IN	Y	15560 FQ	31840 AW	54680 TQ	INBLS	10/01-12/01
	Iowa	Y	18110 FQ	39080 AW	60130 TQ	IABLS	10/01-12/01
	Kansas	Y	13210 FQ	28630 AW	47430 TQ	KSBLS	10/01-12/01
	Topeka MSA, KS	Y	18080 FQ	30500 AW	41290 TQ	KSBLS	10/01-12/01
	Wichita MSA, KS	Y	15010 FQ	28120 AW	34370 TQ	KSBLS	10/01-12/01
	Kentucky	Y	17040 FQ	29750 AW	43690 TQ	KYBLS	10/01-12/01
	Louisville MSA, KY-IN	Y	20530 FQ	32500 AW	45430 TQ	KYBLS	10/01-12/01
	Louisiana	Y	13080 FQ	26810 AW	37750 TQ	LABLS	10/01-12/01
	Baton Rouge MSA, LA	Y	16660 FQ	26970 AW	47360 TQ	LABLS	10/01-12/01
	New Orleans MSA, LA	Y	22890 FQ	30840 AW	40730 TQ	LABLS	10/01-12/01
	Maine	Y	22370 FQ	36380 AW	54970 TQ	MEBLS	10/01-12/01
	Maryland	Y	18240 FQ	39100 AW	67510 TQ	MDBLS	10/01-12/01

AAW	Average annual wage	**AOH**	Average offered, high	**ASH**	Average starting, high	**H**	Hourly	**M**	Monthly	**S**	Special: hourly and annual
AE	Average entry wage	**AOL**	Average offered, low	**ASL**	Average starting, low	**HI**	Highest wage paid	**MTC**	Median total compensation	**TQ**	Third quartile wage
AEX	Average experienced wage	**APH**	Average pay, high range	**AW**	Average wage paid	**HR**	High end range	**MW**	Median wage paid	**W**	Weekly
AO	Average offered	**APL**	Average pay, low range	**FQ**	First quartile wage	**LR**	Low end range	**SQ**	Second quartile wage	**Y**	Yearly

Occupation/Type/Industry	Location	Per	Low	Mid	High	Source	Date
Archivist, Curator, and Museum Technician	Baltimore PMSA, MD	Y	14170 FQ	33980 AW	61800 TQ	MDBLS	10/01-12/01
	Massachusetts	Y	21420 FQ	39280 AW	61340 TQ	MABLS	10/01-12/01
	Boston PMSA, MA-NH	Y	21960 FQ	39840 AW	62120 TQ	MABLS	10/01-12/01
	Springfield MSA, MA	Y	25330 FQ	45360 AW	72250 TQ	MABLS	10/01-12/01
	Michigan	Y	15290 FQ	31560 AW	52800 TQ	MIBLS	10/01-12/01
	Detroit PMSA, MI	Y	15560 FQ	31070 AW	53150 TQ	MIBLS	10/01-12/01
	Grand Rapids-Muskegon-Holland MSA, MI	Y	19390 FQ	33090 AW	53590 TQ	MIBLS	10/01-12/01
	Minnesota	Y	21460 FQ	40990 AW	64200 TQ	MNBLS	10/01-12/01
	Minneapolis-St. Paul MSA, MN-WI	Y	22180 FQ	44520 AW	69240 TQ	MNBLS	10/01-12/01
	Mississippi	Y	15790 FQ	32460 AW	58880 TQ	MSBLS	10/01-12/01
	Missouri	Y	18830 FQ	28230 AW	40660 TQ	MOBLS	10/01-12/01
	Kansas City MSA, MO-KS	Y	19050 FQ	32100 AW	55780 TQ	MOBLS	10/01-12/01
	St. Louis MSA, MO-IL	Y	18750 FQ	26580 AW	35070 TQ	MOBLS	10/01-12/01
	Montana	Y	13490 FQ	27520 AW	44130 TQ	MTBLS	10/01-12/01
	Nebraska	Y	19100 FQ	34660 AW	51010 TQ	NEBLS	10/01-12/01
	Lincoln MSA, NE	Y	23730 FQ	40140 AW	58240 TQ	NEBLS	10/01-12/01
	Omaha MSA, NE-IA	Y	17720 FQ	29830 AW	43610 TQ	NEBLS	10/01-12/01
	Nevada	Y	14780 FQ	32920 AW	53760 TQ	NVBLS	10/01-12/01
	Las Vegas MSA, NV-AZ	Y	13730 FQ	30950 AW	54870 TQ	NVBLS	10/01-12/01
	New Hampshire	Y	17930 FQ	34910 AW	53710 TQ	NHBLS	10/01-12/01
	Portsmouth-Rochester PMSA, NH-ME	Y	15790 FQ	31420 AW	56710 TQ	NHBLS	10/01-12/01
	New Jersey	Y	23440 FQ	39970 AW	59490 TQ	NJBLS	10/01-12/01
	Bergen-Passaic PMSA, NJ	Y	24900 FQ	38510 AW	56740 TQ	NJBLS	10/01-12/01
	Newark PMSA, NJ	Y	23220 FQ	39110 AW	55860 TQ	NJBLS	10/01-12/01
	Trenton PMSA, NJ	Y	29310 FQ	46410 AW	66090 TQ	NJBLS	10/01-12/01
	New Mexico	Y	23870 FQ	38000 AW	54670 TQ	NMBLS	10/01-12/01
	Albuquerque MSA, NM	Y	25300 FQ	40020 AW	58600 TQ	NMBLS	10/01-12/01
	New York	Y	20000 FQ	43030 AW	75350 TQ	NYBLS	10/01-12/01
	Albany-Schenectady-Troy MSA, NY	Y	19890 FQ	38170 AW	61130 TQ	NYBLS	10/01-12/01
	Buffalo-Niagara Falls MSA, NY	Y	15880 FQ	26410 AW	46890 TQ	NYBLS	10/01-12/01
	Nassau-Suffolk PMSA, NY	Y	20390 FQ	42280 AW	74670 TQ	NYBLS	10/01-12/01
	New York PMSA, NY	Y	23220 FQ	48740 AW	87810 TQ	NYBLS	10/01-12/01
	Rochester MSA, NY	Y	19130 FQ	33950 AW	53490 TQ	NYBLS	10/01-12/01
	Syracuse MSA, NY	Y	24450 FQ	36630 AW	47780 TQ	NYBLS	10/01-12/01
	North Carolina	Y	15030 FQ	27030 AW	44200 TQ	NCBLS	10/01-12/01
	Charlotte-Gastonia-Rock Hill MSA, NC-SC	Y	17710 FQ	37130 AW	54660 TQ	NCBLS	10/01-12/01
	Greensboro-Winston-Salem-High Point MSA, NC	Y	18770 FQ	31490 AW	46200 TQ	NCBLS	10/01-12/01
	Raleigh-Durham-Chapel Hill MSA, NC	Y	14730 FQ	24100 AW	42420 TQ	NCBLS	10/01-12/01
	Ohio	Y	20560 FQ	33950 AW	52990 TQ	OHBLS	10/01-12/01
	Cincinnati PMSA, OH-KY-IN	Y	22220 FQ	35370 AW	55910 TQ	OHBLS	10/01-12/01
	Cleveland-Lorain-Elyria PMSA, OH	Y	20840 FQ	38960 AW	72990 TQ	OHBLS	10/01-12/01
	Columbus MSA, OH	Y	22460 FQ	34140 AW	50300 TQ	OHBLS	10/01-12/01
	Dayton-Springfield MSA, OH	Y	18670 FQ	28700 AW	48400 TQ	OHBLS	10/01-12/01
	Toledo MSA, OH	Y	21180 FQ	36220 AW	56430 TQ	OHBLS	10/01-12/01
	Oklahoma	Y	19380 FQ	32610 AW	52070 TQ	OKBLS	10/01-12/01
	Oklahoma City MSA, OK	Y	23480 FQ	34720 AW	53510 TQ	OKBLS	10/01-12/01
	Oregon	Y	18280 FQ	34000 AW	52160 TQ	ORBLS	10/01-12/01
	Portland-Vancouver PMSA, OR-WA	Y	22900 FQ	37170 AW	54860 TQ	ORBLS	10/01-12/01
	Pennsylvania	Y	17260 FQ	34850 AW	56960 TQ	PABLS	10/01-12/01
	Philadelphia PMSA, PA-NJ	Y	18200 FQ	35160 AW	55760 TQ	PABLS	10/01-12/01
	Pittsburgh MSA, PA	Y	18240 FQ	40050 AW	63250 TQ	PABLS	10/01-12/01
	Rhode Island	Y	19750 FQ	42140 AW	65290 TQ	RIBLS	10/01-12/01
	Providence-Fall River-Warwick MSA, RI-MA	Y	27500 FQ	42220 AW	61130 TQ	RIBLS	10/01-12/01
	South Carolina	Y	18990 FQ	32030 AW	46950 TQ	SCBLS	10/01-12/01
	Charleston-North Charleston MSA, SC	Y	15450 FQ	25660 AW	37680 TQ	SCBLS	10/01-12/01
	South Dakota	Y	19810 FQ	32250 AW	49030 TQ	SDBLS	10/01-12/01
	Tennessee	Y	12970 FQ	30150 AW	50150 TQ	TNBLS	10/01-12/01
	Memphis MSA, TN-AR-MS	Y	12050 FQ	27640 AW	51070 TQ	TNBLS	10/01-12/01
	Nashville MSA, TN	Y	18880 FQ	31950 AW	44700 TQ	TNBLS	10/01-12/01

AAW Average annual wage	**AOH** Average offered, high	**ASH** Average starting, high	**H** Hourly	**M** Monthly	**S** Special: hourly and annual
AE Average entry wage	**AOL** Average offered, low	**ASL** Average starting, low	**HI** Highest wage paid	**MTC** Median total compensation	**TQ** Third quartile wage
AEX Average experienced wage	**APH** Average pay, high range	**AW** Average wage paid	**HR** High end range	**MW** Median wage paid	**W** Weekly
AO Average offered	**APL** Average pay, low range	**FQ** First quartile wage	**LR** Low end range	**SQ** Second quartile wage	**Y** Yearly

Occupation/Type/Industry	Location	Per	Low	Mid	High	Source	Date
Archivist, Curator, and Museum Technician	Texas	Y	18710 FQ	37580 AW	60250 TQ	TXBLS	10/01-12/01
	Austin-San Marcos MSA, TX	Y	28650 FQ	38640 AW	55010 TQ	TXBLS	10/01-12/01
	Dallas PMSA, TX	Y	23310 FQ	34920 AW	54420 TQ	TXBLS	10/01-12/01
	Fort Worth-Arlington PMSA, TX	Y	19470 FQ	36190 AW	58530 TQ	TXBLS	10/01-12/01
	Houston PMSA, TX	Y	21610 FQ	49700 AW	99230 TQ	TXBLS	10/01-12/01
	Utah	Y	24240 FQ	35760 AW	53070 TQ	UTBLS	10/01-12/01
	Salt Lake City-Ogden MSA, UT	Y	25520 FQ	34860 AW	48540 TQ	UTBLS	10/01-12/01
	Vermont	Y	18780 FQ	32320 AW	47050 TQ	VTBLS	10/01-12/01
	Virginia	Y	19650 FQ	34880 AW	56780 TQ	VABLS	10/01-12/01
	Norfolk-Virginia Beach-Newport News MSA, VA-NC	Y	18270 FQ	31600 AW	46240 TQ	VABLS	10/01-12/01
	Richmond-Petersburg MSA, VA	Y	22600 FQ	37430 AW	61460 TQ	VABLS	10/01-12/01
	Washington	Y	21030 FQ	38820 AW	58800 TQ	WABLS	10/01-12/01
	Seattle-Bellevue-Everett PMSA, WA	Y	24010 FQ	42760 AW	67460 TQ	WABLS	10/01-12/01
	Tacoma PMSA, WA	Y	23940 FQ	42630 AW	60390 TQ	WABLS	10/01-12/01
	West Virginia	Y	17440 FQ	43250 AW	69930 TQ	WVBLS	10/01-12/01
	Wisconsin	Y	18200 FQ	33480 AW	52040 TQ	WIBLS	10/01-12/01
	Madison MSA, WI	Y	18760 FQ	32570 AW	50400 TQ	WIBLS	10/01-12/01
	Milwaukee-Waukesha PMSA, WI	Y	18400 FQ	35980 AW	54650 TQ	WIBLS	10/01-12/01
	Wyoming	Y	15610 FQ	32630 AW	53060 TQ	WYBLS	10/01-12/01
	Puerto Rico	Y	11480 FQ	19060 AW	32710 TQ	PRBLS	10/01-12/01
	Guam	Y	22460 FQ	34770 AW	49590 TQ	GUBLS	10/01-12/01
Area, Ethnic, and Cultural Studies Teacher							
Postsecondary	California	Y	38310 FQ	66510 AW	91430 TQ	CABLS	10/01-12/01
Postsecondary	Colorado	Y	32270 FQ	56390 AW	95080 TQ	COBLS	10/01-12/01
Postsecondary	Connecticut	Y	39700 FQ	64310 AW	92390 TQ	CTBLS	10/01-12/01
Postsecondary	Florida	Y	37160 FQ	60960 AW	94190 TQ	FLBLS	10/01-12/01
Postsecondary	Georgia	Y	46040 FQ	58710 AW	79970 TQ	GABLS	10/01-12/01
Postsecondary	Hawaii	Y	35590 FQ	57090 AW	87350 TQ	HIBLS	10/01-12/01
Postsecondary	Illinois	Y	24540 FQ	46610 AW	64710 TQ	ILBLS	10/01-12/01
Postsecondary	Indiana	Y	31610 FQ	58610 AW	92480 TQ	INBLS	10/01-12/01
Postsecondary	Kentucky	Y	35540 FQ	54100 AW	84800 TQ	KYBLS	10/01-12/01
Postsecondary	Louisiana	Y	12270 FQ	53790 AW	89740 TQ	LABLS	10/01-12/01
Postsecondary	Maryland	Y	34310 FQ	65840 AW	112980 TQ	MDBLS	10/01-12/01
Postsecondary	Massachusetts	Y	31200 FQ	59770 AW	94240 TQ	MABLS	10/01-12/01
Postsecondary	Michigan	Y	33370 FQ	63310 AW	106260 TQ	MIBLS	10/01-12/01
Postsecondary	Minnesota	Y	30880 FQ	53590 AW	80660 TQ	MNBLS	10/01-12/01
Postsecondary	Mississippi	Y	37570 FQ	45890 AW	56740 TQ	MSBLS	10/01-12/01
Postsecondary	Missouri	Y	29900 FQ	56320 AW	87850 TQ	MOBLS	10/01-12/01
Postsecondary	New Jersey	Y	33200 FQ	60000 AW	94810 TQ	NJBLS	10/01-12/01
Postsecondary	New York	Y	42310 FQ	70570 AW	108210 TQ	NYBLS	10/01-12/01
Postsecondary	North Carolina	Y	29660 FQ	52750 AW	88110 TQ	NCBLS	10/01-12/01
Postsecondary	Ohio	Y	31550 FQ	58820 AW	93890 TQ	OHBLS	10/01-12/01
Postsecondary	Oklahoma	Y	29230 FQ	36560 AW	53890 TQ	OKBLS	10/01-12/01
Postsecondary	Oregon	Y	32070 FQ	57960 AW	97840 TQ	ORBLS	10/01-12/01
Postsecondary	Pennsylvania	Y	31420 FQ	61690 AW	100330 TQ	PABLS	10/01-12/01
Postsecondary	South Carolina	Y	26600 FQ	46080 AW	78710 TQ	SCBLS	10/01-12/01
Postsecondary	Tennessee	Y	36350 FQ	58240 AW	83570 TQ	TNBLS	10/01-12/01
Postsecondary	Texas	Y	30390 FQ	57060 AW	92630 TQ	TXBLS	10/01-12/01
Postsecondary	Vermont	Y	37240 FQ	49230 AW	61550 TQ	VTBLS	10/01-12/01
Postsecondary	Virginia	Y	30450 FQ	55180 AW	87130 TQ	VABLS	10/01-12/01
Postsecondary	Washington	Y	37260 FQ	59780 AW	93090 TQ	WABLS	10/01-12/01
Postsecondary	Puerto Rico	Y	28440 FQ	43450 AW	73640 TQ	PRBLS	10/01-12/01
Art Director	United States	Y	30000 AE			COSGIRL2	1/01-1/02
	Alabama	Y	24220 FQ	44460 AW	80160 TQ	ALBLS	10/01-12/01
	Arizona	Y	30990 FQ	54820 AW	83890 TQ	AZBLS	10/01-12/01
	Phoenix, AZ	Y		50000 AW		TBJ	1/00-1/01
	Arkansas	Y	16360 FQ	37570 AW	61050 TQ	ARBLS	10/01-12/01
	California	Y	37640 FQ	72570 AW	124490 TQ	CABLS	10/01-12/01
	Colorado	Y	25770 FQ	53880 AW	101060 TQ	COBLS	10/01-12/01
	Connecticut	Y	41970 FQ	74990 AW	118670 TQ	CTBLS	10/01-12/01
	District of Columbia	Y	43510 FQ	68710 AW	103180 TQ	DCBLS	10/01-12/01

AAW Average annual wage	**AOH** Average offered, high	**ASH** Average starting, high	**H** Hourly	**M** Monthly	**S** Special: hourly and annual
AE Average entry wage	**AOL** Average offered, low	**ASL** Average starting, low	**HI** Highest wage paid	**MTC** Median total compensation	**TQ** Third quartile wage
AEX Average experienced wage	**APH** Average pay, high range	**AW** Average wage paid	**HR** High end range	**MW** Median wage paid	**W** Weekly
AO Average offered	**APL** Average pay, low range	**FQ** First quartile wage	**LR** Low end range	**SQ** Second quartile wage	**Y** Yearly

Occupation/Type/Industry	Location	Per	Low	Mid	High	Source	Date
Art Director	Florida	Y	31720 FQ	56500 AW	90440 TQ	FLBLS	10/01-12/01
	Georgia	Y	31530 FQ	63200 AW	90080 TQ	GABLS	10/01-12/01
	Hawaii	Y	31570 FQ	54300 AW	88610 TQ	HIBLS	10/01-12/01
	Illinois	Y	29100 FQ	67480 AW	133230 TQ	ILBLS	10/01-12/01
	Indiana	Y	29530 FQ	54740 AW	86120 TQ	INBLS	10/01-12/01
	Iowa	Y	21810 FQ	52240 AW	93800 TQ	IABLS	10/01-12/01
	Kansas	Y	34180 FQ	49290 AW	69300 TQ	KSBLS	10/01-12/01
	Kentucky	Y	20320 FQ	42200 AW	73000 TQ	KYBLS	10/01-12/01
	Louisiana	Y	25260 FQ	42670 AW	61370 TQ	LABLS	10/01-12/01
	Maryland	Y	35720 FQ	60940 AW	93340 TQ	MDBLS	10/01-12/01
	Massachusetts	Y	30220 FQ	56760 AW	91160 TQ	MABLS	10/01-12/01
	Michigan	Y	28840 FQ	78180 AW		MIBLS	10/01-12/01
	Minnesota	Y	39430 FQ	68130 AW	111860 TQ	MNBLS	10/01-12/01
	Mississippi	Y	21820 FQ	43110 AW	80120 TQ	MSBLS	10/01-12/01
	Missouri	Y	31100 FQ	59190 AW	90630 TQ	MOBLS	10/01-12/01
	Nebraska	Y	21380 FQ	44100 AW	77560 TQ	NEBLS	10/01-12/01
	Nevada	Y	31640 FQ	51530 AW	70360 TQ	NVBLS	10/01-12/01
	New Hampshire	Y	36110 FQ	59900 AW	91460 TQ	NHBLS	10/01-12/01
	New Jersey	Y	40430 FQ	68060 AW	104580 TQ	NJBLS	10/01-12/01
	New Mexico	Y	24910 FQ	40350 AW	56520 TQ	NMBLS	10/01-12/01
	New York	Y	42780 FQ	77070 AW	127950 TQ	NYBLS	10/01-12/01
	North Carolina	Y	33520 FQ	54850 AW	83690 TQ	NCBLS	10/01-12/01
	Ohio	Y	38250 FQ	60360 AW	88260 TQ	OHBLS	10/01-12/01
	Oklahoma	Y	18650 FQ	37060 AW	56550 TQ	OKBLS	10/01-12/01
	Oregon	Y	35810 FQ	55700 AW	84370 TQ	ORBLS	10/01-12/01
	Pennsylvania	Y	26700 FQ	55450 AW	91110 TQ	PABLS	10/01-12/01
	Rhode Island	Y	34210 FQ	65770 AW	95250 TQ	RIBLS	10/01-12/01
	South Carolina	Y	36960 FQ	57250 AW	91100 TQ	SCBLS	10/01-12/01
	South Dakota	Y	36670 FQ	49350 AW	80060 TQ	SDBLS	10/01-12/01
	Tennessee	Y	26830 FQ	46240 AW	71930 TQ	TNBLS	10/01-12/01
	Texas	Y	26680 FQ	61530 AW	105360 TQ	TXBLS	10/01-12/01
	Utah	Y	32370 FQ	58470 AW	96640 TQ	UTBLS	10/01-12/01
	Virginia	Y	38330 FQ	59470 AW	85900 TQ	VABLS	10/01-12/01
	Washington	Y	47360 FQ	86640 AW		WABLS	10/01-12/01
	West Virginia	Y	19640 FQ	37930 AW	68180 TQ	WVBLS	10/01-12/01
	Wisconsin	Y	31440 FQ	54790 AW	89380 TQ	WIBLS	10/01-12/01
	Puerto Rico	Y	23080 FQ	30930 AW	48530 TQ	PRBLS	10/01-12/01
Art, Drama, and Music Teacher							
Postsecondary	Alabama	Y	19050 FQ	42060 AW	67260 TQ	ALBLS	10/01-12/01
Postsecondary	Birmingham MSA, AL	Y	29580 FQ	45780 AW	70080 TQ	ALBLS	10/01-12/01
Postsecondary	Mobile MSA, AL	Y	13490 FQ	33100 AW	48530 TQ	ALBLS	10/01-12/01
Postsecondary	Montgomery MSA, AL	Y	29440 FQ	42660 AW	60530 TQ	ALBLS	10/01-12/01
Postsecondary	Arizona	Y	23450 FQ	44750 AW	78670 TQ	AZBLS	10/01-12/01
Postsecondary	Arkansas	Y	20690 FQ	46860 AW	76240 TQ	ARBLS	10/01-12/01
Postsecondary	California	Y	26050 FQ	61540 AW	108630 TQ	CABLS	10/01-12/01
Postsecondary	Fresno MSA, CA	Y	26130 FQ	47680 AW	77350 TQ	CABLS	10/01-12/01
Postsecondary	Los Angeles-Long Beach PMSA, CA	Y	25250 FQ	59170 AW	109260 TQ	CABLS	10/01-12/01
Postsecondary	Oakland PMSA, CA	Y	20990 FQ	62780 AW	111840 TQ	CABLS	10/01-12/01
Postsecondary	Orange County PMSA, CA	Y	28930 FQ	63740 AW	101120 TQ	CABLS	10/01-12/01
Postsecondary	Riverside-San Bernardino PMSA, CA	Y	29990 FQ	55720 AW	98680 TQ	CABLS	10/01-12/01
Postsecondary	Sacramento PMSA, CA	Y	26570 FQ	60340 AW	101750 TQ	CABLS	10/01-12/01
Postsecondary	San Diego MSA, CA	Y	25730 FQ	60390 AW	94160 TQ	CABLS	10/01-12/01
Postsecondary	San Francisco PMSA, CA	Y	32100 FQ	65300 AW	112270 TQ	CABLS	10/01-12/01
Postsecondary	Santa Cruz-Watsonville PMSA, CA	Y	35310 FQ	57250 AW	84770 TQ	CABLS	10/01-12/01
Postsecondary	Colorado	Y	30020 FQ	50480 AW	73900 TQ	COBLS	10/01-12/01
Postsecondary	Denver PMSA, CO	Y	33170 FQ	51630 AW	73060 TQ	COBLS	10/01-12/01
Postsecondary	Connecticut	Y	36870 FQ	62670 AW	94320 TQ	CTBLS	10/01-12/01
Postsecondary	Bridgeport PMSA, CT	Y	41810 FQ	56940 AW	77730 TQ	CTBLS	10/01-12/01
Postsecondary	Hartford MSA, CT	Y	36990 FQ	62970 AW	98270 TQ	CTBLS	10/01-12/01
Postsecondary	New Haven-Meriden PMSA, CT	Y	36640 FQ	65270 AW	93980 TQ	CTBLS	10/01-12/01
Postsecondary	District of Columbia	Y	33170 FQ	62950 AW	89290 TQ	DCBLS	10/01-12/01
Postsecondary	Washington PMSA, DC-MD-VA-WV	Y	29500 FQ	58260 AW	88700 TQ	DCBLS	10/01-12/01
Postsecondary	Florida	Y	27750 FQ	53200 AW	86350 TQ	FLBLS	10/01-12/01
Postsecondary	Fort Lauderdale PMSA, FL	Y	18950 FQ	56840 AW	93970 TQ	FLBLS	10/01-12/01
Postsecondary	Gainesville MSA, FL	Y	37270 FQ	59240 AW	93960 TQ	FLBLS	10/01-12/01
Postsecondary	Jacksonville MSA, FL	Y	34960 FQ	56570 AW	89580 TQ	FLBLS	10/01-12/01
Postsecondary	Miami PMSA, FL	Y	38280 FQ	61150 AW	101200 TQ	FLBLS	10/01-12/01

AAW Average annual wage **AOH** Average offered, high **ASH** Average starting, high **H** Hourly **M** Monthly **S** Special: hourly and annual
AE Average entry wage **AOL** Average offered, low **ASL** Average starting, low **HI** Highest wage paid **MTC** Median total compensation **TQ** Third quartile wage
AEX Average experienced wage **APH** Average pay, high range **AW** Average wage paid **HR** High end range **MW** Median wage paid **W** Weekly
AO Average offered **APL** Average pay, low range **FQ** First quartile wage **LR** Low end range **SQ** Second quartile wage **Y** Yearly

Occupation/Type/Industry	Location	Per	Low	Mid	High	Source	Date
Art, Drama, and Music Teacher							
Postsecondary	Orlando MSA, FL	Y	25580 FQ	49750 AW	84830 TQ	FLBLS	10/01-12/01
Postsecondary	Tallahassee MSA, FL	Y	39790 FQ	62940 AW	95970 TQ	FLBLS	10/01-12/01
Postsecondary	Tampa-St. Petersburg-Clearwater MSA, FL	Y	28360 FQ	48860 AW	79080 TQ	FLBLS	10/01-12/01
Postsecondary	West Palm Beach-Boca Raton MSA, FL	Y	29330 FQ	51640 AW	75860 TQ	FLBLS	10/01-12/01
Postsecondary	Georgia	Y	21910 FQ	48060 AW	73670 TQ	GABLS	10/01-12/01
Postsecondary	Atlanta MSA, GA	Y	22860 FQ	49580 AW	72150 TQ	GABLS	10/01-12/01
Postsecondary	Savannah MSA, GA	Y	13470 FQ	39250 AW	58740 TQ	GABLS	10/01-12/01
Postsecondary	Hawaii	Y	33020 FQ	50350 AW	72160 TQ	HIBLS	10/01-12/01
Postsecondary	Honolulu MSA, HI	Y	32670 FQ	51120 AW	73800 TQ	HIBLS	10/01-12/01
Postsecondary	Idaho	Y	39440 FQ	49510 AW	58700 TQ	IDBLS	10/01-12/01
Postsecondary	Illinois	Y	13510 FQ	52300 AW	90520 TQ	ILBLS	10/01-12/01
Postsecondary	Champaign-Urbana MSA, IL	Y	24080 FQ	55960 AW	89410 TQ	ILBLS	10/01-12/01
Postsecondary	Chicago PMSA, IL	Y	13070 FQ	53980 AW	91940 TQ	ILBLS	10/01-12/01
Postsecondary	Rockford MSA, IL	Y	12590 FQ	36310 AW	59510 TQ	ILBLS	10/01-12/01
Postsecondary	Springfield MSA, IL	Y	12140 FQ	47850 AW	89430 TQ	ILBLS	10/01-12/01
Postsecondary	Indiana	Y	28270 FQ	47670 AW	71730 TQ	INBLS	10/01-12/01
Postsecondary	Lafayette MSA, IN	Y	23480 FQ	46640 AW	75320 TQ	INBLS	10/01-12/01
Postsecondary	South Bend MSA, IN	Y	38550 FQ	51520 AW	71720 TQ	INBLS	10/01-12/01
Postsecondary	Iowa	Y	28460 FQ	57270 AW	115180 TQ	IABLS	10/01-12/01
Postsecondary	Cedar Rapids MSA, IA	Y	22410 FQ	41710 AW	61850 TQ	IABLS	10/01-12/01
Postsecondary	Des Moines MSA, IA	Y	31640 FQ	53890 AW	88540 TQ	IABLS	10/01-12/01
Postsecondary	Kansas	Y	16900 FQ	33880 AW	51480 TQ	KSBLS	10/01-12/01
Postsecondary	Wichita MSA, KS	Y	20710 FQ	34270 AW	48330 TQ	KSBLS	10/01-12/01
Postsecondary	Kentucky	Y	26270 FQ	49740 AW	81620 TQ	KYBLS	10/01-12/01
Postsecondary	Louisville MSA, KY-IN	Y	24890 FQ	48540 AW	79720 TQ	KYBLS	10/01-12/01
Postsecondary	Louisiana	Y	21150 FQ	42610 AW	64680 TQ	LABLS	10/01-12/01
Postsecondary	New Orleans MSA, LA	Y	13450 FQ	41210 AW	68210 TQ	LABLS	10/01-12/01
Postsecondary	Maine	Y	30760 FQ	48660 AW	68760 TQ	MEBLS	10/01-12/01
Postsecondary	Maryland	Y	27250 FQ	50410 AW	82800 TQ	MDBLS	10/01-12/01
Postsecondary	Baltimore PMSA, MD	Y	29830 FQ	49300 AW	81630 TQ	MDBLS	10/01-12/01
Postsecondary	Massachusetts	Y	24220 FQ	49660 AW	71880 TQ	MABLS	10/01-12/01
Postsecondary	Boston PMSA, MA-NH	Y	23750 FQ	49870 AW	71900 TQ	MABLS	10/01-12/01
Postsecondary	Springfield MSA, MA	Y	18170 FQ	48530 AW	73470 TQ	MABLS	10/01-12/01
Postsecondary	Worcester PMSA, MA-CT	Y	30450 FQ	50040 AW	78990 TQ	MABLS	10/01-12/01
Postsecondary	Michigan	Y	27830 FQ	51710 AW	80090 TQ	MIBLS	10/01-12/01
Postsecondary	Ann Arbor PMSA, MI	Y	25670 FQ	48960 AW	77630 TQ	MIBLS	10/01-12/01
Postsecondary	Detroit PMSA, MI	Y	28090 FQ	58520 AW	92300 TQ	MIBLS	10/01-12/01
Postsecondary	Flint PMSA, MI	Y	34690 FQ	47150 AW	69470 TQ	MIBLS	10/01-12/01
Postsecondary	Grand Rapids-Muskegon-Holland MSA, MI	Y	26640 FQ	48180 AW	73270 TQ	MIBLS	10/01-12/01
Postsecondary	Minnesota	Y	28230 FQ	45770 AW	66680 TQ	MNBLS	10/01-12/01
Postsecondary	Duluth-Superior MSA, MN-WI	Y	28150 FQ	45790 AW	67200 TQ	MNBLS	10/01-12/01
Postsecondary	Minneapolis-St. Paul MSA, MN-WI	Y	24640 FQ	45640 AW	68250 TQ	MNBLS	10/01-12/01
Postsecondary	St. Cloud MSA, MN	Y	30520 FQ	45360 AW	57890 TQ	MNBLS	10/01-12/01
Postsecondary	Mississippi	Y	28140 FQ	44150 AW	61120 TQ	MSBLS	10/01-12/01
Postsecondary	Jackson MSA, MS	Y	24250 FQ	37720 AW	51890 TQ	MSBLS	10/01-12/01
Postsecondary	Missouri	Y	24910 FQ	43770 AW	65370 TQ	MOBLS	10/01-12/01
Postsecondary	Kansas City MSA, MO-KS	Y	23410 FQ	42980 AW	65660 TQ	MOBLS	10/01-12/01
Postsecondary	St. Louis MSA, MO-IL	Y	23060 FQ	40720 AW	62640 TQ	MOBLS	10/01-12/01
Postsecondary	Springfield MSA, MO	Y	33710 FQ	50310 AW	71200 TQ	MOBLS	10/01-12/01
Postsecondary	Montana	Y	24350 FQ	48160 AW	75950 TQ	MTBLS	10/01-12/01
Postsecondary	Nebraska	Y	20020 FQ	40960 AW	64930 TQ	NEBLS	10/01-12/01
Postsecondary	Lincoln MSA, NE	Y	16400 FQ	42120 AW	67300 TQ	NEBLS	10/01-12/01
Postsecondary	Omaha MSA, NE-IA	Y	33160 FQ	49160 AW	70430 TQ	NEBLS	10/01-12/01
Postsecondary	Nevada	Y	24990 FQ	47130 AW	74230 TQ	NVBLS	10/01-12/01
Postsecondary	Las Vegas MSA, NV-AZ	Y	26040 FQ	48300 AW	74340 TQ	NVBLS	10/01-12/01
Postsecondary	New Hampshire	Y	31310 FQ	54270 AW	90820 TQ	NHBLS	10/01-12/01
Postsecondary	Manchester PMSA, NH	Y	30820 FQ	49210 AW	81400 TQ	NHBLS	10/01-12/01
Postsecondary	New Jersey	Y	31750 FQ	60740 AW	91690 TQ	NJBLS	10/01-12/01
Postsecondary	Jersey City PMSA, NJ	Y	39410 FQ	66210 AW	97180 TQ	NJBLS	10/01-12/01
Postsecondary	Monmouth-Ocean PMSA, NJ	Y	19560 FQ	52580 AW	86920 TQ	NJBLS	10/01-12/01
Postsecondary	Newark PMSA, NJ	Y	29290 FQ	60710 AW	92180 TQ	NJBLS	10/01-12/01
Postsecondary	Trenton PMSA, NJ	Y	33340 FQ	57020 AW	82610 TQ	NJBLS	10/01-12/01
Postsecondary	New Mexico	Y	20010 FQ	38690 AW	57450 TQ	NMBLS	10/01-12/01
Postsecondary	New York	Y	36300 FQ	64900 AW	122960 TQ	NYBLS	10/01-12/01
Postsecondary	Albany-Schenectady-Troy MSA, NY	Y	36500 FQ	50230 AW	74830 TQ	NYBLS	10/01-12/01
Postsecondary	Nassau-Suffolk PMSA, NY	Y	36340 FQ	60250 AW	91970 TQ	NYBLS	10/01-12/01

AAW	Average annual wage	AOH	Average offered, high	ASH	Average starting, high	H	Hourly	M	Monthly	S	Special: hourly and annual
AE	Average entry wage	AOL	Average offered, low	ASL	Average starting, low	HI	Highest wage paid	MTC	Median total compensation	TQ	Third quartile wage
AEX	Average experienced wage	APH	Average pay, high range	AW	Average wage paid	HR	High end range	MW	Median wage paid	W	Weekly
AO	Average offered	APL	Average pay, low range	FQ	First quartile wage	LR	Low end range	SQ	Second quartile wage	Y	Yearly

Occupation/Type/Industry	Location	Per	Low	Mid	High	Source	Date
Art, Drama, and Music Teacher							
Postsecondary	New York PMSA, NY	Y	40080 FQ	77080 AW		NYBLS	10/01-12/01
Postsecondary	Utica-Rome MSA, NY	Y	27140 FQ	56620 AW	86150 TQ	NYBLS	10/01-12/01
Postsecondary	North Carolina	Y	26620 FQ	44790 AW	66240 TQ	NCBLS	10/01-12/01
Postsecondary	Asheville MSA, NC	Y	26930 FQ	43170 AW	65740 TQ	NCBLS	10/01-12/01
Postsecondary	Charlotte-Gastonia-Rock Hill MSA, NC-SC	Y	25490 FQ	42840 AW	63150 TQ	NCBLS	10/01-12/01
Postsecondary	Fayetteville MSA, NC	Y	32460 FQ	47330 AW	66530 TQ	NCBLS	10/01-12/01
Postsecondary	Greensboro-Winston-Salem-High Point MSA, NC	Y	23710 FQ	41920 AW	60830 TQ	NCBLS	10/01-12/01
Postsecondary	Hickory-Morganton-Lenoir MSA, NC	Y	32040 FQ	41440 AW	54070 TQ	NCBLS	10/01-12/01
Postsecondary	Raleigh-Durham-Chapel Hill MSA, NC	Y	29590 FQ	49790 AW	76530 TQ	NCBLS	10/01-12/01
Postsecondary	Wilmington MSA, NC	Y	26890 FQ	44660 AW	61650 TQ	NCBLS	10/01-12/01
Postsecondary	North Dakota	Y	23980 FQ	37070 AW	52050 TQ	NDBLS	10/01-12/01
Postsecondary	Fargo-Moorhead MSA, ND-MN	Y	25390 FQ	41390 AW	61720 TQ	NDBLS	10/01-12/01
Postsecondary	Ohio	Y	27600 FQ	49150 AW	74480 TQ	OHBLS	10/01-12/01
Postsecondary	Canton-Massillon MSA, OH	Y	29900 FQ	54580 AW	78470 TQ	OHBLS	10/01-12/01
Postsecondary	Cincinnati PMSA, OH-KY-IN	Y	28550 FQ	52510 AW	82590 TQ	OHBLS	10/01-12/01
Postsecondary	Cleveland-Lorain-Elyria PMSA, OH	Y	28250 FQ	51370 AW	81860 TQ	OHBLS	10/01-12/01
Postsecondary	Columbus MSA, OH	Y	25140 FQ	46790 AW	73020 TQ	OHBLS	10/01-12/01
Postsecondary	Dayton-Springfield MSA, OH	Y	32450 FQ	47490 AW	63820 TQ	OHBLS	10/01-12/01
Postsecondary	Toledo MSA, OH	Y	26780 FQ	47990 AW	70320 TQ	OHBLS	10/01-12/01
Postsecondary	Youngstown-Warren MSA, OH	Y	29690 FQ	52250 AW	81880 TQ	OHBLS	10/01-12/01
Postsecondary	Oklahoma	Y	25220 FQ	38200 AW	54980 TQ	OKBLS	10/01-12/01
Postsecondary	Oklahoma City MSA, OK	Y	23930 FQ	36580 AW	56650 TQ	OKBLS	10/01-12/01
Postsecondary	Oregon	Y	33180 FQ	59270 AW	85890 TQ	ORBLS	10/01-12/01
Postsecondary	Eugene-Springfield MSA, OR	Y	32600 FQ	58670 AW	85140 TQ	ORBLS	10/01-12/01
Postsecondary	Portland-Vancouver PMSA, OR-WA	Y	34120 FQ	60770 AW	86410 TQ	ORBLS	10/01-12/01
Postsecondary	Pennsylvania	Y	23910 FQ	56270 AW	91580 TQ	PABLS	10/01-12/01
Postsecondary	Allentown-Bethlehem-Easton MSA, PA	Y	20060 FQ	47060 AW	82870 TQ	PABLS	10/01-12/01
Postsecondary	Harrisburg-Lebanon-Carlisle MSA, PA	Y	23260 FQ	56560 AW	93270 TQ	PABLS	10/01-12/01
Postsecondary	Philadelphia PMSA, PA-NJ	Y	24130 FQ	61600 AW	114040 TQ	PABLS	10/01-12/01
Postsecondary	Pittsburgh MSA, PA	Y	23470 FQ	50760 AW	87420 TQ	PABLS	10/01-12/01
Postsecondary	Reading MSA, PA	Y	26180 FQ	50830 AW	81380 TQ	PABLS	10/01-12/01
Postsecondary	Scranton-Wilkes-Barre-Hazleton MSA, PA	Y	27600 FQ	45820 AW	68810 TQ	PABLS	10/01-12/01
Postsecondary	Rhode Island	Y	31890 FQ	55830 AW	86300 TQ	RIBLS	10/01-12/01
Postsecondary	South Carolina	Y	28170 FQ	48270 AW	73310 TQ	SCBLS	10/01-12/01
Postsecondary	Columbia MSA, SC	Y	29670 FQ	54540 AW	87520 TQ	SCBLS	10/01-12/01
Postsecondary	Greenville-Spartanburg-Anderson MSA, SC	Y	30680 FQ	46860 AW	65690 TQ	SCBLS	10/01-12/01
Postsecondary	South Dakota	Y	29910 FQ	44070 AW	61900 TQ	SDBLS	10/01-12/01
Postsecondary	Tennessee	Y	22240 FQ	43000 AW	67460 TQ	TNBLS	10/01-12/01
Postsecondary	Chattanooga MSA, TN-GA	Y	31400 FQ	44830 AW	58700 TQ	TNBLS	10/01-12/01
Postsecondary	Johnson City-Kingsport-Bristol MSA, TN-VA	Y	24800 FQ	41380 AW	58600 TQ	TNBLS	10/01-12/01
Postsecondary	Knoxville MSA, TN	Y	25050 FQ	43900 AW	65870 TQ	TNBLS	10/01-12/01
Postsecondary	Memphis MSA, TN-AR-MS	Y	12960 FQ	36330 AW	60330 TQ	TNBLS	10/01-12/01
Postsecondary	Nashville MSA, TN	Y	25870 FQ	48460 AW	78260 TQ	TNBLS	10/01-12/01
Postsecondary	Texas	Y	19260 FQ	47140 AW	74150 TQ	TXBLS	10/01-12/01
Postsecondary	Austin-San Marcos MSA, TX	Y	28840 FQ	54600 AW	73560 TQ	TXBLS	10/01-12/01
Postsecondary	Dallas PMSA, TX	Y	19670 FQ	52150 AW	119890 TQ	TXBLS	10/01-12/01
Postsecondary	Fort Worth-Arlington PMSA, TX	Y	16680 FQ	48250 AW	85760 TQ	TXBLS	10/01-12/01
Postsecondary	Houston PMSA, TX	Y	18790 FQ	49630 AW	79140 TQ	TXBLS	10/01-12/01
Postsecondary	Longview-Marshall MSA, TX	Y	13420 FQ	40180 AW	62260 TQ	TXBLS	10/01-12/01
Postsecondary	Odessa-Midland MSA, TX	Y	27560 FQ	46950 AW	71430 TQ	TXBLS	10/01-12/01
Postsecondary	San Antonio MSA, TX	Y	13390 FQ	43560 AW	74120 TQ	TXBLS	10/01-12/01
Postsecondary	Tyler MSA, TX	Y	23160 FQ	37750 AW	54870 TQ	TXBLS	10/01-12/01
Postsecondary	Utah	Y	27530 FQ	51290 AW	78010 TQ	UTBLS	10/01-12/01
Postsecondary	Provo-Orem MSA, UT	Y	17220 FQ	43940 AW	73790 TQ	UTBLS	10/01-12/01
Postsecondary	Salt Lake City-Ogden MSA, UT	Y	31640 FQ	50980 AW	75810 TQ	UTBLS	10/01-12/01
Postsecondary	Vermont	Y	35630 FQ	48120 AW	63900 TQ	VTBLS	10/01-12/01
Postsecondary	Burlington MSA, VT	Y	35710 FQ	48040 AW	67500 TQ	VTBLS	10/01-12/01

AAW	Average annual wage	**AOH**	Average offered, high	**ASH**	Average starting, high	**H**	Hourly	**M**	Monthly	**S**	Special: hourly and annual
AE	Average entry wage	**AOL**	Average offered, low	**ASL**	Average starting, low	**HI**	Highest wage paid	**MTC**	Median total compensation	**TQ**	Third quartile wage
AEX	Average experienced wage	**APH**	Average pay, high range	**AW**	Average wage paid	**HR**	High end range	**MW**	Median wage paid	**W**	Weekly
AO	Average offered	**APL**	Average pay, low range	**FQ**	First quartile wage	**LR**	Low end range	**SQ**	Second quartile wage	**Y**	Yearly

Occupation/Type/Industry	Location	Per	Low	Mid	High	Source	Date
Art, Drama, and Music Teacher							
Postsecondary	Virginia	Y	28270 FQ	48610 AW	70500 TQ	VABLS	10/01-12/01
Postsecondary	Norfolk-Virginia Beach-Newport News MSA, VA-NC	Y	35810 FQ	46990 AW	60400 TQ	VABLS	10/01-12/01
Postsecondary	Richmond-Petersburg MSA, VA	Y	29130 FQ	51580 AW	74530 TQ	VABLS	10/01-12/01
Postsecondary	Roanoke MSA, VA	Y	34320 FQ	48750 AW	67970 TQ	VABLS	10/01-12/01
Postsecondary	Washington	Y	24600 FQ	46630 AW	74770 TQ	WABLS	10/01-12/01
Postsecondary	Bremerton PMSA, WA	Y	17360 FQ	41980 AW	71570 TQ	WABLS	10/01-12/01
Postsecondary	Seattle-Bellevue-Everett PMSA, WA	Y	23130 FQ	48820 AW	79520 TQ	WABLS	10/01-12/01
Postsecondary	Spokane MSA, WA	Y	29460 FQ	41390 AW	56750 TQ	WABLS	10/01-12/01
Postsecondary	Tacoma PMSA, WA	Y	29340 FQ	55110 AW	89970 TQ	WABLS	10/01-12/01
Postsecondary	West Virginia	Y	27480 FQ	52160 AW	75840 TQ	WVBLS	10/01-12/01
Postsecondary	Wisconsin	Y	24060 FQ	42000 AW	63420 TQ	WIBLS	10/01-12/01
Postsecondary	Milwaukee-Waukesha PMSA, WI	Y	28630 FQ	41680 AW	63660 TQ	WIBLS	10/01-12/01
Postsecondary	Wyoming	Y	31390 FQ	45660 AW	63700 TQ	WYBLS	10/01-12/01
Postsecondary	Puerto Rico	Y	25070 FQ	39730 AW	65420 TQ	PRBLS	10/01-12/01
Associate Justice							
State Court	United States	Y		116200 MW		OOH7	1999-2000
Supreme Court of the United States	United States	Y		184400 AW		SCJS	1/1/02
Association Professional							
Mid-Level	United States	Y		44779 AW		AM	1/01-1/02
Astronaut							
NASA	United States	Y	42000 ASL		80000 ASH	AEAC	1/99-1/99
Astronomer	Arizona	Y	34010 FQ	66850 AW	101800 TQ	AZBLS	10/01-12/01
	California	Y	39400 FQ	67130 AW	113190 TQ	CABLS	10/01-12/01
	San Jose PMSA, CA	Y	42820 FQ	77890 AW	118800 TQ	CABLS	10/01-12/01
	Washington PMSA, DC-MD-VA-WV	Y	61010 FQ	87600 AW	112940 TQ	DCBLS	10/01-12/01
	Maryland	Y	71140 FQ	91580 AW	112650 TQ	MDBLS	10/01-12/01
	Massachusetts	Y	73040 FQ	108240 AW	141080 TQ	MABLS	10/01-12/01
	Boston PMSA, MA-NH	Y	73040 FQ	108240 AW	141080 TQ	MABLS	10/01-12/01
	Texas	Y	37520 FQ	84720 AW	122310 TQ	TXBLS	10/01-12/01
	Virginia	Y	39470 FQ	77870 AW	129190 TQ	VABLS	10/01-12/01
Athlete and Sports Competitor	Arizona	Y	27840 FQ	103180 AW		AZBLS	10/01-12/01
	Phoenix-Mesa MSA, AZ	Y	28700 FQ	105470 AW		AZBLS	10/01-12/01
	California	Y	13590 FQ	98350 AW		CABLS	10/01-12/01
	Connecticut	Y	19640 FQ	44530 AW	56750 TQ	CTBLS	10/01-12/01
	Washington PMSA, DC-MD-VA-WV	Y	14120 FQ	94450 AW		DCBLS	10/01-12/01
	Florida	Y	11710 FQ	44030 AW		FLBLS	10/01-12/01
	Georgia	Y	13910 FQ	49610 AW		GABLS	10/01-12/01
	Augusta-Aiken MSA, GA-SC	Y	13130 FQ	35920 AW	99750 TQ	GABLS	10/01-12/01
	Idaho	Y	11780 FQ	30040 AW	64820 TQ	IDBLS	10/01-12/01
	Illinois	Y	12190 FQ	26750 AW	54360 TQ	ILBLS	10/01-12/01
	Iowa	Y	13840 FQ	62260 AW		IABLS	10/01-12/01
	Kansas	Y	22980 FQ	53680 AW	73870 TQ	KSBLS	10/01-12/01
	Kentucky	Y	20360 FQ	32160 AW	44910 TQ	KYBLS	10/01-12/01
	Louisville MSA, KY-IN	Y	20470 FQ	30260 AW	43220 TQ	KYBLS	10/01-12/01
	Maryland	Y	13110 FQ	48750 AW	127110 TQ	MDBLS	10/01-12/01
	Massachusetts	Y	25740 FQ	49520 AW	86260 TQ	MABLS	10/01-12/01
	Boston PMSA, MA-NH	Y	26770 FQ	51990 AW	87490 TQ	MABLS	10/01-12/01
	Springfield MSA, MA	Y	32860 FQ	56860 AW	90400 TQ	MABLS	10/01-12/01
	Michigan	Y	13360 FQ	77360 AW		MIBLS	10/01-12/01
	Detroit PMSA, MI	Y	23110 FQ	86370 AW		MIBLS	10/01-12/01
	Nebraska	Y	12610 FQ	26880 AW	51610 TQ	NEBLS	10/01-12/01
	Nevada	Y	28390 FQ	32860 AW	38100 TQ	NVBLS	10/01-12/01
	Las Vegas MSA, NV-AZ	Y	28390 FQ	32860 AW	38100 TQ	NVBLS	10/01-12/01
	New York	Y	19730 FQ	115930 AW		NYBLS	10/01-12/01
	New York PMSA, NY	Y		142080 AW		NYBLS	10/01-12/01
	Ohio	Y	16660 FQ	32930 AW	63500 TQ	OHBLS	10/01-12/01
	Cincinnati PMSA, OH-KY-IN	Y	16120 FQ	34530 AW	70350 TQ	OHBLS	10/01-12/01
	Cleveland-Lorain-Elyria PMSA, OH	Y	13860 FQ	27210 AW	30120 TQ	OHBLS	10/01-12/01
	Oklahoma	Y	14350 FQ	35260 AW	69150 TQ	OKBLS	10/01-12/01

AAW	Average annual wage	**AOH**	Average offered, high	**ASH**	Average starting, high	**H**	Hourly	**M**	Monthly	**S**	Special: hourly and annual
AE	Average entry wage	**AOL**	Average offered, low	**ASL**	Average starting, low	**HI**	Highest wage paid	**MTC**	Median total compensation	**TQ**	Third quartile wage
AEX	Average experienced wage	**APH**	Average pay, high range	**AW**	Average wage paid	**HR**	High end range	**MW**	Median wage paid	**W**	Weekly
AO	Average offered	**APL**	Average pay, low range	**FQ**	First quartile wage	**LR**	Low end range	**SQ**	Second quartile wage	**Y**	Yearly

Occupation/Type/Industry	Location	Per	Low	Mid	High	Source	Date
Athlete and Sports Competitor	Oregon	Y	14730 FQ	39590 AW		ORBLS	10/01-12/01
	Pennsylvania	Y	23200 FQ	80970 AW		PABLS	10/01-12/01
	Philadelphia PMSA, PA-NJ	Y	24160 FQ	78210 AW		PABLS	10/01-12/01
	Rhode Island	Y	28590 FQ	55080 AW	86420 TQ	RIBLS	10/01-12/01
	Providence-Fall River-Warwick MSA, RI-MA	Y	28550 FQ	55130 AW	86550 TQ	RIBLS	10/01-12/01
	South Carolina	Y	13240 FQ	35910 AW	58590 TQ	SCBLS	10/01-12/01
	Columbia MSA, SC	Y	17950 FQ	32280 AW	55120 TQ	SCBLS	10/01-12/01
	Texas	Y	19400 FQ	69680 AW		TXBLS	10/01-12/01
	Utah	Y	21550 FQ	32500 AW	47680 TQ	UTBLS	10/01-12/01
	Salt Lake City-Ogden MSA, UT	Y	21580 FQ	32410 AW	47470 TQ	UTBLS	10/01-12/01
	Virginia	Y	14110 FQ	93470 AW		VABLS	10/01-12/01
Athletic Trainer	Alabama	Y	15790 FQ	27860 AW	36800 TQ	ALBLS	10/01-12/01
	Arizona	Y	25510 FQ	37780 AW	56090 TQ	AZBLS	10/01-12/01
	Arkansas	Y	16990 FQ	34050 AW	54130 TQ	ARBLS	10/01-12/01
	California	Y	14960 FQ	33340 AW	48100 TQ	CABLS	10/01-12/01
	Colorado	Y	21240 FQ	33960 AW	46790 TQ	COBLS	10/01-12/01
	Connecticut	Y	24300 FQ	34790 AW	45800 TQ	CTBLS	10/01-12/01
	Delaware	Y	31720 FQ	38500 AW	46360 TQ	DEBLS	10/01-12/01
	District of Columbia	Y	23940 FQ	49000 AW	81920 TQ	DCBLS	10/01-12/01
	Florida	Y	24100 FQ	34450 AW	47030 TQ	FLBLS	10/01-12/01
	Georgia	Y	29530 FQ	43150 AW	57800 TQ	GABLS	10/01-12/01
	Hawaii	Y	18880 FQ	35260 AW	44630 TQ	HIBLS	10/01-12/01
	Illinois	Y	12900 FQ	29810 AW	43840 TQ	ILBLS	10/01-12/01
	Indiana	Y	23300 FQ	34200 AW	43990 TQ	INBLS	10/01-12/01
	Iowa	Y	24790 FQ	32970 AW	43150 TQ	IABLS	10/01-12/01
	Kansas	Y	13980 FQ	31910 AW	51090 TQ	KSBLS	10/01-12/01
	Kentucky	Y	18970 FQ	30050 AW	42670 TQ	KYBLS	10/01-12/01
	Louisiana	Y	18660 FQ	31460 AW	41040 TQ	LABLS	10/01-12/01
	Maine	Y	20360 FQ	32420 AW	46140 TQ	MEBLS	10/01-12/01
	Maryland	Y	12590 FQ	29400 AW	45250 TQ	MDBLS	10/01-12/01
	Massachusetts	Y	19690 FQ	30680 AW	44530 TQ	MABLS	10/01-12/01
	Michigan	Y	28450 FQ	39240 AW	50180 TQ	MIBLS	10/01-12/01
	Minnesota	Y	25460 FQ	40040 AW	66920 TQ	MNBLS	10/01-12/01
	Mississippi	Y	17150 FQ	28530 AW	45800 TQ	MSBLS	10/01-12/01
	Missouri	Y	24340 FQ	37570 AW	55840 TQ	MOBLS	10/01-12/01
	Nebraska	Y	24140 FQ	32790 AW	44630 TQ	NEBLS	10/01-12/01
	Nevada	Y	21560 FQ	39480 AW	60550 TQ	NVBLS	10/01-12/01
	New Hampshire	Y	16390 FQ	29060 AW	47730 TQ	NHBLS	10/01-12/01
	New Jersey	Y	30700 FQ	40730 AW	57010 TQ	NJBLS	10/01-12/01
	New Mexico	Y	18840 FQ	31280 AW	43140 TQ	NMBLS	10/01-12/01
	New York	Y	19220 FQ	38100 AW	58440 TQ	NYBLS	10/01-12/01
	North Carolina	Y	18680 FQ	36140 AW	53600 TQ	NCBLS	10/01-12/01
	Ohio	Y	25400 FQ	34800 AW	45450 TQ	OHBLS	10/01-12/01
	Oklahoma	Y	12970 FQ	28210 AW	40780 TQ	OKBLS	10/01-12/01
	Oregon	Y	21390 FQ	36090 AW	51050 TQ	ORBLS	10/01-12/01
	Pennsylvania	Y	17070 FQ	30970 AW	47030 TQ	PABLS	10/01-12/01
	South Carolina	Y	17400 FQ	50050 AW	100310 TQ	SCBLS	10/01-12/01
	South Dakota	Y	22630 FQ	30000 AW	40960 TQ	SDBLS	10/01-12/01
	Tennessee	Y	23150 FQ	33770 AW	47240 TQ	TNBLS	10/01-12/01
	Texas	Y	30720 FQ	43300 AW	57790 TQ	TXBLS	10/01-12/01
	Utah	Y	16370 FQ	35710 AW	55500 TQ	UTBLS	10/01-12/01
	Vermont	Y	22010 FQ	31850 AW	40370 TQ	VTBLS	10/01-12/01
	Virginia	Y	12590 FQ	25710 AW	42530 TQ	VABLS	10/01-12/01
	Washington	Y	24800 FQ	39350 AW	56880 TQ	WABLS	10/01-12/01
	West Virginia	Y	21520 FQ	30940 AW	39660 TQ	WVBLS	10/01-12/01
	Wisconsin	Y	18030 FQ	34930 AW	49740 TQ	WIBLS	10/01-12/01
	Puerto Rico	Y	11870 FQ	19480 AW	27620 TQ	PRBLS	10/01-12/01
Atmospheric and Space Scientist	Alabama	Y	27680 FQ	54630 AW	87010 TQ	ALBLS	10/01-12/01
	Alaska	Y	52220 FQ	76350 AW	103850 TQ	AKBLS	10/01-12/01
	Arizona	Y	41710 FQ	62520 AW	85870 TQ	AZBLS	10/01-12/01
	Arkansas	Y	26020 FQ	55290 AW	95410 TQ	ARBLS	10/01-12/01
	California	Y	38650 FQ	64560 AW	96930 TQ	CABLS	10/01-12/01
	District of Columbia	Y	59270 FQ	87290 AW	117730 TQ	DCBLS	10/01-12/01
	Florida	Y	41230 FQ	68420 AW	97720 TQ	FLBLS	10/01-12/01
	Georgia	Y	30750 FQ	54810 AW	85010 TQ	GABLS	10/01-12/01
	Hawaii	Y	33730 FQ	70630 AW	107520 TQ	HIBLS	10/01-12/01
	Idaho	Y	49070 FQ	67120 AW	86490 TQ	IDBLS	10/01-12/01
	Illinois	Y	25360 FQ	48530 AW	74710 TQ	ILBLS	10/01-12/01
	Indiana	Y	27240 FQ	52340 AW	83260 TQ	INBLS	10/01-12/01

AAW Average annual wage; AE Average entry wage; AEX Average experienced wage; AO Average offered; AOH Average offered, high; AOL Average offered, low; APH Average pay, high range; APL Average pay, low range; ASH Average starting, high; ASL Average starting, low; AW Average wage paid; FQ First quartile wage; H Hourly; HI Highest wage paid; HR High end range; LR Low end range; M Monthly; MTC Median total compensation; MW Median wage paid; SQ Second quartile wage; S Special: hourly and annual; TQ Third quartile wage; W Weekly; Y Yearly

Occupation/Type/Industry	Location	Per	Low	Mid	High	Source	Date
Atmospheric and Space Scientist	Iowa	Y	37730 FQ	63060 AW	87620 TQ	IABLS	10/01-12/01
	Kansas	Y	21530 FQ	52120 AW	79870 TQ	KSBLS	10/01-12/01
	Kentucky	Y	27640 FQ	51950 AW	80520 TQ	KYBLS	10/01-12/01
	Louisiana	Y	30170 FQ	57540 AW	87280 TQ	LABLS	10/01-12/01
	Maine	Y	33100 FQ	56780 AW	80440 TQ	MEBLS	10/01-12/01
	Maryland	Y	36160 FQ	65270 AW	96120 TQ	MDBLS	10/01-12/01
	Massachusetts	Y	31240 FQ	61360 AW	89400 TQ	MABLS	10/01-12/01
	Michigan	Y	30970 FQ	55690 AW	84430 TQ	MIBLS	10/01-12/01
	Minnesota	Y	26660 FQ	55990 AW	85620 TQ	MNBLS	10/01-12/01
	Mississippi	Y	25510 FQ	51280 AW	76690 TQ	MSBLS	10/01-12/01
	Missouri	Y	25530 FQ	54820 AW	84800 TQ	MOBLS	10/01-12/01
	Montana	Y	37610 FQ	59580 AW	74330 TQ	MTBLS	10/01-12/01
	Nebraska	Y	32930 FQ	54120 AW	76150 TQ	NEBLS	10/01-12/01
	Nevada	Y	35740 FQ	64410 AW	87330 TQ	NVBLS	10/01-12/01
	New Jersey	Y	38580 FQ	79790 AW	121030 TQ	NJBLS	10/01-12/01
	New Mexico	Y	45260 FQ	83010 AW	128390 TQ	NMBLS	10/01-12/01
	New York	Y	32800 FQ	61040 AW	93490 TQ	NYBLS	10/01-12/01
	North Carolina	Y	37870 FQ	65250 AW	94610 TQ	NCBLS	10/01-12/01
	North Dakota	Y	22650 FQ	46160 AW	71540 TQ	NDBLS	10/01-12/01
	Ohio	Y	21130 FQ	48400 AW	83000 TQ	OHBLS	10/01-12/01
	Oklahoma	Y	39710 FQ	69850 AW	97650 TQ	OKBLS	10/01-12/01
	Oregon	Y	38710 FQ	67900 AW	89690 TQ	ORBLS	10/01-12/01
	Pennsylvania	Y	28290 FQ	55580 AW	85890 TQ	PABLS	10/01-12/01
	South Carolina	Y	36030 FQ	59390 AW	83250 TQ	SCBLS	10/01-12/01
	South Dakota	Y	34990 FQ	60310 AW	80560 TQ	SDBLS	10/01-12/01
	Tennessee	Y	28780 FQ	58470 AW	87940 TQ	TNBLS	10/01-12/01
	Texas	Y	28920 FQ	51370 AW	80270 TQ	TXBLS	10/01-12/01
	Utah	Y	32140 FQ	65080 AW	100440 TQ	UTBLS	10/01-12/01
	Virginia	Y	33880 FQ	64340 AW	94900 TQ	VABLS	10/01-12/01
	Washington	Y	41090 FQ	65560 AW	90950 TQ	WABLS	10/01-12/01
	West Virginia	Y	32020 FQ	45580 AW	76390 TQ	WVBLS	10/01-12/01
	Wyoming	Y	20560 FQ	46980 AW	74990 TQ	WYBLS	10/01-12/01
Atmospheric, Earth, Marine, and Space Sciences Teacher							
Postsecondary	Alabama	Y	28700 FQ	49300 AW	77530 TQ	ALBLS	10/01-12/01
Postsecondary	Arkansas	Y	20750 FQ	40100 AW	65720 TQ	ARBLS	10/01-12/01
Postsecondary	California	Y	41900 FQ	73320 AW	110360 TQ	CABLS	10/01-12/01
Postsecondary	Colorado	Y	32090 FQ	55420 AW	90330 TQ	COBLS	10/01-12/01
Postsecondary	Connecticut	Y	36770 FQ	68980 AW	107900 TQ	CTBLS	10/01-12/01
Postsecondary	Delaware	Y	40860 FQ	81040 AW	135390 TQ	DEBLS	10/01-12/01
Postsecondary	Florida	Y	33460 FQ	63760 AW	104970 TQ	FLBLS	10/01-12/01
Postsecondary	Georgia	Y	36460 FQ	60220 AW	80440 TQ	GABLS	10/01-12/01
Postsecondary	Hawaii	Y	40650 FQ	75200 AW	115930 TQ	HIBLS	10/01-12/01
Postsecondary	Illinois	Y	20910 FQ	48920 AW	83940 TQ	ILBLS	10/01-12/01
Postsecondary	Indiana	Y	39070 FQ	66760 AW	105880 TQ	INBLS	10/01-12/01
Postsecondary	Iowa	Y	43520 FQ	76720 AW	137580 TQ	IABLS	10/01-12/01
Postsecondary	Kansas	Y	18930 FQ	61710 AW	103910 TQ	KSBLS	10/01-12/01
Postsecondary	Kentucky	Y	39540 FQ	62240 AW	90730 TQ	KYBLS	10/01-12/01
Postsecondary	Louisiana	Y	37740 FQ	58390 AW	95760 TQ	LABLS	10/01-12/01
Postsecondary	Maine	Y	41890 FQ	61990 AW	88380 TQ	MEBLS	10/01-12/01
Postsecondary	Maryland	Y	31110 FQ	78640 AW	137580 TQ	MDBLS	10/01-12/01
Postsecondary	Massachusetts	Y	41450 FQ	72890 AW	114060 TQ	MABLS	10/01-12/01
Postsecondary	Michigan	Y	28220 FQ	59060 AW	94590 TQ	MIBLS	10/01-12/01
Postsecondary	Minnesota	Y	41150 FQ	72370 AW	109450 TQ	MNBLS	10/01-12/01
Postsecondary	Mississippi	Y	28380 FQ	50090 AW	73280 TQ	MSBLS	10/01-12/01
Postsecondary	Missouri	Y	30660 FQ	58690 AW	96320 TQ	MOBLS	10/01-12/01
Postsecondary	New Hampshire	Y	42150 FQ	64620 AW	93820 TQ	NHBLS	10/01-12/01
Postsecondary	New Jersey	Y	40470 FQ	68890 AW	110330 TQ	NJBLS	10/01-12/01
Postsecondary	New Mexico	Y	36260 FQ	52310 AW	74590 TQ	NMBLS	10/01-12/01
Postsecondary	New York	Y	37520 FQ	72790 AW	110150 TQ	NYBLS	10/01-12/01
Postsecondary	North Carolina	Y	35860 FQ	60630 AW	92150 TQ	NCBLS	10/01-12/01
Postsecondary	North Dakota	Y	28450 FQ	52760 AW	84280 TQ	NDBLS	10/01-12/01
Postsecondary	Ohio	Y	27990 FQ	50700 AW	76120 TQ	OHBLS	10/01-12/01
Postsecondary	Oklahoma	Y	28830 FQ	38620 AW	55080 TQ	OKBLS	10/01-12/01
Postsecondary	Oregon	Y	48100 FQ	73950 AW	104140 TQ	ORBLS	10/01-12/01
Postsecondary	Pennsylvania	Y	28530 FQ	62340 AW	98740 TQ	PABLS	10/01-12/01
Postsecondary	Rhode Island	Y	57730 FQ	83890 AW	116340 TQ	RIBLS	10/01-12/01
Postsecondary	South Carolina	Y	38210 FQ	58210 AW	89110 TQ	SCBLS	10/01-12/01
Postsecondary	South Dakota	Y	36580 FQ	57090 AW	85300 TQ	SDBLS	10/01-12/01
Postsecondary	Tennessee	Y	25290 FQ	55760 AW	90290 TQ	TNBLS	10/01-12/01
Postsecondary	Texas	Y	31100 FQ	61610 AW	101950 TQ	TXBLS	10/01-12/01

AAW	Average annual wage	AOH	Average offered, high	ASH	Average starting, high	H	Hourly	M	Monthly	S	Special: hourly and annual
AE	Average entry wage	AOL	Average offered, low	ASL	Average starting, low	HI	Highest wage paid	MTC	Median total compensation	TQ	Third quartile wage
AEX	Average experienced wage	APH	Average pay, high range	AW	Average wage paid	HR	High end range	MW	Median wage paid	W	Weekly
AO	Average offered	APL	Average pay, low range	FQ	First quartile wage	LR	Low end range	SQ	Second quartile wage	Y	Yearly

Occupation/Type/Industry	Location	Per	Low	Mid	High	Source	Date
Atmospheric, Earth, Marine, and Space Sciences Teacher							
Postsecondary	Virginia	Y	32710 FQ	62760 AW	100790 TQ	VABLS	10/01-12/01
Postsecondary	Washington	Y	30440 FQ	66660 AW	114440 TQ	WABLS	10/01-12/01
Audio and Video Equipment Technician	Alabama	Y	15740 FQ	26800 AW	42050 TQ	ALBLS	10/01-12/01
	Alaska	Y	12380 FQ	19290 AW	27970 TQ	AKBLS	10/01-12/01
	Arizona	Y	13200 FQ	26880 AW	48870 TQ	AZBLS	10/01-12/01
	Arkansas	Y	15840 FQ	24240 AW	35410 TQ	ARBLS	10/01-12/01
	California	Y	16720 FQ	41630 AW	74310 TQ	CABLS	10/01-12/01
	Colorado	Y	16940 FQ	30920 AW	47930 TQ	COBLS	10/01-12/01
	Connecticut	Y	19790 FQ	34290 AW	48810 TQ	CTBLS	10/01-12/01
	Delaware	Y	17770 FQ	33840 AW	53230 TQ	DEBLS	10/01-12/01
	District of Columbia	Y	19840 FQ	43660 AW	71500 TQ	DCBLS	10/01-12/01
	Florida	Y	16610 FQ	30760 AW	49590 TQ	FLBLS	10/01-12/01
	Georgia	Y	13480 FQ	25660 AW	38220 TQ	GABLS	10/01-12/01
	Hawaii	Y	18070 FQ	31240 AW	46840 TQ	HIBLS	10/01-12/01
	Idaho	Y	12330 FQ	20890 AW	37710 TQ	IDBLS	10/01-12/01
	Illinois	Y	19270 FQ	35220 AW	57560 TQ	ILBLS	10/01-12/01
	Indiana	Y	18540 FQ	37160 AW	65000 TQ	INBLS	10/01-12/01
	Iowa	Y	12470 FQ	28950 AW	47280 TQ	IABLS	10/01-12/01
	Kansas	Y	13180 FQ	26200 AW	43110 TQ	KSBLS	10/01-12/01
	Kentucky	Y	18960 FQ	32260 AW	48590 TQ	KYBLS	10/01-12/01
	Louisiana	Y	17700 FQ	28030 AW	41830 TQ	LABLS	10/01-12/01
	Maryland	Y	14100 FQ	27520 AW	41960 TQ	MDBLS	10/01-12/01
	Massachusetts	Y	19780 FQ	35380 AW	53530 TQ	MABLS	10/01-12/01
	Michigan	Y	15440 FQ	32100 AW	53400 TQ	MIBLS	10/01-12/01
	Minnesota	Y	20800 FQ	41380 AW	76920 TQ	MNBLS	10/01-12/01
	Mississippi	Y	17500 FQ	30750 AW	59170 TQ	MSBLS	10/01-12/01
	Missouri	Y	19390 FQ	38270 AW	57360 TQ	MOBLS	10/01-12/01
	Montana	Y	13440 FQ	24270 AW	35870 TQ	MTBLS	10/01-12/01
	Nebraska	Y	16230 FQ	29550 AW	50080 TQ	NEBLS	10/01-12/01
	Nevada	Y	22580 FQ	40750 AW	55300 TQ	NVBLS	10/01-12/01
	New Hampshire	Y	16260 FQ	30470 AW	55200 TQ	NHBLS	10/01-12/01
	New Jersey	Y	27920 FQ	65350 AW	116120 TQ	NJBLS	10/01-12/01
	New Mexico	Y	13690 FQ	29910 AW	49960 TQ	NMBLS	10/01-12/01
	New York	Y	18480 FQ	37900 AW	75800 TQ	NYBLS	10/01-12/01
	North Carolina	Y	16940 FQ	28220 AW	42710 TQ	NCBLS	10/01-12/01
	North Dakota	Y	13450 FQ	25890 AW	40380 TQ	NDBLS	10/01-12/01
	Ohio	Y	15150 FQ	28070 AW	44040 TQ	OHBLS	10/01-12/01
	Oklahoma	Y	13330 FQ	25100 AW	38940 TQ	OKBLS	10/01-12/01
	Oregon	Y	18740 FQ	33450 AW	56920 TQ	ORBLS	10/01-12/01
	Pennsylvania	Y	18010 FQ	33470 AW	50130 TQ	PABLS	10/01-12/01
	Rhode Island	Y	18820 FQ	31620 AW	48190 TQ	RIBLS	10/01-12/01
	South Carolina	Y	19330 FQ	28230 AW	39190 TQ	SCBLS	10/01-12/01
	Tennessee	Y	18960 FQ	33480 AW	56240 TQ	TNBLS	10/01-12/01
	Texas	Y	14340 FQ	30290 AW	45030 TQ	TXBLS	10/01-12/01
	Utah	Y	19010 FQ	24940 AW	29850 TQ	UTBLS	10/01-12/01
	Vermont	Y	19730 FQ	27020 AW	34580 TQ	VTBLS	10/01-12/01
	Virginia	Y	18630 FQ	35050 AW	55780 TQ	VABLS	10/01-12/01
	Washington	Y	21060 FQ	39620 AW	58340 TQ	WABLS	10/01-12/01
	West Virginia	Y	12310 FQ	25960 AW	41020 TQ	WVBLS	10/01-12/01
	Wisconsin	Y	14720 FQ	29550 AW	55160 TQ	WIBLS	10/01-12/01
	Puerto Rico	Y	12130 FQ	18570 AW	26830 TQ	PRBLS	10/01-12/01
Audio-Visual Collections Specialist	Alabama	Y	15220 FQ	29260 AW	42720 TQ	ALBLS	10/01-12/01
	Arizona	Y	13130 FQ	43830 AW	84170 TQ	AZBLS	10/01-12/01
	Colorado	Y	19830 FQ	32850 AW	52370 TQ	COBLS	10/01-12/01
	Connecticut	Y	24580 FQ	38140 AW	58020 TQ	CTBLS	10/01-12/01
	District of Columbia	Y	16680 FQ	36240 AW	60310 TQ	DCBLS	10/01-12/01
	Florida	Y	30280 FQ	47520 AW	67920 TQ	FLBLS	10/01-12/01
	Georgia	Y	12610 FQ	24860 AW	38130 TQ	GABLS	10/01-12/01
	Hawaii	Y	16810 FQ	33280 AW	56530 TQ	HIBLS	10/01-12/01
	Idaho	Y	27160 FQ	41600 AW	54940 TQ	IDBLS	10/01-12/01
	Illinois	Y	13300 FQ	27970 AW	46640 TQ	ILBLS	10/01-12/01
	Indiana	Y	20560 FQ	39140 AW	58310 TQ	INBLS	10/01-12/01
	Iowa	Y	17540 FQ	29930 AW	52300 TQ	IABLS	10/01-12/01
	Kansas	Y	12410 FQ	28880 AW	54380 TQ	KSBLS	10/01-12/01
	Kentucky	Y	18610 FQ	35700 AW	55200 TQ	KYBLS	10/01-12/01
	Louisiana	Y	16670 FQ	31220 AW	51780 TQ	LABLS	10/01-12/01

AAW	Average annual wage	**AOH**	Average offered, high	**ASH**	Average starting, high	**H**	Hourly	**M**	Monthly
AE	Average entry wage	**AOL**	Average offered, low	**ASL**	Average starting, low	**HI**	Highest wage paid	**MTC**	Median total compensation
AEX	Average experienced wage	**APH**	Average pay, high range	**AW**	Average wage paid	**HR**	High end range	**MW**	Median wage paid
AO	Average offered	**APL**	Average pay, low range	**FQ**	First quartile wage	**LR**	Low end range	**SQ**	Second quartile wage

S Special: hourly and annual
TQ Third quartile wage
W Weekly
Y Yearly

Occupation/Type/Industry	Location	Per	Low	Mid	High	Source	Date
Audio-Visual Collections Specialist	Maryland	Y	23330 FQ	43520 AW	67850 TQ	MDBLS	10/01-12/01
	Massachusetts	Y	21560 FQ	40460 AW	59140 TQ	MABLS	10/01-12/01
	Michigan	Y	11410 FQ	28200 AW	61640 TQ	MIBLS	10/01-12/01
	Minnesota	Y	31710 FQ	46030 AW	62300 TQ	MNBLS	10/01-12/01
	Missouri	Y	21120 FQ	37890 AW	61730 TQ	MOBLS	10/01-12/01
	Nebraska	Y	13550 FQ	24990 AW	40190 TQ	NEBLS	10/01-12/01
	New Jersey	Y	18740 FQ	31930 AW	51470 TQ	NJBLS	10/01-12/01
	New Mexico	Y	21970 FQ	31320 AW	42940 TQ	NMBLS	10/01-12/01
	New York	Y	19260 FQ	38610 AW	63290 TQ	NYBLS	10/01-12/01
	North Carolina	Y	18900 FQ	33660 AW	46820 TQ	NCBLS	10/01-12/01
	Ohio	Y	15750 FQ	25260 AW	40120 TQ	OHBLS	10/01-12/01
	Oklahoma	Y	14220 FQ	31090 AW	49100 TQ	OKBLS	10/01-12/01
	Oregon	Y	23770 FQ	30630 AW	39460 TQ	ORBLS	10/01-12/01
	Pennsylvania	Y	20110 FQ	34250 AW	57070 TQ	PABLS	10/01-12/01
	South Carolina	Y	14730 FQ	26430 AW	45870 TQ	SCBLS	10/01-12/01
	Tennessee	Y	16600 FQ	32290 AW	48090 TQ	TNBLS	10/01-12/01
	Texas	Y	15700 FQ	26580 AW	44410 TQ	TXBLS	10/01-12/01
	Utah	Y	17460 FQ	44130 AW	72830 TQ	UTBLS	10/01-12/01
	Vermont	Y	19450 FQ	25970 AW	30210 TQ	VTBLS	10/01-12/01
	Virginia	Y	12680 FQ	25690 AW	44530 TQ	VABLS	10/01-12/01
	Washington	Y	14340 FQ	23370 AW	35120 TQ	WABLS	10/01-12/01
	Wisconsin	Y	11850 FQ	26450 AW	56420 TQ	WIBLS	10/01-12/01
	Puerto Rico	Y	15140 FQ	20030 AW	26550 TQ	PRBLS	10/01-12/01
Audiologist	United States	Y		39700 AW		FREEP1	1/00-1/00
	Alabama	Y	28850 FQ	41810 AW	65200 TQ	ALBLS	10/01-12/01
	Alaska	Y	39860 FQ	55530 AW	89050 TQ	AKBLS	10/01-12/01
	Arizona	Y	25300 FQ	41530 AW	64210 TQ	AZBLS	10/01-12/01
	Arkansas	Y	34940 FQ	47060 AW	57170 TQ	ARBLS	10/01-12/01
	California	Y	37200 FQ	54470 AW	72180 TQ	CABLS	10/01-12/01
	Colorado	Y	34770 FQ	43910 AW	55620 TQ	COBLS	10/01-12/01
	Connecticut	Y	28660 FQ	51100 AW	71430 TQ	CTBLS	10/01-12/01
	District of Columbia	Y	31310 FQ	41580 AW	56540 TQ	DCBLS	10/01-12/01
	Florida	Y	30630 FQ	45680 AW	72430 TQ	FLBLS	10/01-12/01
	Georgia	Y	33610 FQ	49330 AW	64630 TQ	GABLS	10/01-12/01
	Hawaii	Y	40390 FQ	50940 AW	63970 TQ	HIBLS	10/01-12/01
	Illinois	Y	32930 FQ	48850 AW	67720 TQ	ILBLS	10/01-12/01
	Indiana	Y	35870 FQ	45300 AW	56760 TQ	INBLS	10/01-12/01
	Iowa	Y	31610 FQ	46380 AW	65160 TQ	IABLS	10/01-12/01
	Kansas	Y	30740 FQ	42390 AW	57350 TQ	KSBLS	10/01-12/01
	Kentucky	Y	31330 FQ	44580 AW	57690 TQ	KYBLS	10/01-12/01
	Louisiana	Y	27980 FQ	47880 AW	73770 TQ	LABLS	10/01-12/01
	Maryland	Y	21120 FQ	53120 AW	126180 TQ	MDBLS	10/01-12/01
	Massachusetts	Y	37760 FQ	53950 AW	69890 TQ	MABLS	10/01-12/01
	Michigan	Y	32580 FQ	53110 AW	72530 TQ	MIBLS	10/01-12/01
	Minnesota	Y	26870 FQ	45510 AW	64080 TQ	MNBLS	10/01-12/01
	Mississippi	Y	28690 FQ	41740 AW	55520 TQ	MSBLS	10/01-12/01
	Missouri	Y	34210 FQ	48710 AW	68360 TQ	MOBLS	10/01-12/01
	Nebraska	Y	28090 FQ	39420 AW	48590 TQ	NEBLS	10/01-12/01
	New Hampshire	Y	41180 FQ	51110 AW	59170 TQ	NHBLS	10/01-12/01
	New Jersey	Y	27000 FQ	50030 AW	68890 TQ	NJBLS	10/01-12/01
	New Mexico	Y	30550 FQ	44790 AW	56580 TQ	NMBLS	10/01-12/01
	New York	Y	33390 FQ	59680 AW	89150 TQ	NYBLS	10/01-12/01
	North Carolina	Y	37780 FQ	50920 AW	76580 TQ	NCBLS	10/01-12/01
	Ohio	Y	32500 FQ	46320 AW	60490 TQ	OHBLS	10/01-12/01
	Oklahoma	Y	30820 FQ	43710 AW	61250 TQ	OKBLS	10/01-12/01
	Oregon	Y	40530 FQ	59230 AW	125700 TQ	ORBLS	10/01-12/01
	Pennsylvania	Y	31170 FQ	48000 AW	70400 TQ	PABLS	10/01-12/01
	Rhode Island	Y	45750 FQ	50190 AW	55770 TQ	RIBLS	10/01-12/01
	South Carolina	Y	35410 FQ	58470 AW	101480 TQ	SCBLS	10/01-12/01
	South Dakota	Y	34110 FQ	44410 AW	55330 TQ	SDBLS	10/01-12/01
	Tennessee	Y	30790 FQ	41760 AW	54580 TQ	TNBLS	10/01-12/01
	Texas	Y	33440 FQ	49270 AW	69160 TQ	TXBLS	10/01-12/01
	Utah	Y	31560 FQ	46200 AW	63880 TQ	UTBLS	10/01-12/01
	Virginia	Y	30660 FQ	44690 AW	62110 TQ	VABLS	10/01-12/01
	Washington	Y	34270 FQ	46170 AW	58230 TQ	WABLS	10/01-12/01
	Wisconsin	Y	29310 FQ	45990 AW	59320 TQ	WIBLS	10/01-12/01
Audit Executive							
Insurance	United States	Y		112595 AW		WW	1/00-1/01

AAW	Average annual wage	**AOH**	Average offered, high	**ASH**	Average starting, high	**H**	Hourly	**M**	Monthly	**S**	Special: hourly and annual
AE	Average entry wage	**AOL**	Average offered, low	**ASL**	Average starting, low	**HI**	Highest wage paid	**MTC**	Median total compensation	**TQ**	Third quartile wage
AEX	Average experienced wage	**APH**	Average pay, high range	**AW**	Average wage paid	**HR**	High end range	**MW**	Median wage paid	**W**	Weekly
AO	Average offered	**APL**	Average pay, low range	**FQ**	First quartile wage	**LR**	Low end range	**SQ**	Second quartile wage	**Y**	Yearly

Occupation/Type/Industry	Location	Per	Low	Mid	High	Source	Date
Auditor							
Quality Control	United States	Y			108000 HI	ASQ	1/00-1/01
Automotive Body and Related Repairer	Alabama	H	7.51 FQ	12.76 AW	20.34 TQ	ALBLS	10/01-12/01
	Birmingham MSA, AL	H	7.31 FQ	10.62 AW	16.63 TQ	ALBLS	10/01-12/01
	Huntsville MSA, AL	H	9.70 FQ	15.40 AW	17.87 TQ	ALBLS	10/01-12/01
	Mobile MSA, AL	H	9.45 FQ	16.74 AW	25.72 TQ	ALBLS	10/01-12/01
	Montgomery MSA, AL	H	8.67 FQ	13.77 AW	22.22 TQ	ALBLS	10/01-12/01
	Alaska	H	12.18 FQ	21.03 AW	29.61 TQ	AKBLS	10/01-12/01
	Anchorage MSA, AK	H	11.70 FQ	21.18 AW	37.75 TQ	AKBLS	10/01-12/01
	Arizona	H	8.48 FQ	18.24 AW	31.72 TQ	AZBLS	10/01-12/01
	Phoenix-Mesa MSA, AZ	H	8.28 FQ	18.62 AW	32.62 TQ	AZBLS	10/01-12/01
	Tucson MSA, AZ	H	8.15 FQ	17.19 AW	31.08 TQ	AZBLS	10/01-12/01
	Arkansas	H	7.71 FQ	14.24 AW	21.09 TQ	ARBLS	10/01-12/01
	Fayetteville-Springdale-Rogers MSA, AR	H	9.25 FQ	12.79 AW	19.52 TQ	ARBLS	10/01-12/01
	Fort Smith MSA, AR-OK	H	9.39 FQ	13.49 AW	18.29 TQ	ARBLS	10/01-12/01
	Little Rock-North Little Rock MSA, AR	H	6.14 FQ	14.10 AW	29.60 TQ	ARBLS	10/01-12/01
	California	H	8.19 FQ	17.05 AW	27.14 TQ	CABLS	10/01-12/01
	Bakersfield MSA, CA	H	7.97 FQ	14.51 AW	23.52 TQ	CABLS	10/01-12/01
	Chico-Paradise MSA, CA	H	11.16 FQ	15.98 AW	25.46 TQ	CABLS	10/01-12/01
	Fresno MSA, CA	H	8.23 FQ	11.98 AW	17.78 TQ	CABLS	10/01-12/01
	Los Angeles-Long Beach PMSA, CA	H	7.76 FQ	15.09 AW	25.75 TQ	CABLS	10/01-12/01
	Merced MSA, CA	H	6.93 FQ	14.58 AW	21.96 TQ	CABLS	10/01-12/01
	Modesto MSA, CA	H	8.03 FQ	18.50 AW	27.22 TQ	CABLS	10/01-12/01
	Oakland PMSA, CA	H	9.08 FQ	20.20 AW	29.32 TQ	CABLS	10/01-12/01
	Orange County PMSA, CA	H	8.39 FQ	19.08 AW	29.12 TQ	CABLS	10/01-12/01
	Redding MSA, CA	H	8.84 FQ	16.22 AW	23.06 TQ	CABLS	10/01-12/01
	Riverside-San Bernardino PMSA, CA	H	7.61 FQ	12.80 AW	20.20 TQ	CABLS	10/01-12/01
	Sacramento PMSA, CA	H	8.42 FQ	20.05 AW	33.02 TQ	CABLS	10/01-12/01
	Salinas MSA, CA	H	11.29 FQ	19.69 AW	26.40 TQ	CABLS	10/01-12/01
	San Diego MSA, CA	H	9.93 FQ	19.37 AW	33.36 TQ	CABLS	10/01-12/01
	San Francisco PMSA, CA	H	8.35 FQ	17.88 AW	26.68 TQ	CABLS	10/01-12/01
	San Jose PMSA, CA	H	7.60 FQ	17.14 AW	27.07 TQ	CABLS	10/01-12/01
	San Luis Obispo-Atascadero-Paso Robles MSA, CA	H	9.61 FQ	14.69 AW	21.95 TQ	CABLS	10/01-12/01
	Santa Barbara-Santa Maria-Lompoc MSA, CA	H	12.13 FQ	22.36 AW	34.36 TQ	CABLS	10/01-12/01
	Santa Cruz-Watsonville PMSA, CA	H	10.96 FQ	19.19 AW	27.13 TQ	CABLS	10/01-12/01
	Santa Rosa PMSA, CA	H	14.11 FQ	21.95 AW	28.37 TQ	CABLS	10/01-12/01
	Stockton-Lodi MSA, CA	H	8.55 FQ	16.59 AW	24.80 TQ	CABLS	10/01-12/01
	Vallejo-Fairfield-Napa PMSA, CA	H	10.74 FQ	18.61 AW	26.51 TQ	CABLS	10/01-12/01
	Ventura PMSA, CA	H	11.76 FQ	18.50 AW	25.99 TQ	CABLS	10/01-12/01
	Visalia-Tulare-Porterville MSA, CA	H	12.28 FQ	19.39 AW	27.26 TQ	CABLS	10/01-12/01
	Colorado	H	11.40 FQ	21.46 AW	34.06 TQ	COBLS	10/01-12/01
	Boulder-Longmont PMSA, CO	H	9.98 FQ	21.85 AW	40.22 TQ	COBLS	10/01-12/01
	Colorado Springs MSA, CO	H	12.41 FQ	20.27 AW	28.91 TQ	COBLS	10/01-12/01
	Denver PMSA, CO	H	14.73 FQ	24.07 AW	37.88 TQ	COBLS	10/01-12/01
	Fort Collins-Loveland MSA, CO	H	8.96 FQ	18.13 AW	30.38 TQ	COBLS	10/01-12/01
	Greeley PMSA, CO	H	12.85 FQ	20.32 AW	30.15 TQ	COBLS	10/01-12/01
	Connecticut	H	11.69 FQ	18.58 AW	27.15 TQ	CTBLS	10/01-12/01
	Bridgeport PMSA, CT	H	12.31 FQ	18.36 AW	24.49 TQ	CTBLS	10/01-12/01
	Danbury PMSA, CT	H	12.04 FQ	21.95 AW	34.28 TQ	CTBLS	10/01-12/01
	Hartford MSA, CT	H	11.52 FQ	19.36 AW	28.70 TQ	CTBLS	10/01-12/01
	New Haven-Meriden PMSA, CT	H	10.86 FQ	16.37 AW	21.66 TQ	CTBLS	10/01-12/01
	New London-Norwich MSA, CT-RI	H	11.33 FQ	15.93 AW	20.85 TQ	CTBLS	10/01-12/01
	Stamford-Norwalk PMSA, CT	H	14.08 FQ	19.95 AW	27.17 TQ	CTBLS	10/01-12/01
	Waterbury PMSA, CT	H	11.24 FQ	14.91 AW	21.12 TQ	CTBLS	10/01-12/01
	Delaware	H	6.76 FQ	15.31 AW	24.43 TQ	DEBLS	10/01-12/01
	Wilmington-Newark PMSA, DE-MD	H	11.66 FQ	17.06 AW	25.65 TQ	DEBLS	10/01-12/01
	District of Columbia	H	9.31 FQ	15.13 AW	21.85 TQ	DCBLS	10/01-12/01

AAW	Average annual wage	**AOH**	Average offered, high	**ASH**	Average starting, high	**H**	Hourly	**M**	Monthly	**S**	Special: hourly and annual
AE	Average entry wage	**AOL**	Average offered, low	**ASL**	Average starting, low	**HI**	Highest wage paid	**MTC**	Median total compensation	**TQ**	Third quartile wage
AEX	Average experienced wage	**APH**	Average pay, high range	**AW**	Average wage paid	**HR**	High end range	**MW**	Median wage paid	**W**	Weekly
AO	Average offered	**APL**	Average pay, low range	**FQ**	First quartile wage	**LR**	Low end range	**SQ**	Second quartile wage	**Y**	Yearly

Occupation/Type/Industry	Location	Per	Low	Mid	High	Source	Date
Automotive Body and Related Repairer	Washington PMSA, DC-MD-VA-WV	H	10.90 FQ	22.73 AW	37.38 TQ	DCBLS	10/01-12/01
	Florida	H	7.17 FQ	16.22 AW	27.62 TQ	FLBLS	10/01-12/01
	Daytona Beach MSA, FL	H	10.67 FQ	17.64 AW	28.30 TQ	FLBLS	10/01-12/01
	Fort Lauderdale PMSA, FL	H	8.06 FQ	17.37 AW	32.32 TQ	FLBLS	10/01-12/01
	Fort Myers-Cape Coral MSA, FL	H	10.12 FQ	19.25 AW	28.08 TQ	FLBLS	10/01-12/01
	Fort Pierce-Port St. Lucie MSA, FL	H	6.13 FQ	12.76 AW	18.97 TQ	FLBLS	10/01-12/01
	Fort Walton Beach MSA, FL	H	5.86 FQ	12.03 AW	20.51 TQ	FLBLS	10/01-12/01
	Gainesville MSA, FL	H	11.50 FQ	19.89 AW	29.29 TQ	FLBLS	10/01-12/01
	Jacksonville MSA, FL	H	9.76 FQ	17.72 AW	30.22 TQ	FLBLS	10/01-12/01
	Lakeland-Winter Haven MSA, FL	H	9.74 FQ	19.32 AW	29.83 TQ	FLBLS	10/01-12/01
	Melbourne-Titusville-Palm Bay MSA, FL	H	11.93 FQ	16.39 AW	22.09 TQ	FLBLS	10/01-12/01
	Miami PMSA, FL	H	10.45 FQ	15.52 AW	23.07 TQ	FLBLS	10/01-12/01
	Naples MSA, FL	H	12.97 FQ	20.48 AW	31.57 TQ	FLBLS	10/01-12/01
	Ocala MSA, FL	H	6.19 FQ	12.70 AW	20.74 TQ	FLBLS	10/01-12/01
	Orlando MSA, FL	H	6.46 FQ	15.70 AW	29.68 TQ	FLBLS	10/01-12/01
	Pensacola MSA, FL	H	5.61 FQ	13.00 AW	24.92 TQ	FLBLS	10/01-12/01
	Sarasota-Bradenton MSA, FL	H	6.49 FQ	14.65 AW	23.44 TQ	FLBLS	10/01-12/01
	Tallahassee MSA, FL	H	11.94 FQ	17.21 AW	21.94 TQ	FLBLS	10/01-12/01
	Tampa-St. Petersburg-Clearwater MSA, FL	H	8.30 FQ	16.82 AW	26.99 TQ	FLBLS	10/01-12/01
	Georgia	H	8.74 FQ	16.70 AW	29.20 TQ	GABLS	10/01-12/01
	Atlanta MSA, GA	H	9.36 FQ	18.71 AW	32.06 TQ	GABLS	10/01-12/01
	Augusta-Aiken MSA, GA-SC	H	9.79 FQ	16.70 AW	26.68 TQ	GABLS	10/01-12/01
	Columbus MSA, GA-AL	H	7.10 FQ	13.03 AW	21.63 TQ	GABLS	10/01-12/01
	Macon MSA, GA	H	10.26 FQ	16.90 AW	24.88 TQ	GABLS	10/01-12/01
	Savannah MSA, GA	H	9.26 FQ	13.68 AW	20.96 TQ	GABLS	10/01-12/01
	Hawaii	H	10.87 FQ	16.81 AW	24.79 TQ	HIBLS	10/01-12/01
	Honolulu MSA, HI	H	11.12 FQ	17.21 AW	25.17 TQ	HIBLS	10/01-12/01
	Idaho	H	8.77 FQ	15.18 AW	25.60 TQ	IDBLS	10/01-12/01
	Boise City MSA, ID	H	11.84 FQ	16.83 AW	26.11 TQ	IDBLS	10/01-12/01
	Illinois	H	9.75 FQ	19.14 AW	32.34 TQ	ILBLS	10/01-12/01
	Champaign-Urbana MSA, IL	H	9.98 FQ	19.29 AW	29.63 TQ	ILBLS	10/01-12/01
	Chicago PMSA, IL	H	11.69 FQ	21.53 AW	34.25 TQ	ILBLS	10/01-12/01
	Peoria-Pekin MSA, IL	H	7.00 FQ	15.54 AW	26.52 TQ	ILBLS	10/01-12/01
	Rockford MSA, IL	H	8.82 FQ	15.67 AW	22.11 TQ	ILBLS	10/01-12/01
	Springfield MSA, IL	H	9.87 FQ	16.71 AW	25.64 TQ	ILBLS	10/01-12/01
	Indiana	H	9.70 FQ	17.95 AW	27.94 TQ	INBLS	10/01-12/01
	Elkhart-Goshen MSA, IN	H	9.16 FQ	15.66 AW	22.44 TQ	INBLS	10/01-12/01
	Evansville-Henderson MSA, IN-KY	H	7.15 FQ	13.82 AW	20.95 TQ	INBLS	10/01-12/01
	Fort Wayne MSA, IN	H	11.91 FQ	17.70 AW	27.29 TQ	INBLS	10/01-12/01
	Gary PMSA, IN	H	8.70 FQ	16.45 AW	25.23 TQ	INBLS	10/01-12/01
	Indianapolis MSA, IN	H	10.35 FQ	19.83 AW	30.50 TQ	INBLS	10/01-12/01
	Lafayette MSA, IN	H	9.80 FQ	17.64 AW	27.02 TQ	INBLS	10/01-12/01
	South Bend MSA, IN	H	10.42 FQ	17.45 AW	22.97 TQ	INBLS	10/01-12/01
	Iowa	H	8.16 FQ	14.68 AW	21.41 TQ	IABLS	10/01-12/01
	Cedar Rapids MSA, IA	H	9.54 FQ	15.96 AW	23.54 TQ	IABLS	10/01-12/01
	Davenport-Moline-Rock Island MSA, IA-IL	H	9.36 FQ	16.66 AW	24.20 TQ	IABLS	10/01-12/01
	Des Moines MSA, IA	H	10.73 FQ	16.50 AW	22.54 TQ	IABLS	10/01-12/01
	Kansas	H	9.07 FQ	16.20 AW	25.74 TQ	KSBLS	10/01-12/01
	Topeka MSA, KS	H	9.87 FQ	18.91 AW	33.88 TQ	KSBLS	10/01-12/01
	Wichita MSA, KS	H	9.58 FQ	16.54 AW	26.44 TQ	KSBLS	10/01-12/01
	Kentucky	H	7.38 FQ	14.98 AW	22.18 TQ	KYBLS	10/01-12/01
	Lexington MSA, KY	H	9.82 FQ	16.42 AW	21.27 TQ	KYBLS	10/01-12/01
	Louisville MSA, KY-IN	H	10.92 FQ	17.64 AW	24.90 TQ	KYBLS	10/01-12/01
	Louisiana	H	7.37 FQ	13.33 AW	20.63 TQ	LABLS	10/01-12/01
	Baton Rouge MSA, LA	H	7.29 FQ	12.18 AW	22.76 TQ	LABLS	10/01-12/01
	Houma MSA, LA	H	8.39 FQ	14.79 AW	23.15 TQ	LABLS	10/01-12/01
	Lafayette MSA, LA	H	9.05 FQ	14.95 AW	20.27 TQ	LABLS	10/01-12/01
	Lake Charles MSA, LA	H	11.76 FQ	17.69 AW	25.31 TQ	LABLS	10/01-12/01
	New Orleans MSA, LA	H	8.81 FQ	14.07 AW	21.23 TQ	LABLS	10/01-12/01
	Shreveport-Bossier City MSA, LA	H	6.06 FQ	12.25 AW	18.31 TQ	LABLS	10/01-12/01
	Maine	H	9.64 FQ	14.67 AW	19.54 TQ	MEBLS	10/01-12/01
	Portland MSA, ME	H	12.01 FQ	16.39 AW	21.02 TQ	MEBLS	10/01-12/01

AAW	Average annual wage	AOH	Average offered, high	ASH	Average starting, high	H	Hourly	M	Monthly	S	Special: hourly and annual
AE	Average entry wage	AOL	Average offered, low	ASL	Average starting, low	HI	Highest wage paid	MTC	Median total compensation	TQ	Third quartile wage
AEX	Average experienced wage	APH	Average pay, high range	AW	Average wage paid	HR	High end range	MW	Median wage paid	W	Weekly
AO	Average offered	APL	Average pay, low range	FQ	First quartile wage	LR	Low end range	SQ	Second quartile wage	Y	Yearly

Occupation/Type/Industry	Location	Per	Low	Mid	High	Source	Date
Automotive Body and Related Repairer	Maryland	H	9.69 FQ	19.48 AW	33.26 TQ	MDBLS	10/01-12/01
	Baltimore PMSA, MD	H	9.30 FQ	17.40 AW	32.64 TQ	MDBLS	10/01-12/01
	Massachusetts	H	9.54 FQ	16.98 AW	26.65 TQ	MABLS	10/01-12/01
	Boston PMSA, MA-NH	H	9.55 FQ	18.06 AW	30.42 TQ	MABLS	10/01-12/01
	Brockton PMSA, MA	H	11.09 FQ	16.20 AW	21.46 TQ	MABLS	10/01-12/01
	Lawrence PMSA, MA-NH	H	11.97 FQ	17.87 AW	24.41 TQ	MABLS	10/01-12/01
	Lowell PMSA, MA-NH	H	10.84 FQ	15.69 AW	24.82 TQ	MABLS	10/01-12/01
	New Bedford PMSA, MA	H	9.32 FQ	15.13 AW	20.67 TQ	MABLS	10/01-12/01
	Springfield MSA, MA	H	9.06 FQ	16.24 AW	21.03 TQ	MABLS	10/01-12/01
	Worcester PMSA, MA-CT	H	10.07 FQ	16.39 AW	22.18 TQ	MABLS	10/01-12/01
	Michigan	H	7.91 FQ	17.54 AW	28.11 TQ	MIBLS	10/01-12/01
	Ann Arbor PMSA, MI	H	7.67 FQ	23.92 AW	43.87 TQ	MIBLS	10/01-12/01
	Detroit PMSA, MI	H	7.60 FQ	17.26 AW	28.85 TQ	MIBLS	10/01-12/01
	Flint PMSA, MI	H	9.85 FQ	20.09 AW	27.48 TQ	MIBLS	10/01-12/01
	Grand Rapids-Muskegon-Holland MSA, MI	H	9.30 FQ	19.00 AW	27.51 TQ	MIBLS	10/01-12/01
	Kalamazoo-Battle Creek MSA, MI	H	11.87 FQ	15.46 AW	20.57 TQ	MIBLS	10/01-12/01
	Lansing-East Lansing MSA, MI	H	9.92 FQ	16.37 AW	26.77 TQ	MIBLS	10/01-12/01
	Saginaw-Bay City-Midland MSA, MI	H	8.48 FQ	15.07 AW	24.54 TQ	MIBLS	10/01-12/01
	Minnesota	H	11.51 FQ	20.80 AW	32.36 TQ	MNBLS	10/01-12/01
	Duluth-Superior MSA, MN-WI	H	6.44 FQ	14.31 AW	23.69 TQ	MNBLS	10/01-12/01
	Minneapolis-St. Paul MSA, MN-WI	H	11.23 FQ	22.83 AW	37.33 TQ	MNBLS	10/01-12/01
	St. Cloud MSA, MN	H	11.28 FQ	14.36 AW	17.44 TQ	MNBLS	10/01-12/01
	Mississippi	H	7.57 FQ	13.42 AW	18.41 TQ	MSBLS	10/01-12/01
	Biloxi-Gulfport-Pascagoula MSA, MS	H	11.42 FQ	16.18 AW	19.34 TQ	MSBLS	10/01-12/01
	Jackson MSA, MS	H	7.87 FQ	14.80 AW	21.07 TQ	MSBLS	10/01-12/01
	Missouri	H	9.64 FQ	17.91 AW	27.76 TQ	MOBLS	10/01-12/01
	Kansas City MSA, MO-KS	H	11.68 FQ	18.21 AW	26.67 TQ	MOBLS	10/01-12/01
	St. Louis MSA, MO-IL	H	11.68 FQ	20.82 AW	32.24 TQ	MOBLS	10/01-12/01
	Springfield MSA, MO	H	8.93 FQ	13.01 AW	21.14 TQ	MOBLS	10/01-12/01
	Montana	H	9.20 FQ	13.73 AW	19.55 TQ	MTBLS	10/01-12/01
	Billings MSA, MT	H	8.29 FQ	15.56 AW	22.21 TQ	MTBLS	10/01-12/01
	Nebraska	H	8.35 FQ	16.71 AW	25.44 TQ	NEBLS	10/01-12/01
	Lincoln MSA, NE	H	11.05 FQ	18.15 AW	25.79 TQ	NEBLS	10/01-12/01
	Omaha MSA, NE-IA	H	11.35 FQ	16.69 AW	25.05 TQ	NEBLS	10/01-12/01
	Nevada	H	10.75 FQ	19.26 AW	30.75 TQ	NVBLS	10/01-12/01
	Las Vegas MSA, NV-AZ	H	10.67 FQ	18.78 AW	29.95 TQ	NVBLS	10/01-12/01
	Reno MSA, NV	H	9.35 FQ	20.20 AW	37.38 TQ	NVBLS	10/01-12/01
	New Hampshire	H	10.09 FQ	15.75 AW	20.98 TQ	NHBLS	10/01-12/01
	Manchester PMSA, NH	H	9.83 FQ	14.02 AW	18.22 TQ	NHBLS	10/01-12/01
	Nashua PMSA, NH	H	6.76 FQ	16.09 AW	26.32 TQ	NHBLS	10/01-12/01
	Portsmouth-Rochester PMSA, NH-ME	H	13.89 FQ	18.22 AW	21.28 TQ	NHBLS	10/01-12/01
	New Jersey	H	11.63 FQ	18.51 AW	26.65 TQ	NJBLS	10/01-12/01
	Atlantic-Cape May PMSA, NJ	H	9.37 FQ	15.09 AW	23.32 TQ	NJBLS	10/01-12/01
	Bergen-Passaic PMSA, NJ	H	13.34 FQ	19.11 AW	25.69 TQ	NJBLS	10/01-12/01
	Jersey City PMSA, NJ	H	11.93 FQ	19.24 AW	26.65 TQ	NJBLS	10/01-12/01
	Middlesex-Somerset-Hunterdon PMSA, NJ	H	11.79 FQ	17.23 AW	22.99 TQ	NJBLS	10/01-12/01
	Monmouth-Ocean PMSA, NJ	H	11.15 FQ	21.20 AW	33.62 TQ	NJBLS	10/01-12/01
	Newark PMSA, NJ	H	11.41 FQ	16.68 AW	22.15 TQ	NJBLS	10/01-12/01
	Trenton PMSA, NJ	H	12.70 FQ	17.83 AW	22.80 TQ	NJBLS	10/01-12/01
	New Mexico	H	12.19 FQ	17.68 AW	26.66 TQ	NMBLS	10/01-12/01
	Albuquerque MSA, NM	H	10.85 FQ	16.14 AW	22.50 TQ	NMBLS	10/01-12/01
	New York	H	8.64 FQ	15.07 AW	22.84 TQ	NYBLS	10/01-12/01
	Albany-Schenectady-Troy MSA, NY	H	11.77 FQ	17.65 AW	21.91 TQ	NYBLS	10/01-12/01
	Binghamton MSA, NY	H	9.04 FQ	12.41 AW	17.49 TQ	NYBLS	10/01-12/01
	Buffalo-Niagara Falls MSA, NY	H	7.15 FQ	14.39 AW	20.67 TQ	NYBLS	10/01-12/01
	Dutchess County PMSA, NY	H	12.18 FQ	18.03 AW	23.30 TQ	NYBLS	10/01-12/01
	Nassau-Suffolk PMSA, NY	H	8.32 FQ	16.94 AW	25.66 TQ	NYBLS	10/01-12/01
	New York PMSA, NY	H	8.98 FQ	15.00 AW	24.68 TQ	NYBLS	10/01-12/01
	Newburgh PMSA, NY-PA	H	9.99 FQ	16.10 AW	21.64 TQ	NYBLS	10/01-12/01
	Rochester MSA, NY	H	10.88 FQ	16.49 AW	24.03 TQ	NYBLS	10/01-12/01
	Syracuse MSA, NY	H	8.69 FQ	12.69 AW	17.34 TQ	NYBLS	10/01-12/01
	Utica-Rome MSA, NY	H	7.51 FQ	12.93 AW	23.63 TQ	NYBLS	10/01-12/01

AAW	Average annual wage	**AOH**	Average offered, high	**ASH**	Average starting, high	**H**	Hourly	**M**	Monthly	**S**	Special: hourly and annual
AE	Average entry wage	**AOL**	Average offered, low	**ASL**	Average starting, low	**HI**	Highest wage paid	**MTC**	Median total compensation	**TQ**	Third quartile wage
AEX	Average experienced wage	**APH**	Average pay, high range	**AW**	Average wage paid	**HR**	High end range	**MW**	Median wage paid	**W**	Weekly
AO	Average offered	**APL**	Average pay, low range	**FQ**	First quartile wage	**LR**	Low end range	**SQ**	Second quartile wage	**Y**	Yearly

Occupation/Type/Industry	Location	Per	Low	Mid	High	Source	Date
Automotive Body and Related Repairer	North Carolina	H	8.87 FQ	17.43 AW	28.17 TQ	NCBLS	10/01-12/01
	Asheville MSA, NC	H	13.37 FQ	16.54 AW	18.28 TQ	NCBLS	10/01-12/01
	Charlotte-Gastonia-Rock Hill MSA, NC-SC	H	11.72 FQ	18.34 AW	27.48 TQ	NCBLS	10/01-12/01
	Fayetteville MSA, NC	H	9.02 FQ	14.63 AW	20.82 TQ	NCBLS	10/01-12/01
	Greensboro-Winston-Salem-High Point MSA, NC	H	7.81 FQ	18.21 AW	31.59 TQ	NCBLS	10/01-12/01
	Hickory-Morganton-Lenoir MSA, NC	H	9.38 FQ	16.16 AW	21.59 TQ	NCBLS	10/01-12/01
	Raleigh-Durham-Chapel Hill MSA, NC	H	9.29 FQ	16.98 AW	30.21 TQ	NCBLS	10/01-12/01
	Wilmington MSA, NC	H	9.29 FQ	12.18 AW	16.21 TQ	NCBLS	10/01-12/01
	North Dakota	H	8.47 FQ	14.48 AW	21.37 TQ	NDBLS	10/01-12/01
	Fargo-Moorhead MSA, ND-MN	H	9.55 FQ	16.24 AW	24.66 TQ	NDBLS	10/01-12/01
	Ohio	H	9.93 FQ	17.18 AW	26.29 TQ	OHBLS	10/01-12/01
	Akron PMSA, OH	H	11.63 FQ	17.42 AW	25.89 TQ	OHBLS	10/01-12/01
	Canton-Massillon MSA, OH	H	8.01 FQ	14.68 AW	25.05 TQ	OHBLS	10/01-12/01
	Cincinnati PMSA, OH-KY-IN	H	7.41 FQ	14.97 AW	23.92 TQ	OHBLS	10/01-12/01
	Cleveland-Lorain-Elyria PMSA, OH	H	12.99 FQ	21.18 AW	27.35 TQ	OHBLS	10/01-12/01
	Columbus MSA, OH	H	11.01 FQ	18.67 AW	27.54 TQ	OHBLS	10/01-12/01
	Dayton-Springfield MSA, OH	H	10.47 FQ	17.42 AW	27.83 TQ	OHBLS	10/01-12/01
	Hamilton-Middletown PMSA, OH	H	11.83 FQ	16.87 AW	25.85 TQ	OHBLS	10/01-12/01
	Mansfield MSA, OH	H	9.91 FQ	13.97 AW	17.87 TQ	OHBLS	10/01-12/01
	Toledo MSA, OH	H	9.17 FQ	17.30 AW	26.89 TQ	OHBLS	10/01-12/01
	Youngstown-Warren MSA, OH	H	8.30 FQ	12.84 AW	17.43 TQ	OHBLS	10/01-12/01
	Oklahoma	H	9.26 FQ	14.89 AW	21.80 TQ	OKBLS	10/01-12/01
	Oklahoma City MSA, OK	H	9.64 FQ	14.85 AW	20.62 TQ	OKBLS	10/01-12/01
	Tulsa MSA, OK	H	11.15 FQ	14.75 AW	19.17 TQ	OKBLS	10/01-12/01
	Oregon	H	9.20 FQ	16.92 AW	26.85 TQ	ORBLS	10/01-12/01
	Eugene-Springfield MSA, OR	H	9.70 FQ	18.77 AW	27.44 TQ	ORBLS	10/01-12/01
	Medford-Ashland MSA, OR	H	14.00 FQ	19.34 AW	26.10 TQ	ORBLS	10/01-12/01
	Portland-Vancouver PMSA, OR-WA	H	10.03 FQ	18.11 AW	27.95 TQ	ORBLS	10/01-12/01
	Salem PMSA, OR	H	9.71 FQ	16.18 AW	25.49 TQ	ORBLS	10/01-12/01
	Pennsylvania	H	9.13 FQ	15.26 AW	22.94 TQ	PABLS	10/01-12/01
	Allentown-Bethlehem-Easton MSA, PA	H	9.80 FQ	15.42 AW	20.20 TQ	PABLS	10/01-12/01
	Erie MSA, PA	H	8.56 FQ	16.69 AW	25.18 TQ	PABLS	10/01-12/01
	Harrisburg-Lebanon-Carlisle MSA, PA	H	10.61 FQ	16.14 AW	23.94 TQ	PABLS	10/01-12/01
	Johnstown MSA, PA	H	8.60 FQ	12.80 AW	19.22 TQ	PABLS	10/01-12/01
	Lancaster MSA, PA	H	9.72 FQ	15.26 AW	22.18 TQ	PABLS	10/01-12/01
	Philadelphia PMSA, PA-NJ	H	10.60 FQ	18.55 AW	26.51 TQ	PABLS	10/01-12/01
	Pittsburgh MSA, PA	H	9.33 FQ	14.31 AW	19.47 TQ	PABLS	10/01-12/01
	Reading MSA, PA	H	7.79 FQ	14.60 AW	19.58 TQ	PABLS	10/01-12/01
	Scranton-Wilkes-Barre-Hazleton MSA, PA	H	6.41 FQ	11.14 AW	15.85 TQ	PABLS	10/01-12/01
	York MSA, PA	H	9.73 FQ	15.43 AW	22.12 TQ	PABLS	10/01-12/01
	Rhode Island	H	9.99 FQ	15.40 AW	20.96 TQ	RIBLS	10/01-12/01
	Providence-Fall River-Warwick MSA, RI-MA	H	9.80 FQ	15.19 AW	20.96 TQ	RIBLS	10/01-12/01
	South Carolina	H	8.56 FQ	13.90 AW	21.20 TQ	SCBLS	10/01-12/01
	Charleston-North Charleston MSA, SC	H	9.02 FQ	15.17 AW	21.43 TQ	SCBLS	10/01-12/01
	Columbia MSA, SC	H	9.06 FQ	15.45 AW	26.33 TQ	SCBLS	10/01-12/01
	Greenville-Spartanburg-Anderson MSA, SC	H	9.10 FQ	14.04 AW	20.62 TQ	SCBLS	10/01-12/01
	Myrtle Beach MSA, SC	H	6.64 FQ	13.97 AW	21.43 TQ	SCBLS	10/01-12/01
	South Dakota	H	9.02 FQ	13.96 AW	20.88 TQ	SDBLS	10/01-12/01
	Sioux Falls MSA, SD	H	10.44 FQ	15.56 AW	25.06 TQ	SDBLS	10/01-12/01
	Tennessee	H	8.42 FQ	15.67 AW	24.93 TQ	TNBLS	10/01-12/01
	Chattanooga MSA, TN-GA	H	10.84 FQ	17.08 AW	23.12 TQ	TNBLS	10/01-12/01
	Clarksville-Hopkinsville MSA, TN-KY	H	9.38 FQ	16.50 AW	26.24 TQ	TNBLS	10/01-12/01
	Johnson City-Kingsport-Bristol MSA, TN-VA	H	9.23 FQ	15.26 AW	23.23 TQ	TNBLS	10/01-12/01
	Knoxville MSA, TN	H	11.29 FQ	16.69 AW	23.12 TQ	TNBLS	10/01-12/01
	Memphis MSA, TN-AR-MS	H	8.21 FQ	17.16 AW	29.63 TQ	TNBLS	10/01-12/01

AAW	Average annual wage	**AOH**	Average offered, high	**ASH**	Average starting, high	**H**	Hourly	**M**	Monthly	**S**	Special: hourly and annual
AE	Average entry wage	**AOL**	Average offered, low	**ASL**	Average starting, low	**HI**	Highest wage paid	**MTC**	Median total compensation	**TQ**	Third quartile wage
AEX	Average experienced wage	**APH**	Average pay, high range	**AW**	Average wage paid	**HR**	High end range	**MW**	Median wage paid	**W**	Weekly
AO	Average offered	**APL**	Average pay, low range	**FQ**	First quartile wage	**LR**	Low end range	**SQ**	Second quartile wage	**Y**	Yearly

Occupation/Type/Industry	Location	Per	Low	Mid	High	Source	Date
Automotive Body and Related Repairer	Nashville MSA, TN	H	7.52 FQ	17.62 AW	30.73 TQ	TNBLS	10/01-12/01
	Texas	H	7.95 FQ	16.87 AW	26.47 TQ	TXBLS	10/01-12/01
	Amarillo MSA, TX	H	6.73 FQ	17.35 AW	27.48 TQ	TXBLS	10/01-12/01
	Austin-San Marcos MSA, TX	H	8.43 FQ	17.92 AW	27.64 TQ	TXBLS	10/01-12/01
	Beaumont-Port Arthur MSA, TX	H	7.46 FQ	15.57 AW	27.18 TQ	TXBLS	10/01-12/01
	Brazoria PMSA, TX	H	5.62 FQ	10.01 AW	19.22 TQ	TXBLS	10/01-12/01
	Brownsville-Harlingen-San Benito MSA, TX	H	6.53 FQ	12.33 AW	17.48 TQ	TXBLS	10/01-12/01
	Corpus Christi MSA, TX	H	8.64 FQ	16.36 AW	30.05 TQ	TXBLS	10/01-12/01
	Dallas PMSA, TX	H	9.00 FQ	17.98 AW	27.09 TQ	TXBLS	10/01-12/01
	El Paso MSA, TX	H	6.45 FQ	12.38 AW	24.07 TQ	TXBLS	10/01-12/01
	Fort Worth-Arlington PMSA, TX	H	12.57 FQ	19.94 AW	26.75 TQ	TXBLS	10/01-12/01
	Galveston-Texas City PMSA, TX	H	11.57 FQ	20.33 AW	27.27 TQ	TXBLS	10/01-12/01
	Houston PMSA, TX	H	9.24 FQ	17.74 AW	27.31 TQ	TXBLS	10/01-12/01
	Killeen-Temple MSA, TX	H	8.68 FQ	17.53 AW	28.49 TQ	TXBLS	10/01-12/01
	Laredo MSA, TX	H	8.25 FQ	13.53 AW	22.47 TQ	TXBLS	10/01-12/01
	Longview-Marshall MSA, TX	H	11.95 FQ	18.11 AW	26.76 TQ	TXBLS	10/01-12/01
	Lubbock MSA, TX	H	8.34 FQ	15.56 AW	24.30 TQ	TXBLS	10/01-12/01
	McAllen-Edinburg-Mission MSA, TX	H	6.01 FQ	9.54 AW	15.86 TQ	TXBLS	10/01-12/01
	Odessa-Midland MSA, TX	H	7.97 FQ	16.33 AW	25.90 TQ	TXBLS	10/01-12/01
	San Antonio MSA, TX	H	7.32 FQ	12.68 AW	17.86 TQ	TXBLS	10/01-12/01
	Tyler MSA, TX	H	6.52 FQ	14.64 AW	24.44 TQ	TXBLS	10/01-12/01
	Waco MSA, TX	H	7.60 FQ	14.53 AW	22.87 TQ	TXBLS	10/01-12/01
	Utah	H	8.67 FQ	16.22 AW	23.97 TQ	UTBLS	10/01-12/01
	Provo-Orem MSA, UT	H	11.05 FQ	17.18 AW	25.08 TQ	UTBLS	10/01-12/01
	Salt Lake City-Ogden MSA, UT	H	8.49 FQ	16.01 AW	24.80 TQ	UTBLS	10/01-12/01
	Vermont	H	11.18 FQ	16.01 AW	21.99 TQ	VTBLS	10/01-12/01
	Burlington MSA, VT	H	10.83 FQ	17.39 AW	22.73 TQ	VTBLS	10/01-12/01
	Virginia	H	9.29 FQ	19.53 AW	36.45 TQ	VABLS	10/01-12/01
	Lynchburg MSA, VA	H	9.29 FQ	15.92 AW	25.66 TQ	VABLS	10/01-12/01
	Norfolk-Virginia Beach-Newport News MSA, VA-NC	H	8.25 FQ	17.91 AW	32.42 TQ	VABLS	10/01-12/01
	Richmond-Petersburg MSA, VA	H	10.31 FQ	16.55 AW	25.36 TQ	VABLS	10/01-12/01
	Roanoke MSA, VA	H	12.21 FQ	23.13 AW	42.10 TQ	VABLS	10/01-12/01
	Washington	H	9.76 FQ	16.28 AW	24.63 TQ	WABLS	10/01-12/01
	Bremerton PMSA, WA	H	10.16 FQ	18.36 AW	26.87 TQ	WABLS	10/01-12/01
	Olympia PMSA, WA	H	8.39 FQ	15.97 AW	24.07 TQ	WABLS	10/01-12/01
	Richland-Kennewick-Pasco MSA, WA	H	9.47 FQ	14.65 AW	21.97 TQ	WABLS	10/01-12/01
	Seattle-Bellevue-Everett PMSA, WA	H	9.48 FQ	14.74 AW	25.22 TQ	WABLS	10/01-12/01
	Spokane MSA, WA	H	14.48 FQ	18.85 AW	22.00 TQ	WABLS	10/01-12/01
	Tacoma PMSA, WA	H	10.06 FQ	18.43 AW	27.57 TQ	WABLS	10/01-12/01
	Yakima MSA, WA	H	10.05 FQ	15.30 AW	20.60 TQ	WABLS	10/01-12/01
	West Virginia	H	7.52 FQ	12.03 AW	18.32 TQ	WVBLS	10/01-12/01
	Charleston MSA, WV	H	7.52 FQ	12.82 AW	20.03 TQ	WVBLS	10/01-12/01
	Huntington-Ashland MSA, WV-KY-OH	H	7.94 FQ	13.68 AW	20.63 TQ	WVBLS	10/01-12/01
	Wisconsin	H	10.26 FQ	16.71 AW	22.40 TQ	WIBLS	10/01-12/01
	Appleton-Oshkosh-Neenah MSA, WI	H	10.58 FQ	16.22 AW	21.59 TQ	WIBLS	10/01-12/01
	Green Bay MSA, WI	H	8.57 FQ	15.90 AW	22.93 TQ	WIBLS	10/01-12/01
	Madison MSA, WI	H	11.29 FQ	16.81 AW	25.78 TQ	WIBLS	10/01-12/01
	Milwaukee-Waukesha PMSA, WI	H	13.59 FQ	19.23 AW	23.56 TQ	WIBLS	10/01-12/01
	Racine PMSA, WI	H	8.45 FQ	14.52 AW	20.97 TQ	WIBLS	10/01-12/01
	Wyoming	H	7.67 FQ	14.13 AW	21.32 TQ	WYBLS	10/01-12/01
	Cheyenne MSA, WY	H	6.81 FQ	15.32 AW	25.40 TQ	WYBLS	10/01-12/01
	Puerto Rico	H	5.74 FQ	8.73 AW	12.54 TQ	PRBLS	10/01-12/01
	Guam	H	7.98 FQ	12.96 AW	18.83 TQ	GUBLS	10/01-12/01
Automotive Body Shop Worker	United States	Y		21000 AW		BSB	1/01-1/02

AAW	Average annual wage	AOH	Average offered, high	ASH	Average starting, high	H	Hourly	M	Monthly	S	Special: hourly and annual
AE	Average entry wage	AOL	Average offered, low	ASL	Average starting, low	HI	Highest wage paid	MTC	Median total compensation	TQ	Third quartile wage
AEX	Average experienced wage	APH	Average pay, high range	AW	Average wage paid	HR	High end range	MW	Median wage paid	W	Weekly
AO	Average offered	APL	Average pay, low range	FQ	First quartile wage	LR	Low end range	SQ	Second quartile wage	Y	Yearly

Occupation/Type/Industry	Location	Per	Low	Mid	High	Source	Date
Automotive Glass Installer and Repairer	Alabama	H	8.50 FQ	12.10 AW	16.70 TQ	ALBLS	10/01-12/01
	Alaska	H	9.49 FQ	15.65 AW	25.12 TQ	AKBLS	10/01-12/01
	Arizona	H	8.70 FQ	11.72 AW	19.48 TQ	AZBLS	10/01-12/01
	Arkansas	H	5.88 FQ	9.59 AW	16.62 TQ	ARBLS	10/01-12/01
	California	H	7.90 FQ	13.40 AW	19.58 TQ	CABLS	10/01-12/01
	Colorado	H	8.01 FQ	12.76 AW	17.25 TQ	COBLS	10/01-12/01
	Connecticut	H	13.50 FQ	21.40 AW	27.75 TQ	CTBLS	10/01-12/01
	Delaware	H	9.10 FQ	10.37 AW	11.12 TQ	DEBLS	10/01-12/01
	Florida	H	8.02 FQ	15.98 AW	26.37 TQ	FLBLS	10/01-12/01
	Georgia	H	8.00 FQ	12.96 AW	18.16 TQ	GABLS	10/01-12/01
	Idaho	H	9.33 FQ	13.48 AW	19.18 TQ	IDBLS	10/01-12/01
	Illinois	H	8.87 FQ	14.49 AW	21.24 TQ	ILBLS	10/01-12/01
	Indiana	H	6.09 FQ	11.46 AW	17.00 TQ	INBLS	10/01-12/01
	Iowa	H	6.45 FQ	12.91 AW	20.08 TQ	IABLS	10/01-12/01
	Kansas	H	11.98 FQ	15.45 AW	17.87 TQ	KSBLS	10/01-12/01
	Kentucky	H	10.55 FQ	16.29 AW	21.46 TQ	KYBLS	10/01-12/01
	Louisiana	H	7.17 FQ	11.31 AW	17.09 TQ	LABLS	10/01-12/01
	Maine	H	7.80 FQ	11.66 AW	15.72 TQ	MEBLS	10/01-12/01
	Maryland	H	8.96 FQ	12.82 AW	18.20 TQ	MDBLS	10/01-12/01
	Massachusetts	H	8.30 FQ	14.88 AW	21.67 TQ	MABLS	10/01-12/01
	Michigan	H	8.46 FQ	14.61 AW	20.25 TQ	MIBLS	10/01-12/01
	Minnesota	H	11.20 FQ	17.10 AW	23.68 TQ	MNBLS	10/01-12/01
	Mississippi	H	7.23 FQ	10.52 AW	16.67 TQ	MSBLS	10/01-12/01
	Missouri	H	7.28 FQ	11.05 AW	15.46 TQ	MOBLS	10/01-12/01
	Montana	H	7.77 FQ	11.48 AW	17.17 TQ	MTBLS	10/01-12/01
	Nebraska	H	7.83 FQ	13.08 AW	17.10 TQ	NEBLS	10/01-12/01
	Nevada	H	9.06 FQ	11.04 AW	15.99 TQ	NVBLS	10/01-12/01
	New Hampshire	H	11.19 FQ	14.51 AW	19.51 TQ	NHBLS	10/01-12/01
	New Jersey	H	9.27 FQ	13.24 AW	19.04 TQ	NJBLS	10/01-12/01
	New Mexico	H	5.93 FQ	10.83 AW	16.73 TQ	NMBLS	10/01-12/01
	New York	H	7.41 FQ	10.95 AW	16.09 TQ	NYBLS	10/01-12/01
	North Carolina	H	8.07 FQ	12.43 AW	17.08 TQ	NCBLS	10/01-12/01
	North Dakota	H	7.71 FQ	14.98 AW	20.12 TQ	NDBLS	10/01-12/01
	Ohio	H	12.00 FQ	16.99 AW	22.79 TQ	OHBLS	10/01-12/01
	Oklahoma	H	8.56 FQ	12.99 AW	18.59 TQ	OKBLS	10/01-12/01
	Oregon	H	9.12 FQ	13.86 AW	19.61 TQ	ORBLS	10/01-12/01
	Pennsylvania	H	8.05 FQ	13.20 AW	16.80 TQ	PABLS	10/01-12/01
	Rhode Island	H	11.52 FQ	13.90 AW	17.04 TQ	RIBLS	10/01-12/01
	South Carolina	H	9.50 FQ	14.60 AW	21.78 TQ	SCBLS	10/01-12/01
	South Dakota	H	9.13 FQ	12.08 AW	16.03 TQ	SDBLS	10/01-12/01
	Tennessee	H	9.22 FQ	13.92 AW	19.57 TQ	TNBLS	10/01-12/01
	Texas	H	8.60 FQ	13.47 AW	20.40 TQ	TXBLS	10/01-12/01
	Utah	H	9.67 FQ	14.89 AW	21.95 TQ	UTBLS	10/01-12/01
	Vermont	H	11.52 FQ	15.45 AW	19.99 TQ	VTBLS	10/01-12/01
	Virginia	H	7.98 FQ	13.50 AW	17.40 TQ	VABLS	10/01-12/01
	Washington	H	12.16 FQ	16.56 AW	21.58 TQ	WABLS	10/01-12/01
	West Virginia	H	7.71 FQ	11.64 AW	17.12 TQ	WVBLS	10/01-12/01
	Wisconsin	H	11.00 FQ	15.22 AW	19.24 TQ	WIBLS	10/01-12/01
	Puerto Rico	H	5.73 FQ	8.08 AW	10.43 TQ	PRBLS	10/01-12/01
Automotive Service Technician and Mechanic	Alabama	H	7.23 FQ	12.84 AW	20.03 TQ	ALBLS	10/01-12/01
	Birmingham MSA, AL	H	8.66 FQ	13.96 AW	20.37 TQ	ALBLS	10/01-12/01
	Huntsville MSA, AL	H	7.76 FQ	14.15 AW	21.04 TQ	ALBLS	10/01-12/01
	Mobile MSA, AL	H	5.99 FQ	12.97 AW	24.04 TQ	ALBLS	10/01-12/01
	Montgomery MSA, AL	H	7.59 FQ	11.57 AW	17.13 TQ	ALBLS	10/01-12/01
	Alaska	H	10.23 FQ	19.85 AW	27.79 TQ	AKBLS	10/01-12/01
	Anchorage MSA, AK	H	8.67 FQ	18.81 AW	27.29 TQ	AKBLS	10/01-12/01
	Arizona	H	7.70 FQ	15.10 AW	24.51 TQ	AZBLS	10/01-12/01
	Phoenix-Mesa MSA, AZ	H	7.56 FQ	14.89 AW	24.66 TQ	AZBLS	10/01-12/01
	Tucson MSA, AZ	H	8.68 FQ	15.53 AW	23.72 TQ	AZBLS	10/01-12/01
	Arkansas	H	7.92 FQ	13.25 AW	20.00 TQ	ARBLS	10/01-12/01
	Fayetteville-Springdale-Rogers MSA, AR	H	8.55 FQ	13.73 AW	21.63 TQ	ARBLS	10/01-12/01
	Fort Smith MSA, AR-OK	H	7.10 FQ	11.88 AW	19.69 TQ	ARBLS	10/01-12/01
	Little Rock-North Little Rock MSA, AR	H	9.21 FQ	14.19 AW	19.80 TQ	ARBLS	10/01-12/01
	California	H	8.81 FQ	16.01 AW	25.67 TQ	CABLS	10/01-12/01
	Bakersfield MSA, CA	H	9.01 FQ	14.94 AW	21.58 TQ	CABLS	10/01-12/01
	Chico-Paradise MSA, CA	H	8.48 FQ	14.37 AW	20.99 TQ	CABLS	10/01-12/01
	Fresno MSA, CA	H	8.82 FQ	15.30 AW	22.95 TQ	CABLS	10/01-12/01

AAW	Average annual wage	**AOH**	Average offered, high	**ASH**	Average starting, high	**H**	Hourly	**M**	Monthly	**S**	Special: hourly and annual
AE	Average entry wage	**AOL**	Average offered, low	**ASL**	Average starting, low	**HI**	Highest wage paid	**MTC**	Median total compensation	**TQ**	Third quartile wage
AEX	Average experienced wage	**APH**	Average pay, high range	**AW**	Average wage paid	**HR**	High end range	**MW**	Median wage paid	**W**	Weekly
AO	Average offered	**APL**	Average pay, low range	**FQ**	First quartile wage	**LR**	Low end range	**SQ**	Second quartile wage	**Y**	Yearly

Occupation/Type/Industry	Location	Per	Low	Mid	High	Source	Date
Automotive Service Technician and Mechanic	Los Angeles-Long Beach PMSA, CA	H	8.15 FQ	14.77 AW	22.05 TQ	CABLS	10/01-12/01
	Merced MSA, CA	H	7.45 FQ	14.18 AW	22.64 TQ	CABLS	10/01-12/01
	Modesto MSA, CA	H	8.04 FQ	15.49 AW	23.11 TQ	CABLS	10/01-12/01
	Oakland PMSA, CA	H	9.28 FQ	14.74 AW	26.15 TQ	CABLS	10/01-12/01
	Orange County PMSA, CA	H	8.09 FQ	16.96 AW	26.93 TQ	CABLS	10/01-12/01
	Redding MSA, CA	H	7.30 FQ	13.52 AW	20.47 TQ	CABLS	10/01-12/01
	Riverside-San Bernardino PMSA, CA	H	8.90 FQ	14.88 AW	23.23 TQ	CABLS	10/01-12/01
	Sacramento PMSA, CA	H	9.22 FQ	17.22 AW	26.73 TQ	CABLS	10/01-12/01
	Salinas MSA, CA	H	11.14 FQ	17.54 AW	26.41 TQ	CABLS	10/01-12/01
	San Diego MSA, CA	H	7.94 FQ	17.02 AW	27.67 TQ	CABLS	10/01-12/01
	San Francisco PMSA, CA	H	12.11 FQ	19.56 AW	27.14 TQ	CABLS	10/01-12/01
	San Jose PMSA, CA	H	9.42 FQ	19.39 AW	28.13 TQ	CABLS	10/01-12/01
	San Luis Obispo-Atascadero-Paso Robles MSA, CA	H	8.91 FQ	16.15 AW	26.02 TQ	CABLS	10/01-12/01
	Santa Barbara-Santa Maria-Lompoc MSA, CA	H	8.27 FQ	16.10 AW	24.78 TQ	CABLS	10/01-12/01
	Santa Cruz-Watsonville PMSA, CA	H	9.90 FQ	18.98 AW	31.43 TQ	CABLS	10/01-12/01
	Santa Rosa PMSA, CA	H	12.19 FQ	19.40 AW	27.64 TQ	CABLS	10/01-12/01
	Stockton-Lodi MSA, CA	H	9.36 FQ	15.89 AW	23.50 TQ	CABLS	10/01-12/01
	Vallejo-Fairfield-Napa PMSA, CA	H	9.02 FQ	17.70 AW	26.41 TQ	CABLS	10/01-12/01
	Ventura PMSA, CA	H	7.71 FQ	17.46 AW	31.87 TQ	CABLS	10/01-12/01
	Visalia-Tulare-Porterville MSA, CA	H	8.19 FQ	15.12 AW	21.71 TQ	CABLS	10/01-12/01
	Colorado	H	8.92 FQ	17.52 AW	27.54 TQ	COBLS	10/01-12/01
	Boulder-Longmont PMSA, CO	H	10.51 FQ	18.95 AW	28.05 TQ	COBLS	10/01-12/01
	Colorado Springs MSA, CO	H	9.47 FQ	16.09 AW	24.96 TQ	COBLS	10/01-12/01
	Denver PMSA, CO	H	10.02 FQ	18.85 AW	29.51 TQ	COBLS	10/01-12/01
	Fort Collins-Loveland MSA, CO	H	8.48 FQ	16.53 AW	27.12 TQ	COBLS	10/01-12/01
	Greeley PMSA, CO	H	8.25 FQ	15.04 AW	23.11 TQ	COBLS	10/01-12/01
	Connecticut	H	9.20 FQ	17.22 AW	26.08 TQ	CTBLS	10/01-12/01
	Bridgeport PMSA, CT	H	6.63 FQ	16.83 AW	26.87 TQ	CTBLS	10/01-12/01
	Danbury PMSA, CT	H	11.24 FQ	21.02 AW	32.07 TQ	CTBLS	10/01-12/01
	Hartford MSA, CT	H	9.12 FQ	17.10 AW	25.85 TQ	CTBLS	10/01-12/01
	New Haven-Meriden PMSA, CT	H	9.45 FQ	17.86 AW	29.67 TQ	CTBLS	10/01-12/01
	New London-Norwich MSA, CT-RI	H	9.17 FQ	15.97 AW	22.16 TQ	CTBLS	10/01-12/01
	Stamford-Norwalk PMSA, CT	H	11.67 FQ	18.26 AW	24.73 TQ	CTBLS	10/01-12/01
	Waterbury PMSA, CT	H	9.29 FQ	15.87 AW	21.95 TQ	CTBLS	10/01-12/01
	District of Columbia	H	11.31 FQ	16.38 AW	24.13 TQ	DCBLS	10/01-12/01
	Washington PMSA, DC-MD-VA-WV	H	9.43 FQ	18.37 AW	28.64 TQ	DCBLS	10/01-12/01
	Florida	H	7.84 FQ	14.98 AW	22.52 TQ	FLBLS	10/01-12/01
	Daytona Beach MSA, FL	H	7.90 FQ	13.47 AW	21.36 TQ	FLBLS	10/01-12/01
	Fort Lauderdale PMSA, FL	H	8.12 FQ	17.04 AW	30.04 TQ	FLBLS	10/01-12/01
	Fort Myers-Cape Coral MSA, FL	H	7.57 FQ	14.04 AW	22.66 TQ	FLBLS	10/01-12/01
	Fort Pierce-Port St. Lucie MSA, FL	H	9.53 FQ	15.14 AW	20.89 TQ	FLBLS	10/01-12/01
	Fort Walton Beach MSA, FL	H	7.34 FQ	12.99 AW	21.70 TQ	FLBLS	10/01-12/01
	Gainesville MSA, FL	H	6.61 FQ	13.83 AW	20.32 TQ	FLBLS	10/01-12/01
	Jacksonville MSA, FL	H	9.97 FQ	17.07 AW	21.35 TQ	FLBLS	10/01-12/01
	Lakeland-Winter Haven MSA, FL	H	7.28 FQ	13.00 AW	20.30 TQ	FLBLS	10/01-12/01
	Melbourne-Titusville-Palm Bay MSA, FL	H	7.83 FQ	14.33 AW	22.16 TQ	FLBLS	10/01-12/01
	Miami PMSA, FL	H	6.78 FQ	13.26 AW	21.34 TQ	FLBLS	10/01-12/01
	Naples MSA, FL	H	7.05 FQ	16.59 AW	25.69 TQ	FLBLS	10/01-12/01
	Ocala MSA, FL	H	7.51 FQ	13.82 AW	21.45 TQ	FLBLS	10/01-12/01
	Orlando MSA, FL	H	9.06 FQ	16.20 AW	24.47 TQ	FLBLS	10/01-12/01
	Pensacola MSA, FL	H	7.55 FQ	13.15 AW	20.45 TQ	FLBLS	10/01-12/01
	Sarasota-Bradenton MSA, FL	H	7.40 FQ	14.81 AW	22.68 TQ	FLBLS	10/01-12/01
	Tallahassee MSA, FL	H	7.69 FQ	14.41 AW	21.66 TQ	FLBLS	10/01-12/01
	Tampa-St. Petersburg-Clearwater MSA, FL	H	8.32 FQ	15.64 AW	22.80 TQ	FLBLS	10/01-12/01

AAW	Average annual wage	**AOH**	Average offered, high	**ASH**	Average starting, high	**H**	Hourly	**M**	Monthly	**S**	Special: hourly and annual
AE	Average entry wage	**AOL**	Average offered, low	**ASL**	Average starting, low	**HI**	Highest wage paid	**MTC**	Median total compensation	**TQ**	Third quartile wage
AEX	Average experienced wage	**APH**	Average pay, high range	**AW**	Average wage paid	**HR**	High end range	**MW**	Median wage paid	**W**	Weekly
AO	Average offered	**APL**	Average pay, low range	**FQ**	First quartile wage	**LR**	Low end range	**SQ**	Second quartile wage	**Y**	Yearly

Occupation/Type/Industry	Location	Per	Low	Mid	High	Source	Date
Automotive Service Technician and Mechanic	West Palm Beach-Boca Raton MSA, FL	H	8.89 FQ	15.50 AW	22.86 TQ	FLBLS	10/01-12/01
	Georgia	H	8.17 FQ	15.81 AW	25.33 TQ	GABLS	10/01-12/01
	Atlanta MSA, GA	H	8.54 FQ	17.03 AW	26.73 TQ	GABLS	10/01-12/01
	Augusta-Aiken MSA, GA-SC	H	7.93 FQ	13.80 AW	21.90 TQ	GABLS	10/01-12/01
	Columbus MSA, GA-AL	H	8.17 FQ	13.83 AW	20.75 TQ	GABLS	10/01-12/01
	Macon MSA, GA	H	6.87 FQ	14.24 AW	23.29 TQ	GABLS	10/01-12/01
	Savannah MSA, GA	H	7.39 FQ	13.96 AW	20.69 TQ	GABLS	10/01-12/01
	Hawaii	H	9.04 FQ	15.59 AW	23.70 TQ	HIBLS	10/01-12/01
	Honolulu MSA, HI	H	9.14 FQ	15.91 AW	24.47 TQ	HIBLS	10/01-12/01
	Idaho	H	8.69 FQ	14.69 AW	21.23 TQ	IDBLS	10/01-12/01
	Boise City MSA, ID	H	10.19 FQ	15.86 AW	21.60 TQ	IDBLS	10/01-12/01
	Illinois	H	8.25 FQ	16.33 AW	27.84 TQ	ILBLS	10/01-12/01
	Champaign-Urbana MSA, IL	H	7.78 FQ	15.30 AW	23.86 TQ	ILBLS	10/01-12/01
	Chicago PMSA, IL	H	8.34 FQ	17.26 AW	30.37 TQ	ILBLS	10/01-12/01
	Peoria-Pekin MSA, IL	H	8.16 FQ	15.17 AW	22.84 TQ	ILBLS	10/01-12/01
	Rockford MSA, IL	H	8.05 FQ	14.20 AW	24.48 TQ	ILBLS	10/01-12/01
	Springfield MSA, IL	H	7.50 FQ	14.75 AW	21.23 TQ	ILBLS	10/01-12/01
	Indiana	H	8.52 FQ	15.19 AW	24.73 TQ	INBLS	10/01-12/01
	Elkhart-Goshen MSA, IN	H	8.33 FQ	13.56 AW	20.31 TQ	INBLS	10/01-12/01
	Evansville-Henderson MSA, IN-KY	H	8.92 FQ	13.96 AW	21.12 TQ	INBLS	10/01-12/01
	Fort Wayne MSA, IN	H	8.46 FQ	15.08 AW	21.90 TQ	INBLS	10/01-12/01
	Gary PMSA, IN	H	8.95 FQ	16.75 AW	26.60 TQ	INBLS	10/01-12/01
	Indianapolis MSA, IN	H	9.34 FQ	17.37 AW	29.92 TQ	INBLS	10/01-12/01
	Lafayette MSA, IN	H	8.35 FQ	14.74 AW	23.77 TQ	INBLS	10/01-12/01
	South Bend MSA, IN	H	8.69 FQ	14.37 AW	21.42 TQ	INBLS	10/01-12/01
	Iowa	H	7.56 FQ	13.13 AW	20.11 TQ	IABLS	10/01-12/01
	Cedar Rapids MSA, IA	H	8.29 FQ	13.80 AW	20.32 TQ	IABLS	10/01-12/01
	Davenport-Moline-Rock Island MSA, IA-IL	H	8.08 FQ	15.60 AW	22.84 TQ	IABLS	10/01-12/01
	Des Moines MSA, IA	H	9.39 FQ	15.74 AW	21.92 TQ	IABLS	10/01-12/01
	Kansas	H	7.88 FQ	14.20 AW	21.57 TQ	KSBLS	10/01-12/01
	Topeka MSA, KS	H	7.75 FQ	13.93 AW	21.39 TQ	KSBLS	10/01-12/01
	Wichita MSA, KS	H	7.96 FQ	13.51 AW	22.31 TQ	KSBLS	10/01-12/01
	Kentucky	H	6.38 FQ	12.38 AW	19.85 TQ	KYBLS	10/01-12/01
	Lexington MSA, KY	H	7.60 FQ	13.77 AW	21.22 TQ	KYBLS	10/01-12/01
	Louisville MSA, KY-IN	H	6.40 FQ	12.97 AW	20.69 TQ	KYBLS	10/01-12/01
	Louisiana	H	7.28 FQ	13.25 AW	20.70 TQ	LABLS	10/01-12/01
	Baton Rouge MSA, LA	H	8.02 FQ	12.32 AW	18.30 TQ	LABLS	10/01-12/01
	Houma MSA, LA	H	7.22 FQ	13.43 AW	20.47 TQ	LABLS	10/01-12/01
	Lafayette MSA, LA	H	6.38 FQ	13.42 AW	22.40 TQ	LABLS	10/01-12/01
	Lake Charles MSA, LA	H	6.93 FQ	12.53 AW	18.32 TQ	LABLS	10/01-12/01
	New Orleans MSA, LA	H	7.76 FQ	14.90 AW	21.54 TQ	LABLS	10/01-12/01
	Shreveport-Bossier City MSA, LA	H	6.48 FQ	12.07 AW	19.53 TQ	LABLS	10/01-12/01
	Maine	H	7.79 FQ	12.94 AW	19.59 TQ	MEBLS	10/01-12/01
	Portland MSA, ME	H	8.49 FQ	14.52 AW	22.07 TQ	MEBLS	10/01-12/01
	Maryland	H	8.90 FQ	16.92 AW	26.79 TQ	MDBLS	10/01-12/01
	Baltimore PMSA, MD	H	8.98 FQ	16.39 AW	25.66 TQ	MDBLS	10/01-12/01
	Massachusetts	H	9.32 FQ	16.62 AW	24.03 TQ	MABLS	10/01-12/01
	Boston PMSA, MA-NH	H	10.08 FQ	17.48 AW	24.77 TQ	MABLS	10/01-12/01
	Brockton PMSA, MA	H	10.37 FQ	16.40 AW	21.97 TQ	MABLS	10/01-12/01
	Lawrence PMSA, MA-NH	H	8.59 FQ	14.37 AW	21.93 TQ	MABLS	10/01-12/01
	Lowell PMSA, MA-NH	H	8.62 FQ	16.57 AW	25.37 TQ	MABLS	10/01-12/01
	New Bedford PMSA, MA	H	7.86 FQ	14.17 AW	22.04 TQ	MABLS	10/01-12/01
	Springfield MSA, MA	H	7.01 FQ	15.61 AW	25.42 TQ	MABLS	10/01-12/01
	Worcester PMSA, MA-CT	H	8.45 FQ	16.04 AW	23.75 TQ	MABLS	10/01-12/01
	Michigan	H	8.28 FQ	17.55 AW	28.06 TQ	MIBLS	10/01-12/01
	Ann Arbor PMSA, MI	H	9.99 FQ	19.02 AW	28.10 TQ	MIBLS	10/01-12/01
	Detroit PMSA, MI	H	8.42 FQ	19.66 AW	31.45 TQ	MIBLS	10/01-12/01
	Flint PMSA, MI	H	8.08 FQ	16.65 AW	29.16 TQ	MIBLS	10/01-12/01
	Grand Rapids-Muskegon-Holland MSA, MI	H	9.45 FQ	18.13 AW	26.51 TQ	MIBLS	10/01-12/01
	Kalamazoo-Battle Creek MSA, MI	H	9.09 FQ	16.62 AW	26.08 TQ	MIBLS	10/01-12/01
	Lansing-East Lansing MSA, MI	H	7.18 FQ	15.81 AW	26.22 TQ	MIBLS	10/01-12/01
	Saginaw-Bay City-Midland MSA, MI	H	7.44 FQ	13.98 AW	22.29 TQ	MIBLS	10/01-12/01
	Minnesota	H	9.22 FQ	15.37 AW	22.10 TQ	MNBLS	10/01-12/01
	Duluth-Superior MSA, MN-WI	H	7.21 FQ	12.81 AW	19.10 TQ	MNBLS	10/01-12/01

AAW	Average annual wage	AOH	Average offered, high	ASH	Average starting, high	H	Hourly	M	Monthly	S	Special: hourly and annual
AE	Average entry wage	AOL	Average offered, low	ASL	Average starting, low	HI	Highest wage paid	MTC	Median total compensation	TQ	Third quartile wage
AEX	Average experienced wage	APH	Average pay, high range	AW	Average wage paid	HR	High end range	MW	Median wage paid	W	Weekly
AO	Average offered	APL	Average pay, low range	FQ	First quartile wage	LR	Low end range	SQ	Second quartile wage	Y	Yearly

Occupation/Type/Industry	Location	Per	Low	Mid	High	Source	Date
Automotive Service Technician and Mechanic	Minneapolis-St. Paul MSA, MN-WI	H	10.08 FQ	16.24 AW	23.20 TQ	MNBLS	10/01-12/01
	St. Cloud MSA, MN	H	9.14 FQ	14.19 AW	18.66 TQ	MNBLS	10/01-12/01
	Mississippi	H	7.08 FQ	13.09 AW	19.37 TQ	MSBLS	10/01-12/01
	Biloxi-Gulfport-Pascagoula MSA, MS	H	7.51 FQ	14.15 AW	20.57 TQ	MSBLS	10/01-12/01
	Jackson MSA, MS	H	9.83 FQ	14.84 AW	20.03 TQ	MSBLS	10/01-12/01
	Missouri	H	7.84 FQ	15.05 AW	22.65 TQ	MOBLS	10/01-12/01
	Kansas City MSA, MO-KS	H	9.21 FQ	16.04 AW	23.64 TQ	MOBLS	10/01-12/01
	St. Louis MSA, MO-IL	H	8.89 FQ	16.38 AW	23.62 TQ	MOBLS	10/01-12/01
	Springfield MSA, MO	H	7.93 FQ	14.51 AW	22.61 TQ	MOBLS	10/01-12/01
	Montana	H	7.22 FQ	14.03 AW	20.84 TQ	MTBLS	10/01-12/01
	Billings MSA, MT	H	7.66 FQ	13.74 AW	20.12 TQ	MTBLS	10/01-12/01
	Nebraska	H	7.75 FQ	14.01 AW	20.82 TQ	NEBLS	10/01-12/01
	Lincoln MSA, NE	H	6.21 FQ	12.73 AW	20.61 TQ	NEBLS	10/01-12/01
	Omaha MSA, NE-IA	H	8.67 FQ	15.47 AW	22.02 TQ	NEBLS	10/01-12/01
	Nevada	H	8.74 FQ	17.04 AW	25.80 TQ	NVBLS	10/01-12/01
	Las Vegas MSA, NV-AZ	H	7.35 FQ	16.44 AW	26.11 TQ	NVBLS	10/01-12/01
	Reno MSA, NV	H	9.76 FQ	17.34 AW	24.58 TQ	NVBLS	10/01-12/01
	New Hampshire	H	9.11 FQ	15.25 AW	21.81 TQ	NHBLS	10/01-12/01
	Manchester PMSA, NH	H	8.79 FQ	17.22 AW	26.71 TQ	NHBLS	10/01-12/01
	Nashua PMSA, NH	H	9.92 FQ	15.85 AW	22.18 TQ	NHBLS	10/01-12/01
	Portsmouth-Rochester PMSA, NH-ME	H	9.63 FQ	15.80 AW	22.22 TQ	NHBLS	10/01-12/01
	New Jersey	H	9.27 FQ	16.94 AW	26.09 TQ	NJBLS	10/01-12/01
	Atlantic-Cape May PMSA, NJ	H	10.34 FQ	16.86 AW	24.65 TQ	NJBLS	10/01-12/01
	Bergen-Passaic PMSA, NJ	H	9.52 FQ	16.85 AW	27.75 TQ	NJBLS	10/01-12/01
	Jersey City PMSA, NJ	H	8.92 FQ	15.08 AW	24.70 TQ	NJBLS	10/01-12/01
	Middlesex-Somerset-Hunterdon PMSA, NJ	H	9.09 FQ	18.44 AW	31.57 TQ	NJBLS	10/01-12/01
	Monmouth-Ocean PMSA, NJ	H	11.12 FQ	17.73 AW	25.72 TQ	NJBLS	10/01-12/01
	Newark PMSA, NJ	H	8.01 FQ	16.42 AW	24.14 TQ	NJBLS	10/01-12/01
	Trenton PMSA, NJ	H	9.70 FQ	17.64 AW	26.48 TQ	NJBLS	10/01-12/01
	New Mexico	H	7.01 FQ	14.30 AW	21.70 TQ	NMBLS	10/01-12/01
	Albuquerque MSA, NM	H	9.65 FQ	16.60 AW	22.68 TQ	NMBLS	10/01-12/01
	Las Cruces MSA, NM	H	5.94 FQ	10.41 AW	16.98 TQ	NMBLS	10/01-12/01
	New York	H	7.02 FQ	14.58 AW	24.99 TQ	NYBLS	10/01-12/01
	Albany-Schenectady-Troy MSA, NY	H	7.42 FQ	14.06 AW	21.30 TQ	NYBLS	10/01-12/01
	Binghamton MSA, NY	H	7.45 FQ	12.77 AW	18.31 TQ	NYBLS	10/01-12/01
	Buffalo-Niagara Falls MSA, NY	H	7.60 FQ	12.63 AW	19.61 TQ	NYBLS	10/01-12/01
	Dutchess County PMSA, NY	H	8.09 FQ	14.25 AW	21.18 TQ	NYBLS	10/01-12/01
	Nassau-Suffolk PMSA, NY	H	7.99 FQ	17.38 AW	27.13 TQ	NYBLS	10/01-12/01
	New York PMSA, NY	H	6.22 FQ	13.97 AW	26.53 TQ	NYBLS	10/01-12/01
	Newburgh PMSA, NY-PA	H	8.92 FQ	15.77 AW	21.79 TQ	NYBLS	10/01-12/01
	Rochester MSA, NY	H	7.94 FQ	15.50 AW	25.41 TQ	NYBLS	10/01-12/01
	Syracuse MSA, NY	H	8.03 FQ	15.40 AW	23.07 TQ	NYBLS	10/01-12/01
	Utica-Rome MSA, NY	H	7.86 FQ	12.56 AW	18.17 TQ	NYBLS	10/01-12/01
	North Carolina	H	8.12 FQ	15.69 AW	25.84 TQ	NCBLS	10/01-12/01
	Asheville MSA, NC	H	8.43 FQ	14.30 AW	22.17 TQ	NCBLS	10/01-12/01
	Charlotte-Gastonia-Rock Hill MSA, NC-SC	H	8.86 FQ	18.85 AW	31.78 TQ	NCBLS	10/01-12/01
	Fayetteville MSA, NC	H	6.54 FQ	12.85 AW	20.11 TQ	NCBLS	10/01-12/01
	Greensboro-Winston-Salem-High Point MSA, NC	H	9.53 FQ	15.79 AW	23.71 TQ	NCBLS	10/01-12/01
	Hickory-Morganton-Lenoir MSA, NC	H	8.89 FQ	14.40 AW	21.38 TQ	NCBLS	10/01-12/01
	Raleigh-Durham-Chapel Hill MSA, NC	H	8.65 FQ	16.64 AW	27.35 TQ	NCBLS	10/01-12/01
	Wilmington MSA, NC	H	8.21 FQ	14.79 AW	21.81 TQ	NCBLS	10/01-12/01
	North Dakota	H	7.48 FQ	13.01 AW	19.59 TQ	NDBLS	10/01-12/01
	Fargo-Moorhead MSA, ND-MN	H	8.68 FQ	14.84 AW	22.31 TQ	NDBLS	10/01-12/01
	Ohio	H	7.69 FQ	14.59 AW	22.33 TQ	OHBLS	10/01-12/01
	Akron PMSA, OH	H	10.13 FQ	15.46 AW	21.36 TQ	OHBLS	10/01-12/01
	Canton-Massillon MSA, OH	H	7.17 FQ	13.32 AW	20.88 TQ	OHBLS	10/01-12/01
	Cincinnati PMSA, OH-KY-IN	H	8.55 FQ	15.59 AW	24.40 TQ	OHBLS	10/01-12/01
	Cleveland-Lorain-Elyria PMSA, OH	H	6.96 FQ	14.90 AW	24.10 TQ	OHBLS	10/01-12/01
	Columbus MSA, OH	H	7.55 FQ	15.59 AW	24.22 TQ	OHBLS	10/01-12/01

Occupation/Type/Industry	Location	Per	Low	Mid	High	Source	Date
Automotive Service Technician and Mechanic	Dayton-Springfield MSA, OH	H	7.54 FQ	13.34 AW	20.93 TQ	OHBLS	10/01-12/01
	Hamilton-Middletown PMSA, OH	H	8.67 FQ	16.39 AW	26.52 TQ	OHBLS	10/01-12/01
	Mansfield MSA, OH	H	7.99 FQ	14.81 AW	21.58 TQ	OHBLS	10/01-12/01
	Toledo MSA, OH	H	8.88 FQ	14.90 AW	21.45 TQ	OHBLS	10/01-12/01
	Youngstown-Warren MSA, OH	H	7.60 FQ	13.79 AW	21.35 TQ	OHBLS	10/01-12/01
	Oklahoma	H	6.91 FQ	12.80 AW	20.36 TQ	OKBLS	10/01-12/01
	Oklahoma City MSA, OK	H	7.63 FQ	13.58 AW	20.13 TQ	OKBLS	10/01-12/01
	Tulsa MSA, OK	H	7.54 FQ	13.97 AW	22.28 TQ	OKBLS	10/01-12/01
	Oregon	H	9.49 FQ	16.26 AW	23.35 TQ	ORBLS	10/01-12/01
	Eugene-Springfield MSA, OR	H	8.89 FQ	15.36 AW	24.78 TQ	ORBLS	10/01-12/01
	Medford-Ashland MSA, OR	H	7.75 FQ	14.06 AW	22.26 TQ	ORBLS	10/01-12/01
	Portland-Vancouver PMSA, OR-WA	H	10.46 FQ	16.98 AW	24.16 TQ	ORBLS	10/01-12/01
	Salem PMSA, OR	H	11.27 FQ	15.12 AW	21.08 TQ	ORBLS	10/01-12/01
	Pennsylvania	H	7.84 FQ	14.40 AW	22.67 TQ	PABLS	10/01-12/01
	Allentown-Bethlehem-Easton MSA, PA	H	9.30 FQ	15.60 AW	22.95 TQ	PABLS	10/01-12/01
	Erie MSA, PA	H	8.24 FQ	14.49 AW	23.60 TQ	PABLS	10/01-12/01
	Harrisburg-Lebanon-Carlisle MSA, PA	H	9.46 FQ	15.10 AW	21.37 TQ	PABLS	10/01-12/01
	Johnstown MSA, PA	H	6.78 FQ	12.15 AW	20.19 TQ	PABLS	10/01-12/01
	Lancaster MSA, PA	H	9.38 FQ	14.23 AW	20.34 TQ	PABLS	10/01-12/01
	Philadelphia PMSA, PA-NJ	H	8.81 FQ	16.25 AW	25.62 TQ	PABLS	10/01-12/01
	Pittsburgh MSA, PA	H	8.78 FQ	14.09 AW	21.11 TQ	PABLS	10/01-12/01
	Reading MSA, PA	H	8.36 FQ	14.77 AW	21.51 TQ	PABLS	10/01-12/01
	Scranton-Wilkes-Barre-Hazleton MSA, PA	H	6.57 FQ	12.46 AW	19.81 TQ	PABLS	10/01-12/01
	York MSA, PA	H	8.88 FQ	13.93 AW	20.26 TQ	PABLS	10/01-12/01
	Rhode Island	H	9.42 FQ	15.32 AW	21.71 TQ	RIBLS	10/01-12/01
	Providence-Fall River-Warwick MSA, RI-MA	H	9.33 FQ	15.25 AW	21.77 TQ	RIBLS	10/01-12/01
	South Carolina	H	8.01 FQ	14.21 AW	22.55 TQ	SCBLS	10/01-12/01
	Charleston-North Charleston MSA, SC	H	7.26 FQ	14.82 AW	26.77 TQ	SCBLS	10/01-12/01
	Columbia MSA, SC	H	8.78 FQ	15.48 AW	24.38 TQ	SCBLS	10/01-12/01
	Greenville-Spartanburg-Anderson MSA, SC	H	8.73 FQ	13.57 AW	20.80 TQ	SCBLS	10/01-12/01
	Myrtle Beach MSA, SC	H	7.99 FQ	15.25 AW	24.40 TQ	SCBLS	10/01-12/01
	South Dakota	H	9.49 FQ	13.65 AW	18.39 TQ	SDBLS	10/01-12/01
	Sioux Falls MSA, SD	H	10.00 FQ	15.07 AW	21.50 TQ	SDBLS	10/01-12/01
	Tennessee	H	7.52 FQ	14.24 AW	22.42 TQ	TNBLS	10/01-12/01
	Chattanooga MSA, TN-GA	H	7.10 FQ	13.59 AW	20.57 TQ	TNBLS	10/01-12/01
	Clarksville-Hopkinsville MSA, TN-KY	H	7.74 FQ	14.98 AW	21.36 TQ	TNBLS	10/01-12/01
	Johnson City-Kingsport-Bristol MSA, TN-VA	H	6.73 FQ	12.58 AW	19.29 TQ	TNBLS	10/01-12/01
	Knoxville MSA, TN	H	6.67 FQ	12.52 AW	20.00 TQ	TNBLS	10/01-12/01
	Memphis MSA, TN-AR-MS	H	8.00 FQ	15.28 AW	23.77 TQ	TNBLS	10/01-12/01
	Nashville MSA, TN	H	9.23 FQ	16.29 AW	26.46 TQ	TNBLS	10/01-12/01
	Texas	H	7.51 FQ	14.90 AW	24.62 TQ	TXBLS	10/01-12/01
	Amarillo MSA, TX	H	6.24 FQ	13.29 AW	21.52 TQ	TXBLS	10/01-12/01
	Austin-San Marcos MSA, TX	H	7.50 FQ	15.92 AW	25.94 TQ	TXBLS	10/01-12/01
	Beaumont-Port Arthur MSA, TX	H	7.40 FQ	13.11 AW	20.53 TQ	TXBLS	10/01-12/01
	Brazoria PMSA, TX	H	6.14 FQ	13.43 AW	22.27 TQ	TXBLS	10/01-12/01
	Brownsville-Harlingen-San Benito MSA, TX	H	6.90 FQ	11.89 AW	18.90 TQ	TXBLS	10/01-12/01
	Corpus Christi MSA, TX	H	7.29 FQ	13.44 AW	20.47 TQ	TXBLS	10/01-12/01
	Dallas PMSA, TX	H	8.23 FQ	14.71 AW	24.62 TQ	TXBLS	10/01-12/01
	El Paso MSA, TX	H	6.89 FQ	12.04 AW	17.96 TQ	TXBLS	10/01-12/01
	Fort Worth-Arlington PMSA, TX	H	8.18 FQ	15.94 AW	25.89 TQ	TXBLS	10/01-12/01
	Galveston-Texas City PMSA, TX	H	9.52 FQ	17.87 AW	27.62 TQ	TXBLS	10/01-12/01
	Houston PMSA, TX	H	7.62 FQ	17.47 AW	27.12 TQ	TXBLS	10/01-12/01
	Killeen-Temple MSA, TX	H	8.55 FQ	13.95 AW	20.43 TQ	TXBLS	10/01-12/01
	Laredo MSA, TX	H	5.92 FQ	11.00 AW	18.42 TQ	TXBLS	10/01-12/01
	Longview-Marshall MSA, TX	H	8.96 FQ	15.09 AW	22.09 TQ	TXBLS	10/01-12/01
	Lubbock MSA, TX	H	7.74 FQ	15.65 AW	24.86 TQ	TXBLS	10/01-12/01

AAW Average annual wage; **AE** Average entry wage; **AEX** Average experienced wage; **AO** Average offered; **AOH** Average offered, high; **AOL** Average offered, low; **APH** Average pay, high range; **APL** Average pay, low range; **ASH** Average starting, high; **ASL** Average starting, low; **AW** Average wage paid; **FQ** First quartile wage; **H** Hourly; **HI** Highest wage paid; **HR** High end range; **LR** Low end range; **M** Monthly; **MTC** Median total compensation; **MW** Median wage paid; **SQ** Second quartile wage; **S** Special: hourly and annual; **TQ** Third quartile wage; **W** Weekly; **Y** Yearly

Occupation/Type/Industry	Location	Per	Low	Mid	High	Source	Date
Automotive Service Technician and Mechanic	McAllen-Edinburg-Mission MSA, TX	H	6.02 FQ	11.53 AW	17.38 TQ	TXBLS	10/01-12/01
	Odessa-Midland MSA, TX	H	7.57 FQ	13.58 AW	21.40 TQ	TXBLS	10/01-12/01
	San Antonio MSA, TX	H	7.43 FQ	14.16 AW	22.23 TQ	TXBLS	10/01-12/01
	Tyler MSA, TX	H	8.10 FQ	15.08 AW	23.76 TQ	TXBLS	10/01-12/01
	Waco MSA, TX	H	9.44 FQ	14.95 AW	21.89 TQ	TXBLS	10/01-12/01
	Utah	H	8.22 FQ	14.91 AW	21.80 TQ	UTBLS	10/01-12/01
	Provo-Orem MSA, UT	H	7.38 FQ	14.63 AW	24.31 TQ	UTBLS	10/01-12/01
	Salt Lake City-Ogden MSA, UT	H	8.78 FQ	15.30 AW	21.64 TQ	UTBLS	10/01-12/01
	Vermont	H	8.50 FQ	13.90 AW	19.92 TQ	VTBLS	10/01-12/01
	Burlington MSA, VT	H	11.67 FQ	16.25 AW	21.32 TQ	VTBLS	10/01-12/01
	Virginia	H	8.72 FQ	16.34 AW	26.08 TQ	VABLS	10/01-12/01
	Lynchburg MSA, VA	H	6.34 FQ	11.34 AW	17.86 TQ	VABLS	10/01-12/01
	Norfolk-Virginia Beach-Newport News MSA, VA-NC	H	8.65 FQ	15.29 AW	22.92 TQ	VABLS	10/01-12/01
	Richmond-Petersburg MSA, VA	H	10.14 FQ	17.34 AW	26.57 TQ	VABLS	10/01-12/01
	Roanoke MSA, VA	H	7.68 FQ	13.21 AW	20.67 TQ	VABLS	10/01-12/01
	Washington	H	9.36 FQ	16.81 AW	24.72 TQ	WABLS	10/01-12/01
	Bremerton PMSA, WA	H	11.09 FQ	21.07 AW	32.61 TQ	WABLS	10/01-12/01
	Olympia PMSA, WA	H	10.96 FQ	16.67 AW	22.83 TQ	WABLS	10/01-12/01
	Richland-Kennewick-Pasco MSA, WA	H	8.69 FQ	15.38 AW	22.57 TQ	WABLS	10/01-12/01
	Seattle-Bellevue-Everett PMSA, WA	H	9.24 FQ	17.92 AW	26.74 TQ	WABLS	10/01-12/01
	Spokane MSA, WA	H	9.53 FQ	15.34 AW	22.13 TQ	WABLS	10/01-12/01
	Tacoma PMSA, WA	H	9.87 FQ	16.14 AW	22.08 TQ	WABLS	10/01-12/01
	Yakima MSA, WA	H	8.94 FQ	14.15 AW	20.96 TQ	WABLS	10/01-12/01
	West Virginia	H	6.34 FQ	11.22 AW	16.93 TQ	WVBLS	10/01-12/01
	Charleston MSA, WV	H	7.84 FQ	13.03 AW	19.22 TQ	WVBLS	10/01-12/01
	Huntington-Ashland MSA, WV-KY-OH	H	6.79 FQ	11.21 AW	17.38 TQ	WVBLS	10/01-12/01
	Wisconsin	H	8.79 FQ	14.85 AW	22.10 TQ	WIBLS	10/01-12/01
	Appleton-Oshkosh-Neenah MSA, WI	H	6.81 FQ	12.91 AW	18.77 TQ	WIBLS	10/01-12/01
	Green Bay MSA, WI	H	9.26 FQ	15.10 AW	20.99 TQ	WIBLS	10/01-12/01
	Madison MSA, WI	H	9.98 FQ	16.64 AW	24.23 TQ	WIBLS	10/01-12/01
	Milwaukee-Waukesha PMSA, WI	H	9.78 FQ	17.63 AW	26.75 TQ	WIBLS	10/01-12/01
	Racine PMSA, WI	H	8.76 FQ	14.40 AW	21.83 TQ	WIBLS	10/01-12/01
	Wyoming	H	6.40 FQ	12.61 AW	20.32 TQ	WYBLS	10/01-12/01
	Cheyenne MSA, WY	H	7.18 FQ	13.67 AW	20.59 TQ	WYBLS	10/01-12/01
	Puerto Rico	H	5.65 FQ	8.04 AW	12.35 TQ	PRBLS	10/01-12/01
	Virgin Islands	H	8.89 FQ	13.43 AW	20.10 TQ	VIBLS	10/01-12/01
	Guam	H	7.46 FQ	12.16 AW	17.48 TQ	GUBLS	10/01-12/01
Aviation Attorney	United States	Y	16000 ASL		120000 ASH	AEAC	1/99-1/99
Aviation Maintenance Director	United States	Y		58100 AW		AVTODAY	1/99-1/99
Aviation Maintenance Technician	United States	Y		47300 AW		AVTODAY	1/99-1/99
	United States	H		22.75 AW		AVTODAY	1/99-1/99
Corporate flight department	United States	Y		60400 AW		AVTODAY	1/99-1/99
Avionics Director	United States	Y		42200 AW		AVTODAY	1/99-1/99
Avionics Specialist	United States	H	9.00 ASL		25.00 ASH	AEAC	1/99-1/99
Avionics Technician	Alabama	H	12.45 FQ	19.19 AW	25.66 TQ	ALBLS	10/01-12/01
	Alaska	H	16.05 FQ	22.16 AW	30.57 TQ	AKBLS	10/01-12/01
	Anchorage MSA, AK	H	16.03 FQ	21.79 AW	29.25 TQ	AKBLS	10/01-12/01
	Arizona	H	15.03 FQ	21.61 AW	27.50 TQ	AZBLS	10/01-12/01
	Phoenix-Mesa MSA, AZ	H	15.37 FQ	22.20 AW	27.66 TQ	AZBLS	10/01-12/01
	Tucson MSA, AZ	H	15.11 FQ	19.31 AW	24.58 TQ	AZBLS	10/01-12/01
	California	H	14.38 FQ	20.95 AW	27.87 TQ	CABLS	10/01-12/01
	Los Angeles-Long Beach PMSA, CA	H	14.66 FQ	21.67 AW	28.59 TQ	CABLS	10/01-12/01
	San Diego MSA, CA	H	17.13 FQ	20.15 AW	25.62 TQ	CABLS	10/01-12/01
	Colorado	H	14.30 FQ	18.27 AW	22.17 TQ	COBLS	10/01-12/01
	Denver PMSA, CO	H	14.93 FQ	18.54 AW	21.95 TQ	COBLS	10/01-12/01

AAW Average annual wage; AE Average entry wage; AEX Average experienced wage; AO Average offered; AOH Average offered, high; AOL Average offered, low; APH Average pay, high range; APL Average pay, low range; ASH Average starting, high; ASL Average starting, low; AW Average wage paid; FQ First quartile wage; H Hourly; HI Highest wage paid; HR High end range; LR Low end range; M Monthly; MTC Median total compensation; MW Median wage paid; SQ Second quartile wage; S Special: hourly and annual; TQ Third quartile wage; W Weekly; Y Yearly

Occupation/Type/Industry	Location	Per	Low	Mid	High	Source	Date
Avionics Technician	Connecticut	H	15.53 FQ	21.70 AW	27.81 TQ	CTBLS	10/01-12/01
	Delaware	H	10.95 FQ	17.94 AW	21.33 TQ	DEBLS	10/01-12/01
	Washington PMSA, DC-MD-VA-WV	H	12.87 FQ	18.68 AW	24.86 TQ	DCBLS	10/01-12/01
	Florida	H	14.78 FQ	20.84 AW	27.34 TQ	FLBLS	10/01-12/01
	Jacksonville MSA, FL	H	14.69 FQ	19.38 AW	23.43 TQ	FLBLS	10/01-12/01
	Melbourne-Titusville-Palm Bay MSA, FL	H	17.69 FQ	20.59 AW	23.18 TQ	FLBLS	10/01-12/01
	Miami PMSA, FL	H	14.92 FQ	22.45 AW	28.45 TQ	FLBLS	10/01-12/01
	Orlando MSA, FL	H	18.46 FQ	21.55 AW	25.64 TQ	FLBLS	10/01-12/01
	Pensacola MSA, FL	H	13.98 FQ	18.81 AW	22.64 TQ	FLBLS	10/01-12/01
	Tampa-St. Petersburg-Clearwater MSA, FL	H	15.88 FQ	22.06 AW	27.85 TQ	FLBLS	10/01-12/01
	Georgia	H	15.44 FQ	21.31 AW	28.40 TQ	GABLS	10/01-12/01
	Atlanta MSA, GA	H	16.17 FQ	22.36 AW	30.52 TQ	GABLS	10/01-12/01
	Macon MSA, GA	H	14.23 FQ	19.57 AW	25.56 TQ	GABLS	10/01-12/01
	Savannah MSA, GA	H	17.21 FQ	21.05 AW	26.02 TQ	GABLS	10/01-12/01
	Idaho	H	11.45 FQ	18.05 AW	31.47 TQ	IDBLS	10/01-12/01
	Boise City MSA, ID	H	13.94 FQ	20.69 AW	32.85 TQ	IDBLS	10/01-12/01
	Illinois	H	14.97 FQ	22.26 AW	28.58 TQ	ILBLS	10/01-12/01
	Indiana	H	13.93 FQ	18.98 AW	24.73 TQ	INBLS	10/01-12/01
	Indianapolis MSA, IN	H	13.64 FQ	18.59 AW	24.13 TQ	INBLS	10/01-12/01
	Iowa	H	11.62 FQ	17.09 AW	24.62 TQ	IABLS	10/01-12/01
	Kansas	H	14.52 FQ	19.60 AW	25.98 TQ	KSBLS	10/01-12/01
	Wichita MSA, KS	H	14.52 FQ	19.58 AW	25.94 TQ	KSBLS	10/01-12/01
	Louisiana	H	13.70 FQ	19.31 AW	24.87 TQ	LABLS	10/01-12/01
	New Orleans MSA, LA	H	12.43 FQ	18.37 AW	25.08 TQ	LABLS	10/01-12/01
	Shreveport-Bossier City MSA, LA	H	13.24 FQ	19.16 AW	22.78 TQ	LABLS	10/01-12/01
	Maryland	H	12.79 FQ	19.54 AW	26.76 TQ	MDBLS	10/01-12/01
	Baltimore PMSA, MD	H	18.11 FQ	21.69 AW	27.08 TQ	MDBLS	10/01-12/01
	Michigan	H	14.51 FQ	19.78 AW	25.74 TQ	MIBLS	10/01-12/01
	Detroit PMSA, MI	H	14.92 FQ	20.09 AW	25.87 TQ	MIBLS	10/01-12/01
	Minnesota	H	11.54 FQ	23.42 AW	38.54 TQ	MNBLS	10/01-12/01
	Minneapolis-St. Paul MSA, MN-WI	H	18.15 FQ	28.66 AW	40.96 TQ	MNBLS	10/01-12/01
	Mississippi	H	15.89 FQ	19.62 AW	23.74 TQ	MSBLS	10/01-12/01
	Missouri	H	13.93 FQ	21.77 AW	28.45 TQ	MOBLS	10/01-12/01
	Kansas City MSA, MO-KS	H	12.26 FQ	21.75 AW	28.70 TQ	MOBLS	10/01-12/01
	St. Louis MSA, MO-IL	H	13.21 FQ	20.63 AW	28.19 TQ	MOBLS	10/01-12/01
	Omaha MSA, NE-IA	H	14.71 FQ	20.58 AW	28.51 TQ	NEBLS	10/01-12/01
	Nevada	H	19.36 FQ	26.86 AW	35.28 TQ	NVBLS	10/01-12/01
	Las Vegas MSA, NV-AZ	H	19.69 FQ	28.84 AW	35.97 TQ	NVBLS	10/01-12/01
	New Jersey	H	13.28 FQ	20.82 AW	26.95 TQ	NJBLS	10/01-12/01
	Bergen-Passaic PMSA, NJ	H	12.48 FQ	22.58 AW	33.10 TQ	NJBLS	10/01-12/01
	New Mexico	H	12.24 FQ	16.69 AW	22.27 TQ	NMBLS	10/01-12/01
	New York	H	14.49 FQ	20.38 AW	28.93 TQ	NYBLS	10/01-12/01
	New York PMSA, NY	H	14.66 FQ	20.61 AW	30.83 TQ	NYBLS	10/01-12/01
	North Carolina	H	12.89 FQ	18.93 AW	25.04 TQ	NCBLS	10/01-12/01
	Charlotte-Gastonia-Rock Hill MSA, NC-SC	H	15.91 FQ	20.53 AW	25.04 TQ	NCBLS	10/01-12/01
	Greensboro-Winston-Salem-High Point MSA, NC	H	11.91 FQ	16.87 AW	21.59 TQ	NCBLS	10/01-12/01
	Raleigh-Durham-Chapel Hill MSA, NC	H	13.78 FQ	22.24 AW	30.47 TQ	NCBLS	10/01-12/01
	North Dakota	H	18.92 FQ	23.46 AW	26.89 TQ	NDBLS	10/01-12/01
	Ohio	H	14.33 FQ	19.74 AW	26.25 TQ	OHBLS	10/01-12/01
	Cincinnati PMSA, OH-KY-IN	H	15.63 FQ	23.04 AW	32.23 TQ	OHBLS	10/01-12/01
	Dayton-Springfield MSA, OH	H	14.43 FQ	18.49 AW	22.12 TQ	OHBLS	10/01-12/01
	Oklahoma	H	11.88 FQ	17.40 AW	21.47 TQ	OKBLS	10/01-12/01
	Oklahoma City MSA, OK	H	12.98 FQ	18.18 AW	21.35 TQ	OKBLS	10/01-12/01
	Oregon	H	17.04 FQ	22.21 AW	26.85 TQ	ORBLS	10/01-12/01
	Portland-Vancouver PMSA, OR-WA	H	17.54 FQ	22.59 AW	26.92 TQ	ORBLS	10/01-12/01
	Pennsylvania	H	12.93 FQ	21.02 AW	33.42 TQ	PABLS	10/01-12/01
	Philadelphia PMSA, PA-NJ	H	14.22 FQ	21.34 AW	32.03 TQ	PABLS	10/01-12/01
	Pittsburgh MSA, PA	H	12.80 FQ	21.95 AW	40.07 TQ	PABLS	10/01-12/01
	South Carolina	H	12.23 FQ	18.55 AW	23.16 TQ	SCBLS	10/01-12/01
	Charleston-North Charleston MSA, SC	H	14.36 FQ	20.35 AW	26.39 TQ	SCBLS	10/01-12/01
	Columbia MSA, SC	H	11.51 FQ	17.10 AW	22.58 TQ	SCBLS	10/01-12/01

AAW	Average annual wage	**AOH**	Average offered, high	**ASH**	Average starting, high	**H**	Hourly	**M**	Monthly	**S**	Special: hourly and annual
AE	Average entry wage	**AOL**	Average offered, low	**ASL**	Average starting, low	**HI**	Highest wage paid	**MTC**	Median total compensation	**TQ**	Third quartile wage
AEX	Average experienced wage	**APH**	Average pay, high range	**AW**	Average wage paid	**HR**	High end range	**MW**	Median wage paid	**W**	Weekly
AO	Average offered	**APL**	Average pay, low range	**FQ**	First quartile wage	**LR**	Low end range	**SQ**	Second quartile wage	**Y**	Yearly

Occupation/Type/Industry	Location	Per	Low	Mid	High	Source	Date
Avionics Technician	Greenville-Spartanburg-Anderson MSA, SC	H	11.56 FQ	17.01 AW	22.58 TQ	SCBLS	10/01-12/01
	Tennessee	H	12.38 FQ	19.25 AW	27.04 TQ	TNBLS	10/01-12/01
	Memphis MSA, TN-AR-MS	H	9.48 FQ	13.89 AW	17.93 TQ	TNBLS	10/01-12/01
	Texas	H	11.46 FQ	17.37 AW	24.25 TQ	TXBLS	10/01-12/01
	Austin-San Marcos MSA, TX	H	11.05 FQ	16.19 AW	21.47 TQ	TXBLS	10/01-12/01
	Corpus Christi MSA, TX	H	17.49 FQ	19.79 AW	23.38 TQ	TXBLS	10/01-12/01
	Dallas PMSA, TX	H	11.25 FQ	15.89 AW	21.39 TQ	TXBLS	10/01-12/01
	Fort Worth-Arlington PMSA, TX	H	12.29 FQ	18.85 AW	25.79 TQ	TXBLS	10/01-12/01
	San Antonio MSA, TX	H	14.70 FQ	19.47 AW	25.32 TQ	TXBLS	10/01-12/01
	Utah	H	12.74 FQ	18.57 AW	22.49 TQ	UTBLS	10/01-12/01
	Salt Lake City-Ogden MSA, UT	H	12.72 FQ	18.56 AW	22.36 TQ	UTBLS	10/01-12/01
	Virginia	H	12.94 FQ	18.73 AW	25.27 TQ	VABLS	10/01-12/01
	Norfolk-Virginia Beach-Newport News MSA, VA-NC	H	13.10 FQ	18.73 AW	25.09 TQ	VABLS	10/01-12/01
	Washington	H	16.75 FQ	24.09 AW	30.96 TQ	WABLS	10/01-12/01
	Seattle-Bellevue-Everett PMSA, WA	H	16.68 FQ	24.22 AW	31.08 TQ	WABLS	10/01-12/01
	Tacoma PMSA, WA	H	10.06 FQ	21.31 AW	29.47 TQ	WABLS	10/01-12/01
Babysitter	North Pole, AK	H		5.00 AW		GDHK	2002
	Menlo Park, CA	H		7.00 AW		GDHK	2002
	Coral Springs, FL	H		6.00 AW		GDHK	2002
	Hawi, HI	H		6.00 AW		GDHK	2002
	St. Louis, MO	H		6.00 AW		GDHK	2002
	Las Vegas, NV	H		2.00 AW		GDHK	2002
	Keene, NH	H		4.00 AW		GDHK	2002
	Montclair, NJ	H		10.00 AW		GDHK	2002
	Chappaqua, NY	H		10.00 AW		GDHK	2002
	Columbus, OH	H		7.50 AW		GDHK	2002
	Spanish Fork, UT	H		1.00 AW		GDHK	2002
	Yellowstone National Park, WY	H		7.00 AW		GDHK	2002
Baggage Porter and Bellhop	Alabama	H	5.56 FQ	6.40 AW	7.60 TQ	ALBLS	10/01-12/01
	Birmingham MSA, AL	H	5.59 FQ	6.51 AW	8.13 TQ	ALBLS	10/01-12/01
	Huntsville MSA, AL	H	5.61 FQ	6.30 AW	7.22 TQ	ALBLS	10/01-12/01
	Mobile MSA, AL	H	5.46 FQ	6.05 AW	6.95 TQ	ALBLS	10/01-12/01
	Alaska	H	6.47 FQ	11.24 AW	21.12 TQ	AKBLS	10/01-12/01
	Anchorage MSA, AK	H	6.49 FQ	11.75 AW	21.44 TQ	AKBLS	10/01-12/01
	Arizona	H	5.64 FQ	7.90 AW	11.72 TQ	AZBLS	10/01-12/01
	Phoenix-Mesa MSA, AZ	H	5.68 FQ	8.55 AW	17.29 TQ	AZBLS	10/01-12/01
	Tucson MSA, AZ	H	5.61 FQ	7.12 AW	8.47 TQ	AZBLS	10/01-12/01
	Arkansas	H	5.71 FQ	7.21 AW	9.30 TQ	ARBLS	10/01-12/01
	Fayetteville-Springdale-Rogers MSA, AR	H	5.54 FQ	6.14 AW	6.94 TQ	ARBLS	10/01-12/01
	Little Rock-North Little Rock MSA, AR	H	6.25 FQ	7.76 AW	10.10 TQ	ARBLS	10/01-12/01
	California	H	6.43 FQ	9.39 AW	16.90 TQ	CABLS	10/01-12/01
	Fresno MSA, CA	H	6.49 FQ	10.22 AW	17.23 TQ	CABLS	10/01-12/01
	Los Angeles-Long Beach PMSA, CA	H	6.46 FQ	9.67 AW	17.79 TQ	CABLS	10/01-12/01
	Oakland PMSA, CA	H	6.49 FQ	9.37 AW	14.82 TQ	CABLS	10/01-12/01
	Orange County PMSA, CA	H	6.33 FQ	7.18 AW	9.33 TQ	CABLS	10/01-12/01
	Riverside-San Bernardino PMSA, CA	H	6.37 FQ	7.27 AW	8.49 TQ	CABLS	10/01-12/01
	Sacramento PMSA, CA	H	6.44 FQ	7.78 AW	9.97 TQ	CABLS	10/01-12/01
	Salinas MSA, CA	H	6.35 FQ	7.36 AW	9.56 TQ	CABLS	10/01-12/01
	San Diego MSA, CA	H	6.40 FQ	8.26 AW	10.22 TQ	CABLS	10/01-12/01
	San Francisco PMSA, CA	H	7.10 FQ	10.17 AW	18.49 TQ	CABLS	10/01-12/01
	San Jose PMSA, CA	H	6.74 FQ	8.83 AW	11.68 TQ	CABLS	10/01-12/01
	Santa Barbara-Santa Maria-Lompoc MSA, CA	H	6.35 FQ	7.52 AW	9.66 TQ	CABLS	10/01-12/01
	Santa Cruz-Watsonville PMSA, CA	H	6.37 FQ	7.56 AW	10.23 TQ	CABLS	10/01-12/01
	Ventura PMSA, CA	H	6.38 FQ	7.32 AW	9.00 TQ	CABLS	10/01-12/01
	Colorado	H	5.89 FQ	10.47 AW	20.51 TQ	COBLS	10/01-12/01
	Boulder-Longmont PMSA, CO	H	5.78 FQ	6.95 AW	8.76 TQ	COBLS	10/01-12/01
	Colorado Springs MSA, CO	H	5.63 FQ	6.53 AW	8.22 TQ	COBLS	10/01-12/01
	Denver PMSA, CO	H	6.03 FQ	12.41 AW	21.82 TQ	COBLS	10/01-12/01

AAW	Average annual wage	**AOH**	Average offered, high	**ASH**	Average starting, high	**H**	Hourly	**M**	Monthly	**S**	Special: hourly and annual
AE	Average entry wage	**AOL**	Average offered, low	**ASL**	Average starting, low	**HI**	Highest wage paid	**MTC**	Median total compensation	**TQ**	Third quartile wage
AEX	Average experienced wage	**APH**	Average pay, high range	**AW**	Average wage paid	**HR**	High end range	**MW**	Median wage paid	**W**	Weekly
AO	Average offered	**APL**	Average pay, low range	**FQ**	First quartile wage	**LR**	Low end range	**SQ**	Second quartile wage	**Y**	Yearly

Occupation/Type/Industry	Location	Per	Low	Mid	High	Source	Date
Baggage Porter and Bellhop	Connecticut	H	6.68 FQ	8.62 AW	11.96 TQ	CTBLS	10/01-12/01
	Hartford MSA, CT	H	6.63 FQ	8.03 AW	10.44 TQ	CTBLS	10/01-12/01
	New London-Norwich MSA, CT-RI	H	6.60 FQ	8.06 AW	10.35 TQ	CTBLS	10/01-12/01
	Delaware	H	6.50 FQ	8.18 AW	10.74 TQ	DEBLS	10/01-12/01
	Wilmington-Newark PMSA, DE-MD	H	6.49 FQ	7.54 AW	9.70 TQ	DEBLS	10/01-12/01
	District of Columbia	H	6.66 FQ	11.12 AW	17.32 TQ	DCBLS	10/01-12/01
	Washington PMSA, DC-MD-VA-WV	H	6.56 FQ	12.30 AW	20.40 TQ	DCBLS	10/01-12/01
	Florida	H	5.77 FQ	9.14 AW	18.10 TQ	FLBLS	10/01-12/01
	Daytona Beach MSA, FL	H	5.70 FQ	6.83 AW	8.78 TQ	FLBLS	10/01-12/01
	Fort Lauderdale PMSA, FL	H	5.86 FQ	9.00 AW	13.19 TQ	FLBLS	10/01-12/01
	Fort Myers-Cape Coral MSA, FL	H	5.88 FQ	8.11 AW	11.98 TQ	FLBLS	10/01-12/01
	Fort Pierce-Port St. Lucie MSA, FL	H	5.58 FQ	6.94 AW	9.29 TQ	FLBLS	10/01-12/01
	Jacksonville MSA, FL	H	5.75 FQ	8.91 AW	17.09 TQ	FLBLS	10/01-12/01
	Miami PMSA, FL	H	5.85 FQ	9.33 AW	14.14 TQ	FLBLS	10/01-12/01
	Naples MSA, FL	H	5.63 FQ	6.72 AW	8.70 TQ	FLBLS	10/01-12/01
	Orlando MSA, FL	H	5.71 FQ	9.47 AW	20.11 TQ	FLBLS	10/01-12/01
	Pensacola MSA, FL	H	5.66 FQ	12.66 AW	24.11 TQ	FLBLS	10/01-12/01
	Sarasota-Bradenton MSA, FL	H	5.83 FQ	7.50 AW	9.60 TQ	FLBLS	10/01-12/01
	Tampa-St. Petersburg-Clearwater MSA, FL	H	5.81 FQ	11.68 AW	21.05 TQ	FLBLS	10/01-12/01
	West Palm Beach-Boca Raton MSA, FL	H	5.84 FQ	7.17 AW	8.88 TQ	FLBLS	10/01-12/01
	Georgia	H	5.97 FQ	12.74 AW	22.56 TQ	GABLS	10/01-12/01
	Atlanta MSA, GA	H	5.85 FQ	11.97 AW	23.79 TQ	GABLS	10/01-12/01
	Hawaii	H	5.71 FQ	8.75 AW	18.00 TQ	HIBLS	10/01-12/01
	Honolulu MSA, HI	H	5.67 FQ	8.63 AW	19.02 TQ	HIBLS	10/01-12/01
	Idaho	H	5.74 FQ	7.77 AW	10.87 TQ	IDBLS	10/01-12/01
	Illinois	H	5.59 FQ	9.08 AW	18.69 TQ	ILBLS	10/01-12/01
	Chicago PMSA, IL	H	5.53 FQ	8.48 AW	17.87 TQ	ILBLS	10/01-12/01
	Indiana	H	6.13 FQ	13.22 AW	21.10 TQ	INBLS	10/01-12/01
	Gary PMSA, IN	H	5.77 FQ	8.04 AW	10.62 TQ	INBLS	10/01-12/01
	Indianapolis MSA, IN	H	5.83 FQ	10.00 AW	20.18 TQ	INBLS	10/01-12/01
	Iowa	H	5.73 FQ	8.38 AW	18.40 TQ	IABLS	10/01-12/01
	Des Moines MSA, IA	H	5.67 FQ	9.29 AW	20.46 TQ	IABLS	10/01-12/01
	Kansas	H	5.95 FQ	10.88 AW	18.89 TQ	KSBLS	10/01-12/01
	Kentucky	H	5.54 FQ	6.66 AW	8.37 TQ	KYBLS	10/01-12/01
	Lexington MSA, KY	H	5.51 FQ	6.19 AW	6.96 TQ	KYBLS	10/01-12/01
	Louisville MSA, KY-IN	H	5.57 FQ	7.02 AW	8.77 TQ	KYBLS	10/01-12/01
	Louisiana	H	5.69 FQ	7.74 AW	11.10 TQ	LABLS	10/01-12/01
	Lafayette MSA, LA	H	5.51 FQ	6.62 AW	8.10 TQ	LABLS	10/01-12/01
	New Orleans MSA, LA	H	5.69 FQ	7.12 AW	9.43 TQ	LABLS	10/01-12/01
	Shreveport-Bossier City MSA, LA	H	5.69 FQ	6.76 AW	8.66 TQ	LABLS	10/01-12/01
	Maine	H	7.60 FQ	13.79 AW	20.83 TQ	MEBLS	10/01-12/01
	Portland MSA, ME	H	7.75 FQ	13.81 AW	21.02 TQ	MEBLS	10/01-12/01
	Maryland	H	5.96 FQ	9.98 AW	20.02 TQ	MDBLS	10/01-12/01
	Baltimore PMSA, MD	H	6.18 FQ	9.91 AW	19.00 TQ	MDBLS	10/01-12/01
	Massachusetts	H	6.87 FQ	11.00 AW	20.30 TQ	MABLS	10/01-12/01
	Boston PMSA, MA-NH	H	6.88 FQ	11.36 AW	20.74 TQ	MABLS	10/01-12/01
	Michigan	H	7.17 FQ	13.41 AW	21.57 TQ	MIBLS	10/01-12/01
	Lansing-East Lansing MSA, MI	H	5.66 FQ	13.16 AW	21.41 TQ	MIBLS	10/01-12/01
	Saginaw-Bay City-Midland MSA, MI	H	5.80 FQ	10.35 AW	20.75 TQ	MIBLS	10/01-12/01
	Minnesota	H	5.82 FQ	11.43 AW	20.93 TQ	MNBLS	10/01-12/01
	Minneapolis-St. Paul MSA, MN-WI	H	5.81 FQ	11.40 AW	20.83 TQ	MNBLS	10/01-12/01
	Mississippi	H	5.58 FQ	7.16 AW	9.59 TQ	MSBLS	10/01-12/01
	Biloxi-Gulfport-Pascagoula MSA, MS	H	5.51 FQ	6.74 AW	8.79 TQ	MSBLS	10/01-12/01
	Missouri	H	5.83 FQ	10.44 AW	19.38 TQ	MOBLS	10/01-12/01
	Kansas City MSA, MO-KS	H	5.99 FQ	12.15 AW	21.33 TQ	MOBLS	10/01-12/01
	St. Louis MSA, MO-IL	H	5.74 FQ	8.47 AW	11.38 TQ	MOBLS	10/01-12/01
	Montana	H	6.01 FQ	12.55 AW	19.46 TQ	MTBLS	10/01-12/01
	Nebraska	H	5.75 FQ	9.16 AW	17.49 TQ	NEBLS	10/01-12/01
	Omaha MSA, NE-IA	H	5.87 FQ	9.13 AW	17.23 TQ	NEBLS	10/01-12/01
	Nevada	H	6.11 FQ	9.49 AW	13.07 TQ	NVBLS	10/01-12/01
	Las Vegas MSA, NV-AZ	H	6.30 FQ	9.81 AW	13.39 TQ	NVBLS	10/01-12/01

AAW Average annual wage; **AE** Average entry wage; **AEX** Average experienced wage; **AO** Average offered; **AOH** Average offered, high; **AOL** Average offered, low; **APH** Average pay, high range; **APL** Average pay, low range; **ASH** Average starting, high; **ASL** Average starting, low; **AW** Average wage paid; **FQ** First quartile wage; **H** Hourly; **HI** Highest wage paid; **HR** High end range; **LR** Low end range; **M** Monthly; **MTC** Median total compensation; **MW** Median wage paid; **SQ** Second quartile wage; **S** Special: hourly and annual; **TQ** Third quartile wage; **W** Weekly; **Y** Yearly

Occupation/Type/Industry	Location	Per	Low	Mid	High	Source	Date
Baggage Porter and Bellhop	Reno MSA, NV	H	5.65 FQ	6.88 AW	8.44 TQ	NVBLS	10/01-12/01
	New Hampshire	H	5.84 FQ	10.81 AW	21.15 TQ	NHBLS	10/01-12/01
	Manchester PMSA, NH	H	5.85 FQ	12.41 AW	21.94 TQ	NHBLS	10/01-12/01
	New Jersey	H	5.91 FQ	11.13 AW	20.17 TQ	NJBLS	10/01-12/01
	Atlantic-Cape May PMSA, NJ	H	5.60 FQ	7.12 AW	8.78 TQ	NJBLS	10/01-12/01
	Bergen-Passaic PMSA, NJ	H	6.16 FQ	12.98 AW	21.87 TQ	NJBLS	10/01-12/01
	Middlesex-Somerset-Hunterdon PMSA, NJ	H	6.16 FQ	8.07 AW	10.67 TQ	NJBLS	10/01-12/01
	Newark PMSA, NJ	H	6.50 FQ	14.25 AW	20.97 TQ	NJBLS	10/01-12/01
	Trenton PMSA, NJ	H	5.77 FQ	7.66 AW	10.01 TQ	NJBLS	10/01-12/01
	New Mexico	H	5.69 FQ	8.33 AW	18.74 TQ	NMBLS	10/01-12/01
	Albuquerque MSA, NM	H	5.82 FQ	10.18 AW	20.72 TQ	NMBLS	10/01-12/01
	New York	H	6.33 FQ	13.80 AW	20.65 TQ	NYBLS	10/01-12/01
	Albany-Schenectady-Troy MSA, NY	H	5.80 FQ	10.60 AW	20.78 TQ	NYBLS	10/01-12/01
	Buffalo-Niagara Falls MSA, NY	H	5.69 FQ	11.17 AW	21.26 TQ	NYBLS	10/01-12/01
	Nassau-Suffolk PMSA, NY	H	5.87 FQ	9.57 AW	18.39 TQ	NYBLS	10/01-12/01
	New York PMSA, NY	H	7.01 FQ	14.79 AW	20.73 TQ	NYBLS	10/01-12/01
	Rochester MSA, NY	H	5.48 FQ	8.69 AW	19.14 TQ	NYBLS	10/01-12/01
	Syracuse MSA, NY	H	5.76 FQ	9.33 AW	19.72 TQ	NYBLS	10/01-12/01
	Utica-Rome MSA, NY	H	5.80 FQ	9.65 AW	14.96 TQ	NYBLS	10/01-12/01
	North Carolina	H	5.96 FQ	12.68 AW	20.98 TQ	NCBLS	10/01-12/01
	Greensboro-Winston-Salem-High Point MSA, NC	H	5.58 FQ	6.84 AW	8.17 TQ	NCBLS	10/01-12/01
	Raleigh-Durham-Chapel Hill MSA, NC	H	5.73 FQ	11.08 AW	21.43 TQ	NCBLS	10/01-12/01
	North Dakota	H	5.96 FQ	8.64 AW	11.07 TQ	NDBLS	10/01-12/01
	Fargo-Moorhead MSA, ND-MN	H	6.17 FQ	8.92 AW	11.59 TQ	NDBLS	10/01-12/01
	Ohio	H	5.79 FQ	9.73 AW	19.25 TQ	OHBLS	10/01-12/01
	Cincinnati PMSA, OH-KY-IN	H	5.64 FQ	6.81 AW	8.65 TQ	OHBLS	10/01-12/01
	Cleveland-Lorain-Elyria PMSA, OH	H	5.86 FQ	9.36 AW	18.63 TQ	OHBLS	10/01-12/01
	Columbus MSA, OH	H	5.86 FQ	10.61 AW	20.29 TQ	OHBLS	10/01-12/01
	Dayton-Springfield MSA, OH	H	5.66 FQ	6.20 AW	7.13 TQ	OHBLS	10/01-12/01
	Toledo MSA, OH	H	5.57 FQ	6.40 AW	7.97 TQ	OHBLS	10/01-12/01
	Oklahoma	H	5.56 FQ	6.36 AW	7.63 TQ	OKBLS	10/01-12/01
	Oklahoma City MSA, OK	H	5.57 FQ	6.50 AW	8.74 TQ	OKBLS	10/01-12/01
	Tulsa MSA, OK	H	5.52 FQ	6.31 AW	7.57 TQ	OKBLS	10/01-12/01
	Oregon	H	6.73 FQ	11.34 AW	18.64 TQ	ORBLS	10/01-12/01
	Portland-Vancouver PMSA, OR-WA	H	6.74 FQ	10.17 AW	19.19 TQ	ORBLS	10/01-12/01
	Pennsylvania	H	5.99 FQ	12.62 AW	21.52 TQ	PABLS	10/01-12/01
	Allentown-Bethlehem-Easton MSA, PA	H	5.72 FQ	6.70 AW	8.21 TQ	PABLS	10/01-12/01
	Harrisburg-Lebanon-Carlisle MSA, PA	H	5.67 FQ	10.42 AW	20.79 TQ	PABLS	10/01-12/01
	Philadelphia PMSA, PA-NJ	H	5.75 FQ	8.03 AW	10.90 TQ	PABLS	10/01-12/01
	Rhode Island	H	6.44 FQ	7.49 AW	9.79 TQ	RIBLS	10/01-12/01
	South Carolina	H	5.77 FQ	8.00 AW	14.05 TQ	SCBLS	10/01-12/01
	Charleston-North Charleston MSA, SC	H	5.86 FQ	8.71 AW	15.32 TQ	SCBLS	10/01-12/01
	Greenville-Spartanburg-Anderson MSA, SC	H	5.69 FQ	6.62 AW	8.45 TQ	SCBLS	10/01-12/01
	Myrtle Beach MSA, SC	H	5.63 FQ	8.35 AW	15.78 TQ	SCBLS	10/01-12/01
	South Dakota	H	5.63 FQ	6.76 AW	9.27 TQ	SDBLS	10/01-12/01
	Chattanooga MSA, TN-GA	H	5.64 FQ	9.86 AW	21.42 TQ	TNBLS	10/01-12/01
	Knoxville MSA, TN	H	5.69 FQ	7.77 AW	17.82 TQ	TNBLS	10/01-12/01
	Nashville MSA, TN	H	5.82 FQ	9.61 AW	20.55 TQ	TNBLS	10/01-12/01
	Texas	H	5.98 FQ	7.94 AW	10.12 TQ	TXBLS	10/01-12/01
	Austin-San Marcos MSA, TX	H	5.68 FQ	7.73 AW	10.66 TQ	TXBLS	10/01-12/01
	Brownsville-Harlingen-San Benito MSA, TX	H	5.86 FQ	7.42 AW	9.99 TQ	TXBLS	10/01-12/01
	Dallas PMSA, TX	H	5.76 FQ	7.67 AW	10.61 TQ	TXBLS	10/01-12/01
	Fort Worth-Arlington PMSA, TX	H	5.67 FQ	10.01 AW	19.36 TQ	TXBLS	10/01-12/01
	Houston PMSA, TX	H	6.81 FQ	7.56 AW	8.39 TQ	TXBLS	10/01-12/01
	San Antonio MSA, TX	H	5.74 FQ	8.78 AW	15.40 TQ	TXBLS	10/01-12/01
	Utah	H	5.80 FQ	8.84 AW	17.27 TQ	UTBLS	10/01-12/01
	Salt Lake City-Ogden MSA, UT	H	5.79 FQ	9.01 AW	18.38 TQ	UTBLS	10/01-12/01

AAW Average annual wage	**AOH** Average offered, high	**ASH** Average starting, high	**H** Hourly	**M** Monthly	**S** Special: hourly and annual
AE Average entry wage	**AOL** Average offered, low	**ASL** Average starting, low	**HI** Highest wage paid	**MTC** Median total compensation	**TQ** Third quartile wage
AEX Average experienced wage	**APH** Average pay, high range	**AW** Average wage paid	**HR** High end range	**MW** Median wage paid	**W** Weekly
AO Average offered	**APL** Average pay, low range	**FQ** First quartile wage	**LR** Low end range	**SQ** Second quartile wage	**Y** Yearly

Occupation/Type/Industry	Location	Per	Low	Mid	High	Source	Date
Baggage Porter and Bellhop	Vermont	H	6.40 FQ	7.23 AW	8.37 TQ	VTBLS	10/01-12/01
	Burlington MSA, VT	H	6.43 FQ	7.28 AW	8.59 TQ	VTBLS	10/01-12/01
	Virginia	H	6.22 FQ	13.21 AW	21.11 TQ	VABLS	10/01-12/01
	Norfolk-Virginia Beach-Newport News MSA, VA-NC	H	5.66 FQ	7.83 AW	10.39 TQ	VABLS	10/01-12/01
	Richmond-Petersburg MSA, VA	H	5.89 FQ	12.44 AW	21.78 TQ	VABLS	10/01-12/01
	Roanoke MSA, VA	H	6.03 FQ	9.77 AW	19.14 TQ	VABLS	10/01-12/01
	Washington	H	6.74 FQ	11.01 AW	20.14 TQ	WABLS	10/01-12/01
	Seattle-Bellevue-Everett PMSA, WA	H	6.75 FQ	10.76 AW	19.86 TQ	WABLS	10/01-12/01
	Spokane MSA, WA	H	6.74 FQ	8.81 AW	12.44 TQ	WABLS	10/01-12/01
	West Virginia	H	5.48 FQ	7.08 AW	10.16 TQ	WVBLS	10/01-12/01
	Wisconsin	H	5.66 FQ	9.42 AW	19.46 TQ	WIBLS	10/01-12/01
	Green Bay MSA, WI	H	5.47 FQ	8.03 AW	12.52 TQ	WIBLS	10/01-12/01
	Madison MSA, WI	H	7.26 FQ	10.64 AW	18.88 TQ	WIBLS	10/01-12/01
	Milwaukee-Waukesha PMSA, WI	H	5.57 FQ	10.62 AW	21.30 TQ	WIBLS	10/01-12/01
	Wyoming	H	5.78 FQ	7.62 AW	10.78 TQ	WYBLS	10/01-12/01
	Puerto Rico	H	5.67 FQ	13.51 AW	26.19 TQ	PRBLS	10/01-12/01
	Virgin Islands	H	5.68 FQ	7.07 AW	8.99 TQ	VIBLS	10/01-12/01
	Guam	H	5.52 FQ	6.76 AW	8.49 TQ	GUBLS	10/01-12/01
Bailiff	Alabama	Y	14290 FQ	22490 AW	33100 TQ	ALBLS	10/01-12/01
	Arizona	Y	20250 FQ	31120 AW	42980 TQ	AZBLS	10/01-12/01
	Phoenix-Mesa MSA, AZ	Y	25580 FQ	33030 AW	38130 TQ	AZBLS	10/01-12/01
	Tucson MSA, AZ	Y	17800 FQ	29490 AW	45830 TQ	AZBLS	10/01-12/01
	Arkansas	Y	13890 FQ	23700 AW	40600 TQ	ARBLS	10/01-12/01
	Fayetteville-Springdale-Rogers MSA, AR	Y	14750 FQ	23560 AW	33440 TQ	ARBLS	10/01-12/01
	California	Y	17170 FQ	34070 AW	51630 TQ	CABLS	10/01-12/01
	Colorado	Y	18340 FQ	24580 AW	39100 TQ	COBLS	10/01-12/01
	Denver PMSA, CO	Y	19110 FQ	30610 AW	45160 TQ	COBLS	10/01-12/01
	Connecticut	Y	39020 FQ	47000 AW	55620 TQ	CTBLS	10/01-12/01
	Washington PMSA, DC-MD-VA-WV	Y	20650 FQ	37360 AW	55670 TQ	DCBLS	10/01-12/01
	Florida	Y	27290 FQ	36930 AW	45460 TQ	FLBLS	10/01-12/01
	Orlando MSA, FL	Y	24140 FQ	33780 AW	45550 TQ	FLBLS	10/01-12/01
	Tallahassee MSA, FL	Y	25300 FQ	36920 AW	44560 TQ	FLBLS	10/01-12/01
	Georgia	Y	12550 FQ	18830 AW	24720 TQ	GABLS	10/01-12/01
	Atlanta MSA, GA	Y	15260 FQ	19430 AW	23240 TQ	GABLS	10/01-12/01
	Hawaii	Y	28470 FQ	35290 AW	50700 TQ	HIBLS	10/01-12/01
	Idaho	Y	17370 FQ	29480 AW	47630 TQ	IDBLS	10/01-12/01
	Illinois	Y	12850 FQ	26150 AW	42990 TQ	ILBLS	10/01-12/01
	Chicago PMSA, IL	Y	13970 FQ	28270 AW	44250 TQ	ILBLS	10/01-12/01
	Indiana	Y	17140 FQ	25110 AW	33230 TQ	INBLS	10/01-12/01
	Kansas	Y	13700 FQ	22610 AW	35780 TQ	KSBLS	10/01-12/01
	Kentucky	Y	15760 FQ	21390 AW	28240 TQ	KYBLS	10/01-12/01
	Louisiana	Y	11950 FQ	21380 AW	36320 TQ	LABLS	10/01-12/01
	Maine	Y	18480 FQ	21510 AW	26580 TQ	MEBLS	10/01-12/01
	Michigan	Y	24380 FQ	35590 AW	48220 TQ	MIBLS	10/01-12/01
	Detroit PMSA, MI	Y	26900 FQ	35570 AW	44910 TQ	MIBLS	10/01-12/01
	Lansing-East Lansing MSA, MI	Y	28840 FQ	38540 AW	46540 TQ	MIBLS	10/01-12/01
	Minnesota	Y	19670 FQ	36520 AW	56720 TQ	MNBLS	10/01-12/01
	Minneapolis-St. Paul MSA, MN-WI	Y	29340 FQ	47290 AW	57950 TQ	MNBLS	10/01-12/01
	Mississippi	Y	12110 FQ	18680 AW	28970 TQ	MSBLS	10/01-12/01
	Missouri	Y	12780 FQ	25030 AW	40990 TQ	MOBLS	10/01-12/01
	Kansas City MSA, MO-KS	Y	15750 FQ	27310 AW	43180 TQ	MOBLS	10/01-12/01
	St. Louis MSA, MO-IL	Y	12060 FQ	25600 AW	37800 TQ	MOBLS	10/01-12/01
	Montana	Y	12220 FQ	18080 AW	27310 TQ	MTBLS	10/01-12/01
	Nebraska	Y	23550 FQ	32920 AW	42970 TQ	NEBLS	10/01-12/01
	New Hampshire	Y	14830 FQ	19260 AW	27420 TQ	NHBLS	10/01-12/01
	New Jersey	Y	15520 FQ	24180 AW	34540 TQ	NJBLS	10/01-12/01
	New Mexico	Y	15570 FQ	19520 AW	22300 TQ	NMBLS	10/01-12/01
	Albuquerque MSA, NM	Y	15860 FQ	19640 AW	22090 TQ	NMBLS	10/01-12/01
	New York	Y	27170 FQ	42020 AW	54630 TQ	NYBLS	10/01-12/01
	Albany-Schenectady-Troy MSA, NY	Y	21370 FQ	34250 AW	49530 TQ	NYBLS	10/01-12/01
	Nassau-Suffolk PMSA, NY	Y	37800 FQ	47030 AW	55590 TQ	NYBLS	10/01-12/01
	New York PMSA, NY	Y	34290 FQ	43910 AW	54630 TQ	NYBLS	10/01-12/01
	Newburgh PMSA, NY-PA	Y	16360 FQ	36630 AW	55250 TQ	NYBLS	10/01-12/01

AAW Average annual wage **AOH** Average offered, high **ASH** Average starting, high **H** Hourly **M** Monthly **S** Special: hourly and annual
AE Average entry wage **AOL** Average offered, low **ASL** Average starting, low **HI** Highest wage paid **MTC** Median total compensation **TQ** Third quartile wage
AEX Average experienced wage **APH** Average pay, high range **AW** Average wage paid **HR** High end range **MW** Median wage paid **W** Weekly
AO Average offered **APL** Average pay, low range **FQ** First quartile wage **LR** Low end range **SQ** Second quartile wage **Y** Yearly

Occupation/Type/Industry	Location	Per	Low	Mid	High	Source	Date
Bailiff	Rochester MSA, NY	Y	13850 FQ	23170 AW	32790 TQ	NYBLS	10/01-12/01
	Syracuse MSA, NY	Y	15970 FQ	25140 AW	33110 TQ	NYBLS	10/01-12/01
	North Carolina	Y	18680 FQ	24820 AW	32020 TQ	NCBLS	10/01-12/01
	Ohio	Y	20580 FQ	32390 AW	46440 TQ	OHBLS	10/01-12/01
	Cleveland-Lorain-Elyria PMSA, OH	Y	23940 FQ	33090 AW	48040 TQ	OHBLS	10/01-12/01
	Dayton-Springfield MSA, OH	Y	25430 FQ	36290 AW	51790 TQ	OHBLS	10/01-12/01
	Toledo MSA, OH	Y	14480 FQ	26460 AW	41390 TQ	OHBLS	10/01-12/01
	Youngstown-Warren MSA, OH	Y	13340 FQ	29060 AW	39670 TQ	OHBLS	10/01-12/01
	Oregon	Y	17360 FQ	28120 AW	38720 TQ	ORBLS	10/01-12/01
	Pennsylvania	Y	13180 FQ	27890 AW	49210 TQ	PABLS	10/01-12/01
	Philadelphia PMSA, PA-NJ	Y	16340 FQ	32260 AW	55440 TQ	PABLS	10/01-12/01
	South Carolina	Y	13110 FQ	20900 AW	31000 TQ	SCBLS	10/01-12/01
	Tennessee	Y	13600 FQ	26930 AW	41600 TQ	TNBLS	10/01-12/01
	Memphis MSA, TN-AR-MS	Y	14430 FQ	27560 AW	42820 TQ	TNBLS	10/01-12/01
	Texas	Y	18840 FQ	29940 AW	42900 TQ	TXBLS	10/01-12/01
	Dallas PMSA, TX	Y	31990 FQ	39610 AW	46320 TQ	TXBLS	10/01-12/01
	Fort Worth-Arlington PMSA, TX	Y	20590 FQ	32160 AW	41980 TQ	TXBLS	10/01-12/01
	Houston PMSA, TX	Y	25920 FQ	34010 AW	44550 TQ	TXBLS	10/01-12/01
	Utah	Y	13750 FQ	28610 AW	38650 TQ	UTBLS	10/01-12/01
	Virginia	Y	24660 FQ	39230 AW	55380 TQ	VABLS	10/01-12/01
	Norfolk-Virginia Beach-Newport News MSA, VA-NC	Y	25540 FQ	40790 AW	56200 TQ	VABLS	10/01-12/01
	Washington	Y	22890 FQ	33110 AW	44470 TQ	WABLS	10/01-12/01
	West Virginia	Y	14740 FQ	23370 AW	33280 TQ	WVBLS	10/01-12/01
	Wisconsin	Y	15950 FQ	40860 AW	57150 TQ	WIBLS	10/01-12/01
	Puerto Rico	Y	18120 FQ	20500 AW	23310 TQ	PRBLS	10/01-12/01
Baker	Alabama	H	6.01 FQ	9.17 AW	13.40 TQ	ALBLS	10/01-12/01
	Birmingham MSA, AL	H	6.07 FQ	9.23 AW	12.81 TQ	ALBLS	10/01-12/01
	Huntsville MSA, AL	H	6.64 FQ	9.96 AW	14.66 TQ	ALBLS	10/01-12/01
	Mobile MSA, AL	H	6.30 FQ	10.14 AW	14.64 TQ	ALBLS	10/01-12/01
	Montgomery MSA, AL	H	5.92 FQ	9.27 AW	14.33 TQ	ALBLS	10/01-12/01
	Alaska	H	7.90 FQ	12.36 AW	18.27 TQ	AKBLS	10/01-12/01
	Anchorage MSA, AK	H	7.80 FQ	12.32 AW	18.00 TQ	AKBLS	10/01-12/01
	Arizona	H	6.64 FQ	10.79 AW	14.34 TQ	AZBLS	10/01-12/01
	Phoenix-Mesa MSA, AZ	H	6.78 FQ	11.09 AW	14.73 TQ	AZBLS	10/01-12/01
	Tucson MSA, AZ	H	7.43 FQ	11.28 AW	14.59 TQ	AZBLS	10/01-12/01
	Arkansas	H	6.15 FQ	9.17 AW	13.14 TQ	ARBLS	10/01-12/01
	Fayetteville-Springdale-Rogers MSA, AR	H	7.06 FQ	10.61 AW	14.28 TQ	ARBLS	10/01-12/01
	Fort Smith MSA, AR-OK	H	6.40 FQ	9.37 AW	12.81 TQ	ARBLS	10/01-12/01
	Little Rock-North Little Rock MSA, AR	H	6.27 FQ	8.76 AW	11.40 TQ	ARBLS	10/01-12/01
	California	H	6.96 FQ	11.54 AW	17.84 TQ	CABLS	10/01-12/01
	Bakersfield MSA, CA	H	7.15 FQ	10.76 AW	15.50 TQ	CABLS	10/01-12/01
	Chico-Paradise MSA, CA	H	6.82 FQ	10.50 AW	17.41 TQ	CABLS	10/01-12/01
	Fresno MSA, CA	H	7.16 FQ	10.25 AW	15.68 TQ	CABLS	10/01-12/01
	Los Angeles-Long Beach PMSA, CA	H	7.06 FQ	11.84 AW	18.66 TQ	CABLS	10/01-12/01
	Merced MSA, CA	H	6.55 FQ	9.82 AW	15.36 TQ	CABLS	10/01-12/01
	Modesto MSA, CA	H	7.02 FQ	10.44 AW	14.98 TQ	CABLS	10/01-12/01
	Oakland PMSA, CA	H	6.67 FQ	11.46 AW	18.06 TQ	CABLS	10/01-12/01
	Orange County PMSA, CA	H	6.68 FQ	10.51 AW	16.45 TQ	CABLS	10/01-12/01
	Redding MSA, CA	H	7.20 FQ	11.46 AW	16.38 TQ	CABLS	10/01-12/01
	Riverside-San Bernardino PMSA, CA	H	7.24 FQ	11.43 AW	16.26 TQ	CABLS	10/01-12/01
	Sacramento PMSA, CA	H	8.46 FQ	12.96 AW	19.30 TQ	CABLS	10/01-12/01
	Salinas MSA, CA	H	7.09 FQ	12.72 AW	22.21 TQ	CABLS	10/01-12/01
	San Diego MSA, CA	H	6.73 FQ	10.82 AW	16.37 TQ	CABLS	10/01-12/01
	San Francisco PMSA, CA	H	7.29 FQ	11.91 AW	19.04 TQ	CABLS	10/01-12/01
	San Jose PMSA, CA	H	7.95 FQ	12.78 AW	19.10 TQ	CABLS	10/01-12/01
	San Luis Obispo-Atascadero-Paso Robles MSA, CA	H	7.19 FQ	11.20 AW	15.56 TQ	CABLS	10/01-12/01
	Santa Barbara-Santa Maria-Lompoc MSA, CA	H	6.77 FQ	9.81 AW	14.80 TQ	CABLS	10/01-12/01
	Santa Cruz-Watsonville PMSA, CA	H	7.76 FQ	10.71 AW	14.97 TQ	CABLS	10/01-12/01
	Santa Rosa PMSA, CA	H	8.25 FQ	11.94 AW	16.65 TQ	CABLS	10/01-12/01
	Stockton-Lodi MSA, CA	H	7.98 FQ	14.64 AW	21.78 TQ	CABLS	10/01-12/01

AAW	Average annual wage	AOH	Average offered, high	ASH	Average starting, high	H	Hourly	M	Monthly	S	Special: hourly and annual
AE	Average entry wage	AOL	Average offered, low	ASL	Average starting, low	HI	Highest wage paid	MTC	Median total compensation	TQ	Third quartile wage
AEX	Average experienced wage	APH	Average pay, high range	AW	Average wage paid	HR	High end range	MW	Median wage paid	W	Weekly
AO	Average offered	APL	Average pay, low range	FQ	First quartile wage	LR	Low end range	SQ	Second quartile wage	Y	Yearly

Occupation/Type/Industry	Location	Per	Low	Mid	High	Source	Date
Baker	Vallejo-Fairfield-Napa PMSA, CA	H	8.24 FQ	12.69 AW	17.24 TQ	CABLS	10/01-12/01
	Ventura PMSA, CA	H	6.68 FQ	10.92 AW	17.21 TQ	CABLS	10/01-12/01
	Visalia-Tulare-Porterville MSA, CA	H	6.60 FQ	9.86 AW	14.72 TQ	CABLS	10/01-12/01
	Colorado	H	7.65 FQ	12.26 AW	16.75 TQ	COBLS	10/01-12/01
	Boulder-Longmont PMSA, CO	H	8.46 FQ	12.37 AW	16.82 TQ	COBLS	10/01-12/01
	Colorado Springs MSA, CO	H	6.36 FQ	11.04 AW	16.28 TQ	COBLS	10/01-12/01
	Denver PMSA, CO	H	8.16 FQ	13.05 AW	16.98 TQ	COBLS	10/01-12/01
	Fort Collins-Loveland MSA, CO	H	7.17 FQ	10.70 AW	14.98 TQ	COBLS	10/01-12/01
	Greeley PMSA, CO	H	6.55 FQ	10.83 AW	14.82 TQ	COBLS	10/01-12/01
	Connecticut	H	7.14 FQ	11.30 AW	16.94 TQ	CTBLS	10/01-12/01
	Bridgeport PMSA, CT	H	6.84 FQ	10.25 AW	15.41 TQ	CTBLS	10/01-12/01
	Danbury PMSA, CT	H	7.67 FQ	12.43 AW	19.97 TQ	CTBLS	10/01-12/01
	Hartford MSA, CT	H	6.96 FQ	10.95 AW	17.12 TQ	CTBLS	10/01-12/01
	New London-Norwich MSA, CT-RI	H	7.45 FQ	10.93 AW	15.49 TQ	CTBLS	10/01-12/01
	Stamford-Norwalk PMSA, CT	H	7.58 FQ	11.35 AW	17.72 TQ	CTBLS	10/01-12/01
	Waterbury PMSA, CT	H	7.21 FQ	9.75 AW	12.98 TQ	CTBLS	10/01-12/01
	Delaware	H	7.48 FQ	10.25 AW	14.79 TQ	DEBLS	10/01-12/01
	Wilmington-Newark PMSA, DE-MD	H	7.37 FQ	9.89 AW	13.54 TQ	DEBLS	10/01-12/01
	District of Columbia	H	8.21 FQ	12.41 AW	16.80 TQ	DCBLS	10/01-12/01
	Washington PMSA, DC-MD-VA-WV	H	7.45 FQ	11.68 AW	16.91 TQ	DCBLS	10/01-12/01
	Florida	H	6.94 FQ	9.72 AW	13.56 TQ	FLBLS	10/01-12/01
	Daytona Beach MSA, FL	H	7.14 FQ	9.17 AW	12.21 TQ	FLBLS	10/01-12/01
	Fort Lauderdale PMSA, FL	H	6.75 FQ	10.76 AW	16.38 TQ	FLBLS	10/01-12/01
	Fort Myers-Cape Coral MSA, FL	H	8.11 FQ	10.13 AW	12.72 TQ	FLBLS	10/01-12/01
	Fort Pierce-Port St. Lucie MSA, FL	H	7.55 FQ	9.38 AW	12.15 TQ	FLBLS	10/01-12/01
	Fort Walton Beach MSA, FL	H	5.84 FQ	8.00 AW	10.59 TQ	FLBLS	10/01-12/01
	Gainesville MSA, FL	H	7.00 FQ	9.16 AW	12.65 TQ	FLBLS	10/01-12/01
	Jacksonville MSA, FL	H	7.56 FQ	10.25 AW	13.41 TQ	FLBLS	10/01-12/01
	Lakeland-Winter Haven MSA, FL	H	6.19 FQ	8.04 AW	9.53 TQ	FLBLS	10/01-12/01
	Melbourne-Titusville-Palm Bay MSA, FL	H	6.93 FQ	9.05 AW	12.88 TQ	FLBLS	10/01-12/01
	Miami PMSA, FL	H	6.94 FQ	10.25 AW	13.73 TQ	FLBLS	10/01-12/01
	Naples MSA, FL	H	7.56 FQ	9.92 AW	13.24 TQ	FLBLS	10/01-12/01
	Ocala MSA, FL	H	7.43 FQ	9.19 AW	11.24 TQ	FLBLS	10/01-12/01
	Orlando MSA, FL	H	7.10 FQ	9.42 AW	13.48 TQ	FLBLS	10/01-12/01
	Pensacola MSA, FL	H	6.02 FQ	8.06 AW	10.88 TQ	FLBLS	10/01-12/01
	Sarasota-Bradenton MSA, FL	H	7.00 FQ	9.78 AW	13.46 TQ	FLBLS	10/01-12/01
	Tallahassee MSA, FL	H	7.34 FQ	9.32 AW	12.74 TQ	FLBLS	10/01-12/01
	Tampa-St. Petersburg-Clearwater MSA, FL	H	6.50 FQ	8.92 AW	11.83 TQ	FLBLS	10/01-12/01
	West Palm Beach-Boca Raton MSA, FL	H	7.54 FQ	10.85 AW	14.34 TQ	FLBLS	10/01-12/01
	Georgia	H	6.93 FQ	10.57 AW	15.50 TQ	GABLS	10/01-12/01
	Atlanta MSA, GA	H	7.27 FQ	10.85 AW	15.69 TQ	GABLS	10/01-12/01
	Augusta-Aiken MSA, GA-SC	H	7.12 FQ	10.44 AW	14.07 TQ	GABLS	10/01-12/01
	Macon MSA, GA	H	5.73 FQ	7.44 AW	10.92 TQ	GABLS	10/01-12/01
	Savannah MSA, GA	H	7.66 FQ	11.05 AW	14.57 TQ	GABLS	10/01-12/01
	Hawaii	H	6.68 FQ	11.76 AW	17.20 TQ	HIBLS	10/01-12/01
	Honolulu MSA, HI	H	6.46 FQ	11.70 AW	17.04 TQ	HIBLS	10/01-12/01
	Idaho	H	6.19 FQ	9.35 AW	14.82 TQ	IDBLS	10/01-12/01
	Boise City MSA, ID	H	7.31 FQ	9.66 AW	13.28 TQ	IDBLS	10/01-12/01
	Illinois	H	6.74 FQ	10.45 AW	16.26 TQ	ILBLS	10/01-12/01
	Champaign-Urbana MSA, IL	H	6.40 FQ	10.06 AW	19.67 TQ	ILBLS	10/01-12/01
	Chicago PMSA, IL	H	7.13 FQ	10.89 AW	16.62 TQ	ILBLS	10/01-12/01
	Peoria-Pekin MSA, IL	H	6.02 FQ	8.11 AW	11.73 TQ	ILBLS	10/01-12/01
	Rockford MSA, IL	H	6.31 FQ	10.34 AW	16.23 TQ	ILBLS	10/01-12/01
	Springfield MSA, IL	H	6.43 FQ	9.94 AW	14.15 TQ	ILBLS	10/01-12/01
	Indiana	H	6.36 FQ	9.24 AW	13.43 TQ	INBLS	10/01-12/01
	Elkhart-Goshen MSA, IN	H	6.69 FQ	8.30 AW	10.38 TQ	INBLS	10/01-12/01
	Evansville-Henderson MSA, IN-KY	H	5.74 FQ	7.86 AW	11.43 TQ	INBLS	10/01-12/01
	Fort Wayne MSA, IN	H	6.31 FQ	9.24 AW	13.26 TQ	INBLS	10/01-12/01
	Gary PMSA, IN	H	6.03 FQ	8.79 AW	13.12 TQ	INBLS	10/01-12/01

AAW Average annual wage **AOH** Average offered, high **ASH** Average starting, high **H** Hourly **M** Monthly **S** Special: hourly and annual
AE Average entry wage **AOL** Average offered, low **ASL** Average starting, low **HI** Highest wage paid **MTC** Median total compensation **TQ** Third quartile wage
AEX Average experienced wage **APH** Average pay, high range **AW** Average wage paid **HR** High end range **MW** Median wage paid **W** Weekly
AO Average offered **APL** Average pay, low range **FQ** First quartile wage **LR** Low end range **SQ** Second quartile wage **Y** Yearly

Occupation/Type/Industry	Location	Per	Low	Mid	High	Source	Date
Baker	Indianapolis MSA, IN	H	6.83 FQ	10.10 AW	13.79 TQ	INBLS	10/01-12/01
	Lafayette MSA, IN	H	6.95 FQ	10.16 AW	14.09 TQ	INBLS	10/01-12/01
	South Bend MSA, IN	H	7.06 FQ	9.56 AW	13.42 TQ	INBLS	10/01-12/01
	Iowa	H	7.17 FQ	9.81 AW	13.15 TQ	IABLS	10/01-12/01
	Cedar Rapids MSA, IA	H	7.44 FQ	10.18 AW	13.04 TQ	IABLS	10/01-12/01
	Davenport-Moline-Rock Island MSA, IA-IL	H	6.28 FQ	9.23 AW	13.71 TQ	IABLS	10/01-12/01
	Des Moines MSA, IA	H	8.79 FQ	10.95 AW	13.61 TQ	IABLS	10/01-12/01
	Kansas	H	6.40 FQ	10.09 AW	15.25 TQ	KSBLS	10/01-12/01
	Topeka MSA, KS	H	6.13 FQ	10.27 AW	16.08 TQ	KSBLS	10/01-12/01
	Wichita MSA, KS	H	5.96 FQ	8.60 AW	12.04 TQ	KSBLS	10/01-12/01
	Kentucky	H	6.12 FQ	9.45 AW	13.37 TQ	KYBLS	10/01-12/01
	Lexington MSA, KY	H	5.73 FQ	7.83 AW	10.71 TQ	KYBLS	10/01-12/01
	Louisville MSA, KY-IN	H	7.02 FQ	9.56 AW	12.96 TQ	KYBLS	10/01-12/01
	Louisiana	H	5.87 FQ	8.89 AW	13.50 TQ	LABLS	10/01-12/01
	Baton Rouge MSA, LA	H	5.88 FQ	9.69 AW	16.55 TQ	LABLS	10/01-12/01
	Houma MSA, LA	H	5.83 FQ	7.94 AW	12.16 TQ	LABLS	10/01-12/01
	Lafayette MSA, LA	H	5.81 FQ	8.24 AW	10.93 TQ	LABLS	10/01-12/01
	Lake Charles MSA, LA	H	5.73 FQ	7.88 AW	11.90 TQ	LABLS	10/01-12/01
	New Orleans MSA, LA	H	5.90 FQ	9.47 AW	14.16 TQ	LABLS	10/01-12/01
	Shreveport-Bossier City MSA, LA	H	5.91 FQ	8.51 AW	12.74 TQ	LABLS	10/01-12/01
	Maine	H	6.95 FQ	9.79 AW	14.49 TQ	MEBLS	10/01-12/01
	Portland MSA, ME	H	7.03 FQ	10.00 AW	14.51 TQ	MEBLS	10/01-12/01
	Maryland	H	6.69 FQ	11.12 AW	16.71 TQ	MDBLS	10/01-12/01
	Baltimore PMSA, MD	H	6.80 FQ	11.44 AW	16.79 TQ	MDBLS	10/01-12/01
	Massachusetts	H	7.52 FQ	11.69 AW	17.39 TQ	MABLS	10/01-12/01
	Boston PMSA, MA-NH	H	7.59 FQ	12.39 AW	18.87 TQ	MABLS	10/01-12/01
	Brockton PMSA, MA	H	7.36 FQ	11.08 AW	16.21 TQ	MABLS	10/01-12/01
	Lawrence PMSA, MA-NH	H	7.30 FQ	10.86 AW	16.76 TQ	MABLS	10/01-12/01
	Lowell PMSA, MA-NH	H	7.63 FQ	12.31 AW	18.48 TQ	MABLS	10/01-12/01
	New Bedford PMSA, MA	H	7.57 FQ	10.83 AW	15.02 TQ	MABLS	10/01-12/01
	Springfield MSA, MA	H	7.45 FQ	10.54 AW	15.28 TQ	MABLS	10/01-12/01
	Worcester PMSA, MA-CT	H	7.33 FQ	11.08 AW	15.69 TQ	MABLS	10/01-12/01
	Michigan	H	7.05 FQ	10.69 AW	15.24 TQ	MIBLS	10/01-12/01
	Ann Arbor PMSA, MI	H	6.85 FQ	10.44 AW	13.82 TQ	MIBLS	10/01-12/01
	Detroit PMSA, MI	H	7.47 FQ	11.52 AW	16.91 TQ	MIBLS	10/01-12/01
	Flint PMSA, MI	H	8.01 FQ	10.83 AW	13.18 TQ	MIBLS	10/01-12/01
	Grand Rapids-Muskegon-Holland MSA, MI	H	7.63 FQ	10.99 AW	14.42 TQ	MIBLS	10/01-12/01
	Kalamazoo-Battle Creek MSA, MI	H	7.50 FQ	10.56 AW	14.85 TQ	MIBLS	10/01-12/01
	Lansing-East Lansing MSA, MI	H	6.48 FQ	10.88 AW	16.34 TQ	MIBLS	10/01-12/01
	Saginaw-Bay City-Midland MSA, MI	H	6.28 FQ	9.85 AW	13.87 TQ	MIBLS	10/01-12/01
	Minnesota	H	7.12 FQ	10.79 AW	15.92 TQ	MNBLS	10/01-12/01
	Duluth-Superior MSA, MN-WI	H	6.12 FQ	9.08 AW	13.15 TQ	MNBLS	10/01-12/01
	Minneapolis-St. Paul MSA, MN-WI	H	7.53 FQ	11.25 AW	16.51 TQ	MNBLS	10/01-12/01
	St. Cloud MSA, MN	H	7.67 FQ	11.69 AW	16.44 TQ	MNBLS	10/01-12/01
	Mississippi	H	5.88 FQ	8.94 AW	14.68 TQ	MSBLS	10/01-12/01
	Biloxi-Gulfport-Pascagoula MSA, MS	H	6.37 FQ	9.31 AW	14.78 TQ	MSBLS	10/01-12/01
	Jackson MSA, MS	H	6.05 FQ	9.00 AW	11.22 TQ	MSBLS	10/01-12/01
	Missouri	H	6.14 FQ	9.97 AW	14.35 TQ	MOBLS	10/01-12/01
	Kansas City MSA, MO-KS	H	6.99 FQ	10.87 AW	15.80 TQ	MOBLS	10/01-12/01
	St. Louis MSA, MO-IL	H	6.51 FQ	10.21 AW	14.23 TQ	MOBLS	10/01-12/01
	Springfield MSA, MO	H	7.46 FQ	11.81 AW	16.45 TQ	MOBLS	10/01-12/01
	Montana	H	6.07 FQ	9.52 AW	15.17 TQ	MTBLS	10/01-12/01
	Billings MSA, MT	H	6.03 FQ	10.49 AW	16.84 TQ	MTBLS	10/01-12/01
	Nebraska	H	6.67 FQ	9.35 AW	12.73 TQ	NEBLS	10/01-12/01
	Lincoln MSA, NE	H	6.37 FQ	9.96 AW	13.69 TQ	NEBLS	10/01-12/01
	Omaha MSA, NE-IA	H	7.54 FQ	10.00 AW	13.05 TQ	NEBLS	10/01-12/01
	Nevada	H	8.50 FQ	12.29 AW	16.66 TQ	NVBLS	10/01-12/01
	Las Vegas MSA, NV-AZ	H	8.19 FQ	12.29 AW	16.67 TQ	NVBLS	10/01-12/01
	Reno MSA, NV	H	9.15 FQ	12.19 AW	16.24 TQ	NVBLS	10/01-12/01
	New Hampshire	H	7.78 FQ	10.99 AW	15.54 TQ	NHBLS	10/01-12/01
	Manchester PMSA, NH	H	8.29 FQ	10.71 AW	14.12 TQ	NHBLS	10/01-12/01
	Nashua PMSA, NH	H	7.61 FQ	9.80 AW	12.25 TQ	NHBLS	10/01-12/01
	Portsmouth-Rochester PMSA, NH-ME	H	8.70 FQ	11.09 AW	14.41 TQ	NHBLS	10/01-12/01
	New Jersey	H	6.85 FQ	11.64 AW	17.40 TQ	NJBLS	10/01-12/01

AAW	Average annual wage	**AOH**	Average offered, high	**ASH**	Average starting, high	**H**	Hourly	**M**	Monthly	**S**	Special: hourly and annual
AE	Average entry wage	**AOL**	Average offered, low	**ASL**	Average starting, low	**HI**	Highest wage paid	**MTC**	Median total compensation	**TQ**	Third quartile wage
AEX	Average experienced wage	**APH**	Average pay, high range	**AW**	Average wage paid	**HR**	High end range	**MW**	Median wage paid	**W**	Weekly
AO	Average offered	**APL**	Average pay, low range	**FQ**	First quartile wage	**LR**	Low end range	**SQ**	Second quartile wage	**Y**	Yearly

Occupation/Type/Industry	Location	Per	Low	Mid	High	Source	Date
Baker	Atlantic-Cape May PMSA, NJ	H	8.73 FQ	12.39 AW	16.73 TQ	NJBLS	10/01-12/01
	Bergen-Passaic PMSA, NJ	H	8.08 FQ	12.98 AW	19.86 TQ	NJBLS	10/01-12/01
	Jersey City PMSA, NJ	H	6.01 FQ	10.53 AW	16.74 TQ	NJBLS	10/01-12/01
	Middlesex-Somerset-Hunterdon PMSA, NJ	H	8.01 FQ	12.11 AW	17.07 TQ	NJBLS	10/01-12/01
	Monmouth-Ocean PMSA, NJ	H	7.35 FQ	10.69 AW	14.53 TQ	NJBLS	10/01-12/01
	Newark PMSA, NJ	H	6.18 FQ	11.58 AW	18.05 TQ	NJBLS	10/01-12/01
	Trenton PMSA, NJ	H	6.61 FQ	10.82 AW	15.94 TQ	NJBLS	10/01-12/01
	New Mexico	H	5.98 FQ	9.00 AW	13.01 TQ	NMBLS	10/01-12/01
	Albuquerque MSA, NM	H	6.52 FQ	10.10 AW	13.86 TQ	NMBLS	10/01-12/01
	Las Cruces MSA, NM	H	5.66 FQ	8.09 AW	12.62 TQ	NMBLS	10/01-12/01
	New York	H	6.89 FQ	10.75 AW	16.79 TQ	NYBLS	10/01-12/01
	Albany-Schenectady-Troy MSA, NY	H	7.37 FQ	11.88 AW	17.33 TQ	NYBLS	10/01-12/01
	Binghamton MSA, NY	H	5.99 FQ	9.19 AW	13.95 TQ	NYBLS	10/01-12/01
	Buffalo-Niagara Falls MSA, NY	H	7.18 FQ	10.37 AW	14.95 TQ	NYBLS	10/01-12/01
	Dutchess County PMSA, NY	H	7.62 FQ	11.40 AW	16.95 TQ	NYBLS	10/01-12/01
	Nassau-Suffolk PMSA, NY	H	6.96 FQ	12.46 AW	20.41 TQ	NYBLS	10/01-12/01
	New York PMSA, NY	H	7.08 FQ	10.24 AW	16.49 TQ	NYBLS	10/01-12/01
	Newburgh PMSA, NY-PA	H	6.13 FQ	10.29 AW	17.45 TQ	NYBLS	10/01-12/01
	Rochester MSA, NY	H	7.23 FQ	10.47 AW	15.97 TQ	NYBLS	10/01-12/01
	Syracuse MSA, NY	H	7.12 FQ	11.13 AW	15.94 TQ	NYBLS	10/01-12/01
	Utica-Rome MSA, NY	H	6.36 FQ	9.79 AW	13.49 TQ	NYBLS	10/01-12/01
	North Carolina	H	6.49 FQ	9.62 AW	13.36 TQ	NCBLS	10/01-12/01
	Asheville MSA, NC	H	7.03 FQ	8.68 AW	10.69 TQ	NCBLS	10/01-12/01
	Charlotte-Gastonia-Rock Hill MSA, NC-SC	H	6.91 FQ	10.00 AW	13.43 TQ	NCBLS	10/01-12/01
	Fayetteville MSA, NC	H	5.72 FQ	7.42 AW	9.07 TQ	NCBLS	10/01-12/01
	Greensboro-Winston-Salem-High Point MSA, NC	H	6.94 FQ	10.51 AW	13.67 TQ	NCBLS	10/01-12/01
	Hickory-Morganton-Lenoir MSA, NC	H	5.65 FQ	8.79 AW	13.31 TQ	NCBLS	10/01-12/01
	Raleigh-Durham-Chapel Hill MSA, NC	H	7.68 FQ	10.71 AW	14.47 TQ	NCBLS	10/01-12/01
	Wilmington MSA, NC	H	6.10 FQ	8.63 AW	11.21 TQ	NCBLS	10/01-12/01
	North Dakota	H	5.93 FQ	8.95 AW	13.35 TQ	NDBLS	10/01-12/01
	Ohio	H	6.03 FQ	9.56 AW	14.58 TQ	OHBLS	10/01-12/01
	Akron PMSA, OH	H	6.59 FQ	9.06 AW	12.54 TQ	OHBLS	10/01-12/01
	Canton-Massillon MSA, OH	H	6.70 FQ	9.98 AW	16.12 TQ	OHBLS	10/01-12/01
	Cincinnati PMSA, OH-KY-IN	H	7.50 FQ	11.33 AW	14.57 TQ	OHBLS	10/01-12/01
	Cleveland-Lorain-Elyria PMSA, OH	H	5.89 FQ	9.24 AW	13.99 TQ	OHBLS	10/01-12/01
	Columbus MSA, OH	H	5.85 FQ	8.41 AW	12.42 TQ	OHBLS	10/01-12/01
	Dayton-Springfield MSA, OH	H	7.17 FQ	9.46 AW	13.28 TQ	OHBLS	10/01-12/01
	Hamilton-Middletown PMSA, OH	H	6.89 FQ	9.24 AW	11.92 TQ	OHBLS	10/01-12/01
	Mansfield MSA, OH	H	6.70 FQ	9.27 AW	13.12 TQ	OHBLS	10/01-12/01
	Toledo MSA, OH	H	7.13 FQ	9.04 AW	10.95 TQ	OHBLS	10/01-12/01
	Youngstown-Warren MSA, OH	H	5.78 FQ	8.83 AW	13.72 TQ	OHBLS	10/01-12/01
	Oklahoma	H	5.97 FQ	8.24 AW	11.09 TQ	OKBLS	10/01-12/01
	Oklahoma City MSA, OK	H	6.46 FQ	8.64 AW	12.20 TQ	OKBLS	10/01-12/01
	Tulsa MSA, OK	H	5.94 FQ	8.09 AW	10.88 TQ	OKBLS	10/01-12/01
	Oregon	H	7.39 FQ	11.11 AW	16.37 TQ	ORBLS	10/01-12/01
	Eugene-Springfield MSA, OR	H	7.81 FQ	11.23 AW	16.28 TQ	ORBLS	10/01-12/01
	Medford-Ashland MSA, OR	H	7.08 FQ	9.71 AW	13.76 TQ	ORBLS	10/01-12/01
	Portland-Vancouver PMSA, OR-WA	H	8.01 FQ	12.50 AW	17.69 TQ	ORBLS	10/01-12/01
	Salem PMSA, OR	H	7.53 FQ	12.27 AW	17.04 TQ	ORBLS	10/01-12/01
	Pennsylvania	H	6.21 FQ	10.38 AW	15.63 TQ	PABLS	10/01-12/01
	Allentown-Bethlehem-Easton MSA, PA	H	8.10 FQ	11.61 AW	15.94 TQ	PABLS	10/01-12/01
	Erie MSA, PA	H	5.80 FQ	8.57 AW	12.19 TQ	PABLS	10/01-12/01
	Harrisburg-Lebanon-Carlisle MSA, PA	H	8.03 FQ	12.32 AW	16.41 TQ	PABLS	10/01-12/01
	Johnstown MSA, PA	H	6.09 FQ	8.81 AW	12.95 TQ	PABLS	10/01-12/01
	Lancaster MSA, PA	H	6.36 FQ	10.84 AW	16.04 TQ	PABLS	10/01-12/01
	Philadelphia PMSA, PA-NJ	H	7.35 FQ	11.59 AW	16.55 TQ	PABLS	10/01-12/01
	Pittsburgh MSA, PA	H	6.05 FQ	9.22 AW	13.17 TQ	PABLS	10/01-12/01
	Reading MSA, PA	H	7.95 FQ	12.08 AW	16.58 TQ	PABLS	10/01-12/01
	Scranton-Wilkes-Barre-Hazleton MSA, PA	H	6.00 FQ	9.70 AW	13.84 TQ	PABLS	10/01-12/01

AAW	Average annual wage	**AOH**	Average offered, high	**ASH**	Average starting, high	**H**	Hourly	**M**	Monthly	**S**	Special: hourly and annual
AE	Average entry wage	**AOL**	Average offered, low	**ASL**	Average starting, low	**HI**	Highest wage paid	**MTC**	Median total compensation	**TQ**	Third quartile wage
AEX	Average experienced wage	**APH**	Average pay, high range	**AW**	Average wage paid	**HR**	High end range	**MW**	Median wage paid	**W**	Weekly
AO	Average offered	**APL**	Average pay, low range	**FQ**	First quartile wage	**LR**	Low end range	**SQ**	Second quartile wage	**Y**	Yearly

Occupation/Type/Industry	Location	Per	Low	Mid	High	Source	Date
Baker	York MSA, PA	H	6.45 FQ	11.64 AW	16.76 TQ	PABLS	10/01-12/01
	Rhode Island	H	7.35 FQ	11.04 AW	14.74 TQ	RIBLS	10/01-12/01
	Providence-Fall River-Warwick MSA, RI-MA	H	7.27 FQ	10.80 AW	14.53 TQ	RIBLS	10/01-12/01
	South Carolina	H	6.17 FQ	8.90 AW	12.77 TQ	SCBLS	10/01-12/01
	Charleston-North Charleston MSA, SC	H	6.25 FQ	8.79 AW	13.02 TQ	SCBLS	10/01-12/01
	Columbia MSA, SC	H	6.88 FQ	9.43 AW	12.72 TQ	SCBLS	10/01-12/01
	Greenville-Spartanburg-Anderson MSA, SC	H	6.08 FQ	8.57 AW	11.62 TQ	SCBLS	10/01-12/01
	Myrtle Beach MSA, SC	H	6.68 FQ	8.76 AW	12.20 TQ	SCBLS	10/01-12/01
	South Dakota	H	6.47 FQ	8.71 AW	11.45 TQ	SDBLS	10/01-12/01
	Sioux Falls MSA, SD	H	7.18 FQ	9.34 AW	12.09 TQ	SDBLS	10/01-12/01
	Tennessee	H	6.27 FQ	9.70 AW	14.54 TQ	TNBLS	10/01-12/01
	Chattanooga MSA, TN-GA	H	6.32 FQ	10.60 AW	16.84 TQ	TNBLS	10/01-12/01
	Johnson City-Kingsport-Bristol MSA, TN-VA	H	5.69 FQ	7.83 AW	11.22 TQ	TNBLS	10/01-12/01
	Knoxville MSA, TN	H	7.39 FQ	9.83 AW	13.45 TQ	TNBLS	10/01-12/01
	Memphis MSA, TN-AR-MS	H	6.13 FQ	9.24 AW	13.94 TQ	TNBLS	10/01-12/01
	Nashville MSA, TN	H	7.10 FQ	10.99 AW	16.48 TQ	TNBLS	10/01-12/01
	Texas	H	6.19 FQ	9.14 AW	13.19 TQ	TXBLS	10/01-12/01
	Amarillo MSA, TX	H	6.07 FQ	8.10 AW	12.03 TQ	TXBLS	10/01-12/01
	Austin-San Marcos MSA, TX	H	6.11 FQ	9.06 AW	13.36 TQ	TXBLS	10/01-12/01
	Beaumont-Port Arthur MSA, TX	H	5.82 FQ	7.61 AW	10.23 TQ	TXBLS	10/01-12/01
	Brazoria PMSA, TX	H	5.67 FQ	7.17 AW	9.16 TQ	TXBLS	10/01-12/01
	Brownsville-Harlingen-San Benito MSA, TX	H	5.59 FQ	6.57 AW	8.37 TQ	TXBLS	10/01-12/01
	Corpus Christi MSA, TX	H	5.66 FQ	8.06 AW	12.12 TQ	TXBLS	10/01-12/01
	Dallas PMSA, TX	H	6.89 FQ	9.55 AW	13.23 TQ	TXBLS	10/01-12/01
	El Paso MSA, TX	H	5.80 FQ	8.92 AW	13.75 TQ	TXBLS	10/01-12/01
	Fort Worth-Arlington PMSA, TX	H	7.30 FQ	9.94 AW	13.02 TQ	TXBLS	10/01-12/01
	Galveston-Texas City PMSA, TX	H	5.95 FQ	8.36 AW	11.13 TQ	TXBLS	10/01-12/01
	Houston PMSA, TX	H	6.39 FQ	8.93 AW	12.69 TQ	TXBLS	10/01-12/01
	Killeen-Temple MSA, TX	H	6.54 FQ	8.87 AW	12.24 TQ	TXBLS	10/01-12/01
	Laredo MSA, TX	H	5.92 FQ	7.74 AW	10.16 TQ	TXBLS	10/01-12/01
	Longview-Marshall MSA, TX	H	6.12 FQ	8.38 AW	11.25 TQ	TXBLS	10/01-12/01
	Lubbock MSA, TX	H	5.99 FQ	8.76 AW	14.04 TQ	TXBLS	10/01-12/01
	McAllen-Edinburg-Mission MSA, TX	H	5.65 FQ	6.95 AW	8.97 TQ	TXBLS	10/01-12/01
	Odessa-Midland MSA, TX	H	5.97 FQ	8.14 AW	10.63 TQ	TXBLS	10/01-12/01
	San Antonio MSA, TX	H	6.50 FQ	9.70 AW	14.05 TQ	TXBLS	10/01-12/01
	Tyler MSA, TX	H	6.52 FQ	9.40 AW	13.27 TQ	TXBLS	10/01-12/01
	Waco MSA, TX	H	5.82 FQ	9.32 AW	13.97 TQ	TXBLS	10/01-12/01
	Utah	H	6.50 FQ	10.38 AW	15.86 TQ	UTBLS	10/01-12/01
	Provo-Orem MSA, UT	H	6.98 FQ	8.54 AW	10.88 TQ	UTBLS	10/01-12/01
	Salt Lake City-Ogden MSA, UT	H	6.40 FQ	11.08 AW	16.29 TQ	UTBLS	10/01-12/01
	Vermont	H	7.44 FQ	10.77 AW	14.93 TQ	VTBLS	10/01-12/01
	Burlington MSA, VT	H	7.55 FQ	10.62 AW	13.78 TQ	VTBLS	10/01-12/01
	Virginia	H	6.65 FQ	10.46 AW	15.52 TQ	VABLS	10/01-12/01
	Lynchburg MSA, VA	H	7.02 FQ	10.06 AW	13.00 TQ	VABLS	10/01-12/01
	Norfolk-Virginia Beach-Newport News MSA, VA-NC	H	6.22 FQ	9.05 AW	11.70 TQ	VABLS	10/01-12/01
	Richmond-Petersburg MSA, VA	H	7.29 FQ	10.73 AW	14.50 TQ	VABLS	10/01-12/01
	Roanoke MSA, VA	H	7.65 FQ	9.90 AW	11.59 TQ	VABLS	10/01-12/01
	Washington	H	7.61 FQ	11.42 AW	16.68 TQ	WABLS	10/01-12/01
	Bremerton PMSA, WA	H	7.27 FQ	11.84 AW	16.64 TQ	WABLS	10/01-12/01
	Olympia PMSA, WA	H	7.43 FQ	10.93 AW	16.04 TQ	WABLS	10/01-12/01
	Richland-Kennewick-Pasco MSA, WA	H	7.41 FQ	10.57 AW	14.20 TQ	WABLS	10/01-12/01
	Seattle-Bellevue-Everett PMSA, WA	H	7.96 FQ	11.47 AW	16.88 TQ	WABLS	10/01-12/01
	Spokane MSA, WA	H	7.16 FQ	10.21 AW	16.18 TQ	WABLS	10/01-12/01
	Tacoma PMSA, WA	H	7.72 FQ	12.37 AW	16.80 TQ	WABLS	10/01-12/01
	Yakima MSA, WA	H	7.16 FQ	10.42 AW	15.37 TQ	WABLS	10/01-12/01
	West Virginia	H	5.80 FQ	9.15 AW	13.44 TQ	WVBLS	10/01-12/01
	Wisconsin	H	7.15 FQ	9.93 AW	13.43 TQ	WIBLS	10/01-12/01

AAW	Average annual wage	**AOH**	Average offered, high	**ASH**	Average starting, high	**H**	Hourly	**M**	Monthly	**S**	Special: hourly and annual
AE	Average entry wage	**AOL**	Average offered, low	**ASL**	Average starting, low	**HI**	Highest wage paid	**MTC**	Median total compensation	**TQ**	Third quartile wage
AEX	Average experienced wage	**APH**	Average pay, high range	**AW**	Average wage paid	**HR**	High end range	**MW**	Median wage paid	**W**	Weekly
AO	Average offered	**APL**	Average pay, low range	**FQ**	First quartile wage	**LR**	Low end range	**SQ**	Second quartile wage	**Y**	Yearly

Occupation/Type/Industry	Location	Per	Low	Mid	High	Source	Date
Baker	Appleton-Oshkosh-Neenah MSA, WI	H	6.83 FQ	11.26 AW	13.95 TQ	WIBLS	10/01-12/01
	Green Bay MSA, WI	H	6.73 FQ	8.72 AW	12.04 TQ	WIBLS	10/01-12/01
	Madison MSA, WI	H	7.32 FQ	9.83 AW	12.44 TQ	WIBLS	10/01-12/01
	Milwaukee-Waukesha PMSA, WI	H	7.43 FQ	10.06 AW	13.44 TQ	WIBLS	10/01-12/01
	Racine PMSA, WI	H	7.71 FQ	11.31 AW	15.08 TQ	WIBLS	10/01-12/01
	Wyoming	H	6.39 FQ	9.80 AW	13.27 TQ	WYBLS	10/01-12/01
	Cheyenne MSA, WY	H	7.37 FQ	10.25 AW	14.46 TQ	WYBLS	10/01-12/01
	Puerto Rico	H	5.61 FQ	6.51 AW	8.07 TQ	PRBLS	10/01-12/01
	Virgin Islands	H	6.42 FQ	9.51 AW	12.86 TQ	VIBLS	10/01-12/01
	Guam	H	5.58 FQ	7.66 AW	11.91 TQ	GUBLS	10/01-12/01
Barber	Alabama	H	5.73 FQ	9.12 AW	15.41 TQ	ALBLS	10/01-12/01
	Montgomery MSA, AL	H	5.73 FQ	8.09 AW	11.76 TQ	ALBLS	10/01-12/01
	Arizona	H	6.55 FQ	10.60 AW	16.29 TQ	AZBLS	10/01-12/01
	Phoenix-Mesa MSA, AZ	H	7.17 FQ	11.29 AW	17.24 TQ	AZBLS	10/01-12/01
	Arkansas	H	6.27 FQ	10.18 AW	16.50 TQ	ARBLS	10/01-12/01
	California	H	6.61 FQ	9.14 AW	13.34 TQ	CABLS	10/01-12/01
	Los Angeles-Long Beach PMSA, CA	H	6.43 FQ	8.49 AW	13.47 TQ	CABLS	10/01-12/01
	Riverside-San Bernardino PMSA, CA	H	6.43 FQ	9.75 AW	15.40 TQ	CABLS	10/01-12/01
	San Francisco PMSA, CA	H	6.93 FQ	11.02 AW	17.59 TQ	CABLS	10/01-12/01
	San Jose PMSA, CA	H	7.17 FQ	8.49 AW	10.94 TQ	CABLS	10/01-12/01
	Colorado	H	6.37 FQ	10.60 AW	15.30 TQ	COBLS	10/01-12/01
	Colorado Springs MSA, CO	H	5.94 FQ	9.72 AW	16.20 TQ	COBLS	10/01-12/01
	Denver PMSA, CO	H	9.02 FQ	10.69 AW	13.29 TQ	COBLS	10/01-12/01
	Connecticut	H	7.67 FQ	11.04 AW	15.58 TQ	CTBLS	10/01-12/01
	Hartford MSA, CT	H	6.66 FQ	11.42 AW	15.17 TQ	CTBLS	10/01-12/01
	New Haven-Meriden PMSA, CT	H	8.81 FQ	9.83 AW	10.98 TQ	CTBLS	10/01-12/01
	Delaware	H	7.28 FQ	13.44 AW	21.09 TQ	DEBLS	10/01-12/01
	District of Columbia	H	7.10 FQ	14.03 AW	29.72 TQ	DCBLS	10/01-12/01
	Washington PMSA, DC-MD-VA-WV	H	6.00 FQ	11.45 AW	21.21 TQ	DCBLS	10/01-12/01
	Florida	H	5.70 FQ	8.25 AW	12.84 TQ	FLBLS	10/01-12/01
	Fort Lauderdale PMSA, FL	H	5.88 FQ	7.39 AW	8.89 TQ	FLBLS	10/01-12/01
	Miami PMSA, FL	H	5.60 FQ	6.94 AW	8.66 TQ	FLBLS	10/01-12/01
	Tampa-St. Petersburg-Clearwater MSA, FL	H	5.74 FQ	8.49 AW	12.62 TQ	FLBLS	10/01-12/01
	Georgia	H	6.03 FQ	10.40 AW	15.81 TQ	GABLS	10/01-12/01
	Atlanta MSA, GA	H	8.10 FQ	12.19 AW	19.28 TQ	GABLS	10/01-12/01
	Hawaii	H	6.02 FQ	11.69 AW	19.75 TQ	HIBLS	10/01-12/01
	Honolulu MSA, HI	H	6.02 FQ	11.69 AW	19.75 TQ	HIBLS	10/01-12/01
	Idaho	H	5.70 FQ	9.37 AW	14.91 TQ	IDBLS	10/01-12/01
	Illinois	H	7.54 FQ	12.27 AW	15.27 TQ	ILBLS	10/01-12/01
	Chicago PMSA, IL	H	7.71 FQ	11.80 AW	14.05 TQ	ILBLS	10/01-12/01
	Springfield MSA, IL	H	9.34 FQ	10.49 AW	11.50 TQ	ILBLS	10/01-12/01
	Indiana	H	5.70 FQ	9.92 AW	16.24 TQ	INBLS	10/01-12/01
	Indianapolis MSA, IN	H	5.68 FQ	10.21 AW	16.82 TQ	INBLS	10/01-12/01
	Iowa	H	6.69 FQ	14.25 AW	21.05 TQ	IABLS	10/01-12/01
	Kansas	H	8.86 FQ	12.71 AW	19.35 TQ	KSBLS	10/01-12/01
	Topeka MSA, KS	H	9.07 FQ	10.11 AW	11.01 TQ	KSBLS	10/01-12/01
	Kentucky	H	6.27 FQ	15.17 AW	26.34 TQ	KYBLS	10/01-12/01
	Louisville MSA, KY-IN	H	6.77 FQ	16.26 AW	26.91 TQ	KYBLS	10/01-12/01
	Louisiana	H	5.74 FQ	7.33 AW	9.11 TQ	LABLS	10/01-12/01
	Baton Rouge MSA, LA	H	5.74 FQ	6.75 AW	7.19 TQ	LABLS	10/01-12/01
	Maryland	H	5.70 FQ	8.54 AW	13.96 TQ	MDBLS	10/01-12/01
	Baltimore PMSA, MD	H	5.69 FQ	8.44 AW	12.85 TQ	MDBLS	10/01-12/01
	Massachusetts	H	7.44 FQ	13.15 AW	18.32 TQ	MABLS	10/01-12/01
	Boston PMSA, MA-NH	H	9.26 FQ	14.83 AW	21.46 TQ	MABLS	10/01-12/01
	Michigan	H	5.83 FQ	9.49 AW	16.67 TQ	MIBLS	10/01-12/01
	Detroit PMSA, MI	H	5.69 FQ	9.35 AW	18.69 TQ	MIBLS	10/01-12/01
	Grand Rapids-Muskegon-Holland MSA, MI	H	6.41 FQ	12.13 AW	17.97 TQ	MIBLS	10/01-12/01
	Minnesota	H	9.56 FQ	17.43 AW	26.94 TQ	MNBLS	10/01-12/01
	Minneapolis-St. Paul MSA, MN-WI	H	9.13 FQ	13.37 AW	18.06 TQ	MNBLS	10/01-12/01
	Mississippi	H	6.03 FQ	13.04 AW	18.05 TQ	MSBLS	10/01-12/01
	Missouri	H	6.18 FQ	11.60 AW	19.23 TQ	MOBLS	10/01-12/01
	Kansas City MSA, MO-KS	H	6.05 FQ	11.56 AW	18.91 TQ	MOBLS	10/01-12/01
	St. Louis MSA, MO-IL	H	8.15 FQ	13.40 AW	23.19 TQ	MOBLS	10/01-12/01

AAW Average annual wage **AE** Average entry wage **AEX** Average experienced wage **AO** Average offered
AOH Average offered, high **AOL** Average offered, low **APH** Average pay, high range **APL** Average pay, low range
ASH Average starting, high **ASL** Average starting, low **AW** Average wage paid **FQ** First quartile wage
H Hourly **HI** Highest wage paid **HR** High end range **LR** Low end range
M Monthly **MTC** Median total compensation **MW** Median wage paid **SQ** Second quartile wage
S Special: hourly and annual **TQ** Third quartile wage **W** Weekly **Y** Yearly

Occupation/Type/Industry	Location	Per	Low	Mid	High	Source	Date
Barber	Montana	H	6.02 FQ	9.44 AW	13.55 TQ	MTBLS	10/01-12/01
	Nebraska	H	6.04 FQ	10.35 AW	16.58 TQ	NEBLS	10/01-12/01
	Omaha MSA, NE-IA	H	6.13 FQ	10.29 AW	16.21 TQ	NEBLS	10/01-12/01
	New Hampshire	H	8.03 FQ	12.02 AW	16.09 TQ	NHBLS	10/01-12/01
	New Jersey	H	6.19 FQ	10.58 AW	15.33 TQ	NJBLS	10/01-12/01
	Bergen-Passaic PMSA, NJ	H	6.49 FQ	11.51 AW	15.89 TQ	NJBLS	10/01-12/01
	Jersey City PMSA, NJ	H	5.68 FQ	8.11 AW	12.63 TQ	NJBLS	10/01-12/01
	Middlesex-Somerset-Hunterdon PMSA, NJ	H	5.80 FQ	8.64 AW	13.12 TQ	NJBLS	10/01-12/01
	Monmouth-Ocean PMSA, NJ	H	6.91 FQ	10.68 AW	15.74 TQ	NJBLS	10/01-12/01
	Newark PMSA, NJ	H	6.01 FQ	11.99 AW	18.82 TQ	NJBLS	10/01-12/01
	Trenton PMSA, NJ	H	7.33 FQ	12.51 AW	16.06 TQ	NJBLS	10/01-12/01
	New Mexico	H	6.07 FQ	8.24 AW	11.21 TQ	NMBLS	10/01-12/01
	New York	H	5.67 FQ	9.08 AW	18.35 TQ	NYBLS	10/01-12/01
	Nassau-Suffolk PMSA, NY	H	5.57 FQ	6.94 AW	9.63 TQ	NYBLS	10/01-12/01
	New York PMSA, NY	H	5.68 FQ	9.70 AW	20.08 TQ	NYBLS	10/01-12/01
	Newburgh PMSA, NY-PA	H	6.52 FQ	14.19 AW	21.29 TQ	NYBLS	10/01-12/01
	Rochester MSA, NY	H	6.15 FQ	8.13 AW	10.67 TQ	NYBLS	10/01-12/01
	North Carolina	H	5.97 FQ	10.68 AW	17.64 TQ	NCBLS	10/01-12/01
	Charlotte-Gastonia-Rock Hill MSA, NC-SC	H	8.60 FQ	14.76 AW	24.38 TQ	NCBLS	10/01-12/01
	Greensboro-Winston-Salem-High Point MSA, NC	H	6.34 FQ	9.45 AW	13.32 TQ	NCBLS	10/01-12/01
	Raleigh-Durham-Chapel Hill MSA, NC	H	6.04 FQ	11.37 AW	14.56 TQ	NCBLS	10/01-12/01
	Ohio	H	6.59 FQ	10.18 AW	13.71 TQ	OHBLS	10/01-12/01
	Cincinnati PMSA, OH-KY-IN	H	7.39 FQ	11.59 AW	16.53 TQ	OHBLS	10/01-12/01
	Cleveland-Lorain-Elyria PMSA, OH	H	6.42 FQ	8.90 AW	11.04 TQ	OHBLS	10/01-12/01
	Oklahoma	H	6.29 FQ	9.94 AW	17.37 TQ	OKBLS	10/01-12/01
	Oklahoma City MSA, OK	H	6.28 FQ	11.14 AW	24.10 TQ	OKBLS	10/01-12/01
	Tulsa MSA, OK	H	6.52 FQ	8.43 AW	10.91 TQ	OKBLS	10/01-12/01
	Pennsylvania	H	5.62 FQ	8.32 AW	13.95 TQ	PABLS	10/01-12/01
	Harrisburg-Lebanon-Carlisle MSA, PA	H	6.09 FQ	11.16 AW	19.25 TQ	PABLS	10/01-12/01
	Lancaster MSA, PA	H	5.56 FQ	7.27 AW	8.96 TQ	PABLS	10/01-12/01
	Philadelphia PMSA, PA-NJ	H	5.64 FQ	8.09 AW	12.99 TQ	PABLS	10/01-12/01
	Pittsburgh MSA, PA	H	5.83 FQ	9.60 AW	16.89 TQ	PABLS	10/01-12/01
	Rhode Island	H	6.62 FQ	10.50 AW	15.98 TQ	RIBLS	10/01-12/01
	South Carolina	H	5.68 FQ	10.15 AW	15.97 TQ	SCBLS	10/01-12/01
	Charleston-North Charleston MSA, SC	H	6.61 FQ	12.25 AW	16.39 TQ	SCBLS	10/01-12/01
	Tennessee	H	7.47 FQ	11.38 AW	16.75 TQ	TNBLS	10/01-12/01
	Knoxville MSA, TN	H	7.93 FQ	12.17 AW	16.42 TQ	TNBLS	10/01-12/01
	Memphis MSA, TN-AR-MS	H	7.47 FQ	8.57 AW	10.01 TQ	TNBLS	10/01-12/01
	Nashville MSA, TN	H	10.15 FQ	13.78 AW	17.38 TQ	TNBLS	10/01-12/01
	Texas	H	6.30 FQ	9.69 AW	15.44 TQ	TXBLS	10/01-12/01
	Austin-San Marcos MSA, TX	H	5.68 FQ	8.29 AW	11.59 TQ	TXBLS	10/01-12/01
	Dallas PMSA, TX	H	10.44 FQ	18.05 AW	23.14 TQ	TXBLS	10/01-12/01
	El Paso MSA, TX	H	6.57 FQ	7.98 AW	9.03 TQ	TXBLS	10/01-12/01
	Fort Worth-Arlington PMSA, TX	H	7.53 FQ	8.92 AW	10.99 TQ	TXBLS	10/01-12/01
	Houston PMSA, TX	H	7.03 FQ	10.26 AW	17.02 TQ	TXBLS	10/01-12/01
	Utah	H	5.68 FQ	8.94 AW	16.32 TQ	UTBLS	10/01-12/01
	Virginia	H	5.72 FQ	9.87 AW	16.27 TQ	VABLS	10/01-12/01
	Norfolk-Virginia Beach-Newport News MSA, VA-NC	H	6.12 FQ	9.45 AW	11.03 TQ	VABLS	10/01-12/01
	Richmond-Petersburg MSA, VA	H	5.56 FQ	8.29 AW	15.32 TQ	VABLS	10/01-12/01
	Washington	H	7.75 FQ	12.43 AW	20.16 TQ	WABLS	10/01-12/01
	Seattle-Bellevue-Everett PMSA, WA	H	9.01 FQ	13.69 AW	21.13 TQ	WABLS	10/01-12/01
	Spokane MSA, WA	H	7.50 FQ	8.81 AW	10.85 TQ	WABLS	10/01-12/01
	West Virginia	H	6.22 FQ	9.53 AW	12.43 TQ	WVBLS	10/01-12/01
	Wisconsin	H	6.06 FQ	10.73 AW	17.65 TQ	WIBLS	10/01-12/01
	Milwaukee-Waukesha PMSA, WI	H	6.48 FQ	11.55 AW	19.48 TQ	WIBLS	10/01-12/01
	Puerto Rico	H	5.50 FQ	7.29 AW	11.66 TQ	PRBLS	10/01-12/01
	Guam	H	5.64 FQ	9.79 AW	14.96 TQ	GUBLS	10/01-12/01
Bartender	Alabama	H	5.58 FQ	6.95 AW	8.66 TQ	ALBLS	10/01-12/01
	Birmingham MSA, AL	H	5.95 FQ	7.47 AW	8.68 TQ	ALBLS	10/01-12/01

AAW	Average annual wage	AOH	Average offered, high	ASH	Average starting, high	H	Hourly	M	Monthly	S	Special: hourly and annual
AE	Average entry wage	AOL	Average offered, low	ASL	Average starting, low	HI	Highest wage paid	MTC	Median total compensation	TQ	Third quartile wage
AEX	Average experienced wage	APH	Average pay, high range	AW	Average wage paid	HR	High end range	MW	Median wage paid	W	Weekly
AO	Average offered	APL	Average pay, low range	FQ	First quartile wage	LR	Low end range	SQ	Second quartile wage	Y	Yearly

Occupation/Type/Industry	Location	Per	Low	Mid	High	Source	Date
Bartender	Huntsville MSA, AL	H	5.65 FQ	8.18 AW	13.75 TQ	ALBLS	10/01-12/01
	Mobile MSA, AL	H	5.39 FQ	6.43 AW	8.10 TQ	ALBLS	10/01-12/01
	Montgomery MSA, AL	H	5.67 FQ	7.60 AW	12.24 TQ	ALBLS	10/01-12/01
	Alaska	H	7.70 FQ	10.10 AW	12.81 TQ	AKBLS	10/01-12/01
	Anchorage MSA, AK	H	7.43 FQ	9.61 AW	12.11 TQ	AKBLS	10/01-12/01
	Arizona	H	5.47 FQ	7.21 AW	11.49 TQ	AZBLS	10/01-12/01
	Phoenix-Mesa MSA, AZ	H	5.44 FQ	7.42 AW	12.27 TQ	AZBLS	10/01-12/01
	Tucson MSA, AZ	H	5.56 FQ	7.35 AW	11.79 TQ	AZBLS	10/01-12/01
	Arkansas	H	5.69 FQ	7.83 AW	11.75 TQ	ARBLS	10/01-12/01
	Fayetteville-Springdale-Rogers MSA, AR	H	5.67 FQ	7.44 AW	10.90 TQ	ARBLS	10/01-12/01
	Fort Smith MSA, AR-OK	H	5.62 FQ	7.24 AW	11.16 TQ	ARBLS	10/01-12/01
	Little Rock-North Little Rock MSA, AR	H	5.97 FQ	8.38 AW	10.99 TQ	ARBLS	10/01-12/01
	California	H	6.40 FQ	8.26 AW	11.60 TQ	CABLS	10/01-12/01
	Bakersfield MSA, CA	H	6.48 FQ	7.99 AW	10.83 TQ	CABLS	10/01-12/01
	Chico-Paradise MSA, CA	H	6.37 FQ	7.31 AW	8.63 TQ	CABLS	10/01-12/01
	Fresno MSA, CA	H	6.51 FQ	7.69 AW	9.36 TQ	CABLS	10/01-12/01
	Los Angeles-Long Beach PMSA, CA	H	6.56 FQ	8.52 AW	11.38 TQ	CABLS	10/01-12/01
	Merced MSA, CA	H	6.41 FQ	8.54 AW	12.56 TQ	CABLS	10/01-12/01
	Modesto MSA, CA	H	6.51 FQ	8.43 AW	10.95 TQ	CABLS	10/01-12/01
	Oakland PMSA, CA	H	6.32 FQ	7.51 AW	10.62 TQ	CABLS	10/01-12/01
	Orange County PMSA, CA	H	6.42 FQ	8.49 AW	13.78 TQ	CABLS	10/01-12/01
	Redding MSA, CA	H	6.45 FQ	8.13 AW	10.91 TQ	CABLS	10/01-12/01
	Riverside-San Bernardino PMSA, CA	H	6.40 FQ	7.44 AW	9.03 TQ	CABLS	10/01-12/01
	Sacramento PMSA, CA	H	6.40 FQ	8.47 AW	11.22 TQ	CABLS	10/01-12/01
	Salinas MSA, CA	H	7.12 FQ	10.30 AW	15.33 TQ	CABLS	10/01-12/01
	San Diego MSA, CA	H	6.32 FQ	7.21 AW	8.59 TQ	CABLS	10/01-12/01
	San Francisco PMSA, CA	H	7.00 FQ	11.03 AW	17.35 TQ	CABLS	10/01-12/01
	San Jose PMSA, CA	H	6.54 FQ	8.94 AW	13.12 TQ	CABLS	10/01-12/01
	San Luis Obispo-Atascadero-Paso Robles MSA, CA	H	6.42 FQ	9.35 AW	14.40 TQ	CABLS	10/01-12/01
	Santa Barbara-Santa Maria-Lompoc MSA, CA	H	6.50 FQ	9.11 AW	13.22 TQ	CABLS	10/01-12/01
	Santa Cruz-Watsonville PMSA, CA	H	6.57 FQ	9.01 AW	14.08 TQ	CABLS	10/01-12/01
	Santa Rosa PMSA, CA	H	6.96 FQ	8.16 AW	9.93 TQ	CABLS	10/01-12/01
	Stockton-Lodi MSA, CA	H	6.37 FQ	7.50 AW	9.59 TQ	CABLS	10/01-12/01
	Vallejo-Fairfield-Napa PMSA, CA	H	6.45 FQ	8.28 AW	10.61 TQ	CABLS	10/01-12/01
	Ventura PMSA, CA	H	6.45 FQ	9.28 AW	17.64 TQ	CABLS	10/01-12/01
	Visalia-Tulare-Porterville MSA, CA	H	6.44 FQ	7.64 AW	9.00 TQ	CABLS	10/01-12/01
	Colorado	H	5.63 FQ	7.72 AW	11.16 TQ	COBLS	10/01-12/01
	Boulder-Longmont PMSA, CO	H	5.67 FQ	7.49 AW	9.96 TQ	COBLS	10/01-12/01
	Colorado Springs MSA, CO	H	5.78 FQ	8.24 AW	11.48 TQ	COBLS	10/01-12/01
	Denver PMSA, CO	H	5.72 FQ	7.96 AW	11.01 TQ	COBLS	10/01-12/01
	Fort Collins-Loveland MSA, CO	H	5.53 FQ	7.63 AW	11.11 TQ	COBLS	10/01-12/01
	Greeley PMSA, CO	H	5.69 FQ	7.34 AW	11.50 TQ	COBLS	10/01-12/01
	Connecticut	H	6.49 FQ	8.42 AW	12.92 TQ	CTBLS	10/01-12/01
	Bridgeport PMSA, CT	H	6.50 FQ	8.38 AW	12.77 TQ	CTBLS	10/01-12/01
	Danbury PMSA, CT	H	6.51 FQ	9.11 AW	14.27 TQ	CTBLS	10/01-12/01
	Hartford MSA, CT	H	6.52 FQ	9.24 AW	15.85 TQ	CTBLS	10/01-12/01
	New Haven-Meriden PMSA, CT	H	6.46 FQ	7.78 AW	10.88 TQ	CTBLS	10/01-12/01
	New London-Norwich MSA, CT-RI	H	6.53 FQ	8.00 AW	10.52 TQ	CTBLS	10/01-12/01
	Stamford-Norwalk PMSA, CT	H	6.49 FQ	8.50 AW	12.76 TQ	CTBLS	10/01-12/01
	Waterbury PMSA, CT	H	6.49 FQ	7.95 AW	11.99 TQ	CTBLS	10/01-12/01
	Delaware	H	6.47 FQ	8.46 AW	12.36 TQ	DEBLS	10/01-12/01
	Wilmington-Newark PMSA, DE-MD	H	6.39 FQ	8.59 AW	12.74 TQ	DEBLS	10/01-12/01
	District of Columbia	H	6.55 FQ	9.89 AW	14.86 TQ	DCBLS	10/01-12/01
	Washington PMSA, DC-MD-VA-WV	H	5.82 FQ	8.47 AW	13.14 TQ	DCBLS	10/01-12/01
	Florida	H	5.59 FQ	7.83 AW	12.95 TQ	FLBLS	10/01-12/01
	Daytona Beach MSA, FL	H	5.67 FQ	6.79 AW	8.69 TQ	FLBLS	10/01-12/01
	Fort Lauderdale PMSA, FL	H	5.81 FQ	8.58 AW	13.00 TQ	FLBLS	10/01-12/01

AAW	Average annual wage	**AOH**	Average offered, high	**ASH**	Average starting, high	**H**	Hourly	**M**	Monthly	**S**	Special: hourly and annual
AE	Average entry wage	**AOL**	Average offered, low	**ASL**	Average starting, low	**HI**	Highest wage paid	**MTC**	Median total compensation	**TQ**	Third quartile wage
AEX	Average experienced wage	**APH**	Average pay, high range	**AW**	Average wage paid	**HR**	High end range	**MW**	Median wage paid	**W**	Weekly
AO	Average offered	**APL**	Average pay, low range	**FQ**	First quartile wage	**LR**	Low end range	**SQ**	Second quartile wage	**Y**	Yearly

Occupation/Type/Industry	Location	Per	Low	Mid	High	Source	Date
Bartender	Fort Myers-Cape Coral MSA, FL	H	6.16 FQ	12.61 AW	16.52 TQ	FLBLS	10/01-12/01
	Fort Pierce-Port St. Lucie MSA, FL	H	5.60 FQ	7.56 AW	10.70 TQ	FLBLS	10/01-12/01
	Fort Walton Beach MSA, FL	H	5.58 FQ	7.18 AW	10.48 TQ	FLBLS	10/01-12/01
	Gainesville MSA, FL	H	5.49 FQ	6.40 AW	6.98 TQ	FLBLS	10/01-12/01
	Jacksonville MSA, FL	H	5.51 FQ	7.25 AW	10.93 TQ	FLBLS	10/01-12/01
	Lakeland-Winter Haven MSA, FL	H	5.65 FQ	7.43 AW	10.76 TQ	FLBLS	10/01-12/01
	Melbourne-Titusville-Palm Bay MSA, FL	H	5.54 FQ	6.53 AW	8.04 TQ	FLBLS	10/01-12/01
	Miami PMSA, FL	H	5.58 FQ	7.37 AW	10.52 TQ	FLBLS	10/01-12/01
	Naples MSA, FL	H	5.84 FQ	9.79 AW	15.66 TQ	FLBLS	10/01-12/01
	Ocala MSA, FL	H	5.59 FQ	6.28 AW	7.18 TQ	FLBLS	10/01-12/01
	Orlando MSA, FL	H	5.55 FQ	6.90 AW	8.61 TQ	FLBLS	10/01-12/01
	Pensacola MSA, FL	H	5.51 FQ	6.23 AW	7.15 TQ	FLBLS	10/01-12/01
	Sarasota-Bradenton MSA, FL	H	5.44 FQ	7.16 AW	11.16 TQ	FLBLS	10/01-12/01
	Tallahassee MSA, FL	H	5.66 FQ	7.59 AW	11.00 TQ	FLBLS	10/01-12/01
	Tampa-St. Petersburg-Clearwater MSA, FL	H	5.64 FQ	7.75 AW	11.38 TQ	FLBLS	10/01-12/01
	West Palm Beach-Boca Raton MSA, FL	H	5.64 FQ	8.41 AW	13.65 TQ	FLBLS	10/01-12/01
	Georgia	H	5.62 FQ	7.80 AW	11.59 TQ	GABLS	10/01-12/01
	Atlanta MSA, GA	H	5.60 FQ	7.77 AW	11.82 TQ	GABLS	10/01-12/01
	Augusta-Aiken MSA, GA-SC	H	5.80 FQ	7.88 AW	10.60 TQ	GABLS	10/01-12/01
	Columbus MSA, GA-AL	H	5.73 FQ	7.52 AW	10.61 TQ	GABLS	10/01-12/01
	Macon MSA, GA	H	5.62 FQ	7.29 AW	10.66 TQ	GABLS	10/01-12/01
	Savannah MSA, GA	H	5.64 FQ	7.49 AW	10.85 TQ	GABLS	10/01-12/01
	Hawaii	H	6.95 FQ	13.00 AW	19.99 TQ	HIBLS	10/01-12/01
	Honolulu MSA, HI	H	6.98 FQ	11.79 AW	18.91 TQ	HIBLS	10/01-12/01
	Idaho	H	5.43 FQ	6.36 AW	7.97 TQ	IDBLS	10/01-12/01
	Boise City MSA, ID	H	5.41 FQ	6.34 AW	8.04 TQ	IDBLS	10/01-12/01
	Illinois	H	5.73 FQ	8.14 AW	11.34 TQ	ILBLS	10/01-12/01
	Champaign-Urbana MSA, IL	H	5.81 FQ	7.89 AW	10.19 TQ	ILBLS	10/01-12/01
	Chicago PMSA, IL	H	5.93 FQ	8.79 AW	14.03 TQ	ILBLS	10/01-12/01
	Peoria-Pekin MSA, IL	H	5.44 FQ	6.64 AW	8.68 TQ	ILBLS	10/01-12/01
	Rockford MSA, IL	H	5.94 FQ	7.66 AW	9.96 TQ	ILBLS	10/01-12/01
	Springfield MSA, IL	H	5.59 FQ	6.98 AW	8.78 TQ	ILBLS	10/01-12/01
	Indiana	H	5.71 FQ	7.82 AW	10.58 TQ	INBLS	10/01-12/01
	Elkhart-Goshen MSA, IN	H	5.58 FQ	8.21 AW	12.29 TQ	INBLS	10/01-12/01
	Evansville-Henderson MSA, IN-KY	H	5.79 FQ	7.48 AW	9.65 TQ	INBLS	10/01-12/01
	Fort Wayne MSA, IN	H	5.89 FQ	7.84 AW	10.43 TQ	INBLS	10/01-12/01
	Gary PMSA, IN	H	5.83 FQ	7.90 AW	10.55 TQ	INBLS	10/01-12/01
	Indianapolis MSA, IN	H	5.88 FQ	8.77 AW	14.28 TQ	INBLS	10/01-12/01
	Lafayette MSA, IN	H	5.61 FQ	6.76 AW	8.46 TQ	INBLS	10/01-12/01
	South Bend MSA, IN	H	5.56 FQ	7.00 AW	8.68 TQ	INBLS	10/01-12/01
	Iowa	H	5.54 FQ	6.97 AW	8.76 TQ	IABLS	10/01-12/01
	Cedar Rapids MSA, IA	H	5.94 FQ	7.80 AW	10.10 TQ	IABLS	10/01-12/01
	Davenport-Moline-Rock Island MSA, IA-IL	H	5.61 FQ	6.86 AW	8.88 TQ	IABLS	10/01-12/01
	Des Moines MSA, IA	H	5.49 FQ	6.80 AW	8.53 TQ	IABLS	10/01-12/01
	Kansas	H	5.57 FQ	6.85 AW	9.43 TQ	KSBLS	10/01-12/01
	Topeka MSA, KS	H	5.85 FQ	9.11 AW	13.69 TQ	KSBLS	10/01-12/01
	Wichita MSA, KS	H	5.58 FQ	6.63 AW	8.46 TQ	KSBLS	10/01-12/01
	Kentucky	H	5.48 FQ	6.92 AW	9.18 TQ	KYBLS	10/01-12/01
	Lexington MSA, KY	H	5.42 FQ	7.20 AW	10.94 TQ	KYBLS	10/01-12/01
	Louisville MSA, KY-IN	H	5.53 FQ	6.90 AW	8.84 TQ	KYBLS	10/01-12/01
	Louisiana	H	5.47 FQ	6.77 AW	9.36 TQ	LABLS	10/01-12/01
	Baton Rouge MSA, LA	H	5.63 FQ	6.70 AW	8.55 TQ	LABLS	10/01-12/01
	Houma MSA, LA	H	5.56 FQ	6.77 AW	9.96 TQ	LABLS	10/01-12/01
	Lafayette MSA, LA	H	5.62 FQ	6.74 AW	8.43 TQ	LABLS	10/01-12/01
	Lake Charles MSA, LA	H	5.50 FQ	6.51 AW	8.10 TQ	LABLS	10/01-12/01
	New Orleans MSA, LA	H	5.45 FQ	6.81 AW	9.63 TQ	LABLS	10/01-12/01
	Shreveport-Bossier City MSA, LA	H	5.56 FQ	7.04 AW	9.75 TQ	LABLS	10/01-12/01
	Maine	H	5.66 FQ	8.07 AW	10.82 TQ	MEBLS	10/01-12/01
	Portland MSA, ME	H	5.69 FQ	8.33 AW	10.62 TQ	MEBLS	10/01-12/01
	Maryland	H	5.73 FQ	8.08 AW	12.70 TQ	MDBLS	10/01-12/01
	Baltimore PMSA, MD	H	5.77 FQ	8.47 AW	13.13 TQ	MDBLS	10/01-12/01
	Massachusetts	H	6.77 FQ	9.14 AW	12.98 TQ	MABLS	10/01-12/01
	Boston PMSA, MA-NH	H	6.85 FQ	9.55 AW	13.54 TQ	MABLS	10/01-12/01

AAW Average annual wage **AE** Average entry wage **AEX** Average experienced wage **AO** Average offered **AOH** Average offered, high **AOL** Average offered, low **APH** Average pay, high range **APL** Average pay, low range **ASH** Average starting, high **ASL** Average starting, low **AW** Average wage paid **FQ** First quartile wage **H** Hourly **HI** Highest wage paid **HR** High end range **LR** Low end range **M** Monthly **MTC** Median total compensation **MW** Median wage paid **SQ** Second quartile wage **S** Special: hourly and annual **TQ** Third quartile wage **W** Weekly **Y** Yearly

Occupation/Type/Industry	Location	Per	Low	Mid	High	Source	Date
Bartender	Brockton PMSA, MA	H	6.94 FQ	10.04 AW	13.02 TQ	MABLS	10/01-12/01
	Lawrence PMSA, MA-NH	H	6.45 FQ	8.51 AW	13.11 TQ	MABLS	10/01-12/01
	Lowell PMSA, MA-NH	H	6.74 FQ	7.50 AW	8.97 TQ	MABLS	10/01-12/01
	New Bedford PMSA, MA	H	6.81 FQ	7.77 AW	9.65 TQ	MABLS	10/01-12/01
	Springfield MSA, MA	H	6.90 FQ	9.30 AW	12.70 TQ	MABLS	10/01-12/01
	Worcester PMSA, MA-CT	H	6.82 FQ	8.42 AW	11.06 TQ	MABLS	10/01-12/01
	Michigan	H	5.61 FQ	7.56 AW	10.61 TQ	MIBLS	10/01-12/01
	Ann Arbor PMSA, MI	H	5.98 FQ	8.58 AW	12.55 TQ	MIBLS	10/01-12/01
	Detroit PMSA, MI	H	5.47 FQ	7.25 AW	10.21 TQ	MIBLS	10/01-12/01
	Flint PMSA, MI	H	5.38 FQ	6.43 AW	8.36 TQ	MIBLS	10/01-12/01
	Grand Rapids-Muskegon-Holland MSA, MI	H	5.95 FQ	8.91 AW	13.28 TQ	MIBLS	10/01-12/01
	Kalamazoo-Battle Creek MSA, MI	H	5.47 FQ	6.73 AW	9.03 TQ	MIBLS	10/01-12/01
	Lansing-East Lansing MSA, MI	H	5.65 FQ	6.92 AW	8.53 TQ	MIBLS	10/01-12/01
	Saginaw-Bay City-Midland MSA, MI	H	5.61 FQ	6.85 AW	9.01 TQ	MIBLS	10/01-12/01
	Minnesota	H	5.74 FQ	7.58 AW	9.97 TQ	MNBLS	10/01-12/01
	Duluth-Superior MSA, MN-WI	H	5.62 FQ	7.13 AW	9.12 TQ	MNBLS	10/01-12/01
	Minneapolis-St. Paul MSA, MN-WI	H	5.77 FQ	7.71 AW	10.19 TQ	MNBLS	10/01-12/01
	St. Cloud MSA, MN	H	5.89 FQ	7.36 AW	8.77 TQ	MNBLS	10/01-12/01
	Mississippi	H	5.41 FQ	6.42 AW	8.09 TQ	MSBLS	10/01-12/01
	Biloxi-Gulfport-Pascagoula MSA, MS	H	5.42 FQ	6.52 AW	8.50 TQ	MSBLS	10/01-12/01
	Jackson MSA, MS	H	5.68 FQ	7.32 AW	10.03 TQ	MSBLS	10/01-12/01
	Missouri	H	5.55 FQ	8.92 AW	11.13 TQ	MOBLS	10/01-12/01
	Kansas City MSA, MO-KS	H	5.86 FQ	8.23 AW	10.70 TQ	MOBLS	10/01-12/01
	St. Louis MSA, MO-IL	H	5.48 FQ	9.72 AW	14.77 TQ	MOBLS	10/01-12/01
	Springfield MSA, MO	H	6.05 FQ	7.87 AW	9.08 TQ	MOBLS	10/01-12/01
	Montana	H	5.62 FQ	7.35 AW	9.76 TQ	MTBLS	10/01-12/01
	Billings MSA, MT	H	5.60 FQ	6.61 AW	8.32 TQ	MTBLS	10/01-12/01
	Nebraska	H	5.50 FQ	6.55 AW	8.51 TQ	NEBLS	10/01-12/01
	Lincoln MSA, NE	H	5.56 FQ	6.30 AW	7.07 TQ	NEBLS	10/01-12/01
	Omaha MSA, NE-IA	H	5.41 FQ	6.54 AW	8.67 TQ	NEBLS	10/01-12/01
	Nevada	H	5.78 FQ	9.59 AW	14.57 TQ	NVBLS	10/01-12/01
	Las Vegas MSA, NV-AZ	H	5.85 FQ	10.11 AW	15.10 TQ	NVBLS	10/01-12/01
	Reno MSA, NV	H	5.73 FQ	7.73 AW	10.87 TQ	NVBLS	10/01-12/01
	New Hampshire	H	5.76 FQ	8.08 AW	12.11 TQ	NHBLS	10/01-12/01
	Manchester PMSA, NH	H	5.80 FQ	7.72 AW	11.06 TQ	NHBLS	10/01-12/01
	Nashua PMSA, NH	H	5.85 FQ	8.25 AW	11.56 TQ	NHBLS	10/01-12/01
	Portsmouth-Rochester PMSA, NH-ME	H	5.73 FQ	8.80 AW	13.32 TQ	NHBLS	10/01-12/01
	New Jersey	H	5.63 FQ	8.69 AW	13.66 TQ	NJBLS	10/01-12/01
	Atlantic-Cape May PMSA, NJ	H	6.03 FQ	11.34 AW	16.51 TQ	NJBLS	10/01-12/01
	Bergen-Passaic PMSA, NJ	H	5.91 FQ	9.37 AW	14.23 TQ	NJBLS	10/01-12/01
	Jersey City PMSA, NJ	H	5.69 FQ	9.22 AW	10.72 TQ	NJBLS	10/01-12/01
	Middlesex-Somerset-Hunterdon PMSA, NJ	H	5.51 FQ	7.99 AW	10.57 TQ	NJBLS	10/01-12/01
	Monmouth-Ocean PMSA, NJ	H	5.90 FQ	8.94 AW	13.57 TQ	NJBLS	10/01-12/01
	Newark PMSA, NJ	H	5.86 FQ	9.14 AW	13.89 TQ	NJBLS	10/01-12/01
	Trenton PMSA, NJ	H	5.98 FQ	9.51 AW	15.06 TQ	NJBLS	10/01-12/01
	New Mexico	H	5.54 FQ	7.03 AW	10.33 TQ	NMBLS	10/01-12/01
	Albuquerque MSA, NM	H	5.59 FQ	7.28 AW	11.72 TQ	NMBLS	10/01-12/01
	Las Cruces MSA, NM	H	5.50 FQ	6.51 AW	8.44 TQ	NMBLS	10/01-12/01
	New York	H	5.62 FQ	8.95 AW	15.63 TQ	NYBLS	10/01-12/01
	Albany-Schenectady-Troy MSA, NY	H	5.65 FQ	7.32 AW	10.66 TQ	NYBLS	10/01-12/01
	Binghamton MSA, NY	H	5.62 FQ	6.77 AW	8.68 TQ	NYBLS	10/01-12/01
	Buffalo-Niagara Falls MSA, NY	H	5.46 FQ	7.14 AW	10.32 TQ	NYBLS	10/01-12/01
	Dutchess County PMSA, NY	H	5.43 FQ	7.33 AW	10.74 TQ	NYBLS	10/01-12/01
	Nassau-Suffolk PMSA, NY	H	5.84 FQ	9.04 AW	13.06 TQ	NYBLS	10/01-12/01
	New York PMSA, NY	H	5.78 FQ	11.22 AW	16.65 TQ	NYBLS	10/01-12/01
	Newburgh PMSA, NY-PA	H	5.65 FQ	7.60 AW	11.89 TQ	NYBLS	10/01-12/01
	Rochester MSA, NY	H	5.66 FQ	7.46 AW	10.16 TQ	NYBLS	10/01-12/01
	Syracuse MSA, NY	H	5.44 FQ	6.63 AW	8.49 TQ	NYBLS	10/01-12/01
	Utica-Rome MSA, NY	H	5.70 FQ	7.33 AW	10.32 TQ	NYBLS	10/01-12/01
	North Carolina	H	5.60 FQ	7.59 AW	11.11 TQ	NCBLS	10/01-12/01
	Asheville MSA, NC	H	5.95 FQ	8.82 AW	13.05 TQ	NCBLS	10/01-12/01
	Charlotte-Gastonia-Rock Hill MSA, NC-SC	H	5.61 FQ	7.29 AW	10.21 TQ	NCBLS	10/01-12/01

AAW	Average annual wage	**AOH**	Average offered, high	**ASH**	Average starting, high	**H**	Hourly	**M**	Monthly	**S**	Special: hourly and annual
AE	Average entry wage	**AOL**	Average offered, low	**ASL**	Average starting, low	**HI**	Highest wage paid	**MTC**	Median total compensation	**TQ**	Third quartile wage
AEX	Average experienced wage	**APH**	Average pay, high range	**AW**	Average wage paid	**HR**	High end range	**MW**	Median wage paid	**W**	Weekly
AO	Average offered	**APL**	Average pay, low range	**FQ**	First quartile wage	**LR**	Low end range	**SQ**	Second quartile wage	**Y**	Yearly

Occupation/Type/Industry	Location	Per	Low	Mid	High	Source	Date
Bartender	Fayetteville MSA, NC	H	5.81 FQ	8.21 AW	13.24 TQ	NCBLS	10/01-12/01
	Greensboro-Winston-Salem-High Point MSA, NC	H	5.46 FQ	7.30 AW	10.56 TQ	NCBLS	10/01-12/01
	Hickory-Morganton-Lenoir MSA, NC	H	5.40 FQ	7.74 AW	13.12 TQ	NCBLS	10/01-12/01
	Raleigh-Durham-Chapel Hill MSA, NC	H	5.85 FQ	8.49 AW	12.96 TQ	NCBLS	10/01-12/01
	Wilmington MSA, NC	H	5.59 FQ	6.66 AW	8.59 TQ	NCBLS	10/01-12/01
	North Dakota	H	5.61 FQ	6.86 AW	8.44 TQ	NDBLS	10/01-12/01
	Fargo-Moorhead MSA, ND-MN	H	5.50 FQ	6.44 AW	8.18 TQ	NDBLS	10/01-12/01
	Ohio	H	5.58 FQ	7.46 AW	10.68 TQ	OHBLS	10/01-12/01
	Akron PMSA, OH	H	5.71 FQ	8.65 AW	12.82 TQ	OHBLS	10/01-12/01
	Canton-Massillon MSA, OH	H	5.74 FQ	7.59 AW	10.27 TQ	OHBLS	10/01-12/01
	Cincinnati PMSA, OH-KY-IN	H	5.39 FQ	6.70 AW	8.68 TQ	OHBLS	10/01-12/01
	Cleveland-Lorain-Elyria PMSA, OH	H	5.58 FQ	7.57 AW	11.03 TQ	OHBLS	10/01-12/01
	Columbus MSA, OH	H	5.71 FQ	7.61 AW	10.79 TQ	OHBLS	10/01-12/01
	Dayton-Springfield MSA, OH	H	5.61 FQ	8.26 AW	12.27 TQ	OHBLS	10/01-12/01
	Hamilton-Middletown PMSA, OH	H	5.81 FQ	7.57 AW	10.15 TQ	OHBLS	10/01-12/01
	Mansfield MSA, OH	H	5.62 FQ	7.45 AW	10.61 TQ	OHBLS	10/01-12/01
	Toledo MSA, OH	H	5.51 FQ	6.87 AW	8.78 TQ	OHBLS	10/01-12/01
	Youngstown-Warren MSA, OH	H	5.64 FQ	7.23 AW	10.40 TQ	OHBLS	10/01-12/01
	Oklahoma	H	5.39 FQ	6.26 AW	7.47 TQ	OKBLS	10/01-12/01
	Oklahoma City MSA, OK	H	5.35 FQ	6.14 AW	6.93 TQ	OKBLS	10/01-12/01
	Tulsa MSA, OK	H	5.60 FQ	6.66 AW	8.59 TQ	OKBLS	10/01-12/01
	Oregon	H	6.76 FQ	8.40 AW	10.79 TQ	ORBLS	10/01-12/01
	Eugene-Springfield MSA, OR	H	6.87 FQ	8.89 AW	11.33 TQ	ORBLS	10/01-12/01
	Medford-Ashland MSA, OR	H	6.83 FQ	7.73 AW	8.90 TQ	ORBLS	10/01-12/01
	Portland-Vancouver PMSA, OR-WA	H	6.97 FQ	8.94 AW	11.05 TQ	ORBLS	10/01-12/01
	Salem PMSA, OR	H	6.83 FQ	7.79 AW	9.30 TQ	ORBLS	10/01-12/01
	Pennsylvania	H	5.51 FQ	7.37 AW	10.17 TQ	PABLS	10/01-12/01
	Allentown-Bethlehem-Easton MSA, PA	H	6.08 FQ	8.21 AW	10.75 TQ	PABLS	10/01-12/01
	Erie MSA, PA	H	5.67 FQ	7.25 AW	10.10 TQ	PABLS	10/01-12/01
	Harrisburg-Lebanon-Carlisle MSA, PA	H	5.64 FQ	7.42 AW	9.87 TQ	PABLS	10/01-12/01
	Johnstown MSA, PA	H	5.52 FQ	6.98 AW	9.93 TQ	PABLS	10/01-12/01
	Lancaster MSA, PA	H	5.48 FQ	6.91 AW	8.70 TQ	PABLS	10/01-12/01
	Philadelphia PMSA, PA-NJ	H	5.45 FQ	7.69 AW	11.85 TQ	PABLS	10/01-12/01
	Pittsburgh MSA, PA	H	5.46 FQ	6.84 AW	8.74 TQ	PABLS	10/01-12/01
	Reading MSA, PA	H	5.90 FQ	8.07 AW	10.84 TQ	PABLS	10/01-12/01
	Scranton-Wilkes-Barre-Hazleton MSA, PA	H	5.68 FQ	7.07 AW	9.68 TQ	PABLS	10/01-12/01
	York MSA, PA	H	6.07 FQ	9.37 AW	14.64 TQ	PABLS	10/01-12/01
	Rhode Island	H	6.40 FQ	8.37 AW	12.00 TQ	RIBLS	10/01-12/01
	Providence-Fall River-Warwick MSA, RI-MA	H	6.43 FQ	8.64 AW	12.85 TQ	RIBLS	10/01-12/01
	South Carolina	H	5.60 FQ	7.16 AW	9.97 TQ	SCBLS	10/01-12/01
	Charleston-North Charleston MSA, SC	H	5.75 FQ	7.73 AW	10.61 TQ	SCBLS	10/01-12/01
	Columbia MSA, SC	H	5.60 FQ	7.08 AW	10.05 TQ	SCBLS	10/01-12/01
	Greenville-Spartanburg-Anderson MSA, SC	H	5.67 FQ	7.27 AW	8.80 TQ	SCBLS	10/01-12/01
	Myrtle Beach MSA, SC	H	5.57 FQ	7.15 AW	11.17 TQ	SCBLS	10/01-12/01
	South Dakota	H	5.66 FQ	7.02 AW	8.44 TQ	SDBLS	10/01-12/01
	Sioux Falls MSA, SD	H	5.72 FQ	7.16 AW	8.78 TQ	SDBLS	10/01-12/01
	Tennessee	H	5.75 FQ	8.13 AW	11.64 TQ	TNBLS	10/01-12/01
	Chattanooga MSA, TN-GA	H	5.76 FQ	8.04 AW	12.56 TQ	TNBLS	10/01-12/01
	Clarksville-Hopkinsville MSA, TN-KY	H	5.70 FQ	6.98 AW	9.38 TQ	TNBLS	10/01-12/01
	Johnson City-Kingsport-Bristol MSA, TN-VA	H	5.72 FQ	7.18 AW	10.22 TQ	TNBLS	10/01-12/01
	Knoxville MSA, TN	H	5.56 FQ	6.79 AW	8.55 TQ	TNBLS	10/01-12/01
	Memphis MSA, TN-AR-MS	H	5.71 FQ	9.19 AW	12.99 TQ	TNBLS	10/01-12/01
	Nashville MSA, TN	H	5.95 FQ	8.60 AW	12.20 TQ	TNBLS	10/01-12/01
	Texas	H	5.64 FQ	8.18 AW	12.85 TQ	TXBLS	10/01-12/01
	Amarillo MSA, TX	H	5.60 FQ	7.53 AW	12.27 TQ	TXBLS	10/01-12/01
	Austin-San Marcos MSA, TX	H	5.69 FQ	7.57 AW	10.80 TQ	TXBLS	10/01-12/01

AAW	Average annual wage	**AOH**	Average offered, high	**ASH**	Average starting, high	**H**	Hourly	**M**	Monthly	**S**	Special: hourly and annual
AE	Average entry wage	**AOL**	Average offered, low	**ASL**	Average starting, low	**HI**	Highest wage paid	**MTC**	Median total compensation	**TQ**	Third quartile wage
AEX	Average experienced wage	**APH**	Average pay, high range	**AW**	Average wage paid	**HR**	High end range	**MW**	Median wage paid	**W**	Weekly
AO	Average offered	**APL**	Average pay, low range	**FQ**	First quartile wage	**LR**	Low end range	**SQ**	Second quartile wage	**Y**	Yearly

Occupation/Type/Industry	Location	Per	Low	Mid	High	Source	Date
Bartender	Beaumont-Port Arthur MSA, TX	H	8.09 FQ	9.44 AW	10.68 TQ	TXBLS	10/01-12/01
	Brazoria PMSA, TX	H	5.62 FQ	7.74 AW	11.80 TQ	TXBLS	10/01-12/01
	Brownsville-Harlingen-San Benito MSA, TX	H	5.60 FQ	6.59 AW	8.19 TQ	TXBLS	10/01-12/01
	Corpus Christi MSA, TX	H	5.51 FQ	6.88 AW	9.81 TQ	TXBLS	10/01-12/01
	Dallas PMSA, TX	H	5.57 FQ	7.66 AW	12.22 TQ	TXBLS	10/01-12/01
	El Paso MSA, TX	H	5.50 FQ	6.74 AW	9.80 TQ	TXBLS	10/01-12/01
	Fort Worth-Arlington PMSA, TX	H	5.80 FQ	9.02 AW	13.17 TQ	TXBLS	10/01-12/01
	Galveston-Texas City PMSA, TX	H	5.59 FQ	7.25 AW	10.72 TQ	TXBLS	10/01-12/01
	Houston PMSA, TX	H	5.76 FQ	10.12 AW	15.24 TQ	TXBLS	10/01-12/01
	Killeen-Temple MSA, TX	H	5.53 FQ	6.16 AW	7.08 TQ	TXBLS	10/01-12/01
	Laredo MSA, TX	H	6.12 FQ	7.82 AW	10.03 TQ	TXBLS	10/01-12/01
	Longview-Marshall MSA, TX	H	5.75 FQ	8.48 AW	13.13 TQ	TXBLS	10/01-12/01
	Lubbock MSA, TX	H	5.62 FQ	6.88 AW	9.63 TQ	TXBLS	10/01-12/01
	McAllen-Edinburg-Mission MSA, TX	H	5.63 FQ	6.77 AW	9.69 TQ	TXBLS	10/01-12/01
	Odessa-Midland MSA, TX	H	5.58 FQ	7.59 AW	12.16 TQ	TXBLS	10/01-12/01
	San Antonio MSA, TX	H	5.57 FQ	7.15 AW	10.71 TQ	TXBLS	10/01-12/01
	Tyler MSA, TX	H	5.72 FQ	7.67 AW	11.87 TQ	TXBLS	10/01-12/01
	Waco MSA, TX	H	5.69 FQ	7.56 AW	11.19 TQ	TXBLS	10/01-12/01
	Utah	H	5.51 FQ	7.46 AW	11.37 TQ	UTBLS	10/01-12/01
	Provo-Orem MSA, UT	H	6.45 FQ	9.67 AW	13.76 TQ	UTBLS	10/01-12/01
	Salt Lake City-Ogden MSA, UT	H	5.46 FQ	7.15 AW	10.95 TQ	UTBLS	10/01-12/01
	Vermont	H	6.52 FQ	8.32 AW	11.88 TQ	VTBLS	10/01-12/01
	Burlington MSA, VT	H	6.42 FQ	8.48 AW	12.31 TQ	VTBLS	10/01-12/01
	Virginia	H	5.62 FQ	7.40 AW	10.67 TQ	VABLS	10/01-12/01
	Lynchburg MSA, VA	H	5.62 FQ	6.71 AW	9.14 TQ	VABLS	10/01-12/01
	Norfolk-Virginia Beach-Newport News MSA, VA-NC	H	5.47 FQ	6.66 AW	8.59 TQ	VABLS	10/01-12/01
	Richmond-Petersburg MSA, VA	H	5.72 FQ	7.62 AW	10.71 TQ	VABLS	10/01-12/01
	Roanoke MSA, VA	H	5.83 FQ	8.56 AW	12.93 TQ	VABLS	10/01-12/01
	Washington	H	6.91 FQ	8.94 AW	11.85 TQ	WABLS	10/01-12/01
	Bremerton PMSA, WA	H	6.82 FQ	7.70 AW	8.89 TQ	WABLS	10/01-12/01
	Olympia PMSA, WA	H	6.90 FQ	8.51 AW	10.81 TQ	WABLS	10/01-12/01
	Richland-Kennewick-Pasco MSA, WA	H	6.95 FQ	8.20 AW	10.12 TQ	WABLS	10/01-12/01
	Seattle-Bellevue-Everett PMSA, WA	H	6.92 FQ	10.81 AW	22.56 TQ	WABLS	10/01-12/01
	Spokane MSA, WA	H	6.84 FQ	9.48 AW	15.88 TQ	WABLS	10/01-12/01
	Tacoma PMSA, WA	H	7.04 FQ	8.20 AW	9.99 TQ	WABLS	10/01-12/01
	Yakima MSA, WA	H	6.85 FQ	7.97 AW	9.74 TQ	WABLS	10/01-12/01
	West Virginia	H	5.48 FQ	6.34 AW	7.54 TQ	WVBLS	10/01-12/01
	Charleston MSA, WV	H	5.69 FQ	6.91 AW	8.71 TQ	WVBLS	10/01-12/01
	Huntington-Ashland MSA, WV-KY-OH	H	5.63 FQ	7.16 AW	10.47 TQ	WVBLS	10/01-12/01
	Wisconsin	H	5.93 FQ	7.81 AW	10.08 TQ	WIBLS	10/01-12/01
	Appleton-Oshkosh-Neenah MSA, WI	H	5.61 FQ	6.95 AW	8.84 TQ	WIBLS	10/01-12/01
	Green Bay MSA, WI	H	5.89 FQ	7.52 AW	9.13 TQ	WIBLS	10/01-12/01
	Madison MSA, WI	H	5.84 FQ	7.83 AW	10.38 TQ	WIBLS	10/01-12/01
	Milwaukee-Waukesha PMSA, WI	H	6.75 FQ	7.58 AW	8.46 TQ	WIBLS	10/01-12/01
	Racine PMSA, WI	H	5.94 FQ	7.32 AW	8.70 TQ	WIBLS	10/01-12/01
	Wyoming	H	5.62 FQ	7.35 AW	10.13 TQ	WYBLS	10/01-12/01
	Cheyenne MSA, WY	H	5.66 FQ	7.09 AW	8.72 TQ	WYBLS	10/01-12/01
	Puerto Rico	H	5.40 FQ	6.89 AW	10.19 TQ	PRBLS	10/01-12/01
	Virgin Islands	H	5.57 FQ	6.51 AW	8.20 TQ	VIBLS	10/01-12/01
	Guam	H	5.61 FQ	7.29 AW	8.89 TQ	GUBLS	10/01-12/01
Basketball Player							
Women's National Basketball Association	United States	Y		40000 MW		WATIMES	7/15/02
Bicycle Repairer	Alabama	H	7.43 FQ	9.14 AW	11.37 TQ	ALBLS	10/01-12/01
	California	H	6.93 FQ	10.01 AW	13.47 TQ	CABLS	10/01-12/01
	Los Angeles-Long Beach PMSA, CA	H	7.00 FQ	10.67 AW	13.56 TQ	CABLS	10/01-12/01
	Oakland PMSA, CA	H	7.54 FQ	9.38 AW	12.12 TQ	CABLS	10/01-12/01

AAW	Average annual wage	**AOH**	Average offered, high	**ASH**	Average starting, high	**H**	Hourly	**M**	Monthly	**S**	Special: hourly and annual
AE	Average entry wage	**AOL**	Average offered, low	**ASL**	Average starting, low	**HI**	Highest wage paid	**MTC**	Median total compensation	**TQ**	Third quartile wage
AEX	Average experienced wage	**APH**	Average pay, high range	**AW**	Average wage paid	**HR**	High end range	**MW**	Median wage paid	**W**	Weekly
AO	Average offered	**APL**	Average pay, low range	**FQ**	First quartile wage	**LR**	Low end range	**SQ**	Second quartile wage	**Y**	Yearly

Occupation/Type/Industry	Location	Per	Low	Mid	High	Source	Date
Bicycle Repairer	Salinas MSA, CA	H	6.48 FQ	7.67 AW	8.99 TQ	CABLS	10/01-12/01
	San Diego MSA, CA	H	6.81 FQ	9.58 AW	13.22 TQ	CABLS	10/01-12/01
	San Francisco PMSA, CA	H	8.01 FQ	10.86 AW	14.76 TQ	CABLS	10/01-12/01
	Santa Cruz-Watsonville PMSA, CA	H	6.69 FQ	11.17 AW	15.46 TQ	CABLS	10/01-12/01
	Santa Rosa PMSA, CA	H	6.63 FQ	10.74 AW	15.42 TQ	CABLS	10/01-12/01
	Ventura PMSA, CA	H	6.88 FQ	9.41 AW	13.54 TQ	CABLS	10/01-12/01
	Colorado	H	7.49 FQ	10.57 AW	14.45 TQ	COBLS	10/01-12/01
	Boulder-Longmont PMSA, CO	H	8.93 FQ	13.53 AW	18.52 TQ	COBLS	10/01-12/01
	Colorado Springs MSA, CO	H	7.71 FQ	10.26 AW	13.65 TQ	COBLS	10/01-12/01
	Denver PMSA, CO	H	7.38 FQ	9.39 AW	13.19 TQ	COBLS	10/01-12/01
	Connecticut	H	9.13 FQ	12.75 AW	13.91 TQ	CTBLS	10/01-12/01
	Hartford MSA, CT	H	9.26 FQ	12.72 AW	13.86 TQ	CTBLS	10/01-12/01
	Washington PMSA, DC-MD-VA-WV	H	6.67 FQ	10.13 AW	14.05 TQ	DCBLS	10/01-12/01
	Florida	H	6.01 FQ	8.22 AW	10.92 TQ	FLBLS	10/01-12/01
	Sarasota-Bradenton MSA, FL	H	7.51 FQ	8.78 AW	12.15 TQ	FLBLS	10/01-12/01
	Georgia	H	5.67 FQ	6.82 AW	8.46 TQ	GABLS	10/01-12/01
	Hawaii	H	5.79 FQ	8.01 AW	12.50 TQ	HIBLS	10/01-12/01
	Idaho	H	6.47 FQ	7.82 AW	8.95 TQ	IDBLS	10/01-12/01
	Illinois	H	6.77 FQ	8.99 AW	12.32 TQ	ILBLS	10/01-12/01
	Indiana	H	6.30 FQ	8.44 AW	11.00 TQ	INBLS	10/01-12/01
	Iowa	H	6.12 FQ	7.74 AW	9.82 TQ	IABLS	10/01-12/01
	Kansas	H	6.91 FQ	8.15 AW	9.88 TQ	KSBLS	10/01-12/01
	Maine	H	8.56 FQ	10.25 AW	13.23 TQ	MEBLS	10/01-12/01
	Maryland	H	5.88 FQ	8.68 AW	13.03 TQ	MDBLS	10/01-12/01
	Massachusetts	H	7.75 FQ	9.70 AW	11.40 TQ	MABLS	10/01-12/01
	Boston PMSA, MA-NH	H	7.79 FQ	9.67 AW	11.39 TQ	MABLS	10/01-12/01
	Michigan	H	6.09 FQ	8.74 AW	11.34 TQ	MIBLS	10/01-12/01
	Kalamazoo-Battle Creek MSA, MI	H	5.92 FQ	7.99 AW	10.66 TQ	MIBLS	10/01-12/01
	Minnesota	H	6.51 FQ	9.72 AW	13.90 TQ	MNBLS	10/01-12/01
	Minneapolis-St. Paul MSA, MN-WI	H	7.08 FQ	9.85 AW	14.79 TQ	MNBLS	10/01-12/01
	Missouri	H	9.36 FQ	10.64 AW	12.91 TQ	MOBLS	10/01-12/01
	Nebraska	H	5.81 FQ	8.88 AW	13.79 TQ	NEBLS	10/01-12/01
	Nevada	H	7.98 FQ	10.28 AW	13.35 TQ	NVBLS	10/01-12/01
	New Hampshire	H	7.18 FQ	9.94 AW	13.47 TQ	NHBLS	10/01-12/01
	Portsmouth-Rochester PMSA, NH-ME	H	7.68 FQ	9.53 AW	11.34 TQ	NHBLS	10/01-12/01
	New Jersey	H	5.69 FQ	7.71 AW	10.66 TQ	NJBLS	10/01-12/01
	New Mexico	H	7.07 FQ	8.25 AW	10.77 TQ	NMBLS	10/01-12/01
	Albuquerque MSA, NM	H	7.11 FQ	8.39 AW	11.50 TQ	NMBLS	10/01-12/01
	New York	H	5.61 FQ	7.25 AW	10.14 TQ	NYBLS	10/01-12/01
	Buffalo-Niagara Falls MSA, NY	H	7.15 FQ	7.88 AW	8.70 TQ	NYBLS	10/01-12/01
	Nassau-Suffolk PMSA, NY	H	5.54 FQ	6.84 AW	9.76 TQ	NYBLS	10/01-12/01
	North Carolina	H	6.20 FQ	9.16 AW	13.35 TQ	NCBLS	10/01-12/01
	Raleigh-Durham-Chapel Hill MSA, NC	H	6.04 FQ	9.80 AW	13.94 TQ	NCBLS	10/01-12/01
	Ohio	H	6.05 FQ	8.22 AW	11.59 TQ	OHBLS	10/01-12/01
	Columbus MSA, OH	H	5.91 FQ	7.64 AW	10.80 TQ	OHBLS	10/01-12/01
	Dayton-Springfield MSA, OH	H	5.85 FQ	7.46 AW	10.52 TQ	OHBLS	10/01-12/01
	Oregon	H	7.61 FQ	9.96 AW	13.27 TQ	ORBLS	10/01-12/01
	Eugene-Springfield MSA, OR	H	7.76 FQ	9.74 AW	12.26 TQ	ORBLS	10/01-12/01
	Portland-Vancouver PMSA, OR-WA	H	7.82 FQ	10.40 AW	13.35 TQ	ORBLS	10/01-12/01
	Pennsylvania	H	6.43 FQ	9.17 AW	13.24 TQ	PABLS	10/01-12/01
	Philadelphia PMSA, PA-NJ	H	5.57 FQ	6.84 AW	9.78 TQ	PABLS	10/01-12/01
	Rhode Island	H	6.59 FQ	8.49 AW	10.94 TQ	RIBLS	10/01-12/01
	Texas	H	7.42 FQ	9.34 AW	11.09 TQ	TXBLS	10/01-12/01
	Austin-San Marcos MSA, TX	H	9.03 FQ	9.91 AW	10.98 TQ	TXBLS	10/01-12/01
	Houston PMSA, TX	H	7.29 FQ	8.85 AW	10.85 TQ	TXBLS	10/01-12/01
	Utah	H	7.37 FQ	9.43 AW	12.81 TQ	UTBLS	10/01-12/01
	Virginia	H	7.39 FQ	9.92 AW	13.37 TQ	VABLS	10/01-12/01
	Washington	H	7.32 FQ	12.91 AW	20.65 TQ	WABLS	10/01-12/01
	Bremerton PMSA, WA	H	8.56 FQ	17.33 AW	21.72 TQ	WABLS	10/01-12/01
	Seattle-Bellevue-Everett PMSA, WA	H	7.91 FQ	11.42 AW	15.79 TQ	WABLS	10/01-12/01
	West Virginia	H	7.11 FQ	9.60 AW	12.76 TQ	WVBLS	10/01-12/01
	Wisconsin	H	6.29 FQ	8.66 AW	11.20 TQ	WIBLS	10/01-12/01

AAW Average annual wage **AOH** Average offered, high **ASH** Average starting, high **H** Hourly **M** Monthly **S** Special: hourly and annual
AE Average entry wage **AOL** Average offered, low **ASL** Average starting, low **HI** Highest wage paid **MTC** Median total compensation **TQ** Third quartile wage
AEX Average experienced wage **APH** Average pay, high range **AW** Average wage paid **HR** High end range **MW** Median wage paid **W** Weekly
AO Average offered **APL** Average pay, low range **FQ** First quartile wage **LR** Low end range **SQ** Second quartile wage **Y** Yearly

Occupation/Type/Industry	Location	Per	Low	Mid	High	Source	Date
Bicycle Repairer	Milwaukee-Waukesha PMSA, WI	H	5.99 FQ	8.45 AW	11.23 TQ	WIBLS	10/01-12/01
	Wyoming	H	5.88 FQ	8.49 AW	12.56 TQ	WYBLS	10/01-12/01
Bill and Account Collector	Alabama	H	7.49 FQ	11.78 AW	18.39 TQ	ALBLS	10/01-12/01
	Birmingham MSA, AL	H	7.87 FQ	12.80 AW	19.55 TQ	ALBLS	10/01-12/01
	Huntsville MSA, AL	H	8.98 FQ	13.81 AW	20.86 TQ	ALBLS	10/01-12/01
	Montgomery MSA, AL	H	7.72 FQ	12.34 AW	19.22 TQ	ALBLS	10/01-12/01
	Alaska	H	10.76 FQ	15.17 AW	19.97 TQ	AKBLS	10/01-12/01
	Anchorage MSA, AK	H	11.78 FQ	15.17 AW	19.15 TQ	AKBLS	10/01-12/01
	Arizona	H	7.85 FQ	12.29 AW	17.40 TQ	AZBLS	10/01-12/01
	Phoenix-Mesa MSA, AZ	H	7.78 FQ	12.23 AW	17.46 TQ	AZBLS	10/01-12/01
	Tucson MSA, AZ	H	9.09 FQ	13.03 AW	17.36 TQ	AZBLS	10/01-12/01
	Arkansas	H	7.26 FQ	10.18 AW	13.57 TQ	ARBLS	10/01-12/01
	Fayetteville-Springdale-Rogers MSA, AR	H	8.24 FQ	10.49 AW	13.58 TQ	ARBLS	10/01-12/01
	Fort Smith MSA, AR-OK	H	7.04 FQ	11.04 AW	16.16 TQ	ARBLS	10/01-12/01
	Little Rock-North Little Rock MSA, AR	H	8.29 FQ	10.66 AW	13.83 TQ	ARBLS	10/01-12/01
	California	H	9.27 FQ	14.63 AW	21.22 TQ	CABLS	10/01-12/01
	Bakersfield MSA, CA	H	7.45 FQ	10.61 AW	15.12 TQ	CABLS	10/01-12/01
	Chico-Paradise MSA, CA	H	7.74 FQ	12.34 AW	18.10 TQ	CABLS	10/01-12/01
	Fresno MSA, CA	H	7.80 FQ	12.50 AW	19.37 TQ	CABLS	10/01-12/01
	Los Angeles-Long Beach PMSA, CA	H	8.99 FQ	14.44 AW	20.99 TQ	CABLS	10/01-12/01
	Merced MSA, CA	H	7.76 FQ	12.17 AW	18.19 TQ	CABLS	10/01-12/01
	Modesto MSA, CA	H	8.73 FQ	12.77 AW	16.98 TQ	CABLS	10/01-12/01
	Oakland PMSA, CA	H	10.03 FQ	15.65 AW	21.44 TQ	CABLS	10/01-12/01
	Orange County PMSA, CA	H	9.81 FQ	14.78 AW	20.69 TQ	CABLS	10/01-12/01
	Redding MSA, CA	H	7.35 FQ	11.22 AW	16.54 TQ	CABLS	10/01-12/01
	Riverside-San Bernardino PMSA, CA	H	9.11 FQ	12.93 AW	17.47 TQ	CABLS	10/01-12/01
	Sacramento PMSA, CA	H	8.78 FQ	13.50 AW	19.40 TQ	CABLS	10/01-12/01
	Salinas MSA, CA	H	9.26 FQ	14.23 AW	20.14 TQ	CABLS	10/01-12/01
	San Diego MSA, CA	H	10.02 FQ	14.42 AW	19.81 TQ	CABLS	10/01-12/01
	San Francisco PMSA, CA	H	12.61 FQ	18.56 AW	25.55 TQ	CABLS	10/01-12/01
	San Jose PMSA, CA	H	10.49 FQ	17.03 AW	24.20 TQ	CABLS	10/01-12/01
	San Luis Obispo-Atascadero-Paso Robles MSA, CA	H	8.81 FQ	11.93 AW	15.96 TQ	CABLS	10/01-12/01
	Santa Barbara-Santa Maria-Lompoc MSA, CA	H	9.35 FQ	13.54 AW	19.68 TQ	CABLS	10/01-12/01
	Santa Cruz-Watsonville PMSA, CA	H	9.86 FQ	13.99 AW	19.31 TQ	CABLS	10/01-12/01
	Santa Rosa PMSA, CA	H	8.89 FQ	15.59 AW	24.57 TQ	CABLS	10/01-12/01
	Stockton-Lodi MSA, CA	H	9.19 FQ	12.79 AW	17.25 TQ	CABLS	10/01-12/01
	Vallejo-Fairfield-Napa PMSA, CA	H	7.12 FQ	12.60 AW	19.33 TQ	CABLS	10/01-12/01
	Ventura PMSA, CA	H	10.08 FQ	14.51 AW	19.83 TQ	CABLS	10/01-12/01
	Visalia-Tulare-Porterville MSA, CA	H	8.07 FQ	12.49 AW	18.70 TQ	CABLS	10/01-12/01
	Colorado	H	8.96 FQ	13.75 AW	20.28 TQ	COBLS	10/01-12/01
	Boulder-Longmont PMSA, CO	H	8.33 FQ	13.42 AW	18.94 TQ	COBLS	10/01-12/01
	Colorado Springs MSA, CO	H	7.08 FQ	12.66 AW	20.24 TQ	COBLS	10/01-12/01
	Denver PMSA, CO	H	9.52 FQ	14.13 AW	20.69 TQ	COBLS	10/01-12/01
	Fort Collins-Loveland MSA, CO	H	8.34 FQ	11.96 AW	16.53 TQ	COBLS	10/01-12/01
	Greeley PMSA, CO	H	9.04 FQ	13.47 AW	20.27 TQ	COBLS	10/01-12/01
	Connecticut	H	10.64 FQ	15.50 AW	21.33 TQ	CTBLS	10/01-12/01
	Bridgeport PMSA, CT	H	11.39 FQ	15.81 AW	21.43 TQ	CTBLS	10/01-12/01
	Danbury PMSA, CT	H	11.55 FQ	17.03 AW	24.63 TQ	CTBLS	10/01-12/01
	Hartford MSA, CT	H	10.88 FQ	15.10 AW	20.13 TQ	CTBLS	10/01-12/01
	New Haven-Meriden PMSA, CT	H	9.99 FQ	14.70 AW	20.79 TQ	CTBLS	10/01-12/01
	New London-Norwich MSA, CT-RI	H	10.72 FQ	15.37 AW	20.72 TQ	CTBLS	10/01-12/01
	Stamford-Norwalk PMSA, CT	H	11.15 FQ	16.85 AW	22.72 TQ	CTBLS	10/01-12/01
	Waterbury PMSA, CT	H	9.90 FQ	14.27 AW	18.25 TQ	CTBLS	10/01-12/01
	Delaware	H	9.03 FQ	12.35 AW	16.92 TQ	DEBLS	10/01-12/01
	Wilmington-Newark PMSA, DE-MD	H	9.06 FQ	12.26 AW	16.79 TQ	DEBLS	10/01-12/01
	District of Columbia	H	10.03 FQ	13.99 AW	18.97 TQ	DCBLS	10/01-12/01
	Washington PMSA, DC-MD-VA-WV	H	9.92 FQ	14.15 AW	19.79 TQ	DCBLS	10/01-12/01

AAW	Average annual wage	**AOH**	Average offered, high	**ASH**	Average starting, high	**H**	Hourly	**M**	Monthly	**S**	Special: hourly and annual
AE	Average entry wage	**AOL**	Average offered, low	**ASL**	Average starting, low	**HI**	Highest wage paid	**MTC**	Median total compensation	**TQ**	Third quartile wage
AEX	Average experienced wage	**APH**	Average pay, high range	**AW**	Average wage paid	**HR**	High end range	**MW**	Median wage paid	**W**	Weekly
AO	Average offered	**APL**	Average pay, low range	**FQ**	First quartile wage	**LR**	Low end range	**SQ**	Second quartile wage	**Y**	Yearly

Occupation/Type/Industry	Location	Per	Low	Mid	High	Source	Date
Bill and Account Collector	Florida	H	8.89 FQ	12.75 AW	17.91 TQ	FLBLS	10/01-12/01
	Daytona Beach MSA, FL	H	7.53 FQ	12.07 AW	17.94 TQ	FLBLS	10/01-12/01
	Fort Lauderdale PMSA, FL	H	9.62 FQ	13.56 AW	18.16 TQ	FLBLS	10/01-12/01
	Fort Myers-Cape Coral MSA, FL	H	8.26 FQ	11.96 AW	17.24 TQ	FLBLS	10/01-12/01
	Fort Pierce-Port St. Lucie MSA, FL	H	8.58 FQ	12.15 AW	16.51 TQ	FLBLS	10/01-12/01
	Fort Walton Beach MSA, FL	H	7.40 FQ	10.43 AW	15.92 TQ	FLBLS	10/01-12/01
	Gainesville MSA, FL	H	8.11 FQ	11.78 AW	16.17 TQ	FLBLS	10/01-12/01
	Jacksonville MSA, FL	H	9.44 FQ	13.22 AW	18.52 TQ	FLBLS	10/01-12/01
	Lakeland-Winter Haven MSA, FL	H	8.68 FQ	11.52 AW	14.52 TQ	FLBLS	10/01-12/01
	Melbourne-Titusville-Palm Bay MSA, FL	H	8.68 FQ	11.35 AW	15.53 TQ	FLBLS	10/01-12/01
	Miami PMSA, FL	H	7.85 FQ	13.64 AW	19.86 TQ	FLBLS	10/01-12/01
	Naples MSA, FL	H	9.70 FQ	13.31 AW	17.27 TQ	FLBLS	10/01-12/01
	Ocala MSA, FL	H	8.66 FQ	11.99 AW	16.60 TQ	FLBLS	10/01-12/01
	Orlando MSA, FL	H	8.34 FQ	11.94 AW	17.19 TQ	FLBLS	10/01-12/01
	Pensacola MSA, FL	H	8.01 FQ	11.54 AW	16.45 TQ	FLBLS	10/01-12/01
	Sarasota-Bradenton MSA, FL	H	8.03 FQ	11.10 AW	14.90 TQ	FLBLS	10/01-12/01
	Tallahassee MSA, FL	H	8.80 FQ	13.16 AW	19.08 TQ	FLBLS	10/01-12/01
	Tampa-St. Petersburg-Clearwater MSA, FL	H	9.12 FQ	12.79 AW	18.09 TQ	FLBLS	10/01-12/01
	West Palm Beach-Boca Raton MSA, FL	H	9.54 FQ	12.55 AW	16.86 TQ	FLBLS	10/01-12/01
	Georgia	H	8.83 FQ	12.78 AW	17.97 TQ	GABLS	10/01-12/01
	Atlanta MSA, GA	H	9.52 FQ	13.45 AW	18.77 TQ	GABLS	10/01-12/01
	Augusta-Aiken MSA, GA-SC	H	7.66 FQ	10.24 AW	13.34 TQ	GABLS	10/01-12/01
	Columbus MSA, GA-AL	H	8.01 FQ	10.99 AW	14.79 TQ	GABLS	10/01-12/01
	Macon MSA, GA	H	8.06 FQ	11.46 AW	15.76 TQ	GABLS	10/01-12/01
	Savannah MSA, GA	H	7.90 FQ	11.91 AW	16.77 TQ	GABLS	10/01-12/01
	Hawaii	H	7.08 FQ	11.67 AW	17.42 TQ	HIBLS	10/01-12/01
	Honolulu MSA, HI	H	9.19 FQ	13.12 AW	19.22 TQ	HIBLS	10/01-12/01
	Idaho	H	7.96 FQ	11.17 AW	14.68 TQ	IDBLS	10/01-12/01
	Boise City MSA, ID	H	8.04 FQ	10.87 AW	14.07 TQ	IDBLS	10/01-12/01
	Illinois	H	8.67 FQ	13.89 AW	19.99 TQ	ILBLS	10/01-12/01
	Champaign-Urbana MSA, IL	H	9.11 FQ	12.66 AW	18.29 TQ	ILBLS	10/01-12/01
	Chicago PMSA, IL	H	9.43 FQ	14.69 AW	20.70 TQ	ILBLS	10/01-12/01
	Peoria-Pekin MSA, IL	H	7.87 FQ	11.28 AW	15.98 TQ	ILBLS	10/01-12/01
	Rockford MSA, IL	H	8.85 FQ	12.40 AW	16.61 TQ	ILBLS	10/01-12/01
	Springfield MSA, IL	H	7.81 FQ	11.02 AW	16.09 TQ	ILBLS	10/01-12/01
	Indiana	H	8.80 FQ	12.74 AW	16.97 TQ	INBLS	10/01-12/01
	Elkhart-Goshen MSA, IN	H	9.42 FQ	14.34 AW	21.11 TQ	INBLS	10/01-12/01
	Evansville-Henderson MSA, IN-KY	H	8.02 FQ	10.91 AW	14.22 TQ	INBLS	10/01-12/01
	Fort Wayne MSA, IN	H	8.74 FQ	11.73 AW	16.03 TQ	INBLS	10/01-12/01
	Gary PMSA, IN	H	7.56 FQ	10.51 AW	14.29 TQ	INBLS	10/01-12/01
	Indianapolis MSA, IN	H	9.44 FQ	14.03 AW	18.18 TQ	INBLS	10/01-12/01
	Lafayette MSA, IN	H	8.94 FQ	12.93 AW	17.83 TQ	INBLS	10/01-12/01
	South Bend MSA, IN	H	9.20 FQ	12.41 AW	16.78 TQ	INBLS	10/01-12/01
	Iowa	H	8.82 FQ	12.43 AW	17.67 TQ	IABLS	10/01-12/01
	Cedar Rapids MSA, IA	H	8.69 FQ	12.44 AW	19.47 TQ	IABLS	10/01-12/01
	Davenport-Moline-Rock Island MSA, IA-IL	H	8.19 FQ	11.86 AW	16.52 TQ	IABLS	10/01-12/01
	Des Moines MSA, IA	H	9.54 FQ	13.07 AW	18.51 TQ	IABLS	10/01-12/01
	Kansas	H	7.59 FQ	10.85 AW	15.27 TQ	KSBLS	10/01-12/01
	Topeka MSA, KS	H	8.43 FQ	10.69 AW	14.44 TQ	KSBLS	10/01-12/01
	Wichita MSA, KS	H	8.61 FQ	11.40 AW	15.99 TQ	KSBLS	10/01-12/01
	Kentucky	H	7.70 FQ	11.29 AW	15.12 TQ	KYBLS	10/01-12/01
	Lexington MSA, KY	H	9.10 FQ	12.78 AW	17.28 TQ	KYBLS	10/01-12/01
	Louisville MSA, KY-IN	H	8.25 FQ	11.41 AW	14.07 TQ	KYBLS	10/01-12/01
	Louisiana	H	7.27 FQ	11.16 AW	16.22 TQ	LABLS	10/01-12/01
	Baton Rouge MSA, LA	H	6.96 FQ	11.18 AW	16.49 TQ	LABLS	10/01-12/01
	Houma MSA, LA	H	7.33 FQ	10.05 AW	13.40 TQ	LABLS	10/01-12/01
	Lafayette MSA, LA	H	7.37 FQ	10.52 AW	14.06 TQ	LABLS	10/01-12/01
	Lake Charles MSA, LA	H	6.73 FQ	10.49 AW	16.00 TQ	LABLS	10/01-12/01
	New Orleans MSA, LA	H	8.69 FQ	12.05 AW	17.74 TQ	LABLS	10/01-12/01
	Shreveport-Bossier City MSA, LA	H	6.69 FQ	11.20 AW	15.75 TQ	LABLS	10/01-12/01
	Maine	H	8.70 FQ	12.71 AW	17.46 TQ	MEBLS	10/01-12/01
	Portland MSA, ME	H	9.16 FQ	12.43 AW	17.73 TQ	MEBLS	10/01-12/01
	Maryland	H	9.07 FQ	12.90 AW	17.60 TQ	MDBLS	10/01-12/01

AAW Average annual wage; **AE** Average entry wage; **AEX** Average experienced wage; **AO** Average offered; **AOH** Average offered, high; **AOL** Average offered, low; **APH** Average pay, high range; **APL** Average pay, low range; **ASH** Average starting, high; **ASL** Average starting, low; **AW** Average wage paid; **FQ** First quartile wage; **H** Hourly; **HI** Highest wage paid; **HR** High end range; **LR** Low end range; **M** Monthly; **MTC** Median total compensation; **MW** Median wage paid; **SQ** Second quartile wage; **S** Special: hourly and annual; **TQ** Third quartile wage; **W** Weekly; **Y** Yearly

Occupation/Type/Industry	Location	Per	Low	Mid	High	Source	Date
Bill and Account Collector	Baltimore PMSA, MD	H	8.95 FQ	12.37 AW	16.72 TQ	MDBLS	10/01-12/01
	Massachusetts	H	9.70 FQ	14.40 AW	20.21 TQ	MABLS	10/01-12/01
	Boston PMSA, MA-NH	H	9.77 FQ	14.46 AW	20.22 TQ	MABLS	10/01-12/01
	Brockton PMSA, MA	H	9.96 FQ	14.06 AW	18.55 TQ	MABLS	10/01-12/01
	Lawrence PMSA, MA-NH	H	10.41 FQ	14.03 AW	18.04 TQ	MABLS	10/01-12/01
	Lowell PMSA, MA-NH	H	9.80 FQ	15.19 AW	20.99 TQ	MABLS	10/01-12/01
	New Bedford PMSA, MA	H	9.47 FQ	14.13 AW	20.52 TQ	MABLS	10/01-12/01
	Springfield MSA, MA	H	9.59 FQ	14.06 AW	20.06 TQ	MABLS	10/01-12/01
	Worcester PMSA, MA-CT	H	10.18 FQ	14.88 AW	20.88 TQ	MABLS	10/01-12/01
	Michigan	H	8.91 FQ	13.58 AW	19.48 TQ	MIBLS	10/01-12/01
	Ann Arbor PMSA, MI	H	9.92 FQ	15.59 AW	20.93 TQ	MIBLS	10/01-12/01
	Detroit PMSA, MI	H	9.63 FQ	14.41 AW	20.34 TQ	MIBLS	10/01-12/01
	Flint PMSA, MI	H	9.46 FQ	13.61 AW	17.01 TQ	MIBLS	10/01-12/01
	Grand Rapids-Muskegon-Holland MSA, MI	H	8.58 FQ	13.02 AW	17.92 TQ	MIBLS	10/01-12/01
	Kalamazoo-Battle Creek MSA, MI	H	9.17 FQ	12.10 AW	16.15 TQ	MIBLS	10/01-12/01
	Lansing-East Lansing MSA, MI	H	7.38 FQ	11.93 AW	18.56 TQ	MIBLS	10/01-12/01
	Saginaw-Bay City-Midland MSA, MI	H	8.88 FQ	12.50 AW	17.07 TQ	MIBLS	10/01-12/01
	Minnesota	H	9.22 FQ	14.72 AW	21.35 TQ	MNBLS	10/01-12/01
	Duluth-Superior MSA, MN-WI	H	9.07 FQ	12.37 AW	16.74 TQ	MNBLS	10/01-12/01
	Minneapolis-St. Paul MSA, MN-WI	H	9.95 FQ	15.58 AW	22.16 TQ	MNBLS	10/01-12/01
	Mississippi	H	7.67 FQ	11.14 AW	15.85 TQ	MSBLS	10/01-12/01
	Biloxi-Gulfport-Pascagoula MSA, MS	H	7.32 FQ	9.95 AW	13.46 TQ	MSBLS	10/01-12/01
	Jackson MSA, MS	H	8.70 FQ	12.71 AW	20.39 TQ	MSBLS	10/01-12/01
	Missouri	H	7.29 FQ	12.06 AW	17.22 TQ	MOBLS	10/01-12/01
	Kansas City MSA, MO-KS	H	8.34 FQ	12.03 AW	16.29 TQ	MOBLS	10/01-12/01
	St. Louis MSA, MO-IL	H	9.32 FQ	13.35 AW	19.01 TQ	MOBLS	10/01-12/01
	Springfield MSA, MO	H	5.44 FQ	8.04 AW	11.68 TQ	MOBLS	10/01-12/01
	Montana	H	7.58 FQ	10.78 AW	14.77 TQ	MTBLS	10/01-12/01
	Billings MSA, MT	H	7.89 FQ	11.38 AW	16.20 TQ	MTBLS	10/01-12/01
	Nebraska	H	8.89 FQ	12.98 AW	19.99 TQ	NEBLS	10/01-12/01
	Lincoln MSA, NE	H	9.17 FQ	12.01 AW	15.32 TQ	NEBLS	10/01-12/01
	Omaha MSA, NE-IA	H	9.30 FQ	13.87 AW	21.55 TQ	NEBLS	10/01-12/01
	Nevada	H	9.30 FQ	12.01 AW	16.20 TQ	NVBLS	10/01-12/01
	Las Vegas MSA, NV-AZ	H	9.27 FQ	11.72 AW	15.72 TQ	NVBLS	10/01-12/01
	Reno MSA, NV	H	9.59 FQ	14.69 AW	21.43 TQ	NVBLS	10/01-12/01
	New Hampshire	H	9.60 FQ	13.09 AW	17.35 TQ	NHBLS	10/01-12/01
	Manchester PMSA, NH	H	10.22 FQ	13.44 AW	17.53 TQ	NHBLS	10/01-12/01
	Nashua PMSA, NH	H	10.17 FQ	13.32 AW	17.12 TQ	NHBLS	10/01-12/01
	Portsmouth-Rochester PMSA, NH-ME	H	9.42 FQ	12.65 AW	17.10 TQ	NHBLS	10/01-12/01
	New Jersey	H	9.75 FQ	14.84 AW	20.69 TQ	NJBLS	10/01-12/01
	Atlantic-Cape May PMSA, NJ	H	11.46 FQ	15.44 AW	21.47 TQ	NJBLS	10/01-12/01
	Bergen-Passaic PMSA, NJ	H	10.06 FQ	14.69 AW	19.86 TQ	NJBLS	10/01-12/01
	Jersey City PMSA, NJ	H	9.93 FQ	15.95 AW	23.06 TQ	NJBLS	10/01-12/01
	Middlesex-Somerset-Hunterdon PMSA, NJ	H	10.66 FQ	15.53 AW	20.69 TQ	NJBLS	10/01-12/01
	Monmouth-Ocean PMSA, NJ	H	9.12 FQ	13.25 AW	18.19 TQ	NJBLS	10/01-12/01
	Newark PMSA, NJ	H	10.44 FQ	16.08 AW	22.90 TQ	NJBLS	10/01-12/01
	Trenton PMSA, NJ	H	9.02 FQ	13.46 AW	19.22 TQ	NJBLS	10/01-12/01
	New Mexico	H	7.98 FQ	11.38 AW	15.07 TQ	NMBLS	10/01-12/01
	Albuquerque MSA, NM	H	8.70 FQ	11.82 AW	15.01 TQ	NMBLS	10/01-12/01
	Las Cruces MSA, NM	H	7.47 FQ	9.94 AW	13.08 TQ	NMBLS	10/01-12/01
	New York	H	9.15 FQ	14.77 AW	20.92 TQ	NYBLS	10/01-12/01
	Albany-Schenectady-Troy MSA, NY	H	9.61 FQ	13.77 AW	19.37 TQ	NYBLS	10/01-12/01
	Binghamton MSA, NY	H	8.90 FQ	11.63 AW	16.66 TQ	NYBLS	10/01-12/01
	Buffalo-Niagara Falls MSA, NY	H	9.27 FQ	13.16 AW	19.84 TQ	NYBLS	10/01-12/01
	Dutchess County PMSA, NY	H	6.75 FQ	12.57 AW	17.41 TQ	NYBLS	10/01-12/01
	Nassau-Suffolk PMSA, NY	H	9.51 FQ	13.56 AW	17.76 TQ	NYBLS	10/01-12/01
	New York PMSA, NY	H	11.80 FQ	17.60 AW	23.59 TQ	NYBLS	10/01-12/01
	Newburgh PMSA, NY-PA	H	9.09 FQ	13.37 AW	17.97 TQ	NYBLS	10/01-12/01
	Rochester MSA, NY	H	8.74 FQ	13.21 AW	19.03 TQ	NYBLS	10/01-12/01
	Syracuse MSA, NY	H	8.68 FQ	12.85 AW	18.15 TQ	NYBLS	10/01-12/01
	Utica-Rome MSA, NY	H	7.80 FQ	11.42 AW	16.84 TQ	NYBLS	10/01-12/01
	North Carolina	H	9.00 FQ	12.67 AW	17.09 TQ	NCBLS	10/01-12/01
	Asheville MSA, NC	H	9.36 FQ	12.92 AW	17.71 TQ	NCBLS	10/01-12/01

AAV	Average annual wage	**AOH**	Average offered, high	**ASH**	Average starting, high	**H**	Hourly	**M**	Monthly	**S**	Special: hourly and annual
AE	Average entry wage	**AOL**	Average offered, low	**ASL**	Average starting, low	**HI**	Highest wage paid	**MTC**	Median total compensation	**TQ**	Third quartile wage
AEX	Average experienced wage	**APH**	Average pay, high range	**AW**	Average wage paid	**HR**	High end range	**MW**	Median wage paid	**W**	Weekly
AO	Average offered	**APL**	Average pay, low range	**FQ**	First quartile wage	**LR**	Low end range	**SQ**	Second quartile wage	**Y**	Yearly

Occupation/Type/Industry	Location	Per	Low	Mid	High	Source	Date
Bill and Account Collector	Charlotte-Gastonia-Rock Hill MSA, NC-SC	H	9.36 FQ	13.44 AW	18.12 TQ	NCBLS	10/01-12/01
	Fayetteville MSA, NC	H	7.13 FQ	10.37 AW	14.37 TQ	NCBLS	10/01-12/01
	Greensboro-Winston-Salem-High Point MSA, NC	H	9.46 FQ	12.62 AW	16.82 TQ	NCBLS	10/01-12/01
	Hickory-Morganton-Lenoir MSA, NC	H	8.11 FQ	12.44 AW	18.64 TQ	NCBLS	10/01-12/01
	Raleigh-Durham-Chapel Hill MSA, NC	H	10.47 FQ	14.30 AW	20.63 TQ	NCBLS	10/01-12/01
	Wilmington MSA, NC	H	8.54 FQ	12.05 AW	16.11 TQ	NCBLS	10/01-12/01
	North Dakota	H	8.01 FQ	12.62 AW	17.92 TQ	NDBLS	10/01-12/01
	Fargo-Moorhead MSA, ND-MN	H	8.24 FQ	13.32 AW	18.59 TQ	NDBLS	10/01-12/01
	Ohio	H	8.97 FQ	12.92 AW	17.92 TQ	OHBLS	10/01-12/01
	Akron PMSA, OH	H	8.27 FQ	11.71 AW	15.79 TQ	OHBLS	10/01-12/01
	Canton-Massillon MSA, OH	H	8.40 FQ	11.82 AW	16.63 TQ	OHBLS	10/01-12/01
	Cincinnati PMSA, OH-KY-IN	H	8.94 FQ	12.89 AW	18.21 TQ	OHBLS	10/01-12/01
	Cleveland-Lorain-Elyria PMSA, OH	H	8.88 FQ	13.16 AW	19.31 TQ	OHBLS	10/01-12/01
	Columbus MSA, OH	H	9.47 FQ	13.53 AW	18.23 TQ	OHBLS	10/01-12/01
	Dayton-Springfield MSA, OH	H	9.07 FQ	12.29 AW	16.56 TQ	OHBLS	10/01-12/01
	Hamilton-Middletown PMSA, OH	H	9.34 FQ	12.96 AW	17.63 TQ	OHBLS	10/01-12/01
	Mansfield MSA, OH	H	8.09 FQ	11.12 AW	14.01 TQ	OHBLS	10/01-12/01
	Toledo MSA, OH	H	9.10 FQ	12.37 AW	16.79 TQ	OHBLS	10/01-12/01
	Youngstown-Warren MSA, OH	H	8.19 FQ	12.10 AW	16.71 TQ	OHBLS	10/01-12/01
	Oklahoma	H	7.00 FQ	11.21 AW	16.95 TQ	OKBLS	10/01-12/01
	Oklahoma City MSA, OK	H	8.12 FQ	12.43 AW	19.79 TQ	OKBLS	10/01-12/01
	Tulsa MSA, OK	H	6.18 FQ	10.45 AW	14.23 TQ	OKBLS	10/01-12/01
	Oregon	H	9.40 FQ	13.35 AW	17.90 TQ	ORBLS	10/01-12/01
	Eugene-Springfield MSA, OR	H	8.26 FQ	12.69 AW	16.82 TQ	ORBLS	10/01-12/01
	Medford-Ashland MSA, OR	H	8.53 FQ	12.24 AW	18.05 TQ	ORBLS	10/01-12/01
	Portland-Vancouver PMSA, OR-WA	H	9.95 FQ	13.76 AW	18.25 TQ	ORBLS	10/01-12/01
	Salem PMSA, OR	H	8.44 FQ	13.83 AW	20.51 TQ	ORBLS	10/01-12/01
	Pennsylvania	H	8.01 FQ	12.19 AW	17.00 TQ	PABLS	10/01-12/01
	Allentown-Bethlehem-Easton MSA, PA	H	8.77 FQ	11.89 AW	14.59 TQ	PABLS	10/01-12/01
	Erie MSA, PA	H	6.94 FQ	10.20 AW	13.44 TQ	PABLS	10/01-12/01
	Harrisburg-Lebanon-Carlisle MSA, PA	H	8.79 FQ	12.33 AW	17.26 TQ	PABLS	10/01-12/01
	Johnstown MSA, PA	H	7.66 FQ	11.09 AW	15.20 TQ	PABLS	10/01-12/01
	Lancaster MSA, PA	H	9.02 FQ	13.97 AW	21.25 TQ	PABLS	10/01-12/01
	Philadelphia PMSA, PA-NJ	H	8.26 FQ	12.79 AW	18.09 TQ	PABLS	10/01-12/01
	Pittsburgh MSA, PA	H	8.91 FQ	12.17 AW	16.54 TQ	PABLS	10/01-12/01
	Reading MSA, PA	H	7.29 FQ	12.02 AW	16.82 TQ	PABLS	10/01-12/01
	Scranton-Wilkes-Barre-Hazleton MSA, PA	H	6.81 FQ	10.64 AW	15.37 TQ	PABLS	10/01-12/01
	York MSA, PA	H	5.80 FQ	10.02 AW	15.03 TQ	PABLS	10/01-12/01
	Rhode Island	H	11.00 FQ	14.91 AW	19.52 TQ	RIBLS	10/01-12/01
	Providence-Fall River-Warwick MSA, RI-MA	H	9.47 FQ	14.05 AW	18.70 TQ	RIBLS	10/01-12/01
	South Carolina	H	8.01 FQ	11.87 AW	16.27 TQ	SCBLS	10/01-12/01
	Charleston-North Charleston MSA, SC	H	7.83 FQ	10.65 AW	14.48 TQ	SCBLS	10/01-12/01
	Columbia MSA, SC	H	8.25 FQ	11.37 AW	14.17 TQ	SCBLS	10/01-12/01
	Greenville-Spartanburg-Anderson MSA, SC	H	8.81 FQ	12.85 AW	17.23 TQ	SCBLS	10/01-12/01
	Myrtle Beach MSA, SC	H	8.27 FQ	12.80 AW	19.97 TQ	SCBLS	10/01-12/01
	South Dakota	H	8.07 FQ	11.29 AW	15.33 TQ	SDBLS	10/01-12/01
	Sioux Falls MSA, SD	H	8.92 FQ	11.70 AW	15.69 TQ	SDBLS	10/01-12/01
	Tennessee	H	8.36 FQ	12.72 AW	17.42 TQ	TNBLS	10/01-12/01
	Chattanooga MSA, TN-GA	H	8.46 FQ	11.66 AW	15.12 TQ	TNBLS	10/01-12/01
	Clarksville-Hopkinsville MSA, TN-KY	H	8.18 FQ	11.93 AW	17.44 TQ	TNBLS	10/01-12/01
	Johnson City-Kingsport-Bristol MSA, TN-VA	H	7.96 FQ	10.86 AW	15.03 TQ	TNBLS	10/01-12/01
	Knoxville MSA, TN	H	8.64 FQ	11.82 AW	15.71 TQ	TNBLS	10/01-12/01
	Memphis MSA, TN-AR-MS	H	8.41 FQ	12.20 AW	16.58 TQ	TNBLS	10/01-12/01
	Nashville MSA, TN	H	9.48 FQ	15.18 AW	24.21 TQ	TNBLS	10/01-12/01
	Texas	H	8.41 FQ	13.17 AW	18.47 TQ	TXBLS	10/01-12/01
	Amarillo MSA, TX	H	7.99 FQ	12.43 AW	17.64 TQ	TXBLS	10/01-12/01

AAW Average annual wage; **AE** Average entry wage; **AEX** Average experienced wage; **AO** Average offered; **AOH** Average offered, high; **AOL** Average offered, low; **APH** Average pay, high range; **APL** Average pay, low range; **ASH** Average starting, high; **ASL** Average starting, low; **AW** Average wage paid; **FQ** First quartile wage; **H** Hourly; **HI** Highest wage paid; **HR** High end range; **LR** Low end range; **M** Monthly; **MTC** Median total compensation; **MW** Median wage paid; **SQ** Second quartile wage; **S** Special: hourly and annual; **TQ** Third quartile wage; **W** Weekly; **Y** Yearly

Occupation/Type/Industry	Location	Per	Low	Mid	High	Source	Date
Bill and Account Collector	Austin-San Marcos MSA, TX	H	9.17 FQ	13.61 AW	19.06 TQ	TXBLS	10/01-12/01
	Beaumont-Port Arthur MSA, TX	H	7.96 FQ	11.08 AW	15.60 TQ	TXBLS	10/01-12/01
	Brazoria PMSA, TX	H	7.61 FQ	11.55 AW	16.46 TQ	TXBLS	10/01-12/01
	Brownsville-Harlingen-San Benito MSA, TX	H	5.91 FQ	9.54 AW	15.28 TQ	TXBLS	10/01-12/01
	Corpus Christi MSA, TX	H	6.84 FQ	9.87 AW	13.94 TQ	TXBLS	10/01-12/01
	Dallas PMSA, TX	H	10.30 FQ	14.84 AW	19.90 TQ	TXBLS	10/01-12/01
	El Paso MSA, TX	H	6.95 FQ	10.17 AW	14.00 TQ	TXBLS	10/01-12/01
	Fort Worth-Arlington PMSA, TX	H	10.00 FQ	15.49 AW	23.90 TQ	TXBLS	10/01-12/01
	Galveston-Texas City PMSA, TX	H	8.91 FQ	13.18 AW	18.26 TQ	TXBLS	10/01-12/01
	Houston PMSA, TX	H	8.50 FQ	12.45 AW	17.24 TQ	TXBLS	10/01-12/01
	Killeen-Temple MSA, TX	H	6.99 FQ	10.55 AW	14.62 TQ	TXBLS	10/01-12/01
	Laredo MSA, TX	H	5.90 FQ	9.49 AW	13.29 TQ	TXBLS	10/01-12/01
	Longview-Marshall MSA, TX	H	7.21 FQ	10.19 AW	14.99 TQ	TXBLS	10/01-12/01
	Lubbock MSA, TX	H	7.45 FQ	10.79 AW	15.91 TQ	TXBLS	10/01-12/01
	McAllen-Edinburg-Mission MSA, TX	H	6.39 FQ	9.64 AW	12.98 TQ	TXBLS	10/01-12/01
	Odessa-Midland MSA, TX	H	6.92 FQ	9.94 AW	14.66 TQ	TXBLS	10/01-12/01
	San Antonio MSA, TX	H	8.64 FQ	11.68 AW	16.01 TQ	TXBLS	10/01-12/01
	Tyler MSA, TX	H	8.09 FQ	12.30 AW	16.71 TQ	TXBLS	10/01-12/01
	Waco MSA, TX	H	7.32 FQ	11.38 AW	16.65 TQ	TXBLS	10/01-12/01
	Utah	H	9.07 FQ	12.95 AW	18.90 TQ	UTBLS	10/01-12/01
	Provo-Orem MSA, UT	H	9.39 FQ	13.28 AW	18.70 TQ	UTBLS	10/01-12/01
	Salt Lake City-Ogden MSA, UT	H	9.18 FQ	13.03 AW	19.86 TQ	UTBLS	10/01-12/01
	Vermont	H	9.08 FQ	12.62 AW	17.70 TQ	VTBLS	10/01-12/01
	Burlington MSA, VT	H	9.43 FQ	13.20 AW	17.61 TQ	VTBLS	10/01-12/01
	Virginia	H	8.46 FQ	12.70 AW	18.04 TQ	VABLS	10/01-12/01
	Lynchburg MSA, VA	H	7.90 FQ	12.18 AW	18.66 TQ	VABLS	10/01-12/01
	Norfolk-Virginia Beach-Newport News MSA, VA-NC	H	7.79 FQ	11.60 AW	17.21 TQ	VABLS	10/01-12/01
	Richmond-Petersburg MSA, VA	H	9.27 FQ	12.93 AW	16.95 TQ	VABLS	10/01-12/01
	Roanoke MSA, VA	H	8.07 FQ	11.80 AW	15.76 TQ	VABLS	10/01-12/01
	Washington	H	9.67 FQ	14.20 AW	19.53 TQ	WABLS	10/01-12/01
	Bremerton PMSA, WA	H	7.57 FQ	11.13 AW	15.96 TQ	WABLS	10/01-12/01
	Olympia PMSA, WA	H	11.18 FQ	15.06 AW	19.88 TQ	WABLS	10/01-12/01
	Richland-Kennewick-Pasco MSA, WA	H	8.84 FQ	11.66 AW	14.67 TQ	WABLS	10/01-12/01
	Seattle-Bellevue-Everett PMSA, WA	H	10.92 FQ	14.88 AW	19.92 TQ	WABLS	10/01-12/01
	Spokane MSA, WA	H	7.48 FQ	11.79 AW	16.59 TQ	WABLS	10/01-12/01
	Tacoma PMSA, WA	H	10.08 FQ	16.09 AW	31.24 TQ	WABLS	10/01-12/01
	Yakima MSA, WA	H	8.82 FQ	12.23 AW	16.66 TQ	WABLS	10/01-12/01
	West Virginia	H	7.43 FQ	10.94 AW	14.84 TQ	WVBLS	10/01-12/01
	Charleston MSA, WV	H	7.56 FQ	11.20 AW	16.55 TQ	WVBLS	10/01-12/01
	Huntington-Ashland MSA, WV-KY-OH	H	8.95 FQ	11.74 AW	15.23 TQ	WVBLS	10/01-12/01
	Wisconsin	H	8.70 FQ	12.42 AW	16.96 TQ	WIBLS	10/01-12/01
	Appleton-Oshkosh-Neenah MSA, WI	H	9.40 FQ	12.28 AW	15.30 TQ	WIBLS	10/01-12/01
	Green Bay MSA, WI	H	9.67 FQ	13.13 AW	17.37 TQ	WIBLS	10/01-12/01
	Madison MSA, WI	H	8.85 FQ	13.11 AW	17.79 TQ	WIBLS	10/01-12/01
	Milwaukee-Waukesha PMSA, WI	H	8.49 FQ	12.65 AW	17.52 TQ	WIBLS	10/01-12/01
	Racine PMSA, WI	H	8.73 FQ	12.00 AW	18.58 TQ	WIBLS	10/01-12/01
	Wyoming	H	7.61 FQ	11.09 AW	14.48 TQ	WYBLS	10/01-12/01
	Cheyenne MSA, WY	H	8.24 FQ	11.00 AW	14.14 TQ	WYBLS	10/01-12/01
	Puerto Rico	H	5.80 FQ	8.22 AW	12.30 TQ	PRBLS	10/01-12/01
	Virgin Islands	H	7.79 FQ	10.63 AW	14.33 TQ	VIBLS	10/01-12/01
	Guam	H	6.72 FQ	10.29 AW	14.43 TQ	GUBLS	10/01-12/01
Billing and Posting Clerk and Machine Operator	Alabama	H	7.68 FQ	11.27 AW	15.54 TQ	ALBLS	10/01-12/01
	Alaska	H	11.26 FQ	14.67 AW	19.54 TQ	AKBLS	10/01-12/01
	Arizona	H	8.55 FQ	11.95 AW	16.23 TQ	AZBLS	10/01-12/01
	Arkansas	H	7.48 FQ	10.58 AW	14.57 TQ	ARBLS	10/01-12/01
	California	H	9.19 FQ	14.06 AW	20.28 TQ	CABLS	10/01-12/01

AAW Average annual wage · **AE** Average entry wage · **AEX** Average experienced wage · **AO** Average offered · **AOH** Average offered, high · **AOL** Average offered, low · **APH** Average pay, high range · **APL** Average pay, low range · **ASH** Average starting, high · **ASL** Average starting, low · **AW** Average wage paid · **FQ** First quartile wage · **H** Hourly · **HI** Highest wage paid · **HR** High end range · **LR** Low end range · **M** Monthly · **MTC** Median total compensation · **MW** Median wage paid · **SQ** Second quartile wage · **S** Special: hourly and annual · **TQ** Third quartile wage · **W** Weekly · **Y** Yearly

Occupation/Type/Industry	Location	Per	Low	Mid	High	Source	Date
Billing and Posting Clerk and Machine Operator	Colorado	H	7.20 FQ	12.20 AW	16.63 TQ	COBLS	10/01-12/01
	Connecticut	H	10.05 FQ	14.47 AW	20.14 TQ	CTBLS	10/01-12/01
	Delaware	H	9.36 FQ	13.42 AW	18.15 TQ	DEBLS	10/01-12/01
	District of Columbia	H	11.65 FQ	16.15 AW	23.19 TQ	DCBLS	10/01-12/01
	Florida	H	8.22 FQ	11.65 AW	16.10 TQ	FLBLS	10/01-12/01
	Georgia	H	8.70 FQ	12.54 AW	17.10 TQ	GABLS	10/01-12/01
	Hawaii	H	8.24 FQ	12.39 AW	17.00 TQ	HIBLS	10/01-12/01
	Idaho	H	8.45 FQ	11.17 AW	14.88 TQ	IDBLS	10/01-12/01
	Illinois	H	8.51 FQ	13.32 AW	18.43 TQ	ILBLS	10/01-12/01
	Indiana	H	8.52 FQ	12.15 AW	16.73 TQ	INBLS	10/01-12/01
	Iowa	H	8.48 FQ	11.81 AW	15.98 TQ	IABLS	10/01-12/01
	Kansas	H	8.02 FQ	12.40 AW	18.40 TQ	KSBLS	10/01-12/01
	Kentucky	H	7.61 FQ	11.25 AW	15.23 TQ	KYBLS	10/01-12/01
	Louisiana	H	7.46 FQ	10.57 AW	13.89 TQ	LABLS	10/01-12/01
	Maine	H	8.57 FQ	11.32 AW	14.63 TQ	MEBLS	10/01-12/01
	Maryland	H	9.20 FQ	13.42 AW	18.19 TQ	MDBLS	10/01-12/01
	Massachusetts	H	9.37 FQ	13.81 AW	19.09 TQ	MABLS	10/01-12/01
	Michigan	H	9.31 FQ	12.94 AW	17.03 TQ	MIBLS	10/01-12/01
	Minnesota	H	9.32 FQ	13.19 AW	17.67 TQ	MNBLS	10/01-12/01
	Mississippi	H	7.46 FQ	10.67 AW	14.22 TQ	MSBLS	10/01-12/01
	Missouri	H	8.03 FQ	11.89 AW	16.30 TQ	MOBLS	10/01-12/01
	Montana	H	7.39 FQ	10.44 AW	14.27 TQ	MTBLS	10/01-12/01
	Nebraska	H	7.75 FQ	11.13 AW	14.53 TQ	NEBLS	10/01-12/01
	Nevada	H	9.38 FQ	12.85 AW	17.34 TQ	NVBLS	10/01-12/01
	New Hampshire	H	9.24 FQ	12.28 AW	16.24 TQ	NHBLS	10/01-12/01
	New Jersey	H	9.43 FQ	13.86 AW	18.86 TQ	NJBLS	10/01-12/01
	New Mexico	H	7.80 FQ	10.78 AW	14.37 TQ	NMBLS	10/01-12/01
	New York	H	9.25 FQ	14.10 AW	20.18 TQ	NYBLS	10/01-12/01
	North Carolina	H	8.62 FQ	12.08 AW	16.44 TQ	NCBLS	10/01-12/01
	North Dakota	H	7.74 FQ	10.62 AW	14.36 TQ	NDBLS	10/01-12/01
	Ohio	H	8.72 FQ	12.01 AW	16.30 TQ	OHBLS	10/01-12/01
	Oklahoma	H	7.46 FQ	10.71 AW	14.84 TQ	OKBLS	10/01-12/01
	Oregon	H	9.44 FQ	13.00 AW	17.03 TQ	ORBLS	10/01-12/01
	Pennsylvania	H	8.51 FQ	12.46 AW	17.24 TQ	PABLS	10/01-12/01
	Rhode Island	H	9.04 FQ	13.10 AW	17.72 TQ	RIBLS	10/01-12/01
	South Carolina	H	7.74 FQ	11.31 AW	16.11 TQ	SCBLS	10/01-12/01
	South Dakota	H	7.58 FQ	10.02 AW	13.06 TQ	SDBLS	10/01-12/01
	Tennessee	H	8.35 FQ	11.99 AW	16.28 TQ	TNBLS	10/01-12/01
	Texas	H	8.06 FQ	12.18 AW	16.85 TQ	TXBLS	10/01-12/01
	Utah	H	8.58 FQ	11.75 AW	15.19 TQ	UTBLS	10/01-12/01
	Vermont	H	8.96 FQ	11.93 AW	15.82 TQ	VTBLS	10/01-12/01
	Virginia	H	8.65 FQ	12.83 AW	18.93 TQ	VABLS	10/01-12/01
	Washington	H	9.49 FQ	13.42 AW	18.13 TQ	WABLS	10/01-12/01
	West Virginia	H	6.93 FQ	9.73 AW	13.51 TQ	WVBLS	10/01-12/01
	Wisconsin	H	8.82 FQ	12.35 AW	16.68 TQ	WIBLS	10/01-12/01
	Wyoming	H	7.60 FQ	10.84 AW	14.71 TQ	WYBLS	10/01-12/01
	Puerto Rico	H	5.69 FQ	7.64 AW	10.81 TQ	PRBLS	10/01-12/01
	Virgin Islands	H	7.29 FQ	9.77 AW	13.13 TQ	VIBLS	10/01-12/01
	Guam	H	6.95 FQ	10.31 AW	14.96 TQ	GUBLS	10/01-12/01
Bindery Worker	Alabama	H	5.95 FQ	10.06 AW	16.45 TQ	ALBLS	10/01-12/01
	Alaska	H	6.24 FQ	12.03 AW	20.22 TQ	AKBLS	10/01-12/01
	Arizona	H	6.98 FQ	10.41 AW	15.79 TQ	AZBLS	10/01-12/01
	Arkansas	H	6.81 FQ	10.82 AW	15.81 TQ	ARBLS	10/01-12/01
	California	H	6.71 FQ	10.97 AW	17.15 TQ	CABLS	10/01-12/01
	Colorado	H	6.26 FQ	10.42 AW	17.12 TQ	COBLS	10/01-12/01
	Connecticut	H	7.44 FQ	12.06 AW	19.19 TQ	CTBLS	10/01-12/01
	Delaware	H	7.85 FQ	11.28 AW	16.71 TQ	DEBLS	10/01-12/01
	District of Columbia	H	8.74 FQ	16.45 AW	26.25 TQ	DCBLS	10/01-12/01
	Florida	H	6.93 FQ	10.66 AW	15.89 TQ	FLBLS	10/01-12/01
	Georgia	H	6.92 FQ	12.44 AW	20.64 TQ	GABLS	10/01-12/01
	Hawaii	H	6.91 FQ	12.98 AW	20.20 TQ	HIBLS	10/01-12/01
	Idaho	H	7.21 FQ	10.01 AW	15.39 TQ	IDBLS	10/01-12/01
	Illinois	H	6.04 FQ	10.87 AW	17.48 TQ	ILBLS	10/01-12/01
	Indiana	H	7.52 FQ	11.91 AW	17.60 TQ	INBLS	10/01-12/01
	Iowa	H	7.30 FQ	10.34 AW	14.89 TQ	IABLS	10/01-12/01
	Kansas	H	6.14 FQ	10.59 AW	18.00 TQ	KSBLS	10/01-12/01
	Kentucky	H	6.08 FQ	10.75 AW	16.75 TQ	KYBLS	10/01-12/01
	Louisiana	H	6.06 FQ	9.02 AW	13.21 TQ	LABLS	10/01-12/01
	Maine	H	7.38 FQ	9.93 AW	14.33 TQ	MEBLS	10/01-12/01
	Maryland	H	7.25 FQ	12.59 AW	19.59 TQ	MDBLS	10/01-12/01

AAW Average annual wage; AE Average entry wage; AEX Average experienced wage; AO Average offered; AOH Average offered, high; AOL Average offered, low; APH Average pay, high range; APL Average pay, low range; ASH Average starting, high; ASL Average starting, low; AW Average wage paid; FQ First quartile wage; H Hourly; HI Highest wage paid; HR High end range; LR Low end range; M Monthly; MTC Median total compensation; MW Median wage paid; SQ Second quartile wage; S Special: hourly and annual; TQ Third quartile wage; W Weekly; Y Yearly

Occupation/Type/Industry	Location	Per	Low	Mid	High	Source	Date
Bindery Worker	Massachusetts	H	7.82 FQ	13.23 AW	20.23 TQ	MABLS	10/01-12/01
	Michigan	H	7.92 FQ	13.12 AW	17.54 TQ	MIBLS	10/01-12/01
	Minnesota	H	8.08 FQ	13.01 AW	19.95 TQ	MNBLS	10/01-12/01
	Missouri	H	6.86 FQ	11.24 AW	18.83 TQ	MOBLS	10/01-12/01
	Montana	H	6.52 FQ	8.94 AW	11.33 TQ	MTBLS	10/01-12/01
	Nebraska	H	6.68 FQ	10.80 AW	15.36 TQ	NEBLS	10/01-12/01
	Nevada	H	7.58 FQ	10.96 AW	17.05 TQ	NVBLS	10/01-12/01
	New Hampshire	H	7.56 FQ	11.30 AW	16.28 TQ	NHBLS	10/01-12/01
	New Jersey	H	6.31 FQ	11.36 AW	19.90 TQ	NJBLS	10/01-12/01
	New Mexico	H	6.29 FQ	9.00 AW	12.29 TQ	NMBLS	10/01-12/01
	New York	H	6.83 FQ	11.96 AW	18.06 TQ	NYBLS	10/01-12/01
	North Carolina	H	7.73 FQ	11.25 AW	16.37 TQ	NCBLS	10/01-12/01
	North Dakota	H	5.91 FQ	8.40 AW	12.19 TQ	NDBLS	10/01-12/01
	Ohio	H	7.16 FQ	11.23 AW	16.74 TQ	OHBLS	10/01-12/01
	Oklahoma	H	5.87 FQ	8.63 AW	13.49 TQ	OKBLS	10/01-12/01
	Oregon	H	6.81 FQ	12.05 AW	18.77 TQ	ORBLS	10/01-12/01
	Pennsylvania	H	7.33 FQ	12.30 AW	18.22 TQ	PABLS	10/01-12/01
	Rhode Island	H	7.16 FQ	12.23 AW	17.08 TQ	RIBLS	10/01-12/01
	South Carolina	H	7.17 FQ	10.76 AW	16.12 TQ	SCBLS	10/01-12/01
	South Dakota	H	7.05 FQ	9.18 AW	13.05 TQ	SDBLS	10/01-12/01
	Tennessee	H	6.91 FQ	10.86 AW	16.25 TQ	TNBLS	10/01-12/01
	Texas	H	6.64 FQ	10.52 AW	15.96 TQ	TXBLS	10/01-12/01
	Utah	H	6.14 FQ	9.64 AW	13.80 TQ	UTBLS	10/01-12/01
	Vermont	H	9.29 FQ	13.11 AW	19.20 TQ	VTBLS	10/01-12/01
	Virginia	H	7.07 FQ	12.06 AW	18.97 TQ	VABLS	10/01-12/01
	Washington	H	7.13 FQ	11.82 AW	18.66 TQ	WABLS	10/01-12/01
	West Virginia	H	5.99 FQ	8.74 AW	12.64 TQ	WVBLS	10/01-12/01
	Wisconsin	H	6.94 FQ	11.10 AW	17.08 TQ	WIBLS	10/01-12/01
	Wyoming	H	5.86 FQ	8.51 AW	12.55 TQ	WYBLS	10/01-12/01
	Puerto Rico	H	5.78 FQ	8.61 AW	13.16 TQ	PRBLS	10/01-12/01
Biochemist and Biophysicist	Alabama	Y	30200 FQ	53440 AW	94770 TQ	ALBLS	10/01-12/01
	Birmingham MSA, AL	Y	29710 FQ	45040 AW	66420 TQ	ALBLS	10/01-12/01
	Phoenix-Mesa MSA, AZ	Y	37250 FQ	58550 AW	97610 TQ	AZBLS	10/01-12/01
	Arkansas	Y	37120 FQ	58090 AW	89080 TQ	ARBLS	10/01-12/01
	California	Y	35970 FQ	63650 AW	104910 TQ	CABLS	10/01-12/01
	Los Angeles-Long Beach PMSA, CA	Y	36960 FQ	63730 AW	99940 TQ	CABLS	10/01-12/01
	Oakland PMSA, CA	Y	39100 FQ	75280 AW	126240 TQ	CABLS	10/01-12/01
	Orange County PMSA, CA	Y	31180 FQ	51240 AW	87010 TQ	CABLS	10/01-12/01
	Sacramento PMSA, CA	Y	45470 FQ	60780 AW	70510 TQ	CABLS	10/01-12/01
	San Diego MSA, CA	Y	33040 FQ	59240 AW	94090 TQ	CABLS	10/01-12/01
	San Francisco PMSA, CA	Y	42520 FQ	75640 AW	106550 TQ	CABLS	10/01-12/01
	San Jose PMSA, CA	Y	38910 FQ	60660 AW	94470 TQ	CABLS	10/01-12/01
	Santa Barbara-Santa Maria-Lompoc MSA, CA	Y	35690 FQ	56140 AW	80560 TQ	CABLS	10/01-12/01
	Denver PMSA, CO	Y	38640 FQ	71670 AW	97910 TQ	COBLS	10/01-12/01
	Connecticut	Y	47280 FQ	69210 AW	107120 TQ	CTBLS	10/01-12/01
	Stamford-Norwalk PMSA, CT	Y	29950 FQ	56210 AW	103800 TQ	CTBLS	10/01-12/01
	Delaware	Y	36500 FQ	67410 AW	101050 TQ	DEBLS	10/01-12/01
	Wilmington-Newark PMSA, DE-MD	Y	36480 FQ	67410 AW	101100 TQ	DEBLS	10/01-12/01
	District of Columbia	Y	36670 FQ	55360 AW	88120 TQ	DCBLS	10/01-12/01
	Washington PMSA, DC-MD-VA-WV	Y	33180 FQ	53800 AW	87860 TQ	DCBLS	10/01-12/01
	Florida	Y	32410 FQ	54280 AW	85670 TQ	FLBLS	10/01-12/01
	Miami PMSA, FL	Y	39280 FQ	65840 AW	97430 TQ	FLBLS	10/01-12/01
	Georgia	Y	24670 FQ	56360 AW	105210 TQ	GABLS	10/01-12/01
	Idaho	Y	40690 FQ	57260 AW	86690 TQ	IDBLS	10/01-12/01
	Illinois	Y	36260 FQ	64650 AW	93530 TQ	ILBLS	10/01-12/01
	Chicago PMSA, IL	Y	38780 FQ	66940 AW	95280 TQ	ILBLS	10/01-12/01
	Indiana	Y	31190 FQ	50080 AW	81370 TQ	INBLS	10/01-12/01
	Fort Wayne MSA, IN	Y	30600 FQ	57460 AW	128700 TQ	INBLS	10/01-12/01
	Indianapolis MSA, IN	Y	28640 FQ	52360 AW	83000 TQ	INBLS	10/01-12/01
	Iowa	Y	34570 FQ	64830 AW	92730 TQ	IABLS	10/01-12/01
	Kansas	Y	24060 FQ	36580 AW	56310 TQ	KSBLS	10/01-12/01
	Kentucky	Y	32070 FQ	64240 AW	108460 TQ	KYBLS	10/01-12/01
	Louisiana	Y	24140 FQ	37560 AW	53940 TQ	LABLS	10/01-12/01
	New Orleans MSA, LA	Y	23410 FQ	38690 AW	66380 TQ	LABLS	10/01-12/01
	Maine	Y	30620 FQ	53850 AW	85430 TQ	MEBLS	10/01-12/01
	Maryland	Y	31870 FQ	51250 AW	86020 TQ	MDBLS	10/01-12/01
	Baltimore PMSA, MD	Y	37270 FQ	63590 AW	114390 TQ	MDBLS	10/01-12/01
	Massachusetts	Y	38170 FQ	66990 AW	101160 TQ	MABLS	10/01-12/01

AAW Average annual wage; AE Average entry wage; AEX Average experienced wage; AO Average offered; AOH Average offered, high; AOL Average offered, low; APH Average pay, high range; APL Average pay, low range; ASH Average starting, high; ASL Average starting, low; AW Average wage paid; FQ First quartile wage; H Hourly; HI Highest wage paid; HR High end range; LR Low end range; M Monthly; MTC Median total compensation; MW Median wage paid; SQ Second quartile wage; S Special: hourly and annual; TQ Third quartile wage; W Weekly; Y Yearly

Occupation/Type/Industry	Location	Per	Low	Mid	High	Source	Date
Biochemist and Biophysicist	Boston PMSA, MA-NH	Y	37290 FQ	66290 AW	101530 TQ	MABLS	10/01-12/01
	Lowell PMSA, MA-NH	Y	41510 FQ	73630 AW	106980 TQ	MABLS	10/01-12/01
	Michigan	Y	32730 FQ	58770 AW	97360 TQ	MIBLS	10/01-12/01
	Ann Arbor PMSA, MI	Y	32900 FQ	59660 AW	100340 TQ	MIBLS	10/01-12/01
	Minnesota	Y	33360 FQ	58160 AW	90190 TQ	MNBLS	10/01-12/01
	Minneapolis-St. Paul MSA, MN-WI	Y	27190 FQ	55600 AW	89060 TQ	MNBLS	10/01-12/01
	Missouri	Y	26680 FQ	51640 AW	85330 TQ	MOBLS	10/01-12/01
	St. Louis MSA, MO-IL	Y	31200 FQ	61650 AW	93660 TQ	MOBLS	10/01-12/01
	Nebraska	Y	27720 FQ	47630 AW	80610 TQ	NEBLS	10/01-12/01
	New Jersey	Y	36180 FQ	67210 AW	117920 TQ	NJBLS	10/01-12/01
	Bergen-Passaic PMSA, NJ	Y	42180 FQ	66060 AW	92450 TQ	NJBLS	10/01-12/01
	Middlesex-Somerset-Hunterdon PMSA, NJ	Y	26650 FQ	66550 AW	95340 TQ	NJBLS	10/01-12/01
	Monmouth-Ocean PMSA, NJ	Y	45110 FQ	76650 AW	122160 TQ	NJBLS	10/01-12/01
	Newark PMSA, NJ	Y	36570 FQ	67150 AW	131040 TQ	NJBLS	10/01-12/01
	New York	Y	33340 FQ	60240 AW	94630 TQ	NYBLS	10/01-12/01
	New York PMSA, NY	Y	33550 FQ	61100 AW	99450 TQ	NYBLS	10/01-12/01
	North Carolina	Y	36140 FQ	61060 AW	93400 TQ	NCBLS	10/01-12/01
	Greensboro-Winston-Salem-High Point MSA, NC	Y	34300 FQ	54020 AW	86220 TQ	NCBLS	10/01-12/01
	Raleigh-Durham-Chapel Hill MSA, NC	Y	35510 FQ	62520 AW	94960 TQ	NCBLS	10/01-12/01
	Ohio	Y	31530 FQ	63390 AW	96130 TQ	OHBLS	10/01-12/01
	Columbus MSA, OH	Y	32020 FQ	66110 AW	97450 TQ	OHBLS	10/01-12/01
	Oregon	Y	27710 FQ	56890 AW	96770 TQ	ORBLS	10/01-12/01
	Pennsylvania	Y	33060 FQ	53360 AW	86820 TQ	PABLS	10/01-12/01
	Philadelphia PMSA, PA-NJ	Y	32850 FQ	51800 AW	83430 TQ	PABLS	10/01-12/01
	Tennessee	Y	30730 FQ	64910 AW	91730 TQ	TNBLS	10/01-12/01
	Texas	Y	32770 FQ	62780 AW	106520 TQ	TXBLS	10/01-12/01
	Houston PMSA, TX	Y	34170 FQ	69390 AW	131000 TQ	TXBLS	10/01-12/01
	Utah	Y	32690 FQ	58470 AW	80580 TQ	UTBLS	10/01-12/01
	Salt Lake City-Ogden MSA, UT	Y	31290 FQ	57050 AW	80430 TQ	UTBLS	10/01-12/01
	Virginia	Y	37200 FQ	62060 AW	105460 TQ	VABLS	10/01-12/01
	Washington	Y	46150 FQ	75520 AW	90120 TQ	WABLS	10/01-12/01
	Seattle-Bellevue-Everett PMSA, WA	Y	58140 FQ	77680 AW	89880 TQ	WABLS	10/01-12/01
	West Virginia	Y	37200 FQ	55370 AW	89570 TQ	WVBLS	10/01-12/01
	Milwaukee-Waukesha PMSA, WI	Y	28560 FQ	59220 AW	93690 TQ	WIBLS	10/01-12/01
Biological Science Teacher							
Postsecondary	Alabama	Y	18820 FQ	60710 AW	116670 TQ	ALBLS	10/01-12/01
Postsecondary	Birmingham MSA, AL	Y	41370 FQ	81430 AW	141630 TQ	ALBLS	10/01-12/01
Postsecondary	Huntsville MSA, AL	Y	24470 FQ	46860 AW	69510 TQ	ALBLS	10/01-12/01
Postsecondary	Mobile MSA, AL	Y	12100 FQ	31550 AW	54850 TQ	ALBLS	10/01-12/01
Postsecondary	Arizona	Y	20030 FQ	39700 AW	67650 TQ	AZBLS	10/01-12/01
Postsecondary	Arkansas	Y	22020 FQ	47760 AW	93550 TQ	ARBLS	10/01-12/01
Postsecondary	California	Y	35970 FQ	70190 AW	107870 TQ	CABLS	10/01-12/01
Postsecondary	Los Angeles-Long Beach PMSA, CA	Y	32280 FQ	66970 AW	105890 TQ	CABLS	10/01-12/01
Postsecondary	Orange County PMSA, CA	Y	33910 FQ	67620 AW	110560 TQ	CABLS	10/01-12/01
Postsecondary	Riverside-San Bernardino PMSA, CA	Y	34570 FQ	64130 AW	103530 TQ	CABLS	10/01-12/01
Postsecondary	San Francisco PMSA, CA	Y	56210 FQ	80130 AW	110910 TQ	CABLS	10/01-12/01
Postsecondary	San Jose PMSA, CA	Y	47070 FQ	62520 AW	81720 TQ	CABLS	10/01-12/01
Postsecondary	Santa Cruz-Watsonville PMSA, CA	Y	34630 FQ	65790 AW	111100 TQ	CABLS	10/01-12/01
Postsecondary	Colorado	Y	32070 FQ	64310 AW	113220 TQ	COBLS	10/01-12/01
Postsecondary	Denver PMSA, CO	Y	31480 FQ	62450 AW	110160 TQ	COBLS	10/01-12/01
Postsecondary	New Haven-Meriden PMSA, CT	Y	31950 FQ	51300 AW	74360 TQ	CTBLS	10/01-12/01
Postsecondary	District of Columbia	Y	39020 FQ	68530 AW	90430 TQ	DCBLS	10/01-12/01
Postsecondary	Washington PMSA, DC-MD-VA-WV	Y	36140 FQ	65700 AW	100580 TQ	DCBLS	10/01-12/01
Postsecondary	Florida	Y	33580 FQ	64300 AW	107280 TQ	FLBLS	10/01-12/01
Postsecondary	Gainesville MSA, FL	Y	40940 FQ	74470 AW	121270 TQ	FLBLS	10/01-12/01
Postsecondary	Miami PMSA, FL	Y	44480 FQ	67200 AW	107580 TQ	FLBLS	10/01-12/01
Postsecondary	Orlando MSA, FL	Y	25650 FQ	56790 AW	95850 TQ	FLBLS	10/01-12/01
Postsecondary	Pensacola MSA, FL	Y	37970 FQ	65650 AW	122520 TQ	FLBLS	10/01-12/01
Postsecondary	Tampa-St. Petersburg-Clearwater MSA, FL	Y	32530 FQ	57370 AW	87890 TQ	FLBLS	10/01-12/01

AAW Average annual wage; **AE** Average entry wage; **AEX** Average experienced wage; **AO** Average offered; **AOH** Average offered, high; **AOL** Average offered, low; **APH** Average pay, high range; **APL** Average pay, low range; **ASH** Average starting, high; **ASL** Average starting, low; **AW** Average wage paid; **FQ** First quartile wage; **H** Hourly; **HI** Highest wage paid; **HR** High end range; **LR** Low end range; **M** Monthly; **MTC** Median total compensation; **MW** Median wage paid; **SQ** Second quartile wage; **S** Special: hourly and annual; **TQ** Third quartile wage; **W** Weekly; **Y** Yearly

Occupation/Type/Industry	Location	Per	Low	Mid	High	Source	Date
Biological Science Teacher							
Postsecondary	West Palm Beach-Boca Raton MSA, FL	Y	45170 FQ	68690 AW	110790 TQ	FLBLS	10/01-12/01
Postsecondary	Hawaii	Y	43630 FQ	83540 AW	117900 TQ	HIBLS	10/01-12/01
Postsecondary	Honolulu MSA, HI	Y	48780 FQ	86250 AW	118700 TQ	HIBLS	10/01-12/01
Postsecondary	Idaho	Y	38360 FQ	57090 AW	75480 TQ	IDBLS	10/01-12/01
Postsecondary	Illinois	Y	19180 FQ	70540 AW		ILBLS	10/01-12/01
Postsecondary	Champaign-Urbana MSA, IL	Y	14500 FQ	48710 AW	91110 TQ	ILBLS	10/01-12/01
Postsecondary	Chicago PMSA, IL	Y	18970 FQ	73150 AW		ILBLS	10/01-12/01
Postsecondary	Springfield MSA, IL	Y	13630 FQ	53100 AW	97320 TQ	ILBLS	10/01-12/01
Postsecondary	Indiana	Y	34490 FQ	65110 AW	111680 TQ	INBLS	10/01-12/01
Postsecondary	South Bend MSA, IN	Y	31360 FQ	53880 AW	71020 TQ	INBLS	10/01-12/01
Postsecondary	Iowa	Y	32680 FQ	69500 AW		IABLS	10/01-12/01
Postsecondary	Cedar Rapids MSA, IA	Y	28590 FQ	42450 AW	59360 TQ	IABLS	10/01-12/01
Postsecondary	Davenport-Moline-Rock Island MSA, IA-IL	Y	26960 FQ	47370 AW	66630 TQ	IABLS	10/01-12/01
Postsecondary	Des Moines MSA, IA	Y	29340 FQ	69630 AW		IABLS	10/01-12/01
Postsecondary	Kansas	Y	26360 FQ	51660 AW	86500 TQ	KSBLS	10/01-12/01
Postsecondary	Kentucky	Y	31010 FQ	47650 AW	72610 TQ	KYBLS	10/01-12/01
Postsecondary	Louisiana	Y	27090 FQ	52400 AW	88670 TQ	LABLS	10/01-12/01
Postsecondary	Maine	Y	33280 FQ	54270 AW	81210 TQ	MEBLS	10/01-12/01
Postsecondary	Maryland	Y	34430 FQ	63330 AW	107830 TQ	MDBLS	10/01-12/01
Postsecondary	Baltimore PMSA, MD	Y	32440 FQ	58180 AW	96780 TQ	MDBLS	10/01-12/01
Postsecondary	Massachusetts	Y	32960 FQ	63030 AW	109250 TQ	MABLS	10/01-12/01
Postsecondary	Boston PMSA, MA-NH	Y	31680 FQ	63120 AW	112840 TQ	MABLS	10/01-12/01
Postsecondary	Springfield MSA, MA	Y	36310 FQ	61380 AW	97470 TQ	MABLS	10/01-12/01
Postsecondary	Worcester PMSA, MA-CT	Y	35490 FQ	64570 AW	104120 TQ	MABLS	10/01-12/01
Postsecondary	Michigan	Y	37980 FQ	68090 AW	103760 TQ	MIBLS	10/01-12/01
Postsecondary	Ann Arbor PMSA, MI	Y	35030 FQ	60790 AW	84750 TQ	MIBLS	10/01-12/01
Postsecondary	Detroit PMSA, MI	Y	24030 FQ	46100 AW	81680 TQ	MIBLS	10/01-12/01
Postsecondary	Minnesota	Y	35910 FQ	62230 AW	102900 TQ	MNBLS	10/01-12/01
Postsecondary	Minneapolis-St. Paul MSA, MN-WI	Y	38560 FQ	70300 AW	115200 TQ	MNBLS	10/01-12/01
Postsecondary	Mississippi	Y	31630 FQ	56590 AW	85340 TQ	MSBLS	10/01-12/01
Postsecondary	Jackson MSA, MS	Y	42760 FQ	70990 AW	102360 TQ	MSBLS	10/01-12/01
Postsecondary	Missouri	Y	25680 FQ	45540 AW	66820 TQ	MOBLS	10/01-12/01
Postsecondary	Kansas City MSA, MO-KS	Y	30150 FQ	44660 AW	61640 TQ	MOBLS	10/01-12/01
Postsecondary	St. Louis MSA, MO-IL	Y	25040 FQ	44860 AW	67140 TQ	MOBLS	10/01-12/01
Postsecondary	Springfield MSA, MO	Y	22390 FQ	47650 AW	70680 TQ	MOBLS	10/01-12/01
Postsecondary	Montana	Y	27310 FQ	62530 AW	113430 TQ	MTBLS	10/01-12/01
Postsecondary	Nebraska	Y	30830 FQ	53220 AW	81290 TQ	NEBLS	10/01-12/01
Postsecondary	Lincoln MSA, NE	Y	40460 FQ	66740 AW	103750 TQ	NEBLS	10/01-12/01
Postsecondary	Omaha MSA, NE-IA	Y	38380 FQ	50880 AW	68120 TQ	NEBLS	10/01-12/01
Postsecondary	Nevada	Y	26800 FQ	57760 AW	98800 TQ	NVBLS	10/01-12/01
Postsecondary	Las Vegas MSA, NV-AZ	Y	26600 FQ	46260 AW	70260 TQ	NVBLS	10/01-12/01
Postsecondary	New Hampshire	Y	35540 FQ	70700 AW	119910 TQ	NHBLS	10/01-12/01
Postsecondary	Manchester PMSA, NH	Y	26280 FQ	44720 AW	69140 TQ	NHBLS	10/01-12/01
Postsecondary	New Jersey	Y	37100 FQ	69270 AW	108330 TQ	NJBLS	10/01-12/01
Postsecondary	Jersey City PMSA, NJ	Y	38050 FQ	70540 AW	110930 TQ	NJBLS	10/01-12/01
Postsecondary	Monmouth-Ocean PMSA, NJ	Y	32700 FQ	57980 AW	92140 TQ	NJBLS	10/01-12/01
Postsecondary	Newark PMSA, NJ	Y	36740 FQ	66120 AW	97060 TQ	NJBLS	10/01-12/01
Postsecondary	New Mexico	Y	37300 FQ	53010 AW	70930 TQ	NMBLS	10/01-12/01
Postsecondary	New York	Y	38830 FQ	72410 AW	112570 TQ	NYBLS	10/01-12/01
Postsecondary	Albany-Schenectady-Troy MSA, NY	Y	39650 FQ	62420 AW	100240 TQ	NYBLS	10/01-12/01
Postsecondary	Buffalo-Niagara Falls MSA, NY	Y	38650 FQ	54960 AW	74750 TQ	NYBLS	10/01-12/01
Postsecondary	Dutchess County PMSA, NY	Y	36230 FQ	61280 AW	110090 TQ	NYBLS	10/01-12/01
Postsecondary	Nassau-Suffolk PMSA, NY	Y	35650 FQ	76940 AW	119580 TQ	NYBLS	10/01-12/01
Postsecondary	New York PMSA, NY	Y	42430 FQ	78500 AW	117720 TQ	NYBLS	10/01-12/01
Postsecondary	Rochester MSA, NY	Y	33860 FQ	59520 AW	100830 TQ	NYBLS	10/01-12/01
Postsecondary	Utica-Rome MSA, NY	Y	25780 FQ	52560 AW	75130 TQ	NYBLS	10/01-12/01
Postsecondary	North Carolina	Y	33060 FQ	57620 AW	93690 TQ	NCBLS	10/01-12/01
Postsecondary	Asheville MSA, NC	Y	36740 FQ	49950 AW	64710 TQ	NCBLS	10/01-12/01
Postsecondary	Charlotte-Gastonia-Rock Hill MSA, NC-SC	Y	33940 FQ	52790 AW	78390 TQ	NCBLS	10/01-12/01
Postsecondary	Fayetteville MSA, NC	Y	29610 FQ	50980 AW	74130 TQ	NCBLS	10/01-12/01
Postsecondary	Greensboro-Winston-Salem-High Point MSA, NC	Y	31550 FQ	53700 AW	86090 TQ	NCBLS	10/01-12/01
Postsecondary	Hickory-Morganton-Lenoir MSA, NC	Y	32840 FQ	41010 AW	48370 TQ	NCBLS	10/01-12/01

AAW Average annual wage; AE Average entry wage; AEX Average experienced wage; AO Average offered; AOH Average offered, high; AOL Average offered, low; APH Average pay, high range; APL Average pay, low range; ASH Average starting, high; ASL Average starting, low; AW Average wage paid; FQ First quartile wage; H Hourly; HI Highest wage paid; HR High end range; LR Low end range; M Monthly; MTC Median total compensation; MW Median wage paid; SQ Second quartile wage; S Special: hourly and annual; TQ Third quartile wage; W Weekly; Y Yearly

Occupation/Type/Industry	Location	Per	Low	Mid	High	Source	Date
Biological Science Teacher							
Postsecondary	Raleigh-Durham-Chapel Hill MSA, NC	Y	36970 FQ	72350 AW	124750 TQ	NCBLS	10/01-12/01
Postsecondary	Wilmington MSA, NC	Y	37490 FQ	60670 AW	91250 TQ	NCBLS	10/01-12/01
Postsecondary	North Dakota	Y	23460 FQ	47230 AW	67970 TQ	NDBLS	10/01-12/01
Postsecondary	Fargo-Moorhead MSA, ND-MN	Y	38060 FQ	55080 AW	76110 TQ	NDBLS	10/01-12/01
Postsecondary	Ohio	Y	31930 FQ	56840 AW	92400 TQ	OHBLS	10/01-12/01
Postsecondary	Akron PMSA, OH	Y	42800 FQ	60470 AW	85300 TQ	OHBLS	10/01-12/01
Postsecondary	Cincinnati PMSA, OH-KY-IN	Y	38680 FQ	69640 AW	112810 TQ	OHBLS	10/01-12/01
Postsecondary	Cleveland-Lorain-Elyria PMSA, OH	Y	37700 FQ	69510 AW	117350 TQ	OHBLS	10/01-12/01
Postsecondary	Columbus MSA, OH	Y	27960 FQ	47440 AW	71740 TQ	OHBLS	10/01-12/01
Postsecondary	Dayton-Springfield MSA, OH	Y	31840 FQ	53330 AW	75150 TQ	OHBLS	10/01-12/01
Postsecondary	Toledo MSA, OH	Y	31980 FQ	56520 AW	84520 TQ	OHBLS	10/01-12/01
Postsecondary	Youngstown-Warren MSA, OH	Y	34880 FQ	54010 AW	97540 TQ	OHBLS	10/01-12/01
Postsecondary	Oklahoma	Y	30450 FQ	44060 AW	64630 TQ	OKBLS	10/01-12/01
Postsecondary	Oklahoma City MSA, OK	Y	29630 FQ	45660 AW	67220 TQ	OKBLS	10/01-12/01
Postsecondary	Oregon	Y	38260 FQ	66560 AW	103780 TQ	ORBLS	10/01-12/01
Postsecondary	Portland-Vancouver PMSA, OR-WA	Y	37110 FQ	65910 AW	108060 TQ	ORBLS	10/01-12/01
Postsecondary	Pennsylvania	Y	28600 FQ	58620 AW	93380 TQ	PABLS	10/01-12/01
Postsecondary	Allentown-Bethlehem-Easton MSA, PA	Y	29210 FQ	46920 AW	70040 TQ	PABLS	10/01-12/01
Postsecondary	Harrisburg-Lebanon-Carlisle MSA, PA	Y	41150 FQ	72790 AW	126080 TQ	PABLS	10/01-12/01
Postsecondary	Lancaster MSA, PA	Y	28560 FQ	63740 AW	94600 TQ	PABLS	10/01-12/01
Postsecondary	Philadelphia PMSA, PA-NJ	Y	30090 FQ	59940 AW	94100 TQ	PABLS	10/01-12/01
Postsecondary	Pittsburgh MSA, PA	Y	26020 FQ	55110 AW	92110 TQ	PABLS	10/01-12/01
Postsecondary	Reading MSA, PA	Y	28840 FQ	56760 AW	89280 TQ	PABLS	10/01-12/01
Postsecondary	Scranton-Wilkes-Barre-Hazleton MSA, PA	Y	33130 FQ	56270 AW	86100 TQ	PABLS	10/01-12/01
Postsecondary	Rhode Island	Y	38840 FQ	71110 AW	110930 TQ	RIBLS	10/01-12/01
Postsecondary	Providence-Fall River-Warwick MSA, RI-MA	Y	38250 FQ	69680 AW	107670 TQ	RIBLS	10/01-12/01
Postsecondary	South Carolina	Y	32710 FQ	49030 AW	72660 TQ	SCBLS	10/01-12/01
Postsecondary	Charleston-North Charleston MSA, SC	Y	31040 FQ	43550 AW	58100 TQ	SCBLS	10/01-12/01
Postsecondary	Columbia MSA, SC	Y	31010 FQ	50760 AW	81510 TQ	SCBLS	10/01-12/01
Postsecondary	Greenville-Spartanburg-Anderson MSA, SC	Y	36390 FQ	52430 AW	80380 TQ	SCBLS	10/01-12/01
Postsecondary	South Dakota	Y	36700 FQ	67750 AW	115230 TQ	SDBLS	10/01-12/01
Postsecondary	Tennessee	Y	30460 FQ	52940 AW	81220 TQ	TNBLS	10/01-12/01
Postsecondary	Chattanooga MSA, TN-GA	Y	30300 FQ	43230 AW	57740 TQ	TNBLS	10/01-12/01
Postsecondary	Johnson City-Kingsport-Bristol MSA, TN-VA	Y	26600 FQ	56810 AW	96610 TQ	TNBLS	10/01-12/01
Postsecondary	Knoxville MSA, TN	Y	36480 FQ	60170 AW	99020 TQ	TNBLS	10/01-12/01
Postsecondary	Memphis MSA, TN-AR-MS	Y	31920 FQ	50990 AW	72760 TQ	TNBLS	10/01-12/01
Postsecondary	Nashville MSA, TN	Y	36080 FQ	54390 AW	76560 TQ	TNBLS	10/01-12/01
Postsecondary	Texas	Y	34750 FQ	73060 AW	139430 TQ	TXBLS	10/01-12/01
Postsecondary	Austin-San Marcos MSA, TX	Y	46860 FQ	62620 AW	76910 TQ	TXBLS	10/01-12/01
Postsecondary	Dallas PMSA, TX	Y	30770 FQ	61440 AW	116170 TQ	TXBLS	10/01-12/01
Postsecondary	El Paso MSA, TX	Y	28710 FQ	60800 AW	113370 TQ	TXBLS	10/01-12/01
Postsecondary	Fort Worth-Arlington PMSA, TX	Y	28320 FQ	53230 AW	81830 TQ	TXBLS	10/01-12/01
Postsecondary	Houston PMSA, TX	Y	35890 FQ	73350 AW	133380 TQ	TXBLS	10/01-12/01
Postsecondary	Odessa-Midland MSA, TX	Y	30020 FQ	46980 AW	80580 TQ	TXBLS	10/01-12/01
Postsecondary	Utah	Y	38760 FQ	66490 AW	108060 TQ	UTBLS	10/01-12/01
Postsecondary	Salt Lake City-Ogden MSA, UT	Y	38000 FQ	64890 AW	113800 TQ	UTBLS	10/01-12/01
Postsecondary	Vermont	Y	36390 FQ	48740 AW	70110 TQ	VTBLS	10/01-12/01
Postsecondary	Burlington MSA, VT	Y	36410 FQ	48620 AW	70170 TQ	VTBLS	10/01-12/01
Postsecondary	Virginia	Y	28940 FQ	60970 AW	101250 TQ	VABLS	10/01-12/01
Postsecondary	Norfolk-Virginia Beach-Newport News MSA, VA-NC	Y	28460 FQ	56530 AW	88540 TQ	VABLS	10/01-12/01
Postsecondary	Richmond-Petersburg MSA, VA	Y	27330 FQ	63600 AW	103630 TQ	VABLS	10/01-12/01
Postsecondary	Washington	Y	33870 FQ	68620 AW	122270 TQ	WABLS	10/01-12/01
Postsecondary	Seattle-Bellevue-Everett PMSA, WA	Y	37940 FQ	76960 AW	134350 TQ	WABLS	10/01-12/01
Postsecondary	Spokane MSA, WA	Y	32490 FQ	58570 AW	95780 TQ	WABLS	10/01-12/01

AAW Average annual wage; **AE** Average entry wage; **AEX** Average experienced wage; **AO** Average offered; **AOH** Average offered, high; **AOL** Average offered, low; **APH** Average pay, high range; **APL** Average pay, low range; **ASH** Average starting, high; **ASL** Average starting, low; **AW** Average wage paid; **FQ** First quartile wage; **H** Hourly; **HI** Highest wage paid; **HR** High end range; **LR** Low end range; **M** Monthly; **MTC** Median total compensation; **MW** Median wage paid; **SQ** Second quartile wage; **S** Special: hourly and annual; **TQ** Third quartile wage; **W** Weekly; **Y** Yearly

Occupation/Type/Industry	Location	Per	Low	Mid	High	Source	Date
Biological Science Teacher							
Postsecondary	Tacoma PMSA, WA	Y	33050 FQ	64870 AW	118970 TQ	WABLS	10/01-12/01
Postsecondary	West Virginia	Y	35990 FQ	59970 AW	90170 TQ	WVBLS	10/01-12/01
Postsecondary	Wisconsin	Y	33960 FQ	62210 AW	108870 TQ	WIBLS	10/01-12/01
Postsecondary	Milwaukee-Waukesha PMSA, WI	Y	32920 FQ	67810 AW	128920 TQ	WIBLS	10/01-12/01
Postsecondary	Wyoming	Y	32540 FQ	54570 AW	84890 TQ	WYBLS	10/01-12/01
Postsecondary	Puerto Rico	Y	28580 FQ	48540 AW	81320 TQ	PRBLS	10/01-12/01
Biological Technician	Alabama	Y	20090 FQ	32390 AW	48280 TQ	ALBLS	10/01-12/01
	Huntsville MSA, AL	Y	20240 FQ	30610 AW	44280 TQ	ALBLS	10/01-12/01
	Mobile MSA, AL	Y	16690 FQ	31660 AW	52660 TQ	ALBLS	10/01-12/01
	Alaska	Y	23250 FQ	29790 AW	38540 TQ	AKBLS	10/01-12/01
	Anchorage MSA, AK	Y	20280 FQ	28850 AW	39720 TQ	AKBLS	10/01-12/01
	Arizona	Y	20640 FQ	29150 AW	41290 TQ	AZBLS	10/01-12/01
	Phoenix-Mesa MSA, AZ	Y	22510 FQ	30200 AW	42180 TQ	AZBLS	10/01-12/01
	Tucson MSA, AZ	Y	19270 FQ	28300 AW	38420 TQ	AZBLS	10/01-12/01
	Arkansas	Y	18010 FQ	30770 AW	43930 TQ	ARBLS	10/01-12/01
	California	Y	21740 FQ	38070 AW	59660 TQ	CABLS	10/01-12/01
	Bakersfield MSA, CA	Y	23060 FQ	34260 AW	51720 TQ	CABLS	10/01-12/01
	Fresno MSA, CA	Y	17380 FQ	30520 AW	47050 TQ	CABLS	10/01-12/01
	Los Angeles-Long Beach PMSA, CA	Y	19560 FQ	36240 AW	60140 TQ	CABLS	10/01-12/01
	Oakland PMSA, CA	Y	25430 FQ	40940 AW	62020 TQ	CABLS	10/01-12/01
	Orange County PMSA, CA	Y	22080 FQ	32050 AW	46520 TQ	CABLS	10/01-12/01
	Riverside-San Bernardino PMSA, CA	Y	23970 FQ	36060 AW	55270 TQ	CABLS	10/01-12/01
	Sacramento PMSA, CA	Y	23270 FQ	29790 AW	38380 TQ	CABLS	10/01-12/01
	Salinas MSA, CA	Y	18690 FQ	27340 AW	47160 TQ	CABLS	10/01-12/01
	San Diego MSA, CA	Y	22800 FQ	36430 AW	55000 TQ	CABLS	10/01-12/01
	San Francisco PMSA, CA	Y	28790 FQ	46370 AW	74060 TQ	CABLS	10/01-12/01
	San Jose PMSA, CA	Y	28520 FQ	44620 AW	60970 TQ	CABLS	10/01-12/01
	Santa Barbara-Santa Maria-Lompoc MSA, CA	Y	19730 FQ	30180 AW	39180 TQ	CABLS	10/01-12/01
	Santa Rosa PMSA, CA	Y	25780 FQ	33350 AW	47280 TQ	CABLS	10/01-12/01
	Vallejo-Fairfield-Napa PMSA, CA	Y	22390 FQ	32700 AW	44370 TQ	CABLS	10/01-12/01
	Ventura PMSA, CA	Y	20570 FQ	43030 AW	71920 TQ	CABLS	10/01-12/01
	Visalia-Tulare-Porterville MSA, CA	Y	18710 FQ	26700 AW	35490 TQ	CABLS	10/01-12/01
	Colorado	Y	20810 FQ	34650 AW	52330 TQ	COBLS	10/01-12/01
	Colorado Springs MSA, CO	Y	21060 FQ	32650 AW	47460 TQ	COBLS	10/01-12/01
	Denver PMSA, CO	Y	21010 FQ	31550 AW	45170 TQ	COBLS	10/01-12/01
	Fort Collins-Loveland MSA, CO	Y	18950 FQ	31140 AW	47520 TQ	COBLS	10/01-12/01
	Connecticut	Y	26210 FQ	37890 AW	51930 TQ	CTBLS	10/01-12/01
	Hartford MSA, CT	Y	24650 FQ	35540 AW	50190 TQ	CTBLS	10/01-12/01
	New Haven-Meriden PMSA, CT	Y	26820 FQ	38310 AW	51530 TQ	CTBLS	10/01-12/01
	Washington PMSA, DC-MD-VA-WV	Y	20690 FQ	34620 AW	49520 TQ	DCBLS	10/01-12/01
	Florida	Y	17470 FQ	27960 AW	39520 TQ	FLBLS	10/01-12/01
	Daytona Beach MSA, FL	Y	23960 FQ	27960 AW	34520 TQ	FLBLS	10/01-12/01
	Fort Lauderdale PMSA, FL	Y	24110 FQ	33420 AW	49900 TQ	FLBLS	10/01-12/01
	Fort Pierce-Port St. Lucie MSA, FL	Y	16040 FQ	24260 AW	34980 TQ	FLBLS	10/01-12/01
	Gainesville MSA, FL	Y	16980 FQ	28950 AW	42620 TQ	FLBLS	10/01-12/01
	Jacksonville MSA, FL	Y	17940 FQ	27930 AW	38570 TQ	FLBLS	10/01-12/01
	Melbourne-Titusville-Palm Bay MSA, FL	Y	19640 FQ	28270 AW	46310 TQ	FLBLS	10/01-12/01
	Miami PMSA, FL	Y	17140 FQ	27770 AW	39390 TQ	FLBLS	10/01-12/01
	Orlando MSA, FL	Y	20490 FQ	27860 AW	38250 TQ	FLBLS	10/01-12/01
	Tallahassee MSA, FL	Y	22470 FQ	31890 AW	50000 TQ	FLBLS	10/01-12/01
	Tampa-St. Petersburg-Clearwater MSA, FL	Y	18830 FQ	28330 AW	37800 TQ	FLBLS	10/01-12/01
	West Palm Beach-Boca Raton MSA, FL	Y	20430 FQ	26970 AW	34450 TQ	FLBLS	10/01-12/01
	Georgia	Y	18810 FQ	31250 AW	48620 TQ	GABLS	10/01-12/01
	Atlanta MSA, GA	Y	20430 FQ	31700 AW	48280 TQ	GABLS	10/01-12/01
	Augusta-Aiken MSA, GA-SC	Y	18680 FQ	29370 AW	43810 TQ	GABLS	10/01-12/01
	Macon MSA, GA	Y	15080 FQ	26510 AW	42850 TQ	GABLS	10/01-12/01
	Hawaii	Y	19990 FQ	30870 AW	43590 TQ	HIBLS	10/01-12/01
	Honolulu MSA, HI	Y	20620 FQ	29980 AW	42660 TQ	HIBLS	10/01-12/01

AAW	Average annual wage	AOH	Average offered, high	ASH	Average starting, high	H	Hourly	M	Monthly	S	Special: hourly and annual
AE	Average entry wage	AOL	Average offered, low	ASL	Average starting, low	HI	Highest wage paid	MTC	Median total compensation	TQ	Third quartile wage
AEX	Average experienced wage	APH	Average pay, high range	AW	Average wage paid	HR	High end range	MW	Median wage paid	W	Weekly
AO	Average offered	APL	Average pay, low range	FQ	First quartile wage	LR	Low end range	SQ	Second quartile wage	Y	Yearly

Occupation/Type/Industry	Location	Per	Low	Mid	High	Source	Date
Biological Technician	Idaho	Y	17900 FQ	29570 AW	46550 TQ	IDBLS	10/01-12/01
	Boise City MSA, ID	Y	18680 FQ	28600 AW	45410 TQ	IDBLS	10/01-12/01
	Illinois	Y	19060 FQ	33520 AW	52170 TQ	ILBLS	10/01-12/01
	Chicago PMSA, IL	Y	19460 FQ	33990 AW	53170 TQ	ILBLS	10/01-12/01
	Peoria-Pekin MSA, IL	Y	18350 FQ	30450 AW	44080 TQ	ILBLS	10/01-12/01
	Indiana	Y	23280 FQ	37490 AW	55570 TQ	INBLS	10/01-12/01
	Elkhart-Goshen MSA, IN	Y	25660 FQ	40310 AW	56230 TQ	INBLS	10/01-12/01
	Indianapolis MSA, IN	Y	26340 FQ	38220 AW	54620 TQ	INBLS	10/01-12/01
	Lafayette MSA, IN	Y	15330 FQ	31320 AW	49960 TQ	INBLS	10/01-12/01
	Iowa	Y	19240 FQ	32420 AW	45730 TQ	IABLS	10/01-12/01
	Des Moines MSA, IA	Y	27930 FQ	41200 AW	56140 TQ	IABLS	10/01-12/01
	Kansas	Y	19000 FQ	29810 AW	43040 TQ	KSBLS	10/01-12/01
	Kentucky	Y	18640 FQ	27870 AW	41300 TQ	KYBLS	10/01-12/01
	Louisiana	Y	17850 FQ	28590 AW	42530 TQ	LABLS	10/01-12/01
	Baton Rouge MSA, LA	Y	16960 FQ	30100 AW	42980 TQ	LABLS	10/01-12/01
	New Orleans MSA, LA	Y	18510 FQ	27730 AW	40160 TQ	LABLS	10/01-12/01
	Maine	Y	20700 FQ	31700 AW	45820 TQ	MEBLS	10/01-12/01
	Portland MSA, ME	Y	19580 FQ	28580 AW	41590 TQ	MEBLS	10/01-12/01
	Maryland	Y	21510 FQ	36330 AW	50960 TQ	MDBLS	10/01-12/01
	Baltimore PMSA, MD	Y	22530 FQ	34110 AW	47270 TQ	MDBLS	10/01-12/01
	Massachusetts	Y	24330 FQ	41550 AW	64520 TQ	MABLS	10/01-12/01
	Boston PMSA, MA-NH	Y	25180 FQ	42230 AW	65450 TQ	MABLS	10/01-12/01
	Lawrence PMSA, MA-NH	Y	22690 FQ	42780 AW	59750 TQ	MABLS	10/01-12/01
	Springfield MSA, MA	Y	18810 FQ	31150 AW	50220 TQ	MABLS	10/01-12/01
	Worcester PMSA, MA-CT	Y	18610 FQ	31750 AW	52000 TQ	MABLS	10/01-12/01
	Michigan	Y	18850 FQ	28370 AW	41810 TQ	MIBLS	10/01-12/01
	Ann Arbor PMSA, MI	Y	17980 FQ	27080 AW	36000 TQ	MIBLS	10/01-12/01
	Detroit PMSA, MI	Y	18310 FQ	24860 AW	34870 TQ	MIBLS	10/01-12/01
	Grand Rapids-Muskegon-Holland MSA, MI	Y	24310 FQ	37860 AW	54640 TQ	MIBLS	10/01-12/01
	Saginaw-Bay City-Midland MSA, MI	Y	17990 FQ	24030 AW	32070 TQ	MIBLS	10/01-12/01
	Minnesota	Y	21520 FQ	33900 AW	44960 TQ	MNBLS	10/01-12/01
	Duluth-Superior MSA, MN-WI	Y	16750 FQ	29810 AW	44260 TQ	MNBLS	10/01-12/01
	Minneapolis-St. Paul MSA, MN-WI	Y	20200 FQ	33540 AW	48950 TQ	MNBLS	10/01-12/01
	Mississippi	Y	14820 FQ	25540 AW	38230 TQ	MSBLS	10/01-12/01
	Missouri	Y	18150 FQ	32690 AW	50660 TQ	MOBLS	10/01-12/01
	Kansas City MSA, MO-KS	Y	20280 FQ	31380 AW	44730 TQ	MOBLS	10/01-12/01
	St. Louis MSA, MO-IL	Y	25740 FQ	37370 AW	52270 TQ	MOBLS	10/01-12/01
	Montana	Y	18850 FQ	28510 AW	41840 TQ	MTBLS	10/01-12/01
	Nebraska	Y	17010 FQ	27570 AW	38090 TQ	NEBLS	10/01-12/01
	Lincoln MSA, NE	Y	15360 FQ	24440 AW	35920 TQ	NEBLS	10/01-12/01
	Omaha MSA, NE-IA	Y	23190 FQ	32770 AW	44460 TQ	NEBLS	10/01-12/01
	Nevada	Y	21670 FQ	28590 AW	35230 TQ	NVBLS	10/01-12/01
	New Hampshire	Y	22610 FQ	34080 AW	51140 TQ	NHBLS	10/01-12/01
	New Jersey	Y	20730 FQ	35640 AW	53690 TQ	NJBLS	10/01-12/01
	Middlesex-Somerset-Hunterdon PMSA, NJ	Y	26800 FQ	40660 AW	56030 TQ	NJBLS	10/01-12/01
	Monmouth-Ocean PMSA, NJ	Y	20940 FQ	37500 AW	56680 TQ	NJBLS	10/01-12/01
	Newark PMSA, NJ	Y	23500 FQ	37960 AW	54800 TQ	NJBLS	10/01-12/01
	New Mexico	Y	19890 FQ	32790 AW	54210 TQ	NMBLS	10/01-12/01
	Albuquerque MSA, NM	Y	18730 FQ	29130 AW	42940 TQ	NMBLS	10/01-12/01
	New York	Y	22130 FQ	35090 AW	51840 TQ	NYBLS	10/01-12/01
	Albany-Schenectady-Troy MSA, NY	Y	20190 FQ	31150 AW	43980 TQ	NYBLS	10/01-12/01
	Buffalo-Niagara Falls MSA, NY	Y	20960 FQ	33610 AW	48070 TQ	NYBLS	10/01-12/01
	Nassau-Suffolk PMSA, NY	Y	24240 FQ	36970 AW	56180 TQ	NYBLS	10/01-12/01
	New York PMSA, NY	Y	23350 FQ	36320 AW	53150 TQ	NYBLS	10/01-12/01
	Rochester MSA, NY	Y	18160 FQ	31110 AW	43420 TQ	NYBLS	10/01-12/01
	North Carolina	Y	24010 FQ	35960 AW	49750 TQ	NCBLS	10/01-12/01
	Charlotte-Gastonia-Rock Hill MSA, NC-SC	Y	24180 FQ	40340 AW	92150 TQ	NCBLS	10/01-12/01
	Greensboro-Winston-Salem-High Point MSA, NC	Y	22100 FQ	29690 AW	38800 TQ	NCBLS	10/01-12/01
	Raleigh-Durham-Chapel Hill MSA, NC	Y	23370 FQ	36590 AW	50210 TQ	NCBLS	10/01-12/01
	North Dakota	Y	18280 FQ	29270 AW	44330 TQ	NDBLS	10/01-12/01
	Fargo-Moorhead MSA, ND-MN	Y	25360 FQ	36850 AW	51490 TQ	NDBLS	10/01-12/01
	Ohio	Y	21500 FQ	34280 AW	50430 TQ	OHBLS	10/01-12/01

AAW	Average annual wage	**AOH**	Average offered, high	**ASH**	Average starting, high	**H**	Hourly	**M**	Monthly	**S**	Special: hourly and annual
AE	Average entry wage	**AOL**	Average offered, low	**ASL**	Average starting, low	**HI**	Highest wage paid	**MTC**	Median total compensation	**TQ**	Third quartile wage
AEX	Average experienced wage	**APH**	Average pay, high range	**AW**	Average wage paid	**HR**	High end range	**MW**	Median wage paid	**W**	Weekly
AO	Average offered	**APL**	Average pay, low range	**FQ**	First quartile wage	**LR**	Low end range	**SQ**	Second quartile wage	**Y**	Yearly

Occupation/Type/Industry	Location	Per	Low	Mid	High	Source	Date
Biological Technician	Akron PMSA, OH	Y	17400 FQ	28290 AW	44080 TQ	OHBLS	10/01-12/01
	Cleveland-Lorain-Elyria PMSA, OH	Y	25010 FQ	39380 AW	55960 TQ	OHBLS	10/01-12/01
	Oklahoma	Y	18330 FQ	27770 AW	40990 TQ	OKBLS	10/01-12/01
	Oklahoma City MSA, OK	Y	18340 FQ	27820 AW	40540 TQ	OKBLS	10/01-12/01
	Tulsa MSA, OK	Y	19490 FQ	26730 AW	37530 TQ	OKBLS	10/01-12/01
	Oregon	Y	19440 FQ	29030 AW	40910 TQ	ORBLS	10/01-12/01
	Eugene-Springfield MSA, OR	Y	19970 FQ	29160 AW	42190 TQ	ORBLS	10/01-12/01
	Medford-Ashland MSA, OR	Y	18300 FQ	26370 AW	35170 TQ	ORBLS	10/01-12/01
	Portland-Vancouver PMSA, OR-WA	Y	21230 FQ	30130 AW	42180 TQ	ORBLS	10/01-12/01
	Pennsylvania	Y	23790 FQ	34960 AW	46160 TQ	PABLS	10/01-12/01
	Lancaster MSA, PA	Y	27760 FQ	36870 AW	43800 TQ	PABLS	10/01-12/01
	Philadelphia PMSA, PA-NJ	Y	24780 FQ	35440 AW	46220 TQ	PABLS	10/01-12/01
	Pittsburgh MSA, PA	Y	24150 FQ	34960 AW	55540 TQ	PABLS	10/01-12/01
	Rhode Island	Y	17850 FQ	29990 AW	43530 TQ	RIBLS	10/01-12/01
	Providence-Fall River-Warwick MSA, RI-MA	Y	18490 FQ	30910 AW	44200 TQ	RIBLS	10/01-12/01
	South Carolina	Y	17610 FQ	32390 AW	50410 TQ	SCBLS	10/01-12/01
	Charleston-North Charleston MSA, SC	Y	15300 FQ	25250 AW	40590 TQ	SCBLS	10/01-12/01
	Columbia MSA, SC	Y	15420 FQ	33260 AW	52650 TQ	SCBLS	10/01-12/01
	South Dakota	Y	17560 FQ	24630 AW	34750 TQ	SDBLS	10/01-12/01
	Tennessee	Y	16610 FQ	27460 AW	39410 TQ	TNBLS	10/01-12/01
	Memphis MSA, TN-AR-MS	Y	17620 FQ	30480 AW	41420 TQ	TNBLS	10/01-12/01
	Nashville MSA, TN	Y	17300 FQ	26630 AW	37690 TQ	TNBLS	10/01-12/01
	Texas	Y	17660 FQ	30440 AW	45650 TQ	TXBLS	10/01-12/01
	Austin-San Marcos MSA, TX	Y	23270 FQ	29880 AW	36650 TQ	TXBLS	10/01-12/01
	Brazoria PMSA, TX	Y	19800 FQ	29630 AW	40900 TQ	TXBLS	10/01-12/01
	Corpus Christi MSA, TX	Y	20550 FQ	31910 AW	50560 TQ	TXBLS	10/01-12/01
	Dallas PMSA, TX	Y	20590 FQ	33300 AW	48350 TQ	TXBLS	10/01-12/01
	Fort Worth-Arlington PMSA, TX	Y	19860 FQ	31840 AW	49860 TQ	TXBLS	10/01-12/01
	Houston PMSA, TX	Y	15380 FQ	26440 AW	44560 TQ	TXBLS	10/01-12/01
	Lubbock MSA, TX	Y	14770 FQ	22620 AW	38800 TQ	TXBLS	10/01-12/01
	McAllen-Edinburg-Mission MSA, TX	Y	16800 FQ	28240 AW	41740 TQ	TXBLS	10/01-12/01
	San Antonio MSA, TX	Y	24660 FQ	36780 AW	54800 TQ	TXBLS	10/01-12/01
	Utah	Y	17120 FQ	28560 AW	43920 TQ	UTBLS	10/01-12/01
	Provo-Orem MSA, UT	Y	18780 FQ	26990 AW	35740 TQ	UTBLS	10/01-12/01
	Salt Lake City-Ogden MSA, UT	Y	19130 FQ	31970 AW	50600 TQ	UTBLS	10/01-12/01
	Vermont	Y	22640 FQ	29440 AW	39960 TQ	VTBLS	10/01-12/01
	Burlington MSA, VT	Y	23300 FQ	30670 AW	40840 TQ	VTBLS	10/01-12/01
	Virginia	Y	20720 FQ	30800 AW	43760 TQ	VABLS	10/01-12/01
	Norfolk-Virginia Beach-Newport News MSA, VA-NC	Y	19080 FQ	31240 AW	52020 TQ	VABLS	10/01-12/01
	Richmond-Petersburg MSA, VA	Y	22380 FQ	30540 AW	44860 TQ	VABLS	10/01-12/01
	Washington	Y	23480 FQ	34850 AW	50020 TQ	WABLS	10/01-12/01
	Olympia PMSA, WA	Y	23450 FQ	31800 AW	41850 TQ	WABLS	10/01-12/01
	Richland-Kennewick-Pasco MSA, WA	Y	21630 FQ	31850 AW	44390 TQ	WABLS	10/01-12/01
	Seattle-Bellevue-Everett PMSA, WA	Y	24960 FQ	36730 AW	53710 TQ	WABLS	10/01-12/01
	Tacoma PMSA, WA	Y	26720 FQ	39500 AW	54740 TQ	WABLS	10/01-12/01
	Yakima MSA, WA	Y	18780 FQ	29580 AW	47530 TQ	WABLS	10/01-12/01
	West Virginia	Y	19090 FQ	31780 AW	49350 TQ	WVBLS	10/01-12/01
	Huntington-Ashland MSA, WV-KY-OH	Y	23880 FQ	41840 AW	56180 TQ	WVBLS	10/01-12/01
	Wisconsin	Y	19720 FQ	29900 AW	44460 TQ	WIBLS	10/01-12/01
	Milwaukee-Waukesha PMSA, WI	Y	19670 FQ	30520 AW	46850 TQ	WIBLS	10/01-12/01
	Wyoming	Y	19810 FQ	28120 AW	36560 TQ	WYBLS	10/01-12/01
	Puerto Rico	Y	15110 FQ	23080 AW	33580 TQ	PRBLS	10/01-12/01
Biomedical Engineer	Alabama	Y	22220 FQ	35270 AW	43500 TQ	ALBLS	10/01-12/01
	Arizona	Y	39160 FQ	57370 AW	88120 TQ	AZBLS	10/01-12/01
	Phoenix-Mesa MSA, AZ	Y	39360 FQ	53910 AW	82780 TQ	AZBLS	10/01-12/01
	Tucson MSA, AZ	Y	34740 FQ	49980 AW	60720 TQ	AZBLS	10/01-12/01
	California	Y	46480 FQ	73980 AW	123220 TQ	CABLS	10/01-12/01

AAW Average annual wage	**AOH** Average offered, high	**ASH** Average starting, high	**H** Hourly	**M** Monthly	**S** Special: hourly and annual
AE Average entry wage	**AOL** Average offered, low	**ASL** Average starting, low	**HI** Highest wage paid	**MTC** Median total compensation	**TQ** Third quartile wage
AEX Average experienced wage	**APH** Average pay, high range	**AW** Average wage paid	**HR** High end range	**MW** Median wage paid	**W** Weekly
AO Average offered	**APL** Average pay, low range	**FQ** First quartile wage	**LR** Low end range	**SQ** Second quartile wage	**Y** Yearly

Occupation/Type/Industry	Location	Per	Low	Mid	High	Source	Date
Biomedical Engineer	Los Angeles-Long Beach PMSA, CA	Y	41870 FQ	62360 AW	87770 TQ	CABLS	10/01-12/01
	Oakland PMSA, CA	Y	48920 FQ	71030 AW	103070 TQ	CABLS	10/01-12/01
	Orange County PMSA, CA	Y	45800 FQ	88240 AW		CABLS	10/01-12/01
	San Diego MSA, CA	Y	46830 FQ	75690 AW	125250 TQ	CABLS	10/01-12/01
	San Francisco PMSA, CA	Y	46360 FQ	80390 AW	136800 TQ	CABLS	10/01-12/01
	San Jose PMSA, CA	Y	54380 FQ	84330 AW	132830 TQ	CABLS	10/01-12/01
	Santa Barbara-Santa Maria-Lompoc MSA, CA	Y	48590 FQ	63300 AW	87270 TQ	CABLS	10/01-12/01
	Colorado	Y	45940 FQ	60880 AW	77280 TQ	COBLS	10/01-12/01
	Denver PMSA, CO	Y	47940 FQ	60870 AW	74300 TQ	COBLS	10/01-12/01
	Connecticut	Y	38780 FQ	54260 AW	73840 TQ	CTBLS	10/01-12/01
	Hartford MSA, CT	Y	39870 FQ	53540 AW	71670 TQ	CTBLS	10/01-12/01
	Wilmington-Newark PMSA, DE-MD	Y	24900 FQ	50630 AW	98600 TQ	DEBLS	10/01-12/01
	Washington PMSA, DC-MD-VA-WV	Y	45250 FQ	70310 AW	102030 TQ	DCBLS	10/01-12/01
	Florida	Y	27410 FQ	53120 AW	85410 TQ	FLBLS	10/01-12/01
	Fort Lauderdale PMSA, FL	Y	25560 FQ	41660 AW	58520 TQ	FLBLS	10/01-12/01
	Jacksonville MSA, FL	Y	16750 FQ	35160 AW	55800 TQ	FLBLS	10/01-12/01
	Miami PMSA, FL	Y	36910 FQ	53310 AW	73600 TQ	FLBLS	10/01-12/01
	Orlando MSA, FL	Y	47070 FQ	66010 AW	100010 TQ	FLBLS	10/01-12/01
	Tampa-St. Petersburg-Clearwater MSA, FL	Y	32190 FQ	49040 AW	67480 TQ	FLBLS	10/01-12/01
	Georgia	Y	33240 FQ	53510 AW	79020 TQ	GABLS	10/01-12/01
	Atlanta MSA, GA	Y	37810 FQ	54710 AW	80690 TQ	GABLS	10/01-12/01
	Illinois	Y	43780 FQ	62550 AW	86080 TQ	ILBLS	10/01-12/01
	Chicago PMSA, IL	Y	45990 FQ	63750 AW	86780 TQ	ILBLS	10/01-12/01
	Indiana	Y	31580 FQ	56800 AW	85550 TQ	INBLS	10/01-12/01
	Indianapolis MSA, IN	Y	26740 FQ	46710 AW	68550 TQ	INBLS	10/01-12/01
	Kentucky	Y	29620 FQ	50240 AW	71490 TQ	KYBLS	10/01-12/01
	Louisiana	Y	31350 FQ	51710 AW	79190 TQ	LABLS	10/01-12/01
	Maine	Y	41340 FQ	68360 AW	95030 TQ	MEBLS	10/01-12/01
	Maryland	Y	38320 FQ	64030 AW	93320 TQ	MDBLS	10/01-12/01
	Baltimore PMSA, MD	Y	35010 FQ	55450 AW	86790 TQ	MDBLS	10/01-12/01
	Massachusetts	Y	39630 FQ	65790 AW	97740 TQ	MABLS	10/01-12/01
	Boston PMSA, MA-NH	Y	44280 FQ	69370 AW	100030 TQ	MABLS	10/01-12/01
	Michigan	Y	37220 FQ	54960 AW	78780 TQ	MIBLS	10/01-12/01
	Minnesota	Y	45040 FQ	64310 AW	89200 TQ	MNBLS	10/01-12/01
	Minneapolis-St. Paul MSA, MN-WI	Y	46500 FQ	65820 AW	90020 TQ	MNBLS	10/01-12/01
	Missouri	Y	40060 FQ	61600 AW	89700 TQ	MOBLS	10/01-12/01
	St. Louis MSA, MO-IL	Y	43090 FQ	64940 AW	92340 TQ	MOBLS	10/01-12/01
	Nebraska	Y	29520 FQ	51560 AW	77400 TQ	NEBLS	10/01-12/01
	New Hampshire	Y	44190 FQ	73090 AW		NHBLS	10/01-12/01
	Nashua PMSA, NH	Y	47280 FQ	76030 AW		NHBLS	10/01-12/01
	New Jersey	Y	48000 FQ	76980 AW	111270 TQ	NJBLS	10/01-12/01
	Newark PMSA, NJ	Y	50360 FQ	79230 AW	114200 TQ	NJBLS	10/01-12/01
	New York	Y	45300 FQ	67480 AW	100040 TQ	NYBLS	10/01-12/01
	Albany-Schenectady-Troy MSA, NY	Y	49500 FQ	57680 AW	70650 TQ	NYBLS	10/01-12/01
	Buffalo-Niagara Falls MSA, NY	Y	44570 FQ	65320 AW	92210 TQ	NYBLS	10/01-12/01
	Nassau-Suffolk PMSA, NY	Y	50090 FQ	95410 AW	142780 TQ	NYBLS	10/01-12/01
	New York PMSA, NY	Y	39890 FQ	61770 AW	89710 TQ	NYBLS	10/01-12/01
	North Carolina	Y	33720 FQ	50940 AW	75970 TQ	NCBLS	10/01-12/01
	Raleigh-Durham-Chapel Hill MSA, NC	Y	33120 FQ	50250 AW	77070 TQ	NCBLS	10/01-12/01
	Ohio	Y	38250 FQ	58480 AW	85210 TQ	OHBLS	10/01-12/01
	Cincinnati PMSA, OH-KY-IN	Y	34640 FQ	52630 AW	73650 TQ	OHBLS	10/01-12/01
	Oklahoma	Y	36320 FQ	52870 AW	71240 TQ	OKBLS	10/01-12/01
	Oklahoma City MSA, OK	Y	36580 FQ	56010 AW	123280 TQ	OKBLS	10/01-12/01
	Tulsa MSA, OK	Y	37400 FQ	51360 AW	70360 TQ	OKBLS	10/01-12/01
	Oregon	Y	36350 FQ	53560 AW	80530 TQ	ORBLS	10/01-12/01
	Portland-Vancouver PMSA, OR-WA	Y	37000 FQ	45970 AW	58650 TQ	ORBLS	10/01-12/01
	Pennsylvania	Y	38800 FQ	61450 AW	86810 TQ	PABLS	10/01-12/01
	Philadelphia PMSA, PA-NJ	Y	38870 FQ	62250 AW	89350 TQ	PABLS	10/01-12/01
	Pittsburgh MSA, PA	Y	44720 FQ	65290 AW	85550 TQ	PABLS	10/01-12/01
	Providence-Fall River-Warwick MSA, RI-MA	Y	43110 FQ	64220 AW	92040 TQ	RIBLS	10/01-12/01
	South Carolina	Y	29500 FQ	45490 AW	72390 TQ	SCBLS	10/01-12/01

AAW	Average annual wage	**AOH**	Average offered, high	**ASH**	Average starting, high	**H**	Hourly	**M**	Monthly	**S**	Special: hourly and annual
AE	Average entry wage	**AOL**	Average offered, low	**ASL**	Average starting, low	**HI**	Highest wage paid	**MTC**	Median total compensation	**TQ**	Third quartile wage
AEX	Average experienced wage	**APH**	Average pay, high range	**AW**	Average wage paid	**HR**	High end range	**MW**	Median wage paid	**W**	Weekly
AO	Average offered	**APL**	Average pay, low range	**FQ**	First quartile wage	**LR**	Low end range	**SQ**	Second quartile wage	**Y**	Yearly

Occupation/Type/Industry	Location	Per	Low	Mid	High	Source	Date
Biomedical Engineer	Tennessee	Y	36590 FQ	63480 AW	105900 TQ	TNBLS	10/01-12/01
	Texas	Y	39600 FQ	66090 AW	98390 TQ	TXBLS	10/01-12/01
	Dallas PMSA, TX	Y	36520 FQ	52140 AW	69740 TQ	TXBLS	10/01-12/01
	Houston PMSA, TX	Y	40440 FQ	67810 AW	123060 TQ	TXBLS	10/01-12/01
	Utah	Y	39590 FQ	49910 AW	65700 TQ	UTBLS	10/01-12/01
	Salt Lake City-Ogden MSA, UT	Y	39660 FQ	48470 AW	60070 TQ	UTBLS	10/01-12/01
	Virginia	Y	51100 FQ	71950 AW	105360 TQ	VABLS	10/01-12/01
	Washington	Y	41970 FQ	70770 AW	119740 TQ	WABLS	10/01-12/01
	Seattle-Bellevue-Everett PMSA, WA	Y	44910 FQ	75020 AW	139960 TQ	WABLS	10/01-12/01
	Wisconsin	Y	31610 FQ	55180 AW	84100 TQ	WIBLS	10/01-12/01
	Milwaukee-Waukesha PMSA, WI	Y	34700 FQ	59180 AW	85420 TQ	WIBLS	10/01-12/01
Biomedical Products Professional	San Diego, CA	Y		46227 AW		SDBJ1	1/99-1/00
Biotechnology Professional	San Diego, CA	Y		70259 AW		SDBJ1	1/99-1/00
Boilermaker	Alabama	H	6.26 FQ	14.59 AW	23.61 TQ	ALBLS	10/01-12/01
	Arizona	H	17.97 FQ	20.46 AW	25.07 TQ	AZBLS	10/01-12/01
	Phoenix-Mesa MSA, AZ	H	17.97 FQ	20.46 AW	25.07 TQ	AZBLS	10/01-12/01
	California	H	14.75 FQ	24.00 AW	35.72 TQ	CABLS	10/01-12/01
	Los Angeles-Long Beach PMSA, CA	H	16.27 FQ	24.23 AW	34.60 TQ	CABLS	10/01-12/01
	Orange County PMSA, CA	H	10.97 FQ	20.95 AW	34.68 TQ	CABLS	10/01-12/01
	Riverside-San Bernardino PMSA, CA	H	17.28 FQ	27.99 AW	39.32 TQ	CABLS	10/01-12/01
	San Diego MSA, CA	H	12.34 FQ	16.53 AW	21.72 TQ	CABLS	10/01-12/01
	Colorado	H	11.76 FQ	16.46 AW	21.17 TQ	COBLS	10/01-12/01
	Connecticut	H	9.37 FQ	17.87 AW	25.51 TQ	CTBLS	10/01-12/01
	Stamford-Norwalk PMSA, CT	H	7.05 FQ	15.42 AW	25.81 TQ	CTBLS	10/01-12/01
	Washington PMSA, DC-MD-VA-WV	H	13.53 FQ	20.72 AW	27.68 TQ	DCBLS	10/01-12/01
	Florida	H	10.81 FQ	16.32 AW	20.87 TQ	FLBLS	10/01-12/01
	Lakeland-Winter Haven MSA, FL	H	15.37 FQ	19.53 AW	22.97 TQ	FLBLS	10/01-12/01
	Tampa-St. Petersburg-Clearwater MSA, FL	H	5.43 FQ	10.50 AW	18.88 TQ	FLBLS	10/01-12/01
	West Palm Beach-Boca Raton MSA, FL	H	13.00 FQ	17.62 AW	21.98 TQ	FLBLS	10/01-12/01
	Georgia	H	13.06 FQ	20.78 AW	28.12 TQ	GABLS	10/01-12/01
	Augusta-Aiken MSA, GA-SC	H	7.77 FQ	17.54 AW	25.64 TQ	GABLS	10/01-12/01
	Hawaii	H	15.55 FQ	23.92 AW	31.91 TQ	HIBLS	10/01-12/01
	Honolulu MSA, HI	H	15.27 FQ	23.78 AW	31.89 TQ	HIBLS	10/01-12/01
	Idaho	H	7.25 FQ	16.21 AW	25.33 TQ	IDBLS	10/01-12/01
	Illinois	H	6.60 FQ	22.23 AW	38.87 TQ	ILBLS	10/01-12/01
	Chicago PMSA, IL	H	13.50 FQ	25.82 AW	40.39 TQ	ILBLS	10/01-12/01
	Peoria-Pekin MSA, IL	H	21.84 FQ	24.37 AW	27.51 TQ	ILBLS	10/01-12/01
	Indiana	H	12.31 FQ	21.30 AW	28.56 TQ	INBLS	10/01-12/01
	Gary PMSA, IN	H	15.26 FQ	20.97 AW	27.13 TQ	INBLS	10/01-12/01
	Iowa	H	14.18 FQ	19.05 AW	26.38 TQ	IABLS	10/01-12/01
	Davenport-Moline-Rock Island MSA, IA-IL	H	11.46 FQ	18.41 AW	26.97 TQ	IABLS	10/01-12/01
	Kansas	H	9.15 FQ	15.34 AW	21.46 TQ	KSBLS	10/01-12/01
	Kentucky	H	14.68 FQ	19.19 AW	22.97 TQ	KYBLS	10/01-12/01
	Lexington MSA, KY	H	15.08 FQ	18.25 AW	22.20 TQ	KYBLS	10/01-12/01
	Louisiana	H	12.71 FQ	17.33 AW	22.15 TQ	LABLS	10/01-12/01
	Baton Rouge MSA, LA	H	13.80 FQ	17.20 AW	20.99 TQ	LABLS	10/01-12/01
	Lake Charles MSA, LA	H	9.19 FQ	16.13 AW	25.86 TQ	LABLS	10/01-12/01
	New Orleans MSA, LA	H	14.37 FQ	18.05 AW	22.11 TQ	LABLS	10/01-12/01
	Maine	H	13.07 FQ	18.69 AW	24.93 TQ	MEBLS	10/01-12/01
	Maryland	H	14.65 FQ	21.76 AW	28.08 TQ	MDBLS	10/01-12/01
	Baltimore PMSA, MD	H	15.78 FQ	21.99 AW	28.12 TQ	MDBLS	10/01-12/01
	Massachusetts	H	11.04 FQ	18.84 AW	26.64 TQ	MABLS	10/01-12/01
	Boston PMSA, MA-NH	H	16.13 FQ	19.81 AW	25.34 TQ	MABLS	10/01-12/01
	Springfield MSA, MA	H	10.58 FQ	15.80 AW	23.27 TQ	MABLS	10/01-12/01
	Michigan	H	15.18 FQ	23.44 AW	30.12 TQ	MIBLS	10/01-12/01
	Detroit PMSA, MI	H	17.80 FQ	24.16 AW	28.44 TQ	MIBLS	10/01-12/01
	Grand Rapids-Muskegon-Holland MSA, MI	H	12.28 FQ	20.89 AW	33.44 TQ	MIBLS	10/01-12/01
	Minnesota	H	19.14 FQ	25.27 AW	31.57 TQ	MNBLS	10/01-12/01

AAW Average annual wage; AE Average entry wage; AEX Average experienced wage; AO Average offered; AOH Average offered, high; AOL Average offered, low; APH Average pay, high range; APL Average pay, low range; ASH Average starting, high; ASL Average starting, low; AW Average wage paid; FQ First quartile wage; H Hourly; HI Highest wage paid; HR High end range; LR Low end range; M Monthly; MTC Median total compensation; MW Median wage paid; SQ Second quartile wage; S Special: hourly and annual; TQ Third quartile wage; W Weekly; Y Yearly

Occupation/Type/Industry	Location	Per	Low	Mid	High	Source	Date
Boilermaker	Minneapolis-St. Paul MSA, MN-WI	H	22.63 FQ	25.95 AW	32.01 TQ	MNBLS	10/01-12/01
	Mississippi	H	11.33 FQ	18.39 AW	22.40 TQ	MSBLS	10/01-12/01
	Missouri	H	13.02 FQ	20.78 AW	28.52 TQ	MOBLS	10/01-12/01
	Kansas City MSA, MO-KS	H	9.49 FQ	20.19 AW	28.76 TQ	MOBLS	10/01-12/01
	Montana	H	19.19 FQ	22.87 AW	26.72 TQ	MTBLS	10/01-12/01
	Omaha MSA, NE-IA	H	13.98 FQ	18.16 AW	21.45 TQ	NEBLS	10/01-12/01
	Nevada	H	18.13 FQ	22.10 AW	32.92 TQ	NVBLS	10/01-12/01
	New Hampshire	H	12.11 FQ	18.72 AW	26.60 TQ	NHBLS	10/01-12/01
	New Jersey	H	22.35 FQ	28.40 AW	35.47 TQ	NJBLS	10/01-12/01
	Middlesex-Somerset-Hunterdon PMSA, NJ	H	20.72 FQ	28.15 AW	34.15 TQ	NJBLS	10/01-12/01
	Newark PMSA, NJ	H	17.88 FQ	30.94 AW	42.13 TQ	NJBLS	10/01-12/01
	New York	H	11.27 FQ	20.04 AW	26.86 TQ	NYBLS	10/01-12/01
	Albany-Schenectady-Troy MSA, NY	H	18.68 FQ	22.39 AW	26.36 TQ	NYBLS	10/01-12/01
	Buffalo-Niagara Falls MSA, NY	H	17.57 FQ	20.68 AW	26.66 TQ	NYBLS	10/01-12/01
	New York PMSA, NY	H	10.04 FQ	19.13 AW	32.36 TQ	NYBLS	10/01-12/01
	North Carolina	H	9.80 FQ	15.01 AW	22.17 TQ	NCBLS	10/01-12/01
	Charlotte-Gastonia-Rock Hill MSA, NC-SC	H	8.96 FQ	15.55 AW	29.11 TQ	NCBLS	10/01-12/01
	Ohio	H	12.87 FQ	20.43 AW	28.70 TQ	OHBLS	10/01-12/01
	Canton-Massillon MSA, OH	H	11.80 FQ	14.53 AW	17.18 TQ	OHBLS	10/01-12/01
	Cincinnati PMSA, OH-KY-IN	H	15.46 FQ	21.49 AW	27.27 TQ	OHBLS	10/01-12/01
	Cleveland-Lorain-Elyria PMSA, OH	H	16.09 FQ	23.95 AW	32.27 TQ	OHBLS	10/01-12/01
	Toledo MSA, OH	H	20.83 FQ	26.52 AW	33.82 TQ	OHBLS	10/01-12/01
	Oklahoma	H	7.62 FQ	12.29 AW	20.22 TQ	OKBLS	10/01-12/01
	Oklahoma City MSA, OK	H	6.61 FQ	9.90 AW	17.76 TQ	OKBLS	10/01-12/01
	Tulsa MSA, OK	H	7.28 FQ	12.29 AW	18.69 TQ	OKBLS	10/01-12/01
	Oregon	H	15.88 FQ	23.70 AW	32.28 TQ	ORBLS	10/01-12/01
	Pennsylvania	H	12.24 FQ	22.50 AW	28.96 TQ	PABLS	10/01-12/01
	Philadelphia PMSA, PA-NJ	H	17.94 FQ	27.13 AW	35.56 TQ	PABLS	10/01-12/01
	York MSA, PA	H	22.08 FQ	25.25 AW	28.76 TQ	PABLS	10/01-12/01
	Providence-Fall River-Warwick MSA, RI-MA	H	12.43 FQ	19.23 AW	32.30 TQ	RIBLS	10/01-12/01
	South Carolina	H	9.39 FQ	15.83 AW	21.05 TQ	SCBLS	10/01-12/01
	Greenville-Spartanburg-Anderson MSA, SC	H	9.12 FQ	11.84 AW	14.78 TQ	SCBLS	10/01-12/01
	Tennessee	H	14.41 FQ	18.88 AW	24.23 TQ	TNBLS	10/01-12/01
	Chattanooga MSA, TN-GA	H	14.76 FQ	18.84 AW	23.91 TQ	TNBLS	10/01-12/01
	Memphis MSA, TN-AR-MS	H	12.02 FQ	17.46 AW	22.09 TQ	TNBLS	10/01-12/01
	Texas	H	9.06 FQ	16.20 AW	21.43 TQ	TXBLS	10/01-12/01
	Beaumont-Port Arthur MSA, TX	H	8.11 FQ	14.96 AW	24.06 TQ	TXBLS	10/01-12/01
	Brazoria PMSA, TX	H	14.11 FQ	15.73 AW	18.02 TQ	TXBLS	10/01-12/01
	Corpus Christi MSA, TX	H	14.44 FQ	18.19 AW	21.27 TQ	TXBLS	10/01-12/01
	Houston PMSA, TX	H	9.64 FQ	17.08 AW	22.69 TQ	TXBLS	10/01-12/01
	San Antonio MSA, TX	H	7.87 FQ	9.57 AW	11.24 TQ	TXBLS	10/01-12/01
	Utah	H	11.62 FQ	19.35 AW	26.15 TQ	UTBLS	10/01-12/01
	Provo-Orem MSA, UT	H	13.46 FQ	20.69 AW	26.27 TQ	UTBLS	10/01-12/01
	Salt Lake City-Ogden MSA, UT	H	11.85 FQ	20.17 AW	26.69 TQ	UTBLS	10/01-12/01
	Virginia	H	12.27 FQ	18.65 AW	26.83 TQ	VABLS	10/01-12/01
	Norfolk-Virginia Beach-Newport News MSA, VA-NC	H	10.81 FQ	17.53 AW	21.69 TQ	VABLS	10/01-12/01
	Richmond-Petersburg MSA, VA	H	18.26 FQ	25.55 AW	33.20 TQ	VABLS	10/01-12/01
	Washington	H	18.13 FQ	24.47 AW	31.22 TQ	WABLS	10/01-12/01
	Seattle-Bellevue-Everett PMSA, WA	H	18.58 FQ	25.17 AW	33.58 TQ	WABLS	10/01-12/01
	West Virginia	H	15.37 FQ	22.31 AW	27.18 TQ	WVBLS	10/01-12/01
	Wisconsin	H	15.06 FQ	20.40 AW	27.16 TQ	WIBLS	10/01-12/01
	Milwaukee-Waukesha PMSA, WI	H	15.01 FQ	20.02 AW	26.73 TQ	WIBLS	10/01-12/01
	Puerto Rico	H	7.07 FQ	14.02 AW	26.60 TQ	PRBLS	10/01-12/01
Bookbinder	Alabama	H	6.48 FQ	11.57 AW	19.12 TQ	ALBLS	10/01-12/01
	Birmingham MSA, AL	H	6.41 FQ	11.18 AW	18.79 TQ	ALBLS	10/01-12/01
	Arizona	H	8.31 FQ	11.96 AW	16.44 TQ	AZBLS	10/01-12/01
	Phoenix-Mesa MSA, AZ	H	8.13 FQ	12.02 AW	16.57 TQ	AZBLS	10/01-12/01

AAW Average annual wage **AOH** Average offered, high **ASH** Average starting, high **H** Hourly **M** Monthly **S** Special: hourly and annual
AE Average entry wage **AOL** Average offered, low **ASL** Average starting, low **HI** Highest wage paid **MTC** Median total compensation **TQ** Third quartile wage
AEX Average experienced wage **APH** Average pay, high range **AW** Average wage paid **HR** High end range **MW** Median wage paid **W** Weekly
AO Average offered **APL** Average pay, low range **FQ** First quartile wage **LR** Low end range **SQ** Second quartile wage **Y** Yearly

Occupation/Type/Industry	Location	Per	Low	Mid	High	Source	Date
Bookbinder	California	H	7.71 FQ	13.67 AW	22.13 TQ	CABLS	10/01-12/01
	Los Angeles-Long Beach PMSA, CA	H	7.39 FQ	11.12 AW	17.10 TQ	CABLS	10/01-12/01
	Sacramento PMSA, CA	H	12.18 FQ	19.44 AW	25.41 TQ	CABLS	10/01-12/01
	San Diego MSA, CA	H	8.07 FQ	11.64 AW	13.79 TQ	CABLS	10/01-12/01
	Connecticut	H	9.86 FQ	16.45 AW	30.19 TQ	CTBLS	10/01-12/01
	New Haven-Meriden PMSA, CT	H	9.71 FQ	18.36 AW	34.52 TQ	CTBLS	10/01-12/01
	District of Columbia	H	27.68 FQ	31.07 AW	38.08 TQ	DCBLS	10/01-12/01
	Washington PMSA, DC-MD-VA-WV	H	10.65 FQ	21.22 AW	32.71 TQ	DCBLS	10/01-12/01
	Florida	H	7.16 FQ	11.18 AW	14.73 TQ	FLBLS	10/01-12/01
	Miami PMSA, FL	H	6.13 FQ	10.21 AW	13.89 TQ	FLBLS	10/01-12/01
	Georgia	H	6.76 FQ	9.97 AW	17.01 TQ	GABLS	10/01-12/01
	Illinois	H	7.06 FQ	12.02 AW	20.34 TQ	ILBLS	10/01-12/01
	Chicago PMSA, IL	H	6.96 FQ	12.18 AW	20.76 TQ	ILBLS	10/01-12/01
	Indiana	H	7.39 FQ	11.69 AW	17.13 TQ	INBLS	10/01-12/01
	Indianapolis MSA, IN	H	7.38 FQ	10.95 AW	16.54 TQ	INBLS	10/01-12/01
	Iowa	H	10.28 FQ	16.29 AW	21.57 TQ	IABLS	10/01-12/01
	Des Moines MSA, IA	H	12.00 FQ	17.67 AW	21.84 TQ	IABLS	10/01-12/01
	Kansas	H	7.38 FQ	14.02 AW	21.10 TQ	KSBLS	10/01-12/01
	Topeka MSA, KS	H	10.16 FQ	15.06 AW	20.30 TQ	KSBLS	10/01-12/01
	Maryland	H	8.08 FQ	18.24 AW	26.41 TQ	MDBLS	10/01-12/01
	Massachusetts	H	8.06 FQ	12.83 AW	19.83 TQ	MABLS	10/01-12/01
	Boston PMSA, MA-NH	H	9.12 FQ	13.85 AW	21.11 TQ	MABLS	10/01-12/01
	Michigan	H	10.55 FQ	19.00 AW	48.17 TQ	MIBLS	10/01-12/01
	Minnesota	H	12.15 FQ	18.15 AW	22.47 TQ	MNBLS	10/01-12/01
	Minneapolis-St. Paul MSA, MN-WI	H	12.62 FQ	18.42 AW	22.51 TQ	MNBLS	10/01-12/01
	Mississippi	H	8.73 FQ	10.82 AW	13.30 TQ	MSBLS	10/01-12/01
	Missouri	H	7.41 FQ	12.65 AW	18.41 TQ	MOBLS	10/01-12/01
	Kansas City MSA, MO-KS	H	8.18 FQ	13.93 AW	20.31 TQ	MOBLS	10/01-12/01
	St. Louis MSA, MO-IL	H	7.34 FQ	12.97 AW	20.16 TQ	MOBLS	10/01-12/01
	Nevada	H	8.05 FQ	11.31 AW	16.61 TQ	NVBLS	10/01-12/01
	New Jersey	H	5.90 FQ	11.54 AW	20.50 TQ	NJBLS	10/01-12/01
	Bergen-Passaic PMSA, NJ	H	5.63 FQ	9.23 AW	15.40 TQ	NJBLS	10/01-12/01
	New York	H	6.62 FQ	10.11 AW	13.92 TQ	NYBLS	10/01-12/01
	Nassau-Suffolk PMSA, NY	H	6.53 FQ	11.34 AW	17.07 TQ	NYBLS	10/01-12/01
	New York PMSA, NY	H	7.31 FQ	10.67 AW	13.75 TQ	NYBLS	10/01-12/01
	North Carolina	H	6.02 FQ	9.18 AW	14.03 TQ	NCBLS	10/01-12/01
	Ohio	H	6.59 FQ	11.75 AW	19.78 TQ	OHBLS	10/01-12/01
	Akron PMSA, OH	H	8.85 FQ	12.94 AW	20.43 TQ	OHBLS	10/01-12/01
	Cincinnati PMSA, OH-KY-IN	H	5.87 FQ	9.43 AW	15.91 TQ	OHBLS	10/01-12/01
	Cleveland-Lorain-Elyria PMSA, OH	H	9.60 FQ	14.25 AW	24.48 TQ	OHBLS	10/01-12/01
	Columbus MSA, OH	H	10.15 FQ	14.73 AW	21.23 TQ	OHBLS	10/01-12/01
	Dayton-Springfield MSA, OH	H	6.61 FQ	9.09 AW	11.95 TQ	OHBLS	10/01-12/01
	Oregon	H	7.92 FQ	13.09 AW	20.83 TQ	ORBLS	10/01-12/01
	Pennsylvania	H	9.18 FQ	14.33 AW	18.83 TQ	PABLS	10/01-12/01
	Philadelphia PMSA, PA-NJ	H	6.06 FQ	14.11 AW	22.96 TQ	PABLS	10/01-12/01
	Rhode Island	H	8.83 FQ	11.13 AW	15.82 TQ	RIBLS	10/01-12/01
	Providence-Fall River-Warwick MSA, RI-MA	H	8.74 FQ	10.98 AW	15.71 TQ	RIBLS	10/01-12/01
	Tennessee	H	9.41 FQ	11.37 AW	14.68 TQ	TNBLS	10/01-12/01
	Memphis MSA, TN-AR-MS	H	9.33 FQ	13.24 AW	20.34 TQ	TNBLS	10/01-12/01
	Nashville MSA, TN	H	9.45 FQ	11.20 AW	14.12 TQ	TNBLS	10/01-12/01
	Texas	H	5.93 FQ	11.51 AW	27.75 TQ	TXBLS	10/01-12/01
	Austin-San Marcos MSA, TX	H	5.86 FQ	10.27 AW	13.58 TQ	TXBLS	10/01-12/01
	Dallas PMSA, TX	H	5.88 FQ	9.15 AW	14.21 TQ	TXBLS	10/01-12/01
	Utah	H	9.95 FQ	13.29 AW	17.21 TQ	UTBLS	10/01-12/01
	Virginia	H	10.28 FQ	14.60 AW	18.31 TQ	VABLS	10/01-12/01
	Washington	H	17.08 FQ	20.56 AW	25.83 TQ	WABLS	10/01-12/01
	Seattle-Bellevue-Everett PMSA, WA	H	17.45 FQ	20.91 AW	26.31 TQ	WABLS	10/01-12/01
	Wisconsin	H	8.65 FQ	14.65 AW	21.12 TQ	WIBLS	10/01-12/01
	Milwaukee-Waukesha PMSA, WI	H	8.56 FQ	16.71 AW	21.58 TQ	WIBLS	10/01-12/01
	Puerto Rico	H	5.55 FQ	7.50 AW	10.63 TQ	PRBLS	10/01-12/01
Bookkeeping, Accounting, and Auditing Clerk	Alabama	H	7.43 FQ	11.87 AW	17.51 TQ	ALBLS	10/01-12/01
	Birmingham MSA, AL	H	8.73 FQ	13.28 AW	19.91 TQ	ALBLS	10/01-12/01

AAW Average annual wage	**AOH** Average offered, high	**ASH** Average starting, high	**H** Hourly
AE Average entry wage	**AOL** Average offered, low	**ASL** Average starting, low	**HI** Highest wage paid
AEX Average experienced wage	**APH** Average pay, high range	**AW** Average wage paid	**HR** High end range
AO Average offered	**APL** Average pay, low range	**FQ** First quartile wage	**LR** Low end range
M Monthly	**S** Special: hourly and annual		
MTC Median total compensation	**TQ** Third quartile wage		
MW Median wage paid	**W** Weekly		
SQ Second quartile wage	**Y** Yearly		

Occupation/Type/Industry	Location	Per	Low	Mid	High	Source	Date
Bookkeeping, Accounting, and Auditing Clerk	Huntsville MSA, AL	H	7.20 FQ	11.59 AW	16.59 TQ	ALBLS	10/01-12/01
	Mobile MSA, AL	H	7.78 FQ	12.05 AW	17.01 TQ	ALBLS	10/01-12/01
	Montgomery MSA, AL	H	7.46 FQ	11.90 AW	17.22 TQ	ALBLS	10/01-12/01
	Alaska	H	10.25 FQ	15.46 AW	21.44 TQ	AKBLS	10/01-12/01
	Anchorage MSA, AK	H	11.11 FQ	15.56 AW	20.95 TQ	AKBLS	10/01-12/01
	Arizona	H	8.18 FQ	13.40 AW	20.84 TQ	AZBLS	10/01-12/01
	Phoenix-Mesa MSA, AZ	H	8.29 FQ	13.94 AW	22.82 TQ	AZBLS	10/01-12/01
	Tucson MSA, AZ	H	8.28 FQ	12.21 AW	16.78 TQ	AZBLS	10/01-12/01
	Arkansas	H	7.59 FQ	11.11 AW	15.60 TQ	ARBLS	10/01-12/01
	Fayetteville-Springdale-Rogers MSA, AR	H	8.19 FQ	10.91 AW	14.36 TQ	ARBLS	10/01-12/01
	Fort Smith MSA, AR-OK	H	7.81 FQ	11.87 AW	16.91 TQ	ARBLS	10/01-12/01
	Little Rock-North Little Rock MSA, AR	H	8.35 FQ	11.75 AW	16.46 TQ	ARBLS	10/01-12/01
	California	H	9.33 FQ	15.32 AW	22.15 TQ	CABLS	10/01-12/01
	Bakersfield MSA, CA	H	8.13 FQ	12.76 AW	17.89 TQ	CABLS	10/01-12/01
	Chico-Paradise MSA, CA	H	8.16 FQ	12.25 AW	16.75 TQ	CABLS	10/01-12/01
	Fresno MSA, CA	H	8.18 FQ	13.16 AW	18.23 TQ	CABLS	10/01-12/01
	Los Angeles-Long Beach PMSA, CA	H	9.22 FQ	15.16 AW	21.76 TQ	CABLS	10/01-12/01
	Merced MSA, CA	H	7.02 FQ	11.96 AW	17.36 TQ	CABLS	10/01-12/01
	Modesto MSA, CA	H	7.75 FQ	13.23 AW	19.39 TQ	CABLS	10/01-12/01
	Oakland PMSA, CA	H	10.70 FQ	17.26 AW	24.52 TQ	CABLS	10/01-12/01
	Orange County PMSA, CA	H	10.05 FQ	15.85 AW	22.31 TQ	CABLS	10/01-12/01
	Redding MSA, CA	H	7.96 FQ	12.40 AW	17.24 TQ	CABLS	10/01-12/01
	Riverside-San Bernardino PMSA, CA	H	9.21 FQ	14.78 AW	21.99 TQ	CABLS	10/01-12/01
	Sacramento PMSA, CA	H	9.00 FQ	14.63 AW	20.58 TQ	CABLS	10/01-12/01
	Salinas MSA, CA	H	9.05 FQ	14.62 AW	21.19 TQ	CABLS	10/01-12/01
	San Diego MSA, CA	H	9.27 FQ	14.23 AW	20.47 TQ	CABLS	10/01-12/01
	San Francisco PMSA, CA	H	11.77 FQ	18.48 AW	26.41 TQ	CABLS	10/01-12/01
	San Jose PMSA, CA	H	11.73 FQ	17.89 AW	25.67 TQ	CABLS	10/01-12/01
	San Luis Obispo-Atascadero-Paso Robles MSA, CA	H	9.28 FQ	14.16 AW	20.72 TQ	CABLS	10/01-12/01
	Santa Barbara-Santa Maria-Lompoc MSA, CA	H	9.27 FQ	15.34 AW	22.99 TQ	CABLS	10/01-12/01
	Santa Cruz-Watsonville PMSA, CA	H	9.58 FQ	15.12 AW	21.90 TQ	CABLS	10/01-12/01
	Santa Rosa PMSA, CA	H	11.00 FQ	15.79 AW	21.32 TQ	CABLS	10/01-12/01
	Stockton-Lodi MSA, CA	H	9.07 FQ	13.82 AW	18.69 TQ	CABLS	10/01-12/01
	Vallejo-Fairfield-Napa PMSA, CA	H	9.00 FQ	14.42 AW	20.30 TQ	CABLS	10/01-12/01
	Ventura PMSA, CA	H	9.91 FQ	15.36 AW	21.18 TQ	CABLS	10/01-12/01
	Visalia-Tulare-Porterville MSA, CA	H	8.22 FQ	13.06 AW	17.88 TQ	CABLS	10/01-12/01
	Colorado	H	9.06 FQ	14.09 AW	20.11 TQ	COBLS	10/01-12/01
	Boulder-Longmont PMSA, CO	H	10.68 FQ	15.18 AW	20.72 TQ	COBLS	10/01-12/01
	Colorado Springs MSA, CO	H	9.25 FQ	13.74 AW	19.91 TQ	COBLS	10/01-12/01
	Denver PMSA, CO	H	9.97 FQ	14.85 AW	20.72 TQ	COBLS	10/01-12/01
	Fort Collins-Loveland MSA, CO	H	9.02 FQ	13.22 AW	18.79 TQ	COBLS	10/01-12/01
	Greeley PMSA, CO	H	8.60 FQ	12.51 AW	17.64 TQ	COBLS	10/01-12/01
	Connecticut	H	10.12 FQ	15.83 AW	22.37 TQ	CTBLS	10/01-12/01
	Bridgeport PMSA, CT	H	9.35 FQ	15.34 AW	21.57 TQ	CTBLS	10/01-12/01
	Danbury PMSA, CT	H	9.64 FQ	16.01 AW	22.89 TQ	CTBLS	10/01-12/01
	Hartford MSA, CT	H	10.72 FQ	15.80 AW	21.82 TQ	CTBLS	10/01-12/01
	New Haven-Meriden PMSA, CT	H	9.96 FQ	15.06 AW	21.09 TQ	CTBLS	10/01-12/01
	New London-Norwich MSA, CT-RI	H	9.40 FQ	13.98 AW	19.90 TQ	CTBLS	10/01-12/01
	Stamford-Norwalk PMSA, CT	H	11.39 FQ	18.24 AW	26.40 TQ	CTBLS	10/01-12/01
	Waterbury PMSA, CT	H	9.80 FQ	14.66 AW	20.51 TQ	CTBLS	10/01-12/01
	Delaware	H	7.61 FQ	14.16 AW	21.77 TQ	DEBLS	10/01-12/01
	Wilmington-Newark PMSA, DE-MD	H	7.45 FQ	14.74 AW	22.93 TQ	DEBLS	10/01-12/01
	District of Columbia	H	11.96 FQ	17.67 AW	24.73 TQ	DCBLS	10/01-12/01
	Washington PMSA, DC-MD-VA-WV	H	9.59 FQ	15.29 AW	21.46 TQ	DCBLS	10/01-12/01
	Florida	H	8.27 FQ	12.31 AW	17.04 TQ	FLBLS	10/01-12/01
	Daytona Beach MSA, FL	H	8.03 FQ	11.80 AW	16.14 TQ	FLBLS	10/01-12/01
	Fort Lauderdale PMSA, FL	H	9.19 FQ	13.40 AW	18.32 TQ	FLBLS	10/01-12/01

AAW	Average annual wage	AOH	Average offered, high	ASH	Average starting, high	H	Hourly	M	Monthly	S	Special: hourly and annual
AE	Average entry wage	AOL	Average offered, low	ASL	Average starting, low	HI	Highest wage paid	MTC	Median total compensation	TQ	Third quartile wage
AEX	Average experienced wage	APH	Average pay, high range	AW	Average wage paid	HR	High end range	MW	Median wage paid	W	Weekly
AO	Average offered	APL	Average pay, low range	FQ	First quartile wage	LR	Low end range	SQ	Second quartile wage	Y	Yearly

Occupation/Type/Industry	Location	Per	Low	Mid	High	Source	Date
Bookkeeping, Accounting, and Auditing Clerk	Fort Myers-Cape Coral MSA, FL	H	8.08 FQ	12.34 AW	17.26 TQ	FLBLS	10/01-12/01
	Fort Pierce-Port St. Lucie MSA, FL	H	7.95 FQ	12.61 AW	17.28 TQ	FLBLS	10/01-12/01
	Fort Walton Beach MSA, FL	H	7.21 FQ	10.60 AW	15.18 TQ	FLBLS	10/01-12/01
	Gainesville MSA, FL	H	8.30 FQ	11.77 AW	15.95 TQ	FLBLS	10/01-12/01
	Jacksonville MSA, FL	H	7.70 FQ	12.10 AW	17.26 TQ	FLBLS	10/01-12/01
	Lakeland-Winter Haven MSA, FL	H	8.18 FQ	11.51 AW	15.83 TQ	FLBLS	10/01-12/01
	Melbourne-Titusville-Palm Bay MSA, FL	H	7.59 FQ	11.58 AW	16.43 TQ	FLBLS	10/01-12/01
	Miami PMSA, FL	H	8.86 FQ	12.73 AW	17.55 TQ	FLBLS	10/01-12/01
	Naples MSA, FL	H	9.49 FQ	13.61 AW	18.16 TQ	FLBLS	10/01-12/01
	Ocala MSA, FL	H	7.36 FQ	11.19 AW	15.71 TQ	FLBLS	10/01-12/01
	Orlando MSA, FL	H	8.13 FQ	11.91 AW	16.58 TQ	FLBLS	10/01-12/01
	Pensacola MSA, FL	H	7.77 FQ	11.20 AW	15.68 TQ	FLBLS	10/01-12/01
	Sarasota-Bradenton MSA, FL	H	7.23 FQ	11.36 AW	16.33 TQ	FLBLS	10/01-12/01
	Tallahassee MSA, FL	H	8.00 FQ	12.51 AW	17.88 TQ	FLBLS	10/01-12/01
	Tampa-St. Petersburg-Clearwater MSA, FL	H	8.89 FQ	12.16 AW	16.52 TQ	FLBLS	10/01-12/01
	West Palm Beach-Boca Raton MSA, FL	H	9.04 FQ	13.54 AW	18.45 TQ	FLBLS	10/01-12/01
	Georgia	H	8.65 FQ	12.47 AW	17.10 TQ	GABLS	10/01-12/01
	Atlanta MSA, GA	H	9.48 FQ	13.04 AW	17.51 TQ	GABLS	10/01-12/01
	Augusta-Aiken MSA, GA-SC	H	6.84 FQ	11.32 AW	16.24 TQ	GABLS	10/01-12/01
	Columbus MSA, GA-AL	H	7.09 FQ	11.28 AW	15.86 TQ	GABLS	10/01-12/01
	Macon MSA, GA	H	7.74 FQ	11.30 AW	16.01 TQ	GABLS	10/01-12/01
	Savannah MSA, GA	H	8.05 FQ	11.92 AW	16.72 TQ	GABLS	10/01-12/01
	Hawaii	H	8.62 FQ	13.36 AW	18.78 TQ	HIBLS	10/01-12/01
	Honolulu MSA, HI	H	8.77 FQ	13.46 AW	19.02 TQ	HIBLS	10/01-12/01
	Idaho	H	7.30 FQ	11.75 AW	16.76 TQ	IDBLS	10/01-12/01
	Boise City MSA, ID	H	8.53 FQ	12.22 AW	16.57 TQ	IDBLS	10/01-12/01
	Illinois	H	8.18 FQ	13.51 AW	19.66 TQ	ILBLS	10/01-12/01
	Champaign-Urbana MSA, IL	H	7.46 FQ	12.57 AW	18.32 TQ	ILBLS	10/01-12/01
	Chicago PMSA, IL	H	8.88 FQ	14.18 AW	20.60 TQ	ILBLS	10/01-12/01
	Peoria-Pekin MSA, IL	H	7.60 FQ	12.74 AW	19.95 TQ	ILBLS	10/01-12/01
	Rockford MSA, IL	H	8.24 FQ	12.72 AW	17.36 TQ	ILBLS	10/01-12/01
	Springfield MSA, IL	H	8.75 FQ	13.52 AW	18.75 TQ	ILBLS	10/01-12/01
	Indiana	H	7.65 FQ	11.89 AW	16.66 TQ	INBLS	10/01-12/01
	Elkhart-Goshen MSA, IN	H	8.58 FQ	12.73 AW	17.45 TQ	INBLS	10/01-12/01
	Evansville-Henderson MSA, IN-KY	H	7.63 FQ	11.48 AW	16.31 TQ	INBLS	10/01-12/01
	Fort Wayne MSA, IN	H	7.77 FQ	12.18 AW	17.01 TQ	INBLS	10/01-12/01
	Gary PMSA, IN	H	6.66 FQ	11.61 AW	17.24 TQ	INBLS	10/01-12/01
	Indianapolis MSA, IN	H	8.60 FQ	12.56 AW	17.16 TQ	INBLS	10/01-12/01
	Lafayette MSA, IN	H	7.62 FQ	11.87 AW	16.60 TQ	INBLS	10/01-12/01
	South Bend MSA, IN	H	7.83 FQ	11.89 AW	16.32 TQ	INBLS	10/01-12/01
	Iowa	H	7.12 FQ	11.50 AW	16.47 TQ	IABLS	10/01-12/01
	Cedar Rapids MSA, IA	H	9.03 FQ	14.10 AW	19.70 TQ	IABLS	10/01-12/01
	Davenport-Moline-Rock Island MSA, IA-IL	H	7.64 FQ	11.75 AW	16.97 TQ	IABLS	10/01-12/01
	Des Moines MSA, IA	H	9.33 FQ	12.95 AW	17.28 TQ	IABLS	10/01-12/01
	Kansas	H	7.11 FQ	11.58 AW	16.58 TQ	KSBLS	10/01-12/01
	Topeka MSA, KS	H	6.56 FQ	11.49 AW	16.34 TQ	KSBLS	10/01-12/01
	Wichita MSA, KS	H	8.06 FQ	12.19 AW	17.18 TQ	KSBLS	10/01-12/01
	Kentucky	H	7.50 FQ	11.86 AW	17.08 TQ	KYBLS	10/01-12/01
	Lexington MSA, KY	H	7.68 FQ	12.13 AW	17.70 TQ	KYBLS	10/01-12/01
	Louisville MSA, KY-IN	H	8.40 FQ	12.54 AW	17.40 TQ	KYBLS	10/01-12/01
	Louisiana	H	7.03 FQ	11.33 AW	16.59 TQ	LABLS	10/01-12/01
	Baton Rouge MSA, LA	H	7.59 FQ	11.64 AW	16.55 TQ	LABLS	10/01-12/01
	Houma MSA, LA	H	6.58 FQ	10.70 AW	16.91 TQ	LABLS	10/01-12/01
	Lafayette MSA, LA	H	6.55 FQ	11.16 AW	16.49 TQ	LABLS	10/01-12/01
	Lake Charles MSA, LA	H	6.20 FQ	10.34 AW	14.79 TQ	LABLS	10/01-12/01
	New Orleans MSA, LA	H	8.09 FQ	12.24 AW	17.55 TQ	LABLS	10/01-12/01
	Shreveport-Bossier City MSA, LA	H	7.47 FQ	11.59 AW	16.85 TQ	LABLS	10/01-12/01
	Maine	H	7.93 FQ	12.13 AW	16.84 TQ	MEBLS	10/01-12/01
	Portland MSA, ME	H	9.24 FQ	13.16 AW	17.45 TQ	MEBLS	10/01-12/01
	Maryland	H	8.95 FQ	14.18 AW	20.55 TQ	MDBLS	10/01-12/01
	Baltimore PMSA, MD	H	8.95 FQ	14.13 AW	20.64 TQ	MDBLS	10/01-12/01
	Massachusetts	H	9.50 FQ	14.92 AW	20.70 TQ	MABLS	10/01-12/01

AAW	Average annual wage	**AOH**	Average offered, high	**ASH**	Average starting, high	**H**	Hourly	**M**	Monthly	**S**	Special: hourly and annual
AE	Average entry wage	**AOL**	Average offered, low	**ASL**	Average starting, low	**HI**	Highest wage paid	**MTC**	Median total compensation	**TQ**	Third quartile wage
AEX	Average experienced wage	**APH**	Average pay, high range	**AW**	Average wage paid	**HR**	High end range	**MW**	Median wage paid	**W**	Weekly
AO	Average offered	**APL**	Average pay, low range	**FQ**	First quartile wage	**LR**	Low end range	**SQ**	Second quartile wage	**Y**	Yearly

Occupation/Type/Industry	Location	Per	Low	Mid	High	Source	Date
Bookkeeping, Accounting, and Auditing Clerk	Boston PMSA, MA-NH	H	10.06 FQ	15.46 AW	21.05 TQ	MABLS	10/01-12/01
	Brockton PMSA, MA	H	9.51 FQ	14.22 AW	19.10 TQ	MABLS	10/01-12/01
	Lawrence PMSA, MA-NH	H	9.33 FQ	14.35 AW	20.09 TQ	MABLS	10/01-12/01
	Lowell PMSA, MA-NH	H	9.77 FQ	15.30 AW	21.78 TQ	MABLS	10/01-12/01
	New Bedford PMSA, MA	H	8.62 FQ	13.08 AW	17.95 TQ	MABLS	10/01-12/01
	Springfield MSA, MA	H	8.88 FQ	13.93 AW	19.48 TQ	MABLS	10/01-12/01
	Worcester PMSA, MA-CT	H	9.04 FQ	13.97 AW	19.41 TQ	MABLS	10/01-12/01
	Michigan	H	8.64 FQ	13.76 AW	20.39 TQ	MIBLS	10/01-12/01
	Ann Arbor PMSA, MI	H	9.03 FQ	14.50 AW	21.35 TQ	MIBLS	10/01-12/01
	Detroit PMSA, MI	H	9.65 FQ	14.84 AW	22.01 TQ	MIBLS	10/01-12/01
	Flint PMSA, MI	H	7.90 FQ	13.51 AW	19.87 TQ	MIBLS	10/01-12/01
	Grand Rapids-Muskegon-Holland MSA, MI	H	8.62 FQ	13.36 AW	18.56 TQ	MIBLS	10/01-12/01
	Kalamazoo-Battle Creek MSA, MI	H	9.30 FQ	13.25 AW	17.90 TQ	MIBLS	10/01-12/01
	Lansing-East Lansing MSA, MI	H	9.21 FQ	13.98 AW	20.06 TQ	MIBLS	10/01-12/01
	Saginaw-Bay City-Midland MSA, MI	H	7.09 FQ	11.26 AW	16.57 TQ	MIBLS	10/01-12/01
	Minnesota	H	9.22 FQ	13.91 AW	19.26 TQ	MNBLS	10/01-12/01
	Duluth-Superior MSA, MN-WI	H	7.66 FQ	12.17 AW	17.21 TQ	MNBLS	10/01-12/01
	Minneapolis-St. Paul MSA, MN-WI	H	10.65 FQ	14.89 AW	20.10 TQ	MNBLS	10/01-12/01
	St. Cloud MSA, MN	H	8.66 FQ	12.56 AW	17.42 TQ	MNBLS	10/01-12/01
	Mississippi	H	7.53 FQ	11.51 AW	16.30 TQ	MSBLS	10/01-12/01
	Biloxi-Gulfport-Pascagoula MSA, MS	H	7.82 FQ	11.47 AW	15.94 TQ	MSBLS	10/01-12/01
	Jackson MSA, MS	H	7.63 FQ	12.54 AW	18.83 TQ	MSBLS	10/01-12/01
	Missouri	H	7.61 FQ	12.18 AW	17.58 TQ	MOBLS	10/01-12/01
	Kansas City MSA, MO-KS	H	8.61 FQ	12.77 AW	17.63 TQ	MOBLS	10/01-12/01
	St. Louis MSA, MO-IL	H	8.57 FQ	13.28 AW	19.16 TQ	MOBLS	10/01-12/01
	Springfield MSA, MO	H	7.25 FQ	10.57 AW	14.06 TQ	MOBLS	10/01-12/01
	Montana	H	6.90 FQ	10.52 AW	14.56 TQ	MTBLS	10/01-12/01
	Billings MSA, MT	H	7.23 FQ	11.17 AW	16.38 TQ	MTBLS	10/01-12/01
	Nebraska	H	7.56 FQ	11.79 AW	16.59 TQ	NEBLS	10/01-12/01
	Lincoln MSA, NE	H	8.36 FQ	11.90 AW	16.54 TQ	NEBLS	10/01-12/01
	Omaha MSA, NE-IA	H	9.04 FQ	13.22 AW	17.99 TQ	NEBLS	10/01-12/01
	Nevada	H	8.98 FQ	13.26 AW	18.14 TQ	NVBLS	10/01-12/01
	Las Vegas MSA, NV-AZ	H	9.16 FQ	13.22 AW	18.12 TQ	NVBLS	10/01-12/01
	Reno MSA, NV	H	8.42 FQ	13.27 AW	17.82 TQ	NVBLS	10/01-12/01
	New Hampshire	H	8.76 FQ	13.07 AW	17.82 TQ	NHBLS	10/01-12/01
	Manchester PMSA, NH	H	9.43 FQ	13.72 AW	18.78 TQ	NHBLS	10/01-12/01
	Nashua PMSA, NH	H	8.56 FQ	13.35 AW	18.22 TQ	NHBLS	10/01-12/01
	Portsmouth-Rochester PMSA, NH-ME	H	9.11 FQ	13.55 AW	18.07 TQ	NHBLS	10/01-12/01
	New Jersey	H	9.59 FQ	15.26 AW	21.93 TQ	NJBLS	10/01-12/01
	Atlantic-Cape May PMSA, NJ	H	8.40 FQ	13.27 AW	19.02 TQ	NJBLS	10/01-12/01
	Bergen-Passaic PMSA, NJ	H	9.67 FQ	15.96 AW	22.75 TQ	NJBLS	10/01-12/01
	Jersey City PMSA, NJ	H	10.11 FQ	16.08 AW	23.45 TQ	NJBLS	10/01-12/01
	Middlesex-Somerset-Hunterdon PMSA, NJ	H	9.59 FQ	15.68 AW	23.10 TQ	NJBLS	10/01-12/01
	Monmouth-Ocean PMSA, NJ	H	9.16 FQ	13.87 AW	19.82 TQ	NJBLS	10/01-12/01
	Newark PMSA, NJ	H	10.18 FQ	15.89 AW	22.63 TQ	NJBLS	10/01-12/01
	Trenton PMSA, NJ	H	10.76 FQ	16.02 AW	21.68 TQ	NJBLS	10/01-12/01
	New Mexico	H	7.34 FQ	11.97 AW	17.89 TQ	NMBLS	10/01-12/01
	Albuquerque MSA, NM	H	7.78 FQ	12.15 AW	17.08 TQ	NMBLS	10/01-12/01
	Las Cruces MSA, NM	H	6.95 FQ	10.32 AW	13.94 TQ	NMBLS	10/01-12/01
	New York	H	8.60 FQ	14.80 AW	21.63 TQ	NYBLS	10/01-12/01
	Albany-Schenectady-Troy MSA, NY	H	8.87 FQ	13.48 AW	18.46 TQ	NYBLS	10/01-12/01
	Binghamton MSA, NY	H	7.63 FQ	11.36 AW	15.98 TQ	NYBLS	10/01-12/01
	Buffalo-Niagara Falls MSA, NY	H	7.52 FQ	12.17 AW	16.82 TQ	NYBLS	10/01-12/01
	Dutchess County PMSA, NY	H	8.68 FQ	13.72 AW	19.57 TQ	NYBLS	10/01-12/01
	Nassau-Suffolk PMSA, NY	H	8.97 FQ	15.18 AW	21.89 TQ	NYBLS	10/01-12/01
	New York PMSA, NY	H	9.13 FQ	16.46 AW	24.82 TQ	NYBLS	10/01-12/01
	Newburgh PMSA, NY-PA	H	8.30 FQ	13.13 AW	18.31 TQ	NYBLS	10/01-12/01
	Rochester MSA, NY	H	8.57 FQ	13.05 AW	18.58 TQ	NYBLS	10/01-12/01
	Syracuse MSA, NY	H	7.86 FQ	12.80 AW	17.91 TQ	NYBLS	10/01-12/01
	Utica-Rome MSA, NY	H	6.94 FQ	11.69 AW	16.62 TQ	NYBLS	10/01-12/01
	North Carolina	H	8.45 FQ	12.88 AW	18.02 TQ	NCBLS	10/01-12/01
	Asheville MSA, NC	H	8.31 FQ	12.47 AW	17.24 TQ	NCBLS	10/01-12/01

AAW Average annual wage; AE Average entry wage; AEX Average experienced wage; AO Average offered; AOH Average offered, high; AOL Average offered, low; APH Average pay, high range; APL Average pay, low range; ASH Average starting, high; ASL Average starting, low; AW Average wage paid; FQ First quartile wage; H Hourly; HI Highest wage paid; HR High end range; LR Low end range; M Monthly; MTC Median total compensation; MW Median wage paid; SQ Second quartile wage; S Special: hourly and annual; TQ Third quartile wage; W Weekly; Y Yearly

Occupation/Type/Industry	Location	Per	Low	Mid	High	Source	Date
Bookkeeping, Accounting, and Auditing Clerk	Charlotte-Gastonia-Rock Hill MSA, NC-SC	H	8.80 FQ	13.71 AW	19.82 TQ	NCBLS	10/01-12/01
	Fayetteville MSA, NC	H	8.32 FQ	12.05 AW	16.80 TQ	NCBLS	10/01-12/01
	Greensboro-Winston-Salem-High Point MSA, NC	H	9.04 FQ	13.33 AW	18.09 TQ	NCBLS	10/01-12/01
	Hickory-Morganton-Lenoir MSA, NC	H	8.29 FQ	13.14 AW	18.18 TQ	NCBLS	10/01-12/01
	Raleigh-Durham-Chapel Hill MSA, NC	H	9.59 FQ	13.99 AW	19.44 TQ	NCBLS	10/01-12/01
	Wilmington MSA, NC	H	6.65 FQ	11.75 AW	16.58 TQ	NCBLS	10/01-12/01
	North Dakota	H	6.60 FQ	10.31 AW	14.45 TQ	NDBLS	10/01-12/01
	Fargo-Moorhead MSA, ND-MN	H	7.63 FQ	11.65 AW	16.10 TQ	NDBLS	10/01-12/01
	Ohio	H	8.12 FQ	12.81 AW	18.09 TQ	OHBLS	10/01-12/01
	Akron PMSA, OH	H	7.88 FQ	12.60 AW	17.44 TQ	OHBLS	10/01-12/01
	Canton-Massillon MSA, OH	H	7.33 FQ	11.81 AW	17.54 TQ	OHBLS	10/01-12/01
	Cincinnati PMSA, OH-KY-IN	H	8.84 FQ	13.35 AW	18.89 TQ	OHBLS	10/01-12/01
	Cleveland-Lorain-Elyria PMSA, OH	H	8.67 FQ	13.34 AW	18.75 TQ	OHBLS	10/01-12/01
	Columbus MSA, OH	H	7.96 FQ	12.98 AW	18.35 TQ	OHBLS	10/01-12/01
	Dayton-Springfield MSA, OH	H	9.02 FQ	13.15 AW	18.96 TQ	OHBLS	10/01-12/01
	Hamilton-Middletown PMSA, OH	H	9.39 FQ	13.63 AW	19.07 TQ	OHBLS	10/01-12/01
	Mansfield MSA, OH	H	7.46 FQ	11.69 AW	16.94 TQ	OHBLS	10/01-12/01
	Toledo MSA, OH	H	8.98 FQ	13.20 AW	18.60 TQ	OHBLS	10/01-12/01
	Youngstown-Warren MSA, OH	H	7.50 FQ	11.47 AW	16.20 TQ	OHBLS	10/01-12/01
	Oklahoma	H	7.46 FQ	11.48 AW	16.41 TQ	OKBLS	10/01-12/01
	Oklahoma City MSA, OK	H	7.71 FQ	11.63 AW	16.66 TQ	OKBLS	10/01-12/01
	Tulsa MSA, OK	H	8.56 FQ	12.53 AW	17.23 TQ	OKBLS	10/01-12/01
	Oregon	H	9.29 FQ	13.31 AW	17.91 TQ	ORBLS	10/01-12/01
	Eugene-Springfield MSA, OR	H	8.81 FQ	13.07 AW	18.65 TQ	ORBLS	10/01-12/01
	Medford-Ashland MSA, OR	H	9.14 FQ	12.50 AW	17.22 TQ	ORBLS	10/01-12/01
	Portland-Vancouver PMSA, OR-WA	H	10.24 FQ	13.88 AW	18.26 TQ	ORBLS	10/01-12/01
	Salem PMSA, OR	H	9.35 FQ	13.22 AW	17.63 TQ	ORBLS	10/01-12/01
	Pennsylvania	H	7.62 FQ	12.73 AW	18.71 TQ	PABLS	10/01-12/01
	Allentown-Bethlehem-Easton MSA, PA	H	8.21 FQ	12.89 AW	17.72 TQ	PABLS	10/01-12/01
	Erie MSA, PA	H	7.51 FQ	11.53 AW	16.31 TQ	PABLS	10/01-12/01
	Harrisburg-Lebanon-Carlisle MSA, PA	H	8.52 FQ	12.97 AW	18.40 TQ	PABLS	10/01-12/01
	Johnstown MSA, PA	H	6.48 FQ	10.32 AW	15.95 TQ	PABLS	10/01-12/01
	Lancaster MSA, PA	H	7.34 FQ	12.03 AW	16.88 TQ	PABLS	10/01-12/01
	Philadelphia PMSA, PA-NJ	H	9.06 FQ	14.35 AW	20.47 TQ	PABLS	10/01-12/01
	Pittsburgh MSA, PA	H	7.67 FQ	11.76 AW	17.08 TQ	PABLS	10/01-12/01
	Reading MSA, PA	H	8.07 FQ	12.19 AW	17.14 TQ	PABLS	10/01-12/01
	Scranton-Wilkes-Barre-Hazleton MSA, PA	H	7.15 FQ	11.41 AW	16.49 TQ	PABLS	10/01-12/01
	York MSA, PA	H	6.40 FQ	11.96 AW	17.53 TQ	PABLS	10/01-12/01
	Rhode Island	H	9.14 FQ	14.00 AW	19.48 TQ	RIBLS	10/01-12/01
	Providence-Fall River-Warwick MSA, RI-MA	H	9.22 FQ	13.89 AW	19.31 TQ	RIBLS	10/01-12/01
	South Carolina	H	7.65 FQ	11.63 AW	16.43 TQ	SCBLS	10/01-12/01
	Charleston-North Charleston MSA, SC	H	8.48 FQ	12.14 AW	16.61 TQ	SCBLS	10/01-12/01
	Columbia MSA, SC	H	7.35 FQ	11.03 AW	16.06 TQ	SCBLS	10/01-12/01
	Greenville-Spartanburg-Anderson MSA, SC	H	8.55 FQ	11.86 AW	16.43 TQ	SCBLS	10/01-12/01
	Myrtle Beach MSA, SC	H	8.34 FQ	12.06 AW	16.63 TQ	SCBLS	10/01-12/01
	South Dakota	H	7.65 FQ	10.25 AW	13.21 TQ	SDBLS	10/01-12/01
	Sioux Falls MSA, SD	H	8.29 FQ	10.84 AW	13.62 TQ	SDBLS	10/01-12/01
	Tennessee	H	7.95 FQ	12.37 AW	17.44 TQ	TNBLS	10/01-12/01
	Chattanooga MSA, TN-GA	H	8.23 FQ	12.58 AW	17.61 TQ	TNBLS	10/01-12/01
	Clarksville-Hopkinsville MSA, TN-KY	H	7.26 FQ	10.97 AW	15.65 TQ	TNBLS	10/01-12/01
	Johnson City-Kingsport-Bristol MSA, TN-VA	H	7.48 FQ	11.25 AW	15.91 TQ	TNBLS	10/01-12/01
	Knoxville MSA, TN	H	7.91 FQ	12.04 AW	17.11 TQ	TNBLS	10/01-12/01
	Memphis MSA, TN-AR-MS	H	8.90 FQ	13.02 AW	18.03 TQ	TNBLS	10/01-12/01
	Nashville MSA, TN	H	8.85 FQ	13.50 AW	19.02 TQ	TNBLS	10/01-12/01
	Texas	H	7.96 FQ	13.26 AW	19.53 TQ	TXBLS	10/01-12/01

AAW	Average annual wage	**AOH**	Average offered, high	**ASH**	Average starting, high	**H**	Hourly	**M**	Monthly	**S**	Special: hourly and annual
AE	Average entry wage	**AOL**	Average offered, low	**ASL**	Average starting, low	**HI**	Highest wage paid	**MTC**	Median total compensation	**TQ**	Third quartile wage
AEX	Average experienced wage	**APH**	Average pay, high range	**AW**	Average wage paid	**HR**	High end range	**MW**	Median wage paid	**W**	Weekly
AO	Average offered	**APL**	Average pay, low range	**FQ**	First quartile wage	**LR**	Low end range	**SQ**	Second quartile wage	**Y**	Yearly

Occupation/Type/Industry	Location	Per	Low	Mid	High	Source	Date
Bookkeeping, Accounting, and Auditing Clerk	Amarillo MSA, TX	H	7.48 FQ	11.92 AW	17.76 TQ	TXBLS	10/01-12/01
	Austin-San Marcos MSA, TX	H	8.98 FQ	13.67 AW	18.54 TQ	TXBLS	10/01-12/01
	Beaumont-Port Arthur MSA, TX	H	7.77 FQ	12.27 AW	19.73 TQ	TXBLS	10/01-12/01
	Brazoria PMSA, TX	H	7.93 FQ	12.40 AW	17.85 TQ	TXBLS	10/01-12/01
	Brownsville-Harlingen-San Benito MSA, TX	H	6.30 FQ	10.42 AW	15.13 TQ	TXBLS	10/01-12/01
	Corpus Christi MSA, TX	H	7.65 FQ	11.78 AW	17.56 TQ	TXBLS	10/01-12/01
	Dallas PMSA, TX	H	9.46 FQ	15.12 AW	21.09 TQ	TXBLS	10/01-12/01
	El Paso MSA, TX	H	7.07 FQ	11.13 AW	15.84 TQ	TXBLS	10/01-12/01
	Fort Worth-Arlington PMSA, TX	H	8.89 FQ	13.07 AW	17.91 TQ	TXBLS	10/01-12/01
	Galveston-Texas City PMSA, TX	H	8.16 FQ	12.45 AW	18.12 TQ	TXBLS	10/01-12/01
	Houston PMSA, TX	H	9.21 FQ	14.38 AW	20.75 TQ	TXBLS	10/01-12/01
	Killeen-Temple MSA, TX	H	7.54 FQ	10.69 AW	14.39 TQ	TXBLS	10/01-12/01
	Laredo MSA, TX	H	6.28 FQ	10.13 AW	15.55 TQ	TXBLS	10/01-12/01
	Longview-Marshall MSA, TX	H	7.20 FQ	11.49 AW	17.34 TQ	TXBLS	10/01-12/01
	Lubbock MSA, TX	H	6.99 FQ	11.05 AW	16.05 TQ	TXBLS	10/01-12/01
	McAllen-Edinburg-Mission MSA, TX	H	6.26 FQ	10.02 AW	14.43 TQ	TXBLS	10/01-12/01
	Odessa-Midland MSA, TX	H	8.01 FQ	12.79 AW	20.93 TQ	TXBLS	10/01-12/01
	San Antonio MSA, TX	H	8.53 FQ	12.96 AW	18.25 TQ	TXBLS	10/01-12/01
	Tyler MSA, TX	H	7.16 FQ	11.70 AW	17.00 TQ	TXBLS	10/01-12/01
	Waco MSA, TX	H	6.93 FQ	11.49 AW	16.69 TQ	TXBLS	10/01-12/01
	Utah	H	7.92 FQ	12.26 AW	17.49 TQ	UTBLS	10/01-12/01
	Provo-Orem MSA, UT	H	7.07 FQ	11.67 AW	16.49 TQ	UTBLS	10/01-12/01
	Salt Lake City-Ogden MSA, UT	H	8.60 FQ	12.57 AW	18.00 TQ	UTBLS	10/01-12/01
	Vermont	H	8.39 FQ	12.84 AW	17.96 TQ	VTBLS	10/01-12/01
	Burlington MSA, VT	H	9.28 FQ	14.08 AW	19.38 TQ	VTBLS	10/01-12/01
	Virginia	H	7.98 FQ	12.91 AW	18.22 TQ	VABLS	10/01-12/01
	Lynchburg MSA, VA	H	7.39 FQ	11.52 AW	16.37 TQ	VABLS	10/01-12/01
	Norfolk-Virginia Beach-Newport News MSA, VA-NC	H	7.64 FQ	12.07 AW	16.88 TQ	VABLS	10/01-12/01
	Richmond-Petersburg MSA, VA	H	8.96 FQ	13.07 AW	17.65 TQ	VABLS	10/01-12/01
	Roanoke MSA, VA	H	7.48 FQ	11.42 AW	16.06 TQ	VABLS	10/01-12/01
	Washington	H	9.34 FQ	14.02 AW	19.25 TQ	WABLS	10/01-12/01
	Bremerton PMSA, WA	H	8.86 FQ	13.42 AW	18.25 TQ	WABLS	10/01-12/01
	Olympia PMSA, WA	H	9.59 FQ	14.20 AW	19.45 TQ	WABLS	10/01-12/01
	Richland-Kennewick-Pasco MSA, WA	H	8.91 FQ	13.27 AW	17.67 TQ	WABLS	10/01-12/01
	Seattle-Bellevue-Everett PMSA, WA	H	10.50 FQ	15.04 AW	20.33 TQ	WABLS	10/01-12/01
	Spokane MSA, WA	H	8.46 FQ	12.75 AW	17.46 TQ	WABLS	10/01-12/01
	Tacoma PMSA, WA	H	9.80 FQ	14.28 AW	19.37 TQ	WABLS	10/01-12/01
	Yakima MSA, WA	H	8.60 FQ	12.63 AW	16.95 TQ	WABLS	10/01-12/01
	West Virginia	H	6.73 FQ	11.01 AW	16.09 TQ	WVBLS	10/01-12/01
	Charleston MSA, WV	H	7.70 FQ	11.71 AW	16.15 TQ	WVBLS	10/01-12/01
	Huntington-Ashland MSA, WV-KY-OH	H	6.28 FQ	10.85 AW	16.38 TQ	WVBLS	10/01-12/01
	Wisconsin	H	8.07 FQ	12.53 AW	17.46 TQ	WIBLS	10/01-12/01
	Appleton-Oshkosh-Neenah MSA, WI	H	7.51 FQ	12.26 AW	17.35 TQ	WIBLS	10/01-12/01
	Green Bay MSA, WI	H	8.17 FQ	12.88 AW	18.03 TQ	WIBLS	10/01-12/01
	Madison MSA, WI	H	9.66 FQ	13.97 AW	18.59 TQ	WIBLS	10/01-12/01
	Milwaukee-Waukesha PMSA, WI	H	9.08 FQ	13.36 AW	18.26 TQ	WIBLS	10/01-12/01
	Racine PMSA, WI	H	8.76 FQ	12.90 AW	17.67 TQ	WIBLS	10/01-12/01
	Wyoming	H	6.64 FQ	10.68 AW	15.58 TQ	WYBLS	10/01-12/01
	Cheyenne MSA, WY	H	7.09 FQ	10.26 AW	14.56 TQ	WYBLS	10/01-12/01
	Puerto Rico	H	6.02 FQ	8.70 AW	12.38 TQ	PRBLS	10/01-12/01
	Virgin Islands	H	7.63 FQ	10.52 AW	13.92 TQ	VIBLS	10/01-12/01
	Guam	H	7.37 FQ	11.71 AW	16.96 TQ	GUBLS	10/01-12/01
Brickmason and Blockmason	Alabama	H	9.68 FQ	15.73 AW	21.67 TQ	ALBLS	10/01-12/01
	Birmingham MSA, AL	H	11.52 FQ	18.22 AW	23.94 TQ	ALBLS	10/01-12/01
	Mobile MSA, AL	H	8.86 FQ	15.37 AW	20.00 TQ	ALBLS	10/01-12/01
	Montgomery MSA, AL	H	11.51 FQ	17.48 AW	23.90 TQ	ALBLS	10/01-12/01

AAW	Average annual wage	**AOH**	Average offered, high	**ASH**	Average starting, high	**H**	Hourly	**M**	Monthly	**S**	Special: hourly and annual
AE	Average entry wage	**AOL**	Average offered, low	**ASL**	Average starting, low	**HI**	Highest wage paid	**MTC**	Median total compensation	**TQ**	Third quartile wage
AEX	Average experienced wage	**APH**	Average pay, high range	**AW**	Average wage paid	**HR**	High end range	**MW**	Median wage paid	**W**	Weekly
AO	Average offered	**APL**	Average pay, low range	**FQ**	First quartile wage	**LR**	Low end range	**SQ**	Second quartile wage	**Y**	Yearly

Occupation/Type/Industry	Location	Per	Low	Mid	High	Source	Date
Brickmason and Blockmason	Alaska	H	15.16 FQ	26.44 AW	35.15 TQ	AKBLS	10/01-12/01
	Anchorage MSA, AK	H	12.72 FQ	24.23 AW	35.41 TQ	AKBLS	10/01-12/01
	Arizona	H	9.85 FQ	15.86 AW	21.27 TQ	AZBLS	10/01-12/01
	Phoenix-Mesa MSA, AZ	H	10.06 FQ	16.50 AW	21.49 TQ	AZBLS	10/01-12/01
	Tucson MSA, AZ	H	8.53 FQ	13.19 AW	17.32 TQ	AZBLS	10/01-12/01
	Arkansas	H	9.93 FQ	16.12 AW	21.40 TQ	ARBLS	10/01-12/01
	Fayetteville-Springdale-Rogers MSA, AR	H	11.71 FQ	15.26 AW	20.54 TQ	ARBLS	10/01-12/01
	Fort Smith MSA, AR-OK	H	7.45 FQ	12.43 AW	23.73 TQ	ARBLS	10/01-12/01
	Little Rock-North Little Rock MSA, AR	H	17.24 FQ	19.81 AW	22.72 TQ	ARBLS	10/01-12/01
	California	H	11.29 FQ	20.66 AW	33.58 TQ	CABLS	10/01-12/01
	Bakersfield MSA, CA	H	10.01 FQ	19.58 AW	27.44 TQ	CABLS	10/01-12/01
	Fresno MSA, CA	H	14.21 FQ	19.44 AW	25.51 TQ	CABLS	10/01-12/01
	Los Angeles-Long Beach PMSA, CA	H	11.02 FQ	19.89 AW	39.19 TQ	CABLS	10/01-12/01
	Modesto MSA, CA	H	10.90 FQ	18.32 AW	31.54 TQ	CABLS	10/01-12/01
	Oakland PMSA, CA	H	12.54 FQ	22.53 AW	34.31 TQ	CABLS	10/01-12/01
	Orange County PMSA, CA	H	8.59 FQ	20.50 AW	32.61 TQ	CABLS	10/01-12/01
	Riverside-San Bernardino PMSA, CA	H	11.63 FQ	18.51 AW	26.02 TQ	CABLS	10/01-12/01
	Sacramento PMSA, CA	H	14.38 FQ	19.29 AW	26.72 TQ	CABLS	10/01-12/01
	Salinas MSA, CA	H	28.92 FQ	31.43 AW	35.08 TQ	CABLS	10/01-12/01
	San Diego MSA, CA	H	12.37 FQ	22.46 AW	33.41 TQ	CABLS	10/01-12/01
	San Francisco PMSA, CA	H	11.38 FQ	27.46 AW	44.53 TQ	CABLS	10/01-12/01
	San Jose PMSA, CA	H	19.67 FQ	26.48 AW	34.71 TQ	CABLS	10/01-12/01
	San Luis Obispo-Atascadero-Paso Robles MSA, CA	H	15.15 FQ	21.46 AW	27.90 TQ	CABLS	10/01-12/01
	Santa Barbara-Santa Maria-Lompoc MSA, CA	H	11.49 FQ	23.98 AW	33.11 TQ	CABLS	10/01-12/01
	Stockton-Lodi MSA, CA	H	14.12 FQ	19.69 AW	25.90 TQ	CABLS	10/01-12/01
	Vallejo-Fairfield-Napa PMSA, CA	H	10.38 FQ	15.99 AW	27.61 TQ	CABLS	10/01-12/01
	Ventura PMSA, CA	H	11.78 FQ	16.86 AW	21.77 TQ	CABLS	10/01-12/01
	Colorado	H	10.42 FQ	19.12 AW	26.73 TQ	COBLS	10/01-12/01
	Boulder-Longmont PMSA, CO	H	15.12 FQ	18.83 AW	25.68 TQ	COBLS	10/01-12/01
	Colorado Springs MSA, CO	H	15.25 FQ	21.22 AW	31.25 TQ	COBLS	10/01-12/01
	Denver PMSA, CO	H	9.55 FQ	19.12 AW	27.14 TQ	COBLS	10/01-12/01
	Fort Collins-Loveland MSA, CO	H	8.12 FQ	16.67 AW	25.32 TQ	COBLS	10/01-12/01
	Greeley PMSA, CO	H	12.31 FQ	15.96 AW	20.08 TQ	COBLS	10/01-12/01
	Connecticut	H	15.13 FQ	23.73 AW	32.64 TQ	CTBLS	10/01-12/01
	Bridgeport PMSA, CT	H	14.91 FQ	24.04 AW	41.63 TQ	CTBLS	10/01-12/01
	Danbury PMSA, CT	H	11.09 FQ	23.17 AW	34.00 TQ	CTBLS	10/01-12/01
	Hartford MSA, CT	H	16.82 FQ	23.77 AW	31.99 TQ	CTBLS	10/01-12/01
	New Haven-Meriden PMSA, CT	H	16.31 FQ	23.78 AW	38.93 TQ	CTBLS	10/01-12/01
	Stamford-Norwalk PMSA, CT	H	19.95 FQ	23.79 AW	27.16 TQ	CTBLS	10/01-12/01
	Waterbury PMSA, CT	H	12.22 FQ	19.83 AW	30.79 TQ	CTBLS	10/01-12/01
	Delaware	H	14.31 FQ	19.96 AW	27.61 TQ	DEBLS	10/01-12/01
	Wilmington-Newark PMSA, DE-MD	H	14.69 FQ	20.70 AW	28.26 TQ	DEBLS	10/01-12/01
	District of Columbia	H	18.33 FQ	22.21 AW	26.38 TQ	DCBLS	10/01-12/01
	Washington PMSA, DC-MD-VA-WV	H	12.46 FQ	18.63 AW	25.30 TQ	DCBLS	10/01-12/01
	Florida	H	9.94 FQ	15.04 AW	20.82 TQ	FLBLS	10/01-12/01
	Daytona Beach MSA, FL	H	12.49 FQ	16.00 AW	19.92 TQ	FLBLS	10/01-12/01
	Fort Lauderdale PMSA, FL	H	9.96 FQ	15.51 AW	22.15 TQ	FLBLS	10/01-12/01
	Fort Myers-Cape Coral MSA, FL	H	12.05 FQ	16.45 AW	20.85 TQ	FLBLS	10/01-12/01
	Fort Pierce-Port St. Lucie MSA, FL	H	12.03 FQ	16.66 AW	21.66 TQ	FLBLS	10/01-12/01
	Fort Walton Beach MSA, FL	H	9.28 FQ	14.63 AW	20.47 TQ	FLBLS	10/01-12/01
	Gainesville MSA, FL	H	10.53 FQ	14.53 AW	18.93 TQ	FLBLS	10/01-12/01
	Jacksonville MSA, FL	H	9.80 FQ	15.82 AW	20.68 TQ	FLBLS	10/01-12/01
	Lakeland-Winter Haven MSA, FL	H	9.27 FQ	12.38 AW	16.94 TQ	FLBLS	10/01-12/01
	Melbourne-Titusville-Palm Bay MSA, FL	H	8.53 FQ	15.30 AW	21.27 TQ	FLBLS	10/01-12/01
	Miami PMSA, FL	H	9.71 FQ	15.92 AW	21.53 TQ	FLBLS	10/01-12/01
	Naples MSA, FL	H	11.68 FQ	14.95 AW	18.57 TQ	FLBLS	10/01-12/01
	Ocala MSA, FL	H	9.44 FQ	14.07 AW	20.01 TQ	FLBLS	10/01-12/01

AAW	Average annual wage	**AOH**	Average offered, high	**ASH**	Average starting, high	**H**	Hourly	**M**	Monthly	**S**	Special: hourly and annual
AE	Average entry wage	**AOL**	Average offered, low	**ASL**	Average starting, low	**HI**	Highest wage paid	**MTC**	Median total compensation	**TQ**	Third quartile wage
AEX	Average experienced wage	**APH**	Average pay, high range	**AW**	Average wage paid	**HR**	High end range	**MW**	Median wage paid	**W**	Weekly
AO	Average offered	**APL**	Average pay, low range	**FQ**	First quartile wage	**LR**	Low end range	**SQ**	Second quartile wage	**Y**	Yearly

Occupation/Type/Industry	Location	Per	Low	Mid	High	Source	Date
Brickmason and Blockmason	Orlando MSA, FL	H	12.06 FQ	17.22 AW	22.03 TQ	FLBLS	10/01-12/01
	Pensacola MSA, FL	H	14.74 FQ	18.62 AW	22.48 TQ	FLBLS	10/01-12/01
	Sarasota-Bradenton MSA, FL	H	11.05 FQ	13.35 AW	18.21 TQ	FLBLS	10/01-12/01
	Tallahassee MSA, FL	H	9.53 FQ	14.18 AW	19.63 TQ	FLBLS	10/01-12/01
	Tampa-St. Petersburg-Clearwater MSA, FL	H	9.00 FQ	13.19 AW	20.11 TQ	FLBLS	10/01-12/01
	West Palm Beach-Boca Raton MSA, FL	H	11.80 FQ	17.84 AW	21.15 TQ	FLBLS	10/01-12/01
	Georgia	H	9.61 FQ	15.98 AW	21.24 TQ	GABLS	10/01-12/01
	Atlanta MSA, GA	H	10.88 FQ	16.88 AW	21.45 TQ	GABLS	10/01-12/01
	Augusta-Aiken MSA, GA-SC	H	9.17 FQ	14.67 AW	21.48 TQ	GABLS	10/01-12/01
	Columbus MSA, GA-AL	H	7.92 FQ	13.05 AW	17.82 TQ	GABLS	10/01-12/01
	Savannah MSA, GA	H	13.30 FQ	17.10 AW	21.59 TQ	GABLS	10/01-12/01
	Hawaii	H	23.02 FQ	26.31 AW	32.53 TQ	HIBLS	10/01-12/01
	Honolulu MSA, HI	H	23.05 FQ	26.46 AW	32.81 TQ	HIBLS	10/01-12/01
	Idaho	H	14.31 FQ	21.89 AW	30.82 TQ	IDBLS	10/01-12/01
	Boise City MSA, ID	H	11.68 FQ	21.94 AW	31.40 TQ	IDBLS	10/01-12/01
	Illinois	H	18.79 FQ	26.87 AW	34.37 TQ	ILBLS	10/01-12/01
	Champaign-Urbana MSA, IL	H	15.50 FQ	23.39 AW	28.94 TQ	ILBLS	10/01-12/01
	Chicago PMSA, IL	H	20.51 FQ	28.00 AW	34.65 TQ	ILBLS	10/01-12/01
	Peoria-Pekin MSA, IL	H	17.52 FQ	22.79 AW	26.94 TQ	ILBLS	10/01-12/01
	Rockford MSA, IL	H	21.90 FQ	24.76 AW	28.23 TQ	ILBLS	10/01-12/01
	Springfield MSA, IL	H	21.68 FQ	25.05 AW	30.23 TQ	ILBLS	10/01-12/01
	Indiana	H	7.87 FQ	18.61 AW	27.37 TQ	INBLS	10/01-12/01
	Evansville-Henderson MSA, IN-KY	H	14.25 FQ	20.75 AW	31.00 TQ	INBLS	10/01-12/01
	Fort Wayne MSA, IN	H	13.57 FQ	21.78 AW	27.52 TQ	INBLS	10/01-12/01
	Gary PMSA, IN	H	14.78 FQ	20.25 AW	26.87 TQ	INBLS	10/01-12/01
	Indianapolis MSA, IN	H	7.18 FQ	15.95 AW	28.31 TQ	INBLS	10/01-12/01
	Iowa	H	10.48 FQ	18.89 AW	27.04 TQ	IABLS	10/01-12/01
	Cedar Rapids MSA, IA	H	18.93 FQ	22.83 AW	27.64 TQ	IABLS	10/01-12/01
	Davenport-Moline-Rock Island MSA, IA-IL	H	17.93 FQ	21.60 AW	26.93 TQ	IABLS	10/01-12/01
	Des Moines MSA, IA	H	9.99 FQ	19.12 AW	28.00 TQ	IABLS	10/01-12/01
	Kansas	H	12.32 FQ	18.97 AW	25.93 TQ	KSBLS	10/01-12/01
	Wichita MSA, KS	H	15.17 FQ	20.79 AW	26.70 TQ	KSBLS	10/01-12/01
	Kentucky	H	12.48 FQ	18.28 AW	22.73 TQ	KYBLS	10/01-12/01
	Lexington MSA, KY	H	14.09 FQ	16.22 AW	20.25 TQ	KYBLS	10/01-12/01
	Louisville MSA, KY-IN	H	12.04 FQ	18.30 AW	22.74 TQ	KYBLS	10/01-12/01
	Louisiana	H	11.14 FQ	16.30 AW	21.33 TQ	LABLS	10/01-12/01
	Baton Rouge MSA, LA	H	13.36 FQ	17.10 AW	21.47 TQ	LABLS	10/01-12/01
	Lafayette MSA, LA	H	12.84 FQ	18.41 AW	22.67 TQ	LABLS	10/01-12/01
	Lake Charles MSA, LA	H	12.68 FQ	16.30 AW	20.76 TQ	LABLS	10/01-12/01
	New Orleans MSA, LA	H	10.30 FQ	15.39 AW	20.97 TQ	LABLS	10/01-12/01
	Shreveport-Bossier City MSA, LA	H	10.42 FQ	16.94 AW	21.90 TQ	LABLS	10/01-12/01
	Maine	H	11.34 FQ	16.00 AW	21.18 TQ	MEBLS	10/01-12/01
	Portland MSA, ME	H	13.27 FQ	17.87 AW	21.87 TQ	MEBLS	10/01-12/01
	Maryland	H	13.54 FQ	19.74 AW	25.85 TQ	MDBLS	10/01-12/01
	Baltimore PMSA, MD	H	14.18 FQ	20.89 AW	26.35 TQ	MDBLS	10/01-12/01
	Massachusetts	H	18.16 FQ	27.49 AW	34.45 TQ	MABLS	10/01-12/01
	Boston PMSA, MA-NH	H	19.78 FQ	28.86 AW	34.47 TQ	MABLS	10/01-12/01
	Brockton PMSA, MA	H	7.73 FQ	22.85 AW	33.34 TQ	MABLS	10/01-12/01
	Lawrence PMSA, MA-NH	H	17.37 FQ	25.76 AW	35.16 TQ	MABLS	10/01-12/01
	Lowell PMSA, MA-NH	H	16.48 FQ	19.55 AW	22.20 TQ	MABLS	10/01-12/01
	New Bedford PMSA, MA	H	21.87 FQ	29.00 AW	37.03 TQ	MABLS	10/01-12/01
	Springfield MSA, MA	H	21.87 FQ	28.25 AW	34.60 TQ	MABLS	10/01-12/01
	Worcester PMSA, MA-CT	H	16.97 FQ	24.28 AW	28.95 TQ	MABLS	10/01-12/01
	Michigan	H	15.12 FQ	22.91 AW	30.79 TQ	MIBLS	10/01-12/01
	Ann Arbor PMSA, MI	H	19.73 FQ	28.57 AW	40.71 TQ	MIBLS	10/01-12/01
	Detroit PMSA, MI	H	15.98 FQ	24.03 AW	31.14 TQ	MIBLS	10/01-12/01
	Flint PMSA, MI	H	15.57 FQ	20.17 AW	26.54 TQ	MIBLS	10/01-12/01
	Grand Rapids-Muskegon-Holland MSA, MI	H	15.68 FQ	21.15 AW	28.05 TQ	MIBLS	10/01-12/01
	Lansing-East Lansing MSA, MI	H	18.55 FQ	25.00 AW	31.76 TQ	MIBLS	10/01-12/01
	Saginaw-Bay City-Midland MSA, MI	H	13.46 FQ	20.02 AW	26.40 TQ	MIBLS	10/01-12/01
	Minnesota	H	18.51 FQ	25.19 AW	31.44 TQ	MNBLS	10/01-12/01
	Minneapolis-St. Paul MSA, MN-WI	H	17.45 FQ	24.92 AW	31.17 TQ	MNBLS	10/01-12/01
	St. Cloud MSA, MN	H	16.97 FQ	26.28 AW	34.57 TQ	MNBLS	10/01-12/01
	Mississippi	H	9.31 FQ	14.29 AW	21.25 TQ	MSBLS	10/01-12/01

AAW	Average annual wage	**AOH**	Average offered, high	**ASH**	Average starting, high	**H**	Hourly	**M**	Monthly	**S**	Special: hourly and annual
AE	Average entry wage	**AOL**	Average offered, low	**ASL**	Average starting, low	**HI**	Highest wage paid	**MTC**	Median total compensation	**TQ**	Third quartile wage
AEX	Average experienced wage	**APH**	Average pay, high range	**AW**	Average wage paid	**HR**	High end range	**MW**	Median wage paid	**W**	Weekly
AO	Average offered	**APL**	Average pay, low range	**FQ**	First quartile wage	**LR**	Low end range	**SQ**	Second quartile wage	**Y**	Yearly

Occupation/Type/Industry	Location	Per	Low	Mid	High	Source	Date
Brickmason and Blockmason	Biloxi-Gulfport-Pascagoula MSA, MS	H	8.92 FQ	10.72 AW	13.21 TQ	MSBLS	10/01-12/01
	Jackson MSA, MS	H	9.78 FQ	14.60 AW	20.14 TQ	MSBLS	10/01-12/01
	Missouri	H	12.90 FQ	20.51 AW	27.34 TQ	MOBLS	10/01-12/01
	Kansas City MSA, MO-KS	H	15.44 FQ	21.99 AW	27.14 TQ	MOBLS	10/01-12/01
	St. Louis MSA, MO-IL	H	14.43 FQ	21.66 AW	27.94 TQ	MOBLS	10/01-12/01
	Montana	H	12.35 FQ	20.27 AW	27.73 TQ	MTBLS	10/01-12/01
	Nebraska	H	12.15 FQ	18.43 AW	25.79 TQ	NEBLS	10/01-12/01
	Lincoln MSA, NE	H	11.97 FQ	20.24 AW	27.29 TQ	NEBLS	10/01-12/01
	Omaha MSA, NE-IA	H	12.48 FQ	18.77 AW	26.11 TQ	NEBLS	10/01-12/01
	Nevada	H	9.60 FQ	17.72 AW	26.86 TQ	NVBLS	10/01-12/01
	Las Vegas MSA, NV-AZ	H	9.51 FQ	16.87 AW	26.35 TQ	NVBLS	10/01-12/01
	Reno MSA, NV	H	18.58 FQ	21.67 AW	26.82 TQ	NVBLS	10/01-12/01
	New Hampshire	H	16.04 FQ	21.11 AW	27.10 TQ	NHBLS	10/01-12/01
	New Jersey	H	13.16 FQ	24.30 AW	34.40 TQ	NJBLS	10/01-12/01
	Atlantic-Cape May PMSA, NJ	H	18.85 FQ	26.59 AW	34.55 TQ	NJBLS	10/01-12/01
	Bergen-Passaic PMSA, NJ	H	15.11 FQ	24.40 AW	33.75 TQ	NJBLS	10/01-12/01
	Jersey City PMSA, NJ	H	15.29 FQ	26.49 AW	36.77 TQ	NJBLS	10/01-12/01
	Middlesex-Somerset-Hunterdon PMSA, NJ	H	23.25 FQ	29.06 AW	34.41 TQ	NJBLS	10/01-12/01
	Monmouth-Ocean PMSA, NJ	H	13.29 FQ	23.02 AW	34.42 TQ	NJBLS	10/01-12/01
	Newark PMSA, NJ	H	10.69 FQ	20.35 AW	32.72 TQ	NJBLS	10/01-12/01
	Trenton PMSA, NJ	H	10.21 FQ	22.94 AW	39.73 TQ	NJBLS	10/01-12/01
	New Mexico	H	8.84 FQ	15.29 AW	22.19 TQ	NMBLS	10/01-12/01
	Albuquerque MSA, NM	H	8.83 FQ	15.79 AW	24.72 TQ	NMBLS	10/01-12/01
	New York	H	12.30 FQ	22.57 AW	34.22 TQ	NYBLS	10/01-12/01
	Albany-Schenectady-Troy MSA, NY	H	15.66 FQ	21.46 AW	27.10 TQ	NYBLS	10/01-12/01
	Buffalo-Niagara Falls MSA, NY	H	15.64 FQ	21.99 AW	27.84 TQ	NYBLS	10/01-12/01
	Dutchess County PMSA, NY	H	22.68 FQ	24.88 AW	27.99 TQ	NYBLS	10/01-12/01
	Nassau-Suffolk PMSA, NY	H	7.62 FQ	20.70 AW	33.95 TQ	NYBLS	10/01-12/01
	New York PMSA, NY	H	13.63 FQ	25.12 AW	36.43 TQ	NYBLS	10/01-12/01
	Newburgh PMSA, NY-PA	H	14.32 FQ	18.23 AW	26.67 TQ	NYBLS	10/01-12/01
	Rochester MSA, NY	H	14.21 FQ	18.51 AW	24.22 TQ	NYBLS	10/01-12/01
	Syracuse MSA, NY	H	15.51 FQ	19.14 AW	22.48 TQ	NYBLS	10/01-12/01
	Utica-Rome MSA, NY	H	18.24 FQ	26.60 AW	33.37 TQ	NYBLS	10/01-12/01
	North Carolina	H	11.77 FQ	16.44 AW	20.96 TQ	NCBLS	10/01-12/01
	Asheville MSA, NC	H	10.07 FQ	16.42 AW	21.37 TQ	NCBLS	10/01-12/01
	Charlotte-Gastonia-Rock Hill MSA, NC-SC	H	12.50 FQ	15.70 AW	19.68 TQ	NCBLS	10/01-12/01
	Fayetteville MSA, NC	H	13.64 FQ	17.83 AW	21.39 TQ	NCBLS	10/01-12/01
	Greensboro-Winston-Salem-High Point MSA, NC	H	16.17 FQ	18.48 AW	21.00 TQ	NCBLS	10/01-12/01
	Raleigh-Durham-Chapel Hill MSA, NC	H	11.36 FQ	17.20 AW	22.28 TQ	NCBLS	10/01-12/01
	Wilmington MSA, NC	H	11.69 FQ	15.60 AW	20.44 TQ	NCBLS	10/01-12/01
	North Dakota	H	15.19 FQ	21.31 AW	27.29 TQ	NDBLS	10/01-12/01
	Ohio	H	12.99 FQ	20.30 AW	27.60 TQ	OHBLS	10/01-12/01
	Akron PMSA, OH	H	16.43 FQ	23.34 AW	28.52 TQ	OHBLS	10/01-12/01
	Canton-Massillon MSA, OH	H	11.66 FQ	18.12 AW	26.26 TQ	OHBLS	10/01-12/01
	Cincinnati PMSA, OH-KY-IN	H	13.42 FQ	18.76 AW	25.24 TQ	OHBLS	10/01-12/01
	Cleveland-Lorain-Elyria PMSA, OH	H	18.00 FQ	21.63 AW	27.45 TQ	OHBLS	10/01-12/01
	Columbus MSA, OH	H	10.38 FQ	19.73 AW	27.54 TQ	OHBLS	10/01-12/01
	Dayton-Springfield MSA, OH	H	9.95 FQ	14.98 AW	24.61 TQ	OHBLS	10/01-12/01
	Hamilton-Middletown PMSA, OH	H	11.27 FQ	17.86 AW	25.57 TQ	OHBLS	10/01-12/01
	Mansfield MSA, OH	H	14.20 FQ	21.70 AW	28.18 TQ	OHBLS	10/01-12/01
	Toledo MSA, OH	H	15.77 FQ	25.13 AW	33.91 TQ	OHBLS	10/01-12/01
	Youngstown-Warren MSA, OH	H	18.48 FQ	22.39 AW	27.78 TQ	OHBLS	10/01-12/01
	Oklahoma	H	9.44 FQ	17.46 AW	24.20 TQ	OKBLS	10/01-12/01
	Oklahoma City MSA, OK	H	12.75 FQ	18.53 AW	22.50 TQ	OKBLS	10/01-12/01
	Tulsa MSA, OK	H	14.60 FQ	19.48 AW	25.66 TQ	OKBLS	10/01-12/01
	Oregon	H	18.92 FQ	25.09 AW	32.43 TQ	ORBLS	10/01-12/01
	Eugene-Springfield MSA, OR	H	20.20 FQ	24.67 AW	28.63 TQ	ORBLS	10/01-12/01
	Portland-Vancouver PMSA, OR-WA	H	16.46 FQ	24.16 AW	32.29 TQ	ORBLS	10/01-12/01
	Salem PMSA, OR	H	22.13 FQ	26.85 AW	33.73 TQ	ORBLS	10/01-12/01
	Pennsylvania	H	12.42 FQ	20.87 AW	31.24 TQ	PABLS	10/01-12/01
	Allentown-Bethlehem-Easton MSA, PA	H	14.32 FQ	20.55 AW	32.22 TQ	PABLS	10/01-12/01

AAW	Average annual wage	**AOH**	Average offered, high	**ASH**	Average starting, high	**H**	Hourly	**M**	Monthly	**S**	Special: hourly and annual
AE	Average entry wage	**AOL**	Average offered, low	**ASL**	Average starting, low	**HI**	Highest wage paid	**MTC**	Median total compensation	**TQ**	Third quartile wage
AEX	Average experienced wage	**APH**	Average pay, high range	**AW**	Average wage paid	**HR**	High end range	**MW**	Median wage paid	**W**	Weekly
AO	Average offered	**APL**	Average pay, low range	**FQ**	First quartile wage	**LR**	Low end range	**SQ**	Second quartile wage	**Y**	Yearly

Occupation/Type/Industry	Location	Per	Low	Mid	High	Source	Date
Brickmason and Blockmason	Erie MSA, PA	H	11.07 FQ	18.41 AW	30.49 TQ	PABLS	10/01-12/01
	Harrisburg-Lebanon-Carlisle MSA, PA	H	15.12 FQ	19.56 AW	25.40 TQ	PABLS	10/01-12/01
	Johnstown MSA, PA	H	9.93 FQ	13.91 AW	17.72 TQ	PABLS	10/01-12/01
	Lancaster MSA, PA	H	13.86 FQ	19.03 AW	26.89 TQ	PABLS	10/01-12/01
	Philadelphia PMSA, PA-NJ	H	14.45 FQ	26.38 AW	36.22 TQ	PABLS	10/01-12/01
	Pittsburgh MSA, PA	H	11.99 FQ	19.18 AW	28.08 TQ	PABLS	10/01-12/01
	Reading MSA, PA	H	15.46 FQ	23.71 AW	31.95 TQ	PABLS	10/01-12/01
	Scranton-Wilkes-Barre-Hazleton MSA, PA	H	13.20 FQ	19.07 AW	29.91 TQ	PABLS	10/01-12/01
	York MSA, PA	H	12.26 FQ	18.03 AW	25.47 TQ	PABLS	10/01-12/01
	Rhode Island	H	15.08 FQ	21.23 AW	26.79 TQ	RIBLS	10/01-12/01
	Providence-Fall River-Warwick MSA, RI-MA	H	15.30 FQ	20.95 AW	26.68 TQ	RIBLS	10/01-12/01
	South Carolina	H	9.98 FQ	16.48 AW	21.34 TQ	SCBLS	10/01-12/01
	Charleston-North Charleston MSA, SC	H	6.26 FQ	14.24 AW	20.52 TQ	SCBLS	10/01-12/01
	Columbia MSA, SC	H	8.36 FQ	15.57 AW	22.35 TQ	SCBLS	10/01-12/01
	Greenville-Spartanburg-Anderson MSA, SC	H	14.74 FQ	18.43 AW	21.37 TQ	SCBLS	10/01-12/01
	Myrtle Beach MSA, SC	H	11.17 FQ	18.26 AW	25.85 TQ	SCBLS	10/01-12/01
	South Dakota	H	13.11 FQ	18.94 AW	25.20 TQ	SDBLS	10/01-12/01
	Sioux Falls MSA, SD	H	12.94 FQ	18.44 AW	22.44 TQ	SDBLS	10/01-12/01
	Tennessee	H	11.40 FQ	17.83 AW	23.27 TQ	TNBLS	10/01-12/01
	Chattanooga MSA, TN-GA	H	11.40 FQ	15.90 AW	20.59 TQ	TNBLS	10/01-12/01
	Clarksville-Hopkinsville MSA, TN-KY	H	12.25 FQ	17.46 AW	24.61 TQ	TNBLS	10/01-12/01
	Johnson City-Kingsport-Bristol MSA, TN-VA	H	16.13 FQ	21.03 AW	25.86 TQ	TNBLS	10/01-12/01
	Knoxville MSA, TN	H	17.94 FQ	20.34 AW	25.14 TQ	TNBLS	10/01-12/01
	Memphis MSA, TN-AR-MS	H	11.35 FQ	19.61 AW	26.61 TQ	TNBLS	10/01-12/01
	Nashville MSA, TN	H	10.18 FQ	16.65 AW	22.24 TQ	TNBLS	10/01-12/01
	Texas	H	9.93 FQ	16.89 AW	21.96 TQ	TXBLS	10/01-12/01
	Amarillo MSA, TX	H	12.76 FQ	18.44 AW	22.21 TQ	TXBLS	10/01-12/01
	Austin-San Marcos MSA, TX	H	11.71 FQ	15.50 AW	20.18 TQ	TXBLS	10/01-12/01
	Beaumont-Port Arthur MSA, TX	H	13.50 FQ	18.50 AW	22.03 TQ	TXBLS	10/01-12/01
	Corpus Christi MSA, TX	H	9.48 FQ	15.13 AW	20.54 TQ	TXBLS	10/01-12/01
	Dallas PMSA, TX	H	11.26 FQ	17.41 AW	21.95 TQ	TXBLS	10/01-12/01
	El Paso MSA, TX	H	17.88 FQ	19.95 AW	22.42 TQ	TXBLS	10/01-12/01
	Fort Worth-Arlington PMSA, TX	H	8.76 FQ	17.66 AW	22.58 TQ	TXBLS	10/01-12/01
	Galveston-Texas City PMSA, TX	H	15.94 FQ	19.24 AW	21.78 TQ	TXBLS	10/01-12/01
	Houston PMSA, TX	H	13.92 FQ	18.59 AW	22.29 TQ	TXBLS	10/01-12/01
	Lubbock MSA, TX	H	14.63 FQ	17.54 AW	21.10 TQ	TXBLS	10/01-12/01
	McAllen-Edinburg-Mission MSA, TX	H	9.18 FQ	14.79 AW	20.84 TQ	TXBLS	10/01-12/01
	Odessa-Midland MSA, TX	H	14.50 FQ	19.09 AW	22.71 TQ	TXBLS	10/01-12/01
	San Antonio MSA, TX	H	7.08 FQ	13.05 AW	20.22 TQ	TXBLS	10/01-12/01
	Waco MSA, TX	H	15.47 FQ	19.36 AW	22.62 TQ	TXBLS	10/01-12/01
	Utah	H	16.66 FQ	25.10 AW	40.55 TQ	UTBLS	10/01-12/01
	Provo-Orem MSA, UT	H	15.95 FQ	27.05 AW	41.69 TQ	UTBLS	10/01-12/01
	Salt Lake City-Ogden MSA, UT	H	18.76 FQ	26.84 AW	41.66 TQ	UTBLS	10/01-12/01
	Vermont	H	14.89 FQ	19.61 AW	22.29 TQ	VTBLS	10/01-12/01
	Burlington MSA, VT	H	14.79 FQ	17.47 AW	21.41 TQ	VTBLS	10/01-12/01
	Virginia	H	12.11 FQ	18.16 AW	23.00 TQ	VABLS	10/01-12/01
	Lynchburg MSA, VA	H	9.76 FQ	17.49 AW	21.41 TQ	VABLS	10/01-12/01
	Norfolk-Virginia Beach-Newport News MSA, VA-NC	H	10.80 FQ	17.77 AW	22.01 TQ	VABLS	10/01-12/01
	Richmond-Petersburg MSA, VA	H	15.65 FQ	19.68 AW	22.98 TQ	VABLS	10/01-12/01
	Roanoke MSA, VA	H	14.96 FQ	19.01 AW	22.30 TQ	VABLS	10/01-12/01
	Washington	H	16.65 FQ	24.29 AW	33.26 TQ	WABLS	10/01-12/01
	Seattle-Bellevue-Everett PMSA, WA	H	16.07 FQ	24.04 AW	33.21 TQ	WABLS	10/01-12/01
	West Virginia	H	10.89 FQ	16.34 AW	25.33 TQ	WVBLS	10/01-12/01
	Charleston MSA, WV	H	10.36 FQ	13.84 AW	17.33 TQ	WVBLS	10/01-12/01
	Huntington-Ashland MSA, WV-KY-OH	H	9.93 FQ	14.09 AW	19.65 TQ	WVBLS	10/01-12/01

AAW Average annual wage; **AE** Average entry wage; **AEX** Average experienced wage; **AO** Average offered; **AOH** Average offered, high; **AOL** Average offered, low; **APH** Average pay, high range; **APL** Average pay, low range; **ASH** Average starting, high; **ASL** Average starting, low; **AW** Average wage paid; **FQ** First quartile wage; **H** Hourly; **HI** Highest wage paid; **HR** High end range; **LR** Low end range; **M** Monthly; **MTC** Median total compensation; **MW** Median wage paid; **SQ** Second quartile wage; **S** Special: hourly and annual; **TQ** Third quartile wage; **W** Weekly; **Y** Yearly

Occupation/Type/Industry	Location	Per	Low	Mid	High	Source	Date
Brickmason and Blockmason	Wisconsin	H	13.33 FQ	21.62 AW	28.89 TQ	WIBLS	10/01-12/01
	Appleton-Oshkosh-Neenah MSA, WI	H	14.75 FQ	20.47 AW	27.25 TQ	WIBLS	10/01-12/01
	Green Bay MSA, WI	H	17.02 FQ	22.73 AW	26.93 TQ	WIBLS	10/01-12/01
	Madison MSA, WI	H	13.48 FQ	22.55 AW	28.63 TQ	WIBLS	10/01-12/01
	Milwaukee-Waukesha PMSA, WI	H	14.19 FQ	22.95 AW	31.34 TQ	WIBLS	10/01-12/01
	Racine PMSA, WI	H	18.14 FQ	24.34 AW	29.05 TQ	WIBLS	10/01-12/01
	Wyoming	H	10.88 FQ	18.10 AW	26.06 TQ	WYBLS	10/01-12/01
	Puerto Rico	H	5.73 FQ	7.34 AW	8.82 TQ	PRBLS	10/01-12/01
	Virgin Islands	H	11.59 FQ	14.73 AW	18.16 TQ	VIBLS	10/01-12/01
	Guam	H	9.64 FQ	11.95 AW	13.73 TQ	GUBLS	10/01-12/01
Bridge and Lock Tender	Alabama	H	15.37 FQ	18.03 AW	20.91 TQ	ALBLS	10/01-12/01
	Arkansas	H	13.18 FQ	15.05 AW	16.98 TQ	ARBLS	10/01-12/01
	California	H	14.79 FQ	17.45 AW	20.72 TQ	CABLS	10/01-12/01
	Connecticut	H	10.70 FQ	15.50 AW	20.81 TQ	CTBLS	10/01-12/01
	Florida	H	6.52 FQ	10.91 AW	18.83 TQ	FLBLS	10/01-12/01
	West Palm Beach-Boca Raton MSA, FL	H	6.31 FQ	10.92 AW	19.48 TQ	FLBLS	10/01-12/01
	Georgia	H	9.86 FQ	15.66 AW	22.32 TQ	GABLS	10/01-12/01
	Illinois	H	15.38 FQ	18.53 AW	21.34 TQ	ILBLS	10/01-12/01
	Chicago PMSA, IL	H	14.49 FQ	18.06 AW	21.26 TQ	ILBLS	10/01-12/01
	Indiana	H	13.81 FQ	17.37 AW	20.89 TQ	INBLS	10/01-12/01
	Iowa	H	17.28 FQ	18.91 AW	21.03 TQ	IABLS	10/01-12/01
	Kentucky	H	16.75 FQ	18.55 AW	21.07 TQ	KYBLS	10/01-12/01
	Louisiana	H	6.86 FQ	11.73 AW	18.88 TQ	LABLS	10/01-12/01
	Houma MSA, LA	H	6.08 FQ	8.32 AW	11.22 TQ	LABLS	10/01-12/01
	Lake Charles MSA, LA	H	9.53 FQ	14.71 AW	18.17 TQ	LABLS	10/01-12/01
	New Orleans MSA, LA	H	7.39 FQ	11.49 AW	17.60 TQ	LABLS	10/01-12/01
	Michigan	H	8.35 FQ	14.12 AW	20.98 TQ	MIBLS	10/01-12/01
	Detroit PMSA, MI	H	7.82 FQ	10.84 AW	14.57 TQ	MIBLS	10/01-12/01
	Minnesota	H	17.13 FQ	19.18 AW	21.41 TQ	MNBLS	10/01-12/01
	Minneapolis-St. Paul MSA, MN-WI	H	17.41 FQ	19.72 AW	23.65 TQ	MNBLS	10/01-12/01
	Mississippi	H	6.13 FQ	14.84 AW	20.74 TQ	MSBLS	10/01-12/01
	Missouri	H	17.50 FQ	20.15 AW	23.44 TQ	MOBLS	10/01-12/01
	St. Louis MSA, MO-IL	H	17.71 FQ	20.89 AW	25.26 TQ	MOBLS	10/01-12/01
	New York	H	9.00 FQ	15.56 AW	20.82 TQ	NYBLS	10/01-12/01
	New York PMSA, NY	H	7.76 FQ	14.49 AW	20.89 TQ	NYBLS	10/01-12/01
	North Carolina	H	5.62 FQ	8.97 AW	19.26 TQ	NCBLS	10/01-12/01
	Ohio	H	13.05 FQ	16.50 AW	20.50 TQ	OHBLS	10/01-12/01
	Pennsylvania	H	14.86 FQ	17.83 AW	20.92 TQ	PABLS	10/01-12/01
	Pittsburgh MSA, PA	H	14.37 FQ	17.81 AW	20.96 TQ	PABLS	10/01-12/01
	Tennessee	H	16.68 FQ	18.63 AW	20.99 TQ	TNBLS	10/01-12/01
	Washington	H	13.92 FQ	18.26 AW	22.95 TQ	WABLS	10/01-12/01
	Seattle-Bellevue-Everett PMSA, WA	H	13.92 FQ	18.44 AW	22.94 TQ	WABLS	10/01-12/01
	West Virginia	H	15.22 FQ	18.26 AW	20.94 TQ	WVBLS	10/01-12/01
	Wisconsin	H	14.62 FQ	17.30 AW	20.85 TQ	WIBLS	10/01-12/01
Broadcast Technician	Alabama	Y	12510 FQ	22690 AW	35970 TQ	ALBLS	10/01-12/01
	Birmingham MSA, AL	Y	12120 FQ	24230 AW	44470 TQ	ALBLS	10/01-12/01
	Huntsville MSA, AL	Y	20880 FQ	24120 AW	27580 TQ	ALBLS	10/01-12/01
	Mobile MSA, AL	Y	14310 FQ	19920 AW	27810 TQ	ALBLS	10/01-12/01
	Montgomery MSA, AL	Y	12810 FQ	23590 AW	39300 TQ	ALBLS	10/01-12/01
	Alaska	Y	16280 FQ	31720 AW	51140 TQ	AKBLS	10/01-12/01
	Anchorage MSA, AK	Y	15720 FQ	28880 AW	45110 TQ	AKBLS	10/01-12/01
	Arizona	Y	13130 FQ	27700 AW	55680 TQ	AZBLS	10/01-12/01
	Phoenix-Mesa MSA, AZ	Y	13580 FQ	27390 AW	52900 TQ	AZBLS	10/01-12/01
	Tucson MSA, AZ	Y	19150 FQ	37210 AW	68980 TQ	AZBLS	10/01-12/01
	Arkansas	Y	12230 FQ	22750 AW	38600 TQ	ARBLS	10/01-12/01
	Little Rock-North Little Rock MSA, AR	Y	18610 FQ	29800 AW	42150 TQ	ARBLS	10/01-12/01
	California	Y	14490 FQ	42550 AW	86530 TQ	CABLS	10/01-12/01
	Bakersfield MSA, CA	Y	14330 FQ	41340 AW	79650 TQ	CABLS	10/01-12/01
	Chico-Paradise MSA, CA	Y	13620 FQ	19230 AW	29980 TQ	CABLS	10/01-12/01
	Fresno MSA, CA	Y	15530 FQ	25850 AW	42720 TQ	CABLS	10/01-12/01
	Los Angeles-Long Beach PMSA, CA	Y	14510 FQ	51250 AW	90620 TQ	CABLS	10/01-12/01
	Oakland PMSA, CA	Y	17710 FQ	41530 AW	57800 TQ	CABLS	10/01-12/01
	Orange County PMSA, CA	Y	14480 FQ	26090 AW	47440 TQ	CABLS	10/01-12/01

AAW Average annual wage **AOH** Average offered, high **ASH** Average starting, high **H** Hourly **M** Monthly **S** Special: hourly and annual
AE Average entry wage **AOL** Average offered, low **ASL** Average starting, low **HI** Highest wage paid **MTC** Median total compensation **TQ** Third quartile wage
AEX Average experienced wage **APH** Average pay, high range **AW** Average wage paid **HR** High end range **MW** Median wage paid **W** Weekly
AO Average offered **APL** Average pay, low range **FQ** First quartile wage **LR** Low end range **SQ** Second quartile wage **Y** Yearly

Occupation/Type/Industry	Location	Per	Low	Mid	High	Source	Date
Broadcast Technician	Riverside-San Bernardino PMSA, CA	Y	14170 FQ	23100 AW	33890 TQ	CABLS	10/01-12/01
	Sacramento PMSA, CA	Y	15860 FQ	34170 AW	75970 TQ	CABLS	10/01-12/01
	San Diego MSA, CA	Y	14600 FQ	28220 AW	52250 TQ	CABLS	10/01-12/01
	San Francisco PMSA, CA	Y	18180 FQ	48300 AW	86590 TQ	CABLS	10/01-12/01
	San Jose PMSA, CA	Y	14570 FQ	28890 AW	52920 TQ	CABLS	10/01-12/01
	Colorado	Y	14940 FQ	31940 AW	54120 TQ	COBLS	10/01-12/01
	Boulder-Longmont PMSA, CO	Y	20670 FQ	33900 AW	53300 TQ	COBLS	10/01-12/01
	Colorado Springs MSA, CO	Y	23840 FQ	30580 AW	43040 TQ	COBLS	10/01-12/01
	Denver PMSA, CO	Y	15190 FQ	33200 AW	57450 TQ	COBLS	10/01-12/01
	Connecticut	Y	18010 FQ	34010 AW	56480 TQ	CTBLS	10/01-12/01
	Hartford MSA, CT	Y	18630 FQ	33940 AW	56870 TQ	CTBLS	10/01-12/01
	Stamford-Norwalk PMSA, CT	Y	18000 FQ	35810 AW	64930 TQ	CTBLS	10/01-12/01
	District of Columbia	Y	16790 FQ	40970 AW	70460 TQ	DCBLS	10/01-12/01
	Washington PMSA, DC-MD-VA-WV	Y	16880 FQ	40720 AW	69830 TQ	DCBLS	10/01-12/01
	Florida	Y	14520 FQ	30160 AW	49350 TQ	FLBLS	10/01-12/01
	Daytona Beach MSA, FL	Y	12850 FQ	27290 AW	49320 TQ	FLBLS	10/01-12/01
	Fort Lauderdale PMSA, FL	Y	13110 FQ	29450 AW	51140 TQ	FLBLS	10/01-12/01
	Fort Myers-Cape Coral MSA, FL	Y	16390 FQ	34650 AW	56540 TQ	FLBLS	10/01-12/01
	Fort Pierce-Port St. Lucie MSA, FL	Y	14030 FQ	18630 AW	26180 TQ	FLBLS	10/01-12/01
	Gainesville MSA, FL	Y	16700 FQ	30180 AW	42700 TQ	FLBLS	10/01-12/01
	Jacksonville MSA, FL	Y	14620 FQ	23280 AW	35910 TQ	FLBLS	10/01-12/01
	Melbourne-Titusville-Palm Bay MSA, FL	Y	13180 FQ	25770 AW	43280 TQ	FLBLS	10/01-12/01
	Miami PMSA, FL	Y	14390 FQ	33350 AW	53160 TQ	FLBLS	10/01-12/01
	Orlando MSA, FL	Y	14640 FQ	29380 AW	44440 TQ	FLBLS	10/01-12/01
	Pensacola MSA, FL	Y	12710 FQ	24920 AW	38440 TQ	FLBLS	10/01-12/01
	Tallahassee MSA, FL	Y	13310 FQ	27100 AW	38880 TQ	FLBLS	10/01-12/01
	Tampa-St. Petersburg-Clearwater MSA, FL	Y	18440 FQ	30680 AW	49880 TQ	FLBLS	10/01-12/01
	West Palm Beach-Boca Raton MSA, FL	Y	13740 FQ	26650 AW	41740 TQ	FLBLS	10/01-12/01
	Georgia	Y	13600 FQ	35330 AW	66710 TQ	GABLS	10/01-12/01
	Atlanta MSA, GA	Y	15190 FQ	38970 AW	70210 TQ	GABLS	10/01-12/01
	Savannah MSA, GA	Y	12080 FQ	27470 AW	44760 TQ	GABLS	10/01-12/01
	Hawaii	Y	15490 FQ	31010 AW	49120 TQ	HIBLS	10/01-12/01
	Honolulu MSA, HI	Y	17190 FQ	31610 AW	48320 TQ	HIBLS	10/01-12/01
	Idaho	Y	11690 FQ	20680 AW	38980 TQ	IDBLS	10/01-12/01
	Boise City MSA, ID	Y	11620 FQ	21500 AW	42590 TQ	IDBLS	10/01-12/01
	Illinois	Y	13780 FQ	30820 AW	56050 TQ	ILBLS	10/01-12/01
	Champaign-Urbana MSA, IL	Y	15040 FQ	24860 AW	41130 TQ	ILBLS	10/01-12/01
	Chicago PMSA, IL	Y	13570 FQ	32690 AW	63310 TQ	ILBLS	10/01-12/01
	Peoria-Pekin MSA, IL	Y	12340 FQ	22030 AW	43240 TQ	ILBLS	10/01-12/01
	Indiana	Y	14170 FQ	26870 AW	49130 TQ	INBLS	10/01-12/01
	Evansville-Henderson MSA, IN-KY	Y	12020 FQ	19730 AW	31690 TQ	INBLS	10/01-12/01
	Fort Wayne MSA, IN	Y	15010 FQ	23000 AW	36770 TQ	INBLS	10/01-12/01
	Indianapolis MSA, IN	Y	14770 FQ	29330 AW	53080 TQ	INBLS	10/01-12/01
	Iowa	Y	12670 FQ	29770 AW	50500 TQ	IABLS	10/01-12/01
	Davenport-Moline-Rock Island MSA, IA-IL	Y	15100 FQ	27750 AW	42370 TQ	IABLS	10/01-12/01
	Kansas	Y	14650 FQ	24920 AW	38510 TQ	KSBLS	10/01-12/01
	Wichita MSA, KS	Y	14830 FQ	24920 AW	35930 TQ	KSBLS	10/01-12/01
	Kentucky	Y	15200 FQ	28680 AW	47490 TQ	KYBLS	10/01-12/01
	Lexington MSA, KY	Y	19010 FQ	33840 AW	52190 TQ	KYBLS	10/01-12/01
	Louisville MSA, KY-IN	Y	14360 FQ	28410 AW	47870 TQ	KYBLS	10/01-12/01
	Louisiana	Y	12500 FQ	24840 AW	51050 TQ	LABLS	10/01-12/01
	Baton Rouge MSA, LA	Y	13540 FQ	26790 AW	52270 TQ	LABLS	10/01-12/01
	New Orleans MSA, LA	Y	13170 FQ	31810 AW	54870 TQ	LABLS	10/01-12/01
	Maine	Y	13840 FQ	24230 AW	39820 TQ	MEBLS	10/01-12/01
	Portland MSA, ME	Y	17990 FQ	30970 AW	56330 TQ	MEBLS	10/01-12/01
	Maryland	Y	16350 FQ	37510 AW	65770 TQ	MDBLS	10/01-12/01
	Baltimore PMSA, MD	Y	16400 FQ	37580 AW	66590 TQ	MDBLS	10/01-12/01
	Massachusetts	Y	15490 FQ	36590 AW	65740 TQ	MABLS	10/01-12/01
	Boston PMSA, MA-NH	Y	16210 FQ	37930 AW	67090 TQ	MABLS	10/01-12/01
	Springfield MSA, MA	Y	15850 FQ	39560 AW	68090 TQ	MABLS	10/01-12/01
	Michigan	Y	15010 FQ	34630 AW	67320 TQ	MIBLS	10/01-12/01
	Detroit PMSA, MI	Y	14070 FQ	38400 AW	70300 TQ	MIBLS	10/01-12/01
	Flint PMSA, MI	Y	15650 FQ	36810 AW	71280 TQ	MIBLS	10/01-12/01

AAW Average annual wage; **AE** Average entry wage; **AEX** Average experienced wage; **AO** Average offered; **AOH** Average offered, high; **AOL** Average offered, low; **APH** Average pay, high range; **APL** Average pay, low range; **ASH** Average starting, high; **ASL** Average starting, low; **AW** Average wage paid; **FQ** First quartile wage; **H** Hourly; **HI** Highest wage paid; **HR** High end range; **LR** Low end range; **M** Monthly; **MTC** Median total compensation; **MW** Median wage paid; **SQ** Second quartile wage; **S** Special: hourly and annual; **TQ** Third quartile wage; **W** Weekly; **Y** Yearly

Occupation/Type/Industry	Location	Per	Low	Mid	High	Source	Date
Broadcast Technician	Grand Rapids-Muskegon-Holland MSA, MI	Y	16050 FQ	28680 AW	50040 TQ	MIBLS	10/01-12/01
	Lansing-East Lansing MSA, MI	Y	14860 FQ	33600 AW	58940 TQ	MIBLS	10/01-12/01
	Minnesota	Y	14910 FQ	29800 AW	52820 TQ	MNBLS	10/01-12/01
	Minneapolis-St. Paul MSA, MN-WI	Y	13880 FQ	32310 AW	55130 TQ	MNBLS	10/01-12/01
	Mississippi	Y	12050 FQ	20740 AW	31940 TQ	MSBLS	10/01-12/01
	Biloxi-Gulfport-Pascagoula MSA, MS	Y	12010 FQ	17630 AW	27340 TQ	MSBLS	10/01-12/01
	Jackson MSA, MS	Y	12270 FQ	22110 AW	30650 TQ	MSBLS	10/01-12/01
	Missouri	Y	13200 FQ	26980 AW	49580 TQ	MOBLS	10/01-12/01
	Kansas City MSA, MO-KS	Y	14080 FQ	27360 AW	47240 TQ	MOBLS	10/01-12/01
	St. Louis MSA, MO-IL	Y	14250 FQ	29740 AW	52560 TQ	MOBLS	10/01-12/01
	Springfield MSA, MO	Y	14330 FQ	26590 AW	46030 TQ	MOBLS	10/01-12/01
	Montana	Y	12990 FQ	21210 AW	28970 TQ	MTBLS	10/01-12/01
	Billings MSA, MT	Y	12280 FQ	20030 AW	29270 TQ	MTBLS	10/01-12/01
	Nebraska	Y	15220 FQ	30310 AW	45510 TQ	NEBLS	10/01-12/01
	Lincoln MSA, NE	Y	17500 FQ	32600 AW	43910 TQ	NEBLS	10/01-12/01
	Omaha MSA, NE-IA	Y	14330 FQ	31140 AW	54160 TQ	NEBLS	10/01-12/01
	Nevada	Y	15410 FQ	25800 AW	40010 TQ	NVBLS	10/01-12/01
	Las Vegas MSA, NV-AZ	Y	16230 FQ	28220 AW	43480 TQ	NVBLS	10/01-12/01
	Reno MSA, NV	Y	14840 FQ	20770 AW	28260 TQ	NVBLS	10/01-12/01
	New Hampshire	Y	15070 FQ	32150 AW	54280 TQ	NHBLS	10/01-12/01
	New Jersey	Y	16390 FQ	31890 AW	58360 TQ	NJBLS	10/01-12/01
	Bergen-Passaic PMSA, NJ	Y	19100 FQ	34920 AW	66700 TQ	NJBLS	10/01-12/01
	Trenton PMSA, NJ	Y	19730 FQ	40360 AW	66980 TQ	NJBLS	10/01-12/01
	New Mexico	Y	14250 FQ	29470 AW	53570 TQ	NMBLS	10/01-12/01
	Albuquerque MSA, NM	Y	15760 FQ	32090 AW	56220 TQ	NMBLS	10/01-12/01
	New York	Y	18520 FQ	45280 AW	73350 TQ	NYBLS	10/01-12/01
	Albany-Schenectady-Troy MSA, NY	Y	18070 FQ	39770 AW	69790 TQ	NYBLS	10/01-12/01
	Binghamton MSA, NY	Y	13060 FQ	27970 AW	53130 TQ	NYBLS	10/01-12/01
	Buffalo-Niagara Falls MSA, NY	Y	19940 FQ	34080 AW	53510 TQ	NYBLS	10/01-12/01
	Nassau-Suffolk PMSA, NY	Y	12240 FQ	37130 AW	72680 TQ	NYBLS	10/01-12/01
	New York PMSA, NY	Y	20510 FQ	49630 AW	75830 TQ	NYBLS	10/01-12/01
	Rochester MSA, NY	Y	19030 FQ	34780 AW	53320 TQ	NYBLS	10/01-12/01
	Syracuse MSA, NY	Y	15970 FQ	30470 AW	52130 TQ	NYBLS	10/01-12/01
	Utica-Rome MSA, NY	Y	15650 FQ	33340 AW	59060 TQ	NYBLS	10/01-12/01
	North Carolina	Y	15000 FQ	29920 AW	48940 TQ	NCBLS	10/01-12/01
	Charlotte-Gastonia-Rock Hill MSA, NC-SC	Y	19560 FQ	34720 AW	53160 TQ	NCBLS	10/01-12/01
	Greensboro-Winston-Salem-High Point MSA, NC	Y	15290 FQ	24450 AW	37740 TQ	NCBLS	10/01-12/01
	Raleigh-Durham-Chapel Hill MSA, NC	Y	19940 FQ	32550 AW	51980 TQ	NCBLS	10/01-12/01
	North Dakota	Y	12620 FQ	26250 AW	46850 TQ	NDBLS	10/01-12/01
	Fargo-Moorhead MSA, ND-MN	Y	16790 FQ	32490 AW	49180 TQ	NDBLS	10/01-12/01
	Ohio	Y	13490 FQ	27910 AW	49060 TQ	OHBLS	10/01-12/01
	Cincinnati PMSA, OH-KY-IN	Y	15840 FQ	31280 AW	51410 TQ	OHBLS	10/01-12/01
	Cleveland-Lorain-Elyria PMSA, OH	Y	13690 FQ	29400 AW	52240 TQ	OHBLS	10/01-12/01
	Columbus MSA, OH	Y	15840 FQ	29250 AW	46090 TQ	OHBLS	10/01-12/01
	Dayton-Springfield MSA, OH	Y	12080 FQ	25950 AW	48720 TQ	OHBLS	10/01-12/01
	Toledo MSA, OH	Y	13260 FQ	25530 AW	43730 TQ	OHBLS	10/01-12/01
	Oklahoma	Y	13050 FQ	28460 AW	46260 TQ	OKBLS	10/01-12/01
	Oklahoma City MSA, OK	Y	14150 FQ	29570 AW	43530 TQ	OKBLS	10/01-12/01
	Tulsa MSA, OK	Y	15720 FQ	31500 AW	56890 TQ	OKBLS	10/01-12/01
	Oregon	Y	15110 FQ	31240 AW	53130 TQ	ORBLS	10/01-12/01
	Eugene-Springfield MSA, OR	Y	14970 FQ	33430 AW	51380 TQ	ORBLS	10/01-12/01
	Medford-Ashland MSA, OR	Y	14550 FQ	28260 AW	45680 TQ	ORBLS	10/01-12/01
	Portland-Vancouver PMSA, OR-WA	Y	18030 FQ	33720 AW	55310 TQ	ORBLS	10/01-12/01
	Pennsylvania	Y	13360 FQ	31080 AW	56160 TQ	PABLS	10/01-12/01
	Allentown-Bethlehem-Easton MSA, PA	Y	13140 FQ	27770 AW	50640 TQ	PABLS	10/01-12/01
	Erie MSA, PA	Y	13630 FQ	22370 AW	35650 TQ	PABLS	10/01-12/01
	Harrisburg-Lebanon-Carlisle MSA, PA	Y	21360 FQ	29840 AW	43850 TQ	PABLS	10/01-12/01
	Johnstown MSA, PA	Y	12230 FQ	17740 AW	31520 TQ	PABLS	10/01-12/01
	Philadelphia PMSA, PA-NJ	Y	14270 FQ	39040 AW	76390 TQ	PABLS	10/01-12/01

AAW	Average annual wage	**AOH**	Average offered, high	**ASH**	Average starting, high	**H**	Hourly	**M**	Monthly	**S**	Special: hourly and annual
AE	Average entry wage	**AOL**	Average offered, low	**ASL**	Average starting, low	**HI**	Highest wage paid	**MTC**	Median total compensation	**TQ**	Third quartile wage
AEX	Average experienced wage	**APH**	Average pay, high range	**AW**	Average wage paid	**HR**	High end range	**MW**	Median wage paid	**W**	Weekly
AO	Average offered	**APL**	Average pay, low range	**FQ**	First quartile wage	**LR**	Low end range	**SQ**	Second quartile wage	**Y**	Yearly

Occupation/Type/Industry	Location	Per	Low	Mid	High	Source	Date
Broadcast Technician	Pittsburgh MSA, PA	Y	13410 FQ	26400 AW	46360 TQ	PABLS	10/01-12/01
	Scranton-Wilkes-Barre-Hazleton MSA, PA	Y	12770 FQ	23420 AW	44130 TQ	PABLS	10/01-12/01
	Rhode Island	Y	15270 FQ	31540 AW	53320 TQ	RIBLS	10/01-12/01
	Providence-Fall River-Warwick MSA, RI-MA	Y	15310 FQ	31400 AW	52630 TQ	RIBLS	10/01-12/01
	South Carolina	Y	14540 FQ	24130 AW	36580 TQ	SCBLS	10/01-12/01
	Charleston-North Charleston MSA, SC	Y	15350 FQ	22370 AW	32160 TQ	SCBLS	10/01-12/01
	Greenville-Spartanburg-Anderson MSA, SC	Y	13300 FQ	25970 AW	40990 TQ	SCBLS	10/01-12/01
	South Dakota	Y	15490 FQ	23820 AW	39760 TQ	SDBLS	10/01-12/01
	Tennessee	Y	12190 FQ	22880 AW	39160 TQ	TNBLS	10/01-12/01
	Chattanooga MSA, TN-GA	Y	14640 FQ	22640 AW	33200 TQ	TNBLS	10/01-12/01
	Johnson City-Kingsport-Bristol MSA, TN-VA	Y	11780 FQ	20570 AW	34640 TQ	TNBLS	10/01-12/01
	Knoxville MSA, TN	Y	12700 FQ	23870 AW	37180 TQ	TNBLS	10/01-12/01
	Memphis MSA, TN-AR-MS	Y	11910 FQ	21360 AW	38780 TQ	TNBLS	10/01-12/01
	Nashville MSA, TN	Y	12530 FQ	26880 AW	43460 TQ	TNBLS	10/01-12/01
	Texas	Y	13320 FQ	29300 AW	51150 TQ	TXBLS	10/01-12/01
	Austin-San Marcos MSA, TX	Y	15330 FQ	26880 AW	49820 TQ	TXBLS	10/01-12/01
	Beaumont-Port Arthur MSA, TX	Y	14400 FQ	27540 AW	44250 TQ	TXBLS	10/01-12/01
	Corpus Christi MSA, TX	Y	12070 FQ	24130 AW	47970 TQ	TXBLS	10/01-12/01
	Dallas PMSA, TX	Y	15010 FQ	32230 AW	48580 TQ	TXBLS	10/01-12/01
	El Paso MSA, TX	Y	12520 FQ	21660 AW	35850 TQ	TXBLS	10/01-12/01
	Houston PMSA, TX	Y	14990 FQ	33940 AW	56790 TQ	TXBLS	10/01-12/01
	Lubbock MSA, TX	Y	12820 FQ	27140 AW	53720 TQ	TXBLS	10/01-12/01
	San Antonio MSA, TX	Y	19560 FQ	35600 AW	51310 TQ	TXBLS	10/01-12/01
	Utah	Y	16170 FQ	28700 AW	44480 TQ	UTBLS	10/01-12/01
	Salt Lake City-Ogden MSA, UT	Y	17150 FQ	30700 AW	48110 TQ	UTBLS	10/01-12/01
	Vermont	Y	15400 FQ	26410 AW	42790 TQ	VTBLS	10/01-12/01
	Burlington MSA, VT	Y	16870 FQ	27990 AW	43380 TQ	VTBLS	10/01-12/01
	Virginia	Y	15140 FQ	25270 AW	42040 TQ	VABLS	10/01-12/01
	Norfolk-Virginia Beach-Newport News MSA, VA-NC	Y	15390 FQ	23450 AW	33470 TQ	VABLS	10/01-12/01
	Richmond-Petersburg MSA, VA	Y	16700 FQ	27130 AW	40880 TQ	VABLS	10/01-12/01
	Roanoke MSA, VA	Y	15480 FQ	24710 AW	40050 TQ	VABLS	10/01-12/01
	Washington	Y	15620 FQ	36510 AW	56130 TQ	WABLS	10/01-12/01
	Seattle-Bellevue-Everett PMSA, WA	Y	16910 FQ	40910 AW	56530 TQ	WABLS	10/01-12/01
	Spokane MSA, WA	Y	15840 FQ	33340 AW	55630 TQ	WABLS	10/01-12/01
	Tacoma PMSA, WA	Y	14500 FQ	40370 AW	67690 TQ	WABLS	10/01-12/01
	Yakima MSA, WA	Y	14500 FQ	23720 AW	48450 TQ	WABLS	10/01-12/01
	West Virginia	Y	11880 FQ	19810 AW	34290 TQ	WVBLS	10/01-12/01
	Wisconsin	Y	15640 FQ	29910 AW	45120 TQ	WIBLS	10/01-12/01
	Green Bay MSA, WI	Y	15870 FQ	22530 AW	33810 TQ	WIBLS	10/01-12/01
	Madison MSA, WI	Y	19860 FQ	32000 AW	43470 TQ	WIBLS	10/01-12/01
	Milwaukee-Waukesha PMSA, WI	Y	16180 FQ	32200 AW	56020 TQ	WIBLS	10/01-12/01
	Puerto Rico	Y	11850 FQ	17360 AW	25630 TQ	PRBLS	10/01-12/01
Brokerage Clerk	Alabama	H	9.43 FQ	13.54 AW	19.32 TQ	ALBLS	10/01-12/01
	Arizona	H	9.28 FQ	14.13 AW	19.85 TQ	AZBLS	10/01-12/01
	Arkansas	H	8.48 FQ	11.97 AW	16.61 TQ	ARBLS	10/01-12/01
	California	H	12.23 FQ	17.72 AW	23.98 TQ	CABLS	10/01-12/01
	Colorado	H	9.34 FQ	15.93 AW	24.40 TQ	COBLS	10/01-12/01
	Connecticut	H	12.23 FQ	19.90 AW	36.03 TQ	CTBLS	10/01-12/01
	Delaware	H	11.05 FQ	16.11 AW	22.21 TQ	DEBLS	10/01-12/01
	District of Columbia	H	10.11 FQ	16.20 AW	25.34 TQ	DCBLS	10/01-12/01
	Florida	H	9.64 FQ	13.52 AW	18.25 TQ	FLBLS	10/01-12/01
	Georgia	H	7.47 FQ	12.56 AW	18.36 TQ	GABLS	10/01-12/01
	Hawaii	H	9.29 FQ	16.29 AW	21.18 TQ	HIBLS	10/01-12/01
	Idaho	H	7.11 FQ	10.84 AW	14.75 TQ	IDBLS	10/01-12/01
	Illinois	H	7.44 FQ	15.20 AW	22.92 TQ	ILBLS	10/01-12/01
	Indiana	H	8.26 FQ	13.53 AW	19.17 TQ	INBLS	10/01-12/01
	Iowa	H	9.52 FQ	14.19 AW	19.11 TQ	IABLS	10/01-12/01
	Kansas	H	8.28 FQ	13.84 AW	20.46 TQ	KSBLS	10/01-12/01
	Kentucky	H	8.60 FQ	12.47 AW	16.79 TQ	KYBLS	10/01-12/01
	Louisiana	H	9.16 FQ	12.69 AW	17.06 TQ	LABLS	10/01-12/01

AAW Average annual wage; AE Average entry wage; AEX Average experienced wage; AO Average offered; AOH Average offered, high; AOL Average offered, low; APH Average pay, high range; APL Average pay, low range; ASH Average starting, high; ASL Average starting, low; AW Average wage paid; FQ First quartile wage; H Hourly; HI Highest wage paid; HR High end range; LR Low end range; M Monthly; MTC Median total compensation; MW Median wage paid; SQ Second quartile wage; S Special: hourly and annual; TQ Third quartile wage; W Weekly; Y Yearly

Occupation/Type/Industry	Location	Per	Low	Mid	High	Source	Date
Brokerage Clerk	Maine	H	10.18 FQ	14.46 AW	19.78 TQ	MEBLS	10/01-12/01
	Maryland	H	11.87 FQ	16.14 AW	21.85 TQ	MDBLS	10/01-12/01
	Massachusetts	H	11.12 FQ	15.48 AW	21.36 TQ	MABLS	10/01-12/01
	Michigan	H	9.82 FQ	15.29 AW	21.53 TQ	MIBLS	10/01-12/01
	Minnesota	H	11.35 FQ	14.83 AW	18.88 TQ	MNBLS	10/01-12/01
	Mississippi	H	9.28 FQ	13.41 AW	18.36 TQ	MSBLS	10/01-12/01
	Missouri	H	9.67 FQ	13.59 AW	17.64 TQ	MOBLS	10/01-12/01
	Montana	H	9.09 FQ	13.05 AW	18.52 TQ	MTBLS	10/01-12/01
	Nebraska	H	9.60 FQ	13.30 AW	18.45 TQ	NEBLS	10/01-12/01
	Nevada	H	11.75 FQ	17.61 AW	26.65 TQ	NVBLS	10/01-12/01
	New Hampshire	H	10.62 FQ	14.33 AW	17.94 TQ	NHBLS	10/01-12/01
	New Jersey	H	11.17 FQ	16.71 AW	24.31 TQ	NJBLS	10/01-12/01
	New Mexico	H	5.66 FQ	9.81 AW	14.05 TQ	NMBLS	10/01-12/01
	New York	H	12.79 FQ	20.96 AW	29.86 TQ	NYBLS	10/01-12/01
	North Carolina	H	10.39 FQ	15.22 AW	20.43 TQ	NCBLS	10/01-12/01
	North Dakota	H	7.28 FQ	9.24 AW	12.81 TQ	NDBLS	10/01-12/01
	Ohio	H	8.92 FQ	14.69 AW	21.05 TQ	OHBLS	10/01-12/01
	Oklahoma	H	8.68 FQ	12.50 AW	17.19 TQ	OKBLS	10/01-12/01
	Oregon	H	9.80 FQ	16.15 AW	22.87 TQ	ORBLS	10/01-12/01
	Pennsylvania	H	9.96 FQ	14.03 AW	18.11 TQ	PABLS	10/01-12/01
	Rhode Island	H	9.47 FQ	14.56 AW	20.39 TQ	RIBLS	10/01-12/01
	South Carolina	H	9.18 FQ	12.77 AW	18.51 TQ	SCBLS	10/01-12/01
	South Dakota	H	8.82 FQ	12.33 AW	16.97 TQ	SDBLS	10/01-12/01
	Tennessee	H	9.59 FQ	15.50 AW	26.06 TQ	TNBLS	10/01-12/01
	Texas	H	9.12 FQ	14.81 AW	21.22 TQ	TXBLS	10/01-12/01
	Utah	H	9.79 FQ	14.16 AW	18.26 TQ	UTBLS	10/01-12/01
	Vermont	H	9.96 FQ	15.42 AW	20.87 TQ	VTBLS	10/01-12/01
	Virginia	H	9.27 FQ	14.58 AW	20.73 TQ	VABLS	10/01-12/01
	Washington	H	11.36 FQ	15.71 AW	21.89 TQ	WABLS	10/01-12/01
	West Virginia	H	9.64 FQ	14.00 AW	19.36 TQ	WVBLS	10/01-12/01
	Wisconsin	H	9.50 FQ	13.68 AW	19.23 TQ	WIBLS	10/01-12/01
	Puerto Rico	H	8.63 FQ	14.44 AW	20.95 TQ	PRBLS	10/01-12/01
Budget Analyst	Alabama	Y	29780 FQ	49500 AW	71330 TQ	ALBLS	10/01-12/01
	Alaska	Y	37900 FQ	56080 AW	77940 TQ	AKBLS	10/01-12/01
	Arizona	Y	32190 FQ	48020 AW	69270 TQ	AZBLS	10/01-12/01
	Arkansas	Y	29780 FQ	47780 AW	70160 TQ	ARBLS	10/01-12/01
	California	Y	38050 FQ	57660 AW	83470 TQ	CABLS	10/01-12/01
	Colorado	Y	33240 FQ	51480 AW	73000 TQ	COBLS	10/01-12/01
	Connecticut	Y	39210 FQ	60520 AW	87910 TQ	CTBLS	10/01-12/01
	Delaware	Y	38830 FQ	58850 AW	87860 TQ	DEBLS	10/01-12/01
	District of Columbia	Y	39470 FQ	63890 AW	88630 TQ	DCBLS	10/01-12/01
	Florida	Y	31740 FQ	49050 AW	70550 TQ	FLBLS	10/01-12/01
	Georgia	Y	32100 FQ	49080 AW	69580 TQ	GABLS	10/01-12/01
	Hawaii	Y	38030 FQ	53190 AW	70960 TQ	HIBLS	10/01-12/01
	Idaho	Y	37160 FQ	53030 AW	73460 TQ	IDBLS	10/01-12/01
	Illinois	Y	30390 FQ	46960 AW	71550 TQ	ILBLS	10/01-12/01
	Indiana	Y	30520 FQ	53180 AW	84200 TQ	INBLS	10/01-12/01
	Iowa	Y	32780 FQ	48530 AW	67420 TQ	IABLS	10/01-12/01
	Kansas	Y	36170 FQ	52060 AW	76770 TQ	KSBLS	10/01-12/01
	Kentucky	Y	33150 FQ	48750 AW	68720 TQ	KYBLS	10/01-12/01
	Louisiana	Y	27570 FQ	46860 AW	70090 TQ	LABLS	10/01-12/01
	Maine	Y	32390 FQ	46600 AW	62010 TQ	MEBLS	10/01-12/01
	Maryland	Y	35730 FQ	54710 AW	79060 TQ	MDBLS	10/01-12/01
	Massachusetts	Y	37600 FQ	59620 AW	89090 TQ	MABLS	10/01-12/01
	Michigan	Y	33580 FQ	52640 AW	75250 TQ	MIBLS	10/01-12/01
	Minnesota	Y	33190 FQ	49560 AW	69220 TQ	MNBLS	10/01-12/01
	Mississippi	Y	25200 FQ	43570 AW	66430 TQ	MSBLS	10/01-12/01
	Missouri	Y	29500 FQ	51390 AW	76070 TQ	MOBLS	10/01-12/01
	Montana	Y	30830 FQ	43860 AW	60190 TQ	MTBLS	10/01-12/01
	Nebraska	Y	29110 FQ	45740 AW	68090 TQ	NEBLS	10/01-12/01
	Nevada	Y	30350 FQ	47640 AW	66810 TQ	NVBLS	10/01-12/01
	New Hampshire	Y	34540 FQ	51390 AW	75550 TQ	NHBLS	10/01-12/01
	New Jersey	Y	36440 FQ	59780 AW	86120 TQ	NJBLS	10/01-12/01
	New Mexico	Y	32090 FQ	47130 AW	66960 TQ	NMBLS	10/01-12/01
	New York	Y	36290 FQ	59800 AW	94470 TQ	NYBLS	10/01-12/01
	North Carolina	Y	32100 FQ	50580 AW	73460 TQ	NCBLS	10/01-12/01
	North Dakota	Y	26130 FQ	42520 AW	59540 TQ	NDBLS	10/01-12/01
	Ohio	Y	33410 FQ	51980 AW	73260 TQ	OHBLS	10/01-12/01
	Oklahoma	Y	26970 FQ	45290 AW	66340 TQ	OKBLS	10/01-12/01
	Oregon	Y	32620 FQ	48010 AW	66530 TQ	ORBLS	10/01-12/01
	Pennsylvania	Y	30050 FQ	50790 AW	73980 TQ	PABLS	10/01-12/01
	Rhode Island	Y	38210 FQ	59030 AW	87880 TQ	RIBLS	10/01-12/01

AAW	Average annual wage	**AOH**	Average offered, high	**ASH**	Average starting, high	**H**	Hourly	**M**	Monthly	**S**	Special: hourly and annual
AE	Average entry wage	**AOL**	Average offered, low	**ASL**	Average starting, low	**HI**	Highest wage paid	**MTC**	Median total compensation	**TQ**	Third quartile wage
AEX	Average experienced wage	**APH**	Average pay, high range	**AW**	Average wage paid	**HR**	High end range	**MW**	Median wage paid	**W**	Weekly
AO	Average offered	**APL**	Average pay, low range	**FQ**	First quartile wage	**LR**	Low end range	**SQ**	Second quartile wage	**Y**	Yearly

Occupation/Type/Industry	Location	Per	Low	Mid	High	Source	Date
Budget Analyst	South Carolina	Y	28560 FQ	52610 AW	84620 TQ	SCBLS	10/01-12/01
	South Dakota	Y	26770 FQ	41170 AW	55730 TQ	SDBLS	10/01-12/01
	Tennessee	Y	26200 FQ	49290 AW	76460 TQ	TNBLS	10/01-12/01
	Texas	Y	30260 FQ	48570 AW	71850 TQ	TXBLS	10/01-12/01
	Utah	Y	34150 FQ	49390 AW	68580 TQ	UTBLS	10/01-12/01
	Vermont	Y	33380 FQ	47800 AW	60180 TQ	VTBLS	10/01-12/01
	Virginia	Y	38380 FQ	56520 AW	80540 TQ	VABLS	10/01-12/01
	Washington	Y	36100 FQ	54260 AW	78270 TQ	WABLS	10/01-12/01
	West Virginia	Y	29140 FQ	48480 AW	73480 TQ	WVBLS	10/01-12/01
	Wisconsin	Y	33210 FQ	49830 AW	70960 TQ	WIBLS	10/01-12/01
	Wyoming	Y	35280 FQ	46160 AW	59040 TQ	WYBLS	10/01-12/01
	Puerto Rico	Y	19760 FQ	32080 AW	49920 TQ	PRBLS	10/01-12/01
	Guam	Y	26010 FQ	44900 AW	64270 TQ	GUBLS	10/01-12/01
Bus and Truck Mechanic and Diesel Engine Specialist	Alabama	H	8.65 FQ	13.66 AW	19.58 TQ	ALBLS	10/01-12/01
	Birmingham MSA, AL	H	10.97 FQ	15.48 AW	21.70 TQ	ALBLS	10/01-12/01
	Huntsville MSA, AL	H	9.86 FQ	14.81 AW	21.99 TQ	ALBLS	10/01-12/01
	Mobile MSA, AL	H	8.77 FQ	13.16 AW	18.12 TQ	ALBLS	10/01-12/01
	Montgomery MSA, AL	H	9.20 FQ	13.62 AW	17.54 TQ	ALBLS	10/01-12/01
	Alaska	H	14.63 FQ	21.75 AW	29.44 TQ	AKBLS	10/01-12/01
	Anchorage MSA, AK	H	14.98 FQ	22.30 AW	30.15 TQ	AKBLS	10/01-12/01
	Arizona	H	10.39 FQ	16.76 AW	23.75 TQ	AZBLS	10/01-12/01
	Phoenix-Mesa MSA, AZ	H	10.81 FQ	17.26 AW	24.61 TQ	AZBLS	10/01-12/01
	Tucson MSA, AZ	H	11.09 FQ	15.82 AW	21.18 TQ	AZBLS	10/01-12/01
	Arkansas	H	9.22 FQ	13.43 AW	18.47 TQ	ARBLS	10/01-12/01
	Fayetteville-Springdale-Rogers MSA, AR	H	9.53 FQ	13.20 AW	17.72 TQ	ARBLS	10/01-12/01
	Fort Smith MSA, AR-OK	H	8.92 FQ	13.20 AW	19.07 TQ	ARBLS	10/01-12/01
	Little Rock-North Little Rock MSA, AR	H	10.15 FQ	14.25 AW	19.08 TQ	ARBLS	10/01-12/01
	California	H	11.67 FQ	19.15 AW	27.31 TQ	CABLS	10/01-12/01
	Bakersfield MSA, CA	H	10.11 FQ	15.85 AW	21.82 TQ	CABLS	10/01-12/01
	Chico-Paradise MSA, CA	H	11.85 FQ	16.90 AW	23.31 TQ	CABLS	10/01-12/01
	Fresno MSA, CA	H	9.64 FQ	17.06 AW	25.20 TQ	CABLS	10/01-12/01
	Los Angeles-Long Beach PMSA, CA	H	11.90 FQ	19.73 AW	28.06 TQ	CABLS	10/01-12/01
	Merced MSA, CA	H	8.86 FQ	16.78 AW	24.59 TQ	CABLS	10/01-12/01
	Modesto MSA, CA	H	12.05 FQ	18.06 AW	25.48 TQ	CABLS	10/01-12/01
	Oakland PMSA, CA	H	14.40 FQ	21.74 AW	30.67 TQ	CABLS	10/01-12/01
	Orange County PMSA, CA	H	12.95 FQ	20.60 AW	28.05 TQ	CABLS	10/01-12/01
	Redding MSA, CA	H	11.67 FQ	16.50 AW	21.44 TQ	CABLS	10/01-12/01
	Riverside-San Bernardino PMSA, CA	H	10.80 FQ	16.92 AW	23.10 TQ	CABLS	10/01-12/01
	Sacramento PMSA, CA	H	13.57 FQ	20.51 AW	27.84 TQ	CABLS	10/01-12/01
	Salinas MSA, CA	H	11.83 FQ	19.21 AW	27.19 TQ	CABLS	10/01-12/01
	San Diego MSA, CA	H	12.00 FQ	19.99 AW	30.27 TQ	CABLS	10/01-12/01
	San Francisco PMSA, CA	H	14.86 FQ	21.87 AW	28.36 TQ	CABLS	10/01-12/01
	San Jose PMSA, CA	H	14.10 FQ	21.72 AW	28.70 TQ	CABLS	10/01-12/01
	San Luis Obispo-Atascadero-Paso Robles MSA, CA	H	11.63 FQ	15.79 AW	21.74 TQ	CABLS	10/01-12/01
	Santa Barbara-Santa Maria-Lompoc MSA, CA	H	9.10 FQ	17.25 AW	23.92 TQ	CABLS	10/01-12/01
	Santa Cruz-Watsonville PMSA, CA	H	15.28 FQ	20.83 AW	26.80 TQ	CABLS	10/01-12/01
	Santa Rosa PMSA, CA	H	13.36 FQ	19.90 AW	27.19 TQ	CABLS	10/01-12/01
	Stockton-Lodi MSA, CA	H	9.90 FQ	16.40 AW	22.11 TQ	CABLS	10/01-12/01
	Vallejo-Fairfield-Napa PMSA, CA	H	13.41 FQ	22.54 AW	33.83 TQ	CABLS	10/01-12/01
	Ventura PMSA, CA	H	11.83 FQ	18.91 AW	26.42 TQ	CABLS	10/01-12/01
	Visalia-Tulare-Porterville MSA, CA	H	6.79 FQ	15.04 AW	21.38 TQ	CABLS	10/01-12/01
	Colorado	H	11.87 FQ	17.38 AW	23.90 TQ	COBLS	10/01-12/01
	Boulder-Longmont PMSA, CO	H	11.69 FQ	17.28 AW	25.21 TQ	COBLS	10/01-12/01
	Colorado Springs MSA, CO	H	11.84 FQ	16.25 AW	21.66 TQ	COBLS	10/01-12/01
	Denver PMSA, CO	H	12.60 FQ	18.19 AW	24.77 TQ	COBLS	10/01-12/01
	Fort Collins-Loveland MSA, CO	H	11.37 FQ	16.56 AW	24.08 TQ	COBLS	10/01-12/01
	Greeley PMSA, CO	H	11.30 FQ	15.11 AW	20.69 TQ	COBLS	10/01-12/01
	Connecticut	H	12.80 FQ	18.99 AW	25.51 TQ	CTBLS	10/01-12/01
	Bridgeport PMSA, CT	H	12.49 FQ	18.89 AW	25.44 TQ	CTBLS	10/01-12/01
	Danbury PMSA, CT	H	12.30 FQ	18.20 AW	24.53 TQ	CTBLS	10/01-12/01

AAW	Average annual wage	**AOH**	Average offered, high	**ASH**	Average starting, high	**H**	Hourly	**M**	Monthly	**S**	Special: hourly and annual
AE	Average entry wage	**AOL**	Average offered, low	**ASL**	Average starting, low	**HI**	Highest wage paid	**MTC**	Median total compensation	**TQ**	Third quartile wage
AEX	Average experienced wage	**APH**	Average pay, high range	**AW**	Average wage paid	**HR**	High end range	**MW**	Median wage paid	**W**	Weekly
AO	Average offered	**APL**	Average pay, low range	**FQ**	First quartile wage	**LR**	Low end range	**SQ**	Second quartile wage	**Y**	Yearly

Occupation/Type/Industry	Location	Per	Low	Mid	High	Source	Date
Bus and Truck Mechanic and Diesel Engine Specialist	Hartford MSA, CT	H	12.65 FQ	18.96 AW	25.78 TQ	CTBLS	10/01-12/01
	New Haven-Meriden PMSA, CT	H	12.72 FQ	18.81 AW	24.95 TQ	CTBLS	10/01-12/01
	New London-Norwich MSA, CT-RI	H	12.19 FQ	17.26 AW	22.65 TQ	CTBLS	10/01-12/01
	Stamford-Norwalk PMSA, CT	H	15.30 FQ	20.57 AW	26.36 TQ	CTBLS	10/01-12/01
	Waterbury PMSA, CT	H	12.69 FQ	19.36 AW	26.36 TQ	CTBLS	10/01-12/01
	Delaware	H	11.44 FQ	17.13 AW	21.99 TQ	DEBLS	10/01-12/01
	Wilmington-Newark PMSA, DE-MD	H	11.67 FQ	18.04 AW	22.46 TQ	DEBLS	10/01-12/01
	District of Columbia	H	13.93 FQ	19.12 AW	25.03 TQ	DCBLS	10/01-12/01
	Washington PMSA, DC-MD-VA-WV	H	11.61 FQ	18.03 AW	26.26 TQ	DCBLS	10/01-12/01
	Florida	H	9.77 FQ	15.18 AW	21.88 TQ	FLBLS	10/01-12/01
	Daytona Beach MSA, FL	H	9.30 FQ	12.33 AW	15.27 TQ	FLBLS	10/01-12/01
	Fort Lauderdale PMSA, FL	H	9.18 FQ	16.22 AW	24.92 TQ	FLBLS	10/01-12/01
	Fort Myers-Cape Coral MSA, FL	H	10.74 FQ	15.05 AW	20.82 TQ	FLBLS	10/01-12/01
	Fort Pierce-Port St. Lucie MSA, FL	H	9.94 FQ	15.49 AW	20.84 TQ	FLBLS	10/01-12/01
	Fort Walton Beach MSA, FL	H	9.69 FQ	14.31 AW	17.54 TQ	FLBLS	10/01-12/01
	Gainesville MSA, FL	H	10.14 FQ	14.96 AW	21.45 TQ	FLBLS	10/01-12/01
	Jacksonville MSA, FL	H	9.89 FQ	15.59 AW	22.11 TQ	FLBLS	10/01-12/01
	Lakeland-Winter Haven MSA, FL	H	9.75 FQ	14.18 AW	19.56 TQ	FLBLS	10/01-12/01
	Melbourne-Titusville-Palm Bay MSA, FL	H	11.36 FQ	20.19 AW	27.41 TQ	FLBLS	10/01-12/01
	Miami PMSA, FL	H	10.09 FQ	14.90 AW	21.19 TQ	FLBLS	10/01-12/01
	Naples MSA, FL	H	10.56 FQ	16.18 AW	24.88 TQ	FLBLS	10/01-12/01
	Ocala MSA, FL	H	9.70 FQ	13.98 AW	19.57 TQ	FLBLS	10/01-12/01
	Orlando MSA, FL	H	9.36 FQ	14.16 AW	20.42 TQ	FLBLS	10/01-12/01
	Pensacola MSA, FL	H	9.50 FQ	14.81 AW	20.50 TQ	FLBLS	10/01-12/01
	Sarasota-Bradenton MSA, FL	H	11.17 FQ	15.04 AW	20.34 TQ	FLBLS	10/01-12/01
	Tallahassee MSA, FL	H	11.14 FQ	15.31 AW	21.26 TQ	FLBLS	10/01-12/01
	Tampa-St. Petersburg-Clearwater MSA, FL	H	9.78 FQ	14.94 AW	20.67 TQ	FLBLS	10/01-12/01
	West Palm Beach-Boca Raton MSA, FL	H	11.33 FQ	16.19 AW	21.74 TQ	FLBLS	10/01-12/01
	Georgia	H	10.06 FQ	15.56 AW	21.72 TQ	GABLS	10/01-12/01
	Atlanta MSA, GA	H	10.58 FQ	16.17 AW	22.10 TQ	GABLS	10/01-12/01
	Augusta-Aiken MSA, GA-SC	H	10.95 FQ	17.51 AW	30.03 TQ	GABLS	10/01-12/01
	Columbus MSA, GA-AL	H	10.06 FQ	14.31 AW	20.15 TQ	GABLS	10/01-12/01
	Macon MSA, GA	H	10.63 FQ	16.52 AW	21.68 TQ	GABLS	10/01-12/01
	Savannah MSA, GA	H	9.27 FQ	15.16 AW	21.88 TQ	GABLS	10/01-12/01
	Hawaii	H	13.45 FQ	19.98 AW	27.39 TQ	HIBLS	10/01-12/01
	Honolulu MSA, HI	H	13.73 FQ	20.18 AW	27.08 TQ	HIBLS	10/01-12/01
	Idaho	H	9.41 FQ	14.61 AW	20.42 TQ	IDBLS	10/01-12/01
	Boise City MSA, ID	H	11.70 FQ	16.34 AW	22.51 TQ	IDBLS	10/01-12/01
	Illinois	H	10.82 FQ	17.64 AW	26.00 TQ	ILBLS	10/01-12/01
	Champaign-Urbana MSA, IL	H	12.71 FQ	17.60 AW	24.90 TQ	ILBLS	10/01-12/01
	Chicago PMSA, IL	H	11.59 FQ	18.64 AW	26.68 TQ	ILBLS	10/01-12/01
	Peoria-Pekin MSA, IL	H	10.96 FQ	15.81 AW	22.72 TQ	ILBLS	10/01-12/01
	Rockford MSA, IL	H	11.79 FQ	19.02 AW	26.44 TQ	ILBLS	10/01-12/01
	Springfield MSA, IL	H	10.59 FQ	18.96 AW	34.24 TQ	ILBLS	10/01-12/01
	Indiana	H	10.61 FQ	16.66 AW	24.54 TQ	INBLS	10/01-12/01
	Elkhart-Goshen MSA, IN	H	11.99 FQ	15.86 AW	20.55 TQ	INBLS	10/01-12/01
	Evansville-Henderson MSA, IN-KY	H	9.42 FQ	14.59 AW	20.42 TQ	INBLS	10/01-12/01
	Fort Wayne MSA, IN	H	11.19 FQ	16.92 AW	22.51 TQ	INBLS	10/01-12/01
	Gary PMSA, IN	H	11.73 FQ	17.08 AW	22.82 TQ	INBLS	10/01-12/01
	Indianapolis MSA, IN	H	11.47 FQ	19.34 AW	29.87 TQ	INBLS	10/01-12/01
	Lafayette MSA, IN	H	13.26 FQ	17.54 AW	24.03 TQ	INBLS	10/01-12/01
	South Bend MSA, IN	H	10.50 FQ	14.83 AW	20.14 TQ	INBLS	10/01-12/01
	Iowa	H	9.45 FQ	14.56 AW	20.65 TQ	IABLS	10/01-12/01
	Cedar Rapids MSA, IA	H	10.95 FQ	15.26 AW	20.68 TQ	IABLS	10/01-12/01
	Davenport-Moline-Rock Island MSA, IA-IL	H	9.75 FQ	15.03 AW	21.08 TQ	IABLS	10/01-12/01
	Des Moines MSA, IA	H	10.02 FQ	14.98 AW	20.42 TQ	IABLS	10/01-12/01
	Kansas	H	10.02 FQ	15.00 AW	20.73 TQ	KSBLS	10/01-12/01
	Topeka MSA, KS	H	10.78 FQ	16.04 AW	23.81 TQ	KSBLS	10/01-12/01
	Wichita MSA, KS	H	10.10 FQ	14.83 AW	20.25 TQ	KSBLS	10/01-12/01

AAW	Average annual wage	**AOH**	Average offered, high	**ASH**	Average starting, high	**H**	Hourly	**M**	Monthly	**S**	Special: hourly and annual
AE	Average entry wage	**AOL**	Average offered, low	**ASL**	Average starting, low	**HI**	Highest wage paid	**MTC**	Median total compensation	**TQ**	Third quartile wage
AEX	Average experienced wage	**APH**	Average pay, high range	**AW**	Average wage paid	**HR**	High end range	**MW**	Median wage paid	**W**	Weekly
AO	Average offered	**APL**	Average pay, low range	**FQ**	First quartile wage	**LR**	Low end range	**SQ**	Second quartile wage	**Y**	Yearly

Occupation/Type/Industry	Location	Per	Low	Mid	High	Source	Date
Bus and Truck Mechanic and Diesel Engine Specialist	Kentucky	H	9.84 FQ	14.74 AW	20.55 TQ	KYBLS	10/01-12/01
	Lexington MSA, KY	H	10.58 FQ	15.87 AW	21.87 TQ	KYBLS	10/01-12/01
	Louisville MSA, KY-IN	H	11.49 FQ	16.62 AW	21.58 TQ	KYBLS	10/01-12/01
	Louisiana	H	9.15 FQ	14.27 AW	20.63 TQ	LABLS	10/01-12/01
	Baton Rouge MSA, LA	H	9.71 FQ	14.66 AW	21.30 TQ	LABLS	10/01-12/01
	Houma MSA, LA	H	8.95 FQ	14.75 AW	21.39 TQ	LABLS	10/01-12/01
	Lafayette MSA, LA	H	9.14 FQ	14.18 AW	20.49 TQ	LABLS	10/01-12/01
	Lake Charles MSA, LA	H	10.76 FQ	14.67 AW	19.66 TQ	LABLS	10/01-12/01
	New Orleans MSA, LA	H	8.09 FQ	14.49 AW	20.78 TQ	LABLS	10/01-12/01
	Shreveport-Bossier City MSA, LA	H	9.22 FQ	14.66 AW	21.52 TQ	LABLS	10/01-12/01
	Maine	H	10.52 FQ	14.81 AW	20.09 TQ	MEBLS	10/01-12/01
	Portland MSA, ME	H	11.51 FQ	15.71 AW	20.77 TQ	MEBLS	10/01-12/01
	Maryland	H	11.00 FQ	17.58 AW	25.64 TQ	MDBLS	10/01-12/01
	Baltimore PMSA, MD	H	10.82 FQ	18.07 AW	25.89 TQ	MDBLS	10/01-12/01
	Massachusetts	H	12.39 FQ	19.02 AW	26.83 TQ	MABLS	10/01-12/01
	Boston PMSA, MA-NH	H	12.30 FQ	20.01 AW	28.82 TQ	MABLS	10/01-12/01
	Brockton PMSA, MA	H	13.77 FQ	19.11 AW	26.45 TQ	MABLS	10/01-12/01
	Lawrence PMSA, MA-NH	H	11.86 FQ	17.18 AW	22.73 TQ	MABLS	10/01-12/01
	Lowell PMSA, MA-NH	H	13.95 FQ	19.62 AW	26.23 TQ	MABLS	10/01-12/01
	New Bedford PMSA, MA	H	12.14 FQ	17.21 AW	22.13 TQ	MABLS	10/01-12/01
	Springfield MSA, MA	H	12.42 FQ	16.79 AW	21.58 TQ	MABLS	10/01-12/01
	Worcester PMSA, MA-CT	H	12.13 FQ	17.99 AW	24.97 TQ	MABLS	10/01-12/01
	Michigan	H	11.48 FQ	18.45 AW	27.14 TQ	MIBLS	10/01-12/01
	Ann Arbor PMSA, MI	H	10.87 FQ	17.90 AW	27.62 TQ	MIBLS	10/01-12/01
	Detroit PMSA, MI	H	14.48 FQ	20.80 AW	28.19 TQ	MIBLS	10/01-12/01
	Flint PMSA, MI	H	12.60 FQ	21.00 AW	31.66 TQ	MIBLS	10/01-12/01
	Grand Rapids-Muskegon-Holland MSA, MI	H	12.01 FQ	17.22 AW	22.34 TQ	MIBLS	10/01-12/01
	Kalamazoo-Battle Creek MSA, MI	H	10.20 FQ	15.03 AW	20.24 TQ	MIBLS	10/01-12/01
	Lansing-East Lansing MSA, MI	H	9.46 FQ	15.91 AW	25.18 TQ	MIBLS	10/01-12/01
	Saginaw-Bay City-Midland MSA, MI	H	11.98 FQ	18.34 AW	27.85 TQ	MIBLS	10/01-12/01
	Minnesota	H	11.85 FQ	17.59 AW	23.14 TQ	MNBLS	10/01-12/01
	Duluth-Superior MSA, MN-WI	H	10.19 FQ	15.90 AW	22.88 TQ	MNBLS	10/01-12/01
	Minneapolis-St. Paul MSA, MN-WI	H	13.87 FQ	18.85 AW	23.98 TQ	MNBLS	10/01-12/01
	St. Cloud MSA, MN	H	11.54 FQ	15.37 AW	20.30 TQ	MNBLS	10/01-12/01
	Mississippi	H	8.88 FQ	13.33 AW	19.38 TQ	MSBLS	10/01-12/01
	Biloxi-Gulfport-Pascagoula MSA, MS	H	11.39 FQ	16.66 AW	21.90 TQ	MSBLS	10/01-12/01
	Jackson MSA, MS	H	9.13 FQ	13.61 AW	19.09 TQ	MSBLS	10/01-12/01
	Missouri	H	9.65 FQ	15.59 AW	21.37 TQ	MOBLS	10/01-12/01
	Kansas City MSA, MO-KS	H	10.11 FQ	15.86 AW	21.22 TQ	MOBLS	10/01-12/01
	St. Louis MSA, MO-IL	H	10.85 FQ	17.30 AW	22.30 TQ	MOBLS	10/01-12/01
	Springfield MSA, MO	H	10.88 FQ	15.26 AW	20.28 TQ	MOBLS	10/01-12/01
	Montana	H	9.90 FQ	14.92 AW	20.56 TQ	MTBLS	10/01-12/01
	Billings MSA, MT	H	11.20 FQ	15.49 AW	20.81 TQ	MTBLS	10/01-12/01
	Nebraska	H	9.42 FQ	13.86 AW	19.56 TQ	NEBLS	10/01-12/01
	Lincoln MSA, NE	H	9.36 FQ	14.30 AW	19.92 TQ	NEBLS	10/01-12/01
	Omaha MSA, NE-IA	H	9.77 FQ	14.88 AW	20.83 TQ	NEBLS	10/01-12/01
	Nevada	H	13.60 FQ	19.26 AW	26.00 TQ	NVBLS	10/01-12/01
	Las Vegas MSA, NV-AZ	H	12.39 FQ	18.85 AW	26.18 TQ	NVBLS	10/01-12/01
	Reno MSA, NV	H	14.66 FQ	19.83 AW	25.71 TQ	NVBLS	10/01-12/01
	New Hampshire	H	11.63 FQ	16.33 AW	21.75 TQ	NHBLS	10/01-12/01
	Manchester PMSA, NH	H	11.91 FQ	16.59 AW	22.06 TQ	NHBLS	10/01-12/01
	Nashua PMSA, NH	H	12.06 FQ	16.90 AW	22.16 TQ	NHBLS	10/01-12/01
	Portsmouth-Rochester PMSA, NH-ME	H	11.51 FQ	15.94 AW	21.06 TQ	NHBLS	10/01-12/01
	New Jersey	H	12.99 FQ	19.23 AW	26.21 TQ	NJBLS	10/01-12/01
	Atlantic-Cape May PMSA, NJ	H	11.17 FQ	17.34 AW	25.21 TQ	NJBLS	10/01-12/01
	Bergen-Passaic PMSA, NJ	H	13.30 FQ	18.59 AW	25.32 TQ	NJBLS	10/01-12/01
	Jersey City PMSA, NJ	H	9.82 FQ	17.77 AW	23.17 TQ	NJBLS	10/01-12/01
	Middlesex-Somerset-Hunterdon PMSA, NJ	H	12.05 FQ	18.80 AW	26.26 TQ	NJBLS	10/01-12/01
	Monmouth-Ocean PMSA, NJ	H	12.70 FQ	17.88 AW	23.20 TQ	NJBLS	10/01-12/01
	Newark PMSA, NJ	H	13.93 FQ	20.66 AW	26.79 TQ	NJBLS	10/01-12/01
	Trenton PMSA, NJ	H	14.05 FQ	18.75 AW	24.21 TQ	NJBLS	10/01-12/01
	New Mexico	H	9.05 FQ	14.15 AW	20.35 TQ	NMBLS	10/01-12/01
	Albuquerque MSA, NM	H	10.92 FQ	15.72 AW	20.95 TQ	NMBLS	10/01-12/01

AAW	Average annual wage	**AOH**	Average offered, high	**ASH**	Average starting, high	**H**	Hourly	**M**	Monthly	**S**	Special: hourly and annual
AE	Average entry wage	**AOL**	Average offered, low	**ASL**	Average starting, low	**HI**	Highest wage paid	**MTC**	Median total compensation	**TQ**	Third quartile wage
AEX	Average experienced wage	**APH**	Average pay, high range	**AW**	Average wage paid	**HR**	High end range	**MW**	Median wage paid	**W**	Weekly
AO	Average offered	**APL**	Average pay, low range	**FQ**	First quartile wage	**LR**	Low end range	**SQ**	Second quartile wage	**Y**	Yearly

Occupation/Type/Industry	Location	Per	Low	Mid	High	Source	Date
Bus and Truck Mechanic and Diesel Engine Specialist	Las Cruces MSA, NM	H	8.61 FQ	12.91 AW	16.90 TQ	NMBLS	10/01-12/01
	New York	H	11.55 FQ	18.98 AW	26.97 TQ	NYBLS	10/01-12/01
	Albany-Schenectady-Troy MSA, NY	H	12.24 FQ	17.57 AW	22.24 TQ	NYBLS	10/01-12/01
	Binghamton MSA, NY	H	9.62 FQ	14.89 AW	21.19 TQ	NYBLS	10/01-12/01
	Buffalo-Niagara Falls MSA, NY	H	10.70 FQ	17.17 AW	23.15 TQ	NYBLS	10/01-12/01
	Dutchess County PMSA, NY	H	12.97 FQ	17.82 AW	23.48 TQ	NYBLS	10/01-12/01
	Nassau-Suffolk PMSA, NY	H	12.51 FQ	18.96 AW	26.34 TQ	NYBLS	10/01-12/01
	New York PMSA, NY	H	14.03 FQ	22.37 AW	30.59 TQ	NYBLS	10/01-12/01
	Newburgh PMSA, NY-PA	H	11.57 FQ	17.75 AW	23.15 TQ	NYBLS	10/01-12/01
	Rochester MSA, NY	H	11.89 FQ	17.59 AW	23.89 TQ	NYBLS	10/01-12/01
	Syracuse MSA, NY	H	9.19 FQ	15.45 AW	22.82 TQ	NYBLS	10/01-12/01
	Utica-Rome MSA, NY	H	10.22 FQ	16.47 AW	27.97 TQ	NYBLS	10/01-12/01
	North Carolina	H	10.36 FQ	15.41 AW	21.23 TQ	NCBLS	10/01-12/01
	Asheville MSA, NC	H	10.95 FQ	14.31 AW	17.97 TQ	NCBLS	10/01-12/01
	Charlotte-Gastonia-Rock Hill MSA, NC-SC	H	11.93 FQ	17.15 AW	22.84 TQ	NCBLS	10/01-12/01
	Fayetteville MSA, NC	H	10.63 FQ	15.47 AW	21.30 TQ	NCBLS	10/01-12/01
	Greensboro-Winston-Salem-High Point MSA, NC	H	10.22 FQ	16.74 AW	24.41 TQ	NCBLS	10/01-12/01
	Hickory-Morganton-Lenoir MSA, NC	H	10.20 FQ	14.31 AW	18.48 TQ	NCBLS	10/01-12/01
	Raleigh-Durham-Chapel Hill MSA, NC	H	10.23 FQ	14.90 AW	20.07 TQ	NCBLS	10/01-12/01
	Wilmington MSA, NC	H	9.88 FQ	14.26 AW	19.43 TQ	NCBLS	10/01-12/01
	North Dakota	H	10.05 FQ	13.99 AW	18.09 TQ	NDBLS	10/01-12/01
	Fargo-Moorhead MSA, ND-MN	H	9.57 FQ	13.59 AW	17.43 TQ	NDBLS	10/01-12/01
	Ohio	H	11.00 FQ	16.63 AW	22.34 TQ	OHBLS	10/01-12/01
	Akron PMSA, OH	H	12.54 FQ	17.67 AW	21.68 TQ	OHBLS	10/01-12/01
	Canton-Massillon MSA, OH	H	10.08 FQ	15.05 AW	20.86 TQ	OHBLS	10/01-12/01
	Cincinnati PMSA, OH-KY-IN	H	10.91 FQ	16.08 AW	21.59 TQ	OHBLS	10/01-12/01
	Cleveland-Lorain-Elyria PMSA, OH	H	12.52 FQ	18.20 AW	23.49 TQ	OHBLS	10/01-12/01
	Columbus MSA, OH	H	11.95 FQ	17.04 AW	22.35 TQ	OHBLS	10/01-12/01
	Dayton-Springfield MSA, OH	H	11.07 FQ	17.00 AW	22.20 TQ	OHBLS	10/01-12/01
	Hamilton-Middletown PMSA, OH	H	11.93 FQ	17.57 AW	22.66 TQ	OHBLS	10/01-12/01
	Mansfield MSA, OH	H	9.72 FQ	15.01 AW	23.32 TQ	OHBLS	10/01-12/01
	Toledo MSA, OH	H	10.95 FQ	17.56 AW	25.95 TQ	OHBLS	10/01-12/01
	Youngstown-Warren MSA, OH	H	10.61 FQ	16.21 AW	24.58 TQ	OHBLS	10/01-12/01
	Oklahoma	H	9.32 FQ	14.46 AW	20.75 TQ	OKBLS	10/01-12/01
	Oklahoma City MSA, OK	H	9.43 FQ	14.87 AW	21.66 TQ	OKBLS	10/01-12/01
	Tulsa MSA, OK	H	10.54 FQ	15.88 AW	22.54 TQ	OKBLS	10/01-12/01
	Oregon	H	11.81 FQ	17.48 AW	22.85 TQ	ORBLS	10/01-12/01
	Eugene-Springfield MSA, OR	H	11.86 FQ	17.23 AW	22.21 TQ	ORBLS	10/01-12/01
	Medford-Ashland MSA, OR	H	10.89 FQ	16.27 AW	21.42 TQ	ORBLS	10/01-12/01
	Portland-Vancouver PMSA, OR-WA	H	13.07 FQ	18.49 AW	23.10 TQ	ORBLS	10/01-12/01
	Salem PMSA, OR	H	11.45 FQ	16.88 AW	23.43 TQ	ORBLS	10/01-12/01
	Pennsylvania	H	10.13 FQ	16.32 AW	23.13 TQ	PABLS	10/01-12/01
	Allentown-Bethlehem-Easton MSA, PA	H	8.51 FQ	15.13 AW	21.32 TQ	PABLS	10/01-12/01
	Erie MSA, PA	H	8.89 FQ	16.03 AW	24.05 TQ	PABLS	10/01-12/01
	Harrisburg-Lebanon-Carlisle MSA, PA	H	11.04 FQ	16.57 AW	22.19 TQ	PABLS	10/01-12/01
	Johnstown MSA, PA	H	9.00 FQ	13.09 AW	18.01 TQ	PABLS	10/01-12/01
	Lancaster MSA, PA	H	10.60 FQ	15.26 AW	20.26 TQ	PABLS	10/01-12/01
	Philadelphia PMSA, PA-NJ	H	12.99 FQ	19.07 AW	26.25 TQ	PABLS	10/01-12/01
	Pittsburgh MSA, PA	H	11.63 FQ	17.65 AW	24.08 TQ	PABLS	10/01-12/01
	Reading MSA, PA	H	10.76 FQ	16.23 AW	21.94 TQ	PABLS	10/01-12/01
	Scranton-Wilkes-Barre-Hazleton MSA, PA	H	9.07 FQ	13.60 AW	19.66 TQ	PABLS	10/01-12/01
	York MSA, PA	H	9.94 FQ	14.86 AW	20.91 TQ	PABLS	10/01-12/01
	Rhode Island	H	12.10 FQ	17.49 AW	22.20 TQ	RIBLS	10/01-12/01
	Providence-Fall River-Warwick MSA, RI-MA	H	12.08 FQ	17.48 AW	22.40 TQ	RIBLS	10/01-12/01
	South Carolina	H	9.70 FQ	14.48 AW	20.52 TQ	SCBLS	10/01-12/01
	Charleston-North Charleston MSA, SC	H	10.86 FQ	15.14 AW	20.07 TQ	SCBLS	10/01-12/01

AAW	Average annual wage	AOH	Average offered, high	ASH	Average starting, high	H	Hourly	M	Monthly	S	Special: hourly and annual
AE	Average entry wage	AOL	Average offered, low	ASL	Average starting, low	HI	Highest wage paid	MTC	Median total compensation	TQ	Third quartile wage
AEX	Average experienced wage	APH	Average pay, high range	AW	Average wage paid	HR	High end range	MW	Median wage paid	W	Weekly
AO	Average offered	APL	Average pay, low range	FQ	First quartile wage	LR	Low end range	SQ	Second quartile wage	Y	Yearly

Occupation/Type/Industry	Location	Per	Low	Mid	High	Source	Date
Bus and Truck Mechanic and Diesel Engine Specialist	Columbia MSA, SC	H	9.89 FQ	14.67 AW	20.33 TQ	SCBLS	10/01-12/01
	Greenville-Spartanburg-Anderson MSA, SC	H	9.57 FQ	13.98 AW	19.77 TQ	SCBLS	10/01-12/01
	Myrtle Beach MSA, SC	H	9.40 FQ	13.17 AW	16.93 TQ	SCBLS	10/01-12/01
	South Dakota	H	9.63 FQ	13.61 AW	18.23 TQ	SDBLS	10/01-12/01
	Sioux Falls MSA, SD	H	10.19 FQ	14.25 AW	19.42 TQ	SDBLS	10/01-12/01
	Tennessee	H	9.69 FQ	14.88 AW	20.70 TQ	TNBLS	10/01-12/01
	Chattanooga MSA, TN-GA	H	10.64 FQ	16.07 AW	20.78 TQ	TNBLS	10/01-12/01
	Clarksville-Hopkinsville MSA, TN-KY	H	10.77 FQ	14.23 AW	18.78 TQ	TNBLS	10/01-12/01
	Johnson City-Kingsport-Bristol MSA, TN-VA	H	9.18 FQ	13.02 AW	17.40 TQ	TNBLS	10/01-12/01
	Knoxville MSA, TN	H	9.51 FQ	13.89 AW	19.13 TQ	TNBLS	10/01-12/01
	Memphis MSA, TN-AR-MS	H	10.06 FQ	15.88 AW	21.56 TQ	TNBLS	10/01-12/01
	Nashville MSA, TN	H	10.82 FQ	15.82 AW	21.11 TQ	TNBLS	10/01-12/01
	Texas	H	9.37 FQ	15.10 AW	21.52 TQ	TXBLS	10/01-12/01
	Amarillo MSA, TX	H	8.89 FQ	14.27 AW	20.72 TQ	TXBLS	10/01-12/01
	Austin-San Marcos MSA, TX	H	9.83 FQ	15.48 AW	21.43 TQ	TXBLS	10/01-12/01
	Beaumont-Port Arthur MSA, TX	H	9.03 FQ	14.72 AW	20.65 TQ	TXBLS	10/01-12/01
	Brazoria PMSA, TX	H	10.03 FQ	13.53 AW	17.27 TQ	TXBLS	10/01-12/01
	Brownsville-Harlingen-San Benito MSA, TX	H	7.29 FQ	11.48 AW	18.39 TQ	TXBLS	10/01-12/01
	Corpus Christi MSA, TX	H	8.51 FQ	13.02 AW	18.36 TQ	TXBLS	10/01-12/01
	Dallas PMSA, TX	H	10.34 FQ	16.11 AW	22.20 TQ	TXBLS	10/01-12/01
	El Paso MSA, TX	H	7.90 FQ	12.85 AW	19.16 TQ	TXBLS	10/01-12/01
	Fort Worth-Arlington PMSA, TX	H	10.78 FQ	16.61 AW	21.66 TQ	TXBLS	10/01-12/01
	Galveston-Texas City PMSA, TX	H	10.73 FQ	15.68 AW	22.61 TQ	TXBLS	10/01-12/01
	Houston PMSA, TX	H	10.29 FQ	15.64 AW	21.99 TQ	TXBLS	10/01-12/01
	Killeen-Temple MSA, TX	H	10.54 FQ	16.01 AW	21.68 TQ	TXBLS	10/01-12/01
	Laredo MSA, TX	H	7.84 FQ	11.91 AW	16.92 TQ	TXBLS	10/01-12/01
	Longview-Marshall MSA, TX	H	9.48 FQ	14.07 AW	21.23 TQ	TXBLS	10/01-12/01
	Lubbock MSA, TX	H	8.98 FQ	14.24 AW	20.86 TQ	TXBLS	10/01-12/01
	McAllen-Edinburg-Mission MSA, TX	H	7.38 FQ	11.90 AW	18.44 TQ	TXBLS	10/01-12/01
	Odessa-Midland MSA, TX	H	10.11 FQ	14.35 AW	22.16 TQ	TXBLS	10/01-12/01
	San Antonio MSA, TX	H	9.78 FQ	16.00 AW	22.15 TQ	TXBLS	10/01-12/01
	Tyler MSA, TX	H	9.57 FQ	14.98 AW	20.67 TQ	TXBLS	10/01-12/01
	Waco MSA, TX	H	10.85 FQ	16.88 AW	22.08 TQ	TXBLS	10/01-12/01
	Utah	H	9.80 FQ	15.51 AW	21.39 TQ	UTBLS	10/01-12/01
	Provo-Orem MSA, UT	H	11.74 FQ	16.49 AW	21.58 TQ	UTBLS	10/01-12/01
	Salt Lake City-Ogden MSA, UT	H	9.67 FQ	15.62 AW	21.43 TQ	UTBLS	10/01-12/01
	Vermont	H	9.95 FQ	14.47 AW	19.86 TQ	VTBLS	10/01-12/01
	Burlington MSA, VT	H	10.17 FQ	14.92 AW	20.33 TQ	VTBLS	10/01-12/01
	Virginia	H	10.15 FQ	15.78 AW	22.27 TQ	VABLS	10/01-12/01
	Lynchburg MSA, VA	H	9.44 FQ	13.37 AW	17.39 TQ	VABLS	10/01-12/01
	Norfolk-Virginia Beach-Newport News MSA, VA-NC	H	9.26 FQ	15.35 AW	21.49 TQ	VABLS	10/01-12/01
	Richmond-Petersburg MSA, VA	H	11.71 FQ	16.58 AW	22.27 TQ	VABLS	10/01-12/01
	Roanoke MSA, VA	H	10.16 FQ	14.81 AW	20.71 TQ	VABLS	10/01-12/01
	Washington	H	13.52 FQ	20.03 AW	27.09 TQ	WABLS	10/01-12/01
	Bremerton PMSA, WA	H	14.87 FQ	19.61 AW	25.74 TQ	WABLS	10/01-12/01
	Olympia PMSA, WA	H	14.14 FQ	20.02 AW	26.75 TQ	WABLS	10/01-12/01
	Richland-Kennewick-Pasco MSA, WA	H	12.49 FQ	17.49 AW	24.02 TQ	WABLS	10/01-12/01
	Seattle-Bellevue-Everett PMSA, WA	H	15.38 FQ	21.86 AW	27.85 TQ	WABLS	10/01-12/01
	Spokane MSA, WA	H	12.60 FQ	17.88 AW	22.02 TQ	WABLS	10/01-12/01
	Tacoma PMSA, WA	H	12.14 FQ	19.00 AW	26.05 TQ	WABLS	10/01-12/01
	Yakima MSA, WA	H	10.17 FQ	14.49 AW	20.03 TQ	WABLS	10/01-12/01
	West Virginia	H	8.83 FQ	13.23 AW	18.27 TQ	WVBLS	10/01-12/01
	Charleston MSA, WV	H	9.34 FQ	14.39 AW	20.30 TQ	WVBLS	10/01-12/01
	Huntington-Ashland MSA, WV-KY-OH	H	6.65 FQ	12.35 AW	17.23 TQ	WVBLS	10/01-12/01
	Wisconsin	H	11.64 FQ	16.75 AW	22.66 TQ	WIBLS	10/01-12/01

AAW	Average annual wage	**AOH**	Average offered, high	**ASH**	Average starting, high	**H**	Hourly	**M**	Monthly	**S**	Special: hourly and annual
AE	Average entry wage	**AOL**	Average offered, low	**ASL**	Average starting, low	**HI**	Highest wage paid	**MTC**	Median total compensation	**TQ**	Third quartile wage
AEX	Average experienced wage	**APH**	Average pay, high range	**AW**	Average wage paid	**HR**	High end range	**MW**	Median wage paid	**W**	Weekly
AO	Average offered	**APL**	Average pay, low range	**FQ**	First quartile wage	**LR**	Low end range	**SQ**	Second quartile wage	**Y**	Yearly

Occupation/Type/Industry	Location	Per	Low	Mid	High	Source	Date
Bus and Truck Mechanic and Diesel Engine Specialist	Appleton-Oshkosh-Neenah MSA, WI	H	11.97 FQ	16.73 AW	21.89 TQ	WIBLS	10/01-12/01
	Green Bay MSA, WI	H	11.32 FQ	15.43 AW	19.92 TQ	WIBLS	10/01-12/01
	Madison MSA, WI	H	10.94 FQ	17.04 AW	22.97 TQ	WIBLS	10/01-12/01
	Milwaukee-Waukesha PMSA, WI	H	12.32 FQ	18.83 AW	26.21 TQ	WIBLS	10/01-12/01
	Racine PMSA, WI	H	12.14 FQ	17.56 AW	22.43 TQ	WIBLS	10/01-12/01
	Wyoming	H	9.83 FQ	16.24 AW	23.44 TQ	WYBLS	10/01-12/01
	Cheyenne MSA, WY	H	7.65 FQ	12.60 AW	18.52 TQ	WYBLS	10/01-12/01
	Puerto Rico	H	5.81 FQ	8.51 AW	12.61 TQ	PRBLS	10/01-12/01
	Virgin Islands	H	12.48 FQ	16.21 AW	20.66 TQ	VIBLS	10/01-12/01
	Guam	H	8.89 FQ	14.21 AW	20.84 TQ	GUBLS	10/01-12/01
Bus Driver	San Diego, CA	H		8.11-16.88 AW		SDUT	1/99-1/00
Metropolitan Transit Development Board	San Diego, CA	H		5.77 AW		SDUT	1/99-1/00
School	Alabama	H	5.51 FQ	6.34 AW	7.27 TQ	ALBLS	10/01-12/01
School	Birmingham MSA, AL	H	5.59 FQ	6.64 AW	8.29 TQ	ALBLS	10/01-12/01
School	Huntsville MSA, AL	H	5.59 FQ	6.30 AW	7.10 TQ	ALBLS	10/01-12/01
School	Arizona	H	6.36 FQ	9.80 AW	13.18 TQ	AZBLS	10/01-12/01
School	Phoenix-Mesa MSA, AZ	H	6.35 FQ	9.90 AW	13.07 TQ	AZBLS	10/01-12/01
School	Tucson MSA, AZ	H	6.21 FQ	9.73 AW	15.40 TQ	AZBLS	10/01-12/01
School	Arkansas	H	5.62 FQ	7.26 AW	11.57 TQ	ARBLS	10/01-12/01
School	Fayetteville-Springdale-Rogers MSA, AR	H	5.62 FQ	7.25 AW	11.77 TQ	ARBLS	10/01-12/01
School	Fort Smith MSA, AR-OK	H	5.57 FQ	6.33 AW	7.14 TQ	ARBLS	10/01-12/01
School	Little Rock-North Little Rock MSA, AR	H	5.71 FQ	8.04 AW	12.40 TQ	ARBLS	10/01-12/01
School	California	H	8.84 FQ	13.03 AW	17.48 TQ	CABLS	10/01-12/01
School	Bakersfield MSA, CA	H	10.61 FQ	13.74 AW	16.73 TQ	CABLS	10/01-12/01
School	Chico-Paradise MSA, CA	H	7.11 FQ	10.69 AW	16.03 TQ	CABLS	10/01-12/01
School	Fresno MSA, CA	H	8.00 FQ	12.43 AW	17.26 TQ	CABLS	10/01-12/01
School	Los Angeles-Long Beach PMSA, CA	H	9.14 FQ	13.00 AW	18.07 TQ	CABLS	10/01-12/01
School	Merced MSA, CA	H	7.55 FQ	11.81 AW	16.82 TQ	CABLS	10/01-12/01
School	Modesto MSA, CA	H	7.89 FQ	12.38 AW	16.72 TQ	CABLS	10/01-12/01
School	Oakland PMSA, CA	H	9.45 FQ	13.12 AW	17.13 TQ	CABLS	10/01-12/01
School	Orange County PMSA, CA	H	10.79 FQ	14.22 AW	17.68 TQ	CABLS	10/01-12/01
School	Redding MSA, CA	H	9.99 FQ	13.37 AW	16.93 TQ	CABLS	10/01-12/01
School	Riverside-San Bernardino PMSA, CA	H	8.78 FQ	12.81 AW	16.86 TQ	CABLS	10/01-12/01
School	Sacramento PMSA, CA	H	7.49 FQ	11.12 AW	15.05 TQ	CABLS	10/01-12/01
School	Salinas MSA, CA	H	8.80 FQ	12.76 AW	17.39 TQ	CABLS	10/01-12/01
School	San Diego MSA, CA	H	9.13 FQ	13.55 AW	17.98 TQ	CABLS	10/01-12/01
School	San Francisco PMSA, CA	H	8.22 FQ	12.98 AW	19.37 TQ	CABLS	10/01-12/01
School	San Jose PMSA, CA	H	9.83 FQ	14.72 AW	18.26 TQ	CABLS	10/01-12/01
School	San Luis Obispo-Atascadero-Paso Robles MSA, CA	H	11.16 FQ	14.33 AW	17.91 TQ	CABLS	10/01-12/01
School	Stockton-Lodi MSA, CA	H	7.97 FQ	12.01 AW	16.96 TQ	CABLS	10/01-12/01
School	Vallejo-Fairfield-Napa PMSA, CA	H	7.76 FQ	10.62 AW	15.25 TQ	CABLS	10/01-12/01
School	Ventura PMSA, CA	H	8.90 FQ	13.00 AW	17.39 TQ	CABLS	10/01-12/01
School	Visalia-Tulare-Porterville MSA, CA	H	9.06 FQ	12.63 AW	16.61 TQ	CABLS	10/01-12/01
School	Colorado	H	7.19 FQ	11.04 AW	15.19 TQ	COBLS	10/01-12/01
School	Boulder-Longmont PMSA, CO	H	6.86 FQ	10.74 AW	14.12 TQ	COBLS	10/01-12/01
School	Colorado Springs MSA, CO	H	8.72 FQ	11.10 AW	14.24 TQ	COBLS	10/01-12/01
School	Denver PMSA, CO	H	8.42 FQ	12.36 AW	16.35 TQ	COBLS	10/01-12/01
School	Fort Collins-Loveland MSA, CO	H	8.30 FQ	10.75 AW	13.87 TQ	COBLS	10/01-12/01
School	Greeley PMSA, CO	H	8.20 FQ	10.43 AW	13.29 TQ	COBLS	10/01-12/01
School	Connecticut	H	9.23 FQ	12.15 AW	15.39 TQ	CTBLS	10/01-12/01
School	Bridgeport PMSA, CT	H	9.79 FQ	12.36 AW	14.43 TQ	CTBLS	10/01-12/01
School	Hartford MSA, CT	H	8.85 FQ	11.69 AW	14.00 TQ	CTBLS	10/01-12/01
School	New Haven-Meriden PMSA, CT	H	9.68 FQ	11.94 AW	13.90 TQ	CTBLS	10/01-12/01
School	New London-Norwich MSA, CT-RI	H	8.90 FQ	11.45 AW	14.99 TQ	CTBLS	10/01-12/01
School	Stamford-Norwalk PMSA, CT	H	10.19 FQ	14.72 AW	19.95 TQ	CTBLS	10/01-12/01
School	Waterbury PMSA, CT	H	8.93 FQ	11.18 AW	13.55 TQ	CTBLS	10/01-12/01
School	Delaware	H	6.81 FQ	10.56 AW	13.84 TQ	DEBLS	10/01-12/01

AAW Average annual wage; **AE** Average entry wage; **AEX** Average experienced wage; **AO** Average offered; **AOH** Average offered, high; **AOL** Average offered, low; **APH** Average pay, high range; **APL** Average pay, low range; **ASH** Average starting, high; **ASL** Average starting, low; **AW** Average wage paid; **FQ** First quartile wage; **H** Hourly; **HI** Highest wage paid; **HR** High end range; **LR** Low end range; **M** Monthly; **MTC** Median total compensation; **MW** Median wage paid; **SQ** Second quartile wage; **S** Special: hourly and annual; **TQ** Third quartile wage; **W** Weekly; **Y** Yearly

Occupation/Type/Industry	Location	Per	Low	Mid	High	Source	Date
Bus Driver							
School	Wilmington-Newark PMSA, DE-MD	H	7.94 FQ	11.29 AW	14.43 TQ	DEBLS	10/01-12/01
School	District of Columbia	H	7.29 FQ	11.58 AW	16.37 TQ	DCBLS	10/01-12/01
School	Washington PMSA, DC-MD-VA-WV	H	6.40 FQ	11.58 AW	17.56 TQ	DCBLS	10/01-12/01
School	Florida	H	6.18 FQ	9.88 AW	13.61 TQ	FLBLS	10/01-12/01
School	Fort Myers-Cape Coral MSA, FL	H	7.17 FQ	10.50 AW	14.01 TQ	FLBLS	10/01-12/01
School	Jacksonville MSA, FL	H	6.71 FQ	9.79 AW	13.23 TQ	FLBLS	10/01-12/01
School	Melbourne-Titusville-Palm Bay MSA, FL	H	5.59 FQ	7.63 AW	10.31 TQ	FLBLS	10/01-12/01
School	Ocala MSA, FL	H	6.94 FQ	7.90 AW	9.55 TQ	FLBLS	10/01-12/01
School	Orlando MSA, FL	H	7.51 FQ	10.59 AW	13.70 TQ	FLBLS	10/01-12/01
School	Pensacola MSA, FL	H	7.64 FQ	11.39 AW	16.10 TQ	FLBLS	10/01-12/01
School	Sarasota-Bradenton MSA, FL	H	5.91 FQ	8.65 AW	12.72 TQ	FLBLS	10/01-12/01
School	Tampa-St. Petersburg-Clearwater MSA, FL	H	8.25 FQ	10.31 AW	12.74 TQ	FLBLS	10/01-12/01
School	Georgia	H	5.54 FQ	6.99 AW	9.65 TQ	GABLS	10/01-12/01
School	Atlanta MSA, GA	H	5.60 FQ	7.53 AW	11.43 TQ	GABLS	10/01-12/01
School	Augusta-Aiken MSA, GA-SC	H	5.49 FQ	7.01 AW	9.56 TQ	GABLS	10/01-12/01
School	Columbus MSA, GA-AL	H	5.61 FQ	7.81 AW	12.57 TQ	GABLS	10/01-12/01
School	Savannah MSA, GA	H	5.87 FQ	9.32 AW	16.27 TQ	GABLS	10/01-12/01
School	Hawaii	H	8.56 FQ	11.43 AW	14.37 TQ	HIBLS	10/01-12/01
School	Honolulu MSA, HI	H	8.20 FQ	10.91 AW	13.84 TQ	HIBLS	10/01-12/01
School	Idaho	H	6.70 FQ	10.96 AW	13.73 TQ	IDBLS	10/01-12/01
School	Boise City MSA, ID	H	6.67 FQ	10.12 AW	11.97 TQ	IDBLS	10/01-12/01
School	Illinois	H	7.14 FQ	12.83 AW	19.63 TQ	ILBLS	10/01-12/01
School	Champaign-Urbana MSA, IL	H	6.22 FQ	10.76 AW	17.14 TQ	ILBLS	10/01-12/01
School	Chicago PMSA, IL	H	9.33 FQ	14.26 AW	20.17 TQ	ILBLS	10/01-12/01
School	Peoria-Pekin MSA, IL	H	6.35 FQ	11.32 AW	16.72 TQ	ILBLS	10/01-12/01
School	Rockford MSA, IL	H	8.91 FQ	12.76 AW	17.02 TQ	ILBLS	10/01-12/01
School	Springfield MSA, IL	H	5.57 FQ	7.54 AW	11.46 TQ	ILBLS	10/01-12/01
School	Indiana	H	6.15 FQ	11.90 AW	17.42 TQ	INBLS	10/01-12/01
School	Elkhart-Goshen MSA, IN	H	6.98 FQ	13.15 AW	17.86 TQ	INBLS	10/01-12/01
School	Evansville-Henderson MSA, IN-KY	H	8.29 FQ	14.27 AW	20.78 TQ	INBLS	10/01-12/01
School	Fort Wayne MSA, IN	H	5.90 FQ	9.36 AW	15.61 TQ	INBLS	10/01-12/01
School	Gary PMSA, IN	H	6.30 FQ	10.17 AW	14.96 TQ	INBLS	10/01-12/01
School	Indianapolis MSA, IN	H	11.81 FQ	14.97 AW	17.51 TQ	INBLS	10/01-12/01
School	Lafayette MSA, IN	H	6.47 FQ	13.14 AW	20.31 TQ	INBLS	10/01-12/01
School	South Bend MSA, IN	H	5.71 FQ	11.28 AW	17.29 TQ	INBLS	10/01-12/01
School	Iowa	H	6.60 FQ	13.04 AW	20.99 TQ	IABLS	10/01-12/01
School	Cedar Rapids MSA, IA	H	11.35 FQ	12.50 AW	13.95 TQ	IABLS	10/01-12/01
School	Davenport-Moline-Rock Island MSA, IA-IL	H	6.24 FQ	11.72 AW	17.93 TQ	IABLS	10/01-12/01
School	Des Moines MSA, IA	H	9.28 FQ	11.42 AW	13.88 TQ	IABLS	10/01-12/01
School	Kansas	H	7.20 FQ	10.56 AW	14.91 TQ	KSBLS	10/01-12/01
School	Topeka MSA, KS	H	8.21 FQ	11.25 AW	15.74 TQ	KSBLS	10/01-12/01
School	Wichita MSA, KS	H	8.56 FQ	10.19 AW	12.71 TQ	KSBLS	10/01-12/01
School	Kentucky	H	8.17 FQ	11.35 AW	14.98 TQ	KYBLS	10/01-12/01
School	Lexington MSA, KY	H	8.84 FQ	11.26 AW	14.24 TQ	KYBLS	10/01-12/01
School	Louisville MSA, KY-IN	H	7.38 FQ	12.59 AW	16.89 TQ	KYBLS	10/01-12/01
School	Louisiana	H	5.63 FQ	7.10 AW	9.65 TQ	LABLS	10/01-12/01
School	Houma MSA, LA	H	5.66 FQ	7.02 AW	8.72 TQ	LABLS	10/01-12/01
School	Lafayette MSA, LA	H	6.14 FQ	10.52 AW	15.32 TQ	LABLS	10/01-12/01
School	New Orleans MSA, LA	H	5.88 FQ	7.67 AW	10.15 TQ	LABLS	10/01-12/01
School	Maine	H	9.05 FQ	11.47 AW	14.33 TQ	MEBLS	10/01-12/01
School	Portland MSA, ME	H	10.89 FQ	12.41 AW	14.48 TQ	MEBLS	10/01-12/01
School	Maryland	H	7.52 FQ	11.00 AW	15.61 TQ	MDBLS	10/01-12/01
School	Baltimore PMSA, MD	H	7.50 FQ	10.78 AW	13.97 TQ	MDBLS	10/01-12/01
School	Massachusetts	H	8.32 FQ	12.08 AW	16.53 TQ	MABLS	10/01-12/01
School	Boston PMSA, MA-NH	H	8.51 FQ	11.97 AW	16.45 TQ	MABLS	10/01-12/01
School	Brockton PMSA, MA	H	7.09 FQ	11.32 AW	16.64 TQ	MABLS	10/01-12/01
School	Lawrence PMSA, MA-NH	H	7.44 FQ	10.66 AW	14.51 TQ	MABLS	10/01-12/01
School	Lowell PMSA, MA-NH	H	7.62 FQ	13.06 AW	17.10 TQ	MABLS	10/01-12/01
School	New Bedford PMSA, MA	H	7.61 FQ	14.17 AW	20.33 TQ	MABLS	10/01-12/01
School	Springfield MSA, MA	H	8.73 FQ	12.76 AW	16.47 TQ	MABLS	10/01-12/01
School	Worcester PMSA, MA-CT	H	8.89 FQ	11.54 AW	14.41 TQ	MABLS	10/01-12/01
School	Michigan	H	7.85 FQ	12.67 AW	16.87 TQ	MIBLS	10/01-12/01
School	Ann Arbor PMSA, MI	H	7.39 FQ	11.59 AW	16.57 TQ	MIBLS	10/01-12/01
School	Detroit PMSA, MI	H	8.88 FQ	12.97 AW	17.01 TQ	MIBLS	10/01-12/01

AAW Average annual wage; **AE** Average entry wage; **AEX** Average experienced wage; **AO** Average offered; **AOH** Average offered, high; **AOL** Average offered, low; **APH** Average pay, high range; **APL** Average pay, low range; **ASH** Average starting, high; **ASL** Average starting, low; **AW** Average wage paid; **FQ** First quartile wage; **H** Hourly; **HI** Highest wage paid; **HR** High end range; **LR** Low end range; **M** Monthly; **MTC** Median total compensation; **MW** Median wage paid; **SQ** Second quartile wage; **S** Special: hourly and annual; **TQ** Third quartile wage; **W** Weekly; **Y** Yearly

Occupation/Type/Industry	Location	Per	Low	Mid	High	Source	Date
Bus Driver							
School	Flint PMSA, MI	H	7.34 FQ	12.30 AW	15.69 TQ	MIBLS	10/01-12/01
School	Grand Rapids-Muskegon-Holland MSA, MI	H	9.97 FQ	14.05 AW	16.83 TQ	MIBLS	10/01-12/01
School	Kalamazoo-Battle Creek MSA, MI	H	8.06 FQ	11.38 AW	15.99 TQ	MIBLS	10/01-12/01
School	Lansing-East Lansing MSA, MI	H	10.06 FQ	14.25 AW	20.47 TQ	MIBLS	10/01-12/01
School	Saginaw-Bay City-Midland MSA, MI	H	5.50 FQ	9.68 AW	16.27 TQ	MIBLS	10/01-12/01
School	Minnesota	H	8.23 FQ	12.00 AW	16.19 TQ	MNBLS	10/01-12/01
School	Duluth-Superior MSA, MN-WI	H	7.64 FQ	12.59 AW	17.20 TQ	MNBLS	10/01-12/01
School	Minneapolis-St. Paul MSA, MN-WI	H	9.39 FQ	12.32 AW	15.41 TQ	MNBLS	10/01-12/01
School	St. Cloud MSA, MN	H	7.16 FQ	11.54 AW	16.08 TQ	MNBLS	10/01-12/01
School	Mississippi	H	5.73 FQ	7.23 AW	8.88 TQ	MSBLS	10/01-12/01
School	Biloxi-Gulfport-Pascagoula MSA, MS	H	5.78 FQ	7.12 AW	9.01 TQ	MSBLS	10/01-12/01
School	Jackson MSA, MS	H	5.75 FQ	7.87 AW	10.65 TQ	MSBLS	10/01-12/01
School	Missouri	H	6.04 FQ	9.84 AW	13.83 TQ	MOBLS	10/01-12/01
School	Kansas City MSA, MO-KS	H	6.38 FQ	10.51 AW	14.12 TQ	MOBLS	10/01-12/01
School	St. Louis MSA, MO-IL	H	6.83 FQ	10.55 AW	14.09 TQ	MOBLS	10/01-12/01
School	Springfield MSA, MO	H	5.62 FQ	7.48 AW	10.49 TQ	MOBLS	10/01-12/01
School	Montana	H	7.08 FQ	10.54 AW	13.98 TQ	MTBLS	10/01-12/01
School	Nebraska	H	6.15 FQ	11.13 AW	17.04 TQ	NEBLS	10/01-12/01
School	Lincoln MSA, NE	H	11.33 FQ	12.96 AW	16.08 TQ	NEBLS	10/01-12/01
School	Omaha MSA, NE-IA	H	6.45 FQ	12.04 AW	19.03 TQ	NEBLS	10/01-12/01
School	Nevada	H	9.56 FQ	13.77 AW	18.19 TQ	NVBLS	10/01-12/01
School	New Hampshire	H	8.36 FQ	10.96 AW	13.93 TQ	NHBLS	10/01-12/01
School	Manchester PMSA, NH	H	7.73 FQ	11.19 AW	13.59 TQ	NHBLS	10/01-12/01
School	Nashua PMSA, NH	H	9.22 FQ	10.67 AW	13.24 TQ	NHBLS	10/01-12/01
School	Portsmouth-Rochester PMSA, NH-ME	H	7.67 FQ	10.56 AW	13.53 TQ	NHBLS	10/01-12/01
School	New Jersey	H	6.81 FQ	11.53 AW	16.31 TQ	NJBLS	10/01-12/01
School	Atlantic-Cape May PMSA, NJ	H	5.92 FQ	9.17 AW	12.12 TQ	NJBLS	10/01-12/01
School	Bergen-Passaic PMSA, NJ	H	9.18 FQ	11.96 AW	15.44 TQ	NJBLS	10/01-12/01
School	Jersey City PMSA, NJ	H	8.02 FQ	11.69 AW	15.57 TQ	NJBLS	10/01-12/01
School	Middlesex-Somerset-Hunterdon PMSA, NJ	H	6.23 FQ	11.64 AW	16.66 TQ	NJBLS	10/01-12/01
School	Monmouth-Ocean PMSA, NJ	H	7.01 FQ	11.88 AW	17.74 TQ	NJBLS	10/01-12/01
School	Newark PMSA, NJ	H	6.86 FQ	11.72 AW	17.03 TQ	NJBLS	10/01-12/01
School	Trenton PMSA, NJ	H	7.01 FQ	12.12 AW	16.46 TQ	NJBLS	10/01-12/01
School	New Mexico	H	5.99 FQ	9.13 AW	12.65 TQ	NMBLS	10/01-12/01
School	Albuquerque MSA, NM	H	7.10 FQ	9.31 AW	11.37 TQ	NMBLS	10/01-12/01
School	New York	H	8.01 FQ	12.50 AW	18.07 TQ	NYBLS	10/01-12/01
School	Albany-Schenectady-Troy MSA, NY	H	7.32 FQ	12.54 AW	17.21 TQ	NYBLS	10/01-12/01
School	Binghamton MSA, NY	H	6.83 FQ	9.10 AW	11.15 TQ	NYBLS	10/01-12/01
School	Buffalo-Niagara Falls MSA, NY	H	7.04 FQ	11.89 AW	18.93 TQ	NYBLS	10/01-12/01
School	Dutchess County PMSA, NY	H	6.67 FQ	10.47 AW	14.57 TQ	NYBLS	10/01-12/01
School	Nassau-Suffolk PMSA, NY	H	9.42 FQ	13.01 AW	18.05 TQ	NYBLS	10/01-12/01
School	New York PMSA, NY	H	9.04 FQ	13.21 AW	20.40 TQ	NYBLS	10/01-12/01
School	Newburgh PMSA, NY-PA	H	7.96 FQ	10.53 AW	13.21 TQ	NYBLS	10/01-12/01
School	Rochester MSA, NY	H	7.47 FQ	11.59 AW	16.56 TQ	NYBLS	10/01-12/01
School	Syracuse MSA, NY	H	6.87 FQ	11.33 AW	17.54 TQ	NYBLS	10/01-12/01
School	Utica-Rome MSA, NY	H	7.82 FQ	11.97 AW	17.43 TQ	NYBLS	10/01-12/01
School	North Carolina	H	7.10 FQ	9.98 AW	13.02 TQ	NCBLS	10/01-12/01
School	Asheville MSA, NC	H	6.84 FQ	9.18 AW	11.16 TQ	NCBLS	10/01-12/01
School	Charlotte-Gastonia-Rock Hill MSA, NC-SC	H	8.66 FQ	10.24 AW	12.83 TQ	NCBLS	10/01-12/01
School	Fayetteville MSA, NC	H	5.96 FQ	8.25 AW	12.31 TQ	NCBLS	10/01-12/01
School	Greensboro-Winston-Salem-High Point MSA, NC	H	7.72 FQ	11.10 AW	13.69 TQ	NCBLS	10/01-12/01
School	Hickory-Morganton-Lenoir MSA, NC	H	6.00 FQ	8.89 AW	12.17 TQ	NCBLS	10/01-12/01
School	Raleigh-Durham-Chapel Hill MSA, NC	H	8.73 FQ	11.10 AW	14.09 TQ	NCBLS	10/01-12/01
School	Wilmington MSA, NC	H	7.05 FQ	9.39 AW	12.22 TQ	NCBLS	10/01-12/01
School	North Dakota	H	8.56 FQ	12.11 AW	16.55 TQ	NDBLS	10/01-12/01
School	Fargo-Moorhead MSA, ND-MN	H	6.62 FQ	10.24 AW	13.92 TQ	NDBLS	10/01-12/01
School	Ohio	H	7.02 FQ	12.35 AW	17.09 TQ	OHBLS	10/01-12/01

AAW	Average annual wage	**AOH**	Average offered, high	**ASH**	Average starting, high	**H**	Hourly	**M**	Monthly	**S**	Special: hourly and annual
AE	Average entry wage	**AOL**	Average offered, low	**ASL**	Average starting, low	**HI**	Highest wage paid	**MTC**	Median total compensation	**TQ**	Third quartile wage
AEX	Average experienced wage	**APH**	Average pay, high range	**AW**	Average wage paid	**HR**	High end range	**MW**	Median wage paid	**W**	Weekly
AO	Average offered	**APL**	Average pay, low range	**FQ**	First quartile wage	**LR**	Low end range	**SQ**	Second quartile wage	**Y**	Yearly

Occupation/Type/Industry	Location	Per	Low	Mid	High	Source	Date
Bus Driver							
School	Akron PMSA, OH	H	9.22 FQ	13.50 AW	17.19 TQ	OHBLS	10/01-12/01
School	Canton-Massillon MSA, OH	H	7.31 FQ	13.08 AW	17.85 TQ	OHBLS	10/01-12/01
School	Cincinnati PMSA, OH-KY-IN	H	7.67 FQ	11.80 AW	16.76 TQ	OHBLS	10/01-12/01
School	Cleveland-Lorain-Elyria PMSA, OH	H	7.66 FQ	13.17 AW	17.63 TQ	OHBLS	10/01-12/01
School	Columbus MSA, OH	H	9.35 FQ	13.55 AW	17.64 TQ	OHBLS	10/01-12/01
School	Dayton-Springfield MSA, OH	H	6.41 FQ	11.51 AW	16.65 TQ	OHBLS	10/01-12/01
School	Hamilton-Middletown PMSA, OH	H	7.42 FQ	11.67 AW	15.64 TQ	OHBLS	10/01-12/01
School	Mansfield MSA, OH	H	5.66 FQ	7.88 AW	12.78 TQ	OHBLS	10/01-12/01
School	Toledo MSA, OH	H	8.85 FQ	13.76 AW	17.02 TQ	OHBLS	10/01-12/01
School	Youngstown-Warren MSA, OH	H	6.96 FQ	11.33 AW	15.41 TQ	OHBLS	10/01-12/01
School	Oklahoma	H	5.64 FQ	7.51 AW	10.63 TQ	OKBLS	10/01-12/01
School	Oklahoma City MSA, OK	H	5.63 FQ	7.59 AW	10.60 TQ	OKBLS	10/01-12/01
School	Tulsa MSA, OK	H	5.94 FQ	8.60 AW	11.05 TQ	OKBLS	10/01-12/01
School	Oregon	H	8.68 FQ	11.43 AW	14.81 TQ	ORBLS	10/01-12/01
School	Eugene-Springfield MSA, OR	H	7.89 FQ	11.58 AW	15.51 TQ	ORBLS	10/01-12/01
School	Portland-Vancouver PMSA, OR-WA	H	9.16 FQ	11.77 AW	15.38 TQ	ORBLS	10/01-12/01
School	Salem PMSA, OR	H	8.76 FQ	10.95 AW	13.70 TQ	ORBLS	10/01-12/01
School	Pennsylvania	H	5.99 FQ	10.40 AW	15.69 TQ	PABLS	10/01-12/01
School	Allentown-Bethlehem-Easton MSA, PA	H	5.86 FQ	10.31 AW	16.06 TQ	PABLS	10/01-12/01
School	Erie MSA, PA	H	6.09 FQ	9.16 AW	12.61 TQ	PABLS	10/01-12/01
School	Harrisburg-Lebanon-Carlisle MSA, PA	H	6.76 FQ	10.09 AW	14.40 TQ	PABLS	10/01-12/01
School	Johnstown MSA, PA	H	5.60 FQ	8.07 AW	11.50 TQ	PABLS	10/01-12/01
School	Lancaster MSA, PA	H	5.68 FQ	8.34 AW	11.91 TQ	PABLS	10/01-12/01
School	Philadelphia PMSA, PA-NJ	H	7.19 FQ	12.00 AW	16.70 TQ	PABLS	10/01-12/01
School	Pittsburgh MSA, PA	H	5.87 FQ	9.95 AW	15.46 TQ	PABLS	10/01-12/01
School	Reading MSA, PA	H	6.52 FQ	10.99 AW	14.05 TQ	PABLS	10/01-12/01
School	Scranton-Wilkes-Barre-Hazleton MSA, PA	H	5.80 FQ	9.42 AW	13.64 TQ	PABLS	10/01-12/01
School	York MSA, PA	H	6.37 FQ	12.26 AW	21.42 TQ	PABLS	10/01-12/01
School	Rhode Island	H	8.95 FQ	11.33 AW	13.86 TQ	RIBLS	10/01-12/01
School	Providence-Fall River-Warwick MSA, RI-MA	H	8.85 FQ	11.48 AW	14.39 TQ	RIBLS	10/01-12/01
School	South Carolina	H	5.71 FQ	7.53 AW	10.16 TQ	SCBLS	10/01-12/01
School	Charleston-North Charleston MSA, SC	H	5.75 FQ	6.86 AW	8.67 TQ	SCBLS	10/01-12/01
School	Columbia MSA, SC	H	5.78 FQ	7.30 AW	9.42 TQ	SCBLS	10/01-12/01
School	Greenville-Spartanburg-Anderson MSA, SC	H	5.73 FQ	7.66 AW	10.32 TQ	SCBLS	10/01-12/01
School	South Dakota	H	8.15 FQ	10.27 AW	13.10 TQ	SDBLS	10/01-12/01
School	Sioux Falls MSA, SD	H	8.88 FQ	11.61 AW	16.81 TQ	SDBLS	10/01-12/01
School	Tennessee	H	5.56 FQ	7.07 AW	10.17 TQ	TNBLS	10/01-12/01
School	Chattanooga MSA, TN-GA	H	5.50 FQ	6.91 AW	9.01 TQ	TNBLS	10/01-12/01
School	Johnson City-Kingsport-Bristol MSA, TN-VA	H	5.59 FQ	6.38 AW	7.24 TQ	TNBLS	10/01-12/01
School	Knoxville MSA, TN	H	5.69 FQ	8.42 AW	12.70 TQ	TNBLS	10/01-12/01
School	Memphis MSA, TN-AR-MS	H	5.49 FQ	7.22 AW	10.40 TQ	TNBLS	10/01-12/01
School	Nashville MSA, TN	H	5.58 FQ	6.99 AW	8.94 TQ	TNBLS	10/01-12/01
School	Texas	H	5.79 FQ	9.02 AW	13.58 TQ	TXBLS	10/01-12/01
School	Austin-San Marcos MSA, TX	H	6.08 FQ	9.87 AW	13.53 TQ	TXBLS	10/01-12/01
School	Beaumont-Port Arthur MSA, TX	H	5.67 FQ	8.19 AW	12.08 TQ	TXBLS	10/01-12/01
School	Brazoria PMSA, TX	H	5.56 FQ	7.15 AW	10.50 TQ	TXBLS	10/01-12/01
School	Brownsville-Harlingen-San Benito MSA, TX	H	5.71 FQ	7.65 AW	10.51 TQ	TXBLS	10/01-12/01
School	Dallas PMSA, TX	H	6.35 FQ	10.56 AW	15.30 TQ	TXBLS	10/01-12/01
School	El Paso MSA, TX	H	5.78 FQ	8.26 AW	10.92 TQ	TXBLS	10/01-12/01
School	Fort Worth-Arlington PMSA, TX	H	5.92 FQ	10.60 AW	15.54 TQ	TXBLS	10/01-12/01
School	Galveston-Texas City PMSA, TX	H	5.95 FQ	9.77 AW	14.99 TQ	TXBLS	10/01-12/01
School	Houston PMSA, TX	H	5.76 FQ	9.43 AW	14.64 TQ	TXBLS	10/01-12/01
School	Killeen-Temple MSA, TX	H	6.80 FQ	9.01 AW	11.23 TQ	TXBLS	10/01-12/01
School	Longview-Marshall MSA, TX	H	5.62 FQ	8.34 AW	12.53 TQ	TXBLS	10/01-12/01
School	Lubbock MSA, TX	H	6.79 FQ	8.59 AW	11.56 TQ	TXBLS	10/01-12/01
School	McAllen-Edinburg-Mission MSA, TX	H	5.79 FQ	8.46 AW	11.07 TQ	TXBLS	10/01-12/01

AAW	Average annual wage	**AOH**	Average offered, high	**ASH**	Average starting, high	**H**	Hourly	**M**	Monthly	**S**	Special: hourly and annual
AE	Average entry wage	**AOL**	Average offered, low	**ASL**	Average starting, low	**HI**	Highest wage paid	**MTC**	Median total compensation	**TQ**	Third quartile wage
AEX	Average experienced wage	**APH**	Average pay, high range	**AW**	Average wage paid	**HR**	High end range	**MW**	Median wage paid	**W**	Weekly
AO	Average offered	**APL**	Average pay, low range	**FQ**	First quartile wage	**LR**	Low end range	**SQ**	Second quartile wage	**Y**	Yearly

Occupation/Type/Industry	Location	Per	Low	Mid	High	Source	Date
Bus Driver							
School	San Antonio MSA, TX	H	6.86 FQ	9.94 AW	13.34 TQ	TXBLS	10/01-12/01
School	Tyler MSA, TX	H	5.60 FQ	8.36 AW	13.83 TQ	TXBLS	10/01-12/01
School	Waco MSA, TX	H	6.54 FQ	10.92 AW	16.50 TQ	TXBLS	10/01-12/01
School	Utah	H	6.94 FQ	11.25 AW	16.07 TQ	UTBLS	10/01-12/01
School	Provo-Orem MSA, UT	H	8.59 FQ	11.75 AW	16.76 TQ	UTBLS	10/01-12/01
School	Salt Lake City-Ogden MSA, UT	H	6.28 FQ	9.69 AW	13.51 TQ	UTBLS	10/01-12/01
School	Vermont	H	7.38 FQ	11.74 AW	17.09 TQ	VTBLS	10/01-12/01
School	Burlington MSA, VT	H	8.40 FQ	11.59 AW	15.81 TQ	VTBLS	10/01-12/01
School	Virginia	H	5.70 FQ	9.95 AW	15.94 TQ	VABLS	10/01-12/01
School	Lynchburg MSA, VA	H	5.74 FQ	8.36 AW	11.42 TQ	VABLS	10/01-12/01
School	Norfolk-Virginia Beach-Newport News MSA, VA-NC	H	5.59 FQ	8.24 AW	12.56 TQ	VABLS	10/01-12/01
School	Richmond-Petersburg MSA, VA	H	5.95 FQ	9.27 AW	13.41 TQ	VABLS	10/01-12/01
School	Washington	H	9.94 FQ	13.52 AW	16.85 TQ	WABLS	10/01-12/01
School	Bremerton PMSA, WA	H	11.50 FQ	14.31 AW	16.75 TQ	WABLS	10/01-12/01
School	Olympia PMSA, WA	H	8.17 FQ	12.25 AW	16.47 TQ	WABLS	10/01-12/01
School	Richland-Kennewick-Pasco MSA, WA	H	10.95 FQ	13.10 AW	16.01 TQ	WABLS	10/01-12/01
School	Seattle-Bellevue-Everett PMSA, WA	H	9.72 FQ	13.68 AW	17.09 TQ	WABLS	10/01-12/01
School	Spokane MSA, WA	H	10.85 FQ	13.49 AW	16.77 TQ	WABLS	10/01-12/01
School	Tacoma PMSA, WA	H	10.29 FQ	13.62 AW	16.74 TQ	WABLS	10/01-12/01
School	Yakima MSA, WA	H	10.19 FQ	13.22 AW	16.25 TQ	WABLS	10/01-12/01
School	West Virginia	H	7.30 FQ	9.27 AW	11.52 TQ	WVBLS	10/01-12/01
School	Huntington-Ashland MSA, WV-KY-OH	H	6.18 FQ	9.21 AW	13.21 TQ	WVBLS	10/01-12/01
School	Wisconsin	H	7.39 FQ	11.05 AW	15.73 TQ	WIBLS	10/01-12/01
School	Appleton-Oshkosh-Neenah MSA, WI	H	6.78 FQ	11.34 AW	18.72 TQ	WIBLS	10/01-12/01
School	Green Bay MSA, WI	H	8.75 FQ	10.02 AW	11.51 TQ	WIBLS	10/01-12/01
School	Madison MSA, WI	H	8.69 FQ	12.83 AW	17.09 TQ	WIBLS	10/01-12/01
School	Milwaukee-Waukesha PMSA, WI	H	7.36 FQ	9.98 AW	12.45 TQ	WIBLS	10/01-12/01
School	Wyoming	H	6.35 FQ	9.61 AW	12.96 TQ	WYBLS	10/01-12/01
School	Puerto Rico	H	5.61 FQ	6.40 AW	7.20 TQ	PRBLS	10/01-12/01
School	Virgin Islands	H	7.72 FQ	10.93 AW	15.88 TQ	VIBLS	10/01-12/01
Transit and Intercity	Alabama	H	5.76 FQ	10.19 AW	18.71 TQ	ALBLS	10/01-12/01
Transit and Intercity	Birmingham MSA, AL	H	5.43 FQ	8.44 AW	14.77 TQ	ALBLS	10/01-12/01
Transit and Intercity	Huntsville MSA, AL	H	7.25 FQ	9.03 AW	11.09 TQ	ALBLS	10/01-12/01
Transit and Intercity	Mobile MSA, AL	H	6.27 FQ	10.88 AW	14.20 TQ	ALBLS	10/01-12/01
Transit and Intercity	Montgomery MSA, AL	H	5.82 FQ	13.15 AW	25.01 TQ	ALBLS	10/01-12/01
Transit and Intercity	Alaska	H	9.03 FQ	15.03 AW	22.01 TQ	AKBLS	10/01-12/01
Transit and Intercity	Arizona	H	8.27 FQ	14.42 AW	25.43 TQ	AZBLS	10/01-12/01
Transit and Intercity	Phoenix-Mesa MSA, AZ	H	9.50 FQ	16.05 AW	26.50 TQ	AZBLS	10/01-12/01
Transit and Intercity	Tucson MSA, AZ	H	7.41 FQ	11.32 AW	16.78 TQ	AZBLS	10/01-12/01
Transit and Intercity	Arkansas	H	5.83 FQ	10.22 AW	15.69 TQ	ARBLS	10/01-12/01
Transit and Intercity	Little Rock-North Little Rock MSA, AR	H	6.54 FQ	11.60 AW	16.42 TQ	ARBLS	10/01-12/01
Transit and Intercity	California	H	8.89 FQ	15.01 AW	22.06 TQ	CABLS	10/01-12/01
Transit and Intercity	Bakersfield MSA, CA	H	7.94 FQ	10.62 AW	15.59 TQ	CABLS	10/01-12/01
Transit and Intercity	Modesto MSA, CA	H	8.14 FQ	11.76 AW	15.99 TQ	CABLS	10/01-12/01
Transit and Intercity	Oakland PMSA, CA	H	9.63 FQ	14.71 AW	18.88 TQ	CABLS	10/01-12/01
Transit and Intercity	Orange County PMSA, CA	H	9.02 FQ	14.44 AW	21.35 TQ	CABLS	10/01-12/01
Transit and Intercity	Redding MSA, CA	H	6.58 FQ	11.96 AW	19.97 TQ	CABLS	10/01-12/01
Transit and Intercity	Riverside-San Bernardino PMSA, CA	H	9.03 FQ	12.58 AW	16.43 TQ	CABLS	10/01-12/01
Transit and Intercity	Sacramento PMSA, CA	H	10.14 FQ	17.13 AW	20.94 TQ	CABLS	10/01-12/01
Transit and Intercity	Salinas MSA, CA	H	12.04 FQ	16.45 AW	21.15 TQ	CABLS	10/01-12/01
Transit and Intercity	San Diego MSA, CA	H	8.34 FQ	13.49 AW	19.40 TQ	CABLS	10/01-12/01
Transit and Intercity	San Francisco PMSA, CA	H	11.56 FQ	15.81 AW	21.48 TQ	CABLS	10/01-12/01
Transit and Intercity	San Jose PMSA, CA	H	10.47 FQ	15.65 AW	21.51 TQ	CABLS	10/01-12/01
Transit and Intercity	San Luis Obispo-Atascadero-Paso Robles MSA, CA	H	9.51 FQ	14.04 AW	18.07 TQ	CABLS	10/01-12/01
Transit and Intercity	Santa Barbara-Santa Maria-Lompoc MSA, CA	H	11.92 FQ	18.51 AW	24.79 TQ	CABLS	10/01-12/01
Transit and Intercity	Santa Rosa PMSA, CA	H	8.67 FQ	12.01 AW	16.40 TQ	CABLS	10/01-12/01
Transit and Intercity	Vallejo-Fairfield-Napa PMSA, CA	H	10.03 FQ	14.92 AW	18.20 TQ	CABLS	10/01-12/01

AAW	Average annual wage	**AOH**	Average offered, high	**ASH**	Average starting, high	**H**	Hourly	**M**	Monthly	**S**	Special: hourly and annual
AE	Average entry wage	**AOL**	Average offered, low	**ASL**	Average starting, low	**HI**	Highest wage paid	**MTC**	Median total compensation	**TQ**	Third quartile wage
AEX	Average experienced wage	**APH**	Average pay, high range	**AW**	Average wage paid	**HR**	High end range	**MW**	Median wage paid	**W**	Weekly
AO	Average offered	**APL**	Average pay, low range	**FQ**	First quartile wage	**LR**	Low end range	**SQ**	Second quartile wage	**Y**	Yearly

Occupation/Type/Industry	Location	Per	Low	Mid	High	Source	Date
Bus Driver							
Transit and Intercity	Ventura PMSA, CA	H	9.76 FQ	15.15 AW	21.09 TQ	CABLS	10/01-12/01
Transit and Intercity	Visalia-Tulare-Porterville MSA, CA	H	8.97 FQ	12.73 AW	17.59 TQ	CABLS	10/01-12/01
Transit and Intercity	Colorado	H	8.93 FQ	13.09 AW	19.23 TQ	COBLS	10/01-12/01
Transit and Intercity	Colorado Springs MSA, CO	H	6.10 FQ	10.47 AW	13.24 TQ	COBLS	10/01-12/01
Transit and Intercity	Denver PMSA, CO	H	9.70 FQ	13.87 AW	20.24 TQ	COBLS	10/01-12/01
Transit and Intercity	Connecticut	H	9.98 FQ	14.52 AW	20.52 TQ	CTBLS	10/01-12/01
Transit and Intercity	Bridgeport PMSA, CT	H	9.30 FQ	12.33 AW	16.21 TQ	CTBLS	10/01-12/01
Transit and Intercity	Hartford MSA, CT	H	11.16 FQ	15.21 AW	20.94 TQ	CTBLS	10/01-12/01
Transit and Intercity	Waterbury PMSA, CT	H	9.24 FQ	13.09 AW	16.98 TQ	CTBLS	10/01-12/01
Transit and Intercity	Delaware	H	8.99 FQ	13.56 AW	20.37 TQ	DEBLS	10/01-12/01
Transit and Intercity	Washington PMSA, DC-MD-VA-WV	H	9.26 FQ	13.61 AW	19.17 TQ	DCBLS	10/01-12/01
Transit and Intercity	Florida	H	7.57 FQ	11.95 AW	17.73 TQ	FLBLS	10/01-12/01
Transit and Intercity	Lakeland-Winter Haven MSA, FL	H	9.25 FQ	10.66 AW	13.16 TQ	FLBLS	10/01-12/01
Transit and Intercity	Melbourne-Titusville-Palm Bay MSA, FL	H	12.05 FQ	15.56 AW	17.86 TQ	FLBLS	10/01-12/01
Transit and Intercity	Miami PMSA, FL	H	7.42 FQ	9.70 AW	13.11 TQ	FLBLS	10/01-12/01
Transit and Intercity	Ocala MSA, FL	H	7.35 FQ	8.42 AW	10.35 TQ	FLBLS	10/01-12/01
Transit and Intercity	Orlando MSA, FL	H	7.46 FQ	10.87 AW	15.87 TQ	FLBLS	10/01-12/01
Transit and Intercity	Tampa-St. Petersburg-Clearwater MSA, FL	H	8.29 FQ	13.00 AW	17.35 TQ	FLBLS	10/01-12/01
Transit and Intercity	West Palm Beach-Boca Raton MSA, FL	H	7.55 FQ	11.75 AW	16.76 TQ	FLBLS	10/01-12/01
Transit and Intercity	Georgia	H	6.87 FQ	10.26 AW	14.42 TQ	GABLS	10/01-12/01
Transit and Intercity	Atlanta MSA, GA	H	7.48 FQ	10.69 AW	16.38 TQ	GABLS	10/01-12/01
Transit and Intercity	Columbus MSA, GA-AL	H	5.82 FQ	9.14 AW	13.14 TQ	GABLS	10/01-12/01
Transit and Intercity	Macon MSA, GA	H	6.78 FQ	10.20 AW	13.18 TQ	GABLS	10/01-12/01
Transit and Intercity	Hawaii	H	9.32 FQ	14.44 AW	20.43 TQ	HIBLS	10/01-12/01
Transit and Intercity	Honolulu MSA, HI	H	9.56 FQ	15.11 AW	20.61 TQ	HIBLS	10/01-12/01
Transit and Intercity	Idaho	H	6.34 FQ	9.49 AW	15.78 TQ	IDBLS	10/01-12/01
Transit and Intercity	Boise City MSA, ID	H	7.20 FQ	11.44 AW	17.08 TQ	IDBLS	10/01-12/01
Transit and Intercity	Rockford MSA, IL	H	11.86 FQ	15.57 AW	20.54 TQ	ILBLS	10/01-12/01
Transit and Intercity	Indiana	H	7.50 FQ	12.20 AW	17.42 TQ	INBLS	10/01-12/01
Transit and Intercity	Evansville-Henderson MSA, IN-KY	H	6.54 FQ	9.80 AW	11.55 TQ	INBLS	10/01-12/01
Transit and Intercity	Fort Wayne MSA, IN	H	9.55 FQ	14.26 AW	24.60 TQ	INBLS	10/01-12/01
Transit and Intercity	Gary PMSA, IN	H	8.15 FQ	12.23 AW	16.99 TQ	INBLS	10/01-12/01
Transit and Intercity	Indianapolis MSA, IN	H	7.59 FQ	12.68 AW	17.56 TQ	INBLS	10/01-12/01
Transit and Intercity	South Bend MSA, IN	H	9.34 FQ	14.02 AW	19.06 TQ	INBLS	10/01-12/01
Transit and Intercity	Iowa	H	6.84 FQ	10.84 AW	16.40 TQ	IABLS	10/01-12/01
Transit and Intercity	Davenport-Moline-Rock Island MSA, IA-IL	H	8.73 FQ	13.46 AW	18.83 TQ	IABLS	10/01-12/01
Transit and Intercity	Des Moines MSA, IA	H	8.78 FQ	13.04 AW	17.87 TQ	IABLS	10/01-12/01
Transit and Intercity	Kansas	H	6.69 FQ	10.66 AW	16.42 TQ	KSBLS	10/01-12/01
Transit and Intercity	Topeka MSA, KS	H	7.66 FQ	10.90 AW	15.52 TQ	KSBLS	10/01-12/01
Transit and Intercity	Wichita MSA, KS	H	7.93 FQ	11.19 AW	13.93 TQ	KSBLS	10/01-12/01
Transit and Intercity	Kentucky	H	7.14 FQ	11.49 AW	17.37 TQ	KYBLS	10/01-12/01
Transit and Intercity	Louisville MSA, KY-IN	H	7.91 FQ	12.79 AW	18.04 TQ	KYBLS	10/01-12/01
Transit and Intercity	Louisiana	H	7.52 FQ	11.29 AW	17.52 TQ	LABLS	10/01-12/01
Transit and Intercity	Baton Rouge MSA, LA	H	8.97 FQ	11.48 AW	13.97 TQ	LABLS	10/01-12/01
Transit and Intercity	Lafayette MSA, LA	H	6.73 FQ	9.34 AW	10.92 TQ	LABLS	10/01-12/01
Transit and Intercity	Lake Charles MSA, LA	H	6.03 FQ	8.87 AW	13.04 TQ	LABLS	10/01-12/01
Transit and Intercity	New Orleans MSA, LA	H	8.58 FQ	11.91 AW	19.05 TQ	LABLS	10/01-12/01
Transit and Intercity	Shreveport-Bossier City MSA, LA	H	6.89 FQ	10.68 AW	18.56 TQ	LABLS	10/01-12/01
Transit and Intercity	Maine	H	8.74 FQ	15.39 AW	21.18 TQ	MEBLS	10/01-12/01
Transit and Intercity	Portland MSA, ME	H	9.40 FQ	16.46 AW	21.52 TQ	MEBLS	10/01-12/01
Transit and Intercity	Maryland	H	9.03 FQ	13.17 AW	20.22 TQ	MDBLS	10/01-12/01
Transit and Intercity	Baltimore PMSA, MD	H	9.13 FQ	13.06 AW	20.47 TQ	MDBLS	10/01-12/01
Transit and Intercity	Massachusetts	H	9.14 FQ	14.21 AW	22.27 TQ	MABLS	10/01-12/01
Transit and Intercity	Lawrence PMSA, MA-NH	H	9.27 FQ	12.44 AW	16.38 TQ	MABLS	10/01-12/01
Transit and Intercity	Lowell PMSA, MA-NH	H	7.90 FQ	13.33 AW	16.96 TQ	MABLS	10/01-12/01
Transit and Intercity	Springfield MSA, MA	H	9.04 FQ	12.83 AW	17.06 TQ	MABLS	10/01-12/01
Transit and Intercity	Michigan	H	8.92 FQ	13.01 AW	17.79 TQ	MIBLS	10/01-12/01
Transit and Intercity	Detroit PMSA, MI	H	9.79 FQ	13.93 AW	18.66 TQ	MIBLS	10/01-12/01
Transit and Intercity	Grand Rapids-Muskegon-Holland MSA, MI	H	8.72 FQ	13.19 AW	17.05 TQ	MIBLS	10/01-12/01
Transit and Intercity	Kalamazoo-Battle Creek MSA, MI	H	8.95 FQ	11.82 AW	15.85 TQ	MIBLS	10/01-12/01

AAW	Average annual wage	**AOH**	Average offered, high	**ASH**	Average starting, high	**H**	Hourly	**M**	Monthly	**S**	Special: hourly and annual
AE	Average entry wage	**AOL**	Average offered, low	**ASL**	Average starting, low	**HI**	Highest wage paid	**MTC**	Median total compensation	**TQ**	Third quartile wage
AEX	Average experienced wage	**APH**	Average pay, high range	**AW**	Average wage paid	**HR**	High end range	**MW**	Median wage paid	**W**	Weekly
AO	Average offered	**APL**	Average pay, low range	**FQ**	First quartile wage	**LR**	Low end range	**SQ**	Second quartile wage	**Y**	Yearly

Occupation/Type/Industry	Location	Per	Low	Mid	High	Source	Date
Bus Driver							
Transit and Intercity	Minnesota	H	9.06 FQ	14.09 AW	20.71 TQ	MNBLS	10/01-12/01
Transit and Intercity	St. Cloud MSA, MN	H	7.81 FQ	11.04 AW	13.77 TQ	MNBLS	10/01-12/01
Transit and Intercity	Mississippi	H	6.92 FQ	10.46 AW	18.40 TQ	MSBLS	10/01-12/01
Transit and Intercity	Biloxi-Gulfport-Pascagoula MSA, MS	H	7.47 FQ	9.06 AW	11.02 TQ	MSBLS	10/01-12/01
Transit and Intercity	Jackson MSA, MS	H	7.71 FQ	15.00 AW	20.73 TQ	MSBLS	10/01-12/01
Transit and Intercity	Missouri	H	7.73 FQ	13.08 AW	19.95 TQ	MOBLS	10/01-12/01
Transit and Intercity	Kansas City MSA, MO-KS	H	7.26 FQ	12.54 AW	18.45 TQ	MOBLS	10/01-12/01
Transit and Intercity	St. Louis MSA, MO-IL	H	8.20 FQ	13.46 AW	20.30 TQ	MOBLS	10/01-12/01
Transit and Intercity	Springfield MSA, MO	H	7.34 FQ	9.79 AW	14.00 TQ	MOBLS	10/01-12/01
Transit and Intercity	Montana	H	6.77 FQ	12.21 AW	18.80 TQ	MTBLS	10/01-12/01
Transit and Intercity	Billings MSA, MT	H	11.17 FQ	15.92 AW	20.74 TQ	MTBLS	10/01-12/01
Transit and Intercity	Nebraska	H	6.01 FQ	11.18 AW	17.05 TQ	NEBLS	10/01-12/01
Transit and Intercity	Nevada	H	8.52 FQ	11.18 AW	16.34 TQ	NVBLS	10/01-12/01
Transit and Intercity	Las Vegas MSA, NV-AZ	H	8.53 FQ	10.76 AW	16.07 TQ	NVBLS	10/01-12/01
Transit and Intercity	Reno MSA, NV	H	8.73 FQ	12.35 AW	16.41 TQ	NVBLS	10/01-12/01
Transit and Intercity	New Hampshire	H	8.76 FQ	10.15 AW	12.65 TQ	NHBLS	10/01-12/01
Transit and Intercity	New Jersey	H	8.91 FQ	14.00 AW	20.46 TQ	NJBLS	10/01-12/01
Transit and Intercity	Atlantic-Cape May PMSA, NJ	H	8.73 FQ	11.11 AW	15.81 TQ	NJBLS	10/01-12/01
Transit and Intercity	Jersey City PMSA, NJ	H	9.24 FQ	12.95 AW	19.15 TQ	NJBLS	10/01-12/01
Transit and Intercity	Middlesex-Somerset-Hunterdon PMSA, NJ	H	9.90 FQ	13.60 AW	19.72 TQ	NJBLS	10/01-12/01
Transit and Intercity	New Mexico	H	7.48 FQ	11.51 AW	16.75 TQ	NMBLS	10/01-12/01
Transit and Intercity	Albuquerque MSA, NM	H	9.36 FQ	12.98 AW	17.33 TQ	NMBLS	10/01-12/01
Transit and Intercity	New York	H	9.20 FQ	18.63 AW	26.08 TQ	NYBLS	10/01-12/01
Transit and Intercity	Albany-Schenectady-Troy MSA, NY	H	8.77 FQ	12.40 AW	19.56 TQ	NYBLS	10/01-12/01
Transit and Intercity	Buffalo-Niagara Falls MSA, NY	H	6.71 FQ	9.60 AW	17.37 TQ	NYBLS	10/01-12/01
Transit and Intercity	Dutchess County PMSA, NY	H	10.02 FQ	14.58 AW	21.01 TQ	NYBLS	10/01-12/01
Transit and Intercity	Nassau-Suffolk PMSA, NY	H	7.97 FQ	12.67 AW	19.49 TQ	NYBLS	10/01-12/01
Transit and Intercity	New York PMSA, NY	H	11.98 FQ	20.38 AW	26.39 TQ	NYBLS	10/01-12/01
Transit and Intercity	Newburgh PMSA, NY-PA	H	9.18 FQ	16.17 AW	25.91 TQ	NYBLS	10/01-12/01
Transit and Intercity	Rochester MSA, NY	H	9.75 FQ	16.49 AW	21.46 TQ	NYBLS	10/01-12/01
Transit and Intercity	Syracuse MSA, NY	H	7.14 FQ	9.60 AW	10.99 TQ	NYBLS	10/01-12/01
Transit and Intercity	Utica-Rome MSA, NY	H	6.18 FQ	9.85 AW	14.28 TQ	NYBLS	10/01-12/01
Transit and Intercity	North Carolina	H	6.99 FQ	11.17 AW	16.69 TQ	NCBLS	10/01-12/01
Transit and Intercity	Asheville MSA, NC	H	6.79 FQ	10.08 AW	13.10 TQ	NCBLS	10/01-12/01
Transit and Intercity	Charlotte-Gastonia-Rock Hill MSA, NC-SC	H	8.26 FQ	13.00 AW	17.23 TQ	NCBLS	10/01-12/01
Transit and Intercity	Fayetteville MSA, NC	H	6.87 FQ	13.36 AW	20.93 TQ	NCBLS	10/01-12/01
Transit and Intercity	Greensboro-Winston-Salem-High Point MSA, NC	H	5.96 FQ	9.55 AW	13.44 TQ	NCBLS	10/01-12/01
Transit and Intercity	Raleigh-Durham-Chapel Hill MSA, NC	H	8.13 FQ	11.58 AW	16.52 TQ	NCBLS	10/01-12/01
Transit and Intercity	North Dakota	H	6.71 FQ	9.43 AW	13.54 TQ	NDBLS	10/01-12/01
Transit and Intercity	Ohio	H	8.50 FQ	15.73 AW	23.75 TQ	OHBLS	10/01-12/01
Transit and Intercity	Cincinnati PMSA, OH-KY-IN	H	8.95 FQ	13.21 AW	17.71 TQ	OHBLS	10/01-12/01
Transit and Intercity	Hamilton-Middletown PMSA, OH	H	10.03 FQ	19.65 AW	27.79 TQ	OHBLS	10/01-12/01
Transit and Intercity	Toledo MSA, OH	H	6.97 FQ	11.24 AW	14.43 TQ	OHBLS	10/01-12/01
Transit and Intercity	Youngstown-Warren MSA, OH	H	6.13 FQ	9.14 AW	12.29 TQ	OHBLS	10/01-12/01
Transit and Intercity	Oklahoma	H	6.25 FQ	10.55 AW	15.78 TQ	OKBLS	10/01-12/01
Transit and Intercity	Oklahoma City MSA, OK	H	6.36 FQ	11.84 AW	16.80 TQ	OKBLS	10/01-12/01
Transit and Intercity	Tulsa MSA, OK	H	6.80 FQ	10.38 AW	13.96 TQ	OKBLS	10/01-12/01
Transit and Intercity	Oregon	H	10.23 FQ	15.92 AW	21.85 TQ	ORBLS	10/01-12/01
Transit and Intercity	Eugene-Springfield MSA, OR	H	8.81 FQ	11.48 AW	19.49 TQ	ORBLS	10/01-12/01
Transit and Intercity	Medford-Ashland MSA, OR	H	10.69 FQ	14.85 AW	18.06 TQ	ORBLS	10/01-12/01
Transit and Intercity	Salem PMSA, OR	H	11.31 FQ	14.71 AW	17.17 TQ	ORBLS	10/01-12/01
Transit and Intercity	Pennsylvania	H	7.84 FQ	15.19 AW	24.36 TQ	PABLS	10/01-12/01
Transit and Intercity	Allentown-Bethlehem-Easton MSA, PA	H	7.88 FQ	13.86 AW	21.53 TQ	PABLS	10/01-12/01
Transit and Intercity	Erie MSA, PA	H	9.27 FQ	13.15 AW	17.55 TQ	PABLS	10/01-12/01
Transit and Intercity	Johnstown MSA, PA	H	6.48 FQ	11.90 AW	16.62 TQ	PABLS	10/01-12/01
Transit and Intercity	Lancaster MSA, PA	H	7.69 FQ	12.16 AW	19.61 TQ	PABLS	10/01-12/01
Transit and Intercity	Reading MSA, PA	H	8.35 FQ	12.47 AW	16.00 TQ	PABLS	10/01-12/01
Transit and Intercity	Scranton-Wilkes-Barre-Hazleton MSA, PA	H	7.68 FQ	12.43 AW	18.04 TQ	PABLS	10/01-12/01
Transit and Intercity	Rhode Island	H	7.77 FQ	11.51 AW	16.57 TQ	RIBLS	10/01-12/01
Transit and Intercity	Providence-Fall River-Warwick MSA, RI-MA	H	7.95 FQ	12.17 AW	18.83 TQ	RIBLS	10/01-12/01

AAW	Average annual wage	AOH	Average offered, high	ASH	Average starting, high	H	Hourly	M	Monthly	S	Special: hourly and annual
AE	Average entry wage	AOL	Average offered, low	ASL	Average starting, low	HI	Highest wage paid	MTC	Median total compensation	TQ	Third quartile wage
AEX	Average experienced wage	APH	Average pay, high range	AW	Average wage paid	HR	High end range	MW	Median wage paid	W	Weekly
AO	Average offered	APL	Average pay, low range	FQ	First quartile wage	LR	Low end range	SQ	Second quartile wage	Y	Yearly

Occupation/Type/Industry	Location	Per	Low	Mid	High	Source	Date
Bus Driver							
Transit and Intercity	South Carolina	H	6.07 FQ	10.62 AW	17.13 TQ	SCBLS	10/01-12/01
Transit and Intercity	Charleston-North Charleston MSA, SC	H	6.17 FQ	11.11 AW	16.90 TQ	SCBLS	10/01-12/01
Transit and Intercity	Columbia MSA, SC	H	5.95 FQ	14.16 AW	25.40 TQ	SCBLS	10/01-12/01
Transit and Intercity	Greenville-Spartanburg-Anderson MSA, SC	H	5.88 FQ	8.56 AW	11.12 TQ	SCBLS	10/01-12/01
Transit and Intercity	South Dakota	H	7.33 FQ	10.06 AW	13.03 TQ	SDBLS	10/01-12/01
Transit and Intercity	Tennessee	H	6.57 FQ	12.75 AW	20.27 TQ	TNBLS	10/01-12/01
Transit and Intercity	Clarksville-Hopkinsville MSA, TN-KY	H	5.82 FQ	8.81 AW	13.22 TQ	TNBLS	10/01-12/01
Transit and Intercity	Johnson City-Kingsport-Bristol MSA, TN-VA	H	5.67 FQ	8.73 AW	12.85 TQ	TNBLS	10/01-12/01
Transit and Intercity	Knoxville MSA, TN	H	6.55 FQ	11.23 AW	18.02 TQ	TNBLS	10/01-12/01
Transit and Intercity	Nashville MSA, TN	H	9.41 FQ	15.08 AW	20.47 TQ	TNBLS	10/01-12/01
Transit and Intercity	Texas	H	7.84 FQ	12.34 AW	16.65 TQ	TXBLS	10/01-12/01
Transit and Intercity	Amarillo MSA, TX	H	13.61 FQ	16.28 AW	22.20 TQ	TXBLS	10/01-12/01
Transit and Intercity	Beaumont-Port Arthur MSA, TX	H	6.05 FQ	11.25 AW	14.11 TQ	TXBLS	10/01-12/01
Transit and Intercity	Brownsville-Harlingen-San Benito MSA, TX	H	7.35 FQ	11.38 AW	16.40 TQ	TXBLS	10/01-12/01
Transit and Intercity	Corpus Christi MSA, TX	H	6.45 FQ	12.10 AW	16.44 TQ	TXBLS	10/01-12/01
Transit and Intercity	Dallas PMSA, TX	H	7.77 FQ	12.22 AW	16.69 TQ	TXBLS	10/01-12/01
Transit and Intercity	El Paso MSA, TX	H	7.60 FQ	11.91 AW	14.46 TQ	TXBLS	10/01-12/01
Transit and Intercity	Fort Worth-Arlington PMSA, TX	H	9.61 FQ	13.71 AW	16.76 TQ	TXBLS	10/01-12/01
Transit and Intercity	Houston PMSA, TX	H	7.70 FQ	12.06 AW	16.83 TQ	TXBLS	10/01-12/01
Transit and Intercity	Killeen-Temple MSA, TX	H	6.94 FQ	10.35 AW	13.06 TQ	TXBLS	10/01-12/01
Transit and Intercity	Laredo MSA, TX	H	8.57 FQ	10.98 AW	16.41 TQ	TXBLS	10/01-12/01
Transit and Intercity	Odessa-Midland MSA, TX	H	7.35 FQ	15.13 AW	36.71 TQ	TXBLS	10/01-12/01
Transit and Intercity	San Antonio MSA, TX	H	8.40 FQ	12.48 AW	16.38 TQ	TXBLS	10/01-12/01
Transit and Intercity	Tyler MSA, TX	H	7.41 FQ	8.75 AW	10.83 TQ	TXBLS	10/01-12/01
Transit and Intercity	Waco MSA, TX	H	9.69 FQ	13.42 AW	17.54 TQ	TXBLS	10/01-12/01
Transit and Intercity	Vermont	H	8.40 FQ	10.82 AW	15.28 TQ	VTBLS	10/01-12/01
Transit and Intercity	Burlington MSA, VT	H	9.13 FQ	12.40 AW	16.57 TQ	VTBLS	10/01-12/01
Transit and Intercity	Virginia	H	6.37 FQ	11.30 AW	16.58 TQ	VABLS	10/01-12/01
Transit and Intercity	Lynchburg MSA, VA	H	9.16 FQ	12.16 AW	14.29 TQ	VABLS	10/01-12/01
Transit and Intercity	Norfolk-Virginia Beach-Newport News MSA, VA-NC	H	5.91 FQ	8.91 AW	14.15 TQ	VABLS	10/01-12/01
Transit and Intercity	Richmond-Petersburg MSA, VA	H	9.05 FQ	13.89 AW	18.14 TQ	VABLS	10/01-12/01
Transit and Intercity	Roanoke MSA, VA	H	6.02 FQ	10.93 AW	16.49 TQ	VABLS	10/01-12/01
Transit and Intercity	Washington	H	10.03 FQ	16.43 AW	21.63 TQ	WABLS	10/01-12/01
Transit and Intercity	Olympia PMSA, WA	H	9.67 FQ	14.37 AW	19.05 TQ	WABLS	10/01-12/01
Transit and Intercity	Yakima MSA, WA	H	8.59 FQ	12.23 AW	17.33 TQ	WABLS	10/01-12/01
Transit and Intercity	West Virginia	H	6.74 FQ	9.27 AW	12.89 TQ	WVBLS	10/01-12/01
Transit and Intercity	Huntington-Ashland MSA, WV-KY-OH	H	7.53 FQ	9.66 AW	12.70 TQ	WVBLS	10/01-12/01
Transit and Intercity	Wisconsin	H	8.24 FQ	14.93 AW	21.12 TQ	WIBLS	10/01-12/01
Transit and Intercity	Appleton-Oshkosh-Neenah MSA, WI	H	8.94 FQ	13.52 AW	17.28 TQ	WIBLS	10/01-12/01
Transit and Intercity	Green Bay MSA, WI	H	7.71 FQ	12.46 AW	17.31 TQ	WIBLS	10/01-12/01
Transit and Intercity	Milwaukee-Waukesha PMSA, WI	H	8.90 FQ	16.03 AW	21.30 TQ	WIBLS	10/01-12/01
Transit and Intercity	Wyoming	H	6.18 FQ	10.62 AW	18.84 TQ	WYBLS	10/01-12/01
Transit and Intercity	Cheyenne MSA, WY	H	7.34 FQ	11.71 AW	19.94 TQ	WYBLS	10/01-12/01
Transit and Intercity	Puerto Rico	H	5.59 FQ	7.80 AW	10.89 TQ	PRBLS	10/01-12/01
Transit and Intercity	Guam	H	5.63 FQ	7.60 AW	10.45 TQ	GUBLS	10/01-12/01
Business Manager							
Web Design	United States	Y		46231 AW		DFMAR	1/01-1/02
Business Teacher							
Postsecondary	Alabama	Y	17440 FQ	49620 AW	86600 TQ	ALBLS	10/01-12/01
Postsecondary	Birmingham MSA, AL	Y	26540 FQ	62440 AW	93730 TQ	ALBLS	10/01-12/01
Postsecondary	Huntsville MSA, AL	Y	17770 FQ	37120 AW	68790 TQ	ALBLS	10/01-12/01
Postsecondary	Mobile MSA, AL	Y	13350 FQ	37040 AW	57490 TQ	ALBLS	10/01-12/01
Postsecondary	Montgomery MSA, AL	Y	38440 FQ	54710 AW	72870 TQ	ALBLS	10/01-12/01
Postsecondary	Arizona	Y	21980 FQ	43240 AW	64590 TQ	AZBLS	10/01-12/01
Postsecondary	Arkansas	Y	21600 FQ	45300 AW	88170 TQ	ARBLS	10/01-12/01
Postsecondary	California	Y	35510 FQ	72270 AW	114450 TQ	CABLS	10/01-12/01
Postsecondary	Fresno MSA, CA	Y	26050 FQ	58280 AW	103210 TQ	CABLS	10/01-12/01

AAW	Average annual wage	**AOH**	Average offered, high	**ASH**	Average starting, high	**H**	Hourly	**M**	Monthly	**S**	Special: hourly and annual
AE	Average entry wage	**AOL**	Average offered, low	**ASL**	Average starting, low	**HI**	Highest wage paid	**MTC**	Median total compensation	**TQ**	Third quartile wage
AEX	Average experienced wage	**APH**	Average pay, high range	**AW**	Average wage paid	**HR**	High end range	**MW**	Median wage paid	**W**	Weekly
AO	Average offered	**APL**	Average pay, low range	**FQ**	First quartile wage	**LR**	Low end range	**SQ**	Second quartile wage	**Y**	Yearly

Occupation/Type/Industry	Location	Per	Low	Mid	High	Source	Date
Business Teacher							
Postsecondary	Los Angeles-Long Beach PMSA, CA	Y	41940 FQ	75830 AW	119480 TQ	CABLS	10/01-12/01
Postsecondary	Oakland PMSA, CA	Y	37040 FQ	72180 AW	114250 TQ	CABLS	10/01-12/01
Postsecondary	Riverside-San Bernardino PMSA, CA	Y	39200 FQ	71130 AW	111840 TQ	CABLS	10/01-12/01
Postsecondary	Sacramento PMSA, CA	Y	33660 FQ	77480 AW	125600 TQ	CABLS	10/01-12/01
Postsecondary	San Diego MSA, CA	Y	24070 FQ	62360 AW	99350 TQ	CABLS	10/01-12/01
Postsecondary	San Francisco PMSA, CA	Y	48910 FQ	83950 AW	118330 TQ	CABLS	10/01-12/01
Postsecondary	San Jose PMSA, CA	Y	37530 FQ	76640 AW	123020 TQ	CABLS	10/01-12/01
Postsecondary	Colorado	Y	27170 FQ	55990 AW	99210 TQ	COBLS	10/01-12/01
Postsecondary	Colorado Springs MSA, CO	Y	23980 FQ	44160 AW	85700 TQ	COBLS	10/01-12/01
Postsecondary	Denver PMSA, CO	Y	30100 FQ	59630 AW	106870 TQ	COBLS	10/01-12/01
Postsecondary	Fort Collins-Loveland MSA, CO	Y	29340 FQ	54800 AW	92360 TQ	COBLS	10/01-12/01
Postsecondary	Connecticut	Y	37750 FQ	73010 AW		CTBLS	10/01-12/01
Postsecondary	Hartford MSA, CT	Y	37640 FQ	82950 AW		CTBLS	10/01-12/01
Postsecondary	New Haven-Meriden PMSA, CT	Y	37330 FQ	49480 AW	59480 TQ	CTBLS	10/01-12/01
Postsecondary	Delaware	Y	39090 FQ	67360 AW	101620 TQ	DEBLS	10/01-12/01
Postsecondary	Wilmington-Newark PMSA, DE-MD	Y	40450 FQ	72490 AW	108200 TQ	DEBLS	10/01-12/01
Postsecondary	District of Columbia	Y	33740 FQ	66860 AW	102940 TQ	DCBLS	10/01-12/01
Postsecondary	Washington PMSA, DC-MD-VA-WV	Y	27580 FQ	63420 AW	107830 TQ	DCBLS	10/01-12/01
Postsecondary	Florida	Y	33400 FQ	67450 AW	113820 TQ	FLBLS	10/01-12/01
Postsecondary	Daytona Beach MSA, FL	Y	35790 FQ	54480 AW	82140 TQ	FLBLS	10/01-12/01
Postsecondary	Fort Lauderdale PMSA, FL	Y	34950 FQ	64690 AW	98520 TQ	FLBLS	10/01-12/01
Postsecondary	Gainesville MSA, FL	Y	35760 FQ	87810 AW		FLBLS	10/01-12/01
Postsecondary	Jacksonville MSA, FL	Y	39000 FQ	55550 AW	90530 TQ	FLBLS	10/01-12/01
Postsecondary	Melbourne-Titusville-Palm Bay MSA, FL	Y	34190 FQ	56520 AW	92580 TQ	FLBLS	10/01-12/01
Postsecondary	Miami PMSA, FL	Y	45910 FQ	74950 AW	122370 TQ	FLBLS	10/01-12/01
Postsecondary	Orlando MSA, FL	Y	28170 FQ	68580 AW	115840 TQ	FLBLS	10/01-12/01
Postsecondary	Pensacola MSA, FL	Y	40300 FQ	64250 AW	96260 TQ	FLBLS	10/01-12/01
Postsecondary	Tallahassee MSA, FL	Y	46180 FQ	78430 AW	115300 TQ	FLBLS	10/01-12/01
Postsecondary	Tampa-St. Petersburg-Clearwater MSA, FL	Y	30240 FQ	61360 AW	108680 TQ	FLBLS	10/01-12/01
Postsecondary	West Palm Beach-Boca Raton MSA, FL	Y	31840 FQ	72290 AW	123090 TQ	FLBLS	10/01-12/01
Postsecondary	Georgia	Y	33260 FQ	60890 AW	102260 TQ	GABLS	10/01-12/01
Postsecondary	Atlanta MSA, GA	Y	35570 FQ	69680 AW	116220 TQ	GABLS	10/01-12/01
Postsecondary	Savannah MSA, GA	Y	12560 FQ	45480 AW	80500 TQ	GABLS	10/01-12/01
Postsecondary	Hawaii	Y	38820 FQ	74150 AW	113250 TQ	HIBLS	10/01-12/01
Postsecondary	Honolulu MSA, HI	Y	38300 FQ	74480 AW	114200 TQ	HIBLS	10/01-12/01
Postsecondary	Idaho	Y	22130 FQ	48910 AW	61280 TQ	IDBLS	10/01-12/01
Postsecondary	Illinois	Y	21240 FQ	61390 AW	108210 TQ	ILBLS	10/01-12/01
Postsecondary	Champaign-Urbana MSA, IL	Y	16960 FQ	57190 AW	93610 TQ	ILBLS	10/01-12/01
Postsecondary	Chicago PMSA, IL	Y	28990 FQ	66930 AW	121060 TQ	ILBLS	10/01-12/01
Postsecondary	Rockford MSA, IL	Y	12520 FQ	47880 AW	74310 TQ	ILBLS	10/01-12/01
Postsecondary	Springfield MSA, IL	Y	13570 FQ	65850 AW	141260 TQ	ILBLS	10/01-12/01
Postsecondary	Indiana	Y	21070 FQ	57730 AW	109420 TQ	INBLS	10/01-12/01
Postsecondary	Fort Wayne MSA, IN	Y	17570 FQ	57150 AW	94020 TQ	INBLS	10/01-12/01
Postsecondary	Gary PMSA, IN	Y	31870 FQ	66350 AW	111970 TQ	INBLS	10/01-12/01
Postsecondary	Indianapolis MSA, IN	Y	27340 FQ	57890 AW	108180 TQ	INBLS	10/01-12/01
Postsecondary	South Bend MSA, IN	Y	28330 FQ	49150 AW	74380 TQ	INBLS	10/01-12/01
Postsecondary	Iowa	Y	26670 FQ	55940 AW	90650 TQ	IABLS	10/01-12/01
Postsecondary	Cedar Rapids MSA, IA	Y	32600 FQ	48460 AW	66730 TQ	IABLS	10/01-12/01
Postsecondary	Des Moines MSA, IA	Y	31150 FQ	49170 AW	72530 TQ	IABLS	10/01-12/01
Postsecondary	Kansas	Y	20820 FQ	43790 AW	77180 TQ	KSBLS	10/01-12/01
Postsecondary	Wichita MSA, KS	Y	25960 FQ	46110 AW	76660 TQ	KSBLS	10/01-12/01
Postsecondary	Kentucky	Y	23260 FQ	60130 AW	107190 TQ	KYBLS	10/01-12/01
Postsecondary	Lexington MSA, KY	Y	31980 FQ	73980 AW	114860 TQ	KYBLS	10/01-12/01
Postsecondary	Louisville MSA, KY-IN	Y	20120 FQ	63950 AW	115940 TQ	KYBLS	10/01-12/01
Postsecondary	Louisiana	Y	17060 FQ	52320 AW	90970 TQ	LABLS	10/01-12/01
Postsecondary	New Orleans MSA, LA	Y	13090 FQ	52350 AW	98030 TQ	LABLS	10/01-12/01
Postsecondary	Shreveport-Bossier City MSA, LA	Y	29980 FQ	53120 AW	81990 TQ	LABLS	10/01-12/01
Postsecondary	Maine	Y	29710 FQ	47360 AW	71320 TQ	MEBLS	10/01-12/01
Postsecondary	Portland MSA, ME	Y	32100 FQ	49950 AW	72380 TQ	MEBLS	10/01-12/01
Postsecondary	Maryland	Y	40490 FQ	71500 AW	124720 TQ	MDBLS	10/01-12/01
Postsecondary	Baltimore PMSA, MD	Y	36090 FQ	64470 AW	101040 TQ	MDBLS	10/01-12/01

AAW	Average annual wage	**AOH**	Average offered, high	**ASH**	Average starting, high	**H**	Hourly	**M**	Monthly	**S**	Special: hourly and annual
AE	Average entry wage	**AOL**	Average offered, low	**ASL**	Average starting, low	**HI**	Highest wage paid	**MTC**	Median total compensation	**TQ**	Third quartile wage
AEX	Average experienced wage	**APH**	Average pay, high range	**AW**	Average wage paid	**HR**	High end range	**MW**	Median wage paid	**W**	Weekly
AO	Average offered	**APL**	Average pay, low range	**FQ**	First quartile wage	**LR**	Low end range	**SQ**	Second quartile wage	**Y**	Yearly

Occupation/Type/Industry	Location	Per	Low	Mid	High	Source	Date
Business Teacher							
Postsecondary	Massachusetts	Y	32170 FQ	67150 AW	111090 TQ	MABLS	10/01-12/01
Postsecondary	Boston PMSA, MA-NH	Y	33350 FQ	70110 AW	113580 TQ	MABLS	10/01-12/01
Postsecondary	Brockton PMSA, MA	Y	43650 FQ	59540 AW	79950 TQ	MABLS	10/01-12/01
Postsecondary	Springfield MSA, MA	Y	20090 FQ	53880 AW	100370 TQ	MABLS	10/01-12/01
Postsecondary	Worcester PMSA, MA-CT	Y	31600 FQ	63090 AW	104500 TQ	MABLS	10/01-12/01
Postsecondary	Michigan	Y	36380 FQ	70430 AW	113570 TQ	MIBLS	10/01-12/01
Postsecondary	Ann Arbor PMSA, MI	Y	35580 FQ	56380 AW	96050 TQ	MIBLS	10/01-12/01
Postsecondary	Detroit PMSA, MI	Y	37110 FQ	78510 AW	118490 TQ	MIBLS	10/01-12/01
Postsecondary	Grand Rapids-Muskegon-Holland MSA, MI	Y	36620 FQ	71960 AW	107470 TQ	MIBLS	10/01-12/01
Postsecondary	Minnesota	Y	39040 FQ	61690 AW	96150 TQ	MNBLS	10/01-12/01
Postsecondary	Duluth-Superior MSA, MN-WI	Y	37540 FQ	56240 AW	82640 TQ	MNBLS	10/01-12/01
Postsecondary	Minneapolis-St. Paul MSA, MN-WI	Y	40110 FQ	69010 AW	114250 TQ	MNBLS	10/01-12/01
Postsecondary	St. Cloud MSA, MN	Y	37910 FQ	49710 AW	63230 TQ	MNBLS	10/01-12/01
Postsecondary	Mississippi	Y	32110 FQ	59280 AW	90790 TQ	MSBLS	10/01-12/01
Postsecondary	Jackson MSA, MS	Y	14360 FQ	44070 AW	76520 TQ	MSBLS	10/01-12/01
Postsecondary	Missouri	Y	21690 FQ	52220 AW	87350 TQ	MOBLS	10/01-12/01
Postsecondary	Kansas City MSA, MO-KS	Y	17330 FQ	47240 AW	71440 TQ	MOBLS	10/01-12/01
Postsecondary	St. Louis MSA, MO-IL	Y	21310 FQ	50170 AW	91250 TQ	MOBLS	10/01-12/01
Postsecondary	Springfield MSA, MO	Y	41620 FQ	71910 AW	97020 TQ	MOBLS	10/01-12/01
Postsecondary	Montana	Y	32580 FQ	65310 AW	113600 TQ	MTBLS	10/01-12/01
Postsecondary	Nebraska	Y	32460 FQ	57640 AW	94530 TQ	NEBLS	10/01-12/01
Postsecondary	Lincoln MSA, NE	Y	36970 FQ	75400 AW	131640 TQ	NEBLS	10/01-12/01
Postsecondary	Omaha MSA, NE-IA	Y	26960 FQ	51270 AW	88120 TQ	NEBLS	10/01-12/01
Postsecondary	Nevada	Y	21080 FQ	50070 AW	92120 TQ	NVBLS	10/01-12/01
Postsecondary	Las Vegas MSA, NV-AZ	Y	20480 FQ	48260 AW	90530 TQ	NVBLS	10/01-12/01
Postsecondary	New Hampshire	Y	29900 FQ	70140 AW	143820 TQ	NHBLS	10/01-12/01
Postsecondary	Nashua PMSA, NH	Y	38540 FQ	53410 AW	92450 TQ	NHBLS	10/01-12/01
Postsecondary	Portsmouth-Rochester PMSA, NH-ME	Y	51980 FQ	77680 AW	106590 TQ	NHBLS	10/01-12/01
Postsecondary	New Jersey	Y	32750 FQ	68210 AW	106280 TQ	NJBLS	10/01-12/01
Postsecondary	Bergen-Passaic PMSA, NJ	Y	31440 FQ	59900 AW	93750 TQ	NJBLS	10/01-12/01
Postsecondary	Jersey City PMSA, NJ	Y	43770 FQ	78140 AW	121570 TQ	NJBLS	10/01-12/01
Postsecondary	Monmouth-Ocean PMSA, NJ	Y	33140 FQ	61100 AW	95210 TQ	NJBLS	10/01-12/01
Postsecondary	Newark PMSA, NJ	Y	22240 FQ	64050 AW	96270 TQ	NJBLS	10/01-12/01
Postsecondary	New Mexico	Y	30000 FQ	49600 AW	76560 TQ	NMBLS	10/01-12/01
Postsecondary	New York	Y	27890 FQ	55050 AW	91800 TQ	NYBLS	10/01-12/01
Postsecondary	Albany-Schenectady-Troy MSA, NY	Y	34440 FQ	48580 AW	70350 TQ	NYBLS	10/01-12/01
Postsecondary	Buffalo-Niagara Falls MSA, NY	Y	21570 FQ	45250 AW	73840 TQ	NYBLS	10/01-12/01
Postsecondary	Nassau-Suffolk PMSA, NY	Y	30990 FQ	60300 AW	98720 TQ	NYBLS	10/01-12/01
Postsecondary	New York PMSA, NY	Y	27310 FQ	54810 AW	90000 TQ	NYBLS	10/01-12/01
Postsecondary	Rochester MSA, NY	Y	25290 FQ	47510 AW	89170 TQ	NYBLS	10/01-12/01
Postsecondary	Syracuse MSA, NY	Y	23160 FQ	49240 AW	104780 TQ	NYBLS	10/01-12/01
Postsecondary	Utica-Rome MSA, NY	Y	28840 FQ	46700 AW	59660 TQ	NYBLS	10/01-12/01
Postsecondary	North Carolina	Y	32130 FQ	54390 AW	87320 TQ	NCBLS	10/01-12/01
Postsecondary	Asheville MSA, NC	Y	33020 FQ	53080 AW	70180 TQ	NCBLS	10/01-12/01
Postsecondary	Charlotte-Gastonia-Rock Hill MSA, NC-SC	Y	31250 FQ	54210 AW	89620 TQ	NCBLS	10/01-12/01
Postsecondary	Fayetteville MSA, NC	Y	42370 FQ	64710 AW	113270 TQ	NCBLS	10/01-12/01
Postsecondary	Greensboro-Winston-Salem-High Point MSA, NC	Y	35440 FQ	60840 AW	93860 TQ	NCBLS	10/01-12/01
Postsecondary	Hickory-Morganton-Lenoir MSA, NC	Y	32390 FQ	42340 AW	55550 TQ	NCBLS	10/01-12/01
Postsecondary	Raleigh-Durham-Chapel Hill MSA, NC	Y	34320 FQ	55610 AW	90600 TQ	NCBLS	10/01-12/01
Postsecondary	Wilmington MSA, NC	Y	38040 FQ	68700 AW	108780 TQ	NCBLS	10/01-12/01
Postsecondary	North Dakota	Y	25320 FQ	49160 AW	77020 TQ	NDBLS	10/01-12/01
Postsecondary	Fargo-Moorhead MSA, ND-MN	Y	39270 FQ	61340 AW	85120 TQ	NDBLS	10/01-12/01
Postsecondary	Ohio	Y	23520 FQ	55170 AW	90780 TQ	OHBLS	10/01-12/01
Postsecondary	Canton-Massillon MSA, OH	Y	24710 FQ	54400 AW	79810 TQ	OHBLS	10/01-12/01
Postsecondary	Cincinnati PMSA, OH-KY-IN	Y	30050 FQ	67150 AW	107800 TQ	OHBLS	10/01-12/01
Postsecondary	Cleveland-Lorain-Elyria PMSA, OH	Y	29230 FQ	63820 AW	101990 TQ	OHBLS	10/01-12/01
Postsecondary	Columbus MSA, OH	Y	29770 FQ	54130 AW	81270 TQ	OHBLS	10/01-12/01
Postsecondary	Dayton-Springfield MSA, OH	Y	17240 FQ	43270 AW	82030 TQ	OHBLS	10/01-12/01
Postsecondary	Toledo MSA, OH	Y	24890 FQ	59910 AW	90020 TQ	OHBLS	10/01-12/01
Postsecondary	Youngstown-Warren MSA, OH	Y	26460 FQ	61510 AW	94120 TQ	OHBLS	10/01-12/01

AAW	Average annual wage	**AOH**	Average offered, high	**ASH**	Average starting, high	**H**	Hourly	**M**	Monthly	**S**	Special: hourly and annual
AE	Average entry wage	**AOL**	Average offered, low	**ASL**	Average starting, low	**HI**	Highest wage paid	**MTC**	Median total compensation	**TQ**	Third quartile wage
AEX	Average experienced wage	**APH**	Average pay, high range	**AW**	Average wage paid	**HR**	High end range	**MW**	Median wage paid	**W**	Weekly
AO	Average offered	**APL**	Average pay, low range	**FQ**	First quartile wage	**LR**	Low end range	**SQ**	Second quartile wage	**Y**	Yearly

Occupation/Type/Industry	Location	Per	Low	Mid	High	Source	Date
Business Teacher							
Postsecondary	Oklahoma	Y	24540 FQ	42640 AW	65440 TQ	OKBLS	10/01-12/01
Postsecondary	Oklahoma City MSA, OK	Y	22800 FQ	38480 AW	63440 TQ	OKBLS	10/01-12/01
Postsecondary	Tulsa MSA, OK	Y	28500 FQ	52610 AW	85800 TQ	OKBLS	10/01-12/01
Postsecondary	Oregon	Y	31640 FQ	68000 AW	119840 TQ	ORBLS	10/01-12/01
Postsecondary	Eugene-Springfield MSA, OR	Y	47290 FQ	94540 AW	138710 TQ	ORBLS	10/01-12/01
Postsecondary	Portland-Vancouver PMSA, OR-WA	Y	27910 FQ	64110 AW	117390 TQ	ORBLS	10/01-12/01
Postsecondary	Pennsylvania	Y	25250 FQ	57470 AW	101820 TQ	PABLS	10/01-12/01
Postsecondary	Allentown-Bethlehem-Easton MSA, PA	Y	22150 FQ	41260 AW	70230 TQ	PABLS	10/01-12/01
Postsecondary	Erie MSA, PA	Y	25430 FQ	54410 AW	89790 TQ	PABLS	10/01-12/01
Postsecondary	Harrisburg-Lebanon-Carlisle MSA, PA	Y	23940 FQ	58890 AW	103680 TQ	PABLS	10/01-12/01
Postsecondary	Johnstown MSA, PA	Y	36160 FQ	54970 AW	74280 TQ	PABLS	10/01-12/01
Postsecondary	Lancaster MSA, PA	Y	39260 FQ	58380 AW	87270 TQ	PABLS	10/01-12/01
Postsecondary	Philadelphia PMSA, PA-NJ	Y	25620 FQ	57080 AW	96870 TQ	PABLS	10/01-12/01
Postsecondary	Pittsburgh MSA, PA	Y	25120 FQ	62580 AW	122640 TQ	PABLS	10/01-12/01
Postsecondary	Reading MSA, PA	Y	25570 FQ	53740 AW	98330 TQ	PABLS	10/01-12/01
Postsecondary	Scranton-Wilkes-Barre-Hazleton MSA, PA	Y	34240 FQ	56480 AW	83240 TQ	PABLS	10/01-12/01
Postsecondary	York MSA, PA	Y	40200 FQ	62090 AW	86120 TQ	PABLS	10/01-12/01
Postsecondary	Rhode Island	Y	36110 FQ	63930 AW	94130 TQ	RIBLS	10/01-12/01
Postsecondary	South Carolina	Y	31430 FQ	49700 AW	69390 TQ	SCBLS	10/01-12/01
Postsecondary	Columbia MSA, SC	Y	30640 FQ	50550 AW	71400 TQ	SCBLS	10/01-12/01
Postsecondary	Greenville-Spartanburg-Anderson MSA, SC	Y	30960 FQ	49910 AW	69060 TQ	SCBLS	10/01-12/01
Postsecondary	South Dakota	Y	28540 FQ	50290 AW	77190 TQ	SDBLS	10/01-12/01
Postsecondary	Sioux Falls MSA, SD	Y	24860 FQ	37940 AW	55600 TQ	SDBLS	10/01-12/01
Postsecondary	Tennessee	Y	24150 FQ	55550 AW	91140 TQ	TNBLS	10/01-12/01
Postsecondary	Chattanooga MSA, TN-GA	Y	21930 FQ	53960 AW	87170 TQ	TNBLS	10/01-12/01
Postsecondary	Clarksville-Hopkinsville MSA, TN-KY	Y	26180 FQ	59710 AW	92710 TQ	TNBLS	10/01-12/01
Postsecondary	Johnson City-Kingsport-Bristol MSA, TN-VA	Y	20980 FQ	47570 AW	86720 TQ	TNBLS	10/01-12/01
Postsecondary	Knoxville MSA, TN	Y	35570 FQ	60670 AW	101260 TQ	TNBLS	10/01-12/01
Postsecondary	Memphis MSA, TN-AR-MS	Y	32690 FQ	62330 AW	93850 TQ	TNBLS	10/01-12/01
Postsecondary	Nashville MSA, TN	Y	32390 FQ	58880 AW	89270 TQ	TNBLS	10/01-12/01
Postsecondary	Texas	Y	26130 FQ	56890 AW	89860 TQ	TXBLS	10/01-12/01
Postsecondary	Austin-San Marcos MSA, TX	Y	33040 FQ	59510 AW	86030 TQ	TXBLS	10/01-12/01
Postsecondary	Beaumont-Port Arthur MSA, TX	Y	30050 FQ	43210 AW	66630 TQ	TXBLS	10/01-12/01
Postsecondary	Dallas PMSA, TX	Y	29710 FQ	58770 AW	90570 TQ	TXBLS	10/01-12/01
Postsecondary	Fort Worth-Arlington PMSA, TX	Y	27940 FQ	57280 AW	88580 TQ	TXBLS	10/01-12/01
Postsecondary	Houston PMSA, TX	Y	25910 FQ	58430 AW	102290 TQ	TXBLS	10/01-12/01
Postsecondary	Odessa-Midland MSA, TX	Y	29560 FQ	51060 AW	78610 TQ	TXBLS	10/01-12/01
Postsecondary	San Antonio MSA, TX	Y	24020 FQ	59560 AW	95970 TQ	TXBLS	10/01-12/01
Postsecondary	Utah	Y	36610 FQ	62830 AW	119990 TQ	UTBLS	10/01-12/01
Postsecondary	Salt Lake City-Ogden MSA, UT	Y	37440 FQ	61890 AW	121940 TQ	UTBLS	10/01-12/01
Postsecondary	Vermont	Y	35380 FQ	52420 AW	68990 TQ	VTBLS	10/01-12/01
Postsecondary	Burlington MSA, VT	Y	34260 FQ	54530 AW	96350 TQ	VTBLS	10/01-12/01
Postsecondary	Virginia	Y	24500 FQ	56090 AW	98550 TQ	VABLS	10/01-12/01
Postsecondary	Lynchburg MSA, VA	Y	21840 FQ	46210 AW	91950 TQ	VABLS	10/01-12/01
Postsecondary	Norfolk-Virginia Beach-Newport News MSA, VA-NC	Y	39130 FQ	66140 AW	100300 TQ	VABLS	10/01-12/01
Postsecondary	Richmond-Petersburg MSA, VA	Y	24670 FQ	56280 AW	99130 TQ	VABLS	10/01-12/01
Postsecondary	Roanoke MSA, VA	Y	33790 FQ	55510 AW	86460 TQ	VABLS	10/01-12/01
Postsecondary	Washington	Y	21580 FQ	62050 AW	125740 TQ	WABLS	10/01-12/01
Postsecondary	Seattle-Bellevue-Everett PMSA, WA	Y	25760 FQ	71300 AW	140970 TQ	WABLS	10/01-12/01
Postsecondary	Spokane MSA, WA	Y	20390 FQ	38170 AW	76130 TQ	WABLS	10/01-12/01
Postsecondary	Tacoma PMSA, WA	Y	23020 FQ	55590 AW	93580 TQ	WABLS	10/01-12/01
Postsecondary	West Virginia	Y	32720 FQ	55530 AW	83890 TQ	WVBLS	10/01-12/01
Postsecondary	Wisconsin	Y	26890 FQ	55360 AW	89730 TQ	WIBLS	10/01-12/01
Postsecondary	Green Bay MSA, WI	Y	23370 FQ	51580 AW	76690 TQ	WIBLS	10/01-12/01
Postsecondary	Milwaukee-Waukesha PMSA, WI	Y	21280 FQ	48360 AW	90870 TQ	WIBLS	10/01-12/01
Postsecondary	Wyoming	Y	27170 FQ	52440 AW	96420 TQ	WYBLS	10/01-12/01

AAW	Average annual wage	**AOH**	Average offered, high	**ASH**	Average starting, high	**H**	Hourly	**M**	Monthly	**S**	Special: hourly and annual
AE	Average entry wage	**AOL**	Average offered, low	**ASL**	Average starting, low	**HI**	Highest wage paid	**MTC**	Median total compensation	**TQ**	Third quartile wage
AEX	Average experienced wage	**APH**	Average pay, high range	**AW**	Average wage paid	**HR**	High end range	**MW**	Median wage paid	**W**	Weekly
AO	Average offered	**APL**	Average pay, low range	**FQ**	First quartile wage	**LR**	Low end range	**SQ**	Second quartile wage	**Y**	Yearly

Occupation/Type/Industry	Location	Per	Low	Mid	High	Source	Date
Business Teacher							
Postsecondary	Puerto Rico	Y	24900 FQ	36060 AW	49140 TQ	PRBLS	10/01-12/01
Butcher and Meat Cutter	Alabama	H	6.27 FQ	10.10 AW	15.40 TQ	ALBLS	10/01-12/01
	Birmingham MSA, AL	H	7.19 FQ	10.95 AW	16.30 TQ	ALBLS	10/01-12/01
	Huntsville MSA, AL	H	6.46 FQ	10.62 AW	15.94 TQ	ALBLS	10/01-12/01
	Mobile MSA, AL	H	6.28 FQ	10.14 AW	15.98 TQ	ALBLS	10/01-12/01
	Montgomery MSA, AL	H	7.21 FQ	10.40 AW	14.34 TQ	ALBLS	10/01-12/01
	Alaska	H	9.46 FQ	15.18 AW	21.59 TQ	AKBLS	10/01-12/01
	Anchorage MSA, AK	H	9.23 FQ	15.82 AW	22.24 TQ	AKBLS	10/01-12/01
	Arizona	H	8.97 FQ	15.07 AW	20.74 TQ	AZBLS	10/01-12/01
	Phoenix-Mesa MSA, AZ	H	8.78 FQ	14.85 AW	20.77 TQ	AZBLS	10/01-12/01
	Tucson MSA, AZ	H	9.75 FQ	15.87 AW	20.83 TQ	AZBLS	10/01-12/01
	Arkansas	H	6.57 FQ	10.00 AW	14.50 TQ	ARBLS	10/01-12/01
	Fayetteville-Springdale-Rogers MSA, AR	H	6.37 FQ	9.65 AW	12.64 TQ	ARBLS	10/01-12/01
	Fort Smith MSA, AR-OK	H	7.58 FQ	9.76 AW	12.51 TQ	ARBLS	10/01-12/01
	Little Rock-North Little Rock MSA, AR	H	7.15 FQ	11.11 AW	15.35 TQ	ARBLS	10/01-12/01
	California	H	7.02 FQ	14.28 AW	21.53 TQ	CABLS	10/01-12/01
	Bakersfield MSA, CA	H	6.71 FQ	12.72 AW	20.64 TQ	CABLS	10/01-12/01
	Chico-Paradise MSA, CA	H	9.84 FQ	16.86 AW	21.63 TQ	CABLS	10/01-12/01
	Fresno MSA, CA	H	6.59 FQ	9.94 AW	17.93 TQ	CABLS	10/01-12/01
	Los Angeles-Long Beach PMSA, CA	H	6.81 FQ	13.11 AW	22.20 TQ	CABLS	10/01-12/01
	Merced MSA, CA	H	6.72 FQ	9.98 AW	14.10 TQ	CABLS	10/01-12/01
	Modesto MSA, CA	H	7.00 FQ	14.82 AW	21.39 TQ	CABLS	10/01-12/01
	Oakland PMSA, CA	H	7.24 FQ	15.69 AW	21.46 TQ	CABLS	10/01-12/01
	Orange County PMSA, CA	H	7.46 FQ	14.19 AW	21.88 TQ	CABLS	10/01-12/01
	Redding MSA, CA	H	10.60 FQ	17.27 AW	21.77 TQ	CABLS	10/01-12/01
	Riverside-San Bernardino PMSA, CA	H	6.72 FQ	13.66 AW	20.97 TQ	CABLS	10/01-12/01
	Sacramento PMSA, CA	H	11.85 FQ	17.85 AW	22.01 TQ	CABLS	10/01-12/01
	Salinas MSA, CA	H	7.90 FQ	15.56 AW	21.42 TQ	CABLS	10/01-12/01
	San Diego MSA, CA	H	7.39 FQ	14.30 AW	21.36 TQ	CABLS	10/01-12/01
	San Francisco PMSA, CA	H	9.18 FQ	17.20 AW	21.73 TQ	CABLS	10/01-12/01
	San Jose PMSA, CA	H	10.57 FQ	18.16 AW	22.44 TQ	CABLS	10/01-12/01
	San Luis Obispo-Atascadero-Paso Robles MSA, CA	H	10.41 FQ	17.28 AW	21.26 TQ	CABLS	10/01-12/01
	Santa Barbara-Santa Maria-Lompoc MSA, CA	H	11.07 FQ	16.94 AW	21.52 TQ	CABLS	10/01-12/01
	Santa Cruz-Watsonville PMSA, CA	H	9.46 FQ	16.49 AW	21.56 TQ	CABLS	10/01-12/01
	Santa Rosa PMSA, CA	H	7.90 FQ	15.69 AW	21.89 TQ	CABLS	10/01-12/01
	Stockton-Lodi MSA, CA	H	8.32 FQ	13.23 AW	20.57 TQ	CABLS	10/01-12/01
	Vallejo-Fairfield-Napa PMSA, CA	H	10.50 FQ	17.90 AW	22.19 TQ	CABLS	10/01-12/01
	Ventura PMSA, CA	H	8.36 FQ	14.29 AW	21.41 TQ	CABLS	10/01-12/01
	Visalia-Tulare-Porterville MSA, CA	H	6.85 FQ	12.08 AW	19.97 TQ	CABLS	10/01-12/01
	Colorado	H	8.69 FQ	14.27 AW	19.09 TQ	COBLS	10/01-12/01
	Boulder-Longmont PMSA, CO	H	10.89 FQ	15.46 AW	18.30 TQ	COBLS	10/01-12/01
	Colorado Springs MSA, CO	H	10.58 FQ	14.74 AW	18.66 TQ	COBLS	10/01-12/01
	Denver PMSA, CO	H	10.01 FQ	15.21 AW	20.06 TQ	COBLS	10/01-12/01
	Fort Collins-Loveland MSA, CO	H	10.23 FQ	14.96 AW	18.26 TQ	COBLS	10/01-12/01
	Greeley PMSA, CO	H	7.61 FQ	12.00 AW	17.26 TQ	COBLS	10/01-12/01
	Connecticut	H	9.73 FQ	18.77 AW	26.85 TQ	CTBLS	10/01-12/01
	Bridgeport PMSA, CT	H	13.98 FQ	18.88 AW	26.45 TQ	CTBLS	10/01-12/01
	Danbury PMSA, CT	H	7.27 FQ	18.01 AW	25.33 TQ	CTBLS	10/01-12/01
	Hartford MSA, CT	H	8.89 FQ	18.10 AW	26.77 TQ	CTBLS	10/01-12/01
	New Haven-Meriden PMSA, CT	H	8.41 FQ	19.08 AW	26.74 TQ	CTBLS	10/01-12/01
	New London-Norwich MSA, CT-RI	H	11.12 FQ	19.54 AW	28.67 TQ	CTBLS	10/01-12/01
	Stamford-Norwalk PMSA, CT	H	13.96 FQ	19.41 AW	26.87 TQ	CTBLS	10/01-12/01
	Waterbury PMSA, CT	H	7.22 FQ	19.51 AW	27.27 TQ	CTBLS	10/01-12/01
	Wilmington-Newark PMSA, DE-MD	H	12.19 FQ	17.67 AW	21.39 TQ	DEBLS	10/01-12/01
	District of Columbia	H	9.30 FQ	13.16 AW	19.53 TQ	DCBLS	10/01-12/01
	Washington PMSA, DC-MD-VA-WV	H	10.75 FQ	16.15 AW	21.18 TQ	DCBLS	10/01-12/01
	Florida	H	7.47 FQ	11.02 AW	14.57 TQ	FLBLS	10/01-12/01

AAW	Average annual wage	AOH	Average offered, high	ASH	Average starting, high	H	Hourly	M	Monthly	S	Special: hourly and annual
AE	Average entry wage	AOL	Average offered, low	ASL	Average starting, low	HI	Highest wage paid	MTC	Median total compensation	TQ	Third quartile wage
AEX	Average experienced wage	APH	Average pay, high range	AW	Average wage paid	HR	High end range	MW	Median wage paid	W	Weekly
AO	Average offered	APL	Average pay, low range	FQ	First quartile wage	LR	Low end range	SQ	Second quartile wage	Y	Yearly

Occupation/Type/Industry	Location	Per	Low	Mid	High	Source	Date
Butcher and Meat Cutter	Daytona Beach MSA, FL	H	8.26 FQ	10.68 AW	13.87 TQ	FLBLS	10/01-12/01
	Fort Lauderdale PMSA, FL	H	7.78 FQ	11.17 AW	14.08 TQ	FLBLS	10/01-12/01
	Fort Myers-Cape Coral MSA, FL	H	7.92 FQ	11.08 AW	13.87 TQ	FLBLS	10/01-12/01
	Fort Pierce-Port St. Lucie MSA, FL	H	7.41 FQ	11.06 AW	15.44 TQ	FLBLS	10/01-12/01
	Fort Walton Beach MSA, FL	H	8.48 FQ	12.56 AW	19.85 TQ	FLBLS	10/01-12/01
	Gainesville MSA, FL	H	7.79 FQ	10.95 AW	15.22 TQ	FLBLS	10/01-12/01
	Jacksonville MSA, FL	H	7.81 FQ	11.12 AW	14.68 TQ	FLBLS	10/01-12/01
	Lakeland-Winter Haven MSA, FL	H	7.56 FQ	10.72 AW	13.75 TQ	FLBLS	10/01-12/01
	Melbourne-Titusville-Palm Bay MSA, FL	H	8.55 FQ	11.73 AW	17.63 TQ	FLBLS	10/01-12/01
	Miami PMSA, FL	H	6.78 FQ	10.26 AW	13.73 TQ	FLBLS	10/01-12/01
	Naples MSA, FL	H	7.87 FQ	10.82 AW	14.25 TQ	FLBLS	10/01-12/01
	Ocala MSA, FL	H	7.50 FQ	10.40 AW	13.61 TQ	FLBLS	10/01-12/01
	Orlando MSA, FL	H	7.90 FQ	11.43 AW	16.40 TQ	FLBLS	10/01-12/01
	Pensacola MSA, FL	H	6.60 FQ	11.41 AW	18.57 TQ	FLBLS	10/01-12/01
	Sarasota-Bradenton MSA, FL	H	8.07 FQ	11.08 AW	13.87 TQ	FLBLS	10/01-12/01
	Tallahassee MSA, FL	H	6.39 FQ	10.06 AW	13.80 TQ	FLBLS	10/01-12/01
	Tampa-St. Petersburg-Clearwater MSA, FL	H	7.85 FQ	12.00 AW	16.97 TQ	FLBLS	10/01-12/01
	West Palm Beach-Boca Raton MSA, FL	H	6.70 FQ	10.80 AW	14.12 TQ	FLBLS	10/01-12/01
	Georgia	H	7.14 FQ	11.19 AW	16.11 TQ	GABLS	10/01-12/01
	Atlanta MSA, GA	H	7.46 FQ	11.56 AW	17.24 TQ	GABLS	10/01-12/01
	Augusta-Aiken MSA, GA-SC	H	8.74 FQ	12.42 AW	16.32 TQ	GABLS	10/01-12/01
	Columbus MSA, GA-AL	H	6.59 FQ	10.12 AW	13.93 TQ	GABLS	10/01-12/01
	Macon MSA, GA	H	6.75 FQ	11.05 AW	16.30 TQ	GABLS	10/01-12/01
	Savannah MSA, GA	H	8.09 FQ	12.48 AW	15.82 TQ	GABLS	10/01-12/01
	Hawaii	H	7.05 FQ	14.53 AW	20.94 TQ	HIBLS	10/01-12/01
	Honolulu MSA, HI	H	7.21 FQ	15.90 AW	21.32 TQ	HIBLS	10/01-12/01
	Idaho	H	6.77 FQ	11.46 AW	17.14 TQ	IDBLS	10/01-12/01
	Illinois	H	7.22 FQ	11.37 AW	16.73 TQ	ILBLS	10/01-12/01
	Champaign-Urbana MSA, IL	H	7.80 FQ	12.51 AW	18.46 TQ	ILBLS	10/01-12/01
	Chicago PMSA, IL	H	7.46 FQ	11.60 AW	16.85 TQ	ILBLS	10/01-12/01
	Peoria-Pekin MSA, IL	H	7.10 FQ	11.10 AW	15.58 TQ	ILBLS	10/01-12/01
	Rockford MSA, IL	H	6.70 FQ	11.19 AW	17.15 TQ	ILBLS	10/01-12/01
	Springfield MSA, IL	H	7.57 FQ	12.38 AW	17.54 TQ	ILBLS	10/01-12/01
	Indiana	H	6.77 FQ	11.47 AW	16.42 TQ	INBLS	10/01-12/01
	Elkhart-Goshen MSA, IN	H	6.21 FQ	10.11 AW	15.16 TQ	INBLS	10/01-12/01
	Evansville-Henderson MSA, IN-KY	H	7.51 FQ	11.34 AW	15.32 TQ	INBLS	10/01-12/01
	Fort Wayne MSA, IN	H	8.57 FQ	12.18 AW	16.46 TQ	INBLS	10/01-12/01
	Gary PMSA, IN	H	7.64 FQ	13.41 AW	18.46 TQ	INBLS	10/01-12/01
	Indianapolis MSA, IN	H	6.91 FQ	12.24 AW	16.61 TQ	INBLS	10/01-12/01
	Lafayette MSA, IN	H	6.40 FQ	11.51 AW	16.31 TQ	INBLS	10/01-12/01
	South Bend MSA, IN	H	7.18 FQ	12.56 AW	16.72 TQ	INBLS	10/01-12/01
	Iowa	H	8.68 FQ	11.24 AW	13.88 TQ	IABLS	10/01-12/01
	Cedar Rapids MSA, IA	H	8.07 FQ	12.74 AW	16.77 TQ	IABLS	10/01-12/01
	Davenport-Moline-Rock Island MSA, IA-IL	H	7.33 FQ	10.52 AW	15.23 TQ	IABLS	10/01-12/01
	Kansas	H	7.49 FQ	12.38 AW	17.57 TQ	KSBLS	10/01-12/01
	Topeka MSA, KS	H	7.54 FQ	12.60 AW	17.82 TQ	KSBLS	10/01-12/01
	Wichita MSA, KS	H	7.91 FQ	12.78 AW	17.41 TQ	KSBLS	10/01-12/01
	Kentucky	H	7.30 FQ	11.10 AW	15.82 TQ	KYBLS	10/01-12/01
	Lexington MSA, KY	H	8.05 FQ	11.98 AW	16.61 TQ	KYBLS	10/01-12/01
	Louisville MSA, KY-IN	H	7.47 FQ	12.27 AW	16.71 TQ	KYBLS	10/01-12/01
	Louisiana	H	5.88 FQ	10.24 AW	15.36 TQ	LABLS	10/01-12/01
	Baton Rouge MSA, LA	H	5.94 FQ	10.88 AW	16.14 TQ	LABLS	10/01-12/01
	Houma MSA, LA	H	5.76 FQ	9.83 AW	14.59 TQ	LABLS	10/01-12/01
	Lafayette MSA, LA	H	5.97 FQ	9.89 AW	14.95 TQ	LABLS	10/01-12/01
	Lake Charles MSA, LA	H	6.21 FQ	11.22 AW	16.31 TQ	LABLS	10/01-12/01
	New Orleans MSA, LA	H	5.75 FQ	10.49 AW	16.27 TQ	LABLS	10/01-12/01
	Shreveport-Bossier City MSA, LA	H	7.61 FQ	11.69 AW	16.75 TQ	LABLS	10/01-12/01
	Maine	H	7.09 FQ	12.49 AW	18.90 TQ	MEBLS	10/01-12/01
	Portland MSA, ME	H	11.68 FQ	15.69 AW	20.37 TQ	MEBLS	10/01-12/01
	Maryland	H	9.53 FQ	14.57 AW	20.39 TQ	MDBLS	10/01-12/01
	Baltimore PMSA, MD	H	9.45 FQ	13.78 AW	19.48 TQ	MDBLS	10/01-12/01
	Massachusetts	H	8.67 FQ	17.65 AW	25.72 TQ	MABLS	10/01-12/01
	Boston PMSA, MA-NH	H	10.08 FQ	18.52 AW	26.47 TQ	MABLS	10/01-12/01

AAW	Average annual wage	**AOH**	Average offered, high	**ASH**	Average starting, high	**H**	Hourly	**M**	Monthly	**S**	Special: hourly and annual
AE	Average entry wage	**AOL**	Average offered, low	**ASL**	Average starting, low	**HI**	Highest wage paid	**MTC**	Median total compensation	**TQ**	Third quartile wage
AEX	Average experienced wage	**APH**	Average pay, high range	**AW**	Average wage paid	**HR**	High end range	**MW**	Median wage paid	**W**	Weekly
AO	Average offered	**APL**	Average pay, low range	**FQ**	First quartile wage	**LR**	Low end range	**SQ**	Second quartile wage	**Y**	Yearly

Occupation/Type/Industry	Location	Per	Low	Mid	High	Source	Date
Butcher and Meat Cutter	Brockton PMSA, MA	H	7.56 FQ	15.32 AW	23.54 TQ	MABLS	10/01-12/01
	Lawrence PMSA, MA-NH	H	12.25 FQ	18.13 AW	24.97 TQ	MABLS	10/01-12/01
	Lowell PMSA, MA-NH	H	13.92 FQ	20.32 AW	26.04 TQ	MABLS	10/01-12/01
	New Bedford PMSA, MA	H	11.24 FQ	18.72 AW	25.94 TQ	MABLS	10/01-12/01
	Springfield MSA, MA	H	7.56 FQ	14.14 AW	24.38 TQ	MABLS	10/01-12/01
	Worcester PMSA, MA-CT	H	7.79 FQ	15.92 AW	22.73 TQ	MABLS	10/01-12/01
	Michigan	H	7.26 FQ	12.33 AW	17.21 TQ	MIBLS	10/01-12/01
	Ann Arbor PMSA, MI	H	8.15 FQ	13.46 AW	17.82 TQ	MIBLS	10/01-12/01
	Detroit PMSA, MI	H	7.63 FQ	13.76 AW	17.78 TQ	MIBLS	10/01-12/01
	Flint PMSA, MI	H	7.73 FQ	12.74 AW	17.31 TQ	MIBLS	10/01-12/01
	Grand Rapids-Muskegon-Holland MSA, MI	H	7.34 FQ	11.73 AW	17.04 TQ	MIBLS	10/01-12/01
	Kalamazoo-Battle Creek MSA, MI	H	7.99 FQ	12.54 AW	17.97 TQ	MIBLS	10/01-12/01
	Lansing-East Lansing MSA, MI	H	7.76 FQ	12.53 AW	16.92 TQ	MIBLS	10/01-12/01
	Saginaw-Bay City-Midland MSA, MI	H	8.76 FQ	11.77 AW	16.19 TQ	MIBLS	10/01-12/01
	Minnesota	H	7.84 FQ	13.82 AW	21.05 TQ	MNBLS	10/01-12/01
	Duluth-Superior MSA, MN-WI	H	7.45 FQ	15.04 AW	21.31 TQ	MNBLS	10/01-12/01
	Minneapolis-St. Paul MSA, MN-WI	H	11.01 FQ	17.05 AW	22.07 TQ	MNBLS	10/01-12/01
	St. Cloud MSA, MN	H	9.58 FQ	14.27 AW	17.35 TQ	MNBLS	10/01-12/01
	Mississippi	H	6.35 FQ	10.29 AW	14.73 TQ	MSBLS	10/01-12/01
	Biloxi-Gulfport-Pascagoula MSA, MS	H	6.20 FQ	10.41 AW	15.65 TQ	MSBLS	10/01-12/01
	Jackson MSA, MS	H	9.25 FQ	12.17 AW	16.08 TQ	MSBLS	10/01-12/01
	Missouri	H	8.01 FQ	11.97 AW	16.97 TQ	MOBLS	10/01-12/01
	Kansas City MSA, MO-KS	H	8.33 FQ	13.71 AW	18.24 TQ	MOBLS	10/01-12/01
	St. Louis MSA, MO-IL	H	7.73 FQ	12.74 AW	19.51 TQ	MOBLS	10/01-12/01
	Springfield MSA, MO	H	8.86 FQ	11.73 AW	16.86 TQ	MOBLS	10/01-12/01
	Montana	H	7.52 FQ	12.16 AW	17.33 TQ	MTBLS	10/01-12/01
	Billings MSA, MT	H	7.97 FQ	12.77 AW	19.25 TQ	MTBLS	10/01-12/01
	Nebraska	H	7.41 FQ	10.82 AW	15.06 TQ	NEBLS	10/01-12/01
	Lincoln MSA, NE	H	6.48 FQ	10.67 AW	14.21 TQ	NEBLS	10/01-12/01
	Omaha MSA, NE-IA	H	9.19 FQ	11.51 AW	16.00 TQ	NEBLS	10/01-12/01
	Nevada	H	10.90 FQ	16.89 AW	21.42 TQ	NVBLS	10/01-12/01
	Las Vegas MSA, NV-AZ	H	10.88 FQ	16.43 AW	21.18 TQ	NVBLS	10/01-12/01
	Reno MSA, NV	H	11.19 FQ	17.22 AW	21.49 TQ	NVBLS	10/01-12/01
	New Hampshire	H	7.84 FQ	13.17 AW	17.55 TQ	NHBLS	10/01-12/01
	Manchester PMSA, NH	H	7.12 FQ	10.35 AW	16.60 TQ	NHBLS	10/01-12/01
	Nashua PMSA, NH	H	8.60 FQ	13.25 AW	17.19 TQ	NHBLS	10/01-12/01
	Portsmouth-Rochester PMSA, NH-ME	H	9.37 FQ	13.75 AW	17.57 TQ	NHBLS	10/01-12/01
	New Jersey	H	9.31 FQ	16.85 AW	22.65 TQ	NJBLS	10/01-12/01
	Atlantic-Cape May PMSA, NJ	H	11.09 FQ	17.11 AW	22.07 TQ	NJBLS	10/01-12/01
	Bergen-Passaic PMSA, NJ	H	9.37 FQ	17.08 AW	24.30 TQ	NJBLS	10/01-12/01
	Jersey City PMSA, NJ	H	12.02 FQ	17.52 AW	22.22 TQ	NJBLS	10/01-12/01
	Middlesex-Somerset-Hunterdon PMSA, NJ	H	11.06 FQ	17.82 AW	23.14 TQ	NJBLS	10/01-12/01
	Monmouth-Ocean PMSA, NJ	H	9.59 FQ	16.72 AW	22.50 TQ	NJBLS	10/01-12/01
	Newark PMSA, NJ	H	7.27 FQ	16.37 AW	22.61 TQ	NJBLS	10/01-12/01
	Trenton PMSA, NJ	H	8.73 FQ	15.21 AW	21.38 TQ	NJBLS	10/01-12/01
	New Mexico	H	6.28 FQ	12.59 AW	20.26 TQ	NMBLS	10/01-12/01
	Albuquerque MSA, NM	H	8.57 FQ	14.61 AW	20.98 TQ	NMBLS	10/01-12/01
	Las Cruces MSA, NM	H	7.91 FQ	12.64 AW	17.88 TQ	NMBLS	10/01-12/01
	New York	H	7.57 FQ	15.77 AW	25.63 TQ	NYBLS	10/01-12/01
	Albany-Schenectady-Troy MSA, NY	H	7.64 FQ	13.11 AW	17.27 TQ	NYBLS	10/01-12/01
	Binghamton MSA, NY	H	8.55 FQ	11.96 AW	16.98 TQ	NYBLS	10/01-12/01
	Buffalo-Niagara Falls MSA, NY	H	9.99 FQ	14.70 AW	17.39 TQ	NYBLS	10/01-12/01
	Dutchess County PMSA, NY	H	10.16 FQ	17.48 AW	22.63 TQ	NYBLS	10/01-12/01
	Nassau-Suffolk PMSA, NY	H	16.19 FQ	22.64 AW	27.34 TQ	NYBLS	10/01-12/01
	New York PMSA, NY	H	7.13 FQ	15.47 AW	26.06 TQ	NYBLS	10/01-12/01
	Newburgh PMSA, NY-PA	H	6.52 FQ	14.51 AW	20.92 TQ	NYBLS	10/01-12/01
	Rochester MSA, NY	H	8.12 FQ	13.80 AW	20.31 TQ	NYBLS	10/01-12/01
	Syracuse MSA, NY	H	6.54 FQ	13.29 AW	17.66 TQ	NYBLS	10/01-12/01
	Utica-Rome MSA, NY	H	8.78 FQ	14.19 AW	17.65 TQ	NYBLS	10/01-12/01
	North Carolina	H	7.62 FQ	11.33 AW	14.54 TQ	NCBLS	10/01-12/01
	Asheville MSA, NC	H	8.94 FQ	11.19 AW	13.34 TQ	NCBLS	10/01-12/01
	Charlotte-Gastonia-Rock Hill MSA, NC-SC	H	5.93 FQ	10.09 AW	14.96 TQ	NCBLS	10/01-12/01

AAW	Average annual wage	**AOH**	Average offered, high	**ASH**	Average starting, high	**H**	Hourly	**M**	Monthly	**S**	Special: hourly and annual
AE	Average entry wage	**AOL**	Average offered, low	**ASL**	Average starting, low	**HI**	Highest wage paid	**MTC**	Median total compensation	**TQ**	Third quartile wage
AEX	Average experienced wage	**APH**	Average pay, high range	**AW**	Average wage paid	**HR**	High end range	**MW**	Median wage paid	**W**	Weekly
AO	Average offered	**APL**	Average pay, low range	**FQ**	First quartile wage	**LR**	Low end range	**SQ**	Second quartile wage	**Y**	Yearly

Occupation/Type/Industry	Location	Per	Low	Mid	High	Source	Date
Butcher and Meat Cutter	Fayetteville MSA, NC	H	9.50 FQ	11.94 AW	14.41 TQ	NCBLS	10/01-12/01
	Greensboro-Winston-Salem-High Point MSA, NC	H	9.52 FQ	12.22 AW	14.86 TQ	NCBLS	10/01-12/01
	Hickory-Morganton-Lenoir MSA, NC	H	9.31 FQ	12.19 AW	14.32 TQ	NCBLS	10/01-12/01
	Raleigh-Durham-Chapel Hill MSA, NC	H	7.54 FQ	10.94 AW	14.48 TQ	NCBLS	10/01-12/01
	Wilmington MSA, NC	H	7.14 FQ	12.08 AW	18.72 TQ	NCBLS	10/01-12/01
	North Dakota	H	6.84 FQ	10.31 AW	14.91 TQ	NDBLS	10/01-12/01
	Fargo-Moorhead MSA, ND-MN	H	8.07 FQ	11.42 AW	16.23 TQ	NDBLS	10/01-12/01
	Ohio	H	7.47 FQ	12.23 AW	16.86 TQ	OHBLS	10/01-12/01
	Akron PMSA, OH	H	9.39 FQ	13.76 AW	17.26 TQ	OHBLS	10/01-12/01
	Canton-Massillon MSA, OH	H	7.68 FQ	11.93 AW	16.40 TQ	OHBLS	10/01-12/01
	Cincinnati PMSA, OH-KY-IN	H	8.08 FQ	12.68 AW	16.61 TQ	OHBLS	10/01-12/01
	Cleveland-Lorain-Elyria PMSA, OH	H	9.70 FQ	14.08 AW	17.37 TQ	OHBLS	10/01-12/01
	Columbus MSA, OH	H	7.40 FQ	12.21 AW	16.80 TQ	OHBLS	10/01-12/01
	Dayton-Springfield MSA, OH	H	6.11 FQ	11.36 AW	16.94 TQ	OHBLS	10/01-12/01
	Hamilton-Middletown PMSA, OH	H	8.26 FQ	12.89 AW	16.81 TQ	OHBLS	10/01-12/01
	Mansfield MSA, OH	H	8.02 FQ	12.59 AW	16.44 TQ	OHBLS	10/01-12/01
	Toledo MSA, OH	H	9.07 FQ	13.50 AW	18.93 TQ	OHBLS	10/01-12/01
	Youngstown-Warren MSA, OH	H	7.66 FQ	12.23 AW	16.25 TQ	OHBLS	10/01-12/01
	Oklahoma	H	6.60 FQ	10.25 AW	14.61 TQ	OKBLS	10/01-12/01
	Oklahoma City MSA, OK	H	7.81 FQ	11.33 AW	15.16 TQ	OKBLS	10/01-12/01
	Tulsa MSA, OK	H	7.76 FQ	10.93 AW	15.64 TQ	OKBLS	10/01-12/01
	Oregon	H	8.63 FQ	14.72 AW	20.58 TQ	ORBLS	10/01-12/01
	Eugene-Springfield MSA, OR	H	11.63 FQ	15.94 AW	21.27 TQ	ORBLS	10/01-12/01
	Medford-Ashland MSA, OR	H	7.46 FQ	13.97 AW	18.36 TQ	ORBLS	10/01-12/01
	Portland-Vancouver PMSA, OR-WA	H	11.19 FQ	16.89 AW	21.32 TQ	ORBLS	10/01-12/01
	Salem PMSA, OR	H	8.49 FQ	14.42 AW	19.92 TQ	ORBLS	10/01-12/01
	Pennsylvania	H	7.47 FQ	12.18 AW	18.71 TQ	PABLS	10/01-12/01
	Allentown-Bethlehem-Easton MSA, PA	H	7.89 FQ	13.66 AW	20.75 TQ	PABLS	10/01-12/01
	Erie MSA, PA	H	8.59 FQ	12.56 AW	16.59 TQ	PABLS	10/01-12/01
	Harrisburg-Lebanon-Carlisle MSA, PA	H	7.99 FQ	12.86 AW	17.85 TQ	PABLS	10/01-12/01
	Johnstown MSA, PA	H	7.27 FQ	10.08 AW	13.06 TQ	PABLS	10/01-12/01
	Lancaster MSA, PA	H	9.09 FQ	12.64 AW	17.58 TQ	PABLS	10/01-12/01
	Philadelphia PMSA, PA-NJ	H	8.08 FQ	14.31 AW	21.06 TQ	PABLS	10/01-12/01
	Pittsburgh MSA, PA	H	7.15 FQ	10.64 AW	15.33 TQ	PABLS	10/01-12/01
	Reading MSA, PA	H	8.84 FQ	14.42 AW	20.83 TQ	PABLS	10/01-12/01
	Scranton-Wilkes-Barre-Hazleton MSA, PA	H	6.85 FQ	10.61 AW	15.47 TQ	PABLS	10/01-12/01
	York MSA, PA	H	9.39 FQ	13.70 AW	17.44 TQ	PABLS	10/01-12/01
	Rhode Island	H	8.58 FQ	14.63 AW	21.57 TQ	RIBLS	10/01-12/01
	Providence-Fall River-Warwick MSA, RI-MA	H	8.74 FQ	14.98 AW	22.10 TQ	RIBLS	10/01-12/01
	South Carolina	H	5.91 FQ	9.43 AW	13.90 TQ	SCBLS	10/01-12/01
	Charleston-North Charleston MSA, SC	H	7.17 FQ	9.96 AW	14.00 TQ	SCBLS	10/01-12/01
	Columbia MSA, SC	H	6.46 FQ	10.92 AW	15.26 TQ	SCBLS	10/01-12/01
	Greenville-Spartanburg-Anderson MSA, SC	H	7.72 FQ	10.93 AW	15.31 TQ	SCBLS	10/01-12/01
	Myrtle Beach MSA, SC	H	9.50 FQ	11.86 AW	14.44 TQ	SCBLS	10/01-12/01
	South Dakota	H	6.79 FQ	10.01 AW	13.96 TQ	SDBLS	10/01-12/01
	Sioux Falls MSA, SD	H	8.65 FQ	11.41 AW	15.65 TQ	SDBLS	10/01-12/01
	Tennessee	H	7.19 FQ	11.46 AW	16.30 TQ	TNBLS	10/01-12/01
	Chattanooga MSA, TN-GA	H	7.53 FQ	11.24 AW	15.19 TQ	TNBLS	10/01-12/01
	Clarksville-Hopkinsville MSA, TN-KY	H	7.29 FQ	11.02 AW	16.12 TQ	TNBLS	10/01-12/01
	Johnson City-Kingsport-Bristol MSA, TN-VA	H	6.30 FQ	10.62 AW	14.31 TQ	TNBLS	10/01-12/01
	Knoxville MSA, TN	H	7.34 FQ	11.97 AW	16.66 TQ	TNBLS	10/01-12/01
	Memphis MSA, TN-AR-MS	H	8.21 FQ	12.47 AW	16.97 TQ	TNBLS	10/01-12/01
	Nashville MSA, TN	H	8.32 FQ	12.03 AW	16.47 TQ	TNBLS	10/01-12/01
	Texas	H	6.61 FQ	11.47 AW	16.92 TQ	TXBLS	10/01-12/01
	Amarillo MSA, TX	H	7.52 FQ	11.78 AW	17.24 TQ	TXBLS	10/01-12/01
	Austin-San Marcos MSA, TX	H	9.55 FQ	12.93 AW	16.69 TQ	TXBLS	10/01-12/01

AAW Average annual wage **AOH** Average offered, high **ASH** Average starting, high **H** Hourly **M** Monthly **S** Special: hourly and annual
AE Average entry wage **AOL** Average offered, low **ASL** Average starting, low **HI** Highest wage paid **MTC** Median total compensation **TQ** Third quartile wage
AEX Average experienced wage **APH** Average pay, high range **AW** Average wage paid **HR** High end range **MW** Median wage paid **W** Weekly
AO Average offered **APL** Average pay, low range **FQ** First quartile wage **LR** Low end range **SQ** Second quartile wage **Y** Yearly

Occupation/Type/Industry	Location	Per	Low	Mid	High	Source	Date
Butcher and Meat Cutter	Beaumont-Port Arthur MSA, TX	H	7.37 FQ	12.27 AW	17.23 TQ	TXBLS	10/01-12/01
	Brazoria PMSA, TX	H	6.67 FQ	11.39 AW	16.54 TQ	TXBLS	10/01-12/01
	Brownsville-Harlingen-San Benito MSA, TX	H	6.09 FQ	9.89 AW	13.69 TQ	TXBLS	10/01-12/01
	Corpus Christi MSA, TX	H	7.44 FQ	11.91 AW	16.65 TQ	TXBLS	10/01-12/01
	Dallas PMSA, TX	H	6.93 FQ	12.73 AW	18.24 TQ	TXBLS	10/01-12/01
	El Paso MSA, TX	H	5.70 FQ	8.90 AW	14.93 TQ	TXBLS	10/01-12/01
	Fort Worth-Arlington PMSA, TX	H	8.36 FQ	12.99 AW	17.20 TQ	TXBLS	10/01-12/01
	Galveston-Texas City PMSA, TX	H	8.78 FQ	12.63 AW	16.42 TQ	TXBLS	10/01-12/01
	Houston PMSA, TX	H	7.39 FQ	12.48 AW	17.17 TQ	TXBLS	10/01-12/01
	Killeen-Temple MSA, TX	H	9.35 FQ	12.56 AW	16.52 TQ	TXBLS	10/01-12/01
	Laredo MSA, TX	H	5.79 FQ	8.11 AW	12.70 TQ	TXBLS	10/01-12/01
	Longview-Marshall MSA, TX	H	7.57 FQ	11.24 AW	15.63 TQ	TXBLS	10/01-12/01
	Lubbock MSA, TX	H	7.63 FQ	11.67 AW	17.39 TQ	TXBLS	10/01-12/01
	McAllen-Edinburg-Mission MSA, TX	H	5.97 FQ	9.58 AW	14.22 TQ	TXBLS	10/01-12/01
	Odessa-Midland MSA, TX	H	6.94 FQ	11.09 AW	16.60 TQ	TXBLS	10/01-12/01
	San Antonio MSA, TX	H	6.17 FQ	12.07 AW	18.15 TQ	TXBLS	10/01-12/01
	Tyler MSA, TX	H	7.58 FQ	11.02 AW	16.23 TQ	TXBLS	10/01-12/01
	Waco MSA, TX	H	6.63 FQ	9.98 AW	15.20 TQ	TXBLS	10/01-12/01
	Utah	H	8.31 FQ	13.51 AW	17.67 TQ	UTBLS	10/01-12/01
	Provo-Orem MSA, UT	H	6.95 FQ	12.19 AW	16.97 TQ	UTBLS	10/01-12/01
	Salt Lake City-Ogden MSA, UT	H	8.86 FQ	14.14 AW	18.21 TQ	UTBLS	10/01-12/01
	Vermont	H	8.63 FQ	14.91 AW	20.12 TQ	VTBLS	10/01-12/01
	Burlington MSA, VT	H	8.18 FQ	13.49 AW	17.94 TQ	VTBLS	10/01-12/01
	Virginia	H	7.07 FQ	11.53 AW	18.32 TQ	VABLS	10/01-12/01
	Lynchburg MSA, VA	H	7.45 FQ	11.47 AW	14.91 TQ	VABLS	10/01-12/01
	Norfolk-Virginia Beach-Newport News MSA, VA-NC	H	6.93 FQ	10.49 AW	16.88 TQ	VABLS	10/01-12/01
	Richmond-Petersburg MSA, VA	H	11.29 FQ	14.63 AW	17.57 TQ	VABLS	10/01-12/01
	Roanoke MSA, VA	H	9.07 FQ	11.44 AW	13.91 TQ	VABLS	10/01-12/01
	Washington	H	9.15 FQ	16.08 AW	21.45 TQ	WABLS	10/01-12/01
	Bremerton PMSA, WA	H	9.62 FQ	16.40 AW	21.10 TQ	WABLS	10/01-12/01
	Olympia PMSA, WA	H	9.15 FQ	16.36 AW	21.62 TQ	WABLS	10/01-12/01
	Richland-Kennewick-Pasco MSA, WA	H	9.26 FQ	14.42 AW	19.97 TQ	WABLS	10/01-12/01
	Seattle-Bellevue-Everett PMSA, WA	H	10.49 FQ	17.34 AW	21.96 TQ	WABLS	10/01-12/01
	Spokane MSA, WA	H	9.36 FQ	14.42 AW	19.41 TQ	WABLS	10/01-12/01
	Tacoma PMSA, WA	H	12.82 FQ	18.28 AW	22.10 TQ	WABLS	10/01-12/01
	Yakima MSA, WA	H	8.35 FQ	15.39 AW	21.31 TQ	WABLS	10/01-12/01
	West Virginia	H	6.20 FQ	10.64 AW	15.31 TQ	WVBLS	10/01-12/01
	Charleston MSA, WV	H	6.57 FQ	10.73 AW	14.26 TQ	WVBLS	10/01-12/01
	Huntington-Ashland MSA, WV-KY-OH	H	6.48 FQ	10.08 AW	14.06 TQ	WVBLS	10/01-12/01
	Wisconsin	H	7.86 FQ	12.40 AW	17.59 TQ	WIBLS	10/01-12/01
	Appleton-Oshkosh-Neenah MSA, WI	H	8.45 FQ	13.13 AW	18.09 TQ	WIBLS	10/01-12/01
	Green Bay MSA, WI	H	7.67 FQ	11.56 AW	16.12 TQ	WIBLS	10/01-12/01
	Madison MSA, WI	H	10.28 FQ	14.86 AW	19.72 TQ	WIBLS	10/01-12/01
	Milwaukee-Waukesha PMSA, WI	H	8.93 FQ	14.01 AW	19.74 TQ	WIBLS	10/01-12/01
	Racine PMSA, WI	H	8.30 FQ	13.36 AW	18.55 TQ	WIBLS	10/01-12/01
	Wyoming	H	7.82 FQ	12.14 AW	16.89 TQ	WYBLS	10/01-12/01
	Cheyenne MSA, WY	H	9.54 FQ	13.37 AW	17.53 TQ	WYBLS	10/01-12/01
	Puerto Rico	H	5.59 FQ	6.79 AW	8.63 TQ	PRBLS	10/01-12/01
	Virgin Islands	H	7.69 FQ	11.73 AW	17.23 TQ	VIBLS	10/01-12/01
	Guam	H	6.33 FQ	10.70 AW	16.42 TQ	GUBLS	10/01-12/01
Cabinetmaker and Bench Carpenter	Alabama	H	7.11 FQ	10.54 AW	15.20 TQ	ALBLS	10/01-12/01
	Birmingham MSA, AL	H	8.63 FQ	11.29 AW	13.85 TQ	ALBLS	10/01-12/01
	Huntsville MSA, AL	H	7.13 FQ	10.99 AW	17.98 TQ	ALBLS	10/01-12/01
	Mobile MSA, AL	H	6.51 FQ	8.75 AW	11.32 TQ	ALBLS	10/01-12/01
	Montgomery MSA, AL	H	10.73 FQ	12.51 AW	14.59 TQ	ALBLS	10/01-12/01
	Alaska	H	8.17 FQ	12.88 AW	18.43 TQ	AKBLS	10/01-12/01

AAW	Average annual wage	**AOH**	Average offered, high	**ASH**	Average starting, high	**H**	Hourly	**M**	Monthly	**S**	Special: hourly and annual
AE	Average entry wage	**AOL**	Average offered, low	**ASL**	Average starting, low	**HI**	Highest wage paid	**MTC**	Median total compensation	**TQ**	Third quartile wage
AEX	Average experienced wage	**APH**	Average pay, high range	**AW**	Average wage paid	**HR**	High end range	**MW**	Median wage paid	**W**	Weekly
AO	Average offered	**APL**	Average pay, low range	**FQ**	First quartile wage	**LR**	Low end range	**SQ**	Second quartile wage	**Y**	Yearly

Occupation/Type/Industry	Location	Per	Low	Mid	High	Source	Date
Cabinetmaker and Bench Carpenter	Anchorage MSA, AK	H	9.22 FQ	13.11 AW	18.47 TQ	AKBLS	10/01-12/01
	Arizona	H	7.40 FQ	11.40 AW	16.84 TQ	AZBLS	10/01-12/01
	Phoenix-Mesa MSA, AZ	H	7.56 FQ	11.87 AW	17.78 TQ	AZBLS	10/01-12/01
	Tucson MSA, AZ	H	7.54 FQ	11.02 AW	15.65 TQ	AZBLS	10/01-12/01
	Arkansas	H	7.27 FQ	10.83 AW	16.25 TQ	ARBLS	10/01-12/01
	Fayetteville-Springdale-Rogers MSA, AR	H	7.92 FQ	10.59 AW	13.57 TQ	ARBLS	10/01-12/01
	Fort Smith MSA, AR-OK	H	7.50 FQ	9.55 AW	12.04 TQ	ARBLS	10/01-12/01
	Little Rock-North Little Rock MSA, AR	H	7.97 FQ	14.06 AW	20.28 TQ	ARBLS	10/01-12/01
	California	H	7.06 FQ	11.68 AW	19.19 TQ	CABLS	10/01-12/01
	Bakersfield MSA, CA	H	7.65 FQ	11.61 AW	17.21 TQ	CABLS	10/01-12/01
	Chico-Paradise MSA, CA	H	7.46 FQ	10.29 AW	14.63 TQ	CABLS	10/01-12/01
	Fresno MSA, CA	H	6.56 FQ	9.76 AW	15.58 TQ	CABLS	10/01-12/01
	Los Angeles-Long Beach PMSA, CA	H	6.90 FQ	10.29 AW	15.90 TQ	CABLS	10/01-12/01
	Merced MSA, CA	H	7.30 FQ	10.17 AW	14.95 TQ	CABLS	10/01-12/01
	Modesto MSA, CA	H	7.15 FQ	10.09 AW	13.59 TQ	CABLS	10/01-12/01
	Oakland PMSA, CA	H	7.70 FQ	16.46 AW	25.85 TQ	CABLS	10/01-12/01
	Orange County PMSA, CA	H	6.79 FQ	10.79 AW	16.86 TQ	CABLS	10/01-12/01
	Redding MSA, CA	H	7.31 FQ	10.59 AW	14.02 TQ	CABLS	10/01-12/01
	Riverside-San Bernardino PMSA, CA	H	7.51 FQ	13.08 AW	20.58 TQ	CABLS	10/01-12/01
	Sacramento PMSA, CA	H	6.87 FQ	10.16 AW	14.98 TQ	CABLS	10/01-12/01
	Salinas MSA, CA	H	7.41 FQ	13.47 AW	20.65 TQ	CABLS	10/01-12/01
	San Diego MSA, CA	H	7.28 FQ	12.31 AW	19.01 TQ	CABLS	10/01-12/01
	San Francisco PMSA, CA	H	8.70 FQ	16.64 AW	26.45 TQ	CABLS	10/01-12/01
	San Jose PMSA, CA	H	8.87 FQ	16.11 AW	25.74 TQ	CABLS	10/01-12/01
	San Luis Obispo-Atascadero-Paso Robles MSA, CA	H	9.06 FQ	11.69 AW	16.84 TQ	CABLS	10/01-12/01
	Santa Barbara-Santa Maria-Lompoc MSA, CA	H	8.28 FQ	15.27 AW	23.39 TQ	CABLS	10/01-12/01
	Santa Cruz-Watsonville PMSA, CA	H	9.47 FQ	16.38 AW	23.10 TQ	CABLS	10/01-12/01
	Santa Rosa PMSA, CA	H	8.47 FQ	13.94 AW	20.03 TQ	CABLS	10/01-12/01
	Stockton-Lodi MSA, CA	H	7.47 FQ	13.32 AW	24.37 TQ	CABLS	10/01-12/01
	Vallejo-Fairfield-Napa PMSA, CA	H	9.04 FQ	14.25 AW	20.39 TQ	CABLS	10/01-12/01
	Ventura PMSA, CA	H	8.92 FQ	12.01 AW	16.51 TQ	CABLS	10/01-12/01
	Visalia-Tulare-Porterville MSA, CA	H	6.85 FQ	10.53 AW	13.84 TQ	CABLS	10/01-12/01
	Colorado	H	8.57 FQ	13.09 AW	18.89 TQ	COBLS	10/01-12/01
	Boulder-Longmont PMSA, CO	H	10.84 FQ	14.65 AW	19.27 TQ	COBLS	10/01-12/01
	Colorado Springs MSA, CO	H	8.81 FQ	13.83 AW	18.74 TQ	COBLS	10/01-12/01
	Denver PMSA, CO	H	8.94 FQ	12.78 AW	18.12 TQ	COBLS	10/01-12/01
	Fort Collins-Loveland MSA, CO	H	5.90 FQ	11.06 AW	17.79 TQ	COBLS	10/01-12/01
	Greeley PMSA, CO	H	8.95 FQ	13.90 AW	19.85 TQ	COBLS	10/01-12/01
	Connecticut	H	10.16 FQ	16.18 AW	22.38 TQ	CTBLS	10/01-12/01
	Bridgeport PMSA, CT	H	10.28 FQ	17.48 AW	25.42 TQ	CTBLS	10/01-12/01
	Hartford MSA, CT	H	10.37 FQ	15.79 AW	21.43 TQ	CTBLS	10/01-12/01
	New Haven-Meriden PMSA, CT	H	9.14 FQ	15.17 AW	22.28 TQ	CTBLS	10/01-12/01
	New London-Norwich MSA, CT-RI	H	9.61 FQ	13.53 AW	17.71 TQ	CTBLS	10/01-12/01
	Stamford-Norwalk PMSA, CT	H	13.13 FQ	20.27 AW	27.65 TQ	CTBLS	10/01-12/01
	Waterbury PMSA, CT	H	11.18 FQ	16.26 AW	21.79 TQ	CTBLS	10/01-12/01
	Delaware	H	8.82 FQ	12.16 AW	17.42 TQ	DEBLS	10/01-12/01
	Wilmington-Newark PMSA, DE-MD	H	9.62 FQ	15.16 AW	20.52 TQ	DEBLS	10/01-12/01
	District of Columbia	H	9.47 FQ	17.88 AW	25.49 TQ	DCBLS	10/01-12/01
	Washington PMSA, DC-MD-VA-WV	H	9.55 FQ	15.30 AW	21.39 TQ	DCBLS	10/01-12/01
	Florida	H	7.39 FQ	11.40 AW	16.75 TQ	FLBLS	10/01-12/01
	Daytona Beach MSA, FL	H	6.85 FQ	10.32 AW	13.72 TQ	FLBLS	10/01-12/01
	Fort Lauderdale PMSA, FL	H	8.61 FQ	13.07 AW	19.39 TQ	FLBLS	10/01-12/01
	Fort Myers-Cape Coral MSA, FL	H	7.07 FQ	11.26 AW	18.86 TQ	FLBLS	10/01-12/01
	Fort Pierce-Port St. Lucie MSA, FL	H	9.54 FQ	15.00 AW	21.61 TQ	FLBLS	10/01-12/01
	Fort Walton Beach MSA, FL	H	7.75 FQ	10.91 AW	14.49 TQ	FLBLS	10/01-12/01

AAW	Average annual wage	**AOH**	Average offered, high	**ASH**	Average starting, high	**H**	Hourly	**M**	Monthly	**S**	Special: hourly and annual
AE	Average entry wage	**AOL**	Average offered, low	**ASL**	Average starting, low	**HI**	Highest wage paid	**MTC**	Median total compensation	**TQ**	Third quartile wage
AEX	Average experienced wage	**APH**	Average pay, high range	**AW**	Average wage paid	**HR**	High end range	**MW**	Median wage paid	**W**	Weekly
AO	Average offered	**APL**	Average pay, low range	**FQ**	First quartile wage	**LR**	Low end range	**SQ**	Second quartile wage	**Y**	Yearly

Occupation/Type/Industry	Location	Per	Low	Mid	High	Source	Date
Cabinetmaker and Bench Carpenter	Gainesville MSA, FL	H	8.61 FQ	12.06 AW	16.39 TQ	FLBLS	10/01-12/01
	Jacksonville MSA, FL	H	8.29 FQ	12.58 AW	17.41 TQ	FLBLS	10/01-12/01
	Lakeland-Winter Haven MSA, FL	H	9.28 FQ	11.44 AW	13.65 TQ	FLBLS	10/01-12/01
	Melbourne-Titusville-Palm Bay MSA, FL	H	8.70 FQ	12.15 AW	16.33 TQ	FLBLS	10/01-12/01
	Miami PMSA, FL	H	7.38 FQ	10.99 AW	17.36 TQ	FLBLS	10/01-12/01
	Naples MSA, FL	H	10.45 FQ	14.15 AW	19.13 TQ	FLBLS	10/01-12/01
	Ocala MSA, FL	H	6.86 FQ	11.19 AW	17.80 TQ	FLBLS	10/01-12/01
	Orlando MSA, FL	H	6.05 FQ	10.86 AW	16.58 TQ	FLBLS	10/01-12/01
	Pensacola MSA, FL	H	7.77 FQ	10.53 AW	13.77 TQ	FLBLS	10/01-12/01
	Sarasota-Bradenton MSA, FL	H	8.71 FQ	12.43 AW	16.73 TQ	FLBLS	10/01-12/01
	Tallahassee MSA, FL	H	8.88 FQ	11.31 AW	15.54 TQ	FLBLS	10/01-12/01
	Tampa-St. Petersburg-Clearwater MSA, FL	H	7.08 FQ	10.26 AW	14.07 TQ	FLBLS	10/01-12/01
	West Palm Beach-Boca Raton MSA, FL	H	8.36 FQ	13.03 AW	17.78 TQ	FLBLS	10/01-12/01
	Georgia	H	7.36 FQ	10.74 AW	15.94 TQ	GABLS	10/01-12/01
	Atlanta MSA, GA	H	7.39 FQ	10.98 AW	16.71 TQ	GABLS	10/01-12/01
	Augusta-Aiken MSA, GA-SC	H	7.51 FQ	10.32 AW	15.08 TQ	GABLS	10/01-12/01
	Columbus MSA, GA-AL	H	7.51 FQ	9.96 AW	13.56 TQ	GABLS	10/01-12/01
	Macon MSA, GA	H	6.66 FQ	10.51 AW	16.83 TQ	GABLS	10/01-12/01
	Savannah MSA, GA	H	7.49 FQ	11.52 AW	17.86 TQ	GABLS	10/01-12/01
	Hawaii	H	8.83 FQ	16.10 AW	24.31 TQ	HIBLS	10/01-12/01
	Honolulu MSA, HI	H	8.63 FQ	15.83 AW	23.38 TQ	HIBLS	10/01-12/01
	Idaho	H	7.09 FQ	10.35 AW	14.45 TQ	IDBLS	10/01-12/01
	Boise City MSA, ID	H	8.09 FQ	11.35 AW	16.40 TQ	IDBLS	10/01-12/01
	Illinois	H	8.37 FQ	13.61 AW	20.05 TQ	ILBLS	10/01-12/01
	Chicago PMSA, IL	H	9.15 FQ	14.80 AW	21.44 TQ	ILBLS	10/01-12/01
	Peoria-Pekin MSA, IL	H	9.06 FQ	13.53 AW	19.79 TQ	ILBLS	10/01-12/01
	Rockford MSA, IL	H	7.82 FQ	11.10 AW	15.81 TQ	ILBLS	10/01-12/01
	Indiana	H	8.16 FQ	13.04 AW	20.12 TQ	INBLS	10/01-12/01
	Elkhart-Goshen MSA, IN	H	9.50 FQ	14.74 AW	20.84 TQ	INBLS	10/01-12/01
	Evansville-Henderson MSA, IN-KY	H	8.68 FQ	11.24 AW	15.01 TQ	INBLS	10/01-12/01
	Fort Wayne MSA, IN	H	7.76 FQ	12.11 AW	17.34 TQ	INBLS	10/01-12/01
	Gary PMSA, IN	H	7.33 FQ	9.71 AW	14.78 TQ	INBLS	10/01-12/01
	Indianapolis MSA, IN	H	9.40 FQ	12.39 AW	16.13 TQ	INBLS	10/01-12/01
	South Bend MSA, IN	H	7.67 FQ	11.93 AW	19.79 TQ	INBLS	10/01-12/01
	Iowa	H	8.92 FQ	12.62 AW	16.84 TQ	IABLS	10/01-12/01
	Cedar Rapids MSA, IA	H	8.76 FQ	12.77 AW	16.81 TQ	IABLS	10/01-12/01
	Davenport-Moline-Rock Island MSA, IA-IL	H	8.81 FQ	13.09 AW	17.93 TQ	IABLS	10/01-12/01
	Des Moines MSA, IA	H	9.16 FQ	12.98 AW	17.89 TQ	IABLS	10/01-12/01
	Kansas	H	8.06 FQ	11.33 AW	15.30 TQ	KSBLS	10/01-12/01
	Wichita MSA, KS	H	8.66 FQ	11.49 AW	15.46 TQ	KSBLS	10/01-12/01
	Kentucky	H	7.48 FQ	10.67 AW	14.56 TQ	KYBLS	10/01-12/01
	Lexington MSA, KY	H	8.80 FQ	12.28 AW	16.75 TQ	KYBLS	10/01-12/01
	Louisville MSA, KY-IN	H	9.98 FQ	17.22 AW	22.50 TQ	KYBLS	10/01-12/01
	Louisiana	H	7.30 FQ	11.19 AW	16.62 TQ	LABLS	10/01-12/01
	Baton Rouge MSA, LA	H	7.11 FQ	9.80 AW	13.47 TQ	LABLS	10/01-12/01
	Lafayette MSA, LA	H	8.18 FQ	12.87 AW	19.35 TQ	LABLS	10/01-12/01
	New Orleans MSA, LA	H	6.83 FQ	11.07 AW	16.66 TQ	LABLS	10/01-12/01
	Shreveport-Bossier City MSA, LA	H	7.35 FQ	11.04 AW	15.43 TQ	LABLS	10/01-12/01
	Maine	H	8.93 FQ	12.29 AW	16.48 TQ	MEBLS	10/01-12/01
	Portland MSA, ME	H	9.58 FQ	13.87 AW	17.93 TQ	MEBLS	10/01-12/01
	Maryland	H	9.67 FQ	14.79 AW	20.60 TQ	MDBLS	10/01-12/01
	Baltimore PMSA, MD	H	9.68 FQ	14.27 AW	19.80 TQ	MDBLS	10/01-12/01
	Massachusetts	H	9.35 FQ	14.37 AW	20.54 TQ	MABLS	10/01-12/01
	Boston PMSA, MA-NH	H	10.19 FQ	15.29 AW	21.07 TQ	MABLS	10/01-12/01
	Brockton PMSA, MA	H	9.34 FQ	13.82 AW	19.39 TQ	MABLS	10/01-12/01
	Lawrence PMSA, MA-NH	H	8.99 FQ	13.13 AW	18.32 TQ	MABLS	10/01-12/01
	Springfield MSA, MA	H	9.03 FQ	14.07 AW	19.86 TQ	MABLS	10/01-12/01
	Worcester PMSA, MA-CT	H	9.69 FQ	14.30 AW	20.60 TQ	MABLS	10/01-12/01
	Michigan	H	8.66 FQ	13.95 AW	20.84 TQ	MIBLS	10/01-12/01
	Ann Arbor PMSA, MI	H	10.54 FQ	14.95 AW	20.31 TQ	MIBLS	10/01-12/01
	Detroit PMSA, MI	H	9.11 FQ	14.79 AW	22.14 TQ	MIBLS	10/01-12/01
	Flint PMSA, MI	H	11.53 FQ	14.29 AW	17.36 TQ	MIBLS	10/01-12/01
	Grand Rapids-Muskegon-Holland MSA, MI	H	8.95 FQ	14.29 AW	20.47 TQ	MIBLS	10/01-12/01

AAW	Average annual wage	AOH	Average offered, high	ASH	Average starting, high	H	Hourly	M	Monthly	S	Special: hourly and annual
AE	Average entry wage	AOL	Average offered, low	ASL	Average starting, low	HI	Highest wage paid	MTC	Median total compensation	TQ	Third quartile wage
AEX	Average experienced wage	APH	Average pay, high range	AW	Average wage paid	HR	High end range	MW	Median wage paid	W	Weekly
AO	Average offered	APL	Average pay, low range	FQ	First quartile wage	LR	Low end range	SQ	Second quartile wage	Y	Yearly

Occupation/Type/Industry	Location	Per	Low	Mid	High	Source	Date
Cabinetmaker and Bench Carpenter	Kalamazoo-Battle Creek MSA, MI	H	8.03 FQ	11.63 AW	16.47 TQ	MIBLS	10/01-12/01
	Saginaw-Bay City-Midland MSA, MI	H	8.47 FQ	12.54 AW	17.71 TQ	MIBLS	10/01-12/01
	Minnesota	H	9.17 FQ	13.22 AW	17.80 TQ	MNBLS	10/01-12/01
	Duluth-Superior MSA, MN-WI	H	9.07 FQ	13.24 AW	19.71 TQ	MNBLS	10/01-12/01
	Minneapolis-St. Paul MSA, MN-WI	H	10.51 FQ	14.29 AW	19.03 TQ	MNBLS	10/01-12/01
	St. Cloud MSA, MN	H	9.02 FQ	12.14 AW	16.47 TQ	MNBLS	10/01-12/01
	Mississippi	H	7.63 FQ	10.79 AW	14.92 TQ	MSBLS	10/01-12/01
	Biloxi-Gulfport-Pascagoula MSA, MS	H	8.15 FQ	12.42 AW	17.48 TQ	MSBLS	10/01-12/01
	Jackson MSA, MS	H	7.31 FQ	10.72 AW	15.32 TQ	MSBLS	10/01-12/01
	Missouri	H	7.33 FQ	11.19 AW	15.86 TQ	MOBLS	10/01-12/01
	Kansas City MSA, MO-KS	H	7.96 FQ	11.67 AW	16.24 TQ	MOBLS	10/01-12/01
	St. Louis MSA, MO-IL	H	8.92 FQ	12.86 AW	16.90 TQ	MOBLS	10/01-12/01
	Springfield MSA, MO	H	7.35 FQ	9.91 AW	13.02 TQ	MOBLS	10/01-12/01
	Montana	H	7.78 FQ	11.87 AW	16.61 TQ	MTBLS	10/01-12/01
	Billings MSA, MT	H	8.37 FQ	11.91 AW	16.70 TQ	MTBLS	10/01-12/01
	Nebraska	H	8.66 FQ	12.30 AW	15.98 TQ	NEBLS	10/01-12/01
	Lincoln MSA, NE	H	8.40 FQ	14.52 AW	24.60 TQ	NEBLS	10/01-12/01
	Omaha MSA, NE-IA	H	9.56 FQ	12.52 AW	15.46 TQ	NEBLS	10/01-12/01
	Nevada	H	7.85 FQ	14.96 AW	24.33 TQ	NVBLS	10/01-12/01
	Las Vegas MSA, NV-AZ	H	7.22 FQ	13.95 AW	23.95 TQ	NVBLS	10/01-12/01
	Reno MSA, NV	H	9.06 FQ	13.90 AW	19.86 TQ	NVBLS	10/01-12/01
	New Hampshire	H	9.14 FQ	14.14 AW	19.81 TQ	NHBLS	10/01-12/01
	Manchester PMSA, NH	H	10.91 FQ	13.86 AW	17.26 TQ	NHBLS	10/01-12/01
	Nashua PMSA, NH	H	8.05 FQ	14.40 AW	20.76 TQ	NHBLS	10/01-12/01
	Portsmouth-Rochester PMSA, NH-ME	H	9.15 FQ	14.09 AW	19.91 TQ	NHBLS	10/01-12/01
	New Jersey	H	7.67 FQ	14.19 AW	21.97 TQ	NJBLS	10/01-12/01
	Atlantic-Cape May PMSA, NJ	H	5.99 FQ	10.81 AW	17.23 TQ	NJBLS	10/01-12/01
	Bergen-Passaic PMSA, NJ	H	7.76 FQ	13.07 AW	18.49 TQ	NJBLS	10/01-12/01
	Jersey City PMSA, NJ	H	14.13 FQ	18.74 AW	22.27 TQ	NJBLS	10/01-12/01
	Middlesex-Somerset-Hunterdon PMSA, NJ	H	7.16 FQ	13.44 AW	23.13 TQ	NJBLS	10/01-12/01
	Monmouth-Ocean PMSA, NJ	H	11.67 FQ	16.58 AW	23.46 TQ	NJBLS	10/01-12/01
	Newark PMSA, NJ	H	7.68 FQ	14.45 AW	23.02 TQ	NJBLS	10/01-12/01
	Trenton PMSA, NJ	H	13.05 FQ	18.56 AW	23.00 TQ	NJBLS	10/01-12/01
	New Mexico	H	6.94 FQ	11.15 AW	17.06 TQ	NMBLS	10/01-12/01
	Albuquerque MSA, NM	H	6.33 FQ	10.43 AW	16.14 TQ	NMBLS	10/01-12/01
	Las Cruces MSA, NM	H	6.88 FQ	9.99 AW	14.80 TQ	NMBLS	10/01-12/01
	New York	H	8.15 FQ	14.00 AW	22.16 TQ	NYBLS	10/01-12/01
	Albany-Schenectady-Troy MSA, NY	H	7.80 FQ	11.98 AW	16.36 TQ	NYBLS	10/01-12/01
	Binghamton MSA, NY	H	7.09 FQ	10.74 AW	16.18 TQ	NYBLS	10/01-12/01
	Buffalo-Niagara Falls MSA, NY	H	7.72 FQ	12.25 AW	16.95 TQ	NYBLS	10/01-12/01
	Dutchess County PMSA, NY	H	7.98 FQ	12.87 AW	20.32 TQ	NYBLS	10/01-12/01
	Nassau-Suffolk PMSA, NY	H	8.39 FQ	14.91 AW	24.20 TQ	NYBLS	10/01-12/01
	New York PMSA, NY	H	8.68 FQ	16.75 AW	25.52 TQ	NYBLS	10/01-12/01
	Newburgh PMSA, NY-PA	H	8.84 FQ	15.07 AW	21.64 TQ	NYBLS	10/01-12/01
	Rochester MSA, NY	H	8.63 FQ	12.00 AW	16.64 TQ	NYBLS	10/01-12/01
	Syracuse MSA, NY	H	8.57 FQ	11.54 AW	15.16 TQ	NYBLS	10/01-12/01
	Utica-Rome MSA, NY	H	7.56 FQ	11.68 AW	16.70 TQ	NYBLS	10/01-12/01
	North Carolina	H	8.04 FQ	11.06 AW	14.82 TQ	NCBLS	10/01-12/01
	Charlotte-Gastonia-Rock Hill MSA, NC-SC	H	7.68 FQ	11.07 AW	15.36 TQ	NCBLS	10/01-12/01
	Greensboro-Winston-Salem-High Point MSA, NC	H	8.76 FQ	11.28 AW	14.48 TQ	NCBLS	10/01-12/01
	Hickory-Morganton-Lenoir MSA, NC	H	8.33 FQ	11.35 AW	15.14 TQ	NCBLS	10/01-12/01
	Raleigh-Durham-Chapel Hill MSA, NC	H	8.48 FQ	10.98 AW	15.53 TQ	NCBLS	10/01-12/01
	Wilmington MSA, NC	H	5.81 FQ	9.73 AW	16.56 TQ	NCBLS	10/01-12/01
	North Dakota	H	7.57 FQ	10.34 AW	13.51 TQ	NDBLS	10/01-12/01
	Fargo-Moorhead MSA, ND-MN	H	7.44 FQ	10.60 AW	14.07 TQ	NDBLS	10/01-12/01
	Ohio	H	8.68 FQ	12.70 AW	17.35 TQ	OHBLS	10/01-12/01
	Akron PMSA, OH	H	8.94 FQ	16.13 AW	24.98 TQ	OHBLS	10/01-12/01
	Cincinnati PMSA, OH-KY-IN	H	9.57 FQ	13.60 AW	18.37 TQ	OHBLS	10/01-12/01

AAW	Average annual wage	**AOH**	Average offered, high	**ASH**	Average starting, high	**H**	Hourly	**M**	Monthly	**S**	Special: hourly and annual
AE	Average entry wage	**AOL**	Average offered, low	**ASL**	Average starting, low	**HI**	Highest wage paid	**MTC**	Median total compensation	**TQ**	Third quartile wage
AEX	Average experienced wage	**APH**	Average pay, high range	**AW**	Average wage paid	**HR**	High end range	**MW**	Median wage paid	**W**	Weekly
AO	Average offered	**APL**	Average pay, low range	**FQ**	First quartile wage	**LR**	Low end range	**SQ**	Second quartile wage	**Y**	Yearly

Occupation/Type/Industry	Location	Per	Low	Mid	High	Source	Date
Cabinetmaker and Bench Carpenter	Cleveland-Lorain-Elyria PMSA, OH	H	11.12 FQ	14.92 AW	19.65 TQ	OHBLS	10/01-12/01
	Columbus MSA, OH	H	10.15 FQ	13.84 AW	17.26 TQ	OHBLS	10/01-12/01
	Dayton-Springfield MSA, OH	H	9.77 FQ	14.39 AW	18.93 TQ	OHBLS	10/01-12/01
	Hamilton-Middletown PMSA, OH	H	8.38 FQ	13.19 AW	18.47 TQ	OHBLS	10/01-12/01
	Mansfield MSA, OH	H	9.08 FQ	12.33 AW	16.19 TQ	OHBLS	10/01-12/01
	Toledo MSA, OH	H	8.62 FQ	12.21 AW	16.38 TQ	OHBLS	10/01-12/01
	Youngstown-Warren MSA, OH	H	8.38 FQ	13.55 AW	19.25 TQ	OHBLS	10/01-12/01
	Oklahoma	H	7.33 FQ	11.07 AW	15.40 TQ	OKBLS	10/01-12/01
	Oklahoma City MSA, OK	H	7.52 FQ	11.05 AW	14.25 TQ	OKBLS	10/01-12/01
	Tulsa MSA, OK	H	7.90 FQ	11.98 AW	16.79 TQ	OKBLS	10/01-12/01
	Oregon	H	8.52 FQ	12.45 AW	17.11 TQ	ORBLS	10/01-12/01
	Eugene-Springfield MSA, OR	H	9.33 FQ	12.51 AW	16.29 TQ	ORBLS	10/01-12/01
	Medford-Ashland MSA, OR	H	7.32 FQ	11.99 AW	17.03 TQ	ORBLS	10/01-12/01
	Portland-Vancouver PMSA, OR-WA	H	8.29 FQ	12.80 AW	17.46 TQ	ORBLS	10/01-12/01
	Salem PMSA, OR	H	8.55 FQ	11.70 AW	16.22 TQ	ORBLS	10/01-12/01
	Pennsylvania	H	7.43 FQ	12.46 AW	18.32 TQ	PABLS	10/01-12/01
	Allentown-Bethlehem-Easton MSA, PA	H	9.71 FQ	12.90 AW	16.54 TQ	PABLS	10/01-12/01
	Erie MSA, PA	H	6.00 FQ	9.89 AW	14.75 TQ	PABLS	10/01-12/01
	Harrisburg-Lebanon-Carlisle MSA, PA	H	8.07 FQ	11.21 AW	14.51 TQ	PABLS	10/01-12/01
	Johnstown MSA, PA	H	7.36 FQ	10.05 AW	13.20 TQ	PABLS	10/01-12/01
	Lancaster MSA, PA	H	10.16 FQ	13.35 AW	16.95 TQ	PABLS	10/01-12/01
	Philadelphia PMSA, PA-NJ	H	9.05 FQ	15.10 AW	21.28 TQ	PABLS	10/01-12/01
	Pittsburgh MSA, PA	H	6.25 FQ	12.37 AW	17.38 TQ	PABLS	10/01-12/01
	Reading MSA, PA	H	6.16 FQ	12.71 AW	20.57 TQ	PABLS	10/01-12/01
	Scranton-Wilkes-Barre-Hazleton MSA, PA	H	6.07 FQ	10.05 AW	15.87 TQ	PABLS	10/01-12/01
	York MSA, PA	H	9.19 FQ	12.66 AW	17.58 TQ	PABLS	10/01-12/01
	Rhode Island	H	9.51 FQ	14.51 AW	20.36 TQ	RIBLS	10/01-12/01
	Providence-Fall River-Warwick MSA, RI-MA	H	9.30 FQ	14.29 AW	20.51 TQ	RIBLS	10/01-12/01
	South Carolina	H	6.97 FQ	10.85 AW	15.92 TQ	SCBLS	10/01-12/01
	Charleston-North Charleston MSA, SC	H	8.46 FQ	12.24 AW	16.60 TQ	SCBLS	10/01-12/01
	Columbia MSA, SC	H	7.79 FQ	12.52 AW	17.80 TQ	SCBLS	10/01-12/01
	Greenville-Spartanburg-Anderson MSA, SC	H	8.14 FQ	11.86 AW	16.14 TQ	SCBLS	10/01-12/01
	South Dakota	H	7.94 FQ	9.93 AW	12.62 TQ	SDBLS	10/01-12/01
	Sioux Falls MSA, SD	H	8.46 FQ	10.09 AW	12.70 TQ	SDBLS	10/01-12/01
	Tennessee	H	7.24 FQ	10.80 AW	15.41 TQ	TNBLS	10/01-12/01
	Chattanooga MSA, TN-GA	H	7.53 FQ	10.59 AW	14.24 TQ	TNBLS	10/01-12/01
	Clarksville-Hopkinsville MSA, TN-KY	H	7.60 FQ	11.00 AW	13.74 TQ	TNBLS	10/01-12/01
	Knoxville MSA, TN	H	7.73 FQ	10.25 AW	13.62 TQ	TNBLS	10/01-12/01
	Memphis MSA, TN-AR-MS	H	7.33 FQ	11.73 AW	17.56 TQ	TNBLS	10/01-12/01
	Nashville MSA, TN	H	9.63 FQ	13.77 AW	19.49 TQ	TNBLS	10/01-12/01
	Texas	H	6.78 FQ	10.50 AW	15.24 TQ	TXBLS	10/01-12/01
	Amarillo MSA, TX	H	7.57 FQ	10.00 AW	13.37 TQ	TXBLS	10/01-12/01
	Austin-San Marcos MSA, TX	H	7.81 FQ	11.86 AW	16.83 TQ	TXBLS	10/01-12/01
	Beaumont-Port Arthur MSA, TX	H	7.47 FQ	10.95 AW	15.79 TQ	TXBLS	10/01-12/01
	Brownsville-Harlingen-San Benito MSA, TX	H	6.22 FQ	9.32 AW	16.36 TQ	TXBLS	10/01-12/01
	Corpus Christi MSA, TX	H	6.19 FQ	9.76 AW	13.88 TQ	TXBLS	10/01-12/01
	Dallas PMSA, TX	H	7.27 FQ	10.99 AW	16.02 TQ	TXBLS	10/01-12/01
	El Paso MSA, TX	H	5.96 FQ	8.45 AW	13.03 TQ	TXBLS	10/01-12/01
	Fort Worth-Arlington PMSA, TX	H	7.15 FQ	11.07 AW	14.89 TQ	TXBLS	10/01-12/01
	Houston PMSA, TX	H	7.29 FQ	11.27 AW	16.12 TQ	TXBLS	10/01-12/01
	Killeen-Temple MSA, TX	H	6.15 FQ	9.02 AW	12.39 TQ	TXBLS	10/01-12/01
	Longview-Marshall MSA, TX	H	6.27 FQ	10.01 AW	14.57 TQ	TXBLS	10/01-12/01
	Lubbock MSA, TX	H	8.00 FQ	10.53 AW	13.72 TQ	TXBLS	10/01-12/01
	McAllen-Edinburg-Mission MSA, TX	H	5.81 FQ	8.07 AW	11.52 TQ	TXBLS	10/01-12/01
	Odessa-Midland MSA, TX	H	6.66 FQ	10.07 AW	15.67 TQ	TXBLS	10/01-12/01
	San Antonio MSA, TX	H	6.42 FQ	10.01 AW	14.55 TQ	TXBLS	10/01-12/01
	Tyler MSA, TX	H	7.07 FQ	10.51 AW	14.87 TQ	TXBLS	10/01-12/01

AAW Average annual wage **AOH** Average offered, high **ASH** Average starting, high **H** Hourly **M** Monthly **S** Special: hourly and annual
AE Average entry wage **AOL** Average offered, low **ASL** Average starting, low **HI** Highest wage paid **MTC** Median total compensation **TQ** Third quartile wage
AEX Average experienced wage **APH** Average pay, high range **AW** Average wage paid **HR** High end range **MW** Median wage paid **W** Weekly
AO Average offered **APL** Average pay, low range **FQ** First quartile wage **LR** Low end range **SQ** Second quartile wage **Y** Yearly

Occupation/Type/Industry	Location	Per	Low	Mid	High	Source	Date
Cabinetmaker and Bench Carpenter	Waco MSA, TX	H	6.29 FQ	9.93 AW	15.05 TQ	TXBLS	10/01-12/01
	Utah	H	7.53 FQ	11.33 AW	16.07 TQ	UTBLS	10/01-12/01
	Provo-Orem MSA, UT	H	7.77 FQ	10.52 AW	13.49 TQ	UTBLS	10/01-12/01
	Salt Lake City-Ogden MSA, UT	H	7.50 FQ	11.84 AW	17.06 TQ	UTBLS	10/01-12/01
	Vermont	H	8.68 FQ	12.57 AW	17.25 TQ	VTBLS	10/01-12/01
	Burlington MSA, VT	H	8.90 FQ	12.98 AW	19.48 TQ	VTBLS	10/01-12/01
	Virginia	H	7.80 FQ	11.92 AW	17.79 TQ	VABLS	10/01-12/01
	Norfolk-Virginia Beach-Newport News MSA, VA-NC	H	7.77 FQ	13.14 AW	19.66 TQ	VABLS	10/01-12/01
	Richmond-Petersburg MSA, VA	H	9.18 FQ	12.44 AW	15.97 TQ	VABLS	10/01-12/01
	Roanoke MSA, VA	H	7.39 FQ	10.79 AW	14.08 TQ	VABLS	10/01-12/01
	Washington	H	8.61 FQ	13.01 AW	17.95 TQ	WABLS	10/01-12/01
	Bremerton PMSA, WA	H	9.95 FQ	15.76 AW	24.10 TQ	WABLS	10/01-12/01
	Seattle-Bellevue-Everett PMSA, WA	H	9.27 FQ	13.78 AW	18.76 TQ	WABLS	10/01-12/01
	Spokane MSA, WA	H	8.91 FQ	11.21 AW	14.47 TQ	WABLS	10/01-12/01
	Tacoma PMSA, WA	H	8.51 FQ	12.38 AW	17.14 TQ	WABLS	10/01-12/01
	West Virginia	H	7.79 FQ	10.65 AW	13.38 TQ	WVBLS	10/01-12/01
	Charleston MSA, WV	H	6.51 FQ	9.32 AW	13.26 TQ	WVBLS	10/01-12/01
	Wisconsin	H	8.90 FQ	13.33 AW	19.22 TQ	WIBLS	10/01-12/01
	Appleton-Oshkosh-Neenah MSA, WI	H	9.77 FQ	14.48 AW	19.31 TQ	WIBLS	10/01-12/01
	Green Bay MSA, WI	H	7.93 FQ	11.66 AW	16.68 TQ	WIBLS	10/01-12/01
	Madison MSA, WI	H	8.83 FQ	14.23 AW	20.20 TQ	WIBLS	10/01-12/01
	Milwaukee-Waukesha PMSA, WI	H	9.51 FQ	15.07 AW	21.32 TQ	WIBLS	10/01-12/01
	Racine PMSA, WI	H	7.83 FQ	11.21 AW	16.95 TQ	WIBLS	10/01-12/01
	Wyoming	H	8.81 FQ	13.39 AW	17.44 TQ	WYBLS	10/01-12/01
	Cheyenne MSA, WY	H	8.66 FQ	12.76 AW	17.96 TQ	WYBLS	10/01-12/01
	Puerto Rico	H	5.61 FQ	6.58 AW	8.04 TQ	PRBLS	10/01-12/01
Call Center Professional							
Airlines	Hawaii	H		9.31 AW		HIBUS	1/00-1/01
Hotels	Hawaii	H		9.56 AW		HIBUS	1/00-1/01
Utilities	Hawaii	H		16.03 AW		HIBUS	1/00-1/01
Camera and Photographic Equipment Repairer	Alabama	H	7.76 FQ	11.08 AW	14.29 TQ	ALBLS	10/01-12/01
	Arizona	H	11.00 FQ	14.20 AW	21.12 TQ	AZBLS	10/01-12/01
	Phoenix-Mesa MSA, AZ	H	10.89 FQ	13.95 AW	22.29 TQ	AZBLS	10/01-12/01
	California	H	12.67 FQ	19.37 AW	26.92 TQ	CABLS	10/01-12/01
	Los Angeles-Long Beach PMSA, CA	H	17.20 FQ	20.97 AW	28.20 TQ	CABLS	10/01-12/01
	San Francisco PMSA, CA	H	11.05 FQ	21.10 AW	33.45 TQ	CABLS	10/01-12/01
	Colorado	H	10.00 FQ	15.36 AW	20.98 TQ	COBLS	10/01-12/01
	Colorado Springs MSA, CO	H	12.43 FQ	15.32 AW	17.45 TQ	COBLS	10/01-12/01
	Denver PMSA, CO	H	11.44 FQ	16.56 AW	21.73 TQ	COBLS	10/01-12/01
	Washington PMSA, DC-MD-VA-WV	H	8.49 FQ	13.19 AW	18.09 TQ	DCBLS	10/01-12/01
	Florida	H	7.96 FQ	11.89 AW	16.09 TQ	FLBLS	10/01-12/01
	Miami PMSA, FL	H	7.34 FQ	11.43 AW	20.23 TQ	FLBLS	10/01-12/01
	Orlando MSA, FL	H	8.59 FQ	10.07 AW	10.73 TQ	FLBLS	10/01-12/01
	Tampa-St. Petersburg-Clearwater MSA, FL	H	8.90 FQ	11.57 AW	13.22 TQ	FLBLS	10/01-12/01
	Georgia	H	6.66 FQ	15.70 AW	25.49 TQ	GABLS	10/01-12/01
	Atlanta MSA, GA	H	6.76 FQ	15.80 AW	25.55 TQ	GABLS	10/01-12/01
	Illinois	H	7.94 FQ	15.21 AW	22.31 TQ	ILBLS	10/01-12/01
	Chicago PMSA, IL	H	12.30 FQ	17.49 AW	23.37 TQ	ILBLS	10/01-12/01
	Indiana	H	9.12 FQ	14.74 AW	21.50 TQ	INBLS	10/01-12/01
	Kentucky	H	9.59 FQ	17.72 AW	22.72 TQ	KYBLS	10/01-12/01
	Louisville MSA, KY-IN	H	9.66 FQ	18.02 AW	22.69 TQ	KYBLS	10/01-12/01
	Louisiana	H	7.50 FQ	13.91 AW	26.73 TQ	LABLS	10/01-12/01
	Maryland	H	9.67 FQ	14.00 AW	18.34 TQ	MDBLS	10/01-12/01
	Michigan	H	8.99 FQ	16.81 AW	33.23 TQ	MIBLS	10/01-12/01
	Detroit PMSA, MI	H	8.86 FQ	17.39 AW	33.72 TQ	MIBLS	10/01-12/01
	Minnesota	H	8.53 FQ	20.20 AW	28.32 TQ	MNBLS	10/01-12/01
	Minneapolis-St. Paul MSA, MN-WI	H	6.75 FQ	17.09 AW	27.95 TQ	MNBLS	10/01-12/01

AAW Average annual wage	**AOH** Average offered, high	**ASH** Average starting, high	**H** Hourly	**M** Monthly	**S** Special: hourly and annual
AE Average entry wage	**AOL** Average offered, low	**ASL** Average starting, low	**HI** Highest wage paid	**MTC** Median total compensation	**TQ** Third quartile wage
AEX Average experienced wage	**APH** Average pay, high range	**AW** Average wage paid	**HR** High end range	**MW** Median wage paid	**W** Weekly
AO Average offered	**APL** Average pay, low range	**FQ** First quartile wage	**LR** Low end range	**SQ** Second quartile wage	**Y** Yearly

Occupation/Type/Industry	Location	Per	Low	Mid	High	Source	Date
Camera and Photographic Equipment Repairer	Nebraska	H	7.95 FQ	12.07 AW	19.52 TQ	NEBLS	10/01-12/01
	Omaha MSA, NE-IA	H	7.53 FQ	9.86 AW	11.32 TQ	NEBLS	10/01-12/01
	New Hampshire	H	11.78 FQ	15.54 AW	23.44 TQ	NHBLS	10/01-12/01
	New Jersey	H	9.17 FQ	16.62 AW	22.34 TQ	NJBLS	10/01-12/01
	Bergen-Passaic PMSA, NJ	H	10.44 FQ	17.24 AW	22.31 TQ	NJBLS	10/01-12/01
	Jersey City PMSA, NJ	H	8.26 FQ	14.40 AW	21.47 TQ	NJBLS	10/01-12/01
	Middlesex-Somerset-Hunterdon PMSA, NJ	H	12.18 FQ	18.45 AW	30.95 TQ	NJBLS	10/01-12/01
	Newark PMSA, NJ	H	10.11 FQ	18.32 AW	24.45 TQ	NJBLS	10/01-12/01
	New York	H	7.35 FQ	15.07 AW	23.65 TQ	NYBLS	10/01-12/01
	Nassau-Suffolk PMSA, NY	H	9.66 FQ	15.74 AW	21.93 TQ	NYBLS	10/01-12/01
	New York PMSA, NY	H	6.13 FQ	14.39 AW	25.00 TQ	NYBLS	10/01-12/01
	North Carolina	H	9.02 FQ	14.21 AW	19.82 TQ	NCBLS	10/01-12/01
	Charlotte-Gastonia-Rock Hill MSA, NC-SC	H	9.15 FQ	14.47 AW	20.04 TQ	NCBLS	10/01-12/01
	Ohio	H	9.35 FQ	15.80 AW	25.13 TQ	OHBLS	10/01-12/01
	Cleveland-Lorain-Elyria PMSA, OH	H	9.04 FQ	17.68 AW	25.69 TQ	OHBLS	10/01-12/01
	Oklahoma	H	5.92 FQ	17.99 AW	29.20 TQ	OKBLS	10/01-12/01
	Oregon	H	9.15 FQ	13.73 AW	23.25 TQ	ORBLS	10/01-12/01
	Portland-Vancouver PMSA, OR-WA	H	9.04 FQ	13.28 AW	24.09 TQ	ORBLS	10/01-12/01
	Pennsylvania	H	9.24 FQ	14.29 AW	20.83 TQ	PABLS	10/01-12/01
	Philadelphia PMSA, PA-NJ	H	7.81 FQ	12.58 AW	19.50 TQ	PABLS	10/01-12/01
	South Carolina	H	8.21 FQ	12.75 AW	19.20 TQ	SCBLS	10/01-12/01
	Columbia MSA, SC	H	6.97 FQ	12.53 AW	19.83 TQ	SCBLS	10/01-12/01
	Myrtle Beach MSA, SC	H	8.19 FQ	12.63 AW	17.76 TQ	SCBLS	10/01-12/01
	Tennessee	H	8.91 FQ	14.23 AW	18.93 TQ	TNBLS	10/01-12/01
	Texas	H	7.25 FQ	11.06 AW	21.23 TQ	TXBLS	10/01-12/01
	Dallas PMSA, TX	H	7.23 FQ	9.52 AW	15.95 TQ	TXBLS	10/01-12/01
	Virginia	H	6.72 FQ	13.07 AW	19.78 TQ	VABLS	10/01-12/01
	Richmond-Petersburg MSA, VA	H	6.60 FQ	12.05 AW	14.01 TQ	VABLS	10/01-12/01
	Washington	H	6.90 FQ	14.72 AW	23.08 TQ	WABLS	10/01-12/01
	Wisconsin	H	10.98 FQ	14.98 AW	20.00 TQ	WIBLS	10/01-12/01
Camera Operator							
Television, Video, and Motion Picture	Alabama	Y	13550 FQ	25210 AW	44510 TQ	ALBLS	10/01-12/01
Television, Video, and Motion Picture	Mobile MSA, AL	Y	16410 FQ	23740 AW	36790 TQ	ALBLS	10/01-12/01
Television, Video, and Motion Picture	Alaska	Y	16250 FQ	24000 AW	32440 TQ	AKBLS	10/01-12/01
Television, Video, and Motion Picture	Arizona	Y	14460 FQ	33270 AW	66180 TQ	AZBLS	10/01-12/01
Television, Video, and Motion Picture	Phoenix-Mesa MSA, AZ	Y	15390 FQ	35680 AW	73230 TQ	AZBLS	10/01-12/01
Television, Video, and Motion Picture	Tucson MSA, AZ	Y	16130 FQ	32340 AW	64810 TQ	AZBLS	10/01-12/01
Television, Video, and Motion Picture	Arkansas	Y	12180 FQ	21900 AW	41120 TQ	ARBLS	10/01-12/01
Television, Video, and Motion Picture	Fayetteville-Springdale-Rogers MSA, AR	Y	11750 FQ	18930 AW	36110 TQ	ARBLS	10/01-12/01
Television, Video, and Motion Picture	Little Rock-North Little Rock MSA, AR	Y	12430 FQ	24860 AW	43060 TQ	ARBLS	10/01-12/01
Television, Video, and Motion Picture	California	Y	21800 FQ	49470 AW	72960 TQ	CABLS	10/01-12/01
Television, Video, and Motion Picture	Bakersfield MSA, CA	Y	24930 FQ	47850 AW	69540 TQ	CABLS	10/01-12/01
Television, Video, and Motion Picture	Fresno MSA, CA	Y	13540 FQ	26490 AW	40100 TQ	CABLS	10/01-12/01
Television, Video, and Motion Picture	Los Angeles-Long Beach PMSA, CA	Y	29290 FQ	52630 AW	77110 TQ	CABLS	10/01-12/01
Television, Video, and Motion Picture	Oakland PMSA, CA	Y	47610 FQ	58890 AW	72230 TQ	CABLS	10/01-12/01
Television, Video, and Motion Picture	Orange County PMSA, CA	Y	20550 FQ	48990 AW	83420 TQ	CABLS	10/01-12/01
Television, Video, and Motion Picture	Riverside-San Bernardino PMSA, CA	Y	21550 FQ	36520 AW	54520 TQ	CABLS	10/01-12/01
Television, Video, and Motion Picture	Sacramento PMSA, CA	Y	13800 FQ	43080 AW	68260 TQ	CABLS	10/01-12/01
Television, Video, and Motion Picture	San Diego MSA, CA	Y	20460 FQ	34430 AW	53250 TQ	CABLS	10/01-12/01
Television, Video, and Motion Picture	San Francisco PMSA, CA	Y	14550 FQ	46060 AW	66520 TQ	CABLS	10/01-12/01
Television, Video, and Motion Picture	San Jose PMSA, CA	Y	27750 FQ	52970 AW	82820 TQ	CABLS	10/01-12/01
Television, Video, and Motion Picture	Santa Barbara-Santa Maria-Lompoc MSA, CA	Y	29720 FQ	43390 AW	56240 TQ	CABLS	10/01-12/01
Television, Video, and Motion Picture	Ventura PMSA, CA	Y	15300 FQ	34120 AW	68040 TQ	CABLS	10/01-12/01
Television, Video, and Motion Picture	Colorado	Y	18620 FQ	34220 AW	56660 TQ	COBLS	10/01-12/01
Television, Video, and Motion Picture	Denver PMSA, CO	Y	19780 FQ	34260 AW	55710 TQ	COBLS	10/01-12/01
Television, Video, and Motion Picture	Connecticut	Y	20660 FQ	37130 AW	57770 TQ	CTBLS	10/01-12/01
Television, Video, and Motion Picture	Hartford MSA, CT	Y	21510 FQ	36010 AW	54710 TQ	CTBLS	10/01-12/01
Television, Video, and Motion Picture	Delaware	Y	17590 FQ	28610 AW	52390 TQ	DEBLS	10/01-12/01
Television, Video, and Motion Picture	Wilmington-Newark PMSA, DE-MD	Y	19030 FQ	30220 AW	56320 TQ	DEBLS	10/01-12/01

AAW	Average annual wage	**AOH**	Average offered, high	**ASH**	Average starting, high	**H**	Hourly	**M**	Monthly	**S**	Special: hourly and annual
AE	Average entry wage	**AOL**	Average offered, low	**ASL**	Average starting, low	**HI**	Highest wage paid	**MTC**	Median total compensation	**TQ**	Third quartile wage
AEX	Average experienced wage	**APH**	Average pay, high range	**AW**	Average wage paid	**HR**	High end range	**MW**	Median wage paid	**W**	Weekly
AO	Average offered	**APL**	Average pay, low range	**FQ**	First quartile wage	**LR**	Low end range	**SQ**	Second quartile wage	**Y**	Yearly

Occupation/Type/Industry	Location	Per	Low	Mid	High	Source	Date
Camera Operator							
Television, Video, and Motion Picture	District of Columbia	Y	14940 FQ	39350 AW	66110 TQ	DCBLS	10/01-12/01
Television, Video, and Motion Picture	Washington PMSA, DC-MD-VA-WV	Y	15600 FQ	36720 AW	64110 TQ	DCBLS	10/01-12/01
Television, Video, and Motion Picture	Florida	Y	15510 FQ	29210 AW	46300 TQ	FLBLS	10/01-12/01
Television, Video, and Motion Picture	Fort Lauderdale PMSA, FL	Y	16670 FQ	30710 AW	42310 TQ	FLBLS	10/01-12/01
Television, Video, and Motion Picture	Fort Myers-Cape Coral MSA, FL	Y	19500 FQ	27160 AW	39150 TQ	FLBLS	10/01-12/01
Television, Video, and Motion Picture	Jacksonville MSA, FL	Y	12550 FQ	23990 AW	37340 TQ	FLBLS	10/01-12/01
Television, Video, and Motion Picture	Miami PMSA, FL	Y	18480 FQ	32970 AW	55900 TQ	FLBLS	10/01-12/01
Television, Video, and Motion Picture	Orlando MSA, FL	Y	18520 FQ	30210 AW	44610 TQ	FLBLS	10/01-12/01
Television, Video, and Motion Picture	Tallahassee MSA, FL	Y	21460 FQ	31450 AW	45680 TQ	FLBLS	10/01-12/01
Television, Video, and Motion Picture	Tampa-St. Petersburg-Clearwater MSA, FL	Y	13910 FQ	28010 AW	44790 TQ	FLBLS	10/01-12/01
Television, Video, and Motion Picture	West Palm Beach-Boca Raton MSA, FL	Y	16150 FQ	29600 AW	45380 TQ	FLBLS	10/01-12/01
Television, Video, and Motion Picture	Georgia	Y	18360 FQ	24470 AW	40210 TQ	GABLS	10/01-12/01
Television, Video, and Motion Picture	Atlanta MSA, GA	Y	18510 FQ	24080 AW	38850 TQ	GABLS	10/01-12/01
Television, Video, and Motion Picture	Macon MSA, GA	Y	18450 FQ	26630 AW	42030 TQ	GABLS	10/01-12/01
Television, Video, and Motion Picture	Savannah MSA, GA	Y	12050 FQ	22720 AW	38460 TQ	GABLS	10/01-12/01
Television, Video, and Motion Picture	Hawaii	Y	19630 FQ	34780 AW	60340 TQ	HIBLS	10/01-12/01
Television, Video, and Motion Picture	Honolulu MSA, HI	Y	19550 FQ	34670 AW	58680 TQ	HIBLS	10/01-12/01
Television, Video, and Motion Picture	Idaho	Y	11300 FQ	18330 AW	36590 TQ	IDBLS	10/01-12/01
Television, Video, and Motion Picture	Boise City MSA, ID	Y	11280 FQ	18370 AW	35180 TQ	IDBLS	10/01-12/01
Television, Video, and Motion Picture	Illinois	Y	14720 FQ	29870 AW	44550 TQ	ILBLS	10/01-12/01
Television, Video, and Motion Picture	Chicago PMSA, IL	Y	15120 FQ	30190 AW	44100 TQ	ILBLS	10/01-12/01
Television, Video, and Motion Picture	Indiana	Y	12740 FQ	28550 AW	54440 TQ	INBLS	10/01-12/01
Television, Video, and Motion Picture	Evansville-Henderson MSA, IN-KY	Y	14110 FQ	23670 AW	35520 TQ	INBLS	10/01-12/01
Television, Video, and Motion Picture	Fort Wayne MSA, IN	Y	13590 FQ	29460 AW	53400 TQ	INBLS	10/01-12/01
Television, Video, and Motion Picture	Indianapolis MSA, IN	Y	14850 FQ	34500 AW	58850 TQ	INBLS	10/01-12/01
Television, Video, and Motion Picture	Iowa	Y	12230 FQ	23730 AW	43310 TQ	IABLS	10/01-12/01
Television, Video, and Motion Picture	Des Moines MSA, IA	Y	14050 FQ	34930 AW	65490 TQ	IABLS	10/01-12/01
Television, Video, and Motion Picture	Kansas	Y	13570 FQ	27480 AW	52950 TQ	KSBLS	10/01-12/01
Television, Video, and Motion Picture	Wichita MSA, KS	Y	15520 FQ	28950 AW	59900 TQ	KSBLS	10/01-12/01
Television, Video, and Motion Picture	Kentucky	Y	13070 FQ	25390 AW	41940 TQ	KYBLS	10/01-12/01
Television, Video, and Motion Picture	Lexington MSA, KY	Y	18220 FQ	27310 AW	40970 TQ	KYBLS	10/01-12/01
Television, Video, and Motion Picture	Louisville MSA, KY-IN	Y	15920 FQ	26590 AW	42270 TQ	KYBLS	10/01-12/01
Television, Video, and Motion Picture	Louisiana	Y	12500 FQ	24950 AW	36010 TQ	LABLS	10/01-12/01
Television, Video, and Motion Picture	Baton Rouge MSA, LA	Y	12020 FQ	20000 AW	28120 TQ	LABLS	10/01-12/01
Television, Video, and Motion Picture	New Orleans MSA, LA	Y	13410 FQ	28160 AW	36230 TQ	LABLS	10/01-12/01
Television, Video, and Motion Picture	Maine	Y	12610 FQ	19840 AW	34260 TQ	MEBLS	10/01-12/01
Television, Video, and Motion Picture	Portland MSA, ME	Y	14600 FQ	24150 AW	38000 TQ	MEBLS	10/01-12/01
Television, Video, and Motion Picture	Maryland	Y	17610 FQ	35770 AW	63580 TQ	MDBLS	10/01-12/01
Television, Video, and Motion Picture	Baltimore PMSA, MD	Y	20430 FQ	37990 AW	64980 TQ	MDBLS	10/01-12/01
Television, Video, and Motion Picture	Massachusetts	Y	17870 FQ	37750 AW	61530 TQ	MABLS	10/01-12/01
Television, Video, and Motion Picture	Boston PMSA, MA-NH	Y	18230 FQ	38310 AW	60410 TQ	MABLS	10/01-12/01
Television, Video, and Motion Picture	Michigan	Y	15800 FQ	36910 AW	60830 TQ	MIBLS	10/01-12/01
Television, Video, and Motion Picture	Detroit PMSA, MI	Y	23330 FQ	41930 AW	63140 TQ	MIBLS	10/01-12/01
Television, Video, and Motion Picture	Grand Rapids-Muskegon-Holland MSA, MI	Y	15010 FQ	28200 AW	50740 TQ	MIBLS	10/01-12/01
Television, Video, and Motion Picture	Kalamazoo-Battle Creek MSA, MI	Y	25750 FQ	30610 AW	34740 TQ	MIBLS	10/01-12/01
Television, Video, and Motion Picture	Minnesota	Y	14920 FQ	37300 AW	57860 TQ	MNBLS	10/01-12/01
Television, Video, and Motion Picture	Duluth-Superior MSA, MN-WI	Y	12600 FQ	25360 AW	56610 TQ	MNBLS	10/01-12/01
Television, Video, and Motion Picture	Minneapolis-St. Paul MSA, MN-WI	Y	16920 FQ	40720 AW	59460 TQ	MNBLS	10/01-12/01
Television, Video, and Motion Picture	Mississippi	Y	15500 FQ	23920 AW	31380 TQ	MSBLS	10/01-12/01
Television, Video, and Motion Picture	Missouri	Y	14640 FQ	31480 AW	51760 TQ	MOBLS	10/01-12/01
Television, Video, and Motion Picture	Kansas City MSA, MO-KS	Y	16140 FQ	33490 AW	55720 TQ	MOBLS	10/01-12/01
Television, Video, and Motion Picture	St. Louis MSA, MO-IL	Y	23560 FQ	32790 AW	48000 TQ	MOBLS	10/01-12/01
Television, Video, and Motion Picture	Montana	Y	12010 FQ	22400 AW	35790 TQ	MTBLS	10/01-12/01
Television, Video, and Motion Picture	Nebraska	Y	13750 FQ	27730 AW	45050 TQ	NEBLS	10/01-12/01
Television, Video, and Motion Picture	Nevada	Y	18370 FQ	41870 AW	69640 TQ	NVBLS	10/01-12/01
Television, Video, and Motion Picture	Las Vegas MSA, NV-AZ	Y	19000 FQ	42090 AW	70140 TQ	NVBLS	10/01-12/01
Television, Video, and Motion Picture	New Hampshire	Y	13370 FQ	27860 AW	50640 TQ	NHBLS	10/01-12/01
Television, Video, and Motion Picture	New Jersey	Y	18420 FQ	41320 AW	77650 TQ	NJBLS	10/01-12/01
Television, Video, and Motion Picture	Bergen-Passaic PMSA, NJ	Y	20450 FQ	42700 AW	66460 TQ	NJBLS	10/01-12/01
Television, Video, and Motion Picture	Middlesex-Somerset-Hunterdon PMSA, NJ	Y	19550 FQ	36820 AW	79590 TQ	NJBLS	10/01-12/01
Television, Video, and Motion Picture	Newark PMSA, NJ	Y	20870 FQ	64610 AW	90760 TQ	NJBLS	10/01-12/01
Television, Video, and Motion Picture	Trenton PMSA, NJ	Y	20850 FQ	43200 AW	67800 TQ	NJBLS	10/01-12/01

AAW	Average annual wage	AOH	Average offered, high	ASH	Average starting, high	H	Hourly	M	Monthly	S	Special: hourly and annual
AE	Average entry wage	AOL	Average offered, low	ASL	Average starting, low	HI	Highest wage paid	MTC	Median total compensation	TQ	Third quartile wage
AEX	Average experienced wage	APH	Average pay, high range	AW	Average wage paid	HR	High end range	MW	Median wage paid	W	Weekly
AO	Average offered	APL	Average pay, low range	FQ	First quartile wage	LR	Low end range	SQ	Second quartile wage	Y	Yearly

Occupation/Type/Industry	Location	Per	Low	Mid	High	Source	Date
Camera Operator							
Television, Video, and Motion Picture	New Mexico	Y	18430 FQ	32710 AW	54190 TQ	NMBLS	10/01-12/01
Television, Video, and Motion Picture	Albuquerque MSA, NM	Y	16950 FQ	28370 AW	48490 TQ	NMBLS	10/01-12/01
Television, Video, and Motion Picture	New York	Y	15680 FQ	36880 AW	70830 TQ	NYBLS	10/01-12/01
Television, Video, and Motion Picture	Albany-Schenectady-Troy MSA, NY	Y	14220 FQ	31180 AW	50910 TQ	NYBLS	10/01-12/01
Television, Video, and Motion Picture	Nassau-Suffolk PMSA, NY	Y	16020 FQ	37080 AW	67280 TQ	NYBLS	10/01-12/01
Television, Video, and Motion Picture	New York PMSA, NY	Y	16070 FQ	37830 AW	79670 TQ	NYBLS	10/01-12/01
Television, Video, and Motion Picture	Rochester MSA, NY	Y	15170 FQ	32350 AW	58050 TQ	NYBLS	10/01-12/01
Television, Video, and Motion Picture	Syracuse MSA, NY	Y	12760 FQ	30150 AW	49980 TQ	NYBLS	10/01-12/01
Television, Video, and Motion Picture	North Carolina	Y	12900 FQ	27760 AW	49460 TQ	NCBLS	10/01-12/01
Television, Video, and Motion Picture	Charlotte-Gastonia-Rock Hill MSA, NC-SC	Y	16440 FQ	29580 AW	44030 TQ	NCBLS	10/01-12/01
Television, Video, and Motion Picture	Greensboro-Winston-Salem-High Point MSA, NC	Y	12300 FQ	23510 AW	48640 TQ	NCBLS	10/01-12/01
Television, Video, and Motion Picture	Raleigh-Durham-Chapel Hill MSA, NC	Y	14120 FQ	29810 AW	50090 TQ	NCBLS	10/01-12/01
Television, Video, and Motion Picture	North Dakota	Y	11650 FQ	17000 AW	28440 TQ	NDBLS	10/01-12/01
Television, Video, and Motion Picture	Fargo-Moorhead MSA, ND-MN	Y	11710 FQ	17260 AW	29230 TQ	NDBLS	10/01-12/01
Television, Video, and Motion Picture	Ohio	Y	15120 FQ	30930 AW	52410 TQ	OHBLS	10/01-12/01
Television, Video, and Motion Picture	Akron PMSA, OH	Y	19940 FQ	26060 AW	36180 TQ	OHBLS	10/01-12/01
Television, Video, and Motion Picture	Canton-Massillon MSA, OH	Y	11270 FQ	16720 AW	31250 TQ	OHBLS	10/01-12/01
Television, Video, and Motion Picture	Cincinnati PMSA, OH-KY-IN	Y	17790 FQ	36120 AW	54650 TQ	OHBLS	10/01-12/01
Television, Video, and Motion Picture	Cleveland-Lorain-Elyria PMSA, OH	Y	23410 FQ	39360 AW	55420 TQ	OHBLS	10/01-12/01
Television, Video, and Motion Picture	Columbus MSA, OH	Y	22590 FQ	32430 AW	43310 TQ	OHBLS	10/01-12/01
Television, Video, and Motion Picture	Dayton-Springfield MSA, OH	Y	24220 FQ	42300 AW	55790 TQ	OHBLS	10/01-12/01
Television, Video, and Motion Picture	Toledo MSA, OH	Y	14800 FQ	29670 AW	53230 TQ	OHBLS	10/01-12/01
Television, Video, and Motion Picture	Oklahoma	Y	14740 FQ	22820 AW	37340 TQ	OKBLS	10/01-12/01
Television, Video, and Motion Picture	Oklahoma City MSA, OK	Y	15650 FQ	24550 AW	39850 TQ	OKBLS	10/01-12/01
Television, Video, and Motion Picture	Tulsa MSA, OK	Y	15000 FQ	21280 AW	33060 TQ	OKBLS	10/01-12/01
Television, Video, and Motion Picture	Oregon	Y	15080 FQ	35080 AW	56780 TQ	ORBLS	10/01-12/01
Television, Video, and Motion Picture	Portland-Vancouver PMSA, OR-WA	Y	16770 FQ	39930 AW	57750 TQ	ORBLS	10/01-12/01
Television, Video, and Motion Picture	Pennsylvania	Y	14140 FQ	29650 AW	58230 TQ	PABLS	10/01-12/01
Television, Video, and Motion Picture	Allentown-Bethlehem-Easton MSA, PA	Y	14660 FQ	24220 AW	48200 TQ	PABLS	10/01-12/01
Television, Video, and Motion Picture	Erie MSA, PA	Y	12490 FQ	24560 AW	56350 TQ	PABLS	10/01-12/01
Television, Video, and Motion Picture	Harrisburg-Lebanon-Carlisle MSA, PA	Y	17720 FQ	26220 AW	37010 TQ	PABLS	10/01-12/01
Television, Video, and Motion Picture	Johnstown MSA, PA	Y	13350 FQ	17040 AW	26030 TQ	PABLS	10/01-12/01
Television, Video, and Motion Picture	Philadelphia PMSA, PA-NJ	Y	15890 FQ	37490 AW	72640 TQ	PABLS	10/01-12/01
Television, Video, and Motion Picture	Pittsburgh MSA, PA	Y	14210 FQ	27720 AW	49770 TQ	PABLS	10/01-12/01
Television, Video, and Motion Picture	South Carolina	Y	14810 FQ	26390 AW	44200 TQ	SCBLS	10/01-12/01
Television, Video, and Motion Picture	Charleston-North Charleston MSA, SC	Y	20080 FQ	30700 AW	43600 TQ	SCBLS	10/01-12/01
Television, Video, and Motion Picture	Columbia MSA, SC	Y	18240 FQ	31140 AW	54890 TQ	SCBLS	10/01-12/01
Television, Video, and Motion Picture	Greenville-Spartanburg-Anderson MSA, SC	Y	13370 FQ	21470 AW	35910 TQ	SCBLS	10/01-12/01
Television, Video, and Motion Picture	South Dakota	Y	14470 FQ	18320 AW	24010 TQ	SDBLS	10/01-12/01
Television, Video, and Motion Picture	Tennessee	Y	13280 FQ	26810 AW	43320 TQ	TNBLS	10/01-12/01
Television, Video, and Motion Picture	Chattanooga MSA, TN-GA	Y	13440 FQ	23060 AW	40530 TQ	TNBLS	10/01-12/01
Television, Video, and Motion Picture	Johnson City-Kingsport-Bristol MSA, TN-VA	Y	13040 FQ	23190 AW	35870 TQ	TNBLS	10/01-12/01
Television, Video, and Motion Picture	Knoxville MSA, TN	Y	16190 FQ	30130 AW	60110 TQ	TNBLS	10/01-12/01
Television, Video, and Motion Picture	Memphis MSA, TN-AR-MS	Y	12770 FQ	27510 AW	37750 TQ	TNBLS	10/01-12/01
Television, Video, and Motion Picture	Nashville MSA, TN	Y	12830 FQ	28310 AW	46140 TQ	TNBLS	10/01-12/01
Television, Video, and Motion Picture	Texas	Y	13320 FQ	25910 AW	41910 TQ	TXBLS	10/01-12/01
Television, Video, and Motion Picture	Amarillo MSA, TX	Y	12250 FQ	22210 AW	40560 TQ	TXBLS	10/01-12/01
Television, Video, and Motion Picture	Austin-San Marcos MSA, TX	Y	14330 FQ	22920 AW	32620 TQ	TXBLS	10/01-12/01
Television, Video, and Motion Picture	Dallas PMSA, TX	Y	13510 FQ	29540 AW	53730 TQ	TXBLS	10/01-12/01
Television, Video, and Motion Picture	Fort Worth-Arlington PMSA, TX	Y	15830 FQ	32200 AW	51880 TQ	TXBLS	10/01-12/01
Television, Video, and Motion Picture	Houston PMSA, TX	Y	18470 FQ	28460 AW	42130 TQ	TXBLS	10/01-12/01
Television, Video, and Motion Picture	Lubbock MSA, TX	Y	12720 FQ	18420 AW	25430 TQ	TXBLS	10/01-12/01
Television, Video, and Motion Picture	San Antonio MSA, TX	Y	14770 FQ	27440 AW	41860 TQ	TXBLS	10/01-12/01
Television, Video, and Motion Picture	Utah	Y	15360 FQ	25670 AW	46710 TQ	UTBLS	10/01-12/01
Television, Video, and Motion Picture	Salt Lake City-Ogden MSA, UT	Y	15410 FQ	25090 AW	43890 TQ	UTBLS	10/01-12/01
Television, Video, and Motion Picture	Virginia	Y	14640 FQ	31230 AW	57790 TQ	VABLS	10/01-12/01
Television, Video, and Motion Picture	Lynchburg MSA, VA	Y	12770 FQ	20670 AW	30830 TQ	VABLS	10/01-12/01

AAW Average annual wage **AOH** Average offered, high **ASH** Average starting, high **H** Hourly **M** Monthly **S** Special: hourly and annual
AE Average entry wage **AOL** Average offered, low **ASL** Average starting, low **HI** Highest wage paid **MTC** Median total compensation **TQ** Third quartile wage
AEX Average experienced wage **APH** Average pay, high range **AW** Average wage paid **HR** High end range **MW** Median wage paid **W** Weekly
AO Average offered **APL** Average pay, low range **FQ** First quartile wage **LR** Low end range **SQ** Second quartile wage **Y** Yearly

Occupation/Type/Industry	Location	Per	Low	Mid	High	Source	Date
Camera Operator							
Television, Video, and Motion Picture	Norfolk-Virginia Beach-Newport News MSA, VA-NC	Y	13830 FQ	33000 AW	64500 TQ	VABLS	10/01-12/01
Television, Video, and Motion Picture	Richmond-Petersburg MSA, VA	Y	15400 FQ	26770 AW	44920 TQ	VABLS	10/01-12/01
Television, Video, and Motion Picture	Washington	Y	16090 FQ	35600 AW	53320 TQ	WABLS	10/01-12/01
Television, Video, and Motion Picture	Seattle-Bellevue-Everett PMSA, WA	Y	23140 FQ	40320 AW	54880 TQ	WABLS	10/01-12/01
Television, Video, and Motion Picture	Spokane MSA, WA	Y	14380 FQ	22840 AW	42480 TQ	WABLS	10/01-12/01
Television, Video, and Motion Picture	West Virginia	Y	14700 FQ	21820 AW	33700 TQ	WVBLS	10/01-12/01
Television, Video, and Motion Picture	Wisconsin	Y	12580 FQ	30520 AW	57070 TQ	WIBLS	10/01-12/01
Television, Video, and Motion Picture	Green Bay MSA, WI	Y	13300 FQ	23320 AW	38620 TQ	WIBLS	10/01-12/01
Television, Video, and Motion Picture	Madison MSA, WI	Y	13930 FQ	38830 AW	58630 TQ	WIBLS	10/01-12/01
Television, Video, and Motion Picture	Milwaukee-Waukesha PMSA, WI	Y	16670 FQ	42560 AW	60550 TQ	WIBLS	10/01-12/01
Television, Video, and Motion Picture	Puerto Rico	Y	19110 FQ	24750 AW	37130 TQ	PRBLS	10/01-12/01
Captain							
Aviation Department, Corporations	United States	Y		64580 AW		AWST	2001-2001
Tugboat	Jacksonville, FL	Y		60000-65000 AEX		FLTU	2002
Captain, Mate, and Pilot							
Water Vessel	Alabama	H	13.18 FQ	26.61 AW	40.63 TQ	ALBLS	10/01-12/01
Water Vessel	Alaska	H	12.75 FQ	25.11 AW	37.78 TQ	AKBLS	10/01-12/01
Water Vessel	Arizona	H	6.06 FQ	15.65 AW	31.03 TQ	AZBLS	10/01-12/01
Water Vessel	Arkansas	H	11.12 FQ	19.09 AW	29.50 TQ	ARBLS	10/01-12/01
Water Vessel	California	H	11.60 FQ	24.65 AW	35.71 TQ	CABLS	10/01-12/01
Water Vessel	Connecticut	H	9.88 FQ	21.09 AW	33.52 TQ	CTBLS	10/01-12/01
Water Vessel	Delaware	H	14.75 FQ	26.02 AW	42.94 TQ	DEBLS	10/01-12/01
Water Vessel	Florida	H	7.21 FQ	18.88 AW	31.79 TQ	FLBLS	10/01-12/01
Water Vessel	Georgia	H	5.91 FQ	18.08 AW	27.71 TQ	GABLS	10/01-12/01
Water Vessel	Hawaii	H	13.52 FQ	20.27 AW	30.19 TQ	HIBLS	10/01-12/01
Water Vessel	Idaho	H	9.31 FQ	18.39 AW	32.77 TQ	IDBLS	10/01-12/01
Water Vessel	Illinois	H	17.57 FQ	26.66 AW	35.70 TQ	ILBLS	10/01-12/01
Water Vessel	Indiana	H	12.32 FQ	25.28 AW	36.01 TQ	INBLS	10/01-12/01
Water Vessel	Kentucky	H	13.06 FQ	32.75 AW		KYBLS	10/01-12/01
Water Vessel	Louisiana	H	12.86 FQ	23.64 AW	35.11 TQ	LABLS	10/01-12/01
Water Vessel	Maine	H	12.01 FQ	22.41 AW	39.95 TQ	MEBLS	10/01-12/01
Water Vessel	Maryland	H	7.78 FQ	19.47 AW	36.43 TQ	MDBLS	10/01-12/01
Water Vessel	Massachusetts	H	12.66 FQ	23.36 AW	38.49 TQ	MABLS	10/01-12/01
Water Vessel	Michigan	H	9.83 FQ	20.40 AW	34.46 TQ	MIBLS	10/01-12/01
Water Vessel	Minnesota	H	17.03 FQ	21.54 AW	27.37 TQ	MNBLS	10/01-12/01
Water Vessel	Mississippi	H	14.53 FQ	22.36 AW	33.78 TQ	MSBLS	10/01-12/01
Water Vessel	Missouri	H	14.61 FQ	23.13 AW	33.14 TQ	MOBLS	10/01-12/01
Water Vessel	Nevada	H	11.44 FQ	18.41 AW	27.19 TQ	NVBLS	10/01-12/01
Water Vessel	New Jersey	H	12.20 FQ	25.18 AW	41.19 TQ	NJBLS	10/01-12/01
Water Vessel	New York	H	15.14 FQ	25.87 AW	37.58 TQ	NYBLS	10/01-12/01
Water Vessel	North Carolina	H	11.22 FQ	17.05 AW	27.81 TQ	NCBLS	10/01-12/01
Water Vessel	Ohio	H	14.15 FQ	23.54 AW	40.68 TQ	OHBLS	10/01-12/01
Water Vessel	Oregon	H	15.65 FQ	25.95 AW	29.53 TQ	ORBLS	10/01-12/01
Water Vessel	Pennsylvania	H	14.29 FQ	24.80 AW	35.87 TQ	PABLS	10/01-12/01
Water Vessel	Rhode Island	H	8.95 FQ	17.94 AW	26.42 TQ	RIBLS	10/01-12/01
Water Vessel	South Carolina	H	9.02 FQ	19.11 AW	28.23 TQ	SCBLS	10/01-12/01
Water Vessel	Tennessee	H	10.71 FQ	23.59 AW	33.58 TQ	TNBLS	10/01-12/01
Water Vessel	Texas	H	14.62 FQ	22.77 AW	30.64 TQ	TXBLS	10/01-12/01
Water Vessel	Virginia	H	16.44 FQ	27.22 AW	45.10 TQ	VABLS	10/01-12/01
Water Vessel	Washington	H	17.99 FQ	28.78 AW	40.91 TQ	WABLS	10/01-12/01
Water Vessel	West Virginia	H	11.08 FQ	21.72 AW	32.73 TQ	WVBLS	10/01-12/01
Water Vessel	Wisconsin	H	10.33 FQ	21.56 AW	33.37 TQ	WIBLS	10/01-12/01
Water Vessel	Puerto Rico	H	11.53 FQ	16.29 AW	28.74 TQ	PRBLS	10/01-12/01
Water Vessel	Virgin Islands	H	11.87 FQ	16.71 AW	22.82 TQ	VIBLS	10/01-12/01
Water Vessel	Guam	H	6.36 FQ	17.44 AW	26.21 TQ	GUBLS	10/01-12/01
Card Dealer							
Casino	Buffalo, NY	Y	25000-35000 AE			BUFNEWS	7/30/02
Cardiologist	United States	Y		267000 AW		HHN	1/01-1/02
Cardiovascular Technologist and Technician	United States	Y		33350 MW		OOH4	1999-2000

AAW	Average annual wage	AOH	Average offered, high	ASH	Average starting, high	H	Hourly	M	Monthly	S	Special: hourly and annual
AE	Average entry wage	AOL	Average offered, low	ASL	Average starting, low	HI	Highest wage paid	MTC	Median total compensation	TQ	Third quartile wage
AEX	Average experienced wage	APH	Average pay, high range	AW	Average wage paid	HR	High end range	MW	Median wage paid	W	Weekly
AO	Average offered	APL	Average pay, low range	FQ	First quartile wage	LR	Low end range	SQ	Second quartile wage	Y	Yearly

Occupation/Type/Industry	Location	Per	Low	Mid	High	Source	Date
Cardiovascular Technologist and Technician	Alabama	Y	16580 FQ	36460 AW	70810 TQ	ALBLS	10/01-12/01
	Birmingham MSA, AL	Y	18910 FQ	44320 AW	79810 TQ	ALBLS	10/01-12/01
	Mobile MSA, AL	Y	14790 FQ	23030 AW	38070 TQ	ALBLS	10/01-12/01
	Montgomery MSA, AL	Y	17920 FQ	36060 AW	65140 TQ	ALBLS	10/01-12/01
	Alaska	Y	25900 FQ	43780 AW	59030 TQ	AKBLS	10/01-12/01
	Anchorage MSA, AK	Y	27480 FQ	46270 AW	59490 TQ	AKBLS	10/01-12/01
	Arizona	Y	20960 FQ	36320 AW	55510 TQ	AZBLS	10/01-12/01
	Phoenix-Mesa MSA, AZ	Y	21390 FQ	34440 AW	51240 TQ	AZBLS	10/01-12/01
	Tucson MSA, AZ	Y	20640 FQ	37680 AW	55180 TQ	AZBLS	10/01-12/01
	Arkansas	Y	19120 FQ	33980 AW	50190 TQ	ARBLS	10/01-12/01
	Fayetteville-Springdale-Rogers MSA, AR	Y	17640 FQ	32250 AW	49180 TQ	ARBLS	10/01-12/01
	Fort Smith MSA, AR-OK	Y	19380 FQ	32840 AW	50960 TQ	ARBLS	10/01-12/01
	California	Y	24800 FQ	40190 AW	58220 TQ	CABLS	10/01-12/01
	Bakersfield MSA, CA	Y	26940 FQ	40060 AW	57540 TQ	CABLS	10/01-12/01
	Chico-Paradise MSA, CA	Y	28830 FQ	43210 AW	55320 TQ	CABLS	10/01-12/01
	Fresno MSA, CA	Y	24240 FQ	36330 AW	52640 TQ	CABLS	10/01-12/01
	Los Angeles-Long Beach PMSA, CA	Y	25360 FQ	40030 AW	57270 TQ	CABLS	10/01-12/01
	Oakland PMSA, CA	Y	32220 FQ	44600 AW	62610 TQ	CABLS	10/01-12/01
	Orange County PMSA, CA	Y	25910 FQ	41420 AW	57400 TQ	CABLS	10/01-12/01
	Riverside-San Bernardino PMSA, CA	Y	23560 FQ	34040 AW	54480 TQ	CABLS	10/01-12/01
	Sacramento PMSA, CA	Y	25920 FQ	39900 AW	55580 TQ	CABLS	10/01-12/01
	San Diego MSA, CA	Y	25070 FQ	37530 AW	55420 TQ	CABLS	10/01-12/01
	San Francisco PMSA, CA	Y	30800 FQ	46870 AW	67710 TQ	CABLS	10/01-12/01
	San Jose PMSA, CA	Y	23340 FQ	35290 AW	54490 TQ	CABLS	10/01-12/01
	Santa Barbara-Santa Maria-Lompoc MSA, CA	Y	22540 FQ	37600 AW	67210 TQ	CABLS	10/01-12/01
	Stockton-Lodi MSA, CA	Y	23530 FQ	49750 AW	87590 TQ	CABLS	10/01-12/01
	Vallejo-Fairfield-Napa PMSA, CA	Y	26070 FQ	45030 AW	66650 TQ	CABLS	10/01-12/01
	Ventura PMSA, CA	Y	26190 FQ	42740 AW	62540 TQ	CABLS	10/01-12/01
	Colorado	Y	21370 FQ	35950 AW	53800 TQ	COBLS	10/01-12/01
	Boulder-Longmont PMSA, CO	Y	22360 FQ	36710 AW	55590 TQ	COBLS	10/01-12/01
	Denver PMSA, CO	Y	23260 FQ	38520 AW	55850 TQ	COBLS	10/01-12/01
	Connecticut	Y	29840 FQ	52680 AW	73140 TQ	CTBLS	10/01-12/01
	Bridgeport PMSA, CT	Y	35300 FQ	58010 AW	70030 TQ	CTBLS	10/01-12/01
	Hartford MSA, CT	Y	23690 FQ	38760 AW	57190 TQ	CTBLS	10/01-12/01
	New London-Norwich MSA, CT-RI	Y	25800 FQ	41680 AW	58410 TQ	CTBLS	10/01-12/01
	Stamford-Norwalk PMSA, CT	Y	57300 FQ	67940 AW	86540 TQ	CTBLS	10/01-12/01
	Delaware	Y	22570 FQ	39460 AW	54780 TQ	DEBLS	10/01-12/01
	Wilmington-Newark PMSA, DE-MD	Y	28440 FQ	40160 AW	55210 TQ	DEBLS	10/01-12/01
	District of Columbia	Y	24050 FQ	41080 AW	58150 TQ	DCBLS	10/01-12/01
	Washington PMSA, DC-MD-VA-WV	Y	25220 FQ	42830 AW	65250 TQ	DCBLS	10/01-12/01
	Florida	Y	18580 FQ	33220 AW	49430 TQ	FLBLS	10/01-12/01
	Daytona Beach MSA, FL	Y	17150 FQ	29880 AW	46520 TQ	FLBLS	10/01-12/01
	Fort Lauderdale PMSA, FL	Y	20530 FQ	33740 AW	48550 TQ	FLBLS	10/01-12/01
	Fort Pierce-Port St. Lucie MSA, FL	Y	19350 FQ	32360 AW	50400 TQ	FLBLS	10/01-12/01
	Jacksonville MSA, FL	Y	19320 FQ	34340 AW	53300 TQ	FLBLS	10/01-12/01
	Lakeland-Winter Haven MSA, FL	Y	19090 FQ	31920 AW	45930 TQ	FLBLS	10/01-12/01
	Melbourne-Titusville-Palm Bay MSA, FL	Y	17140 FQ	31980 AW	48790 TQ	FLBLS	10/01-12/01
	Miami PMSA, FL	Y	18260 FQ	30980 AW	46810 TQ	FLBLS	10/01-12/01
	Ocala MSA, FL	Y	18070 FQ	34480 AW	49550 TQ	FLBLS	10/01-12/01
	Orlando MSA, FL	Y	19310 FQ	32960 AW	49830 TQ	FLBLS	10/01-12/01
	Pensacola MSA, FL	Y	20090 FQ	35510 AW	46720 TQ	FLBLS	10/01-12/01
	Sarasota-Bradenton MSA, FL	Y	20420 FQ	38030 AW	54950 TQ	FLBLS	10/01-12/01
	Tampa-St. Petersburg-Clearwater MSA, FL	Y	17750 FQ	31760 AW	46450 TQ	FLBLS	10/01-12/01
	West Palm Beach-Boca Raton MSA, FL	Y	18350 FQ	31160 AW	46170 TQ	FLBLS	10/01-12/01
	Georgia	Y	14440 FQ	32160 AW	53380 TQ	GABLS	10/01-12/01
	Atlanta MSA, GA	Y	13660 FQ	30800 AW	53020 TQ	GABLS	10/01-12/01
	Columbus MSA, GA-AL	Y	17760 FQ	33800 AW	53850 TQ	GABLS	10/01-12/01
	Macon MSA, GA	Y	14050 FQ	34560 AW	56890 TQ	GABLS	10/01-12/01

AAW	Average annual wage	**AOH**	Average offered, high	**ASH**	Average starting, high	**H**	Hourly	**M**	Monthly	**S**	Special: hourly and annual
AE	Average entry wage	**AOL**	Average offered, low	**ASL**	Average starting, low	**HI**	Highest wage paid	**MTC**	Median total compensation	**TQ**	Third quartile wage
AEX	Average experienced wage	**APH**	Average pay, high range	**AW**	Average wage paid	**HR**	High end range	**MW**	Median wage paid	**W**	Weekly
AO	Average offered	**APL**	Average pay, low range	**FQ**	First quartile wage	**LR**	Low end range	**SQ**	Second quartile wage	**Y**	Yearly

Occupation/Type/Industry	Location	Per	Low	Mid	High	Source	Date
Cardiovascular Technologist and Technician	Hawaii	Y	25930 FQ	39650 AW	56030 TQ	HIBLS	10/01-12/01
	Honolulu MSA, HI	Y	26860 FQ	39180 AW	55620 TQ	HIBLS	10/01-12/01
	Idaho	Y	18490 FQ	33950 AW	50300 TQ	IDBLS	10/01-12/01
	Illinois	Y	21200 FQ	36220 AW	53460 TQ	ILBLS	10/01-12/01
	Chicago PMSA, IL	Y	21400 FQ	35930 AW	54350 TQ	ILBLS	10/01-12/01
	Rockford MSA, IL	Y	21830 FQ	39910 AW	54450 TQ	ILBLS	10/01-12/01
	Springfield MSA, IL	Y	21220 FQ	32920 AW	48200 TQ	ILBLS	10/01-12/01
	Indiana	Y	19700 FQ	30370 AW	45980 TQ	INBLS	10/01-12/01
	Evansville-Henderson MSA, IN-KY	Y	19860 FQ	29390 AW	42730 TQ	INBLS	10/01-12/01
	Fort Wayne MSA, IN	Y	20330 FQ	32180 AW	51780 TQ	INBLS	10/01-12/01
	Gary PMSA, IN	Y	19570 FQ	28800 AW	43760 TQ	INBLS	10/01-12/01
	Indianapolis MSA, IN	Y	19610 FQ	30650 AW	46880 TQ	INBLS	10/01-12/01
	South Bend MSA, IN	Y	20570 FQ	30060 AW	43700 TQ	INBLS	10/01-12/01
	Iowa	Y	20340 FQ	32300 AW	47460 TQ	IABLS	10/01-12/01
	Cedar Rapids MSA, IA	Y	22400 FQ	28830 AW	35680 TQ	IABLS	10/01-12/01
	Kansas	Y	20210 FQ	34850 AW	50700 TQ	KSBLS	10/01-12/01
	Wichita MSA, KS	Y	18440 FQ	33020 AW	50180 TQ	KSBLS	10/01-12/01
	Kentucky	Y	20180 FQ	34450 AW	48110 TQ	KYBLS	10/01-12/01
	Lexington MSA, KY	Y	20100 FQ	47740 AW	111660 TQ	KYBLS	10/01-12/01
	Louisville MSA, KY-IN	Y	20770 FQ	32290 AW	45220 TQ	KYBLS	10/01-12/01
	Louisiana	Y	15350 FQ	29420 AW	47450 TQ	LABLS	10/01-12/01
	Baton Rouge MSA, LA	Y	14580 FQ	24610 AW	48330 TQ	LABLS	10/01-12/01
	Houma MSA, LA	Y	14920 FQ	31750 AW	51750 TQ	LABLS	10/01-12/01
	Lafayette MSA, LA	Y	17280 FQ	31700 AW	46880 TQ	LABLS	10/01-12/01
	New Orleans MSA, LA	Y	16630 FQ	32980 AW	53380 TQ	LABLS	10/01-12/01
	Shreveport-Bossier City MSA, LA	Y	16120 FQ	24990 AW	32840 TQ	LABLS	10/01-12/01
	Maine	Y	21910 FQ	32140 AW	49760 TQ	MEBLS	10/01-12/01
	Portland MSA, ME	Y	24060 FQ	32050 AW	52120 TQ	MEBLS	10/01-12/01
	Maryland	Y	27960 FQ	40880 AW	54630 TQ	MDBLS	10/01-12/01
	Baltimore PMSA, MD	Y	29550 FQ	42550 AW	55030 TQ	MDBLS	10/01-12/01
	Massachusetts	Y	24460 FQ	43340 AW	62520 TQ	MABLS	10/01-12/01
	Boston PMSA, MA-NH	Y	25150 FQ	44940 AW	63560 TQ	MABLS	10/01-12/01
	Lawrence PMSA, MA-NH	Y	29290 FQ	44860 AW	58400 TQ	MABLS	10/01-12/01
	Lowell PMSA, MA-NH	Y	26820 FQ	46660 AW	57390 TQ	MABLS	10/01-12/01
	Worcester PMSA, MA-CT	Y	21730 FQ	37300 AW	57300 TQ	MABLS	10/01-12/01
	Michigan	Y	24610 FQ	38880 AW	54520 TQ	MIBLS	10/01-12/01
	Detroit PMSA, MI	Y	25370 FQ	40650 AW	55440 TQ	MIBLS	10/01-12/01
	Flint PMSA, MI	Y	25850 FQ	38550 AW	53100 TQ	MIBLS	10/01-12/01
	Grand Rapids-Muskegon-Holland MSA, MI	Y	24100 FQ	38520 AW	53530 TQ	MIBLS	10/01-12/01
	Kalamazoo-Battle Creek MSA, MI	Y	25400 FQ	37650 AW	48360 TQ	MIBLS	10/01-12/01
	Lansing-East Lansing MSA, MI	Y	27610 FQ	41870 AW	55780 TQ	MIBLS	10/01-12/01
	Saginaw-Bay City-Midland MSA, MI	Y	21300 FQ	32690 AW	44800 TQ	MIBLS	10/01-12/01
	Minneapolis-St. Paul MSA, MN-WI	Y	22400 FQ	37780 AW	54960 TQ	MNBLS	10/01-12/01
	Mississippi	Y	16030 FQ	28370 AW	43200 TQ	MSBLS	10/01-12/01
	Jackson MSA, MS	Y	16080 FQ	28020 AW	43530 TQ	MSBLS	10/01-12/01
	Missouri	Y	19700 FQ	32380 AW	48800 TQ	MOBLS	10/01-12/01
	Kansas City MSA, MO-KS	Y	20100 FQ	33790 AW	50800 TQ	MOBLS	10/01-12/01
	St. Louis MSA, MO-IL	Y	20190 FQ	33600 AW	49650 TQ	MOBLS	10/01-12/01
	Montana	Y	22950 FQ	40340 AW	56740 TQ	MTBLS	10/01-12/01
	Nebraska	Y	20090 FQ	35830 AW	53490 TQ	NEBLS	10/01-12/01
	Omaha MSA, NE-IA	Y	19440 FQ	32990 AW	50540 TQ	NEBLS	10/01-12/01
	Nevada	Y	22310 FQ	32560 AW	45400 TQ	NVBLS	10/01-12/01
	Las Vegas MSA, NV-AZ	Y	23150 FQ	32320 AW	45370 TQ	NVBLS	10/01-12/01
	Reno MSA, NV	Y	21390 FQ	32570 AW	44940 TQ	NVBLS	10/01-12/01
	New Hampshire	Y	24400 FQ	41880 AW	58110 TQ	NHBLS	10/01-12/01
	Portsmouth-Rochester PMSA, NH-ME	Y	22890 FQ	44120 AW	59690 TQ	NHBLS	10/01-12/01
	New Jersey	Y	23080 FQ	41450 AW	57930 TQ	NJBLS	10/01-12/01
	Atlantic-Cape May PMSA, NJ	Y	27450 FQ	56500 AW	86630 TQ	NJBLS	10/01-12/01
	Bergen-Passaic PMSA, NJ	Y	13690 FQ	36200 AW	58070 TQ	NJBLS	10/01-12/01
	Jersey City PMSA, NJ	Y	21660 FQ	34560 AW	51170 TQ	NJBLS	10/01-12/01
	Middlesex-Somerset-Hunterdon PMSA, NJ	Y	30660 FQ	47820 AW	56200 TQ	NJBLS	10/01-12/01
	Monmouth-Ocean PMSA, NJ	Y	23490 FQ	41340 AW	64420 TQ	NJBLS	10/01-12/01
	Newark PMSA, NJ	Y	22990 FQ	38880 AW	55870 TQ	NJBLS	10/01-12/01

AAW Average annual wage; **AE** Average entry wage; **AEX** Average experienced wage; **AO** Average offered; **AOH** Average offered, high; **AOL** Average offered, low; **APH** Average pay, high range; **APL** Average pay, low range; **ASH** Average starting, high; **ASL** Average starting, low; **AW** Average wage paid; **FQ** First quartile wage; **H** Hourly; **HI** Highest wage paid; **HR** High end range; **LR** Low end range; **M** Monthly; **MTC** Median total compensation; **MW** Median wage paid; **SQ** Second quartile wage; **S** Special: hourly and annual; **TQ** Third quartile wage; **W** Weekly; **Y** Yearly

Occupation/Type/Industry	Location	Per	Low	Mid	High	Source	Date
Cardiovascular Technologist and Technician	Trenton PMSA, NJ	Y	36540 FQ	57950 AW	103660 TQ	NJBLS	10/01-12/01
	New Mexico	Y	18950 FQ	33870 AW	50180 TQ	NMBLS	10/01-12/01
	Albuquerque MSA, NM	Y	22230 FQ	31540 AW	41780 TQ	NMBLS	10/01-12/01
	New York	Y	24180 FQ	41490 AW	65300 TQ	NYBLS	10/01-12/01
	Albany-Schenectady-Troy MSA, NY	Y	17780 FQ	33720 AW	52350 TQ	NYBLS	10/01-12/01
	Binghamton MSA, NY	Y	22640 FQ	39780 AW	52450 TQ	NYBLS	10/01-12/01
	Buffalo-Niagara Falls MSA, NY	Y	23410 FQ	34520 AW	51500 TQ	NYBLS	10/01-12/01
	Nassau-Suffolk PMSA, NY	Y	29200 FQ	44110 AW	63800 TQ	NYBLS	10/01-12/01
	New York PMSA, NY	Y	26820 FQ	44520 AW	69390 TQ	NYBLS	10/01-12/01
	Newburgh PMSA, NY-PA	Y	24330 FQ	46370 AW	102290 TQ	NYBLS	10/01-12/01
	Rochester MSA, NY	Y	20470 FQ	38650 AW	58590 TQ	NYBLS	10/01-12/01
	Syracuse MSA, NY	Y	27050 FQ	43560 AW	60570 TQ	NYBLS	10/01-12/01
	Utica-Rome MSA, NY	Y	19830 FQ	34850 AW	52130 TQ	NYBLS	10/01-12/01
	North Carolina	Y	21050 FQ	36080 AW	52980 TQ	NCBLS	10/01-12/01
	Charlotte-Gastonia-Rock Hill MSA, NC-SC	Y	27800 FQ	42700 AW	56210 TQ	NCBLS	10/01-12/01
	Greensboro-Winston-Salem-High Point MSA, NC	Y	19980 FQ	33200 AW	46520 TQ	NCBLS	10/01-12/01
	Raleigh-Durham-Chapel Hill MSA, NC	Y	21260 FQ	35500 AW	51730 TQ	NCBLS	10/01-12/01
	North Dakota	Y	16780 FQ	28920 AW	44920 TQ	NDBLS	10/01-12/01
	Ohio	Y	22320 FQ	36090 AW	49650 TQ	OHBLS	10/01-12/01
	Akron PMSA, OH	Y	22150 FQ	37270 AW	53150 TQ	OHBLS	10/01-12/01
	Cincinnati PMSA, OH-KY-IN	Y	23200 FQ	36760 AW	51210 TQ	OHBLS	10/01-12/01
	Cleveland-Lorain-Elyria PMSA, OH	Y	25280 FQ	37780 AW	49750 TQ	OHBLS	10/01-12/01
	Columbus MSA, OH	Y	22880 FQ	41340 AW	67630 TQ	OHBLS	10/01-12/01
	Dayton-Springfield MSA, OH	Y	18630 FQ	30410 AW	44130 TQ	OHBLS	10/01-12/01
	Toledo MSA, OH	Y	26350 FQ	37630 AW	47790 TQ	OHBLS	10/01-12/01
	Youngstown-Warren MSA, OH	Y	22940 FQ	33920 AW	47110 TQ	OHBLS	10/01-12/01
	Oklahoma	Y	16830 FQ	26570 AW	44430 TQ	OKBLS	10/01-12/01
	Oklahoma City MSA, OK	Y	17130 FQ	29200 AW	50790 TQ	OKBLS	10/01-12/01
	Tulsa MSA, OK	Y	18010 FQ	24870 AW	39480 TQ	OKBLS	10/01-12/01
	Oregon	Y	21490 FQ	36980 AW	55350 TQ	ORBLS	10/01-12/01
	Portland-Vancouver PMSA, OR-WA	Y	23560 FQ	43870 AW	66530 TQ	ORBLS	10/01-12/01
	Salem PMSA, OR	Y	24700 FQ	35190 AW	55940 TQ	ORBLS	10/01-12/01
	Pennsylvania	Y	19550 FQ	32220 AW	48590 TQ	PABLS	10/01-12/01
	Allentown-Bethlehem-Easton MSA, PA	Y	11250 FQ	19010 AW	34680 TQ	PABLS	10/01-12/01
	Erie MSA, PA	Y	22120 FQ	35660 AW	51270 TQ	PABLS	10/01-12/01
	Harrisburg-Lebanon-Carlisle MSA, PA	Y	18600 FQ	26750 AW	44170 TQ	PABLS	10/01-12/01
	Johnstown MSA, PA	Y	21470 FQ	31700 AW	46510 TQ	PABLS	10/01-12/01
	Philadelphia PMSA, PA-NJ	Y	22060 FQ	35000 AW	52620 TQ	PABLS	10/01-12/01
	Pittsburgh MSA, PA	Y	21610 FQ	32040 AW	45530 TQ	PABLS	10/01-12/01
	Reading MSA, PA	Y	20410 FQ	39310 AW	56790 TQ	PABLS	10/01-12/01
	Scranton-Wilkes-Barre-Hazleton MSA, PA	Y	23720 FQ	35550 AW	47770 TQ	PABLS	10/01-12/01
	Rhode Island	Y	21970 FQ	38340 AW	57290 TQ	RIBLS	10/01-12/01
	Providence-Fall River-Warwick MSA, RI-MA	Y	22180 FQ	39570 AW	61120 TQ	RIBLS	10/01-12/01
	South Carolina	Y	18960 FQ	40370 AW	74550 TQ	SCBLS	10/01-12/01
	Charleston-North Charleston MSA, SC	Y	20850 FQ	42300 AW	69930 TQ	SCBLS	10/01-12/01
	Columbia MSA, SC	Y	20450 FQ	49940 AW	87010 TQ	SCBLS	10/01-12/01
	Greenville-Spartanburg-Anderson MSA, SC	Y	18720 FQ	40070 AW	78150 TQ	SCBLS	10/01-12/01
	South Dakota	Y	21110 FQ	33940 AW	51660 TQ	SDBLS	10/01-12/01
	Tennessee	Y	16810 FQ	30170 AW	47230 TQ	TNBLS	10/01-12/01
	Clarksville-Hopkinsville MSA, TN-KY	Y	22380 FQ	33780 AW	43600 TQ	TNBLS	10/01-12/01
	Johnson City-Kingsport-Bristol MSA, TN-VA	Y	15620 FQ	27870 AW	45770 TQ	TNBLS	10/01-12/01
	Knoxville MSA, TN	Y	16320 FQ	27850 AW	43950 TQ	TNBLS	10/01-12/01
	Memphis MSA, TN-AR-MS	Y	18880 FQ	31870 AW	49320 TQ	TNBLS	10/01-12/01
	Nashville MSA, TN	Y	17160 FQ	30380 AW	48780 TQ	TNBLS	10/01-12/01
	Texas	Y	18280 FQ	32110 AW	48370 TQ	TXBLS	10/01-12/01
	Austin-San Marcos MSA, TX	Y	22430 FQ	34780 AW	46380 TQ	TXBLS	10/01-12/01

AAW Average annual wage; **AE** Average entry wage; **AEX** Average experienced wage; **AO** Average offered; **AOH** Average offered, high; **AOL** Average offered, low; **APH** Average pay, high range; **APL** Average pay, low range; **ASH** Average starting, high; **ASL** Average starting, low; **AW** Average wage paid; **FQ** First quartile wage; **H** Hourly; **HI** Highest wage paid; **HR** High end range; **LR** Low end range; **M** Monthly; **MTC** Median total compensation; **MW** Median wage paid; **SQ** Second quartile wage; **S** Special: hourly and annual; **TQ** Third quartile wage; **W** Weekly; **Y** Yearly

Occupation/Type/Industry	Location	Per	Low	Mid	High	Source	Date
Cardiovascular Technologist and Technician	Corpus Christi MSA, TX	Y	16580 FQ	28760 AW	44560 TQ	TXBLS	10/01-12/01
	Dallas PMSA, TX	Y	18360 FQ	30890 AW	46070 TQ	TXBLS	10/01-12/01
	Fort Worth-Arlington PMSA, TX	Y	18090 FQ	33250 AW	51100 TQ	TXBLS	10/01-12/01
	Houston PMSA, TX	Y	19600 FQ	33510 AW	47840 TQ	TXBLS	10/01-12/01
	McAllen-Edinburg-Mission MSA, TX	Y	17590 FQ	35480 AW	55290 TQ	TXBLS	10/01-12/01
	San Antonio MSA, TX	Y	17970 FQ	31850 AW	47590 TQ	TXBLS	10/01-12/01
	Tyler MSA, TX	Y	16510 FQ	30150 AW	48210 TQ	TXBLS	10/01-12/01
	Utah	Y	21980 FQ	38110 AW	54710 TQ	UTBLS	10/01-12/01
	Salt Lake City-Ogden MSA, UT	Y	22620 FQ	38280 AW	54860 TQ	UTBLS	10/01-12/01
	Vermont	Y	20550 FQ	34180 AW	47900 TQ	VTBLS	10/01-12/01
	Virginia	Y	21610 FQ	39170 AW	63380 TQ	VABLS	10/01-12/01
	Norfolk-Virginia Beach-Newport News MSA, VA-NC	Y	22270 FQ	37230 AW	49380 TQ	VABLS	10/01-12/01
	Richmond-Petersburg MSA, VA	Y	20530 FQ	34880 AW	52420 TQ	VABLS	10/01-12/01
	Washington	Y	29320 FQ	44630 AW	64900 TQ	WABLS	10/01-12/01
	Olympia PMSA, WA	Y	20770 FQ	35020 AW	49560 TQ	WABLS	10/01-12/01
	Seattle-Bellevue-Everett PMSA, WA	Y	29210 FQ	46830 AW	65310 TQ	WABLS	10/01-12/01
	Spokane MSA, WA	Y	26940 FQ	41040 AW	56080 TQ	WABLS	10/01-12/01
	Tacoma PMSA, WA	Y	30970 FQ	40510 AW	53270 TQ	WABLS	10/01-12/01
	West Virginia	Y	18270 FQ	33610 AW	51210 TQ	WVBLS	10/01-12/01
	Charleston MSA, WV	Y	15330 FQ	26580 AW	47830 TQ	WVBLS	10/01-12/01
	Huntington-Ashland MSA, WV-KY-OH	Y	21390 FQ	31840 AW	48270 TQ	WVBLS	10/01-12/01
	Wisconsin	Y	21140 FQ	34790 AW	53160 TQ	WIBLS	10/01-12/01
	Appleton-Oshkosh-Neenah MSA, WI	Y	21150 FQ	38470 AW	55740 TQ	WIBLS	10/01-12/01
	Madison MSA, WI	Y	20980 FQ	36990 AW	56570 TQ	WIBLS	10/01-12/01
	Milwaukee-Waukesha PMSA, WI	Y	23260 FQ	34200 AW	50640 TQ	WIBLS	10/01-12/01
	Puerto Rico	Y	13330 FQ	19180 AW	27730 TQ	PRBLS	10/01-12/01
Hospitals	United States	Y		32860 MW		OOH4	1999-2000
Medical Offices and Clinics	United States	Y		33100 MW		OOH4	1999-2000
Cargo and Freight Agent	Alabama	H	7.32 FQ	12.67 AW	19.05 TQ	ALBLS	10/01-12/01
	Birmingham MSA, AL	H	9.00 FQ	12.81 AW	16.90 TQ	ALBLS	10/01-12/01
	Mobile MSA, AL	H	6.88 FQ	10.56 AW	16.45 TQ	ALBLS	10/01-12/01
	Alaska	H	6.47 FQ	12.27 AW	18.99 TQ	AKBLS	10/01-12/01
	Anchorage MSA, AK	H	9.00 FQ	13.70 AW	22.24 TQ	AKBLS	10/01-12/01
	Arizona	H	10.73 FQ	17.66 AW	22.93 TQ	AZBLS	10/01-12/01
	Phoenix-Mesa MSA, AZ	H	11.34 FQ	17.53 AW	22.74 TQ	AZBLS	10/01-12/01
	Tucson MSA, AZ	H	6.28 FQ	13.10 AW	21.04 TQ	AZBLS	10/01-12/01
	Arkansas	H	10.13 FQ	16.54 AW	27.11 TQ	ARBLS	10/01-12/01
	Fayetteville-Springdale-Rogers MSA, AR	H	11.32 FQ	15.83 AW	26.62 TQ	ARBLS	10/01-12/01
	Fort Smith MSA, AR-OK	H	8.75 FQ	15.49 AW	36.50 TQ	ARBLS	10/01-12/01
	Little Rock-North Little Rock MSA, AR	H	12.88 FQ	18.56 AW	23.38 TQ	ARBLS	10/01-12/01
	California	H	9.54 FQ	17.06 AW	26.62 TQ	CABLS	10/01-12/01
	Bakersfield MSA, CA	H	7.31 FQ	9.03 AW	10.84 TQ	CABLS	10/01-12/01
	Fresno MSA, CA	H	7.38 FQ	12.27 AW	20.53 TQ	CABLS	10/01-12/01
	Los Angeles-Long Beach PMSA, CA	H	10.54 FQ	18.18 AW	28.38 TQ	CABLS	10/01-12/01
	Oakland PMSA, CA	H	10.61 FQ	17.38 AW	30.60 TQ	CABLS	10/01-12/01
	Orange County PMSA, CA	H	10.69 FQ	15.79 AW	22.35 TQ	CABLS	10/01-12/01
	Riverside-San Bernardino PMSA, CA	H	9.83 FQ	15.04 AW	21.00 TQ	CABLS	10/01-12/01
	Sacramento PMSA, CA	H	7.96 FQ	13.37 AW	19.48 TQ	CABLS	10/01-12/01
	Salinas MSA, CA	H	8.32 FQ	17.52 AW	31.43 TQ	CABLS	10/01-12/01
	San Diego MSA, CA	H	8.58 FQ	14.43 AW	21.43 TQ	CABLS	10/01-12/01
	San Francisco PMSA, CA	H	11.29 FQ	17.91 AW	26.14 TQ	CABLS	10/01-12/01
	San Jose PMSA, CA	H	10.45 FQ	16.61 AW	22.30 TQ	CABLS	10/01-12/01
	Stockton-Lodi MSA, CA	H	11.28 FQ	20.19 AW	31.22 TQ	CABLS	10/01-12/01
	Ventura PMSA, CA	H	10.64 FQ	18.65 AW	26.14 TQ	CABLS	10/01-12/01
	Colorado	H	9.00 FQ	14.91 AW	20.86 TQ	COBLS	10/01-12/01
	Boulder-Longmont PMSA, CO	H	8.16 FQ	12.19 AW	17.38 TQ	COBLS	10/01-12/01

AAW	Average annual wage	AOH	Average offered, high	ASH	Average starting, high	H	Hourly	M	Monthly	S	Special: hourly and annual
AE	Average entry wage	AOL	Average offered, low	ASL	Average starting, low	HI	Highest wage paid	MTC	Median total compensation	TQ	Third quartile wage
AEX	Average experienced wage	APH	Average pay, high range	AW	Average wage paid	HR	High end range	MW	Median wage paid	W	Weekly
AO	Average offered	APL	Average pay, low range	FQ	First quartile wage	LR	Low end range	SQ	Second quartile wage	Y	Yearly

Occupation/Type/Industry	Location	Per	Low	Mid	High	Source	Date
Cargo and Freight Agent	Colorado Springs MSA, CO	H	8.81 FQ	13.66 AW	18.74 TQ	COBLS	10/01-12/01
	Denver PMSA, CO	H	11.18 FQ	15.81 AW	21.19 TQ	COBLS	10/01-12/01
	Connecticut	H	8.93 FQ	20.54 AW	52.60 TQ	CTBLS	10/01-12/01
	Hartford MSA, CT	H	8.66 FQ	13.78 AW	21.51 TQ	CTBLS	10/01-12/01
	New Haven-Meriden PMSA, CT	H	9.46 FQ	23.59 AW	52.46 TQ	CTBLS	10/01-12/01
	New London-Norwich MSA, CT-RI	H	8.64 FQ	15.12 AW	19.41 TQ	CTBLS	10/01-12/01
	Stamford-Norwalk PMSA, CT	H	10.69 FQ	31.06 AW	66.58 TQ	CTBLS	10/01-12/01
	Delaware	H	7.02 FQ	14.32 AW	21.96 TQ	DEBLS	10/01-12/01
	Wilmington-Newark PMSA, DE-MD	H	9.36 FQ	15.56 AW	22.50 TQ	DEBLS	10/01-12/01
	Washington PMSA, DC-MD-VA-WV	H	9.67 FQ	17.13 AW	27.16 TQ	DCBLS	10/01-12/01
	Florida	H	8.87 FQ	14.29 AW	21.07 TQ	FLBLS	10/01-12/01
	Fort Lauderdale PMSA, FL	H	10.58 FQ	19.84 AW	33.75 TQ	FLBLS	10/01-12/01
	Fort Myers-Cape Coral MSA, FL	H	9.46 FQ	14.84 AW	21.38 TQ	FLBLS	10/01-12/01
	Gainesville MSA, FL	H	9.06 FQ	14.98 AW	17.57 TQ	FLBLS	10/01-12/01
	Jacksonville MSA, FL	H	9.76 FQ	15.55 AW	24.54 TQ	FLBLS	10/01-12/01
	Lakeland-Winter Haven MSA, FL	H	6.03 FQ	15.89 AW	33.43 TQ	FLBLS	10/01-12/01
	Melbourne-Titusville-Palm Bay MSA, FL	H	11.04 FQ	14.83 AW	21.09 TQ	FLBLS	10/01-12/01
	Miami PMSA, FL	H	9.26 FQ	13.07 AW	17.19 TQ	FLBLS	10/01-12/01
	Orlando MSA, FL	H	8.17 FQ	14.76 AW	21.10 TQ	FLBLS	10/01-12/01
	Tampa-St. Petersburg-Clearwater MSA, FL	H	7.90 FQ	13.94 AW	21.25 TQ	FLBLS	10/01-12/01
	West Palm Beach-Boca Raton MSA, FL	H	10.19 FQ	15.64 AW	21.84 TQ	FLBLS	10/01-12/01
	Georgia	H	10.81 FQ	17.12 AW	23.00 TQ	GABLS	10/01-12/01
	Atlanta MSA, GA	H	11.56 FQ	17.72 AW	23.48 TQ	GABLS	10/01-12/01
	Savannah MSA, GA	H	9.59 FQ	14.80 AW	21.28 TQ	GABLS	10/01-12/01
	Hawaii	H	7.98 FQ	13.34 AW	20.71 TQ	HIBLS	10/01-12/01
	Honolulu MSA, HI	H	7.98 FQ	13.16 AW	20.16 TQ	HIBLS	10/01-12/01
	Idaho	H	7.32 FQ	12.78 AW	19.86 TQ	IDBLS	10/01-12/01
	Boise City MSA, ID	H	7.75 FQ	11.98 AW	18.98 TQ	IDBLS	10/01-12/01
	Illinois	H	7.67 FQ	15.59 AW	23.01 TQ	ILBLS	10/01-12/01
	Chicago PMSA, IL	H	8.21 FQ	16.37 AW	23.47 TQ	ILBLS	10/01-12/01
	Rockford MSA, IL	H	7.34 FQ	14.17 AW	19.24 TQ	ILBLS	10/01-12/01
	Indiana	H	8.54 FQ	14.93 AW	24.61 TQ	INBLS	10/01-12/01
	Fort Wayne MSA, IN	H	9.13 FQ	15.44 AW	24.58 TQ	INBLS	10/01-12/01
	Gary PMSA, IN	H	7.22 FQ	13.71 AW	20.94 TQ	INBLS	10/01-12/01
	Indianapolis MSA, IN	H	8.68 FQ	13.64 AW	21.15 TQ	INBLS	10/01-12/01
	South Bend MSA, IN	H	12.01 FQ	18.61 AW	26.09 TQ	INBLS	10/01-12/01
	Iowa	H	6.71 FQ	13.21 AW	20.78 TQ	IABLS	10/01-12/01
	Cedar Rapids MSA, IA	H	7.75 FQ	13.29 AW	19.52 TQ	IABLS	10/01-12/01
	Des Moines MSA, IA	H	6.93 FQ	16.45 AW	22.30 TQ	IABLS	10/01-12/01
	Kansas	H	10.88 FQ	16.63 AW	22.47 TQ	KSBLS	10/01-12/01
	Wichita MSA, KS	H	11.20 FQ	14.69 AW	21.09 TQ	KSBLS	10/01-12/01
	Kentucky	H	9.41 FQ	14.74 AW	21.56 TQ	KYBLS	10/01-12/01
	Lexington MSA, KY	H	8.53 FQ	11.88 AW	15.19 TQ	KYBLS	10/01-12/01
	Louisville MSA, KY-IN	H	9.22 FQ	13.90 AW	20.73 TQ	KYBLS	10/01-12/01
	Louisiana	H	8.23 FQ	14.65 AW	21.11 TQ	LABLS	10/01-12/01
	Houma MSA, LA	H	6.99 FQ	12.54 AW	16.83 TQ	LABLS	10/01-12/01
	Lafayette MSA, LA	H	5.90 FQ	10.95 AW	13.94 TQ	LABLS	10/01-12/01
	New Orleans MSA, LA	H	11.74 FQ	16.14 AW	21.92 TQ	LABLS	10/01-12/01
	Maine	H	7.49 FQ	13.99 AW	21.61 TQ	MEBLS	10/01-12/01
	Portland MSA, ME	H	7.75 FQ	12.31 AW	20.86 TQ	MEBLS	10/01-12/01
	Maryland	H	8.80 FQ	17.62 AW	28.07 TQ	MDBLS	10/01-12/01
	Baltimore PMSA, MD	H	7.43 FQ	14.12 AW	21.45 TQ	MDBLS	10/01-12/01
	Massachusetts	H	10.45 FQ	18.76 AW	26.95 TQ	MABLS	10/01-12/01
	Boston PMSA, MA-NH	H	10.84 FQ	19.10 AW	27.11 TQ	MABLS	10/01-12/01
	Michigan	H	9.13 FQ	16.20 AW	22.37 TQ	MIBLS	10/01-12/01
	Detroit PMSA, MI	H	9.71 FQ	17.28 AW	26.24 TQ	MIBLS	10/01-12/01
	Flint PMSA, MI	H	12.04 FQ	16.30 AW	20.53 TQ	MIBLS	10/01-12/01
	Grand Rapids-Muskegon-Holland MSA, MI	H	9.61 FQ	15.11 AW	20.95 TQ	MIBLS	10/01-12/01
	Kalamazoo-Battle Creek MSA, MI	H	6.18 FQ	13.42 AW	21.17 TQ	MIBLS	10/01-12/01
	Saginaw-Bay City-Midland MSA, MI	H	7.19 FQ	13.52 AW	17.66 TQ	MIBLS	10/01-12/01

AAW	Average annual wage	**AOH**	Average offered, high	**ASH**	Average starting, high	**H**	Hourly	**M**	Monthly	**S**	Special: hourly and annual
AE	Average entry wage	**AOL**	Average offered, low	**ASL**	Average starting, low	**HI**	Highest wage paid	**MTC**	Median total compensation	**TQ**	Third quartile wage
AEX	Average experienced wage	**APH**	Average pay, high range	**AW**	Average wage paid	**HR**	High end range	**MW**	Median wage paid	**W**	Weekly
AO	Average offered	**APL**	Average pay, low range	**FQ**	First quartile wage	**LR**	Low end range	**SQ**	Second quartile wage	**Y**	Yearly

Occupation/Type/Industry	Location	Per	Low	Mid	High	Source	Date
Cargo and Freight Agent	Minnesota	H	10.90 FQ	16.54 AW	24.90 TQ	MNBLS	10/01-12/01
	Minneapolis-St. Paul MSA, MN-WI	H	11.60 FQ	16.71 AW	24.22 TQ	MNBLS	10/01-12/01
	Mississippi	H	6.72 FQ	12.04 AW	17.27 TQ	MSBLS	10/01-12/01
	Biloxi-Gulfport-Pascagoula MSA, MS	H	7.09 FQ	11.16 AW	14.41 TQ	MSBLS	10/01-12/01
	Jackson MSA, MS	H	8.59 FQ	13.83 AW	24.70 TQ	MSBLS	10/01-12/01
	Missouri	H	8.17 FQ	15.40 AW	27.53 TQ	MOBLS	10/01-12/01
	Kansas City MSA, MO-KS	H	8.59 FQ	14.30 AW	21.14 TQ	MOBLS	10/01-12/01
	St. Louis MSA, MO-IL	H	9.14 FQ	17.58 AW	30.79 TQ	MOBLS	10/01-12/01
	Springfield MSA, MO	H	7.81 FQ	10.45 AW	13.81 TQ	MOBLS	10/01-12/01
	Montana	H	10.95 FQ	14.75 AW	20.45 TQ	MTBLS	10/01-12/01
	Nebraska	H	9.36 FQ	15.48 AW	23.38 TQ	NEBLS	10/01-12/01
	Omaha MSA, NE-IA	H	9.27 FQ	16.13 AW	27.02 TQ	NEBLS	10/01-12/01
	Nevada	H	14.82 FQ	16.72 AW	20.12 TQ	NVBLS	10/01-12/01
	Las Vegas MSA, NV-AZ	H	7.20 FQ	13.96 AW	23.20 TQ	NVBLS	10/01-12/01
	Reno MSA, NV	H	15.02 FQ	16.97 AW	19.92 TQ	NVBLS	10/01-12/01
	New Hampshire	H	9.26 FQ	18.11 AW	28.02 TQ	NHBLS	10/01-12/01
	Manchester PMSA, NH	H	10.30 FQ	16.84 AW	21.85 TQ	NHBLS	10/01-12/01
	Portsmouth-Rochester PMSA, NH-ME	H	13.64 FQ	18.42 AW	22.03 TQ	NHBLS	10/01-12/01
	New Jersey	H	9.90 FQ	18.00 AW	26.88 TQ	NJBLS	10/01-12/01
	Bergen-Passaic PMSA, NJ	H	10.60 FQ	16.33 AW	20.95 TQ	NJBLS	10/01-12/01
	Jersey City PMSA, NJ	H	12.78 FQ	21.05 AW	32.11 TQ	NJBLS	10/01-12/01
	Middlesex-Somerset-Hunterdon PMSA, NJ	H	12.55 FQ	20.18 AW	27.33 TQ	NJBLS	10/01-12/01
	Monmouth-Ocean PMSA, NJ	H	12.54 FQ	22.16 AW	27.89 TQ	NJBLS	10/01-12/01
	Newark PMSA, NJ	H	9.23 FQ	15.25 AW	23.00 TQ	NJBLS	10/01-12/01
	Trenton PMSA, NJ	H	7.92 FQ	18.82 AW	28.35 TQ	NJBLS	10/01-12/01
	New Mexico	H	9.89 FQ	13.78 AW	20.03 TQ	NMBLS	10/01-12/01
	Albuquerque MSA, NM	H	9.71 FQ	12.76 AW	18.58 TQ	NMBLS	10/01-12/01
	New York	H	8.88 FQ	15.19 AW	23.02 TQ	NYBLS	10/01-12/01
	Albany-Schenectady-Troy MSA, NY	H	9.12 FQ	14.59 AW	20.62 TQ	NYBLS	10/01-12/01
	Buffalo-Niagara Falls MSA, NY	H	8.88 FQ	14.80 AW	21.32 TQ	NYBLS	10/01-12/01
	Nassau-Suffolk PMSA, NY	H	11.25 FQ	17.78 AW	25.29 TQ	NYBLS	10/01-12/01
	New York PMSA, NY	H	8.77 FQ	14.91 AW	23.07 TQ	NYBLS	10/01-12/01
	Newburgh PMSA, NY-PA	H	9.57 FQ	16.48 AW	24.56 TQ	NYBLS	10/01-12/01
	Rochester MSA, NY	H	9.01 FQ	13.74 AW	20.01 TQ	NYBLS	10/01-12/01
	Syracuse MSA, NY	H	8.51 FQ	14.09 AW	20.47 TQ	NYBLS	10/01-12/01
	North Carolina	H	9.91 FQ	17.05 AW	25.66 TQ	NCBLS	10/01-12/01
	Charlotte-Gastonia-Rock Hill MSA, NC-SC	H	10.50 FQ	16.91 AW	25.58 TQ	NCBLS	10/01-12/01
	Greensboro-Winston-Salem-High Point MSA, NC	H	9.43 FQ	17.47 AW	25.86 TQ	NCBLS	10/01-12/01
	Raleigh-Durham-Chapel Hill MSA, NC	H	10.10 FQ	14.31 AW	19.00 TQ	NCBLS	10/01-12/01
	North Dakota	H	7.04 FQ	14.63 AW	20.86 TQ	NDBLS	10/01-12/01
	Fargo-Moorhead MSA, ND-MN	H	6.91 FQ	14.95 AW	21.13 TQ	NDBLS	10/01-12/01
	Ohio	H	8.04 FQ	14.50 AW	21.65 TQ	OHBLS	10/01-12/01
	Akron PMSA, OH	H	6.11 FQ	9.83 AW	14.26 TQ	OHBLS	10/01-12/01
	Cincinnati PMSA, OH-KY-IN	H	10.33 FQ	16.95 AW	26.06 TQ	OHBLS	10/01-12/01
	Cleveland-Lorain-Elyria PMSA, OH	H	9.12 FQ	13.05 AW	19.78 TQ	OHBLS	10/01-12/01
	Columbus MSA, OH	H	9.56 FQ	14.44 AW	20.63 TQ	OHBLS	10/01-12/01
	Dayton-Springfield MSA, OH	H	9.43 FQ	18.18 AW	26.98 TQ	OHBLS	10/01-12/01
	Youngstown-Warren MSA, OH	H	10.56 FQ	15.46 AW	20.88 TQ	OHBLS	10/01-12/01
	Oklahoma	H	7.51 FQ	12.58 AW	20.11 TQ	OKBLS	10/01-12/01
	Oklahoma City MSA, OK	H	7.31 FQ	14.73 AW	24.06 TQ	OKBLS	10/01-12/01
	Tulsa MSA, OK	H	7.84 FQ	12.61 AW	20.11 TQ	OKBLS	10/01-12/01
	Oregon	H	7.74 FQ	15.20 AW	26.14 TQ	ORBLS	10/01-12/01
	Eugene-Springfield MSA, OR	H	8.64 FQ	15.56 AW	20.15 TQ	ORBLS	10/01-12/01
	Medford-Ashland MSA, OR	H	7.92 FQ	14.96 AW	24.64 TQ	ORBLS	10/01-12/01
	Portland-Vancouver PMSA, OR-WA	H	7.72 FQ	15.35 AW	26.40 TQ	ORBLS	10/01-12/01
	Pennsylvania	H	8.31 FQ	12.73 AW	20.63 TQ	PABLS	10/01-12/01
	Harrisburg-Lebanon-Carlisle MSA, PA	H	10.92 FQ	15.12 AW	21.00 TQ	PABLS	10/01-12/01
	Philadelphia PMSA, PA-NJ	H	8.56 FQ	12.90 AW	21.45 TQ	PABLS	10/01-12/01
	Pittsburgh MSA, PA	H	8.24 FQ	14.46 AW	22.08 TQ	PABLS	10/01-12/01

AAW	Average annual wage	**AOH**	Average offered, high	**ASH**	Average starting, high	**H**	Hourly	**M**	Monthly	**S**	Special: hourly and annual
AE	Average entry wage	**AOL**	Average offered, low	**ASL**	Average starting, low	**HI**	Highest wage paid	**MTC**	Median total compensation	**TQ**	Third quartile wage
AEX	Average experienced wage	**APH**	Average pay, high range	**AW**	Average wage paid	**HR**	High end range	**MW**	Median wage paid	**W**	Weekly
AO	Average offered	**APL**	Average pay, low range	**FQ**	First quartile wage	**LR**	Low end range	**SQ**	Second quartile wage	**Y**	Yearly

Occupation/Type/Industry	Location	Per	Low	Mid	High	Source	Date
Cargo and Freight Agent	Reading MSA, PA	H	8.67 FQ	13.90 AW	20.76 TQ	PABLS	10/01-12/01
	Rhode Island	H	8.92 FQ	16.93 AW	29.06 TQ	RIBLS	10/01-12/01
	Providence-Fall River-Warwick MSA, RI-MA	H	8.92 FQ	15.63 AW	24.41 TQ	RIBLS	10/01-12/01
	South Carolina	H	5.72 FQ	9.06 AW	15.46 TQ	SCBLS	10/01-12/01
	Charleston-North Charleston MSA, SC	H	7.48 FQ	13.33 AW	19.68 TQ	SCBLS	10/01-12/01
	South Dakota	H	11.68 FQ	19.55 AW	25.76 TQ	SDBLS	10/01-12/01
	Sioux Falls MSA, SD	H	14.30 FQ	20.38 AW	26.01 TQ	SDBLS	10/01-12/01
	Nashville MSA, TN	H	9.36 FQ	14.02 AW	20.03 TQ	TNBLS	10/01-12/01
	Texas	H	8.40 FQ	14.07 AW	20.98 TQ	TXBLS	10/01-12/01
	Brownsville-Harlingen-San Benito MSA, TX	H	5.82 FQ	8.61 AW	13.39 TQ	TXBLS	10/01-12/01
	Dallas PMSA, TX	H	9.89 FQ	15.09 AW	21.22 TQ	TXBLS	10/01-12/01
	El Paso MSA, TX	H	6.51 FQ	10.57 AW	16.11 TQ	TXBLS	10/01-12/01
	Fort Worth-Arlington PMSA, TX	H	11.58 FQ	18.32 AW	22.70 TQ	TXBLS	10/01-12/01
	Houston PMSA, TX	H	8.92 FQ	14.01 AW	20.12 TQ	TXBLS	10/01-12/01
	Killeen-Temple MSA, TX	H	8.46 FQ	13.36 AW	20.36 TQ	TXBLS	10/01-12/01
	Laredo MSA, TX	H	7.52 FQ	11.09 AW	17.74 TQ	TXBLS	10/01-12/01
	Lubbock MSA, TX	H	10.14 FQ	14.35 AW	19.44 TQ	TXBLS	10/01-12/01
	McAllen-Edinburg-Mission MSA, TX	H	8.84 FQ	15.26 AW	23.90 TQ	TXBLS	10/01-12/01
	San Antonio MSA, TX	H	11.32 FQ	14.83 AW	19.32 TQ	TXBLS	10/01-12/01
	Utah	H	8.94 FQ	12.91 AW	19.12 TQ	UTBLS	10/01-12/01
	Salt Lake City-Ogden MSA, UT	H	8.95 FQ	12.91 AW	19.13 TQ	UTBLS	10/01-12/01
	Vermont	H	7.81 FQ	11.98 AW	16.91 TQ	VTBLS	10/01-12/01
	Virginia	H	9.70 FQ	15.62 AW	22.89 TQ	VABLS	10/01-12/01
	Norfolk-Virginia Beach-Newport News MSA, VA-NC	H	9.73 FQ	14.76 AW	20.91 TQ	VABLS	10/01-12/01
	Richmond-Petersburg MSA, VA	H	9.95 FQ	16.62 AW	25.13 TQ	VABLS	10/01-12/01
	Washington	H	9.54 FQ	16.36 AW	23.23 TQ	WABLS	10/01-12/01
	Seattle-Bellevue-Everett PMSA, WA	H	9.89 FQ	16.16 AW	22.58 TQ	WABLS	10/01-12/01
	Spokane MSA, WA	H	10.87 FQ	14.90 AW	21.33 TQ	WABLS	10/01-12/01
	Tacoma PMSA, WA	H	11.13 FQ	18.01 AW	27.84 TQ	WABLS	10/01-12/01
	Yakima MSA, WA	H	9.64 FQ	17.58 AW	27.18 TQ	WABLS	10/01-12/01
	West Virginia	H	6.10 FQ	9.68 AW	15.42 TQ	WVBLS	10/01-12/01
	Charleston MSA, WV	H	7.26 FQ	12.38 AW	20.94 TQ	WVBLS	10/01-12/01
	Wisconsin	H	8.85 FQ	15.75 AW	27.81 TQ	WIBLS	10/01-12/01
	Appleton-Oshkosh-Neenah MSA, WI	H	9.18 FQ	13.33 AW	19.63 TQ	WIBLS	10/01-12/01
	Green Bay MSA, WI	H	11.70 FQ	15.11 AW	18.10 TQ	WIBLS	10/01-12/01
	Milwaukee-Waukesha PMSA, WI	H	9.14 FQ	17.16 AW	32.55 TQ	WIBLS	10/01-12/01
	Puerto Rico	H	5.68 FQ	8.62 AW	16.04 TQ	PRBLS	10/01-12/01
Carpenter	Alabama	H	8.51 FQ	12.69 AW	17.80 TQ	ALBLS	10/01-12/01
	Birmingham MSA, AL	H	8.95 FQ	13.97 AW	20.44 TQ	ALBLS	10/01-12/01
	Huntsville MSA, AL	H	9.06 FQ	13.28 AW	18.07 TQ	ALBLS	10/01-12/01
	Mobile MSA, AL	H	8.29 FQ	12.31 AW	17.06 TQ	ALBLS	10/01-12/01
	Montgomery MSA, AL	H	8.22 FQ	12.47 AW	16.68 TQ	ALBLS	10/01-12/01
	Alaska	H	14.54 FQ	22.54 AW	32.06 TQ	AKBLS	10/01-12/01
	Anchorage MSA, AK	H	12.94 FQ	21.08 AW	28.27 TQ	AKBLS	10/01-12/01
	Arizona	H	9.51 FQ	15.52 AW	22.17 TQ	AZBLS	10/01-12/01
	Phoenix-Mesa MSA, AZ	H	9.44 FQ	15.91 AW	22.85 TQ	AZBLS	10/01-12/01
	Tucson MSA, AZ	H	9.77 FQ	14.01 AW	19.98 TQ	AZBLS	10/01-12/01
	Arkansas	H	9.41 FQ	13.46 AW	17.75 TQ	ARBLS	10/01-12/01
	Fayetteville-Springdale-Rogers MSA, AR	H	9.00 FQ	14.07 AW	22.38 TQ	ARBLS	10/01-12/01
	Fort Smith MSA, AR-OK	H	8.76 FQ	13.52 AW	18.60 TQ	ARBLS	10/01-12/01
	Little Rock-North Little Rock MSA, AR	H	10.03 FQ	13.73 AW	17.47 TQ	ARBLS	10/01-12/01
	California	H	10.40 FQ	20.21 AW	31.46 TQ	CABLS	10/01-12/01
	Bakersfield MSA, CA	H	10.19 FQ	17.01 AW	26.01 TQ	CABLS	10/01-12/01
	Chico-Paradise MSA, CA	H	8.97 FQ	16.36 AW	25.42 TQ	CABLS	10/01-12/01
	Fresno MSA, CA	H	9.11 FQ	17.05 AW	26.40 TQ	CABLS	10/01-12/01
	Los Angeles-Long Beach PMSA, CA	H	10.74 FQ	20.57 AW	32.02 TQ	CABLS	10/01-12/01
	Merced MSA, CA	H	8.47 FQ	15.91 AW	24.99 TQ	CABLS	10/01-12/01

AAW	Average annual wage	**AOH**	Average offered, high	**ASH**	Average starting, high	**H**	Hourly	**M**	Monthly	**S**	Special: hourly and annual
AE	Average entry wage	**AOL**	Average offered, low	**ASL**	Average starting, low	**HI**	Highest wage paid	**MTC**	Median total compensation	**TQ**	Third quartile wage
AEX	Average experienced wage	**APH**	Average pay, high range	**AW**	Average wage paid	**HR**	High end range	**MW**	Median wage paid	**W**	Weekly
AO	Average offered	**APL**	Average pay, low range	**FQ**	First quartile wage	**LR**	Low end range	**SQ**	Second quartile wage	**Y**	Yearly

Occupation/Type/Industry	Location	Per	Low	Mid	High	Source	Date
Carpenter	Modesto MSA, CA	H	8.88 FQ	16.93 AW	25.93 TQ	CABLS	10/01-12/01
	Oakland PMSA, CA	H	11.01 FQ	22.56 AW	33.55 TQ	CABLS	10/01-12/01
	Orange County PMSA, CA	H	11.58 FQ	21.07 AW	31.86 TQ	CABLS	10/01-12/01
	Redding MSA, CA	H	10.83 FQ	19.40 AW	28.78 TQ	CABLS	10/01-12/01
	Riverside-San Bernardino PMSA, CA	H	9.45 FQ	17.78 AW	26.30 TQ	CABLS	10/01-12/01
	Sacramento PMSA, CA	H	11.30 FQ	20.11 AW	31.14 TQ	CABLS	10/01-12/01
	Salinas MSA, CA	H	10.11 FQ	21.14 AW	30.18 TQ	CABLS	10/01-12/01
	San Diego MSA, CA	H	9.05 FQ	17.47 AW	26.74 TQ	CABLS	10/01-12/01
	San Francisco PMSA, CA	H	16.27 FQ	26.03 AW	34.65 TQ	CABLS	10/01-12/01
	San Jose PMSA, CA	H	12.30 FQ	21.37 AW	33.00 TQ	CABLS	10/01-12/01
	San Luis Obispo-Atascadero-Paso Robles MSA, CA	H	7.74 FQ	16.85 AW	26.90 TQ	CABLS	10/01-12/01
	Santa Barbara-Santa Maria-Lompoc MSA, CA	H	12.01 FQ	22.20 AW	33.07 TQ	CABLS	10/01-12/01
	Santa Cruz-Watsonville PMSA, CA	H	14.20 FQ	22.96 AW	31.45 TQ	CABLS	10/01-12/01
	Santa Rosa PMSA, CA	H	12.54 FQ	21.53 AW	32.48 TQ	CABLS	10/01-12/01
	Stockton-Lodi MSA, CA	H	14.40 FQ	20.45 AW	27.62 TQ	CABLS	10/01-12/01
	Vallejo-Fairfield-Napa PMSA, CA	H	11.19 FQ	22.42 AW	33.03 TQ	CABLS	10/01-12/01
	Ventura PMSA, CA	H	9.71 FQ	17.36 AW	26.53 TQ	CABLS	10/01-12/01
	Visalia-Tulare-Porterville MSA, CA	H	8.39 FQ	15.78 AW	26.05 TQ	CABLS	10/01-12/01
	Colorado	H	10.56 FQ	17.02 AW	23.30 TQ	COBLS	10/01-12/01
	Boulder-Longmont PMSA, CO	H	12.25 FQ	17.16 AW	21.67 TQ	COBLS	10/01-12/01
	Colorado Springs MSA, CO	H	9.21 FQ	14.89 AW	20.83 TQ	COBLS	10/01-12/01
	Denver PMSA, CO	H	10.65 FQ	17.20 AW	23.46 TQ	COBLS	10/01-12/01
	Fort Collins-Loveland MSA, CO	H	9.61 FQ	14.02 AW	20.01 TQ	COBLS	10/01-12/01
	Greeley PMSA, CO	H	10.36 FQ	15.51 AW	20.85 TQ	COBLS	10/01-12/01
	Connecticut	H	13.56 FQ	19.90 AW	26.83 TQ	CTBLS	10/01-12/01
	Bridgeport PMSA, CT	H	12.48 FQ	20.26 AW	27.37 TQ	CTBLS	10/01-12/01
	Danbury PMSA, CT	H	14.73 FQ	20.12 AW	27.17 TQ	CTBLS	10/01-12/01
	Hartford MSA, CT	H	13.61 FQ	19.15 AW	25.97 TQ	CTBLS	10/01-12/01
	New Haven-Meriden PMSA, CT	H	13.69 FQ	20.84 AW	27.23 TQ	CTBLS	10/01-12/01
	New London-Norwich MSA, CT-RI	H	12.83 FQ	18.72 AW	25.13 TQ	CTBLS	10/01-12/01
	Stamford-Norwalk PMSA, CT	H	16.00 FQ	22.21 AW	28.76 TQ	CTBLS	10/01-12/01
	Waterbury PMSA, CT	H	12.95 FQ	19.75 AW	26.77 TQ	CTBLS	10/01-12/01
	Delaware	H	10.84 FQ	17.05 AW	24.98 TQ	DEBLS	10/01-12/01
	Wilmington-Newark PMSA, DE-MD	H	11.90 FQ	17.96 AW	25.83 TQ	DEBLS	10/01-12/01
	District of Columbia	H	15.01 FQ	20.36 AW	25.68 TQ	DCBLS	10/01-12/01
	Washington PMSA, DC-MD-VA-WV	H	11.57 FQ	17.11 AW	22.69 TQ	DCBLS	10/01-12/01
	Florida	H	8.66 FQ	13.68 AW	19.29 TQ	FLBLS	10/01-12/01
	Daytona Beach MSA, FL	H	6.96 FQ	11.81 AW	17.16 TQ	FLBLS	10/01-12/01
	Fort Lauderdale PMSA, FL	H	10.51 FQ	15.11 AW	20.07 TQ	FLBLS	10/01-12/01
	Fort Myers-Cape Coral MSA, FL	H	9.08 FQ	13.62 AW	18.60 TQ	FLBLS	10/01-12/01
	Fort Pierce-Port St. Lucie MSA, FL	H	7.11 FQ	13.00 AW	18.33 TQ	FLBLS	10/01-12/01
	Fort Walton Beach MSA, FL	H	6.64 FQ	12.02 AW	17.95 TQ	FLBLS	10/01-12/01
	Gainesville MSA, FL	H	9.81 FQ	13.65 AW	17.13 TQ	FLBLS	10/01-12/01
	Jacksonville MSA, FL	H	9.66 FQ	13.54 AW	17.51 TQ	FLBLS	10/01-12/01
	Lakeland-Winter Haven MSA, FL	H	8.34 FQ	13.25 AW	20.57 TQ	FLBLS	10/01-12/01
	Melbourne-Titusville-Palm Bay MSA, FL	H	8.85 FQ	13.43 AW	19.90 TQ	FLBLS	10/01-12/01
	Miami PMSA, FL	H	6.23 FQ	12.58 AW	18.29 TQ	FLBLS	10/01-12/01
	Naples MSA, FL	H	8.59 FQ	15.26 AW	22.75 TQ	FLBLS	10/01-12/01
	Ocala MSA, FL	H	7.93 FQ	11.83 AW	16.24 TQ	FLBLS	10/01-12/01
	Orlando MSA, FL	H	10.17 FQ	14.91 AW	19.96 TQ	FLBLS	10/01-12/01
	Pensacola MSA, FL	H	8.39 FQ	11.60 AW	15.78 TQ	FLBLS	10/01-12/01
	Sarasota-Bradenton MSA, FL	H	8.33 FQ	13.32 AW	19.44 TQ	FLBLS	10/01-12/01
	Tallahassee MSA, FL	H	10.45 FQ	15.08 AW	20.72 TQ	FLBLS	10/01-12/01
	Tampa-St. Petersburg-Clearwater MSA, FL	H	8.86 FQ	13.24 AW	18.31 TQ	FLBLS	10/01-12/01
	West Palm Beach-Boca Raton MSA, FL	H	10.22 FQ	14.87 AW	20.33 TQ	FLBLS	10/01-12/01

AAW	Average annual wage	**AOH**	Average offered, high	**ASH**	Average starting, high	**H**	Hourly	**M**	Monthly	**S**	Special: hourly and annual
AE	Average entry wage	**AOL**	Average offered, low	**ASL**	Average starting, low	**HI**	Highest wage paid	**MTC**	Median total compensation	**TQ**	Third quartile wage
AEX	Average experienced wage	**APH**	Average pay, high range	**AW**	Average wage paid	**HR**	High end range	**MW**	Median wage paid	**W**	Weekly
AO	Average offered	**APL**	Average pay, low range	**FQ**	First quartile wage	**LR**	Low end range	**SQ**	Second quartile wage	**Y**	Yearly

Occupation/Type/Industry	Location	Per	Low	Mid	High	Source	Date
Carpenter	Georgia	H	9.59 FQ	14.90 AW	20.59 TQ	GABLS	10/01-12/01
	Atlanta MSA, GA	H	11.43 FQ	15.66 AW	20.84 TQ	GABLS	10/01-12/01
	Augusta-Aiken MSA, GA-SC	H	9.93 FQ	14.44 AW	21.61 TQ	GABLS	10/01-12/01
	Columbus MSA, GA-AL	H	8.32 FQ	11.87 AW	16.58 TQ	GABLS	10/01-12/01
	Macon MSA, GA	H	9.91 FQ	14.20 AW	19.98 TQ	GABLS	10/01-12/01
	Savannah MSA, GA	H	10.23 FQ	14.16 AW	17.76 TQ	GABLS	10/01-12/01
	Hawaii	H	14.09 FQ	24.69 AW	34.49 TQ	HIBLS	10/01-12/01
	Honolulu MSA, HI	H	14.36 FQ	25.37 AW	34.84 TQ	HIBLS	10/01-12/01
	Idaho	H	9.12 FQ	13.75 AW	20.18 TQ	IDBLS	10/01-12/01
	Boise City MSA, ID	H	8.73 FQ	14.37 AW	21.03 TQ	IDBLS	10/01-12/01
	Illinois	H	11.89 FQ	22.07 AW	33.00 TQ	ILBLS	10/01-12/01
	Champaign-Urbana MSA, IL	H	9.85 FQ	19.54 AW	29.84 TQ	ILBLS	10/01-12/01
	Chicago PMSA, IL	H	12.35 FQ	23.17 AW	33.58 TQ	ILBLS	10/01-12/01
	Peoria-Pekin MSA, IL	H	12.59 FQ	20.35 AW	27.48 TQ	ILBLS	10/01-12/01
	Springfield MSA, IL	H	10.00 FQ	18.49 AW	28.87 TQ	ILBLS	10/01-12/01
	Indiana	H	10.46 FQ	17.02 AW	25.40 TQ	INBLS	10/01-12/01
	Elkhart-Goshen MSA, IN	H	11.03 FQ	17.20 AW	22.54 TQ	INBLS	10/01-12/01
	Evansville-Henderson MSA, IN-KY	H	10.14 FQ	16.34 AW	22.71 TQ	INBLS	10/01-12/01
	Fort Wayne MSA, IN	H	10.78 FQ	15.33 AW	21.39 TQ	INBLS	10/01-12/01
	Gary PMSA, IN	H	13.41 FQ	21.97 AW	28.88 TQ	INBLS	10/01-12/01
	Indianapolis MSA, IN	H	11.20 FQ	17.57 AW	25.79 TQ	INBLS	10/01-12/01
	Lafayette MSA, IN	H	9.86 FQ	16.52 AW	22.97 TQ	INBLS	10/01-12/01
	South Bend MSA, IN	H	11.68 FQ	17.90 AW	25.00 TQ	INBLS	10/01-12/01
	Iowa	H	9.48 FQ	14.35 AW	21.05 TQ	IABLS	10/01-12/01
	Cedar Rapids MSA, IA	H	10.88 FQ	16.70 AW	23.64 TQ	IABLS	10/01-12/01
	Davenport-Moline-Rock Island MSA, IA-IL	H	9.76 FQ	17.10 AW	25.63 TQ	IABLS	10/01-12/01
	Des Moines MSA, IA	H	8.98 FQ	14.74 AW	21.60 TQ	IABLS	10/01-12/01
	Kansas	H	10.02 FQ	15.96 AW	23.86 TQ	KSBLS	10/01-12/01
	Topeka MSA, KS	H	11.81 FQ	15.60 AW	20.61 TQ	KSBLS	10/01-12/01
	Wichita MSA, KS	H	10.63 FQ	15.64 AW	21.51 TQ	KSBLS	10/01-12/01
	Kentucky	H	9.53 FQ	14.99 AW	21.75 TQ	KYBLS	10/01-12/01
	Lexington MSA, KY	H	10.33 FQ	14.68 AW	20.09 TQ	KYBLS	10/01-12/01
	Louisville MSA, KY-IN	H	10.20 FQ	16.05 AW	22.27 TQ	KYBLS	10/01-12/01
	Louisiana	H	8.72 FQ	13.52 AW	17.93 TQ	LABLS	10/01-12/01
	Baton Rouge MSA, LA	H	11.23 FQ	14.64 AW	17.79 TQ	LABLS	10/01-12/01
	Houma MSA, LA	H	6.68 FQ	13.86 AW	20.48 TQ	LABLS	10/01-12/01
	Lafayette MSA, LA	H	8.15 FQ	12.75 AW	18.10 TQ	LABLS	10/01-12/01
	Lake Charles MSA, LA	H	11.07 FQ	16.89 AW	25.43 TQ	LABLS	10/01-12/01
	New Orleans MSA, LA	H	7.79 FQ	12.49 AW	17.23 TQ	LABLS	10/01-12/01
	Shreveport-Bossier City MSA, LA	H	9.11 FQ	13.00 AW	17.04 TQ	LABLS	10/01-12/01
	Maine	H	9.11 FQ	13.56 AW	20.14 TQ	MEBLS	10/01-12/01
	Portland MSA, ME	H	10.03 FQ	15.55 AW	25.04 TQ	MEBLS	10/01-12/01
	Maryland	H	11.85 FQ	16.46 AW	21.44 TQ	MDBLS	10/01-12/01
	Baltimore PMSA, MD	H	11.86 FQ	15.96 AW	20.62 TQ	MDBLS	10/01-12/01
	Massachusetts	H	13.19 FQ	20.89 AW	29.56 TQ	MABLS	10/01-12/01
	Boston PMSA, MA-NH	H	14.33 FQ	22.26 AW	31.02 TQ	MABLS	10/01-12/01
	Brockton PMSA, MA	H	13.25 FQ	19.19 AW	28.66 TQ	MABLS	10/01-12/01
	Lawrence PMSA, MA-NH	H	13.39 FQ	20.68 AW	28.21 TQ	MABLS	10/01-12/01
	Lowell PMSA, MA-NH	H	13.92 FQ	21.10 AW	30.69 TQ	MABLS	10/01-12/01
	New Bedford PMSA, MA	H	10.97 FQ	18.56 AW	26.31 TQ	MABLS	10/01-12/01
	Springfield MSA, MA	H	13.51 FQ	18.80 AW	25.76 TQ	MABLS	10/01-12/01
	Worcester PMSA, MA-CT	H	9.85 FQ	16.39 AW	23.04 TQ	MABLS	10/01-12/01
	Michigan	H	10.98 FQ	18.89 AW	27.36 TQ	MIBLS	10/01-12/01
	Ann Arbor PMSA, MI	H	11.79 FQ	20.73 AW	31.21 TQ	MIBLS	10/01-12/01
	Detroit PMSA, MI	H	13.73 FQ	21.60 AW	27.92 TQ	MIBLS	10/01-12/01
	Flint PMSA, MI	H	10.96 FQ	19.67 AW	27.73 TQ	MIBLS	10/01-12/01
	Grand Rapids-Muskegon-Holland MSA, MI	H	9.84 FQ	15.72 AW	23.84 TQ	MIBLS	10/01-12/01
	Kalamazoo-Battle Creek MSA, MI	H	11.61 FQ	16.14 AW	23.19 TQ	MIBLS	10/01-12/01
	Lansing-East Lansing MSA, MI	H	11.57 FQ	19.70 AW	28.23 TQ	MIBLS	10/01-12/01
	Saginaw-Bay City-Midland MSA, MI	H	10.65 FQ	17.48 AW	26.98 TQ	MIBLS	10/01-12/01
	Minnesota	H	11.35 FQ	18.65 AW	26.98 TQ	MNBLS	10/01-12/01
	Duluth-Superior MSA, MN-WI	H	10.69 FQ	17.13 AW	25.12 TQ	MNBLS	10/01-12/01
	Minneapolis-St. Paul MSA, MN-WI	H	12.58 FQ	19.97 AW	27.66 TQ	MNBLS	10/01-12/01
	St. Cloud MSA, MN	H	9.99 FQ	15.36 AW	22.11 TQ	MNBLS	10/01-12/01
	Mississippi	H	8.26 FQ	12.71 AW	17.58 TQ	MSBLS	10/01-12/01

AAW	Average annual wage	**AOH**	Average offered, high	**ASH**	Average starting, high	**H**	Hourly	**M**	Monthly	**S**	Special: hourly and annual
AE	Average entry wage	**AOL**	Average offered, low	**ASL**	Average starting, low	**HI**	Highest wage paid	**MTC**	Median total compensation	**TQ**	Third quartile wage
AEX	Average experienced wage	**APH**	Average pay, high range	**AW**	Average wage paid	**HR**	High end range	**MW**	Median wage paid	**W**	Weekly
AO	Average offered	**APL**	Average pay, low range	**FQ**	First quartile wage	**LR**	Low end range	**SQ**	Second quartile wage	**Y**	Yearly

Occupation/Type/Industry	Location	Per	Low	Mid	High	Source	Date
Carpenter	Biloxi-Gulfport-Pascagoula MSA, MS	H	9.29 FQ	13.47 AW	17.39 TQ	MSBLS	10/01-12/01
	Jackson MSA, MS	H	8.84 FQ	14.01 AW	20.12 TQ	MSBLS	10/01-12/01
	Missouri	H	10.20 FQ	18.82 AW	29.20 TQ	MOBLS	10/01-12/01
	Kansas City MSA, MO-KS	H	12.08 FQ	19.26 AW	27.25 TQ	MOBLS	10/01-12/01
	St. Louis MSA, MO-IL	H	12.80 FQ	21.50 AW	31.37 TQ	MOBLS	10/01-12/01
	Springfield MSA, MO	H	9.00 FQ	13.55 AW	18.97 TQ	MOBLS	10/01-12/01
	Montana	H	11.08 FQ	14.48 AW	18.64 TQ	MTBLS	10/01-12/01
	Billings MSA, MT	H	10.90 FQ	14.73 AW	21.30 TQ	MTBLS	10/01-12/01
	Nebraska	H	9.39 FQ	14.46 AW	20.32 TQ	NEBLS	10/01-12/01
	Lincoln MSA, NE	H	8.34 FQ	13.58 AW	19.03 TQ	NEBLS	10/01-12/01
	Omaha MSA, NE-IA	H	11.53 FQ	16.08 AW	21.07 TQ	NEBLS	10/01-12/01
	Nevada	H	12.87 FQ	20.04 AW	27.81 TQ	NVBLS	10/01-12/01
	Las Vegas MSA, NV-AZ	H	12.42 FQ	19.44 AW	27.56 TQ	NVBLS	10/01-12/01
	Reno MSA, NV	H	14.96 FQ	22.16 AW	29.60 TQ	NVBLS	10/01-12/01
	New Hampshire	H	9.90 FQ	14.89 AW	19.91 TQ	NHBLS	10/01-12/01
	Manchester PMSA, NH	H	11.78 FQ	16.14 AW	21.12 TQ	NHBLS	10/01-12/01
	Nashua PMSA, NH	H	12.45 FQ	17.04 AW	23.67 TQ	NHBLS	10/01-12/01
	Portsmouth-Rochester PMSA, NH-ME	H	10.37 FQ	14.42 AW	18.76 TQ	NHBLS	10/01-12/01
	New Jersey	H	11.73 FQ	22.71 AW	34.92 TQ	NJBLS	10/01-12/01
	Atlantic-Cape May PMSA, NJ	H	12.17 FQ	22.41 AW	34.46 TQ	NJBLS	10/01-12/01
	Bergen-Passaic PMSA, NJ	H	10.96 FQ	26.53 AW	58.89 TQ	NJBLS	10/01-12/01
	Jersey City PMSA, NJ	H	10.93 FQ	22.16 AW	34.20 TQ	NJBLS	10/01-12/01
	Middlesex-Somerset-Hunterdon PMSA, NJ	H	10.80 FQ	19.58 AW	32.63 TQ	NJBLS	10/01-12/01
	Monmouth-Ocean PMSA, NJ	H	11.40 FQ	21.17 AW	36.97 TQ	NJBLS	10/01-12/01
	Newark PMSA, NJ	H	12.90 FQ	23.47 AW	33.89 TQ	NJBLS	10/01-12/01
	Trenton PMSA, NJ	H	14.54 FQ	22.21 AW	33.08 TQ	NJBLS	10/01-12/01
	New Mexico	H	8.78 FQ	14.27 AW	20.60 TQ	NMBLS	10/01-12/01
	Albuquerque MSA, NM	H	8.49 FQ	14.26 AW	20.72 TQ	NMBLS	10/01-12/01
	Las Cruces MSA, NM	H	6.71 FQ	11.32 AW	17.49 TQ	NMBLS	10/01-12/01
	New York	H	9.58 FQ	19.82 AW	34.14 TQ	NYBLS	10/01-12/01
	Albany-Schenectady-Troy MSA, NY	H	10.55 FQ	17.71 AW	23.55 TQ	NYBLS	10/01-12/01
	Binghamton MSA, NY	H	9.15 FQ	15.14 AW	22.82 TQ	NYBLS	10/01-12/01
	Buffalo-Niagara Falls MSA, NY	H	9.11 FQ	15.64 AW	22.21 TQ	NYBLS	10/01-12/01
	Dutchess County PMSA, NY	H	12.45 FQ	20.50 AW	29.27 TQ	NYBLS	10/01-12/01
	Nassau-Suffolk PMSA, NY	H	6.53 FQ	20.12 AW	34.18 TQ	NYBLS	10/01-12/01
	New York PMSA, NY	H	9.99 FQ	22.53 AW	37.45 TQ	NYBLS	10/01-12/01
	Newburgh PMSA, NY-PA	H	8.13 FQ	16.12 AW	25.10 TQ	NYBLS	10/01-12/01
	Rochester MSA, NY	H	10.14 FQ	15.79 AW	24.03 TQ	NYBLS	10/01-12/01
	Syracuse MSA, NY	H	7.61 FQ	15.20 AW	22.75 TQ	NYBLS	10/01-12/01
	Utica-Rome MSA, NY	H	12.00 FQ	16.68 AW	21.43 TQ	NYBLS	10/01-12/01
	North Carolina	H	8.99 FQ	13.42 AW	18.51 TQ	NCBLS	10/01-12/01
	Asheville MSA, NC	H	9.44 FQ	12.78 AW	16.71 TQ	NCBLS	10/01-12/01
	Charlotte-Gastonia-Rock Hill MSA, NC-SC	H	8.73 FQ	15.31 AW	22.32 TQ	NCBLS	10/01-12/01
	Fayetteville MSA, NC	H	8.02 FQ	11.79 AW	16.17 TQ	NCBLS	10/01-12/01
	Greensboro-Winston-Salem-High Point MSA, NC	H	9.59 FQ	13.16 AW	16.92 TQ	NCBLS	10/01-12/01
	Hickory-Morganton-Lenoir MSA, NC	H	7.00 FQ	13.37 AW	17.41 TQ	NCBLS	10/01-12/01
	Raleigh-Durham-Chapel Hill MSA, NC	H	8.58 FQ	13.48 AW	18.01 TQ	NCBLS	10/01-12/01
	Wilmington MSA, NC	H	8.23 FQ	13.39 AW	19.46 TQ	NCBLS	10/01-12/01
	North Dakota	H	8.88 FQ	13.06 AW	18.35 TQ	NDBLS	10/01-12/01
	Fargo-Moorhead MSA, ND-MN	H	10.42 FQ	14.83 AW	20.33 TQ	NDBLS	10/01-12/01
	Ohio	H	9.74 FQ	16.75 AW	25.50 TQ	OHBLS	10/01-12/01
	Akron PMSA, OH	H	9.89 FQ	16.82 AW	25.01 TQ	OHBLS	10/01-12/01
	Canton-Massillon MSA, OH	H	9.80 FQ	16.21 AW	22.30 TQ	OHBLS	10/01-12/01
	Cincinnati PMSA, OH-KY-IN	H	9.84 FQ	16.82 AW	23.65 TQ	OHBLS	10/01-12/01
	Cleveland-Lorain-Elyria PMSA, OH	H	11.71 FQ	21.07 AW	30.58 TQ	OHBLS	10/01-12/01
	Columbus MSA, OH	H	9.25 FQ	15.17 AW	21.73 TQ	OHBLS	10/01-12/01
	Dayton-Springfield MSA, OH	H	9.14 FQ	15.44 AW	21.68 TQ	OHBLS	10/01-12/01
	Hamilton-Middletown PMSA, OH	H	11.12 FQ	16.83 AW	25.53 TQ	OHBLS	10/01-12/01
	Mansfield MSA, OH	H	8.04 FQ	14.35 AW	21.98 TQ	OHBLS	10/01-12/01
	Toledo MSA, OH	H	12.06 FQ	18.63 AW	25.58 TQ	OHBLS	10/01-12/01

AAW Average annual wage; **AE** Average entry wage; **AEX** Average experienced wage; **AO** Average offered; **AOH** Average offered, high; **AOL** Average offered, low; **APH** Average pay, high range; **APL** Average pay, low range; **ASH** Average starting, high; **ASL** Average starting, low; **AW** Average wage paid; **FQ** First quartile wage; **H** Hourly; **HI** Highest wage paid; **HR** High end range; **LR** Low end range; **M** Monthly; **MTC** Median total compensation; **MW** Median wage paid; **SQ** Second quartile wage; **S** Special: hourly and annual; **TQ** Third quartile wage; **W** Weekly; **Y** Yearly

Occupation/Type/Industry	Location	Per	Low	Mid	High	Source	Date
Carpenter	Youngstown-Warren MSA, OH	H	11.48 FQ	18.06 AW	24.73 TQ	OHBLS	10/01-12/01
	Oklahoma	H	7.82 FQ	12.56 AW	18.15 TQ	OKBLS	10/01-12/01
	Oklahoma City MSA, OK	H	7.80 FQ	12.49 AW	18.17 TQ	OKBLS	10/01-12/01
	Tulsa MSA, OK	H	9.73 FQ	13.65 AW	17.48 TQ	OKBLS	10/01-12/01
	Oregon	H	10.18 FQ	17.82 AW	26.66 TQ	ORBLS	10/01-12/01
	Eugene-Springfield MSA, OR	H	8.80 FQ	15.56 AW	23.09 TQ	ORBLS	10/01-12/01
	Medford-Ashland MSA, OR	H	10.59 FQ	16.51 AW	23.35 TQ	ORBLS	10/01-12/01
	Portland-Vancouver PMSA, OR-WA	H	11.15 FQ	19.26 AW	27.71 TQ	ORBLS	10/01-12/01
	Salem PMSA, OR	H	8.32 FQ	16.58 AW	26.73 TQ	ORBLS	10/01-12/01
	Pennsylvania	H	10.06 FQ	17.50 AW	27.47 TQ	PABLS	10/01-12/01
	Erie MSA, PA	H	9.11 FQ	15.72 AW	25.97 TQ	PABLS	10/01-12/01
	Harrisburg-Lebanon-Carlisle MSA, PA	H	10.38 FQ	16.13 AW	22.39 TQ	PABLS	10/01-12/01
	Johnstown MSA, PA	H	7.95 FQ	12.03 AW	19.20 TQ	PABLS	10/01-12/01
	Lancaster MSA, PA	H	10.79 FQ	15.68 AW	21.01 TQ	PABLS	10/01-12/01
	Philadelphia PMSA, PA-NJ	H	12.18 FQ	21.42 AW	33.01 TQ	PABLS	10/01-12/01
	Pittsburgh MSA, PA	H	11.37 FQ	19.85 AW	28.33 TQ	PABLS	10/01-12/01
	Reading MSA, PA	H	7.89 FQ	15.31 AW	21.57 TQ	PABLS	10/01-12/01
	Scranton-Wilkes-Barre-Hazleton MSA, PA	H	10.41 FQ	15.91 AW	21.88 TQ	PABLS	10/01-12/01
	York MSA, PA	H	11.49 FQ	16.39 AW	24.39 TQ	PABLS	10/01-12/01
	Rhode Island	H	11.65 FQ	18.52 AW	27.29 TQ	RIBLS	10/01-12/01
	Providence-Fall River-Warwick MSA, RI-MA	H	11.62 FQ	18.39 AW	27.29 TQ	RIBLS	10/01-12/01
	South Carolina	H	9.19 FQ	14.49 AW	21.83 TQ	SCBLS	10/01-12/01
	Charleston-North Charleston MSA, SC	H	9.57 FQ	13.75 AW	18.82 TQ	SCBLS	10/01-12/01
	Columbia MSA, SC	H	9.44 FQ	12.94 AW	16.92 TQ	SCBLS	10/01-12/01
	Greenville-Spartanburg-Anderson MSA, SC	H	9.59 FQ	13.70 AW	17.51 TQ	SCBLS	10/01-12/01
	Myrtle Beach MSA, SC	H	9.14 FQ	13.19 AW	19.85 TQ	SCBLS	10/01-12/01
	South Dakota	H	8.83 FQ	11.93 AW	15.63 TQ	SDBLS	10/01-12/01
	Sioux Falls MSA, SD	H	9.17 FQ	12.84 AW	16.94 TQ	SDBLS	10/01-12/01
	Tennessee	H	9.28 FQ	13.56 AW	18.17 TQ	TNBLS	10/01-12/01
	Chattanooga MSA, TN-GA	H	10.18 FQ	14.61 AW	19.46 TQ	TNBLS	10/01-12/01
	Clarksville-Hopkinsville MSA, TN-KY	H	9.92 FQ	14.05 AW	18.55 TQ	TNBLS	10/01-12/01
	Johnson City-Kingsport-Bristol MSA, TN-VA	H	8.42 FQ	12.05 AW	16.44 TQ	TNBLS	10/01-12/01
	Knoxville MSA, TN	H	9.39 FQ	12.97 AW	17.22 TQ	TNBLS	10/01-12/01
	Memphis MSA, TN-AR-MS	H	7.58 FQ	14.43 AW	20.37 TQ	TNBLS	10/01-12/01
	Nashville MSA, TN	H	9.97 FQ	14.19 AW	18.73 TQ	TNBLS	10/01-12/01
	Texas	H	8.78 FQ	13.21 AW	18.00 TQ	TXBLS	10/01-12/01
	Amarillo MSA, TX	H	10.05 FQ	14.39 AW	17.54 TQ	TXBLS	10/01-12/01
	Austin-San Marcos MSA, TX	H	8.83 FQ	13.97 AW	19.87 TQ	TXBLS	10/01-12/01
	Beaumont-Port Arthur MSA, TX	H	11.23 FQ	15.34 AW	20.48 TQ	TXBLS	10/01-12/01
	Brazoria PMSA, TX	H	9.51 FQ	14.48 AW	19.21 TQ	TXBLS	10/01-12/01
	Brownsville-Harlingen-San Benito MSA, TX	H	6.74 FQ	10.49 AW	15.26 TQ	TXBLS	10/01-12/01
	Corpus Christi MSA, TX	H	8.13 FQ	11.82 AW	16.47 TQ	TXBLS	10/01-12/01
	Dallas PMSA, TX	H	9.34 FQ	13.48 AW	17.92 TQ	TXBLS	10/01-12/01
	El Paso MSA, TX	H	5.94 FQ	9.52 AW	13.66 TQ	TXBLS	10/01-12/01
	Fort Worth-Arlington PMSA, TX	H	8.51 FQ	12.88 AW	18.12 TQ	TXBLS	10/01-12/01
	Galveston-Texas City PMSA, TX	H	7.35 FQ	15.16 AW	24.98 TQ	TXBLS	10/01-12/01
	Houston PMSA, TX	H	9.58 FQ	13.84 AW	18.20 TQ	TXBLS	10/01-12/01
	Killeen-Temple MSA, TX	H	8.54 FQ	12.70 AW	17.58 TQ	TXBLS	10/01-12/01
	Laredo MSA, TX	H	7.16 FQ	10.05 AW	14.83 TQ	TXBLS	10/01-12/01
	Longview-Marshall MSA, TX	H	9.22 FQ	12.66 AW	16.84 TQ	TXBLS	10/01-12/01
	Lubbock MSA, TX	H	7.49 FQ	11.83 AW	15.12 TQ	TXBLS	10/01-12/01
	McAllen-Edinburg-Mission MSA, TX	H	6.21 FQ	9.61 AW	14.44 TQ	TXBLS	10/01-12/01
	Odessa-Midland MSA, TX	H	9.35 FQ	14.33 AW	20.73 TQ	TXBLS	10/01-12/01
	San Antonio MSA, TX	H	8.96 FQ	13.23 AW	17.99 TQ	TXBLS	10/01-12/01
	Tyler MSA, TX	H	8.38 FQ	11.74 AW	15.71 TQ	TXBLS	10/01-12/01
	Utah	H	10.23 FQ	15.35 AW	21.06 TQ	UTBLS	10/01-12/01
	Provo-Orem MSA, UT	H	9.42 FQ	14.73 AW	20.97 TQ	UTBLS	10/01-12/01
	Salt Lake City-Ogden MSA, UT	H	10.87 FQ	15.86 AW	21.31 TQ	UTBLS	10/01-12/01

AAW	Average annual wage	AOH	Average offered, high	ASH	Average starting, high	H	Hourly	M	Monthly	S	Special: hourly and annual
AE	Average entry wage	AOL	Average offered, low	ASL	Average starting, low	HI	Highest wage paid	MTC	Median total compensation	TQ	Third quartile wage
AEX	Average experienced wage	APH	Average pay, high range	AW	Average wage paid	HR	High end range	MW	Median wage paid	W	Weekly
AO	Average offered	APL	Average pay, low range	FQ	First quartile wage	LR	Low end range	SQ	Second quartile wage	Y	Yearly

Occupation/Type/Industry	Location	Per	Low	Mid	High	Source	Date
Carpenter	Vermont	H	11.37 FQ	14.85 AW	19.84 TQ	VTBLS	10/01-12/01
	Burlington MSA, VT	H	11.63 FQ	14.99 AW	19.81 TQ	VTBLS	10/01-12/01
	Virginia	H	9.42 FQ	14.17 AW	19.47 TQ	VABLS	10/01-12/01
	Lynchburg MSA, VA	H	8.15 FQ	11.74 AW	16.43 TQ	VABLS	10/01-12/01
	Norfolk-Virginia Beach-Newport News MSA, VA-NC	H	10.09 FQ	14.41 AW	18.95 TQ	VABLS	10/01-12/01
	Richmond-Petersburg MSA, VA	H	10.44 FQ	14.75 AW	18.91 TQ	VABLS	10/01-12/01
	Roanoke MSA, VA	H	9.61 FQ	13.42 AW	19.64 TQ	VABLS	10/01-12/01
	Washington	H	12.16 FQ	20.39 AW	28.45 TQ	WABLS	10/01-12/01
	Bremerton PMSA, WA	H	9.62 FQ	16.39 AW	24.94 TQ	WABLS	10/01-12/01
	Olympia PMSA, WA	H	9.34 FQ	16.71 AW	24.47 TQ	WABLS	10/01-12/01
	Richland-Kennewick-Pasco MSA, WA	H	10.80 FQ	18.33 AW	26.63 TQ	WABLS	10/01-12/01
	Seattle-Bellevue-Everett PMSA, WA	H	15.04 FQ	22.47 AW	29.42 TQ	WABLS	10/01-12/01
	Spokane MSA, WA	H	10.72 FQ	17.77 AW	27.76 TQ	WABLS	10/01-12/01
	Tacoma PMSA, WA	H	12.65 FQ	21.23 AW	30.82 TQ	WABLS	10/01-12/01
	Yakima MSA, WA	H	11.59 FQ	17.27 AW	23.85 TQ	WABLS	10/01-12/01
	West Virginia	H	7.75 FQ	13.77 AW	23.13 TQ	WVBLS	10/01-12/01
	Charleston MSA, WV	H	9.11 FQ	15.73 AW	25.35 TQ	WVBLS	10/01-12/01
	Huntington-Ashland MSA, WV-KY-OH	H	9.30 FQ	14.72 AW	23.04 TQ	WVBLS	10/01-12/01
	Wisconsin	H	9.69 FQ	17.22 AW	26.58 TQ	WIBLS	10/01-12/01
	Appleton-Oshkosh-Neenah MSA, WI	H	11.73 FQ	18.56 AW	26.16 TQ	WIBLS	10/01-12/01
	Green Bay MSA, WI	H	9.85 FQ	17.93 AW	27.16 TQ	WIBLS	10/01-12/01
	Madison MSA, WI	H	12.19 FQ	19.20 AW	26.20 TQ	WIBLS	10/01-12/01
	Milwaukee-Waukesha PMSA, WI	H	11.02 FQ	20.06 AW	28.91 TQ	WIBLS	10/01-12/01
	Racine PMSA, WI	H	10.26 FQ	18.88 AW	27.00 TQ	WIBLS	10/01-12/01
	Wyoming	H	11.51 FQ	17.26 AW	23.27 TQ	WYBLS	10/01-12/01
	Cheyenne MSA, WY	H	12.77 FQ	16.15 AW	19.30 TQ	WYBLS	10/01-12/01
	Puerto Rico	H	5.80 FQ	7.38 AW	8.88 TQ	PRBLS	10/01-12/01
	Virgin Islands	H	12.14 FQ	15.13 AW	17.98 TQ	VIBLS	10/01-12/01
	Guam	H	10.15 FQ	12.57 AW	14.46 TQ	GUBLS	10/01-12/01
Carpet Installer	Alabama	H	8.34 FQ	14.90 AW	24.44 TQ	ALBLS	10/01-12/01
	Alaska	H	11.63 FQ	15.76 AW	24.57 TQ	AKBLS	10/01-12/01
	Arizona	H	9.08 FQ	14.57 AW	21.28 TQ	AZBLS	10/01-12/01
	Arkansas	H	6.57 FQ	10.85 AW	15.52 TQ	ARBLS	10/01-12/01
	California	H	8.41 FQ	16.72 AW	27.95 TQ	CABLS	10/01-12/01
	Colorado	H	9.27 FQ	15.68 AW	24.24 TQ	COBLS	10/01-12/01
	Connecticut	H	14.68 FQ	17.67 AW	21.79 TQ	CTBLS	10/01-12/01
	Delaware	H	10.01 FQ	15.15 AW	20.60 TQ	DEBLS	10/01-12/01
	Florida	H	8.64 FQ	14.30 AW	21.23 TQ	FLBLS	10/01-12/01
	Georgia	H	8.97 FQ	14.97 AW	23.90 TQ	GABLS	10/01-12/01
	Hawaii	H	9.88 FQ	20.23 AW	31.43 TQ	HIBLS	10/01-12/01
	Idaho	H	8.72 FQ	13.68 AW	17.89 TQ	IDBLS	10/01-12/01
	Illinois	H	8.64 FQ	21.51 AW	33.21 TQ	ILBLS	10/01-12/01
	Indiana	H	7.80 FQ	14.95 AW	22.23 TQ	INBLS	10/01-12/01
	Iowa	H	9.19 FQ	14.16 AW	20.37 TQ	IABLS	10/01-12/01
	Kansas	H	9.28 FQ	15.22 AW	21.77 TQ	KSBLS	10/01-12/01
	Kentucky	H	7.88 FQ	13.40 AW	20.12 TQ	KYBLS	10/01-12/01
	Louisiana	H	7.65 FQ	11.90 AW	17.02 TQ	LABLS	10/01-12/01
	Maine	H	8.56 FQ	12.54 AW	16.75 TQ	MEBLS	10/01-12/01
	Maryland	H	10.63 FQ	17.05 AW	22.87 TQ	MDBLS	10/01-12/01
	Massachusetts	H	12.74 FQ	22.88 AW	32.24 TQ	MABLS	10/01-12/01
	Michigan	H	9.31 FQ	15.05 AW	23.78 TQ	MIBLS	10/01-12/01
	Minnesota	H	11.41 FQ	19.93 AW	27.67 TQ	MNBLS	10/01-12/01
	Mississippi	H	7.78 FQ	12.40 AW	17.04 TQ	MSBLS	10/01-12/01
	Missouri	H	11.11 FQ	19.28 AW	26.82 TQ	MOBLS	10/01-12/01
	Montana	H	22.45 FQ	23.83 AW	27.67 TQ	MTBLS	10/01-12/01
	Nebraska	H	11.23 FQ	16.59 AW	22.31 TQ	NEBLS	10/01-12/01
	Nevada	H	9.09 FQ	20.79 AW	28.53 TQ	NVBLS	10/01-12/01
	New Hampshire	H	12.50 FQ	17.49 AW	24.42 TQ	NHBLS	10/01-12/01
	New Jersey	H	11.05 FQ	18.40 AW	31.21 TQ	NJBLS	10/01-12/01
	New Mexico	H	9.22 FQ	14.15 AW	17.49 TQ	NMBLS	10/01-12/01
	New York	H	7.03 FQ	20.28 AW	34.62 TQ	NYBLS	10/01-12/01
	North Carolina	H	8.76 FQ	13.72 AW	17.67 TQ	NCBLS	10/01-12/01
	North Dakota	H	7.76 FQ	11.09 AW	15.91 TQ	NDBLS	10/01-12/01
	Ohio	H	9.58 FQ	16.10 AW	24.50 TQ	OHBLS	10/01-12/01

AAW Average annual wage **AE** Average entry wage **AEX** Average experienced wage **AO** Average offered **AOH** Average offered, high **AOL** Average offered, low **APH** Average pay, high range **APL** Average pay, low range **ASH** Average starting, high **ASL** Average starting, low **AW** Average wage paid **FQ** First quartile wage **H** Hourly **HI** Highest wage paid **HR** High end range **LR** Low end range **M** Monthly **MTC** Median total compensation **MW** Median wage paid **SQ** Second quartile wage **S** Special: hourly and annual **TQ** Third quartile wage **W** Weekly **Y** Yearly

Occupation/Type/Industry	Location	Per	Low	Mid	High	Source	Date
Carpet Installer	Oklahoma	H	7.34 FQ	12.13 AW	18.02 TQ	OKBLS	10/01-12/01
	Oregon	H	7.66 FQ	16.04 AW	26.08 TQ	ORBLS	10/01-12/01
	Pennsylvania	H	7.16 FQ	13.70 AW	21.87 TQ	PABLS	10/01-12/01
	Rhode Island	H	15.47 FQ	26.49 AW	34.47 TQ	RIBLS	10/01-12/01
	South Carolina	H	7.47 FQ	9.43 AW	11.54 TQ	SCBLS	10/01-12/01
	South Dakota	H	9.12 FQ	11.63 AW	15.24 TQ	SDBLS	10/01-12/01
	Tennessee	H	7.22 FQ	11.53 AW	17.16 TQ	TNBLS	10/01-12/01
	Texas	H	7.90 FQ	13.37 AW	18.34 TQ	TXBLS	10/01-12/01
	Utah	H	8.22 FQ	13.29 AW	19.37 TQ	UTBLS	10/01-12/01
	Vermont	H	8.46 FQ	14.44 AW	23.44 TQ	VTBLS	10/01-12/01
	Virginia	H	8.39 FQ	14.61 AW	23.92 TQ	VABLS	10/01-12/01
	Washington	H	11.53 FQ	20.55 AW	27.93 TQ	WABLS	10/01-12/01
	West Virginia	H	5.82 FQ	9.83 AW	16.83 TQ	WVBLS	10/01-12/01
	Wisconsin	H	9.70 FQ	17.44 AW	26.91 TQ	WIBLS	10/01-12/01
	Wyoming	H	9.15 FQ	13.31 AW	20.31 TQ	WYBLS	10/01-12/01
	Puerto Rico	H	5.35 FQ	6.10 AW	7.27 TQ	PRBLS	10/01-12/01
Cartographer	United States	Y	16000 ASL		48000 ASH	AEAC	1/99-1/99
Cartographer and Photogrammetrist	Alabama	Y	28160 FQ	41560 AW	53960 TQ	ALBLS	10/01-12/01
	Alaska	Y	31570 FQ	47540 AW	65640 TQ	AKBLS	10/01-12/01
	Arizona	Y	28130 FQ	42640 AW	58770 TQ	AZBLS	10/01-12/01
	Arkansas	Y	24230 FQ	34640 AW	51630 TQ	ARBLS	10/01-12/01
	California	Y	28300 FQ	50300 AW	76120 TQ	CABLS	10/01-12/01
	Colorado	Y	33340 FQ	51550 AW	69190 TQ	COBLS	10/01-12/01
	Connecticut	Y	32920 FQ	42320 AW	53860 TQ	CTBLS	10/01-12/01
	District of Columbia	Y	45300 FQ	52120 AW	62030 TQ	DCBLS	10/01-12/01
	Florida	Y	23670 FQ	34240 AW	46410 TQ	FLBLS	10/01-12/01
	Georgia	Y	29330 FQ	40310 AW	57170 TQ	GABLS	10/01-12/01
	Hawaii	Y	23490 FQ	41380 AW	65910 TQ	HIBLS	10/01-12/01
	Idaho	Y	26110 FQ	34720 AW	44480 TQ	IDBLS	10/01-12/01
	Illinois	Y	15440 FQ	35190 AW	71420 TQ	ILBLS	10/01-12/01
	Indiana	Y	23640 FQ	39320 AW	68760 TQ	INBLS	10/01-12/01
	Kansas	Y	19520 FQ	34720 AW	53340 TQ	KSBLS	10/01-12/01
	Kentucky	Y	20790 FQ	33690 AW	51130 TQ	KYBLS	10/01-12/01
	Louisiana	Y	27250 FQ	41800 AW	61300 TQ	LABLS	10/01-12/01
	Maine	Y	26620 FQ	43050 AW	72390 TQ	MEBLS	10/01-12/01
	Maryland	Y	26310 FQ	48320 AW	70330 TQ	MDBLS	10/01-12/01
	Massachusetts	Y	23760 FQ	44620 AW	64410 TQ	MABLS	10/01-12/01
	Michigan	Y	32120 FQ	46350 AW	64700 TQ	MIBLS	10/01-12/01
	Minnesota	Y	31600 FQ	43880 AW	58370 TQ	MNBLS	10/01-12/01
	Missouri	Y	25260 FQ	44390 AW	69050 TQ	MOBLS	10/01-12/01
	Montana	Y	24970 FQ	36740 AW	53180 TQ	MTBLS	10/01-12/01
	Nebraska	Y	29230 FQ	41560 AW	59870 TQ	NEBLS	10/01-12/01
	Nevada	Y	19300 FQ	41940 AW	59680 TQ	NVBLS	10/01-12/01
	New Hampshire	Y	25700 FQ	34910 AW	48700 TQ	NHBLS	10/01-12/01
	New Jersey	Y	27110 FQ	41220 AW	58990 TQ	NJBLS	10/01-12/01
	New Mexico	Y	27010 FQ	39780 AW	58380 TQ	NMBLS	10/01-12/01
	New York	Y	25140 FQ	41670 AW	61000 TQ	NYBLS	10/01-12/01
	North Carolina	Y	31280 FQ	47230 AW	68070 TQ	NCBLS	10/01-12/01
	Ohio	Y	20870 FQ	40720 AW	59330 TQ	OHBLS	10/01-12/01
	Oklahoma	Y	27080 FQ	44790 AW	65730 TQ	OKBLS	10/01-12/01
	Oregon	Y	30150 FQ	44240 AW	60700 TQ	ORBLS	10/01-12/01
	Pennsylvania	Y	23170 FQ	41860 AW	66190 TQ	PABLS	10/01-12/01
	South Carolina	Y	25530 FQ	40660 AW	58380 TQ	SCBLS	10/01-12/01
	Tennessee	Y	21420 FQ	37160 AW	54670 TQ	TNBLS	10/01-12/01
	Texas	Y	23310 FQ	36260 AW	54680 TQ	TXBLS	10/01-12/01
	Utah	Y	23540 FQ	41630 AW	64660 TQ	UTBLS	10/01-12/01
	Vermont	Y	36480 FQ	43000 AW	53100 TQ	VTBLS	10/01-12/01
	Virginia	Y	27170 FQ	53960 AW	85900 TQ	VABLS	10/01-12/01
	Washington	Y	33770 FQ	48620 AW	60570 TQ	WABLS	10/01-12/01
	Wisconsin	Y	24430 FQ	36860 AW	54840 TQ	WIBLS	10/01-12/01
Cashier	Alabama	Y	11560 FQ	14040 AW	17780 TQ	ALBLS	10/01-12/01
	Birmingham MSA, AL	Y	11590 FQ	14310 AW	18400 TQ	ALBLS	10/01-12/01
	Huntsville MSA, AL	Y	11530 FQ	14290 AW	18300 TQ	ALBLS	10/01-12/01
	Mobile MSA, AL	Y	11640 FQ	14290 AW	17900 TQ	ALBLS	10/01-12/01
	Montgomery MSA, AL	Y	11590 FQ	14290 AW	18100 TQ	ALBLS	10/01-12/01
	Alaska	Y	14230 FQ	19560 AW	26980 TQ	AKBLS	10/01-12/01
	Anchorage MSA, AK	Y	14160 FQ	18570 AW	23520 TQ	AKBLS	10/01-12/01
	Arizona	Y	12070 FQ	17480 AW	27280 TQ	AZBLS	10/01-12/01

AAW	Average annual wage	**AOH**	Average offered, high	**ASH**	Average starting, high	**H**	Hourly	**M**	Monthly	**S**	Special: hourly and annual
AE	Average entry wage	**AOL**	Average offered, low	**ASL**	Average starting, low	**HI**	Highest wage paid	**MTC**	Median total compensation	**TQ**	Third quartile wage
AEX	Average experienced wage	**APH**	Average pay, high range	**AW**	Average wage paid	**HR**	High end range	**MW**	Median wage paid	**W**	Weekly
AO	Average offered	**APL**	Average pay, low range	**FQ**	First quartile wage	**LR**	Low end range	**SQ**	Second quartile wage	**Y**	Yearly

Occupation/Type/Industry	Location	Per	Low	Mid	High	Source	Date
Cashier	Phoenix-Mesa MSA, AZ	Y	12310 FQ	17620 AW	26390 TQ	AZBLS	10/01-12/01
	Tucson MSA, AZ	Y	11980 FQ	18390 AW	31250 TQ	AZBLS	10/01-12/01
	Arkansas	Y	11530 FQ	14020 AW	17800 TQ	ARBLS	10/01-12/01
	Fayetteville-Springdale-Rogers MSA, AR	Y	11480 FQ	13870 AW	17410 TQ	ARBLS	10/01-12/01
	Fort Smith MSA, AR-OK	Y	11640 FQ	14070 AW	17470 TQ	ARBLS	10/01-12/01
	Little Rock-North Little Rock MSA, AR	Y	11700 FQ	14860 AW	19360 TQ	ARBLS	10/01-12/01
	California	Y	13510 FQ	19670 AW	33620 TQ	CABLS	10/01-12/01
	Bakersfield MSA, CA	Y	13300 FQ	17830 AW	28730 TQ	CABLS	10/01-12/01
	Chico-Paradise MSA, CA	Y	13500 FQ	19540 AW	35650 TQ	CABLS	10/01-12/01
	Fresno MSA, CA	Y	13340 FQ	17120 AW	24920 TQ	CABLS	10/01-12/01
	Los Angeles-Long Beach PMSA, CA	Y	13420 FQ	19510 AW	33430 TQ	CABLS	10/01-12/01
	Merced MSA, CA	Y	13400 FQ	18530 AW	30380 TQ	CABLS	10/01-12/01
	Modesto MSA, CA	Y	13380 FQ	18610 AW	29110 TQ	CABLS	10/01-12/01
	Oakland PMSA, CA	Y	13690 FQ	20320 AW	34150 TQ	CABLS	10/01-12/01
	Orange County PMSA, CA	Y	13560 FQ	19690 AW	34110 TQ	CABLS	10/01-12/01
	Redding MSA, CA	Y	13440 FQ	18690 AW	30910 TQ	CABLS	10/01-12/01
	Riverside-San Bernardino PMSA, CA	Y	13560 FQ	19770 AW	34770 TQ	CABLS	10/01-12/01
	Sacramento PMSA, CA	Y	13570 FQ	20380 AW	37680 TQ	CABLS	10/01-12/01
	Salinas MSA, CA	Y	13830 FQ	19410 AW	29110 TQ	CABLS	10/01-12/01
	San Diego MSA, CA	Y	13450 FQ	19270 AW	33540 TQ	CABLS	10/01-12/01
	San Francisco PMSA, CA	Y	14210 FQ	22130 AW	36100 TQ	CABLS	10/01-12/01
	San Jose PMSA, CA	Y	13860 FQ	20370 AW	33320 TQ	CABLS	10/01-12/01
	San Luis Obispo-Atascadero-Paso Robles MSA, CA	Y	13530 FQ	20860 AW	38690 TQ	CABLS	10/01-12/01
	Santa Barbara-Santa Maria-Lompoc MSA, CA	Y	13730 FQ	19100 AW	29470 TQ	CABLS	10/01-12/01
	Santa Cruz-Watsonville PMSA, CA	Y	13800 FQ	20270 AW	36550 TQ	CABLS	10/01-12/01
	Santa Rosa PMSA, CA	Y	14040 FQ	21920 AW	39250 TQ	CABLS	10/01-12/01
	Stockton-Lodi MSA, CA	Y	13380 FQ	18130 AW	26920 TQ	CABLS	10/01-12/01
	Vallejo-Fairfield-Napa PMSA, CA	Y	13720 FQ	20110 AW	35140 TQ	CABLS	10/01-12/01
	Ventura PMSA, CA	Y	13530 FQ	20130 AW	36740 TQ	CABLS	10/01-12/01
	Visalia-Tulare-Porterville MSA, CA	Y	13360 FQ	17440 AW	25360 TQ	CABLS	10/01-12/01
	Colorado	Y	12460 FQ	18510 AW	29540 TQ	COBLS	10/01-12/01
	Boulder-Longmont PMSA, CO	Y	14360 FQ	20050 AW	31660 TQ	COBLS	10/01-12/01
	Colorado Springs MSA, CO	Y	12270 FQ	17440 AW	26240 TQ	COBLS	10/01-12/01
	Denver PMSA, CO	Y	13010 FQ	18840 AW	29660 TQ	COBLS	10/01-12/01
	Fort Collins-Loveland MSA, CO	Y	11720 FQ	17200 AW	28750 TQ	COBLS	10/01-12/01
	Greeley PMSA, CO	Y	12300 FQ	18820 AW	29820 TQ	COBLS	10/01-12/01
	Connecticut	Y	13770 FQ	17410 AW	22420 TQ	CTBLS	10/01-12/01
	Bridgeport PMSA, CT	Y	13720 FQ	17280 AW	22410 TQ	CTBLS	10/01-12/01
	Danbury PMSA, CT	Y	13790 FQ	18160 AW	24840 TQ	CTBLS	10/01-12/01
	Hartford MSA, CT	Y	13790 FQ	17050 AW	21520 TQ	CTBLS	10/01-12/01
	New Haven-Meriden PMSA, CT	Y	13710 FQ	16990 AW	21790 TQ	CTBLS	10/01-12/01
	New London-Norwich MSA, CT-RI	Y	13870 FQ	17220 AW	21660 TQ	CTBLS	10/01-12/01
	Stamford-Norwalk PMSA, CT	Y	14020 FQ	19610 AW	29800 TQ	CTBLS	10/01-12/01
	Waterbury PMSA, CT	Y	13600 FQ	16890 AW	22720 TQ	CTBLS	10/01-12/01
	Delaware	Y	13500 FQ	16870 AW	22140 TQ	DEBLS	10/01-12/01
	Wilmington-Newark PMSA, DE-MD	Y	13400 FQ	17020 AW	22760 TQ	DEBLS	10/01-12/01
	District of Columbia	Y	14460 FQ	20450 AW	28400 TQ	DCBLS	10/01-12/01
	Washington PMSA, DC-MD-VA-WV	Y	12360 FQ	18070 AW	28200 TQ	DCBLS	10/01-12/01
	Florida	Y	11770 FQ	15460 AW	21380 TQ	FLBLS	10/01-12/01
	Daytona Beach MSA, FL	Y	11800 FQ	15400 AW	21800 TQ	FLBLS	10/01-12/01
	Fort Lauderdale PMSA, FL	Y	11840 FQ	15790 AW	22260 TQ	FLBLS	10/01-12/01
	Fort Myers-Cape Coral MSA, FL	Y	11840 FQ	16070 AW	22460 TQ	FLBLS	10/01-12/01
	Fort Pierce-Port St. Lucie MSA, FL	Y	11820 FQ	15710 AW	21420 TQ	FLBLS	10/01-12/01
	Fort Walton Beach MSA, FL	Y	11680 FQ	14820 AW	18770 TQ	FLBLS	10/01-12/01
	Gainesville MSA, FL	Y	11730 FQ	15810 AW	24310 TQ	FLBLS	10/01-12/01
	Jacksonville MSA, FL	Y	11710 FQ	15060 AW	19960 TQ	FLBLS	10/01-12/01

AAW Average annual wage **AOH** Average offered, high **ASH** Average starting, high **H** Hourly **M** Monthly **S** Special: hourly and annual
AE Average entry wage **AOL** Average offered, low **ASL** Average starting, low **HI** Highest wage paid **MTC** Median total compensation **TQ** Third quartile wage
AEX Average experienced wage **APH** Average pay, high range **AW** Average wage paid **HR** High end range **MW** Median wage paid **W** Weekly
AO Average offered **APL** Average pay, low range **FQ** First quartile wage **LR** Low end range **SQ** Second quartile wage **Y** Yearly

Occupation/Type/Industry	Location	Per	Low	Mid	High	Source	Date
Cashier	Lakeland-Winter Haven MSA, FL	Y	11590 FQ	14330 AW	18410 TQ	FLBLS	10/01-12/01
	Melbourne-Titusville-Palm Bay MSA, FL	Y	11740 FQ	15270 AW	21370 TQ	FLBLS	10/01-12/01
	Miami PMSA, FL	Y	11730 FQ	15620 AW	22050 TQ	FLBLS	10/01-12/01
	Naples MSA, FL	Y	12060 FQ	17230 AW	25120 TQ	FLBLS	10/01-12/01
	Ocala MSA, FL	Y	11650 FQ	15090 AW	22320 TQ	FLBLS	10/01-12/01
	Orlando MSA, FL	Y	11900 FQ	15670 AW	21050 TQ	FLBLS	10/01-12/01
	Pensacola MSA, FL	Y	11510 FQ	14210 AW	17940 TQ	FLBLS	10/01-12/01
	Sarasota-Bradenton MSA, FL	Y	11890 FQ	16400 AW	23850 TQ	FLBLS	10/01-12/01
	Tallahassee MSA, FL	Y	11670 FQ	16240 AW	25210 TQ	FLBLS	10/01-12/01
	Tampa-St. Petersburg-Clearwater MSA, FL	Y	11780 FQ	15300 AW	20690 TQ	FLBLS	10/01-12/01
	West Palm Beach-Boca Raton MSA, FL	Y	11850 FQ	15320 AW	20280 TQ	FLBLS	10/01-12/01
	Georgia	Y	11740 FQ	15280 AW	20290 TQ	GABLS	10/01-12/01
	Atlanta MSA, GA	Y	12150 FQ	16370 AW	21880 TQ	GABLS	10/01-12/01
	Augusta-Aiken MSA, GA-SC	Y	11600 FQ	14210 AW	18010 TQ	GABLS	10/01-12/01
	Columbus MSA, GA-AL	Y	11650 FQ	14480 AW	18940 TQ	GABLS	10/01-12/01
	Macon MSA, GA	Y	11540 FQ	14100 AW	18030 TQ	GABLS	10/01-12/01
	Savannah MSA, GA	Y	11580 FQ	14250 AW	18010 TQ	GABLS	10/01-12/01
	Hawaii	Y	12530 FQ	19000 AW	29570 TQ	HIBLS	10/01-12/01
	Honolulu MSA, HI	Y	12510 FQ	19430 AW	31060 TQ	HIBLS	10/01-12/01
	Idaho	Y	11720 FQ	15550 AW	21930 TQ	IDBLS	10/01-12/01
	Boise City MSA, ID	Y	11990 FQ	16650 AW	22840 TQ	IDBLS	10/01-12/01
	Illinois	Y	11790 FQ	15830 AW	21300 TQ	ILBLS	10/01-12/01
	Champaign-Urbana MSA, IL	Y	11750 FQ	15100 AW	18650 TQ	ILBLS	10/01-12/01
	Chicago PMSA, IL	Y	11960 FQ	16440 AW	21890 TQ	ILBLS	10/01-12/01
	Peoria-Pekin MSA, IL	Y	11600 FQ	14870 AW	20300 TQ	ILBLS	10/01-12/01
	Rockford MSA, IL	Y	11730 FQ	15490 AW	20880 TQ	ILBLS	10/01-12/01
	Springfield MSA, IL	Y	11610 FQ	15320 AW	20610 TQ	ILBLS	10/01-12/01
	Indiana	Y	11790 FQ	15230 AW	20410 TQ	INBLS	10/01-12/01
	Elkhart-Goshen MSA, IN	Y	12020 FQ	15830 AW	20750 TQ	INBLS	10/01-12/01
	Evansville-Henderson MSA, IN-KY	Y	11720 FQ	15460 AW	21120 TQ	INBLS	10/01-12/01
	Fort Wayne MSA, IN	Y	11870 FQ	15240 AW	19880 TQ	INBLS	10/01-12/01
	Gary PMSA, IN	Y	11770 FQ	15120 AW	20320 TQ	INBLS	10/01-12/01
	Indianapolis MSA, IN	Y	11970 FQ	15970 AW	21810 TQ	INBLS	10/01-12/01
	Lafayette MSA, IN	Y	11800 FQ	15050 AW	19470 TQ	INBLS	10/01-12/01
	South Bend MSA, IN	Y	11680 FQ	14980 AW	19940 TQ	INBLS	10/01-12/01
	Iowa	Y	11660 FQ	14620 AW	18750 TQ	IABLS	10/01-12/01
	Cedar Rapids MSA, IA	Y	11880 FQ	15360 AW	20080 TQ	IABLS	10/01-12/01
	Davenport-Moline-Rock Island MSA, IA-IL	Y	11640 FQ	14190 AW	17750 TQ	IABLS	10/01-12/01
	Des Moines MSA, IA	Y	11950 FQ	15720 AW	21350 TQ	IABLS	10/01-12/01
	Kansas	Y	11690 FQ	14660 AW	18350 TQ	KSBLS	10/01-12/01
	Topeka MSA, KS	Y	11850 FQ	15250 AW	19510 TQ	KSBLS	10/01-12/01
	Wichita MSA, KS	Y	11870 FQ	15180 AW	18740 TQ	KSBLS	10/01-12/01
	Kentucky	Y	11680 FQ	15000 AW	19310 TQ	KYBLS	10/01-12/01
	Lexington MSA, KY	Y	11940 FQ	16600 AW	23570 TQ	KYBLS	10/01-12/01
	Louisville MSA, KY-IN	Y	11960 FQ	15470 AW	19950 TQ	KYBLS	10/01-12/01
	Louisiana	Y	11480 FQ	13950 AW	17700 TQ	LABLS	10/01-12/01
	Baton Rouge MSA, LA	Y	11540 FQ	14260 AW	17970 TQ	LABLS	10/01-12/01
	Houma MSA, LA	Y	11440 FQ	13580 AW	17090 TQ	LABLS	10/01-12/01
	Lafayette MSA, LA	Y	11490 FQ	14010 AW	17690 TQ	LABLS	10/01-12/01
	Lake Charles MSA, LA	Y	11600 FQ	14190 AW	18080 TQ	LABLS	10/01-12/01
	New Orleans MSA, LA	Y	11440 FQ	13800 AW	17530 TQ	LABLS	10/01-12/01
	Shreveport-Bossier City MSA, LA	Y	11630 FQ	14690 AW	19560 TQ	LABLS	10/01-12/01
	Maine	Y	11890 FQ	15660 AW	20770 TQ	MEBLS	10/01-12/01
	Portland MSA, ME	Y	12680 FQ	16640 AW	21630 TQ	MEBLS	10/01-12/01
	Maryland	Y	12170 FQ	17940 AW	29660 TQ	MDBLS	10/01-12/01
	Baltimore PMSA, MD	Y	12230 FQ	18000 AW	28980 TQ	MDBLS	10/01-12/01
	Massachusetts	Y	14270 FQ	17430 AW	22050 TQ	MABLS	10/01-12/01
	Boston PMSA, MA-NH	Y	14270 FQ	17490 AW	22120 TQ	MABLS	10/01-12/01
	Brockton PMSA, MA	Y	14280 FQ	17360 AW	21940 TQ	MABLS	10/01-12/01
	Lawrence PMSA, MA-NH	Y	14050 FQ	17230 AW	21990 TQ	MABLS	10/01-12/01
	Lowell PMSA, MA-NH	Y	14220 FQ	17280 AW	22060 TQ	MABLS	10/01-12/01
	New Bedford PMSA, MA	Y	14270 FQ	16870 AW	21010 TQ	MABLS	10/01-12/01
	Springfield MSA, MA	Y	14250 FQ	17060 AW	21510 TQ	MABLS	10/01-12/01
	Worcester PMSA, MA-CT	Y	14270 FQ	17300 AW	22110 TQ	MABLS	10/01-12/01
	Michigan	Y	11910 FQ	16290 AW	22480 TQ	MIBLS	10/01-12/01

AAW	Average annual wage	**AOH**	Average offered, high	**ASH**	Average starting, high	**H**	Hourly	**M**	Monthly	**S**	Special: hourly and annual
AE	Average entry wage	**AOL**	Average offered, low	**ASL**	Average starting, low	**HI**	Highest wage paid	**MTC**	Median total compensation	**TQ**	Third quartile wage
AEX	Average experienced wage	**APH**	Average pay, high range	**AW**	Average wage paid	**HR**	High end range	**MW**	Median wage paid	**W**	Weekly
AO	Average offered	**APL**	Average pay, low range	**FQ**	First quartile wage	**LR**	Low end range	**SQ**	Second quartile wage	**Y**	Yearly

Occupation/Type/Industry	Location	Per	Low	Mid	High	Source	Date
Cashier	Ann Arbor PMSA, MI	Y	12750 FQ	18180 AW	26270 TQ	MIBLS	10/01-12/01
	Detroit PMSA, MI	Y	11930 FQ	16680 AW	23950 TQ	MIBLS	10/01-12/01
	Flint PMSA, MI	Y	11790 FQ	16250 AW	22370 TQ	MIBLS	10/01-12/01
	Grand Rapids-Muskegon-Holland MSA, MI	Y	12040 FQ	16270 AW	22020 TQ	MIBLS	10/01-12/01
	Kalamazoo-Battle Creek MSA, MI	Y	12000 FQ	16040 AW	21770 TQ	MIBLS	10/01-12/01
	Lansing-East Lansing MSA, MI	Y	11980 FQ	15840 AW	22110 TQ	MIBLS	10/01-12/01
	Saginaw-Bay City-Midland MSA, MI	Y	11660 FQ	15440 AW	21330 TQ	MIBLS	10/01-12/01
	Minnesota	Y	12180 FQ	16510 AW	21810 TQ	MNBLS	10/01-12/01
	Duluth-Superior MSA, MN-WI	Y	11810 FQ	15310 AW	21770 TQ	MNBLS	10/01-12/01
	Minneapolis-St. Paul MSA, MN-WI	Y	13220 FQ	17500 AW	22590 TQ	MNBLS	10/01-12/01
	St. Cloud MSA, MN	Y	11850 FQ	14970 AW	18710 TQ	MNBLS	10/01-12/01
	Mississippi	Y	11510 FQ	14020 AW	17940 TQ	MSBLS	10/01-12/01
	Biloxi-Gulfport-Pascagoula MSA, MS	Y	11590 FQ	13940 AW	17630 TQ	MSBLS	10/01-12/01
	Jackson MSA, MS	Y	11630 FQ	14500 AW	18380 TQ	MSBLS	10/01-12/01
	Missouri	Y	11760 FQ	15140 AW	19600 TQ	MOBLS	10/01-12/01
	Kansas City MSA, MO-KS	Y	11990 FQ	15790 AW	20410 TQ	MOBLS	10/01-12/01
	St. Louis MSA, MO-IL	Y	11950 FQ	15710 AW	20580 TQ	MOBLS	10/01-12/01
	Springfield MSA, MO	Y	11750 FQ	15270 AW	20010 TQ	MOBLS	10/01-12/01
	Montana	Y	11730 FQ	15520 AW	21190 TQ	MTBLS	10/01-12/01
	Billings MSA, MT	Y	11780 FQ	15800 AW	21690 TQ	MTBLS	10/01-12/01
	Nebraska	Y	11740 FQ	14740 AW	18660 TQ	NEBLS	10/01-12/01
	Lincoln MSA, NE	Y	11650 FQ	14460 AW	18150 TQ	NEBLS	10/01-12/01
	Omaha MSA, NE-IA	Y	12120 FQ	15960 AW	20800 TQ	NEBLS	10/01-12/01
	Nevada	Y	12000 FQ	18200 AW	28400 TQ	NVBLS	10/01-12/01
	Las Vegas MSA, NV-AZ	Y	11930 FQ	17950 AW	27910 TQ	NVBLS	10/01-12/01
	Reno MSA, NV	Y	12640 FQ	19600 AW	30480 TQ	NVBLS	10/01-12/01
	New Hampshire	Y	12270 FQ	16120 AW	21060 TQ	NHBLS	10/01-12/01
	Manchester PMSA, NH	Y	12460 FQ	16580 AW	21610 TQ	NHBLS	10/01-12/01
	Nashua PMSA, NH	Y	13380 FQ	17040 AW	21740 TQ	NHBLS	10/01-12/01
	Portsmouth-Rochester PMSA, NH-ME	Y	13190 FQ	17310 AW	22210 TQ	NHBLS	10/01-12/01
	New Jersey	Y	11840 FQ	16670 AW	23150 TQ	NJBLS	10/01-12/01
	Atlantic-Cape May PMSA, NJ	Y	11980 FQ	17120 AW	23840 TQ	NJBLS	10/01-12/01
	Bergen-Passaic PMSA, NJ	Y	11930 FQ	16910 AW	23280 TQ	NJBLS	10/01-12/01
	Jersey City PMSA, NJ	Y	11610 FQ	15870 AW	22360 TQ	NJBLS	10/01-12/01
	Middlesex-Somerset-Hunterdon PMSA, NJ	Y	11930 FQ	16770 AW	23050 TQ	NJBLS	10/01-12/01
	Monmouth-Ocean PMSA, NJ	Y	11910 FQ	16800 AW	22890 TQ	NJBLS	10/01-12/01
	Newark PMSA, NJ	Y	11720 FQ	16620 AW	24110 TQ	NJBLS	10/01-12/01
	Trenton PMSA, NJ	Y	11980 FQ	17280 AW	24890 TQ	NJBLS	10/01-12/01
	New Mexico	Y	11700 FQ	15600 AW	22510 TQ	NMBLS	10/01-12/01
	Albuquerque MSA, NM	Y	11890 FQ	16420 AW	24170 TQ	NMBLS	10/01-12/01
	Las Cruces MSA, NM	Y	11670 FQ	15160 AW	20610 TQ	NMBLS	10/01-12/01
	New York	Y	11660 FQ	15670 AW	21610 TQ	NYBLS	10/01-12/01
	Albany-Schenectady-Troy MSA, NY	Y	11820 FQ	15500 AW	20540 TQ	NYBLS	10/01-12/01
	Binghamton MSA, NY	Y	11530 FQ	13890 AW	17560 TQ	NYBLS	10/01-12/01
	Buffalo-Niagara Falls MSA, NY	Y	11510 FQ	14310 AW	18780 TQ	NYBLS	10/01-12/01
	Dutchess County PMSA, NY	Y	11860 FQ	15330 AW	20490 TQ	NYBLS	10/01-12/01
	Nassau-Suffolk PMSA, NY	Y	12130 FQ	17130 AW	22300 TQ	NYBLS	10/01-12/01
	New York PMSA, NY	Y	11660 FQ	16400 AW	24270 TQ	NYBLS	10/01-12/01
	Newburgh PMSA, NY-PA	Y	11760 FQ	15600 AW	21360 TQ	NYBLS	10/01-12/01
	Rochester MSA, NY	Y	11470 FQ	14230 AW	18000 TQ	NYBLS	10/01-12/01
	Syracuse MSA, NY	Y	11470 FQ	13920 AW	17530 TQ	NYBLS	10/01-12/01
	Utica-Rome MSA, NY	Y	11570 FQ	14210 AW	18070 TQ	NYBLS	10/01-12/01
	North Carolina	Y	11780 FQ	15190 AW	19920 TQ	NCBLS	10/01-12/01
	Asheville MSA, NC	Y	11880 FQ	15500 AW	20470 TQ	NCBLS	10/01-12/01
	Charlotte-Gastonia-Rock Hill MSA, NC-SC	Y	12060 FQ	15840 AW	20660 TQ	NCBLS	10/01-12/01
	Fayetteville MSA, NC	Y	11560 FQ	13970 AW	17750 TQ	NCBLS	10/01-12/01
	Greensboro-Winston-Salem-High Point MSA, NC	Y	11810 FQ	15410 AW	20240 TQ	NCBLS	10/01-12/01
	Hickory-Morganton-Lenoir MSA, NC	Y	11850 FQ	15180 AW	18980 TQ	NCBLS	10/01-12/01
	Raleigh-Durham-Chapel Hill MSA, NC	Y	12220 FQ	16200 AW	21350 TQ	NCBLS	10/01-12/01

AAW	Average annual wage	AOH	Average offered, high	ASH	Average starting, high	H	Hourly	M	Monthly	S	Special: hourly and annual
AE	Average entry wage	AOL	Average offered, low	ASL	Average starting, low	HI	Highest wage paid	MTC	Median total compensation	TQ	Third quartile wage
AEX	Average experienced wage	APH	Average pay, high range	AW	Average wage paid	HR	High end range	MW	Median wage paid	W	Weekly
AO	Average offered	APL	Average pay, low range	FQ	First quartile wage	LR	Low end range	SQ	Second quartile wage	Y	Yearly

Occupation/Type/Industry	Location	Per	Low	Mid	High	Source	Date
Cashier	Wilmington MSA, NC	Y	11840 FQ	15030 AW	19250 TQ	NCBLS	10/01-12/01
	North Dakota	Y	11690 FQ	14380 AW	17950 TQ	NDBLS	10/01-12/01
	Fargo-Moorhead MSA, ND-MN	Y	11900 FQ	15130 AW	18530 TQ	NDBLS	10/01-12/01
	Ohio	Y	11760 FQ	15290 AW	20470 TQ	OHBLS	10/01-12/01
	Akron PMSA, OH	Y	11800 FQ	16050 AW	22980 TQ	OHBLS	10/01-12/01
	Canton-Massillon MSA, OH	Y	11580 FQ	14120 AW	17670 TQ	OHBLS	10/01-12/01
	Cincinnati PMSA, OH-KY-IN	Y	11840 FQ	15820 AW	22050 TQ	OHBLS	10/01-12/01
	Cleveland-Lorain-Elyria PMSA, OH	Y	11810 FQ	15340 AW	19940 TQ	OHBLS	10/01-12/01
	Columbus MSA, OH	Y	12270 FQ	16180 AW	21180 TQ	OHBLS	10/01-12/01
	Dayton-Springfield MSA, OH	Y	11820 FQ	15370 AW	20490 TQ	OHBLS	10/01-12/01
	Hamilton-Middletown PMSA, OH	Y	11840 FQ	15640 AW	21650 TQ	OHBLS	10/01-12/01
	Mansfield MSA, OH	Y	11800 FQ	15120 AW	19620 TQ	OHBLS	10/01-12/01
	Toledo MSA, OH	Y	11700 FQ	15300 AW	20990 TQ	OHBLS	10/01-12/01
	Youngstown-Warren MSA, OH	Y	11570 FQ	14060 AW	17860 TQ	OHBLS	10/01-12/01
	Oklahoma	Y	11540 FQ	14050 AW	17780 TQ	OKBLS	10/01-12/01
	Oklahoma City MSA, OK	Y	11600 FQ	14390 AW	18250 TQ	OKBLS	10/01-12/01
	Tulsa MSA, OK	Y	11670 FQ	14890 AW	19700 TQ	OKBLS	10/01-12/01
	Oregon	Y	14440 FQ	19100 AW	27800 TQ	ORBLS	10/01-12/01
	Eugene-Springfield MSA, OR	Y	14230 FQ	18370 AW	26090 TQ	ORBLS	10/01-12/01
	Medford-Ashland MSA, OR	Y	14380 FQ	18770 AW	26610 TQ	ORBLS	10/01-12/01
	Portland-Vancouver PMSA, OR-WA	Y	14560 FQ	20000 AW	30910 TQ	ORBLS	10/01-12/01
	Salem PMSA, OR	Y	14410 FQ	18440 AW	25970 TQ	ORBLS	10/01-12/01
	Pennsylvania	Y	11670 FQ	15320 AW	20220 TQ	PABLS	10/01-12/01
	Allentown-Bethlehem-Easton MSA, PA	Y	11720 FQ	15160 AW	19550 TQ	PABLS	10/01-12/01
	Erie MSA, PA	Y	11490 FQ	14050 AW	17810 TQ	PABLS	10/01-12/01
	Harrisburg-Lebanon-Carlisle MSA, PA	Y	11810 FQ	16990 AW	28510 TQ	PABLS	10/01-12/01
	Johnstown MSA, PA	Y	11520 FQ	13610 AW	16980 TQ	PABLS	10/01-12/01
	Lancaster MSA, PA	Y	11850 FQ	15420 AW	19760 TQ	PABLS	10/01-12/01
	Philadelphia PMSA, PA-NJ	Y	11790 FQ	16520 AW	23290 TQ	PABLS	10/01-12/01
	Pittsburgh MSA, PA	Y	11650 FQ	14580 AW	18020 TQ	PABLS	10/01-12/01
	Reading MSA, PA	Y	11710 FQ	14920 AW	19530 TQ	PABLS	10/01-12/01
	Scranton-Wilkes-Barre-Hazleton MSA, PA	Y	11620 FQ	14360 AW	18400 TQ	PABLS	10/01-12/01
	York MSA, PA	Y	11710 FQ	14710 AW	18700 TQ	PABLS	10/01-12/01
	Rhode Island	Y	13410 FQ	16590 AW	21160 TQ	RIBLS	10/01-12/01
	Providence-Fall River-Warwick MSA, RI-MA	Y	13520 FQ	16770 AW	21470 TQ	RIBLS	10/01-12/01
	South Carolina	Y	11640 FQ	14750 AW	19230 TQ	SCBLS	10/01-12/01
	Charleston-North Charleston MSA, SC	Y	11650 FQ	14560 AW	18450 TQ	SCBLS	10/01-12/01
	Columbia MSA, SC	Y	11770 FQ	15140 AW	20140 TQ	SCBLS	10/01-12/01
	Greenville-Spartanburg-Anderson MSA, SC	Y	11780 FQ	15170 AW	19860 TQ	SCBLS	10/01-12/01
	Myrtle Beach MSA, SC	Y	11610 FQ	15130 AW	20460 TQ	SCBLS	10/01-12/01
	South Dakota	Y	11690 FQ	14380 AW	17780 TQ	SDBLS	10/01-12/01
	Sioux Falls MSA, SD	Y	11810 FQ	14880 AW	18220 TQ	SDBLS	10/01-12/01
	Tennessee	Y	11690 FQ	15170 AW	20620 TQ	TNBLS	10/01-12/01
	Chattanooga MSA, TN-GA	Y	11770 FQ	14790 AW	18680 TQ	TNBLS	10/01-12/01
	Clarksville-Hopkinsville MSA, TN-KY	Y	11830 FQ	14820 AW	18190 TQ	TNBLS	10/01-12/01
	Johnson City-Kingsport-Bristol MSA, TN-VA	Y	11510 FQ	14290 AW	18530 TQ	TNBLS	10/01-12/01
	Knoxville MSA, TN	Y	12030 FQ	16210 AW	22220 TQ	TNBLS	10/01-12/01
	Memphis MSA, TN-AR-MS	Y	11710 FQ	15250 AW	20780 TQ	TNBLS	10/01-12/01
	Nashville MSA, TN	Y	11930 FQ	16120 AW	21790 TQ	TNBLS	10/01-12/01
	Texas	Y	11710 FQ	15390 AW	20750 TQ	TXBLS	10/01-12/01
	Amarillo MSA, TX	Y	11650 FQ	14760 AW	18610 TQ	TXBLS	10/01-12/01
	Austin-San Marcos MSA, TX	Y	12560 FQ	16870 AW	21780 TQ	TXBLS	10/01-12/01
	Beaumont-Port Arthur MSA, TX	Y	11530 FQ	14230 AW	18890 TQ	TXBLS	10/01-12/01
	Brazoria PMSA, TX	Y	11510 FQ	14340 AW	19000 TQ	TXBLS	10/01-12/01
	Brownsville-Harlingen-San Benito MSA, TX	Y	11520 FQ	14590 AW	20090 TQ	TXBLS	10/01-12/01
	Corpus Christi MSA, TX	Y	11540 FQ	15370 AW	20010 TQ	TXBLS	10/01-12/01
	Dallas PMSA, TX	Y	12270 FQ	16840 AW	22270 TQ	TXBLS	10/01-12/01
	El Paso MSA, TX	Y	11490 FQ	14040 AW	17940 TQ	TXBLS	10/01-12/01

AAW	Average annual wage	**AOH**	Average offered, high	**ASH**	Average starting, high	**H**	Hourly	**M**	Monthly	**S**	Special: hourly and annual
AE	Average entry wage	**AOL**	Average offered, low	**ASL**	Average starting, low	**HI**	Highest wage paid	**MTC**	Median total compensation	**TQ**	Third quartile wage
AEX	Average experienced wage	**APH**	Average pay, high range	**AW**	Average wage paid	**HR**	High end range	**MW**	Median wage paid	**W**	Weekly
AO	Average offered	**APL**	Average pay, low range	**FQ**	First quartile wage	**LR**	Low end range	**SQ**	Second quartile wage	**Y**	Yearly

Occupation/Type/Industry	Location	Per	Low	Mid	High	Source	Date
Cashier	Fort Worth-Arlington PMSA, TX	Y	11980 FQ	16070 AW	21230 TQ	TXBLS	10/01-12/01
	Galveston-Texas City PMSA, TX	Y	11550 FQ	14460 AW	18690 TQ	TXBLS	10/01-12/01
	Houston PMSA, TX	Y	11760 FQ	15250 AW	20620 TQ	TXBLS	10/01-12/01
	Killeen-Temple MSA, TX	Y	11570 FQ	14660 AW	19270 TQ	TXBLS	10/01-12/01
	Laredo MSA, TX	Y	11480 FQ	15110 AW	21110 TQ	TXBLS	10/01-12/01
	Longview-Marshall MSA, TX	Y	11380 FQ	13680 AW	17180 TQ	TXBLS	10/01-12/01
	Lubbock MSA, TX	Y	11600 FQ	14180 AW	18070 TQ	TXBLS	10/01-12/01
	McAllen-Edinburg-Mission MSA, TX	Y	11470 FQ	14370 AW	19240 TQ	TXBLS	10/01-12/01
	Odessa-Midland MSA, TX	Y	11520 FQ	14770 AW	20030 TQ	TXBLS	10/01-12/01
	San Antonio MSA, TX	Y	11910 FQ	16000 AW	21240 TQ	TXBLS	10/01-12/01
	Tyler MSA, TX	Y	11730 FQ	15290 AW	20470 TQ	TXBLS	10/01-12/01
	Waco MSA, TX	Y	11840 FQ	15410 AW	20200 TQ	TXBLS	10/01-12/01
	Utah	Y	11810 FQ	15590 AW	20840 TQ	UTBLS	10/01-12/01
	Provo-Orem MSA, UT	Y	11790 FQ	15380 AW	20170 TQ	UTBLS	10/01-12/01
	Salt Lake City-Ogden MSA, UT	Y	11970 FQ	16140 AW	21530 TQ	UTBLS	10/01-12/01
	Vermont	Y	13350 FQ	15930 AW	19940 TQ	VTBLS	10/01-12/01
	Burlington MSA, VT	Y	13570 FQ	16660 AW	21140 TQ	VTBLS	10/01-12/01
	Virginia	Y	11760 FQ	15370 AW	20420 TQ	VABLS	10/01-12/01
	Lynchburg MSA, VA	Y	11570 FQ	14360 AW	17750 TQ	VABLS	10/01-12/01
	Norfolk-Virginia Beach-Newport News MSA, VA-NC	Y	11660 FQ	14220 AW	17960 TQ	VABLS	10/01-12/01
	Richmond-Petersburg MSA, VA	Y	11960 FQ	15730 AW	20170 TQ	VABLS	10/01-12/01
	Roanoke MSA, VA	Y	11880 FQ	15540 AW	20720 TQ	VABLS	10/01-12/01
	Washington	Y	14380 FQ	20140 AW	31350 TQ	WABLS	10/01-12/01
	Bremerton PMSA, WA	Y	14170 FQ	20240 AW	32820 TQ	WABLS	10/01-12/01
	Olympia PMSA, WA	Y	14250 FQ	19870 AW	31510 TQ	WABLS	10/01-12/01
	Richland-Kennewick-Pasco MSA, WA	Y	14150 FQ	17870 AW	24820 TQ	WABLS	10/01-12/01
	Seattle-Bellevue-Everett PMSA, WA	Y	14920 FQ	21250 AW	32680 TQ	WABLS	10/01-12/01
	Spokane MSA, WA	Y	14370 FQ	18720 AW	27350 TQ	WABLS	10/01-12/01
	Tacoma PMSA, WA	Y	14220 FQ	19680 AW	31110 TQ	WABLS	10/01-12/01
	Yakima MSA, WA	Y	14240 FQ	19260 AW	30660 TQ	WABLS	10/01-12/01
	West Virginia	Y	11490 FQ	13800 AW	17250 TQ	WVBLS	10/01-12/01
	Charleston MSA, WV	Y	11450 FQ	14470 AW	19000 TQ	WVBLS	10/01-12/01
	Huntington-Ashland MSA, WV-KY-OH	Y	11500 FQ	13560 AW	16930 TQ	WVBLS	10/01-12/01
	Wisconsin	Y	11980 FQ	15780 AW	21000 TQ	WIBLS	10/01-12/01
	Appleton-Oshkosh-Neenah MSA, WI	Y	12190 FQ	16440 AW	21900 TQ	WIBLS	10/01-12/01
	Green Bay MSA, WI	Y	12000 FQ	15620 AW	20150 TQ	WIBLS	10/01-12/01
	Madison MSA, WI	Y	12540 FQ	16990 AW	22730 TQ	WIBLS	10/01-12/01
	Milwaukee-Waukesha PMSA, WI	Y	12270 FQ	16170 AW	21190 TQ	WIBLS	10/01-12/01
	Racine PMSA, WI	Y	11850 FQ	15640 AW	21320 TQ	WIBLS	10/01-12/01
	Wyoming	Y	11650 FQ	15410 AW	21380 TQ	WYBLS	10/01-12/01
	Cheyenne MSA, WY	Y	11670 FQ	16000 AW	23290 TQ	WYBLS	10/01-12/01
	Puerto Rico	Y	11440 FQ	12990 AW	14620 TQ	PRBLS	10/01-12/01
	Virgin Islands	Y	11560 FQ	14120 AW	18080 TQ	VIBLS	10/01-12/01
	Guam	Y	11570 FQ	14900 AW	20820 TQ	GUBLS	10/01-12/01
Hardware Store	United States	H		7.11 AW		DIYR	1/01-1/02
CBT and WEB and Multimedia Designer	Central	Y		49250 AW		TRAIN	1/01-1/02
	East North Central	Y		60338 AW		TRAIN	1/01-1/02
	Northeast	Y		65283 AW		TRAIN	1/01-1/02
	Pacific	Y		63570 AW		TRAIN	1/01-1/02
	Southeast	Y		56011 AW		TRAIN	1/01-1/02
	West Central	Y		64853 AW		TRAIN	1/01-1/02
Cement Mason and Concrete Finisher	Alabama	H	8.43 FQ	11.76 AW	15.88 TQ	ALBLS	10/01-12/01
	Birmingham MSA, AL	H	8.82 FQ	11.94 AW	16.05 TQ	ALBLS	10/01-12/01
	Huntsville MSA, AL	H	10.11 FQ	13.34 AW	17.60 TQ	ALBLS	10/01-12/01
	Mobile MSA, AL	H	9.00 FQ	11.42 AW	14.27 TQ	ALBLS	10/01-12/01
	Montgomery MSA, AL	H	7.45 FQ	10.21 AW	13.37 TQ	ALBLS	10/01-12/01

AAW	Average annual wage	AOH	Average offered, high	ASH	Average starting, high	H	Hourly	M	Monthly	S	Special: hourly and annual
AE	Average entry wage	AOL	Average offered, low	ASL	Average starting, low	HI	Highest wage paid	MTC	Median total compensation	TQ	Third quartile wage
AEX	Average experienced wage	APH	Average pay, high range	AW	Average wage paid	HR	High end range	MW	Median wage paid	W	Weekly
AO	Average offered	APL	Average pay, low range	FQ	First quartile wage	LR	Low end range	SQ	Second quartile wage	Y	Yearly

Occupation/Type/Industry	Location	Per	Low	Mid	High	Source	Date
Cement Mason and Concrete Finisher	Alaska	H	10.30 FQ	27.71 AW	42.69 TQ	AKBLS	10/01-12/01
	Anchorage MSA, AK	H	9.38 FQ	27.67 AW	44.03 TQ	AKBLS	10/01-12/01
	Arizona	H	10.35 FQ	14.76 AW	20.12 TQ	AZBLS	10/01-12/01
	Phoenix-Mesa MSA, AZ	H	10.46 FQ	14.83 AW	20.27 TQ	AZBLS	10/01-12/01
	Tucson MSA, AZ	H	10.04 FQ	14.61 AW	20.03 TQ	AZBLS	10/01-12/01
	Arkansas	H	7.93 FQ	11.70 AW	15.73 TQ	ARBLS	10/01-12/01
	Fayetteville-Springdale-Rogers MSA, AR	H	9.82 FQ	12.57 AW	15.33 TQ	ARBLS	10/01-12/01
	Fort Smith MSA, AR-OK	H	9.38 FQ	12.63 AW	16.30 TQ	ARBLS	10/01-12/01
	Little Rock-North Little Rock MSA, AR	H	7.54 FQ	11.34 AW	17.07 TQ	ARBLS	10/01-12/01
	California	H	6.85 FQ	16.99 AW	26.95 TQ	CABLS	10/01-12/01
	Bakersfield MSA, CA	H	9.78 FQ	14.53 AW	19.73 TQ	CABLS	10/01-12/01
	Chico-Paradise MSA, CA	H	11.94 FQ	17.00 AW	22.67 TQ	CABLS	10/01-12/01
	Fresno MSA, CA	H	9.06 FQ	15.94 AW	23.09 TQ	CABLS	10/01-12/01
	Los Angeles-Long Beach PMSA, CA	H	6.45 FQ	12.04 AW	23.56 TQ	CABLS	10/01-12/01
	Merced MSA, CA	H	9.59 FQ	13.65 AW	20.27 TQ	CABLS	10/01-12/01
	Modesto MSA, CA	H	7.70 FQ	13.60 AW	22.95 TQ	CABLS	10/01-12/01
	Oakland PMSA, CA	H	13.09 FQ	22.98 AW	30.55 TQ	CABLS	10/01-12/01
	Orange County PMSA, CA	H	11.00 FQ	19.41 AW	27.07 TQ	CABLS	10/01-12/01
	Redding MSA, CA	H	11.38 FQ	15.13 AW	20.64 TQ	CABLS	10/01-12/01
	Riverside-San Bernardino PMSA, CA	H	11.57 FQ	18.84 AW	27.23 TQ	CABLS	10/01-12/01
	Sacramento PMSA, CA	H	14.09 FQ	21.77 AW	32.31 TQ	CABLS	10/01-12/01
	Salinas MSA, CA	H	15.43 FQ	24.36 AW	33.98 TQ	CABLS	10/01-12/01
	San Diego MSA, CA	H	14.80 FQ	22.17 AW	28.22 TQ	CABLS	10/01-12/01
	San Francisco PMSA, CA	H	12.07 FQ	21.27 AW	28.34 TQ	CABLS	10/01-12/01
	San Jose PMSA, CA	H	10.40 FQ	19.40 AW	27.29 TQ	CABLS	10/01-12/01
	San Luis Obispo-Atascadero-Paso Robles MSA, CA	H	11.57 FQ	18.25 AW	25.68 TQ	CABLS	10/01-12/01
	Santa Barbara-Santa Maria-Lompoc MSA, CA	H	11.17 FQ	18.35 AW	24.80 TQ	CABLS	10/01-12/01
	Santa Cruz-Watsonville PMSA, CA	H	9.39 FQ	16.81 AW	25.78 TQ	CABLS	10/01-12/01
	Santa Rosa PMSA, CA	H	12.40 FQ	18.92 AW	26.13 TQ	CABLS	10/01-12/01
	Stockton-Lodi MSA, CA	H	11.41 FQ	18.86 AW	26.74 TQ	CABLS	10/01-12/01
	Vallejo-Fairfield-Napa PMSA, CA	H	9.44 FQ	18.37 AW	26.84 TQ	CABLS	10/01-12/01
	Ventura PMSA, CA	H	12.89 FQ	23.43 AW	36.51 TQ	CABLS	10/01-12/01
	Visalia-Tulare-Porterville MSA, CA	H	8.54 FQ	13.15 AW	18.79 TQ	CABLS	10/01-12/01
	Colorado	H	9.57 FQ	14.97 AW	21.06 TQ	COBLS	10/01-12/01
	Boulder-Longmont PMSA, CO	H	14.39 FQ	18.49 AW	22.33 TQ	COBLS	10/01-12/01
	Colorado Springs MSA, CO	H	11.42 FQ	16.25 AW	21.18 TQ	COBLS	10/01-12/01
	Denver PMSA, CO	H	9.45 FQ	15.47 AW	21.86 TQ	COBLS	10/01-12/01
	Fort Collins-Loveland MSA, CO	H	10.21 FQ	16.42 AW	22.30 TQ	COBLS	10/01-12/01
	Greeley PMSA, CO	H	9.09 FQ	12.88 AW	18.68 TQ	COBLS	10/01-12/01
	Connecticut	H	10.94 FQ	19.87 AW	29.84 TQ	CTBLS	10/01-12/01
	Bridgeport PMSA, CT	H	10.03 FQ	22.16 AW	34.35 TQ	CTBLS	10/01-12/01
	Danbury PMSA, CT	H	10.54 FQ	21.51 AW	33.36 TQ	CTBLS	10/01-12/01
	Hartford MSA, CT	H	13.51 FQ	19.96 AW	26.87 TQ	CTBLS	10/01-12/01
	New Haven-Meriden PMSA, CT	H	10.47 FQ	18.53 AW	25.65 TQ	CTBLS	10/01-12/01
	New London-Norwich MSA, CT-RI	H	9.57 FQ	15.33 AW	21.36 TQ	CTBLS	10/01-12/01
	Stamford-Norwalk PMSA, CT	H	14.78 FQ	21.65 AW	29.27 TQ	CTBLS	10/01-12/01
	Waterbury PMSA, CT	H	15.47 FQ	21.23 AW	29.81 TQ	CTBLS	10/01-12/01
	Delaware	H	11.30 FQ	17.19 AW	25.36 TQ	DEBLS	10/01-12/01
	Wilmington-Newark PMSA, DE-MD	H	10.72 FQ	17.73 AW	25.71 TQ	DEBLS	10/01-12/01
	District of Columbia	H	9.12 FQ	14.39 AW	20.49 TQ	DCBLS	10/01-12/01
	Washington PMSA, DC-MD-VA-WV	H	11.23 FQ	16.37 AW	21.66 TQ	DCBLS	10/01-12/01
	Florida	H	8.33 FQ	13.23 AW	18.72 TQ	FLBLS	10/01-12/01
	Daytona Beach MSA, FL	H	6.07 FQ	12.82 AW	19.85 TQ	FLBLS	10/01-12/01
	Fort Lauderdale PMSA, FL	H	11.24 FQ	14.75 AW	19.96 TQ	FLBLS	10/01-12/01
	Fort Myers-Cape Coral MSA, FL	H	9.80 FQ	16.72 AW	30.64 TQ	FLBLS	10/01-12/01

AAW Average annual wage **AE** Average entry wage **AEX** Average experienced wage **AO** Average offered **AOH** Average offered, high **AOL** Average offered, low **APH** Average pay, high range **APL** Average pay, low range **ASH** Average starting, high **ASL** Average starting, low **AW** Average wage paid **FQ** First quartile wage **H** Hourly **HI** Highest wage paid **HR** High end range **LR** Low end range **M** Monthly **MTC** Median total compensation **MW** Median wage paid **SQ** Second quartile wage **S** Special: hourly and annual **TQ** Third quartile wage **W** Weekly **Y** Yearly

Occupation/Type/Industry	Location	Per	Low	Mid	High	Source	Date
Cement Mason and Concrete Finisher	Fort Pierce-Port St. Lucie MSA, FL	H	8.38 FQ	17.58 AW	30.21 TQ	FLBLS	10/01-12/01
	Fort Walton Beach MSA, FL	H	8.12 FQ	11.56 AW	15.71 TQ	FLBLS	10/01-12/01
	Gainesville MSA, FL	H	7.85 FQ	11.23 AW	15.14 TQ	FLBLS	10/01-12/01
	Jacksonville MSA, FL	H	9.42 FQ	13.83 AW	19.60 TQ	FLBLS	10/01-12/01
	Lakeland-Winter Haven MSA, FL	H	8.23 FQ	11.47 AW	16.44 TQ	FLBLS	10/01-12/01
	Melbourne-Titusville-Palm Bay MSA, FL	H	10.51 FQ	15.89 AW	23.65 TQ	FLBLS	10/01-12/01
	Miami PMSA, FL	H	7.65 FQ	11.52 AW	17.39 TQ	FLBLS	10/01-12/01
	Naples MSA, FL	H	9.25 FQ	13.12 AW	16.94 TQ	FLBLS	10/01-12/01
	Ocala MSA, FL	H	8.31 FQ	12.44 AW	17.35 TQ	FLBLS	10/01-12/01
	Orlando MSA, FL	H	7.98 FQ	12.90 AW	18.04 TQ	FLBLS	10/01-12/01
	Pensacola MSA, FL	H	7.57 FQ	11.36 AW	16.88 TQ	FLBLS	10/01-12/01
	Sarasota-Bradenton MSA, FL	H	8.62 FQ	12.78 AW	17.63 TQ	FLBLS	10/01-12/01
	Tallahassee MSA, FL	H	7.84 FQ	11.85 AW	15.85 TQ	FLBLS	10/01-12/01
	Tampa-St. Petersburg-Clearwater MSA, FL	H	8.72 FQ	12.26 AW	16.75 TQ	FLBLS	10/01-12/01
	West Palm Beach-Boca Raton MSA, FL	H	9.90 FQ	14.08 AW	17.50 TQ	FLBLS	10/01-12/01
	Georgia	H	8.99 FQ	12.68 AW	18.40 TQ	GABLS	10/01-12/01
	Atlanta MSA, GA	H	9.52 FQ	13.15 AW	19.13 TQ	GABLS	10/01-12/01
	Augusta-Aiken MSA, GA-SC	H	9.16 FQ	14.39 AW	20.61 TQ	GABLS	10/01-12/01
	Columbus MSA, GA-AL	H	6.92 FQ	11.32 AW	16.97 TQ	GABLS	10/01-12/01
	Macon MSA, GA	H	8.58 FQ	11.59 AW	15.10 TQ	GABLS	10/01-12/01
	Savannah MSA, GA	H	9.45 FQ	12.32 AW	15.17 TQ	GABLS	10/01-12/01
	Hawaii	H	15.35 FQ	24.62 AW	33.24 TQ	HIBLS	10/01-12/01
	Honolulu MSA, HI	H	14.96 FQ	23.95 AW	31.53 TQ	HIBLS	10/01-12/01
	Idaho	H	8.15 FQ	13.22 AW	18.27 TQ	IDBLS	10/01-12/01
	Boise City MSA, ID	H	9.24 FQ	14.60 AW	19.72 TQ	IDBLS	10/01-12/01
	Illinois	H	12.94 FQ	23.15 AW	32.49 TQ	ILBLS	10/01-12/01
	Champaign-Urbana MSA, IL	H	11.34 FQ	21.31 AW	27.87 TQ	ILBLS	10/01-12/01
	Chicago PMSA, IL	H	14.75 FQ	25.05 AW	33.27 TQ	ILBLS	10/01-12/01
	Peoria-Pekin MSA, IL	H	11.51 FQ	18.56 AW	27.16 TQ	ILBLS	10/01-12/01
	Rockford MSA, IL	H	17.43 FQ	21.65 AW	27.41 TQ	ILBLS	10/01-12/01
	Springfield MSA, IL	H	11.59 FQ	20.62 AW	26.24 TQ	ILBLS	10/01-12/01
	Indiana	H	9.54 FQ	16.07 AW	25.12 TQ	INBLS	10/01-12/01
	Elkhart-Goshen MSA, IN	H	13.17 FQ	18.06 AW	22.30 TQ	INBLS	10/01-12/01
	Evansville-Henderson MSA, IN-KY	H	13.71 FQ	18.59 AW	22.60 TQ	INBLS	10/01-12/01
	Fort Wayne MSA, IN	H	9.28 FQ	12.97 AW	18.08 TQ	INBLS	10/01-12/01
	Gary PMSA, IN	H	16.33 FQ	23.68 AW	29.25 TQ	INBLS	10/01-12/01
	Indianapolis MSA, IN	H	9.35 FQ	13.53 AW	20.64 TQ	INBLS	10/01-12/01
	Lafayette MSA, IN	H	12.75 FQ	19.05 AW	25.69 TQ	INBLS	10/01-12/01
	South Bend MSA, IN	H	12.64 FQ	18.46 AW	22.88 TQ	INBLS	10/01-12/01
	Iowa	H	8.99 FQ	12.99 AW	18.98 TQ	IABLS	10/01-12/01
	Cedar Rapids MSA, IA	H	11.95 FQ	17.09 AW	22.23 TQ	IABLS	10/01-12/01
	Davenport-Moline-Rock Island MSA, IA-IL	H	9.05 FQ	15.64 AW	23.71 TQ	IABLS	10/01-12/01
	Des Moines MSA, IA	H	9.52 FQ	13.57 AW	19.94 TQ	IABLS	10/01-12/01
	Kansas	H	9.01 FQ	14.29 AW	21.16 TQ	KSBLS	10/01-12/01
	Topeka MSA, KS	H	12.72 FQ	17.21 AW	21.64 TQ	KSBLS	10/01-12/01
	Wichita MSA, KS	H	9.70 FQ	12.83 AW	16.61 TQ	KSBLS	10/01-12/01
	Kentucky	H	9.41 FQ	13.78 AW	20.94 TQ	KYBLS	10/01-12/01
	Lexington MSA, KY	H	9.71 FQ	13.64 AW	18.27 TQ	KYBLS	10/01-12/01
	Louisville MSA, KY-IN	H	9.20 FQ	12.56 AW	17.43 TQ	KYBLS	10/01-12/01
	Louisiana	H	7.63 FQ	12.45 AW	17.07 TQ	LABLS	10/01-12/01
	Baton Rouge MSA, LA	H	6.65 FQ	12.43 AW	16.96 TQ	LABLS	10/01-12/01
	Houma MSA, LA	H	5.84 FQ	8.51 AW	13.35 TQ	LABLS	10/01-12/01
	Lafayette MSA, LA	H	8.54 FQ	11.33 AW	16.00 TQ	LABLS	10/01-12/01
	Lake Charles MSA, LA	H	9.48 FQ	14.94 AW	20.37 TQ	LABLS	10/01-12/01
	New Orleans MSA, LA	H	7.91 FQ	12.84 AW	17.10 TQ	LABLS	10/01-12/01
	Shreveport-Bossier City MSA, LA	H	8.91 FQ	13.55 AW	18.03 TQ	LABLS	10/01-12/01
	Maine	H	9.81 FQ	12.83 AW	16.36 TQ	MEBLS	10/01-12/01
	Portland MSA, ME	H	11.78 FQ	13.93 AW	17.16 TQ	MEBLS	10/01-12/01
	Maryland	H	10.73 FQ	16.28 AW	23.40 TQ	MDBLS	10/01-12/01
	Baltimore PMSA, MD	H	11.43 FQ	16.76 AW	24.86 TQ	MDBLS	10/01-12/01
	Massachusetts	H	12.73 FQ	22.20 AW	33.30 TQ	MABLS	10/01-12/01
	Boston PMSA, MA-NH	H	12.98 FQ	23.23 AW	33.98 TQ	MABLS	10/01-12/01
	Brockton PMSA, MA	H	15.90 FQ	22.10 AW	33.31 TQ	MABLS	10/01-12/01

AAW Average annual wage; AE Average entry wage; AEX Average experienced wage; AO Average offered; AOH Average offered, high; AOL Average offered, low; APH Average pay, high range; APL Average pay, low range; ASH Average starting, high; ASL Average starting, low; AW Average wage paid; FQ First quartile wage; H Hourly; HI Highest wage paid; HR High end range; LR Low end range; M Monthly; MTC Median total compensation; MW Median wage paid; SQ Second quartile wage; S Special: hourly and annual; TQ Third quartile wage; W Weekly; Y Yearly

Occupation/Type/Industry	Location	Per	Low	Mid	High	Source	Date
Cement Mason and Concrete Finisher	Lawrence PMSA, MA-NH	H	9.64 FQ	14.23 AW	23.68 TQ	MABLS	10/01-12/01
	Lowell PMSA, MA-NH	H	18.81 FQ	20.76 AW	22.71 TQ	MABLS	10/01-12/01
	New Bedford PMSA, MA	H	12.24 FQ	17.59 AW	21.13 TQ	MABLS	10/01-12/01
	Springfield MSA, MA	H	16.51 FQ	24.47 AW	31.30 TQ	MABLS	10/01-12/01
	Worcester PMSA, MA-CT	H	11.37 FQ	17.59 AW	21.92 TQ	MABLS	10/01-12/01
	Michigan	H	10.69 FQ	17.58 AW	25.65 TQ	MIBLS	10/01-12/01
	Ann Arbor PMSA, MI	H	11.57 FQ	18.31 AW	26.74 TQ	MIBLS	10/01-12/01
	Detroit PMSA, MI	H	13.43 FQ	20.53 AW	26.84 TQ	MIBLS	10/01-12/01
	Flint PMSA, MI	H	12.62 FQ	20.66 AW	26.67 TQ	MIBLS	10/01-12/01
	Grand Rapids-Muskegon-Holland MSA, MI	H	11.28 FQ	15.05 AW	20.24 TQ	MIBLS	10/01-12/01
	Kalamazoo-Battle Creek MSA, MI	H	10.78 FQ	16.42 AW	21.50 TQ	MIBLS	10/01-12/01
	Lansing-East Lansing MSA, MI	H	11.90 FQ	17.80 AW	25.73 TQ	MIBLS	10/01-12/01
	Saginaw-Bay City-Midland MSA, MI	H	11.48 FQ	15.34 AW	20.39 TQ	MIBLS	10/01-12/01
	Minnesota	H	12.08 FQ	20.17 AW	26.73 TQ	MNBLS	10/01-12/01
	Duluth-Superior MSA, MN-WI	H	12.87 FQ	19.58 AW	26.63 TQ	MNBLS	10/01-12/01
	Minneapolis-St. Paul MSA, MN-WI	H	16.59 FQ	21.61 AW	27.02 TQ	MNBLS	10/01-12/01
	St. Cloud MSA, MN	H	13.76 FQ	19.40 AW	25.64 TQ	MNBLS	10/01-12/01
	Mississippi	H	8.78 FQ	11.62 AW	16.11 TQ	MSBLS	10/01-12/01
	Biloxi-Gulfport-Pascagoula MSA, MS	H	8.86 FQ	11.32 AW	14.00 TQ	MSBLS	10/01-12/01
	Jackson MSA, MS	H	7.83 FQ	10.80 AW	15.87 TQ	MSBLS	10/01-12/01
	Missouri	H	9.24 FQ	16.53 AW	25.46 TQ	MOBLS	10/01-12/01
	Kansas City MSA, MO-KS	H	12.71 FQ	18.13 AW	24.01 TQ	MOBLS	10/01-12/01
	St. Louis MSA, MO-IL	H	13.22 FQ	20.94 AW	27.62 TQ	MOBLS	10/01-12/01
	Springfield MSA, MO	H	6.99 FQ	13.81 AW	18.95 TQ	MOBLS	10/01-12/01
	Montana	H	11.18 FQ	15.26 AW	21.56 TQ	MTBLS	10/01-12/01
	Billings MSA, MT	H	9.28 FQ	14.52 AW	22.72 TQ	MTBLS	10/01-12/01
	Nebraska	H	9.38 FQ	14.07 AW	19.76 TQ	NEBLS	10/01-12/01
	Lincoln MSA, NE	H	9.67 FQ	13.12 AW	17.16 TQ	NEBLS	10/01-12/01
	Omaha MSA, NE-IA	H	10.60 FQ	16.11 AW	21.38 TQ	NEBLS	10/01-12/01
	Nevada	H	13.54 FQ	19.81 AW	26.66 TQ	NVBLS	10/01-12/01
	Las Vegas MSA, NV-AZ	H	13.47 FQ	19.64 AW	26.64 TQ	NVBLS	10/01-12/01
	Reno MSA, NV	H	10.10 FQ	18.33 AW	25.85 TQ	NVBLS	10/01-12/01
	New Hampshire	H	10.81 FQ	16.23 AW	24.21 TQ	NHBLS	10/01-12/01
	Manchester PMSA, NH	H	13.98 FQ	20.25 AW	27.03 TQ	NHBLS	10/01-12/01
	Nashua PMSA, NH	H	11.86 FQ	16.43 AW	21.27 TQ	NHBLS	10/01-12/01
	New Jersey	H	11.57 FQ	20.84 AW	32.78 TQ	NJBLS	10/01-12/01
	Atlantic-Cape May PMSA, NJ	H	10.09 FQ	24.64 AW	34.79 TQ	NJBLS	10/01-12/01
	Bergen-Passaic PMSA, NJ	H	13.19 FQ	18.91 AW	28.95 TQ	NJBLS	10/01-12/01
	Jersey City PMSA, NJ	H	11.67 FQ	15.09 AW	19.04 TQ	NJBLS	10/01-12/01
	Middlesex-Somerset-Hunterdon PMSA, NJ	H	15.16 FQ	24.62 AW	34.84 TQ	NJBLS	10/01-12/01
	Monmouth-Ocean PMSA, NJ	H	12.47 FQ	19.18 AW	26.93 TQ	NJBLS	10/01-12/01
	Newark PMSA, NJ	H	10.74 FQ	24.66 AW	33.66 TQ	NJBLS	10/01-12/01
	Trenton PMSA, NJ	H	15.79 FQ	21.50 AW	29.15 TQ	NJBLS	10/01-12/01
	New Mexico	H	8.94 FQ	12.75 AW	16.77 TQ	NMBLS	10/01-12/01
	Albuquerque MSA, NM	H	9.26 FQ	13.02 AW	17.08 TQ	NMBLS	10/01-12/01
	Las Cruces MSA, NM	H	7.86 FQ	9.95 AW	12.35 TQ	NMBLS	10/01-12/01
	New York	H	9.54 FQ	18.73 AW	32.92 TQ	NYBLS	10/01-12/01
	Albany-Schenectady-Troy MSA, NY	H	14.91 FQ	20.45 AW	25.79 TQ	NYBLS	10/01-12/01
	Binghamton MSA, NY	H	9.92 FQ	18.59 AW	27.10 TQ	NYBLS	10/01-12/01
	Buffalo-Niagara Falls MSA, NY	H	11.81 FQ	21.24 AW	28.67 TQ	NYBLS	10/01-12/01
	Nassau-Suffolk PMSA, NY	H	14.52 FQ	23.89 AW	39.89 TQ	NYBLS	10/01-12/01
	New York PMSA, NY	H	9.64 FQ	18.02 AW	33.07 TQ	NYBLS	10/01-12/01
	Newburgh PMSA, NY-PA	H	13.20 FQ	19.86 AW	27.62 TQ	NYBLS	10/01-12/01
	Rochester MSA, NY	H	9.19 FQ	16.28 AW	21.56 TQ	NYBLS	10/01-12/01
	Syracuse MSA, NY	H	5.81 FQ	14.22 AW	22.23 TQ	NYBLS	10/01-12/01
	Utica-Rome MSA, NY	H	5.93 FQ	11.88 AW	22.72 TQ	NYBLS	10/01-12/01
	North Carolina	H	8.30 FQ	12.52 AW	17.21 TQ	NCBLS	10/01-12/01
	Asheville MSA, NC	H	11.27 FQ	14.45 AW	18.61 TQ	NCBLS	10/01-12/01
	Charlotte-Gastonia-Rock Hill MSA, NC-SC	H	9.72 FQ	12.76 AW	16.07 TQ	NCBLS	10/01-12/01
	Fayetteville MSA, NC	H	9.60 FQ	13.70 AW	17.49 TQ	NCBLS	10/01-12/01
	Greensboro-Winston-Salem-High Point MSA, NC	H	9.93 FQ	13.39 AW	18.31 TQ	NCBLS	10/01-12/01

AAW	Average annual wage	**AOH**	Average offered, high	**ASH**	Average starting, high	**H**	Hourly	**M**	Monthly	**S**	Special: hourly and annual
AE	Average entry wage	**AOL**	Average offered, low	**ASL**	Average starting, low	**HI**	Highest wage paid	**MTC**	Median total compensation	**TQ**	Third quartile wage
AEX	Average experienced wage	**APH**	Average pay, high range	**AW**	Average wage paid	**HR**	High end range	**MW**	Median wage paid	**W**	Weekly
AO	Average offered	**APL**	Average pay, low range	**FQ**	First quartile wage	**LR**	Low end range	**SQ**	Second quartile wage	**Y**	Yearly

Occupation/Type/Industry	Location	Per	Low	Mid	High	Source	Date
Cement Mason and Concrete Finisher	Hickory-Morganton-Lenoir MSA, NC	H	10.84 FQ	14.60 AW	20.78 TQ	NCBLS	10/01-12/01
	Raleigh-Durham-Chapel Hill MSA, NC	H	7.76 FQ	13.50 AW	20.88 TQ	NCBLS	10/01-12/01
	Wilmington MSA, NC	H	8.45 FQ	12.61 AW	16.96 TQ	NCBLS	10/01-12/01
	North Dakota	H	9.72 FQ	13.68 AW	18.27 TQ	NDBLS	10/01-12/01
	Fargo-Moorhead MSA, ND-MN	H	11.17 FQ	14.22 AW	17.27 TQ	NDBLS	10/01-12/01
	Ohio	H	11.02 FQ	18.49 AW	26.61 TQ	OHBLS	10/01-12/01
	Akron PMSA, OH	H	12.65 FQ	20.00 AW	27.39 TQ	OHBLS	10/01-12/01
	Canton-Massillon MSA, OH	H	14.08 FQ	17.13 AW	25.06 TQ	OHBLS	10/01-12/01
	Cincinnati PMSA, OH-KY-IN	H	11.72 FQ	17.27 AW	25.18 TQ	OHBLS	10/01-12/01
	Cleveland-Lorain-Elyria PMSA, OH	H	13.34 FQ	24.56 AW	28.34 TQ	OHBLS	10/01-12/01
	Columbus MSA, OH	H	9.62 FQ	15.35 AW	21.02 TQ	OHBLS	10/01-12/01
	Dayton-Springfield MSA, OH	H	11.20 FQ	15.49 AW	22.43 TQ	OHBLS	10/01-12/01
	Hamilton-Middletown PMSA, OH	H	11.15 FQ	17.16 AW	23.48 TQ	OHBLS	10/01-12/01
	Mansfield MSA, OH	H	11.61 FQ	16.64 AW	21.34 TQ	OHBLS	10/01-12/01
	Toledo MSA, OH	H	11.07 FQ	17.10 AW	25.80 TQ	OHBLS	10/01-12/01
	Youngstown-Warren MSA, OH	H	10.02 FQ	18.33 AW	27.42 TQ	OHBLS	10/01-12/01
	Oklahoma	H	8.29 FQ	12.12 AW	16.84 TQ	OKBLS	10/01-12/01
	Oklahoma City MSA, OK	H	7.64 FQ	11.30 AW	16.04 TQ	OKBLS	10/01-12/01
	Tulsa MSA, OK	H	9.58 FQ	13.66 AW	18.09 TQ	OKBLS	10/01-12/01
	Oregon	H	8.30 FQ	16.66 AW	25.87 TQ	ORBLS	10/01-12/01
	Eugene-Springfield MSA, OR	H	11.60 FQ	15.96 AW	22.66 TQ	ORBLS	10/01-12/01
	Medford-Ashland MSA, OR	H	14.00 FQ	17.25 AW	25.43 TQ	ORBLS	10/01-12/01
	Portland-Vancouver PMSA, OR-WA	H	7.74 FQ	17.92 AW	28.25 TQ	ORBLS	10/01-12/01
	Salem PMSA, OR	H	10.60 FQ	17.27 AW	25.28 TQ	ORBLS	10/01-12/01
	Pennsylvania	H	10.44 FQ	17.70 AW	26.14 TQ	PABLS	10/01-12/01
	Allentown-Bethlehem-Easton MSA, PA	H	11.16 FQ	15.38 AW	20.91 TQ	PABLS	10/01-12/01
	Erie MSA, PA	H	10.68 FQ	14.56 AW	17.75 TQ	PABLS	10/01-12/01
	Harrisburg-Lebanon-Carlisle MSA, PA	H	13.17 FQ	18.26 AW	22.93 TQ	PABLS	10/01-12/01
	Johnstown MSA, PA	H	8.54 FQ	11.01 AW	16.07 TQ	PABLS	10/01-12/01
	Lancaster MSA, PA	H	8.72 FQ	13.67 AW	18.33 TQ	PABLS	10/01-12/01
	Philadelphia PMSA, PA-NJ	H	10.87 FQ	19.31 AW	27.85 TQ	PABLS	10/01-12/01
	Pittsburgh MSA, PA	H	10.84 FQ	17.04 AW	22.92 TQ	PABLS	10/01-12/01
	Reading MSA, PA	H	11.69 FQ	17.33 AW	25.05 TQ	PABLS	10/01-12/01
	Scranton-Wilkes-Barre-Hazleton MSA, PA	H	10.14 FQ	18.90 AW	26.18 TQ	PABLS	10/01-12/01
	York MSA, PA	H	11.67 FQ	16.06 AW	24.21 TQ	PABLS	10/01-12/01
	Rhode Island	H	9.03 FQ	14.67 AW	24.67 TQ	RIBLS	10/01-12/01
	Providence-Fall River-Warwick MSA, RI-MA	H	9.29 FQ	16.68 AW	27.02 TQ	RIBLS	10/01-12/01
	South Carolina	H	8.60 FQ	12.44 AW	16.71 TQ	SCBLS	10/01-12/01
	Charleston-North Charleston MSA, SC	H	10.04 FQ	14.02 AW	19.12 TQ	SCBLS	10/01-12/01
	Columbia MSA, SC	H	7.45 FQ	10.54 AW	13.35 TQ	SCBLS	10/01-12/01
	Greenville-Spartanburg-Anderson MSA, SC	H	8.68 FQ	12.76 AW	16.64 TQ	SCBLS	10/01-12/01
	Myrtle Beach MSA, SC	H	9.38 FQ	12.10 AW	14.95 TQ	SCBLS	10/01-12/01
	South Dakota	H	9.13 FQ	12.10 AW	16.18 TQ	SDBLS	10/01-12/01
	Sioux Falls MSA, SD	H	9.60 FQ	12.51 AW	16.41 TQ	SDBLS	10/01-12/01
	Tennessee	H	9.79 FQ	13.31 AW	17.19 TQ	TNBLS	10/01-12/01
	Chattanooga MSA, TN-GA	H	10.98 FQ	14.18 AW	19.16 TQ	TNBLS	10/01-12/01
	Clarksville-Hopkinsville MSA, TN-KY	H	8.66 FQ	11.11 AW	14.76 TQ	TNBLS	10/01-12/01
	Johnson City-Kingsport-Bristol MSA, TN-VA	H	9.51 FQ	12.99 AW	16.55 TQ	TNBLS	10/01-12/01
	Knoxville MSA, TN	H	9.40 FQ	12.16 AW	15.90 TQ	TNBLS	10/01-12/01
	Memphis MSA, TN-AR-MS	H	9.49 FQ	13.32 AW	17.50 TQ	TNBLS	10/01-12/01
	Nashville MSA, TN	H	10.16 FQ	13.98 AW	17.41 TQ	TNBLS	10/01-12/01
	Texas	H	7.68 FQ	11.33 AW	15.62 TQ	TXBLS	10/01-12/01
	Amarillo MSA, TX	H	8.31 FQ	12.50 AW	16.94 TQ	TXBLS	10/01-12/01
	Austin-San Marcos MSA, TX	H	7.74 FQ	12.06 AW	16.81 TQ	TXBLS	10/01-12/01
	Beaumont-Port Arthur MSA, TX	H	8.43 FQ	12.11 AW	16.43 TQ	TXBLS	10/01-12/01
	Brazoria PMSA, TX	H	8.12 FQ	12.25 AW	16.39 TQ	TXBLS	10/01-12/01

AAW Average annual wage; AE Average entry wage; AEX Average experienced wage; AO Average offered; AOH Average offered, high; AOL Average offered, low; APH Average pay, high range; APL Average pay, low range; ASH Average starting, high; ASL Average starting, low; AW Average wage paid; FQ First quartile wage; H Hourly; HI Highest wage paid; HR High end range; LR Low end range; M Monthly; MTC Median total compensation; MW Median wage paid; SQ Second quartile wage; S Special: hourly and annual; TQ Third quartile wage; W Weekly; Y Yearly

Occupation/Type/Industry	Location	Per	Low	Mid	High	Source	Date
Cement Mason and Concrete Finisher	Brownsville-Harlingen-San Benito MSA, TX	H	6.70 FQ	8.80 AW	10.69 TQ	TXBLS	10/01-12/01
	Corpus Christi MSA, TX	H	6.91 FQ	10.24 AW	15.25 TQ	TXBLS	10/01-12/01
	Dallas PMSA, TX	H	8.02 FQ	11.64 AW	15.95 TQ	TXBLS	10/01-12/01
	El Paso MSA, TX	H	7.56 FQ	10.26 AW	13.70 TQ	TXBLS	10/01-12/01
	Fort Worth-Arlington PMSA, TX	H	7.65 FQ	11.48 AW	15.25 TQ	TXBLS	10/01-12/01
	Galveston-Texas City PMSA, TX	H	7.55 FQ	10.65 AW	14.64 TQ	TXBLS	10/01-12/01
	Houston PMSA, TX	H	7.91 FQ	11.47 AW	15.42 TQ	TXBLS	10/01-12/01
	Killeen-Temple MSA, TX	H	7.80 FQ	10.98 AW	14.33 TQ	TXBLS	10/01-12/01
	Laredo MSA, TX	H	7.05 FQ	8.53 AW	11.00 TQ	TXBLS	10/01-12/01
	Longview-Marshall MSA, TX	H	7.42 FQ	10.80 AW	14.05 TQ	TXBLS	10/01-12/01
	Lubbock MSA, TX	H	9.59 FQ	12.46 AW	15.35 TQ	TXBLS	10/01-12/01
	McAllen-Edinburg-Mission MSA, TX	H	6.58 FQ	9.34 AW	13.14 TQ	TXBLS	10/01-12/01
	Odessa-Midland MSA, TX	H	7.75 FQ	10.19 AW	13.56 TQ	TXBLS	10/01-12/01
	San Antonio MSA, TX	H	8.71 FQ	11.78 AW	16.46 TQ	TXBLS	10/01-12/01
	Tyler MSA, TX	H	8.10 FQ	12.48 AW	19.77 TQ	TXBLS	10/01-12/01
	Waco MSA, TX	H	6.25 FQ	9.43 AW	13.44 TQ	TXBLS	10/01-12/01
	Utah	H	8.74 FQ	14.64 AW	19.75 TQ	UTBLS	10/01-12/01
	Provo-Orem MSA, UT	H	9.65 FQ	13.56 AW	18.30 TQ	UTBLS	10/01-12/01
	Salt Lake City-Ogden MSA, UT	H	7.74 FQ	15.29 AW	20.34 TQ	UTBLS	10/01-12/01
	Vermont	H	9.66 FQ	13.59 AW	18.44 TQ	VTBLS	10/01-12/01
	Burlington MSA, VT	H	9.94 FQ	14.28 AW	20.07 TQ	VTBLS	10/01-12/01
	Virginia	H	9.40 FQ	13.78 AW	19.80 TQ	VABLS	10/01-12/01
	Lynchburg MSA, VA	H	7.52 FQ	10.82 AW	16.06 TQ	VABLS	10/01-12/01
	Norfolk-Virginia Beach-Newport News MSA, VA-NC	H	9.44 FQ	12.92 AW	16.90 TQ	VABLS	10/01-12/01
	Richmond-Petersburg MSA, VA	H	9.46 FQ	11.81 AW	14.17 TQ	VABLS	10/01-12/01
	Roanoke MSA, VA	H	9.44 FQ	13.92 AW	19.98 TQ	VABLS	10/01-12/01
	Washington	H	11.80 FQ	20.10 AW	28.74 TQ	WABLS	10/01-12/01
	Olympia PMSA, WA	H	17.91 FQ	22.40 AW	27.28 TQ	WABLS	10/01-12/01
	Richland-Kennewick-Pasco MSA, WA	H	11.84 FQ	15.78 AW	22.48 TQ	WABLS	10/01-12/01
	Seattle-Bellevue-Everett PMSA, WA	H	14.65 FQ	23.11 AW	28.72 TQ	WABLS	10/01-12/01
	Spokane MSA, WA	H	8.09 FQ	18.40 AW	28.56 TQ	WABLS	10/01-12/01
	Tacoma PMSA, WA	H	12.95 FQ	18.61 AW	28.17 TQ	WABLS	10/01-12/01
	Yakima MSA, WA	H	11.20 FQ	16.95 AW	28.01 TQ	WABLS	10/01-12/01
	West Virginia	H	9.97 FQ	16.39 AW	25.44 TQ	WVBLS	10/01-12/01
	Charleston MSA, WV	H	10.81 FQ	20.21 AW	26.59 TQ	WVBLS	10/01-12/01
	Huntington-Ashland MSA, WV-KY-OH	H	11.18 FQ	14.72 AW	20.30 TQ	WVBLS	10/01-12/01
	Wisconsin	H	12.01 FQ	18.69 AW	26.79 TQ	WIBLS	10/01-12/01
	Appleton-Oshkosh-Neenah MSA, WI	H	13.91 FQ	21.11 AW	37.61 TQ	WIBLS	10/01-12/01
	Green Bay MSA, WI	H	11.95 FQ	16.03 AW	24.15 TQ	WIBLS	10/01-12/01
	Madison MSA, WI	H	12.37 FQ	20.11 AW	27.17 TQ	WIBLS	10/01-12/01
	Milwaukee-Waukesha PMSA, WI	H	11.80 FQ	19.82 AW	27.78 TQ	WIBLS	10/01-12/01
	Racine PMSA, WI	H	11.87 FQ	19.44 AW	26.65 TQ	WIBLS	10/01-12/01
	Wyoming	H	9.39 FQ	13.55 AW	18.19 TQ	WYBLS	10/01-12/01
	Cheyenne MSA, WY	H	6.18 FQ	11.57 AW	14.55 TQ	WYBLS	10/01-12/01
	Puerto Rico	H	5.71 FQ	7.35 AW	9.15 TQ	PRBLS	10/01-12/01
	Virgin Islands	H	10.08 FQ	12.93 AW	17.53 TQ	VIBLS	10/01-12/01
	Guam	H	11.22 FQ	12.60 AW	14.24 TQ	GUBLS	10/01-12/01
Cementing and Gluing Machine Operator and Tender	Alabama	H	8.11 FQ	12.20 AW	18.72 TQ	ALBLS	10/01-12/01
	Arizona	H	7.63 FQ	10.30 AW	13.36 TQ	AZBLS	10/01-12/01
	Arkansas	H	7.28 FQ	12.16 AW	20.83 TQ	ARBLS	10/01-12/01
	California	H	6.86 FQ	10.04 AW	16.38 TQ	CABLS	10/01-12/01
	Colorado	H	7.76 FQ	13.29 AW	20.33 TQ	COBLS	10/01-12/01
	Connecticut	H	7.64 FQ	12.47 AW	17.55 TQ	CTBLS	10/01-12/01
	Florida	H	8.43 FQ	11.87 AW	15.19 TQ	FLBLS	10/01-12/01
	Georgia	H	5.95 FQ	9.57 AW	15.92 TQ	GABLS	10/01-12/01
	Idaho	H	8.40 FQ	12.65 AW	16.97 TQ	IDBLS	10/01-12/01

AAW	Average annual wage	AOH	Average offered, high	ASH	Average starting, high	H	Hourly	M	Monthly	S	Special: hourly and annual
AE	Average entry wage	AOL	Average offered, low	ASL	Average starting, low	HI	Highest wage paid	MTC	Median total compensation	TQ	Third quartile wage
AEX	Average experienced wage	APH	Average pay, high range	AW	Average wage paid	HR	High end range	MW	Median wage paid	W	Weekly
AO	Average offered	APL	Average pay, low range	FQ	First quartile wage	LR	Low end range	SQ	Second quartile wage	Y	Yearly

Occupation/Type/Industry	Location	Per	Low	Mid	High	Source	Date
Cementing and Gluing Machine Operator and Tender	Illinois	H	7.69 FQ	11.94 AW	16.76 TQ	ILBLS	10/01-12/01
	Indiana	H	7.90 FQ	11.57 AW	16.36 TQ	INBLS	10/01-12/01
	Iowa	H	7.63 FQ	11.97 AW	16.69 TQ	IABLS	10/01-12/01
	Kansas	H	7.85 FQ	12.05 AW	24.30 TQ	KSBLS	10/01-12/01
	Kentucky	H	7.61 FQ	10.49 AW	15.64 TQ	KYBLS	10/01-12/01
	Louisiana	H	10.54 FQ	12.31 AW	13.96 TQ	LABLS	10/01-12/01
	Maine	H	7.64 FQ	10.44 AW	13.62 TQ	MEBLS	10/01-12/01
	Maryland	H	9.95 FQ	14.15 AW	19.10 TQ	MDBLS	10/01-12/01
	Massachusetts	H	8.35 FQ	12.74 AW	16.84 TQ	MABLS	10/01-12/01
	Michigan	H	8.30 FQ	10.79 AW	13.82 TQ	MIBLS	10/01-12/01
	Minnesota	H	6.17 FQ	12.02 AW	18.06 TQ	MNBLS	10/01-12/01
	Mississippi	H	6.72 FQ	9.92 AW	13.97 TQ	MSBLS	10/01-12/01
	Missouri	H	7.06 FQ	11.48 AW	16.82 TQ	MOBLS	10/01-12/01
	Montana	H	11.74 FQ	14.17 AW	16.90 TQ	MTBLS	10/01-12/01
	New Jersey	H	6.26 FQ	12.55 AW	23.88 TQ	NJBLS	10/01-12/01
	New Mexico	H	7.34 FQ	9.52 AW	12.73 TQ	NMBLS	10/01-12/01
	New York	H	7.06 FQ	12.11 AW	17.82 TQ	NYBLS	10/01-12/01
	North Carolina	H	7.87 FQ	11.05 AW	14.72 TQ	NCBLS	10/01-12/01
	North Dakota	H	7.41 FQ	9.99 AW	13.61 TQ	NDBLS	10/01-12/01
	Ohio	H	8.15 FQ	12.20 AW	16.68 TQ	OHBLS	10/01-12/01
	Oregon	H	9.86 FQ	14.01 AW	17.24 TQ	ORBLS	10/01-12/01
	Pennsylvania	H	7.18 FQ	11.18 AW	16.69 TQ	PABLS	10/01-12/01
	Rhode Island	H	6.90 FQ	10.33 AW	14.39 TQ	RIBLS	10/01-12/01
	South Carolina	H	7.43 FQ	10.46 AW	13.43 TQ	SCBLS	10/01-12/01
	South Dakota	H	8.08 FQ	11.06 AW	14.06 TQ	SDBLS	10/01-12/01
	Tennessee	H	8.21 FQ	11.03 AW	14.02 TQ	TNBLS	10/01-12/01
	Texas	H	6.39 FQ	10.92 AW	16.10 TQ	TXBLS	10/01-12/01
	Utah	H	6.48 FQ	9.49 AW	13.36 TQ	UTBLS	10/01-12/01
	Vermont	H	8.12 FQ	10.48 AW	13.32 TQ	VTBLS	10/01-12/01
	Virginia	H	8.61 FQ	11.43 AW	15.76 TQ	VABLS	10/01-12/01
	Washington	H	8.97 FQ	12.70 AW	18.19 TQ	WABLS	10/01-12/01
	West Virginia	H	6.51 FQ	12.03 AW	15.67 TQ	WVBLS	10/01-12/01
	Wisconsin	H	8.34 FQ	12.67 AW	17.56 TQ	WIBLS	10/01-12/01
	Puerto Rico	H	5.72 FQ	7.63 AW	10.46 TQ	PRBLS	10/01-12/01
Central Services Professional							
Health care	Central	Y		43539 Y		HPN	8/02
Health care	Mountain	Y		50714 Y		HPN	8/02
Health care	Northeast	Y		47791 Y		HPN	8/02
Health care	Pacific	Y		53482 Y		HPN	8/02
Health care	Southeast	Y		47536 Y		HPN	8/02
Certified Protection Professional							
10,000+ employees	United States	Y		85852 AAW		CSE	1/01-1/01
Architectural and engineering firms	United States	Y		76800 AAW		CSE	1/01-1/01
Educational facilities, museums, libraries	United States	Y		52000 AAW		CSE	1/01-1/01
Fewer than 1,000 employees	United States	Y		58590 AAW		CSE	1/01-1/01
Utilities and energy industry	United States	Y		87320 AAW		CSE	1/01-1/01
Certified Safety Professional							
Concrete production	United States	Y		69218 AAW		CP	1/97-1/98
Environment	United States	Y		70000 AW		SAFEDIR	2001
Chef							
Executive, Golf Course	St. Louis, MO	Y		69500 AW		SLBJ	1/00-1/01
Chef and Head Cook	Alabama	H	7.54 FQ	12.99 AW	21.30 TQ	ALBLS	10/01-12/01
	Birmingham MSA, AL	H	8.65 FQ	14.14 AW	24.71 TQ	ALBLS	10/01-12/01
	Huntsville MSA, AL	H	7.46 FQ	12.71 AW	20.99 TQ	ALBLS	10/01-12/01
	Mobile MSA, AL	H	11.88 FQ	15.40 AW	21.76 TQ	ALBLS	10/01-12/01
	Montgomery MSA, AL	H	7.54 FQ	13.07 AW	22.25 TQ	ALBLS	10/01-12/01
	Alaska	H	9.32 FQ	14.87 AW	24.16 TQ	AKBLS	10/01-12/01
	Anchorage MSA, AK	H	8.65 FQ	14.99 AW	24.92 TQ	AKBLS	10/01-12/01
	Arizona	H	9.42 FQ	16.84 AW	23.69 TQ	AZBLS	10/01-12/01
	Phoenix-Mesa MSA, AZ	H	11.78 FQ	18.68 AW	24.81 TQ	AZBLS	10/01-12/01
	Tucson MSA, AZ	H	10.49 FQ	16.44 AW	24.58 TQ	AZBLS	10/01-12/01
	Arkansas	H	7.39 FQ	12.39 AW	20.68 TQ	ARBLS	10/01-12/01
	Fort Smith MSA, AR-OK	H	7.47 FQ	11.16 AW	18.92 TQ	ARBLS	10/01-12/01
	Little Rock-North Little Rock MSA, AR	H	8.53 FQ	11.94 AW	17.68 TQ	ARBLS	10/01-12/01
	California	H	9.37 FQ	17.29 AW	26.62 TQ	CABLS	10/01-12/01
	Bakersfield MSA, CA	H	10.20 FQ	16.66 AW	20.94 TQ	CABLS	10/01-12/01

AAW	Average annual wage	**AOH**	Average offered, high	**ASH**	Average starting, high	**H**	Hourly	**M**	Monthly	**S**	Special: hourly and annual
AE	Average entry wage	**AOL**	Average offered, low	**ASL**	Average starting, low	**HI**	Highest wage paid	**MTC**	Median total compensation	**TQ**	Third quartile wage
AEX	Average experienced wage	**APH**	Average pay, high range	**AW**	Average wage paid	**HR**	High end range	**MW**	Median wage paid	**W**	Weekly
AO	Average offered	**APL**	Average pay, low range	**FQ**	First quartile wage	**LR**	Low end range	**SQ**	Second quartile wage	**Y**	Yearly

Occupation/Type/Industry	Location	Per	Low	Mid	High	Source	Date
Chef and Head Cook	Chico-Paradise MSA, CA	H	9.07 FQ	13.31 AW	20.80 TQ	CABLS	10/01-12/01
	Fresno MSA, CA	H	7.54 FQ	13.50 AW	20.24 TQ	CABLS	10/01-12/01
	Los Angeles-Long Beach PMSA, CA	H	11.10 FQ	17.97 AW	28.65 TQ	CABLS	10/01-12/01
	Modesto MSA, CA	H	7.59 FQ	13.08 AW	22.60 TQ	CABLS	10/01-12/01
	Oakland PMSA, CA	H	8.70 FQ	18.68 AW	28.23 TQ	CABLS	10/01-12/01
	Orange County PMSA, CA	H	9.21 FQ	17.86 AW	26.90 TQ	CABLS	10/01-12/01
	Redding MSA, CA	H	8.02 FQ	18.21 AW	41.40 TQ	CABLS	10/01-12/01
	Riverside-San Bernardino PMSA, CA	H	6.96 FQ	15.75 AW	22.71 TQ	CABLS	10/01-12/01
	Sacramento PMSA, CA	H	10.73 FQ	19.04 AW	26.86 TQ	CABLS	10/01-12/01
	Salinas MSA, CA	H	9.90 FQ	17.06 AW	25.04 TQ	CABLS	10/01-12/01
	San Diego MSA, CA	H	9.85 FQ	16.79 AW	25.97 TQ	CABLS	10/01-12/01
	San Francisco PMSA, CA	H	10.08 FQ	20.09 AW	31.59 TQ	CABLS	10/01-12/01
	San Jose PMSA, CA	H	10.37 FQ	17.73 AW	27.98 TQ	CABLS	10/01-12/01
	San Luis Obispo-Atascadero-Paso Robles MSA, CA	H	9.91 FQ	15.45 AW	21.04 TQ	CABLS	10/01-12/01
	Santa Barbara-Santa Maria-Lompoc MSA, CA	H	7.89 FQ	14.90 AW	24.60 TQ	CABLS	10/01-12/01
	Santa Cruz-Watsonville PMSA, CA	H	9.22 FQ	15.06 AW	24.61 TQ	CABLS	10/01-12/01
	Santa Rosa PMSA, CA	H	14.06 FQ	18.38 AW	24.62 TQ	CABLS	10/01-12/01
	Stockton-Lodi MSA, CA	H	8.85 FQ	15.61 AW	21.05 TQ	CABLS	10/01-12/01
	Vallejo-Fairfield-Napa PMSA, CA	H	10.06 FQ	18.11 AW	29.37 TQ	CABLS	10/01-12/01
	Ventura PMSA, CA	H	9.43 FQ	15.99 AW	25.98 TQ	CABLS	10/01-12/01
	Visalia-Tulare-Porterville MSA, CA	H	6.60 FQ	12.05 AW	18.37 TQ	CABLS	10/01-12/01
	Colorado	H	9.15 FQ	15.69 AW	24.34 TQ	COBLS	10/01-12/01
	Boulder-Longmont PMSA, CO	H	11.07 FQ	19.04 AW	27.85 TQ	COBLS	10/01-12/01
	Colorado Springs MSA, CO	H	8.05 FQ	11.44 AW	16.71 TQ	COBLS	10/01-12/01
	Denver PMSA, CO	H	11.07 FQ	16.01 AW	22.37 TQ	COBLS	10/01-12/01
	Fort Collins-Loveland MSA, CO	H	7.98 FQ	14.88 AW	21.69 TQ	COBLS	10/01-12/01
	Greeley PMSA, CO	H	7.39 FQ	12.53 AW	20.95 TQ	COBLS	10/01-12/01
	Connecticut	H	10.68 FQ	18.90 AW	26.73 TQ	CTBLS	10/01-12/01
	Bridgeport PMSA, CT	H	8.22 FQ	15.02 AW	24.32 TQ	CTBLS	10/01-12/01
	Danbury PMSA, CT	H	12.15 FQ	17.32 AW	25.72 TQ	CTBLS	10/01-12/01
	Hartford MSA, CT	H	11.40 FQ	18.61 AW	26.04 TQ	CTBLS	10/01-12/01
	New Haven-Meriden PMSA, CT	H	8.58 FQ	16.79 AW	24.64 TQ	CTBLS	10/01-12/01
	New London-Norwich MSA, CT-RI	H	12.49 FQ	21.35 AW	27.54 TQ	CTBLS	10/01-12/01
	Stamford-Norwalk PMSA, CT	H	19.19 FQ	32.38 AW	59.27 TQ	CTBLS	10/01-12/01
	Waterbury PMSA, CT	H	11.81 FQ	17.23 AW	25.98 TQ	CTBLS	10/01-12/01
	Delaware	H	7.16 FQ	12.68 AW	21.10 TQ	DEBLS	10/01-12/01
	Wilmington-Newark PMSA, DE-MD	H	6.87 FQ	14.33 AW	23.37 TQ	DEBLS	10/01-12/01
	District of Columbia	H	8.95 FQ	21.26 AW	36.05 TQ	DCBLS	10/01-12/01
	Washington PMSA, DC-MD-VA-WV	H	8.99 FQ	18.10 AW	29.24 TQ	DCBLS	10/01-12/01
	Florida	H	8.68 FQ	16.45 AW	26.81 TQ	FLBLS	10/01-12/01
	Daytona Beach MSA, FL	H	7.86 FQ	12.18 AW	17.33 TQ	FLBLS	10/01-12/01
	Fort Lauderdale PMSA, FL	H	9.30 FQ	15.26 AW	25.58 TQ	FLBLS	10/01-12/01
	Fort Myers-Cape Coral MSA, FL	H	11.48 FQ	16.77 AW	25.15 TQ	FLBLS	10/01-12/01
	Fort Pierce-Port St. Lucie MSA, FL	H	7.60 FQ	14.99 AW	24.02 TQ	FLBLS	10/01-12/01
	Fort Walton Beach MSA, FL	H	10.80 FQ	15.39 AW	24.53 TQ	FLBLS	10/01-12/01
	Gainesville MSA, FL	H	7.99 FQ	18.62 AW	28.22 TQ	FLBLS	10/01-12/01
	Jacksonville MSA, FL	H	9.30 FQ	15.03 AW	24.11 TQ	FLBLS	10/01-12/01
	Lakeland-Winter Haven MSA, FL	H	9.94 FQ	15.27 AW	25.60 TQ	FLBLS	10/01-12/01
	Melbourne-Titusville-Palm Bay MSA, FL	H	10.39 FQ	12.88 AW	14.45 TQ	FLBLS	10/01-12/01
	Miami PMSA, FL	H	12.38 FQ	21.10 AW	27.76 TQ	FLBLS	10/01-12/01
	Naples MSA, FL	H	12.39 FQ	21.81 AW	34.19 TQ	FLBLS	10/01-12/01
	Orlando MSA, FL	H	7.82 FQ	15.63 AW	26.06 TQ	FLBLS	10/01-12/01
	Pensacola MSA, FL	H	7.09 FQ	11.81 AW	16.67 TQ	FLBLS	10/01-12/01
	Sarasota-Bradenton MSA, FL	H	9.18 FQ	14.10 AW	24.37 TQ	FLBLS	10/01-12/01
	Tallahassee MSA, FL	H	7.47 FQ	13.23 AW	21.12 TQ	FLBLS	10/01-12/01

AAW	Average annual wage	**AOH**	Average offered, high	**ASH**	Average starting, high	**H**	Hourly	**M**	Monthly	**S**	Special: hourly and annual
AE	Average entry wage	**AOL**	Average offered, low	**ASL**	Average starting, low	**HI**	Highest wage paid	**MTC**	Median total compensation	**TQ**	Third quartile wage
AEX	Average experienced wage	**APH**	Average pay, high range	**AW**	Average wage paid	**HR**	High end range	**MW**	Median wage paid	**W**	Weekly
AO	Average offered	**APL**	Average pay, low range	**FQ**	First quartile wage	**LR**	Low end range	**SQ**	Second quartile wage	**Y**	Yearly

Occupation/Type/Industry	Location	Per	Low	Mid	High	Source	Date
Chef and Head Cook	Tampa-St. Petersburg-Clearwater MSA, FL	H	9.24 FQ	14.61 AW	21.06 TQ	FLBLS	10/01-12/01
	West Palm Beach-Boca Raton MSA, FL	H	6.14 FQ	17.44 AW	29.20 TQ	FLBLS	10/01-12/01
	Georgia	H	8.07 FQ	13.21 AW	20.15 TQ	GABLS	10/01-12/01
	Atlanta MSA, GA	H	9.34 FQ	15.04 AW	21.59 TQ	GABLS	10/01-12/01
	Augusta-Aiken MSA, GA-SC	H	7.19 FQ	12.15 AW	16.77 TQ	GABLS	10/01-12/01
	Columbus MSA, GA-AL	H	10.56 FQ	14.30 AW	20.45 TQ	GABLS	10/01-12/01
	Macon MSA, GA	H	9.06 FQ	11.46 AW	15.74 TQ	GABLS	10/01-12/01
	Savannah MSA, GA	H	10.68 FQ	15.01 AW	22.79 TQ	GABLS	10/01-12/01
	Hawaii	H	11.71 FQ	18.39 AW	27.04 TQ	HIBLS	10/01-12/01
	Honolulu MSA, HI	H	12.02 FQ	17.99 AW	25.88 TQ	HIBLS	10/01-12/01
	Idaho	H	7.62 FQ	11.74 AW	16.38 TQ	IDBLS	10/01-12/01
	Boise City MSA, ID	H	11.21 FQ	14.33 AW	17.32 TQ	IDBLS	10/01-12/01
	Illinois	H	5.94 FQ	13.30 AW	24.26 TQ	ILBLS	10/01-12/01
	Champaign-Urbana MSA, IL	H	11.11 FQ	15.41 AW	24.36 TQ	ILBLS	10/01-12/01
	Chicago PMSA, IL	H	10.20 FQ	17.28 AW	26.95 TQ	ILBLS	10/01-12/01
	Peoria-Pekin MSA, IL	H	5.98 FQ	11.93 AW	23.26 TQ	ILBLS	10/01-12/01
	Rockford MSA, IL	H	7.28 FQ	11.31 AW	16.86 TQ	ILBLS	10/01-12/01
	Springfield MSA, IL	H	9.06 FQ	15.08 AW	22.37 TQ	ILBLS	10/01-12/01
	Indiana	H	7.62 FQ	12.69 AW	19.43 TQ	INBLS	10/01-12/01
	Elkhart-Goshen MSA, IN	H	8.20 FQ	12.16 AW	16.90 TQ	INBLS	10/01-12/01
	Evansville-Henderson MSA, IN-KY	H	6.92 FQ	13.79 AW	23.63 TQ	INBLS	10/01-12/01
	Fort Wayne MSA, IN	H	6.01 FQ	10.59 AW	15.85 TQ	INBLS	10/01-12/01
	Gary PMSA, IN	H	11.26 FQ	15.61 AW	21.68 TQ	INBLS	10/01-12/01
	Indianapolis MSA, IN	H	9.26 FQ	12.78 AW	18.30 TQ	INBLS	10/01-12/01
	Lafayette MSA, IN	H	7.30 FQ	10.33 AW	13.83 TQ	INBLS	10/01-12/01
	South Bend MSA, IN	H	7.53 FQ	10.76 AW	13.19 TQ	INBLS	10/01-12/01
	Iowa	H	6.74 FQ	13.53 AW	23.22 TQ	IABLS	10/01-12/01
	Cedar Rapids MSA, IA	H	5.82 FQ	11.55 AW	17.46 TQ	IABLS	10/01-12/01
	Davenport-Moline-Rock Island MSA, IA-IL	H	5.73 FQ	10.85 AW	19.82 TQ	IABLS	10/01-12/01
	Des Moines MSA, IA	H	8.32 FQ	21.01 AW	36.26 TQ	IABLS	10/01-12/01
	Kansas	H	8.18 FQ	12.50 AW	19.18 TQ	KSBLS	10/01-12/01
	Topeka MSA, KS	H	7.94 FQ	12.10 AW	20.67 TQ	KSBLS	10/01-12/01
	Wichita MSA, KS	H	9.22 FQ	11.52 AW	15.83 TQ	KSBLS	10/01-12/01
	Kentucky	H	7.67 FQ	12.76 AW	19.25 TQ	KYBLS	10/01-12/01
	Lexington MSA, KY	H	9.51 FQ	16.15 AW	22.95 TQ	KYBLS	10/01-12/01
	Louisville MSA, KY-IN	H	8.38 FQ	12.82 AW	17.71 TQ	KYBLS	10/01-12/01
	Louisiana	H	5.66 FQ	11.50 AW	19.37 TQ	LABLS	10/01-12/01
	Baton Rouge MSA, LA	H	5.42 FQ	9.44 AW	16.43 TQ	LABLS	10/01-12/01
	Houma MSA, LA	H	10.82 FQ	11.98 AW	13.35 TQ	LABLS	10/01-12/01
	Lafayette MSA, LA	H	9.83 FQ	14.45 AW	18.13 TQ	LABLS	10/01-12/01
	Lake Charles MSA, LA	H	8.78 FQ	17.93 AW	22.54 TQ	LABLS	10/01-12/01
	New Orleans MSA, LA	H	5.53 FQ	10.07 AW	17.10 TQ	LABLS	10/01-12/01
	Shreveport-Bossier City MSA, LA	H	9.17 FQ	13.99 AW	19.58 TQ	LABLS	10/01-12/01
	Maine	H	7.89 FQ	13.13 AW	19.85 TQ	MEBLS	10/01-12/01
	Portland MSA, ME	H	11.46 FQ	14.13 AW	17.52 TQ	MEBLS	10/01-12/01
	Maryland	H	7.91 FQ	15.92 AW	24.39 TQ	MDBLS	10/01-12/01
	Baltimore PMSA, MD	H	8.74 FQ	16.45 AW	22.24 TQ	MDBLS	10/01-12/01
	Massachusetts	H	8.50 FQ	15.00 AW	24.05 TQ	MABLS	10/01-12/01
	Boston PMSA, MA-NH	H	11.36 FQ	17.43 AW	26.96 TQ	MABLS	10/01-12/01
	Brockton PMSA, MA	H	17.18 FQ	27.82 AW	36.62 TQ	MABLS	10/01-12/01
	Lawrence PMSA, MA-NH	H	11.34 FQ	17.51 AW	31.00 TQ	MABLS	10/01-12/01
	Lowell PMSA, MA-NH	H	7.17 FQ	12.38 AW	18.06 TQ	MABLS	10/01-12/01
	New Bedford PMSA, MA	H	9.08 FQ	12.80 AW	17.94 TQ	MABLS	10/01-12/01
	Springfield MSA, MA	H	7.54 FQ	11.27 AW	16.37 TQ	MABLS	10/01-12/01
	Worcester PMSA, MA-CT	H	9.28 FQ	14.02 AW	22.11 TQ	MABLS	10/01-12/01
	Michigan	H	8.36 FQ	16.23 AW	30.92 TQ	MIBLS	10/01-12/01
	Ann Arbor PMSA, MI	H	8.92 FQ	14.52 AW	24.65 TQ	MIBLS	10/01-12/01
	Detroit PMSA, MI	H	9.18 FQ	19.57 AW	32.57 TQ	MIBLS	10/01-12/01
	Flint PMSA, MI	H	6.97 FQ	9.40 AW	13.08 TQ	MIBLS	10/01-12/01
	Grand Rapids-Muskegon-Holland MSA, MI	H	9.93 FQ	15.32 AW	23.19 TQ	MIBLS	10/01-12/01
	Kalamazoo-Battle Creek MSA, MI	H	9.54 FQ	14.62 AW	21.72 TQ	MIBLS	10/01-12/01
	Lansing-East Lansing MSA, MI	H	7.73 FQ	13.94 AW	22.02 TQ	MIBLS	10/01-12/01
	Saginaw-Bay City-Midland MSA, MI	H	7.38 FQ	12.07 AW	17.90 TQ	MIBLS	10/01-12/01
	Minnesota	H	7.63 FQ	13.97 AW	21.44 TQ	MNBLS	10/01-12/01

AAW	Average annual wage	**AOH**	Average offered, high	**ASH**	Average starting, high	**H**	Hourly	**M**	Monthly	**S**	Special: hourly and annual
AE	Average entry wage	**AOL**	Average offered, low	**ASL**	Average starting, low	**HI**	Highest wage paid	**MTC**	Median total compensation	**TQ**	Third quartile wage
AEX	Average experienced wage	**APH**	Average pay, high range	**AW**	Average wage paid	**HR**	High end range	**MW**	Median wage paid	**W**	Weekly
AO	Average offered	**APL**	Average pay, low range	**FQ**	First quartile wage	**LR**	Low end range	**SQ**	Second quartile wage	**Y**	Yearly

Occupation/Type/Industry	Location	Per	Low	Mid	High	Source	Date
Chef and Head Cook	Duluth-Superior MSA, MN-WI	H	8.54 FQ	14.42 AW	20.03 TQ	MNBLS	10/01-12/01
	Minneapolis-St. Paul MSA, MN-WI	H	9.10 FQ	15.78 AW	23.17 TQ	MNBLS	10/01-12/01
	St. Cloud MSA, MN	H	6.37 FQ	11.67 AW	17.04 TQ	MNBLS	10/01-12/01
	Mississippi	H	6.03 FQ	12.11 AW	18.93 TQ	MSBLS	10/01-12/01
	Biloxi-Gulfport-Pascagoula MSA, MS	H	9.33 FQ	15.12 AW	26.94 TQ	MSBLS	10/01-12/01
	Jackson MSA, MS	H	6.07 FQ	10.49 AW	17.04 TQ	MSBLS	10/01-12/01
	Missouri	H	5.70 FQ	10.47 AW	17.43 TQ	MOBLS	10/01-12/01
	Kansas City MSA, MO-KS	H	9.18 FQ	14.72 AW	22.25 TQ	MOBLS	10/01-12/01
	St. Louis MSA, MO-IL	H	5.54 FQ	10.18 AW	17.62 TQ	MOBLS	10/01-12/01
	Springfield MSA, MO	H	7.96 FQ	12.75 AW	19.47 TQ	MOBLS	10/01-12/01
	Montana	H	5.43 FQ	8.70 AW	14.86 TQ	MTBLS	10/01-12/01
	Billings MSA, MT	H	8.66 FQ	10.84 AW	15.77 TQ	MTBLS	10/01-12/01
	Nebraska	H	9.20 FQ	13.89 AW	21.01 TQ	NEBLS	10/01-12/01
	Lincoln MSA, NE	H	8.94 FQ	14.01 AW	21.23 TQ	NEBLS	10/01-12/01
	Omaha MSA, NE-IA	H	9.63 FQ	14.48 AW	21.85 TQ	NEBLS	10/01-12/01
	Nevada	H	8.01 FQ	16.15 AW	25.78 TQ	NVBLS	10/01-12/01
	Las Vegas MSA, NV-AZ	H	7.89 FQ	16.08 AW	25.81 TQ	NVBLS	10/01-12/01
	Reno MSA, NV	H	11.60 FQ	17.11 AW	25.98 TQ	NVBLS	10/01-12/01
	New Hampshire	H	6.86 FQ	15.16 AW	22.50 TQ	NHBLS	10/01-12/01
	Manchester PMSA, NH	H	5.84 FQ	10.14 AW	17.88 TQ	NHBLS	10/01-12/01
	Nashua PMSA, NH	H	6.36 FQ	13.49 AW	21.89 TQ	NHBLS	10/01-12/01
	Portsmouth-Rochester PMSA, NH-ME	H	11.76 FQ	17.50 AW	22.91 TQ	NHBLS	10/01-12/01
	New Jersey	H	14.68 FQ	22.46 AW	32.77 TQ	NJBLS	10/01-12/01
	Atlantic-Cape May PMSA, NJ	H	15.15 FQ	22.96 AW	31.34 TQ	NJBLS	10/01-12/01
	Bergen-Passaic PMSA, NJ	H	13.37 FQ	22.42 AW	31.72 TQ	NJBLS	10/01-12/01
	Jersey City PMSA, NJ	H	12.60 FQ	21.33 AW	30.20 TQ	NJBLS	10/01-12/01
	Middlesex-Somerset-Hunterdon PMSA, NJ	H	15.74 FQ	23.96 AW	33.18 TQ	NJBLS	10/01-12/01
	Monmouth-Ocean PMSA, NJ	H	15.53 FQ	22.28 AW	36.30 TQ	NJBLS	10/01-12/01
	Newark PMSA, NJ	H	15.37 FQ	24.12 AW	37.70 TQ	NJBLS	10/01-12/01
	Trenton PMSA, NJ	H	12.39 FQ	20.56 AW	27.17 TQ	NJBLS	10/01-12/01
	New Mexico	H	7.18 FQ	12.79 AW	20.60 TQ	NMBLS	10/01-12/01
	Albuquerque MSA, NM	H	11.74 FQ	16.40 AW	22.02 TQ	NMBLS	10/01-12/01
	Las Cruces MSA, NM	H	5.97 FQ	7.70 AW	9.38 TQ	NMBLS	10/01-12/01
	New York	H	8.55 FQ	16.24 AW	27.98 TQ	NYBLS	10/01-12/01
	Albany-Schenectady-Troy MSA, NY	H	7.75 FQ	13.75 AW	20.73 TQ	NYBLS	10/01-12/01
	Binghamton MSA, NY	H	8.17 FQ	11.65 AW	19.43 TQ	NYBLS	10/01-12/01
	Buffalo-Niagara Falls MSA, NY	H	8.17 FQ	14.20 AW	21.39 TQ	NYBLS	10/01-12/01
	Dutchess County PMSA, NY	H	8.40 FQ	17.78 AW	37.95 TQ	NYBLS	10/01-12/01
	Nassau-Suffolk PMSA, NY	H	8.97 FQ	17.33 AW	28.83 TQ	NYBLS	10/01-12/01
	New York PMSA, NY	H	6.69 FQ	17.16 AW	32.55 TQ	NYBLS	10/01-12/01
	Newburgh PMSA, NY-PA	H	7.90 FQ	15.63 AW	25.84 TQ	NYBLS	10/01-12/01
	Rochester MSA, NY	H	8.77 FQ	14.10 AW	23.57 TQ	NYBLS	10/01-12/01
	Syracuse MSA, NY	H	10.20 FQ	16.14 AW	21.66 TQ	NYBLS	10/01-12/01
	Utica-Rome MSA, NY	H	9.40 FQ	12.44 AW	19.49 TQ	NYBLS	10/01-12/01
	North Carolina	H	7.82 FQ	13.82 AW	23.65 TQ	NCBLS	10/01-12/01
	Asheville MSA, NC	H	9.25 FQ	13.59 AW	19.94 TQ	NCBLS	10/01-12/01
	Charlotte-Gastonia-Rock Hill MSA, NC-SC	H	8.23 FQ	14.68 AW	24.11 TQ	NCBLS	10/01-12/01
	Fayetteville MSA, NC	H	8.51 FQ	11.94 AW	17.05 TQ	NCBLS	10/01-12/01
	Greensboro-Winston-Salem-High Point MSA, NC	H	8.92 FQ	16.35 AW	31.64 TQ	NCBLS	10/01-12/01
	Hickory-Morganton-Lenoir MSA, NC	H	6.00 FQ	8.95 AW	10.92 TQ	NCBLS	10/01-12/01
	Raleigh-Durham-Chapel Hill MSA, NC	H	9.68 FQ	14.83 AW	22.03 TQ	NCBLS	10/01-12/01
	Wilmington MSA, NC	H	8.72 FQ	15.23 AW	23.22 TQ	NCBLS	10/01-12/01
	North Dakota	H	6.79 FQ	9.52 AW	13.48 TQ	NDBLS	10/01-12/01
	Fargo-Moorhead MSA, ND-MN	H	6.25 FQ	10.04 AW	15.90 TQ	NDBLS	10/01-12/01
	Ohio	H	7.18 FQ	12.93 AW	20.11 TQ	OHBLS	10/01-12/01
	Akron PMSA, OH	H	7.41 FQ	12.47 AW	24.72 TQ	OHBLS	10/01-12/01
	Canton-Massillon MSA, OH	H	6.22 FQ	10.52 AW	16.63 TQ	OHBLS	10/01-12/01
	Cincinnati PMSA, OH-KY-IN	H	7.94 FQ	13.57 AW	21.17 TQ	OHBLS	10/01-12/01
	Cleveland-Lorain-Elyria PMSA, OH	H	7.35 FQ	13.27 AW	18.01 TQ	OHBLS	10/01-12/01
	Columbus MSA, OH	H	10.55 FQ	15.33 AW	21.33 TQ	OHBLS	10/01-12/01

AAW	Average annual wage	**AOH**	Average offered, high	**ASH**	Average starting, high	**H**	Hourly	**M**	Monthly	**S**	Special: hourly and annual
AE	Average entry wage	**AOL**	Average offered, low	**ASL**	Average starting, low	**HI**	Highest wage paid	**MTC**	Median total compensation	**TQ**	Third quartile wage
AEX	Average experienced wage	**APH**	Average pay, high range	**AW**	Average wage paid	**HR**	High end range	**MW**	Median wage paid	**W**	Weekly
AO	Average offered	**APL**	Average pay, low range	**FQ**	First quartile wage	**LR**	Low end range	**SQ**	Second quartile wage	**Y**	Yearly

Occupation/Type/Industry	Location	Per	Low	Mid	High	Source	Date
Chef and Head Cook	Dayton-Springfield MSA, OH	H	7.47 FQ	13.45 AW	27.58 TQ	OHBLS	10/01-12/01
	Hamilton-Middletown PMSA, OH	H	10.55 FQ	15.31 AW	23.00 TQ	OHBLS	10/01-12/01
	Toledo MSA, OH	H	5.97 FQ	9.50 AW	14.97 TQ	OHBLS	10/01-12/01
	Youngstown-Warren MSA, OH	H	11.00 FQ	14.78 AW	21.58 TQ	OHBLS	10/01-12/01
	Oklahoma	H	5.97 FQ	10.29 AW	17.08 TQ	OKBLS	10/01-12/01
	Oklahoma City MSA, OK	H	6.01 FQ	9.69 AW	13.65 TQ	OKBLS	10/01-12/01
	Tulsa MSA, OK	H	6.16 FQ	10.00 AW	14.10 TQ	OKBLS	10/01-12/01
	Oregon	H	9.13 FQ	15.39 AW	25.19 TQ	ORBLS	10/01-12/01
	Eugene-Springfield MSA, OR	H	8.27 FQ	15.33 AW	21.95 TQ	ORBLS	10/01-12/01
	Medford-Ashland MSA, OR	H	7.67 FQ	12.25 AW	18.45 TQ	ORBLS	10/01-12/01
	Portland-Vancouver PMSA, OR-WA	H	9.36 FQ	15.16 AW	25.87 TQ	ORBLS	10/01-12/01
	Salem PMSA, OR	H	8.40 FQ	12.01 AW	19.23 TQ	ORBLS	10/01-12/01
	Pennsylvania	H	9.17 FQ	16.95 AW	26.00 TQ	PABLS	10/01-12/01
	Allentown-Bethlehem-Easton MSA, PA	H	9.08 FQ	12.68 AW	20.50 TQ	PABLS	10/01-12/01
	Erie MSA, PA	H	9.04 FQ	14.13 AW	19.00 TQ	PABLS	10/01-12/01
	Harrisburg-Lebanon-Carlisle MSA, PA	H	9.34 FQ	16.07 AW	24.55 TQ	PABLS	10/01-12/01
	Johnstown MSA, PA	H	7.71 FQ	11.53 AW	22.47 TQ	PABLS	10/01-12/01
	Lancaster MSA, PA	H	7.92 FQ	14.85 AW	24.92 TQ	PABLS	10/01-12/01
	Philadelphia PMSA, PA-NJ	H	9.95 FQ	19.84 AW	27.92 TQ	PABLS	10/01-12/01
	Pittsburgh MSA, PA	H	10.46 FQ	17.51 AW	21.80 TQ	PABLS	10/01-12/01
	Reading MSA, PA	H	9.81 FQ	15.16 AW	21.02 TQ	PABLS	10/01-12/01
	Scranton-Wilkes-Barre-Hazleton MSA, PA	H	11.30 FQ	16.05 AW	20.71 TQ	PABLS	10/01-12/01
	York MSA, PA	H	11.97 FQ	20.64 AW	27.41 TQ	PABLS	10/01-12/01
	Rhode Island	H	8.87 FQ	15.72 AW	24.13 TQ	RIBLS	10/01-12/01
	Providence-Fall River-Warwick MSA, RI-MA	H	7.91 FQ	14.40 AW	22.32 TQ	RIBLS	10/01-12/01
	South Carolina	H	7.72 FQ	12.61 AW	20.48 TQ	SCBLS	10/01-12/01
	Charleston-North Charleston MSA, SC	H	8.59 FQ	13.89 AW	22.91 TQ	SCBLS	10/01-12/01
	Columbia MSA, SC	H	7.48 FQ	10.00 AW	12.80 TQ	SCBLS	10/01-12/01
	Greenville-Spartanburg-Anderson MSA, SC	H	7.10 FQ	10.96 AW	17.26 TQ	SCBLS	10/01-12/01
	Myrtle Beach MSA, SC	H	7.95 FQ	12.91 AW	19.75 TQ	SCBLS	10/01-12/01
	South Dakota	H	9.70 FQ	13.12 AW	18.83 TQ	SDBLS	10/01-12/01
	Tennessee	H	6.73 FQ	11.69 AW	18.20 TQ	TNBLS	10/01-12/01
	Chattanooga MSA, TN-GA	H	8.07 FQ	12.45 AW	19.03 TQ	TNBLS	10/01-12/01
	Clarksville-Hopkinsville MSA, TN-KY	H	5.76 FQ	8.88 AW	15.26 TQ	TNBLS	10/01-12/01
	Johnson City-Kingsport-Bristol MSA, TN-VA	H	6.08 FQ	9.25 AW	13.08 TQ	TNBLS	10/01-12/01
	Memphis MSA, TN-AR-MS	H	8.03 FQ	13.53 AW	20.13 TQ	TNBLS	10/01-12/01
	Nashville MSA, TN	H	13.48 FQ	19.55 AW	28.32 TQ	TNBLS	10/01-12/01
	Texas	H	7.19 FQ	12.25 AW	21.13 TQ	TXBLS	10/01-12/01
	Amarillo MSA, TX	H	8.54 FQ	17.23 AW	29.44 TQ	TXBLS	10/01-12/01
	Austin-San Marcos MSA, TX	H	7.19 FQ	11.93 AW	19.32 TQ	TXBLS	10/01-12/01
	Beaumont-Port Arthur MSA, TX	H	6.36 FQ	16.36 AW	25.94 TQ	TXBLS	10/01-12/01
	Brownsville-Harlingen-San Benito MSA, TX	H	5.76 FQ	8.56 AW	11.38 TQ	TXBLS	10/01-12/01
	Corpus Christi MSA, TX	H	7.63 FQ	13.00 AW	21.19 TQ	TXBLS	10/01-12/01
	Dallas PMSA, TX	H	7.06 FQ	16.70 AW	25.85 TQ	TXBLS	10/01-12/01
	El Paso MSA, TX	H	5.42 FQ	8.58 AW	14.91 TQ	TXBLS	10/01-12/01
	Fort Worth-Arlington PMSA, TX	H	8.50 FQ	15.02 AW	19.92 TQ	TXBLS	10/01-12/01
	Galveston-Texas City PMSA, TX	H	9.52 FQ	17.26 AW	29.37 TQ	TXBLS	10/01-12/01
	Houston PMSA, TX	H	7.41 FQ	11.13 AW	19.97 TQ	TXBLS	10/01-12/01
	Killeen-Temple MSA, TX	H	5.76 FQ	11.09 AW	15.97 TQ	TXBLS	10/01-12/01
	Laredo MSA, TX	H	7.20 FQ	8.15 AW	8.73 TQ	TXBLS	10/01-12/01
	Longview-Marshall MSA, TX	H	7.42 FQ	11.42 AW	17.89 TQ	TXBLS	10/01-12/01
	Lubbock MSA, TX	H	7.12 FQ	11.38 AW	18.65 TQ	TXBLS	10/01-12/01
	McAllen-Edinburg-Mission MSA, TX	H	7.30 FQ	11.78 AW	22.47 TQ	TXBLS	10/01-12/01
	Odessa-Midland MSA, TX	H	7.38 FQ	11.63 AW	17.81 TQ	TXBLS	10/01-12/01
	San Antonio MSA, TX	H	7.35 FQ	12.66 AW	21.47 TQ	TXBLS	10/01-12/01
	Tyler MSA, TX	H	7.80 FQ	13.82 AW	17.63 TQ	TXBLS	10/01-12/01
	Waco MSA, TX	H	7.37 FQ	9.98 AW	18.09 TQ	TXBLS	10/01-12/01

AAW	Average annual wage	**AOH**	Average offered, high	**ASH**	Average starting, high	**H**	Hourly	**M**	Monthly	**S**	Special: hourly and annual
AE	Average entry wage	**AOL**	Average offered, low	**ASL**	Average starting, low	**HI**	Highest wage paid	**MTC**	Median total compensation	**TQ**	Third quartile wage
AEX	Average experienced wage	**APH**	Average pay, high range	**AW**	Average wage paid	**HR**	High end range	**MW**	Median wage paid	**W**	Weekly
AO	Average offered	**APL**	Average pay, low range	**FQ**	First quartile wage	**LR**	Low end range	**SQ**	Second quartile wage	**Y**	Yearly

Occupation/Type/Industry	Location	Per	Low	Mid	High	Source	Date
Chef and Head Cook	Utah	H	6.56 FQ	10.69 AW	16.74 TQ	UTBLS	10/01-12/01
	Provo-Orem MSA, UT	H	6.41 FQ	11.52 AW	16.88 TQ	UTBLS	10/01-12/01
	Salt Lake City-Ogden MSA, UT	H	6.48 FQ	11.60 AW	19.64 TQ	UTBLS	10/01-12/01
	Vermont	H	10.34 FQ	17.60 AW	26.18 TQ	VTBLS	10/01-12/01
	Burlington MSA, VT	H	12.39 FQ	22.07 AW	37.85 TQ	VTBLS	10/01-12/01
	Virginia	H	7.92 FQ	15.38 AW	26.10 TQ	VABLS	10/01-12/01
	Lynchburg MSA, VA	H	8.98 FQ	12.42 AW	17.63 TQ	VABLS	10/01-12/01
	Norfolk-Virginia Beach-Newport News MSA, VA-NC	H	6.63 FQ	12.96 AW	21.40 TQ	VABLS	10/01-12/01
	Richmond-Petersburg MSA, VA	H	10.79 FQ	16.45 AW	24.69 TQ	VABLS	10/01-12/01
	Roanoke MSA, VA	H	7.86 FQ	13.68 AW	22.05 TQ	VABLS	10/01-12/01
	Washington	H	9.64 FQ	15.75 AW	23.98 TQ	WABLS	10/01-12/01
	Bremerton PMSA, WA	H	10.54 FQ	14.26 AW	17.86 TQ	WABLS	10/01-12/01
	Olympia PMSA, WA	H	7.03 FQ	11.65 AW	15.52 TQ	WABLS	10/01-12/01
	Seattle-Bellevue-Everett PMSA, WA	H	13.50 FQ	18.78 AW	26.76 TQ	WABLS	10/01-12/01
	Spokane MSA, WA	H	10.62 FQ	16.63 AW	24.61 TQ	WABLS	10/01-12/01
	Tacoma PMSA, WA	H	11.56 FQ	17.76 AW	27.12 TQ	WABLS	10/01-12/01
	Yakima MSA, WA	H	7.63 FQ	10.30 AW	17.34 TQ	WABLS	10/01-12/01
	West Virginia	H	6.22 FQ	10.14 AW	17.82 TQ	WVBLS	10/01-12/01
	Charleston MSA, WV	H	5.79 FQ	10.02 AW	16.58 TQ	WVBLS	10/01-12/01
	Huntington-Ashland MSA, WV-KY-OH	H	6.19 FQ	11.30 AW	22.47 TQ	WVBLS	10/01-12/01
	Wisconsin	H	7.92 FQ	12.08 AW	18.78 TQ	WIBLS	10/01-12/01
	Appleton-Oshkosh-Neenah MSA, WI	H	9.22 FQ	11.88 AW	15.45 TQ	WIBLS	10/01-12/01
	Green Bay MSA, WI	H	9.35 FQ	12.88 AW	18.17 TQ	WIBLS	10/01-12/01
	Madison MSA, WI	H	7.30 FQ	10.80 AW	13.79 TQ	WIBLS	10/01-12/01
	Milwaukee-Waukesha PMSA, WI	H	7.74 FQ	13.16 AW	21.50 TQ	WIBLS	10/01-12/01
	Racine PMSA, WI	H	7.59 FQ	13.62 AW	20.66 TQ	WIBLS	10/01-12/01
	Wyoming	H	7.37 FQ	10.98 AW	16.54 TQ	WYBLS	10/01-12/01
	Puerto Rico	H	8.74 FQ	13.62 AW	19.49 TQ	PRBLS	10/01-12/01
	Virgin Islands	H	14.54 FQ	20.07 AW	27.03 TQ	VIBLS	10/01-12/01
	Guam	H	8.35 FQ	14.86 AW	23.88 TQ	GUBLS	10/01-12/01
Chemical Engineer	Alabama	Y	45310 FQ	71240 AW	102070 TQ	ALBLS	10/01-12/01
	Huntsville MSA, AL	Y	48730 FQ	75850 AW	108220 TQ	ALBLS	10/01-12/01
	Mobile MSA, AL	Y	41800 FQ	72060 AW	103680 TQ	ALBLS	10/01-12/01
	Arizona	Y	42550 FQ	73490 AW	123970 TQ	AZBLS	10/01-12/01
	Phoenix-Mesa MSA, AZ	Y	41260 FQ	73400 AW	124360 TQ	AZBLS	10/01-12/01
	Arkansas	Y	42800 FQ	59420 AW	83180 TQ	ARBLS	10/01-12/01
	Little Rock-North Little Rock MSA, AR	Y	47150 FQ	55040 AW	69410 TQ	ARBLS	10/01-12/01
	California	Y	50990 FQ	91450 AW		CABLS	10/01-12/01
	Oakland PMSA, CA	Y	43580 FQ	79570 AW	140440 TQ	CABLS	10/01-12/01
	Orange County PMSA, CA	Y	52410 FQ	75090 AW	97840 TQ	CABLS	10/01-12/01
	Riverside-San Bernardino PMSA, CA	Y	40220 FQ	71530 AW	105340 TQ	CABLS	10/01-12/01
	San Diego MSA, CA	Y	56540 FQ	75930 AW	107870 TQ	CABLS	10/01-12/01
	San Francisco PMSA, CA	Y	50380 FQ	79310 AW	127500 TQ	CABLS	10/01-12/01
	San Jose PMSA, CA	Y	48850 FQ	75070 AW	119620 TQ	CABLS	10/01-12/01
	Ventura PMSA, CA	Y	52470 FQ	78270 AW	103320 TQ	CABLS	10/01-12/01
	San Diego, CA	Y		90000 AW		SDBJ	1/01-1/02
	Colorado	Y	47510 FQ	73200 AW	107190 TQ	COBLS	10/01-12/01
	Boulder-Longmont PMSA, CO	Y	46590 FQ	71760 AW	105500 TQ	COBLS	10/01-12/01
	Denver PMSA, CO	Y	49160 FQ	76120 AW	109320 TQ	COBLS	10/01-12/01
	Connecticut	Y	49940 FQ	75440 AW	109230 TQ	CTBLS	10/01-12/01
	Danbury PMSA, CT	Y	57390 FQ	84350 AW	127200 TQ	CTBLS	10/01-12/01
	Hartford MSA, CT	Y	48020 FQ	67660 AW	92440 TQ	CTBLS	10/01-12/01
	New Haven-Meriden PMSA, CT	Y	50130 FQ	80450 AW	121340 TQ	CTBLS	10/01-12/01
	Delaware	Y	47020 FQ	70140 AW	97860 TQ	DEBLS	10/01-12/01
	Wilmington-Newark PMSA, DE-MD	Y	46920 FQ	70220 AW	98190 TQ	DEBLS	10/01-12/01
	Washington PMSA, DC-MD-VA-WV	Y	50920 FQ	74520 AW	102650 TQ	DCBLS	10/01-12/01
	Florida	Y	39190 FQ	69340 AW	104880 TQ	FLBLS	10/01-12/01
	Lakeland-Winter Haven MSA, FL	Y	51960 FQ	80360 AW	118150 TQ	FLBLS	10/01-12/01

AAW	Average annual wage	**AOH**	Average offered, high	**ASH**	Average starting, high	**H**	Hourly	**M**	Monthly	**S**	Special: hourly and annual
AE	Average entry wage	**AOL**	Average offered, low	**ASL**	Average starting, low	**HI**	Highest wage paid	**MTC**	Median total compensation	**TQ**	Third quartile wage
AEX	Average experienced wage	**APH**	Average pay, high range	**AW**	Average wage paid	**HR**	High end range	**MW**	Median wage paid	**W**	Weekly
AO	Average offered	**APL**	Average pay, low range	**FQ**	First quartile wage	**LR**	Low end range	**SQ**	Second quartile wage	**Y**	Yearly

Occupation/Type/Industry	Location	Per	Low	Mid	High	Source	Date
Chemical Engineer	Melbourne-Titusville-Palm Bay MSA, FL	Y	31920 FQ	55990 AW	84440 TQ	FLBLS	10/01-12/01
	Pensacola MSA, FL	Y	39560 FQ	71700 AW	113710 TQ	FLBLS	10/01-12/01
	Tampa-St. Petersburg-Clearwater MSA, FL	Y	42400 FQ	66970 AW	95730 TQ	FLBLS	10/01-12/01
	Georgia	Y	47960 FQ	69820 AW	96280 TQ	GABLS	10/01-12/01
	Atlanta MSA, GA	Y	48710 FQ	73770 AW	104790 TQ	GABLS	10/01-12/01
	Idaho	Y	50350 FQ	71370 AW	93400 TQ	IDBLS	10/01-12/01
	Illinois	Y	47510 FQ	67560 AW	90620 TQ	ILBLS	10/01-12/01
	Chicago PMSA, IL	Y	47350 FQ	67100 AW	89740 TQ	ILBLS	10/01-12/01
	Indiana	Y	33140 FQ	59350 AW	87490 TQ	INBLS	10/01-12/01
	Evansville-Henderson MSA, IN-KY	Y	37790 FQ	51180 AW	77820 TQ	INBLS	10/01-12/01
	Fort Wayne MSA, IN	Y	36520 FQ	64520 AW	90920 TQ	INBLS	10/01-12/01
	Indianapolis MSA, IN	Y	30930 FQ	52740 AW	83030 TQ	INBLS	10/01-12/01
	Iowa	Y	42350 FQ	62740 AW	88650 TQ	IABLS	10/01-12/01
	Kansas	Y	47510 FQ	68860 AW	100150 TQ	KSBLS	10/01-12/01
	Wichita MSA, KS	Y	44830 FQ	68530 AW	102560 TQ	KSBLS	10/01-12/01
	Kentucky	Y	49580 FQ	71230 AW	99400 TQ	KYBLS	10/01-12/01
	Louisville MSA, KY-IN	Y	47560 FQ	68540 AW	95670 TQ	KYBLS	10/01-12/01
	Louisiana	Y	50620 FQ	74020 AW	107000 TQ	LABLS	10/01-12/01
	Baton Rouge MSA, LA	Y	49420 FQ	74030 AW	107260 TQ	LABLS	10/01-12/01
	Lake Charles MSA, LA	Y	56790 FQ	74850 AW	99430 TQ	LABLS	10/01-12/01
	New Orleans MSA, LA	Y	53490 FQ	81820 AW	118250 TQ	LABLS	10/01-12/01
	Maine	Y	46040 FQ	64810 AW	91150 TQ	MEBLS	10/01-12/01
	Maryland	Y	50400 FQ	78110 AW	114640 TQ	MDBLS	10/01-12/01
	Baltimore PMSA, MD	Y	53570 FQ	81270 AW	121900 TQ	MDBLS	10/01-12/01
	Massachusetts	Y	43410 FQ	70710 AW	101320 TQ	MABLS	10/01-12/01
	Boston PMSA, MA-NH	Y	42480 FQ	68750 AW	97140 TQ	MABLS	10/01-12/01
	Lawrence PMSA, MA-NH	Y	51030 FQ	83160 AW	132890 TQ	MABLS	10/01-12/01
	Lowell PMSA, MA-NH	Y	40840 FQ	70340 AW	103640 TQ	MABLS	10/01-12/01
	Michigan	Y	46820 FQ	67060 AW	94830 TQ	MIBLS	10/01-12/01
	Ann Arbor PMSA, MI	Y	48730 FQ	68040 AW	90880 TQ	MIBLS	10/01-12/01
	Detroit PMSA, MI	Y	45190 FQ	63910 AW	96010 TQ	MIBLS	10/01-12/01
	Grand Rapids-Muskegon-Holland MSA, MI	Y	35920 FQ	59020 AW	86700 TQ	MIBLS	10/01-12/01
	Kalamazoo-Battle Creek MSA, MI	Y	40370 FQ	59420 AW	91550 TQ	MIBLS	10/01-12/01
	Saginaw-Bay City-Midland MSA, MI	Y	58840 FQ	72030 AW	95800 TQ	MIBLS	10/01-12/01
	Minnesota	Y	46720 FQ	65690 AW	89850 TQ	MNBLS	10/01-12/01
	Minneapolis-St. Paul MSA, MN-WI	Y	48660 FQ	67530 AW	90900 TQ	MNBLS	10/01-12/01
	Mississippi	Y	43110 FQ	67030 AW	97410 TQ	MSBLS	10/01-12/01
	Biloxi-Gulfport-Pascagoula MSA, MS	Y	51780 FQ	81070 AW	120660 TQ	MSBLS	10/01-12/01
	Missouri	Y	44100 FQ	72830 AW	108610 TQ	MOBLS	10/01-12/01
	Kansas City MSA, MO-KS	Y	41080 FQ	62680 AW	92520 TQ	MOBLS	10/01-12/01
	St. Louis MSA, MO-IL	Y	51390 FQ	80670 AW	111860 TQ	MOBLS	10/01-12/01
	Montana	Y	47520 FQ	66290 AW	91850 TQ	MTBLS	10/01-12/01
	Nebraska	Y	46830 FQ	62560 AW	81870 TQ	NEBLS	10/01-12/01
	Omaha MSA, NE-IA	Y	40500 FQ	59940 AW	77000 TQ	NEBLS	10/01-12/01
	Nevada	Y	48440 FQ	66500 AW	101190 TQ	NVBLS	10/01-12/01
	Las Vegas MSA, NV-AZ	Y	50820 FQ	72120 AW	115520 TQ	NVBLS	10/01-12/01
	New Hampshire	Y	44350 FQ	66590 AW	93190 TQ	NHBLS	10/01-12/01
	New Jersey	Y	50120 FQ	78490 AW	114860 TQ	NJBLS	10/01-12/01
	Bergen-Passaic PMSA, NJ	Y	49520 FQ	77550 AW	124010 TQ	NJBLS	10/01-12/01
	Jersey City PMSA, NJ	Y	49500 FQ	76540 AW	108600 TQ	NJBLS	10/01-12/01
	Middlesex-Somerset-Hunterdon PMSA, NJ	Y	52960 FQ	82750 AW	117110 TQ	NJBLS	10/01-12/01
	Monmouth-Ocean PMSA, NJ	Y	44930 FQ	67260 AW	99010 TQ	NJBLS	10/01-12/01
	Newark PMSA, NJ	Y	49770 FQ	78690 AW	116770 TQ	NJBLS	10/01-12/01
	Trenton PMSA, NJ	Y	56810 FQ	78430 AW	104650 TQ	NJBLS	10/01-12/01
	New Mexico	Y	52130 FQ	84880 AW	117610 TQ	NMBLS	10/01-12/01
	Albuquerque MSA, NM	Y	53480 FQ	83720 AW	114950 TQ	NMBLS	10/01-12/01
	New York	Y	49720 FQ	77030 AW	111860 TQ	NYBLS	10/01-12/01
	Albany-Schenectady-Troy MSA, NY	Y	57800 FQ	79450 AW	109970 TQ	NYBLS	10/01-12/01
	Buffalo-Niagara Falls MSA, NY	Y	47270 FQ	71380 AW	103420 TQ	NYBLS	10/01-12/01
	Nassau-Suffolk PMSA, NY	Y	49370 FQ	71660 AW	95940 TQ	NYBLS	10/01-12/01
	New York PMSA, NY	Y	49350 FQ	75520 AW	112790 TQ	NYBLS	10/01-12/01

AAW	Average annual wage	**AOH**	Average offered, high	**ASH**	Average starting, high	**H**	Hourly	**M**	Monthly	**S**	Special: hourly and annual
AE	Average entry wage	**AOL**	Average offered, low	**ASL**	Average starting, low	**HI**	Highest wage paid	**MTC**	Median total compensation	**TQ**	Third quartile wage
AEX	Average experienced wage	**APH**	Average pay, high range	**AW**	Average wage paid	**HR**	High end range	**MW**	Median wage paid	**W**	Weekly
AO	Average offered	**APL**	Average pay, low range	**FQ**	First quartile wage	**LR**	Low end range	**SQ**	Second quartile wage	**Y**	Yearly

Occupation/Type/Industry	Location	Per	Low	Mid	High	Source	Date
Chemical Engineer	North Carolina	Y	49880 FQ	70240 AW	92960 TQ	NCBLS	10/01-12/01
	Charlotte-Gastonia-Rock Hill MSA, NC-SC	Y	53520 FQ	73570 AW	92390 TQ	NCBLS	10/01-12/01
	Greensboro-Winston-Salem-High Point MSA, NC	Y	47350 FQ	69860 AW	96350 TQ	NCBLS	10/01-12/01
	Raleigh-Durham-Chapel Hill MSA, NC	Y	50450 FQ	69030 AW	90840 TQ	NCBLS	10/01-12/01
	North Dakota	Y	46460 FQ	64970 AW	84000 TQ	NDBLS	10/01-12/01
	Ohio	Y	45470 FQ	66670 AW	92520 TQ	OHBLS	10/01-12/01
	Akron PMSA, OH	Y	49320 FQ	68410 AW	89510 TQ	OHBLS	10/01-12/01
	Cincinnati PMSA, OH-KY-IN	Y	48660 FQ	70700 AW	96820 TQ	OHBLS	10/01-12/01
	Cleveland-Lorain-Elyria PMSA, OH	Y	43740 FQ	63050 AW	86800 TQ	OHBLS	10/01-12/01
	Columbus MSA, OH	Y	44160 FQ	64610 AW	92380 TQ	OHBLS	10/01-12/01
	Dayton-Springfield MSA, OH	Y	49250 FQ	71020 AW	102840 TQ	OHBLS	10/01-12/01
	Toledo MSA, OH	Y	40890 FQ	64680 AW	91590 TQ	OHBLS	10/01-12/01
	Youngstown-Warren MSA, OH	Y	46180 FQ	68720 AW	103460 TQ	OHBLS	10/01-12/01
	Oklahoma	Y	48570 FQ	74410 AW	106940 TQ	OKBLS	10/01-12/01
	Oklahoma City MSA, OK	Y	46550 FQ	68710 AW	93090 TQ	OKBLS	10/01-12/01
	Tulsa MSA, OK	Y	49380 FQ	80100 AW	119310 TQ	OKBLS	10/01-12/01
	Oregon	Y	54870 FQ	73610 AW	93570 TQ	ORBLS	10/01-12/01
	Portland-Vancouver PMSA, OR-WA	Y	58010 FQ	74580 AW	93280 TQ	ORBLS	10/01-12/01
	Pennsylvania	Y	43000 FQ	61570 AW	87190 TQ	PABLS	10/01-12/01
	Allentown-Bethlehem-Easton MSA, PA	Y	43800 FQ	58540 AW	73250 TQ	PABLS	10/01-12/01
	Philadelphia PMSA, PA-NJ	Y	45580 FQ	66240 AW	92860 TQ	PABLS	10/01-12/01
	Pittsburgh MSA, PA	Y	38100 FQ	63200 AW	88360 TQ	PABLS	10/01-12/01
	Rhode Island	Y	44140 FQ	68080 AW	93600 TQ	RIBLS	10/01-12/01
	Providence-Fall River-Warwick MSA, RI-MA	Y	45330 FQ	69270 AW	93320 TQ	RIBLS	10/01-12/01
	South Carolina	Y	50490 FQ	75400 AW	101270 TQ	SCBLS	10/01-12/01
	Charleston-North Charleston MSA, SC	Y	47600 FQ	69200 AW	100030 TQ	SCBLS	10/01-12/01
	Greenville-Spartanburg-Anderson MSA, SC	Y	51540 FQ	77890 AW	110600 TQ	SCBLS	10/01-12/01
	Tennessee	Y	49110 FQ	76360 AW	112250 TQ	TNBLS	10/01-12/01
	Chattanooga MSA, TN-GA	Y	41730 FQ	63240 AW	89780 TQ	TNBLS	10/01-12/01
	Johnson City-Kingsport-Bristol MSA, TN-VA	Y	53280 FQ	82740 AW	116370 TQ	TNBLS	10/01-12/01
	Memphis MSA, TN-AR-MS	Y	34880 FQ	66440 AW	96930 TQ	TNBLS	10/01-12/01
	Nashville MSA, TN	Y	37990 FQ	81760 AW	130050 TQ	TNBLS	10/01-12/01
	Texas	Y	49720 FQ	74240 AW	105320 TQ	TXBLS	10/01-12/01
	Austin-San Marcos MSA, TX	Y	38370 FQ	63780 AW	97520 TQ	TXBLS	10/01-12/01
	Beaumont-Port Arthur MSA, TX	Y	53350 FQ	75430 AW	103870 TQ	TXBLS	10/01-12/01
	Brazoria PMSA, TX	Y	52160 FQ	79790 AW	119930 TQ	TXBLS	10/01-12/01
	Corpus Christi MSA, TX	Y	57230 FQ	78460 AW	106230 TQ	TXBLS	10/01-12/01
	Dallas PMSA, TX	Y	51990 FQ	72750 AW	99320 TQ	TXBLS	10/01-12/01
	Fort Worth-Arlington PMSA, TX	Y	44070 FQ	71840 AW	105810 TQ	TXBLS	10/01-12/01
	Galveston-Texas City PMSA, TX	Y	51720 FQ	73110 AW	92670 TQ	TXBLS	10/01-12/01
	Houston PMSA, TX	Y	51560 FQ	77160 AW	111410 TQ	TXBLS	10/01-12/01
	Longview-Marshall MSA, TX	Y	47300 FQ	75030 AW	106280 TQ	TXBLS	10/01-12/01
	San Antonio MSA, TX	Y	55060 FQ	73950 AW	93440 TQ	TXBLS	10/01-12/01
	Tyler MSA, TX	Y	53340 FQ	78090 AW	106620 TQ	TXBLS	10/01-12/01
	Utah	Y	47580 FQ	65780 AW	90510 TQ	UTBLS	10/01-12/01
	Provo-Orem MSA, UT	Y	47420 FQ	62960 AW	86750 TQ	UTBLS	10/01-12/01
	Salt Lake City-Ogden MSA, UT	Y	47880 FQ	68020 AW	91850 TQ	UTBLS	10/01-12/01
	Vermont	Y	30710 FQ	55380 AW	82550 TQ	VTBLS	10/01-12/01
	Virginia	Y	46920 FQ	67530 AW	90840 TQ	VABLS	10/01-12/01
	Norfolk-Virginia Beach-Newport News MSA, VA-NC	Y	46480 FQ	67420 AW	90100 TQ	VABLS	10/01-12/01
	Washington	Y	47350 FQ	73140 AW	101370 TQ	WABLS	10/01-12/01
	Richland-Kennewick-Pasco MSA, WA	Y	57720 FQ	80390 AW	107540 TQ	WABLS	10/01-12/01
	Seattle-Bellevue-Everett PMSA, WA	Y	35630 FQ	64290 AW	91150 TQ	WABLS	10/01-12/01
	West Virginia	Y	48890 FQ	69130 AW	93350 TQ	WVBLS	10/01-12/01

AAW	Average annual wage	**AOH**	Average offered, high	**ASH**	Average starting, high	**H**	Hourly	**M**	Monthly	**S**	Special: hourly and annual
AE	Average entry wage	**AOL**	Average offered, low	**ASL**	Average starting, low	**HI**	Highest wage paid	**MTC**	Median total compensation	**TQ**	Third quartile wage
AEX	Average experienced wage	**APH**	Average pay, high range	**AW**	Average wage paid	**HR**	High end range	**MW**	Median wage paid	**W**	Weekly
AO	Average offered	**APL**	Average pay, low range	**FQ**	First quartile wage	**LR**	Low end range	**SQ**	Second quartile wage	**Y**	Yearly

Occupation/Type/Industry	Location	Per	Low	Mid	High	Source	Date
Chemical Engineer	Charleston MSA, WV	Y	50190 FQ	68180 AW	90350 TQ	WVBLS	10/01-12/01
	Huntington-Ashland MSA, WV-KY-OH	Y	52350 FQ	69490 AW	94640 TQ	WVBLS	10/01-12/01
	Wisconsin	Y	47590 FQ	67520 AW	91230 TQ	WIBLS	10/01-12/01
	Appleton-Oshkosh-Neenah MSA, WI	Y	49430 FQ	64280 AW	86970 TQ	WIBLS	10/01-12/01
	Madison MSA, WI	Y	43220 FQ	68740 AW	101500 TQ	WIBLS	10/01-12/01
	Milwaukee-Waukesha PMSA, WI	Y	46000 FQ	65960 AW	91040 TQ	WIBLS	10/01-12/01
	Wyoming	Y	46310 FQ	66180 AW	89660 TQ	WYBLS	10/01-12/01
	Puerto Rico	Y	28420 FQ	50400 AW	75640 TQ	PRBLS	10/01-12/01
Chemical Equipment Operator and Tender	Alabama	H	11.27 FQ	16.84 AW	23.39 TQ	ALBLS	10/01-12/01
	Birmingham MSA, AL	H	11.81 FQ	15.19 AW	20.00 TQ	ALBLS	10/01-12/01
	Huntsville MSA, AL	H	9.44 FQ	14.39 AW	20.51 TQ	ALBLS	10/01-12/01
	Mobile MSA, AL	H	14.43 FQ	20.12 AW	26.07 TQ	ALBLS	10/01-12/01
	Arizona	H	9.06 FQ	14.82 AW	21.47 TQ	AZBLS	10/01-12/01
	Phoenix-Mesa MSA, AZ	H	9.09 FQ	15.10 AW	21.69 TQ	AZBLS	10/01-12/01
	Arkansas	H	11.50 FQ	15.23 AW	20.40 TQ	ARBLS	10/01-12/01
	Little Rock-North Little Rock MSA, AR	H	11.80 FQ	15.46 AW	20.39 TQ	ARBLS	10/01-12/01
	California	H	8.16 FQ	15.15 AW	22.41 TQ	CABLS	10/01-12/01
	Los Angeles-Long Beach PMSA, CA	H	7.38 FQ	11.85 AW	18.77 TQ	CABLS	10/01-12/01
	Merced MSA, CA	H	9.72 FQ	15.17 AW	21.73 TQ	CABLS	10/01-12/01
	Oakland PMSA, CA	H	8.47 FQ	15.78 AW	21.23 TQ	CABLS	10/01-12/01
	Orange County PMSA, CA	H	8.80 FQ	13.62 AW	20.36 TQ	CABLS	10/01-12/01
	Riverside-San Bernardino PMSA, CA	H	11.19 FQ	15.69 AW	20.57 TQ	CABLS	10/01-12/01
	Sacramento PMSA, CA	H	11.82 FQ	18.19 AW	25.51 TQ	CABLS	10/01-12/01
	San Diego MSA, CA	H	9.55 FQ	15.49 AW	22.01 TQ	CABLS	10/01-12/01
	San Francisco PMSA, CA	H	14.42 FQ	23.30 AW	35.79 TQ	CABLS	10/01-12/01
	San Jose PMSA, CA	H	8.68 FQ	16.30 AW	24.30 TQ	CABLS	10/01-12/01
	Santa Rosa PMSA, CA	H	9.52 FQ	14.06 AW	20.41 TQ	CABLS	10/01-12/01
	Stockton-Lodi MSA, CA	H	12.27 FQ	18.86 AW	25.62 TQ	CABLS	10/01-12/01
	Colorado	H	9.43 FQ	15.93 AW	24.47 TQ	COBLS	10/01-12/01
	Denver PMSA, CO	H	11.92 FQ	16.36 AW	21.26 TQ	COBLS	10/01-12/01
	Connecticut	H	12.61 FQ	20.31 AW	27.18 TQ	CTBLS	10/01-12/01
	Bridgeport PMSA, CT	H	10.79 FQ	16.80 AW	20.90 TQ	CTBLS	10/01-12/01
	Danbury PMSA, CT	H	12.80 FQ	20.21 AW	27.78 TQ	CTBLS	10/01-12/01
	Hartford MSA, CT	H	12.43 FQ	19.47 AW	26.14 TQ	CTBLS	10/01-12/01
	New Haven-Meriden PMSA, CT	H	11.70 FQ	18.41 AW	24.25 TQ	CTBLS	10/01-12/01
	Stamford-Norwalk PMSA, CT	H	11.40 FQ	14.74 AW	20.88 TQ	CTBLS	10/01-12/01
	Waterbury PMSA, CT	H	14.27 FQ	20.39 AW	26.79 TQ	CTBLS	10/01-12/01
	Delaware	H	14.23 FQ	19.91 AW	26.97 TQ	DEBLS	10/01-12/01
	Wilmington-Newark PMSA, DE-MD	H	14.11 FQ	19.98 AW	27.14 TQ	DEBLS	10/01-12/01
	Washington PMSA, DC-MD-VA-WV	H	12.07 FQ	18.30 AW	26.58 TQ	DCBLS	10/01-12/01
	Florida	H	9.83 FQ	16.00 AW	22.17 TQ	FLBLS	10/01-12/01
	Jacksonville MSA, FL	H	14.03 FQ	17.99 AW	25.48 TQ	FLBLS	10/01-12/01
	Lakeland-Winter Haven MSA, FL	H	10.96 FQ	15.98 AW	20.17 TQ	FLBLS	10/01-12/01
	Miami PMSA, FL	H	9.18 FQ	12.80 AW	19.52 TQ	FLBLS	10/01-12/01
	Tampa-St. Petersburg-Clearwater MSA, FL	H	9.23 FQ	13.17 AW	17.18 TQ	FLBLS	10/01-12/01
	Georgia	H	10.80 FQ	17.02 AW	25.65 TQ	GABLS	10/01-12/01
	Atlanta MSA, GA	H	11.00 FQ	16.65 AW	24.58 TQ	GABLS	10/01-12/01
	Savannah MSA, GA	H	12.47 FQ	16.88 AW	23.85 TQ	GABLS	10/01-12/01
	Idaho	H	11.37 FQ	18.27 AW	22.14 TQ	IDBLS	10/01-12/01
	Illinois	H	10.62 FQ	16.63 AW	23.18 TQ	ILBLS	10/01-12/01
	Chicago PMSA, IL	H	8.45 FQ	15.83 AW	21.79 TQ	ILBLS	10/01-12/01
	Peoria-Pekin MSA, IL	H	8.28 FQ	17.57 AW	26.06 TQ	ILBLS	10/01-12/01
	Indiana	H	11.14 FQ	18.11 AW	22.09 TQ	INBLS	10/01-12/01
	Elkhart-Goshen MSA, IN	H	10.21 FQ	17.27 AW	20.92 TQ	INBLS	10/01-12/01
	Evansville-Henderson MSA, IN-KY	H	16.31 FQ	19.47 AW	22.15 TQ	INBLS	10/01-12/01
	Gary PMSA, IN	H	15.45 FQ	19.96 AW	25.30 TQ	INBLS	10/01-12/01
	Indianapolis MSA, IN	H	10.18 FQ	18.27 AW	22.18 TQ	INBLS	10/01-12/01
	Lafayette MSA, IN	H	12.88 FQ	17.68 AW	21.86 TQ	INBLS	10/01-12/01

Occupation/Type/Industry	Location	Per	Low	Mid	High	Source	Date
Chemical Equipment Operator and Tender	South Bend MSA, IN	H	12.15 FQ	15.68 AW	19.30 TQ	INBLS	10/01-12/01
	Iowa	H	11.20 FQ	15.30 AW	19.67 TQ	IABLS	10/01-12/01
	Kansas	H	10.63 FQ	17.62 AW	26.09 TQ	KSBLS	10/01-12/01
	Kentucky	H	16.29 FQ	22.32 AW	26.95 TQ	KYBLS	10/01-12/01
	Lexington MSA, KY	H	9.41 FQ	14.63 AW	17.42 TQ	KYBLS	10/01-12/01
	Louisville MSA, KY-IN	H	16.67 FQ	22.13 AW	26.90 TQ	KYBLS	10/01-12/01
	Louisiana	H	14.42 FQ	21.05 AW	27.42 TQ	LABLS	10/01-12/01
	Baton Rouge MSA, LA	H	14.51 FQ	20.96 AW	27.41 TQ	LABLS	10/01-12/01
	Lake Charles MSA, LA	H	18.29 FQ	22.67 AW	27.20 TQ	LABLS	10/01-12/01
	New Orleans MSA, LA	H	16.49 FQ	22.49 AW	27.71 TQ	LABLS	10/01-12/01
	Shreveport-Bossier City MSA, LA	H	7.84 FQ	16.94 AW	25.87 TQ	LABLS	10/01-12/01
	Maine	H	11.42 FQ	17.75 AW	25.91 TQ	MEBLS	10/01-12/01
	Maryland	H	12.80 FQ	20.13 AW	26.20 TQ	MDBLS	10/01-12/01
	Baltimore PMSA, MD	H	12.83 FQ	20.60 AW	26.19 TQ	MDBLS	10/01-12/01
	Massachusetts	H	11.34 FQ	17.91 AW	28.32 TQ	MABLS	10/01-12/01
	Boston PMSA, MA-NH	H	11.64 FQ	18.79 AW	31.55 TQ	MABLS	10/01-12/01
	Michigan	H	11.59 FQ	16.35 AW	24.14 TQ	MIBLS	10/01-12/01
	Ann Arbor PMSA, MI	H	14.16 FQ	18.54 AW	25.96 TQ	MIBLS	10/01-12/01
	Detroit PMSA, MI	H	11.66 FQ	17.73 AW	25.81 TQ	MIBLS	10/01-12/01
	Grand Rapids-Muskegon-Holland MSA, MI	H	14.06 FQ	17.36 AW	24.48 TQ	MIBLS	10/01-12/01
	Kalamazoo-Battle Creek MSA, MI	H	14.34 FQ	19.80 AW	27.20 TQ	MIBLS	10/01-12/01
	Minnesota	H	10.73 FQ	16.67 AW	22.40 TQ	MNBLS	10/01-12/01
	Minneapolis-St. Paul MSA, MN-WI	H	11.58 FQ	18.01 AW	24.27 TQ	MNBLS	10/01-12/01
	Mississippi	H	11.59 FQ	18.10 AW	22.37 TQ	MSBLS	10/01-12/01
	Missouri	H	11.96 FQ	17.88 AW	21.92 TQ	MOBLS	10/01-12/01
	Kansas City MSA, MO-KS	H	11.90 FQ	18.76 AW	22.63 TQ	MOBLS	10/01-12/01
	St. Louis MSA, MO-IL	H	12.75 FQ	19.43 AW	23.23 TQ	MOBLS	10/01-12/01
	Montana	H	10.35 FQ	17.52 AW	26.27 TQ	MTBLS	10/01-12/01
	Nebraska	H	9.10 FQ	13.27 AW	18.62 TQ	NEBLS	10/01-12/01
	Omaha MSA, NE-IA	H	10.16 FQ	15.22 AW	19.86 TQ	NEBLS	10/01-12/01
	New Hampshire	H	10.94 FQ	15.83 AW	21.83 TQ	NHBLS	10/01-12/01
	New Jersey	H	10.95 FQ	17.88 AW	24.80 TQ	NJBLS	10/01-12/01
	Bergen-Passaic PMSA, NJ	H	8.63 FQ	16.99 AW	22.72 TQ	NJBLS	10/01-12/01
	Jersey City PMSA, NJ	H	12.59 FQ	17.77 AW	22.15 TQ	NJBLS	10/01-12/01
	Middlesex-Somerset-Hunterdon PMSA, NJ	H	14.03 FQ	20.74 AW	26.27 TQ	NJBLS	10/01-12/01
	Monmouth-Ocean PMSA, NJ	H	9.19 FQ	12.44 AW	17.95 TQ	NJBLS	10/01-12/01
	Newark PMSA, NJ	H	11.82 FQ	17.06 AW	21.49 TQ	NJBLS	10/01-12/01
	Trenton PMSA, NJ	H	13.44 FQ	19.76 AW	26.49 TQ	NJBLS	10/01-12/01
	New Mexico	H	11.12 FQ	16.03 AW	21.52 TQ	NMBLS	10/01-12/01
	New York	H	12.31 FQ	18.50 AW	25.72 TQ	NYBLS	10/01-12/01
	Buffalo-Niagara Falls MSA, NY	H	13.66 FQ	18.41 AW	23.29 TQ	NYBLS	10/01-12/01
	Nassau-Suffolk PMSA, NY	H	11.22 FQ	16.44 AW	21.97 TQ	NYBLS	10/01-12/01
	Newburgh PMSA, NY-PA	H	12.15 FQ	15.46 AW	17.99 TQ	NYBLS	10/01-12/01
	Syracuse MSA, NY	H	11.42 FQ	16.77 AW	24.02 TQ	NYBLS	10/01-12/01
	North Carolina	H	12.24 FQ	17.66 AW	22.88 TQ	NCBLS	10/01-12/01
	Charlotte-Gastonia-Rock Hill MSA, NC-SC	H	11.94 FQ	17.11 AW	21.77 TQ	NCBLS	10/01-12/01
	Greensboro-Winston-Salem-High Point MSA, NC	H	11.98 FQ	14.87 AW	17.39 TQ	NCBLS	10/01-12/01
	Hickory-Morganton-Lenoir MSA, NC	H	9.74 FQ	14.53 AW	21.39 TQ	NCBLS	10/01-12/01
	Raleigh-Durham-Chapel Hill MSA, NC	H	13.79 FQ	15.51 AW	17.81 TQ	NCBLS	10/01-12/01
	Ohio	H	10.96 FQ	17.69 AW	24.27 TQ	OHBLS	10/01-12/01
	Cincinnati PMSA, OH-KY-IN	H	8.32 FQ	16.84 AW	22.00 TQ	OHBLS	10/01-12/01
	Cleveland-Lorain-Elyria PMSA, OH	H	11.48 FQ	16.30 AW	21.40 TQ	OHBLS	10/01-12/01
	Columbus MSA, OH	H	9.80 FQ	21.50 AW	30.52 TQ	OHBLS	10/01-12/01
	Dayton-Springfield MSA, OH	H	11.62 FQ	16.69 AW	21.43 TQ	OHBLS	10/01-12/01
	Toledo MSA, OH	H	11.76 FQ	16.61 AW	25.11 TQ	OHBLS	10/01-12/01
	Youngstown-Warren MSA, OH	H	13.44 FQ	19.44 AW	22.42 TQ	OHBLS	10/01-12/01
	Oklahoma	H	12.25 FQ	16.07 AW	20.46 TQ	OKBLS	10/01-12/01
	Oklahoma City MSA, OK	H	11.70 FQ	15.19 AW	20.01 TQ	OKBLS	10/01-12/01
	Oregon	H	11.85 FQ	18.87 AW	25.40 TQ	ORBLS	10/01-12/01

AAW Average annual wage; AE Average entry wage; AEX Average experienced wage; AO Average offered; AOH Average offered, high; AOL Average offered, low; APH Average pay, high range; APL Average pay, low range; ASH Average starting, high; ASL Average starting, low; AW Average wage paid; FQ First quartile wage; H Hourly; HI Highest wage paid; HR High end range; LR Low end range; M Monthly; MTC Median total compensation; MW Median wage paid; SQ Second quartile wage; S Special: hourly and annual; TQ Third quartile wage; W Weekly; Y Yearly

Occupation/Type/Industry	Location	Per	Low	Mid	High	Source	Date
Chemical Equipment Operator and Tender	Portland-Vancouver PMSA, OR-WA	H	9.94 FQ	16.70 AW	24.76 TQ	ORBLS	10/01-12/01
	Pennsylvania	H	10.65 FQ	16.83 AW	22.15 TQ	PABLS	10/01-12/01
	Allentown-Bethlehem-Easton MSA, PA	H	9.56 FQ	13.52 AW	17.68 TQ	PABLS	10/01-12/01
	Philadelphia PMSA, PA-NJ	H	12.96 FQ	18.99 AW	26.00 TQ	PABLS	10/01-12/01
	Pittsburgh MSA, PA	H	11.30 FQ	17.46 AW	21.83 TQ	PABLS	10/01-12/01
	Reading MSA, PA	H	8.23 FQ	15.60 AW	22.05 TQ	PABLS	10/01-12/01
	York MSA, PA	H	10.38 FQ	14.72 AW	20.22 TQ	PABLS	10/01-12/01
	Rhode Island	H	12.20 FQ	16.92 AW	21.70 TQ	RIBLS	10/01-12/01
	Providence-Fall River-Warwick MSA, RI-MA	H	11.90 FQ	16.66 AW	21.61 TQ	RIBLS	10/01-12/01
	South Carolina	H	12.08 FQ	18.31 AW	31.29 TQ	SCBLS	10/01-12/01
	Charleston-North Charleston MSA, SC	H	11.83 FQ	16.29 AW	24.09 TQ	SCBLS	10/01-12/01
	Greenville-Spartanburg-Anderson MSA, SC	H	11.33 FQ	14.25 AW	17.27 TQ	SCBLS	10/01-12/01
	South Dakota	H	8.92 FQ	10.10 AW	11.91 TQ	SDBLS	10/01-12/01
	Tennessee	H	10.88 FQ	16.35 AW	22.19 TQ	TNBLS	10/01-12/01
	Memphis MSA, TN-AR-MS	H	11.36 FQ	18.57 AW	24.86 TQ	TNBLS	10/01-12/01
	Nashville MSA, TN	H	10.77 FQ	13.34 AW	16.46 TQ	TNBLS	10/01-12/01
	Texas	H	13.96 FQ	20.30 AW	26.89 TQ	TXBLS	10/01-12/01
	Beaumont-Port Arthur MSA, TX	H	18.09 FQ	22.74 AW	27.46 TQ	TXBLS	10/01-12/01
	Dallas PMSA, TX	H	9.12 FQ	16.14 AW	23.13 TQ	TXBLS	10/01-12/01
	Fort Worth-Arlington PMSA, TX	H	11.34 FQ	16.35 AW	20.89 TQ	TXBLS	10/01-12/01
	Houston PMSA, TX	H	14.29 FQ	20.29 AW	26.88 TQ	TXBLS	10/01-12/01
	San Antonio MSA, TX	H	11.44 FQ	21.49 AW	27.54 TQ	TXBLS	10/01-12/01
	Utah	H	7.82 FQ	11.97 AW	17.17 TQ	UTBLS	10/01-12/01
	Salt Lake City-Ogden MSA, UT	H	7.78 FQ	11.56 AW	16.95 TQ	UTBLS	10/01-12/01
	Virginia	H	11.80 FQ	17.96 AW	26.07 TQ	VABLS	10/01-12/01
	Norfolk-Virginia Beach-Newport News MSA, VA-NC	H	11.76 FQ	15.90 AW	24.91 TQ	VABLS	10/01-12/01
	Richmond-Petersburg MSA, VA	H	12.61 FQ	20.65 AW	26.57 TQ	VABLS	10/01-12/01
	Washington	H	9.86 FQ	20.74 AW	36.27 TQ	WABLS	10/01-12/01
	Richland-Kennewick-Pasco MSA, WA	H	7.82 FQ	31.48 AW	44.04 TQ	WABLS	10/01-12/01
	Seattle-Bellevue-Everett PMSA, WA	H	10.68 FQ	19.27 AW	27.48 TQ	WABLS	10/01-12/01
	West Virginia	H	13.48 FQ	20.00 AW	26.53 TQ	WVBLS	10/01-12/01
	Charleston MSA, WV	H	15.21 FQ	20.56 AW	26.72 TQ	WVBLS	10/01-12/01
	Wisconsin	H	11.02 FQ	17.52 AW	26.30 TQ	WIBLS	10/01-12/01
	Appleton-Oshkosh-Neenah MSA, WI	H	10.45 FQ	18.10 AW	28.24 TQ	WIBLS	10/01-12/01
	Madison MSA, WI	H	11.65 FQ	15.89 AW	21.39 TQ	WIBLS	10/01-12/01
	Milwaukee-Waukesha PMSA, WI	H	10.41 FQ	15.15 AW	25.07 TQ	WIBLS	10/01-12/01
	Puerto Rico	H	9.24 FQ	13.86 AW	17.46 TQ	PRBLS	10/01-12/01
Chemical Plant and System Operator	Alabama	H	14.88 FQ	19.96 AW	27.26 TQ	ALBLS	10/01-12/01
	Arizona	H	9.84 FQ	15.90 AW	25.28 TQ	AZBLS	10/01-12/01
	Arkansas	H	14.66 FQ	19.31 AW	22.62 TQ	ARBLS	10/01-12/01
	California	H	14.64 FQ	20.91 AW	27.28 TQ	CABLS	10/01-12/01
	Colorado	H	11.05 FQ	15.74 AW	21.11 TQ	COBLS	10/01-12/01
	Connecticut	H	11.82 FQ	19.62 AW	25.98 TQ	CTBLS	10/01-12/01
	Delaware	H	17.25 FQ	21.15 AW	26.18 TQ	DEBLS	10/01-12/01
	Florida	H	10.19 FQ	16.51 AW	22.25 TQ	FLBLS	10/01-12/01
	Georgia	H	12.10 FQ	18.99 AW	26.15 TQ	GABLS	10/01-12/01
	Idaho	H	8.97 FQ	16.85 AW	22.18 TQ	IDBLS	10/01-12/01
	Illinois	H	10.57 FQ	18.64 AW	26.84 TQ	ILBLS	10/01-12/01
	Indiana	H	13.80 FQ	19.69 AW	26.24 TQ	INBLS	10/01-12/01
	Iowa	H	14.78 FQ	18.93 AW	22.24 TQ	IABLS	10/01-12/01
	Kansas	H	12.34 FQ	16.45 AW	21.47 TQ	KSBLS	10/01-12/01
	Kentucky	H	14.27 FQ	20.84 AW	27.12 TQ	KYBLS	10/01-12/01
	Louisiana	H	18.31 FQ	23.52 AW	27.94 TQ	LABLS	10/01-12/01
	Maryland	H	11.14 FQ	18.05 AW	22.70 TQ	MDBLS	10/01-12/01

AAW	Average annual wage	AOH	Average offered, high	ASH	Average starting, high	H	Hourly	M	Monthly	S	Special: hourly and annual
AE	Average entry wage	AOL	Average offered, low	ASL	Average starting, low	HI	Highest wage paid	MTC	Median total compensation	TQ	Third quartile wage
AEX	Average experienced wage	APH	Average pay, high range	AW	Average wage paid	HR	High end range	MW	Median wage paid	W	Weekly
AO	Average offered	APL	Average pay, low range	FQ	First quartile wage	LR	Low end range	SQ	Second quartile wage	Y	Yearly

Occupation/Type/Industry	Location	Per	Low	Mid	High	Source	Date
Chemical Plant and System Operator	Massachusetts	H	11.74 FQ	17.17 AW	21.85 TQ	MABLS	10/01-12/01
	Michigan	H	14.30 FQ	19.51 AW	26.92 TQ	MIBLS	10/01-12/01
	Minnesota	H	12.45 FQ	20.42 AW	27.97 TQ	MNBLS	10/01-12/01
	Mississippi	H	13.76 FQ	19.55 AW	25.66 TQ	MSBLS	10/01-12/01
	Missouri	H	12.28 FQ	17.94 AW	25.52 TQ	MOBLS	10/01-12/01
	Montana	H	8.58 FQ	15.47 AW	25.50 TQ	MTBLS	10/01-12/01
	Nebraska	H	13.58 FQ	18.21 AW	23.23 TQ	NEBLS	10/01-12/01
	Nevada	H	15.17 FQ	19.54 AW	24.16 TQ	NVBLS	10/01-12/01
	New Jersey	H	13.75 FQ	20.61 AW	26.68 TQ	NJBLS	10/01-12/01
	New Mexico	H	10.77 FQ	17.44 AW	25.77 TQ	NMBLS	10/01-12/01
	New York	H	13.15 FQ	18.68 AW	23.98 TQ	NYBLS	10/01-12/01
	North Carolina	H	13.22 FQ	17.97 AW	22.27 TQ	NCBLS	10/01-12/01
	Ohio	H	12.07 FQ	18.07 AW	23.84 TQ	OHBLS	10/01-12/01
	Oklahoma	H	14.49 FQ	19.45 AW	25.91 TQ	OKBLS	10/01-12/01
	Oregon	H	14.82 FQ	20.21 AW	26.50 TQ	ORBLS	10/01-12/01
	Pennsylvania	H	13.12 FQ	20.20 AW	26.74 TQ	PABLS	10/01-12/01
	Rhode Island	H	13.12 FQ	17.12 AW	21.28 TQ	RIBLS	10/01-12/01
	South Carolina	H	10.33 FQ	15.64 AW	21.24 TQ	SCBLS	10/01-12/01
	Tennessee	H	14.89 FQ	19.26 AW	24.88 TQ	TNBLS	10/01-12/01
	Texas	H	13.88 FQ	23.19 AW	30.63 TQ	TXBLS	10/01-12/01
	Utah	H	14.00 FQ	17.19 AW	21.78 TQ	UTBLS	10/01-12/01
	Virginia	H	12.12 FQ	18.68 AW	25.13 TQ	VABLS	10/01-12/01
	Washington	H	8.26 FQ	19.72 AW	27.20 TQ	WABLS	10/01-12/01
	West Virginia	H	17.48 FQ	21.86 AW	26.70 TQ	WVBLS	10/01-12/01
	Wisconsin	H	12.33 FQ	17.23 AW	25.96 TQ	WIBLS	10/01-12/01
	Puerto Rico	H	10.06 FQ	14.30 AW	17.12 TQ	PRBLS	10/01-12/01
Chemical Technician	Alabama	Y	21780 FQ	35390 AW	51140 TQ	ALBLS	10/01-12/01
	Birmingham MSA, AL	Y	21910 FQ	37400 AW	54150 TQ	ALBLS	10/01-12/01
	Huntsville MSA, AL	Y	20350 FQ	30420 AW	43190 TQ	ALBLS	10/01-12/01
	Mobile MSA, AL	Y	20480 FQ	36290 AW	50640 TQ	ALBLS	10/01-12/01
	Arizona	Y	23750 FQ	43830 AW	75530 TQ	AZBLS	10/01-12/01
	Phoenix-Mesa MSA, AZ	Y	26480 FQ	48550 AW	80520 TQ	AZBLS	10/01-12/01
	Tucson MSA, AZ	Y	15490 FQ	31580 AW	48450 TQ	AZBLS	10/01-12/01
	Arkansas	Y	20370 FQ	31870 AW	45120 TQ	ARBLS	10/01-12/01
	Fayetteville-Springdale-Rogers MSA, AR	Y	18610 FQ	30650 AW	52330 TQ	ARBLS	10/01-12/01
	Little Rock-North Little Rock MSA, AR	Y	22050 FQ	29430 AW	36190 TQ	ARBLS	10/01-12/01
	California	Y	21510 FQ	36370 AW	55870 TQ	CABLS	10/01-12/01
	Bakersfield MSA, CA	Y	26160 FQ	43380 AW	66970 TQ	CABLS	10/01-12/01
	Fresno MSA, CA	Y	18410 FQ	28470 AW	42350 TQ	CABLS	10/01-12/01
	Los Angeles-Long Beach PMSA, CA	Y	22520 FQ	37210 AW	55760 TQ	CABLS	10/01-12/01
	Merced MSA, CA	Y	20080 FQ	45260 AW	86840 TQ	CABLS	10/01-12/01
	Modesto MSA, CA	Y	17490 FQ	25640 AW	40400 TQ	CABLS	10/01-12/01
	Oakland PMSA, CA	Y	22780 FQ	36840 AW	54650 TQ	CABLS	10/01-12/01
	Orange County PMSA, CA	Y	19900 FQ	32200 AW	50710 TQ	CABLS	10/01-12/01
	Riverside-San Bernardino PMSA, CA	Y	18590 FQ	31630 AW	46630 TQ	CABLS	10/01-12/01
	Sacramento PMSA, CA	Y	24170 FQ	36770 AW	54460 TQ	CABLS	10/01-12/01
	San Diego MSA, CA	Y	21400 FQ	38120 AW	60600 TQ	CABLS	10/01-12/01
	San Francisco PMSA, CA	Y	25620 FQ	44420 AW	66420 TQ	CABLS	10/01-12/01
	San Jose PMSA, CA	Y	24100 FQ	36740 AW	52700 TQ	CABLS	10/01-12/01
	Santa Barbara-Santa Maria-Lompoc MSA, CA	Y	18940 FQ	35150 AW	57840 TQ	CABLS	10/01-12/01
	Santa Cruz-Watsonville PMSA, CA	Y	20450 FQ	31980 AW	42620 TQ	CABLS	10/01-12/01
	Santa Rosa PMSA, CA	Y	20850 FQ	33070 AW	49840 TQ	CABLS	10/01-12/01
	Vallejo-Fairfield-Napa PMSA, CA	Y	24240 FQ	31480 AW	36080 TQ	CABLS	10/01-12/01
	Colorado	Y	23790 FQ	36710 AW	53000 TQ	COBLS	10/01-12/01
	Boulder-Longmont PMSA, CO	Y	30620 FQ	40010 AW	57290 TQ	COBLS	10/01-12/01
	Colorado Springs MSA, CO	Y	21050 FQ	31790 AW	41440 TQ	COBLS	10/01-12/01
	Denver PMSA, CO	Y	24160 FQ	36740 AW	53230 TQ	COBLS	10/01-12/01
	Fort Collins-Loveland MSA, CO	Y	20520 FQ	33090 AW	46260 TQ	COBLS	10/01-12/01
	Greeley PMSA, CO	Y	21380 FQ	33330 AW	49060 TQ	COBLS	10/01-12/01
	Connecticut	Y	25250 FQ	39870 AW	55930 TQ	CTBLS	10/01-12/01
	Bridgeport PMSA, CT	Y	24540 FQ	40120 AW	54680 TQ	CTBLS	10/01-12/01
	Danbury PMSA, CT	Y	21450 FQ	36900 AW	54450 TQ	CTBLS	10/01-12/01

AAW	Average annual wage	**AOH**	Average offered, high	**ASH**	Average starting, high	**H**	Hourly	**M**	Monthly	**S**	Special: hourly and annual
AE	Average entry wage	**AOL**	Average offered, low	**ASL**	Average starting, low	**HI**	Highest wage paid	**MTC**	Median total compensation	**TQ**	Third quartile wage
AEX	Average experienced wage	**APH**	Average pay, high range	**AW**	Average wage paid	**HR**	High end range	**MW**	Median wage paid	**W**	Weekly
AO	Average offered	**APL**	Average pay, low range	**FQ**	First quartile wage	**LR**	Low end range	**SQ**	Second quartile wage	**Y**	Yearly

Occupation/Type/Industry	Location	Per	Low	Mid	High	Source	Date
Chemical Technician	Hartford MSA, CT	Y	23560 FQ	37880 AW	52980 TQ	CTBLS	10/01-12/01
	New Haven-Meriden PMSA, CT	Y	24500 FQ	34210 AW	52400 TQ	CTBLS	10/01-12/01
	Stamford-Norwalk PMSA, CT	Y	32150 FQ	44130 AW	56540 TQ	CTBLS	10/01-12/01
	Delaware	Y	30650 FQ	47680 AW	59060 TQ	DEBLS	10/01-12/01
	Wilmington-Newark PMSA, DE-MD	Y	32830 FQ	48590 AW	59100 TQ	DEBLS	10/01-12/01
	District of Columbia	Y	25130 FQ	39950 AW	61730 TQ	DCBLS	10/01-12/01
	Washington PMSA, DC-MD-VA-WV	Y	20990 FQ	35080 AW	51160 TQ	DCBLS	10/01-12/01
	Florida	Y	19820 FQ	33190 AW	50390 TQ	FLBLS	10/01-12/01
	Daytona Beach MSA, FL	Y	20130 FQ	30010 AW	43000 TQ	FLBLS	10/01-12/01
	Fort Lauderdale PMSA, FL	Y	19900 FQ	35160 AW	61060 TQ	FLBLS	10/01-12/01
	Gainesville MSA, FL	Y	18270 FQ	28750 AW	52490 TQ	FLBLS	10/01-12/01
	Jacksonville MSA, FL	Y	20660 FQ	34280 AW	45780 TQ	FLBLS	10/01-12/01
	Lakeland-Winter Haven MSA, FL	Y	17290 FQ	27960 AW	43230 TQ	FLBLS	10/01-12/01
	Melbourne-Titusville-Palm Bay MSA, FL	Y	22470 FQ	32880 AW	51790 TQ	FLBLS	10/01-12/01
	Miami PMSA, FL	Y	18450 FQ	31440 AW	43970 TQ	FLBLS	10/01-12/01
	Orlando MSA, FL	Y	18180 FQ	30150 AW	48950 TQ	FLBLS	10/01-12/01
	Tampa-St. Petersburg-Clearwater MSA, FL	Y	22890 FQ	36410 AW	53340 TQ	FLBLS	10/01-12/01
	West Palm Beach-Boca Raton MSA, FL	Y	18250 FQ	28860 AW	44390 TQ	FLBLS	10/01-12/01
	Georgia	Y	19650 FQ	31730 AW	45510 TQ	GABLS	10/01-12/01
	Atlanta MSA, GA	Y	19660 FQ	31740 AW	45500 TQ	GABLS	10/01-12/01
	Augusta-Aiken MSA, GA-SC	Y	17220 FQ	33720 AW	53590 TQ	GABLS	10/01-12/01
	Columbus MSA, GA-AL	Y	22420 FQ	30350 AW	41410 TQ	GABLS	10/01-12/01
	Macon MSA, GA	Y	16410 FQ	26020 AW	40650 TQ	GABLS	10/01-12/01
	Savannah MSA, GA	Y	19700 FQ	33800 AW	48130 TQ	GABLS	10/01-12/01
	Hawaii	Y	19420 FQ	45170 AW	84770 TQ	HIBLS	10/01-12/01
	Honolulu MSA, HI	Y	19420 FQ	45170 AW	84770 TQ	HIBLS	10/01-12/01
	Idaho	Y	16550 FQ	29470 AW	44010 TQ	IDBLS	10/01-12/01
	Boise City MSA, ID	Y	24330 FQ	27090 AW	30270 TQ	IDBLS	10/01-12/01
	Illinois	Y	24370 FQ	36930 AW	52590 TQ	ILBLS	10/01-12/01
	Chicago PMSA, IL	Y	24580 FQ	36100 AW	49770 TQ	ILBLS	10/01-12/01
	Peoria-Pekin MSA, IL	Y	31150 FQ	44880 AW	57970 TQ	ILBLS	10/01-12/01
	Rockford MSA, IL	Y	19790 FQ	36650 AW	49270 TQ	ILBLS	10/01-12/01
	Indiana	Y	21170 FQ	34300 AW	46160 TQ	INBLS	10/01-12/01
	Elkhart-Goshen MSA, IN	Y	22790 FQ	35740 AW	48760 TQ	INBLS	10/01-12/01
	Evansville-Henderson MSA, IN-KY	Y	28750 FQ	35890 AW	44350 TQ	INBLS	10/01-12/01
	Fort Wayne MSA, IN	Y	18220 FQ	31160 AW	50440 TQ	INBLS	10/01-12/01
	Gary PMSA, IN	Y	25600 FQ	37290 AW	45410 TQ	INBLS	10/01-12/01
	Indianapolis MSA, IN	Y	20610 FQ	33790 AW	46640 TQ	INBLS	10/01-12/01
	Lafayette MSA, IN	Y	24750 FQ	36380 AW	44730 TQ	INBLS	10/01-12/01
	Iowa	Y	21220 FQ	35080 AW	50800 TQ	IABLS	10/01-12/01
	Davenport-Moline-Rock Island MSA, IA-IL	Y	20890 FQ	32790 AW	44100 TQ	IABLS	10/01-12/01
	Kansas	Y	19370 FQ	35320 AW	55940 TQ	KSBLS	10/01-12/01
	Wichita MSA, KS	Y	20470 FQ	40390 AW	57880 TQ	KSBLS	10/01-12/01
	Kentucky	Y	19320 FQ	34590 AW	52630 TQ	KYBLS	10/01-12/01
	Lexington MSA, KY	Y	24240 FQ	32820 AW	44800 TQ	KYBLS	10/01-12/01
	Louisville MSA, KY-IN	Y	25260 FQ	36130 AW	48820 TQ	KYBLS	10/01-12/01
	Louisiana	Y	28010 FQ	48340 AW	65000 TQ	LABLS	10/01-12/01
	Baton Rouge MSA, LA	Y	39080 FQ	50350 AW	60470 TQ	LABLS	10/01-12/01
	Houma MSA, LA	Y	36180 FQ	53010 AW	81490 TQ	LABLS	10/01-12/01
	Lafayette MSA, LA	Y	15300 FQ	38830 AW	69600 TQ	LABLS	10/01-12/01
	Lake Charles MSA, LA	Y	26500 FQ	44040 AW	59970 TQ	LABLS	10/01-12/01
	New Orleans MSA, LA	Y	26110 FQ	43740 AW	68110 TQ	LABLS	10/01-12/01
	Shreveport-Bossier City MSA, LA	Y	25900 FQ	44600 AW	58370 TQ	LABLS	10/01-12/01
	Maine	Y	21950 FQ	30370 AW	41090 TQ	MEBLS	10/01-12/01
	Maryland	Y	24910 FQ	39500 AW	54330 TQ	MDBLS	10/01-12/01
	Baltimore PMSA, MD	Y	27420 FQ	40280 AW	54290 TQ	MDBLS	10/01-12/01
	Massachusetts	Y	26340 FQ	38730 AW	58480 TQ	MABLS	10/01-12/01
	Boston PMSA, MA-NH	Y	27090 FQ	38780 AW	58930 TQ	MABLS	10/01-12/01
	Lawrence PMSA, MA-NH	Y	29290 FQ	47990 AW	67940 TQ	MABLS	10/01-12/01
	Lowell PMSA, MA-NH	Y	26520 FQ	39730 AW	55640 TQ	MABLS	10/01-12/01
	Springfield MSA, MA	Y	22290 FQ	38040 AW	57030 TQ	MABLS	10/01-12/01
	Worcester PMSA, MA-CT	Y	28590 FQ	36190 AW	45740 TQ	MABLS	10/01-12/01

AAW	Average annual wage	AOH	Average offered, high	ASH	Average starting, high	H	Hourly	M	Monthly	S	Special: hourly and annual
AE	Average entry wage	AOL	Average offered, low	ASL	Average starting, low	HI	Highest wage paid	MTC	Median total compensation	TQ	Third quartile wage
AEX	Average experienced wage	APH	Average pay, high range	AW	Average wage paid	HR	High end range	MW	Median wage paid	W	Weekly
AO	Average offered	APL	Average pay, low range	FQ	First quartile wage	LR	Low end range	SQ	Second quartile wage	Y	Yearly

Occupation/Type/Industry	Location	Per	Low	Mid	High	Source	Date
Chemical Technician	Michigan	Y	25750 FQ	39460 AW	56160 TQ	MIBLS	10/01-12/01
	Ann Arbor PMSA, MI	Y	23370 FQ	34890 AW	48640 TQ	MIBLS	10/01-12/01
	Detroit PMSA, MI	Y	23600 FQ	41410 AW	61170 TQ	MIBLS	10/01-12/01
	Grand Rapids-Muskegon-Holland MSA, MI	Y	25860 FQ	39310 AW	57830 TQ	MIBLS	10/01-12/01
	Kalamazoo-Battle Creek MSA, MI	Y	25300 FQ	42710 AW	58690 TQ	MIBLS	10/01-12/01
	Lansing-East Lansing MSA, MI	Y	24630 FQ	42390 AW	58880 TQ	MIBLS	10/01-12/01
	Saginaw-Bay City-Midland MSA, MI	Y	30480 FQ	38440 AW	48530 TQ	MIBLS	10/01-12/01
	Minnesota	Y	23830 FQ	33520 AW	45190 TQ	MNBLS	10/01-12/01
	Minneapolis-St. Paul MSA, MN-WI	Y	24610 FQ	34380 AW	45430 TQ	MNBLS	10/01-12/01
	Mississippi	Y	20120 FQ	34080 AW	50880 TQ	MSBLS	10/01-12/01
	Biloxi-Gulfport-Pascagoula MSA, MS	Y	22670 FQ	38460 AW	53840 TQ	MSBLS	10/01-12/01
	Missouri	Y	26790 FQ	41260 AW	59040 TQ	MOBLS	10/01-12/01
	Kansas City MSA, MO-KS	Y	23910 FQ	36700 AW	53280 TQ	MOBLS	10/01-12/01
	St. Louis MSA, MO-IL	Y	28530 FQ	42010 AW	58450 TQ	MOBLS	10/01-12/01
	Montana	Y	16560 FQ	30010 AW	44790 TQ	MTBLS	10/01-12/01
	Billings MSA, MT	Y	15870 FQ	28090 AW	45090 TQ	MTBLS	10/01-12/01
	Nebraska	Y	19730 FQ	29060 AW	40840 TQ	NEBLS	10/01-12/01
	Lincoln MSA, NE	Y	18340 FQ	25160 AW	33680 TQ	NEBLS	10/01-12/01
	Omaha MSA, NE-IA	Y	22920 FQ	33700 AW	50170 TQ	NEBLS	10/01-12/01
	Nevada	Y	23970 FQ	38440 AW	55440 TQ	NVBLS	10/01-12/01
	Las Vegas MSA, NV-AZ	Y	21110 FQ	39030 AW	56230 TQ	NVBLS	10/01-12/01
	Reno MSA, NV	Y	22820 FQ	27950 AW	34150 TQ	NVBLS	10/01-12/01
	New Hampshire	Y	23390 FQ	36700 AW	52320 TQ	NHBLS	10/01-12/01
	Nashua PMSA, NH	Y	22910 FQ	36530 AW	55720 TQ	NHBLS	10/01-12/01
	Portsmouth-Rochester PMSA, NH-ME	Y	28110 FQ	37430 AW	47480 TQ	NHBLS	10/01-12/01
	New Jersey	Y	26370 FQ	41400 AW	57290 TQ	NJBLS	10/01-12/01
	Bergen-Passaic PMSA, NJ	Y	27540 FQ	41210 AW	57220 TQ	NJBLS	10/01-12/01
	Jersey City PMSA, NJ	Y	27180 FQ	40240 AW	54930 TQ	NJBLS	10/01-12/01
	Middlesex-Somerset-Hunterdon PMSA, NJ	Y	28070 FQ	39620 AW	54410 TQ	NJBLS	10/01-12/01
	Monmouth-Ocean PMSA, NJ	Y	27140 FQ	41220 AW	55790 TQ	NJBLS	10/01-12/01
	Newark PMSA, NJ	Y	22880 FQ	42460 AW	63450 TQ	NJBLS	10/01-12/01
	Trenton PMSA, NJ	Y	25070 FQ	39410 AW	57440 TQ	NJBLS	10/01-12/01
	New Mexico	Y	25280 FQ	43880 AW	63600 TQ	NMBLS	10/01-12/01
	Albuquerque MSA, NM	Y	25520 FQ	39200 AW	55570 TQ	NMBLS	10/01-12/01
	New York	Y	19390 FQ	34650 AW	53560 TQ	NYBLS	10/01-12/01
	Albany-Schenectady-Troy MSA, NY	Y	20680 FQ	33120 AW	50810 TQ	NYBLS	10/01-12/01
	Binghamton MSA, NY	Y	19790 FQ	27280 AW	34700 TQ	NYBLS	10/01-12/01
	Buffalo-Niagara Falls MSA, NY	Y	21440 FQ	36740 AW	52970 TQ	NYBLS	10/01-12/01
	Nassau-Suffolk PMSA, NY	Y	22390 FQ	34290 AW	53140 TQ	NYBLS	10/01-12/01
	New York PMSA, NY	Y	17350 FQ	29520 AW	43980 TQ	NYBLS	10/01-12/01
	Syracuse MSA, NY	Y	17460 FQ	31250 AW	59980 TQ	NYBLS	10/01-12/01
	North Carolina	Y	23660 FQ	36330 AW	53140 TQ	NCBLS	10/01-12/01
	Charlotte-Gastonia-Rock Hill MSA, NC-SC	Y	24580 FQ	37000 AW	53910 TQ	NCBLS	10/01-12/01
	Greensboro-Winston-Salem-High Point MSA, NC	Y	24390 FQ	38910 AW	57790 TQ	NCBLS	10/01-12/01
	Hickory-Morganton-Lenoir MSA, NC	Y	20670 FQ	33710 AW	46410 TQ	NCBLS	10/01-12/01
	Raleigh-Durham-Chapel Hill MSA, NC	Y	25860 FQ	36110 AW	48090 TQ	NCBLS	10/01-12/01
	Wilmington MSA, NC	Y	29230 FQ	39640 AW	54670 TQ	NCBLS	10/01-12/01
	North Dakota	Y	20900 FQ	40980 AW	57640 TQ	NDBLS	10/01-12/01
	Ohio	Y	22150 FQ	33830 AW	47220 TQ	OHBLS	10/01-12/01
	Akron PMSA, OH	Y	20680 FQ	31830 AW	44670 TQ	OHBLS	10/01-12/01
	Canton-Massillon MSA, OH	Y	21890 FQ	33080 AW	49370 TQ	OHBLS	10/01-12/01
	Cincinnati PMSA, OH-KY-IN	Y	24510 FQ	36020 AW	47980 TQ	OHBLS	10/01-12/01
	Cleveland-Lorain-Elyria PMSA, OH	Y	24250 FQ	34250 AW	45900 TQ	OHBLS	10/01-12/01
	Columbus MSA, OH	Y	20930 FQ	32960 AW	47930 TQ	OHBLS	10/01-12/01
	Dayton-Springfield MSA, OH	Y	20850 FQ	29960 AW	44040 TQ	OHBLS	10/01-12/01
	Hamilton-Middletown PMSA, OH	Y	21590 FQ	34310 AW	46470 TQ	OHBLS	10/01-12/01
	Toledo MSA, OH	Y	23250 FQ	37280 AW	55450 TQ	OHBLS	10/01-12/01

AAW	Average annual wage	AOH	Average offered, high	ASH	Average starting, high	H	Hourly	M	Monthly	S	Special: hourly and annual
AE	Average entry wage	AOL	Average offered, low	ASL	Average starting, low	HI	Highest wage paid	MTC	Median total compensation	TQ	Third quartile wage
AEX	Average experienced wage	APH	Average pay, high range	AW	Average wage paid	HR	High end range	MW	Median wage paid	W	Weekly
AO	Average offered	APL	Average pay, low range	FQ	First quartile wage	LR	Low end range	SQ	Second quartile wage	Y	Yearly

Occupation/Type/Industry	Location	Per	Low	Mid	High	Source	Date
Chemical Technician	Youngstown-Warren MSA, OH	Y	20860 FQ	34360 AW	56260 TQ	OHBLS	10/01-12/01
	Oklahoma	Y	22910 FQ	37330 AW	54940 TQ	OKBLS	10/01-12/01
	Oklahoma City MSA, OK	Y	21840 FQ	34720 AW	48260 TQ	OKBLS	10/01-12/01
	Tulsa MSA, OK	Y	25600 FQ	41260 AW	56380 TQ	OKBLS	10/01-12/01
	Oregon	Y	23270 FQ	33400 AW	46990 TQ	ORBLS	10/01-12/01
	Eugene-Springfield MSA, OR	Y	22830 FQ	32410 AW	46220 TQ	ORBLS	10/01-12/01
	Portland-Vancouver PMSA, OR-WA	Y	24970 FQ	37120 AW	49040 TQ	ORBLS	10/01-12/01
	Pennsylvania	Y	20470 FQ	37660 AW	59590 TQ	PABLS	10/01-12/01
	Allentown-Bethlehem-Easton MSA, PA	Y	23470 FQ	35510 AW	54540 TQ	PABLS	10/01-12/01
	Harrisburg-Lebanon-Carlisle MSA, PA	Y	22440 FQ	32890 AW	51740 TQ	PABLS	10/01-12/01
	Lancaster MSA, PA	Y	15680 FQ	28000 AW	45430 TQ	PABLS	10/01-12/01
	Philadelphia PMSA, PA-NJ	Y	21550 FQ	43250 AW	68280 TQ	PABLS	10/01-12/01
	Pittsburgh MSA, PA	Y	22470 FQ	33680 AW	44320 TQ	PABLS	10/01-12/01
	Reading MSA, PA	Y	22570 FQ	34350 AW	48100 TQ	PABLS	10/01-12/01
	Scranton-Wilkes-Barre-Hazleton MSA, PA	Y	24930 FQ	47540 AW	73570 TQ	PABLS	10/01-12/01
	York MSA, PA	Y	19090 FQ	28790 AW	37170 TQ	PABLS	10/01-12/01
	Rhode Island	Y	21000 FQ	33440 AW	48180 TQ	RIBLS	10/01-12/01
	Providence-Fall River-Warwick MSA, RI-MA	Y	20850 FQ	32910 AW	47390 TQ	RIBLS	10/01-12/01
	South Carolina	Y	23860 FQ	35200 AW	48910 TQ	SCBLS	10/01-12/01
	Charleston-North Charleston MSA, SC	Y	26910 FQ	41300 AW	67270 TQ	SCBLS	10/01-12/01
	Columbia MSA, SC	Y	22060 FQ	37010 AW	55560 TQ	SCBLS	10/01-12/01
	Greenville-Spartanburg-Anderson MSA, SC	Y	24080 FQ	33130 AW	44320 TQ	SCBLS	10/01-12/01
	South Dakota	Y	20060 FQ	26280 AW	34390 TQ	SDBLS	10/01-12/01
	Tennessee	Y	23890 FQ	40370 AW	57170 TQ	TNBLS	10/01-12/01
	Chattanooga MSA, TN-GA	Y	18850 FQ	28830 AW	40380 TQ	TNBLS	10/01-12/01
	Clarksville-Hopkinsville MSA, TN-KY	Y	24840 FQ	34300 AW	47710 TQ	TNBLS	10/01-12/01
	Johnson City-Kingsport-Bristol MSA, TN-VA	Y	39250 FQ	48220 AW	58910 TQ	TNBLS	10/01-12/01
	Knoxville MSA, TN	Y	23290 FQ	33740 AW	47680 TQ	TNBLS	10/01-12/01
	Memphis MSA, TN-AR-MS	Y	21850 FQ	37300 AW	56280 TQ	TNBLS	10/01-12/01
	Texas	Y	21280 FQ	41730 AW	61780 TQ	TXBLS	10/01-12/01
	Austin-San Marcos MSA, TX	Y	15830 FQ	26710 AW	37730 TQ	TXBLS	10/01-12/01
	Beaumont-Port Arthur MSA, TX	Y	36660 FQ	50320 AW	67090 TQ	TXBLS	10/01-12/01
	Brazoria PMSA, TX	Y	40190 FQ	52790 AW	64660 TQ	TXBLS	10/01-12/01
	Corpus Christi MSA, TX	Y	24760 FQ	44450 AW	61650 TQ	TXBLS	10/01-12/01
	Dallas PMSA, TX	Y	18850 FQ	36180 AW	57440 TQ	TXBLS	10/01-12/01
	El Paso MSA, TX	Y	27810 FQ	39700 AW	60210 TQ	TXBLS	10/01-12/01
	Fort Worth-Arlington PMSA, TX	Y	19970 FQ	36720 AW	65020 TQ	TXBLS	10/01-12/01
	Galveston-Texas City PMSA, TX	Y	30750 FQ	45930 AW	61150 TQ	TXBLS	10/01-12/01
	Houston PMSA, TX	Y	21850 FQ	40950 AW	60780 TQ	TXBLS	10/01-12/01
	Odessa-Midland MSA, TX	Y	13450 FQ	27270 AW	54600 TQ	TXBLS	10/01-12/01
	San Antonio MSA, TX	Y	19500 FQ	37400 AW	61890 TQ	TXBLS	10/01-12/01
	Utah	Y	20500 FQ	34080 AW	50480 TQ	UTBLS	10/01-12/01
	Provo-Orem MSA, UT	Y	21840 FQ	30480 AW	40250 TQ	UTBLS	10/01-12/01
	Salt Lake City-Ogden MSA, UT	Y	19840 FQ	33260 AW	52370 TQ	UTBLS	10/01-12/01
	Vermont	Y	22620 FQ	33720 AW	52630 TQ	VTBLS	10/01-12/01
	Virginia	Y	22810 FQ	37120 AW	51660 TQ	VABLS	10/01-12/01
	Norfolk-Virginia Beach-Newport News MSA, VA-NC	Y	24360 FQ	37550 AW	51070 TQ	VABLS	10/01-12/01
	Richmond-Petersburg MSA, VA	Y	28130 FQ	41990 AW	54370 TQ	VABLS	10/01-12/01
	Roanoke MSA, VA	Y	22820 FQ	34860 AW	48790 TQ	VABLS	10/01-12/01
	Washington	Y	26450 FQ	41960 AW	61490 TQ	WABLS	10/01-12/01
	Seattle-Bellevue-Everett PMSA, WA	Y	28850 FQ	43700 AW	66250 TQ	WABLS	10/01-12/01
	Spokane MSA, WA	Y	24800 FQ	40510 AW	59760 TQ	WABLS	10/01-12/01
	Tacoma PMSA, WA	Y	23800 FQ	34570 AW	45710 TQ	WABLS	10/01-12/01
	West Virginia	Y	18180 FQ	40690 AW	59360 TQ	WVBLS	10/01-12/01
	Charleston MSA, WV	Y	16790 FQ	41820 AW	58590 TQ	WVBLS	10/01-12/01

AAW	Average annual wage	**AOH**	Average offered, high	**ASH**	Average starting, high	**H**	Hourly	**M**	Monthly	**S**	Special: hourly and annual
AE	Average entry wage	**AOL**	Average offered, low	**ASL**	Average starting, low	**HI**	Highest wage paid	**MTC**	Median total compensation	**TQ**	Third quartile wage
AEX	Average experienced wage	**APH**	Average pay, high range	**AW**	Average wage paid	**HR**	High end range	**MW**	Median wage paid	**W**	Weekly
AO	Average offered	**APL**	Average pay, low range	**FQ**	First quartile wage	**LR**	Low end range	**SQ**	Second quartile wage	**Y**	Yearly

Occupation/Type/Industry	Location	Per	Low	Mid	High	Source	Date
Chemical Technician	Huntington-Ashland MSA, WV-KY-OH	Y	13300 FQ	36180 AW	58880 TQ	WVBLS	10/01-12/01
	Wisconsin	Y	21930 FQ	32130 AW	43900 TQ	WIBLS	10/01-12/01
	Appleton-Oshkosh-Neenah MSA, WI	Y	20410 FQ	34870 AW	46140 TQ	WIBLS	10/01-12/01
	Green Bay MSA, WI	Y	19230 FQ	28830 AW	36470 TQ	WIBLS	10/01-12/01
	Madison MSA, WI	Y	21770 FQ	30530 AW	41040 TQ	WIBLS	10/01-12/01
	Milwaukee-Waukesha PMSA, WI	Y	24150 FQ	32560 AW	42730 TQ	WIBLS	10/01-12/01
	Racine PMSA, WI	Y	25100 FQ	33070 AW	44830 TQ	WIBLS	10/01-12/01
	Wyoming	Y	16190 FQ	26770 AW	42020 TQ	WYBLS	10/01-12/01
	Puerto Rico	Y	16950 FQ	26530 AW	35350 TQ	PRBLS	10/01-12/01
	Virgin Islands	Y	28560 FQ	42330 AW	63420 TQ	VIBLS	10/01-12/01
Chemist	United States	Y		76500 MW		CEN	3/01-3/02
	Alabama	Y	27740 FQ	54310 AW	89040 TQ	ALBLS	10/01-12/01
	Birmingham MSA, AL	Y	30920 FQ	48950 AW	81480 TQ	ALBLS	10/01-12/01
	Huntsville MSA, AL	Y	33790 FQ	61570 AW	91870 TQ	ALBLS	10/01-12/01
	Mobile MSA, AL	Y	24430 FQ	51580 AW	92970 TQ	ALBLS	10/01-12/01
	Montgomery MSA, AL	Y	23680 FQ	41070 AW	67590 TQ	ALBLS	10/01-12/01
	Alaska	Y	28030 FQ	52830 AW	77240 TQ	AKBLS	10/01-12/01
	Anchorage MSA, AK	Y	25740 FQ	48250 AW	74860 TQ	AKBLS	10/01-12/01
	Arizona	Y	25930 FQ	47030 AW	74780 TQ	AZBLS	10/01-12/01
	Phoenix-Mesa MSA, AZ	Y	25670 FQ	46710 AW	76050 TQ	AZBLS	10/01-12/01
	Tucson MSA, AZ	Y	22620 FQ	47970 AW	77340 TQ	AZBLS	10/01-12/01
	Arkansas	Y	27030 FQ	48490 AW	73350 TQ	ARBLS	10/01-12/01
	Fayetteville-Springdale-Rogers MSA, AR	Y	24220 FQ	45300 AW	84080 TQ	ARBLS	10/01-12/01
	Little Rock-North Little Rock MSA, AR	Y	28190 FQ	43330 AW	56910 TQ	ARBLS	10/01-12/01
	California	Y	28730 FQ	52880 AW	87350 TQ	CABLS	10/01-12/01
	Bakersfield MSA, CA	Y	36490 FQ	64140 AW	97690 TQ	CABLS	10/01-12/01
	Fresno MSA, CA	Y	18270 FQ	40710 AW	68040 TQ	CABLS	10/01-12/01
	Los Angeles-Long Beach PMSA, CA	Y	30730 FQ	53650 AW	91960 TQ	CABLS	10/01-12/01
	Oakland PMSA, CA	Y	32660 FQ	57490 AW	89120 TQ	CABLS	10/01-12/01
	Orange County PMSA, CA	Y	31650 FQ	48590 AW	69510 TQ	CABLS	10/01-12/01
	Redding MSA, CA	Y	28420 FQ	39760 AW	54500 TQ	CABLS	10/01-12/01
	Riverside-San Bernardino PMSA, CA	Y	23510 FQ	42650 AW	76750 TQ	CABLS	10/01-12/01
	Sacramento PMSA, CA	Y	28670 FQ	52740 AW	72730 TQ	CABLS	10/01-12/01
	San Diego MSA, CA	Y	24060 FQ	51980 AW	93530 TQ	CABLS	10/01-12/01
	San Francisco PMSA, CA	Y	36830 FQ	57200 AW	85750 TQ	CABLS	10/01-12/01
	San Jose PMSA, CA	Y	35700 FQ	59250 AW	87760 TQ	CABLS	10/01-12/01
	San Luis Obispo-Atascadero-Paso Robles MSA, CA	Y	24800 FQ	43370 AW	76360 TQ	CABLS	10/01-12/01
	Santa Barbara-Santa Maria-Lompoc MSA, CA	Y	30580 FQ	45760 AW	67910 TQ	CABLS	10/01-12/01
	Santa Rosa PMSA, CA	Y	31140 FQ	46400 AW	68150 TQ	CABLS	10/01-12/01
	Vallejo-Fairfield-Napa PMSA, CA	Y	31780 FQ	48550 AW	71010 TQ	CABLS	10/01-12/01
	Ventura PMSA, CA	Y	31680 FQ	51620 AW	80510 TQ	CABLS	10/01-12/01
	Colorado	Y	27150 FQ	50820 AW	84800 TQ	COBLS	10/01-12/01
	Boulder-Longmont PMSA, CO	Y	25670 FQ	49210 AW	89240 TQ	COBLS	10/01-12/01
	Denver PMSA, CO	Y	28290 FQ	52690 AW	85410 TQ	COBLS	10/01-12/01
	Fort Collins-Loveland MSA, CO	Y	35470 FQ	51740 AW	73410 TQ	COBLS	10/01-12/01
	Connecticut	Y	39240 FQ	67850 AW	98540 TQ	CTBLS	10/01-12/01
	Bridgeport PMSA, CT	Y	33250 FQ	60770 AW	94350 TQ	CTBLS	10/01-12/01
	Danbury PMSA, CT	Y	28070 FQ	65150 AW	110850 TQ	CTBLS	10/01-12/01
	Hartford MSA, CT	Y	35730 FQ	54620 AW	74830 TQ	CTBLS	10/01-12/01
	New Haven-Meriden PMSA, CT	Y	36220 FQ	60980 AW	94680 TQ	CTBLS	10/01-12/01
	Stamford-Norwalk PMSA, CT	Y	42230 FQ	70020 AW	101460 TQ	CTBLS	10/01-12/01
	Delaware	Y	45140 FQ	78400 AW	118550 TQ	DEBLS	10/01-12/01
	Wilmington-Newark PMSA, DE-MD	Y	46210 FQ	79500 AW	118540 TQ	DEBLS	10/01-12/01
	District of Columbia	Y	48160 FQ	73740 AW	104450 TQ	DCBLS	10/01-12/01
	Washington PMSA, DC-MD-VA-WV	Y	44300 FQ	74260 AW	109700 TQ	DCBLS	10/01-12/01
	Florida	Y	26170 FQ	43640 AW	67950 TQ	FLBLS	10/01-12/01
	Daytona Beach MSA, FL	Y	27300 FQ	40780 AW	62920 TQ	FLBLS	10/01-12/01
	Fort Lauderdale PMSA, FL	Y	25600 FQ	45040 AW	70570 TQ	FLBLS	10/01-12/01

AAW	Average annual wage	**AOH**	Average offered, high	**ASH**	Average starting, high	**H**	Hourly	**M**	Monthly	**S**	Special: hourly and annual
AE	Average entry wage	**AOL**	Average offered, low	**ASL**	Average starting, low	**HI**	Highest wage paid	**MTC**	Median total compensation	**TQ**	Third quartile wage
AEX	Average experienced wage	**APH**	Average pay, high range	**AW**	Average wage paid	**HR**	High end range	**MW**	Median wage paid	**W**	Weekly
AO	Average offered	**APL**	Average pay, low range	**FQ**	First quartile wage	**LR**	Low end range	**SQ**	Second quartile wage	**Y**	Yearly

Occupation/Type/Industry	Location	Per	Low	Mid	High	Source	Date
Chemist	Gainesville MSA, FL	Y	28250 FQ	40130 AW	55700 TQ	FLBLS	10/01-12/01
	Jacksonville MSA, FL	Y	26850 FQ	45270 AW	69170 TQ	FLBLS	10/01-12/01
	Lakeland-Winter Haven MSA, FL	Y	28210 FQ	46250 AW	69630 TQ	FLBLS	10/01-12/01
	Melbourne-Titusville-Palm Bay MSA, FL	Y	30660 FQ	49640 AW	70120 TQ	FLBLS	10/01-12/01
	Miami PMSA, FL	Y	25490 FQ	41850 AW	63010 TQ	FLBLS	10/01-12/01
	Orlando MSA, FL	Y	24800 FQ	35540 AW	46040 TQ	FLBLS	10/01-12/01
	Pensacola MSA, FL	Y	24940 FQ	40280 AW	58440 TQ	FLBLS	10/01-12/01
	Tallahassee MSA, FL	Y	29460 FQ	50460 AW	83030 TQ	FLBLS	10/01-12/01
	Tampa-St. Petersburg-Clearwater MSA, FL	Y	28530 FQ	45770 AW	68930 TQ	FLBLS	10/01-12/01
	West Palm Beach-Boca Raton MSA, FL	Y	22600 FQ	36980 AW	57740 TQ	FLBLS	10/01-12/01
	Georgia	Y	33000 FQ	56820 AW	84030 TQ	GABLS	10/01-12/01
	Atlanta MSA, GA	Y	34460 FQ	58750 AW	86820 TQ	GABLS	10/01-12/01
	Columbus MSA, GA-AL	Y	38000 FQ	64940 AW	88950 TQ	GABLS	10/01-12/01
	Macon MSA, GA	Y	40780 FQ	58370 AW	70630 TQ	GABLS	10/01-12/01
	Savannah MSA, GA	Y	22220 FQ	43280 AW	68370 TQ	GABLS	10/01-12/01
	Hawaii	Y	24890 FQ	44650 AW	69300 TQ	HIBLS	10/01-12/01
	Honolulu MSA, HI	Y	24380 FQ	43690 AW	68380 TQ	HIBLS	10/01-12/01
	Idaho	Y	32550 FQ	59050 AW	91820 TQ	IDBLS	10/01-12/01
	Boise City MSA, ID	Y	29580 FQ	48140 AW	69380 TQ	IDBLS	10/01-12/01
	Illinois	Y	30040 FQ	57870 AW	90500 TQ	ILBLS	10/01-12/01
	Champaign-Urbana MSA, IL	Y	30480 FQ	46860 AW	72970 TQ	ILBLS	10/01-12/01
	Chicago PMSA, IL	Y	29580 FQ	58340 AW	92980 TQ	ILBLS	10/01-12/01
	Peoria-Pekin MSA, IL	Y	29710 FQ	59370 AW	86570 TQ	ILBLS	10/01-12/01
	Rockford MSA, IL	Y	25860 FQ	47410 AW	81500 TQ	ILBLS	10/01-12/01
	Indiana	Y	28660 FQ	48740 AW	73150 TQ	INBLS	10/01-12/01
	Elkhart-Goshen MSA, IN	Y	32490 FQ	49640 AW	72570 TQ	INBLS	10/01-12/01
	Evansville-Henderson MSA, IN-KY	Y	31410 FQ	49440 AW	71170 TQ	INBLS	10/01-12/01
	Fort Wayne MSA, IN	Y	25280 FQ	42000 AW	73060 TQ	INBLS	10/01-12/01
	Gary PMSA, IN	Y	30760 FQ	53300 AW	70700 TQ	INBLS	10/01-12/01
	Indianapolis MSA, IN	Y	27990 FQ	47140 AW	75950 TQ	INBLS	10/01-12/01
	Lafayette MSA, IN	Y	38140 FQ	65150 AW	113730 TQ	INBLS	10/01-12/01
	South Bend MSA, IN	Y	26820 FQ	41020 AW	56990 TQ	INBLS	10/01-12/01
	Iowa	Y	25870 FQ	45470 AW	76420 TQ	IABLS	10/01-12/01
	Davenport-Moline-Rock Island MSA, IA-IL	Y	22520 FQ	47340 AW	79120 TQ	IABLS	10/01-12/01
	Des Moines MSA, IA	Y	30670 FQ	49750 AW	75410 TQ	IABLS	10/01-12/01
	Kansas	Y	29000 FQ	48200 AW	70570 TQ	KSBLS	10/01-12/01
	Topeka MSA, KS	Y	29870 FQ	39750 AW	52950 TQ	KSBLS	10/01-12/01
	Wichita MSA, KS	Y	37870 FQ	56700 AW	76450 TQ	KSBLS	10/01-12/01
	Kentucky	Y	31310 FQ	54770 AW	81720 TQ	KYBLS	10/01-12/01
	Lexington MSA, KY	Y	31710 FQ	55960 AW	83010 TQ	KYBLS	10/01-12/01
	Louisville MSA, KY-IN	Y	33370 FQ	56080 AW	82820 TQ	KYBLS	10/01-12/01
	Louisiana	Y	29030 FQ	54630 AW	82930 TQ	LABLS	10/01-12/01
	Baton Rouge MSA, LA	Y	25400 FQ	50490 AW	78230 TQ	LABLS	10/01-12/01
	Lafayette MSA, LA	Y	21150 FQ	49490 AW	77980 TQ	LABLS	10/01-12/01
	Lake Charles MSA, LA	Y	38930 FQ	58770 AW	82990 TQ	LABLS	10/01-12/01
	New Orleans MSA, LA	Y	37230 FQ	59970 AW	88120 TQ	LABLS	10/01-12/01
	Maine	Y	25150 FQ	47750 AW	72670 TQ	MEBLS	10/01-12/01
	Maryland	Y	36570 FQ	68220 AW	107110 TQ	MDBLS	10/01-12/01
	Baltimore PMSA, MD	Y	27330 FQ	53300 AW	85260 TQ	MDBLS	10/01-12/01
	Massachusetts	Y	39360 FQ	65230 AW	94320 TQ	MABLS	10/01-12/01
	Boston PMSA, MA-NH	Y	39710 FQ	65430 AW	93950 TQ	MABLS	10/01-12/01
	Brockton PMSA, MA	Y	39200 FQ	60440 AW	90750 TQ	MABLS	10/01-12/01
	Lawrence PMSA, MA-NH	Y	53000 FQ	83330 AW	113220 TQ	MABLS	10/01-12/01
	Lowell PMSA, MA-NH	Y	39050 FQ	65710 AW	114110 TQ	MABLS	10/01-12/01
	Springfield MSA, MA	Y	29960 FQ	54020 AW	86390 TQ	MABLS	10/01-12/01
	Worcester PMSA, MA-CT	Y	39800 FQ	63350 AW	94420 TQ	MABLS	10/01-12/01
	Michigan	Y	32920 FQ	56030 AW	85360 TQ	MIBLS	10/01-12/01
	Ann Arbor PMSA, MI	Y	38020 FQ	61120 AW	93650 TQ	MIBLS	10/01-12/01
	Detroit PMSA, MI	Y	33450 FQ	56420 AW	85380 TQ	MIBLS	10/01-12/01
	Grand Rapids-Muskegon-Holland MSA, MI	Y	27710 FQ	53980 AW	85800 TQ	MIBLS	10/01-12/01
	Kalamazoo-Battle Creek MSA, MI	Y	29320 FQ	53000 AW	81200 TQ	MIBLS	10/01-12/01
	Saginaw-Bay City-Midland MSA, MI	Y	38130 FQ	55570 AW	81040 TQ	MIBLS	10/01-12/01
	Minnesota	Y	33020 FQ	55230 AW	79370 TQ	MNBLS	10/01-12/01

AAW Average annual wage **AOH** Average offered, high **ASH** Average starting, high **H** Hourly **M** Monthly **S** Special: hourly and annual
AE Average entry wage **AOL** Average offered, low **ASL** Average starting, low **HI** Highest wage paid **MTC** Median total compensation **TQ** Third quartile wage
AEX Average experienced wage **APH** Average pay, high range **AW** Average wage paid **HR** High end range **MW** Median wage paid **W** Weekly
AO Average offered **APL** Average pay, low range **FQ** First quartile wage **LR** Low end range **SQ** Second quartile wage **Y** Yearly

Occupation/Type/Industry	Location	Per	Low	Mid	High	Source	Date
Chemist	Duluth-Superior MSA, MN-WI	Y	31230 FQ	50230 AW	71430 TQ	MNBLS	10/01-12/01
	Minneapolis-St. Paul MSA, MN-WI	Y	33530 FQ	56070 AW	80730 TQ	MNBLS	10/01-12/01
	Mississippi	Y	30130 FQ	50840 AW	72290 TQ	MSBLS	10/01-12/01
	Biloxi-Gulfport-Pascagoula MSA, MS	Y	37150 FQ	54230 AW	76750 TQ	MSBLS	10/01-12/01
	Jackson MSA, MS	Y	25520 FQ	38560 AW	56680 TQ	MSBLS	10/01-12/01
	Missouri	Y	27830 FQ	51130 AW	79410 TQ	MOBLS	10/01-12/01
	Kansas City MSA, MO-KS	Y	31110 FQ	54060 AW	78320 TQ	MOBLS	10/01-12/01
	St. Louis MSA, MO-IL	Y	32060 FQ	55710 AW	82710 TQ	MOBLS	10/01-12/01
	Montana	Y	27340 FQ	47250 AW	74780 TQ	MTBLS	10/01-12/01
	Nebraska	Y	27820 FQ	46480 AW	68980 TQ	NEBLS	10/01-12/01
	Lincoln MSA, NE	Y	29240 FQ	45020 AW	66100 TQ	NEBLS	10/01-12/01
	Omaha MSA, NE-IA	Y	29200 FQ	47850 AW	70480 TQ	NEBLS	10/01-12/01
	Nevada	Y	27440 FQ	51060 AW	76850 TQ	NVBLS	10/01-12/01
	Las Vegas MSA, NV-AZ	Y	43550 FQ	62990 AW	88150 TQ	NVBLS	10/01-12/01
	Reno MSA, NV	Y	22760 FQ	40420 AW	60800 TQ	NVBLS	10/01-12/01
	New Hampshire	Y	37000 FQ	59790 AW	89400 TQ	NHBLS	10/01-12/01
	Manchester PMSA, NH	Y	38670 FQ	58020 AW	96290 TQ	NHBLS	10/01-12/01
	Nashua PMSA, NH	Y	36690 FQ	61510 AW	89250 TQ	NHBLS	10/01-12/01
	Portsmouth-Rochester PMSA, NH-ME	Y	45160 FQ	58010 AW	70590 TQ	NHBLS	10/01-12/01
	New Jersey	Y	36830 FQ	64410 AW	101220 TQ	NJBLS	10/01-12/01
	Atlantic-Cape May PMSA, NJ	Y	38820 FQ	63120 AW	95240 TQ	NJBLS	10/01-12/01
	Bergen-Passaic PMSA, NJ	Y	37180 FQ	66330 AW	113220 TQ	NJBLS	10/01-12/01
	Jersey City PMSA, NJ	Y	36640 FQ	57760 AW	87050 TQ	NJBLS	10/01-12/01
	Middlesex-Somerset-Hunterdon PMSA, NJ	Y	36050 FQ	62910 AW	92560 TQ	NJBLS	10/01-12/01
	Monmouth-Ocean PMSA, NJ	Y	31080 FQ	54130 AW	80060 TQ	NJBLS	10/01-12/01
	Newark PMSA, NJ	Y	38120 FQ	66170 AW	107730 TQ	NJBLS	10/01-12/01
	Albuquerque MSA, NM	Y	29000 FQ	54300 AW	99660 TQ	NMBLS	10/01-12/01
	New York	Y	33140 FQ	54560 AW	82850 TQ	NYBLS	10/01-12/01
	Albany-Schenectady-Troy MSA, NY	Y	31910 FQ	52190 AW	73510 TQ	NYBLS	10/01-12/01
	Buffalo-Niagara Falls MSA, NY	Y	33140 FQ	52350 AW	83590 TQ	NYBLS	10/01-12/01
	Nassau-Suffolk PMSA, NY	Y	30140 FQ	52860 AW	82460 TQ	NYBLS	10/01-12/01
	New York PMSA, NY	Y	36550 FQ	55960 AW	83380 TQ	NYBLS	10/01-12/01
	Newburgh PMSA, NY-PA	Y	32460 FQ	49050 AW	69020 TQ	NYBLS	10/01-12/01
	Rochester MSA, NY	Y	32500 FQ	61330 AW	92430 TQ	NYBLS	10/01-12/01
	Syracuse MSA, NY	Y	30840 FQ	53090 AW	77280 TQ	NYBLS	10/01-12/01
	North Carolina	Y	32840 FQ	58170 AW	91750 TQ	NCBLS	10/01-12/01
	Charlotte-Gastonia-Rock Hill MSA, NC-SC	Y	32100 FQ	58170 AW	91470 TQ	NCBLS	10/01-12/01
	Greensboro-Winston-Salem-High Point MSA, NC	Y	32700 FQ	58100 AW	92560 TQ	NCBLS	10/01-12/01
	Hickory-Morganton-Lenoir MSA, NC	Y	30630 FQ	51470 AW	72480 TQ	NCBLS	10/01-12/01
	Raleigh-Durham-Chapel Hill MSA, NC	Y	36110 FQ	61660 AW	95090 TQ	NCBLS	10/01-12/01
	Wilmington MSA, NC	Y	27960 FQ	60450 AW	94480 TQ	NCBLS	10/01-12/01
	North Dakota	Y	24350 FQ	47020 AW	79540 TQ	NDBLS	10/01-12/01
	Fargo-Moorhead MSA, ND-MN	Y	25150 FQ	49120 AW	84650 TQ	NDBLS	10/01-12/01
	Ohio	Y	30240 FQ	52700 AW	83430 TQ	OHBLS	10/01-12/01
	Akron PMSA, OH	Y	25620 FQ	47410 AW	78370 TQ	OHBLS	10/01-12/01
	Canton-Massillon MSA, OH	Y	31670 FQ	50810 AW	69490 TQ	OHBLS	10/01-12/01
	Cincinnati PMSA, OH-KY-IN	Y	30040 FQ	53590 AW	85080 TQ	OHBLS	10/01-12/01
	Cleveland-Lorain-Elyria PMSA, OH	Y	32080 FQ	51980 AW	78380 TQ	OHBLS	10/01-12/01
	Columbus MSA, OH	Y	32670 FQ	55600 AW	83900 TQ	OHBLS	10/01-12/01
	Dayton-Springfield MSA, OH	Y	31490 FQ	56820 AW	102210 TQ	OHBLS	10/01-12/01
	Hamilton-Middletown PMSA, OH	Y	30620 FQ	46270 AW	68710 TQ	OHBLS	10/01-12/01
	Toledo MSA, OH	Y	26500 FQ	50420 AW	74450 TQ	OHBLS	10/01-12/01
	Oklahoma	Y	28940 FQ	48060 AW	85350 TQ	OKBLS	10/01-12/01
	Oklahoma City MSA, OK	Y	28700 FQ	38370 AW	59680 TQ	OKBLS	10/01-12/01
	Oregon	Y	26760 FQ	49770 AW	77960 TQ	ORBLS	10/01-12/01
	Portland-Vancouver PMSA, OR-WA	Y	26030 FQ	45790 AW	72030 TQ	ORBLS	10/01-12/01
	Pennsylvania	Y	27840 FQ	47240 AW	72450 TQ	PABLS	10/01-12/01

AAW	Average annual wage	**AOH**	Average offered, high	**ASH**	Average starting, high	**H**	Hourly	**M**	Monthly	**S**	Special: hourly and annual
AE	Average entry wage	**AOL**	Average offered, low	**ASL**	Average starting, low	**HI**	Highest wage paid	**MTC**	Median total compensation	**TQ**	Third quartile wage
AEX	Average experienced wage	**APH**	Average pay, high range	**AW**	Average wage paid	**HR**	High end range	**MW**	Median wage paid	**W**	Weekly
AO	Average offered	**APL**	Average pay, low range	**FQ**	First quartile wage	**LR**	Low end range	**SQ**	Second quartile wage	**Y**	Yearly

Occupation/Type/Industry	Location	Per	Low	Mid	High	Source	Date
Chemist	Allentown-Bethlehem-Easton MSA, PA	Y	26500 FQ	56810 AW	123450 TQ	PABLS	10/01-12/01
	Johnstown MSA, PA	Y	27960 FQ	40140 AW	61960 TQ	PABLS	10/01-12/01
	Philadelphia PMSA, PA-NJ	Y	29620 FQ	49790 AW	77660 TQ	PABLS	10/01-12/01
	Pittsburgh MSA, PA	Y	27660 FQ	45430 AW	70110 TQ	PABLS	10/01-12/01
	Reading MSA, PA	Y	28390 FQ	47000 AW	70250 TQ	PABLS	10/01-12/01
	Scranton-Wilkes-Barre-Hazleton MSA, PA	Y	30190 FQ	56510 AW	88230 TQ	PABLS	10/01-12/01
	York MSA, PA	Y	20870 FQ	40400 AW	57120 TQ	PABLS	10/01-12/01
	Rhode Island	Y	31430 FQ	57810 AW	87910 TQ	RIBLS	10/01-12/01
	Providence-Fall River-Warwick MSA, RI-MA	Y	31870 FQ	56170 AW	86560 TQ	RIBLS	10/01-12/01
	South Carolina	Y	31470 FQ	58420 AW	92960 TQ	SCBLS	10/01-12/01
	Charleston-North Charleston MSA, SC	Y	33800 FQ	55840 AW	83850 TQ	SCBLS	10/01-12/01
	Greenville-Spartanburg-Anderson MSA, SC	Y	31520 FQ	50000 AW	72440 TQ	SCBLS	10/01-12/01
	South Dakota	Y	29520 FQ	43180 AW	56140 TQ	SDBLS	10/01-12/01
	Tennessee	Y	26060 FQ	57230 AW	98390 TQ	TNBLS	10/01-12/01
	Chattanooga MSA, TN-GA	Y	32300 FQ	54380 AW	79530 TQ	TNBLS	10/01-12/01
	Johnson City-Kingsport-Bristol MSA, TN-VA	Y	49570 FQ	76600 AW	112620 TQ	TNBLS	10/01-12/01
	Memphis MSA, TN-AR-MS	Y	27410 FQ	46760 AW	71370 TQ	TNBLS	10/01-12/01
	Nashville MSA, TN	Y	23360 FQ	39340 AW	76270 TQ	TNBLS	10/01-12/01
	Texas	Y	27200 FQ	51800 AW	87430 TQ	TXBLS	10/01-12/01
	Austin-San Marcos MSA, TX	Y	25060 FQ	41390 AW	57350 TQ	TXBLS	10/01-12/01
	Beaumont-Port Arthur MSA, TX	Y	33850 FQ	61350 AW	89720 TQ	TXBLS	10/01-12/01
	Brazoria PMSA, TX	Y	45740 FQ	66760 AW	93300 TQ	TXBLS	10/01-12/01
	Corpus Christi MSA, TX	Y	29750 FQ	61930 AW	96560 TQ	TXBLS	10/01-12/01
	Dallas PMSA, TX	Y	20660 FQ	49280 AW	84770 TQ	TXBLS	10/01-12/01
	El Paso MSA, TX	Y	29330 FQ	38360 AW	51480 TQ	TXBLS	10/01-12/01
	Fort Worth-Arlington PMSA, TX	Y	23550 FQ	43370 AW	67430 TQ	TXBLS	10/01-12/01
	Galveston-Texas City PMSA, TX	Y	32570 FQ	55820 AW	84440 TQ	TXBLS	10/01-12/01
	Houston PMSA, TX	Y	27900 FQ	50950 AW	89820 TQ	TXBLS	10/01-12/01
	Longview-Marshall MSA, TX	Y	27840 FQ	60190 AW	90590 TQ	TXBLS	10/01-12/01
	Lubbock MSA, TX	Y	19280 FQ	31980 AW	45420 TQ	TXBLS	10/01-12/01
	Odessa-Midland MSA, TX	Y	23400 FQ	53230 AW	91570 TQ	TXBLS	10/01-12/01
	San Antonio MSA, TX	Y	30530 FQ	51830 AW	79580 TQ	TXBLS	10/01-12/01
	Utah	Y	30690 FQ	48740 AW	73840 TQ	UTBLS	10/01-12/01
	Provo-Orem MSA, UT	Y	32480 FQ	50310 AW	80470 TQ	UTBLS	10/01-12/01
	Salt Lake City-Ogden MSA, UT	Y	29810 FQ	46840 AW	70340 TQ	UTBLS	10/01-12/01
	Vermont	Y	33150 FQ	50460 AW	71040 TQ	VTBLS	10/01-12/01
	Burlington MSA, VT	Y	32410 FQ	46880 AW	65610 TQ	VTBLS	10/01-12/01
	Virginia	Y	30450 FQ	58050 AW	97270 TQ	VABLS	10/01-12/01
	Norfolk-Virginia Beach-Newport News MSA, VA-NC	Y	32210 FQ	52490 AW	74200 TQ	VABLS	10/01-12/01
	Richmond-Petersburg MSA, VA	Y	29770 FQ	52650 AW	78210 TQ	VABLS	10/01-12/01
	Roanoke MSA, VA	Y	25590 FQ	46240 AW	77330 TQ	VABLS	10/01-12/01
	Washington	Y	37090 FQ	60120 AW	87070 TQ	WABLS	10/01-12/01
	Richland-Kennewick-Pasco MSA, WA	Y	42490 FQ	65750 AW	88300 TQ	WABLS	10/01-12/01
	Seattle-Bellevue-Everett PMSA, WA	Y	39560 FQ	63960 AW	91340 TQ	WABLS	10/01-12/01
	Spokane MSA, WA	Y	26120 FQ	45780 AW	70690 TQ	WABLS	10/01-12/01
	Tacoma PMSA, WA	Y	33760 FQ	45230 AW	59680 TQ	WABLS	10/01-12/01
	West Virginia	Y	33900 FQ	60810 AW	100000 TQ	WVBLS	10/01-12/01
	Charleston MSA, WV	Y	31770 FQ	53980 AW	87660 TQ	WVBLS	10/01-12/01
	Huntington-Ashland MSA, WV-KY-OH	Y	33600 FQ	55590 AW	83330 TQ	WVBLS	10/01-12/01
	Wisconsin	Y	29190 FQ	46550 AW	73570 TQ	WIBLS	10/01-12/01
	Green Bay MSA, WI	Y	31900 FQ	43790 AW	56430 TQ	WIBLS	10/01-12/01
	Milwaukee-Waukesha PMSA, WI	Y	31790 FQ	49220 AW	76350 TQ	WIBLS	10/01-12/01
	Racine PMSA, WI	Y	26930 FQ	46560 AW	73760 TQ	WIBLS	10/01-12/01
	Wyoming	Y	29270 FQ	44140 AW	66740 TQ	WYBLS	10/01-12/01
	Puerto Rico	Y	24340 FQ	35940 AW	52200 TQ	PRBLS	10/01-12/01

AAW	Average annual wage	**AOH**	Average offered, high	**ASH**	Average starting, high	**H**	Hourly	**M**	Monthly	**S**	Special: hourly and annual
AE	Average entry wage	**AOL**	Average offered, low	**ASL**	Average starting, low	**HI**	Highest wage paid	**MTC**	Median total compensation	**TQ**	Third quartile wage
AEX	Average experienced wage	**APH**	Average pay, high range	**AW**	Average wage paid	**HR**	High end range	**MW**	Median wage paid	**W**	Weekly
AO	Average offered	**APL**	Average pay, low range	**FQ**	First quartile wage	**LR**	Low end range	**SQ**	Second quartile wage	**Y**	Yearly

Occupation/Type/Industry	Location	Per	Low	Mid	High	Source	Date
Chemist							
Bachelor's Degree	United States	Y		35900 MW		CEN	3/01-3/02
Bachelor's Degree	East North Central	Y		59000 MW		CEN	3/01-3/02
Bachelor's Degree	East South Central	Y		53800 MW		CEN	3/01-3/02
Bachelor's Degree	Middle Atlantic	Y		60000 MW		CEN	3/01-3/02
Bachelor's Degree	Mountain	Y		52700 MW		CEN	3/01-3/02
Bachelor's Degree	New England	Y		61000 MW		CEN	3/01-3/02
Bachelor's Degree	Pacific	Y		60000 MW		CEN	3/01-3/02
Bachelor's Degree	South Atlantic	Y		56500 MW		CEN	3/01-3/02
Bachelor's Degree	West North Central	Y		52000 MW		CEN	3/01-3/02
Bachelor's Degree	West South Central	Y		60300 MW		CEN	3/01-3/02
Chemistry Teacher							
Postsecondary	Alabama	Y	23140 FQ	63780 AW	129250 TQ	ALBLS	10/01-12/01
Postsecondary	Birmingham MSA, AL	Y	33890 FQ	80760 AW	145310 TQ	ALBLS	10/01-12/01
Postsecondary	Arizona	Y	23660 FQ	37980 AW	55700 TQ	AZBLS	10/01-12/01
Postsecondary	Arkansas	Y	25940 FQ	50140 AW	86030 TQ	ARBLS	10/01-12/01
Postsecondary	California	Y	40670 FQ	69480 AW	107100 TQ	CABLS	10/01-12/01
Postsecondary	Los Angeles-Long Beach PMSA, CA	Y	40460 FQ	72600 AW	112850 TQ	CABLS	10/01-12/01
Postsecondary	Riverside-San Bernardino PMSA, CA	Y	35220 FQ	57750 AW	86370 TQ	CABLS	10/01-12/01
Postsecondary	San Francisco PMSA, CA	Y	51120 FQ	77040 AW	110550 TQ	CABLS	10/01-12/01
Postsecondary	San Jose PMSA, CA	Y	39630 FQ	62880 AW	89030 TQ	CABLS	10/01-12/01
Postsecondary	Santa Cruz-Watsonville PMSA, CA	Y	34570 FQ	63300 AW	100310 TQ	CABLS	10/01-12/01
Postsecondary	Colorado	Y	35100 FQ	57940 AW	89350 TQ	COBLS	10/01-12/01
Postsecondary	Denver PMSA, CO	Y	34910 FQ	58100 AW	90370 TQ	COBLS	10/01-12/01
Postsecondary	Connecticut	Y	31080 FQ	59350 AW	93790 TQ	CTBLS	10/01-12/01
Postsecondary	Delaware	Y	43590 FQ	75150 AW	117110 TQ	DEBLS	10/01-12/01
Postsecondary	District of Columbia	Y	35660 FQ	60510 AW	92750 TQ	DCBLS	10/01-12/01
Postsecondary	Washington PMSA, DC-MD-VA-WV	Y	32140 FQ	63930 AW	109420 TQ	DCBLS	10/01-12/01
Postsecondary	Florida	Y	41480 FQ	67960 AW	110850 TQ	FLBLS	10/01-12/01
Postsecondary	Gainesville MSA, FL	Y	46960 FQ	74960 AW	120190 TQ	FLBLS	10/01-12/01
Postsecondary	Miami PMSA, FL	Y	46820 FQ	65710 AW	102370 TQ	FLBLS	10/01-12/01
Postsecondary	Orlando MSA, FL	Y	26950 FQ	58850 AW	100290 TQ	FLBLS	10/01-12/01
Postsecondary	Tallahassee MSA, FL	Y	48010 FQ	75180 AW	125570 TQ	FLBLS	10/01-12/01
Postsecondary	Tampa-St. Petersburg-Clearwater MSA, FL	Y	39040 FQ	62410 AW	102070 TQ	FLBLS	10/01-12/01
Postsecondary	West Palm Beach-Boca Raton MSA, FL	Y	40620 FQ	65600 AW	99210 TQ	FLBLS	10/01-12/01
Postsecondary	Georgia	Y	39340 FQ	60070 AW	90780 TQ	GABLS	10/01-12/01
Postsecondary	Atlanta MSA, GA	Y	39650 FQ	62010 AW	111100 TQ	GABLS	10/01-12/01
Postsecondary	Hawaii	Y	41070 FQ	62490 AW	93190 TQ	HIBLS	10/01-12/01
Postsecondary	Honolulu MSA, HI	Y	40730 FQ	63530 AW	94780 TQ	HIBLS	10/01-12/01
Postsecondary	Idaho	Y	40470 FQ	54740 AW	69820 TQ	IDBLS	10/01-12/01
Postsecondary	Illinois	Y	19610 FQ	50450 AW	84420 TQ	ILBLS	10/01-12/01
Postsecondary	Champaign-Urbana MSA, IL	Y	14710 FQ	41580 AW	61650 TQ	ILBLS	10/01-12/01
Postsecondary	Chicago PMSA, IL	Y	22060 FQ	53760 AW	95890 TQ	ILBLS	10/01-12/01
Postsecondary	Indiana	Y	32620 FQ	57520 AW	91970 TQ	INBLS	10/01-12/01
Postsecondary	South Bend MSA, IN	Y	31860 FQ	50960 AW	75040 TQ	INBLS	10/01-12/01
Postsecondary	Iowa	Y	32190 FQ	58530 AW	99910 TQ	IABLS	10/01-12/01
Postsecondary	Kansas	Y	26420 FQ	48380 AW	77400 TQ	KSBLS	10/01-12/01
Postsecondary	Kentucky	Y	33160 FQ	55350 AW	86520 TQ	KYBLS	10/01-12/01
Postsecondary	Lexington MSA, KY	Y	36600 FQ	60740 AW	89800 TQ	KYBLS	10/01-12/01
Postsecondary	Louisiana	Y	28990 FQ	50020 AW	80650 TQ	LABLS	10/01-12/01
Postsecondary	New Orleans MSA, LA	Y	31200 FQ	54270 AW	91690 TQ	LABLS	10/01-12/01
Postsecondary	Maine	Y	33000 FQ	50630 AW	73220 TQ	MEBLS	10/01-12/01
Postsecondary	Maryland	Y	31990 FQ	64060 AW	109680 TQ	MDBLS	10/01-12/01
Postsecondary	Baltimore PMSA, MD	Y	34950 FQ	60080 AW	93150 TQ	MDBLS	10/01-12/01
Postsecondary	Massachusetts	Y	37510 FQ	62090 AW	94370 TQ	MABLS	10/01-12/01
Postsecondary	Boston PMSA, MA-NH	Y	36660 FQ	61640 AW	94280 TQ	MABLS	10/01-12/01
Postsecondary	Springfield MSA, MA	Y	40560 FQ	61730 AW	87770 TQ	MABLS	10/01-12/01
Postsecondary	Michigan	Y	38450 FQ	62360 AW	93000 TQ	MIBLS	10/01-12/01
Postsecondary	Detroit PMSA, MI	Y	32430 FQ	58870 AW	89560 TQ	MIBLS	10/01-12/01
Postsecondary	Grand Rapids-Muskegon-Holland MSA, MI	Y	39430 FQ	56270 AW	85540 TQ	MIBLS	10/01-12/01
Postsecondary	Minnesota	Y	37050 FQ	56420 AW	88700 TQ	MNBLS	10/01-12/01
Postsecondary	Minneapolis-St. Paul MSA, MN-WI	Y	39610 FQ	62720 AW	103320 TQ	MNBLS	10/01-12/01
Postsecondary	Mississippi	Y	36480 FQ	51770 AW	71090 TQ	MSBLS	10/01-12/01
Postsecondary	Jackson MSA, MS	Y	31410 FQ	45950 AW	65470 TQ	MSBLS	10/01-12/01

AAW	Average annual wage	**AOH**	Average offered, high	**ASH**	Average starting, high	**H**	Hourly	**M**	Monthly	**S**	Special: hourly and annual
AE	Average entry wage	**AOL**	Average offered, low	**ASL**	Average starting, low	**HI**	Highest wage paid	**MTC**	Median total compensation	**TQ**	Third quartile wage
AEX	Average experienced wage	**APH**	Average pay, high range	**AW**	Average wage paid	**HR**	High end range	**MW**	Median wage paid	**W**	Weekly
AO	Average offered	**APL**	Average pay, low range	**FQ**	First quartile wage	**LR**	Low end range	**SQ**	Second quartile wage	**Y**	Yearly

Occupation/Type/Industry	Location	Per	Low	Mid	High	Source	Date
Chemistry Teacher							
Postsecondary	Missouri	Y	34690 FQ	51590 AW	73070 TQ	MOBLS	10/01-12/01
Postsecondary	Kansas City MSA, MO-KS	Y	34270 FQ	49500 AW	69790 TQ	MOBLS	10/01-12/01
Postsecondary	St. Louis MSA, MO-IL	Y	33220 FQ	50770 AW	72390 TQ	MOBLS	10/01-12/01
Postsecondary	Springfield MSA, MO	Y	41060 FQ	60230 AW	86630 TQ	MOBLS	10/01-12/01
Postsecondary	Montana	Y	34200 FQ	65040 AW	110230 TQ	MTBLS	10/01-12/01
Postsecondary	Nebraska	Y	34040 FQ	56370 AW	89520 TQ	NEBLS	10/01-12/01
Postsecondary	Lincoln MSA, NE	Y	37110 FQ	69990 AW	123730 TQ	NEBLS	10/01-12/01
Postsecondary	Nevada	Y	26470 FQ	52280 AW	80910 TQ	NVBLS	10/01-12/01
Postsecondary	Las Vegas MSA, NV-AZ	Y	25780 FQ	48790 AW	74610 TQ	NVBLS	10/01-12/01
Postsecondary	New Hampshire	Y	38170 FQ	67700 AW	111900 TQ	NHBLS	10/01-12/01
Postsecondary	New Jersey	Y	39690 FQ	72740 AW	118380 TQ	NJBLS	10/01-12/01
Postsecondary	Jersey City PMSA, NJ	Y	39530 FQ	72950 AW	118980 TQ	NJBLS	10/01-12/01
Postsecondary	Newark PMSA, NJ	Y	40860 FQ	69320 AW	98600 TQ	NJBLS	10/01-12/01
Postsecondary	New Mexico	Y	30740 FQ	49500 AW	66870 TQ	NMBLS	10/01-12/01
Postsecondary	New York	Y	44990 FQ	71890 AW	110080 TQ	NYBLS	10/01-12/01
Postsecondary	Albany-Schenectady-Troy MSA, NY	Y	45060 FQ	70900 AW	109450 TQ	NYBLS	10/01-12/01
Postsecondary	Nassau-Suffolk PMSA, NY	Y	41100 FQ	67970 AW	101630 TQ	NYBLS	10/01-12/01
Postsecondary	New York PMSA, NY	Y	46960 FQ	73140 AW	113030 TQ	NYBLS	10/01-12/01
Postsecondary	North Carolina	Y	34700 FQ	53950 AW	82770 TQ	NCBLS	10/01-12/01
Postsecondary	Asheville MSA, NC	Y	47820 FQ	60370 AW	86270 TQ	NCBLS	10/01-12/01
Postsecondary	Charlotte-Gastonia-Rock Hill MSA, NC-SC	Y	31830 FQ	53910 AW	83510 TQ	NCBLS	10/01-12/01
Postsecondary	Greensboro-Winston-Salem-High Point MSA, NC	Y	35550 FQ	53250 AW	81810 TQ	NCBLS	10/01-12/01
Postsecondary	Raleigh-Durham-Chapel Hill MSA, NC	Y	36880 FQ	56790 AW	88660 TQ	NCBLS	10/01-12/01
Postsecondary	Wilmington MSA, NC	Y	39310 FQ	65140 AW	102480 TQ	NCBLS	10/01-12/01
Postsecondary	North Dakota	Y	36060 FQ	50080 AW	73110 TQ	NDBLS	10/01-12/01
Postsecondary	Fargo-Moorhead MSA, ND-MN	Y	35370 FQ	52750 AW	76800 TQ	NDBLS	10/01-12/01
Postsecondary	Ohio	Y	33740 FQ	57680 AW	88760 TQ	OHBLS	10/01-12/01
Postsecondary	Cincinnati PMSA, OH-KY-IN	Y	37910 FQ	65240 AW	103430 TQ	OHBLS	10/01-12/01
Postsecondary	Cleveland-Lorain-Elyria PMSA, OH	Y	28870 FQ	53540 AW	82320 TQ	OHBLS	10/01-12/01
Postsecondary	Columbus MSA, OH	Y	37290 FQ	56930 AW	82250 TQ	OHBLS	10/01-12/01
Postsecondary	Dayton-Springfield MSA, OH	Y	22120 FQ	50260 AW	71830 TQ	OHBLS	10/01-12/01
Postsecondary	Toledo MSA, OH	Y	32240 FQ	58360 AW	87830 TQ	OHBLS	10/01-12/01
Postsecondary	Youngstown-Warren MSA, OH	Y	39550 FQ	56560 AW	87850 TQ	OHBLS	10/01-12/01
Postsecondary	Oklahoma	Y	29500 FQ	43330 AW	58920 TQ	OKBLS	10/01-12/01
Postsecondary	Oklahoma City MSA, OK	Y	27850 FQ	41220 AW	57660 TQ	OKBLS	10/01-12/01
Postsecondary	Oregon	Y	41640 FQ	73990 AW	114000 TQ	ORBLS	10/01-12/01
Postsecondary	Portland-Vancouver PMSA, OR-WA	Y	37680 FQ	65650 AW	99740 TQ	ORBLS	10/01-12/01
Postsecondary	Pennsylvania	Y	34630 FQ	61660 AW	94130 TQ	PABLS	10/01-12/01
Postsecondary	Allentown-Bethlehem-Easton MSA, PA	Y	30590 FQ	48850 AW	69930 TQ	PABLS	10/01-12/01
Postsecondary	Harrisburg-Lebanon-Carlisle MSA, PA	Y	41880 FQ	72900 AW	111360 TQ	PABLS	10/01-12/01
Postsecondary	Lancaster MSA, PA	Y	42770 FQ	66450 AW	96490 TQ	PABLS	10/01-12/01
Postsecondary	Philadelphia PMSA, PA-NJ	Y	38400 FQ	62460 AW	93080 TQ	PABLS	10/01-12/01
Postsecondary	Pittsburgh MSA, PA	Y	27400 FQ	61030 AW	104990 TQ	PABLS	10/01-12/01
Postsecondary	Scranton-Wilkes-Barre-Hazleton MSA, PA	Y	31970 FQ	58740 AW	87190 TQ	PABLS	10/01-12/01
Postsecondary	Rhode Island	Y	42420 FQ	61890 AW	89070 TQ	RIBLS	10/01-12/01
Postsecondary	South Carolina	Y	29380 FQ	51410 AW	85060 TQ	SCBLS	10/01-12/01
Postsecondary	Charleston-North Charleston MSA, SC	Y	23960 FQ	48590 AW	81540 TQ	SCBLS	10/01-12/01
Postsecondary	Columbia MSA, SC	Y	30810 FQ	53380 AW	87790 TQ	SCBLS	10/01-12/01
Postsecondary	Greenville-Spartanburg-Anderson MSA, SC	Y	27360 FQ	50350 AW	83490 TQ	SCBLS	10/01-12/01
Postsecondary	South Dakota	Y	34150 FQ	49380 AW	69360 TQ	SDBLS	10/01-12/01
Postsecondary	Tennessee	Y	32610 FQ	55750 AW	86550 TQ	TNBLS	10/01-12/01
Postsecondary	Johnson City-Kingsport-Bristol MSA, TN-VA	Y	32740 FQ	56730 AW	91130 TQ	TNBLS	10/01-12/01
Postsecondary	Knoxville MSA, TN	Y	36710 FQ	63160 AW	103850 TQ	TNBLS	10/01-12/01
Postsecondary	Memphis MSA, TN-AR-MS	Y	39270 FQ	54330 AW	78150 TQ	TNBLS	10/01-12/01
Postsecondary	Nashville MSA, TN	Y	38050 FQ	57270 AW	83730 TQ	TNBLS	10/01-12/01
Postsecondary	Texas	Y	33620 FQ	57340 AW	85680 TQ	TXBLS	10/01-12/01
Postsecondary	Austin-San Marcos MSA, TX	Y	41910 FQ	57370 AW	72750 TQ	TXBLS	10/01-12/01
Postsecondary	Dallas PMSA, TX	Y	33030 FQ	55580 AW	83070 TQ	TXBLS	10/01-12/01

AAW	Average annual wage	AOH	Average offered, high	ASH	Average starting, high	H	Hourly	M	Monthly	S	Special: hourly and annual
AE	Average entry wage	AOL	Average offered, low	ASL	Average starting, low	HI	Highest wage paid	MTC	Median total compensation	TQ	Third quartile wage
AEX	Average experienced wage	APH	Average pay, high range	AW	Average wage paid	HR	High end range	MW	Median wage paid	W	Weekly
AO	Average offered	APL	Average pay, low range	FQ	First quartile wage	LR	Low end range	SQ	Second quartile wage	Y	Yearly

Occupation/Type/Industry	Location	Per	Low	Mid	High	Source	Date
Chemistry Teacher							
Postsecondary	Fort Worth-Arlington PMSA, TX	Y	35020 FQ	55070 AW	78800 TQ	TXBLS	10/01-12/01
Postsecondary	Houston PMSA, TX	Y	39840 FQ	68440 AW	120790 TQ	TXBLS	10/01-12/01
Postsecondary	San Antonio MSA, TX	Y	30580 FQ	60460 AW	95590 TQ	TXBLS	10/01-12/01
Postsecondary	Utah	Y	38520 FQ	77210 AW	132860 TQ	UTBLS	10/01-12/01
Postsecondary	Vermont	Y	28420 FQ	51900 AW	87400 TQ	VTBLS	10/01-12/01
Postsecondary	Virginia	Y	36970 FQ	64180 AW	106230 TQ	VABLS	10/01-12/01
Postsecondary	Norfolk-Virginia Beach-Newport News MSA, VA-NC	Y	44610 FQ	63250 AW	88280 TQ	VABLS	10/01-12/01
Postsecondary	Richmond-Petersburg MSA, VA	Y	24950 FQ	61890 AW	102410 TQ	VABLS	10/01-12/01
Postsecondary	Washington	Y	31030 FQ	61300 AW	112900 TQ	WABLS	10/01-12/01
Postsecondary	Seattle-Bellevue-Everett PMSA, WA	Y	33700 FQ	66680 AW	119200 TQ	WABLS	10/01-12/01
Postsecondary	Tacoma PMSA, WA	Y	26770 FQ	55190 AW	95030 TQ	WABLS	10/01-12/01
Postsecondary	West Virginia	Y	32980 FQ	55370 AW	80400 TQ	WVBLS	10/01-12/01
Postsecondary	Wisconsin	Y	37020 FQ	55100 AW	85410 TQ	WIBLS	10/01-12/01
Postsecondary	Milwaukee-Waukesha PMSA, WI	Y	35590 FQ	47930 AW	66030 TQ	WIBLS	10/01-12/01
Postsecondary	Wyoming	Y	35870 FQ	59710 AW	91380 TQ	WYBLS	10/01-12/01
Postsecondary	Puerto Rico	Y	30650 FQ	46180 AW	66220 TQ	PRBLS	10/01-12/01
Chief Airplane Maintenance Technician	United States	Y		98000 AW		BCAVIA	1/01-1/01
Chief Architect							
Information Technology Systems	United States	Y		104873 AW		INFO1	1/01-1/02
Chief Executive	Alabama	Y	46510 FQ	103350 AW		ALBLS	10/01-12/01
	Birmingham MSA, AL	Y	57120 FQ	108950 AW		ALBLS	10/01-12/01
	Huntsville MSA, AL	Y	38780 FQ	101200 AW		ALBLS	10/01-12/01
	Mobile MSA, AL	Y	57980 FQ	108890 AW		ALBLS	10/01-12/01
	Montgomery MSA, AL	Y	53820 FQ	112940 AW		ALBLS	10/01-12/01
	Alaska	Y	54740 FQ	101220 AW		AKBLS	10/01-12/01
	Anchorage MSA, AK	Y	65520 FQ	108840 AW		AKBLS	10/01-12/01
	Arizona	Y	55320 FQ	107000 AW		AZBLS	10/01-12/01
	Phoenix-Mesa MSA, AZ	Y	58650 FQ	111160 AW		AZBLS	10/01-12/01
	Tucson MSA, AZ	Y	46410 FQ	96500 AW		AZBLS	10/01-12/01
	Arkansas	Y	52320 FQ	101640 AW		ARBLS	10/01-12/01
	Fayetteville-Springdale-Rogers MSA, AR	Y	36940 FQ	94100 AW		ARBLS	10/01-12/01
	Fort Smith MSA, AR-OK	Y	33230 FQ	98090 AW		ARBLS	10/01-12/01
	Little Rock-North Little Rock MSA, AR	Y	64060 FQ	109800 AW		ARBLS	10/01-12/01
	California	Y	67490 FQ	119190 AW		CABLS	10/01-12/01
	Bakersfield MSA, CA	Y	61050 FQ	111250 AW		CABLS	10/01-12/01
	Chico-Paradise MSA, CA	Y	52160 FQ	90370 AW		CABLS	10/01-12/01
	Fresno MSA, CA	Y	57250 FQ	104020 AW		CABLS	10/01-12/01
	Los Angeles-Long Beach PMSA, CA	Y	71040 FQ	121300 AW		CABLS	10/01-12/01
	Merced MSA, CA	Y	58630 FQ	101430 AW		CABLS	10/01-12/01
	Modesto MSA, CA	Y	59110 FQ	103710 AW		CABLS	10/01-12/01
	Oakland PMSA, CA	Y	66430 FQ	119020 AW		CABLS	10/01-12/01
	Orange County PMSA, CA	Y	79000 FQ	126130 AW		CABLS	10/01-12/01
	Redding MSA, CA	Y	61160 FQ	107260 AW		CABLS	10/01-12/01
	Riverside-San Bernardino PMSA, CA	Y	49290 FQ	105270 AW		CABLS	10/01-12/01
	Sacramento PMSA, CA	Y	66490 FQ	110710 AW		CABLS	10/01-12/01
	Salinas MSA, CA	Y	53170 FQ	102010 AW		CABLS	10/01-12/01
	San Diego MSA, CA	Y	63090 FQ	115090 AW		CABLS	10/01-12/01
	San Francisco PMSA, CA	Y	81550 FQ	128030 AW		CABLS	10/01-12/01
	San Jose PMSA, CA	Y	90740 FQ	132640 AW		CABLS	10/01-12/01
	San Luis Obispo-Atascadero-Paso Robles MSA, CA	Y	57800 FQ	100290 AW		CABLS	10/01-12/01
	Santa Barbara-Santa Maria-Lompoc MSA, CA	Y	67070 FQ	114120 AW		CABLS	10/01-12/01
	Santa Cruz-Watsonville PMSA, CA	Y	69740 FQ	120660 AW		CABLS	10/01-12/01
	Santa Rosa PMSA, CA	Y	57730 FQ	108170 AW		CABLS	10/01-12/01
	Stockton-Lodi MSA, CA	Y	62040 FQ	108610 AW		CABLS	10/01-12/01

AAW	Average annual wage	AOH	Average offered, high	ASH	Average starting, high	H	Hourly	M	Monthly	S	Special: hourly and annual
AE	Average entry wage	AOL	Average offered, low	ASL	Average starting, low	HI	Highest wage paid	MTC	Median total compensation	TQ	Third quartile wage
AEX	Average experienced wage	APH	Average pay, high range	AW	Average wage paid	HR	High end range	MW	Median wage paid	W	Weekly
AO	Average offered	APL	Average pay, low range	FQ	First quartile wage	LR	Low end range	SQ	Second quartile wage	Y	Yearly

Occupation/Type/Industry	Location	Per	Low	Mid	High	Source	Date
Chief Executive	Vallejo-Fairfield-Napa PMSA, CA	Y	61290 FQ	109890 AW		CABLS	10/01-12/01
	Ventura PMSA, CA	Y	70440 FQ	121010 AW		CABLS	10/01-12/01
	Visalia-Tulare-Porterville MSA, CA	Y	80220 FQ	113360 AW		CABLS	10/01-12/01
	Colorado	Y	63990 FQ	116300 AW		COBLS	10/01-12/01
	Boulder-Longmont PMSA, CO	Y	81100 FQ	128260 AW		COBLS	10/01-12/01
	Colorado Springs MSA, CO	Y	60530 FQ	110570 AW		COBLS	10/01-12/01
	Denver PMSA, CO	Y	73650 FQ	123030 AW		COBLS	10/01-12/01
	Fort Collins-Loveland MSA, CO	Y	70630 FQ	119690 AW		COBLS	10/01-12/01
	Greeley PMSA, CO	Y	48070 FQ	89870 AW		COBLS	10/01-12/01
	Connecticut	Y	69720 FQ	123130 AW		CTBLS	10/01-12/01
	Bridgeport PMSA, CT	Y	56380 FQ	112860 AW		CTBLS	10/01-12/01
	Danbury PMSA, CT	Y	49390 FQ	103460 AW		CTBLS	10/01-12/01
	Hartford MSA, CT	Y	85510 FQ	128930 AW		CTBLS	10/01-12/01
	New Haven-Meriden PMSA, CT	Y	88230 FQ	122930 AW		CTBLS	10/01-12/01
	New London-Norwich MSA, CT-RI	Y	40040 FQ	114690 AW		CTBLS	10/01-12/01
	Stamford-Norwalk PMSA, CT	Y	77180 FQ	128650 AW		CTBLS	10/01-12/01
	Waterbury PMSA, CT	Y	81280 FQ	131040 AW		CTBLS	10/01-12/01
	Delaware	Y	31740 FQ	101060 AW		DEBLS	10/01-12/01
	Wilmington-Newark PMSA, DE-MD	Y	32660 FQ	103500 AW		DEBLS	10/01-12/01
	District of Columbia	Y	36370 FQ	98030 AW		DCBLS	10/01-12/01
	Washington PMSA, DC-MD-VA-WV	Y	49730 FQ	109110 AW		DCBLS	10/01-12/01
	Florida	Y	53630 FQ	111230 AW		FLBLS	10/01-12/01
	Daytona Beach MSA, FL	Y	41130 FQ	103610 AW		FLBLS	10/01-12/01
	Fort Lauderdale PMSA, FL	Y	64050 FQ	117780 AW		FLBLS	10/01-12/01
	Fort Myers-Cape Coral MSA, FL	Y	45720 FQ	110980 AW		FLBLS	10/01-12/01
	Fort Pierce-Port St. Lucie MSA, FL	Y	41150 FQ	89750 AW		FLBLS	10/01-12/01
	Fort Walton Beach MSA, FL	Y	59360 FQ	102270 AW		FLBLS	10/01-12/01
	Gainesville MSA, FL	Y	47330 FQ	106890 AW		FLBLS	10/01-12/01
	Jacksonville MSA, FL	Y	35040 FQ	106460 AW		FLBLS	10/01-12/01
	Lakeland-Winter Haven MSA, FL	Y	42810 FQ	101800 AW		FLBLS	10/01-12/01
	Melbourne-Titusville-Palm Bay MSA, FL	Y	47150 FQ	100890 AW		FLBLS	10/01-12/01
	Miami PMSA, FL	Y	75510 FQ	122950 AW		FLBLS	10/01-12/01
	Naples MSA, FL	Y	33480 FQ	92110 AW		FLBLS	10/01-12/01
	Ocala MSA, FL	Y	27050 FQ	94880 AW		FLBLS	10/01-12/01
	Orlando MSA, FL	Y	54070 FQ	113610 AW		FLBLS	10/01-12/01
	Pensacola MSA, FL	Y	57140 FQ	113050 AW		FLBLS	10/01-12/01
	Sarasota-Bradenton MSA, FL	Y	58600 FQ	106160 AW		FLBLS	10/01-12/01
	Tallahassee MSA, FL	Y	55620 FQ	111770 AW		FLBLS	10/01-12/01
	Tampa-St. Petersburg-Clearwater MSA, FL	Y	53940 FQ	108650 AW		FLBLS	10/01-12/01
	West Palm Beach-Boca Raton MSA, FL	Y	58530 FQ	113830 AW		FLBLS	10/01-12/01
	Georgia	Y	56040 FQ	113410 AW		GABLS	10/01-12/01
	Atlanta MSA, GA	Y	71830 FQ	121640 AW		GABLS	10/01-12/01
	Augusta-Aiken MSA, GA-SC	Y	37900 FQ	86120 AW		GABLS	10/01-12/01
	Columbus MSA, GA-AL	Y	39320 FQ	96640 AW		GABLS	10/01-12/01
	Macon MSA, GA	Y	42540 FQ	91550 AW		GABLS	10/01-12/01
	Savannah MSA, GA	Y	41290 FQ	86880 AW		GABLS	10/01-12/01
	Hawaii	Y	67240 FQ	114490 AW		HIBLS	10/01-12/01
	Honolulu MSA, HI	Y	70920 FQ	117470 AW		HIBLS	10/01-12/01
	Idaho	Y	31410 FQ	82300 AW		IDBLS	10/01-12/01
	Boise City MSA, ID	Y	47120 FQ	98980 AW		IDBLS	10/01-12/01
	Illinois	Y	47110 FQ	102400 AW		ILBLS	10/01-12/01
	Champaign-Urbana MSA, IL	Y	41480 FQ	90120 AW		ILBLS	10/01-12/01
	Chicago PMSA, IL	Y	54620 FQ	109640 AW		ILBLS	10/01-12/01
	Peoria-Pekin MSA, IL	Y	22800 FQ	79040 AW		ILBLS	10/01-12/01
	Rockford MSA, IL	Y	22610 FQ	85550 AW		ILBLS	10/01-12/01
	Springfield MSA, IL	Y	26090 FQ	78630 AW		ILBLS	10/01-12/01
	Indiana	Y	52060 FQ	110740 AW		INBLS	10/01-12/01
	Elkhart-Goshen MSA, IN	Y	40370 FQ	107780 AW		INBLS	10/01-12/01

AAW	Average annual wage	**AOH**	Average offered, high	**ASH**	Average starting, high	**H**	Hourly	**M**	Monthly	**S**	Special: hourly and annual
AE	Average entry wage	**AOL**	Average offered, low	**ASL**	Average starting, low	**HI**	Highest wage paid	**MTC**	Median total compensation	**TQ**	Third quartile wage
AEX	Average experienced wage	**APH**	Average pay, high range	**AW**	Average wage paid	**HR**	High end range	**MW**	Median wage paid	**W**	Weekly
AO	Average offered	**APL**	Average pay, low range	**FQ**	First quartile wage	**LR**	Low end range	**SQ**	Second quartile wage	**Y**	Yearly

Occupation/Type/Industry	Location	Per	Low	Mid	High	Source	Date
Chief Executive	Evansville-Henderson MSA, IN-KY	Y	46260 FQ	105390 AW		INBLS	10/01-12/01
	Fort Wayne MSA, IN	Y	55220 FQ	109690 AW		INBLS	10/01-12/01
	Gary PMSA, IN	Y	54390 FQ	110380 AW		INBLS	10/01-12/01
	Indianapolis MSA, IN	Y	76490 FQ	123360 AW		INBLS	10/01-12/01
	Lafayette MSA, IN	Y	60120 FQ	116550 AW		INBLS	10/01-12/01
	South Bend MSA, IN	Y	43990 FQ	105840 AW		INBLS	10/01-12/01
	Iowa	Y	29990 FQ	91700 AW		IABLS	10/01-12/01
	Cedar Rapids MSA, IA	Y	23040 FQ	89390 AW		IABLS	10/01-12/01
	Davenport-Moline-Rock Island MSA, IA-IL	Y	27570 FQ	84230 AW		IABLS	10/01-12/01
	Des Moines MSA, IA	Y	44610 FQ	104580 AW		IABLS	10/01-12/01
	Kansas	Y	54610 FQ	105140 AW		KSBLS	10/01-12/01
	Topeka MSA, KS	Y	51060 FQ	97440 AW		KSBLS	10/01-12/01
	Wichita MSA, KS	Y	59410 FQ	107590 AW		KSBLS	10/01-12/01
	Kentucky	Y	52130 FQ	103090 AW		KYBLS	10/01-12/01
	Lexington MSA, KY	Y	64570 FQ	110750 AW		KYBLS	10/01-12/01
	Louisville MSA, KY-IN	Y	59110 FQ	110870 AW		KYBLS	10/01-12/01
	Louisiana	Y	33190 FQ	90320 AW		LABLS	10/01-12/01
	Baton Rouge MSA, LA	Y	50470 FQ	101390 AW		LABLS	10/01-12/01
	Houma MSA, LA	Y	15760 FQ	84670 AW		LABLS	10/01-12/01
	Lafayette MSA, LA	Y	35010 FQ	90460 AW		LABLS	10/01-12/01
	Lake Charles MSA, LA	Y	39290 FQ	75490 AW		LABLS	10/01-12/01
	New Orleans MSA, LA	Y	42990 FQ	97330 AW		LABLS	10/01-12/01
	Shreveport-Bossier City MSA, LA	Y	29450 FQ	66440 AW		LABLS	10/01-12/01
	Maine	Y	49290 FQ	96480 AW		MEBLS	10/01-12/01
	Portland MSA, ME	Y	58700 FQ	105910 AW		MEBLS	10/01-12/01
	Maryland	Y	53470 FQ	113100 AW		MDBLS	10/01-12/01
	Baltimore PMSA, MD	Y	48090 FQ	112340 AW		MDBLS	10/01-12/01
	Massachusetts	Y	64260 FQ	118990 AW		MABLS	10/01-12/01
	Boston PMSA, MA-NH	Y	75760 FQ	125140 AW		MABLS	10/01-12/01
	Brockton PMSA, MA	Y	50960 FQ	105140 AW		MABLS	10/01-12/01
	Lawrence PMSA, MA-NH	Y	73590 FQ	121700 AW		MABLS	10/01-12/01
	Lowell PMSA, MA-NH	Y	64620 FQ	119030 AW		MABLS	10/01-12/01
	New Bedford PMSA, MA	Y	47640 FQ	99130 AW		MABLS	10/01-12/01
	Springfield MSA, MA	Y	61310 FQ	107200 AW		MABLS	10/01-12/01
	Worcester PMSA, MA-CT	Y	57370 FQ	113710 AW		MABLS	10/01-12/01
	Michigan	Y	69390 FQ	119000 AW		MIBLS	10/01-12/01
	Ann Arbor PMSA, MI	Y	67530 FQ	118830 AW		MIBLS	10/01-12/01
	Detroit PMSA, MI	Y	84840 FQ	126750 AW		MIBLS	10/01-12/01
	Flint PMSA, MI	Y	61650 FQ	110510 AW		MIBLS	10/01-12/01
	Grand Rapids-Muskegon-Holland MSA, MI	Y	66980 FQ	118330 AW		MIBLS	10/01-12/01
	Kalamazoo-Battle Creek MSA, MI	Y	62300 FQ	111000 AW		MIBLS	10/01-12/01
	Lansing-East Lansing MSA, MI	Y	66560 FQ	115800 AW		MIBLS	10/01-12/01
	Saginaw-Bay City-Midland MSA, MI	Y	54580 FQ	105310 AW		MIBLS	10/01-12/01
	Minnesota	Y	72510 FQ	120460 AW		MNBLS	10/01-12/01
	Duluth-Superior MSA, MN-WI	Y	51560 FQ	98980 AW		MNBLS	10/01-12/01
	Minneapolis-St. Paul MSA, MN-WI	Y	82690 FQ	126920 AW		MNBLS	10/01-12/01
	St. Cloud MSA, MN	Y	27170 FQ	94640 AW		MNBLS	10/01-12/01
	Mississippi	Y	37030 FQ	88460 AW		MSBLS	10/01-12/01
	Biloxi-Gulfport-Pascagoula MSA, MS	Y	43660 FQ	95210 AW		MSBLS	10/01-12/01
	Jackson MSA, MS	Y	46780 FQ	90560 AW		MSBLS	10/01-12/01
	Missouri	Y	34650 FQ	98490 AW		MOBLS	10/01-12/01
	Kansas City MSA, MO-KS	Y	54690 FQ	110650 AW		MOBLS	10/01-12/01
	St. Louis MSA, MO-IL	Y	48970 FQ	104090 AW		MOBLS	10/01-12/01
	Springfield MSA, MO	Y	42110 FQ	93300 AW		MOBLS	10/01-12/01
	Montana	Y	36300 FQ	83380 AW		MTBLS	10/01-12/01
	Billings MSA, MT	Y	39710 FQ	85080 AW		MTBLS	10/01-12/01
	Nebraska	Y	24940 FQ	79400 AW		NEBLS	10/01-12/01
	Lincoln MSA, NE	Y	30590 FQ	85950 AW		NEBLS	10/01-12/01
	Omaha MSA, NE-IA	Y	33600 FQ	91080 AW		NEBLS	10/01-12/01
	Nevada	Y	57310 FQ	115370 AW		NVBLS	10/01-12/01
	Las Vegas MSA, NV-AZ	Y	59430 FQ	116750 AW		NVBLS	10/01-12/01
	Reno MSA, NV	Y	44590 FQ	110020 AW		NVBLS	10/01-12/01
	New Hampshire	Y	44620 FQ	102180 AW		NHBLS	10/01-12/01
	Manchester PMSA, NH	Y	50170 FQ	105310 AW		NHBLS	10/01-12/01

AAW	Average annual wage	**AOH**	Average offered, high	**ASH**	Average starting, high	**H**	Hourly	**M**	Monthly	**S**	Special: hourly and annual
AE	Average entry wage	**AOL**	Average offered, low	**ASL**	Average starting, low	**HI**	Highest wage paid	**MTC**	Median total compensation	**TQ**	Third quartile wage
AEX	Average experienced wage	**APH**	Average pay, high range	**AW**	Average wage paid	**HR**	High end range	**MW**	Median wage paid	**W**	Weekly
AO	Average offered	**APL**	Average pay, low range	**FQ**	First quartile wage	**LR**	Low end range	**SQ**	Second quartile wage	**Y**	Yearly

Occupation/Type/Industry	Location	Per	Low	Mid	High	Source	Date
Chief Executive	Nashua PMSA, NH	Y	54190 FQ	110020 AW		NHBLS	10/01-12/01
	Portsmouth-Rochester PMSA, NH-ME	Y	50310 FQ	103280 AW		NHBLS	10/01-12/01
	New Jersey	Y	84100 FQ	128300 AW		NJBLS	10/01-12/01
	Atlantic-Cape May PMSA, NJ	Y	64950 FQ	118840 AW		NJBLS	10/01-12/01
	Bergen-Passaic PMSA, NJ	Y	91980 FQ	131980 AW		NJBLS	10/01-12/01
	Jersey City PMSA, NJ	Y	100300 FQ	130540 AW		NJBLS	10/01-12/01
	Middlesex-Somerset-Hunterdon PMSA, NJ	Y	71670 FQ	126680 AW		NJBLS	10/01-12/01
	Monmouth-Ocean PMSA, NJ	Y	83180 FQ	128330 AW		NJBLS	10/01-12/01
	Newark PMSA, NJ	Y	79300 FQ	128320 AW		NJBLS	10/01-12/01
	Trenton PMSA, NJ	Y	89250 FQ	121010 AW		NJBLS	10/01-12/01
	New Mexico	Y	40880 FQ	97540 AW		NMBLS	10/01-12/01
	Albuquerque MSA, NM	Y	41810 FQ	108310 AW		NMBLS	10/01-12/01
	Las Cruces MSA, NM	Y	61080 FQ	105320 AW		NMBLS	10/01-12/01
	New York	Y	74900 FQ	123840 AW		NYBLS	10/01-12/01
	Albany-Schenectady-Troy MSA, NY	Y	51420 FQ	101110 AW		NYBLS	10/01-12/01
	Binghamton MSA, NY	Y	50050 FQ	101290 AW		NYBLS	10/01-12/01
	Buffalo-Niagara Falls MSA, NY	Y	57250 FQ	110440 AW		NYBLS	10/01-12/01
	Dutchess County PMSA, NY	Y	65120 FQ	108120 AW		NYBLS	10/01-12/01
	Nassau-Suffolk PMSA, NY	Y	73390 FQ	122510 AW		NYBLS	10/01-12/01
	New York PMSA, NY	Y	100910 FQ	133550 AW		NYBLS	10/01-12/01
	Newburgh PMSA, NY-PA	Y	39480 FQ	93040 AW		NYBLS	10/01-12/01
	Rochester MSA, NY	Y	63760 FQ	114240 AW		NYBLS	10/01-12/01
	Syracuse MSA, NY	Y	64060 FQ	112720 AW		NYBLS	10/01-12/01
	Utica-Rome MSA, NY	Y	27890 FQ	99210 AW		NYBLS	10/01-12/01
	North Carolina	Y	40960 FQ	106370 AW		NCBLS	10/01-12/01
	Asheville MSA, NC	Y	36680 FQ	100080 AW		NCBLS	10/01-12/01
	Charlotte-Gastonia-Rock Hill MSA, NC-SC	Y	56250 FQ	112770 AW		NCBLS	10/01-12/01
	Fayetteville MSA, NC	Y	42760 FQ	100610 AW		NCBLS	10/01-12/01
	Greensboro-Winston-Salem-High Point MSA, NC	Y	34940 FQ	110150 AW		NCBLS	10/01-12/01
	Hickory-Morganton-Lenoir MSA, NC	Y	23060 FQ	105540 AW		NCBLS	10/01-12/01
	Raleigh-Durham-Chapel Hill MSA, NC	Y	31990 FQ	105600 AW		NCBLS	10/01-12/01
	Wilmington MSA, NC	Y	32840 FQ	98320 AW		NCBLS	10/01-12/01
	North Dakota	Y	27120 FQ	87940 AW		NDBLS	10/01-12/01
	Fargo-Moorhead MSA, ND-MN	Y	50880 FQ	103140 AW		NDBLS	10/01-12/01
	Ohio	Y	56210 FQ	108920 AW		OHBLS	10/01-12/01
	Akron PMSA, OH	Y	59940 FQ	110000 AW		OHBLS	10/01-12/01
	Canton-Massillon MSA, OH	Y	35840 FQ	97690 AW		OHBLS	10/01-12/01
	Cincinnati PMSA, OH-KY-IN	Y	57560 FQ	111460 AW		OHBLS	10/01-12/01
	Cleveland-Lorain-Elyria PMSA, OH	Y	59510 FQ	115740 AW		OHBLS	10/01-12/01
	Columbus MSA, OH	Y	61700 FQ	113140 AW		OHBLS	10/01-12/01
	Dayton-Springfield MSA, OH	Y	62460 FQ	110020 AW		OHBLS	10/01-12/01
	Hamilton-Middletown PMSA, OH	Y	57790 FQ	101310 AW		OHBLS	10/01-12/01
	Mansfield MSA, OH	Y	45550 FQ	89080 AW		OHBLS	10/01-12/01
	Toledo MSA, OH	Y	51680 FQ	106620 AW		OHBLS	10/01-12/01
	Youngstown-Warren MSA, OH	Y	34530 FQ	98610 AW		OHBLS	10/01-12/01
	Oklahoma	Y	31050 FQ	82770 AW		OKBLS	10/01-12/01
	Oklahoma City MSA, OK	Y	29850 FQ	80560 AW		OKBLS	10/01-12/01
	Tulsa MSA, OK	Y	40920 FQ	97080 AW		OKBLS	10/01-12/01
	Oregon	Y	72240 FQ	117250 AW		ORBLS	10/01-12/01
	Eugene-Springfield MSA, OR	Y	76650 FQ	112020 AW		ORBLS	10/01-12/01
	Medford-Ashland MSA, OR	Y	58680 FQ	111850 AW		ORBLS	10/01-12/01
	Portland-Vancouver PMSA, OR-WA	Y	77210 FQ	124750 AW		ORBLS	10/01-12/01
	Salem PMSA, OR	Y	77430 FQ	108630 AW		ORBLS	10/01-12/01
	Pennsylvania	Y	40880 FQ	100820 AW		PABLS	10/01-12/01
	Allentown-Bethlehem-Easton MSA, PA	Y	40050 FQ	97140 AW		PABLS	10/01-12/01
	Erie MSA, PA	Y	31900 FQ	88450 AW		PABLS	10/01-12/01
	Harrisburg-Lebanon-Carlisle MSA, PA	Y	53380 FQ	102820 AW		PABLS	10/01-12/01
	Johnstown MSA, PA	Y	43440 FQ	85520 AW		PABLS	10/01-12/01

AAW	Average annual wage	**AOH**	Average offered, high	**ASH**	Average starting, high	**H**	Hourly	**M**	Monthly	**S**	Special: hourly and annual
AE	Average entry wage	**AOL**	Average offered, low	**ASL**	Average starting, low	**HI**	Highest wage paid	**MTC**	Median total compensation	**TQ**	Third quartile wage
AEX	Average experienced wage	**APH**	Average pay, high range	**AW**	Average wage paid	**HR**	High end range	**MW**	Median wage paid	**W**	Weekly
AO	Average offered	**APL**	Average pay, low range	**FQ**	First quartile wage	**LR**	Low end range	**SQ**	Second quartile wage	**Y**	Yearly

Occupation/Type/Industry	Location	Per	Low	Mid	High	Source	Date
Chief Executive	Lancaster MSA, PA	Y	37800 FQ	93590 AW		PABLS	10/01-12/01
	Philadelphia PMSA, PA-NJ	Y	52400 FQ	109770 AW		PABLS	10/01-12/01
	Pittsburgh MSA, PA	Y	32730 FQ	100880 AW		PABLS	10/01-12/01
	Reading MSA, PA	Y	36900 FQ	98780 AW		PABLS	10/01-12/01
	Scranton-Wilkes-Barre-Hazleton MSA, PA	Y	31700 FQ	85530 AW		PABLS	10/01-12/01
	York MSA, PA	Y	40340 FQ	102770 AW		PABLS	10/01-12/01
	Rhode Island	Y	90770 FQ	130240 AW		RIBLS	10/01-12/01
	Providence-Fall River-Warwick MSA, RI-MA	Y	62400 FQ	119740 AW		RIBLS	10/01-12/01
	South Carolina	Y	36730 FQ	90180 AW		SCBLS	10/01-12/01
	Charleston-North Charleston MSA, SC	Y	36170 FQ	90520 AW		SCBLS	10/01-12/01
	Columbia MSA, SC	Y	50170 FQ	98770 AW		SCBLS	10/01-12/01
	Greenville-Spartanburg-Anderson MSA, SC	Y	40990 FQ	92510 AW		SCBLS	10/01-12/01
	Myrtle Beach MSA, SC	Y	31190 FQ	77930 AW		SCBLS	10/01-12/01
	South Dakota	Y	27190 FQ	81860 AW		SDBLS	10/01-12/01
	Sioux Falls MSA, SD	Y	64910 FQ	115310 AW		SDBLS	10/01-12/01
	Tennessee	Y	46090 FQ	103810 AW		TNBLS	10/01-12/01
	Chattanooga MSA, TN-GA	Y	47740 FQ	97540 AW		TNBLS	10/01-12/01
	Clarksville-Hopkinsville MSA, TN-KY	Y	30740 FQ	87380 AW		TNBLS	10/01-12/01
	Johnson City-Kingsport-Bristol MSA, TN-VA	Y	37150 FQ	87600 AW		TNBLS	10/01-12/01
	Knoxville MSA, TN	Y	47570 FQ	104600 AW		TNBLS	10/01-12/01
	Memphis MSA, TN-AR-MS	Y	51390 FQ	108740 AW		TNBLS	10/01-12/01
	Nashville MSA, TN	Y	58790 FQ	113950 AW		TNBLS	10/01-12/01
	Texas	Y	39820 FQ	101510 AW		TXBLS	10/01-12/01
	Amarillo MSA, TX	Y	40490 FQ	91320 AW		TXBLS	10/01-12/01
	Austin-San Marcos MSA, TX	Y	46130 FQ	97840 AW		TXBLS	10/01-12/01
	Beaumont-Port Arthur MSA, TX	Y	24960 FQ	76590 AW		TXBLS	10/01-12/01
	Brazoria PMSA, TX	Y	37650 FQ	91810 AW		TXBLS	10/01-12/01
	Brownsville-Harlingen-San Benito MSA, TX	Y	34290 FQ	79960 AW		TXBLS	10/01-12/01
	Corpus Christi MSA, TX	Y	24630 FQ	80130 AW		TXBLS	10/01-12/01
	Dallas PMSA, TX	Y	56900 FQ	115400 AW		TXBLS	10/01-12/01
	El Paso MSA, TX	Y	32580 FQ	90040 AW		TXBLS	10/01-12/01
	Fort Worth-Arlington PMSA, TX	Y	42640 FQ	109580 AW		TXBLS	10/01-12/01
	Galveston-Texas City PMSA, TX	Y	29460 FQ	84420 AW		TXBLS	10/01-12/01
	Houston PMSA, TX	Y	47130 FQ	106650 AW		TXBLS	10/01-12/01
	Killeen-Temple MSA, TX	Y	28330 FQ	75860 AW		TXBLS	10/01-12/01
	Laredo MSA, TX	Y	32850 FQ	87420 AW		TXBLS	10/01-12/01
	Longview-Marshall MSA, TX	Y	36900 FQ	84560 AW		TXBLS	10/01-12/01
	Lubbock MSA, TX	Y	32840 FQ	84770 AW		TXBLS	10/01-12/01
	McAllen-Edinburg-Mission MSA, TX	Y	27180 FQ	80740 AW		TXBLS	10/01-12/01
	Odessa-Midland MSA, TX	Y	39380 FQ	85580 AW		TXBLS	10/01-12/01
	San Antonio MSA, TX	Y	34380 FQ	97590 AW		TXBLS	10/01-12/01
	Tyler MSA, TX	Y	43050 FQ	94330 AW		TXBLS	10/01-12/01
	Waco MSA, TX	Y	31270 FQ	90640 AW		TXBLS	10/01-12/01
	Utah	Y	40460 FQ	98820 AW		UTBLS	10/01-12/01
	Provo-Orem MSA, UT	Y	32980 FQ	97670 AW		UTBLS	10/01-12/01
	Salt Lake City-Ogden MSA, UT	Y	50290 FQ	105050 AW		UTBLS	10/01-12/01
	Vermont	Y	39590 FQ	103730 AW		VTBLS	10/01-12/01
	Burlington MSA, VT	Y	37500 FQ	100690 AW		VTBLS	10/01-12/01
	Virginia	Y	57890 FQ	110280 AW		VABLS	10/01-12/01
	Lynchburg MSA, VA	Y	50120 FQ	100930 AW		VABLS	10/01-12/01
	Norfolk-Virginia Beach-Newport News MSA, VA-NC	Y	45340 FQ	101040 AW		VABLS	10/01-12/01
	Richmond-Petersburg MSA, VA	Y	52880 FQ	110120 AW		VABLS	10/01-12/01
	Roanoke MSA, VA	Y	46410 FQ	92800 AW		VABLS	10/01-12/01
	Washington	Y	72980 FQ	122500 AW		WABLS	10/01-12/01
	Bremerton PMSA, WA	Y	77180 FQ	119910 AW		WABLS	10/01-12/01
	Olympia PMSA, WA	Y	57880 FQ	103470 AW		WABLS	10/01-12/01

AAW Average annual wage **AOH** Average offered, high **ASH** Average starting, high **H** Hourly **M** Monthly **S** Special: hourly and annual
AE Average entry wage **AOL** Average offered, low **ASL** Average starting, low **HI** Highest wage paid **MTC** Median total compensation **TQ** Third quartile wage
AEX Average experienced wage **APH** Average pay, high range **AW** Average wage paid **HR** High end range **MW** Median wage paid **W** Weekly
AO Average offered **APL** Average pay, low range **FQ** First quartile wage **LR** Low end range **SQ** Second quartile wage **Y** Yearly

Occupation/Type/Industry	Location	Per	Low	Mid	High	Source	Date
Chief Executive	Richland-Kennewick-Pasco MSA, WA	Y	76460 FQ	121770 AW		WABLS	10/01-12/01
	Seattle-Bellevue-Everett PMSA, WA	Y	78790 FQ	127850 AW		WABLS	10/01-12/01
	Spokane MSA, WA	Y	70410 FQ	120280 AW		WABLS	10/01-12/01
	Tacoma PMSA, WA	Y	72540 FQ	114480 AW		WABLS	10/01-12/01
	Yakima MSA, WA	Y	58520 FQ	103740 AW		WABLS	10/01-12/01
	West Virginia	Y	32960 FQ	77190 AW		WVBLS	10/01-12/01
	Charleston MSA, WV	Y	41120 FQ	82020 AW		WVBLS	10/01-12/01
	Huntington-Ashland MSA, WV-KY-OH	Y	38670 FQ	88850 AW		WVBLS	10/01-12/01
	Wisconsin	Y	49060 FQ	105790 AW		WIBLS	10/01-12/01
	Appleton-Oshkosh-Neenah MSA, WI	Y	40340 FQ	103880 AW		WIBLS	10/01-12/01
	Green Bay MSA, WI	Y	16580 FQ	103440 AW		WIBLS	10/01-12/01
	Madison MSA, WI	Y	64740 FQ	114360 AW		WIBLS	10/01-12/01
	Milwaukee-Waukesha PMSA, WI	Y	59190 FQ	113140 AW		WIBLS	10/01-12/01
	Racine PMSA, WI	Y	77550 FQ	114310 AW		WIBLS	10/01-12/01
	Wyoming	Y	23820 FQ	76590 AW		WYBLS	10/01-12/01
	Cheyenne MSA, WY	Y	35560 FQ	74840 AW	143820 TQ	WYBLS	10/01-12/01
	Puerto Rico	Y	45440 FQ	93280 AW		PRBLS	10/01-12/01
	Virgin Islands	Y	51270 FQ	83190 AW		VIBLS	10/01-12/01
	Guam	Y	23220 FQ	75110 AW		GUBLS	10/01-12/01
Chief Information Officer	United States	Y		122250-200750 AW		WW	1/00-1/01
E-Commerce	United States	Y		122900 AW		INFO4	1/01-1/02
Chief Information Officer/Vice President of Information Systems	United States	Y		140184 AW		INFO1	1/01-1/02
Chief Justice of the United States	United States	Y		192600 AW		SCJS	1/1/02
Chief of Police	United States	Y	97215 AE			SCJS	1/99-1/00
250,000 to 349,999 population	United States	Y	87989 AE			SCJS	1/99-1/00
350,000 to 499,999 population	United States	Y	89050 AE			SCJS	1/99-1/00
500,000 to 999,999 population	United States	Y	105488 AE			SCJS	1/99-1/00
1,000,000 or more population	United States	Y	105524 AE			SCJS	1/99-1/00
Chief Pilot	United States	Y		95500 AW		BCAVIA	1/01-1/01
Chief Technology Officer	United States	Y		72857 AW		ACC	1/99-1/00
	United States	Y		98750-152500 AW		WW	1/00-1/01
	United States	Y		143802 AW		INFO1	1/01-1/02
Advertising Agency	East	Y		94000 AW		ADAGE	1/00-1/01
Advertising Agency	Midwest	Y		68000 AW		ADAGE	1/00-1/01
Advertising Agency	South	Y		59000 AW		ADAGE	1/00-1/01
Advertising Agency	West	Y		80000 AW		ADAGE	1/00-1/01
County Government	United States	Y		73000 AW		ACC	1/99-1/00
Municipal Government	United States	Y		67857 AW		ACC	1/99-1/00
Child Care Worker	Alabama	H	5.61 FQ	7.14 AW	9.33 TQ	ALBLS	10/01-12/01
	Birmingham MSA, AL	H	5.63 FQ	7.02 AW	8.66 TQ	ALBLS	10/01-12/01
	Huntsville MSA, AL	H	5.74 FQ	7.07 AW	9.54 TQ	ALBLS	10/01-12/01
	Mobile MSA, AL	H	5.60 FQ	7.24 AW	9.46 TQ	ALBLS	10/01-12/01
	Montgomery MSA, AL	H	5.66 FQ	7.10 AW	8.72 TQ	ALBLS	10/01-12/01
	Alaska	H	6.55 FQ	9.13 AW	13.04 TQ	AKBLS	10/01-12/01
	Anchorage MSA, AK	H	6.41 FQ	8.95 AW	12.36 TQ	AKBLS	10/01-12/01
	Arizona	H	5.70 FQ	7.33 AW	9.58 TQ	AZBLS	10/01-12/01
	Phoenix-Mesa MSA, AZ	H	5.69 FQ	7.36 AW	9.64 TQ	AZBLS	10/01-12/01
	Tucson MSA, AZ	H	5.80 FQ	7.24 AW	8.89 TQ	AZBLS	10/01-12/01
	Arkansas	H	5.61 FQ	6.62 AW	8.24 TQ	ARBLS	10/01-12/01
	Fayetteville-Springdale-Rogers MSA, AR	H	5.65 FQ	6.64 AW	8.21 TQ	ARBLS	10/01-12/01
	Fort Smith MSA, AR-OK	H	5.68 FQ	6.70 AW	8.42 TQ	ARBLS	10/01-12/01
	Little Rock-North Little Rock MSA, AR	H	5.76 FQ	7.50 AW	8.79 TQ	ARBLS	10/01-12/01
	California	H	6.69 FQ	9.68 AW	13.65 TQ	CABLS	10/01-12/01
	Bakersfield MSA, CA	H	6.89 FQ	9.17 AW	11.52 TQ	CABLS	10/01-12/01
	Chico-Paradise MSA, CA	H	6.62 FQ	7.93 AW	9.95 TQ	CABLS	10/01-12/01

AAW Average annual wage; AE Average entry wage; AEX Average experienced wage; AO Average offered; AOH Average offered, high; AOL Average offered, low; APH Average pay, high range; APL Average pay, low range; ASH Average starting, high; ASL Average starting, low; AW Average wage paid; FQ First quartile wage; H Hourly; HI Highest wage paid; HR High end range; LR Low end range; M Monthly; MTC Median total compensation; MW Median wage paid; SQ Second quartile wage; S Special: hourly and annual; TQ Third quartile wage; W Weekly; Y Yearly

Occupation/Type/Industry	Location	Per	Low	Mid	High	Source	Date
Child Care Worker	Fresno MSA, CA	H	6.57 FQ	8.49 AW	10.83 TQ	CABLS	10/01-12/01
	Los Angeles-Long Beach PMSA, CA	H	6.70 FQ	9.69 AW	13.80 TQ	CABLS	10/01-12/01
	Modesto MSA, CA	H	6.71 FQ	8.76 AW	11.89 TQ	CABLS	10/01-12/01
	Oakland PMSA, CA	H	6.66 FQ	9.59 AW	13.96 TQ	CABLS	10/01-12/01
	Orange County PMSA, CA	H	6.48 FQ	9.30 AW	13.23 TQ	CABLS	10/01-12/01
	Redding MSA, CA	H	6.76 FQ	8.74 AW	12.43 TQ	CABLS	10/01-12/01
	Riverside-San Bernardino PMSA, CA	H	6.59 FQ	8.91 AW	12.43 TQ	CABLS	10/01-12/01
	Sacramento PMSA, CA	H	6.62 FQ	8.35 AW	10.73 TQ	CABLS	10/01-12/01
	Salinas MSA, CA	H	6.67 FQ	8.34 AW	10.66 TQ	CABLS	10/01-12/01
	San Diego MSA, CA	H	6.72 FQ	9.60 AW	13.34 TQ	CABLS	10/01-12/01
	San Francisco PMSA, CA	H	8.00 FQ	14.31 AW	20.27 TQ	CABLS	10/01-12/01
	San Jose PMSA, CA	H	7.13 FQ	10.80 AW	13.48 TQ	CABLS	10/01-12/01
	San Luis Obispo-Atascadero-Paso Robles MSA, CA	H	6.41 FQ	8.46 AW	12.30 TQ	CABLS	10/01-12/01
	Santa Barbara-Santa Maria-Lompoc MSA, CA	H	6.81 FQ	8.90 AW	10.83 TQ	CABLS	10/01-12/01
	Santa Cruz-Watsonville PMSA, CA	H	6.56 FQ	8.69 AW	11.35 TQ	CABLS	10/01-12/01
	Santa Rosa PMSA, CA	H	7.32 FQ	10.03 AW	13.02 TQ	CABLS	10/01-12/01
	Stockton-Lodi MSA, CA	H	6.71 FQ	8.82 AW	12.11 TQ	CABLS	10/01-12/01
	Vallejo-Fairfield-Napa PMSA, CA	H	6.85 FQ	11.30 AW	17.16 TQ	CABLS	10/01-12/01
	Ventura PMSA, CA	H	6.57 FQ	9.52 AW	13.48 TQ	CABLS	10/01-12/01
	Visalia-Tulare-Porterville MSA, CA	H	7.05 FQ	9.12 AW	12.19 TQ	CABLS	10/01-12/01
	Colorado	H	5.85 FQ	7.96 AW	10.67 TQ	COBLS	10/01-12/01
	Boulder-Longmont PMSA, CO	H	6.22 FQ	8.96 AW	11.50 TQ	COBLS	10/01-12/01
	Colorado Springs MSA, CO	H	5.79 FQ	7.19 AW	8.59 TQ	COBLS	10/01-12/01
	Denver PMSA, CO	H	5.97 FQ	8.12 AW	10.74 TQ	COBLS	10/01-12/01
	Fort Collins-Loveland MSA, CO	H	6.03 FQ	7.83 AW	10.04 TQ	COBLS	10/01-12/01
	Greeley PMSA, CO	H	5.72 FQ	7.86 AW	10.66 TQ	COBLS	10/01-12/01
	Connecticut	H	6.93 FQ	9.64 AW	13.43 TQ	CTBLS	10/01-12/01
	Bridgeport PMSA, CT	H	7.12 FQ	9.66 AW	13.41 TQ	CTBLS	10/01-12/01
	Danbury PMSA, CT	H	6.50 FQ	7.91 AW	10.22 TQ	CTBLS	10/01-12/01
	Hartford MSA, CT	H	7.12 FQ	9.91 AW	14.02 TQ	CTBLS	10/01-12/01
	New Haven-Meriden PMSA, CT	H	7.05 FQ	9.71 AW	13.18 TQ	CTBLS	10/01-12/01
	New London-Norwich MSA, CT-RI	H	6.87 FQ	9.08 AW	12.49 TQ	CTBLS	10/01-12/01
	Stamford-Norwalk PMSA, CT	H	7.57 FQ	10.25 AW	13.62 TQ	CTBLS	10/01-12/01
	Waterbury PMSA, CT	H	6.82 FQ	8.71 AW	11.36 TQ	CTBLS	10/01-12/01
	Delaware	H	6.52 FQ	8.04 AW	10.16 TQ	DEBLS	10/01-12/01
	Wilmington-Newark PMSA, DE-MD	H	6.62 FQ	8.35 AW	10.54 TQ	DEBLS	10/01-12/01
	District of Columbia	H	6.85 FQ	8.94 AW	11.85 TQ	DCBLS	10/01-12/01
	Washington PMSA, DC-MD-VA-WV	H	6.24 FQ	9.41 AW	14.05 TQ	DCBLS	10/01-12/01
	Florida	H	5.61 FQ	7.20 AW	9.45 TQ	FLBLS	10/01-12/01
	Daytona Beach MSA, FL	H	6.02 FQ	7.74 AW	9.73 TQ	FLBLS	10/01-12/01
	Fort Lauderdale PMSA, FL	H	6.42 FQ	7.67 AW	8.67 TQ	FLBLS	10/01-12/01
	Fort Myers-Cape Coral MSA, FL	H	5.76 FQ	7.68 AW	10.25 TQ	FLBLS	10/01-12/01
	Fort Pierce-Port St. Lucie MSA, FL	H	5.83 FQ	7.24 AW	8.52 TQ	FLBLS	10/01-12/01
	Fort Walton Beach MSA, FL	H	5.55 FQ	6.77 AW	8.54 TQ	FLBLS	10/01-12/01
	Gainesville MSA, FL	H	5.60 FQ	7.71 AW	10.97 TQ	FLBLS	10/01-12/01
	Jacksonville MSA, FL	H	5.59 FQ	7.25 AW	9.66 TQ	FLBLS	10/01-12/01
	Lakeland-Winter Haven MSA, FL	H	5.61 FQ	7.33 AW	10.05 TQ	FLBLS	10/01-12/01
	Melbourne-Titusville-Palm Bay MSA, FL	H	5.46 FQ	7.16 AW	9.10 TQ	FLBLS	10/01-12/01
	Miami PMSA, FL	H	5.53 FQ	6.59 AW	8.60 TQ	FLBLS	10/01-12/01
	Naples MSA, FL	H	5.67 FQ	7.78 AW	10.43 TQ	FLBLS	10/01-12/01
	Ocala MSA, FL	H	6.02 FQ	8.17 AW	10.61 TQ	FLBLS	10/01-12/01
	Orlando MSA, FL	H	5.58 FQ	7.31 AW	9.98 TQ	FLBLS	10/01-12/01
	Pensacola MSA, FL	H	5.57 FQ	6.44 AW	7.93 TQ	FLBLS	10/01-12/01
	Sarasota-Bradenton MSA, FL	H	5.86 FQ	7.75 AW	10.36 TQ	FLBLS	10/01-12/01
	Tallahassee MSA, FL	H	5.54 FQ	6.89 AW	8.62 TQ	FLBLS	10/01-12/01

AAW	Average annual wage	AOH	Average offered, high	ASH	Average starting, high	H	Hourly	M	Monthly	S	Special: hourly and annual
AE	Average entry wage	AOL	Average offered, low	ASL	Average starting, low	HI	Highest wage paid	MTC	Median total compensation	TQ	Third quartile wage
AEX	Average experienced wage	APH	Average pay, high range	AW	Average wage paid	HR	High end range	MW	Median wage paid	W	Weekly
AO	Average offered	APL	Average pay, low range	FQ	First quartile wage	LR	Low end range	SQ	Second quartile wage	Y	Yearly

Occupation/Type/Industry	Location	Per	Low	Mid	High	Source	Date
Child Care Worker	Tampa-St. Petersburg-Clearwater MSA, FL	H	5.53 FQ	7.44 AW	10.12 TQ	FLBLS	10/01-12/01
	West Palm Beach-Boca Raton MSA, FL	H	5.92 FQ	7.60 AW	9.63 TQ	FLBLS	10/01-12/01
	Georgia	H	5.62 FQ	7.18 AW	8.95 TQ	GABLS	10/01-12/01
	Atlanta MSA, GA	H	5.82 FQ	7.67 AW	9.76 TQ	GABLS	10/01-12/01
	Augusta-Aiken MSA, GA-SC	H	5.58 FQ	6.70 AW	8.46 TQ	GABLS	10/01-12/01
	Columbus MSA, GA-AL	H	5.48 FQ	6.60 AW	8.16 TQ	GABLS	10/01-12/01
	Macon MSA, GA	H	5.64 FQ	6.98 AW	9.00 TQ	GABLS	10/01-12/01
	Savannah MSA, GA	H	5.71 FQ	7.07 AW	9.52 TQ	GABLS	10/01-12/01
	Hawaii	H	5.68 FQ	7.30 AW	9.88 TQ	HIBLS	10/01-12/01
	Honolulu MSA, HI	H	5.67 FQ	7.35 AW	10.11 TQ	HIBLS	10/01-12/01
	Idaho	H	5.72 FQ	7.53 AW	9.72 TQ	IDBLS	10/01-12/01
	Boise City MSA, ID	H	6.11 FQ	7.97 AW	10.05 TQ	IDBLS	10/01-12/01
	Illinois	H	5.97 FQ	8.53 AW	11.40 TQ	ILBLS	10/01-12/01
	Champaign-Urbana MSA, IL	H	5.68 FQ	8.76 AW	17.67 TQ	ILBLS	10/01-12/01
	Chicago PMSA, IL	H	6.09 FQ	8.73 AW	11.66 TQ	ILBLS	10/01-12/01
	Peoria-Pekin MSA, IL	H	5.98 FQ	8.10 AW	10.35 TQ	ILBLS	10/01-12/01
	Rockford MSA, IL	H	5.60 FQ	7.05 AW	9.81 TQ	ILBLS	10/01-12/01
	Springfield MSA, IL	H	6.64 FQ	8.76 AW	11.82 TQ	ILBLS	10/01-12/01
	Indiana	H	5.83 FQ	7.89 AW	10.65 TQ	INBLS	10/01-12/01
	Elkhart-Goshen MSA, IN	H	6.94 FQ	9.19 AW	12.28 TQ	INBLS	10/01-12/01
	Evansville-Henderson MSA, IN-KY	H	5.74 FQ	7.59 AW	10.85 TQ	INBLS	10/01-12/01
	Fort Wayne MSA, IN	H	6.13 FQ	8.34 AW	11.22 TQ	INBLS	10/01-12/01
	Gary PMSA, IN	H	5.53 FQ	7.26 AW	10.97 TQ	INBLS	10/01-12/01
	Indianapolis MSA, IN	H	5.97 FQ	8.22 AW	10.71 TQ	INBLS	10/01-12/01
	Lafayette MSA, IN	H	5.95 FQ	8.58 AW	11.74 TQ	INBLS	10/01-12/01
	South Bend MSA, IN	H	5.63 FQ	8.22 AW	11.46 TQ	INBLS	10/01-12/01
	Iowa	H	5.61 FQ	6.95 AW	9.00 TQ	IABLS	10/01-12/01
	Cedar Rapids MSA, IA	H	5.98 FQ	8.41 AW	11.06 TQ	IABLS	10/01-12/01
	Davenport-Moline-Rock Island MSA, IA-IL	H	5.66 FQ	7.61 AW	10.58 TQ	IABLS	10/01-12/01
	Des Moines MSA, IA	H	6.00 FQ	7.91 AW	10.25 TQ	IABLS	10/01-12/01
	Kansas	H	5.85 FQ	7.48 AW	9.32 TQ	KSBLS	10/01-12/01
	Topeka MSA, KS	H	5.97 FQ	7.91 AW	10.04 TQ	KSBLS	10/01-12/01
	Wichita MSA, KS	H	5.80 FQ	7.15 AW	8.64 TQ	KSBLS	10/01-12/01
	Kentucky	H	5.72 FQ	7.33 AW	9.37 TQ	KYBLS	10/01-12/01
	Lexington MSA, KY	H	5.80 FQ	7.60 AW	10.03 TQ	KYBLS	10/01-12/01
	Louisville MSA, KY-IN	H	5.87 FQ	7.45 AW	9.05 TQ	KYBLS	10/01-12/01
	Louisiana	H	5.53 FQ	6.45 AW	8.11 TQ	LABLS	10/01-12/01
	Baton Rouge MSA, LA	H	5.57 FQ	6.60 AW	8.40 TQ	LABLS	10/01-12/01
	Houma MSA, LA	H	5.56 FQ	6.59 AW	8.28 TQ	LABLS	10/01-12/01
	Lafayette MSA, LA	H	5.52 FQ	6.27 AW	7.13 TQ	LABLS	10/01-12/01
	Lake Charles MSA, LA	H	5.53 FQ	6.78 AW	9.32 TQ	LABLS	10/01-12/01
	New Orleans MSA, LA	H	5.57 FQ	6.24 AW	6.99 TQ	LABLS	10/01-12/01
	Shreveport-Bossier City MSA, LA	H	5.53 FQ	6.50 AW	8.30 TQ	LABLS	10/01-12/01
	Maine	H	5.89 FQ	7.90 AW	10.41 TQ	MEBLS	10/01-12/01
	Portland MSA, ME	H	6.47 FQ	8.62 AW	11.03 TQ	MEBLS	10/01-12/01
	Maryland	H	6.17 FQ	9.35 AW	13.04 TQ	MDBLS	10/01-12/01
	Baltimore PMSA, MD	H	6.23 FQ	8.93 AW	11.34 TQ	MDBLS	10/01-12/01
	Massachusetts	H	7.12 FQ	9.88 AW	13.16 TQ	MABLS	10/01-12/01
	Boston PMSA, MA-NH	H	7.29 FQ	10.17 AW	13.36 TQ	MABLS	10/01-12/01
	Brockton PMSA, MA	H	6.97 FQ	8.15 AW	10.24 TQ	MABLS	10/01-12/01
	Lawrence PMSA, MA-NH	H	7.37 FQ	9.81 AW	12.94 TQ	MABLS	10/01-12/01
	Lowell PMSA, MA-NH	H	7.20 FQ	9.71 AW	12.75 TQ	MABLS	10/01-12/01
	New Bedford PMSA, MA	H	6.95 FQ	9.58 AW	13.05 TQ	MABLS	10/01-12/01
	Springfield MSA, MA	H	7.06 FQ	9.40 AW	12.40 TQ	MABLS	10/01-12/01
	Worcester PMSA, MA-CT	H	6.97 FQ	9.16 AW	12.49 TQ	MABLS	10/01-12/01
	Michigan	H	6.12 FQ	8.87 AW	12.29 TQ	MIBLS	10/01-12/01
	Ann Arbor PMSA, MI	H	6.05 FQ	8.59 AW	11.45 TQ	MIBLS	10/01-12/01
	Detroit PMSA, MI	H	6.81 FQ	9.41 AW	12.91 TQ	MIBLS	10/01-12/01
	Flint PMSA, MI	H	5.77 FQ	8.31 AW	11.05 TQ	MIBLS	10/01-12/01
	Grand Rapids-Muskegon-Holland MSA, MI	H	5.89 FQ	8.53 AW	12.26 TQ	MIBLS	10/01-12/01
	Kalamazoo-Battle Creek MSA, MI	H	6.45 FQ	8.49 AW	11.15 TQ	MIBLS	10/01-12/01
	Lansing-East Lansing MSA, MI	H	6.14 FQ	8.62 AW	11.75 TQ	MIBLS	10/01-12/01
	Saginaw-Bay City-Midland MSA, MI	H	5.49 FQ	7.11 AW	10.51 TQ	MIBLS	10/01-12/01
	Minnesota	H	5.86 FQ	8.31 AW	11.71 TQ	MNBLS	10/01-12/01

AAW	Average annual wage	**AOH**	Average offered, high	**ASH**	Average starting, high	**H**	Hourly	**M**	Monthly	**S**	Special: hourly and annual
AE	Average entry wage	**AOL**	Average offered, low	**ASL**	Average starting, low	**HI**	Highest wage paid	**MTC**	Median total compensation	**TQ**	Third quartile wage
AEX	Average experienced wage	**APH**	Average pay, high range	**AW**	Average wage paid	**HR**	High end range	**MW**	Median wage paid	**W**	Weekly
AO	Average offered	**APL**	Average pay, low range	**FQ**	First quartile wage	**LR**	Low end range	**SQ**	Second quartile wage	**Y**	Yearly

Occupation/Type/Industry	Location	Per	Low	Mid	High	Source	Date
Child Care Worker	Duluth-Superior MSA, MN-WI	H	5.72 FQ	7.77 AW	10.25 TQ	MNBLS	10/01-12/01
	Minneapolis-St. Paul MSA, MN-WI	H	5.95 FQ	8.57 AW	12.03 TQ	MNBLS	10/01-12/01
	St. Cloud MSA, MN	H	5.75 FQ	7.40 AW	10.17 TQ	MNBLS	10/01-12/01
	Mississippi	H	5.58 FQ	6.77 AW	8.71 TQ	MSBLS	10/01-12/01
	Biloxi-Gulfport-Pascagoula MSA, MS	H	5.75 FQ	7.11 AW	9.67 TQ	MSBLS	10/01-12/01
	Jackson MSA, MS	H	5.82 FQ	7.27 AW	8.94 TQ	MSBLS	10/01-12/01
	Missouri	H	5.74 FQ	7.79 AW	10.66 TQ	MOBLS	10/01-12/01
	Kansas City MSA, MO-KS	H	5.83 FQ	7.87 AW	10.52 TQ	MOBLS	10/01-12/01
	St. Louis MSA, MO-IL	H	5.90 FQ	8.16 AW	10.94 TQ	MOBLS	10/01-12/01
	Springfield MSA, MO	H	5.59 FQ	7.65 AW	11.40 TQ	MOBLS	10/01-12/01
	Montana	H	5.69 FQ	7.13 AW	9.16 TQ	MTBLS	10/01-12/01
	Billings MSA, MT	H	5.73 FQ	7.07 AW	8.99 TQ	MTBLS	10/01-12/01
	Nebraska	H	5.66 FQ	7.29 AW	9.91 TQ	NEBLS	10/01-12/01
	Lincoln MSA, NE	H	5.82 FQ	7.68 AW	10.21 TQ	NEBLS	10/01-12/01
	Omaha MSA, NE-IA	H	5.69 FQ	7.50 AW	10.18 TQ	NEBLS	10/01-12/01
	Nevada	H	5.82 FQ	8.20 AW	11.55 TQ	NVBLS	10/01-12/01
	Las Vegas MSA, NV-AZ	H	5.96 FQ	8.45 AW	11.88 TQ	NVBLS	10/01-12/01
	Reno MSA, NV	H	5.61 FQ	7.65 AW	10.53 TQ	NVBLS	10/01-12/01
	New Hampshire	H	6.16 FQ	8.34 AW	10.77 TQ	NHBLS	10/01-12/01
	Manchester PMSA, NH	H	5.66 FQ	7.50 AW	9.69 TQ	NHBLS	10/01-12/01
	Nashua PMSA, NH	H	6.78 FQ	8.68 AW	11.85 TQ	NHBLS	10/01-12/01
	Portsmouth-Rochester PMSA, NH-ME	H	6.50 FQ	8.66 AW	10.79 TQ	NHBLS	10/01-12/01
	New Jersey	H	5.87 FQ	8.27 AW	11.09 TQ	NJBLS	10/01-12/01
	Atlantic-Cape May PMSA, NJ	H	5.68 FQ	7.72 AW	10.37 TQ	NJBLS	10/01-12/01
	Bergen-Passaic PMSA, NJ	H	6.54 FQ	8.77 AW	11.55 TQ	NJBLS	10/01-12/01
	Jersey City PMSA, NJ	H	5.62 FQ	7.28 AW	9.49 TQ	NJBLS	10/01-12/01
	Middlesex-Somerset-Hunterdon PMSA, NJ	H	6.16 FQ	8.90 AW	11.25 TQ	NJBLS	10/01-12/01
	Monmouth-Ocean PMSA, NJ	H	5.76 FQ	8.21 AW	12.16 TQ	NJBLS	10/01-12/01
	Newark PMSA, NJ	H	5.94 FQ	8.38 AW	11.23 TQ	NJBLS	10/01-12/01
	Trenton PMSA, NJ	H	6.03 FQ	8.17 AW	10.74 TQ	NJBLS	10/01-12/01
	New Mexico	H	5.57 FQ	6.83 AW	9.32 TQ	NMBLS	10/01-12/01
	Albuquerque MSA, NM	H	5.58 FQ	6.74 AW	8.75 TQ	NMBLS	10/01-12/01
	Las Cruces MSA, NM	H	5.44 FQ	6.37 AW	8.02 TQ	NMBLS	10/01-12/01
	New York	H	6.32 FQ	9.37 AW	12.37 TQ	NYBLS	10/01-12/01
	Albany-Schenectady-Troy MSA, NY	H	6.48 FQ	9.69 AW	13.59 TQ	NYBLS	10/01-12/01
	Binghamton MSA, NY	H	5.87 FQ	7.83 AW	10.55 TQ	NYBLS	10/01-12/01
	Buffalo-Niagara Falls MSA, NY	H	5.77 FQ	8.37 AW	11.88 TQ	NYBLS	10/01-12/01
	Dutchess County PMSA, NY	H	5.96 FQ	8.75 AW	12.23 TQ	NYBLS	10/01-12/01
	Nassau-Suffolk PMSA, NY	H	6.58 FQ	9.36 AW	12.88 TQ	NYBLS	10/01-12/01
	New York PMSA, NY	H	7.47 FQ	10.01 AW	12.62 TQ	NYBLS	10/01-12/01
	Newburgh PMSA, NY-PA	H	6.14 FQ	8.35 AW	10.88 TQ	NYBLS	10/01-12/01
	Rochester MSA, NY	H	5.80 FQ	8.21 AW	10.96 TQ	NYBLS	10/01-12/01
	Syracuse MSA, NY	H	5.91 FQ	8.19 AW	10.71 TQ	NYBLS	10/01-12/01
	Utica-Rome MSA, NY	H	5.68 FQ	8.11 AW	12.85 TQ	NYBLS	10/01-12/01
	North Carolina	H	5.80 FQ	7.61 AW	9.96 TQ	NCBLS	10/01-12/01
	Asheville MSA, NC	H	6.10 FQ	7.86 AW	9.86 TQ	NCBLS	10/01-12/01
	Charlotte-Gastonia-Rock Hill MSA, NC-SC	H	5.77 FQ	7.43 AW	9.97 TQ	NCBLS	10/01-12/01
	Fayetteville MSA, NC	H	5.58 FQ	6.57 AW	8.08 TQ	NCBLS	10/01-12/01
	Greensboro-Winston-Salem-High Point MSA, NC	H	5.96 FQ	8.28 AW	10.96 TQ	NCBLS	10/01-12/01
	Hickory-Morganton-Lenoir MSA, NC	H	5.86 FQ	7.63 AW	10.44 TQ	NCBLS	10/01-12/01
	Raleigh-Durham-Chapel Hill MSA, NC	H	5.99 FQ	8.13 AW	10.29 TQ	NCBLS	10/01-12/01
	Wilmington MSA, NC	H	5.91 FQ	8.00 AW	10.25 TQ	NCBLS	10/01-12/01
	North Dakota	H	5.61 FQ	7.19 AW	10.04 TQ	NDBLS	10/01-12/01
	Fargo-Moorhead MSA, ND-MN	H	5.57 FQ	6.98 AW	9.40 TQ	NDBLS	10/01-12/01
	Ohio	H	5.87 FQ	8.25 AW	11.16 TQ	OHBLS	10/01-12/01
	Akron PMSA, OH	H	5.76 FQ	8.25 AW	12.30 TQ	OHBLS	10/01-12/01
	Canton-Massillon MSA, OH	H	5.68 FQ	7.25 AW	10.07 TQ	OHBLS	10/01-12/01
	Cincinnati PMSA, OH-KY-IN	H	5.98 FQ	8.53 AW	11.78 TQ	OHBLS	10/01-12/01
	Cleveland-Lorain-Elyria PMSA, OH	H	5.85 FQ	7.96 AW	10.57 TQ	OHBLS	10/01-12/01
	Columbus MSA, OH	H	6.14 FQ	8.60 AW	11.00 TQ	OHBLS	10/01-12/01

AAW	Average annual wage	AOH	Average offered, high	ASH	Average starting, high	H	Hourly	M	Monthly	S	Special: hourly and annual
AE	Average entry wage	AOL	Average offered, low	ASL	Average starting, low	HI	Highest wage paid	MTC	Median total compensation	TQ	Third quartile wage
AEX	Average experienced wage	APH	Average pay, high range	AW	Average wage paid	HR	High end range	MW	Median wage paid	W	Weekly
AO	Average offered	APL	Average pay, low range	FQ	First quartile wage	LR	Low end range	SQ	Second quartile wage	Y	Yearly

Occupation/Type/Industry	Location	Per	Low	Mid	High	Source	Date
Child Care Worker	Dayton-Springfield MSA, OH	H	6.00 FQ	8.31 AW	10.79 TQ	OHBLS	10/01-12/01
	Hamilton-Middletown PMSA, OH	H	5.95 FQ	8.22 AW	11.25 TQ	OHBLS	10/01-12/01
	Mansfield MSA, OH	H	5.60 FQ	7.13 AW	9.65 TQ	OHBLS	10/01-12/01
	Toledo MSA, OH	H	5.74 FQ	8.68 AW	12.55 TQ	OHBLS	10/01-12/01
	Youngstown-Warren MSA, OH	H	5.89 FQ	8.33 AW	11.04 TQ	OHBLS	10/01-12/01
	Oklahoma	H	5.59 FQ	6.70 AW	8.47 TQ	OKBLS	10/01-12/01
	Oklahoma City MSA, OK	H	5.63 FQ	6.63 AW	8.30 TQ	OKBLS	10/01-12/01
	Tulsa MSA, OK	H	5.57 FQ	6.80 AW	8.82 TQ	OKBLS	10/01-12/01
	Oregon	H	6.82 FQ	8.29 AW	10.73 TQ	ORBLS	10/01-12/01
	Eugene-Springfield MSA, OR	H	6.80 FQ	7.70 AW	9.11 TQ	ORBLS	10/01-12/01
	Medford-Ashland MSA, OR	H	6.88 FQ	8.64 AW	11.50 TQ	ORBLS	10/01-12/01
	Portland-Vancouver PMSA, OR-WA	H	6.88 FQ	8.36 AW	10.60 TQ	ORBLS	10/01-12/01
	Salem PMSA, OR	H	6.71 FQ	9.43 AW	13.22 TQ	ORBLS	10/01-12/01
	Pennsylvania	H	5.76 FQ	7.82 AW	10.70 TQ	PABLS	10/01-12/01
	Allentown-Bethlehem-Easton MSA, PA	H	5.72 FQ	7.28 AW	9.40 TQ	PABLS	10/01-12/01
	Erie MSA, PA	H	5.58 FQ	7.22 AW	9.95 TQ	PABLS	10/01-12/01
	Harrisburg-Lebanon-Carlisle MSA, PA	H	5.65 FQ	7.31 AW	9.32 TQ	PABLS	10/01-12/01
	Johnstown MSA, PA	H	5.72 FQ	6.74 AW	8.38 TQ	PABLS	10/01-12/01
	Lancaster MSA, PA	H	5.56 FQ	7.33 AW	10.25 TQ	PABLS	10/01-12/01
	Philadelphia PMSA, PA-NJ	H	5.93 FQ	8.11 AW	10.72 TQ	PABLS	10/01-12/01
	Pittsburgh MSA, PA	H	5.57 FQ	7.27 AW	10.17 TQ	PABLS	10/01-12/01
	Reading MSA, PA	H	5.84 FQ	8.09 AW	10.74 TQ	PABLS	10/01-12/01
	Scranton-Wilkes-Barre-Hazleton MSA, PA	H	5.82 FQ	7.63 AW	10.71 TQ	PABLS	10/01-12/01
	York MSA, PA	H	5.67 FQ	6.83 AW	8.44 TQ	PABLS	10/01-12/01
	Rhode Island	H	6.77 FQ	8.93 AW	11.69 TQ	RIBLS	10/01-12/01
	Providence-Fall River-Warwick MSA, RI-MA	H	6.79 FQ	8.89 AW	11.54 TQ	RIBLS	10/01-12/01
	South Carolina	H	5.61 FQ	6.93 AW	8.63 TQ	SCBLS	10/01-12/01
	Charleston-North Charleston MSA, SC	H	5.68 FQ	6.97 AW	9.46 TQ	SCBLS	10/01-12/01
	Columbia MSA, SC	H	5.65 FQ	7.04 AW	9.16 TQ	SCBLS	10/01-12/01
	Greenville-Spartanburg-Anderson MSA, SC	H	5.58 FQ	6.70 AW	8.37 TQ	SCBLS	10/01-12/01
	Myrtle Beach MSA, SC	H	5.79 FQ	7.06 AW	8.70 TQ	SCBLS	10/01-12/01
	South Dakota	H	5.69 FQ	7.29 AW	9.53 TQ	SDBLS	10/01-12/01
	Sioux Falls MSA, SD	H	5.90 FQ	7.79 AW	10.33 TQ	SDBLS	10/01-12/01
	Tennessee	H	5.53 FQ	6.98 AW	9.16 TQ	TNBLS	10/01-12/01
	Chattanooga MSA, TN-GA	H	5.41 FQ	6.33 AW	7.86 TQ	TNBLS	10/01-12/01
	Clarksville-Hopkinsville MSA, TN-KY	H	5.54 FQ	6.51 AW	8.31 TQ	TNBLS	10/01-12/01
	Johnson City-Kingsport-Bristol MSA, TN-VA	H	5.62 FQ	6.75 AW	8.38 TQ	TNBLS	10/01-12/01
	Knoxville MSA, TN	H	5.93 FQ	8.10 AW	10.55 TQ	TNBLS	10/01-12/01
	Memphis MSA, TN-AR-MS	H	5.44 FQ	6.54 AW	8.26 TQ	TNBLS	10/01-12/01
	Nashville MSA, TN	H	5.68 FQ	7.39 AW	9.83 TQ	TNBLS	10/01-12/01
	Texas	H	5.58 FQ	7.13 AW	9.91 TQ	TXBLS	10/01-12/01
	Amarillo MSA, TX	H	5.59 FQ	6.49 AW	7.74 TQ	TXBLS	10/01-12/01
	Austin-San Marcos MSA, TX	H	6.60 FQ	8.86 AW	10.69 TQ	TXBLS	10/01-12/01
	Beaumont-Port Arthur MSA, TX	H	5.37 FQ	6.00 AW	6.73 TQ	TXBLS	10/01-12/01
	Brazoria PMSA, TX	H	5.63 FQ	6.63 AW	8.13 TQ	TXBLS	10/01-12/01
	Brownsville-Harlingen-San Benito MSA, TX	H	5.66 FQ	6.85 AW	8.50 TQ	TXBLS	10/01-12/01
	Corpus Christi MSA, TX	H	5.76 FQ	7.10 AW	8.76 TQ	TXBLS	10/01-12/01
	Dallas PMSA, TX	H	5.61 FQ	7.44 AW	11.23 TQ	TXBLS	10/01-12/01
	El Paso MSA, TX	H	5.51 FQ	6.56 AW	8.32 TQ	TXBLS	10/01-12/01
	Fort Worth-Arlington PMSA, TX	H	5.55 FQ	7.30 AW	9.73 TQ	TXBLS	10/01-12/01
	Galveston-Texas City PMSA, TX	H	5.59 FQ	7.04 AW	10.07 TQ	TXBLS	10/01-12/01
	Houston PMSA, TX	H	5.58 FQ	6.76 AW	8.75 TQ	TXBLS	10/01-12/01
	Killeen-Temple MSA, TX	H	5.58 FQ	6.68 AW	8.85 TQ	TXBLS	10/01-12/01
	Laredo MSA, TX	H	5.75 FQ	7.62 AW	10.16 TQ	TXBLS	10/01-12/01
	Longview-Marshall MSA, TX	H	5.42 FQ	6.25 AW	7.72 TQ	TXBLS	10/01-12/01
	Lubbock MSA, TX	H	5.57 FQ	6.35 AW	7.31 TQ	TXBLS	10/01-12/01
	McAllen-Edinburg-Mission MSA, TX	H	5.53 FQ	6.40 AW	7.42 TQ	TXBLS	10/01-12/01

AAW	Average annual wage	AOH	Average offered, high	ASH	Average starting, high	H	Hourly	M	Monthly	S	Special: hourly and annual
AE	Average entry wage	AOL	Average offered, low	ASL	Average starting, low	HI	Highest wage paid	MTC	Median total compensation	TQ	Third quartile wage
AEX	Average experienced wage	APH	Average pay, high range	AW	Average wage paid	HR	High end range	MW	Median wage paid	W	Weekly
AO	Average offered	APL	Average pay, low range	FQ	First quartile wage	LR	Low end range	SQ	Second quartile wage	Y	Yearly

Occupation/Type/Industry	Location	Per	Low	Mid	High	Source	Date
Child Care Worker	Odessa-Midland MSA, TX	H	5.50 FQ	6.19 AW	7.05 TQ	TXBLS	10/01-12/01
	San Antonio MSA, TX	H	5.58 FQ	7.39 AW	10.08 TQ	TXBLS	10/01-12/01
	Tyler MSA, TX	H	5.63 FQ	6.96 AW	8.95 TQ	TXBLS	10/01-12/01
	Waco MSA, TX	H	5.66 FQ	7.17 AW	9.77 TQ	TXBLS	10/01-12/01
	Utah	H	5.64 FQ	7.55 AW	9.91 TQ	UTBLS	10/01-12/01
	Provo-Orem MSA, UT	H	5.71 FQ	7.26 AW	9.03 TQ	UTBLS	10/01-12/01
	Salt Lake City-Ogden MSA, UT	H	5.77 FQ	7.70 AW	9.48 TQ	UTBLS	10/01-12/01
	Vermont	H	6.50 FQ	8.12 AW	10.75 TQ	VTBLS	10/01-12/01
	Burlington MSA, VT	H	6.48 FQ	8.05 AW	10.62 TQ	VTBLS	10/01-12/01
	Virginia	H	5.77 FQ	8.00 AW	10.70 TQ	VABLS	10/01-12/01
	Lynchburg MSA, VA	H	5.70 FQ	7.47 AW	9.48 TQ	VABLS	10/01-12/01
	Norfolk-Virginia Beach-Newport News MSA, VA-NC	H	5.56 FQ	7.08 AW	8.89 TQ	VABLS	10/01-12/01
	Richmond-Petersburg MSA, VA	H	5.72 FQ	7.34 AW	10.03 TQ	VABLS	10/01-12/01
	Roanoke MSA, VA	H	5.59 FQ	7.32 AW	9.86 TQ	VABLS	10/01-12/01
	Washington	H	6.90 FQ	8.59 AW	11.07 TQ	WABLS	10/01-12/01
	Bremerton PMSA, WA	H	7.04 FQ	8.14 AW	9.10 TQ	WABLS	10/01-12/01
	Olympia PMSA, WA	H	7.01 FQ	8.34 AW	10.40 TQ	WABLS	10/01-12/01
	Richland-Kennewick-Pasco MSA, WA	H	6.74 FQ	7.71 AW	10.09 TQ	WABLS	10/01-12/01
	Seattle-Bellevue-Everett PMSA, WA	H	6.96 FQ	9.07 AW	12.27 TQ	WABLS	10/01-12/01
	Spokane MSA, WA	H	6.90 FQ	8.16 AW	10.41 TQ	WABLS	10/01-12/01
	Tacoma PMSA, WA	H	6.79 FQ	8.13 AW	10.42 TQ	WABLS	10/01-12/01
	Yakima MSA, WA	H	6.91 FQ	8.14 AW	10.24 TQ	WABLS	10/01-12/01
	West Virginia	H	5.63 FQ	6.82 AW	8.54 TQ	WVBLS	10/01-12/01
	Charleston MSA, WV	H	5.72 FQ	6.94 AW	8.52 TQ	WVBLS	10/01-12/01
	Huntington-Ashland MSA, WV-KY-OH	H	5.66 FQ	7.36 AW	9.81 TQ	WVBLS	10/01-12/01
	Wisconsin	H	5.93 FQ	8.09 AW	10.76 TQ	WIBLS	10/01-12/01
	Appleton-Oshkosh-Neenah MSA, WI	H	6.18 FQ	7.96 AW	10.01 TQ	WIBLS	10/01-12/01
	Green Bay MSA, WI	H	6.08 FQ	7.35 AW	8.52 TQ	WIBLS	10/01-12/01
	Madison MSA, WI	H	6.49 FQ	9.28 AW	11.54 TQ	WIBLS	10/01-12/01
	Milwaukee-Waukesha PMSA, WI	H	6.03 FQ	8.27 AW	11.38 TQ	WIBLS	10/01-12/01
	Racine PMSA, WI	H	6.76 FQ	9.31 AW	14.15 TQ	WIBLS	10/01-12/01
	Wyoming	H	5.58 FQ	7.28 AW	9.98 TQ	WYBLS	10/01-12/01
	Cheyenne MSA, WY	H	5.52 FQ	6.83 AW	9.13 TQ	WYBLS	10/01-12/01
	Puerto Rico	H	5.57 FQ	6.61 AW	8.19 TQ	PRBLS	10/01-12/01
	Virgin Islands	H	5.65 FQ	6.41 AW	7.78 TQ	VIBLS	10/01-12/01
	Guam	H	5.52 FQ	6.69 AW	8.44 TQ	GUBLS	10/01-12/01
Child, Family, and School Social Worker	Alabama	Y	18590 FQ	28970 AW	42870 TQ	ALBLS	10/01-12/01
	Birmingham MSA, AL	Y	20260 FQ	29250 AW	41260 TQ	ALBLS	10/01-12/01
	Huntsville MSA, AL	Y	18760 FQ	28380 AW	45310 TQ	ALBLS	10/01-12/01
	Mobile MSA, AL	Y	22680 FQ	33820 AW	43670 TQ	ALBLS	10/01-12/01
	Montgomery MSA, AL	Y	16910 FQ	33460 AW	52810 TQ	ALBLS	10/01-12/01
	Alaska	Y	24270 FQ	36850 AW	53230 TQ	AKBLS	10/01-12/01
	Arizona	Y	20000 FQ	31580 AW	46720 TQ	AZBLS	10/01-12/01
	Phoenix-Mesa MSA, AZ	Y	20540 FQ	32150 AW	47530 TQ	AZBLS	10/01-12/01
	Tucson MSA, AZ	Y	21250 FQ	32910 AW	50290 TQ	AZBLS	10/01-12/01
	Arkansas	Y	18520 FQ	28390 AW	41490 TQ	ARBLS	10/01-12/01
	Fayetteville-Springdale-Rogers MSA, AR	Y	15360 FQ	25200 AW	36480 TQ	ARBLS	10/01-12/01
	Fort Smith MSA, AR-OK	Y	22160 FQ	30420 AW	46240 TQ	ARBLS	10/01-12/01
	Little Rock-North Little Rock MSA, AR	Y	23430 FQ	32140 AW	45390 TQ	ARBLS	10/01-12/01
	California	Y	20190 FQ	37130 AW	53210 TQ	CABLS	10/01-12/01
	Bakersfield MSA, CA	Y	17930 FQ	32600 AW	48880 TQ	CABLS	10/01-12/01
	Chico-Paradise MSA, CA	Y	21750 FQ	31470 AW	47500 TQ	CABLS	10/01-12/01
	Fresno MSA, CA	Y	24320 FQ	40090 AW	48980 TQ	CABLS	10/01-12/01
	Los Angeles-Long Beach PMSA, CA	Y	21130 FQ	38050 AW	48150 TQ	CABLS	10/01-12/01
	Merced MSA, CA	Y	19940 FQ	30300 AW	41000 TQ	CABLS	10/01-12/01
	Modesto MSA, CA	Y	20690 FQ	36260 AW	51080 TQ	CABLS	10/01-12/01
	Oakland PMSA, CA	Y	16830 FQ	32000 AW	45460 TQ	CABLS	10/01-12/01
	Orange County PMSA, CA	Y	23870 FQ	38430 AW	53260 TQ	CABLS	10/01-12/01

AAW	Average annual wage	**AOH**	Average offered, high	**ASH**	Average starting, high	**H**	Hourly	**M**	Monthly	**S**	Special: hourly and annual
AE	Average entry wage	**AOL**	Average offered, low	**ASL**	Average starting, low	**HI**	Highest wage paid	**MTC**	Median total compensation	**TQ**	Third quartile wage
AEX	Average experienced wage	**APH**	Average pay, high range	**AW**	Average wage paid	**HR**	High end range	**MW**	Median wage paid	**W**	Weekly
AO	Average offered	**APL**	Average pay, low range	**FQ**	First quartile wage	**LR**	Low end range	**SQ**	Second quartile wage	**Y**	Yearly

Occupation/Type/Industry	Location	Per	Low	Mid	High	Source	Date
Child, Family, and School Social Worker	Redding MSA, CA	Y	26180 FQ	37670 AW	47560 TQ	CABLS	10/01-12/01
	Riverside-San Bernardino PMSA, CA	Y	15510 FQ	34840 AW	64490 TQ	CABLS	10/01-12/01
	Sacramento PMSA, CA	Y	24750 FQ	34680 AW	46220 TQ	CABLS	10/01-12/01
	Salinas MSA, CA	Y	14520 FQ	32620 AW	46680 TQ	CABLS	10/01-12/01
	San Diego MSA, CA	Y	16980 FQ	32320 AW	50170 TQ	CABLS	10/01-12/01
	San Francisco PMSA, CA	Y	21020 FQ	38190 AW	58850 TQ	CABLS	10/01-12/01
	San Jose PMSA, CA	Y	19010 FQ	34500 AW	46830 TQ	CABLS	10/01-12/01
	San Luis Obispo-Atascadero-Paso Robles MSA, CA	Y	21620 FQ	46000 AW	69320 TQ	CABLS	10/01-12/01
	Santa Barbara-Santa Maria-Lompoc MSA, CA	Y	27210 FQ	39080 AW	47280 TQ	CABLS	10/01-12/01
	Santa Cruz-Watsonville PMSA, CA	Y	26840 FQ	40650 AW	52540 TQ	CABLS	10/01-12/01
	Santa Rosa PMSA, CA	Y	20260 FQ	33160 AW	47690 TQ	CABLS	10/01-12/01
	Stockton-Lodi MSA, CA	Y	28150 FQ	46740 AW	67530 TQ	CABLS	10/01-12/01
	Vallejo-Fairfield-Napa PMSA, CA	Y	20690 FQ	41070 AW	58980 TQ	CABLS	10/01-12/01
	Ventura PMSA, CA	Y	26390 FQ	41270 AW	62910 TQ	CABLS	10/01-12/01
	Visalia-Tulare-Porterville MSA, CA	Y	16850 FQ	35450 AW	51060 TQ	CABLS	10/01-12/01
	Colorado	Y	24390 FQ	38580 AW	56100 TQ	COBLS	10/01-12/01
	Boulder-Longmont PMSA, CO	Y	19260 FQ	38100 AW	54640 TQ	COBLS	10/01-12/01
	Colorado Springs MSA, CO	Y	25350 FQ	38110 AW	54980 TQ	COBLS	10/01-12/01
	Denver PMSA, CO	Y	25900 FQ	41410 AW	60060 TQ	COBLS	10/01-12/01
	Greeley PMSA, CO	Y	24660 FQ	36000 AW	46400 TQ	COBLS	10/01-12/01
	Connecticut	Y	29340 FQ	47330 AW	67400 TQ	CTBLS	10/01-12/01
	Bridgeport PMSA, CT	Y	35410 FQ	48630 AW	66850 TQ	CTBLS	10/01-12/01
	Danbury PMSA, CT	Y	35600 FQ	47590 AW	66310 TQ	CTBLS	10/01-12/01
	New Haven-Meriden PMSA, CT	Y	30530 FQ	47860 AW	67630 TQ	CTBLS	10/01-12/01
	New London-Norwich MSA, CT-RI	Y	30280 FQ	48820 AW	68090 TQ	CTBLS	10/01-12/01
	Stamford-Norwalk PMSA, CT	Y	26450 FQ	43940 AW	68210 TQ	CTBLS	10/01-12/01
	Waterbury PMSA, CT	Y	23090 FQ	42680 AW	65310 TQ	CTBLS	10/01-12/01
	Delaware	Y	25470 FQ	35870 AW	51390 TQ	DEBLS	10/01-12/01
	District of Columbia	Y	28240 FQ	41360 AW	70090 TQ	DCBLS	10/01-12/01
	Washington PMSA, DC-MD-VA-WV	Y	26600 FQ	43610 AW	64830 TQ	DCBLS	10/01-12/01
	Florida	Y	21000 FQ	31350 AW	43700 TQ	FLBLS	10/01-12/01
	Daytona Beach MSA, FL	Y	20360 FQ	33760 AW	58270 TQ	FLBLS	10/01-12/01
	Fort Lauderdale PMSA, FL	Y	22570 FQ	32530 AW	44900 TQ	FLBLS	10/01-12/01
	Fort Myers-Cape Coral MSA, FL	Y	20780 FQ	27730 AW	34710 TQ	FLBLS	10/01-12/01
	Fort Pierce-Port St. Lucie MSA, FL	Y	18970 FQ	28920 AW	42100 TQ	FLBLS	10/01-12/01
	Fort Walton Beach MSA, FL	Y	22230 FQ	30670 AW	40470 TQ	FLBLS	10/01-12/01
	Gainesville MSA, FL	Y	20480 FQ	29770 AW	39760 TQ	FLBLS	10/01-12/01
	Jacksonville MSA, FL	Y	21410 FQ	31100 AW	43150 TQ	FLBLS	10/01-12/01
	Lakeland-Winter Haven MSA, FL	Y	19830 FQ	29950 AW	42880 TQ	FLBLS	10/01-12/01
	Melbourne-Titusville-Palm Bay MSA, FL	Y	19960 FQ	28340 AW	35750 TQ	FLBLS	10/01-12/01
	Miami PMSA, FL	Y	22120 FQ	32320 AW	43580 TQ	FLBLS	10/01-12/01
	Naples MSA, FL	Y	19570 FQ	32480 AW	44350 TQ	FLBLS	10/01-12/01
	Ocala MSA, FL	Y	20010 FQ	29040 AW	34870 TQ	FLBLS	10/01-12/01
	Orlando MSA, FL	Y	25140 FQ	34210 AW	45880 TQ	FLBLS	10/01-12/01
	Pensacola MSA, FL	Y	19920 FQ	27650 AW	35250 TQ	FLBLS	10/01-12/01
	Sarasota-Bradenton MSA, FL	Y	20480 FQ	27430 AW	35640 TQ	FLBLS	10/01-12/01
	Tallahassee MSA, FL	Y	23640 FQ	32640 AW	43190 TQ	FLBLS	10/01-12/01
	Tampa-St. Petersburg-Clearwater MSA, FL	Y	20350 FQ	31950 AW	48850 TQ	FLBLS	10/01-12/01
	West Palm Beach-Boca Raton MSA, FL	Y	20650 FQ	30480 AW	42510 TQ	FLBLS	10/01-12/01
	Georgia	Y	19520 FQ	32190 AW	47990 TQ	GABLS	10/01-12/01
	Atlanta MSA, GA	Y	22540 FQ	34550 AW	54660 TQ	GABLS	10/01-12/01
	Augusta-Aiken MSA, GA-SC	Y	18110 FQ	28420 AW	43520 TQ	GABLS	10/01-12/01
	Columbus MSA, GA-AL	Y	12150 FQ	26210 AW	41030 TQ	GABLS	10/01-12/01
	Macon MSA, GA	Y	25790 FQ	38180 AW	51760 TQ	GABLS	10/01-12/01
	Savannah MSA, GA	Y	23420 FQ	30910 AW	42860 TQ	GABLS	10/01-12/01
	Hawaii	Y	26920 FQ	41220 AW	56600 TQ	HIBLS	10/01-12/01

AAW	Average annual wage	**AOH**	Average offered, high	**ASH**	Average starting, high	**H**	Hourly	**M**	Monthly	**S**	Special: hourly and annual
AE	Average entry wage	**AOL**	Average offered, low	**ASL**	Average starting, low	**HI**	Highest wage paid	**MTC**	Median total compensation	**TQ**	Third quartile wage
AEX	Average experienced wage	**APH**	Average pay, high range	**AW**	Average wage paid	**HR**	High end range	**MW**	Median wage paid	**W**	Weekly
AO	Average offered	**APL**	Average pay, low range	**FQ**	First quartile wage	**LR**	Low end range	**SQ**	Second quartile wage	**Y**	Yearly

Occupation/Type/Industry	Location	Per	Low	Mid	High	Source	Date
Child, Family, and School Social Worker	Honolulu MSA, HI	Y	31320 FQ	44610 AW	60520 TQ	HIBLS	10/01-12/01
	Idaho	Y	20590 FQ	37410 AW	55920 TQ	IDBLS	10/01-12/01
	Boise City MSA, ID	Y	22290 FQ	42030 AW	56360 TQ	IDBLS	10/01-12/01
	Illinois	Y	21150 FQ	36730 AW	53450 TQ	ILBLS	10/01-12/01
	Chicago PMSA, IL	Y	21950 FQ	37950 AW	55160 TQ	ILBLS	10/01-12/01
	Peoria-Pekin MSA, IL	Y	19920 FQ	32890 AW	49730 TQ	ILBLS	10/01-12/01
	Rockford MSA, IL	Y	16740 FQ	36030 AW	51640 TQ	ILBLS	10/01-12/01
	Springfield MSA, IL	Y	21610 FQ	34710 AW	48870 TQ	ILBLS	10/01-12/01
	Indiana	Y	20010 FQ	29180 AW	39400 TQ	INBLS	10/01-12/01
	Elkhart-Goshen MSA, IN	Y	19410 FQ	26970 AW	35190 TQ	INBLS	10/01-12/01
	Evansville-Henderson MSA, IN-KY	Y	18620 FQ	28860 AW	40640 TQ	INBLS	10/01-12/01
	Fort Wayne MSA, IN	Y	21290 FQ	31570 AW	43730 TQ	INBLS	10/01-12/01
	Gary PMSA, IN	Y	20540 FQ	30480 AW	43080 TQ	INBLS	10/01-12/01
	Indianapolis MSA, IN	Y	20100 FQ	29520 AW	40150 TQ	INBLS	10/01-12/01
	Lafayette MSA, IN	Y	20420 FQ	27950 AW	35560 TQ	INBLS	10/01-12/01
	South Bend MSA, IN	Y	21700 FQ	31150 AW	43700 TQ	INBLS	10/01-12/01
	Iowa	Y	20480 FQ	34570 AW	46960 TQ	IABLS	10/01-12/01
	Cedar Rapids MSA, IA	Y	20140 FQ	30810 AW	43170 TQ	IABLS	10/01-12/01
	Davenport-Moline-Rock Island MSA, IA-IL	Y	16630 FQ	31980 AW	48830 TQ	IABLS	10/01-12/01
	Des Moines MSA, IA	Y	26960 FQ	38830 AW	51330 TQ	IABLS	10/01-12/01
	Kansas	Y	20240 FQ	29520 AW	42010 TQ	KSBLS	10/01-12/01
	Topeka MSA, KS	Y	19050 FQ	27930 AW	39730 TQ	KSBLS	10/01-12/01
	Wichita MSA, KS	Y	19770 FQ	28910 AW	38810 TQ	KSBLS	10/01-12/01
	Kentucky	Y	20150 FQ	31350 AW	44090 TQ	KYBLS	10/01-12/01
	Louisiana	Y	16870 FQ	31180 AW	47330 TQ	LABLS	10/01-12/01
	Baton Rouge MSA, LA	Y	12970 FQ	26610 AW	47960 TQ	LABLS	10/01-12/01
	Houma MSA, LA	Y	20050 FQ	31870 AW	45590 TQ	LABLS	10/01-12/01
	Lafayette MSA, LA	Y	17890 FQ	30260 AW	50310 TQ	LABLS	10/01-12/01
	Lake Charles MSA, LA	Y	21800 FQ	38380 AW	55480 TQ	LABLS	10/01-12/01
	New Orleans MSA, LA	Y	20460 FQ	33760 AW	46910 TQ	LABLS	10/01-12/01
	Shreveport-Bossier City MSA, LA	Y	18990 FQ	29000 AW	44800 TQ	LABLS	10/01-12/01
	Maine	Y	20920 FQ	32630 AW	47550 TQ	MEBLS	10/01-12/01
	Portland MSA, ME	Y	24240 FQ	35800 AW	52240 TQ	MEBLS	10/01-12/01
	Maryland	Y	21920 FQ	38090 AW	54020 TQ	MDBLS	10/01-12/01
	Baltimore PMSA, MD	Y	22680 FQ	38460 AW	52860 TQ	MDBLS	10/01-12/01
	Massachusetts	Y	20110 FQ	39210 AW	55500 TQ	MABLS	10/01-12/01
	Boston PMSA, MA-NH	Y	19360 FQ	38930 AW	55590 TQ	MABLS	10/01-12/01
	Springfield MSA, MA	Y	24030 FQ	40630 AW	55350 TQ	MABLS	10/01-12/01
	Worcester PMSA, MA-CT	Y	19270 FQ	37320 AW	54440 TQ	MABLS	10/01-12/01
	Michigan	Y	25140 FQ	39490 AW	55270 TQ	MIBLS	10/01-12/01
	Ann Arbor PMSA, MI	Y	28820 FQ	42560 AW	60030 TQ	MIBLS	10/01-12/01
	Detroit PMSA, MI	Y	26300 FQ	41250 AW	58710 TQ	MIBLS	10/01-12/01
	Grand Rapids-Muskegon-Holland MSA, MI	Y	22930 FQ	37360 AW	53580 TQ	MIBLS	10/01-12/01
	Kalamazoo-Battle Creek MSA, MI	Y	16830 FQ	35740 AW	51610 TQ	MIBLS	10/01-12/01
	Lansing-East Lansing MSA, MI	Y	32370 FQ	42820 AW	56620 TQ	MIBLS	10/01-12/01
	Saginaw-Bay City-Midland MSA, MI	Y	25140 FQ	37870 AW	51160 TQ	MIBLS	10/01-12/01
	Minnesota	Y	22050 FQ	37710 AW	57790 TQ	MNBLS	10/01-12/01
	Minneapolis-St. Paul MSA, MN-WI	Y	21490 FQ	38080 AW	59570 TQ	MNBLS	10/01-12/01
	Mississippi	Y	20460 FQ	28130 AW	37200 TQ	MSBLS	10/01-12/01
	Biloxi-Gulfport-Pascagoula MSA, MS	Y	18200 FQ	26750 AW	34660 TQ	MSBLS	10/01-12/01
	Jackson MSA, MS	Y	22440 FQ	30220 AW	41960 TQ	MSBLS	10/01-12/01
	Missouri	Y	18810 FQ	28910 AW	38070 TQ	MOBLS	10/01-12/01
	Kansas City MSA, MO-KS	Y	21140 FQ	32730 AW	55920 TQ	MOBLS	10/01-12/01
	St. Louis MSA, MO-IL	Y	18220 FQ	30950 AW	44610 TQ	MOBLS	10/01-12/01
	Springfield MSA, MO	Y	12580 FQ	27670 AW	46990 TQ	MOBLS	10/01-12/01
	Montana	Y	18770 FQ	27570 AW	40050 TQ	MTBLS	10/01-12/01
	Billings MSA, MT	Y	16520 FQ	28110 AW	47820 TQ	MTBLS	10/01-12/01
	Nebraska	Y	17180 FQ	27890 AW	39950 TQ	NEBLS	10/01-12/01
	Lincoln MSA, NE	Y	18440 FQ	30230 AW	42440 TQ	NEBLS	10/01-12/01
	Omaha MSA, NE-IA	Y	20810 FQ	30260 AW	41100 TQ	NEBLS	10/01-12/01
	Nevada	Y	24260 FQ	40200 AW	59730 TQ	NVBLS	10/01-12/01
	Las Vegas MSA, NV-AZ	Y	22060 FQ	40980 AW	65420 TQ	NVBLS	10/01-12/01
	Reno MSA, NV	Y	26160 FQ	36450 AW	51930 TQ	NVBLS	10/01-12/01

AAW	Average annual wage	**AOH**	Average offered, high	**ASH**	Average starting, high	**H**	Hourly	**M**	Monthly	**S**	Special: hourly and annual
AE	Average entry wage	**AOL**	Average offered, low	**ASL**	Average starting, low	**HI**	Highest wage paid	**MTC**	Median total compensation	**TQ**	Third quartile wage
AEX	Average experienced wage	**APH**	Average pay, high range	**AW**	Average wage paid	**HR**	High end range	**MW**	Median wage paid	**W**	Weekly
AO	Average offered	**APL**	Average pay, low range	**FQ**	First quartile wage	**LR**	Low end range	**SQ**	Second quartile wage	**Y**	Yearly

Occupation/Type/Industry	Location	Per	Low	Mid	High	Source	Date
Child, Family, and School Social Worker	New Hampshire	Y	17590 FQ	34830 AW	53740 TQ	NHBLS	10/01-12/01
	Manchester PMSA, NH	Y	21970 FQ	30420 AW	40880 TQ	NHBLS	10/01-12/01
	Nashua PMSA, NH	Y	24890 FQ	61920 AW	114840 TQ	NHBLS	10/01-12/01
	Portsmouth-Rochester PMSA, NH-ME	Y	15590 FQ	31000 AW	46820 TQ	NHBLS	10/01-12/01
	New Jersey	Y	25570 FQ	45830 AW	73270 TQ	NJBLS	10/01-12/01
	Atlantic-Cape May PMSA, NJ	Y	24550 FQ	40160 AW	66970 TQ	NJBLS	10/01-12/01
	Bergen-Passaic PMSA, NJ	Y	26560 FQ	50630 AW	80150 TQ	NJBLS	10/01-12/01
	Jersey City PMSA, NJ	Y	27960 FQ	43430 AW	77840 TQ	NJBLS	10/01-12/01
	Middlesex-Somerset-Hunterdon PMSA, NJ	Y	29830 FQ	48300 AW	69130 TQ	NJBLS	10/01-12/01
	Monmouth-Ocean PMSA, NJ	Y	28740 FQ	47790 AW	77580 TQ	NJBLS	10/01-12/01
	Newark PMSA, NJ	Y	23060 FQ	43520 AW	71780 TQ	NJBLS	10/01-12/01
	Trenton PMSA, NJ	Y	25320 FQ	43840 AW	65140 TQ	NJBLS	10/01-12/01
	New Mexico	Y	19610 FQ	29760 AW	42550 TQ	NMBLS	10/01-12/01
	Albuquerque MSA, NM	Y	21200 FQ	31710 AW	44470 TQ	NMBLS	10/01-12/01
	Las Cruces MSA, NM	Y	19750 FQ	28480 AW	40040 TQ	NMBLS	10/01-12/01
	New York	Y	24550 FQ	41510 AW	72440 TQ	NYBLS	10/01-12/01
	Albany-Schenectady-Troy MSA, NY	Y	21470 FQ	38040 AW	59530 TQ	NYBLS	10/01-12/01
	Binghamton MSA, NY	Y	23920 FQ	36570 AW	44610 TQ	NYBLS	10/01-12/01
	Buffalo-Niagara Falls MSA, NY	Y	22390 FQ	32820 AW	47250 TQ	NYBLS	10/01-12/01
	Dutchess County PMSA, NY	Y	28440 FQ	42130 AW	58980 TQ	NYBLS	10/01-12/01
	Nassau-Suffolk PMSA, NY	Y	23940 FQ	42560 AW	71050 TQ	NYBLS	10/01-12/01
	New York PMSA, NY	Y	26700 FQ	45110 AW	83760 TQ	NYBLS	10/01-12/01
	Newburgh PMSA, NY-PA	Y	20710 FQ	38700 AW	62080 TQ	NYBLS	10/01-12/01
	Rochester MSA, NY	Y	21750 FQ	34470 AW	53550 TQ	NYBLS	10/01-12/01
	Syracuse MSA, NY	Y	21960 FQ	36670 AW	52440 TQ	NYBLS	10/01-12/01
	Utica-Rome MSA, NY	Y	17570 FQ	34370 AW	69630 TQ	NYBLS	10/01-12/01
	North Carolina	Y	24090 FQ	33460 AW	44900 TQ	NCBLS	10/01-12/01
	Asheville MSA, NC	Y	25140 FQ	31940 AW	38160 TQ	NCBLS	10/01-12/01
	Charlotte-Gastonia-Rock Hill MSA, NC-SC	Y	24790 FQ	35350 AW	48490 TQ	NCBLS	10/01-12/01
	Greensboro-Winston-Salem-High Point MSA, NC	Y	24430 FQ	35260 AW	47250 TQ	NCBLS	10/01-12/01
	Hickory-Morganton-Lenoir MSA, NC	Y	25480 FQ	34090 AW	44690 TQ	NCBLS	10/01-12/01
	Raleigh-Durham-Chapel Hill MSA, NC	Y	28360 FQ	37040 AW	48050 TQ	NCBLS	10/01-12/01
	Wilmington MSA, NC	Y	20080 FQ	32080 AW	43580 TQ	NCBLS	10/01-12/01
	North Dakota	Y	21630 FQ	31500 AW	42870 TQ	NDBLS	10/01-12/01
	Fargo-Moorhead MSA, ND-MN	Y	25770 FQ	35550 AW	47910 TQ	NDBLS	10/01-12/01
	Ohio	Y	19950 FQ	31970 AW	47560 TQ	OHBLS	10/01-12/01
	Akron PMSA, OH	Y	18800 FQ	30750 AW	49210 TQ	OHBLS	10/01-12/01
	Canton-Massillon MSA, OH	Y	19830 FQ	30720 AW	44410 TQ	OHBLS	10/01-12/01
	Cincinnati PMSA, OH-KY-IN	Y	20830 FQ	31160 AW	42410 TQ	OHBLS	10/01-12/01
	Cleveland-Lorain-Elyria PMSA, OH	Y	14750 FQ	31450 AW	49710 TQ	OHBLS	10/01-12/01
	Columbus MSA, OH	Y	22150 FQ	34570 AW	56740 TQ	OHBLS	10/01-12/01
	Dayton-Springfield MSA, OH	Y	21060 FQ	29340 AW	39110 TQ	OHBLS	10/01-12/01
	Hamilton-Middletown PMSA, OH	Y	17500 FQ	26690 AW	35310 TQ	OHBLS	10/01-12/01
	Toledo MSA, OH	Y	24450 FQ	37420 AW	53100 TQ	OHBLS	10/01-12/01
	Youngstown-Warren MSA, OH	Y	18860 FQ	28530 AW	40760 TQ	OHBLS	10/01-12/01
	Oklahoma	Y	20420 FQ	28340 AW	34950 TQ	OKBLS	10/01-12/01
	Oregon	Y	21210 FQ	33880 AW	45860 TQ	ORBLS	10/01-12/01
	Eugene-Springfield MSA, OR	Y	18910 FQ	32400 AW	50050 TQ	ORBLS	10/01-12/01
	Medford-Ashland MSA, OR	Y	22640 FQ	34660 AW	46170 TQ	ORBLS	10/01-12/01
	Portland-Vancouver PMSA, OR-WA	Y	23110 FQ	34540 AW	46850 TQ	ORBLS	10/01-12/01
	Pennsylvania	Y	20320 FQ	32870 AW	50480 TQ	PABLS	10/01-12/01
	Allentown-Bethlehem-Easton MSA, PA	Y	20390 FQ	38910 AW	62410 TQ	PABLS	10/01-12/01
	Erie MSA, PA	Y	21800 FQ	40770 AW	67410 TQ	PABLS	10/01-12/01
	Harrisburg-Lebanon-Carlisle MSA, PA	Y	20860 FQ	31260 AW	44940 TQ	PABLS	10/01-12/01
	Lancaster MSA, PA	Y	21140 FQ	32420 AW	51120 TQ	PABLS	10/01-12/01
	Philadelphia PMSA, PA-NJ	Y	24880 FQ	39410 AW	63700 TQ	PABLS	10/01-12/01
	Pittsburgh MSA, PA	Y	19850 FQ	29410 AW	43800 TQ	PABLS	10/01-12/01

AAW	Average annual wage	**AOH**	Average offered, high	**ASH**	Average starting, high	**H**	Hourly	**M**	Monthly	**S**	Special: hourly and annual
AE	Average entry wage	**AOL**	Average offered, low	**ASL**	Average starting, low	**HI**	Highest wage paid	**MTC**	Median total compensation	**TQ**	Third quartile wage
AEX	Average experienced wage	**APH**	Average pay, high range	**AW**	Average wage paid	**HR**	High end range	**MW**	Median wage paid	**W**	Weekly
AO	Average offered	**APL**	Average pay, low range	**FQ**	First quartile wage	**LR**	Low end range	**SQ**	Second quartile wage	**Y**	Yearly

Occupation/Type/Industry	Location	Per	Low	Mid	High	Source	Date
Choreographer	Indiana	Y	12620 FQ	25740 AW	41830 TQ	INBLS	10/01-12/01
	Iowa	Y	11830 FQ	20580 AW	38420 TQ	IABLS	10/01-12/01
	Kansas	Y	12270 FQ	27410 AW	50970 TQ	KSBLS	10/01-12/01
	Kentucky	Y	13340 FQ	25770 AW	46790 TQ	KYBLS	10/01-12/01
	Louisiana	Y	12560 FQ	31250 AW	57540 TQ	LABLS	10/01-12/01
	Maryland	Y	12250 FQ	25550 AW	40680 TQ	MDBLS	10/01-12/01
	Massachusetts	Y	24180 FQ	36800 AW	57220 TQ	MABLS	10/01-12/01
	Michigan	Y	13190 FQ	22420 AW	41160 TQ	MIBLS	10/01-12/01
	Minnesota	Y	15550 FQ	34850 AW	60430 TQ	MNBLS	10/01-12/01
	Mississippi	Y	12640 FQ	19160 AW	26940 TQ	MSBLS	10/01-12/01
	Missouri	Y	11980 FQ	26610 AW	51870 TQ	MOBLS	10/01-12/01
	Nebraska	Y	20020 FQ	29390 AW	47210 TQ	NEBLS	10/01-12/01
	Nevada	Y	12300 FQ	37520 AW	59200 TQ	NVBLS	10/01-12/01
	New Jersey	Y	23650 FQ	41410 AW	71230 TQ	NJBLS	10/01-12/01
	New Mexico	Y	12510 FQ	29340 AW	54940 TQ	NMBLS	10/01-12/01
	New York	Y	14830 FQ	44380 AW	91820 TQ	NYBLS	10/01-12/01
	North Carolina	Y	13580 FQ	32180 AW	54830 TQ	NCBLS	10/01-12/01
	Ohio	Y	15220 FQ	37660 AW	66000 TQ	OHBLS	10/01-12/01
	Oklahoma	Y	12780 FQ	23820 AW	36730 TQ	OKBLS	10/01-12/01
	Oregon	Y	18200 FQ	36010 AW	52630 TQ	ORBLS	10/01-12/01
	Pennsylvania	Y	12680 FQ	28980 AW	67810 TQ	PABLS	10/01-12/01
	South Carolina	Y	13450 FQ	28830 AW	46370 TQ	SCBLS	10/01-12/01
	South Dakota	Y	14720 FQ	19560 AW	27570 TQ	SDBLS	10/01-12/01
	Tennessee	Y	26480 FQ	69650 AW	95030 TQ	TNBLS	10/01-12/01
	Texas	Y	13040 FQ	31980 AW	53850 TQ	TXBLS	10/01-12/01
	Utah	Y	19820 FQ	30830 AW	47920 TQ	UTBLS	10/01-12/01
	Vermont	Y	24320 FQ	53830 AW	87440 TQ	VTBLS	10/01-12/01
	Virginia	Y	20260 FQ	43690 AW	70390 TQ	VABLS	10/01-12/01
	Washington	Y	25260 FQ	46400 AW	79360 TQ	WABLS	10/01-12/01
	West Virginia	Y	16190 FQ	25940 AW	39130 TQ	WVBLS	10/01-12/01
	Wisconsin	Y	16310 FQ	41310 AW	86630 TQ	WIBLS	10/01-12/01
Civil Engineer	United States	Y		76940 AW		STLOUPD1	1/01-1/02
	Alabama	Y	33320 FQ	56000 AW	86530 TQ	ALBLS	10/01-12/01
	Birmingham MSA, AL	Y	31500 FQ	55200 AW	88530 TQ	ALBLS	10/01-12/01
	Huntsville MSA, AL	Y	36090 FQ	57960 AW	86970 TQ	ALBLS	10/01-12/01
	Mobile MSA, AL	Y	38160 FQ	61050 AW	92370 TQ	ALBLS	10/01-12/01
	Montgomery MSA, AL	Y	30960 FQ	52290 AW	84340 TQ	ALBLS	10/01-12/01
	Alaska	Y	42370 FQ	68890 AW	100030 TQ	AKBLS	10/01-12/01
	Anchorage MSA, AK	Y	42840 FQ	71090 AW	105100 TQ	AKBLS	10/01-12/01
	Arizona	Y	34320 FQ	52170 AW	81380 TQ	AZBLS	10/01-12/01
	Phoenix-Mesa MSA, AZ	Y	32590 FQ	52760 AW	84550 TQ	AZBLS	10/01-12/01
	Arkansas	Y	34650 FQ	56040 AW	81420 TQ	ARBLS	10/01-12/01
	Fayetteville-Springdale-Rogers MSA, AR	Y	20770 FQ	40840 AW	67240 TQ	ARBLS	10/01-12/01
	Fort Smith MSA, AR-OK	Y	32340 FQ	51690 AW	72860 TQ	ARBLS	10/01-12/01
	Little Rock-North Little Rock MSA, AR	Y	40440 FQ	57380 AW	79780 TQ	ARBLS	10/01-12/01
	California	Y	46050 FQ	66470 AW	93350 TQ	CABLS	10/01-12/01
	Bakersfield MSA, CA	Y	44980 FQ	67460 AW	91590 TQ	CABLS	10/01-12/01
	Chico-Paradise MSA, CA	Y	42750 FQ	58270 AW	77880 TQ	CABLS	10/01-12/01
	Fresno MSA, CA	Y	45150 FQ	60290 AW	83370 TQ	CABLS	10/01-12/01
	Los Angeles-Long Beach PMSA, CA	Y	45430 FQ	63820 AW	88760 TQ	CABLS	10/01-12/01
	Modesto MSA, CA	Y	41070 FQ	60530 AW	83790 TQ	CABLS	10/01-12/01
	Oakland PMSA, CA	Y	47900 FQ	69390 AW	97610 TQ	CABLS	10/01-12/01
	Orange County PMSA, CA	Y	42830 FQ	70100 AW	103110 TQ	CABLS	10/01-12/01
	Redding MSA, CA	Y	44920 FQ	61360 AW	81140 TQ	CABLS	10/01-12/01
	Riverside-San Bernardino PMSA, CA	Y	46860 FQ	65190 AW	90420 TQ	CABLS	10/01-12/01
	Sacramento PMSA, CA	Y	47290 FQ	65620 AW	87420 TQ	CABLS	10/01-12/01
	Salinas MSA, CA	Y	50010 FQ	67000 AW	88740 TQ	CABLS	10/01-12/01
	San Diego MSA, CA	Y	46830 FQ	65420 AW	88930 TQ	CABLS	10/01-12/01
	San Francisco PMSA, CA	Y	48170 FQ	71560 AW	105830 TQ	CABLS	10/01-12/01
	San Jose PMSA, CA	Y	40450 FQ	65640 AW	99480 TQ	CABLS	10/01-12/01
	San Luis Obispo-Atascadero-Paso Robles MSA, CA	Y	41910 FQ	60260 AW	83760 TQ	CABLS	10/01-12/01
	Santa Barbara-Santa Maria-Lompoc MSA, CA	Y	47620 FQ	70470 AW	97690 TQ	CABLS	10/01-12/01
	Santa Cruz-Watsonville PMSA, CA	Y	49310 FQ	69750 AW	93860 TQ	CABLS	10/01-12/01
	Santa Rosa PMSA, CA	Y	48420 FQ	68170 AW	93480 TQ	CABLS	10/01-12/01
	Stockton-Lodi MSA, CA	Y	45560 FQ	61740 AW	83090 TQ	CABLS	10/01-12/01

AAW	Average annual wage	**AOH**	Average offered, high	**ASH**	Average starting, high	**H**	Hourly	**M**	Monthly	**S**	Special: hourly and annual
AE	Average entry wage	**AOL**	Average offered, low	**ASL**	Average starting, low	**HI**	Highest wage paid	**MTC**	Median total compensation	**TQ**	Third quartile wage
AEX	Average experienced wage	**APH**	Average pay, high range	**AW**	Average wage paid	**HR**	High end range	**MW**	Median wage paid	**W**	Weekly
AO	Average offered	**APL**	Average pay, low range	**FQ**	First quartile wage	**LR**	Low end range	**SQ**	Second quartile wage	**Y**	Yearly

Occupation/Type/Industry	Location	Per	Low	Mid	High	Source	Date
Civil Engineer	Vallejo-Fairfield-Napa PMSA, CA	Y	46390 FQ	73310 AW	107120 TQ	CABLS	10/01-12/01
	Ventura PMSA, CA	Y	47300 FQ	70870 AW	123250 TQ	CABLS	10/01-12/01
	Visalia-Tulare-Porterville MSA, CA	Y	40170 FQ	56150 AW	78120 TQ	CABLS	10/01-12/01
	Colorado	Y	39310 FQ	59410 AW	87950 TQ	COBLS	10/01-12/01
	Boulder-Longmont PMSA, CO	Y	38520 FQ	54460 AW	81560 TQ	COBLS	10/01-12/01
	Colorado Springs MSA, CO	Y	34950 FQ	56990 AW	88320 TQ	COBLS	10/01-12/01
	Denver PMSA, CO	Y	40120 FQ	60550 AW	89070 TQ	COBLS	10/01-12/01
	Fort Collins-Loveland MSA, CO	Y	38520 FQ	54220 AW	77900 TQ	COBLS	10/01-12/01
	Greeley PMSA, CO	Y	40210 FQ	60030 AW	87470 TQ	COBLS	10/01-12/01
	Connecticut	Y	39960 FQ	59830 AW	85480 TQ	CTBLS	10/01-12/01
	Bridgeport PMSA, CT	Y	38310 FQ	61310 AW	98310 TQ	CTBLS	10/01-12/01
	Danbury PMSA, CT	Y	44470 FQ	67860 AW	94410 TQ	CTBLS	10/01-12/01
	Hartford MSA, CT	Y	40240 FQ	60010 AW	84240 TQ	CTBLS	10/01-12/01
	New Haven-Meriden PMSA, CT	Y	39260 FQ	57520 AW	84010 TQ	CTBLS	10/01-12/01
	New London-Norwich MSA, CT-RI	Y	41080 FQ	58690 AW	77490 TQ	CTBLS	10/01-12/01
	Stamford-Norwalk PMSA, CT	Y	49230 FQ	68030 AW	104940 TQ	CTBLS	10/01-12/01
	Delaware	Y	33880 FQ	55600 AW	82710 TQ	DEBLS	10/01-12/01
	Wilmington-Newark PMSA, DE-MD	Y	33750 FQ	56980 AW	85600 TQ	DEBLS	10/01-12/01
	District of Columbia	Y	44020 FQ	70330 AW	101950 TQ	DCBLS	10/01-12/01
	Washington PMSA, DC-MD-VA-WV	Y	40690 FQ	64920 AW	91170 TQ	DCBLS	10/01-12/01
	Florida	Y	38870 FQ	62370 AW	90770 TQ	FLBLS	10/01-12/01
	Daytona Beach MSA, FL	Y	41980 FQ	60960 AW	92040 TQ	FLBLS	10/01-12/01
	Fort Lauderdale PMSA, FL	Y	40100 FQ	70840 AW	113370 TQ	FLBLS	10/01-12/01
	Fort Myers-Cape Coral MSA, FL	Y	40580 FQ	67030 AW	96560 TQ	FLBLS	10/01-12/01
	Fort Pierce-Port St. Lucie MSA, FL	Y	36140 FQ	57720 AW	85910 TQ	FLBLS	10/01-12/01
	Fort Walton Beach MSA, FL	Y	32460 FQ	60830 AW	98860 TQ	FLBLS	10/01-12/01
	Gainesville MSA, FL	Y	36790 FQ	55010 AW	80970 TQ	FLBLS	10/01-12/01
	Jacksonville MSA, FL	Y	42290 FQ	62550 AW	84590 TQ	FLBLS	10/01-12/01
	Lakeland-Winter Haven MSA, FL	Y	38900 FQ	56440 AW	80960 TQ	FLBLS	10/01-12/01
	Melbourne-Titusville-Palm Bay MSA, FL	Y	43870 FQ	59930 AW	78420 TQ	FLBLS	10/01-12/01
	Miami PMSA, FL	Y	38830 FQ	60870 AW	88960 TQ	FLBLS	10/01-12/01
	Naples MSA, FL	Y	41400 FQ	69320 AW	95770 TQ	FLBLS	10/01-12/01
	Ocala MSA, FL	Y	39790 FQ	57340 AW	76540 TQ	FLBLS	10/01-12/01
	Orlando MSA, FL	Y	37390 FQ	60960 AW	87650 TQ	FLBLS	10/01-12/01
	Pensacola MSA, FL	Y	34030 FQ	55130 AW	81640 TQ	FLBLS	10/01-12/01
	Sarasota-Bradenton MSA, FL	Y	37880 FQ	61380 AW	94520 TQ	FLBLS	10/01-12/01
	Tallahassee MSA, FL	Y	39100 FQ	64740 AW	92360 TQ	FLBLS	10/01-12/01
	Tampa-St. Petersburg-Clearwater MSA, FL	Y	38750 FQ	57960 AW	84220 TQ	FLBLS	10/01-12/01
	West Palm Beach-Boca Raton MSA, FL	Y	37710 FQ	68010 AW	102190 TQ	FLBLS	10/01-12/01
	Georgia	Y	36380 FQ	56990 AW	86190 TQ	GABLS	10/01-12/01
	Atlanta MSA, GA	Y	37500 FQ	57500 AW	86800 TQ	GABLS	10/01-12/01
	Augusta-Aiken MSA, GA-SC	Y	50110 FQ	73290 AW	96090 TQ	GABLS	10/01-12/01
	Columbus MSA, GA-AL	Y	33700 FQ	50060 AW	67740 TQ	GABLS	10/01-12/01
	Macon MSA, GA	Y	33220 FQ	50360 AW	70800 TQ	GABLS	10/01-12/01
	Savannah MSA, GA	Y	38360 FQ	58040 AW	81380 TQ	GABLS	10/01-12/01
	Hawaii	Y	39120 FQ	58860 AW	83560 TQ	HIBLS	10/01-12/01
	Honolulu MSA, HI	Y	39100 FQ	57900 AW	80620 TQ	HIBLS	10/01-12/01
	Idaho	Y	38120 FQ	55930 AW	79320 TQ	IDBLS	10/01-12/01
	Boise City MSA, ID	Y	39830 FQ	59710 AW	84980 TQ	IDBLS	10/01-12/01
	Illinois	Y	39930 FQ	61900 AW	87700 TQ	ILBLS	10/01-12/01
	Champaign-Urbana MSA, IL	Y	40360 FQ	60580 AW	87110 TQ	ILBLS	10/01-12/01
	Chicago PMSA, IL	Y	39890 FQ	62840 AW	89130 TQ	ILBLS	10/01-12/01
	Peoria-Pekin MSA, IL	Y	41990 FQ	60030 AW	80680 TQ	ILBLS	10/01-12/01
	Rockford MSA, IL	Y	39360 FQ	64580 AW	94920 TQ	ILBLS	10/01-12/01
	Springfield MSA, IL	Y	39950 FQ	59850 AW	87340 TQ	ILBLS	10/01-12/01
	Indiana	Y	33660 FQ	52700 AW	73940 TQ	INBLS	10/01-12/01
	Elkhart-Goshen MSA, IN	Y	26760 FQ	48000 AW	66050 TQ	INBLS	10/01-12/01
	Evansville-Henderson MSA, IN-KY	Y	33540 FQ	52580 AW	74010 TQ	INBLS	10/01-12/01

AAW	Average annual wage	**AOH**	Average offered, high	**ASH**	Average starting, high	**H**	Hourly	**M**	Monthly	**S**	Special: hourly and annual
AE	Average entry wage	**AOL**	Average offered, low	**ASL**	Average starting, low	**HI**	Highest wage paid	**MTC**	Median total compensation	**TQ**	Third quartile wage
AEX	Average experienced wage	**APH**	Average pay, high range	**AW**	Average wage paid	**HR**	High end range	**MW**	Median wage paid	**W**	Weekly
AO	Average offered	**APL**	Average pay, low range	**FQ**	First quartile wage	**LR**	Low end range	**SQ**	Second quartile wage	**Y**	Yearly

Occupation/Type/Industry	Location	Per	Low	Mid	High	Source	Date
Civil Engineer	Fort Wayne MSA, IN	Y	33270 FQ	50460 AW	70000 TQ	INBLS	10/01-12/01
	Gary PMSA, IN	Y	32950 FQ	56210 AW	86690 TQ	INBLS	10/01-12/01
	Indianapolis MSA, IN	Y	38410 FQ	53810 AW	74650 TQ	INBLS	10/01-12/01
	South Bend MSA, IN	Y	31950 FQ	53360 AW	81550 TQ	INBLS	10/01-12/01
	Iowa	Y	38520 FQ	57470 AW	77830 TQ	IABLS	10/01-12/01
	Cedar Rapids MSA, IA	Y	40990 FQ	58800 AW	80020 TQ	IABLS	10/01-12/01
	Davenport-Moline-Rock Island MSA, IA-IL	Y	40960 FQ	63220 AW	88530 TQ	IABLS	10/01-12/01
	Des Moines MSA, IA	Y	37820 FQ	57200 AW	77870 TQ	IABLS	10/01-12/01
	Kansas	Y	39020 FQ	57050 AW	82300 TQ	KSBLS	10/01-12/01
	Topeka MSA, KS	Y	45330 FQ	59350 AW	76450 TQ	KSBLS	10/01-12/01
	Wichita MSA, KS	Y	34980 FQ	54400 AW	84010 TQ	KSBLS	10/01-12/01
	Kentucky	Y	36290 FQ	56870 AW	82580 TQ	KYBLS	10/01-12/01
	Lexington MSA, KY	Y	35080 FQ	52680 AW	81190 TQ	KYBLS	10/01-12/01
	Louisville MSA, KY-IN	Y	38820 FQ	58360 AW	80250 TQ	KYBLS	10/01-12/01
	Louisiana	Y	33850 FQ	62320 AW	93230 TQ	LABLS	10/01-12/01
	Baton Rouge MSA, LA	Y	24450 FQ	54280 AW	89430 TQ	LABLS	10/01-12/01
	Lafayette MSA, LA	Y	32250 FQ	52490 AW	75830 TQ	LABLS	10/01-12/01
	Lake Charles MSA, LA	Y	41720 FQ	71680 AW	103950 TQ	LABLS	10/01-12/01
	New Orleans MSA, LA	Y	38640 FQ	65620 AW	94390 TQ	LABLS	10/01-12/01
	Shreveport-Bossier City MSA, LA	Y	41650 FQ	60130 AW	85170 TQ	LABLS	10/01-12/01
	Maine	Y	36720 FQ	51840 AW	71040 TQ	MEBLS	10/01-12/01
	Portland MSA, ME	Y	36800 FQ	49070 AW	68470 TQ	MEBLS	10/01-12/01
	Maryland	Y	37090 FQ	53870 AW	78440 TQ	MDBLS	10/01-12/01
	Baltimore PMSA, MD	Y	37160 FQ	52670 AW	76200 TQ	MDBLS	10/01-12/01
	Massachusetts	Y	39520 FQ	60350 AW	87680 TQ	MABLS	10/01-12/01
	Boston PMSA, MA-NH	Y	40510 FQ	61480 AW	89160 TQ	MABLS	10/01-12/01
	Brockton PMSA, MA	Y	43120 FQ	65080 AW	86370 TQ	MABLS	10/01-12/01
	Lawrence PMSA, MA-NH	Y	39440 FQ	55080 AW	82150 TQ	MABLS	10/01-12/01
	Lowell PMSA, MA-NH	Y	30890 FQ	52230 AW	81250 TQ	MABLS	10/01-12/01
	New Bedford PMSA, MA	Y	37100 FQ	49800 AW	68090 TQ	MABLS	10/01-12/01
	Springfield MSA, MA	Y	40310 FQ	60000 AW	85780 TQ	MABLS	10/01-12/01
	Worcester PMSA, MA-CT	Y	39030 FQ	55840 AW	73200 TQ	MABLS	10/01-12/01
	Michigan	Y	37840 FQ	55920 AW	76890 TQ	MIBLS	10/01-12/01
	Ann Arbor PMSA, MI	Y	42800 FQ	60740 AW	86470 TQ	MIBLS	10/01-12/01
	Detroit PMSA, MI	Y	38190 FQ	55450 AW	75530 TQ	MIBLS	10/01-12/01
	Flint PMSA, MI	Y	36970 FQ	57400 AW	85710 TQ	MIBLS	10/01-12/01
	Grand Rapids-Muskegon-Holland MSA, MI	Y	38770 FQ	56850 AW	78430 TQ	MIBLS	10/01-12/01
	Kalamazoo-Battle Creek MSA, MI	Y	26580 FQ	46760 AW	69050 TQ	MIBLS	10/01-12/01
	Lansing-East Lansing MSA, MI	Y	39920 FQ	56350 AW	73610 TQ	MIBLS	10/01-12/01
	Saginaw-Bay City-Midland MSA, MI	Y	37350 FQ	58710 AW	86160 TQ	MIBLS	10/01-12/01
	Minnesota	Y	37400 FQ	56930 AW	82390 TQ	MNBLS	10/01-12/01
	Duluth-Superior MSA, MN-WI	Y	38310 FQ	51180 AW	68200 TQ	MNBLS	10/01-12/01
	Minneapolis-St. Paul MSA, MN-WI	Y	37640 FQ	57950 AW	84420 TQ	MNBLS	10/01-12/01
	St. Cloud MSA, MN	Y	36680 FQ	54760 AW	73090 TQ	MNBLS	10/01-12/01
	Mississippi	Y	30990 FQ	54560 AW	85680 TQ	MSBLS	10/01-12/01
	Biloxi-Gulfport-Pascagoula MSA, MS	Y	31680 FQ	47790 AW	71880 TQ	MSBLS	10/01-12/01
	Jackson MSA, MS	Y	26930 FQ	51420 AW	82920 TQ	MSBLS	10/01-12/01
	Missouri	Y	38790 FQ	57530 AW	79070 TQ	MOBLS	10/01-12/01
	Kansas City MSA, MO-KS	Y	39230 FQ	58030 AW	80710 TQ	MOBLS	10/01-12/01
	St. Louis MSA, MO-IL	Y	39630 FQ	58780 AW	83740 TQ	MOBLS	10/01-12/01
	Springfield MSA, MO	Y	33470 FQ	54790 AW	75170 TQ	MOBLS	10/01-12/01
	Montana	Y	31570 FQ	51690 AW	76030 TQ	MTBLS	10/01-12/01
	Billings MSA, MT	Y	33820 FQ	55890 AW	81330 TQ	MTBLS	10/01-12/01
	Nebraska	Y	37350 FQ	59120 AW	85640 TQ	NEBLS	10/01-12/01
	Lincoln MSA, NE	Y	35210 FQ	52580 AW	72360 TQ	NEBLS	10/01-12/01
	Omaha MSA, NE-IA	Y	39330 FQ	61280 AW	87590 TQ	NEBLS	10/01-12/01
	Nevada	Y	45280 FQ	65230 AW	88890 TQ	NVBLS	10/01-12/01
	Las Vegas MSA, NV-AZ	Y	45470 FQ	68640 AW	91510 TQ	NVBLS	10/01-12/01
	Reno MSA, NV	Y	45440 FQ	62150 AW	85640 TQ	NVBLS	10/01-12/01
	New Hampshire	Y	37820 FQ	55680 AW	78680 TQ	NHBLS	10/01-12/01
	Manchester PMSA, NH	Y	40130 FQ	57700 AW	81890 TQ	NHBLS	10/01-12/01
	Nashua PMSA, NH	Y	30970 FQ	61450 AW		NHBLS	10/01-12/01
	Portsmouth-Rochester PMSA, NH-ME	Y	37900 FQ	52950 AW	77380 TQ	NHBLS	10/01-12/01
	New Jersey	Y	43570 FQ	65460 AW	93740 TQ	NJBLS	10/01-12/01

AAW	Average annual wage	**AOH**	Average offered, high	**ASH**	Average starting, high	**H**	Hourly	**M**	Monthly	**S**	Special: hourly and annual
AE	Average entry wage	**AOL**	Average offered, low	**ASL**	Average starting, low	**HI**	Highest wage paid	**MTC**	Median total compensation	**TQ**	Third quartile wage
AEX	Average experienced wage	**APH**	Average pay, high range	**AW**	Average wage paid	**HR**	High end range	**MW**	Median wage paid	**W**	Weekly
AO	Average offered	**APL**	Average pay, low range	**FQ**	First quartile wage	**LR**	Low end range	**SQ**	Second quartile wage	**Y**	Yearly

Occupation/Type/Industry	Location	Per	Low	Mid	High	Source	Date
Civil Engineer	Atlantic-Cape May PMSA, NJ	Y	44770 FQ	64430 AW	93130 TQ	NJBLS	10/01-12/01
	Bergen-Passaic PMSA, NJ	Y	43670 FQ	69920 AW	100520 TQ	NJBLS	10/01-12/01
	Jersey City PMSA, NJ	Y	47170 FQ	68450 AW	94550 TQ	NJBLS	10/01-12/01
	Middlesex-Somerset-Hunterdon PMSA, NJ	Y	41390 FQ	67930 AW	100710 TQ	NJBLS	10/01-12/01
	Monmouth-Ocean PMSA, NJ	Y	43330 FQ	65200 AW	90740 TQ	NJBLS	10/01-12/01
	Newark PMSA, NJ	Y	46670 FQ	64310 AW	96410 TQ	NJBLS	10/01-12/01
	New Mexico	Y	37220 FQ	57580 AW	85440 TQ	NMBLS	10/01-12/01
	Albuquerque MSA, NM	Y	39030 FQ	58760 AW	85210 TQ	NMBLS	10/01-12/01
	Las Cruces MSA, NM	Y	35120 FQ	50990 AW	68550 TQ	NMBLS	10/01-12/01
	New York	Y	41970 FQ	63520 AW	93240 TQ	NYBLS	10/01-12/01
	Albany-Schenectady-Troy MSA, NY	Y	44880 FQ	64900 AW	99410 TQ	NYBLS	10/01-12/01
	Binghamton MSA, NY	Y	41170 FQ	54310 AW	70720 TQ	NYBLS	10/01-12/01
	Buffalo-Niagara Falls MSA, NY	Y	39490 FQ	57600 AW	82170 TQ	NYBLS	10/01-12/01
	Dutchess County PMSA, NY	Y	45220 FQ	57480 AW	75960 TQ	NYBLS	10/01-12/01
	Nassau-Suffolk PMSA, NY	Y	42660 FQ	63940 AW	92390 TQ	NYBLS	10/01-12/01
	New York PMSA, NY	Y	42330 FQ	66720 AW	100660 TQ	NYBLS	10/01-12/01
	Newburgh PMSA, NY-PA	Y	42850 FQ	72860 AW	126050 TQ	NYBLS	10/01-12/01
	Rochester MSA, NY	Y	41420 FQ	59810 AW	83760 TQ	NYBLS	10/01-12/01
	Syracuse MSA, NY	Y	39690 FQ	56600 AW	79030 TQ	NYBLS	10/01-12/01
	Utica-Rome MSA, NY	Y	36000 FQ	53530 AW	74930 TQ	NYBLS	10/01-12/01
	North Carolina	Y	38490 FQ	56400 AW	77470 TQ	NCBLS	10/01-12/01
	Asheville MSA, NC	Y	28980 FQ	51090 AW	70080 TQ	NCBLS	10/01-12/01
	Charlotte-Gastonia-Rock Hill MSA, NC-SC	Y	36650 FQ	55790 AW	78300 TQ	NCBLS	10/01-12/01
	Fayetteville MSA, NC	Y	35480 FQ	51040 AW	68260 TQ	NCBLS	10/01-12/01
	Greensboro-Winston-Salem-High Point MSA, NC	Y	38480 FQ	56920 AW	84590 TQ	NCBLS	10/01-12/01
	Hickory-Morganton-Lenoir MSA, NC	Y	44240 FQ	53380 AW	66650 TQ	NCBLS	10/01-12/01
	Raleigh-Durham-Chapel Hill MSA, NC	Y	39930 FQ	57740 AW	78940 TQ	NCBLS	10/01-12/01
	Wilmington MSA, NC	Y	44380 FQ	58410 AW	76500 TQ	NCBLS	10/01-12/01
	North Dakota	Y	35430 FQ	51170 AW	76290 TQ	NDBLS	10/01-12/01
	Fargo-Moorhead MSA, ND-MN	Y	37320 FQ	55410 AW	83340 TQ	NDBLS	10/01-12/01
	Ohio	Y	37120 FQ	55930 AW	80860 TQ	OHBLS	10/01-12/01
	Akron PMSA, OH	Y	38050 FQ	54840 AW	78330 TQ	OHBLS	10/01-12/01
	Canton-Massillon MSA, OH	Y	35110 FQ	47780 AW	67960 TQ	OHBLS	10/01-12/01
	Cincinnati PMSA, OH-KY-IN	Y	37520 FQ	61270 AW	87010 TQ	OHBLS	10/01-12/01
	Cleveland-Lorain-Elyria PMSA, OH	Y	38130 FQ	53980 AW	72430 TQ	OHBLS	10/01-12/01
	Columbus MSA, OH	Y	37820 FQ	57300 AW	84100 TQ	OHBLS	10/01-12/01
	Dayton-Springfield MSA, OH	Y	38120 FQ	58260 AW	91240 TQ	OHBLS	10/01-12/01
	Hamilton-Middletown PMSA, OH	Y	28130 FQ	48220 AW	70150 TQ	OHBLS	10/01-12/01
	Mansfield MSA, OH	Y	36200 FQ	48710 AW	68510 TQ	OHBLS	10/01-12/01
	Toledo MSA, OH	Y	36030 FQ	49310 AW	69980 TQ	OHBLS	10/01-12/01
	Youngstown-Warren MSA, OH	Y	36120 FQ	55680 AW	83530 TQ	OHBLS	10/01-12/01
	Oklahoma	Y	40130 FQ	65120 AW	117930 TQ	OKBLS	10/01-12/01
	Oklahoma City MSA, OK	Y	41640 FQ	71820 AW	130760 TQ	OKBLS	10/01-12/01
	Tulsa MSA, OK	Y	40010 FQ	60860 AW	84840 TQ	OKBLS	10/01-12/01
	Oregon	Y	40240 FQ	58570 AW	82730 TQ	ORBLS	10/01-12/01
	Eugene-Springfield MSA, OR	Y	39830 FQ	58960 AW	86530 TQ	ORBLS	10/01-12/01
	Portland-Vancouver PMSA, OR-WA	Y	40440 FQ	59800 AW	84950 TQ	ORBLS	10/01-12/01
	Pennsylvania	Y	38710 FQ	61100 AW	90100 TQ	PABLS	10/01-12/01
	Allentown-Bethlehem-Easton MSA, PA	Y	13350 FQ	51790 AW	82270 TQ	PABLS	10/01-12/01
	Erie MSA, PA	Y	37640 FQ	54720 AW	73700 TQ	PABLS	10/01-12/01
	Harrisburg-Lebanon-Carlisle MSA, PA	Y	39710 FQ	58540 AW	83080 TQ	PABLS	10/01-12/01
	Johnstown MSA, PA	Y	46050 FQ	71300 AW	105700 TQ	PABLS	10/01-12/01
	Lancaster MSA, PA	Y	45770 FQ	71400 AW	93960 TQ	PABLS	10/01-12/01
	Philadelphia PMSA, PA-NJ	Y	41030 FQ	63770 AW	93950 TQ	PABLS	10/01-12/01
	Pittsburgh MSA, PA	Y	38610 FQ	59110 AW	86150 TQ	PABLS	10/01-12/01
	Reading MSA, PA	Y	39260 FQ	61400 AW	89800 TQ	PABLS	10/01-12/01
	Scranton-Wilkes-Barre-Hazleton MSA, PA	Y	36420 FQ	54320 AW	76200 TQ	PABLS	10/01-12/01
	York MSA, PA	Y	40050 FQ	59840 AW	84860 TQ	PABLS	10/01-12/01

AAW	Average annual wage	**AOH**	Average offered, high	**ASH**	Average starting, high	**H**	Hourly	**M**	Monthly	**S**	Special: hourly and annual
AE	Average entry wage	**AOL**	Average offered, low	**ASL**	Average starting, low	**HI**	Highest wage paid	**MTC**	Median total compensation	**TQ**	Third quartile wage
AEX	Average experienced wage	**APH**	Average pay, high range	**AW**	Average wage paid	**HR**	High end range	**MW**	Median wage paid	**W**	Weekly
AO	Average offered	**APL**	Average pay, low range	**FQ**	First quartile wage	**LR**	Low end range	**SQ**	Second quartile wage	**Y**	Yearly

Occupation/Type/Industry	Location	Per	Low	Mid	High	Source	Date
Civil Engineer	Rhode Island	Y	36080 FQ	60330 AW	84900 TQ	RIBLS	10/01-12/01
	Providence-Fall River-Warwick MSA, RI-MA	Y	35930 FQ	59910 AW	84170 TQ	RIBLS	10/01-12/01
	South Carolina	Y	37560 FQ	57680 AW	87940 TQ	SCBLS	10/01-12/01
	Charleston-North Charleston MSA, SC	Y	38470 FQ	57670 AW	81800 TQ	SCBLS	10/01-12/01
	Columbia MSA, SC	Y	35910 FQ	54960 AW	82310 TQ	SCBLS	10/01-12/01
	Greenville-Spartanburg-Anderson MSA, SC	Y	32240 FQ	56660 AW	89460 TQ	SCBLS	10/01-12/01
	Myrtle Beach MSA, SC	Y	37250 FQ	54990 AW	83180 TQ	SCBLS	10/01-12/01
	South Dakota	Y	37830 FQ	52710 AW	72720 TQ	SDBLS	10/01-12/01
	Sioux Falls MSA, SD	Y	39150 FQ	56700 AW	85170 TQ	SDBLS	10/01-12/01
	Tennessee	Y	34850 FQ	58490 AW	86020 TQ	TNBLS	10/01-12/01
	Chattanooga MSA, TN-GA	Y	34720 FQ	58580 AW	85880 TQ	TNBLS	10/01-12/01
	Clarksville-Hopkinsville MSA, TN-KY	Y	34910 FQ	49440 AW	68740 TQ	TNBLS	10/01-12/01
	Johnson City-Kingsport-Bristol MSA, TN-VA	Y	33630 FQ	52510 AW	71570 TQ	TNBLS	10/01-12/01
	Knoxville MSA, TN	Y	40930 FQ	61430 AW	86650 TQ	TNBLS	10/01-12/01
	Memphis MSA, TN-AR-MS	Y	34870 FQ	57820 AW	83830 TQ	TNBLS	10/01-12/01
	Nashville MSA, TN	Y	33110 FQ	57530 AW	86820 TQ	TNBLS	10/01-12/01
	Texas	Y	40640 FQ	65910 AW	103390 TQ	TXBLS	10/01-12/01
	Amarillo MSA, TX	Y	38190 FQ	51830 AW	78620 TQ	TXBLS	10/01-12/01
	Austin-San Marcos MSA, TX	Y	39500 FQ	57300 AW	77380 TQ	TXBLS	10/01-12/01
	Beaumont-Port Arthur MSA, TX	Y	35580 FQ	68610 AW	113470 TQ	TXBLS	10/01-12/01
	Brazoria PMSA, TX	Y	40960 FQ	77960 AW	131080 TQ	TXBLS	10/01-12/01
	Brownsville-Harlingen-San Benito MSA, TX	Y	21100 FQ	50390 AW	73860 TQ	TXBLS	10/01-12/01
	Corpus Christi MSA, TX	Y	36470 FQ	70480 AW	113390 TQ	TXBLS	10/01-12/01
	Dallas PMSA, TX	Y	38540 FQ	59080 AW	89150 TQ	TXBLS	10/01-12/01
	El Paso MSA, TX	Y	27800 FQ	47180 AW	66210 TQ	TXBLS	10/01-12/01
	Fort Worth-Arlington PMSA, TX	Y	36620 FQ	56030 AW	83010 TQ	TXBLS	10/01-12/01
	Galveston-Texas City PMSA, TX	Y	45640 FQ	67120 AW	90570 TQ	TXBLS	10/01-12/01
	Houston PMSA, TX	Y	46470 FQ	71980 AW	110440 TQ	TXBLS	10/01-12/01
	Killeen-Temple MSA, TX	Y	42260 FQ	56780 AW	71720 TQ	TXBLS	10/01-12/01
	Laredo MSA, TX	Y	35790 FQ	53240 AW	74960 TQ	TXBLS	10/01-12/01
	Longview-Marshall MSA, TX	Y	33670 FQ	50440 AW	72950 TQ	TXBLS	10/01-12/01
	Lubbock MSA, TX	Y	39110 FQ	55270 AW	69310 TQ	TXBLS	10/01-12/01
	McAllen-Edinburg-Mission MSA, TX	Y	42790 FQ	70900 AW	93080 TQ	TXBLS	10/01-12/01
	Odessa-Midland MSA, TX	Y	43180 FQ	76550 AW	116310 TQ	TXBLS	10/01-12/01
	San Antonio MSA, TX	Y	39100 FQ	63340 AW	94220 TQ	TXBLS	10/01-12/01
	Tyler MSA, TX	Y	37740 FQ	54350 AW	81980 TQ	TXBLS	10/01-12/01
	Waco MSA, TX	Y	34140 FQ	57750 AW	96170 TQ	TXBLS	10/01-12/01
	Utah	Y	36770 FQ	55670 AW	82730 TQ	UTBLS	10/01-12/01
	Provo-Orem MSA, UT	Y	36620 FQ	53150 AW	77130 TQ	UTBLS	10/01-12/01
	Salt Lake City-Ogden MSA, UT	Y	37950 FQ	57030 AW	83880 TQ	UTBLS	10/01-12/01
	Vermont	Y	31710 FQ	51880 AW	72350 TQ	VTBLS	10/01-12/01
	Burlington MSA, VT	Y	30240 FQ	49730 AW	70880 TQ	VTBLS	10/01-12/01
	Virginia	Y	38880 FQ	60800 AW	86960 TQ	VABLS	10/01-12/01
	Lynchburg MSA, VA	Y	38010 FQ	53630 AW	70580 TQ	VABLS	10/01-12/01
	Norfolk-Virginia Beach-Newport News MSA, VA-NC	Y	40350 FQ	59710 AW	83280 TQ	VABLS	10/01-12/01
	Richmond-Petersburg MSA, VA	Y	36460 FQ	54250 AW	74700 TQ	VABLS	10/01-12/01
	Roanoke MSA, VA	Y	32340 FQ	47320 AW	67980 TQ	VABLS	10/01-12/01
	Washington	Y	44610 FQ	66610 AW	99670 TQ	WABLS	10/01-12/01
	Bremerton PMSA, WA	Y	46100 FQ	64090 AW	90260 TQ	WABLS	10/01-12/01
	Olympia PMSA, WA	Y	47150 FQ	59980 AW	74020 TQ	WABLS	10/01-12/01
	Richland-Kennewick-Pasco MSA, WA	Y	45210 FQ	72310 AW	103570 TQ	WABLS	10/01-12/01
	Seattle-Bellevue-Everett PMSA, WA	Y	45210 FQ	70580 AW	106370 TQ	WABLS	10/01-12/01
	Spokane MSA, WA	Y	36770 FQ	53390 AW	70700 TQ	WABLS	10/01-12/01
	Tacoma PMSA, WA	Y	44800 FQ	60820 AW	84410 TQ	WABLS	10/01-12/01
	Yakima MSA, WA	Y	44910 FQ	57310 AW	73790 TQ	WABLS	10/01-12/01
	West Virginia	Y	30170 FQ	51490 AW	72760 TQ	WVBLS	10/01-12/01

AAW	Average annual wage	**AOH**	Average offered, high	**ASH**	Average starting, high	**H**	Hourly	**M**	Monthly	**S**	Special: hourly and annual
AE	Average entry wage	**AOL**	Average offered, low	**ASL**	Average starting, low	**HI**	Highest wage paid	**MTC**	Median total compensation	**TQ**	Third quartile wage
AEX	Average experienced wage	**APH**	Average pay, high range	**AW**	Average wage paid	**HR**	High end range	**MW**	Median wage paid	**W**	Weekly
AO	Average offered	**APL**	Average pay, low range	**FQ**	First quartile wage	**LR**	Low end range	**SQ**	Second quartile wage	**Y**	Yearly

Occupation/Type/Industry	Location	Per	Low	Mid	High	Source	Date
Civil Engineer	Huntington-Ashland MSA, WV-KY-OH	Y	37180 FQ	57480 AW	74370 TQ	WVBLS	10/01-12/01
	Wisconsin	Y	37220 FQ	53930 AW	73640 TQ	WIBLS	10/01-12/01
	Appleton-Oshkosh-Neenah MSA, WI	Y	41370 FQ	59850 AW	83300 TQ	WIBLS	10/01-12/01
	Green Bay MSA, WI	Y	38590 FQ	52770 AW	69280 TQ	WIBLS	10/01-12/01
	Madison MSA, WI	Y	30720 FQ	53520 AW	73760 TQ	WIBLS	10/01-12/01
	Milwaukee-Waukesha PMSA, WI	Y	38320 FQ	53400 AW	72010 TQ	WIBLS	10/01-12/01
	Racine PMSA, WI	Y	41060 FQ	62430 AW	87820 TQ	WIBLS	10/01-12/01
	Wyoming	Y	31590 FQ	49330 AW	70640 TQ	WYBLS	10/01-12/01
	Cheyenne MSA, WY	Y	36000 FQ	53230 AW	69220 TQ	WYBLS	10/01-12/01
	Puerto Rico	Y	28110 FQ	42300 AW	62400 TQ	PRBLS	10/01-12/01
	Guam	Y	29270 FQ	46840 AW	76830 TQ	GUBLS	10/01-12/01
Private Sector	Missouri	H		37.00 AW		STLOUPD1	1/01-1/02
State Department of Transportation	Missouri	Y		60094 AW		STLOUPD1	1/01-1/02
State Department of Transportation	Missouri	H		29.00 AW		STLOUPD1	1/01-1/02
Civil Engineering Technician	Alabama	Y	22170 FQ	38410 AW	61800 TQ	ALBLS	10/01-12/01
	Alaska	Y	36050 FQ	50330 AW	67400 TQ	AKBLS	10/01-12/01
	Arizona	Y	23060 FQ	38940 AW	59820 TQ	AZBLS	10/01-12/01
	Arkansas	Y	15630 FQ	32470 AW	53680 TQ	ARBLS	10/01-12/01
	California	Y	30190 FQ	48220 AW	70050 TQ	CABLS	10/01-12/01
	Colorado	Y	23270 FQ	40680 AW	58810 TQ	COBLS	10/01-12/01
	Connecticut	Y	31600 FQ	48130 AW	66500 TQ	CTBLS	10/01-12/01
	Delaware	Y	23970 FQ	34020 AW	46380 TQ	DEBLS	10/01-12/01
	District of Columbia	Y	29710 FQ	49800 AW	73200 TQ	DCBLS	10/01-12/01
	Florida	Y	23740 FQ	36860 AW	52530 TQ	FLBLS	10/01-12/01
	Georgia	Y	20030 FQ	32230 AW	47350 TQ	GABLS	10/01-12/01
	Hawaii	Y	29200 FQ	39720 AW	51440 TQ	HIBLS	10/01-12/01
	Idaho	Y	25490 FQ	34830 AW	43570 TQ	IDBLS	10/01-12/01
	Illinois	Y	26280 FQ	42430 AW	59160 TQ	ILBLS	10/01-12/01
	Indiana	Y	19160 FQ	32960 AW	51800 TQ	INBLS	10/01-12/01
	Iowa	Y	24970 FQ	36680 AW	51030 TQ	IABLS	10/01-12/01
	Kansas	Y	22640 FQ	34490 AW	49650 TQ	KSBLS	10/01-12/01
	Kentucky	Y	23340 FQ	40270 AW	61440 TQ	KYBLS	10/01-12/01
	Louisiana	Y	19420 FQ	34410 AW	60260 TQ	LABLS	10/01-12/01
	Maine	Y	23970 FQ	36760 AW	51580 TQ	MEBLS	10/01-12/01
	Maryland	Y	19170 FQ	34360 AW	47620 TQ	MDBLS	10/01-12/01
	Massachusetts	Y	29150 FQ	42050 AW	56170 TQ	MABLS	10/01-12/01
	Michigan	Y	24950 FQ	38600 AW	54190 TQ	MIBLS	10/01-12/01
	Minnesota	Y	28920 FQ	41450 AW	54950 TQ	MNBLS	10/01-12/01
	Mississippi	Y	18130 FQ	27990 AW	39430 TQ	MSBLS	10/01-12/01
	Missouri	Y	23450 FQ	38760 AW	56860 TQ	MOBLS	10/01-12/01
	Montana	Y	18580 FQ	33440 AW	50310 TQ	MTBLS	10/01-12/01
	Nebraska	Y	22550 FQ	33280 AW	49000 TQ	NEBLS	10/01-12/01
	Nevada	Y	30000 FQ	43740 AW	59670 TQ	NVBLS	10/01-12/01
	New Hampshire	Y	17010 FQ	28290 AW	43330 TQ	NHBLS	10/01-12/01
	New Jersey	Y	24630 FQ	41690 AW	57740 TQ	NJBLS	10/01-12/01
	New Mexico	Y	20120 FQ	32530 AW	49800 TQ	NMBLS	10/01-12/01
	New York	Y	24960 FQ	44930 AW	62010 TQ	NYBLS	10/01-12/01
	North Carolina	Y	23790 FQ	35260 AW	48220 TQ	NCBLS	10/01-12/01
	North Dakota	Y	22450 FQ	32150 AW	44250 TQ	NDBLS	10/01-12/01
	Ohio	Y	23320 FQ	38550 AW	56610 TQ	OHBLS	10/01-12/01
	Oklahoma	Y	26680 FQ	39090 AW	54450 TQ	OKBLS	10/01-12/01
	Oregon	Y	28770 FQ	40890 AW	55680 TQ	ORBLS	10/01-12/01
	Pennsylvania	Y	24160 FQ	39940 AW	56100 TQ	PABLS	10/01-12/01
	Rhode Island	Y	28780 FQ	39030 AW	52740 TQ	RIBLS	10/01-12/01
	South Carolina	Y	22480 FQ	41030 AW	66610 TQ	SCBLS	10/01-12/01
	South Dakota	Y	24210 FQ	31190 AW	40200 TQ	SDBLS	10/01-12/01
	Tennessee	Y	19030 FQ	32070 AW	45390 TQ	TNBLS	10/01-12/01
	Texas	Y	20180 FQ	33430 AW	49520 TQ	TXBLS	10/01-12/01
	Utah	Y	24450 FQ	37330 AW	51180 TQ	UTBLS	10/01-12/01
	Vermont	Y	26380 FQ	39380 AW	53820 TQ	VTBLS	10/01-12/01
	Virginia	Y	19860 FQ	34990 AW	52480 TQ	VABLS	10/01-12/01
	Washington	Y	32600 FQ	44680 AW	58620 TQ	WABLS	10/01-12/01
	West Virginia	Y	21390 FQ	32670 AW	45350 TQ	WVBLS	10/01-12/01
	Wisconsin	Y	27360 FQ	39210 AW	53960 TQ	WIBLS	10/01-12/01
	Wyoming	Y	18760 FQ	31520 AW	46840 TQ	WYBLS	10/01-12/01
	Puerto Rico	Y	14770 FQ	23980 AW	37650 TQ	PRBLS	10/01-12/01
	Guam	Y	21830 FQ	33390 AW	49560 TQ	GUBLS	10/01-12/01

AAW	Average annual wage	**AOH**	Average offered, high	**ASH**	Average starting, high	**H**	Hourly	**M**	Monthly	**S**	Special: hourly and annual
AE	Average entry wage	**AOL**	Average offered, low	**ASL**	Average starting, low	**HI**	Highest wage paid	**MTC**	Median total compensation	**TQ**	Third quartile wage
AEX	Average experienced wage	**APH**	Average pay, high range	**AW**	Average wage paid	**HR**	High end range	**MW**	Median wage paid	**W**	Weekly
AO	Average offered	**APL**	Average pay, low range	**FQ**	First quartile wage	**LR**	Low end range	**SQ**	Second quartile wage	**Y**	Yearly

Occupation/Type/Industry	Location	Per	Low	Mid	High	Source	Date
Claims Adjuster, Examiner, and Investigator	Alabama	Y	24420 FQ	42240 AW	68970 TQ	ALBLS	10/01-12/01
	Birmingham MSA, AL	Y	24180 FQ	42310 AW	69410 TQ	ALBLS	10/01-12/01
	Huntsville MSA, AL	Y	27010 FQ	43970 AW	68140 TQ	ALBLS	10/01-12/01
	Montgomery MSA, AL	Y	27480 FQ	46130 AW	75130 TQ	ALBLS	10/01-12/01
	Alaska	Y	32070 FQ	61500 AW	105120 TQ	AKBLS	10/01-12/01
	Anchorage MSA, AK	Y	33140 FQ	63910 AW	107600 TQ	AKBLS	10/01-12/01
	Arizona	Y	28230 FQ	44490 AW	65660 TQ	AZBLS	10/01-12/01
	Phoenix-Mesa MSA, AZ	Y	28250 FQ	44490 AW	65340 TQ	AZBLS	10/01-12/01
	Tucson MSA, AZ	Y	28260 FQ	46150 AW	69520 TQ	AZBLS	10/01-12/01
	Arkansas	Y	24890 FQ	44560 AW	67950 TQ	ARBLS	10/01-12/01
	Fort Smith MSA, AR-OK	Y	14820 FQ	38590 AW	70130 TQ	ARBLS	10/01-12/01
	Little Rock-North Little Rock MSA, AR	Y	24580 FQ	42840 AW	64690 TQ	ARBLS	10/01-12/01
	California	Y	28790 FQ	49650 AW	73750 TQ	CABLS	10/01-12/01
	Chico-Paradise MSA, CA	Y	24510 FQ	39280 AW	61920 TQ	CABLS	10/01-12/01
	Fresno MSA, CA	Y	21540 FQ	41980 AW	67550 TQ	CABLS	10/01-12/01
	Los Angeles-Long Beach PMSA, CA	Y	29300 FQ	49870 AW	73020 TQ	CABLS	10/01-12/01
	Modesto MSA, CA	Y	27950 FQ	47860 AW	68880 TQ	CABLS	10/01-12/01
	Oakland PMSA, CA	Y	30790 FQ	51950 AW	78280 TQ	CABLS	10/01-12/01
	Orange County PMSA, CA	Y	28870 FQ	48920 AW	77750 TQ	CABLS	10/01-12/01
	Redding MSA, CA	Y	30820 FQ	53040 AW	81260 TQ	CABLS	10/01-12/01
	Riverside-San Bernardino PMSA, CA	Y	32400 FQ	49980 AW	67090 TQ	CABLS	10/01-12/01
	Sacramento PMSA, CA	Y	32110 FQ	53910 AW	75960 TQ	CABLS	10/01-12/01
	Salinas MSA, CA	Y	36990 FQ	59500 AW	85260 TQ	CABLS	10/01-12/01
	San Diego MSA, CA	Y	26120 FQ	39670 AW	57250 TQ	CABLS	10/01-12/01
	San Francisco PMSA, CA	Y	30720 FQ	57960 AW	78020 TQ	CABLS	10/01-12/01
	San Jose PMSA, CA	Y	30170 FQ	47390 AW	68470 TQ	CABLS	10/01-12/01
	San Luis Obispo-Atascadero-Paso Robles MSA, CA	Y	21020 FQ	53090 AW	73590 TQ	CABLS	10/01-12/01
	Santa Barbara-Santa Maria-Lompoc MSA, CA	Y	27560 FQ	52750 AW	71090 TQ	CABLS	10/01-12/01
	Santa Rosa PMSA, CA	Y	32060 FQ	45270 AW	59880 TQ	CABLS	10/01-12/01
	Stockton-Lodi MSA, CA	Y	24730 FQ	46420 AW	71330 TQ	CABLS	10/01-12/01
	Vallejo-Fairfield-Napa PMSA, CA	Y	25220 FQ	38850 AW	59360 TQ	CABLS	10/01-12/01
	Ventura PMSA, CA	Y	24710 FQ	50530 AW	81160 TQ	CABLS	10/01-12/01
	Visalia-Tulare-Porterville MSA, CA	Y	36080 FQ	52990 AW	73630 TQ	CABLS	10/01-12/01
	Colorado	Y	31830 FQ	48000 AW	68860 TQ	COBLS	10/01-12/01
	Boulder-Longmont PMSA, CO	Y	35020 FQ	47790 AW	73190 TQ	COBLS	10/01-12/01
	Colorado Springs MSA, CO	Y	33310 FQ	48510 AW	68670 TQ	COBLS	10/01-12/01
	Denver PMSA, CO	Y	31430 FQ	48220 AW	69730 TQ	COBLS	10/01-12/01
	Connecticut	Y	32650 FQ	50640 AW	72020 TQ	CTBLS	10/01-12/01
	Bridgeport PMSA, CT	Y	30850 FQ	74470 AW	136350 TQ	CTBLS	10/01-12/01
	Danbury PMSA, CT	Y	26680 FQ	34610 AW	45290 TQ	CTBLS	10/01-12/01
	Hartford MSA, CT	Y	32500 FQ	47690 AW	68220 TQ	CTBLS	10/01-12/01
	New Haven-Meriden PMSA, CT	Y	33450 FQ	49140 AW	66910 TQ	CTBLS	10/01-12/01
	Stamford-Norwalk PMSA, CT	Y	35160 FQ	62610 AW	102920 TQ	CTBLS	10/01-12/01
	Waterbury PMSA, CT	Y	37260 FQ	56380 AW	78450 TQ	CTBLS	10/01-12/01
	Delaware	Y	27130 FQ	44940 AW	70520 TQ	DEBLS	10/01-12/01
	Wilmington-Newark PMSA, DE-MD	Y	27960 FQ	45850 AW	70760 TQ	DEBLS	10/01-12/01
	District of Columbia	Y	23870 FQ	41050 AW	70830 TQ	DCBLS	10/01-12/01
	Washington PMSA, DC-MD-VA-WV	Y	29000 FQ	45000 AW	67610 TQ	DCBLS	10/01-12/01
	Florida	Y	25880 FQ	45270 AW	71740 TQ	FLBLS	10/01-12/01
	Daytona Beach MSA, FL	Y	26070 FQ	41050 AW	57550 TQ	FLBLS	10/01-12/01
	Fort Lauderdale PMSA, FL	Y	26850 FQ	43510 AW	65310 TQ	FLBLS	10/01-12/01
	Fort Myers-Cape Coral MSA, FL	Y	31520 FQ	50540 AW	76880 TQ	FLBLS	10/01-12/01
	Gainesville MSA, FL	Y	25940 FQ	49000 AW	78280 TQ	FLBLS	10/01-12/01
	Jacksonville MSA, FL	Y	27470 FQ	47860 AW	73380 TQ	FLBLS	10/01-12/01
	Melbourne-Titusville-Palm Bay MSA, FL	Y	29540 FQ	46170 AW	70360 TQ	FLBLS	10/01-12/01
	Miami PMSA, FL	Y	25420 FQ	43370 AW	70260 TQ	FLBLS	10/01-12/01
	Ocala MSA, FL	Y	14560 FQ	48710 AW	88670 TQ	FLBLS	10/01-12/01
	Orlando MSA, FL	Y	29590 FQ	49760 AW	75630 TQ	FLBLS	10/01-12/01
	Pensacola MSA, FL	Y	24990 FQ	43990 AW	68560 TQ	FLBLS	10/01-12/01

AAW Average annual wage; **AE** Average entry wage; **AEX** Average experienced wage; **AO** Average offered; **AOH** Average offered, high; **AOL** Average offered, low; **APH** Average pay, high range; **APL** Average pay, low range; **ASH** Average starting, high; **ASL** Average starting, low; **AW** Average wage paid; **FQ** First quartile wage; **H** Hourly; **HI** Highest wage paid; **HR** High end range; **LR** Low end range; **M** Monthly; **MTC** Median total compensation; **MW** Median wage paid; **SQ** Second quartile wage; **S** Special: hourly and annual; **TQ** Third quartile wage; **W** Weekly; **Y** Yearly

Occupation/Type/Industry	Location	Per	Low	Mid	High	Source	Date
Claims Adjuster, Examiner, and Investigator	Sarasota-Bradenton MSA, FL	Y	30260 FQ	43910 AW	61340 TQ	FLBLS	10/01-12/01
	Tallahassee MSA, FL	Y	21040 FQ	58360 AW	88610 TQ	FLBLS	10/01-12/01
	Tampa-St. Petersburg-Clearwater MSA, FL	Y	28420 FQ	44520 AW	66890 TQ	FLBLS	10/01-12/01
	West Palm Beach-Boca Raton MSA, FL	Y	31320 FQ	53800 AW	78820 TQ	FLBLS	10/01-12/01
	Georgia	Y	28150 FQ	46580 AW	72710 TQ	GABLS	10/01-12/01
	Atlanta MSA, GA	Y	27150 FQ	45430 AW	72840 TQ	GABLS	10/01-12/01
	Augusta-Aiken MSA, GA-SC	Y	34210 FQ	55890 AW	72260 TQ	GABLS	10/01-12/01
	Columbus MSA, GA-AL	Y	30910 FQ	48790 AW	72140 TQ	GABLS	10/01-12/01
	Macon MSA, GA	Y	33290 FQ	51530 AW	74670 TQ	GABLS	10/01-12/01
	Savannah MSA, GA	Y	32930 FQ	49100 AW	70850 TQ	GABLS	10/01-12/01
	Hawaii	Y	23890 FQ	45610 AW	71640 TQ	HIBLS	10/01-12/01
	Honolulu MSA, HI	Y	23750 FQ	45430 AW	71860 TQ	HIBLS	10/01-12/01
	Idaho	Y	21770 FQ	41690 AW	68120 TQ	IDBLS	10/01-12/01
	Boise City MSA, ID	Y	20450 FQ	39500 AW	67000 TQ	IDBLS	10/01-12/01
	Illinois	Y	24330 FQ	39510 AW	60080 TQ	ILBLS	10/01-12/01
	Champaign-Urbana MSA, IL	Y	24880 FQ	42060 AW	68540 TQ	ILBLS	10/01-12/01
	Chicago PMSA, IL	Y	24560 FQ	38560 AW	56740 TQ	ILBLS	10/01-12/01
	Peoria-Pekin MSA, IL	Y	19380 FQ	38100 AW	61220 TQ	ILBLS	10/01-12/01
	Rockford MSA, IL	Y	24400 FQ	41890 AW	63110 TQ	ILBLS	10/01-12/01
	Springfield MSA, IL	Y	20390 FQ	35920 AW	54400 TQ	ILBLS	10/01-12/01
	Indiana	Y	27280 FQ	43650 AW	66590 TQ	INBLS	10/01-12/01
	Elkhart-Goshen MSA, IN	Y	27690 FQ	33570 AW	42180 TQ	INBLS	10/01-12/01
	Evansville-Henderson MSA, IN-KY	Y	23100 FQ	45650 AW	80420 TQ	INBLS	10/01-12/01
	Fort Wayne MSA, IN	Y	24070 FQ	40020 AW	64080 TQ	INBLS	10/01-12/01
	Gary PMSA, IN	Y	34730 FQ	51530 AW	74720 TQ	INBLS	10/01-12/01
	Indianapolis MSA, IN	Y	26960 FQ	42290 AW	58280 TQ	INBLS	10/01-12/01
	South Bend MSA, IN	Y	21420 FQ	40500 AW	68990 TQ	INBLS	10/01-12/01
	Iowa	Y	21200 FQ	38920 AW	59050 TQ	IABLS	10/01-12/01
	Cedar Rapids MSA, IA	Y	25350 FQ	42150 AW	57760 TQ	IABLS	10/01-12/01
	Davenport-Moline-Rock Island MSA, IA-IL	Y	20920 FQ	39730 AW	64310 TQ	IABLS	10/01-12/01
	Des Moines MSA, IA	Y	21080 FQ	38120 AW	58270 TQ	IABLS	10/01-12/01
	Kansas	Y	28530 FQ	46340 AW	67810 TQ	KSBLS	10/01-12/01
	Topeka MSA, KS	Y	25620 FQ	40110 AW	53540 TQ	KSBLS	10/01-12/01
	Wichita MSA, KS	Y	33370 FQ	48650 AW	68260 TQ	KSBLS	10/01-12/01
	Kentucky	Y	28800 FQ	44600 AW	67700 TQ	KYBLS	10/01-12/01
	Lexington MSA, KY	Y	28170 FQ	49100 AW	72770 TQ	KYBLS	10/01-12/01
	Louisville MSA, KY-IN	Y	27010 FQ	41340 AW	58060 TQ	KYBLS	10/01-12/01
	Louisiana	Y	23900 FQ	40850 AW	65000 TQ	LABLS	10/01-12/01
	Baton Rouge MSA, LA	Y	26760 FQ	43740 AW	66350 TQ	LABLS	10/01-12/01
	Lafayette MSA, LA	Y	21790 FQ	42380 AW	64470 TQ	LABLS	10/01-12/01
	New Orleans MSA, LA	Y	22760 FQ	39460 AW	68230 TQ	LABLS	10/01-12/01
	Shreveport-Bossier City MSA, LA	Y	21190 FQ	37140 AW	60770 TQ	LABLS	10/01-12/01
	Maine	Y	28940 FQ	45580 AW	70270 TQ	MEBLS	10/01-12/01
	Maryland	Y	26280 FQ	44190 AW	68830 TQ	MDBLS	10/01-12/01
	Baltimore PMSA, MD	Y	25250 FQ	43790 AW	69980 TQ	MDBLS	10/01-12/01
	Massachusetts	Y	29120 FQ	43660 AW	61850 TQ	MABLS	10/01-12/01
	Boston PMSA, MA-NH	Y	30980 FQ	45520 AW	64070 TQ	MABLS	10/01-12/01
	Lawrence PMSA, MA-NH	Y	25510 FQ	38220 AW	69060 TQ	MABLS	10/01-12/01
	Lowell PMSA, MA-NH	Y	29860 FQ	44090 AW	65210 TQ	MABLS	10/01-12/01
	Worcester PMSA, MA-CT	Y	29800 FQ	42070 AW	57080 TQ	MABLS	10/01-12/01
	Michigan	Y	27570 FQ	47230 AW	74700 TQ	MIBLS	10/01-12/01
	Detroit PMSA, MI	Y	27700 FQ	50390 AW	83350 TQ	MIBLS	10/01-12/01
	Flint PMSA, MI	Y	35240 FQ	51610 AW	78420 TQ	MIBLS	10/01-12/01
	Grand Rapids-Muskegon-Holland MSA, MI	Y	26290 FQ	42250 AW	64730 TQ	MIBLS	10/01-12/01
	Kalamazoo-Battle Creek MSA, MI	Y	24840 FQ	44360 AW	73730 TQ	MIBLS	10/01-12/01
	Lansing-East Lansing MSA, MI	Y	30920 FQ	43680 AW	60650 TQ	MIBLS	10/01-12/01
	Minnesota	Y	28210 FQ	44760 AW	69450 TQ	MNBLS	10/01-12/01
	Duluth-Superior MSA, MN-WI	Y	29110 FQ	39610 AW	56070 TQ	MNBLS	10/01-12/01
	Minneapolis-St. Paul MSA, MN-WI	Y	28640 FQ	46180 AW	77350 TQ	MNBLS	10/01-12/01
	St. Cloud MSA, MN	Y	30400 FQ	40590 AW	54830 TQ	MNBLS	10/01-12/01
	Mississippi	Y	21170 FQ	38990 AW	60880 TQ	MSBLS	10/01-12/01
	Missouri	Y	22700 FQ	39330 AW	61110 TQ	MOBLS	10/01-12/01
	Kansas City MSA, MO-KS	Y	26420 FQ	44780 AW	68470 TQ	MOBLS	10/01-12/01

AAW	Average annual wage	**AOH**	Average offered, high	**ASH**	Average starting, high	**H**	Hourly	**M**	Monthly	**S**	Special: hourly and annual
AE	Average entry wage	**AOL**	Average offered, low	**ASL**	Average starting, low	**HI**	Highest wage paid	**MTC**	Median total compensation	**TQ**	Third quartile wage
AEX	Average experienced wage	**APH**	Average pay, high range	**AW**	Average wage paid	**HR**	High end range	**MW**	Median wage paid	**W**	Weekly
AO	Average offered	**APL**	Average pay, low range	**FQ**	First quartile wage	**LR**	Low end range	**SQ**	Second quartile wage	**Y**	Yearly

Occupation/Type/Industry	Location	Per	Low	Mid	High	Source	Date
Claims Adjuster, Examiner, and Investigator	St. Louis MSA, MO-IL	Y	21910 FQ	40260 AW	62180 TQ	MOBLS	10/01-12/01
	Springfield MSA, MO	Y	21430 FQ	34710 AW	54150 TQ	MOBLS	10/01-12/01
	Montana	Y	23660 FQ	44090 AW	69550 TQ	MTBLS	10/01-12/01
	Billings MSA, MT	Y	24230 FQ	47500 AW	70950 TQ	MTBLS	10/01-12/01
	Nebraska	Y	24500 FQ	39550 AW	58590 TQ	NEBLS	10/01-12/01
	Lincoln MSA, NE	Y	27770 FQ	40200 AW	57730 TQ	NEBLS	10/01-12/01
	Omaha MSA, NE-IA	Y	23800 FQ	38240 AW	56510 TQ	NEBLS	10/01-12/01
	Nevada	Y	27680 FQ	43710 AW	63250 TQ	NVBLS	10/01-12/01
	Las Vegas MSA, NV-AZ	Y	32270 FQ	46640 AW	66200 TQ	NVBLS	10/01-12/01
	Reno MSA, NV	Y	25080 FQ	37020 AW	56020 TQ	NVBLS	10/01-12/01
	New Hampshire	Y	33830 FQ	59420 AW	95000 TQ	NHBLS	10/01-12/01
	Manchester PMSA, NH	Y	37050 FQ	53490 AW	82390 TQ	NHBLS	10/01-12/01
	New Jersey	Y	27060 FQ	46500 AW	73900 TQ	NJBLS	10/01-12/01
	Bergen-Passaic PMSA, NJ	Y	26990 FQ	49110 AW	75020 TQ	NJBLS	10/01-12/01
	Jersey City PMSA, NJ	Y	24680 FQ	45570 AW	75670 TQ	NJBLS	10/01-12/01
	Middlesex-Somerset-Hunterdon PMSA, NJ	Y	29110 FQ	45320 AW	72470 TQ	NJBLS	10/01-12/01
	Monmouth-Ocean PMSA, NJ	Y	32700 FQ	55360 AW	83370 TQ	NJBLS	10/01-12/01
	Newark PMSA, NJ	Y	24860 FQ	44220 AW	70680 TQ	NJBLS	10/01-12/01
	Trenton PMSA, NJ	Y	30240 FQ	43200 AW	59870 TQ	NJBLS	10/01-12/01
	New Mexico	Y	25940 FQ	42380 AW	64140 TQ	NMBLS	10/01-12/01
	Albuquerque MSA, NM	Y	25650 FQ	41770 AW	62030 TQ	NMBLS	10/01-12/01
	New York	Y	28050 FQ	50760 AW	82280 TQ	NYBLS	10/01-12/01
	Albany-Schenectady-Troy MSA, NY	Y	28220 FQ	50310 AW	83230 TQ	NYBLS	10/01-12/01
	Binghamton MSA, NY	Y	28830 FQ	47790 AW	64360 TQ	NYBLS	10/01-12/01
	Buffalo-Niagara Falls MSA, NY	Y	28190 FQ	46910 AW	70500 TQ	NYBLS	10/01-12/01
	Nassau-Suffolk PMSA, NY	Y	28090 FQ	49950 AW	81480 TQ	NYBLS	10/01-12/01
	New York PMSA, NY	Y	33330 FQ	57410 AW	87930 TQ	NYBLS	10/01-12/01
	Rochester MSA, NY	Y	29640 FQ	47050 AW	72610 TQ	NYBLS	10/01-12/01
	Syracuse MSA, NY	Y	26840 FQ	45040 AW	71410 TQ	NYBLS	10/01-12/01
	North Carolina	Y	25990 FQ	42200 AW	62680 TQ	NCBLS	10/01-12/01
	Asheville MSA, NC	Y	32810 FQ	43270 AW	61990 TQ	NCBLS	10/01-12/01
	Charlotte-Gastonia-Rock Hill MSA, NC-SC	Y	26060 FQ	42720 AW	62100 TQ	NCBLS	10/01-12/01
	Greensboro-Winston-Salem-High Point MSA, NC	Y	24570 FQ	41400 AW	62170 TQ	NCBLS	10/01-12/01
	Hickory-Morganton-Lenoir MSA, NC	Y	24940 FQ	40950 AW	67650 TQ	NCBLS	10/01-12/01
	Raleigh-Durham-Chapel Hill MSA, NC	Y	28090 FQ	42370 AW	63340 TQ	NCBLS	10/01-12/01
	Wilmington MSA, NC	Y	30540 FQ	39110 AW	48950 TQ	NCBLS	10/01-12/01
	North Dakota	Y	24780 FQ	37050 AW	53990 TQ	NDBLS	10/01-12/01
	Fargo-Moorhead MSA, ND-MN	Y	27070 FQ	38390 AW	54910 TQ	NDBLS	10/01-12/01
	Ohio	Y	25060 FQ	40810 AW	64760 TQ	OHBLS	10/01-12/01
	Canton-Massillon MSA, OH	Y	28540 FQ	43740 AW	63450 TQ	OHBLS	10/01-12/01
	Cincinnati PMSA, OH-KY-IN	Y	27880 FQ	45420 AW	71460 TQ	OHBLS	10/01-12/01
	Cleveland-Lorain-Elyria PMSA, OH	Y	24050 FQ	40080 AW	68700 TQ	OHBLS	10/01-12/01
	Columbus MSA, OH	Y	23950 FQ	37430 AW	56100 TQ	OHBLS	10/01-12/01
	Dayton-Springfield MSA, OH	Y	29140 FQ	46980 AW	60410 TQ	OHBLS	10/01-12/01
	Mansfield MSA, OH	Y	26030 FQ	37860 AW	59870 TQ	OHBLS	10/01-12/01
	Toledo MSA, OH	Y	22160 FQ	38890 AW	60550 TQ	OHBLS	10/01-12/01
	Youngstown-Warren MSA, OH	Y	23210 FQ	35560 AW	60520 TQ	OHBLS	10/01-12/01
	Oklahoma	Y	26390 FQ	46040 AW	70140 TQ	OKBLS	10/01-12/01
	Oklahoma City MSA, OK	Y	29730 FQ	48350 AW	71130 TQ	OKBLS	10/01-12/01
	Oregon	Y	30050 FQ	45280 AW	63070 TQ	ORBLS	10/01-12/01
	Eugene-Springfield MSA, OR	Y	36530 FQ	50780 AW	68690 TQ	ORBLS	10/01-12/01
	Portland-Vancouver PMSA, OR-WA	Y	29700 FQ	44920 AW	63050 TQ	ORBLS	10/01-12/01
	Salem PMSA, OR	Y	31390 FQ	45150 AW	58870 TQ	ORBLS	10/01-12/01
	Pennsylvania	Y	25700 FQ	44510 AW	68740 TQ	PABLS	10/01-12/01
	Allentown-Bethlehem-Easton MSA, PA	Y	30800 FQ	48350 AW	69420 TQ	PABLS	10/01-12/01
	Harrisburg-Lebanon-Carlisle MSA, PA	Y	26480 FQ	42660 AW	63450 TQ	PABLS	10/01-12/01
	Lancaster MSA, PA	Y	20410 FQ	33040 AW	52000 TQ	PABLS	10/01-12/01
	Philadelphia PMSA, PA-NJ	Y	26440 FQ	46330 AW	76510 TQ	PABLS	10/01-12/01
	Pittsburgh MSA, PA	Y	24330 FQ	43380 AW	66420 TQ	PABLS	10/01-12/01

AAW	Average annual wage	**AOH**	Average offered, high	**ASH**	Average starting, high	**H**	Hourly	**M**	Monthly	**S**	Special: hourly and annual
AE	Average entry wage	**AOL**	Average offered, low	**ASL**	Average starting, low	**HI**	Highest wage paid	**MTC**	Median total compensation	**TQ**	Third quartile wage
AEX	Average experienced wage	**APH**	Average pay, high range	**AW**	Average wage paid	**HR**	High end range	**MW**	Median wage paid	**W**	Weekly
AO	Average offered	**APL**	Average pay, low range	**FQ**	First quartile wage	**LR**	Low end range	**SQ**	Second quartile wage	**Y**	Yearly

Occupation/Type/Industry	Location	Per	Low	Mid	High	Source	Date
Claims Adjuster, Examiner, and Investigator							
	Scranton-Wilkes-Barre-Hazleton MSA, PA	Y	22300 FQ	35280 AW	54220 TQ	PABLS	10/01-12/01
	York MSA, PA	Y	28740 FQ	44640 AW	69120 TQ	PABLS	10/01-12/01
	Rhode Island	Y	24610 FQ	48970 AW	77970 TQ	RIBLS	10/01-12/01
	Providence-Fall River-Warwick MSA, RI-MA	Y	24800 FQ	48520 AW	77030 TQ	RIBLS	10/01-12/01
	South Carolina	Y	23520 FQ	40350 AW	66220 TQ	SCBLS	10/01-12/01
	Charleston-North Charleston MSA, SC	Y	19990 FQ	40750 AW	65590 TQ	SCBLS	10/01-12/01
	Columbia MSA, SC	Y	23740 FQ	38020 AW	57790 TQ	SCBLS	10/01-12/01
	Greenville-Spartanburg-Anderson MSA, SC	Y	29250 FQ	51280 AW	75500 TQ	SCBLS	10/01-12/01
	South Dakota	Y	29040 FQ	42550 AW	60290 TQ	SDBLS	10/01-12/01
	Sioux Falls MSA, SD	Y	30400 FQ	40700 AW	55880 TQ	SDBLS	10/01-12/01
	Tennessee	Y	27480 FQ	46720 AW	73950 TQ	TNBLS	10/01-12/01
	Chattanooga MSA, TN-GA	Y	28180 FQ	49230 AW	80160 TQ	TNBLS	10/01-12/01
	Johnson City-Kingsport-Bristol MSA, TN-VA	Y	21500 FQ	44860 AW	72500 TQ	TNBLS	10/01-12/01
	Knoxville MSA, TN	Y	26220 FQ	44780 AW	68720 TQ	TNBLS	10/01-12/01
	Memphis MSA, TN-AR-MS	Y	28530 FQ	47520 AW	75390 TQ	TNBLS	10/01-12/01
	Nashville MSA, TN	Y	27450 FQ	45480 AW	71280 TQ	TNBLS	10/01-12/01
	Texas	Y	28890 FQ	47440 AW	70490 TQ	TXBLS	10/01-12/01
	Amarillo MSA, TX	Y	29680 FQ	48410 AW	69200 TQ	TXBLS	10/01-12/01
	Austin-San Marcos MSA, TX	Y	28630 FQ	47620 AW	69880 TQ	TXBLS	10/01-12/01
	Beaumont-Port Arthur MSA, TX	Y	24330 FQ	40910 AW	59770 TQ	TXBLS	10/01-12/01
	Brownsville-Harlingen-San Benito MSA, TX	Y	22850 FQ	36180 AW	65070 TQ	TXBLS	10/01-12/01
	Corpus Christi MSA, TX	Y	25370 FQ	44970 AW	70480 TQ	TXBLS	10/01-12/01
	Dallas PMSA, TX	Y	27800 FQ	45870 AW	69410 TQ	TXBLS	10/01-12/01
	El Paso MSA, TX	Y	32260 FQ	53380 AW	74490 TQ	TXBLS	10/01-12/01
	Fort Worth-Arlington PMSA, TX	Y	32780 FQ	49470 AW	68220 TQ	TXBLS	10/01-12/01
	Galveston-Texas City PMSA, TX	Y	26610 FQ	43780 AW	66190 TQ	TXBLS	10/01-12/01
	Houston PMSA, TX	Y	30160 FQ	49720 AW	79410 TQ	TXBLS	10/01-12/01
	Killeen-Temple MSA, TX	Y	30180 FQ	43770 AW	62070 TQ	TXBLS	10/01-12/01
	Laredo MSA, TX	Y	24530 FQ	44430 AW	69170 TQ	TXBLS	10/01-12/01
	Longview-Marshall MSA, TX	Y	22630 FQ	37890 AW	58110 TQ	TXBLS	10/01-12/01
	Lubbock MSA, TX	Y	44120 FQ	66060 AW	86280 TQ	TXBLS	10/01-12/01
	McAllen-Edinburg-Mission MSA, TX	Y	29470 FQ	42680 AW	66110 TQ	TXBLS	10/01-12/01
	Odessa-Midland MSA, TX	Y	30140 FQ	47160 AW	69030 TQ	TXBLS	10/01-12/01
	San Antonio MSA, TX	Y	31270 FQ	47750 AW	69240 TQ	TXBLS	10/01-12/01
	Tyler MSA, TX	Y	31530 FQ	52160 AW	75610 TQ	TXBLS	10/01-12/01
	Utah	Y	23020 FQ	43410 AW	72750 TQ	UTBLS	10/01-12/01
	Salt Lake City-Ogden MSA, UT	Y	23090 FQ	42960 AW	71900 TQ	UTBLS	10/01-12/01
	Vermont	Y	28300 FQ	47240 AW	70020 TQ	VTBLS	10/01-12/01
	Burlington MSA, VT	Y	25660 FQ	42650 AW	69370 TQ	VTBLS	10/01-12/01
	Virginia	Y	25250 FQ	41600 AW	64330 TQ	VABLS	10/01-12/01
	Lynchburg MSA, VA	Y	30090 FQ	44270 AW	64130 TQ	VABLS	10/01-12/01
	Richmond-Petersburg MSA, VA	Y	25470 FQ	41140 AW	62130 TQ	VABLS	10/01-12/01
	Roanoke MSA, VA	Y	27900 FQ	45910 AW	70950 TQ	VABLS	10/01-12/01
	Washington	Y	31340 FQ	48690 AW	70720 TQ	WABLS	10/01-12/01
	Olympia PMSA, WA	Y	28540 FQ	50350 AW	71450 TQ	WABLS	10/01-12/01
	Richland-Kennewick-Pasco MSA, WA	Y	40230 FQ	61700 AW	86010 TQ	WABLS	10/01-12/01
	Seattle-Bellevue-Everett PMSA, WA	Y	32460 FQ	50190 AW	71890 TQ	WABLS	10/01-12/01
	Spokane MSA, WA	Y	23750 FQ	40490 AW	58470 TQ	WABLS	10/01-12/01
	Tacoma PMSA, WA	Y	31250 FQ	47090 AW	68970 TQ	WABLS	10/01-12/01
	Yakima MSA, WA	Y	36000 FQ	51430 AW	73910 TQ	WABLS	10/01-12/01
	West Virginia	Y	21700 FQ	39330 AW	65380 TQ	WVBLS	10/01-12/01
	Charleston MSA, WV	Y	23300 FQ	39890 AW	67360 TQ	WVBLS	10/01-12/01
	Huntington-Ashland MSA, WV-KY-OH	Y	19910 FQ	39910 AW	60900 TQ	WVBLS	10/01-12/01
	Wisconsin	Y	20790 FQ	37080 AW	55860 TQ	WIBLS	10/01-12/01
	Appleton-Oshkosh-Neenah MSA, WI	Y	24790 FQ	38100 AW	53830 TQ	WIBLS	10/01-12/01

AAW	Average annual wage	**AOH**	Average offered, high	**ASH**	Average starting, high	**H**	Hourly	**M**	Monthly	**S**	Special: hourly and annual
AE	Average entry wage	**AOL**	Average offered, low	**ASL**	Average starting, low	**HI**	Highest wage paid	**MTC**	Median total compensation	**TQ**	Third quartile wage
AEX	Average experienced wage	**APH**	Average pay, high range	**AW**	Average wage paid	**HR**	High end range	**MW**	Median wage paid	**W**	Weekly
AO	Average offered	**APL**	Average pay, low range	**FQ**	First quartile wage	**LR**	Low end range	**SQ**	Second quartile wage	**Y**	Yearly

Occupation/Type/Industry	Location	Per	Low	Mid	High	Source	Date
Claims Adjuster, Examiner, and Investigator	Madison MSA, WI	Y	19760 FQ	35350 AW	55290 TQ	WIBLS	10/01-12/01
	Milwaukee-Waukesha PMSA, WI	Y	24160 FQ	40500 AW	58860 TQ	WIBLS	10/01-12/01
	Wyoming	Y	29550 FQ	44090 AW	67060 TQ	WYBLS	10/01-12/01
	Puerto Rico	Y	14000 FQ	23850 AW	38120 TQ	PRBLS	10/01-12/01
	Guam	Y	16400 FQ	31460 AW	47770 TQ	GUBLS	10/01-12/01
Claims Executive							
Insurance	United States	Y		116826 AW		WW	1/00-1/01
Classroom Instructor							
Computers	Central	Y		49909 AW		TRAIN	1/01-1/02
Computers	East North Central	Y		59590 AW		TRAIN	1/01-1/02
Computers	Northeast	Y		55187 AW		TRAIN	1/01-1/02
Computers	Pacific	Y		54571 AW		TRAIN	1/01-1/02
Computers	Southeast	Y		49211 AW		TRAIN	1/01-1/02
Computers	West Central	Y		57158 AW		TRAIN	1/01-1/02
Cleaner of Vehicle and Equipment	Alabama	H	5.78 FQ	8.58 AW	12.83 TQ	ALBLS	10/01-12/01
	Alaska	H	7.09 FQ	9.17 AW	11.69 TQ	AKBLS	10/01-12/01
	Arizona	H	5.63 FQ	7.46 AW	10.16 TQ	AZBLS	10/01-12/01
	Arkansas	H	6.24 FQ	8.96 AW	11.71 TQ	ARBLS	10/01-12/01
	California	H	6.47 FQ	8.65 AW	12.51 TQ	CABLS	10/01-12/01
	Colorado	H	6.33 FQ	9.76 AW	14.17 TQ	COBLS	10/01-12/01
	Connecticut	H	6.70 FQ	9.68 AW	14.59 TQ	CTBLS	10/01-12/01
	Delaware	H	6.80 FQ	9.96 AW	15.01 TQ	DEBLS	10/01-12/01
	District of Columbia	H	7.00 FQ	11.06 AW	16.90 TQ	DCBLS	10/01-12/01
	Florida	H	5.82 FQ	8.07 AW	11.38 TQ	FLBLS	10/01-12/01
	Georgia	H	5.86 FQ	8.39 AW	11.74 TQ	GABLS	10/01-12/01
	Hawaii	H	5.94 FQ	9.18 AW	14.91 TQ	HIBLS	10/01-12/01
	Idaho	H	5.77 FQ	7.75 AW	10.49 TQ	IDBLS	10/01-12/01
	Illinois	H	5.72 FQ	8.46 AW	13.58 TQ	ILBLS	10/01-12/01
	Indiana	H	5.89 FQ	9.34 AW	14.60 TQ	INBLS	10/01-12/01
	Iowa	H	5.83 FQ	8.88 AW	13.17 TQ	IABLS	10/01-12/01
	Kansas	H	5.88 FQ	8.18 AW	10.89 TQ	KSBLS	10/01-12/01
	Kentucky	H	5.79 FQ	8.78 AW	13.40 TQ	KYBLS	10/01-12/01
	Louisiana	H	5.64 FQ	7.56 AW	10.97 TQ	LABLS	10/01-12/01
	Maine	H	6.04 FQ	8.58 AW	12.03 TQ	MEBLS	10/01-12/01
	Maryland	H	6.00 FQ	10.50 AW	19.13 TQ	MDBLS	10/01-12/01
	Massachusetts	H	7.01 FQ	10.24 AW	14.79 TQ	MABLS	10/01-12/01
	Michigan	H	5.94 FQ	10.21 AW	18.66 TQ	MIBLS	10/01-12/01
	Minnesota	H	6.38 FQ	9.54 AW	14.41 TQ	MNBLS	10/01-12/01
	Mississippi	H	5.94 FQ	8.40 AW	11.44 TQ	MSBLS	10/01-12/01
	Missouri	H	5.91 FQ	8.66 AW	12.33 TQ	MOBLS	10/01-12/01
	Montana	H	5.78 FQ	8.19 AW	12.68 TQ	MTBLS	10/01-12/01
	Nebraska	H	5.97 FQ	8.51 AW	11.56 TQ	NEBLS	10/01-12/01
	Nevada	H	5.78 FQ	8.23 AW	11.63 TQ	NVBLS	10/01-12/01
	New Hampshire	H	7.38 FQ	9.60 AW	12.92 TQ	NHBLS	10/01-12/01
	New Jersey	H	5.89 FQ	9.08 AW	13.42 TQ	NJBLS	10/01-12/01
	New Mexico	H	5.60 FQ	7.11 AW	9.13 TQ	NMBLS	10/01-12/01
	New York	H	5.78 FQ	9.59 AW	16.94 TQ	NYBLS	10/01-12/01
	North Carolina	H	5.86 FQ	8.63 AW	12.45 TQ	NCBLS	10/01-12/01
	North Dakota	H	5.69 FQ	7.59 AW	10.66 TQ	NDBLS	10/01-12/01
	Ohio	H	5.85 FQ	9.48 AW	15.10 TQ	OHBLS	10/01-12/01
	Oklahoma	H	5.70 FQ	8.39 AW	12.84 TQ	OKBLS	10/01-12/01
	Oregon	H	7.06 FQ	9.29 AW	13.29 TQ	ORBLS	10/01-12/01
	Pennsylvania	H	5.79 FQ	8.49 AW	12.36 TQ	PABLS	10/01-12/01
	Rhode Island	H	6.82 FQ	10.00 AW	13.93 TQ	RIBLS	10/01-12/01
	South Carolina	H	5.83 FQ	8.10 AW	10.83 TQ	SCBLS	10/01-12/01
	South Dakota	H	5.71 FQ	7.34 AW	9.22 TQ	SDBLS	10/01-12/01
	Tennessee	H	5.97 FQ	9.02 AW	13.26 TQ	TNBLS	10/01-12/01
	Texas	H	5.71 FQ	7.92 AW	11.29 TQ	TXBLS	10/01-12/01
	Utah	H	5.89 FQ	8.10 AW	11.18 TQ	UTBLS	10/01-12/01
	Vermont	H	6.87 FQ	9.51 AW	12.49 TQ	VTBLS	10/01-12/01
	Virginia	H	6.01 FQ	8.57 AW	12.07 TQ	VABLS	10/01-12/01
	Washington	H	6.94 FQ	10.02 AW	15.86 TQ	WABLS	10/01-12/01
	West Virginia	H	5.63 FQ	7.36 AW	10.26 TQ	WVBLS	10/01-12/01
	Wisconsin	H	6.04 FQ	8.89 AW	12.70 TQ	WIBLS	10/01-12/01
	Wyoming	H	5.74 FQ	8.35 AW	11.76 TQ	WYBLS	10/01-12/01
	Puerto Rico	H	5.52 FQ	6.65 AW	8.21 TQ	PRBLS	10/01-12/01

AAW Average annual wage; **AE** Average entry wage; **AEX** Average experienced wage; **AO** Average offered; **AOH** Average offered, high; **AOL** Average offered, low; **APH** Average pay, high range; **APL** Average pay, low range; **ASH** Average starting, high; **ASL** Average starting, low; **AW** Average wage paid; **FQ** First quartile wage; **H** Hourly; **HI** Highest wage paid; **HR** High end range; **LR** Low end range; **M** Monthly; **MTC** Median total compensation; **MW** Median wage paid; **SQ** Second quartile wage; **S** Special: hourly and annual; **TQ** Third quartile wage; **W** Weekly; **Y** Yearly

Occupation/Type/Industry	Location	Per	Low	Mid	High	Source	Date
Cleaner of Vehicle and Equipment	Virgin Islands	H	5.65 FQ	6.89 AW	9.31 TQ	VIBLS	10/01-12/01
	Guam	H	5.76 FQ	7.27 AW	9.33 TQ	GUBLS	10/01-12/01
Cleaning, Washing, and Metal Pickling Equipment Operator and Tender	Alabama	H	7.24 FQ	10.75 AW	17.75 TQ	ALBLS	10/01-12/01
	Arizona	H	5.95 FQ	9.18 AW	14.34 TQ	AZBLS	10/01-12/01
	Arkansas	H	7.40 FQ	10.86 AW	17.10 TQ	ARBLS	10/01-12/01
	California	H	6.90 FQ	10.93 AW	16.84 TQ	CABLS	10/01-12/01
	Colorado	H	7.32 FQ	10.90 AW	16.92 TQ	COBLS	10/01-12/01
	Connecticut	H	8.32 FQ	13.05 AW	17.28 TQ	CTBLS	10/01-12/01
	Florida	H	6.58 FQ	10.03 AW	14.36 TQ	FLBLS	10/01-12/01
	Georgia	H	7.42 FQ	10.00 AW	14.30 TQ	GABLS	10/01-12/01
	Illinois	H	6.41 FQ	11.02 AW	18.95 TQ	ILBLS	10/01-12/01
	Indiana	H	8.53 FQ	13.85 AW	20.14 TQ	INBLS	10/01-12/01
	Iowa	H	8.33 FQ	12.38 AW	19.01 TQ	IABLS	10/01-12/01
	Kansas	H	8.89 FQ	12.96 AW	16.96 TQ	KSBLS	10/01-12/01
	Kentucky	H	7.55 FQ	10.89 AW	15.81 TQ	KYBLS	10/01-12/01
	Louisiana	H	6.26 FQ	10.92 AW	16.62 TQ	LABLS	10/01-12/01
	Maine	H	9.14 FQ	12.01 AW	16.97 TQ	MEBLS	10/01-12/01
	Maryland	H	7.62 FQ	11.16 AW	16.21 TQ	MDBLS	10/01-12/01
	Massachusetts	H	7.68 FQ	12.52 AW	17.41 TQ	MABLS	10/01-12/01
	Michigan	H	8.62 FQ	12.04 AW	16.07 TQ	MIBLS	10/01-12/01
	Minnesota	H	7.15 FQ	12.63 AW	17.47 TQ	MNBLS	10/01-12/01
	Mississippi	H	6.33 FQ	9.88 AW	13.46 TQ	MSBLS	10/01-12/01
	Missouri	H	8.52 FQ	12.21 AW	16.64 TQ	MOBLS	10/01-12/01
	Montana	H	7.90 FQ	11.76 AW	18.82 TQ	MTBLS	10/01-12/01
	Nebraska	H	8.74 FQ	11.83 AW	19.00 TQ	NEBLS	10/01-12/01
	New Hampshire	H	9.16 FQ	11.31 AW	15.73 TQ	NHBLS	10/01-12/01
	New Jersey	H	6.01 FQ	10.24 AW	15.69 TQ	NJBLS	10/01-12/01
	New Mexico	H	7.55 FQ	11.02 AW	16.32 TQ	NMBLS	10/01-12/01
	New York	H	7.98 FQ	13.08 AW	19.22 TQ	NYBLS	10/01-12/01
	North Carolina	H	6.53 FQ	9.69 AW	14.82 TQ	NCBLS	10/01-12/01
	Ohio	H	8.25 FQ	12.97 AW	18.09 TQ	OHBLS	10/01-12/01
	Oklahoma	H	7.46 FQ	9.49 AW	11.80 TQ	OKBLS	10/01-12/01
	Oregon	H	7.69 FQ	12.16 AW	21.10 TQ	ORBLS	10/01-12/01
	Pennsylvania	H	9.26 FQ	13.86 AW	20.54 TQ	PABLS	10/01-12/01
	Rhode Island	H	7.68 FQ	9.83 AW	12.32 TQ	RIBLS	10/01-12/01
	South Carolina	H	6.82 FQ	11.64 AW	16.26 TQ	SCBLS	10/01-12/01
	South Dakota	H	7.94 FQ	11.26 AW	14.87 TQ	SDBLS	10/01-12/01
	Tennessee	H	9.20 FQ	15.76 AW	25.98 TQ	TNBLS	10/01-12/01
	Texas	H	6.00 FQ	9.64 AW	15.26 TQ	TXBLS	10/01-12/01
	Vermont	H	8.61 FQ	12.24 AW	16.80 TQ	VTBLS	10/01-12/01
	Virginia	H	8.06 FQ	15.88 AW	25.94 TQ	VABLS	10/01-12/01
	Washington	H	7.30 FQ	9.91 AW	13.18 TQ	WABLS	10/01-12/01
	West Virginia	H	6.75 FQ	12.87 AW	20.13 TQ	WVBLS	10/01-12/01
	Wisconsin	H	7.85 FQ	11.34 AW	15.44 TQ	WIBLS	10/01-12/01
Clergy	Alabama	Y	18930 FQ	34570 AW	59390 TQ	ALBLS	10/01-12/01
	Birmingham MSA, AL	Y	18350 FQ	34470 AW	56230 TQ	ALBLS	10/01-12/01
	Alaska	Y	12570 FQ	28680 AW	48550 TQ	AKBLS	10/01-12/01
	Arizona	Y	18170 FQ	36070 AW	55770 TQ	AZBLS	10/01-12/01
	Phoenix-Mesa MSA, AZ	Y	20110 FQ	36690 AW	53980 TQ	AZBLS	10/01-12/01
	Tucson MSA, AZ	Y	28110 FQ	40120 AW	66880 TQ	AZBLS	10/01-12/01
	Arkansas	Y	23030 FQ	33700 AW	48700 TQ	ARBLS	10/01-12/01
	Little Rock-North Little Rock MSA, AR	Y	23580 FQ	34350 AW	51400 TQ	ARBLS	10/01-12/01
	California	Y	15180 FQ	44180 AW	76040 TQ	CABLS	10/01-12/01
	Bakersfield MSA, CA	Y	22860 FQ	41450 AW	64450 TQ	CABLS	10/01-12/01
	Fresno MSA, CA	Y	13380 FQ	36530 AW	67370 TQ	CABLS	10/01-12/01
	Los Angeles-Long Beach PMSA, CA	Y	31520 FQ	57890 AW	85820 TQ	CABLS	10/01-12/01
	Modesto MSA, CA	Y	13380 FQ	25460 AW	49410 TQ	CABLS	10/01-12/01
	Oakland PMSA, CA	Y	19260 FQ	41170 AW	83020 TQ	CABLS	10/01-12/01
	Orange County PMSA, CA	Y	36470 FQ	46980 AW	63470 TQ	CABLS	10/01-12/01
	Riverside-San Bernardino PMSA, CA	Y	21470 FQ	42140 AW	63750 TQ	CABLS	10/01-12/01
	Sacramento PMSA, CA	Y	19560 FQ	34700 AW	54780 TQ	CABLS	10/01-12/01
	San Diego MSA, CA	Y	13320 FQ	22470 AW	44650 TQ	CABLS	10/01-12/01
	San Francisco PMSA, CA	Y	20850 FQ	58640 AW	103930 TQ	CABLS	10/01-12/01
	San Jose PMSA, CA	Y	24900 FQ	41980 AW	64630 TQ	CABLS	10/01-12/01

AAW	Average annual wage	AOH	Average offered, high	ASH	Average starting, high	H	Hourly	M	Monthly	S	Special: hourly and annual
AE	Average entry wage	AOL	Average offered, low	ASL	Average starting, low	HI	Highest wage paid	MTC	Median total compensation	TQ	Third quartile wage
AEX	Average experienced wage	APH	Average pay, high range	AW	Average wage paid	HR	High end range	MW	Median wage paid	W	Weekly
AO	Average offered	APL	Average pay, low range	FQ	First quartile wage	LR	Low end range	SQ	Second quartile wage	Y	Yearly

Occupation/Type/Industry	Location	Per	Low	Mid	High	Source	Date
Clergy	San Luis Obispo-Atascadero-Paso Robles MSA, CA	Y	36920 FQ	47060 AW	62270 TQ	CABLS	10/01-12/01
	Santa Barbara-Santa Maria-Lompoc MSA, CA	Y	38410 FQ	52150 AW	68360 TQ	CABLS	10/01-12/01
	Stockton-Lodi MSA, CA	Y	13830 FQ	35440 AW	63530 TQ	CABLS	10/01-12/01
	Vallejo-Fairfield-Napa PMSA, CA	Y	13970 FQ	41750 AW	56470 TQ	CABLS	10/01-12/01
	Ventura PMSA, CA	Y	16560 FQ	38410 AW	61240 TQ	CABLS	10/01-12/01
	Colorado	Y	12960 FQ	36370 AW	62540 TQ	COBLS	10/01-12/01
	Colorado Springs MSA, CO	Y	21800 FQ	48860 AW		COBLS	10/01-12/01
	Denver PMSA, CO	Y	12250 FQ	29290 AW	53550 TQ	COBLS	10/01-12/01
	Connecticut	Y	21250 FQ	44810 AW	67670 TQ	CTBLS	10/01-12/01
	Hartford MSA, CT	Y	20280 FQ	42420 AW	65990 TQ	CTBLS	10/01-12/01
	New Haven-Meriden PMSA, CT	Y	25440 FQ	52140 AW	71200 TQ	CTBLS	10/01-12/01
	Delaware	Y	31550 FQ	41150 AW	54800 TQ	DEBLS	10/01-12/01
	Wilmington-Newark PMSA, DE-MD	Y	32240 FQ	43700 AW	61760 TQ	DEBLS	10/01-12/01
	District of Columbia	Y	26270 FQ	54040 AW	83990 TQ	DCBLS	10/01-12/01
	Washington PMSA, DC-MD-VA-WV	Y	12580 FQ	32140 AW	61510 TQ	DCBLS	10/01-12/01
	Florida	Y	13760 FQ	30370 AW	49890 TQ	FLBLS	10/01-12/01
	Daytona Beach MSA, FL	Y	18900 FQ	33850 AW	51440 TQ	FLBLS	10/01-12/01
	Fort Lauderdale PMSA, FL	Y	15580 FQ	34040 AW	55130 TQ	FLBLS	10/01-12/01
	Fort Myers-Cape Coral MSA, FL	Y	18490 FQ	27720 AW	35320 TQ	FLBLS	10/01-12/01
	Gainesville MSA, FL	Y	15670 FQ	33230 AW	52110 TQ	FLBLS	10/01-12/01
	Jacksonville MSA, FL	Y	17650 FQ	24590 AW	35150 TQ	FLBLS	10/01-12/01
	Lakeland-Winter Haven MSA, FL	Y	15470 FQ	28100 AW	50080 TQ	FLBLS	10/01-12/01
	Melbourne-Titusville-Palm Bay MSA, FL	Y	23080 FQ	27700 AW	38800 TQ	FLBLS	10/01-12/01
	Miami PMSA, FL	Y	14770 FQ	29110 AW	47560 TQ	FLBLS	10/01-12/01
	Orlando MSA, FL	Y	19940 FQ	30790 AW	44740 TQ	FLBLS	10/01-12/01
	Pensacola MSA, FL	Y	12220 FQ	21340 AW	33350 TQ	FLBLS	10/01-12/01
	Sarasota-Bradenton MSA, FL	Y	12230 FQ	24650 AW	36140 TQ	FLBLS	10/01-12/01
	Tallahassee MSA, FL	Y	23020 FQ	37860 AW	61500 TQ	FLBLS	10/01-12/01
	Tampa-St. Petersburg-Clearwater MSA, FL	Y	12100 FQ	27760 AW	51460 TQ	FLBLS	10/01-12/01
	West Palm Beach-Boca Raton MSA, FL	Y	29940 FQ	47580 AW	68380 TQ	FLBLS	10/01-12/01
	Georgia	Y	24400 FQ	39350 AW	57250 TQ	GABLS	10/01-12/01
	Atlanta MSA, GA	Y	23590 FQ	41010 AW	59050 TQ	GABLS	10/01-12/01
	Hawaii	Y	19950 FQ	35750 AW	53780 TQ	HIBLS	10/01-12/01
	Honolulu MSA, HI	Y	19320 FQ	35430 AW	47410 TQ	HIBLS	10/01-12/01
	Idaho	Y	30400 FQ	38280 AW	50250 TQ	IDBLS	10/01-12/01
	Boise City MSA, ID	Y	31010 FQ	36850 AW	44750 TQ	IDBLS	10/01-12/01
	Illinois	Y	16710 FQ	35770 AW	57330 TQ	ILBLS	10/01-12/01
	Chicago PMSA, IL	Y	18560 FQ	37210 AW	58320 TQ	ILBLS	10/01-12/01
	Peoria-Pekin MSA, IL	Y	24090 FQ	38940 AW	51350 TQ	ILBLS	10/01-12/01
	Rockford MSA, IL	Y	12210 FQ	21000 AW	34190 TQ	ILBLS	10/01-12/01
	Indiana	Y	17340 FQ	31150 AW	45530 TQ	INBLS	10/01-12/01
	Evansville-Henderson MSA, IN-KY	Y	23740 FQ	27060 AW	32340 TQ	INBLS	10/01-12/01
	Fort Wayne MSA, IN	Y	14630 FQ	25530 AW	32500 TQ	INBLS	10/01-12/01
	Gary PMSA, IN	Y	12560 FQ	30040 AW	55390 TQ	INBLS	10/01-12/01
	Indianapolis MSA, IN	Y	21060 FQ	32340 AW	46390 TQ	INBLS	10/01-12/01
	South Bend MSA, IN	Y	29760 FQ	36970 AW	45200 TQ	INBLS	10/01-12/01
	Iowa	Y	17970 FQ	32370 AW	52100 TQ	IABLS	10/01-12/01
	Davenport-Moline-Rock Island MSA, IA-IL	Y	20220 FQ	33260 AW	52090 TQ	IABLS	10/01-12/01
	Des Moines MSA, IA	Y	12390 FQ	29010 AW	44240 TQ	IABLS	10/01-12/01
	Kansas	Y	20310 FQ	35890 AW	54570 TQ	KSBLS	10/01-12/01
	Wichita MSA, KS	Y	22870 FQ	36540 AW	52670 TQ	KSBLS	10/01-12/01
	Kentucky	Y	22980 FQ	35270 AW	47710 TQ	KYBLS	10/01-12/01
	Lexington MSA, KY	Y	18350 FQ	32070 AW	44730 TQ	KYBLS	10/01-12/01
	Louisville MSA, KY-IN	Y	24310 FQ	34680 AW	45020 TQ	KYBLS	10/01-12/01
	Louisiana	Y	19970 FQ	35700 AW	52620 TQ	LABLS	10/01-12/01
	New Orleans MSA, LA	Y	20520 FQ	36140 AW	55090 TQ	LABLS	10/01-12/01
	Maine	Y	23430 FQ	38400 AW	50630 TQ	MEBLS	10/01-12/01
	Maryland	Y	22970 FQ	37070 AW	54300 TQ	MDBLS	10/01-12/01
	Baltimore PMSA, MD	Y	22390 FQ	35340 AW	53970 TQ	MDBLS	10/01-12/01

AAW Average annual wage · **AE** Average entry wage · **AEX** Average experienced wage · **AO** Average offered · **AOH** Average offered, high · **AOL** Average offered, low · **APH** Average pay, high range · **APL** Average pay, low range · **ASH** Average starting, high · **ASL** Average starting, low · **AW** Average wage paid · **FQ** First quartile wage · **H** Hourly · **HI** Highest wage paid · **HR** High end range · **LR** Low end range · **M** Monthly · **MTC** Median total compensation · **MW** Median wage paid · **SQ** Second quartile wage · **S** Special: hourly and annual · **TQ** Third quartile wage · **W** Weekly · **Y** Yearly

Occupation/Type/Industry	Location	Per	Low	Mid	High	Source	Date
Clergy	Massachusetts	Y	25550 FQ	39960 AW	57510 TQ	MABLS	10/01-12/01
	Boston PMSA, MA-NH	Y	25890 FQ	40790 AW	57990 TQ	MABLS	10/01-12/01
	Springfield MSA, MA	Y	22300 FQ	36830 AW	53780 TQ	MABLS	10/01-12/01
	Michigan	Y	15980 FQ	29320 AW	46940 TQ	MIBLS	10/01-12/01
	Ann Arbor PMSA, MI	Y	22710 FQ	38340 AW	58480 TQ	MIBLS	10/01-12/01
	Detroit PMSA, MI	Y	15810 FQ	28050 AW	46870 TQ	MIBLS	10/01-12/01
	Flint PMSA, MI	Y	24570 FQ	33610 AW	45710 TQ	MIBLS	10/01-12/01
	Grand Rapids-Muskegon-Holland MSA, MI	Y	21180 FQ	31270 AW	45110 TQ	MIBLS	10/01-12/01
	Kalamazoo-Battle Creek MSA, MI	Y	12600 FQ	27600 AW	47510 TQ	MIBLS	10/01-12/01
	Lansing-East Lansing MSA, MI	Y	23130 FQ	31960 AW	42210 TQ	MIBLS	10/01-12/01
	Saginaw-Bay City-Midland MSA, MI	Y	14270 FQ	28090 AW	45770 TQ	MIBLS	10/01-12/01
	Minnesota	Y	16010 FQ	37090 AW	55750 TQ	MNBLS	10/01-12/01
	Minneapolis-St. Paul MSA, MN-WI	Y	15220 FQ	36080 AW	55580 TQ	MNBLS	10/01-12/01
	Mississippi	Y	19260 FQ	32110 AW	47260 TQ	MSBLS	10/01-12/01
	Jackson MSA, MS	Y	18790 FQ	30400 AW	50490 TQ	MSBLS	10/01-12/01
	Missouri	Y	20790 FQ	38770 AW	61130 TQ	MOBLS	10/01-12/01
	Kansas City MSA, MO-KS	Y	17760 FQ	34290 AW	55180 TQ	MOBLS	10/01-12/01
	St. Louis MSA, MO-IL	Y	21470 FQ	41530 AW	66450 TQ	MOBLS	10/01-12/01
	Springfield MSA, MO	Y	26340 FQ	38810 AW	57110 TQ	MOBLS	10/01-12/01
	Montana	Y	19270 FQ	29090 AW	45740 TQ	MTBLS	10/01-12/01
	Billings MSA, MT	Y	23420 FQ	32350 AW	51500 TQ	MTBLS	10/01-12/01
	Nebraska	Y	19060 FQ	34100 AW	46270 TQ	NEBLS	10/01-12/01
	Lincoln MSA, NE	Y	12840 FQ	30080 AW	44260 TQ	NEBLS	10/01-12/01
	Omaha MSA, NE-IA	Y	20420 FQ	36170 AW	46080 TQ	NEBLS	10/01-12/01
	Nevada	Y	27210 FQ	66210 AW	116190 TQ	NVBLS	10/01-12/01
	New Hampshire	Y	26430 FQ	39180 AW	55910 TQ	NHBLS	10/01-12/01
	New Jersey	Y	16310 FQ	40330 AW	65350 TQ	NJBLS	10/01-12/01
	Bergen-Passaic PMSA, NJ	Y	13550 FQ	38480 AW	56760 TQ	NJBLS	10/01-12/01
	Jersey City PMSA, NJ	Y	12460 FQ	43520 AW	86380 TQ	NJBLS	10/01-12/01
	Middlesex-Somerset-Hunterdon PMSA, NJ	Y	27190 FQ	49530 AW	69700 TQ	NJBLS	10/01-12/01
	Monmouth-Ocean PMSA, NJ	Y	14470 FQ	36310 AW	56600 TQ	NJBLS	10/01-12/01
	Newark PMSA, NJ	Y	21990 FQ	42160 AW	67500 TQ	NJBLS	10/01-12/01
	New Mexico	Y	16570 FQ	31990 AW	45870 TQ	NMBLS	10/01-12/01
	Albuquerque MSA, NM	Y	29380 FQ	36930 AW	51650 TQ	NMBLS	10/01-12/01
	New York	Y	14960 FQ	36180 AW	64720 TQ	NYBLS	10/01-12/01
	Albany-Schenectady-Troy MSA, NY	Y	13340 FQ	36820 AW	59030 TQ	NYBLS	10/01-12/01
	Binghamton MSA, NY	Y	14420 FQ	34050 AW	55910 TQ	NYBLS	10/01-12/01
	Buffalo-Niagara Falls MSA, NY	Y	14930 FQ	29000 AW	56890 TQ	NYBLS	10/01-12/01
	Dutchess County PMSA, NY	Y	15410 FQ	43880 AW	67610 TQ	NYBLS	10/01-12/01
	Nassau-Suffolk PMSA, NY	Y	13100 FQ	40610 AW	58870 TQ	NYBLS	10/01-12/01
	New York PMSA, NY	Y	17910 FQ	36370 AW	71170 TQ	NYBLS	10/01-12/01
	Newburgh PMSA, NY-PA	Y	15850 FQ	33860 AW	59660 TQ	NYBLS	10/01-12/01
	Rochester MSA, NY	Y	23190 FQ	38420 AW	59020 TQ	NYBLS	10/01-12/01
	Syracuse MSA, NY	Y	12560 FQ	34280 AW	57870 TQ	NYBLS	10/01-12/01
	Utica-Rome MSA, NY	Y	12040 FQ	25370 AW	61610 TQ	NYBLS	10/01-12/01
	North Carolina	Y	21250 FQ	36640 AW	54780 TQ	NCBLS	10/01-12/01
	Charlotte-Gastonia-Rock Hill MSA, NC-SC	Y	22880 FQ	38490 AW	58220 TQ	NCBLS	10/01-12/01
	Greensboro-Winston-Salem-High Point MSA, NC	Y	30990 FQ	47880 AW	79670 TQ	NCBLS	10/01-12/01
	Raleigh-Durham-Chapel Hill MSA, NC	Y	20240 FQ	32730 AW	51010 TQ	NCBLS	10/01-12/01
	North Dakota	Y	14390 FQ	30830 AW	46020 TQ	NDBLS	10/01-12/01
	Ohio	Y	16380 FQ	29480 AW	49030 TQ	OHBLS	10/01-12/01
	Akron PMSA, OH	Y	13700 FQ	28970 AW	54990 TQ	OHBLS	10/01-12/01
	Canton-Massillon MSA, OH	Y	13240 FQ	24920 AW	39490 TQ	OHBLS	10/01-12/01
	Cincinnati PMSA, OH-KY-IN	Y	15530 FQ	31370 AW	56450 TQ	OHBLS	10/01-12/01
	Cleveland-Lorain-Elyria PMSA, OH	Y	19520 FQ	32500 AW	54370 TQ	OHBLS	10/01-12/01
	Columbus MSA, OH	Y	22550 FQ	39020 AW	52800 TQ	OHBLS	10/01-12/01
	Dayton-Springfield MSA, OH	Y	19380 FQ	33710 AW	55180 TQ	OHBLS	10/01-12/01
	Hamilton-Middletown PMSA, OH	Y	18460 FQ	23980 AW	32320 TQ	OHBLS	10/01-12/01
	Toledo MSA, OH	Y	16050 FQ	24040 AW	42090 TQ	OHBLS	10/01-12/01
	Youngstown-Warren MSA, OH	Y	17220 FQ	31280 AW	43680 TQ	OHBLS	10/01-12/01

AAW Average annual wage; **AE** Average entry wage; **AEX** Average experienced wage; **AO** Average offered; **AOH** Average offered, high; **AOL** Average offered, low; **APH** Average pay, high range; **APL** Average pay, low range; **ASH** Average starting, high; **ASL** Average starting, low; **AW** Average wage paid; **FQ** First quartile wage; **H** Hourly; **HI** Highest wage paid; **HR** High end range; **LR** Low end range; **M** Monthly; **MTC** Median total compensation; **MW** Median wage paid; **SQ** Second quartile wage; **S** Special: hourly and annual; **TQ** Third quartile wage; **W** Weekly; **Y** Yearly

Occupation/Type/Industry	Location	Per	Low	Mid	High	Source	Date
Clergy	Oklahoma	Y	19790 FQ	34760 AW	57660 TQ	OKBLS	10/01-12/01
	Oklahoma City MSA, OK	Y	24450 FQ	40920 AW	76630 TQ	OKBLS	10/01-12/01
	Oregon	Y	21310 FQ	37750 AW	53490 TQ	ORBLS	10/01-12/01
	Eugene-Springfield MSA, OR	Y	19250 FQ	32200 AW	45580 TQ	ORBLS	10/01-12/01
	Medford-Ashland MSA, OR	Y	23580 FQ	42520 AW	60660 TQ	ORBLS	10/01-12/01
	Portland-Vancouver PMSA, OR-WA	Y	26790 FQ	39760 AW	54760 TQ	ORBLS	10/01-12/01
	Salem PMSA, OR	Y	24440 FQ	37750 AW	53770 TQ	ORBLS	10/01-12/01
	Pennsylvania	Y	15660 FQ	32910 AW	56300 TQ	PABLS	10/01-12/01
	Allentown-Bethlehem-Easton MSA, PA	Y	17460 FQ	30920 AW	44700 TQ	PABLS	10/01-12/01
	Harrisburg-Lebanon-Carlisle MSA, PA	Y	20010 FQ	35690 AW	55470 TQ	PABLS	10/01-12/01
	Lancaster MSA, PA	Y	23610 FQ	33750 AW	46340 TQ	PABLS	10/01-12/01
	Philadelphia PMSA, PA-NJ	Y	14770 FQ	34200 AW	59730 TQ	PABLS	10/01-12/01
	Pittsburgh MSA, PA	Y	16310 FQ	35860 AW	60570 TQ	PABLS	10/01-12/01
	Scranton-Wilkes-Barre-Hazleton MSA, PA	Y	15180 FQ	26810 AW	36690 TQ	PABLS	10/01-12/01
	Rhode Island	Y	15890 FQ	32990 AW	61720 TQ	RIBLS	10/01-12/01
	Providence-Fall River-Warwick MSA, RI-MA	Y	15750 FQ	33500 AW	63000 TQ	RIBLS	10/01-12/01
	South Carolina	Y	13420 FQ	31300 AW	53620 TQ	SCBLS	10/01-12/01
	Columbia MSA, SC	Y	21280 FQ	37240 AW	57380 TQ	SCBLS	10/01-12/01
	Greenville-Spartanburg-Anderson MSA, SC	Y	24400 FQ	39810 AW	55490 TQ	SCBLS	10/01-12/01
	South Dakota	Y	22940 FQ	34450 AW	46840 TQ	SDBLS	10/01-12/01
	Tennessee	Y	19930 FQ	35680 AW	55490 TQ	TNBLS	10/01-12/01
	Knoxville MSA, TN	Y	19240 FQ	30870 AW	48960 TQ	TNBLS	10/01-12/01
	Memphis MSA, TN-AR-MS	Y	22970 FQ	36880 AW	51720 TQ	TNBLS	10/01-12/01
	Nashville MSA, TN	Y	19010 FQ	35610 AW	59850 TQ	TNBLS	10/01-12/01
	Texas	Y	20990 FQ	34610 AW	52690 TQ	TXBLS	10/01-12/01
	Austin-San Marcos MSA, TX	Y	28430 FQ	34790 AW	45440 TQ	TXBLS	10/01-12/01
	Dallas PMSA, TX	Y	20580 FQ	33800 AW	52480 TQ	TXBLS	10/01-12/01
	Fort Worth-Arlington PMSA, TX	Y	17410 FQ	35780 AW	56950 TQ	TXBLS	10/01-12/01
	Houston PMSA, TX	Y	21180 FQ	35370 AW	53620 TQ	TXBLS	10/01-12/01
	Killeen-Temple MSA, TX	Y	19030 FQ	30110 AW	54080 TQ	TXBLS	10/01-12/01
	San Antonio MSA, TX	Y	20590 FQ	37430 AW	62690 TQ	TXBLS	10/01-12/01
	Tyler MSA, TX	Y	21690 FQ	35240 AW	52260 TQ	TXBLS	10/01-12/01
	Utah	Y	14620 FQ	37630 AW	63860 TQ	UTBLS	10/01-12/01
	Virginia	Y	12600 FQ	28110 AW	49790 TQ	VABLS	10/01-12/01
	Norfolk-Virginia Beach-Newport News MSA, VA-NC	Y	15790 FQ	36340 AW	59910 TQ	VABLS	10/01-12/01
	Richmond-Petersburg MSA, VA	Y	14780 FQ	35130 AW	55160 TQ	VABLS	10/01-12/01
	Roanoke MSA, VA	Y	17300 FQ	35930 AW	53620 TQ	VABLS	10/01-12/01
	Washington	Y	25680 FQ	41070 AW	55730 TQ	WABLS	10/01-12/01
	Seattle-Bellevue-Everett PMSA, WA	Y	25860 FQ	41250 AW	55920 TQ	WABLS	10/01-12/01
	Tacoma PMSA, WA	Y	29370 FQ	41860 AW	55980 TQ	WABLS	10/01-12/01
	West Virginia	Y	20290 FQ	39470 AW	57990 TQ	WVBLS	10/01-12/01
	Wisconsin	Y	25730 FQ	40850 AW	57670 TQ	WIBLS	10/01-12/01
	Green Bay MSA, WI	Y	31170 FQ	37870 AW	45840 TQ	WIBLS	10/01-12/01
	Milwaukee-Waukesha PMSA, WI	Y	27890 FQ	47560 AW	77200 TQ	WIBLS	10/01-12/01
	Puerto Rico	Y	12670 FQ	25690 AW	44870 TQ	PRBLS	10/01-12/01
	Guam	Y	17070 FQ	37440 AW	57570 TQ	GUBLS	10/01-12/01
Clerical Worker Association	United States	Y		29248 AW		AM	1/01-1/02
Clerical Worker G-2 Federal Government	Washington MSA, DC-MD-VA-WV	Y	20975 AE			OPM1	2003
Clerical Worker G-3 Federal Government	Washington MSA, DC-MD-VA-WV	Y	22396 AE			OPM1	2003
Clerical Worker G-4 Federal Government	Washington MSA, DC-MD-VA-WV	Y	23744 AE			OPM1	2003

AAW	Average annual wage	**AOH**	Average offered, high	**ASH**	Average starting, high	**H**	Hourly	**M**	Monthly	**S**	Special: hourly and annual
AE	Average entry wage	**AOL**	Average offered, low	**ASL**	Average starting, low	**HI**	Highest wage paid	**MTC**	Median total compensation	**TQ**	Third quartile wage
AEX	Average experienced wage	**APH**	Average pay, high range	**AW**	Average wage paid	**HR**	High end range	**MW**	Median wage paid	**W**	Weekly
AO	Average offered	**APL**	Average pay, low range	**FQ**	First quartile wage	**LR**	Low end range	**SQ**	Second quartile wage	**Y**	Yearly

Occupation/Type/Industry	Location	Per	Low	Mid	High	Source	Date
Clerical Worker G-5							
Federal Government	Washington MSA, DC-MD-VA-WV	Y	25785 AE			OPM1	2003
Clerical Worker G-6							
Federal Government	Washington MSA, DC-MD-VA-WV	Y	27872 AE			OPM1	2003
Clerical Worker G-7							
Federal Government	Washington MSA, DC-MD-VA-WV	Y	30005 AE			OPM1	2003
Clerk							
Convenience Store	United States	H			7.33 MW	BEVA	1/01-1/02
Clinical, Counseling, and School Psychologist	Alabama	Y	22560 FQ	44170 AW	65770 TQ	ALBLS	10/01-12/01
	Alaska	Y	39950 FQ	58760 AW	84250 TQ	AKBLS	10/01-12/01
	Arizona	Y	26520 FQ	46200 AW	70970 TQ	AZBLS	10/01-12/01
	Arkansas	Y	27910 FQ	44230 AW	60840 TQ	ARBLS	10/01-12/01
	California	Y	33080 FQ	62870 AW	89880 TQ	CABLS	10/01-12/01
	Colorado	Y	29750 FQ	47890 AW	69200 TQ	COBLS	10/01-12/01
	Connecticut	Y	34290 FQ	56030 AW	79830 TQ	CTBLS	10/01-12/01
	Delaware	Y	30700 FQ	52280 AW	83780 TQ	DEBLS	10/01-12/01
	District of Columbia	Y	28680 FQ	54930 AW	85130 TQ	DCBLS	10/01-12/01
	Florida	Y	30160 FQ	49550 AW	70940 TQ	FLBLS	10/01-12/01
	Georgia	Y	26660 FQ	49920 AW	74540 TQ	GABLS	10/01-12/01
	Hawaii	Y	35710 FQ	51150 AW	70720 TQ	HIBLS	10/01-12/01
	Idaho	Y	25990 FQ	42710 AW	63580 TQ	IDBLS	10/01-12/01
	Illinois	Y	29910 FQ	47260 AW	70970 TQ	ILBLS	10/01-12/01
	Indiana	Y	27330 FQ	48590 AW	77210 TQ	INBLS	10/01-12/01
	Iowa	Y	29840 FQ	47700 AW	66100 TQ	IABLS	10/01-12/01
	Kansas	Y	31310 FQ	42950 AW	56300 TQ	KSBLS	10/01-12/01
	Kentucky	Y	26820 FQ	42640 AW	60970 TQ	KYBLS	10/01-12/01
	Louisiana	Y	28740 FQ	43390 AW	63160 TQ	LABLS	10/01-12/01
	Maine	Y	26740 FQ	56670 AW	109420 TQ	MEBLS	10/01-12/01
	Maryland	Y	29780 FQ	48600 AW	68670 TQ	MDBLS	10/01-12/01
	Massachusetts	Y	26130 FQ	48850 AW	76630 TQ	MABLS	10/01-12/01
	Michigan	Y	34000 FQ	61310 AW	94270 TQ	MIBLS	10/01-12/01
	Minnesota	Y	31230 FQ	51280 AW	76900 TQ	MNBLS	10/01-12/01
	Mississippi	Y	25880 FQ	39360 AW	54280 TQ	MSBLS	10/01-12/01
	Missouri	Y	28790 FQ	56230 AW	115570 TQ	MOBLS	10/01-12/01
	Montana	Y	29810 FQ	39690 AW	52960 TQ	MTBLS	10/01-12/01
	Nebraska	Y	31990 FQ	49340 AW	68960 TQ	NEBLS	10/01-12/01
	Nevada	Y	38770 FQ	58020 AW	79050 TQ	NVBLS	10/01-12/01
	New Hampshire	Y	25430 FQ	48380 AW	87150 TQ	NHBLS	10/01-12/01
	New Jersey	Y	38120 FQ	59370 AW	85360 TQ	NJBLS	10/01-12/01
	New Mexico	Y	28710 FQ	39520 AW	55600 TQ	NMBLS	10/01-12/01
	New York	Y	38260 FQ	66270 AW	106470 TQ	NYBLS	10/01-12/01
	North Carolina	Y	32770 FQ	53380 AW	74050 TQ	NCBLS	10/01-12/01
	North Dakota	Y	26330 FQ	46800 AW	69810 TQ	NDBLS	10/01-12/01
	Ohio	Y	29780 FQ	53240 AW	81430 TQ	OHBLS	10/01-12/01
	Oklahoma	Y	25120 FQ	38270 AW	56410 TQ	OKBLS	10/01-12/01
	Oregon	Y	31510 FQ	54870 AW	80730 TQ	ORBLS	10/01-12/01
	Pennsylvania	Y	23820 FQ	47620 AW	74470 TQ	PABLS	10/01-12/01
	Rhode Island	Y	32110 FQ	57400 AW	77540 TQ	RIBLS	10/01-12/01
	South Carolina	Y	23970 FQ	37810 AW	56670 TQ	SCBLS	10/01-12/01
	South Dakota	Y	40050 FQ	57500 AW	81670 TQ	SDBLS	10/01-12/01
	Tennessee	Y	24220 FQ	53810 AW	115200 TQ	TNBLS	10/01-12/01
	Texas	Y	29820 FQ	45890 AW	66100 TQ	TXBLS	10/01-12/01
	Utah	Y	28080 FQ	44170 AW	60120 TQ	UTBLS	10/01-12/01
	Vermont	Y	25800 FQ	55750 AW		VTBLS	10/01-12/01
	Virginia	Y	32940 FQ	55300 AW	84580 TQ	VABLS	10/01-12/01
	Washington	Y	38380 FQ	58150 AW	84920 TQ	WABLS	10/01-12/01
	West Virginia	Y	18740 FQ	38260 AW	61800 TQ	WVBLS	10/01-12/01
	Wisconsin	Y	29740 FQ	56240 AW	89210 TQ	WIBLS	10/01-12/01
	Wyoming	Y	33670 FQ	47720 AW	64440 TQ	WYBLS	10/01-12/01
	Puerto Rico	Y	22400 FQ	39160 AW	64380 TQ	PRBLS	10/01-12/01
Co-Pilot	United States	Y		56000 AW		BCAVIA	1/01-1/01
American Airlines	United States	H		126.83 AW		NYT	6/01
American Eagle Airlines	United States	H		33.93 AW		NYT	6/01
Comair (Delta)	United States	H		35.02 AW		NYT	6/01

AAW	Average annual wage	**AOH**	Average offered, high	**ASH**	Average starting, high	**H**	Hourly	**M**	Monthly	**S**	Special: hourly and annual
AE	Average entry wage	**AOL**	Average offered, low	**ASL**	Average starting, low	**HI**	Highest wage paid	**MTC**	Median total compensation	**TQ**	Third quartile wage
AEX	Average experienced wage	**APH**	Average pay, high range	**AW**	Average wage paid	**HR**	High end range	**MW**	Median wage paid	**W**	Weekly
AO	Average offered	**APL**	Average pay, low range	**FQ**	First quartile wage	**LR**	Low end range	**SQ**	Second quartile wage	**Y**	Yearly

Occupation/Type/Industry	Location	Per	Low	Mid	High	Source	Date
Co-Pilot							
Continental Airlines	United States	H		107.04 AW		NYT	6/01
Continental Express Airlines	United States	H		31.99 AW		NYT	6/01
Corporations	United States	Y		37170 AW		AWST	2001-2001
Delta Airlines	United States	H		137.73 AW		NYT	6/01
Southwest Airlines	United States	H		90.86 AW		NYT	6/01
United Airlines	United States	H		135.61 AW		NYT	6/01
Coach and Scout	Alabama	Y	14360 FQ	33730 AW	57450 TQ	ALBLS	10/01-12/01
	Birmingham MSA, AL	Y	13190 FQ	31420 AW	57650 TQ	ALBLS	10/01-12/01
	Huntsville MSA, AL	Y	12260 FQ	27280 AW	48100 TQ	ALBLS	10/01-12/01
	Mobile MSA, AL	Y	18620 FQ	35840 AW	52960 TQ	ALBLS	10/01-12/01
	Montgomery MSA, AL	Y	16490 FQ	31410 AW	46940 TQ	ALBLS	10/01-12/01
	Alaska	Y	12890 FQ	28270 AW	49530 TQ	AKBLS	10/01-12/01
	Arizona	Y	16910 FQ	33880 AW	57630 TQ	AZBLS	10/01-12/01
	Phoenix-Mesa MSA, AZ	Y	19340 FQ	37260 AW	60450 TQ	AZBLS	10/01-12/01
	Tucson MSA, AZ	Y	16090 FQ	29480 AW	54970 TQ	AZBLS	10/01-12/01
	Arkansas	Y	21270 FQ	42450 AW	70820 TQ	ARBLS	10/01-12/01
	Little Rock-North Little Rock MSA, AR	Y	20190 FQ	40460 AW	66420 TQ	ARBLS	10/01-12/01
	California	Y	15150 FQ	39900 AW	82940 TQ	CABLS	10/01-12/01
	Bakersfield MSA, CA	Y	13840 FQ	28370 AW	59700 TQ	CABLS	10/01-12/01
	Fresno MSA, CA	Y	21740 FQ	61340 AW	90780 TQ	CABLS	10/01-12/01
	Los Angeles-Long Beach PMSA, CA	Y	15670 FQ	41130 AW	81270 TQ	CABLS	10/01-12/01
	Oakland PMSA, CA	Y	14350 FQ	33700 AW	65530 TQ	CABLS	10/01-12/01
	Orange County PMSA, CA	Y	15180 FQ	36470 AW	78710 TQ	CABLS	10/01-12/01
	Redding MSA, CA	Y	13320 FQ	18000 AW	29120 TQ	CABLS	10/01-12/01
	Riverside-San Bernardino PMSA, CA	Y	14860 FQ	30000 AW	49270 TQ	CABLS	10/01-12/01
	Sacramento PMSA, CA	Y	15780 FQ	33170 AW	74440 TQ	CABLS	10/01-12/01
	Salinas MSA, CA	Y	24270 FQ	41920 AW	74150 TQ	CABLS	10/01-12/01
	San Diego MSA, CA	Y	14540 FQ	48890 AW	144170 TQ	CABLS	10/01-12/01
	San Francisco PMSA, CA	Y	13830 FQ	43970 AW	81120 TQ	CABLS	10/01-12/01
	San Jose PMSA, CA	Y	16940 FQ	45300 AW	93220 TQ	CABLS	10/01-12/01
	San Luis Obispo-Atascadero-Paso Robles MSA, CA	Y	14610 FQ	21250 AW	23350 TQ	CABLS	10/01-12/01
	Santa Barbara-Santa Maria-Lompoc MSA, CA	Y	14530 FQ	43500 AW	93890 TQ	CABLS	10/01-12/01
	Ventura PMSA, CA	Y	13390 FQ	31720 AW	72270 TQ	CABLS	10/01-12/01
	Colorado	Y	14850 FQ	39430 AW	68870 TQ	COBLS	10/01-12/01
	Boulder-Longmont PMSA, CO	Y	13310 FQ	25150 AW	42210 TQ	COBLS	10/01-12/01
	Colorado Springs MSA, CO	Y	23160 FQ	52280 AW	69610 TQ	COBLS	10/01-12/01
	Denver PMSA, CO	Y	16820 FQ	37240 AW	60600 TQ	COBLS	10/01-12/01
	Connecticut	Y	19940 FQ	41880 AW	75260 TQ	CTBLS	10/01-12/01
	Bridgeport PMSA, CT	Y	20290 FQ	34950 AW	55420 TQ	CTBLS	10/01-12/01
	Hartford MSA, CT	Y	19950 FQ	52410 AW	93470 TQ	CTBLS	10/01-12/01
	New Haven-Meriden PMSA, CT	Y	21580 FQ	43190 AW	67130 TQ	CTBLS	10/01-12/01
	Stamford-Norwalk PMSA, CT	Y	21310 FQ	30840 AW	36230 TQ	CTBLS	10/01-12/01
	Delaware	Y	21050 FQ	38520 AW	64440 TQ	DEBLS	10/01-12/01
	Wilmington-Newark PMSA, DE-MD	Y	20340 FQ	39480 AW	64850 TQ	DEBLS	10/01-12/01
	District of Columbia	Y	20480 FQ	52660 AW	107380 TQ	DCBLS	10/01-12/01
	Washington PMSA, DC-MD-VA-WV	Y	15910 FQ	40620 AW	62380 TQ	DCBLS	10/01-12/01
	Florida	Y	17170 FQ	37740 AW	67940 TQ	FLBLS	10/01-12/01
	Daytona Beach MSA, FL	Y	19320 FQ	32390 AW	45160 TQ	FLBLS	10/01-12/01
	Fort Lauderdale PMSA, FL	Y	16770 FQ	35200 AW	54530 TQ	FLBLS	10/01-12/01
	Fort Myers-Cape Coral MSA, FL	Y	19090 FQ	35000 AW	68210 TQ	FLBLS	10/01-12/01
	Fort Pierce-Port St. Lucie MSA, FL	Y	14640 FQ	31460 AW	50160 TQ	FLBLS	10/01-12/01
	Fort Walton Beach MSA, FL	Y	15640 FQ	27570 AW	57210 TQ	FLBLS	10/01-12/01
	Gainesville MSA, FL	Y	21280 FQ	50530 AW	107520 TQ	FLBLS	10/01-12/01
	Jacksonville MSA, FL	Y	14880 FQ	26960 AW	44450 TQ	FLBLS	10/01-12/01
	Lakeland-Winter Haven MSA, FL	Y	20590 FQ	49200 AW	85590 TQ	FLBLS	10/01-12/01
	Melbourne-Titusville-Palm Bay MSA, FL	Y	20770 FQ	27600 AW	35670 TQ	FLBLS	10/01-12/01
	Miami PMSA, FL	Y	19400 FQ	44540 AW	98060 TQ	FLBLS	10/01-12/01
	Naples MSA, FL	Y	17990 FQ	33390 AW	62080 TQ	FLBLS	10/01-12/01
	Orlando MSA, FL	Y	20140 FQ	39760 AW	66300 TQ	FLBLS	10/01-12/01

AAW	Average annual wage	**AOH**	Average offered, high	**ASH**	Average starting, high	**H**	Hourly	**M**	Monthly	**S**	Special: hourly and annual
AE	Average entry wage	**AOL**	Average offered, low	**ASL**	Average starting, low	**HI**	Highest wage paid	**MTC**	Median total compensation	**TQ**	Third quartile wage
AEX	Average experienced wage	**APH**	Average pay, high range	**AW**	Average wage paid	**HR**	High end range	**MW**	Median wage paid	**W**	Weekly
AO	Average offered	**APL**	Average pay, low range	**FQ**	First quartile wage	**LR**	Low end range	**SQ**	Second quartile wage	**Y**	Yearly

Occupation/Type/Industry	Location	Per	Low	Mid	High	Source	Date
Coach and Scout	Pensacola MSA, FL	Y	12940 FQ	36610 AW	56930 TQ	FLBLS	10/01-12/01
	Sarasota-Bradenton MSA, FL	Y	15520 FQ	35590 AW	77110 TQ	FLBLS	10/01-12/01
	Tallahassee MSA, FL	Y	17370 FQ	45030 AW	92060 TQ	FLBLS	10/01-12/01
	Tampa-St. Petersburg-Clearwater MSA, FL	Y	15140 FQ	39160 AW	66740 TQ	FLBLS	10/01-12/01
	West Palm Beach-Boca Raton MSA, FL	Y	19530 FQ	41790 AW	69350 TQ	FLBLS	10/01-12/01
	Georgia	Y	19190 FQ	38780 AW	72390 TQ	GABLS	10/01-12/01
	Atlanta MSA, GA	Y	19230 FQ	31940 AW	58070 TQ	GABLS	10/01-12/01
	Augusta-Aiken MSA, GA-SC	Y	18310 FQ	39370 AW	67160 TQ	GABLS	10/01-12/01
	Macon MSA, GA	Y	12500 FQ	24910 AW	35680 TQ	GABLS	10/01-12/01
	Savannah MSA, GA	Y	24860 FQ	43350 AW	68940 TQ	GABLS	10/01-12/01
	Hawaii	Y	19880 FQ	41960 AW	67810 TQ	HIBLS	10/01-12/01
	Honolulu MSA, HI	Y	17220 FQ	43050 AW	76680 TQ	HIBLS	10/01-12/01
	Idaho	Y	13570 FQ	26280 AW	40820 TQ	IDBLS	10/01-12/01
	Boise City MSA, ID	Y	12480 FQ	25020 AW	36600 TQ	IDBLS	10/01-12/01
	Illinois	Y	11410 FQ	24530 AW	54050 TQ	ILBLS	10/01-12/01
	Champaign-Urbana MSA, IL	Y	12310 FQ	27020 AW	55770 TQ	ILBLS	10/01-12/01
	Chicago PMSA, IL	Y	11280 FQ	24030 AW	55600 TQ	ILBLS	10/01-12/01
	Peoria-Pekin MSA, IL	Y	11890 FQ	20440 AW	27990 TQ	ILBLS	10/01-12/01
	Indiana	Y	12460 FQ	27560 AW	54270 TQ	INBLS	10/01-12/01
	Evansville-Henderson MSA, IN-KY	Y	11450 FQ	20190 AW	38900 TQ	INBLS	10/01-12/01
	Fort Wayne MSA, IN	Y	13050 FQ	27620 AW	47830 TQ	INBLS	10/01-12/01
	Gary PMSA, IN	Y	15880 FQ	30870 AW	57210 TQ	INBLS	10/01-12/01
	Indianapolis MSA, IN	Y	15130 FQ	29110 AW	53590 TQ	INBLS	10/01-12/01
	Lafayette MSA, IN	Y	11900 FQ	24500 AW	43590 TQ	INBLS	10/01-12/01
	Iowa	Y	11710 FQ	22800 AW	41990 TQ	IABLS	10/01-12/01
	Cedar Rapids MSA, IA	Y	11600 FQ	17760 AW	29350 TQ	IABLS	10/01-12/01
	Davenport-Moline-Rock Island MSA, IA-IL	Y	12060 FQ	21410 AW	41750 TQ	IABLS	10/01-12/01
	Des Moines MSA, IA	Y	13850 FQ	28210 AW	42930 TQ	IABLS	10/01-12/01
	Kansas	Y	11910 FQ	23320 AW	40040 TQ	KSBLS	10/01-12/01
	Topeka MSA, KS	Y	13270 FQ	24920 AW	37080 TQ	KSBLS	10/01-12/01
	Wichita MSA, KS	Y	12040 FQ	22660 AW	36500 TQ	KSBLS	10/01-12/01
	Kentucky	Y	12270 FQ	31510 AW	59790 TQ	KYBLS	10/01-12/01
	Lexington MSA, KY	Y	12660 FQ	36200 AW	73680 TQ	KYBLS	10/01-12/01
	Louisville MSA, KY-IN	Y	12220 FQ	31140 AW	59430 TQ	KYBLS	10/01-12/01
	Louisiana	Y	17800 FQ	49540 AW	100130 TQ	LABLS	10/01-12/01
	Baton Rouge MSA, LA	Y	24730 FQ	54390 AW	103120 TQ	LABLS	10/01-12/01
	Houma MSA, LA	Y	20360 FQ	38640 AW	66590 TQ	LABLS	10/01-12/01
	Lafayette MSA, LA	Y	19280 FQ	45950 AW	70900 TQ	LABLS	10/01-12/01
	Lake Charles MSA, LA	Y	15910 FQ	26370 AW	41220 TQ	LABLS	10/01-12/01
	New Orleans MSA, LA	Y	15670 FQ	56300 AW		LABLS	10/01-12/01
	Maine	Y	14670 FQ	35440 AW	58710 TQ	MEBLS	10/01-12/01
	Portland MSA, ME	Y	17950 FQ	34440 AW	53950 TQ	MEBLS	10/01-12/01
	Maryland	Y	15160 FQ	30910 AW	54040 TQ	MDBLS	10/01-12/01
	Baltimore PMSA, MD	Y	14930 FQ	30660 AW	56760 TQ	MDBLS	10/01-12/01
	Massachusetts	Y	14270 FQ	28610 AW	50580 TQ	MABLS	10/01-12/01
	Boston PMSA, MA-NH	Y	14170 FQ	29160 AW	48950 TQ	MABLS	10/01-12/01
	Brockton PMSA, MA	Y	14790 FQ	23960 AW	48910 TQ	MABLS	10/01-12/01
	Springfield MSA, MA	Y	14090 FQ	28960 AW	57020 TQ	MABLS	10/01-12/01
	Worcester PMSA, MA-CT	Y	16910 FQ	35930 AW	56670 TQ	MABLS	10/01-12/01
	Michigan	Y	13760 FQ	34910 AW	59060 TQ	MIBLS	10/01-12/01
	Ann Arbor PMSA, MI	Y	13190 FQ	28110 AW	51960 TQ	MIBLS	10/01-12/01
	Detroit PMSA, MI	Y	13690 FQ	39050 AW	72250 TQ	MIBLS	10/01-12/01
	Flint PMSA, MI	Y	18250 FQ	41620 AW	58550 TQ	MIBLS	10/01-12/01
	Grand Rapids-Muskegon-Holland MSA, MI	Y	16190 FQ	28910 AW	55640 TQ	MIBLS	10/01-12/01
	Kalamazoo-Battle Creek MSA, MI	Y	18410 FQ	38580 AW	58870 TQ	MIBLS	10/01-12/01
	Minnesota	Y	13390 FQ	31400 AW	55520 TQ	MNBLS	10/01-12/01
	Duluth-Superior MSA, MN-WI	Y	18680 FQ	35830 AW	56560 TQ	MNBLS	10/01-12/01
	Minneapolis-St. Paul MSA, MN-WI	Y	13600 FQ	31790 AW	59370 TQ	MNBLS	10/01-12/01
	St. Cloud MSA, MN	Y	11890 FQ	25020 AW	51550 TQ	MNBLS	10/01-12/01
	Mississippi	Y	19310 FQ	43590 AW	71870 TQ	MSBLS	10/01-12/01
	Jackson MSA, MS	Y	15000 FQ	38700 AW	65570 TQ	MSBLS	10/01-12/01
	Missouri	Y	14000 FQ	36150 AW	57070 TQ	MOBLS	10/01-12/01
	Kansas City MSA, MO-KS	Y	13170 FQ	32800 AW	55810 TQ	MOBLS	10/01-12/01
	St. Louis MSA, MO-IL	Y	16000 FQ	43350 AW	65950 TQ	MOBLS	10/01-12/01
	Springfield MSA, MO	Y	13190 FQ	34780 AW	54820 TQ	MOBLS	10/01-12/01

AAW	Average annual wage	**AOH**	Average offered, high	**ASH**	Average starting, high	**H**	Hourly	**M**	Monthly	**S**	Special: hourly and annual
AE	Average entry wage	**AOL**	Average offered, low	**ASL**	Average starting, low	**HI**	Highest wage paid	**MTC**	Median total compensation	**TQ**	Third quartile wage
AEX	Average experienced wage	**APH**	Average pay, high range	**AW**	Average wage paid	**HR**	High end range	**MW**	Median wage paid	**W**	Weekly
AO	Average offered	**APL**	Average pay, low range	**FQ**	First quartile wage	**LR**	Low end range	**SQ**	Second quartile wage	**Y**	Yearly

Occupation/Type/Industry	Location	Per	Low	Mid	High	Source	Date
Coach and Scout	Montana	Y	12160 FQ	28100 AW	52520 TQ	MTBLS	10/01-12/01
	Nebraska	Y	13000 FQ	33500 AW	60640 TQ	NEBLS	10/01-12/01
	Lincoln MSA, NE	Y	12930 FQ	37160 AW	91120 TQ	NEBLS	10/01-12/01
	Omaha MSA, NE-IA	Y	14400 FQ	34870 AW	58680 TQ	NEBLS	10/01-12/01
	Nevada	Y	20580 FQ	35390 AW	56090 TQ	NVBLS	10/01-12/01
	Las Vegas MSA, NV-AZ	Y	21200 FQ	35020 AW	52070 TQ	NVBLS	10/01-12/01
	Reno MSA, NV	Y	19820 FQ	37750 AW	64850 TQ	NVBLS	10/01-12/01
	New Hampshire	Y	15960 FQ	33120 AW	56720 TQ	NHBLS	10/01-12/01
	Manchester PMSA, NH	Y	15160 FQ	30530 AW	52110 TQ	NHBLS	10/01-12/01
	Nashua PMSA, NH	Y	15050 FQ	20530 AW	30460 TQ	NHBLS	10/01-12/01
	Portsmouth-Rochester PMSA, NH-ME	Y	19810 FQ	34470 AW	57440 TQ	NHBLS	10/01-12/01
	New Jersey	Y	18130 FQ	44070 AW	80670 TQ	NJBLS	10/01-12/01
	Atlantic-Cape May PMSA, NJ	Y	19240 FQ	30370 AW	49650 TQ	NJBLS	10/01-12/01
	Bergen-Passaic PMSA, NJ	Y	13450 FQ	53190 AW		NJBLS	10/01-12/01
	Jersey City PMSA, NJ	Y	17980 FQ	47170 AW	61020 TQ	NJBLS	10/01-12/01
	Monmouth-Ocean PMSA, NJ	Y	24400 FQ	43400 AW	68090 TQ	NJBLS	10/01-12/01
	Newark PMSA, NJ	Y	21130 FQ	42030 AW	74730 TQ	NJBLS	10/01-12/01
	Trenton PMSA, NJ	Y	18070 FQ	42650 AW	76330 TQ	NJBLS	10/01-12/01
	New Mexico	Y	24410 FQ	49110 AW	74750 TQ	NMBLS	10/01-12/01
	Albuquerque MSA, NM	Y	25040 FQ	53480 AW	82040 TQ	NMBLS	10/01-12/01
	New York	Y	16190 FQ	40970 AW	72840 TQ	NYBLS	10/01-12/01
	Albany-Schenectady-Troy MSA, NY	Y	12170 FQ	24730 AW	46610 TQ	NYBLS	10/01-12/01
	Buffalo-Niagara Falls MSA, NY	Y	14100 FQ	47980 AW		NYBLS	10/01-12/01
	Dutchess County PMSA, NY	Y	13530 FQ	34610 AW	52270 TQ	NYBLS	10/01-12/01
	Nassau-Suffolk PMSA, NY	Y	20790 FQ	48540 AW	98920 TQ	NYBLS	10/01-12/01
	New York PMSA, NY	Y	22670 FQ	43760 AW	74470 TQ	NYBLS	10/01-12/01
	Rochester MSA, NY	Y	18450 FQ	26230 AW	40590 TQ	NYBLS	10/01-12/01
	Syracuse MSA, NY	Y	13640 FQ	44210 AW	86960 TQ	NYBLS	10/01-12/01
	North Carolina	Y	15540 FQ	39340 AW	77220 TQ	NCBLS	10/01-12/01
	Asheville MSA, NC	Y	20420 FQ	34550 AW	46850 TQ	NCBLS	10/01-12/01
	Charlotte-Gastonia-Rock Hill MSA, NC-SC	Y	19460 FQ	43030 AW	84170 TQ	NCBLS	10/01-12/01
	Greensboro-Winston-Salem-High Point MSA, NC	Y	14200 FQ	34290 AW	68740 TQ	NCBLS	10/01-12/01
	Raleigh-Durham-Chapel Hill MSA, NC	Y	15290 FQ	50290 AW	102800 TQ	NCBLS	10/01-12/01
	Wilmington MSA, NC	Y	23900 FQ	40150 AW	57850 TQ	NCBLS	10/01-12/01
	North Dakota	Y	12270 FQ	25500 AW	47430 TQ	NDBLS	10/01-12/01
	Fargo-Moorhead MSA, ND-MN	Y	12260 FQ	26350 AW	49350 TQ	NDBLS	10/01-12/01
	Ohio	Y	14860 FQ	34480 AW	61150 TQ	OHBLS	10/01-12/01
	Akron PMSA, OH	Y	17950 FQ	29490 AW	42090 TQ	OHBLS	10/01-12/01
	Canton-Massillon MSA, OH	Y	16810 FQ	38540 AW	67520 TQ	OHBLS	10/01-12/01
	Cincinnati PMSA, OH-KY-IN	Y	12760 FQ	28670 AW	51470 TQ	OHBLS	10/01-12/01
	Cleveland-Lorain-Elyria PMSA, OH	Y	15540 FQ	37410 AW	68290 TQ	OHBLS	10/01-12/01
	Columbus MSA, OH	Y	19220 FQ	32820 AW	57190 TQ	OHBLS	10/01-12/01
	Dayton-Springfield MSA, OH	Y	18500 FQ	35220 AW	53680 TQ	OHBLS	10/01-12/01
	Hamilton-Middletown PMSA, OH	Y	13120 FQ	35540 AW	66060 TQ	OHBLS	10/01-12/01
	Toledo MSA, OH	Y	12390 FQ	35420 AW	55590 TQ	OHBLS	10/01-12/01
	Oklahoma	Y	12900 FQ	32830 AW	57310 TQ	OKBLS	10/01-12/01
	Oklahoma City MSA, OK	Y	12430 FQ	31470 AW	54400 TQ	OKBLS	10/01-12/01
	Tulsa MSA, OK	Y	13970 FQ	39130 AW	67810 TQ	OKBLS	10/01-12/01
	Oregon	Y	15000 FQ	32010 AW	52940 TQ	ORBLS	10/01-12/01
	Eugene-Springfield MSA, OR	Y	20810 FQ	47360 AW	87920 TQ	ORBLS	10/01-12/01
	Portland-Vancouver PMSA, OR-WA	Y	15120 FQ	27630 AW	42290 TQ	ORBLS	10/01-12/01
	Salem PMSA, OR	Y	17090 FQ	28580 AW	42570 TQ	ORBLS	10/01-12/01
	Pennsylvania	Y	12400 FQ	32580 AW	66630 TQ	PABLS	10/01-12/01
	Allentown-Bethlehem-Easton MSA, PA	Y	12630 FQ	25520 AW	44140 TQ	PABLS	10/01-12/01
	Erie MSA, PA	Y	11570 FQ	24430 AW	54440 TQ	PABLS	10/01-12/01
	Harrisburg-Lebanon-Carlisle MSA, PA	Y	12470 FQ	27380 AW	51340 TQ	PABLS	10/01-12/01
	Lancaster MSA, PA	Y	12350 FQ	23610 AW	37480 TQ	PABLS	10/01-12/01
	Philadelphia PMSA, PA-NJ	Y	13260 FQ	38910 AW	86530 TQ	PABLS	10/01-12/01
	Pittsburgh MSA, PA	Y	12370 FQ	40240 AW	79420 TQ	PABLS	10/01-12/01
	Reading MSA, PA	Y	11500 FQ	19420 AW	32250 TQ	PABLS	10/01-12/01

AAW Average annual wage **AOH** Average offered, high **ASH** Average starting, high **H** Hourly **M** Monthly **S** Special: hourly and annual
AE Average entry wage **AOL** Average offered, low **ASL** Average starting, low **HI** Highest wage paid **MTC** Median total compensation **TQ** Third quartile wage
AEX Average experienced wage **APH** Average pay, high range **AW** Average wage paid **HR** High end range **MW** Median wage paid **W** Weekly
AO Average offered **APL** Average pay, low range **FQ** First quartile wage **LR** Low end range **SQ** Second quartile wage **Y** Yearly

Occupation/Type/Industry	Location	Per	Low	Mid	High	Source	Date
Coach and Scout	Scranton-Wilkes-Barre-Hazleton MSA, PA	Y	11720 FQ	22720 AW	38230 TQ	PABLS	10/01-12/01
	York MSA, PA	Y	12200 FQ	17630 AW	27250 TQ	PABLS	10/01-12/01
	Rhode Island	Y	13230 FQ	31640 AW	54380 TQ	RIBLS	10/01-12/01
	Providence-Fall River-Warwick MSA, RI-MA	Y	13300 FQ	31550 AW	53050 TQ	RIBLS	10/01-12/01
	South Carolina	Y	14440 FQ	31240 AW	56150 TQ	SCBLS	10/01-12/01
	Charleston-North Charleston MSA, SC	Y	14550 FQ	33240 AW	56830 TQ	SCBLS	10/01-12/01
	Columbia MSA, SC	Y	15020 FQ	25200 AW	48730 TQ	SCBLS	10/01-12/01
	Greenville-Spartanburg-Anderson MSA, SC	Y	13920 FQ	39710 AW	73350 TQ	SCBLS	10/01-12/01
	Myrtle Beach MSA, SC	Y	12350 FQ	24990 AW	52570 TQ	SCBLS	10/01-12/01
	South Dakota	Y	18550 FQ	28090 AW	41960 TQ	SDBLS	10/01-12/01
	Sioux Falls MSA, SD	Y	15240 FQ	25100 AW	38400 TQ	SDBLS	10/01-12/01
	Tennessee	Y	13550 FQ	39660 AW	80740 TQ	TNBLS	10/01-12/01
	Chattanooga MSA, TN-GA	Y	16980 FQ	33380 AW	54080 TQ	TNBLS	10/01-12/01
	Johnson City-Kingsport-Bristol MSA, TN-VA	Y	11380 FQ	23160 AW	56370 TQ	TNBLS	10/01-12/01
	Knoxville MSA, TN	Y	22100 FQ	57190 AW	112830 TQ	TNBLS	10/01-12/01
	Memphis MSA, TN-AR-MS	Y	19310 FQ	46340 AW	94890 TQ	TNBLS	10/01-12/01
	Nashville MSA, TN	Y	23650 FQ	44110 AW	91170 TQ	TNBLS	10/01-12/01
	Texas	Y	14020 FQ	34340 AW	56480 TQ	TXBLS	10/01-12/01
	Austin-San Marcos MSA, TX	Y	16300 FQ	32450 AW	47560 TQ	TXBLS	10/01-12/01
	Brownsville-Harlingen-San Benito MSA, TX	Y	16870 FQ	35640 AW	63060 TQ	TXBLS	10/01-12/01
	Corpus Christi MSA, TX	Y	12680 FQ	30890 AW	54030 TQ	TXBLS	10/01-12/01
	Dallas PMSA, TX	Y	14060 FQ	31710 AW	52900 TQ	TXBLS	10/01-12/01
	Fort Worth-Arlington PMSA, TX	Y	14450 FQ	35480 AW	57670 TQ	TXBLS	10/01-12/01
	Galveston-Texas City PMSA, TX	Y	20840 FQ	31760 AW	35320 TQ	TXBLS	10/01-12/01
	Houston PMSA, TX	Y	16470 FQ	44420 AW	78710 TQ	TXBLS	10/01-12/01
	Killeen-Temple MSA, TX	Y	13190 FQ	30430 AW	48280 TQ	TXBLS	10/01-12/01
	Longview-Marshall MSA, TX	Y	12310 FQ	31280 AW	52800 TQ	TXBLS	10/01-12/01
	Lubbock MSA, TX	Y	14530 FQ	30370 AW	47910 TQ	TXBLS	10/01-12/01
	Odessa-Midland MSA, TX	Y	22540 FQ	33890 AW	44590 TQ	TXBLS	10/01-12/01
	San Antonio MSA, TX	Y	12650 FQ	29790 AW	57870 TQ	TXBLS	10/01-12/01
	Utah	Y	15490 FQ	39550 AW	67830 TQ	UTBLS	10/01-12/01
	Salt Lake City-Ogden MSA, UT	Y	16900 FQ	40620 AW	68100 TQ	UTBLS	10/01-12/01
	Vermont	Y	14460 FQ	33590 AW	52100 TQ	VTBLS	10/01-12/01
	Burlington MSA, VT	Y	14590 FQ	35270 AW	47990 TQ	VTBLS	10/01-12/01
	Virginia	Y	13050 FQ	37010 AW	61480 TQ	VABLS	10/01-12/01
	Norfolk-Virginia Beach-Newport News MSA, VA-NC	Y	13420 FQ	34800 AW	59820 TQ	VABLS	10/01-12/01
	Richmond-Petersburg MSA, VA	Y	12350 FQ	37680 AW	71030 TQ	VABLS	10/01-12/01
	Roanoke MSA, VA	Y	14630 FQ	27960 AW	44350 TQ	VABLS	10/01-12/01
	Washington	Y	18740 FQ	33370 AW	48900 TQ	WABLS	10/01-12/01
	Bremerton PMSA, WA	Y	18390 FQ	25120 AW	34810 TQ	WABLS	10/01-12/01
	Olympia PMSA, WA	Y	17460 FQ	28590 AW	43620 TQ	WABLS	10/01-12/01
	Seattle-Bellevue-Everett PMSA, WA	Y	24310 FQ	43100 AW	66500 TQ	WABLS	10/01-12/01
	Spokane MSA, WA	Y	17170 FQ	33230 AW	49020 TQ	WABLS	10/01-12/01
	Tacoma PMSA, WA	Y	20130 FQ	26990 AW	36330 TQ	WABLS	10/01-12/01
	Yakima MSA, WA	Y	19560 FQ	28980 AW	36090 TQ	WABLS	10/01-12/01
	West Virginia	Y	14350 FQ	36590 AW	61860 TQ	WVBLS	10/01-12/01
	Charleston MSA, WV	Y	14240 FQ	33390 AW	55230 TQ	WVBLS	10/01-12/01
	Wisconsin	Y	12330 FQ	28850 AW	56630 TQ	WIBLS	10/01-12/01
	Appleton-Oshkosh-Neenah MSA, WI	Y	13580 FQ	28590 AW	59390 TQ	WIBLS	10/01-12/01
	Madison MSA, WI	Y	11930 FQ	26310 AW	51680 TQ	WIBLS	10/01-12/01
	Milwaukee-Waukesha PMSA, WI	Y	17150 FQ	33460 AW	50240 TQ	WIBLS	10/01-12/01
	Wyoming	Y	12060 FQ	19860 AW	45390 TQ	WYBLS	10/01-12/01
	Puerto Rico	Y	11520 FQ	19110 AW	29750 TQ	PRBLS	10/01-12/01
	Virgin Islands	Y	21240 FQ	36700 AW	52510 TQ	VIBLS	10/01-12/01
Coal Miner	Kentucky	Y		61000 Y		MINQ	2002

AAW	Average annual wage	**AOH**	Average offered, high	**ASH**	Average starting, high	**H**	Hourly	**M**	Monthly	**S**	Special: hourly and annual
AE	Average entry wage	**AOL**	Average offered, low	**ASL**	Average starting, low	**HI**	Highest wage paid	**MTC**	Median total compensation	**TQ**	Third quartile wage
AEX	Average experienced wage	**APH**	Average pay, high range	**AW**	Average wage paid	**HR**	High end range	**MW**	Median wage paid	**W**	Weekly
AO	Average offered	**APL**	Average pay, low range	**FQ**	First quartile wage	**LR**	Low end range	**SQ**	Second quartile wage	**Y**	Yearly

Occupation/Type/Industry	Location	Per	Low	Mid	High	Source	Date
Coating, Painting, and Spraying Machine Setter, Operator, and Tender	Alabama	H	7.57 FQ	11.02 AW	15.77 TQ	ALBLS	10/01-12/01
	Arizona	H	6.68 FQ	10.35 AW	14.11 TQ	AZBLS	10/01-12/01
	Arkansas	H	7.18 FQ	11.23 AW	16.28 TQ	ARBLS	10/01-12/01
	California	H	7.17 FQ	11.17 AW	16.63 TQ	CABLS	10/01-12/01
	Colorado	H	8.09 FQ	11.84 AW	16.08 TQ	COBLS	10/01-12/01
	Connecticut	H	9.47 FQ	13.83 AW	19.20 TQ	CTBLS	10/01-12/01
	Delaware	H	10.98 FQ	14.09 AW	17.20 TQ	DEBLS	10/01-12/01
	Florida	H	7.39 FQ	11.39 AW	16.29 TQ	FLBLS	10/01-12/01
	Georgia	H	7.79 FQ	11.91 AW	16.59 TQ	GABLS	10/01-12/01
	Idaho	H	7.20 FQ	10.62 AW	14.56 TQ	IDBLS	10/01-12/01
	Illinois	H	7.98 FQ	12.67 AW	19.17 TQ	ILBLS	10/01-12/01
	Indiana	H	8.26 FQ	11.72 AW	16.20 TQ	INBLS	10/01-12/01
	Iowa	H	8.91 FQ	13.31 AW	19.25 TQ	IABLS	10/01-12/01
	Kansas	H	7.65 FQ	12.87 AW	21.10 TQ	KSBLS	10/01-12/01
	Kentucky	H	7.95 FQ	12.10 AW	16.80 TQ	KYBLS	10/01-12/01
	Louisiana	H	7.20 FQ	11.82 AW	18.25 TQ	LABLS	10/01-12/01
	Maine	H	9.23 FQ	17.39 AW	25.44 TQ	MEBLS	10/01-12/01
	Maryland	H	9.17 FQ	14.59 AW	21.29 TQ	MDBLS	10/01-12/01
	Massachusetts	H	9.34 FQ	13.58 AW	18.77 TQ	MABLS	10/01-12/01
	Michigan	H	8.64 FQ	14.35 AW	25.06 TQ	MIBLS	10/01-12/01
	Minnesota	H	9.61 FQ	14.38 AW	20.26 TQ	MNBLS	10/01-12/01
	Mississippi	H	7.66 FQ	11.03 AW	14.22 TQ	MSBLS	10/01-12/01
	Missouri	H	8.03 FQ	13.97 AW	25.23 TQ	MOBLS	10/01-12/01
	Montana	H	7.92 FQ	12.82 AW	19.28 TQ	MTBLS	10/01-12/01
	Nebraska	H	9.09 FQ	11.68 AW	15.20 TQ	NEBLS	10/01-12/01
	Nevada	H	7.61 FQ	12.81 AW	18.23 TQ	NVBLS	10/01-12/01
	New Hampshire	H	9.13 FQ	13.03 AW	16.93 TQ	NHBLS	10/01-12/01
	New Jersey	H	8.72 FQ	13.79 AW	20.34 TQ	NJBLS	10/01-12/01
	New Mexico	H	6.42 FQ	9.83 AW	13.36 TQ	NMBLS	10/01-12/01
	New York	H	8.15 FQ	13.94 AW	21.25 TQ	NYBLS	10/01-12/01
	North Carolina	H	8.59 FQ	11.55 AW	15.73 TQ	NCBLS	10/01-12/01
	North Dakota	H	8.22 FQ	11.11 AW	13.91 TQ	NDBLS	10/01-12/01
	Ohio	H	8.49 FQ	13.17 AW	18.94 TQ	OHBLS	10/01-12/01
	Oklahoma	H	7.68 FQ	12.78 AW	17.48 TQ	OKBLS	10/01-12/01
	Oregon	H	7.25 FQ	12.03 AW	17.77 TQ	ORBLS	10/01-12/01
	Pennsylvania	H	8.68 FQ	13.14 AW	17.99 TQ	PABLS	10/01-12/01
	Rhode Island	H	7.65 FQ	12.03 AW	16.12 TQ	RIBLS	10/01-12/01
	South Carolina	H	9.07 FQ	13.59 AW	20.24 TQ	SCBLS	10/01-12/01
	South Dakota	H	8.00 FQ	11.01 AW	13.99 TQ	SDBLS	10/01-12/01
	Tennessee	H	8.07 FQ	10.89 AW	13.98 TQ	TNBLS	10/01-12/01
	Texas	H	7.13 FQ	10.33 AW	14.40 TQ	TXBLS	10/01-12/01
	Utah	H	8.11 FQ	11.40 AW	15.19 TQ	UTBLS	10/01-12/01
	Vermont	H	8.25 FQ	13.57 AW	18.90 TQ	VTBLS	10/01-12/01
	Virginia	H	8.39 FQ	14.44 AW	25.87 TQ	VABLS	10/01-12/01
	Washington	H	8.29 FQ	13.81 AW	21.32 TQ	WABLS	10/01-12/01
	West Virginia	H	7.23 FQ	12.39 AW	18.12 TQ	WVBLS	10/01-12/01
	Wisconsin	H	9.31 FQ	13.37 AW	18.57 TQ	WIBLS	10/01-12/01
	Puerto Rico	H	5.67 FQ	7.17 AW	8.99 TQ	PRBLS	10/01-12/01
Coil Winder, Taper, and Finisher	Alabama	H	7.59 FQ	11.93 AW	20.09 TQ	ALBLS	10/01-12/01
	Birmingham MSA, AL	H	7.47 FQ	9.59 AW	13.48 TQ	ALBLS	10/01-12/01
	Arizona	H	8.00 FQ	12.75 AW	18.11 TQ	AZBLS	10/01-12/01
	Tucson MSA, AZ	H	7.64 FQ	12.88 AW	20.97 TQ	AZBLS	10/01-12/01
	Arkansas	H	8.75 FQ	11.76 AW	15.93 TQ	ARBLS	10/01-12/01
	California	H	6.65 FQ	10.02 AW	15.43 TQ	CABLS	10/01-12/01
	Los Angeles-Long Beach PMSA, CA	H	6.45 FQ	8.33 AW	11.19 TQ	CABLS	10/01-12/01
	Oakland PMSA, CA	H	7.15 FQ	13.92 AW	21.10 TQ	CABLS	10/01-12/01
	Orange County PMSA, CA	H	7.33 FQ	10.25 AW	14.13 TQ	CABLS	10/01-12/01
	Riverside-San Bernardino PMSA, CA	H	7.42 FQ	10.71 AW	15.78 TQ	CABLS	10/01-12/01
	San Diego MSA, CA	H	6.71 FQ	8.86 AW	11.07 TQ	CABLS	10/01-12/01
	San Francisco PMSA, CA	H	8.98 FQ	18.06 AW	26.82 TQ	CABLS	10/01-12/01
	San Jose PMSA, CA	H	7.23 FQ	11.25 AW	20.45 TQ	CABLS	10/01-12/01
	Ventura PMSA, CA	H	7.93 FQ	10.25 AW	13.43 TQ	CABLS	10/01-12/01
	Colorado	H	7.02 FQ	11.46 AW	16.89 TQ	COBLS	10/01-12/01
	Denver PMSA, CO	H	7.75 FQ	12.65 AW	21.39 TQ	COBLS	10/01-12/01
	Connecticut	H	7.45 FQ	12.43 AW	17.13 TQ	CTBLS	10/01-12/01
	Danbury PMSA, CT	H	11.54 FQ	14.66 AW	17.57 TQ	CTBLS	10/01-12/01
	Hartford MSA, CT	H	6.93 FQ	11.91 AW	17.41 TQ	CTBLS	10/01-12/01

AAW Average annual wage; **AE** Average entry wage; **AEX** Average experienced wage; **AO** Average offered; **AOH** Average offered, high; **AOL** Average offered, low; **APH** Average pay, high range; **APL** Average pay, low range; **ASH** Average starting, high; **ASL** Average starting, low; **AW** Average wage paid; **FQ** First quartile wage; **H** Hourly; **HI** Highest wage paid; **HR** High end range; **LR** Low end range; **M** Monthly; **MTC** Median total compensation; **MW** Median wage paid; **SQ** Second quartile wage; **S** Special: hourly and annual; **TQ** Third quartile wage; **W** Weekly; **Y** Yearly

Occupation/Type/Industry	Location	Per	Low	Mid	High	Source	Date
Coil Winder, Taper, and Finisher	New Haven-Meriden PMSA, CT	H	7.87 FQ	13.10 AW	17.24 TQ	CTBLS	10/01-12/01
	Delaware	H	7.79 FQ	11.84 AW	16.46 TQ	DEBLS	10/01-12/01
	Washington PMSA, DC-MD-VA-WV	H	7.42 FQ	10.28 AW	13.97 TQ	DCBLS	10/01-12/01
	Florida	H	6.82 FQ	10.93 AW	18.84 TQ	FLBLS	10/01-12/01
	Fort Lauderdale PMSA, FL	H	7.19 FQ	9.42 AW	12.72 TQ	FLBLS	10/01-12/01
	Miami PMSA, FL	H	6.45 FQ	9.29 AW	13.63 TQ	FLBLS	10/01-12/01
	Orlando MSA, FL	H	6.01 FQ	10.42 AW	19.17 TQ	FLBLS	10/01-12/01
	Tampa-St. Petersburg-Clearwater MSA, FL	H	6.92 FQ	10.08 AW	14.11 TQ	FLBLS	10/01-12/01
	West Palm Beach-Boca Raton MSA, FL	H	8.26 FQ	14.35 AW	22.45 TQ	FLBLS	10/01-12/01
	Georgia	H	8.12 FQ	11.68 AW	16.14 TQ	GABLS	10/01-12/01
	Atlanta MSA, GA	H	8.19 FQ	11.77 AW	16.23 TQ	GABLS	10/01-12/01
	Idaho	H	7.39 FQ	11.59 AW	16.00 TQ	IDBLS	10/01-12/01
	Illinois	H	6.69 FQ	10.31 AW	14.91 TQ	ILBLS	10/01-12/01
	Chicago PMSA, IL	H	6.68 FQ	9.97 AW	14.36 TQ	ILBLS	10/01-12/01
	Rockford MSA, IL	H	7.36 FQ	9.42 AW	12.60 TQ	ILBLS	10/01-12/01
	Indiana	H	7.30 FQ	10.44 AW	15.58 TQ	INBLS	10/01-12/01
	Evansville-Henderson MSA, IN-KY	H	9.25 FQ	10.36 AW	11.44 TQ	INBLS	10/01-12/01
	Fort Wayne MSA, IN	H	8.07 FQ	10.66 AW	13.55 TQ	INBLS	10/01-12/01
	Indianapolis MSA, IN	H	7.81 FQ	12.39 AW	22.70 TQ	INBLS	10/01-12/01
	South Bend MSA, IN	H	6.32 FQ	9.02 AW	12.50 TQ	INBLS	10/01-12/01
	Iowa	H	6.57 FQ	10.60 AW	16.40 TQ	IABLS	10/01-12/01
	Kansas	H	7.42 FQ	10.07 AW	14.24 TQ	KSBLS	10/01-12/01
	Kentucky	H	7.02 FQ	10.47 AW	13.99 TQ	KYBLS	10/01-12/01
	Louisiana	H	11.08 FQ	16.05 AW	20.79 TQ	LABLS	10/01-12/01
	Maryland	H	7.43 FQ	9.65 AW	12.60 TQ	MDBLS	10/01-12/01
	Baltimore PMSA, MD	H	7.61 FQ	9.79 AW	12.67 TQ	MDBLS	10/01-12/01
	Massachusetts	H	6.97 FQ	11.60 AW	15.26 TQ	MABLS	10/01-12/01
	Boston PMSA, MA-NH	H	6.89 FQ	11.13 AW	15.79 TQ	MABLS	10/01-12/01
	Lowell PMSA, MA-NH	H	8.85 FQ	11.02 AW	13.97 TQ	MABLS	10/01-12/01
	Springfield MSA, MA	H	11.39 FQ	13.71 AW	16.08 TQ	MABLS	10/01-12/01
	Worcester PMSA, MA-CT	H	6.94 FQ	11.57 AW	15.79 TQ	MABLS	10/01-12/01
	Michigan	H	9.32 FQ	14.63 AW	18.13 TQ	MIBLS	10/01-12/01
	Ann Arbor PMSA, MI	H	10.77 FQ	19.10 AW	27.26 TQ	MIBLS	10/01-12/01
	Detroit PMSA, MI	H	8.83 FQ	14.36 AW	25.56 TQ	MIBLS	10/01-12/01
	Grand Rapids-Muskegon-Holland MSA, MI	H	11.92 FQ	15.65 AW	17.88 TQ	MIBLS	10/01-12/01
	Minnesota	H	8.28 FQ	12.93 AW	17.51 TQ	MNBLS	10/01-12/01
	Minneapolis-St. Paul MSA, MN-WI	H	8.38 FQ	14.85 AW	19.85 TQ	MNBLS	10/01-12/01
	Mississippi	H	7.21 FQ	10.27 AW	15.51 TQ	MSBLS	10/01-12/01
	Missouri	H	8.80 FQ	11.50 AW	15.27 TQ	MOBLS	10/01-12/01
	Kansas City MSA, MO-KS	H	8.77 FQ	10.26 AW	12.19 TQ	MOBLS	10/01-12/01
	St. Louis MSA, MO-IL	H	9.83 FQ	12.80 AW	16.61 TQ	MOBLS	10/01-12/01
	Nebraska	H	6.76 FQ	8.28 AW	10.44 TQ	NEBLS	10/01-12/01
	Portsmouth-Rochester PMSA, NH-ME	H	7.94 FQ	12.36 AW	16.58 TQ	NHBLS	10/01-12/01
	New Jersey	H	8.72 FQ	11.82 AW	16.10 TQ	NJBLS	10/01-12/01
	Bergen-Passaic PMSA, NJ	H	8.54 FQ	11.93 AW	17.03 TQ	NJBLS	10/01-12/01
	Middlesex-Somerset-Hunterdon PMSA, NJ	H	8.45 FQ	11.19 AW	15.36 TQ	NJBLS	10/01-12/01
	Newark PMSA, NJ	H	9.10 FQ	11.90 AW	15.03 TQ	NJBLS	10/01-12/01
	Trenton PMSA, NJ	H	9.01 FQ	12.04 AW	17.17 TQ	NJBLS	10/01-12/01
	New York	H	6.98 FQ	9.89 AW	14.06 TQ	NYBLS	10/01-12/01
	Binghamton MSA, NY	H	6.49 FQ	8.94 AW	12.37 TQ	NYBLS	10/01-12/01
	Buffalo-Niagara Falls MSA, NY	H	7.93 FQ	13.73 AW	24.01 TQ	NYBLS	10/01-12/01
	Dutchess County PMSA, NY	H	7.82 FQ	10.45 AW	13.77 TQ	NYBLS	10/01-12/01
	Nassau-Suffolk PMSA, NY	H	7.83 FQ	12.25 AW	19.25 TQ	NYBLS	10/01-12/01
	New York PMSA, NY	H	6.56 FQ	9.63 AW	13.48 TQ	NYBLS	10/01-12/01
	Rochester MSA, NY	H	7.54 FQ	10.16 AW	13.54 TQ	NYBLS	10/01-12/01
	Syracuse MSA, NY	H	7.92 FQ	9.52 AW	10.81 TQ	NYBLS	10/01-12/01
	North Carolina	H	8.53 FQ	11.73 AW	16.45 TQ	NCBLS	10/01-12/01
	Asheville MSA, NC	H	9.00 FQ	11.07 AW	15.82 TQ	NCBLS	10/01-12/01
	Charlotte-Gastonia-Rock Hill MSA, NC-SC	H	10.84 FQ	15.88 AW	21.36 TQ	NCBLS	10/01-12/01
	Raleigh-Durham-Chapel Hill MSA, NC	H	7.90 FQ	10.89 AW	15.12 TQ	NCBLS	10/01-12/01

AAW Average annual wage; AE Average entry wage; AEX Average experienced wage; AO Average offered; AOH Average offered, high; AOL Average offered, low; APH Average pay, high range; APL Average pay, low range; ASH Average starting, high; ASL Average starting, low; AW Average wage paid; FQ First quartile wage; H Hourly; HI Highest wage paid; HR High end range; LR Low end range; M Monthly; MTC Median total compensation; MW Median wage paid; SQ Second quartile wage; S Special: hourly and annual; TQ Third quartile wage; W Weekly; Y Yearly

Occupation/Type/Industry	Location	Per	Low	Mid	High	Source	Date
Coil Winder, Taper, and Finisher	Ohio	H	8.40 FQ	12.67 AW	17.85 TQ	OHBLS	10/01-12/01
	Akron PMSA, OH	H	7.89 FQ	14.06 AW	25.61 TQ	OHBLS	10/01-12/01
	Cincinnati PMSA, OH-KY-IN	H	8.16 FQ	12.32 AW	16.89 TQ	OHBLS	10/01-12/01
	Cleveland-Lorain-Elyria PMSA, OH	H	7.82 FQ	11.65 AW	16.56 TQ	OHBLS	10/01-12/01
	Dayton-Springfield MSA, OH	H	8.93 FQ	11.23 AW	15.05 TQ	OHBLS	10/01-12/01
	Oklahoma	H	8.56 FQ	11.59 AW	15.74 TQ	OKBLS	10/01-12/01
	Oklahoma City MSA, OK	H	9.34 FQ	12.82 AW	16.26 TQ	OKBLS	10/01-12/01
	Tulsa MSA, OK	H	8.53 FQ	10.90 AW	14.54 TQ	OKBLS	10/01-12/01
	Oregon	H	8.69 FQ	11.40 AW	15.95 TQ	ORBLS	10/01-12/01
	Portland-Vancouver PMSA, OR-WA	H	8.61 FQ	10.31 AW	13.33 TQ	ORBLS	10/01-12/01
	Pennsylvania	H	8.53 FQ	14.29 AW	21.00 TQ	PABLS	10/01-12/01
	Allentown-Bethlehem-Easton MSA, PA	H	9.69 FQ	12.70 AW	16.15 TQ	PABLS	10/01-12/01
	Philadelphia PMSA, PA-NJ	H	7.61 FQ	11.13 AW	15.86 TQ	PABLS	10/01-12/01
	Pittsburgh MSA, PA	H	9.14 FQ	13.46 AW	20.15 TQ	PABLS	10/01-12/01
	Reading MSA, PA	H	8.31 FQ	12.19 AW	18.24 TQ	PABLS	10/01-12/01
	Scranton-Wilkes-Barre-Hazleton MSA, PA	H	7.47 FQ	9.97 AW	13.39 TQ	PABLS	10/01-12/01
	York MSA, PA	H	6.42 FQ	9.08 AW	12.51 TQ	PABLS	10/01-12/01
	Rhode Island	H	7.12 FQ	10.72 AW	15.14 TQ	RIBLS	10/01-12/01
	Providence-Fall River-Warwick MSA, RI-MA	H	6.89 FQ	10.75 AW	15.57 TQ	RIBLS	10/01-12/01
	South Carolina	H	9.44 FQ	12.68 AW	16.86 TQ	SCBLS	10/01-12/01
	Greenville-Spartanburg-Anderson MSA, SC	H	8.34 FQ	10.42 AW	13.32 TQ	SCBLS	10/01-12/01
	Tennessee	H	8.17 FQ	11.26 AW	14.52 TQ	TNBLS	10/01-12/01
	Memphis MSA, TN-AR-MS	H	8.16 FQ	10.52 AW	13.27 TQ	TNBLS	10/01-12/01
	Nashville MSA, TN	H	7.29 FQ	10.73 AW	15.69 TQ	TNBLS	10/01-12/01
	Texas	H	6.61 FQ	9.53 AW	13.28 TQ	TXBLS	10/01-12/01
	Austin-San Marcos MSA, TX	H	7.24 FQ	9.13 AW	12.79 TQ	TXBLS	10/01-12/01
	Beaumont-Port Arthur MSA, TX	H	7.94 FQ	12.03 AW	16.19 TQ	TXBLS	10/01-12/01
	Dallas PMSA, TX	H	7.43 FQ	9.36 AW	11.66 TQ	TXBLS	10/01-12/01
	El Paso MSA, TX	H	5.83 FQ	8.31 AW	11.61 TQ	TXBLS	10/01-12/01
	Fort Worth-Arlington PMSA, TX	H	6.76 FQ	8.76 AW	11.50 TQ	TXBLS	10/01-12/01
	Houston PMSA, TX	H	6.15 FQ	9.91 AW	13.74 TQ	TXBLS	10/01-12/01
	Utah	H	7.50 FQ	9.99 AW	13.28 TQ	UTBLS	10/01-12/01
	Salt Lake City-Ogden MSA, UT	H	7.53 FQ	9.86 AW	13.22 TQ	UTBLS	10/01-12/01
	Virginia	H	7.07 FQ	11.03 AW	16.12 TQ	VABLS	10/01-12/01
	Lynchburg MSA, VA	H	6.35 FQ	9.73 AW	15.24 TQ	VABLS	10/01-12/01
	Washington	H	7.76 FQ	12.77 AW	17.96 TQ	WABLS	10/01-12/01
	Seattle-Bellevue-Everett PMSA, WA	H	7.69 FQ	12.89 AW	18.12 TQ	WABLS	10/01-12/01
	West Virginia	H	8.96 FQ	13.72 AW	22.52 TQ	WVBLS	10/01-12/01
	Wisconsin	H	8.13 FQ	12.94 AW	20.15 TQ	WIBLS	10/01-12/01
	Madison MSA, WI	H	9.36 FQ	11.78 AW	14.00 TQ	WIBLS	10/01-12/01
	Milwaukee-Waukesha PMSA, WI	H	8.36 FQ	14.02 AW	20.52 TQ	WIBLS	10/01-12/01
	Puerto Rico	H	5.83 FQ	7.21 AW	8.69 TQ	PRBLS	10/01-12/01
Coin, Vending, and Amusement Machine Servicer and Repairer	Alabama	H	8.94 FQ	12.22 AW	16.27 TQ	ALBLS	10/01-12/01
	Alaska	H	9.64 FQ	13.58 AW	19.69 TQ	AKBLS	10/01-12/01
	Arizona	H	9.05 FQ	13.87 AW	17.67 TQ	AZBLS	10/01-12/01
	Arkansas	H	8.91 FQ	11.44 AW	14.29 TQ	ARBLS	10/01-12/01
	California	H	8.03 FQ	13.98 AW	20.92 TQ	CABLS	10/01-12/01
	Colorado	H	8.46 FQ	12.99 AW	17.69 TQ	COBLS	10/01-12/01
	Connecticut	H	7.83 FQ	12.58 AW	16.90 TQ	CTBLS	10/01-12/01
	Delaware	H	9.14 FQ	12.47 AW	16.66 TQ	DEBLS	10/01-12/01
	Florida	H	7.45 FQ	13.54 AW	20.80 TQ	FLBLS	10/01-12/01
	Georgia	H	8.08 FQ	12.90 AW	16.91 TQ	GABLS	10/01-12/01
	Hawaii	H	7.73 FQ	12.84 AW	20.79 TQ	HIBLS	10/01-12/01
	Idaho	H	8.16 FQ	13.40 AW	17.88 TQ	IDBLS	10/01-12/01
	Illinois	H	8.03 FQ	14.65 AW	23.62 TQ	ILBLS	10/01-12/01
	Indiana	H	7.94 FQ	12.66 AW	17.56 TQ	INBLS	10/01-12/01
	Iowa	H	8.91 FQ	13.08 AW	17.73 TQ	IABLS	10/01-12/01
	Kansas	H	7.91 FQ	14.40 AW	24.06 TQ	KSBLS	10/01-12/01
	Kentucky	H	7.22 FQ	12.38 AW	17.15 TQ	KYBLS	10/01-12/01

AAW	Average annual wage	**AOH**	Average offered, high	**ASH**	Average starting, high	**H**	Hourly	**M**	Monthly	**S**	Special: hourly and annual
AE	Average entry wage	**AOL**	Average offered, low	**ASL**	Average starting, low	**HI**	Highest wage paid	**MTC**	Median total compensation	**TQ**	Third quartile wage
AEX	Average experienced wage	**APH**	Average pay, high range	**AW**	Average wage paid	**HR**	High end range	**MW**	Median wage paid	**W**	Weekly
AO	Average offered	**APL**	Average pay, low range	**FQ**	First quartile wage	**LR**	Low end range	**SQ**	Second quartile wage	**Y**	Yearly

Occupation/Type/Industry	Location	Per	Low	Mid	High	Source	Date
Coin, Vending, and Amusement Machine Servicer and Repairer	Louisiana	H	9.26 FQ	13.44 AW	18.11 TQ	LABLS	10/01-12/01
	Maine	H	7.71 FQ	11.01 AW	16.36 TQ	MEBLS	10/01-12/01
	Maryland	H	8.18 FQ	13.04 AW	19.43 TQ	MDBLS	10/01-12/01
	Massachusetts	H	9.31 FQ	14.05 AW	19.20 TQ	MABLS	10/01-12/01
	Michigan	H	8.58 FQ	12.52 AW	18.09 TQ	MIBLS	10/01-12/01
	Minnesota	H	7.42 FQ	14.13 AW	21.07 TQ	MNBLS	10/01-12/01
	Mississippi	H	8.83 FQ	12.93 AW	17.35 TQ	MSBLS	10/01-12/01
	Missouri	H	6.17 FQ	11.89 AW	18.85 TQ	MOBLS	10/01-12/01
	Montana	H	6.77 FQ	12.33 AW	18.65 TQ	MTBLS	10/01-12/01
	Nebraska	H	9.09 FQ	12.79 AW	17.07 TQ	NEBLS	10/01-12/01
	Nevada	H	9.36 FQ	15.78 AW	24.32 TQ	NVBLS	10/01-12/01
	New Hampshire	H	9.59 FQ	13.04 AW	16.72 TQ	NHBLS	10/01-12/01
	New Jersey	H	9.31 FQ	15.56 AW	23.43 TQ	NJBLS	10/01-12/01
	New Mexico	H	7.68 FQ	10.90 AW	15.51 TQ	NMBLS	10/01-12/01
	New York	H	6.14 FQ	14.46 AW	25.82 TQ	NYBLS	10/01-12/01
	North Carolina	H	8.05 FQ	12.91 AW	17.95 TQ	NCBLS	10/01-12/01
	North Dakota	H	7.87 FQ	11.82 AW	16.10 TQ	NDBLS	10/01-12/01
	Ohio	H	6.45 FQ	11.66 AW	17.22 TQ	OHBLS	10/01-12/01
	Oklahoma	H	7.19 FQ	13.55 AW	23.57 TQ	OKBLS	10/01-12/01
	Oregon	H	11.04 FQ	15.59 AW	20.37 TQ	ORBLS	10/01-12/01
	Pennsylvania	H	7.35 FQ	12.82 AW	19.24 TQ	PABLS	10/01-12/01
	Rhode Island	H	9.30 FQ	13.43 AW	19.47 TQ	RIBLS	10/01-12/01
	South Carolina	H	6.83 FQ	10.34 AW	16.65 TQ	SCBLS	10/01-12/01
	South Dakota	H	8.78 FQ	11.71 AW	15.68 TQ	SDBLS	10/01-12/01
	Tennessee	H	6.48 FQ	11.65 AW	16.13 TQ	TNBLS	10/01-12/01
	Texas	H	6.89 FQ	11.78 AW	16.68 TQ	TXBLS	10/01-12/01
	Utah	H	8.88 FQ	13.99 AW	23.90 TQ	UTBLS	10/01-12/01
	Vermont	H	9.30 FQ	12.51 AW	16.43 TQ	VTBLS	10/01-12/01
	Virginia	H	7.51 FQ	12.01 AW	17.01 TQ	VABLS	10/01-12/01
	Washington	H	11.46 FQ	15.13 AW	19.97 TQ	WABLS	10/01-12/01
	West Virginia	H	7.06 FQ	10.59 AW	14.21 TQ	WVBLS	10/01-12/01
	Wisconsin	H	8.22 FQ	14.12 AW	20.38 TQ	WIBLS	10/01-12/01
	Wyoming	H	7.24 FQ	9.02 AW	13.04 TQ	WYBLS	10/01-12/01
	Puerto Rico	H	5.44 FQ	7.36 AW	11.61 TQ	PRBLS	10/01-12/01
Commercial and Industrial Designer	Alabama	Y	24360 FQ	42970 AW	69550 TQ	ALBLS	10/01-12/01
	Birmingham MSA, AL	Y	23890 FQ	44090 AW	68050 TQ	ALBLS	10/01-12/01
	Huntsville MSA, AL	Y	22370 FQ	46200 AW	72520 TQ	ALBLS	10/01-12/01
	Montgomery MSA, AL	Y	28390 FQ	32190 AW	35350 TQ	ALBLS	10/01-12/01
	Arizona	Y	30060 FQ	45690 AW	59340 TQ	AZBLS	10/01-12/01
	Phoenix-Mesa MSA, AZ	Y	31040 FQ	46820 AW	59730 TQ	AZBLS	10/01-12/01
	Tucson MSA, AZ	Y	29670 FQ	41080 AW	57120 TQ	AZBLS	10/01-12/01
	Arkansas	Y	27030 FQ	42280 AW	62320 TQ	ARBLS	10/01-12/01
	Little Rock-North Little Rock MSA, AR	Y	26900 FQ	43580 AW	62450 TQ	ARBLS	10/01-12/01
	California	Y	31290 FQ	55440 AW	87210 TQ	CABLS	10/01-12/01
	Fresno MSA, CA	Y	28100 FQ	47610 AW	70040 TQ	CABLS	10/01-12/01
	Los Angeles-Long Beach PMSA, CA	Y	35140 FQ	58680 AW	92320 TQ	CABLS	10/01-12/01
	Oakland PMSA, CA	Y	31100 FQ	51660 AW	70970 TQ	CABLS	10/01-12/01
	Orange County PMSA, CA	Y	28140 FQ	53460 AW	84080 TQ	CABLS	10/01-12/01
	Riverside-San Bernardino PMSA, CA	Y	26350 FQ	50670 AW	85320 TQ	CABLS	10/01-12/01
	Sacramento PMSA, CA	Y	33600 FQ	55500 AW	78660 TQ	CABLS	10/01-12/01
	San Diego MSA, CA	Y	27690 FQ	51790 AW	82290 TQ	CABLS	10/01-12/01
	San Francisco PMSA, CA	Y	36190 FQ	49640 AW	79360 TQ	CABLS	10/01-12/01
	San Jose PMSA, CA	Y	45790 FQ	68180 AW	104890 TQ	CABLS	10/01-12/01
	Santa Rosa PMSA, CA	Y	30720 FQ	42610 AW	57930 TQ	CABLS	10/01-12/01
	Stockton-Lodi MSA, CA	Y	31580 FQ	41060 AW	47840 TQ	CABLS	10/01-12/01
	Ventura PMSA, CA	Y	29210 FQ	45140 AW	69370 TQ	CABLS	10/01-12/01
	Colorado	Y	28560 FQ	44110 AW	65090 TQ	COBLS	10/01-12/01
	Boulder-Longmont PMSA, CO	Y	36140 FQ	47610 AW	67770 TQ	COBLS	10/01-12/01
	Colorado Springs MSA, CO	Y	24480 FQ	38020 AW	60270 TQ	COBLS	10/01-12/01
	Denver PMSA, CO	Y	29070 FQ	42500 AW	61080 TQ	COBLS	10/01-12/01
	Connecticut	Y	33550 FQ	71790 AW		CTBLS	10/01-12/01
	Hartford MSA, CT	Y	30440 FQ	47850 AW	66990 TQ	CTBLS	10/01-12/01
	New Haven-Meriden PMSA, CT	Y	32170 FQ	46410 AW	58280 TQ	CTBLS	10/01-12/01
	New London-Norwich MSA, CT-RI	Y	26320 FQ	43460 AW	62010 TQ	CTBLS	10/01-12/01

AAW	Average annual wage	AOH	Average offered, high	ASH	Average starting, high	H	Hourly	M	Monthly	S	Special: hourly and annual
AE	Average entry wage	AOL	Average offered, low	ASL	Average starting, low	HI	Highest wage paid	MTC	Median total compensation	TQ	Third quartile wage
AEX	Average experienced wage	APH	Average pay, high range	AW	Average wage paid	HR	High end range	MW	Median wage paid	W	Weekly
AO	Average offered	APL	Average pay, low range	FQ	First quartile wage	LR	Low end range	SQ	Second quartile wage	Y	Yearly

Occupation/Type/Industry	Location	Per	Low	Mid	High	Source	Date
Commercial and Industrial Designer	Stamford-Norwalk PMSA, CT	Y	34050 FQ	53730 AW	70240 TQ	CTBLS	10/01-12/01
	Delaware	Y	30290 FQ	53380 AW	74360 TQ	DEBLS	10/01-12/01
	District of Columbia	Y	21840 FQ	50490 AW	75660 TQ	DCBLS	10/01-12/01
	Washington PMSA, DC-MD-VA-WV	Y	31530 FQ	49020 AW	70150 TQ	DCBLS	10/01-12/01
	Florida	Y	18310 FQ	42530 AW	67830 TQ	FLBLS	10/01-12/01
	Melbourne-Titusville-Palm Bay MSA, FL	Y	37160 FQ	41810 AW	51140 TQ	FLBLS	10/01-12/01
	Miami PMSA, FL	Y	24570 FQ	45770 AW	70810 TQ	FLBLS	10/01-12/01
	Orlando MSA, FL	Y	16100 FQ	37420 AW	71000 TQ	FLBLS	10/01-12/01
	Sarasota-Bradenton MSA, FL	Y	30920 FQ	53360 AW	71230 TQ	FLBLS	10/01-12/01
	Tampa-St. Petersburg-Clearwater MSA, FL	Y	21810 FQ	38870 AW	62500 TQ	FLBLS	10/01-12/01
	West Palm Beach-Boca Raton MSA, FL	Y	29640 FQ	54670 AW		FLBLS	10/01-12/01
	Georgia	Y	25840 FQ	42640 AW	66570 TQ	GABLS	10/01-12/01
	Atlanta MSA, GA	Y	25500 FQ	41920 AW	66140 TQ	GABLS	10/01-12/01
	Augusta-Aiken MSA, GA-SC	Y	35910 FQ	39740 AW	44160 TQ	GABLS	10/01-12/01
	Idaho	Y	22460 FQ	41420 AW	60670 TQ	IDBLS	10/01-12/01
	Boise City MSA, ID	Y	25330 FQ	41820 AW	58450 TQ	IDBLS	10/01-12/01
	Illinois	Y	19110 FQ	48850 AW	73760 TQ	ILBLS	10/01-12/01
	Champaign-Urbana MSA, IL	Y	35670 FQ	50800 AW	84420 TQ	ILBLS	10/01-12/01
	Chicago PMSA, IL	Y	16410 FQ	48360 AW	73500 TQ	ILBLS	10/01-12/01
	Peoria-Pekin MSA, IL	Y	31950 FQ	54670 AW	71510 TQ	ILBLS	10/01-12/01
	Rockford MSA, IL	Y	30070 FQ	40290 AW	59010 TQ	ILBLS	10/01-12/01
	Indiana	Y	24660 FQ	45630 AW	68160 TQ	INBLS	10/01-12/01
	Elkhart-Goshen MSA, IN	Y	32940 FQ	49390 AW	70730 TQ	INBLS	10/01-12/01
	Evansville-Henderson MSA, IN-KY	Y	24900 FQ	38660 AW	55250 TQ	INBLS	10/01-12/01
	Fort Wayne MSA, IN	Y	19670 FQ	36700 AW	58160 TQ	INBLS	10/01-12/01
	Indianapolis MSA, IN	Y	24970 FQ	46350 AW	66220 TQ	INBLS	10/01-12/01
	Iowa	Y	25390 FQ	42480 AW	63640 TQ	IABLS	10/01-12/01
	Des Moines MSA, IA	Y	20870 FQ	42310 AW	68640 TQ	IABLS	10/01-12/01
	Kansas	Y	20330 FQ	37490 AW	56230 TQ	KSBLS	10/01-12/01
	Wichita MSA, KS	Y	25400 FQ	39680 AW	54980 TQ	KSBLS	10/01-12/01
	Kentucky	Y	23130 FQ	45540 AW	73900 TQ	KYBLS	10/01-12/01
	Louisville MSA, KY-IN	Y	32030 FQ	51870 AW	79350 TQ	KYBLS	10/01-12/01
	Louisiana	Y	33730 FQ	46920 AW	67770 TQ	LABLS	10/01-12/01
	New Orleans MSA, LA	Y	35160 FQ	47590 AW	68400 TQ	LABLS	10/01-12/01
	Maryland	Y	27270 FQ	48580 AW	65210 TQ	MDBLS	10/01-12/01
	Baltimore PMSA, MD	Y	25880 FQ	45980 AW	58810 TQ	MDBLS	10/01-12/01
	Massachusetts	Y	35910 FQ	60400 AW	85580 TQ	MABLS	10/01-12/01
	Boston PMSA, MA-NH	Y	41560 FQ	62440 AW	86190 TQ	MABLS	10/01-12/01
	Lawrence PMSA, MA-NH	Y	30390 FQ	50230 AW	79830 TQ	MABLS	10/01-12/01
	Lowell PMSA, MA-NH	Y	31760 FQ	49060 AW	69820 TQ	MABLS	10/01-12/01
	Springfield MSA, MA	Y	29680 FQ	42070 AW	60620 TQ	MABLS	10/01-12/01
	Worcester PMSA, MA-CT	Y	34040 FQ	56190 AW	79310 TQ	MABLS	10/01-12/01
	Michigan	Y	44040 FQ	64050 AW	87400 TQ	MIBLS	10/01-12/01
	Ann Arbor PMSA, MI	Y	46190 FQ	61960 AW	77690 TQ	MIBLS	10/01-12/01
	Detroit PMSA, MI	Y	49930 FQ	68120 AW	91190 TQ	MIBLS	10/01-12/01
	Grand Rapids-Muskegon-Holland MSA, MI	Y	37050 FQ	56190 AW	76010 TQ	MIBLS	10/01-12/01
	Kalamazoo-Battle Creek MSA, MI	Y	26770 FQ	48310 AW	70260 TQ	MIBLS	10/01-12/01
	Saginaw-Bay City-Midland MSA, MI	Y	20780 FQ	38900 AW	65210 TQ	MIBLS	10/01-12/01
	Minnesota	Y	30390 FQ	48330 AW	73580 TQ	MNBLS	10/01-12/01
	Minneapolis-St. Paul MSA, MN-WI	Y	29280 FQ	50380 AW	76510 TQ	MNBLS	10/01-12/01
	St. Cloud MSA, MN	Y	30590 FQ	39720 AW	52940 TQ	MNBLS	10/01-12/01
	Mississippi	Y	22530 FQ	36610 AW	56280 TQ	MSBLS	10/01-12/01
	Missouri	Y	26390 FQ	47210 AW	72380 TQ	MOBLS	10/01-12/01
	Kansas City MSA, MO-KS	Y	27410 FQ	50320 AW	75250 TQ	MOBLS	10/01-12/01
	St. Louis MSA, MO-IL	Y	25830 FQ	49730 AW	75330 TQ	MOBLS	10/01-12/01
	Montana	Y	24110 FQ	32290 AW	36650 TQ	MTBLS	10/01-12/01
	Nevada	Y	22800 FQ	41730 AW	59790 TQ	NVBLS	10/01-12/01
	Las Vegas MSA, NV-AZ	Y	21820 FQ	39090 AW	56380 TQ	NVBLS	10/01-12/01
	New Hampshire	Y	25980 FQ	43080 AW	61480 TQ	NHBLS	10/01-12/01
	New Jersey	Y	27450 FQ	50100 AW	79620 TQ	NJBLS	10/01-12/01
	Bergen-Passaic PMSA, NJ	Y	32830 FQ	52570 AW	83990 TQ	NJBLS	10/01-12/01

AAW	Average annual wage	AOH	Average offered, high	ASH	Average starting, high	H	Hourly	M	Monthly	S	Special: hourly and annual
AE	Average entry wage	AOL	Average offered, low	ASL	Average starting, low	HI	Highest wage paid	MTC	Median total compensation	TQ	Third quartile wage
AEX	Average experienced wage	APH	Average pay, high range	AW	Average wage paid	HR	High end range	MW	Median wage paid	W	Weekly
AO	Average offered	APL	Average pay, low range	FQ	First quartile wage	LR	Low end range	SQ	Second quartile wage	Y	Yearly

Occupation/Type/Industry	Location	Per	Low	Mid	High	Source	Date
Commercial and Industrial Designer	Middlesex-Somerset-Hunterdon PMSA, NJ	Y	31580 FQ	60940 AW	109160 TQ	NJBLS	10/01-12/01
	Newark PMSA, NJ	Y	21800 FQ	40780 AW	67830 TQ	NJBLS	10/01-12/01
	New Mexico	Y	12520 FQ	31530 AW	78550 TQ	NMBLS	10/01-12/01
	Albuquerque MSA, NM	Y	21620 FQ	54530 AW	91340 TQ	NMBLS	10/01-12/01
	New York	Y	31940 FQ	59190 AW	94880 TQ	NYBLS	10/01-12/01
	Albany-Schenectady-Troy MSA, NY	Y	27600 FQ	44120 AW	73540 TQ	NYBLS	10/01-12/01
	Buffalo-Niagara Falls MSA, NY	Y	27420 FQ	59410 AW	104010 TQ	NYBLS	10/01-12/01
	Nassau-Suffolk PMSA, NY	Y	38930 FQ	60770 AW	84010 TQ	NYBLS	10/01-12/01
	New York PMSA, NY	Y	34080 FQ	63370 AW	124270 TQ	NYBLS	10/01-12/01
	Rochester MSA, NY	Y	36280 FQ	58770 AW	78200 TQ	NYBLS	10/01-12/01
	North Carolina	Y	24690 FQ	49970 AW	87060 TQ	NCBLS	10/01-12/01
	Charlotte-Gastonia-Rock Hill MSA, NC-SC	Y	26370 FQ	40630 AW	57490 TQ	NCBLS	10/01-12/01
	Greensboro-Winston-Salem-High Point MSA, NC	Y	34000 FQ	53890 AW	77130 TQ	NCBLS	10/01-12/01
	Raleigh-Durham-Chapel Hill MSA, NC	Y	23560 FQ	48910 AW	105160 TQ	NCBLS	10/01-12/01
	North Dakota	Y	16940 FQ	31480 AW	44690 TQ	NDBLS	10/01-12/01
	Fargo-Moorhead MSA, ND-MN	Y	15110 FQ	25920 AW	40350 TQ	NDBLS	10/01-12/01
	Ohio	Y	30140 FQ	50960 AW	73450 TQ	OHBLS	10/01-12/01
	Akron PMSA, OH	Y	27660 FQ	54620 AW	79610 TQ	OHBLS	10/01-12/01
	Canton-Massillon MSA, OH	Y	24940 FQ	43760 AW	68570 TQ	OHBLS	10/01-12/01
	Cincinnati PMSA, OH-KY-IN	Y	26210 FQ	49820 AW	84360 TQ	OHBLS	10/01-12/01
	Cleveland-Lorain-Elyria PMSA, OH	Y	28950 FQ	56040 AW	87300 TQ	OHBLS	10/01-12/01
	Columbus MSA, OH	Y	36070 FQ	49110 AW	67710 TQ	OHBLS	10/01-12/01
	Dayton-Springfield MSA, OH	Y	35380 FQ	56260 AW	77110 TQ	OHBLS	10/01-12/01
	Toledo MSA, OH	Y	29670 FQ	55560 AW	74480 TQ	OHBLS	10/01-12/01
	Youngstown-Warren MSA, OH	Y	31050 FQ	43050 AW	67040 TQ	OHBLS	10/01-12/01
	Oklahoma	Y	23570 FQ	41060 AW	63030 TQ	OKBLS	10/01-12/01
	Oklahoma City MSA, OK	Y	23580 FQ	39910 AW	64020 TQ	OKBLS	10/01-12/01
	Tulsa MSA, OK	Y	23170 FQ	41420 AW	56660 TQ	OKBLS	10/01-12/01
	Oregon	Y	30650 FQ	52420 AW	73730 TQ	ORBLS	10/01-12/01
	Portland-Vancouver PMSA, OR-WA	Y	30940 FQ	53610 AW	75120 TQ	ORBLS	10/01-12/01
	Pennsylvania	Y	22180 FQ	43970 AW	70350 TQ	PABLS	10/01-12/01
	Allentown-Bethlehem-Easton MSA, PA	Y	24740 FQ	42970 AW	57450 TQ	PABLS	10/01-12/01
	Harrisburg-Lebanon-Carlisle MSA, PA	Y	30070 FQ	45630 AW	66940 TQ	PABLS	10/01-12/01
	Philadelphia PMSA, PA-NJ	Y	24440 FQ	46380 AW	78190 TQ	PABLS	10/01-12/01
	Pittsburgh MSA, PA	Y	18370 FQ	42160 AW	68380 TQ	PABLS	10/01-12/01
	Reading MSA, PA	Y	24350 FQ	40030 AW	60090 TQ	PABLS	10/01-12/01
	Rhode Island	Y	26190 FQ	49680 AW	84580 TQ	RIBLS	10/01-12/01
	Providence-Fall River-Warwick MSA, RI-MA	Y	24290 FQ	46090 AW	75900 TQ	RIBLS	10/01-12/01
	South Carolina	Y	27880 FQ	47480 AW	74240 TQ	SCBLS	10/01-12/01
	Charleston-North Charleston MSA, SC	Y	31050 FQ	52190 AW	77300 TQ	SCBLS	10/01-12/01
	Columbia MSA, SC	Y	19570 FQ	34470 AW	51680 TQ	SCBLS	10/01-12/01
	Greenville-Spartanburg-Anderson MSA, SC	Y	30090 FQ	47090 AW	73900 TQ	SCBLS	10/01-12/01
	South Dakota	Y	20170 FQ	28540 AW	38760 TQ	SDBLS	10/01-12/01
	Sioux Falls MSA, SD	Y	19870 FQ	27170 AW	36170 TQ	SDBLS	10/01-12/01
	Tennessee	Y	26620 FQ	45600 AW	65900 TQ	TNBLS	10/01-12/01
	Knoxville MSA, TN	Y	27260 FQ	41520 AW	63600 TQ	TNBLS	10/01-12/01
	Memphis MSA, TN-AR-MS	Y	20830 FQ	47560 AW	73990 TQ	TNBLS	10/01-12/01
	Nashville MSA, TN	Y	25990 FQ	46550 AW	62470 TQ	TNBLS	10/01-12/01
	Texas	Y	27880 FQ	57400 AW	89740 TQ	TXBLS	10/01-12/01
	Austin-San Marcos MSA, TX	Y	29600 FQ	66650 AW	122530 TQ	TXBLS	10/01-12/01
	Dallas PMSA, TX	Y	36290 FQ	62350 AW	90240 TQ	TXBLS	10/01-12/01
	El Paso MSA, TX	Y	25890 FQ	39950 AW	53970 TQ	TXBLS	10/01-12/01
	Fort Worth-Arlington PMSA, TX	Y	24540 FQ	45180 AW	69280 TQ	TXBLS	10/01-12/01
	Houston PMSA, TX	Y	38230 FQ	61940 AW	92630 TQ	TXBLS	10/01-12/01
	San Antonio MSA, TX	Y	14910 FQ	35560 AW	61890 TQ	TXBLS	10/01-12/01
	Utah	Y	23530 FQ	42330 AW	71070 TQ	UTBLS	10/01-12/01

AAW	Average annual wage	AOH	Average offered, high	ASH	Average starting, high	H	Hourly	M	Monthly	S	Special: hourly and annual
AE	Average entry wage	AOL	Average offered, low	ASL	Average starting, low	HI	Highest wage paid	MTC	Median total compensation	TQ	Third quartile wage
AEX	Average experienced wage	APH	Average pay, high range	AW	Average wage paid	HR	High end range	MW	Median wage paid	W	Weekly
AO	Average offered	APL	Average pay, low range	FQ	First quartile wage	LR	Low end range	SQ	Second quartile wage	Y	Yearly

Occupation/Type/Industry	Location	Per	Low	Mid	High	Source	Date
Commercial and Industrial Designer	Provo-Orem MSA, UT	Y	18010 FQ	37350 AW	82130 TQ	UTBLS	10/01-12/01
	Salt Lake City-Ogden MSA, UT	Y	30030 FQ	44810 AW	70310 TQ	UTBLS	10/01-12/01
	Vermont	Y	31770 FQ	46500 AW	60840 TQ	VTBLS	10/01-12/01
	Virginia	Y	27810 FQ	45850 AW	69670 TQ	VABLS	10/01-12/01
	Norfolk-Virginia Beach-Newport News MSA, VA-NC	Y	20650 FQ	42010 AW	69860 TQ	VABLS	10/01-12/01
	Richmond-Petersburg MSA, VA	Y	29430 FQ	43320 AW	64060 TQ	VABLS	10/01-12/01
	Roanoke MSA, VA	Y	29400 FQ	49690 AW	76120 TQ	VABLS	10/01-12/01
	Washington	Y	35450 FQ	51340 AW	71060 TQ	WABLS	10/01-12/01
	Seattle-Bellevue-Everett PMSA, WA	Y	35970 FQ	51550 AW	70880 TQ	WABLS	10/01-12/01
	Wisconsin	Y	27780 FQ	48470 AW	70390 TQ	WIBLS	10/01-12/01
	Appleton-Oshkosh-Neenah MSA, WI	Y	33020 FQ	53470 AW	72620 TQ	WIBLS	10/01-12/01
	Madison MSA, WI	Y	29770 FQ	49980 AW	72680 TQ	WIBLS	10/01-12/01
	Milwaukee-Waukesha PMSA, WI	Y	31720 FQ	52400 AW	72520 TQ	WIBLS	10/01-12/01
	Racine PMSA, WI	Y	35800 FQ	49760 AW	68990 TQ	WIBLS	10/01-12/01
	Puerto Rico	Y	15350 FQ	30560 AW	55460 TQ	PRBLS	10/01-12/01
Commercial Diver	Alabama	H	9.47 FQ	13.86 AW	16.97 TQ	ALBLS	10/01-12/01
	California	H	10.43 FQ	23.96 AW	34.82 TQ	CABLS	10/01-12/01
	Florida	H	8.07 FQ	14.68 AW	20.78 TQ	FLBLS	10/01-12/01
	Hawaii	H	11.77 FQ	18.34 AW	26.03 TQ	HIBLS	10/01-12/01
	Indiana	H	10.01 FQ	14.31 AW	17.67 TQ	INBLS	10/01-12/01
	Kentucky	H	6.34 FQ	40.94 AW		KYBLS	10/01-12/01
	Louisiana	H	14.27 FQ	16.88 AW	20.76 TQ	LABLS	10/01-12/01
	New York	H	9.03 FQ	15.25 AW	27.16 TQ	NYBLS	10/01-12/01
	Texas	H	12.27 FQ	15.96 AW	20.41 TQ	TXBLS	10/01-12/01
	Virginia	H	11.00 FQ	14.88 AW	23.46 TQ	VABLS	10/01-12/01
	Washington	H	25.27 FQ	51.40 AW		WABLS	10/01-12/01
Commercial Pilot	Alabama	Y	39540 FQ	61600 AW	100520 TQ	ALBLS	10/01-12/01
	Alaska	Y	27660 FQ	51070 AW	81130 TQ	AKBLS	10/01-12/01
	Arizona	Y	29380 FQ	49040 AW	78800 TQ	AZBLS	10/01-12/01
	Arkansas	Y	22690 FQ	61610 AW	105300 TQ	ARBLS	10/01-12/01
	California	Y	28550 FQ	61840 AW		CABLS	10/01-12/01
	Colorado	Y	23940 FQ	45740 AW	82880 TQ	COBLS	10/01-12/01
	Connecticut	Y	37110 FQ	69250 AW	112710 TQ	CTBLS	10/01-12/01
	Florida	Y	24280 FQ	46960 AW	81120 TQ	FLBLS	10/01-12/01
	Georgia	Y	28170 FQ	57290 AW	91860 TQ	GABLS	10/01-12/01
	Hawaii	Y	33100 FQ	55480 AW	80390 TQ	HIBLS	10/01-12/01
	Idaho	Y	25980 FQ	43190 AW	71640 TQ	IDBLS	10/01-12/01
	Illinois	Y	32670 FQ	57980 AW	94520 TQ	ILBLS	10/01-12/01
	Indiana	Y	20310 FQ	38320 AW	59020 TQ	INBLS	10/01-12/01
	Iowa	Y	20060 FQ	47100 AW	81030 TQ	IABLS	10/01-12/01
	Kansas	Y	30340 FQ	62920 AW	105490 TQ	KSBLS	10/01-12/01
	Kentucky	Y	21990 FQ	45570 AW	75340 TQ	KYBLS	10/01-12/01
	Louisiana	Y	31300 FQ	60190 AW	94040 TQ	LABLS	10/01-12/01
	Maine	Y	23850 FQ	38980 AW	56110 TQ	MEBLS	10/01-12/01
	Maryland	Y	22010 FQ	54000 AW	83880 TQ	MDBLS	10/01-12/01
	Massachusetts	Y	28260 FQ	51360 AW	73200 TQ	MABLS	10/01-12/01
	Michigan	Y	24680 FQ	39070 AW	58050 TQ	MIBLS	10/01-12/01
	Minnesota	Y	25620 FQ	44670 AW	75280 TQ	MNBLS	10/01-12/01
	Mississippi	Y	28110 FQ	61790 AW	127450 TQ	MSBLS	10/01-12/01
	Missouri	Y	17020 FQ	37840 AW	60990 TQ	MOBLS	10/01-12/01
	Montana	Y	25380 FQ	37240 AW	54810 TQ	MTBLS	10/01-12/01
	Nebraska	Y	27250 FQ	49730 AW	79720 TQ	NEBLS	10/01-12/01
	Nevada	Y	29130 FQ	45030 AW	61700 TQ	NVBLS	10/01-12/01
	New Hampshire	Y	29450 FQ	50890 AW	91900 TQ	NHBLS	10/01-12/01
	New Jersey	Y	29880 FQ	56880 AW	94000 TQ	NJBLS	10/01-12/01
	New Mexico	Y	30530 FQ	53110 AW	80660 TQ	NMBLS	10/01-12/01
	North Carolina	Y	26770 FQ	69990 AW	133370 TQ	NCBLS	10/01-12/01
	North Dakota	Y	27840 FQ	47730 AW	70150 TQ	NDBLS	10/01-12/01
	Oklahoma	Y	27390 FQ	55180 AW	89970 TQ	OKBLS	10/01-12/01
	Oregon	Y	29710 FQ	49330 AW	82850 TQ	ORBLS	10/01-12/01
	Pennsylvania	Y	20160 FQ	46730 AW	73070 TQ	PABLS	10/01-12/01
	South Carolina	Y	28570 FQ	45540 AW	66920 TQ	SCBLS	10/01-12/01

AAW	Average annual wage	**AOH**	Average offered, high	**ASH**	Average starting, high	**H**	Hourly	**M**	Monthly	**S**	Special: hourly and annual
AE	Average entry wage	**AOL**	Average offered, low	**ASL**	Average starting, low	**HI**	Highest wage paid	**MTC**	Median total compensation	**TQ**	Third quartile wage
AEX	Average experienced wage	**APH**	Average pay, high range	**AW**	Average wage paid	**HR**	High end range	**MW**	Median wage paid	**W**	Weekly
AO	Average offered	**APL**	Average pay, low range	**FQ**	First quartile wage	**LR**	Low end range	**SQ**	Second quartile wage	**Y**	Yearly

Occupation/Type/Industry	Location	Per	Low	Mid	High	Source	Date
Commercial Pilot	South Dakota	Y	23840 FQ	38050 AW	55010 TQ	SDBLS	10/01-12/01
	Tennessee	Y	31770 FQ	50590 AW	77430 TQ	TNBLS	10/01-12/01
	Texas	Y	27300 FQ	55310 AW	96540 TQ	TXBLS	10/01-12/01
	Utah	Y	25480 FQ	42520 AW	58990 TQ	UTBLS	10/01-12/01
	Virginia	Y	22420 FQ	46030 AW	87750 TQ	VABLS	10/01-12/01
	Washington	Y	28610 FQ	56490 AW	124240 TQ	WABLS	10/01-12/01
	West Virginia	Y	28360 FQ	43950 AW	58010 TQ	WVBLS	10/01-12/01
	Wisconsin	Y	28660 FQ	46290 AW	65480 TQ	WIBLS	10/01-12/01
	Wyoming	Y	22550 FQ	44150 AW	69060 TQ	WYBLS	10/01-12/01
	Puerto Rico	Y	23630 FQ	34330 AW	47190 TQ	PRBLS	10/01-12/01
Communications Professional	San Diego, CA	Y		116301 AW		SDBJ1	1/99-1/00
Communications Teacher							
Postsecondary	Alabama	Y	19290 FQ	40550 AW	66250 TQ	ALBLS	10/01-12/01
Postsecondary	Arkansas	Y	23880 FQ	43350 AW	72940 TQ	ARBLS	10/01-12/01
Postsecondary	California	Y	30290 FQ	57910 AW	91990 TQ	CABLS	10/01-12/01
Postsecondary	Colorado	Y	28750 FQ	48840 AW	73860 TQ	COBLS	10/01-12/01
Postsecondary	Connecticut	Y	34420 FQ	62040 AW	99490 TQ	CTBLS	10/01-12/01
Postsecondary	Delaware	Y	27250 FQ	52440 AW	84550 TQ	DEBLS	10/01-12/01
Postsecondary	District of Columbia	Y	37120 FQ	57740 AW	86190 TQ	DCBLS	10/01-12/01
Postsecondary	Florida	Y	34090 FQ	59770 AW	93330 TQ	FLBLS	10/01-12/01
Postsecondary	Georgia	Y	33880 FQ	55250 AW	79460 TQ	GABLS	10/01-12/01
Postsecondary	Hawaii	Y	33610 FQ	50850 AW	74120 TQ	HIBLS	10/01-12/01
Postsecondary	Illinois	Y	15840 FQ	49780 AW	90380 TQ	ILBLS	10/01-12/01
Postsecondary	Indiana	Y	30400 FQ	49200 AW	73880 TQ	INBLS	10/01-12/01
Postsecondary	Iowa	Y	31710 FQ	51390 AW	74410 TQ	IABLS	10/01-12/01
Postsecondary	Kansas	Y	16070 FQ	38340 AW	56300 TQ	KSBLS	10/01-12/01
Postsecondary	Kentucky	Y	23820 FQ	43510 AW	68580 TQ	KYBLS	10/01-12/01
Postsecondary	Louisiana	Y	30290 FQ	45470 AW	70940 TQ	LABLS	10/01-12/01
Postsecondary	Maine	Y	35810 FQ	47710 AW	61860 TQ	MEBLS	10/01-12/01
Postsecondary	Maryland	Y	35270 FQ	62650 AW	120520 TQ	MDBLS	10/01-12/01
Postsecondary	Massachusetts	Y	30810 FQ	50230 AW	74660 TQ	MABLS	10/01-12/01
Postsecondary	Michigan	Y	30600 FQ	54740 AW	83380 TQ	MIBLS	10/01-12/01
Postsecondary	Minnesota	Y	30010 FQ	49050 AW	71850 TQ	MNBLS	10/01-12/01
Postsecondary	Mississippi	Y	22530 FQ	43930 AW	63880 TQ	MSBLS	10/01-12/01
Postsecondary	Missouri	Y	26640 FQ	43860 AW	65600 TQ	MOBLS	10/01-12/01
Postsecondary	Montana	Y	25010 FQ	54560 AW	93170 TQ	MTBLS	10/01-12/01
Postsecondary	Nebraska	Y	27610 FQ	42130 AW	65100 TQ	NEBLS	10/01-12/01
Postsecondary	Nevada	Y	23670 FQ	46480 AW	77030 TQ	NVBLS	10/01-12/01
Postsecondary	New Hampshire	Y	28790 FQ	49060 AW	82490 TQ	NHBLS	10/01-12/01
Postsecondary	New Jersey	Y	33010 FQ	56690 AW	89010 TQ	NJBLS	10/01-12/01
Postsecondary	New Mexico	Y	21790 FQ	41960 AW	59490 TQ	NMBLS	10/01-12/01
Postsecondary	New York	Y	34080 FQ	57480 AW	88370 TQ	NYBLS	10/01-12/01
Postsecondary	North Carolina	Y	27340 FQ	45640 AW	65850 TQ	NCBLS	10/01-12/01
Postsecondary	North Dakota	Y	21740 FQ	37860 AW	56420 TQ	NDBLS	10/01-12/01
Postsecondary	Ohio	Y	26220 FQ	46570 AW	73890 TQ	OHBLS	10/01-12/01
Postsecondary	Oklahoma	Y	25900 FQ	40050 AW	59990 TQ	OKBLS	10/01-12/01
Postsecondary	Oregon	Y	34190 FQ	60370 AW	88580 TQ	ORBLS	10/01-12/01
Postsecondary	Pennsylvania	Y	27110 FQ	50810 AW	81960 TQ	PABLS	10/01-12/01
Postsecondary	Rhode Island	Y	34850 FQ	55820 AW	76930 TQ	RIBLS	10/01-12/01
Postsecondary	South Carolina	Y	28670 FQ	45570 AW	71020 TQ	SCBLS	10/01-12/01
Postsecondary	South Dakota	Y	28300 FQ	42870 AW	64690 TQ	SDBLS	10/01-12/01
Postsecondary	Tennessee	Y	23450 FQ	47280 AW	71700 TQ	TNBLS	10/01-12/01
Postsecondary	Texas	Y	23310 FQ	45780 AW	70340 TQ	TXBLS	10/01-12/01
Postsecondary	Utah	Y	33680 FQ	57930 AW	92200 TQ	UTBLS	10/01-12/01
Postsecondary	Vermont	Y	41820 FQ	63360 AW	92690 TQ	VTBLS	10/01-12/01
Postsecondary	Virginia	Y	26990 FQ	50610 AW	77540 TQ	VABLS	10/01-12/01
Postsecondary	Washington	Y	23390 FQ	46390 AW	74660 TQ	WABLS	10/01-12/01
Postsecondary	West Virginia	Y	33210 FQ	53160 AW	76290 TQ	WVBLS	10/01-12/01
Postsecondary	Wisconsin	Y	28150 FQ	46980 AW	68970 TQ	WIBLS	10/01-12/01
Postsecondary	Wyoming	Y	31080 FQ	46470 AW	67970 TQ	WYBLS	10/01-12/01
Postsecondary	Puerto Rico	Y	24990 FQ	42250 AW	62740 TQ	PRBLS	10/01-12/01
Compensation, Benefits, and Job Analysis Specialist	Alabama	Y	21840 FQ	38590 AW	54870 TQ	ALBLS	10/01-12/01
	Birmingham MSA, AL	Y	19670 FQ	37520 AW	54850 TQ	ALBLS	10/01-12/01
	Huntsville MSA, AL	Y	27910 FQ	41880 AW	63840 TQ	ALBLS	10/01-12/01
	Mobile MSA, AL	Y	20960 FQ	36670 AW	51840 TQ	ALBLS	10/01-12/01
	Montgomery MSA, AL	Y	25580 FQ	39450 AW	53770 TQ	ALBLS	10/01-12/01
	Alaska	Y	32120 FQ	59030 AW	92510 TQ	AKBLS	10/01-12/01
	Anchorage MSA, AK	Y	31990 FQ	58870 AW	92080 TQ	AKBLS	10/01-12/01

AAW	Average annual wage	**AOH**	Average offered, high	**ASH**	Average starting, high	**H**	Hourly	**M**	Monthly	**S**	Special: hourly and annual
AE	Average entry wage	**AOL**	Average offered, low	**ASL**	Average starting, low	**HI**	Highest wage paid	**MTC**	Median total compensation	**TQ**	Third quartile wage
AEX	Average experienced wage	**APH**	Average pay, high range	**AW**	Average wage paid	**HR**	High end range	**MW**	Median wage paid	**W**	Weekly
AO	Average offered	**APL**	Average pay, low range	**FQ**	First quartile wage	**LR**	Low end range	**SQ**	Second quartile wage	**Y**	Yearly

Occupation/Type/Industry	Location	Per	Low	Mid	High	Source	Date
Compensation, Benefits, and Job Analysis Specialist	Arizona	Y	24540 FQ	39900 AW	59490 TQ	AZBLS	10/01-12/01
	Phoenix-Mesa MSA, AZ	Y	24390 FQ	40310 AW	61110 TQ	AZBLS	10/01-12/01
	Tucson MSA, AZ	Y	25120 FQ	37620 AW	52860 TQ	AZBLS	10/01-12/01
	Arkansas	Y	19010 FQ	31140 AW	48200 TQ	ARBLS	10/01-12/01
	Fayetteville-Springdale-Rogers MSA, AR	Y	17310 FQ	28010 AW	41760 TQ	ARBLS	10/01-12/01
	Fort Smith MSA, AR-OK	Y	20930 FQ	34550 AW	53800 TQ	ARBLS	10/01-12/01
	Little Rock-North Little Rock MSA, AR	Y	22490 FQ	36090 AW	53780 TQ	ARBLS	10/01-12/01
	California	Y	32830 FQ	51200 AW	74490 TQ	CABLS	10/01-12/01
	Bakersfield MSA, CA	Y	28080 FQ	46630 AW	66330 TQ	CABLS	10/01-12/01
	Fresno MSA, CA	Y	28790 FQ	45270 AW	63810 TQ	CABLS	10/01-12/01
	Los Angeles-Long Beach PMSA, CA	Y	30450 FQ	48250 AW	70110 TQ	CABLS	10/01-12/01
	Modesto MSA, CA	Y	28420 FQ	47380 AW	70280 TQ	CABLS	10/01-12/01
	Oakland PMSA, CA	Y	37160 FQ	56050 AW	81050 TQ	CABLS	10/01-12/01
	Orange County PMSA, CA	Y	33940 FQ	51360 AW	75240 TQ	CABLS	10/01-12/01
	Riverside-San Bernardino PMSA, CA	Y	31000 FQ	46730 AW	60720 TQ	CABLS	10/01-12/01
	Sacramento PMSA, CA	Y	31930 FQ	48670 AW	68660 TQ	CABLS	10/01-12/01
	San Diego MSA, CA	Y	32300 FQ	49130 AW	67900 TQ	CABLS	10/01-12/01
	San Francisco PMSA, CA	Y	38870 FQ	58010 AW	85180 TQ	CABLS	10/01-12/01
	San Jose PMSA, CA	Y	37090 FQ	56080 AW	83390 TQ	CABLS	10/01-12/01
	San Luis Obispo-Atascadero-Paso Robles MSA, CA	Y	29460 FQ	49100 AW	81400 TQ	CABLS	10/01-12/01
	Santa Barbara-Santa Maria-Lompoc MSA, CA	Y	31110 FQ	50110 AW	74200 TQ	CABLS	10/01-12/01
	Santa Rosa PMSA, CA	Y	32570 FQ	50250 AW	72380 TQ	CABLS	10/01-12/01
	Stockton-Lodi MSA, CA	Y	30850 FQ	49140 AW	72700 TQ	CABLS	10/01-12/01
	Vallejo-Fairfield-Napa PMSA, CA	Y	32100 FQ	49030 AW	71160 TQ	CABLS	10/01-12/01
	Ventura PMSA, CA	Y	33280 FQ	53810 AW	81640 TQ	CABLS	10/01-12/01
	Visalia-Tulare-Porterville MSA, CA	Y	22270 FQ	40280 AW	56780 TQ	CABLS	10/01-12/01
	Colorado	Y	29100 FQ	49410 AW	73970 TQ	COBLS	10/01-12/01
	Boulder-Longmont PMSA, CO	Y	31470 FQ	47190 AW	69010 TQ	COBLS	10/01-12/01
	Colorado Springs MSA, CO	Y	25110 FQ	47890 AW	84480 TQ	COBLS	10/01-12/01
	Denver PMSA, CO	Y	31390 FQ	51780 AW	75290 TQ	COBLS	10/01-12/01
	Fort Collins-Loveland MSA, CO	Y	27940 FQ	43040 AW	64610 TQ	COBLS	10/01-12/01
	Greeley PMSA, CO	Y	28080 FQ	46780 AW	69250 TQ	COBLS	10/01-12/01
	Connecticut	Y	33850 FQ	52550 AW	74740 TQ	CTBLS	10/01-12/01
	Bridgeport PMSA, CT	Y	34290 FQ	57360 AW	85730 TQ	CTBLS	10/01-12/01
	Danbury PMSA, CT	Y	31620 FQ	50900 AW	79730 TQ	CTBLS	10/01-12/01
	Hartford MSA, CT	Y	34040 FQ	51450 AW	73480 TQ	CTBLS	10/01-12/01
	New Haven-Meriden PMSA, CT	Y	36830 FQ	54400 AW	78700 TQ	CTBLS	10/01-12/01
	New London-Norwich MSA, CT-RI	Y	29740 FQ	47440 AW	67670 TQ	CTBLS	10/01-12/01
	Stamford-Norwalk PMSA, CT	Y	35800 FQ	55000 AW	75300 TQ	CTBLS	10/01-12/01
	Delaware	Y	27150 FQ	42950 AW	65700 TQ	DEBLS	10/01-12/01
	Wilmington-Newark PMSA, DE-MD	Y	26560 FQ	43220 AW	68920 TQ	DEBLS	10/01-12/01
	District of Columbia	Y	37040 FQ	55830 AW	80160 TQ	DCBLS	10/01-12/01
	Washington PMSA, DC-MD-VA-WV	Y	31630 FQ	52930 AW	79350 TQ	DCBLS	10/01-12/01
	Florida	Y	24880 FQ	41160 AW	64740 TQ	FLBLS	10/01-12/01
	Daytona Beach MSA, FL	Y	24400 FQ	34720 AW	50710 TQ	FLBLS	10/01-12/01
	Fort Lauderdale PMSA, FL	Y	25810 FQ	41300 AW	63020 TQ	FLBLS	10/01-12/01
	Fort Myers-Cape Coral MSA, FL	Y	28610 FQ	38110 AW	52500 TQ	FLBLS	10/01-12/01
	Fort Pierce-Port St. Lucie MSA, FL	Y	23390 FQ	38450 AW	55000 TQ	FLBLS	10/01-12/01
	Fort Walton Beach MSA, FL	Y	22190 FQ	31290 AW	46790 TQ	FLBLS	10/01-12/01
	Gainesville MSA, FL	Y	23190 FQ	38910 AW	63560 TQ	FLBLS	10/01-12/01
	Jacksonville MSA, FL	Y	17140 FQ	36390 AW	57220 TQ	FLBLS	10/01-12/01
	Lakeland-Winter Haven MSA, FL	Y	25190 FQ	42570 AW	66540 TQ	FLBLS	10/01-12/01
	Melbourne-Titusville-Palm Bay MSA, FL	Y	25720 FQ	42030 AW	70930 TQ	FLBLS	10/01-12/01
	Miami PMSA, FL	Y	14140 FQ	39270 AW	66200 TQ	FLBLS	10/01-12/01

AAW	Average annual wage	**AOH**	Average offered, high	**ASH**	Average starting, high	**H**	Hourly	**M**	Monthly	**S**	Special: hourly and annual
AE	Average entry wage	**AOL**	Average offered, low	**ASL**	Average starting, low	**HI**	Highest wage paid	**MTC**	Median total compensation	**TQ**	Third quartile wage
AEX	Average experienced wage	**APH**	Average pay, high range	**AW**	Average wage paid	**HR**	High end range	**MW**	Median wage paid	**W**	Weekly
AO	Average offered	**APL**	Average pay, low range	**FQ**	First quartile wage	**LR**	Low end range	**SQ**	Second quartile wage	**Y**	Yearly

Occupation/Type/Industry	Location	Per	Low	Mid	High	Source	Date
Compensation, Benefits, and Job Analysis Specialist	Naples MSA, FL	Y	29190 FQ	39870 AW	57200 TQ	FLBLS	10/01-12/01
	Ocala MSA, FL	Y	25030 FQ	39550 AW	56930 TQ	FLBLS	10/01-12/01
	Orlando MSA, FL	Y	26660 FQ	41540 AW	58640 TQ	FLBLS	10/01-12/01
	Pensacola MSA, FL	Y	26360 FQ	38520 AW	54490 TQ	FLBLS	10/01-12/01
	Sarasota-Bradenton MSA, FL	Y	27210 FQ	40870 AW	59200 TQ	FLBLS	10/01-12/01
	Tallahassee MSA, FL	Y	26090 FQ	41510 AW	68970 TQ	FLBLS	10/01-12/01
	Tampa-St. Petersburg-Clearwater MSA, FL	Y	29100 FQ	45790 AW	78100 TQ	FLBLS	10/01-12/01
	West Palm Beach-Boca Raton MSA, FL	Y	29280 FQ	46800 AW	70870 TQ	FLBLS	10/01-12/01
	Georgia	Y	26470 FQ	45510 AW	70900 TQ	GABLS	10/01-12/01
	Atlanta MSA, GA	Y	27670 FQ	47790 AW	74870 TQ	GABLS	10/01-12/01
	Columbus MSA, GA-AL	Y	26970 FQ	40690 AW	57480 TQ	GABLS	10/01-12/01
	Macon MSA, GA	Y	27150 FQ	44570 AW	68070 TQ	GABLS	10/01-12/01
	Savannah MSA, GA	Y	29520 FQ	41320 AW	64340 TQ	GABLS	10/01-12/01
	Hawaii	Y	29460 FQ	43120 AW	55860 TQ	HIBLS	10/01-12/01
	Honolulu MSA, HI	Y	30640 FQ	44450 AW	56760 TQ	HIBLS	10/01-12/01
	Idaho	Y	24840 FQ	40910 AW	59100 TQ	IDBLS	10/01-12/01
	Boise City MSA, ID	Y	25090 FQ	39750 AW	55390 TQ	IDBLS	10/01-12/01
	Illinois	Y	30230 FQ	49930 AW	81500 TQ	ILBLS	10/01-12/01
	Chicago PMSA, IL	Y	31370 FQ	49670 AW	76970 TQ	ILBLS	10/01-12/01
	Peoria-Pekin MSA, IL	Y	23190 FQ	42260 AW	63910 TQ	ILBLS	10/01-12/01
	Rockford MSA, IL	Y	26400 FQ	41070 AW	56270 TQ	ILBLS	10/01-12/01
	Springfield MSA, IL	Y	23320 FQ	46210 AW	71580 TQ	ILBLS	10/01-12/01
	Indiana	Y	21140 FQ	42420 AW	61810 TQ	INBLS	10/01-12/01
	Elkhart-Goshen MSA, IN	Y	18110 FQ	34430 AW	56580 TQ	INBLS	10/01-12/01
	Evansville-Henderson MSA, IN-KY	Y	12190 FQ	24040 AW	46020 TQ	INBLS	10/01-12/01
	Fort Wayne MSA, IN	Y	23570 FQ	38880 AW	57910 TQ	INBLS	10/01-12/01
	Gary PMSA, IN	Y	32110 FQ	45150 AW	58560 TQ	INBLS	10/01-12/01
	Indianapolis MSA, IN	Y	20850 FQ	40270 AW	65450 TQ	INBLS	10/01-12/01
	Lafayette MSA, IN	Y	23480 FQ	39030 AW	55290 TQ	INBLS	10/01-12/01
	South Bend MSA, IN	Y	25150 FQ	63410 AW		INBLS	10/01-12/01
	Iowa	Y	19100 FQ	35450 AW	55960 TQ	IABLS	10/01-12/01
	Cedar Rapids MSA, IA	Y	21270 FQ	33720 AW	54310 TQ	IABLS	10/01-12/01
	Davenport-Moline-Rock Island MSA, IA-IL	Y	25470 FQ	41550 AW	63030 TQ	IABLS	10/01-12/01
	Des Moines MSA, IA	Y	13180 FQ	36200 AW	58530 TQ	IABLS	10/01-12/01
	Kansas	Y	24770 FQ	41560 AW	63320 TQ	KSBLS	10/01-12/01
	Topeka MSA, KS	Y	25120 FQ	36140 AW	51010 TQ	KSBLS	10/01-12/01
	Wichita MSA, KS	Y	26300 FQ	45100 AW	72070 TQ	KSBLS	10/01-12/01
	Kentucky	Y	24340 FQ	40070 AW	60780 TQ	KYBLS	10/01-12/01
	Lexington MSA, KY	Y	25480 FQ	40030 AW	58010 TQ	KYBLS	10/01-12/01
	Louisville MSA, KY-IN	Y	25720 FQ	41900 AW	62270 TQ	KYBLS	10/01-12/01
	Louisiana	Y	19550 FQ	33730 AW	52270 TQ	LABLS	10/01-12/01
	Baton Rouge MSA, LA	Y	21180 FQ	30640 AW	41130 TQ	LABLS	10/01-12/01
	Lafayette MSA, LA	Y	22660 FQ	34440 AW	49960 TQ	LABLS	10/01-12/01
	Lake Charles MSA, LA	Y	22970 FQ	37880 AW	66470 TQ	LABLS	10/01-12/01
	New Orleans MSA, LA	Y	23330 FQ	42690 AW	72120 TQ	LABLS	10/01-12/01
	Shreveport-Bossier City MSA, LA	Y	12670 FQ	30790 AW	55000 TQ	LABLS	10/01-12/01
	Maine	Y	28150 FQ	41220 AW	59140 TQ	MEBLS	10/01-12/01
	Portland MSA, ME	Y	29510 FQ	43100 AW	60740 TQ	MEBLS	10/01-12/01
	Maryland	Y	29400 FQ	47570 AW	70070 TQ	MDBLS	10/01-12/01
	Baltimore PMSA, MD	Y	31180 FQ	46280 AW	65320 TQ	MDBLS	10/01-12/01
	Massachusetts	Y	30340 FQ	51580 AW	80020 TQ	MABLS	10/01-12/01
	Boston PMSA, MA-NH	Y	31240 FQ	53300 AW	82270 TQ	MABLS	10/01-12/01
	Brockton PMSA, MA	Y	25870 FQ	38680 AW	52910 TQ	MABLS	10/01-12/01
	Lawrence PMSA, MA-NH	Y	29020 FQ	47140 AW	70450 TQ	MABLS	10/01-12/01
	Lowell PMSA, MA-NH	Y	31420 FQ	51470 AW	80040 TQ	MABLS	10/01-12/01
	Springfield MSA, MA	Y	28540 FQ	47550 AW	70310 TQ	MABLS	10/01-12/01
	Worcester PMSA, MA-CT	Y	30420 FQ	49140 AW	74350 TQ	MABLS	10/01-12/01
	Michigan	Y	29980 FQ	46810 AW	67930 TQ	MIBLS	10/01-12/01
	Ann Arbor PMSA, MI	Y	32540 FQ	49150 AW	70530 TQ	MIBLS	10/01-12/01
	Detroit PMSA, MI	Y	30540 FQ	48390 AW	69650 TQ	MIBLS	10/01-12/01
	Flint PMSA, MI	Y	30350 FQ	51060 AW	73100 TQ	MIBLS	10/01-12/01
	Grand Rapids-Muskegon-Holland MSA, MI	Y	29600 FQ	44200 AW	60910 TQ	MIBLS	10/01-12/01
	Saginaw-Bay City-Midland MSA, MI	Y	28600 FQ	46220 AW	82650 TQ	MIBLS	10/01-12/01
	Minnesota	Y	27920 FQ	42670 AW	63700 TQ	MNBLS	10/01-12/01

AAW	Average annual wage	AOH	Average offered, high	ASH	Average starting, high	H	Hourly	M	Monthly	S	Special: hourly and annual
AE	Average entry wage	AOL	Average offered, low	ASL	Average starting, low	HI	Highest wage paid	MTC	Median total compensation	TQ	Third quartile wage
AEX	Average experienced wage	APH	Average pay, high range	AW	Average wage paid	HR	High end range	MW	Median wage paid	W	Weekly
AO	Average offered	APL	Average pay, low range	FQ	First quartile wage	LR	Low end range	SQ	Second quartile wage	Y	Yearly

Occupation/Type/Industry	Location	Per	Low	Mid	High	Source	Date
Compensation, Benefits, and Job Analysis Specialist	Duluth-Superior MSA, MN-WI	Y	24190 FQ	40400 AW	59850 TQ	MNBLS	10/01-12/01
	Minneapolis-St. Paul MSA, MN-WI	Y	27950 FQ	43150 AW	64830 TQ	MNBLS	10/01-12/01
	St. Cloud MSA, MN	Y	29120 FQ	37950 AW	50270 TQ	MNBLS	10/01-12/01
	Mississippi	Y	19320 FQ	30790 AW	51720 TQ	MSBLS	10/01-12/01
	Biloxi-Gulfport-Pascagoula MSA, MS	Y	20390 FQ	30250 AW	46810 TQ	MSBLS	10/01-12/01
	Jackson MSA, MS	Y	19210 FQ	31810 AW	57380 TQ	MSBLS	10/01-12/01
	Missouri	Y	19920 FQ	42530 AW	69570 TQ	MOBLS	10/01-12/01
	Kansas City MSA, MO-KS	Y	28730 FQ	46160 AW	68380 TQ	MOBLS	10/01-12/01
	St. Louis MSA, MO-IL	Y	14110 FQ	41480 AW	70610 TQ	MOBLS	10/01-12/01
	Springfield MSA, MO	Y	21890 FQ	37500 AW	53820 TQ	MOBLS	10/01-12/01
	Montana	Y	21760 FQ	34970 AW	55310 TQ	MTBLS	10/01-12/01
	Nebraska	Y	24530 FQ	39380 AW	60990 TQ	NEBLS	10/01-12/01
	Lincoln MSA, NE	Y	25200 FQ	37880 AW	53600 TQ	NEBLS	10/01-12/01
	Omaha MSA, NE-IA	Y	23700 FQ	38800 AW	61290 TQ	NEBLS	10/01-12/01
	Nevada	Y	23970 FQ	42320 AW	62600 TQ	NVBLS	10/01-12/01
	Las Vegas MSA, NV-AZ	Y	22710 FQ	40870 AW	63870 TQ	NVBLS	10/01-12/01
	Reno MSA, NV	Y	31290 FQ	46460 AW	62750 TQ	NVBLS	10/01-12/01
	New Hampshire	Y	27290 FQ	40790 AW	56020 TQ	NHBLS	10/01-12/01
	Manchester PMSA, NH	Y	26180 FQ	43900 AW	58580 TQ	NHBLS	10/01-12/01
	Portsmouth-Rochester PMSA, NH-ME	Y	26390 FQ	41020 AW	59410 TQ	NHBLS	10/01-12/01
	New Jersey	Y	28420 FQ	50330 AW	76370 TQ	NJBLS	10/01-12/01
	Atlantic-Cape May PMSA, NJ	Y	27060 FQ	44590 AW	70980 TQ	NJBLS	10/01-12/01
	Bergen-Passaic PMSA, NJ	Y	33580 FQ	53170 AW	81040 TQ	NJBLS	10/01-12/01
	Jersey City PMSA, NJ	Y	33850 FQ	48630 AW	70720 TQ	NJBLS	10/01-12/01
	Middlesex-Somerset-Hunterdon PMSA, NJ	Y	35160 FQ	53670 AW	74130 TQ	NJBLS	10/01-12/01
	Monmouth-Ocean PMSA, NJ	Y	33350 FQ	67570 AW	122550 TQ	NJBLS	10/01-12/01
	Newark PMSA, NJ	Y	27100 FQ	49520 AW	73850 TQ	NJBLS	10/01-12/01
	Trenton PMSA, NJ	Y	21330 FQ	41240 AW	66410 TQ	NJBLS	10/01-12/01
	New Mexico	Y	24590 FQ	40670 AW	64850 TQ	NMBLS	10/01-12/01
	Albuquerque MSA, NM	Y	25860 FQ	44390 AW	67920 TQ	NMBLS	10/01-12/01
	New York	Y	36840 FQ	52800 AW	72010 TQ	NYBLS	10/01-12/01
	Albany-Schenectady-Troy MSA, NY	Y	31610 FQ	46840 AW	65520 TQ	NYBLS	10/01-12/01
	Buffalo-Niagara Falls MSA, NY	Y	27600 FQ	43480 AW	65050 TQ	NYBLS	10/01-12/01
	Nassau-Suffolk PMSA, NY	Y	33380 FQ	51730 AW	75990 TQ	NYBLS	10/01-12/01
	New York PMSA, NY	Y	39700 FQ	54460 AW	72960 TQ	NYBLS	10/01-12/01
	Newburgh PMSA, NY-PA	Y	28570 FQ	43530 AW	60730 TQ	NYBLS	10/01-12/01
	Rochester MSA, NY	Y	29110 FQ	44630 AW	66970 TQ	NYBLS	10/01-12/01
	Syracuse MSA, NY	Y	27590 FQ	45540 AW	66480 TQ	NYBLS	10/01-12/01
	Utica-Rome MSA, NY	Y	26430 FQ	42490 AW	65310 TQ	NYBLS	10/01-12/01
	North Carolina	Y	27420 FQ	45320 AW	69920 TQ	NCBLS	10/01-12/01
	Asheville MSA, NC	Y	32880 FQ	53930 AW	73650 TQ	NCBLS	10/01-12/01
	Charlotte-Gastonia-Rock Hill MSA, NC-SC	Y	28870 FQ	51790 AW	87330 TQ	NCBLS	10/01-12/01
	Fayetteville MSA, NC	Y	29340 FQ	36060 AW	45490 TQ	NCBLS	10/01-12/01
	Greensboro-Winston-Salem-High Point MSA, NC	Y	30060 FQ	44960 AW	66240 TQ	NCBLS	10/01-12/01
	Hickory-Morganton-Lenoir MSA, NC	Y	25550 FQ	41010 AW	62530 TQ	NCBLS	10/01-12/01
	Raleigh-Durham-Chapel Hill MSA, NC	Y	30850 FQ	44970 AW	60960 TQ	NCBLS	10/01-12/01
	Wilmington MSA, NC	Y	26190 FQ	40490 AW	65820 TQ	NCBLS	10/01-12/01
	North Dakota	Y	27330 FQ	39810 AW	54920 TQ	NDBLS	10/01-12/01
	Fargo-Moorhead MSA, ND-MN	Y	26000 FQ	38440 AW	61800 TQ	NDBLS	10/01-12/01
	Ohio	Y	27250 FQ	45260 AW	69110 TQ	OHBLS	10/01-12/01
	Akron PMSA, OH	Y	28520 FQ	42700 AW	64750 TQ	OHBLS	10/01-12/01
	Canton-Massillon MSA, OH	Y	25120 FQ	44130 AW	68300 TQ	OHBLS	10/01-12/01
	Cincinnati PMSA, OH-KY-IN	Y	27060 FQ	47280 AW	71630 TQ	OHBLS	10/01-12/01
	Cleveland-Lorain-Elyria PMSA, OH	Y	30420 FQ	47520 AW	71610 TQ	OHBLS	10/01-12/01
	Columbus MSA, OH	Y	26410 FQ	43480 AW	61600 TQ	OHBLS	10/01-12/01
	Dayton-Springfield MSA, OH	Y	28310 FQ	45670 AW	67800 TQ	OHBLS	10/01-12/01
	Hamilton-Middletown PMSA, OH	Y	29950 FQ	42270 AW	57310 TQ	OHBLS	10/01-12/01
	Mansfield MSA, OH	Y	29690 FQ	44060 AW	58700 TQ	OHBLS	10/01-12/01

AAW	Average annual wage	AOH	Average offered, high	ASH	Average starting, high	H	Hourly	M	Monthly	S	Special: hourly and annual
AE	Average entry wage	AOL	Average offered, low	ASL	Average starting, low	HI	Highest wage paid	MTC	Median total compensation	TQ	Third quartile wage
AEX	Average experienced wage	APH	Average pay, high range	AW	Average wage paid	HR	High end range	MW	Median wage paid	W	Weekly
AO	Average offered	APL	Average pay, low range	FQ	First quartile wage	LR	Low end range	SQ	Second quartile wage	Y	Yearly

Occupation/Type/Industry	Location	Per	Low	Mid	High	Source	Date
Compensation, Benefits, and Job Analysis Specialist	Toledo MSA, OH	Y	29910 FQ	42020 AW	58970 TQ	OHBLS	10/01-12/01
	Youngstown-Warren MSA, OH	Y	24840 FQ	39660 AW	61360 TQ	OHBLS	10/01-12/01
	Oklahoma	Y	23240 FQ	39530 AW	64440 TQ	OKBLS	10/01-12/01
	Oklahoma City MSA, OK	Y	25300 FQ	44140 AW	67370 TQ	OKBLS	10/01-12/01
	Tulsa MSA, OK	Y	23880 FQ	38610 AW	55530 TQ	OKBLS	10/01-12/01
	Oregon	Y	29180 FQ	47090 AW	77700 TQ	ORBLS	10/01-12/01
	Eugene-Springfield MSA, OR	Y	30880 FQ	45130 AW	64610 TQ	ORBLS	10/01-12/01
	Portland-Vancouver PMSA, OR-WA	Y	29710 FQ	48540 AW	81000 TQ	ORBLS	10/01-12/01
	Salem PMSA, OR	Y	27100 FQ	42720 AW	57860 TQ	ORBLS	10/01-12/01
	Pennsylvania	Y	25100 FQ	41660 AW	65570 TQ	PABLS	10/01-12/01
	Allentown-Bethlehem-Easton MSA, PA	Y	24270 FQ	40890 AW	67620 TQ	PABLS	10/01-12/01
	Erie MSA, PA	Y	13160 FQ	35770 AW	60430 TQ	PABLS	10/01-12/01
	Harrisburg-Lebanon-Carlisle MSA, PA	Y	24460 FQ	38100 AW	55600 TQ	PABLS	10/01-12/01
	Lancaster MSA, PA	Y	29900 FQ	45150 AW	68280 TQ	PABLS	10/01-12/01
	Philadelphia PMSA, PA-NJ	Y	26680 FQ	44840 AW	69510 TQ	PABLS	10/01-12/01
	Pittsburgh MSA, PA	Y	28060 FQ	44920 AW	68420 TQ	PABLS	10/01-12/01
	Reading MSA, PA	Y	25100 FQ	36540 AW	53360 TQ	PABLS	10/01-12/01
	Scranton-Wilkes-Barre-Hazleton MSA, PA	Y	24280 FQ	34980 AW	46040 TQ	PABLS	10/01-12/01
	York MSA, PA	Y	25350 FQ	33920 AW	45990 TQ	PABLS	10/01-12/01
	Rhode Island	Y	28930 FQ	44350 AW	60330 TQ	RIBLS	10/01-12/01
	Providence-Fall River-Warwick MSA, RI-MA	Y	28680 FQ	44300 AW	60650 TQ	RIBLS	10/01-12/01
	South Carolina	Y	24660 FQ	48300 AW	98810 TQ	SCBLS	10/01-12/01
	Charleston-North Charleston MSA, SC	Y	27820 FQ	38820 AW	54370 TQ	SCBLS	10/01-12/01
	Columbia MSA, SC	Y	23500 FQ	33010 AW	46490 TQ	SCBLS	10/01-12/01
	Greenville-Spartanburg-Anderson MSA, SC	Y	24350 FQ	39260 AW	57560 TQ	SCBLS	10/01-12/01
	South Dakota	Y	26450 FQ	38810 AW	55990 TQ	SDBLS	10/01-12/01
	Sioux Falls MSA, SD	Y	27730 FQ	39870 AW	56190 TQ	SDBLS	10/01-12/01
	Tennessee	Y	19600 FQ	37220 AW	58450 TQ	TNBLS	10/01-12/01
	Chattanooga MSA, TN-GA	Y	13620 FQ	32650 AW	54880 TQ	TNBLS	10/01-12/01
	Johnson City-Kingsport-Bristol MSA, TN-VA	Y	24310 FQ	34880 AW	48340 TQ	TNBLS	10/01-12/01
	Knoxville MSA, TN	Y	29540 FQ	39880 AW	61430 TQ	TNBLS	10/01-12/01
	Memphis MSA, TN-AR-MS	Y	25220 FQ	50680 AW	75200 TQ	TNBLS	10/01-12/01
	Nashville MSA, TN	Y	23910 FQ	38850 AW	54880 TQ	TNBLS	10/01-12/01
	Texas	Y	27330 FQ	47800 AW	73800 TQ	TXBLS	10/01-12/01
	Amarillo MSA, TX	Y	24830 FQ	38570 AW	54200 TQ	TXBLS	10/01-12/01
	Austin-San Marcos MSA, TX	Y	27620 FQ	51870 AW	101560 TQ	TXBLS	10/01-12/01
	Beaumont-Port Arthur MSA, TX	Y	24140 FQ	45580 AW	70410 TQ	TXBLS	10/01-12/01
	Corpus Christi MSA, TX	Y	24640 FQ	38890 AW	57280 TQ	TXBLS	10/01-12/01
	Dallas PMSA, TX	Y	29020 FQ	48860 AW	74850 TQ	TXBLS	10/01-12/01
	El Paso MSA, TX	Y	25770 FQ	43690 AW	64860 TQ	TXBLS	10/01-12/01
	Fort Worth-Arlington PMSA, TX	Y	27140 FQ	47160 AW	72170 TQ	TXBLS	10/01-12/01
	Galveston-Texas City PMSA, TX	Y	33240 FQ	45810 AW	57540 TQ	TXBLS	10/01-12/01
	Houston PMSA, TX	Y	31120 FQ	50850 AW	77740 TQ	TXBLS	10/01-12/01
	Laredo MSA, TX	Y	23240 FQ	31850 AW	47070 TQ	TXBLS	10/01-12/01
	Longview-Marshall MSA, TX	Y	27670 FQ	41260 AW	56160 TQ	TXBLS	10/01-12/01
	Lubbock MSA, TX	Y	19210 FQ	34670 AW	55400 TQ	TXBLS	10/01-12/01
	San Antonio MSA, TX	Y	26470 FQ	45090 AW	70750 TQ	TXBLS	10/01-12/01
	Tyler MSA, TX	Y	26980 FQ	53470 AW	88670 TQ	TXBLS	10/01-12/01
	Waco MSA, TX	Y	25030 FQ	43140 AW	69170 TQ	TXBLS	10/01-12/01
	Utah	Y	27140 FQ	42480 AW	62570 TQ	UTBLS	10/01-12/01
	Provo-Orem MSA, UT	Y	28240 FQ	40510 AW	55240 TQ	UTBLS	10/01-12/01
	Salt Lake City-Ogden MSA, UT	Y	28420 FQ	43640 AW	63580 TQ	UTBLS	10/01-12/01
	Vermont	Y	28630 FQ	42070 AW	62900 TQ	VTBLS	10/01-12/01
	Burlington MSA, VT	Y	30760 FQ	45130 AW	66580 TQ	VTBLS	10/01-12/01
	Virginia	Y	29460 FQ	47260 AW	71060 TQ	VABLS	10/01-12/01
	Lynchburg MSA, VA	Y	26010 FQ	40170 AW	62270 TQ	VABLS	10/01-12/01
	Norfolk-Virginia Beach-Newport News MSA, VA-NC	Y	28010 FQ	42360 AW	63720 TQ	VABLS	10/01-12/01

AAW	Average annual wage	AOH	Average offered, high	ASH	Average starting, high	H	Hourly	M	Monthly	S	Special: hourly and annual
AE	Average entry wage	AOL	Average offered, low	ASL	Average starting, low	HI	Highest wage paid	MTC	Median total compensation	TQ	Third quartile wage
AEX	Average experienced wage	APH	Average pay, high range	AW	Average wage paid	HR	High end range	MW	Median wage paid	W	Weekly
AO	Average offered	APL	Average pay, low range	FQ	First quartile wage	LR	Low end range	SQ	Second quartile wage	Y	Yearly

Occupation/Type/Industry	Location	Per	Low	Mid	High	Source	Date
Compensation, Benefits, and Job Analysis Specialist	Richmond-Petersburg MSA, VA	Y	30710 FQ	44540 AW	63820 TQ	VABLS	10/01-12/01
	Roanoke MSA, VA	Y	26830 FQ	42640 AW	68890 TQ	VABLS	10/01-12/01
	Washington	Y	33170 FQ	50300 AW	71690 TQ	WABLS	10/01-12/01
	Olympia PMSA, WA	Y	31800 FQ	41300 AW	57070 TQ	WABLS	10/01-12/01
	Richland-Kennewick-Pasco MSA, WA	Y	30190 FQ	47270 AW	69050 TQ	WABLS	10/01-12/01
	Seattle-Bellevue-Everett PMSA, WA	Y	37300 FQ	53800 AW	74020 TQ	WABLS	10/01-12/01
	Spokane MSA, WA	Y	27770 FQ	51130 AW	86340 TQ	WABLS	10/01-12/01
	Tacoma PMSA, WA	Y	31230 FQ	43090 AW	60550 TQ	WABLS	10/01-12/01
	Yakima MSA, WA	Y	28490 FQ	50710 AW	78830 TQ	WABLS	10/01-12/01
	West Virginia	Y	22380 FQ	36870 AW	55650 TQ	WVBLS	10/01-12/01
	Huntington-Ashland MSA, WV-KY-OH	Y	22730 FQ	39350 AW	67570 TQ	WVBLS	10/01-12/01
	Wisconsin	Y	25340 FQ	38370 AW	54540 TQ	WIBLS	10/01-12/01
	Appleton-Oshkosh-Neenah MSA, WI	Y	28180 FQ	39140 AW	54730 TQ	WIBLS	10/01-12/01
	Green Bay MSA, WI	Y	25160 FQ	37240 AW	53220 TQ	WIBLS	10/01-12/01
	Madison MSA, WI	Y	27730 FQ	39640 AW	54510 TQ	WIBLS	10/01-12/01
	Milwaukee-Waukesha PMSA, WI	Y	26400 FQ	39260 AW	55450 TQ	WIBLS	10/01-12/01
	Racine PMSA, WI	Y	23550 FQ	38980 AW	54830 TQ	WIBLS	10/01-12/01
	Puerto Rico	Y	18400 FQ	28710 AW	45890 TQ	PRBLS	10/01-12/01
Compliance Officer							
Except Agriculture, Construction, Health and Safety, and Transportation	Alabama	Y	24540 FQ	38010 AW	55580 TQ	ALBLS	10/01-12/01
Except Agriculture, Construction, Health and Safety, and Transportation	Alaska	Y	31420 FQ	50120 AW	74050 TQ	AKBLS	10/01-12/01
Except Agriculture, Construction, Health and Safety, and Transportation	Arizona	Y	27180 FQ	43010 AW	63960 TQ	AZBLS	10/01-12/01
Except Agriculture, Construction, Health and Safety, and Transportation	Arkansas	Y	21930 FQ	34310 AW	48230 TQ	ARBLS	10/01-12/01
Except Agriculture, Construction, Health and Safety, and Transportation	California	Y	27750 FQ	47680 AW	76850 TQ	CABLS	10/01-12/01
Except Agriculture, Construction, Health and Safety, and Transportation	Colorado	Y	28290 FQ	47130 AW	69670 TQ	COBLS	10/01-12/01
Except Agriculture, Construction, Health and Safety, and Transportation	Connecticut	Y	36120 FQ	59870 AW	90440 TQ	CTBLS	10/01-12/01
Except Agriculture, Construction, Health and Safety, and Transportation	Delaware	Y	28270 FQ	45930 AW	76800 TQ	DEBLS	10/01-12/01
Except Agriculture, Construction, Health and Safety, and Transportation	District of Columbia	Y	36410 FQ	62020 AW	89530 TQ	DCBLS	10/01-12/01
Except Agriculture, Construction, Health and Safety, and Transportation	Florida	Y	25650 FQ	43410 AW	68000 TQ	FLBLS	10/01-12/01
Except Agriculture, Construction, Health and Safety, and Transportation	Georgia	Y	24790 FQ	42640 AW	67920 TQ	GABLS	10/01-12/01
Except Agriculture, Construction, Health and Safety, and Transportation	Hawaii	Y	31760 FQ	46130 AW	64720 TQ	HIBLS	10/01-12/01
Except Agriculture, Construction, Health and Safety, and Transportation	Idaho	Y	12590 FQ	36150 AW	59930 TQ	IDBLS	10/01-12/01
Except Agriculture, Construction, Health and Safety, and Transportation	Illinois	Y	23890 FQ	45690 AW	69640 TQ	ILBLS	10/01-12/01
Except Agriculture, Construction, Health and Safety, and Transportation	Indiana	Y	23090 FQ	43650 AW	68620 TQ	INBLS	10/01-12/01
Except Agriculture, Construction, Health and Safety, and Transportation	Iowa	Y	25110 FQ	40620 AW	63750 TQ	IABLS	10/01-12/01
Except Agriculture, Construction, Health and Safety, and Transportation	Kansas	Y	26050 FQ	41930 AW	67690 TQ	KSBLS	10/01-12/01
Except Agriculture, Construction, Health and Safety, and Transportation	Kentucky	Y	25100 FQ	42230 AW	64670 TQ	KYBLS	10/01-12/01
Except Agriculture, Construction, Health and Safety, and Transportation	Louisiana	Y	24620 FQ	43720 AW	68670 TQ	LABLS	10/01-12/01
Except Agriculture, Construction, Health and Safety, and Transportation	Maine	Y	26540 FQ	40080 AW	55320 TQ	MEBLS	10/01-12/01
Except Agriculture, Construction, Health and Safety, and Transportation	Maryland	Y	27890 FQ	44180 AW	67100 TQ	MDBLS	10/01-12/01
Except Agriculture, Construction, Health and Safety, and Transportation	Massachusetts	Y	33380 FQ	52640 AW	78990 TQ	MABLS	10/01-12/01

AAW	Average annual wage	**AOH**	Average offered, high	**ASH**	Average starting, high	**H**	Hourly	**M**	Monthly	**S**	Special: hourly and annual
AE	Average entry wage	**AOL**	Average offered, low	**ASL**	Average starting, low	**HI**	Highest wage paid	**MTC**	Median total compensation	**TQ**	Third quartile wage
AEX	Average experienced wage	**APH**	Average pay, high range	**AW**	Average wage paid	**HR**	High end range	**MW**	Median wage paid	**W**	Weekly
AO	Average offered	**APL**	Average pay, low range	**FQ**	First quartile wage	**LR**	Low end range	**SQ**	Second quartile wage	**Y**	Yearly

Occupation/Type/Industry	Location	Per	Low	Mid	High	Source	Date
Compliance Officer							
Except Agriculture, Construction, Health and Safety, and Transportation	Michigan	Y	32470 FQ	52100 AW	79570 TQ	MIBLS	10/01-12/01
Except Agriculture, Construction, Health and Safety, and Transportation	Minnesota	Y	33400 FQ	50220 AW	70350 TQ	MNBLS	10/01-12/01
Except Agriculture, Construction, Health and Safety, and Transportation	Mississippi	Y	20460 FQ	33430 AW	48470 TQ	MSBLS	10/01-12/01
Except Agriculture, Construction, Health and Safety, and Transportation	Missouri	Y	25620 FQ	45430 AW	71660 TQ	MOBLS	10/01-12/01
Except Agriculture, Construction, Health and Safety, and Transportation	Montana	Y	22630 FQ	34680 AW	50140 TQ	MTBLS	10/01-12/01
Except Agriculture, Construction, Health and Safety, and Transportation	Nebraska	Y	23910 FQ	39990 AW	64820 TQ	NEBLS	10/01-12/01
Except Agriculture, Construction, Health and Safety, and Transportation	Nevada	Y	34040 FQ	48550 AW	64730 TQ	NVBLS	10/01-12/01
Except Agriculture, Construction, Health and Safety, and Transportation	New Hampshire	Y	28640 FQ	43470 AW	67900 TQ	NHBLS	10/01-12/01
Except Agriculture, Construction, Health and Safety, and Transportation	New Jersey	Y	31480 FQ	52680 AW	81400 TQ	NJBLS	10/01-12/01
Except Agriculture, Construction, Health and Safety, and Transportation	New Mexico	Y	24800 FQ	41540 AW	66330 TQ	NMBLS	10/01-12/01
Except Agriculture, Construction, Health and Safety, and Transportation	New York	Y	27470 FQ	51200 AW	82950 TQ	NYBLS	10/01-12/01
Except Agriculture, Construction, Health and Safety, and Transportation	North Carolina	Y	25590 FQ	42140 AW	66310 TQ	NCBLS	10/01-12/01
Except Agriculture, Construction, Health and Safety, and Transportation	North Dakota	Y	24530 FQ	39490 AW	55760 TQ	NDBLS	10/01-12/01
Except Agriculture, Construction, Health and Safety, and Transportation	Ohio	Y	27340 FQ	47510 AW	69260 TQ	OHBLS	10/01-12/01
Except Agriculture, Construction, Health and Safety, and Transportation	Oklahoma	Y	19970 FQ	38110 AW	62700 TQ	OKBLS	10/01-12/01
Except Agriculture, Construction, Health and Safety, and Transportation	Oregon	Y	30280 FQ	46760 AW	67860 TQ	ORBLS	10/01-12/01
Except Agriculture, Construction, Health and Safety, and Transportation	Pennsylvania	Y	22780 FQ	44180 AW	69080 TQ	PABLS	10/01-12/01
Except Agriculture, Construction, Health and Safety, and Transportation	Rhode Island	Y	26690 FQ	49910 AW	74730 TQ	RIBLS	10/01-12/01
Except Agriculture, Construction, Health and Safety, and Transportation	South Carolina	Y	23520 FQ	38290 AW	61930 TQ	SCBLS	10/01-12/01
Except Agriculture, Construction, Health and Safety, and Transportation	South Dakota	Y	23850 FQ	35800 AW	50550 TQ	SDBLS	10/01-12/01
Except Agriculture, Construction, Health and Safety, and Transportation	Tennessee	Y	24180 FQ	40610 AW	62070 TQ	TNBLS	10/01-12/01
Except Agriculture, Construction, Health and Safety, and Transportation	Texas	Y	28400 FQ	46110 AW	70010 TQ	TXBLS	10/01-12/01
Except Agriculture, Construction, Health and Safety, and Transportation	Utah	Y	26890 FQ	41520 AW	57380 TQ	UTBLS	10/01-12/01
Except Agriculture, Construction, Health and Safety, and Transportation	Vermont	Y	26000 FQ	42200 AW	65290 TQ	VTBLS	10/01-12/01
Except Agriculture, Construction, Health and Safety, and Transportation	Virginia	Y	27700 FQ	44740 AW	69950 TQ	VABLS	10/01-12/01
Except Agriculture, Construction, Health and Safety, and Transportation	Washington	Y	32120 FQ	47730 AW	67940 TQ	WABLS	10/01-12/01
Except Agriculture, Construction, Health and Safety, and Transportation	West Virginia	Y	23990 FQ	46500 AW	85530 TQ	WVBLS	10/01-12/01
Except Agriculture, Construction, Health and Safety, and Transportation	Wisconsin	Y	14350 FQ	43020 AW	71730 TQ	WIBLS	10/01-12/01
Except Agriculture, Construction, Health and Safety, and Transportation	Wyoming	Y	19630 FQ	42260 AW	68520 TQ	WYBLS	10/01-12/01
Except Agriculture, Construction, Health and Safety, and Transportation	Puerto Rico	Y	15060 FQ	29530 AW	50780 TQ	PRBLS	10/01-12/01
Except Agriculture, Construction, Health and Safety, and Transportation	Virgin Islands	Y	24220 FQ	37620 AW	53540 TQ	VIBLS	10/01-12/01
Except Agriculture, Construction, Health and Safety, and Transportation	Guam	Y	26830 FQ	39750 AW	54660 TQ	GUBLS	10/01-12/01
Computer and Electronics Manufacturing Professional	San Diego, CA	Y		72616 AW		SDBJ1	1/99-1/00
Computer and Information Scientist							
Research	United States	Y		39700 AW		FREEP1	1/00-1/00

AAW Average annual wage; AE Average entry wage; AEX Average experienced wage; AO Average offered; AOH Average offered, high; AOL Average offered, low; APH Average pay, high range; APL Average pay, low range; ASH Average starting, high; ASL Average starting, low; AW Average wage paid; FQ First quartile wage; H Hourly; HI Highest wage paid; HR High end range; LR Low end range; M Monthly; MTC Median total compensation; MW Median wage paid; SQ Second quartile wage; S Special: hourly and annual; TQ Third quartile wage; W Weekly; Y Yearly

Occupation/Type/Industry	Location	Per	Low	Mid	High	Source	Date
Computer and Information Scientist							
Research	Alabama	Y	33790 FQ	65570 AW	95000 TQ	ALBLS	10/01-12/01
Research	Arizona	Y	26470 FQ	68910 AW	110060 TQ	AZBLS	10/01-12/01
Research	California	Y	51830 FQ	89350 AW	138280 TQ	CABLS	10/01-12/01
Research	Colorado	Y	49810 FQ	84970 AW		COBLS	10/01-12/01
Research	Connecticut	Y	50930 FQ	81950 AW	113150 TQ	CTBLS	10/01-12/01
Research	District of Columbia	Y	45590 FQ	75420 AW	110560 TQ	DCBLS	10/01-12/01
Research	Florida	Y	42400 FQ	75180 AW	126700 TQ	FLBLS	10/01-12/01
Research	Georgia	Y	42030 FQ	64860 AW	91770 TQ	GABLS	10/01-12/01
Research	Hawaii	Y	40900 FQ	64310 AW	86410 TQ	HIBLS	10/01-12/01
Research	Illinois	Y	35830 FQ	69570 AW	109110 TQ	ILBLS	10/01-12/01
Research	Indiana	Y	37690 FQ	59300 AW	79970 TQ	INBLS	10/01-12/01
Research	Iowa	Y	32630 FQ	59230 AW	93470 TQ	IABLS	10/01-12/01
Research	Kansas	Y	50400 FQ	72600 AW	94770 TQ	KSBLS	10/01-12/01
Research	Kentucky	Y	46020 FQ	67680 AW	93570 TQ	KYBLS	10/01-12/01
Research	Louisiana	Y	31450 FQ	50940 AW	70060 TQ	LABLS	10/01-12/01
Research	Maryland	Y	48380 FQ	75810 AW	110870 TQ	MDBLS	10/01-12/01
Research	Massachusetts	Y	45440 FQ	77340 AW	115670 TQ	MABLS	10/01-12/01
Research	Michigan	Y	38440 FQ	61480 AW	96600 TQ	MIBLS	10/01-12/01
Research	Mississippi	Y	43890 FQ	64510 AW	87410 TQ	MSBLS	10/01-12/01
Research	Missouri	Y	14500 FQ	65250 AW	100240 TQ	MOBLS	10/01-12/01
Research	Montana	Y	24910 FQ	36770 AW	51310 TQ	MTBLS	10/01-12/01
Research	Nebraska	Y	29700 FQ	45080 AW	68410 TQ	NEBLS	10/01-12/01
Research	New Hampshire	Y	41670 FQ	70510 AW	112110 TQ	NHBLS	10/01-12/01
Research	New Jersey	Y	55920 FQ	87800 AW	127260 TQ	NJBLS	10/01-12/01
Research	New Mexico	Y	44790 FQ	76620 AW	108050 TQ	NMBLS	10/01-12/01
Research	New York	Y	34120 FQ	69540 AW	119800 TQ	NYBLS	10/01-12/01
Research	Ohio	Y	45950 FQ	72690 AW	107790 TQ	OHBLS	10/01-12/01
Research	Oklahoma	Y	35550 FQ	58440 AW	73530 TQ	OKBLS	10/01-12/01
Research	Oregon	Y	50920 FQ	84670 AW	118230 TQ	ORBLS	10/01-12/01
Research	Pennsylvania	Y	39080 FQ	70710 AW	109680 TQ	PABLS	10/01-12/01
Research	Rhode Island	Y	47340 FQ	67960 AW	88700 TQ	RIBLS	10/01-12/01
Research	South Carolina	Y	33150 FQ	49750 AW	76170 TQ	SCBLS	10/01-12/01
Research	Tennessee	Y	39920 FQ	69040 AW	105380 TQ	TNBLS	10/01-12/01
Research	Texas	Y	43750 FQ	78540 AW	119610 TQ	TXBLS	10/01-12/01
Research	Utah	Y	38440 FQ	67070 AW	94100 TQ	UTBLS	10/01-12/01
Research	Virginia	Y	47200 FQ	77330 AW	129320 TQ	VABLS	10/01-12/01
Research	Washington	Y	58980 FQ	103480 AW		WABLS	10/01-12/01
Research	Wisconsin	Y	39900 FQ	65200 AW	108230 TQ	WIBLS	10/01-12/01
Computer and Information Systems Manager	United States	Y		39700 AW		FREEP1	1/00-1/00
	Alabama	Y	35660 FQ	65360 AW	96490 TQ	ALBLS	10/01-12/01
	Birmingham MSA, AL	Y	35350 FQ	63720 AW	94490 TQ	ALBLS	10/01-12/01
	Huntsville MSA, AL	Y	42500 FQ	73590 AW	106320 TQ	ALBLS	10/01-12/01
	Mobile MSA, AL	Y	34040 FQ	61640 AW	91840 TQ	ALBLS	10/01-12/01
	Montgomery MSA, AL	Y	39390 FQ	67550 AW	93780 TQ	ALBLS	10/01-12/01
	Alaska	Y	47950 FQ	74380 AW	111690 TQ	AKBLS	10/01-12/01
	Anchorage MSA, AK	Y	44060 FQ	74800 AW	121070 TQ	AKBLS	10/01-12/01
	Arizona	Y	43220 FQ	77570 AW	113380 TQ	AZBLS	10/01-12/01
	Phoenix-Mesa MSA, AZ	Y	45910 FQ	79700 AW	114040 TQ	AZBLS	10/01-12/01
	Tucson MSA, AZ	Y	34700 FQ	68220 AW	108760 TQ	AZBLS	10/01-12/01
	Arkansas	Y	36950 FQ	68370 AW	108880 TQ	ARBLS	10/01-12/01
	Fayetteville-Springdale-Rogers MSA, AR	Y	37400 FQ	67420 AW	101930 TQ	ARBLS	10/01-12/01
	Fort Smith MSA, AR-OK	Y	37090 FQ	63230 AW	88790 TQ	ARBLS	10/01-12/01
	Little Rock-North Little Rock MSA, AR	Y	43680 FQ	75260 AW	118490 TQ	ARBLS	10/01-12/01
	California	Y	54370 FQ	94700 AW		CABLS	10/01-12/01
	Bakersfield MSA, CA	Y	47340 FQ	78450 AW	116910 TQ	CABLS	10/01-12/01
	Chico-Paradise MSA, CA	Y	34590 FQ	57570 AW	89740 TQ	CABLS	10/01-12/01
	Fresno MSA, CA	Y	46670 FQ	76100 AW	127610 TQ	CABLS	10/01-12/01
	Los Angeles-Long Beach PMSA, CA	Y	49670 FQ	86420 AW	132950 TQ	CABLS	10/01-12/01
	Merced MSA, CA	Y	49440 FQ	75070 AW	110050 TQ	CABLS	10/01-12/01
	Modesto MSA, CA	Y	39830 FQ	74350 AW		CABLS	10/01-12/01
	Oakland PMSA, CA	Y	57140 FQ	92960 AW	138830 TQ	CABLS	10/01-12/01
	Orange County PMSA, CA	Y	54670 FQ	90530 AW	136600 TQ	CABLS	10/01-12/01
	Redding MSA, CA	Y	39600 FQ	61340 AW	91130 TQ	CABLS	10/01-12/01
	Riverside-San Bernardino PMSA, CA	Y	39790 FQ	65670 AW	96230 TQ	CABLS	10/01-12/01

AAW	Average annual wage	AOH	Average offered, high	ASH	Average starting, high	H	Hourly	M	Monthly	S	Special: hourly and annual
AE	Average entry wage	AOL	Average offered, low	ASL	Average starting, low	HI	Highest wage paid	MTC	Median total compensation	TQ	Third quartile wage
AEX	Average experienced wage	APH	Average pay, high range	AW	Average wage paid	HR	High end range	MW	Median wage paid	W	Weekly
AO	Average offered	APL	Average pay, low range	FQ	First quartile wage	LR	Low end range	SQ	Second quartile wage	Y	Yearly

Occupation/Type/Industry	Location	Per	Low	Mid	High	Source	Date
Computer and Information Systems Manager	Sacramento PMSA, CA	Y	58840 FQ	93070 AW		CABLS	10/01-12/01
	Salinas MSA, CA	Y	54370 FQ	89800 AW	133270 TQ	CABLS	10/01-12/01
	San Diego MSA, CA	Y	52280 FQ	83530 AW	122840 TQ	CABLS	10/01-12/01
	San Francisco PMSA, CA	Y	63130 FQ	108960 AW		CABLS	10/01-12/01
	San Jose PMSA, CA	Y	80990 FQ	113810 AW		CABLS	10/01-12/01
	San Luis Obispo-Atascadero-Paso Robles MSA, CA	Y	37190 FQ	63440 AW	91660 TQ	CABLS	10/01-12/01
	Santa Barbara-Santa Maria-Lompoc MSA, CA	Y	51550 FQ	91430 AW	138020 TQ	CABLS	10/01-12/01
	Santa Cruz-Watsonville PMSA, CA	Y	40900 FQ	88710 AW	139600 TQ	CABLS	10/01-12/01
	Santa Rosa PMSA, CA	Y	47910 FQ	88360 AW		CABLS	10/01-12/01
	Stockton-Lodi MSA, CA	Y	41700 FQ	70850 AW	101910 TQ	CABLS	10/01-12/01
	Vallejo-Fairfield-Napa PMSA, CA	Y	48830 FQ	72890 AW	111110 TQ	CABLS	10/01-12/01
	Ventura PMSA, CA	Y	51170 FQ	87260 AW	140220 TQ	CABLS	10/01-12/01
	Visalia-Tulare-Porterville MSA, CA	Y	38930 FQ	70300 AW	104700 TQ	CABLS	10/01-12/01
	Colorado	Y	54960 FQ	89480 AW	135000 TQ	COBLS	10/01-12/01
	Boulder-Longmont PMSA, CO	Y	63490 FQ	96880 AW	141700 TQ	COBLS	10/01-12/01
	Colorado Springs MSA, CO	Y	56860 FQ	87330 AW	133610 TQ	COBLS	10/01-12/01
	Denver PMSA, CO	Y	57600 FQ	90390 AW	133460 TQ	COBLS	10/01-12/01
	Fort Collins-Loveland MSA, CO	Y	45650 FQ	86290 AW	133680 TQ	COBLS	10/01-12/01
	Greeley PMSA, CO	Y	27190 FQ	66890 AW	110110 TQ	COBLS	10/01-12/01
	Connecticut	Y	60340 FQ	95190 AW		CTBLS	10/01-12/01
	Bridgeport PMSA, CT	Y	62450 FQ	93420 AW	130890 TQ	CTBLS	10/01-12/01
	Danbury PMSA, CT	Y	53610 FQ	97460 AW		CTBLS	10/01-12/01
	Hartford MSA, CT	Y	62610 FQ	94820 AW		CTBLS	10/01-12/01
	New Haven-Meriden PMSA, CT	Y	53160 FQ	80580 AW	114390 TQ	CTBLS	10/01-12/01
	New London-Norwich MSA, CT-RI	Y	49900 FQ	90800 AW	136070 TQ	CTBLS	10/01-12/01
	Stamford-Norwalk PMSA, CT	Y	63960 FQ	103120 AW		CTBLS	10/01-12/01
	Delaware	Y	39970 FQ	79780 AW	119250 TQ	DEBLS	10/01-12/01
	Wilmington-Newark PMSA, DE-MD	Y	41850 FQ	81320 AW	119560 TQ	DEBLS	10/01-12/01
	District of Columbia	Y	55670 FQ	87410 AW	116860 TQ	DCBLS	10/01-12/01
	Washington PMSA, DC-MD-VA-WV	Y	57490 FQ	91120 AW	134180 TQ	DCBLS	10/01-12/01
	Florida	Y	45340 FQ	80700 AW	134160 TQ	FLBLS	10/01-12/01
	Daytona Beach MSA, FL	Y	45630 FQ	70900 AW	99200 TQ	FLBLS	10/01-12/01
	Fort Lauderdale PMSA, FL	Y	49230 FQ	85780 AW	134400 TQ	FLBLS	10/01-12/01
	Fort Myers-Cape Coral MSA, FL	Y	36760 FQ	67090 AW	111730 TQ	FLBLS	10/01-12/01
	Fort Pierce-Port St. Lucie MSA, FL	Y	48330 FQ	75140 AW	121290 TQ	FLBLS	10/01-12/01
	Fort Walton Beach MSA, FL	Y	47820 FQ	71730 AW	95980 TQ	FLBLS	10/01-12/01
	Gainesville MSA, FL	Y	47120 FQ	74790 AW	116540 TQ	FLBLS	10/01-12/01
	Jacksonville MSA, FL	Y	53910 FQ	84310 AW	126940 TQ	FLBLS	10/01-12/01
	Lakeland-Winter Haven MSA, FL	Y	34050 FQ	63880 AW	107190 TQ	FLBLS	10/01-12/01
	Melbourne-Titusville-Palm Bay MSA, FL	Y	51220 FQ	76300 AW	129380 TQ	FLBLS	10/01-12/01
	Miami PMSA, FL	Y	48620 FQ	85150 AW		FLBLS	10/01-12/01
	Naples MSA, FL	Y	39790 FQ	66080 AW	96270 TQ	FLBLS	10/01-12/01
	Ocala MSA, FL	Y	31660 FQ	70340 AW	114460 TQ	FLBLS	10/01-12/01
	Orlando MSA, FL	Y	36830 FQ	78120 AW	122900 TQ	FLBLS	10/01-12/01
	Pensacola MSA, FL	Y	32000 FQ	62340 AW	96500 TQ	FLBLS	10/01-12/01
	Sarasota-Bradenton MSA, FL	Y	33810 FQ	73740 AW	127980 TQ	FLBLS	10/01-12/01
	Tallahassee MSA, FL	Y	46860 FQ	80110 AW	136750 TQ	FLBLS	10/01-12/01
	Tampa-St. Petersburg-Clearwater MSA, FL	Y	48080 FQ	83270 AW		FLBLS	10/01-12/01
	West Palm Beach-Boca Raton MSA, FL	Y	46790 FQ	83750 AW	136470 TQ	FLBLS	10/01-12/01
	Georgia	Y	50660 FQ	85810 AW	131710 TQ	GABLS	10/01-12/01
	Atlanta MSA, GA	Y	57180 FQ	89670 AW	136240 TQ	GABLS	10/01-12/01
	Columbus MSA, GA-AL	Y	47960 FQ	71510 AW	99580 TQ	GABLS	10/01-12/01
	Macon MSA, GA	Y	42660 FQ	73210 AW	113490 TQ	GABLS	10/01-12/01
	Savannah MSA, GA	Y	35390 FQ	66730 AW	101790 TQ	GABLS	10/01-12/01
	Hawaii	Y	47670 FQ	69240 AW	101550 TQ	HIBLS	10/01-12/01

AAW Average annual wage	**AOH** Average offered, high	**ASH** Average starting, high	**H** Hourly	**M** Monthly	**S** Special: hourly and annual
AE Average entry wage	**AOL** Average offered, low	**ASL** Average starting, low	**HI** Highest wage paid	**MTC** Median total compensation	**TQ** Third quartile wage
AEX Average experienced wage	**APH** Average pay, high range	**AW** Average wage paid	**HR** High end range	**MW** Median wage paid	**W** Weekly
AO Average offered	**APL** Average pay, low range	**FQ** First quartile wage	**LR** Low end range	**SQ** Second quartile wage	**Y** Yearly

Occupation/Type/Industry	Location	Per	Low	Mid	High	Source	Date
Computer and Information Systems Manager	Honolulu MSA, HI	Y	48380 FQ	70100 AW	101480 TQ	HIBLS	10/01-12/01
	Idaho	Y	37670 FQ	68710 AW	108830 TQ	IDBLS	10/01-12/01
	Boise City MSA, ID	Y	42900 FQ	73890 AW	113480 TQ	IDBLS	10/01-12/01
	Illinois	Y	42400 FQ	81060 AW	132470 TQ	ILBLS	10/01-12/01
	Champaign-Urbana MSA, IL	Y	40680 FQ	85470 AW		ILBLS	10/01-12/01
	Chicago PMSA, IL	Y	48460 FQ	84110 AW	134480 TQ	ILBLS	10/01-12/01
	Peoria-Pekin MSA, IL	Y	37760 FQ	67080 AW	94200 TQ	ILBLS	10/01-12/01
	Rockford MSA, IL	Y	39790 FQ	65770 AW	93310 TQ	ILBLS	10/01-12/01
	Springfield MSA, IL	Y	41350 FQ	83710 AW	145590 TQ	ILBLS	10/01-12/01
	Indiana	Y	42200 FQ	70380 AW	103830 TQ	INBLS	10/01-12/01
	Elkhart-Goshen MSA, IN	Y	38760 FQ	66850 AW	91780 TQ	INBLS	10/01-12/01
	Evansville-Henderson MSA, IN-KY	Y	38360 FQ	58410 AW	79070 TQ	INBLS	10/01-12/01
	Fort Wayne MSA, IN	Y	35370 FQ	64840 AW	104820 TQ	INBLS	10/01-12/01
	Gary PMSA, IN	Y	36040 FQ	71510 AW		INBLS	10/01-12/01
	Indianapolis MSA, IN	Y	51590 FQ	76490 AW	110520 TQ	INBLS	10/01-12/01
	Lafayette MSA, IN	Y	45560 FQ	67650 AW	93970 TQ	INBLS	10/01-12/01
	South Bend MSA, IN	Y	44980 FQ	77970 AW	112560 TQ	INBLS	10/01-12/01
	Iowa	Y	39010 FQ	67180 AW	97930 TQ	IABLS	10/01-12/01
	Cedar Rapids MSA, IA	Y	50200 FQ	73340 AW	99720 TQ	IABLS	10/01-12/01
	Davenport-Moline-Rock Island MSA, IA-IL	Y	32550 FQ	60130 AW	94170 TQ	IABLS	10/01-12/01
	Des Moines MSA, IA	Y	48500 FQ	74750 AW	108670 TQ	IABLS	10/01-12/01
	Kansas	Y	44100 FQ	75200 AW	112820 TQ	KSBLS	10/01-12/01
	Topeka MSA, KS	Y	45950 FQ	74470 AW	108480 TQ	KSBLS	10/01-12/01
	Wichita MSA, KS	Y	50530 FQ	71550 AW	100390 TQ	KSBLS	10/01-12/01
	Kentucky	Y	39260 FQ	69910 AW	105170 TQ	KYBLS	10/01-12/01
	Lexington MSA, KY	Y	43860 FQ	73870 AW	113440 TQ	KYBLS	10/01-12/01
	Louisville MSA, KY-IN	Y	43540 FQ	72280 AW	104840 TQ	KYBLS	10/01-12/01
	Louisiana	Y	29430 FQ	60100 AW	93100 TQ	LABLS	10/01-12/01
	Baton Rouge MSA, LA	Y	26510 FQ	51670 AW	81110 TQ	LABLS	10/01-12/01
	Houma MSA, LA	Y	37040 FQ	54090 AW	81630 TQ	LABLS	10/01-12/01
	Lafayette MSA, LA	Y	29740 FQ	55330 AW	88410 TQ	LABLS	10/01-12/01
	Lake Charles MSA, LA	Y	31750 FQ	62370 AW	104000 TQ	LABLS	10/01-12/01
	New Orleans MSA, LA	Y	38360 FQ	69930 AW	106780 TQ	LABLS	10/01-12/01
	Shreveport-Bossier City MSA, LA	Y	33420 FQ	61210 AW	89870 TQ	LABLS	10/01-12/01
	Maine	Y	34790 FQ	66590 AW	105250 TQ	MEBLS	10/01-12/01
	Portland MSA, ME	Y	38940 FQ	73230 AW	110080 TQ	MEBLS	10/01-12/01
	Maryland	Y	46000 FQ	83130 AW	119300 TQ	MDBLS	10/01-12/01
	Baltimore PMSA, MD	Y	42260 FQ	80360 AW	115140 TQ	MDBLS	10/01-12/01
	Massachusetts	Y	52210 FQ	88070 AW	140310 TQ	MABLS	10/01-12/01
	Boston PMSA, MA-NH	Y	53680 FQ	89450 AW	140530 TQ	MABLS	10/01-12/01
	Brockton PMSA, MA	Y	52360 FQ	79720 AW	122000 TQ	MABLS	10/01-12/01
	Lawrence PMSA, MA-NH	Y	58330 FQ	96300 AW		MABLS	10/01-12/01
	Lowell PMSA, MA-NH	Y	56710 FQ	89850 AW	137710 TQ	MABLS	10/01-12/01
	New Bedford PMSA, MA	Y	44830 FQ	72190 AW	100800 TQ	MABLS	10/01-12/01
	Springfield MSA, MA	Y	44510 FQ	76390 AW	112530 TQ	MABLS	10/01-12/01
	Worcester PMSA, MA-CT	Y	50100 FQ	83740 AW	145090 TQ	MABLS	10/01-12/01
	Michigan	Y	49230 FQ	81470 AW	119990 TQ	MIBLS	10/01-12/01
	Ann Arbor PMSA, MI	Y	57630 FQ	85480 AW	127860 TQ	MIBLS	10/01-12/01
	Detroit PMSA, MI	Y	50530 FQ	85480 AW	129050 TQ	MIBLS	10/01-12/01
	Flint PMSA, MI	Y	52330 FQ	79060 AW	111830 TQ	MIBLS	10/01-12/01
	Grand Rapids-Muskegon-Holland MSA, MI	Y	53650 FQ	81920 AW	117970 TQ	MIBLS	10/01-12/01
	Kalamazoo-Battle Creek MSA, MI	Y	48240 FQ	77620 AW	118080 TQ	MIBLS	10/01-12/01
	Lansing-East Lansing MSA, MI	Y	44480 FQ	75480 AW	110940 TQ	MIBLS	10/01-12/01
	Saginaw-Bay City-Midland MSA, MI	Y	47280 FQ	73530 AW	110380 TQ	MIBLS	10/01-12/01
	Minnesota	Y	57040 FQ	88480 AW	131200 TQ	MNBLS	10/01-12/01
	Duluth-Superior MSA, MN-WI	Y	48490 FQ	75630 AW	113260 TQ	MNBLS	10/01-12/01
	Minneapolis-St. Paul MSA, MN-WI	Y	60290 FQ	90340 AW	132770 TQ	MNBLS	10/01-12/01
	St. Cloud MSA, MN	Y	39380 FQ	67820 AW	97920 TQ	MNBLS	10/01-12/01
	Mississippi	Y	31340 FQ	58200 AW	87920 TQ	MSBLS	10/01-12/01
	Biloxi-Gulfport-Pascagoula MSA, MS	Y	28890 FQ	61440 AW	100030 TQ	MSBLS	10/01-12/01
	Jackson MSA, MS	Y	32630 FQ	61310 AW	89680 TQ	MSBLS	10/01-12/01
	Missouri	Y	42900 FQ	71950 AW	108040 TQ	MOBLS	10/01-12/01
	Kansas City MSA, MO-KS	Y	45330 FQ	75750 AW	114260 TQ	MOBLS	10/01-12/01

AAW	Average annual wage	**AOH**	Average offered, high	**ASH**	Average starting, high	**H**	Hourly	**M**	Monthly	**S**	Special: hourly and annual
AE	Average entry wage	**AOL**	Average offered, low	**ASL**	Average starting, low	**HI**	Highest wage paid	**MTC**	Median total compensation	**TQ**	Third quartile wage
AEX	Average experienced wage	**APH**	Average pay, high range	**AW**	Average wage paid	**HR**	High end range	**MW**	Median wage paid	**W**	Weekly
AO	Average offered	**APL**	Average pay, low range	**FQ**	First quartile wage	**LR**	Low end range	**SQ**	Second quartile wage	**Y**	Yearly

Occupation/Type/Industry	Location	Per	Low	Mid	High	Source	Date
Computer and Information Systems Manager	St. Louis MSA, MO-IL	Y	47090 FQ	76090 AW	112070 TQ	MOBLS	10/01-12/01
	Springfield MSA, MO	Y	35260 FQ	60410 AW	94720 TQ	MOBLS	10/01-12/01
	Montana	Y	31780 FQ	55390 AW	81540 TQ	MTBLS	10/01-12/01
	Billings MSA, MT	Y	30940 FQ	53030 AW	80540 TQ	MTBLS	10/01-12/01
	Nebraska	Y	45190 FQ	73510 AW	106750 TQ	NEBLS	10/01-12/01
	Lincoln MSA, NE	Y	43070 FQ	69250 AW	101860 TQ	NEBLS	10/01-12/01
	Omaha MSA, NE-IA	Y	46640 FQ	75290 AW	107890 TQ	NEBLS	10/01-12/01
	Nevada	Y	44220 FQ	75430 AW	118110 TQ	NVBLS	10/01-12/01
	Las Vegas MSA, NV-AZ	Y	45000 FQ	76610 AW	118650 TQ	NVBLS	10/01-12/01
	Reno MSA, NV	Y	41150 FQ	73370 AW	128660 TQ	NVBLS	10/01-12/01
	New Hampshire	Y	43660 FQ	74950 AW	115390 TQ	NHBLS	10/01-12/01
	Manchester PMSA, NH	Y	36080 FQ	73210 AW	113710 TQ	NHBLS	10/01-12/01
	Nashua PMSA, NH	Y	47150 FQ	82600 AW	121650 TQ	NHBLS	10/01-12/01
	Portsmouth-Rochester PMSA, NH-ME	Y	39780 FQ	69670 AW	102790 TQ	NHBLS	10/01-12/01
	New Jersey	Y	64220 FQ	101150 AW		NJBLS	10/01-12/01
	Atlantic-Cape May PMSA, NJ	Y	60210 FQ	99830 AW		NJBLS	10/01-12/01
	Bergen-Passaic PMSA, NJ	Y	62150 FQ	102160 AW		NJBLS	10/01-12/01
	Jersey City PMSA, NJ	Y	64570 FQ	105480 AW		NJBLS	10/01-12/01
	Middlesex-Somerset-Hunterdon PMSA, NJ	Y	75020 FQ	107390 AW		NJBLS	10/01-12/01
	Monmouth-Ocean PMSA, NJ	Y	70060 FQ	104180 AW	142240 TQ	NJBLS	10/01-12/01
	Newark PMSA, NJ	Y	63320 FQ	99840 AW		NJBLS	10/01-12/01
	Trenton PMSA, NJ	Y	56480 FQ	83000 AW	121780 TQ	NJBLS	10/01-12/01
	New Mexico	Y	37240 FQ	68210 AW	108170 TQ	NMBLS	10/01-12/01
	Albuquerque MSA, NM	Y	38430 FQ	70330 AW	108330 TQ	NMBLS	10/01-12/01
	Las Cruces MSA, NM	Y	37940 FQ	60200 AW	87400 TQ	NMBLS	10/01-12/01
	New York	Y	59380 FQ	100250 AW		NYBLS	10/01-12/01
	Albany-Schenectady-Troy MSA, NY	Y	54650 FQ	79410 AW	110450 TQ	NYBLS	10/01-12/01
	Binghamton MSA, NY	Y	52210 FQ	91240 AW	139520 TQ	NYBLS	10/01-12/01
	Buffalo-Niagara Falls MSA, NY	Y	47130 FQ	78900 AW	117010 TQ	NYBLS	10/01-12/01
	Nassau-Suffolk PMSA, NY	Y	59280 FQ	96270 AW		NYBLS	10/01-12/01
	New York PMSA, NY	Y	65920 FQ	108070 AW		NYBLS	10/01-12/01
	Newburgh PMSA, NY-PA	Y	45280 FQ	78470 AW	123560 TQ	NYBLS	10/01-12/01
	Rochester MSA, NY	Y	52800 FQ	84960 AW	131980 TQ	NYBLS	10/01-12/01
	Syracuse MSA, NY	Y	49160 FQ	81520 AW	131290 TQ	NYBLS	10/01-12/01
	Utica-Rome MSA, NY	Y	44020 FQ	74300 AW	113130 TQ	NYBLS	10/01-12/01
	North Carolina	Y	46190 FQ	83290 AW	131760 TQ	NCBLS	10/01-12/01
	Asheville MSA, NC	Y	40230 FQ	67900 AW	106070 TQ	NCBLS	10/01-12/01
	Charlotte-Gastonia-Rock Hill MSA, NC-SC	Y	50980 FQ	87360 AW		NCBLS	10/01-12/01
	Fayetteville MSA, NC	Y	35740 FQ	59330 AW	88270 TQ	NCBLS	10/01-12/01
	Greensboro-Winston-Salem-High Point MSA, NC	Y	46950 FQ	79710 AW	120990 TQ	NCBLS	10/01-12/01
	Hickory-Morganton-Lenoir MSA, NC	Y	34110 FQ	63780 AW	95090 TQ	NCBLS	10/01-12/01
	Raleigh-Durham-Chapel Hill MSA, NC	Y	61200 FQ	93440 AW	136590 TQ	NCBLS	10/01-12/01
	Wilmington MSA, NC	Y	35580 FQ	68160 AW	100940 TQ	NCBLS	10/01-12/01
	North Dakota	Y	32570 FQ	57840 AW	88840 TQ	NDBLS	10/01-12/01
	Fargo-Moorhead MSA, ND-MN	Y	39160 FQ	62800 AW	91110 TQ	NDBLS	10/01-12/01
	Ohio	Y	43820 FQ	75430 AW	114110 TQ	OHBLS	10/01-12/01
	Akron PMSA, OH	Y	46510 FQ	74430 AW	112870 TQ	OHBLS	10/01-12/01
	Canton-Massillon MSA, OH	Y	32410 FQ	62170 AW	102050 TQ	OHBLS	10/01-12/01
	Cincinnati PMSA, OH-KY-IN	Y	47780 FQ	79920 AW	116320 TQ	OHBLS	10/01-12/01
	Cleveland-Lorain-Elyria PMSA, OH	Y	45470 FQ	77970 AW	121900 TQ	OHBLS	10/01-12/01
	Columbus MSA, OH	Y	47630 FQ	79860 AW	121240 TQ	OHBLS	10/01-12/01
	Dayton-Springfield MSA, OH	Y	43490 FQ	73100 AW	102170 TQ	OHBLS	10/01-12/01
	Hamilton-Middletown PMSA, OH	Y	42740 FQ	73700 AW	124260 TQ	OHBLS	10/01-12/01
	Mansfield MSA, OH	Y	29680 FQ	59970 AW	91210 TQ	OHBLS	10/01-12/01
	Toledo MSA, OH	Y	41580 FQ	67210 AW	97360 TQ	OHBLS	10/01-12/01
	Youngstown-Warren MSA, OH	Y	36120 FQ	67360 AW	105640 TQ	OHBLS	10/01-12/01
	Oklahoma	Y	31210 FQ	62740 AW	99380 TQ	OKBLS	10/01-12/01
	Oklahoma City MSA, OK	Y	34280 FQ	67120 AW	100990 TQ	OKBLS	10/01-12/01
	Tulsa MSA, OK	Y	34750 FQ	65580 AW	107040 TQ	OKBLS	10/01-12/01
	Oregon	Y	48460 FQ	81830 AW	126690 TQ	ORBLS	10/01-12/01

AAW	Average annual wage	**AOH**	Average offered, high	**ASH**	Average starting, high	**H**	Hourly	**M**	Monthly	**S**	Special: hourly and annual
AE	Average entry wage	**AOL**	Average offered, low	**ASL**	Average starting, low	**HI**	Highest wage paid	**MTC**	Median total compensation	**TQ**	Third quartile wage
AEX	Average experienced wage	**APH**	Average pay, high range	**AW**	Average wage paid	**HR**	High end range	**MW**	Median wage paid	**W**	Weekly
AO	Average offered	**APL**	Average pay, low range	**FQ**	First quartile wage	**LR**	Low end range	**SQ**	Second quartile wage	**Y**	Yearly

Occupation/Type/Industry	Location	Per	Low	Mid	High	Source	Date
Computer and Information Systems Manager	Eugene-Springfield MSA, OR	Y	46780 FQ	88130 AW		ORBLS	10/01-12/01
	Medford-Ashland MSA, OR	Y	46350 FQ	67720 AW	103120 TQ	ORBLS	10/01-12/01
	Portland-Vancouver PMSA, OR-WA	Y	55490 FQ	87300 AW	131190 TQ	ORBLS	10/01-12/01
	Salem PMSA, OR	Y	45020 FQ	75540 AW	106710 TQ	ORBLS	10/01-12/01
	Pennsylvania	Y	40280 FQ	74300 AW	115400 TQ	PABLS	10/01-12/01
	Allentown-Bethlehem-Easton MSA, PA	Y	39810 FQ	68240 AW	95850 TQ	PABLS	10/01-12/01
	Erie MSA, PA	Y	30680 FQ	55970 AW	92580 TQ	PABLS	10/01-12/01
	Harrisburg-Lebanon-Carlisle MSA, PA	Y	39240 FQ	67230 AW	102010 TQ	PABLS	10/01-12/01
	Johnstown MSA, PA	Y	33570 FQ	60510 AW	87410 TQ	PABLS	10/01-12/01
	Lancaster MSA, PA	Y	37510 FQ	68270 AW	103800 TQ	PABLS	10/01-12/01
	Philadelphia PMSA, PA-NJ	Y	43630 FQ	81270 AW	131760 TQ	PABLS	10/01-12/01
	Pittsburgh MSA, PA	Y	43600 FQ	76120 AW	113330 TQ	PABLS	10/01-12/01
	Reading MSA, PA	Y	41910 FQ	69060 AW	90910 TQ	PABLS	10/01-12/01
	Scranton-Wilkes-Barre-Hazleton MSA, PA	Y	33210 FQ	67910 AW	108010 TQ	PABLS	10/01-12/01
	York MSA, PA	Y	42680 FQ	70290 AW	100710 TQ	PABLS	10/01-12/01
	Rhode Island	Y	54470 FQ	86840 AW	121820 TQ	RIBLS	10/01-12/01
	Providence-Fall River-Warwick MSA, RI-MA	Y	49770 FQ	84110 AW	119890 TQ	RIBLS	10/01-12/01
	South Carolina	Y	35330 FQ	68590 AW	104810 TQ	SCBLS	10/01-12/01
	Charleston-North Charleston MSA, SC	Y	39790 FQ	63360 AW	90790 TQ	SCBLS	10/01-12/01
	Columbia MSA, SC	Y	39870 FQ	66910 AW	92790 TQ	SCBLS	10/01-12/01
	Greenville-Spartanburg-Anderson MSA, SC	Y	35900 FQ	65000 AW	95190 TQ	SCBLS	10/01-12/01
	Myrtle Beach MSA, SC	Y	23280 FQ	60480 AW	109070 TQ	SCBLS	10/01-12/01
	South Dakota	Y	56460 FQ	83410 AW	132960 TQ	SDBLS	10/01-12/01
	Sioux Falls MSA, SD	Y	62840 FQ	90480 AW	137080 TQ	SDBLS	10/01-12/01
	Tennessee	Y	33230 FQ	68180 AW	110040 TQ	TNBLS	10/01-12/01
	Chattanooga MSA, TN-GA	Y	30590 FQ	61870 AW	98390 TQ	TNBLS	10/01-12/01
	Clarksville-Hopkinsville MSA, TN-KY	Y	30010 FQ	59390 AW	95270 TQ	TNBLS	10/01-12/01
	Johnson City-Kingsport-Bristol MSA, TN-VA	Y	32310 FQ	61530 AW	99340 TQ	TNBLS	10/01-12/01
	Knoxville MSA, TN	Y	34050 FQ	66680 AW	107000 TQ	TNBLS	10/01-12/01
	Memphis MSA, TN-AR-MS	Y	39650 FQ	77020 AW	119360 TQ	TNBLS	10/01-12/01
	Nashville MSA, TN	Y	34410 FQ	68540 AW	111060 TQ	TNBLS	10/01-12/01
	Texas	Y	41900 FQ	80210 AW	125100 TQ	TXBLS	10/01-12/01
	Amarillo MSA, TX	Y	30430 FQ	58030 AW	91290 TQ	TXBLS	10/01-12/01
	Austin-San Marcos MSA, TX	Y	48460 FQ	88100 AW		TXBLS	10/01-12/01
	Beaumont-Port Arthur MSA, TX	Y	36040 FQ	69220 AW	116720 TQ	TXBLS	10/01-12/01
	Brazoria PMSA, TX	Y	38670 FQ	71390 AW	102970 TQ	TXBLS	10/01-12/01
	Brownsville-Harlingen-San Benito MSA, TX	Y	35340 FQ	63590 AW	100700 TQ	TXBLS	10/01-12/01
	Corpus Christi MSA, TX	Y	32560 FQ	62640 AW	105580 TQ	TXBLS	10/01-12/01
	Dallas PMSA, TX	Y	52110 FQ	88490 AW	134240 TQ	TXBLS	10/01-12/01
	El Paso MSA, TX	Y	26580 FQ	57450 AW	97050 TQ	TXBLS	10/01-12/01
	Fort Worth-Arlington PMSA, TX	Y	39630 FQ	73180 AW	119690 TQ	TXBLS	10/01-12/01
	Galveston-Texas City PMSA, TX	Y	39410 FQ	58270 AW	102460 TQ	TXBLS	10/01-12/01
	Houston PMSA, TX	Y	43870 FQ	79010 AW	119470 TQ	TXBLS	10/01-12/01
	Killeen-Temple MSA, TX	Y	38130 FQ	64830 AW	96490 TQ	TXBLS	10/01-12/01
	Laredo MSA, TX	Y	26140 FQ	64280 AW	109520 TQ	TXBLS	10/01-12/01
	Longview-Marshall MSA, TX	Y	31580 FQ	57540 AW	93020 TQ	TXBLS	10/01-12/01
	Lubbock MSA, TX	Y	27990 FQ	61990 AW	93020 TQ	TXBLS	10/01-12/01
	McAllen-Edinburg-Mission MSA, TX	Y	32680 FQ	58070 AW	87150 TQ	TXBLS	10/01-12/01
	Odessa-Midland MSA, TX	Y	32290 FQ	64000 AW	108940 TQ	TXBLS	10/01-12/01
	San Antonio MSA, TX	Y	39930 FQ	70140 AW	100860 TQ	TXBLS	10/01-12/01
	Tyler MSA, TX	Y	35070 FQ	63710 AW	93030 TQ	TXBLS	10/01-12/01
	Waco MSA, TX	Y	38230 FQ	66140 AW	96270 TQ	TXBLS	10/01-12/01
	Utah	Y	31170 FQ	70340 AW	114710 TQ	UTBLS	10/01-12/01
	Provo-Orem MSA, UT	Y	27690 FQ	68150 AW	107210 TQ	UTBLS	10/01-12/01
	Salt Lake City-Ogden MSA, UT	Y	33120 FQ	71870 AW	118480 TQ	UTBLS	10/01-12/01
	Vermont	Y	52480 FQ	82610 AW	133350 TQ	VTBLS	10/01-12/01

AAW Average annual wage; **AE** Average entry wage; **AEX** Average experienced wage; **AO** Average offered; **AOH** Average offered, high; **AOL** Average offered, low; **APH** Average pay, high range; **APL** Average pay, low range; **ASH** Average starting, high; **ASL** Average starting, low; **AW** Average wage paid; **FQ** First quartile wage; **H** Hourly; **HI** Highest wage paid; **HR** High end range; **LR** Low end range; **M** Monthly; **MTC** Median total compensation; **MW** Median wage paid; **SQ** Second quartile wage; **S** Special: hourly and annual; **TQ** Third quartile wage; **W** Weekly; **Y** Yearly

Occupation/Type/Industry	Location	Per	Low	Mid	High	Source	Date
Computer and Information Systems Manager	Burlington MSA, VT	Y	60400 FQ	92090 AW		VTBLS	10/01-12/01
	Virginia	Y	53340 FQ	88920 AW	135740 TQ	VABLS	10/01-12/01
	Lynchburg MSA, VA	Y	44960 FQ	75380 AW	111980 TQ	VABLS	10/01-12/01
	Norfolk-Virginia Beach-Newport News MSA, VA-NC	Y	45040 FQ	73280 AW	108030 TQ	VABLS	10/01-12/01
	Richmond-Petersburg MSA, VA	Y	39970 FQ	81190 AW	127350 TQ	VABLS	10/01-12/01
	Roanoke MSA, VA	Y	49520 FQ	78300 AW	116590 TQ	VABLS	10/01-12/01
	Washington	Y	54740 FQ	91210 AW	138790 TQ	WABLS	10/01-12/01
	Bremerton PMSA, WA	Y	56290 FQ	75540 AW	93130 TQ	WABLS	10/01-12/01
	Olympia PMSA, WA	Y	51960 FQ	81410 AW	114140 TQ	WABLS	10/01-12/01
	Richland-Kennewick-Pasco MSA, WA	Y	63330 FQ	90310 AW	119330 TQ	WABLS	10/01-12/01
	Seattle-Bellevue-Everett PMSA, WA	Y	59170 FQ	94450 AW	142310 TQ	WABLS	10/01-12/01
	Spokane MSA, WA	Y	35220 FQ	76850 AW	138880 TQ	WABLS	10/01-12/01
	Tacoma PMSA, WA	Y	47880 FQ	78480 AW	123790 TQ	WABLS	10/01-12/01
	West Virginia	Y	30650 FQ	61860 AW	97390 TQ	WVBLS	10/01-12/01
	Charleston MSA, WV	Y	31040 FQ	53360 AW	76760 TQ	WVBLS	10/01-12/01
	Huntington-Ashland MSA, WV-KY-OH	Y	32200 FQ	60100 AW	95130 TQ	WVBLS	10/01-12/01
	Wisconsin	Y	42570 FQ	72820 AW	107570 TQ	WIBLS	10/01-12/01
	Appleton-Oshkosh-Neenah MSA, WI	Y	46230 FQ	70080 AW	101520 TQ	WIBLS	10/01-12/01
	Green Bay MSA, WI	Y	38480 FQ	66800 AW	104620 TQ	WIBLS	10/01-12/01
	Madison MSA, WI	Y	52190 FQ	77130 AW	108850 TQ	WIBLS	10/01-12/01
	Milwaukee-Waukesha PMSA, WI	Y	51480 FQ	80310 AW	114190 TQ	WIBLS	10/01-12/01
	Racine PMSA, WI	Y	41800 FQ	72940 AW	112350 TQ	WIBLS	10/01-12/01
	Wyoming	Y	29400 FQ	50630 AW	71700 TQ	WYBLS	10/01-12/01
	Cheyenne MSA, WY	Y	36710 FQ	52740 AW	70810 TQ	WYBLS	10/01-12/01
	Puerto Rico	Y	31860 FQ	59410 AW	91930 TQ	PRBLS	10/01-12/01
	Guam	Y	41210 FQ	63140 AW	89690 TQ	GUBLS	10/01-12/01
Computer, Automated Teller, and Office Machine Repairer	Alabama	H	7.78 FQ	14.55 AW	22.11 TQ	ALBLS	10/01-12/01
	Alaska	H	11.80 FQ	18.70 AW	27.21 TQ	AKBLS	10/01-12/01
	Arizona	H	10.54 FQ	15.68 AW	23.31 TQ	AZBLS	10/01-12/01
	Arkansas	H	9.11 FQ	15.42 AW	25.41 TQ	ARBLS	10/01-12/01
	California	H	9.87 FQ	16.88 AW	24.87 TQ	CABLS	10/01-12/01
	Colorado	H	10.38 FQ	16.70 AW	23.47 TQ	COBLS	10/01-12/01
	Connecticut	H	11.25 FQ	18.82 AW	26.65 TQ	CTBLS	10/01-12/01
	Delaware	H	9.31 FQ	15.57 AW	25.03 TQ	DEBLS	10/01-12/01
	District of Columbia	H	11.15 FQ	18.27 AW	26.08 TQ	DCBLS	10/01-12/01
	Florida	H	8.70 FQ	14.37 AW	21.60 TQ	FLBLS	10/01-12/01
	Georgia	H	11.47 FQ	18.07 AW	27.14 TQ	GABLS	10/01-12/01
	Hawaii	H	9.84 FQ	16.26 AW	22.66 TQ	HIBLS	10/01-12/01
	Idaho	H	10.05 FQ	16.21 AW	22.97 TQ	IDBLS	10/01-12/01
	Illinois	H	10.36 FQ	16.24 AW	24.22 TQ	ILBLS	10/01-12/01
	Indiana	H	10.26 FQ	17.03 AW	25.15 TQ	INBLS	10/01-12/01
	Iowa	H	9.65 FQ	15.83 AW	23.81 TQ	IABLS	10/01-12/01
	Kansas	H	9.62 FQ	16.89 AW	25.58 TQ	KSBLS	10/01-12/01
	Kentucky	H	9.58 FQ	15.00 AW	23.81 TQ	KYBLS	10/01-12/01
	Louisiana	H	6.88 FQ	14.74 AW	23.14 TQ	LABLS	10/01-12/01
	Maine	H	8.46 FQ	14.49 AW	23.85 TQ	MEBLS	10/01-12/01
	Maryland	H	10.82 FQ	16.94 AW	25.03 TQ	MDBLS	10/01-12/01
	Massachusetts	H	10.54 FQ	18.63 AW	27.12 TQ	MABLS	10/01-12/01
	Michigan	H	10.44 FQ	16.66 AW	24.77 TQ	MIBLS	10/01-12/01
	Minnesota	H	10.97 FQ	17.69 AW	26.34 TQ	MNBLS	10/01-12/01
	Mississippi	H	9.55 FQ	14.27 AW	20.51 TQ	MSBLS	10/01-12/01
	Missouri	H	9.26 FQ	15.18 AW	21.24 TQ	MOBLS	10/01-12/01
	Montana	H	8.85 FQ	14.51 AW	21.85 TQ	MTBLS	10/01-12/01
	Nebraska	H	9.68 FQ	15.55 AW	22.28 TQ	NEBLS	10/01-12/01
	Nevada	H	9.40 FQ	16.22 AW	25.19 TQ	NVBLS	10/01-12/01
	New Hampshire	H	10.96 FQ	16.25 AW	22.71 TQ	NHBLS	10/01-12/01
	New Jersey	H	11.99 FQ	18.94 AW	26.62 TQ	NJBLS	10/01-12/01
	New Mexico	H	9.42 FQ	15.09 AW	21.96 TQ	NMBLS	10/01-12/01
	New York	H	10.85 FQ	17.07 AW	24.51 TQ	NYBLS	10/01-12/01
	North Carolina	H	10.96 FQ	16.76 AW	24.79 TQ	NCBLS	10/01-12/01
	North Dakota	H	9.91 FQ	15.48 AW	24.11 TQ	NDBLS	10/01-12/01

AAW	Average annual wage	**AOH**	Average offered, high	**ASH**	Average starting, high	**H**	Hourly	**M**	Monthly	**S**	Special: hourly and annual
AE	Average entry wage	**AOL**	Average offered, low	**ASL**	Average starting, low	**HI**	Highest wage paid	**MTC**	Median total compensation	**TQ**	Third quartile wage
AEX	Average experienced wage	**APH**	Average pay, high range	**AW**	Average wage paid	**HR**	High end range	**MW**	Median wage paid	**W**	Weekly
AO	Average offered	**APL**	Average pay, low range	**FQ**	First quartile wage	**LR**	Low end range	**SQ**	Second quartile wage	**Y**	Yearly

Occupation/Type/Industry	Location	Per	Low	Mid	High	Source	Date
Computer, Automated Teller, and Office Machine Repairer	Ohio	H	9.35 FQ	15.65 AW	23.29 TQ	OHBLS	10/01-12/01
	Oklahoma	H	6.70 FQ	13.80 AW	21.39 TQ	OKBLS	10/01-12/01
	Oregon	H	10.54 FQ	17.22 AW	25.85 TQ	ORBLS	10/01-12/01
	Pennsylvania	H	9.96 FQ	16.66 AW	24.94 TQ	PABLS	10/01-12/01
	Rhode Island	H	8.31 FQ	14.86 AW	21.29 TQ	RIBLS	10/01-12/01
	South Carolina	H	9.37 FQ	14.60 AW	20.74 TQ	SCBLS	10/01-12/01
	South Dakota	H	10.23 FQ	15.91 AW	23.79 TQ	SDBLS	10/01-12/01
	Tennessee	H	9.48 FQ	14.58 AW	20.93 TQ	TNBLS	10/01-12/01
	Texas	H	9.33 FQ	15.86 AW	22.10 TQ	TXBLS	10/01-12/01
	Utah	H	10.50 FQ	18.79 AW	27.00 TQ	UTBLS	10/01-12/01
	Vermont	H	11.40 FQ	17.03 AW	24.05 TQ	VTBLS	10/01-12/01
	Virginia	H	9.89 FQ	15.22 AW	21.16 TQ	VABLS	10/01-12/01
	Washington	H	10.59 FQ	17.36 AW	24.99 TQ	WABLS	10/01-12/01
	West Virginia	H	9.02 FQ	16.31 AW	25.23 TQ	WVBLS	10/01-12/01
	Wisconsin	H	10.05 FQ	16.86 AW	23.93 TQ	WIBLS	10/01-12/01
	Wyoming	H	6.15 FQ	14.35 AW	30.85 TQ	WYBLS	10/01-12/01
	Puerto Rico	H	6.37 FQ	11.07 AW	19.25 TQ	PRBLS	10/01-12/01
	Guam	H	6.10 FQ	11.59 AW	16.46 TQ	GUBLS	10/01-12/01
Computer-Controlled Machine Tool Operator							
Metals and Plastics	Alabama	H	8.19 FQ	11.97 AW	16.81 TQ	ALBLS	10/01-12/01
Metals and Plastics	Arizona	H	9.08 FQ	14.36 AW	20.83 TQ	AZBLS	10/01-12/01
Metals and Plastics	Arkansas	H	9.33 FQ	12.89 AW	16.96 TQ	ARBLS	10/01-12/01
Metals and Plastics	California	H	7.72 FQ	14.85 AW	23.04 TQ	CABLS	10/01-12/01
Metals and Plastics	Colorado	H	9.95 FQ	15.27 AW	20.89 TQ	COBLS	10/01-12/01
Metals and Plastics	Connecticut	H	9.91 FQ	16.10 AW	21.99 TQ	CTBLS	10/01-12/01
Metals and Plastics	Florida	H	8.33 FQ	12.92 AW	17.34 TQ	FLBLS	10/01-12/01
Metals and Plastics	Georgia	H	9.31 FQ	13.36 AW	17.24 TQ	GABLS	10/01-12/01
Metals and Plastics	Idaho	H	8.13 FQ	12.76 AW	18.95 TQ	IDBLS	10/01-12/01
Metals and Plastics	Illinois	H	8.39 FQ	14.75 AW	22.73 TQ	ILBLS	10/01-12/01
Metals and Plastics	Indiana	H	9.02 FQ	13.58 AW	19.90 TQ	INBLS	10/01-12/01
Metals and Plastics	Iowa	H	7.50 FQ	12.51 AW	17.25 TQ	IABLS	10/01-12/01
Metals and Plastics	Kansas	H	10.21 FQ	16.20 AW	22.42 TQ	KSBLS	10/01-12/01
Metals and Plastics	Kentucky	H	9.16 FQ	12.95 AW	17.46 TQ	KYBLS	10/01-12/01
Metals and Plastics	Louisiana	H	9.13 FQ	13.32 AW	19.45 TQ	LABLS	10/01-12/01
Metals and Plastics	Maine	H	9.92 FQ	15.45 AW	20.92 TQ	MEBLS	10/01-12/01
Metals and Plastics	Maryland	H	7.83 FQ	12.63 AW	19.75 TQ	MDBLS	10/01-12/01
Metals and Plastics	Massachusetts	H	9.66 FQ	15.78 AW	21.69 TQ	MABLS	10/01-12/01
Metals and Plastics	Michigan	H	9.43 FQ	14.89 AW	21.68 TQ	MIBLS	10/01-12/01
Metals and Plastics	Minnesota	H	10.55 FQ	16.03 AW	21.52 TQ	MNBLS	10/01-12/01
Metals and Plastics	Mississippi	H	7.52 FQ	11.89 AW	16.62 TQ	MSBLS	10/01-12/01
Metals and Plastics	Missouri	H	9.12 FQ	13.38 AW	19.12 TQ	MOBLS	10/01-12/01
Metals and Plastics	Nebraska	H	9.67 FQ	13.80 AW	19.33 TQ	NEBLS	10/01-12/01
Metals and Plastics	Nevada	H	7.60 FQ	12.10 AW	18.61 TQ	NVBLS	10/01-12/01
Metals and Plastics	New Hampshire	H	10.72 FQ	14.61 AW	19.15 TQ	NHBLS	10/01-12/01
Metals and Plastics	New Jersey	H	8.85 FQ	16.35 AW	23.36 TQ	NJBLS	10/01-12/01
Metals and Plastics	New Mexico	H	8.26 FQ	12.46 AW	17.09 TQ	NMBLS	10/01-12/01
Metals and Plastics	New York	H	7.67 FQ	13.20 AW	19.96 TQ	NYBLS	10/01-12/01
Metals and Plastics	North Carolina	H	9.77 FQ	13.89 AW	17.98 TQ	NCBLS	10/01-12/01
Metals and Plastics	North Dakota	H	8.49 FQ	11.96 AW	17.23 TQ	NDBLS	10/01-12/01
Metals and Plastics	Ohio	H	9.16 FQ	14.33 AW	20.36 TQ	OHBLS	10/01-12/01
Metals and Plastics	Oklahoma	H	8.48 FQ	12.69 AW	17.17 TQ	OKBLS	10/01-12/01
Metals and Plastics	Oregon	H	10.21 FQ	15.63 AW	21.66 TQ	ORBLS	10/01-12/01
Metals and Plastics	Pennsylvania	H	8.77 FQ	13.90 AW	19.75 TQ	PABLS	10/01-12/01
Metals and Plastics	Rhode Island	H	8.33 FQ	14.32 AW	20.77 TQ	RIBLS	10/01-12/01
Metals and Plastics	South Carolina	H	9.85 FQ	14.85 AW	20.22 TQ	SCBLS	10/01-12/01
Metals and Plastics	South Dakota	H	10.38 FQ	13.46 AW	16.94 TQ	SDBLS	10/01-12/01
Metals and Plastics	Tennessee	H	7.65 FQ	12.26 AW	17.14 TQ	TNBLS	10/01-12/01
Metals and Plastics	Texas	H	8.74 FQ	13.48 AW	20.26 TQ	TXBLS	10/01-12/01
Metals and Plastics	Utah	H	9.58 FQ	13.99 AW	19.06 TQ	UTBLS	10/01-12/01
Metals and Plastics	Virginia	H	11.28 FQ	14.16 AW	17.71 TQ	VABLS	10/01-12/01
Metals and Plastics	Washington	H	10.29 FQ	15.55 AW	21.91 TQ	WABLS	10/01-12/01
Metals and Plastics	West Virginia	H	9.22 FQ	13.04 AW	18.80 TQ	WVBLS	10/01-12/01
Metals and Plastics	Wisconsin	H	9.79 FQ	14.74 AW	20.93 TQ	WIBLS	10/01-12/01
Metals and Plastics	Puerto Rico	H	5.62 FQ	7.80 AW	11.00 TQ	PRBLS	10/01-12/01
Computer Graphics Professional	Texas	Y		27820 AW		SAEN	1/01-1/02
Computer Hardware Engineer	Alabama	Y	46540 FQ	73280 AW	106690 TQ	ALBLS	10/01-12/01
	Arkansas	Y	38190 FQ	57590 AW	85150 TQ	ARBLS	10/01-12/01

AAW	Average annual wage	**AOH**	Average offered, high	**ASH**	Average starting, high	**H**	Hourly	**M**	Monthly	**S**	Special: hourly and annual
AE	Average entry wage	**AOL**	Average offered, low	**ASL**	Average starting, low	**HI**	Highest wage paid	**MTC**	Median total compensation	**TQ**	Third quartile wage
AEX	Average experienced wage	**APH**	Average pay, high range	**AW**	Average wage paid	**HR**	High end range	**MW**	Median wage paid	**W**	Weekly
AO	Average offered	**APL**	Average pay, low range	**FQ**	First quartile wage	**LR**	Low end range	**SQ**	Second quartile wage	**Y**	Yearly

Occupation/Type/Industry	Location	Per	Low	Mid	High	Source	Date
Computer Hardware Engineer	California	Y	51350 FQ	84370 AW	129880 TQ	CABLS	10/01-12/01
	Colorado	Y	53550 FQ	78860 AW	112450 TQ	COBLS	10/01-12/01
	Connecticut	Y	45340 FQ	70270 AW	97870 TQ	CTBLS	10/01-12/01
	Delaware	Y	45370 FQ	67760 AW	108050 TQ	DEBLS	10/01-12/01
	District of Columbia	Y	45950 FQ	52940 AW	60440 TQ	DCBLS	10/01-12/01
	Florida	Y	47680 FQ	66720 AW	90170 TQ	FLBLS	10/01-12/01
	Georgia	Y	49620 FQ	76050 AW	96710 TQ	GABLS	10/01-12/01
	Illinois	Y	39960 FQ	66530 AW	97510 TQ	ILBLS	10/01-12/01
	Indiana	Y	28330 FQ	58390 AW	94360 TQ	INBLS	10/01-12/01
	Kansas	Y	34340 FQ	59410 AW	85960 TQ	KSBLS	10/01-12/01
	Louisiana	Y	41540 FQ	60330 AW	88920 TQ	LABLS	10/01-12/01
	Maryland	Y	46040 FQ	72350 AW	104010 TQ	MDBLS	10/01-12/01
	Massachusetts	Y	57660 FQ	85460 AW	119900 TQ	MABLS	10/01-12/01
	Michigan	Y	45140 FQ	73270 AW	106830 TQ	MIBLS	10/01-12/01
	Minnesota	Y	48980 FQ	73600 AW	113240 TQ	MNBLS	10/01-12/01
	Mississippi	Y	28760 FQ	55460 AW	85130 TQ	MSBLS	10/01-12/01
	Missouri	Y	40500 FQ	62230 AW	90810 TQ	MOBLS	10/01-12/01
	Montana	Y	42800 FQ	70370 AW	96350 TQ	MTBLS	10/01-12/01
	Nebraska	Y	38190 FQ	64610 AW	97530 TQ	NEBLS	10/01-12/01
	Nevada	Y	40430 FQ	59080 AW	75860 TQ	NVBLS	10/01-12/01
	New Jersey	Y	48950 FQ	75900 AW	112180 TQ	NJBLS	10/01-12/01
	New Mexico	Y	48050 FQ	67760 AW	96200 TQ	NMBLS	10/01-12/01
	New York	Y	46100 FQ	81010 AW	131180 TQ	NYBLS	10/01-12/01
	North Carolina	Y	42740 FQ	75920 AW	117930 TQ	NCBLS	10/01-12/01
	Ohio	Y	39410 FQ	64310 AW	93850 TQ	OHBLS	10/01-12/01
	Oklahoma	Y	39690 FQ	66820 AW	97550 TQ	OKBLS	10/01-12/01
	Pennsylvania	Y	44650 FQ	68310 AW	96830 TQ	PABLS	10/01-12/01
	Rhode Island	Y	44100 FQ	64730 AW	91680 TQ	RIBLS	10/01-12/01
	South Carolina	Y	28110 FQ	58600 AW	87970 TQ	SCBLS	10/01-12/01
	South Dakota	Y	30840 FQ	47810 AW	73730 TQ	SDBLS	10/01-12/01
	Tennessee	Y	30640 FQ	56440 AW	77300 TQ	TNBLS	10/01-12/01
	Texas	Y	43100 FQ	68850 AW	107480 TQ	TXBLS	10/01-12/01
	Utah	Y	37340 FQ	59590 AW	93790 TQ	UTBLS	10/01-12/01
	Virginia	Y	44800 FQ	69380 AW	103890 TQ	VABLS	10/01-12/01
	Washington	Y	45880 FQ	69450 AW	102700 TQ	WABLS	10/01-12/01
	West Virginia	Y	33700 FQ	47630 AW	67570 TQ	WVBLS	10/01-12/01
	Wisconsin	Y	32440 FQ	59820 AW	90270 TQ	WIBLS	10/01-12/01
	Puerto Rico	Y	27010 FQ	43450 AW	66100 TQ	PRBLS	10/01-12/01
Computer Operator	Alabama	H	7.22 FQ	12.98 AW	20.26 TQ	ALBLS	10/01-12/01
	Alaska	H	11.88 FQ	19.65 AW	28.62 TQ	AKBLS	10/01-12/01
	Arizona	H	8.31 FQ	12.96 AW	18.88 TQ	AZBLS	10/01-12/01
	Arkansas	H	8.10 FQ	12.33 AW	17.33 TQ	ARBLS	10/01-12/01
	California	H	9.67 FQ	16.87 AW	24.96 TQ	CABLS	10/01-12/01
	Colorado	H	10.39 FQ	15.91 AW	22.11 TQ	COBLS	10/01-12/01
	Connecticut	H	10.73 FQ	16.42 AW	23.09 TQ	CTBLS	10/01-12/01
	Delaware	H	9.38 FQ	14.91 AW	20.88 TQ	DEBLS	10/01-12/01
	District of Columbia	H	10.01 FQ	15.82 AW	22.82 TQ	DCBLS	10/01-12/01
	Florida	H	8.50 FQ	13.39 AW	20.17 TQ	FLBLS	10/01-12/01
	Georgia	H	7.64 FQ	14.29 AW	21.48 TQ	GABLS	10/01-12/01
	Hawaii	H	11.23 FQ	15.17 AW	19.75 TQ	HIBLS	10/01-12/01
	Idaho	H	6.66 FQ	12.52 AW	19.25 TQ	IDBLS	10/01-12/01
	Illinois	H	8.45 FQ	17.18 AW	25.00 TQ	ILBLS	10/01-12/01
	Indiana	H	8.35 FQ	12.89 AW	18.60 TQ	INBLS	10/01-12/01
	Iowa	H	7.75 FQ	12.64 AW	17.74 TQ	IABLS	10/01-12/01
	Kansas	H	8.75 FQ	14.18 AW	20.36 TQ	KSBLS	10/01-12/01
	Kentucky	H	9.04 FQ	13.94 AW	20.25 TQ	KYBLS	10/01-12/01
	Louisiana	H	7.62 FQ	12.95 AW	19.56 TQ	LABLS	10/01-12/01
	Maine	H	8.54 FQ	13.86 AW	20.23 TQ	MEBLS	10/01-12/01
	Maryland	H	9.13 FQ	15.67 AW	24.16 TQ	MDBLS	10/01-12/01
	Massachusetts	H	10.35 FQ	17.37 AW	25.05 TQ	MABLS	10/01-12/01
	Michigan	H	9.06 FQ	14.88 AW	21.15 TQ	MIBLS	10/01-12/01
	Minnesota	H	9.84 FQ	15.59 AW	21.40 TQ	MNBLS	10/01-12/01
	Mississippi	H	7.91 FQ	12.29 AW	17.38 TQ	MSBLS	10/01-12/01
	Missouri	H	8.58 FQ	14.03 AW	20.76 TQ	MOBLS	10/01-12/01
	Montana	H	6.83 FQ	11.19 AW	16.39 TQ	MTBLS	10/01-12/01
	Nebraska	H	8.11 FQ	13.91 AW	21.62 TQ	NEBLS	10/01-12/01
	Nevada	H	9.29 FQ	14.16 AW	20.66 TQ	NVBLS	10/01-12/01
	New Hampshire	H	10.19 FQ	15.49 AW	20.69 TQ	NHBLS	10/01-12/01
	New Jersey	H	10.50 FQ	16.96 AW	24.97 TQ	NJBLS	10/01-12/01
	New Mexico	H	8.45 FQ	12.43 AW	17.93 TQ	NMBLS	10/01-12/01
	New York	H	8.95 FQ	16.20 AW	24.97 TQ	NYBLS	10/01-12/01
	North Carolina	H	9.32 FQ	14.73 AW	20.94 TQ	NCBLS	10/01-12/01

AAW	Average annual wage	**AOH**	Average offered, high	**ASH**	Average starting, high	**H**	Hourly	**M**	Monthly	**S**	Special: hourly and annual
AE	Average entry wage	**AOL**	Average offered, low	**ASL**	Average starting, low	**HI**	Highest wage paid	**MTC**	Median total compensation	**TQ**	Third quartile wage
AEX	Average experienced wage	**APH**	Average pay, high range	**AW**	Average wage paid	**HR**	High end range	**MW**	Median wage paid	**W**	Weekly
AO	Average offered	**APL**	Average pay, low range	**FQ**	First quartile wage	**LR**	Low end range	**SQ**	Second quartile wage	**Y**	Yearly

Occupation/Type/Industry	Location	Per	Low	Mid	High	Source	Date
Computer Operator	North Dakota	H	7.67 FQ	12.76 AW	19.40 TQ	NDBLS	10/01-12/01
	Ohio	H	7.49 FQ	12.72 AW	19.48 TQ	OHBLS	10/01-12/01
	Oklahoma	H	7.05 FQ	12.03 AW	18.77 TQ	OKBLS	10/01-12/01
	Oregon	H	10.29 FQ	15.22 AW	21.50 TQ	ORBLS	10/01-12/01
	Pennsylvania	H	7.96 FQ	13.65 AW	20.66 TQ	PABLS	10/01-12/01
	Rhode Island	H	8.13 FQ	14.70 AW	21.30 TQ	RIBLS	10/01-12/01
	South Carolina	H	9.02 FQ	13.95 AW	20.19 TQ	SCBLS	10/01-12/01
	South Dakota	H	8.29 FQ	11.22 AW	15.02 TQ	SDBLS	10/01-12/01
	Tennessee	H	8.95 FQ	13.96 AW	20.57 TQ	TNBLS	10/01-12/01
	Texas	H	8.62 FQ	14.33 AW	21.26 TQ	TXBLS	10/01-12/01
	Utah	H	7.26 FQ	13.02 AW	21.01 TQ	UTBLS	10/01-12/01
	Vermont	H	8.85 FQ	12.62 AW	17.51 TQ	VTBLS	10/01-12/01
	Virginia	H	8.15 FQ	14.01 AW	20.98 TQ	VABLS	10/01-12/01
	Washington	H	10.04 FQ	16.24 AW	23.17 TQ	WABLS	10/01-12/01
	West Virginia	H	7.43 FQ	12.06 AW	17.66 TQ	WVBLS	10/01-12/01
	Wisconsin	H	9.26 FQ	13.75 AW	20.01 TQ	WIBLS	10/01-12/01
	Wyoming	H	8.33 FQ	12.16 AW	17.05 TQ	WYBLS	10/01-12/01
	Puerto Rico	H	6.06 FQ	9.45 AW	14.55 TQ	PRBLS	10/01-12/01
	Virgin Islands	H	9.09 FQ	11.69 AW	15.15 TQ	VIBLS	10/01-12/01
	Guam	H	7.24 FQ	12.90 AW	18.03 TQ	GUBLS	10/01-12/01
Computer Programmer	Alabama	Y	30360 FQ	52080 AW	82050 TQ	ALBLS	10/01-12/01
	Birmingham MSA, AL	Y	31040 FQ	50780 AW	76520 TQ	ALBLS	10/01-12/01
	Huntsville MSA, AL	Y	31410 FQ	58740 AW	89470 TQ	ALBLS	10/01-12/01
	Mobile MSA, AL	Y	26730 FQ	50820 AW	83940 TQ	ALBLS	10/01-12/01
	Montgomery MSA, AL	Y	31250 FQ	49980 AW	69880 TQ	ALBLS	10/01-12/01
	Alaska	Y	38690 FQ	57990 AW	78730 TQ	AKBLS	10/01-12/01
	Anchorage MSA, AK	Y	39230 FQ	59130 AW	82970 TQ	AKBLS	10/01-12/01
	Arizona	Y	30490 FQ	55730 AW	85320 TQ	AZBLS	10/01-12/01
	Phoenix-Mesa MSA, AZ	Y	31190 FQ	57060 AW	86440 TQ	AZBLS	10/01-12/01
	Tucson MSA, AZ	Y	28630 FQ	49460 AW	76180 TQ	AZBLS	10/01-12/01
	Arkansas	Y	19930 FQ	43880 AW	71230 TQ	ARBLS	10/01-12/01
	Fayetteville-Springdale-Rogers MSA, AR	Y	18710 FQ	32690 AW	55790 TQ	ARBLS	10/01-12/01
	Fort Smith MSA, AR-OK	Y	26660 FQ	43540 AW	68520 TQ	ARBLS	10/01-12/01
	Little Rock-North Little Rock MSA, AR	Y	27460 FQ	49280 AW	71430 TQ	ARBLS	10/01-12/01
	California	Y	39290 FQ	69920 AW	108250 TQ	CABLS	10/01-12/01
	Bakersfield MSA, CA	Y	38880 FQ	60150 AW	85420 TQ	CABLS	10/01-12/01
	Chico-Paradise MSA, CA	Y	25670 FQ	52780 AW	86770 TQ	CABLS	10/01-12/01
	Fresno MSA, CA	Y	28640 FQ	53780 AW	82250 TQ	CABLS	10/01-12/01
	Los Angeles-Long Beach PMSA, CA	Y	40540 FQ	64930 AW	94960 TQ	CABLS	10/01-12/01
	Merced MSA, CA	Y	30390 FQ	47480 AW	69820 TQ	CABLS	10/01-12/01
	Modesto MSA, CA	Y	31740 FQ	55850 AW	77160 TQ	CABLS	10/01-12/01
	Oakland PMSA, CA	Y	47430 FQ	75120 AW	110010 TQ	CABLS	10/01-12/01
	Orange County PMSA, CA	Y	43740 FQ	72030 AW	108140 TQ	CABLS	10/01-12/01
	Redding MSA, CA	Y	34670 FQ	66000 AW	95340 TQ	CABLS	10/01-12/01
	Riverside-San Bernardino PMSA, CA	Y	33020 FQ	65350 AW	105040 TQ	CABLS	10/01-12/01
	Sacramento PMSA, CA	Y	39580 FQ	65460 AW	95370 TQ	CABLS	10/01-12/01
	Salinas MSA, CA	Y	25120 FQ	65800 AW	125920 TQ	CABLS	10/01-12/01
	San Diego MSA, CA	Y	35700 FQ	63930 AW	96570 TQ	CABLS	10/01-12/01
	San Francisco PMSA, CA	Y	43940 FQ	75990 AW	117210 TQ	CABLS	10/01-12/01
	San Jose PMSA, CA	Y	31920 FQ	73190 AW	114300 TQ	CABLS	10/01-12/01
	San Luis Obispo-Atascadero-Paso Robles MSA, CA	Y	27620 FQ	49630 AW	82970 TQ	CABLS	10/01-12/01
	Santa Barbara-Santa Maria-Lompoc MSA, CA	Y	33920 FQ	57530 AW	85110 TQ	CABLS	10/01-12/01
	Santa Cruz-Watsonville PMSA, CA	Y	37680 FQ	65990 AW	110060 TQ	CABLS	10/01-12/01
	Santa Rosa PMSA, CA	Y	30980 FQ	56370 AW	82760 TQ	CABLS	10/01-12/01
	Stockton-Lodi MSA, CA	Y	28090 FQ	49400 AW	74020 TQ	CABLS	10/01-12/01
	Vallejo-Fairfield-Napa PMSA, CA	Y	34560 FQ	62290 AW	97280 TQ	CABLS	10/01-12/01
	Ventura PMSA, CA	Y	37400 FQ	70270 AW	113650 TQ	CABLS	10/01-12/01
	Visalia-Tulare-Porterville MSA, CA	Y	32280 FQ	52760 AW	76790 TQ	CABLS	10/01-12/01
	Colorado	Y	39730 FQ	65850 AW	92830 TQ	COBLS	10/01-12/01
	Boulder-Longmont PMSA, CO	Y	35540 FQ	67260 AW	94050 TQ	COBLS	10/01-12/01
	Colorado Springs MSA, CO	Y	42440 FQ	62300 AW	88200 TQ	COBLS	10/01-12/01
	Denver PMSA, CO	Y	42650 FQ	68330 AW	94240 TQ	COBLS	10/01-12/01

AAW Average annual wage; **AE** Average entry wage; **AEX** Average experienced wage; **AO** Average offered; **AOH** Average offered, high; **AOL** Average offered, low; **APH** Average pay, high range; **APL** Average pay, low range; **ASH** Average starting, high; **ASL** Average starting, low; **AW** Average wage paid; **FQ** First quartile wage; **H** Hourly; **HI** Highest wage paid; **HR** High end range; **LR** Low end range; **M** Monthly; **MTC** Median total compensation; **MW** Median wage paid; **SQ** Second quartile wage; **S** Special: hourly and annual; **TQ** Third quartile wage; **W** Weekly; **Y** Yearly

Occupation/Type/Industry	Location	Per	Low	Mid	High	Source	Date
Computer Programmer	Fort Collins-Loveland MSA, CO	Y	27840 FQ	56260 AW	86490 TQ	COBLS	10/01-12/01
	Greeley PMSA, CO	Y	32950 FQ	50460 AW	68540 TQ	COBLS	10/01-12/01
	Connecticut	Y	38670 FQ	67110 AW	107080 TQ	CTBLS	10/01-12/01
	Bridgeport PMSA, CT	Y	36540 FQ	61010 AW	86280 TQ	CTBLS	10/01-12/01
	Danbury PMSA, CT	Y	41720 FQ	73120 AW	111800 TQ	CTBLS	10/01-12/01
	Hartford MSA, CT	Y	36940 FQ	66160 AW	113200 TQ	CTBLS	10/01-12/01
	New Haven-Meriden PMSA, CT	Y	36440 FQ	54890 AW	76300 TQ	CTBLS	10/01-12/01
	New London-Norwich MSA, CT-RI	Y	43240 FQ	64520 AW	87950 TQ	CTBLS	10/01-12/01
	Stamford-Norwalk PMSA, CT	Y	46040 FQ	70660 AW	100270 TQ	CTBLS	10/01-12/01
	Delaware	Y	40090 FQ	71070 AW	108970 TQ	DEBLS	10/01-12/01
	Wilmington-Newark PMSA, DE-MD	Y	41930 FQ	72130 AW	110070 TQ	DEBLS	10/01-12/01
	District of Columbia	Y	39530 FQ	60440 AW	88720 TQ	DCBLS	10/01-12/01
	Washington PMSA, DC-MD-VA-WV	Y	40900 FQ	65280 AW	92500 TQ	DCBLS	10/01-12/01
	Florida	Y	31860 FQ	57850 AW	88340 TQ	FLBLS	10/01-12/01
	Daytona Beach MSA, FL	Y	29580 FQ	46140 AW	67850 TQ	FLBLS	10/01-12/01
	Fort Lauderdale PMSA, FL	Y	36140 FQ	63900 AW	94640 TQ	FLBLS	10/01-12/01
	Fort Myers-Cape Coral MSA, FL	Y	30650 FQ	55260 AW	88800 TQ	FLBLS	10/01-12/01
	Fort Pierce-Port St. Lucie MSA, FL	Y	28630 FQ	43430 AW	64710 TQ	FLBLS	10/01-12/01
	Fort Walton Beach MSA, FL	Y	30670 FQ	49800 AW	75840 TQ	FLBLS	10/01-12/01
	Gainesville MSA, FL	Y	30520 FQ	47670 AW	68130 TQ	FLBLS	10/01-12/01
	Jacksonville MSA, FL	Y	36160 FQ	60680 AW	89080 TQ	FLBLS	10/01-12/01
	Lakeland-Winter Haven MSA, FL	Y	29650 FQ	47790 AW	70340 TQ	FLBLS	10/01-12/01
	Melbourne-Titusville-Palm Bay MSA, FL	Y	21900 FQ	51800 AW	81130 TQ	FLBLS	10/01-12/01
	Miami PMSA, FL	Y	37450 FQ	57200 AW	85620 TQ	FLBLS	10/01-12/01
	Naples MSA, FL	Y	35250 FQ	63420 AW	93040 TQ	FLBLS	10/01-12/01
	Ocala MSA, FL	Y	26990 FQ	46730 AW	67460 TQ	FLBLS	10/01-12/01
	Orlando MSA, FL	Y	33530 FQ	59020 AW	90020 TQ	FLBLS	10/01-12/01
	Pensacola MSA, FL	Y	30120 FQ	50830 AW	69270 TQ	FLBLS	10/01-12/01
	Sarasota-Bradenton MSA, FL	Y	31330 FQ	58100 AW	115110 TQ	FLBLS	10/01-12/01
	Tallahassee MSA, FL	Y	32400 FQ	60160 AW	90720 TQ	FLBLS	10/01-12/01
	Tampa-St. Petersburg-Clearwater MSA, FL	Y	31520 FQ	57490 AW	87300 TQ	FLBLS	10/01-12/01
	West Palm Beach-Boca Raton MSA, FL	Y	22280 FQ	58270 AW	92210 TQ	FLBLS	10/01-12/01
	Georgia	Y	34600 FQ	57410 AW	86740 TQ	GABLS	10/01-12/01
	Atlanta MSA, GA	Y	37770 FQ	59770 AW	89060 TQ	GABLS	10/01-12/01
	Augusta-Aiken MSA, GA-SC	Y	34330 FQ	67530 AW	98220 TQ	GABLS	10/01-12/01
	Columbus MSA, GA-AL	Y	28780 FQ	41590 AW	64190 TQ	GABLS	10/01-12/01
	Macon MSA, GA	Y	33650 FQ	50990 AW	70650 TQ	GABLS	10/01-12/01
	Savannah MSA, GA	Y	32260 FQ	50380 AW	73650 TQ	GABLS	10/01-12/01
	Hawaii	Y	30360 FQ	45550 AW	66320 TQ	HIBLS	10/01-12/01
	Honolulu MSA, HI	Y	30850 FQ	45940 AW	66440 TQ	HIBLS	10/01-12/01
	Idaho	Y	31240 FQ	59780 AW	109680 TQ	IDBLS	10/01-12/01
	Boise City MSA, ID	Y	33670 FQ	61670 AW	112490 TQ	IDBLS	10/01-12/01
	Illinois	Y	35720 FQ	58960 AW	89580 TQ	ILBLS	10/01-12/01
	Champaign-Urbana MSA, IL	Y	30010 FQ	49490 AW	73970 TQ	ILBLS	10/01-12/01
	Chicago PMSA, IL	Y	37010 FQ	59540 AW	89730 TQ	ILBLS	10/01-12/01
	Peoria-Pekin MSA, IL	Y	30850 FQ	48790 AW	71980 TQ	ILBLS	10/01-12/01
	Rockford MSA, IL	Y	28480 FQ	52810 AW	75700 TQ	ILBLS	10/01-12/01
	Springfield MSA, IL	Y	29530 FQ	48640 AW	74620 TQ	ILBLS	10/01-12/01
	Indiana	Y	30000 FQ	51970 AW	78640 TQ	INBLS	10/01-12/01
	Elkhart-Goshen MSA, IN	Y	30960 FQ	46940 AW	65440 TQ	INBLS	10/01-12/01
	Evansville-Henderson MSA, IN-KY	Y	30670 FQ	48020 AW	70130 TQ	INBLS	10/01-12/01
	Fort Wayne MSA, IN	Y	23600 FQ	47740 AW	71290 TQ	INBLS	10/01-12/01
	Gary PMSA, IN	Y	36100 FQ	58320 AW	84720 TQ	INBLS	10/01-12/01
	Indianapolis MSA, IN	Y	33160 FQ	55710 AW	83830 TQ	INBLS	10/01-12/01
	Lafayette MSA, IN	Y	22350 FQ	40980 AW	58330 TQ	INBLS	10/01-12/01
	South Bend MSA, IN	Y	33680 FQ	56760 AW	84690 TQ	INBLS	10/01-12/01
	Iowa	Y	31600 FQ	50820 AW	72520 TQ	IABLS	10/01-12/01
	Cedar Rapids MSA, IA	Y	34250 FQ	52020 AW	74270 TQ	IABLS	10/01-12/01
	Davenport-Moline-Rock Island MSA, IA-IL	Y	25920 FQ	55580 AW	90390 TQ	IABLS	10/01-12/01

AAW	Average annual wage	**AOH**	Average offered, high	**ASH**	Average starting, high	**H**	Hourly	**M**	Monthly	**S**	Special: hourly and annual
AE	Average entry wage	**AOL**	Average offered, low	**ASL**	Average starting, low	**HI**	Highest wage paid	**MTC**	Median total compensation	**TQ**	Third quartile wage
AEX	Average experienced wage	**APH**	Average pay, high range	**AW**	Average wage paid	**HR**	High end range	**MW**	Median wage paid	**W**	Weekly
AO	Average offered	**APL**	Average pay, low range	**FQ**	First quartile wage	**LR**	Low end range	**SQ**	Second quartile wage	**Y**	Yearly

Occupation/Type/Industry	Location	Per	Low	Mid	High	Source	Date
Computer Programmer	Kansas	Y	37090 FQ	58600 AW	85310 TQ	KSBLS	10/01-12/01
	Topeka MSA, KS	Y	34400 FQ	52180 AW	70780 TQ	KSBLS	10/01-12/01
	Wichita MSA, KS	Y	39250 FQ	57980 AW	76280 TQ	KSBLS	10/01-12/01
	Kentucky	Y	32520 FQ	53930 AW	80770 TQ	KYBLS	10/01-12/01
	Lexington MSA, KY	Y	38380 FQ	61960 AW	93100 TQ	KYBLS	10/01-12/01
	Louisville MSA, KY-IN	Y	32300 FQ	52760 AW	76470 TQ	KYBLS	10/01-12/01
	Louisiana	Y	29270 FQ	49970 AW	73280 TQ	LABLS	10/01-12/01
	Baton Rouge MSA, LA	Y	29120 FQ	45420 AW	64520 TQ	LABLS	10/01-12/01
	Houma MSA, LA	Y	27020 FQ	47290 AW	67640 TQ	LABLS	10/01-12/01
	Lafayette MSA, LA	Y	26660 FQ	46970 AW	70380 TQ	LABLS	10/01-12/01
	Lake Charles MSA, LA	Y	26800 FQ	45650 AW	70000 TQ	LABLS	10/01-12/01
	New Orleans MSA, LA	Y	31810 FQ	56490 AW	86100 TQ	LABLS	10/01-12/01
	Shreveport-Bossier City MSA, LA	Y	28170 FQ	50040 AW	82260 TQ	LABLS	10/01-12/01
	Maine	Y	29510 FQ	50890 AW	76270 TQ	MEBLS	10/01-12/01
	Portland MSA, ME	Y	38130 FQ	56990 AW	77440 TQ	MEBLS	10/01-12/01
	Maryland	Y	29250 FQ	59490 AW	93380 TQ	MDBLS	10/01-12/01
	Baltimore PMSA, MD	Y	24220 FQ	52790 AW	85140 TQ	MDBLS	10/01-12/01
	Massachusetts	Y	40780 FQ	69700 AW	109660 TQ	MABLS	10/01-12/01
	Boston PMSA, MA-NH	Y	41190 FQ	70210 AW	110630 TQ	MABLS	10/01-12/01
	Brockton PMSA, MA	Y	39160 FQ	60660 AW	87640 TQ	MABLS	10/01-12/01
	Lawrence PMSA, MA-NH	Y	42110 FQ	71290 AW	110610 TQ	MABLS	10/01-12/01
	Lowell PMSA, MA-NH	Y	41090 FQ	74050 AW	112360 TQ	MABLS	10/01-12/01
	New Bedford PMSA, MA	Y	32370 FQ	56390 AW	74910 TQ	MABLS	10/01-12/01
	Springfield MSA, MA	Y	35970 FQ	64180 AW	103060 TQ	MABLS	10/01-12/01
	Worcester PMSA, MA-CT	Y	40000 FQ	61720 AW	88720 TQ	MABLS	10/01-12/01
	Michigan	Y	37100 FQ	59900 AW	87600 TQ	MIBLS	10/01-12/01
	Ann Arbor PMSA, MI	Y	37060 FQ	59580 AW	89870 TQ	MIBLS	10/01-12/01
	Detroit PMSA, MI	Y	40410 FQ	63380 AW	90170 TQ	MIBLS	10/01-12/01
	Grand Rapids-Muskegon-Holland MSA, MI	Y	36280 FQ	56280 AW	76450 TQ	MIBLS	10/01-12/01
	Kalamazoo-Battle Creek MSA, MI	Y	33490 FQ	50600 AW	69680 TQ	MIBLS	10/01-12/01
	Lansing-East Lansing MSA, MI	Y	33250 FQ	52620 AW	77300 TQ	MIBLS	10/01-12/01
	Saginaw-Bay City-Midland MSA, MI	Y	26300 FQ	45930 AW	67180 TQ	MIBLS	10/01-12/01
	Minnesota	Y	36420 FQ	61670 AW	92600 TQ	MNBLS	10/01-12/01
	Duluth-Superior MSA, MN-WI	Y	23220 FQ	41190 AW	67920 TQ	MNBLS	10/01-12/01
	Minneapolis-St. Paul MSA, MN-WI	Y	38120 FQ	62830 AW	92620 TQ	MNBLS	10/01-12/01
	St. Cloud MSA, MN	Y	31270 FQ	45950 AW	65680 TQ	MNBLS	10/01-12/01
	Mississippi	Y	26140 FQ	43370 AW	65370 TQ	MSBLS	10/01-12/01
	Biloxi-Gulfport-Pascagoula MSA, MS	Y	27090 FQ	42980 AW	61320 TQ	MSBLS	10/01-12/01
	Jackson MSA, MS	Y	28530 FQ	46460 AW	69230 TQ	MSBLS	10/01-12/01
	Missouri	Y	33700 FQ	59270 AW	88460 TQ	MOBLS	10/01-12/01
	Kansas City MSA, MO-KS	Y	38770 FQ	59850 AW	85480 TQ	MOBLS	10/01-12/01
	St. Louis MSA, MO-IL	Y	37740 FQ	62420 AW	89910 TQ	MOBLS	10/01-12/01
	Springfield MSA, MO	Y	19590 FQ	42810 AW	66820 TQ	MOBLS	10/01-12/01
	Montana	Y	23760 FQ	47390 AW	73080 TQ	MTBLS	10/01-12/01
	Billings MSA, MT	Y	21930 FQ	43110 AW	68200 TQ	MTBLS	10/01-12/01
	Nebraska	Y	32220 FQ	53180 AW	79290 TQ	NEBLS	10/01-12/01
	Lincoln MSA, NE	Y	32250 FQ	52800 AW	75920 TQ	NEBLS	10/01-12/01
	Omaha MSA, NE-IA	Y	34600 FQ	54130 AW	80310 TQ	NEBLS	10/01-12/01
	Nevada	Y	35060 FQ	55130 AW	81540 TQ	NVBLS	10/01-12/01
	Las Vegas MSA, NV-AZ	Y	33430 FQ	54970 AW	82420 TQ	NVBLS	10/01-12/01
	Reno MSA, NV	Y	37350 FQ	56650 AW	86310 TQ	NVBLS	10/01-12/01
	New Hampshire	Y	32360 FQ	51750 AW	75350 TQ	NHBLS	10/01-12/01
	Manchester PMSA, NH	Y	40010 FQ	63660 AW	94810 TQ	NHBLS	10/01-12/01
	Nashua PMSA, NH	Y	35800 FQ	55010 AW	75620 TQ	NHBLS	10/01-12/01
	Portsmouth-Rochester PMSA, NH-ME	Y	31160 FQ	43730 AW	67280 TQ	NHBLS	10/01-12/01
	New Jersey	Y	42200 FQ	69040 AW	104180 TQ	NJBLS	10/01-12/01
	Atlantic-Cape May PMSA, NJ	Y	38740 FQ	58780 AW	84540 TQ	NJBLS	10/01-12/01
	Bergen-Passaic PMSA, NJ	Y	39930 FQ	61380 AW	89190 TQ	NJBLS	10/01-12/01
	Jersey City PMSA, NJ	Y	46940 FQ	74330 AW	107410 TQ	NJBLS	10/01-12/01
	Middlesex-Somerset-Hunterdon PMSA, NJ	Y	46920 FQ	75560 AW	111490 TQ	NJBLS	10/01-12/01
	Monmouth-Ocean PMSA, NJ	Y	37910 FQ	65170 AW	95850 TQ	NJBLS	10/01-12/01
	Newark PMSA, NJ	Y	45960 FQ	73830 AW	111750 TQ	NJBLS	10/01-12/01
	Trenton PMSA, NJ	Y	40910 FQ	63800 AW	87850 TQ	NJBLS	10/01-12/01
	New Mexico	Y	32690 FQ	56140 AW	87040 TQ	NMBLS	10/01-12/01

AAW	Average annual wage	**AOH**	Average offered, high	**ASH**	Average starting, high	**H**	Hourly	**M**	Monthly	**S**	Special: hourly and annual
AE	Average entry wage	**AOL**	Average offered, low	**ASL**	Average starting, low	**HI**	Highest wage paid	**MTC**	Median total compensation	**TQ**	Third quartile wage
AEX	Average experienced wage	**APH**	Average pay, high range	**AW**	Average wage paid	**HR**	High end range	**MW**	Median wage paid	**W**	Weekly
AO	Average offered	**APL**	Average pay, low range	**FQ**	First quartile wage	**LR**	Low end range	**SQ**	Second quartile wage	**Y**	Yearly

Occupation/Type/Industry	Location	Per	Low	Mid	High	Source	Date
Computer Programmer	Albuquerque MSA, NM	Y	36010 FQ	58190 AW	88150 TQ	NMBLS	10/01-12/01
	Las Cruces MSA, NM	Y	28670 FQ	43950 AW	58380 TQ	NMBLS	10/01-12/01
	New York	Y	38430 FQ	67720 AW	105060 TQ	NYBLS	10/01-12/01
	Albany-Schenectady-Troy MSA, NY	Y	37250 FQ	54830 AW	73590 TQ	NYBLS	10/01-12/01
	Buffalo-Niagara Falls MSA, NY	Y	27820 FQ	50960 AW	79880 TQ	NYBLS	10/01-12/01
	Nassau-Suffolk PMSA, NY	Y	38470 FQ	64590 AW	89570 TQ	NYBLS	10/01-12/01
	New York PMSA, NY	Y	44650 FQ	73080 AW	110320 TQ	NYBLS	10/01-12/01
	Rochester MSA, NY	Y	37900 FQ	57940 AW	80670 TQ	NYBLS	10/01-12/01
	Syracuse MSA, NY	Y	30490 FQ	50290 AW	73470 TQ	NYBLS	10/01-12/01
	Utica-Rome MSA, NY	Y	28940 FQ	46800 AW	67780 TQ	NYBLS	10/01-12/01
	North Carolina	Y	38520 FQ	65560 AW	100780 TQ	NCBLS	10/01-12/01
	Asheville MSA, NC	Y	33590 FQ	51870 AW	81210 TQ	NCBLS	10/01-12/01
	Charlotte-Gastonia-Rock Hill MSA, NC-SC	Y	39810 FQ	66110 AW	96280 TQ	NCBLS	10/01-12/01
	Fayetteville MSA, NC	Y	30140 FQ	48630 AW	71400 TQ	NCBLS	10/01-12/01
	Greensboro-Winston-Salem-High Point MSA, NC	Y	35540 FQ	57470 AW	86480 TQ	NCBLS	10/01-12/01
	Hickory-Morganton-Lenoir MSA, NC	Y	30200 FQ	51110 AW	78510 TQ	NCBLS	10/01-12/01
	Raleigh-Durham-Chapel Hill MSA, NC	Y	41880 FQ	70790 AW	110260 TQ	NCBLS	10/01-12/01
	Wilmington MSA, NC	Y	39830 FQ	63380 AW	92490 TQ	NCBLS	10/01-12/01
	North Dakota	Y	25860 FQ	42420 AW	56460 TQ	NDBLS	10/01-12/01
	Fargo-Moorhead MSA, ND-MN	Y	24430 FQ	38530 AW	54820 TQ	NDBLS	10/01-12/01
	Ohio	Y	34740 FQ	57600 AW	85530 TQ	OHBLS	10/01-12/01
	Akron PMSA, OH	Y	34760 FQ	62180 AW	105020 TQ	OHBLS	10/01-12/01
	Canton-Massillon MSA, OH	Y	27780 FQ	48580 AW	72970 TQ	OHBLS	10/01-12/01
	Cincinnati PMSA, OH-KY-IN	Y	33650 FQ	55010 AW	76860 TQ	OHBLS	10/01-12/01
	Cleveland-Lorain-Elyria PMSA, OH	Y	38300 FQ	60650 AW	89180 TQ	OHBLS	10/01-12/01
	Columbus MSA, OH	Y	38550 FQ	59670 AW	84620 TQ	OHBLS	10/01-12/01
	Dayton-Springfield MSA, OH	Y	34770 FQ	53660 AW	76750 TQ	OHBLS	10/01-12/01
	Hamilton-Middletown PMSA, OH	Y	36310 FQ	65910 AW	108190 TQ	OHBLS	10/01-12/01
	Mansfield MSA, OH	Y	31810 FQ	49590 AW	72440 TQ	OHBLS	10/01-12/01
	Toledo MSA, OH	Y	30960 FQ	49230 AW	70550 TQ	OHBLS	10/01-12/01
	Youngstown-Warren MSA, OH	Y	23540 FQ	49290 AW	74310 TQ	OHBLS	10/01-12/01
	Oklahoma	Y	27510 FQ	50760 AW	80420 TQ	OKBLS	10/01-12/01
	Oklahoma City MSA, OK	Y	22090 FQ	47480 AW	73860 TQ	OKBLS	10/01-12/01
	Tulsa MSA, OK	Y	33920 FQ	59980 AW	90540 TQ	OKBLS	10/01-12/01
	Oregon	Y	15580 FQ	47920 AW	79270 TQ	ORBLS	10/01-12/01
	Eugene-Springfield MSA, OR	Y	31140 FQ	50290 AW	73800 TQ	ORBLS	10/01-12/01
	Medford-Ashland MSA, OR	Y	37230 FQ	51920 AW	68340 TQ	ORBLS	10/01-12/01
	Portland-Vancouver PMSA, OR-WA	Y	15300 FQ	47990 AW	81890 TQ	ORBLS	10/01-12/01
	Salem PMSA, OR	Y	33650 FQ	53790 AW	78640 TQ	ORBLS	10/01-12/01
	Pennsylvania	Y	30780 FQ	57310 AW	89220 TQ	PABLS	10/01-12/01
	Allentown-Bethlehem-Easton MSA, PA	Y	25980 FQ	52510 AW	76920 TQ	PABLS	10/01-12/01
	Erie MSA, PA	Y	27060 FQ	44980 AW	70840 TQ	PABLS	10/01-12/01
	Harrisburg-Lebanon-Carlisle MSA, PA	Y	35490 FQ	58500 AW	87470 TQ	PABLS	10/01-12/01
	Johnstown MSA, PA	Y	21610 FQ	40790 AW	65990 TQ	PABLS	10/01-12/01
	Lancaster MSA, PA	Y	26110 FQ	48280 AW	70750 TQ	PABLS	10/01-12/01
	Philadelphia PMSA, PA-NJ	Y	31800 FQ	60620 AW	92520 TQ	PABLS	10/01-12/01
	Pittsburgh MSA, PA	Y	34010 FQ	56530 AW	86990 TQ	PABLS	10/01-12/01
	Reading MSA, PA	Y	26810 FQ	51480 AW	78560 TQ	PABLS	10/01-12/01
	Scranton-Wilkes-Barre-Hazleton MSA, PA	Y	31020 FQ	49810 AW	72850 TQ	PABLS	10/01-12/01
	York MSA, PA	Y	31130 FQ	49960 AW	70040 TQ	PABLS	10/01-12/01
	Rhode Island	Y	36130 FQ	55490 AW	78900 TQ	RIBLS	10/01-12/01
	Providence-Fall River-Warwick MSA, RI-MA	Y	36020 FQ	55260 AW	79240 TQ	RIBLS	10/01-12/01
	South Carolina	Y	29720 FQ	51330 AW	81990 TQ	SCBLS	10/01-12/01
	Charleston-North Charleston MSA, SC	Y	28780 FQ	42060 AW	60390 TQ	SCBLS	10/01-12/01
	Columbia MSA, SC	Y	29840 FQ	51590 AW	78790 TQ	SCBLS	10/01-12/01
	Greenville-Spartanburg-Anderson MSA, SC	Y	31030 FQ	53720 AW	85910 TQ	SCBLS	10/01-12/01

AAW Average annual wage **AE** Average entry wage **AEX** Average experienced wage **AO** Average offered **AOH** Average offered, high **AOL** Average offered, low **APH** Average pay, high range **APL** Average pay, low range **ASH** Average starting, high **ASL** Average starting, low **AW** Average wage paid **FQ** First quartile wage **H** Hourly **HI** Highest wage paid **HR** High end range **LR** Low end range **M** Monthly **MTC** Median total compensation **MW** Median wage paid **SQ** Second quartile wage **S** Special: hourly and annual **TQ** Third quartile wage **W** Weekly **Y** Yearly

Occupation/Type/Industry	Location	Per	Low	Mid	High	Source	Date
Computer Programmer	Myrtle Beach MSA, SC	Y	29270 FQ	45280 AW	70510 TQ	SCBLS	10/01-12/01
	South Dakota	Y	29810 FQ	43260 AW	60570 TQ	SDBLS	10/01-12/01
	Sioux Falls MSA, SD	Y	31920 FQ	45500 AW	63000 TQ	SDBLS	10/01-12/01
	Tennessee	Y	30550 FQ	55020 AW	84180 TQ	TNBLS	10/01-12/01
	Chattanooga MSA, TN-GA	Y	22700 FQ	43250 AW	68330 TQ	TNBLS	10/01-12/01
	Clarksville-Hopkinsville MSA, TN-KY	Y	37560 FQ	56860 AW	83640 TQ	TNBLS	10/01-12/01
	Johnson City-Kingsport-Bristol MSA, TN-VA	Y	21650 FQ	37330 AW	61980 TQ	TNBLS	10/01-12/01
	Knoxville MSA, TN	Y	30250 FQ	50990 AW	77670 TQ	TNBLS	10/01-12/01
	Memphis MSA, TN-AR-MS	Y	37980 FQ	59300 AW	86160 TQ	TNBLS	10/01-12/01
	Nashville MSA, TN	Y	34360 FQ	57890 AW	85040 TQ	TNBLS	10/01-12/01
	Texas	Y	38570 FQ	70860 AW	113560 TQ	TXBLS	10/01-12/01
	Amarillo MSA, TX	Y	29880 FQ	51350 AW	75570 TQ	TXBLS	10/01-12/01
	Austin-San Marcos MSA, TX	Y	40570 FQ	69400 AW	107630 TQ	TXBLS	10/01-12/01
	Beaumont-Port Arthur MSA, TX	Y	25830 FQ	50980 AW	82540 TQ	TXBLS	10/01-12/01
	Brazoria PMSA, TX	Y	36140 FQ	58510 AW	77310 TQ	TXBLS	10/01-12/01
	Brownsville-Harlingen-San Benito MSA, TX	Y	14260 FQ	37420 AW	68730 TQ	TXBLS	10/01-12/01
	Corpus Christi MSA, TX	Y	31010 FQ	55980 AW	90690 TQ	TXBLS	10/01-12/01
	Dallas PMSA, TX	Y	44920 FQ	76020 AW	111600 TQ	TXBLS	10/01-12/01
	El Paso MSA, TX	Y	29020 FQ	74290 AW	140270 TQ	TXBLS	10/01-12/01
	Fort Worth-Arlington PMSA, TX	Y	15960 FQ	60470 AW	112190 TQ	TXBLS	10/01-12/01
	Galveston-Texas City PMSA, TX	Y	13010 FQ	45150 AW	74210 TQ	TXBLS	10/01-12/01
	Houston PMSA, TX	Y	40510 FQ	76370 AW	141050 TQ	TXBLS	10/01-12/01
	Killeen-Temple MSA, TX	Y	26970 FQ	49450 AW	73430 TQ	TXBLS	10/01-12/01
	Laredo MSA, TX	Y	25080 FQ	45820 AW	81370 TQ	TXBLS	10/01-12/01
	Longview-Marshall MSA, TX	Y	30150 FQ	44220 AW	57090 TQ	TXBLS	10/01-12/01
	Lubbock MSA, TX	Y	19670 FQ	45500 AW	73000 TQ	TXBLS	10/01-12/01
	McAllen-Edinburg-Mission MSA, TX	Y	26940 FQ	45570 AW	61150 TQ	TXBLS	10/01-12/01
	Odessa-Midland MSA, TX	Y	31710 FQ	55330 AW	93330 TQ	TXBLS	10/01-12/01
	San Antonio MSA, TX	Y	28660 FQ	48550 AW	74460 TQ	TXBLS	10/01-12/01
	Tyler MSA, TX	Y	16990 FQ	40890 AW	66130 TQ	TXBLS	10/01-12/01
	Waco MSA, TX	Y	26460 FQ	45430 AW	66880 TQ	TXBLS	10/01-12/01
	Utah	Y	34030 FQ	57740 AW	87990 TQ	UTBLS	10/01-12/01
	Provo-Orem MSA, UT	Y	31930 FQ	52920 AW	84400 TQ	UTBLS	10/01-12/01
	Salt Lake City-Ogden MSA, UT	Y	37830 FQ	60040 AW	89400 TQ	UTBLS	10/01-12/01
	Vermont	Y	31700 FQ	53950 AW	83480 TQ	VTBLS	10/01-12/01
	Burlington MSA, VT	Y	32770 FQ	58730 AW	89170 TQ	VTBLS	10/01-12/01
	Virginia	Y	37650 FQ	61400 AW	89400 TQ	VABLS	10/01-12/01
	Lynchburg MSA, VA	Y	31590 FQ	54890 AW	83870 TQ	VABLS	10/01-12/01
	Norfolk-Virginia Beach-Newport News MSA, VA-NC	Y	35960 FQ	51610 AW	69000 TQ	VABLS	10/01-12/01
	Richmond-Petersburg MSA, VA	Y	37100 FQ	57700 AW	89840 TQ	VABLS	10/01-12/01
	Roanoke MSA, VA	Y	31210 FQ	51060 AW	74230 TQ	VABLS	10/01-12/01
	Washington	Y	43600 FQ	70740 AW	104760 TQ	WABLS	10/01-12/01
	Bremerton PMSA, WA	Y	45060 FQ	68220 AW	95410 TQ	WABLS	10/01-12/01
	Olympia PMSA, WA	Y	39100 FQ	55630 AW	70540 TQ	WABLS	10/01-12/01
	Richland-Kennewick-Pasco MSA, WA	Y	27780 FQ	55420 AW	83530 TQ	WABLS	10/01-12/01
	Seattle-Bellevue-Everett PMSA, WA	Y	47140 FQ	75180 AW	109730 TQ	WABLS	10/01-12/01
	Spokane MSA, WA	Y	34410 FQ	51030 AW	70080 TQ	WABLS	10/01-12/01
	Tacoma PMSA, WA	Y	39470 FQ	59310 AW	97210 TQ	WABLS	10/01-12/01
	Yakima MSA, WA	Y	30590 FQ	43560 AW	64260 TQ	WABLS	10/01-12/01
	West Virginia	Y	28090 FQ	45320 AW	70220 TQ	WVBLS	10/01-12/01
	Charleston MSA, WV	Y	28830 FQ	46420 AW	69540 TQ	WVBLS	10/01-12/01
	Huntington-Ashland MSA, WV-KY-OH	Y	19380 FQ	38070 AW	65330 TQ	WVBLS	10/01-12/01
	Wisconsin	Y	33190 FQ	53740 AW	77500 TQ	WIBLS	10/01-12/01
	Appleton-Oshkosh-Neenah MSA, WI	Y	37940 FQ	54850 AW	77000 TQ	WIBLS	10/01-12/01
	Green Bay MSA, WI	Y	23210 FQ	49420 AW	74410 TQ	WIBLS	10/01-12/01
	Madison MSA, WI	Y	37780 FQ	58420 AW	87010 TQ	WIBLS	10/01-12/01

AAW Average annual wage; **AE** Average entry wage; **AEX** Average experienced wage; **AO** Average offered; **AOH** Average offered, high; **AOL** Average offered, low; **APH** Average pay, high range; **APL** Average pay, low range; **ASH** Average starting, high; **ASL** Average starting, low; **AW** Average wage paid; **FQ** First quartile wage; **H** Hourly; **HI** Highest wage paid; **HR** High end range; **LR** Low end range; **M** Monthly; **MTC** Median total compensation; **MW** Median wage paid; **SQ** Second quartile wage; **S** Special: hourly and annual; **TQ** Third quartile wage; **W** Weekly; **Y** Yearly

Occupation/Type/Industry	Location	Per	Low	Mid	High	Source	Date
Computer Programmer	Milwaukee-Waukesha PMSA, WI	Y	32220 FQ	54670 AW	77990 TQ	WIBLS	10/01-12/01
	Racine PMSA, WI	Y	30480 FQ	57000 AW	81670 TQ	WIBLS	10/01-12/01
	Wyoming	Y	21140 FQ	41620 AW	60800 TQ	WYBLS	10/01-12/01
	Cheyenne MSA, WY	Y	30370 FQ	43920 AW	56590 TQ	WYBLS	10/01-12/01
	Puerto Rico	Y	18210 FQ	32270 AW	50280 TQ	PRBLS	10/01-12/01
	Virgin Islands	Y	28270 FQ	40790 AW	55260 TQ	VIBLS	10/01-12/01
	Guam	Y	25280 FQ	41200 AW	55880 TQ	GUBLS	10/01-12/01
Computer Programmer I							
Private Sector	Florida	Y		52000 AW		TALL	1/01-1/02
Public Sector	Florida	Y		41000 AW		TALL	1/01-1/02
State Government	Florida	Y		38000 AW		TALL	1/01-1/02
Computer Science Teacher							
Postsecondary	Alabama	Y	18290 FQ	49160 AW	81370 TQ	ALBLS	10/01-12/01
Postsecondary	Huntsville MSA, AL	Y	27520 FQ	55150 AW	85480 TQ	ALBLS	10/01-12/01
Postsecondary	Montgomery MSA, AL	Y	38560 FQ	54480 AW	71180 TQ	ALBLS	10/01-12/01
Postsecondary	Alaska	Y	32210 FQ	53890 AW	81980 TQ	AKBLS	10/01-12/01
Postsecondary	Arizona	Y	24880 FQ	42860 AW	68560 TQ	AZBLS	10/01-12/01
Postsecondary	Arkansas	Y	20140 FQ	44100 AW	81200 TQ	ARBLS	10/01-12/01
Postsecondary	California	Y	33620 FQ	63570 AW	101340 TQ	CABLS	10/01-12/01
Postsecondary	Los Angeles-Long Beach PMSA, CA	Y	37540 FQ	68470 AW	104290 TQ	CABLS	10/01-12/01
Postsecondary	Orange County PMSA, CA	Y	31400 FQ	57570 AW	89590 TQ	CABLS	10/01-12/01
Postsecondary	Riverside-San Bernardino PMSA, CA	Y	33830 FQ	59550 AW	101740 TQ	CABLS	10/01-12/01
Postsecondary	San Francisco PMSA, CA	Y	31850 FQ	62310 AW	101340 TQ	CABLS	10/01-12/01
Postsecondary	San Jose PMSA, CA	Y	32570 FQ	61250 AW	93410 TQ	CABLS	10/01-12/01
Postsecondary	Santa Cruz-Watsonville PMSA, CA	Y	34680 FQ	59180 AW	92470 TQ	CABLS	10/01-12/01
Postsecondary	Colorado	Y	29090 FQ	49260 AW	86920 TQ	COBLS	10/01-12/01
Postsecondary	Denver PMSA, CO	Y	28730 FQ	45700 AW	79450 TQ	COBLS	10/01-12/01
Postsecondary	Connecticut	Y	27740 FQ	64990 AW	132600 TQ	CTBLS	10/01-12/01
Postsecondary	Bridgeport PMSA, CT	Y	24680 FQ	57580 AW	86010 TQ	CTBLS	10/01-12/01
Postsecondary	Hartford MSA, CT	Y	34570 FQ	83580 AW		CTBLS	10/01-12/01
Postsecondary	Delaware	Y	39480 FQ	62670 AW	96070 TQ	DEBLS	10/01-12/01
Postsecondary	Wilmington-Newark PMSA, DE-MD	Y	38090 FQ	63890 AW	97760 TQ	DEBLS	10/01-12/01
Postsecondary	District of Columbia	Y	32590 FQ	56470 AW	85070 TQ	DCBLS	10/01-12/01
Postsecondary	Washington PMSA, DC-MD-VA-WV	Y	23680 FQ	47370 AW	81280 TQ	DCBLS	10/01-12/01
Postsecondary	Florida	Y	29080 FQ	62050 AW	103920 TQ	FLBLS	10/01-12/01
Postsecondary	Fort Lauderdale PMSA, FL	Y	26100 FQ	46630 AW	82870 TQ	FLBLS	10/01-12/01
Postsecondary	Gainesville MSA, FL	Y	44830 FQ	77070 AW	115320 TQ	FLBLS	10/01-12/01
Postsecondary	Jacksonville MSA, FL	Y	33470 FQ	62460 AW	96170 TQ	FLBLS	10/01-12/01
Postsecondary	Melbourne-Titusville-Palm Bay MSA, FL	Y	30440 FQ	67890 AW	116070 TQ	FLBLS	10/01-12/01
Postsecondary	Miami PMSA, FL	Y	40890 FQ	72440 AW	115080 TQ	FLBLS	10/01-12/01
Postsecondary	Orlando MSA, FL	Y	25530 FQ	59740 AW	104440 TQ	FLBLS	10/01-12/01
Postsecondary	Pensacola MSA, FL	Y	33450 FQ	61550 AW	101590 TQ	FLBLS	10/01-12/01
Postsecondary	Tallahassee MSA, FL	Y	50840 FQ	74990 AW	107030 TQ	FLBLS	10/01-12/01
Postsecondary	Tampa-St. Petersburg-Clearwater MSA, FL	Y	31930 FQ	55980 AW	93400 TQ	FLBLS	10/01-12/01
Postsecondary	West Palm Beach-Boca Raton MSA, FL	Y	27980 FQ	64290 AW	110630 TQ	FLBLS	10/01-12/01
Postsecondary	Georgia	Y	33360 FQ	59400 AW	94970 TQ	GABLS	10/01-12/01
Postsecondary	Atlanta MSA, GA	Y	33770 FQ	65600 AW	115300 TQ	GABLS	10/01-12/01
Postsecondary	Savannah MSA, GA	Y	15130 FQ	49530 AW	78080 TQ	GABLS	10/01-12/01
Postsecondary	Hawaii	Y	27030 FQ	53920 AW	85990 TQ	HIBLS	10/01-12/01
Postsecondary	Honolulu MSA, HI	Y	26270 FQ	54390 AW	87670 TQ	HIBLS	10/01-12/01
Postsecondary	Illinois	Y	22380 FQ	51010 AW	91480 TQ	ILBLS	10/01-12/01
Postsecondary	Champaign-Urbana MSA, IL	Y	15190 FQ	56130 AW	93530 TQ	ILBLS	10/01-12/01
Postsecondary	Chicago PMSA, IL	Y	23810 FQ	53320 AW	93500 TQ	ILBLS	10/01-12/01
Postsecondary	Rockford MSA, IL	Y	11850 FQ	31960 AW	60470 TQ	ILBLS	10/01-12/01
Postsecondary	Indiana	Y	21160 FQ	46960 AW	83560 TQ	INBLS	10/01-12/01
Postsecondary	South Bend MSA, IN	Y	20710 FQ	36000 AW	60320 TQ	INBLS	10/01-12/01
Postsecondary	Iowa	Y	32960 FQ	53980 AW	83860 TQ	IABLS	10/01-12/01
Postsecondary	Davenport-Moline-Rock Island MSA, IA-IL	Y	31800 FQ	49970 AW	73520 TQ	IABLS	10/01-12/01
Postsecondary	Des Moines MSA, IA	Y	30720 FQ	47700 AW	69440 TQ	IABLS	10/01-12/01
Postsecondary	Kansas	Y	21000 FQ	43570 AW	81490 TQ	KSBLS	10/01-12/01
Postsecondary	Kentucky	Y	24400 FQ	53400 AW	91540 TQ	KYBLS	10/01-12/01

AAW Average annual wage; AE Average entry wage; AEX Average experienced wage; AO Average offered; AOH Average offered, high; AOL Average offered, low; APH Average pay, high range; APL Average pay, low range; ASH Average starting, high; ASL Average starting, low; AW Average wage paid; FQ First quartile wage; H Hourly; HI Highest wage paid; HR High end range; LR Low end range; M Monthly; MTC Median total compensation; MW Median wage paid; SQ Second quartile wage; S Special: hourly and annual; TQ Third quartile wage; W Weekly; Y Yearly

Occupation/Type/Industry	Location	Per	Low	Mid	High	Source	Date
Computer Science Teacher							
Postsecondary	Lexington MSA, KY	Y	33950 FQ	61250 AW	88800 TQ	KYBLS	10/01-12/01
Postsecondary	Louisville MSA, KY-IN	Y	22220 FQ	57860 AW	101320 TQ	KYBLS	10/01-12/01
Postsecondary	Louisiana	Y	29500 FQ	50970 AW	75700 TQ	LABLS	10/01-12/01
Postsecondary	New Orleans MSA, LA	Y	13120 FQ	46540 AW	71680 TQ	LABLS	10/01-12/01
Postsecondary	Maine	Y	30420 FQ	47090 AW	68460 TQ	MEBLS	10/01-12/01
Postsecondary	Maryland	Y	38740 FQ	63320 AW	103660 TQ	MDBLS	10/01-12/01
Postsecondary	Baltimore PMSA, MD	Y	38850 FQ	62880 AW	92900 TQ	MDBLS	10/01-12/01
Postsecondary	Massachusetts	Y	32720 FQ	58980 AW	92480 TQ	MABLS	10/01-12/01
Postsecondary	Boston PMSA, MA-NH	Y	31790 FQ	60850 AW	95410 TQ	MABLS	10/01-12/01
Postsecondary	Brockton PMSA, MA	Y	32010 FQ	50680 AW	74480 TQ	MABLS	10/01-12/01
Postsecondary	Springfield MSA, MA	Y	40140 FQ	62620 AW	90830 TQ	MABLS	10/01-12/01
Postsecondary	Michigan	Y	27900 FQ	54670 AW	88280 TQ	MIBLS	10/01-12/01
Postsecondary	Ann Arbor PMSA, MI	Y	28580 FQ	48540 AW	77660 TQ	MIBLS	10/01-12/01
Postsecondary	Detroit PMSA, MI	Y	25020 FQ	47670 AW	83030 TQ	MIBLS	10/01-12/01
Postsecondary	Grand Rapids-Muskegon-Holland MSA, MI	Y	31340 FQ	59000 AW	89930 TQ	MIBLS	10/01-12/01
Postsecondary	Kalamazoo-Battle Creek MSA, MI	Y	31830 FQ	62570 AW	97120 TQ	MIBLS	10/01-12/01
Postsecondary	Minnesota	Y	35890 FQ	56970 AW	83040 TQ	MNBLS	10/01-12/01
Postsecondary	Duluth-Superior MSA, MN-WI	Y	47340 FQ	56310 AW	71420 TQ	MNBLS	10/01-12/01
Postsecondary	Minneapolis-St. Paul MSA, MN-WI	Y	38100 FQ	58400 AW	86440 TQ	MNBLS	10/01-12/01
Postsecondary	St. Cloud MSA, MN	Y	33470 FQ	47260 AW	58580 TQ	MNBLS	10/01-12/01
Postsecondary	Mississippi	Y	30110 FQ	51300 AW	74910 TQ	MSBLS	10/01-12/01
Postsecondary	Jackson MSA, MS	Y	30950 FQ	47030 AW	69380 TQ	MSBLS	10/01-12/01
Postsecondary	Missouri	Y	22200 FQ	45420 AW	71810 TQ	MOBLS	10/01-12/01
Postsecondary	Kansas City MSA, MO-KS	Y	19610 FQ	38810 AW	65390 TQ	MOBLS	10/01-12/01
Postsecondary	St. Louis MSA, MO-IL	Y	24200 FQ	43470 AW	69600 TQ	MOBLS	10/01-12/01
Postsecondary	Springfield MSA, MO	Y	35980 FQ	62370 AW	90400 TQ	MOBLS	10/01-12/01
Postsecondary	Montana	Y	16770 FQ	44150 AW	80440 TQ	MTBLS	10/01-12/01
Postsecondary	Nebraska	Y	30600 FQ	54460 AW	89610 TQ	NEBLS	10/01-12/01
Postsecondary	Omaha MSA, NE-IA	Y	34310 FQ	59560 AW	92260 TQ	NEBLS	10/01-12/01
Postsecondary	Nevada	Y	21360 FQ	45460 AW	78950 TQ	NVBLS	10/01-12/01
Postsecondary	Las Vegas MSA, NV-AZ	Y	20810 FQ	40010 AW	76300 TQ	NVBLS	10/01-12/01
Postsecondary	New Hampshire	Y	30460 FQ	55630 AW	89810 TQ	NHBLS	10/01-12/01
Postsecondary	Manchester PMSA, NH	Y	26580 FQ	40370 AW	59920 TQ	NHBLS	10/01-12/01
Postsecondary	New Jersey	Y	33410 FQ	61870 AW	96850 TQ	NJBLS	10/01-12/01
Postsecondary	Bergen-Passaic PMSA, NJ	Y	36140 FQ	57510 AW	87300 TQ	NJBLS	10/01-12/01
Postsecondary	Jersey City PMSA, NJ	Y	33670 FQ	68240 AW	113110 TQ	NJBLS	10/01-12/01
Postsecondary	Middlesex-Somerset-Hunterdon PMSA, NJ	Y	38550 FQ	71400 AW	114440 TQ	NJBLS	10/01-12/01
Postsecondary	Monmouth-Ocean PMSA, NJ	Y	39060 FQ	59480 AW	88610 TQ	NJBLS	10/01-12/01
Postsecondary	Newark PMSA, NJ	Y	22490 FQ	58460 AW	93120 TQ	NJBLS	10/01-12/01
Postsecondary	New Mexico	Y	28760 FQ	46560 AW	68270 TQ	NMBLS	10/01-12/01
Postsecondary	New York	Y	35370 FQ	65280 AW	107370 TQ	NYBLS	10/01-12/01
Postsecondary	Dutchess County PMSA, NY	Y	35010 FQ	59880 AW	94840 TQ	NYBLS	10/01-12/01
Postsecondary	Nassau-Suffolk PMSA, NY	Y	41590 FQ	65980 AW	104060 TQ	NYBLS	10/01-12/01
Postsecondary	New York PMSA, NY	Y	39880 FQ	67960 AW	109080 TQ	NYBLS	10/01-12/01
Postsecondary	Utica-Rome MSA, NY	Y	31530 FQ	50860 AW	76950 TQ	NYBLS	10/01-12/01
Postsecondary	North Carolina	Y	31040 FQ	48110 AW	70950 TQ	NCBLS	10/01-12/01
Postsecondary	Asheville MSA, NC	Y	41900 FQ	54380 AW	68820 TQ	NCBLS	10/01-12/01
Postsecondary	Charlotte-Gastonia-Rock Hill MSA, NC-SC	Y	36720 FQ	53780 AW	73280 TQ	NCBLS	10/01-12/01
Postsecondary	Fayetteville MSA, NC	Y	32390 FQ	53630 AW	89950 TQ	NCBLS	10/01-12/01
Postsecondary	Greensboro-Winston-Salem-High Point MSA, NC	Y	31940 FQ	46420 AW	64150 TQ	NCBLS	10/01-12/01
Postsecondary	Hickory-Morganton-Lenoir MSA, NC	Y	30510 FQ	35830 AW	43720 TQ	NCBLS	10/01-12/01
Postsecondary	Raleigh-Durham-Chapel Hill MSA, NC	Y	34230 FQ	50960 AW	80640 TQ	NCBLS	10/01-12/01
Postsecondary	Wilmington MSA, NC	Y	33450 FQ	66320 AW	105650 TQ	NCBLS	10/01-12/01
Postsecondary	North Dakota	Y	20370 FQ	40570 AW	67090 TQ	NDBLS	10/01-12/01
Postsecondary	Ohio	Y	22460 FQ	48780 AW	83490 TQ	OHBLS	10/01-12/01
Postsecondary	Akron PMSA, OH	Y	30140 FQ	46880 AW	78990 TQ	OHBLS	10/01-12/01
Postsecondary	Cincinnati PMSA, OH-KY-IN	Y	30380 FQ	63550 AW	95780 TQ	OHBLS	10/01-12/01
Postsecondary	Cleveland-Lorain-Elyria PMSA, OH	Y	25490 FQ	51640 AW	82630 TQ	OHBLS	10/01-12/01
Postsecondary	Columbus MSA, OH	Y	27310 FQ	48100 AW	71320 TQ	OHBLS	10/01-12/01
Postsecondary	Dayton-Springfield MSA, OH	Y	17010 FQ	42460 AW	80780 TQ	OHBLS	10/01-12/01
Postsecondary	Toledo MSA, OH	Y	28540 FQ	60350 AW	97280 TQ	OHBLS	10/01-12/01
Postsecondary	Oklahoma	Y	26840 FQ	42670 AW	68020 TQ	OKBLS	10/01-12/01

AAW	Average annual wage	**AOH**	Average offered, high	**ASH**	Average starting, high	**H**	Hourly	**M**	Monthly	**S**	Special: hourly and annual
AE	Average entry wage	**AOL**	Average offered, low	**ASL**	Average starting, low	**HI**	Highest wage paid	**MTC**	Median total compensation	**TQ**	Third quartile wage
AEX	Average experienced wage	**APH**	Average pay, high range	**AW**	Average wage paid	**HR**	High end range	**MW**	Median wage paid	**W**	Weekly
AO	Average offered	**APL**	Average pay, low range	**FQ**	First quartile wage	**LR**	Low end range	**SQ**	Second quartile wage	**Y**	Yearly

Occupation/Type/Industry	Location	Per	Low	Mid	High	Source	Date
Computer Science Teacher							
Postsecondary	Oklahoma City MSA, OK	Y	24500 FQ	40420 AW	72000 TQ	OKBLS	10/01-12/01
Postsecondary	Tulsa MSA, OK	Y	32050 FQ	50360 AW	86810 TQ	OKBLS	10/01-12/01
Postsecondary	Oregon	Y	33160 FQ	66960 AW	116910 TQ	ORBLS	10/01-12/01
Postsecondary	Portland-Vancouver PMSA, OR-WA	Y	33360 FQ	63810 AW	112080 TQ	ORBLS	10/01-12/01
Postsecondary	Pennsylvania	Y	27060 FQ	60780 AW	104270 TQ	PABLS	10/01-12/01
Postsecondary	Allentown-Bethlehem-Easton MSA, PA	Y	28150 FQ	49860 AW	82980 TQ	PABLS	10/01-12/01
Postsecondary	Philadelphia PMSA, PA-NJ	Y	30210 FQ	62330 AW	98930 TQ	PABLS	10/01-12/01
Postsecondary	Pittsburgh MSA, PA	Y	24910 FQ	56560 AW	105150 TQ	PABLS	10/01-12/01
Postsecondary	Scranton-Wilkes-Barre-Hazleton MSA, PA	Y	25910 FQ	47650 AW	72790 TQ	PABLS	10/01-12/01
Postsecondary	Rhode Island	Y	30030 FQ	58690 AW	95210 TQ	RIBLS	10/01-12/01
Postsecondary	South Carolina	Y	26850 FQ	46200 AW	66300 TQ	SCBLS	10/01-12/01
Postsecondary	Charleston-North Charleston MSA, SC	Y	31050 FQ	48370 AW	67590 TQ	SCBLS	10/01-12/01
Postsecondary	Columbia MSA, SC	Y	25350 FQ	43240 AW	63990 TQ	SCBLS	10/01-12/01
Postsecondary	Greenville-Spartanburg-Anderson MSA, SC	Y	25650 FQ	46330 AW	68740 TQ	SCBLS	10/01-12/01
Postsecondary	South Dakota	Y	27570 FQ	45800 AW	65300 TQ	SDBLS	10/01-12/01
Postsecondary	Sioux Falls MSA, SD	Y	24650 FQ	40210 AW	58400 TQ	SDBLS	10/01-12/01
Postsecondary	Tennessee	Y	21700 FQ	46820 AW	73230 TQ	TNBLS	10/01-12/01
Postsecondary	Chattanooga MSA, TN-GA	Y	20640 FQ	38220 AW	53950 TQ	TNBLS	10/01-12/01
Postsecondary	Clarksville-Hopkinsville MSA, TN-KY	Y	22770 FQ	43360 AW	71990 TQ	TNBLS	10/01-12/01
Postsecondary	Johnson City-Kingsport-Bristol MSA, TN-VA	Y	21000 FQ	40170 AW	72090 TQ	TNBLS	10/01-12/01
Postsecondary	Knoxville MSA, TN	Y	33400 FQ	61600 AW	92190 TQ	TNBLS	10/01-12/01
Postsecondary	Memphis MSA, TN-AR-MS	Y	29620 FQ	46980 AW	72250 TQ	TNBLS	10/01-12/01
Postsecondary	Nashville MSA, TN	Y	32610 FQ	53350 AW	74450 TQ	TNBLS	10/01-12/01
Postsecondary	Texas	Y	27940 FQ	50420 AW	73630 TQ	TXBLS	10/01-12/01
Postsecondary	Austin-San Marcos MSA, TX	Y	35280 FQ	54830 AW	71750 TQ	TXBLS	10/01-12/01
Postsecondary	Dallas PMSA, TX	Y	29930 FQ	54060 AW	76840 TQ	TXBLS	10/01-12/01
Postsecondary	El Paso MSA, TX	Y	27360 FQ	53860 AW	81890 TQ	TXBLS	10/01-12/01
Postsecondary	Fort Worth-Arlington PMSA, TX	Y	20070 FQ	49370 AW	73860 TQ	TXBLS	10/01-12/01
Postsecondary	Houston PMSA, TX	Y	25940 FQ	48460 AW	75730 TQ	TXBLS	10/01-12/01
Postsecondary	Killeen-Temple MSA, TX	Y	30660 FQ	46870 AW	67400 TQ	TXBLS	10/01-12/01
Postsecondary	McAllen-Edinburg-Mission MSA, TX	Y	28160 FQ	51930 AW	70730 TQ	TXBLS	10/01-12/01
Postsecondary	Odessa-Midland MSA, TX	Y	30980 FQ	48200 AW	69980 TQ	TXBLS	10/01-12/01
Postsecondary	San Antonio MSA, TX	Y	28750 FQ	54280 AW	84920 TQ	TXBLS	10/01-12/01
Postsecondary	Tyler MSA, TX	Y	29870 FQ	43120 AW	68880 TQ	TXBLS	10/01-12/01
Postsecondary	Utah	Y	36020 FQ	71940 AW	137010 TQ	UTBLS	10/01-12/01
Postsecondary	Salt Lake City-Ogden MSA, UT	Y	36160 FQ	79160 AW		UTBLS	10/01-12/01
Postsecondary	Vermont	Y	33470 FQ	47590 AW	59310 TQ	VTBLS	10/01-12/01
Postsecondary	Virginia	Y	23250 FQ	46490 AW	86340 TQ	VABLS	10/01-12/01
Postsecondary	Norfolk-Virginia Beach-Newport News MSA, VA-NC	Y	37370 FQ	63100 AW	94480 TQ	VABLS	10/01-12/01
Postsecondary	Richmond-Petersburg MSA, VA	Y	18510 FQ	40590 AW	81090 TQ	VABLS	10/01-12/01
Postsecondary	Roanoke MSA, VA	Y	29140 FQ	58280 AW	91380 TQ	VABLS	10/01-12/01
Postsecondary	Washington	Y	24370 FQ	53420 AW	108850 TQ	WABLS	10/01-12/01
Postsecondary	Seattle-Bellevue-Everett PMSA, WA	Y	27150 FQ	59050 AW	120620 TQ	WABLS	10/01-12/01
Postsecondary	Spokane MSA, WA	Y	23070 FQ	40790 AW	67100 TQ	WABLS	10/01-12/01
Postsecondary	West Virginia	Y	27580 FQ	51000 AW	81010 TQ	WVBLS	10/01-12/01
Postsecondary	Wisconsin	Y	25630 FQ	51970 AW	86780 TQ	WIBLS	10/01-12/01
Postsecondary	Appleton-Oshkosh-Neenah MSA, WI	Y	30070 FQ	54890 AW	89480 TQ	WIBLS	10/01-12/01
Postsecondary	Milwaukee-Waukesha PMSA, WI	Y	21090 FQ	47000 AW	75520 TQ	WIBLS	10/01-12/01
Postsecondary	Wyoming	Y	27250 FQ	54400 AW	89680 TQ	WYBLS	10/01-12/01
Postsecondary	Puerto Rico	Y	20360 FQ	31220 AW	44130 TQ	PRBLS	10/01-12/01
Computer Scientist	United States	Y	52259 AE			TIME	1/00-1/01
	United States	Y		49596 AW		RTM	1/01-1/02
Computer Software Engineer							
Applications	United States	Y		39700 AW		FREEP1	1/00-1/00

AAW	Average annual wage	**AOH**	Average offered, high	**ASH**	Average starting, high	**H**	Hourly	**M**	Monthly	**S**	Special: hourly and annual
AE	Average entry wage	**AOL**	Average offered, low	**ASL**	Average starting, low	**HI**	Highest wage paid	**MTC**	Median total compensation	**TQ**	Third quartile wage
AEX	Average experienced wage	**APH**	Average pay, high range	**AW**	Average wage paid	**HR**	High end range	**MW**	Median wage paid	**W**	Weekly
AO	Average offered	**APL**	Average pay, low range	**FQ**	First quartile wage	**LR**	Low end range	**SQ**	Second quartile wage	**Y**	Yearly

Occupation/Type/Industry	Location	Per	Low	Mid	High	Source	Date
Computer Software Engineer							
Applications	Alabama	Y	41140 FQ	65390 AW	91170 TQ	ALBLS	10/01-12/01
Applications	Birmingham MSA, AL	Y	45300 FQ	67600 AW	94290 TQ	ALBLS	10/01-12/01
Applications	Huntsville MSA, AL	Y	43060 FQ	66820 AW	91270 TQ	ALBLS	10/01-12/01
Applications	Mobile MSA, AL	Y	34450 FQ	53680 AW	80960 TQ	ALBLS	10/01-12/01
Applications	Montgomery MSA, AL	Y	40000 FQ	58410 AW	79160 TQ	ALBLS	10/01-12/01
Applications	Alaska	Y	46200 FQ	66270 AW	92630 TQ	AKBLS	10/01-12/01
Applications	Anchorage MSA, AK	Y	43880 FQ	61060 AW	82690 TQ	AKBLS	10/01-12/01
Applications	Arizona	Y	38960 FQ	82820 AW	141140 TQ	AZBLS	10/01-12/01
Applications	Phoenix-Mesa MSA, AZ	Y	40970 FQ	87520 AW	142230 TQ	AZBLS	10/01-12/01
Applications	Tucson MSA, AZ	Y	38180 FQ	64990 AW	95010 TQ	AZBLS	10/01-12/01
Applications	Arkansas	Y	25190 FQ	49300 AW	80880 TQ	ARBLS	10/01-12/01
Applications	Fort Smith MSA, AR-OK	Y	27810 FQ	50020 AW	74070 TQ	ARBLS	10/01-12/01
Applications	California	Y	50790 FQ	81450 AW	118440 TQ	CABLS	10/01-12/01
Applications	Bakersfield MSA, CA	Y	35240 FQ	61130 AW	95200 TQ	CABLS	10/01-12/01
Applications	Chico-Paradise MSA, CA	Y	22830 FQ	69450 AW		CABLS	10/01-12/01
Applications	Fresno MSA, CA	Y	34930 FQ	58150 AW	88600 TQ	CABLS	10/01-12/01
Applications	Los Angeles-Long Beach PMSA, CA	Y	40400 FQ	77630 AW	128590 TQ	CABLS	10/01-12/01
Applications	Oakland PMSA, CA	Y	58900 FQ	85020 AW	123330 TQ	CABLS	10/01-12/01
Applications	Orange County PMSA, CA	Y	51950 FQ	77780 AW	110260 TQ	CABLS	10/01-12/01
Applications	Riverside-San Bernardino PMSA, CA	Y	45940 FQ	72500 AW	103900 TQ	CABLS	10/01-12/01
Applications	Sacramento PMSA, CA	Y	51280 FQ	76410 AW	113260 TQ	CABLS	10/01-12/01
Applications	Salinas MSA, CA	Y	47320 FQ	78930 AW	128150 TQ	CABLS	10/01-12/01
Applications	San Diego MSA, CA	Y	44120 FQ	72120 AW	109180 TQ	CABLS	10/01-12/01
Applications	San Francisco PMSA, CA	Y	59450 FQ	86670 AW	121270 TQ	CABLS	10/01-12/01
Applications	San Jose PMSA, CA	Y	60350 FQ	88600 AW	121500 TQ	CABLS	10/01-12/01
Applications	San Luis Obispo-Atascadero-Paso Robles MSA, CA	Y	38580 FQ	61870 AW	86500 TQ	CABLS	10/01-12/01
Applications	Santa Barbara-Santa Maria-Lompoc MSA, CA	Y	40810 FQ	68140 AW	97290 TQ	CABLS	10/01-12/01
Applications	Santa Cruz-Watsonville PMSA, CA	Y	62000 FQ	91180 AW	117520 TQ	CABLS	10/01-12/01
Applications	Santa Rosa PMSA, CA	Y	54540 FQ	88280 AW	134710 TQ	CABLS	10/01-12/01
Applications	Stockton-Lodi MSA, CA	Y	38630 FQ	58460 AW	89740 TQ	CABLS	10/01-12/01
Applications	Vallejo-Fairfield-Napa PMSA, CA	Y	60130 FQ	89100 AW	124990 TQ	CABLS	10/01-12/01
Applications	Ventura PMSA, CA	Y	44780 FQ	72350 AW	106060 TQ	CABLS	10/01-12/01
Applications	Visalia-Tulare-Porterville MSA, CA	Y	33760 FQ	57150 AW	88220 TQ	CABLS	10/01-12/01
Applications	Colorado	Y	42600 FQ	75810 AW	119250 TQ	COBLS	10/01-12/01
Applications	Boulder-Longmont PMSA, CO	Y	51730 FQ	77260 AW	108020 TQ	COBLS	10/01-12/01
Applications	Colorado Springs MSA, CO	Y	45450 FQ	70250 AW	99370 TQ	COBLS	10/01-12/01
Applications	Denver PMSA, CO	Y	41640 FQ	78160 AW		COBLS	10/01-12/01
Applications	Fort Collins-Loveland MSA, CO	Y	41010 FQ	67610 AW	97350 TQ	COBLS	10/01-12/01
Applications	Greeley PMSA, CO	Y	14500 FQ	59640 AW	87030 TQ	COBLS	10/01-12/01
Applications	Connecticut	Y	49770 FQ	75320 AW	108860 TQ	CTBLS	10/01-12/01
Applications	Bridgeport PMSA, CT	Y	54590 FQ	82300 AW	112630 TQ	CTBLS	10/01-12/01
Applications	Danbury PMSA, CT	Y	44250 FQ	77000 AW	110120 TQ	CTBLS	10/01-12/01
Applications	Hartford MSA, CT	Y	48450 FQ	72360 AW	104700 TQ	CTBLS	10/01-12/01
Applications	New Haven-Meriden PMSA, CT	Y	47890 FQ	68210 AW	98710 TQ	CTBLS	10/01-12/01
Applications	New London-Norwich MSA, CT-RI	Y	50240 FQ	79690 AW	112260 TQ	CTBLS	10/01-12/01
Applications	Stamford-Norwalk PMSA, CT	Y	55070 FQ	81790 AW	114210 TQ	CTBLS	10/01-12/01
Applications	Waterbury PMSA, CT	Y	46020 FQ	74870 AW	111890 TQ	CTBLS	10/01-12/01
Applications	Delaware	Y	47490 FQ	73440 AW	99660 TQ	DEBLS	10/01-12/01
Applications	Wilmington-Newark PMSA, DE-MD	Y	49530 FQ	73730 AW	97390 TQ	DEBLS	10/01-12/01
Applications	District of Columbia	Y	44960 FQ	62070 AW	86330 TQ	DCBLS	10/01-12/01
Applications	Washington PMSA, DC-MD-VA-WV	Y	47160 FQ	73050 AW	102790 TQ	DCBLS	10/01-12/01
Applications	Florida	Y	43000 FQ	65260 AW	93920 TQ	FLBLS	10/01-12/01
Applications	Daytona Beach MSA, FL	Y	25820 FQ	45200 AW	69670 TQ	FLBLS	10/01-12/01
Applications	Fort Lauderdale PMSA, FL	Y	43000 FQ	66850 AW	104530 TQ	FLBLS	10/01-12/01
Applications	Fort Myers-Cape Coral MSA, FL	Y	47680 FQ	71010 AW	108870 TQ	FLBLS	10/01-12/01
Applications	Fort Pierce-Port St. Lucie MSA, FL	Y	38860 FQ	61670 AW	90730 TQ	FLBLS	10/01-12/01
Applications	Gainesville MSA, FL	Y	34230 FQ	61210 AW	99400 TQ	FLBLS	10/01-12/01

AAW	Average annual wage	AOH	Average offered, high	ASH	Average starting, high	H	Hourly	M	Monthly	S	Special: hourly and annual
AE	Average entry wage	AOL	Average offered, low	ASL	Average starting, low	HI	Highest wage paid	MTC	Median total compensation	TQ	Third quartile wage
AEX	Average experienced wage	APH	Average pay, high range	AW	Average wage paid	HR	High end range	MW	Median wage paid	W	Weekly
AO	Average offered	APL	Average pay, low range	FQ	First quartile wage	LR	Low end range	SQ	Second quartile wage	Y	Yearly

Occupation/Type/Industry	Location	Per	Low	Mid	High	Source	Date
Computer Software Engineer							
Applications	Jacksonville MSA, FL	Y	46410 FQ	78450 AW	114200 TQ	FLBLS	10/01-12/01
Applications	Lakeland-Winter Haven MSA, FL	Y	39410 FQ	58790 AW	85930 TQ	FLBLS	10/01-12/01
Applications	Melbourne-Titusville-Palm Bay MSA, FL	Y	45490 FQ	67260 AW	91760 TQ	FLBLS	10/01-12/01
Applications	Miami PMSA, FL	Y	40060 FQ	57460 AW	77620 TQ	FLBLS	10/01-12/01
Applications	Naples MSA, FL	Y	46810 FQ	67600 AW	95290 TQ	FLBLS	10/01-12/01
Applications	Ocala MSA, FL	Y	33460 FQ	49590 AW	73770 TQ	FLBLS	10/01-12/01
Applications	Orlando MSA, FL	Y	44540 FQ	64640 AW	89300 TQ	FLBLS	10/01-12/01
Applications	Pensacola MSA, FL	Y	43760 FQ	52280 AW	62420 TQ	FLBLS	10/01-12/01
Applications	Sarasota-Bradenton MSA, FL	Y	39230 FQ	57770 AW	84680 TQ	FLBLS	10/01-12/01
Applications	Tallahassee MSA, FL	Y	43450 FQ	65500 AW	88750 TQ	FLBLS	10/01-12/01
Applications	Tampa-St. Petersburg-Clearwater MSA, FL	Y	43700 FQ	63890 AW	85330 TQ	FLBLS	10/01-12/01
Applications	West Palm Beach-Boca Raton MSA, FL	Y	47260 FQ	70860 AW	113800 TQ	FLBLS	10/01-12/01
Applications	Georgia	Y	43660 FQ	75020 AW	133560 TQ	GABLS	10/01-12/01
Applications	Atlanta MSA, GA	Y	46080 FQ	78460 AW	136870 TQ	GABLS	10/01-12/01
Applications	Columbus MSA, GA-AL	Y	34680 FQ	55840 AW	73480 TQ	GABLS	10/01-12/01
Applications	Macon MSA, GA	Y	35800 FQ	55910 AW	82960 TQ	GABLS	10/01-12/01
Applications	Savannah MSA, GA	Y	47070 FQ	59290 AW	81890 TQ	GABLS	10/01-12/01
Applications	Hawaii	Y	39710 FQ	65040 AW	97450 TQ	HIBLS	10/01-12/01
Applications	Honolulu MSA, HI	Y	39640 FQ	64900 AW	98250 TQ	HIBLS	10/01-12/01
Applications	Idaho	Y	44280 FQ	65480 AW	93780 TQ	IDBLS	10/01-12/01
Applications	Boise City MSA, ID	Y	45340 FQ	64690 AW	92100 TQ	IDBLS	10/01-12/01
Applications	Illinois	Y	40070 FQ	65320 AW	93160 TQ	ILBLS	10/01-12/01
Applications	Champaign-Urbana MSA, IL	Y	37560 FQ	56810 AW	82270 TQ	ILBLS	10/01-12/01
Applications	Chicago PMSA, IL	Y	43360 FQ	66880 AW	94350 TQ	ILBLS	10/01-12/01
Applications	Peoria-Pekin MSA, IL	Y	34470 FQ	53470 AW	76610 TQ	ILBLS	10/01-12/01
Applications	Rockford MSA, IL	Y	36360 FQ	58810 AW	86850 TQ	ILBLS	10/01-12/01
Applications	Springfield MSA, IL	Y	34080 FQ	59090 AW	81980 TQ	ILBLS	10/01-12/01
Applications	Indiana	Y	39140 FQ	59950 AW	85170 TQ	INBLS	10/01-12/01
Applications	Elkhart-Goshen MSA, IN	Y	41620 FQ	59970 AW	71710 TQ	INBLS	10/01-12/01
Applications	Evansville-Henderson MSA, IN-KY	Y	32520 FQ	52440 AW	71410 TQ	INBLS	10/01-12/01
Applications	Fort Wayne MSA, IN	Y	42880 FQ	63620 AW	89920 TQ	INBLS	10/01-12/01
Applications	Gary PMSA, IN	Y	42400 FQ	68260 AW	99340 TQ	INBLS	10/01-12/01
Applications	Indianapolis MSA, IN	Y	41590 FQ	59120 AW	78610 TQ	INBLS	10/01-12/01
Applications	Lafayette MSA, IN	Y	38440 FQ	63030 AW	118210 TQ	INBLS	10/01-12/01
Applications	South Bend MSA, IN	Y	41300 FQ	60080 AW	82140 TQ	INBLS	10/01-12/01
Applications	Iowa	Y	39160 FQ	65710 AW	100680 TQ	IABLS	10/01-12/01
Applications	Davenport-Moline-Rock Island MSA, IA-IL	Y	32770 FQ	66680 AW	113100 TQ	IABLS	10/01-12/01
Applications	Des Moines MSA, IA	Y	45580 FQ	65940 AW	92650 TQ	IABLS	10/01-12/01
Applications	Kansas	Y	37270 FQ	59700 AW	84590 TQ	KSBLS	10/01-12/01
Applications	Topeka MSA, KS	Y	36500 FQ	59250 AW	84700 TQ	KSBLS	10/01-12/01
Applications	Wichita MSA, KS	Y	37610 FQ	67670 AW	123000 TQ	KSBLS	10/01-12/01
Applications	Kentucky	Y	40810 FQ	62170 AW	89370 TQ	KYBLS	10/01-12/01
Applications	Lexington MSA, KY	Y	46160 FQ	73720 AW	101500 TQ	KYBLS	10/01-12/01
Applications	Louisville MSA, KY-IN	Y	39820 FQ	57070 AW	79410 TQ	KYBLS	10/01-12/01
Applications	Louisiana	Y	37270 FQ	61010 AW	87230 TQ	LABLS	10/01-12/01
Applications	Baton Rouge MSA, LA	Y	38690 FQ	62960 AW	91160 TQ	LABLS	10/01-12/01
Applications	Lafayette MSA, LA	Y	28140 FQ	50880 AW	80440 TQ	LABLS	10/01-12/01
Applications	New Orleans MSA, LA	Y	45250 FQ	63910 AW	87790 TQ	LABLS	10/01-12/01
Applications	Shreveport-Bossier City MSA, LA	Y	35810 FQ	53910 AW	74560 TQ	LABLS	10/01-12/01
Applications	Maine	Y	38150 FQ	55520 AW	74670 TQ	MEBLS	10/01-12/01
Applications	Portland MSA, ME	Y	36820 FQ	56240 AW	80100 TQ	MEBLS	10/01-12/01
Applications	Maryland	Y	44430 FQ	75410 AW	112050 TQ	MDBLS	10/01-12/01
Applications	Baltimore PMSA, MD	Y	51170 FQ	82330 AW	125100 TQ	MDBLS	10/01-12/01
Applications	Massachusetts	Y	53250 FQ	82470 AW	119080 TQ	MABLS	10/01-12/01
Applications	Boston PMSA, MA-NH	Y	53800 FQ	82930 AW	118780 TQ	MABLS	10/01-12/01
Applications	Brockton PMSA, MA	Y	42660 FQ	70770 AW	106390 TQ	MABLS	10/01-12/01
Applications	Lawrence PMSA, MA-NH	Y	52650 FQ	85160 AW	119080 TQ	MABLS	10/01-12/01
Applications	Lowell PMSA, MA-NH	Y	54810 FQ	83400 AW	117270 TQ	MABLS	10/01-12/01
Applications	Springfield MSA, MA	Y	31650 FQ	72800 AW	124380 TQ	MABLS	10/01-12/01
Applications	Worcester PMSA, MA-CT	Y	48920 FQ	71240 AW	103720 TQ	MABLS	10/01-12/01
Applications	Michigan	Y	42950 FQ	68420 AW	98000 TQ	MIBLS	10/01-12/01
Applications	Ann Arbor PMSA, MI	Y	43030 FQ	71440 AW	111970 TQ	MIBLS	10/01-12/01
Applications	Detroit PMSA, MI	Y	46550 FQ	70240 AW	97250 TQ	MIBLS	10/01-12/01
Applications	Flint PMSA, MI	Y	35810 FQ	57390 AW	82590 TQ	MIBLS	10/01-12/01

AAW	Average annual wage	AOH	Average offered, high	ASH	Average starting, high	H	Hourly	M	Monthly	S	Special: hourly and annual
AE	Average entry wage	AOL	Average offered, low	ASL	Average starting, low	HI	Highest wage paid	MTC	Median total compensation	TQ	Third quartile wage
AEX	Average experienced wage	APH	Average pay, high range	AW	Average wage paid	HR	High end range	MW	Median wage paid	W	Weekly
AO	Average offered	APL	Average pay, low range	FQ	First quartile wage	LR	Low end range	SQ	Second quartile wage	Y	Yearly

Occupation/Type/Industry	Location	Per	Low	Mid	High	Source	Date
Computer Software Engineer							
Applications	Grand Rapids-Muskegon-Holland MSA, MI	Y	37370 FQ	57360 AW	90040 TQ	MIBLS	10/01-12/01
Applications	Kalamazoo-Battle Creek MSA, MI	Y	42140 FQ	76600 AW	112100 TQ	MIBLS	10/01-12/01
Applications	Lansing-East Lansing MSA, MI	Y	42730 FQ	61930 AW	84970 TQ	MIBLS	10/01-12/01
Applications	Saginaw-Bay City-Midland MSA, MI	Y	28200 FQ	50820 AW	77560 TQ	MIBLS	10/01-12/01
Applications	Minnesota	Y	42480 FQ	68210 AW	97450 TQ	MNBLS	10/01-12/01
Applications	Duluth-Superior MSA, MN-WI	Y	38510 FQ	61900 AW	88280 TQ	MNBLS	10/01-12/01
Applications	Minneapolis-St. Paul MSA, MN-WI	Y	42820 FQ	67660 AW	96150 TQ	MNBLS	10/01-12/01
Applications	St. Cloud MSA, MN	Y	35590 FQ	53090 AW	77810 TQ	MNBLS	10/01-12/01
Applications	Mississippi	Y	34560 FQ	49920 AW	73830 TQ	MSBLS	10/01-12/01
Applications	Biloxi-Gulfport-Pascagoula MSA, MS	Y	37940 FQ	46820 AW	55520 TQ	MSBLS	10/01-12/01
Applications	Jackson MSA, MS	Y	33400 FQ	48680 AW	70620 TQ	MSBLS	10/01-12/01
Applications	Missouri	Y	45210 FQ	66760 AW	92130 TQ	MOBLS	10/01-12/01
Applications	Kansas City MSA, MO-KS	Y	39240 FQ	61120 AW	85710 TQ	MOBLS	10/01-12/01
Applications	St. Louis MSA, MO-IL	Y	40090 FQ	65590 AW	92580 TQ	MOBLS	10/01-12/01
Applications	Springfield MSA, MO	Y	21750 FQ	54280 AW	91220 TQ	MOBLS	10/01-12/01
Applications	Montana	Y	32480 FQ	49370 AW	70370 TQ	MTBLS	10/01-12/01
Applications	Billings MSA, MT	Y	45330 FQ	53250 AW	66840 TQ	MTBLS	10/01-12/01
Applications	Nebraska	Y	40810 FQ	59460 AW	81820 TQ	NEBLS	10/01-12/01
Applications	Lincoln MSA, NE	Y	34570 FQ	53210 AW	78050 TQ	NEBLS	10/01-12/01
Applications	Omaha MSA, NE-IA	Y	45560 FQ	61150 AW	81980 TQ	NEBLS	10/01-12/01
Applications	Nevada	Y	37530 FQ	62730 AW	93200 TQ	NVBLS	10/01-12/01
Applications	Las Vegas MSA, NV-AZ	Y	41180 FQ	64160 AW	91800 TQ	NVBLS	10/01-12/01
Applications	Reno MSA, NV	Y	32130 FQ	51520 AW	75680 TQ	NVBLS	10/01-12/01
Applications	New Hampshire	Y	45890 FQ	74120 AW	105350 TQ	NHBLS	10/01-12/01
Applications	Manchester PMSA, NH	Y	47650 FQ	73130 AW	112350 TQ	NHBLS	10/01-12/01
Applications	Nashua PMSA, NH	Y	51510 FQ	79880 AW	105260 TQ	NHBLS	10/01-12/01
Applications	Portsmouth-Rochester PMSA, NH-ME	Y	45300 FQ	73300 AW	111250 TQ	NHBLS	10/01-12/01
Applications	New Jersey	Y	48920 FQ	76100 AW	109440 TQ	NJBLS	10/01-12/01
Applications	Atlantic-Cape May PMSA, NJ	Y	38810 FQ	66030 AW	93320 TQ	NJBLS	10/01-12/01
Applications	Bergen-Passaic PMSA, NJ	Y	46670 FQ	70610 AW	96070 TQ	NJBLS	10/01-12/01
Applications	Jersey City PMSA, NJ	Y	50360 FQ	77660 AW	112000 TQ	NJBLS	10/01-12/01
Applications	Middlesex-Somerset-Hunterdon PMSA, NJ	Y	49610 FQ	77590 AW	107340 TQ	NJBLS	10/01-12/01
Applications	Monmouth-Ocean PMSA, NJ	Y	51890 FQ	76810 AW	109400 TQ	NJBLS	10/01-12/01
Applications	Newark PMSA, NJ	Y	50360 FQ	80500 AW	120340 TQ	NJBLS	10/01-12/01
Applications	Trenton PMSA, NJ	Y	49520 FQ	75250 AW	103100 TQ	NJBLS	10/01-12/01
Applications	New Mexico	Y	41220 FQ	64990 AW	93640 TQ	NMBLS	10/01-12/01
Applications	Albuquerque MSA, NM	Y	41260 FQ	63980 AW	94230 TQ	NMBLS	10/01-12/01
Applications	Las Cruces MSA, NM	Y	22360 FQ	52240 AW	78040 TQ	NMBLS	10/01-12/01
Applications	New York	Y	42000 FQ	70800 AW	108690 TQ	NYBLS	10/01-12/01
Applications	Albany-Schenectady-Troy MSA, NY	Y	37220 FQ	53270 AW	74030 TQ	NYBLS	10/01-12/01
Applications	Buffalo-Niagara Falls MSA, NY	Y	38010 FQ	60470 AW	92490 TQ	NYBLS	10/01-12/01
Applications	Nassau-Suffolk PMSA, NY	Y	42300 FQ	74890 AW	124060 TQ	NYBLS	10/01-12/01
Applications	New York PMSA, NY	Y	48340 FQ	76230 AW	112440 TQ	NYBLS	10/01-12/01
Applications	Newburgh PMSA, NY-PA	Y	31190 FQ	55690 AW	92000 TQ	NYBLS	10/01-12/01
Applications	Rochester MSA, NY	Y	41390 FQ	69740 AW	106890 TQ	NYBLS	10/01-12/01
Applications	Syracuse MSA, NY	Y	39270 FQ	64920 AW	97610 TQ	NYBLS	10/01-12/01
Applications	Utica-Rome MSA, NY	Y	41840 FQ	59240 AW	82830 TQ	NYBLS	10/01-12/01
Applications	North Carolina	Y	44280 FQ	71120 AW	106020 TQ	NCBLS	10/01-12/01
Applications	Charlotte-Gastonia-Rock Hill MSA, NC-SC	Y	42720 FQ	69040 AW	104380 TQ	NCBLS	10/01-12/01
Applications	Greensboro-Winston-Salem-High Point MSA, NC	Y	39640 FQ	64650 AW	90550 TQ	NCBLS	10/01-12/01
Applications	Hickory-Morganton-Lenoir MSA, NC	Y	37250 FQ	58340 AW	79400 TQ	NCBLS	10/01-12/01
Applications	Raleigh-Durham-Chapel Hill MSA, NC	Y	47280 FQ	72790 AW	106560 TQ	NCBLS	10/01-12/01
Applications	Wilmington MSA, NC	Y	20440 FQ	40950 AW	73280 TQ	NCBLS	10/01-12/01
Applications	North Dakota	Y	36430 FQ	55190 AW	81590 TQ	NDBLS	10/01-12/01
Applications	Fargo-Moorhead MSA, ND-MN	Y	39750 FQ	59750 AW	90030 TQ	NDBLS	10/01-12/01
Applications	Ohio	Y	42360 FQ	64990 AW	90270 TQ	OHBLS	10/01-12/01
Applications	Akron PMSA, OH	Y	23980 FQ	47310 AW	75920 TQ	OHBLS	10/01-12/01

AAW	Average annual wage	**AOH**	Average offered, high	**ASH**	Average starting, high	**H**	Hourly	**M**	Monthly	**S**	Special: hourly and annual
AE	Average entry wage	**AOL**	Average offered, low	**ASL**	Average starting, low	**HI**	Highest wage paid	**MTC**	Median total compensation	**TQ**	Third quartile wage
AEX	Average experienced wage	**APH**	Average pay, high range	**AW**	Average wage paid	**HR**	High end range	**MW**	Median wage paid	**W**	Weekly
AO	Average offered	**APL**	Average pay, low range	**FQ**	First quartile wage	**LR**	Low end range	**SQ**	Second quartile wage	**Y**	Yearly

Occupation/Type/Industry	Location	Per	Low	Mid	High	Source	Date
Computer Software Engineer							
Applications	Canton-Massillon MSA, OH	Y	39430 FQ	59130 AW	84450 TQ	OHBLS	10/01-12/01
Applications	Cincinnati PMSA, OH-KY-IN	Y	46470 FQ	64760 AW	87770 TQ	OHBLS	10/01-12/01
Applications	Cleveland-Lorain-Elyria PMSA, OH	Y	38730 FQ	65440 AW	94510 TQ	OHBLS	10/01-12/01
Applications	Columbus MSA, OH	Y	46970 FQ	68940 AW	95740 TQ	OHBLS	10/01-12/01
Applications	Dayton-Springfield MSA, OH	Y	44540 FQ	62530 AW	86410 TQ	OHBLS	10/01-12/01
Applications	Hamilton-Middletown PMSA, OH	Y	52330 FQ	76160 AW	92650 TQ	OHBLS	10/01-12/01
Applications	Toledo MSA, OH	Y	31650 FQ	54330 AW	84220 TQ	OHBLS	10/01-12/01
Applications	Youngstown-Warren MSA, OH	Y	42890 FQ	71080 AW	102590 TQ	OHBLS	10/01-12/01
Applications	Oklahoma	Y	34880 FQ	55160 AW	75330 TQ	OKBLS	10/01-12/01
Applications	Oklahoma City MSA, OK	Y	33890 FQ	51830 AW	73500 TQ	OKBLS	10/01-12/01
Applications	Tulsa MSA, OK	Y	41720 FQ	61060 AW	78590 TQ	OKBLS	10/01-12/01
Applications	Oregon	Y	49050 FQ	74020 AW	106280 TQ	ORBLS	10/01-12/01
Applications	Eugene-Springfield MSA, OR	Y	36460 FQ	55980 AW	83780 TQ	ORBLS	10/01-12/01
Applications	Medford-Ashland MSA, OR	Y	39040 FQ	58710 AW	95750 TQ	ORBLS	10/01-12/01
Applications	Portland-Vancouver PMSA, OR-WA	Y	50590 FQ	75370 AW	106820 TQ	ORBLS	10/01-12/01
Applications	Salem PMSA, OR	Y	45790 FQ	65790 AW	93560 TQ	ORBLS	10/01-12/01
Applications	Pennsylvania	Y	40600 FQ	65500 AW	93370 TQ	PABLS	10/01-12/01
Applications	Allentown-Bethlehem-Easton MSA, PA	Y	37250 FQ	63190 AW	92470 TQ	PABLS	10/01-12/01
Applications	Erie MSA, PA	Y	31350 FQ	48900 AW	77660 TQ	PABLS	10/01-12/01
Applications	Harrisburg-Lebanon-Carlisle MSA, PA	Y	47060 FQ	76410 AW	109010 TQ	PABLS	10/01-12/01
Applications	Johnstown MSA, PA	Y	32480 FQ	50760 AW	74850 TQ	PABLS	10/01-12/01
Applications	Lancaster MSA, PA	Y	21960 FQ	46680 AW	73540 TQ	PABLS	10/01-12/01
Applications	Philadelphia PMSA, PA-NJ	Y	47260 FQ	70220 AW	97460 TQ	PABLS	10/01-12/01
Applications	Pittsburgh MSA, PA	Y	38190 FQ	59220 AW	84930 TQ	PABLS	10/01-12/01
Applications	Reading MSA, PA	Y	44610 FQ	65210 AW	87200 TQ	PABLS	10/01-12/01
Applications	Scranton-Wilkes-Barre-Hazleton MSA, PA	Y	40400 FQ	61210 AW	75500 TQ	PABLS	10/01-12/01
Applications	York MSA, PA	Y	30510 FQ	50690 AW	70970 TQ	PABLS	10/01-12/01
Applications	Rhode Island	Y	41120 FQ	65210 AW	91570 TQ	RIBLS	10/01-12/01
Applications	Providence-Fall River-Warwick MSA, RI-MA	Y	41420 FQ	64890 AW	90870 TQ	RIBLS	10/01-12/01
Applications	South Carolina	Y	36800 FQ	61410 AW	90220 TQ	SCBLS	10/01-12/01
Applications	Charleston-North Charleston MSA, SC	Y	36940 FQ	55410 AW	73640 TQ	SCBLS	10/01-12/01
Applications	Columbia MSA, SC	Y	27260 FQ	50140 AW	70680 TQ	SCBLS	10/01-12/01
Applications	Greenville-Spartanburg-Anderson MSA, SC	Y	40630 FQ	60880 AW	83610 TQ	SCBLS	10/01-12/01
Applications	South Dakota	Y	35390 FQ	58000 AW	83150 TQ	SDBLS	10/01-12/01
Applications	Sioux Falls MSA, SD	Y	39390 FQ	61790 AW	84530 TQ	SDBLS	10/01-12/01
Applications	Tennessee	Y	37740 FQ	61560 AW	89630 TQ	TNBLS	10/01-12/01
Applications	Chattanooga MSA, TN-GA	Y	27910 FQ	51530 AW	74140 TQ	TNBLS	10/01-12/01
Applications	Johnson City-Kingsport-Bristol MSA, TN-VA	Y	34460 FQ	51470 AW	74950 TQ	TNBLS	10/01-12/01
Applications	Knoxville MSA, TN	Y	42150 FQ	65150 AW	89950 TQ	TNBLS	10/01-12/01
Applications	Memphis MSA, TN-AR-MS	Y	35670 FQ	63420 AW	93600 TQ	TNBLS	10/01-12/01
Applications	Nashville MSA, TN	Y	39830 FQ	62680 AW	90360 TQ	TNBLS	10/01-12/01
Applications	Texas	Y	42750 FQ	68530 AW	99790 TQ	TXBLS	10/01-12/01
Applications	Amarillo MSA, TX	Y	50870 FQ	68260 AW	90120 TQ	TXBLS	10/01-12/01
Applications	Austin-San Marcos MSA, TX	Y	46260 FQ	68260 AW	98420 TQ	TXBLS	10/01-12/01
Applications	Beaumont-Port Arthur MSA, TX	Y	40360 FQ	69570 AW	93490 TQ	TXBLS	10/01-12/01
Applications	Brazoria PMSA, TX	Y	58190 FQ	73430 AW	101590 TQ	TXBLS	10/01-12/01
Applications	Dallas PMSA, TX	Y	45020 FQ	72330 AW	104710 TQ	TXBLS	10/01-12/01
Applications	Fort Worth-Arlington PMSA, TX	Y	43370 FQ	72170 AW	107930 TQ	TXBLS	10/01-12/01
Applications	Galveston-Texas City PMSA, TX	Y	32890 FQ	56140 AW	76430 TQ	TXBLS	10/01-12/01
Applications	Houston PMSA, TX	Y	41900 FQ	67550 AW	98750 TQ	TXBLS	10/01-12/01
Applications	Killeen-Temple MSA, TX	Y	33780 FQ	50760 AW	71590 TQ	TXBLS	10/01-12/01
Applications	Lubbock MSA, TX	Y	30470 FQ	52720 AW	78350 TQ	TXBLS	10/01-12/01
Applications	San Antonio MSA, TX	Y	37660 FQ	59930 AW	86680 TQ	TXBLS	10/01-12/01
Applications	Utah	Y	45640 FQ	71340 AW	107040 TQ	UTBLS	10/01-12/01
Applications	Provo-Orem MSA, UT	Y	50270 FQ	74270 AW	106520 TQ	UTBLS	10/01-12/01
Applications	Salt Lake City-Ogden MSA, UT	Y	44910 FQ	71450 AW	108020 TQ	UTBLS	10/01-12/01
Applications	Vermont	Y	42580 FQ	72900 AW	107580 TQ	VTBLS	10/01-12/01

AAW	Average annual wage	**AOH**	Average offered, high	**ASH**	Average starting, high	**H**	Hourly	**M**	Monthly	**S**	Special: hourly and annual
AE	Average entry wage	**AOL**	Average offered, low	**ASL**	Average starting, low	**HI**	Highest wage paid	**MTC**	Median total compensation	**TQ**	Third quartile wage
AEX	Average experienced wage	**APH**	Average pay, high range	**AW**	Average wage paid	**HR**	High end range	**MW**	Median wage paid	**W**	Weekly
AO	Average offered	**APL**	Average pay, low range	**FQ**	First quartile wage	**LR**	Low end range	**SQ**	Second quartile wage	**Y**	Yearly

Occupation/Type/Industry	Location	Per	Low	Mid	High	Source	Date
Computer Software Engineer							
Applications	Burlington MSA, VT	Y	42950 FQ	73940 AW	108000 TQ	VTBLS	10/01-12/01
Applications	Virginia	Y	46690 FQ	70930 AW	100790 TQ	VABLS	10/01-12/01
Applications	Lynchburg MSA, VA	Y	41160 FQ	63580 AW	89230 TQ	VABLS	10/01-12/01
Applications	Norfolk-Virginia Beach-Newport News MSA, VA-NC	Y	42850 FQ	57680 AW	80420 TQ	VABLS	10/01-12/01
Applications	Richmond-Petersburg MSA, VA	Y	41930 FQ	65660 AW	93740 TQ	VABLS	10/01-12/01
Applications	Roanoke MSA, VA	Y	43520 FQ	67300 AW	96860 TQ	VABLS	10/01-12/01
Applications	Washington	Y	48920 FQ	75690 AW	110570 TQ	WABLS	10/01-12/01
Applications	Bremerton PMSA, WA	Y	45300 FQ	58010 AW	78230 TQ	WABLS	10/01-12/01
Applications	Olympia PMSA, WA	Y	45230 FQ	62340 AW	81120 TQ	WABLS	10/01-12/01
Applications	Richland-Kennewick-Pasco MSA, WA	Y	42650 FQ	70970 AW	101530 TQ	WABLS	10/01-12/01
Applications	Seattle-Bellevue-Everett PMSA, WA	Y	50900 FQ	77550 AW	111790 TQ	WABLS	10/01-12/01
Applications	Spokane MSA, WA	Y	35590 FQ	63390 AW	93690 TQ	WABLS	10/01-12/01
Applications	Tacoma PMSA, WA	Y	22620 FQ	49600 AW	70060 TQ	WABLS	10/01-12/01
Applications	Yakima MSA, WA	Y	37640 FQ	57110 AW	83460 TQ	WABLS	10/01-12/01
Applications	West Virginia	Y	39800 FQ	59800 AW	72870 TQ	WVBLS	10/01-12/01
Applications	Charleston MSA, WV	Y	22970 FQ	49310 AW	79770 TQ	WVBLS	10/01-12/01
Applications	Wisconsin	Y	41300 FQ	62790 AW	88680 TQ	WIBLS	10/01-12/01
Applications	Appleton-Oshkosh-Neenah MSA, WI	Y	39130 FQ	65020 AW	91380 TQ	WIBLS	10/01-12/01
Applications	Green Bay MSA, WI	Y	32470 FQ	54660 AW	80830 TQ	WIBLS	10/01-12/01
Applications	Madison MSA, WI	Y	45790 FQ	63280 AW	86710 TQ	WIBLS	10/01-12/01
Applications	Milwaukee-Waukesha PMSA, WI	Y	43520 FQ	64400 AW	89630 TQ	WIBLS	10/01-12/01
Applications	Wyoming	Y	32460 FQ	54090 AW	83050 TQ	WYBLS	10/01-12/01
Applications	Puerto Rico	Y	32850 FQ	60200 AW	89530 TQ	PRBLS	10/01-12/01
Systems software	United States	Y		39700 AW		FREEP1	1/00-1/00
Systems Software	Alabama	Y	39880 FQ	66470 AW	94950 TQ	ALBLS	10/01-12/01
Systems Software	Birmingham MSA, AL	Y	38220 FQ	71610 AW	107850 TQ	ALBLS	10/01-12/01
Systems Software	Huntsville MSA, AL	Y	46380 FQ	67240 AW	92140 TQ	ALBLS	10/01-12/01
Systems Software	Mobile MSA, AL	Y	42390 FQ	70620 AW	104580 TQ	ALBLS	10/01-12/01
Systems Software	Montgomery MSA, AL	Y	27190 FQ	49400 AW	72790 TQ	ALBLS	10/01-12/01
Systems Software	Arizona	Y	45720 FQ	70320 AW	94670 TQ	AZBLS	10/01-12/01
Systems Software	Phoenix-Mesa MSA, AZ	Y	46040 FQ	71370 AW	94750 TQ	AZBLS	10/01-12/01
Systems Software	Tucson MSA, AZ	Y	48650 FQ	69520 AW	95050 TQ	AZBLS	10/01-12/01
Systems Software	Arkansas	Y	27540 FQ	54340 AW	88910 TQ	ARBLS	10/01-12/01
Systems Software	Fayetteville-Springdale-Rogers MSA, AR	Y	24930 FQ	48760 AW	88990 TQ	ARBLS	10/01-12/01
Systems Software	Little Rock-North Little Rock MSA, AR	Y	36850 FQ	58230 AW	85800 TQ	ARBLS	10/01-12/01
Systems Software	California	Y	50300 FQ	83070 AW	119940 TQ	CABLS	10/01-12/01
Systems Software	Bakersfield MSA, CA	Y	37380 FQ	57410 AW	87810 TQ	CABLS	10/01-12/01
Systems Software	Fresno MSA, CA	Y	32800 FQ	55870 AW	88780 TQ	CABLS	10/01-12/01
Systems Software	Los Angeles-Long Beach PMSA, CA	Y	46300 FQ	73640 AW	110320 TQ	CABLS	10/01-12/01
Systems Software	Modesto MSA, CA	Y	54330 FQ	84800 AW	113060 TQ	CABLS	10/01-12/01
Systems Software	Oakland PMSA, CA	Y	47450 FQ	80730 AW	113490 TQ	CABLS	10/01-12/01
Systems Software	Orange County PMSA, CA	Y	47230 FQ	78380 AW	112620 TQ	CABLS	10/01-12/01
Systems Software	Riverside-San Bernardino PMSA, CA	Y	37290 FQ	60900 AW	87700 TQ	CABLS	10/01-12/01
Systems Software	Sacramento PMSA, CA	Y	57140 FQ	83780 AW	112100 TQ	CABLS	10/01-12/01
Systems Software	Salinas MSA, CA	Y	39390 FQ	66790 AW	95810 TQ	CABLS	10/01-12/01
Systems Software	San Diego MSA, CA	Y	49200 FQ	78230 AW	112250 TQ	CABLS	10/01-12/01
Systems Software	San Francisco PMSA, CA	Y	52240 FQ	81190 AW	117590 TQ	CABLS	10/01-12/01
Systems Software	San Jose PMSA, CA	Y	59600 FQ	91660 AW	133230 TQ	CABLS	10/01-12/01
Systems Software	San Luis Obispo-Atascadero-Paso Robles MSA, CA	Y	37330 FQ	77980 AW	116840 TQ	CABLS	10/01-12/01
Systems Software	Santa Barbara-Santa Maria-Lompoc MSA, CA	Y	46710 FQ	73070 AW	107920 TQ	CABLS	10/01-12/01
Systems Software	Santa Cruz-Watsonville PMSA, CA	Y	55880 FQ	91660 AW	126010 TQ	CABLS	10/01-12/01
Systems Software	Santa Rosa PMSA, CA	Y	32910 FQ	71260 AW	119360 TQ	CABLS	10/01-12/01
Systems Software	Stockton-Lodi MSA, CA	Y	27610 FQ	55970 AW	77600 TQ	CABLS	10/01-12/01
Systems Software	Ventura PMSA, CA	Y	46460 FQ	69180 AW	107250 TQ	CABLS	10/01-12/01
Systems Software	Visalia-Tulare-Porterville MSA, CA	Y	48320 FQ	80060 AW	112790 TQ	CABLS	10/01-12/01
Systems Software	Colorado	Y	50530 FQ	73650 AW	102130 TQ	COBLS	10/01-12/01

AAW	Average annual wage	**AOH**	Average offered, high	**ASH**	Average starting, high	**H**	Hourly	**M**	Monthly	**S**	Special: hourly and annual
AE	Average entry wage	**AOL**	Average offered, low	**ASL**	Average starting, low	**HI**	Highest wage paid	**MTC**	Median total compensation	**TQ**	Third quartile wage
AEX	Average experienced wage	**APH**	Average pay, high range	**AW**	Average wage paid	**HR**	High end range	**MW**	Median wage paid	**W**	Weekly
AO	Average offered	**APL**	Average pay, low range	**FQ**	First quartile wage	**LR**	Low end range	**SQ**	Second quartile wage	**Y**	Yearly

Occupation/Type/Industry	Location	Per	Low	Mid	High	Source	Date
Computer Software Engineer							
Systems Software	Boulder-Longmont PMSA, CO	Y	50550 FQ	77330 AW	110840 TQ	COBLS	10/01-12/01
Systems Software	Colorado Springs MSA, CO	Y	51640 FQ	73940 AW	97920 TQ	COBLS	10/01-12/01
Systems Software	Denver PMSA, CO	Y	49130 FQ	71870 AW	99190 TQ	COBLS	10/01-12/01
Systems Software	Fort Collins-Loveland MSA, CO	Y	59430 FQ	76630 AW	105760 TQ	COBLS	10/01-12/01
Systems Software	Greeley PMSA, CO	Y	60160 FQ	67370 AW	74210 TQ	COBLS	10/01-12/01
Systems Software	Connecticut	Y	47320 FQ	68910 AW	97570 TQ	CTBLS	10/01-12/01
Systems Software	Bridgeport PMSA, CT	Y	48940 FQ	74110 AW	106550 TQ	CTBLS	10/01-12/01
Systems Software	Danbury PMSA, CT	Y	49270 FQ	72630 AW	100580 TQ	CTBLS	10/01-12/01
Systems Software	Hartford MSA, CT	Y	45060 FQ	68680 AW	94250 TQ	CTBLS	10/01-12/01
Systems Software	New Haven-Meriden PMSA, CT	Y	47950 FQ	66490 AW	92780 TQ	CTBLS	10/01-12/01
Systems Software	New London-Norwich MSA, CT-RI	Y	50660 FQ	71220 AW	92260 TQ	CTBLS	10/01-12/01
Systems Software	Stamford-Norwalk PMSA, CT	Y	46470 FQ	67450 AW	98370 TQ	CTBLS	10/01-12/01
Systems Software	Delaware	Y	46880 FQ	71650 AW	102300 TQ	DEBLS	10/01-12/01
Systems Software	Wilmington-Newark PMSA, DE-MD	Y	47380 FQ	72000 AW	101950 TQ	DEBLS	10/01-12/01
Systems Software	District of Columbia	Y	50070 FQ	79000 AW	111340 TQ	DCBLS	10/01-12/01
Systems Software	Washington PMSA, DC-MD-VA-WV	Y	49210 FQ	77010 AW	110800 TQ	DCBLS	10/01-12/01
Systems Software	Florida	Y	38070 FQ	66920 AW	98110 TQ	FLBLS	10/01-12/01
Systems Software	Daytona Beach MSA, FL	Y	34720 FQ	61700 AW	89240 TQ	FLBLS	10/01-12/01
Systems Software	Fort Lauderdale PMSA, FL	Y	51980 FQ	86420 AW	127920 TQ	FLBLS	10/01-12/01
Systems Software	Fort Myers-Cape Coral MSA, FL	Y	40190 FQ	68770 AW	105620 TQ	FLBLS	10/01-12/01
Systems Software	Fort Walton Beach MSA, FL	Y	45500 FQ	62720 AW	83060 TQ	FLBLS	10/01-12/01
Systems Software	Gainesville MSA, FL	Y	46170 FQ	71970 AW	100790 TQ	FLBLS	10/01-12/01
Systems Software	Jacksonville MSA, FL	Y	49320 FQ	71130 AW	93840 TQ	FLBLS	10/01-12/01
Systems Software	Lakeland-Winter Haven MSA, FL	Y	41020 FQ	63870 AW	88650 TQ	FLBLS	10/01-12/01
Systems Software	Melbourne-Titusville-Palm Bay MSA, FL	Y	39270 FQ	66170 AW	92630 TQ	FLBLS	10/01-12/01
Systems Software	Miami PMSA, FL	Y	25230 FQ	55800 AW	91840 TQ	FLBLS	10/01-12/01
Systems Software	Naples MSA, FL	Y	48690 FQ	70960 AW	98750 TQ	FLBLS	10/01-12/01
Systems Software	Orlando MSA, FL	Y	45470 FQ	71330 AW	97910 TQ	FLBLS	10/01-12/01
Systems Software	Pensacola MSA, FL	Y	35760 FQ	50220 AW	68300 TQ	FLBLS	10/01-12/01
Systems Software	Sarasota-Bradenton MSA, FL	Y	45190 FQ	97800 AW		FLBLS	10/01-12/01
Systems Software	Tallahassee MSA, FL	Y	46080 FQ	57700 AW	73340 TQ	FLBLS	10/01-12/01
Systems Software	Tampa-St. Petersburg-Clearwater MSA, FL	Y	31810 FQ	61990 AW	91270 TQ	FLBLS	10/01-12/01
Systems Software	West Palm Beach-Boca Raton MSA, FL	Y	44900 FQ	76030 AW	119290 TQ	FLBLS	10/01-12/01
Systems Software	Georgia	Y	47130 FQ	70310 AW	97000 TQ	GABLS	10/01-12/01
Systems Software	Atlanta MSA, GA	Y	47360 FQ	68660 AW	93890 TQ	GABLS	10/01-12/01
Systems Software	Columbus MSA, GA-AL	Y	38810 FQ	58350 AW	82940 TQ	GABLS	10/01-12/01
Systems Software	Macon MSA, GA	Y	38580 FQ	59420 AW	83630 TQ	GABLS	10/01-12/01
Systems Software	Savannah MSA, GA	Y	46410 FQ	62260 AW	84500 TQ	GABLS	10/01-12/01
Systems Software	Hawaii	Y	37600 FQ	63690 AW	88920 TQ	HIBLS	10/01-12/01
Systems Software	Honolulu MSA, HI	Y	36810 FQ	62200 AW	87430 TQ	HIBLS	10/01-12/01
Systems Software	Illinois	Y	45060 FQ	79180 AW	123720 TQ	ILBLS	10/01-12/01
Systems Software	Champaign-Urbana MSA, IL	Y	34250 FQ	72070 AW	129010 TQ	ILBLS	10/01-12/01
Systems Software	Chicago PMSA, IL	Y	46990 FQ	81010 AW	125360 TQ	ILBLS	10/01-12/01
Systems Software	Peoria-Pekin MSA, IL	Y	38970 FQ	63820 AW	88670 TQ	ILBLS	10/01-12/01
Systems Software	Rockford MSA, IL	Y	33210 FQ	48520 AW	73550 TQ	ILBLS	10/01-12/01
Systems Software	Indiana	Y	40960 FQ	64070 AW	91320 TQ	INBLS	10/01-12/01
Systems Software	Fort Wayne MSA, IN	Y	35160 FQ	63980 AW	90460 TQ	INBLS	10/01-12/01
Systems Software	Gary PMSA, IN	Y	38210 FQ	56210 AW	81050 TQ	INBLS	10/01-12/01
Systems Software	Indianapolis MSA, IN	Y	45260 FQ	67100 AW	92230 TQ	INBLS	10/01-12/01
Systems Software	Lafayette MSA, IN	Y	45400 FQ	59340 AW	86230 TQ	INBLS	10/01-12/01
Systems Software	South Bend MSA, IN	Y	23690 FQ	56260 AW	87530 TQ	INBLS	10/01-12/01
Systems Software	Davenport-Moline-Rock Island MSA, IA-IL	Y	35240 FQ	53470 AW	74370 TQ	IABLS	10/01-12/01
Systems Software	Des Moines MSA, IA	Y	47240 FQ	83600 AW	134940 TQ	IABLS	10/01-12/01
Systems Software	Kansas	Y	37410 FQ	68630 AW	114650 TQ	KSBLS	10/01-12/01
Systems Software	Topeka MSA, KS	Y	37050 FQ	55570 AW	77810 TQ	KSBLS	10/01-12/01
Systems Software	Wichita MSA, KS	Y	44430 FQ	67350 AW	93120 TQ	KSBLS	10/01-12/01
Systems Software	Kentucky	Y	39510 FQ	62470 AW	87540 TQ	KYBLS	10/01-12/01
Systems Software	Lexington MSA, KY	Y	21350 FQ	58250 AW	90840 TQ	KYBLS	10/01-12/01
Systems Software	Louisville MSA, KY-IN	Y	40550 FQ	62620 AW	85720 TQ	KYBLS	10/01-12/01
Systems Software	Louisiana	Y	38750 FQ	63560 AW	91650 TQ	LABLS	10/01-12/01

AAW	Average annual wage	**AOH**	Average offered, high	**ASH**	Average starting, high	**H**	Hourly	**M**	Monthly	**S**	Special: hourly and annual
AE	Average entry wage	**AOL**	Average offered, low	**ASL**	Average starting, low	**HI**	Highest wage paid	**MTC**	Median total compensation	**TQ**	Third quartile wage
AEX	Average experienced wage	**APH**	Average pay, high range	**AW**	Average wage paid	**HR**	High end range	**MW**	Median wage paid	**W**	Weekly
AO	Average offered	**APL**	Average pay, low range	**FQ**	First quartile wage	**LR**	Low end range	**SQ**	Second quartile wage	**Y**	Yearly

Occupation/Type/Industry	Location	Per	Low	Mid	High	Source	Date
Computer Software Engineer							
Systems Software	Baton Rouge MSA, LA	Y	28370 FQ	52910 AW	79330 TQ	LABLS	10/01-12/01
Systems Software	Lafayette MSA, LA	Y	40380 FQ	60450 AW	85890 TQ	LABLS	10/01-12/01
Systems Software	New Orleans MSA, LA	Y	40550 FQ	66640 AW	95200 TQ	LABLS	10/01-12/01
Systems Software	Maine	Y	44660 FQ	67420 AW	91010 TQ	MEBLS	10/01-12/01
Systems Software	Portland MSA, ME	Y	42880 FQ	63570 AW	85590 TQ	MEBLS	10/01-12/01
Systems Software	Maryland	Y	51230 FQ	78810 AW	116700 TQ	MDBLS	10/01-12/01
Systems Software	Baltimore PMSA, MD	Y	51260 FQ	77740 AW	109330 TQ	MDBLS	10/01-12/01
Systems Software	Massachusetts	Y	53080 FQ	82230 AW	117310 TQ	MABLS	10/01-12/01
Systems Software	Boston PMSA, MA-NH	Y	57470 FQ	85560 AW	121190 TQ	MABLS	10/01-12/01
Systems Software	Brockton PMSA, MA	Y	58880 FQ	78390 AW	110770 TQ	MABLS	10/01-12/01
Systems Software	Lawrence PMSA, MA-NH	Y	53090 FQ	80550 AW	111460 TQ	MABLS	10/01-12/01
Systems Software	Lowell PMSA, MA-NH	Y	54630 FQ	82940 AW	114680 TQ	MABLS	10/01-12/01
Systems Software	Springfield MSA, MA	Y	52430 FQ	78330 AW	111940 TQ	MABLS	10/01-12/01
Systems Software	Worcester PMSA, MA-CT	Y	30550 FQ	57140 AW	88100 TQ	MABLS	10/01-12/01
Systems Software	Michigan	Y	46320 FQ	72660 AW	106930 TQ	MIBLS	10/01-12/01
Systems Software	Ann Arbor PMSA, MI	Y	48430 FQ	68590 AW	91580 TQ	MIBLS	10/01-12/01
Systems Software	Detroit PMSA, MI	Y	47190 FQ	74820 AW	109860 TQ	MIBLS	10/01-12/01
Systems Software	Grand Rapids-Muskegon-Holland MSA, MI	Y	42850 FQ	65110 AW	93330 TQ	MIBLS	10/01-12/01
Systems Software	Lansing-East Lansing MSA, MI	Y	39780 FQ	59810 AW	78330 TQ	MIBLS	10/01-12/01
Systems Software	Minnesota	Y	49600 FQ	72780 AW	103130 TQ	MNBLS	10/01-12/01
Systems Software	Minneapolis-St. Paul MSA, MN-WI	Y	49660 FQ	73400 AW	104250 TQ	MNBLS	10/01-12/01
Systems Software	Mississippi	Y	46770 FQ	73360 AW	105160 TQ	MSBLS	10/01-12/01
Systems Software	Biloxi-Gulfport-Pascagoula MSA, MS	Y	51180 FQ	79720 AW	109490 TQ	MSBLS	10/01-12/01
Systems Software	Jackson MSA, MS	Y	46050 FQ	70630 AW	101610 TQ	MSBLS	10/01-12/01
Systems Software	Missouri	Y	41160 FQ	66210 AW	92480 TQ	MOBLS	10/01-12/01
Systems Software	Kansas City MSA, MO-KS	Y	36220 FQ	67510 AW	108700 TQ	MOBLS	10/01-12/01
Systems Software	St. Louis MSA, MO-IL	Y	44320 FQ	67550 AW	92610 TQ	MOBLS	10/01-12/01
Systems Software	Springfield MSA, MO	Y	45060 FQ	75750 AW	130850 TQ	MOBLS	10/01-12/01
Systems Software	Montana	Y	36020 FQ	60130 AW	81920 TQ	MTBLS	10/01-12/01
Systems Software	Nebraska	Y	44480 FQ	67870 AW	91240 TQ	NEBLS	10/01-12/01
Systems Software	Lincoln MSA, NE	Y	22390 FQ	56190 AW	86360 TQ	NEBLS	10/01-12/01
Systems Software	Omaha MSA, NE-IA	Y	45750 FQ	67600 AW	90820 TQ	NEBLS	10/01-12/01
Systems Software	Nevada	Y	38520 FQ	68290 AW	108120 TQ	NVBLS	10/01-12/01
Systems Software	Las Vegas MSA, NV-AZ	Y	37420 FQ	68280 AW	110280 TQ	NVBLS	10/01-12/01
Systems Software	Reno MSA, NV	Y	44220 FQ	67890 AW	94430 TQ	NVBLS	10/01-12/01
Systems Software	New Hampshire	Y	40960 FQ	71640 AW	113900 TQ	NHBLS	10/01-12/01
Systems Software	Manchester PMSA, NH	Y	39130 FQ	68680 AW	105500 TQ	NHBLS	10/01-12/01
Systems Software	Nashua PMSA, NH	Y	44260 FQ	78730 AW	123320 TQ	NHBLS	10/01-12/01
Systems Software	Portsmouth-Rochester PMSA, NH-ME	Y	37080 FQ	61840 AW	87890 TQ	NHBLS	10/01-12/01
Systems Software	New Jersey	Y	53580 FQ	82560 AW	117000 TQ	NJBLS	10/01-12/01
Systems Software	Atlantic-Cape May PMSA, NJ	Y	52380 FQ	78290 AW	113960 TQ	NJBLS	10/01-12/01
Systems Software	Bergen-Passaic PMSA, NJ	Y	49250 FQ	78060 AW	112480 TQ	NJBLS	10/01-12/01
Systems Software	Jersey City PMSA, NJ	Y	52530 FQ	83760 AW	129760 TQ	NJBLS	10/01-12/01
Systems Software	Middlesex-Somerset-Hunterdon PMSA, NJ	Y	54520 FQ	82940 AW	122240 TQ	NJBLS	10/01-12/01
Systems Software	Newark PMSA, NJ	Y	56220 FQ	86980 AW	124770 TQ	NJBLS	10/01-12/01
Systems Software	Trenton PMSA, NJ	Y	45210 FQ	70830 AW	106090 TQ	NJBLS	10/01-12/01
Systems Software	New Mexico	Y	38550 FQ	65940 AW	102620 TQ	NMBLS	10/01-12/01
Systems Software	Albuquerque MSA, NM	Y	38330 FQ	64840 AW	102750 TQ	NMBLS	10/01-12/01
Systems Software	New York	Y	33530 FQ	68830 AW	107350 TQ	NYBLS	10/01-12/01
Systems Software	Albany-Schenectady-Troy MSA, NY	Y	39100 FQ	65170 AW	102150 TQ	NYBLS	10/01-12/01
Systems Software	Buffalo-Niagara Falls MSA, NY	Y	32550 FQ	50830 AW	74480 TQ	NYBLS	10/01-12/01
Systems Software	Nassau-Suffolk PMSA, NY	Y	47930 FQ	72230 AW	102730 TQ	NYBLS	10/01-12/01
Systems Software	New York PMSA, NY	Y	31190 FQ	66080 AW	107400 TQ	NYBLS	10/01-12/01
Systems Software	Rochester MSA, NY	Y	43870 FQ	68720 AW	98690 TQ	NYBLS	10/01-12/01
Systems Software	Syracuse MSA, NY	Y	43870 FQ	64370 AW	89310 TQ	NYBLS	10/01-12/01
Systems Software	Utica-Rome MSA, NY	Y	37050 FQ	61760 AW	90670 TQ	NYBLS	10/01-12/01
Systems Software	North Carolina	Y	47280 FQ	73160 AW	105850 TQ	NCBLS	10/01-12/01
Systems Software	Charlotte-Gastonia-Rock Hill MSA, NC-SC	Y	47000 FQ	72170 AW	99110 TQ	NCBLS	10/01-12/01
Systems Software	Fayetteville MSA, NC	Y	31910 FQ	41230 AW	51000 TQ	NCBLS	10/01-12/01
Systems Software	Greensboro-Winston-Salem-High Point MSA, NC	Y	41200 FQ	64230 AW	100040 TQ	NCBLS	10/01-12/01
Systems Software	Wilmington MSA, NC	Y	34500 FQ	75340 AW	118180 TQ	NCBLS	10/01-12/01
Systems Software	North Dakota	Y	34460 FQ	57510 AW	91330 TQ	NDBLS	10/01-12/01

AAW	Average annual wage	**AOH**	Average offered, high	**ASH**	Average starting, high	**H**	Hourly	**M**	Monthly	**S**	Special: hourly and annual
AE	Average entry wage	**AOL**	Average offered, low	**ASL**	Average starting, low	**HI**	Highest wage paid	**MTC**	Median total compensation	**TQ**	Third quartile wage
AEX	Average experienced wage	**APH**	Average pay, high range	**AW**	Average wage paid	**HR**	High end range	**MW**	Median wage paid	**W**	Weekly
AO	Average offered	**APL**	Average pay, low range	**FQ**	First quartile wage	**LR**	Low end range	**SQ**	Second quartile wage	**Y**	Yearly

Occupation/Type/Industry	Location	Per	Low	Mid	High	Source	Date
Computer Software Engineer							
Systems Software	Ohio	Y	41530 FQ	64190 AW	89460 TQ	OHBLS	10/01-12/01
Systems Software	Akron PMSA, OH	Y	43590 FQ	70290 AW	102750 TQ	OHBLS	10/01-12/01
Systems Software	Canton-Massillon MSA, OH	Y	40170 FQ	56570 AW	81340 TQ	OHBLS	10/01-12/01
Systems Software	Cincinnati PMSA, OH-KY-IN	Y	41120 FQ	62570 AW	86960 TQ	OHBLS	10/01-12/01
Systems Software	Cleveland-Lorain-Elyria PMSA, OH	Y	39460 FQ	63900 AW	90700 TQ	OHBLS	10/01-12/01
Systems Software	Columbus MSA, OH	Y	42220 FQ	64060 AW	87570 TQ	OHBLS	10/01-12/01
Systems Software	Dayton-Springfield MSA, OH	Y	43010 FQ	63590 AW	87730 TQ	OHBLS	10/01-12/01
Systems Software	Hamilton-Middletown PMSA, OH	Y	37520 FQ	58600 AW	79520 TQ	OHBLS	10/01-12/01
Systems Software	Toledo MSA, OH	Y	36090 FQ	57490 AW	78340 TQ	OHBLS	10/01-12/01
Systems Software	Youngstown-Warren MSA, OH	Y	33100 FQ	61320 AW	87030 TQ	OHBLS	10/01-12/01
Systems Software	Oklahoma	Y	35960 FQ	63420 AW	90510 TQ	OKBLS	10/01-12/01
Systems Software	Oklahoma City MSA, OK	Y	30780 FQ	55690 AW	80570 TQ	OKBLS	10/01-12/01
Systems Software	Tulsa MSA, OK	Y	45940 FQ	68110 AW	93700 TQ	OKBLS	10/01-12/01
Systems Software	Oregon	Y	46210 FQ	72390 AW	107420 TQ	ORBLS	10/01-12/01
Systems Software	Eugene-Springfield MSA, OR	Y	47960 FQ	65590 AW	89890 TQ	ORBLS	10/01-12/01
Systems Software	Medford-Ashland MSA, OR	Y	55640 FQ	70030 AW	89890 TQ	ORBLS	10/01-12/01
Systems Software	Portland-Vancouver PMSA, OR-WA	Y	46130 FQ	72150 AW	107250 TQ	ORBLS	10/01-12/01
Systems Software	Pennsylvania	Y	47080 FQ	70350 AW	97980 TQ	PABLS	10/01-12/01
Systems Software	Allentown-Bethlehem-Easton MSA, PA	Y	48090 FQ	67760 AW	91740 TQ	PABLS	10/01-12/01
Systems Software	Harrisburg-Lebanon-Carlisle MSA, PA	Y	50250 FQ	70190 AW	95590 TQ	PABLS	10/01-12/01
Systems Software	Lancaster MSA, PA	Y	46490 FQ	63160 AW	81970 TQ	PABLS	10/01-12/01
Systems Software	Philadelphia PMSA, PA-NJ	Y	48380 FQ	72620 AW	103480 TQ	PABLS	10/01-12/01
Systems Software	Pittsburgh MSA, PA	Y	45180 FQ	69410 AW	95340 TQ	PABLS	10/01-12/01
Systems Software	Reading MSA, PA	Y	52100 FQ	68140 AW	87790 TQ	PABLS	10/01-12/01
Systems Software	Scranton-Wilkes-Barre-Hazleton MSA, PA	Y	40000 FQ	61610 AW	86410 TQ	PABLS	10/01-12/01
Systems Software	York MSA, PA	Y	31570 FQ	52250 AW	77260 TQ	PABLS	10/01-12/01
Systems Software	Rhode Island	Y	48510 FQ	68610 AW	91280 TQ	RIBLS	10/01-12/01
Systems Software	Providence-Fall River-Warwick MSA, RI-MA	Y	48880 FQ	69010 AW	91280 TQ	RIBLS	10/01-12/01
Systems Software	South Carolina	Y	38030 FQ	57020 AW	86670 TQ	SCBLS	10/01-12/01
Systems Software	Charleston-North Charleston MSA, SC	Y	37530 FQ	49680 AW	74270 TQ	SCBLS	10/01-12/01
Systems Software	Columbia MSA, SC	Y	35580 FQ	54660 AW	87130 TQ	SCBLS	10/01-12/01
Systems Software	Greenville-Spartanburg-Anderson MSA, SC	Y	39610 FQ	59940 AW	85740 TQ	SCBLS	10/01-12/01
Systems Software	South Dakota	Y	44450 FQ	65240 AW	95630 TQ	SDBLS	10/01-12/01
Systems Software	Sioux Falls MSA, SD	Y	46270 FQ	61390 AW	89510 TQ	SDBLS	10/01-12/01
Systems Software	Tennessee	Y	31140 FQ	56680 AW	86750 TQ	TNBLS	10/01-12/01
Systems Software	Chattanooga MSA, TN-GA	Y	26300 FQ	65280 AW	97790 TQ	TNBLS	10/01-12/01
Systems Software	Clarksville-Hopkinsville MSA, TN-KY	Y	28220 FQ	45460 AW	70010 TQ	TNBLS	10/01-12/01
Systems Software	Johnson City-Kingsport-Bristol MSA, TN-VA	Y	27070 FQ	77870 AW	128580 TQ	TNBLS	10/01-12/01
Systems Software	Knoxville MSA, TN	Y	49790 FQ	66480 AW	88850 TQ	TNBLS	10/01-12/01
Systems Software	Memphis MSA, TN-AR-MS	Y	30270 FQ	50420 AW	80660 TQ	TNBLS	10/01-12/01
Systems Software	Nashville MSA, TN	Y	29980 FQ	53320 AW	87560 TQ	TNBLS	10/01-12/01
Systems Software	Texas	Y	47350 FQ	72970 AW	108260 TQ	TXBLS	10/01-12/01
Systems Software	Austin-San Marcos MSA, TX	Y	50890 FQ	80060 AW	121570 TQ	TXBLS	10/01-12/01
Systems Software	Brownsville-Harlingen-San Benito MSA, TX	Y	32950 FQ	65140 AW	97790 TQ	TXBLS	10/01-12/01
Systems Software	Dallas PMSA, TX	Y	46010 FQ	71870 AW	106590 TQ	TXBLS	10/01-12/01
Systems Software	El Paso MSA, TX	Y	40280 FQ	73850 AW	119470 TQ	TXBLS	10/01-12/01
Systems Software	Fort Worth-Arlington PMSA, TX	Y	47830 FQ	69890 AW	94060 TQ	TXBLS	10/01-12/01
Systems Software	Galveston-Texas City PMSA, TX	Y	31570 FQ	68060 AW	103650 TQ	TXBLS	10/01-12/01
Systems Software	Houston PMSA, TX	Y	48970 FQ	72470 AW	104160 TQ	TXBLS	10/01-12/01
Systems Software	Killeen-Temple MSA, TX	Y	46150 FQ	68150 AW	93010 TQ	TXBLS	10/01-12/01
Systems Software	Lubbock MSA, TX	Y	17080 FQ	50940 AW	89980 TQ	TXBLS	10/01-12/01
Systems Software	San Antonio MSA, TX	Y	44350 FQ	64730 AW	94000 TQ	TXBLS	10/01-12/01
Systems Software	Tyler MSA, TX	Y	45300 FQ	90950 AW	142250 TQ	TXBLS	10/01-12/01
Systems Software	Waco MSA, TX	Y	28470 FQ	63590 AW	103810 TQ	TXBLS	10/01-12/01
Systems Software	Utah	Y	32190 FQ	60240 AW	89860 TQ	UTBLS	10/01-12/01
Systems Software	Provo-Orem MSA, UT	Y	18530 FQ	54660 AW	88210 TQ	UTBLS	10/01-12/01

AAW	Average annual wage	**AOH**	Average offered, high	**ASH**	Average starting, high	**H**	Hourly	**M**	Monthly	**S**	Special: hourly and annual
AE	Average entry wage	**AOL**	Average offered, low	**ASL**	Average starting, low	**HI**	Highest wage paid	**MTC**	Median total compensation	**TQ**	Third quartile wage
AEX	Average experienced wage	**APH**	Average pay, high range	**AW**	Average wage paid	**HR**	High end range	**MW**	Median wage paid	**W**	Weekly
AO	Average offered	**APL**	Average pay, low range	**FQ**	First quartile wage	**LR**	Low end range	**SQ**	Second quartile wage	**Y**	Yearly

Occupation/Type/Industry	Location	Per	Low	Mid	High	Source	Date
Computer Software Engineer							
Systems Software	Salt Lake City-Ogden MSA, UT	Y	35620 FQ	62010 AW	90540 TQ	UTBLS	10/01-12/01
Systems Software	Vermont	Y	45590 FQ	69920 AW	100010 TQ	VTBLS	10/01-12/01
Systems Software	Virginia	Y	44200 FQ	72090 AW	101330 TQ	VABLS	10/01-12/01
Systems Software	Lynchburg MSA, VA	Y	44680 FQ	68610 AW	92040 TQ	VABLS	10/01-12/01
Systems Software	Norfolk-Virginia Beach-Newport News MSA, VA-NC	Y	45320 FQ	62900 AW	90110 TQ	VABLS	10/01-12/01
Systems Software	Richmond-Petersburg MSA, VA	Y	42210 FQ	66920 AW	91140 TQ	VABLS	10/01-12/01
Systems Software	Roanoke MSA, VA	Y	48030 FQ	72610 AW	95340 TQ	VABLS	10/01-12/01
Systems Software	Washington	Y	51320 FQ	77650 AW	110480 TQ	WABLS	10/01-12/01
Systems Software	Bremerton PMSA, WA	Y	47080 FQ	62580 AW	100470 TQ	WABLS	10/01-12/01
Systems Software	Richland-Kennewick-Pasco MSA, WA	Y	45600 FQ	71070 AW	104420 TQ	WABLS	10/01-12/01
Systems Software	Seattle-Bellevue-Everett PMSA, WA	Y	51980 FQ	78200 AW	111010 TQ	WABLS	10/01-12/01
Systems Software	Spokane MSA, WA	Y	39240 FQ	64980 AW	96800 TQ	WABLS	10/01-12/01
Systems Software	Tacoma PMSA, WA	Y	58620 FQ	80260 AW	108940 TQ	WABLS	10/01-12/01
Systems Software	Yakima MSA, WA	Y	47320 FQ	70100 AW	93470 TQ	WABLS	10/01-12/01
Systems Software	West Virginia	Y	40940 FQ	63230 AW	89520 TQ	WVBLS	10/01-12/01
Systems Software	Charleston MSA, WV	Y	48970 FQ	72800 AW	96840 TQ	WVBLS	10/01-12/01
Systems Software	Huntington-Ashland MSA, WV-KY-OH	Y	38830 FQ	57300 AW	85730 TQ	WVBLS	10/01-12/01
Systems Software	Wisconsin	Y	38300 FQ	60290 AW	87000 TQ	WIBLS	10/01-12/01
Systems Software	Appleton-Oshkosh-Neenah MSA, WI	Y	45030 FQ	64230 AW	88920 TQ	WIBLS	10/01-12/01
Systems Software	Green Bay MSA, WI	Y	27800 FQ	47480 AW	70290 TQ	WIBLS	10/01-12/01
Systems Software	Madison MSA, WI	Y	39460 FQ	63080 AW	95350 TQ	WIBLS	10/01-12/01
Systems Software	Milwaukee-Waukesha PMSA, WI	Y	43110 FQ	62830 AW	86660 TQ	WIBLS	10/01-12/01
Systems Software	Racine PMSA, WI	Y	41200 FQ	61190 AW	86780 TQ	WIBLS	10/01-12/01
Systems Software	Wyoming	Y	29910 FQ	44480 AW	56700 TQ	WYBLS	10/01-12/01
Systems Software	Puerto Rico	Y	35200 FQ	59400 AW	88290 TQ	PRBLS	10/01-12/01
Computer Support Specialist	United States	Y		25760-39660 AW		FREEP1	1/00-1/00
	Alabama	Y	18500 FQ	36120 AW	56320 TQ	ALBLS	10/01-12/01
	Alaska	Y	25810 FQ	41370 AW	56430 TQ	AKBLS	10/01-12/01
	Arizona	Y	22150 FQ	41320 AW	64600 TQ	AZBLS	10/01-12/01
	Arkansas	Y	18970 FQ	29530 AW	43290 TQ	ARBLS	10/01-12/01
	California	Y	26800 FQ	47000 AW	73060 TQ	CABLS	10/01-12/01
	Colorado	Y	25790 FQ	43870 AW	76470 TQ	COBLS	10/01-12/01
	Connecticut	Y	29360 FQ	45130 AW	64300 TQ	CTBLS	10/01-12/01
	Delaware	Y	17870 FQ	42400 AW	67770 TQ	DEBLS	10/01-12/01
	District of Columbia	Y	21720 FQ	41720 AW	59750 TQ	DCBLS	10/01-12/01
	Florida	Y	20520 FQ	34940 AW	54130 TQ	FLBLS	10/01-12/01
	Georgia	Y	24390 FQ	41260 AW	65490 TQ	GABLS	10/01-12/01
	Hawaii	Y	22390 FQ	46630 AW	81450 TQ	HIBLS	10/01-12/01
	Idaho	Y	21260 FQ	35760 AW	55130 TQ	IDBLS	10/01-12/01
	Illinois	Y	21900 FQ	42980 AW	70120 TQ	ILBLS	10/01-12/01
	Indiana	Y	20800 FQ	35940 AW	52790 TQ	INBLS	10/01-12/01
	Iowa	Y	22830 FQ	37370 AW	57300 TQ	IABLS	10/01-12/01
	Kansas	Y	22450 FQ	40690 AW	60150 TQ	KSBLS	10/01-12/01
	Kentucky	Y	17000 FQ	33130 AW	50820 TQ	KYBLS	10/01-12/01
	Louisiana	Y	22930 FQ	39150 AW	57260 TQ	LABLS	10/01-12/01
	Maine	Y	20960 FQ	32690 AW	45980 TQ	MEBLS	10/01-12/01
	Maryland	Y	26870 FQ	46290 AW	70760 TQ	MDBLS	10/01-12/01
	Massachusetts	Y	28400 FQ	48990 AW	77000 TQ	MABLS	10/01-12/01
	Michigan	Y	24920 FQ	41290 AW	58680 TQ	MIBLS	10/01-12/01
	Minnesota	Y	25830 FQ	40390 AW	57680 TQ	MNBLS	10/01-12/01
	Mississippi	Y	17950 FQ	33600 AW	53500 TQ	MSBLS	10/01-12/01
	Missouri	Y	21560 FQ	39840 AW	64130 TQ	MOBLS	10/01-12/01
	Montana	Y	20490 FQ	33450 AW	49500 TQ	MTBLS	10/01-12/01
	Nebraska	Y	21430 FQ	37090 AW	57480 TQ	NEBLS	10/01-12/01
	Nevada	Y	19790 FQ	31110 AW	48460 TQ	NVBLS	10/01-12/01
	New Hampshire	Y	23360 FQ	37270 AW	54880 TQ	NHBLS	10/01-12/01
	New Jersey	Y	27810 FQ	47330 AW	72880 TQ	NJBLS	10/01-12/01
	New Mexico	Y	21130 FQ	36460 AW	60250 TQ	NMBLS	10/01-12/01
	New York	Y	26340 FQ	48980 AW	75340 TQ	NYBLS	10/01-12/01
	North Carolina	Y	25710 FQ	45770 AW	77180 TQ	NCBLS	10/01-12/01
	North Dakota	Y	17750 FQ	25650 AW	39920 TQ	NDBLS	10/01-12/01

AAW	Average annual wage	**AOH**	Average offered, high	**ASH**	Average starting, high	**H**	Hourly	**M**	Monthly	**S**	Special: hourly and annual
AE	Average entry wage	**AOL**	Average offered, low	**ASL**	Average starting, low	**HI**	Highest wage paid	**MTC**	Median total compensation	**TQ**	Third quartile wage
AEX	Average experienced wage	**APH**	Average pay, high range	**AW**	Average wage paid	**HR**	High end range	**MW**	Median wage paid	**W**	Weekly
AO	Average offered	**APL**	Average pay, low range	**FQ**	First quartile wage	**LR**	Low end range	**SQ**	Second quartile wage	**Y**	Yearly

Occupation/Type/Industry	Location	Per	Low	Mid	High	Source	Date
Computer Support Specialist	Ohio	Y	25930 FQ	42690 AW	63400 TQ	OHBLS	10/01-12/01
	Oklahoma	Y	15820 FQ	26910 AW	43470 TQ	OKBLS	10/01-12/01
	Oregon	Y	20960 FQ	34610 AW	52330 TQ	ORBLS	10/01-12/01
	Pennsylvania	Y	22270 FQ	38980 AW	58850 TQ	PABLS	10/01-12/01
	Rhode Island	Y	25370 FQ	39400 AW	56130 TQ	RIBLS	10/01-12/01
	South Carolina	Y	19650 FQ	35170 AW	53630 TQ	SCBLS	10/01-12/01
	South Dakota	Y	20600 FQ	29030 AW	39620 TQ	SDBLS	10/01-12/01
	Tennessee	Y	19630 FQ	34280 AW	51820 TQ	TNBLS	10/01-12/01
	Texas	Y	20570 FQ	42250 AW	74040 TQ	TXBLS	10/01-12/01
	Utah	Y	15920 FQ	25700 AW	41450 TQ	UTBLS	10/01-12/01
	Vermont	Y	24710 FQ	39250 AW	56560 TQ	VTBLS	10/01-12/01
	Virginia	Y	25040 FQ	46320 AW	79090 TQ	VABLS	10/01-12/01
	Washington	Y	25500 FQ	42500 AW	61810 TQ	WABLS	10/01-12/01
	West Virginia	Y	15620 FQ	28000 AW	45260 TQ	WVBLS	10/01-12/01
	Wisconsin	Y	24440 FQ	39840 AW	57030 TQ	WIBLS	10/01-12/01
	Wyoming	Y	15720 FQ	29080 AW	47530 TQ	WYBLS	10/01-12/01
	Puerto Rico	Y	15240 FQ	25500 AW	40650 TQ	PRBLS	10/01-12/01
	Guam	Y	20280 FQ	31740 AW	48050 TQ	GUBLS	10/01-12/01
Computer Systems Analyst	United States	Y		39700 AW		FREEP1	1/00-1/00
	Alabama	Y	35950 FQ	58120 AW	84900 TQ	ALBLS	10/01-12/01
	Birmingham MSA, AL	Y	36000 FQ	58640 AW	87050 TQ	ALBLS	10/01-12/01
	Huntsville MSA, AL	Y	37100 FQ	60530 AW	86500 TQ	ALBLS	10/01-12/01
	Mobile MSA, AL	Y	36470 FQ	57220 AW	83160 TQ	ALBLS	10/01-12/01
	Montgomery MSA, AL	Y	37910 FQ	56030 AW	71550 TQ	ALBLS	10/01-12/01
	Alaska	Y	43190 FQ	63650 AW	86700 TQ	AKBLS	10/01-12/01
	Anchorage MSA, AK	Y	44310 FQ	63860 AW	85650 TQ	AKBLS	10/01-12/01
	Arizona	Y	38910 FQ	68910 AW	97480 TQ	AZBLS	10/01-12/01
	Phoenix-Mesa MSA, AZ	Y	39950 FQ	71370 AW	100130 TQ	AZBLS	10/01-12/01
	Tucson MSA, AZ	Y	34830 FQ	52210 AW	72040 TQ	AZBLS	10/01-12/01
	Arkansas	Y	29230 FQ	48130 AW	70460 TQ	ARBLS	10/01-12/01
	Fayetteville-Springdale-Rogers MSA, AR	Y	26230 FQ	44010 AW	70840 TQ	ARBLS	10/01-12/01
	Fort Smith MSA, AR-OK	Y	37410 FQ	54090 AW	76680 TQ	ARBLS	10/01-12/01
	Little Rock-North Little Rock MSA, AR	Y	32530 FQ	50240 AW	70280 TQ	ARBLS	10/01-12/01
	California	Y	41850 FQ	67340 AW	98130 TQ	CABLS	10/01-12/01
	Bakersfield MSA, CA	Y	40890 FQ	64510 AW	88300 TQ	CABLS	10/01-12/01
	Chico-Paradise MSA, CA	Y	36400 FQ	57230 AW	90930 TQ	CABLS	10/01-12/01
	Fresno MSA, CA	Y	37850 FQ	55490 AW	72890 TQ	CABLS	10/01-12/01
	Los Angeles-Long Beach PMSA, CA	Y	39430 FQ	63190 AW	89840 TQ	CABLS	10/01-12/01
	Merced MSA, CA	Y	30060 FQ	52670 AW	72980 TQ	CABLS	10/01-12/01
	Modesto MSA, CA	Y	38810 FQ	69980 AW	129250 TQ	CABLS	10/01-12/01
	Oakland PMSA, CA	Y	46950 FQ	71480 AW	105200 TQ	CABLS	10/01-12/01
	Orange County PMSA, CA	Y	45840 FQ	66960 AW	93100 TQ	CABLS	10/01-12/01
	Redding MSA, CA	Y	31730 FQ	45030 AW	59310 TQ	CABLS	10/01-12/01
	Riverside-San Bernardino PMSA, CA	Y	38630 FQ	56040 AW	76890 TQ	CABLS	10/01-12/01
	Sacramento PMSA, CA	Y	39300 FQ	60640 AW	82830 TQ	CABLS	10/01-12/01
	Salinas MSA, CA	Y	47810 FQ	71200 AW	99720 TQ	CABLS	10/01-12/01
	San Diego MSA, CA	Y	43130 FQ	65380 AW	94000 TQ	CABLS	10/01-12/01
	San Francisco PMSA, CA	Y	47250 FQ	74660 AW	109620 TQ	CABLS	10/01-12/01
	San Jose PMSA, CA	Y	41350 FQ	74970 AW	117680 TQ	CABLS	10/01-12/01
	San Luis Obispo-Atascadero-Paso Robles MSA, CA	Y	30550 FQ	52590 AW	75770 TQ	CABLS	10/01-12/01
	Santa Barbara-Santa Maria-Lompoc MSA, CA	Y	42810 FQ	67680 AW	97640 TQ	CABLS	10/01-12/01
	Santa Cruz-Watsonville PMSA, CA	Y	38530 FQ	66200 AW	104790 TQ	CABLS	10/01-12/01
	Santa Rosa PMSA, CA	Y	39420 FQ	77430 AW	127550 TQ	CABLS	10/01-12/01
	Stockton-Lodi MSA, CA	Y	36080 FQ	57070 AW	82510 TQ	CABLS	10/01-12/01
	Vallejo-Fairfield-Napa PMSA, CA	Y	40080 FQ	57240 AW	85560 TQ	CABLS	10/01-12/01
	Ventura PMSA, CA	Y	43390 FQ	65550 AW	90880 TQ	CABLS	10/01-12/01
	Visalia-Tulare-Porterville MSA, CA	Y	38630 FQ	53400 AW	72000 TQ	CABLS	10/01-12/01
	Colorado	Y	44760 FQ	69790 AW	91050 TQ	COBLS	10/01-12/01
	Boulder-Longmont PMSA, CO	Y	42400 FQ	64510 AW	91860 TQ	COBLS	10/01-12/01
	Colorado Springs MSA, CO	Y	41480 FQ	70310 AW	107950 TQ	COBLS	10/01-12/01
	Denver PMSA, CO	Y	45950 FQ	71590 AW	90660 TQ	COBLS	10/01-12/01
	Fort Collins-Loveland MSA, CO	Y	42440 FQ	65430 AW	94350 TQ	COBLS	10/01-12/01

AAW	Average annual wage	**AOH**	Average offered, high	**ASH**	Average starting, high	**H**	Hourly	**M**	Monthly	**S**	Special: hourly and annual
AE	Average entry wage	**AOL**	Average offered, low	**ASL**	Average starting, low	**HI**	Highest wage paid	**MTC**	Median total compensation	**TQ**	Third quartile wage
AEX	Average experienced wage	**APH**	Average pay, high range	**AW**	Average wage paid	**HR**	High end range	**MW**	Median wage paid	**W**	Weekly
AO	Average offered	**APL**	Average pay, low range	**FQ**	First quartile wage	**LR**	Low end range	**SQ**	Second quartile wage	**Y**	Yearly

Occupation/Type/Industry	Location	Per	Low	Mid	High	Source	Date
Computer Systems Analyst	Greeley PMSA, CO	Y	39290 FQ	63510 AW	90910 TQ	COBLS	10/01-12/01
	Connecticut	Y	42410 FQ	65950 AW	91400 TQ	CTBLS	10/01-12/01
	Bridgeport PMSA, CT	Y	47180 FQ	76030 AW	124950 TQ	CTBLS	10/01-12/01
	Danbury PMSA, CT	Y	47650 FQ	71270 AW	106030 TQ	CTBLS	10/01-12/01
	Hartford MSA, CT	Y	40650 FQ	63570 AW	90570 TQ	CTBLS	10/01-12/01
	New Haven-Meriden PMSA, CT	Y	47010 FQ	71250 AW	90530 TQ	CTBLS	10/01-12/01
	New London-Norwich MSA, CT-RI	Y	41160 FQ	61110 AW	87750 TQ	CTBLS	10/01-12/01
	Stamford-Norwalk PMSA, CT	Y	44850 FQ	68580 AW	93750 TQ	CTBLS	10/01-12/01
	Delaware	Y	39930 FQ	65070 AW	92050 TQ	DEBLS	10/01-12/01
	Wilmington-Newark PMSA, DE-MD	Y	40360 FQ	65160 AW	92050 TQ	DEBLS	10/01-12/01
	District of Columbia	Y	48290 FQ	70670 AW	95850 TQ	DCBLS	10/01-12/01
	Washington PMSA, DC-MD-VA-WV	Y	43890 FQ	66990 AW	92980 TQ	DCBLS	10/01-12/01
	Florida	Y	35020 FQ	57920 AW	85790 TQ	FLBLS	10/01-12/01
	Daytona Beach MSA, FL	Y	31290 FQ	46360 AW	67850 TQ	FLBLS	10/01-12/01
	Fort Lauderdale PMSA, FL	Y	37730 FQ	58130 AW	85540 TQ	FLBLS	10/01-12/01
	Fort Myers-Cape Coral MSA, FL	Y	36030 FQ	54900 AW	80980 TQ	FLBLS	10/01-12/01
	Fort Pierce-Port St. Lucie MSA, FL	Y	38590 FQ	49360 AW	66400 TQ	FLBLS	10/01-12/01
	Fort Walton Beach MSA, FL	Y	38540 FQ	57120 AW	83570 TQ	FLBLS	10/01-12/01
	Gainesville MSA, FL	Y	30690 FQ	46690 AW	71870 TQ	FLBLS	10/01-12/01
	Jacksonville MSA, FL	Y	38090 FQ	59890 AW	86110 TQ	FLBLS	10/01-12/01
	Lakeland-Winter Haven MSA, FL	Y	33780 FQ	50920 AW	70500 TQ	FLBLS	10/01-12/01
	Melbourne-Titusville-Palm Bay MSA, FL	Y	31680 FQ	49860 AW	73290 TQ	FLBLS	10/01-12/01
	Miami PMSA, FL	Y	35940 FQ	59360 AW	85800 TQ	FLBLS	10/01-12/01
	Naples MSA, FL	Y	33030 FQ	52930 AW	76640 TQ	FLBLS	10/01-12/01
	Ocala MSA, FL	Y	32370 FQ	45740 AW	63090 TQ	FLBLS	10/01-12/01
	Orlando MSA, FL	Y	37370 FQ	61140 AW	88780 TQ	FLBLS	10/01-12/01
	Pensacola MSA, FL	Y	32790 FQ	54380 AW	70330 TQ	FLBLS	10/01-12/01
	Sarasota-Bradenton MSA, FL	Y	31470 FQ	55720 AW	84120 TQ	FLBLS	10/01-12/01
	Tallahassee MSA, FL	Y	31750 FQ	57840 AW	90110 TQ	FLBLS	10/01-12/01
	Tampa-St. Petersburg-Clearwater MSA, FL	Y	35410 FQ	58560 AW	88160 TQ	FLBLS	10/01-12/01
	West Palm Beach-Boca Raton MSA, FL	Y	34240 FQ	58700 AW	86960 TQ	FLBLS	10/01-12/01
	Georgia	Y	41540 FQ	64890 AW	92390 TQ	GABLS	10/01-12/01
	Atlanta MSA, GA	Y	43670 FQ	67710 AW	95790 TQ	GABLS	10/01-12/01
	Augusta-Aiken MSA, GA-SC	Y	36470 FQ	60410 AW	89650 TQ	GABLS	10/01-12/01
	Columbus MSA, GA-AL	Y	34550 FQ	54610 AW	73850 TQ	GABLS	10/01-12/01
	Macon MSA, GA	Y	48750 FQ	58560 AW	72620 TQ	GABLS	10/01-12/01
	Savannah MSA, GA	Y	34280 FQ	47440 AW	67350 TQ	GABLS	10/01-12/01
	Hawaii	Y	40320 FQ	58060 AW	81200 TQ	HIBLS	10/01-12/01
	Honolulu MSA, HI	Y	40530 FQ	58260 AW	81270 TQ	HIBLS	10/01-12/01
	Idaho	Y	33060 FQ	51980 AW	72580 TQ	IDBLS	10/01-12/01
	Boise City MSA, ID	Y	32890 FQ	52540 AW	75210 TQ	IDBLS	10/01-12/01
	Illinois	Y	40810 FQ	68960 AW	106170 TQ	ILBLS	10/01-12/01
	Champaign-Urbana MSA, IL	Y	30720 FQ	56610 AW	88240 TQ	ILBLS	10/01-12/01
	Chicago PMSA, IL	Y	40970 FQ	69480 AW	106630 TQ	ILBLS	10/01-12/01
	Peoria-Pekin MSA, IL	Y	45460 FQ	58000 AW	72960 TQ	ILBLS	10/01-12/01
	Springfield MSA, IL	Y	39170 FQ	57920 AW	74930 TQ	ILBLS	10/01-12/01
	Indiana	Y	36660 FQ	53780 AW	75600 TQ	INBLS	10/01-12/01
	Elkhart-Goshen MSA, IN	Y	36820 FQ	54150 AW	76300 TQ	INBLS	10/01-12/01
	Evansville-Henderson MSA, IN-KY	Y	32150 FQ	57720 AW	85070 TQ	INBLS	10/01-12/01
	Fort Wayne MSA, IN	Y	38020 FQ	56600 AW	77480 TQ	INBLS	10/01-12/01
	Gary PMSA, IN	Y	39730 FQ	60890 AW	84650 TQ	INBLS	10/01-12/01
	Indianapolis MSA, IN	Y	37170 FQ	53650 AW	76280 TQ	INBLS	10/01-12/01
	Lafayette MSA, IN	Y	30720 FQ	48890 AW	69900 TQ	INBLS	10/01-12/01
	South Bend MSA, IN	Y	34290 FQ	57880 AW	84430 TQ	INBLS	10/01-12/01
	Iowa	Y	33090 FQ	53240 AW	73600 TQ	IABLS	10/01-12/01
	Cedar Rapids MSA, IA	Y	33920 FQ	55660 AW	79960 TQ	IABLS	10/01-12/01
	Davenport-Moline-Rock Island MSA, IA-IL	Y	36410 FQ	55460 AW	76060 TQ	IABLS	10/01-12/01
	Des Moines MSA, IA	Y	33690 FQ	54420 AW	74630 TQ	IABLS	10/01-12/01
	Kansas	Y	35350 FQ	58020 AW	87220 TQ	KSBLS	10/01-12/01
	Topeka MSA, KS	Y	33980 FQ	54180 AW	75530 TQ	KSBLS	10/01-12/01

AAW Average annual wage; **AE** Average entry wage; **AEX** Average experienced wage; **AO** Average offered; **AOH** Average offered, high; **AOL** Average offered, low; **APH** Average pay, high range; **APL** Average pay, low range; **ASH** Average starting, high; **ASL** Average starting, low; **AW** Average wage paid; **FQ** First quartile wage; **H** Hourly; **HI** Highest wage paid; **HR** High end range; **LR** Low end range; **M** Monthly; **MTC** Median total compensation; **MW** Median wage paid; **SQ** Second quartile wage; **S** Special: hourly and annual; **TQ** Third quartile wage; **W** Weekly; **Y** Yearly

Occupation/Type/Industry	Location	Per	Low	Mid	High	Source	Date
Computer Systems Analyst	Wichita MSA, KS	Y	42150 FQ	61720 AW	86630 TQ	KSBLS	10/01-12/01
	Kentucky	Y	37970 FQ	58800 AW	83680 TQ	KYBLS	10/01-12/01
	Lexington MSA, KY	Y	38650 FQ	60020 AW	87230 TQ	KYBLS	10/01-12/01
	Louisville MSA, KY-IN	Y	37200 FQ	54630 AW	72060 TQ	KYBLS	10/01-12/01
	Louisiana	Y	34360 FQ	52140 AW	73490 TQ	LABLS	10/01-12/01
	Baton Rouge MSA, LA	Y	31310 FQ	51530 AW	79210 TQ	LABLS	10/01-12/01
	Houma MSA, LA	Y	30420 FQ	44550 AW	68530 TQ	LABLS	10/01-12/01
	Lafayette MSA, LA	Y	29120 FQ	53740 AW	81760 TQ	LABLS	10/01-12/01
	Lake Charles MSA, LA	Y	36230 FQ	55690 AW	79410 TQ	LABLS	10/01-12/01
	New Orleans MSA, LA	Y	35720 FQ	51990 AW	71260 TQ	LABLS	10/01-12/01
	Shreveport-Bossier City MSA, LA	Y	33270 FQ	51630 AW	74820 TQ	LABLS	10/01-12/01
	Maine	Y	37880 FQ	56700 AW	80740 TQ	MEBLS	10/01-12/01
	Portland MSA, ME	Y	40160 FQ	60000 AW	85810 TQ	MEBLS	10/01-12/01
	Maryland	Y	44400 FQ	65340 AW	89060 TQ	MDBLS	10/01-12/01
	Baltimore PMSA, MD	Y	45340 FQ	66500 AW	89430 TQ	MDBLS	10/01-12/01
	Massachusetts	Y	43460 FQ	66710 AW	95200 TQ	MABLS	10/01-12/01
	Boston PMSA, MA-NH	Y	44210 FQ	67350 AW	95060 TQ	MABLS	10/01-12/01
	Brockton PMSA, MA	Y	41270 FQ	61080 AW	87640 TQ	MABLS	10/01-12/01
	Lawrence PMSA, MA-NH	Y	45120 FQ	65770 AW	91440 TQ	MABLS	10/01-12/01
	Lowell PMSA, MA-NH	Y	38190 FQ	65050 AW	91580 TQ	MABLS	10/01-12/01
	New Bedford PMSA, MA	Y	38700 FQ	59070 AW	86700 TQ	MABLS	10/01-12/01
	Worcester PMSA, MA-CT	Y	43780 FQ	63070 AW	90540 TQ	MABLS	10/01-12/01
	Michigan	Y	37620 FQ	58410 AW	83520 TQ	MIBLS	10/01-12/01
	Ann Arbor PMSA, MI	Y	36500 FQ	61260 AW	102700 TQ	MIBLS	10/01-12/01
	Detroit PMSA, MI	Y	38660 FQ	61020 AW	86640 TQ	MIBLS	10/01-12/01
	Flint PMSA, MI	Y	42440 FQ	59450 AW	79110 TQ	MIBLS	10/01-12/01
	Grand Rapids-Muskegon-Holland MSA, MI	Y	35860 FQ	54860 AW	75930 TQ	MIBLS	10/01-12/01
	Kalamazoo-Battle Creek MSA, MI	Y	40090 FQ	59370 AW	81620 TQ	MIBLS	10/01-12/01
	Saginaw-Bay City-Midland MSA, MI	Y	37380 FQ	51160 AW	72920 TQ	MIBLS	10/01-12/01
	Minnesota	Y	40520 FQ	63340 AW	90870 TQ	MNBLS	10/01-12/01
	Duluth-Superior MSA, MN-WI	Y	34910 FQ	55680 AW	83880 TQ	MNBLS	10/01-12/01
	Minneapolis-St. Paul MSA, MN-WI	Y	40870 FQ	63900 AW	91280 TQ	MNBLS	10/01-12/01
	St. Cloud MSA, MN	Y	37860 FQ	55320 AW	74130 TQ	MNBLS	10/01-12/01
	Mississippi	Y	30810 FQ	46630 AW	66530 TQ	MSBLS	10/01-12/01
	Biloxi-Gulfport-Pascagoula MSA, MS	Y	31090 FQ	48740 AW	69710 TQ	MSBLS	10/01-12/01
	Jackson MSA, MS	Y	31940 FQ	47810 AW	66780 TQ	MSBLS	10/01-12/01
	Missouri	Y	37870 FQ	58420 AW	81140 TQ	MOBLS	10/01-12/01
	Kansas City MSA, MO-KS	Y	36930 FQ	57630 AW	84250 TQ	MOBLS	10/01-12/01
	St. Louis MSA, MO-IL	Y	39850 FQ	60130 AW	82730 TQ	MOBLS	10/01-12/01
	Springfield MSA, MO	Y	31930 FQ	50710 AW	71410 TQ	MOBLS	10/01-12/01
	Montana	Y	34940 FQ	51130 AW	70200 TQ	MTBLS	10/01-12/01
	Billings MSA, MT	Y	35920 FQ	49650 AW	68240 TQ	MTBLS	10/01-12/01
	Nebraska	Y	31300 FQ	55400 AW	79960 TQ	NEBLS	10/01-12/01
	Lincoln MSA, NE	Y	33220 FQ	53580 AW	75170 TQ	NEBLS	10/01-12/01
	Omaha MSA, NE-IA	Y	30610 FQ	55800 AW	80690 TQ	NEBLS	10/01-12/01
	Nevada	Y	41170 FQ	61550 AW	89100 TQ	NVBLS	10/01-12/01
	Las Vegas MSA, NV-AZ	Y	41780 FQ	61490 AW	82990 TQ	NVBLS	10/01-12/01
	Reno MSA, NV	Y	43730 FQ	64360 AW	104300 TQ	NVBLS	10/01-12/01
	New Hampshire	Y	41910 FQ	65000 AW	100860 TQ	NHBLS	10/01-12/01
	Manchester PMSA, NH	Y	38860 FQ	59710 AW	86500 TQ	NHBLS	10/01-12/01
	Nashua PMSA, NH	Y	45070 FQ	70290 AW	107600 TQ	NHBLS	10/01-12/01
	Portsmouth-Rochester PMSA, NH-ME	Y	43620 FQ	72660 AW	112870 TQ	NHBLS	10/01-12/01
	New Jersey	Y	44490 FQ	75230 AW	115430 TQ	NJBLS	10/01-12/01
	Atlantic-Cape May PMSA, NJ	Y	46390 FQ	70990 AW	93410 TQ	NJBLS	10/01-12/01
	Bergen-Passaic PMSA, NJ	Y	41810 FQ	69120 AW	97930 TQ	NJBLS	10/01-12/01
	Jersey City PMSA, NJ	Y	46350 FQ	78480 AW	125980 TQ	NJBLS	10/01-12/01
	Middlesex-Somerset-Hunterdon PMSA, NJ	Y	50690 FQ	83930 AW		NJBLS	10/01-12/01
	Monmouth-Ocean PMSA, NJ	Y	44110 FQ	71230 AW	105040 TQ	NJBLS	10/01-12/01
	Newark PMSA, NJ	Y	47590 FQ	74850 AW	110570 TQ	NJBLS	10/01-12/01
	Trenton PMSA, NJ	Y	38880 FQ	59260 AW	85620 TQ	NJBLS	10/01-12/01
	New Mexico	Y	37150 FQ	55470 AW	78340 TQ	NMBLS	10/01-12/01
	Albuquerque MSA, NM	Y	38210 FQ	57570 AW	82690 TQ	NMBLS	10/01-12/01
	Las Cruces MSA, NM	Y	35030 FQ	52010 AW	69120 TQ	NMBLS	10/01-12/01
	New York	Y	40440 FQ	69410 AW	105060 TQ	NYBLS	10/01-12/01

AAW	Average annual wage	AOH	Average offered, high	ASH	Average starting, high	H	Hourly	M	Monthly	S	Special: hourly and annual
AE	Average entry wage	AOL	Average offered, low	ASL	Average starting, low	HI	Highest wage paid	MTC	Median total compensation	TQ	Third quartile wage
AEX	Average experienced wage	APH	Average pay, high range	AW	Average wage paid	HR	High end range	MW	Median wage paid	W	Weekly
AO	Average offered	APL	Average pay, low range	FQ	First quartile wage	LR	Low end range	SQ	Second quartile wage	Y	Yearly

Occupation/Type/Industry	Location	Per	Low	Mid	High	Source	Date
Computer Systems Analyst	Albany-Schenectady-Troy MSA, NY	Y	37190 FQ	64720 AW	111550 TQ	NYBLS	10/01-12/01
	Buffalo-Niagara Falls MSA, NY	Y	36800 FQ	54600 AW	72970 TQ	NYBLS	10/01-12/01
	Dutchess County PMSA, NY	Y	45500 FQ	71330 AW	103830 TQ	NYBLS	10/01-12/01
	Nassau-Suffolk PMSA, NY	Y	39250 FQ	64680 AW	92450 TQ	NYBLS	10/01-12/01
	New York PMSA, NY	Y	43950 FQ	74560 AW	111990 TQ	NYBLS	10/01-12/01
	Newburgh PMSA, NY-PA	Y	39920 FQ	60740 AW	86120 TQ	NYBLS	10/01-12/01
	Rochester MSA, NY	Y	38560 FQ	61440 AW	87760 TQ	NYBLS	10/01-12/01
	Syracuse MSA, NY	Y	36090 FQ	60760 AW	87270 TQ	NYBLS	10/01-12/01
	Utica-Rome MSA, NY	Y	28830 FQ	49710 AW	69810 TQ	NYBLS	10/01-12/01
	North Carolina	Y	36130 FQ	60480 AW	89490 TQ	NCBLS	10/01-12/01
	Asheville MSA, NC	Y	32510 FQ	52840 AW	70060 TQ	NCBLS	10/01-12/01
	Charlotte-Gastonia-Rock Hill MSA, NC-SC	Y	36470 FQ	60990 AW	91870 TQ	NCBLS	10/01-12/01
	Fayetteville MSA, NC	Y	19750 FQ	37560 AW	66280 TQ	NCBLS	10/01-12/01
	Greensboro-Winston-Salem-High Point MSA, NC	Y	39460 FQ	60600 AW	84060 TQ	NCBLS	10/01-12/01
	Hickory-Morganton-Lenoir MSA, NC	Y	33760 FQ	49450 AW	66540 TQ	NCBLS	10/01-12/01
	Raleigh-Durham-Chapel Hill MSA, NC	Y	38620 FQ	64280 AW	94370 TQ	NCBLS	10/01-12/01
	Wilmington MSA, NC	Y	30010 FQ	49540 AW	73210 TQ	NCBLS	10/01-12/01
	North Dakota	Y	29100 FQ	45010 AW	61520 TQ	NDBLS	10/01-12/01
	Fargo-Moorhead MSA, ND-MN	Y	31710 FQ	47300 AW	65500 TQ	NDBLS	10/01-12/01
	Ohio	Y	38830 FQ	60040 AW	85280 TQ	OHBLS	10/01-12/01
	Akron PMSA, OH	Y	39050 FQ	59600 AW	85940 TQ	OHBLS	10/01-12/01
	Canton-Massillon MSA, OH	Y	37450 FQ	55330 AW	75750 TQ	OHBLS	10/01-12/01
	Cincinnati PMSA, OH-KY-IN	Y	39750 FQ	61950 AW	88110 TQ	OHBLS	10/01-12/01
	Cleveland-Lorain-Elyria PMSA, OH	Y	42210 FQ	62160 AW	85710 TQ	OHBLS	10/01-12/01
	Columbus MSA, OH	Y	38620 FQ	60450 AW	86280 TQ	OHBLS	10/01-12/01
	Dayton-Springfield MSA, OH	Y	39800 FQ	59390 AW	82040 TQ	OHBLS	10/01-12/01
	Hamilton-Middletown PMSA, OH	Y	32410 FQ	52240 AW	75500 TQ	OHBLS	10/01-12/01
	Mansfield MSA, OH	Y	36520 FQ	56150 AW	81440 TQ	OHBLS	10/01-12/01
	Toledo MSA, OH	Y	31360 FQ	52390 AW	74060 TQ	OHBLS	10/01-12/01
	Oklahoma	Y	13910 FQ	49030 AW	73280 TQ	OKBLS	10/01-12/01
	Oklahoma City MSA, OK	Y	12460 FQ	47460 AW	72090 TQ	OKBLS	10/01-12/01
	Tulsa MSA, OK	Y	32290 FQ	50700 AW	71580 TQ	OKBLS	10/01-12/01
	Oregon	Y	39480 FQ	60430 AW	86070 TQ	ORBLS	10/01-12/01
	Eugene-Springfield MSA, OR	Y	37210 FQ	54940 AW	71970 TQ	ORBLS	10/01-12/01
	Medford-Ashland MSA, OR	Y	30460 FQ	50520 AW	69940 TQ	ORBLS	10/01-12/01
	Portland-Vancouver PMSA, OR-WA	Y	40000 FQ	61260 AW	88030 TQ	ORBLS	10/01-12/01
	Salem PMSA, OR	Y	40080 FQ	60380 AW	82980 TQ	ORBLS	10/01-12/01
	Pennsylvania	Y	39020 FQ	61690 AW	90430 TQ	PABLS	10/01-12/01
	Allentown-Bethlehem-Easton MSA, PA	Y	40510 FQ	60850 AW	86270 TQ	PABLS	10/01-12/01
	Erie MSA, PA	Y	34670 FQ	56610 AW	80180 TQ	PABLS	10/01-12/01
	Harrisburg-Lebanon-Carlisle MSA, PA	Y	42650 FQ	60820 AW	83400 TQ	PABLS	10/01-12/01
	Johnstown MSA, PA	Y	33540 FQ	54250 AW	75270 TQ	PABLS	10/01-12/01
	Lancaster MSA, PA	Y	39580 FQ	57250 AW	79040 TQ	PABLS	10/01-12/01
	Philadelphia PMSA, PA-NJ	Y	38420 FQ	66930 AW	106310 TQ	PABLS	10/01-12/01
	Pittsburgh MSA, PA	Y	39700 FQ	62100 AW	91170 TQ	PABLS	10/01-12/01
	Reading MSA, PA	Y	34090 FQ	56680 AW	81310 TQ	PABLS	10/01-12/01
	Scranton-Wilkes-Barre-Hazleton MSA, PA	Y	36080 FQ	53740 AW	71500 TQ	PABLS	10/01-12/01
	York MSA, PA	Y	29210 FQ	52050 AW	71020 TQ	PABLS	10/01-12/01
	Rhode Island	Y	40250 FQ	60510 AW	83050 TQ	RIBLS	10/01-12/01
	Providence-Fall River-Warwick MSA, RI-MA	Y	39090 FQ	60620 AW	84230 TQ	RIBLS	10/01-12/01
	South Carolina	Y	27640 FQ	48720 AW	72410 TQ	SCBLS	10/01-12/01
	Charleston-North Charleston MSA, SC	Y	33720 FQ	49650 AW	69700 TQ	SCBLS	10/01-12/01
	Greenville-Spartanburg-Anderson MSA, SC	Y	24850 FQ	47210 AW	72920 TQ	SCBLS	10/01-12/01
	Myrtle Beach MSA, SC	Y	31110 FQ	47860 AW	71750 TQ	SCBLS	10/01-12/01
	South Dakota	Y	40050 FQ	56760 AW	76430 TQ	SDBLS	10/01-12/01
	Sioux Falls MSA, SD	Y	43350 FQ	60230 AW	81200 TQ	SDBLS	10/01-12/01

AAW	Average annual wage	**AOH**	Average offered, high	**ASH**	Average starting, high	**H**	Hourly	**M**	Monthly	**S**	Special: hourly and annual
AE	Average entry wage	**AOL**	Average offered, low	**ASL**	Average starting, low	**HI**	Highest wage paid	**MTC**	Median total compensation	**TQ**	Third quartile wage
AEX	Average experienced wage	**APH**	Average pay, high range	**AW**	Average wage paid	**HR**	High end range	**MW**	Median wage paid	**W**	Weekly
AO	Average offered	**APL**	Average pay, low range	**FQ**	First quartile wage	**LR**	Low end range	**SQ**	Second quartile wage	**Y**	Yearly

Occupation/Type/Industry	Location	Per	Low	Mid	High	Source	Date
Computer Systems Analyst	Tennessee	Y	34250 FQ	56200 AW	81790 TQ	TNBLS	10/01-12/01
	Chattanooga MSA, TN-GA	Y	33890 FQ	56870 AW	75850 TQ	TNBLS	10/01-12/01
	Clarksville-Hopkinsville MSA, TN-KY	Y	40080 FQ	56410 AW	73410 TQ	TNBLS	10/01-12/01
	Johnson City-Kingsport-Bristol MSA, TN-VA	Y	33330 FQ	52170 AW	74810 TQ	TNBLS	10/01-12/01
	Knoxville MSA, TN	Y	36750 FQ	54910 AW	74740 TQ	TNBLS	10/01-12/01
	Memphis MSA, TN-AR-MS	Y	36110 FQ	55840 AW	77090 TQ	TNBLS	10/01-12/01
	Nashville MSA, TN	Y	32610 FQ	58860 AW	97430 TQ	TNBLS	10/01-12/01
	Texas	Y	33200 FQ	59230 AW	89700 TQ	TXBLS	10/01-12/01
	Amarillo MSA, TX	Y	34510 FQ	52750 AW	74150 TQ	TXBLS	10/01-12/01
	Austin-San Marcos MSA, TX	Y	36990 FQ	57140 AW	83060 TQ	TXBLS	10/01-12/01
	Beaumont-Port Arthur MSA, TX	Y	31820 FQ	56340 AW	85900 TQ	TXBLS	10/01-12/01
	Brazoria PMSA, TX	Y	32590 FQ	53520 AW	86240 TQ	TXBLS	10/01-12/01
	Brownsville-Harlingen-San Benito MSA, TX	Y	26430 FQ	49900 AW	75650 TQ	TXBLS	10/01-12/01
	Corpus Christi MSA, TX	Y	33220 FQ	55920 AW	83530 TQ	TXBLS	10/01-12/01
	Dallas PMSA, TX	Y	39460 FQ	65480 AW	95010 TQ	TXBLS	10/01-12/01
	El Paso MSA, TX	Y	29980 FQ	49920 AW	73420 TQ	TXBLS	10/01-12/01
	Fort Worth-Arlington PMSA, TX	Y	34810 FQ	59800 AW	89330 TQ	TXBLS	10/01-12/01
	Galveston-Texas City PMSA, TX	Y	40410 FQ	60990 AW	86800 TQ	TXBLS	10/01-12/01
	Houston PMSA, TX	Y	39010 FQ	63280 AW	90900 TQ	TXBLS	10/01-12/01
	Killeen-Temple MSA, TX	Y	29190 FQ	46430 AW	76580 TQ	TXBLS	10/01-12/01
	Laredo MSA, TX	Y	25380 FQ	49580 AW	74370 TQ	TXBLS	10/01-12/01
	Longview-Marshall MSA, TX	Y	29700 FQ	48790 AW	76000 TQ	TXBLS	10/01-12/01
	Lubbock MSA, TX	Y	31280 FQ	50290 AW	75620 TQ	TXBLS	10/01-12/01
	McAllen-Edinburg-Mission MSA, TX	Y	27380 FQ	44880 AW	66820 TQ	TXBLS	10/01-12/01
	Odessa-Midland MSA, TX	Y	31750 FQ	58360 AW	87510 TQ	TXBLS	10/01-12/01
	San Antonio MSA, TX	Y	24370 FQ	41950 AW	66670 TQ	TXBLS	10/01-12/01
	Tyler MSA, TX	Y	31630 FQ	51730 AW	77440 TQ	TXBLS	10/01-12/01
	Waco MSA, TX	Y	30910 FQ	47730 AW	72570 TQ	TXBLS	10/01-12/01
	Utah	Y	33950 FQ	53790 AW	73440 TQ	UTBLS	10/01-12/01
	Provo-Orem MSA, UT	Y	24850 FQ	47490 AW	78360 TQ	UTBLS	10/01-12/01
	Salt Lake City-Ogden MSA, UT	Y	36660 FQ	54770 AW	73200 TQ	UTBLS	10/01-12/01
	Vermont	Y	33510 FQ	53160 AW	76820 TQ	VTBLS	10/01-12/01
	Burlington MSA, VT	Y	37650 FQ	55240 AW	80260 TQ	VTBLS	10/01-12/01
	Virginia	Y	39890 FQ	63370 AW	91260 TQ	VABLS	10/01-12/01
	Lynchburg MSA, VA	Y	41810 FQ	63270 AW	85450 TQ	VABLS	10/01-12/01
	Norfolk-Virginia Beach-Newport News MSA, VA-NC	Y	34750 FQ	53850 AW	74140 TQ	VABLS	10/01-12/01
	Richmond-Petersburg MSA, VA	Y	39300 FQ	59610 AW	84870 TQ	VABLS	10/01-12/01
	Roanoke MSA, VA	Y	37610 FQ	61480 AW	94740 TQ	VABLS	10/01-12/01
	Washington	Y	43760 FQ	64840 AW	89280 TQ	WABLS	10/01-12/01
	Bremerton PMSA, WA	Y	40920 FQ	59970 AW	87320 TQ	WABLS	10/01-12/01
	Olympia PMSA, WA	Y	43410 FQ	60510 AW	70620 TQ	WABLS	10/01-12/01
	Richland-Kennewick-Pasco MSA, WA	Y	39980 FQ	64150 AW	93480 TQ	WABLS	10/01-12/01
	Seattle-Bellevue-Everett PMSA, WA	Y	45740 FQ	66740 AW	90420 TQ	WABLS	10/01-12/01
	Spokane MSA, WA	Y	35970 FQ	56150 AW	76660 TQ	WABLS	10/01-12/01
	Tacoma PMSA, WA	Y	39470 FQ	55590 AW	74310 TQ	WABLS	10/01-12/01
	Yakima MSA, WA	Y	39410 FQ	53270 AW	70410 TQ	WABLS	10/01-12/01
	West Virginia	Y	37570 FQ	57880 AW	84250 TQ	WVBLS	10/01-12/01
	Charleston MSA, WV	Y	32270 FQ	53660 AW	81390 TQ	WVBLS	10/01-12/01
	Huntington-Ashland MSA, WV-KY-OH	Y	36020 FQ	53580 AW	74430 TQ	WVBLS	10/01-12/01
	Wisconsin	Y	39960 FQ	70090 AW	106010 TQ	WIBLS	10/01-12/01
	Appleton-Oshkosh-Neenah MSA, WI	Y	36020 FQ	51700 AW	71060 TQ	WIBLS	10/01-12/01
	Green Bay MSA, WI	Y	37180 FQ	56580 AW	77300 TQ	WIBLS	10/01-12/01
	Madison MSA, WI	Y	37460 FQ	53820 AW	73570 TQ	WIBLS	10/01-12/01
	Milwaukee-Waukesha PMSA, WI	Y	49740 FQ	81350 AW	109550 TQ	WIBLS	10/01-12/01
	Racine PMSA, WI	Y	41040 FQ	59430 AW	81180 TQ	WIBLS	10/01-12/01
	Wyoming	Y	25020 FQ	45630 AW	68150 TQ	WYBLS	10/01-12/01

AAW	Average annual wage	AOH	Average offered, high	ASH	Average starting, high	H	Hourly	M	Monthly	S	Special: hourly and annual
AE	Average entry wage	AOL	Average offered, low	ASL	Average starting, low	HI	Highest wage paid	MTC	Median total compensation	TQ	Third quartile wage
AEX	Average experienced wage	APH	Average pay, high range	AW	Average wage paid	HR	High end range	MW	Median wage paid	W	Weekly
AO	Average offered	APL	Average pay, low range	FQ	First quartile wage	LR	Low end range	SQ	Second quartile wage	Y	Yearly

Occupation/Type/Industry	Location	Per	Low	Mid	High	Source	Date
Computer Systems Analyst	Cheyenne MSA, WY	Y	26980 FQ	46620 AW	67420 TQ	WYBLS	10/01-12/01
	Puerto Rico	Y	25030 FQ	44070 AW	66130 TQ	PRBLS	10/01-12/01
	Virgin Islands	Y	30680 FQ	45150 AW	67020 TQ	VIBLS	10/01-12/01
	Guam	Y	22810 FQ	47820 AW	73510 TQ	GUBLS	10/01-12/01
Concession Worker	United States	H	8.00 ASL			AEAC	1/99-1/99
Concierge	Alabama	H	5.45 FQ	7.97 AW	15.05 TQ	ALBLS	10/01-12/01
	Arizona	H	6.45 FQ	8.80 AW	10.93 TQ	AZBLS	10/01-12/01
	Arkansas	H	5.69 FQ	7.60 AW	10.65 TQ	ARBLS	10/01-12/01
	California	H	7.76 FQ	12.32 AW	17.83 TQ	CABLS	10/01-12/01
	Colorado	H	7.90 FQ	10.95 AW	15.14 TQ	COBLS	10/01-12/01
	Connecticut	H	7.89 FQ	10.82 AW	14.90 TQ	CTBLS	10/01-12/01
	District of Columbia	H	7.63 FQ	11.84 AW	16.77 TQ	DCBLS	10/01-12/01
	Florida	H	6.96 FQ	9.01 AW	11.14 TQ	FLBLS	10/01-12/01
	Georgia	H	6.27 FQ	9.14 AW	12.25 TQ	GABLS	10/01-12/01
	Hawaii	H	9.48 FQ	15.05 AW	24.41 TQ	HIBLS	10/01-12/01
	Illinois	H	5.90 FQ	9.36 AW	12.41 TQ	ILBLS	10/01-12/01
	Indiana	H	7.38 FQ	9.45 AW	12.22 TQ	INBLS	10/01-12/01
	Iowa	H	6.25 FQ	8.08 AW	9.95 TQ	IABLS	10/01-12/01
	Kansas	H	5.86 FQ	7.18 AW	9.05 TQ	KSBLS	10/01-12/01
	Kentucky	H	6.03 FQ	8.32 AW	10.24 TQ	KYBLS	10/01-12/01
	Louisiana	H	5.98 FQ	8.20 AW	10.77 TQ	LABLS	10/01-12/01
	Maryland	H	7.25 FQ	10.49 AW	13.95 TQ	MDBLS	10/01-12/01
	Massachusetts	H	8.62 FQ	11.12 AW	14.41 TQ	MABLS	10/01-12/01
	Michigan	H	7.28 FQ	10.98 AW	13.62 TQ	MIBLS	10/01-12/01
	Minnesota	H	5.97 FQ	9.37 AW	13.40 TQ	MNBLS	10/01-12/01
	Mississippi	H	6.15 FQ	9.13 AW	13.36 TQ	MSBLS	10/01-12/01
	Missouri	H	5.97 FQ	8.07 AW	10.59 TQ	MOBLS	10/01-12/01
	Nebraska	H	7.39 FQ	10.02 AW	15.32 TQ	NEBLS	10/01-12/01
	Nevada	H	8.40 FQ	13.27 AW	16.92 TQ	NVBLS	10/01-12/01
	New Hampshire	H	6.55 FQ	9.60 AW	12.77 TQ	NHBLS	10/01-12/01
	New Jersey	H	7.91 FQ	11.44 AW	16.26 TQ	NJBLS	10/01-12/01
	New Mexico	H	7.23 FQ	9.55 AW	11.72 TQ	NMBLS	10/01-12/01
	New York	H	12.76 FQ	15.37 AW	17.94 TQ	NYBLS	10/01-12/01
	North Carolina	H	5.82 FQ	8.62 AW	12.64 TQ	NCBLS	10/01-12/01
	Ohio	H	6.04 FQ	9.15 AW	12.49 TQ	OHBLS	10/01-12/01
	Oklahoma	H	5.50 FQ	6.91 AW	8.51 TQ	OKBLS	10/01-12/01
	Oregon	H	7.16 FQ	10.63 AW	14.46 TQ	ORBLS	10/01-12/01
	Pennsylvania	H	6.34 FQ	9.09 AW	12.33 TQ	PABLS	10/01-12/01
	Rhode Island	H	6.86 FQ	10.90 AW	14.18 TQ	RIBLS	10/01-12/01
	South Carolina	H	5.51 FQ	8.21 AW	11.39 TQ	SCBLS	10/01-12/01
	Tennessee	H	6.32 FQ	8.29 AW	10.73 TQ	TNBLS	10/01-12/01
	Texas	H	6.75 FQ	10.67 AW	16.90 TQ	TXBLS	10/01-12/01
	Utah	H	6.50 FQ	8.97 AW	11.98 TQ	UTBLS	10/01-12/01
	Vermont	H	7.00 FQ	9.52 AW	12.70 TQ	VTBLS	10/01-12/01
	Virginia	H	6.46 FQ	8.98 AW	11.89 TQ	VABLS	10/01-12/01
	Washington	H	8.63 FQ	10.82 AW	14.54 TQ	WABLS	10/01-12/01
	West Virginia	H	5.82 FQ	10.19 AW	16.79 TQ	WVBLS	10/01-12/01
	Wisconsin	H	7.24 FQ	9.27 AW	11.30 TQ	WIBLS	10/01-12/01
	Puerto Rico	H	6.00 FQ	7.95 AW	10.21 TQ	PRBLS	10/01-12/01
	Guam	H	8.25 FQ	13.01 AW	16.85 TQ	GUBLS	10/01-12/01
Conservation Scientist	Alabama	Y	38550 FQ	52010 AW	69350 TQ	ALBLS	10/01-12/01
	Alaska	Y	34010 FQ	58530 AW	85200 TQ	AKBLS	10/01-12/01
	Arizona	Y	36460 FQ	47930 AW	62870 TQ	AZBLS	10/01-12/01
	Arkansas	Y	33440 FQ	50100 AW	67260 TQ	ARBLS	10/01-12/01
	California	Y	37600 FQ	55470 AW	70920 TQ	CABLS	10/01-12/01
	Colorado	Y	33100 FQ	52080 AW	78130 TQ	COBLS	10/01-12/01
	Connecticut	Y	27990 FQ	60600 AW	103860 TQ	CTBLS	10/01-12/01
	Florida	Y	31090 FQ	52360 AW	77190 TQ	FLBLS	10/01-12/01
	Georgia	Y	32230 FQ	52880 AW	71180 TQ	GABLS	10/01-12/01
	Hawaii	Y	36880 FQ	55970 AW	82360 TQ	HIBLS	10/01-12/01
	Idaho	Y	34390 FQ	48270 AW	65810 TQ	IDBLS	10/01-12/01
	Illinois	Y	33060 FQ	50710 AW	68290 TQ	ILBLS	10/01-12/01
	Indiana	Y	26670 FQ	45820 AW	63550 TQ	INBLS	10/01-12/01
	Iowa	Y	28510 FQ	45500 AW	63490 TQ	IABLS	10/01-12/01
	Kansas	Y	36910 FQ	49350 AW	62700 TQ	KSBLS	10/01-12/01
	Kentucky	Y	37110 FQ	51710 AW	68050 TQ	KYBLS	10/01-12/01
	Louisiana	Y	37700 FQ	54490 AW	72550 TQ	LABLS	10/01-12/01
	Maine	Y	34330 FQ	75290 AW	108960 TQ	MEBLS	10/01-12/01
	Massachusetts	Y	32010 FQ	54110 AW	82370 TQ	MABLS	10/01-12/01
	Michigan	Y	28710 FQ	50370 AW	74040 TQ	MIBLS	10/01-12/01

AAW Average annual wage **AE** Average entry wage **AEX** Average experienced wage **AO** Average offered **AOH** Average offered, high **AOL** Average offered, low **APH** Average pay, high range **APL** Average pay, low range **ASH** Average starting, high **ASL** Average starting, low **AW** Average wage paid **FQ** First quartile wage **H** Hourly **HI** Highest wage paid **HR** High end range **LR** Low end range **M** Monthly **MTC** Median total compensation **MW** Median wage paid **SQ** Second quartile wage **S** Special: hourly and annual **TQ** Third quartile wage **W** Weekly **Y** Yearly

Occupation/Type/Industry	Location	Per	Low	Mid	High	Source	Date
Conservation Scientist	Minnesota	Y	36800 FQ	49150 AW	64650 TQ	MNBLS	10/01-12/01
	Mississippi	Y	24040 FQ	38750 AW	60410 TQ	MSBLS	10/01-12/01
	Missouri	Y	20480 FQ	43200 AW	65230 TQ	MOBLS	10/01-12/01
	Montana	Y	33640 FQ	47680 AW	63130 TQ	MTBLS	10/01-12/01
	Nebraska	Y	36280 FQ	50810 AW	68750 TQ	NEBLS	10/01-12/01
	Nevada	Y	31380 FQ	46140 AW	60290 TQ	NVBLS	10/01-12/01
	New Hampshire	Y	25820 FQ	44870 AW	65820 TQ	NHBLS	10/01-12/01
	New Jersey	Y	30110 FQ	47470 AW	68440 TQ	NJBLS	10/01-12/01
	New Mexico	Y	36970 FQ	50730 AW	67170 TQ	NMBLS	10/01-12/01
	New York	Y	35620 FQ	47670 AW	62380 TQ	NYBLS	10/01-12/01
	North Carolina	Y	28900 FQ	44320 AW	58080 TQ	NCBLS	10/01-12/01
	North Dakota	Y	31770 FQ	45610 AW	62940 TQ	NDBLS	10/01-12/01
	Ohio	Y	26890 FQ	43720 AW	63520 TQ	OHBLS	10/01-12/01
	Oklahoma	Y	19710 FQ	38450 AW	60990 TQ	OKBLS	10/01-12/01
	Oregon	Y	26910 FQ	47490 AW	71490 TQ	ORBLS	10/01-12/01
	Pennsylvania	Y	26370 FQ	45000 AW	65190 TQ	PABLS	10/01-12/01
	South Carolina	Y	36860 FQ	52080 AW	68600 TQ	SCBLS	10/01-12/01
	South Dakota	Y	35910 FQ	48090 AW	63340 TQ	SDBLS	10/01-12/01
	Tennessee	Y	34080 FQ	51830 AW	70020 TQ	TNBLS	10/01-12/01
	Texas	Y	32770 FQ	48220 AW	66060 TQ	TXBLS	10/01-12/01
	Utah	Y	34850 FQ	49350 AW	67520 TQ	UTBLS	10/01-12/01
	Vermont	Y	33140 FQ	43580 AW	55840 TQ	VTBLS	10/01-12/01
	Virginia	Y	28840 FQ	48940 AW	73340 TQ	VABLS	10/01-12/01
	Washington	Y	35100 FQ	52930 AW	72710 TQ	WABLS	10/01-12/01
	West Virginia	Y	32180 FQ	50300 AW	69520 TQ	WVBLS	10/01-12/01
	Wisconsin	Y	32650 FQ	45940 AW	60470 TQ	WIBLS	10/01-12/01
	Wyoming	Y	36500 FQ	49120 AW	62380 TQ	WYBLS	10/01-12/01
Construction and Building Inspector	Alabama	H	10.90 FQ	17.60 AW	25.60 TQ	ALBLS	10/01-12/01
	Birmingham MSA, AL	H	10.84 FQ	18.57 AW	26.61 TQ	ALBLS	10/01-12/01
	Huntsville MSA, AL	H	12.71 FQ	18.15 AW	24.42 TQ	ALBLS	10/01-12/01
	Mobile MSA, AL	H	10.99 FQ	17.01 AW	24.45 TQ	ALBLS	10/01-12/01
	Montgomery MSA, AL	H	12.91 FQ	18.52 AW	25.63 TQ	ALBLS	10/01-12/01
	Alaska	H	16.58 FQ	27.07 AW	39.27 TQ	AKBLS	10/01-12/01
	Anchorage MSA, AK	H	16.31 FQ	28.70 AW	43.72 TQ	AKBLS	10/01-12/01
	Arizona	H	12.46 FQ	19.55 AW	28.12 TQ	AZBLS	10/01-12/01
	Phoenix-Mesa MSA, AZ	H	12.62 FQ	21.03 AW	28.97 TQ	AZBLS	10/01-12/01
	Tucson MSA, AZ	H	12.28 FQ	16.38 AW	21.26 TQ	AZBLS	10/01-12/01
	Arkansas	H	12.29 FQ	16.36 AW	21.27 TQ	ARBLS	10/01-12/01
	Fayetteville-Springdale-Rogers MSA, AR	H	10.98 FQ	15.49 AW	20.86 TQ	ARBLS	10/01-12/01
	Little Rock-North Little Rock MSA, AR	H	11.83 FQ	16.55 AW	21.66 TQ	ARBLS	10/01-12/01
	California	H	16.40 FQ	25.12 AW	34.20 TQ	CABLS	10/01-12/01
	Bakersfield MSA, CA	H	11.02 FQ	18.46 AW	29.59 TQ	CABLS	10/01-12/01
	Chico-Paradise MSA, CA	H	13.47 FQ	20.93 AW	28.56 TQ	CABLS	10/01-12/01
	Los Angeles-Long Beach PMSA, CA	H	14.70 FQ	24.97 AW	34.71 TQ	CABLS	10/01-12/01
	Merced MSA, CA	H	14.59 FQ	22.71 AW	31.49 TQ	CABLS	10/01-12/01
	Modesto MSA, CA	H	11.50 FQ	21.71 AW	34.45 TQ	CABLS	10/01-12/01
	Oakland PMSA, CA	H	19.00 FQ	26.80 AW	35.33 TQ	CABLS	10/01-12/01
	Orange County PMSA, CA	H	17.91 FQ	25.93 AW	34.40 TQ	CABLS	10/01-12/01
	Riverside-San Bernardino PMSA, CA	H	18.31 FQ	23.04 AW	28.93 TQ	CABLS	10/01-12/01
	Sacramento PMSA, CA	H	12.39 FQ	22.92 AW	32.38 TQ	CABLS	10/01-12/01
	Salinas MSA, CA	H	22.31 FQ	28.05 AW	34.07 TQ	CABLS	10/01-12/01
	San Diego MSA, CA	H	18.94 FQ	25.93 AW	33.75 TQ	CABLS	10/01-12/01
	San Francisco PMSA, CA	H	23.77 FQ	29.78 AW	36.29 TQ	CABLS	10/01-12/01
	San Jose PMSA, CA	H	20.58 FQ	27.90 AW	36.47 TQ	CABLS	10/01-12/01
	San Luis Obispo-Atascadero-Paso Robles MSA, CA	H	15.37 FQ	22.33 AW	31.25 TQ	CABLS	10/01-12/01
	Santa Barbara-Santa Maria-Lompoc MSA, CA	H	17.50 FQ	24.29 AW	31.70 TQ	CABLS	10/01-12/01
	Santa Cruz-Watsonville PMSA, CA	H	17.92 FQ	23.85 AW	31.00 TQ	CABLS	10/01-12/01
	Santa Rosa PMSA, CA	H	19.38 FQ	26.97 AW	36.82 TQ	CABLS	10/01-12/01
	Stockton-Lodi MSA, CA	H	11.74 FQ	20.49 AW	27.01 TQ	CABLS	10/01-12/01
	Vallejo-Fairfield-Napa PMSA, CA	H	18.96 FQ	25.89 AW	33.20 TQ	CABLS	10/01-12/01
	Ventura PMSA, CA	H	16.97 FQ	24.23 AW	32.29 TQ	CABLS	10/01-12/01

AAW Average annual wage	**AOH** Average offered, high	**ASH** Average starting, high	**H** Hourly	**M** Monthly	**S** Special: hourly and annual
AE Average entry wage	**AOL** Average offered, low	**ASL** Average starting, low	**HI** Highest wage paid	**MTC** Median total compensation	**TQ** Third quartile wage
AEX Average experienced wage	**APH** Average pay, high range	**AW** Average wage paid	**HR** High end range	**MW** Median wage paid	**W** Weekly
AO Average offered	**APL** Average pay, low range	**FQ** First quartile wage	**LR** Low end range	**SQ** Second quartile wage	**Y** Yearly

Occupation/Type/Industry	Location	Per	Low	Mid	High	Source	Date
Construction and Building Inspector	Visalia-Tulare-Porterville MSA, CA	H	16.59 FQ	23.13 AW	28.48 TQ	CABLS	10/01-12/01
	Colorado	H	12.11 FQ	18.69 AW	26.70 TQ	COBLS	10/01-12/01
	Boulder-Longmont PMSA, CO	H	18.17 FQ	21.73 AW	26.38 TQ	COBLS	10/01-12/01
	Colorado Springs MSA, CO	H	12.64 FQ	19.40 AW	27.74 TQ	COBLS	10/01-12/01
	Denver PMSA, CO	H	11.48 FQ	18.57 AW	26.92 TQ	COBLS	10/01-12/01
	Fort Collins-Loveland MSA, CO	H	13.11 FQ	18.93 AW	26.34 TQ	COBLS	10/01-12/01
	Greeley PMSA, CO	H	9.69 FQ	19.24 AW	27.00 TQ	COBLS	10/01-12/01
	Connecticut	H	15.73 FQ	22.71 AW	29.44 TQ	CTBLS	10/01-12/01
	Bridgeport PMSA, CT	H	7.62 FQ	19.21 AW	27.94 TQ	CTBLS	10/01-12/01
	Danbury PMSA, CT	H	17.85 FQ	22.72 AW	29.27 TQ	CTBLS	10/01-12/01
	Hartford MSA, CT	H	17.08 FQ	23.17 AW	28.65 TQ	CTBLS	10/01-12/01
	New Haven-Meriden PMSA, CT	H	16.01 FQ	23.83 AW	33.11 TQ	CTBLS	10/01-12/01
	New London-Norwich MSA, CT-RI	H	14.69 FQ	20.77 AW	27.52 TQ	CTBLS	10/01-12/01
	Stamford-Norwalk PMSA, CT	H	17.79 FQ	24.04 AW	31.33 TQ	CTBLS	10/01-12/01
	Delaware	H	13.75 FQ	19.52 AW	29.70 TQ	DEBLS	10/01-12/01
	Wilmington-Newark PMSA, DE-MD	H	13.93 FQ	19.48 AW	29.00 TQ	DEBLS	10/01-12/01
	District of Columbia	H	23.53 FQ	30.04 AW	40.49 TQ	DCBLS	10/01-12/01
	Washington PMSA, DC-MD-VA-WV	H	12.50 FQ	20.01 AW	27.59 TQ	DCBLS	10/01-12/01
	Florida	H	12.55 FQ	18.87 AW	26.68 TQ	FLBLS	10/01-12/01
	Daytona Beach MSA, FL	H	11.16 FQ	15.36 AW	21.17 TQ	FLBLS	10/01-12/01
	Fort Lauderdale PMSA, FL	H	15.54 FQ	21.93 AW	29.08 TQ	FLBLS	10/01-12/01
	Fort Myers-Cape Coral MSA, FL	H	14.09 FQ	18.69 AW	24.78 TQ	FLBLS	10/01-12/01
	Fort Pierce-Port St. Lucie MSA, FL	H	12.11 FQ	18.32 AW	25.68 TQ	FLBLS	10/01-12/01
	Fort Walton Beach MSA, FL	H	11.97 FQ	16.60 AW	23.98 TQ	FLBLS	10/01-12/01
	Gainesville MSA, FL	H	12.21 FQ	18.12 AW	24.86 TQ	FLBLS	10/01-12/01
	Jacksonville MSA, FL	H	13.75 FQ	18.74 AW	26.21 TQ	FLBLS	10/01-12/01
	Lakeland-Winter Haven MSA, FL	H	11.82 FQ	15.88 AW	21.21 TQ	FLBLS	10/01-12/01
	Melbourne-Titusville-Palm Bay MSA, FL	H	13.87 FQ	18.21 AW	22.90 TQ	FLBLS	10/01-12/01
	Miami PMSA, FL	H	12.08 FQ	20.15 AW	32.14 TQ	FLBLS	10/01-12/01
	Naples MSA, FL	H	14.72 FQ	20.10 AW	27.79 TQ	FLBLS	10/01-12/01
	Ocala MSA, FL	H	11.83 FQ	16.07 AW	21.00 TQ	FLBLS	10/01-12/01
	Orlando MSA, FL	H	12.18 FQ	17.51 AW	24.37 TQ	FLBLS	10/01-12/01
	Pensacola MSA, FL	H	11.86 FQ	15.35 AW	19.30 TQ	FLBLS	10/01-12/01
	Sarasota-Bradenton MSA, FL	H	13.34 FQ	18.06 AW	23.13 TQ	FLBLS	10/01-12/01
	Tallahassee MSA, FL	H	12.47 FQ	20.29 AW	27.40 TQ	FLBLS	10/01-12/01
	Tampa-St. Petersburg-Clearwater MSA, FL	H	14.19 FQ	19.64 AW	26.15 TQ	FLBLS	10/01-12/01
	West Palm Beach-Boca Raton MSA, FL	H	14.60 FQ	20.28 AW	27.66 TQ	FLBLS	10/01-12/01
	Georgia	H	11.40 FQ	17.35 AW	23.99 TQ	GABLS	10/01-12/01
	Atlanta MSA, GA	H	12.35 FQ	19.00 AW	26.07 TQ	GABLS	10/01-12/01
	Augusta-Aiken MSA, GA-SC	H	11.97 FQ	17.31 AW	23.95 TQ	GABLS	10/01-12/01
	Columbus MSA, GA-AL	H	10.90 FQ	13.24 AW	16.70 TQ	GABLS	10/01-12/01
	Macon MSA, GA	H	9.39 FQ	13.88 AW	20.39 TQ	GABLS	10/01-12/01
	Savannah MSA, GA	H	11.72 FQ	15.30 AW	18.26 TQ	GABLS	10/01-12/01
	Hawaii	H	15.19 FQ	21.10 AW	26.99 TQ	HIBLS	10/01-12/01
	Honolulu MSA, HI	H	15.49 FQ	21.49 AW	27.21 TQ	HIBLS	10/01-12/01
	Idaho	H	11.82 FQ	17.82 AW	24.16 TQ	IDBLS	10/01-12/01
	Boise City MSA, ID	H	10.51 FQ	17.46 AW	24.42 TQ	IDBLS	10/01-12/01
	Illinois	H	13.47 FQ	21.74 AW	29.92 TQ	ILBLS	10/01-12/01
	Champaign-Urbana MSA, IL	H	12.93 FQ	20.42 AW	28.32 TQ	ILBLS	10/01-12/01
	Chicago PMSA, IL	H	14.33 FQ	22.73 AW	31.64 TQ	ILBLS	10/01-12/01
	Peoria-Pekin MSA, IL	H	12.60 FQ	19.81 AW	27.53 TQ	ILBLS	10/01-12/01
	Springfield MSA, IL	H	16.86 FQ	21.48 AW	27.45 TQ	ILBLS	10/01-12/01
	Indiana	H	9.28 FQ	15.36 AW	22.23 TQ	INBLS	10/01-12/01
	Elkhart-Goshen MSA, IN	H	13.18 FQ	20.52 AW	31.85 TQ	INBLS	10/01-12/01
	Fort Wayne MSA, IN	H	9.09 FQ	13.09 AW	21.15 TQ	INBLS	10/01-12/01
	Gary PMSA, IN	H	6.43 FQ	13.93 AW	20.64 TQ	INBLS	10/01-12/01
	Indianapolis MSA, IN	H	9.47 FQ	14.91 AW	23.89 TQ	INBLS	10/01-12/01
	Lafayette MSA, IN	H	9.73 FQ	15.29 AW	21.87 TQ	INBLS	10/01-12/01
	Iowa	H	9.52 FQ	16.27 AW	24.33 TQ	IABLS	10/01-12/01

AAW	Average annual wage	**AOH**	Average offered, high	**ASH**	Average starting, high	**H**	Hourly	**M**	Monthly	**S**	Special: hourly and annual
AE	Average entry wage	**AOL**	Average offered, low	**ASL**	Average starting, low	**HI**	Highest wage paid	**MTC**	Median total compensation	**TQ**	Third quartile wage
AEX	Average experienced wage	**APH**	Average pay, high range	**AW**	Average wage paid	**HR**	High end range	**MW**	Median wage paid	**W**	Weekly
AO	Average offered	**APL**	Average pay, low range	**FQ**	First quartile wage	**LR**	Low end range	**SQ**	Second quartile wage	**Y**	Yearly

Occupation/Type/Industry	Location	Per	Low	Mid	High	Source	Date
Construction and Building Inspector	Davenport-Moline-Rock Island MSA, IA-IL	H	14.49 FQ	19.87 AW	26.81 TQ	IABLS	10/01-12/01
	Des Moines MSA, IA	H	17.27 FQ	22.14 AW	26.88 TQ	IABLS	10/01-12/01
	Kansas	H	9.70 FQ	16.65 AW	21.70 TQ	KSBLS	10/01-12/01
	Topeka MSA, KS	H	14.50 FQ	18.63 AW	22.01 TQ	KSBLS	10/01-12/01
	Wichita MSA, KS	H	9.12 FQ	16.02 AW	21.06 TQ	KSBLS	10/01-12/01
	Kentucky	H	10.23 FQ	17.30 AW	25.30 TQ	KYBLS	10/01-12/01
	Lexington MSA, KY	H	11.78 FQ	17.58 AW	24.61 TQ	KYBLS	10/01-12/01
	Louisville MSA, KY-IN	H	10.22 FQ	18.35 AW	27.06 TQ	KYBLS	10/01-12/01
	Louisiana	H	9.77 FQ	16.54 AW	24.70 TQ	LABLS	10/01-12/01
	Baton Rouge MSA, LA	H	9.31 FQ	18.38 AW	30.43 TQ	LABLS	10/01-12/01
	Lake Charles MSA, LA	H	7.73 FQ	19.30 AW	28.48 TQ	LABLS	10/01-12/01
	New Orleans MSA, LA	H	10.14 FQ	16.04 AW	22.19 TQ	LABLS	10/01-12/01
	Maine	H	11.57 FQ	18.91 AW	25.63 TQ	MEBLS	10/01-12/01
	Portland MSA, ME	H	14.48 FQ	25.36 AW	52.75 TQ	MEBLS	10/01-12/01
	Maryland	H	12.29 FQ	18.20 AW	26.14 TQ	MDBLS	10/01-12/01
	Baltimore PMSA, MD	H	13.70 FQ	17.81 AW	24.22 TQ	MDBLS	10/01-12/01
	Massachusetts	H	12.16 FQ	19.69 AW	27.50 TQ	MABLS	10/01-12/01
	Boston PMSA, MA-NH	H	11.99 FQ	19.58 AW	27.49 TQ	MABLS	10/01-12/01
	Brockton PMSA, MA	H	13.56 FQ	19.92 AW	27.00 TQ	MABLS	10/01-12/01
	Lawrence PMSA, MA-NH	H	14.35 FQ	20.61 AW	28.76 TQ	MABLS	10/01-12/01
	Lowell PMSA, MA-NH	H	6.47 FQ	19.64 AW	30.14 TQ	MABLS	10/01-12/01
	New Bedford PMSA, MA	H	11.94 FQ	22.14 AW	33.52 TQ	MABLS	10/01-12/01
	Springfield MSA, MA	H	15.52 FQ	20.62 AW	26.66 TQ	MABLS	10/01-12/01
	Worcester PMSA, MA-CT	H	12.27 FQ	19.19 AW	25.27 TQ	MABLS	10/01-12/01
	Michigan	H	12.75 FQ	19.73 AW	26.69 TQ	MIBLS	10/01-12/01
	Ann Arbor PMSA, MI	H	14.95 FQ	21.55 AW	31.49 TQ	MIBLS	10/01-12/01
	Detroit PMSA, MI	H	13.36 FQ	20.37 AW	26.82 TQ	MIBLS	10/01-12/01
	Flint PMSA, MI	H	11.41 FQ	19.38 AW	28.58 TQ	MIBLS	10/01-12/01
	Grand Rapids-Muskegon-Holland MSA, MI	H	11.12 FQ	18.01 AW	25.24 TQ	MIBLS	10/01-12/01
	Kalamazoo-Battle Creek MSA, MI	H	14.29 FQ	19.54 AW	25.48 TQ	MIBLS	10/01-12/01
	Lansing-East Lansing MSA, MI	H	12.93 FQ	23.03 AW	29.89 TQ	MIBLS	10/01-12/01
	Saginaw-Bay City-Midland MSA, MI	H	12.35 FQ	18.11 AW	23.74 TQ	MIBLS	10/01-12/01
	Minnesota	H	16.55 FQ	23.42 AW	31.86 TQ	MNBLS	10/01-12/01
	Duluth-Superior MSA, MN-WI	H	14.58 FQ	21.39 AW	31.03 TQ	MNBLS	10/01-12/01
	Minneapolis-St. Paul MSA, MN-WI	H	17.73 FQ	24.45 AW	32.90 TQ	MNBLS	10/01-12/01
	Mississippi	H	7.13 FQ	14.62 AW	23.39 TQ	MSBLS	10/01-12/01
	Biloxi-Gulfport-Pascagoula MSA, MS	H	7.83 FQ	12.72 AW	17.00 TQ	MSBLS	10/01-12/01
	Jackson MSA, MS	H	11.85 FQ	20.10 AW	30.48 TQ	MSBLS	10/01-12/01
	Missouri	H	7.41 FQ	17.54 AW	27.09 TQ	MOBLS	10/01-12/01
	Kansas City MSA, MO-KS	H	11.53 FQ	18.86 AW	26.76 TQ	MOBLS	10/01-12/01
	St. Louis MSA, MO-IL	H	11.65 FQ	19.95 AW	28.26 TQ	MOBLS	10/01-12/01
	Springfield MSA, MO	H	11.96 FQ	18.77 AW	27.57 TQ	MOBLS	10/01-12/01
	Montana	H	11.84 FQ	16.55 AW	21.25 TQ	MTBLS	10/01-12/01
	Nebraska	H	11.18 FQ	17.12 AW	22.65 TQ	NEBLS	10/01-12/01
	Lincoln MSA, NE	H	11.61 FQ	17.18 AW	23.75 TQ	NEBLS	10/01-12/01
	Omaha MSA, NE-IA	H	13.52 FQ	18.60 AW	23.40 TQ	NEBLS	10/01-12/01
	Nevada	H	15.23 FQ	24.54 AW	33.83 TQ	NVBLS	10/01-12/01
	Las Vegas MSA, NV-AZ	H	14.63 FQ	24.85 AW	34.28 TQ	NVBLS	10/01-12/01
	Reno MSA, NV	H	15.25 FQ	22.46 AW	27.98 TQ	NVBLS	10/01-12/01
	New Hampshire	H	8.68 FQ	17.22 AW	25.35 TQ	NHBLS	10/01-12/01
	Manchester PMSA, NH	H	11.68 FQ	17.42 AW	28.54 TQ	NHBLS	10/01-12/01
	Portsmouth-Rochester PMSA, NH-ME	H	14.34 FQ	20.31 AW	27.57 TQ	NHBLS	10/01-12/01
	New Jersey	H	14.09 FQ	22.29 AW	31.48 TQ	NJBLS	10/01-12/01
	Atlantic-Cape May PMSA, NJ	H	17.11 FQ	22.85 AW	28.96 TQ	NJBLS	10/01-12/01
	Bergen-Passaic PMSA, NJ	H	14.69 FQ	22.70 AW	30.50 TQ	NJBLS	10/01-12/01
	Jersey City PMSA, NJ	H	11.52 FQ	22.20 AW	32.82 TQ	NJBLS	10/01-12/01
	Middlesex-Somerset-Hunterdon PMSA, NJ	H	14.24 FQ	23.78 AW	33.26 TQ	NJBLS	10/01-12/01
	Monmouth-Ocean PMSA, NJ	H	13.07 FQ	21.21 AW	28.05 TQ	NJBLS	10/01-12/01
	Newark PMSA, NJ	H	15.40 FQ	22.58 AW	32.36 TQ	NJBLS	10/01-12/01
	Trenton PMSA, NJ	H	18.54 FQ	25.23 AW	33.61 TQ	NJBLS	10/01-12/01
	New Mexico	H	11.43 FQ	17.80 AW	24.78 TQ	NMBLS	10/01-12/01
	Albuquerque MSA, NM	H	14.43 FQ	19.89 AW	26.01 TQ	NMBLS	10/01-12/01
	Las Cruces MSA, NM	H	10.58 FQ	16.74 AW	22.65 TQ	NMBLS	10/01-12/01

AAW Average annual wage	**AOH** Average offered, high	**ASH** Average starting, high	**H** Hourly	**M** Monthly	**S** Special: hourly and annual
AE Average entry wage	**AOL** Average offered, low	**ASL** Average starting, low	**HI** Highest wage paid	**MTC** Median total compensation	**TQ** Third quartile wage
AEX Average experienced wage	**APH** Average pay, high range	**AW** Average wage paid	**HR** High end range	**MW** Median wage paid	**W** Weekly
AO Average offered	**APL** Average pay, low range	**FQ** First quartile wage	**LR** Low end range	**SQ** Second quartile wage	**Y** Yearly

Occupation/Type/Industry	Location	Per	Low	Mid	High	Source	Date
Construction and Building Inspector	New York	H	13.12 FQ	22.50 AW	33.19 TQ	NYBLS	10/01-12/01
	Albany-Schenectady-Troy MSA, NY	H	14.10 FQ	20.56 AW	29.02 TQ	NYBLS	10/01-12/01
	Binghamton MSA, NY	H	9.47 FQ	16.58 AW	24.65 TQ	NYBLS	10/01-12/01
	Buffalo-Niagara Falls MSA, NY	H	13.93 FQ	22.89 AW	32.25 TQ	NYBLS	10/01-12/01
	Dutchess County PMSA, NY	H	13.24 FQ	19.82 AW	27.18 TQ	NYBLS	10/01-12/01
	Nassau-Suffolk PMSA, NY	H	14.04 FQ	24.63 AW	35.49 TQ	NYBLS	10/01-12/01
	New York PMSA, NY	H	16.43 FQ	23.89 AW	34.06 TQ	NYBLS	10/01-12/01
	Newburgh PMSA, NY-PA	H	12.68 FQ	22.36 AW	33.81 TQ	NYBLS	10/01-12/01
	Rochester MSA, NY	H	13.61 FQ	23.58 AW	36.51 TQ	NYBLS	10/01-12/01
	Syracuse MSA, NY	H	11.82 FQ	17.73 AW	25.37 TQ	NYBLS	10/01-12/01
	Utica-Rome MSA, NY	H	9.53 FQ	16.93 AW	26.55 TQ	NYBLS	10/01-12/01
	North Carolina	H	14.01 FQ	18.64 AW	24.82 TQ	NCBLS	10/01-12/01
	Asheville MSA, NC	H	14.30 FQ	17.97 AW	23.57 TQ	NCBLS	10/01-12/01
	Charlotte-Gastonia-Rock Hill MSA, NC-SC	H	14.92 FQ	19.61 AW	25.60 TQ	NCBLS	10/01-12/01
	Fayetteville MSA, NC	H	14.14 FQ	17.51 AW	22.87 TQ	NCBLS	10/01-12/01
	Greensboro-Winston-Salem-High Point MSA, NC	H	14.94 FQ	19.72 AW	25.62 TQ	NCBLS	10/01-12/01
	Hickory-Morganton-Lenoir MSA, NC	H	12.36 FQ	17.00 AW	21.62 TQ	NCBLS	10/01-12/01
	Raleigh-Durham-Chapel Hill MSA, NC	H	14.49 FQ	19.97 AW	26.61 TQ	NCBLS	10/01-12/01
	Wilmington MSA, NC	H	14.11 FQ	16.97 AW	21.23 TQ	NCBLS	10/01-12/01
	North Dakota	H	13.18 FQ	18.61 AW	25.32 TQ	NDBLS	10/01-12/01
	Fargo-Moorhead MSA, ND-MN	H	15.09 FQ	19.81 AW	25.80 TQ	NDBLS	10/01-12/01
	Ohio	H	11.18 FQ	17.85 AW	24.99 TQ	OHBLS	10/01-12/01
	Akron PMSA, OH	H	10.29 FQ	15.75 AW	22.16 TQ	OHBLS	10/01-12/01
	Canton-Massillon MSA, OH	H	9.46 FQ	15.54 AW	22.02 TQ	OHBLS	10/01-12/01
	Cincinnati PMSA, OH-KY-IN	H	14.55 FQ	20.09 AW	26.68 TQ	OHBLS	10/01-12/01
	Cleveland-Lorain-Elyria PMSA, OH	H	11.05 FQ	18.04 AW	24.81 TQ	OHBLS	10/01-12/01
	Columbus MSA, OH	H	11.76 FQ	18.20 AW	25.16 TQ	OHBLS	10/01-12/01
	Dayton-Springfield MSA, OH	H	14.08 FQ	19.03 AW	26.41 TQ	OHBLS	10/01-12/01
	Hamilton-Middletown PMSA, OH	H	12.33 FQ	17.30 AW	24.38 TQ	OHBLS	10/01-12/01
	Mansfield MSA, OH	H	11.39 FQ	14.75 AW	19.47 TQ	OHBLS	10/01-12/01
	Toledo MSA, OH	H	10.12 FQ	17.37 AW	23.75 TQ	OHBLS	10/01-12/01
	Youngstown-Warren MSA, OH	H	5.77 FQ	12.65 AW	20.88 TQ	OHBLS	10/01-12/01
	Oklahoma	H	10.48 FQ	16.07 AW	20.90 TQ	OKBLS	10/01-12/01
	Oklahoma City MSA, OK	H	13.04 FQ	17.55 AW	21.24 TQ	OKBLS	10/01-12/01
	Tulsa MSA, OK	H	10.87 FQ	15.81 AW	20.38 TQ	OKBLS	10/01-12/01
	Oregon	H	13.20 FQ	21.25 AW	27.49 TQ	ORBLS	10/01-12/01
	Eugene-Springfield MSA, OR	H	15.03 FQ	21.22 AW	27.69 TQ	ORBLS	10/01-12/01
	Portland-Vancouver PMSA, OR-WA	H	12.88 FQ	21.16 AW	27.57 TQ	ORBLS	10/01-12/01
	Pennsylvania	H	12.91 FQ	18.36 AW	25.36 TQ	PABLS	10/01-12/01
	Allentown-Bethlehem-Easton MSA, PA	H	14.05 FQ	19.02 AW	23.10 TQ	PABLS	10/01-12/01
	Harrisburg-Lebanon-Carlisle MSA, PA	H	14.33 FQ	20.26 AW	27.00 TQ	PABLS	10/01-12/01
	Johnstown MSA, PA	H	10.16 FQ	15.55 AW	21.10 TQ	PABLS	10/01-12/01
	Lancaster MSA, PA	H	14.13 FQ	19.23 AW	32.02 TQ	PABLS	10/01-12/01
	Philadelphia PMSA, PA-NJ	H	12.47 FQ	19.57 AW	26.92 TQ	PABLS	10/01-12/01
	Pittsburgh MSA, PA	H	12.60 FQ	17.80 AW	24.00 TQ	PABLS	10/01-12/01
	Reading MSA, PA	H	11.73 FQ	16.57 AW	21.11 TQ	PABLS	10/01-12/01
	Scranton-Wilkes-Barre-Hazleton MSA, PA	H	11.28 FQ	15.91 AW	22.82 TQ	PABLS	10/01-12/01
	York MSA, PA	H	6.79 FQ	17.84 AW	25.91 TQ	PABLS	10/01-12/01
	Rhode Island	H	11.58 FQ	18.98 AW	27.75 TQ	RIBLS	10/01-12/01
	Providence-Fall River-Warwick MSA, RI-MA	H	14.78 FQ	20.72 AW	28.46 TQ	RIBLS	10/01-12/01
	South Carolina	H	11.33 FQ	17.29 AW	25.08 TQ	SCBLS	10/01-12/01
	Charleston-North Charleston MSA, SC	H	13.83 FQ	18.32 AW	24.95 TQ	SCBLS	10/01-12/01
	Columbia MSA, SC	H	10.45 FQ	17.57 AW	29.02 TQ	SCBLS	10/01-12/01
	Greenville-Spartanburg-Anderson MSA, SC	H	12.21 FQ	16.22 AW	21.29 TQ	SCBLS	10/01-12/01
	Myrtle Beach MSA, SC	H	9.91 FQ	16.78 AW	24.57 TQ	SCBLS	10/01-12/01

AAW	Average annual wage	AOH	Average offered, high	ASH	Average starting, high	H	Hourly	M	Monthly	S	Special: hourly and annual
AE	Average entry wage	AOL	Average offered, low	ASL	Average starting, low	HI	Highest wage paid	MTC	Median total compensation	TQ	Third quartile wage
AEX	Average experienced wage	APH	Average pay, high range	AW	Average wage paid	HR	High end range	MW	Median wage paid	W	Weekly
AO	Average offered	APL	Average pay, low range	FQ	First quartile wage	LR	Low end range	SQ	Second quartile wage	Y	Yearly

Occupation/Type/Industry	Location	Per	Low	Mid	High	Source	Date
Construction and Building Inspector	South Dakota	H	10.22 FQ	14.81 AW	20.94 TQ	SDBLS	10/01-12/01
	Sioux Falls MSA, SD	H	13.83 FQ	18.09 AW	25.59 TQ	SDBLS	10/01-12/01
	Tennessee	H	11.09 FQ	16.95 AW	24.07 TQ	TNBLS	10/01-12/01
	Chattanooga MSA, TN-GA	H	8.31 FQ	15.40 AW	21.62 TQ	TNBLS	10/01-12/01
	Clarksville-Hopkinsville MSA, TN-KY	H	9.85 FQ	14.74 AW	23.51 TQ	TNBLS	10/01-12/01
	Johnson City-Kingsport-Bristol MSA, TN-VA	H	6.73 FQ	14.71 AW	21.37 TQ	TNBLS	10/01-12/01
	Knoxville MSA, TN	H	11.82 FQ	17.09 AW	23.87 TQ	TNBLS	10/01-12/01
	Memphis MSA, TN-AR-MS	H	11.56 FQ	16.31 AW	23.63 TQ	TNBLS	10/01-12/01
	Nashville MSA, TN	H	13.11 FQ	18.66 AW	24.04 TQ	TNBLS	10/01-12/01
	Texas	H	10.90 FQ	18.45 AW	26.90 TQ	TXBLS	10/01-12/01
	Austin-San Marcos MSA, TX	H	12.51 FQ	18.06 AW	22.24 TQ	TXBLS	10/01-12/01
	Beaumont-Port Arthur MSA, TX	H	9.83 FQ	15.91 AW	25.14 TQ	TXBLS	10/01-12/01
	Brazoria PMSA, TX	H	12.44 FQ	17.79 AW	22.95 TQ	TXBLS	10/01-12/01
	Brownsville-Harlingen-San Benito MSA, TX	H	8.56 FQ	13.23 AW	19.54 TQ	TXBLS	10/01-12/01
	Corpus Christi MSA, TX	H	6.24 FQ	15.69 AW	28.36 TQ	TXBLS	10/01-12/01
	Dallas PMSA, TX	H	14.35 FQ	19.38 AW	25.94 TQ	TXBLS	10/01-12/01
	El Paso MSA, TX	H	7.72 FQ	14.03 AW	21.50 TQ	TXBLS	10/01-12/01
	Fort Worth-Arlington PMSA, TX	H	14.84 FQ	20.86 AW	29.17 TQ	TXBLS	10/01-12/01
	Galveston-Texas City PMSA, TX	H	10.54 FQ	16.02 AW	21.00 TQ	TXBLS	10/01-12/01
	Houston PMSA, TX	H	12.44 FQ	21.51 AW	31.74 TQ	TXBLS	10/01-12/01
	Killeen-Temple MSA, TX	H	8.48 FQ	15.41 AW	23.99 TQ	TXBLS	10/01-12/01
	Lubbock MSA, TX	H	11.42 FQ	16.58 AW	20.99 TQ	TXBLS	10/01-12/01
	McAllen-Edinburg-Mission MSA, TX	H	6.65 FQ	12.42 AW	21.67 TQ	TXBLS	10/01-12/01
	San Antonio MSA, TX	H	8.69 FQ	14.87 AW	21.84 TQ	TXBLS	10/01-12/01
	Utah	H	12.34 FQ	18.54 AW	24.07 TQ	UTBLS	10/01-12/01
	Provo-Orem MSA, UT	H	15.58 FQ	19.45 AW	22.51 TQ	UTBLS	10/01-12/01
	Salt Lake City-Ogden MSA, UT	H	11.79 FQ	19.02 AW	25.69 TQ	UTBLS	10/01-12/01
	Vermont	H	11.17 FQ	15.66 AW	25.10 TQ	VTBLS	10/01-12/01
	Burlington MSA, VT	H	15.56 FQ	21.68 AW	27.21 TQ	VTBLS	10/01-12/01
	Virginia	H	11.24 FQ	17.76 AW	25.49 TQ	VABLS	10/01-12/01
	Lynchburg MSA, VA	H	11.77 FQ	16.73 AW	22.38 TQ	VABLS	10/01-12/01
	Norfolk-Virginia Beach-Newport News MSA, VA-NC	H	11.96 FQ	17.92 AW	23.10 TQ	VABLS	10/01-12/01
	Richmond-Petersburg MSA, VA	H	12.44 FQ	18.26 AW	25.86 TQ	VABLS	10/01-12/01
	Roanoke MSA, VA	H	9.56 FQ	12.50 AW	17.51 TQ	VABLS	10/01-12/01
	Washington	H	17.56 FQ	24.38 AW	32.58 TQ	WABLS	10/01-12/01
	Olympia PMSA, WA	H	18.48 FQ	23.07 AW	26.94 TQ	WABLS	10/01-12/01
	Richland-Kennewick-Pasco MSA, WA	H	17.90 FQ	23.16 AW	29.42 TQ	WABLS	10/01-12/01
	Seattle-Bellevue-Everett PMSA, WA	H	18.16 FQ	25.78 AW	35.29 TQ	WABLS	10/01-12/01
	Spokane MSA, WA	H	18.45 FQ	22.74 AW	27.15 TQ	WABLS	10/01-12/01
	Tacoma PMSA, WA	H	20.63 FQ	24.49 AW	28.41 TQ	WABLS	10/01-12/01
	Yakima MSA, WA	H	15.72 FQ	21.10 AW	26.60 TQ	WABLS	10/01-12/01
	West Virginia	H	9.30 FQ	14.28 AW	20.30 TQ	WVBLS	10/01-12/01
	Charleston MSA, WV	H	12.25 FQ	15.49 AW	18.86 TQ	WVBLS	10/01-12/01
	Wisconsin	H	11.87 FQ	20.11 AW	27.58 TQ	WIBLS	10/01-12/01
	Appleton-Oshkosh-Neenah MSA, WI	H	15.29 FQ	21.87 AW	26.95 TQ	WIBLS	10/01-12/01
	Green Bay MSA, WI	H	15.06 FQ	20.20 AW	26.30 TQ	WIBLS	10/01-12/01
	Madison MSA, WI	H	13.69 FQ	20.82 AW	27.01 TQ	WIBLS	10/01-12/01
	Milwaukee-Waukesha PMSA, WI	H	11.72 FQ	20.96 AW	28.70 TQ	WIBLS	10/01-12/01
	Wyoming	H	12.85 FQ	18.20 AW	23.56 TQ	WYBLS	10/01-12/01
	Puerto Rico	H	5.89 FQ	11.20 AW	17.52 TQ	PRBLS	10/01-12/01
	Guam	H	13.25 FQ	20.24 AW	34.22 TQ	GUBLS	10/01-12/01
Construction Laborer	Alabama	H	6.58 FQ	9.55 AW	13.32 TQ	ALBLS	10/01-12/01
	Birmingham MSA, AL	H	7.18 FQ	10.77 AW	15.73 TQ	ALBLS	10/01-12/01
	Huntsville MSA, AL	H	7.37 FQ	9.55 AW	12.40 TQ	ALBLS	10/01-12/01
	Mobile MSA, AL	H	6.18 FQ	8.82 AW	11.60 TQ	ALBLS	10/01-12/01

AAW	Average annual wage	AOH	Average offered, high	ASH	Average starting, high	H	Hourly	M	Monthly	S	Special: hourly and annual
AE	Average entry wage	AOL	Average offered, low	ASL	Average starting, low	HI	Highest wage paid	MTC	Median total compensation	TQ	Third quartile wage
AEX	Average experienced wage	APH	Average pay, high range	AW	Average wage paid	HR	High end range	MW	Median wage paid	W	Weekly
AO	Average offered	APL	Average pay, low range	FQ	First quartile wage	LR	Low end range	SQ	Second quartile wage	Y	Yearly

Occupation/Type/Industry	Location	Per	Low	Mid	High	Source	Date
Construction Laborer	Montgomery MSA, AL	H	6.79 FQ	8.84 AW	11.02 TQ	ALBLS	10/01-12/01
	Alaska	H	10.93 FQ	19.11 AW	30.30 TQ	AKBLS	10/01-12/01
	Anchorage MSA, AK	H	10.56 FQ	18.46 AW	27.77 TQ	AKBLS	10/01-12/01
	Arizona	H	6.38 FQ	10.46 AW	15.78 TQ	AZBLS	10/01-12/01
	Phoenix-Mesa MSA, AZ	H	6.35 FQ	10.70 AW	16.25 TQ	AZBLS	10/01-12/01
	Tucson MSA, AZ	H	6.27 FQ	9.76 AW	13.46 TQ	AZBLS	10/01-12/01
	Arkansas	H	7.32 FQ	9.64 AW	12.92 TQ	ARBLS	10/01-12/01
	Fayetteville-Springdale-Rogers MSA, AR	H	7.71 FQ	10.04 AW	13.05 TQ	ARBLS	10/01-12/01
	Fort Smith MSA, AR-OK	H	6.28 FQ	9.03 AW	11.11 TQ	ARBLS	10/01-12/01
	Little Rock-North Little Rock MSA, AR	H	7.47 FQ	9.72 AW	13.32 TQ	ARBLS	10/01-12/01
	California	H	8.53 FQ	16.09 AW	26.25 TQ	CABLS	10/01-12/01
	Bakersfield MSA, CA	H	7.39 FQ	11.71 AW	17.58 TQ	CABLS	10/01-12/01
	Chico-Paradise MSA, CA	H	7.67 FQ	14.01 AW	28.83 TQ	CABLS	10/01-12/01
	Fresno MSA, CA	H	7.71 FQ	13.01 AW	22.79 TQ	CABLS	10/01-12/01
	Los Angeles-Long Beach PMSA, CA	H	8.27 FQ	15.98 AW	25.61 TQ	CABLS	10/01-12/01
	Merced MSA, CA	H	7.47 FQ	11.22 AW	18.02 TQ	CABLS	10/01-12/01
	Modesto MSA, CA	H	8.15 FQ	14.88 AW	22.06 TQ	CABLS	10/01-12/01
	Oakland PMSA, CA	H	9.13 FQ	19.30 AW	28.64 TQ	CABLS	10/01-12/01
	Orange County PMSA, CA	H	8.02 FQ	14.90 AW	22.82 TQ	CABLS	10/01-12/01
	Redding MSA, CA	H	8.91 FQ	15.55 AW	22.39 TQ	CABLS	10/01-12/01
	Riverside-San Bernardino PMSA, CA	H	8.05 FQ	14.52 AW	22.86 TQ	CABLS	10/01-12/01
	Sacramento PMSA, CA	H	8.77 FQ	14.70 AW	23.66 TQ	CABLS	10/01-12/01
	Salinas MSA, CA	H	8.92 FQ	16.72 AW	25.77 TQ	CABLS	10/01-12/01
	San Diego MSA, CA	H	9.39 FQ	15.66 AW	24.22 TQ	CABLS	10/01-12/01
	San Francisco PMSA, CA	H	10.10 FQ	19.55 AW	27.15 TQ	CABLS	10/01-12/01
	San Jose PMSA, CA	H	9.70 FQ	19.60 AW	31.94 TQ	CABLS	10/01-12/01
	San Luis Obispo-Atascadero-Paso Robles MSA, CA	H	9.28 FQ	15.54 AW	23.16 TQ	CABLS	10/01-12/01
	Santa Barbara-Santa Maria-Lompoc MSA, CA	H	8.27 FQ	13.85 AW	21.04 TQ	CABLS	10/01-12/01
	Santa Cruz-Watsonville PMSA, CA	H	8.29 FQ	13.38 AW	21.12 TQ	CABLS	10/01-12/01
	Santa Rosa PMSA, CA	H	8.23 FQ	13.66 AW	22.77 TQ	CABLS	10/01-12/01
	Stockton-Lodi MSA, CA	H	8.97 FQ	16.02 AW	25.37 TQ	CABLS	10/01-12/01
	Vallejo-Fairfield-Napa PMSA, CA	H	8.56 FQ	17.92 AW	27.40 TQ	CABLS	10/01-12/01
	Ventura PMSA, CA	H	9.08 FQ	15.87 AW	25.31 TQ	CABLS	10/01-12/01
	Visalia-Tulare-Porterville MSA, CA	H	7.62 FQ	12.29 AW	18.27 TQ	CABLS	10/01-12/01
	Colorado	H	7.68 FQ	11.79 AW	16.77 TQ	COBLS	10/01-12/01
	Boulder-Longmont PMSA, CO	H	8.07 FQ	11.46 AW	15.96 TQ	COBLS	10/01-12/01
	Colorado Springs MSA, CO	H	8.47 FQ	12.10 AW	16.48 TQ	COBLS	10/01-12/01
	Denver PMSA, CO	H	7.41 FQ	11.82 AW	17.20 TQ	COBLS	10/01-12/01
	Fort Collins-Loveland MSA, CO	H	7.73 FQ	11.48 AW	15.96 TQ	COBLS	10/01-12/01
	Greeley PMSA, CO	H	7.28 FQ	10.83 AW	15.79 TQ	COBLS	10/01-12/01
	Connecticut	H	10.43 FQ	16.19 AW	21.97 TQ	CTBLS	10/01-12/01
	Bridgeport PMSA, CT	H	12.06 FQ	17.30 AW	22.59 TQ	CTBLS	10/01-12/01
	Danbury PMSA, CT	H	9.53 FQ	14.35 AW	20.44 TQ	CTBLS	10/01-12/01
	Hartford MSA, CT	H	10.23 FQ	16.02 AW	21.87 TQ	CTBLS	10/01-12/01
	New Haven-Meriden PMSA, CT	H	10.71 FQ	16.33 AW	21.49 TQ	CTBLS	10/01-12/01
	New London-Norwich MSA, CT-RI	H	8.21 FQ	14.90 AW	21.49 TQ	CTBLS	10/01-12/01
	Stamford-Norwalk PMSA, CT	H	11.04 FQ	17.53 AW	22.54 TQ	CTBLS	10/01-12/01
	Waterbury PMSA, CT	H	8.81 FQ	15.80 AW	24.38 TQ	CTBLS	10/01-12/01
	Delaware	H	7.73 FQ	12.06 AW	16.75 TQ	DEBLS	10/01-12/01
	Wilmington-Newark PMSA, DE-MD	H	7.69 FQ	12.22 AW	16.90 TQ	DEBLS	10/01-12/01
	District of Columbia	H	10.12 FQ	13.78 AW	18.04 TQ	DCBLS	10/01-12/01
	Washington PMSA, DC-MD-VA-WV	H	8.35 FQ	12.07 AW	16.91 TQ	DCBLS	10/01-12/01
	Florida	H	6.01 FQ	9.60 AW	13.63 TQ	FLBLS	10/01-12/01
	Daytona Beach MSA, FL	H	6.25 FQ	9.22 AW	13.15 TQ	FLBLS	10/01-12/01
	Fort Lauderdale PMSA, FL	H	5.80 FQ	9.54 AW	14.07 TQ	FLBLS	10/01-12/01
	Fort Myers-Cape Coral MSA, FL	H	6.30 FQ	9.50 AW	13.59 TQ	FLBLS	10/01-12/01

AAW	Average annual wage	AOH	Average offered, high	ASH	Average starting, high	H	Hourly	M	Monthly	S	Special: hourly and annual
AE	Average entry wage	AOL	Average offered, low	ASL	Average starting, low	HI	Highest wage paid	MTC	Median total compensation	TQ	Third quartile wage
AEX	Average experienced wage	APH	Average pay, high range	AW	Average wage paid	HR	High end range	MW	Median wage paid	W	Weekly
AO	Average offered	APL	Average pay, low range	FQ	First quartile wage	LR	Low end range	SQ	Second quartile wage	Y	Yearly

Occupation/Type/Industry	Location	Per	Low	Mid	High	Source	Date
Construction Laborer	Fort Pierce-Port St. Lucie MSA, FL	H	6.56 FQ	9.50 AW	12.74 TQ	FLBLS	10/01-12/01
	Fort Walton Beach MSA, FL	H	6.98 FQ	9.33 AW	12.12 TQ	FLBLS	10/01-12/01
	Gainesville MSA, FL	H	5.56 FQ	7.28 AW	9.42 TQ	FLBLS	10/01-12/01
	Jacksonville MSA, FL	H	6.84 FQ	9.86 AW	13.53 TQ	FLBLS	10/01-12/01
	Lakeland-Winter Haven MSA, FL	H	5.72 FQ	9.25 AW	13.53 TQ	FLBLS	10/01-12/01
	Melbourne-Titusville-Palm Bay MSA, FL	H	7.43 FQ	9.99 AW	13.23 TQ	FLBLS	10/01-12/01
	Miami PMSA, FL	H	5.90 FQ	9.71 AW	13.70 TQ	FLBLS	10/01-12/01
	Naples MSA, FL	H	8.40 FQ	11.27 AW	14.78 TQ	FLBLS	10/01-12/01
	Ocala MSA, FL	H	6.16 FQ	8.75 AW	11.13 TQ	FLBLS	10/01-12/01
	Orlando MSA, FL	H	5.91 FQ	9.83 AW	14.06 TQ	FLBLS	10/01-12/01
	Pensacola MSA, FL	H	6.19 FQ	8.47 AW	11.43 TQ	FLBLS	10/01-12/01
	Sarasota-Bradenton MSA, FL	H	5.64 FQ	8.76 AW	12.51 TQ	FLBLS	10/01-12/01
	Tallahassee MSA, FL	H	7.12 FQ	10.56 AW	16.48 TQ	FLBLS	10/01-12/01
	Tampa-St. Petersburg-Clearwater MSA, FL	H	5.86 FQ	9.27 AW	13.54 TQ	FLBLS	10/01-12/01
	West Palm Beach-Boca Raton MSA, FL	H	7.16 FQ	10.88 AW	14.96 TQ	FLBLS	10/01-12/01
	Georgia	H	7.50 FQ	10.59 AW	14.29 TQ	GABLS	10/01-12/01
	Atlanta MSA, GA	H	8.43 FQ	11.11 AW	14.65 TQ	GABLS	10/01-12/01
	Augusta-Aiken MSA, GA-SC	H	7.09 FQ	9.88 AW	13.53 TQ	GABLS	10/01-12/01
	Columbus MSA, GA-AL	H	6.21 FQ	8.48 AW	11.07 TQ	GABLS	10/01-12/01
	Macon MSA, GA	H	6.10 FQ	8.86 AW	12.32 TQ	GABLS	10/01-12/01
	Savannah MSA, GA	H	7.73 FQ	9.91 AW	12.26 TQ	GABLS	10/01-12/01
	Hawaii	H	10.48 FQ	19.68 AW	29.02 TQ	HIBLS	10/01-12/01
	Honolulu MSA, HI	H	11.30 FQ	21.25 AW	30.29 TQ	HIBLS	10/01-12/01
	Idaho	H	7.30 FQ	10.88 AW	15.60 TQ	IDBLS	10/01-12/01
	Boise City MSA, ID	H	7.49 FQ	10.88 AW	14.01 TQ	IDBLS	10/01-12/01
	Illinois	H	6.65 FQ	17.75 AW	27.00 TQ	ILBLS	10/01-12/01
	Champaign-Urbana MSA, IL	H	9.09 FQ	17.36 AW	22.67 TQ	ILBLS	10/01-12/01
	Chicago PMSA, IL	H	6.35 FQ	18.67 AW	27.71 TQ	ILBLS	10/01-12/01
	Peoria-Pekin MSA, IL	H	9.42 FQ	15.95 AW	21.63 TQ	ILBLS	10/01-12/01
	Rockford MSA, IL	H	6.48 FQ	16.07 AW	25.35 TQ	ILBLS	10/01-12/01
	Springfield MSA, IL	H	6.73 FQ	17.28 AW	22.32 TQ	ILBLS	10/01-12/01
	Indiana	H	8.62 FQ	14.61 AW	22.02 TQ	INBLS	10/01-12/01
	Elkhart-Goshen MSA, IN	H	9.40 FQ	14.08 AW	19.50 TQ	INBLS	10/01-12/01
	Evansville-Henderson MSA, IN-KY	H	8.94 FQ	15.33 AW	21.09 TQ	INBLS	10/01-12/01
	Fort Wayne MSA, IN	H	6.36 FQ	13.08 AW	19.97 TQ	INBLS	10/01-12/01
	Gary PMSA, IN	H	7.23 FQ	16.28 AW	26.71 TQ	INBLS	10/01-12/01
	Indianapolis MSA, IN	H	9.09 FQ	14.49 AW	21.73 TQ	INBLS	10/01-12/01
	Lafayette MSA, IN	H	9.60 FQ	13.78 AW	20.21 TQ	INBLS	10/01-12/01
	South Bend MSA, IN	H	10.50 FQ	17.10 AW	22.44 TQ	INBLS	10/01-12/01
	Iowa	H	8.24 FQ	12.48 AW	18.41 TQ	IABLS	10/01-12/01
	Cedar Rapids MSA, IA	H	9.01 FQ	14.78 AW	20.50 TQ	IABLS	10/01-12/01
	Davenport-Moline-Rock Island MSA, IA-IL	H	9.16 FQ	15.79 AW	22.18 TQ	IABLS	10/01-12/01
	Des Moines MSA, IA	H	9.00 FQ	14.21 AW	20.18 TQ	IABLS	10/01-12/01
	Kansas	H	7.47 FQ	11.67 AW	17.33 TQ	KSBLS	10/01-12/01
	Topeka MSA, KS	H	8.59 FQ	12.40 AW	16.60 TQ	KSBLS	10/01-12/01
	Wichita MSA, KS	H	7.65 FQ	10.43 AW	13.45 TQ	KSBLS	10/01-12/01
	Kentucky	H	6.74 FQ	11.42 AW	16.93 TQ	KYBLS	10/01-12/01
	Lexington MSA, KY	H	7.82 FQ	10.83 AW	14.30 TQ	KYBLS	10/01-12/01
	Louisville MSA, KY-IN	H	6.56 FQ	12.19 AW	17.76 TQ	KYBLS	10/01-12/01
	Louisiana	H	6.78 FQ	10.00 AW	13.82 TQ	LABLS	10/01-12/01
	Baton Rouge MSA, LA	H	6.30 FQ	9.17 AW	12.44 TQ	LABLS	10/01-12/01
	Houma MSA, LA	H	7.05 FQ	10.39 AW	16.38 TQ	LABLS	10/01-12/01
	Lafayette MSA, LA	H	7.16 FQ	9.94 AW	13.22 TQ	LABLS	10/01-12/01
	Lake Charles MSA, LA	H	7.14 FQ	10.93 AW	14.98 TQ	LABLS	10/01-12/01
	New Orleans MSA, LA	H	6.75 FQ	10.06 AW	14.04 TQ	LABLS	10/01-12/01
	Shreveport-Bossier City MSA, LA	H	7.22 FQ	9.67 AW	12.66 TQ	LABLS	10/01-12/01
	Maine	H	7.38 FQ	10.08 AW	13.26 TQ	MEBLS	10/01-12/01
	Portland MSA, ME	H	8.52 FQ	10.84 AW	13.69 TQ	MEBLS	10/01-12/01
	Maryland	H	8.79 FQ	12.12 AW	16.50 TQ	MDBLS	10/01-12/01
	Baltimore PMSA, MD	H	8.89 FQ	12.23 AW	16.42 TQ	MDBLS	10/01-12/01
	Massachusetts	H	11.62 FQ	19.43 AW	27.41 TQ	MABLS	10/01-12/01
	Boston PMSA, MA-NH	H	12.13 FQ	21.29 AW	28.97 TQ	MABLS	10/01-12/01
	Brockton PMSA, MA	H	11.27 FQ	16.06 AW	24.62 TQ	MABLS	10/01-12/01
	Lawrence PMSA, MA-NH	H	10.29 FQ	16.87 AW	26.38 TQ	MABLS	10/01-12/01

AAW	Average annual wage	**AOH**	Average offered, high	**ASH**	Average starting, high	**H**	Hourly	**M**	Monthly	**S**	Special: hourly and annual
AE	Average entry wage	**AOL**	Average offered, low	**ASL**	Average starting, low	**HI**	Highest wage paid	**MTC**	Median total compensation	**TQ**	Third quartile wage
AEX	Average experienced wage	**APH**	Average pay, high range	**AW**	Average wage paid	**HR**	High end range	**MW**	Median wage paid	**W**	Weekly
AO	Average offered	**APL**	Average pay, low range	**FQ**	First quartile wage	**LR**	Low end range	**SQ**	Second quartile wage	**Y**	Yearly

Occupation/Type/Industry	Location	Per	Low	Mid	High	Source	Date
Construction Laborer	Lowell PMSA, MA-NH	H	11.16 FQ	17.35 AW	25.71 TQ	MABLS	10/01-12/01
	New Bedford PMSA, MA	H	10.44 FQ	17.11 AW	22.84 TQ	MABLS	10/01-12/01
	Springfield MSA, MA	H	10.85 FQ	16.48 AW	22.61 TQ	MABLS	10/01-12/01
	Worcester PMSA, MA-CT	H	11.15 FQ	16.43 AW	23.97 TQ	MABLS	10/01-12/01
	Michigan	H	9.12 FQ	15.88 AW	22.26 TQ	MIBLS	10/01-12/01
	Ann Arbor PMSA, MI	H	10.20 FQ	17.24 AW	24.03 TQ	MIBLS	10/01-12/01
	Detroit PMSA, MI	H	11.00 FQ	17.68 AW	23.54 TQ	MIBLS	10/01-12/01
	Flint PMSA, MI	H	11.57 FQ	17.74 AW	22.16 TQ	MIBLS	10/01-12/01
	Grand Rapids-Muskegon-Holland MSA, MI	H	7.32 FQ	12.08 AW	17.88 TQ	MIBLS	10/01-12/01
	Kalamazoo-Battle Creek MSA, MI	H	9.22 FQ	14.57 AW	20.14 TQ	MIBLS	10/01-12/01
	Lansing-East Lansing MSA, MI	H	11.12 FQ	16.63 AW	22.09 TQ	MIBLS	10/01-12/01
	Saginaw-Bay City-Midland MSA, MI	H	8.67 FQ	15.02 AW	22.09 TQ	MIBLS	10/01-12/01
	Minnesota	H	9.81 FQ	17.44 AW	26.08 TQ	MNBLS	10/01-12/01
	Duluth-Superior MSA, MN-WI	H	9.45 FQ	16.34 AW	21.95 TQ	MNBLS	10/01-12/01
	Minneapolis-St. Paul MSA, MN-WI	H	11.63 FQ	19.44 AW	26.86 TQ	MNBLS	10/01-12/01
	St. Cloud MSA, MN	H	7.72 FQ	12.52 AW	17.58 TQ	MNBLS	10/01-12/01
	Mississippi	H	7.03 FQ	9.57 AW	12.78 TQ	MSBLS	10/01-12/01
	Biloxi-Gulfport-Pascagoula MSA, MS	H	7.54 FQ	9.47 AW	11.97 TQ	MSBLS	10/01-12/01
	Jackson MSA, MS	H	7.14 FQ	11.01 AW	17.92 TQ	MSBLS	10/01-12/01
	Missouri	H	8.63 FQ	16.37 AW	25.80 TQ	MOBLS	10/01-12/01
	Kansas City MSA, MO-KS	H	8.87 FQ	15.53 AW	22.21 TQ	MOBLS	10/01-12/01
	St. Louis MSA, MO-IL	H	10.50 FQ	19.11 AW	26.94 TQ	MOBLS	10/01-12/01
	Springfield MSA, MO	H	6.98 FQ	12.19 AW	18.52 TQ	MOBLS	10/01-12/01
	Montana	H	7.62 FQ	12.93 AW	20.20 TQ	MTBLS	10/01-12/01
	Billings MSA, MT	H	8.11 FQ	15.23 AW	20.81 TQ	MTBLS	10/01-12/01
	Nebraska	H	6.79 FQ	10.61 AW	15.56 TQ	NEBLS	10/01-12/01
	Lincoln MSA, NE	H	6.09 FQ	10.20 AW	14.43 TQ	NEBLS	10/01-12/01
	Omaha MSA, NE-IA	H	6.52 FQ	10.81 AW	16.01 TQ	NEBLS	10/01-12/01
	Nevada	H	8.20 FQ	14.08 AW	21.52 TQ	NVBLS	10/01-12/01
	Las Vegas MSA, NV-AZ	H	8.12 FQ	13.23 AW	20.90 TQ	NVBLS	10/01-12/01
	Reno MSA, NV	H	9.54 FQ	16.59 AW	23.08 TQ	NVBLS	10/01-12/01
	New Hampshire	H	8.76 FQ	12.98 AW	18.32 TQ	NHBLS	10/01-12/01
	Manchester PMSA, NH	H	9.85 FQ	13.07 AW	16.81 TQ	NHBLS	10/01-12/01
	Nashua PMSA, NH	H	10.03 FQ	13.16 AW	17.14 TQ	NHBLS	10/01-12/01
	Portsmouth-Rochester PMSA, NH-ME	H	9.39 FQ	12.95 AW	17.31 TQ	NHBLS	10/01-12/01
	New Jersey	H	9.98 FQ	18.91 AW	27.50 TQ	NJBLS	10/01-12/01
	Atlantic-Cape May PMSA, NJ	H	11.32 FQ	21.54 AW	31.57 TQ	NJBLS	10/01-12/01
	Bergen-Passaic PMSA, NJ	H	10.48 FQ	21.20 AW	31.17 TQ	NJBLS	10/01-12/01
	Jersey City PMSA, NJ	H	12.12 FQ	21.43 AW	30.32 TQ	NJBLS	10/01-12/01
	Middlesex-Somerset-Hunterdon PMSA, NJ	H	11.98 FQ	20.21 AW	26.91 TQ	NJBLS	10/01-12/01
	Monmouth-Ocean PMSA, NJ	H	9.29 FQ	14.96 AW	23.14 TQ	NJBLS	10/01-12/01
	Newark PMSA, NJ	H	13.75 FQ	20.13 AW	27.23 TQ	NJBLS	10/01-12/01
	Trenton PMSA, NJ	H	11.06 FQ	19.77 AW	27.71 TQ	NJBLS	10/01-12/01
	New Mexico	H	6.71 FQ	9.85 AW	13.64 TQ	NMBLS	10/01-12/01
	Albuquerque MSA, NM	H	7.53 FQ	10.01 AW	13.25 TQ	NMBLS	10/01-12/01
	Las Cruces MSA, NM	H	6.40 FQ	8.85 AW	11.17 TQ	NMBLS	10/01-12/01
	New York	H	9.43 FQ	18.52 AW	29.52 TQ	NYBLS	10/01-12/01
	Albany-Schenectady-Troy MSA, NY	H	8.40 FQ	15.21 AW	22.34 TQ	NYBLS	10/01-12/01
	Binghamton MSA, NY	H	8.12 FQ	15.77 AW	26.23 TQ	NYBLS	10/01-12/01
	Buffalo-Niagara Falls MSA, NY	H	8.09 FQ	15.24 AW	24.43 TQ	NYBLS	10/01-12/01
	Dutchess County PMSA, NY	H	9.99 FQ	17.15 AW	26.69 TQ	NYBLS	10/01-12/01
	Nassau-Suffolk PMSA, NY	H	10.57 FQ	20.53 AW	30.54 TQ	NYBLS	10/01-12/01
	New York PMSA, NY	H	10.26 FQ	20.91 AW	32.71 TQ	NYBLS	10/01-12/01
	Newburgh PMSA, NY-PA	H	9.66 FQ	15.53 AW	24.10 TQ	NYBLS	10/01-12/01
	Rochester MSA, NY	H	9.04 FQ	14.48 AW	20.28 TQ	NYBLS	10/01-12/01
	Syracuse MSA, NY	H	7.80 FQ	15.01 AW	21.48 TQ	NYBLS	10/01-12/01
	Utica-Rome MSA, NY	H	9.82 FQ	15.70 AW	21.94 TQ	NYBLS	10/01-12/01
	North Carolina	H	7.34 FQ	10.26 AW	13.79 TQ	NCBLS	10/01-12/01
	Asheville MSA, NC	H	6.22 FQ	9.09 AW	11.64 TQ	NCBLS	10/01-12/01
	Charlotte-Gastonia-Rock Hill MSA, NC-SC	H	7.56 FQ	10.68 AW	14.87 TQ	NCBLS	10/01-12/01
	Fayetteville MSA, NC	H	6.77 FQ	9.22 AW	12.65 TQ	NCBLS	10/01-12/01

AAW Average annual wage; **AE** Average entry wage; **AEX** Average experienced wage; **AO** Average offered; **AOH** Average offered, high; **AOL** Average offered, low; **APH** Average pay, high range; **APL** Average pay, low range; **ASH** Average starting, high; **ASL** Average starting, low; **AW** Average wage paid; **FQ** First quartile wage; **H** Hourly; **HI** Highest wage paid; **HR** High end range; **LR** Low end range; **M** Monthly; **MTC** Median total compensation; **MW** Median wage paid; **SQ** Second quartile wage; **S** Special: hourly and annual; **TQ** Third quartile wage; **W** Weekly; **Y** Yearly

Occupation/Type/Industry	Location	Per	Low	Mid	High	Source	Date
Construction Laborer	Greensboro-Winston-Salem-High Point MSA, NC	H	6.34 FQ	9.96 AW	13.73 TQ	NCBLS	10/01-12/01
	Hickory-Morganton-Lenoir MSA, NC	H	7.88 FQ	10.75 AW	13.85 TQ	NCBLS	10/01-12/01
	Raleigh-Durham-Chapel Hill MSA, NC	H	7.76 FQ	10.93 AW	14.01 TQ	NCBLS	10/01-12/01
	Wilmington MSA, NC	H	8.37 FQ	10.61 AW	13.74 TQ	NCBLS	10/01-12/01
	North Dakota	H	7.91 FQ	10.73 AW	14.23 TQ	NDBLS	10/01-12/01
	Fargo-Moorhead MSA, ND-MN	H	8.07 FQ	11.16 AW	14.53 TQ	NDBLS	10/01-12/01
	Ohio	H	8.04 FQ	15.20 AW	22.62 TQ	OHBLS	10/01-12/01
	Akron PMSA, OH	H	9.58 FQ	15.83 AW	22.83 TQ	OHBLS	10/01-12/01
	Canton-Massillon MSA, OH	H	8.75 FQ	13.89 AW	20.46 TQ	OHBLS	10/01-12/01
	Cincinnati PMSA, OH-KY-IN	H	6.76 FQ	13.73 AW	21.04 TQ	OHBLS	10/01-12/01
	Cleveland-Lorain-Elyria PMSA, OH	H	8.08 FQ	16.52 AW	25.45 TQ	OHBLS	10/01-12/01
	Columbus MSA, OH	H	8.48 FQ	13.92 AW	21.01 TQ	OHBLS	10/01-12/01
	Dayton-Springfield MSA, OH	H	7.28 FQ	14.35 AW	22.32 TQ	OHBLS	10/01-12/01
	Hamilton-Middletown PMSA, OH	H	9.47 FQ	16.01 AW	21.61 TQ	OHBLS	10/01-12/01
	Mansfield MSA, OH	H	8.84 FQ	14.47 AW	21.27 TQ	OHBLS	10/01-12/01
	Toledo MSA, OH	H	7.85 FQ	15.70 AW	22.36 TQ	OHBLS	10/01-12/01
	Youngstown-Warren MSA, OH	H	7.38 FQ	16.16 AW	22.31 TQ	OHBLS	10/01-12/01
	Oklahoma	H	7.57 FQ	10.57 AW	13.44 TQ	OKBLS	10/01-12/01
	Oklahoma City MSA, OK	H	7.64 FQ	10.96 AW	13.40 TQ	OKBLS	10/01-12/01
	Tulsa MSA, OK	H	7.82 FQ	10.64 AW	13.33 TQ	OKBLS	10/01-12/01
	Oregon	H	8.80 FQ	14.77 AW	23.89 TQ	ORBLS	10/01-12/01
	Eugene-Springfield MSA, OR	H	7.78 FQ	12.67 AW	18.39 TQ	ORBLS	10/01-12/01
	Medford-Ashland MSA, OR	H	8.17 FQ	12.09 AW	18.89 TQ	ORBLS	10/01-12/01
	Portland-Vancouver PMSA, OR-WA	H	9.13 FQ	15.34 AW	24.55 TQ	ORBLS	10/01-12/01
	Salem PMSA, OR	H	9.17 FQ	16.39 AW	26.70 TQ	ORBLS	10/01-12/01
	Pennsylvania	H	8.89 FQ	14.41 AW	21.50 TQ	PABLS	10/01-12/01
	Allentown-Bethlehem-Easton MSA, PA	H	9.58 FQ	13.53 AW	17.90 TQ	PABLS	10/01-12/01
	Erie MSA, PA	H	7.72 FQ	11.50 AW	17.49 TQ	PABLS	10/01-12/01
	Harrisburg-Lebanon-Carlisle MSA, PA	H	9.63 FQ	13.14 AW	18.38 TQ	PABLS	10/01-12/01
	Johnstown MSA, PA	H	7.63 FQ	13.43 AW	20.08 TQ	PABLS	10/01-12/01
	Lancaster MSA, PA	H	9.51 FQ	13.36 AW	19.14 TQ	PABLS	10/01-12/01
	Philadelphia PMSA, PA-NJ	H	9.12 FQ	16.34 AW	25.54 TQ	PABLS	10/01-12/01
	Pittsburgh MSA, PA	H	9.07 FQ	13.90 AW	20.77 TQ	PABLS	10/01-12/01
	Reading MSA, PA	H	10.29 FQ	14.63 AW	19.82 TQ	PABLS	10/01-12/01
	Scranton-Wilkes-Barre-Hazleton MSA, PA	H	8.66 FQ	13.16 AW	18.45 TQ	PABLS	10/01-12/01
	York MSA, PA	H	9.15 FQ	13.26 AW	19.12 TQ	PABLS	10/01-12/01
	Rhode Island	H	10.28 FQ	16.29 AW	21.95 TQ	RIBLS	10/01-12/01
	Providence-Fall River-Warwick MSA, RI-MA	H	10.91 FQ	16.73 AW	22.26 TQ	RIBLS	10/01-12/01
	South Carolina	H	7.01 FQ	9.53 AW	12.72 TQ	SCBLS	10/01-12/01
	Charleston-North Charleston MSA, SC	H	6.87 FQ	9.16 AW	12.16 TQ	SCBLS	10/01-12/01
	Columbia MSA, SC	H	6.43 FQ	9.28 AW	13.09 TQ	SCBLS	10/01-12/01
	Greenville-Spartanburg-Anderson MSA, SC	H	7.56 FQ	9.73 AW	12.22 TQ	SCBLS	10/01-12/01
	Myrtle Beach MSA, SC	H	7.46 FQ	9.92 AW	12.96 TQ	SCBLS	10/01-12/01
	South Dakota	H	7.69 FQ	10.26 AW	13.60 TQ	SDBLS	10/01-12/01
	Sioux Falls MSA, SD	H	8.72 FQ	10.83 AW	13.78 TQ	SDBLS	10/01-12/01
	Tennessee	H	7.51 FQ	10.51 AW	13.88 TQ	TNBLS	10/01-12/01
	Chattanooga MSA, TN-GA	H	8.21 FQ	10.86 AW	13.93 TQ	TNBLS	10/01-12/01
	Clarksville-Hopkinsville MSA, TN-KY	H	7.82 FQ	11.48 AW	17.05 TQ	TNBLS	10/01-12/01
	Johnson City-Kingsport-Bristol MSA, TN-VA	H	6.08 FQ	9.06 AW	11.93 TQ	TNBLS	10/01-12/01
	Knoxville MSA, TN	H	8.28 FQ	10.84 AW	13.70 TQ	TNBLS	10/01-12/01
	Memphis MSA, TN-AR-MS	H	7.60 FQ	10.54 AW	14.15 TQ	TNBLS	10/01-12/01
	Nashville MSA, TN	H	7.82 FQ	11.07 AW	14.66 TQ	TNBLS	10/01-12/01
	Texas	H	6.58 FQ	9.60 AW	13.43 TQ	TXBLS	10/01-12/01
	Amarillo MSA, TX	H	6.97 FQ	10.11 AW	14.81 TQ	TXBLS	10/01-12/01
	Austin-San Marcos MSA, TX	H	7.07 FQ	9.65 AW	13.26 TQ	TXBLS	10/01-12/01
	Beaumont-Port Arthur MSA, TX	H	6.19 FQ	8.93 AW	11.96 TQ	TXBLS	10/01-12/01

AAW	Average annual wage	**AOH**	Average offered, high	**ASH**	Average starting, high	**H**	Hourly	**M**	Monthly	**S**	Special: hourly and annual
AE	Average entry wage	**AOL**	Average offered, low	**ASL**	Average starting, low	**HI**	Highest wage paid	**MTC**	Median total compensation	**TQ**	Third quartile wage
AEX	Average experienced wage	**APH**	Average pay, high range	**AW**	Average wage paid	**HR**	High end range	**MW**	Median wage paid	**W**	Weekly
AO	Average offered	**APL**	Average pay, low range	**FQ**	First quartile wage	**LR**	Low end range	**SQ**	Second quartile wage	**Y**	Yearly

Occupation/Type/Industry	Location	Per	Low	Mid	High	Source	Date
Construction Laborer	Brazoria PMSA, TX	H	7.02 FQ	9.65 AW	13.35 TQ	TXBLS	10/01-12/01
	Brownsville-Harlingen-San Benito MSA, TX	H	5.78 FQ	7.60 AW	10.09 TQ	TXBLS	10/01-12/01
	Corpus Christi MSA, TX	H	6.29 FQ	9.49 AW	15.03 TQ	TXBLS	10/01-12/01
	Dallas PMSA, TX	H	6.94 FQ	10.01 AW	13.36 TQ	TXBLS	10/01-12/01
	El Paso MSA, TX	H	5.84 FQ	8.29 AW	11.55 TQ	TXBLS	10/01-12/01
	Fort Worth-Arlington PMSA, TX	H	7.62 FQ	11.37 AW	17.03 TQ	TXBLS	10/01-12/01
	Galveston-Texas City PMSA, TX	H	7.47 FQ	10.62 AW	13.69 TQ	TXBLS	10/01-12/01
	Houston PMSA, TX	H	6.43 FQ	9.69 AW	13.84 TQ	TXBLS	10/01-12/01
	Killeen-Temple MSA, TX	H	6.50 FQ	8.47 AW	10.65 TQ	TXBLS	10/01-12/01
	Laredo MSA, TX	H	5.88 FQ	8.44 AW	13.52 TQ	TXBLS	10/01-12/01
	Longview-Marshall MSA, TX	H	7.29 FQ	9.68 AW	12.88 TQ	TXBLS	10/01-12/01
	Lubbock MSA, TX	H	6.66 FQ	9.09 AW	12.60 TQ	TXBLS	10/01-12/01
	McAllen-Edinburg-Mission MSA, TX	H	5.69 FQ	7.13 AW	9.23 TQ	TXBLS	10/01-12/01
	Odessa-Midland MSA, TX	H	5.98 FQ	9.05 AW	12.84 TQ	TXBLS	10/01-12/01
	San Antonio MSA, TX	H	6.91 FQ	9.19 AW	12.67 TQ	TXBLS	10/01-12/01
	Tyler MSA, TX	H	6.29 FQ	9.01 AW	11.20 TQ	TXBLS	10/01-12/01
	Waco MSA, TX	H	6.46 FQ	8.86 AW	11.51 TQ	TXBLS	10/01-12/01
	Utah	H	7.64 FQ	11.18 AW	16.14 TQ	UTBLS	10/01-12/01
	Provo-Orem MSA, UT	H	7.46 FQ	9.75 AW	13.14 TQ	UTBLS	10/01-12/01
	Salt Lake City-Ogden MSA, UT	H	8.06 FQ	11.85 AW	17.39 TQ	UTBLS	10/01-12/01
	Vermont	H	8.10 FQ	10.79 AW	14.21 TQ	VTBLS	10/01-12/01
	Burlington MSA, VT	H	8.68 FQ	11.03 AW	13.87 TQ	VTBLS	10/01-12/01
	Virginia	H	7.39 FQ	10.38 AW	13.91 TQ	VABLS	10/01-12/01
	Lynchburg MSA, VA	H	6.62 FQ	9.08 AW	12.11 TQ	VABLS	10/01-12/01
	Norfolk-Virginia Beach-Newport News MSA, VA-NC	H	7.34 FQ	9.55 AW	12.54 TQ	VABLS	10/01-12/01
	Richmond-Petersburg MSA, VA	H	7.88 FQ	10.24 AW	13.18 TQ	VABLS	10/01-12/01
	Roanoke MSA, VA	H	7.51 FQ	9.20 AW	11.08 TQ	VABLS	10/01-12/01
	Washington	H	9.20 FQ	17.33 AW	26.55 TQ	WABLS	10/01-12/01
	Bremerton PMSA, WA	H	9.38 FQ	15.02 AW	24.13 TQ	WABLS	10/01-12/01
	Olympia PMSA, WA	H	9.29 FQ	15.82 AW	26.21 TQ	WABLS	10/01-12/01
	Richland-Kennewick-Pasco MSA, WA	H	9.20 FQ	15.41 AW	21.76 TQ	WABLS	10/01-12/01
	Seattle-Bellevue-Everett PMSA, WA	H	8.66 FQ	18.89 AW	27.25 TQ	WABLS	10/01-12/01
	Spokane MSA, WA	H	9.29 FQ	15.06 AW	22.39 TQ	WABLS	10/01-12/01
	Tacoma PMSA, WA	H	10.95 FQ	16.02 AW	23.82 TQ	WABLS	10/01-12/01
	Yakima MSA, WA	H	8.86 FQ	12.77 AW	16.91 TQ	WABLS	10/01-12/01
	West Virginia	H	7.26 FQ	12.56 AW	21.41 TQ	WVBLS	10/01-12/01
	Charleston MSA, WV	H	8.04 FQ	15.15 AW	23.30 TQ	WVBLS	10/01-12/01
	Huntington-Ashland MSA, WV-KY-OH	H	6.73 FQ	11.57 AW	17.99 TQ	WVBLS	10/01-12/01
	Wisconsin	H	10.19 FQ	16.15 AW	23.30 TQ	WIBLS	10/01-12/01
	Appleton-Oshkosh-Neenah MSA, WI	H	9.84 FQ	13.82 AW	17.91 TQ	WIBLS	10/01-12/01
	Green Bay MSA, WI	H	11.53 FQ	17.73 AW	25.70 TQ	WIBLS	10/01-12/01
	Madison MSA, WI	H	11.55 FQ	16.78 AW	23.24 TQ	WIBLS	10/01-12/01
	Milwaukee-Waukesha PMSA, WI	H	11.88 FQ	17.41 AW	25.09 TQ	WIBLS	10/01-12/01
	Racine PMSA, WI	H	9.46 FQ	15.78 AW	21.24 TQ	WIBLS	10/01-12/01
	Wyoming	H	7.24 FQ	10.87 AW	14.72 TQ	WYBLS	10/01-12/01
	Cheyenne MSA, WY	H	8.27 FQ	12.56 AW	18.10 TQ	WYBLS	10/01-12/01
	Puerto Rico	H	5.54 FQ	6.42 AW	7.69 TQ	PRBLS	10/01-12/01
	Virgin Islands	H	6.89 FQ	9.44 AW	13.17 TQ	VIBLS	10/01-12/01
	Guam	H	7.07 FQ	8.54 AW	11.12 TQ	GUBLS	10/01-12/01
Construction Manager	Alabama	Y	35000 FQ	57740 AW	89000 TQ	ALBLS	10/01-12/01
	Birmingham MSA, AL	Y	36940 FQ	60450 AW	93930 TQ	ALBLS	10/01-12/01
	Huntsville MSA, AL	Y	28930 FQ	55780 AW	101010 TQ	ALBLS	10/01-12/01
	Mobile MSA, AL	Y	40130 FQ	63840 AW	89410 TQ	ALBLS	10/01-12/01
	Montgomery MSA, AL	Y	34310 FQ	59620 AW	88470 TQ	ALBLS	10/01-12/01
	Alaska	Y	48570 FQ	74120 AW	112270 TQ	AKBLS	10/01-12/01
	Anchorage MSA, AK	Y	48420 FQ	79830 AW	120900 TQ	AKBLS	10/01-12/01
	Arizona	Y	46430 FQ	70580 AW	100930 TQ	AZBLS	10/01-12/01
	Phoenix-Mesa MSA, AZ	Y	48310 FQ	72720 AW	104710 TQ	AZBLS	10/01-12/01
	Tucson MSA, AZ	Y	40280 FQ	63870 AW	91250 TQ	AZBLS	10/01-12/01

AAW Average annual wage; AE Average entry wage; AEX Average experienced wage; AO Average offered; AOH Average offered, high; AOL Average offered, low; APH Average pay, high range; APL Average pay, low range; ASH Average starting, high; ASL Average starting, low; AW Average wage paid; FQ First quartile wage; H Hourly; HI Highest wage paid; HR High end range; LR Low end range; M Monthly; MTC Median total compensation; MW Median wage paid; SQ Second quartile wage; S Special: hourly and annual; TQ Third quartile wage; W Weekly; Y Yearly

Occupation/Type/Industry	Location	Per	Low	Mid	High	Source	Date
Construction Manager	Arkansas	Y	26320 FQ	47320 AW	79740 TQ	ARBLS	10/01-12/01
	Fayetteville-Springdale-Rogers MSA, AR	Y	19900 FQ	45580 AW	105230 TQ	ARBLS	10/01-12/01
	Fort Smith MSA, AR-OK	Y	32550 FQ	54470 AW	81850 TQ	ARBLS	10/01-12/01
	Little Rock-North Little Rock MSA, AR	Y	30070 FQ	47490 AW	78910 TQ	ARBLS	10/01-12/01
	California	Y	47270 FQ	76860 AW	116990 TQ	CABLS	10/01-12/01
	Bakersfield MSA, CA	Y	46660 FQ	68080 AW	96810 TQ	CABLS	10/01-12/01
	Chico-Paradise MSA, CA	Y	38270 FQ	57500 AW	82210 TQ	CABLS	10/01-12/01
	Fresno MSA, CA	Y	38630 FQ	63280 AW	89950 TQ	CABLS	10/01-12/01
	Los Angeles-Long Beach PMSA, CA	Y	49460 FQ	79760 AW	116830 TQ	CABLS	10/01-12/01
	Merced MSA, CA	Y	39040 FQ	54080 AW	72610 TQ	CABLS	10/01-12/01
	Modesto MSA, CA	Y	30530 FQ	56460 AW	86840 TQ	CABLS	10/01-12/01
	Oakland PMSA, CA	Y	55040 FQ	81390 AW	123890 TQ	CABLS	10/01-12/01
	Orange County PMSA, CA	Y	48820 FQ	75170 AW	116620 TQ	CABLS	10/01-12/01
	Redding MSA, CA	Y	39060 FQ	52180 AW	80500 TQ	CABLS	10/01-12/01
	Riverside-San Bernardino PMSA, CA	Y	44600 FQ	76510 AW	118460 TQ	CABLS	10/01-12/01
	Sacramento PMSA, CA	Y	45330 FQ	72090 AW	110120 TQ	CABLS	10/01-12/01
	Salinas MSA, CA	Y	47240 FQ	78480 AW	122730 TQ	CABLS	10/01-12/01
	San Diego MSA, CA	Y	43190 FQ	73180 AW	106200 TQ	CABLS	10/01-12/01
	San Francisco PMSA, CA	Y	56340 FQ	96740 AW		CABLS	10/01-12/01
	San Jose PMSA, CA	Y	49010 FQ	81610 AW	120990 TQ	CABLS	10/01-12/01
	San Luis Obispo-Atascadero-Paso Robles MSA, CA	Y	45380 FQ	67460 AW	88420 TQ	CABLS	10/01-12/01
	Santa Barbara-Santa Maria-Lompoc MSA, CA	Y	49130 FQ	86800 AW	140080 TQ	CABLS	10/01-12/01
	Santa Cruz-Watsonville PMSA, CA	Y	48320 FQ	72520 AW	99400 TQ	CABLS	10/01-12/01
	Santa Rosa PMSA, CA	Y	43220 FQ	77720 AW		CABLS	10/01-12/01
	Stockton-Lodi MSA, CA	Y	46370 FQ	67870 AW	94370 TQ	CABLS	10/01-12/01
	Vallejo-Fairfield-Napa PMSA, CA	Y	50920 FQ	80250 AW	135390 TQ	CABLS	10/01-12/01
	Ventura PMSA, CA	Y	48370 FQ	74210 AW	108460 TQ	CABLS	10/01-12/01
	Visalia-Tulare-Porterville MSA, CA	Y	44790 FQ	67210 AW	91480 TQ	CABLS	10/01-12/01
	Colorado	Y	40080 FQ	66890 AW	101470 TQ	COBLS	10/01-12/01
	Boulder-Longmont PMSA, CO	Y	32670 FQ	74430 AW		COBLS	10/01-12/01
	Colorado Springs MSA, CO	Y	42140 FQ	63900 AW	88860 TQ	COBLS	10/01-12/01
	Denver PMSA, CO	Y	43450 FQ	69280 AW	103310 TQ	COBLS	10/01-12/01
	Fort Collins-Loveland MSA, CO	Y	42380 FQ	60260 AW	84550 TQ	COBLS	10/01-12/01
	Greeley PMSA, CO	Y	45640 FQ	62530 AW	88300 TQ	COBLS	10/01-12/01
	Connecticut	Y	44930 FQ	80140 AW		CTBLS	10/01-12/01
	Bridgeport PMSA, CT	Y	43300 FQ	72140 AW	116400 TQ	CTBLS	10/01-12/01
	Danbury PMSA, CT	Y	52120 FQ	84260 AW		CTBLS	10/01-12/01
	Hartford MSA, CT	Y	29010 FQ	70900 AW	113330 TQ	CTBLS	10/01-12/01
	New Haven-Meriden PMSA, CT	Y	46210 FQ	73060 AW	134460 TQ	CTBLS	10/01-12/01
	New London-Norwich MSA, CT-RI	Y	27140 FQ	67120 AW	112160 TQ	CTBLS	10/01-12/01
	Stamford-Norwalk PMSA, CT	Y	64570 FQ	114720 AW		CTBLS	10/01-12/01
	Waterbury PMSA, CT	Y	45680 FQ	66570 AW	89760 TQ	CTBLS	10/01-12/01
	Delaware	Y	26470 FQ	54560 AW	86480 TQ	DEBLS	10/01-12/01
	Wilmington-Newark PMSA, DE-MD	Y	27150 FQ	57030 AW	88780 TQ	DEBLS	10/01-12/01
	District of Columbia	Y	41960 FQ	73110 AW	123640 TQ	DCBLS	10/01-12/01
	Washington PMSA, DC-MD-VA-WV	Y	40730 FQ	69600 AW	111000 TQ	DCBLS	10/01-12/01
	Florida	Y	32140 FQ	62080 AW	108140 TQ	FLBLS	10/01-12/01
	Daytona Beach MSA, FL	Y	25380 FQ	43890 AW	79950 TQ	FLBLS	10/01-12/01
	Fort Lauderdale PMSA, FL	Y	42820 FQ	68700 AW	106730 TQ	FLBLS	10/01-12/01
	Fort Myers-Cape Coral MSA, FL	Y	38790 FQ	66500 AW	112310 TQ	FLBLS	10/01-12/01
	Fort Pierce-Port St. Lucie MSA, FL	Y	32400 FQ	54720 AW	85840 TQ	FLBLS	10/01-12/01
	Fort Walton Beach MSA, FL	Y	25530 FQ	47910 AW	73030 TQ	FLBLS	10/01-12/01
	Gainesville MSA, FL	Y	29980 FQ	46950 AW	77580 TQ	FLBLS	10/01-12/01
	Jacksonville MSA, FL	Y	34880 FQ	65150 AW	108520 TQ	FLBLS	10/01-12/01
	Lakeland-Winter Haven MSA, FL	Y	25660 FQ	48810 AW	74720 TQ	FLBLS	10/01-12/01

AAW	Average annual wage	**AOH**	Average offered, high	**ASH**	Average starting, high	**H**	Hourly	**M**	Monthly	**S**	Special: hourly and annual
AE	Average entry wage	**AOL**	Average offered, low	**ASL**	Average starting, low	**HI**	Highest wage paid	**MTC**	Median total compensation	**TQ**	Third quartile wage
AEX	Average experienced wage	**APH**	Average pay, high range	**AW**	Average wage paid	**HR**	High end range	**MW**	Median wage paid	**W**	Weekly
AO	Average offered	**APL**	Average pay, low range	**FQ**	First quartile wage	**LR**	Low end range	**SQ**	Second quartile wage	**Y**	Yearly

Occupation/Type/Industry	Location	Per	Low	Mid	High	Source	Date
Construction Manager	Melbourne-Titusville-Palm Bay MSA, FL	Y	33900 FQ	62250 AW	100310 TQ	FLBLS	10/01-12/01
	Miami PMSA, FL	Y	34210 FQ	61130 AW	93570 TQ	FLBLS	10/01-12/01
	Naples MSA, FL	Y	37340 FQ	64600 AW	97770 TQ	FLBLS	10/01-12/01
	Ocala MSA, FL	Y	32080 FQ	50270 AW	73240 TQ	FLBLS	10/01-12/01
	Orlando MSA, FL	Y	38670 FQ	58730 AW	93520 TQ	FLBLS	10/01-12/01
	Pensacola MSA, FL	Y	32360 FQ	57400 AW	83630 TQ	FLBLS	10/01-12/01
	Sarasota-Bradenton MSA, FL	Y	36670 FQ	50440 AW	73170 TQ	FLBLS	10/01-12/01
	Tallahassee MSA, FL	Y	33800 FQ	59370 AW	84430 TQ	FLBLS	10/01-12/01
	Tampa-St. Petersburg-Clearwater MSA, FL	Y	35420 FQ	75370 AW		FLBLS	10/01-12/01
	West Palm Beach-Boca Raton MSA, FL	Y	27410 FQ	64580 AW	111920 TQ	FLBLS	10/01-12/01
	Georgia	Y	36200 FQ	59750 AW	90070 TQ	GABLS	10/01-12/01
	Atlanta MSA, GA	Y	39890 FQ	62770 AW	92200 TQ	GABLS	10/01-12/01
	Augusta-Aiken MSA, GA-SC	Y	35840 FQ	66920 AW	95870 TQ	GABLS	10/01-12/01
	Columbus MSA, GA-AL	Y	31590 FQ	56490 AW	93980 TQ	GABLS	10/01-12/01
	Macon MSA, GA	Y	39530 FQ	53120 AW	70620 TQ	GABLS	10/01-12/01
	Savannah MSA, GA	Y	31170 FQ	50680 AW	90570 TQ	GABLS	10/01-12/01
	Hawaii	Y	45940 FQ	77790 AW	118820 TQ	HIBLS	10/01-12/01
	Honolulu MSA, HI	Y	45250 FQ	78690 AW	119920 TQ	HIBLS	10/01-12/01
	Idaho	Y	31580 FQ	56950 AW	96120 TQ	IDBLS	10/01-12/01
	Boise City MSA, ID	Y	36920 FQ	61140 AW	101880 TQ	IDBLS	10/01-12/01
	Illinois	Y	38330 FQ	67870 AW	97980 TQ	ILBLS	10/01-12/01
	Champaign-Urbana MSA, IL	Y	33620 FQ	58780 AW	86620 TQ	ILBLS	10/01-12/01
	Chicago PMSA, IL	Y	45320 FQ	71110 AW	101970 TQ	ILBLS	10/01-12/01
	Peoria-Pekin MSA, IL	Y	36820 FQ	56350 AW	75170 TQ	ILBLS	10/01-12/01
	Rockford MSA, IL	Y	47760 FQ	74710 AW	110980 TQ	ILBLS	10/01-12/01
	Springfield MSA, IL	Y	18280 FQ	51310 AW	90190 TQ	ILBLS	10/01-12/01
	Indiana	Y	39270 FQ	64480 AW	97400 TQ	INBLS	10/01-12/01
	Elkhart-Goshen MSA, IN	Y	39510 FQ	65810 AW	108040 TQ	INBLS	10/01-12/01
	Evansville-Henderson MSA, IN-KY	Y	23410 FQ	58750 AW	87840 TQ	INBLS	10/01-12/01
	Fort Wayne MSA, IN	Y	13940 FQ	53350 AW	85960 TQ	INBLS	10/01-12/01
	Gary PMSA, IN	Y	44460 FQ	67230 AW	94450 TQ	INBLS	10/01-12/01
	Indianapolis MSA, IN	Y	43490 FQ	69190 AW	105910 TQ	INBLS	10/01-12/01
	Lafayette MSA, IN	Y	44380 FQ	65540 AW	95300 TQ	INBLS	10/01-12/01
	South Bend MSA, IN	Y	40350 FQ	64560 AW	107120 TQ	INBLS	10/01-12/01
	Iowa	Y	31150 FQ	53920 AW	84120 TQ	IABLS	10/01-12/01
	Cedar Rapids MSA, IA	Y	35090 FQ	67020 AW	131340 TQ	IABLS	10/01-12/01
	Davenport-Moline-Rock Island MSA, IA-IL	Y	35250 FQ	53250 AW	70340 TQ	IABLS	10/01-12/01
	Des Moines MSA, IA	Y	33560 FQ	57930 AW	92790 TQ	IABLS	10/01-12/01
	Kansas	Y	32890 FQ	57240 AW	88550 TQ	KSBLS	10/01-12/01
	Topeka MSA, KS	Y	30320 FQ	43870 AW	69860 TQ	KSBLS	10/01-12/01
	Wichita MSA, KS	Y	35460 FQ	57750 AW	98660 TQ	KSBLS	10/01-12/01
	Kentucky	Y	33950 FQ	59030 AW	88420 TQ	KYBLS	10/01-12/01
	Lexington MSA, KY	Y	37470 FQ	58600 AW	84810 TQ	KYBLS	10/01-12/01
	Louisville MSA, KY-IN	Y	39150 FQ	66820 AW	119240 TQ	KYBLS	10/01-12/01
	Louisiana	Y	29080 FQ	54350 AW	85560 TQ	LABLS	10/01-12/01
	Baton Rouge MSA, LA	Y	36250 FQ	55990 AW	81510 TQ	LABLS	10/01-12/01
	Houma MSA, LA	Y	38060 FQ	61320 AW	102080 TQ	LABLS	10/01-12/01
	Lafayette MSA, LA	Y	34970 FQ	68220 AW	105510 TQ	LABLS	10/01-12/01
	Lake Charles MSA, LA	Y	30520 FQ	63270 AW	92460 TQ	LABLS	10/01-12/01
	New Orleans MSA, LA	Y	34960 FQ	53320 AW	79850 TQ	LABLS	10/01-12/01
	Shreveport-Bossier City MSA, LA	Y	28670 FQ	49570 AW	82910 TQ	LABLS	10/01-12/01
	Maine	Y	30970 FQ	53900 AW	79360 TQ	MEBLS	10/01-12/01
	Portland MSA, ME	Y	32550 FQ	59830 AW	119970 TQ	MEBLS	10/01-12/01
	Maryland	Y	40180 FQ	69340 AW	109430 TQ	MDBLS	10/01-12/01
	Baltimore PMSA, MD	Y	42780 FQ	73070 AW	128950 TQ	MDBLS	10/01-12/01
	Massachusetts	Y	45210 FQ	70320 AW	104900 TQ	MABLS	10/01-12/01
	Boston PMSA, MA-NH	Y	47270 FQ	73490 AW	108300 TQ	MABLS	10/01-12/01
	Brockton PMSA, MA	Y	44220 FQ	59630 AW	79630 TQ	MABLS	10/01-12/01
	Lawrence PMSA, MA-NH	Y	38570 FQ	73970 AW	140180 TQ	MABLS	10/01-12/01
	Lowell PMSA, MA-NH	Y	33960 FQ	57770 AW	89300 TQ	MABLS	10/01-12/01
	New Bedford PMSA, MA	Y	39860 FQ	63270 AW	89670 TQ	MABLS	10/01-12/01
	Springfield MSA, MA	Y	37180 FQ	56770 AW	83370 TQ	MABLS	10/01-12/01
	Worcester PMSA, MA-CT	Y	40960 FQ	63130 AW	97430 TQ	MABLS	10/01-12/01
	Michigan	Y	42090 FQ	73860 AW	123830 TQ	MIBLS	10/01-12/01
	Ann Arbor PMSA, MI	Y	49610 FQ	95640 AW		MIBLS	10/01-12/01
	Detroit PMSA, MI	Y	53260 FQ	79450 AW	122160 TQ	MIBLS	10/01-12/01

AAW	Average annual wage	**AOH**	Average offered, high	**ASH**	Average starting, high	**H**	Hourly	**M**	Monthly	**S**	Special: hourly and annual
AE	Average entry wage	**AOL**	Average offered, low	**ASL**	Average starting, low	**HI**	Highest wage paid	**MTC**	Median total compensation	**TQ**	Third quartile wage
AEX	Average experienced wage	**APH**	Average pay, high range	**AW**	Average wage paid	**HR**	High end range	**MW**	Median wage paid	**W**	Weekly
AO	Average offered	**APL**	Average pay, low range	**FQ**	First quartile wage	**LR**	Low end range	**SQ**	Second quartile wage	**Y**	Yearly

Occupation/Type/Industry	Location	Per	Low	Mid	High	Source	Date
Construction Manager	Flint PMSA, MI	Y	41070 FQ	78550 AW	118230 TQ	MIBLS	10/01-12/01
	Grand Rapids-Muskegon-Holland MSA, MI	Y	43040 FQ	73350 AW	134880 TQ	MIBLS	10/01-12/01
	Kalamazoo-Battle Creek MSA, MI	Y	40790 FQ	57830 AW	74820 TQ	MIBLS	10/01-12/01
	Lansing-East Lansing MSA, MI	Y	44460 FQ	72470 AW	116630 TQ	MIBLS	10/01-12/01
	Saginaw-Bay City-Midland MSA, MI	Y	41430 FQ	69430 AW	113040 TQ	MIBLS	10/01-12/01
	Minnesota	Y	44530 FQ	70550 AW	113390 TQ	MNBLS	10/01-12/01
	Duluth-Superior MSA, MN-WI	Y	31950 FQ	56520 AW	78200 TQ	MNBLS	10/01-12/01
	Minneapolis-St. Paul MSA, MN-WI	Y	47670 FQ	73940 AW	119910 TQ	MNBLS	10/01-12/01
	St. Cloud MSA, MN	Y	44680 FQ	61090 AW	79850 TQ	MNBLS	10/01-12/01
	Mississippi	Y	27130 FQ	51290 AW	78590 TQ	MSBLS	10/01-12/01
	Biloxi-Gulfport-Pascagoula MSA, MS	Y	26630 FQ	52820 AW	82580 TQ	MSBLS	10/01-12/01
	Jackson MSA, MS	Y	25820 FQ	54000 AW	100600 TQ	MSBLS	10/01-12/01
	Missouri	Y	32880 FQ	59550 AW	90660 TQ	MOBLS	10/01-12/01
	Kansas City MSA, MO-KS	Y	37750 FQ	61790 AW	88560 TQ	MOBLS	10/01-12/01
	St. Louis MSA, MO-IL	Y	39000 FQ	65340 AW	93910 TQ	MOBLS	10/01-12/01
	Springfield MSA, MO	Y	29740 FQ	47570 AW	70730 TQ	MOBLS	10/01-12/01
	Montana	Y	25660 FQ	47250 AW	71700 TQ	MTBLS	10/01-12/01
	Billings MSA, MT	Y	28690 FQ	46360 AW	68340 TQ	MTBLS	10/01-12/01
	Nebraska	Y	37060 FQ	73430 AW	143230 TQ	NEBLS	10/01-12/01
	Lincoln MSA, NE	Y	35940 FQ	56970 AW	93060 TQ	NEBLS	10/01-12/01
	Omaha MSA, NE-IA	Y	38940 FQ	83270 AW		NEBLS	10/01-12/01
	Nevada	Y	46800 FQ	68890 AW	104560 TQ	NVBLS	10/01-12/01
	Las Vegas MSA, NV-AZ	Y	45400 FQ	69360 AW	105160 TQ	NVBLS	10/01-12/01
	Reno MSA, NV	Y	50310 FQ	72500 AW	107180 TQ	NVBLS	10/01-12/01
	New Hampshire	Y	36380 FQ	59580 AW	96350 TQ	NHBLS	10/01-12/01
	Manchester PMSA, NH	Y	36980 FQ	63540 AW	93900 TQ	NHBLS	10/01-12/01
	Nashua PMSA, NH	Y	41450 FQ	60620 AW	90680 TQ	NHBLS	10/01-12/01
	Portsmouth-Rochester PMSA, NH-ME	Y	41200 FQ	71590 AW	111630 TQ	NHBLS	10/01-12/01
	New Jersey	Y	55620 FQ	84560 AW	128340 TQ	NJBLS	10/01-12/01
	Atlantic-Cape May PMSA, NJ	Y	61050 FQ	87960 AW	128640 TQ	NJBLS	10/01-12/01
	Bergen-Passaic PMSA, NJ	Y	53670 FQ	92920 AW	137370 TQ	NJBLS	10/01-12/01
	Jersey City PMSA, NJ	Y	56840 FQ	90710 AW		NJBLS	10/01-12/01
	Middlesex-Somerset-Hunterdon PMSA, NJ	Y	54720 FQ	86900 AW	123700 TQ	NJBLS	10/01-12/01
	Monmouth-Ocean PMSA, NJ	Y	51650 FQ	85070 AW	129050 TQ	NJBLS	10/01-12/01
	Newark PMSA, NJ	Y	62770 FQ	84350 AW	134100 TQ	NJBLS	10/01-12/01
	Trenton PMSA, NJ	Y	49430 FQ	71710 AW	109160 TQ	NJBLS	10/01-12/01
	New Mexico	Y	34710 FQ	66770 AW		NMBLS	10/01-12/01
	Albuquerque MSA, NM	Y	37640 FQ	56460 AW	77230 TQ	NMBLS	10/01-12/01
	Las Cruces MSA, NM	Y	31730 FQ	41900 AW	53240 TQ	NMBLS	10/01-12/01
	New York	Y	48480 FQ	89440 AW		NYBLS	10/01-12/01
	Albany-Schenectady-Troy MSA, NY	Y	43550 FQ	75990 AW	131740 TQ	NYBLS	10/01-12/01
	Binghamton MSA, NY	Y	35110 FQ	59630 AW	88980 TQ	NYBLS	10/01-12/01
	Buffalo-Niagara Falls MSA, NY	Y	43020 FQ	68540 AW	114640 TQ	NYBLS	10/01-12/01
	Dutchess County PMSA, NY	Y	48400 FQ	83660 AW		NYBLS	10/01-12/01
	Nassau-Suffolk PMSA, NY	Y	57490 FQ	102780 AW		NYBLS	10/01-12/01
	New York PMSA, NY	Y	51430 FQ	95370 AW		NYBLS	10/01-12/01
	Newburgh PMSA, NY-PA	Y	40880 FQ	70470 AW		NYBLS	10/01-12/01
	Rochester MSA, NY	Y	46730 FQ	79440 AW		NYBLS	10/01-12/01
	Syracuse MSA, NY	Y	45510 FQ	81140 AW		NYBLS	10/01-12/01
	Utica-Rome MSA, NY	Y	42170 FQ	82540 AW		NYBLS	10/01-12/01
	North Carolina	Y	31920 FQ	56320 AW	87600 TQ	NCBLS	10/01-12/01
	Asheville MSA, NC	Y	38340 FQ	60810 AW	90040 TQ	NCBLS	10/01-12/01
	Charlotte-Gastonia-Rock Hill MSA, NC-SC	Y	34670 FQ	59390 AW	92280 TQ	NCBLS	10/01-12/01
	Fayetteville MSA, NC	Y	31550 FQ	50960 AW	71530 TQ	NCBLS	10/01-12/01
	Greensboro-Winston-Salem-High Point MSA, NC	Y	36710 FQ	60070 AW	88770 TQ	NCBLS	10/01-12/01
	Hickory-Morganton-Lenoir MSA, NC	Y	32270 FQ	54030 AW	77840 TQ	NCBLS	10/01-12/01
	Raleigh-Durham-Chapel Hill MSA, NC	Y	37310 FQ	60910 AW	90920 TQ	NCBLS	10/01-12/01
	Wilmington MSA, NC	Y	31660 FQ	49790 AW	71210 TQ	NCBLS	10/01-12/01
	North Dakota	Y	30090 FQ	50920 AW	82330 TQ	NDBLS	10/01-12/01

AAW Average annual wage **AE** Average entry wage **AEX** Average experienced wage **AO** Average offered **AOH** Average offered, high **AOL** Average offered, low **APH** Average pay, high range **APL** Average pay, low range **ASH** Average starting, high **ASL** Average starting, low **AW** Average wage paid **FQ** First quartile wage **H** Hourly **HI** Highest wage paid **HR** High end range **LR** Low end range **M** Monthly **MTC** Median total compensation **MW** Median wage paid **SQ** Second quartile wage **S** Special: hourly and annual **TQ** Third quartile wage **W** Weekly **Y** Yearly

Occupation/Type/Industry	Location	Per	Low	Mid	High	Source	Date
Construction Manager	Fargo-Moorhead MSA, ND-MN	Y	32710 FQ	53770 AW	84040 TQ	NDBLS	10/01-12/01
	Ohio	Y	37510 FQ	63240 AW	99420 TQ	OHBLS	10/01-12/01
	Akron PMSA, OH	Y	38010 FQ	61820 AW	88510 TQ	OHBLS	10/01-12/01
	Canton-Massillon MSA, OH	Y	38860 FQ	55880 AW	75610 TQ	OHBLS	10/01-12/01
	Cincinnati PMSA, OH-KY-IN	Y	35860 FQ	60100 AW	89700 TQ	OHBLS	10/01-12/01
	Cleveland-Lorain-Elyria PMSA, OH	Y	41150 FQ	64760 AW	96240 TQ	OHBLS	10/01-12/01
	Columbus MSA, OH	Y	36650 FQ	66040 AW	110030 TQ	OHBLS	10/01-12/01
	Dayton-Springfield MSA, OH	Y	39160 FQ	64710 AW	102800 TQ	OHBLS	10/01-12/01
	Hamilton-Middletown PMSA, OH	Y	35410 FQ	69470 AW	119050 TQ	OHBLS	10/01-12/01
	Mansfield MSA, OH	Y	25110 FQ	60560 AW	107980 TQ	OHBLS	10/01-12/01
	Toledo MSA, OH	Y	40460 FQ	69520 AW	111510 TQ	OHBLS	10/01-12/01
	Youngstown-Warren MSA, OH	Y	28980 FQ	56810 AW	91970 TQ	OHBLS	10/01-12/01
	Oklahoma	Y	31220 FQ	51630 AW	80550 TQ	OKBLS	10/01-12/01
	Oklahoma City MSA, OK	Y	31260 FQ	48170 AW	81980 TQ	OKBLS	10/01-12/01
	Tulsa MSA, OK	Y	40420 FQ	59350 AW	83410 TQ	OKBLS	10/01-12/01
	Oregon	Y	33020 FQ	68200 AW	117340 TQ	ORBLS	10/01-12/01
	Eugene-Springfield MSA, OR	Y	42000 FQ	71060 AW	130280 TQ	ORBLS	10/01-12/01
	Medford-Ashland MSA, OR	Y	45880 FQ	67020 AW	114350 TQ	ORBLS	10/01-12/01
	Portland-Vancouver PMSA, OR-WA	Y	34200 FQ	72650 AW	128110 TQ	ORBLS	10/01-12/01
	Salem PMSA, OR	Y	38020 FQ	61080 AW	91220 TQ	ORBLS	10/01-12/01
	Pennsylvania	Y	39910 FQ	65020 AW	95730 TQ	PABLS	10/01-12/01
	Allentown-Bethlehem-Easton MSA, PA	Y	41120 FQ	61400 AW	90070 TQ	PABLS	10/01-12/01
	Erie MSA, PA	Y	39350 FQ	54900 AW	79680 TQ	PABLS	10/01-12/01
	Harrisburg-Lebanon-Carlisle MSA, PA	Y	34550 FQ	56400 AW	82560 TQ	PABLS	10/01-12/01
	Johnstown MSA, PA	Y	28330 FQ	53940 AW	77100 TQ	PABLS	10/01-12/01
	Lancaster MSA, PA	Y	35650 FQ	58720 AW	88520 TQ	PABLS	10/01-12/01
	Philadelphia PMSA, PA-NJ	Y	49550 FQ	74210 AW	104550 TQ	PABLS	10/01-12/01
	Pittsburgh MSA, PA	Y	40520 FQ	63950 AW	97290 TQ	PABLS	10/01-12/01
	Reading MSA, PA	Y	44360 FQ	64950 AW	96210 TQ	PABLS	10/01-12/01
	Scranton-Wilkes-Barre-Hazleton MSA, PA	Y	31810 FQ	52240 AW	77410 TQ	PABLS	10/01-12/01
	York MSA, PA	Y	37380 FQ	58580 AW	92180 TQ	PABLS	10/01-12/01
	Rhode Island	Y	50020 FQ	78230 AW	115080 TQ	RIBLS	10/01-12/01
	Providence-Fall River-Warwick MSA, RI-MA	Y	45360 FQ	74410 AW	111270 TQ	RIBLS	10/01-12/01
	South Carolina	Y	31030 FQ	53800 AW	86630 TQ	SCBLS	10/01-12/01
	Charleston-North Charleston MSA, SC	Y	31540 FQ	48090 AW	68690 TQ	SCBLS	10/01-12/01
	Columbia MSA, SC	Y	36410 FQ	59230 AW	89340 TQ	SCBLS	10/01-12/01
	Greenville-Spartanburg-Anderson MSA, SC	Y	32060 FQ	53750 AW	85220 TQ	SCBLS	10/01-12/01
	Myrtle Beach MSA, SC	Y	34250 FQ	54990 AW	85560 TQ	SCBLS	10/01-12/01
	South Dakota	Y	42210 FQ	58890 AW	75380 TQ	SDBLS	10/01-12/01
	Sioux Falls MSA, SD	Y	39270 FQ	58260 AW	80010 TQ	SDBLS	10/01-12/01
	Tennessee	Y	32590 FQ	57110 AW	88280 TQ	TNBLS	10/01-12/01
	Chattanooga MSA, TN-GA	Y	37220 FQ	56250 AW	74670 TQ	TNBLS	10/01-12/01
	Clarksville-Hopkinsville MSA, TN-KY	Y	35920 FQ	54300 AW	79670 TQ	TNBLS	10/01-12/01
	Johnson City-Kingsport-Bristol MSA, TN-VA	Y	26020 FQ	46500 AW	75870 TQ	TNBLS	10/01-12/01
	Knoxville MSA, TN	Y	31300 FQ	58960 AW	94100 TQ	TNBLS	10/01-12/01
	Memphis MSA, TN-AR-MS	Y	33970 FQ	61000 AW	95240 TQ	TNBLS	10/01-12/01
	Nashville MSA, TN	Y	34850 FQ	57200 AW	87300 TQ	TNBLS	10/01-12/01
	Texas	Y	36110 FQ	60900 AW	92680 TQ	TXBLS	10/01-12/01
	Amarillo MSA, TX	Y	28620 FQ	52200 AW	77640 TQ	TXBLS	10/01-12/01
	Austin-San Marcos MSA, TX	Y	40610 FQ	65030 AW	99120 TQ	TXBLS	10/01-12/01
	Beaumont-Port Arthur MSA, TX	Y	36400 FQ	58160 AW	80920 TQ	TXBLS	10/01-12/01
	Brazoria PMSA, TX	Y	38220 FQ	63980 AW	127650 TQ	TXBLS	10/01-12/01
	Brownsville-Harlingen-San Benito MSA, TX	Y	21080 FQ	41870 AW	69960 TQ	TXBLS	10/01-12/01
	Corpus Christi MSA, TX	Y	33410 FQ	56540 AW	99110 TQ	TXBLS	10/01-12/01
	Dallas PMSA, TX	Y	40320 FQ	69240 AW	113340 TQ	TXBLS	10/01-12/01
	El Paso MSA, TX	Y	33570 FQ	47730 AW	76810 TQ	TXBLS	10/01-12/01
	Fort Worth-Arlington PMSA, TX	Y	39700 FQ	61970 AW	90540 TQ	TXBLS	10/01-12/01

AAW	Average annual wage	**AOH**	Average offered, high	**ASH**	Average starting, high	**H**	Hourly	**M**	Monthly	**S**	Special: hourly and annual
AE	Average entry wage	**AOL**	Average offered, low	**ASL**	Average starting, low	**HI**	Highest wage paid	**MTC**	Median total compensation	**TQ**	Third quartile wage
AEX	Average experienced wage	**APH**	Average pay, high range	**AW**	Average wage paid	**HR**	High end range	**MW**	Median wage paid	**W**	Weekly
AO	Average offered	**APL**	Average pay, low range	**FQ**	First quartile wage	**LR**	Low end range	**SQ**	Second quartile wage	**Y**	Yearly

Occupation/Type/Industry	Location	Per	Low	Mid	High	Source	Date
Construction Manager	Galveston-Texas City PMSA, TX	Y	26470 FQ	57450 AW	93850 TQ	TXBLS	10/01-12/01
	Houston PMSA, TX	Y	38610 FQ	61370 AW	89050 TQ	TXBLS	10/01-12/01
	Killeen-Temple MSA, TX	Y	32070 FQ	47190 AW	69720 TQ	TXBLS	10/01-12/01
	Laredo MSA, TX	Y	21200 FQ	60460 AW	128670 TQ	TXBLS	10/01-12/01
	Longview-Marshall MSA, TX	Y	31980 FQ	55170 AW	87950 TQ	TXBLS	10/01-12/01
	Lubbock MSA, TX	Y	34490 FQ	58270 AW	98930 TQ	TXBLS	10/01-12/01
	McAllen-Edinburg-Mission MSA, TX	Y	27220 FQ	50670 AW	86840 TQ	TXBLS	10/01-12/01
	Odessa-Midland MSA, TX	Y	35720 FQ	54460 AW	70930 TQ	TXBLS	10/01-12/01
	San Antonio MSA, TX	Y	31460 FQ	55880 AW	96460 TQ	TXBLS	10/01-12/01
	Tyler MSA, TX	Y	36410 FQ	60740 AW	124840 TQ	TXBLS	10/01-12/01
	Waco MSA, TX	Y	31520 FQ	47670 AW	80490 TQ	TXBLS	10/01-12/01
	Utah	Y	35800 FQ	59750 AW	90210 TQ	UTBLS	10/01-12/01
	Provo-Orem MSA, UT	Y	32140 FQ	56550 AW	81600 TQ	UTBLS	10/01-12/01
	Salt Lake City-Ogden MSA, UT	Y	38610 FQ	63770 AW	93730 TQ	UTBLS	10/01-12/01
	Vermont	Y	41440 FQ	69660 AW	121500 TQ	VTBLS	10/01-12/01
	Burlington MSA, VT	Y	41300 FQ	66310 AW	99720 TQ	VTBLS	10/01-12/01
	Virginia	Y	38880 FQ	65400 AW	106360 TQ	VABLS	10/01-12/01
	Lynchburg MSA, VA	Y	34420 FQ	58410 AW	96030 TQ	VABLS	10/01-12/01
	Norfolk-Virginia Beach-Newport News MSA, VA-NC	Y	39120 FQ	62650 AW	95980 TQ	VABLS	10/01-12/01
	Richmond-Petersburg MSA, VA	Y	37910 FQ	60300 AW	89630 TQ	VABLS	10/01-12/01
	Roanoke MSA, VA	Y	37470 FQ	62080 AW	105860 TQ	VABLS	10/01-12/01
	Washington	Y	40780 FQ	68040 AW	106550 TQ	WABLS	10/01-12/01
	Bremerton PMSA, WA	Y	50080 FQ	70310 AW	103670 TQ	WABLS	10/01-12/01
	Olympia PMSA, WA	Y	40950 FQ	68040 AW	93480 TQ	WABLS	10/01-12/01
	Richland-Kennewick-Pasco MSA, WA	Y	45700 FQ	73110 AW	111610 TQ	WABLS	10/01-12/01
	Seattle-Bellevue-Everett PMSA, WA	Y	40290 FQ	66700 AW	103880 TQ	WABLS	10/01-12/01
	Spokane MSA, WA	Y	44390 FQ	67610 AW	113950 TQ	WABLS	10/01-12/01
	Tacoma PMSA, WA	Y	51270 FQ	81770 AW	128070 TQ	WABLS	10/01-12/01
	Yakima MSA, WA	Y	39960 FQ	69610 AW		WABLS	10/01-12/01
	West Virginia	Y	25330 FQ	41360 AW	68830 TQ	WVBLS	10/01-12/01
	Charleston MSA, WV	Y	33590 FQ	51370 AW	83040 TQ	WVBLS	10/01-12/01
	Huntington-Ashland MSA, WV-KY-OH	Y	30870 FQ	45950 AW	60510 TQ	WVBLS	10/01-12/01
	Wisconsin	Y	38050 FQ	63410 AW	99220 TQ	WIBLS	10/01-12/01
	Appleton-Oshkosh-Neenah MSA, WI	Y	39200 FQ	68260 AW	110360 TQ	WIBLS	10/01-12/01
	Green Bay MSA, WI	Y	40200 FQ	58510 AW	81930 TQ	WIBLS	10/01-12/01
	Madison MSA, WI	Y	39780 FQ	69600 AW	118930 TQ	WIBLS	10/01-12/01
	Milwaukee-Waukesha PMSA, WI	Y	41210 FQ	68250 AW	106570 TQ	WIBLS	10/01-12/01
	Racine PMSA, WI	Y	32790 FQ	66020 AW	114990 TQ	WIBLS	10/01-12/01
	Wyoming	Y	31010 FQ	53870 AW	85840 TQ	WYBLS	10/01-12/01
	Cheyenne MSA, WY	Y	38500 FQ	63860 AW	110180 TQ	WYBLS	10/01-12/01
	Puerto Rico	Y	28470 FQ	49450 AW	91080 TQ	PRBLS	10/01-12/01
	Virgin Islands	Y	38830 FQ	61840 AW	88550 TQ	VIBLS	10/01-12/01
	Guam	Y	24660 FQ	65470 AW	115630 TQ	GUBLS	10/01-12/01
Consultant							
Quality Control	United States	Y			240000 HI	ASQ	1/00-1/01
Continuous Mining Machine Operator	Alabama	H	10.11 FQ	12.45 AW	15.62 TQ	ALBLS	10/01-12/01
	Arizona	H	15.28 FQ	18.80 AW	22.16 TQ	AZBLS	10/01-12/01
	Arkansas	H	10.06 FQ	13.63 AW	16.60 TQ	ARBLS	10/01-12/01
	Colorado	H	11.88 FQ	17.91 AW	25.99 TQ	COBLS	10/01-12/01
	Florida	H	7.94 FQ	12.56 AW	16.85 TQ	FLBLS	10/01-12/01
	Georgia	H	10.45 FQ	13.85 AW	19.33 TQ	GABLS	10/01-12/01
	Idaho	H	7.87 FQ	14.14 AW	20.80 TQ	IDBLS	10/01-12/01
	Illinois	H	12.95 FQ	19.21 AW	22.82 TQ	ILBLS	10/01-12/01
	Indiana	H	11.16 FQ	16.83 AW	26.12 TQ	INBLS	10/01-12/01
	Iowa	H	10.70 FQ	14.03 AW	16.88 TQ	IABLS	10/01-12/01
	Kansas	H	9.05 FQ	13.13 AW	19.81 TQ	KSBLS	10/01-12/01
	Kentucky	H	12.49 FQ	15.72 AW	18.34 TQ	KYBLS	10/01-12/01
	Michigan	H	10.04 FQ	15.38 AW	19.99 TQ	MIBLS	10/01-12/01

AAW	Average annual wage	AOH	Average offered, high	ASH	Average starting, high	H	Hourly	M	Monthly	S	Special: hourly and annual
AE	Average entry wage	AOL	Average offered, low	ASL	Average starting, low	HI	Highest wage paid	MTC	Median total compensation	TQ	Third quartile wage
AEX	Average experienced wage	APH	Average pay, high range	AW	Average wage paid	HR	High end range	MW	Median wage paid	W	Weekly
AO	Average offered	APL	Average pay, low range	FQ	First quartile wage	LR	Low end range	SQ	Second quartile wage	Y	Yearly

Occupation/Type/Industry	Location	Per	Low	Mid	High	Source	Date
Continuous Mining Machine Operator	Missouri	H	8.77 FQ	12.53 AW	16.66 TQ	MOBLS	10/01-12/01
	Nevada	H	17.67 FQ	19.71 AW	22.30 TQ	NVBLS	10/01-12/01
	North Carolina	H	9.34 FQ	12.92 AW	17.13 TQ	NCBLS	10/01-12/01
	Ohio	H	11.26 FQ	16.69 AW	23.08 TQ	OHBLS	10/01-12/01
	Oklahoma	H	8.29 FQ	12.48 AW	17.74 TQ	OKBLS	10/01-12/01
	Pennsylvania	H	9.74 FQ	17.10 AW	26.22 TQ	PABLS	10/01-12/01
	South Carolina	H	11.07 FQ	13.65 AW	17.05 TQ	SCBLS	10/01-12/01
	Tennessee	H	11.07 FQ	13.69 AW	17.05 TQ	TNBLS	10/01-12/01
	Texas	H	8.99 FQ	12.51 AW	15.78 TQ	TXBLS	10/01-12/01
	Virginia	H	10.68 FQ	16.03 AW	23.78 TQ	VABLS	10/01-12/01
	West Virginia	H	14.56 FQ	17.51 AW	21.20 TQ	WVBLS	10/01-12/01
	Wisconsin	H	11.19 FQ	13.85 AW	17.16 TQ	WIBLS	10/01-12/01
	Wyoming	H	12.64 FQ	21.80 AW	27.17 TQ	WYBLS	10/01-12/01
	Puerto Rico	H	5.71 FQ	7.20 AW	8.97 TQ	PRBLS	10/01-12/01
Control and Valve Installer and Repairer							
Except Mechanical Door	Alabama	H	9.65 FQ	16.87 AW	24.60 TQ	ALBLS	10/01-12/01
Except Mechanical Door	Alaska	H	19.15 FQ	32.94 AW	55.77 TQ	AKBLS	10/01-12/01
Except Mechanical Door	Arizona	H	12.08 FQ	19.85 AW	30.79 TQ	AZBLS	10/01-12/01
Except Mechanical Door	Arkansas	H	9.74 FQ	16.96 AW	24.64 TQ	ARBLS	10/01-12/01
Except Mechanical Door	California	H	16.11 FQ	23.61 AW	31.28 TQ	CABLS	10/01-12/01
Except Mechanical Door	Colorado	H	5.73 FQ	17.44 AW	28.72 TQ	COBLS	10/01-12/01
Except Mechanical Door	Connecticut	H	17.74 FQ	23.73 AW	29.86 TQ	CTBLS	10/01-12/01
Except Mechanical Door	Delaware	H	12.54 FQ	22.78 AW	32.73 TQ	DEBLS	10/01-12/01
Except Mechanical Door	Florida	H	9.91 FQ	16.32 AW	23.10 TQ	FLBLS	10/01-12/01
Except Mechanical Door	Georgia	H	10.11 FQ	16.18 AW	21.79 TQ	GABLS	10/01-12/01
Except Mechanical Door	Hawaii	H	13.73 FQ	20.94 AW	32.62 TQ	HIBLS	10/01-12/01
Except Mechanical Door	Idaho	H	13.14 FQ	22.34 AW	29.23 TQ	IDBLS	10/01-12/01
Except Mechanical Door	Illinois	H	15.39 FQ	26.17 AW	42.99 TQ	ILBLS	10/01-12/01
Except Mechanical Door	Indiana	H	12.45 FQ	21.55 AW	30.92 TQ	INBLS	10/01-12/01
Except Mechanical Door	Iowa	H	15.64 FQ	22.11 AW	29.60 TQ	IABLS	10/01-12/01
Except Mechanical Door	Kansas	H	11.07 FQ	19.66 AW	26.68 TQ	KSBLS	10/01-12/01
Except Mechanical Door	Kentucky	H	8.08 FQ	14.41 AW	21.50 TQ	KYBLS	10/01-12/01
Except Mechanical Door	Louisiana	H	8.38 FQ	17.78 AW	27.02 TQ	LABLS	10/01-12/01
Except Mechanical Door	Maine	H	13.68 FQ	20.68 AW	27.86 TQ	MEBLS	10/01-12/01
Except Mechanical Door	Maryland	H	11.89 FQ	20.16 AW	28.07 TQ	MDBLS	10/01-12/01
Except Mechanical Door	Massachusetts	H	14.74 FQ	22.18 AW	31.26 TQ	MABLS	10/01-12/01
Except Mechanical Door	Michigan	H	14.66 FQ	20.98 AW	27.06 TQ	MIBLS	10/01-12/01
Except Mechanical Door	Minnesota	H	14.28 FQ	22.46 AW	31.68 TQ	MNBLS	10/01-12/01
Except Mechanical Door	Mississippi	H	9.23 FQ	15.02 AW	21.46 TQ	MSBLS	10/01-12/01
Except Mechanical Door	Missouri	H	11.79 FQ	17.76 AW	24.41 TQ	MOBLS	10/01-12/01
Except Mechanical Door	Montana	H	6.01 FQ	13.82 AW	23.27 TQ	MTBLS	10/01-12/01
Except Mechanical Door	Nebraska	H	14.53 FQ	19.72 AW	26.32 TQ	NEBLS	10/01-12/01
Except Mechanical Door	Nevada	H	15.51 FQ	22.51 AW	30.13 TQ	NVBLS	10/01-12/01
Except Mechanical Door	New Hampshire	H	10.87 FQ	17.30 AW	25.88 TQ	NHBLS	10/01-12/01
Except Mechanical Door	New Jersey	H	15.17 FQ	22.92 AW	29.54 TQ	NJBLS	10/01-12/01
Except Mechanical Door	New Mexico	H	9.11 FQ	16.64 AW	25.35 TQ	NMBLS	10/01-12/01
Except Mechanical Door	New York	H	15.90 FQ	25.36 AW	33.18 TQ	NYBLS	10/01-12/01
Except Mechanical Door	North Carolina	H	11.36 FQ	18.32 AW	26.34 TQ	NCBLS	10/01-12/01
Except Mechanical Door	North Dakota	H	13.69 FQ	21.71 AW	30.11 TQ	NDBLS	10/01-12/01
Except Mechanical Door	Ohio	H	10.35 FQ	18.70 AW	28.15 TQ	OHBLS	10/01-12/01
Except Mechanical Door	Oklahoma	H	11.63 FQ	18.15 AW	24.90 TQ	OKBLS	10/01-12/01
Except Mechanical Door	Oregon	H	14.78 FQ	22.39 AW	30.54 TQ	ORBLS	10/01-12/01
Except Mechanical Door	Pennsylvania	H	13.36 FQ	23.72 AW	31.69 TQ	PABLS	10/01-12/01
Except Mechanical Door	Rhode Island	H	14.01 FQ	19.77 AW	26.77 TQ	RIBLS	10/01-12/01
Except Mechanical Door	South Carolina	H	9.29 FQ	16.84 AW	30.91 TQ	SCBLS	10/01-12/01
Except Mechanical Door	South Dakota	H	12.16 FQ	18.38 AW	25.15 TQ	SDBLS	10/01-12/01
Except Mechanical Door	Tennessee	H	10.80 FQ	17.28 AW	24.97 TQ	TNBLS	10/01-12/01
Except Mechanical Door	Texas	H	10.63 FQ	17.89 AW	26.19 TQ	TXBLS	10/01-12/01
Except Mechanical Door	Utah	H	13.43 FQ	18.59 AW	24.96 TQ	UTBLS	10/01-12/01
Except Mechanical Door	Vermont	H	11.73 FQ	17.97 AW	25.07 TQ	VTBLS	10/01-12/01
Except Mechanical Door	Virginia	H	8.67 FQ	17.61 AW	25.32 TQ	VABLS	10/01-12/01
Except Mechanical Door	Washington	H	12.04 FQ	20.80 AW	28.09 TQ	WABLS	10/01-12/01
Except Mechanical Door	West Virginia	H	10.48 FQ	18.40 AW	26.33 TQ	WVBLS	10/01-12/01
Except Mechanical Door	Wisconsin	H	13.88 FQ	21.92 AW	29.33 TQ	WIBLS	10/01-12/01
Except Mechanical Door	Wyoming	H	14.03 FQ	19.72 AW	27.18 TQ	WYBLS	10/01-12/01
Controller	United States	Y		68000 SQ		CR	1/00-1/01
	Central	Y		62500 SQ		CR	1/00-1/01
	East Central	Y		65000 SQ		CR	1/00-1/01

AAW	Average annual wage	**AOH**	Average offered, high	**ASH**	Average starting, high	**H**	Hourly	**M**	Monthly	**S**	Special: hourly and annual
AE	Average entry wage	**AOL**	Average offered, low	**ASL**	Average starting, low	**HI**	Highest wage paid	**MTC**	Median total compensation	**TQ**	Third quartile wage
AEX	Average experienced wage	**APH**	Average pay, high range	**AW**	Average wage paid	**HR**	High end range	**MW**	Median wage paid	**W**	Weekly
AO	Average offered	**APL**	Average pay, low range	**FQ**	First quartile wage	**LR**	Low end range	**SQ**	Second quartile wage	**Y**	Yearly

Occupation/Type/Industry	Location	Per	Low	Mid	High	Source	Date
Controller	Far West	Y		70000 SQ		CR	1/00-1/01
	Northeast	Y		71000 SQ		CR	1/00-1/01
	South	Y		67200 SQ		CR	1/00-1/01
	Tulsa, Ok	Y			77095 TQ	IOMA6	1/01-1/02
	Phoenix, AZ	Y			179630 TQ	IOMA6	1/01-1/02
	Chattanooga, TN	Y			70340 TQ	IOMA6	1/01-1/02
	Provo, UT	Y			81477 TQ	IOMA6	1/01-1/02
	Laramie, WY	Y			164680 TQ	IOMA6	1/01-1/02
Golf Course	St. Louis, MO	Y		48500 AW		SLBJ	1/00-1/01
Conveyor Operator and Tender	Alabama	H	7.96 FQ	10.95 AW	15.73 TQ	ALBLS	10/01-12/01
	Arizona	H	8.44 FQ	14.59 AW	20.99 TQ	AZBLS	10/01-12/01
	Arkansas	H	7.85 FQ	11.52 AW	15.75 TQ	ARBLS	10/01-12/01
	California	H	7.19 FQ	11.45 AW	17.15 TQ	CABLS	10/01-12/01
	Colorado	H	8.46 FQ	12.94 AW	20.97 TQ	COBLS	10/01-12/01
	Connecticut	H	8.63 FQ	12.82 AW	17.80 TQ	CTBLS	10/01-12/01
	Florida	H	7.03 FQ	11.37 AW	18.17 TQ	FLBLS	10/01-12/01
	Georgia	H	7.38 FQ	10.69 AW	14.15 TQ	GABLS	10/01-12/01
	Hawaii	H	7.80 FQ	11.23 AW	14.27 TQ	HIBLS	10/01-12/01
	Idaho	H	6.49 FQ	10.41 AW	15.74 TQ	IDBLS	10/01-12/01
	Illinois	H	7.21 FQ	13.63 AW	20.96 TQ	ILBLS	10/01-12/01
	Indiana	H	9.18 FQ	12.60 AW	17.33 TQ	INBLS	10/01-12/01
	Iowa	H	8.99 FQ	12.42 AW	16.62 TQ	IABLS	10/01-12/01
	Kansas	H	7.55 FQ	10.57 AW	13.95 TQ	KSBLS	10/01-12/01
	Kentucky	H	7.65 FQ	12.03 AW	17.69 TQ	KYBLS	10/01-12/01
	Louisiana	H	6.31 FQ	10.43 AW	15.07 TQ	LABLS	10/01-12/01
	Maine	H	7.53 FQ	11.30 AW	15.67 TQ	MEBLS	10/01-12/01
	Maryland	H	8.33 FQ	11.79 AW	16.50 TQ	MDBLS	10/01-12/01
	Massachusetts	H	9.05 FQ	12.84 AW	17.01 TQ	MABLS	10/01-12/01
	Michigan	H	8.73 FQ	13.42 AW	19.42 TQ	MIBLS	10/01-12/01
	Minnesota	H	6.48 FQ	11.89 AW	18.23 TQ	MNBLS	10/01-12/01
	Mississippi	H	6.68 FQ	11.25 AW	18.92 TQ	MSBLS	10/01-12/01
	Missouri	H	7.72 FQ	12.57 AW	17.65 TQ	MOBLS	10/01-12/01
	Montana	H	6.69 FQ	12.21 AW	17.50 TQ	MTBLS	10/01-12/01
	Nebraska	H	7.43 FQ	11.77 AW	20.49 TQ	NEBLS	10/01-12/01
	Nevada	H	7.23 FQ	11.75 AW	17.98 TQ	NVBLS	10/01-12/01
	New Hampshire	H	8.36 FQ	12.30 AW	16.94 TQ	NHBLS	10/01-12/01
	New Jersey	H	7.96 FQ	13.00 AW	19.11 TQ	NJBLS	10/01-12/01
	New Mexico	H	6.23 FQ	13.59 AW	29.61 TQ	NMBLS	10/01-12/01
	New York	H	7.79 FQ	11.78 AW	16.93 TQ	NYBLS	10/01-12/01
	North Carolina	H	7.85 FQ	10.68 AW	13.79 TQ	NCBLS	10/01-12/01
	North Dakota	H	9.18 FQ	13.05 AW	18.18 TQ	NDBLS	10/01-12/01
	Ohio	H	9.26 FQ	13.05 AW	18.84 TQ	OHBLS	10/01-12/01
	Oklahoma	H	6.08 FQ	10.08 AW	15.37 TQ	OKBLS	10/01-12/01
	Oregon	H	7.74 FQ	13.11 AW	17.58 TQ	ORBLS	10/01-12/01
	Pennsylvania	H	8.26 FQ	14.27 AW	21.73 TQ	PABLS	10/01-12/01
	Rhode Island	H	7.66 FQ	11.71 AW	16.19 TQ	RIBLS	10/01-12/01
	South Carolina	H	8.95 FQ	11.60 AW	15.18 TQ	SCBLS	10/01-12/01
	South Dakota	H	8.09 FQ	10.16 AW	12.77 TQ	SDBLS	10/01-12/01
	Tennessee	H	9.05 FQ	12.67 AW	16.79 TQ	TNBLS	10/01-12/01
	Texas	H	7.49 FQ	10.47 AW	14.22 TQ	TXBLS	10/01-12/01
	Utah	H	8.28 FQ	12.25 AW	17.15 TQ	UTBLS	10/01-12/01
	Vermont	H	7.68 FQ	10.36 AW	13.94 TQ	VTBLS	10/01-12/01
	Virginia	H	8.08 FQ	11.62 AW	16.20 TQ	VABLS	10/01-12/01
	Washington	H	8.07 FQ	14.03 AW	20.67 TQ	WABLS	10/01-12/01
	West Virginia	H	9.31 FQ	16.86 AW	23.12 TQ	WVBLS	10/01-12/01
	Wisconsin	H	7.67 FQ	10.95 AW	16.41 TQ	WIBLS	10/01-12/01
	Wyoming	H	11.77 FQ	20.87 AW	26.48 TQ	WYBLS	10/01-12/01
	Puerto Rico	H	6.28 FQ	9.80 AW	13.97 TQ	PRBLS	10/01-12/01
Cook							
Fast Food	Alabama	H	5.58 FQ	6.39 AW	7.70 TQ	ALBLS	10/01-12/01
Fast Food	Birmingham MSA, AL	H	5.50 FQ	6.51 AW	8.05 TQ	ALBLS	10/01-12/01
Fast Food	Huntsville MSA, AL	H	5.55 FQ	6.22 AW	6.98 TQ	ALBLS	10/01-12/01
Fast Food	Mobile MSA, AL	H	5.59 FQ	6.29 AW	7.23 TQ	ALBLS	10/01-12/01
Fast Food	Montgomery MSA, AL	H	5.69 FQ	6.75 AW	8.12 TQ	ALBLS	10/01-12/01
Fast Food	Alaska	H	7.75 FQ	10.08 AW	13.28 TQ	AKBLS	10/01-12/01
Fast Food	Anchorage MSA, AK	H	7.84 FQ	10.21 AW	13.44 TQ	AKBLS	10/01-12/01
Fast Food	Arizona	H	5.68 FQ	7.33 AW	9.36 TQ	AZBLS	10/01-12/01
Fast Food	Phoenix-Mesa MSA, AZ	H	5.76 FQ	7.52 AW	9.61 TQ	AZBLS	10/01-12/01
Fast Food	Tucson MSA, AZ	H	5.51 FQ	6.70 AW	8.40 TQ	AZBLS	10/01-12/01
Fast Food	Arkansas	H	5.48 FQ	6.51 AW	8.30 TQ	ARBLS	10/01-12/01

AAW	Average annual wage	**AOH**	Average offered, high	**ASH**	Average starting, high	**H**	Hourly	**M**	Monthly	**S**	Special: hourly and annual
AE	Average entry wage	**AOL**	Average offered, low	**ASL**	Average starting, low	**HI**	Highest wage paid	**MTC**	Median total compensation	**TQ**	Third quartile wage
AEX	Average experienced wage	**APH**	Average pay, high range	**AW**	Average wage paid	**HR**	High end range	**MW**	Median wage paid	**W**	Weekly
AO	Average offered	**APL**	Average pay, low range	**FQ**	First quartile wage	**LR**	Low end range	**SQ**	Second quartile wage	**Y**	Yearly

Occupation/Type/Industry	Location	Per	Low	Mid	High	Source	Date
Cook							
Fast Food	Fayetteville-Springdale-Rogers MSA, AR	H	5.59 FQ	6.81 AW	8.82 TQ	ARBLS	10/01-12/01
Fast Food	Fort Smith MSA, AR-OK	H	6.05 FQ	8.14 AW	10.84 TQ	ARBLS	10/01-12/01
Fast Food	Little Rock-North Little Rock MSA, AR	H	5.68 FQ	7.25 AW	9.73 TQ	ARBLS	10/01-12/01
Fast Food	California	H	6.49 FQ	7.60 AW	8.76 TQ	CABLS	10/01-12/01
Fast Food	Bakersfield MSA, CA	H	6.38 FQ	7.07 AW	8.16 TQ	CABLS	10/01-12/01
Fast Food	Chico-Paradise MSA, CA	H	6.34 FQ	6.94 AW	8.00 TQ	CABLS	10/01-12/01
Fast Food	Fresno MSA, CA	H	6.46 FQ	7.69 AW	9.87 TQ	CABLS	10/01-12/01
Fast Food	Los Angeles-Long Beach PMSA, CA	H	6.81 FQ	7.61 AW	8.43 TQ	CABLS	10/01-12/01
Fast Food	Merced MSA, CA	H	6.35 FQ	7.08 AW	8.25 TQ	CABLS	10/01-12/01
Fast Food	Modesto MSA, CA	H	6.42 FQ	7.30 AW	8.30 TQ	CABLS	10/01-12/01
Fast Food	Oakland PMSA, CA	H	6.41 FQ	7.62 AW	8.49 TQ	CABLS	10/01-12/01
Fast Food	Orange County PMSA, CA	H	6.52 FQ	8.05 AW	10.14 TQ	CABLS	10/01-12/01
Fast Food	Redding MSA, CA	H	6.33 FQ	6.77 AW	7.12 TQ	CABLS	10/01-12/01
Fast Food	Riverside-San Bernardino PMSA, CA	H	6.64 FQ	7.54 AW	8.44 TQ	CABLS	10/01-12/01
Fast Food	Sacramento PMSA, CA	H	6.40 FQ	7.65 AW	9.76 TQ	CABLS	10/01-12/01
Fast Food	Salinas MSA, CA	H	6.37 FQ	7.67 AW	10.31 TQ	CABLS	10/01-12/01
Fast Food	San Diego MSA, CA	H	6.40 FQ	7.35 AW	8.43 TQ	CABLS	10/01-12/01
Fast Food	San Francisco PMSA, CA	H	6.49 FQ	8.34 AW	10.87 TQ	CABLS	10/01-12/01
Fast Food	San Jose PMSA, CA	H	6.35 FQ	7.36 AW	9.12 TQ	CABLS	10/01-12/01
Fast Food	San Luis Obispo-Atascadero-Paso Robles MSA, CA	H	6.86 FQ	7.87 AW	9.47 TQ	CABLS	10/01-12/01
Fast Food	Santa Barbara-Santa Maria-Lompoc MSA, CA	H	6.37 FQ	7.17 AW	8.43 TQ	CABLS	10/01-12/01
Fast Food	Santa Cruz-Watsonville PMSA, CA	H	6.47 FQ	7.70 AW	9.97 TQ	CABLS	10/01-12/01
Fast Food	Santa Rosa PMSA, CA	H	6.64 FQ	8.10 AW	10.36 TQ	CABLS	10/01-12/01
Fast Food	Stockton Lodi MSA, CA	H	6.38 FQ	7.16 AW	8.25 TQ	CABLS	10/01-12/01
Fast Food	Vallejo-Fairfield-Napa PMSA, CA	H	6.43 FQ	7.32 AW	8.35 TQ	CABLS	10/01-12/01
Fast Food	Ventura PMSA, CA	H	6.47 FQ	7.40 AW	8.40 TQ	CABLS	10/01-12/01
Fast Food	Visalia-Tulare-Porterville MSA, CA	H	6.37 FQ	7.08 AW	8.14 TQ	CABLS	10/01-12/01
Fast Food	Colorado	H	5.79 FQ	8.04 AW	11.08 TQ	COBLS	10/01-12/01
Fast Food	Boulder-Longmont PMSA, CO	H	7.13 FQ	8.94 AW	10.83 TQ	COBLS	10/01-12/01
Fast Food	Colorado Springs MSA, CO	H	5.80 FQ	7.96 AW	11.13 TQ	COBLS	10/01-12/01
Fast Food	Denver PMSA, CO	H	5.97 FQ	8.76 AW	12.37 TQ	COBLS	10/01-12/01
Fast Food	Fort Collins-Loveland MSA, CO	H	6.15 FQ	7.97 AW	10.16 TQ	COBLS	10/01-12/01
Fast Food	Greeley PMSA, CO	H	5.74 FQ	7.65 AW	10.55 TQ	COBLS	10/01-12/01
Fast Food	Connecticut	H	6.60 FQ	8.49 AW	12.05 TQ	CTBLS	10/01-12/01
Fast Food	Bridgeport PMSA, CT	H	6.77 FQ	8.36 AW	9.09 TQ	CTBLS	10/01-12/01
Fast Food	Danbury PMSA, CT	H	6.59 FQ	8.83 AW	10.46 TQ	CTBLS	10/01-12/01
Fast Food	Hartford MSA, CT	H	6.56 FQ	7.85 AW	9.32 TQ	CTBLS	10/01-12/01
Fast Food	New Haven-Meriden PMSA, CT	H	7.08 FQ	9.65 AW	14.53 TQ	CTBLS	10/01-12/01
Fast Food	Stamford-Norwalk PMSA, CT	H	6.68 FQ	10.60 AW	13.18 TQ	CTBLS	10/01-12/01
Fast Food	Waterbury PMSA, CT	H	6.57 FQ	7.78 AW	9.30 TQ	CTBLS	10/01-12/01
Fast Food	Delaware	H	6.55 FQ	7.60 AW	8.81 TQ	DEBLS	10/01-12/01
Fast Food	Wilmington-Newark PMSA, DE-MD	H	6.11 FQ	7.32 AW	8.57 TQ	DEBLS	10/01-12/01
Fast Food	District of Columbia	H	7.46 FQ	8.45 AW	9.56 TQ	DCBLS	10/01-12/01
Fast Food	Washington PMSA, DC-MD-VA-WV	H	5.77 FQ	7.98 AW	11.43 TQ	DCBLS	10/01-12/01
Fast Food	Florida	H	5.52 FQ	6.80 AW	8.46 TQ	FLBLS	10/01-12/01
Fast Food	Daytona Beach MSA, FL	H	5.75 FQ	7.30 AW	9.05 TQ	FLBLS	10/01-12/01
Fast Food	Fort Lauderdale PMSA, FL	H	5.71 FQ	7.58 AW	10.10 TQ	FLBLS	10/01-12/01
Fast Food	Fort Myers-Cape Coral MSA, FL	H	5.62 FQ	6.86 AW	8.34 TQ	FLBLS	10/01-12/01
Fast Food	Fort Pierce-Port St. Lucie MSA, FL	H	5.51 FQ	6.72 AW	8.31 TQ	FLBLS	10/01-12/01
Fast Food	Fort Walton Beach MSA, FL	H	5.52 FQ	6.27 AW	7.29 TQ	FLBLS	10/01-12/01
Fast Food	Gainesville MSA, FL	H	5.70 FQ	6.61 AW	8.16 TQ	FLBLS	10/01-12/01
Fast Food	Jacksonville MSA, FL	H	5.54 FQ	6.74 AW	8.33 TQ	FLBLS	10/01-12/01
Fast Food	Lakeland-Winter Haven MSA, FL	H	5.44 FQ	6.53 AW	8.10 TQ	FLBLS	10/01-12/01
Fast Food	Melbourne-Titusville-Palm Bay MSA, FL	H	5.39 FQ	6.22 AW	7.63 TQ	FLBLS	10/01-12/01

AAW	Average annual wage	AOH	Average offered, high	ASH	Average starting, high	H	Hourly	M	Monthly	S	Special: hourly and annual
AE	Average entry wage	AOL	Average offered, low	ASL	Average starting, low	HI	Highest wage paid	MTC	Median total compensation	TQ	Third quartile wage
AEX	Average experienced wage	APH	Average pay, high range	AW	Average wage paid	HR	High end range	MW	Median wage paid	W	Weekly
AO	Average offered	APL	Average pay, low range	FQ	First quartile wage	LR	Low end range	SQ	Second quartile wage	Y	Yearly

Occupation/Type/Industry	Location	Per	Low	Mid	High	Source	Date
Cook							
Fast Food	Miami PMSA, FL	H	5.36 FQ	6.14 AW	7.05 TQ	FLBLS	10/01-12/01
Fast Food	Naples MSA, FL	H	5.99 FQ	11.88 AW	16.44 TQ	FLBLS	10/01-12/01
Fast Food	Ocala MSA, FL	H	5.41 FQ	6.41 AW	8.31 TQ	FLBLS	10/01-12/01
Fast Food	Orlando MSA, FL	H	5.64 FQ	7.07 AW	8.53 TQ	FLBLS	10/01-12/01
Fast Food	Pensacola MSA, FL	H	5.60 FQ	7.22 AW	10.13 TQ	FLBLS	10/01-12/01
Fast Food	Sarasota-Bradenton MSA, FL	H	5.57 FQ	7.11 AW	8.63 TQ	FLBLS	10/01-12/01
Fast Food	Tallahassee MSA, FL	H	5.69 FQ	7.18 AW	10.21 TQ	FLBLS	10/01-12/01
Fast Food	Tampa-St. Petersburg-Clearwater MSA, FL	H	5.55 FQ	6.64 AW	8.30 TQ	FLBLS	10/01-12/01
Fast Food	West Palm Beach-Boca Raton MSA, FL	H	5.59 FQ	6.98 AW	8.50 TQ	FLBLS	10/01-12/01
Fast Food	Georgia	H	5.43 FQ	6.25 AW	7.53 TQ	GABLS	10/01-12/01
Fast Food	Atlanta MSA, GA	H	5.39 FQ	6.15 AW	7.29 TQ	GABLS	10/01-12/01
Fast Food	Augusta-Aiken MSA, GA-SC	H	5.48 FQ	6.16 AW	7.02 TQ	GABLS	10/01-12/01
Fast Food	Columbus MSA, GA-AL	H	5.53 FQ	6.44 AW	7.91 TQ	GABLS	10/01-12/01
Fast Food	Macon MSA, GA	H	5.54 FQ	6.40 AW	7.75 TQ	GABLS	10/01-12/01
Fast Food	Savannah MSA, GA	H	5.61 FQ	6.32 AW	7.28 TQ	GABLS	10/01-12/01
Fast Food	Hawaii	H	5.72 FQ	7.89 AW	11.28 TQ	HIBLS	10/01-12/01
Fast Food	Honolulu MSA, HI	H	5.56 FQ	7.15 AW	9.35 TQ	HIBLS	10/01-12/01
Fast Food	Idaho	H	5.61 FQ	7.01 AW	8.60 TQ	IDBLS	10/01-12/01
Fast Food	Boise City MSA, ID	H	5.61 FQ	6.66 AW	8.29 TQ	IDBLS	10/01-12/01
Fast Food	Illinois	H	5.55 FQ	7.28 AW	9.75 TQ	ILBLS	10/01-12/01
Fast Food	Champaign-Urbana MSA, IL	H	5.86 FQ	7.82 AW	10.20 TQ	ILBLS	10/01-12/01
Fast Food	Chicago PMSA, IL	H	5.64 FQ	7.62 AW	10.18 TQ	ILBLS	10/01-12/01
Fast Food	Peoria-Pekin MSA, IL	H	5.66 FQ	7.41 AW	10.09 TQ	ILBLS	10/01-12/01
Fast Food	Rockford MSA, IL	H	5.52 FQ	6.82 AW	8.60 TQ	ILBLS	10/01-12/01
Fast Food	Springfield MSA, IL	H	5.55 FQ	7.62 AW	10.50 TQ	ILBLS	10/01-12/01
Fast Food	Indiana	H	5.61 FQ	6.94 AW	8.46 TQ	INBLS	10/01-12/01
Fast Food	Elkhart-Goshen MSA, IN	H	5.45 FQ	6.35 AW	7.90 TQ	INBLS	10/01-12/01
Fast Food	Evansville-Henderson MSA, IN-KY	H	5.60 FQ	6.62 AW	8.08 TQ	INBLS	10/01-12/01
Fast Food	Fort Wayne MSA, IN	H	5.62 FQ	7.06 AW	8.42 TQ	INBLS	10/01-12/01
Fast Food	Gary PMSA, IN	H	5.50 FQ	6.48 AW	8.07 TQ	INBLS	10/01-12/01
Fast Food	Indianapolis MSA, IN	H	5.89 FQ	7.45 AW	8.93 TQ	INBLS	10/01-12/01
Fast Food	Lafayette MSA, IN	H	5.62 FQ	6.91 AW	8.40 TQ	INBLS	10/01-12/01
Fast Food	South Bend MSA, IN	H	5.69 FQ	7.35 AW	10.26 TQ	INBLS	10/01-12/01
Fast Food	Iowa	H	5.42 FQ	6.48 AW	8.24 TQ	IABLS	10/01-12/01
Fast Food	Davenport-Moline-Rock Island MSA, IA-IL	H	5.51 FQ	6.93 AW	9.35 TQ	IABLS	10/01-12/01
Fast Food	Des Moines MSA, IA	H	6.77 FQ	8.46 AW	12.04 TQ	IABLS	10/01-12/01
Fast Food	Kansas	H	5.55 FQ	7.01 AW	9.32 TQ	KSBLS	10/01-12/01
Fast Food	Topeka MSA, KS	H	5.57 FQ	6.63 AW	8.30 TQ	KSBLS	10/01-12/01
Fast Food	Kentucky	H	5.57 FQ	6.97 AW	8.75 TQ	KYBLS	10/01-12/01
Fast Food	Lexington MSA, KY	H	5.97 FQ	7.85 AW	10.13 TQ	KYBLS	10/01-12/01
Fast Food	Louisville MSA, KY-IN	H	5.65 FQ	7.34 AW	8.91 TQ	KYBLS	10/01-12/01
Fast Food	Louisiana	H	5.51 FQ	6.49 AW	8.27 TQ	LABLS	10/01-12/01
Fast Food	Baton Rouge MSA, LA	H	5.58 FQ	6.41 AW	7.64 TQ	LABLS	10/01-12/01
Fast Food	Houma MSA, LA	H	5.56 FQ	6.25 AW	7.22 TQ	LABLS	10/01-12/01
Fast Food	Lafayette MSA, LA	H	5.45 FQ	6.41 AW	8.06 TQ	LABLS	10/01-12/01
Fast Food	Lake Charles MSA, LA	H	5.53 FQ	6.26 AW	7.06 TQ	LABLS	10/01-12/01
Fast Food	New Orleans MSA, LA	H	5.45 FQ	6.18 AW	7.19 TQ	LABLS	10/01-12/01
Fast Food	Shreveport-Bossier City MSA, LA	H	5.76 FQ	7.59 AW	10.28 TQ	LABLS	10/01-12/01
Fast Food	Maine	H	5.51 FQ	7.03 AW	8.99 TQ	MEBLS	10/01-12/01
Fast Food	Portland MSA, ME	H	5.76 FQ	7.27 AW	8.66 TQ	MEBLS	10/01-12/01
Fast Food	Maryland	H	5.84 FQ	8.02 AW	11.55 TQ	MDBLS	10/01-12/01
Fast Food	Baltimore PMSA, MD	H	5.77 FQ	7.61 AW	9.89 TQ	MDBLS	10/01-12/01
Fast Food	Massachusetts	H	6.99 FQ	9.32 AW	12.85 TQ	MABLS	10/01-12/01
Fast Food	Boston PMSA, MA-NH	H	6.94 FQ	9.47 AW	13.29 TQ	MABLS	10/01-12/01
Fast Food	Brockton PMSA, MA	H	7.22 FQ	9.45 AW	13.11 TQ	MABLS	10/01-12/01
Fast Food	Lawrence PMSA, MA-NH	H	7.49 FQ	9.34 AW	10.76 TQ	MABLS	10/01-12/01
Fast Food	Lowell PMSA, MA-NH	H	7.78 FQ	10.02 AW	12.95 TQ	MABLS	10/01-12/01
Fast Food	New Bedford PMSA, MA	H	6.95 FQ	8.14 AW	10.14 TQ	MABLS	10/01-12/01
Fast Food	Springfield MSA, MA	H	7.08 FQ	8.82 AW	11.40 TQ	MABLS	10/01-12/01
Fast Food	Worcester PMSA, MA-CT	H	7.05 FQ	8.79 AW	11.33 TQ	MABLS	10/01-12/01
Fast Food	Michigan	H	5.52 FQ	6.89 AW	8.73 TQ	MIBLS	10/01-12/01
Fast Food	Ann Arbor PMSA, MI	H	5.93 FQ	7.69 AW	9.87 TQ	MIBLS	10/01-12/01
Fast Food	Detroit PMSA, MI	H	5.45 FQ	6.76 AW	8.49 TQ	MIBLS	10/01-12/01
Fast Food	Flint PMSA, MI	H	6.04 FQ	7.94 AW	10.17 TQ	MIBLS	10/01-12/01
Fast Food	Grand Rapids-Muskegon-Holland MSA, MI	H	5.71 FQ	6.90 AW	8.59 TQ	MIBLS	10/01-12/01

AAW	Average annual wage	AOH	Average offered, high	ASH	Average starting, high	H	Hourly	M	Monthly	S	Special: hourly and annual
AE	Average entry wage	AOL	Average offered, low	ASL	Average starting, low	HI	Highest wage paid	MTC	Median total compensation	TQ	Third quartile wage
AEX	Average experienced wage	APH	Average pay, high range	AW	Average wage paid	HR	High end range	MW	Median wage paid	W	Weekly
AO	Average offered	APL	Average pay, low range	FQ	First quartile wage	LR	Low end range	SQ	Second quartile wage	Y	Yearly

Occupation/Type/Industry	Location	Per	Low	Mid	High	Source	Date
Cook							
Fast Food	Kalamazoo-Battle Creek MSA, MI	H	5.52 FQ	7.12 AW	9.98 TQ	MIBLS	10/01-12/01
Fast Food	Lansing-East Lansing MSA, MI	H	5.61 FQ	6.94 AW	8.41 TQ	MIBLS	10/01-12/01
Fast Food	Saginaw-Bay City-Midland MSA, MI	H	5.52 FQ	6.14 AW	6.93 TQ	MIBLS	10/01-12/01
Fast Food	Minnesota	H	5.84 FQ	7.46 AW	9.80 TQ	MNBLS	10/01-12/01
Fast Food	Duluth-Superior MSA, MN-WI	H	5.62 FQ	7.60 AW	10.37 TQ	MNBLS	10/01-12/01
Fast Food	Minneapolis-St. Paul MSA, MN-WI	H	5.96 FQ	7.64 AW	10.16 TQ	MNBLS	10/01-12/01
Fast Food	St. Cloud MSA, MN	H	5.60 FQ	6.70 AW	8.36 TQ	MNBLS	10/01-12/01
Fast Food	Mississippi	H	5.54 FQ	6.52 AW	8.26 TQ	MSBLS	10/01-12/01
Fast Food	Biloxi-Gulfport-Pascagoula MSA, MS	H	5.83 FQ	7.28 AW	8.93 TQ	MSBLS	10/01-12/01
Fast Food	Jackson MSA, MS	H	5.68 FQ	6.91 AW	8.69 TQ	MSBLS	10/01-12/01
Fast Food	Missouri	H	5.44 FQ	6.71 AW	8.91 TQ	MOBLS	10/01-12/01
Fast Food	Kansas City MSA, MO-KS	H	5.56 FQ	7.27 AW	9.86 TQ	MOBLS	10/01-12/01
Fast Food	St. Louis MSA, MO-IL	H	5.52 FQ	7.25 AW	9.97 TQ	MOBLS	10/01-12/01
Fast Food	Springfield MSA, MO	H	5.56 FQ	6.36 AW	7.41 TQ	MOBLS	10/01-12/01
Fast Food	Montana	H	5.51 FQ	6.43 AW	8.05 TQ	MTBLS	10/01-12/01
Fast Food	Billings MSA, MT	H	5.67 FQ	6.36 AW	7.26 TQ	MTBLS	10/01-12/01
Fast Food	Nebraska	H	5.65 FQ	6.98 AW	8.57 TQ	NEBLS	10/01-12/01
Fast Food	Lincoln MSA, NE	H	5.77 FQ	7.32 AW	8.72 TQ	NEBLS	10/01-12/01
Fast Food	Omaha MSA, NE-IA	H	5.71 FQ	7.17 AW	8.59 TQ	NEBLS	10/01-12/01
Fast Food	Nevada	H	5.61 FQ	6.98 AW	9.00 TQ	NVBLS	10/01-12/01
Fast Food	Las Vegas MSA, NV-AZ	H	5.64 FQ	7.15 AW	9.04 TQ	NVBLS	10/01-12/01
Fast Food	Reno MSA, NV	H	5.64 FQ	6.50 AW	7.79 TQ	NVBLS	10/01-12/01
Fast Food	New Hampshire	H	5.68 FQ	7.67 AW	10.49 TQ	NHBLS	10/01-12/01
Fast Food	Manchester PMSA, NH	H	5.76 FQ	8.38 AW	10.91 TQ	NHBLS	10/01-12/01
Fast Food	Nashua PMSA, NH	H	6.49 FQ	7.81 AW	8.96 TQ	NHBLS	10/01-12/01
Fast Food	Portsmouth-Rochester PMSA, NH-ME	H	6.07 FQ	9.16 AW	13.23 TQ	NHBLS	10/01-12/01
Fast Food	New Jersey	H	5.63 FQ	7.79 AW	10.89 TQ	NJBLS	10/01-12/01
Fast Food	Atlantic-Cape May PMSA, NJ	H	5.63 FQ	7.69 AW	11.73 TQ	NJBLS	10/01-12/01
Fast Food	Bergen-Passaic PMSA, NJ	H	5.83 FQ	9.22 AW	12.48 TQ	NJBLS	10/01-12/01
Fast Food	Jersey City PMSA, NJ	H	5.43 FQ	6.61 AW	8.56 TQ	NJBLS	10/01-12/01
Fast Food	Middlesex-Somerset-Hunterdon PMSA, NJ	H	5.58 FQ	7.12 AW	9.37 TQ	NJBLS	10/01-12/01
Fast Food	Monmouth-Ocean PMSA, NJ	H	5.92 FQ	7.51 AW	9.31 TQ	NJBLS	10/01-12/01
Fast Food	Newark PMSA, NJ	H	5.62 FQ	7.31 AW	9.99 TQ	NJBLS	10/01-12/01
Fast Food	Trenton PMSA, NJ	H	5.53 FQ	6.88 AW	9.41 TQ	NJBLS	10/01-12/01
Fast Food	New Mexico	H	5.47 FQ	6.17 AW	6.92 TQ	NMBLS	10/01-12/01
Fast Food	Albuquerque MSA, NM	H	5.58 FQ	6.36 AW	7.07 TQ	NMBLS	10/01-12/01
Fast Food	Las Cruces MSA, NM	H	5.63 FQ	6.14 AW	6.99 TQ	NMBLS	10/01-12/01
Fast Food	New York	H	5.60 FQ	7.29 AW	9.98 TQ	NYBLS	10/01-12/01
Fast Food	Albany-Schenectady-Troy MSA, NY	H	5.80 FQ	7.86 AW	10.29 TQ	NYBLS	10/01-12/01
Fast Food	Binghamton MSA, NY	H	5.74 FQ	7.08 AW	8.38 TQ	NYBLS	10/01-12/01
Fast Food	Buffalo-Niagara Falls MSA, NY	H	5.53 FQ	7.12 AW	9.93 TQ	NYBLS	10/01-12/01
Fast Food	Dutchess County PMSA, NY	H	5.73 FQ	6.57 AW	7.90 TQ	NYBLS	10/01-12/01
Fast Food	Nassau-Suffolk PMSA, NY	H	6.96 FQ	8.98 AW	11.22 TQ	NYBLS	10/01-12/01
Fast Food	New York PMSA, NY	H	5.50 FQ	6.35 AW	6.99 TQ	NYBLS	10/01-12/01
Fast Food	Newburgh PMSA, NY-PA	H	5.79 FQ	7.85 AW	10.23 TQ	NYBLS	10/01-12/01
Fast Food	Rochester MSA, NY	H	5.88 FQ	8.14 AW	10.34 TQ	NYBLS	10/01-12/01
Fast Food	Syracuse MSA, NY	H	5.54 FQ	7.39 AW	10.04 TQ	NYBLS	10/01-12/01
Fast Food	Utica-Rome MSA, NY	H	6.00 FQ	7.40 AW	8.48 TQ	NYBLS	10/01-12/01
Fast Food	North Carolina	H	5.47 FQ	6.62 AW	8.47 TQ	NCBLS	10/01-12/01
Fast Food	Asheville MSA, NC	H	5.57 FQ	6.97 AW	9.01 TQ	NCBLS	10/01-12/01
Fast Food	Charlotte-Gastonia-Rock Hill MSA, NC-SC	H	5.53 FQ	6.99 AW	9.07 TQ	NCBLS	10/01-12/01
Fast Food	Fayetteville MSA, NC	H	5.47 FQ	6.14 AW	6.98 TQ	NCBLS	10/01-12/01
Fast Food	Greensboro-Winston-Salem-High Point MSA, NC	H	5.40 FQ	6.57 AW	8.83 TQ	NCBLS	10/01-12/01
Fast Food	Hickory-Morganton-Lenoir MSA, NC	H	5.63 FQ	6.68 AW	8.36 TQ	NCBLS	10/01-12/01
Fast Food	Raleigh-Durham-Chapel Hill MSA, NC	H	6.88 FQ	8.64 AW	10.74 TQ	NCBLS	10/01-12/01
Fast Food	Wilmington MSA, NC	H	5.38 FQ	6.18 AW	7.37 TQ	NCBLS	10/01-12/01
Fast Food	North Dakota	H	5.60 FQ	6.83 AW	8.32 TQ	NDBLS	10/01-12/01
Fast Food	Fargo-Moorhead MSA, ND-MN	H	5.69 FQ	6.88 AW	8.38 TQ	NDBLS	10/01-12/01

AAW	Average annual wage	**AOH**	Average offered, high	**ASH**	Average starting, high	**H**	Hourly	**M**	Monthly	**S**	Special: hourly and annual
AE	Average entry wage	**AOL**	Average offered, low	**ASL**	Average starting, low	**HI**	Highest wage paid	**MTC**	Median total compensation	**TQ**	Third quartile wage
AEX	Average experienced wage	**APH**	Average pay, high range	**AW**	Average wage paid	**HR**	High end range	**MW**	Median wage paid	**W**	Weekly
AO	Average offered	**APL**	Average pay, low range	**FQ**	First quartile wage	**LR**	Low end range	**SQ**	Second quartile wage	**Y**	Yearly

Occupation/Type/Industry	Location	Per	Low	Mid	High	Source	Date
Cook							
Fast Food	Ohio	H	5.55 FQ	6.84 AW	8.70 TQ	OHBLS	10/01-12/01
Fast Food	Akron PMSA, OH	H	5.55 FQ	6.31 AW	7.61 TQ	OHBLS	10/01-12/01
Fast Food	Canton-Massillon MSA, OH	H	5.57 FQ	7.06 AW	8.43 TQ	OHBLS	10/01-12/01
Fast Food	Cincinnati PMSA, OH-KY-IN	H	5.79 FQ	7.66 AW	9.92 TQ	OHBLS	10/01-12/01
Fast Food	Cleveland-Lorain-Elyria PMSA, OH	H	5.54 FQ	6.59 AW	8.09 TQ	OHBLS	10/01-12/01
Fast Food	Columbus MSA, OH	H	6.13 FQ	7.88 AW	9.35 TQ	OHBLS	10/01-12/01
Fast Food	Dayton-Springfield MSA, OH	H	6.34 FQ	7.66 AW	9.48 TQ	OHBLS	10/01-12/01
Fast Food	Hamilton-Middletown PMSA, OH	H	5.58 FQ	7.00 AW	9.80 TQ	OHBLS	10/01-12/01
Fast Food	Mansfield MSA, OH	H	5.72 FQ	6.48 AW	7.77 TQ	OHBLS	10/01-12/01
Fast Food	Toledo MSA, OH	H	5.63 FQ	7.07 AW	9.29 TQ	OHBLS	10/01-12/01
Fast Food	Youngstown-Warren MSA, OH	H	5.39 FQ	6.07 AW	6.95 TQ	OHBLS	10/01-12/01
Fast Food	Oklahoma	H	5.53 FQ	6.73 AW	8.41 TQ	OKBLS	10/01-12/01
Fast Food	Oklahoma City MSA, OK	H	5.61 FQ	7.21 AW	9.28 TQ	OKBLS	10/01-12/01
Fast Food	Tulsa MSA, OK	H	5.57 FQ	6.54 AW	8.17 TQ	OKBLS	10/01-12/01
Fast Food	Oregon	H	6.78 FQ	7.82 AW	9.16 TQ	ORBLS	10/01-12/01
Fast Food	Eugene-Springfield MSA, OR	H	7.04 FQ	7.89 AW	9.04 TQ	ORBLS	10/01-12/01
Fast Food	Medford-Ashland MSA, OR	H	6.79 FQ	7.81 AW	8.81 TQ	ORBLS	10/01-12/01
Fast Food	Portland-Vancouver PMSA, OR-WA	H	6.81 FQ	7.68 AW	8.67 TQ	ORBLS	10/01-12/01
Fast Food	Salem PMSA, OR	H	6.96 FQ	7.53 AW	8.56 TQ	ORBLS	10/01-12/01
Fast Food	Pennsylvania	H	5.46 FQ	6.55 AW	8.23 TQ	PABLS	10/01-12/01
Fast Food	Allentown-Bethlehem-Easton MSA, PA	H	6.06 FQ	7.27 AW	8.38 TQ	PABLS	10/01-12/01
Fast Food	Erie MSA, PA	H	5.61 FQ	6.61 AW	8.31 TQ	PABLS	10/01-12/01
Fast Food	Harrisburg-Lebanon-Carlisle MSA, PA	H	5.58 FQ	6.84 AW	8.66 TQ	PABLS	10/01-12/01
Fast Food	Johnstown MSA, PA	H	5.57 FQ	6.34 AW	7.56 TQ	PABLS	10/01-12/01
Fast Food	Lancaster MSA, PA	H	5.51 FQ	6.40 AW	7.06 TQ	PABLS	10/01-12/01
Fast Food	Philadelphia PMSA, PA-NJ	H	5.54 FQ	7.35 AW	11.38 TQ	PABLS	10/01-12/01
Fast Food	Pittsburgh MSA, PA	H	5.38 FQ	6.26 AW	7.58 TQ	PABLS	10/01-12/01
Fast Food	Reading MSA, PA	H	5.51 FQ	6.27 AW	7.43 TQ	PABLS	10/01-12/01
Fast Food	Scranton-Wilkes-Barre-Hazleton MSA, PA	H	5.58 FQ	6.54 AW	8.17 TQ	PABLS	10/01-12/01
Fast Food	York MSA, PA	H	5.57 FQ	6.63 AW	8.25 TQ	PABLS	10/01-12/01
Fast Food	Rhode Island	H	6.55 FQ	7.89 AW	10.09 TQ	RIBLS	10/01-12/01
Fast Food	Providence-Fall River-Warwick MSA, RI-MA	H	6.55 FQ	7.94 AW	10.34 TQ	RIBLS	10/01-12/01
Fast Food	South Carolina	H	5.46 FQ	6.39 AW	7.87 TQ	SCBLS	10/01-12/01
Fast Food	Charleston-North Charleston MSA, SC	H	5.42 FQ	6.58 AW	8.06 TQ	SCBLS	10/01-12/01
Fast Food	Columbia MSA, SC	H	5.47 FQ	6.25 AW	7.49 TQ	SCBLS	10/01-12/01
Fast Food	Greenville-Spartanburg-Anderson MSA, SC	H	5.48 FQ	6.55 AW	8.19 TQ	SCBLS	10/01-12/01
Fast Food	Myrtle Beach MSA, SC	H	5.36 FQ	6.32 AW	7.81 TQ	SCBLS	10/01-12/01
Fast Food	South Dakota	H	5.71 FQ	6.72 AW	8.41 TQ	SDBLS	10/01-12/01
Fast Food	Sioux Falls MSA, SD	H	5.78 FQ	6.90 AW	8.63 TQ	SDBLS	10/01-12/01
Fast Food	Tennessee	H	5.60 FQ	6.72 AW	8.51 TQ	TNBLS	10/01-12/01
Fast Food	Chattanooga MSA, TN-GA	H	5.74 FQ	6.33 AW	7.22 TQ	TNBLS	10/01-12/01
Fast Food	Clarksville-Hopkinsville MSA, TN-KY	H	5.58 FQ	6.10 AW	6.92 TQ	TNBLS	10/01-12/01
Fast Food	Johnson City-Kingsport-Bristol MSA, TN-VA	H	5.63 FQ	6.74 AW	8.37 TQ	TNBLS	10/01-12/01
Fast Food	Knoxville MSA, TN	H	5.57 FQ	6.67 AW	8.34 TQ	TNBLS	10/01-12/01
Fast Food	Memphis MSA, TN-AR-MS	H	5.64 FQ	6.61 AW	8.24 TQ	TNBLS	10/01-12/01
Fast Food	Nashville MSA, TN	H	5.66 FQ	7.10 AW	9.00 TQ	TNBLS	10/01-12/01
Fast Food	Texas	H	5.47 FQ	6.52 AW	8.14 TQ	TXBLS	10/01-12/01
Fast Food	Amarillo MSA, TX	H	5.52 FQ	6.30 AW	7.59 TQ	TXBLS	10/01-12/01
Fast Food	Austin-San Marcos MSA, TX	H	5.43 FQ	6.73 AW	8.44 TQ	TXBLS	10/01-12/01
Fast Food	Beaumont-Port Arthur MSA, TX	H	5.40 FQ	6.28 AW	7.85 TQ	TXBLS	10/01-12/01
Fast Food	Brazoria PMSA, TX	H	5.34 FQ	6.09 AW	7.31 TQ	TXBLS	10/01-12/01
Fast Food	Brownsville-Harlingen-San Benito MSA, TX	H	5.55 FQ	6.14 AW	7.09 TQ	TXBLS	10/01-12/01
Fast Food	Corpus Christi MSA, TX	H	5.38 FQ	6.22 AW	7.68 TQ	TXBLS	10/01-12/01
Fast Food	Dallas PMSA, TX	H	5.50 FQ	6.66 AW	8.35 TQ	TXBLS	10/01-12/01
Fast Food	El Paso MSA, TX	H	5.48 FQ	6.31 AW	7.67 TQ	TXBLS	10/01-12/01
Fast Food	Fort Worth-Arlington PMSA, TX	H	5.40 FQ	6.28 AW	7.77 TQ	TXBLS	10/01-12/01

AAW	Average annual wage	AOH	Average offered, high	ASH	Average starting, high	H	Hourly	M	Monthly	S	Special: hourly and annual
AE	Average entry wage	AOL	Average offered, low	ASL	Average starting, low	HI	Highest wage paid	MTC	Median total compensation	TQ	Third quartile wage
AEX	Average experienced wage	APH	Average pay, high range	AW	Average wage paid	HR	High end range	MW	Median wage paid	W	Weekly
AO	Average offered	APL	Average pay, low range	FQ	First quartile wage	LR	Low end range	SQ	Second quartile wage	Y	Yearly

Occupation/Type/Industry	Location	Per	Low	Mid	High	Source	Date
Cook							
Fast Food	Galveston-Texas City PMSA, TX	H	5.45 FQ	6.36 AW	7.92 TQ	TXBLS	10/01-12/01
Fast Food	Houston PMSA, TX	H	5.47 FQ	6.49 AW	8.05 TQ	TXBLS	10/01-12/01
Fast Food	Killeen-Temple MSA, TX	H	5.62 FQ	6.90 AW	8.43 TQ	TXBLS	10/01-12/01
Fast Food	Laredo MSA, TX	H	5.48 FQ	6.17 AW	7.18 TQ	TXBLS	10/01-12/01
Fast Food	Longview-Marshall MSA, TX	H	5.40 FQ	6.14 AW	7.25 TQ	TXBLS	10/01-12/01
Fast Food	Lubbock MSA, TX	H	5.41 FQ	6.25 AW	7.62 TQ	TXBLS	10/01-12/01
Fast Food	McAllen-Edinburg-Mission MSA, TX	H	5.58 FQ	6.28 AW	7.25 TQ	TXBLS	10/01-12/01
Fast Food	Odessa-Midland MSA, TX	H	5.57 FQ	6.36 AW	7.72 TQ	TXBLS	10/01-12/01
Fast Food	San Antonio MSA, TX	H	5.58 FQ	6.95 AW	8.48 TQ	TXBLS	10/01-12/01
Fast Food	Tyler MSA, TX	H	5.61 FQ	6.33 AW	7.46 TQ	TXBLS	10/01-12/01
Fast Food	Waco MSA, TX	H	5.57 FQ	6.41 AW	7.97 TQ	TXBLS	10/01-12/01
Fast Food	Utah	H	5.50 FQ	6.75 AW	8.39 TQ	UTBLS	10/01-12/01
Fast Food	Provo-Orem MSA, UT	H	5.49 FQ	6.72 AW	8.28 TQ	UTBLS	10/01-12/01
Fast Food	Salt Lake City-Ogden MSA, UT	H	5.53 FQ	7.00 AW	8.53 TQ	UTBLS	10/01-12/01
Fast Food	Vermont	H	6.45 FQ	7.95 AW	10.18 TQ	VTBLS	10/01-12/01
Fast Food	Burlington MSA, VT	H	6.49 FQ	8.06 AW	10.33 TQ	VTBLS	10/01-12/01
Fast Food	Virginia	H	5.48 FQ	6.64 AW	8.36 TQ	VABLS	10/01-12/01
Fast Food	Lynchburg MSA, VA	H	5.57 FQ	6.54 AW	8.46 TQ	VABLS	10/01-12/01
Fast Food	Norfolk-Virginia Beach-Newport News MSA, VA-NC	H	5.51 FQ	6.55 AW	8.15 TQ	VABLS	10/01-12/01
Fast Food	Richmond-Petersburg MSA, VA	H	5.69 FQ	7.37 AW	9.81 TQ	VABLS	10/01-12/01
Fast Food	Roanoke MSA, VA	H	5.45 FQ	6.21 AW	6.97 TQ	VABLS	10/01-12/01
Fast Food	Washington	H	6.82 FQ	8.24 AW	10.56 TQ	WABLS	10/01-12/01
Fast Food	Bremerton PMSA, WA	H	6.90 FQ	8.11 AW	9.90 TQ	WABLS	10/01-12/01
Fast Food	Olympia PMSA, WA	H	6.83 FQ	7.35 AW	8.34 TQ	WABLS	10/01-12/01
Fast Food	Richland-Kennewick-Pasco MSA, WA	H	6.80 FQ	7.70 AW	9.17 TQ	WABLS	10/01-12/01
Fast Food	Seattle-Bellevue-Everett PMSA, WA	H	6.77 FQ	9.14 AW	12.04 TQ	WABLS	10/01-12/01
Fast Food	Spokane MSA, WA	H	6.96 FQ	8.02 AW	9.40 TQ	WABLS	10/01-12/01
Fast Food	Tacoma PMSA, WA	H	6.88 FQ	7.90 AW	8.97 TQ	WABLS	10/01-12/01
Fast Food	Yakima MSA, WA	H	6.82 FQ	7.35 AW	8.40 TQ	WABLS	10/01-12/01
Fast Food	West Virginia	H	5.54 FQ	6.29 AW	7.25 TQ	WVBLS	10/01-12/01
Fast Food	Charleston MSA, WV	H	5.59 FQ	6.11 AW	7.02 TQ	WVBLS	10/01-12/01
Fast Food	Huntington-Ashland MSA, WV-KY-OH	H	5.49 FQ	6.14 AW	7.11 TQ	WVBLS	10/01-12/01
Fast Food	Wisconsin	H	5.64 FQ	7.18 AW	9.02 TQ	WIBLS	10/01-12/01
Fast Food	Appleton-Oshkosh-Neenah MSA, WI	H	5.64 FQ	7.15 AW	9.61 TQ	WIBLS	10/01-12/01
Fast Food	Green Bay MSA, WI	H	5.75 FQ	6.89 AW	8.66 TQ	WIBLS	10/01-12/01
Fast Food	Madison MSA, WI	H	5.86 FQ	7.61 AW	9.83 TQ	WIBLS	10/01-12/01
Fast Food	Milwaukee-Waukesha PMSA, WI	H	7.04 FQ	8.14 AW	10.10 TQ	WIBLS	10/01-12/01
Fast Food	Racine PMSA, WI	H	5.70 FQ	6.81 AW	8.64 TQ	WIBLS	10/01-12/01
Fast Food	Wyoming	H	5.36 FQ	5.98 AW	6.73 TQ	WYBLS	10/01-12/01
Fast Food	Cheyenne MSA, WY	H	5.47 FQ	6.12 AW	7.10 TQ	WYBLS	10/01-12/01
Fast Food	Puerto Rico	H	5.57 FQ	6.08 AW	6.99 TQ	PRBLS	10/01-12/01
Fast Food	Virgin Islands	H	5.56 FQ	6.68 AW	8.20 TQ	VIBLS	10/01-12/01
Fast Food	Guam	H	5.40 FQ	6.39 AW	8.13 TQ	GUBLS	10/01-12/01
Institution and Cafeteria	Alabama	H	5.62 FQ	7.05 AW	9.48 TQ	ALBLS	10/01-12/01
Institution and Cafeteria	Birmingham MSA, AL	H	5.81 FQ	7.81 AW	10.83 TQ	ALBLS	10/01-12/01
Institution and Cafeteria	Huntsville MSA, AL	H	5.60 FQ	7.27 AW	11.29 TQ	ALBLS	10/01-12/01
Institution and Cafeteria	Montgomery MSA, AL	H	5.63 FQ	6.79 AW	8.84 TQ	ALBLS	10/01-12/01
Institution and Cafeteria	Alaska	H	8.85 FQ	14.46 AW	21.14 TQ	AKBLS	10/01-12/01
Institution and Cafeteria	Anchorage MSA, AK	H	8.74 FQ	13.09 AW	17.83 TQ	AKBLS	10/01-12/01
Institution and Cafeteria	Arizona	H	6.64 FQ	9.55 AW	12.97 TQ	AZBLS	10/01-12/01
Institution and Cafeteria	Phoenix-Mesa MSA, AZ	H	6.84 FQ	9.65 AW	12.95 TQ	AZBLS	10/01-12/01
Institution and Cafeteria	Tucson MSA, AZ	H	6.49 FQ	9.39 AW	12.67 TQ	AZBLS	10/01-12/01
Institution and Cafeteria	Arkansas	H	5.70 FQ	7.05 AW	8.99 TQ	ARBLS	10/01-12/01
Institution and Cafeteria	Fayetteville-Springdale-Rogers MSA, AR	H	5.71 FQ	7.35 AW	9.74 TQ	ARBLS	10/01-12/01
Institution and Cafeteria	Fort Smith MSA, AR-OK	H	5.64 FQ	6.69 AW	8.57 TQ	ARBLS	10/01-12/01
Institution and Cafeteria	Little Rock-North Little Rock MSA, AR	H	5.83 FQ	7.72 AW	10.41 TQ	ARBLS	10/01-12/01
Institution and Cafeteria	California	H	7.27 FQ	10.89 AW	15.40 TQ	CABLS	10/01-12/01
Institution and Cafeteria	Bakersfield MSA, CA	H	8.34 FQ	11.87 AW	17.32 TQ	CABLS	10/01-12/01

AAW	Average annual wage	**AOH**	Average offered, high	**ASH**	Average starting, high	**H**	Hourly	**M**	Monthly	**S**	Special: hourly and annual
AE	Average entry wage	**AOL**	Average offered, low	**ASL**	Average starting, low	**HI**	Highest wage paid	**MTC**	Median total compensation	**TQ**	Third quartile wage
AEX	Average experienced wage	**APH**	Average pay, high range	**AW**	Average wage paid	**HR**	High end range	**MW**	Median wage paid	**W**	Weekly
AO	Average offered	**APL**	Average pay, low range	**FQ**	First quartile wage	**LR**	Low end range	**SQ**	Second quartile wage	**Y**	Yearly

Occupation/Type/Industry	Location	Per	Low	Mid	High	Source	Date
Cook							
Institution and Cafeteria	Chico-Paradise MSA, CA	H	6.92 FQ	10.46 AW	14.32 TQ	CABLS	10/01-12/01
Institution and Cafeteria	Fresno MSA, CA	H	6.72 FQ	9.33 AW	12.31 TQ	CABLS	10/01-12/01
Institution and Cafeteria	Los Angeles-Long Beach PMSA, CA	H	7.28 FQ	10.35 AW	14.01 TQ	CABLS	10/01-12/01
Institution and Cafeteria	Merced MSA, CA	H	6.82 FQ	9.58 AW	13.62 TQ	CABLS	10/01-12/01
Institution and Cafeteria	Modesto MSA, CA	H	7.40 FQ	10.17 AW	14.28 TQ	CABLS	10/01-12/01
Institution and Cafeteria	Oakland PMSA, CA	H	7.80 FQ	12.15 AW	17.32 TQ	CABLS	10/01-12/01
Institution and Cafeteria	Orange County PMSA, CA	H	6.60 FQ	10.96 AW	17.01 TQ	CABLS	10/01-12/01
Institution and Cafeteria	Redding MSA, CA	H	7.56 FQ	10.97 AW	17.30 TQ	CABLS	10/01-12/01
Institution and Cafeteria	Riverside-San Bernardino PMSA, CA	H	7.40 FQ	10.74 AW	14.15 TQ	CABLS	10/01-12/01
Institution and Cafeteria	Sacramento PMSA, CA	H	7.35 FQ	10.26 AW	13.73 TQ	CABLS	10/01-12/01
Institution and Cafeteria	Salinas MSA, CA	H	8.68 FQ	11.75 AW	16.36 TQ	CABLS	10/01-12/01
Institution and Cafeteria	San Diego MSA, CA	H	7.22 FQ	10.71 AW	15.28 TQ	CABLS	10/01-12/01
Institution and Cafeteria	San Francisco PMSA, CA	H	9.29 FQ	13.41 AW	18.08 TQ	CABLS	10/01-12/01
Institution and Cafeteria	San Jose PMSA, CA	H	6.94 FQ	11.47 AW	15.82 TQ	CABLS	10/01-12/01
Institution and Cafeteria	San Luis Obispo-Atascadero-Paso Robles MSA, CA	H	7.47 FQ	11.62 AW	17.57 TQ	CABLS	10/01-12/01
Institution and Cafeteria	Santa Barbara-Santa Maria-Lompoc MSA, CA	H	7.70 FQ	11.08 AW	14.12 TQ	CABLS	10/01-12/01
Institution and Cafeteria	Santa Cruz-Watsonville PMSA, CA	H	7.35 FQ	10.57 AW	14.70 TQ	CABLS	10/01-12/01
Institution and Cafeteria	Santa Rosa PMSA, CA	H	8.91 FQ	12.29 AW	16.67 TQ	CABLS	10/01-12/01
Institution and Cafeteria	Stockton-Lodi MSA, CA	H	7.16 FQ	11.39 AW	17.26 TQ	CABLS	10/01-12/01
Institution and Cafeteria	Vallejo-Fairfield-Napa PMSA, CA	H	7.93 FQ	11.62 AW	16.69 TQ	CABLS	10/01-12/01
Institution and Cafeteria	Ventura PMSA, CA	H	7.51 FQ	10.38 AW	13.85 TQ	CABLS	10/01-12/01
Institution and Cafeteria	Visalia-Tulare-Porterville MSA, CA	H	7.48 FQ	10.18 AW	13.89 TQ	CABLS	10/01-12/01
Institution and Cafeteria	Colorado	H	6.83 FQ	9.59 AW	13.23 TQ	COBLS	10/01-12/01
Institution and Cafeteria	Boulder-Longmont PMSA, CO	H	7.59 FQ	10.07 AW	13.32 TQ	COBLS	10/01-12/01
Institution and Cafeteria	Colorado Springs MSA, CO	H	6.38 FQ	9.77 AW	13.46 TQ	COBLS	10/01-12/01
Institution and Cafeteria	Denver PMSA, CO	H	7.52 FQ	10.23 AW	13.60 TQ	COBLS	10/01-12/01
Institution and Cafeteria	Fort Collins-Loveland MSA, CO	H	6.50 FQ	9.00 AW	12.16 TQ	COBLS	10/01-12/01
Institution and Cafeteria	Greeley PMSA, CO	H	5.83 FQ	7.52 AW	9.89 TQ	COBLS	10/01-12/01
Institution and Cafeteria	Connecticut	H	8.58 FQ	12.66 AW	17.34 TQ	CTBLS	10/01-12/01
Institution and Cafeteria	Bridgeport PMSA, CT	H	11.18 FQ	14.38 AW	18.80 TQ	CTBLS	10/01-12/01
Institution and Cafeteria	Danbury PMSA, CT	H	9.17 FQ	12.13 AW	16.83 TQ	CTBLS	10/01-12/01
Institution and Cafeteria	Hartford MSA, CT	H	6.90 FQ	11.99 AW	16.79 TQ	CTBLS	10/01-12/01
Institution and Cafeteria	New Haven-Meriden PMSA, CT	H	8.95 FQ	13.21 AW	17.27 TQ	CTBLS	10/01-12/01
Institution and Cafeteria	New London-Norwich MSA, CT-RI	H	8.44 FQ	11.43 AW	15.18 TQ	CTBLS	10/01-12/01
Institution and Cafeteria	Stamford-Norwalk PMSA, CT	H	10.48 FQ	14.11 AW	19.99 TQ	CTBLS	10/01-12/01
Institution and Cafeteria	Waterbury PMSA, CT	H	9.29 FQ	13.55 AW	18.75 TQ	CTBLS	10/01-12/01
Institution and Cafeteria	Delaware	H	6.92 FQ	10.67 AW	14.72 TQ	DEBLS	10/01-12/01
Institution and Cafeteria	Wilmington-Newark PMSA, DE-MD	H	7.24 FQ	11.35 AW	15.98 TQ	DEBLS	10/01-12/01
Institution and Cafeteria	District of Columbia	H	7.25 FQ	12.19 AW	17.82 TQ	DCBLS	10/01-12/01
Institution and Cafeteria	Washington PMSA, DC-MD-VA-WV	H	7.41 FQ	11.35 AW	16.45 TQ	DCBLS	10/01-12/01
Institution and Cafeteria	Florida	H	6.10 FQ	8.83 AW	11.72 TQ	FLBLS	10/01-12/01
Institution and Cafeteria	Daytona Beach MSA, FL	H	7.37 FQ	9.25 AW	11.58 TQ	FLBLS	10/01-12/01
Institution and Cafeteria	Fort Lauderdale PMSA, FL	H	7.69 FQ	9.92 AW	12.50 TQ	FLBLS	10/01-12/01
Institution and Cafeteria	Fort Myers-Cape Coral MSA, FL	H	7.49 FQ	10.02 AW	11.83 TQ	FLBLS	10/01-12/01
Institution and Cafeteria	Fort Pierce-Port St. Lucie MSA, FL	H	7.09 FQ	9.60 AW	12.39 TQ	FLBLS	10/01-12/01
Institution and Cafeteria	Fort Walton Beach MSA, FL	H	5.86 FQ	8.37 AW	10.93 TQ	FLBLS	10/01-12/01
Institution and Cafeteria	Gainesville MSA, FL	H	6.01 FQ	8.25 AW	10.81 TQ	FLBLS	10/01-12/01
Institution and Cafeteria	Jacksonville MSA, FL	H	6.67 FQ	9.09 AW	11.58 TQ	FLBLS	10/01-12/01
Institution and Cafeteria	Lakeland-Winter Haven MSA, FL	H	6.23 FQ	9.24 AW	12.68 TQ	FLBLS	10/01-12/01
Institution and Cafeteria	Melbourne-Titusville-Palm Bay MSA, FL	H	6.50 FQ	8.93 AW	10.84 TQ	FLBLS	10/01-12/01
Institution and Cafeteria	Naples MSA, FL	H	7.16 FQ	10.03 AW	12.90 TQ	FLBLS	10/01-12/01
Institution and Cafeteria	Ocala MSA, FL	H	7.06 FQ	8.53 AW	10.34 TQ	FLBLS	10/01-12/01
Institution and Cafeteria	Orlando MSA, FL	H	7.29 FQ	9.41 AW	11.69 TQ	FLBLS	10/01-12/01
Institution and Cafeteria	Pensacola MSA, FL	H	5.84 FQ	8.38 AW	12.15 TQ	FLBLS	10/01-12/01
Institution and Cafeteria	Sarasota-Bradenton MSA, FL	H	5.89 FQ	7.83 AW	10.73 TQ	FLBLS	10/01-12/01

AAW Average annual wage; AE Average entry wage; AEX Average experienced wage; AO Average offered; AOH Average offered, high; AOL Average offered, low; APH Average pay, high range; APL Average pay, low range; ASH Average starting, high; ASL Average starting, low; AW Average wage paid; FQ First quartile wage; H Hourly; HI Highest wage paid; HR High end range; LR Low end range; M Monthly; MTC Median total compensation; MW Median wage paid; SQ Second quartile wage; S Special: hourly and annual; TQ Third quartile wage; W Weekly; Y Yearly

Occupation/Type/Industry	Location	Per	Low	Mid	High	Source	Date
Cook							
Institution and Cafeteria	Tallahassee MSA, FL	H	6.32 FQ	8.84 AW	11.50 TQ	FLBLS	10/01-12/01
Institution and Cafeteria	Tampa-St. Petersburg-Clearwater MSA, FL	H	7.43 FQ	9.21 AW	12.58 TQ	FLBLS	10/01-12/01
Institution and Cafeteria	West Palm Beach-Boca Raton MSA, FL	H	6.45 FQ	9.45 AW	13.17 TQ	FLBLS	10/01-12/01
Institution and Cafeteria	Georgia	H	5.71 FQ	7.67 AW	10.61 TQ	GABLS	10/01-12/01
Institution and Cafeteria	Atlanta MSA, GA	H	5.84 FQ	8.35 AW	11.03 TQ	GABLS	10/01-12/01
Institution and Cafeteria	Augusta-Aiken MSA, GA-SC	H	5.66 FQ	7.34 AW	10.29 TQ	GABLS	10/01-12/01
Institution and Cafeteria	Columbus MSA, GA-AL	H	5.58 FQ	6.99 AW	9.37 TQ	GABLS	10/01-12/01
Institution and Cafeteria	Macon MSA, GA	H	5.76 FQ	7.44 AW	9.88 TQ	GABLS	10/01-12/01
Institution and Cafeteria	Savannah MSA, GA	H	6.02 FQ	7.78 AW	10.20 TQ	GABLS	10/01-12/01
Institution and Cafeteria	Hawaii	H	7.18 FQ	11.89 AW	16.70 TQ	HIBLS	10/01-12/01
Institution and Cafeteria	Honolulu MSA, HI	H	7.06 FQ	11.64 AW	16.83 TQ	HIBLS	10/01-12/01
Institution and Cafeteria	Idaho	H	7.13 FQ	9.03 AW	11.56 TQ	IDBLS	10/01-12/01
Institution and Cafeteria	Boise City MSA, ID	H	7.16 FQ	8.95 AW	11.58 TQ	IDBLS	10/01-12/01
Institution and Cafeteria	Illinois	H	6.02 FQ	8.99 AW	12.77 TQ	ILBLS	10/01-12/01
Institution and Cafeteria	Champaign-Urbana MSA, IL	H	7.44 FQ	10.63 AW	14.45 TQ	ILBLS	10/01-12/01
Institution and Cafeteria	Chicago PMSA, IL	H	6.32 FQ	9.63 AW	13.41 TQ	ILBLS	10/01-12/01
Institution and Cafeteria	Peoria-Pekin MSA, IL	H	6.41 FQ	8.64 AW	10.96 TQ	ILBLS	10/01-12/01
Institution and Cafeteria	Rockford MSA, IL	H	6.45 FQ	9.03 AW	11.77 TQ	ILBLS	10/01-12/01
Institution and Cafeteria	Springfield MSA, IL	H	5.87 FQ	8.09 AW	11.83 TQ	ILBLS	10/01-12/01
Institution and Cafeteria	Indiana	H	6.36 FQ	8.86 AW	11.43 TQ	INBLS	10/01-12/01
Institution and Cafeteria	Elkhart-Goshen MSA, IN	H	8.04 FQ	9.96 AW	12.02 TQ	INBLS	10/01-12/01
Institution and Cafeteria	Evansville-Henderson MSA, IN-KY	H	6.41 FQ	8.96 AW	11.95 TQ	INBLS	10/01-12/01
Institution and Cafeteria	Fort Wayne MSA, IN	H	7.45 FQ	9.53 AW	11.37 TQ	INBLS	10/01-12/01
Institution and Cafeteria	Gary PMSA, IN	H	5.70 FQ	8.18 AW	11.68 TQ	INBLS	10/01-12/01
Institution and Cafeteria	Indianapolis MSA, IN	H	7.43 FQ	9.49 AW	12.24 TQ	INBLS	10/01-12/01
Institution and Cafeteria	Lafayette MSA, IN	H	7.16 FQ	9.34 AW	11.14 TQ	INBLS	10/01-12/01
Institution and Cafeteria	South Bend MSA, IN	H	7.07 FQ	9.35 AW	12.22 TQ	INBLS	10/01-12/01
Institution and Cafeteria	Iowa	H	6.42 FQ	8.64 AW	11.04 TQ	IABLS	10/01-12/01
Institution and Cafeteria	Cedar Rapids MSA, IA	H	7.53 FQ	10.16 AW	13.14 TQ	IABLS	10/01-12/01
Institution and Cafeteria	Davenport-Moline-Rock Island MSA, IA-IL	H	6.00 FQ	8.52 AW	11.32 TQ	IABLS	10/01-12/01
Institution and Cafeteria	Des Moines MSA, IA	H	7.36 FQ	9.89 AW	13.03 TQ	IABLS	10/01-12/01
Institution and Cafeteria	Kansas	H	6.08 FQ	8.26 AW	10.83 TQ	KSBLS	10/01-12/01
Institution and Cafeteria	Topeka MSA, KS	H	7.23 FQ	9.57 AW	12.45 TQ	KSBLS	10/01-12/01
Institution and Cafeteria	Wichita MSA, KS	H	5.98 FQ	8.28 AW	11.01 TQ	KSBLS	10/01-12/01
Institution and Cafeteria	Kentucky	H	5.93 FQ	8.06 AW	10.66 TQ	KYBLS	10/01-12/01
Institution and Cafeteria	Lexington MSA, KY	H	6.94 FQ	9.01 AW	11.98 TQ	KYBLS	10/01-12/01
Institution and Cafeteria	Louisville MSA, KY-IN	H	7.34 FQ	9.38 AW	11.88 TQ	KYBLS	10/01-12/01
Institution and Cafeteria	Louisiana	H	5.61 FQ	6.85 AW	8.88 TQ	LABLS	10/01-12/01
Institution and Cafeteria	Baton Rouge MSA, LA	H	5.73 FQ	7.10 AW	8.80 TQ	LABLS	10/01-12/01
Institution and Cafeteria	Houma MSA, LA	H	5.67 FQ	7.33 AW	8.80 TQ	LABLS	10/01-12/01
Institution and Cafeteria	Lafayette MSA, LA	H	5.55 FQ	6.71 AW	8.70 TQ	LABLS	10/01-12/01
Institution and Cafeteria	New Orleans MSA, LA	H	5.66 FQ	7.23 AW	10.29 TQ	LABLS	10/01-12/01
Institution and Cafeteria	Shreveport-Bossier City MSA, LA	H	5.49 FQ	6.50 AW	8.17 TQ	LABLS	10/01-12/01
Institution and Cafeteria	Maine	H	7.36 FQ	9.56 AW	12.18 TQ	MEBLS	10/01-12/01
Institution and Cafeteria	Portland MSA, ME	H	8.19 FQ	10.55 AW	13.28 TQ	MEBLS	10/01-12/01
Institution and Cafeteria	Maryland	H	7.72 FQ	11.55 AW	16.38 TQ	MDBLS	10/01-12/01
Institution and Cafeteria	Baltimore PMSA, MD	H	7.73 FQ	11.28 AW	15.88 TQ	MDBLS	10/01-12/01
Institution and Cafeteria	Massachusetts	H	7.74 FQ	11.10 AW	14.49 TQ	MABLS	10/01-12/01
Institution and Cafeteria	Boston PMSA, MA-NH	H	7.99 FQ	11.35 AW	15.07 TQ	MABLS	10/01-12/01
Institution and Cafeteria	Brockton PMSA, MA	H	6.90 FQ	11.16 AW	15.66 TQ	MABLS	10/01-12/01
Institution and Cafeteria	Lawrence PMSA, MA-NH	H	7.01 FQ	10.57 AW	15.12 TQ	MABLS	10/01-12/01
Institution and Cafeteria	Lowell PMSA, MA-NH	H	7.42 FQ	10.86 AW	13.93 TQ	MABLS	10/01-12/01
Institution and Cafeteria	New Bedford PMSA, MA	H	7.63 FQ	9.99 AW	12.93 TQ	MABLS	10/01-12/01
Institution and Cafeteria	Springfield MSA, MA	H	7.93 FQ	10.82 AW	13.67 TQ	MABLS	10/01-12/01
Institution and Cafeteria	Worcester PMSA, MA-CT	H	7.91 FQ	11.14 AW	14.22 TQ	MABLS	10/01-12/01
Institution and Cafeteria	Michigan	H	7.23 FQ	10.30 AW	13.77 TQ	MIBLS	10/01-12/01
Institution and Cafeteria	Ann Arbor PMSA, MI	H	6.60 FQ	10.19 AW	14.56 TQ	MIBLS	10/01-12/01
Institution and Cafeteria	Detroit PMSA, MI	H	8.37 FQ	10.92 AW	14.03 TQ	MIBLS	10/01-12/01
Institution and Cafeteria	Flint PMSA, MI	H	5.72 FQ	8.32 AW	12.67 TQ	MIBLS	10/01-12/01
Institution and Cafeteria	Grand Rapids-Muskegon-Holland MSA, MI	H	7.81 FQ	10.48 AW	13.37 TQ	MIBLS	10/01-12/01
Institution and Cafeteria	Kalamazoo-Battle Creek MSA, MI	H	7.43 FQ	10.38 AW	13.77 TQ	MIBLS	10/01-12/01
Institution and Cafeteria	Lansing-East Lansing MSA, MI	H	7.64 FQ	11.18 AW	15.50 TQ	MIBLS	10/01-12/01
Institution and Cafeteria	Saginaw-Bay City-Midland MSA, MI	H	6.53 FQ	8.83 AW	11.90 TQ	MIBLS	10/01-12/01

AAW	Average annual wage	AOH	Average offered, high	ASH	Average starting, high	H	Hourly	M	Monthly	S	Special: hourly and annual
AE	Average entry wage	AOL	Average offered, low	ASL	Average starting, low	HI	Highest wage paid	MTC	Median total compensation	TQ	Third quartile wage
AEX	Average experienced wage	APH	Average pay, high range	AW	Average wage paid	HR	High end range	MW	Median wage paid	W	Weekly
AO	Average offered	APL	Average pay, low range	FQ	First quartile wage	LR	Low end range	SQ	Second quartile wage	Y	Yearly

Occupation/Type/Industry	Location	Per	Low	Mid	High	Source	Date
Cook							
Institution and Cafeteria	Minnesota	H	8.01 FQ	11.21 AW	15.31 TQ	MNBLS	10/01-12/01
Institution and Cafeteria	Duluth-Superior MSA, MN-WI	H	7.56 FQ	10.38 AW	13.76 TQ	MNBLS	10/01-12/01
Institution and Cafeteria	Minneapolis-St. Paul MSA, MN-WI	H	8.84 FQ	12.15 AW	16.30 TQ	MNBLS	10/01-12/01
Institution and Cafeteria	St. Cloud MSA, MN	H	8.81 FQ	11.14 AW	14.20 TQ	MNBLS	10/01-12/01
Institution and Cafeteria	Mississippi	H	5.65 FQ	6.99 AW	9.26 TQ	MSBLS	10/01-12/01
Institution and Cafeteria	Biloxi-Gulfport-Pascagoula MSA, MS	H	5.64 FQ	7.01 AW	8.71 TQ	MSBLS	10/01-12/01
Institution and Cafeteria	Jackson MSA, MS	H	5.77 FQ	7.64 AW	10.27 TQ	MSBLS	10/01-12/01
Institution and Cafeteria	Missouri	H	5.86 FQ	8.10 AW	10.97 TQ	MOBLS	10/01-12/01
Institution and Cafeteria	Kansas City MSA, MO-KS	H	6.08 FQ	8.73 AW	11.45 TQ	MOBLS	10/01-12/01
Institution and Cafeteria	St. Louis MSA, MO-IL	H	6.23 FQ	8.81 AW	11.78 TQ	MOBLS	10/01-12/01
Institution and Cafeteria	Springfield MSA, MO	H	5.73 FQ	7.89 AW	10.85 TQ	MOBLS	10/01-12/01
Institution and Cafeteria	Montana	H	6.13 FQ	8.55 AW	10.97 TQ	MTBLS	10/01-12/01
Institution and Cafeteria	Billings MSA, MT	H	6.35 FQ	8.77 AW	10.91 TQ	MTBLS	10/01-12/01
Institution and Cafeteria	Nebraska	H	5.90 FQ	8.03 AW	10.78 TQ	NEBLS	10/01-12/01
Institution and Cafeteria	Lincoln MSA, NE	H	6.37 FQ	8.95 AW	11.12 TQ	NEBLS	10/01-12/01
Institution and Cafeteria	Omaha MSA, NE-IA	H	6.18 FQ	9.19 AW	12.78 TQ	NEBLS	10/01-12/01
Institution and Cafeteria	Nevada	H	7.30 FQ	10.88 AW	15.38 TQ	NVBLS	10/01-12/01
Institution and Cafeteria	Las Vegas MSA, NV-AZ	H	7.32 FQ	11.01 AW	15.48 TQ	NVBLS	10/01-12/01
Institution and Cafeteria	Reno MSA, NV	H	8.22 FQ	11.76 AW	17.18 TQ	NVBLS	10/01-12/01
Institution and Cafeteria	New Hampshire	H	6.70 FQ	10.41 AW	13.94 TQ	NHBLS	10/01-12/01
Institution and Cafeteria	Manchester PMSA, NH	H	7.60 FQ	10.78 AW	14.22 TQ	NHBLS	10/01-12/01
Institution and Cafeteria	Nashua PMSA, NH	H	6.35 FQ	10.79 AW	15.63 TQ	NHBLS	10/01-12/01
Institution and Cafeteria	Portsmouth-Rochester PMSA, NH-ME	H	7.18 FQ	10.74 AW	13.75 TQ	NHBLS	10/01-12/01
Institution and Cafeteria	New Jersey	H	7.22 FQ	11.67 AW	16.56 TQ	NJBLS	10/01-12/01
Institution and Cafeteria	Atlantic-Cape May PMSA, NJ	H	6.96 FQ	11.85 AW	16.50 TQ	NJBLS	10/01-12/01
Institution and Cafeteria	Bergen-Passaic PMSA, NJ	H	8.05 FQ	12.15 AW	16.92 TQ	NJBLS	10/01-12/01
Institution and Cafeteria	Jersey City PMSA, NJ	H	7.52 FQ	11.55 AW	16.67 TQ	NJBLS	10/01-12/01
Institution and Cafeteria	Middlesex-Somerset-Hunterdon PMSA, NJ	H	9.21 FQ	13.13 AW	17.63 TQ	NJBLS	10/01-12/01
Institution and Cafeteria	Monmouth-Ocean PMSA, NJ	H	7.95 FQ	11.74 AW	16.27 TQ	NJBLS	10/01-12/01
Institution and Cafeteria	Newark PMSA, NJ	H	6.54 FQ	11.54 AW	16.00 TQ	NJBLS	10/01-12/01
Institution and Cafeteria	Trenton PMSA, NJ	H	6.85 FQ	12.38 AW	18.37 TQ	NJBLS	10/01-12/01
Institution and Cafeteria	New Mexico	H	5.73 FQ	7.91 AW	10.77 TQ	NMBLS	10/01-12/01
Institution and Cafeteria	Albuquerque MSA, NM	H	6.14 FQ	8.43 AW	10.96 TQ	NMBLS	10/01-12/01
Institution and Cafeteria	Las Cruces MSA, NM	H	5.63 FQ	6.93 AW	9.49 TQ	NMBLS	10/01-12/01
Institution and Cafeteria	New York	H	7.07 FQ	11.36 AW	16.29 TQ	NYBLS	10/01-12/01
Institution and Cafeteria	Albany-Schenectady-Troy MSA, NY	H	6.84 FQ	9.93 AW	13.35 TQ	NYBLS	10/01-12/01
Institution and Cafeteria	Binghamton MSA, NY	H	6.09 FQ	9.19 AW	13.00 TQ	NYBLS	10/01-12/01
Institution and Cafeteria	Buffalo-Niagara Falls MSA, NY	H	7.13 FQ	10.65 AW	15.71 TQ	NYBLS	10/01-12/01
Institution and Cafeteria	Dutchess County PMSA, NY	H	6.11 FQ	10.70 AW	17.22 TQ	NYBLS	10/01-12/01
Institution and Cafeteria	Nassau-Suffolk PMSA, NY	H	7.55 FQ	12.29 AW	16.71 TQ	NYBLS	10/01-12/01
Institution and Cafeteria	New York PMSA, NY	H	8.68 FQ	13.16 AW	18.05 TQ	NYBLS	10/01-12/01
Institution and Cafeteria	Newburgh PMSA, NY-PA	H	8.57 FQ	9.81 AW	11.06 TQ	NYBLS	10/01-12/01
Institution and Cafeteria	Rochester MSA, NY	H	6.21 FQ	9.87 AW	14.47 TQ	NYBLS	10/01-12/01
Institution and Cafeteria	Syracuse MSA, NY	H	6.18 FQ	9.23 AW	13.14 TQ	NYBLS	10/01-12/01
Institution and Cafeteria	Utica-Rome MSA, NY	H	5.99 FQ	8.94 AW	13.44 TQ	NYBLS	10/01-12/01
Institution and Cafeteria	North Carolina	H	6.06 FQ	8.24 AW	10.87 TQ	NCBLS	10/01-12/01
Institution and Cafeteria	Asheville MSA, NC	H	6.82 FQ	8.70 AW	11.36 TQ	NCBLS	10/01-12/01
Institution and Cafeteria	Charlotte-Gastonia-Rock Hill MSA, NC-SC	H	6.58 FQ	8.71 AW	11.18 TQ	NCBLS	10/01-12/01
Institution and Cafeteria	Fayetteville MSA, NC	H	6.53 FQ	8.68 AW	11.24 TQ	NCBLS	10/01-12/01
Institution and Cafeteria	Greensboro-Winston-Salem-High Point MSA, NC	H	6.50 FQ	8.92 AW	11.53 TQ	NCBLS	10/01-12/01
Institution and Cafeteria	Hickory-Morganton-Lenoir MSA, NC	H	6.21 FQ	8.06 AW	10.51 TQ	NCBLS	10/01-12/01
Institution and Cafeteria	Raleigh-Durham-Chapel Hill MSA, NC	H	6.32 FQ	8.80 AW	11.55 TQ	NCBLS	10/01-12/01
Institution and Cafeteria	Wilmington MSA, NC	H	5.70 FQ	7.70 AW	10.55 TQ	NCBLS	10/01-12/01
Institution and Cafeteria	North Dakota	H	6.03 FQ	8.50 AW	11.02 TQ	NDBLS	10/01-12/01
Institution and Cafeteria	Fargo-Moorhead MSA, ND-MN	H	5.77 FQ	8.93 AW	12.32 TQ	NDBLS	10/01-12/01
Institution and Cafeteria	Ohio	H	6.45 FQ	9.69 AW	13.28 TQ	OHBLS	10/01-12/01
Institution and Cafeteria	Akron PMSA, OH	H	7.04 FQ	9.77 AW	12.90 TQ	OHBLS	10/01-12/01
Institution and Cafeteria	Canton-Massillon MSA, OH	H	6.58 FQ	9.18 AW	11.41 TQ	OHBLS	10/01-12/01
Institution and Cafeteria	Cincinnati PMSA, OH-KY-IN	H	6.10 FQ	9.50 AW	13.32 TQ	OHBLS	10/01-12/01

AAW	Average annual wage	AOH	Average offered, high	ASH	Average starting, high	H	Hourly	M	Monthly	S	Special: hourly and annual
AE	Average entry wage	AOL	Average offered, low	ASL	Average starting, low	HI	Highest wage paid	MTC	Median total compensation	TQ	Third quartile wage
AEX	Average experienced wage	APH	Average pay, high range	AW	Average wage paid	HR	High end range	MW	Median wage paid	W	Weekly
AO	Average offered	APL	Average pay, low range	FQ	First quartile wage	LR	Low end range	SQ	Second quartile wage	Y	Yearly

Occupation/Type/Industry	Location	Per	Low	Mid	High	Source	Date
Cook							
Institution and Cafeteria	Cleveland-Lorain-Elyria PMSA, OH	H	6.38 FQ	9.97 AW	13.65 TQ	OHBLS	10/01-12/01
Institution and Cafeteria	Columbus MSA, OH	H	7.66 FQ	10.80 AW	14.16 TQ	OHBLS	10/01-12/01
Institution and Cafeteria	Dayton-Springfield MSA, OH	H	6.56 FQ	9.54 AW	12.87 TQ	OHBLS	10/01-12/01
Institution and Cafeteria	Hamilton-Middletown PMSA, OH	H	7.54 FQ	9.79 AW	12.60 TQ	OHBLS	10/01-12/01
Institution and Cafeteria	Mansfield MSA, OH	H	6.34 FQ	9.68 AW	13.75 TQ	OHBLS	10/01-12/01
Institution and Cafeteria	Toledo MSA, OH	H	7.24 FQ	9.87 AW	13.15 TQ	OHBLS	10/01-12/01
Institution and Cafeteria	Youngstown-Warren MSA, OH	H	6.03 FQ	8.45 AW	11.12 TQ	OHBLS	10/01-12/01
Institution and Cafeteria	Oklahoma	H	5.66 FQ	7.14 AW	9.52 TQ	OKBLS	10/01-12/01
Institution and Cafeteria	Oklahoma City MSA, OK	H	5.67 FQ	7.43 AW	10.24 TQ	OKBLS	10/01-12/01
Institution and Cafeteria	Tulsa MSA, OK	H	5.80 FQ	7.55 AW	10.20 TQ	OKBLS	10/01-12/01
Institution and Cafeteria	Oregon	H	7.47 FQ	10.04 AW	13.39 TQ	ORBLS	10/01-12/01
Institution and Cafeteria	Eugene-Springfield MSA, OR	H	7.71 FQ	10.35 AW	13.74 TQ	ORBLS	10/01-12/01
Institution and Cafeteria	Medford-Ashland MSA, OR	H	7.48 FQ	10.01 AW	14.00 TQ	ORBLS	10/01-12/01
Institution and Cafeteria	Portland-Vancouver PMSA, OR-WA	H	7.50 FQ	10.24 AW	13.75 TQ	ORBLS	10/01-12/01
Institution and Cafeteria	Salem PMSA, OR	H	7.44 FQ	10.22 AW	13.68 TQ	ORBLS	10/01-12/01
Institution and Cafeteria	Pennsylvania	H	6.60 FQ	9.72 AW	13.45 TQ	PABLS	10/01-12/01
Institution and Cafeteria	Allentown-Bethlehem-Easton MSA, PA	H	7.36 FQ	9.68 AW	13.32 TQ	PABLS	10/01-12/01
Institution and Cafeteria	Erie MSA, PA	H	7.06 FQ	9.51 AW	12.73 TQ	PABLS	10/01-12/01
Institution and Cafeteria	Harrisburg-Lebanon-Carlisle MSA, PA	H	6.01 FQ	8.98 AW	12.76 TQ	PABLS	10/01-12/01
Institution and Cafeteria	Johnstown MSA, PA	H	5.97 FQ	7.80 AW	9.78 TQ	PABLS	10/01-12/01
Institution and Cafeteria	Lancaster MSA, PA	H	7.60 FQ	10.09 AW	12.97 TQ	PABLS	10/01-12/01
Institution and Cafeteria	Philadelphia PMSA, PA-NJ	H	7.34 FQ	10.78 AW	15.23 TQ	PABLS	10/01-12/01
Institution and Cafeteria	Pittsburgh MSA, PA	H	6.63 FQ	9.74 AW	13.40 TQ	PABLS	10/01-12/01
Institution and Cafeteria	Reading MSA, PA	H	7.54 FQ	10.74 AW	13.94 TQ	PABLS	10/01-12/01
Institution and Cafeteria	Scranton-Wilkes-Barre-Hazleton MSA, PA	H	6.02 FQ	8.99 AW	12.42 TQ	PABLS	10/01-12/01
Institution and Cafeteria	York MSA, PA	H	7.17 FQ	9.83 AW	13.13 TQ	PABLS	10/01 12/01
Institution and Cafeteria	Rhode Island	H	8.10 FQ	12.40 AW	16.55 TQ	RIBLS	10/01-12/01
Institution and Cafeteria	Providence-Fall River-Warwick MSA, RI-MA	H	7.84 FQ	11.69 AW	15.91 TQ	RIBLS	10/01-12/01
Institution and Cafeteria	South Carolina	H	5.75 FQ	7.85 AW	10.86 TQ	SCBLS	10/01-12/01
Institution and Cafeteria	Charleston-North Charleston MSA, SC	H	6.27 FQ	8.23 AW	10.42 TQ	SCBLS	10/01-12/01
Institution and Cafeteria	Columbia MSA, SC	H	5.79 FQ	7.72 AW	10.45 TQ	SCBLS	10/01-12/01
Institution and Cafeteria	Greenville-Spartanburg-Anderson MSA, SC	H	6.01 FQ	8.57 AW	11.36 TQ	SCBLS	10/01-12/01
Institution and Cafeteria	Myrtle Beach MSA, SC	H	6.04 FQ	8.56 AW	11.42 TQ	SCBLS	10/01-12/01
Institution and Cafeteria	South Dakota	H	7.03 FQ	8.87 AW	10.98 TQ	SDBLS	10/01-12/01
Institution and Cafeteria	Sioux Falls MSA, SD	H	7.06 FQ	9.22 AW	11.55 TQ	SDBLS	10/01-12/01
Institution and Cafeteria	Tennessee	H	5.73 FQ	7.56 AW	10.15 TQ	TNBLS	10/01-12/01
Institution and Cafeteria	Chattanooga MSA, TN-GA	H	5.99 FQ	8.17 AW	10.68 TQ	TNBLS	10/01-12/01
Institution and Cafeteria	Clarksville-Hopkinsville MSA, TN-KY	H	5.71 FQ	7.58 AW	9.92 TQ	TNBLS	10/01-12/01
Institution and Cafeteria	Johnson City-Kingsport-Bristol MSA, TN-VA	H	5.71 FQ	7.51 AW	10.20 TQ	TNBLS	10/01-12/01
Institution and Cafeteria	Knoxville MSA, TN	H	5.84 FQ	8.18 AW	11.15 TQ	TNBLS	10/01-12/01
Institution and Cafeteria	Memphis MSA, TN-AR-MS	H	5.75 FQ	7.71 AW	10.28 TQ	TNBLS	10/01-12/01
Institution and Cafeteria	Nashville MSA, TN	H	5.85 FQ	7.80 AW	10.44 TQ	TNBLS	10/01-12/01
Institution and Cafeteria	Texas	H	5.72 FQ	7.71 AW	10.56 TQ	TXBLS	10/01-12/01
Institution and Cafeteria	Austin-San Marcos MSA, TX	H	5.83 FQ	8.34 AW	11.43 TQ	TXBLS	10/01-12/01
Institution and Cafeteria	Beaumont-Port Arthur MSA, TX	H	5.62 FQ	7.19 AW	9.82 TQ	TXBLS	10/01-12/01
Institution and Cafeteria	Brazoria PMSA, TX	H	5.64 FQ	7.03 AW	9.10 TQ	TXBLS	10/01-12/01
Institution and Cafeteria	Brownsville-Harlingen-San Benito MSA, TX	H	5.57 FQ	7.54 AW	9.97 TQ	TXBLS	10/01-12/01
Institution and Cafeteria	Corpus Christi MSA, TX	H	5.54 FQ	7.05 AW	9.12 TQ	TXBLS	10/01-12/01
Institution and Cafeteria	Dallas PMSA, TX	H	5.80 FQ	8.34 AW	11.90 TQ	TXBLS	10/01-12/01
Institution and Cafeteria	El Paso MSA, TX	H	5.86 FQ	8.00 AW	10.91 TQ	TXBLS	10/01-12/01
Institution and Cafeteria	Fort Worth-Arlington PMSA, TX	H	5.80 FQ	7.98 AW	10.61 TQ	TXBLS	10/01-12/01
Institution and Cafeteria	Galveston-Texas City PMSA, TX	H	5.78 FQ	7.44 AW	9.40 TQ	TXBLS	10/01-12/01
Institution and Cafeteria	Houston PMSA, TX	H	5.81 FQ	8.04 AW	10.95 TQ	TXBLS	10/01-12/01
Institution and Cafeteria	Killeen-Temple MSA, TX	H	5.63 FQ	7.35 AW	10.43 TQ	TXBLS	10/01-12/01
Institution and Cafeteria	Laredo MSA, TX	H	5.70 FQ	7.21 AW	9.68 TQ	TXBLS	10/01-12/01
Institution and Cafeteria	Longview-Marshall MSA, TX	H	5.72 FQ	7.06 AW	8.73 TQ	TXBLS	10/01-12/01

AAW Average annual wage; **AE** Average entry wage; **AEX** Average experienced wage; **AO** Average offered; **AOH** Average offered, high; **AOL** Average offered, low; **APH** Average pay, high range; **APL** Average pay, low range; **ASH** Average starting, high; **ASL** Average starting, low; **AW** Average wage paid; **FQ** First quartile wage; **H** Hourly; **HI** Highest wage paid; **HR** High end range; **LR** Low end range; **M** Monthly; **MTC** Median total compensation; **MW** Median wage paid; **SQ** Second quartile wage; **S** Special: hourly and annual; **TQ** Third quartile wage; **W** Weekly; **Y** Yearly

Occupation/Type/Industry	Location	Per	Low	Mid	High	Source	Date
Cook							
Institution and Cafeteria	Lubbock MSA, TX	H	6.05 FQ	8.22 AW	10.55 TQ	TXBLS	10/01-12/01
Institution and Cafeteria	McAllen-Edinburg-Mission MSA, TX	H	5.72 FQ	7.35 AW	9.53 TQ	TXBLS	10/01-12/01
Institution and Cafeteria	Odessa-Midland MSA, TX	H	5.55 FQ	6.61 AW	8.37 TQ	TXBLS	10/01-12/01
Institution and Cafeteria	San Antonio MSA, TX	H	6.30 FQ	8.42 AW	10.99 TQ	TXBLS	10/01-12/01
Institution and Cafeteria	Tyler MSA, TX	H	5.68 FQ	7.23 AW	9.48 TQ	TXBLS	10/01-12/01
Institution and Cafeteria	Waco MSA, TX	H	5.62 FQ	6.78 AW	8.62 TQ	TXBLS	10/01-12/01
Institution and Cafeteria	Utah	H	6.14 FQ	8.81 AW	12.31 TQ	UTBLS	10/01-12/01
Institution and Cafeteria	Provo-Orem MSA, UT	H	6.09 FQ	7.73 AW	10.00 TQ	UTBLS	10/01-12/01
Institution and Cafeteria	Salt Lake City-Ogden MSA, UT	H	6.22 FQ	9.11 AW	12.55 TQ	UTBLS	10/01-12/01
Institution and Cafeteria	Vermont	H	7.08 FQ	10.48 AW	13.98 TQ	VTBLS	10/01-12/01
Institution and Cafeteria	Burlington MSA, VT	H	7.85 FQ	10.77 AW	14.12 TQ	VTBLS	10/01-12/01
Institution and Cafeteria	Virginia	H	5.89 FQ	8.65 AW	12.23 TQ	VABLS	10/01-12/01
Institution and Cafeteria	Lynchburg MSA, VA	H	6.89 FQ	8.82 AW	12.05 TQ	VABLS	10/01-12/01
Institution and Cafeteria	Norfolk-Virginia Beach-Newport News MSA, VA-NC	H	5.79 FQ	9.03 AW	13.70 TQ	VABLS	10/01-12/01
Institution and Cafeteria	Richmond-Petersburg MSA, VA	H	5.99 FQ	8.44 AW	11.23 TQ	VABLS	10/01-12/01
Institution and Cafeteria	Roanoke MSA, VA	H	6.42 FQ	8.78 AW	11.81 TQ	VABLS	10/01-12/01
Institution and Cafeteria	Washington	H	7.96 FQ	10.97 AW	14.23 TQ	WABLS	10/01-12/01
Institution and Cafeteria	Bremerton PMSA, WA	H	8.62 FQ	11.48 AW	14.31 TQ	WABLS	10/01-12/01
Institution and Cafeteria	Olympia PMSA, WA	H	8.84 FQ	11.59 AW	14.55 TQ	WABLS	10/01-12/01
Institution and Cafeteria	Richland-Kennewick-Pasco MSA, WA	H	7.46 FQ	10.22 AW	13.56 TQ	WABLS	10/01-12/01
Institution and Cafeteria	Seattle-Bellevue-Everett PMSA, WA	H	8.80 FQ	11.78 AW	14.97 TQ	WABLS	10/01-12/01
Institution and Cafeteria	Spokane MSA, WA	H	7.78 FQ	10.16 AW	13.32 TQ	WABLS	10/01-12/01
Institution and Cafeteria	Tacoma PMSA, WA	H	7.89 FQ	11.21 AW	14.77 TQ	WABLS	10/01-12/01
Institution and Cafeteria	Yakima MSA, WA	H	7.85 FQ	10.98 AW	13.76 TQ	WABLS	10/01-12/01
Institution and Cafeteria	West Virginia	H	6.19 FQ	8.23 AW	10.60 TQ	WVBLS	10/01-12/01
Institution and Cafeteria	Charleston MSA, WV	H	6.16 FQ	8.25 AW	10.68 TQ	WVBLS	10/01-12/01
Institution and Cafeteria	Huntington-Ashland MSA, WV-KY-OH	H	5.86 FQ	7.71 AW	10.15 TQ	WVBLS	10/01-12/01
Institution and Cafeteria	Wisconsin	H	7.23 FQ	9.76 AW	13.06 TQ	WIBLS	10/01-12/01
Institution and Cafeteria	Appleton-Oshkosh-Neenah MSA, WI	H	6.48 FQ	8.96 AW	11.54 TQ	WIBLS	10/01-12/01
Institution and Cafeteria	Green Bay MSA, WI	H	7.44 FQ	9.52 AW	11.52 TQ	WIBLS	10/01-12/01
Institution and Cafeteria	Madison MSA, WI	H	8.21 FQ	10.83 AW	14.58 TQ	WIBLS	10/01-12/01
Institution and Cafeteria	Milwaukee-Waukesha PMSA, WI	H	7.52 FQ	10.16 AW	13.57 TQ	WIBLS	10/01-12/01
Institution and Cafeteria	Racine PMSA, WI	H	7.37 FQ	9.55 AW	12.98 TQ	WIBLS	10/01-12/01
Institution and Cafeteria	Wyoming	H	5.87 FQ	8.17 AW	10.82 TQ	WYBLS	10/01-12/01
Institution and Cafeteria	Cheyenne MSA, WY	H	5.56 FQ	7.37 AW	10.20 TQ	WYBLS	10/01-12/01
Institution and Cafeteria	Virgin Islands	H	6.06 FQ	8.16 AW	10.38 TQ	VIBLS	10/01-12/01
Institution and Cafeteria	Guam	H	6.45 FQ	9.34 AW	12.97 TQ	GUBLS	10/01-12/01
Restaurant	Alabama	H	5.69 FQ	7.66 AW	10.56 TQ	ALBLS	10/01-12/01
Restaurant	Birmingham MSA, AL	H	5.80 FQ	8.26 AW	11.39 TQ	ALBLS	10/01-12/01
Restaurant	Huntsville MSA, AL	H	5.62 FQ	7.19 AW	9.38 TQ	ALBLS	10/01-12/01
Restaurant	Mobile MSA, AL	H	5.88 FQ	8.20 AW	11.15 TQ	ALBLS	10/01-12/01
Restaurant	Montgomery MSA, AL	H	5.54 FQ	7.45 AW	10.13 TQ	ALBLS	10/01-12/01
Restaurant	Alaska	H	8.90 FQ	11.66 AW	14.46 TQ	AKBLS	10/01-12/01
Restaurant	Anchorage MSA, AK	H	8.91 FQ	11.59 AW	14.11 TQ	AKBLS	10/01-12/01
Restaurant	Arizona	H	6.77 FQ	9.28 AW	12.54 TQ	AZBLS	10/01-12/01
Restaurant	Phoenix-Mesa MSA, AZ	H	6.74 FQ	9.29 AW	12.45 TQ	AZBLS	10/01-12/01
Restaurant	Tucson MSA, AZ	H	7.42 FQ	10.14 AW	13.24 TQ	AZBLS	10/01-12/01
Restaurant	Arkansas	H	5.81 FQ	7.91 AW	10.61 TQ	ARBLS	10/01-12/01
Restaurant	Fayetteville-Springdale-Rogers MSA, AR	H	6.41 FQ	8.97 AW	11.53 TQ	ARBLS	10/01-12/01
Restaurant	Fort Smith MSA, AR-OK	H	5.94 FQ	8.26 AW	10.66 TQ	ARBLS	10/01-12/01
Restaurant	Little Rock-North Little Rock MSA, AR	H	5.82 FQ	8.09 AW	10.94 TQ	ARBLS	10/01-12/01
Restaurant	California	H	7.00 FQ	9.82 AW	13.17 TQ	CABLS	10/01-12/01
Restaurant	Bakersfield MSA, CA	H	6.80 FQ	8.94 AW	11.04 TQ	CABLS	10/01-12/01
Restaurant	Chico-Paradise MSA, CA	H	7.02 FQ	8.74 AW	11.18 TQ	CABLS	10/01-12/01
Restaurant	Fresno MSA, CA	H	6.82 FQ	8.03 AW	9.93 TQ	CABLS	10/01-12/01
Restaurant	Los Angeles-Long Beach PMSA, CA	H	6.71 FQ	9.05 AW	12.49 TQ	CABLS	10/01-12/01
Restaurant	Merced MSA, CA	H	6.61 FQ	8.53 AW	10.90 TQ	CABLS	10/01-12/01
Restaurant	Modesto MSA, CA	H	7.24 FQ	9.01 AW	10.74 TQ	CABLS	10/01-12/01

AAW	Average annual wage	AOH	Average offered, high	ASH	Average starting, high	H	Hourly	M	Monthly	S	Special: hourly and annual
AE	Average entry wage	AOL	Average offered, low	ASL	Average starting, low	HI	Highest wage paid	MTC	Median total compensation	TQ	Third quartile wage
AEX	Average experienced wage	APH	Average pay, high range	AW	Average wage paid	HR	High end range	MW	Median wage paid	W	Weekly
AO	Average offered	APL	Average pay, low range	FQ	First quartile wage	LR	Low end range	SQ	Second quartile wage	Y	Yearly

Occupation/Type/Industry	Location	Per	Low	Mid	High	Source	Date
Cook							
Restaurant	Oakland PMSA, CA	H	7.61 FQ	11.81 AW	16.21 TQ	CABLS	10/01-12/01
Restaurant	Orange County PMSA, CA	H	7.46 FQ	9.68 AW	11.78 TQ	CABLS	10/01-12/01
Restaurant	Redding MSA, CA	H	6.69 FQ	8.77 AW	11.03 TQ	CABLS	10/01-12/01
Restaurant	Riverside-San Bernardino PMSA, CA	H	6.68 FQ	8.99 AW	11.61 TQ	CABLS	10/01-12/01
Restaurant	Sacramento PMSA, CA	H	7.51 FQ	10.08 AW	13.31 TQ	CABLS	10/01-12/01
Restaurant	Salinas MSA, CA	H	7.13 FQ	10.18 AW	14.56 TQ	CABLS	10/01-12/01
Restaurant	San Diego MSA, CA	H	7.37 FQ	9.67 AW	12.43 TQ	CABLS	10/01-12/01
Restaurant	San Francisco PMSA, CA	H	7.30 FQ	12.85 AW	20.88 TQ	CABLS	10/01-12/01
Restaurant	San Jose PMSA, CA	H	8.29 FQ	11.44 AW	15.89 TQ	CABLS	10/01-12/01
Restaurant	San Luis Obispo-Atascadero-Paso Robles MSA, CA	H	7.66 FQ	9.50 AW	11.43 TQ	CABLS	10/01-12/01
Restaurant	Santa Barbara-Santa Maria-Lompoc MSA, CA	H	7.75 FQ	10.70 AW	14.91 TQ	CABLS	10/01-12/01
Restaurant	Santa Cruz-Watsonville PMSA, CA	H	7.39 FQ	10.20 AW	13.32 TQ	CABLS	10/01-12/01
Restaurant	Santa Rosa PMSA, CA	H	7.11 FQ	9.88 AW	13.36 TQ	CABLS	10/01-12/01
Restaurant	Stockton-Lodi MSA, CA	H	6.64 FQ	9.22 AW	12.51 TQ	CABLS	10/01-12/01
Restaurant	Vallejo-Fairfield-Napa PMSA, CA	H	7.21 FQ	9.61 AW	13.45 TQ	CABLS	10/01-12/01
Restaurant	Ventura PMSA, CA	H	8.00 FQ	9.74 AW	11.55 TQ	CABLS	10/01-12/01
Restaurant	Visalia-Tulare-Porterville MSA, CA	H	6.61 FQ	8.64 AW	10.75 TQ	CABLS	10/01-12/01
Restaurant	Colorado	H	6.45 FQ	9.67 AW	13.40 TQ	COBLS	10/01-12/01
Restaurant	Boulder-Longmont PMSA, CO	H	8.65 FQ	10.71 AW	14.05 TQ	COBLS	10/01-12/01
Restaurant	Colorado Springs MSA, CO	H	6.37 FQ	9.25 AW	12.61 TQ	COBLS	10/01-12/01
Restaurant	Denver PMSA, CO	H	6.64 FQ	10.11 AW	13.86 TQ	COBLS	10/01-12/01
Restaurant	Fort Collins-Loveland MSA, CO	H	6.12 FQ	8.65 AW	11.11 TQ	COBLS	10/01-12/01
Restaurant	Greeley PMSA, CO	H	5.91 FQ	7.73 AW	10.43 TQ	COBLS	10/01-12/01
Restaurant	Connecticut	H	7.62 FQ	11.40 AW	15.44 TQ	CTBLS	10/01-12/01
Restaurant	Bridgeport PMSA, CT	H	8.74 FQ	12.56 AW	16.25 TQ	CTBLS	10/01-12/01
Restaurant	Danbury PMSA, CT	H	7.91 FQ	12.12 AW	16.88 TQ	CTBLS	10/01-12/01
Restaurant	Hartford MSA, CT	H	7.57 FQ	11.19 AW	14.53 TQ	CTBLS	10/01-12/01
Restaurant	New Haven-Meriden PMSA, CT	H	8.58 FQ	11.32 AW	13.69 TQ	CTBLS	10/01-12/01
Restaurant	New London-Norwich MSA, CT-RI	H	7.84 FQ	11.49 AW	15.68 TQ	CTBLS	10/01-12/01
Restaurant	Stamford-Norwalk PMSA, CT	H	7.17 FQ	11.47 AW	17.44 TQ	CTBLS	10/01-12/01
Restaurant	Waterbury PMSA, CT	H	7.92 FQ	10.71 AW	14.14 TQ	CTBLS	10/01-12/01
Restaurant	Delaware	H	7.24 FQ	9.83 AW	12.61 TQ	DEBLS	10/01-12/01
Restaurant	Wilmington-Newark PMSA, DE-MD	H	7.24 FQ	9.96 AW	12.74 TQ	DEBLS	10/01-12/01
Restaurant	District of Columbia	H	8.69 FQ	11.51 AW	15.74 TQ	DCBLS	10/01-12/01
Restaurant	Washington PMSA, DC-MD-VA-WV	H	6.61 FQ	10.08 AW	13.66 TQ	DCBLS	10/01-12/01
Restaurant	Florida	H	7.00 FQ	9.63 AW	12.93 TQ	FLBLS	10/01-12/01
Restaurant	Daytona Beach MSA, FL	H	7.14 FQ	9.07 AW	11.28 TQ	FLBLS	10/01-12/01
Restaurant	Fort Lauderdale PMSA, FL	H	6.23 FQ	9.27 AW	12.42 TQ	FLBLS	10/01-12/01
Restaurant	Fort Myers-Cape Coral MSA, FL	H	7.75 FQ	10.43 AW	13.41 TQ	FLBLS	10/01-12/01
Restaurant	Fort Pierce-Port St. Lucie MSA, FL	H	6.97 FQ	9.09 AW	12.14 TQ	FLBLS	10/01-12/01
Restaurant	Fort Walton Beach MSA, FL	H	7.04 FQ	8.65 AW	10.86 TQ	FLBLS	10/01-12/01
Restaurant	Gainesville MSA, FL	H	6.15 FQ	8.62 AW	11.16 TQ	FLBLS	10/01-12/01
Restaurant	Jacksonville MSA, FL	H	6.91 FQ	9.29 AW	12.46 TQ	FLBLS	10/01-12/01
Restaurant	Lakeland-Winter Haven MSA, FL	H	7.49 FQ	9.02 AW	10.88 TQ	FLBLS	10/01-12/01
Restaurant	Melbourne-Titusville-Palm Bay MSA, FL	H	6.85 FQ	8.90 AW	11.78 TQ	FLBLS	10/01-12/01
Restaurant	Miami PMSA, FL	H	6.74 FQ	9.73 AW	12.96 TQ	FLBLS	10/01-12/01
Restaurant	Naples MSA, FL	H	8.77 FQ	11.96 AW	15.72 TQ	FLBLS	10/01-12/01
Restaurant	Ocala MSA, FL	H	6.89 FQ	8.39 AW	10.60 TQ	FLBLS	10/01-12/01
Restaurant	Orlando MSA, FL	H	7.41 FQ	10.22 AW	13.31 TQ	FLBLS	10/01-12/01
Restaurant	Pensacola MSA, FL	H	6.55 FQ	8.28 AW	10.67 TQ	FLBLS	10/01-12/01
Restaurant	Sarasota-Bradenton MSA, FL	H	7.31 FQ	9.40 AW	12.27 TQ	FLBLS	10/01-12/01
Restaurant	Tallahassee MSA, FL	H	5.89 FQ	8.38 AW	11.24 TQ	FLBLS	10/01-12/01
Restaurant	Tampa-St. Petersburg-Clearwater MSA, FL	H	6.82 FQ	9.22 AW	11.62 TQ	FLBLS	10/01-12/01
Restaurant	West Palm Beach-Boca Raton MSA, FL	H	7.70 FQ	10.77 AW	14.05 TQ	FLBLS	10/01-12/01

AAW Average annual wage		**AOH** Average offered, high		**ASH** Average starting, high		**H** Hourly		**M** Monthly		**S** Special: hourly and annual		
AE Average entry wage		**AOL** Average offered, low		**ASL** Average starting, low		**HI** Highest wage paid		**MTC** Median total compensation		**TQ** Third quartile wage		
AEX Average experienced wage		**APH** Average pay, high range		**AW** Average wage paid		**HR** High end range		**MW** Median wage paid		**W** Weekly		
AO Average offered		**APL** Average pay, low range		**FQ** First quartile wage		**LR** Low end range		**SQ** Second quartile wage		**Y** Yearly		

Occupation/Type/Industry	Location	Per	Low	Mid	High	Source	Date
Cook							
Restaurant	Georgia	H	6.08 FQ	8.16 AW	10.64 TQ	GABLS	10/01-12/01
Restaurant	Atlanta MSA, GA	H	7.07 FQ	8.81 AW	11.05 TQ	GABLS	10/01-12/01
Restaurant	Augusta-Aiken MSA, GA-SC	H	5.80 FQ	7.28 AW	9.76 TQ	GABLS	10/01-12/01
Restaurant	Columbus MSA, GA-AL	H	5.83 FQ	7.34 AW	10.10 TQ	GABLS	10/01-12/01
Restaurant	Macon MSA, GA	H	5.72 FQ	6.80 AW	9.27 TQ	GABLS	10/01-12/01
Restaurant	Savannah MSA, GA	H	5.87 FQ	7.56 AW	10.27 TQ	GABLS	10/01-12/01
Restaurant	Hawaii	H	7.65 FQ	12.28 AW	17.54 TQ	HIBLS	10/01-12/01
Restaurant	Honolulu MSA, HI	H	7.24 FQ	11.62 AW	16.89 TQ	HIBLS	10/01-12/01
Restaurant	Idaho	H	6.48 FQ	8.80 AW	11.82 TQ	IDBLS	10/01-12/01
Restaurant	Boise City MSA, ID	H	6.40 FQ	9.02 AW	12.67 TQ	IDBLS	10/01-12/01
Restaurant	Illinois	H	6.11 FQ	8.91 AW	11.99 TQ	ILBLS	10/01-12/01
Restaurant	Champaign-Urbana MSA, IL	H	7.16 FQ	8.97 AW	11.21 TQ	ILBLS	10/01-12/01
Restaurant	Chicago PMSA, IL	H	6.22 FQ	9.21 AW	12.38 TQ	ILBLS	10/01-12/01
Restaurant	Peoria-Pekin MSA, IL	H	6.90 FQ	8.34 AW	10.37 TQ	ILBLS	10/01-12/01
Restaurant	Rockford MSA, IL	H	6.51 FQ	9.17 AW	13.57 TQ	ILBLS	10/01-12/01
Restaurant	Springfield MSA, IL	H	6.68 FQ	8.49 AW	10.74 TQ	ILBLS	10/01-12/01
Restaurant	Indiana	H	6.79 FQ	9.16 AW	11.97 TQ	INBLS	10/01-12/01
Restaurant	Elkhart-Goshen MSA, IN	H	7.14 FQ	8.95 AW	10.89 TQ	INBLS	10/01-12/01
Restaurant	Evansville-Henderson MSA, IN-KY	H	6.84 FQ	8.95 AW	11.44 TQ	INBLS	10/01-12/01
Restaurant	Fort Wayne MSA, IN	H	6.75 FQ	8.61 AW	10.80 TQ	INBLS	10/01-12/01
Restaurant	Gary PMSA, IN	H	6.52 FQ	8.81 AW	11.55 TQ	INBLS	10/01-12/01
Restaurant	Indianapolis MSA, IN	H	7.02 FQ	9.63 AW	12.46 TQ	INBLS	10/01-12/01
Restaurant	Lafayette MSA, IN	H	7.26 FQ	9.41 AW	11.54 TQ	INBLS	10/01-12/01
Restaurant	South Bend MSA, IN	H	7.01 FQ	9.40 AW	12.84 TQ	INBLS	10/01-12/01
Restaurant	Iowa	H	5.73 FQ	8.11 AW	11.15 TQ	IABLS	10/01-12/01
Restaurant	Cedar Rapids MSA, IA	H	6.06 FQ	8.67 AW	11.39 TQ	IABLS	10/01-12/01
Restaurant	Davenport-Moline-Rock Island MSA, IA-IL	H	5.85 FQ	7.60 AW	9.88 TQ	IABLS	10/01-12/01
Restaurant	Des Moines MSA, IA	H	6.99 FQ	9.70 AW	12.87 TQ	IABLS	10/01-12/01
Restaurant	Kansas	H	5.74 FQ	7.83 AW	10.80 TQ	KSBLS	10/01-12/01
Restaurant	Topeka MSA, KS	H	7.36 FQ	9.22 AW	12.19 TQ	KSBLS	10/01-12/01
Restaurant	Wichita MSA, KS	H	7.22 FQ	8.70 AW	10.99 TQ	KSBLS	10/01-12/01
Restaurant	Kentucky	H	5.97 FQ	8.66 AW	11.50 TQ	KYBLS	10/01-12/01
Restaurant	Lexington MSA, KY	H	7.16 FQ	9.18 AW	11.37 TQ	KYBLS	10/01-12/01
Restaurant	Louisville MSA, KY-IN	H	7.32 FQ	9.57 AW	12.15 TQ	KYBLS	10/01-12/01
Restaurant	Louisiana	H	5.90 FQ	8.53 AW	12.11 TQ	LABLS	10/01-12/01
Restaurant	Baton Rouge MSA, LA	H	5.77 FQ	7.66 AW	10.16 TQ	LABLS	10/01-12/01
Restaurant	Houma MSA, LA	H	5.90 FQ	8.17 AW	10.98 TQ	LABLS	10/01-12/01
Restaurant	Lafayette MSA, LA	H	5.77 FQ	7.09 AW	8.62 TQ	LABLS	10/01-12/01
Restaurant	Lake Charles MSA, LA	H	5.92 FQ	7.86 AW	10.03 TQ	LABLS	10/01-12/01
Restaurant	New Orleans MSA, LA	H	6.22 FQ	9.01 AW	12.93 TQ	LABLS	10/01-12/01
Restaurant	Shreveport-Bossier City MSA, LA	H	5.45 FQ	7.20 AW	10.20 TQ	LABLS	10/01-12/01
Restaurant	Maine	H	6.76 FQ	9.35 AW	12.66 TQ	MEBLS	10/01-12/01
Restaurant	Portland MSA, ME	H	6.97 FQ	9.91 AW	13.16 TQ	MEBLS	10/01-12/01
Restaurant	Maryland	H	5.60 FQ	8.52 AW	11.91 TQ	MDBLS	10/01-12/01
Restaurant	Baltimore PMSA, MD	H	5.45 FQ	7.82 AW	11.01 TQ	MDBLS	10/01-12/01
Restaurant	Massachusetts	H	8.23 FQ	11.04 AW	14.08 TQ	MABLS	10/01-12/01
Restaurant	Boston PMSA, MA-NH	H	8.22 FQ	11.11 AW	14.12 TQ	MABLS	10/01-12/01
Restaurant	Brockton PMSA, MA	H	8.81 FQ	10.79 AW	13.88 TQ	MABLS	10/01-12/01
Restaurant	Lawrence PMSA, MA-NH	H	7.87 FQ	10.71 AW	14.12 TQ	MABLS	10/01-12/01
Restaurant	Lowell PMSA, MA-NH	H	8.65 FQ	11.05 AW	13.81 TQ	MABLS	10/01-12/01
Restaurant	New Bedford PMSA, MA	H	8.49 FQ	12.06 AW	15.94 TQ	MABLS	10/01-12/01
Restaurant	Springfield MSA, MA	H	7.85 FQ	10.62 AW	13.87 TQ	MABLS	10/01-12/01
Restaurant	Worcester PMSA, MA-CT	H	8.28 FQ	11.55 AW	14.31 TQ	MABLS	10/01-12/01
Restaurant	Michigan	H	6.40 FQ	9.30 AW	13.05 TQ	MIBLS	10/01-12/01
Restaurant	Ann Arbor PMSA, MI	H	7.16 FQ	9.25 AW	11.99 TQ	MIBLS	10/01-12/01
Restaurant	Detroit PMSA, MI	H	6.75 FQ	10.49 AW	15.33 TQ	MIBLS	10/01-12/01
Restaurant	Flint PMSA, MI	H	6.73 FQ	9.03 AW	11.57 TQ	MIBLS	10/01-12/01
Restaurant	Grand Rapids-Muskegon-Holland MSA, MI	H	5.95 FQ	8.06 AW	10.55 TQ	MIBLS	10/01-12/01
Restaurant	Kalamazoo-Battle Creek MSA, MI	H	6.60 FQ	8.36 AW	10.78 TQ	MIBLS	10/01-12/01
Restaurant	Lansing-East Lansing MSA, MI	H	6.95 FQ	8.82 AW	10.97 TQ	MIBLS	10/01-12/01
Restaurant	Saginaw-Bay City-Midland MSA, MI	H	6.87 FQ	8.36 AW	10.67 TQ	MIBLS	10/01-12/01
Restaurant	Minnesota	H	6.82 FQ	9.62 AW	12.84 TQ	MNBLS	10/01-12/01
Restaurant	Duluth-Superior MSA, MN-WI	H	5.96 FQ	7.92 AW	10.50 TQ	MNBLS	10/01-12/01
Restaurant	Minneapolis-St. Paul MSA, MN-WI	H	7.16 FQ	10.04 AW	13.13 TQ	MNBLS	10/01-12/01

AAW	Average annual wage	**AOH**	Average offered, high	**ASH**	Average starting, high	**H**	Hourly	**M**	Monthly	**S**	Special: hourly and annual
AE	Average entry wage	**AOL**	Average offered, low	**ASL**	Average starting, low	**HI**	Highest wage paid	**MTC**	Median total compensation	**TQ**	Third quartile wage
AEX	Average experienced wage	**APH**	Average pay, high range	**AW**	Average wage paid	**HR**	High end range	**MW**	Median wage paid	**W**	Weekly
AO	Average offered	**APL**	Average pay, low range	**FQ**	First quartile wage	**LR**	Low end range	**SQ**	Second quartile wage	**Y**	Yearly

Occupation/Type/Industry	Location	Per	Low	Mid	High	Source	Date
Cook							
Restaurant	St. Cloud MSA, MN	H	6.12 FQ	8.26 AW	10.79 TQ	MNBLS	10/01-12/01
Restaurant	Mississippi	H	5.52 FQ	7.15 AW	9.67 TQ	MSBLS	10/01-12/01
Restaurant	Biloxi-Gulfport-Pascagoula MSA, MS	H	5.76 FQ	7.85 AW	11.12 TQ	MSBLS	10/01-12/01
Restaurant	Jackson MSA, MS	H	5.70 FQ	7.82 AW	10.64 TQ	MSBLS	10/01-12/01
Restaurant	Missouri	H	6.87 FQ	9.08 AW	11.93 TQ	MOBLS	10/01-12/01
Restaurant	Kansas City MSA, MO-KS	H	7.32 FQ	10.02 AW	13.23 TQ	MOBLS	10/01-12/01
Restaurant	St. Louis MSA, MO-IL	H	6.40 FQ	8.92 AW	11.83 TQ	MOBLS	10/01-12/01
Restaurant	Springfield MSA, MO	H	7.29 FQ	8.10 AW	9.09 TQ	MOBLS	10/01-12/01
Restaurant	Montana	H	6.13 FQ	8.19 AW	10.75 TQ	MTBLS	10/01-12/01
Restaurant	Billings MSA, MT	H	6.28 FQ	7.89 AW	10.11 TQ	MTBLS	10/01-12/01
Restaurant	Nebraska	H	5.93 FQ	8.41 AW	11.38 TQ	NEBLS	10/01-12/01
Restaurant	Lincoln MSA, NE	H	6.05 FQ	8.38 AW	11.21 TQ	NEBLS	10/01-12/01
Restaurant	Omaha MSA, NE-IA	H	7.42 FQ	9.81 AW	12.52 TQ	NEBLS	10/01-12/01
Restaurant	Nevada	H	7.79 FQ	11.66 AW	16.27 TQ	NVBLS	10/01-12/01
Restaurant	Las Vegas MSA, NV-AZ	H	7.93 FQ	12.13 AW	16.54 TQ	NVBLS	10/01-12/01
Restaurant	Reno MSA, NV	H	7.97 FQ	10.24 AW	13.08 TQ	NVBLS	10/01-12/01
Restaurant	New Hampshire	H	8.07 FQ	11.24 AW	14.44 TQ	NHBLS	10/01-12/01
Restaurant	Manchester PMSA, NH	H	8.59 FQ	11.63 AW	14.26 TQ	NHBLS	10/01-12/01
Restaurant	Nashua PMSA, NH	H	9.17 FQ	11.47 AW	13.94 TQ	NHBLS	10/01-12/01
Restaurant	Portsmouth-Rochester PMSA, NH-ME	H	7.77 FQ	10.09 AW	12.96 TQ	NHBLS	10/01-12/01
Restaurant	New Jersey	H	8.04 FQ	12.07 AW	17.35 TQ	NJBLS	10/01-12/01
Restaurant	Atlantic-Cape May PMSA, NJ	H	8.96 FQ	13.88 AW	18.29 TQ	NJBLS	10/01-12/01
Restaurant	Bergen-Passaic PMSA, NJ	H	8.65 FQ	11.86 AW	17.07 TQ	NJBLS	10/01-12/01
Restaurant	Jersey City PMSA, NJ	H	8.14 FQ	11.33 AW	15.11 TQ	NJBLS	10/01-12/01
Restaurant	Middlesex-Somerset-Hunterdon PMSA, NJ	H	8.43 FQ	11.11 AW	14.69 TQ	NJBLS	10/01-12/01
Restaurant	Monmouth-Ocean PMSA, NJ	H	8.89 FQ	11.06 AW	14.66 TQ	NJBLS	10/01-12/01
Restaurant	Newark PMSA, NJ	H	7.49 FQ	12.69 AW	18.02 TQ	NJBLS	10/01-12/01
Restaurant	Trenton PMSA, NJ	H	7.88 FQ	11.92 AW	18.78 TQ	NJBLS	10/01-12/01
Restaurant	New Mexico	H	5.83 FQ	7.97 AW	10.42 TQ	NMBLS	10/01-12/01
Restaurant	Albuquerque MSA, NM	H	7.01 FQ	8.37 AW	10.55 TQ	NMBLS	10/01-12/01
Restaurant	Las Cruces MSA, NM	H	5.72 FQ	7.18 AW	8.88 TQ	NMBLS	10/01-12/01
Restaurant	New York	H	7.07 FQ	11.52 AW	17.96 TQ	NYBLS	10/01-12/01
Restaurant	Albany-Schenectady-Troy MSA, NY	H	7.27 FQ	10.75 AW	14.38 TQ	NYBLS	10/01-12/01
Restaurant	Binghamton MSA, NY	H	7.28 FQ	10.19 AW	13.67 TQ	NYBLS	10/01-12/01
Restaurant	Buffalo-Niagara Falls MSA, NY	H	6.79 FQ	8.86 AW	10.89 TQ	NYBLS	10/01-12/01
Restaurant	Dutchess County PMSA, NY	H	7.69 FQ	11.75 AW	16.86 TQ	NYBLS	10/01-12/01
Restaurant	Nassau-Suffolk PMSA, NY	H	8.06 FQ	11.94 AW	16.61 TQ	NYBLS	10/01-12/01
Restaurant	New York PMSA, NY	H	7.49 FQ	12.87 AW	19.66 TQ	NYBLS	10/01-12/01
Restaurant	Newburgh PMSA, NY-PA	H	6.07 FQ	9.61 AW	14.21 TQ	NYBLS	10/01-12/01
Restaurant	Rochester MSA, NY	H	6.51 FQ	10.07 AW	14.64 TQ	NYBLS	10/01-12/01
Restaurant	Syracuse MSA, NY	H	7.04 FQ	9.72 AW	12.93 TQ	NYBLS	10/01-12/01
Restaurant	Utica-Rome MSA, NY	H	5.86 FQ	8.45 AW	11.54 TQ	NYBLS	10/01-12/01
Restaurant	North Carolina	H	6.06 FQ	8.80 AW	11.41 TQ	NCBLS	10/01-12/01
Restaurant	Asheville MSA, NC	H	7.15 FQ	8.91 AW	10.93 TQ	NCBLS	10/01-12/01
Restaurant	Charlotte-Gastonia-Rock Hill MSA, NC-SC	H	7.13 FQ	10.01 AW	12.41 TQ	NCBLS	10/01-12/01
Restaurant	Fayetteville MSA, NC	H	5.88 FQ	8.48 AW	11.27 TQ	NCBLS	10/01-12/01
Restaurant	Greensboro-Winston-Salem-High Point MSA, NC	H	7.23 FQ	9.84 AW	12.95 TQ	NCBLS	10/01-12/01
Restaurant	Hickory-Morganton-Lenoir MSA, NC	H	7.28 FQ	8.92 AW	11.17 TQ	NCBLS	10/01-12/01
Restaurant	Raleigh-Durham-Chapel Hill MSA, NC	H	7.28 FQ	9.25 AW	11.17 TQ	NCBLS	10/01-12/01
Restaurant	Wilmington MSA, NC	H	5.76 FQ	8.25 AW	11.42 TQ	NCBLS	10/01-12/01
Restaurant	North Dakota	H	6.27 FQ	8.13 AW	10.40 TQ	NDBLS	10/01-12/01
Restaurant	Fargo-Moorhead MSA, ND-MN	H	6.91 FQ	8.32 AW	10.51 TQ	NDBLS	10/01-12/01
Restaurant	Ohio	H	6.15 FQ	8.67 AW	11.47 TQ	OHBLS	10/01-12/01
Restaurant	Akron PMSA, OH	H	6.88 FQ	8.92 AW	11.82 TQ	OHBLS	10/01-12/01
Restaurant	Canton-Massillon MSA, OH	H	6.31 FQ	8.16 AW	10.41 TQ	OHBLS	10/01-12/01
Restaurant	Cincinnati PMSA, OH-KY-IN	H	6.45 FQ	9.20 AW	12.48 TQ	OHBLS	10/01-12/01
Restaurant	Cleveland-Lorain-Elyria PMSA, OH	H	6.88 FQ	9.02 AW	11.81 TQ	OHBLS	10/01-12/01
Restaurant	Columbus MSA, OH	H	7.04 FQ	9.19 AW	11.91 TQ	OHBLS	10/01-12/01
Restaurant	Dayton-Springfield MSA, OH	H	7.09 FQ	8.99 AW	11.26 TQ	OHBLS	10/01-12/01

AAW	Average annual wage	AOH	Average offered, high	ASH	Average starting, high	H	Hourly	M	Monthly	S	Special: hourly and annual
AE	Average entry wage	AOL	Average offered, low	ASL	Average starting, low	HI	Highest wage paid	MTC	Median total compensation	TQ	Third quartile wage
AEX	Average experienced wage	APH	Average pay, high range	AW	Average wage paid	HR	High end range	MW	Median wage paid	W	Weekly
AO	Average offered	APL	Average pay, low range	FQ	First quartile wage	LR	Low end range	SQ	Second quartile wage	Y	Yearly

Occupation/Type/Industry	Location	Per	Low	Mid	High	Source	Date
Cook							
Restaurant	Hamilton-Middletown PMSA, OH	H	7.05 FQ	9.17 AW	10.67 TQ	OHBLS	10/01-12/01
Restaurant	Mansfield MSA, OH	H	6.21 FQ	8.76 AW	11.32 TQ	OHBLS	10/01-12/01
Restaurant	Toledo MSA, OH	H	5.96 FQ	8.60 AW	11.59 TQ	OHBLS	10/01-12/01
Restaurant	Youngstown-Warren MSA, OH	H	5.89 FQ	7.98 AW	10.65 TQ	OHBLS	10/01-12/01
Restaurant	Oklahoma	H	5.79 FQ	7.53 AW	9.68 TQ	OKBLS	10/01-12/01
Restaurant	Oklahoma City MSA, OK	H	6.33 FQ	8.18 AW	10.40 TQ	OKBLS	10/01-12/01
Restaurant	Tulsa MSA, OK	H	5.76 FQ	7.40 AW	9.86 TQ	OKBLS	10/01-12/01
Restaurant	Oregon	H	7.23 FQ	9.40 AW	12.44 TQ	ORBLS	10/01-12/01
Restaurant	Eugene-Springfield MSA, OR	H	7.42 FQ	9.00 AW	11.12 TQ	ORBLS	10/01-12/01
Restaurant	Medford-Ashland MSA, OR	H	7.59 FQ	9.70 AW	12.38 TQ	ORBLS	10/01-12/01
Restaurant	Portland-Vancouver PMSA, OR-WA	H	7.32 FQ	9.54 AW	12.24 TQ	ORBLS	10/01-12/01
Restaurant	Salem PMSA, OR	H	7.23 FQ	10.11 AW	14.46 TQ	ORBLS	10/01-12/01
Restaurant	Pennsylvania	H	5.91 FQ	8.55 AW	11.59 TQ	PABLS	10/01-12/01
Restaurant	Allentown-Bethlehem-Easton MSA, PA	H	6.62 FQ	8.80 AW	11.00 TQ	PABLS	10/01-12/01
Restaurant	Erie MSA, PA	H	5.89 FQ	8.07 AW	10.48 TQ	PABLS	10/01-12/01
Restaurant	Harrisburg-Lebanon-Carlisle MSA, PA	H	6.52 FQ	9.57 AW	13.02 TQ	PABLS	10/01-12/01
Restaurant	Johnstown MSA, PA	H	5.55 FQ	6.58 AW	8.37 TQ	PABLS	10/01-12/01
Restaurant	Lancaster MSA, PA	H	6.42 FQ	8.47 AW	10.86 TQ	PABLS	10/01-12/01
Restaurant	Philadelphia PMSA, PA-NJ	H	5.83 FQ	9.17 AW	13.40 TQ	PABLS	10/01-12/01
Restaurant	Pittsburgh MSA, PA	H	6.53 FQ	8.74 AW	11.02 TQ	PABLS	10/01-12/01
Restaurant	Reading MSA, PA	H	7.37 FQ	9.62 AW	11.75 TQ	PABLS	10/01-12/01
Restaurant	Scranton-Wilkes-Barre-Hazleton MSA, PA	H	6.28 FQ	8.99 AW	12.41 TQ	PABLS	10/01-12/01
Restaurant	York MSA, PA	H	7.11 FQ	8.94 AW	11.01 TQ	PABLS	10/01-12/01
Restaurant	Rhode Island	H	7.52 FQ	10.11 AW	13.21 TQ	RIBLS	10/01-12/01
Restaurant	Providence-Fall River-Warwick MSA, RI-MA	H	7.43 FQ	9.84 AW	12.90 TQ	RIBLS	10/01-12/01
Restaurant	South Carolina	H	6.01 FQ	8.63 AW	10.85 TQ	SCBLS	10/01-12/01
Restaurant	Charleston-North Charleston MSA, SC	H	6.97 FQ	8.82 AW	10.67 TQ	SCBLS	10/01-12/01
Restaurant	Columbia MSA, SC	H	5.84 FQ	8.53 AW	11.04 TQ	SCBLS	10/01-12/01
Restaurant	Greenville-Spartanburg-Anderson MSA, SC	H	6.20 FQ	8.40 AW	10.59 TQ	SCBLS	10/01-12/01
Restaurant	Myrtle Beach MSA, SC	H	7.32 FQ	8.89 AW	10.64 TQ	SCBLS	10/01-12/01
Restaurant	South Dakota	H	6.78 FQ	8.23 AW	10.43 TQ	SDBLS	10/01-12/01
Restaurant	Sioux Falls MSA, SD	H	6.35 FQ	8.61 AW	10.97 TQ	SDBLS	10/01-12/01
Restaurant	Tennessee	H	5.96 FQ	8.76 AW	11.71 TQ	TNBLS	10/01-12/01
Restaurant	Chattanooga MSA, TN-GA	H	6.30 FQ	8.98 AW	11.66 TQ	TNBLS	10/01-12/01
Restaurant	Clarksville-Hopkinsville MSA, TN-KY	H	6.29 FQ	8.38 AW	10.78 TQ	TNBLS	10/01-12/01
Restaurant	Johnson City-Kingsport-Bristol MSA, TN-VA	H	5.56 FQ	7.25 AW	10.34 TQ	TNBLS	10/01-12/01
Restaurant	Knoxville MSA, TN	H	7.39 FQ	9.43 AW	12.00 TQ	TNBLS	10/01-12/01
Restaurant	Memphis MSA, TN-AR-MS	H	6.02 FQ	8.82 AW	12.41 TQ	TNBLS	10/01-12/01
Restaurant	Nashville MSA, TN	H	7.57 FQ	9.76 AW	12.05 TQ	TNBLS	10/01-12/01
Restaurant	Texas	H	5.82 FQ	8.00 AW	10.66 TQ	TXBLS	10/01-12/01
Restaurant	Amarillo MSA, TX	H	7.15 FQ	8.56 AW	10.74 TQ	TXBLS	10/01-12/01
Restaurant	Austin-San Marcos MSA, TX	H	6.02 FQ	8.56 AW	11.53 TQ	TXBLS	10/01-12/01
Restaurant	Beaumont-Port Arthur MSA, TX	H	5.96 FQ	7.94 AW	10.25 TQ	TXBLS	10/01-12/01
Restaurant	Brazoria PMSA, TX	H	5.64 FQ	7.64 AW	11.06 TQ	TXBLS	10/01-12/01
Restaurant	Brownsville-Harlingen-San Benito MSA, TX	H	6.84 FQ	8.24 AW	10.31 TQ	TXBLS	10/01-12/01
Restaurant	Corpus Christi MSA, TX	H	5.71 FQ	6.98 AW	8.80 TQ	TXBLS	10/01-12/01
Restaurant	Dallas PMSA, TX	H	6.41 FQ	8.53 AW	11.15 TQ	TXBLS	10/01-12/01
Restaurant	El Paso MSA, TX	H	5.61 FQ	7.03 AW	9.07 TQ	TXBLS	10/01-12/01
Restaurant	Fort Worth-Arlington PMSA, TX	H	6.09 FQ	8.14 AW	10.62 TQ	TXBLS	10/01-12/01
Restaurant	Galveston-Texas City PMSA, TX	H	5.72 FQ	7.52 AW	10.27 TQ	TXBLS	10/01-12/01
Restaurant	Houston PMSA, TX	H	5.70 FQ	8.26 AW	10.96 TQ	TXBLS	10/01-12/01
Restaurant	Killeen-Temple MSA, TX	H	5.63 FQ	7.45 AW	9.53 TQ	TXBLS	10/01-12/01
Restaurant	Laredo MSA, TX	H	5.55 FQ	6.93 AW	8.62 TQ	TXBLS	10/01-12/01
Restaurant	Longview-Marshall MSA, TX	H	5.87 FQ	7.60 AW	10.11 TQ	TXBLS	10/01-12/01
Restaurant	Lubbock MSA, TX	H	6.08 FQ	7.80 AW	9.84 TQ	TXBLS	10/01-12/01
Restaurant	McAllen-Edinburg-Mission MSA, TX	H	5.57 FQ	7.09 AW	9.02 TQ	TXBLS	10/01-12/01

AAW Average annual wage; **AE** Average entry wage; **AEX** Average experienced wage; **AO** Average offered; **AOH** Average offered, high; **AOL** Average offered, low; **APH** Average pay, high range; **APL** Average pay, low range; **ASH** Average starting, high; **ASL** Average starting, low; **AW** Average wage paid; **FQ** First quartile wage; **H** Hourly; **HI** Highest wage paid; **HR** High end range; **LR** Low end range; **M** Monthly; **MTC** Median total compensation; **MW** Median wage paid; **SQ** Second quartile wage; **S** Special: hourly and annual; **TQ** Third quartile wage; **W** Weekly; **Y** Yearly

Occupation/Type/Industry	Location	Per	Low	Mid	High	Source	Date
Cook							
Restaurant	Odessa-Midland MSA, TX	H	6.28 FQ	7.85 AW	9.50 TQ	TXBLS	10/01-12/01
Restaurant	San Antonio MSA, TX	H	6.37 FQ	8.26 AW	10.73 TQ	TXBLS	10/01-12/01
Restaurant	Tyler MSA, TX	H	5.83 FQ	7.54 AW	9.38 TQ	TXBLS	10/01-12/01
Restaurant	Waco MSA, TX	H	6.70 FQ	8.11 AW	10.15 TQ	TXBLS	10/01-12/01
Restaurant	Utah	H	7.17 FQ	9.18 AW	11.11 TQ	UTBLS	10/01-12/01
Restaurant	Provo-Orem MSA, UT	H	7.27 FQ	9.07 AW	10.72 TQ	UTBLS	10/01-12/01
Restaurant	Salt Lake City-Ogden MSA, UT	H	7.38 FQ	9.42 AW	11.24 TQ	UTBLS	10/01-12/01
Restaurant	Vermont	H	7.49 FQ	10.68 AW	14.32 TQ	VTBLS	10/01-12/01
Restaurant	Burlington MSA, VT	H	6.65 FQ	9.91 AW	13.27 TQ	VTBLS	10/01-12/01
Restaurant	Virginia	H	5.90 FQ	8.73 AW	12.12 TQ	VABLS	10/01-12/01
Restaurant	Lynchburg MSA, VA	H	6.19 FQ	8.96 AW	12.08 TQ	VABLS	10/01-12/01
Restaurant	Norfolk-Virginia Beach-Newport News MSA, VA-NC	H	5.76 FQ	8.06 AW	10.86 TQ	VABLS	10/01-12/01
Restaurant	Richmond-Petersburg MSA, VA	H	7.23 FQ	9.60 AW	12.18 TQ	VABLS	10/01-12/01
Restaurant	Roanoke MSA, VA	H	6.35 FQ	8.96 AW	12.37 TQ	VABLS	10/01-12/01
Restaurant	Washington	H	7.72 FQ	10.12 AW	13.08 TQ	WABLS	10/01-12/01
Restaurant	Bremerton PMSA, WA	H	7.50 FQ	9.30 AW	11.41 TQ	WABLS	10/01-12/01
Restaurant	Olympia PMSA, WA	H	7.06 FQ	9.40 AW	11.87 TQ	WABLS	10/01-12/01
Restaurant	Richland-Kennewick-Pasco MSA, WA	H	7.47 FQ	9.57 AW	11.17 TQ	WABLS	10/01-12/01
Restaurant	Seattle-Bellevue-Everett PMSA, WA	H	8.81 FQ	10.95 AW	13.54 TQ	WABLS	10/01-12/01
Restaurant	Spokane MSA, WA	H	7.32 FQ	8.74 AW	10.62 TQ	WABLS	10/01-12/01
Restaurant	Tacoma PMSA, WA	H	7.58 FQ	10.08 AW	13.62 TQ	WABLS	10/01-12/01
Restaurant	Yakima MSA, WA	H	7.02 FQ	8.77 AW	10.79 TQ	WABLS	10/01-12/01
Restaurant	West Virginia	H	5.77 FQ	7.69 AW	10.48 TQ	WVBLS	10/01-12/01
Restaurant	Charleston MSA, WV	H	5.88 FQ	8.03 AW	10.60 TQ	WVBLS	10/01-12/01
Restaurant	Huntington-Ashland MSA, WV-KY-OH	H	5.71 FQ	7.96 AW	11.28 TQ	WVBLS	10/01-12/01
Restaurant	Wisconsin	H	6.45 FQ	9.10 AW	12.19 TQ	WIBLS	10/01-12/01
Restaurant	Appleton-Oshkosh-Neenah MSA, WI	H	7.48 FQ	9.50 AW	12.00 TQ	WIBLS	10/01-12/01
Restaurant	Green Bay MSA, WI	H	7.71 FQ	9.98 AW	13.23 TQ	WIBLS	10/01-12/01
Restaurant	Madison MSA, WI	H	7.83 FQ	9.76 AW	11.24 TQ	WIBLS	10/01-12/01
Restaurant	Milwaukee-Waukesha PMSA, WI	H	7.16 FQ	9.58 AW	13.53 TQ	WIBLS	10/01-12/01
Restaurant	Racine PMSA, WI	H	6.45 FQ	9.20 AW	11.44 TQ	WIBLS	10/01-12/01
Restaurant	Wyoming	H	5.97 FQ	8.60 AW	12.58 TQ	WYBLS	10/01-12/01
Restaurant	Cheyenne MSA, WY	H	6.00 FQ	7.61 AW	9.08 TQ	WYBLS	10/01-12/01
Restaurant	Puerto Rico	H	5.43 FQ	6.80 AW	8.92 TQ	PRBLS	10/01-12/01
Restaurant	Virgin Islands	H	7.61 FQ	9.82 AW	12.63 TQ	VIBLS	10/01-12/01
Restaurant	Guam	H	5.84 FQ	7.68 AW	10.00 TQ	GUBLS	10/01-12/01
Short Order	Alabama	H	5.60 FQ	6.95 AW	8.45 TQ	ALBLS	10/01-12/01
Short Order	Birmingham MSA, AL	H	6.87 FQ	7.62 AW	8.43 TQ	ALBLS	10/01-12/01
Short Order	Huntsville MSA, AL	H	6.65 FQ	7.62 AW	8.75 TQ	ALBLS	10/01-12/01
Short Order	Mobile MSA, AL	H	5.60 FQ	7.06 AW	8.70 TQ	ALBLS	10/01-12/01
Short Order	Montgomery MSA, AL	H	5.63 FQ	6.79 AW	8.46 TQ	ALBLS	10/01-12/01
Short Order	Alaska	H	7.61 FQ	11.38 AW	16.67 TQ	AKBLS	10/01-12/01
Short Order	Anchorage MSA, AK	H	7.60 FQ	11.53 AW	16.84 TQ	AKBLS	10/01-12/01
Short Order	Arizona	H	6.17 FQ	7.83 AW	9.97 TQ	AZBLS	10/01-12/01
Short Order	Phoenix-Mesa MSA, AZ	H	6.77 FQ	7.88 AW	9.56 TQ	AZBLS	10/01-12/01
Short Order	Tucson MSA, AZ	H	5.95 FQ	7.85 AW	10.50 TQ	AZBLS	10/01-12/01
Short Order	Arkansas	H	5.90 FQ	7.24 AW	8.43 TQ	ARBLS	10/01-12/01
Short Order	Fayetteville-Springdale-Rogers MSA, AR	H	6.92 FQ	7.59 AW	8.36 TQ	ARBLS	10/01-12/01
Short Order	Fort Smith MSA, AR-OK	H	5.69 FQ	7.09 AW	8.45 TQ	ARBLS	10/01-12/01
Short Order	Little Rock-North Little Rock MSA, AR	H	6.21 FQ	8.01 AW	10.28 TQ	ARBLS	10/01-12/01
Short Order	California	H	6.38 FQ	8.17 AW	10.59 TQ	CABLS	10/01-12/01
Short Order	Bakersfield MSA, CA	H	6.78 FQ	7.88 AW	9.75 TQ	CABLS	10/01-12/01
Short Order	Chico-Paradise MSA, CA	H	6.83 FQ	8.21 AW	10.37 TQ	CABLS	10/01-12/01
Short Order	Fresno MSA, CA	H	6.67 FQ	8.48 AW	10.98 TQ	CABLS	10/01-12/01
Short Order	Los Angeles-Long Beach PMSA, CA	H	6.97 FQ	9.67 AW	13.25 TQ	CABLS	10/01-12/01
Short Order	Merced MSA, CA	H	6.70 FQ	8.77 AW	11.88 TQ	CABLS	10/01-12/01
Short Order	Oakland PMSA, CA	H	7.01 FQ	8.54 AW	10.43 TQ	CABLS	10/01-12/01
Short Order	Orange County PMSA, CA	H	6.51 FQ	8.58 AW	11.33 TQ	CABLS	10/01-12/01
Short Order	Redding MSA, CA	H	6.51 FQ	7.87 AW	9.98 TQ	CABLS	10/01-12/01

AAW Average annual wage	**AOH** Average offered, high	**ASH** Average starting, high	**H** Hourly	**M** Monthly	**S** Special: hourly and annual
AE Average entry wage	**AOL** Average offered, low	**ASL** Average starting, low	**HI** Highest wage paid	**MTC** Median total compensation	**TQ** Third quartile wage
AEX Average experienced wage	**APH** Average pay, high range	**AW** Average wage paid	**HR** High end range	**MW** Median wage paid	**W** Weekly
AO Average offered	**APL** Average pay, low range	**FQ** First quartile wage	**LR** Low end range	**SQ** Second quartile wage	**Y** Yearly

Occupation/Type/Industry	Location	Per	Low	Mid	High	Source	Date
Cook							
Short Order	Riverside-San Bernardino PMSA, CA	H	6.58 FQ	9.29 AW	12.42 TQ	CABLS	10/01-12/01
Short Order	Sacramento PMSA, CA	H	6.99 FQ	8.54 AW	11.56 TQ	CABLS	10/01-12/01
Short Order	Salinas MSA, CA	H	6.74 FQ	10.07 AW	13.64 TQ	CABLS	10/01-12/01
Short Order	San Diego MSA, CA	H	6.30 FQ	6.76 AW	6.74 TQ	CABLS	10/01-12/01
Short Order	San Francisco PMSA, CA	H	6.56 FQ	9.01 AW	10.59 TQ	CABLS	10/01-12/01
Short Order	San Jose PMSA, CA	H	6.38 FQ	8.11 AW	10.56 TQ	CABLS	10/01-12/01
Short Order	San Luis Obispo-Atascadero-Paso Robles MSA, CA	H	7.40 FQ	8.61 AW	10.65 TQ	CABLS	10/01-12/01
Short Order	Santa Barbara-Santa Maria-Lompoc MSA, CA	H	6.98 FQ	10.16 AW	13.32 TQ	CABLS	10/01-12/01
Short Order	Santa Cruz-Watsonville PMSA, CA	H	8.58 FQ	9.60 AW	10.74 TQ	CABLS	10/01-12/01
Short Order	Santa Rosa PMSA, CA	H	6.64 FQ	10.58 AW	19.07 TQ	CABLS	10/01-12/01
Short Order	Stockton-Lodi MSA, CA	H	7.38 FQ	9.18 AW	10.74 TQ	CABLS	10/01-12/01
Short Order	Vallejo-Fairfield-Napa PMSA, CA	H	7.34 FQ	9.78 AW	13.26 TQ	CABLS	10/01-12/01
Short Order	Ventura PMSA, CA	H	6.87 FQ	8.71 AW	12.25 TQ	CABLS	10/01-12/01
Short Order	Visalia-Tulare-Porterville MSA, CA	H	6.38 FQ	7.64 AW	10.03 TQ	CABLS	10/01-12/01
Short Order	Colorado	H	6.43 FQ	8.58 AW	10.57 TQ	COBLS	10/01-12/01
Short Order	Colorado Springs MSA, CO	H	6.90 FQ	8.14 AW	10.25 TQ	COBLS	10/01-12/01
Short Order	Denver PMSA, CO	H	7.64 FQ	9.26 AW	10.61 TQ	COBLS	10/01-12/01
Short Order	Fort Collins-Loveland MSA, CO	H	5.80 FQ	7.80 AW	10.12 TQ	COBLS	10/01-12/01
Short Order	Greeley PMSA, CO	H	6.62 FQ	9.03 AW	11.38 TQ	COBLS	10/01-12/01
Short Order	Connecticut	H	7.39 FQ	10.67 AW	16.53 TQ	CTBLS	10/01-12/01
Short Order	Bridgeport PMSA, CT	H	7.46 FQ	9.45 AW	12.73 TQ	CTBLS	10/01-12/01
Short Order	Danbury PMSA, CT	H	7.88 FQ	10.10 AW	12.99 TQ	CTBLS	10/01-12/01
Short Order	Hartford MSA, CT	H	7.11 FQ	9.66 AW	12.95 TQ	CTBLS	10/01-12/01
Short Order	New Haven-Meriden PMSA, CT	H	7.22 FQ	9.41 AW	13.01 TQ	CTBLS	10/01-12/01
Short Order	New London-Norwich MSA, CT-RI	H	7.35 FQ	9.89 AW	13.77 TQ	CTBLS	10/01-12/01
Short Order	Stamford-Norwalk PMSA, CT	H	9.68 FQ	14.99 AW	20.60 TQ	CTBLS	10/01-12/01
Short Order	Waterbury PMSA, CT	H	7.72 FQ	10.12 AW	13.10 TQ	CTBLS	10/01-12/01
Short Order	Delaware	H	6.62 FQ	9.30 AW	12.60 TQ	DEBLS	10/01-12/01
Short Order	Wilmington-Newark PMSA, DE-MD	H	7.21 FQ	9.93 AW	12.97 TQ	DEBLS	10/01-12/01
Short Order	District of Columbia	H	7.88 FQ	11.82 AW	20.50 TQ	DCBLS	10/01-12/01
Short Order	Washington PMSA, DC-MD-VA-WV	H	5.91 FQ	9.46 AW	13.36 TQ	DCBLS	10/01-12/01
Short Order	Florida	H	5.55 FQ	7.75 AW	11.08 TQ	FLBLS	10/01-12/01
Short Order	Daytona Beach MSA, FL	H	5.88 FQ	7.21 AW	8.84 TQ	FLBLS	10/01-12/01
Short Order	Fort Lauderdale PMSA, FL	H	6.72 FQ	9.74 AW	12.87 TQ	FLBLS	10/01-12/01
Short Order	Fort Myers-Cape Coral MSA, FL	H	8.61 FQ	9.49 AW	10.64 TQ	FLBLS	10/01-12/01
Short Order	Fort Pierce-Port St. Lucie MSA, FL	H	5.62 FQ	7.05 AW	9.59 TQ	FLBLS	10/01-12/01
Short Order	Fort Walton Beach MSA, FL	H	6.30 FQ	8.91 AW	10.93 TQ	FLBLS	10/01-12/01
Short Order	Gainesville MSA, FL	H	7.33 FQ	9.14 AW	11.00 TQ	FLBLS	10/01-12/01
Short Order	Jacksonville MSA, FL	H	7.00 FQ	9.55 AW	12.50 TQ	FLBLS	10/01-12/01
Short Order	Lakeland-Winter Haven MSA, FL	H	5.60 FQ	7.10 AW	8.56 TQ	FLBLS	10/01-12/01
Short Order	Melbourne-Titusville-Palm Bay MSA, FL	H	7.65 FQ	9.43 AW	10.91 TQ	FLBLS	10/01-12/01
Short Order	Miami PMSA, FL	H	6.04 FQ	8.71 AW	12.71 TQ	FLBLS	10/01-12/01
Short Order	Naples MSA, FL	H	5.87 FQ	8.46 AW	11.49 TQ	FLBLS	10/01-12/01
Short Order	Ocala MSA, FL	H	5.72 FQ	6.98 AW	8.70 TQ	FLBLS	10/01-12/01
Short Order	Orlando MSA, FL	H	5.87 FQ	8.87 AW	13.40 TQ	FLBLS	10/01-12/01
Short Order	Pensacola MSA, FL	H	5.70 FQ	7.20 AW	9.57 TQ	FLBLS	10/01-12/01
Short Order	Sarasota-Bradenton MSA, FL	H	7.40 FQ	9.40 AW	11.12 TQ	FLBLS	10/01-12/01
Short Order	Tallahassee MSA, FL	H	5.96 FQ	7.87 AW	10.41 TQ	FLBLS	10/01-12/01
Short Order	Tampa-St. Petersburg-Clearwater MSA, FL	H	5.36 FQ	6.45 AW	8.53 TQ	FLBLS	10/01-12/01
Short Order	West Palm Beach-Boca Raton MSA, FL	H	6.69 FQ	10.26 AW	14.49 TQ	FLBLS	10/01-12/01
Short Order	Georgia	H	6.11 FQ	8.45 AW	11.69 TQ	GABLS	10/01-12/01
Short Order	Atlanta MSA, GA	H	7.14 FQ	9.47 AW	12.63 TQ	GABLS	10/01-12/01
Short Order	Augusta-Aiken MSA, GA-SC	H	5.73 FQ	7.21 AW	9.06 TQ	GABLS	10/01-12/01
Short Order	Columbus MSA, GA-AL	H	6.11 FQ	7.34 AW	8.42 TQ	GABLS	10/01-12/01

AAW Average annual wage **AOH** Average offered, high **ASH** Average starting, high **H** Hourly **M** Monthly **S** Special: hourly and annual
AE Average entry wage **AOL** Average offered, low **ASL** Average starting, low **HI** Highest wage paid **MTC** Median total compensation **TQ** Third quartile wage
AEX Average experienced wage **APH** Average pay, high range **AW** Average wage paid **HR** High end range **MW** Median wage paid **W** Weekly
AO Average offered **APL** Average pay, low range **FQ** First quartile wage **LR** Low end range **SQ** Second quartile wage **Y** Yearly

Occupation/Type/Industry	Location	Per	Low	Mid	High	Source	Date
Cook							
Short Order	Macon MSA, GA	H	5.78 FQ	7.60 AW	9.73 TQ	GABLS	10/01-12/01
Short Order	Savannah MSA, GA	H	5.97 FQ	7.79 AW	9.80 TQ	GABLS	10/01-12/01
Short Order	Hawaii	H	7.69 FQ	10.48 AW	14.98 TQ	HIBLS	10/01-12/01
Short Order	Honolulu MSA, HI	H	9.10 FQ	11.27 AW	15.78 TQ	HIBLS	10/01-12/01
Short Order	Idaho	H	5.60 FQ	7.41 AW	10.14 TQ	IDBLS	10/01-12/01
Short Order	Boise City MSA, ID	H	5.54 FQ	6.40 AW	7.53 TQ	IDBLS	10/01-12/01
Short Order	Illinois	H	5.75 FQ	7.90 AW	10.78 TQ	ILBLS	10/01-12/01
Short Order	Champaign-Urbana MSA, IL	H	5.79 FQ	6.96 AW	8.56 TQ	ILBLS	10/01-12/01
Short Order	Chicago PMSA, IL	H	6.33 FQ	9.02 AW	11.59 TQ	ILBLS	10/01-12/01
Short Order	Peoria-Pekin MSA, IL	H	5.75 FQ	7.26 AW	10.09 TQ	ILBLS	10/01-12/01
Short Order	Rockford MSA, IL	H	6.53 FQ	8.44 AW	10.69 TQ	ILBLS	10/01-12/01
Short Order	Springfield MSA, IL	H	7.06 FQ	7.93 AW	8.86 TQ	ILBLS	10/01-12/01
Short Order	Indiana	H	5.59 FQ	7.54 AW	11.00 TQ	INBLS	10/01-12/01
Short Order	Elkhart-Goshen MSA, IN	H	5.79 FQ	8.89 AW	16.40 TQ	INBLS	10/01-12/01
Short Order	Evansville-Henderson MSA, IN-KY	H	5.49 FQ	7.49 AW	11.85 TQ	INBLS	10/01-12/01
Short Order	Fort Wayne MSA, IN	H	5.52 FQ	7.40 AW	10.34 TQ	INBLS	10/01-12/01
Short Order	Gary PMSA, IN	H	6.10 FQ	8.31 AW	11.06 TQ	INBLS	10/01-12/01
Short Order	Indianapolis MSA, IN	H	5.68 FQ	8.22 AW	12.48 TQ	INBLS	10/01-12/01
Short Order	Lafayette MSA, IN	H	5.73 FQ	7.48 AW	9.83 TQ	INBLS	10/01-12/01
Short Order	South Bend MSA, IN	H	5.60 FQ	6.88 AW	8.44 TQ	INBLS	10/01-12/01
Short Order	Iowa	H	5.77 FQ	7.69 AW	10.29 TQ	IABLS	10/01-12/01
Short Order	Cedar Rapids MSA, IA	H	5.72 FQ	6.94 AW	9.41 TQ	IABLS	10/01-12/01
Short Order	Davenport-Moline-Rock Island MSA, IA-IL	H	5.66 FQ	7.18 AW	9.37 TQ	IABLS	10/01-12/01
Short Order	Des Moines MSA, IA	H	7.11 FQ	9.22 AW	10.89 TQ	IABLS	10/01-12/01
Short Order	Kansas	H	5.65 FQ	7.33 AW	10.28 TQ	KSBLS	10/01-12/01
Short Order	Wichita MSA, KS	H	5.73 FQ	7.10 AW	9.56 TQ	KSBLS	10/01-12/01
Short Order	Kentucky	H	5.56 FQ	7.01 AW	8.90 TQ	KYBLS	10/01-12/01
Short Order	Lexington MSA, KY	H	6.38 FQ	8.06 AW	10.17 TQ	KYBLS	10/01-12/01
Short Order	Louisville MSA, KY-IN	H	5.65 FQ	7.00 AW	9.54 TQ	KYBLS	10/01-12/01
Short Order	Louisiana	H	5.52 FQ	6.73 AW	8.61 TQ	LABLS	10/01-12/01
Short Order	Baton Rouge MSA, LA	H	5.53 FQ	6.59 AW	8.27 TQ	LABLS	10/01-12/01
Short Order	Houma MSA, LA	H	5.52 FQ	6.43 AW	8.04 TQ	LABLS	10/01-12/01
Short Order	Lafayette MSA, LA	H	5.43 FQ	7.01 AW	11.09 TQ	LABLS	10/01-12/01
Short Order	Lake Charles MSA, LA	H	5.54 FQ	6.55 AW	8.12 TQ	LABLS	10/01-12/01
Short Order	New Orleans MSA, LA	H	5.63 FQ	7.49 AW	9.90 TQ	LABLS	10/01-12/01
Short Order	Shreveport-Bossier City MSA, LA	H	5.62 FQ	6.70 AW	8.33 TQ	LABLS	10/01-12/01
Short Order	Maine	H	6.05 FQ	8.74 AW	12.01 TQ	MEBLS	10/01-12/01
Short Order	Portland MSA, ME	H	7.31 FQ	9.30 AW	12.34 TQ	MEBLS	10/01-12/01
Short Order	Maryland	H	5.75 FQ	8.37 AW	12.38 TQ	MDBLS	10/01-12/01
Short Order	Baltimore PMSA, MD	H	5.97 FQ	8.76 AW	12.74 TQ	MDBLS	10/01-12/01
Short Order	Massachusetts	H	7.19 FQ	10.14 AW	13.68 TQ	MABLS	10/01-12/01
Short Order	Boston PMSA, MA-NH	H	8.60 FQ	11.14 AW	14.32 TQ	MABLS	10/01-12/01
Short Order	Brockton PMSA, MA	H	7.25 FQ	10.59 AW	13.56 TQ	MABLS	10/01-12/01
Short Order	Lawrence PMSA, MA-NH	H	6.77 FQ	8.28 AW	10.60 TQ	MABLS	10/01-12/01
Short Order	Lowell PMSA, MA-NH	H	8.03 FQ	10.44 AW	13.51 TQ	MABLS	10/01-12/01
Short Order	New Bedford PMSA, MA	H	7.49 FQ	9.74 AW	12.91 TQ	MABLS	10/01-12/01
Short Order	Springfield MSA, MA	H	7.44 FQ	9.73 AW	13.19 TQ	MABLS	10/01-12/01
Short Order	Worcester PMSA, MA-CT	H	6.86 FQ	9.54 AW	13.55 TQ	MABLS	10/01-12/01
Short Order	Michigan	H	5.99 FQ	8.42 AW	10.76 TQ	MIBLS	10/01-12/01
Short Order	Ann Arbor PMSA, MI	H	6.14 FQ	9.19 AW	11.91 TQ	MIBLS	10/01-12/01
Short Order	Detroit PMSA, MI	H	7.08 FQ	9.37 AW	11.60 TQ	MIBLS	10/01-12/01
Short Order	Flint PMSA, MI	H	5.63 FQ	8.56 AW	13.04 TQ	MIBLS	10/01-12/01
Short Order	Grand Rapids-Muskegon-Holland MSA, MI	H	6.00 FQ	8.42 AW	11.02 TQ	MIBLS	10/01-12/01
Short Order	Kalamazoo-Battle Creek MSA, MI	H	5.88 FQ	7.42 AW	8.83 TQ	MIBLS	10/01-12/01
Short Order	Lansing-East Lansing MSA, MI	H	6.00 FQ	7.94 AW	10.24 TQ	MIBLS	10/01-12/01
Short Order	Saginaw-Bay City-Midland MSA, MI	H	5.41 FQ	6.59 AW	8.19 TQ	MIBLS	10/01-12/01
Short Order	Minnesota	H	5.71 FQ	8.27 AW	11.77 TQ	MNBLS	10/01-12/01
Short Order	Duluth-Superior MSA, MN-WI	H	5.99 FQ	8.24 AW	10.58 TQ	MNBLS	10/01-12/01
Short Order	Minneapolis-St. Paul MSA, MN-WI	H	5.81 FQ	8.54 AW	12.25 TQ	MNBLS	10/01-12/01
Short Order	St. Cloud MSA, MN	H	5.66 FQ	7.38 AW	9.96 TQ	MNBLS	10/01-12/01
Short Order	Mississippi	H	5.61 FQ	6.84 AW	8.98 TQ	MSBLS	10/01-12/01
Short Order	Jackson MSA, MS	H	5.67 FQ	6.97 AW	8.80 TQ	MSBLS	10/01-12/01
Short Order	Missouri	H	5.78 FQ	7.96 AW	10.74 TQ	MOBLS	10/01-12/01
Short Order	Kansas City MSA, MO-KS	H	5.81 FQ	8.05 AW	11.07 TQ	MOBLS	10/01-12/01

AAW	Average annual wage	**AOH**	Average offered, high	**ASH**	Average starting, high	**H**	Hourly	**M**	Monthly	**S**	Special: hourly and annual
AE	Average entry wage	**AOL**	Average offered, low	**ASL**	Average starting, low	**HI**	Highest wage paid	**MTC**	Median total compensation	**TQ**	Third quartile wage
AEX	Average experienced wage	**APH**	Average pay, high range	**AW**	Average wage paid	**HR**	High end range	**MW**	Median wage paid	**W**	Weekly
AO	Average offered	**APL**	Average pay, low range	**FQ**	First quartile wage	**LR**	Low end range	**SQ**	Second quartile wage	**Y**	Yearly

Occupation/Type/Industry	Location	Per	Low	Mid	High	Source	Date
Cook							
Short Order	St. Louis MSA, MO-IL	H	5.87 FQ	8.34 AW	10.96 TQ	MOBLS	10/01-12/01
Short Order	Springfield MSA, MO	H	5.85 FQ	7.99 AW	10.77 TQ	MOBLS	10/01-12/01
Short Order	Montana	H	6.04 FQ	8.46 AW	10.42 TQ	MTBLS	10/01-12/01
Short Order	Billings MSA, MT	H	5.99 FQ	7.41 AW	8.80 TQ	MTBLS	10/01-12/01
Short Order	Nebraska	H	5.66 FQ	7.50 AW	10.38 TQ	NEBLS	10/01-12/01
Short Order	Lincoln MSA, NE	H	6.59 FQ	7.98 AW	10.00 TQ	NEBLS	10/01-12/01
Short Order	Omaha MSA, NE-IA	H	5.80 FQ	7.07 AW	8.98 TQ	NEBLS	10/01-12/01
Short Order	Nevada	H	5.50 FQ	8.31 AW	13.22 TQ	NVBLS	10/01-12/01
Short Order	Las Vegas MSA, NV-AZ	H	6.94 FQ	10.92 AW	15.53 TQ	NVBLS	10/01-12/01
Short Order	New Hampshire	H	6.04 FQ	7.90 AW	10.30 TQ	NHBLS	10/01-12/01
Short Order	Manchester PMSA, NH	H	5.96 FQ	8.19 AW	10.96 TQ	NHBLS	10/01-12/01
Short Order	Nashua PMSA, NH	H	5.93 FQ	7.36 AW	8.93 TQ	NHBLS	10/01-12/01
Short Order	Portsmouth-Rochester PMSA, NH-ME	H	6.58 FQ	8.28 AW	10.49 TQ	NHBLS	10/01-12/01
Short Order	New Jersey	H	7.02 FQ	9.82 AW	14.07 TQ	NJBLS	10/01-12/01
Short Order	Atlantic-Cape May PMSA, NJ	H	6.68 FQ	10.11 AW	13.37 TQ	NJBLS	10/01-12/01
Short Order	Bergen-Passaic PMSA, NJ	H	7.54 FQ	11.97 AW	17.01 TQ	NJBLS	10/01-12/01
Short Order	Jersey City PMSA, NJ	H	5.68 FQ	9.38 AW	13.12 TQ	NJBLS	10/01-12/01
Short Order	Middlesex-Somerset-Hunterdon PMSA, NJ	H	6.13 FQ	10.44 AW	15.79 TQ	NJBLS	10/01-12/01
Short Order	Monmouth-Ocean PMSA, NJ	H	7.49 FQ	9.53 AW	11.33 TQ	NJBLS	10/01-12/01
Short Order	Newark PMSA, NJ	H	7.20 FQ	9.63 AW	14.12 TQ	NJBLS	10/01-12/01
Short Order	Trenton PMSA, NJ	H	7.21 FQ	9.04 AW	12.98 TQ	NJBLS	10/01-12/01
Short Order	New Mexico	H	5.65 FQ	7.23 AW	9.99 TQ	NMBLS	10/01-12/01
Short Order	Albuquerque MSA, NM	H	5.86 FQ	7.51 AW	10.21 TQ	NMBLS	10/01-12/01
Short Order	Las Cruces MSA, NM	H	5.74 FQ	7.19 AW	10.03 TQ	NMBLS	10/01-12/01
Short Order	New York	H	5.87 FQ	9.00 AW	12.95 TQ	NYBLS	10/01-12/01
Short Order	Albany-Schenectady-Troy MSA, NY	H	5.59 FQ	8.05 AW	10.88 TQ	NYBLS	10/01-12/01
Short Order	Binghamton MSA, NY	H	5.76 FQ	7.49 AW	9.51 TQ	NYBLS	10/01-12/01
Short Order	Buffalo-Niagara Falls MSA, NY	H	5.51 FQ	6.77 AW	9.23 TQ	NYBLS	10/01-12/01
Short Order	Dutchess County PMSA, NY	H	5.49 FQ	7.75 AW	10.55 TQ	NYBLS	10/01-12/01
Short Order	Nassau-Suffolk PMSA, NY	H	7.44 FQ	10.88 AW	14.60 TQ	NYBLS	10/01-12/01
Short Order	New York PMSA, NY	H	6.84 FQ	10.51 AW	14.02 TQ	NYBLS	10/01-12/01
Short Order	Newburgh PMSA, NY-PA	H	5.62 FQ	7.48 AW	10.82 TQ	NYBLS	10/01-12/01
Short Order	Rochester MSA, NY	H	7.24 FQ	8.81 AW	10.70 TQ	NYBLS	10/01-12/01
Short Order	Syracuse MSA, NY	H	6.84 FQ	9.09 AW	10.69 TQ	NYBLS	10/01-12/01
Short Order	Utica-Rome MSA, NY	H	5.36 FQ	6.28 AW	8.01 TQ	NYBLS	10/01-12/01
Short Order	North Carolina	H	5.48 FQ	7.19 AW	9.95 TQ	NCBLS	10/01-12/01
Short Order	Asheville MSA, NC	H	5.62 FQ	7.07 AW	8.81 TQ	NCBLS	10/01-12/01
Short Order	Charlotte-Gastonia-Rock Hill MSA, NC-SC	H	5.92 FQ	8.07 AW	10.69 TQ	NCBLS	10/01-12/01
Short Order	Fayetteville MSA, NC	H	5.47 FQ	6.72 AW	8.36 TQ	NCBLS	10/01-12/01
Short Order	Greensboro-Winston-Salem-High Point MSA, NC	H	6.80 FQ	8.47 AW	11.54 TQ	NCBLS	10/01-12/01
Short Order	Hickory-Morganton-Lenoir MSA, NC	H	6.70 FQ	7.81 AW	9.13 TQ	NCBLS	10/01-12/01
Short Order	Raleigh-Durham-Chapel Hill MSA, NC	H	5.57 FQ	8.16 AW	12.25 TQ	NCBLS	10/01-12/01
Short Order	Wilmington MSA, NC	H	5.75 FQ	6.99 AW	8.74 TQ	NCBLS	10/01-12/01
Short Order	North Dakota	H	6.17 FQ	7.91 AW	10.38 TQ	NDBLS	10/01-12/01
Short Order	Fargo-Moorhead MSA, ND-MN	H	6.05 FQ	8.40 AW	11.52 TQ	NDBLS	10/01-12/01
Short Order	Ohio	H	5.71 FQ	7.61 AW	10.24 TQ	OHBLS	10/01-12/01
Short Order	Akron PMSA, OH	H	6.23 FQ	8.09 AW	10.41 TQ	OHBLS	10/01-12/01
Short Order	Canton-Massillon MSA, OH	H	5.74 FQ	7.31 AW	9.01 TQ	OHBLS	10/01-12/01
Short Order	Cincinnati PMSA, OH-KY-IN	H	6.18 FQ	8.76 AW	10.83 TQ	OHBLS	10/01-12/01
Short Order	Cleveland-Lorain-Elyria PMSA, OH	H	6.95 FQ	8.51 AW	10.92 TQ	OHBLS	10/01-12/01
Short Order	Columbus MSA, OH	H	6.94 FQ	8.39 AW	10.47 TQ	OHBLS	10/01-12/01
Short Order	Dayton-Springfield MSA, OH	H	5.54 FQ	7.05 AW	8.87 TQ	OHBLS	10/01-12/01
Short Order	Hamilton-Middletown PMSA, OH	H	5.50 FQ	6.85 AW	8.61 TQ	OHBLS	10/01-12/01
Short Order	Mansfield MSA, OH	H	5.99 FQ	7.39 AW	8.76 TQ	OHBLS	10/01-12/01
Short Order	Toledo MSA, OH	H	5.64 FQ	7.56 AW	10.25 TQ	OHBLS	10/01-12/01
Short Order	Youngstown-Warren MSA, OH	H	5.73 FQ	7.68 AW	10.31 TQ	OHBLS	10/01-12/01
Short Order	Oklahoma	H	5.51 FQ	6.71 AW	8.68 TQ	OKBLS	10/01-12/01
Short Order	Oklahoma City MSA, OK	H	5.58 FQ	6.58 AW	8.48 TQ	OKBLS	10/01-12/01
Short Order	Tulsa MSA, OK	H	5.50 FQ	7.17 AW	9.90 TQ	OKBLS	10/01-12/01
Short Order	Oregon	H	6.83 FQ	8.80 AW	10.72 TQ	ORBLS	10/01-12/01

AAW Average annual wage; AE Average entry wage; AEX Average experienced wage; AO Average offered; AOH Average offered, high; AOL Average offered, low; APH Average pay, high range; APL Average pay, low range; ASH Average starting, high; ASL Average starting, low; AW Average wage paid; FQ First quartile wage; H Hourly; HI Highest wage paid; HR High end range; LR Low end range; M Monthly; MTC Median total compensation; MW Median wage paid; SQ Second quartile wage; S Special: hourly and annual; TQ Third quartile wage; W Weekly; Y Yearly

Occupation/Type/Industry	Location	Per	Low	Mid	High	Source	Date
Cook							
Short Order	Eugene-Springfield MSA, OR	H	7.11 FQ	9.35 AW	11.38 TQ	ORBLS	10/01-12/01
Short Order	Medford-Ashland MSA, OR	H	6.88 FQ	8.26 AW	10.42 TQ	ORBLS	10/01-12/01
Short Order	Portland-Vancouver PMSA, OR-WA	H	7.40 FQ	9.47 AW	11.49 TQ	ORBLS	10/01-12/01
Short Order	Salem PMSA, OR	H	6.85 FQ	7.91 AW	8.78 TQ	ORBLS	10/01-12/01
Short Order	Pennsylvania	H	5.74 FQ	7.74 AW	10.41 TQ	PABLS	10/01-12/01
Short Order	Allentown-Bethlehem-Easton MSA, PA	H	5.70 FQ	7.16 AW	8.72 TQ	PABLS	10/01-12/01
Short Order	Erie MSA, PA	H	5.88 FQ	7.53 AW	9.08 TQ	PABLS	10/01-12/01
Short Order	Harrisburg-Lebanon-Carlisle MSA, PA	H	6.49 FQ	8.01 AW	10.19 TQ	PABLS	10/01-12/01
Short Order	Johnstown MSA, PA	H	5.74 FQ	7.03 AW	8.56 TQ	PABLS	10/01-12/01
Short Order	Lancaster MSA, PA	H	6.81 FQ	8.86 AW	10.59 TQ	PABLS	10/01-12/01
Short Order	Philadelphia PMSA, PA-NJ	H	5.55 FQ	7.89 AW	11.38 TQ	PABLS	10/01-12/01
Short Order	Pittsburgh MSA, PA	H	5.97 FQ	8.08 AW	10.78 TQ	PABLS	10/01-12/01
Short Order	Reading MSA, PA	H	6.43 FQ	8.31 AW	10.57 TQ	PABLS	10/01-12/01
Short Order	Scranton-Wilkes-Barre-Hazleton MSA, PA	H	6.04 FQ	7.66 AW	9.89 TQ	PABLS	10/01-12/01
Short Order	York MSA, PA	H	6.27 FQ	8.52 AW	12.51 TQ	PABLS	10/01-12/01
Short Order	Rhode Island	H	7.13 FQ	8.95 AW	10.66 TQ	RIBLS	10/01-12/01
Short Order	Providence-Fall River-Warwick MSA, RI-MA	H	7.08 FQ	8.84 AW	10.55 TQ	RIBLS	10/01-12/01
Short Order	South Carolina	H	5.70 FQ	7.38 AW	9.88 TQ	SCBLS	10/01-12/01
Short Order	Charleston-North Charleston MSA, SC	H	5.96 FQ	7.61 AW	9.13 TQ	SCBLS	10/01-12/01
Short Order	Columbia MSA, SC	H	5.97 FQ	8.02 AW	10.72 TQ	SCBLS	10/01-12/01
Short Order	Greenville-Spartanburg-Anderson MSA, SC	H	5.59 FQ	6.59 AW	8.35 TQ	SCBLS	10/01-12/01
Short Order	Myrtle Beach MSA, SC	H	6.28 FQ	8.85 AW	11.98 TQ	SCBLS	10/01-12/01
Short Order	South Dakota	H	5.74 FQ	7.25 AW	9.51 TQ	SDBLS	10/01-12/01
Short Order	Sioux Falls MSA, SD	H	6.17 FQ	8.25 AW	10.83 TQ	SDBLS	10/01-12/01
Short Order	Tennessee	H	5.85 FQ	7.72 AW	10.18 TQ	TNBLS	10/01-12/01
Short Order	Chattanooga MSA, TN-GA	H	5.85 FQ	7.08 AW	8.53 TQ	TNBLS	10/01-12/01
Short Order	Clarksville-Hopkinsville MSA, TN-KY	H	5.91 FQ	7.83 AW	10.41 TQ	TNBLS	10/01-12/01
Short Order	Johnson City-Kingsport-Bristol MSA, TN-VA	H	5.65 FQ	6.98 AW	8.65 TQ	TNBLS	10/01-12/01
Short Order	Knoxville MSA, TN	H	5.76 FQ	7.50 AW	10.16 TQ	TNBLS	10/01-12/01
Short Order	Memphis MSA, TN-AR-MS	H	5.60 FQ	6.62 AW	8.33 TQ	TNBLS	10/01-12/01
Short Order	Nashville MSA, TN	H	6.89 FQ	8.52 AW	11.00 TQ	TNBLS	10/01-12/01
Short Order	Texas	H	5.73 FQ	7.54 AW	10.00 TQ	TXBLS	10/01-12/01
Short Order	Amarillo MSA, TX	H	5.59 FQ	6.75 AW	8.66 TQ	TXBLS	10/01-12/01
Short Order	Austin-San Marcos MSA, TX	H	7.45 FQ	9.61 AW	12.36 TQ	TXBLS	10/01-12/01
Short Order	Beaumont-Port Arthur MSA, TX	H	5.59 FQ	6.99 AW	9.41 TQ	TXBLS	10/01-12/01
Short Order	Brazoria PMSA, TX	H	5.79 FQ	6.86 AW	8.58 TQ	TXBLS	10/01-12/01
Short Order	Brownsville-Harlingen-San Benito MSA, TX	H	5.69 FQ	7.36 AW	9.09 TQ	TXBLS	10/01-12/01
Short Order	Corpus Christi MSA, TX	H	5.56 FQ	6.29 AW	7.23 TQ	TXBLS	10/01-12/01
Short Order	Dallas PMSA, TX	H	7.00 FQ	8.31 AW	10.50 TQ	TXBLS	10/01-12/01
Short Order	El Paso MSA, TX	H	5.71 FQ	7.53 AW	11.02 TQ	TXBLS	10/01-12/01
Short Order	Fort Worth-Arlington PMSA, TX	H	6.36 FQ	7.70 AW	9.27 TQ	TXBLS	10/01-12/01
Short Order	Galveston-Texas City PMSA, TX	H	5.60 FQ	6.83 AW	8.68 TQ	TXBLS	10/01-12/01
Short Order	Houston PMSA, TX	H	5.70 FQ	7.51 AW	9.61 TQ	TXBLS	10/01-12/01
Short Order	Killeen-Temple MSA, TX	H	5.67 FQ	7.26 AW	9.10 TQ	TXBLS	10/01-12/01
Short Order	Laredo MSA, TX	H	5.60 FQ	6.72 AW	8.76 TQ	TXBLS	10/01-12/01
Short Order	Longview-Marshall MSA, TX	H	5.37 FQ	6.23 AW	6.88 TQ	TXBLS	10/01-12/01
Short Order	Lubbock MSA, TX	H	5.65 FQ	6.96 AW	8.65 TQ	TXBLS	10/01-12/01
Short Order	McAllen-Edinburg-Mission MSA, TX	H	5.46 FQ	6.15 AW	7.01 TQ	TXBLS	10/01-12/01
Short Order	Odessa-Midland MSA, TX	H	5.82 FQ	7.82 AW	10.55 TQ	TXBLS	10/01-12/01
Short Order	San Antonio MSA, TX	H	5.68 FQ	7.34 AW	9.89 TQ	TXBLS	10/01-12/01
Short Order	Tyler MSA, TX	H	5.73 FQ	7.39 AW	9.08 TQ	TXBLS	10/01-12/01
Short Order	Utah	H	5.93 FQ	7.26 AW	8.54 TQ	UTBLS	10/01-12/01
Short Order	Provo-Orem MSA, UT	H	6.25 FQ	7.48 AW	8.66 TQ	UTBLS	10/01-12/01
Short Order	Salt Lake City-Ogden MSA, UT	H	6.37 FQ	7.60 AW	8.62 TQ	UTBLS	10/01-12/01
Short Order	Vermont	H	6.86 FQ	8.96 AW	12.18 TQ	VTBLS	10/01-12/01
Short Order	Burlington MSA, VT	H	7.35 FQ	9.64 AW	12.47 TQ	VTBLS	10/01-12/01

AAW	Average annual wage	AOH	Average offered, high	ASH	Average starting, high	H	Hourly	M	Monthly	S	Special: hourly and annual
AE	Average entry wage	AOL	Average offered, low	ASL	Average starting, low	HI	Highest wage paid	MTC	Median total compensation	TQ	Third quartile wage
AEX	Average experienced wage	APH	Average pay, high range	AW	Average wage paid	HR	High end range	MW	Median wage paid	W	Weekly
AO	Average offered	APL	Average pay, low range	FQ	First quartile wage	LR	Low end range	SQ	Second quartile wage	Y	Yearly

Occupation/Type/Industry	Location	Per	Low	Mid	High	Source	Date
Cook							
Short Order	Virginia	H	5.94 FQ	8.00 AW	10.48 TQ	VABLS	10/01-12/01
Short Order	Norfolk-Virginia Beach-Newport News MSA, VA-NC	H	6.31 FQ	8.13 AW	10.43 TQ	VABLS	10/01-12/01
Short Order	Richmond-Petersburg MSA, VA	H	5.89 FQ	8.31 AW	11.08 TQ	VABLS	10/01-12/01
Short Order	Roanoke MSA, VA	H	5.87 FQ	7.46 AW	8.83 TQ	VABLS	10/01-12/01
Short Order	Washington	H	7.14 FQ	9.78 AW	12.99 TQ	WABLS	10/01-12/01
Short Order	Bremerton PMSA, WA	H	6.84 FQ	7.80 AW	9.75 TQ	WABLS	10/01-12/01
Short Order	Olympia PMSA, WA	H	6.86 FQ	8.29 AW	11.22 TQ	WABLS	10/01-12/01
Short Order	Richland-Kennewick-Pasco MSA, WA	H	6.88 FQ	8.35 AW	10.73 TQ	WABLS	10/01-12/01
Short Order	Seattle-Bellevue-Everett PMSA, WA	H	8.77 FQ	10.79 AW	13.40 TQ	WABLS	10/01-12/01
Short Order	Spokane MSA, WA	H	7.09 FQ	9.01 AW	11.01 TQ	WABLS	10/01-12/01
Short Order	Tacoma PMSA, WA	H	7.33 FQ	9.04 AW	10.84 TQ	WABLS	10/01-12/01
Short Order	Yakima MSA, WA	H	6.88 FQ	9.27 AW	12.75 TQ	WABLS	10/01-12/01
Short Order	West Virginia	H	5.45 FQ	6.20 AW	7.18 TQ	WVBLS	10/01-12/01
Short Order	Charleston MSA, WV	H	5.51 FQ	6.77 AW	8.89 TQ	WVBLS	10/01-12/01
Short Order	Huntington-Ashland MSA, WV-KY-OH	H	5.44 FQ	6.08 AW	6.99 TQ	WVBLS	10/01-12/01
Short Order	Wisconsin	H	5.67 FQ	7.86 AW	10.69 TQ	WIBLS	10/01-12/01
Short Order	Appleton-Oshkosh-Neenah MSA, WI	H	7.23 FQ	8.92 AW	10.78 TQ	WIBLS	10/01-12/01
Short Order	Green Bay MSA, WI	H	5.96 FQ	8.37 AW	11.02 TQ	WIBLS	10/01-12/01
Short Order	Madison MSA, WI	H	6.11 FQ	7.78 AW	9.93 TQ	WIBLS	10/01-12/01
Short Order	Milwaukee-Waukesha PMSA, WI	H	5.51 FQ	8.45 AW	12.92 TQ	WIBLS	10/01-12/01
Short Order	Racine PMSA, WI	H	7.31 FQ	10.32 AW	16.34 TQ	WIBLS	10/01-12/01
Short Order	Wyoming	H	6.00 FQ	7.69 AW	9.31 TQ	WYBLS	10/01-12/01
Short Order	Cheyenne MSA, WY	H	5.82 FQ	7.40 AW	8.92 TQ	WYBLS	10/01-12/01
Short Order	Puerto Rico	H	5.57 FQ	6.37 AW	7.26 TQ	PRBLS	10/01-12/01
Short Order	Virgin Islands	H	5.84 FQ	7.50 AW	9.61 TQ	VIBLS	10/01-12/01
Short Order	Guam	H	5.71 FQ	8.06 AW	12.25 TQ	GUBLS	10/01-12/01
Cooling and Freezing Equipment Operator and Tender	Alaska	H	10.08 FQ	16.17 AW	21.86 TQ	AKBLS	10/01-12/01
	Arizona	H	6.37 FQ	9.40 AW	13.52 TQ	AZBLS	10/01-12/01
	Phoenix-Mesa MSA, AZ	H	6.25 FQ	9.36 AW	14.56 TQ	AZBLS	10/01-12/01
	Arkansas	H	7.60 FQ	9.60 AW	11.21 TQ	ARBLS	10/01-12/01
	Fayetteville-Springdale-Rogers MSA, AR	H	8.25 FQ	10.00 AW	12.01 TQ	ARBLS	10/01-12/01
	California	H	7.88 FQ	13.53 AW	20.39 TQ	CABLS	10/01-12/01
	Bakersfield MSA, CA	H	8.30 FQ	14.52 AW	21.48 TQ	CABLS	10/01-12/01
	Fresno MSA, CA	H	9.82 FQ	13.51 AW	17.75 TQ	CABLS	10/01-12/01
	Los Angeles-Long Beach PMSA, CA	H	8.26 FQ	14.66 AW	20.40 TQ	CABLS	10/01-12/01
	Sacramento PMSA, CA	H	7.66 FQ	10.12 AW	13.42 TQ	CABLS	10/01-12/01
	Salinas MSA, CA	H	9.59 FQ	14.99 AW	20.91 TQ	CABLS	10/01-12/01
	Santa Barbara-Santa Maria-Lompoc MSA, CA	H	8.45 FQ	11.60 AW	14.23 TQ	CABLS	10/01-12/01
	Colorado	H	8.47 FQ	13.12 AW	18.83 TQ	COBLS	10/01-12/01
	Denver PMSA, CO	H	10.73 FQ	13.33 AW	17.00 TQ	COBLS	10/01-12/01
	Connecticut	H	9.71 FQ	13.74 AW	18.55 TQ	CTBLS	10/01-12/01
	Hartford MSA, CT	H	9.67 FQ	13.70 AW	18.67 TQ	CTBLS	10/01-12/01
	Florida	H	7.26 FQ	12.62 AW	18.49 TQ	FLBLS	10/01-12/01
	Lakeland-Winter Haven MSA, FL	H	6.44 FQ	10.51 AW	16.11 TQ	FLBLS	10/01-12/01
	Georgia	H	7.28 FQ	9.95 AW	15.57 TQ	GABLS	10/01-12/01
	Atlanta MSA, GA	H	7.47 FQ	11.60 AW	20.74 TQ	GABLS	10/01-12/01
	Illinois	H	7.59 FQ	14.39 AW	20.66 TQ	ILBLS	10/01-12/01
	Chicago PMSA, IL	H	8.18 FQ	15.43 AW	20.80 TQ	ILBLS	10/01-12/01
	Indiana	H	7.87 FQ	13.38 AW	25.45 TQ	INBLS	10/01-12/01
	Iowa	H	8.91 FQ	11.44 AW	15.89 TQ	IABLS	10/01-12/01
	Kansas	H	8.75 FQ	11.97 AW	16.33 TQ	KSBLS	10/01-12/01
	Kentucky	H	5.98 FQ	9.24 AW	13.39 TQ	KYBLS	10/01-12/01
	Louisiana	H	5.77 FQ	8.49 AW	16.45 TQ	LABLS	10/01-12/01
	Massachusetts	H	7.58 FQ	14.02 AW	20.67 TQ	MABLS	10/01-12/01
	New Bedford PMSA, MA	H	7.03 FQ	8.94 AW	10.70 TQ	MABLS	10/01-12/01
	Michigan	H	10.59 FQ	16.01 AW	20.41 TQ	MIBLS	10/01-12/01
	Minnesota	H	7.54 FQ	12.73 AW	20.65 TQ	MNBLS	10/01-12/01

AAW Average annual wage	**AOH** Average offered, high	**ASH** Average starting, high	**H** Hourly	**M** Monthly	**S** Special: hourly and annual
AE Average entry wage	**AOL** Average offered, low	**ASL** Average starting, low	**HI** Highest wage paid	**MTC** Median total compensation	**TQ** Third quartile wage
AEX Average experienced wage	**APH** Average pay, high range	**AW** Average wage paid	**HR** High end range	**MW** Median wage paid	**W** Weekly
AO Average offered	**APL** Average pay, low range	**FQ** First quartile wage	**LR** Low end range	**SQ** Second quartile wage	**Y** Yearly

Occupation/Type/Industry	Location	Per	Low	Mid	High	Source	Date
Cooling and Freezing Equipment Operator and Tender	Mississippi	H	5.80 FQ	7.84 AW	10.40 TQ	MSBLS	10/01-12/01
	Missouri	H	8.45 FQ	10.67 AW	13.31 TQ	MOBLS	10/01-12/01
	Nebraska	H	10.33 FQ	13.05 AW	15.94 TQ	NEBLS	10/01-12/01
	Omaha MSA, NE-IA	H	11.48 FQ	13.12 AW	15.50 TQ	NEBLS	10/01-12/01
	New Jersey	H	5.61 FQ	8.20 AW	13.32 TQ	NJBLS	10/01-12/01
	New York	H	7.66 FQ	12.41 AW	19.37 TQ	NYBLS	10/01-12/01
	Rochester MSA, NY	H	7.39 FQ	12.89 AW	20.80 TQ	NYBLS	10/01-12/01
	North Carolina	H	7.49 FQ	11.61 AW	24.48 TQ	NCBLS	10/01-12/01
	Ohio	H	9.84 FQ	13.89 AW	19.23 TQ	OHBLS	10/01-12/01
	Oklahoma	H	7.98 FQ	11.11 AW	15.79 TQ	OKBLS	10/01-12/01
	Oregon	H	7.62 FQ	13.46 AW	24.15 TQ	ORBLS	10/01-12/01
	Salem PMSA, OR	H	7.43 FQ	8.65 AW	10.68 TQ	ORBLS	10/01-12/01
	Pennsylvania	H	9.22 FQ	13.95 AW	21.75 TQ	PABLS	10/01-12/01
	Lancaster MSA, PA	H	9.87 FQ	16.86 AW	24.89 TQ	PABLS	10/01-12/01
	Philadelphia PMSA, PA-NJ	H	8.85 FQ	11.10 AW	14.41 TQ	PABLS	10/01-12/01
	South Carolina	H	7.94 FQ	10.92 AW	17.40 TQ	SCBLS	10/01-12/01
	South Dakota	H	8.52 FQ	10.74 AW	13.22 TQ	SDBLS	10/01-12/01
	Tennessee	H	7.56 FQ	10.20 AW	14.16 TQ	TNBLS	10/01-12/01
	Texas	H	5.71 FQ	9.31 AW	14.13 TQ	TXBLS	10/01-12/01
	Utah	H	7.34 FQ	10.89 AW	15.76 TQ	UTBLS	10/01-12/01
	Virginia	H	7.04 FQ	8.84 AW	10.81 TQ	VABLS	10/01-12/01
	Richmond-Petersburg MSA, VA	H	6.04 FQ	8.61 AW	10.73 TQ	VABLS	10/01-12/01
	Washington	H	6.94 FQ	13.55 AW	20.71 TQ	WABLS	10/01-12/01
	Wisconsin	H	6.49 FQ	13.65 AW	20.24 TQ	WIBLS	10/01-12/01
	Puerto Rico	H	5.62 FQ	6.70 AW	9.43 TQ	PRBLS	10/01-12/01
Copywriter							
Advertising	East	Y		62000 AW		ADAGE	1/00-1/01
Advertising	Midwest	Y		53000 AW		ADAGE	1/00-1/01
Advertising	South	Y		50000 AW		ADAGE	1/00-1/01
Advertising	West	Y		59000 AW		ADAGE	1/00-1/01
Marketing, Medical	United States	Y		75100 AW		MM&M	1/01-1/02
Correctional Officer and Jailer	Alabama	Y	16970 FQ	25710 AW	35430 TQ	ALBLS	10/01-12/01
	Birmingham MSA, AL	Y	20120 FQ	27100 AW	35520 TQ	ALBLS	10/01-12/01
	Huntsville MSA, AL	Y	17730 FQ	22010 AW	27530 TQ	ALBLS	10/01-12/01
	Mobile MSA, AL	Y	18580 FQ	23570 AW	29810 TQ	ALBLS	10/01-12/01
	Montgomery MSA, AL	Y	21520 FQ	31580 AW	44970 TQ	ALBLS	10/01-12/01
	Alaska	Y	24210 FQ	41630 AW	55510 TQ	AKBLS	10/01-12/01
	Arizona	Y	22660 FQ	28770 AW	35310 TQ	AZBLS	10/01-12/01
	Phoenix-Mesa MSA, AZ	Y	22820 FQ	29010 AW	35180 TQ	AZBLS	10/01-12/01
	Arkansas	Y	17230 FQ	23080 AW	31710 TQ	ARBLS	10/01-12/01
	Fayetteville-Springdale-Rogers MSA, AR	Y	19220 FQ	22820 AW	28450 TQ	ARBLS	10/01-12/01
	Fort Smith MSA, AR-OK	Y	16040 FQ	20680 AW	24820 TQ	ARBLS	10/01-12/01
	Little Rock-North Little Rock MSA, AR	Y	19470 FQ	25750 AW	33200 TQ	ARBLS	10/01-12/01
	California	Y	34510 FQ	46650 AW	58430 TQ	CABLS	10/01-12/01
	Bakersfield MSA, CA	Y	29540 FQ	45560 AW	56240 TQ	CABLS	10/01-12/01
	Los Angeles-Long Beach PMSA, CA	Y	35690 FQ	46290 AW	56480 TQ	CABLS	10/01-12/01
	Oakland PMSA, CA	Y	34250 FQ	43680 AW	55170 TQ	CABLS	10/01-12/01
	Orange County PMSA, CA	Y	17070 FQ	39950 AW	58260 TQ	CABLS	10/01-12/01
	Riverside-San Bernardino PMSA, CA	Y	35780 FQ	47890 AW	56640 TQ	CABLS	10/01-12/01
	Sacramento PMSA, CA	Y	24660 FQ	43080 AW	58210 TQ	CABLS	10/01-12/01
	San Diego MSA, CA	Y	37390 FQ	42830 AW	52150 TQ	CABLS	10/01-12/01
	San Francisco PMSA, CA	Y	37110 FQ	51530 AW	68790 TQ	CABLS	10/01-12/01
	Vallejo-Fairfield-Napa PMSA, CA	Y	40670 FQ	49380 AW	57620 TQ	CABLS	10/01-12/01
	Colorado	Y	27400 FQ	38190 AW	51920 TQ	COBLS	10/01-12/01
	Colorado Springs MSA, CO	Y	26060 FQ	36650 AW	48560 TQ	COBLS	10/01-12/01
	Denver PMSA, CO	Y	27700 FQ	39540 AW	54270 TQ	COBLS	10/01-12/01
	Greeley PMSA, CO	Y	20940 FQ	35680 AW	45330 TQ	COBLS	10/01-12/01
	Connecticut	Y	30240 FQ	37350 AW	43700 TQ	CTBLS	10/01-12/01
	Delaware	Y	23350 FQ	28740 AW	36470 TQ	DEBLS	10/01-12/01
	Washington PMSA, DC-MD-VA-WV	Y	21660 FQ	36740 AW	56600 TQ	DCBLS	10/01-12/01
	Florida	Y	24170 FQ	31560 AW	40490 TQ	FLBLS	10/01-12/01
	Daytona Beach MSA, FL	Y	23210 FQ	29540 AW	35320 TQ	FLBLS	10/01-12/01

AAW	Average annual wage	**AOH**	Average offered, high	**ASH**	Average starting, high	**H**	Hourly	**M**	Monthly	**S**	Special: hourly and annual
AE	Average entry wage	**AOL**	Average offered, low	**ASL**	Average starting, low	**HI**	Highest wage paid	**MTC**	Median total compensation	**TQ**	Third quartile wage
AEX	Average experienced wage	**APH**	Average pay, high range	**AW**	Average wage paid	**HR**	High end range	**MW**	Median wage paid	**W**	Weekly
AO	Average offered	**APL**	Average pay, low range	**FQ**	First quartile wage	**LR**	Low end range	**SQ**	Second quartile wage	**Y**	Yearly

Occupation/Type/Industry	Location	Per	Low	Mid	High	Source	Date
Correctional Officer and Jailer	Fort Lauderdale PMSA, FL	Y	24750 FQ	33190 AW	43480 TQ	FLBLS	10/01-12/01
	Fort Pierce-Port St. Lucie MSA, FL	Y	25120 FQ	30820 AW	37280 TQ	FLBLS	10/01-12/01
	Fort Walton Beach MSA, FL	Y	24560 FQ	31790 AW	41200 TQ	FLBLS	10/01-12/01
	Lakeland-Winter Haven MSA, FL	Y	23920 FQ	31200 AW	41200 TQ	FLBLS	10/01-12/01
	Melbourne-Titusville-Palm Bay MSA, FL	Y	18830 FQ	28730 AW	42130 TQ	FLBLS	10/01-12/01
	Miami PMSA, FL	Y	28480 FQ	33390 AW	41160 TQ	FLBLS	10/01-12/01
	Ocala MSA, FL	Y	23860 FQ	29740 AW	34930 TQ	FLBLS	10/01-12/01
	Orlando MSA, FL	Y	23500 FQ	31980 AW	43140 TQ	FLBLS	10/01-12/01
	Pensacola MSA, FL	Y	23900 FQ	29600 AW	35240 TQ	FLBLS	10/01-12/01
	Tallahassee MSA, FL	Y	23850 FQ	31790 AW	41740 TQ	FLBLS	10/01-12/01
	Tampa-St. Petersburg-Clearwater MSA, FL	Y	26940 FQ	33170 AW	38800 TQ	FLBLS	10/01-12/01
	Georgia	Y	20880 FQ	26110 AW	33680 TQ	GABLS	10/01-12/01
	Atlanta MSA, GA	Y	21110 FQ	28090 AW	39850 TQ	GABLS	10/01-12/01
	Augusta-Aiken MSA, GA-SC	Y	22610 FQ	27460 AW	36110 TQ	GABLS	10/01-12/01
	Columbus MSA, GA-AL	Y	22250 FQ	25640 AW	31710 TQ	GABLS	10/01-12/01
	Macon MSA, GA	Y	21360 FQ	25260 AW	30220 TQ	GABLS	10/01-12/01
	Savannah MSA, GA	Y	22380 FQ	26490 AW	32500 TQ	GABLS	10/01-12/01
	Hawaii	Y	27340 FQ	32660 AW	40930 TQ	HIBLS	10/01-12/01
	Honolulu MSA, HI	Y	27110 FQ	32820 AW	41410 TQ	HIBLS	10/01-12/01
	Idaho	Y	19670 FQ	26430 AW	34130 TQ	IDBLS	10/01-12/01
	Boise City MSA, ID	Y	22830 FQ	26570 AW	32800 TQ	IDBLS	10/01-12/01
	Illinois	Y	28390 FQ	35910 AW	43770 TQ	ILBLS	10/01-12/01
	Chicago PMSA, IL	Y	26760 FQ	33990 AW	42700 TQ	ILBLS	10/01-12/01
	Peoria-Pekin MSA, IL	Y	26990 FQ	35060 AW	43210 TQ	ILBLS	10/01-12/01
	Rockford MSA, IL	Y	25270 FQ	32700 AW	42000 TQ	ILBLS	10/01-12/01
	Indiana	Y	18850 FQ	24550 AW	32240 TQ	INBLS	10/01-12/01
	Evansville-Henderson MSA, IN-KY	Y	14660 FQ	22910 AW	31750 TQ	INBLS	10/01-12/01
	Fort Wayne MSA, IN	Y	21540 FQ	26970 AW	33220 TQ	INBLS	10/01-12/01
	Gary PMSA, IN	Y	15120 FQ	22180 AW	29200 TQ	INBLS	10/01-12/01
	Iowa	Y	19950 FQ	31880 AW	42640 TQ	IABLS	10/01-12/01
	Davenport-Moline-Rock Island MSA, IA-IL	Y	25940 FQ	34740 AW	43260 TQ	IABLS	10/01-12/01
	Kansas	Y	19180 FQ	26990 AW	36540 TQ	KSBLS	10/01-12/01
	Topeka MSA, KS	Y	20520 FQ	28360 AW	40150 TQ	KSBLS	10/01-12/01
	Wichita MSA, KS	Y	23030 FQ	27210 AW	34050 TQ	KSBLS	10/01-12/01
	Kentucky	Y	15440 FQ	23430 AW	35030 TQ	KYBLS	10/01-12/01
	Lexington MSA, KY	Y	19810 FQ	30100 AW	43870 TQ	KYBLS	10/01-12/01
	Louisville MSA, KY-IN	Y	17690 FQ	23080 AW	31250 TQ	KYBLS	10/01-12/01
	Louisiana	Y	15290 FQ	23340 AW	33580 TQ	LABLS	10/01-12/01
	Baton Rouge MSA, LA	Y	18450 FQ	26280 AW	34170 TQ	LABLS	10/01-12/01
	Houma MSA, LA	Y	16480 FQ	26810 AW	34380 TQ	LABLS	10/01-12/01
	Lafayette MSA, LA	Y	14640 FQ	25320 AW	39910 TQ	LABLS	10/01-12/01
	New Orleans MSA, LA	Y	15570 FQ	22600 AW	32580 TQ	LABLS	10/01-12/01
	Shreveport-Bossier City MSA, LA	Y	17840 FQ	21150 AW	26930 TQ	LABLS	10/01-12/01
	Maine	Y	17740 FQ	24170 AW	30180 TQ	MEBLS	10/01-12/01
	Portland MSA, ME	Y	21380 FQ	25770 AW	31250 TQ	MEBLS	10/01-12/01
	Maryland	Y	25770 FQ	34640 AW	43740 TQ	MDBLS	10/01-12/01
	Massachusetts	Y	37890 FQ	48900 AW	61120 TQ	MABLS	10/01-12/01
	Boston PMSA, MA-NH	Y	37000 FQ	48050 AW	60720 TQ	MABLS	10/01-12/01
	Michigan	Y	27660 FQ	36560 AW	43740 TQ	MIBLS	10/01-12/01
	Ann Arbor PMSA, MI	Y	29250 FQ	37630 AW	44160 TQ	MIBLS	10/01-12/01
	Detroit PMSA, MI	Y	28580 FQ	36820 AW	43640 TQ	MIBLS	10/01-12/01
	Kalamazoo-Battle Creek MSA, MI	Y	26910 FQ	38150 AW	47690 TQ	MIBLS	10/01-12/01
	Lansing-East Lansing MSA, MI	Y	30170 FQ	40050 AW	50310 TQ	MIBLS	10/01-12/01
	Minnesota	Y	25550 FQ	36110 AW	48880 TQ	MNBLS	10/01-12/01
	Duluth-Superior MSA, MN-WI	Y	30610 FQ	38020 AW	45470 TQ	MNBLS	10/01-12/01
	Minneapolis-St. Paul MSA, MN-WI	Y	28570 FQ	38410 AW	51770 TQ	MNBLS	10/01-12/01
	Mississippi	Y	14730 FQ	21810 AW	31840 TQ	MSBLS	10/01-12/01
	Biloxi-Gulfport-Pascagoula MSA, MS	Y	12170 FQ	18560 AW	27300 TQ	MSBLS	10/01-12/01
	Jackson MSA, MS	Y	15890 FQ	21130 AW	27350 TQ	MSBLS	10/01-12/01
	Kansas City MSA, MO-KS	Y	12920 FQ	26570 AW	41180 TQ	MOBLS	10/01-12/01
	St. Louis MSA, MO-IL	Y	21880 FQ	34620 AW	49610 TQ	MOBLS	10/01-12/01
	Montana	Y	17690 FQ	25140 AW	34380 TQ	MTBLS	10/01-12/01

AAW Average annual wage **AE** Average entry wage **AEX** Average experienced wage **AO** Average offered **AOH** Average offered, high **AOL** Average offered, low **APH** Average pay, high range **APL** Average pay, low range **ASH** Average starting, high **ASL** Average starting, low **AW** Average wage paid **FQ** First quartile wage **H** Hourly **HI** Highest wage paid **HR** High end range **LR** Low end range **M** Monthly **MTC** Median total compensation **MW** Median wage paid **SQ** Second quartile wage **S** Special: hourly and annual **TQ** Third quartile wage **W** Weekly **Y** Yearly

Occupation/Type/Industry	Location	Per	Low	Mid	High	Source	Date
Correctional Officer and Jailer	Nebraska	Y	22440 FQ	27300 AW	34400 TQ	NEBLS	10/01-12/01
	Omaha MSA, NE-IA	Y	20920 FQ	27880 AW	35690 TQ	NEBLS	10/01-12/01
	Nevada	Y	29600 FQ	41120 AW	56660 TQ	NVBLS	10/01-12/01
	Las Vegas MSA, NV-AZ	Y	31010 FQ	45100 AW	60000 TQ	NVBLS	10/01-12/01
	New Hampshire	Y	23960 FQ	30510 AW	38070 TQ	NHBLS	10/01-12/01
	New Jersey	Y	27120 FQ	47940 AW	68620 TQ	NJBLS	10/01-12/01
	Atlantic-Cape May PMSA, NJ	Y	24980 FQ	41170 AW	65300 TQ	NJBLS	10/01-12/01
	Bergen-Passaic PMSA, NJ	Y	25870 FQ	54510 AW	80900 TQ	NJBLS	10/01-12/01
	Monmouth-Ocean PMSA, NJ	Y	24610 FQ	42330 AW	73060 TQ	NJBLS	10/01-12/01
	Newark PMSA, NJ	Y	25750 FQ	47700 AW	68940 TQ	NJBLS	10/01-12/01
	New Mexico	Y	15900 FQ	23070 AW	32550 TQ	NMBLS	10/01-12/01
	Albuquerque MSA, NM	Y	15590 FQ	20940 AW	29370 TQ	NMBLS	10/01-12/01
	Las Cruces MSA, NM	Y	20440 FQ	25390 AW	32360 TQ	NMBLS	10/01-12/01
	New York	Y	32540 FQ	45090 AW	57460 TQ	NYBLS	10/01-12/01
	Albany-Schenectady-Troy MSA, NY	Y	25980 FQ	43210 AW	57640 TQ	NYBLS	10/01-12/01
	Buffalo-Niagara Falls MSA, NY	Y	36000 FQ	43860 AW	54310 TQ	NYBLS	10/01-12/01
	Newburgh PMSA, NY-PA	Y	25710 FQ	40330 AW	53930 TQ	NYBLS	10/01-12/01
	Rochester MSA, NY	Y	33100 FQ	42030 AW	53710 TQ	NYBLS	10/01-12/01
	Syracuse MSA, NY	Y	31760 FQ	41650 AW	54520 TQ	NYBLS	10/01-12/01
	Utica-Rome MSA, NY	Y	33330 FQ	41360 AW	53030 TQ	NYBLS	10/01-12/01
	North Carolina	Y	22720 FQ	26740 AW	33650 TQ	NCBLS	10/01-12/01
	Asheville MSA, NC	Y	23410 FQ	26390 AW	30380 TQ	NCBLS	10/01-12/01
	Charlotte-Gastonia-Rock Hill MSA, NC-SC	Y	23600 FQ	28600 AW	34930 TQ	NCBLS	10/01-12/01
	Greensboro-Winston-Salem-High Point MSA, NC	Y	23080 FQ	27290 AW	34420 TQ	NCBLS	10/01-12/01
	Hickory-Morganton-Lenoir MSA, NC	Y	22890 FQ	26210 AW	31740 TQ	NCBLS	10/01-12/01
	Raleigh-Durham-Chapel Hill MSA, NC	Y	23110 FQ	27390 AW	33840 TQ	NCBLS	10/01-12/01
	North Dakota	Y	18500 FQ	24750 AW	32600 TQ	NDBLS	10/01-12/01
	Fargo-Moorhead MSA, ND-MN	Y	20020 FQ	28190 AW	43670 TQ	NDBLS	10/01-12/01
	Ohio	Y	23070 FQ	33270 AW	42710 TQ	OHBLS	10/01-12/01
	Canton-Massillon MSA, OH	Y	20070 FQ	29480 AW	41250 TQ	OHBLS	10/01-12/01
	Cincinnati PMSA, OH-KY-IN	Y	23210 FQ	31150 AW	40970 TQ	OHBLS	10/01-12/01
	Cleveland-Lorain-Elyria PMSA, OH	Y	23600 FQ	32470 AW	42490 TQ	OHBLS	10/01-12/01
	Columbus MSA, OH	Y	29380 FQ	36050 AW	43230 TQ	OHBLS	10/01-12/01
	Dayton-Springfield MSA, OH	Y	19470 FQ	30590 AW	42930 TQ	OHBLS	10/01-12/01
	Toledo MSA, OH	Y	21320 FQ	29350 AW	36970 TQ	OHBLS	10/01-12/01
	Youngstown-Warren MSA, OH	Y	20270 FQ	31830 AW	42520 TQ	OHBLS	10/01-12/01
	Oklahoma	Y	15500 FQ	20700 AW	28280 TQ	OKBLS	10/01-12/01
	Oklahoma City MSA, OK	Y	15890 FQ	24690 AW	41250 TQ	OKBLS	10/01-12/01
	Tulsa MSA, OK	Y	14860 FQ	18940 AW	23800 TQ	OKBLS	10/01-12/01
	Oregon	Y	29480 FQ	38200 AW	50150 TQ	ORBLS	10/01-12/01
	Portland-Vancouver PMSA, OR-WA	Y	30040 FQ	40690 AW	54170 TQ	ORBLS	10/01-12/01
	Pennsylvania	Y	24370 FQ	36770 AW	52470 TQ	PABLS	10/01-12/01
	Lancaster MSA, PA	Y	23790 FQ	34890 AW	50350 TQ	PABLS	10/01-12/01
	Philadelphia PMSA, PA-NJ	Y	28450 FQ	41140 AW	63340 TQ	PABLS	10/01-12/01
	Pittsburgh MSA, PA	Y	24560 FQ	39290 AW	55020 TQ	PABLS	10/01-12/01
	Rhode Island	Y	28970 FQ	37520 AW	44390 TQ	RIBLS	10/01-12/01
	Providence-Fall River-Warwick MSA, RI-MA	Y	28920 FQ	37510 AW	44380 TQ	RIBLS	10/01-12/01
	South Carolina	Y	19060 FQ	25140 AW	33270 TQ	SCBLS	10/01-12/01
	Greenville-Spartanburg-Anderson MSA, SC	Y	20000 FQ	25760 AW	32610 TQ	SCBLS	10/01-12/01
	South Dakota	Y	18390 FQ	25880 AW	34700 TQ	SDBLS	10/01-12/01
	Tennessee	Y	16370 FQ	24530 AW	36700 TQ	TNBLS	10/01-12/01
	Chattanooga MSA, TN-GA	Y	16000 FQ	21910 AW	27420 TQ	TNBLS	10/01-12/01
	Johnson City-Kingsport-Bristol MSA, TN-VA	Y	19060 FQ	25770 AW	34530 TQ	TNBLS	10/01-12/01
	Memphis MSA, TN-AR-MS	Y	18130 FQ	28440 AW	42820 TQ	TNBLS	10/01-12/01
	Texas	Y	20120 FQ	27610 AW	34550 TQ	TXBLS	10/01-12/01
	Austin-San Marcos MSA, TX	Y	17950 FQ	27220 AW	41940 TQ	TXBLS	10/01-12/01
	Dallas PMSA, TX	Y	22120 FQ	27180 AW	32230 TQ	TXBLS	10/01-12/01
	El Paso MSA, TX	Y	23370 FQ	31390 AW	41520 TQ	TXBLS	10/01-12/01
	Fort Worth-Arlington PMSA, TX	Y	20040 FQ	29470 AW	43060 TQ	TXBLS	10/01-12/01

AAW	Average annual wage	**AOH**	Average offered, high	**ASH**	Average starting, high	**H**	Hourly	**M**	Monthly	**S**	Special: hourly and annual
AE	Average entry wage	**AOL**	Average offered, low	**ASL**	Average starting, low	**HI**	Highest wage paid	**MTC**	Median total compensation	**TQ**	Third quartile wage
AEX	Average experienced wage	**APH**	Average pay, high range	**AW**	Average wage paid	**HR**	High end range	**MW**	Median wage paid	**W**	Weekly
AO	Average offered	**APL**	Average pay, low range	**FQ**	First quartile wage	**LR**	Low end range	**SQ**	Second quartile wage	**Y**	Yearly

Occupation/Type/Industry	Location	Per	Low	Mid	High	Source	Date
Correctional Officer and Jailer	Houston PMSA, TX	Y	18950 FQ	28150 AW	38300 TQ	TXBLS	10/01-12/01
	San Antonio MSA, TX	Y	17070 FQ	25320 AW	33680 TQ	TXBLS	10/01-12/01
	Utah	Y	24340 FQ	31080 AW	38130 TQ	UTBLS	10/01-12/01
	Salt Lake City-Ogden MSA, UT	Y	24330 FQ	31160 AW	38700 TQ	UTBLS	10/01-12/01
	Virginia	Y	22970 FQ	27870 AW	36250 TQ	VABLS	10/01-12/01
	Lynchburg MSA, VA	Y	23550 FQ	26970 AW	32270 TQ	VABLS	10/01-12/01
	Norfolk-Virginia Beach-Newport News MSA, VA-NC	Y	23110 FQ	27150 AW	33400 TQ	VABLS	10/01-12/01
	Richmond-Petersburg MSA, VA	Y	23330 FQ	29070 AW	38910 TQ	VABLS	10/01-12/01
	Washington	Y	28430 FQ	36690 AW	45540 TQ	WABLS	10/01-12/01
	Seattle-Bellevue-Everett PMSA, WA	Y	29570 FQ	40210 AW	53880 TQ	WABLS	10/01-12/01
	Tacoma PMSA, WA	Y	28500 FQ	35370 AW	43050 TQ	WABLS	10/01-12/01
	Yakima MSA, WA	Y	27650 FQ	36020 AW	45290 TQ	WABLS	10/01-12/01
	West Virginia	Y	18490 FQ	24660 AW	34870 TQ	WVBLS	10/01-12/01
	Huntington-Ashland MSA, WV-KY-OH	Y	17180 FQ	29920 AW	43360 TQ	WVBLS	10/01-12/01
	Wisconsin	Y	24590 FQ	31910 AW	40710 TQ	WIBLS	10/01-12/01
	Milwaukee-Waukesha PMSA, WI	Y	25060 FQ	32130 AW	38890 TQ	WIBLS	10/01-12/01
	Wyoming	Y	22530 FQ	28460 AW	36750 TQ	WYBLS	10/01-12/01
Corrections Officer	California	M		2809-4573 AW		CORPRO	1/01-1/02
	Cumberland County, ME	Y		23000-31000 AW		CORPRO	1/01-1/02
Correspondence Clerk	Alabama	H	7.97 FQ	12.12 AW	17.40 TQ	ALBLS	10/01-12/01
	Arizona	H	9.09 FQ	11.87 AW	15.82 TQ	AZBLS	10/01-12/01
	Arkansas	H	7.95 FQ	10.30 AW	13.25 TQ	ARBLS	10/01-12/01
	California	H	9.59 FQ	14.06 AW	19.65 TQ	CABLS	10/01-12/01
	Colorado	H	9.22 FQ	13.29 AW	19.16 TQ	COBLS	10/01-12/01
	Connecticut	H	9.20 FQ	13.91 AW	20.05 TQ	CTBLS	10/01-12/01
	Delaware	H	9.26 FQ	12.72 AW	16.89 TQ	DEBLS	10/01-12/01
	District of Columbia	H	9.84 FQ	13.60 AW	18.07 TQ	DCBLS	10/01-12/01
	Florida	H	8.60 FQ	11.34 AW	14.65 TQ	FLBLS	10/01-12/01
	Georgia	H	8.90 FQ	12.72 AW	17.05 TQ	GABLS	10/01-12/01
	Idaho	H	9.00 FQ	13.47 AW	20.19 TQ	IDBLS	10/01-12/01
	Illinois	H	9.14 FQ	12.95 AW	17.86 TQ	ILBLS	10/01-12/01
	Indiana	H	9.09 FQ	12.12 AW	16.32 TQ	INBLS	10/01-12/01
	Iowa	H	7.50 FQ	10.69 AW	15.60 TQ	IABLS	10/01-12/01
	Kansas	H	8.70 FQ	11.33 AW	14.09 TQ	KSBLS	10/01-12/01
	Kentucky	H	8.55 FQ	12.86 AW	17.03 TQ	KYBLS	10/01-12/01
	Louisiana	H	8.32 FQ	12.16 AW	15.77 TQ	LABLS	10/01-12/01
	Maine	H	9.51 FQ	12.22 AW	14.47 TQ	MEBLS	10/01-12/01
	Maryland	H	8.10 FQ	14.18 AW	23.39 TQ	MDBLS	10/01-12/01
	Massachusetts	H	9.74 FQ	13.95 AW	20.02 TQ	MABLS	10/01-12/01
	Michigan	H	9.03 FQ	12.38 AW	16.55 TQ	MIBLS	10/01-12/01
	Minnesota	H	9.91 FQ	13.06 AW	17.01 TQ	MNBLS	10/01-12/01
	Mississippi	H	8.23 FQ	11.30 AW	14.61 TQ	MSBLS	10/01-12/01
	Missouri	H	8.42 FQ	12.00 AW	17.43 TQ	MOBLS	10/01-12/01
	Nebraska	H	8.06 FQ	10.91 AW	14.28 TQ	NEBLS	10/01-12/01
	Nevada	H	9.16 FQ	11.45 AW	15.33 TQ	NVBLS	10/01-12/01
	New Hampshire	H	8.61 FQ	12.35 AW	18.00 TQ	NHBLS	10/01-12/01
	New Jersey	H	9.34 FQ	13.96 AW	19.14 TQ	NJBLS	10/01-12/01
	New Mexico	H	7.22 FQ	10.57 AW	14.36 TQ	NMBLS	10/01-12/01
	New York	H	9.32 FQ	12.77 AW	18.07 TQ	NYBLS	10/01-12/01
	North Carolina	H	8.57 FQ	11.77 AW	15.74 TQ	NCBLS	10/01-12/01
	Ohio	H	8.97 FQ	11.89 AW	16.12 TQ	OHBLS	10/01-12/01
	Oklahoma	H	8.24 FQ	11.80 AW	15.98 TQ	OKBLS	10/01-12/01
	Pennsylvania	H	8.75 FQ	12.40 AW	17.40 TQ	PABLS	10/01-12/01
	Rhode Island	H	10.08 FQ	13.75 AW	17.72 TQ	RIBLS	10/01-12/01
	South Carolina	H	7.28 FQ	11.32 AW	16.72 TQ	SCBLS	10/01-12/01
	South Dakota	H	7.77 FQ	10.67 AW	13.97 TQ	SDBLS	10/01-12/01
	Tennessee	H	9.07 FQ	12.70 AW	16.97 TQ	TNBLS	10/01-12/01
	Texas	H	7.92 FQ	12.17 AW	17.61 TQ	TXBLS	10/01-12/01
	Utah	H	9.22 FQ	12.60 AW	16.53 TQ	UTBLS	10/01-12/01
	Virginia	H	8.81 FQ	13.73 AW	20.46 TQ	VABLS	10/01-12/01
	Washington	H	9.78 FQ	14.00 AW	19.52 TQ	WABLS	10/01-12/01
	West Virginia	H	8.35 FQ	13.05 AW	17.17 TQ	WVBLS	10/01-12/01

AAW	Average annual wage	**AOH**	Average offered, high	**ASH**	Average starting, high	**H**	Hourly	**M**	Monthly	**S**	Special: hourly and annual
AE	Average entry wage	**AOL**	Average offered, low	**ASL**	Average starting, low	**HI**	Highest wage paid	**MTC**	Median total compensation	**TQ**	Third quartile wage
AEX	Average experienced wage	**APH**	Average pay, high range	**AW**	Average wage paid	**HR**	High end range	**MW**	Median wage paid	**W**	Weekly
AO	Average offered	**APL**	Average pay, low range	**FQ**	First quartile wage	**LR**	Low end range	**SQ**	Second quartile wage	**Y**	Yearly

Occupation/Type/Industry	Location	Per	Low	Mid	High	Source	Date
Correspondence Clerk	Wisconsin	H	9.45 FQ	13.35 AW	18.08 TQ	WIBLS	10/01-12/01
	Puerto Rico	H	6.61 FQ	9.91 AW	13.71 TQ	PRBLS	10/01-12/01
Cost Estimator	Alabama	Y	26830 FQ	45840 AW	68200 TQ	ALBLS	10/01-12/01
	Birmingham MSA, AL	Y	29530 FQ	45970 AW	67710 TQ	ALBLS	10/01-12/01
	Huntsville MSA, AL	Y	30190 FQ	47630 AW	71610 TQ	ALBLS	10/01-12/01
	Mobile MSA, AL	Y	31680 FQ	49220 AW	71080 TQ	ALBLS	10/01-12/01
	Montgomery MSA, AL	Y	28700 FQ	47780 AW	69190 TQ	ALBLS	10/01-12/01
	Alaska	Y	33140 FQ	62420 AW	91600 TQ	AKBLS	10/01-12/01
	Anchorage MSA, AK	Y	32170 FQ	61380 AW	91420 TQ	AKBLS	10/01-12/01
	Arizona	Y	24710 FQ	49550 AW	89710 TQ	AZBLS	10/01-12/01
	Phoenix-Mesa MSA, AZ	Y	24930 FQ	51300 AW	94610 TQ	AZBLS	10/01-12/01
	Tucson MSA, AZ	Y	22990 FQ	44970 AW	76440 TQ	AZBLS	10/01-12/01
	Arkansas	Y	23460 FQ	47520 AW	96920 TQ	ARBLS	10/01-12/01
	Fayetteville-Springdale-Rogers MSA, AR	Y	25210 FQ	39980 AW	54920 TQ	ARBLS	10/01-12/01
	Fort Smith MSA, AR-OK	Y	25170 FQ	46040 AW	66820 TQ	ARBLS	10/01-12/01
	Little Rock-North Little Rock MSA, AR	Y	28370 FQ	60970 AW	131890 TQ	ARBLS	10/01-12/01
	California	Y	30880 FQ	57170 AW	89820 TQ	CABLS	10/01-12/01
	Bakersfield MSA, CA	Y	26720 FQ	47540 AW	70900 TQ	CABLS	10/01-12/01
	Chico-Paradise MSA, CA	Y	22580 FQ	46840 AW	73660 TQ	CABLS	10/01-12/01
	Fresno MSA, CA	Y	30690 FQ	50950 AW	76860 TQ	CABLS	10/01-12/01
	Los Angeles-Long Beach PMSA, CA	Y	27130 FQ	54440 AW	87300 TQ	CABLS	10/01-12/01
	Merced MSA, CA	Y	30440 FQ	52420 AW	73210 TQ	CABLS	10/01-12/01
	Modesto MSA, CA	Y	30200 FQ	50600 AW	78240 TQ	CABLS	10/01-12/01
	Oakland PMSA, CA	Y	39440 FQ	67370 AW	104340 TQ	CABLS	10/01-12/01
	Orange County PMSA, CA	Y	33380 FQ	57340 AW	84970 TQ	CABLS	10/01-12/01
	Redding MSA, CA	Y	24870 FQ	47080 AW	77670 TQ	CABLS	10/01-12/01
	Riverside-San Bernardino PMSA, CA	Y	30830 FQ	53440 AW	88010 TQ	CABLS	10/01-12/01
	Sacramento PMSA, CA	Y	31410 FQ	52880 AW	79180 TQ	CABLS	10/01-12/01
	Salinas MSA, CA	Y	32890 FQ	55300 AW	79540 TQ	CABLS	10/01-12/01
	San Diego MSA, CA	Y	29190 FQ	52540 AW	84890 TQ	CABLS	10/01-12/01
	San Francisco PMSA, CA	Y	37050 FQ	68170 AW	102280 TQ	CABLS	10/01-12/01
	San Jose PMSA, CA	Y	38850 FQ	70450 AW	105280 TQ	CABLS	10/01-12/01
	San Luis Obispo-Atascadero-Paso Robles MSA, CA	Y	25830 FQ	47620 AW	74070 TQ	CABLS	10/01-12/01
	Santa Barbara-Santa Maria-Lompoc MSA, CA	Y	31850 FQ	50920 AW	73080 TQ	CABLS	10/01-12/01
	Santa Cruz-Watsonville PMSA, CA	Y	34280 FQ	51390 AW	69630 TQ	CABLS	10/01-12/01
	Santa Rosa PMSA, CA	Y	31440 FQ	53440 AW	83610 TQ	CABLS	10/01-12/01
	Stockton-Lodi MSA, CA	Y	28770 FQ	51820 AW	70820 TQ	CABLS	10/01-12/01
	Vallejo-Fairfield-Napa PMSA, CA	Y	36220 FQ	55270 AW	79180 TQ	CABLS	10/01-12/01
	Ventura PMSA, CA	Y	30580 FQ	53150 AW	86630 TQ	CABLS	10/01-12/01
	Visalia-Tulare-Porterville MSA, CA	Y	23850 FQ	49740 AW	78020 TQ	CABLS	10/01-12/01
	Colorado	Y	31810 FQ	50470 AW	71730 TQ	COBLS	10/01-12/01
	Boulder-Longmont PMSA, CO	Y	32660 FQ	48900 AW	68950 TQ	COBLS	10/01-12/01
	Colorado Springs MSA, CO	Y	31520 FQ	50690 AW	70870 TQ	COBLS	10/01-12/01
	Denver PMSA, CO	Y	32780 FQ	52060 AW	72710 TQ	COBLS	10/01-12/01
	Fort Collins-Loveland MSA, CO	Y	31310 FQ	50050 AW	73230 TQ	COBLS	10/01-12/01
	Greeley PMSA, CO	Y	29130 FQ	46130 AW	72120 TQ	COBLS	10/01-12/01
	Connecticut	Y	36710 FQ	60520 AW	88440 TQ	CTBLS	10/01-12/01
	Bridgeport PMSA, CT	Y	37080 FQ	56660 AW	83120 TQ	CTBLS	10/01-12/01
	Danbury PMSA, CT	Y	37680 FQ	60630 AW	110610 TQ	CTBLS	10/01-12/01
	Hartford MSA, CT	Y	37140 FQ	60350 AW	88740 TQ	CTBLS	10/01-12/01
	New Haven-Meriden PMSA, CT	Y	39200 FQ	62280 AW	85300 TQ	CTBLS	10/01-12/01
	New London-Norwich MSA, CT-RI	Y	32100 FQ	51650 AW	77300 TQ	CTBLS	10/01-12/01
	Stamford-Norwalk PMSA, CT	Y	39840 FQ	67940 AW	98080 TQ	CTBLS	10/01-12/01
	Waterbury PMSA, CT	Y	32510 FQ	61180 AW	90930 TQ	CTBLS	10/01-12/01
	Delaware	Y	34500 FQ	55650 AW	82660 TQ	DEBLS	10/01-12/01
	Wilmington-Newark PMSA, DE-MD	Y	35630 FQ	56180 AW	82600 TQ	DEBLS	10/01-12/01
	District of Columbia	Y	28090 FQ	53690 AW	72450 TQ	DCBLS	10/01-12/01
	Washington PMSA, DC-MD-VA-WV	Y	30730 FQ	53770 AW	79880 TQ	DCBLS	10/01-12/01

AAW	Average annual wage	AOH	Average offered, high	ASH	Average starting, high	H	Hourly	M	Monthly	S	Special: hourly and annual
AE	Average entry wage	AOL	Average offered, low	ASL	Average starting, low	HI	Highest wage paid	MTC	Median total compensation	TQ	Third quartile wage
AEX	Average experienced wage	APH	Average pay, high range	AW	Average wage paid	HR	High end range	MW	Median wage paid	W	Weekly
AO	Average offered	APL	Average pay, low range	FQ	First quartile wage	LR	Low end range	SQ	Second quartile wage	Y	Yearly

Occupation/Type/Industry	Location	Per	Low	Mid	High	Source	Date
Cost Estimator	Florida	Y	26400 FQ	44780 AW	67790 TQ	FLBLS	10/01-12/01
	Daytona Beach MSA, FL	Y	27120 FQ	40530 AW	61250 TQ	FLBLS	10/01-12/01
	Fort Lauderdale PMSA, FL	Y	23480 FQ	43380 AW	67910 TQ	FLBLS	10/01-12/01
	Fort Myers-Cape Coral MSA, FL	Y	29630 FQ	40900 AW	56270 TQ	FLBLS	10/01-12/01
	Fort Pierce-Port St. Lucie MSA, FL	Y	25290 FQ	46510 AW	75970 TQ	FLBLS	10/01-12/01
	Fort Walton Beach MSA, FL	Y	30110 FQ	43150 AW	56420 TQ	FLBLS	10/01-12/01
	Gainesville MSA, FL	Y	26250 FQ	39470 AW	61280 TQ	FLBLS	10/01-12/01
	Jacksonville MSA, FL	Y	30320 FQ	51590 AW	78340 TQ	FLBLS	10/01-12/01
	Lakeland-Winter Haven MSA, FL	Y	25450 FQ	45610 AW	75460 TQ	FLBLS	10/01-12/01
	Melbourne-Titusville-Palm Bay MSA, FL	Y	20090 FQ	39130 AW	57680 TQ	FLBLS	10/01-12/01
	Miami PMSA, FL	Y	28150 FQ	45190 AW	67880 TQ	FLBLS	10/01-12/01
	Naples MSA, FL	Y	26870 FQ	50040 AW	79170 TQ	FLBLS	10/01-12/01
	Ocala MSA, FL	Y	21220 FQ	41200 AW	66040 TQ	FLBLS	10/01-12/01
	Orlando MSA, FL	Y	30320 FQ	48950 AW	72740 TQ	FLBLS	10/01-12/01
	Pensacola MSA, FL	Y	20780 FQ	38600 AW	55400 TQ	FLBLS	10/01-12/01
	Sarasota-Bradenton MSA, FL	Y	25760 FQ	41920 AW	59420 TQ	FLBLS	10/01-12/01
	Tallahassee MSA, FL	Y	23480 FQ	42200 AW	66590 TQ	FLBLS	10/01-12/01
	Tampa-St. Petersburg-Clearwater MSA, FL	Y	25740 FQ	43020 AW	58910 TQ	FLBLS	10/01-12/01
	West Palm Beach-Boca Raton MSA, FL	Y	31910 FQ	49400 AW	72850 TQ	FLBLS	10/01-12/01
	Georgia	Y	28870 FQ	52640 AW	84730 TQ	GABLS	10/01-12/01
	Atlanta MSA, GA	Y	31080 FQ	57080 AW	90290 TQ	GABLS	10/01-12/01
	Augusta-Aiken MSA, GA-SC	Y	35440 FQ	57960 AW	76410 TQ	GABLS	10/01-12/01
	Columbus MSA, GA-AL	Y	20250 FQ	41810 AW	64560 TQ	GABLS	10/01-12/01
	Macon MSA, GA	Y	29590 FQ	49320 AW	77780 TQ	GABLS	10/01-12/01
	Savannah MSA, GA	Y	31930 FQ	46990 AW	70970 TQ	GABLS	10/01-12/01
	Hawaii	Y	30050 FQ	56270 AW	88700 TQ	HIBLS	10/01-12/01
	Honolulu MSA, HI	Y	33650 FQ	58860 AW	91430 TQ	HIBLS	10/01-12/01
	Idaho	Y	23560 FQ	41520 AW	63580 TQ	IDBLS	10/01-12/01
	Boise City MSA, ID	Y	18120 FQ	39200 AW	60270 TQ	IDBLS	10/01-12/01
	Illinois	Y	26290 FQ	48900 AW	77930 TQ	ILBLS	10/01-12/01
	Champaign-Urbana MSA, IL	Y	25960 FQ	46740 AW	70070 TQ	ILBLS	10/01-12/01
	Chicago PMSA, IL	Y	26820 FQ	49610 AW	80420 TQ	ILBLS	10/01-12/01
	Peoria-Pekin MSA, IL	Y	29800 FQ	48950 AW	69530 TQ	ILBLS	10/01-12/01
	Rockford MSA, IL	Y	32640 FQ	54140 AW	81100 TQ	ILBLS	10/01-12/01
	Springfield MSA, IL	Y	30340 FQ	52450 AW	86810 TQ	ILBLS	10/01-12/01
	Indiana	Y	27810 FQ	47360 AW	72340 TQ	INBLS	10/01-12/01
	Elkhart-Goshen MSA, IN	Y	16830 FQ	35760 AW	59580 TQ	INBLS	10/01-12/01
	Evansville-Henderson MSA, IN-KY	Y	31210 FQ	50190 AW	71810 TQ	INBLS	10/01-12/01
	Fort Wayne MSA, IN	Y	29340 FQ	51980 AW	83050 TQ	INBLS	10/01-12/01
	Gary PMSA, IN	Y	26700 FQ	52890 AW	73680 TQ	INBLS	10/01-12/01
	Indianapolis MSA, IN	Y	30310 FQ	49230 AW	74760 TQ	INBLS	10/01-12/01
	Lafayette MSA, IN	Y	25800 FQ	44910 AW	76220 TQ	INBLS	10/01-12/01
	South Bend MSA, IN	Y	29510 FQ	45340 AW	58090 TQ	INBLS	10/01-12/01
	Iowa	Y	25980 FQ	47290 AW	70590 TQ	IABLS	10/01-12/01
	Cedar Rapids MSA, IA	Y	38280 FQ	65290 AW	137600 TQ	IABLS	10/01-12/01
	Davenport-Moline-Rock Island MSA, IA-IL	Y	25290 FQ	49180 AW	70530 TQ	IABLS	10/01-12/01
	Des Moines MSA, IA	Y	29770 FQ	48500 AW	71390 TQ	IABLS	10/01-12/01
	Kansas	Y	27370 FQ	46800 AW	69480 TQ	KSBLS	10/01-12/01
	Topeka MSA, KS	Y	29880 FQ	44710 AW	62960 TQ	KSBLS	10/01-12/01
	Wichita MSA, KS	Y	27620 FQ	47460 AW	71940 TQ	KSBLS	10/01-12/01
	Kentucky	Y	25710 FQ	43950 AW	67640 TQ	KYBLS	10/01-12/01
	Lexington MSA, KY	Y	29090 FQ	44790 AW	67650 TQ	KYBLS	10/01-12/01
	Louisville MSA, KY-IN	Y	28330 FQ	47070 AW	70270 TQ	KYBLS	10/01-12/01
	Louisiana	Y	26720 FQ	45390 AW	68150 TQ	LABLS	10/01-12/01
	Baton Rouge MSA, LA	Y	28900 FQ	45640 AW	64470 TQ	LABLS	10/01-12/01
	Houma MSA, LA	Y	27720 FQ	51930 AW	89760 TQ	LABLS	10/01-12/01
	Lafayette MSA, LA	Y	22980 FQ	42950 AW	68010 TQ	LABLS	10/01-12/01
	Lake Charles MSA, LA	Y	30970 FQ	50050 AW	68180 TQ	LABLS	10/01-12/01
	New Orleans MSA, LA	Y	30900 FQ	46350 AW	68650 TQ	LABLS	10/01-12/01
	Shreveport-Bossier City MSA, LA	Y	25090 FQ	40790 AW	61690 TQ	LABLS	10/01-12/01
	Maine	Y	25030 FQ	43960 AW	65820 TQ	MEBLS	10/01-12/01
	Portland MSA, ME	Y	25440 FQ	44590 AW	72150 TQ	MEBLS	10/01-12/01
	Maryland	Y	29460 FQ	49690 AW	72540 TQ	MDBLS	10/01-12/01

AAW	Average annual wage	**AOH**	Average offered, high	**ASH**	Average starting, high	**H**	Hourly	**M**	Monthly	**S**	Special: hourly and annual
AE	Average entry wage	**AOL**	Average offered, low	**ASL**	Average starting, low	**HI**	Highest wage paid	**MTC**	Median total compensation	**TQ**	Third quartile wage
AEX	Average experienced wage	**APH**	Average pay, high range	**AW**	Average wage paid	**HR**	High end range	**MW**	Median wage paid	**W**	Weekly
AO	Average offered	**APL**	Average pay, low range	**FQ**	First quartile wage	**LR**	Low end range	**SQ**	Second quartile wage	**Y**	Yearly

Occupation/Type/Industry	Location	Per	Low	Mid	High	Source	Date
Cost Estimator	Baltimore PMSA, MD	Y	30650 FQ	50290 AW	72460 TQ	MDBLS	10/01-12/01
	Massachusetts	Y	33240 FQ	58670 AW	87230 TQ	MABLS	10/01-12/01
	Boston PMSA, MA-NH	Y	36690 FQ	62270 AW	89830 TQ	MABLS	10/01-12/01
	Brockton PMSA, MA	Y	32100 FQ	51430 AW	71630 TQ	MABLS	10/01-12/01
	Lawrence PMSA, MA-NH	Y	36150 FQ	52300 AW	73350 TQ	MABLS	10/01-12/01
	Lowell PMSA, MA-NH	Y	29320 FQ	56450 AW	80660 TQ	MABLS	10/01-12/01
	New Bedford PMSA, MA	Y	33000 FQ	56890 AW	84610 TQ	MABLS	10/01-12/01
	Springfield MSA, MA	Y	29220 FQ	47410 AW	66910 TQ	MABLS	10/01-12/01
	Worcester PMSA, MA-CT	Y	32490 FQ	50470 AW	72810 TQ	MABLS	10/01-12/01
	Michigan	Y	29300 FQ	52520 AW	83450 TQ	MIBLS	10/01-12/01
	Ann Arbor PMSA, MI	Y	27010 FQ	51440 AW	82450 TQ	MIBLS	10/01-12/01
	Detroit PMSA, MI	Y	32070 FQ	58070 AW	89500 TQ	MIBLS	10/01-12/01
	Flint PMSA, MI	Y	29430 FQ	54480 AW	94640 TQ	MIBLS	10/01-12/01
	Grand Rapids-Muskegon-Holland MSA, MI	Y	32450 FQ	51950 AW	74430 TQ	MIBLS	10/01-12/01
	Kalamazoo-Battle Creek MSA, MI	Y	25460 FQ	45780 AW	71540 TQ	MIBLS	10/01-12/01
	Lansing-East Lansing MSA, MI	Y	30320 FQ	52240 AW	80240 TQ	MIBLS	10/01-12/01
	Saginaw-Bay City-Midland MSA, MI	Y	28640 FQ	47930 AW	73680 TQ	MIBLS	10/01-12/01
	Minnesota	Y	29710 FQ	47620 AW	70690 TQ	MNBLS	10/01-12/01
	Duluth-Superior MSA, MN-WI	Y	24590 FQ	41000 AW	64820 TQ	MNBLS	10/01-12/01
	Minneapolis-St. Paul MSA, MN-WI	Y	31170 FQ	49740 AW	72130 TQ	MNBLS	10/01-12/01
	St. Cloud MSA, MN	Y	28150 FQ	43240 AW	63970 TQ	MNBLS	10/01-12/01
	Mississippi	Y	25260 FQ	43200 AW	67630 TQ	MSBLS	10/01-12/01
	Biloxi-Gulfport-Pascagoula MSA, MS	Y	27000 FQ	42140 AW	63770 TQ	MSBLS	10/01-12/01
	Jackson MSA, MS	Y	23960 FQ	43160 AW	69990 TQ	MSBLS	10/01-12/01
	Missouri	Y	28350 FQ	49820 AW	74280 TQ	MOBLS	10/01-12/01
	Kansas City MSA, MO-KS	Y	30620 FQ	51990 AW	74490 TQ	MOBLS	10/01-12/01
	St. Louis MSA, MO-IL	Y	30140 FQ	51920 AW	75490 TQ	MOBLS	10/01-12/01
	Springfield MSA, MO	Y	24250 FQ	48370 AW	80090 TQ	MOBLS	10/01-12/01
	Montana	Y	22410 FQ	37510 AW	54770 TQ	MTBLS	10/01-12/01
	Billings MSA, MT	Y	18570 FQ	36250 AW	49670 TQ	MTBLS	10/01-12/01
	Nebraska	Y	23750 FQ	41180 AW	63160 TQ	NEBLS	10/01-12/01
	Lincoln MSA, NE	Y	20900 FQ	37410 AW	58060 TQ	NEBLS	10/01-12/01
	Omaha MSA, NE-IA	Y	29240 FQ	44740 AW	65000 TQ	NEBLS	10/01-12/01
	Nevada	Y	32730 FQ	52720 AW	75880 TQ	NVBLS	10/01-12/01
	Las Vegas MSA, NV-AZ	Y	31880 FQ	52800 AW	75960 TQ	NVBLS	10/01-12/01
	Reno MSA, NV	Y	33590 FQ	52000 AW	75950 TQ	NVBLS	10/01-12/01
	New Hampshire	Y	30840 FQ	50610 AW	72940 TQ	NHBLS	10/01-12/01
	Manchester PMSA, NH	Y	31350 FQ	50820 AW	81730 TQ	NHBLS	10/01-12/01
	Nashua PMSA, NH	Y	31810 FQ	59130 AW		NHBLS	10/01-12/01
	Portsmouth-Rochester PMSA, NH-ME	Y	30500 FQ	49280 AW	73520 TQ	NHBLS	10/01-12/01
	New Jersey	Y	32670 FQ	56050 AW	83840 TQ	NJBLS	10/01-12/01
	Atlantic-Cape May PMSA, NJ	Y	31770 FQ	52990 AW	75700 TQ	NJBLS	10/01-12/01
	Bergen-Passaic PMSA, NJ	Y	33110 FQ	56300 AW	84000 TQ	NJBLS	10/01-12/01
	Jersey City PMSA, NJ	Y	22140 FQ	54640 AW	89660 TQ	NJBLS	10/01-12/01
	Middlesex-Somerset-Hunterdon PMSA, NJ	Y	31840 FQ	55290 AW	86580 TQ	NJBLS	10/01-12/01
	Monmouth-Ocean PMSA, NJ	Y	33700 FQ	54450 AW	81240 TQ	NJBLS	10/01-12/01
	Newark PMSA, NJ	Y	36440 FQ	60000 AW	87170 TQ	NJBLS	10/01-12/01
	Trenton PMSA, NJ	Y	36040 FQ	51960 AW	68880 TQ	NJBLS	10/01-12/01
	New Mexico	Y	26450 FQ	43890 AW	66040 TQ	NMBLS	10/01-12/01
	Albuquerque MSA, NM	Y	27590 FQ	43530 AW	64390 TQ	NMBLS	10/01-12/01
	Las Cruces MSA, NM	Y	21450 FQ	38820 AW	62050 TQ	NMBLS	10/01-12/01
	New York	Y	27340 FQ	53860 AW	88640 TQ	NYBLS	10/01-12/01
	Albany-Schenectady-Troy MSA, NY	Y	20860 FQ	42140 AW	62620 TQ	NYBLS	10/01-12/01
	Binghamton MSA, NY	Y	23480 FQ	36200 AW	53220 TQ	NYBLS	10/01-12/01
	Buffalo-Niagara Falls MSA, NY	Y	28360 FQ	46210 AW	66180 TQ	NYBLS	10/01-12/01
	Dutchess County PMSA, NY	Y	32600 FQ	47920 AW	72040 TQ	NYBLS	10/01-12/01
	Nassau-Suffolk PMSA, NY	Y	24880 FQ	49640 AW	82800 TQ	NYBLS	10/01-12/01
	New York PMSA, NY	Y	36030 FQ	64030 AW	97360 TQ	NYBLS	10/01-12/01
	Newburgh PMSA, NY-PA	Y	30000 FQ	54060 AW	84550 TQ	NYBLS	10/01-12/01
	Rochester MSA, NY	Y	25500 FQ	46570 AW	74600 TQ	NYBLS	10/01-12/01
	Syracuse MSA, NY	Y	31370 FQ	47280 AW	67730 TQ	NYBLS	10/01-12/01
	Utica-Rome MSA, NY	Y	23190 FQ	38830 AW	55650 TQ	NYBLS	10/01-12/01
	North Carolina	Y	28420 FQ	45740 AW	69030 TQ	NCBLS	10/01-12/01

AAW	Average annual wage	**AOH**	Average offered, high	**ASH**	Average starting, high	**H**	Hourly	**M**	Monthly	**S**	Special: hourly and annual
AE	Average entry wage	**AOL**	Average offered, low	**ASL**	Average starting, low	**HI**	Highest wage paid	**MTC**	Median total compensation	**TQ**	Third quartile wage
AEX	Average experienced wage	**APH**	Average pay, high range	**AW**	Average wage paid	**HR**	High end range	**MW**	Median wage paid	**W**	Weekly
AO	Average offered	**APL**	Average pay, low range	**FQ**	First quartile wage	**LR**	Low end range	**SQ**	Second quartile wage	**Y**	Yearly

Occupation/Type/Industry	Location	Per	Low	Mid	High	Source	Date
Cost Estimator	Asheville MSA, NC	Y	19100 FQ	39670 AW	58750 TQ	NCBLS	10/01-12/01
	Charlotte-Gastonia-Rock Hill MSA, NC-SC	Y	31750 FQ	49120 AW	70500 TQ	NCBLS	10/01-12/01
	Fayetteville MSA, NC	Y	23230 FQ	42390 AW	67840 TQ	NCBLS	10/01-12/01
	Greensboro-Winston-Salem-High Point MSA, NC	Y	29050 FQ	44180 AW	66990 TQ	NCBLS	10/01-12/01
	Hickory-Morganton-Lenoir MSA, NC	Y	29820 FQ	43490 AW	59310 TQ	NCBLS	10/01-12/01
	Raleigh-Durham-Chapel Hill MSA, NC	Y	28160 FQ	46440 AW	70500 TQ	NCBLS	10/01-12/01
	Wilmington MSA, NC	Y	23570 FQ	46980 AW	73260 TQ	NCBLS	10/01-12/01
	North Dakota	Y	23650 FQ	40110 AW	57880 TQ	NDBLS	10/01-12/01
	Fargo-Moorhead MSA, ND-MN	Y	25010 FQ	41350 AW	61700 TQ	NDBLS	10/01-12/01
	Ohio	Y	26820 FQ	45780 AW	69070 TQ	OHBLS	10/01-12/01
	Akron PMSA, OH	Y	30170 FQ	47460 AW	69160 TQ	OHBLS	10/01-12/01
	Canton-Massillon MSA, OH	Y	24640 FQ	39000 AW	56560 TQ	OHBLS	10/01-12/01
	Cincinnati PMSA, OH-KY-IN	Y	26970 FQ	46850 AW	73060 TQ	OHBLS	10/01-12/01
	Cleveland-Lorain-Elyria PMSA, OH	Y	31910 FQ	50420 AW	71660 TQ	OHBLS	10/01-12/01
	Columbus MSA, OH	Y	21300 FQ	42050 AW	59530 TQ	OHBLS	10/01-12/01
	Dayton-Springfield MSA, OH	Y	28660 FQ	47330 AW	70530 TQ	OHBLS	10/01-12/01
	Hamilton-Middletown PMSA, OH	Y	21980 FQ	48470 AW	70990 TQ	OHBLS	10/01-12/01
	Mansfield MSA, OH	Y	22820 FQ	38910 AW	57870 TQ	OHBLS	10/01-12/01
	Toledo MSA, OH	Y	28390 FQ	48310 AW	72260 TQ	OHBLS	10/01-12/01
	Youngstown-Warren MSA, OH	Y	25840 FQ	44280 AW	60440 TQ	OHBLS	10/01-12/01
	Oklahoma	Y	24950 FQ	42470 AW	61360 TQ	OKBLS	10/01-12/01
	Oklahoma City MSA, OK	Y	27420 FQ	45000 AW	64110 TQ	OKBLS	10/01-12/01
	Tulsa MSA, OK	Y	24250 FQ	40470 AW	59460 TQ	OKBLS	10/01-12/01
	Oregon	Y	29800 FQ	49090 AW	71840 TQ	ORBLS	10/01-12/01
	Eugene-Springfield MSA, OR	Y	28280 FQ	44380 AW	69330 TQ	ORBLS	10/01-12/01
	Medford-Ashland MSA, OR	Y	26810 FQ	45640 AW	67910 TQ	ORBLS	10/01-12/01
	Portland-Vancouver PMSA, OR-WA	Y	31890 FQ	51500 AW	72960 TQ	ORBLS	10/01-12/01
	Salem PMSA, OR	Y	29330 FQ	51030 AW	72520 TQ	ORBLS	10/01-12/01
	Pennsylvania	Y	28820 FQ	48770 AW	75240 TQ	PABLS	10/01-12/01
	Allentown-Bethlehem-Easton MSA, PA	Y	28260 FQ	47170 AW	70990 TQ	PABLS	10/01-12/01
	Erie MSA, PA	Y	27160 FQ	43020 AW	65710 TQ	PABLS	10/01-12/01
	Harrisburg-Lebanon-Carlisle MSA, PA	Y	27320 FQ	45670 AW	70340 TQ	PABLS	10/01-12/01
	Johnstown MSA, PA	Y	24050 FQ	35560 AW	51980 TQ	PABLS	10/01-12/01
	Lancaster MSA, PA	Y	30780 FQ	46600 AW	72400 TQ	PABLS	10/01-12/01
	Philadelphia PMSA, PA-NJ	Y	33000 FQ	55070 AW	84200 TQ	PABLS	10/01-12/01
	Pittsburgh MSA, PA	Y	29730 FQ	49210 AW	73700 TQ	PABLS	10/01-12/01
	Reading MSA, PA	Y	27440 FQ	46060 AW	68210 TQ	PABLS	10/01-12/01
	Scranton-Wilkes-Barre-Hazleton MSA, PA	Y	28870 FQ	47430 AW	68290 TQ	PABLS	10/01-12/01
	York MSA, PA	Y	28130 FQ	45210 AW	68090 TQ	PABLS	10/01-12/01
	Rhode Island	Y	33650 FQ	56890 AW	89670 TQ	RIBLS	10/01-12/01
	Providence-Fall River-Warwick MSA, RI-MA	Y	31210 FQ	55390 AW	88710 TQ	RIBLS	10/01-12/01
	South Carolina	Y	25460 FQ	44250 AW	70010 TQ	SCBLS	10/01-12/01
	Charleston-North Charleston MSA, SC	Y	25770 FQ	41830 AW	63730 TQ	SCBLS	10/01-12/01
	Columbia MSA, SC	Y	24970 FQ	40080 AW	61380 TQ	SCBLS	10/01-12/01
	Greenville-Spartanburg-Anderson MSA, SC	Y	25760 FQ	46700 AW	68920 TQ	SCBLS	10/01-12/01
	Myrtle Beach MSA, SC	Y	26110 FQ	38930 AW	55120 TQ	SCBLS	10/01-12/01
	South Dakota	Y	28030 FQ	38680 AW	52930 TQ	SDBLS	10/01-12/01
	Sioux Falls MSA, SD	Y	29910 FQ	40020 AW	53860 TQ	SDBLS	10/01-12/01
	Tennessee	Y	27800 FQ	46840 AW	70660 TQ	TNBLS	10/01-12/01
	Chattanooga MSA, TN-GA	Y	28560 FQ	46780 AW	71760 TQ	TNBLS	10/01-12/01
	Clarksville-Hopkinsville MSA, TN-KY	Y	21410 FQ	40760 AW	64650 TQ	TNBLS	10/01-12/01
	Johnson City-Kingsport-Bristol MSA, TN-VA	Y	24110 FQ	41210 AW	60910 TQ	TNBLS	10/01-12/01
	Knoxville MSA, TN	Y	28830 FQ	50730 AW	72820 TQ	TNBLS	10/01-12/01
	Memphis MSA, TN-AR-MS	Y	30230 FQ	48590 AW	72720 TQ	TNBLS	10/01-12/01
	Nashville MSA, TN	Y	29680 FQ	47680 AW	71580 TQ	TNBLS	10/01-12/01
	Texas	Y	29280 FQ	50270 AW	75350 TQ	TXBLS	10/01-12/01

AAW	Average annual wage	**AOH**	Average offered, high	**ASH**	Average starting, high	**H**	Hourly	**M**	Monthly	**S**	Special: hourly and annual
AE	Average entry wage	**AOL**	Average offered, low	**ASL**	Average starting, low	**HI**	Highest wage paid	**MTC**	Median total compensation	**TQ**	Third quartile wage
AEX	Average experienced wage	**APH**	Average pay, high range	**AW**	Average wage paid	**HR**	High end range	**MW**	Median wage paid	**W**	Weekly
AO	Average offered	**APL**	Average pay, low range	**FQ**	First quartile wage	**LR**	Low end range	**SQ**	Second quartile wage	**Y**	Yearly

Occupation/Type/Industry	Location	Per	Low	Mid	High	Source	Date
Cost Estimator	Amarillo MSA, TX	Y	21030 FQ	42120 AW	64460 TQ	TXBLS	10/01-12/01
	Austin-San Marcos MSA, TX	Y	29340 FQ	49590 AW	72490 TQ	TXBLS	10/01-12/01
	Beaumont-Port Arthur MSA, TX	Y	35740 FQ	51540 AW	71390 TQ	TXBLS	10/01-12/01
	Brazoria PMSA, TX	Y	37380 FQ	54190 AW	73950 TQ	TXBLS	10/01-12/01
	Brownsville-Harlingen-San Benito MSA, TX	Y	23790 FQ	38680 AW	55310 TQ	TXBLS	10/01-12/01
	Corpus Christi MSA, TX	Y	30310 FQ	48350 AW	70770 TQ	TXBLS	10/01-12/01
	Dallas PMSA, TX	Y	33130 FQ	53300 AW	79720 TQ	TXBLS	10/01-12/01
	El Paso MSA, TX	Y	24830 FQ	43080 AW	68840 TQ	TXBLS	10/01-12/01
	Fort Worth-Arlington PMSA, TX	Y	30670 FQ	50120 AW	74540 TQ	TXBLS	10/01-12/01
	Galveston-Texas City PMSA, TX	Y	31070 FQ	49980 AW	75450 TQ	TXBLS	10/01-12/01
	Houston PMSA, TX	Y	31230 FQ	53540 AW	80450 TQ	TXBLS	10/01-12/01
	Killeen-Temple MSA, TX	Y	23310 FQ	43380 AW	65760 TQ	TXBLS	10/01-12/01
	Laredo MSA, TX	Y	23570 FQ	43330 AW	70230 TQ	TXBLS	10/01-12/01
	Longview-Marshall MSA, TX	Y	23440 FQ	46600 AW	73700 TQ	TXBLS	10/01-12/01
	Lubbock MSA, TX	Y	28720 FQ	51120 AW	71450 TQ	TXBLS	10/01-12/01
	McAllen-Edinburg-Mission MSA, TX	Y	17390 FQ	37090 AW	54510 TQ	TXBLS	10/01-12/01
	Odessa-Midland MSA, TX	Y	28460 FQ	45450 AW	63190 TQ	TXBLS	10/01-12/01
	San Antonio MSA, TX	Y	26020 FQ	46490 AW	74820 TQ	TXBLS	10/01-12/01
	Tyler MSA, TX	Y	19050 FQ	39250 AW	64160 TQ	TXBLS	10/01-12/01
	Waco MSA, TX	Y	25890 FQ	43510 AW	72750 TQ	TXBLS	10/01-12/01
	Utah	Y	22980 FQ	46060 AW	72850 TQ	UTBLS	10/01-12/01
	Provo-Orem MSA, UT	Y	27520 FQ	48460 AW	71560 TQ	UTBLS	10/01-12/01
	Salt Lake City-Ogden MSA, UT	Y	27170 FQ	47420 AW	73390 TQ	UTBLS	10/01-12/01
	Vermont	Y	28790 FQ	44770 AW	63970 TQ	VTBLS	10/01-12/01
	Burlington MSA, VT	Y	30260 FQ	46490 AW	69410 TQ	VTBLS	10/01-12/01
	Virginia	Y	29590 FQ	50360 AW	77310 TQ	VABLS	10/01-12/01
	Lynchburg MSA, VA	Y	24500 FQ	43440 AW	63520 TQ	VABLS	10/01-12/01
	Norfolk-Virginia Beach-Newport News MSA, VA-NC	Y	28350 FQ	47700 AW	75300 TQ	VABLS	10/01-12/01
	Richmond-Petersburg MSA, VA	Y	30360 FQ	46370 AW	69990 TQ	VABLS	10/01-12/01
	Roanoke MSA, VA	Y	27090 FQ	44920 AW	67600 TQ	VABLS	10/01-12/01
	Washington	Y	31880 FQ	52840 AW	79370 TQ	WABLS	10/01-12/01
	Bremerton PMSA, WA	Y	33470 FQ	49800 AW	73640 TQ	WABLS	10/01-12/01
	Olympia PMSA, WA	Y	29890 FQ	50390 AW	72470 TQ	WABLS	10/01-12/01
	Richland-Kennewick-Pasco MSA, WA	Y	31670 FQ	63180 AW	101380 TQ	WABLS	10/01-12/01
	Seattle-Bellevue-Everett PMSA, WA	Y	34700 FQ	55330 AW	79270 TQ	WABLS	10/01-12/01
	Spokane MSA, WA	Y	28800 FQ	43120 AW	62230 TQ	WABLS	10/01-12/01
	Tacoma PMSA, WA	Y	32440 FQ	53710 AW	83600 TQ	WABLS	10/01-12/01
	Yakima MSA, WA	Y	29180 FQ	41550 AW	58320 TQ	WABLS	10/01-12/01
	West Virginia	Y	23230 FQ	42470 AW	61310 TQ	WVBLS	10/01-12/01
	Charleston MSA, WV	Y	23570 FQ	43050 AW	61200 TQ	WVBLS	10/01-12/01
	Huntington-Ashland MSA, WV-KY-OH	Y	22600 FQ	43290 AW	68960 TQ	WVBLS	10/01-12/01
	Wisconsin	Y	27980 FQ	45870 AW	70450 TQ	WIBLS	10/01-12/01
	Appleton-Oshkosh-Neenah MSA, WI	Y	28210 FQ	45440 AW	65920 TQ	WIBLS	10/01-12/01
	Green Bay MSA, WI	Y	30940 FQ	51870 AW	73590 TQ	WIBLS	10/01-12/01
	Madison MSA, WI	Y	27840 FQ	46270 AW	74360 TQ	WIBLS	10/01-12/01
	Milwaukee-Waukesha PMSA, WI	Y	29420 FQ	49950 AW	77790 TQ	WIBLS	10/01-12/01
	Racine PMSA, WI	Y	28530 FQ	41700 AW	59020 TQ	WIBLS	10/01-12/01
	Wyoming	Y	26800 FQ	46570 AW	68150 TQ	WYBLS	10/01-12/01
	Cheyenne MSA, WY	Y	21890 FQ	41360 AW	59050 TQ	WYBLS	10/01-12/01
	Puerto Rico	Y	18520 FQ	34770 AW	55930 TQ	PRBLS	10/01-12/01
	Guam	Y	19810 FQ	34470 AW	50610 TQ	GUBLS	10/01-12/01
Costume Attendant	Arizona	H	6.65 FQ	10.53 AW	14.17 TQ	AZBLS	10/01-12/01
	California	H	7.94 FQ	15.03 AW	22.94 TQ	CABLS	10/01-12/01
	Connecticut	H	7.53 FQ	10.51 AW	15.71 TQ	CTBLS	10/01-12/01
	Florida	H	6.06 FQ	9.58 AW	13.69 TQ	FLBLS	10/01-12/01
	Illinois	H	7.76 FQ	12.81 AW	20.23 TQ	ILBLS	10/01-12/01
	Indiana	H	6.67 FQ	13.70 AW	25.33 TQ	INBLS	10/01-12/01
	Minnesota	H	8.45 FQ	14.15 AW	17.50 TQ	MNBLS	10/01-12/01

AAW Average annual wage; AE Average entry wage; AEX Average experienced wage; AO Average offered; AOH Average offered, high; AOL Average offered, low; APH Average pay, high range; APL Average pay, low range; ASH Average starting, high; ASL Average starting, low; AW Average wage paid; FQ First quartile wage; H Hourly; HI Highest wage paid; HR High end range; LR Low end range; M Monthly; MTC Median total compensation; MW Median wage paid; SQ Second quartile wage; S Special: hourly and annual; TQ Third quartile wage; W Weekly; Y Yearly

Occupation/Type/Industry	Location	Per	Low	Mid	High	Source	Date
Costume Attendant	Mississippi	H	6.89 FQ	10.61 AW	13.94 TQ	MSBLS	10/01-12/01
	Missouri	H	7.63 FQ	13.09 AW	20.92 TQ	MOBLS	10/01-12/01
	Nevada	H	7.25 FQ	11.53 AW	15.34 TQ	NVBLS	10/01-12/01
	New Jersey	H	7.67 FQ	13.02 AW	18.54 TQ	NJBLS	10/01-12/01
	New York	H	9.14 FQ	19.79 AW	29.09 TQ	NYBLS	10/01-12/01
	Ohio	H	7.29 FQ	10.69 AW	15.90 TQ	OHBLS	10/01-12/01
	Oklahoma	H	11.84 FQ	12.83 AW	14.30 TQ	OKBLS	10/01-12/01
	Pennsylvania	H	6.14 FQ	10.24 AW	17.05 TQ	PABLS	10/01-12/01
	South Carolina	H	6.50 FQ	8.32 AW	10.64 TQ	SCBLS	10/01-12/01
	Texas	H	6.08 FQ	11.61 AW	17.96 TQ	TXBLS	10/01-12/01
	Virginia	H	8.37 FQ	12.09 AW	17.75 TQ	VABLS	10/01-12/01
	Washington	H	10.13 FQ	13.29 AW	16.59 TQ	WABLS	10/01-12/01
	Wisconsin	H	5.82 FQ	8.14 AW	11.12 TQ	WIBLS	10/01-12/01
Counter and Rental Clerk	Alabama	Y	11750 FQ	17750 AW	28250 TQ	ALBLS	10/01-12/01
	Birmingham MSA, AL	Y	12170 FQ	19510 AW	32220 TQ	ALBLS	10/01-12/01
	Huntsville MSA, AL	Y	12040 FQ	17640 AW	25790 TQ	ALBLS	10/01-12/01
	Mobile MSA, AL	Y	11710 FQ	17050 AW	25320 TQ	ALBLS	10/01-12/01
	Montgomery MSA, AL	Y	11880 FQ	17780 AW	26610 TQ	ALBLS	10/01-12/01
	Alaska	Y	12640 FQ	18990 AW	29820 TQ	AKBLS	10/01-12/01
	Anchorage MSA, AK	Y	15180 FQ	22710 AW	33410 TQ	AKBLS	10/01-12/01
	Arizona	Y	12090 FQ	21350 AW	32860 TQ	AZBLS	10/01-12/01
	Phoenix-Mesa MSA, AZ	Y	12030 FQ	21860 AW	34800 TQ	AZBLS	10/01-12/01
	Tucson MSA, AZ	Y	12410 FQ	19750 AW	28630 TQ	AZBLS	10/01-12/01
	Arkansas	Y	11630 FQ	15440 AW	21740 TQ	ARBLS	10/01-12/01
	Fayetteville-Springdale-Rogers MSA, AR	Y	11650 FQ	15300 AW	20700 TQ	ARBLS	10/01-12/01
	Fort Smith MSA, AR-OK	Y	11660 FQ	15260 AW	21120 TQ	ARBLS	10/01-12/01
	Little Rock-North Little Rock MSA, AR	Y	11700 FQ	15670 AW	22120 TQ	ARBLS	10/01-12/01
	California	Y	13970 FQ	21610 AW	32980 TQ	CABLS	10/01-12/01
	Bakersfield MSA, CA	Y	13830 FQ	19380 AW	27970 TQ	CABLS	10/01-12/01
	Chico-Paradise MSA, CA	Y	13480 FQ	20060 AW	27930 TQ	CABLS	10/01-12/01
	Fresno MSA, CA	Y	14090 FQ	21300 AW	34240 TQ	CABLS	10/01-12/01
	Los Angeles-Long Beach PMSA, CA	Y	14010 FQ	21500 AW	33010 TQ	CABLS	10/01-12/01
	Merced MSA, CA	Y	13470 FQ	19190 AW	27880 TQ	CABLS	10/01-12/01
	Modesto MSA, CA	Y	13830 FQ	19790 AW	28470 TQ	CABLS	10/01-12/01
	Oakland PMSA, CA	Y	14400 FQ	22450 AW	34200 TQ	CABLS	10/01-12/01
	Orange County PMSA, CA	Y	13790 FQ	21590 AW	32700 TQ	CABLS	10/01-12/01
	Redding MSA, CA	Y	13540 FQ	18370 AW	27110 TQ	CABLS	10/01-12/01
	Riverside-San Bernardino PMSA, CA	Y	14210 FQ	20760 AW	27600 TQ	CABLS	10/01-12/01
	Sacramento PMSA, CA	Y	13820 FQ	21590 AW	34250 TQ	CABLS	10/01-12/01
	Salinas MSA, CA	Y	13710 FQ	20980 AW	33010 TQ	CABLS	10/01-12/01
	San Diego MSA, CA	Y	14200 FQ	21730 AW	33450 TQ	CABLS	10/01-12/01
	San Francisco PMSA, CA	Y	13970 FQ	23930 AW	35640 TQ	CABLS	10/01-12/01
	San Jose PMSA, CA	Y	15170 FQ	25400 AW	39820 TQ	CABLS	10/01-12/01
	San Luis Obispo-Atascadero-Paso Robles MSA, CA	Y	13610 FQ	21010 AW	39080 TQ	CABLS	10/01-12/01
	Santa Barbara-Santa Maria-Lompoc MSA, CA	Y	13440 FQ	18510 AW	25960 TQ	CABLS	10/01-12/01
	Santa Cruz-Watsonville PMSA, CA	Y	14130 FQ	24490 AW	47880 TQ	CABLS	10/01-12/01
	Santa Rosa PMSA, CA	Y	13730 FQ	20940 AW	28720 TQ	CABLS	10/01-12/01
	Stockton-Lodi MSA, CA	Y	13560 FQ	20180 AW	30630 TQ	CABLS	10/01-12/01
	Vallejo-Fairfield-Napa PMSA, CA	Y	14140 FQ	22120 AW	33650 TQ	CABLS	10/01-12/01
	Ventura PMSA, CA	Y	13520 FQ	21480 AW	33880 TQ	CABLS	10/01-12/01
	Visalia-Tulare-Porterville MSA, CA	Y	14110 FQ	18780 AW	23650 TQ	CABLS	10/01-12/01
	Colorado	Y	12350 FQ	19520 AW	30790 TQ	COBLS	10/01-12/01
	Boulder-Longmont PMSA, CO	Y	12680 FQ	21530 AW	35480 TQ	COBLS	10/01-12/01
	Colorado Springs MSA, CO	Y	12400 FQ	20680 AW	36830 TQ	COBLS	10/01-12/01
	Denver PMSA, CO	Y	12700 FQ	19840 AW	31120 TQ	COBLS	10/01-12/01
	Fort Collins-Loveland MSA, CO	Y	11760 FQ	17730 AW	27560 TQ	COBLS	10/01-12/01
	Greeley PMSA, CO	Y	12410 FQ	17840 AW	26200 TQ	COBLS	10/01-12/01
	Connecticut	Y	13800 FQ	21440 AW	35240 TQ	CTBLS	10/01-12/01
	Bridgeport PMSA, CT	Y	13640 FQ	23490 AW	41920 TQ	CTBLS	10/01-12/01
	Danbury PMSA, CT	Y	14900 FQ	23140 AW	30150 TQ	CTBLS	10/01-12/01
	Hartford MSA, CT	Y	13860 FQ	20820 AW	34210 TQ	CTBLS	10/01-12/01

AAW	Average annual wage	**AOH**	Average offered, high	**ASH**	Average starting, high	**H**	Hourly	**M**	Monthly	**S**	Special: hourly and annual
AE	Average entry wage	**AOL**	Average offered, low	**ASL**	Average starting, low	**HI**	Highest wage paid	**MTC**	Median total compensation	**TQ**	Third quartile wage
AEX	Average experienced wage	**APH**	Average pay, high range	**AW**	Average wage paid	**HR**	High end range	**MW**	Median wage paid	**W**	Weekly
AO	Average offered	**APL**	Average pay, low range	**FQ**	First quartile wage	**LR**	Low end range	**SQ**	Second quartile wage	**Y**	Yearly

Occupation/Type/Industry	Location	Per	Low	Mid	High	Source	Date
Counter and Rental Clerk	New Haven-Meriden PMSA, CT	Y	13730 FQ	22180 AW	45520 TQ	CTBLS	10/01-12/01
	New London-Norwich MSA, CT-RI	Y	14200 FQ	21080 AW	32710 TQ	CTBLS	10/01-12/01
	Stamford-Norwalk PMSA, CT	Y	14580 FQ	25420 AW	40810 TQ	CTBLS	10/01-12/01
	Waterbury PMSA, CT	Y	14060 FQ	19400 AW	26900 TQ	CTBLS	10/01-12/01
	Delaware	Y	13550 FQ	19870 AW	30200 TQ	DEBLS	10/01-12/01
	Wilmington-Newark PMSA, DE-MD	Y	13760 FQ	21480 AW	35050 TQ	DEBLS	10/01-12/01
	District of Columbia	Y	14500 FQ	19830 AW	28830 TQ	DCBLS	10/01-12/01
	Washington PMSA, DC-MD-VA-WV	Y	12500 FQ	19730 AW	32530 TQ	DCBLS	10/01-12/01
	Florida	Y	11820 FQ	18400 AW	28920 TQ	FLBLS	10/01-12/01
	Daytona Beach MSA, FL	Y	13630 FQ	17510 AW	21980 TQ	FLBLS	10/01-12/01
	Fort Myers-Cape Coral MSA, FL	Y	12770 FQ	20290 AW	30710 TQ	FLBLS	10/01-12/01
	Fort Pierce-Port St. Lucie MSA, FL	Y	12800 FQ	19510 AW	27590 TQ	FLBLS	10/01-12/01
	Fort Walton Beach MSA, FL	Y	11850 FQ	16840 AW	23570 TQ	FLBLS	10/01-12/01
	Gainesville MSA, FL	Y	11780 FQ	16230 AW	22130 TQ	FLBLS	10/01-12/01
	Jacksonville MSA, FL	Y	11780 FQ	18720 AW	30100 TQ	FLBLS	10/01-12/01
	Lakeland-Winter Haven MSA, FL	Y	11400 FQ	15800 AW	22620 TQ	FLBLS	10/01-12/01
	Melbourne-Titusville-Palm Bay MSA, FL	Y	11800 FQ	19020 AW	31320 TQ	FLBLS	10/01-12/01
	Miami PMSA, FL	Y	11590 FQ	17990 AW	28550 TQ	FLBLS	10/01-12/01
	Naples MSA, FL	Y	12750 FQ	23620 AW	42140 TQ	FLBLS	10/01-12/01
	Ocala MSA, FL	Y	11880 FQ	19330 AW	32230 TQ	FLBLS	10/01-12/01
	Orlando MSA, FL	Y	11810 FQ	18190 AW	28860 TQ	FLBLS	10/01-12/01
	Pensacola MSA, FL	Y	12290 FQ	18120 AW	27580 TQ	FLBLS	10/01-12/01
	Sarasota-Bradenton MSA, FL	Y	12270 FQ	21340 AW	39240 TQ	FLBLS	10/01-12/01
	Tallahassee MSA, FL	Y	11390 FQ	14180 AW	18120 TQ	FLBLS	10/01-12/01
	Tampa-St. Petersburg-Clearwater MSA, FL	Y	12980 FQ	21490 AW	33570 TQ	FLBLS	10/01-12/01
	West Palm Beach-Boca Raton MSA, FL	Y	12210 FQ	20280 AW	29280 TQ	FLBLS	10/01-12/01
	Georgia	Y	11900 FQ	17280 AW	25900 TQ	GABLS	10/01-12/01
	Atlanta MSA, GA	Y	12160 FQ	17910 AW	26340 TQ	GABLS	10/01-12/01
	Augusta-Aiken MSA, GA-SC	Y	11870 FQ	17080 AW	24860 TQ	GABLS	10/01-12/01
	Columbus MSA, GA-AL	Y	11790 FQ	16200 AW	25620 TQ	GABLS	10/01-12/01
	Macon MSA, GA	Y	11720 FQ	16210 AW	23800 TQ	GABLS	10/01-12/01
	Savannah MSA, GA	Y	12020 FQ	17440 AW	25450 TQ	GABLS	10/01-12/01
	Hawaii	Y	12390 FQ	20180 AW	28580 TQ	HIBLS	10/01-12/01
	Honolulu MSA, HI	Y	12190 FQ	19310 AW	27480 TQ	HIBLS	10/01-12/01
	Idaho	Y	12140 FQ	18540 AW	28040 TQ	IDBLS	10/01-12/01
	Boise City MSA, ID	Y	12580 FQ	19970 AW	33610 TQ	IDBLS	10/01-12/01
	Illinois	Y	12470 FQ	19310 AW	26790 TQ	ILBLS	10/01-12/01
	Champaign-Urbana MSA, IL	Y	12020 FQ	19680 AW	35480 TQ	ILBLS	10/01-12/01
	Chicago PMSA, IL	Y	13540 FQ	20400 AW	27170 TQ	ILBLS	10/01-12/01
	Peoria-Pekin MSA, IL	Y	11730 FQ	16990 AW	24610 TQ	ILBLS	10/01-12/01
	Rockford MSA, IL	Y	11830 FQ	19860 AW	33310 TQ	ILBLS	10/01-12/01
	Springfield MSA, IL	Y	11720 FQ	16030 AW	23940 TQ	ILBLS	10/01-12/01
	Indiana	Y	11640 FQ	17420 AW	26890 TQ	INBLS	10/01-12/01
	Elkhart-Goshen MSA, IN	Y	11800 FQ	17720 AW	28420 TQ	INBLS	10/01-12/01
	Evansville-Henderson MSA, IN-KY	Y	11810 FQ	17670 AW	26970 TQ	INBLS	10/01-12/01
	Fort Wayne MSA, IN	Y	11740 FQ	18880 AW	29750 TQ	INBLS	10/01-12/01
	Gary PMSA, IN	Y	11600 FQ	19800 AW	38040 TQ	INBLS	10/01-12/01
	Indianapolis MSA, IN	Y	11850 FQ	17550 AW	24180 TQ	INBLS	10/01-12/01
	Lafayette MSA, IN	Y	11640 FQ	17520 AW	29230 TQ	INBLS	10/01-12/01
	South Bend MSA, IN	Y	11310 FQ	15190 AW	21170 TQ	INBLS	10/01-12/01
	Iowa	Y	11730 FQ	16480 AW	23600 TQ	IABLS	10/01-12/01
	Cedar Rapids MSA, IA	Y	11900 FQ	17370 AW	26110 TQ	IABLS	10/01-12/01
	Davenport-Moline-Rock Island MSA, IA-IL	Y	11830 FQ	17600 AW	27010 TQ	IABLS	10/01-12/01
	Des Moines MSA, IA	Y	12220 FQ	18150 AW	24610 TQ	IABLS	10/01-12/01
	Kansas	Y	11910 FQ	17890 AW	27770 TQ	KSBLS	10/01-12/01
	Topeka MSA, KS	Y	11940 FQ	21410 AW	44270 TQ	KSBLS	10/01-12/01
	Wichita MSA, KS	Y	12960 FQ	19590 AW	27380 TQ	KSBLS	10/01-12/01
	Kentucky	Y	11610 FQ	17040 AW	26890 TQ	KYBLS	10/01-12/01
	Lexington MSA, KY	Y	11670 FQ	17430 AW	26150 TQ	KYBLS	10/01-12/01
	Louisville MSA, KY-IN	Y	12090 FQ	18530 AW	28380 TQ	KYBLS	10/01-12/01

AAW	Average annual wage	**AOH**	Average offered, high	**ASH**	Average starting, high	**H**	Hourly	**M**	Monthly	**S**	Special: hourly and annual
AE	Average entry wage	**AOL**	Average offered, low	**ASL**	Average starting, low	**HI**	Highest wage paid	**MTC**	Median total compensation	**TQ**	Third quartile wage
AEX	Average experienced wage	**APH**	Average pay, high range	**AW**	Average wage paid	**HR**	High end range	**MW**	Median wage paid	**W**	Weekly
AO	Average offered	**APL**	Average pay, low range	**FQ**	First quartile wage	**LR**	Low end range	**SQ**	Second quartile wage	**Y**	Yearly

Occupation/Type/Industry	Location	Per	Low	Mid	High	Source	Date
Counter and Rental Clerk	Louisiana	Y	11910 FQ	17920 AW	26550 TQ	LABLS	10/01-12/01
	Baton Rouge MSA, LA	Y	11820 FQ	17040 AW	23590 TQ	LABLS	10/01-12/01
	Houma MSA, LA	Y	11660 FQ	16670 AW	24000 TQ	LABLS	10/01-12/01
	Lafayette MSA, LA	Y	11840 FQ	17100 AW	24750 TQ	LABLS	10/01-12/01
	Lake Charles MSA, LA	Y	12280 FQ	17270 AW	22910 TQ	LABLS	10/01-12/01
	New Orleans MSA, LA	Y	12120 FQ	19500 AW	28030 TQ	LABLS	10/01-12/01
	Shreveport-Bossier City MSA, LA	Y	12230 FQ	20590 AW	37460 TQ	LABLS	10/01-12/01
	Maine	Y	12240 FQ	19450 AW	28380 TQ	MEBLS	10/01-12/01
	Portland MSA, ME	Y	13620 FQ	19910 AW	27480 TQ	MEBLS	10/01-12/01
	Maryland	Y	12400 FQ	20540 AW	33810 TQ	MDBLS	10/01-12/01
	Baltimore PMSA, MD	Y	12450 FQ	21550 AW	34400 TQ	MDBLS	10/01-12/01
	Massachusetts	Y	14320 FQ	20940 AW	33920 TQ	MABLS	10/01-12/01
	Boston PMSA, MA-NH	Y	14330 FQ	21370 AW	34380 TQ	MABLS	10/01-12/01
	Brockton PMSA, MA	Y	14430 FQ	26220 AW	42940 TQ	MABLS	10/01-12/01
	Lawrence PMSA, MA-NH	Y	13680 FQ	18750 AW	27630 TQ	MABLS	10/01-12/01
	Lowell PMSA, MA-NH	Y	14380 FQ	23810 AW	37000 TQ	MABLS	10/01-12/01
	New Bedford PMSA, MA	Y	14210 FQ	18440 AW	23070 TQ	MABLS	10/01-12/01
	Springfield MSA, MA	Y	14450 FQ	18370 AW	26820 TQ	MABLS	10/01-12/01
	Worcester PMSA, MA-CT	Y	14230 FQ	21030 AW	35540 TQ	MABLS	10/01-12/01
	Michigan	Y	12220 FQ	19300 AW	29310 TQ	MIBLS	10/01-12/01
	Ann Arbor PMSA, MI	Y	12240 FQ	21210 AW	35330 TQ	MIBLS	10/01-12/01
	Detroit PMSA, MI	Y	12710 FQ	20270 AW	29900 TQ	MIBLS	10/01-12/01
	Flint PMSA, MI	Y	11880 FQ	17220 AW	26250 TQ	MIBLS	10/01-12/01
	Grand Rapids-Muskegon-Holland MSA, MI	Y	12180 FQ	20010 AW	32230 TQ	MIBLS	10/01-12/01
	Kalamazoo-Battle Creek MSA, MI	Y	12470 FQ	19660 AW	31520 TQ	MIBLS	10/01-12/01
	Lansing-East Lansing MSA, MI	Y	11910 FQ	18430 AW	29580 TQ	MIBLS	10/01-12/01
	Saginaw-Bay City-Midland MSA, MI	Y	12150 FQ	16900 AW	23340 TQ	MIBLS	10/01-12/01
	Minnesota	Y	11780 FQ	17780 AW	27560 TQ	MNBLS	10/01-12/01
	Duluth-Superior MSA, MN-WI	Y	11750 FQ	16590 AW	25130 TQ	MNBLS	10/01-12/01
	Minneapolis-St. Paul MSA, MN-WI	Y	11880 FQ	18630 AW	30030 TQ	MNBLS	10/01-12/01
	St. Cloud MSA, MN	Y	11930 FQ	16900 AW	23220 TQ	MNBLS	10/01-12/01
	Mississippi	Y	11970 FQ	17140 AW	25550 TQ	MSBLS	10/01-12/01
	Biloxi-Gulfport-Pascagoula MSA, MS	Y	12230 FQ	17920 AW	28360 TQ	MSBLS	10/01-12/01
	Jackson MSA, MS	Y	12200 FQ	17970 AW	26520 TQ	MSBLS	10/01-12/01
	Missouri	Y	11910 FQ	18890 AW	30580 TQ	MOBLS	10/01-12/01
	Kansas City MSA, MO-KS	Y	12050 FQ	18970 AW	30140 TQ	MOBLS	10/01-12/01
	St. Louis MSA, MO-IL	Y	11980 FQ	19270 AW	37580 TQ	MOBLS	10/01-12/01
	Springfield MSA, MO	Y	12020 FQ	19190 AW	27280 TQ	MOBLS	10/01-12/01
	Montana	Y	11700 FQ	15580 AW	21260 TQ	MTBLS	10/01-12/01
	Billings MSA, MT	Y	12530 FQ	16870 AW	22720 TQ	MTBLS	10/01-12/01
	Nebraska	Y	11790 FQ	16980 AW	24860 TQ	NEBLS	10/01-12/01
	Lincoln MSA, NE	Y	12500 FQ	18840 AW	30140 TQ	NEBLS	10/01-12/01
	Omaha MSA, NE-IA	Y	11790 FQ	18280 AW	26530 TQ	NEBLS	10/01-12/01
	Nevada	Y	12090 FQ	21430 AW	34300 TQ	NVBLS	10/01-12/01
	Las Vegas MSA, NV-AZ	Y	12020 FQ	21710 AW	34890 TQ	NVBLS	10/01-12/01
	Reno MSA, NV	Y	12490 FQ	20540 AW	32920 TQ	NVBLS	10/01-12/01
	New Hampshire	Y	12540 FQ	19790 AW	31100 TQ	NHBLS	10/01-12/01
	Manchester PMSA, NH	Y	12630 FQ	19850 AW	30750 TQ	NHBLS	10/01-12/01
	Nashua PMSA, NH	Y	13200 FQ	21600 AW	33980 TQ	NHBLS	10/01-12/01
	Portsmouth-Rochester PMSA, NH-ME	Y	12790 FQ	21300 AW	33850 TQ	NHBLS	10/01-12/01
	New Jersey	Y	12120 FQ	19210 AW	30260 TQ	NJBLS	10/01-12/01
	Atlantic-Cape May PMSA, NJ	Y	11930 FQ	17380 AW	26880 TQ	NJBLS	10/01-12/01
	Bergen-Passaic PMSA, NJ	Y	11950 FQ	19070 AW	31640 TQ	NJBLS	10/01-12/01
	Jersey City PMSA, NJ	Y	12960 FQ	19050 AW	23720 TQ	NJBLS	10/01-12/01
	Middlesex-Somerset-Hunterdon PMSA, NJ	Y	11940 FQ	19690 AW	36920 TQ	NJBLS	10/01-12/01
	Monmouth-Ocean PMSA, NJ	Y	11660 FQ	17060 AW	28520 TQ	NJBLS	10/01-12/01
	Newark PMSA, NJ	Y	12700 FQ	20080 AW	30470 TQ	NJBLS	10/01-12/01
	Trenton PMSA, NJ	Y	11720 FQ	17380 AW	24240 TQ	NJBLS	10/01-12/01
	New Mexico	Y	12130 FQ	18940 AW	28260 TQ	NMBLS	10/01-12/01
	Albuquerque MSA, NM	Y	12920 FQ	20640 AW	29220 TQ	NMBLS	10/01-12/01
	Las Cruces MSA, NM	Y	12800 FQ	18710 AW	27120 TQ	NMBLS	10/01-12/01
	New York	Y	12070 FQ	20020 AW	33410 TQ	NYBLS	10/01-12/01
	Albany-Schenectady-Troy MSA, NY	Y	12320 FQ	19620 AW	31050 TQ	NYBLS	10/01-12/01

AAW Average annual wage; AE Average entry wage; AEX Average experienced wage; AO Average offered; AOH Average offered, high; AOL Average offered, low; APH Average pay, high range; APL Average pay, low range; ASH Average starting, high; ASL Average starting, low; AW Average wage paid; FQ First quartile wage; H Hourly; HI Highest wage paid; HR High end range; LR Low end range; M Monthly; MTC Median total compensation; MW Median wage paid; SQ Second quartile wage; S Special: hourly and annual; TQ Third quartile wage; W Weekly; Y Yearly

Occupation/Type/Industry	Location	Per	Low	Mid	High	Source	Date
Counter and Rental Clerk	Binghamton MSA, NY	Y	11820 FQ	17500 AW	28480 TQ	NYBLS	10/01-12/01
	Buffalo-Niagara Falls MSA, NY	Y	11940 FQ	18010 AW	28670 TQ	NYBLS	10/01-12/01
	Dutchess County PMSA, NY	Y	12320 FQ	18760 AW	27370 TQ	NYBLS	10/01-12/01
	Nassau-Suffolk PMSA, NY	Y	12320 FQ	22790 AW	41470 TQ	NYBLS	10/01-12/01
	New York PMSA, NY	Y	12330 FQ	21290 AW	36380 TQ	NYBLS	10/01-12/01
	Newburgh PMSA, NY-PA	Y	12080 FQ	21010 AW	33990 TQ	NYBLS	10/01-12/01
	Rochester MSA, NY	Y	11790 FQ	19120 AW	31570 TQ	NYBLS	10/01-12/01
	Syracuse MSA, NY	Y	12030 FQ	17160 AW	24950 TQ	NYBLS	10/01-12/01
	Utica-Rome MSA, NY	Y	12030 FQ	17900 AW	26260 TQ	NYBLS	10/01-12/01
	North Carolina	Y	12400 FQ	20430 AW	31620 TQ	NCBLS	10/01-12/01
	Asheville MSA, NC	Y	12790 FQ	19170 AW	30590 TQ	NCBLS	10/01-12/01
	Charlotte-Gastonia-Rock Hill MSA, NC-SC	Y	12590 FQ	20680 AW	31740 TQ	NCBLS	10/01-12/01
	Fayetteville MSA, NC	Y	14660 FQ	18530 AW	25510 TQ	NCBLS	10/01-12/01
	Greensboro-Winston-Salem-High Point MSA, NC	Y	12990 FQ	22760 AW	37950 TQ	NCBLS	10/01-12/01
	Hickory-Morganton-Lenoir MSA, NC	Y	13770 FQ	21490 AW	33170 TQ	NCBLS	10/01-12/01
	Raleigh-Durham-Chapel Hill MSA, NC	Y	11860 FQ	20900 AW	37500 TQ	NCBLS	10/01-12/01
	Wilmington MSA, NC	Y	11930 FQ	18160 AW	27300 TQ	NCBLS	10/01-12/01
	North Dakota	Y	11670 FQ	16580 AW	25360 TQ	NDBLS	10/01-12/01
	Fargo-Moorhead MSA, ND-MN	Y	11960 FQ	17910 AW	28230 TQ	NDBLS	10/01-12/01
	Ohio	Y	12100 FQ	18380 AW	27670 TQ	OHBLS	10/01-12/01
	Akron PMSA, OH	Y	11660 FQ	17770 AW	27790 TQ	OHBLS	10/01-12/01
	Canton-Massillon MSA, OH	Y	12110 FQ	19880 AW	33040 TQ	OHBLS	10/01-12/01
	Cincinnati PMSA, OH-KY-IN	Y	12150 FQ	19710 AW	32350 TQ	OHBLS	10/01-12/01
	Cleveland-Lorain-Elyria PMSA, OH	Y	11810 FQ	17730 AW	27130 TQ	OHBLS	10/01-12/01
	Columbus MSA, OH	Y	13100 FQ	20370 AW	30800 TQ	OHBLS	10/01-12/01
	Dayton-Springfield MSA, OH	Y	12460 FQ	16940 AW	23130 TQ	OHBLS	10/01-12/01
	Hamilton-Middletown PMSA, OH	Y	12440 FQ	18010 AW	23730 TQ	OHBLS	10/01-12/01
	Mansfield MSA, OH	Y	11870 FQ	16460 AW	24450 TQ	OHBLS	10/01-12/01
	Toledo MSA, OH	Y	11900 FQ	17730 AW	25420 TQ	OHBLS	10/01-12/01
	Youngstown-Warren MSA, OH	Y	11810 FQ	16100 AW	23680 TQ	OHBLS	10/01-12/01
	Oklahoma	Y	12040 FQ	18500 AW	27430 TQ	OKBLS	10/01-12/01
	Oklahoma City MSA, OK	Y	12670 FQ	20160 AW	27730 TQ	OKBLS	10/01-12/01
	Tulsa MSA, OK	Y	12130 FQ	18110 AW	26710 TQ	OKBLS	10/01-12/01
	Oregon	Y	13990 FQ	20960 AW	35480 TQ	ORBLS	10/01-12/01
	Eugene-Springfield MSA, OR	Y	13970 FQ	20110 AW	36570 TQ	ORBLS	10/01-12/01
	Medford-Ashland MSA, OR	Y	13830 FQ	18560 AW	27190 TQ	ORBLS	10/01-12/01
	Portland-Vancouver PMSA, OR-WA	Y	14030 FQ	21390 AW	35250 TQ	ORBLS	10/01-12/01
	Salem PMSA, OR	Y	14240 FQ	21110 AW	34620 TQ	ORBLS	10/01-12/01
	Pennsylvania	Y	11780 FQ	17480 AW	27460 TQ	PABLS	10/01-12/01
	Allentown-Bethlehem-Easton MSA, PA	Y	11660 FQ	17020 AW	28180 TQ	PABLS	10/01-12/01
	Erie MSA, PA	Y	11830 FQ	17620 AW	29810 TQ	PABLS	10/01-12/01
	Harrisburg-Lebanon-Carlisle MSA, PA	Y	12130 FQ	19600 AW	34380 TQ	PABLS	10/01-12/01
	Johnstown MSA, PA	Y	11760 FQ	16160 AW	22880 TQ	PABLS	10/01-12/01
	Lancaster MSA, PA	Y	11700 FQ	18170 AW	28760 TQ	PABLS	10/01-12/01
	Philadelphia PMSA, PA-NJ	Y	12130 FQ	19500 AW	31190 TQ	PABLS	10/01-12/01
	Pittsburgh MSA, PA	Y	11660 FQ	15980 AW	23250 TQ	PABLS	10/01-12/01
	Reading MSA, PA	Y	11770 FQ	16280 AW	24270 TQ	PABLS	10/01-12/01
	Scranton-Wilkes-Barre-Hazleton MSA, PA	Y	12130 FQ	18700 AW	28190 TQ	PABLS	10/01-12/01
	York MSA, PA	Y	11680 FQ	15930 AW	21880 TQ	PABLS	10/01-12/01
	Rhode Island	Y	13830 FQ	23170 AW	35420 TQ	RIBLS	10/01-12/01
	Providence-Fall River-Warwick MSA, RI-MA	Y	14030 FQ	22850 AW	35200 TQ	RIBLS	10/01-12/01
	South Carolina	Y	12030 FQ	17340 AW	25320 TQ	SCBLS	10/01-12/01
	Charleston-North Charleston MSA, SC	Y	11770 FQ	15900 AW	23090 TQ	SCBLS	10/01-12/01
	Columbia MSA, SC	Y	12470 FQ	18620 AW	28490 TQ	SCBLS	10/01-12/01
	Greenville-Spartanburg-Anderson MSA, SC	Y	12180 FQ	18500 AW	25350 TQ	SCBLS	10/01-12/01
	Myrtle Beach MSA, SC	Y	12410 FQ	19270 AW	27930 TQ	SCBLS	10/01-12/01
	South Dakota	Y	11640 FQ	15310 AW	21860 TQ	SDBLS	10/01-12/01

AAW Average annual wage; AE Average entry wage; AEX Average experienced wage; AO Average offered; AOH Average offered, high; AOL Average offered, low; APH Average pay, high range; APL Average pay, low range; ASH Average starting, high; ASL Average starting, low; AW Average wage paid; FQ First quartile wage; H Hourly; HI Highest wage paid; HR High end range; LR Low end range; M Monthly; MTC Median total compensation; MW Median wage paid; SQ Second quartile wage; S Special: hourly and annual; TQ Third quartile wage; W Weekly; Y Yearly

Occupation/Type/Industry	Location	Per	Low	Mid	High	Source	Date
Counter and Rental Clerk	Sioux Falls MSA, SD	Y	12080 FQ	17400 AW	25720 TQ	SDBLS	10/01-12/01
	Tennessee	Y	11920 FQ	17510 AW	25470 TQ	TNBLS	10/01-12/01
	Chattanooga MSA, TN-GA	Y	12560 FQ	17910 AW	23470 TQ	TNBLS	10/01-12/01
	Clarksville-Hopkinsville MSA, TN-KY	Y	11500 FQ	19090 AW	33700 TQ	TNBLS	10/01-12/01
	Johnson City-Kingsport-Bristol MSA, TN-VA	Y	11480 FQ	15670 AW	23160 TQ	TNBLS	10/01-12/01
	Knoxville MSA, TN	Y	12110 FQ	17120 AW	23120 TQ	TNBLS	10/01-12/01
	Memphis MSA, TN-AR-MS	Y	13100 FQ	21350 AW	32420 TQ	TNBLS	10/01-12/01
	Nashville MSA, TN	Y	11990 FQ	17350 AW	23960 TQ	TNBLS	10/01-12/01
	Texas	Y	12040 FQ	19690 AW	32190 TQ	TXBLS	10/01-12/01
	Amarillo MSA, TX	Y	11740 FQ	17850 AW	27300 TQ	TXBLS	10/01-12/01
	Austin-San Marcos MSA, TX	Y	12220 FQ	19400 AW	32790 TQ	TXBLS	10/01-12/01
	Beaumont-Port Arthur MSA, TX	Y	11550 FQ	19540 AW	40510 TQ	TXBLS	10/01-12/01
	Brazoria PMSA, TX	Y	13610 FQ	23530 AW	43900 TQ	TXBLS	10/01-12/01
	Brownsville-Harlingen-San Benito MSA, TX	Y	11890 FQ	18260 AW	27990 TQ	TXBLS	10/01-12/01
	Corpus Christi MSA, TX	Y	11590 FQ	15970 AW	21860 TQ	TXBLS	10/01-12/01
	Dallas PMSA, TX	Y	13070 FQ	20500 AW	28950 TQ	TXBLS	10/01-12/01
	El Paso MSA, TX	Y	11840 FQ	17650 AW	27190 TQ	TXBLS	10/01-12/01
	Fort Worth-Arlington PMSA, TX	Y	12640 FQ	20460 AW	30330 TQ	TXBLS	10/01-12/01
	Galveston-Texas City PMSA, TX	Y	11700 FQ	19050 AW	28620 TQ	TXBLS	10/01-12/01
	Houston PMSA, TX	Y	11910 FQ	20690 AW	35300 TQ	TXBLS	10/01-12/01
	Killeen-Temple MSA, TX	Y	11620 FQ	15910 AW	23470 TQ	TXBLS	10/01-12/01
	Laredo MSA, TX	Y	11490 FQ	16940 AW	29460 TQ	TXBLS	10/01-12/01
	Longview-Marshall MSA, TX	Y	11490 FQ	16990 AW	26550 TQ	TXBLS	10/01-12/01
	Lubbock MSA, TX	Y	11980 FQ	18020 AW	27680 TQ	TXBLS	10/01-12/01
	McAllen-Edinburg-Mission MSA, TX	Y	11520 FQ	18300 AW	35850 TQ	TXBLS	10/01-12/01
	Odessa-Midland MSA, TX	Y	11880 FQ	18440 AW	34370 TQ	TXBLS	10/01-12/01
	San Antonio MSA, TX	Y	12520 FQ	20280 AW	34300 TQ	TXBLS	10/01-12/01
	Tyler MSA, TX	Y	11770 FQ	17430 AW	27010 TQ	TXBLS	10/01-12/01
	Waco MSA, TX	Y	11550 FQ	18330 AW	25310 TQ	TXBLS	10/01-12/01
	Utah	Y	12330 FQ	17950 AW	26210 TQ	UTBLS	10/01-12/01
	Provo-Orem MSA, UT	Y	12140 FQ	17030 AW	26980 TQ	UTBLS	10/01-12/01
	Salt Lake City-Ogden MSA, UT	Y	12450 FQ	17840 AW	24810 TQ	UTBLS	10/01-12/01
	Vermont	Y	13810 FQ	18940 AW	27330 TQ	VTBLS	10/01-12/01
	Burlington MSA, VT	Y	14430 FQ	18700 AW	24760 TQ	VTBLS	10/01-12/01
	Virginia	Y	11890 FQ	18370 AW	28700 TQ	VABLS	10/01-12/01
	Lynchburg MSA, VA	Y	12230 FQ	15690 AW	20120 TQ	VABLS	10/01-12/01
	Norfolk-Virginia Beach-Newport News MSA, VA-NC	Y	11710 FQ	17250 AW	25250 TQ	VABLS	10/01-12/01
	Richmond-Petersburg MSA, VA	Y	11820 FQ	19270 AW	31770 TQ	VABLS	10/01-12/01
	Roanoke MSA, VA	Y	12560 FQ	19700 AW	31750 TQ	VABLS	10/01-12/01
	Washington	Y	14040 FQ	20010 AW	29760 TQ	WABLS	10/01-12/01
	Bremerton PMSA, WA	Y	14210 FQ	18710 AW	26360 TQ	WABLS	10/01-12/01
	Olympia PMSA, WA	Y	14050 FQ	21580 AW	36100 TQ	WABLS	10/01-12/01
	Richland-Kennewick-Pasco MSA, WA	Y	14020 FQ	18730 AW	27350 TQ	WABLS	10/01-12/01
	Seattle-Bellevue-Everett PMSA, WA	Y	14030 FQ	20490 AW	30190 TQ	WABLS	10/01-12/01
	Spokane MSA, WA	Y	14220 FQ	19200 AW	27600 TQ	WABLS	10/01-12/01
	Tacoma PMSA, WA	Y	14070 FQ	19630 AW	30450 TQ	WABLS	10/01-12/01
	Yakima MSA, WA	Y	14020 FQ	17820 AW	23590 TQ	WABLS	10/01-12/01
	West Virginia	Y	11640 FQ	16070 AW	25610 TQ	WVBLS	10/01-12/01
	Charleston MSA, WV	Y	11430 FQ	15910 AW	26110 TQ	WVBLS	10/01-12/01
	Huntington-Ashland MSA, WV-KY-OH	Y	11650 FQ	14370 AW	18030 TQ	WVBLS	10/01-12/01
	Wisconsin	Y	11960 FQ	18320 AW	27820 TQ	WIBLS	10/01-12/01
	Appleton-Oshkosh-Neenah MSA, WI	Y	13540 FQ	20060 AW	29250 TQ	WIBLS	10/01-12/01
	Green Bay MSA, WI	Y	12340 FQ	17320 AW	23380 TQ	WIBLS	10/01-12/01
	Madison MSA, WI	Y	13860 FQ	19730 AW	27930 TQ	WIBLS	10/01-12/01
	Milwaukee-Waukesha PMSA, WI	Y	12460 FQ	21290 AW	39140 TQ	WIBLS	10/01-12/01
	Racine PMSA, WI	Y	11590 FQ	15280 AW	21300 TQ	WIBLS	10/01-12/01

AAW Average annual wage; AE Average entry wage; AEX Average experienced wage; AO Average offered; AOH Average offered, high; AOL Average offered, low; APH Average pay, high range; APL Average pay, low range; ASH Average starting, high; ASL Average starting, low; AW Average wage paid; FQ First quartile wage; H Hourly; HI Highest wage paid; HR High end range; LR Low end range; M Monthly; MTC Median total compensation; MW Median wage paid; SQ Second quartile wage; S Special: hourly and annual; TQ Third quartile wage; W Weekly; Y Yearly

Occupation/Type/Industry	Location	Per	Low	Mid	High	Source	Date
Counter and Rental Clerk	Wyoming	Y	11660 FQ	16840 AW	26460 TQ	WYBLS	10/01-12/01
	Cheyenne MSA, WY	Y	11690 FQ	17380 AW	25810 TQ	WYBLS	10/01-12/01
	Puerto Rico	Y	11560 FQ	14730 AW	20790 TQ	PRBLS	10/01-12/01
	Virgin Islands	Y	11730 FQ	15350 AW	21040 TQ	VIBLS	10/01-12/01
	Guam	Y	11660 FQ	15780 AW	22350 TQ	GUBLS	10/01-12/01
Counter Attendant							
Cafeteria, Food, Coffee Shop	Alabama	H	5.48 FQ	6.39 AW	7.95 TQ	ALBLS	10/01-12/01
Cafeteria, Food, Coffee Shop	Alaska	H	6.26 FQ	8.91 AW	12.61 TQ	AKBLS	10/01-12/01
Cafeteria, Food, Coffee Shop	Arizona	H	5.75 FQ	7.36 AW	9.78 TQ	AZBLS	10/01-12/01
Cafeteria, Food, Coffee Shop	Arkansas	H	5.64 FQ	6.74 AW	8.39 TQ	ARBLS	10/01-12/01
Cafeteria, Food, Coffee Shop	California	H	6.51 FQ	8.48 AW	12.01 TQ	CABLS	10/01-12/01
Cafeteria, Food, Coffee Shop	Colorado	H	5.77 FQ	7.66 AW	10.32 TQ	COBLS	10/01-12/01
Cafeteria, Food, Coffee Shop	Connecticut	H	6.59 FQ	8.23 AW	11.11 TQ	CTBLS	10/01-12/01
Cafeteria, Food, Coffee Shop	Delaware	H	6.50 FQ	8.01 AW	10.79 TQ	DEBLS	10/01-12/01
Cafeteria, Food, Coffee Shop	District of Columbia	H	6.91 FQ	8.08 AW	9.96 TQ	DCBLS	10/01-12/01
Cafeteria, Food, Coffee Shop	Florida	H	5.64 FQ	6.98 AW	8.79 TQ	FLBLS	10/01-12/01
Cafeteria, Food, Coffee Shop	Georgia	H	5.72 FQ	8.12 AW	12.04 TQ	GABLS	10/01-12/01
Cafeteria, Food, Coffee Shop	Hawaii	H	5.57 FQ	7.35 AW	11.83 TQ	HIBLS	10/01-12/01
Cafeteria, Food, Coffee Shop	Idaho	H	5.65 FQ	7.04 AW	9.20 TQ	IDBLS	10/01-12/01
Cafeteria, Food, Coffee Shop	Illinois	H	5.69 FQ	7.59 AW	10.53 TQ	ILBLS	10/01-12/01
Cafeteria, Food, Coffee Shop	Indiana	H	5.65 FQ	7.14 AW	9.47 TQ	INBLS	10/01-12/01
Cafeteria, Food, Coffee Shop	Iowa	H	5.65 FQ	6.83 AW	8.49 TQ	IABLS	10/01-12/01
Cafeteria, Food, Coffee Shop	Kansas	H	5.72 FQ	7.11 AW	8.55 TQ	KSBLS	10/01-12/01
Cafeteria, Food, Coffee Shop	Kentucky	H	5.59 FQ	6.81 AW	8.59 TQ	KYBLS	10/01-12/01
Cafeteria, Food, Coffee Shop	Louisiana	H	5.56 FQ	6.39 AW	7.60 TQ	LABLS	10/01-12/01
Cafeteria, Food, Coffee Shop	Maine	H	5.85 FQ	7.55 AW	9.40 TQ	MEBLS	10/01-12/01
Cafeteria, Food, Coffee Shop	Maryland	H	5.74 FQ	7.92 AW	11.51 TQ	MDBLS	10/01-12/01
Cafeteria, Food, Coffee Shop	Massachusetts	H	6.87 FQ	7.92 AW	9.72 TQ	MABLS	10/01-12/01
Cafeteria, Food, Coffee Shop	Michigan	H	5.61 FQ	7.14 AW	9.31 TQ	MIBLS	10/01-12/01
Cafeteria, Food, Coffee Shop	Minnesota	H	5.72 FQ	7.26 AW	9.30 TQ	MNBLS	10/01-12/01
Cafeteria, Food, Coffee Shop	Mississippi	H	5.58 FQ	6.72 AW	8.78 TQ	MSBLS	10/01-12/01
Cafeteria, Food, Coffee Shop	Missouri	H	5.76 FQ	7.92 AW	11.44 TQ	MOBLS	10/01-12/01
Cafeteria, Food, Coffee Shop	Montana	H	5.65 FQ	7.04 AW	8.62 TQ	MTBLS	10/01-12/01
Cafeteria, Food, Coffee Shop	Nebraska	H	5.69 FQ	6.98 AW	8.88 TQ	NEBLS	10/01-12/01
Cafeteria, Food, Coffee Shop	Nevada	H	5.92 FQ	8.93 AW	12.80 TQ	NVBLS	10/01-12/01
Cafeteria, Food, Coffee Shop	New Hampshire	H	5.93 FQ	7.92 AW	10.42 TQ	NHBLS	10/01-12/01
Cafeteria, Food, Coffee Shop	New Jersey	H	5.57 FQ	7.17 AW	9.39 TQ	NJBLS	10/01-12/01
Cafeteria, Food, Coffee Shop	New Mexico	H	5.59 FQ	6.61 AW	8.43 TQ	NMBLS	10/01-12/01
Cafeteria, Food, Coffee Shop	New York	H	5.74 FQ	7.31 AW	8.88 TQ	NYBLS	10/01-12/01
Cafeteria, Food, Coffee Shop	North Carolina	H	5.60 FQ	6.77 AW	8.58 TQ	NCBLS	10/01-12/01
Cafeteria, Food, Coffee Shop	North Dakota	H	5.64 FQ	7.37 AW	9.78 TQ	NDBLS	10/01-12/01
Cafeteria, Food, Coffee Shop	Ohio	H	5.70 FQ	7.46 AW	10.35 TQ	OHBLS	10/01-12/01
Cafeteria, Food, Coffee Shop	Oklahoma	H	5.55 FQ	6.46 AW	7.98 TQ	OKBLS	10/01-12/01
Cafeteria, Food, Coffee Shop	Oregon	H	6.74 FQ	7.66 AW	8.48 TQ	ORBLS	10/01-12/01
Cafeteria, Food, Coffee Shop	Pennsylvania	H	5.58 FQ	6.96 AW	9.46 TQ	PABLS	10/01-12/01
Cafeteria, Food, Coffee Shop	Rhode Island	H	6.44 FQ	7.40 AW	8.66 TQ	RIBLS	10/01-12/01
Cafeteria, Food, Coffee Shop	South Carolina	H	5.63 FQ	6.80 AW	8.62 TQ	SCBLS	10/01-12/01
Cafeteria, Food, Coffee Shop	South Dakota	H	5.65 FQ	7.01 AW	8.76 TQ	SDBLS	10/01-12/01
Cafeteria, Food, Coffee Shop	Tennessee	H	5.62 FQ	7.07 AW	8.86 TQ	TNBLS	10/01-12/01
Cafeteria, Food, Coffee Shop	Texas	H	5.60 FQ	7.15 AW	8.79 TQ	TXBLS	10/01-12/01
Cafeteria, Food, Coffee Shop	Utah	H	5.60 FQ	6.97 AW	8.52 TQ	UTBLS	10/01-12/01
Cafeteria, Food, Coffee Shop	Vermont	H	6.53 FQ	7.92 AW	9.89 TQ	VTBLS	10/01-12/01
Cafeteria, Food, Coffee Shop	Virginia	H	5.72 FQ	8.19 AW	10.62 TQ	VABLS	10/01-12/01
Cafeteria, Food, Coffee Shop	Washington	H	6.84 FQ	8.75 AW	12.54 TQ	WABLS	10/01-12/01
Cafeteria, Food, Coffee Shop	West Virginia	H	5.50 FQ	6.31 AW	7.60 TQ	WVBLS	10/01-12/01
Cafeteria, Food, Coffee Shop	Wisconsin	H	5.69 FQ	7.17 AW	9.18 TQ	WIBLS	10/01-12/01
Cafeteria, Food, Coffee Shop	Wyoming	H	5.58 FQ	6.77 AW	8.99 TQ	WYBLS	10/01-12/01
Cafeteria, Food, Coffee Shop	Puerto Rico	H	5.40 FQ	5.98 AW	6.75 TQ	PRBLS	10/01-12/01
Cafeteria, Food, Coffee Shop	Virgin Islands	H	5.63 FQ	6.61 AW	8.27 TQ	VIBLS	10/01-12/01
Cafeteria, Food, Coffee Shop	Guam	H	5.56 FQ	6.33 AW	7.51 TQ	GUBLS	10/01-12/01
Courier and Messenger	Alabama	H	5.79 FQ	7.99 AW	10.60 TQ	ALBLS	10/01-12/01
	Birmingham MSA, AL	H	6.49 FQ	8.47 AW	10.65 TQ	ALBLS	10/01-12/01
	Huntsville MSA, AL	H	5.69 FQ	7.40 AW	10.05 TQ	ALBLS	10/01-12/01
	Mobile MSA, AL	H	5.69 FQ	8.34 AW	13.19 TQ	ALBLS	10/01-12/01
	Montgomery MSA, AL	H	5.84 FQ	7.98 AW	10.26 TQ	ALBLS	10/01-12/01
	Alaska	H	9.03 FQ	13.11 AW	21.57 TQ	AKBLS	10/01-12/01
	Anchorage MSA, AK	H	9.09 FQ	12.12 AW	16.77 TQ	AKBLS	10/01-12/01
	Arizona	H	6.52 FQ	9.16 AW	11.27 TQ	AZBLS	10/01-12/01
	Phoenix-Mesa MSA, AZ	H	6.79 FQ	9.24 AW	11.26 TQ	AZBLS	10/01-12/01
	Tucson MSA, AZ	H	6.13 FQ	9.03 AW	11.58 TQ	AZBLS	10/01-12/01
	Arkansas	H	6.18 FQ	8.69 AW	10.61 TQ	ARBLS	10/01-12/01

AAW	Average annual wage	**AOH**	Average offered, high	**ASH**	Average starting, high	**H**	Hourly	**M**	Monthly	**S**	Special: hourly and annual
AE	Average entry wage	**AOL**	Average offered, low	**ASL**	Average starting, low	**HI**	Highest wage paid	**MTC**	Median total compensation	**TQ**	Third quartile wage
AEX	Average experienced wage	**APH**	Average pay, high range	**AW**	Average wage paid	**HR**	High end range	**MW**	Median wage paid	**W**	Weekly
AO	Average offered	**APL**	Average pay, low range	**FQ**	First quartile wage	**LR**	Low end range	**SQ**	Second quartile wage	**Y**	Yearly

Occupation/Type/Industry	Location	Per	Low	Mid	High	Source	Date
Courier and Messenger	Fayetteville-Springdale-Rogers MSA, AR	H	6.01 FQ	8.36 AW	11.02 TQ	ARBLS	10/01-12/01
	Fort Smith MSA, AR-OK	H	5.75 FQ	7.54 AW	10.15 TQ	ARBLS	10/01-12/01
	Little Rock-North Little Rock MSA, AR	H	7.60 FQ	9.38 AW	10.66 TQ	ARBLS	10/01-12/01
	California	H	6.62 FQ	10.46 AW	17.91 TQ	CABLS	10/01-12/01
	Bakersfield MSA, CA	H	6.95 FQ	9.54 AW	18.67 TQ	CABLS	10/01-12/01
	Chico-Paradise MSA, CA	H	7.39 FQ	8.60 AW	10.53 TQ	CABLS	10/01-12/01
	Fresno MSA, CA	H	6.51 FQ	8.41 AW	11.73 TQ	CABLS	10/01-12/01
	Los Angeles-Long Beach PMSA, CA	H	6.49 FQ	9.48 AW	14.90 TQ	CABLS	10/01-12/01
	Modesto MSA, CA	H	7.16 FQ	8.93 AW	11.06 TQ	CABLS	10/01-12/01
	Oakland PMSA, CA	H	7.51 FQ	12.40 AW	19.84 TQ	CABLS	10/01-12/01
	Orange County PMSA, CA	H	6.48 FQ	8.99 AW	13.73 TQ	CABLS	10/01-12/01
	Riverside-San Bernardino PMSA, CA	H	6.46 FQ	8.75 AW	12.71 TQ	CABLS	10/01-12/01
	Sacramento PMSA, CA	H	7.47 FQ	10.36 AW	13.86 TQ	CABLS	10/01-12/01
	Salinas MSA, CA	H	6.98 FQ	13.09 AW	20.44 TQ	CABLS	10/01-12/01
	San Diego MSA, CA	H	7.23 FQ	10.92 AW	17.44 TQ	CABLS	10/01-12/01
	San Francisco PMSA, CA	H	7.57 FQ	14.57 AW	21.73 TQ	CABLS	10/01-12/01
	San Jose PMSA, CA	H	8.21 FQ	12.77 AW	18.89 TQ	CABLS	10/01-12/01
	San Luis Obispo-Atascadero-Paso Robles MSA, CA	H	6.59 FQ	8.46 AW	11.13 TQ	CABLS	10/01-12/01
	Santa Barbara-Santa Maria-Lompoc MSA, CA	H	6.93 FQ	10.47 AW	16.85 TQ	CABLS	10/01-12/01
	Santa Cruz-Watsonville PMSA, CA	H	9.30 FQ	12.14 AW	15.84 TQ	CABLS	10/01-12/01
	Santa Rosa PMSA, CA	H	8.21 FQ	12.47 AW	20.62 TQ	CABLS	10/01-12/01
	Stockton-Lodi MSA, CA	H	7.30 FQ	10.75 AW	19.22 TQ	CABLS	10/01-12/01
	Vallejo-Fairfield-Napa PMSA, CA	H	6.93 FQ	10.43 AW	15.54 TQ	CABLS	10/01-12/01
	Ventura PMSA, CA	H	7.12 FQ	9.17 AW	13.00 TQ	CABLS	10/01-12/01
	Visalia-Tulare-Porterville MSA, CA	H	7.27 FQ	9.47 AW	13.33 TQ	CABLS	10/01-12/01
	Colorado	H	7.03 FQ	9.90 AW	13.57 TQ	COBLS	10/01-12/01
	Boulder-Longmont PMSA, CO	H	7.27 FQ	9.62 AW	12.57 TQ	COBLS	10/01-12/01
	Colorado Springs MSA, CO	H	7.48 FQ	9.99 AW	12.51 TQ	COBLS	10/01-12/01
	Denver PMSA, CO	H	6.96 FQ	9.87 AW	13.62 TQ	COBLS	10/01-12/01
	Fort Collins-Loveland MSA, CO	H	7.84 FQ	11.98 AW	20.23 TQ	COBLS	10/01-12/01
	Connecticut	H	7.69 FQ	11.29 AW	14.55 TQ	CTBLS	10/01-12/01
	Bridgeport PMSA, CT	H	9.10 FQ	11.21 AW	15.05 TQ	CTBLS	10/01-12/01
	Danbury PMSA, CT	H	6.66 FQ	11.32 AW	16.58 TQ	CTBLS	10/01-12/01
	Hartford MSA, CT	H	7.55 FQ	11.12 AW	14.33 TQ	CTBLS	10/01-12/01
	New Haven-Meriden PMSA, CT	H	7.98 FQ	12.29 AW	19.46 TQ	CTBLS	10/01-12/01
	New London-Norwich MSA, CT-RI	H	7.37 FQ	10.75 AW	14.75 TQ	CTBLS	10/01-12/01
	Stamford-Norwalk PMSA, CT	H	7.82 FQ	11.51 AW	14.57 TQ	CTBLS	10/01-12/01
	Waterbury PMSA, CT	H	7.91 FQ	11.89 AW	15.94 TQ	CTBLS	10/01-12/01
	Delaware	H	7.22 FQ	9.94 AW	13.98 TQ	DEBLS	10/01-12/01
	Wilmington-Newark PMSA, DE-MD	H	7.43 FQ	10.59 AW	15.24 TQ	DEBLS	10/01-12/01
	District of Columbia	H	6.84 FQ	10.80 AW	17.53 TQ	DCBLS	10/01-12/01
	Washington PMSA, DC-MD-VA-WV	H	7.14 FQ	11.11 AW	16.37 TQ	DCBLS	10/01-12/01
	Florida	H	6.50 FQ	9.89 AW	14.81 TQ	FLBLS	10/01-12/01
	Daytona Beach MSA, FL	H	5.82 FQ	8.23 AW	11.07 TQ	FLBLS	10/01-12/01
	Fort Lauderdale PMSA, FL	H	7.22 FQ	10.79 AW	16.32 TQ	FLBLS	10/01-12/01
	Fort Myers-Cape Coral MSA, FL	H	6.92 FQ	9.08 AW	11.09 TQ	FLBLS	10/01-12/01
	Fort Pierce-Port St. Lucie MSA, FL	H	6.67 FQ	9.31 AW	12.09 TQ	FLBLS	10/01-12/01
	Fort Walton Beach MSA, FL	H	6.64 FQ	8.65 AW	12.28 TQ	FLBLS	10/01-12/01
	Gainesville MSA, FL	H	7.10 FQ	11.06 AW	16.29 TQ	FLBLS	10/01-12/01
	Jacksonville MSA, FL	H	6.00 FQ	8.70 AW	11.87 TQ	FLBLS	10/01-12/01
	Lakeland-Winter Haven MSA, FL	H	6.92 FQ	8.60 AW	10.95 TQ	FLBLS	10/01-12/01
	Melbourne-Titusville-Palm Bay MSA, FL	H	6.00 FQ	9.15 AW	13.23 TQ	FLBLS	10/01-12/01
	Miami PMSA, FL	H	7.37 FQ	11.57 AW	18.53 TQ	FLBLS	10/01-12/01
	Naples MSA, FL	H	6.99 FQ	9.85 AW	13.75 TQ	FLBLS	10/01-12/01

AAW	Average annual wage	AOH	Average offered, high	ASH	Average starting, high	H	Hourly	M	Monthly	S	Special: hourly and annual
AE	Average entry wage	AOL	Average offered, low	ASL	Average starting, low	HI	Highest wage paid	MTC	Median total compensation	TQ	Third quartile wage
AEX	Average experienced wage	APH	Average pay, high range	AW	Average wage paid	HR	High end range	MW	Median wage paid	W	Weekly
AO	Average offered	APL	Average pay, low range	FQ	First quartile wage	LR	Low end range	SQ	Second quartile wage	Y	Yearly

Occupation/Type/Industry	Location	Per	Low	Mid	High	Source	Date
Courier and Messenger	Ocala MSA, FL	H	6.45 FQ	7.96 AW	9.84 TQ	FLBLS	10/01-12/01
	Orlando MSA, FL	H	6.87 FQ	9.15 AW	12.73 TQ	FLBLS	10/01-12/01
	Pensacola MSA, FL	H	5.80 FQ	7.77 AW	10.46 TQ	FLBLS	10/01-12/01
	Sarasota-Bradenton MSA, FL	H	7.09 FQ	9.31 AW	12.44 TQ	FLBLS	10/01-12/01
	Tallahassee MSA, FL	H	6.11 FQ	8.86 AW	12.25 TQ	FLBLS	10/01-12/01
	Tampa-St. Petersburg-Clearwater MSA, FL	H	6.58 FQ	9.77 AW	13.18 TQ	FLBLS	10/01-12/01
	West Palm Beach-Boca Raton MSA, FL	H	7.12 FQ	11.12 AW	16.63 TQ	FLBLS	10/01-12/01
	Georgia	H	6.24 FQ	9.83 AW	13.68 TQ	GABLS	10/01-12/01
	Atlanta MSA, GA	H	6.38 FQ	10.54 AW	13.98 TQ	GABLS	10/01-12/01
	Augusta-Aiken MSA, GA-SC	H	5.71 FQ	8.21 AW	11.22 TQ	GABLS	10/01-12/01
	Columbus MSA, GA-AL	H	6.76 FQ	8.19 AW	10.27 TQ	GABLS	10/01-12/01
	Macon MSA, GA	H	6.50 FQ	9.19 AW	13.04 TQ	GABLS	10/01-12/01
	Savannah MSA, GA	H	6.48 FQ	9.22 AW	12.81 TQ	GABLS	10/01-12/01
	Hawaii	H	6.77 FQ	9.84 AW	13.40 TQ	HIBLS	10/01-12/01
	Honolulu MSA, HI	H	6.59 FQ	9.69 AW	13.43 TQ	HIBLS	10/01-12/01
	Idaho	H	6.56 FQ	8.68 AW	11.05 TQ	IDBLS	10/01-12/01
	Boise City MSA, ID	H	7.35 FQ	8.86 AW	11.11 TQ	IDBLS	10/01-12/01
	Illinois	H	6.78 FQ	10.62 AW	15.26 TQ	ILBLS	10/01-12/01
	Champaign-Urbana MSA, IL	H	5.90 FQ	8.22 AW	11.33 TQ	ILBLS	10/01-12/01
	Chicago PMSA, IL	H	7.06 FQ	10.98 AW	15.73 TQ	ILBLS	10/01-12/01
	Peoria-Pekin MSA, IL	H	6.53 FQ	10.56 AW	14.12 TQ	ILBLS	10/01-12/01
	Rockford MSA, IL	H	5.68 FQ	7.86 AW	10.39 TQ	ILBLS	10/01-12/01
	Springfield MSA, IL	H	5.90 FQ	8.25 AW	11.24 TQ	ILBLS	10/01-12/01
	Indiana	H	6.24 FQ	9.08 AW	12.75 TQ	INBLS	10/01-12/01
	Elkhart-Goshen MSA, IN	H	6.68 FQ	8.94 AW	11.53 TQ	INBLS	10/01-12/01
	Evansville-Henderson MSA, IN-KY	H	6.08 FQ	8.51 AW	11.10 TQ	INBLS	10/01-12/01
	Fort Wayne MSA, IN	H	7.14 FQ	8.81 AW	11.28 TQ	INBLS	10/01-12/01
	Gary PMSA, IN	H	5.94 FQ	8.58 AW	14.52 TQ	INBLS	10/01-12/01
	Indianapolis MSA, IN	H	6.44 FQ	9.40 AW	13.07 TQ	INBLS	10/01-12/01
	Lafayette MSA, IN	H	7.22 FQ	9.58 AW	13.30 TQ	INBLS	10/01-12/01
	South Bend MSA, IN	H	7.00 FQ	9.43 AW	12.70 TQ	INBLS	10/01-12/01
	Iowa	H	6.63 FQ	8.85 AW	11.52 TQ	IABLS	10/01-12/01
	Cedar Rapids MSA, IA	H	5.83 FQ	8.54 AW	11.18 TQ	IABLS	10/01-12/01
	Des Moines MSA, IA	H	7.14 FQ	9.12 AW	11.11 TQ	IABLS	10/01-12/01
	Kansas	H	6.70 FQ	9.20 AW	11.47 TQ	KSBLS	10/01-12/01
	Topeka MSA, KS	H	7.26 FQ	9.11 AW	10.92 TQ	KSBLS	10/01-12/01
	Wichita MSA, KS	H	6.33 FQ	8.94 AW	10.96 TQ	KSBLS	10/01-12/01
	Kentucky	H	6.77 FQ	9.66 AW	12.82 TQ	KYBLS	10/01-12/01
	Lexington MSA, KY	H	7.02 FQ	8.69 AW	10.72 TQ	KYBLS	10/01-12/01
	Louisville MSA, KY-IN	H	6.53 FQ	9.07 AW	10.69 TQ	KYBLS	10/01-12/01
	Louisiana	H	5.81 FQ	8.25 AW	11.41 TQ	LABLS	10/01-12/01
	Baton Rouge MSA, LA	H	5.85 FQ	8.58 AW	12.05 TQ	LABLS	10/01-12/01
	Houma MSA, LA	H	6.08 FQ	10.73 AW	17.37 TQ	LABLS	10/01-12/01
	Lafayette MSA, LA	H	5.49 FQ	7.14 AW	10.00 TQ	LABLS	10/01-12/01
	Lake Charles MSA, LA	H	5.85 FQ	7.71 AW	9.48 TQ	LABLS	10/01-12/01
	New Orleans MSA, LA	H	5.91 FQ	8.27 AW	11.57 TQ	LABLS	10/01-12/01
	Shreveport-Bossier City MSA, LA	H	5.78 FQ	7.45 AW	9.15 TQ	LABLS	10/01-12/01
	Maine	H	6.64 FQ	9.42 AW	13.01 TQ	MEBLS	10/01-12/01
	Maryland	H	7.15 FQ	11.27 AW	16.38 TQ	MDBLS	10/01-12/01
	Baltimore PMSA, MD	H	6.86 FQ	11.48 AW	17.84 TQ	MDBLS	10/01-12/01
	Massachusetts	H	7.41 FQ	10.98 AW	14.65 TQ	MABLS	10/01-12/01
	Boston PMSA, MA-NH	H	7.52 FQ	11.23 AW	15.66 TQ	MABLS	10/01-12/01
	Brockton PMSA, MA	H	7.31 FQ	10.35 AW	13.55 TQ	MABLS	10/01-12/01
	Lawrence PMSA, MA-NH	H	6.97 FQ	10.52 AW	14.15 TQ	MABLS	10/01-12/01
	Lowell PMSA, MA-NH	H	7.11 FQ	10.10 AW	13.06 TQ	MABLS	10/01-12/01
	Springfield MSA, MA	H	8.41 FQ	11.43 AW	14.81 TQ	MABLS	10/01-12/01
	Worcester PMSA, MA-CT	H	7.64 FQ	10.25 AW	13.29 TQ	MABLS	10/01-12/01
	Michigan	H	7.36 FQ	10.01 AW	13.15 TQ	MIBLS	10/01-12/01
	Ann Arbor PMSA, MI	H	6.94 FQ	10.44 AW	15.19 TQ	MIBLS	10/01-12/01
	Detroit PMSA, MI	H	7.81 FQ	10.01 AW	11.94 TQ	MIBLS	10/01-12/01
	Flint PMSA, MI	H	7.03 FQ	10.55 AW	14.14 TQ	MIBLS	10/01-12/01
	Grand Rapids-Muskegon-Holland MSA, MI	H	6.20 FQ	9.69 AW	13.19 TQ	MIBLS	10/01-12/01
	Kalamazoo-Battle Creek MSA, MI	H	7.21 FQ	9.48 AW	13.87 TQ	MIBLS	10/01-12/01
	Lansing-East Lansing MSA, MI	H	7.64 FQ	9.95 AW	11.52 TQ	MIBLS	10/01-12/01
	Saginaw-Bay City-Midland MSA, MI	H	6.66 FQ	9.74 AW	13.55 TQ	MIBLS	10/01-12/01

AAW	Average annual wage	AOH	Average offered, high	ASH	Average starting, high	H	Hourly	M	Monthly	S	Special: hourly and annual
AE	Average entry wage	AOL	Average offered, low	ASL	Average starting, low	HI	Highest wage paid	MTC	Median total compensation	TQ	Third quartile wage
AEX	Average experienced wage	APH	Average pay, high range	AW	Average wage paid	HR	High end range	MW	Median wage paid	W	Weekly
AO	Average offered	APL	Average pay, low range	FQ	First quartile wage	LR	Low end range	SQ	Second quartile wage	Y	Yearly

Occupation/Type/Industry	Location	Per	Low	Mid	High	Source	Date
Courier and Messenger	Minnesota	H	6.26 FQ	10.05 AW	14.60 TQ	MNBLS	10/01-12/01
	Minneapolis-St. Paul MSA, MN-WI	H	7.34 FQ	11.25 AW	16.48 TQ	MNBLS	10/01-12/01
	St. Cloud MSA, MN	H	7.58 FQ	10.12 AW	14.76 TQ	MNBLS	10/01-12/01
	Mississippi	H	5.78 FQ	7.65 AW	10.28 TQ	MSBLS	10/01-12/01
	Biloxi-Gulfport-Pascagoula MSA, MS	H	5.77 FQ	7.82 AW	10.33 TQ	MSBLS	10/01-12/01
	Jackson MSA, MS	H	5.75 FQ	7.49 AW	10.21 TQ	MSBLS	10/01-12/01
	Missouri	H	5.97 FQ	9.41 AW	13.49 TQ	MOBLS	10/01-12/01
	Kansas City MSA, MO-KS	H	7.60 FQ	10.81 AW	15.07 TQ	MOBLS	10/01-12/01
	St. Louis MSA, MO-IL	H	5.78 FQ	9.31 AW	13.47 TQ	MOBLS	10/01-12/01
	Springfield MSA, MO	H	5.82 FQ	7.86 AW	10.80 TQ	MOBLS	10/01-12/01
	Montana	H	5.66 FQ	7.80 AW	11.34 TQ	MTBLS	10/01-12/01
	Billings MSA, MT	H	5.55 FQ	7.44 AW	10.51 TQ	MTBLS	10/01-12/01
	Nebraska	H	6.95 FQ	9.11 AW	11.32 TQ	NEBLS	10/01-12/01
	Lincoln MSA, NE	H	7.13 FQ	9.05 AW	11.01 TQ	NEBLS	10/01-12/01
	Omaha MSA, NE-IA	H	7.17 FQ	9.25 AW	11.35 TQ	NEBLS	10/01-12/01
	Nevada	H	7.16 FQ	9.97 AW	13.52 TQ	NVBLS	10/01-12/01
	Las Vegas MSA, NV-AZ	H	7.53 FQ	10.21 AW	13.48 TQ	NVBLS	10/01-12/01
	Reno MSA, NV	H	6.43 FQ	9.32 AW	13.42 TQ	NVBLS	10/01-12/01
	New Hampshire	H	6.20 FQ	9.35 AW	12.80 TQ	NHBLS	10/01-12/01
	Manchester PMSA, NH	H	5.86 FQ	8.72 AW	11.56 TQ	NHBLS	10/01-12/01
	Portsmouth-Rochester PMSA, NH-ME	H	8.95 FQ	10.72 AW	13.97 TQ	NHBLS	10/01-12/01
	New Jersey	H	7.57 FQ	11.09 AW	15.75 TQ	NJBLS	10/01-12/01
	Atlantic-Cape May PMSA, NJ	H	7.62 FQ	10.28 AW	14.78 TQ	NJBLS	10/01-12/01
	Bergen-Passaic PMSA, NJ	H	8.80 FQ	11.39 AW	14.94 TQ	NJBLS	10/01-12/01
	Jersey City PMSA, NJ	H	7.51 FQ	10.62 AW	14.00 TQ	NJBLS	10/01-12/01
	Middlesex-Somerset-Hunterdon PMSA, NJ	H	7.88 FQ	12.24 AW	18.45 TQ	NJBLS	10/01-12/01
	Monmouth-Ocean PMSA, NJ	H	7.77 FQ	11.06 AW	15.76 TQ	NJBLS	10/01-12/01
	Newark PMSA, NJ	H	8.14 FQ	11.10 AW	15.52 TQ	NJBLS	10/01-12/01
	Trenton PMSA, NJ	H	5.99 FQ	10.32 AW	15.92 TQ	NJBLS	10/01-12/01
	New Mexico	H	5.97 FQ	8.10 AW	10.82 TQ	NMBLS	10/01-12/01
	Albuquerque MSA, NM	H	6.10 FQ	8.48 AW	11.10 TQ	NMBLS	10/01-12/01
	Las Cruces MSA, NM	H	5.89 FQ	7.33 AW	9.04 TQ	NMBLS	10/01-12/01
	New York	H	5.87 FQ	9.88 AW	15.49 TQ	NYBLS	10/01-12/01
	Albany-Schenectady-Troy MSA, NY	H	6.42 FQ	10.05 AW	14.35 TQ	NYBLS	10/01-12/01
	Binghamton MSA, NY	H	6.21 FQ	10.32 AW	17.08 TQ	NYBLS	10/01-12/01
	Buffalo-Niagara Falls MSA, NY	H	6.05 FQ	9.00 AW	13.33 TQ	NYBLS	10/01-12/01
	Dutchess County PMSA, NY	H	7.40 FQ	9.98 AW	13.23 TQ	NYBLS	10/01-12/01
	Nassau-Suffolk PMSA, NY	H	7.14 FQ	11.89 AW	16.91 TQ	NYBLS	10/01-12/01
	New York PMSA, NY	H	5.77 FQ	9.64 AW	15.12 TQ	NYBLS	10/01-12/01
	Newburgh PMSA, NY-PA	H	6.17 FQ	9.39 AW	13.88 TQ	NYBLS	10/01-12/01
	Rochester MSA, NY	H	6.35 FQ	11.02 AW	19.27 TQ	NYBLS	10/01-12/01
	Syracuse MSA, NY	H	5.82 FQ	8.18 AW	11.74 TQ	NYBLS	10/01-12/01
	Utica-Rome MSA, NY	H	6.43 FQ	8.60 AW	10.93 TQ	NYBLS	10/01-12/01
	North Carolina	H	6.81 FQ	10.10 AW	13.43 TQ	NCBLS	10/01-12/01
	Charlotte-Gastonia-Rock Hill MSA, NC-SC	H	7.37 FQ	10.50 AW	13.47 TQ	NCBLS	10/01-12/01
	Greensboro-Winston-Salem-High Point MSA, NC	H	7.56 FQ	10.37 AW	13.26 TQ	NCBLS	10/01-12/01
	Raleigh-Durham-Chapel Hill MSA, NC	H	6.63 FQ	10.31 AW	13.88 TQ	NCBLS	10/01-12/01
	North Dakota	H	6.15 FQ	8.63 AW	11.65 TQ	NDBLS	10/01-12/01
	Ohio	H	6.60 FQ	10.13 AW	15.63 TQ	OHBLS	10/01-12/01
	Akron PMSA, OH	H	6.42 FQ	8.38 AW	10.53 TQ	OHBLS	10/01-12/01
	Canton-Massillon MSA, OH	H	6.66 FQ	8.95 AW	11.62 TQ	OHBLS	10/01-12/01
	Cincinnati PMSA, OH-KY-IN	H	6.87 FQ	9.77 AW	13.82 TQ	OHBLS	10/01-12/01
	Cleveland-Lorain-Elyria PMSA, OH	H	7.53 FQ	11.53 AW	16.25 TQ	OHBLS	10/01-12/01
	Columbus MSA, OH	H	7.44 FQ	11.02 AW	16.46 TQ	OHBLS	10/01-12/01
	Dayton-Springfield MSA, OH	H	7.41 FQ	10.37 AW	15.87 TQ	OHBLS	10/01-12/01
	Hamilton-Middletown PMSA, OH	H	5.56 FQ	6.60 AW	8.75 TQ	OHBLS	10/01-12/01
	Toledo MSA, OH	H	6.11 FQ	9.23 AW	13.57 TQ	OHBLS	10/01-12/01
	Youngstown-Warren MSA, OH	H	5.75 FQ	8.18 AW	11.35 TQ	OHBLS	10/01-12/01
	Oklahoma	H	6.02 FQ	8.46 AW	10.86 TQ	OKBLS	10/01-12/01
	Oklahoma City MSA, OK	H	5.92 FQ	8.23 AW	10.76 TQ	OKBLS	10/01-12/01
	Tulsa MSA, OK	H	6.84 FQ	9.29 AW	11.29 TQ	OKBLS	10/01-12/01

AAW	Average annual wage	AOH	Average offered, high	ASH	Average starting, high	H	Hourly	M	Monthly	S	Special: hourly and annual
AE	Average entry wage	AOL	Average offered, low	ASL	Average starting, low	HI	Highest wage paid	MTC	Median total compensation	TQ	Third quartile wage
AEX	Average experienced wage	APH	Average pay, high range	AW	Average wage paid	HR	High end range	MW	Median wage paid	W	Weekly
AO	Average offered	APL	Average pay, low range	FQ	First quartile wage	LR	Low end range	SQ	Second quartile wage	Y	Yearly

Occupation/Type/Industry	Location	Per	Low	Mid	High	Source	Date
Courier and Messenger	Oregon	H	7.03 FQ	10.44 AW	14.85 TQ	ORBLS	10/01-12/01
	Eugene-Springfield MSA, OR	H	7.66 FQ	10.32 AW	13.18 TQ	ORBLS	10/01-12/01
	Medford-Ashland MSA, OR	H	7.22 FQ	9.53 AW	13.21 TQ	ORBLS	10/01-12/01
	Portland-Vancouver PMSA, OR-WA	H	6.87 FQ	10.54 AW	15.20 TQ	ORBLS	10/01-12/01
	Salem PMSA, OR	H	7.49 FQ	10.94 AW	13.56 TQ	ORBLS	10/01-12/01
	Pennsylvania	H	6.83 FQ	9.98 AW	15.09 TQ	PABLS	10/01-12/01
	Allentown-Bethlehem-Easton MSA, PA	H	6.22 FQ	9.19 AW	11.86 TQ	PABLS	10/01-12/01
	Erie MSA, PA	H	6.02 FQ	8.49 AW	12.79 TQ	PABLS	10/01-12/01
	Harrisburg-Lebanon-Carlisle MSA, PA	H	7.18 FQ	9.32 AW	12.16 TQ	PABLS	10/01-12/01
	Johnstown MSA, PA	H	6.13 FQ	8.50 AW	11.46 TQ	PABLS	10/01-12/01
	Lancaster MSA, PA	H	6.53 FQ	11.37 AW	17.42 TQ	PABLS	10/01-12/01
	Philadelphia PMSA, PA-NJ	H	7.11 FQ	10.36 AW	14.21 TQ	PABLS	10/01-12/01
	Pittsburgh MSA, PA	H	6.64 FQ	9.66 AW	14.50 TQ	PABLS	10/01-12/01
	Reading MSA, PA	H	5.84 FQ	8.27 AW	11.46 TQ	PABLS	10/01-12/01
	Scranton-Wilkes-Barre-Hazleton MSA, PA	H	6.53 FQ	8.68 AW	11.70 TQ	PABLS	10/01-12/01
	York MSA, PA	H	8.18 FQ	11.93 AW	19.70 TQ	PABLS	10/01-12/01
	Rhode Island	H	6.64 FQ	9.53 AW	13.64 TQ	RIBLS	10/01-12/01
	Providence-Fall River-Warwick MSA, RI-MA	H	6.67 FQ	9.54 AW	13.50 TQ	RIBLS	10/01-12/01
	South Carolina	H	6.03 FQ	8.90 AW	11.59 TQ	SCBLS	10/01-12/01
	Charleston-North Charleston MSA, SC	H	5.87 FQ	7.86 AW	10.31 TQ	SCBLS	10/01-12/01
	Columbia MSA, SC	H	5.90 FQ	8.16 AW	10.65 TQ	SCBLS	10/01-12/01
	Greenville-Spartanburg-Anderson MSA, SC	H	6.92 FQ	9.05 AW	11.11 TQ	SCBLS	10/01-12/01
	Myrtle Beach MSA, SC	H	5.72 FQ	7.40 AW	9.91 TQ	SCBLS	10/01-12/01
	South Dakota	H	6.22 FQ	8.54 AW	10.88 TQ	SDBLS	10/01-12/01
	Tennessee	H	5.92 FQ	9.08 AW	13.06 TQ	TNBLS	10/01-12/01
	Chattanooga MSA, TN-GA	H	7.11 FQ	8.84 AW	11.49 TQ	TNBLS	10/01-12/01
	Johnson City-Kingsport-Bristol MSA, TN-VA	H	5.97 FQ	8.53 AW	11.84 TQ	TNBLS	10/01-12/01
	Knoxville MSA, TN	H	5.51 FQ	7.72 AW	10.67 TQ	TNBLS	10/01-12/01
	Memphis MSA, TN-AR-MS	H	7.22 FQ	10.28 AW	13.50 TQ	TNBLS	10/01-12/01
	Nashville MSA, TN	H	6.41 FQ	9.77 AW	14.02 TQ	TNBLS	10/01-12/01
	Texas	H	6.19 FQ	9.14 AW	12.79 TQ	TXBLS	10/01-12/01
	Amarillo MSA, TX	H	5.89 FQ	7.89 AW	10.47 TQ	TXBLS	10/01-12/01
	Austin-San Marcos MSA, TX	H	6.07 FQ	8.77 AW	11.56 TQ	TXBLS	10/01-12/01
	Beaumont-Port Arthur MSA, TX	H	5.84 FQ	8.93 AW	15.62 TQ	TXBLS	10/01-12/01
	Brownsville-Harlingen-San Benito MSA, TX	H	6.02 FQ	8.01 AW	10.57 TQ	TXBLS	10/01-12/01
	Corpus Christi MSA, TX	H	5.84 FQ	8.71 AW	11.48 TQ	TXBLS	10/01-12/01
	Dallas PMSA, TX	H	6.02 FQ	9.45 AW	13.61 TQ	TXBLS	10/01-12/01
	El Paso MSA, TX	H	5.66 FQ	7.78 AW	11.10 TQ	TXBLS	10/01-12/01
	Fort Worth-Arlington PMSA, TX	H	7.01 FQ	8.80 AW	11.23 TQ	TXBLS	10/01-12/01
	Galveston-Texas City PMSA, TX	H	6.03 FQ	8.61 AW	12.04 TQ	TXBLS	10/01-12/01
	Houston PMSA, TX	H	7.06 FQ	10.40 AW	17.57 TQ	TXBLS	10/01-12/01
	Killeen-Temple MSA, TX	H	6.83 FQ	8.23 AW	10.31 TQ	TXBLS	10/01-12/01
	Laredo MSA, TX	H	5.76 FQ	7.76 AW	11.71 TQ	TXBLS	10/01-12/01
	Longview-Marshall MSA, TX	H	6.04 FQ	8.84 AW	10.08 TQ	TXBLS	10/01-12/01
	Lubbock MSA, TX	H	6.75 FQ	8.12 AW	9.70 TQ	TXBLS	10/01-12/01
	McAllen-Edinburg-Mission MSA, TX	H	5.87 FQ	7.83 AW	11.18 TQ	TXBLS	10/01-12/01
	Odessa-Midland MSA, TX	H	6.49 FQ	8.50 AW	10.82 TQ	TXBLS	10/01-12/01
	San Antonio MSA, TX	H	6.90 FQ	9.13 AW	11.42 TQ	TXBLS	10/01-12/01
	Tyler MSA, TX	H	5.89 FQ	8.08 AW	11.30 TQ	TXBLS	10/01-12/01
	Waco MSA, TX	H	5.74 FQ	7.75 AW	10.84 TQ	TXBLS	10/01-12/01
	Utah	H	5.92 FQ	8.51 AW	12.09 TQ	UTBLS	10/01-12/01
	Provo-Orem MSA, UT	H	6.85 FQ	8.52 AW	11.07 TQ	UTBLS	10/01-12/01
	Salt Lake City-Ogden MSA, UT	H	5.88 FQ	8.43 AW	11.86 TQ	UTBLS	10/01-12/01
	Vermont	H	6.40 FQ	8.79 AW	13.37 TQ	VTBLS	10/01-12/01
	Burlington MSA, VT	H	6.38 FQ	8.33 AW	13.04 TQ	VTBLS	10/01-12/01
	Virginia	H	6.95 FQ	10.05 AW	14.71 TQ	VABLS	10/01-12/01

AAW	Average annual wage	**AOH**	Average offered, high	**ASH**	Average starting, high	**H**	Hourly	**M**	Monthly	**S**	Special: hourly and annual
AE	Average entry wage	**AOL**	Average offered, low	**ASL**	Average starting, low	**HI**	Highest wage paid	**MTC**	Median total compensation	**TQ**	Third quartile wage
AEX	Average experienced wage	**APH**	Average pay, high range	**AW**	Average wage paid	**HR**	High end range	**MW**	Median wage paid	**W**	Weekly
AO	Average offered	**APL**	Average pay, low range	**FQ**	First quartile wage	**LR**	Low end range	**SQ**	Second quartile wage	**Y**	Yearly

Occupation/Type/Industry	Location	Per	Low	Mid	High	Source	Date
Courier and Messenger	Norfolk-Virginia Beach-Newport News MSA, VA-NC	H	6.96 FQ	9.52 AW	14.07 TQ	VABLS	10/01-12/01
	Richmond-Petersburg MSA, VA	H	6.86 FQ	10.47 AW	15.85 TQ	VABLS	10/01-12/01
	Roanoke MSA, VA	H	6.04 FQ	8.35 AW	11.17 TQ	VABLS	10/01-12/01
	Washington	H	7.48 FQ	10.79 AW	15.13 TQ	WABLS	10/01-12/01
	Bremerton PMSA, WA	H	7.43 FQ	10.24 AW	13.15 TQ	WABLS	10/01-12/01
	Olympia PMSA, WA	H	7.49 FQ	9.66 AW	12.57 TQ	WABLS	10/01-12/01
	Richland-Kennewick-Pasco MSA, WA	H	7.28 FQ	9.46 AW	12.57 TQ	WABLS	10/01-12/01
	Seattle-Bellevue-Everett PMSA, WA	H	7.35 FQ	11.23 AW	16.24 TQ	WABLS	10/01-12/01
	Spokane MSA, WA	H	8.33 FQ	10.56 AW	13.26 TQ	WABLS	10/01-12/01
	Tacoma PMSA, WA	H	8.01 FQ	10.70 AW	13.68 TQ	WABLS	10/01-12/01
	West Virginia	H	5.97 FQ	9.14 AW	12.97 TQ	WVBLS	10/01-12/01
	Charleston MSA, WV	H	7.06 FQ	10.75 AW	13.26 TQ	WVBLS	10/01-12/01
	Huntington-Ashland MSA, WV-KY-OH	H	6.01 FQ	8.74 AW	13.11 TQ	WVBLS	10/01-12/01
	Wisconsin	H	6.64 FQ	9.73 AW	13.25 TQ	WIBLS	10/01-12/01
	Appleton-Oshkosh-Neenah MSA, WI	H	5.87 FQ	8.81 AW	11.56 TQ	WIBLS	10/01-12/01
	Green Bay MSA, WI	H	6.80 FQ	10.18 AW	14.14 TQ	WIBLS	10/01-12/01
	Madison MSA, WI	H	7.76 FQ	10.33 AW	13.35 TQ	WIBLS	10/01-12/01
	Milwaukee-Waukesha PMSA, WI	H	6.62 FQ	10.22 AW	14.23 TQ	WIBLS	10/01-12/01
	Wyoming	H	6.08 FQ	8.20 AW	10.66 TQ	WYBLS	10/01-12/01
	Puerto Rico	H	5.60 FQ	7.15 AW	9.77 TQ	PRBLS	10/01-12/01
	Virgin Islands	H	6.45 FQ	8.24 AW	10.50 TQ	VIBLS	10/01-12/01
	Guam	H	6.32 FQ	9.30 AW	13.45 TQ	GUBLS	10/01-12/01
Court, Municipal, and License Clerk	Alabama	H	7.02 FQ	11.59 AW	16.53 TQ	ALBLS	10/01-12/01
	Birmingham MSA, AL	H	6.06 FQ	10.60 AW	16.06 TQ	ALBLS	10/01-12/01
	Huntsville MSA, AL	H	9.64 FQ	13.35 AW	17.56 TQ	ALBLS	10/01-12/01
	Mobile MSA, AL	H	8.27 FQ	11.59 AW	15.64 TQ	ALBLS	10/01-12/01
	Montgomery MSA, AL	H	8.72 FQ	13.02 AW	16.60 TQ	ALBLS	10/01-12/01
	Alaska	H	11.80 FQ	16.83 AW	23.28 TQ	AKBLS	10/01-12/01
	Arizona	H	9.18 FQ	12.33 AW	16.51 TQ	AZBLS	10/01-12/01
	Phoenix-Mesa MSA, AZ	H	9.21 FQ	12.56 AW	16.84 TQ	AZBLS	10/01-12/01
	Tucson MSA, AZ	H	9.30 FQ	11.15 AW	13.63 TQ	AZBLS	10/01-12/01
	Arkansas	H	5.98 FQ	9.72 AW	14.27 TQ	ARBLS	10/01-12/01
	Fayetteville-Springdale-Rogers MSA, AR	H	7.96 FQ	11.32 AW	16.30 TQ	ARBLS	10/01-12/01
	Fort Smith MSA, AR-OK	H	6.11 FQ	11.09 AW	16.97 TQ	ARBLS	10/01-12/01
	Little Rock-North Little Rock MSA, AR	H	8.44 FQ	11.78 AW	16.10 TQ	ARBLS	10/01-12/01
	California	H	12.17 FQ	17.32 AW	24.50 TQ	CABLS	10/01-12/01
	Fresno MSA, CA	H	12.18 FQ	16.69 AW	22.79 TQ	CABLS	10/01-12/01
	Oakland PMSA, CA	H	12.22 FQ	16.80 AW	22.91 TQ	CABLS	10/01-12/01
	Riverside-San Bernardino PMSA, CA	H	11.79 FQ	17.66 AW	26.57 TQ	CABLS	10/01-12/01
	Sacramento PMSA, CA	H	12.38 FQ	16.96 AW	22.84 TQ	CABLS	10/01-12/01
	San Francisco PMSA, CA	H	16.73 FQ	24.75 AW	30.99 TQ	CABLS	10/01-12/01
	San Jose PMSA, CA	H	12.49 FQ	19.49 AW	28.47 TQ	CABLS	10/01-12/01
	Ventura PMSA, CA	H	12.29 FQ	17.26 AW	23.32 TQ	CABLS	10/01-12/01
	Colorado	H	10.78 FQ	14.59 AW	20.01 TQ	COBLS	10/01-12/01
	Boulder-Longmont PMSA, CO	H	11.39 FQ	16.27 AW	21.16 TQ	COBLS	10/01-12/01
	Colorado Springs MSA, CO	H	11.13 FQ	14.79 AW	19.85 TQ	COBLS	10/01-12/01
	Denver PMSA, CO	H	11.37 FQ	15.18 AW	20.30 TQ	COBLS	10/01-12/01
	Greeley PMSA, CO	H	10.77 FQ	14.61 AW	19.96 TQ	COBLS	10/01-12/01
	Connecticut	H	10.02 FQ	16.00 AW	23.66 TQ	CTBLS	10/01-12/01
	Danbury PMSA, CT	H	10.36 FQ	16.03 AW	23.31 TQ	CTBLS	10/01-12/01
	Hartford MSA, CT	H	10.84 FQ	16.09 AW	22.79 TQ	CTBLS	10/01-12/01
	New Haven-Meriden PMSA, CT	H	9.92 FQ	15.42 AW	23.36 TQ	CTBLS	10/01-12/01
	New London-Norwich MSA, CT-RI	H	6.67 FQ	14.78 AW	24.44 TQ	CTBLS	10/01-12/01
	Stamford-Norwalk PMSA, CT	H	10.55 FQ	17.00 AW	24.22 TQ	CTBLS	10/01-12/01
	Delaware	H	11.11 FQ	13.48 AW	16.59 TQ	DEBLS	10/01-12/01
	Washington PMSA, DC-MD-VA-WV	H	11.24 FQ	16.37 AW	22.36 TQ	DCBLS	10/01-12/01

AAW	Average annual wage	**AOH**	Average offered, high	**ASH**	Average starting, high	**H**	Hourly	**M**	Monthly	**S**	Special: hourly and annual
AE	Average entry wage	**AOL**	Average offered, low	**ASL**	Average starting, low	**HI**	Highest wage paid	**MTC**	Median total compensation	**TQ**	Third quartile wage
AEX	Average experienced wage	**APH**	Average pay, high range	**AW**	Average wage paid	**HR**	High end range	**MW**	Median wage paid	**W**	Weekly
AO	Average offered	**APL**	Average pay, low range	**FQ**	First quartile wage	**LR**	Low end range	**SQ**	Second quartile wage	**Y**	Yearly

Occupation/Type/Industry	Location	Per	Low	Mid	High	Source	Date
Court, Municipal, and License Clerk	Florida	H	8.50 FQ	13.62 AW	23.48 TQ	FLBLS	10/01-12/01
	Fort Lauderdale PMSA, FL	H	8.60 FQ	13.31 AW	22.35 TQ	FLBLS	10/01-12/01
	Fort Myers-Cape Coral MSA, FL	H	9.56 FQ	15.04 AW	24.51 TQ	FLBLS	10/01-12/01
	Lakeland-Winter Haven MSA, FL	H	9.28 FQ	18.33 AW	27.93 TQ	FLBLS	10/01-12/01
	Miami PMSA, FL	H	13.20 FQ	22.97 AW	29.25 TQ	FLBLS	10/01-12/01
	Ocala MSA, FL	H	7.59 FQ	11.04 AW	15.92 TQ	FLBLS	10/01-12/01
	Orlando MSA, FL	H	8.22 FQ	12.72 AW	21.91 TQ	FLBLS	10/01-12/01
	Pensacola MSA, FL	H	8.31 FQ	14.26 AW	26.24 TQ	FLBLS	10/01-12/01
	Tallahassee MSA, FL	H	9.75 FQ	14.19 AW	20.21 TQ	FLBLS	10/01-12/01
	Tampa-St. Petersburg-Clearwater MSA, FL	H	10.16 FQ	15.17 AW	23.53 TQ	FLBLS	10/01-12/01
	Georgia	H	8.31 FQ	12.45 AW	17.67 TQ	GABLS	10/01-12/01
	Atlanta MSA, GA	H	9.62 FQ	13.72 AW	18.35 TQ	GABLS	10/01-12/01
	Augusta-Aiken MSA, GA-SC	H	7.90 FQ	10.76 AW	15.09 TQ	GABLS	10/01-12/01
	Macon MSA, GA	H	7.12 FQ	9.55 AW	14.23 TQ	GABLS	10/01-12/01
	Savannah MSA, GA	H	9.07 FQ	11.49 AW	15.90 TQ	GABLS	10/01-12/01
	Hawaii	H	11.72 FQ	15.94 AW	21.08 TQ	HIBLS	10/01-12/01
	Idaho	H	8.63 FQ	11.53 AW	14.55 TQ	IDBLS	10/01-12/01
	Illinois	H	8.57 FQ	13.60 AW	19.27 TQ	ILBLS	10/01-12/01
	Chicago PMSA, IL	H	8.96 FQ	13.98 AW	19.59 TQ	ILBLS	10/01-12/01
	Indiana	H	6.82 FQ	10.43 AW	13.88 TQ	INBLS	10/01-12/01
	Elkhart-Goshen MSA, IN	H	5.72 FQ	9.11 AW	13.74 TQ	INBLS	10/01-12/01
	Evansville-Henderson MSA, IN-KY	H	8.69 FQ	11.42 AW	14.38 TQ	INBLS	10/01-12/01
	Fort Wayne MSA, IN	H	9.75 FQ	12.70 AW	16.31 TQ	INBLS	10/01-12/01
	Gary PMSA, IN	H	8.28 FQ	11.64 AW	14.50 TQ	INBLS	10/01-12/01
	Indianapolis MSA, IN	H	7.11 FQ	9.98 AW	13.02 TQ	INBLS	10/01-12/01
	Lafayette MSA, IN	H	7.07 FQ	11.35 AW	15.71 TQ	INBLS	10/01-12/01
	South Bend MSA, IN	H	7.76 FQ	10.47 AW	13.54 TQ	INBLS	10/01-12/01
	Iowa	H	9.28 FQ	12.91 AW	16.33 TQ	IABLS	10/01-12/01
	Davenport-Moline-Rock Island MSA, IA-IL	H	8.35 FQ	13.56 AW	18.09 TQ	IABLS	10/01-12/01
	Kansas	H	8.51 FQ	11.34 AW	15.72 TQ	KSBLS	10/01-12/01
	Wichita MSA, KS	H	8.85 FQ	11.64 AW	16.30 TQ	KSBLS	10/01-12/01
	Kentucky	H	8.34 FQ	12.24 AW	16.92 TQ	KYBLS	10/01-12/01
	Louisiana	H	6.42 FQ	11.08 AW	16.72 TQ	LABLS	10/01-12/01
	Baton Rouge MSA, LA	H	6.96 FQ	11.17 AW	16.14 TQ	LABLS	10/01-12/01
	Lafayette MSA, LA	H	6.11 FQ	10.10 AW	15.29 TQ	LABLS	10/01-12/01
	Lake Charles MSA, LA	H	7.60 FQ	12.37 AW	19.83 TQ	LABLS	10/01-12/01
	New Orleans MSA, LA	H	7.44 FQ	12.97 AW	21.15 TQ	LABLS	10/01-12/01
	Shreveport-Bossier City MSA, LA	H	6.49 FQ	11.64 AW	17.39 TQ	LABLS	10/01-12/01
	Maine	H	9.11 FQ	12.72 AW	16.75 TQ	MEBLS	10/01-12/01
	Portland MSA, ME	H	9.19 FQ	12.26 AW	15.98 TQ	MEBLS	10/01-12/01
	Maryland	H	9.17 FQ	14.54 AW	20.03 TQ	MDBLS	10/01-12/01
	Baltimore PMSA, MD	H	10.26 FQ	14.59 AW	18.97 TQ	MDBLS	10/01-12/01
	Massachusetts	H	8.29 FQ	16.28 AW	23.98 TQ	MABLS	10/01-12/01
	Boston PMSA, MA-NH	H	8.04 FQ	15.71 AW	23.34 TQ	MABLS	10/01-12/01
	Lawrence PMSA, MA-NH	H	9.93 FQ	15.84 AW	22.22 TQ	MABLS	10/01-12/01
	Lowell PMSA, MA-NH	H	8.15 FQ	14.18 AW	19.86 TQ	MABLS	10/01-12/01
	New Bedford PMSA, MA	H	8.28 FQ	14.94 AW	21.39 TQ	MABLS	10/01-12/01
	Worcester PMSA, MA-CT	H	12.41 FQ	19.28 AW	26.76 TQ	MABLS	10/01-12/01
	Michigan	H	11.37 FQ	15.50 AW	20.43 TQ	MIBLS	10/01-12/01
	Ann Arbor PMSA, MI	H	13.33 FQ	16.58 AW	20.22 TQ	MIBLS	10/01-12/01
	Detroit PMSA, MI	H	11.97 FQ	15.98 AW	20.76 TQ	MIBLS	10/01-12/01
	Flint PMSA, MI	H	12.41 FQ	16.05 AW	20.29 TQ	MIBLS	10/01-12/01
	Grand Rapids-Muskegon-Holland MSA, MI	H	11.90 FQ	16.04 AW	20.58 TQ	MIBLS	10/01-12/01
	Kalamazoo-Battle Creek MSA, MI	H	11.34 FQ	14.64 AW	19.77 TQ	MIBLS	10/01-12/01
	Lansing-East Lansing MSA, MI	H	13.48 FQ	16.93 AW	22.17 TQ	MIBLS	10/01-12/01
	Saginaw-Bay City-Midland MSA, MI	H	13.52 FQ	16.62 AW	20.34 TQ	MIBLS	10/01-12/01
	Minnesota	H	10.45 FQ	14.33 AW	19.17 TQ	MNBLS	10/01-12/01
	Minneapolis-St. Paul MSA, MN-WI	H	10.68 FQ	14.52 AW	19.05 TQ	MNBLS	10/01-12/01
	Mississippi	H	7.54 FQ	11.95 AW	17.65 TQ	MSBLS	10/01-12/01
	Biloxi-Gulfport-Pascagoula MSA, MS	H	7.93 FQ	10.79 AW	14.35 TQ	MSBLS	10/01-12/01

AAW	Average annual wage	AOH	Average offered, high	ASH	Average starting, high	H	Hourly	M	Monthly	S	Special: hourly and annual
AE	Average entry wage	AOL	Average offered, low	ASL	Average starting, low	HI	Highest wage paid	MTC	Median total compensation	TQ	Third quartile wage
AEX	Average experienced wage	APH	Average pay, high range	AW	Average wage paid	HR	High end range	MW	Median wage paid	W	Weekly
AO	Average offered	APL	Average pay, low range	FQ	First quartile wage	LR	Low end range	SQ	Second quartile wage	Y	Yearly

Occupation/Type/Industry	Location	Per	Low	Mid	High	Source	Date
Court, Municipal, and License Clerk	Jackson MSA, MS	H	7.93 FQ	13.67 AW	20.36 TQ	MSBLS	10/01-12/01
	Kansas City MSA, MO-KS	H	8.37 FQ	12.19 AW	17.33 TQ	MOBLS	10/01-12/01
	St. Louis MSA, MO-IL	H	8.60 FQ	13.00 AW	18.73 TQ	MOBLS	10/01-12/01
	Montana	H	7.07 FQ	10.32 AW	13.95 TQ	MTBLS	10/01-12/01
	Nebraska	H	7.97 FQ	11.73 AW	16.17 TQ	NEBLS	10/01-12/01
	Nevada	H	11.65 FQ	16.46 AW	22.23 TQ	NVBLS	10/01-12/01
	Las Vegas MSA, NV-AZ	H	11.52 FQ	16.96 AW	23.62 TQ	NVBLS	10/01-12/01
	New Hampshire	H	8.75 FQ	11.63 AW	15.61 TQ	NHBLS	10/01-12/01
	Nashua PMSA, NH	H	9.33 FQ	12.61 AW	16.80 TQ	NHBLS	10/01-12/01
	Portsmouth-Rochester PMSA, NH-ME	H	7.87 FQ	13.00 AW	18.65 TQ	NHBLS	10/01-12/01
	New Jersey	H	8.67 FQ	15.15 AW	22.96 TQ	NJBLS	10/01-12/01
	Atlantic-Cape May PMSA, NJ	H	10.12 FQ	15.46 AW	21.30 TQ	NJBLS	10/01-12/01
	Bergen-Passaic PMSA, NJ	H	9.73 FQ	16.42 AW	24.34 TQ	NJBLS	10/01-12/01
	Middlesex-Somerset-Hunterdon PMSA, NJ	H	9.04 FQ	14.61 AW	23.00 TQ	NJBLS	10/01-12/01
	Monmouth-Ocean PMSA, NJ	H	6.13 FQ	13.91 AW	21.80 TQ	NJBLS	10/01-12/01
	Newark PMSA, NJ	H	9.64 FQ	16.03 AW	24.78 TQ	NJBLS	10/01-12/01
	Trenton PMSA, NJ	H	9.94 FQ	16.14 AW	21.38 TQ	NJBLS	10/01-12/01
	New Mexico	H	8.83 FQ	12.32 AW	16.83 TQ	NMBLS	10/01-12/01
	Albuquerque MSA, NM	H	9.75 FQ	12.67 AW	17.07 TQ	NMBLS	10/01-12/01
	Las Cruces MSA, NM	H	9.29 FQ	12.56 AW	17.46 TQ	NMBLS	10/01-12/01
	New York	H	9.88 FQ	19.15 AW	32.17 TQ	NYBLS	10/01-12/01
	Albany-Schenectady-Troy MSA, NY	H	8.92 FQ	14.86 AW	21.55 TQ	NYBLS	10/01-12/01
	Binghamton MSA, NY	H	6.82 FQ	11.46 AW	19.49 TQ	NYBLS	10/01-12/01
	Buffalo-Niagara Falls MSA, NY	H	8.95 FQ	14.54 AW	21.72 TQ	NYBLS	10/01-12/01
	Dutchess County PMSA, NY	H	7.21 FQ	15.67 AW	27.95 TQ	NYBLS	10/01-12/01
	Nassau-Suffolk PMSA, NY	H	11.75 FQ	20.99 AW	33.33 TQ	NYBLS	10/01-12/01
	New York PMSA, NY	H	12.71 FQ	23.87 AW	34.06 TQ	NYBLS	10/01-12/01
	Newburgh PMSA, NY-PA	H	9.03 FQ	15.37 AW	28.72 TQ	NYBLS	10/01-12/01
	Rochester MSA, NY	H	8.59 FQ	15.63 AW	24.51 TQ	NYBLS	10/01-12/01
	Syracuse MSA, NY	H	10.13 FQ	15.15 AW	23.13 TQ	NYBLS	10/01-12/01
	Utica-Rome MSA, NY	H	7.07 FQ	15.32 AW	25.75 TQ	NYBLS	10/01-12/01
	North Carolina	H	8.89 FQ	12.08 AW	16.16 TQ	NCBLS	10/01-12/01
	Charlotte-Gastonia-Rock Hill MSA, NC-SC	H	9.44 FQ	13.44 AW	19.75 TQ	NCBLS	10/01-12/01
	Greensboro-Winston-Salem-High Point MSA, NC	H	8.56 FQ	11.74 AW	15.30 TQ	NCBLS	10/01-12/01
	Hickory-Morganton-Lenoir MSA, NC	H	7.95 FQ	11.60 AW	15.01 TQ	NCBLS	10/01-12/01
	Raleigh-Durham-Chapel Hill MSA, NC	H	9.71 FQ	12.94 AW	17.35 TQ	NCBLS	10/01-12/01
	North Dakota	H	7.63 FQ	11.06 AW	14.44 TQ	NDBLS	10/01-12/01
	Ohio	H	8.28 FQ	13.23 AW	19.22 TQ	OHBLS	10/01-12/01
	Akron PMSA, OH	H	10.87 FQ	16.33 AW	24.00 TQ	OHBLS	10/01-12/01
	Canton-Massillon MSA, OH	H	7.86 FQ	13.07 AW	18.86 TQ	OHBLS	10/01-12/01
	Cincinnati PMSA, OH-KY-IN	H	8.22 FQ	12.69 AW	18.75 TQ	OHBLS	10/01-12/01
	Cleveland-Lorain-Elyria PMSA, OH	H	9.45 FQ	14.08 AW	19.85 TQ	OHBLS	10/01-12/01
	Dayton-Springfield MSA, OH	H	8.67 FQ	13.54 AW	19.39 TQ	OHBLS	10/01-12/01
	Hamilton-Middletown PMSA, OH	H	10.61 FQ	15.17 AW	20.17 TQ	OHBLS	10/01-12/01
	Mansfield MSA, OH	H	7.03 FQ	10.28 AW	15.95 TQ	OHBLS	10/01-12/01
	Toledo MSA, OH	H	8.57 FQ	12.18 AW	17.45 TQ	OHBLS	10/01-12/01
	Youngstown-Warren MSA, OH	H	8.94 FQ	12.63 AW	18.28 TQ	OHBLS	10/01-12/01
	Oklahoma	H	7.45 FQ	10.84 AW	14.26 TQ	OKBLS	10/01-12/01
	Oklahoma City MSA, OK	H	9.14 FQ	11.88 AW	14.67 TQ	OKBLS	10/01-12/01
	Tulsa MSA, OK	H	9.55 FQ	12.56 AW	16.53 TQ	OKBLS	10/01-12/01
	Oregon	H	11.29 FQ	14.45 AW	17.02 TQ	ORBLS	10/01-12/01
	Portland-Vancouver PMSA, OR-WA	H	11.42 FQ	14.47 AW	18.09 TQ	ORBLS	10/01-12/01
	Pennsylvania	H	6.83 FQ	13.35 AW	21.11 TQ	PABLS	10/01-12/01
	Erie MSA, PA	H	7.30 FQ	12.71 AW	17.57 TQ	PABLS	10/01-12/01
	Harrisburg-Lebanon-Carlisle MSA, PA	H	7.87 FQ	15.69 AW	23.74 TQ	PABLS	10/01-12/01
	Philadelphia PMSA, PA-NJ	H	9.28 FQ	14.60 AW	20.50 TQ	PABLS	10/01-12/01
	Pittsburgh MSA, PA	H	7.21 FQ	11.78 AW	16.71 TQ	PABLS	10/01-12/01
	Scranton-Wilkes-Barre-Hazleton MSA, PA	H	5.98 FQ	12.87 AW	25.93 TQ	PABLS	10/01-12/01

Occupation/Type/Industry	Location	Per	Low	Mid	High	Source	Date
Court, Municipal, and License Clerk	York MSA, PA	H	12.04 FQ	13.99 AW	16.75 TQ	PABLS	10/01-12/01
	Rhode Island	H	11.18 FQ	15.63 AW	21.38 TQ	RIBLS	10/01-12/01
	Providence-Fall River-Warwick MSA, RI-MA	H	11.22 FQ	15.73 AW	21.44 TQ	RIBLS	10/01-12/01
	South Carolina	H	7.68 FQ	11.42 AW	16.41 TQ	SCBLS	10/01-12/01
	Charleston-North Charleston MSA, SC	H	7.06 FQ	11.61 AW	19.68 TQ	SCBLS	10/01-12/01
	Columbia MSA, SC	H	8.14 FQ	12.06 AW	16.34 TQ	SCBLS	10/01-12/01
	Greenville-Spartanburg-Anderson MSA, SC	H	7.72 FQ	11.00 AW	15.54 TQ	SCBLS	10/01-12/01
	South Dakota	H	6.18 FQ	8.99 AW	12.65 TQ	SDBLS	10/01-12/01
	Sioux Falls MSA, SD	H	7.53 FQ	10.99 AW	13.71 TQ	SDBLS	10/01-12/01
	Tennessee	H	7.89 FQ	12.48 AW	17.91 TQ	TNBLS	10/01-12/01
	Chattanooga MSA, TN-GA	H	8.40 FQ	11.49 AW	14.16 TQ	TNBLS	10/01-12/01
	Johnson City-Kingsport-Bristol MSA, TN-VA	H	7.66 FQ	11.74 AW	16.09 TQ	TNBLS	10/01-12/01
	Knoxville MSA, TN	H	8.67 FQ	13.04 AW	17.81 TQ	TNBLS	10/01-12/01
	Memphis MSA, TN-AR-MS	H	7.29 FQ	12.57 AW	17.75 TQ	TNBLS	10/01-12/01
	Texas	H	7.82 FQ	11.36 AW	16.09 TQ	TXBLS	10/01-12/01
	Brazoria PMSA, TX	H	8.52 FQ	11.22 AW	15.70 TQ	TXBLS	10/01-12/01
	Brownsville-Harlingen-San Benito MSA, TX	H	6.95 FQ	9.34 AW	11.18 TQ	TXBLS	10/01-12/01
	Corpus Christi MSA, TX	H	7.39 FQ	8.59 AW	10.66 TQ	TXBLS	10/01-12/01
	Dallas PMSA, TX	H	9.51 FQ	13.11 AW	16.48 TQ	TXBLS	10/01-12/01
	El Paso MSA, TX	H	8.96 FQ	10.96 AW	14.02 TQ	TXBLS	10/01-12/01
	Fort Worth-Arlington PMSA, TX	H	9.43 FQ	12.30 AW	15.61 TQ	TXBLS	10/01-12/01
	Galveston-Texas City PMSA, TX	H	9.66 FQ	13.68 AW	18.47 TQ	TXBLS	10/01-12/01
	Houston PMSA, TX	H	7.63 FQ	9.77 AW	13.72 TQ	TXBLS	10/01-12/01
	Killeen-Temple MSA, TX	H	7.59 FQ	9.10 AW	10.86 TQ	TXBLS	10/01-12/01
	Longview-Marshall MSA, TX	H	7.42 FQ	9.66 AW	12.78 TQ	TXBLS	10/01-12/01
	McAllen-Edinburg-Mission MSA, TX	H	7.68 FQ	9.92 AW	13.16 TQ	TXBLS	10/01-12/01
	San Antonio MSA, TX	H	8.99 FQ	11.04 AW	13.69 TQ	TXBLS	10/01-12/01
	Waco MSA, TX	H	9.27 FQ	11.47 AW	15.09 TQ	TXBLS	10/01-12/01
	Utah	H	5.68 FQ	10.33 AW	15.94 TQ	UTBLS	10/01-12/01
	Provo-Orem MSA, UT	H	5.33 FQ	6.64 AW	10.15 TQ	UTBLS	10/01-12/01
	Vermont	H	9.10 FQ	12.55 AW	16.70 TQ	VTBLS	10/01-12/01
	Burlington MSA, VT	H	10.86 FQ	13.79 AW	17.40 TQ	VTBLS	10/01-12/01
	Virginia	H	9.64 FQ	14.72 AW	20.61 TQ	VABLS	10/01-12/01
	Lynchburg MSA, VA	H	10.19 FQ	15.21 AW	19.90 TQ	VABLS	10/01-12/01
	Norfolk-Virginia Beach-Newport News MSA, VA-NC	H	9.75 FQ	14.00 AW	18.88 TQ	VABLS	10/01-12/01
	Richmond-Petersburg MSA, VA	H	10.07 FQ	14.23 AW	20.34 TQ	VABLS	10/01-12/01
	Roanoke MSA, VA	H	9.47 FQ	13.31 AW	18.31 TQ	VABLS	10/01-12/01
	Washington	H	12.35 FQ	16.20 AW	20.56 TQ	WABLS	10/01-12/01
	Bremerton PMSA, WA	H	12.20 FQ	15.67 AW	19.49 TQ	WABLS	10/01-12/01
	Olympia PMSA, WA	H	10.22 FQ	15.31 AW	19.75 TQ	WABLS	10/01-12/01
	Tacoma PMSA, WA	H	14.09 FQ	17.36 AW	21.25 TQ	WABLS	10/01-12/01
	Yakima MSA, WA	H	12.42 FQ	15.42 AW	18.66 TQ	WABLS	10/01-12/01
	West Virginia	H	6.30 FQ	9.36 AW	12.07 TQ	WVBLS	10/01-12/01
	Charleston MSA, WV	H	6.23 FQ	9.69 AW	11.68 TQ	WVBLS	10/01-12/01
	Huntington-Ashland MSA, WV-KY-OH	H	7.61 FQ	11.53 AW	17.37 TQ	WVBLS	10/01-12/01
	Wisconsin	H	6.09 FQ	11.90 AW	18.74 TQ	WIBLS	10/01-12/01
	Appleton-Oshkosh-Neenah MSA, WI	H	9.85 FQ	14.77 AW	20.09 TQ	WIBLS	10/01-12/01
	Green Bay MSA, WI	H	10.55 FQ	12.99 AW	14.62 TQ	WIBLS	10/01-12/01
	Milwaukee-Waukesha PMSA, WI	H	12.08 FQ	16.42 AW	21.58 TQ	WIBLS	10/01-12/01
	Racine PMSA, WI	H	11.21 FQ	14.36 AW	18.14 TQ	WIBLS	10/01-12/01
	Wyoming	H	6.25 FQ	11.22 AW	16.21 TQ	WYBLS	10/01-12/01
	Puerto Rico	H	5.42 FQ	7.73 AW	12.69 TQ	PRBLS	10/01-12/01
Court Reporter	Alabama	Y	12160 FQ	26920 AW	54590 TQ	ALBLS	10/01-12/01
	Montgomery MSA, AL	Y	13260 FQ	34270 AW	59200 TQ	ALBLS	10/01-12/01
	Arizona	Y	27170 FQ	43270 AW	55500 TQ	AZBLS	10/01-12/01
	Phoenix-Mesa MSA, AZ	Y	13950 FQ	42370 AW	55530 TQ	AZBLS	10/01-12/01

AAW Average annual wage; AE Average entry wage; AEX Average experienced wage; AO Average offered; AOH Average offered, high; AOL Average offered, low; APH Average pay, high range; APL Average pay, low range; ASH Average starting, high; ASL Average starting, low; AW Average wage paid; FQ First quartile wage; H Hourly; HI Highest wage paid; HR High end range; LR Low end range; M Monthly; MTC Median total compensation; MW Median wage paid; SQ Second quartile wage; S Special: hourly and annual; TQ Third quartile wage; W Weekly; Y Yearly

Occupation/Type/Industry	Location	Per	Low	Mid	High	Source	Date
Court Reporter	Arkansas	Y	12860 FQ	24540 AW	47340 TQ	ARBLS	10/01-12/01
	California	Y	26020 FQ	49700 AW	73630 TQ	CABLS	10/01-12/01
	Bakersfield MSA, CA	Y	53450 FQ	64630 AW	79790 TQ	CABLS	10/01-12/01
	Fresno MSA, CA	Y	29610 FQ	48350 AW	71020 TQ	CABLS	10/01-12/01
	Los Angeles-Long Beach PMSA, CA	Y	25220 FQ	43700 AW	62670 TQ	CABLS	10/01-12/01
	Orange County PMSA, CA	Y	26650 FQ	45840 AW	68610 TQ	CABLS	10/01-12/01
	Sacramento PMSA, CA	Y	38660 FQ	52790 AW	68500 TQ	CABLS	10/01-12/01
	San Jose PMSA, CA	Y	46910 FQ	94930 AW	117200 TQ	CABLS	10/01-12/01
	Stockton-Lodi MSA, CA	Y	44920 FQ	55660 AW	69770 TQ	CABLS	10/01-12/01
	Colorado	Y	30080 FQ	42720 AW	55450 TQ	COBLS	10/01-12/01
	Denver PMSA, CO	Y	29650 FQ	42480 AW	56120 TQ	COBLS	10/01-12/01
	Connecticut	Y	24410 FQ	34300 AW	45950 TQ	CTBLS	10/01-12/01
	Delaware	Y	42870 FQ	55150 AW	73650 TQ	DEBLS	10/01-12/01
	District of Columbia	Y	26800 FQ	40580 AW	56950 TQ	DCBLS	10/01-12/01
	Washington PMSA, DC-MD-VA-WV	Y	23920 FQ	37280 AW	59220 TQ	DCBLS	10/01-12/01
	Florida	Y	15650 FQ	35690 AW	69950 TQ	FLBLS	10/01-12/01
	Fort Pierce-Port St. Lucie MSA, FL	Y	11900 FQ	17050 AW	25390 TQ	FLBLS	10/01-12/01
	Jacksonville MSA, FL	Y	20090 FQ	38170 AW	69310 TQ	FLBLS	10/01-12/01
	Lakeland-Winter Haven MSA, FL	Y	18310 FQ	40150 AW	79850 TQ	FLBLS	10/01-12/01
	Miami PMSA, FL	Y	31900 FQ	47270 AW	65540 TQ	FLBLS	10/01-12/01
	Orlando MSA, FL	Y	13350 FQ	43450 AW	83350 TQ	FLBLS	10/01-12/01
	Sarasota-Bradenton MSA, FL	Y	14820 FQ	34630 AW	85340 TQ	FLBLS	10/01-12/01
	Tampa-St. Petersburg-Clearwater MSA, FL	Y	20660 FQ	34490 AW	69020 TQ	FLBLS	10/01-12/01
	West Palm Beach-Boca Raton MSA, FL	Y	23720 FQ	31270 AW	46790 TQ	FLBLS	10/01-12/01
	Georgia	Y	12470 FQ	40330 AW	74240 TQ	GABLS	10/01-12/01
	Atlanta MSA, GA	Y	19050 FQ	55620 AW	77080 TQ	GABLS	10/01-12/01
	Hawaii	Y	32710 FQ	45010 AW	56280 TQ	HIBLS	10/01-12/01
	Honolulu MSA, HI	Y	33860 FQ	46720 AW	59680 TQ	HIBLS	10/01-12/01
	Idaho	Y	25040 FQ	52570 AW	86960 TQ	IDBLS	10/01-12/01
	Illinois	Y	12090 FQ	18810 AW	42200 TQ	ILBLS	10/01-12/01
	Chicago PMSA, IL	Y	12060 FQ	16340 AW	15250 TQ	ILBLS	10/01-12/01
	Indiana	Y	20800 FQ	28120 AW	35410 TQ	INBLS	10/01-12/01
	Fort Wayne MSA, IN	Y	20870 FQ	32620 AW	37680 TQ	INBLS	10/01-12/01
	Indianapolis MSA, IN	Y	24090 FQ	28680 AW	34910 TQ	INBLS	10/01-12/01
	Iowa	Y	35790 FQ	48310 AW	57330 TQ	IABLS	10/01-12/01
	Davenport-Moline-Rock Island MSA, IA-IL	Y	25680 FQ	44320 AW	61360 TQ	IABLS	10/01-12/01
	Kansas	Y	27580 FQ	44580 AW	59300 TQ	KSBLS	10/01-12/01
	Wichita MSA, KS	Y	21040 FQ	39580 AW	60950 TQ	KSBLS	10/01-12/01
	Kentucky	Y	17580 FQ	40230 AW	58700 TQ	KYBLS	10/01-12/01
	Louisiana	Y	14130 FQ	34060 AW	54580 TQ	LABLS	10/01-12/01
	Baton Rouge MSA, LA	Y	21050 FQ	43300 AW	57880 TQ	LABLS	10/01-12/01
	New Orleans MSA, LA	Y	15680 FQ	38660 AW	55730 TQ	LABLS	10/01-12/01
	Maine	Y	36240 FQ	52340 AW	68900 TQ	MEBLS	10/01-12/01
	Maryland	Y	29610 FQ	45760 AW	65510 TQ	MDBLS	10/01-12/01
	Baltimore PMSA, MD	Y	36750 FQ	44940 AW	55810 TQ	MDBLS	10/01-12/01
	Massachusetts	Y	30070 FQ	48050 AW	66870 TQ	MABLS	10/01-12/01
	Boston PMSA, MA-NH	Y	32970 FQ	49270 AW	67900 TQ	MABLS	10/01-12/01
	Michigan	Y	28470 FQ	41420 AW	56710 TQ	MIBLS	10/01-12/01
	Detroit PMSA, MI	Y	35590 FQ	46220 AW	58250 TQ	MIBLS	10/01-12/01
	Flint PMSA, MI	Y	34440 FQ	48620 AW	74490 TQ	MIBLS	10/01-12/01
	Lansing-East Lansing MSA, MI	Y	31550 FQ	41800 AW	56370 TQ	MIBLS	10/01-12/01
	Minnesota	Y	33430 FQ	46440 AW	56270 TQ	MNBLS	10/01-12/01
	Minneapolis-St. Paul MSA, MN-WI	Y	34100 FQ	47780 AW	58240 TQ	MNBLS	10/01-12/01
	Mississippi	Y	14180 FQ	30690 AW	44670 TQ	MSBLS	10/01-12/01
	Missouri	Y	20420 FQ	39330 AW	55320 TQ	MOBLS	10/01-12/01
	Kansas City MSA, MO-KS	Y	30660 FQ	48140 AW	65100 TQ	MOBLS	10/01-12/01
	St. Louis MSA, MO-IL	Y	19530 FQ	24520 AW	29970 TQ	MOBLS	10/01-12/01
	Montana	Y	24200 FQ	32760 AW	41670 TQ	MTBLS	10/01-12/01
	Nevada	Y	28010 FQ	55110 AW	85730 TQ	NVBLS	10/01-12/01
	Newark PMSA, NJ	Y	19330 FQ	37610 AW	67230 TQ	NJBLS	10/01-12/01
	New Mexico	Y	17300 FQ	33850 AW	51350 TQ	NMBLS	10/01-12/01
	New York	Y	36330 FQ	63700 AW	88050 TQ	NYBLS	10/01-12/01
	Albany-Schenectady-Troy MSA, NY	Y	36670 FQ	51930 AW	78420 TQ	NYBLS	10/01-12/01

AAW	Average annual wage	**AOH**	Average offered, high	**ASH**	Average starting, high	**H**	Hourly	**M**	Monthly	**S**	Special: hourly and annual
AE	Average entry wage	**AOL**	Average offered, low	**ASL**	Average starting, low	**HI**	Highest wage paid	**MTC**	Median total compensation	**TQ**	Third quartile wage
AEX	Average experienced wage	**APH**	Average pay, high range	**AW**	Average wage paid	**HR**	High end range	**MW**	Median wage paid	**W**	Weekly
AO	Average offered	**APL**	Average pay, low range	**FQ**	First quartile wage	**LR**	Low end range	**SQ**	Second quartile wage	**Y**	Yearly

Occupation/Type/Industry	Location	Per	Low	Mid	High	Source	Date
Court Reporter	Buffalo-Niagara Falls MSA, NY	Y	25020 FQ	48070 AW	78040 TQ	NYBLS	10/01-12/01
	Nassau-Suffolk PMSA, NY	Y	36500 FQ	60030 AW	85270 TQ	NYBLS	10/01-12/01
	New York PMSA, NY	Y	38020 FQ	65920 AW	89310 TQ	NYBLS	10/01-12/01
	Rochester MSA, NY	Y	33900 FQ	60210 AW	86470 TQ	NYBLS	10/01-12/01
	Syracuse MSA, NY	Y	29860 FQ	52820 AW	83610 TQ	NYBLS	10/01-12/01
	North Carolina	Y	18810 FQ	34280 AW	48200 TQ	NCBLS	10/01-12/01
	Greensboro-Winston-Salem-High Point MSA, NC	Y	12360 FQ	26850 AW	41640 TQ	NCBLS	10/01-12/01
	Ohio	Y	25760 FQ	44900 AW	70920 TQ	OHBLS	10/01-12/01
	Cleveland-Lorain-Elyria PMSA, OH	Y	31580 FQ	49830 AW	75510 TQ	OHBLS	10/01-12/01
	Columbus MSA, OH	Y	23990 FQ	43170 AW	68850 TQ	OHBLS	10/01-12/01
	Dayton-Springfield MSA, OH	Y	28640 FQ	54970 AW	87570 TQ	OHBLS	10/01-12/01
	Toledo MSA, OH	Y	25890 FQ	44800 AW	72040 TQ	OHBLS	10/01-12/01
	Oklahoma	Y	28390 FQ	37110 AW	44390 TQ	OKBLS	10/01-12/01
	Oregon	Y	20580 FQ	45100 AW	77950 TQ	ORBLS	10/01-12/01
	Portland-Vancouver PMSA, OR-WA	Y	20430 FQ	48780 AW	96870 TQ	ORBLS	10/01-12/01
	Pennsylvania	Y	24730 FQ	36410 AW	46230 TQ	PABLS	10/01-12/01
	Erie MSA, PA	Y	22090 FQ	32550 AW	42410 TQ	PABLS	10/01-12/01
	Philadelphia PMSA, PA-NJ	Y	27660 FQ	38970 AW	60740 TQ	PABLS	10/01-12/01
	Pittsburgh MSA, PA	Y	26200 FQ	40650 AW	53380 TQ	PABLS	10/01-12/01
	Scranton-Wilkes-Barre-Hazleton MSA, PA	Y	13010 FQ	31230 AW	42950 TQ	PABLS	10/01-12/01
	Rhode Island	Y	42940 FQ	56180 AW	69810 TQ	RIBLS	10/01-12/01
	Providence-Fall River-Warwick MSA, RI-MA	Y	41570 FQ	55620 AW	69670 TQ	RIBLS	10/01-12/01
	South Carolina	Y	19700 FQ	29820 AW	40930 TQ	SCBLS	10/01-12/01
	South Dakota	Y	30850 FQ	39410 AW	44930 TQ	SDBLS	10/01-12/01
	Tennessee	Y	16470 FQ	37510 AW	67750 TQ	TNBLS	10/01-12/01
	Texas	Y	22580 FQ	44240 AW	67850 TQ	TXBLS	10/01-12/01
	Dallas PMSA, TX	Y	30730 FQ	45780 AW	72550 TQ	TXBLS	10/01-12/01
	Fort Worth-Arlington PMSA, TX	Y	27520 FQ	43830 AW	59370 TQ	TXBLS	10/01-12/01
	Houston PMSA, TX	Y	27840 FQ	45940 AW	61270 TQ	TXBLS	10/01-12/01
	San Antonio MSA, TX	Y	18780 FQ	33120 AW	62460 TQ	TXBLS	10/01-12/01
	Utah	Y	21610 FQ	31570 AW	49660 TQ	UTBLS	10/01-12/01
	Virginia	Y	20040 FQ	28850 AW	50340 TQ	VABLS	10/01-12/01
	Norfolk-Virginia Beach-Newport News MSA, VA-NC	Y	19960 FQ	26920 AW	38190 TQ	VABLS	10/01-12/01
	Washington	Y	37320 FQ	49180 AW	60320 TQ	WABLS	10/01-12/01
	West Virginia	Y	25610 FQ	43250 AW	72340 TQ	WVBLS	10/01-12/01
	Wisconsin	Y	25770 FQ	40780 AW	57780 TQ	WIBLS	10/01-12/01
	Milwaukee-Waukesha PMSA, WI	Y	25680 FQ	41700 AW	58080 TQ	WIBLS	10/01-12/01
	Puerto Rico	Y	14340 FQ	18580 AW	22390 TQ	PRBLS	10/01-12/01
Supreme Court, Unionized	New York	Y		91200 AW		WSJ	1/01-1/02
Crane and Tower Operator	Alabama	H	11.61 FQ	16.80 AW	21.49 TQ	ALBLS	10/01-12/01
	Birmingham MSA, AL	H	12.08 FQ	17.25 AW	21.63 TQ	ALBLS	10/01-12/01
	Mobile MSA, AL	H	13.52 FQ	16.78 AW	22.32 TQ	ALBLS	10/01-12/01
	Montgomery MSA, AL	H	11.57 FQ	16.76 AW	21.78 TQ	ALBLS	10/01-12/01
	Alaska	H	15.97 FQ	23.59 AW	33.08 TQ	AKBLS	10/01-12/01
	Arizona	H	10.97 FQ	16.83 AW	23.72 TQ	AZBLS	10/01-12/01
	Phoenix-Mesa MSA, AZ	H	11.59 FQ	17.31 AW	24.94 TQ	AZBLS	10/01-12/01
	Arkansas	H	9.82 FQ	14.17 AW	18.90 TQ	ARBLS	10/01-12/01
	Fort Smith MSA, AR-OK	H	10.24 FQ	14.83 AW	19.30 TQ	ARBLS	10/01-12/01
	Little Rock-North Little Rock MSA, AR	H	10.90 FQ	13.68 AW	16.86 TQ	ARBLS	10/01-12/01
	California	H	11.81 FQ	23.97 AW	34.82 TQ	CABLS	10/01-12/01
	Bakersfield MSA, CA	H	13.58 FQ	20.49 AW	28.04 TQ	CABLS	10/01-12/01
	Fresno MSA, CA	H	8.99 FQ	18.11 AW	33.63 TQ	CABLS	10/01-12/01
	Oakland PMSA, CA	H	9.46 FQ	19.92 AW	32.60 TQ	CABLS	10/01-12/01
	Orange County PMSA, CA	H	8.13 FQ	20.42 AW	28.65 TQ	CABLS	10/01-12/01
	Riverside-San Bernardino PMSA, CA	H	14.32 FQ	21.44 AW	28.53 TQ	CABLS	10/01-12/01
	Sacramento PMSA, CA	H	13.25 FQ	24.64 AW	41.36 TQ	CABLS	10/01-12/01
	San Diego MSA, CA	H	16.88 FQ	22.74 AW	28.25 TQ	CABLS	10/01-12/01
	San Francisco PMSA, CA	H	15.50 FQ	24.77 AW	34.15 TQ	CABLS	10/01-12/01
	San Jose PMSA, CA	H	12.52 FQ	23.02 AW	44.95 TQ	CABLS	10/01-12/01
	Stockton-Lodi MSA, CA	H	9.89 FQ	20.11 AW	32.64 TQ	CABLS	10/01-12/01

AAW	Average annual wage	**AOH**	Average offered, high	**ASH**	Average starting, high	**H**	Hourly	**M**	Monthly	**S**	Special: hourly and annual
AE	Average entry wage	**AOL**	Average offered, low	**ASL**	Average starting, low	**HI**	Highest wage paid	**MTC**	Median total compensation	**TQ**	Third quartile wage
AEX	Average experienced wage	**APH**	Average pay, high range	**AW**	Average wage paid	**HR**	High end range	**MW**	Median wage paid	**W**	Weekly
AO	Average offered	**APL**	Average pay, low range	**FQ**	First quartile wage	**LR**	Low end range	**SQ**	Second quartile wage	**Y**	Yearly

Occupation/Type/Industry	Location	Per	Low	Mid	High	Source	Date
Crane and Tower Operator	Ventura PMSA, CA	H	19.44 FQ	26.32 AW	33.34 TQ	CABLS	10/01-12/01
	Colorado	H	14.22 FQ	21.24 AW	27.09 TQ	COBLS	10/01-12/01
	Colorado Springs MSA, CO	H	11.72 FQ	16.43 AW	21.47 TQ	COBLS	10/01-12/01
	Denver PMSA, CO	H	17.70 FQ	22.61 AW	27.38 TQ	COBLS	10/01-12/01
	Fort Collins-Loveland MSA, CO	H	10.72 FQ	17.12 AW	22.42 TQ	COBLS	10/01-12/01
	Connecticut	H	12.10 FQ	20.34 AW	28.92 TQ	CTBLS	10/01-12/01
	Hartford MSA, CT	H	15.36 FQ	22.27 AW	32.85 TQ	CTBLS	10/01-12/01
	New Haven-Meriden PMSA, CT	H	12.61 FQ	18.72 AW	26.64 TQ	CTBLS	10/01-12/01
	New London-Norwich MSA, CT-RI	H	10.89 FQ	23.23 AW	46.30 TQ	CTBLS	10/01-12/01
	Delaware	H	10.65 FQ	16.55 AW	22.33 TQ	DEBLS	10/01-12/01
	Wilmington-Newark PMSA, DE-MD	H	11.79 FQ	16.81 AW	22.09 TQ	DEBLS	10/01-12/01
	District of Columbia	H	21.39 FQ	27.69 AW	34.33 TQ	DCBLS	10/01-12/01
	Washington PMSA, DC-MD-VA-WV	H	13.84 FQ	19.77 AW	27.49 TQ	DCBLS	10/01-12/01
	Florida	H	10.16 FQ	16.19 AW	23.20 TQ	FLBLS	10/01-12/01
	Daytona Beach MSA, FL	H	9.67 FQ	13.37 AW	17.98 TQ	FLBLS	10/01-12/01
	Fort Lauderdale PMSA, FL	H	12.21 FQ	17.99 AW	24.96 TQ	FLBLS	10/01-12/01
	Fort Myers-Cape Coral MSA, FL	H	12.38 FQ	22.92 AW	33.68 TQ	FLBLS	10/01-12/01
	Jacksonville MSA, FL	H	9.28 FQ	14.03 AW	19.98 TQ	FLBLS	10/01-12/01
	Melbourne-Titusville-Palm Bay MSA, FL	H	10.47 FQ	15.45 AW	20.86 TQ	FLBLS	10/01-12/01
	Miami PMSA, FL	H	9.85 FQ	17.24 AW	26.28 TQ	FLBLS	10/01-12/01
	Orlando MSA, FL	H	9.87 FQ	15.91 AW	21.19 TQ	FLBLS	10/01-12/01
	Pensacola MSA, FL	H	11.42 FQ	17.55 AW	27.09 TQ	FLBLS	10/01-12/01
	Sarasota-Bradenton MSA, FL	H	9.15 FQ	14.36 AW	19.92 TQ	FLBLS	10/01-12/01
	Tampa-St. Petersburg-Clearwater MSA, FL	H	9.93 FQ	15.90 AW	20.74 TQ	FLBLS	10/01-12/01
	West Palm Beach-Boca Raton MSA, FL	H	11.23 FQ	15.71 AW	21.81 TQ	FLBLS	10/01-12/01
	Georgia	H	10.25 FQ	16.29 AW	21.68 TQ	GABLS	10/01-12/01
	Atlanta MSA, GA	H	10.69 FQ	17.16 AW	21.82 TQ	GABLS	10/01-12/01
	Augusta-Aiken MSA, GA-SC	H	9.29 FQ	18.14 AW	30.70 TQ	GABLS	10/01-12/01
	Columbus MSA, GA-AL	H	9.35 FQ	13.81 AW	18.61 TQ	GABLS	10/01-12/01
	Macon MSA, GA	H	9.81 FQ	15.94 AW	20.94 TQ	GABLS	10/01-12/01
	Savannah MSA, GA	H	12.67 FQ	18.87 AW	30.43 TQ	GABLS	10/01-12/01
	Hawaii	H	21.52 FQ	27.71 AW	34.96 TQ	HIBLS	10/01-12/01
	Honolulu MSA, HI	H	21.73 FQ	28.22 AW	35.27 TQ	HIBLS	10/01-12/01
	Idaho	H	11.69 FQ	16.53 AW	22.13 TQ	IDBLS	10/01-12/01
	Boise City MSA, ID	H	12.22 FQ	16.43 AW	21.80 TQ	IDBLS	10/01-12/01
	Illinois	H	11.88 FQ	19.36 AW	31.73 TQ	ILBLS	10/01-12/01
	Chicago PMSA, IL	H	12.37 FQ	20.87 AW	33.48 TQ	ILBLS	10/01-12/01
	Peoria-Pekin MSA, IL	H	10.19 FQ	16.72 AW	25.40 TQ	ILBLS	10/01-12/01
	Rockford MSA, IL	H	10.58 FQ	20.40 AW	33.47 TQ	ILBLS	10/01-12/01
	Indiana	H	12.04 FQ	18.07 AW	25.56 TQ	INBLS	10/01-12/01
	Elkhart-Goshen MSA, IN	H	11.24 FQ	13.00 AW	14.10 TQ	INBLS	10/01-12/01
	Evansville-Henderson MSA, IN-KY	H	12.15 FQ	15.32 AW	18.54 TQ	INBLS	10/01-12/01
	Fort Wayne MSA, IN	H	11.75 FQ	17.08 AW	24.49 TQ	INBLS	10/01-12/01
	Gary PMSA, IN	H	13.17 FQ	18.87 AW	25.00 TQ	INBLS	10/01-12/01
	Indianapolis MSA, IN	H	11.09 FQ	18.33 AW	27.12 TQ	INBLS	10/01-12/01
	Lafayette MSA, IN	H	12.84 FQ	19.84 AW	27.02 TQ	INBLS	10/01-12/01
	South Bend MSA, IN	H	13.20 FQ	18.61 AW	26.74 TQ	INBLS	10/01-12/01
	Iowa	H	10.08 FQ	18.16 AW	26.32 TQ	IABLS	10/01-12/01
	Cedar Rapids MSA, IA	H	17.94 FQ	22.44 AW	25.67 TQ	IABLS	10/01-12/01
	Davenport-Moline-Rock Island MSA, IA-IL	H	10.94 FQ	16.09 AW	22.08 TQ	IABLS	10/01-12/01
	Des Moines MSA, IA	H	10.48 FQ	15.36 AW	21.15 TQ	IABLS	10/01-12/01
	Kansas	H	9.60 FQ	15.74 AW	24.81 TQ	KSBLS	10/01-12/01
	Kentucky	H	10.35 FQ	16.31 AW	23.41 TQ	KYBLS	10/01-12/01
	Lexington MSA, KY	H	9.36 FQ	14.87 AW	23.56 TQ	KYBLS	10/01-12/01
	Louisville MSA, KY-IN	H	9.91 FQ	16.96 AW	26.65 TQ	KYBLS	10/01-12/01
	Louisiana	H	10.51 FQ	15.54 AW	21.77 TQ	LABLS	10/01-12/01
	Baton Rouge MSA, LA	H	11.30 FQ	15.18 AW	19.08 TQ	LABLS	10/01-12/01
	Houma MSA, LA	H	12.02 FQ	18.25 AW	25.92 TQ	LABLS	10/01-12/01
	Lafayette MSA, LA	H	11.35 FQ	15.10 AW	18.47 TQ	LABLS	10/01-12/01
	Lake Charles MSA, LA	H	12.24 FQ	16.90 AW	24.20 TQ	LABLS	10/01-12/01
	New Orleans MSA, LA	H	10.04 FQ	14.65 AW	20.28 TQ	LABLS	10/01-12/01

AAW	Average annual wage	**AOH**	Average offered, high	**ASH**	Average starting, high	**H**	Hourly	**M**	Monthly	**S**	Special: hourly and annual
AE	Average entry wage	**AOL**	Average offered, low	**ASL**	Average starting, low	**HI**	Highest wage paid	**MTC**	Median total compensation	**TQ**	Third quartile wage
AEX	Average experienced wage	**APH**	Average pay, high range	**AW**	Average wage paid	**HR**	High end range	**MW**	Median wage paid	**W**	Weekly
AO	Average offered	**APL**	Average pay, low range	**FQ**	First quartile wage	**LR**	Low end range	**SQ**	Second quartile wage	**Y**	Yearly

Occupation/Type/Industry	Location	Per	Low	Mid	High	Source	Date
Crane and Tower Operator	Maine	H	10.71 FQ	16.34 AW	21.38 TQ	MEBLS	10/01-12/01
	Portland MSA, ME	H	12.59 FQ	17.07 AW	21.34 TQ	MEBLS	10/01-12/01
	Maryland	H	12.52 FQ	18.36 AW	24.96 TQ	MDBLS	10/01-12/01
	Baltimore PMSA, MD	H	12.06 FQ	18.36 AW	25.00 TQ	MDBLS	10/01-12/01
	Massachusetts	H	11.69 FQ	21.39 AW	32.63 TQ	MABLS	10/01-12/01
	Boston PMSA, MA-NH	H	12.00 FQ	22.04 AW	34.21 TQ	MABLS	10/01-12/01
	Lowell PMSA, MA-NH	H	16.21 FQ	23.74 AW	32.47 TQ	MABLS	10/01-12/01
	Springfield MSA, MA	H	14.02 FQ	22.83 AW	27.48 TQ	MABLS	10/01-12/01
	Worcester PMSA, MA-CT	H	9.40 FQ	13.34 AW	17.83 TQ	MABLS	10/01-12/01
	Michigan	H	10.81 FQ	18.85 AW	28.16 TQ	MIBLS	10/01-12/01
	Ann Arbor PMSA, MI	H	15.07 FQ	23.51 AW	31.17 TQ	MIBLS	10/01-12/01
	Detroit PMSA, MI	H	11.06 FQ	18.89 AW	29.21 TQ	MIBLS	10/01-12/01
	Grand Rapids-Muskegon-Holland MSA, MI	H	10.96 FQ	17.15 AW	26.31 TQ	MIBLS	10/01-12/01
	Kalamazoo-Battle Creek MSA, MI	H	8.90 FQ	15.76 AW	25.63 TQ	MIBLS	10/01-12/01
	Lansing-East Lansing MSA, MI	H	11.87 FQ	19.26 AW	27.75 TQ	MIBLS	10/01-12/01
	Saginaw-Bay City-Midland MSA, MI	H	9.72 FQ	18.83 AW	28.54 TQ	MIBLS	10/01-12/01
	Minnesota	H	11.97 FQ	18.26 AW	26.52 TQ	MNBLS	10/01-12/01
	Duluth-Superior MSA, MN-WI	H	11.59 FQ	18.16 AW	26.50 TQ	MNBLS	10/01-12/01
	Minneapolis-St. Paul MSA, MN-WI	H	12.96 FQ	19.04 AW	26.84 TQ	MNBLS	10/01-12/01
	St. Cloud MSA, MN	H	12.07 FQ	20.24 AW	27.39 TQ	MNBLS	10/01-12/01
	Mississippi	H	10.46 FQ	14.74 AW	20.02 TQ	MSBLS	10/01-12/01
	Jackson MSA, MS	H	10.55 FQ	13.99 AW	17.55 TQ	MSBLS	10/01-12/01
	Missouri	H	10.85 FQ	18.99 AW	27.56 TQ	MOBLS	10/01-12/01
	Kansas City MSA, MO-KS	H	10.72 FQ	16.61 AW	24.65 TQ	MOBLS	10/01-12/01
	St. Louis MSA, MO-IL	H	13.46 FQ	17.43 AW	24.74 TQ	MOBLS	10/01-12/01
	Springfield MSA, MO	H	9.55 FQ	15.93 AW	24.93 TQ	MOBLS	10/01-12/01
	Montana	H	12.99 FQ	19.95 AW	29.55 TQ	MTBLS	10/01-12/01
	Nebraska	H	9.54 FQ	13.88 AW	20.20 TQ	NEBLS	10/01-12/01
	Omaha MSA, NE-IA	H	11.33 FQ	15.84 AW	20.90 TQ	NEBLS	10/01-12/01
	Nevada	H	12.22 FQ	23.85 AW	35.24 TQ	NVBLS	10/01-12/01
	Las Vegas MSA, NV-AZ	H	14.69 FQ	24.84 AW	35.67 TQ	NVBLS	10/01-12/01
	New Hampshire	H	12.07 FQ	17.76 AW	25.15 TQ	NHBLS	10/01-12/01
	Portsmouth-Rochester PMSA, NH-ME	H	17.49 FQ	19.87 AW	23.94 TQ	NHBLS	10/01-12/01
	New Jersey	H	12.20 FQ	19.87 AW	31.76 TQ	NJBLS	10/01-12/01
	Bergen-Passaic PMSA, NJ	H	10.99 FQ	18.38 AW	31.82 TQ	NJBLS	10/01-12/01
	Jersey City PMSA, NJ	H	11.18 FQ	16.29 AW	22.42 TQ	NJBLS	10/01-12/01
	Middlesex-Somerset-Hunterdon PMSA, NJ	H	11.94 FQ	20.68 AW	31.67 TQ	NJBLS	10/01-12/01
	Newark PMSA, NJ	H	13.79 FQ	22.27 AW	34.48 TQ	NJBLS	10/01-12/01
	New Mexico	H	9.63 FQ	14.30 AW	19.89 TQ	NMBLS	10/01-12/01
	Albuquerque MSA, NM	H	9.37 FQ	12.31 AW	15.93 TQ	NMBLS	10/01-12/01
	New York	H	12.35 FQ	22.17 AW	38.51 TQ	NYBLS	10/01-12/01
	Albany-Schenectady-Troy MSA, NY	H	12.64 FQ	18.15 AW	22.75 TQ	NYBLS	10/01-12/01
	Buffalo-Niagara Falls MSA, NY	H	13.31 FQ	19.15 AW	26.24 TQ	NYBLS	10/01-12/01
	New York PMSA, NY	H	9.60 FQ	33.70 AW	69.62 TQ	NYBLS	10/01-12/01
	Rochester MSA, NY	H	13.79 FQ	19.51 AW	25.52 TQ	NYBLS	10/01-12/01
	Syracuse MSA, NY	H	11.30 FQ	17.33 AW	24.11 TQ	NYBLS	10/01-12/01
	Utica-Rome MSA, NY	H	13.54 FQ	16.86 AW	21.40 TQ	NYBLS	10/01-12/01
	North Carolina	H	10.12 FQ	15.58 AW	22.85 TQ	NCBLS	10/01-12/01
	Charlotte-Gastonia-Rock Hill MSA, NC-SC	H	10.06 FQ	14.90 AW	20.84 TQ	NCBLS	10/01-12/01
	Greensboro-Winston-Salem-High Point MSA, NC	H	9.66 FQ	15.86 AW	25.70 TQ	NCBLS	10/01-12/01
	Hickory-Morganton-Lenoir MSA, NC	H	10.78 FQ	12.45 AW	15.33 TQ	NCBLS	10/01-12/01
	Raleigh-Durham-Chapel Hill MSA, NC	H	10.10 FQ	17.58 AW	25.39 TQ	NCBLS	10/01-12/01
	Wilmington MSA, NC	H	13.37 FQ	20.31 AW	28.93 TQ	NCBLS	10/01-12/01
	North Dakota	H	10.75 FQ	17.53 AW	23.17 TQ	NDBLS	10/01-12/01
	Fargo-Moorhead MSA, ND-MN	H	10.00 FQ	14.84 AW	21.45 TQ	NDBLS	10/01-12/01
	Ohio	H	11.38 FQ	17.30 AW	25.79 TQ	OHBLS	10/01-12/01
	Akron PMSA, OH	H	11.30 FQ	19.45 AW	27.44 TQ	OHBLS	10/01-12/01
	Canton-Massillon MSA, OH	H	12.14 FQ	17.32 AW	22.97 TQ	OHBLS	10/01-12/01
	Cincinnati PMSA, OH-KY-IN	H	11.37 FQ	16.35 AW	21.19 TQ	OHBLS	10/01-12/01

AAW	Average annual wage	**AOH**	Average offered, high	**ASH**	Average starting, high	**H**	Hourly	**M**	Monthly	**S**	Special: hourly and annual
AE	Average entry wage	**AOL**	Average offered, low	**ASL**	Average starting, low	**HI**	Highest wage paid	**MTC**	Median total compensation	**TQ**	Third quartile wage
AEX	Average experienced wage	**APH**	Average pay, high range	**AW**	Average wage paid	**HR**	High end range	**MW**	Median wage paid	**W**	Weekly
AO	Average offered	**APL**	Average pay, low range	**FQ**	First quartile wage	**LR**	Low end range	**SQ**	Second quartile wage	**Y**	Yearly

Occupation/Type/Industry	Location	Per	Low	Mid	High	Source	Date
Crane and Tower Operator	Cleveland-Lorain-Elyria PMSA, OH	H	11.69 FQ	18.93 AW	26.89 TQ	OHBLS	10/01-12/01
	Columbus MSA, OH	H	11.04 FQ	14.02 AW	22.22 TQ	OHBLS	10/01-12/01
	Dayton-Springfield MSA, OH	H	11.17 FQ	17.49 AW	26.74 TQ	OHBLS	10/01-12/01
	Mansfield MSA, OH	H	11.27 FQ	23.25 AW	28.55 TQ	OHBLS	10/01-12/01
	Toledo MSA, OH	H	11.50 FQ	20.02 AW	26.96 TQ	OHBLS	10/01-12/01
	Youngstown-Warren MSA, OH	H	10.03 FQ	14.16 AW	17.92 TQ	OHBLS	10/01-12/01
	Oklahoma	H	10.86 FQ	16.62 AW	25.19 TQ	OKBLS	10/01-12/01
	Oklahoma City MSA, OK	H	12.29 FQ	19.43 AW	25.63 TQ	OKBLS	10/01-12/01
	Tulsa MSA, OK	H	10.97 FQ	16.25 AW	26.23 TQ	OKBLS	10/01-12/01
	Oregon	H	7.73 FQ	15.56 AW	24.70 TQ	ORBLS	10/01-12/01
	Portland-Vancouver PMSA, OR-WA	H	10.89 FQ	17.86 AW	29.28 TQ	ORBLS	10/01-12/01
	Pennsylvania	H	11.00 FQ	16.49 AW	22.41 TQ	PABLS	10/01-12/01
	Allentown-Bethlehem-Easton MSA, PA	H	11.46 FQ	15.02 AW	20.65 TQ	PABLS	10/01-12/01
	Johnstown MSA, PA	H	13.10 FQ	17.30 AW	21.94 TQ	PABLS	10/01-12/01
	Lancaster MSA, PA	H	14.05 FQ	17.14 AW	21.37 TQ	PABLS	10/01-12/01
	Philadelphia PMSA, PA-NJ	H	12.13 FQ	18.02 AW	26.46 TQ	PABLS	10/01-12/01
	Pittsburgh MSA, PA	H	12.19 FQ	16.52 AW	21.23 TQ	PABLS	10/01-12/01
	Reading MSA, PA	H	11.14 FQ	17.75 AW	23.90 TQ	PABLS	10/01-12/01
	Scranton-Wilkes-Barre-Hazleton MSA, PA	H	9.10 FQ	17.77 AW	26.66 TQ	PABLS	10/01-12/01
	York MSA, PA	H	7.78 FQ	12.35 AW	17.83 TQ	PABLS	10/01-12/01
	Rhode Island	H	10.39 FQ	17.08 AW	26.52 TQ	RIBLS	10/01-12/01
	Providence-Fall River-Warwick MSA, RI-MA	H	10.33 FQ	17.03 AW	30.98 TQ	RIBLS	10/01-12/01
	South Carolina	H	10.56 FQ	17.08 AW	26.24 TQ	SCBLS	10/01-12/01
	Charleston-North Charleston MSA, SC	H	11.09 FQ	15.46 AW	21.36 TQ	SCBLS	10/01-12/01
	Columbia MSA, SC	H	11.75 FQ	16.54 AW	21.80 TQ	SCBLS	10/01-12/01
	Greenville-Spartanburg-Anderson MSA, SC	H	11.21 FQ	18.39 AW	26.77 TQ	SCBLS	10/01-12/01
	South Dakota	H	12.12 FQ	16.39 AW	20.96 TQ	SDBLS	10/01-12/01
	Tennessee	H	10.28 FQ	14.47 AW	19.89 TQ	TNBLS	10/01-12/01
	Chattanooga MSA, TN-GA	H	7.13 FQ	12.69 AW	19.78 TQ	TNBLS	10/01-12/01
	Clarksville-Hopkinsville MSA, TN-KY	H	16.07 FQ	22.17 AW	26.47 TQ	TNBLS	10/01-12/01
	Johnson City-Kingsport-Bristol MSA, TN-VA	H	10.04 FQ	13.71 AW	17.99 TQ	TNBLS	10/01-12/01
	Knoxville MSA, TN	H	11.40 FQ	13.57 AW	17.86 TQ	TNBLS	10/01-12/01
	Memphis MSA, TN-AR-MS	H	10.00 FQ	14.74 AW	22.72 TQ	TNBLS	10/01-12/01
	Nashville MSA, TN	H	11.74 FQ	15.33 AW	20.09 TQ	TNBLS	10/01-12/01
	Texas	H	9.49 FQ	14.35 AW	20.12 TQ	TXBLS	10/01-12/01
	Amarillo MSA, TX	H	7.71 FQ	12.49 AW	16.69 TQ	TXBLS	10/01-12/01
	Austin-San Marcos MSA, TX	H	9.66 FQ	13.67 AW	19.60 TQ	TXBLS	10/01-12/01
	Beaumont-Port Arthur MSA, TX	H	11.34 FQ	16.02 AW	21.91 TQ	TXBLS	10/01-12/01
	Brazoria PMSA, TX	H	11.41 FQ	15.04 AW	18.25 TQ	TXBLS	10/01-12/01
	Brownsville-Harlingen-San Benito MSA, TX	H	8.39 FQ	10.26 AW	12.79 TQ	TXBLS	10/01-12/01
	Corpus Christi MSA, TX	H	9.86 FQ	14.75 AW	20.27 TQ	TXBLS	10/01-12/01
	Dallas PMSA, TX	H	9.43 FQ	13.87 AW	19.56 TQ	TXBLS	10/01-12/01
	El Paso MSA, TX	H	9.79 FQ	14.94 AW	20.96 TQ	TXBLS	10/01-12/01
	Fort Worth-Arlington PMSA, TX	H	10.56 FQ	15.53 AW	20.78 TQ	TXBLS	10/01-12/01
	Galveston-Texas City PMSA, TX	H	12.60 FQ	18.40 AW	22.26 TQ	TXBLS	10/01-12/01
	Houston PMSA, TX	H	10.27 FQ	15.45 AW	20.52 TQ	TXBLS	10/01-12/01
	Longview-Marshall MSA, TX	H	10.26 FQ	13.32 AW	16.89 TQ	TXBLS	10/01-12/01
	McAllen-Edinburg-Mission MSA, TX	H	7.39 FQ	10.63 AW	14.47 TQ	TXBLS	10/01-12/01
	Odessa-Midland MSA, TX	H	10.26 FQ	13.88 AW	20.84 TQ	TXBLS	10/01-12/01
	San Antonio MSA, TX	H	9.15 FQ	12.85 AW	17.96 TQ	TXBLS	10/01-12/01
	Utah	H	11.92 FQ	18.24 AW	23.83 TQ	UTBLS	10/01-12/01
	Provo-Orem MSA, UT	H	9.94 FQ	16.46 AW	26.36 TQ	UTBLS	10/01-12/01
	Salt Lake City-Ogden MSA, UT	H	12.51 FQ	18.13 AW	22.27 TQ	UTBLS	10/01-12/01
	Vermont	H	11.86 FQ	17.67 AW	24.98 TQ	VTBLS	10/01-12/01
	Burlington MSA, VT	H	11.80 FQ	15.59 AW	19.59 TQ	VTBLS	10/01-12/01
	Virginia	H	12.20 FQ	17.48 AW	23.67 TQ	VABLS	10/01-12/01
	Lynchburg MSA, VA	H	11.65 FQ	14.91 AW	19.51 TQ	VABLS	10/01-12/01

AAW Average annual wage **AE** Average entry wage **AEX** Average experienced wage **AO** Average offered **AOH** Average offered, high **AOL** Average offered, low **APH** Average pay, high range **APL** Average pay, low range **ASH** Average starting, high **ASL** Average starting, low **AW** Average wage paid **FQ** First quartile wage **H** Hourly **HI** Highest wage paid **HR** High end range **LR** Low end range **M** Monthly **MTC** Median total compensation **MW** Median wage paid **SQ** Second quartile wage **S** Special: hourly and annual **TQ** Third quartile wage **W** Weekly **Y** Yearly

Occupation/Type/Industry	Location	Per	Low	Mid	High	Source	Date
Crane and Tower Operator	Norfolk-Virginia Beach-Newport News MSA, VA-NC	H	12.92 FQ	17.00 AW	21.31 TQ	VABLS	10/01-12/01
	Richmond-Petersburg MSA, VA	H	10.72 FQ	17.05 AW	22.09 TQ	VABLS	10/01-12/01
	Roanoke MSA, VA	H	10.39 FQ	13.83 AW	17.46 TQ	VABLS	10/01-12/01
	Washington	H	13.63 FQ	23.23 AW	32.97 TQ	WABLS	10/01-12/01
	Bremerton PMSA, WA	H	21.83 FQ	23.73 AW	26.64 TQ	WABLS	10/01-12/01
	Seattle-Bellevue-Everett PMSA, WA	H	16.56 FQ	24.54 AW	32.70 TQ	WABLS	10/01-12/01
	Spokane MSA, WA	H	9.88 FQ	15.04 AW	25.70 TQ	WABLS	10/01-12/01
	Tacoma PMSA, WA	H	12.65 FQ	23.24 AW	34.84 TQ	WABLS	10/01-12/01
	West Virginia	H	9.06 FQ	15.03 AW	22.20 TQ	WVBLS	10/01-12/01
	Charleston MSA, WV	H	9.20 FQ	12.70 AW	20.03 TQ	WVBLS	10/01-12/01
	Huntington-Ashland MSA, WV-KY-OH	H	11.58 FQ	16.23 AW	22.00 TQ	WVBLS	10/01-12/01
	Wisconsin	H	10.98 FQ	15.96 AW	23.89 TQ	WIBLS	10/01-12/01
	Appleton-Oshkosh-Neenah MSA, WI	H	11.31 FQ	15.80 AW	24.28 TQ	WIBLS	10/01-12/01
	Green Bay MSA, WI	H	11.76 FQ	16.62 AW	24.11 TQ	WIBLS	10/01-12/01
	Madison MSA, WI	H	12.97 FQ	17.05 AW	25.24 TQ	WIBLS	10/01-12/01
	Milwaukee-Waukesha PMSA, WI	H	12.26 FQ	16.27 AW	20.75 TQ	WIBLS	10/01-12/01
	Wyoming	H	11.29 FQ	20.20 AW	30.97 TQ	WYBLS	10/01-12/01
	Puerto Rico	H	6.50 FQ	11.68 AW	22.87 TQ	PRBLS	10/01-12/01
	Virgin Islands	H	12.72 FQ	16.58 AW	21.06 TQ	VIBLS	10/01-12/01
Creative Director	Phoenix, AZ	Y		70000 AW		TBJ	1/00-1/01
Advertising Agency	East	Y		133000 AW		ADAGE	1/00-1/01
Advertising Agency	Midwest	Y		113000 AW		ADAGE	1/00-1/01
Advertising Agency	South	Y		97000 AW		ADAGE	1/00-1/01
Advertising Agency	West	Y		120000 AW		ADAGE	1/00-1/01
Creative Director of Copywriting							
Marketing, Medical	United States	Y		108100 AW		MM&M	1/01-1/02
Credit Analyst	Alabama	Y	25200 FQ	39290 AW	57550 TQ	ALBLS	10/01-12/01
	Alaska	Y	24280 FQ	51260 AW	105750 TQ	AKBLS	10/01-12/01
	Arizona	Y	23080 FQ	32530 AW	54160 TQ	AZBLS	10/01-12/01
	Arkansas	Y	22040 FQ	35600 AW	56680 TQ	ARBLS	10/01-12/01
	California	Y	26530 FQ	52080 AW	87930 TQ	CABLS	10/01-12/01
	Colorado	Y	24830 FQ	43820 AW	61320 TQ	COBLS	10/01-12/01
	Connecticut	Y	32490 FQ	57200 AW	86460 TQ	CTBLS	10/01-12/01
	Delaware	Y	23050 FQ	35290 AW	53390 TQ	DEBLS	10/01-12/01
	District of Columbia	Y	33100 FQ	47670 AW	66160 TQ	DCBLS	10/01-12/01
	Florida	Y	23540 FQ	49020 AW	83000 TQ	FLBLS	10/01-12/01
	Georgia	Y	30340 FQ	51360 AW	87260 TQ	GABLS	10/01-12/01
	Hawaii	Y	30220 FQ	45740 AW	75130 TQ	HIBLS	10/01-12/01
	Idaho	Y	25150 FQ	42840 AW	63710 TQ	IDBLS	10/01-12/01
	Illinois	Y	25920 FQ	43510 AW	66890 TQ	ILBLS	10/01-12/01
	Indiana	Y	26190 FQ	42930 AW	65040 TQ	INBLS	10/01-12/01
	Iowa	Y	21370 FQ	37760 AW	59390 TQ	IABLS	10/01-12/01
	Kansas	Y	26660 FQ	46260 AW	69330 TQ	KSBLS	10/01-12/01
	Kentucky	Y	23750 FQ	42210 AW	69650 TQ	KYBLS	10/01-12/01
	Louisiana	Y	24480 FQ	52260 AW	124400 TQ	LABLS	10/01-12/01
	Maryland	Y	21450 FQ	44360 AW	70780 TQ	MDBLS	10/01-12/01
	Massachusetts	Y	29660 FQ	51250 AW	79390 TQ	MABLS	10/01-12/01
	Michigan	Y	24690 FQ	41700 AW	65980 TQ	MIBLS	10/01-12/01
	Minnesota	Y	27210 FQ	45710 AW	68980 TQ	MNBLS	10/01-12/01
	Mississippi	Y	23270 FQ	41720 AW	74190 TQ	MSBLS	10/01-12/01
	Missouri	Y	25890 FQ	42990 AW	66730 TQ	MOBLS	10/01-12/01
	Montana	Y	19400 FQ	31880 AW	52610 TQ	MTBLS	10/01-12/01
	Nebraska	Y	21450 FQ	37740 AW	56770 TQ	NEBLS	10/01-12/01
	Nevada	Y	25160 FQ	45160 AW	72220 TQ	NVBLS	10/01-12/01
	New Hampshire	Y	28890 FQ	41570 AW	62140 TQ	NHBLS	10/01-12/01
	New Jersey	Y	28880 FQ	51630 AW	78420 TQ	NJBLS	10/01-12/01
	New Mexico	Y	19100 FQ	37550 AW	61710 TQ	NMBLS	10/01-12/01
	New York	Y	31950 FQ	62300 AW	106920 TQ	NYBLS	10/01-12/01
	North Carolina	Y	29380 FQ	58300 AW	125680 TQ	NCBLS	10/01-12/01
	North Dakota	Y	28010 FQ	44160 AW	78040 TQ	NDBLS	10/01-12/01
	Ohio	Y	28680 FQ	43790 AW	63820 TQ	OHBLS	10/01-12/01
	Oklahoma	Y	22420 FQ	35990 AW	57690 TQ	OKBLS	10/01-12/01
	Oregon	Y	29770 FQ	43250 AW	63370 TQ	ORBLS	10/01-12/01

AAW	Average annual wage	AOH	Average offered, high	ASH	Average starting, high	H	Hourly	M	Monthly	S	Special: hourly and annual
AE	Average entry wage	AOL	Average offered, low	ASL	Average starting, low	HI	Highest wage paid	MTC	Median total compensation	TQ	Third quartile wage
AEX	Average experienced wage	APH	Average pay, high range	AW	Average wage paid	HR	High end range	MW	Median wage paid	W	Weekly
AO	Average offered	APL	Average pay, low range	FQ	First quartile wage	LR	Low end range	SQ	Second quartile wage	Y	Yearly

Occupation/Type/Industry	Location	Per	Low	Mid	High	Source	Date
Credit Analyst	Pennsylvania	Y	24530 FQ	41020 AW	61510 TQ	PABLS	10/01-12/01
	Rhode Island	Y	28690 FQ	49540 AW	80890 TQ	RIBLS	10/01-12/01
	South Carolina	Y	24640 FQ	38940 AW	57550 TQ	SCBLS	10/01-12/01
	South Dakota	Y	24620 FQ	40070 AW	62850 TQ	SDBLS	10/01-12/01
	Tennessee	Y	23820 FQ	43650 AW	71010 TQ	TNBLS	10/01-12/01
	Texas	Y	26400 FQ	46280 AW	73380 TQ	TXBLS	10/01-12/01
	Utah	Y	20720 FQ	42280 AW	92470 TQ	UTBLS	10/01-12/01
	Vermont	Y	30670 FQ	46420 AW	77570 TQ	VTBLS	10/01-12/01
	Virginia	Y	29220 FQ	49270 AW	77990 TQ	VABLS	10/01-12/01
	Washington	Y	30920 FQ	54530 AW	91650 TQ	WABLS	10/01-12/01
	West Virginia	Y	23550 FQ	35990 AW	55950 TQ	WVBLS	10/01-12/01
	Wisconsin	Y	24540 FQ	38860 AW	57070 TQ	WIBLS	10/01-12/01
	Puerto Rico	Y	18470 FQ	33990 AW	52510 TQ	PRBLS	10/01-12/01
Credit Authorizer, Checker, and Clerk	Alabama	H	5.61 FQ	10.50 AW	16.82 TQ	ALBLS	10/01-12/01
	Alaska	H	7.87 FQ	14.29 AW	21.63 TQ	AKBLS	10/01-12/01
	Arizona	H	8.05 FQ	12.18 AW	17.94 TQ	AZBLS	10/01-12/01
	Arkansas	H	7.42 FQ	11.59 AW	16.91 TQ	ARBLS	10/01-12/01
	California	H	8.92 FQ	15.03 AW	22.29 TQ	CABLS	10/01-12/01
	Colorado	H	9.06 FQ	14.73 AW	20.76 TQ	COBLS	10/01-12/01
	Connecticut	H	9.94 FQ	15.33 AW	21.30 TQ	CTBLS	10/01-12/01
	Delaware	H	9.34 FQ	13.90 AW	20.80 TQ	DEBLS	10/01-12/01
	District of Columbia	H	9.65 FQ	15.56 AW	22.33 TQ	DCBLS	10/01-12/01
	Florida	H	9.25 FQ	13.35 AW	18.64 TQ	FLBLS	10/01-12/01
	Georgia	H	8.95 FQ	13.20 AW	18.43 TQ	GABLS	10/01-12/01
	Hawaii	H	9.57 FQ	14.94 AW	22.50 TQ	HIBLS	10/01-12/01
	Idaho	H	7.45 FQ	15.41 AW	24.82 TQ	IDBLS	10/01-12/01
	Illinois	H	7.75 FQ	14.06 AW	21.67 TQ	ILBLS	10/01-12/01
	Indiana	H	8.63 FQ	12.19 AW	16.94 TQ	INBLS	10/01-12/01
	Iowa	H	7.89 FQ	11.94 AW	18.76 TQ	IABLS	10/01-12/01
	Kansas	H	9.19 FQ	13.02 AW	17.89 TQ	KSBLS	10/01-12/01
	Kentucky	H	9.09 FQ	14.13 AW	21.45 TQ	KYBLS	10/01-12/01
	Louisiana	H	7.29 FQ	10.39 AW	15.07 TQ	LABLS	10/01-12/01
	Maine	H	8.91 FQ	12.32 AW	16.81 TQ	MEBLS	10/01-12/01
	Maryland	H	8.08 FQ	12.65 AW	17.47 TQ	MDBLS	10/01-12/01
	Massachusetts	H	9.15 FQ	14.08 AW	21.06 TQ	MABLS	10/01-12/01
	Michigan	H	8.19 FQ	13.50 AW	20.23 TQ	MIBLS	10/01-12/01
	Minnesota	H	9.53 FQ	14.85 AW	21.22 TQ	MNBLS	10/01-12/01
	Mississippi	H	7.51 FQ	11.47 AW	16.98 TQ	MSBLS	10/01-12/01
	Missouri	H	7.49 FQ	13.74 AW	20.46 TQ	MOBLS	10/01-12/01
	Montana	H	8.17 FQ	12.03 AW	16.63 TQ	MTBLS	10/01-12/01
	Nebraska	H	6.91 FQ	11.38 AW	16.26 TQ	NEBLS	10/01-12/01
	Nevada	H	8.29 FQ	12.28 AW	17.79 TQ	NVBLS	10/01-12/01
	New Hampshire	H	8.21 FQ	12.50 AW	18.70 TQ	NHBLS	10/01-12/01
	New Jersey	H	10.09 FQ	16.12 AW	23.18 TQ	NJBLS	10/01-12/01
	New Mexico	H	8.01 FQ	12.97 AW	20.54 TQ	NMBLS	10/01-12/01
	New York	H	9.42 FQ	15.03 AW	21.00 TQ	NYBLS	10/01-12/01
	North Carolina	H	9.20 FQ	13.57 AW	18.88 TQ	NCBLS	10/01-12/01
	North Dakota	H	8.83 FQ	13.88 AW	18.33 TQ	NDBLS	10/01-12/01
	Ohio	H	8.38 FQ	12.78 AW	18.88 TQ	OHBLS	10/01-12/01
	Oklahoma	H	7.01 FQ	11.39 AW	17.74 TQ	OKBLS	10/01-12/01
	Oregon	H	9.25 FQ	14.85 AW	22.73 TQ	ORBLS	10/01-12/01
	Pennsylvania	H	7.54 FQ	12.08 AW	17.08 TQ	PABLS	10/01-12/01
	Rhode Island	H	8.09 FQ	13.75 AW	20.71 TQ	RIBLS	10/01-12/01
	South Carolina	H	8.27 FQ	12.22 AW	18.63 TQ	SCBLS	10/01-12/01
	South Dakota	H	8.33 FQ	10.77 AW	13.68 TQ	SDBLS	10/01-12/01
	Tennessee	H	8.73 FQ	13.42 AW	18.78 TQ	TNBLS	10/01-12/01
	Texas	H	8.53 FQ	12.37 AW	18.94 TQ	TXBLS	10/01-12/01
	Utah	H	6.94 FQ	12.16 AW	18.44 TQ	UTBLS	10/01-12/01
	Vermont	H	8.76 FQ	11.93 AW	16.31 TQ	VTBLS	10/01-12/01
	Virginia	H	8.96 FQ	12.75 AW	16.61 TQ	VABLS	10/01-12/01
	Washington	H	10.10 FQ	14.45 AW	20.44 TQ	WABLS	10/01-12/01
	West Virginia	H	7.64 FQ	11.31 AW	16.79 TQ	WVBLS	10/01-12/01
	Wisconsin	H	8.18 FQ	13.03 AW	19.62 TQ	WIBLS	10/01-12/01
	Wyoming	H	7.42 FQ	12.64 AW	20.64 TQ	WYBLS	10/01-12/01
	Puerto Rico	H	6.29 FQ	10.23 AW	14.54 TQ	PRBLS	10/01-12/01
Criminal Justice and Law Enforcement Teacher							
Postsecondary	Alabama	Y	18140 FQ	41070 AW	69730 TQ	ALBLS	10/01-12/01
Postsecondary	California	Y	33180 FQ	62420 AW	104910 TQ	CABLS	10/01-12/01

AAW	Average annual wage	**AOH**	Average offered, high	**ASH**	Average starting, high	**H**	Hourly	**M**	Monthly	**S**	Special: hourly and annual
AE	Average entry wage	**AOL**	Average offered, low	**ASL**	Average starting, low	**HI**	Highest wage paid	**MTC**	Median total compensation	**TQ**	Third quartile wage
AEX	Average experienced wage	**APH**	Average pay, high range	**AW**	Average wage paid	**HR**	High end range	**MW**	Median wage paid	**W**	Weekly
AO	Average offered	**APL**	Average pay, low range	**FQ**	First quartile wage	**LR**	Low end range	**SQ**	Second quartile wage	**Y**	Yearly

Occupation/Type/Industry	Location	Per	Low	Mid	High	Source	Date
Criminal Justice and Law Enforcement Teacher							
Postsecondary	Colorado	Y	27980 FQ	68700 AW	137730 TQ	COBLS	10/01-12/01
Postsecondary	Connecticut	Y	19270 FQ	47610 AW	79670 TQ	CTBLS	10/01-12/01
Postsecondary	Delaware	Y	39710 FQ	56540 AW	83550 TQ	DEBLS	10/01-12/01
Postsecondary	Florida	Y	18260 FQ	40030 AW	70560 TQ	FLBLS	10/01-12/01
Postsecondary	Georgia	Y	22700 FQ	47010 AW	68690 TQ	GABLS	10/01-12/01
Postsecondary	Illinois	Y	23180 FQ	52460 AW	90160 TQ	ILBLS	10/01-12/01
Postsecondary	Indiana	Y	26680 FQ	46880 AW	78060 TQ	INBLS	10/01-12/01
Postsecondary	Iowa	Y	37120 FQ	58210 AW	90300 TQ	IABLS	10/01-12/01
Postsecondary	Kansas	Y	16610 FQ	36200 AW	53050 TQ	KSBLS	10/01-12/01
Postsecondary	Kentucky	Y	22790 FQ	51790 AW	82320 TQ	KYBLS	10/01-12/01
Postsecondary	Louisiana	Y	27200 FQ	42910 AW	54630 TQ	LABLS	10/01-12/01
Postsecondary	Maryland	Y	24390 FQ	54520 AW	100730 TQ	MDBLS	10/01-12/01
Postsecondary	Massachusetts	Y	21370 FQ	46600 AW	76560 TQ	MABLS	10/01-12/01
Postsecondary	Michigan	Y	23540 FQ	46840 AW	76130 TQ	MIBLS	10/01-12/01
Postsecondary	Minnesota	Y	35920 FQ	48460 AW	58640 TQ	MNBLS	10/01-12/01
Postsecondary	Mississippi	Y	13340 FQ	39620 AW	57660 TQ	MSBLS	10/01-12/01
Postsecondary	Missouri	Y	25180 FQ	44630 AW	66870 TQ	MOBLS	10/01-12/01
Postsecondary	Nebraska	Y	34890 FQ	51380 AW	70570 TQ	NEBLS	10/01-12/01
Postsecondary	Nevada	Y	24090 FQ	41380 AW	73190 TQ	NVBLS	10/01-12/01
Postsecondary	New Hampshire	Y	17730 FQ	39160 AW	59880 TQ	NHBLS	10/01-12/01
Postsecondary	New Jersey	Y	32160 FQ	58430 AW	89170 TQ	NJBLS	10/01-12/01
Postsecondary	New Mexico	Y	21570 FQ	31620 AW	42320 TQ	NMBLS	10/01-12/01
Postsecondary	New York	Y	30440 FQ	58760 AW	112000 TQ	NYBLS	10/01-12/01
Postsecondary	North Carolina	Y	29380 FQ	40290 AW	54600 TQ	NCBLS	10/01-12/01
Postsecondary	North Dakota	Y	16290 FQ	24820 AW	35490 TQ	NDBLS	10/01-12/01
Postsecondary	Ohio	Y	22120 FQ	43640 AW	68020 TQ	OHBLS	10/01-12/01
Postsecondary	Oklahoma	Y	26810 FQ	36720 AW	48450 TQ	OKBLS	10/01-12/01
Postsecondary	Oregon	Y	16740 FQ	43160 AW	79200 TQ	ORBLS	10/01-12/01
Postsecondary	Pennsylvania	Y	28900 FQ	59900 AW	113600 TQ	PABLS	10/01-12/01
Postsecondary	Rhode Island	Y	29320 FQ	50520 AW	83880 TQ	RIBLS	10/01-12/01
Postsecondary	South Carolina	Y	25690 FQ	44460 AW	68060 TQ	SCBLS	10/01-12/01
Postsecondary	Tennessee	Y	16650 FQ	39830 AW	65240 TQ	TNBLS	10/01-12/01
Postsecondary	Texas	Y	22910 FQ	49580 AW	72810 TQ	TXBLS	10/01-12/01
Postsecondary	Virginia	Y	24550 FQ	42430 AW	59890 TQ	VABLS	10/01-12/01
Postsecondary	Washington	Y	21710 FQ	35860 AW	52130 TQ	WABLS	10/01-12/01
Postsecondary	West Virginia	Y	24720 FQ	42440 AW	60450 TQ	WVBLS	10/01-12/01
Postsecondary	Wisconsin	Y	23390 FQ	44680 AW	68880 TQ	WIBLS	10/01-12/01
Postsecondary	Puerto Rico	Y	28870 FQ	41790 AW	57110 TQ	PRBLS	10/01-12/01
Crossing Guard	Alabama	Y	11700 FQ	14800 AW	21200 TQ	ALBLS	10/01-12/01
	Alaska	Y	20730 FQ	40920 AW	56660 TQ	AKBLS	10/01-12/01
	Arizona	Y	12060 FQ	15590 AW	18840 TQ	AZBLS	10/01-12/01
	Phoenix-Mesa MSA, AZ	Y	12160 FQ	15930 AW	19420 TQ	AZBLS	10/01-12/01
	Tucson MSA, AZ	Y	11850 FQ	13670 AW	16650 TQ	AZBLS	10/01-12/01
	Arkansas	Y	12070 FQ	16060 AW	20380 TQ	ARBLS	10/01-12/01
	Fayetteville-Springdale-Rogers MSA, AR	Y	11890 FQ	15660 AW	22080 TQ	ARBLS	10/01-12/01
	California	Y	13700 FQ	18750 AW	25780 TQ	CABLS	10/01-12/01
	Bakersfield MSA, CA	Y	13240 FQ	15950 AW	20680 TQ	CABLS	10/01-12/01
	Modesto MSA, CA	Y	13230 FQ	15670 AW	21460 TQ	CABLS	10/01-12/01
	Oakland PMSA, CA	Y	13890 FQ	19930 AW	28900 TQ	CABLS	10/01-12/01
	Orange County PMSA, CA	Y	15160 FQ	18440 AW	21750 TQ	CABLS	10/01-12/01
	Riverside-San Bernardino PMSA, CA	Y	14020 FQ	19050 AW	23540 TQ	CABLS	10/01-12/01
	Salinas MSA, CA	Y	14100 FQ	19590 AW	25700 TQ	CABLS	10/01-12/01
	San Diego MSA, CA	Y	13370 FQ	16430 AW	21710 TQ	CABLS	10/01-12/01
	San Francisco PMSA, CA	Y	15020 FQ	24850 AW	34920 TQ	CABLS	10/01-12/01
	San Jose PMSA, CA	Y	13380 FQ	18410 AW	26490 TQ	CABLS	10/01-12/01
	San Luis Obispo-Atascadero-Paso Robles MSA, CA	Y	13260 FQ	16040 AW	21400 TQ	CABLS	10/01-12/01
	Santa Barbara-Santa Maria-Lompoc MSA, CA	Y	13500 FQ	15490 AW	17400 TQ	CABLS	10/01-12/01
	Santa Rosa PMSA, CA	Y	13350 FQ	18560 AW	29410 TQ	CABLS	10/01-12/01
	Ventura PMSA, CA	Y	14520 FQ	17520 AW	21970 TQ	CABLS	10/01-12/01
	Visalia-Tulare-Porterville MSA, CA	Y	13920 FQ	18690 AW	23220 TQ	CABLS	10/01-12/01
	Colorado	Y	14850 FQ	23470 AW	34090 TQ	COBLS	10/01-12/01
	Boulder-Longmont PMSA, CO	Y	12070 FQ	15790 AW	22550 TQ	COBLS	10/01-12/01
	Colorado Springs MSA, CO	Y	19530 FQ	22700 AW	29420 TQ	COBLS	10/01-12/01
	Denver PMSA, CO	Y	15450 FQ	21030 AW	30130 TQ	COBLS	10/01-12/01

AAW Average annual wage	AOH Average offered, high	ASH Average starting, high	H Hourly	M Monthly	S Special: hourly and annual
AE Average entry wage	AOL Average offered, low	ASL Average starting, low	HI Highest wage paid	MTC Median total compensation	TQ Third quartile wage
AEX Average experienced wage	APH Average pay, high range	AW Average wage paid	HR High end range	MW Median wage paid	W Weekly
AO Average offered	APL Average pay, low range	FQ First quartile wage	LR Low end range	SQ Second quartile wage	Y Yearly

Occupation/Type/Industry	Location	Per	Low	Mid	High	Source	Date
Crossing Guard	Connecticut	Y	14870 FQ	21780 AW	32380 TQ	CTBLS	10/01-12/01
	Bridgeport PMSA, CT	Y	13960 FQ	17110 AW	20050 TQ	CTBLS	10/01-12/01
	Danbury PMSA, CT	Y	14560 FQ	20430 AW	28730 TQ	CTBLS	10/01-12/01
	Hartford MSA, CT	Y	16680 FQ	26220 AW	40010 TQ	CTBLS	10/01-12/01
	New Haven-Meriden PMSA, CT	Y	13910 FQ	21110 AW	28620 TQ	CTBLS	10/01-12/01
	New London-Norwich MSA, CT-RI	Y	14990 FQ	20740 AW	29040 TQ	CTBLS	10/01-12/01
	Stamford-Norwalk PMSA, CT	Y	15530 FQ	17850 AW	19020 TQ	CTBLS	10/01-12/01
	Waterbury PMSA, CT	Y	18570 FQ	25060 AW	41010 TQ	CTBLS	10/01-12/01
	Washington PMSA, DC-MD-VA-WV	Y	15100 FQ	43840 AW	84570 TQ	DCBLS	10/01-12/01
	Florida	Y	12240 FQ	16800 AW	22470 TQ	FLBLS	10/01-12/01
	Fort Lauderdale PMSA, FL	Y	11850 FQ	16840 AW	31030 TQ	FLBLS	10/01-12/01
	Fort Pierce-Port St. Lucie MSA, FL	Y	15520 FQ	22180 AW	32880 TQ	FLBLS	10/01-12/01
	Jacksonville MSA, FL	Y	11950 FQ	14110 AW	19280 TQ	FLBLS	10/01-12/01
	Melbourne-Titusville-Palm Bay MSA, FL	Y	13180 FQ	17990 AW	22920 TQ	FLBLS	10/01-12/01
	Miami PMSA, FL	Y	12100 FQ	16270 AW	21600 TQ	FLBLS	10/01-12/01
	Naples MSA, FL	Y	13440 FQ	20780 AW	30290 TQ	FLBLS	10/01-12/01
	Orlando MSA, FL	Y	14630 FQ	17470 AW	21550 TQ	FLBLS	10/01-12/01
	Tallahassee MSA, FL	Y	12340 FQ	16570 AW	21190 TQ	FLBLS	10/01-12/01
	West Palm Beach-Boca Raton MSA, FL	Y	14750 FQ	20150 AW	27330 TQ	FLBLS	10/01-12/01
	Georgia	Y	12130 FQ	17680 AW	27040 TQ	GABLS	10/01-12/01
	Atlanta MSA, GA	Y	12790 FQ	19140 AW	32760 TQ	GABLS	10/01-12/01
	Macon MSA, GA	Y	11960 FQ	15610 AW	23000 TQ	GABLS	10/01-12/01
	Savannah MSA, GA	Y	12070 FQ	15060 AW	21780 TQ	GABLS	10/01-12/01
	Hawaii	Y	15130 FQ	17820 AW	21230 TQ	HIBLS	10/01-12/01
	Honolulu MSA, HI	Y	15030 FQ	17350 AW	20740 TQ	HIBLS	10/01-12/01
	Illinois	Y	12280 FQ	20330 AW	28520 TQ	ILBLS	10/01-12/01
	Peoria-Pekin MSA, IL	Y	13300 FQ	17290 AW	22160 TQ	ILBLS	10/01-12/01
	Rockford MSA, IL	Y	12610 FQ	24560 AW	34940 TQ	ILBLS	10/01-12/01
	Indiana	Y	11950 FQ	20680 AW	38400 TQ	INBLS	10/01-12/01
	Gary PMSA, IN	Y	12970 FQ	16690 AW	21540 TQ	INBLS	10/01-12/01
	Indianapolis MSA, IN	Y	11920 FQ	19800 AW	39750 TQ	INBLS	10/01-12/01
	South Bend MSA, IN	Y	11680 FQ	17140 AW	27280 TQ	INBLS	10/01-12/01
	Iowa	Y	14070 FQ	21100 AW	31230 TQ	IABLS	10/01-12/01
	Cedar Rapids MSA, IA	Y	18110 FQ	20810 AW	22090 TQ	IABLS	10/01-12/01
	Des Moines MSA, IA	Y	17940 FQ	20090 AW	22980 TQ	IABLS	10/01-12/01
	Kansas	Y	12430 FQ	16300 AW	21280 TQ	KSBLS	10/01-12/01
	Wichita MSA, KS	Y	12080 FQ	14880 AW	18440 TQ	KSBLS	10/01-12/01
	Kentucky	Y	12170 FQ	15770 AW	21420 TQ	KYBLS	10/01-12/01
	Louisville MSA, KY-IN	Y	11990 FQ	14490 AW	17620 TQ	KYBLS	10/01-12/01
	Louisiana	Y	11780 FQ	14110 AW	19650 TQ	LABLS	10/01-12/01
	Baton Rouge MSA, LA	Y	11380 FQ	15600 AW	22560 TQ	LABLS	10/01-12/01
	Houma MSA, LA	Y	11340 FQ	15120 AW	21270 TQ	LABLS	10/01-12/01
	New Orleans MSA, LA	Y	11890 FQ	13850 AW	19080 TQ	LABLS	10/01-12/01
	Maine	Y	12770 FQ	15720 AW	18780 TQ	MEBLS	10/01-12/01
	Maryland	Y	13450 FQ	21540 AW	31990 TQ	MDBLS	10/01-12/01
	Baltimore PMSA, MD	Y	13330 FQ	19880 AW	28530 TQ	MDBLS	10/01-12/01
	Massachusetts	Y	14270 FQ	18880 AW	27570 TQ	MABLS	10/01-12/01
	Boston PMSA, MA-NH	Y	14260 FQ	19120 AW	29580 TQ	MABLS	10/01-12/01
	Brockton PMSA, MA	Y	14120 FQ	20810 AW	33720 TQ	MABLS	10/01-12/01
	Lawrence PMSA, MA-NH	Y	14280 FQ	18070 AW	23080 TQ	MABLS	10/01-12/01
	Lowell PMSA, MA-NH	Y	14090 FQ	16390 AW	25030 TQ	MABLS	10/01-12/01
	Springfield MSA, MA	Y	15220 FQ	20050 AW	29290 TQ	MABLS	10/01-12/01
	Worcester PMSA, MA-CT	Y	14260 FQ	17540 AW	25290 TQ	MABLS	10/01-12/01
	Michigan	Y	12560 FQ	17380 AW	23090 TQ	MIBLS	10/01-12/01
	Ann Arbor PMSA, MI	Y	13750 FQ	19930 AW	26830 TQ	MIBLS	10/01-12/01
	Detroit PMSA, MI	Y	13860 FQ	17550 AW	22870 TQ	MIBLS	10/01-12/01
	Grand Rapids-Muskegon-Holland MSA, MI	Y	12490 FQ	18160 AW	23920 TQ	MIBLS	10/01-12/01
	Kalamazoo-Battle Creek MSA, MI	Y	11850 FQ	16120 AW	21660 TQ	MIBLS	10/01-12/01
	Saginaw-Bay City-Midland MSA, MI	Y	12050 FQ	15270 AW	18290 TQ	MIBLS	10/01-12/01
	Minnesota	Y	12050 FQ	16300 AW	23670 TQ	MNBLS	10/01-12/01
	Minneapolis-St. Paul MSA, MN-WI	Y	11990 FQ	15070 AW	22500 TQ	MNBLS	10/01-12/01
	Mississippi	Y	12020 FQ	17460 AW	23940 TQ	MSBLS	10/01-12/01

AAW	Average annual wage	AOH	Average offered, high	ASH	Average starting, high	H	Hourly	M	Monthly	S	Special: hourly and annual
AE	Average entry wage	AOL	Average offered, low	ASL	Average starting, low	HI	Highest wage paid	MTC	Median total compensation	TQ	Third quartile wage
AEX	Average experienced wage	APH	Average pay, high range	AW	Average wage paid	HR	High end range	MW	Median wage paid	W	Weekly
AO	Average offered	APL	Average pay, low range	FQ	First quartile wage	LR	Low end range	SQ	Second quartile wage	Y	Yearly

Occupation/Type/Industry	Location	Per	Low	Mid	High	Source	Date
Crossing Guard	Biloxi-Gulfport-Pascagoula MSA, MS	Y	14340 FQ	23240 AW	34420 TQ	MSBLS	10/01-12/01
	Jackson MSA, MS	Y	12620 FQ	15750 AW	18530 TQ	MSBLS	10/01-12/01
	Missouri	Y	12340 FQ	20250 AW	29400 TQ	MOBLS	10/01-12/01
	Kansas City MSA, MO-KS	Y	12450 FQ	18050 AW	26540 TQ	MOBLS	10/01-12/01
	St. Louis MSA, MO-IL	Y	12300 FQ	20670 AW	29840 TQ	MOBLS	10/01-12/01
	Montana	Y	12530 FQ	19910 AW	33440 TQ	MTBLS	10/01-12/01
	Nevada	Y	15460 FQ	20330 AW	23580 TQ	NVBLS	10/01-12/01
	Las Vegas MSA, NV-AZ	Y	15650 FQ	19450 AW	23320 TQ	NVBLS	10/01-12/01
	New Hampshire	Y	12720 FQ	17520 AW	22730 TQ	NHBLS	10/01-12/01
	New Jersey	Y	12160 FQ	20880 AW	29600 TQ	NJBLS	10/01-12/01
	Atlantic-Cape May PMSA, NJ	Y	13570 FQ	21760 AW	28850 TQ	NJBLS	10/01-12/01
	Bergen-Passaic PMSA, NJ	Y	12050 FQ	20270 AW	27870 TQ	NJBLS	10/01-12/01
	Jersey City PMSA, NJ	Y	13100 FQ	21120 AW	30940 TQ	NJBLS	10/01-12/01
	Middlesex-Somerset-Hunterdon PMSA, NJ	Y	13010 FQ	23800 AW	38060 TQ	NJBLS	10/01-12/01
	Monmouth-Ocean PMSA, NJ	Y	12670 FQ	23430 AW	47000 TQ	NJBLS	10/01-12/01
	Newark PMSA, NJ	Y	11740 FQ	19550 AW	28850 TQ	NJBLS	10/01-12/01
	Trenton PMSA, NJ	Y	24370 FQ	33070 AW	50400 TQ	NJBLS	10/01-12/01
	New Mexico	Y	12270 FQ	18190 AW	29200 TQ	NMBLS	10/01-12/01
	Albuquerque MSA, NM	Y	12310 FQ	17030 AW	22600 TQ	NMBLS	10/01-12/01
	New York	Y	13850 FQ	23870 AW	30160 TQ	NYBLS	10/01-12/01
	Albany-Schenectady-Troy MSA, NY	Y	11740 FQ	16530 AW	28180 TQ	NYBLS	10/01-12/01
	Binghamton MSA, NY	Y	11460 FQ	13840 AW	17090 TQ	NYBLS	10/01-12/01
	Newburgh PMSA, NY-PA	Y	15200 FQ	20820 AW	27400 TQ	NYBLS	10/01-12/01
	Rochester MSA, NY	Y	13040 FQ	17990 AW	21990 TQ	NYBLS	10/01-12/01
	Syracuse MSA, NY	Y	11500 FQ	14080 AW	18090 TQ	NYBLS	10/01-12/01
	Utica-Rome MSA, NY	Y	11640 FQ	12710 AW	14450 TQ	NYBLS	10/01-12/01
	North Carolina	Y	12180 FQ	17520 AW	23490 TQ	NCBLS	10/01-12/01
	Charlotte-Gastonia-Rock Hill MSA, NC-SC	Y	12130 FQ	16800 AW	21730 TQ	NCBLS	10/01-12/01
	Greensboro-Winston-Salem-High Point MSA, NC	Y	12000 FQ	16500 AW	23300 TQ	NCBLS	10/01-12/01
	Raleigh-Durham-Chapel Hill MSA, NC	Y	13420 FQ	18290 AW	22100 TQ	NCBLS	10/01-12/01
	North Dakota	Y	17810 FQ	24400 AW	36860 TQ	NDBLS	10/01-12/01
	Ohio	Y	12620 FQ	21150 AW	40100 TQ	OHBLS	10/01-12/01
	Akron PMSA, OH	Y	13010 FQ	22520 AW	44240 TQ	OHBLS	10/01-12/01
	Cincinnati PMSA, OH-KY-IN	Y	12200 FQ	17880 AW	23010 TQ	OHBLS	10/01-12/01
	Cleveland-Lorain-Elyria PMSA, OH	Y	15000 FQ	26060 AW	43400 TQ	OHBLS	10/01-12/01
	Columbus MSA, OH	Y	12300 FQ	18530 AW	26590 TQ	OHBLS	10/01-12/01
	Toledo MSA, OH	Y	12340 FQ	15900 AW	18960 TQ	OHBLS	10/01-12/01
	Youngstown-Warren MSA, OH	Y	11830 FQ	14850 AW	20600 TQ	OHBLS	10/01-12/01
	Oklahoma	Y	12350 FQ	21740 AW	29420 TQ	OKBLS	10/01-12/01
	Tulsa MSA, OK	Y	12340 FQ	22400 AW	29570 TQ	OKBLS	10/01-12/01
	Oregon	Y	16590 FQ	25030 AW	44530 TQ	ORBLS	10/01-12/01
	Eugene-Springfield MSA, OR	Y	18410 FQ	31970 AW	47980 TQ	ORBLS	10/01-12/01
	Portland-Vancouver PMSA, OR-WA	Y	16420 FQ	25270 AW	48790 TQ	ORBLS	10/01-12/01
	Salem PMSA, OR	Y	15970 FQ	24510 AW	49400 TQ	ORBLS	10/01-12/01
	Pennsylvania	Y	11930 FQ	16690 AW	23120 TQ	PABLS	10/01-12/01
	Allentown-Bethlehem-Easton MSA, PA	Y	11930 FQ	15560 AW	20550 TQ	PABLS	10/01-12/01
	Erie MSA, PA	Y	12220 FQ	16400 AW	21120 TQ	PABLS	10/01-12/01
	Harrisburg-Lebanon-Carlisle MSA, PA	Y	11860 FQ	14790 AW	18180 TQ	PABLS	10/01-12/01
	Lancaster MSA, PA	Y	11960 FQ	18330 AW	30280 TQ	PABLS	10/01-12/01
	Philadelphia PMSA, PA-NJ	Y	12200 FQ	17740 AW	25540 TQ	PABLS	10/01-12/01
	Pittsburgh MSA, PA	Y	11880 FQ	17180 AW	22490 TQ	PABLS	10/01-12/01
	Scranton-Wilkes-Barre-Hazleton MSA, PA	Y	11700 FQ	13960 AW	15120 TQ	PABLS	10/01-12/01
	York MSA, PA	Y	11880 FQ	17780 AW	23390 TQ	PABLS	10/01-12/01
	Rhode Island	Y	13860 FQ	22950 AW	35500 TQ	RIBLS	10/01-12/01
	Providence-Fall River-Warwick MSA, RI-MA	Y	14010 FQ	21830 AW	34890 TQ	RIBLS	10/01-12/01
	South Carolina	Y	12400 FQ	20860 AW	29050 TQ	SCBLS	10/01-12/01
	Charleston-North Charleston MSA, SC	Y	13360 FQ	24860 AW	37240 TQ	SCBLS	10/01-12/01
	Columbia MSA, SC	Y	13400 FQ	20170 AW	28010 TQ	SCBLS	10/01-12/01
	South Dakota	Y	13800 FQ	17140 AW	21480 TQ	SDBLS	10/01-12/01

AAW	Average annual wage	**AOH**	Average offered, high	**ASH**	Average starting, high	**H**	Hourly	**M**	Monthly	**S**	Special: hourly and annual
AE	Average entry wage	**AOL**	Average offered, low	**ASL**	Average starting, low	**HI**	Highest wage paid	**MTC**	Median total compensation	**TQ**	Third quartile wage
AEX	Average experienced wage	**APH**	Average pay, high range	**AW**	Average wage paid	**HR**	High end range	**MW**	Median wage paid	**W**	Weekly
AO	Average offered	**APL**	Average pay, low range	**FQ**	First quartile wage	**LR**	Low end range	**SQ**	Second quartile wage	**Y**	Yearly

Occupation/Type/Industry	Location	Per	Low	Mid	High	Source	Date
Crossing Guard	Tennessee	Y	14300 FQ	19920 AW	27980 TQ	TNBLS	10/01-12/01
	Chattanooga MSA, TN-GA	Y	12510 FQ	19990 AW	26990 TQ	TNBLS	10/01-12/01
	Johnson City-Kingsport-Bristol MSA, TN-VA	Y	11720 FQ	15920 AW	23410 TQ	TNBLS	10/01-12/01
	Knoxville MSA, TN	Y	15390 FQ	21350 AW	37780 TQ	TNBLS	10/01-12/01
	Memphis MSA, TN-AR-MS	Y	14770 FQ	19550 AW	28360 TQ	TNBLS	10/01-12/01
	Nashville MSA, TN	Y	15230 FQ	20070 AW	27700 TQ	TNBLS	10/01-12/01
	Texas	Y	12160 FQ	16720 AW	22580 TQ	TXBLS	10/01-12/01
	Austin-San Marcos MSA, TX	Y	14190 FQ	19510 AW	22860 TQ	TXBLS	10/01-12/01
	Brazoria PMSA, TX	Y	13030 FQ	18610 AW	22560 TQ	TXBLS	10/01-12/01
	Corpus Christi MSA, TX	Y	11900 FQ	13200 AW	15070 TQ	TXBLS	10/01-12/01
	Dallas PMSA, TX	Y	12580 FQ	17790 AW	22930 TQ	TXBLS	10/01-12/01
	El Paso MSA, TX	Y	11790 FQ	15760 AW	22040 TQ	TXBLS	10/01-12/01
	Fort Worth-Arlington PMSA, TX	Y	12020 FQ	14870 AW	18430 TQ	TXBLS	10/01-12/01
	Galveston-Texas City PMSA, TX	Y	13400 FQ	19590 AW	24820 TQ	TXBLS	10/01-12/01
	Houston PMSA, TX	Y	12050 FQ	16600 AW	23580 TQ	TXBLS	10/01-12/01
	McAllen-Edinburg-Mission MSA, TX	Y	11480 FQ	15370 AW	21360 TQ	TXBLS	10/01-12/01
	San Antonio MSA, TX	Y	14900 FQ	17860 AW	21860 TQ	TXBLS	10/01-12/01
	Utah	Y	12040 FQ	16710 AW	23210 TQ	UTBLS	10/01-12/01
	Provo-Orem MSA, UT	Y	12190 FQ	15500 AW	18550 TQ	UTBLS	10/01-12/01
	Salt Lake City-Ogden MSA, UT	Y	11860 FQ	16290 AW	22700 TQ	UTBLS	10/01-12/01
	Vermont	Y	14320 FQ	19410 AW	24260 TQ	VTBLS	10/01-12/01
	Burlington MSA, VT	Y	16770 FQ	23280 AW	28070 TQ	VTBLS	10/01-12/01
	Virginia	Y	12560 FQ	21920 AW	34860 TQ	VABLS	10/01-12/01
	Lynchburg MSA, VA	Y	14700 FQ	18290 AW	23610 TQ	VABLS	10/01-12/01
	Norfolk-Virginia Beach-Newport News MSA, VA-NC	Y	12280 FQ	20000 AW	33310 TQ	VABLS	10/01-12/01
	Richmond-Petersburg MSA, VA	Y	12550 FQ	24660 AW	45990 TQ	VABLS	10/01-12/01
	Washington	Y	15890 FQ	27260 AW	45340 TQ	WABLS	10/01-12/01
	Olympia PMSA, WA	Y	18060 FQ	29020 AW	50620 TQ	WABLS	10/01-12/01
	Seattle-Bellevue-Everett PMSA, WA	Y	15280 FQ	23250 AW	39620 TQ	WABLS	10/01-12/01
	Tacoma PMSA, WA	Y	20780 FQ	30190 AW	44300 TQ	WABLS	10/01-12/01
	West Virginia	Y	11850 FQ	18690 AW	38780 TQ	WVBLS	10/01-12/01
	Charleston MSA, WV	Y	12120 FQ	16170 AW	22500 TQ	WVBLS	10/01-12/01
	Wisconsin	Y	13850 FQ	19370 AW	25020 TQ	WIBLS	10/01-12/01
	Appleton-Oshkosh-Neenah MSA, WI	Y	12240 FQ	17890 AW	26690 TQ	WIBLS	10/01-12/01
	Green Bay MSA, WI	Y	19200 FQ	23590 AW	39270 TQ	WIBLS	10/01-12/01
	Madison MSA, WI	Y	15840 FQ	21380 AW	28360 TQ	WIBLS	10/01-12/01
	Milwaukee-Waukesha PMSA, WI	Y	13890 FQ	18980 AW	23790 TQ	WIBLS	10/01-12/01
	Wyoming	Y	12190 FQ	19240 AW	28240 TQ	WYBLS	10/01-12/01
	Puerto Rico	Y	11480 FQ	14230 AW	17890 TQ	PRBLS	10/01-12/01
Crushing, Grinding, and Polishing Machine Setter, Operator, and Tender	Alabama	H	8.48 FQ	12.88 AW	22.70 TQ	ALBLS	10/01-12/01
	Birmingham MSA, AL	H	8.54 FQ	10.79 AW	13.46 TQ	ALBLS	10/01-12/01
	Huntsville MSA, AL	H	7.91 FQ	13.81 AW	18.00 TQ	ALBLS	10/01-12/01
	Mobile MSA, AL	H	7.65 FQ	16.15 AW	29.73 TQ	ALBLS	10/01-12/01
	Arizona	H	7.36 FQ	13.23 AW	20.51 TQ	AZBLS	10/01-12/01
	Phoenix-Mesa MSA, AZ	H	6.82 FQ	13.30 AW	20.59 TQ	AZBLS	10/01-12/01
	Tucson MSA, AZ	H	7.32 FQ	9.49 AW	13.95 TQ	AZBLS	10/01-12/01
	Arkansas	H	7.38 FQ	11.00 AW	15.47 TQ	ARBLS	10/01-12/01
	Fayetteville-Springdale-Rogers MSA, AR	H	7.68 FQ	11.30 AW	15.57 TQ	ARBLS	10/01-12/01
	Fort Smith MSA, AR-OK	H	7.39 FQ	11.50 AW	23.60 TQ	ARBLS	10/01-12/01
	Little Rock-North Little Rock MSA, AR	H	8.31 FQ	13.45 AW	16.54 TQ	ARBLS	10/01-12/01
	California	H	7.36 FQ	12.28 AW	19.51 TQ	CABLS	10/01-12/01
	Bakersfield MSA, CA	H	6.59 FQ	11.68 AW	21.43 TQ	CABLS	10/01-12/01
	Fresno MSA, CA	H	7.05 FQ	10.17 AW	15.29 TQ	CABLS	10/01-12/01
	Los Angeles-Long Beach PMSA, CA	H	7.79 FQ	12.76 AW	19.70 TQ	CABLS	10/01-12/01
	Modesto MSA, CA	H	7.52 FQ	12.21 AW	17.05 TQ	CABLS	10/01-12/01

AAW Average annual wage; AE Average entry wage; AEX Average experienced wage; AO Average offered; AOH Average offered, high; AOL Average offered, low; APH Average pay, high range; APL Average pay, low range; ASH Average starting, high; ASL Average starting, low; AW Average wage paid; FQ First quartile wage; H Hourly; HI Highest wage paid; HR High end range; LR Low end range; M Monthly; MTC Median total compensation; MW Median wage paid; SQ Second quartile wage; S Special: hourly and annual; TQ Third quartile wage; W Weekly; Y Yearly

Occupation/Type/Industry	Location	Per	Low	Mid	High	Source	Date
Crushing, Grinding, and Polishing Machine Setter, Operator, and Tender	Oakland PMSA, CA	H	7.72 FQ	12.69 AW	20.44 TQ	CABLS	10/01-12/01
	Orange County PMSA, CA	H	6.82 FQ	9.80 AW	13.88 TQ	CABLS	10/01-12/01
	Riverside-San Bernardino PMSA, CA	H	6.73 FQ	11.99 AW	19.68 TQ	CABLS	10/01-12/01
	Sacramento PMSA, CA	H	10.54 FQ	15.32 AW	18.04 TQ	CABLS	10/01-12/01
	San Diego MSA, CA	H	7.33 FQ	10.08 AW	15.95 TQ	CABLS	10/01-12/01
	San Francisco PMSA, CA	H	9.64 FQ	14.81 AW	19.99 TQ	CABLS	10/01-12/01
	San Jose PMSA, CA	H	8.35 FQ	11.61 AW	16.11 TQ	CABLS	10/01-12/01
	Santa Barbara-Santa Maria-Lompoc MSA, CA	H	8.55 FQ	11.32 AW	15.40 TQ	CABLS	10/01-12/01
	Stockton-Lodi MSA, CA	H	7.28 FQ	16.00 AW	26.21 TQ	CABLS	10/01-12/01
	Ventura PMSA, CA	H	8.22 FQ	15.05 AW	25.34 TQ	CABLS	10/01-12/01
	Colorado	H	9.16 FQ	14.16 AW	20.72 TQ	COBLS	10/01-12/01
	Boulder-Longmont PMSA, CO	H	9.00 FQ	12.82 AW	19.73 TQ	COBLS	10/01-12/01
	Denver PMSA, CO	H	9.47 FQ	14.61 AW	20.40 TQ	COBLS	10/01-12/01
	Fort Collins-Loveland MSA, CO	H	8.83 FQ	11.55 AW	15.05 TQ	COBLS	10/01-12/01
	Connecticut	H	8.95 FQ	13.84 AW	20.62 TQ	CTBLS	10/01-12/01
	Bridgeport PMSA, CT	H	10.21 FQ	18.78 AW	27.00 TQ	CTBLS	10/01-12/01
	Danbury PMSA, CT	H	11.55 FQ	15.69 AW	21.45 TQ	CTBLS	10/01-12/01
	Hartford MSA, CT	H	8.53 FQ	12.82 AW	18.55 TQ	CTBLS	10/01-12/01
	New Haven-Meriden PMSA, CT	H	11.38 FQ	14.77 AW	19.24 TQ	CTBLS	10/01-12/01
	Delaware	H	10.39 FQ	13.52 AW	18.00 TQ	DEBLS	10/01-12/01
	Wilmington-Newark PMSA, DE-MD	H	10.57 FQ	13.60 AW	17.90 TQ	DEBLS	10/01-12/01
	Washington PMSA, DC-MD-VA-WV	H	8.87 FQ	13.91 AW	19.66 TQ	DCBLS	10/01-12/01
	Florida	H	7.57 FQ	10.65 AW	14.36 TQ	FLBLS	10/01-12/01
	Daytona Beach MSA, FL	H	7.14 FQ	9.36 AW	12.70 TQ	FLBLS	10/01-12/01
	Fort Lauderdale PMSA, FL	H	8.53 FQ	11.20 AW	15.18 TQ	FLBLS	10/01-12/01
	Fort Myers-Cape Coral MSA, FL	H	9.32 FQ	11.63 AW	14.26 TQ	FLBLS	10/01-12/01
	Jacksonville MSA, FL	H	9.02 FQ	10.99 AW	13.55 TQ	FLBLS	10/01-12/01
	Miami PMSA, FL	H	7.05 FQ	9.89 AW	13.41 TQ	FLBLS	10/01-12/01
	Orlando MSA, FL	H	6.55 FQ	11.42 AW	16.47 TQ	FLBLS	10/01-12/01
	Sarasota-Bradenton MSA, FL	H	6.63 FQ	9.15 AW	12.25 TQ	FLBLS	10/01-12/01
	Tampa-St. Petersburg-Clearwater MSA, FL	H	7.58 FQ	10.88 AW	14.81 TQ	FLBLS	10/01-12/01
	West Palm Beach-Boca Raton MSA, FL	H	6.16 FQ	9.28 AW	12.26 TQ	FLBLS	10/01-12/01
	Georgia	H	7.99 FQ	12.90 AW	18.24 TQ	GABLS	10/01-12/01
	Atlanta MSA, GA	H	7.71 FQ	12.56 AW	17.17 TQ	GABLS	10/01-12/01
	Augusta-Aiken MSA, GA-SC	H	12.02 FQ	18.05 AW	24.40 TQ	GABLS	10/01-12/01
	Macon MSA, GA	H	7.39 FQ	11.72 AW	17.75 TQ	GABLS	10/01-12/01
	Savannah MSA, GA	H	10.45 FQ	15.61 AW	20.83 TQ	GABLS	10/01-12/01
	Hawaii	H	8.37 FQ	16.23 AW	24.83 TQ	HIBLS	10/01-12/01
	Honolulu MSA, HI	H	8.10 FQ	16.20 AW	23.76 TQ	HIBLS	10/01-12/01
	Idaho	H	6.23 FQ	11.33 AW	18.65 TQ	IDBLS	10/01-12/01
	Boise City MSA, ID	H	7.76 FQ	13.07 AW	23.11 TQ	IDBLS	10/01-12/01
	Illinois	H	8.06 FQ	13.31 AW	19.98 TQ	ILBLS	10/01-12/01
	Chicago PMSA, IL	H	7.65 FQ	12.78 AW	19.58 TQ	ILBLS	10/01-12/01
	Rockford MSA, IL	H	7.90 FQ	13.34 AW	16.82 TQ	ILBLS	10/01-12/01
	Indiana	H	8.85 FQ	14.38 AW	21.33 TQ	INBLS	10/01-12/01
	Elkhart-Goshen MSA, IN	H	7.81 FQ	13.01 AW	19.96 TQ	INBLS	10/01-12/01
	Evansville-Henderson MSA, IN-KY	H	8.17 FQ	13.02 AW	20.54 TQ	INBLS	10/01-12/01
	Fort Wayne MSA, IN	H	9.21 FQ	15.39 AW	21.87 TQ	INBLS	10/01-12/01
	Gary PMSA, IN	H	9.38 FQ	16.15 AW	21.50 TQ	INBLS	10/01-12/01
	Indianapolis MSA, IN	H	8.68 FQ	13.94 AW	20.56 TQ	INBLS	10/01-12/01
	South Bend MSA, IN	H	8.59 FQ	11.40 AW	17.19 TQ	INBLS	10/01-12/01
	Iowa	H	9.30 FQ	12.98 AW	17.08 TQ	IABLS	10/01-12/01
	Cedar Rapids MSA, IA	H	9.38 FQ	12.13 AW	15.83 TQ	IABLS	10/01-12/01
	Davenport-Moline-Rock Island MSA, IA-IL	H	10.15 FQ	13.26 AW	17.39 TQ	IABLS	10/01-12/01
	Des Moines MSA, IA	H	9.13 FQ	13.58 AW	17.46 TQ	IABLS	10/01-12/01
	Kansas	H	8.71 FQ	11.55 AW	15.58 TQ	KSBLS	10/01-12/01
	Topeka MSA, KS	H	8.85 FQ	11.55 AW	18.88 TQ	KSBLS	10/01-12/01
	Wichita MSA, KS	H	8.10 FQ	11.57 AW	15.78 TQ	KSBLS	10/01-12/01
	Kentucky	H	8.69 FQ	12.13 AW	16.44 TQ	KYBLS	10/01-12/01

AAW Average annual wage · **AE** Average entry wage · **AEX** Average experienced wage · **AO** Average offered · **AOH** Average offered, high · **AOL** Average offered, low · **APH** Average pay, high range · **APL** Average pay, low range · **ASH** Average starting, high · **ASL** Average starting, low · **AW** Average wage paid · **FQ** First quartile wage · **H** Hourly · **HI** Highest wage paid · **HR** High end range · **LR** Low end range · **M** Monthly · **MTC** Median total compensation · **MW** Median wage paid · **SQ** Second quartile wage · **S** Special: hourly and annual · **TQ** Third quartile wage · **W** Weekly · **Y** Yearly

Occupation/Type/Industry	Location	Per	Low	Mid	High	Source	Date
Crushing, Grinding, and Polishing Machine Setter, Operator, and Tender	Lexington MSA, KY	H	8.39 FQ	11.62 AW	16.26 TQ	KYBLS	10/01-12/01
	Louisville MSA, KY-IN	H	9.08 FQ	12.66 AW	16.06 TQ	KYBLS	10/01-12/01
	Louisiana	H	7.46 FQ	13.01 AW	20.58 TQ	LABLS	10/01-12/01
	New Orleans MSA, LA	H	7.81 FQ	14.00 AW	23.17 TQ	LABLS	10/01-12/01
	Maine	H	9.48 FQ	14.29 AW	19.70 TQ	MEBLS	10/01-12/01
	Maryland	H	10.12 FQ	16.03 AW	21.18 TQ	MDBLS	10/01-12/01
	Baltimore PMSA, MD	H	10.05 FQ	14.78 AW	20.25 TQ	MDBLS	10/01-12/01
	Massachusetts	H	9.42 FQ	14.72 AW	21.26 TQ	MABLS	10/01-12/01
	Boston PMSA, MA-NH	H	10.88 FQ	17.17 AW	27.92 TQ	MABLS	10/01-12/01
	Lowell PMSA, MA-NH	H	10.26 FQ	14.30 AW	20.40 TQ	MABLS	10/01-12/01
	Springfield MSA, MA	H	10.13 FQ	13.67 AW	17.82 TQ	MABLS	10/01-12/01
	Worcester PMSA, MA-CT	H	9.08 FQ	12.31 AW	16.75 TQ	MABLS	10/01-12/01
	Michigan	H	9.34 FQ	13.58 AW	19.51 TQ	MIBLS	10/01-12/01
	Detroit PMSA, MI	H	9.30 FQ	13.02 AW	17.78 TQ	MIBLS	10/01-12/01
	Grand Rapids-Muskegon-Holland MSA, MI	H	9.28 FQ	14.33 AW	20.93 TQ	MIBLS	10/01-12/01
	Kalamazoo-Battle Creek MSA, MI	H	8.79 FQ	12.64 AW	16.56 TQ	MIBLS	10/01-12/01
	Lansing-East Lansing MSA, MI	H	9.16 FQ	11.28 AW	14.75 TQ	MIBLS	10/01-12/01
	Saginaw-Bay City-Midland MSA, MI	H	8.20 FQ	15.57 AW	25.67 TQ	MIBLS	10/01-12/01
	Minnesota	H	9.17 FQ	14.50 AW	21.21 TQ	MNBLS	10/01-12/01
	Duluth-Superior MSA, MN-WI	H	15.28 FQ	19.24 AW	22.69 TQ	MNBLS	10/01-12/01
	Minneapolis-St. Paul MSA, MN-WI	H	9.46 FQ	15.36 AW	22.06 TQ	MNBLS	10/01-12/01
	Mississippi	H	7.69 FQ	11.85 AW	18.97 TQ	MSBLS	10/01-12/01
	Jackson MSA, MS	H	7.13 FQ	8.76 AW	10.69 TQ	MSBLS	10/01-12/01
	Missouri	H	8.37 FQ	12.89 AW	17.33 TQ	MOBLS	10/01-12/01
	Kansas City MSA, MO-KS	H	8.56 FQ	12.36 AW	16.39 TQ	MOBLS	10/01-12/01
	St. Louis MSA, MO-IL	H	8.75 FQ	13.14 AW	18.10 TQ	MOBLS	10/01-12/01
	Montana	H	9.03 FQ	15.95 AW	24.64 TQ	MTBLS	10/01-12/01
	Nebraska	H	7.61 FQ	12.95 AW	20.62 TQ	NEBLS	10/01-12/01
	Omaha MSA, NE-IA	H	7.70 FQ	14.36 AW	22.18 TQ	NEBLS	10/01-12/01
	Nevada	H	7.66 FQ	13.93 AW	20.92 TQ	NVBLS	10/01-12/01
	Las Vegas MSA, NV-AZ	H	9.62 FQ	15.14 AW	20.95 TQ	NVBLS	10/01-12/01
	Reno MSA, NV	H	6.33 FQ	10.44 AW	16.92 TQ	NVBLS	10/01-12/01
	New Hampshire	H	9.74 FQ	13.57 AW	17.82 TQ	NHBLS	10/01-12/01
	Nashua PMSA, NH	H	9.59 FQ	14.67 AW	20.39 TQ	NHBLS	10/01-12/01
	New Jersey	H	8.46 FQ	13.54 AW	18.45 TQ	NJBLS	10/01-12/01
	Bergen-Passaic PMSA, NJ	H	7.58 FQ	11.12 AW	15.37 TQ	NJBLS	10/01-12/01
	Jersey City PMSA, NJ	H	7.63 FQ	13.02 AW	17.25 TQ	NJBLS	10/01-12/01
	Middlesex-Somerset-Hunterdon PMSA, NJ	H	9.43 FQ	12.76 AW	16.77 TQ	NJBLS	10/01-12/01
	Monmouth-Ocean PMSA, NJ	H	7.79 FQ	13.14 AW	19.14 TQ	NJBLS	10/01-12/01
	Newark PMSA, NJ	H	9.36 FQ	14.11 AW	18.13 TQ	NJBLS	10/01-12/01
	New Mexico	H	8.15 FQ	13.26 AW	17.92 TQ	NMBLS	10/01-12/01
	New York	H	7.69 FQ	13.04 AW	19.53 TQ	NYBLS	10/01-12/01
	Albany-Schenectady-Troy MSA, NY	H	9.08 FQ	14.19 AW	20.50 TQ	NYBLS	10/01-12/01
	Buffalo-Niagara Falls MSA, NY	H	8.82 FQ	13.60 AW	20.81 TQ	NYBLS	10/01-12/01
	Dutchess County PMSA, NY	H	8.28 FQ	14.61 AW	17.71 TQ	NYBLS	10/01-12/01
	Nassau-Suffolk PMSA, NY	H	5.84 FQ	8.85 AW	14.27 TQ	NYBLS	10/01-12/01
	New York PMSA, NY	H	7.31 FQ	12.19 AW	17.39 TQ	NYBLS	10/01-12/01
	Rochester MSA, NY	H	8.42 FQ	13.12 AW	18.56 TQ	NYBLS	10/01-12/01
	Utica-Rome MSA, NY	H	7.48 FQ	10.93 AW	15.04 TQ	NYBLS	10/01-12/01
	North Carolina	H	8.13 FQ	11.43 AW	15.81 TQ	NCBLS	10/01-12/01
	Charlotte-Gastonia-Rock Hill MSA, NC-SC	H	9.23 FQ	11.71 AW	13.95 TQ	NCBLS	10/01-12/01
	Greensboro-Winston-Salem-High Point MSA, NC	H	8.22 FQ	10.19 AW	13.12 TQ	NCBLS	10/01-12/01
	Hickory-Morganton-Lenoir MSA, NC	H	8.58 FQ	11.07 AW	17.08 TQ	NCBLS	10/01-12/01
	Raleigh-Durham-Chapel Hill MSA, NC	H	10.41 FQ	12.54 AW	15.36 TQ	NCBLS	10/01-12/01
	North Dakota	H	8.89 FQ	12.16 AW	16.15 TQ	NDBLS	10/01-12/01
	Fargo-Moorhead MSA, ND-MN	H	11.05 FQ	16.36 AW	20.66 TQ	NDBLS	10/01-12/01
	Ohio	H	8.70 FQ	13.34 AW	19.51 TQ	OHBLS	10/01-12/01
	Akron PMSA, OH	H	9.06 FQ	12.78 AW	18.90 TQ	OHBLS	10/01-12/01

AAW	Average annual wage	**AOH**	Average offered, high	**ASH**	Average starting, high	**H**	Hourly	**M**	Monthly	**S**	Special: hourly and annual
AE	Average entry wage	**AOL**	Average offered, low	**ASL**	Average starting, low	**HI**	Highest wage paid	**MTC**	Median total compensation	**TQ**	Third quartile wage
AEX	Average experienced wage	**APH**	Average pay, high range	**AW**	Average wage paid	**HR**	High end range	**MW**	Median wage paid	**W**	Weekly
AO	Average offered	**APL**	Average pay, low range	**FQ**	First quartile wage	**LR**	Low end range	**SQ**	Second quartile wage	**Y**	Yearly

Occupation/Type/Industry	Location	Per	Low	Mid	High	Source	Date
Crushing, Grinding, and Polishing Machine Setter, Operator, and Tender	Canton-Massillon MSA, OH	H	11.00 FQ	14.13 AW	21.70 TQ	OHBLS	10/01-12/01
	Cincinnati PMSA, OH-KY-IN	H	8.34 FQ	13.04 AW	17.70 TQ	OHBLS	10/01-12/01
	Cleveland-Lorain-Elyria PMSA, OH	H	9.69 FQ	13.37 AW	17.55 TQ	OHBLS	10/01-12/01
	Columbus MSA, OH	H	8.88 FQ	13.10 AW	20.84 TQ	OHBLS	10/01-12/01
	Dayton-Springfield MSA, OH	H	8.13 FQ	13.24 AW	19.33 TQ	OHBLS	10/01-12/01
	Toledo MSA, OH	H	8.42 FQ	13.45 AW	17.78 TQ	OHBLS	10/01-12/01
	Youngstown-Warren MSA, OH	H	6.12 FQ	11.52 AW	17.26 TQ	OHBLS	10/01-12/01
	Oklahoma	H	7.51 FQ	10.23 AW	14.09 TQ	OKBLS	10/01-12/01
	Oklahoma City MSA, OK	H	7.44 FQ	9.91 AW	13.10 TQ	OKBLS	10/01-12/01
	Tulsa MSA, OK	H	8.94 FQ	10.61 AW	13.63 TQ	OKBLS	10/01-12/01
	Oregon	H	8.16 FQ	14.21 AW	20.84 TQ	ORBLS	10/01-12/01
	Eugene-Springfield MSA, OR	H	9.06 FQ	12.39 AW	16.81 TQ	ORBLS	10/01-12/01
	Portland-Vancouver PMSA, OR-WA	H	8.97 FQ	15.14 AW	21.11 TQ	ORBLS	10/01-12/01
	Salem PMSA, OR	H	8.34 FQ	13.66 AW	17.84 TQ	ORBLS	10/01-12/01
	Pennsylvania	H	8.11 FQ	13.04 AW	17.81 TQ	PABLS	10/01-12/01
	Allentown-Bethlehem-Easton MSA, PA	H	7.91 FQ	12.67 AW	18.24 TQ	PABLS	10/01-12/01
	Erie MSA, PA	H	6.47 FQ	11.47 AW	17.01 TQ	PABLS	10/01-12/01
	Harrisburg-Lebanon-Carlisle MSA, PA	H	10.95 FQ	13.35 AW	16.63 TQ	PABLS	10/01-12/01
	Lancaster MSA, PA	H	8.40 FQ	12.54 AW	17.52 TQ	PABLS	10/01-12/01
	Philadelphia PMSA, PA-NJ	H	9.65 FQ	15.38 AW	21.17 TQ	PABLS	10/01-12/01
	Pittsburgh MSA, PA	H	6.42 FQ	11.88 AW	17.81 TQ	PABLS	10/01-12/01
	Reading MSA, PA	H	9.98 FQ	14.05 AW	17.58 TQ	PABLS	10/01-12/01
	Scranton-Wilkes-Barre-Hazleton MSA, PA	H	9.69 FQ	14.45 AW	17.10 TQ	PABLS	10/01-12/01
	York MSA, PA	H	11.27 FQ	13.92 AW	17.09 TQ	PABLS	10/01-12/01
	Rhode Island	H	6.97 FQ	9.83 AW	15.75 TQ	RIBLS	10/01-12/01
	Providence-Fall River-Warwick MSA, RI-MA	H	6.98 FQ	9.98 AW	15.90 TQ	RIBLS	10/01-12/01
	South Carolina	H	9.06 FQ	12.90 AW	17.22 TQ	SCBLS	10/01-12/01
	Charleston-North Charleston MSA, SC	H	8.73 FQ	12.68 AW	20.51 TQ	SCBLS	10/01-12/01
	Columbia MSA, SC	H	10.35 FQ	13.30 AW	17.25 TQ	SCBLS	10/01-12/01
	South Dakota	H	8.92 FQ	12.03 AW	17.23 TQ	SDBLS	10/01-12/01
	Tennessee	H	7.58 FQ	12.17 AW	16.79 TQ	TNBLS	10/01-12/01
	Chattanooga MSA, TN-GA	H	8.75 FQ	11.60 AW	14.12 TQ	TNBLS	10/01-12/01
	Clarksville-Hopkinsville MSA, TN-KY	H	7.70 FQ	10.00 AW	12.79 TQ	TNBLS	10/01-12/01
	Johnson City-Kingsport-Bristol MSA, TN-VA	H	6.30 FQ	9.64 AW	12.90 TQ	TNBLS	10/01-12/01
	Knoxville MSA, TN	H	7.21 FQ	10.25 AW	13.65 TQ	TNBLS	10/01-12/01
	Memphis MSA, TN-AR-MS	H	7.43 FQ	10.53 AW	15.27 TQ	TNBLS	10/01-12/01
	Nashville MSA, TN	H	7.80 FQ	13.71 AW	25.88 TQ	TNBLS	10/01-12/01
	Texas	H	7.10 FQ	11.62 AW	18.10 TQ	TXBLS	10/01-12/01
	Amarillo MSA, TX	H	6.76 FQ	9.47 AW	12.41 TQ	TXBLS	10/01-12/01
	Austin-San Marcos MSA, TX	H	8.61 FQ	11.06 AW	13.29 TQ	TXBLS	10/01-12/01
	Beaumont-Port Arthur MSA, TX	H	5.67 FQ	8.46 AW	13.14 TQ	TXBLS	10/01-12/01
	Corpus Christi MSA, TX	H	5.96 FQ	9.42 AW	13.23 TQ	TXBLS	10/01-12/01
	Dallas PMSA, TX	H	7.50 FQ	11.95 AW	16.57 TQ	TXBLS	10/01-12/01
	El Paso MSA, TX	H	5.84 FQ	8.27 AW	11.27 TQ	TXBLS	10/01-12/01
	Fort Worth-Arlington PMSA, TX	H	8.01 FQ	12.28 AW	19.33 TQ	TXBLS	10/01-12/01
	Houston PMSA, TX	H	7.67 FQ	13.29 AW	20.84 TQ	TXBLS	10/01-12/01
	Longview-Marshall MSA, TX	H	5.89 FQ	8.73 AW	12.58 TQ	TXBLS	10/01-12/01
	McAllen-Edinburg-Mission MSA, TX	H	5.79 FQ	8.04 AW	10.51 TQ	TXBLS	10/01-12/01
	San Antonio MSA, TX	H	7.59 FQ	11.98 AW	16.53 TQ	TXBLS	10/01-12/01
	Waco MSA, TX	H	7.02 FQ	9.24 AW	12.70 TQ	TXBLS	10/01-12/01
	Utah	H	9.52 FQ	15.68 AW	21.19 TQ	UTBLS	10/01-12/01
	Provo-Orem MSA, UT	H	5.91 FQ	9.02 AW	13.08 TQ	UTBLS	10/01-12/01
	Salt Lake City-Ogden MSA, UT	H	10.68 FQ	16.86 AW	21.47 TQ	UTBLS	10/01-12/01
	Vermont	H	9.47 FQ	13.55 AW	17.26 TQ	VTBLS	10/01-12/01
	Burlington MSA, VT	H	10.00 FQ	14.66 AW	19.46 TQ	VTBLS	10/01-12/01
	Virginia	H	8.89 FQ	12.99 AW	17.46 TQ	VABLS	10/01-12/01
	Lynchburg MSA, VA	H	9.23 FQ	11.88 AW	14.68 TQ	VABLS	10/01-12/01

AAW Average annual wage; **AE** Average entry wage; **AEX** Average experienced wage; **AO** Average offered; **AOH** Average offered, high; **AOL** Average offered, low; **APH** Average pay, high range; **APL** Average pay, low range; **ASH** Average starting, high; **ASL** Average starting, low; **AW** Average wage paid; **FQ** First quartile wage; **H** Hourly; **HI** Highest wage paid; **HR** High end range; **LR** Low end range; **M** Monthly; **MTC** Median total compensation; **MW** Median wage paid; **SQ** Second quartile wage; **S** Special: hourly and annual; **TQ** Third quartile wage; **W** Weekly; **Y** Yearly

Occupation/Type/Industry	Location	Per	Low	Mid	High	Source	Date
Crushing, Grinding, and Polishing Machine Setter, Operator, and Tender	Richmond-Petersburg MSA, VA	H	8.03 FQ	12.97 AW	19.08 TQ	VABLS	10/01-12/01
	Roanoke MSA, VA	H	8.04 FQ	11.39 AW	16.06 TQ	VABLS	10/01-12/01
	Washington	H	8.53 FQ	13.82 AW	20.42 TQ	WABLS	10/01-12/01
	Seattle-Bellevue-Everett PMSA, WA	H	9.51 FQ	14.87 AW	20.46 TQ	WABLS	10/01-12/01
	Spokane MSA, WA	H	7.80 FQ	12.37 AW	24.00 TQ	WABLS	10/01-12/01
	Yakima MSA, WA	H	7.52 FQ	10.45 AW	14.35 TQ	WABLS	10/01-12/01
	West Virginia	H	7.60 FQ	14.30 AW	21.73 TQ	WVBLS	10/01-12/01
	Wisconsin	H	9.48 FQ	13.69 AW	19.68 TQ	WIBLS	10/01-12/01
	Appleton-Oshkosh-Neenah MSA, WI	H	9.85 FQ	14.38 AW	18.95 TQ	WIBLS	10/01-12/01
	Green Bay MSA, WI	H	11.20 FQ	15.59 AW	23.17 TQ	WIBLS	10/01-12/01
	Milwaukee-Waukesha PMSA, WI	H	10.03 FQ	14.50 AW	20.55 TQ	WIBLS	10/01-12/01
	Racine PMSA, WI	H	10.18 FQ	12.82 AW	17.37 TQ	WIBLS	10/01-12/01
	Wyoming	H	11.14 FQ	20.41 AW	27.34 TQ	WYBLS	10/01-12/01
	Puerto Rico	H	5.65 FQ	8.02 AW	12.12 TQ	PRBLS	10/01-12/01
Customer Service Representative	Alabama	H	7.60 FQ	11.81 AW	17.68 TQ	ALBLS	10/01-12/01
	Alaska	H	9.66 FQ	15.01 AW	21.26 TQ	AKBLS	10/01-12/01
	Arizona	H	7.82 FQ	11.57 AW	16.59 TQ	AZBLS	10/01-12/01
	Arkansas	H	7.20 FQ	11.59 AW	17.63 TQ	ARBLS	10/01-12/01
	California	H	9.17 FQ	15.46 AW	23.40 TQ	CABLS	10/01-12/01
	Colorado	H	8.42 FQ	13.18 AW	19.08 TQ	COBLS	10/01-12/01
	Connecticut	H	9.22 FQ	14.92 AW	21.13 TQ	CTBLS	10/01-12/01
	Delaware	H	8.72 FQ	14.02 AW	21.18 TQ	DEBLS	10/01-12/01
	District of Columbia	H	9.53 FQ	15.44 AW	25.61 TQ	DCBLS	10/01-12/01
	Florida	H	7.95 FQ	12.07 AW	17.27 TQ	FLBLS	10/01-12/01
	Georgia	H	8.65 FQ	13.12 AW	18.97 TQ	GABLS	10/01-12/01
	Hawaii	H	9.14 FQ	13.49 AW	19.33 TQ	HIBLS	10/01-12/01
	Idaho	H	7.09 FQ	10.57 AW	15.97 TQ	IDBLS	10/01-12/01
	Illinois	H	8.16 FQ	13.53 AW	20.41 TQ	ILBLS	10/01-12/01
	Indiana	H	8.10 FQ	12.93 AW	18.99 TQ	INBLS	10/01-12/01
	Iowa	H	7.23 FQ	11.24 AW	16.38 TQ	IABLS	10/01-12/01
	Kansas	H	7.67 FQ	12.29 AW	18.21 TQ	KSBLS	10/01-12/01
	Kentucky	H	7.46 FQ	11.79 AW	17.07 TQ	KYBLS	10/01-12/01
	Louisiana	H	6.15 FQ	10.29 AW	16.27 TQ	LABLS	10/01-12/01
	Maine	H	8.03 FQ	12.16 AW	17.25 TQ	MEBLS	10/01-12/01
	Maryland	H	7.76 FQ	12.89 AW	18.99 TQ	MDBLS	10/01-12/01
	Massachusetts	H	9.60 FQ	15.21 AW	22.30 TQ	MABLS	10/01-12/01
	Michigan	H	8.73 FQ	14.19 AW	22.26 TQ	MIBLS	10/01-12/01
	Minnesota	H	8.70 FQ	13.51 AW	19.78 TQ	MNBLS	10/01-12/01
	Mississippi	H	7.39 FQ	10.75 AW	15.17 TQ	MSBLS	10/01-12/01
	Missouri	H	7.67 FQ	12.44 AW	19.41 TQ	MOBLS	10/01-12/01
	Montana	H	7.01 FQ	10.31 AW	15.28 TQ	MTBLS	10/01-12/01
	Nebraska	H	7.14 FQ	11.38 AW	17.60 TQ	NEBLS	10/01-12/01
	Nevada	H	8.95 FQ	12.75 AW	17.86 TQ	NVBLS	10/01-12/01
	New Hampshire	H	8.53 FQ	13.04 AW	18.53 TQ	NHBLS	10/01-12/01
	New Jersey	H	9.49 FQ	14.96 AW	21.93 TQ	NJBLS	10/01-12/01
	New Mexico	H	7.48 FQ	10.93 AW	14.87 TQ	NMBLS	10/01-12/01
	New York	H	8.34 FQ	15.17 AW	25.00 TQ	NYBLS	10/01-12/01
	North Carolina	H	7.65 FQ	12.75 AW	18.31 TQ	NCBLS	10/01-12/01
	North Dakota	H	7.64 FQ	11.57 AW	18.22 TQ	NDBLS	10/01-12/01
	Ohio	H	8.33 FQ	13.14 AW	20.02 TQ	OHBLS	10/01-12/01
	Oklahoma	H	7.27 FQ	11.52 AW	17.29 TQ	OKBLS	10/01-12/01
	Oregon	H	8.27 FQ	12.42 AW	17.96 TQ	ORBLS	10/01-12/01
	Pennsylvania	H	7.79 FQ	12.55 AW	19.13 TQ	PABLS	10/01-12/01
	Rhode Island	H	7.99 FQ	12.95 AW	17.60 TQ	RIBLS	10/01-12/01
	South Carolina	H	7.68 FQ	11.80 AW	16.72 TQ	SCBLS	10/01-12/01
	South Dakota	H	7.75 FQ	10.51 AW	13.76 TQ	SDBLS	10/01-12/01
	Tennessee	H	8.04 FQ	12.08 AW	17.14 TQ	TNBLS	10/01-12/01
	Texas	H	7.52 FQ	12.29 AW	18.45 TQ	TXBLS	10/01-12/01
	Utah	H	7.91 FQ	11.28 AW	15.57 TQ	UTBLS	10/01-12/01
	Vermont	H	9.05 FQ	12.90 AW	17.89 TQ	VTBLS	10/01-12/01
	Virginia	H	7.58 FQ	12.61 AW	19.13 TQ	VABLS	10/01-12/01
	Washington	H	9.25 FQ	14.19 AW	20.48 TQ	WABLS	10/01-12/01
	West Virginia	H	7.36 FQ	10.79 AW	15.30 TQ	WVBLS	10/01-12/01
	Wisconsin	H	8.16 FQ	13.61 AW	21.27 TQ	WIBLS	10/01-12/01
	Wyoming	H	6.75 FQ	10.52 AW	15.33 TQ	WYBLS	10/01-12/01

Occupation/Type/Industry	Location	Per	Low	Mid	High	Source	Date
Customer Service Representative	Puerto Rico	H	6.03 FQ	9.45 AW	14.52 TQ	PRBLS	10/01-12/01
	Virgin Islands	H	8.03 FQ	11.48 AW	16.26 TQ	VIBLS	10/01-12/01
	Guam	H	6.18 FQ	10.74 AW	16.23 TQ	GUBLS	10/01-12/01
Customs Agent	United States	Y	23000 ASL		44000 ASH	AEAC	1/99-1/99
Cutter and Trimmer							
Hand	Alabama	H	8.01 FQ	13.27 AW	18.17 TQ	ALBLS	10/01-12/01
Hand	Arizona	H	6.19 FQ	9.98 AW	13.14 TQ	AZBLS	10/01-12/01
Hand	Arkansas	H	5.77 FQ	7.40 AW	10.45 TQ	ARBLS	10/01-12/01
Hand	California	H	6.55 FQ	9.33 AW	13.42 TQ	CABLS	10/01-12/01
Hand	Colorado	H	6.32 FQ	10.20 AW	17.20 TQ	COBLS	10/01-12/01
Hand	Connecticut	H	7.48 FQ	10.72 AW	16.61 TQ	CTBLS	10/01-12/01
Hand	Delaware	H	9.60 FQ	13.33 AW	20.87 TQ	DEBLS	10/01-12/01
Hand	Florida	H	5.93 FQ	9.92 AW	14.80 TQ	FLBLS	10/01-12/01
Hand	Georgia	H	7.28 FQ	11.27 AW	17.02 TQ	GABLS	10/01-12/01
Hand	Hawaii	H	5.89 FQ	8.64 AW	13.14 TQ	HIBLS	10/01-12/01
Hand	Idaho	H	5.83 FQ	8.70 AW	13.28 TQ	IDBLS	10/01-12/01
Hand	Illinois	H	8.02 FQ	13.16 AW	21.37 TQ	ILBLS	10/01-12/01
Hand	Indiana	H	8.27 FQ	11.96 AW	14.37 TQ	INBLS	10/01-12/01
Hand	Iowa	H	7.52 FQ	12.16 AW	18.73 TQ	IABLS	10/01-12/01
Hand	Kansas	H	7.73 FQ	9.82 AW	12.19 TQ	KSBLS	10/01-12/01
Hand	Kentucky	H	7.28 FQ	14.28 AW	25.16 TQ	KYBLS	10/01-12/01
Hand	Louisiana	H	7.88 FQ	9.82 AW	11.19 TQ	LABLS	10/01-12/01
Hand	Maine	H	6.68 FQ	9.60 AW	11.40 TQ	MEBLS	10/01-12/01
Hand	Massachusetts	H	7.36 FQ	11.14 AW	15.50 TQ	MABLS	10/01-12/01
Hand	Michigan	H	7.20 FQ	14.71 AW	27.24 TQ	MIBLS	10/01-12/01
Hand	Minnesota	H	9.04 FQ	17.64 AW	27.58 TQ	MNBLS	10/01-12/01
Hand	Mississippi	H	7.35 FQ	11.23 AW	14.98 TQ	MSBLS	10/01-12/01
Hand	Missouri	H	10.17 FQ	19.69 AW	27.85 TQ	MOBLS	10/01-12/01
Hand	Montana	H	5.91 FQ	9.50 AW	13.78 TQ	MTBLS	10/01-12/01
Hand	Nebraska	H	6.72 FQ	9.21 AW	13.19 TQ	NEBLS	10/01-12/01
Hand	Nevada	II	7.20 FQ	11.34 AW	16.19 TQ	NVBLS	10/01-12/01
Hand	New Hampshire	H	7.83 FQ	11.22 AW	14.26 TQ	NHBLS	10/01-12/01
Hand	New Jersey	H	5.87 FQ	10.98 AW	21.37 TQ	NJBLS	10/01-12/01
Hand	New Mexico	H	5.75 FQ	7.33 AW	10.76 TQ	NMBLS	10/01-12/01
Hand	New York	H	5.80 FQ	10.29 AW	17.77 TQ	NYBLS	10/01-12/01
Hand	North Carolina	H	8.21 FQ	13.62 AW	19.93 TQ	NCBLS	10/01-12/01
Hand	Ohio	H	7.74 FQ	10.93 AW	14.79 TQ	OHBLS	10/01-12/01
Hand	Oklahoma	H	6.80 FQ	11.32 AW	19.82 TQ	OKBLS	10/01-12/01
Hand	Oregon	H	7.20 FQ	9.92 AW	13.60 TQ	ORBLS	10/01-12/01
Hand	Pennsylvania	H	6.44 FQ	10.32 AW	15.15 TQ	PABLS	10/01-12/01
Hand	Rhode Island	H	8.27 FQ	10.16 AW	12.57 TQ	RIBLS	10/01-12/01
Hand	South Carolina	H	6.45 FQ	10.31 AW	17.67 TQ	SCBLS	10/01-12/01
Hand	South Dakota	H	7.09 FQ	9.44 AW	12.62 TQ	SDBLS	10/01-12/01
Hand	Tennessee	H	7.28 FQ	10.37 AW	14.70 TQ	TNBLS	10/01-12/01
Hand	Texas	H	6.46 FQ	9.07 AW	12.65 TQ	TXBLS	10/01-12/01
Hand	Utah	H	7.00 FQ	9.49 AW	13.22 TQ	UTBLS	10/01-12/01
Hand	Vermont	H	7.71 FQ	12.15 AW	16.82 TQ	VTBLS	10/01-12/01
Hand	Virginia	H	7.20 FQ	11.80 AW	24.10 TQ	VABLS	10/01-12/01
Hand	Washington	H	7.38 FQ	10.55 AW	13.49 TQ	WABLS	10/01-12/01
Hand	Wisconsin	H	8.02 FQ	11.95 AW	16.20 TQ	WIBLS	10/01-12/01
Hand	Puerto Rico	H	5.54 FQ	6.62 AW	9.06 TQ	PRBLS	10/01-12/01
Cutting and Slicing Machine Setter, Operator, and Tender	Alabama	H	7.56 FQ	11.63 AW	17.25 TQ	ALBLS	10/01-12/01
	Birmingham MSA, AL	H	7.48 FQ	11.70 AW	19.41 TQ	ALBLS	10/01-12/01
	Huntsville MSA, AL	H	8.38 FQ	15.56 AW	21.01 TQ	ALBLS	10/01-12/01
	Mobile MSA, AL	H	7.28 FQ	12.03 AW	16.59 TQ	ALBLS	10/01-12/01
	Montgomery MSA, AL	H	7.69 FQ	10.92 AW	13.15 TQ	ALBLS	10/01-12/01
	Phoenix-Mesa MSA, AZ	H	7.47 FQ	10.78 AW	16.21 TQ	AZBLS	10/01-12/01
	Tucson MSA, AZ	H	7.83 FQ	11.56 AW	17.02 TQ	AZBLS	10/01-12/01
	Arkansas	H	7.53 FQ	11.02 AW	16.37 TQ	ARBLS	10/01-12/01
	Fayetteville-Springdale-Rogers MSA, AR	H	7.59 FQ	10.08 AW	13.72 TQ	ARBLS	10/01-12/01
	Fort Smith MSA, AR-OK	H	7.18 FQ	9.12 AW	11.67 TQ	ARBLS	10/01-12/01
	Little Rock-North Little Rock MSA, AR	H	8.09 FQ	12.84 AW	17.27 TQ	ARBLS	10/01-12/01
	California	H	6.96 FQ	11.39 AW	18.60 TQ	CABLS	10/01-12/01
	Bakersfield MSA, CA	H	7.39 FQ	8.22 AW	8.95 TQ	CABLS	10/01-12/01
	Chico-Paradise MSA, CA	H	7.60 FQ	10.76 AW	13.39 TQ	CABLS	10/01-12/01
	Fresno MSA, CA	H	6.90 FQ	10.28 AW	16.60 TQ	CABLS	10/01-12/01

AAW	Average annual wage	**AOH**	Average offered, high	**ASH**	Average starting, high	**H**	Hourly	**M**	Monthly	**S**	Special: hourly and annual
AE	Average entry wage	**AOL**	Average offered, low	**ASL**	Average starting, low	**HI**	Highest wage paid	**MTC**	Median total compensation	**TQ**	Third quartile wage
AEX	Average experienced wage	**APH**	Average pay, high range	**AW**	Average wage paid	**HR**	High end range	**MW**	Median wage paid	**W**	Weekly
AO	Average offered	**APL**	Average pay, low range	**FQ**	First quartile wage	**LR**	Low end range	**SQ**	Second quartile wage	**Y**	Yearly

Occupation/Type/Industry	Location	Per	Low	Mid	High	Source	Date
Cutting and Slicing Machine Setter, Operator, and Tender	Los Angeles-Long Beach PMSA, CA	H	6.77 FQ	10.85 AW	16.81 TQ	CABLS	10/01-12/01
	Oakland PMSA, CA	H	9.53 FQ	14.63 AW	20.96 TQ	CABLS	10/01-12/01
	Orange County PMSA, CA	H	7.26 FQ	11.62 AW	17.59 TQ	CABLS	10/01-12/01
	Riverside-San Bernardino PMSA, CA	H	7.16 FQ	11.71 AW	18.44 TQ	CABLS	10/01-12/01
	Sacramento PMSA, CA	H	9.02 FQ	12.97 AW	19.15 TQ	CABLS	10/01-12/01
	San Diego MSA, CA	H	6.59 FQ	9.98 AW	16.62 TQ	CABLS	10/01-12/01
	San Francisco PMSA, CA	H	6.81 FQ	14.77 AW	22.12 TQ	CABLS	10/01-12/01
	San Jose PMSA, CA	H	7.83 FQ	13.26 AW	21.54 TQ	CABLS	10/01-12/01
	Santa Rosa PMSA, CA	H	8.14 FQ	12.62 AW	17.88 TQ	CABLS	10/01-12/01
	Stockton-Lodi MSA, CA	H	7.85 FQ	12.24 AW	16.85 TQ	CABLS	10/01-12/01
	Ventura PMSA, CA	H	7.28 FQ	12.47 AW	20.45 TQ	CABLS	10/01-12/01
	Visalia-Tulare-Porterville MSA, CA	H	6.76 FQ	8.84 AW	12.08 TQ	CABLS	10/01-12/01
	Colorado	H	8.77 FQ	13.18 AW	18.94 TQ	COBLS	10/01-12/01
	Colorado Springs MSA, CO	H	7.56 FQ	9.81 AW	12.85 TQ	COBLS	10/01-12/01
	Denver PMSA, CO	H	8.90 FQ	14.05 AW	19.94 TQ	COBLS	10/01-12/01
	Connecticut	H	9.55 FQ	13.88 AW	18.31 TQ	CTBLS	10/01-12/01
	Bridgeport PMSA, CT	H	9.68 FQ	13.71 AW	17.99 TQ	CTBLS	10/01-12/01
	Danbury PMSA, CT	H	9.02 FQ	11.42 AW	15.37 TQ	CTBLS	10/01-12/01
	Hartford MSA, CT	H	10.10 FQ	14.62 AW	19.46 TQ	CTBLS	10/01-12/01
	New Haven-Meriden PMSA, CT	H	8.88 FQ	12.60 AW	16.55 TQ	CTBLS	10/01-12/01
	New London-Norwich MSA, CT-RI	H	9.75 FQ	14.89 AW	20.01 TQ	CTBLS	10/01-12/01
	Stamford-Norwalk PMSA, CT	H	8.79 FQ	13.88 AW	20.56 TQ	CTBLS	10/01-12/01
	Waterbury PMSA, CT	H	11.19 FQ	14.89 AW	19.57 TQ	CTBLS	10/01-12/01
	Delaware	H	10.50 FQ	13.73 AW	16.92 TQ	DEBLS	10/01-12/01
	Wilmington-Newark PMSA, DE-MD	H	9.49 FQ	13.62 AW	17.01 TQ	DEBLS	10/01-12/01
	Washington PMSA, DC-MD-VA-WV	H	6.69 FQ	13.43 AW	20.46 TQ	DCBLS	10/01-12/01
	Florida	H	7.63 FQ	11.33 AW	15.86 TQ	FLBLS	10/01-12/01
	Daytona Beach MSA, FL	H	6.78 FQ	9.23 AW	12.39 TQ	FLBLS	10/01-12/01
	Fort Lauderdale PMSA, FL	H	6.88 FQ	11.41 AW	14.20 TQ	FLBLS	10/01-12/01
	Jacksonville MSA, FL	H	9.92 FQ	12.30 AW	15.21 TQ	FLBLS	10/01-12/01
	Lakeland-Winter Haven MSA, FL	H	8.19 FQ	12.68 AW	16.41 TQ	FLBLS	10/01-12/01
	Miami PMSA, FL	H	7.17 FQ	11.76 AW	19.02 TQ	FLBLS	10/01-12/01
	Orlando MSA, FL	H	8.21 FQ	12.35 AW	17.18 TQ	FLBLS	10/01-12/01
	Sarasota-Bradenton MSA, FL	H	7.07 FQ	11.24 AW	16.23 TQ	FLBLS	10/01-12/01
	Tallahassee MSA, FL	H	7.82 FQ	9.80 AW	11.66 TQ	FLBLS	10/01-12/01
	Tampa-St. Petersburg-Clearwater MSA, FL	H	7.49 FQ	10.10 AW	13.67 TQ	FLBLS	10/01-12/01
	West Palm Beach-Boca Raton MSA, FL	H	6.84 FQ	10.61 AW	15.22 TQ	FLBLS	10/01-12/01
	Georgia	H	7.73 FQ	11.78 AW	17.04 TQ	GABLS	10/01-12/01
	Atlanta MSA, GA	H	7.87 FQ	12.05 AW	16.84 TQ	GABLS	10/01-12/01
	Augusta-Aiken MSA, GA-SC	H	9.38 FQ	12.34 AW	15.68 TQ	GABLS	10/01-12/01
	Columbus MSA, GA-AL	H	7.15 FQ	10.38 AW	13.62 TQ	GABLS	10/01-12/01
	Macon MSA, GA	H	9.18 FQ	12.61 AW	19.82 TQ	GABLS	10/01-12/01
	Savannah MSA, GA	H	10.79 FQ	17.82 AW	23.73 TQ	GABLS	10/01-12/01
	Hawaii	H	7.68 FQ	15.77 AW	22.05 TQ	HIBLS	10/01-12/01
	Honolulu MSA, HI	H	6.90 FQ	14.65 AW	20.67 TQ	HIBLS	10/01-12/01
	Idaho	H	8.23 FQ	12.85 AW	17.32 TQ	IDBLS	10/01-12/01
	Boise City MSA, ID	H	7.56 FQ	12.00 AW	15.90 TQ	IDBLS	10/01-12/01
	Illinois	H	7.54 FQ	12.95 AW	18.40 TQ	ILBLS	10/01-12/01
	Chicago PMSA, IL	H	7.31 FQ	12.94 AW	19.09 TQ	ILBLS	10/01-12/01
	Rockford MSA, IL	H	8.70 FQ	13.75 AW	16.86 TQ	ILBLS	10/01-12/01
	Indiana	H	8.95 FQ	12.93 AW	18.33 TQ	INBLS	10/01-12/01
	Elkhart-Goshen MSA, IN	H	9.02 FQ	11.24 AW	13.81 TQ	INBLS	10/01-12/01
	Evansville-Henderson MSA, IN-KY	H	8.30 FQ	13.88 AW	20.45 TQ	INBLS	10/01-12/01
	Fort Wayne MSA, IN	H	10.20 FQ	15.18 AW	21.25 TQ	INBLS	10/01-12/01
	Gary PMSA, IN	H	8.63 FQ	16.89 AW	24.85 TQ	INBLS	10/01-12/01
	Indianapolis MSA, IN	H	9.15 FQ	13.13 AW	18.17 TQ	INBLS	10/01-12/01
	South Bend MSA, IN	H	8.48 FQ	10.79 AW	13.14 TQ	INBLS	10/01-12/01
	Iowa	H	9.30 FQ	14.25 AW	20.31 TQ	IABLS	10/01-12/01
	Davenport-Moline-Rock Island MSA, IA-IL	H	9.44 FQ	13.40 AW	17.11 TQ	IABLS	10/01-12/01

AAW Average annual wage; AE Average entry wage; AEX Average experienced wage; AO Average offered; AOH Average offered, high; AOL Average offered, low; APH Average pay, high range; APL Average pay, low range; ASH Average starting, high; ASL Average starting, low; AW Average wage paid; FQ First quartile wage; H Hourly; HI Highest wage paid; HR High end range; LR Low end range; M Monthly; MTC Median total compensation; MW Median wage paid; SQ Second quartile wage; S Special: hourly and annual; TQ Third quartile wage; W Weekly; Y Yearly

Occupation/Type/Industry	Location	Per	Low	Mid	High	Source	Date
Cutting and Slicing Machine Setter, Operator, and Tender	Des Moines MSA, IA	H	11.03 FQ	15.34 AW	19.96 TQ	IABLS	10/01-12/01
	Kansas	H	8.53 FQ	11.77 AW	16.46 TQ	KSBLS	10/01-12/01
	Topeka MSA, KS	H	7.78 FQ	11.02 AW	15.26 TQ	KSBLS	10/01-12/01
	Wichita MSA, KS	H	8.48 FQ	11.53 AW	16.90 TQ	KSBLS	10/01-12/01
	Kentucky	H	7.96 FQ	13.40 AW	19.97 TQ	KYBLS	10/01-12/01
	Lexington MSA, KY	H	9.35 FQ	13.54 AW	17.34 TQ	KYBLS	10/01-12/01
	Louisville MSA, KY-IN	H	9.75 FQ	14.58 AW	21.75 TQ	KYBLS	10/01-12/01
	Louisiana	H	7.85 FQ	12.13 AW	16.32 TQ	LABLS	10/01-12/01
	New Orleans MSA, LA	H	7.23 FQ	10.25 AW	14.14 TQ	LABLS	10/01-12/01
	Shreveport-Bossier City MSA, LA	H	7.98 FQ	13.03 AW	17.09 TQ	LABLS	10/01-12/01
	Maine	H	8.78 FQ	12.94 AW	22.74 TQ	MEBLS	10/01-12/01
	Portland MSA, ME	H	9.15 FQ	11.23 AW	13.60 TQ	MEBLS	10/01-12/01
	Maryland	H	6.94 FQ	12.42 AW	18.69 TQ	MDBLS	10/01-12/01
	Baltimore PMSA, MD	H	7.16 FQ	12.80 AW	18.28 TQ	MDBLS	10/01-12/01
	Massachusetts	H	9.99 FQ	14.20 AW	18.41 TQ	MABLS	10/01-12/01
	Boston PMSA, MA-NH	H	10.06 FQ	14.52 AW	20.05 TQ	MABLS	10/01-12/01
	Brockton PMSA, MA	H	8.97 FQ	13.68 AW	21.33 TQ	MABLS	10/01-12/01
	Lawrence PMSA, MA-NH	H	8.89 FQ	12.81 AW	19.06 TQ	MABLS	10/01-12/01
	Lowell PMSA, MA-NH	H	9.92 FQ	14.23 AW	19.89 TQ	MABLS	10/01-12/01
	Springfield MSA, MA	H	8.69 FQ	12.88 AW	16.79 TQ	MABLS	10/01-12/01
	Worcester PMSA, MA-CT	H	11.32 FQ	14.09 AW	17.17 TQ	MABLS	10/01-12/01
	Michigan	H	9.18 FQ	13.95 AW	20.38 TQ	MIBLS	10/01-12/01
	Ann Arbor PMSA, MI	H	8.55 FQ	13.02 AW	16.87 TQ	MIBLS	10/01-12/01
	Detroit PMSA, MI	H	8.59 FQ	15.32 AW	24.21 TQ	MIBLS	10/01-12/01
	Grand Rapids-Muskegon-Holland MSA, MI	H	9.52 FQ	12.87 AW	17.13 TQ	MIBLS	10/01-12/01
	Kalamazoo-Battle Creek MSA, MI	H	10.59 FQ	14.95 AW	20.61 TQ	MIBLS	10/01-12/01
	Minnesota	H	9.53 FQ	14.07 AW	19.53 TQ	MNBLS	10/01-12/01
	Minneapolis-St. Paul MSA, MN-WI	H	11.11 FQ	15.42 AW	20.92 TQ	MNBLS	10/01-12/01
	Mississippi	H	7.42 FQ	10.87 AW	15.02 TQ	MSBLS	10/01-12/01
	Jackson MSA, MS	H	7.26 FQ	10.27 AW	15.51 TQ	MSBLS	10/01-12/01
	Missouri	H	7.60 FQ	11.63 AW	16.98 TQ	MOBLS	10/01-12/01
	Kansas City MSA, MO-KS	H	8.58 FQ	12.82 AW	19.75 TQ	MOBLS	10/01-12/01
	St. Louis MSA, MO-IL	H	8.62 FQ	13.11 AW	17.91 TQ	MOBLS	10/01-12/01
	Springfield MSA, MO	H	7.78 FQ	10.42 AW	13.29 TQ	MOBLS	10/01-12/01
	Montana	H	5.74 FQ	11.74 AW	19.10 TQ	MTBLS	10/01-12/01
	Nebraska	H	7.75 FQ	12.43 AW	18.01 TQ	NEBLS	10/01-12/01
	Lincoln MSA, NE	H	10.39 FQ	16.31 AW	21.31 TQ	NEBLS	10/01-12/01
	Omaha MSA, NE-IA	H	8.89 FQ	12.32 AW	16.19 TQ	NEBLS	10/01-12/01
	Nevada	H	7.68 FQ	12.72 AW	16.91 TQ	NVBLS	10/01-12/01
	Las Vegas MSA, NV-AZ	H	8.15 FQ	13.03 AW	16.88 TQ	NVBLS	10/01-12/01
	New Hampshire	H	8.91 FQ	12.49 AW	16.89 TQ	NHBLS	10/01-12/01
	Manchester PMSA, NH	H	9.89 FQ	12.54 AW	14.96 TQ	NHBLS	10/01-12/01
	Nashua PMSA, NH	H	8.05 FQ	11.39 AW	16.50 TQ	NHBLS	10/01-12/01
	Portsmouth-Rochester PMSA, NH-ME	H	11.48 FQ	14.68 AW	17.53 TQ	NHBLS	10/01-12/01
	New Jersey	H	7.76 FQ	13.06 AW	18.84 TQ	NJBLS	10/01-12/01
	Bergen-Passaic PMSA, NJ	H	8.48 FQ	13.94 AW	20.67 TQ	NJBLS	10/01-12/01
	Jersey City PMSA, NJ	H	7.79 FQ	12.65 AW	19.38 TQ	NJBLS	10/01-12/01
	Middlesex-Somerset-Hunterdon PMSA, NJ	H	8.25 FQ	12.83 AW	17.22 TQ	NJBLS	10/01-12/01
	Monmouth-Ocean PMSA, NJ	H	7.42 FQ	11.08 AW	17.45 TQ	NJBLS	10/01-12/01
	Newark PMSA, NJ	H	7.23 FQ	12.65 AW	20.01 TQ	NJBLS	10/01-12/01
	Trenton PMSA, NJ	H	8.97 FQ	12.73 AW	16.79 TQ	NJBLS	10/01-12/01
	New Mexico	H	6.09 FQ	9.79 AW	16.24 TQ	NMBLS	10/01-12/01
	Albuquerque MSA, NM	H	7.52 FQ	11.55 AW	19.48 TQ	NMBLS	10/01-12/01
	New York	H	7.70 FQ	13.69 AW	20.91 TQ	NYBLS	10/01-12/01
	Albany-Schenectady-Troy MSA, NY	H	7.66 FQ	13.01 AW	19.24 TQ	NYBLS	10/01-12/01
	Buffalo-Niagara Falls MSA, NY	H	9.02 FQ	14.66 AW	20.67 TQ	NYBLS	10/01-12/01
	Dutchess County PMSA, NY	H	11.73 FQ	12.97 AW	14.22 TQ	NYBLS	10/01-12/01
	Nassau-Suffolk PMSA, NY	H	8.13 FQ	13.55 AW	20.12 TQ	NYBLS	10/01-12/01
	New York PMSA, NY	H	6.67 FQ	12.70 AW	21.98 TQ	NYBLS	10/01-12/01
	Newburgh PMSA, NY-PA	H	6.45 FQ	11.33 AW	19.05 TQ	NYBLS	10/01-12/01
	Rochester MSA, NY	H	11.22 FQ	16.66 AW	22.12 TQ	NYBLS	10/01-12/01
	Syracuse MSA, NY	H	7.88 FQ	11.63 AW	16.47 TQ	NYBLS	10/01-12/01
	North Carolina	H	8.84 FQ	13.38 AW	19.75 TQ	NCBLS	10/01-12/01

AAW	Average annual wage	**AOH**	Average offered, high	**ASH**	Average starting, high	**H**	Hourly	**M**	Monthly	**S**	Special: hourly and annual
AE	Average entry wage	**AOL**	Average offered, low	**ASL**	Average starting, low	**HI**	Highest wage paid	**MTC**	Median total compensation	**TQ**	Third quartile wage
AEX	Average experienced wage	**APH**	Average pay, high range	**AW**	Average wage paid	**HR**	High end range	**MW**	Median wage paid	**W**	Weekly
AO	Average offered	**APL**	Average pay, low range	**FQ**	First quartile wage	**LR**	Low end range	**SQ**	Second quartile wage	**Y**	Yearly

Occupation/Type/Industry	Location	Per	Low	Mid	High	Source	Date
Cutting and Slicing Machine Setter, Operator, and Tender	Charlotte-Gastonia-Rock Hill MSA, NC-SC	H	9.42 FQ	13.28 AW	16.98 TQ	NCBLS	10/01-12/01
	Greensboro-Winston-Salem-High Point MSA, NC	H	9.23 FQ	14.90 AW	21.73 TQ	NCBLS	10/01-12/01
	Hickory-Morganton-Lenoir MSA, NC	H	8.24 FQ	10.77 AW	13.59 TQ	NCBLS	10/01-12/01
	Raleigh-Durham-Chapel Hill MSA, NC	H	8.30 FQ	12.09 AW	17.24 TQ	NCBLS	10/01-12/01
	Wilmington MSA, NC	H	7.83 FQ	9.78 AW	11.61 TQ	NCBLS	10/01-12/01
	North Dakota	H	9.24 FQ	13.55 AW	19.36 TQ	NDBLS	10/01-12/01
	Ohio	H	8.16 FQ	12.29 AW	17.02 TQ	OHBLS	10/01-12/01
	Akron PMSA, OH	H	9.10 FQ	13.46 AW	19.19 TQ	OHBLS	10/01-12/01
	Canton-Massillon MSA, OH	H	7.43 FQ	10.71 AW	16.02 TQ	OHBLS	10/01-12/01
	Cincinnati PMSA, OH-KY-IN	H	9.14 FQ	13.50 AW	19.29 TQ	OHBLS	10/01-12/01
	Cleveland-Lorain-Elyria PMSA, OH	H	8.34 FQ	13.43 AW	17.98 TQ	OHBLS	10/01-12/01
	Columbus MSA, OH	H	8.71 FQ	12.47 AW	16.70 TQ	OHBLS	10/01-12/01
	Dayton-Springfield MSA, OH	H	8.35 FQ	11.97 AW	16.32 TQ	OHBLS	10/01-12/01
	Hamilton-Middletown PMSA, OH	H	11.49 FQ	15.77 AW	20.75 TQ	OHBLS	10/01-12/01
	Mansfield MSA, OH	H	8.58 FQ	10.68 AW	12.93 TQ	OHBLS	10/01-12/01
	Youngstown-Warren MSA, OH	H	9.18 FQ	12.11 AW	15.96 TQ	OHBLS	10/01-12/01
	Oklahoma	H	7.17 FQ	11.16 AW	15.81 TQ	OKBLS	10/01-12/01
	Oklahoma City MSA, OK	H	6.24 FQ	10.53 AW	14.65 TQ	OKBLS	10/01-12/01
	Tulsa MSA, OK	H	8.72 FQ	11.84 AW	15.54 TQ	OKBLS	10/01-12/01
	Oregon	H	8.00 FQ	12.54 AW	19.18 TQ	ORBLS	10/01-12/01
	Eugene-Springfield MSA, OR	H	9.13 FQ	14.80 AW	21.46 TQ	ORBLS	10/01-12/01
	Portland-Vancouver PMSA, OR-WA	H	8.12 FQ	12.73 AW	19.40 TQ	ORBLS	10/01-12/01
	Salem PMSA, OR	H	9.56 FQ	13.43 AW	19.73 TQ	ORBLS	10/01-12/01
	Pennsylvania	H	7.74 FQ	12.59 AW	17.61 TQ	PABLS	10/01-12/01
	Allentown-Bethlehem-Easton MSA, PA	H	9.36 FQ	13.84 AW	16.70 TQ	PABLS	10/01-12/01
	Erie MSA, PA	H	8.76 FQ	11.00 AW	17.68 TQ	PABLS	10/01-12/01
	Harrisburg-Lebanon-Carlisle MSA, PA	H	8.68 FQ	13.80 AW	17.31 TQ	PABLS	10/01-12/01
	Lancaster MSA, PA	H	9.07 FQ	12.67 AW	16.76 TQ	PABLS	10/01-12/01
	Philadelphia PMSA, PA-NJ	H	6.64 FQ	12.34 AW	17.80 TQ	PABLS	10/01-12/01
	Pittsburgh MSA, PA	H	9.24 FQ	13.62 AW	19.75 TQ	PABLS	10/01-12/01
	Reading MSA, PA	H	9.27 FQ	11.80 AW	14.17 TQ	PABLS	10/01-12/01
	Scranton-Wilkes-Barre-Hazleton MSA, PA	H	8.61 FQ	12.68 AW	16.25 TQ	PABLS	10/01-12/01
	Rhode Island	H	7.98 FQ	11.89 AW	16.70 TQ	RIBLS	10/01-12/01
	Providence-Fall River-Warwick MSA, RI-MA	H	8.17 FQ	12.36 AW	16.99 TQ	RIBLS	10/01-12/01
	South Carolina	H	8.19 FQ	12.74 AW	17.87 TQ	SCBLS	10/01-12/01
	Greenville-Spartanburg-Anderson MSA, SC	H	7.61 FQ	11.97 AW	17.95 TQ	SCBLS	10/01-12/01
	South Dakota	H	7.71 FQ	10.67 AW	13.45 TQ	SDBLS	10/01-12/01
	Sioux Falls MSA, SD	H	10.97 FQ	12.78 AW	15.74 TQ	SDBLS	10/01-12/01
	Tennessee	H	8.47 FQ	12.51 AW	17.10 TQ	TNBLS	10/01-12/01
	Chattanooga MSA, TN-GA	H	9.31 FQ	12.26 AW	15.92 TQ	TNBLS	10/01-12/01
	Johnson City-Kingsport-Bristol MSA, TN-VA	H	7.17 FQ	10.32 AW	14.57 TQ	TNBLS	10/01-12/01
	Knoxville MSA, TN	H	8.00 FQ	10.57 AW	13.20 TQ	TNBLS	10/01-12/01
	Memphis MSA, TN-AR-MS	H	8.01 FQ	12.65 AW	16.82 TQ	TNBLS	10/01-12/01
	Nashville MSA, TN	H	8.32 FQ	14.52 AW	23.80 TQ	TNBLS	10/01-12/01
	Texas	H	7.36 FQ	11.51 AW	16.86 TQ	TXBLS	10/01-12/01
	Amarillo MSA, TX	H	6.72 FQ	9.16 AW	12.14 TQ	TXBLS	10/01-12/01
	Austin-San Marcos MSA, TX	H	7.37 FQ	10.30 AW	14.42 TQ	TXBLS	10/01-12/01
	Brownsville-Harlingen-San Benito MSA, TX	H	6.40 FQ	11.54 AW	22.51 TQ	TXBLS	10/01-12/01
	Dallas PMSA, TX	H	7.88 FQ	12.75 AW	17.69 TQ	TXBLS	10/01-12/01
	El Paso MSA, TX	H	6.91 FQ	10.09 AW	15.79 TQ	TXBLS	10/01-12/01
	Fort Worth-Arlington PMSA, TX	H	7.73 FQ	10.87 AW	14.87 TQ	TXBLS	10/01-12/01
	Houston PMSA, TX	H	7.29 FQ	12.45 AW	17.43 TQ	TXBLS	10/01-12/01
	McAllen-Edinburg-Mission MSA, TX	H	7.07 FQ	9.33 AW	12.81 TQ	TXBLS	10/01-12/01
	Odessa-Midland MSA, TX	H	7.10 FQ	8.91 AW	12.42 TQ	TXBLS	10/01-12/01
	San Antonio MSA, TX	H	7.76 FQ	10.63 AW	13.87 TQ	TXBLS	10/01-12/01

AAW Average annual wage **AOH** Average offered, high **ASH** Average starting, high **H** Hourly **M** Monthly **S** Special: hourly and annual
AE Average entry wage **AOL** Average offered, low **ASL** Average starting, low **HI** Highest wage paid **MTC** Median total compensation **TQ** Third quartile wage
AEX Average experienced wage **APH** Average pay, high range **AW** Average wage paid **HR** High end range **MW** Median wage paid **W** Weekly
AO Average offered **APL** Average pay, low range **FQ** First quartile wage **LR** Low end range **SQ** Second quartile wage **Y** Yearly

Occupation/Type/Industry	Location	Per	Low	Mid	High	Source	Date
Cutting and Slicing Machine Setter, Operator, and Tender	Waco MSA, TX	H	7.59 FQ	12.61 AW	16.78 TQ	TXBLS	10/01-12/01
	Utah	H	7.61 FQ	11.41 AW	17.57 TQ	UTBLS	10/01-12/01
	Provo-Orem MSA, UT	H	7.25 FQ	8.95 AW	11.23 TQ	UTBLS	10/01-12/01
	Salt Lake City-Ogden MSA, UT	H	9.04 FQ	13.22 AW	19.43 TQ	UTBLS	10/01-12/01
	Vermont	H	8.70 FQ	11.95 AW	15.66 TQ	VTBLS	10/01-12/01
	Virginia	H	8.57 FQ	12.31 AW	17.21 TQ	VABLS	10/01-12/01
	Lynchburg MSA, VA	H	7.23 FQ	12.16 AW	17.84 TQ	VABLS	10/01-12/01
	Norfolk-Virginia Beach-Newport News MSA, VA-NC	H	8.44 FQ	11.80 AW	16.16 TQ	VABLS	10/01-12/01
	Richmond-Petersburg MSA, VA	H	8.86 FQ	11.98 AW	17.05 TQ	VABLS	10/01-12/01
	Roanoke MSA, VA	H	7.22 FQ	10.16 AW	13.74 TQ	VABLS	10/01-12/01
	Washington	H	8.87 FQ	12.96 AW	19.47 TQ	WABLS	10/01-12/01
	Richland-Kennewick-Pasco MSA, WA	H	8.46 FQ	10.73 AW	13.48 TQ	WABLS	10/01-12/01
	Seattle-Bellevue-Everett PMSA, WA	H	9.69 FQ	14.47 AW	20.69 TQ	WABLS	10/01-12/01
	Tacoma PMSA, WA	H	8.79 FQ	14.95 AW	21.01 TQ	WABLS	10/01-12/01
	West Virginia	H	8.53 FQ	13.46 AW	19.80 TQ	WVBLS	10/01-12/01
	Huntington-Ashland MSA, WV-KY-OH	H	7.67 FQ	11.04 AW	15.77 TQ	WVBLS	10/01-12/01
	Wisconsin	H	7.90 FQ	12.26 AW	17.24 TQ	WIBLS	10/01-12/01
	Appleton-Oshkosh-Neenah MSA, WI	H	10.09 FQ	14.28 AW	17.70 TQ	WIBLS	10/01-12/01
	Green Bay MSA, WI	H	7.97 FQ	11.70 AW	16.35 TQ	WIBLS	10/01-12/01
	Madison MSA, WI	H	9.76 FQ	13.93 AW	17.77 TQ	WIBLS	10/01-12/01
	Milwaukee-Waukesha PMSA, WI	H	7.17 FQ	11.92 AW	18.96 TQ	WIBLS	10/01-12/01
	Racine PMSA, WI	H	8.09 FQ	12.31 AW	19.00 TQ	WIBLS	10/01-12/01
	Wyoming	H	8.85 FQ	10.49 AW	13.01 TQ	WYBLS	10/01-12/01
	Puerto Rico	H	5.67 FQ	7.58 AW	10.90 TQ	PRBLS	10/01-12/01
Cutting, Punching, and Press Machine Setter, Operator, and Tender							
Metals and Plastics	Alabama	H	8.02 FQ	11.72 AW	16.13 TQ	ALBLS	10/01-12/01
Metals and Plastics	Birmingham MSA, AL	H	7.88 FQ	11.49 AW	16.23 TQ	ALBLS	10/01-12/01
Metals and Plastics	Huntsville MSA, AL	H	8.15 FQ	11.87 AW	15.79 TQ	ALBLS	10/01-12/01
Metals and Plastics	Mobile MSA, AL	H	7.65 FQ	10.74 AW	15.69 TQ	ALBLS	10/01-12/01
Metals and Plastics	Montgomery MSA, AL	H	7.91 FQ	12.70 AW	19.05 TQ	ALBLS	10/01-12/01
Metals and Plastics	Arizona	H	6.69 FQ	10.10 AW	14.37 TQ	AZBLS	10/01-12/01
Metals and Plastics	Phoenix-Mesa MSA, AZ	H	6.92 FQ	10.36 AW	14.87 TQ	AZBLS	10/01-12/01
Metals and Plastics	Tucson MSA, AZ	H	6.28 FQ	9.46 AW	13.29 TQ	AZBLS	10/01-12/01
Metals and Plastics	Arkansas	H	7.70 FQ	11.38 AW	15.64 TQ	ARBLS	10/01-12/01
Metals and Plastics	Fayetteville-Springdale-Rogers MSA, AR	H	9.47 FQ	12.87 AW	16.59 TQ	ARBLS	10/01-12/01
Metals and Plastics	Fort Smith MSA, AR-OK	H	9.31 FQ	13.38 AW	16.78 TQ	ARBLS	10/01-12/01
Metals and Plastics	Little Rock-North Little Rock MSA, AR	H	7.75 FQ	10.89 AW	14.08 TQ	ARBLS	10/01-12/01
Metals and Plastics	California	H	7.14 FQ	11.74 AW	17.72 TQ	CABLS	10/01-12/01
Metals and Plastics	Bakersfield MSA, CA	H	7.24 FQ	10.81 AW	17.07 TQ	CABLS	10/01-12/01
Metals and Plastics	Chico-Paradise MSA, CA	H	7.36 FQ	11.85 AW	18.73 TQ	CABLS	10/01-12/01
Metals and Plastics	Fresno MSA, CA	H	8.44 FQ	11.50 AW	15.64 TQ	CABLS	10/01-12/01
Metals and Plastics	Los Angeles-Long Beach PMSA, CA	H	7.08 FQ	11.35 AW	17.00 TQ	CABLS	10/01-12/01
Metals and Plastics	Merced MSA, CA	H	6.43 FQ	9.54 AW	14.13 TQ	CABLS	10/01-12/01
Metals and Plastics	Modesto MSA, CA	H	9.57 FQ	13.73 AW	19.27 TQ	CABLS	10/01-12/01
Metals and Plastics	Oakland PMSA, CA	H	8.98 FQ	15.44 AW	23.80 TQ	CABLS	10/01-12/01
Metals and Plastics	Orange County PMSA, CA	H	6.89 FQ	11.12 AW	16.83 TQ	CABLS	10/01-12/01
Metals and Plastics	Riverside-San Bernardino PMSA, CA	H	6.84 FQ	10.59 AW	15.77 TQ	CABLS	10/01-12/01
Metals and Plastics	Sacramento PMSA, CA	H	8.06 FQ	11.33 AW	15.00 TQ	CABLS	10/01-12/01
Metals and Plastics	Salinas MSA, CA	H	6.95 FQ	8.25 AW	8.76 TQ	CABLS	10/01-12/01
Metals and Plastics	San Diego MSA, CA	H	7.32 FQ	11.17 AW	16.61 TQ	CABLS	10/01-12/01
Metals and Plastics	San Francisco PMSA, CA	H	9.02 FQ	16.35 AW	24.99 TQ	CABLS	10/01-12/01
Metals and Plastics	San Jose PMSA, CA	H	8.51 FQ	14.72 AW	21.14 TQ	CABLS	10/01-12/01
Metals and Plastics	San Luis Obispo-Atascadero-Paso Robles MSA, CA	H	7.61 FQ	11.16 AW	16.07 TQ	CABLS	10/01-12/01

Occupation/Type/Industry	Location	Per	Low	Mid	High	Source	Date
Cutting, Punching, and Press Machine Setter, Operator, and Tender							
Metals and Plastics	Santa Barbara-Santa Maria-Lompoc MSA, CA	H	8.29 FQ	11.51 AW	15.78 TQ	CABLS	10/01-12/01
Metals and Plastics	Santa Cruz-Watsonville PMSA, CA	H	7.83 FQ	12.30 AW	18.12 TQ	CABLS	10/01-12/01
Metals and Plastics	Santa Rosa PMSA, CA	H	9.21 FQ	13.38 AW	18.81 TQ	CABLS	10/01-12/01
Metals and Plastics	Stockton-Lodi MSA, CA	H	7.86 FQ	11.56 AW	16.79 TQ	CABLS	10/01-12/01
Metals and Plastics	Vallejo-Fairfield-Napa PMSA, CA	H	7.76 FQ	11.63 AW	16.44 TQ	CABLS	10/01-12/01
Metals and Plastics	Ventura PMSA, CA	H	7.09 FQ	10.69 AW	16.56 TQ	CABLS	10/01-12/01
Metals and Plastics	Visalia-Tulare-Porterville MSA, CA	H	6.73 FQ	10.58 AW	15.22 TQ	CABLS	10/01-12/01
Metals and Plastics	Colorado	H	8.53 FQ	14.37 AW	22.08 TQ	COBLS	10/01-12/01
Metals and Plastics	Boulder-Longmont PMSA, CO	H	8.14 FQ	12.49 AW	18.98 TQ	COBLS	10/01-12/01
Metals and Plastics	Colorado Springs MSA, CO	H	8.65 FQ	11.72 AW	16.21 TQ	COBLS	10/01-12/01
Metals and Plastics	Denver PMSA, CO	H	9.01 FQ	15.59 AW	23.77 TQ	COBLS	10/01-12/01
Metals and Plastics	Fort Collins-Loveland MSA, CO	H	7.39 FQ	10.84 AW	15.54 TQ	COBLS	10/01-12/01
Metals and Plastics	Connecticut	H	9.03 FQ	13.94 AW	20.14 TQ	CTBLS	10/01-12/01
Metals and Plastics	Bridgeport PMSA, CT	H	7.94 FQ	13.19 AW	20.67 TQ	CTBLS	10/01-12/01
Metals and Plastics	Danbury PMSA, CT	H	10.16 FQ	15.16 AW	21.21 TQ	CTBLS	10/01-12/01
Metals and Plastics	Hartford MSA, CT	H	9.62 FQ	14.66 AW	20.90 TQ	CTBLS	10/01-12/01
Metals and Plastics	New Haven-Meriden PMSA, CT	H	9.20 FQ	13.53 AW	17.51 TQ	CTBLS	10/01-12/01
Metals and Plastics	New London-Norwich MSA, CT-RI	H	9.46 FQ	13.37 AW	17.74 TQ	CTBLS	10/01-12/01
Metals and Plastics	Stamford-Norwalk PMSA, CT	H	9.65 FQ	14.80 AW	20.49 TQ	CTBLS	10/01-12/01
Metals and Plastics	Waterbury PMSA, CT	H	9.45 FQ	13.11 AW	17.21 TQ	CTBLS	10/01-12/01
Metals and Plastics	Delaware	H	8.97 FQ	13.20 AW	17.29 TQ	DEBLS	10/01-12/01
Metals and Plastics	Wilmington-Newark PMSA, DE-MD	H	8.51 FQ	13.71 AW	17.73 TQ	DEBLS	10/01-12/01
Metals and Plastics	Washington PMSA, DC-MD-VA-WV	H	8.04 FQ	13.36 AW	18.23 TQ	DCBLS	10/01-12/01
Metals and Plastics	Florida	H	7.23 FQ	10.63 AW	15.65 TQ	FLBLS	10/01-12/01
Metals and Plastics	Daytona Beach MSA, FL	H	7.42 FQ	11.22 AW	15.48 TQ	FLBLS	10/01-12/01
Metals and Plastics	Fort Lauderdale PMSA, FL	H	7.10 FQ	11.14 AW	16.46 TQ	FLBLS	10/01-12/01
Metals and Plastics	Fort Myers-Cape Coral MSA, FL	H	7.88 FQ	10.47 AW	13.37 TQ	FLBLS	10/01-12/01
Metals and Plastics	Fort Pierce-Port St. Lucie MSA, FL	H	8.54 FQ	11.54 AW	15.70 TQ	FLBLS	10/01-12/01
Metals and Plastics	Fort Walton Beach MSA, FL	H	7.46 FQ	10.35 AW	15.91 TQ	FLBLS	10/01-12/01
Metals and Plastics	Jacksonville MSA, FL	H	7.53 FQ	9.92 AW	12.86 TQ	FLBLS	10/01-12/01
Metals and Plastics	Lakeland-Winter Haven MSA, FL	H	7.90 FQ	10.52 AW	13.48 TQ	FLBLS	10/01-12/01
Metals and Plastics	Melbourne-Titusville-Palm Bay MSA, FL	H	7.63 FQ	10.20 AW	13.22 TQ	FLBLS	10/01-12/01
Metals and Plastics	Miami PMSA, FL	H	6.26 FQ	10.21 AW	15.15 TQ	FLBLS	10/01-12/01
Metals and Plastics	Ocala MSA, FL	H	6.30 FQ	9.54 AW	13.40 TQ	FLBLS	10/01-12/01
Metals and Plastics	Orlando MSA, FL	H	7.58 FQ	10.95 AW	15.99 TQ	FLBLS	10/01-12/01
Metals and Plastics	Pensacola MSA, FL	H	6.51 FQ	8.88 AW	12.30 TQ	FLBLS	10/01-12/01
Metals and Plastics	Sarasota-Bradenton MSA, FL	H	7.98 FQ	10.80 AW	13.60 TQ	FLBLS	10/01-12/01
Metals and Plastics	Tampa-St. Petersburg-Clearwater MSA, FL	H	6.64 FQ	9.87 AW	14.52 TQ	FLBLS	10/01-12/01
Metals and Plastics	West Palm Beach-Boca Raton MSA, FL	H	9.27 FQ	13.41 AW	18.21 TQ	FLBLS	10/01-12/01
Metals and Plastics	Georgia	H	8.03 FQ	11.65 AW	16.22 TQ	GABLS	10/01-12/01
Metals and Plastics	Atlanta MSA, GA	H	8.56 FQ	12.17 AW	17.05 TQ	GABLS	10/01-12/01
Metals and Plastics	Augusta-Aiken MSA, GA-SC	H	8.29 FQ	12.76 AW	16.94 TQ	GABLS	10/01-12/01
Metals and Plastics	Macon MSA, GA	H	7.30 FQ	13.85 AW	20.99 TQ	GABLS	10/01-12/01
Metals and Plastics	Savannah MSA, GA	H	7.67 FQ	10.34 AW	13.31 TQ	GABLS	10/01-12/01
Metals and Plastics	Hawaii	H	9.54 FQ	15.06 AW	21.90 TQ	HIBLS	10/01-12/01
Metals and Plastics	Honolulu MSA, HI	H	9.43 FQ	14.50 AW	21.05 TQ	HIBLS	10/01-12/01
Metals and Plastics	Idaho	H	7.49 FQ	10.34 AW	13.75 TQ	IDBLS	10/01-12/01
Metals and Plastics	Boise City MSA, ID	H	7.43 FQ	9.98 AW	13.60 TQ	IDBLS	10/01-12/01
Metals and Plastics	Illinois	H	7.37 FQ	11.74 AW	16.69 TQ	ILBLS	10/01-12/01
Metals and Plastics	Champaign-Urbana MSA, IL	H	10.04 FQ	12.84 AW	15.94 TQ	ILBLS	10/01-12/01
Metals and Plastics	Chicago PMSA, IL	H	7.43 FQ	11.65 AW	16.51 TQ	ILBLS	10/01-12/01
Metals and Plastics	Peoria-Pekin MSA, IL	H	8.24 FQ	11.85 AW	16.43 TQ	ILBLS	10/01-12/01
Metals and Plastics	Rockford MSA, IL	H	6.94 FQ	11.50 AW	16.53 TQ	ILBLS	10/01-12/01
Metals and Plastics	Indiana	H	8.57 FQ	13.00 AW	19.62 TQ	INBLS	10/01-12/01

AAW	Average annual wage	**AOH**	Average offered, high	**ASH**	Average starting, high	**H**	Hourly	**M**	Monthly	**S**	Special: hourly and annual
AE	Average entry wage	**AOL**	Average offered, low	**ASL**	Average starting, low	**HI**	Highest wage paid	**MTC**	Median total compensation	**TQ**	Third quartile wage
AEX	Average experienced wage	**APH**	Average pay, high range	**AW**	Average wage paid	**HR**	High end range	**MW**	Median wage paid	**W**	Weekly
AO	Average offered	**APL**	Average pay, low range	**FQ**	First quartile wage	**LR**	Low end range	**SQ**	Second quartile wage	**Y**	Yearly

Occupation/Type/Industry	Location	Per	Low	Mid	High	Source	Date
Cutting, Punching, and Press Machine Setter, Operator, and Tender							
Metals and Plastics	Elkhart-Goshen MSA, IN	H	7.58 FQ	10.97 AW	14.78 TQ	INBLS	10/01-12/01
Metals and Plastics	Evansville-Henderson MSA, IN-KY	H	9.19 FQ	11.61 AW	13.98 TQ	INBLS	10/01-12/01
Metals and Plastics	Fort Wayne MSA, IN	H	8.88 FQ	12.54 AW	17.00 TQ	INBLS	10/01-12/01
Metals and Plastics	Gary PMSA, IN	H	10.16 FQ	16.90 AW	21.75 TQ	INBLS	10/01-12/01
Metals and Plastics	Indianapolis MSA, IN	H	7.83 FQ	13.70 AW	24.84 TQ	INBLS	10/01-12/01
Metals and Plastics	Lafayette MSA, IN	H	8.77 FQ	12.61 AW	17.91 TQ	INBLS	10/01-12/01
Metals and Plastics	South Bend MSA, IN	H	8.74 FQ	10.57 AW	13.38 TQ	INBLS	10/01-12/01
Metals and Plastics	Iowa	H	8.63 FQ	12.64 AW	16.96 TQ	IABLS	10/01-12/01
Metals and Plastics	Cedar Rapids MSA, IA	H	9.78 FQ	15.46 AW	21.04 TQ	IABLS	10/01-12/01
Metals and Plastics	Davenport-Moline-Rock Island MSA, IA-IL	H	9.01 FQ	12.01 AW	16.29 TQ	IABLS	10/01-12/01
Metals and Plastics	Des Moines MSA, IA	H	7.92 FQ	11.63 AW	16.72 TQ	IABLS	10/01-12/01
Metals and Plastics	Kansas	H	8.04 FQ	13.01 AW	19.99 TQ	KSBLS	10/01-12/01
Metals and Plastics	Topeka MSA, KS	H	10.50 FQ	13.33 AW	16.72 TQ	KSBLS	10/01-12/01
Metals and Plastics	Wichita MSA, KS	H	9.46 FQ	15.83 AW	24.85 TQ	KSBLS	10/01-12/01
Metals and Plastics	Kentucky	H	7.74 FQ	11.69 AW	16.38 TQ	KYBLS	10/01-12/01
Metals and Plastics	Lexington MSA, KY	H	7.62 FQ	11.91 AW	16.82 TQ	KYBLS	10/01-12/01
Metals and Plastics	Louisville MSA, KY-IN	H	7.66 FQ	11.34 AW	15.83 TQ	KYBLS	10/01-12/01
Metals and Plastics	Louisiana	H	6.93 FQ	10.24 AW	13.87 TQ	LABLS	10/01-12/01
Metals and Plastics	Baton Rouge MSA, LA	H	6.40 FQ	9.79 AW	13.84 TQ	LABLS	10/01-12/01
Metals and Plastics	Lafayette MSA, LA	H	7.47 FQ	10.43 AW	14.84 TQ	LABLS	10/01-12/01
Metals and Plastics	New Orleans MSA, LA	H	7.13 FQ	10.97 AW	15.71 TQ	LABLS	10/01-12/01
Metals and Plastics	Shreveport-Bossier City MSA, LA	H	6.65 FQ	9.67 AW	13.02 TQ	LABLS	10/01-12/01
Metals and Plastics	Maine	H	8.25 FQ	12.50 AW	16.77 TQ	MEBLS	10/01-12/01
Metals and Plastics	Portland MSA, ME	H	8.22 FQ	11.81 AW	16.75 TQ	MEBLS	10/01-12/01
Metals and Plastics	Maryland	H	8.95 FQ	13.65 AW	20.00 TQ	MDBLS	10/01-12/01
Metals and Plastics	Baltimore PMSA, MD	H	9.09 FQ	13.48 AW	19.07 TQ	MDBLS	10/01-12/01
Metals and Plastics	Massachusetts	H	8.52 FQ	13.37 AW	19.10 TQ	MABLS	10/01-12/01
Metals and Plastics	Boston PMSA, MA-NH	H	8.60 FQ	13.98 AW	20.36 TQ	MABLS	10/01-12/01
Metals and Plastics	Brockton PMSA, MA	H	9.22 FQ	13.24 AW	18.92 TQ	MABLS	10/01-12/01
Metals and Plastics	Lawrence PMSA, MA-NH	H	8.12 FQ	12.09 AW	17.14 TQ	MABLS	10/01-12/01
Metals and Plastics	Lowell PMSA, MA-NH	H	8.54 FQ	14.57 AW	20.82 TQ	MABLS	10/01-12/01
Metals and Plastics	New Bedford PMSA, MA	H	8.97 FQ	14.37 AW	20.16 TQ	MABLS	10/01-12/01
Metals and Plastics	Springfield MSA, MA	H	8.66 FQ	13.42 AW	18.64 TQ	MABLS	10/01-12/01
Metals and Plastics	Worcester PMSA, MA-CT	H	8.63 FQ	12.49 AW	16.68 TQ	MABLS	10/01-12/01
Metals and Plastics	Michigan	H	8.07 FQ	13.04 AW	21.04 TQ	MIBLS	10/01-12/01
Metals and Plastics	Ann Arbor PMSA, MI	H	8.85 FQ	12.80 AW	23.16 TQ	MIBLS	10/01-12/01
Metals and Plastics	Detroit PMSA, MI	H	7.79 FQ	12.88 AW	24.48 TQ	MIBLS	10/01-12/01
Metals and Plastics	Flint PMSA, MI	H	7.70 FQ	18.63 AW	27.76 TQ	MIBLS	10/01-12/01
Metals and Plastics	Grand Rapids-Muskegon-Holland MSA, MI	H	8.31 FQ	12.68 AW	17.14 TQ	MIBLS	10/01-12/01
Metals and Plastics	Kalamazoo-Battle Creek MSA, MI	H	8.21 FQ	11.65 AW	15.43 TQ	MIBLS	10/01-12/01
Metals and Plastics	Lansing-East Lansing MSA, MI	H	9.07 FQ	14.08 AW	20.12 TQ	MIBLS	10/01-12/01
Metals and Plastics	Saginaw-Bay City-Midland MSA, MI	H	9.43 FQ	16.89 AW	26.23 TQ	MIBLS	10/01-12/01
Metals and Plastics	Minnesota	H	9.12 FQ	12.70 AW	17.38 TQ	MNBLS	10/01-12/01
Metals and Plastics	Duluth-Superior MSA, MN-WI	H	8.05 FQ	12.61 AW	19.52 TQ	MNBLS	10/01-12/01
Metals and Plastics	Minneapolis-St. Paul MSA, MN-WI	H	9.25 FQ	13.70 AW	18.52 TQ	MNBLS	10/01-12/01
Metals and Plastics	Mississippi	H	7.62 FQ	10.65 AW	13.67 TQ	MSBLS	10/01-12/01
Metals and Plastics	Biloxi-Gulfport-Pascagoula MSA, MS	H	8.88 FQ	11.26 AW	15.25 TQ	MSBLS	10/01-12/01
Metals and Plastics	Jackson MSA, MS	H	7.07 FQ	9.39 AW	12.94 TQ	MSBLS	10/01-12/01
Metals and Plastics	Missouri	H	7.71 FQ	11.52 AW	16.10 TQ	MOBLS	10/01-12/01
Metals and Plastics	Kansas City MSA, MO-KS	H	7.66 FQ	12.39 AW	17.75 TQ	MOBLS	10/01-12/01
Metals and Plastics	St. Louis MSA, MO-IL	H	7.26 FQ	11.44 AW	16.16 TQ	MOBLS	10/01-12/01
Metals and Plastics	Springfield MSA, MO	H	9.12 FQ	12.91 AW	17.26 TQ	MOBLS	10/01-12/01
Metals and Plastics	Montana	H	7.28 FQ	11.47 AW	17.00 TQ	MTBLS	10/01-12/01
Metals and Plastics	Billings MSA, MT	H	7.73 FQ	13.64 AW	20.87 TQ	MTBLS	10/01-12/01
Metals and Plastics	Nebraska	H	7.89 FQ	11.62 AW	15.86 TQ	NEBLS	10/01-12/01
Metals and Plastics	Lincoln MSA, NE	H	8.54 FQ	12.00 AW	18.78 TQ	NEBLS	10/01-12/01
Metals and Plastics	Omaha MSA, NE-IA	H	7.26 FQ	11.73 AW	18.20 TQ	NEBLS	10/01-12/01
Metals and Plastics	Nevada	H	8.08 FQ	12.67 AW	18.42 TQ	NVBLS	10/01-12/01
Metals and Plastics	Las Vegas MSA, NV-AZ	H	7.59 FQ	12.50 AW	18.23 TQ	NVBLS	10/01-12/01
Metals and Plastics	Reno MSA, NV	H	9.22 FQ	13.21 AW	18.93 TQ	NVBLS	10/01-12/01
Metals and Plastics	New Hampshire	H	7.93 FQ	11.26 AW	15.25 TQ	NHBLS	10/01-12/01

AAW	Average annual wage	**AOH**	Average offered, high	**ASH**	Average starting, high	**H**	Hourly	**M**	Monthly	**S**	Special: hourly and annual
AE	Average entry wage	**AOL**	Average offered, low	**ASL**	Average starting, low	**HI**	Highest wage paid	**MTC**	Median total compensation	**TQ**	Third quartile wage
AEX	Average experienced wage	**APH**	Average pay, high range	**AW**	Average wage paid	**HR**	High end range	**MW**	Median wage paid	**W**	Weekly
AO	Average offered	**APL**	Average pay, low range	**FQ**	First quartile wage	**LR**	Low end range	**SQ**	Second quartile wage	**Y**	Yearly

Occupation/Type/Industry	Location	Per	Low	Mid	High	Source	Date
Cutting, Punching, and Press Machine Setter, Operator, and Tender							
Metals and Plastics	Manchester PMSA, NH	H	7.81 FQ	11.04 AW	13.88 TQ	NHBLS	10/01-12/01
Metals and Plastics	Nashua PMSA, NH	H	7.97 FQ	11.48 AW	15.77 TQ	NHBLS	10/01-12/01
Metals and Plastics	Portsmouth-Rochester PMSA, NH-ME	H	8.34 FQ	11.69 AW	15.45 TQ	NHBLS	10/01-12/01
Metals and Plastics	New Jersey	H	7.35 FQ	12.12 AW	17.98 TQ	NJBLS	10/01-12/01
Metals and Plastics	Bergen-Passaic PMSA, NJ	H	7.63 FQ	12.78 AW	18.86 TQ	NJBLS	10/01-12/01
Metals and Plastics	Jersey City PMSA, NJ	H	6.71 FQ	11.54 AW	17.20 TQ	NJBLS	10/01-12/01
Metals and Plastics	Middlesex-Somerset-Hunterdon PMSA, NJ	H	7.27 FQ	11.51 AW	17.13 TQ	NJBLS	10/01-12/01
Metals and Plastics	Monmouth-Ocean PMSA, NJ	H	7.45 FQ	11.26 AW	17.32 TQ	NJBLS	10/01-12/01
Metals and Plastics	Newark PMSA, NJ	H	7.10 FQ	11.66 AW	17.37 TQ	NJBLS	10/01-12/01
Metals and Plastics	Trenton PMSA, NJ	H	7.69 FQ	12.42 AW	17.08 TQ	NJBLS	10/01-12/01
Metals and Plastics	New Mexico	H	7.22 FQ	10.37 AW	14.04 TQ	NMBLS	10/01-12/01
Metals and Plastics	Albuquerque MSA, NM	H	7.58 FQ	11.10 AW	15.16 TQ	NMBLS	10/01-12/01
Metals and Plastics	New York	H	7.28 FQ	11.74 AW	17.40 TQ	NYBLS	10/01-12/01
Metals and Plastics	Albany-Schenectady-Troy MSA, NY	H	8.10 FQ	13.02 AW	23.13 TQ	NYBLS	10/01-12/01
Metals and Plastics	Binghamton MSA, NY	H	7.54 FQ	10.20 AW	13.36 TQ	NYBLS	10/01-12/01
Metals and Plastics	Buffalo-Niagara Falls MSA, NY	H	7.64 FQ	12.12 AW	18.03 TQ	NYBLS	10/01-12/01
Metals and Plastics	Dutchess County PMSA, NY	H	6.56 FQ	13.77 AW	22.15 TQ	NYBLS	10/01-12/01
Metals and Plastics	Nassau-Suffolk PMSA, NY	H	7.02 FQ	11.85 AW	18.19 TQ	NYBLS	10/01-12/01
Metals and Plastics	New York PMSA, NY	H	6.46 FQ	10.38 AW	15.90 TQ	NYBLS	10/01-12/01
Metals and Plastics	Newburgh PMSA, NY-PA	H	7.85 FQ	14.61 AW	24.07 TQ	NYBLS	10/01-12/01
Metals and Plastics	Rochester MSA, NY	H	7.78 FQ	11.77 AW	17.32 TQ	NYBLS	10/01-12/01
Metals and Plastics	Syracuse MSA, NY	H	7.65 FQ	12.41 AW	16.79 TQ	NYBLS	10/01-12/01
Metals and Plastics	Utica-Rome MSA, NY	H	7.59 FQ	12.83 AW	17.78 TQ	NYBLS	10/01-12/01
Metals and Plastics	North Carolina	H	7.75 FQ	11.48 AW	15.93 TQ	NCBLS	10/01-12/01
Metals and Plastics	Asheville MSA, NC	H	8.29 FQ	12.33 AW	16.76 TQ	NCBLS	10/01-12/01
Metals and Plastics	Charlotte-Gastonia-Rock Hill MSA, NC-SC	H	8.19 FQ	11.97 AW	16.56 TQ	NCBLS	10/01-12/01
Metals and Plastics	Greensboro-Winston-Salem-High Point MSA, NC	H	7.87 FQ	11.50 AW	15.89 TQ	NCBLS	10/01-12/01
Metals and Plastics	Hickory-Morganton-Lenoir MSA, NC	H	7.72 FQ	10.84 AW	15.11 TQ	NCBLS	10/01-12/01
Metals and Plastics	Raleigh-Durham-Chapel Hill MSA, NC	H	7.79 FQ	11.62 AW	16.56 TQ	NCBLS	10/01-12/01
Metals and Plastics	Wilmington MSA, NC	H	7.75 FQ	10.39 AW	13.49 TQ	NCBLS	10/01-12/01
Metals and Plastics	North Dakota	H	7.54 FQ	11.17 AW	16.49 TQ	NDBLS	10/01-12/01
Metals and Plastics	Fargo-Moorhead MSA, ND-MN	H	7.38 FQ	9.30 AW	12.44 TQ	NDBLS	10/01-12/01
Metals and Plastics	Ohio	H	8.25 FQ	12.80 AW	17.85 TQ	OHBLS	10/01-12/01
Metals and Plastics	Akron PMSA, OH	H	8.15 FQ	11.74 AW	16.76 TQ	OHBLS	10/01-12/01
Metals and Plastics	Canton-Massillon MSA, OH	H	7.80 FQ	12.50 AW	16.91 TQ	OHBLS	10/01-12/01
Metals and Plastics	Cincinnati PMSA, OH-KY-IN	H	8.81 FQ	13.63 AW	19.35 TQ	OHBLS	10/01-12/01
Metals and Plastics	Cleveland-Lorain-Elyria PMSA, OH	H	8.18 FQ	12.83 AW	17.73 TQ	OHBLS	10/01-12/01
Metals and Plastics	Columbus MSA, OH	H	7.82 FQ	12.23 AW	19.41 TQ	OHBLS	10/01-12/01
Metals and Plastics	Dayton-Springfield MSA, OH	H	7.88 FQ	12.49 AW	21.70 TQ	OHBLS	10/01-12/01
Metals and Plastics	Hamilton-Middletown PMSA, OH	H	9.80 FQ	14.68 AW	20.54 TQ	OHBLS	10/01-12/01
Metals and Plastics	Mansfield MSA, OH	H	7.92 FQ	13.64 AW	25.75 TQ	OHBLS	10/01-12/01
Metals and Plastics	Toledo MSA, OH	H	8.56 FQ	13.75 AW	18.70 TQ	OHBLS	10/01-12/01
Metals and Plastics	Youngstown-Warren MSA, OH	H	8.30 FQ	14.95 AW	25.75 TQ	OHBLS	10/01-12/01
Metals and Plastics	Oklahoma	H	7.46 FQ	11.05 AW	15.83 TQ	OKBLS	10/01-12/01
Metals and Plastics	Oklahoma City MSA, OK	H	7.51 FQ	12.20 AW	17.27 TQ	OKBLS	10/01-12/01
Metals and Plastics	Tulsa MSA, OK	H	8.19 FQ	11.50 AW	15.67 TQ	OKBLS	10/01-12/01
Metals and Plastics	Oregon	H	9.08 FQ	13.29 AW	18.19 TQ	ORBLS	10/01-12/01
Metals and Plastics	Eugene-Springfield MSA, OR	H	8.49 FQ	11.05 AW	14.01 TQ	ORBLS	10/01-12/01
Metals and Plastics	Medford-Ashland MSA, OR	H	9.38 FQ	13.34 AW	17.25 TQ	ORBLS	10/01-12/01
Metals and Plastics	Portland-Vancouver PMSA, OR-WA	H	8.96 FQ	13.67 AW	19.49 TQ	ORBLS	10/01-12/01
Metals and Plastics	Salem PMSA, OR	H	8.45 FQ	12.77 AW	17.54 TQ	ORBLS	10/01-12/01
Metals and Plastics	Pennsylvania	H	8.64 FQ	13.25 AW	18.61 TQ	PABLS	10/01-12/01
Metals and Plastics	Allentown-Bethlehem-Easton MSA, PA	H	7.72 FQ	11.53 AW	16.74 TQ	PABLS	10/01-12/01
Metals and Plastics	Erie MSA, PA	H	7.88 FQ	10.89 AW	14.73 TQ	PABLS	10/01-12/01
Metals and Plastics	Harrisburg-Lebanon-Carlisle MSA, PA	H	8.52 FQ	13.95 AW	18.06 TQ	PABLS	10/01-12/01

AAW Average annual wage **AOH** Average offered, high **ASH** Average starting, high **H** Hourly **M** Monthly **S** Special: hourly and annual
AE Average entry wage **AOL** Average offered, low **ASL** Average starting, low **HI** Highest wage paid **MTC** Median total compensation **TQ** Third quartile wage
AEX Average experienced wage **APH** Average pay, high range **AW** Average wage paid **HR** High end range **MW** Median wage paid **W** Weekly
AO Average offered **APL** Average pay, low range **FQ** First quartile wage **LR** Low end range **SQ** Second quartile wage **Y** Yearly

Occupation/Type/Industry	Location	Per	Low	Mid	High	Source	Date
Cutting, Punching, and Press Machine Setter, Operator, and Tender							
Metals and Plastics	Johnstown MSA, PA	H	9.49 FQ	12.75 AW	16.64 TQ	PABLS	10/01-12/01
Metals and Plastics	Lancaster MSA, PA	H	9.59 FQ	14.59 AW	20.07 TQ	PABLS	10/01-12/01
Metals and Plastics	Philadelphia PMSA, PA-NJ	H	9.31 FQ	14.43 AW	20.02 TQ	PABLS	10/01-12/01
Metals and Plastics	Pittsburgh MSA, PA	H	8.34 FQ	13.00 AW	19.64 TQ	PABLS	10/01-12/01
Metals and Plastics	Reading MSA, PA	H	9.18 FQ	13.99 AW	17.38 TQ	PABLS	10/01-12/01
Metals and Plastics	Scranton-Wilkes-Barre-Hazleton MSA, PA	H	8.73 FQ	14.00 AW	19.39 TQ	PABLS	10/01-12/01
Metals and Plastics	York MSA, PA	H	9.18 FQ	13.54 AW	20.17 TQ	PABLS	10/01-12/01
Metals and Plastics	Rhode Island	H	7.28 FQ	10.38 AW	15.44 TQ	RIBLS	10/01-12/01
Metals and Plastics	Providence-Fall River-Warwick MSA, RI-MA	H	7.38 FQ	10.93 AW	16.10 TQ	RIBLS	10/01-12/01
Metals and Plastics	South Carolina	H	8.00 FQ	12.49 AW	17.07 TQ	SCBLS	10/01-12/01
Metals and Plastics	Charleston-North Charleston MSA, SC	H	7.32 FQ	11.36 AW	19.66 TQ	SCBLS	10/01-12/01
Metals and Plastics	Columbia MSA, SC	H	9.33 FQ	14.83 AW	22.61 TQ	SCBLS	10/01-12/01
Metals and Plastics	Greenville-Spartanburg-Anderson MSA, SC	H	7.76 FQ	12.08 AW	16.77 TQ	SCBLS	10/01-12/01
Metals and Plastics	South Dakota	H	9.13 FQ	12.21 AW	16.34 TQ	SDBLS	10/01-12/01
Metals and Plastics	Sioux Falls MSA, SD	H	9.27 FQ	12.78 AW	17.88 TQ	SDBLS	10/01-12/01
Metals and Plastics	Tennessee	H	7.79 FQ	11.19 AW	14.81 TQ	TNBLS	10/01-12/01
Metals and Plastics	Chattanooga MSA, TN-GA	H	9.05 FQ	11.29 AW	14.00 TQ	TNBLS	10/01-12/01
Metals and Plastics	Clarksville-Hopkinsville MSA, TN-KY	H	9.49 FQ	12.17 AW	14.70 TQ	TNBLS	10/01-12/01
Metals and Plastics	Johnson City-Kingsport-Bristol MSA, TN-VA	H	6.86 FQ	9.85 AW	13.86 TQ	TNBLS	10/01-12/01
Metals and Plastics	Knoxville MSA, TN	H	7.66 FQ	11.40 AW	15.75 TQ	TNBLS	10/01-12/01
Metals and Plastics	Memphis MSA, TN-AR-MS	H	7.72 FQ	11.25 AW	14.27 TQ	TNBLS	10/01-12/01
Metals and Plastics	Nashville MSA, TN	H	8.01 FQ	11.76 AW	15.16 TQ	TNBLS	10/01-12/01
Metals and Plastics	Texas	H	7.35 FQ	10.35 AW	14.39 TQ	TXBLS	10/01-12/01
Metals and Plastics	Austin-San Marcos MSA, TX	H	7.66 FQ	11.16 AW	16.37 TQ	TXBLS	10/01-12/01
Metals and Plastics	Beaumont-Port Arthur MSA, TX	H	8.09 FQ	10.49 AW	13.27 TQ	TXBLS	10/01-12/01
Metals and Plastics	Brazoria PMSA, TX	H	6.54 FQ	10.01 AW	13.02 TQ	TXBLS	10/01-12/01
Metals and Plastics	Brownsville-Harlingen-San Benito MSA, TX	H	6.66 FQ	8.67 AW	11.72 TQ	TXBLS	10/01-12/01
Metals and Plastics	Corpus Christi MSA, TX	H	6.15 FQ	9.01 AW	11.92 TQ	TXBLS	10/01-12/01
Metals and Plastics	Dallas PMSA, TX	H	7.63 FQ	10.95 AW	15.47 TQ	TXBLS	10/01-12/01
Metals and Plastics	El Paso MSA, TX	H	6.09 FQ	9.11 AW	13.42 TQ	TXBLS	10/01-12/01
Metals and Plastics	Fort Worth-Arlington PMSA, TX	H	7.53 FQ	10.27 AW	13.89 TQ	TXBLS	10/01-12/01
Metals and Plastics	Houston PMSA, TX	H	7.30 FQ	10.28 AW	14.50 TQ	TXBLS	10/01-12/01
Metals and Plastics	Killeen-Temple MSA, TX	H	7.02 FQ	9.12 AW	11.08 TQ	TXBLS	10/01-12/01
Metals and Plastics	Longview-Marshall MSA, TX	H	5.88 FQ	9.02 AW	13.09 TQ	TXBLS	10/01-12/01
Metals and Plastics	Lubbock MSA, TX	H	7.15 FQ	9.97 AW	13.82 TQ	TXBLS	10/01-12/01
Metals and Plastics	Odessa-Midland MSA, TX	H	7.37 FQ	9.44 AW	12.88 TQ	TXBLS	10/01-12/01
Metals and Plastics	San Antonio MSA, TX	H	7.34 FQ	9.14 AW	11.96 TQ	TXBLS	10/01-12/01
Metals and Plastics	Tyler MSA, TX	H	6.48 FQ	10.15 AW	13.58 TQ	TXBLS	10/01-12/01
Metals and Plastics	Utah	H	8.15 FQ	11.29 AW	14.72 TQ	UTBLS	10/01-12/01
Metals and Plastics	Provo-Orem MSA, UT	H	8.98 FQ	12.54 AW	17.13 TQ	UTBLS	10/01-12/01
Metals and Plastics	Salt Lake City-Ogden MSA, UT	H	8.04 FQ	11.01 AW	14.12 TQ	UTBLS	10/01-12/01
Metals and Plastics	Vermont	H	7.65 FQ	10.97 AW	14.67 TQ	VTBLS	10/01-12/01
Metals and Plastics	Burlington MSA, VT	H	8.93 FQ	11.41 AW	14.24 TQ	VTBLS	10/01-12/01
Metals and Plastics	Virginia	H	8.52 FQ	12.17 AW	16.68 TQ	VABLS	10/01-12/01
Metals and Plastics	Lynchburg MSA, VA	H	8.52 FQ	11.97 AW	15.19 TQ	VABLS	10/01-12/01
Metals and Plastics	Norfolk-Virginia Beach-Newport News MSA, VA-NC	H	7.60 FQ	12.16 AW	17.01 TQ	VABLS	10/01-12/01
Metals and Plastics	Richmond-Petersburg MSA, VA	H	9.29 FQ	12.50 AW	16.78 TQ	VABLS	10/01-12/01
Metals and Plastics	Roanoke MSA, VA	H	8.28 FQ	12.48 AW	16.55 TQ	VABLS	10/01-12/01
Metals and Plastics	Washington	H	8.65 FQ	13.27 AW	19.16 TQ	WABLS	10/01-12/01
Metals and Plastics	Seattle-Bellevue-Everett PMSA, WA	H	9.47 FQ	13.65 AW	19.09 TQ	WABLS	10/01-12/01
Metals and Plastics	Spokane MSA, WA	H	7.56 FQ	11.05 AW	15.44 TQ	WABLS	10/01-12/01
Metals and Plastics	Tacoma PMSA, WA	H	8.91 FQ	13.56 AW	23.52 TQ	WABLS	10/01-12/01
Metals and Plastics	Yakima MSA, WA	H	7.95 FQ	11.82 AW	16.65 TQ	WABLS	10/01-12/01
Metals and Plastics	West Virginia	H	7.32 FQ	10.86 AW	16.08 TQ	WVBLS	10/01-12/01
Metals and Plastics	Charleston MSA, WV	H	7.20 FQ	8.37 AW	9.23 TQ	WVBLS	10/01-12/01

AAW Average annual wage; AE Average entry wage; AEX Average experienced wage; AO Average offered; AOH Average offered, high; AOL Average offered, low; APH Average pay, high range; APL Average pay, low range; ASH Average starting, high; ASL Average starting, low; AW Average wage paid; FQ First quartile wage; H Hourly; HI Highest wage paid; HR High end range; LR Low end range; M Monthly; MTC Median total compensation; MW Median wage paid; SQ Second quartile wage; S Special: hourly and annual; TQ Third quartile wage; W Weekly; Y Yearly

Occupation/Type/Industry	Location	Per	Low	Mid	High	Source	Date
Cutting, Punching, and Press Machine Setter, Operator, and Tender							
Metals and Plastics	Huntington-Ashland MSA, WV-KY-OH	H	7.34 FQ	11.77 AW	16.74 TQ	WVBLS	10/01-12/01
Metals and Plastics	Wisconsin	H	8.91 FQ	12.84 AW	17.41 TQ	WIBLS	10/01-12/01
Metals and Plastics	Appleton-Oshkosh-Neenah MSA, WI	H	9.97 FQ	13.52 AW	17.27 TQ	WIBLS	10/01-12/01
Metals and Plastics	Green Bay MSA, WI	H	9.79 FQ	12.97 AW	16.56 TQ	WIBLS	10/01-12/01
Metals and Plastics	Madison MSA, WI	H	9.14 FQ	12.75 AW	16.95 TQ	WIBLS	10/01-12/01
Metals and Plastics	Milwaukee-Waukesha PMSA, WI	H	8.83 FQ	13.16 AW	19.63 TQ	WIBLS	10/01-12/01
Metals and Plastics	Racine PMSA, WI	H	8.26 FQ	12.59 AW	19.37 TQ	WIBLS	10/01-12/01
Metals and Plastics	Wyoming	H	7.42 FQ	10.65 AW	13.81 TQ	WYBLS	10/01-12/01
Metals and Plastics	Puerto Rico	H	5.82 FQ	7.80 AW	10.56 TQ	PRBLS	10/01-12/01
Dancer	Arizona	Y	11810 FQ	17100 AW	26950 TQ	AZBLS	10/01-12/01
	Phoenix-Mesa MSA, AZ	Y	11610 FQ	19500 AW	28640 TQ	AZBLS	10/01-12/01
	California	Y	13320 FQ	26640 AW	55370 TQ	CABLS	10/01-12/01
	Los Angeles-Long Beach PMSA, CA	Y	13280 FQ	21400 AW	43230 TQ	CABLS	10/01-12/01
	Orange County PMSA, CA	Y	16730 FQ	45020 AW	71890 TQ	CABLS	10/01-12/01
	Sacramento PMSA, CA	Y	18950 FQ	31860 AW	52100 TQ	CABLS	10/01-12/01
	San Francisco PMSA, CA	Y	14100 FQ	39590 AW	57400 TQ	CABLS	10/01-12/01
	San Jose PMSA, CA	Y	14320 FQ	37400 AW	75900 TQ	CABLS	10/01-12/01
	Connecticut	Y	25040 FQ	41070 AW	60180 TQ	CTBLS	10/01-12/01
	Hartford MSA, CT	Y	26530 FQ	42580 AW	60270 TQ	CTBLS	10/01-12/01
	Washington PMSA, DC-MD-VA-WV	Y	20070 FQ	41750 AW	60850 TQ	DCBLS	10/01-12/01
	Florida	Y	13080 FQ	24370 AW	30340 TQ	FLBLS	10/01-12/01
	Miami PMSA, FL	Y	11680 FQ	16100 AW	26310 TQ	FLBLS	10/01-12/01
	Orlando MSA, FL	Y	12600 FQ	24210 AW	35820 TQ	FLBLS	10/01-12/01
	Tampa-St. Petersburg-Clearwater MSA, FL	Y	23550 FQ	26180 AW	29820 TQ	FLBLS	10/01-12/01
	Georgia	Y	15660 FQ	28260 AW	41580 TQ	GABLS	10/01-12/01
	Atlanta MSA, GA	Y	16300 FQ	29050 AW	42120 TQ	GABLS	10/01-12/01
	Hawaii	Y	12530 FQ	31250 AW	52880 TQ	HIBLS	10/01-12/01
	Honolulu MSA, HI	Y	12290 FQ	26310 AW	46010 TQ	HIBLS	10/01-12/01
	Illinois	Y	11850 FQ	23010 AW	44470 TQ	ILBLS	10/01-12/01
	Chicago PMSA, IL	Y	11800 FQ	23310 AW	45840 TQ	ILBLS	10/01-12/01
	Indiana	Y	11930 FQ	14000 AW	15980 TQ	INBLS	10/01-12/01
	Indianapolis MSA, IN	Y	11960 FQ	13620 AW	15170 TQ	INBLS	10/01-12/01
	Iowa	Y	11840 FQ	20570 AW	35690 TQ	IABLS	10/01-12/01
	Des Moines MSA, IA	Y	11740 FQ	19400 AW	36740 TQ	IABLS	10/01-12/01
	Kentucky	Y	12600 FQ	27370 AW	57070 TQ	KYBLS	10/01-12/01
	Louisiana	Y	11570 FQ	21690 AW	49170 TQ	LABLS	10/01-12/01
	Lake Charles MSA, LA	Y	11130 FQ	14730 AW	21910 TQ	LABLS	10/01-12/01
	New Orleans MSA, LA	Y	15670 FQ	31000 AW	55520 TQ	LABLS	10/01-12/01
	Massachusetts	Y	14370 FQ	30560 AW	45120 TQ	MABLS	10/01-12/01
	Michigan	Y	13600 FQ	31270 AW	44420 TQ	MIBLS	10/01-12/01
	Detroit PMSA, MI	Y	24370 FQ	35000 AW	45170 TQ	MIBLS	10/01-12/01
	Minnesota	Y	12680 FQ	25890 AW	49580 TQ	MNBLS	10/01-12/01
	Minneapolis-St. Paul MSA, MN-WI	Y	13030 FQ	26860 AW	53370 TQ	MNBLS	10/01-12/01
	Missouri	Y	14200 FQ	27930 AW	54030 TQ	MOBLS	10/01-12/01
	Kansas City MSA, MO-KS	Y	15980 FQ	20020 AW	22130 TQ	MOBLS	10/01-12/01
	St. Louis MSA, MO-IL	Y	12430 FQ	38460 AW	67550 TQ	MOBLS	10/01-12/01
	Nevada	Y	30230 FQ	36640 AW	45610 TQ	NVBLS	10/01-12/01
	Las Vegas MSA, NV-AZ	Y	30090 FQ	36750 AW	45950 TQ	NVBLS	10/01-12/01
	New Jersey	Y	13300 FQ	24740 AW	42190 TQ	NJBLS	10/01-12/01
	New Mexico	Y	11670 FQ	19690 AW	35600 TQ	NMBLS	10/01-12/01
	New York	Y	15470 FQ	34450 AW	66750 TQ	NYBLS	10/01-12/01
	New York PMSA, NY	Y	21780 FQ	49470 AW	84090 TQ	NYBLS	10/01-12/01
	North Carolina	Y	12340 FQ	21530 AW	41400 TQ	NCBLS	10/01-12/01
	Charlotte-Gastonia-Rock Hill MSA, NC-SC	Y	19010 FQ	27320 AW	42990 TQ	NCBLS	10/01-12/01
	Ohio	Y	12920 FQ	25770 AW	36040 TQ	OHBLS	10/01-12/01
	Oregon	Y	14720 FQ	26990 AW	55420 TQ	ORBLS	10/01-12/01
	Pennsylvania	Y	13110 FQ	30700 AW	55660 TQ	PABLS	10/01-12/01
	Philadelphia PMSA, PA-NJ	Y	12740 FQ	28640 AW	51900 TQ	PABLS	10/01-12/01
	Pittsburgh MSA, PA	Y	18980 FQ	22460 AW	27880 TQ	PABLS	10/01-12/01
	South Carolina	Y	16840 FQ	24300 AW	40180 TQ	SCBLS	10/01-12/01

AAW	Average annual wage	**AOH**	Average offered, high	**ASH**	Average starting, high	**H**	Hourly	**M**	Monthly	**S**	Special: hourly and annual		
AE	Average entry wage	**AOL**	Average offered, low	**ASL**	Average starting, low	**HI**	Highest wage paid	**MTC**	Median total compensation	**TQ**	Third quartile wage		
AEX	Average experienced wage	**APH**	Average pay, high range	**AW**	Average wage paid	**HR**	High end range	**MW**	Median wage paid	**W**	Weekly		
AO	Average offered	**APL**	Average pay, low range	**FQ**	First quartile wage	**LR**	Low end range	**SQ**	Second quartile wage	**Y**	Yearly		

Occupation/Type/Industry	Location	Per	Low	Mid	High	Source	Date
Dancer	Tennessee	Y	14000 FQ	24340 AW	33060 TQ	TNBLS	10/01-12/01
	Memphis MSA, TN-AR-MS	Y	12190 FQ	20290 AW	30840 TQ	TNBLS	10/01-12/01
	Nashville MSA, TN	Y	19580 FQ	26940 AW	35870 TQ	TNBLS	10/01-12/01
	Texas	Y	12570 FQ	20250 AW	32810 TQ	TXBLS	10/01-12/01
	Fort Worth-Arlington PMSA, TX	Y	14570 FQ	26580 AW	37450 TQ	TXBLS	10/01-12/01
	Utah	Y	12410 FQ	22900 AW	39830 TQ	UTBLS	10/01-12/01
	Salt Lake City-Ogden MSA, UT	Y	12420 FQ	22230 AW	38380 TQ	UTBLS	10/01-12/01
	Virginia	Y	12470 FQ	33510 AW	57470 TQ	VABLS	10/01-12/01
	Norfolk-Virginia Beach-Newport News MSA, VA-NC	Y	12830 FQ	29040 AW	49970 TQ	VABLS	10/01-12/01
	Richmond-Petersburg MSA, VA	Y	12070 FQ	39610 AW	82810 TQ	VABLS	10/01-12/01
	Washington	Y	13990 FQ	26510 AW	55760 TQ	WABLS	10/01-12/01
	Seattle-Bellevue-Everett PMSA, WA	Y	13990 FQ	27070 AW	56550 TQ	WABLS	10/01-12/01
	Puerto Rico	Y	12640 FQ	17520 AW	24910 TQ	PRBLS	10/01-12/01
Data Entry Keyer	Alabama	H	6.93 FQ	10.17 AW	14.65 TQ	ALBLS	10/01-12/01
	Birmingham MSA, AL	H	7.59 FQ	11.35 AW	15.94 TQ	ALBLS	10/01-12/01
	Huntsville MSA, AL	H	6.53 FQ	9.65 AW	13.09 TQ	ALBLS	10/01-12/01
	Mobile MSA, AL	H	7.02 FQ	9.36 AW	12.78 TQ	ALBLS	10/01-12/01
	Montgomery MSA, AL	H	6.23 FQ	9.57 AW	13.36 TQ	ALBLS	10/01-12/01
	Alaska	H	8.24 FQ	12.28 AW	17.71 TQ	AKBLS	10/01-12/01
	Anchorage MSA, AK	H	7.86 FQ	11.10 AW	15.50 TQ	AKBLS	10/01-12/01
	Arizona	H	7.68 FQ	10.61 AW	13.95 TQ	AZBLS	10/01-12/01
	Phoenix-Mesa MSA, AZ	H	7.79 FQ	10.65 AW	13.89 TQ	AZBLS	10/01-12/01
	Tucson MSA, AZ	H	7.51 FQ	10.70 AW	14.67 TQ	AZBLS	10/01-12/01
	Arkansas	H	7.00 FQ	9.89 AW	13.11 TQ	ARBLS	10/01-12/01
	Fayetteville-Springdale-Rogers MSA, AR	H	7.49 FQ	9.61 AW	12.11 TQ	ARBLS	10/01-12/01
	Fort Smith MSA, AR-OK	H	5.71 FQ	8.66 AW	11.46 TQ	ARBLS	10/01-12/01
	Little Rock-North Little Rock MSA, AR	H	7.65 FQ	10.74 AW	14.38 TQ	ARBLS	10/01-12/01
	California	H	8.19 FQ	11.85 AW	16.42 TQ	CABLS	10/01-12/01
	Bakersfield MSA, CA	H	7.80 FQ	11.43 AW	16.19 TQ	CABLS	10/01-12/01
	Chico-Paradise MSA, CA	H	7.16 FQ	9.26 AW	12.34 TQ	CABLS	10/01-12/01
	Fresno MSA, CA	H	7.66 FQ	11.13 AW	14.27 TQ	CABLS	10/01-12/01
	Los Angeles-Long Beach PMSA, CA	H	7.78 FQ	11.24 AW	15.19 TQ	CABLS	10/01-12/01
	Merced MSA, CA	H	7.62 FQ	10.99 AW	15.28 TQ	CABLS	10/01-12/01
	Modesto MSA, CA	H	8.02 FQ	11.76 AW	15.13 TQ	CABLS	10/01-12/01
	Oakland PMSA, CA	H	7.22 FQ	12.31 AW	16.81 TQ	CABLS	10/01-12/01
	Orange County PMSA, CA	H	8.67 FQ	12.23 AW	16.80 TQ	CABLS	10/01-12/01
	Redding MSA, CA	H	7.87 FQ	11.69 AW	16.66 TQ	CABLS	10/01-12/01
	Riverside-San Bernardino PMSA, CA	H	8.34 FQ	11.19 AW	14.61 TQ	CABLS	10/01-12/01
	Sacramento PMSA, CA	H	7.99 FQ	11.88 AW	16.07 TQ	CABLS	10/01-12/01
	Salinas MSA, CA	H	7.60 FQ	11.74 AW	16.27 TQ	CABLS	10/01-12/01
	San Diego MSA, CA	H	8.52 FQ	11.74 AW	16.24 TQ	CABLS	10/01-12/01
	San Francisco PMSA, CA	H	9.67 FQ	13.91 AW	18.28 TQ	CABLS	10/01-12/01
	San Jose PMSA, CA	H	9.02 FQ	13.04 AW	17.60 TQ	CABLS	10/01-12/01
	San Luis Obispo-Atascadero-Paso Robles MSA, CA	H	7.77 FQ	11.61 AW	16.37 TQ	CABLS	10/01-12/01
	Santa Barbara-Santa Maria-Lompoc MSA, CA	H	8.27 FQ	11.62 AW	15.79 TQ	CABLS	10/01-12/01
	Santa Cruz-Watsonville PMSA, CA	H	8.37 FQ	11.95 AW	16.91 TQ	CABLS	10/01-12/01
	Santa Rosa PMSA, CA	H	8.47 FQ	12.57 AW	18.21 TQ	CABLS	10/01-12/01
	Stockton-Lodi MSA, CA	H	7.52 FQ	10.73 AW	14.83 TQ	CABLS	10/01-12/01
	Vallejo-Fairfield-Napa PMSA, CA	H	7.57 FQ	11.23 AW	15.15 TQ	CABLS	10/01-12/01
	Ventura PMSA, CA	H	8.99 FQ	12.75 AW	20.21 TQ	CABLS	10/01-12/01
	Visalia-Tulare-Porterville MSA, CA	H	7.66 FQ	10.80 AW	15.32 TQ	CABLS	10/01-12/01
	Colorado	H	7.62 FQ	11.11 AW	14.82 TQ	COBLS	10/01-12/01
	Boulder-Longmont PMSA, CO	H	8.86 FQ	11.91 AW	14.62 TQ	COBLS	10/01-12/01
	Colorado Springs MSA, CO	H	7.47 FQ	10.02 AW	13.67 TQ	COBLS	10/01-12/01
	Denver PMSA, CO	H	7.67 FQ	11.12 AW	15.00 TQ	COBLS	10/01-12/01
	Fort Collins-Loveland MSA, CO	H	7.64 FQ	9.90 AW	14.02 TQ	COBLS	10/01-12/01

AAW	Average annual wage	**AOH**	Average offered, high	**ASH**	Average starting, high	**H**	Hourly	**M**	Monthly	**S**	Special: hourly and annual
AE	Average entry wage	**AOL**	Average offered, low	**ASL**	Average starting, low	**HI**	Highest wage paid	**MTC**	Median total compensation	**TQ**	Third quartile wage
AEX	Average experienced wage	**APH**	Average pay, high range	**AW**	Average wage paid	**HR**	High end range	**MW**	Median wage paid	**W**	Weekly
AO	Average offered	**APL**	Average pay, low range	**FQ**	First quartile wage	**LR**	Low end range	**SQ**	Second quartile wage	**Y**	Yearly

Occupation/Type/Industry	Location	Per	Low	Mid	High	Source	Date
Data Entry Keyer	Greeley PMSA, CO	H	7.67 FQ	11.13 AW	14.26 TQ	COBLS	10/01-12/01
	Connecticut	H	8.84 FQ	12.46 AW	17.22 TQ	CTBLS	10/01-12/01
	Bridgeport PMSA, CT	H	9.30 FQ	12.26 AW	15.76 TQ	CTBLS	10/01-12/01
	Danbury PMSA, CT	H	9.40 FQ	14.91 AW	22.54 TQ	CTBLS	10/01-12/01
	Hartford MSA, CT	H	9.06 FQ	12.63 AW	17.82 TQ	CTBLS	10/01-12/01
	New Haven-Meriden PMSA, CT	H	9.12 FQ	12.00 AW	16.44 TQ	CTBLS	10/01-12/01
	New London-Norwich MSA, CT-RI	H	9.09 FQ	11.35 AW	14.50 TQ	CTBLS	10/01-12/01
	Stamford-Norwalk PMSA, CT	H	7.31 FQ	12.19 AW	18.17 TQ	CTBLS	10/01-12/01
	Waterbury PMSA, CT	H	8.88 FQ	12.30 AW	16.42 TQ	CTBLS	10/01-12/01
	Delaware	H	8.19 FQ	11.23 AW	15.14 TQ	DEBLS	10/01-12/01
	Wilmington-Newark PMSA, DE-MD	H	8.29 FQ	11.37 AW	15.47 TQ	DEBLS	10/01-12/01
	District of Columbia	H	10.01 FQ	13.73 AW	17.42 TQ	DCBLS	10/01-12/01
	Washington PMSA, DC-MD-VA-WV	H	7.93 FQ	12.07 AW	16.36 TQ	DCBLS	10/01-12/01
	Florida	H	7.35 FQ	9.81 AW	13.16 TQ	FLBLS	10/01-12/01
	Daytona Beach MSA, FL	H	6.48 FQ	9.02 AW	12.64 TQ	FLBLS	10/01-12/01
	Fort Lauderdale PMSA, FL	H	7.51 FQ	10.14 AW	13.59 TQ	FLBLS	10/01-12/01
	Fort Myers-Cape Coral MSA, FL	H	7.52 FQ	9.33 AW	11.47 TQ	FLBLS	10/01-12/01
	Fort Pierce-Port St. Lucie MSA, FL	H	5.81 FQ	8.30 AW	11.35 TQ	FLBLS	10/01-12/01
	Fort Walton Beach MSA, FL	H	7.19 FQ	8.63 AW	10.60 TQ	FLBLS	10/01-12/01
	Gainesville MSA, FL	H	7.15 FQ	9.35 AW	12.31 TQ	FLBLS	10/01-12/01
	Jacksonville MSA, FL	H	7.80 FQ	10.19 AW	12.99 TQ	FLBLS	10/01-12/01
	Lakeland-Winter Haven MSA, FL	H	7.52 FQ	9.95 AW	13.18 TQ	FLBLS	10/01-12/01
	Melbourne-Titusville-Palm Bay MSA, FL	H	7.38 FQ	9.91 AW	13.35 TQ	FLBLS	10/01-12/01
	Miami PMSA, FL	H	6.41 FQ	10.10 AW	14.59 TQ	FLBLS	10/01-12/01
	Naples MSA, FL	H	7.84 FQ	10.26 AW	13.31 TQ	FLBLS	10/01-12/01
	Ocala MSA, FL	H	6.60 FQ	8.80 AW	11.57 TQ	FLBLS	10/01-12/01
	Orlando MSA, FL	H	7.46 FQ	9.48 AW	12.46 TQ	FLBLS	10/01-12/01
	Pensacola MSA, FL	H	6.96 FQ	9.47 AW	13.03 TQ	FLBLS	10/01-12/01
	Sarasota-Bradenton MSA, FL	H	7.50 FQ	9.17 AW	11.31 TQ	FLBLS	10/01-12/01
	Tallahassee MSA, FL	H	8.31 FQ	10.72 AW	14.30 TQ	FLBLS	10/01-12/01
	Tampa-St. Petersburg-Clearwater MSA, FL	H	7.45 FQ	9.99 AW	13.20 TQ	FLBLS	10/01-12/01
	West Palm Beach-Boca Raton MSA, FL	H	8.05 FQ	10.82 AW	13.97 TQ	FLBLS	10/01-12/01
	Georgia	H	7.83 FQ	10.76 AW	14.26 TQ	GABLS	10/01-12/01
	Atlanta MSA, GA	H	8.06 FQ	11.01 AW	14.46 TQ	GABLS	10/01-12/01
	Augusta-Aiken MSA, GA-SC	H	7.68 FQ	10.17 AW	13.17 TQ	GABLS	10/01-12/01
	Columbus MSA, GA-AL	H	7.48 FQ	9.98 AW	13.24 TQ	GABLS	10/01-12/01
	Macon MSA, GA	H	7.84 FQ	10.08 AW	12.91 TQ	GABLS	10/01-12/01
	Savannah MSA, GA	H	7.76 FQ	9.71 AW	11.53 TQ	GABLS	10/01-12/01
	Hawaii	H	8.22 FQ	11.42 AW	15.30 TQ	HIBLS	10/01-12/01
	Honolulu MSA, HI	H	7.72 FQ	11.21 AW	14.94 TQ	HIBLS	10/01-12/01
	Idaho	H	7.53 FQ	10.78 AW	14.82 TQ	IDBLS	10/01-12/01
	Boise City MSA, ID	H	8.44 FQ	12.05 AW	16.61 TQ	IDBLS	10/01-12/01
	Illinois	H	7.57 FQ	11.45 AW	15.98 TQ	ILBLS	10/01-12/01
	Champaign-Urbana MSA, IL	H	6.55 FQ	10.06 AW	13.84 TQ	ILBLS	10/01-12/01
	Chicago PMSA, IL	H	8.38 FQ	11.82 AW	16.21 TQ	ILBLS	10/01-12/01
	Peoria-Pekin MSA, IL	H	7.83 FQ	11.63 AW	14.97 TQ	ILBLS	10/01-12/01
	Rockford MSA, IL	H	7.08 FQ	9.00 AW	11.88 TQ	ILBLS	10/01-12/01
	Springfield MSA, IL	H	5.98 FQ	10.17 AW	15.24 TQ	ILBLS	10/01-12/01
	Indiana	H	7.43 FQ	10.31 AW	13.49 TQ	INBLS	10/01-12/01
	Elkhart-Goshen MSA, IN	H	7.62 FQ	10.54 AW	14.00 TQ	INBLS	10/01-12/01
	Evansville-Henderson MSA, IN-KY	H	7.31 FQ	9.74 AW	12.93 TQ	INBLS	10/01-12/01
	Fort Wayne MSA, IN	H	8.22 FQ	11.29 AW	14.29 TQ	INBLS	10/01-12/01
	Gary PMSA, IN	H	6.62 FQ	9.86 AW	13.89 TQ	INBLS	10/01-12/01
	Indianapolis MSA, IN	H	8.25 FQ	10.76 AW	13.88 TQ	INBLS	10/01-12/01
	Lafayette MSA, IN	H	7.43 FQ	9.65 AW	13.44 TQ	INBLS	10/01-12/01
	South Bend MSA, IN	H	7.55 FQ	10.46 AW	13.64 TQ	INBLS	10/01-12/01
	Iowa	H	6.77 FQ	9.97 AW	13.67 TQ	IABLS	10/01-12/01
	Cedar Rapids MSA, IA	H	8.08 FQ	10.74 AW	13.72 TQ	IABLS	10/01-12/01
	Davenport-Moline-Rock Island MSA, IA-IL	H	7.12 FQ	9.55 AW	12.52 TQ	IABLS	10/01-12/01
	Des Moines MSA, IA	H	6.47 FQ	10.21 AW	14.04 TQ	IABLS	10/01-12/01

AAW	Average annual wage	**AOH**	Average offered, high	**ASH**	Average starting, high	**H**	Hourly	**M**	Monthly	**S**	Special: hourly and annual
AE	Average entry wage	**AOL**	Average offered, low	**ASL**	Average starting, low	**HI**	Highest wage paid	**MTC**	Median total compensation	**TQ**	Third quartile wage
AEX	Average experienced wage	**APH**	Average pay, high range	**AW**	Average wage paid	**HR**	High end range	**MW**	Median wage paid	**W**	Weekly
AO	Average offered	**APL**	Average pay, low range	**FQ**	First quartile wage	**LR**	Low end range	**SQ**	Second quartile wage	**Y**	Yearly

Occupation/Type/Industry	Location	Per	Low	Mid	High	Source	Date
Data Entry Keyer	Kansas	H	7.25 FQ	10.56 AW	13.51 TQ	KSBLS	10/01-12/01
	Topeka MSA, KS	H	7.11 FQ	9.74 AW	13.06 TQ	KSBLS	10/01-12/01
	Wichita MSA, KS	H	8.16 FQ	11.52 AW	13.91 TQ	KSBLS	10/01-12/01
	Kentucky	H	6.42 FQ	9.45 AW	13.14 TQ	KYBLS	10/01-12/01
	Lexington MSA, KY	H	7.68 FQ	9.79 AW	12.59 TQ	KYBLS	10/01-12/01
	Louisville MSA, KY-IN	H	7.74 FQ	10.51 AW	13.82 TQ	KYBLS	10/01-12/01
	Louisiana	H	6.36 FQ	9.03 AW	12.41 TQ	LABLS	10/01-12/01
	Baton Rouge MSA, LA	H	7.27 FQ	9.49 AW	13.19 TQ	LABLS	10/01-12/01
	Houma MSA, LA	H	5.84 FQ	7.99 AW	11.50 TQ	LABLS	10/01-12/01
	Lafayette MSA, LA	H	6.05 FQ	8.59 AW	12.33 TQ	LABLS	10/01-12/01
	Lake Charles MSA, LA	H	5.95 FQ	8.09 AW	10.75 TQ	LABLS	10/01-12/01
	New Orleans MSA, LA	H	7.35 FQ	9.56 AW	12.66 TQ	LABLS	10/01-12/01
	Shreveport-Bossier City MSA, LA	H	6.28 FQ	9.04 AW	12.90 TQ	LABLS	10/01-12/01
	Maine	H	6.92 FQ	9.81 AW	13.39 TQ	MEBLS	10/01-12/01
	Portland MSA, ME	H	8.05 FQ	10.64 AW	13.40 TQ	MEBLS	10/01-12/01
	Maryland	H	7.38 FQ	10.82 AW	15.14 TQ	MDBLS	10/01-12/01
	Baltimore PMSA, MD	H	7.79 FQ	10.96 AW	14.67 TQ	MDBLS	10/01-12/01
	Massachusetts	H	8.20 FQ	11.66 AW	15.88 TQ	MABLS	10/01-12/01
	Boston PMSA, MA-NH	H	8.53 FQ	11.88 AW	16.07 TQ	MABLS	10/01-12/01
	Brockton PMSA, MA	H	7.87 FQ	11.44 AW	16.36 TQ	MABLS	10/01-12/01
	Lawrence PMSA, MA-NH	H	8.84 FQ	11.96 AW	15.96 TQ	MABLS	10/01-12/01
	Lowell PMSA, MA-NH	H	9.38 FQ	12.24 AW	16.79 TQ	MABLS	10/01-12/01
	New Bedford PMSA, MA	H	7.43 FQ	10.09 AW	13.93 TQ	MABLS	10/01-12/01
	Springfield MSA, MA	H	7.63 FQ	10.66 AW	14.37 TQ	MABLS	10/01-12/01
	Worcester PMSA, MA-CT	H	7.57 FQ	11.20 AW	14.96 TQ	MABLS	10/01-12/01
	Michigan	H	7.82 FQ	11.03 AW	14.88 TQ	MIBLS	10/01-12/01
	Ann Arbor PMSA, MI	H	8.68 FQ	12.07 AW	16.80 TQ	MIBLS	10/01-12/01
	Detroit PMSA, MI	H	8.03 FQ	11.14 AW	14.56 TQ	MIBLS	10/01-12/01
	Flint PMSA, MI	H	7.29 FQ	9.82 AW	15.07 TQ	MIBLS	10/01-12/01
	Grand Rapids-Muskegon-Holland MSA, MI	H	7.95 FQ	10.68 AW	14.04 TQ	MIBLS	10/01-12/01
	Kalamazoo-Battle Creek MSA, MI	H	7.60 FQ	10.48 AW	14.21 TQ	MIBLS	10/01-12/01
	Lansing-East Lansing MSA, MI	H	7.72 FQ	11.54 AW	16.16 TQ	MIBLS	10/01-12/01
	Saginaw-Bay City-Midland MSA, MI	H	7.61 FQ	10.82 AW	18.01 TQ	MIBLS	10/01-12/01
	Minnesota	H	7.94 FQ	11.18 AW	14.46 TQ	MNBLS	10/01-12/01
	Duluth-Superior MSA, MN-WI	H	8.82 FQ	11.65 AW	13.40 TQ	MNBLS	10/01-12/01
	Minneapolis-St. Paul MSA, MN-WI	H	9.32 FQ	11.85 AW	15.19 TQ	MNBLS	10/01-12/01
	St. Cloud MSA, MN	H	7.82 FQ	10.05 AW	13.23 TQ	MNBLS	10/01-12/01
	Mississippi	H	6.46 FQ	9.31 AW	12.75 TQ	MSBLS	10/01-12/01
	Biloxi-Gulfport-Pascagoula MSA, MS	H	6.09 FQ	9.22 AW	13.27 TQ	MSBLS	10/01-12/01
	Jackson MSA, MS	H	7.32 FQ	9.96 AW	13.12 TQ	MSBLS	10/01-12/01
	Missouri	H	7.10 FQ	10.11 AW	13.92 TQ	MOBLS	10/01-12/01
	Kansas City MSA, MO-KS	H	7.95 FQ	10.71 AW	13.96 TQ	MOBLS	10/01-12/01
	St. Louis MSA, MO-IL	H	6.81 FQ	10.25 AW	14.42 TQ	MOBLS	10/01-12/01
	Springfield MSA, MO	H	6.48 FQ	9.68 AW	14.27 TQ	MOBLS	10/01-12/01
	Montana	H	7.16 FQ	9.27 AW	12.41 TQ	MTBLS	10/01-12/01
	Billings MSA, MT	H	7.01 FQ	8.75 AW	10.75 TQ	MTBLS	10/01-12/01
	Nebraska	H	7.28 FQ	9.55 AW	12.49 TQ	NEBLS	10/01-12/01
	Lincoln MSA, NE	H	7.45 FQ	9.50 AW	11.40 TQ	NEBLS	10/01-12/01
	Omaha MSA, NE-IA	H	7.39 FQ	9.90 AW	13.07 TQ	NEBLS	10/01-12/01
	Nevada	H	7.64 FQ	10.20 AW	14.29 TQ	NVBLS	10/01-12/01
	Las Vegas MSA, NV-AZ	H	7.68 FQ	10.25 AW	14.30 TQ	NVBLS	10/01-12/01
	Reno MSA, NV	H	7.58 FQ	10.33 AW	14.68 TQ	NVBLS	10/01-12/01
	New Hampshire	H	7.86 FQ	10.68 AW	13.77 TQ	NHBLS	10/01-12/01
	Manchester PMSA, NH	H	8.68 FQ	11.11 AW	14.19 TQ	NHBLS	10/01-12/01
	Nashua PMSA, NH	H	7.41 FQ	10.42 AW	14.56 TQ	NHBLS	10/01-12/01
	Portsmouth-Rochester PMSA, NH-ME	H	8.42 FQ	11.07 AW	13.39 TQ	NHBLS	10/01-12/01
	New Jersey	H	8.75 FQ	12.24 AW	16.75 TQ	NJBLS	10/01-12/01
	Atlantic-Cape May PMSA, NJ	H	8.88 FQ	12.32 AW	16.97 TQ	NJBLS	10/01-12/01
	Bergen-Passaic PMSA, NJ	H	8.21 FQ	11.90 AW	16.75 TQ	NJBLS	10/01-12/01
	Jersey City PMSA, NJ	H	9.11 FQ	11.99 AW	16.25 TQ	NJBLS	10/01-12/01
	Middlesex-Somerset-Hunterdon PMSA, NJ	H	9.15 FQ	12.33 AW	16.58 TQ	NJBLS	10/01-12/01
	Monmouth-Ocean PMSA, NJ	H	8.95 FQ	12.29 AW	16.55 TQ	NJBLS	10/01-12/01
	Newark PMSA, NJ	H	8.47 FQ	12.66 AW	17.60 TQ	NJBLS	10/01-12/01
	Trenton PMSA, NJ	H	9.90 FQ	12.97 AW	16.89 TQ	NJBLS	10/01-12/01

AAW	Average annual wage	**AOH**	Average offered, high	**ASH**	Average starting, high	**H**	Hourly	**M**	Monthly	**S**	Special: hourly and annual
AE	Average entry wage	**AOL**	Average offered, low	**ASL**	Average starting, low	**HI**	Highest wage paid	**MTC**	Median total compensation	**TQ**	Third quartile wage
AEX	Average experienced wage	**APH**	Average pay, high range	**AW**	Average wage paid	**HR**	High end range	**MW**	Median wage paid	**W**	Weekly
AO	Average offered	**APL**	Average pay, low range	**FQ**	First quartile wage	**LR**	Low end range	**SQ**	Second quartile wage	**Y**	Yearly

Occupation/Type/Industry	Location	Per	Low	Mid	High	Source	Date
Data Entry Keyer	New Mexico	H	6.67 FQ	9.49 AW	13.09 TQ	NMBLS	10/01-12/01
	Albuquerque MSA, NM	H	7.33 FQ	10.02 AW	13.58 TQ	NMBLS	10/01-12/01
	Las Cruces MSA, NM	H	6.88 FQ	8.89 AW	11.02 TQ	NMBLS	10/01-12/01
	New York	H	8.17 FQ	12.29 AW	17.05 TQ	NYBLS	10/01-12/01
	Albany-Schenectady-Troy MSA, NY	H	7.93 FQ	11.52 AW	14.94 TQ	NYBLS	10/01-12/01
	Binghamton MSA, NY	H	7.01 FQ	9.44 AW	13.05 TQ	NYBLS	10/01-12/01
	Buffalo-Niagara Falls MSA, NY	H	7.64 FQ	10.78 AW	14.48 TQ	NYBLS	10/01-12/01
	Dutchess County PMSA, NY	H	7.13 FQ	9.86 AW	12.99 TQ	NYBLS	10/01-12/01
	Nassau-Suffolk PMSA, NY	H	8.61 FQ	11.90 AW	16.19 TQ	NYBLS	10/01-12/01
	New York PMSA, NY	H	9.13 FQ	13.50 AW	18.18 TQ	NYBLS	10/01-12/01
	Newburgh PMSA, NY-PA	H	6.67 FQ	10.44 AW	15.87 TQ	NYBLS	10/01-12/01
	Rochester MSA, NY	H	7.47 FQ	10.30 AW	13.86 TQ	NYBLS	10/01-12/01
	Syracuse MSA, NY	H	7.17 FQ	11.29 AW	15.69 TQ	NYBLS	10/01-12/01
	Utica-Rome MSA, NY	H	7.27 FQ	10.62 AW	14.29 TQ	NYBLS	10/01-12/01
	North Carolina	H	7.89 FQ	10.85 AW	14.02 TQ	NCBLS	10/01-12/01
	Asheville MSA, NC	H	7.11 FQ	9.99 AW	13.02 TQ	NCBLS	10/01-12/01
	Charlotte-Gastonia-Rock Hill MSA, NC-SC	H	8.33 FQ	11.20 AW	14.50 TQ	NCBLS	10/01-12/01
	Fayetteville MSA, NC	H	9.71 FQ	11.86 AW	13.40 TQ	NCBLS	10/01-12/01
	Greensboro-Winston-Salem-High Point MSA, NC	H	8.28 FQ	11.35 AW	16.25 TQ	NCBLS	10/01-12/01
	Hickory-Morganton-Lenoir MSA, NC	H	7.69 FQ	10.10 AW	13.21 TQ	NCBLS	10/01-12/01
	Raleigh-Durham-Chapel Hill MSA, NC	H	8.73 FQ	11.27 AW	14.25 TQ	NCBLS	10/01-12/01
	Wilmington MSA, NC	H	7.79 FQ	10.62 AW	14.18 TQ	NCBLS	10/01-12/01
	North Dakota	H	7.13 FQ	9.41 AW	12.69 TQ	NDBLS	10/01-12/01
	Fargo-Moorhead MSA, ND-MN	H	7.48 FQ	10.07 AW	13.00 TQ	NDBLS	10/01-12/01
	Ohio	H	7.60 FQ	10.80 AW	14.28 TQ	OHBLS	10/01-12/01
	Akron PMSA, OH	H	7.40 FQ	10.77 AW	13.49 TQ	OHBLS	10/01-12/01
	Canton-Massillon MSA, OH	H	6.40 FQ	9.79 AW	13.54 TQ	OHBLS	10/01-12/01
	Cincinnati PMSA, OH-KY-IN	H	7.84 FQ	11.27 AW	15.49 TQ	OHBLS	10/01-12/01
	Cleveland-Lorain-Elyria PMSA, OH	H	7.59 FQ	11.12 AW	14.71 TQ	OHBLS	10/01-12/01
	Columbus MSA, OH	H	8.58 FQ	11.03 AW	14.12 TQ	OHBLS	10/01-12/01
	Dayton-Springfield MSA, OH	H	7.93 FQ	10.87 AW	13.46 TQ	OHBLS	10/01-12/01
	Hamilton-Middletown PMSA, OH	H	7.65 FQ	10.83 AW	14.29 TQ	OHBLS	10/01-12/01
	Mansfield MSA, OH	H	5.94 FQ	8.58 AW	11.37 TQ	OHBLS	10/01-12/01
	Toledo MSA, OH	H	7.51 FQ	10.05 AW	13.24 TQ	OHBLS	10/01-12/01
	Youngstown-Warren MSA, OH	H	7.52 FQ	9.94 AW	13.78 TQ	OHBLS	10/01-12/01
	Oklahoma	H	7.01 FQ	9.70 AW	13.06 TQ	OKBLS	10/01-12/01
	Oklahoma City MSA, OK	H	7.03 FQ	9.72 AW	12.61 TQ	OKBLS	10/01-12/01
	Tulsa MSA, OK	H	7.63 FQ	10.35 AW	14.01 TQ	OKBLS	10/01-12/01
	Oregon	H	8.15 FQ	10.95 AW	14.43 TQ	ORBLS	10/01-12/01
	Eugene-Springfield MSA, OR	H	7.61 FQ	10.80 AW	14.30 TQ	ORBLS	10/01-12/01
	Medford-Ashland MSA, OR	H	6.64 FQ	8.94 AW	12.91 TQ	ORBLS	10/01-12/01
	Portland-Vancouver PMSA, OR-WA	H	8.41 FQ	11.15 AW	14.70 TQ	ORBLS	10/01-12/01
	Salem PMSA, OR	H	8.50 FQ	10.58 AW	14.29 TQ	ORBLS	10/01-12/01
	Pennsylvania	H	7.04 FQ	10.26 AW	13.79 TQ	PABLS	10/01-12/01
	Allentown-Bethlehem-Easton MSA, PA	H	7.07 FQ	9.87 AW	13.29 TQ	PABLS	10/01-12/01
	Erie MSA, PA	H	7.52 FQ	10.95 AW	15.70 TQ	PABLS	10/01-12/01
	Harrisburg-Lebanon-Carlisle MSA, PA	H	7.42 FQ	10.01 AW	13.45 TQ	PABLS	10/01-12/01
	Johnstown MSA, PA	H	5.94 FQ	7.82 AW	10.51 TQ	PABLS	10/01-12/01
	Lancaster MSA, PA	H	7.64 FQ	10.38 AW	14.26 TQ	PABLS	10/01-12/01
	Philadelphia PMSA, PA-NJ	H	7.54 FQ	11.05 AW	14.63 TQ	PABLS	10/01-12/01
	Pittsburgh MSA, PA	H	6.53 FQ	9.92 AW	13.20 TQ	PABLS	10/01-12/01
	Reading MSA, PA	H	7.55 FQ	10.29 AW	13.75 TQ	PABLS	10/01-12/01
	Scranton-Wilkes-Barre-Hazleton MSA, PA	H	7.04 FQ	9.01 AW	11.52 TQ	PABLS	10/01-12/01
	York MSA, PA	H	7.44 FQ	9.95 AW	13.04 TQ	PABLS	10/01-12/01
	Rhode Island	H	8.96 FQ	11.46 AW	15.60 TQ	RIBLS	10/01-12/01
	Providence-Fall River-Warwick MSA, RI-MA	H	8.85 FQ	11.40 AW	15.55 TQ	RIBLS	10/01-12/01
	South Carolina	H	6.88 FQ	10.13 AW	13.54 TQ	SCBLS	10/01-12/01

AAW	Average annual wage	**AOH**	Average offered, high	**ASH**	Average starting, high	**H**	Hourly	**M**	Monthly	**S**	Special: hourly and annual
AE	Average entry wage	**AOL**	Average offered, low	**ASL**	Average starting, low	**HI**	Highest wage paid	**MTC**	Median total compensation	**TQ**	Third quartile wage
AEX	Average experienced wage	**APH**	Average pay, high range	**AW**	Average wage paid	**HR**	High end range	**MW**	Median wage paid	**W**	Weekly
AO	Average offered	**APL**	Average pay, low range	**FQ**	First quartile wage	**LR**	Low end range	**SQ**	Second quartile wage	**Y**	Yearly

Occupation/Type/Industry	Location	Per	Low	Mid	High	Source	Date
Data Entry Keyer	Charleston-North Charleston MSA, SC	H	7.70 FQ	10.02 AW	13.40 TQ	SCBLS	10/01-12/01
	Columbia MSA, SC	H	6.56 FQ	10.57 AW	13.82 TQ	SCBLS	10/01-12/01
	Greenville-Spartanburg-Anderson MSA, SC	H	7.47 FQ	10.09 AW	13.37 TQ	SCBLS	10/01-12/01
	Myrtle Beach MSA, SC	H	7.49 FQ	9.72 AW	12.64 TQ	SCBLS	10/01-12/01
	South Dakota	H	6.52 FQ	8.79 AW	12.06 TQ	SDBLS	10/01-12/01
	Sioux Falls MSA, SD	H	6.92 FQ	9.32 AW	12.92 TQ	SDBLS	10/01-12/01
	Tennessee	H	7.34 FQ	10.38 AW	13.97 TQ	TNBLS	10/01-12/01
	Chattanooga MSA, TN-GA	H	7.83 FQ	11.60 AW	16.32 TQ	TNBLS	10/01-12/01
	Clarksville-Hopkinsville MSA, TN-KY	H	6.30 FQ	9.20 AW	12.90 TQ	TNBLS	10/01-12/01
	Johnson City-Kingsport-Bristol MSA, TN-VA	H	7.19 FQ	9.56 AW	12.76 TQ	TNBLS	10/01-12/01
	Knoxville MSA, TN	H	7.25 FQ	9.70 AW	13.25 TQ	TNBLS	10/01-12/01
	Memphis MSA, TN-AR-MS	H	7.03 FQ	9.81 AW	12.93 TQ	TNBLS	10/01-12/01
	Nashville MSA, TN	H	6.86 FQ	11.01 AW	15.99 TQ	TNBLS	10/01-12/01
	Texas	H	7.37 FQ	10.41 AW	13.75 TQ	TXBLS	10/01-12/01
	Amarillo MSA, TX	H	6.33 FQ	8.88 AW	11.55 TQ	TXBLS	10/01-12/01
	Austin-San Marcos MSA, TX	H	7.76 FQ	10.73 AW	14.39 TQ	TXBLS	10/01-12/01
	Beaumont-Port Arthur MSA, TX	H	8.37 FQ	11.75 AW	13.49 TQ	TXBLS	10/01-12/01
	Brazoria PMSA, TX	H	7.40 FQ	9.55 AW	11.60 TQ	TXBLS	10/01-12/01
	Brownsville-Harlingen-San Benito MSA, TX	H	5.78 FQ	8.17 AW	11.20 TQ	TXBLS	10/01-12/01
	Corpus Christi MSA, TX	H	6.93 FQ	9.60 AW	12.99 TQ	TXBLS	10/01-12/01
	Dallas PMSA, TX	H	8.01 FQ	10.72 AW	13.83 TQ	TXBLS	10/01-12/01
	El Paso MSA, TX	H	6.05 FQ	8.50 AW	11.55 TQ	TXBLS	10/01-12/01
	Fort Worth-Arlington PMSA, TX	H	8.13 FQ	11.09 AW	15.41 TQ	TXBLS	10/01-12/01
	Galveston-Texas City PMSA, TX	H	7.81 FQ	10.85 AW	14.65 TQ	TXBLS	10/01-12/01
	Houston PMSA, TX	H	7.63 FQ	10.81 AW	13.87 TQ	TXBLS	10/01 12/01
	Killeen-Temple MSA, TX	H	7.05 FQ	9.39 AW	12.07 TQ	TXBLS	10/01-12/01
	Laredo MSA, TX	H	5.92 FQ	8.45 AW	11.89 TQ	TXBLS	10/01-12/01
	Longview-Marshall MSA, TX	H	6.78 FQ	8.94 AW	11.89 TQ	TXBLS	10/01-12/01
	Lubbock MSA, TX	H	6.48 FQ	9.43 AW	12.63 TQ	TXBLS	10/01-12/01
	McAllen-Edinburg-Mission MSA, TX	H	5.74 FQ	7.98 AW	11.43 TQ	TXBLS	10/01-12/01
	Odessa-Midland MSA, TX	H	5.53 FQ	8.52 AW	12.72 TQ	TXBLS	10/01-12/01
	San Antonio MSA, TX	H	7.48 FQ	10.23 AW	13.77 TQ	TXBLS	10/01-12/01
	Tyler MSA, TX	H	7.08 FQ	9.19 AW	11.46 TQ	TXBLS	10/01-12/01
	Waco MSA, TX	H	5.94 FQ	8.88 AW	12.39 TQ	TXBLS	10/01-12/01
	Utah	H	7.51 FQ	9.87 AW	12.65 TQ	UTBLS	10/01-12/01
	Provo-Orem MSA, UT	H	7.25 FQ	8.89 AW	10.93 TQ	UTBLS	10/01-12/01
	Vermont	H	7.35 FQ	10.02 AW	13.33 TQ	VTBLS	10/01-12/01
	Burlington MSA, VT	H	7.25 FQ	10.04 AW	13.41 TQ	VTBLS	10/01-12/01
	Virginia	H	7.10 FQ	10.53 AW	14.09 TQ	VABLS	10/01-12/01
	Lynchburg MSA, VA	H	7.02 FQ	9.78 AW	13.54 TQ	VABLS	10/01-12/01
	Norfolk-Virginia Beach-Newport News MSA, VA-NC	H	6.18 FQ	9.02 AW	12.84 TQ	VABLS	10/01-12/01
	Richmond-Petersburg MSA, VA	H	7.05 FQ	9.75 AW	13.22 TQ	VABLS	10/01-12/01
	Roanoke MSA, VA	H	6.36 FQ	10.09 AW	13.63 TQ	VABLS	10/01-12/01
	Washington	H	8.37 FQ	11.57 AW	15.31 TQ	WABLS	10/01-12/01
	Bremerton PMSA, WA	H	8.27 FQ	10.66 AW	13.38 TQ	WABLS	10/01-12/01
	Olympia PMSA, WA	H	7.58 FQ	10.61 AW	14.66 TQ	WABLS	10/01-12/01
	Richland-Kennewick-Pasco MSA, WA	H	6.89 FQ	10.63 AW	16.26 TQ	WABLS	10/01-12/01
	Seattle-Bellevue-Everett PMSA, WA	H	9.49 FQ	12.32 AW	16.16 TQ	WABLS	10/01-12/01
	Spokane MSA, WA	H	7.45 FQ	10.01 AW	13.16 TQ	WABLS	10/01-12/01
	Tacoma PMSA, WA	H	6.92 FQ	10.12 AW	13.96 TQ	WABLS	10/01-12/01
	Yakima MSA, WA	H	7.65 FQ	10.27 AW	13.65 TQ	WABLS	10/01-12/01
	West Virginia	H	6.36 FQ	9.78 AW	13.31 TQ	WVBLS	10/01-12/01
	Charleston MSA, WV	H	6.67 FQ	10.61 AW	13.66 TQ	WVBLS	10/01-12/01
	Huntington-Ashland MSA, WV-KY-OH	H	5.98 FQ	8.82 AW	12.81 TQ	WVBLS	10/01-12/01
	Wisconsin	H	7.60 FQ	10.37 AW	13.78 TQ	WIBLS	10/01-12/01
	Appleton-Oshkosh-Neenah MSA, WI	H	7.21 FQ	10.27 AW	15.31 TQ	WIBLS	10/01-12/01

AAW	Average annual wage	AOH	Average offered, high	ASH	Average starting, high	H	Hourly	M	Monthly	S	Special: hourly and annual
AE	Average entry wage	AOL	Average offered, low	ASL	Average starting, low	HI	Highest wage paid	MTC	Median total compensation	TQ	Third quartile wage
AEX	Average experienced wage	APH	Average pay, high range	AW	Average wage paid	HR	High end range	MW	Median wage paid	W	Weekly
AO	Average offered	APL	Average pay, low range	FQ	First quartile wage	LR	Low end range	SQ	Second quartile wage	Y	Yearly

Occupation/Type/Industry	Location	Per	Low	Mid	High	Source	Date
Data Entry Keyer	Green Bay MSA, WI	H	7.44 FQ	9.85 AW	13.12 TQ	WIBLS	10/01-12/01
	Madison MSA, WI	H	8.09 FQ	10.99 AW	14.12 TQ	WIBLS	10/01-12/01
	Milwaukee-Waukesha PMSA, WI	H	7.86 FQ	10.64 AW	13.87 TQ	WIBLS	10/01-12/01
	Racine PMSA, WI	H	8.64 FQ	11.34 AW	14.82 TQ	WIBLS	10/01-12/01
	Wyoming	H	6.30 FQ	8.62 AW	11.30 TQ	WYBLS	10/01-12/01
	Cheyenne MSA, WY	H	6.16 FQ	8.70 AW	11.34 TQ	WYBLS	10/01-12/01
	Puerto Rico	H	5.72 FQ	7.72 AW	10.73 TQ	PRBLS	10/01-12/01
	Virgin Islands	H	7.44 FQ	9.44 AW	11.45 TQ	VIBLS	10/01-12/01
	Guam	H	6.36 FQ	8.69 AW	12.43 TQ	GUBLS	10/01-12/01
Data Mining and Warehousing Professional							
Information Technology	United States	Y	62500 AOL			IOMA5	1/01-1/02
Database Administrator	United States	Y		39700 AW		FREEP1	1/00-1/00
	Alabama	Y	28780 FQ	48550 AW	74000 TQ	ALBLS	10/01-12/01
	Birmingham MSA, AL	Y	31500 FQ	54460 AW	82560 TQ	ALBLS	10/01-12/01
	Huntsville MSA, AL	Y	29920 FQ	46620 AW	72960 TQ	ALBLS	10/01-12/01
	Mobile MSA, AL	Y	29510 FQ	48950 AW	73910 TQ	ALBLS	10/01-12/01
	Montgomery MSA, AL	Y	26310 FQ	46590 AW	66760 TQ	ALBLS	10/01-12/01
	Alaska	Y	30560 FQ	54330 AW	83530 TQ	AKBLS	10/01-12/01
	Anchorage MSA, AK	Y	33040 FQ	57730 AW	88600 TQ	AKBLS	10/01-12/01
	Arizona	Y	30980 FQ	58080 AW	90430 TQ	AZBLS	10/01-12/01
	Phoenix-Mesa MSA, AZ	Y	32060 FQ	58930 AW	91890 TQ	AZBLS	10/01-12/01
	Tucson MSA, AZ	Y	29080 FQ	55880 AW	84820 TQ	AZBLS	10/01-12/01
	Fayetteville-Springdale-Rogers MSA, AR	Y	23640 FQ	45250 AW	82340 TQ	ARBLS	10/01-12/01
	Fort Smith MSA, AR-OK	Y	25520 FQ	51730 AW	80510 TQ	ARBLS	10/01-12/01
	California	Y	32760 FQ	64220 AW	104870 TQ	CABLS	10/01-12/01
	Bakersfield MSA, CA	Y	30590 FQ	52670 AW	85750 TQ	CABLS	10/01-12/01
	Fresno MSA, CA	Y	31830 FQ	56950 AW	86640 TQ	CABLS	10/01-12/01
	Los Angeles-Long Beach PMSA, CA	Y	32900 FQ	59220 AW	95020 TQ	CABLS	10/01-12/01
	Modesto MSA, CA	Y	24730 FQ	45450 AW	71370 TQ	CABLS	10/01-12/01
	Oakland PMSA, CA	Y	32340 FQ	60060 AW	94820 TQ	CABLS	10/01-12/01
	Orange County PMSA, CA	Y	31550 FQ	56120 AW	89190 TQ	CABLS	10/01-12/01
	Riverside-San Bernardino PMSA, CA	Y	25820 FQ	49000 AW	80880 TQ	CABLS	10/01-12/01
	Sacramento PMSA, CA	Y	29580 FQ	56600 AW	92070 TQ	CABLS	10/01-12/01
	Salinas MSA, CA	Y	26300 FQ	56660 AW	92250 TQ	CABLS	10/01-12/01
	San Diego MSA, CA	Y	31320 FQ	59810 AW	98200 TQ	CABLS	10/01-12/01
	San Francisco PMSA, CA	Y	35610 FQ	71770 AW	110760 TQ	CABLS	10/01-12/01
	San Jose PMSA, CA	Y	48800 FQ	81140 AW	116720 TQ	CABLS	10/01-12/01
	San Luis Obispo-Atascadero-Paso Robles MSA, CA	Y	31180 FQ	50220 AW	76140 TQ	CABLS	10/01-12/01
	Santa Barbara-Santa Maria-Lompoc MSA, CA	Y	30540 FQ	62520 AW	106510 TQ	CABLS	10/01-12/01
	Santa Cruz-Watsonville PMSA, CA	Y	26950 FQ	59160 AW	102620 TQ	CABLS	10/01-12/01
	Santa Rosa PMSA, CA	Y	24950 FQ	52020 AW	94170 TQ	CABLS	10/01-12/01
	Stockton-Lodi MSA, CA	Y	21560 FQ	48950 AW	86310 TQ	CABLS	10/01-12/01
	Vallejo-Fairfield-Napa PMSA, CA	Y	37120 FQ	56320 AW	85920 TQ	CABLS	10/01-12/01
	Ventura PMSA, CA	Y	25680 FQ	65410 AW	113680 TQ	CABLS	10/01-12/01
	Visalia-Tulare-Porterville MSA, CA	Y	39220 FQ	69390 AW	122390 TQ	CABLS	10/01-12/01
	Colorado	Y	32470 FQ	58310 AW	89230 TQ	COBLS	10/01-12/01
	Boulder-Longmont PMSA, CO	Y	34530 FQ	61900 AW	91110 TQ	COBLS	10/01-12/01
	Colorado Springs MSA, CO	Y	26430 FQ	53490 AW	88170 TQ	COBLS	10/01-12/01
	Denver PMSA, CO	Y	35250 FQ	59900 AW	90180 TQ	COBLS	10/01-12/01
	Fort Collins-Loveland MSA, CO	Y	33330 FQ	56600 AW	82190 TQ	COBLS	10/01-12/01
	Greeley PMSA, CO	Y	32260 FQ	56110 AW	81390 TQ	COBLS	10/01-12/01
	Connecticut	Y	35810 FQ	62330 AW	93780 TQ	CTBLS	10/01-12/01
	Bridgeport PMSA, CT	Y	31930 FQ	65350 AW	98950 TQ	CTBLS	10/01-12/01
	Danbury PMSA, CT	Y	35660 FQ	66510 AW	104930 TQ	CTBLS	10/01-12/01
	Hartford MSA, CT	Y	38480 FQ	62680 AW	90090 TQ	CTBLS	10/01-12/01
	New Haven-Meriden PMSA, CT	Y	35960 FQ	61590 AW	92610 TQ	CTBLS	10/01-12/01
	New London-Norwich MSA, CT-RI	Y	29660 FQ	52350 AW	77270 TQ	CTBLS	10/01-12/01

AAW	Average annual wage	AOH	Average offered, high	ASH	Average starting, high	H	Hourly	M	Monthly	S	Special: hourly and annual
AE	Average entry wage	AOL	Average offered, low	ASL	Average starting, low	HI	Highest wage paid	MTC	Median total compensation	TQ	Third quartile wage
AEX	Average experienced wage	APH	Average pay, high range	AW	Average wage paid	HR	High end range	MW	Median wage paid	W	Weekly
AO	Average offered	APL	Average pay, low range	FQ	First quartile wage	LR	Low end range	SQ	Second quartile wage	Y	Yearly

Occupation/Type/Industry	Location	Per	Low	Mid	High	Source	Date
Database Administrator	Stamford-Norwalk PMSA, CT	Y	35700 FQ	62180 AW	104860 TQ	CTBLS	10/01-12/01
	Waterbury PMSA, CT	Y	39060 FQ	67130 AW	103920 TQ	CTBLS	10/01-12/01
	Delaware	Y	30370 FQ	59100 AW	90610 TQ	DEBLS	10/01-12/01
	Wilmington-Newark PMSA, DE-MD	Y	30410 FQ	59370 AW	90860 TQ	DEBLS	10/01-12/01
	District of Columbia	Y	34520 FQ	62050 AW	104510 TQ	DCBLS	10/01-12/01
	Washington PMSA, DC-MD-VA-WV	Y	37230 FQ	60750 AW	90880 TQ	DCBLS	10/01-12/01
	Florida	Y	29400 FQ	53500 AW	86040 TQ	FLBLS	10/01-12/01
	Daytona Beach MSA, FL	Y	28380 FQ	41300 AW	56530 TQ	FLBLS	10/01-12/01
	Fort Lauderdale PMSA, FL	Y	30760 FQ	61910 AW	136190 TQ	FLBLS	10/01-12/01
	Fort Myers-Cape Coral MSA, FL	Y	26820 FQ	42480 AW	66090 TQ	FLBLS	10/01-12/01
	Gainesville MSA, FL	Y	27670 FQ	46040 AW	67740 TQ	FLBLS	10/01-12/01
	Jacksonville MSA, FL	Y	34930 FQ	67190 AW	92950 TQ	FLBLS	10/01-12/01
	Lakeland-Winter Haven MSA, FL	Y	26220 FQ	42390 AW	73870 TQ	FLBLS	10/01-12/01
	Melbourne-Titusville-Palm Bay MSA, FL	Y	27790 FQ	47020 AW	74230 TQ	FLBLS	10/01-12/01
	Miami PMSA, FL	Y	28350 FQ	50060 AW	84820 TQ	FLBLS	10/01-12/01
	Naples MSA, FL	Y	32360 FQ	49780 AW	78850 TQ	FLBLS	10/01-12/01
	Ocala MSA, FL	Y	33380 FQ	48750 AW	72280 TQ	FLBLS	10/01-12/01
	Orlando MSA, FL	Y	27570 FQ	50060 AW	76360 TQ	FLBLS	10/01-12/01
	Pensacola MSA, FL	Y	28060 FQ	50570 AW	70220 TQ	FLBLS	10/01-12/01
	Sarasota-Bradenton MSA, FL	Y	23740 FQ	43930 AW	78750 TQ	FLBLS	10/01-12/01
	Tallahassee MSA, FL	Y	30470 FQ	67130 AW	121090 TQ	FLBLS	10/01-12/01
	Tampa-St. Petersburg-Clearwater MSA, FL	Y	30360 FQ	49660 AW	73190 TQ	FLBLS	10/01-12/01
	West Palm Beach-Boca Raton MSA, FL	Y	28470 FQ	48840 AW	75640 TQ	FLBLS	10/01-12/01
	Georgia	Y	28380 FQ	60520 AW	94560 TQ	GABLS	10/01-12/01
	Atlanta MSA, GA	Y	29330 FQ	63620 AW	97490 TQ	GABLS	10/01-12/01
	Augusta-Aiken MSA, GA-SC	Y	18720 FQ	43670 AW	68120 TQ	GABLS	10/01-12/01
	Macon MSA, GA	Y	28300 FQ	59810 AW	93620 TQ	GABLS	10/01-12/01
	Savannah MSA, GA	Y	28510 FQ	50710 AW	74800 TQ	GABLS	10/01-12/01
	Hawaii	Y	31230 FQ	46960 AW	65830 TQ	HIBLS	10/01-12/01
	Honolulu MSA, HI	Y	30480 FQ	46060 AW	64150 TQ	HIBLS	10/01-12/01
	Idaho	Y	26270 FQ	46060 AW	72460 TQ	IDBLS	10/01-12/01
	Boise City MSA, ID	Y	25780 FQ	44380 AW	64880 TQ	IDBLS	10/01-12/01
	Illinois	Y	29970 FQ	55370 AW	88560 TQ	ILBLS	10/01-12/01
	Champaign-Urbana MSA, IL	Y	26750 FQ	46940 AW	72210 TQ	ILBLS	10/01-12/01
	Chicago PMSA, IL	Y	31160 FQ	56820 AW	89430 TQ	ILBLS	10/01-12/01
	Peoria-Pekin MSA, IL	Y	23480 FQ	46510 AW	72780 TQ	ILBLS	10/01-12/01
	Rockford MSA, IL	Y	26780 FQ	45970 AW	71550 TQ	ILBLS	10/01-12/01
	Springfield MSA, IL	Y	28280 FQ	48010 AW	90690 TQ	ILBLS	10/01-12/01
	Indiana	Y	30260 FQ	50000 AW	77510 TQ	INBLS	10/01-12/01
	Elkhart-Goshen MSA, IN	Y	30160 FQ	43720 AW	65060 TQ	INBLS	10/01-12/01
	Evansville-Henderson MSA, IN-KY	Y	28830 FQ	42590 AW	60890 TQ	INBLS	10/01-12/01
	Fort Wayne MSA, IN	Y	27490 FQ	47050 AW	67150 TQ	INBLS	10/01-12/01
	Gary PMSA, IN	Y	25180 FQ	49000 AW	89350 TQ	INBLS	10/01-12/01
	Indianapolis MSA, IN	Y	32760 FQ	54190 AW	85000 TQ	INBLS	10/01-12/01
	South Bend MSA, IN	Y	31510 FQ	49810 AW	73340 TQ	INBLS	10/01-12/01
	Iowa	Y	29060 FQ	50100 AW	76040 TQ	IABLS	10/01-12/01
	Cedar Rapids MSA, IA	Y	32550 FQ	52310 AW	76530 TQ	IABLS	10/01-12/01
	Davenport-Moline-Rock Island MSA, IA-IL	Y	27050 FQ	50360 AW	83180 TQ	IABLS	10/01-12/01
	Des Moines MSA, IA	Y	29510 FQ	52690 AW	83400 TQ	IABLS	10/01-12/01
	Kansas	Y	30420 FQ	56340 AW	89140 TQ	KSBLS	10/01-12/01
	Topeka MSA, KS	Y	29930 FQ	52240 AW	80430 TQ	KSBLS	10/01-12/01
	Wichita MSA, KS	Y	30520 FQ	59220 AW	92730 TQ	KSBLS	10/01-12/01
	Kentucky	Y	24970 FQ	48870 AW	77890 TQ	KYBLS	10/01-12/01
	Lexington MSA, KY	Y	24990 FQ	46970 AW	73110 TQ	KYBLS	10/01-12/01
	Louisville MSA, KY-IN	Y	31230 FQ	53460 AW	80500 TQ	KYBLS	10/01-12/01
	Louisiana	Y	24130 FQ	47070 AW	74440 TQ	LABLS	10/01-12/01
	Baton Rouge MSA, LA	Y	22910 FQ	41590 AW	70430 TQ	LABLS	10/01-12/01
	Lafayette MSA, LA	Y	35020 FQ	56880 AW	82780 TQ	LABLS	10/01-12/01
	New Orleans MSA, LA	Y	24730 FQ	47830 AW	74610 TQ	LABLS	10/01-12/01
	Shreveport-Bossier City MSA, LA	Y	26510 FQ	52550 AW	82680 TQ	LABLS	10/01-12/01
	Maine	Y	29280 FQ	52510 AW	80110 TQ	MEBLS	10/01-12/01
	Portland MSA, ME	Y	31870 FQ	60540 AW	88130 TQ	MEBLS	10/01-12/01

AAW Average annual wage **AE** Average entry wage **AEX** Average experienced wage **AO** Average offered **AOH** Average offered, high **AOL** Average offered, low **APH** Average pay, high range **APL** Average pay, low range **ASH** Average starting, high **ASL** Average starting, low **AW** Average wage paid **FQ** First quartile wage **H** Hourly **HI** Highest wage paid **HR** High end range **LR** Low end range **M** Monthly **MTC** Median total compensation **MW** Median wage paid **SQ** Second quartile wage **S** Special: hourly and annual **TQ** Third quartile wage **W** Weekly **Y** Yearly

Occupation/Type/Industry	Location	Per	Low	Mid	High	Source	Date
Database Administrator	Maryland	Y	31620 FQ	63100 AW	97760 TQ	MDBLS	10/01-12/01
	Baltimore PMSA, MD	Y	33240 FQ	61920 AW	96490 TQ	MDBLS	10/01-12/01
	Massachusetts	Y	33640 FQ	62780 AW	94290 TQ	MABLS	10/01-12/01
	Boston PMSA, MA-NH	Y	34990 FQ	64600 AW	96150 TQ	MABLS	10/01-12/01
	Brockton PMSA, MA	Y	43550 FQ	61960 AW	79310 TQ	MABLS	10/01-12/01
	Lawrence PMSA, MA-NH	Y	34620 FQ	58660 AW	83590 TQ	MABLS	10/01-12/01
	Lowell PMSA, MA-NH	Y	34230 FQ	61210 AW	91790 TQ	MABLS	10/01-12/01
	Springfield MSA, MA	Y	22860 FQ	44240 AW	73790 TQ	MABLS	10/01-12/01
	Worcester PMSA, MA-CT	Y	32070 FQ	58090 AW	99090 TQ	MABLS	10/01-12/01
	Michigan	Y	29700 FQ	50650 AW	80300 TQ	MIBLS	10/01-12/01
	Ann Arbor PMSA, MI	Y	33040 FQ	54840 AW	82920 TQ	MIBLS	10/01-12/01
	Detroit PMSA, MI	Y	31290 FQ	53220 AW	84810 TQ	MIBLS	10/01-12/01
	Flint PMSA, MI	Y	24670 FQ	37550 AW	55730 TQ	MIBLS	10/01-12/01
	Grand Rapids-Muskegon-Holland MSA, MI	Y	30590 FQ	47450 AW	70590 TQ	MIBLS	10/01-12/01
	Kalamazoo-Battle Creek MSA, MI	Y	28990 FQ	52480 AW	80660 TQ	MIBLS	10/01-12/01
	Lansing-East Lansing MSA, MI	Y	33290 FQ	54960 AW	82350 TQ	MIBLS	10/01-12/01
	Minnesota	Y	30290 FQ	58650 AW	90280 TQ	MNBLS	10/01-12/01
	Duluth-Superior MSA, MN-WI	Y	24960 FQ	47910 AW	74500 TQ	MNBLS	10/01-12/01
	Minneapolis-St. Paul MSA, MN-WI	Y	31650 FQ	60560 AW	91500 TQ	MNBLS	10/01-12/01
	St. Cloud MSA, MN	Y	31950 FQ	49360 AW	67580 TQ	MNBLS	10/01-12/01
	Mississippi	Y	21970 FQ	45350 AW	70510 TQ	MSBLS	10/01-12/01
	Biloxi-Gulfport-Pascagoula MSA, MS	Y	21560 FQ	43040 AW	67570 TQ	MSBLS	10/01-12/01
	Jackson MSA, MS	Y	30610 FQ	54960 AW	84690 TQ	MSBLS	10/01-12/01
	Missouri	Y	28520 FQ	55800 AW	87300 TQ	MOBLS	10/01-12/01
	Kansas City MSA, MO-KS	Y	30870 FQ	58350 AW	90060 TQ	MOBLS	10/01-12/01
	St. Louis MSA, MO-IL	Y	30770 FQ	57360 AW	86730 TQ	MOBLS	10/01-12/01
	Springfield MSA, MO	Y	28860 FQ	51170 AW	74060 TQ	MOBLS	10/01-12/01
	Montana	Y	22690 FQ	36470 AW	56090 TQ	MTBLS	10/01-12/01
	Billings MSA, MT	Y	20750 FQ	33910 AW	53180 TQ	MTBLS	10/01-12/01
	Nebraska	Y	32640 FQ	56330 AW	85450 TQ	NEBLS	10/01-12/01
	Lincoln MSA, NE	Y	25720 FQ	48160 AW	71520 TQ	NEBLS	10/01-12/01
	Omaha MSA, NE-IA	Y	35380 FQ	58670 AW	87530 TQ	NEBLS	10/01-12/01
	Nevada	Y	36710 FQ	59300 AW	88870 TQ	NVBLS	10/01-12/01
	Las Vegas MSA, NV-AZ	Y	38490 FQ	57130 AW	83060 TQ	NVBLS	10/01-12/01
	Reno MSA, NV	Y	30840 FQ	49960 AW	74020 TQ	NVBLS	10/01-12/01
	New Hampshire	Y	32900 FQ	55260 AW	81250 TQ	NHBLS	10/01-12/01
	Manchester PMSA, NH	Y	36400 FQ	59070 AW	84090 TQ	NHBLS	10/01-12/01
	Nashua PMSA, NH	Y	39440 FQ	61310 AW	82230 TQ	NHBLS	10/01-12/01
	Portsmouth-Rochester PMSA, NH-ME	Y	28530 FQ	51310 AW	83250 TQ	NHBLS	10/01-12/01
	New Jersey	Y	37090 FQ	67770 AW	108000 TQ	NJBLS	10/01-12/01
	Atlantic-Cape May PMSA, NJ	Y	30580 FQ	65970 AW	113170 TQ	NJBLS	10/01-12/01
	Bergen-Passaic PMSA, NJ	Y	38580 FQ	68040 AW	103650 TQ	NJBLS	10/01-12/01
	Jersey City PMSA, NJ	Y	39600 FQ	74540 AW	116930 TQ	NJBLS	10/01-12/01
	Middlesex-Somerset-Hunterdon PMSA, NJ	Y	40180 FQ	72710 AW	118400 TQ	NJBLS	10/01-12/01
	Monmouth-Ocean PMSA, NJ	Y	37050 FQ	59830 AW	92170 TQ	NJBLS	10/01-12/01
	Newark PMSA, NJ	Y	35590 FQ	66520 AW	106580 TQ	NJBLS	10/01-12/01
	Trenton PMSA, NJ	Y	36540 FQ	66000 AW	89740 TQ	NJBLS	10/01-12/01
	New Mexico	Y	27090 FQ	45730 AW	67840 TQ	NMBLS	10/01-12/01
	Albuquerque MSA, NM	Y	27640 FQ	46170 AW	68290 TQ	NMBLS	10/01-12/01
	New York	Y	36910 FQ	68310 AW	107220 TQ	NYBLS	10/01-12/01
	Albany-Schenectady-Troy MSA, NY	Y	32270 FQ	60260 AW	86700 TQ	NYBLS	10/01-12/01
	Binghamton MSA, NY	Y	28720 FQ	50580 AW	77120 TQ	NYBLS	10/01-12/01
	Buffalo-Niagara Falls MSA, NY	Y	31180 FQ	53470 AW	87390 TQ	NYBLS	10/01-12/01
	Nassau-Suffolk PMSA, NY	Y	35390 FQ	62520 AW	90690 TQ	NYBLS	10/01-12/01
	New York PMSA, NY	Y	43340 FQ	76050 AW	113910 TQ	NYBLS	10/01-12/01
	Rochester MSA, NY	Y	28030 FQ	58810 AW	88930 TQ	NYBLS	10/01-12/01
	Syracuse MSA, NY	Y	37460 FQ	56070 AW	81630 TQ	NYBLS	10/01-12/01
	Utica-Rome MSA, NY	Y	29450 FQ	42100 AW	69580 TQ	NYBLS	10/01-12/01
	North Carolina	Y	29270 FQ	57700 AW	92320 TQ	NCBLS	10/01-12/01
	Charlotte-Gastonia-Rock Hill MSA, NC-SC	Y	29150 FQ	61130 AW	114060 TQ	NCBLS	10/01-12/01
	Greensboro-Winston-Salem-High Point MSA, NC	Y	32610 FQ	57580 AW	90970 TQ	NCBLS	10/01-12/01

AAW	Average annual wage	**AOH**	Average offered, high	**ASH**	Average starting, high	**H**	Hourly	**M**	Monthly	**S**	Special: hourly and annual
AE	Average entry wage	**AOL**	Average offered, low	**ASL**	Average starting, low	**HI**	Highest wage paid	**MTC**	Median total compensation	**TQ**	Third quartile wage
AEX	Average experienced wage	**APH**	Average pay, high range	**AW**	Average wage paid	**HR**	High end range	**MW**	Median wage paid	**W**	Weekly
AO	Average offered	**APL**	Average pay, low range	**FQ**	First quartile wage	**LR**	Low end range	**SQ**	Second quartile wage	**Y**	Yearly

Occupation/Type/Industry	Location	Per	Low	Mid	High	Source	Date
Database Administrator	Raleigh-Durham-Chapel Hill MSA, NC	Y	33020 FQ	61160 AW	91840 TQ	NCBLS	10/01-12/01
	Wilmington MSA, NC	Y	24670 FQ	38400 AW	64440 TQ	NCBLS	10/01-12/01
	North Dakota	Y	25330 FQ	43000 AW	59710 TQ	NDBLS	10/01-12/01
	Fargo-Moorhead MSA, ND-MN	Y	23530 FQ	44820 AW	80600 TQ	NDBLS	10/01-12/01
	Ohio	Y	27500 FQ	57820 AW	92160 TQ	OHBLS	10/01-12/01
	Akron PMSA, OH	Y	28790 FQ	58000 AW	92050 TQ	OHBLS	10/01-12/01
	Canton-Massillon MSA, OH	Y	35360 FQ	53120 AW	73830 TQ	OHBLS	10/01-12/01
	Cincinnati PMSA, OH-KY-IN	Y	31130 FQ	59240 AW	90350 TQ	OHBLS	10/01-12/01
	Cleveland-Lorain-Elyria PMSA, OH	Y	29150 FQ	55990 AW	90560 TQ	OHBLS	10/01-12/01
	Columbus MSA, OH	Y	36960 FQ	62230 AW	91430 TQ	OHBLS	10/01-12/01
	Dayton-Springfield MSA, OH	Y	36430 FQ	62180 AW	93130 TQ	OHBLS	10/01-12/01
	Toledo MSA, OH	Y	19090 FQ	29600 AW	55680 TQ	OHBLS	10/01-12/01
	Youngstown-Warren MSA, OH	Y	29940 FQ	53140 AW	82790 TQ	OHBLS	10/01-12/01
	Oklahoma	Y	26610 FQ	47030 AW	74990 TQ	OKBLS	10/01-12/01
	Oklahoma City MSA, OK	Y	27530 FQ	46150 AW	76900 TQ	OKBLS	10/01-12/01
	Tulsa MSA, OK	Y	29390 FQ	51450 AW	74900 TQ	OKBLS	10/01-12/01
	Oregon	Y	30930 FQ	52820 AW	81290 TQ	ORBLS	10/01-12/01
	Eugene-Springfield MSA, OR	Y	33350 FQ	51330 AW	69440 TQ	ORBLS	10/01-12/01
	Portland-Vancouver PMSA, OR-WA	Y	32160 FQ	54660 AW	83540 TQ	ORBLS	10/01-12/01
	Salem PMSA, OR	Y	25560 FQ	51300 AW	99970 TQ	ORBLS	10/01-12/01
	Pennsylvania	Y	27760 FQ	55870 AW	90520 TQ	PABLS	10/01-12/01
	Allentown-Bethlehem-Easton MSA, PA	Y	31550 FQ	65560 AW	106210 TQ	PABLS	10/01-12/01
	Erie MSA, PA	Y	21790 FQ	41800 AW	63970 TQ	PABLS	10/01-12/01
	Lancaster MSA, PA	Y	29550 FQ	49720 AW	80300 TQ	PABLS	10/01-12/01
	Philadelphia PMSA, PA-NJ	Y	30900 FQ	60440 AW	101450 TQ	PABLS	10/01-12/01
	Pittsburgh MSA, PA	Y	24020 FQ	52710 AW	86960 TQ	PABLS	10/01-12/01
	Reading MSA, PA	Y	27900 FQ	55290 AW	86400 TQ	PABLS	10/01-12/01
	Scranton-Wilkes-Barre-Hazleton MSA, PA	Y	26440 FQ	49100 AW	80510 TQ	PABLS	10/01-12/01
	York MSA, PA	Y	24740 FQ	42570 AW	73730 TQ	PABLS	10/01-12/01
	Rhode Island	Y	31750 FQ	54470 AW	80690 TQ	RIBLS	10/01-12/01
	Providence-Fall River-Warwick MSA, RI-MA	Y	33700 FQ	56220 AW	81900 TQ	RIBLS	10/01-12/01
	South Carolina	Y	23370 FQ	46120 AW	72220 TQ	SCBLS	10/01-12/01
	Charleston-North Charleston MSA, SC	Y	16590 FQ	36780 AW	63640 TQ	SCBLS	10/01-12/01
	Columbia MSA, SC	Y	27200 FQ	53450 AW	77260 TQ	SCBLS	10/01-12/01
	Greenville-Spartanburg-Anderson MSA, SC	Y	28030 FQ	49910 AW	72900 TQ	SCBLS	10/01-12/01
	South Dakota	Y	33220 FQ	53970 AW	84990 TQ	SDBLS	10/01-12/01
	Sioux Falls MSA, SD	Y	29050 FQ	49570 AW	75870 TQ	SDBLS	10/01-12/01
	Tennessee	Y	25630 FQ	50790 AW	77980 TQ	TNBLS	10/01-12/01
	Chattanooga MSA, TN-GA	Y	23300 FQ	45990 AW	74000 TQ	TNBLS	10/01-12/01
	Johnson City-Kingsport-Bristol MSA, TN-VA	Y	23250 FQ	49850 AW	84850 TQ	TNBLS	10/01-12/01
	Knoxville MSA, TN	Y	28320 FQ	53040 AW	74040 TQ	TNBLS	10/01-12/01
	Memphis MSA, TN-AR-MS	Y	27250 FQ	54200 AW	83220 TQ	TNBLS	10/01-12/01
	Nashville MSA, TN	Y	26180 FQ	50820 AW	78120 TQ	TNBLS	10/01-12/01
	Texas	Y	28470 FQ	55360 AW	87930 TQ	TXBLS	10/01-12/01
	Amarillo MSA, TX	Y	29120 FQ	47490 AW	68130 TQ	TXBLS	10/01-12/01
	Austin-San Marcos MSA, TX	Y	32200 FQ	60490 AW	90480 TQ	TXBLS	10/01-12/01
	Beaumont-Port Arthur MSA, TX	Y	38690 FQ	54030 AW	72680 TQ	TXBLS	10/01-12/01
	Corpus Christi MSA, TX	Y	26030 FQ	44060 AW	67980 TQ	TXBLS	10/01-12/01
	Dallas PMSA, TX	Y	33620 FQ	62120 AW	92520 TQ	TXBLS	10/01-12/01
	El Paso MSA, TX	Y	24220 FQ	52690 AW	83100 TQ	TXBLS	10/01-12/01
	Fort Worth-Arlington PMSA, TX	Y	29290 FQ	54740 AW	83580 TQ	TXBLS	10/01-12/01
	Houston PMSA, TX	Y	24350 FQ	49600 AW	84770 TQ	TXBLS	10/01-12/01
	Killeen-Temple MSA, TX	Y	21920 FQ	42350 AW	70480 TQ	TXBLS	10/01-12/01
	Lubbock MSA, TX	Y	16520 FQ	44950 AW	69510 TQ	TXBLS	10/01-12/01
	McAllen-Edinburg-Mission MSA, TX	Y	24050 FQ	40320 AW	57400 TQ	TXBLS	10/01-12/01
	San Antonio MSA, TX	Y	30160 FQ	50090 AW	75270 TQ	TXBLS	10/01-12/01
	Waco MSA, TX	Y	21320 FQ	46140 AW	71900 TQ	TXBLS	10/01-12/01
	Utah	Y	32990 FQ	55680 AW	85110 TQ	UTBLS	10/01-12/01
	Provo-Orem MSA, UT	Y	37560 FQ	56700 AW	86230 TQ	UTBLS	10/01-12/01

AAW	Average annual wage	**AOH**	Average offered, high	**ASH**	Average starting, high	**H**	Hourly	**M**	Monthly	**S**	Special: hourly and annual
AE	Average entry wage	**AOL**	Average offered, low	**ASL**	Average starting, low	**HI**	Highest wage paid	**MTC**	Median total compensation	**TQ**	Third quartile wage
AEX	Average experienced wage	**APH**	Average pay, high range	**AW**	Average wage paid	**HR**	High end range	**MW**	Median wage paid	**W**	Weekly
AO	Average offered	**APL**	Average pay, low range	**FQ**	First quartile wage	**LR**	Low end range	**SQ**	Second quartile wage	**Y**	Yearly

Occupation/Type/Industry	Location	Per	Low	Mid	High	Source	Date
Database Administrator	Salt Lake City-Ogden MSA, UT	Y	32960 FQ	56160 AW	85070 TQ	UTBLS	10/01-12/01
	Vermont	Y	35680 FQ	50530 AW	70090 TQ	VTBLS	10/01-12/01
	Burlington MSA, VT	Y	36320 FQ	54050 AW	80850 TQ	VTBLS	10/01-12/01
	Virginia	Y	36790 FQ	56460 AW	87160 TQ	VABLS	10/01-12/01
	Lynchburg MSA, VA	Y	31780 FQ	50510 AW	81070 TQ	VABLS	10/01-12/01
	Norfolk-Virginia Beach-Newport News MSA, VA-NC	Y	35810 FQ	48730 AW	70110 TQ	VABLS	10/01-12/01
	Richmond-Petersburg MSA, VA	Y	31260 FQ	57830 AW	89320 TQ	VABLS	10/01-12/01
	Roanoke MSA, VA	Y	24220 FQ	48740 AW	84860 TQ	VABLS	10/01-12/01
	Washington	Y	35900 FQ	61640 AW	93630 TQ	WABLS	10/01-12/01
	Bremerton PMSA, WA	Y	29930 FQ	49520 AW	71270 TQ	WABLS	10/01-12/01
	Olympia PMSA, WA	Y	31290 FQ	56440 AW	81020 TQ	WABLS	10/01-12/01
	Richland-Kennewick-Pasco MSA, WA	Y	34080 FQ	54230 AW	86490 TQ	WABLS	10/01-12/01
	Seattle-Bellevue-Everett PMSA, WA	Y	37890 FQ	64430 AW	97460 TQ	WABLS	10/01-12/01
	Spokane MSA, WA	Y	30780 FQ	50550 AW	73370 TQ	WABLS	10/01-12/01
	Tacoma PMSA, WA	Y	31610 FQ	51610 AW	80210 TQ	WABLS	10/01-12/01
	Yakima MSA, WA	Y	25970 FQ	49000 AW	85790 TQ	WABLS	10/01-12/01
	West Virginia	Y	27400 FQ	44430 AW	67400 TQ	WVBLS	10/01-12/01
	Charleston MSA, WV	Y	30580 FQ	46160 AW	66140 TQ	WVBLS	10/01-12/01
	Huntington-Ashland MSA, WV-KY-OH	Y	24240 FQ	36670 AW	54690 TQ	WVBLS	10/01-12/01
	Wisconsin	Y	28280 FQ	50550 AW	77270 TQ	WIBLS	10/01-12/01
	Appleton-Oshkosh-Neenah MSA, WI	Y	29960 FQ	52720 AW	85440 TQ	WIBLS	10/01-12/01
	Green Bay MSA, WI	Y	32850 FQ	53440 AW	81810 TQ	WIBLS	10/01-12/01
	Madison MSA, WI	Y	32410 FQ	53830 AW	79350 TQ	WIBLS	10/01-12/01
	Milwaukee-Waukesha PMSA, WI	Y	30510 FQ	51640 AW	79450 TQ	WIBLS	10/01-12/01
	Wyoming	Y	18680 FQ	40880 AW	81750 TQ	WYBLS	10/01-12/01
	Puerto Rico	Y	25250 FQ	40160 AW	62050 TQ	PRBLS	10/01-12/01
Deckhand							
Tugboat	Jacksonville, FL	Y	20000 AE	30000 AW		FLTU	2002
Defense and Transportation Manufacturer	San Diego, CA	Y		53111 AW		SDBJ1	1/99-1/00
Delivery Technician							
Home Care	United States	Y	25243 AOL			HCM	1/01-1/02
Demonstrator and Product Promoter	Alabama	Y	12700 FQ	26910 AW	56170 TQ	ALBLS	10/01-12/01
	Alaska	Y	15170 FQ	20700 AW	26370 TQ	AKBLS	10/01-12/01
	Arizona	Y	15770 FQ	27700 AW	41160 TQ	AZBLS	10/01-12/01
	Arkansas	Y	12400 FQ	23270 AW	37810 TQ	ARBLS	10/01-12/01
	California	Y	14920 FQ	24940 AW	43710 TQ	CABLS	10/01-12/01
	Colorado	Y	15490 FQ	24010 AW	37130 TQ	COBLS	10/01-12/01
	Connecticut	Y	15140 FQ	31290 AW	60700 TQ	CTBLS	10/01-12/01
	Delaware	Y	14880 FQ	26910 AW	49170 TQ	DEBLS	10/01-12/01
	Florida	Y	13930 FQ	27540 AW	44270 TQ	FLBLS	10/01-12/01
	Georgia	Y	14770 FQ	22920 AW	39570 TQ	GABLS	10/01-12/01
	Idaho	Y	12660 FQ	17400 AW	20890 TQ	IDBLS	10/01-12/01
	Illinois	Y	15540 FQ	28160 AW	46390 TQ	ILBLS	10/01-12/01
	Indiana	Y	13060 FQ	23580 AW	44080 TQ	INBLS	10/01-12/01
	Iowa	Y	13460 FQ	27490 AW	49790 TQ	IABLS	10/01-12/01
	Kansas	Y	14180 FQ	18620 AW	22920 TQ	KSBLS	10/01-12/01
	Kentucky	Y	15470 FQ	26530 AW	45420 TQ	KYBLS	10/01-12/01
	Louisiana	Y	14590 FQ	23500 AW	41870 TQ	LABLS	10/01-12/01
	Maine	Y	12200 FQ	22380 AW	41270 TQ	MEBLS	10/01-12/01
	Maryland	Y	14840 FQ	25290 AW	41090 TQ	MDBLS	10/01-12/01
	Massachusetts	Y	17080 FQ	31160 AW	56020 TQ	MABLS	10/01-12/01
	Michigan	Y	14550 FQ	25310 AW	46590 TQ	MIBLS	10/01-12/01
	Minnesota	Y	14150 FQ	22070 AW	37380 TQ	MNBLS	10/01-12/01
	Mississippi	Y	12270 FQ	18570 AW	26830 TQ	MSBLS	10/01-12/01
	Missouri	Y	12040 FQ	26200 AW	49950 TQ	MOBLS	10/01-12/01
	Montana	Y	12900 FQ	17010 AW	18770 TQ	MTBLS	10/01-12/01
	Nebraska	Y	11920 FQ	18530 AW	30220 TQ	NEBLS	10/01-12/01

AAW Average annual wage **AOH** Average offered, high **ASH** Average starting, high **H** Hourly **M** Monthly **S** Special: hourly and annual
AE Average entry wage **AOL** Average offered, low **ASL** Average starting, low **HI** Highest wage paid **MTC** Median total compensation **TQ** Third quartile wage
AEX Average experienced wage **APH** Average pay, high range **AW** Average wage paid **HR** High end range **MW** Median wage paid **W** Weekly
AO Average offered **APL** Average pay, low range **FQ** First quartile wage **LR** Low end range **SQ** Second quartile wage **Y** Yearly

Occupation/Type/Industry	Location	Per	Low	Mid	High	Source	Date
Demonstrator and Product Promoter	Nevada	Y	14750 FQ	32120 AW	69690 TQ	NVBLS	10/01-12/01
	New Hampshire	Y	13320 FQ	25650 AW	42140 TQ	NHBLS	10/01-12/01
	New Jersey	Y	15360 FQ	27060 AW	49120 TQ	NJBLS	10/01-12/01
	New Mexico	Y	14450 FQ	19720 AW	29320 TQ	NMBLS	10/01-12/01
	New York	Y	14350 FQ	33310 AW	55130 TQ	NYBLS	10/01-12/01
	North Carolina	Y	14010 FQ	25940 AW	48440 TQ	NCBLS	10/01-12/01
	North Dakota	Y	13020 FQ	18320 AW	25430 TQ	NDBLS	10/01-12/01
	Ohio	Y	15420 FQ	31970 AW	50080 TQ	OHBLS	10/01-12/01
	Oklahoma	Y	13600 FQ	22910 AW	36910 TQ	OKBLS	10/01-12/01
	Oregon	Y	14590 FQ	18430 AW	24180 TQ	ORBLS	10/01-12/01
	Pennsylvania	Y	14570 FQ	30060 AW	62060 TQ	PABLS	10/01-12/01
	Rhode Island	Y	14840 FQ	27970 AW	44880 TQ	RIBLS	10/01-12/01
	South Carolina	Y	14400 FQ	27140 AW	43600 TQ	SCBLS	10/01-12/01
	South Dakota	Y	12270 FQ	16710 AW	23220 TQ	SDBLS	10/01-12/01
	Tennessee	Y	13460 FQ	25480 AW	42460 TQ	TNBLS	10/01-12/01
	Texas	Y	15290 FQ	24910 AW	38530 TQ	TXBLS	10/01-12/01
	Utah	Y	16230 FQ	22290 AW	30130 TQ	UTBLS	10/01-12/01
	Vermont	Y	13190 FQ	27140 AW	68250 TQ	VTBLS	10/01-12/01
	Virginia	Y	12640 FQ	21570 AW	33720 TQ	VABLS	10/01-12/01
	Washington	Y	14540 FQ	24390 AW	41580 TQ	WABLS	10/01-12/01
	West Virginia	Y	15000 FQ	24600 AW	41930 TQ	WVBLS	10/01-12/01
	Wisconsin	Y	12880 FQ	22580 AW	39960 TQ	WIBLS	10/01-12/01
	Wyoming	Y	14260 FQ	18980 AW	29810 TQ	WYBLS	10/01-12/01
	Puerto Rico	Y	11920 FQ	16520 AW	22210 TQ	PRBLS	10/01-12/01
Dental Assistant	United States	Y		25760-39660 AW		FREEP1	1/00-1/00
	Alabama	H	7.01 FQ	10.45 AW	14.67 TQ	ALBLS	10/01-12/01
	Alaska	H	8.37 FQ	15.26 AW	20.71 TQ	AKBLS	10/01-12/01
	Arizona	H	6.94 FQ	10.84 AW	15.21 TQ	AZBLS	10/01-12/01
	Arkansas	H	7.36 FQ	9.82 AW	12.93 TQ	ARBLS	10/01-12/01
	California	H	10.77 FQ	15.58 AW	20.81 TQ	CABLS	10/01-12/01
	Colorado	H	10.57 FQ	17.04 AW	23.22 TQ	COBLS	10/01-12/01
	Connecticut	H	11.81 FQ	15.79 AW	20.43 TQ	CTBLS	10/01-12/01
	Delaware	H	8.27 FQ	12.57 AW	17.19 TQ	DEBLS	10/01-12/01
	District of Columbia	H	13.99 FQ	18.54 AW	23.50 TQ	DCBLS	10/01-12/01
	Florida	H	8.69 FQ	12.08 AW	15.99 TQ	FLBLS	10/01-12/01
	Georgia	H	7.41 FQ	12.33 AW	18.22 TQ	GABLS	10/01-12/01
	Hawaii	H	11.14 FQ	14.01 AW	17.14 TQ	HIBLS	10/01-12/01
	Idaho	H	8.29 FQ	12.49 AW	19.12 TQ	IDBLS	10/01-12/01
	Illinois	H	7.11 FQ	10.23 AW	16.10 TQ	ILBLS	10/01-12/01
	Indiana	H	9.24 FQ	12.33 AW	16.12 TQ	INBLS	10/01-12/01
	Iowa	H	9.35 FQ	12.55 AW	16.61 TQ	IABLS	10/01-12/01
	Kansas	H	8.58 FQ	11.98 AW	16.41 TQ	KSBLS	10/01-12/01
	Kentucky	H	7.95 FQ	11.66 AW	16.55 TQ	KYBLS	10/01-12/01
	Louisiana	H	6.27 FQ	8.88 AW	11.61 TQ	LABLS	10/01-12/01
	Maine	H	9.13 FQ	11.81 AW	14.56 TQ	MEBLS	10/01-12/01
	Maryland	H	10.29 FQ	15.51 AW	20.87 TQ	MDBLS	10/01-12/01
	Massachusetts	H	11.40 FQ	15.06 AW	19.42 TQ	MABLS	10/01-12/01
	Michigan	H	8.79 FQ	13.14 AW	16.84 TQ	MIBLS	10/01-12/01
	Minnesota	H	10.69 FQ	15.24 AW	20.33 TQ	MNBLS	10/01-12/01
	Mississippi	H	6.69 FQ	11.08 AW	14.49 TQ	MSBLS	10/01-12/01
	Missouri	H	8.09 FQ	11.99 AW	16.46 TQ	MOBLS	10/01-12/01
	Montana	H	8.96 FQ	11.34 AW	14.05 TQ	MTBLS	10/01-12/01
	Nebraska	H	7.96 FQ	11.44 AW	14.37 TQ	NEBLS	10/01-12/01
	Nevada	H	8.65 FQ	15.58 AW	21.20 TQ	NVBLS	10/01-12/01
	New Hampshire	H	8.42 FQ	13.21 AW	18.46 TQ	NHBLS	10/01-12/01
	New Jersey	H	9.74 FQ	14.43 AW	19.64 TQ	NJBLS	10/01-12/01
	New Mexico	H	8.05 FQ	11.31 AW	14.47 TQ	NMBLS	10/01-12/01
	New York	H	9.09 FQ	14.47 AW	20.26 TQ	NYBLS	10/01-12/01
	North Carolina	H	8.15 FQ	12.69 AW	17.10 TQ	NCBLS	10/01-12/01
	North Dakota	H	9.92 FQ	12.24 AW	14.06 TQ	NDBLS	10/01-12/01
	Ohio	H	8.84 FQ	11.80 AW	15.86 TQ	OHBLS	10/01-12/01
	Oklahoma	H	8.84 FQ	11.61 AW	15.86 TQ	OKBLS	10/01-12/01
	Oregon	H	9.24 FQ	14.07 AW	19.70 TQ	ORBLS	10/01-12/01
	Pennsylvania	H	8.45 FQ	11.75 AW	17.57 TQ	PABLS	10/01-12/01
	Rhode Island	H	11.36 FQ	14.74 AW	17.35 TQ	RIBLS	10/01-12/01
	South Carolina	H	8.12 FQ	11.84 AW	16.36 TQ	SCBLS	10/01-12/01
	South Dakota	H	7.63 FQ	11.24 AW	15.80 TQ	SDBLS	10/01-12/01
	Tennessee	H	8.99 FQ	12.40 AW	16.68 TQ	TNBLS	10/01-12/01
	Texas	H	8.33 FQ	14.07 AW	20.57 TQ	TXBLS	10/01-12/01

AAW Average annual wage; **AE** Average entry wage; **AEX** Average experienced wage; **AO** Average offered; **AOH** Average offered, high; **AOL** Average offered, low; **APH** Average pay, high range; **APL** Average pay, low range; **ASH** Average starting, high; **ASL** Average starting, low; **AW** Average wage paid; **FQ** First quartile wage; **H** Hourly; **HI** Highest wage paid; **HR** High end range; **LR** Low end range; **M** Monthly; **MTC** Median total compensation; **MW** Median wage paid; **SQ** Second quartile wage; **S** Special: hourly and annual; **TQ** Third quartile wage; **W** Weekly; **Y** Yearly

Occupation/Type/Industry	Location	Per	Low	Mid	High	Source	Date
Dental Assistant	Utah	H	7.09 FQ	9.75 AW	12.97 TQ	UTBLS	10/01-12/01
	Vermont	H	9.50 FQ	14.14 AW	19.58 TQ	VTBLS	10/01-12/01
	Virginia	H	8.71 FQ	12.95 AW	18.01 TQ	VABLS	10/01-12/01
	Washington	H	10.67 FQ	15.59 AW	20.86 TQ	WABLS	10/01-12/01
	West Virginia	H	6.64 FQ	9.43 AW	12.17 TQ	WVBLS	10/01-12/01
	Wisconsin	H	8.89 FQ	11.61 AW	15.58 TQ	WIBLS	10/01-12/01
	Wyoming	H	8.06 FQ	10.87 AW	14.20 TQ	WYBLS	10/01-12/01
	Puerto Rico	H	5.49 FQ	6.31 AW	7.24 TQ	PRBLS	10/01-12/01
	Guam	H	8.41 FQ	12.55 AW	16.92 TQ	GUBLS	10/01-12/01
Dental Hygienist	United States	Y		39700 AW		FREEP1	1/00-1/00
	Alabama	Y	23310 FQ	32370 AW	41980 TQ	ALBLS	10/01-12/01
	Birmingham MSA, AL	Y	27450 FQ	35830 AW	43380 TQ	ALBLS	10/01-12/01
	Huntsville MSA, AL	Y	28700 FQ	35330 AW	42940 TQ	ALBLS	10/01-12/01
	Mobile MSA, AL	Y	14930 FQ	31340 AW	40790 TQ	ALBLS	10/01-12/01
	Montgomery MSA, AL	Y	28000 FQ	34030 AW	38420 TQ	ALBLS	10/01-12/01
	Alaska	Y	20200 FQ	63290 AW	90200 TQ	AKBLS	10/01-12/01
	Anchorage MSA, AK	Y	59470 FQ	73320 AW	91270 TQ	AKBLS	10/01-12/01
	Arizona	Y	35430 FQ	63520 AW	86730 TQ	AZBLS	10/01-12/01
	Phoenix-Mesa MSA, AZ	Y	34580 FQ	64860 AW	87550 TQ	AZBLS	10/01-12/01
	Tucson MSA, AZ	Y	37000 FQ	54070 AW	70450 TQ	AZBLS	10/01-12/01
	Arkansas	Y	18680 FQ	43080 AW	58480 TQ	ARBLS	10/01-12/01
	Fayetteville-Springdale-Rogers MSA, AR	Y	37750 FQ	41740 AW	46050 TQ	ARBLS	10/01-12/01
	Fort Smith MSA, AR-OK	Y	21150 FQ	42960 AW	68710 TQ	ARBLS	10/01-12/01
	Little Rock-North Little Rock MSA, AR	Y	45160 FQ	50590 AW	57940 TQ	ARBLS	10/01-12/01
	California	Y	37080 FQ	80250 AW		CABLS	10/01-12/01
	Bakersfield MSA, CA	Y	62460 FQ	91340 AW	140440 TQ	CABLS	10/01-12/01
	Chico-Paradise MSA, CA	Y	38400 FQ	59840 AW	85410 TQ	CABLS	10/01-12/01
	Fresno MSA, CA	Y	46310 FQ	59690 AW	71870 TQ	CABLS	10/01-12/01
	Modesto MSA, CA	Y	75310 FQ	93330 AW	112110 TQ	CABLS	10/01-12/01
	Oakland PMSA, CA	Y	43140 FQ	75870 AW	113450 TQ	CABLS	10/01-12/01
	Riverside-San Bernardino PMSA, CA	Y	46850 FQ	59500 AW	84790 TQ	CABLS	10/01-12/01
	Sacramento PMSA, CA	Y	15270 FQ	26650 AW	42030 TQ	CABLS	10/01-12/01
	Salinas MSA, CA	Y	31280 FQ	49050 AW	69350 TQ	CABLS	10/01-12/01
	San Diego MSA, CA	Y	75090 FQ	80400 AW	92300 TQ	CABLS	10/01-12/01
	San Francisco PMSA, CA	Y	38210 FQ	64790 AW	90620 TQ	CABLS	10/01-12/01
	San Jose PMSA, CA	Y	37560 FQ	90510 AW	133890 TQ	CABLS	10/01-12/01
	San Luis Obispo-Atascadero-Paso Robles MSA, CA	Y	47180 FQ	64010 AW	87910 TQ	CABLS	10/01-12/01
	Santa Barbara-Santa Maria-Lompoc MSA, CA	Y	71370 FQ	125700 AW		CABLS	10/01-12/01
	Santa Cruz-Watsonville PMSA, CA	Y	76430 FQ	82600 AW	92450 TQ	CABLS	10/01-12/01
	Santa Rosa PMSA, CA	Y	78170 FQ	92280 AW	112670 TQ	CABLS	10/01-12/01
	Stockton-Lodi MSA, CA	Y	25040 FQ	59780 AW	107970 TQ	CABLS	10/01-12/01
	Vallejo-Fairfield-Napa PMSA, CA	Y	47460 FQ	58760 AW	91170 TQ	CABLS	10/01-12/01
	Ventura PMSA, CA	Y	33370 FQ	65180 AW	90640 TQ	CABLS	10/01-12/01
	Visalia-Tulare-Porterville MSA, CA	Y	30560 FQ	49390 AW	73100 TQ	CABLS	10/01-12/01
	Colorado	Y	37260 FQ	63480 AW	86620 TQ	COBLS	10/01-12/01
	Boulder-Longmont PMSA, CO	Y	74570 FQ	80910 AW	92200 TQ	COBLS	10/01-12/01
	Colorado Springs MSA, CO	Y	39730 FQ	57090 AW	70740 TQ	COBLS	10/01-12/01
	Denver PMSA, CO	Y	19380 FQ	61960 AW	86300 TQ	COBLS	10/01-12/01
	Fort Collins-Loveland MSA, CO	Y	57770 FQ	63420 AW	70990 TQ	COBLS	10/01-12/01
	Greeley PMSA, CO	Y	49920 FQ	65340 AW	87250 TQ	COBLS	10/01-12/01
	Connecticut	Y	46640 FQ	57540 AW	70470 TQ	CTBLS	10/01-12/01
	Bridgeport PMSA, CT	Y	46550 FQ	52840 AW	64720 TQ	CTBLS	10/01-12/01
	Danbury PMSA, CT	Y	50440 FQ	61180 AW	72750 TQ	CTBLS	10/01-12/01
	Hartford MSA, CT	Y	50230 FQ	60730 AW	70660 TQ	CTBLS	10/01-12/01
	New Haven-Meriden PMSA, CT	Y	27530 FQ	49720 AW	69030 TQ	CTBLS	10/01-12/01
	New London-Norwich MSA, CT-RI	Y	39940 FQ	57030 AW	70080 TQ	CTBLS	10/01-12/01
	Stamford-Norwalk PMSA, CT	Y	53300 FQ	63200 AW	72720 TQ	CTBLS	10/01-12/01
	Waterbury PMSA, CT	Y	48030 FQ	57200 AW	70870 TQ	CTBLS	10/01-12/01
	Delaware	Y	24800 FQ	47340 AW	70380 TQ	DEBLS	10/01-12/01
	Wilmington-Newark PMSA, DE-MD	Y	23740 FQ	44630 AW	70580 TQ	DEBLS	10/01-12/01

AAW Average annual wage **AOH** Average offered, high **ASH** Average starting, high **H** Hourly **M** Monthly **S** Special: hourly and annual
AE Average entry wage **AOL** Average offered, low **ASL** Average starting, low **HI** Highest wage paid **MTC** Median total compensation **TQ** Third quartile wage
AEX Average experienced wage **APH** Average pay, high range **AW** Average wage paid **HR** High end range **MW** Median wage paid **W** Weekly
AO Average offered **APL** Average pay, low range **FQ** First quartile wage **LR** Low end range **SQ** Second quartile wage **Y** Yearly

Occupation/Type/Industry	Location	Per	Low	Mid	High	Source	Date
Dental Hygienist	District of Columbia	Y	22750 FQ	48850 AW	74480 TQ	DCBLS	10/01-12/01
	Washington PMSA, DC-MD-VA-WV	Y	50410 FQ	68610 AW	89880 TQ	DCBLS	10/01-12/01
	Florida	Y	35920 FQ	54200 AW	69070 TQ	FLBLS	10/01-12/01
	Daytona Beach MSA, FL	Y	32350 FQ	38470 AW	44830 TQ	FLBLS	10/01-12/01
	Fort Lauderdale PMSA, FL	Y	29960 FQ	36160 AW	49850 TQ	FLBLS	10/01-12/01
	Fort Myers-Cape Coral MSA, FL	Y	42380 FQ	54510 AW	68950 TQ	FLBLS	10/01-12/01
	Fort Pierce-Port St. Lucie MSA, FL	Y	36080 FQ	41460 AW	51780 TQ	FLBLS	10/01-12/01
	Fort Walton Beach MSA, FL	Y	33890 FQ	48300 AW	57320 TQ	FLBLS	10/01-12/01
	Jacksonville MSA, FL	Y	45390 FQ	50470 AW	55990 TQ	FLBLS	10/01-12/01
	Lakeland-Winter Haven MSA, FL	Y	34360 FQ	56150 AW	76960 TQ	FLBLS	10/01-12/01
	Melbourne-Titusville-Palm Bay MSA, FL	Y	26020 FQ	39630 AW	56130 TQ	FLBLS	10/01-12/01
	Miami PMSA, FL	Y	40590 FQ	48750 AW	55620 TQ	FLBLS	10/01-12/01
	Naples MSA, FL	Y	59830 FQ	63480 AW	73150 TQ	FLBLS	10/01-12/01
	Ocala MSA, FL	Y	39740 FQ	47520 AW	55030 TQ	FLBLS	10/01-12/01
	Pensacola MSA, FL	Y	33710 FQ	39320 AW	44990 TQ	FLBLS	10/01-12/01
	Sarasota-Bradenton MSA, FL	Y	55530 FQ	62920 AW	70820 TQ	FLBLS	10/01-12/01
	Tallahassee MSA, FL	Y	24150 FQ	45840 AW	58460 TQ	FLBLS	10/01-12/01
	Tampa-St. Petersburg-Clearwater MSA, FL	Y	36960 FQ	46950 AW	60780 TQ	FLBLS	10/01-12/01
	West Palm Beach-Boca Raton MSA, FL	Y	37870 FQ	47010 AW	58030 TQ	FLBLS	10/01-12/01
	Georgia	Y	33080 FQ	48330 AW	60280 TQ	GABLS	10/01-12/01
	Atlanta MSA, GA	Y	46840 FQ	52790 AW	63720 TQ	GABLS	10/01-12/01
	Augusta-Aiken MSA, GA-SC	Y	30940 FQ	42780 AW	64070 TQ	GABLS	10/01-12/01
	Columbus MSA, GA-AL	Y	30410 FQ	36360 AW	45380 TQ	GABLS	10/01-12/01
	Macon MSA, GA	Y	35780 FQ	44990 AW	55550 TQ	GABLS	10/01-12/01
	Savannah MSA, GA	Y	31120 FQ	37000 AW	43590 TQ	GABLS	10/01-12/01
	Hawaii	Y	31070 FQ	45820 AW	62620 TQ	HIBLS	10/01-12/01
	Honolulu MSA, HI	Y	30800 FQ	44060 AW	58510 TQ	HIBLS	10/01-12/01
	Idaho	Y	39510 FQ	53370 AW	69690 TQ	IDBLS	10/01-12/01
	Boise City MSA, ID	Y	38750 FQ	53110 AW	69670 TQ	IDBLS	10/01-12/01
	Illinois	Y	29200 FQ	49810 AW	69890 TQ	ILBLS	10/01-12/01
	Champaign-Urbana MSA, IL	Y	36500 FQ	41430 AW	49510 TQ	ILBLS	10/01-12/01
	Chicago PMSA, IL	Y	34210 FQ	56110 AW	71630 TQ	ILBLS	10/01-12/01
	Peoria-Pekin MSA, IL	Y	24190 FQ	35310 AW	54600 TQ	ILBLS	10/01-12/01
	Rockford MSA, IL	Y	47290 FQ	55030 AW	67370 TQ	ILBLS	10/01-12/01
	Springfield MSA, IL	Y	19670 FQ	40440 AW	48750 TQ	ILBLS	10/01-12/01
	Indiana	Y	29100 FQ	47260 AW	66450 TQ	INBLS	10/01-12/01
	Elkhart-Goshen MSA, IN	Y	41090 FQ	50970 AW	57700 TQ	INBLS	10/01-12/01
	Evansville-Henderson MSA, IN-KY	Y	31850 FQ	41600 AW	52770 TQ	INBLS	10/01-12/01
	Fort Wayne MSA, IN	Y	31020 FQ	41170 AW	54280 TQ	INBLS	10/01-12/01
	Gary PMSA, IN	Y	22400 FQ	39960 AW	65650 TQ	INBLS	10/01-12/01
	Indianapolis MSA, IN	Y	60140 FQ	66140 AW	74190 TQ	INBLS	10/01-12/01
	Lafayette MSA, IN	Y	28540 FQ	37400 AW	57050 TQ	INBLS	10/01-12/01
	South Bend MSA, IN	Y	41360 FQ	51330 AW	60610 TQ	INBLS	10/01-12/01
	Iowa	Y	37940 FQ	48570 AW	59010 TQ	IABLS	10/01-12/01
	Cedar Rapids MSA, IA	Y	37100 FQ	43250 AW	54160 TQ	IABLS	10/01-12/01
	Davenport-Moline-Rock Island MSA, IA-IL	Y	17310 FQ	39030 AW	56000 TQ	IABLS	10/01-12/01
	Des Moines MSA, IA	Y	47220 FQ	54740 AW	67000 TQ	IABLS	10/01-12/01
	Kansas	Y	40650 FQ	50740 AW	60630 TQ	KSBLS	10/01-12/01
	Topeka MSA, KS	Y	46870 FQ	54500 AW	65920 TQ	KSBLS	10/01-12/01
	Wichita MSA, KS	Y	37770 FQ	43400 AW	53080 TQ	KSBLS	10/01-12/01
	Kentucky	Y	18780 FQ	40990 AW	56610 TQ	KYBLS	10/01-12/01
	Lexington MSA, KY	Y	12010 FQ	21080 AW	38770 TQ	KYBLS	10/01-12/01
	Louisville MSA, KY-IN	Y	39410 FQ	53060 AW	79380 TQ	KYBLS	10/01-12/01
	Louisiana	Y	24070 FQ	43210 AW	57900 TQ	LABLS	10/01-12/01
	Baton Rouge MSA, LA	Y	27000 FQ	46270 AW	57170 TQ	LABLS	10/01-12/01
	Houma MSA, LA	Y	23340 FQ	32160 AW	47160 TQ	LABLS	10/01-12/01
	Lafayette MSA, LA	Y	46720 FQ	60860 AW	70080 TQ	LABLS	10/01-12/01
	Lake Charles MSA, LA	Y	33970 FQ	38800 AW	44410 TQ	LABLS	10/01-12/01
	New Orleans MSA, LA	Y	23960 FQ	41950 AW	55450 TQ	LABLS	10/01-12/01
	Shreveport-Bossier City MSA, LA	Y	35950 FQ	45810 AW	56700 TQ	LABLS	10/01-12/01
	Maine	Y	37580 FQ	48860 AW	61050 TQ	MEBLS	10/01-12/01
	Portland MSA, ME	Y	38250 FQ	45800 AW	54800 TQ	MEBLS	10/01-12/01

AAW Average annual wage **AE** Average entry wage **AEX** Average experienced wage **AO** Average offered **AOH** Average offered, high **AOL** Average offered, low **APH** Average pay, high range **APL** Average pay, low range **ASH** Average starting, high **ASL** Average starting, low **AW** Average wage paid **FQ** First quartile wage **H** Hourly **HI** Highest wage paid **HR** High end range **LR** Low end range **M** Monthly **MTC** Median total compensation **MW** Median wage paid **SQ** Second quartile wage **S** Special: hourly and annual **TQ** Third quartile wage **W** Weekly **Y** Yearly

Occupation/Type/Industry	Location	Per	Low	Mid	High	Source	Date
Dental Hygienist	Maryland	Y	36170 FQ	53240 AW	69260 TQ	MDBLS	10/01-12/01
	Baltimore PMSA, MD	Y	32670 FQ	46900 AW	58190 TQ	MDBLS	10/01-12/01
	Massachusetts	Y	44900 FQ	58170 AW	70260 TQ	MABLS	10/01-12/01
	Boston PMSA, MA-NH	Y	42570 FQ	57870 AW	70100 TQ	MABLS	10/01-12/01
	Brockton PMSA, MA	Y	45800 FQ	56970 AW	69870 TQ	MABLS	10/01-12/01
	Lawrence PMSA, MA-NH	Y	44470 FQ	54280 AW	66640 TQ	MABLS	10/01-12/01
	Lowell PMSA, MA-NH	Y	45930 FQ	56880 AW	69690 TQ	MABLS	10/01-12/01
	New Bedford PMSA, MA	Y	47490 FQ	59590 AW	71920 TQ	MABLS	10/01-12/01
	Springfield MSA, MA	Y	58090 FQ	62920 AW	70240 TQ	MABLS	10/01-12/01
	Worcester PMSA, MA-CT	Y	49380 FQ	60270 AW	70700 TQ	MABLS	10/01-12/01
	Michigan	Y	38200 FQ	49330 AW	58710 TQ	MIBLS	10/01-12/01
	Ann Arbor PMSA, MI	Y	49700 FQ	66930 AW	86740 TQ	MIBLS	10/01-12/01
	Detroit PMSA, MI	Y	46270 FQ	51000 AW	58440 TQ	MIBLS	10/01-12/01
	Flint PMSA, MI	Y	33100 FQ	45260 AW	55440 TQ	MIBLS	10/01-12/01
	Grand Rapids-Muskegon-Holland MSA, MI	Y	26090 FQ	43810 AW	55430 TQ	MIBLS	10/01-12/01
	Kalamazoo-Battle Creek MSA, MI	Y	37000 FQ	47590 AW	64420 TQ	MIBLS	10/01-12/01
	Lansing-East Lansing MSA, MI	Y	39270 FQ	46990 AW	55330 TQ	MIBLS	10/01-12/01
	Saginaw-Bay City-Midland MSA, MI	Y	33900 FQ	44070 AW	56110 TQ	MIBLS	10/01-12/01
	Minnesota	Y	39440 FQ	54660 AW	69650 TQ	MNBLS	10/01-12/01
	Duluth-Superior MSA, MN-WI	Y	39780 FQ	48430 AW	56720 TQ	MNBLS	10/01-12/01
	Minneapolis-St. Paul MSA, MN-WI	Y	39200 FQ	55980 AW	70240 TQ	MNBLS	10/01-12/01
	St. Cloud MSA, MN	Y	46430 FQ	50290 AW	58160 TQ	MNBLS	10/01-12/01
	Mississippi	Y	22390 FQ	33480 AW	48070 TQ	MSBLS	10/01-12/01
	Biloxi-Gulfport-Pascagoula MSA, MS	Y	36080 FQ	44440 AW	55120 TQ	MSBLS	10/01-12/01
	Jackson MSA, MS	Y	23410 FQ	33230 AW	51110 TQ	MSBLS	10/01-12/01
	Missouri	Y	39730 FQ	54620 AW	71110 TQ	MOBLS	10/01-12/01
	Kansas City MSA, MO-KS	Y	44480 FQ	55680 AW	70520 TQ	MOBLS	10/01-12/01
	St. Louis MSA, MO-IL	Y	37890 FQ	52680 AW	70490 TQ	MOBLS	10/01-12/01
	Springfield MSA, MO	Y	18900 FQ	44070 AW	55990 TQ	MOBLS	10/01-12/01
	Montana	Y	37690 FQ	48150 AW	57020 TQ	MTBLS	10/01-12/01
	Billings MSA, MT	Y	45710 FQ	49840 AW	55460 TQ	MTBLS	10/01-12/01
	Nebraska	Y	28400 FQ	44970 AW	66350 TQ	NEBLS	10/01-12/01
	Lincoln MSA, NE	Y	48040 FQ	60190 AW	74180 TQ	NEBLS	10/01-12/01
	Omaha MSA, NE-IA	Y	28710 FQ	41740 AW	57460 TQ	NEBLS	10/01-12/01
	Nevada	Y	60940 FQ	74510 AW	90580 TQ	NVBLS	10/01-12/01
	Las Vegas MSA, NV-AZ	Y	62710 FQ	76260 AW	91180 TQ	NVBLS	10/01-12/01
	Reno MSA, NV	Y	60360 FQ	71650 AW	88930 TQ	NVBLS	10/01-12/01
	New Hampshire	Y	42620 FQ	56590 AW	74050 TQ	NHBLS	10/01-12/01
	Manchester PMSA, NH	Y	48440 FQ	65410 AW	86940 TQ	NHBLS	10/01-12/01
	Nashua PMSA, NH	Y	49400 FQ	61330 AW	73410 TQ	NHBLS	10/01-12/01
	Portsmouth-Rochester PMSA, NH-ME	Y	37760 FQ	46920 AW	56310 TQ	NHBLS	10/01-12/01
	New Jersey	Y	38020 FQ	54000 AW	69940 TQ	NJBLS	10/01-12/01
	Atlantic-Cape May PMSA, NJ	Y	47750 FQ	60860 AW	80600 TQ	NJBLS	10/01-12/01
	Bergen-Passaic PMSA, NJ	Y	37580 FQ	48760 AW	65790 TQ	NJBLS	10/01-12/01
	Middlesex-Somerset-Hunterdon PMSA, NJ	Y	45360 FQ	60630 AW	71060 TQ	NJBLS	10/01-12/01
	Monmouth-Ocean PMSA, NJ	Y	49880 FQ	60590 AW	71930 TQ	NJBLS	10/01-12/01
	Newark PMSA, NJ	Y	21210 FQ	46190 AW	64880 TQ	NJBLS	10/01-12/01
	Trenton PMSA, NJ	Y	57790 FQ	63340 AW	71320 TQ	NJBLS	10/01-12/01
	New Mexico	Y	31370 FQ	53100 AW	73440 TQ	NMBLS	10/01-12/01
	Albuquerque MSA, NM	Y	48500 FQ	62120 AW	90070 TQ	NMBLS	10/01-12/01
	Las Cruces MSA, NM	Y	29760 FQ	42410 AW	60920 TQ	NMBLS	10/01-12/01
	New York	Y	38300 FQ	54130 AW	73830 TQ	NYBLS	10/01-12/01
	Albany-Schenectady-Troy MSA, NY	Y	40800 FQ	48350 AW	56080 TQ	NYBLS	10/01-12/01
	Binghamton MSA, NY	Y	34070 FQ	39370 AW	44480 TQ	NYBLS	10/01-12/01
	Buffalo-Niagara Falls MSA, NY	Y	35770 FQ	40200 AW	45110 TQ	NYBLS	10/01-12/01
	Dutchess County PMSA, NY	Y	47100 FQ	51350 AW	57770 TQ	NYBLS	10/01-12/01
	Nassau-Suffolk PMSA, NY	Y	37410 FQ	51260 AW	68540 TQ	NYBLS	10/01-12/01
	New York PMSA, NY	Y	51130 FQ	64880 AW	83620 TQ	NYBLS	10/01-12/01
	Newburgh PMSA, NY-PA	Y	46860 FQ	50810 AW	57440 TQ	NYBLS	10/01-12/01
	Rochester MSA, NY	Y	36450 FQ	44250 AW	55820 TQ	NYBLS	10/01-12/01
	Syracuse MSA, NY	Y	37470 FQ	42290 AW	49500 TQ	NYBLS	10/01-12/01
	Utica-Rome MSA, NY	Y	37910 FQ	46500 AW	56650 TQ	NYBLS	10/01-12/01
	New York, NY	H		35.00 AW		CRAINNY	2002

AAW	Average annual wage	**AOH**	Average offered, high	**ASH**	Average starting, high	**H**	Hourly	**M**	Monthly	**S**	Special: hourly and annual
AE	Average entry wage	**AOL**	Average offered, low	**ASL**	Average starting, low	**HI**	Highest wage paid	**MTC**	Median total compensation	**TQ**	Third quartile wage
AEX	Average experienced wage	**APH**	Average pay, high range	**AW**	Average wage paid	**HR**	High end range	**MW**	Median wage paid	**W**	Weekly
AO	Average offered	**APL**	Average pay, low range	**FQ**	First quartile wage	**LR**	Low end range	**SQ**	Second quartile wage	**Y**	Yearly

Occupation/Type/Industry	Location	Per	Low	Mid	High	Source	Date
Dental Hygienist	North Carolina	Y	17160 FQ	45960 AW	68740 TQ	NCBLS	10/01-12/01
	Asheville MSA, NC	Y	38530 FQ	46720 AW	60500 TQ	NCBLS	10/01-12/01
	Charlotte-Gastonia-Rock Hill MSA, NC-SC	Y	15150 FQ	27740 AW	54860 TQ	NCBLS	10/01-12/01
	Fayetteville MSA, NC	Y	33340 FQ	45120 AW	55550 TQ	NCBLS	10/01-12/01
	Greensboro-Winston-Salem-High Point MSA, NC	Y	51770 FQ	63710 AW	73580 TQ	NCBLS	10/01-12/01
	Hickory-Morganton-Lenoir MSA, NC	Y	40530 FQ	47600 AW	55180 TQ	NCBLS	10/01-12/01
	Raleigh-Durham-Chapel Hill MSA, NC	Y	42250 FQ	50620 AW	60500 TQ	NCBLS	10/01-12/01
	Wilmington MSA, NC	Y	46720 FQ	49910 AW	57600 TQ	NCBLS	10/01-12/01
	North Dakota	Y	40170 FQ	49260 AW	57720 TQ	NDBLS	10/01-12/01
	Fargo-Moorhead MSA, ND-MN	Y	40140 FQ	48690 AW	57100 TQ	NDBLS	10/01-12/01
	Ohio	Y	42400 FQ	51820 AW	63340 TQ	OHBLS	10/01-12/01
	Akron PMSA, OH	Y	40940 FQ	51090 AW	64080 TQ	OHBLS	10/01-12/01
	Canton-Massillon MSA, OH	Y	50120 FQ	60630 AW	70950 TQ	OHBLS	10/01-12/01
	Cincinnati PMSA, OH-KY-IN	Y	47590 FQ	52740 AW	58560 TQ	OHBLS	10/01-12/01
	Cleveland-Lorain-Elyria PMSA, OH	Y	46700 FQ	51050 AW	58340 TQ	OHBLS	10/01-12/01
	Columbus MSA, OH	Y	44820 FQ	52650 AW	64810 TQ	OHBLS	10/01-12/01
	Dayton-Springfield MSA, OH	Y	49420 FQ	60200 AW	70710 TQ	OHBLS	10/01-12/01
	Hamilton-Middletown PMSA, OH	Y	47390 FQ	56020 AW	68430 TQ	OHBLS	10/01-12/01
	Mansfield MSA, OH	Y	37890 FQ	42990 AW	51750 TQ	OHBLS	10/01-12/01
	Toledo MSA, OH	Y	41540 FQ	51940 AW	71330 TQ	OHBLS	10/01-12/01
	Youngstown-Warren MSA, OH	Y	36340 FQ	42870 AW	54410 TQ	OHBLS	10/01-12/01
	Oklahoma	Y	39670 FQ	49830 AW	58230 TQ	OKBLS	10/01-12/01
	Oklahoma City MSA, OK	Y	47150 FQ	51160 AW	58120 TQ	OKBLS	10/01-12/01
	Tulsa MSA, OK	Y	36210 FQ	46030 AW	57680 TQ	OKBLS	10/01-12/01
	Oregon	Y	49000 FQ	60550 AW	72810 TQ	ORBLS	10/01-12/01
	Eugene-Springfield MSA, OR	Y	58910 FQ	64420 AW	73560 TQ	ORBLS	10/01-12/01
	Medford-Ashland MSA, OR	Y	58540 FQ	63680 AW	71190 TQ	ORBLS	10/01-12/01
	Portland-Vancouver PMSA, OR-WA	Y	50440 FQ	60720 AW	72700 TQ	ORBLS	10/01-12/01
	Salem PMSA, OR	Y	51440 FQ	60930 AW	70610 TQ	ORBLS	10/01-12/01
	Pennsylvania	Y	34720 FQ	47300 AW	65210 TQ	PABLS	10/01-12/01
	Allentown-Bethlehem-Easton MSA, PA	Y	32930 FQ	46060 AW	56960 TQ	PABLS	10/01-12/01
	Erie MSA, PA	Y	35820 FQ	40490 AW	49430 TQ	PABLS	10/01-12/01
	Harrisburg-Lebanon-Carlisle MSA, PA	Y	36860 FQ	47360 AW	56060 TQ	PABLS	10/01-12/01
	Johnstown MSA, PA	Y	24360 FQ	41110 AW	57390 TQ	PABLS	10/01-12/01
	Lancaster MSA, PA	Y	46780 FQ	51480 AW	60100 TQ	PABLS	10/01-12/01
	Philadelphia PMSA, PA-NJ	Y	46620 FQ	55980 AW	69550 TQ	PABLS	10/01-12/01
	Pittsburgh MSA, PA	Y	36120 FQ	40130 AW	44600 TQ	PABLS	10/01-12/01
	Reading MSA, PA	Y	41440 FQ	48450 AW	55550 TQ	PABLS	10/01-12/01
	Scranton-Wilkes-Barre-Hazleton MSA, PA	Y	12500 FQ	28540 AW	45680 TQ	PABLS	10/01-12/01
	York MSA, PA	Y	39960 FQ	48740 AW	56660 TQ	PABLS	10/01-12/01
	Rhode Island	Y	45580 FQ	52350 AW	62420 TQ	RIBLS	10/01-12/01
	Providence-Fall River-Warwick MSA, RI-MA	Y	46700 FQ	55070 AW	68020 TQ	RIBLS	10/01-12/01
	South Carolina	Y	30560 FQ	47130 AW	74100 TQ	SCBLS	10/01-12/01
	Charleston-North Charleston MSA, SC	Y	38440 FQ	47960 AW	57150 TQ	SCBLS	10/01-12/01
	Columbia MSA, SC	Y	29240 FQ	37480 AW	60500 TQ	SCBLS	10/01-12/01
	Greenville-Spartanburg-Anderson MSA, SC	Y	36460 FQ	51160 AW	86980 TQ	SCBLS	10/01-12/01
	Myrtle Beach MSA, SC	Y	24080 FQ	31870 AW	43060 TQ	SCBLS	10/01-12/01
	South Dakota	Y	32090 FQ	44860 AW	58730 TQ	SDBLS	10/01-12/01
	Sioux Falls MSA, SD	Y	39150 FQ	45630 AW	54990 TQ	SDBLS	10/01-12/01
	Tennessee	Y	31540 FQ	56140 AW	84780 TQ	TNBLS	10/01-12/01
	Chattanooga MSA, TN-GA	Y	24540 FQ	33620 AW	49930 TQ	TNBLS	10/01-12/01
	Clarksville-Hopkinsville MSA, TN-KY	Y	37020 FQ	48750 AW	65780 TQ	TNBLS	10/01-12/01
	Johnson City-Kingsport-Bristol MSA, TN-VA	Y	37850 FQ	44100 AW	54090 TQ	TNBLS	10/01-12/01
	Knoxville MSA, TN	Y	42640 FQ	72960 AW	91670 TQ	TNBLS	10/01-12/01
	Memphis MSA, TN-AR-MS	Y	44980 FQ	55260 AW	68850 TQ	TNBLS	10/01-12/01
	Texas	Y	40490 FQ	60750 AW	83880 TQ	TXBLS	10/01-12/01

AAW	Average annual wage	AOH	Average offered, high	ASH	Average starting, high	H	Hourly	M	Monthly	S	Special: hourly and annual
AE	Average entry wage	AOL	Average offered, low	ASL	Average starting, low	HI	Highest wage paid	MTC	Median total compensation	TQ	Third quartile wage
AEX	Average experienced wage	APH	Average pay, high range	AW	Average wage paid	HR	High end range	MW	Median wage paid	W	Weekly
AO	Average offered	APL	Average pay, low range	FQ	First quartile wage	LR	Low end range	SQ	Second quartile wage	Y	Yearly

Occupation/Type/Industry	Location	Per	Low	Mid	High	Source	Date
Dental Hygienist	Austin-San Marcos MSA, TX	Y	47800 FQ	61650 AW	89960 TQ	TXBLS	10/01-12/01
	Beaumont-Port Arthur MSA, TX	Y	45110 FQ	49380 AW	55440 TQ	TXBLS	10/01-12/01
	Brazoria PMSA, TX	Y	45100 FQ	49670 AW	55800 TQ	TXBLS	10/01-12/01
	Brownsville-Harlingen-San Benito MSA, TX	Y	48190 FQ	63060 AW	84240 TQ	TXBLS	10/01-12/01
	Corpus Christi MSA, TX	Y	46740 FQ	50570 AW	57480 TQ	TXBLS	10/01-12/01
	Dallas PMSA, TX	Y	57840 FQ	63950 AW	71700 TQ	TXBLS	10/01-12/01
	El Paso MSA, TX	Y	26640 FQ	37780 AW	66440 TQ	TXBLS	10/01-12/01
	Fort Worth-Arlington PMSA, TX	Y	44850 FQ	57850 AW	69690 TQ	TXBLS	10/01-12/01
	Galveston-Texas City PMSA, TX	Y	46250 FQ	53890 AW	68490 TQ	TXBLS	10/01-12/01
	Houston PMSA, TX	Y	59370 FQ	72710 AW	88360 TQ	TXBLS	10/01-12/01
	Killeen-Temple MSA, TX	Y	43390 FQ	51390 AW	65250 TQ	TXBLS	10/01-12/01
	Longview-Marshall MSA, TX	Y	39090 FQ	47760 AW	57040 TQ	TXBLS	10/01-12/01
	Lubbock MSA, TX	Y	47470 FQ	52060 AW	58060 TQ	TXBLS	10/01-12/01
	McAllen-Edinburg-Mission MSA, TX	Y	45140 FQ	56180 AW	72070 TQ	TXBLS	10/01-12/01
	Odessa-Midland MSA, TX	Y	38690 FQ	53190 AW	69880 TQ	TXBLS	10/01-12/01
	San Antonio MSA, TX	Y	36220 FQ	45230 AW	55140 TQ	TXBLS	10/01-12/01
	Tyler MSA, TX	Y	45900 FQ	51120 AW	56570 TQ	TXBLS	10/01-12/01
	Utah	Y	46380 FQ	69260 AW	129980 TQ	UTBLS	10/01-12/01
	Provo-Orem MSA, UT	Y	36310 FQ	47740 AW	55540 TQ	UTBLS	10/01-12/01
	Salt Lake City-Ogden MSA, UT	Y	61160 FQ	88340 AW	140660 TQ	UTBLS	10/01-12/01
	Vermont	Y	34750 FQ	48480 AW	64770 TQ	VTBLS	10/01-12/01
	Burlington MSA, VT	Y	36920 FQ	49410 AW	61390 TQ	VTBLS	10/01-12/01
	Virginia	Y	39740 FQ	61410 AW	87600 TQ	VABLS	10/01-12/01
	Lynchburg MSA, VA	Y	38680 FQ	45270 AW	55200 TQ	VABLS	10/01-12/01
	Norfolk-Virginia Beach-Newport News MSA, VA-NC	Y	45720 FQ	51490 AW	58700 TQ	VABLS	10/01-12/01
	Richmond-Petersburg MSA, VA	Y	31540 FQ	51780 AW	71230 TQ	VABLS	10/01-12/01
	Washington	Y	60200 FQ	69740 AW	87010 TQ	WABLS	10/01-12/01
	Bremerton PMSA, WA	Y	54280 FQ	75860 AW	92850 TQ	WABLS	10/01-12/01
	Olympia PMSA, WA	Y	53130 FQ	68010 AW	86840 TQ	WABLS	10/01-12/01
	Richland-Kennewick-Pasco MSA, WA	Y	60090 FQ	76490 AW	93520 TQ	WABLS	10/01-12/01
	Seattle-Bellevue-Everett PMSA, WA	Y	60820 FQ	69480 AW	85750 TQ	WABLS	10/01-12/01
	Spokane MSA, WA	Y	60540 FQ	70650 AW	89530 TQ	WABLS	10/01-12/01
	Tacoma PMSA, WA	Y	60160 FQ	66760 AW	75600 TQ	WABLS	10/01-12/01
	Yakima MSA, WA	Y	49840 FQ	65480 AW	87870 TQ	WABLS	10/01-12/01
	West Virginia	Y	24570 FQ	37330 AW	52910 TQ	WVBLS	10/01-12/01
	Charleston MSA, WV	Y	32380 FQ	42590 AW	50440 TQ	WVBLS	10/01-12/01
	Huntington-Ashland MSA, WV-KY-OH	Y	25530 FQ	41000 AW	53730 TQ	WVBLS	10/01-12/01
	Wisconsin	Y	40140 FQ	49270 AW	57540 TQ	WIBLS	10/01-12/01
	Appleton-Oshkosh-Neenah MSA, WI	Y	46690 FQ	51110 AW	57310 TQ	WIBLS	10/01-12/01
	Green Bay MSA, WI	Y	45860 FQ	51240 AW	58110 TQ	WIBLS	10/01-12/01
	Madison MSA, WI	Y	45270 FQ	49760 AW	56060 TQ	WIBLS	10/01-12/01
	Milwaukee-Waukesha PMSA, WI	Y	31870 FQ	48410 AW	61210 TQ	WIBLS	10/01-12/01
	Racine PMSA, WI	Y	39630 FQ	47860 AW	56290 TQ	WIBLS	10/01-12/01
	Wyoming	Y	38060 FQ	49270 AW	59420 TQ	WYBLS	10/01-12/01
	Cheyenne MSA, WY	Y	46910 FQ	51210 AW	57550 TQ	WYBLS	10/01-12/01
	Puerto Rico	Y	14320 FQ	25240 AW	34440 TQ	PRBLS	10/01-12/01
	Guam	Y	18000 FQ	27990 AW	48400 TQ	GUBLS	10/01-12/01
Dental Laboratory Technician	Alabama	H	6.55 FQ	12.19 AW	18.69 TQ	ALBLS	10/01-12/01
	Alaska	H	9.64 FQ	19.56 AW	34.29 TQ	AKBLS	10/01-12/01
	Arizona	H	9.06 FQ	13.40 AW	19.08 TQ	AZBLS	10/01-12/01
	Arkansas	H	8.97 FQ	14.11 AW	21.48 TQ	ARBLS	10/01-12/01
	California	H	8.67 FQ	14.69 AW	22.13 TQ	CABLS	10/01-12/01
	Colorado	H	7.85 FQ	14.55 AW	23.97 TQ	COBLS	10/01-12/01
	Connecticut	H	9.14 FQ	17.28 AW	25.14 TQ	CTBLS	10/01-12/01
	District of Columbia	H	13.69 FQ	19.00 AW	26.01 TQ	DCBLS	10/01-12/01
	Florida	H	9.18 FQ	15.94 AW	25.06 TQ	FLBLS	10/01-12/01
	Georgia	H	7.66 FQ	13.92 AW	19.99 TQ	GABLS	10/01-12/01
	Hawaii	H	7.94 FQ	13.82 AW	21.46 TQ	HIBLS	10/01-12/01

AAW	Average annual wage	**AOH**	Average offered, high	**ASH**	Average starting, high	**H**	Hourly	**M**	Monthly	**S**	Special: hourly and annual
AE	Average entry wage	**AOL**	Average offered, low	**ASL**	Average starting, low	**HI**	Highest wage paid	**MTC**	Median total compensation	**TQ**	Third quartile wage
AEX	Average experienced wage	**APH**	Average pay, high range	**AW**	Average wage paid	**HR**	High end range	**MW**	Median wage paid	**W**	Weekly
AO	Average offered	**APL**	Average pay, low range	**FQ**	First quartile wage	**LR**	Low end range	**SQ**	Second quartile wage	**Y**	Yearly

Occupation/Type/Industry	Location	Per	Low	Mid	High	Source	Date
Dental Laboratory Technician	Idaho	H	6.21 FQ	13.20 AW	26.45 TQ	IDBLS	10/01-12/01
	Illinois	H	9.41 FQ	15.60 AW	22.90 TQ	ILBLS	10/01-12/01
	Indiana	H	8.30 FQ	15.14 AW	21.37 TQ	INBLS	10/01-12/01
	Iowa	H	8.39 FQ	14.07 AW	21.16 TQ	IABLS	10/01-12/01
	Kansas	H	9.31 FQ	13.77 AW	20.14 TQ	KSBLS	10/01-12/01
	Kentucky	H	8.59 FQ	12.99 AW	20.73 TQ	KYBLS	10/01-12/01
	Louisiana	H	7.13 FQ	12.85 AW	29.07 TQ	LABLS	10/01-12/01
	Maine	H	9.68 FQ	15.09 AW	22.32 TQ	MEBLS	10/01-12/01
	Maryland	H	5.59 FQ	10.82 AW	19.60 TQ	MDBLS	10/01-12/01
	Massachusetts	H	10.78 FQ	14.69 AW	20.87 TQ	MABLS	10/01-12/01
	Michigan	H	8.87 FQ	14.70 AW	21.78 TQ	MIBLS	10/01-12/01
	Minnesota	H	7.22 FQ	13.77 AW	22.30 TQ	MNBLS	10/01-12/01
	Mississippi	H	6.91 FQ	12.41 AW	18.98 TQ	MSBLS	10/01-12/01
	Missouri	H	6.51 FQ	14.34 AW	25.73 TQ	MOBLS	10/01-12/01
	Montana	H	7.43 FQ	17.80 AW	35.69 TQ	MTBLS	10/01-12/01
	Nebraska	H	9.53 FQ	14.68 AW	20.92 TQ	NEBLS	10/01-12/01
	Nevada	H	9.10 FQ	15.59 AW	22.27 TQ	NVBLS	10/01-12/01
	New Jersey	H	8.34 FQ	16.64 AW	27.29 TQ	NJBLS	10/01-12/01
	New Mexico	H	8.37 FQ	14.13 AW	19.26 TQ	NMBLS	10/01-12/01
	New York	H	8.02 FQ	16.42 AW	26.24 TQ	NYBLS	10/01-12/01
	North Carolina	H	8.11 FQ	14.60 AW	21.81 TQ	NCBLS	10/01-12/01
	North Dakota	H	8.06 FQ	12.66 AW	19.07 TQ	NDBLS	10/01-12/01
	Ohio	H	8.59 FQ	16.51 AW	27.07 TQ	OHBLS	10/01-12/01
	Oklahoma	H	8.19 FQ	12.54 AW	17.13 TQ	OKBLS	10/01-12/01
	Oregon	H	8.65 FQ	15.36 AW	22.74 TQ	ORBLS	10/01-12/01
	Pennsylvania	H	8.23 FQ	13.50 AW	19.53 TQ	PABLS	10/01-12/01
	Rhode Island	H	8.58 FQ	16.26 AW	25.51 TQ	RIBLS	10/01-12/01
	South Carolina	H	8.00 FQ	14.69 AW	24.33 TQ	SCBLS	10/01-12/01
	South Dakota	H	8.24 FQ	10.56 AW	13.40 TQ	SDBLS	10/01-12/01
	Tennessee	H	7.80 FQ	11.99 AW	17.47 TQ	TNBLS	10/01-12/01
	Texas	H	7.34 FQ	12.55 AW	19.40 TQ	TXBLS	10/01-12/01
	Utah	H	7.04 FQ	11.23 AW	20.12 TQ	UTBLS	10/01-12/01
	Vermont	H	6.66 FQ	12.18 AW	19.60 TQ	VTBLS	10/01-12/01
	Virginia	H	8.47 FQ	16.71 AW	26.05 TQ	VABLS	10/01-12/01
	Washington	H	10.78 FQ	16.33 AW	24.25 TQ	WABLS	10/01-12/01
	West Virginia	H	7.77 FQ	11.08 AW	16.19 TQ	WVBLS	10/01-12/01
	Wisconsin	H	9.15 FQ	15.07 AW	20.29 TQ	WIBLS	10/01-12/01
	Puerto Rico	H	5.58 FQ	8.58 AW	16.79 TQ	PRBLS	10/01-12/01
Dentist	Alabama	Y	53800 FQ	115910 AW		ALBLS	10/01-12/01
	Huntsville MSA, AL	Y	53540 FQ	107090 AW		ALBLS	10/01-12/01
	Mobile MSA, AL	Y	46070 FQ	103910 AW		ALBLS	10/01-12/01
	Montgomery MSA, AL	Y	66520 FQ	123060 AW		ALBLS	10/01-12/01
	Alaska	Y	66030 FQ	123250 AW		AKBLS	10/01-12/01
	Anchorage MSA, AK	Y	108910 FQ	134170 AW		AKBLS	10/01-12/01
	Arizona	Y	97990 FQ	135150 AW		AZBLS	10/01-12/01
	Phoenix-Mesa MSA, AZ	Y	118340 FQ	139250 AW		AZBLS	10/01-12/01
	Tucson MSA, AZ	Y	79090 FQ	115330 AW		AZBLS	10/01-12/01
	Arkansas	Y	78280 FQ	115560 AW		ARBLS	10/01-12/01
	Fayetteville-Springdale-Rogers MSA, AR	Y	80050 FQ	118220 AW		ARBLS	10/01-12/01
	Little Rock-North Little Rock MSA, AR	Y	91420 FQ	126550 AW		ARBLS	10/01-12/01
	California	Y	84200 FQ	124160 AW		CABLS	10/01-12/01
	Bakersfield MSA, CA	Y	80360 FQ	111390 AW		CABLS	10/01-12/01
	Chico-Paradise MSA, CA	Y	116820 FQ	134840 AW		CABLS	10/01-12/01
	Fresno MSA, CA	Y	93200 FQ	126240 AW		CABLS	10/01-12/01
	Los Angeles-Long Beach PMSA, CA	Y	92080 FQ	131940 AW		CABLS	10/01-12/01
	Modesto MSA, CA	Y	93830 FQ	110700 AW	143770 TQ	CABLS	10/01-12/01
	Oakland PMSA, CA	Y	100280 FQ	132190 AW		CABLS	10/01-12/01
	Orange County PMSA, CA	Y	65300 FQ	118990 AW		CABLS	10/01-12/01
	Riverside-San Bernardino PMSA, CA	Y	70580 FQ	117290 AW		CABLS	10/01-12/01
	Sacramento PMSA, CA	Y	96010 FQ	113680 AW		CABLS	10/01-12/01
	Salinas MSA, CA	Y	74270 FQ	112580 AW		CABLS	10/01-12/01
	San Francisco PMSA, CA	Y	77480 FQ	98400 AW	135930 TQ	CABLS	10/01-12/01
	San Jose PMSA, CA	Y	122030 FQ	137670 AW		CABLS	10/01-12/01
	San Luis Obispo-Atascadero-Paso Robles MSA, CA	Y	82280 FQ	118680 AW		CABLS	10/01-12/01
	Santa Barbara-Santa Maria-Lompoc MSA, CA	Y	76300 FQ	92100 AW	144440 TQ	CABLS	10/01-12/01
	Santa Rosa PMSA, CA	Y	99170 FQ	118880 AW	141590 TQ	CABLS	10/01-12/01

AAW Average annual wage	**AOH** Average offered, high	**ASH** Average starting, high	**H** Hourly	**M** Monthly	**S** Special: hourly and annual
AE Average entry wage	**AOL** Average offered, low	**ASL** Average starting, low	**HI** Highest wage paid	**MTC** Median total compensation	**TQ** Third quartile wage
AEX Average experienced wage	**APH** Average pay, high range	**AW** Average wage paid	**HR** High end range	**MW** Median wage paid	**W** Weekly
AO Average offered	**APL** Average pay, low range	**FQ** First quartile wage	**LR** Low end range	**SQ** Second quartile wage	**Y** Yearly

Occupation/Type/Industry	Location	Per	Low	Mid	High	Source	Date
Dentist	Stockton-Lodi MSA, CA	Y	81160 FQ	121990 AW		CABLS	10/01-12/01
	Vallejo-Fairfield-Napa PMSA, CA	Y	81120 FQ	112450 AW		CABLS	10/01-12/01
	Ventura PMSA, CA	Y	93860 FQ	113720 AW		CABLS	10/01-12/01
	Visalia-Tulare-Porterville MSA, CA	Y	66030 FQ	121950 AW		CABLS	10/01-12/01
	Colorado	Y	106790 FQ	133040 AW		COBLS	10/01-12/01
	Colorado Springs MSA, CO	Y	127250 FQ	139070 AW		COBLS	10/01-12/01
	Fort Collins-Loveland MSA, CO	Y	119420 FQ	134980 AW		COBLS	10/01-12/01
	Connecticut	Y	62280 FQ	107120 AW		CTBLS	10/01-12/01
	Bridgeport PMSA, CT	Y	67140 FQ	101020 AW	141320 TQ	CTBLS	10/01-12/01
	Danbury PMSA, CT	Y	110160 FQ	133430 AW		CTBLS	10/01-12/01
	Hartford MSA, CT	Y	43780 FQ	103740 AW		CTBLS	10/01-12/01
	New Haven-Meriden PMSA, CT	Y	59510 FQ	108360 AW		CTBLS	10/01-12/01
	New London-Norwich MSA, CT-RI	Y	59250 FQ	88120 AW		CTBLS	10/01-12/01
	Stamford-Norwalk PMSA, CT	Y	78340 FQ	111490 AW		CTBLS	10/01-12/01
	Waterbury PMSA, CT	Y	121330 FQ	136850 AW		CTBLS	10/01-12/01
	Delaware	Y	37750 FQ	98470 AW		DEBLS	10/01-12/01
	Wilmington-Newark PMSA, DE-MD	Y	37920 FQ	94100 AW		DEBLS	10/01-12/01
	District of Columbia	Y	57280 FQ	93590 AW		DCBLS	10/01-12/01
	Washington PMSA, DC-MD-VA-WV	Y	66650 FQ	129670 AW		DCBLS	10/01-12/01
	Florida	Y	43010 FQ	109270 AW		FLBLS	10/01-12/01
	Daytona Beach MSA, FL	Y	37790 FQ	47200 AW	52950 TQ	FLBLS	10/01-12/01
	Fort Lauderdale PMSA, FL	Y	123040 FQ	135410 AW		FLBLS	10/01-12/01
	Fort Myers-Cape Coral MSA, FL	Y	105030 FQ	134810 AW		FLBLS	10/01-12/01
	Fort Pierce-Port St. Lucie MSA, FL	Y	119290 FQ	133920 AW		FLBLS	10/01-12/01
	Fort Walton Beach MSA, FL	Y	39130 FQ	73430 AW		FLBLS	10/01-12/01
	Gainesville MSA, FL	Y	110910 FQ	130890 AW		FLBLS	10/01-12/01
	Jacksonville MSA, FL	Y	76440 FQ	129950 AW		FLBLS	10/01-12/01
	Lakeland-Winter Haven MSA, FL	Y	78470 FQ	114130 AW		FLBLS	10/01-12/01
	Orlando MSA, FL	Y	90230 FQ	129780 AW		FLBLS	10/01-12/01
	Pensacola MSA, FL	Y	84160 FQ	128090 AW		FLBLS	10/01-12/01
	Sarasota-Bradenton MSA, FL	Y	65290 FQ	117260 AW		FLBLS	10/01-12/01
	Tallahassee MSA, FL	Y	79080 FQ	112780 AW		FLBLS	10/01-12/01
	Tampa-St. Petersburg-Clearwater MSA, FL	Y	38030 FQ	67550 AW	89750 TQ	FLBLS	10/01-12/01
	West Palm Beach-Boca Raton MSA, FL	Y	61340 FQ	92230 AW		FLBLS	10/01-12/01
	Georgia	Y	45760 FQ	103550 AW		GABLS	10/01-12/01
	Atlanta MSA, GA	Y	74590 FQ	96600 AW		GABLS	10/01-12/01
	Augusta-Aiken MSA, GA-SC	Y	77970 FQ	119750 AW		GABLS	10/01-12/01
	Macon MSA, GA	Y	78620 FQ	123980 AW		GABLS	10/01-12/01
	Savannah MSA, GA	Y	47830 FQ	113860 AW		GABLS	10/01-12/01
	Hawaii	Y	96420 FQ	115720 AW		HIBLS	10/01-12/01
	Honolulu MSA, HI	Y	96780 FQ	111740 AW		HIBLS	10/01-12/01
	Idaho	Y	74420 FQ	128640 AW		IDBLS	10/01-12/01
	Illinois	Y	44450 FQ	76740 AW		ILBLS	10/01-12/01
	Chicago PMSA, IL	Y	45180 FQ	71050 AW		ILBLS	10/01-12/01
	Peoria-Pekin MSA, IL	Y	59910 FQ	86440 AW		ILBLS	10/01-12/01
	Rockford MSA, IL	Y	42330 FQ	91410 AW		ILBLS	10/01-12/01
	Springfield MSA, IL	Y	38490 FQ	54270 AW	71700 TQ	ILBLS	10/01-12/01
	Indiana	Y	48550 FQ	106040 AW		INBLS	10/01-12/01
	Elkhart-Goshen MSA, IN	Y	38390 FQ	103840 AW		INBLS	10/01-12/01
	Evansville-Henderson MSA, IN-KY	Y	76650 FQ	118780 AW		INBLS	10/01-12/01
	Fort Wayne MSA, IN	Y	17280 FQ	104410 AW		INBLS	10/01-12/01
	Gary PMSA, IN	Y	52800 FQ	106330 AW		INBLS	10/01-12/01
	Indianapolis MSA, IN	Y	61180 FQ	104020 AW		INBLS	10/01-12/01
	South Bend MSA, IN	Y	61350 FQ	124290 AW		INBLS	10/01-12/01
	Iowa	Y	69170 FQ	123880 AW		IABLS	10/01-12/01
	Cedar Rapids MSA, IA	Y	75370 FQ	111520 AW		IABLS	10/01-12/01
	Davenport-Moline-Rock Island MSA, IA-IL	Y	70970 FQ	128680 AW		IABLS	10/01-12/01
	Des Moines MSA, IA	Y	56470 FQ	125550 AW		IABLS	10/01-12/01

AAW	Average annual wage	**AOH**	Average offered, high	**ASH**	Average starting, high	**H**	Hourly	**M**	Monthly	**S**	Special: hourly and annual
AE	Average entry wage	**AOL**	Average offered, low	**ASL**	Average starting, low	**HI**	Highest wage paid	**MTC**	Median total compensation	**TQ**	Third quartile wage
AEX	Average experienced wage	**APH**	Average pay, high range	**AW**	Average wage paid	**HR**	High end range	**MW**	Median wage paid	**W**	Weekly
AO	Average offered	**APL**	Average pay, low range	**FQ**	First quartile wage	**LR**	Low end range	**SQ**	Second quartile wage	**Y**	Yearly

Occupation/Type/Industry	Location	Per	Low	Mid	High	Source	Date
Dentist	Kansas	Y	77970 FQ	104740 AW		KSBLS	10/01-12/01
	Topeka MSA, KS	Y	75350 FQ	110630 AW		KSBLS	10/01-12/01
	Wichita MSA, KS	Y	76940 FQ	93680 AW		KSBLS	10/01-12/01
	Kentucky	Y	62530 FQ	105280 AW		KYBLS	10/01-12/01
	Lexington MSA, KY	Y	59870 FQ	76990 AW	108560 TQ	KYBLS	10/01-12/01
	Louisville MSA, KY-IN	Y	64770 FQ	109280 AW		KYBLS	10/01-12/01
	Louisiana	Y	29110 FQ	105740 AW		LABLS	10/01-12/01
	Baton Rouge MSA, LA	Y	112710 FQ	128230 AW		LABLS	10/01-12/01
	Houma MSA, LA	Y	47280 FQ	93680 AW		LABLS	10/01-12/01
	Lafayette MSA, LA	Y	21310 FQ	83040 AW		LABLS	10/01-12/01
	New Orleans MSA, LA	Y	65550 FQ	111690 AW		LABLS	10/01-12/01
	Maine	Y	59430 FQ	86050 AW		MEBLS	10/01-12/01
	Portland MSA, ME	Y	62090 FQ	101830 AW		MEBLS	10/01-12/01
	Maryland	Y	72090 FQ	118260 AW		MDBLS	10/01-12/01
	Baltimore PMSA, MD	Y	75690 FQ	98670 AW		MDBLS	10/01-12/01
	Massachusetts	Y	53670 FQ	111520 AW		MABLS	10/01-12/01
	Boston PMSA, MA-NH	Y	52160 FQ	104190 AW		MABLS	10/01-12/01
	Lawrence PMSA, MA-NH	Y	73160 FQ	124710 AW		MABLS	10/01-12/01
	Lowell PMSA, MA-NH	Y	43240 FQ	87710 AW		MABLS	10/01-12/01
	New Bedford PMSA, MA	Y	82250 FQ	119910 AW		MABLS	10/01-12/01
	Worcester PMSA, MA-CT	Y	122360 FQ	133670 AW		MABLS	10/01-12/01
	Michigan	Y	82360 FQ	123230 AW		MIBLS	10/01-12/01
	Detroit PMSA, MI	Y	94760 FQ	125040 AW		MIBLS	10/01-12/01
	Flint PMSA, MI	Y	54070 FQ	123270 AW		MIBLS	10/01-12/01
	Grand Rapids-Muskegon-Holland MSA, MI	Y	100690 FQ	131990 AW		MIBLS	10/01-12/01
	Lansing-East Lansing MSA, MI	Y	119880 FQ	133660 AW		MIBLS	10/01-12/01
	Saginaw-Bay City-Midland MSA, MI	Y	111600 FQ	129390 AW		MIBLS	10/01-12/01
	Minnesota	Y	65110 FQ	114120 AW		MNBLS	10/01-12/01
	Minneapolis-St. Paul MSA, MN-WI	Y	74970 FQ	116180 AW		MNBLS	10/01-12/01
	St. Cloud MSA, MN	Y	118330 FQ	135460 AW		MNBLS	10/01-12/01
	Mississippi	Y	33350 FQ	79090 AW		MSBLS	10/01-12/01
	Biloxi-Gulfport-Pascagoula MSA, MS	Y	46090 FQ	69290 AW		MSBLS	10/01-12/01
	Jackson MSA, MS	Y	59200 FQ	83150 AW		MSBLS	10/01-12/01
	Missouri	Y	55290 FQ	111690 AW		MOBLS	10/01-12/01
	Kansas City MSA, MO-KS	Y	56980 FQ	111040 AW		MOBLS	10/01-12/01
	St. Louis MSA, MO-IL	Y	79020 FQ	122050 AW		MOBLS	10/01-12/01
	Montana	Y	40510 FQ	90240 AW	145100 TQ	MTBLS	10/01-12/01
	Billings MSA, MT	Y	118170 FQ	128550 AW	145230 TQ	MTBLS	10/01-12/01
	Nebraska	Y	96070 FQ	119560 AW		NEBLS	10/01-12/01
	Lincoln MSA, NE	Y	95730 FQ	121640 AW		NEBLS	10/01-12/01
	Omaha MSA, NE-IA	Y	97430 FQ	116690 AW		NEBLS	10/01-12/01
	Nevada	Y	73660 FQ	132100 AW		NVBLS	10/01-12/01
	Las Vegas MSA, NV-AZ	Y	132460 FQ	140450 AW		NVBLS	10/01-12/01
	New Hampshire	Y	38300 FQ	102920 AW		NHBLS	10/01-12/01
	Nashua PMSA, NH	Y	88980 FQ	120620 AW		NHBLS	10/01-12/01
	Portsmouth-Rochester PMSA, NH-ME	Y	85950 FQ	118410 AW		NHBLS	10/01-12/01
	New Jersey	Y	61020 FQ	114900 AW		NJBLS	10/01-12/01
	Atlantic-Cape May PMSA, NJ	Y	93360 FQ	111900 AW		NJBLS	10/01-12/01
	Bergen-Passaic PMSA, NJ	Y	96620 FQ	129880 AW		NJBLS	10/01-12/01
	Middlesex-Somerset-Hunterdon PMSA, NJ	Y	56290 FQ	118920 AW		NJBLS	10/01-12/01
	Monmouth-Ocean PMSA, NJ	Y	58950 FQ	89710 AW		NJBLS	10/01-12/01
	Newark PMSA, NJ	Y	74900 FQ	119020 AW		NJBLS	10/01-12/01
	Trenton PMSA, NJ	Y	50440 FQ	102260 AW		NJBLS	10/01-12/01
	New Mexico	Y	52410 FQ	100430 AW		NMBLS	10/01-12/01
	Albuquerque MSA, NM	Y	81540 FQ	113450 AW		NMBLS	10/01-12/01
	Las Cruces MSA, NM	Y	75300 FQ	106380 AW		NMBLS	10/01-12/01
	New York	Y	60310 FQ	110600 AW		NYBLS	10/01-12/01
	Albany-Schenectady-Troy MSA, NY	Y	48330 FQ	85310 AW		NYBLS	10/01-12/01
	Binghamton MSA, NY	Y	53590 FQ	117830 AW		NYBLS	10/01-12/01
	Buffalo-Niagara Falls MSA, NY	Y	74650 FQ	107150 AW		NYBLS	10/01-12/01
	Dutchess County PMSA, NY	Y	53600 FQ	93980 AW		NYBLS	10/01-12/01
	Nassau-Suffolk PMSA, NY	Y	81950 FQ	109830 AW		NYBLS	10/01-12/01
	New York PMSA, NY	Y	65050 FQ	117590 AW		NYBLS	10/01-12/01
	Newburgh PMSA, NY-PA	Y	43140 FQ	87250 AW		NYBLS	10/01-12/01

AAW Average annual wage; **AE** Average entry wage; **AEX** Average experienced wage; **AO** Average offered; **AOH** Average offered, high; **AOL** Average offered, low; **APH** Average pay, high range; **APL** Average pay, low range; **ASH** Average starting, high; **ASL** Average starting, low; **AW** Average wage paid; **FQ** First quartile wage; **H** Hourly; **HI** Highest wage paid; **HR** High end range; **LR** Low end range; **M** Monthly; **MTC** Median total compensation; **MW** Median wage paid; **SQ** Second quartile wage; **S** Special: hourly and annual; **TQ** Third quartile wage; **W** Weekly; **Y** Yearly

Occupation/Type/Industry	Location	Per	Low	Mid	High	Source	Date
Dentist	Rochester MSA, NY	Y	45280 FQ	94590 AW		NYBLS	10/01-12/01
	Syracuse MSA, NY	Y	62740 FQ	90970 AW		NYBLS	10/01-12/01
	Utica-Rome MSA, NY	Y	39220 FQ	92730 AW		NYBLS	10/01-12/01
	North Carolina	Y	39500 FQ	104340 AW		NCBLS	10/01-12/01
	Asheville MSA, NC	Y	68100 FQ	115450 AW		NCBLS	10/01-12/01
	Fayetteville MSA, NC	Y	64030 FQ	117840 AW		NCBLS	10/01-12/01
	Greensboro-Winston-Salem-High Point MSA, NC	Y	23390 FQ	77700 AW		NCBLS	10/01-12/01
	Wilmington MSA, NC	Y	47260 FQ	117020 AW		NCBLS	10/01-12/01
	North Dakota	Y	22000 FQ	103340 AW		NDBLS	10/01-12/01
	Fargo-Moorhead MSA, ND-MN	Y	77070 FQ	121650 AW		NDBLS	10/01-12/01
	Ohio	Y	73750 FQ	121220 AW		OHBLS	10/01-12/01
	Akron PMSA, OH	Y	79870 FQ	109710 AW		OHBLS	10/01-12/01
	Cincinnati PMSA, OH-KY-IN	Y	76410 FQ	112390 AW		OHBLS	10/01-12/01
	Dayton-Springfield MSA, OH	Y	115890 FQ	127300 AW		OHBLS	10/01-12/01
	Toledo MSA, OH	Y	73550 FQ	101770 AW		OHBLS	10/01-12/01
	Youngstown-Warren MSA, OH	Y	35030 FQ	119380 AW		OHBLS	10/01-12/01
	Oklahoma	Y	40470 FQ	114700 AW		OKBLS	10/01-12/01
	Eugene-Springfield MSA, OR	Y	109020 FQ	133160 AW		ORBLS	10/01-12/01
	Salem PMSA, OR	Y	73070 FQ	92480 AW		ORBLS	10/01-12/01
	Pennsylvania	Y	56020 FQ	97580 AW		PABLS	10/01-12/01
	Allentown-Bethlehem-Easton MSA, PA	Y	37750 FQ	70490 AW		PABLS	10/01-12/01
	Erie MSA, PA	Y	84450 FQ	124790 AW		PABLS	10/01-12/01
	Harrisburg-Lebanon-Carlisle MSA, PA	Y	79310 FQ	122320 AW		PABLS	10/01-12/01
	Lancaster MSA, PA	Y	101400 FQ	126500 AW		PABLS	10/01-12/01
	Philadelphia PMSA, PA-NJ	Y	72410 FQ	122920 AW		PABLS	10/01-12/01
	Pittsburgh MSA, PA	Y	57110 FQ	73200 AW	127940 TQ	PABLS	10/01-12/01
	Reading MSA, PA	Y	44670 FQ	98740 AW		PABLS	10/01-12/01
	Scranton-Wilkes-Barre-Hazleton MSA, PA	Y	64700 FQ	88720 AW	116480 TQ	PABLS	10/01-12/01
	Rhode Island	Y	85620 FQ	120160 AW		RIBLS	10/01-12/01
	Providence-Fall River-Warwick MSA, RI-MA	Y	75970 FQ	115250 AW		RIBLS	10/01-12/01
	South Carolina	Y	77810 FQ	114350 AW		SCBLS	10/01-12/01
	Charleston-North Charleston MSA, SC	Y	99990 FQ	126980 AW		SCBLS	10/01-12/01
	Columbia MSA, SC	Y	95870 FQ	110690 AW		SCBLS	10/01-12/01
	South Dakota	Y	51920 FQ	92800 AW		SDBLS	10/01-12/01
	Tennessee	Y	33150 FQ	77490 AW		TNBLS	10/01-12/01
	Knoxville MSA, TN	Y	36470 FQ	117450 AW		TNBLS	10/01-12/01
	Memphis MSA, TN-AR-MS	Y	65280 FQ	127760 AW		TNBLS	10/01-12/01
	Texas	Y	50530 FQ	110040 AW		TXBLS	10/01-12/01
	Amarillo MSA, TX	Y	116010 FQ	126690 AW	145580 TQ	TXBLS	10/01-12/01
	Austin-San Marcos MSA, TX	Y	71130 FQ	127200 AW		TXBLS	10/01-12/01
	Brownsville-Harlingen-San Benito MSA, TX	Y	27440 FQ	83470 AW		TXBLS	10/01-12/01
	Corpus Christi MSA, TX	Y	115390 FQ	131870 AW		TXBLS	10/01-12/01
	Dallas PMSA, TX	Y	62530 FQ	97880 AW		TXBLS	10/01-12/01
	Fort Worth-Arlington PMSA, TX	Y	37400 FQ	72960 AW		TXBLS	10/01-12/01
	Killeen-Temple MSA, TX	Y	38100 FQ	113340 AW		TXBLS	10/01-12/01
	McAllen-Edinburg-Mission MSA, TX	Y	79440 FQ	120590 AW		TXBLS	10/01-12/01
	San Antonio MSA, TX	Y	62750 FQ	101030 AW	143610 TQ	TXBLS	10/01-12/01
	Waco MSA, TX	Y	102420 FQ	129840 AW		TXBLS	10/01-12/01
	Utah	Y	32830 FQ	100200 AW		UTBLS	10/01-12/01
	Salt Lake City-Ogden MSA, UT	Y	61110 FQ	109560 AW		UTBLS	10/01-12/01
	Vermont	Y	69900 FQ	103700 AW		VTBLS	10/01-12/01
	Burlington MSA, VT	Y	44690 FQ	100570 AW		VTBLS	10/01-12/01
	Virginia	Y	45220 FQ	120070 AW		VABLS	10/01-12/01
	Lynchburg MSA, VA	Y	83050 FQ	126220 AW		VABLS	10/01-12/01
	Richmond-Petersburg MSA, VA	Y	55130 FQ	90690 AW		VABLS	10/01-12/01
	Washington	Y	84560 FQ	126550 AW		WABLS	10/01-12/01
	Olympia PMSA, WA	Y	83640 FQ	110270 AW		WABLS	10/01-12/01
	Richland-Kennewick-Pasco MSA, WA	Y	128280 FQ	141410 AW		WABLS	10/01-12/01

AAW	Average annual wage	AOH	Average offered, high	ASH	Average starting, high	H	Hourly	M	Monthly	S	Special: hourly and annual
AE	Average entry wage	AOL	Average offered, low	ASL	Average starting, low	HI	Highest wage paid	MTC	Median total compensation	TQ	Third quartile wage
AEX	Average experienced wage	APH	Average pay, high range	AW	Average wage paid	HR	High end range	MW	Median wage paid	W	Weekly
AO	Average offered	APL	Average pay, low range	FQ	First quartile wage	LR	Low end range	SQ	Second quartile wage	Y	Yearly

Occupation/Type/Industry	Location	Per	Low	Mid	High	Source	Date
Dentist	Seattle-Bellevue-Everett PMSA, WA	Y	68680 FQ	107020 AW		WABLS	10/01-12/01
	Spokane MSA, WA	Y	126420 FQ	139900 AW		WABLS	10/01-12/01
	Tacoma PMSA, WA	Y	85140 FQ	119350 AW		WABLS	10/01-12/01
	Yakima MSA, WA	Y	122950 FQ	138140 AW		WABLS	10/01-12/01
	West Virginia	Y	25480 FQ	96760 AW		WVBLS	10/01-12/01
	Charleston MSA, WV	Y	65920 FQ	118920 AW		WVBLS	10/01-12/01
	Huntington-Ashland MSA, WV-KY-OH	Y	36960 FQ	88780 AW		WVBLS	10/01-12/01
	Wisconsin	Y	29490 FQ	79130 AW		WIBLS	10/01-12/01
	Appleton-Oshkosh-Neenah MSA, WI	Y		143790 AW		WIBLS	10/01-12/01
	Green Bay MSA, WI	Y	98670 FQ	135520 AW		WIBLS	10/01-12/01
	Madison MSA, WI	Y	34570 FQ	88830 AW		WIBLS	10/01-12/01
	Racine PMSA, WI	Y	113100 FQ	131470 AW		WIBLS	10/01-12/01
	Wyoming	Y	74240 FQ	109690 AW		WYBLS	10/01-12/01
	Puerto Rico	Y	29740 FQ	49380 AW	75510 TQ	PRBLS	10/01-12/01
	Guam	Y	79610 FQ	116560 AW		GUBLS	10/01-12/01
Derrick Operator							
Oil and Gas	Alabama	H	9.41 FQ	12.30 AW	16.08 TQ	ALBLS	10/01-12/01
Oil and Gas	Arkansas	H	11.36 FQ	15.66 AW	25.13 TQ	ARBLS	10/01-12/01
Oil and Gas	California	H	11.21 FQ	15.87 AW	21.27 TQ	CABLS	10/01-12/01
Oil and Gas	Colorado	H	12.15 FQ	15.51 AW	18.72 TQ	COBLS	10/01-12/01
Oil and Gas	Kansas	H	9.24 FQ	12.51 AW	19.11 TQ	KSBLS	10/01-12/01
Oil and Gas	Louisiana	H	11.68 FQ	18.11 AW	26.97 TQ	LABLS	10/01-12/01
Oil and Gas	Michigan	H	11.76 FQ	16.85 AW	26.41 TQ	MIBLS	10/01-12/01
Oil and Gas	New Mexico	H	9.85 FQ	13.51 AW	18.07 TQ	NMBLS	10/01-12/01
Oil and Gas	North Dakota	H	10.98 FQ	14.06 AW	17.60 TQ	NDBLS	10/01-12/01
Oil and Gas	Oklahoma	H	9.40 FQ	12.35 AW	16.66 TQ	OKBLS	10/01-12/01
Oil and Gas	Pennsylvania	H	9.52 FQ	12.22 AW	17.25 TQ	PABLS	10/01-12/01
Oil and Gas	Texas	H	9.61 FQ	14.58 AW	22.50 TQ	TXBLS	10/01-12/01
Oil and Gas	Utah	H	11.90 FQ	14.73 AW	19.93 TQ	UTBLS	10/01-12/01
Oil and Gas	Virginia	H	9.16 FQ	13.31 AW	21.94 TQ	VABLS	10/01-12/01
Oil and Gas	West Virginia	H	9.26 FQ	11.06 AW	13.04 TQ	WVBLS	10/01-12/01
Oil and Gas	Wyoming	H	11.58 FQ	17.14 AW	21.66 TQ	WYBLS	10/01-12/01
Design Engineer	United States	Y		50000-80000 AW		DN	1/01-1/02
	Mountain	Y		70000 AW		DN	1/01-1/02
	Pacific	Y		70000 AW		DN	1/01-1/02
Telecommunications	United States	Y		78200 MW		DN	1/01-1/02
Designer	Phoenix, AZ	Y	28000 AE	35500 AW		TBJ	1/00-1/01
Desktop Publisher	United States	Y		25760-39660 AW		FREEP1	1/00-1/00
	Alabama	H	8.04 FQ	12.35 AW	16.97 TQ	ALBLS	10/01-12/01
	Arizona	H	9.22 FQ	17.79 AW	27.29 TQ	AZBLS	10/01-12/01
	Arkansas	H	6.99 FQ	10.55 AW	15.55 TQ	ARBLS	10/01-12/01
	California	H	9.82 FQ	17.63 AW	27.07 TQ	CABLS	10/01-12/01
	Colorado	H	10.94 FQ	16.05 AW	21.84 TQ	COBLS	10/01-12/01
	Connecticut	H	10.54 FQ	17.79 AW	25.09 TQ	CTBLS	10/01-12/01
	Delaware	H	9.70 FQ	13.71 AW	17.90 TQ	DEBLS	10/01-12/01
	District of Columbia	H	11.35 FQ	20.04 AW	30.57 TQ	DCBLS	10/01-12/01
	Florida	H	8.99 FQ	14.40 AW	21.57 TQ	FLBLS	10/01-12/01
	Georgia	H	9.06 FQ	14.05 AW	21.26 TQ	GABLS	10/01-12/01
	Hawaii	H	9.43 FQ	15.97 AW	23.15 TQ	HIBLS	10/01-12/01
	Idaho	H	7.40 FQ	11.19 AW	16.94 TQ	IDBLS	10/01-12/01
	Illinois	H	8.05 FQ	20.37 AW	41.10 TQ	ILBLS	10/01-12/01
	Indiana	H	7.88 FQ	12.72 AW	19.15 TQ	INBLS	10/01-12/01
	Iowa	H	8.21 FQ	12.47 AW	17.33 TQ	IABLS	10/01-12/01
	Kentucky	H	7.85 FQ	12.56 AW	19.50 TQ	KYBLS	10/01-12/01
	Louisiana	H	7.51 FQ	12.78 AW	19.30 TQ	LABLS	10/01-12/01
	Maine	H	8.12 FQ	13.54 AW	20.31 TQ	MEBLS	10/01-12/01
	Maryland	H	11.43 FQ	18.11 AW	26.52 TQ	MDBLS	10/01-12/01
	Massachusetts	H	12.37 FQ	18.95 AW	25.82 TQ	MABLS	10/01-12/01
	Michigan	H	8.41 FQ	15.04 AW	21.46 TQ	MIBLS	10/01-12/01
	Minnesota	H	9.33 FQ	16.55 AW	24.77 TQ	MNBLS	10/01-12/01
	Mississippi	H	7.59 FQ	11.81 AW	16.29 TQ	MSBLS	10/01-12/01
	Missouri	H	6.21 FQ	12.79 AW	21.74 TQ	MOBLS	10/01-12/01
	Montana	H	7.47 FQ	11.43 AW	16.90 TQ	MTBLS	10/01-12/01

AAW Average annual wage; AE Average entry wage; AEX Average experienced wage; AO Average offered; AOH Average offered, high; AOL Average offered, low; APH Average pay, high range; APL Average pay, low range; ASH Average starting, high; ASL Average starting, low; AW Average wage paid; FQ First quartile wage; H Hourly; HI Highest wage paid; HR High end range; LR Low end range; M Monthly; MTC Median total compensation; MW Median wage paid; SQ Second quartile wage; S Special: hourly and annual; TQ Third quartile wage; W Weekly; Y Yearly

Occupation/Type/Industry	Location	Per	Low	Mid	High	Source	Date
Desktop Publisher	Nebraska	H	8.98 FQ	14.80 AW	23.54 TQ	NEBLS	10/01-12/01
	Nevada	H	11.11 FQ	15.46 AW	21.04 TQ	NVBLS	10/01-12/01
	New Hampshire	H	10.18 FQ	15.06 AW	20.47 TQ	NHBLS	10/01-12/01
	New Jersey	H	11.04 FQ	19.46 AW	28.21 TQ	NJBLS	10/01-12/01
	New Mexico	H	6.66 FQ	12.29 AW	18.10 TQ	NMBLS	10/01-12/01
	New York	H	10.32 FQ	20.22 AW	32.57 TQ	NYBLS	10/01-12/01
	North Carolina	H	9.08 FQ	14.07 AW	20.51 TQ	NCBLS	10/01-12/01
	North Dakota	H	9.01 FQ	12.21 AW	17.02 TQ	NDBLS	10/01-12/01
	Ohio	H	8.91 FQ	14.38 AW	19.62 TQ	OHBLS	10/01-12/01
	Oklahoma	H	6.36 FQ	12.00 AW	18.25 TQ	OKBLS	10/01-12/01
	Oregon	H	9.82 FQ	15.39 AW	22.85 TQ	ORBLS	10/01-12/01
	Pennsylvania	H	8.32 FQ	14.28 AW	21.13 TQ	PABLS	10/01-12/01
	Rhode Island	H	10.70 FQ	16.66 AW	21.42 TQ	RIBLS	10/01-12/01
	South Carolina	H	9.83 FQ	13.82 AW	20.08 TQ	SCBLS	10/01-12/01
	South Dakota	H	7.45 FQ	9.50 AW	12.41 TQ	SDBLS	10/01-12/01
	Tennessee	H	7.77 FQ	13.22 AW	20.04 TQ	TNBLS	10/01-12/01
	Texas	H	7.53 FQ	14.40 AW	21.57 TQ	TXBLS	10/01-12/01
	Utah	H	8.78 FQ	13.00 AW	19.15 TQ	UTBLS	10/01-12/01
	Vermont	H	9.55 FQ	13.72 AW	18.85 TQ	VTBLS	10/01-12/01
	Virginia	H	7.68 FQ	14.85 AW	21.80 TQ	VABLS	10/01-12/01
	Washington	H	9.34 FQ	15.23 AW	21.76 TQ	WABLS	10/01-12/01
	West Virginia	H	7.42 FQ	10.25 AW	13.38 TQ	WVBLS	10/01-12/01
	Wisconsin	H	8.57 FQ	16.00 AW	24.69 TQ	WIBLS	10/01-12/01
	Puerto Rico	H	6.63 FQ	12.51 AW	22.63 TQ	PRBLS	10/01-12/01
Detective and Criminal Investigator	United States	Y		48870 MW		OOH2	1/99-1/00
	Alabama	Y	23950 FQ	38570 AW	64380 TQ	ALBLS	10/01-12/01
	Birmingham MSA, AL	Y	23100 FQ	47170 AW	71430 TQ	ALBLS	10/01-12/01
	Huntsville MSA, AL	Y	33320 FQ	50650 AW	75850 TQ	ALBLS	10/01-12/01
	Montgomery MSA, AL	Y	25720 FQ	42070 AW	68450 TQ	ALBLS	10/01-12/01
	Alaska	Y	37030 FQ	54860 AW	78030 TQ	AKBLS	10/01-12/01
	Arizona	Y	31610 FQ	46090 AW	68390 TQ	AZBLS	10/01-12/01
	Phoenix-Mesa MSA, AZ	Y	31410 FQ	45980 AW	68960 TQ	AZBLS	10/01-12/01
	Tucson MSA, AZ	Y	32380 FQ	49780 AW	71390 TQ	AZBLS	10/01-12/01
	Arkansas	Y	22860 FQ	37150 AW	65080 TQ	ARBLS	10/01-12/01
	Fayetteville-Springdale-Rogers MSA, AR	Y	25040 FQ	38380 AW	65310 TQ	ARBLS	10/01-12/01
	Fort Smith MSA, AR-OK	Y	25500 FQ	46020 AW	78110 TQ	ARBLS	10/01-12/01
	Little Rock-North Little Rock MSA, AR	Y	24070 FQ	44260 AW	69600 TQ	ARBLS	10/01-12/01
	California	Y	41950 FQ	61580 AW	84450 TQ	CABLS	10/01-12/01
	Bakersfield MSA, CA	Y	47290 FQ	61520 AW	80880 TQ	CABLS	10/01-12/01
	Fresno MSA, CA	Y	37920 FQ	60060 AW	76790 TQ	CABLS	10/01-12/01
	Los Angeles-Long Beach PMSA, CA	Y	42990 FQ	62100 AW	83620 TQ	CABLS	10/01-12/01
	Merced MSA, CA	Y	42660 FQ	62370 AW	86190 TQ	CABLS	10/01-12/01
	Modesto MSA, CA	Y	38820 FQ	53210 AW	70000 TQ	CABLS	10/01-12/01
	Oakland PMSA, CA	Y	46650 FQ	64120 AW	87550 TQ	CABLS	10/01-12/01
	Orange County PMSA, CA	Y	44960 FQ	69930 AW	92000 TQ	CABLS	10/01-12/01
	Redding MSA, CA	Y	42000 FQ	61650 AW	83610 TQ	CABLS	10/01-12/01
	Riverside-San Bernardino PMSA, CA	Y	48880 FQ	61310 AW	81080 TQ	CABLS	10/01-12/01
	Sacramento PMSA, CA	Y	36690 FQ	52720 AW	72400 TQ	CABLS	10/01-12/01
	Salinas MSA, CA	Y	42490 FQ	59010 AW	77060 TQ	CABLS	10/01-12/01
	San Diego MSA, CA	Y	43840 FQ	61690 AW	82270 TQ	CABLS	10/01-12/01
	San Francisco PMSA, CA	Y	42380 FQ	62230 AW	84420 TQ	CABLS	10/01-12/01
	San Jose PMSA, CA	Y	44040 FQ	63150 AW	86160 TQ	CABLS	10/01-12/01
	San Luis Obispo-Atascadero-Paso Robles MSA, CA	Y	39630 FQ	47720 AW	58200 TQ	CABLS	10/01-12/01
	Santa Barbara-Santa Maria-Lompoc MSA, CA	Y	47930 FQ	62440 AW	76820 TQ	CABLS	10/01-12/01
	Santa Cruz-Watsonville PMSA, CA	Y	48640 FQ	65420 AW	86280 TQ	CABLS	10/01-12/01
	Santa Rosa PMSA, CA	Y	47620 FQ	63100 AW	76480 TQ	CABLS	10/01-12/01
	Stockton-Lodi MSA, CA	Y	37240 FQ	56960 AW	72910 TQ	CABLS	10/01-12/01
	Vallejo-Fairfield-Napa PMSA, CA	Y	45400 FQ	66200 AW	87930 TQ	CABLS	10/01-12/01
	Ventura PMSA, CA	Y	48180 FQ	63260 AW	83590 TQ	CABLS	10/01-12/01
	Colorado	Y	37930 FQ	57280 AW	75670 TQ	COBLS	10/01-12/01
	Boulder-Longmont PMSA, CO	Y	43680 FQ	56910 AW	71200 TQ	COBLS	10/01-12/01
	Colorado Springs MSA, CO	Y	32850 FQ	53020 AW	82610 TQ	COBLS	10/01-12/01

AAW Average annual wage; AE Average entry wage; AEX Average experienced wage; AO Average offered; AOH Average offered, high; AOL Average offered, low; APH Average pay, high range; APL Average pay, low range; ASH Average starting, high; ASL Average starting, low; AW Average wage paid; FQ First quartile wage; H Hourly; HI Highest wage paid; HR High end range; LR Low end range; M Monthly; MTC Median total compensation; MW Median wage paid; SQ Second quartile wage; S Special: hourly and annual; TQ Third quartile wage; W Weekly; Y Yearly

Occupation/Type/Industry	Location	Per	Low	Mid	High	Source	Date
Detective and Criminal Investigator	Denver PMSA, CO	Y	45970 FQ	61580 AW	77300 TQ	COBLS	10/01-12/01
	Connecticut	Y	46820 FQ	54030 AW	64650 TQ	CTBLS	10/01-12/01
	Bridgeport PMSA, CT	Y	48450 FQ	54320 AW	61820 TQ	CTBLS	10/01-12/01
	Danbury PMSA, CT	Y	41940 FQ	51020 AW	59490 TQ	CTBLS	10/01-12/01
	Hartford MSA, CT	Y	45920 FQ	54000 AW	65830 TQ	CTBLS	10/01-12/01
	New Haven-Meriden PMSA, CT	Y	46990 FQ	54640 AW	68300 TQ	CTBLS	10/01-12/01
	New London-Norwich MSA, CT-RI	Y	48090 FQ	54610 AW	64590 TQ	CTBLS	10/01-12/01
	Stamford-Norwalk PMSA, CT	Y	48580 FQ	54080 AW	60550 TQ	CTBLS	10/01-12/01
	Delaware	Y	25930 FQ	42810 AW	66450 TQ	DEBLS	10/01-12/01
	Washington PMSA, DC-MD-VA-WV	Y	46420 FQ	68000 AW	89360 TQ	DCBLS	10/01-12/01
	Florida	Y	33090 FQ	57540 AW	88440 TQ	FLBLS	10/01-12/01
	Daytona Beach MSA, FL	Y	29900 FQ	59680 AW	108740 TQ	FLBLS	10/01-12/01
	Fort Lauderdale PMSA, FL	Y	42140 FQ	65140 AW	90880 TQ	FLBLS	10/01-12/01
	Fort Myers-Cape Coral MSA, FL	Y	32160 FQ	55420 AW	90890 TQ	FLBLS	10/01-12/01
	Fort Pierce-Port St. Lucie MSA, FL	Y	29230 FQ	47860 AW	77750 TQ	FLBLS	10/01-12/01
	Fort Walton Beach MSA, FL	Y	29920 FQ	57870 AW	99650 TQ	FLBLS	10/01-12/01
	Gainesville MSA, FL	Y	35350 FQ	57470 AW	90090 TQ	FLBLS	10/01-12/01
	Jacksonville MSA, FL	Y	36440 FQ	64310 AW	94010 TQ	FLBLS	10/01-12/01
	Lakeland-Winter Haven MSA, FL	Y	28990 FQ	62880 AW	111000 TQ	FLBLS	10/01-12/01
	Melbourne-Titusville-Palm Bay MSA, FL	Y	31170 FQ	50960 AW	89590 TQ	FLBLS	10/01-12/01
	Miami PMSA, FL	Y	38240 FQ	58470 AW	82900 TQ	FLBLS	10/01-12/01
	Orlando MSA, FL	Y	31810 FQ	58480 AW	90200 TQ	FLBLS	10/01-12/01
	Pensacola MSA, FL	Y	28700 FQ	62090 AW	99310 TQ	FLBLS	10/01-12/01
	Sarasota-Bradenton MSA, FL	Y	32220 FQ	50050 AW	82670 TQ	FLBLS	10/01-12/01
	Tallahassee MSA, FL	Y	32760 FQ	51980 AW	85490 TQ	FLBLS	10/01-12/01
	Tampa-St. Petersburg-Clearwater MSA, FL	Y	32900 FQ	57640 AW	85540 TQ	FLBLS	10/01-12/01
	West Palm Beach-Boca Raton MSA, FL	Y	39680 FQ	64180 AW	106880 TQ	FLBLS	10/01-12/01
	Georgia	Y	26670 FQ	42650 AW	67800 TQ	GABLS	10/01-12/01
	Atlanta MSA, GA	Y	30770 FQ	46400 AW	69780 TQ	GABLS	10/01-12/01
	Augusta-Aiken MSA, GA-SC	Y	26290 FQ	41920 AW	65620 TQ	GABLS	10/01-12/01
	Macon MSA, GA	Y	28180 FQ	45720 AW	71660 TQ	GABLS	10/01-12/01
	Savannah MSA, GA	Y	28310 FQ	51160 AW	78760 TQ	GABLS	10/01-12/01
	Hawaii	Y	43560 FQ	55360 AW	80180 TQ	HIBLS	10/01-12/01
	Honolulu MSA, HI	Y	43550 FQ	56490 AW	82010 TQ	HIBLS	10/01-12/01
	Idaho	Y	28420 FQ	42150 AW	63750 TQ	IDBLS	10/01-12/01
	Boise City MSA, ID	Y	21290 FQ	44270 AW	69350 TQ	IDBLS	10/01-12/01
	Illinois	Y	35670 FQ	53860 AW	74140 TQ	ILBLS	10/01-12/01
	Chicago PMSA, IL	Y	36830 FQ	55230 AW	74620 TQ	ILBLS	10/01-12/01
	Peoria-Pekin MSA, IL	Y	33650 FQ	51490 AW	71970 TQ	ILBLS	10/01-12/01
	Springfield MSA, IL	Y	35550 FQ	51970 AW	72940 TQ	ILBLS	10/01-12/01
	Indiana	Y	28220 FQ	40910 AW	62320 TQ	INBLS	10/01-12/01
	Elkhart-Goshen MSA, IN	Y	31180 FQ	38300 AW	44720 TQ	INBLS	10/01-12/01
	Evansville-Henderson MSA, IN-KY	Y	24310 FQ	46830 AW	77190 TQ	INBLS	10/01-12/01
	Fort Wayne MSA, IN	Y	32770 FQ	44450 AW	65160 TQ	INBLS	10/01-12/01
	Gary PMSA, IN	Y	31880 FQ	46150 AW	69580 TQ	INBLS	10/01-12/01
	Indianapolis MSA, IN	Y	28290 FQ	42990 AW	67670 TQ	INBLS	10/01-12/01
	Lafayette MSA, IN	Y	30160 FQ	38230 AW	46130 TQ	INBLS	10/01-12/01
	South Bend MSA, IN	Y	28970 FQ	39840 AW	57460 TQ	INBLS	10/01-12/01
	Iowa	Y	29340 FQ	45870 AW	64360 TQ	IABLS	10/01-12/01
	Cedar Rapids MSA, IA	Y	39990 FQ	52550 AW	65730 TQ	IABLS	10/01-12/01
	Davenport-Moline-Rock Island MSA, IA-IL	Y	42370 FQ	58150 AW	73010 TQ	IABLS	10/01-12/01
	Des Moines MSA, IA	Y	34440 FQ	47820 AW	66970 TQ	IABLS	10/01-12/01
	Kansas	Y	25820 FQ	40750 AW	57920 TQ	KSBLS	10/01-12/01
	Topeka MSA, KS	Y	24790 FQ	41560 AW	57720 TQ	KSBLS	10/01-12/01
	Kentucky	Y	27690 FQ	44970 AW	69600 TQ	KYBLS	10/01-12/01
	Lexington MSA, KY	Y	30060 FQ	47170 AW	70980 TQ	KYBLS	10/01-12/01
	Louisville MSA, KY-IN	Y	26540 FQ	46760 AW	74440 TQ	KYBLS	10/01-12/01
	Louisiana	Y	22520 FQ	37540 AW	65850 TQ	LABLS	10/01-12/01
	Baton Rouge MSA, LA	Y	28850 FQ	42070 AW	68980 TQ	LABLS	10/01-12/01
	Houma MSA, LA	Y	22570 FQ	30730 AW	35130 TQ	LABLS	10/01-12/01

AAW	Average annual wage	AOH	Average offered, high	ASH	Average starting, high	H	Hourly	M	Monthly	S	Special: hourly and annual
AE	Average entry wage	AOL	Average offered, low	ASL	Average starting, low	HI	Highest wage paid	MTC	Median total compensation	TQ	Third quartile wage
AEX	Average experienced wage	APH	Average pay, high range	AW	Average wage paid	HR	High end range	MW	Median wage paid	W	Weekly
AO	Average offered	APL	Average pay, low range	FQ	First quartile wage	LR	Low end range	SQ	Second quartile wage	Y	Yearly

Occupation/Type/Industry	Location	Per	Low	Mid	High	Source	Date
Detective and Criminal Investigator	Lafayette MSA, LA	Y	23610 FQ	42060 AW	64240 TQ	LABLS	10/01-12/01
	Lake Charles MSA, LA	Y	18310 FQ	31030 AW	46290 TQ	LABLS	10/01-12/01
	New Orleans MSA, LA	Y	25260 FQ	41980 AW	70940 TQ	LABLS	10/01-12/01
	Shreveport-Bossier City MSA, LA	Y	19570 FQ	39560 AW	66590 TQ	LABLS	10/01-12/01
	Maine	Y	30110 FQ	41510 AW	60750 TQ	MEBLS	10/01-12/01
	Portland MSA, ME	Y	33460 FQ	48700 AW	70030 TQ	MEBLS	10/01-12/01
	Maryland	Y	32120 FQ	55610 AW	78550 TQ	MDBLS	10/01-12/01
	Baltimore PMSA, MD	Y	31200 FQ	52990 AW	72560 TQ	MDBLS	10/01-12/01
	Massachusetts	Y	39700 FQ	56040 AW	78180 TQ	MABLS	10/01-12/01
	Boston PMSA, MA-NH	Y	45170 FQ	58620 AW	80790 TQ	MABLS	10/01-12/01
	Lawrence PMSA, MA-NH	Y	36670 FQ	51250 AW	71500 TQ	MABLS	10/01-12/01
	Springfield MSA, MA	Y	34190 FQ	50720 AW	70320 TQ	MABLS	10/01-12/01
	Worcester PMSA, MA-CT	Y	42550 FQ	56570 AW	75400 TQ	MABLS	10/01-12/01
	Michigan	Y	39330 FQ	52710 AW	71420 TQ	MIBLS	10/01-12/01
	Ann Arbor PMSA, MI	Y	40550 FQ	52660 AW	68500 TQ	MIBLS	10/01-12/01
	Detroit PMSA, MI	Y	43790 FQ	55610 AW	75480 TQ	MIBLS	10/01-12/01
	Grand Rapids-Muskegon-Holland MSA, MI	Y	39630 FQ	54190 AW	73910 TQ	MIBLS	10/01-12/01
	Kalamazoo-Battle Creek MSA, MI	Y	37570 FQ	49990 AW	60500 TQ	MIBLS	10/01-12/01
	Lansing-East Lansing MSA, MI	Y	41380 FQ	50620 AW	60030 TQ	MIBLS	10/01-12/01
	Saginaw-Bay City-Midland MSA, MI	Y	37180 FQ	46410 AW	57200 TQ	MIBLS	10/01-12/01
	Minnesota	Y	39430 FQ	53130 AW	69610 TQ	MNBLS	10/01-12/01
	Duluth-Superior MSA, MN-WI	Y	39940 FQ	49420 AW	58270 TQ	MNBLS	10/01-12/01
	Minneapolis-St. Paul MSA, MN-WI	Y	40420 FQ	55440 AW	73260 TQ	MNBLS	10/01-12/01
	Mississippi	Y	22400 FQ	33990 AW	54290 TQ	MSBLS	10/01-12/01
	Biloxi-Gulfport-Pascagoula MSA, MS	Y	22640 FQ	38270 AW	65830 TQ	MSBLS	10/01-12/01
	Jackson MSA, MS	Y	23830 FQ	36270 AW	58710 TQ	MSBLS	10/01-12/01
	Missouri	Y	25810 FQ	44150 AW	70830 TQ	MOBLS	10/01-12/01
	Kansas City MSA, MO-KS	Y	30930 FQ	48340 AW	70910 TQ	MOBLS	10/01-12/01
	St. Louis MSA, MO-IL	Y	30720 FQ	50850 AW	77000 TQ	MOBLS	10/01-12/01
	Springfield MSA, MO	Y	14590 FQ	36900 AW	66170 TQ	MOBLS	10/01-12/01
	Montana	Y	28940 FQ	48220 AW	70290 TQ	MTBLS	10/01-12/01
	Billings MSA, MT	Y	35790 FQ	49250 AW	73650 TQ	MTBLS	10/01-12/01
	Nebraska	Y	29400 FQ	43800 AW	61490 TQ	NEBLS	10/01-12/01
	Lincoln MSA, NE	Y	32550 FQ	45170 AW	56960 TQ	NEBLS	10/01-12/01
	Omaha MSA, NE-IA	Y	36920 FQ	50040 AW	66920 TQ	NEBLS	10/01-12/01
	Nevada	Y	38580 FQ	52960 AW	70080 TQ	NVBLS	10/01-12/01
	Las Vegas MSA, NV-AZ	Y	39270 FQ	54340 AW	70570 TQ	NVBLS	10/01-12/01
	Reno MSA, NV	Y	38440 FQ	53820 AW	73360 TQ	NVBLS	10/01-12/01
	New Hampshire	Y	32660 FQ	44900 AW	59440 TQ	NHBLS	10/01-12/01
	Nashua PMSA, NH	Y	38190 FQ	48850 AW	57760 TQ	NHBLS	10/01-12/01
	Portsmouth-Rochester PMSA, NH-ME	Y	32970 FQ	44560 AW	70610 TQ	NHBLS	10/01-12/01
	New Jersey	Y	40190 FQ	64120 AW	87760 TQ	NJBLS	10/01-12/01
	Atlantic-Cape May PMSA, NJ	Y	38530 FQ	56680 AW	72540 TQ	NJBLS	10/01-12/01
	Bergen-Passaic PMSA, NJ	Y	43670 FQ	72480 AW	101030 TQ	NJBLS	10/01-12/01
	Jersey City PMSA, NJ	Y	30340 FQ	62350 AW	90710 TQ	NJBLS	10/01-12/01
	Middlesex-Somerset-Hunterdon PMSA, NJ	Y	48700 FQ	67400 AW	92190 TQ	NJBLS	10/01-12/01
	Monmouth-Ocean PMSA, NJ	Y	54430 FQ	72960 AW	89650 TQ	NJBLS	10/01-12/01
	Newark PMSA, NJ	Y	41080 FQ	62310 AW	83730 TQ	NJBLS	10/01-12/01
	Trenton PMSA, NJ	Y	47230 FQ	63090 AW	79290 TQ	NJBLS	10/01-12/01
	New Mexico	Y	29190 FQ	42770 AW	60370 TQ	NMBLS	10/01-12/01
	Albuquerque MSA, NM	Y	28840 FQ	47730 AW	64040 TQ	NMBLS	10/01-12/01
	Las Cruces MSA, NM	Y	30800 FQ	41240 AW	64620 TQ	NMBLS	10/01-12/01
	New York	Y	32930 FQ	56030 AW	86170 TQ	NYBLS	10/01-12/01
	Albany-Schenectady-Troy MSA, NY	Y	42140 FQ	57730 AW	70250 TQ	NYBLS	10/01-12/01
	Buffalo-Niagara Falls MSA, NY	Y	36530 FQ	52400 AW	70470 TQ	NYBLS	10/01-12/01
	Dutchess County PMSA, NY	Y	27300 FQ	48390 AW	61010 TQ	NYBLS	10/01-12/01
	New York PMSA, NY	Y	31810 FQ	49980 AW	77540 TQ	NYBLS	10/01-12/01
	Newburgh PMSA, NY-PA	Y	34260 FQ	54990 AW	78370 TQ	NYBLS	10/01-12/01
	Rochester MSA, NY	Y	37150 FQ	52800 AW	71890 TQ	NYBLS	10/01-12/01
	Syracuse MSA, NY	Y	32820 FQ	52640 AW	74500 TQ	NYBLS	10/01-12/01
	North Carolina	Y	25960 FQ	39040 AW	58880 TQ	NCBLS	10/01-12/01

AAW	Average annual wage	AOH	Average offered, high	ASH	Average starting, high	H	Hourly	M	Monthly	S	Special: hourly and annual
AE	Average entry wage	AOL	Average offered, low	ASL	Average starting, low	HI	Highest wage paid	MTC	Median total compensation	TQ	Third quartile wage
AEX	Average experienced wage	APH	Average pay, high range	AW	Average wage paid	HR	High end range	MW	Median wage paid	W	Weekly
AO	Average offered	APL	Average pay, low range	FQ	First quartile wage	LR	Low end range	SQ	Second quartile wage	Y	Yearly

Occupation/Type/Industry	Location	Per	Low	Mid	High	Source	Date
Detective and Criminal Investigator	Asheville MSA, NC	Y	28920 FQ	40740 AW	63900 TQ	NCBLS	10/01-12/01
	Charlotte-Gastonia-Rock Hill MSA, NC-SC	Y	26110 FQ	42120 AW	67410 TQ	NCBLS	10/01-12/01
	Fayetteville MSA, NC	Y	26090 FQ	43660 AW	69720 TQ	NCBLS	10/01-12/01
	Greensboro-Winston-Salem-High Point MSA, NC	Y	28930 FQ	40590 AW	63980 TQ	NCBLS	10/01-12/01
	Hickory-Morganton-Lenoir MSA, NC	Y	25170 FQ	35850 AW	51880 TQ	NCBLS	10/01-12/01
	Raleigh-Durham-Chapel Hill MSA, NC	Y	28930 FQ	42910 AW	59640 TQ	NCBLS	10/01-12/01
	Wilmington MSA, NC	Y	26030 FQ	38790 AW	65380 TQ	NCBLS	10/01-12/01
	North Dakota	Y	26900 FQ	40510 AW	61500 TQ	NDBLS	10/01-12/01
	Fargo-Moorhead MSA, ND-MN	Y	35750 FQ	47830 AW	70630 TQ	NDBLS	10/01-12/01
	Ohio	Y	29510 FQ	47540 AW	67600 TQ	OHBLS	10/01-12/01
	Akron PMSA, OH	Y	36500 FQ	51720 AW	73790 TQ	OHBLS	10/01-12/01
	Canton-Massillon MSA, OH	Y	31480 FQ	42190 AW	48180 TQ	OHBLS	10/01-12/01
	Cincinnati PMSA, OH-KY-IN	Y	32760 FQ	50330 AW	72690 TQ	OHBLS	10/01-12/01
	Cleveland-Lorain-Elyria PMSA, OH	Y	38600 FQ	53600 AW	72750 TQ	OHBLS	10/01-12/01
	Columbus MSA, OH	Y	38490 FQ	53480 AW	70450 TQ	OHBLS	10/01-12/01
	Dayton-Springfield MSA, OH	Y	39630 FQ	51570 AW	68130 TQ	OHBLS	10/01-12/01
	Toledo MSA, OH	Y	33280 FQ	47080 AW	68480 TQ	OHBLS	10/01-12/01
	Youngstown-Warren MSA, OH	Y	30450 FQ	46340 AW	67040 TQ	OHBLS	10/01-12/01
	Oklahoma	Y	25590 FQ	45590 AW	64770 TQ	OKBLS	10/01-12/01
	Tulsa MSA, OK	Y	24340 FQ	47050 AW	71380 TQ	OKBLS	10/01-12/01
	Oregon	Y	37420 FQ	51270 AW	69780 TQ	ORBLS	10/01-12/01
	Portland-Vancouver PMSA, OR-WA	Y	37910 FQ	53240 AW	72110 TQ	ORBLS	10/01-12/01
	Pennsylvania	Y	40170 FQ	58980 AW	88200 TQ	PABLS	10/01-12/01
	Allentown-Bethlehem-Easton MSA, PA	Y	38650 FQ	52280 AW	70020 TQ	PABLS	10/01-12/01
	Erie MSA, PA	Y	38240 FQ	51440 AW	72430 TQ	PABLS	10/01-12/01
	Lancaster MSA, PA	Y	41940 FQ	57170 AW	82610 TQ	PABLS	10/01-12/01
	Philadelphia PMSA, PA-NJ	Y	44080 FQ	57410 AW	77950 TQ	PABLS	10/01-12/01
	Pittsburgh MSA, PA	Y	42670 FQ	64450 AW	87340 TQ	PABLS	10/01-12/01
	Scranton-Wilkes-Barre-Hazleton MSA, PA	Y	36920 FQ	54970 AW	76850 TQ	PABLS	10/01-12/01
	York MSA, PA	Y	40520 FQ	51100 AW	59020 TQ	PABLS	10/01-12/01
	Rhode Island	Y	38840 FQ	50890 AW	68880 TQ	RIBLS	10/01-12/01
	Providence-Fall River-Warwick MSA, RI-MA	Y	34220 FQ	48060 AW	64170 TQ	RIBLS	10/01-12/01
	South Carolina	Y	20820 FQ	37210 AW	63940 TQ	SCBLS	10/01-12/01
	Charleston-North Charleston MSA, SC	Y	24670 FQ	47920 AW	71260 TQ	SCBLS	10/01-12/01
	Greenville-Spartanburg-Anderson MSA, SC	Y	29890 FQ	40340 AW	61670 TQ	SCBLS	10/01-12/01
	South Dakota	Y	29970 FQ	42280 AW	65280 TQ	SDBLS	10/01-12/01
	Sioux Falls MSA, SD	Y	36090 FQ	57810 AW	80450 TQ	SDBLS	10/01-12/01
	Tennessee	Y	26250 FQ	42310 AW	67380 TQ	TNBLS	10/01-12/01
	Chattanooga MSA, TN-GA	Y	28610 FQ	46880 AW	73940 TQ	TNBLS	10/01-12/01
	Johnson City-Kingsport-Bristol MSA, TN-VA	Y	27430 FQ	40500 AW	66950 TQ	TNBLS	10/01-12/01
	Knoxville MSA, TN	Y	31090 FQ	45030 AW	69390 TQ	TNBLS	10/01-12/01
	Memphis MSA, TN-AR-MS	Y	25320 FQ	44670 AW	70790 TQ	TNBLS	10/01-12/01
	Nashville MSA, TN	Y	31380 FQ	47250 AW	70170 TQ	TNBLS	10/01-12/01
	Texas	Y	29250 FQ	47250 AW	68360 TQ	TXBLS	10/01-12/01
	Austin-San Marcos MSA, TX	Y	31840 FQ	48490 AW	59730 TQ	TXBLS	10/01-12/01
	Beaumont-Port Arthur MSA, TX	Y	30250 FQ	42700 AW	60980 TQ	TXBLS	10/01-12/01
	Brazoria PMSA, TX	Y	31830 FQ	43830 AW	61960 TQ	TXBLS	10/01-12/01
	Brownsville-Harlingen-San Benito MSA, TX	Y	26980 FQ	47050 AW	69050 TQ	TXBLS	10/01-12/01
	Corpus Christi MSA, TX	Y	28680 FQ	47760 AW	61030 TQ	TXBLS	10/01-12/01
	Dallas PMSA, TX	Y	29380 FQ	50060 AW	71610 TQ	TXBLS	10/01-12/01
	El Paso MSA, TX	Y	33870 FQ	47120 AW	68260 TQ	TXBLS	10/01-12/01
	Fort Worth-Arlington PMSA, TX	Y	34520 FQ	48750 AW	60910 TQ	TXBLS	10/01-12/01
	Galveston-Texas City PMSA, TX	Y	25790 FQ	41330 AW	62150 TQ	TXBLS	10/01-12/01
	Houston PMSA, TX	Y	31120 FQ	53320 AW	81150 TQ	TXBLS	10/01-12/01

Occupation/Type/Industry	Location	Per	Low	Mid	High	Source	Date
Detective and Criminal Investigator	Killeen-Temple MSA, TX	Y	24640 FQ	32560 AW	42080 TQ	TXBLS	10/01-12/01
	Laredo MSA, TX	Y	29230 FQ	44250 AW	65300 TQ	TXBLS	10/01-12/01
	Longview-Marshall MSA, TX	Y	27210 FQ	33820 AW	41110 TQ	TXBLS	10/01-12/01
	Lubbock MSA, TX	Y	27250 FQ	46820 AW	73450 TQ	TXBLS	10/01-12/01
	McAllen-Edinburg-Mission MSA, TX	Y	23280 FQ	43180 AW	68610 TQ	TXBLS	10/01-12/01
	San Antonio MSA, TX	Y	32130 FQ	49170 AW	63340 TQ	TXBLS	10/01-12/01
	Tyler MSA, TX	Y	31580 FQ	44310 AW	65280 TQ	TXBLS	10/01-12/01
	Waco MSA, TX	Y	26880 FQ	42850 AW	64780 TQ	TXBLS	10/01-12/01
	Utah	Y	30400 FQ	43670 AW	65590 TQ	UTBLS	10/01-12/01
	Provo-Orem MSA, UT	Y	31650 FQ	37770 AW	45800 TQ	UTBLS	10/01-12/01
	Salt Lake City-Ogden MSA, UT	Y	32900 FQ	48830 AW	70260 TQ	UTBLS	10/01-12/01
	Vermont	Y	31420 FQ	46620 AW	68110 TQ	VTBLS	10/01-12/01
	Burlington MSA, VT	Y	32640 FQ	51000 AW	71650 TQ	VTBLS	10/01-12/01
	Virginia	Y	35450 FQ	59230 AW	83560 TQ	VABLS	10/01-12/01
	Lynchburg MSA, VA	Y	32760 FQ	47610 AW	65900 TQ	VABLS	10/01-12/01
	Norfolk-Virginia Beach-Newport News MSA, VA-NC	Y	35620 FQ	56150 AW	75480 TQ	VABLS	10/01-12/01
	Richmond-Petersburg MSA, VA	Y	35840 FQ	53520 AW	71430 TQ	VABLS	10/01-12/01
	Roanoke MSA, VA	Y	35140 FQ	53700 AW	75840 TQ	VABLS	10/01-12/01
	Washington	Y	38100 FQ	57010 AW	74540 TQ	WABLS	10/01-12/01
	Bremerton PMSA, WA	Y	36250 FQ	54430 AW	81050 TQ	WABLS	10/01-12/01
	Richland-Kennewick-Pasco MSA, WA	Y	37030 FQ	49370 AW	67660 TQ	WABLS	10/01-12/01
	Seattle-Bellevue-Everett PMSA, WA	Y	42540 FQ	62610 AW	77080 TQ	WABLS	10/01-12/01
	Spokane MSA, WA	Y	31400 FQ	51640 AW	69990 TQ	WABLS	10/01-12/01
	Tacoma PMSA, WA	Y	38110 FQ	55620 AW	72250 TQ	WABLS	10/01-12/01
	Yakima MSA, WA	Y	39580 FQ	57040 AW	72420 TQ	WABLS	10/01-12/01
	West Virginia	Y	24100 FQ	38150 AW	64810 TQ	WVBLS	10/01-12/01
	Huntington-Ashland MSA, WV-KY-OH	Y	24130 FQ	37270 AW	62480 TQ	WVBLS	10/01-12/01
	Wisconsin	Y	36600 FQ	49470 AW	62000 TQ	WIBLS	10/01-12/01
	Appleton-Oshkosh-Neenah MSA, WI	Y	39800 FQ	48220 AW	56490 TQ	WIBLS	10/01-12/01
	Green Bay MSA, WI	Y	39030 FQ	45450 AW	55560 TQ	WIBLS	10/01-12/01
	Madison MSA, WI	Y	37640 FQ	50300 AW	65340 TQ	WIBLS	10/01-12/01
	Milwaukee-Waukesha PMSA, WI	Y	41630 FQ	53930 AW	67600 TQ	WIBLS	10/01-12/01
	Wyoming	Y	30200 FQ	43520 AW	65680 TQ	WYBLS	10/01-12/01
	Cheyenne MSA, WY	Y	32200 FQ	50670 AW	71660 TQ	WYBLS	10/01-12/01
	Puerto Rico	Y	17760 FQ	34410 AW	64980 TQ	PRBLS	10/01-12/01
Federal government	United States	Y		61180 MW		OOH2	1/99-1/00
Local government	United States	Y		46340 MW		OOH2	1/99-1/00
State government	United States	Y		43050 MW		OOH2	1/99-1/00
Diagnostic Medical Sonographer	Alabama	Y	25410 FQ	39000 AW	53600 TQ	ALBLS	10/01-12/01
	Alaska	Y	46930 FQ	59760 AW	83590 TQ	AKBLS	10/01-12/01
	Arizona	Y	36310 FQ	55220 AW	82230 TQ	AZBLS	10/01-12/01
	Arkansas	Y	30390 FQ	41270 AW	56270 TQ	ARBLS	10/01-12/01
	California	Y	37010 FQ	52760 AW	72330 TQ	CABLS	10/01-12/01
	Colorado	Y	44770 FQ	58980 AW	84660 TQ	COBLS	10/01-12/01
	Connecticut	Y	40310 FQ	56280 AW	74740 TQ	CTBLS	10/01-12/01
	Delaware	Y	34310 FQ	46170 AW	61420 TQ	DEBLS	10/01-12/01
	District of Columbia	Y	39950 FQ	51030 AW	63220 TQ	DCBLS	10/01-12/01
	Florida	Y	29390 FQ	45610 AW	58470 TQ	FLBLS	10/01-12/01
	Georgia	Y	31940 FQ	43840 AW	57060 TQ	GABLS	10/01-12/01
	Hawaii	Y	37430 FQ	46760 AW	57800 TQ	HIBLS	10/01-12/01
	Idaho	Y	36050 FQ	45670 AW	56300 TQ	IDBLS	10/01-12/01
	Illinois	Y	34220 FQ	54610 AW	85490 TQ	ILBLS	10/01-12/01
	Indiana	Y	32620 FQ	43520 AW	55490 TQ	INBLS	10/01-12/01
	Iowa	Y	28290 FQ	43260 AW	55920 TQ	IABLS	10/01-12/01
	Kansas	Y	33200 FQ	46170 AW	65220 TQ	KSBLS	10/01-12/01
	Kentucky	Y	31850 FQ	44030 AW	56240 TQ	KYBLS	10/01-12/01
	Louisiana	Y	27270 FQ	41440 AW	54920 TQ	LABLS	10/01-12/01
	Maine	Y	34580 FQ	45700 AW	56170 TQ	MEBLS	10/01-12/01
	Maryland	Y	37650 FQ	53200 AW	68310 TQ	MDBLS	10/01-12/01
	Massachusetts	Y	37940 FQ	53640 AW	77000 TQ	MABLS	10/01-12/01

AAW	Average annual wage	AOH	Average offered, high	ASH	Average starting, high	H	Hourly	M	Monthly	S	Special: hourly and annual
AE	Average entry wage	AOL	Average offered, low	ASL	Average starting, low	HI	Highest wage paid	MTC	Median total compensation	TQ	Third quartile wage
AEX	Average experienced wage	APH	Average pay, high range	AW	Average wage paid	HR	High end range	MW	Median wage paid	W	Weekly
AO	Average offered	APL	Average pay, low range	FQ	First quartile wage	LR	Low end range	SQ	Second quartile wage	Y	Yearly

Occupation/Type/Industry	Location	Per	Low	Mid	High	Source	Date
Diagnostic Medical Sonographer	Michigan	Y	27480 FQ	41630 AW	54460 TQ	MIBLS	10/01-12/01
	Minnesota	Y	37370 FQ	50800 AW	68090 TQ	MNBLS	10/01-12/01
	Mississippi	Y	25340 FQ	43040 AW	56190 TQ	MSBLS	10/01-12/01
	Missouri	Y	34490 FQ	47270 AW	56900 TQ	MOBLS	10/01-12/01
	Montana	Y	37150 FQ	46140 AW	56490 TQ	MTBLS	10/01-12/01
	Nebraska	Y	31430 FQ	41700 AW	53960 TQ	NEBLS	10/01-12/01
	Nevada	Y	39830 FQ	51670 AW	65890 TQ	NVBLS	10/01-12/01
	New Hampshire	Y	29970 FQ	44020 AW	56690 TQ	NHBLS	10/01-12/01
	New Jersey	Y	35020 FQ	51320 AW	74040 TQ	NJBLS	10/01-12/01
	New Mexico	Y	40780 FQ	50660 AW	59930 TQ	NMBLS	10/01-12/01
	New York	Y	38150 FQ	49890 AW	65820 TQ	NYBLS	10/01-12/01
	North Carolina	Y	33970 FQ	46120 AW	57630 TQ	NCBLS	10/01-12/01
	North Dakota	Y	37620 FQ	46470 AW	58990 TQ	NDBLS	10/01-12/01
	Ohio	Y	33270 FQ	43400 AW	55640 TQ	OHBLS	10/01-12/01
	Oklahoma	Y	22340 FQ	44980 AW	58020 TQ	OKBLS	10/01-12/01
	Oregon	Y	45500 FQ	56240 AW	70400 TQ	ORBLS	10/01-12/01
	Pennsylvania	Y	32480 FQ	44570 AW	55530 TQ	PABLS	10/01-12/01
	Rhode Island	Y	39950 FQ	49530 AW	58030 TQ	RIBLS	10/01-12/01
	South Carolina	Y	34400 FQ	45550 AW	58140 TQ	SCBLS	10/01-12/01
	South Dakota	Y	29330 FQ	39160 AW	50720 TQ	SDBLS	10/01-12/01
	Tennessee	Y	32750 FQ	44940 AW	57760 TQ	TNBLS	10/01-12/01
	Texas	Y	34290 FQ	45640 AW	58360 TQ	TXBLS	10/01-12/01
	Utah	Y	37490 FQ	46190 AW	55680 TQ	UTBLS	10/01-12/01
	Vermont	Y	37940 FQ	46630 AW	56400 TQ	VTBLS	10/01-12/01
	Virginia	Y	36380 FQ	46350 AW	58850 TQ	VABLS	10/01-12/01
	Washington	Y	41970 FQ	53860 AW	67470 TQ	WABLS	10/01-12/01
	West Virginia	Y	31570 FQ	43870 AW	58070 TQ	WVBLS	10/01-12/01
	Wisconsin	Y	35270 FQ	52770 AW	71340 TQ	WIBLS	10/01-12/01
	Wyoming	Y	36860 FQ	44230 AW	54780 TQ	WYBLS	10/01-12/01
	Puerto Rico	Y	14750 FQ	19720 AW	26620 TQ	PRBLS	10/01-12/01
Dietetic Technician	Alabama	Y	12590 FQ	20700 AW	34300 TQ	ALBLS	10/01-12/01
	Arizona	Y	15740 FQ	22770 AW	32860 TQ	AZBLS	10/01-12/01
	Arkansas	Y	14470 FQ	23170 AW	34600 TQ	ARBLS	10/01-12/01
	California	Y	16130 FQ	26220 AW	35760 TQ	CABLS	10/01-12/01
	Colorado	Y	13070 FQ	21510 AW	32050 TQ	COBLS	10/01-12/01
	Connecticut	Y	19330 FQ	27050 AW	36510 TQ	CTBLS	10/01-12/01
	Delaware	Y	14210 FQ	20470 AW	29500 TQ	DEBLS	10/01-12/01
	District of Columbia	Y	15110 FQ	24780 AW	36060 TQ	DCBLS	10/01-12/01
	Florida	Y	13220 FQ	22330 AW	32790 TQ	FLBLS	10/01-12/01
	Georgia	Y	14360 FQ	30630 AW	37380 TQ	GABLS	10/01-12/01
	Idaho	Y	12560 FQ	18240 AW	23190 TQ	IDBLS	10/01-12/01
	Illinois	Y	12890 FQ	19530 AW	29010 TQ	ILBLS	10/01-12/01
	Indiana	Y	14330 FQ	22890 AW	32470 TQ	INBLS	10/01-12/01
	Iowa	Y	12580 FQ	16560 AW	21360 TQ	IABLS	10/01-12/01
	Kansas	Y	12820 FQ	19020 AW	25240 TQ	KSBLS	10/01-12/01
	Kentucky	Y	15500 FQ	23520 AW	31470 TQ	KYBLS	10/01-12/01
	Louisiana	Y	12010 FQ	16060 AW	24040 TQ	LABLS	10/01-12/01
	Maine	Y	16580 FQ	22900 AW	30650 TQ	MEBLS	10/01-12/01
	Maryland	Y	17640 FQ	24720 AW	30000 TQ	MDBLS	10/01-12/01
	Massachusetts	Y	16760 FQ	23580 AW	32770 TQ	MABLS	10/01-12/01
	Michigan	Y	15950 FQ	24750 AW	35200 TQ	MIBLS	10/01-12/01
	Minnesota	Y	23460 FQ	29570 AW	37600 TQ	MNBLS	10/01-12/01
	Mississippi	Y	12620 FQ	19150 AW	27240 TQ	MSBLS	10/01-12/01
	Missouri	Y	13630 FQ	18460 AW	25660 TQ	MOBLS	10/01-12/01
	Nebraska	Y	12450 FQ	17760 AW	23790 TQ	NEBLS	10/01-12/01
	Nevada	Y	15670 FQ	25730 AW	39740 TQ	NVBLS	10/01-12/01
	New Hampshire	Y	17210 FQ	24550 AW	31060 TQ	NHBLS	10/01-12/01
	New Jersey	Y	17310 FQ	29250 AW	40720 TQ	NJBLS	10/01-12/01
	New Mexico	Y	13550 FQ	19220 AW	28920 TQ	NMBLS	10/01-12/01
	New York	Y	19920 FQ	29430 AW	43090 TQ	NYBLS	10/01-12/01
	North Carolina	Y	13020 FQ	21880 AW	28370 TQ	NCBLS	10/01-12/01
	North Dakota	Y	14930 FQ	19420 AW	26600 TQ	NDBLS	10/01-12/01
	Ohio	Y	16310 FQ	26460 AW	36440 TQ	OHBLS	10/01-12/01
	Oklahoma	Y	12370 FQ	16710 AW	22180 TQ	OKBLS	10/01-12/01
	Oregon	Y	13920 FQ	24450 AW	34520 TQ	ORBLS	10/01-12/01
	Pennsylvania	Y	13630 FQ	23230 AW	36530 TQ	PABLS	10/01-12/01
	Rhode Island	Y	15820 FQ	23500 AW	34580 TQ	RIBLS	10/01-12/01
	South Carolina	Y	14200 FQ	26900 AW	34780 TQ	SCBLS	10/01-12/01
	Tennessee	Y	14280 FQ	21590 AW	31760 TQ	TNBLS	10/01-12/01
	Texas	Y	12660 FQ	19740 AW	31170 TQ	TXBLS	10/01-12/01
	Utah	Y	12820 FQ	18940 AW	27880 TQ	UTBLS	10/01-12/01
	Virginia	Y	13770 FQ	18640 AW	26070 TQ	VABLS	10/01-12/01

AAW	Average annual wage	**AOH**	Average offered, high	**ASH**	Average starting, high	**H**	Hourly	**M**	Monthly	**S**	Special: hourly and annual
AE	Average entry wage	**AOL**	Average offered, low	**ASL**	Average starting, low	**HI**	Highest wage paid	**MTC**	Median total compensation	**TQ**	Third quartile wage
AEX	Average experienced wage	**APH**	Average pay, high range	**AW**	Average wage paid	**HR**	High end range	**MW**	Median wage paid	**W**	Weekly
AO	Average offered	**APL**	Average pay, low range	**FQ**	First quartile wage	**LR**	Low end range	**SQ**	Second quartile wage	**Y**	Yearly

Occupation/Type/Industry	Location	Per	Low	Mid	High	Source	Date
Dietetic Technician	Washington	Y	20650 FQ	28310 AW	36540 TQ	WABLS	10/01-12/01
	West Virginia	Y	15290 FQ	23130 AW	32800 TQ	WVBLS	10/01-12/01
	Wisconsin	Y	14580 FQ	23180 AW	33330 TQ	WIBLS	10/01-12/01
	Puerto Rico	Y	11700 FQ	14900 AW	20140 TQ	PRBLS	10/01-12/01
Dietitian and Nutritionist	Alabama	Y	21230 FQ	38350 AW	54970 TQ	ALBLS	10/01-12/01
	Alaska	Y	41090 FQ	54010 AW	69160 TQ	AKBLS	10/01-12/01
	Arizona	Y	25190 FQ	40310 AW	57360 TQ	AZBLS	10/01-12/01
	Arkansas	Y	25040 FQ	38340 AW	53570 TQ	ARBLS	10/01-12/01
	California	Y	32540 FQ	49750 AW	69980 TQ	CABLS	10/01-12/01
	Colorado	Y	27720 FQ	39990 AW	54550 TQ	COBLS	10/01-12/01
	Connecticut	Y	32530 FQ	48310 AW	66970 TQ	CTBLS	10/01-12/01
	Delaware	Y	28950 FQ	48070 AW	69450 TQ	DEBLS	10/01-12/01
	District of Columbia	Y	29570 FQ	45470 AW	74710 TQ	DCBLS	10/01-12/01
	Florida	Y	25140 FQ	39800 AW	55030 TQ	FLBLS	10/01-12/01
	Georgia	Y	26480 FQ	41810 AW	56740 TQ	GABLS	10/01-12/01
	Hawaii	Y	35480 FQ	46340 AW	59820 TQ	HIBLS	10/01-12/01
	Idaho	Y	19310 FQ	39020 AW	56670 TQ	IDBLS	10/01-12/01
	Illinois	Y	22710 FQ	36560 AW	53570 TQ	ILBLS	10/01-12/01
	Indiana	Y	27700 FQ	39110 AW	54010 TQ	INBLS	10/01-12/01
	Iowa	Y	22910 FQ	36250 AW	48070 TQ	IABLS	10/01-12/01
	Kansas	Y	26810 FQ	39050 AW	52010 TQ	KSBLS	10/01-12/01
	Kentucky	Y	30880 FQ	40980 AW	52410 TQ	KYBLS	10/01-12/01
	Louisiana	Y	21320 FQ	37870 AW	55580 TQ	LABLS	10/01-12/01
	Maine	Y	14430 FQ	30980 AW	45880 TQ	MEBLS	10/01-12/01
	Maryland	Y	17390 FQ	38190 AW	56110 TQ	MDBLS	10/01-12/01
	Massachusetts	Y	30380 FQ	43630 AW	67430 TQ	MABLS	10/01-12/01
	Michigan	Y	29580 FQ	41930 AW	55110 TQ	MIBLS	10/01-12/01
	Minnesota	Y	32510 FQ	44130 AW	56240 TQ	MNBLS	10/01-12/01
	Mississippi	Y	24580 FQ	36420 AW	52080 TQ	MSBLS	10/01-12/01
	Missouri	Y	26780 FQ	37320 AW	49130 TQ	MOBLS	10/01-12/01
	Montana	Y	25530 FQ	37930 AW	51850 TQ	MTBLS	10/01-12/01
	Nebraska	Y	13860 FQ	26630 AW	44920 TQ	NEBLS	10/01-12/01
	Nevada	Y	17270 FQ	43300 AW	58650 TQ	NVBLS	10/01-12/01
	New Hampshire	Y	29280 FQ	42810 AW	58330 TQ	NHBLS	10/01-12/01
	New Jersey	Y	33960 FQ	45980 AW	59180 TQ	NJBLS	10/01-12/01
	New Mexico	Y	23320 FQ	33430 AW	48920 TQ	NMBLS	10/01-12/01
	New York	Y	31230 FQ	45520 AW	65910 TQ	NYBLS	10/01-12/01
	North Carolina	Y	30250 FQ	38840 AW	52080 TQ	NCBLS	10/01-12/01
	North Dakota	Y	25970 FQ	37610 AW	50210 TQ	NDBLS	10/01-12/01
	Ohio	Y	26190 FQ	39720 AW	53680 TQ	OHBLS	10/01-12/01
	Oklahoma	Y	14010 FQ	36440 AW	58520 TQ	OKBLS	10/01-12/01
	Oregon	Y	30460 FQ	43650 AW	55700 TQ	ORBLS	10/01-12/01
	Pennsylvania	Y	17910 FQ	36150 AW	52960 TQ	PABLS	10/01-12/01
	Rhode Island	Y	28720 FQ	43350 AW	58150 TQ	RIBLS	10/01-12/01
	South Carolina	Y	17360 FQ	33810 AW	49050 TQ	SCBLS	10/01-12/01
	South Dakota	Y	29070 FQ	37810 AW	47860 TQ	SDBLS	10/01-12/01
	Tennessee	Y	21670 FQ	36400 AW	49510 TQ	TNBLS	10/01-12/01
	Texas	Y	25430 FQ	40000 AW	54590 TQ	TXBLS	10/01-12/01
	Utah	Y	27190 FQ	38430 AW	54220 TQ	UTBLS	10/01-12/01
	Vermont	Y	29090 FQ	39260 AW	50390 TQ	VTBLS	10/01-12/01
	Virginia	Y	28070 FQ	43630 AW	60560 TQ	VABLS	10/01-12/01
	Washington	Y	36340 FQ	45310 AW	56160 TQ	WABLS	10/01-12/01
	West Virginia	Y	23530 FQ	37670 AW	58120 TQ	WVBLS	10/01-12/01
	Wisconsin	Y	22420 FQ	39660 AW	54950 TQ	WIBLS	10/01-12/01
	Wyoming	Y	29650 FQ	40510 AW	54000 TQ	WYBLS	10/01-12/01
	Puerto Rico	Y	19660 FQ	27110 AW	38110 TQ	PRBLS	10/01-12/01
Dining Room and Cafeteria Attendant and Bartender Helper	Alabama	H	5.61 FQ	6.74 AW	8.46 TQ	ALBLS	10/01-12/01
	Alaska	H	6.11 FQ	8.33 AW	12.47 TQ	AKBLS	10/01-12/01
	Arizona	H	5.53 FQ	6.65 AW	8.59 TQ	AZBLS	10/01-12/01
	Arkansas	H	5.59 FQ	6.35 AW	7.58 TQ	ARBLS	10/01-12/01
	California	H	6.37 FQ	7.47 AW	9.08 TQ	CABLS	10/01-12/01
	Colorado	H	5.64 FQ	7.00 AW	8.74 TQ	COBLS	10/01-12/01
	Connecticut	H	6.54 FQ	8.57 AW	12.54 TQ	CTBLS	10/01-12/01
	Delaware	H	6.45 FQ	7.90 AW	10.65 TQ	DEBLS	10/01-12/01
	District of Columbia	H	6.52 FQ	9.46 AW	13.24 TQ	DCBLS	10/01-12/01
	Florida	H	5.65 FQ	6.99 AW	8.76 TQ	FLBLS	10/01-12/01
	Georgia	H	5.70 FQ	7.15 AW	8.84 TQ	GABLS	10/01-12/01
	Hawaii	H	5.96 FQ	9.34 AW	14.45 TQ	HIBLS	10/01-12/01

AAW Average annual wage; AE Average entry wage; AEX Average experienced wage; AO Average offered; AOH Average offered, high; AOL Average offered, low; APH Average pay, high range; APL Average pay, low range; ASH Average starting, high; ASL Average starting, low; AW Average wage paid; FQ First quartile wage; H Hourly; HI Highest wage paid; HR High end range; LR Low end range; M Monthly; MTC Median total compensation; MW Median wage paid; SQ Second quartile wage; S Special: hourly and annual; TQ Third quartile wage; W Weekly; Y Yearly

Occupation/Type/Industry	Location	Per	Low	Mid	High	Source	Date
Dining Room and Cafeteria Attendant and Bartender Helper	Idaho	H	5.66 FQ	6.41 AW	7.27 TQ	IDBLS	10/01-12/01
	Illinois	H	5.46 FQ	6.73 AW	8.78 TQ	ILBLS	10/01-12/01
	Indiana	H	5.61 FQ	6.70 AW	8.40 TQ	INBLS	10/01-12/01
	Iowa	H	5.66 FQ	6.77 AW	8.48 TQ	IABLS	10/01-12/01
	Kansas	H	5.70 FQ	6.87 AW	8.57 TQ	KSBLS	10/01-12/01
	Kentucky	H	5.72 FQ	7.19 AW	9.21 TQ	KYBLS	10/01-12/01
	Louisiana	H	5.61 FQ	6.44 AW	7.88 TQ	LABLS	10/01-12/01
	Maine	H	5.64 FQ	7.22 AW	9.70 TQ	MEBLS	10/01-12/01
	Maryland	H	5.61 FQ	6.86 AW	8.71 TQ	MDBLS	10/01-12/01
	Massachusetts	H	6.86 FQ	8.76 AW	11.50 TQ	MABLS	10/01-12/01
	Michigan	H	5.54 FQ	7.03 AW	9.39 TQ	MIBLS	10/01-12/01
	Minnesota	H	5.68 FQ	7.34 AW	10.04 TQ	MNBLS	10/01-12/01
	Mississippi	H	5.50 FQ	6.41 AW	7.96 TQ	MSBLS	10/01-12/01
	Missouri	H	5.62 FQ	6.93 AW	8.70 TQ	MOBLS	10/01-12/01
	Montana	H	5.59 FQ	6.45 AW	7.91 TQ	MTBLS	10/01-12/01
	Nebraska	H	5.83 FQ	7.24 AW	8.71 TQ	NEBLS	10/01-12/01
	Nevada	H	5.79 FQ	8.36 AW	11.56 TQ	NVBLS	10/01-12/01
	New Hampshire	H	5.63 FQ	7.00 AW	9.02 TQ	NHBLS	10/01-12/01
	New Jersey	H	5.61 FQ	7.49 AW	10.82 TQ	NJBLS	10/01-12/01
	New Mexico	H	5.51 FQ	6.31 AW	7.56 TQ	NMBLS	10/01-12/01
	New York	H	5.66 FQ	7.83 AW	11.71 TQ	NYBLS	10/01-12/01
	North Carolina	H	5.62 FQ	6.94 AW	8.69 TQ	NCBLS	10/01-12/01
	North Dakota	H	5.65 FQ	6.80 AW	8.83 TQ	NDBLS	10/01-12/01
	Ohio	H	5.60 FQ	6.83 AW	8.67 TQ	OHBLS	10/01-12/01
	Oklahoma	H	5.60 FQ	6.53 AW	8.07 TQ	OKBLS	10/01-12/01
	Oregon	H	6.63 FQ	7.44 AW	8.71 TQ	ORBLS	10/01-12/01
	Pennsylvania	H	5.64 FQ	7.23 AW	9.80 TQ	PABLS	10/01-12/01
	Rhode Island	H	6.44 FQ	7.68 AW	9.65 TQ	RIBLS	10/01-12/01
	South Carolina	H	5.67 FQ	7.15 AW	9.34 TQ	SCBLS	10/01-12/01
	South Dakota	H	5.58 FQ	6.37 AW	7.74 TQ	SDBLS	10/01-12/01
	Tennessee	H	5.71 FQ	7.10 AW	9.04 TQ	TNBLS	10/01-12/01
	Texas	H	5.59 FQ	6.64 AW	8.21 TQ	TXBLS	10/01-12/01
	Utah	H	5.70 FQ	6.90 AW	8.57 TQ	UTBLS	10/01-12/01
	Vermont	H	6.39 FQ	7.44 AW	8.99 TQ	VTBLS	10/01-12/01
	Virginia	H	5.69 FQ	7.20 AW	9.14 TQ	VABLS	10/01-12/01
	Washington	H	6.77 FQ	7.69 AW	9.36 TQ	WABLS	10/01-12/01
	West Virginia	H	5.61 FQ	6.35 AW	7.43 TQ	WVBLS	10/01-12/01
	Wisconsin	H	5.63 FQ	7.05 AW	9.24 TQ	WIBLS	10/01-12/01
	Wyoming	H	5.61 FQ	6.55 AW	8.33 TQ	WYBLS	10/01-12/01
	Puerto Rico	H	5.61 FQ	6.51 AW	7.97 TQ	PRBLS	10/01-12/01
	Virgin Islands	H	5.52 FQ	6.15 AW	6.96 TQ	VIBLS	10/01-12/01
	Guam	H	5.44 FQ	6.91 AW	10.18 TQ	GUBLS	10/01-12/01
Director							
Religious Activities and Education	Alaska	Y	14470 FQ	23240 AW	34460 TQ	AKBLS	10/01-12/01
Religious Activities and Education	Arizona	Y	19060 FQ	34880 AW	54490 TQ	AZBLS	10/01-12/01
Religious Activities and Education	Phoenix-Mesa MSA, AZ	Y	19630 FQ	35760 AW	55170 TQ	AZBLS	10/01-12/01
Religious Activities and Education	California	Y	14900 FQ	32670 AW	57580 TQ	CABLS	10/01-12/01
Religious Activities and Education	Fresno MSA, CA	Y	13600 FQ	22890 AW	32210 TQ	CABLS	10/01-12/01
Religious Activities and Education	Los Angeles-Long Beach PMSA, CA	Y	18320 FQ	33040 AW	58480 TQ	CABLS	10/01-12/01
Religious Activities and Education	Oakland PMSA, CA	Y	14160 FQ	30830 AW	45250 TQ	CABLS	10/01-12/01
Religious Activities and Education	Orange County PMSA, CA	Y	19420 FQ	30170 AW	52400 TQ	CABLS	10/01-12/01
Religious Activities and Education	Riverside-San Bernardino PMSA, CA	Y	16070 FQ	29660 AW	44880 TQ	CABLS	10/01-12/01
Religious Activities and Education	San Diego MSA, CA	Y	13950 FQ	25950 AW	41610 TQ	CABLS	10/01-12/01
Religious Activities and Education	San Francisco PMSA, CA	Y	29360 FQ	52670 AW	82300 TQ	CABLS	10/01-12/01
Religious Activities and Education	San Jose PMSA, CA	Y	16030 FQ	30690 AW	50800 TQ	CABLS	10/01-12/01
Religious Activities and Education	Santa Cruz-Watsonville PMSA, CA	Y	13240 FQ	19600 AW	35070 TQ	CABLS	10/01-12/01
Religious Activities and Education	Vallejo-Fairfield-Napa PMSA, CA	Y	19960 FQ	26740 AW	33400 TQ	CABLS	10/01-12/01
Religious Activities and Education	Ventura PMSA, CA	Y	14830 FQ	26430 AW	41770 TQ	CABLS	10/01-12/01
Religious Activities and Education	Colorado	Y	13730 FQ	31660 AW	44860 TQ	COBLS	10/01-12/01
Religious Activities and Education	Denver PMSA, CO	Y	12640 FQ	29860 AW	36420 TQ	COBLS	10/01-12/01
Religious Activities and Education	Connecticut	Y	23260 FQ	38740 AW	72170 TQ	CTBLS	10/01-12/01
Religious Activities and Education	Hartford MSA, CT	Y	24970 FQ	35530 AW	59330 TQ	CTBLS	10/01-12/01
Religious Activities and Education	District of Columbia	Y	14310 FQ	22250 AW	39560 TQ	DCBLS	10/01-12/01
Religious Activities and Education	Washington PMSA, DC-MD-VA-WV	Y	13330 FQ	26460 AW	44220 TQ	DCBLS	10/01-12/01

AAW Average annual wage; AE Average entry wage; AEX Average experienced wage; AO Average offered; AOH Average offered, high; AOL Average offered, low; APH Average pay, high range; APL Average pay, low range; ASH Average starting, high; ASL Average starting, low; AW Average wage paid; FQ First quartile wage; H Hourly; HI Highest wage paid; HR High end range; LR Low end range; M Monthly; MTC Median total compensation; MW Median wage paid; SQ Second quartile wage; S Special: hourly and annual; TQ Third quartile wage; W Weekly; Y Yearly

Occupation/Type/Industry	Location	Per	Low	Mid	High	Source	Date
Director							
Religious Activities and Education	Florida	Y	15130 FQ	28570 AW	44590 TQ	FLBLS	10/01-12/01
Religious Activities and Education	Fort Lauderdale PMSA, FL	Y	18220 FQ	24550 AW	41150 TQ	FLBLS	10/01-12/01
Religious Activities and Education	Fort Myers-Cape Coral MSA, FL	Y	18040 FQ	25820 AW	30030 TQ	FLBLS	10/01-12/01
Religious Activities and Education	Jacksonville MSA, FL	Y	12510 FQ	26200 AW	42640 TQ	FLBLS	10/01-12/01
Religious Activities and Education	Miami PMSA, FL	Y	15250 FQ	28270 AW	60030 TQ	FLBLS	10/01-12/01
Religious Activities and Education	Orlando MSA, FL	Y	20880 FQ	32840 AW	44960 TQ	FLBLS	10/01-12/01
Religious Activities and Education	Pensacola MSA, FL	Y	12580 FQ	21300 AW	29570 TQ	FLBLS	10/01-12/01
Religious Activities and Education	Sarasota-Bradenton MSA, FL	Y	12480 FQ	21960 AW	35450 TQ	FLBLS	10/01-12/01
Religious Activities and Education	Tampa-St. Petersburg-Clearwater MSA, FL	Y	16750 FQ	32430 AW	58530 TQ	FLBLS	10/01-12/01
Religious Activities and Education	West Palm Beach-Boca Raton MSA, FL	Y	23380 FQ	43480 AW	111570 TQ	FLBLS	10/01-12/01
Religious Activities and Education	Georgia	Y	22800 FQ	41990 AW	66670 TQ	GABLS	10/01-12/01
Religious Activities and Education	Atlanta MSA, GA	Y	23560 FQ	41710 AW	65060 TQ	GABLS	10/01-12/01
Religious Activities and Education	Hawaii	Y	14450 FQ	30380 AW	53500 TQ	HIBLS	10/01-12/01
Religious Activities and Education	Honolulu MSA, HI	Y	14290 FQ	29760 AW	52590 TQ	HIBLS	10/01-12/01
Religious Activities and Education	Illinois	Y	16500 FQ	32350 AW	50370 TQ	ILBLS	10/01-12/01
Religious Activities and Education	Chicago PMSA, IL	Y	16870 FQ	33400 AW	51820 TQ	ILBLS	10/01-12/01
Religious Activities and Education	Indiana	Y	12520 FQ	25150 AW	38460 TQ	INBLS	10/01-12/01
Religious Activities and Education	Gary PMSA, IN	Y	11550 FQ	14990 AW	21700 TQ	INBLS	10/01-12/01
Religious Activities and Education	Iowa	Y	20020 FQ	32170 AW	47350 TQ	IABLS	10/01-12/01
Religious Activities and Education	Kansas	Y	13900 FQ	28070 AW	36170 TQ	KSBLS	10/01-12/01
Religious Activities and Education	Kentucky	Y	18150 FQ	24790 AW	29920 TQ	KYBLS	10/01-12/01
Religious Activities and Education	Maryland	Y	12970 FQ	27320 AW	51050 TQ	MDBLS	10/01-12/01
Religious Activities and Education	Baltimore PMSA, MD	Y	12340 FQ	27060 AW	50930 TQ	MDBLS	10/01-12/01
Religious Activities and Education	Massachusetts	Y	30720 FQ	42180 AW	54530 TQ	MABLS	10/01-12/01
Religious Activities and Education	Boston PMSA, MA-NH	Y	30440 FQ	41450 AW	47910 TQ	MABLS	10/01-12/01
Religious Activities and Education	Michigan	Y	13670 FQ	24640 AW	37580 TQ	MIBLS	10/01-12/01
Religious Activities and Education	Ann Arbor PMSA, MI	Y	14200 FQ	28110 AW	44080 TQ	MIBLS	10/01-12/01
Religious Activities and Education	Detroit PMSA, MI	Y	13770 FQ	24930 AW	37170 TQ	MIBLS	10/01-12/01
Religious Activities and Education	Grand Rapids-Muskegon-Holland MSA, MI	Y	14110 FQ	24020 AW	40140 TQ	MIBLS	10/01-12/01
Religious Activities and Education	Kalamazoo-Battle Creek MSA, MI	Y	19520 FQ	31260 AW	45150 TQ	MIBLS	10/01-12/01
Religious Activities and Education	Saginaw-Bay City-Midland MSA, MI	Y	12450 FQ	20410 AW	30220 TQ	MIBLS	10/01-12/01
Religious Activities and Education	Minnesota	Y	18790 FQ	32070 AW	47840 TQ	MNBLS	10/01-12/01
Religious Activities and Education	Minneapolis-St. Paul MSA, MN-WI	Y	22980 FQ	35980 AW	51390 TQ	MNBLS	10/01-12/01
Religious Activities and Education	Missouri	Y	26930 FQ	49180 AW	72220 TQ	MOBLS	10/01-12/01
Religious Activities and Education	St. Louis MSA, MO-IL	Y	14820 FQ	35070 AW	69590 TQ	MOBLS	10/01-12/01
Religious Activities and Education	Montana	Y	12330 FQ	19690 AW	28260 TQ	MTBLS	10/01-12/01
Religious Activities and Education	New Jersey	Y	28200 FQ	60150 AW	117610 TQ	NJBLS	10/01-12/01
Religious Activities and Education	Middlesex-Somerset-Hunterdon PMSA, NJ	Y	29510 FQ	70470 AW	139790 TQ	NJBLS	10/01-12/01
Religious Activities and Education	Newark PMSA, NJ	Y	37150 FQ	52940 AW	81030 TQ	NJBLS	10/01-12/01
Religious Activities and Education	New York	Y	18590 FQ	35080 AW	58530 TQ	NYBLS	10/01-12/01
Religious Activities and Education	Albany-Schenectady-Troy MSA, NY	Y	21630 FQ	29010 AW	42730 TQ	NYBLS	10/01-12/01
Religious Activities and Education	Binghamton MSA, NY	Y	20180 FQ	25300 AW	28830 TQ	NYBLS	10/01-12/01
Religious Activities and Education	Buffalo-Niagara Falls MSA, NY	Y	17490 FQ	24410 AW	27580 TQ	NYBLS	10/01-12/01
Religious Activities and Education	Nassau-Suffolk PMSA, NY	Y	13510 FQ	39940 AW	62230 TQ	NYBLS	10/01-12/01
Religious Activities and Education	New York PMSA, NY	Y	25210 FQ	47790 AW	72470 TQ	NYBLS	10/01-12/01
Religious Activities and Education	Rochester MSA, NY	Y	23730 FQ	26270 AW	29020 TQ	NYBLS	10/01-12/01
Religious Activities and Education	Syracuse MSA, NY	Y	21640 FQ	27770 AW	34770 TQ	NYBLS	10/01-12/01
Religious Activities and Education	North Carolina	Y	14140 FQ	27910 AW	36440 TQ	NCBLS	10/01-12/01
Religious Activities and Education	Ohio	Y	14170 FQ	28930 AW	43670 TQ	OHBLS	10/01-12/01
Religious Activities and Education	Cincinnati PMSA, OH-KY-IN	Y	13680 FQ	30800 AW	45450 TQ	OHBLS	10/01-12/01
Religious Activities and Education	Cleveland-Lorain-Elyria PMSA, OH	Y	21650 FQ	33260 AW	45620 TQ	OHBLS	10/01-12/01
Religious Activities and Education	Dayton-Springfield MSA, OH	Y	18050 FQ	27460 AW	38730 TQ	OHBLS	10/01-12/01
Religious Activities and Education	Toledo MSA, OH	Y	30780 FQ	34520 AW	37740 TQ	OHBLS	10/01-12/01
Religious Activities and Education	Oregon	Y	15470 FQ	33060 AW	54380 TQ	ORBLS	10/01-12/01
Religious Activities and Education	Eugene-Springfield MSA, OR	Y	15360 FQ	21910 AW	33600 TQ	ORBLS	10/01-12/01
Religious Activities and Education	Portland-Vancouver PMSA, OR-WA	Y	14450 FQ	39300 AW	56570 TQ	ORBLS	10/01-12/01
Religious Activities and Education	Salem PMSA, OR	Y	24850 FQ	29380 AW	36340 TQ	ORBLS	10/01-12/01
Religious Activities and Education	Pennsylvania	Y	12540 FQ	25320 AW	44060 TQ	PABLS	10/01-12/01
Religious Activities and Education	Philadelphia PMSA, PA-NJ	Y	14560 FQ	35130 AW	57430 TQ	PABLS	10/01-12/01

AAW Average annual wage; AE Average entry wage; AEX Average experienced wage; AO Average offered; AOH Average offered, high; AOL Average offered, low; APH Average pay, high range; APL Average pay, low range; ASH Average starting, high; ASL Average starting, low; AW Average wage paid; FQ First quartile wage; H Hourly; HI Highest wage paid; HR High end range; LR Low end range; M Monthly; MTC Median total compensation; MW Median wage paid; SQ Second quartile wage; S Special: hourly and annual; TQ Third quartile wage; W Weekly; Y Yearly

Occupation/Type/Industry	Location	Per	Low	Mid	High	Source	Date
Director							
Religious Activities and Education	Pittsburgh MSA, PA	Y	12300 FQ	17490 AW	27120 TQ	PABLS	10/01-12/01
Religious Activities and Education	Rhode Island	Y	20240 FQ	30930 AW	44610 TQ	RIBLS	10/01-12/01
Religious Activities and Education	Providence-Fall River-Warwick MSA, RI-MA	Y	20250 FQ	30820 AW	44660 TQ	RIBLS	10/01-12/01
Religious Activities and Education	South Carolina	Y	22030 FQ	33700 AW	45060 TQ	SCBLS	10/01-12/01
Religious Activities and Education	Tennessee	Y	13320 FQ	29050 AW	40460 TQ	TNBLS	10/01-12/01
Religious Activities and Education	Texas	Y	12820 FQ	29940 AW	54650 TQ	TXBLS	10/01-12/01
Religious Activities and Education	Dallas PMSA, TX	Y	12590 FQ	27230 AW	51430 TQ	TXBLS	10/01-12/01
Religious Activities and Education	Utah	Y	24740 FQ	43620 AW	72030 TQ	UTBLS	10/01-12/01
Religious Activities and Education	Salt Lake City-Ogden MSA, UT	Y	26370 FQ	44680 AW	72630 TQ	UTBLS	10/01-12/01
Religious Activities and Education	Virginia	Y	12310 FQ	26340 AW	41450 TQ	VABLS	10/01-12/01
Religious Activities and Education	Norfolk-Virginia Beach-Newport News MSA, VA-NC	Y	11600 FQ	22490 AW	38760 TQ	VABLS	10/01-12/01
Religious Activities and Education	Richmond-Petersburg MSA, VA	Y	13040 FQ	28230 AW	41240 TQ	VABLS	10/01-12/01
Religious Activities and Education	Washington	Y	25310 FQ	38190 AW	54710 TQ	WABLS	10/01-12/01
Religious Activities and Education	Seattle-Bellevue-Everett PMSA, WA	Y	26430 FQ	38460 AW	54820 TQ	WABLS	10/01-12/01
Director and Manager of E-Commerce	United States	Y		86100 AW		INFO4	1/01-1/02
Director of Aviation	United States	Y		130000 AW		BCAVIA	1/01-1/01
Director of Information Systems	Baltimore, MD	Y		136240 AW		INFO5	1/00-1/01
Director of Information Systems/ Information Technology	United States	Y		99589 AW		INFO1	1/01-1/02
Director of New Business Development							
Marketing, Medical	United States	Y		126800 AW		MM&M	1/01-1/02
Dishwasher	Alabama	H	5.59 FQ	6.62 AW	8.23 TQ	ALBLS	10/01-12/01
	Birmingham MSA, AL	H	5.70 FQ	6.94 AW	8.42 TQ	ALBLS	10/01-12/01
	Huntsville MSA, AL	H	5.86 FQ	7.18 AW	8.56 TQ	ALBLS	10/01-12/01
	Mobile MSA, AL	H	5.68 FQ	6.52 AW	8.04 TQ	ALBLS	10/01-12/01
	Montgomery MSA, AL	H	5.47 FQ	6.45 AW	8.03 TQ	ALBLS	10/01-12/01
	Alaska	H	6.70 FQ	8.71 AW	11.60 TQ	AKBLS	10/01-12/01
	Anchorage MSA, AK	H	6.99 FQ	9.34 AW	12.28 TQ	AKBLS	10/01-12/01
	Arizona	H	5.50 FQ	6.33 AW	7.72 TQ	AZBLS	10/01-12/01
	Phoenix-Mesa MSA, AZ	H	5.49 FQ	6.33 AW	7.75 TQ	AZBLS	10/01-12/01
	Tucson MSA, AZ	H	5.52 FQ	6.41 AW	7.96 TQ	AZBLS	10/01-12/01
	Arkansas	H	5.58 FQ	6.57 AW	8.26 TQ	ARBLS	10/01-12/01
	Fayetteville-Springdale-Rogers MSA, AR	H	5.68 FQ	6.77 AW	8.31 TQ	ARBLS	10/01-12/01
	Fort Smith MSA, AR-OK	H	5.40 FQ	6.36 AW	8.15 TQ	ARBLS	10/01-12/01
	Little Rock-North Little Rock MSA, AR	H	5.68 FQ	6.80 AW	8.41 TQ	ARBLS	10/01-12/01
	California	H	6.40 FQ	7.45 AW	8.77 TQ	CABLS	10/01-12/01
	Bakersfield MSA, CA	H	6.44 FQ	7.34 AW	8.42 TQ	CABLS	10/01-12/01
	Chico-Paradise MSA, CA	H	6.42 FQ	7.18 AW	8.24 TQ	CABLS	10/01-12/01
	Fresno MSA, CA	H	6.36 FQ	7.12 AW	8.37 TQ	CABLS	10/01-12/01
	Los Angeles-Long Beach PMSA, CA	H	6.36 FQ	7.19 AW	8.45 TQ	CABLS	10/01-12/01
	Merced MSA, CA	H	6.34 FQ	6.92 AW	8.00 TQ	CABLS	10/01-12/01
	Modesto MSA, CA	H	6.40 FQ	7.22 AW	8.39 TQ	CABLS	10/01-12/01
	Oakland PMSA, CA	H	6.63 FQ	8.04 AW	10.28 TQ	CABLS	10/01-12/01
	Orange County PMSA, CA	H	6.41 FQ	7.20 AW	8.31 TQ	CABLS	10/01-12/01
	Redding MSA, CA	H	6.37 FQ	7.06 AW	8.24 TQ	CABLS	10/01-12/01
	Riverside-San Bernardino PMSA, CA	H	6.37 FQ	7.11 AW	8.27 TQ	CABLS	10/01-12/01
	Sacramento PMSA, CA	H	6.40 FQ	7.38 AW	8.49 TQ	CABLS	10/01-12/01
	Salinas MSA, CA	H	6.44 FQ	7.70 AW	9.32 TQ	CABLS	10/01-12/01
	San Diego MSA, CA	H	6.45 FQ	7.61 AW	9.06 TQ	CABLS	10/01-12/01
	San Francisco PMSA, CA	H	6.67 FQ	8.47 AW	11.64 TQ	CABLS	10/01-12/01
	San Jose PMSA, CA	H	6.43 FQ	7.61 AW	9.17 TQ	CABLS	10/01-12/01
	San Luis Obispo-Atascadero-Paso Robles MSA, CA	H	6.50 FQ	7.49 AW	8.61 TQ	CABLS	10/01-12/01

AAW	Average annual wage	AOH	Average offered, high	ASH	Average starting, high	H	Hourly	M	Monthly	S	Special: hourly and annual
AE	Average entry wage	AOL	Average offered, low	ASL	Average starting, low	HI	Highest wage paid	MTC	Median total compensation	TQ	Third quartile wage
AEX	Average experienced wage	APH	Average pay, high range	AW	Average wage paid	HR	High end range	MW	Median wage paid	W	Weekly
AO	Average offered	APL	Average pay, low range	FQ	First quartile wage	LR	Low end range	SQ	Second quartile wage	Y	Yearly

Occupation/Type/Industry	Location	Per	Low	Mid	High	Source	Date
Dishwasher	Santa Barbara-Santa Maria-Lompoc MSA, CA	H	6.37 FQ	7.20 AW	8.55 TQ	CABLS	10/01-12/01
	Santa Cruz-Watsonville PMSA, CA	H	6.45 FQ	7.72 AW	9.11 TQ	CABLS	10/01-12/01
	Santa Rosa PMSA, CA	H	6.50 FQ	7.88 AW	9.94 TQ	CABLS	10/01-12/01
	Stockton-Lodi MSA, CA	H	6.35 FQ	7.05 AW	8.28 TQ	CABLS	10/01-12/01
	Vallejo-Fairfield-Napa PMSA, CA	H	6.46 FQ	7.62 AW	9.06 TQ	CABLS	10/01-12/01
	Ventura PMSA, CA	H	6.44 FQ	7.84 AW	9.98 TQ	CABLS	10/01-12/01
	Visalia-Tulare-Porterville MSA, CA	H	6.38 FQ	7.18 AW	8.36 TQ	CABLS	10/01-12/01
	Colorado	H	5.88 FQ	7.51 AW	9.19 TQ	COBLS	10/01-12/01
	Boulder-Longmont PMSA, CO	H	5.74 FQ	7.15 AW	9.63 TQ	COBLS	10/01-12/01
	Colorado Springs MSA, CO	H	5.87 FQ	7.33 AW	8.79 TQ	COBLS	10/01-12/01
	Denver PMSA, CO	H	6.95 FQ	7.97 AW	9.48 TQ	COBLS	10/01-12/01
	Fort Collins-Loveland MSA, CO	H	5.69 FQ	7.04 AW	8.44 TQ	COBLS	10/01-12/01
	Greeley PMSA, CO	H	5.70 FQ	6.88 AW	8.43 TQ	COBLS	10/01-12/01
	Connecticut	H	6.80 FQ	8.48 AW	10.65 TQ	CTBLS	10/01-12/01
	Bridgeport PMSA, CT	H	6.83 FQ	8.28 AW	10.64 TQ	CTBLS	10/01-12/01
	Danbury PMSA, CT	H	7.01 FQ	8.41 AW	10.60 TQ	CTBLS	10/01-12/01
	Hartford MSA, CT	H	6.67 FQ	8.16 AW	10.25 TQ	CTBLS	10/01-12/01
	New Haven-Meriden PMSA, CT	H	7.21 FQ	8.99 AW	11.82 TQ	CTBLS	10/01-12/01
	New London-Norwich MSA, CT-RI	H	6.71 FQ	8.21 AW	10.37 TQ	CTBLS	10/01-12/01
	Stamford-Norwalk PMSA, CT	H	6.86 FQ	9.24 AW	12.93 TQ	CTBLS	10/01-12/01
	Waterbury PMSA, CT	H	7.03 FQ	8.71 AW	10.84 TQ	CTBLS	10/01-12/01
	Delaware	H	6.48 FQ	7.63 AW	9.11 TQ	DEBLS	10/01-12/01
	Wilmington-Newark PMSA, DE-MD	H	6.39 FQ	7.52 AW	9.38 TQ	DEBLS	10/01-12/01
	District of Columbia	H	6.80 FQ	8.90 AW	12.35 TQ	DCBLS	10/01-12/01
	Washington PMSA, DC-MD-VA-WV	H	6.09 FQ	8.05 AW	10.61 TQ	DCBLS	10/01-12/01
	Florida	H	5.68 FQ	7.12 AW	9.06 TQ	FLBLS	10/01-12/01
	Daytona Beach MSA, FL	H	5.69 FQ	6.63 AW	8.22 TQ	FLBLS	10/01-12/01
	Fort Lauderdale PMSA, FL	H	5.72 FQ	7.01 AW	8.87 TQ	FLBLS	10/01-12/01
	Fort Myers-Cape Coral MSA, FL	H	6.01 FQ	7.57 AW	9.14 TQ	FLBLS	10/01-12/01
	Fort Pierce-Port St. Lucie MSA, FL	H	5.78 FQ	7.19 AW	8.65 TQ	FLBLS	10/01-12/01
	Fort Walton Beach MSA, FL	H	5.55 FQ	6.89 AW	8.63 TQ	FLBLS	10/01-12/01
	Gainesville MSA, FL	H	5.50 FQ	6.52 AW	8.18 TQ	FLBLS	10/01-12/01
	Jacksonville MSA, FL	H	5.69 FQ	7.11 AW	9.03 TQ	FLBLS	10/01-12/01
	Lakeland-Winter Haven MSA, FL	H	5.61 FQ	6.81 AW	8.36 TQ	FLBLS	10/01-12/01
	Melbourne-Titusville-Palm Bay MSA, FL	H	5.67 FQ	7.03 AW	8.77 TQ	FLBLS	10/01-12/01
	Miami PMSA, FL	H	5.57 FQ	6.81 AW	8.65 TQ	FLBLS	10/01-12/01
	Naples MSA, FL	H	6.86 FQ	8.38 AW	10.34 TQ	FLBLS	10/01-12/01
	Ocala MSA, FL	H	5.65 FQ	6.43 AW	7.88 TQ	FLBLS	10/01-12/01
	Orlando MSA, FL	H	5.74 FQ	7.46 AW	10.15 TQ	FLBLS	10/01-12/01
	Pensacola MSA, FL	H	5.88 FQ	8.03 AW	10.73 TQ	FLBLS	10/01-12/01
	Sarasota-Bradenton MSA, FL	H	5.73 FQ	7.15 AW	8.84 TQ	FLBLS	10/01-12/01
	Tallahassee MSA, FL	H	5.48 FQ	6.55 AW	8.45 TQ	FLBLS	10/01-12/01
	Tampa-St. Petersburg-Clearwater MSA, FL	H	5.70 FQ	7.00 AW	8.65 TQ	FLBLS	10/01-12/01
	West Palm Beach-Boca Raton MSA, FL	H	5.67 FQ	7.21 AW	9.15 TQ	FLBLS	10/01-12/01
	Georgia	H	5.82 FQ	7.30 AW	8.81 TQ	GABLS	10/01-12/01
	Atlanta MSA, GA	H	6.30 FQ	7.65 AW	9.22 TQ	GABLS	10/01-12/01
	Augusta-Aiken MSA, GA-SC	H	5.59 FQ	6.63 AW	8.32 TQ	GABLS	10/01-12/01
	Columbus MSA, GA-AL	H	5.68 FQ	6.46 AW	7.83 TQ	GABLS	10/01-12/01
	Macon MSA, GA	H	5.73 FQ	6.74 AW	8.12 TQ	GABLS	10/01-12/01
	Savannah MSA, GA	H	5.68 FQ	6.63 AW	8.17 TQ	GABLS	10/01-12/01
	Hawaii	H	6.21 FQ	9.19 AW	13.14 TQ	HIBLS	10/01-12/01
	Honolulu MSA, HI	H	6.09 FQ	9.10 AW	13.07 TQ	HIBLS	10/01-12/01
	Idaho	H	5.57 FQ	6.47 AW	8.04 TQ	IDBLS	10/01-12/01
	Boise City MSA, ID	H	5.60 FQ	6.56 AW	8.24 TQ	IDBLS	10/01-12/01
	Illinois	H	5.63 FQ	6.96 AW	8.64 TQ	ILBLS	10/01-12/01
	Champaign-Urbana MSA, IL	H	5.59 FQ	7.60 AW	11.08 TQ	ILBLS	10/01-12/01
	Chicago PMSA, IL	H	5.64 FQ	7.03 AW	8.69 TQ	ILBLS	10/01-12/01

AAW	Average annual wage	**AOH**	Average offered, high	**ASH**	Average starting, high	**H**	Hourly	**M**	Monthly	**S**	Special: hourly and annual
AE	Average entry wage	**AOL**	Average offered, low	**ASL**	Average starting, low	**HI**	Highest wage paid	**MTC**	Median total compensation	**TQ**	Third quartile wage
AEX	Average experienced wage	**APH**	Average pay, high range	**AW**	Average wage paid	**HR**	High end range	**MW**	Median wage paid	**W**	Weekly
AO	Average offered	**APL**	Average pay, low range	**FQ**	First quartile wage	**LR**	Low end range	**SQ**	Second quartile wage	**Y**	Yearly

Occupation/Type/Industry	Location	Per	Low	Mid	High	Source	Date
Dishwasher	Peoria-Pekin MSA, IL	H	5.68 FQ	6.65 AW	8.35 TQ	ILBLS	10/01-12/01
	Rockford MSA, IL	H	5.74 FQ	6.98 AW	8.61 TQ	ILBLS	10/01-12/01
	Springfield MSA, IL	H	5.76 FQ	7.31 AW	9.88 TQ	ILBLS	10/01-12/01
	Indiana	H	5.61 FQ	6.96 AW	8.83 TQ	INBLS	10/01-12/01
	Elkhart-Goshen MSA, IN	H	5.66 FQ	6.86 AW	8.57 TQ	INBLS	10/01-12/01
	Evansville-Henderson MSA, IN-KY	H	5.67 FQ	6.60 AW	8.26 TQ	INBLS	10/01-12/01
	Fort Wayne MSA, IN	H	5.64 FQ	6.84 AW	8.48 TQ	INBLS	10/01-12/01
	Gary PMSA, IN	H	5.59 FQ	6.62 AW	8.28 TQ	INBLS	10/01-12/01
	Indianapolis MSA, IN	H	5.60 FQ	7.27 AW	10.05 TQ	INBLS	10/01-12/01
	Lafayette MSA, IN	H	5.60 FQ	6.72 AW	8.51 TQ	INBLS	10/01-12/01
	South Bend MSA, IN	H	5.63 FQ	7.09 AW	8.48 TQ	INBLS	10/01-12/01
	Iowa	H	5.56 FQ	6.74 AW	8.61 TQ	IABLS	10/01-12/01
	Cedar Rapids MSA, IA	H	5.65 FQ	6.88 AW	8.59 TQ	IABLS	10/01-12/01
	Davenport-Moline-Rock Island MSA, IA-IL	H	5.60 FQ	6.56 AW	8.20 TQ	IABLS	10/01-12/01
	Des Moines MSA, IA	H	5.99 FQ	7.64 AW	9.43 TQ	IABLS	10/01-12/01
	Kansas	H	5.65 FQ	6.72 AW	8.40 TQ	KSBLS	10/01-12/01
	Topeka MSA, KS	H	5.86 FQ	7.22 AW	8.75 TQ	KSBLS	10/01-12/01
	Wichita MSA, KS	H	5.66 FQ	6.72 AW	8.52 TQ	KSBLS	10/01-12/01
	Kentucky	H	5.76 FQ	7.35 AW	9.36 TQ	KYBLS	10/01-12/01
	Lexington MSA, KY	H	6.01 FQ	8.00 AW	10.46 TQ	KYBLS	10/01-12/01
	Louisville MSA, KY-IN	H	5.97 FQ	7.70 AW	9.80 TQ	KYBLS	10/01-12/01
	Louisiana	H	5.51 FQ	6.31 AW	7.65 TQ	LABLS	10/01-12/01
	Baton Rouge MSA, LA	H	5.48 FQ	6.23 AW	7.27 TQ	LABLS	10/01-12/01
	Houma MSA, LA	H	5.66 FQ	6.63 AW	8.41 TQ	LABLS	10/01-12/01
	Lafayette MSA, LA	H	5.47 FQ	6.14 AW	7.05 TQ	LABLS	10/01-12/01
	Lake Charles MSA, LA	H	5.53 FQ	6.17 AW	7.15 TQ	LABLS	10/01-12/01
	New Orleans MSA, LA	H	5.51 FQ	6.39 AW	7.91 TQ	LABLS	10/01-12/01
	Shreveport-Bossier City MSA, LA	H	5.52 FQ	6.29 AW	7.44 TQ	LABLS	10/01-12/01
	Maine	H	5.65 FQ	6.95 AW	8.74 TQ	MEBLS	10/01-12/01
	Portland MSA, ME	H	5.90 FQ	7.57 AW	9.40 TQ	MEBLS	10/01-12/01
	Maryland	H	5.67 FQ	7.08 AW	8.81 TQ	MDBLS	10/01-12/01
	Baltimore PMSA, MD	H	5.59 FQ	6.72 AW	8.51 TQ	MDBLS	10/01-12/01
	Massachusetts	H	6.99 FQ	8.46 AW	10.69 TQ	MABLS	10/01-12/01
	Boston PMSA, MA-NH	H	7.11 FQ	8.69 AW	11.11 TQ	MABLS	10/01-12/01
	Brockton PMSA, MA	H	7.37 FQ	9.15 AW	11.17 TQ	MABLS	10/01-12/01
	Lawrence PMSA, MA-NH	H	6.78 FQ	8.13 AW	10.36 TQ	MABLS	10/01-12/01
	Lowell PMSA, MA-NH	H	7.07 FQ	8.89 AW	12.00 TQ	MABLS	10/01-12/01
	New Bedford PMSA, MA	H	6.85 FQ	7.83 AW	9.29 TQ	MABLS	10/01-12/01
	Springfield MSA, MA	H	6.97 FQ	8.05 AW	9.50 TQ	MABLS	10/01-12/01
	Worcester PMSA, MA-CT	H	6.93 FQ	8.20 AW	10.07 TQ	MABLS	10/01-12/01
	Michigan	H	5.72 FQ	7.51 AW	9.88 TQ	MIBLS	10/01-12/01
	Ann Arbor PMSA, MI	H	5.63 FQ	7.43 AW	9.84 TQ	MIBLS	10/01-12/01
	Detroit PMSA, MI	H	6.27 FQ	8.17 AW	10.73 TQ	MIBLS	10/01-12/01
	Flint PMSA, MI	H	5.56 FQ	6.95 AW	8.40 TQ	MIBLS	10/01-12/01
	Grand Rapids-Muskegon-Holland MSA, MI	H	5.71 FQ	7.15 AW	8.67 TQ	MIBLS	10/01-12/01
	Kalamazoo-Battle Creek MSA, MI	H	5.50 FQ	6.72 AW	8.74 TQ	MIBLS	10/01-12/01
	Lansing-East Lansing MSA, MI	H	5.69 FQ	7.17 AW	8.99 TQ	MIBLS	10/01-12/01
	Saginaw-Bay City-Midland MSA, MI	H	5.60 FQ	6.62 AW	8.39 TQ	MIBLS	10/01-12/01
	Minnesota	H	5.68 FQ	7.41 AW	10.03 TQ	MNBLS	10/01-12/01
	Duluth-Superior MSA, MN-WI	H	5.45 FQ	6.20 AW	7.09 TQ	MNBLS	10/01-12/01
	Minneapolis-St. Paul MSA, MN-WI	H	5.84 FQ	7.89 AW	10.37 TQ	MNBLS	10/01-12/01
	St. Cloud MSA, MN	H	5.66 FQ	6.50 AW	7.99 TQ	MNBLS	10/01-12/01
	Mississippi	H	5.50 FQ	6.31 AW	7.61 TQ	MSBLS	10/01-12/01
	Biloxi-Gulfport-Pascagoula MSA, MS	H	5.52 FQ	6.46 AW	8.09 TQ	MSBLS	10/01-12/01
	Jackson MSA, MS	H	5.61 FQ	6.35 AW	7.46 TQ	MSBLS	10/01-12/01
	Missouri	H	5.61 FQ	6.99 AW	8.81 TQ	MOBLS	10/01-12/01
	Kansas City MSA, MO-KS	H	5.84 FQ	7.43 AW	9.09 TQ	MOBLS	10/01-12/01
	St. Louis MSA, MO-IL	H	5.61 FQ	7.11 AW	9.12 TQ	MOBLS	10/01-12/01
	Springfield MSA, MO	H	5.73 FQ	6.92 AW	8.63 TQ	MOBLS	10/01-12/01
	Montana	H	5.55 FQ	6.25 AW	7.20 TQ	MTBLS	10/01-12/01
	Billings MSA, MT	H	5.48 FQ	6.10 AW	6.98 TQ	MTBLS	10/01-12/01
	Nebraska	H	5.78 FQ	7.02 AW	8.67 TQ	NEBLS	10/01-12/01
	Lincoln MSA, NE	H	5.95 FQ	7.58 AW	9.12 TQ	NEBLS	10/01-12/01
	Omaha MSA, NE-IA	H	6.02 FQ	7.47 AW	8.84 TQ	NEBLS	10/01-12/01

AAW	Average annual wage	**AOH**	Average offered, high	**ASH**	Average starting, high	**H**	Hourly	**M**	Monthly	**S**	Special: hourly and annual
AE	Average entry wage	**AOL**	Average offered, low	**ASL**	Average starting, low	**HI**	Highest wage paid	**MTC**	Median total compensation	**TQ**	Third quartile wage
AEX	Average experienced wage	**APH**	Average pay, high range	**AW**	Average wage paid	**HR**	High end range	**MW**	Median wage paid	**W**	Weekly
AO	Average offered	**APL**	Average pay, low range	**FQ**	First quartile wage	**LR**	Low end range	**SQ**	Second quartile wage	**Y**	Yearly

Occupation/Type/Industry	Location	Per	Low	Mid	High	Source	Date
Dishwasher	Nevada	H	5.99 FQ	9.24 AW	13.11 TQ	NVBLS	10/01-12/01
	Las Vegas MSA, NV-AZ	H	6.12 FQ	9.79 AW	13.30 TQ	NVBLS	10/01-12/01
	Reno MSA, NV	H	5.81 FQ	7.38 AW	9.18 TQ	NVBLS	10/01-12/01
	New Hampshire	H	5.79 FQ	7.43 AW	10.03 TQ	NHBLS	10/01-12/01
	Manchester PMSA, NH	H	7.10 FQ	8.53 AW	10.71 TQ	NHBLS	10/01-12/01
	Nashua PMSA, NH	H	6.38 FQ	8.52 AW	10.70 TQ	NHBLS	10/01-12/01
	Portsmouth-Rochester PMSA, NH-ME	H	5.74 FQ	7.86 AW	10.58 TQ	NHBLS	10/01-12/01
	New Jersey	H	5.80 FQ	8.00 AW	11.73 TQ	NJBLS	10/01-12/01
	Atlantic-Cape May PMSA, NJ	H	6.25 FQ	9.62 AW	13.22 TQ	NJBLS	10/01-12/01
	Bergen-Passaic PMSA, NJ	H	5.88 FQ	8.02 AW	11.01 TQ	NJBLS	10/01-12/01
	Jersey City PMSA, NJ	H	6.05 FQ	7.92 AW	10.22 TQ	NJBLS	10/01-12/01
	Middlesex-Somerset-Hunterdon PMSA, NJ	H	5.87 FQ	7.47 AW	9.40 TQ	NJBLS	10/01-12/01
	Monmouth-Ocean PMSA, NJ	H	5.63 FQ	6.94 AW	8.94 TQ	NJBLS	10/01-12/01
	Newark PMSA, NJ	H	5.80 FQ	7.58 AW	10.09 TQ	NJBLS	10/01-12/01
	Trenton PMSA, NJ	H	5.69 FQ	7.98 AW	11.01 TQ	NJBLS	10/01-12/01
	New Mexico	H	5.57 FQ	6.57 AW	8.34 TQ	NMBLS	10/01-12/01
	Albuquerque MSA, NM	H	5.63 FQ	6.70 AW	8.53 TQ	NMBLS	10/01-12/01
	Las Cruces MSA, NM	H	5.66 FQ	6.23 AW	7.14 TQ	NMBLS	10/01-12/01
	New York	H	5.58 FQ	7.45 AW	10.39 TQ	NYBLS	10/01-12/01
	Albany-Schenectady-Troy MSA, NY	H	5.77 FQ	7.44 AW	9.03 TQ	NYBLS	10/01-12/01
	Binghamton MSA, NY	H	5.56 FQ	6.55 AW	8.08 TQ	NYBLS	10/01-12/01
	Buffalo-Niagara Falls MSA, NY	H	5.47 FQ	6.30 AW	7.65 TQ	NYBLS	10/01-12/01
	Dutchess County PMSA, NY	H	5.59 FQ	7.34 AW	10.06 TQ	NYBLS	10/01-12/01
	Nassau-Suffolk PMSA, NY	H	5.80 FQ	7.68 AW	10.74 TQ	NYBLS	10/01-12/01
	New York PMSA, NY	H	5.58 FQ	7.95 AW	10.95 TQ	NYBLS	10/01-12/01
	Newburgh PMSA, NY-PA	H	5.76 FQ	7.14 AW	8.79 TQ	NYBLS	10/01-12/01
	Rochester MSA, NY	H	5.55 FQ	6.60 AW	8.23 TQ	NYBLS	10/01-12/01
	Syracuse MSA, NY	H	5.60 FQ	6.70 AW	8.32 TQ	NYBLS	10/01-12/01
	Utica-Rome MSA, NY	H	5.47 FQ	6.52 AW	8.49 TQ	NYBLS	10/01-12/01
	North Carolina	H	5.65 FQ	7.25 AW	9.10 TQ	NCBLS	10/01-12/01
	Asheville MSA, NC	H	6.06 FQ	7.43 AW	8.73 TQ	NCBLS	10/01-12/01
	Charlotte-Gastonia-Rock Hill MSA, NC-SC	H	5.96 FQ	7.57 AW	9.04 TQ	NCBLS	10/01-12/01
	Fayetteville MSA, NC	H	5.73 FQ	7.11 AW	9.33 TQ	NCBLS	10/01-12/01
	Greensboro-Winston-Salem-High Point MSA, NC	H	5.65 FQ	7.34 AW	8.67 TQ	NCBLS	10/01-12/01
	Hickory-Morganton-Lenoir MSA, NC	H	5.64 FQ	6.74 AW	8.41 TQ	NCBLS	10/01-12/01
	Raleigh-Durham-Chapel Hill MSA, NC	H	5.96 FQ	7.98 AW	10.37 TQ	NCBLS	10/01-12/01
	Wilmington MSA, NC	H	5.68 FQ	6.82 AW	8.81 TQ	NCBLS	10/01-12/01
	North Dakota	H	5.60 FQ	6.52 AW	8.12 TQ	NDBLS	10/01-12/01
	Fargo-Moorhead MSA, ND-MN	H	5.63 FQ	6.60 AW	8.30 TQ	NDBLS	10/01-12/01
	Ohio	H	5.64 FQ	7.11 AW	9.17 TQ	OHBLS	10/01-12/01
	Akron PMSA, OH	H	5.69 FQ	7.02 AW	8.57 TQ	OHBLS	10/01-12/01
	Canton-Massillon MSA, OH	H	5.62 FQ	6.72 AW	8.42 TQ	OHBLS	10/01-12/01
	Cincinnati PMSA, OH-KY-IN	H	5.87 FQ	7.46 AW	9.53 TQ	OHBLS	10/01-12/01
	Cleveland-Lorain-Elyria PMSA, OH	H	5.55 FQ	7.09 AW	9.37 TQ	OHBLS	10/01-12/01
	Columbus MSA, OH	H	5.87 FQ	7.92 AW	10.34 TQ	OHBLS	10/01-12/01
	Dayton-Springfield MSA, OH	H	5.60 FQ	6.75 AW	8.42 TQ	OHBLS	10/01-12/01
	Hamilton-Middletown PMSA, OH	H	5.81 FQ	7.14 AW	8.71 TQ	OHBLS	10/01-12/01
	Mansfield MSA, OH	H	5.44 FQ	6.43 AW	8.24 TQ	OHBLS	10/01-12/01
	Toledo MSA, OH	H	5.72 FQ	7.25 AW	9.45 TQ	OHBLS	10/01-12/01
	Youngstown-Warren MSA, OH	H	5.56 FQ	6.29 AW	7.24 TQ	OHBLS	10/01-12/01
	Oklahoma	H	5.58 FQ	6.53 AW	8.20 TQ	OKBLS	10/01-12/01
	Oklahoma City MSA, OK	H	5.67 FQ	6.73 AW	8.41 TQ	OKBLS	10/01-12/01
	Tulsa MSA, OK	H	5.63 FQ	6.57 AW	8.19 TQ	OKBLS	10/01-12/01
	Oregon	H	6.73 FQ	7.50 AW	8.63 TQ	ORBLS	10/01-12/01
	Eugene-Springfield MSA, OR	H	6.96 FQ	7.74 AW	8.79 TQ	ORBLS	10/01-12/01
	Medford-Ashland MSA, OR	H	6.84 FQ	7.70 AW	8.85 TQ	ORBLS	10/01-12/01
	Portland-Vancouver PMSA, OR-WA	H	6.80 FQ	7.61 AW	8.71 TQ	ORBLS	10/01-12/01
	Salem PMSA, OR	H	6.78 FQ	7.59 AW	8.69 TQ	ORBLS	10/01-12/01
	Pennsylvania	H	5.62 FQ	7.07 AW	8.98 TQ	PABLS	10/01-12/01

AAW	Average annual wage	**AOH**	Average offered, high	**ASH**	Average starting, high	**H**	Hourly	**M**	Monthly	**S**	Special: hourly and annual
AE	Average entry wage	**AOL**	Average offered, low	**ASL**	Average starting, low	**HI**	Highest wage paid	**MTC**	Median total compensation	**TQ**	Third quartile wage
AEX	Average experienced wage	**APH**	Average pay, high range	**AW**	Average wage paid	**HR**	High end range	**MW**	Median wage paid	**W**	Weekly
AO	Average offered	**APL**	Average pay, low range	**FQ**	First quartile wage	**LR**	Low end range	**SQ**	Second quartile wage	**Y**	Yearly

Occupation/Type/Industry	Location	Per	Low	Mid	High	Source	Date
Dishwasher	Allentown-Bethlehem-Easton MSA, PA	H	5.63 FQ	6.50 AW	8.04 TQ	PABLS	10/01-12/01
	Erie MSA, PA	H	5.41 FQ	6.39 AW	8.09 TQ	PABLS	10/01-12/01
	Harrisburg-Lebanon-Carlisle MSA, PA	H	5.68 FQ	7.15 AW	8.95 TQ	PABLS	10/01-12/01
	Johnstown MSA, PA	H	5.59 FQ	6.41 AW	7.98 TQ	PABLS	10/01-12/01
	Lancaster MSA, PA	H	5.73 FQ	7.25 AW	8.73 TQ	PABLS	10/01-12/01
	Philadelphia PMSA, PA-NJ	H	5.74 FQ	7.55 AW	9.96 TQ	PABLS	10/01-12/01
	Pittsburgh MSA, PA	H	5.68 FQ	7.36 AW	9.49 TQ	PABLS	10/01-12/01
	Reading MSA, PA	H	5.66 FQ	6.71 AW	8.40 TQ	PABLS	10/01-12/01
	Scranton-Wilkes-Barre-Hazleton MSA, PA	H	5.58 FQ	6.76 AW	8.54 TQ	PABLS	10/01-12/01
	York MSA, PA	H	5.67 FQ	7.22 AW	9.16 TQ	PABLS	10/01-12/01
	Rhode Island	H	6.49 FQ	7.44 AW	9.03 TQ	RIBLS	10/01-12/01
	Providence-Fall River-Warwick MSA, RI-MA	H	6.53 FQ	7.43 AW	8.91 TQ	RIBLS	10/01-12/01
	South Carolina	H	5.62 FQ	6.79 AW	8.47 TQ	SCBLS	10/01-12/01
	Charleston-North Charleston MSA, SC	H	5.63 FQ	6.71 AW	8.34 TQ	SCBLS	10/01-12/01
	Columbia MSA, SC	H	5.61 FQ	6.71 AW	8.39 TQ	SCBLS	10/01-12/01
	Greenville-Spartanburg-Anderson MSA, SC	H	5.68 FQ	6.84 AW	8.46 TQ	SCBLS	10/01-12/01
	Myrtle Beach MSA, SC	H	5.74 FQ	7.10 AW	8.73 TQ	SCBLS	10/01-12/01
	South Dakota	H	5.52 FQ	6.42 AW	8.00 TQ	SDBLS	10/01-12/01
	Sioux Falls MSA, SD	H	5.76 FQ	7.35 AW	9.63 TQ	SDBLS	10/01-12/01
	Tennessee	H	5.69 FQ	7.23 AW	9.06 TQ	TNBLS	10/01-12/01
	Chattanooga MSA, TN-GA	H	5.72 FQ	7.19 AW	8.67 TQ	TNBLS	10/01-12/01
	Clarksville-Hopkinsville MSA, TN-KY	H	5.78 FQ	7.20 AW	9.33 TQ	TNBLS	10/01-12/01
	Johnson City-Kingsport-Bristol MSA, TN-VA	H	5.61 FQ	6.65 AW	8.36 TQ	TNBLS	10/01-12/01
	Knoxville MSA, TN	H	6.00 FQ	7.68 AW	9.23 TQ	TNBLS	10/01-12/01
	Memphis MSA, TN-AR-MS	H	5.80 FQ	7.21 AW	9.10 TQ	TNBLS	10/01-12/01
	Nashville MSA, TN	H	5.90 FQ	7.80 AW	10.18 TQ	TNBLS	10/01-12/01
	Texas	H	5.56 FQ	6.62 AW	8.30 TQ	TXBLS	10/01-12/01
	Amarillo MSA, TX	H	5.59 FQ	6.89 AW	8.98 TQ	TXBLS	10/01-12/01
	Austin-San Marcos MSA, TX	H	5.75 FQ	7.13 AW	8.67 TQ	TXBLS	10/01-12/01
	Beaumont-Port Arthur MSA, TX	H	5.61 FQ	6.63 AW	8.28 TQ	TXBLS	10/01-12/01
	Brazoria PMSA, TX	H	5.56 FQ	6.41 AW	7.97 TQ	TXBLS	10/01-12/01
	Brownsville-Harlingen-San Benito MSA, TX	H	5.51 FQ	6.06 AW	6.92 TQ	TXBLS	10/01-12/01
	Corpus Christi MSA, TX	H	5.60 FQ	6.19 AW	7.13 TQ	TXBLS	10/01-12/01
	Dallas PMSA, TX	H	5.59 FQ	6.72 AW	8.25 TQ	TXBLS	10/01-12/01
	El Paso MSA, TX	H	5.55 FQ	6.18 AW	7.13 TQ	TXBLS	10/01-12/01
	Fort Worth-Arlington PMSA, TX	H	5.67 FQ	7.09 AW	8.80 TQ	TXBLS	10/01-12/01
	Galveston-Texas City PMSA, TX	H	5.63 FQ	6.69 AW	8.41 TQ	TXBLS	10/01-12/01
	Houston PMSA, TX	H	5.48 FQ	6.54 AW	8.66 TQ	TXBLS	10/01-12/01
	Killeen-Temple MSA, TX	H	5.64 FQ	6.79 AW	8.45 TQ	TXBLS	10/01-12/01
	Laredo MSA, TX	H	5.41 FQ	6.24 AW	6.95 TQ	TXBLS	10/01-12/01
	Longview-Marshall MSA, TX	H	5.51 FQ	6.50 AW	8.01 TQ	TXBLS	10/01-12/01
	Lubbock MSA, TX	H	5.57 FQ	6.34 AW	7.64 TQ	TXBLS	10/01-12/01
	McAllen-Edinburg-Mission MSA, TX	H	5.51 FQ	6.54 AW	8.06 TQ	TXBLS	10/01-12/01
	Odessa-Midland MSA, TX	H	5.46 FQ	6.42 AW	8.03 TQ	TXBLS	10/01-12/01
	San Antonio MSA, TX	H	5.63 FQ	6.75 AW	8.49 TQ	TXBLS	10/01-12/01
	Tyler MSA, TX	H	5.56 FQ	6.59 AW	8.16 TQ	TXBLS	10/01-12/01
	Waco MSA, TX	H	5.66 FQ	6.43 AW	7.59 TQ	TXBLS	10/01-12/01
	Utah	H	5.69 FQ	6.95 AW	8.43 TQ	UTBLS	10/01-12/01
	Provo-Orem MSA, UT	H	5.68 FQ	7.10 AW	8.47 TQ	UTBLS	10/01-12/01
	Salt Lake City-Ogden MSA, UT	H	5.80 FQ	7.15 AW	8.50 TQ	UTBLS	10/01-12/01
	Vermont	H	6.41 FQ	7.49 AW	8.89 TQ	VTBLS	10/01-12/01
	Burlington MSA, VT	H	6.77 FQ	8.23 AW	10.35 TQ	VTBLS	10/01-12/01
	Virginia	H	5.68 FQ	7.22 AW	9.33 TQ	VABLS	10/01-12/01
	Lynchburg MSA, VA	H	5.58 FQ	6.68 AW	8.43 TQ	VABLS	10/01-12/01
	Norfolk-Virginia Beach-Newport News MSA, VA-NC	H	5.65 FQ	7.13 AW	9.84 TQ	VABLS	10/01-12/01

AAW	Average annual wage	AOH	Average offered, high	ASH	Average starting, high	H	Hourly	M	Monthly	S	Special: hourly and annual
AE	Average entry wage	AOL	Average offered, low	ASL	Average starting, low	HI	Highest wage paid	MTC	Median total compensation	TQ	Third quartile wage
AEX	Average experienced wage	APH	Average pay, high range	AW	Average wage paid	HR	High end range	MW	Median wage paid	W	Weekly
AO	Average offered	APL	Average pay, low range	FQ	First quartile wage	LR	Low end range	SQ	Second quartile wage	Y	Yearly

Occupation/Type/Industry	Location	Per	Low	Mid	High	Source	Date
Dishwasher	Richmond-Petersburg MSA, VA	H	5.64 FQ	6.67 AW	8.48 TQ	VABLS	10/01-12/01
	Roanoke MSA, VA	H	5.56 FQ	6.64 AW	8.46 TQ	VABLS	10/01-12/01
	Washington	H	6.80 FQ	7.99 AW	9.97 TQ	WABLS	10/01-12/01
	Bremerton PMSA, WA	H	6.80 FQ	7.58 AW	9.27 TQ	WABLS	10/01-12/01
	Olympia PMSA, WA	H	6.84 FQ	7.62 AW	8.63 TQ	WABLS	10/01-12/01
	Richland-Kennewick-Pasco MSA, WA	H	6.75 FQ	7.65 AW	8.55 TQ	WABLS	10/01-12/01
	Seattle-Bellevue-Everett PMSA, WA	H	6.93 FQ	8.36 AW	10.33 TQ	WABLS	10/01-12/01
	Spokane MSA, WA	H	6.83 FQ	8.04 AW	10.29 TQ	WABLS	10/01-12/01
	Tacoma PMSA, WA	H	6.82 FQ	7.78 AW	9.10 TQ	WABLS	10/01-12/01
	Yakima MSA, WA	H	6.78 FQ	7.35 AW	8.36 TQ	WABLS	10/01-12/01
	West Virginia	H	5.59 FQ	6.31 AW	7.38 TQ	WVBLS	10/01-12/01
	Charleston MSA, WV	H	5.66 FQ	6.52 AW	8.12 TQ	WVBLS	10/01-12/01
	Huntington-Ashland MSA, WV-KY-OH	H	5.63 FQ	6.70 AW	8.79 TQ	WVBLS	10/01-12/01
	Wisconsin	H	5.58 FQ	6.85 AW	8.60 TQ	WIBLS	10/01-12/01
	Appleton-Oshkosh-Neenah MSA, WI	H	5.68 FQ	7.14 AW	9.31 TQ	WIBLS	10/01-12/01
	Green Bay MSA, WI	H	5.70 FQ	7.00 AW	8.74 TQ	WIBLS	10/01-12/01
	Madison MSA, WI	H	5.60 FQ	7.10 AW	8.98 TQ	WIBLS	10/01-12/01
	Milwaukee-Waukesha PMSA, WI	H	5.79 FQ	7.18 AW	8.63 TQ	WIBLS	10/01-12/01
	Racine PMSA, WI	H	5.60 FQ	6.86 AW	8.60 TQ	WIBLS	10/01-12/01
	Wyoming	H	5.65 FQ	6.65 AW	8.24 TQ	WYBLS	10/01-12/01
	Cheyenne MSA, WY	H	5.71 FQ	6.64 AW	8.22 TQ	WYBLS	10/01-12/01
	Puerto Rico	H	5.57 FQ	6.17 AW	7.01 TQ	PRBLS	10/01-12/01
	Virgin Islands	H	5.62 FQ	6.78 AW	8.39 TQ	VIBLS	10/01-12/01
	Guam	H	5.51 FQ	6.16 AW	7.02 TQ	GUBLS	10/01-12/01
Dispatcher							
Except Police, Fire, and Ambulance	Alabama	H	7.42 FQ	14.46 AW	24.06 TQ	ALBLS	10/01-12/01
Except Police, Fire, and Ambulance	Birmingham MSA, AL	H	7.89 FQ	15.93 AW	26.01 TQ	ALBLS	10/01-12/01
Except Police, Fire, and Ambulance	Huntsville MSA, AL	H	7.33 FQ	13.07 AW	18.47 TQ	ALBLS	10/01-12/01
Except Police, Fire, and Ambulance	Mobile MSA, AL	H	7.69 FQ	13.81 AW	24.04 TQ	ALBLS	10/01-12/01
Except Police, Fire, and Ambulance	Montgomery MSA, AL	H	8.64 FQ	13.84 AW	20.83 TQ	ALBLS	10/01-12/01
Except Police, Fire, and Ambulance	Alaska	H	8.28 FQ	16.49 AW	26.05 TQ	AKBLS	10/01-12/01
Except Police, Fire, and Ambulance	Anchorage MSA, AK	H	11.47 FQ	17.34 AW	27.07 TQ	AKBLS	10/01-12/01
Except Police, Fire, and Ambulance	Arizona	H	8.54 FQ	14.22 AW	21.16 TQ	AZBLS	10/01-12/01
Except Police, Fire, and Ambulance	Phoenix-Mesa MSA, AZ	H	9.04 FQ	14.76 AW	21.45 TQ	AZBLS	10/01-12/01
Except Police, Fire, and Ambulance	Tucson MSA, AZ	H	7.86 FQ	12.87 AW	19.82 TQ	AZBLS	10/01-12/01
Except Police, Fire, and Ambulance	Arkansas	H	8.50 FQ	15.36 AW	22.36 TQ	ARBLS	10/01-12/01
Except Police, Fire, and Ambulance	Fayetteville-Springdale-Rogers MSA, AR	H	9.57 FQ	15.99 AW	22.06 TQ	ARBLS	10/01-12/01
Except Police, Fire, and Ambulance	Fort Smith MSA, AR-OK	H	7.37 FQ	13.27 AW	20.92 TQ	ARBLS	10/01-12/01
Except Police, Fire, and Ambulance	Little Rock-North Little Rock MSA, AR	H	9.51 FQ	16.42 AW	29.60 TQ	ARBLS	10/01-12/01
Except Police, Fire, and Ambulance	California	H	8.72 FQ	15.56 AW	24.51 TQ	CABLS	10/01-12/01
Except Police, Fire, and Ambulance	Bakersfield MSA, CA	H	9.47 FQ	15.45 AW	23.28 TQ	CABLS	10/01-12/01
Except Police, Fire, and Ambulance	Chico-Paradise MSA, CA	H	7.57 FQ	12.49 AW	18.40 TQ	CABLS	10/01-12/01
Except Police, Fire, and Ambulance	Fresno MSA, CA	H	8.14 FQ	14.81 AW	21.99 TQ	CABLS	10/01-12/01
Except Police, Fire, and Ambulance	Los Angeles-Long Beach PMSA, CA	H	8.73 FQ	15.16 AW	23.59 TQ	CABLS	10/01-12/01
Except Police, Fire, and Ambulance	Merced MSA, CA	H	10.05 FQ	17.28 AW	26.15 TQ	CABLS	10/01-12/01
Except Police, Fire, and Ambulance	Modesto MSA, CA	H	8.02 FQ	14.66 AW	23.07 TQ	CABLS	10/01-12/01
Except Police, Fire, and Ambulance	Oakland PMSA, CA	H	11.16 FQ	17.89 AW	28.03 TQ	CABLS	10/01-12/01
Except Police, Fire, and Ambulance	Orange County PMSA, CA	H	9.44 FQ	16.32 AW	24.88 TQ	CABLS	10/01-12/01
Except Police, Fire, and Ambulance	Redding MSA, CA	H	8.64 FQ	14.98 AW	24.11 TQ	CABLS	10/01-12/01
Except Police, Fire, and Ambulance	Riverside-San Bernardino PMSA, CA	H	7.96 FQ	15.20 AW	22.92 TQ	CABLS	10/01-12/01
Except Police, Fire, and Ambulance	Sacramento PMSA, CA	H	9.08 FQ	14.52 AW	22.20 TQ	CABLS	10/01-12/01
Except Police, Fire, and Ambulance	Salinas MSA, CA	H	8.83 FQ	16.42 AW	27.88 TQ	CABLS	10/01-12/01
Except Police, Fire, and Ambulance	San Diego MSA, CA	H	7.94 FQ	13.20 AW	20.81 TQ	CABLS	10/01-12/01
Except Police, Fire, and Ambulance	San Francisco PMSA, CA	H	9.52 FQ	17.19 AW	26.42 TQ	CABLS	10/01-12/01
Except Police, Fire, and Ambulance	San Jose PMSA, CA	H	10.02 FQ	17.99 AW	28.63 TQ	CABLS	10/01-12/01
Except Police, Fire, and Ambulance	San Luis Obispo-Atascadero-Paso Robles MSA, CA	H	10.62 FQ	16.63 AW	22.24 TQ	CABLS	10/01-12/01
Except Police, Fire, and Ambulance	Santa Barbara-Santa Maria-Lompoc MSA, CA	H	8.75 FQ	14.62 AW	21.53 TQ	CABLS	10/01-12/01
Except Police, Fire, and Ambulance	Santa Cruz-Watsonville PMSA, CA	H	8.24 FQ	13.85 AW	21.00 TQ	CABLS	10/01-12/01
Except Police, Fire, and Ambulance	Santa Rosa PMSA, CA	H	10.66 FQ	19.64 AW	29.69 TQ	CABLS	10/01-12/01

AAW	Average annual wage	**AOH**	Average offered, high	**ASH**	Average starting, high	**H**	Hourly	**M**	Monthly	**S**	Special: hourly and annual
AE	Average entry wage	**AOL**	Average offered, low	**ASL**	Average starting, low	**HI**	Highest wage paid	**MTC**	Median total compensation	**TQ**	Third quartile wage
AEX	Average experienced wage	**APH**	Average pay, high range	**AW**	Average wage paid	**HR**	High end range	**MW**	Median wage paid	**W**	Weekly
AO	Average offered	**APL**	Average pay, low range	**FQ**	First quartile wage	**LR**	Low end range	**SQ**	Second quartile wage	**Y**	Yearly

Occupation/Type/Industry	Location	Per	Low	Mid	High	Source	Date
Dispatcher							
Except Police, Fire, and Ambulance	Stockton-Lodi MSA, CA	H	8.68 FQ	16.68 AW	26.62 TQ	CABLS	10/01-12/01
Except Police, Fire, and Ambulance	Vallejo-Fairfield-Napa PMSA, CA	H	10.26 FQ	16.84 AW	23.99 TQ	CABLS	10/01-12/01
Except Police, Fire, and Ambulance	Ventura PMSA, CA	H	7.44 FQ	15.53 AW	27.51 TQ	CABLS	10/01-12/01
Except Police, Fire, and Ambulance	Visalia-Tulare-Porterville MSA, CA	H	9.62 FQ	14.84 AW	22.88 TQ	CABLS	10/01-12/01
Except Police, Fire, and Ambulance	Colorado	H	9.67 FQ	15.30 AW	21.69 TQ	COBLS	10/01-12/01
Except Police, Fire, and Ambulance	Colorado Springs MSA, CO	H	8.13 FQ	12.71 AW	17.25 TQ	COBLS	10/01-12/01
Except Police, Fire, and Ambulance	Denver PMSA, CO	H	10.48 FQ	16.15 AW	22.24 TQ	COBLS	10/01-12/01
Except Police, Fire, and Ambulance	Fort Collins-Loveland MSA, CO	H	9.28 FQ	13.99 AW	17.99 TQ	COBLS	10/01-12/01
Except Police, Fire, and Ambulance	Greeley PMSA, CO	H	9.54 FQ	15.55 AW	22.68 TQ	COBLS	10/01-12/01
Except Police, Fire, and Ambulance	Connecticut	H	9.67 FQ	16.26 AW	24.69 TQ	CTBLS	10/01-12/01
Except Police, Fire, and Ambulance	Bridgeport PMSA, CT	H	10.13 FQ	16.16 AW	23.65 TQ	CTBLS	10/01-12/01
Except Police, Fire, and Ambulance	Danbury PMSA, CT	H	9.71 FQ	15.60 AW	24.40 TQ	CTBLS	10/01-12/01
Except Police, Fire, and Ambulance	Hartford MSA, CT	H	10.09 FQ	16.95 AW	25.21 TQ	CTBLS	10/01-12/01
Except Police, Fire, and Ambulance	New Haven-Meriden PMSA, CT	H	9.62 FQ	15.38 AW	24.75 TQ	CTBLS	10/01-12/01
Except Police, Fire, and Ambulance	New London-Norwich MSA, CT-RI	H	8.16 FQ	14.42 AW	21.08 TQ	CTBLS	10/01-12/01
Except Police, Fire, and Ambulance	Stamford-Norwalk PMSA, CT	H	10.21 FQ	17.62 AW	28.14 TQ	CTBLS	10/01-12/01
Except Police, Fire, and Ambulance	Waterbury PMSA, CT	H	6.55 FQ	14.89 AW	24.56 TQ	CTBLS	10/01-12/01
Except Police, Fire, and Ambulance	Delaware	H	8.66 FQ	14.50 AW	21.41 TQ	DEBLS	10/01-12/01
Except Police, Fire, and Ambulance	Wilmington-Newark PMSA, DE-MD	H	8.70 FQ	14.44 AW	22.40 TQ	DEBLS	10/01-12/01
Except Police, Fire, and Ambulance	District of Columbia	H	9.44 FQ	13.86 AW	18.70 TQ	DCBLS	10/01-12/01
Except Police, Fire, and Ambulance	Washington PMSA, DC-MD-VA-WV	H	8.53 FQ	14.36 AW	21.93 TQ	DCBLS	10/01-12/01
Except Police, Fire, and Ambulance	Florida	H	8.24 FQ	13.40 AW	20.51 TQ	FLBLS	10/01-12/01
Except Police, Fire, and Ambulance	Daytona Beach MSA, FL	H	8.03 FQ	12.15 AW	17.83 TQ	FLBLS	10/01-12/01
Except Police, Fire, and Ambulance	Fort Lauderdale PMSA, FL	H	8.27 FQ	13.39 AW	20.47 TQ	FLBLS	10/01-12/01
Except Police, Fire, and Ambulance	Fort Myers-Cape Coral MSA, FL	H	6.92 FQ	12.01 AW	17.58 TQ	FLBLS	10/01-12/01
Except Police, Fire, and Ambulance	Fort Pierce-Port St. Lucie MSA, FL	H	9.08 FQ	14.71 AW	21.39 TQ	FLBLS	10/01-12/01
Except Police, Fire, and Ambulance	Fort Walton Beach MSA, FL	H	7.90 FQ	12.21 AW	16.75 TQ	FLBLS	10/01-12/01
Except Police, Fire, and Ambulance	Gainesville MSA, FL	H	7.66 FQ	12.48 AW	16.95 TQ	FLBLS	10/01-12/01
Except Police, Fire, and Ambulance	Jacksonville MSA, FL	H	9.44 FQ	13.60 AW	20.33 TQ	FLBLS	10/01-12/01
Except Police, Fire, and Ambulance	Lakeland-Winter Haven MSA, FL	H	8.96 FQ	15.51 AW	22.58 TQ	FLBLS	10/01-12/01
Except Police, Fire, and Ambulance	Melbourne-Titusville-Palm Bay MSA, FL	H	8.25 FQ	13.04 AW	19.56 TQ	FLBLS	10/01-12/01
Except Police, Fire, and Ambulance	Miami PMSA, FL	H	7.65 FQ	12.67 AW	18.91 TQ	FLBLS	10/01-12/01
Except Police, Fire, and Ambulance	Naples MSA, FL	H	8.81 FQ	14.25 AW	20.98 TQ	FLBLS	10/01-12/01
Except Police, Fire, and Ambulance	Ocala MSA, FL	H	8.39 FQ	13.32 AW	19.89 TQ	FLBLS	10/01-12/01
Except Police, Fire, and Ambulance	Orlando MSA, FL	H	8.35 FQ	13.49 AW	19.99 TQ	FLBLS	10/01-12/01
Except Police, Fire, and Ambulance	Pensacola MSA, FL	H	6.22 FQ	11.67 AW	19.81 TQ	FLBLS	10/01-12/01
Except Police, Fire, and Ambulance	Sarasota-Bradenton MSA, FL	H	8.93 FQ	14.47 AW	21.25 TQ	FLBLS	10/01-12/01
Except Police, Fire, and Ambulance	Tallahassee MSA, FL	H	5.76 FQ	11.90 AW	18.63 TQ	FLBLS	10/01-12/01
Except Police, Fire, and Ambulance	Tampa-St. Petersburg-Clearwater MSA, FL	H	8.87 FQ	14.03 AW	21.59 TQ	FLBLS	10/01-12/01
Except Police, Fire, and Ambulance	West Palm Beach-Boca Raton MSA, FL	H	8.90 FQ	13.48 AW	20.16 TQ	FLBLS	10/01-12/01
Except Police, Fire, and Ambulance	Georgia	H	9.41 FQ	15.83 AW	23.17 TQ	GABLS	10/01-12/01
Except Police, Fire, and Ambulance	Atlanta MSA, GA	H	10.45 FQ	16.03 AW	22.70 TQ	GABLS	10/01-12/01
Except Police, Fire, and Ambulance	Augusta-Aiken MSA, GA-SC	H	7.49 FQ	15.17 AW	26.25 TQ	GABLS	10/01-12/01
Except Police, Fire, and Ambulance	Columbus MSA, GA-AL	H	6.59 FQ	13.22 AW	21.14 TQ	GABLS	10/01-12/01
Except Police, Fire, and Ambulance	Macon MSA, GA	H	7.40 FQ	12.77 AW	20.60 TQ	GABLS	10/01-12/01
Except Police, Fire, and Ambulance	Savannah MSA, GA	H	7.08 FQ	13.26 AW	20.23 TQ	GABLS	10/01-12/01
Except Police, Fire, and Ambulance	Hawaii	H	7.92 FQ	13.69 AW	21.55 TQ	HIBLS	10/01-12/01
Except Police, Fire, and Ambulance	Honolulu MSA, HI	H	7.61 FQ	13.77 AW	21.67 TQ	HIBLS	10/01-12/01
Except Police, Fire, and Ambulance	Idaho	H	8.10 FQ	16.19 AW	22.59 TQ	IDBLS	10/01-12/01
Except Police, Fire, and Ambulance	Boise City MSA, ID	H	9.52 FQ	17.17 AW	22.12 TQ	IDBLS	10/01-12/01
Except Police, Fire, and Ambulance	Illinois	H	7.89 FQ	15.91 AW	26.12 TQ	ILBLS	10/01-12/01
Except Police, Fire, and Ambulance	Champaign-Urbana MSA, IL	H	6.03 FQ	11.92 AW	20.69 TQ	ILBLS	10/01-12/01
Except Police, Fire, and Ambulance	Chicago PMSA, IL	H	8.41 FQ	16.38 AW	26.91 TQ	ILBLS	10/01-12/01
Except Police, Fire, and Ambulance	Peoria-Pekin MSA, IL	H	7.57 FQ	14.98 AW	23.62 TQ	ILBLS	10/01-12/01
Except Police, Fire, and Ambulance	Rockford MSA, IL	H	9.93 FQ	17.76 AW	26.49 TQ	ILBLS	10/01-12/01
Except Police, Fire, and Ambulance	Springfield MSA, IL	H	9.28 FQ	14.99 AW	21.64 TQ	ILBLS	10/01-12/01
Except Police, Fire, and Ambulance	Indiana	H	9.40 FQ	15.12 AW	22.81 TQ	INBLS	10/01-12/01
Except Police, Fire, and Ambulance	Elkhart-Goshen MSA, IN	H	9.89 FQ	16.69 AW	25.66 TQ	INBLS	10/01-12/01

AAW	Average annual wage	AOH	Average offered, high	ASH	Average starting, high	H	Hourly	M	Monthly	S	Special: hourly and annual
AE	Average entry wage	AOL	Average offered, low	ASL	Average starting, low	HI	Highest wage paid	MTC	Median total compensation	TQ	Third quartile wage
AEX	Average experienced wage	APH	Average pay, high range	AW	Average wage paid	HR	High end range	MW	Median wage paid	W	Weekly
AO	Average offered	APL	Average pay, low range	FQ	First quartile wage	LR	Low end range	SQ	Second quartile wage	Y	Yearly

Occupation/Type/Industry	Location	Per	Low	Mid	High	Source	Date
Dispatcher							
Except Police, Fire, and Ambulance	Evansville-Henderson MSA, IN-KY	H	7.59 FQ	14.36 AW	22.17 TQ	INBLS	10/01-12/01
Except Police, Fire, and Ambulance	Gary PMSA, IN	H	9.68 FQ	17.02 AW	25.49 TQ	INBLS	10/01-12/01
Except Police, Fire, and Ambulance	Indianapolis MSA, IN	H	10.16 FQ	13.99 AW	20.34 TQ	INBLS	10/01-12/01
Except Police, Fire, and Ambulance	Lafayette MSA, IN	H	8.59 FQ	16.89 AW	25.48 TQ	INBLS	10/01-12/01
Except Police, Fire, and Ambulance	South Bend MSA, IN	H	10.36 FQ	16.68 AW	21.47 TQ	INBLS	10/01-12/01
Except Police, Fire, and Ambulance	Iowa	H	9.37 FQ	14.94 AW	20.97 TQ	IABLS	10/01-12/01
Except Police, Fire, and Ambulance	Cedar Rapids MSA, IA	H	8.50 FQ	14.01 AW	20.28 TQ	IABLS	10/01-12/01
Except Police, Fire, and Ambulance	Davenport-Moline-Rock Island MSA, IA-IL	H	6.90 FQ	13.61 AW	20.41 TQ	IABLS	10/01-12/01
Except Police, Fire, and Ambulance	Des Moines MSA, IA	H	10.80 FQ	16.48 AW	21.06 TQ	IABLS	10/01-12/01
Except Police, Fire, and Ambulance	Kansas	H	8.99 FQ	15.16 AW	21.82 TQ	KSBLS	10/01-12/01
Except Police, Fire, and Ambulance	Topeka MSA, KS	H	7.87 FQ	13.97 AW	21.59 TQ	KSBLS	10/01-12/01
Except Police, Fire, and Ambulance	Wichita MSA, KS	H	9.40 FQ	14.94 AW	23.67 TQ	KSBLS	10/01-12/01
Except Police, Fire, and Ambulance	Kentucky	H	7.59 FQ	14.00 AW	20.76 TQ	KYBLS	10/01-12/01
Except Police, Fire, and Ambulance	Lexington MSA, KY	H	6.33 FQ	12.81 AW	20.72 TQ	KYBLS	10/01-12/01
Except Police, Fire, and Ambulance	Louisville MSA, KY-IN	H	9.40 FQ	14.24 AW	20.66 TQ	KYBLS	10/01-12/01
Except Police, Fire, and Ambulance	Louisiana	H	8.03 FQ	15.04 AW	25.17 TQ	LABLS	10/01-12/01
Except Police, Fire, and Ambulance	Baton Rouge MSA, LA	H	8.90 FQ	14.72 AW	25.41 TQ	LABLS	10/01-12/01
Except Police, Fire, and Ambulance	Houma MSA, LA	H	8.72 FQ	12.13 AW	18.73 TQ	LABLS	10/01-12/01
Except Police, Fire, and Ambulance	Lafayette MSA, LA	H	9.70 FQ	19.16 AW	27.15 TQ	LABLS	10/01-12/01
Except Police, Fire, and Ambulance	Lake Charles MSA, LA	H	9.19 FQ	15.17 AW	22.74 TQ	LABLS	10/01-12/01
Except Police, Fire, and Ambulance	New Orleans MSA, LA	H	7.48 FQ	12.26 AW	19.50 TQ	LABLS	10/01-12/01
Except Police, Fire, and Ambulance	Shreveport-Bossier City MSA, LA	H	7.59 FQ	14.06 AW	21.29 TQ	LABLS	10/01-12/01
Except Police, Fire, and Ambulance	Maine	H	8.39 FQ	13.48 AW	20.13 TQ	MEBLS	10/01-12/01
Except Police, Fire, and Ambulance	Portland MSA, ME	H	9.07 FQ	14.55 AW	21.30 TQ	MEBLS	10/01-12/01
Except Police, Fire, and Ambulance	Maryland	H	9.13 FQ	15.01 AW	22.99 TQ	MDBLS	10/01-12/01
Except Police, Fire, and Ambulance	Baltimore PMSA, MD	H	9.05 FQ	13.91 AW	21.06 TQ	MDBLS	10/01-12/01
Except Police, Fire, and Ambulance	Massachusetts	H	9.67 FQ	17.57 AW	29.31 TQ	MABLS	10/01-12/01
Except Police, Fire, and Ambulance	Boston PMSA, MA-NH	H	10.32 FQ	18.86 AW	31.16 TQ	MABLS	10/01-12/01
Except Police, Fire, and Ambulance	Brockton PMSA, MA	H	9.53 FQ	15.75 AW	22.20 TQ	MABLS	10/01-12/01
Except Police, Fire, and Ambulance	Lawrence PMSA, MA-NH	H	10.10 FQ	16.75 AW	26.34 TQ	MABLS	10/01-12/01
Except Police, Fire, and Ambulance	Lowell PMSA, MA-NH	H	9.80 FQ	16.28 AW	24.17 TQ	MABLS	10/01-12/01
Except Police, Fire, and Ambulance	Springfield MSA, MA	H	8.19 FQ	13.17 AW	19.90 TQ	MABLS	10/01-12/01
Except Police, Fire, and Ambulance	Worcester PMSA, MA-CT	H	9.13 FQ	14.54 AW	22.59 TQ	MABLS	10/01-12/01
Except Police, Fire, and Ambulance	Michigan	H	8.63 FQ	15.32 AW	23.94 TQ	MIBLS	10/01-12/01
Except Police, Fire, and Ambulance	Ann Arbor PMSA, MI	H	7.63 FQ	15.72 AW	26.60 TQ	MIBLS	10/01-12/01
Except Police, Fire, and Ambulance	Detroit PMSA, MI	H	8.04 FQ	15.12 AW	24.37 TQ	MIBLS	10/01-12/01
Except Police, Fire, and Ambulance	Flint PMSA, MI	H	8.55 FQ	15.33 AW	24.35 TQ	MIBLS	10/01-12/01
Except Police, Fire, and Ambulance	Grand Rapids-Muskegon-Holland MSA, MI	H	10.16 FQ	16.57 AW	22.72 TQ	MIBLS	10/01-12/01
Except Police, Fire, and Ambulance	Kalamazoo-Battle Creek MSA, MI	H	9.60 FQ	15.63 AW	21.08 TQ	MIBLS	10/01-12/01
Except Police, Fire, and Ambulance	Lansing-East Lansing MSA, MI	H	9.22 FQ	14.10 AW	21.45 TQ	MIBLS	10/01-12/01
Except Police, Fire, and Ambulance	Saginaw-Bay City-Midland MSA, MI	H	7.66 FQ	12.93 AW	20.32 TQ	MIBLS	10/01-12/01
Except Police, Fire, and Ambulance	Minnesota	H	10.55 FQ	18.14 AW	25.53 TQ	MNBLS	10/01-12/01
Except Police, Fire, and Ambulance	Duluth-Superior MSA, MN-WI	H	10.36 FQ	17.28 AW	21.98 TQ	MNBLS	10/01-12/01
Except Police, Fire, and Ambulance	Minneapolis-St. Paul MSA, MN-WI	H	11.37 FQ	19.04 AW	26.15 TQ	MNBLS	10/01-12/01
Except Police, Fire, and Ambulance	St. Cloud MSA, MN	H	8.10 FQ	14.02 AW	21.81 TQ	MNBLS	10/01-12/01
Except Police, Fire, and Ambulance	Mississippi	H	7.34 FQ	13.62 AW	23.05 TQ	MSBLS	10/01-12/01
Except Police, Fire, and Ambulance	Biloxi-Gulfport-Pascagoula MSA, MS	H	7.09 FQ	11.83 AW	16.65 TQ	MSBLS	10/01-12/01
Except Police, Fire, and Ambulance	Jackson MSA, MS	H	7.59 FQ	13.50 AW	21.61 TQ	MSBLS	10/01-12/01
Except Police, Fire, and Ambulance	Missouri	H	9.07 FQ	16.83 AW	27.65 TQ	MOBLS	10/01-12/01
Except Police, Fire, and Ambulance	Kansas City MSA, MO-KS	H	11.03 FQ	18.68 AW	28.92 TQ	MOBLS	10/01-12/01
Except Police, Fire, and Ambulance	St. Louis MSA, MO-IL	H	8.59 FQ	14.54 AW	23.98 TQ	MOBLS	10/01-12/01
Except Police, Fire, and Ambulance	Springfield MSA, MO	H	6.65 FQ	18.98 AW	39.94 TQ	MOBLS	10/01-12/01
Except Police, Fire, and Ambulance	Montana	H	7.67 FQ	12.87 AW	19.48 TQ	MTBLS	10/01-12/01
Except Police, Fire, and Ambulance	Billings MSA, MT	H	9.16 FQ	11.91 AW	16.71 TQ	MTBLS	10/01-12/01
Except Police, Fire, and Ambulance	Nebraska	H	8.87 FQ	20.46 AW	35.82 TQ	NEBLS	10/01-12/01
Except Police, Fire, and Ambulance	Lincoln MSA, NE	H	9.47 FQ	16.84 AW	24.03 TQ	NEBLS	10/01-12/01
Except Police, Fire, and Ambulance	Omaha MSA, NE-IA	H	8.53 FQ	16.81 AW	25.81 TQ	NEBLS	10/01-12/01
Except Police, Fire, and Ambulance	Nevada	H	8.32 FQ	13.41 AW	20.49 TQ	NVBLS	10/01-12/01
Except Police, Fire, and Ambulance	Las Vegas MSA, NV-AZ	H	8.39 FQ	12.93 AW	19.23 TQ	NVBLS	10/01-12/01
Except Police, Fire, and Ambulance	Reno MSA, NV	H	8.06 FQ	15.46 AW	22.96 TQ	NVBLS	10/01-12/01
Except Police, Fire, and Ambulance	New Hampshire	H	8.15 FQ	14.16 AW	20.79 TQ	NHBLS	10/01-12/01
Except Police, Fire, and Ambulance	Manchester PMSA, NH	H	10.51 FQ	15.70 AW	21.07 TQ	NHBLS	10/01-12/01
Except Police, Fire, and Ambulance	Nashua PMSA, NH	H	9.27 FQ	15.51 AW	21.32 TQ	NHBLS	10/01-12/01

AAW Average annual wage; AE Average entry wage; AEX Average experienced wage; AO Average offered; AOH Average offered, high; AOL Average offered, low; APH Average pay, high range; APL Average pay, low range; ASH Average starting, high; ASL Average starting, low; AW Average wage paid; FQ First quartile wage; H Hourly; HI Highest wage paid; HR High end range; LR Low end range; M Monthly; MTC Median total compensation; MW Median wage paid; SQ Second quartile wage; S Special: hourly and annual; TQ Third quartile wage; W Weekly; Y Yearly

Occupation/Type/Industry	Location	Per	Low	Mid	High	Source	Date
Dispatcher							
Except Police, Fire, and Ambulance	Portsmouth-Rochester PMSA, NH-ME	H	8.50 FQ	14.14 AW	20.73 TQ	NHBLS	10/01-12/01
Except Police, Fire, and Ambulance	New Jersey	H	10.02 FQ	17.04 AW	26.21 TQ	NJBLS	10/01-12/01
Except Police, Fire, and Ambulance	Atlantic-Cape May PMSA, NJ	H	8.25 FQ	16.57 AW	26.87 TQ	NJBLS	10/01-12/01
Except Police, Fire, and Ambulance	Bergen-Passaic PMSA, NJ	H	11.35 FQ	16.34 AW	22.40 TQ	NJBLS	10/01-12/01
Except Police, Fire, and Ambulance	Jersey City PMSA, NJ	H	9.02 FQ	16.18 AW	25.85 TQ	NJBLS	10/01-12/01
Except Police, Fire, and Ambulance	Middlesex-Somerset-Hunterdon PMSA, NJ	H	9.87 FQ	16.73 AW	25.43 TQ	NJBLS	10/01-12/01
Except Police, Fire, and Ambulance	Monmouth-Ocean PMSA, NJ	H	11.26 FQ	17.88 AW	28.52 TQ	NJBLS	10/01-12/01
Except Police, Fire, and Ambulance	Newark PMSA, NJ	H	9.68 FQ	17.32 AW	26.79 TQ	NJBLS	10/01-12/01
Except Police, Fire, and Ambulance	Trenton PMSA, NJ	H	10.26 FQ	16.80 AW	23.60 TQ	NJBLS	10/01-12/01
Except Police, Fire, and Ambulance	New Mexico	H	8.53 FQ	14.26 AW	21.57 TQ	NMBLS	10/01-12/01
Except Police, Fire, and Ambulance	Albuquerque MSA, NM	H	9.82 FQ	15.61 AW	21.97 TQ	NMBLS	10/01-12/01
Except Police, Fire, and Ambulance	Las Cruces MSA, NM	H	7.89 FQ	12.07 AW	18.13 TQ	NMBLS	10/01-12/01
Except Police, Fire, and Ambulance	New York	H	9.67 FQ	19.25 AW	31.86 TQ	NYBLS	10/01-12/01
Except Police, Fire, and Ambulance	Albany-Schenectady-Troy MSA, NY	H	8.71 FQ	14.42 AW	20.96 TQ	NYBLS	10/01-12/01
Except Police, Fire, and Ambulance	Binghamton MSA, NY	H	7.84 FQ	12.31 AW	17.28 TQ	NYBLS	10/01-12/01
Except Police, Fire, and Ambulance	Buffalo-Niagara Falls MSA, NY	H	7.15 FQ	14.54 AW	22.03 TQ	NYBLS	10/01-12/01
Except Police, Fire, and Ambulance	Dutchess County PMSA, NY	H	7.82 FQ	14.29 AW	22.45 TQ	NYBLS	10/01-12/01
Except Police, Fire, and Ambulance	Nassau-Suffolk PMSA, NY	H	10.15 FQ	16.40 AW	25.55 TQ	NYBLS	10/01-12/01
Except Police, Fire, and Ambulance	New York PMSA, NY	H	11.09 FQ	21.75 AW	33.01 TQ	NYBLS	10/01-12/01
Except Police, Fire, and Ambulance	Newburgh PMSA, NY-PA	H	8.70 FQ	15.12 AW	24.46 TQ	NYBLS	10/01-12/01
Except Police, Fire, and Ambulance	Rochester MSA, NY	H	8.18 FQ	14.44 AW	21.11 TQ	NYBLS	10/01-12/01
Except Police, Fire, and Ambulance	Syracuse MSA, NY	H	6.80 FQ	14.77 AW	24.86 TQ	NYBLS	10/01-12/01
Except Police, Fire, and Ambulance	Utica-Rome MSA, NY	H	7.29 FQ	12.45 AW	19.61 TQ	NYBLS	10/01-12/01
Except Police, Fire, and Ambulance	North Carolina	H	8.58 FQ	14.81 AW	21.55 TQ	NCBLS	10/01-12/01
Except Police, Fire, and Ambulance	Asheville MSA, NC	H	7.68 FQ	10.54 AW	14.54 TQ	NCBLS	10/01-12/01
Except Police, Fire, and Ambulance	Charlotte-Gastonia-Rock Hill MSA, NC-SC	H	9.57 FQ	15.96 AW	23.74 TQ	NCBLS	10/01-12/01
Except Police, Fire, and Ambulance	Fayetteville MSA, NC	H	7.01 FQ	15.22 AW	22.05 TQ	NCBLS	10/01-12/01
Except Police, Fire, and Ambulance	Greensboro-Winston-Salem-High Point MSA, NC	H	9.47 FQ	15.60 AW	22.51 TQ	NCBLS	10/01-12/01
Except Police, Fire, and Ambulance	Hickory-Morganton-Lenoir MSA, NC	H	10.13 FQ	15.92 AW	21.68 TQ	NCBLS	10/01-12/01
Except Police, Fire, and Ambulance	Raleigh-Durham-Chapel Hill MSA, NC	H	8.43 FQ	15.50 AW	24.98 TQ	NCBLS	10/01-12/01
Except Police, Fire, and Ambulance	Wilmington MSA, NC	H	7.47 FQ	11.74 AW	16.84 TQ	NCBLS	10/01-12/01
Except Police, Fire, and Ambulance	North Dakota	H	8.34 FQ	14.22 AW	20.38 TQ	NDBLS	10/01-12/01
Except Police, Fire, and Ambulance	Fargo-Moorhead MSA, ND-MN	H	9.68 FQ	15.05 AW	21.66 TQ	NDBLS	10/01-12/01
Except Police, Fire, and Ambulance	Ohio	H	9.21 FQ	15.08 AW	22.68 TQ	OHBLS	10/01-12/01
Except Police, Fire, and Ambulance	Akron PMSA, OH	H	8.45 FQ	15.08 AW	21.81 TQ	OHBLS	10/01-12/01
Except Police, Fire, and Ambulance	Canton-Massillon MSA, OH	H	9.35 FQ	16.28 AW	24.20 TQ	OHBLS	10/01-12/01
Except Police, Fire, and Ambulance	Cincinnati PMSA, OH-KY-IN	H	9.01 FQ	14.43 AW	22.19 TQ	OHBLS	10/01-12/01
Except Police, Fire, and Ambulance	Cleveland-Lorain-Elyria PMSA, OH	H	9.52 FQ	16.48 AW	25.42 TQ	OHBLS	10/01-12/01
Except Police, Fire, and Ambulance	Columbus MSA, OH	H	8.27 FQ	14.50 AW	22.21 TQ	OHBLS	10/01-12/01
Except Police, Fire, and Ambulance	Dayton-Springfield MSA, OH	H	8.00 FQ	13.67 AW	20.29 TQ	OHBLS	10/01-12/01
Except Police, Fire, and Ambulance	Hamilton-Middletown PMSA, OH	H	11.99 FQ	17.21 AW	22.48 TQ	OHBLS	10/01-12/01
Except Police, Fire, and Ambulance	Mansfield MSA, OH	H	9.95 FQ	16.39 AW	23.11 TQ	OHBLS	10/01-12/01
Except Police, Fire, and Ambulance	Toledo MSA, OH	H	9.45 FQ	14.08 AW	21.94 TQ	OHBLS	10/01-12/01
Except Police, Fire, and Ambulance	Youngstown-Warren MSA, OH	H	9.80 FQ	17.00 AW	28.36 TQ	OHBLS	10/01-12/01
Except Police, Fire, and Ambulance	Oklahoma	H	8.02 FQ	13.41 AW	21.29 TQ	OKBLS	10/01-12/01
Except Police, Fire, and Ambulance	Oklahoma City MSA, OK	H	8.34 FQ	13.71 AW	21.65 TQ	OKBLS	10/01-12/01
Except Police, Fire, and Ambulance	Tulsa MSA, OK	H	9.34 FQ	14.50 AW	23.57 TQ	OKBLS	10/01-12/01
Except Police, Fire, and Ambulance	Oregon	H	8.06 FQ	14.87 AW	22.95 TQ	ORBLS	10/01-12/01
Except Police, Fire, and Ambulance	Eugene-Springfield MSA, OR	H	9.95 FQ	14.85 AW	21.36 TQ	ORBLS	10/01-12/01
Except Police, Fire, and Ambulance	Medford-Ashland MSA, OR	H	8.66 FQ	15.24 AW	24.28 TQ	ORBLS	10/01-12/01
Except Police, Fire, and Ambulance	Portland-Vancouver PMSA, OR-WA	H	7.27 FQ	14.48 AW	23.19 TQ	ORBLS	10/01-12/01
Except Police, Fire, and Ambulance	Salem PMSA, OR	H	8.94 FQ	15.56 AW	24.21 TQ	ORBLS	10/01-12/01
Except Police, Fire, and Ambulance	Pennsylvania	H	8.13 FQ	14.83 AW	22.79 TQ	PABLS	10/01-12/01
Except Police, Fire, and Ambulance	Allentown-Bethlehem-Easton MSA, PA	H	8.97 FQ	15.15 AW	22.89 TQ	PABLS	10/01-12/01
Except Police, Fire, and Ambulance	Erie MSA, PA	H	9.74 FQ	14.94 AW	20.25 TQ	PABLS	10/01-12/01
Except Police, Fire, and Ambulance	Harrisburg-Lebanon-Carlisle MSA, PA	H	10.32 FQ	16.70 AW	25.47 TQ	PABLS	10/01-12/01
Except Police, Fire, and Ambulance	Johnstown MSA, PA	H	6.30 FQ	11.36 AW	16.38 TQ	PABLS	10/01-12/01

AAW Average annual wage **AOH** Average offered, high **ASH** Average starting, high **H** Hourly **M** Monthly **S** Special: hourly and annual
AE Average entry wage **AOL** Average offered, low **ASL** Average starting, low **HI** Highest wage paid **MTC** Median total compensation **TQ** Third quartile wage
AEX Average experienced wage **APH** Average pay, high range **AW** Average wage paid **HR** High end range **MW** Median wage paid **W** Weekly
AO Average offered **APL** Average pay, low range **FQ** First quartile wage **LR** Low end range **SQ** Second quartile wage **Y** Yearly

Occupation/Type/Industry	Location	Per	Low	Mid	High	Source	Date
Dispatcher							
Except Police, Fire, and Ambulance	Lancaster MSA, PA	H	7.77 FQ	12.39 AW	18.26 TQ	PABLS	10/01-12/01
Except Police, Fire, and Ambulance	Philadelphia PMSA, PA-NJ	H	8.55 FQ	15.59 AW	23.76 TQ	PABLS	10/01-12/01
Except Police, Fire, and Ambulance	Pittsburgh MSA, PA	H	8.56 FQ	15.09 AW	21.99 TQ	PABLS	10/01-12/01
Except Police, Fire, and Ambulance	Reading MSA, PA	H	8.05 FQ	14.74 AW	22.34 TQ	PABLS	10/01-12/01
Except Police, Fire, and Ambulance	Scranton-Wilkes-Barre-Hazleton MSA, PA	H	6.42 FQ	12.79 AW	20.32 TQ	PABLS	10/01-12/01
Except Police, Fire, and Ambulance	York MSA, PA	H	9.51 FQ	14.71 AW	20.94 TQ	PABLS	10/01-12/01
Except Police, Fire, and Ambulance	Rhode Island	H	8.96 FQ	14.32 AW	21.58 TQ	RIBLS	10/01-12/01
Except Police, Fire, and Ambulance	Providence-Fall River-Warwick MSA, RI-MA	H	9.07 FQ	14.37 AW	21.13 TQ	RIBLS	10/01-12/01
Except Police, Fire, and Ambulance	South Carolina	H	8.02 FQ	14.10 AW	22.21 TQ	SCBLS	10/01-12/01
Except Police, Fire, and Ambulance	Charleston-North Charleston MSA, SC	H	9.25 FQ	13.94 AW	20.86 TQ	SCBLS	10/01-12/01
Except Police, Fire, and Ambulance	Columbia MSA, SC	H	8.38 FQ	14.86 AW	22.35 TQ	SCBLS	10/01-12/01
Except Police, Fire, and Ambulance	Greenville-Spartanburg-Anderson MSA, SC	H	8.30 FQ	15.66 AW	26.16 TQ	SCBLS	10/01-12/01
Except Police, Fire, and Ambulance	Myrtle Beach MSA, SC	H	7.09 FQ	14.24 AW	21.95 TQ	SCBLS	10/01-12/01
Except Police, Fire, and Ambulance	South Dakota	H	8.09 FQ	11.90 AW	16.67 TQ	SDBLS	10/01-12/01
Except Police, Fire, and Ambulance	Sioux Falls MSA, SD	H	9.10 FQ	13.21 AW	18.75 TQ	SDBLS	10/01-12/01
Except Police, Fire, and Ambulance	Tennessee	H	7.54 FQ	14.65 AW	22.73 TQ	TNBLS	10/01-12/01
Except Police, Fire, and Ambulance	Chattanooga MSA, TN-GA	H	9.49 FQ	17.28 AW	25.17 TQ	TNBLS	10/01-12/01
Except Police, Fire, and Ambulance	Clarksville-Hopkinsville MSA, TN-KY	H	6.46 FQ	11.50 AW	17.04 TQ	TNBLS	10/01-12/01
Except Police, Fire, and Ambulance	Johnson City-Kingsport-Bristol MSA, TN-VA	H	7.08 FQ	12.24 AW	18.63 TQ	TNBLS	10/01-12/01
Except Police, Fire, and Ambulance	Knoxville MSA, TN	H	8.12 FQ	15.21 AW	21.39 TQ	TNBLS	10/01-12/01
Except Police, Fire, and Ambulance	Memphis MSA, TN-AR-MS	H	9.68 FQ	16.52 AW	23.34 TQ	TNBLS	10/01-12/01
Except Police, Fire, and Ambulance	Nashville MSA, TN	H	7.83 FQ	13.51 AW	21.72 TQ	TNBLS	10/01-12/01
Except Police, Fire, and Ambulance	Texas	H	8.24 FQ	13.95 AW	21.35 TQ	TXBLS	10/01-12/01
Except Police, Fire, and Ambulance	Amarillo MSA, TX	H	6.40 FQ	13.64 AW	22.97 TQ	TXBLS	10/01-12/01
Except Police, Fire, and Ambulance	Austin-San Marcos MSA, TX	H	9.09 FQ	14.29 AW	21.07 TQ	TXBLS	10/01-12/01
Except Police, Fire, and Ambulance	Beaumont-Port Arthur MSA, TX	H	7.75 FQ	13.45 AW	18.74 TQ	TXBLS	10/01-12/01
Except Police, Fire, and Ambulance	Brazoria PMSA, TX	H	8.38 FQ	16.12 AW	25.65 TQ	TXBLS	10/01-12/01
Except Police, Fire, and Ambulance	Brownsville-Harlingen-San Benito MSA, TX	H	7.02 FQ	11.09 AW	17.64 TQ	TXBLS	10/01-12/01
Except Police, Fire, and Ambulance	Corpus Christi MSA, TX	H	7.58 FQ	13.32 AW	18.28 TQ	TXBLS	10/01-12/01
Except Police, Fire, and Ambulance	Dallas PMSA, TX	H	9.24 FQ	14.54 AW	20.82 TQ	TXBLS	10/01-12/01
Except Police, Fire, and Ambulance	El Paso MSA, TX	H	6.00 FQ	10.65 AW	17.40 TQ	TXBLS	10/01-12/01
Except Police, Fire, and Ambulance	Fort Worth-Arlington PMSA, TX	H	9.10 FQ	15.11 AW	23.55 TQ	TXBLS	10/01-12/01
Except Police, Fire, and Ambulance	Galveston-Texas City PMSA, TX	H	7.57 FQ	11.52 AW	17.16 TQ	TXBLS	10/01-12/01
Except Police, Fire, and Ambulance	Houston PMSA, TX	H	8.68 FQ	13.78 AW	21.44 TQ	TXBLS	10/01-12/01
Except Police, Fire, and Ambulance	Killeen-Temple MSA, TX	H	6.05 FQ	10.15 AW	14.35 TQ	TXBLS	10/01-12/01
Except Police, Fire, and Ambulance	Laredo MSA, TX	H	6.27 FQ	11.33 AW	19.75 TQ	TXBLS	10/01-12/01
Except Police, Fire, and Ambulance	Longview-Marshall MSA, TX	H	8.89 FQ	15.42 AW	22.16 TQ	TXBLS	10/01-12/01
Except Police, Fire, and Ambulance	Lubbock MSA, TX	H	7.76 FQ	14.06 AW	21.63 TQ	TXBLS	10/01-12/01
Except Police, Fire, and Ambulance	McAllen-Edinburg-Mission MSA, TX	H	7.18 FQ	12.44 AW	18.92 TQ	TXBLS	10/01-12/01
Except Police, Fire, and Ambulance	Odessa-Midland MSA, TX	H	10.56 FQ	16.41 AW	22.17 TQ	TXBLS	10/01-12/01
Except Police, Fire, and Ambulance	San Antonio MSA, TX	H	8.98 FQ	13.96 AW	22.22 TQ	TXBLS	10/01-12/01
Except Police, Fire, and Ambulance	Tyler MSA, TX	H	7.48 FQ	12.28 AW	17.72 TQ	TXBLS	10/01-12/01
Except Police, Fire, and Ambulance	Waco MSA, TX	H	7.31 FQ	12.17 AW	17.56 TQ	TXBLS	10/01-12/01
Except Police, Fire, and Ambulance	Utah	H	9.98 FQ	17.27 AW	22.90 TQ	UTBLS	10/01-12/01
Except Police, Fire, and Ambulance	Provo-Orem MSA, UT	H	9.84 FQ	13.89 AW	18.57 TQ	UTBLS	10/01-12/01
Except Police, Fire, and Ambulance	Salt Lake City-Ogden MSA, UT	H	10.07 FQ	17.62 AW	22.86 TQ	UTBLS	10/01-12/01
Except Police, Fire, and Ambulance	Vermont	H	9.21 FQ	14.07 AW	20.36 TQ	VTBLS	10/01-12/01
Except Police, Fire, and Ambulance	Burlington MSA, VT	H	9.18 FQ	14.66 AW	21.20 TQ	VTBLS	10/01-12/01
Except Police, Fire, and Ambulance	Virginia	H	8.08 FQ	13.82 AW	21.05 TQ	VABLS	10/01-12/01
Except Police, Fire, and Ambulance	Lynchburg MSA, VA	H	7.00 FQ	12.95 AW	20.30 TQ	VABLS	10/01-12/01
Except Police, Fire, and Ambulance	Norfolk-Virginia Beach-Newport News MSA, VA-NC	H	7.33 FQ	12.33 AW	19.59 TQ	VABLS	10/01-12/01
Except Police, Fire, and Ambulance	Richmond-Petersburg MSA, VA	H	8.89 FQ	14.84 AW	22.38 TQ	VABLS	10/01-12/01
Except Police, Fire, and Ambulance	Roanoke MSA, VA	H	8.10 FQ	12.34 AW	16.99 TQ	VABLS	10/01-12/01
Except Police, Fire, and Ambulance	Washington	H	9.71 FQ	17.43 AW	22.99 TQ	WABLS	10/01-12/01
Except Police, Fire, and Ambulance	Bremerton PMSA, WA	H	7.99 FQ	14.56 AW	21.45 TQ	WABLS	10/01-12/01
Except Police, Fire, and Ambulance	Olympia PMSA, WA	H	8.21 FQ	14.71 AW	21.55 TQ	WABLS	10/01-12/01

AAW Average annual wage **AOH** Average offered, high **ASH** Average starting, high **H** Hourly **M** Monthly **S** Special: hourly and annual
AE Average entry wage **AOL** Average offered, low **ASL** Average starting, low **HI** Highest wage paid **MTC** Median total compensation **TQ** Third quartile wage
AEX Average experienced wage **APH** Average pay, high range **AW** Average wage paid **HR** High end range **MW** Median wage paid **W** Weekly
AO Average offered **APL** Average pay, low range **FQ** First quartile wage **LR** Low end range **SQ** Second quartile wage **Y** Yearly

Occupation/Type/Industry	Location	Per	Low	Mid	High	Source	Date
Dispatcher							
Except Police, Fire, and Ambulance	Richland-Kennewick-Pasco MSA, WA	H	11.79 FQ	20.26 AW	30.95 TQ	WABLS	10/01-12/01
Except Police, Fire, and Ambulance	Seattle-Bellevue-Everett PMSA, WA	H	12.82 FQ	18.66 AW	22.41 TQ	WABLS	10/01-12/01
Except Police, Fire, and Ambulance	Spokane MSA, WA	H	8.51 FQ	15.65 AW	23.99 TQ	WABLS	10/01-12/01
Except Police, Fire, and Ambulance	Tacoma PMSA, WA	H	8.52 FQ	17.29 AW	25.07 TQ	WABLS	10/01-12/01
Except Police, Fire, and Ambulance	Yakima MSA, WA	H	7.46 FQ	13.95 AW	21.91 TQ	WABLS	10/01-12/01
Except Police, Fire, and Ambulance	West Virginia	H	6.15 FQ	13.50 AW	23.98 TQ	WVBLS	10/01-12/01
Except Police, Fire, and Ambulance	Charleston MSA, WV	H	7.12 FQ	14.72 AW	22.25 TQ	WVBLS	10/01-12/01
Except Police, Fire, and Ambulance	Huntington-Ashland MSA, WV-KY-OH	H	7.11 FQ	13.46 AW	22.97 TQ	WVBLS	10/01-12/01
Except Police, Fire, and Ambulance	Wisconsin	H	9.14 FQ	15.78 AW	23.79 TQ	WIBLS	10/01-12/01
Except Police, Fire, and Ambulance	Appleton-Oshkosh-Neenah MSA, WI	H	8.44 FQ	14.33 AW	20.18 TQ	WIBLS	10/01-12/01
Except Police, Fire, and Ambulance	Green Bay MSA, WI	H	12.08 FQ	18.38 AW	28.07 TQ	WIBLS	10/01-12/01
Except Police, Fire, and Ambulance	Madison MSA, WI	H	10.01 FQ	16.45 AW	25.69 TQ	WIBLS	10/01-12/01
Except Police, Fire, and Ambulance	Milwaukee-Waukesha PMSA, WI	H	8.62 FQ	15.71 AW	23.33 TQ	WIBLS	10/01-12/01
Except Police, Fire, and Ambulance	Wyoming	H	7.59 FQ	14.99 AW	21.01 TQ	WYBLS	10/01-12/01
Except Police, Fire, and Ambulance	Puerto Rico	H	5.84 FQ	10.57 AW	18.32 TQ	PRBLS	10/01-12/01
Except Police, Fire, and Ambulance	Virgin Islands	H	7.22 FQ	10.42 AW	14.28 TQ	VIBLS	10/01-12/01
Except Police, Fire, and Ambulance	Guam	H	7.17 FQ	12.26 AW	20.63 TQ	GUBLS	10/01-12/01
Docking Master							
Tugboat	Jacksonville, FL	Y		100000 AEX		FLTU	2002
Door-To-Door Sales Worker, News and Street Vendor, and Related Worker	Alabama	Y	15100 FQ	34800 AW	62680 TQ	ALBLS	10/01-12/01
	Arizona	Y	12350 FQ	21900 AW	33220 TQ	AZBLS	10/01-12/01
	Arkansas	Y	12450 FQ	19850 AW	32550 TQ	ARBLS	10/01-12/01
	California	Y	13510 FQ	24700 AW	44250 TQ	CABLS	10/01-12/01
	Connecticut	Y	14900 FQ	35080 AW	56600 TQ	CTBLS	10/01-12/01
	Delaware	Y	14200 FQ	31680 AW	64670 TQ	DEBLS	10/01-12/01
	District of Columbia	Y	13260 FQ	23450 AW	41960 TQ	DCBLS	10/01-12/01
	Florida	Y	15010 FQ	31570 AW	54380 TQ	FLBLS	10/01-12/01
	Georgia	Y	13770 FQ	30550 AW	49630 TQ	GABLS	10/01-12/01
	Hawaii	Y	12420 FQ	25600 AW	43530 TQ	HIBLS	10/01-12/01
	Idaho	Y	13070 FQ	35750 AW	83860 TQ	IDBLS	10/01-12/01
	Illinois	Y	13350 FQ	24700 AW	46570 TQ	ILBLS	10/01-12/01
	Indiana	Y	12850 FQ	32350 AW	54860 TQ	INBLS	10/01-12/01
	Iowa	Y	12190 FQ	29030 AW	53040 TQ	IABLS	10/01-12/01
	Kansas	Y	11850 FQ	19630 AW	28230 TQ	KSBLS	10/01-12/01
	Kentucky	Y	16630 FQ	33620 AW	54300 TQ	KYBLS	10/01-12/01
	Louisiana	Y	18670 FQ	33440 AW	48900 TQ	LABLS	10/01-12/01
	Maine	Y	15290 FQ	29550 AW	49090 TQ	MEBLS	10/01-12/01
	Maryland	Y	13230 FQ	33260 AW	66580 TQ	MDBLS	10/01-12/01
	Massachusetts	Y	16520 FQ	32600 AW	54580 TQ	MABLS	10/01-12/01
	Michigan	Y	13640 FQ	29180 AW	44170 TQ	MIBLS	10/01-12/01
	Minnesota	Y	15400 FQ	28040 AW	46920 TQ	MNBLS	10/01-12/01
	Mississippi	Y	24530 FQ	42280 AW	65190 TQ	MSBLS	10/01-12/01
	Missouri	Y	13050 FQ	40110 AW	89680 TQ	MOBLS	10/01-12/01
	Montana	Y	11720 FQ	24750 AW	41250 TQ	MTBLS	10/01-12/01
	Nebraska	Y	13770 FQ	29340 AW	44750 TQ	NEBLS	10/01-12/01
	Nevada	Y	14980 FQ	30040 AW	51930 TQ	NVBLS	10/01-12/01
	New Hampshire	Y	23000 FQ	36610 AW	56340 TQ	NHBLS	10/01-12/01
	New Jersey	Y	14860 FQ	23990 AW	34100 TQ	NJBLS	10/01-12/01
	New York	Y	11520 FQ	19950 AW	39190 TQ	NYBLS	10/01-12/01
	North Carolina	Y	13450 FQ	39430 AW	70470 TQ	NCBLS	10/01-12/01
	North Dakota	Y	12060 FQ	25170 AW	42800 TQ	NDBLS	10/01-12/01
	Ohio	Y	16770 FQ	30180 AW	46010 TQ	OHBLS	10/01-12/01
	Oklahoma	Y	13080 FQ	35350 AW	59960 TQ	OKBLS	10/01-12/01
	Oregon	Y	14020 FQ	27960 AW	50600 TQ	ORBLS	10/01-12/01
	Pennsylvania	Y	15820 FQ	37290 AW	58370 TQ	PABLS	10/01-12/01
	Rhode Island	Y	15330 FQ	43810 AW	110250 TQ	RIBLS	10/01-12/01
	South Carolina	Y	16500 FQ	40690 AW	82700 TQ	SCBLS	10/01-12/01
	Tennessee	Y	13350 FQ	36190 AW	71650 TQ	TNBLS	10/01-12/01
	Texas	Y	12680 FQ	34470 AW	68860 TQ	TXBLS	10/01-12/01
	Utah	Y	11940 FQ	24810 AW	50170 TQ	UTBLS	10/01-12/01
	Vermont	Y	13190 FQ	18500 AW	36650 TQ	VTBLS	10/01-12/01
	Virginia	Y	12940 FQ	25680 AW	43420 TQ	VABLS	10/01-12/01

AAW Average annual wage **AE** Average entry wage **AEX** Average experienced wage **AO** Average offered **AOH** Average offered, high **AOL** Average offered, low **APH** Average pay, high range **APL** Average pay, low range **ASH** Average starting, high **ASL** Average starting, low **AW** Average wage paid **FQ** First quartile wage **H** Hourly **HI** Highest wage paid **HR** High end range **LR** Low end range **M** Monthly **MTC** Median total compensation **MW** Median wage paid **SQ** Second quartile wage **S** Special: hourly and annual **TQ** Third quartile wage **W** Weekly **Y** Yearly

Occupation/Type/Industry	Location	Per	Low	Mid	High	Source	Date
Door-To-Door Sales Worker, News and Street Vendor, and Related Worker	Washington	Y	17390 FQ	32700 AW	50760 TQ	WABLS	10/01-12/01
	West Virginia	Y	13580 FQ	29000 AW	46290 TQ	WVBLS	10/01-12/01
	Wisconsin	Y	11530 FQ	19770 AW	37830 TQ	WIBLS	10/01-12/01
	Puerto Rico	Y	11760 FQ	17320 AW	29760 TQ	PRBLS	10/01-12/01
Dredge Operator	Alabama	H	7.45 FQ	9.87 AW	12.80 TQ	ALBLS	10/01-12/01
	California	H	18.51 FQ	24.05 AW	28.18 TQ	CABLS	10/01-12/01
	Connecticut	H	12.21 FQ	15.70 AW	18.04 TQ	CTBLS	10/01-12/01
	Florida	H	7.88 FQ	15.82 AW	23.06 TQ	FLBLS	10/01-12/01
	Illinois	H	10.50 FQ	14.31 AW	22.11 TQ	ILBLS	10/01-12/01
	Indiana	H	10.21 FQ	15.78 AW	25.55 TQ	INBLS	10/01-12/01
	Iowa	H	9.25 FQ	12.38 AW	16.38 TQ	IABLS	10/01-12/01
	Kansas	H	7.53 FQ	12.20 AW	19.76 TQ	KSBLS	10/01-12/01
	Louisiana	H	6.36 FQ	11.04 AW	13.49 TQ	LABLS	10/01-12/01
	Michigan	H	7.52 FQ	13.01 AW	16.76 TQ	MIBLS	10/01-12/01
	Minnesota	H	14.27 FQ	20.55 AW	27.19 TQ	MNBLS	10/01-12/01
	Mississippi	H	10.95 FQ	15.73 AW	20.61 TQ	MSBLS	10/01-12/01
	Missouri	H	8.21 FQ	16.21 AW	26.83 TQ	MOBLS	10/01-12/01
	Nebraska	H	7.60 FQ	11.19 AW	16.85 TQ	NEBLS	10/01-12/01
	New Jersey	H	11.73 FQ	15.64 AW	20.29 TQ	NJBLS	10/01-12/01
	North Carolina	H	7.43 FQ	10.15 AW	13.54 TQ	NCBLS	10/01-12/01
	Ohio	H	11.47 FQ	15.63 AW	18.71 TQ	OHBLS	10/01-12/01
	Oklahoma	H	6.88 FQ	13.37 AW	21.14 TQ	OKBLS	10/01-12/01
	Pennsylvania	H	9.37 FQ	13.21 AW	17.63 TQ	PABLS	10/01-12/01
	Tennessee	H	9.53 FQ	11.68 AW	14.24 TQ	TNBLS	10/01-12/01
	Virginia	H	12.67 FQ	17.59 AW	22.16 TQ	VABLS	10/01-12/01
	Puerto Rico	H	5.92 FQ	7.64 AW	9.12 TQ	PRBLS	10/01-12/01
Drilling and Boring Machine Tool Setter, Operator, and Tender							
Metals and Plastics	Alabama	H	8.61 FQ	12.86 AW	16.85 TQ	ALBLS	10/01-12/01
Metals and Plastics	Birmingham MSA, AL	H	9.14 FQ	12.39 AW	16.01 TQ	ALBLS	10/01-12/01
Metals and Plastics	Huntsville MSA, AL	H	10.05 FQ	13.00 AW	16.38 TQ	ALBLS	10/01-12/01
Metals and Plastics	Phoenix-Mesa MSA, AZ	H	7.18 FQ	11.30 AW	16.83 TQ	AZBLS	10/01-12/01
Metals and Plastics	Tucson MSA, AZ	H	9.71 FQ	13.86 AW	19.71 TQ	AZBLS	10/01-12/01
Metals and Plastics	Arkansas	H	7.19 FQ	11.59 AW	16.19 TQ	ARBLS	10/01-12/01
Metals and Plastics	Fayetteville-Springdale-Rogers MSA, AR	H	10.76 FQ	12.97 AW	16.32 TQ	ARBLS	10/01-12/01
Metals and Plastics	Little Rock-North Little Rock MSA, AR	H	7.00 FQ	13.35 AW	17.57 TQ	ARBLS	10/01-12/01
Metals and Plastics	California	H	7.34 FQ	12.05 AW	18.65 TQ	CABLS	10/01-12/01
Metals and Plastics	Fresno MSA, CA	H	8.06 FQ	13.49 AW	23.04 TQ	CABLS	10/01-12/01
Metals and Plastics	Los Angeles-Long Beach PMSA, CA	H	7.05 FQ	11.34 AW	18.88 TQ	CABLS	10/01-12/01
Metals and Plastics	Oakland PMSA, CA	H	9.54 FQ	15.63 AW	22.52 TQ	CABLS	10/01-12/01
Metals and Plastics	Orange County PMSA, CA	H	7.44 FQ	11.26 AW	16.04 TQ	CABLS	10/01-12/01
Metals and Plastics	Riverside-San Bernardino PMSA, CA	H	8.34 FQ	13.43 AW	20.04 TQ	CABLS	10/01-12/01
Metals and Plastics	San Diego MSA, CA	H	7.75 FQ	11.51 AW	16.91 TQ	CABLS	10/01-12/01
Metals and Plastics	San Francisco PMSA, CA	H	8.00 FQ	14.98 AW	29.09 TQ	CABLS	10/01-12/01
Metals and Plastics	San Jose PMSA, CA	H	8.96 FQ	14.88 AW	21.36 TQ	CABLS	10/01-12/01
Metals and Plastics	Vallejo-Fairfield-Napa PMSA, CA	H	9.17 FQ	12.09 AW	16.31 TQ	CABLS	10/01-12/01
Metals and Plastics	Ventura PMSA, CA	H	7.48 FQ	12.07 AW	16.14 TQ	CABLS	10/01-12/01
Metals and Plastics	Visalia-Tulare-Porterville MSA, CA	H	6.76 FQ	9.51 AW	15.85 TQ	CABLS	10/01-12/01
Metals and Plastics	Colorado	H	9.72 FQ	13.29 AW	17.50 TQ	COBLS	10/01-12/01
Metals and Plastics	Boulder-Longmont PMSA, CO	H	9.64 FQ	13.65 AW	16.99 TQ	COBLS	10/01-12/01
Metals and Plastics	Colorado Springs MSA, CO	H	9.88 FQ	14.53 AW	20.30 TQ	COBLS	10/01-12/01
Metals and Plastics	Denver PMSA, CO	H	10.83 FQ	13.61 AW	18.15 TQ	COBLS	10/01-12/01
Metals and Plastics	Connecticut	H	8.64 FQ	13.16 AW	18.42 TQ	CTBLS	10/01-12/01
Metals and Plastics	Bridgeport PMSA, CT	H	8.68 FQ	12.89 AW	19.21 TQ	CTBLS	10/01-12/01
Metals and Plastics	Danbury PMSA, CT	H	10.21 FQ	13.93 AW	17.53 TQ	CTBLS	10/01-12/01
Metals and Plastics	Hartford MSA, CT	H	9.32 FQ	13.63 AW	18.96 TQ	CTBLS	10/01-12/01
Metals and Plastics	New Haven-Meriden PMSA, CT	H	9.81 FQ	14.06 AW	17.38 TQ	CTBLS	10/01-12/01
Metals and Plastics	Stamford-Norwalk PMSA, CT	H	10.88 FQ	17.48 AW	24.39 TQ	CTBLS	10/01-12/01
Metals and Plastics	Waterbury PMSA, CT	H	7.51 FQ	10.12 AW	13.44 TQ	CTBLS	10/01-12/01
Metals and Plastics	Washington PMSA, DC-MD-VA-WV	H	8.86 FQ	11.52 AW	15.50 TQ	DCBLS	10/01-12/01

AAW	Average annual wage	**AOH**	Average offered, high	**ASH**	Average starting, high	**H**	Hourly	**M**	Monthly	**S**	Special: hourly and annual
AE	Average entry wage	**AOL**	Average offered, low	**ASL**	Average starting, low	**HI**	Highest wage paid	**MTC**	Median total compensation	**TQ**	Third quartile wage
AEX	Average experienced wage	**APH**	Average pay, high range	**AW**	Average wage paid	**HR**	High end range	**MW**	Median wage paid	**W**	Weekly
AO	Average offered	**APL**	Average pay, low range	**FQ**	First quartile wage	**LR**	Low end range	**SQ**	Second quartile wage	**Y**	Yearly

Occupation/Type/Industry	Location	Per	Low	Mid	High	Source	Date
Drilling and Boring Machine Tool Setter, Operator, and Tender							
Metals and Plastics	Florida	H	7.46 FQ	11.09 AW	16.16 TQ	FLBLS	10/01-12/01
Metals and Plastics	Fort Lauderdale PMSA, FL	H	7.56 FQ	11.72 AW	17.08 TQ	FLBLS	10/01-12/01
Metals and Plastics	Jacksonville MSA, FL	H	7.70 FQ	11.51 AW	16.27 TQ	FLBLS	10/01-12/01
Metals and Plastics	Melbourne-Titusville-Palm Bay MSA, FL	H	8.49 FQ	12.69 AW	16.93 TQ	FLBLS	10/01-12/01
Metals and Plastics	Miami PMSA, FL	H	6.36 FQ	8.90 AW	11.44 TQ	FLBLS	10/01-12/01
Metals and Plastics	Orlando MSA, FL	H	7.52 FQ	11.07 AW	15.88 TQ	FLBLS	10/01-12/01
Metals and Plastics	Sarasota-Bradenton MSA, FL	H	7.66 FQ	10.00 AW	12.33 TQ	FLBLS	10/01-12/01
Metals and Plastics	Tampa-St. Petersburg-Clearwater MSA, FL	H	7.84 FQ	11.70 AW	16.97 TQ	FLBLS	10/01-12/01
Metals and Plastics	Georgia	H	9.02 FQ	12.88 AW	17.08 TQ	GABLS	10/01-12/01
Metals and Plastics	Atlanta MSA, GA	H	8.99 FQ	12.43 AW	17.07 TQ	GABLS	10/01-12/01
Metals and Plastics	Macon MSA, GA	H	9.75 FQ	14.67 AW	17.85 TQ	GABLS	10/01-12/01
Metals and Plastics	Idaho	H	8.11 FQ	10.47 AW	13.12 TQ	IDBLS	10/01-12/01
Metals and Plastics	Boise City MSA, ID	H	8.98 FQ	10.46 AW	12.90 TQ	IDBLS	10/01-12/01
Metals and Plastics	Illinois	H	8.75 FQ	13.87 AW	19.55 TQ	ILBLS	10/01-12/01
Metals and Plastics	Champaign-Urbana MSA, IL	H	9.28 FQ	15.62 AW	25.12 TQ	ILBLS	10/01-12/01
Metals and Plastics	Chicago PMSA, IL	H	8.20 FQ	13.00 AW	17.35 TQ	ILBLS	10/01-12/01
Metals and Plastics	Peoria-Pekin MSA, IL	H	13.90 FQ	21.10 AW	27.55 TQ	ILBLS	10/01-12/01
Metals and Plastics	Rockford MSA, IL	H	14.65 FQ	17.13 AW	21.36 TQ	ILBLS	10/01-12/01
Metals and Plastics	Indiana	H	9.10 FQ	15.70 AW	25.50 TQ	INBLS	10/01-12/01
Metals and Plastics	Elkhart-Goshen MSA, IN	H	8.27 FQ	16.51 AW	25.60 TQ	INBLS	10/01-12/01
Metals and Plastics	Fort Wayne MSA, IN	H	9.40 FQ	11.92 AW	16.44 TQ	INBLS	10/01-12/01
Metals and Plastics	Gary PMSA, IN	H	9.69 FQ	14.45 AW	20.48 TQ	INBLS	10/01-12/01
Metals and Plastics	Indianapolis MSA, IN	H	9.23 FQ	17.37 AW	26.05 TQ	INBLS	10/01-12/01
Metals and Plastics	South Bend MSA, IN	H	8.98 FQ	11.12 AW	14.63 TQ	INBLS	10/01-12/01
Metals and Plastics	Iowa	H	9.11 FQ	14.19 AW	19.78 TQ	IABLS	10/01-12/01
Metals and Plastics	Davenport-Moline-Rock Island MSA, IA-IL	H	9.60 FQ	12.84 AW	16.53 TQ	IABLS	10/01-12/01
Metals and Plastics	Kansas	H	6.89 FQ	14.08 AW	30.43 TQ	KSBLS	10/01-12/01
Metals and Plastics	Wichita MSA, KS	H	10.21 FQ	21.59 AW	33.72 TQ	KSBLS	10/01-12/01
Metals and Plastics	Kentucky	H	8.63 FQ	12.62 AW	16.57 TQ	KYBLS	10/01-12/01
Metals and Plastics	Lexington MSA, KY	H	9.55 FQ	12.38 AW	14.27 TQ	KYBLS	10/01-12/01
Metals and Plastics	Louisville MSA, KY-IN	H	10.53 FQ	12.92 AW	16.11 TQ	KYBLS	10/01-12/01
Metals and Plastics	Louisiana	H	6.64 FQ	11.60 AW	16.84 TQ	LABLS	10/01-12/01
Metals and Plastics	Baton Rouge MSA, LA	H	6.06 FQ	9.79 AW	15.40 TQ	LABLS	10/01-12/01
Metals and Plastics	Maine	H	9.26 FQ	13.24 AW	18.85 TQ	MEBLS	10/01-12/01
Metals and Plastics	Portland MSA, ME	H	9.54 FQ	13.18 AW	17.03 TQ	MEBLS	10/01-12/01
Metals and Plastics	Maryland	H	9.65 FQ	16.49 AW	25.15 TQ	MDBLS	10/01-12/01
Metals and Plastics	Massachusetts	H	8.45 FQ	15.15 AW	25.45 TQ	MABLS	10/01-12/01
Metals and Plastics	Boston PMSA, MA-NH	H	9.19 FQ	17.54 AW	30.53 TQ	MABLS	10/01-12/01
Metals and Plastics	Lowell PMSA, MA-NH	H	9.88 FQ	16.11 AW	22.05 TQ	MABLS	10/01-12/01
Metals and Plastics	Springfield MSA, MA	H	7.88 FQ	12.41 AW	17.44 TQ	MABLS	10/01-12/01
Metals and Plastics	Worcester PMSA, MA-CT	H	7.60 FQ	13.88 AW	20.95 TQ	MABLS	10/01-12/01
Metals and Plastics	Michigan	H	9.42 FQ	15.66 AW	25.90 TQ	MIBLS	10/01-12/01
Metals and Plastics	Ann Arbor PMSA, MI	H	10.30 FQ	18.38 AW	27.10 TQ	MIBLS	10/01-12/01
Metals and Plastics	Detroit PMSA, MI	H	10.15 FQ	17.34 AW	26.90 TQ	MIBLS	10/01-12/01
Metals and Plastics	Grand Rapids-Muskegon-Holland MSA, MI	H	8.90 FQ	14.51 AW	24.50 TQ	MIBLS	10/01-12/01
Metals and Plastics	Kalamazoo-Battle Creek MSA, MI	H	7.56 FQ	11.36 AW	16.53 TQ	MIBLS	10/01-12/01
Metals and Plastics	Lansing-East Lansing MSA, MI	H	12.46 FQ	15.63 AW	19.01 TQ	MIBLS	10/01-12/01
Metals and Plastics	Saginaw-Bay City-Midland MSA, MI	H	8.04 FQ	14.20 AW	20.48 TQ	MIBLS	10/01-12/01
Metals and Plastics	Minnesota	H	10.17 FQ	14.66 AW	20.44 TQ	MNBLS	10/01-12/01
Metals and Plastics	Minneapolis-St. Paul MSA, MN-WI	H	11.09 FQ	15.41 AW	21.00 TQ	MNBLS	10/01-12/01
Metals and Plastics	Mississippi	H	8.47 FQ	11.99 AW	14.32 TQ	MSBLS	10/01-12/01
Metals and Plastics	Jackson MSA, MS	H	9.72 FQ	11.73 AW	13.55 TQ	MSBLS	10/01-12/01
Metals and Plastics	Missouri	H	8.46 FQ	13.26 AW	18.47 TQ	MOBLS	10/01-12/01
Metals and Plastics	Kansas City MSA, MO-KS	H	8.29 FQ	11.82 AW	16.61 TQ	MOBLS	10/01-12/01
Metals and Plastics	St. Louis MSA, MO-IL	H	8.06 FQ	13.19 AW	18.13 TQ	MOBLS	10/01-12/01
Metals and Plastics	Nebraska	H	9.10 FQ	13.82 AW	20.51 TQ	NEBLS	10/01-12/01
Metals and Plastics	Lincoln MSA, NE	H	11.94 FQ	15.45 AW	17.96 TQ	NEBLS	10/01-12/01
Metals and Plastics	Nevada	H	8.24 FQ	12.10 AW	17.56 TQ	NVBLS	10/01-12/01
Metals and Plastics	Reno MSA, NV	H	8.70 FQ	12.16 AW	17.49 TQ	NVBLS	10/01-12/01
Metals and Plastics	New Hampshire	H	10.05 FQ	13.73 AW	17.60 TQ	NHBLS	10/01-12/01
Metals and Plastics	Nashua PMSA, NH	H	10.27 FQ	14.29 AW	17.54 TQ	NHBLS	10/01-12/01
Metals and Plastics	New Jersey	H	6.46 FQ	11.52 AW	17.52 TQ	NJBLS	10/01-12/01
Metals and Plastics	Bergen-Passaic PMSA, NJ	H	6.50 FQ	11.86 AW	18.20 TQ	NJBLS	10/01-12/01

AAW	Average annual wage	AOH	Average offered, high	ASH	Average starting, high	H	Hourly	M	Monthly	S	Special: hourly and annual
AE	Average entry wage	AOL	Average offered, low	ASL	Average starting, low	HI	Highest wage paid	MTC	Median total compensation	TQ	Third quartile wage
AEX	Average experienced wage	APH	Average pay, high range	AW	Average wage paid	HR	High end range	MW	Median wage paid	W	Weekly
AO	Average offered	APL	Average pay, low range	FQ	First quartile wage	LR	Low end range	SQ	Second quartile wage	Y	Yearly

Occupation/Type/Industry	Location	Per	Low	Mid	High	Source	Date
Drilling and Boring Machine Tool Setter, Operator, and Tender							
Metals and Plastics	Middlesex-Somerset-Hunterdon PMSA, NJ	H	7.69 FQ	11.96 AW	17.78 TQ	NJBLS	10/01-12/01
Metals and Plastics	Monmouth-Ocean PMSA, NJ	H	6.94 FQ	13.32 AW	24.62 TQ	NJBLS	10/01-12/01
Metals and Plastics	Newark PMSA, NJ	H	6.01 FQ	10.07 AW	15.12 TQ	NJBLS	10/01-12/01
Metals and Plastics	New Mexico	H	9.31 FQ	16.31 AW	27.26 TQ	NMBLS	10/01-12/01
Metals and Plastics	New York	H	7.66 FQ	12.87 AW	18.56 TQ	NYBLS	10/01-12/01
Metals and Plastics	Buffalo-Niagara Falls MSA, NY	H	8.25 FQ	12.76 AW	17.68 TQ	NYBLS	10/01-12/01
Metals and Plastics	Nassau-Suffolk PMSA, NY	H	7.35 FQ	13.12 AW	21.20 TQ	NYBLS	10/01-12/01
Metals and Plastics	New York PMSA, NY	H	6.12 FQ	12.93 AW	24.21 TQ	NYBLS	10/01-12/01
Metals and Plastics	Rochester MSA, NY	H	7.70 FQ	12.59 AW	19.18 TQ	NYBLS	10/01-12/01
Metals and Plastics	Syracuse MSA, NY	H	9.39 FQ	12.37 AW	15.80 TQ	NYBLS	10/01-12/01
Metals and Plastics	Utica-Rome MSA, NY	H	8.40 FQ	12.60 AW	16.88 TQ	NYBLS	10/01-12/01
Metals and Plastics	North Carolina	H	8.67 FQ	13.47 AW	18.04 TQ	NCBLS	10/01-12/01
Metals and Plastics	Asheville MSA, NC	H	10.34 FQ	12.65 AW	14.94 TQ	NCBLS	10/01-12/01
Metals and Plastics	Charlotte-Gastonia-Rock Hill MSA, NC-SC	H	7.49 FQ	12.73 AW	19.48 TQ	NCBLS	10/01-12/01
Metals and Plastics	Greensboro-Winston-Salem-High Point MSA, NC	H	8.97 FQ	14.53 AW	21.07 TQ	NCBLS	10/01-12/01
Metals and Plastics	North Dakota	H	9.97 FQ	13.96 AW	17.23 TQ	NDBLS	10/01-12/01
Metals and Plastics	Ohio	H	8.95 FQ	14.81 AW	21.14 TQ	OHBLS	10/01-12/01
Metals and Plastics	Akron PMSA, OH	H	9.74 FQ	13.95 AW	17.39 TQ	OHBLS	10/01-12/01
Metals and Plastics	Cincinnati PMSA, OH-KY-IN	H	9.12 FQ	14.68 AW	20.96 TQ	OHBLS	10/01-12/01
Metals and Plastics	Cleveland-Lorain-Elyria PMSA, OH	H	8.52 FQ	13.41 AW	19.84 TQ	OHBLS	10/01-12/01
Metals and Plastics	Columbus MSA, OH	H	8.91 FQ	12.12 AW	16.10 TQ	OHBLS	10/01-12/01
Metals and Plastics	Dayton-Springfield MSA, OH	H	12.09 FQ	18.84 AW	25.29 TQ	OHBLS	10/01-12/01
Metals and Plastics	Hamilton-Middletown PMSA, OH	H	9.31 FQ	13.45 AW	18.13 TQ	OHBLS	10/01-12/01
Metals and Plastics	Mansfield MSA, OH	H	6.71 FQ	11.79 AW	18.00 TQ	OHBLS	10/01-12/01
Metals and Plastics	Toledo MSA, OH	H	9.53 FQ	14.75 AW	21.12 TQ	OHBLS	10/01-12/01
Metals and Plastics	Youngstown-Warren MSA, OH	H	6.78 FQ	16.01 AW	30.49 TQ	OHBLS	10/01-12/01
Metals and Plastics	Oklahoma	H	8.90 FQ	12.82 AW	16.77 TQ	OKBLS	10/01-12/01
Metals and Plastics	Oklahoma City MSA, OK	H	9.54 FQ	13.47 AW	17.55 TQ	OKBLS	10/01-12/01
Metals and Plastics	Tulsa MSA, OK	H	8.30 FQ	12.94 AW	16.83 TQ	OKBLS	10/01-12/01
Metals and Plastics	Oregon	H	9.72 FQ	15.75 AW	26.10 TQ	ORBLS	10/01-12/01
Metals and Plastics	Portland-Vancouver PMSA, OR-WA	H	10.11 FQ	16.82 AW	26.79 TQ	ORBLS	10/01-12/01
Metals and Plastics	Pennsylvania	H	9.40 FQ	14.19 AW	20.98 TQ	PABLS	10/01-12/01
Metals and Plastics	Allentown-Bethlehem-Easton MSA, PA	H	8.55 FQ	11.77 AW	15.93 TQ	PABLS	10/01-12/01
Metals and Plastics	Erie MSA, PA	H	9.34 FQ	14.11 AW	20.22 TQ	PABLS	10/01-12/01
Metals and Plastics	Harrisburg-Lebanon-Carlisle MSA, PA	H	10.06 FQ	17.50 AW	27.22 TQ	PABLS	10/01-12/01
Metals and Plastics	Lancaster MSA, PA	H	9.55 FQ	14.01 AW	20.47 TQ	PABLS	10/01-12/01
Metals and Plastics	Philadelphia PMSA, PA-NJ	H	10.99 FQ	17.41 AW	27.09 TQ	PABLS	10/01-12/01
Metals and Plastics	Pittsburgh MSA, PA	H	9.14 FQ	13.32 AW	19.24 TQ	PABLS	10/01-12/01
Metals and Plastics	Reading MSA, PA	H	12.90 FQ	17.31 AW	21.46 TQ	PABLS	10/01-12/01
Metals and Plastics	Scranton-Wilkes-Barre-Hazleton MSA, PA	H	11.38 FQ	13.81 AW	16.82 TQ	PABLS	10/01-12/01
Metals and Plastics	Rhode Island	H	8.85 FQ	12.14 AW	19.04 TQ	RIBLS	10/01-12/01
Metals and Plastics	Providence-Fall River-Warwick MSA, RI-MA	H	8.84 FQ	12.38 AW	18.81 TQ	RIBLS	10/01-12/01
Metals and Plastics	South Carolina	H	7.69 FQ	11.56 AW	16.49 TQ	SCBLS	10/01-12/01
Metals and Plastics	Columbia MSA, SC	H	9.34 FQ	11.50 AW	15.37 TQ	SCBLS	10/01-12/01
Metals and Plastics	Greenville-Spartanburg-Anderson MSA, SC	H	7.48 FQ	11.85 AW	17.89 TQ	SCBLS	10/01-12/01
Metals and Plastics	Myrtle Beach MSA, SC	H	10.30 FQ	12.40 AW	15.49 TQ	SCBLS	10/01-12/01
Metals and Plastics	South Dakota	H	8.73 FQ	11.74 AW	15.30 TQ	SDBLS	10/01-12/01
Metals and Plastics	Tennessee	H	8.37 FQ	12.29 AW	16.64 TQ	TNBLS	10/01-12/01
Metals and Plastics	Chattanooga MSA, TN-GA	H	9.28 FQ	13.36 AW	17.18 TQ	TNBLS	10/01-12/01
Metals and Plastics	Johnson City-Kingsport-Bristol MSA, TN-VA	H	9.18 FQ	13.06 AW	16.86 TQ	TNBLS	10/01-12/01
Metals and Plastics	Knoxville MSA, TN	H	9.13 FQ	12.88 AW	16.55 TQ	TNBLS	10/01-12/01
Metals and Plastics	Memphis MSA, TN-AR-MS	H	7.00 FQ	11.19 AW	14.51 TQ	TNBLS	10/01-12/01
Metals and Plastics	Nashville MSA, TN	H	9.99 FQ	13.16 AW	16.94 TQ	TNBLS	10/01-12/01
Metals and Plastics	Texas	H	7.70 FQ	11.79 AW	17.52 TQ	TXBLS	10/01-12/01
Metals and Plastics	Austin-San Marcos MSA, TX	H	7.39 FQ	8.77 AW	10.86 TQ	TXBLS	10/01-12/01
Metals anu Plastics	Beaumont-Port Arthur MSA, TX	H	7.85 FQ	11.71 AW	16.24 TQ	TXBLS	10/01-12/01

AAW Average annual wage; AE Average entry wage; AEX Average experienced wage; AO Average offered; AOH Average offered, high; AOL Average offered, low; APH Average pay, high range; APL Average pay, low range; ASH Average starting, high; ASL Average starting, low; AW Average wage paid; FQ First quartile wage; H Hourly; HI Highest wage paid; HR High end range; LR Low end range; M Monthly; MTC Median total compensation; MW Median wage paid; SQ Second quartile wage; S Special: hourly and annual; TQ Third quartile wage; W Weekly; Y Yearly

Drilling and Boring Machine Tool Setter, Operator, and Tender

Occupation/Type/Industry	Location	Per	Low	Mid	High	Source	Date
Metals and Plastics	Dallas PMSA, TX	H	7.97 FQ	12.37 AW	18.92 TQ	TXBLS	10/01-12/01
Metals and Plastics	El Paso MSA, TX	H	6.45 FQ	8.94 AW	12.51 TQ	TXBLS	10/01-12/01
Metals and Plastics	Fort Worth-Arlington PMSA, TX	H	7.61 FQ	15.07 AW	25.25 TQ	TXBLS	10/01-12/01
Metals and Plastics	Houston PMSA, TX	H	8.02 FQ	11.87 AW	16.75 TQ	TXBLS	10/01-12/01
Metals and Plastics	Longview-Marshall MSA, TX	H	6.87 FQ	11.16 AW	15.22 TQ	TXBLS	10/01-12/01
Metals and Plastics	Odessa-Midland MSA, TX	H	7.95 FQ	11.71 AW	15.72 TQ	TXBLS	10/01-12/01
Metals and Plastics	San Antonio MSA, TX	H	7.65 FQ	14.41 AW	20.54 TQ	TXBLS	10/01-12/01
Metals and Plastics	Utah	H	7.73 FQ	11.32 AW	16.99 TQ	UTBLS	10/01-12/01
Metals and Plastics	Vermont	H	8.33 FQ	12.70 AW	16.66 TQ	VTBLS	10/01-12/01
Metals and Plastics	Virginia	H	9.16 FQ	12.82 AW	16.82 TQ	VABLS	10/01-12/01
Metals and Plastics	Lynchburg MSA, VA	H	8.76 FQ	11.66 AW	15.09 TQ	VABLS	10/01-12/01
Metals and Plastics	Norfolk-Virginia Beach-Newport News MSA, VA-NC	H	9.43 FQ	13.28 AW	16.90 TQ	VABLS	10/01-12/01
Metals and Plastics	Washington	H	8.90 FQ	15.65 AW	25.85 TQ	WABLS	10/01-12/01
Metals and Plastics	Seattle-Bellevue-Everett PMSA, WA	H	8.70 FQ	17.14 AW	26.73 TQ	WABLS	10/01-12/01
Metals and Plastics	Spokane MSA, WA	H	9.38 FQ	13.61 AW	20.12 TQ	WABLS	10/01-12/01
Metals and Plastics	West Virginia	H	7.57 FQ	11.31 AW	16.61 TQ	WVBLS	10/01-12/01
Metals and Plastics	Huntington-Ashland MSA, WV-KY-OH	H	7.98 FQ	14.89 AW	21.69 TQ	WVBLS	10/01-12/01
Metals and Plastics	Wisconsin	H	8.98 FQ	13.92 AW	20.10 TQ	WIBLS	10/01-12/01
Metals and Plastics	Appleton-Oshkosh-Neenah MSA, WI	H	11.36 FQ	14.87 AW	18.35 TQ	WIBLS	10/01-12/01
Metals and Plastics	Green Bay MSA, WI	H	8.40 FQ	13.66 AW	20.77 TQ	WIBLS	10/01-12/01
Metals and Plastics	Milwaukee-Waukesha PMSA, WI	H	9.51 FQ	14.90 AW	21.31 TQ	WIBLS	10/01-12/01
Metals and Plastics	Racine PMSA, WI	H	9.02 FQ	14.32 AW	20.77 TQ	WIBLS	10/01-12/01
Metals and Plastics	Puerto Rico	H	5.82 FQ	8.05 AW	10.60 TQ	PRBLS	10/01-12/01

Driver/Sales Worker

Occupation/Type/Industry	Location	Per	Low	Mid	High	Source	Date
	Alabama	H	5.85 FQ	11.53 AW	20.03 TQ	ALBLS	10/01-12/01
	Alaska	H	7.18 FQ	11.71 AW	18.80 TQ	AKBLS	10/01-12/01
	Arizona	H	5.75 FQ	9.65 AW	16.63 TQ	AZBLS	10/01-12/01
	Arkansas	H	6.89 FQ	11.97 AW	17.64 TQ	ARBLS	10/01-12/01
	California	H	6.73 FQ	10.98 AW	19.12 TQ	CABLS	10/01-12/01
	Colorado	H	5.80 FQ	11.35 AW	20.04 TQ	COBLS	10/01-12/01
	Connecticut	H	6.72 FQ	12.02 AW	20.41 TQ	CTBLS	10/01-12/01
	Delaware	H	6.45 FQ	11.83 AW	22.67 TQ	DEBLS	10/01-12/01
	District of Columbia	H	7.69 FQ	11.57 AW	16.43 TQ	DCBLS	10/01-12/01
	Florida	H	5.65 FQ	9.59 AW	17.11 TQ	FLBLS	10/01-12/01
	Georgia	H	5.84 FQ	11.12 AW	18.22 TQ	GABLS	10/01-12/01
	Hawaii	H	7.07 FQ	12.14 AW	20.16 TQ	HIBLS	10/01-12/01
	Idaho	H	5.83 FQ	10.12 AW	16.79 TQ	IDBLS	10/01-12/01
	Illinois	H	6.18 FQ	12.53 AW	20.34 TQ	ILBLS	10/01-12/01
	Indiana	H	6.23 FQ	12.65 AW	20.50 TQ	INBLS	10/01-12/01
	Iowa	H	6.75 FQ	12.59 AW	19.68 TQ	IABLS	10/01-12/01
	Kansas	H	5.85 FQ	10.83 AW	18.11 TQ	KSBLS	10/01-12/01
	Kentucky	H	6.93 FQ	12.51 AW	18.31 TQ	KYBLS	10/01-12/01
	Louisiana	H	6.43 FQ	10.94 AW	16.78 TQ	LABLS	10/01-12/01
	Maine	H	7.68 FQ	12.26 AW	19.34 TQ	MEBLS	10/01-12/01
	Maryland	H	5.94 FQ	11.56 AW	19.58 TQ	MDBLS	10/01-12/01
	Massachusetts	H	7.52 FQ	13.39 AW	21.26 TQ	MABLS	10/01-12/01
	Michigan	H	5.83 FQ	11.65 AW	20.70 TQ	MIBLS	10/01-12/01
	Minnesota	H	5.82 FQ	10.01 AW	16.56 TQ	MNBLS	10/01-12/01
	Mississippi	H	6.18 FQ	10.29 AW	16.48 TQ	MSBLS	10/01-12/01
	Missouri	H	6.09 FQ	11.90 AW	19.20 TQ	MOBLS	10/01-12/01
	Montana	H	5.70 FQ	9.33 AW	15.98 TQ	MTBLS	10/01-12/01
	Nebraska	H	5.70 FQ	10.00 AW	19.18 TQ	NEBLS	10/01-12/01
	Nevada	H	6.86 FQ	11.85 AW	17.38 TQ	NVBLS	10/01-12/01
	New Hampshire	H	6.52 FQ	13.05 AW	21.14 TQ	NHBLS	10/01-12/01
	New Jersey	H	7.57 FQ	16.20 AW	25.88 TQ	NJBLS	10/01-12/01
	New Mexico	H	5.73 FQ	9.60 AW	15.91 TQ	NMBLS	10/01-12/01
	New York	H	6.10 FQ	13.00 AW	21.34 TQ	NYBLS	10/01-12/01
	North Carolina	H	5.85 FQ	12.58 AW	20.44 TQ	NCBLS	10/01-12/01
	North Dakota	H	5.49 FQ	8.55 AW	14.74 TQ	NDBLS	10/01-12/01
	Ohio	H	5.63 FQ	10.02 AW	17.63 TQ	OHBLS	10/01-12/01
	Oklahoma	H	5.79 FQ	10.70 AW	18.11 TQ	OKBLS	10/01-12/01
	Oregon	H	7.23 FQ	13.48 AW	20.60 TQ	ORBLS	10/01-12/01
	Pennsylvania	H	5.75 FQ	11.01 AW	19.93 TQ	PABLS	10/01-12/01

AAW	Average annual wage	**AOH**	Average offered, high	**ASH**	Average starting, high	**H**	Hourly	**M**	Monthly	**S**	Special: hourly and annual
AE	Average entry wage	**AOL**	Average offered, low	**ASL**	Average starting, low	**HI**	Highest wage paid	**MTC**	Median total compensation	**TQ**	Third quartile wage
AEX	Average experienced wage	**APH**	Average pay, high range	**AW**	Average wage paid	**HR**	High end range	**MW**	Median wage paid	**W**	Weekly
AO	Average offered	**APL**	Average pay, low range	**FQ**	First quartile wage	**LR**	Low end range	**SQ**	Second quartile wage	**Y**	Yearly

Occupation/Type/Industry	Location	Per	Low	Mid	High	Source	Date
Driver/Sales Worker	Rhode Island	H	6.68 FQ	11.39 AW	20.70 TQ	RIBLS	10/01-12/01
	South Carolina	H	6.29 FQ	11.67 AW	17.86 TQ	SCBLS	10/01-12/01
	South Dakota	H	5.82 FQ	11.78 AW	19.75 TQ	SDBLS	10/01-12/01
	Tennessee	H	6.17 FQ	12.22 AW	19.84 TQ	TNBLS	10/01-12/01
	Texas	H	5.71 FQ	9.55 AW	16.25 TQ	TXBLS	10/01-12/01
	Utah	H	5.79 FQ	11.59 AW	20.22 TQ	UTBLS	10/01-12/01
	Vermont	H	6.75 FQ	13.59 AW	20.46 TQ	VTBLS	10/01-12/01
	Virginia	H	5.69 FQ	10.02 AW	16.68 TQ	VABLS	10/01-12/01
	Washington	H	6.93 FQ	10.91 AW	17.82 TQ	WABLS	10/01-12/01
	West Virginia	H	5.63 FQ	10.12 AW	17.44 TQ	WVBLS	10/01-12/01
	Wisconsin	H	6.40 FQ	12.33 AW	19.29 TQ	WIBLS	10/01-12/01
	Wyoming	H	5.84 FQ	10.47 AW	17.91 TQ	WYBLS	10/01-12/01
	Puerto Rico	H	5.61 FQ	6.78 AW	8.47 TQ	PRBLS	10/01-12/01
	Guam	H	5.51 FQ	7.69 AW	11.82 TQ	GUBLS	10/01-12/01
Drywall and Ceiling Tile Installer	Alabama	H	7.26 FQ	11.76 AW	16.08 TQ	ALBLS	10/01-12/01
	Birmingham MSA, AL	H	9.44 FQ	13.51 AW	17.41 TQ	ALBLS	10/01-12/01
	Mobile MSA, AL	H	7.86 FQ	12.22 AW	16.24 TQ	ALBLS	10/01-12/01
	Montgomery MSA, AL	H	8.30 FQ	10.99 AW	15.00 TQ	ALBLS	10/01-12/01
	Alaska	H	13.64 FQ	25.50 AW	34.70 TQ	AKBLS	10/01-12/01
	Anchorage MSA, AK	H	14.29 FQ	26.01 AW	34.81 TQ	AKBLS	10/01-12/01
	Arizona	H	8.00 FQ	13.17 AW	18.28 TQ	AZBLS	10/01-12/01
	Phoenix-Mesa MSA, AZ	H	8.05 FQ	13.27 AW	18.52 TQ	AZBLS	10/01-12/01
	Tucson MSA, AZ	H	8.83 FQ	12.62 AW	16.92 TQ	AZBLS	10/01-12/01
	Arkansas	H	9.14 FQ	12.19 AW	15.92 TQ	ARBLS	10/01-12/01
	Fayetteville-Springdale-Rogers MSA, AR	H	9.05 FQ	12.31 AW	16.52 TQ	ARBLS	10/01-12/01
	Little Rock-North Little Rock MSA, AR	H	10.81 FQ	12.99 AW	16.10 TQ	ARBLS	10/01-12/01
	California	H	10.35 FQ	19.36 AW	29.77 TQ	CABLS	10/01-12/01
	Bakersfield MSA, CA	H	11.58 FQ	15.84 AW	21.10 TQ	CABLS	10/01-12/01
	Chico-Paradise MSA, CA	H	8.32 FQ	16.90 AW	28.65 TQ	CABLS	10/01-12/01
	Fresno MSA, CA	H	7.52 FQ	15.13 AW	26.09 TQ	CABLS	10/01-12/01
	Los Angeles-Long Beach PMSA, CA	H	9.60 FQ	18.21 AW	27.34 TQ	CABLS	10/01-12/01
	Merced MSA, CA	H	12.56 FQ	18.89 AW	25.83 TQ	CABLS	10/01-12/01
	Modesto MSA, CA	H	14.38 FQ	19.63 AW	30.24 TQ	CABLS	10/01-12/01
	Oakland PMSA, CA	H	11.37 FQ	22.86 AW	33.19 TQ	CABLS	10/01-12/01
	Orange County PMSA, CA	H	10.59 FQ	20.38 AW	31.28 TQ	CABLS	10/01-12/01
	Redding MSA, CA	H	11.37 FQ	16.32 AW	21.28 TQ	CABLS	10/01-12/01
	Riverside-San Bernardino PMSA, CA	H	11.41 FQ	19.05 AW	27.01 TQ	CABLS	10/01-12/01
	Sacramento PMSA, CA	H	8.79 FQ	16.13 AW	24.14 TQ	CABLS	10/01-12/01
	Salinas MSA, CA	H	16.84 FQ	25.48 AW	34.16 TQ	CABLS	10/01-12/01
	San Diego MSA, CA	H	10.18 FQ	17.44 AW	25.13 TQ	CABLS	10/01-12/01
	San Francisco PMSA, CA	H	16.87 FQ	25.65 AW	34.38 TQ	CABLS	10/01-12/01
	San Jose PMSA, CA	H	17.85 FQ	26.05 AW	36.34 TQ	CABLS	10/01-12/01
	San Luis Obispo-Atascadero-Paso Robles MSA, CA	H	10.98 FQ	16.38 AW	22.22 TQ	CABLS	10/01-12/01
	Santa Barbara-Santa Maria-Lompoc MSA, CA	H	11.93 FQ	18.07 AW	23.92 TQ	CABLS	10/01-12/01
	Santa Cruz-Watsonville PMSA, CA	H	9.96 FQ	19.48 AW	31.43 TQ	CABLS	10/01-12/01
	Santa Rosa PMSA, CA	H	9.52 FQ	18.32 AW	28.03 TQ	CABLS	10/01-12/01
	Stockton-Lodi MSA, CA	H	12.37 FQ	18.43 AW	24.48 TQ	CABLS	10/01-12/01
	Vallejo-Fairfield-Napa PMSA, CA	H	12.62 FQ	19.28 AW	24.89 TQ	CABLS	10/01-12/01
	Ventura PMSA, CA	H	12.18 FQ	22.08 AW	39.08 TQ	CABLS	10/01-12/01
	Visalia-Tulare-Porterville MSA, CA	H	11.36 FQ	20.43 AW	33.96 TQ	CABLS	10/01-12/01
	Colorado	H	8.74 FQ	14.96 AW	20.64 TQ	COBLS	10/01-12/01
	Colorado Springs MSA, CO	H	7.92 FQ	12.20 AW	18.16 TQ	COBLS	10/01-12/01
	Denver PMSA, CO	H	8.63 FQ	15.09 AW	20.78 TQ	COBLS	10/01-12/01
	Fort Collins-Loveland MSA, CO	H	11.44 FQ	16.05 AW	21.08 TQ	COBLS	10/01-12/01
	Greeley PMSA, CO	H	11.35 FQ	16.10 AW	20.37 TQ	COBLS	10/01-12/01
	Connecticut	H	18.40 FQ	23.18 AW	27.53 TQ	CTBLS	10/01-12/01
	Danbury PMSA, CT	H	22.41 FQ	25.26 AW	29.72 TQ	CTBLS	10/01-12/01
	Hartford MSA, CT	H	17.00 FQ	23.06 AW	27.55 TQ	CTBLS	10/01-12/01
	New Haven-Meriden PMSA, CT	H	18.65 FQ	23.20 AW	27.23 TQ	CTBLS	10/01-12/01
	Stamford-Norwalk PMSA, CT	H	21.91 FQ	24.26 AW	27.57 TQ	CTBLS	10/01-12/01
	Delaware	H	11.05 FQ	16.39 AW	25.53 TQ	DEBLS	10/01-12/01

AAW	Average annual wage	**AOH**	Average offered, high	**ASH**	Average starting, high	**H**	Hourly	**M**	Monthly	**S**	Special: hourly and annual
AE	Average entry wage	**AOL**	Average offered, low	**ASL**	Average starting, low	**HI**	Highest wage paid	**MTC**	Median total compensation	**TQ**	Third quartile wage
AEX	Average experienced wage	**APH**	Average pay, high range	**AW**	Average wage paid	**HR**	High end range	**MW**	Median wage paid	**W**	Weekly
AO	Average offered	**APL**	Average pay, low range	**FQ**	First quartile wage	**LR**	Low end range	**SQ**	Second quartile wage	**Y**	Yearly

Occupation/Type/Industry	Location	Per	Low	Mid	High	Source	Date
Drywall and Ceiling Tile Installer	Wilmington-Newark PMSA, DE-MD	H	13.14 FQ	18.20 AW	26.11 TQ	DEBLS	10/01-12/01
	District of Columbia	H	17.99 FQ	19.53 AW	21.87 TQ	DCBLS	10/01-12/01
	Washington PMSA, DC-MD-VA-WV	H	12.10 FQ	15.93 AW	20.41 TQ	DCBLS	10/01-12/01
	Florida	H	9.43 FQ	14.00 AW	19.44 TQ	FLBLS	10/01-12/01
	Fort Lauderdale PMSA, FL	H	11.99 FQ	15.37 AW	17.81 TQ	FLBLS	10/01-12/01
	Fort Myers-Cape Coral MSA, FL	H	11.29 FQ	16.64 AW	21.64 TQ	FLBLS	10/01-12/01
	Fort Pierce-Port St. Lucie MSA, FL	H	11.98 FQ	14.97 AW	20.43 TQ	FLBLS	10/01-12/01
	Jacksonville MSA, FL	H	10.69 FQ	15.14 AW	21.58 TQ	FLBLS	10/01-12/01
	Melbourne-Titusville-Palm Bay MSA, FL	H	8.79 FQ	12.07 AW	13.71 TQ	FLBLS	10/01-12/01
	Miami PMSA, FL	H	10.09 FQ	15.03 AW	20.92 TQ	FLBLS	10/01-12/01
	Naples MSA, FL	H	9.24 FQ	14.51 AW	20.35 TQ	FLBLS	10/01-12/01
	Orlando MSA, FL	H	9.64 FQ	14.20 AW	18.20 TQ	FLBLS	10/01-12/01
	Pensacola MSA, FL	H	9.43 FQ	12.50 AW	15.17 TQ	FLBLS	10/01-12/01
	Sarasota-Bradenton MSA, FL	H	8.05 FQ	13.96 AW	19.43 TQ	FLBLS	10/01-12/01
	Tallahassee MSA, FL	H	9.22 FQ	12.50 AW	17.26 TQ	FLBLS	10/01-12/01
	Tampa-St. Petersburg-Clearwater MSA, FL	H	8.59 FQ	12.71 AW	16.90 TQ	FLBLS	10/01-12/01
	West Palm Beach-Boca Raton MSA, FL	H	9.32 FQ	13.32 AW	19.15 TQ	FLBLS	10/01-12/01
	Georgia	H	10.56 FQ	15.58 AW	21.16 TQ	GABLS	10/01-12/01
	Atlanta MSA, GA	H	11.66 FQ	16.70 AW	21.62 TQ	GABLS	10/01-12/01
	Augusta-Aiken MSA, GA-SC	H	8.02 FQ	11.86 AW	15.91 TQ	GABLS	10/01-12/01
	Columbus MSA, GA-AL	H	9.55 FQ	12.59 AW	16.02 TQ	GABLS	10/01-12/01
	Macon MSA, GA	H	11.23 FQ	13.45 AW	16.44 TQ	GABLS	10/01-12/01
	Savannah MSA, GA	H	10.90 FQ	14.65 AW	17.52 TQ	GABLS	10/01-12/01
	Hawaii	H	15.07 FQ	26.84 AW	34.89 TQ	HIBLS	10/01-12/01
	Honolulu MSA, HI	H	16.25 FQ	26.68 AW	34.43 TQ	HIBLS	10/01-12/01
	Idaho	H	9.50 FQ	15.35 AW	18.61 TQ	IDBLS	10/01-12/01
	Boise City MSA, ID	H	11.36 FQ	16.26 AW	20.50 TQ	IDBLS	10/01-12/01
	Illinois	H	6.42 FQ	20.11 AW	31.65 TQ	ILBLS	10/01-12/01
	Champaign-Urbana MSA, IL	H	11.26 FQ	15.86 AW	22.47 TQ	ILBLS	10/01-12/01
	Chicago PMSA, IL	H	6.25 FQ	19.89 AW	31.60 TQ	ILBLS	10/01-12/01
	Peoria-Pekin MSA, IL	H	22.06 FQ	29.54 AW	36.08 TQ	ILBLS	10/01-12/01
	Springfield MSA, IL	H	13.92 FQ	19.84 AW	22.65 TQ	ILBLS	10/01-12/01
	Indiana	H	10.99 FQ	18.71 AW	26.95 TQ	INBLS	10/01-12/01
	Elkhart-Goshen MSA, IN	H	10.58 FQ	16.45 AW	21.88 TQ	INBLS	10/01-12/01
	Evansville-Henderson MSA, IN-KY	H	13.96 FQ	18.20 AW	21.31 TQ	INBLS	10/01-12/01
	Fort Wayne MSA, IN	H	5.72 FQ	9.63 AW	16.37 TQ	INBLS	10/01-12/01
	Indianapolis MSA, IN	H	14.42 FQ	21.75 AW	27.85 TQ	INBLS	10/01-12/01
	Lafayette MSA, IN	H	11.58 FQ	14.74 AW	20.86 TQ	INBLS	10/01-12/01
	Iowa	H	10.67 FQ	16.52 AW	22.10 TQ	IABLS	10/01-12/01
	Des Moines MSA, IA	H	11.48 FQ	17.36 AW	22.33 TQ	IABLS	10/01-12/01
	Kansas	H	11.38 FQ	15.90 AW	22.86 TQ	KSBLS	10/01-12/01
	Wichita MSA, KS	H	11.20 FQ	16.14 AW	21.50 TQ	KSBLS	10/01-12/01
	Kentucky	H	9.88 FQ	14.07 AW	18.48 TQ	KYBLS	10/01-12/01
	Lexington MSA, KY	H	9.82 FQ	12.69 AW	16.88 TQ	KYBLS	10/01-12/01
	Louisville MSA, KY-IN	H	11.24 FQ	15.00 AW	20.08 TQ	KYBLS	10/01-12/01
	Louisiana	H	9.08 FQ	13.02 AW	17.19 TQ	LABLS	10/01-12/01
	Baton Rouge MSA, LA	H	9.40 FQ	12.40 AW	16.68 TQ	LABLS	10/01-12/01
	Lafayette MSA, LA	H	9.78 FQ	13.28 AW	17.28 TQ	LABLS	10/01-12/01
	New Orleans MSA, LA	H	6.31 FQ	12.54 AW	17.13 TQ	LABLS	10/01-12/01
	Shreveport-Bossier City MSA, LA	H	11.45 FQ	13.54 AW	16.61 TQ	LABLS	10/01-12/01
	Maine	H	7.33 FQ	14.09 AW	19.87 TQ	MEBLS	10/01-12/01
	Portland MSA, ME	H	11.96 FQ	15.77 AW	20.99 TQ	MEBLS	10/01-12/01
	Maryland	H	9.54 FQ	14.36 AW	19.57 TQ	MDBLS	10/01-12/01
	Baltimore PMSA, MD	H	9.00 FQ	12.35 AW	18.15 TQ	MDBLS	10/01-12/01
	Massachusetts	H	13.15 FQ	21.44 AW	28.42 TQ	MABLS	10/01-12/01
	Boston PMSA, MA-NH	H	13.53 FQ	22.60 AW	29.28 TQ	MABLS	10/01-12/01
	Lowell PMSA, MA-NH	H	12.97 FQ	20.66 AW	27.20 TQ	MABLS	10/01-12/01
	New Bedford PMSA, MA	H	9.97 FQ	16.31 AW	24.60 TQ	MABLS	10/01-12/01
	Worcester PMSA, MA-CT	H	15.38 FQ	19.06 AW	22.38 TQ	MABLS	10/01-12/01
	Michigan	H	11.56 FQ	18.78 AW	27.05 TQ	MIBLS	10/01-12/01
	Ann Arbor PMSA, MI	H	19.71 FQ	25.52 AW	32.05 TQ	MIBLS	10/01-12/01
	Detroit PMSA, MI	H	12.83 FQ	21.73 AW	27.92 TQ	MIBLS	10/01-12/01

AAW	Average annual wage	**AOH**	Average offered, high	**ASH**	Average starting, high	**H**	Hourly	**M**	Monthly	**S**	Special: hourly and annual
AE	Average entry wage	**AOL**	Average offered, low	**ASL**	Average starting, low	**HI**	Highest wage paid	**MTC**	Median total compensation	**TQ**	Third quartile wage
AEX	Average experienced wage	**APH**	Average pay, high range	**AW**	Average wage paid	**HR**	High end range	**MW**	Median wage paid	**W**	Weekly
AO	Average offered	**APL**	Average pay, low range	**FQ**	First quartile wage	**LR**	Low end range	**SQ**	Second quartile wage	**Y**	Yearly

Occupation/Type/Industry	Location	Per	Low	Mid	High	Source	Date
Drywall and Ceiling Tile Installer	Grand Rapids-Muskegon-Holland MSA, MI	H	12.82 FQ	15.61 AW	19.82 TQ	MIBLS	10/01-12/01
	Minnesota	H	14.49 FQ	22.40 AW	30.62 TQ	MNBLS	10/01-12/01
	Minneapolis-St. Paul MSA, MN-WI	H	16.01 FQ	23.90 AW	31.80 TQ	MNBLS	10/01-12/01
	St. Cloud MSA, MN	H	11.63 FQ	18.36 AW	26.38 TQ	MNBLS	10/01-12/01
	Mississippi	H	8.16 FQ	12.09 AW	17.18 TQ	MSBLS	10/01-12/01
	Biloxi-Gulfport-Pascagoula MSA, MS	H	6.34 FQ	14.12 AW	19.18 TQ	MSBLS	10/01-12/01
	Missouri	H	10.38 FQ	19.80 AW	30.15 TQ	MOBLS	10/01-12/01
	Kansas City MSA, MO-KS	H	12.69 FQ	19.59 AW	26.82 TQ	MOBLS	10/01-12/01
	St. Louis MSA, MO-IL	H	17.32 FQ	25.14 AW	32.88 TQ	MOBLS	10/01-12/01
	Springfield MSA, MO	H	9.34 FQ	13.02 AW	17.56 TQ	MOBLS	10/01-12/01
	Montana	H	11.88 FQ	16.21 AW	21.74 TQ	MTBLS	10/01-12/01
	Billings MSA, MT	H	14.23 FQ	17.50 AW	23.68 TQ	MTBLS	10/01-12/01
	Nebraska	H	10.24 FQ	15.09 AW	20.99 TQ	NEBLS	10/01-12/01
	Lincoln MSA, NE	H	10.11 FQ	14.38 AW	18.47 TQ	NEBLS	10/01-12/01
	Omaha MSA, NE-IA	H	12.70 FQ	17.27 AW	22.37 TQ	NEBLS	10/01-12/01
	Nevada	H	11.65 FQ	17.07 AW	25.33 TQ	NVBLS	10/01-12/01
	Las Vegas MSA, NV-AZ	H	10.26 FQ	16.72 AW	26.51 TQ	NVBLS	10/01-12/01
	Reno MSA, NV	H	12.20 FQ	15.78 AW	20.66 TQ	NVBLS	10/01-12/01
	New Hampshire	H	10.83 FQ	16.69 AW	22.17 TQ	NHBLS	10/01-12/01
	Manchester PMSA, NH	H	8.50 FQ	14.41 AW	20.85 TQ	NHBLS	10/01-12/01
	Nashua PMSA, NH	H	14.51 FQ	19.15 AW	26.67 TQ	NHBLS	10/01-12/01
	Portsmouth-Rochester PMSA, NH-ME	H	9.84 FQ	12.57 AW	14.46 TQ	NHBLS	10/01-12/01
	New Jersey	H	10.93 FQ	21.28 AW	33.56 TQ	NJBLS	10/01-12/01
	Atlantic-Cape May PMSA, NJ	H	11.18 FQ	15.70 AW	22.23 TQ	NJBLS	10/01-12/01
	Bergen-Passaic PMSA, NJ	H	15.05 FQ	25.46 AW	34.60 TQ	NJBLS	10/01-12/01
	Middlesex-Somerset-Hunterdon PMSA, NJ	H	16.64 FQ	26.62 AW	34.98 TQ	NJBLS	10/01-12/01
	Monmouth-Ocean PMSA, NJ	H	10.21 FQ	19.95 AW	32.48 TQ	NJBLS	10/01-12/01
	Newark PMSA, NJ	H	10.20 FQ	18.37 AW	33.32 TQ	NJBLS	10/01-12/01
	New Mexico	H	9.20 FQ	13.89 AW	20.76 TQ	NMBLS	10/01-12/01
	Albuquerque MSA, NM	H	9.17 FQ	14.29 AW	21.12 TQ	NMBLS	10/01-12/01
	New York	H	12.99 FQ	26.13 AW	46.83 TQ	NYBLS	10/01-12/01
	Albany-Schenectady-Troy MSA, NY	H	17.78 FQ	21.77 AW	27.72 TQ	NYBLS	10/01-12/01
	Buffalo-Niagara Falls MSA, NY	H	9.13 FQ	14.97 AW	24.51 TQ	NYBLS	10/01-12/01
	Nassau-Suffolk PMSA, NY	H	17.58 FQ	27.16 AW	35.13 TQ	NYBLS	10/01-12/01
	New York PMSA, NY	H	13.64 FQ	31.30 AW	52.94 TQ	NYBLS	10/01-12/01
	Rochester MSA, NY	H	12.18 FQ	18.68 AW	25.55 TQ	NYBLS	10/01-12/01
	Syracuse MSA, NY	H	11.43 FQ	18.06 AW	22.23 TQ	NYBLS	10/01-12/01
	North Carolina	H	9.31 FQ	13.58 AW	18.69 TQ	NCBLS	10/01-12/01
	Asheville MSA, NC	H	9.06 FQ	12.38 AW	15.89 TQ	NCBLS	10/01-12/01
	Charlotte-Gastonia-Rock Hill MSA, NC-SC	H	9.43 FQ	14.12 AW	20.03 TQ	NCBLS	10/01-12/01
	Greensboro-Winston-Salem-High Point MSA, NC	H	10.96 FQ	14.13 AW	18.46 TQ	NCBLS	10/01-12/01
	Raleigh-Durham-Chapel Hill MSA, NC	H	8.96 FQ	13.03 AW	17.17 TQ	NCBLS	10/01-12/01
	Wilmington MSA, NC	H	9.03 FQ	12.21 AW	16.19 TQ	NCBLS	10/01-12/01
	North Dakota	H	11.90 FQ	19.84 AW	25.97 TQ	NDBLS	10/01-12/01
	Fargo-Moorhead MSA, ND-MN	H	14.82 FQ	20.38 AW	25.99 TQ	NDBLS	10/01-12/01
	Ohio	H	6.99 FQ	15.74 AW	23.59 TQ	OHBLS	10/01-12/01
	Akron PMSA, OH	H	6.55 FQ	14.21 AW	21.20 TQ	OHBLS	10/01-12/01
	Canton-Massillon MSA, OH	H	12.17 FQ	18.91 AW	24.70 TQ	OHBLS	10/01-12/01
	Cincinnati PMSA, OH-KY-IN	H	10.72 FQ	17.23 AW	22.03 TQ	OHBLS	10/01-12/01
	Cleveland-Lorain-Elyria PMSA, OH	H	9.91 FQ	15.98 AW	24.46 TQ	OHBLS	10/01-12/01
	Columbus MSA, OH	H	5.82 FQ	11.48 AW	18.22 TQ	OHBLS	10/01-12/01
	Dayton-Springfield MSA, OH	H	9.76 FQ	14.98 AW	20.34 TQ	OHBLS	10/01-12/01
	Hamilton-Middletown PMSA, OH	H	11.32 FQ	14.97 AW	18.69 TQ	OHBLS	10/01-12/01
	Toledo MSA, OH	H	9.30 FQ	18.25 AW	26.70 TQ	OHBLS	10/01-12/01
	Youngstown-Warren MSA, OH	H	10.39 FQ	20.63 AW	32.20 TQ	OHBLS	10/01-12/01
	Oklahoma	H	10.76 FQ	14.59 AW	18.98 TQ	OKBLS	10/01-12/01
	Oklahoma City MSA, OK	H	11.39 FQ	14.68 AW	18.11 TQ	OKBLS	10/01-12/01
	Tulsa MSA, OK	H	11.68 FQ	15.29 AW	19.77 TQ	OKBLS	10/01-12/01
	Oregon	H	11.67 FQ	19.96 AW	28.61 TQ	ORBLS	10/01-12/01

AAW	Average annual wage	**AOH**	Average offered, high	**ASH**	Average starting, high	**H**	Hourly	**M**	Monthly	**S**	Special: hourly and annual
AE	Average entry wage	**AOL**	Average offered, low	**ASL**	Average starting, low	**HI**	Highest wage paid	**MTC**	Median total compensation	**TQ**	Third quartile wage
AEX	Average experienced wage	**APH**	Average pay, high range	**AW**	Average wage paid	**HR**	High end range	**MW**	Median wage paid	**W**	Weekly
AO	Average offered	**APL**	Average pay, low range	**FQ**	First quartile wage	**LR**	Low end range	**SQ**	Second quartile wage	**Y**	Yearly

Occupation/Type/Industry	Location	Per	Low	Mid	High	Source	Date
Drywall and Ceiling Tile Installer	Eugene-Springfield MSA, OR	H	15.88 FQ	21.18 AW	27.35 TQ	ORBLS	10/01-12/01
	Medford-Ashland MSA, OR	H	8.52 FQ	19.55 AW	34.03 TQ	ORBLS	10/01-12/01
	Portland-Vancouver PMSA, OR-WA	H	12.44 FQ	20.31 AW	28.06 TQ	ORBLS	10/01-12/01
	Salem PMSA, OR	H	10.01 FQ	22.49 AW	34.27 TQ	ORBLS	10/01-12/01
	Pennsylvania	H	9.08 FQ	17.23 AW	28.24 TQ	PABLS	10/01-12/01
	Allentown-Bethlehem-Easton MSA, PA	H	11.16 FQ	16.30 AW	21.96 TQ	PABLS	10/01-12/01
	Harrisburg-Lebanon-Carlisle MSA, PA	H	12.42 FQ	17.71 AW	21.72 TQ	PABLS	10/01-12/01
	Lancaster MSA, PA	H	6.19 FQ	13.80 AW	21.83 TQ	PABLS	10/01-12/01
	Philadelphia PMSA, PA-NJ	H	12.15 FQ	23.04 AW	33.11 TQ	PABLS	10/01-12/01
	Pittsburgh MSA, PA	H	8.16 FQ	13.19 AW	21.01 TQ	PABLS	10/01-12/01
	Rhode Island	H	13.84 FQ	18.24 AW	22.44 TQ	RIBLS	10/01-12/01
	Providence-Fall River-Warwick MSA, RI-MA	H	12.02 FQ	18.29 AW	23.49 TQ	RIBLS	10/01-12/01
	South Carolina	H	8.92 FQ	13.25 AW	18.98 TQ	SCBLS	10/01-12/01
	Charleston-North Charleston MSA, SC	H	8.65 FQ	12.10 AW	16.72 TQ	SCBLS	10/01-12/01
	Columbia MSA, SC	H	10.28 FQ	15.57 AW	20.54 TQ	SCBLS	10/01-12/01
	Greenville-Spartanburg-Anderson MSA, SC	H	10.13 FQ	13.60 AW	17.32 TQ	SCBLS	10/01-12/01
	South Dakota	H	9.29 FQ	12.64 AW	17.83 TQ	SDBLS	10/01-12/01
	Sioux Falls MSA, SD	H	9.25 FQ	12.32 AW	18.29 TQ	SDBLS	10/01-12/01
	Tennessee	H	10.80 FQ	14.32 AW	17.61 TQ	TNBLS	10/01-12/01
	Chattanooga MSA, TN-GA	H	11.33 FQ	15.10 AW	17.89 TQ	TNBLS	10/01-12/01
	Johnson City-Kingsport-Bristol MSA, TN-VA	H	9.76 FQ	12.73 AW	16.49 TQ	TNBLS	10/01-12/01
	Knoxville MSA, TN	H	10.27 FQ	12.95 AW	16.42 TQ	TNBLS	10/01-12/01
	Memphis MSA, TN-AR-MS	H	10.19 FQ	15.25 AW	19.00 TQ	TNBLS	10/01-12/01
	Nashville MSA, TN	H	12.43 FQ	15.43 AW	17.82 TQ	TNBLS	10/01-12/01
	Texas	H	8.63 FQ	12.34 AW	16.63 TQ	TXBLS	10/01-12/01
	Amarillo MSA, TX	H	10.16 FQ	13.01 AW	16.68 TQ	TXBLS	10/01-12/01
	Austin-San Marcos MSA, TX	H	9.08 FQ	13.11 AW	17.13 TQ	TXBLS	10/01-12/01
	Beaumont-Port Arthur MSA, TX	H	9.72 FQ	13.49 AW	17.45 TQ	TXBLS	10/01-12/01
	Corpus Christi MSA, TX	H	7.60 FQ	9.53 AW	11.43 TQ	TXBLS	10/01-12/01
	Dallas PMSA, TX	H	9.36 FQ	13.11 AW	17.06 TQ	TXBLS	10/01-12/01
	El Paso MSA, TX	H	9.13 FQ	11.25 AW	15.17 TQ	TXBLS	10/01-12/01
	Fort Worth-Arlington PMSA, TX	H	8.41 FQ	12.28 AW	16.40 TQ	TXBLS	10/01-12/01
	Houston PMSA, TX	H	8.65 FQ	12.67 AW	17.25 TQ	TXBLS	10/01-12/01
	Killeen-Temple MSA, TX	H	5.84 FQ	9.51 AW	15.19 TQ	TXBLS	10/01-12/01
	Lubbock MSA, TX	H	9.23 FQ	12.19 AW	14.52 TQ	TXBLS	10/01-12/01
	McAllen-Edinburg-Mission MSA, TX	H	6.43 FQ	8.24 AW	10.82 TQ	TXBLS	10/01-12/01
	Odessa-Midland MSA, TX	H	6.35 FQ	11.77 AW	15.81 TQ	TXBLS	10/01-12/01
	San Antonio MSA, TX	H	7.67 FQ	10.74 AW	14.39 TQ	TXBLS	10/01-12/01
	Waco MSA, TX	H	10.27 FQ	12.99 AW	16.07 TQ	TXBLS	10/01-12/01
	Utah	H	9.76 FQ	14.54 AW	19.92 TQ	UTBLS	10/01-12/01
	Provo-Orem MSA, UT	H	9.31 FQ	13.84 AW	19.31 TQ	UTBLS	10/01-12/01
	Salt Lake City-Ogden MSA, UT	H	10.05 FQ	15.11 AW	20.58 TQ	UTBLS	10/01-12/01
	Vermont	H	12.04 FQ	16.53 AW	21.16 TQ	VTBLS	10/01-12/01
	Burlington MSA, VT	H	11.52 FQ	15.89 AW	20.55 TQ	VTBLS	10/01-12/01
	Virginia	H	9.02 FQ	14.08 AW	18.19 TQ	VABLS	10/01-12/01
	Norfolk-Virginia Beach-Newport News MSA, VA-NC	H	7.09 FQ	13.40 AW	17.56 TQ	VABLS	10/01-12/01
	Richmond-Petersburg MSA, VA	H	9.33 FQ	13.90 AW	17.55 TQ	VABLS	10/01-12/01
	Roanoke MSA, VA	H	10.26 FQ	13.36 AW	16.96 TQ	VABLS	10/01-12/01
	Washington	H	13.78 FQ	23.70 AW	32.93 TQ	WABLS	10/01-12/01
	Bremerton PMSA, WA	H	15.94 FQ	23.24 AW	34.58 TQ	WABLS	10/01-12/01
	Olympia PMSA, WA	H	14.59 FQ	20.99 AW	29.43 TQ	WABLS	10/01-12/01
	Richland-Kennewick-Pasco MSA, WA	H	17.29 FQ	19.83 AW	22.98 TQ	WABLS	10/01-12/01
	Seattle-Bellevue-Everett PMSA, WA	H	16.81 FQ	25.66 AW	33.77 TQ	WABLS	10/01-12/01
	Spokane MSA, WA	H	12.35 FQ	19.18 AW	27.73 TQ	WABLS	10/01-12/01
	Tacoma PMSA, WA	H	15.53 FQ	22.17 AW	28.76 TQ	WABLS	10/01-12/01
	Yakima MSA, WA	H	12.05 FQ	21.71 AW	32.55 TQ	WABLS	10/01-12/01

AAW Average annual wage; AE Average entry wage; AEX Average experienced wage; AO Average offered; AOH Average offered, high; AOL Average offered, low; APH Average pay, high range; APL Average pay, low range; ASH Average starting, high; ASL Average starting, low; AW Average wage paid; FQ First quartile wage; H Hourly; HI Highest wage paid; HR High end range; LR Low end range; M Monthly; MTC Median total compensation; MW Median wage paid; SQ Second quartile wage; S Special: hourly and annual; TQ Third quartile wage; W Weekly; Y Yearly

Occupation/Type/Industry	Location	Per	Low	Mid	High	Source	Date
Drywall and Ceiling Tile Installer	West Virginia	H	8.34 FQ	15.78 AW	26.06 TQ	WVBLS	10/01-12/01
	Huntington-Ashland MSA, WV-KY-OH	H	7.25 FQ	9.37 AW	13.01 TQ	WVBLS	10/01-12/01
	Wisconsin	H	12.60 FQ	20.28 AW	27.08 TQ	WIBLS	10/01-12/01
	Appleton-Oshkosh-Neenah MSA, WI	H	14.23 FQ	19.26 AW	24.53 TQ	WIBLS	10/01-12/01
	Green Bay MSA, WI	H	10.18 FQ	17.16 AW	25.01 TQ	WIBLS	10/01-12/01
	Madison MSA, WI	H	14.23 FQ	21.44 AW	27.36 TQ	WIBLS	10/01-12/01
	Milwaukee-Waukesha PMSA, WI	H	17.62 FQ	22.99 AW	27.84 TQ	WIBLS	10/01-12/01
	Wyoming	H	9.17 FQ	13.69 AW	18.96 TQ	WYBLS	10/01-12/01
	Puerto Rico	H	6.00 FQ	10.68 AW	18.57 TQ	PRBLS	10/01-12/01
E-Mail Administrator							
Internet and E-Commerce	United States	Y		47000-67250 AW		IW	1/00-1/01
E-Procurement Manager and Analyst	United States	Y		64100 AW		INFO4	1/01-1/02
Earth Driller							
Except Oil and Gas	Alabama	H	8.24 FQ	14.27 AW	23.51 TQ	ALBLS	10/01-12/01
Except Oil and Gas	Alaska	H	14.93 FQ	24.34 AW	37.06 TQ	AKBLS	10/01-12/01
Except Oil and Gas	Arizona	H	9.49 FQ	15.33 AW	20.96 TQ	AZBLS	10/01-12/01
Except Oil and Gas	Arkansas	H	9.35 FQ	12.73 AW	16.97 TQ	ARBLS	10/01-12/01
Except Oil and Gas	California	H	11.28 FQ	19.51 AW	31.34 TQ	CABLS	10/01-12/01
Except Oil and Gas	Colorado	H	11.22 FQ	17.35 AW	26.17 TQ	COBLS	10/01-12/01
Except Oil and Gas	Connecticut	H	14.23 FQ	17.78 AW	23.13 TQ	CTBLS	10/01-12/01
Except Oil and Gas	Florida	H	9.06 FQ	13.13 AW	18.17 TQ	FLBLS	10/01-12/01
Except Oil and Gas	Georgia	H	9.29 FQ	14.83 AW	19.84 TQ	GABLS	10/01-12/01
Except Oil and Gas	Hawaii	H	18.56 FQ	25.96 AW	38.40 TQ	HIBLS	10/01-12/01
Except Oil and Gas	Idaho	H	12.97 FQ	18.05 AW	24.14 TQ	IDBLS	10/01-12/01
Except Oil and Gas	Illinois	H	11.16 FQ	18.74 AW	27.18 TQ	ILBLS	10/01-12/01
Except Oil and Gas	Indiana	H	8.90 FQ	15.06 AW	21.26 TQ	INBLS	10/01-12/01
Except Oil and Gas	Iowa	H	9.83 FQ	15.01 AW	21.33 TQ	IABLS	10/01-12/01
Except Oil and Gas	Kansas	H	9.46 FQ	13.12 AW	17.91 TQ	KSBLS	10/01-12/01
Except Oil and Gas	Kentucky	H	10.22 FQ	13.51 AW	18.40 TQ	KYBLS	10/01-12/01
Except Oil and Gas	Louisiana	H	10.77 FQ	18.20 AW	22.46 TQ	LABLS	10/01-12/01
Except Oil and Gas	Maine	H	9.81 FQ	13.93 AW	17.83 TQ	MEBLS	10/01-12/01
Except Oil and Gas	Maryland	H	9.80 FQ	15.69 AW	20.94 TQ	MDBLS	10/01-12/01
Except Oil and Gas	Massachusetts	H	18.23 FQ	24.43 AW	31.83 TQ	MABLS	10/01-12/01
Except Oil and Gas	Michigan	H	9.50 FQ	16.58 AW	26.00 TQ	MIBLS	10/01-12/01
Except Oil and Gas	Minnesota	H	11.51 FQ	16.63 AW	21.50 TQ	MNBLS	10/01-12/01
Except Oil and Gas	Mississippi	H	9.66 FQ	12.75 AW	15.96 TQ	MSBLS	10/01-12/01
Except Oil and Gas	Missouri	H	9.29 FQ	14.49 AW	20.10 TQ	MOBLS	10/01-12/01
Except Oil and Gas	Montana	H	11.10 FQ	16.03 AW	22.29 TQ	MTBLS	10/01-12/01
Except Oil and Gas	Nebraska	H	8.91 FQ	13.19 AW	17.87 TQ	NEBLS	10/01-12/01
Except Oil and Gas	Nevada	H	11.03 FQ	18.23 AW	22.01 TQ	NVBLS	10/01-12/01
Except Oil and Gas	New Hampshire	H	12.00 FQ	17.21 AW	23.06 TQ	NHBLS	10/01-12/01
Except Oil and Gas	New Jersey	H	13.48 FQ	21.61 AW	32.43 TQ	NJBLS	10/01-12/01
Except Oil and Gas	New Mexico	H	9.74 FQ	17.20 AW	21.96 TQ	NMBLS	10/01-12/01
Except Oil and Gas	New York	H	10.50 FQ	17.45 AW	26.68 TQ	NYBLS	10/01-12/01
Except Oil and Gas	North Carolina	H	10.46 FQ	14.73 AW	19.53 TQ	NCBLS	10/01-12/01
Except Oil and Gas	North Dakota	H	13.83 FQ	16.83 AW	24.76 TQ	NDBLS	10/01-12/01
Except Oil and Gas	Ohio	H	9.75 FQ	16.46 AW	26.68 TQ	OHBLS	10/01-12/01
Except Oil and Gas	Oklahoma	H	7.99 FQ	13.00 AW	18.71 TQ	OKBLS	10/01-12/01
Except Oil and Gas	Oregon	H	11.86 FQ	18.57 AW	29.09 TQ	ORBLS	10/01-12/01
Except Oil and Gas	Pennsylvania	H	9.57 FQ	14.30 AW	20.08 TQ	PABLS	10/01-12/01
Except Oil and Gas	South Carolina	H	8.82 FQ	13.49 AW	19.18 TQ	SCBLS	10/01-12/01
Except Oil and Gas	South Dakota	H	10.44 FQ	14.82 AW	20.37 TQ	SDBLS	10/01-12/01
Except Oil and Gas	Tennessee	H	6.83 FQ	11.46 AW	18.36 TQ	TNBLS	10/01-12/01
Except Oil and Gas	Texas	H	8.92 FQ	13.91 AW	19.68 TQ	TXBLS	10/01-12/01
Except Oil and Gas	Utah	H	10.87 FQ	16.47 AW	22.49 TQ	UTBLS	10/01-12/01
Except Oil and Gas	Vermont	H	11.34 FQ	13.90 AW	17.21 TQ	VTBLS	10/01-12/01
Except Oil and Gas	Virginia	H	9.58 FQ	16.00 AW	24.61 TQ	VABLS	10/01-12/01
Except Oil and Gas	Washington	H	10.31 FQ	17.48 AW	25.10 TQ	WABLS	10/01-12/01
Except Oil and Gas	West Virginia	H	9.72 FQ	16.58 AW	25.23 TQ	WVBLS	10/01-12/01
Except Oil and Gas	Wisconsin	H	12.95 FQ	18.10 AW	24.77 TQ	WIBLS	10/01-12/01
Except Oil and Gas	Wyoming	H	10.56 FQ	16.94 AW	25.90 TQ	WYBLS	10/01-12/01
Except Oil and Gas	Puerto Rico	H	5.80 FQ	9.16 AW	15.81 TQ	PRBLS	10/01-12/01
Economics Teacher							
Postsecondary	Alabama	Y	17400 FQ	54210 AW	89090 TQ	ALBLS	10/01-12/01

AAW	Average annual wage	AOH	Average offered, high	ASH	Average starting, high	H	Hourly	M	Monthly	S	Special: hourly and annual
AE	Average entry wage	AOL	Average offered, low	ASL	Average starting, low	HI	Highest wage paid	MTC	Median total compensation	TQ	Third quartile wage
AEX	Average experienced wage	APH	Average pay, high range	AW	Average wage paid	HR	High end range	MW	Median wage paid	W	Weekly
AO	Average offered	APL	Average pay, low range	FQ	First quartile wage	LR	Low end range	SQ	Second quartile wage	Y	Yearly

Occupation/Type/Industry	Location	Per	Low	Mid	High	Source	Date
Economics Teacher							
Postsecondary	Arizona	Y	25420 FQ	56450 AW	118870 TQ	AZBLS	10/01-12/01
Postsecondary	California	Y	46870 FQ	70670 AW	106050 TQ	CABLS	10/01-12/01
Postsecondary	Los Angeles-Long Beach PMSA, CA	Y	48020 FQ	77740 AW	125380 TQ	CABLS	10/01-12/01
Postsecondary	San Diego MSA, CA	Y	47080 FQ	60600 AW	85910 TQ	CABLS	10/01-12/01
Postsecondary	San Francisco PMSA, CA	Y	50690 FQ	70150 AW	97750 TQ	CABLS	10/01-12/01
Postsecondary	Colorado	Y	32530 FQ	61620 AW	92710 TQ	COBLS	10/01-12/01
Postsecondary	Denver PMSA, CO	Y	31740 FQ	60230 AW	91990 TQ	COBLS	10/01-12/01
Postsecondary	Connecticut	Y	36750 FQ	68470 AW	103010 TQ	CTBLS	10/01-12/01
Postsecondary	District of Columbia	Y	39070 FQ	61850 AW	89160 TQ	DCBLS	10/01-12/01
Postsecondary	Washington PMSA, DC-MD-VA-WV	Y	36930 FQ	68850 AW	118990 TQ	DCBLS	10/01-12/01
Postsecondary	Florida	Y	42780 FQ	76340 AW	126360 TQ	FLBLS	10/01-12/01
Postsecondary	Gainesville MSA, FL	Y	53330 FQ	95410 AW		FLBLS	10/01-12/01
Postsecondary	Miami PMSA, FL	Y	47910 FQ	71100 AW	101350 TQ	FLBLS	10/01-12/01
Postsecondary	Orlando MSA, FL	Y	28590 FQ	66910 AW	108270 TQ	FLBLS	10/01-12/01
Postsecondary	Tallahassee MSA, FL	Y	52810 FQ	83110 AW	131600 TQ	FLBLS	10/01-12/01
Postsecondary	Tampa-St. Petersburg-Clearwater MSA, FL	Y	40520 FQ	72930 AW	110870 TQ	FLBLS	10/01-12/01
Postsecondary	Georgia	Y	37900 FQ	65520 AW	93980 TQ	GABLS	10/01-12/01
Postsecondary	Atlanta MSA, GA	Y	45090 FQ	70310 AW	108250 TQ	GABLS	10/01-12/01
Postsecondary	Hawaii	Y	41420 FQ	63970 AW	89320 TQ	HIBLS	10/01-12/01
Postsecondary	Honolulu MSA, HI	Y	41880 FQ	64970 AW	90360 TQ	HIBLS	10/01-12/01
Postsecondary	Illinois	Y	17920 FQ	63250 AW	96750 TQ	ILBLS	10/01-12/01
Postsecondary	Champaign-Urbana MSA, IL	Y	14130 FQ	64000 AW	95920 TQ	ILBLS	10/01-12/01
Postsecondary	Chicago PMSA, IL	Y	24390 FQ	63200 AW	97840 TQ	ILBLS	10/01-12/01
Postsecondary	Indiana	Y	33850 FQ	61940 AW	97330 TQ	INBLS	10/01-12/01
Postsecondary	South Bend MSA, IN	Y	44280 FQ	56430 AW	70890 TQ	INBLS	10/01-12/01
Postsecondary	Iowa	Y	40930 FQ	74570 AW		IABLS	10/01-12/01
Postsecondary	Kansas	Y	23210 FQ	60720 AW	100110 TQ	KSBLS	10/01-12/01
Postsecondary	Kentucky	Y	40080 FQ	72080 AW	110850 TQ	KYBLS	10/01-12/01
Postsecondary	Louisiana	Y	34480 FQ	58840 AW	87480 TQ	LABLS	10/01-12/01
Postsecondary	Maine	Y	38960 FQ	63590 AW	93030 TQ	MEBLS	10/01-12/01
Postsecondary	Maryland	Y	37360 FQ	71670 AW	122240 TQ	MDBLS	10/01-12/01
Postsecondary	Baltimore PMSA, MD	Y	34930 FQ	62490 AW	94080 TQ	MDBLS	10/01-12/01
Postsecondary	Massachusetts	Y	34900 FQ	67960 AW	113050 TQ	MABLS	10/01-12/01
Postsecondary	Boston PMSA, MA-NH	Y	34230 FQ	69540 AW	115810 TQ	MABLS	10/01-12/01
Postsecondary	Springfield MSA, MA	Y	45440 FQ	66740 AW	98920 TQ	MABLS	10/01-12/01
Postsecondary	Worcester PMSA, MA-CT	Y	33620 FQ	66320 AW	110370 TQ	MABLS	10/01-12/01
Postsecondary	Michigan	Y	42920 FQ	73410 AW	111230 TQ	MIBLS	10/01-12/01
Postsecondary	Minnesota	Y	42740 FQ	66920 AW	110490 TQ	MNBLS	10/01-12/01
Postsecondary	Minneapolis-St. Paul MSA, MN-WI	Y	44640 FQ	74060 AW	121160 TQ	MNBLS	10/01-12/01
Postsecondary	Mississippi	Y	32400 FQ	51390 AW	79900 TQ	MSBLS	10/01-12/01
Postsecondary	Missouri	Y	34710 FQ	58350 AW	76920 TQ	MOBLS	10/01-12/01
Postsecondary	Kansas City MSA, MO-KS	Y	22690 FQ	47830 AW	74490 TQ	MOBLS	10/01-12/01
Postsecondary	St. Louis MSA, MO-IL	Y	35270 FQ	58930 AW	77500 TQ	MOBLS	10/01-12/01
Postsecondary	Nebraska	Y	38090 FQ	72680 AW	110140 TQ	NEBLS	10/01-12/01
Postsecondary	Nevada	Y	21800 FQ	61040 AW	100690 TQ	NVBLS	10/01-12/01
Postsecondary	Las Vegas MSA, NV-AZ	Y	20110 FQ	50440 AW	89030 TQ	NVBLS	10/01-12/01
Postsecondary	New Hampshire	Y	48430 FQ	75600 AW	115010 TQ	NHBLS	10/01-12/01
Postsecondary	New Jersey	Y	35850 FQ	68370 AW	108330 TQ	NJBLS	10/01-12/01
Postsecondary	Jersey City PMSA, NJ	Y	34450 FQ	64830 AW	97070 TQ	NJBLS	10/01-12/01
Postsecondary	Newark PMSA, NJ	Y	34330 FQ	61550 AW	90310 TQ	NJBLS	10/01-12/01
Postsecondary	New Mexico	Y	36090 FQ	56330 AW	77130 TQ	NMBLS	10/01-12/01
Postsecondary	New York	Y	47600 FQ	74210 AW	111770 TQ	NYBLS	10/01-12/01
Postsecondary	New York PMSA, NY	Y	51730 FQ	76260 AW	111380 TQ	NYBLS	10/01-12/01
Postsecondary	North Carolina	Y	36990 FQ	63270 AW	93420 TQ	NCBLS	10/01-12/01
Postsecondary	Charlotte-Gastonia-Rock Hill MSA, NC-SC	Y	39110 FQ	61210 AW	89350 TQ	NCBLS	10/01-12/01
Postsecondary	Greensboro-Winston-Salem-High Point MSA, NC	Y	27900 FQ	58840 AW	88270 TQ	NCBLS	10/01-12/01
Postsecondary	Raleigh-Durham-Chapel Hill MSA, NC	Y	38650 FQ	73390 AW	118320 TQ	NCBLS	10/01-12/01
Postsecondary	North Dakota	Y	35820 FQ	54840 AW	92000 TQ	NDBLS	10/01-12/01
Postsecondary	Ohio	Y	34030 FQ	62090 AW	91980 TQ	OHBLS	10/01-12/01
Postsecondary	Cincinnati PMSA, OH-KY-IN	Y	38570 FQ	67120 AW	96370 TQ	OHBLS	10/01-12/01
Postsecondary	Cleveland-Lorain-Elyria PMSA, OH	Y	43430 FQ	71110 AW	102060 TQ	OHBLS	10/01-12/01
Postsecondary	Columbus MSA, OH	Y	31230 FQ	59890 AW	94150 TQ	OHBLS	10/01-12/01
Postsecondary	Dayton-Springfield MSA, OH	Y	22870 FQ	55540 AW	93000 TQ	OHBLS	10/01-12/01

AAW	Average annual wage	**AOH**	Average offered, high	**ASH**	Average starting, high	**H**	Hourly	**M**	Monthly	**S**	Special: hourly and annual
AE	Average entry wage	**AOL**	Average offered, low	**ASL**	Average starting, low	**HI**	Highest wage paid	**MTC**	Median total compensation	**TQ**	Third quartile wage
AEX	Average experienced wage	**APH**	Average pay, high range	**AW**	Average wage paid	**HR**	High end range	**MW**	Median wage paid	**W**	Weekly
AO	Average offered	**APL**	Average pay, low range	**FQ**	First quartile wage	**LR**	Low end range	**SQ**	Second quartile wage	**Y**	Yearly

Occupation/Type/Industry	Location	Per	Low	Mid	High	Source	Date
Economics Teacher							
Postsecondary	Oklahoma	Y	23820 FQ	43040 AW	71920 TQ	OKBLS	10/01-12/01
Postsecondary	Oklahoma City MSA, OK	Y	22700 FQ	35540 AW	65920 TQ	OKBLS	10/01-12/01
Postsecondary	Oregon	Y	49320 FQ	76050 AW	107740 TQ	ORBLS	10/01-12/01
Postsecondary	Portland-Vancouver PMSA, OR-WA	Y	38130 FQ	68720 AW	103450 TQ	ORBLS	10/01-12/01
Postsecondary	Pennsylvania	Y	38240 FQ	72100 AW	122440 TQ	PABLS	10/01-12/01
Postsecondary	Allentown-Bethlehem-Easton MSA, PA	Y	31080 FQ	55770 AW	76280 TQ	PABLS	10/01-12/01
Postsecondary	Philadelphia PMSA, PA-NJ	Y	39680 FQ	74590 AW	125240 TQ	PABLS	10/01-12/01
Postsecondary	Pittsburgh MSA, PA	Y	36010 FQ	69930 AW	127410 TQ	PABLS	10/01-12/01
Postsecondary	Scranton-Wilkes-Barre-Hazleton MSA, PA	Y	30220 FQ	59550 AW	88200 TQ	PABLS	10/01-12/01
Postsecondary	Rhode Island	Y	37160 FQ	65960 AW	94710 TQ	RIBLS	10/01-12/01
Postsecondary	South Carolina	Y	25360 FQ	53290 AW	85560 TQ	SCBLS	10/01-12/01
Postsecondary	Tennessee	Y	34680 FQ	64750 AW	107610 TQ	TNBLS	10/01-12/01
Postsecondary	Nashville MSA, TN	Y	46030 FQ	75100 AW	124600 TQ	TNBLS	10/01-12/01
Postsecondary	Texas	Y	32930 FQ	64800 AW	116770 TQ	TXBLS	10/01-12/01
Postsecondary	Austin-San Marcos MSA, TX	Y	45350 FQ	62810 AW	76210 TQ	TXBLS	10/01-12/01
Postsecondary	Dallas PMSA, TX	Y	30930 FQ	71100 AW		TXBLS	10/01-12/01
Postsecondary	Fort Worth-Arlington PMSA, TX	Y	29150 FQ	51750 AW	76960 TQ	TXBLS	10/01-12/01
Postsecondary	Houston PMSA, TX	Y	39960 FQ	73990 AW	138780 TQ	TXBLS	10/01-12/01
Postsecondary	San Antonio MSA, TX	Y	37320 FQ	66690 AW	116250 TQ	TXBLS	10/01-12/01
Postsecondary	Utah	Y	42120 FQ	75440 AW	110870 TQ	UTBLS	10/01-12/01
Postsecondary	Vermont	Y	42220 FQ	56580 AW	81150 TQ	VTBLS	10/01-12/01
Postsecondary	Virginia	Y	28830 FQ	65670 AW	108560 TQ	VABLS	10/01-12/01
Postsecondary	Norfolk-Virginia Beach-Newport News MSA, VA-NC	Y	40580 FQ	71120 AW	110840 TQ	VABLS	10/01-12/01
Postsecondary	Richmond-Petersburg MSA, VA	Y	27510 FQ	65750 AW	100780 TQ	VABLS	10/01-12/01
Postsecondary	Washington	Y	23820 FQ	61090 AW	108180 TQ	WABLS	10/01-12/01
Postsecondary	Seattle-Bellevue-Everett PMSA, WA	Y	32470 FQ	64130 AW	122770 TQ	WABLS	10/01-12/01
Postsecondary	West Virginia	Y	35230 FQ	60830 AW	90000 TQ	WVBLS	10/01-12/01
Postsecondary	Wisconsin	Y	30890 FQ	62160 AW	98620 TQ	WIBLS	10/01-12/01
Postsecondary	Milwaukee-Waukesha PMSA, WI	Y	24940 FQ	56820 AW	90030 TQ	WIBLS	10/01-12/01
Postsecondary	Puerto Rico	Y	23940 FQ	42430 AW	76700 TQ	PRBLS	10/01-12/01
Economist	Alabama	Y	36890 FQ	61780 AW	90080 TQ	ALBLS	10/01-12/01
	Alaska	Y	36180 FQ	66280 AW	107160 TQ	AKBLS	10/01-12/01
	Anchorage MSA, AK	Y	35300 FQ	67910 AW	108370 TQ	AKBLS	10/01-12/01
	Arizona	Y	33410 FQ	64250 AW	96590 TQ	AZBLS	10/01-12/01
	Phoenix-Mesa MSA, AZ	Y	36820 FQ	66160 AW	97370 TQ	AZBLS	10/01-12/01
	Arkansas	Y	33570 FQ	54580 AW	74560 TQ	ARBLS	10/01-12/01
	Little Rock-North Little Rock MSA, AR	Y	31240 FQ	52450 AW	77840 TQ	ARBLS	10/01-12/01
	California	Y	48950 FQ	98710 AW		CABLS	10/01-12/01
	Los Angeles-Long Beach PMSA, CA	Y	44620 FQ	72400 AW	118580 TQ	CABLS	10/01-12/01
	Sacramento PMSA, CA	Y	46820 FQ	62520 AW	73910 TQ	CABLS	10/01-12/01
	San Francisco PMSA, CA	Y	38060 FQ	68410 AW	104550 TQ	CABLS	10/01-12/01
	San Jose PMSA, CA	Y	94520 FQ	119270 AW		CABLS	10/01-12/01
	Colorado	Y	43060 FQ	64140 AW	86230 TQ	COBLS	10/01-12/01
	Denver PMSA, CO	Y	42060 FQ	60900 AW	77690 TQ	COBLS	10/01-12/01
	Stamford-Norwalk PMSA, CT	Y	70040 FQ	112340 AW		CTBLS	10/01-12/01
	Delaware	Y	40630 FQ	64820 AW	111070 TQ	DEBLS	10/01-12/01
	Wilmington-Newark PMSA, DE-MD	Y	42340 FQ	73760 AW	133060 TQ	DEBLS	10/01-12/01
	District of Columbia	Y	44000 FQ	76780 AW	112450 TQ	DCBLS	10/01-12/01
	Washington PMSA, DC-MD-VA-WV	Y	43430 FQ	77210 AW	112030 TQ	DCBLS	10/01-12/01
	Florida	Y	38640 FQ	64670 AW	104640 TQ	FLBLS	10/01-12/01
	Jacksonville MSA, FL	Y	40730 FQ	53660 AW	68040 TQ	FLBLS	10/01-12/01
	Miami PMSA, FL	Y	48790 FQ	61170 AW	72610 TQ	FLBLS	10/01-12/01
	Tampa-St. Petersburg-Clearwater MSA, FL	Y	31930 FQ	53940 AW	80590 TQ	FLBLS	10/01-12/01
	Georgia	Y	36770 FQ	56930 AW	83990 TQ	GABLS	10/01-12/01
	Atlanta MSA, GA	Y	36730 FQ	57320 AW	84270 TQ	GABLS	10/01-12/01
	Idaho	Y	37040 FQ	50710 AW	69630 TQ	IDBLS	10/01-12/01
	Illinois	Y	34480 FQ	69360 AW		ILBLS	10/01-12/01

AAW	Average annual wage	**AOH**	Average offered, high	**ASH**	Average starting, high	**H**	Hourly	**M**	Monthly	**S**	Special: hourly and annual
AE	Average entry wage	**AOL**	Average offered, low	**ASL**	Average starting, low	**HI**	Highest wage paid	**MTC**	Median total compensation	**TQ**	Third quartile wage
AEX	Average experienced wage	**APH**	Average pay, high range	**AW**	Average wage paid	**HR**	High end range	**MW**	Median wage paid	**W**	Weekly
AO	Average offered	**APL**	Average pay, low range	**FQ**	First quartile wage	**LR**	Low end range	**SQ**	Second quartile wage	**Y**	Yearly

Occupation/Type/Industry	Location	Per	Low	Mid	High	Source	Date
Economist	Chicago PMSA, IL	Y	36020 FQ	71910 AW		ILBLS	10/01-12/01
	Indiana	Y	42440 FQ	62570 AW	96830 TQ	INBLS	10/01-12/01
	Iowa	Y	32320 FQ	47060 AW	70870 TQ	IABLS	10/01-12/01
	Louisiana	Y	38540 FQ	57920 AW	80500 TQ	LABLS	10/01-12/01
	New Orleans MSA, LA	Y	39320 FQ	58600 AW	77440 TQ	LABLS	10/01-12/01
	Maine	Y	30090 FQ	43000 AW	58370 TQ	MEBLS	10/01-12/01
	Maryland	Y	35290 FQ	71740 AW	110400 TQ	MDBLS	10/01-12/01
	Baltimore PMSA, MD	Y	47120 FQ	69580 AW	104930 TQ	MDBLS	10/01-12/01
	Massachusetts	Y	35840 FQ	68000 AW	119540 TQ	MABLS	10/01-12/01
	Boston PMSA, MA-NH	Y	35720 FQ	68310 AW	122330 TQ	MABLS	10/01-12/01
	Michigan	Y	45560 FQ	80700 AW		MIBLS	10/01-12/01
	Detroit PMSA, MI	Y	38420 FQ	65630 AW	106090 TQ	MIBLS	10/01-12/01
	Grand Rapids-Muskegon-Holland MSA, MI	Y	57810 FQ	63460 AW	70480 TQ	MIBLS	10/01-12/01
	Minnesota	Y	36070 FQ	56100 AW	82410 TQ	MNBLS	10/01-12/01
	Minneapolis-St. Paul MSA, MN-WI	Y	36350 FQ	56980 AW	83850 TQ	MNBLS	10/01-12/01
	Mississippi	Y	13250 FQ	57360 AW	92940 TQ	MSBLS	10/01-12/01
	Missouri	Y	39570 FQ	87930 AW		MOBLS	10/01-12/01
	Kansas City MSA, MO-KS	Y	39530 FQ	77770 AW		MOBLS	10/01-12/01
	Montana	Y	34610 FQ	58840 AW	72820 TQ	MTBLS	10/01-12/01
	Nebraska	Y	33390 FQ	60190 AW	88980 TQ	NEBLS	10/01-12/01
	Nevada	Y	38760 FQ	59300 AW	85250 TQ	NVBLS	10/01-12/01
	Middlesex-Somerset-Hunterdon PMSA, NJ	Y	41720 FQ	83270 AW	123290 TQ	NJBLS	10/01-12/01
	New Mexico	Y	33130 FQ	50090 AW	86290 TQ	NMBLS	10/01-12/01
	New York	Y	36440 FQ	75210 AW		NYBLS	10/01-12/01
	Albany-Schenectady-Troy MSA, NY	Y	40640 FQ	59390 AW	83440 TQ	NYBLS	10/01-12/01
	New York PMSA, NY	Y	38590 FQ	84090 AW		NYBLS	10/01-12/01
	North Carolina	Y	34990 FQ	66100 AW	106050 TQ	NCBLS	10/01-12/01
	Charlotte-Gastonia-Rock Hill MSA, NC-SC	Y	48570 FQ	89730 AW		NCBLS	10/01-12/01
	Raleigh-Durham-Chapel Hill MSA, NC	Y	33760 FQ	58740 AW	89260 TQ	NCBLS	10/01-12/01
	Ohio	Y	30680 FQ	57520 AW	87370 TQ	OHBLS	10/01-12/01
	Cleveland-Lorain-Elyria PMSA, OH	Y	32880 FQ	63600 AW	98460 TQ	OHBLS	10/01-12/01
	Columbus MSA, OH	Y	28730 FQ	54500 AW	75250 TQ	OHBLS	10/01-12/01
	Oklahoma	Y	29770 FQ	58040 AW	92590 TQ	OKBLS	10/01-12/01
	Oregon	Y	38920 FQ	67540 AW	128970 TQ	ORBLS	10/01-12/01
	Portland-Vancouver PMSA, OR-WA	Y	40260 FQ	68940 AW	130430 TQ	ORBLS	10/01-12/01
	Pennsylvania	Y	35510 FQ	64530 AW	106770 TQ	PABLS	10/01-12/01
	Philadelphia PMSA, PA-NJ	Y	36800 FQ	64210 AW	104510 TQ	PABLS	10/01-12/01
	Pittsburgh MSA, PA	Y	27550 FQ	57600 AW	85970 TQ	PABLS	10/01-12/01
	Tennessee	Y	29070 FQ	59180 AW	104360 TQ	TNBLS	10/01-12/01
	Memphis MSA, TN-AR-MS	Y	25790 FQ	54060 AW	118940 TQ	TNBLS	10/01-12/01
	Texas	Y	39420 FQ	70830 AW	113750 TQ	TXBLS	10/01-12/01
	Austin-San Marcos MSA, TX	Y	37460 FQ	67940 AW	113070 TQ	TXBLS	10/01-12/01
	Dallas PMSA, TX	Y	49010 FQ	77330 AW	131930 TQ	TXBLS	10/01-12/01
	San Antonio MSA, TX	Y	34810 FQ	59060 AW	94490 TQ	TXBLS	10/01-12/01
	Utah	Y	37720 FQ	51020 AW	69160 TQ	UTBLS	10/01-12/01
	Salt Lake City-Ogden MSA, UT	Y	37420 FQ	50780 AW	71210 TQ	UTBLS	10/01-12/01
	Vermont	Y	37940 FQ	63460 AW	97520 TQ	VTBLS	10/01-12/01
	Burlington MSA, VT	Y	35490 FQ	62490 AW	100940 TQ	VTBLS	10/01-12/01
	Virginia	Y	46160 FQ	75700 AW	103370 TQ	VABLS	10/01-12/01
	Norfolk-Virginia Beach-Newport News MSA, VA-NC	Y	26490 FQ	55800 AW	102850 TQ	VABLS	10/01-12/01
	Washington	Y	42010 FQ	61680 AW	86470 TQ	WABLS	10/01-12/01
	Olympia PMSA, WA	Y	40660 FQ	55330 AW	69450 TQ	WABLS	10/01-12/01
	Seattle-Bellevue-Everett PMSA, WA	Y	41940 FQ	66010 AW	97830 TQ	WABLS	10/01-12/01
	Wisconsin	Y	25740 FQ	52120 AW	87130 TQ	WIBLS	10/01-12/01
	Madison MSA, WI	Y	26020 FQ	54340 AW	94430 TQ	WIBLS	10/01-12/01
	Milwaukee-Waukesha PMSA, WI	Y	26770 FQ	56180 AW	94820 TQ	WIBLS	10/01-12/01
	Wyoming	Y	37370 FQ	46660 AW	55540 TQ	WYBLS	10/01-12/01
	Puerto Rico	Y	18150 FQ	28230 AW	47760 TQ	PRBLS	10/01-12/01
Editor	Alabama	Y	21380 FQ	36220 AW	54610 TQ	ALBLS	10/01-12/01

AAW	Average annual wage	**AOH**	Average offered, high	**ASH**	Average starting, high	**H**	Hourly	**M**	Monthly	**S**	Special: hourly and annual
AE	Average entry wage	**AOL**	Average offered, low	**ASL**	Average starting, low	**HI**	Highest wage paid	**MTC**	Median total compensation	**TQ**	Third quartile wage
AEX	Average experienced wage	**APH**	Average pay, high range	**AW**	Average wage paid	**HR**	High end range	**MW**	Median wage paid	**W**	Weekly
AO	Average offered	**APL**	Average pay, low range	**FQ**	First quartile wage	**LR**	Low end range	**SQ**	Second quartile wage	**Y**	Yearly

Occupation/Type/Industry	Location	Per	Low	Mid	High	Source	Date
Editor	Birmingham MSA, AL	Y	21580 FQ	38300 AW	58010 TQ	ALBLS	10/01-12/01
	Huntsville MSA, AL	Y	21820 FQ	36010 AW	54610 TQ	ALBLS	10/01-12/01
	Mobile MSA, AL	Y	22560 FQ	31350 AW	47720 TQ	ALBLS	10/01-12/01
	Montgomery MSA, AL	Y	22020 FQ	34590 AW	50560 TQ	ALBLS	10/01-12/01
	Alaska	Y	25570 FQ	43890 AW	68280 TQ	AKBLS	10/01-12/01
	Anchorage MSA, AK	Y	29250 FQ	48140 AW	70740 TQ	AKBLS	10/01-12/01
	Arizona	Y	24490 FQ	45650 AW	71510 TQ	AZBLS	10/01-12/01
	Phoenix-Mesa MSA, AZ	Y	27120 FQ	49820 AW	77200 TQ	AZBLS	10/01-12/01
	Tucson MSA, AZ	Y	25040 FQ	42110 AW	63960 TQ	AZBLS	10/01-12/01
	Arkansas	Y	16200 FQ	32790 AW	48660 TQ	ARBLS	10/01-12/01
	Fayetteville-Springdale-Rogers MSA, AR	Y	20340 FQ	28800 AW	38430 TQ	ARBLS	10/01-12/01
	Little Rock-North Little Rock MSA, AR	Y	15940 FQ	37500 AW	61050 TQ	ARBLS	10/01-12/01
	California	Y	25630 FQ	49110 AW	78500 TQ	CABLS	10/01-12/01
	Chico-Paradise MSA, CA	Y	19580 FQ	33700 AW	59020 TQ	CABLS	10/01-12/01
	Fresno MSA, CA	Y	19930 FQ	39970 AW	71970 TQ	CABLS	10/01-12/01
	Los Angeles-Long Beach PMSA, CA	Y	25420 FQ	44690 AW	71890 TQ	CABLS	10/01-12/01
	Modesto MSA, CA	Y	24590 FQ	39720 AW	63730 TQ	CABLS	10/01-12/01
	Oakland PMSA, CA	Y	29880 FQ	49310 AW	79300 TQ	CABLS	10/01-12/01
	Orange County PMSA, CA	Y	28710 FQ	47840 AW	70570 TQ	CABLS	10/01-12/01
	Riverside-San Bernardino PMSA, CA	Y	25660 FQ	44090 AW	68330 TQ	CABLS	10/01-12/01
	Sacramento PMSA, CA	Y	26830 FQ	46530 AW	69150 TQ	CABLS	10/01-12/01
	Salinas MSA, CA	Y	28070 FQ	43570 AW	60720 TQ	CABLS	10/01-12/01
	San Diego MSA, CA	Y	21730 FQ	51650 AW	128260 TQ	CABLS	10/01-12/01
	San Francisco PMSA, CA	Y	30040 FQ	53640 AW	82170 TQ	CABLS	10/01-12/01
	San Jose PMSA, CA	Y	31260 FQ	64050 AW	107650 TQ	CABLS	10/01-12/01
	San Luis Obispo-Atascadero-Paso Robles MSA, CA	Y	27710 FQ	39440 AW	52730 TQ	CABLS	10/01-12/01
	Santa Cruz-Watsonville PMSA, CA	Y	27190 FQ	44330 AW	65100 TQ	CABLS	10/01-12/01
	Santa Rosa PMSA, CA	Y	20520 FQ	50860 AW	83220 TQ	CABLS	10/01-12/01
	Stockton-Lodi MSA, CA	Y	27000 FQ	41440 AW	57100 TQ	CABLS	10/01-12/01
	Vallejo-Fairfield-Napa PMSA, CA	Y	30910 FQ	52060 AW	68990 TQ	CABLS	10/01-12/01
	Ventura PMSA, CA	Y	26430 FQ	44050 AW	66650 TQ	CABLS	10/01-12/01
	Colorado	Y	23760 FQ	40990 AW	65590 TQ	COBLS	10/01-12/01
	Boulder-Longmont PMSA, CO	Y	21580 FQ	32380 AW	51640 TQ	COBLS	10/01-12/01
	Colorado Springs MSA, CO	Y	24090 FQ	39900 AW	58440 TQ	COBLS	10/01-12/01
	Denver PMSA, CO	Y	27150 FQ	47110 AW	70880 TQ	COBLS	10/01-12/01
	Fort Collins-Loveland MSA, CO	Y	24940 FQ	40320 AW	61470 TQ	COBLS	10/01-12/01
	Connecticut	Y	28700 FQ	51910 AW	82140 TQ	CTBLS	10/01-12/01
	Bridgeport PMSA, CT	Y	25330 FQ	52170 AW	89590 TQ	CTBLS	10/01-12/01
	Danbury PMSA, CT	Y	32190 FQ	51750 AW	76190 TQ	CTBLS	10/01-12/01
	Hartford MSA, CT	Y	26100 FQ	48070 AW	77110 TQ	CTBLS	10/01-12/01
	New Haven-Meriden PMSA, CT	Y	14870 FQ	53870 AW	122230 TQ	CTBLS	10/01-12/01
	New London-Norwich MSA, CT-RI	Y	32370 FQ	53250 AW	82030 TQ	CTBLS	10/01-12/01
	Stamford-Norwalk PMSA, CT	Y	33550 FQ	54390 AW	82310 TQ	CTBLS	10/01-12/01
	Waterbury PMSA, CT	Y	27970 FQ	39670 AW	57170 TQ	CTBLS	10/01-12/01
	Delaware	Y	20450 FQ	42560 AW	69000 TQ	DEBLS	10/01-12/01
	Wilmington-Newark PMSA, DE-MD	Y	21310 FQ	40520 AW	61160 TQ	DEBLS	10/01-12/01
	District of Columbia	Y	25800 FQ	50200 AW	74980 TQ	DCBLS	10/01-12/01
	Washington PMSA, DC-MD-VA-WV	Y	27700 FQ	49640 AW	76820 TQ	DCBLS	10/01-12/01
	Florida	Y	20920 FQ	40490 AW	66530 TQ	FLBLS	10/01-12/01
	Daytona Beach MSA, FL	Y	12140 FQ	32200 AW	46130 TQ	FLBLS	10/01-12/01
	Fort Lauderdale PMSA, FL	Y	18560 FQ	32290 AW	54560 TQ	FLBLS	10/01-12/01
	Fort Walton Beach MSA, FL	Y	30500 FQ	50400 AW	86160 TQ	FLBLS	10/01-12/01
	Gainesville MSA, FL	Y	23540 FQ	35170 AW	50300 TQ	FLBLS	10/01-12/01
	Jacksonville MSA, FL	Y	26630 FQ	43420 AW	63150 TQ	FLBLS	10/01-12/01
	Melbourne-Titusville-Palm Bay MSA, FL	Y	27440 FQ	50840 AW	102730 TQ	FLBLS	10/01-12/01
	Miami PMSA, FL	Y	28830 FQ	50670 AW	88350 TQ	FLBLS	10/01-12/01
	Naples MSA, FL	Y	22100 FQ	36150 AW	61230 TQ	FLBLS	10/01-12/01
	Orlando MSA, FL	Y	24010 FQ	43790 AW	69170 TQ	FLBLS	10/01-12/01
	Pensacola MSA, FL	Y	21840 FQ	38060 AW	56540 TQ	FLBLS	10/01-12/01

AAW Average annual wage **AOH** Average offered, high **ASH** Average starting, high **H** Hourly **M** Monthly **S** Special: hourly and annual
AE Average entry wage **AOL** Average offered, low **ASL** Average starting, low **HI** Highest wage paid **MTC** Median total compensation **TQ** Third quartile wage
AEX Average experienced wage **APH** Average pay, high range **AW** Average wage paid **HR** High end range **MW** Median wage paid **W** Weekly
AO Average offered **APL** Average pay, low range **FQ** First quartile wage **LR** Low end range **SQ** Second quartile wage **Y** Yearly

Occupation/Type/Industry	Location	Per	Low	Mid	High	Source	Date
Editor	Sarasota-Bradenton MSA, FL	Y	24080 FQ	33840 AW	46430 TQ	FLBLS	10/01-12/01
	Tallahassee MSA, FL	Y	21140 FQ	36960 AW	61430 TQ	FLBLS	10/01-12/01
	Tampa-St. Petersburg-Clearwater MSA, FL	Y	18260 FQ	35440 AW	65260 TQ	FLBLS	10/01-12/01
	West Palm Beach-Boca Raton MSA, FL	Y	26010 FQ	46950 AW	68170 TQ	FLBLS	10/01-12/01
	Georgia	Y	24010 FQ	37180 AW	57850 TQ	GABLS	10/01-12/01
	Atlanta MSA, GA	Y	24600 FQ	38250 AW	59900 TQ	GABLS	10/01-12/01
	Augusta-Aiken MSA, GA-SC	Y	22510 FQ	33630 AW	49860 TQ	GABLS	10/01-12/01
	Macon MSA, GA	Y	24580 FQ	36960 AW	55970 TQ	GABLS	10/01-12/01
	Savannah MSA, GA	Y	18810 FQ	30510 AW	54310 TQ	GABLS	10/01-12/01
	Hawaii	Y	28460 FQ	51200 AW	78880 TQ	HIBLS	10/01-12/01
	Honolulu MSA, HI	Y	28560 FQ	52890 AW	81010 TQ	HIBLS	10/01-12/01
	Idaho	Y	16700 FQ	33780 AW	50480 TQ	IDBLS	10/01-12/01
	Boise City MSA, ID	Y	16430 FQ	33370 AW	50890 TQ	IDBLS	10/01-12/01
	Illinois	Y	24410 FQ	47560 AW	73780 TQ	ILBLS	10/01-12/01
	Champaign-Urbana MSA, IL	Y	18500 FQ	34830 AW	55450 TQ	ILBLS	10/01-12/01
	Chicago PMSA, IL	Y	28920 FQ	51530 AW	81030 TQ	ILBLS	10/01-12/01
	Peoria-Pekin MSA, IL	Y	24050 FQ	38620 AW	54940 TQ	ILBLS	10/01-12/01
	Rockford MSA, IL	Y	25860 FQ	44500 AW	61290 TQ	ILBLS	10/01-12/01
	Springfield MSA, IL	Y	22910 FQ	39340 AW	61380 TQ	ILBLS	10/01-12/01
	Indiana	Y	21740 FQ	36600 AW	55740 TQ	INBLS	10/01-12/01
	Elkhart-Goshen MSA, IN	Y	20050 FQ	33100 AW	52210 TQ	INBLS	10/01-12/01
	Evansville-Henderson MSA, IN-KY	Y	21110 FQ	35840 AW	54280 TQ	INBLS	10/01-12/01
	Fort Wayne MSA, IN	Y	20160 FQ	41150 AW	68930 TQ	INBLS	10/01-12/01
	Gary PMSA, IN	Y	28430 FQ	39840 AW	56360 TQ	INBLS	10/01-12/01
	Indianapolis MSA, IN	Y	22580 FQ	37780 AW	56020 TQ	INBLS	10/01-12/01
	Lafayette MSA, IN	Y	20890 FQ	33600 AW	45760 TQ	INBLS	10/01-12/01
	South Bend MSA, IN	Y	20330 FQ	37620 AW	62160 TQ	INBLS	10/01-12/01
	Iowa	Y	20750 FQ	40070 AW	66400 TQ	IABLS	10/01-12/01
	Davenport-Moline-Rock Island MSA, IA-IL	Y	19330 FQ	37150 AW	55600 TQ	IABLS	10/01-12/01
	Des Moines MSA, IA	Y	27710 FQ	49310 AW	75420 TQ	IABLS	10/01-12/01
	Kansas	Y	16110 FQ	37740 AW	59630 TQ	KSBLS	10/01-12/01
	Topeka MSA, KS	Y	12830 FQ	34940 AW	65810 TQ	KSBLS	10/01-12/01
	Wichita MSA, KS	Y	25290 FQ	43910 AW	59390 TQ	KSBLS	10/01-12/01
	Kentucky	Y	18490 FQ	34850 AW	62430 TQ	KYBLS	10/01-12/01
	Lexington MSA, KY	Y	20400 FQ	37370 AW	67210 TQ	KYBLS	10/01-12/01
	Louisville MSA, KY-IN	Y	18870 FQ	37880 AW	69870 TQ	KYBLS	10/01-12/01
	Louisiana	Y	17550 FQ	34410 AW	54000 TQ	LABLS	10/01-12/01
	Baton Rouge MSA, LA	Y	26800 FQ	40690 AW	53920 TQ	LABLS	10/01-12/01
	Lafayette MSA, LA	Y	18020 FQ	32580 AW	52940 TQ	LABLS	10/01-12/01
	Lake Charles MSA, LA	Y	11360 FQ	20950 AW	38840 TQ	LABLS	10/01-12/01
	New Orleans MSA, LA	Y	16310 FQ	32420 AW	54630 TQ	LABLS	10/01-12/01
	Maine	Y	15650 FQ	34500 AW	57930 TQ	MEBLS	10/01-12/01
	Portland MSA, ME	Y	17170 FQ	43470 AW	70140 TQ	MEBLS	10/01-12/01
	Maryland	Y	26070 FQ	42730 AW	65700 TQ	MDBLS	10/01-12/01
	Baltimore PMSA, MD	Y	24900 FQ	42370 AW	66630 TQ	MDBLS	10/01-12/01
	Massachusetts	Y	27010 FQ	49690 AW	82490 TQ	MABLS	10/01-12/01
	Boston PMSA, MA-NH	Y	27500 FQ	50830 AW	86190 TQ	MABLS	10/01-12/01
	Lawrence PMSA, MA-NH	Y	24770 FQ	41020 AW	57290 TQ	MABLS	10/01-12/01
	Lowell PMSA, MA-NH	Y	26440 FQ	44660 AW	68380 TQ	MABLS	10/01-12/01
	Springfield MSA, MA	Y	26170 FQ	46090 AW	67750 TQ	MABLS	10/01-12/01
	Michigan	Y	24640 FQ	44070 AW	73020 TQ	MIBLS	10/01-12/01
	Ann Arbor PMSA, MI	Y	24670 FQ	38110 AW	60060 TQ	MIBLS	10/01-12/01
	Detroit PMSA, MI	Y	26050 FQ	46810 AW	76960 TQ	MIBLS	10/01-12/01
	Flint PMSA, MI	Y	19040 FQ	35310 AW	55810 TQ	MIBLS	10/01-12/01
	Grand Rapids-Muskegon-Holland MSA, MI	Y	22480 FQ	42140 AW	74310 TQ	MIBLS	10/01-12/01
	Kalamazoo-Battle Creek MSA, MI	Y	27760 FQ	56570 AW	96230 TQ	MIBLS	10/01-12/01
	Lansing-East Lansing MSA, MI	Y	28160 FQ	42050 AW	59370 TQ	MIBLS	10/01-12/01
	Saginaw-Bay City-Midland MSA, MI	Y	19780 FQ	41160 AW	68240 TQ	MIBLS	10/01-12/01
	Minnesota	Y	25450 FQ	41560 AW	65860 TQ	MNBLS	10/01-12/01
	Duluth-Superior MSA, MN-WI	Y	23520 FQ	35140 AW	48510 TQ	MNBLS	10/01-12/01
	Minneapolis-St. Paul MSA, MN-WI	Y	29300 FQ	44060 AW	68230 TQ	MNBLS	10/01-12/01
	St. Cloud MSA, MN	Y	18990 FQ	30540 AW	43170 TQ	MNBLS	10/01-12/01
	Mississippi	Y	21920 FQ	33000 AW	45660 TQ	MSBLS	10/01-12/01

AAW	Average annual wage	**AOH**	Average offered, high	**ASH**	Average starting, high	**H**	Hourly	**M**	Monthly	**S**	Special: hourly and annual
AE	Average entry wage	**AOL**	Average offered, low	**ASL**	Average starting, low	**HI**	Highest wage paid	**MTC**	Median total compensation	**TQ**	Third quartile wage
AEX	Average experienced wage	**APH**	Average pay, high range	**AW**	Average wage paid	**HR**	High end range	**MW**	Median wage paid	**W**	Weekly
AO	Average offered	**APL**	Average pay, low range	**FQ**	First quartile wage	**LR**	Low end range	**SQ**	Second quartile wage	**Y**	Yearly

Occupation/Type/Industry	Location	Per	Low	Mid	High	Source	Date
Editor	Biloxi-Gulfport-Pascagoula MSA, MS	Y	24010 FQ	36980 AW	53110 TQ	MSBLS	10/01-12/01
	Jackson MSA, MS	Y	19680 FQ	31780 AW	44100 TQ	MSBLS	10/01-12/01
	Missouri	Y	18440 FQ	38650 AW	67090 TQ	MOBLS	10/01-12/01
	Kansas City MSA, MO-KS	Y	19630 FQ	42680 AW	72170 TQ	MOBLS	10/01-12/01
	St. Louis MSA, MO-IL	Y	24270 FQ	40050 AW	59740 TQ	MOBLS	10/01-12/01
	Springfield MSA, MO	Y	14420 FQ	28040 AW	41340 TQ	MOBLS	10/01-12/01
	Montana	Y	20330 FQ	34450 AW	51270 TQ	MTBLS	10/01-12/01
	Nebraska	Y	17020 FQ	31050 AW	51100 TQ	NEBLS	10/01-12/01
	Lincoln MSA, NE	Y	13390 FQ	32270 AW	52420 TQ	NEBLS	10/01-12/01
	Omaha MSA, NE-IA	Y	16980 FQ	35740 AW	54340 TQ	NEBLS	10/01-12/01
	Nevada	Y	20860 FQ	43380 AW	67150 TQ	NVBLS	10/01-12/01
	Las Vegas MSA, NV-AZ	Y	21360 FQ	44380 AW	67230 TQ	NVBLS	10/01-12/01
	Reno MSA, NV	Y	19600 FQ	40960 AW	68430 TQ	NVBLS	10/01-12/01
	New Hampshire	Y	25750 FQ	44690 AW	70400 TQ	NHBLS	10/01-12/01
	Nashua PMSA, NH	Y	30290 FQ	49400 AW	81620 TQ	NHBLS	10/01-12/01
	Portsmouth-Rochester PMSA, NH-ME	Y	24370 FQ	42210 AW	74040 TQ	NHBLS	10/01-12/01
	New Jersey	Y	26340 FQ	48290 AW	76530 TQ	NJBLS	10/01-12/01
	Atlantic-Cape May PMSA, NJ	Y	17210 FQ	42090 AW	69680 TQ	NJBLS	10/01-12/01
	Bergen-Passaic PMSA, NJ	Y	29310 FQ	53860 AW	91750 TQ	NJBLS	10/01-12/01
	Jersey City PMSA, NJ	Y	25600 FQ	54840 AW	89760 TQ	NJBLS	10/01-12/01
	Middlesex-Somerset-Hunterdon PMSA, NJ	Y	25780 FQ	45900 AW	71240 TQ	NJBLS	10/01-12/01
	Monmouth-Ocean PMSA, NJ	Y	27380 FQ	46460 AW	69250 TQ	NJBLS	10/01-12/01
	Newark PMSA, NJ	Y	25860 FQ	45640 AW	76740 TQ	NJBLS	10/01-12/01
	Trenton PMSA, NJ	Y	24370 FQ	44620 AW	69320 TQ	NJBLS	10/01-12/01
	New Mexico	Y	24440 FQ	40410 AW	61240 TQ	NMBLS	10/01-12/01
	Albuquerque MSA, NM	Y	26840 FQ	41260 AW	61230 TQ	NMBLS	10/01-12/01
	Las Cruces MSA, NM	Y	20340 FQ	38300 AW	63420 TQ	NMBLS	10/01-12/01
	New York	Y	22740 FQ	50480 AW	91130 TQ	NYBLS	10/01-12/01
	Albany-Schenectady-Troy MSA, NY	Y	18750 FQ	38510 AW	66280 TQ	NYBLS	10/01-12/01
	Binghamton MSA, NY	Y	15060 FQ	31740 AW	51580 TQ	NYBLS	10/01-12/01
	Buffalo-Niagara Falls MSA, NY	Y	18500 FQ	33560 AW	58090 TQ	NYBLS	10/01-12/01
	Nassau-Suffolk PMSA, NY	Y	20380 FQ	43950 AW	86070 TQ	NYBLS	10/01-12/01
	New York PMSA, NY	Y	25360 FQ	53760 AW	95110 TQ	NYBLS	10/01-12/01
	Newburgh PMSA, NY-PA	Y	24570 FQ	42530 AW	67280 TQ	NYBLS	10/01-12/01
	Rochester MSA, NY	Y	24430 FQ	42180 AW	69760 TQ	NYBLS	10/01-12/01
	Syracuse MSA, NY	Y	12460 FQ	22810 AW	36360 TQ	NYBLS	10/01-12/01
	Utica-Rome MSA, NY	Y	17600 FQ	35120 AW	65740 TQ	NYBLS	10/01-12/01
	North Carolina	Y	24290 FQ	41040 AW	63660 TQ	NCBLS	10/01-12/01
	Asheville MSA, NC	Y	21620 FQ	37430 AW	53440 TQ	NCBLS	10/01-12/01
	Charlotte-Gastonia-Rock Hill MSA, NC-SC	Y	25900 FQ	50770 AW	82500 TQ	NCBLS	10/01-12/01
	Greensboro-Winston-Salem-High Point MSA, NC	Y	25460 FQ	36820 AW	51980 TQ	NCBLS	10/01-12/01
	Raleigh-Durham-Chapel Hill MSA, NC	Y	27440 FQ	43310 AW	66860 TQ	NCBLS	10/01-12/01
	North Dakota	Y	19990 FQ	30280 AW	44830 TQ	NDBLS	10/01-12/01
	Fargo-Moorhead MSA, ND-MN	Y	19230 FQ	31980 AW	51990 TQ	NDBLS	10/01-12/01
	Ohio	Y	23520 FQ	41740 AW	66900 TQ	OHBLS	10/01-12/01
	Akron PMSA, OH	Y	25060 FQ	45340 AW	68720 TQ	OHBLS	10/01-12/01
	Canton-Massillon MSA, OH	Y	24710 FQ	38680 AW	64300 TQ	OHBLS	10/01-12/01
	Cincinnati PMSA, OH-KY-IN	Y	24630 FQ	42020 AW	65610 TQ	OHBLS	10/01-12/01
	Cleveland-Lorain-Elyria PMSA, OH	Y	22680 FQ	41550 AW	62000 TQ	OHBLS	10/01-12/01
	Columbus MSA, OH	Y	25700 FQ	46700 AW	78530 TQ	OHBLS	10/01-12/01
	Dayton-Springfield MSA, OH	Y	24570 FQ	39300 AW	58940 TQ	OHBLS	10/01-12/01
	Youngstown-Warren MSA, OH	Y	21300 FQ	43750 AW	60090 TQ	OHBLS	10/01-12/01
	Oklahoma	Y	14380 FQ	29840 AW	50120 TQ	OKBLS	10/01-12/01
	Oklahoma City MSA, OK	Y	14250 FQ	34180 AW	56720 TQ	OKBLS	10/01-12/01
	Tulsa MSA, OK	Y	19430 FQ	31160 AW	51780 TQ	OKBLS	10/01-12/01
	Oregon	Y	20720 FQ	39470 AW	57260 TQ	ORBLS	10/01-12/01
	Eugene-Springfield MSA, OR	Y	14990 FQ	31200 AW	52020 TQ	ORBLS	10/01-12/01
	Medford-Ashland MSA, OR	Y	14980 FQ	29720 AW	47410 TQ	ORBLS	10/01-12/01
	Portland-Vancouver PMSA, OR-WA	Y	27000 FQ	43500 AW	58810 TQ	ORBLS	10/01-12/01
	Salem PMSA, OR	Y	28580 FQ	43670 AW	61910 TQ	ORBLS	10/01-12/01
	Pennsylvania	Y	23680 FQ	42360 AW	67930 TQ	PABLS	10/01-12/01

AAW Average annual wage; AE Average entry wage; AEX Average experienced wage; AO Average offered; AOH Average offered, high; AOL Average offered, low; APH Average pay, high range; APL Average pay, low range; ASH Average starting, high; ASL Average starting, low; AW Average wage paid; FQ First quartile wage; H Hourly; HI Highest wage paid; HR High end range; LR Low end range; M Monthly; MTC Median total compensation; MW Median wage paid; SQ Second quartile wage; S Special: hourly and annual; TQ Third quartile wage; W Weekly; Y Yearly

Occupation/Type/Industry	Location	Per	Low	Mid	High	Source	Date
Editor	Allentown-Bethlehem-Easton MSA, PA	Y	19540 FQ	40050 AW	61690 TQ	PABLS	10/01-12/01
	Erie MSA, PA	Y	22620 FQ	39020 AW	59740 TQ	PABLS	10/01-12/01
	Harrisburg-Lebanon-Carlisle MSA, PA	Y	24490 FQ	42260 AW	63230 TQ	PABLS	10/01-12/01
	Johnstown MSA, PA	Y	12410 FQ	32050 AW	57710 TQ	PABLS	10/01-12/01
	Lancaster MSA, PA	Y	13540 FQ	39560 AW	60590 TQ	PABLS	10/01-12/01
	Philadelphia PMSA, PA-NJ	Y	26140 FQ	44910 AW	71270 TQ	PABLS	10/01-12/01
	Pittsburgh MSA, PA	Y	23430 FQ	35540 AW	53430 TQ	PABLS	10/01-12/01
	Reading MSA, PA	Y	24200 FQ	38150 AW	56650 TQ	PABLS	10/01-12/01
	Scranton-Wilkes-Barre-Hazleton MSA, PA	Y	18850 FQ	31450 AW	50780 TQ	PABLS	10/01-12/01
	York MSA, PA	Y	25190 FQ	38510 AW	52060 TQ	PABLS	10/01-12/01
	South Carolina	Y	24030 FQ	42440 AW	62480 TQ	SCBLS	10/01-12/01
	Columbia MSA, SC	Y	23630 FQ	41580 AW	58510 TQ	SCBLS	10/01-12/01
	Greenville-Spartanburg-Anderson MSA, SC	Y	29510 FQ	46230 AW	79830 TQ	SCBLS	10/01-12/01
	South Dakota	Y	20530 FQ	32780 AW	45890 TQ	SDBLS	10/01-12/01
	Tennessee	Y	21850 FQ	39320 AW	60450 TQ	TNBLS	10/01-12/01
	Chattanooga MSA, TN-GA	Y	22660 FQ	38690 AW	55630 TQ	TNBLS	10/01-12/01
	Johnson City-Kingsport-Bristol MSA, TN-VA	Y	19820 FQ	34560 AW	51670 TQ	TNBLS	10/01-12/01
	Knoxville MSA, TN	Y	24240 FQ	41020 AW	60850 TQ	TNBLS	10/01-12/01
	Memphis MSA, TN-AR-MS	Y	23690 FQ	44420 AW	66970 TQ	TNBLS	10/01-12/01
	Nashville MSA, TN	Y	23940 FQ	39590 AW	59130 TQ	TNBLS	10/01-12/01
	Texas	Y	18970 FQ	38970 AW	63840 TQ	TXBLS	10/01-12/01
	Austin-San Marcos MSA, TX	Y	24970 FQ	40410 AW	59650 TQ	TXBLS	10/01-12/01
	Beaumont-Port Arthur MSA, TX	Y	13620 FQ	28100 AW	38600 TQ	TXBLS	10/01-12/01
	Brownsville-Harlingen-San Benito MSA, TX	Y	19560 FQ	31970 AW	49850 TQ	TXBLS	10/01-12/01
	Corpus Christi MSA, TX	Y	18620 FQ	32500 AW	53260 TQ	TXBLS	10/01-12/01
	Dallas PMSA, TX	Y	19410 FQ	39820 AW	64980 TQ	TXBLS	10/01-12/01
	El Paso MSA, TX	Y	18370 FQ	29110 AW	52330 TQ	TXBLS	10/01-12/01
	Fort Worth-Arlington PMSA, TX	Y	24380 FQ	46380 AW	70650 TQ	TXBLS	10/01-12/01
	Houston PMSA, TX	Y	19550 FQ	44200 AW	69900 TQ	TXBLS	10/01-12/01
	Killeen-Temple MSA, TX	Y	23060 FQ	35980 AW	46660 TQ	TXBLS	10/01-12/01
	Longview-Marshall MSA, TX	Y	18210 FQ	32880 AW	55010 TQ	TXBLS	10/01-12/01
	Lubbock MSA, TX	Y	15990 FQ	33530 AW	52510 TQ	TXBLS	10/01-12/01
	McAllen-Edinburg-Mission MSA, TX	Y	14830 FQ	28960 AW	64330 TQ	TXBLS	10/01-12/01
	Odessa-Midland MSA, TX	Y	13350 FQ	28620 AW	45300 TQ	TXBLS	10/01-12/01
	San Antonio MSA, TX	Y	23490 FQ	40310 AW	60590 TQ	TXBLS	10/01-12/01
	Tyler MSA, TX	Y	12640 FQ	29320 AW	62430 TQ	TXBLS	10/01-12/01
	Waco MSA, TX	Y	18110 FQ	27990 AW	39350 TQ	TXBLS	10/01-12/01
	Utah	Y	22740 FQ	42890 AW	67160 TQ	UTBLS	10/01-12/01
	Provo-Orem MSA, UT	Y	25250 FQ	50420 AW	78710 TQ	UTBLS	10/01-12/01
	Salt Lake City-Ogden MSA, UT	Y	22350 FQ	39620 AW	59170 TQ	UTBLS	10/01-12/01
	Vermont	Y	24020 FQ	42880 AW	64590 TQ	VTBLS	10/01-12/01
	Burlington MSA, VT	Y	24650 FQ	47410 AW	66600 TQ	VTBLS	10/01-12/01
	Virginia	Y	26140 FQ	48560 AW	83770 TQ	VABLS	10/01-12/01
	Norfolk-Virginia Beach-Newport News MSA, VA-NC	Y	24420 FQ	46920 AW	80270 TQ	VABLS	10/01-12/01
	Richmond-Petersburg MSA, VA	Y	21720 FQ	46370 AW	86190 TQ	VABLS	10/01-12/01
	Roanoke MSA, VA	Y	28540 FQ	39160 AW	59900 TQ	VABLS	10/01-12/01
	Washington	Y	22180 FQ	49880 AW	79560 TQ	WABLS	10/01-12/01
	Bremerton PMSA, WA	Y	32120 FQ	53220 AW	78920 TQ	WABLS	10/01-12/01
	Richland-Kennewick-Pasco MSA, WA	Y	26890 FQ	52900 AW	77600 TQ	WABLS	10/01-12/01
	Seattle-Bellevue-Everett PMSA, WA	Y	21380 FQ	52610 AW	84030 TQ	WABLS	10/01-12/01
	Spokane MSA, WA	Y	27060 FQ	47600 AW	72100 TQ	WABLS	10/01-12/01
	Tacoma PMSA, WA	Y	18350 FQ	45290 AW	65540 TQ	WABLS	10/01-12/01
	West Virginia	Y	12380 FQ	33760 AW	61150 TQ	WVBLS	10/01-12/01
	Charleston MSA, WV	Y	12010 FQ	31810 AW	48320 TQ	WVBLS	10/01-12/01
	Wisconsin	Y	22550 FQ	41650 AW	63390 TQ	WIBLS	10/01-12/01
	Appleton-Oshkosh-Neenah MSA, WI	Y	22250 FQ	38190 AW	59120 TQ	WIBLS	10/01-12/01

Occupation/Type/Industry	Location	Per	Low	Mid	High	Source	Date
Editor	Green Bay MSA, WI	Y	21460 FQ	33890 AW	50890 TQ	WIBLS	10/01-12/01
	Madison MSA, WI	Y	22990 FQ	40190 AW	59900 TQ	WIBLS	10/01-12/01
	Milwaukee-Waukesha PMSA, WI	Y	24230 FQ	47140 AW	77160 TQ	WIBLS	10/01-12/01
	Wyoming	Y	18470 FQ	30300 AW	44020 TQ	WYBLS	10/01-12/01
	Puerto Rico	Y	22080 FQ	40470 AW	66870 TQ	PRBLS	10/01-12/01
Fashion Magazine	United States	Y		35000-80000 AW		COSGIRL	1/01-1/02
Film and Video	Alabama	Y	17190 FQ	30760 AW	52070 TQ	ALBLS	10/01-12/01
Film and Video	Arizona	Y	15720 FQ	36310 AW	56350 TQ	AZBLS	10/01-12/01
Film and Video	Arkansas	Y	17210 FQ	28950 AW	46720 TQ	ARBLS	10/01-12/01
Film and Video	California	Y	21580 FQ	48040 AW	87660 TQ	CABLS	10/01-12/01
Film and Video	Colorado	Y	21810 FQ	43440 AW	76690 TQ	COBLS	10/01-12/01
Film and Video	Connecticut	Y	23860 FQ	46590 AW	73890 TQ	CTBLS	10/01-12/01
Film and Video	District of Columbia	Y	22350 FQ	42540 AW	64150 TQ	DCBLS	10/01-12/01
Film and Video	Florida	Y	16190 FQ	35310 AW	66620 TQ	FLBLS	10/01-12/01
Film and Video	Georgia	Y	20690 FQ	40300 AW	69960 TQ	GABLS	10/01-12/01
Film and Video	Hawaii	Y	18120 FQ	32270 AW	51900 TQ	HIBLS	10/01-12/01
Film and Video	Illinois	Y	19700 FQ	38570 AW	55820 TQ	ILBLS	10/01-12/01
Film and Video	Indiana	Y	21390 FQ	39130 AW	67190 TQ	INBLS	10/01-12/01
Film and Video	Iowa	Y	12950 FQ	27640 AW	47070 TQ	IABLS	10/01-12/01
Film and Video	Kansas	Y	18760 FQ	37830 AW	55860 TQ	KSBLS	10/01-12/01
Film and Video	Kentucky	Y	18450 FQ	25250 AW	39430 TQ	KYBLS	10/01-12/01
Film and Video	Louisiana	Y	15270 FQ	35570 AW	65090 TQ	LABLS	10/01-12/01
Film and Video	Maine	Y	13040 FQ	27280 AW	43230 TQ	MEBLS	10/01-12/01
Film and Video	Maryland	Y	23610 FQ	42790 AW	69320 TQ	MDBLS	10/01-12/01
Film and Video	Massachusetts	Y	21300 FQ	47170 AW	70900 TQ	MABLS	10/01-12/01
Film and Video	Michigan	Y	24690 FQ	52260 AW	82650 TQ	MIBLS	10/01-12/01
Film and Video	Minnesota	Y	22090 FQ	49190 AW	86380 TQ	MNBLS	10/01-12/01
Film and Video	Missouri	Y	19530 FQ	39680 AW	67500 TQ	MOBLS	10/01-12/01
Film and Video	Montana	Y	21800 FQ	38840 AW	62290 TQ	MTBLS	10/01-12/01
Film and Video	Nevada	Y	23030 FQ	34340 AW	53490 TQ	NVBLS	10/01-12/01
Film and Video	New Jersey	Y	25190 FQ	55720 AW	84470 TQ	NJBLS	10/01-12/01
Film and Video	New Mexico	Y	17650 FQ	34800 AW	58260 TQ	NMBLS	10/01-12/01
Film and Video	New York	Y	19780 FQ	43600 AW	71290 TQ	NYBLS	10/01-12/01
Film and Video	North Carolina	Y	20270 FQ	33090 AW	46830 TQ	NCBLS	10/01-12/01
Film and Video	Ohio	Y	19990 FQ	38970 AW	71840 TQ	OHBLS	10/01-12/01
Film and Video	Oklahoma	Y	15240 FQ	31360 AW	54170 TQ	OKBLS	10/01-12/01
Film and Video	Oregon	Y	22960 FQ	37680 AW	56440 TQ	ORBLS	10/01-12/01
Film and Video	Pennsylvania	Y	12170 FQ	40710 AW	82530 TQ	PABLS	10/01-12/01
Film and Video	South Carolina	Y	15930 FQ	27530 AW	44640 TQ	SCBLS	10/01-12/01
Film and Video	Tennessee	Y	22650 FQ	37850 AW	76240 TQ	TNBLS	10/01-12/01
Film and Video	Texas	Y	18690 FQ	31330 AW	47250 TQ	TXBLS	10/01-12/01
Film and Video	Utah	Y	17030 FQ	33570 AW	63900 TQ	UTBLS	10/01-12/01
Film and Video	Vermont	Y	26320 FQ	41330 AW	66830 TQ	VTBLS	10/01-12/01
Film and Video	Virginia	Y	17350 FQ	35660 AW	69260 TQ	VABLS	10/01-12/01
Film and Video	Washington	Y	20650 FQ	42950 AW	71520 TQ	WABLS	10/01-12/01
Film and Video	Wisconsin	Y	19020 FQ	37250 AW	44470 TQ	WIBLS	10/01-12/01
Film and Video	Puerto Rico	Y	15780 FQ	28610 AW	46480 TQ	PRBLS	10/01-12/01
Editorial Assistant							
Fashion Magazine	United States	Y		25000 AW		COSGIRL	1/01-1/02
Education Administrator							
Elementary and Secondary School	Alabama	Y	46050 FQ	60290 AW	74180 TQ	ALBLS	10/01-12/01
Elementary and Secondary School	Birmingham MSA, AL	Y	50100 FQ	63320 AW	78170 TQ	ALBLS	10/01-12/01
Elementary and Secondary School	Huntsville MSA, AL	Y	48820 FQ	63250 AW	82270 TQ	ALBLS	10/01-12/01
Elementary and Secondary School	Montgomery MSA, AL	Y	24720 FQ	42980 AW	69380 TQ	ALBLS	10/01-12/01
Elementary and Secondary School	Alaska	Y	61180 FQ	74520 AW	91290 TQ	AKBLS	10/01-12/01
Elementary and Secondary School	Arizona	Y	45160 FQ	67690 AW	96600 TQ	AZBLS	10/01-12/01
Elementary and Secondary School	Phoenix-Mesa MSA, AZ	Y	47620 FQ	72370 AW	105470 TQ	AZBLS	10/01-12/01
Elementary and Secondary School	Tucson MSA, AZ	Y	42050 FQ	62200 AW	76100 TQ	AZBLS	10/01-12/01
Elementary and Secondary School	Arkansas	Y	42580 FQ	57140 AW	74810 TQ	ARBLS	10/01-12/01
Elementary and Secondary School	Fayetteville-Springdale-Rogers MSA, AR	Y	47960 FQ	61270 AW	79920 TQ	ARBLS	10/01-12/01
Elementary and Secondary School	Fort Smith MSA, AR-OK	Y	46960 FQ	60020 AW	74760 TQ	ARBLS	10/01-12/01
Elementary and Secondary School	Little Rock-North Little Rock MSA, AR	Y	45220 FQ	60750 AW	84130 TQ	ARBLS	10/01-12/01
Elementary and Secondary School	California	Y	60630 FQ	82660 AW	109920 TQ	CABLS	10/01-12/01
Elementary and Secondary School	Bakersfield MSA, CA	Y	56430 FQ	76510 AW	97310 TQ	CABLS	10/01-12/01
Elementary and Secondary School	Chico-Paradise MSA, CA	Y	65050 FQ	82330 AW	101970 TQ	CABLS	10/01-12/01
Elementary and Secondary School	Fresno MSA, CA	Y	61790 FQ	77000 AW	98660 TQ	CABLS	10/01-12/01

AAW	Average annual wage	AOH	Average offered, high	ASH	Average starting, high	H	Hourly	M	Monthly	S	Special: hourly and annual
AE	Average entry wage	AOL	Average offered, low	ASL	Average starting, low	HI	Highest wage paid	MTC	Median total compensation	TQ	Third quartile wage
AEX	Average experienced wage	APH	Average pay, high range	AW	Average wage paid	HR	High end range	MW	Median wage paid	W	Weekly
AO	Average offered	APL	Average pay, low range	FQ	First quartile wage	LR	Low end range	SQ	Second quartile wage	Y	Yearly

Occupation/Type/Industry	Location	Per	Low	Mid	High	Source	Date
Education Administrator							
Elementary and Secondary School	Los Angeles-Long Beach PMSA, CA	Y	72390 FQ	87690 AW	111010 TQ	CABLS	10/01-12/01
Elementary and Secondary School	Merced MSA, CA	Y	33930 FQ	74820 AW	95010 TQ	CABLS	10/01-12/01
Elementary and Secondary School	Modesto MSA, CA	Y	62930 FQ	82620 AW	107810 TQ	CABLS	10/01-12/01
Elementary and Secondary School	Oakland PMSA, CA	Y	42490 FQ	77120 AW	114580 TQ	CABLS	10/01-12/01
Elementary and Secondary School	Orange County PMSA, CA	Y	65450 FQ	87090 AW	113710 TQ	CABLS	10/01-12/01
Elementary and Secondary School	Redding MSA, CA	Y	50190 FQ	65970 AW	85080 TQ	CABLS	10/01-12/01
Elementary and Secondary School	Riverside-San Bernardino PMSA, CA	Y	56590 FQ	81790 AW	107890 TQ	CABLS	10/01-12/01
Elementary and Secondary School	Sacramento PMSA, CA	Y	59370 FQ	86950 AW	131290 TQ	CABLS	10/01-12/01
Elementary and Secondary School	Salinas MSA, CA	Y	62260 FQ	81250 AW	103910 TQ	CABLS	10/01-12/01
Elementary and Secondary School	San Diego MSA, CA	Y	62290 FQ	82070 AW	107020 TQ	CABLS	10/01-12/01
Elementary and Secondary School	San Francisco PMSA, CA	Y	59500 FQ	84720 AW	111750 TQ	CABLS	10/01-12/01
Elementary and Secondary School	San Jose PMSA, CA	Y	66180 FQ	91960 AW	120040 TQ	CABLS	10/01-12/01
Elementary and Secondary School	San Luis Obispo-Atascadero-Paso Robles MSA, CA	Y	62030 FQ	78510 AW	94180 TQ	CABLS	10/01-12/01
Elementary and Secondary School	Santa Barbara-Santa Maria-Lompoc MSA, CA	Y	56480 FQ	83320 AW	120480 TQ	CABLS	10/01-12/01
Elementary and Secondary School	Santa Rosa PMSA, CA	Y	62480 FQ	77170 AW	94100 TQ	CABLS	10/01-12/01
Elementary and Secondary School	Stockton-Lodi MSA, CA	Y	51800 FQ	80140 AW	110170 TQ	CABLS	10/01-12/01
Elementary and Secondary School	Vallejo-Fairfield-Napa PMSA, CA	Y	54470 FQ	69470 AW	89110 TQ	CABLS	10/01-12/01
Elementary and Secondary School	Ventura PMSA, CA	Y	66940 FQ	84290 AW	107530 TQ	CABLS	10/01-12/01
Elementary and Secondary School	Visalia-Tulare-Porterville MSA, CA	Y	61980 FQ	78570 AW	93740 TQ	CABLS	10/01-12/01
Elementary and Secondary School	Colorado	Y	47220 FQ	64920 AW	86820 TQ	COBLS	10/01-12/01
Elementary and Secondary School	Boulder-Longmont PMSA, CO	Y	48280 FQ	67610 AW	90590 TQ	COBLS	10/01-12/01
Elementary and Secondary School	Colorado Springs MSA, CO	Y	49400 FQ	66630 AW	87710 TQ	COBLS	10/01-12/01
Elementary and Secondary School	Denver PMSA, CO	Y	48620 FQ	67080 AW	88230 TQ	COBLS	10/01-12/01
Elementary and Secondary School	Fort Collins-Loveland MSA, CO	Y	50220 FQ	67370 AW	88830 TQ	COBLS	10/01-12/01
Elementary and Secondary School	Greeley PMSA, CO	Y	47540 FQ	62070 AW	82030 TQ	COBLS	10/01-12/01
Elementary and Secondary School	Connecticut	Y	64640 FQ	86410 AW	113360 TQ	CTBLS	10/01-12/01
Elementary and Secondary School	Bridgeport PMSA, CT	Y	69600 FQ	91070 AW	117340 TQ	CTBLS	10/01-12/01
Elementary and Secondary School	Danbury PMSA, CT	Y	63500 FQ	88690 AW	113580 TQ	CTBLS	10/01-12/01
Elementary and Secondary School	Hartford MSA, CT	Y	60310 FQ	83750 AW	110510 TQ	CTBLS	10/01-12/01
Elementary and Secondary School	New Haven-Meriden PMSA, CT	Y	72240 FQ	87210 AW	111680 TQ	CTBLS	10/01-12/01
Elementary and Secondary School	New London-Norwich MSA, CT-RI	Y	70610 FQ	87900 AW	113310 TQ	CTBLS	10/01-12/01
Elementary and Secondary School	Stamford-Norwalk PMSA, CT	Y	54610 FQ	93030 AW	120940 TQ	CTBLS	10/01-12/01
Elementary and Secondary School	Waterbury PMSA, CT	Y	67250 FQ	84240 AW	105380 TQ	CTBLS	10/01-12/01
Elementary and Secondary School	Delaware	Y	51980 FQ	82020 AW	112610 TQ	DEBLS	10/01-12/01
Elementary and Secondary School	Wilmington-Newark PMSA, DE-MD	Y	57020 FQ	82200 AW	108110 TQ	DEBLS	10/01-12/01
Elementary and Secondary School	District of Columbia	Y	73770 FQ	96000 AW		DCBLS	10/01-12/01
Elementary and Secondary School	Washington PMSA, DC-MD-VA-WV	Y	49680 FQ	77060 AW	107030 TQ	DCBLS	10/01-12/01
Elementary and Secondary School	Florida	Y	46300 FQ	64520 AW	86860 TQ	FLBLS	10/01-12/01
Elementary and Secondary School	Fort Myers-Cape Coral MSA, FL	Y	28370 FQ	49180 AW	83510 TQ	FLBLS	10/01-12/01
Elementary and Secondary School	Jacksonville MSA, FL	Y	50460 FQ	66630 AW	87220 TQ	FLBLS	10/01-12/01
Elementary and Secondary School	Melbourne-Titusville-Palm Bay MSA, FL	Y	43500 FQ	57710 AW	74300 TQ	FLBLS	10/01-12/01
Elementary and Secondary School	Ocala MSA, FL	Y	45450 FQ	58050 AW	71470 TQ	FLBLS	10/01-12/01
Elementary and Secondary School	Orlando MSA, FL	Y	48090 FQ	62180 AW	81230 TQ	FLBLS	10/01-12/01
Elementary and Secondary School	Pensacola MSA, FL	Y	49550 FQ	65700 AW	86850 TQ	FLBLS	10/01-12/01
Elementary and Secondary School	Sarasota-Bradenton MSA, FL	Y	23880 FQ	64390 AW	94320 TQ	FLBLS	10/01-12/01
Elementary and Secondary School	Tallahassee MSA, FL	Y	43620 FQ	91010 AW		FLBLS	10/01-12/01
Elementary and Secondary School	Tampa-St. Petersburg-Clearwater MSA, FL	Y	55920 FQ	69450 AW	88110 TQ	FLBLS	10/01-12/01
Elementary and Secondary School	Georgia	Y	50320 FQ	70200 AW	92480 TQ	GABLS	10/01-12/01
Elementary and Secondary School	Atlanta MSA, GA	Y	53060 FQ	74330 AW	95810 TQ	GABLS	10/01-12/01
Elementary and Secondary School	Augusta-Aiken MSA, GA-SC	Y	51680 FQ	68130 AW	87680 TQ	GABLS	10/01-12/01
Elementary and Secondary School	Columbus MSA, GA-AL	Y	33740 FQ	62660 AW	90690 TQ	GABLS	10/01-12/01
Elementary and Secondary School	Macon MSA, GA	Y	41420 FQ	63990 AW	86650 TQ	GABLS	10/01-12/01
Elementary and Secondary School	Savannah MSA, GA	Y	43790 FQ	56470 AW	72440 TQ	GABLS	10/01-12/01
Elementary and Secondary School	Hawaii	Y	48260 FQ	65670 AW	87220 TQ	HIBLS	10/01-12/01
Elementary and Secondary School	Honolulu MSA, HI	Y	48640 FQ	67540 AW	89130 TQ	HIBLS	10/01-12/01
Elementary and Secondary School	Idaho	Y	49320 FQ	61310 AW	73500 TQ	IDBLS	10/01-12/01
Elementary and Secondary School	Boise City MSA, ID	Y	50930 FQ	64870 AW	81090 TQ	IDBLS	10/01-12/01

AAW	Average annual wage	**AOH**	Average offered, high	**ASH**	Average starting, high	**H**	Hourly	**M**	Monthly	**S**	Special: hourly and annual
AE	Average entry wage	**AOL**	Average offered, low	**ASL**	Average starting, low	**HI**	Highest wage paid	**MTC**	Median total compensation	**TQ**	Third quartile wage
AEX	Average experienced wage	**APH**	Average pay, high range	**AW**	Average wage paid	**HR**	High end range	**MW**	Median wage paid	**W**	Weekly
AO	Average offered	**APL**	Average pay, low range	**FQ**	First quartile wage	**LR**	Low end range	**SQ**	Second quartile wage	**Y**	Yearly

Occupation/Type/Industry	Location	Per	Low	Mid	High	Source	Date
Education Administrator							
Elementary and Secondary School	Illinois	Y	45690 FQ	75210 AW	108710 TQ	ILBLS	10/01-12/01
Elementary and Secondary School	Champaign-Urbana MSA, IL	Y	50050 FQ	70950 AW	95670 TQ	ILBLS	10/01-12/01
Elementary and Secondary School	Chicago PMSA, IL	Y	49730 FQ	82220 AW	111570 TQ	ILBLS	10/01-12/01
Elementary and Secondary School	Peoria-Pekin MSA, IL	Y	55400 FQ	75860 AW	120100 TQ	ILBLS	10/01-12/01
Elementary and Secondary School	Rockford MSA, IL	Y	51740 FQ	69780 AW	93500 TQ	ILBLS	10/01-12/01
Elementary and Secondary School	Springfield MSA, IL	Y	49950 FQ	67570 AW	92110 TQ	ILBLS	10/01-12/01
Elementary and Secondary School	Indiana	Y	49640 FQ	67450 AW	88500 TQ	INBLS	10/01-12/01
Elementary and Secondary School	Elkhart-Goshen MSA, IN	Y	58260 FQ	79440 AW	117810 TQ	INBLS	10/01-12/01
Elementary and Secondary School	Evansville-Henderson MSA, IN-KY	Y	45480 FQ	64630 AW	84910 TQ	INBLS	10/01-12/01
Elementary and Secondary School	Fort Wayne MSA, IN	Y	56590 FQ	69300 AW	87400 TQ	INBLS	10/01-12/01
Elementary and Secondary School	Gary PMSA, IN	Y	41850 FQ	62950 AW	86410 TQ	INBLS	10/01-12/01
Elementary and Secondary School	Indianapolis MSA, IN	Y	48670 FQ	69500 AW	92650 TQ	INBLS	10/01-12/01
Elementary and Secondary School	Lafayette MSA, IN	Y	49670 FQ	67150 AW	95860 TQ	INBLS	10/01-12/01
Elementary and Secondary School	South Bend MSA, IN	Y	43270 FQ	67660 AW	87490 TQ	INBLS	10/01-12/01
Elementary and Secondary School	Iowa	Y	47780 FQ	63360 AW	86640 TQ	IABLS	10/01-12/01
Elementary and Secondary School	Cedar Rapids MSA, IA	Y	41400 FQ	60940 AW	87870 TQ	IABLS	10/01-12/01
Elementary and Secondary School	Davenport-Moline-Rock Island MSA, IA-IL	Y	58250 FQ	72440 AW	90910 TQ	IABLS	10/01-12/01
Elementary and Secondary School	Des Moines MSA, IA	Y	48310 FQ	67550 AW	92870 TQ	IABLS	10/01-12/01
Elementary and Secondary School	Kansas	Y	46230 FQ	59640 AW	73970 TQ	KSBLS	10/01-12/01
Elementary and Secondary School	Wichita MSA, KS	Y	43250 FQ	59170 AW	74250 TQ	KSBLS	10/01-12/01
Elementary and Secondary School	Kentucky	Y	46270 FQ	62180 AW	82870 TQ	KYBLS	10/01-12/01
Elementary and Secondary School	Lexington MSA, KY	Y	49840 FQ	66190 AW	84900 TQ	KYBLS	10/01-12/01
Elementary and Secondary School	Louisville MSA, KY-IN	Y	47310 FQ	71250 AW	92180 TQ	KYBLS	10/01-12/01
Elementary and Secondary School	Louisiana	Y	40530 FQ	54390 AW	70680 TQ	LABLS	10/01-12/01
Elementary and Secondary School	Baton Rouge MSA, LA	Y	47030 FQ	59140 AW	73430 TQ	LABLS	10/01-12/01
Elementary and Secondary School	Houma MSA, LA	Y	39220 FQ	51600 AW	66960 TQ	LABLS	10/01-12/01
Elementary and Secondary School	Lafayette MSA, LA	Y	43050 FQ	55980 AW	70190 TQ	LABLS	10/01-12/01
Elementary and Secondary School	New Orleans MSA, LA	Y	40440 FQ	55080 AW	72770 TQ	LABLS	10/01-12/01
Elementary and Secondary School	Maine	Y	45490 FQ	56310 AW	71320 TQ	MEBLS	10/01-12/01
Elementary and Secondary School	Portland MSA, ME	Y	49380 FQ	62250 AW	75830 TQ	MEBLS	10/01-12/01
Elementary and Secondary School	Maryland	Y	54220 FQ	76510 AW	104160 TQ	MDBLS	10/01-12/01
Elementary and Secondary School	Baltimore PMSA, MD	Y	56820 FQ	80630 AW	111080 TQ	MDBLS	10/01-12/01
Elementary and Secondary School	Massachusetts	Y	48540 FQ	70930 AW	92090 TQ	MABLS	10/01-12/01
Elementary and Secondary School	Boston PMSA, MA-NH	Y	51560 FQ	72090 AW	92820 TQ	MABLS	10/01-12/01
Elementary and Secondary School	Brockton PMSA, MA	Y	54060 FQ	73220 AW	94300 TQ	MABLS	10/01-12/01
Elementary and Secondary School	Lawrence PMSA, MA-NH	Y	52310 FQ	74620 AW	95460 TQ	MABLS	10/01-12/01
Elementary and Secondary School	Lowell PMSA, MA-NH	Y	58060 FQ	75250 AW	92760 TQ	MABLS	10/01-12/01
Elementary and Secondary School	New Bedford PMSA, MA	Y	58140 FQ	72770 AW	91680 TQ	MABLS	10/01-12/01
Elementary and Secondary School	Springfield MSA, MA	Y	31200 FQ	60750 AW	88370 TQ	MABLS	10/01-12/01
Elementary and Secondary School	Worcester PMSA, MA-CT	Y	58770 FQ	72750 AW	89830 TQ	MABLS	10/01-12/01
Elementary and Secondary School	Michigan	Y	57860 FQ	76480 AW	100630 TQ	MIBLS	10/01-12/01
Elementary and Secondary School	Ann Arbor PMSA, MI	Y	60380 FQ	77730 AW	93970 TQ	MIBLS	10/01-12/01
Elementary and Secondary School	Detroit PMSA, MI	Y	66440 FQ	84900 AW	109620 TQ	MIBLS	10/01-12/01
Elementary and Secondary School	Flint PMSA, MI	Y	56170 FQ	76550 AW	101070 TQ	MIBLS	10/01-12/01
Elementary and Secondary School	Grand Rapids-Muskegon-Holland MSA, MI	Y	57060 FQ	72320 AW	90290 TQ	MIBLS	10/01-12/01
Elementary and Secondary School	Kalamazoo-Battle Creek MSA, MI	Y	50060 FQ	66900 AW	89450 TQ	MIBLS	10/01-12/01
Elementary and Secondary School	Lansing-East Lansing MSA, MI	Y	53770 FQ	72140 AW	93870 TQ	MIBLS	10/01-12/01
Elementary and Secondary School	Saginaw-Bay City-Midland MSA, MI	Y	59380 FQ	75800 AW	94920 TQ	MIBLS	10/01-12/01
Elementary and Secondary School	Minnesota	Y	52500 FQ	73500 AW	95440 TQ	MNBLS	10/01-12/01
Elementary and Secondary School	Duluth-Superior MSA, MN-WI	Y	37090 FQ	67110 AW	87560 TQ	MNBLS	10/01-12/01
Elementary and Secondary School	Minneapolis-St. Paul MSA, MN-WI	Y	56900 FQ	77990 AW	98110 TQ	MNBLS	10/01-12/01
Elementary and Secondary School	St. Cloud MSA, MN	Y	57260 FQ	74610 AW	93700 TQ	MNBLS	10/01-12/01
Elementary and Secondary School	Mississippi	Y	41030 FQ	56570 AW	73340 TQ	MSBLS	10/01-12/01
Elementary and Secondary School	Biloxi-Gulfport-Pascagoula MSA, MS	Y	49100 FQ	61170 AW	74360 TQ	MSBLS	10/01-12/01
Elementary and Secondary School	Jackson MSA, MS	Y	39710 FQ	54270 AW	71040 TQ	MSBLS	10/01-12/01
Elementary and Secondary School	Missouri	Y	43800 FQ	65290 AW	90990 TQ	MOBLS	10/01-12/01
Elementary and Secondary School	Kansas City MSA, MO-KS	Y	50150 FQ	66430 AW	86790 TQ	MOBLS	10/01-12/01
Elementary and Secondary School	St. Louis MSA, MO-IL	Y	48130 FQ	72390 AW	99900 TQ	MOBLS	10/01-12/01
Elementary and Secondary School	Springfield MSA, MO	Y	38780 FQ	56600 AW	76760 TQ	MOBLS	10/01-12/01
Elementary and Secondary School	Montana	Y	41200 FQ	54050 AW	69980 TQ	MTBLS	10/01-12/01
Elementary and Secondary School	Nebraska	Y	46970 FQ	62150 AW	84450 TQ	NEBLS	10/01-12/01
Elementary and Secondary School	Lincoln MSA, NE	Y	28150 FQ	63180 AW	87530 TQ	NEBLS	10/01-12/01
Elementary and Secondary School	Omaha MSA, NE-IA	Y	45100 FQ	63780 AW	86910 TQ	NEBLS	10/01-12/01
Elementary and Secondary School	New Hampshire	Y	48940 FQ	61690 AW	76350 TQ	NHBLS	10/01-12/01

AAW Average annual wage **AOH** Average offered, high **ASH** Average starting, high **H** Hourly **M** Monthly **S** Special: hourly and annual
AE Average entry wage **AOL** Average offered, low **ASL** Average starting, low **HI** Highest wage paid **MTC** Median total compensation **TQ** Third quartile wage
AEX Average experienced wage **APH** Average pay, high range **AW** Average wage paid **HR** High end range **MW** Median wage paid **W** Weekly
AO Average offered **APL** Average pay, low range **FQ** First quartile wage **LR** Low end range **SQ** Second quartile wage **Y** Yearly

Occupation/Type/Industry	Location	Per	Low	Mid	High	Source	Date
Education Administrator							
Elementary and Secondary School	Nashua PMSA, NH	Y	45300 FQ	64880 AW	86460 TQ	NHBLS	10/01-12/01
Elementary and Secondary School	Portsmouth-Rochester PMSA, NH-ME	Y	49700 FQ	63390 AW	79010 TQ	NHBLS	10/01-12/01
Elementary and Secondary School	New Jersey	Y	64190 FQ	89900 AW	117920 TQ	NJBLS	10/01-12/01
Elementary and Secondary School	Atlantic-Cape May PMSA, NJ	Y	55910 FQ	79270 AW	106240 TQ	NJBLS	10/01-12/01
Elementary and Secondary School	Bergen-Passaic PMSA, NJ	Y	74040 FQ	96670 AW	120260 TQ	NJBLS	10/01-12/01
Elementary and Secondary School	Jersey City PMSA, NJ	Y	77670 FQ	100330 AW	122300 TQ	NJBLS	10/01-12/01
Elementary and Secondary School	Middlesex-Somerset-Hunterdon PMSA, NJ	Y	73070 FQ	92780 AW	119040 TQ	NJBLS	10/01-12/01
Elementary and Secondary School	Monmouth-Ocean PMSA, NJ	Y	71390 FQ	88830 AW	114890 TQ	NJBLS	10/01-12/01
Elementary and Secondary School	Newark PMSA, NJ	Y	55350 FQ	87790 AW	121960 TQ	NJBLS	10/01-12/01
Elementary and Secondary School	Trenton PMSA, NJ	Y	50750 FQ	80990 AW	113580 TQ	NJBLS	10/01-12/01
Elementary and Secondary School	New Mexico	Y	43490 FQ	57380 AW	74260 TQ	NMBLS	10/01-12/01
Elementary and Secondary School	Las Cruces MSA, NM	Y	42750 FQ	62730 AW	93400 TQ	NMBLS	10/01-12/01
Elementary and Secondary School	New York	Y	58930 FQ	99550 AW		NYBLS	10/01-12/01
Elementary and Secondary School	Albany-Schenectady-Troy MSA, NY	Y	46420 FQ	77590 AW	109760 TQ	NYBLS	10/01-12/01
Elementary and Secondary School	Binghamton MSA, NY	Y	49840 FQ	76120 AW	112450 TQ	NYBLS	10/01-12/01
Elementary and Secondary School	Buffalo-Niagara Falls MSA, NY	Y	60620 FQ	78990 AW	105690 TQ	NYBLS	10/01-12/01
Elementary and Secondary School	Dutchess County PMSA, NY	Y	55440 FQ	84570 AW	133130 TQ	NYBLS	10/01-12/01
Elementary and Secondary School	Nassau-Suffolk PMSA, NY	Y	69040 FQ	96920 AW	132360 TQ	NYBLS	10/01-12/01
Elementary and Secondary School	Newburgh PMSA, NY-PA	Y	59330 FQ	77880 AW	103880 TQ	NYBLS	10/01-12/01
Elementary and Secondary School	Rochester MSA, NY	Y	50960 FQ	78360 AW	105470 TQ	NYBLS	10/01-12/01
Elementary and Secondary School	Syracuse MSA, NY	Y	49940 FQ	70750 AW	91830 TQ	NYBLS	10/01-12/01
Elementary and Secondary School	Utica-Rome MSA, NY	Y	55110 FQ	71090 AW	90830 TQ	NYBLS	10/01-12/01
Elementary and Secondary School	North Carolina	Y	40010 FQ	61090 AW	87050 TQ	NCBLS	10/01-12/01
Elementary and Secondary School	Asheville MSA, NC	Y	38910 FQ	56760 AW	73800 TQ	NCBLS	10/01-12/01
Elementary and Secondary School	Charlotte-Gastonia-Rock Hill MSA, NC-SC	Y	40930 FQ	65640 AW	93100 TQ	NCBLS	10/01-12/01
Elementary and Secondary School	Fayetteville MSA, NC	Y	38560 FQ	58020 AW	85240 TQ	NCBLS	10/01-12/01
Elementary and Secondary School	Greensboro-Winston-Salem-High Point MSA, NC	Y	40620 FQ	64950 AW	99320 TQ	NCBLS	10/01-12/01
Elementary and Secondary School	Hickory-Morganton-Lenoir MSA, NC	Y	30490 FQ	58270 AW	75560 TQ	NCBLS	10/01-12/01
Elementary and Secondary School	Raleigh-Durham-Chapel Hill MSA, NC	Y	44410 FQ	63770 AW	89530 TQ	NCBLS	10/01-12/01
Elementary and Secondary School	Wilmington MSA, NC	Y	39580 FQ	56890 AW	77640 TQ	NCBLS	10/01-12/01
Elementary and Secondary School	North Dakota	Y	35940 FQ	50090 AW	69350 TQ	NDBLS	10/01-12/01
Elementary and Secondary School	Fargo-Moorhead MSA, ND-MN	Y	46820 FQ	61840 AW	80420 TQ	NDBLS	10/01-12/01
Elementary and Secondary School	Ohio	Y	48850 FQ	67710 AW	90400 TQ	OHBLS	10/01-12/01
Elementary and Secondary School	Akron PMSA, OH	Y	50510 FQ	67720 AW	87900 TQ	OHBLS	10/01-12/01
Elementary and Secondary School	Canton-Massillon MSA, OH	Y	48770 FQ	67130 AW	89500 TQ	OHBLS	10/01-12/01
Elementary and Secondary School	Cincinnati PMSA, OH-KY-IN	Y	46450 FQ	67710 AW	89570 TQ	OHBLS	10/01-12/01
Elementary and Secondary School	Cleveland-Lorain-Elyria PMSA, OH	Y	51090 FQ	72040 AW	95210 TQ	OHBLS	10/01-12/01
Elementary and Secondary School	Columbus MSA, OH	Y	54320 FQ	74450 AW	95360 TQ	OHBLS	10/01-12/01
Elementary and Secondary School	Dayton-Springfield MSA, OH	Y	51790 FQ	68170 AW	88900 TQ	OHBLS	10/01-12/01
Elementary and Secondary School	Hamilton-Middletown PMSA, OH	Y	53810 FQ	75810 AW	105660 TQ	OHBLS	10/01-12/01
Elementary and Secondary School	Mansfield MSA, OH	Y	37010 FQ	61520 AW	76010 TQ	OHBLS	10/01-12/01
Elementary and Secondary School	Toledo MSA, OH	Y	37270 FQ	63740 AW	86900 TQ	OHBLS	10/01-12/01
Elementary and Secondary School	Youngstown-Warren MSA, OH	Y	46890 FQ	61760 AW	80590 TQ	OHBLS	10/01-12/01
Elementary and Secondary School	Oklahoma	Y	39300 FQ	53550 AW	70140 TQ	OKBLS	10/01-12/01
Elementary and Secondary School	Oklahoma City MSA, OK	Y	32260 FQ	51250 AW	70290 TQ	OKBLS	10/01-12/01
Elementary and Secondary School	Tulsa MSA, OK	Y	39490 FQ	54450 AW	72640 TQ	OKBLS	10/01-12/01
Elementary and Secondary School	Oregon	Y	53020 FQ	70920 AW	90390 TQ	ORBLS	10/01-12/01
Elementary and Secondary School	Eugene-Springfield MSA, OR	Y	55980 FQ	66770 AW	83820 TQ	ORBLS	10/01-12/01
Elementary and Secondary School	Medford-Ashland MSA, OR	Y	48250 FQ	69520 AW	88610 TQ	ORBLS	10/01-12/01
Elementary and Secondary School	Portland-Vancouver PMSA, OR-WA	Y	55560 FQ	75040 AW	92490 TQ	ORBLS	10/01-12/01
Elementary and Secondary School	Salem PMSA, OR	Y	53760 FQ	70080 AW	89910 TQ	ORBLS	10/01-12/01
Elementary and Secondary School	Pennsylvania	Y	44450 FQ	70750 AW	96460 TQ	PABLS	10/01-12/01
Elementary and Secondary School	Allentown-Bethlehem-Easton MSA, PA	Y	44030 FQ	70640 AW	93070 TQ	PABLS	10/01-12/01
Elementary and Secondary School	Erie MSA, PA	Y	51990 FQ	70840 AW	88690 TQ	PABLS	10/01-12/01
Elementary and Secondary School	Harrisburg-Lebanon-Carlisle MSA, PA	Y	49950 FQ	68110 AW	87600 TQ	PABLS	10/01-12/01
Elementary and Secondary School	Johnstown MSA, PA	Y	52110 FQ	67010 AW	86120 TQ	PABLS	10/01-12/01
Elementary and Secondary School	Lancaster MSA, PA	Y	51340 FQ	68710 AW	88210 TQ	PABLS	10/01-12/01

AAW	Average annual wage	AOH	Average offered, high	ASH	Average starting, high	H	Hourly	M	Monthly	S	Special: hourly and annual
AE	Average entry wage	AOL	Average offered, low	ASL	Average starting, low	HI	Highest wage paid	MTC	Median total compensation	TQ	Third quartile wage
AEX	Average experienced wage	APH	Average pay, high range	AW	Average wage paid	HR	High end range	MW	Median wage paid	W	Weekly
AO	Average offered	APL	Average pay, low range	FQ	First quartile wage	LR	Low end range	SQ	Second quartile wage	Y	Yearly

Occupation/Type/Industry	Location	Per	Low	Mid	High	Source	Date
Education Administrator							
Elementary and Secondary School	Philadelphia PMSA, PA-NJ	Y	38340 FQ	75950 AW	108850 TQ	PABLS	10/01-12/01
Elementary and Secondary School	Pittsburgh MSA, PA	Y	58500 FQ	78880 AW	106360 TQ	PABLS	10/01-12/01
Elementary and Secondary School	Reading MSA, PA	Y	35360 FQ	73390 AW	103750 TQ	PABLS	10/01-12/01
Elementary and Secondary School	Scranton-Wilkes-Barre-Hazleton MSA, PA	Y	23780 FQ	59480 AW	89910 TQ	PABLS	10/01-12/01
Elementary and Secondary School	York MSA, PA	Y	36620 FQ	65520 AW	87350 TQ	PABLS	10/01-12/01
Elementary and Secondary School	Rhode Island	Y	43920 FQ	72620 AW	92340 TQ	RIBLS	10/01-12/01
Elementary and Secondary School	Providence-Fall River-Warwick MSA, RI-MA	Y	50930 FQ	71100 AW	90600 TQ	RIBLS	10/01-12/01
Elementary and Secondary School	South Carolina	Y	40090 FQ	62100 AW	86050 TQ	SCBLS	10/01-12/01
Elementary and Secondary School	Charleston-North Charleston MSA, SC	Y	43800 FQ	66820 AW	87860 TQ	SCBLS	10/01-12/01
Elementary and Secondary School	Columbia MSA, SC	Y	48970 FQ	65070 AW	88870 TQ	SCBLS	10/01-12/01
Elementary and Secondary School	Greenville-Spartanburg-Anderson MSA, SC	Y	33180 FQ	58550 AW	86180 TQ	SCBLS	10/01-12/01
Elementary and Secondary School	South Dakota	Y	40160 FQ	54010 AW	70690 TQ	SDBLS	10/01-12/01
Elementary and Secondary School	Tennessee	Y	39540 FQ	57170 AW	74860 TQ	TNBLS	10/01-12/01
Elementary and Secondary School	Chattanooga MSA, TN-GA	Y	44860 FQ	64990 AW	88560 TQ	TNBLS	10/01-12/01
Elementary and Secondary School	Johnson City-Kingsport-Bristol MSA, TN-VA	Y	38180 FQ	54970 AW	71480 TQ	TNBLS	10/01-12/01
Elementary and Secondary School	Knoxville MSA, TN	Y	45550 FQ	60770 AW	79140 TQ	TNBLS	10/01-12/01
Elementary and Secondary School	Memphis MSA, TN-AR-MS	Y	40250 FQ	60480 AW	76480 TQ	TNBLS	10/01-12/01
Elementary and Secondary School	Nashville MSA, TN	Y	37990 FQ	54270 AW	73210 TQ	TNBLS	10/01-12/01
Elementary and Secondary School	Texas	Y	46850 FQ	60920 AW	79820 TQ	TXBLS	10/01-12/01
Elementary and Secondary School	Austin-San Marcos MSA, TX	Y	45780 FQ	64540 AW	90170 TQ	TXBLS	10/01-12/01
Elementary and Secondary School	Beaumont-Port Arthur MSA, TX	Y	46450 FQ	57470 AW	71100 TQ	TXBLS	10/01-12/01
Elementary and Secondary School	Brazoria PMSA, TX	Y	49070 FQ	63890 AW	84600 TQ	TXBLS	10/01-12/01
Elementary and Secondary School	Brownsville-Harlingen-San Benito MSA, TX	Y	48360 FQ	61120 AW	78170 TQ	TXBLS	10/01-12/01
Elementary and Secondary School	Corpus Christi MSA, TX	Y	49770 FQ	65340 AW	85930 TQ	TXBLS	10/01-12/01
Elementary and Secondary School	Dallas PMSA, TX	Y	48600 FQ	63140 AW	83210 TQ	TXBLS	10/01-12/01
Elementary and Secondary School	El Paso MSA, TX	Y	46770 FQ	60810 AW	74200 TQ	TXBLS	10/01-12/01
Elementary and Secondary School	Fort Worth-Arlington PMSA, TX	Y	44130 FQ	63130 AW	86000 TQ	TXBLS	10/01-12/01
Elementary and Secondary School	Galveston-Texas City PMSA, TX	Y	48740 FQ	61470 AW	75360 TQ	TXBLS	10/01-12/01
Elementary and Secondary School	Houston PMSA, TX	Y	48520 FQ	63220 AW	83130 TQ	TXBLS	10/01-12/01
Elementary and Secondary School	Killeen-Temple MSA, TX	Y	45230 FQ	63460 AW	88290 TQ	TXBLS	10/01-12/01
Elementary and Secondary School	Laredo MSA, TX	Y	47640 FQ	61100 AW	77200 TQ	TXBLS	10/01-12/01
Elementary and Secondary School	Longview-Marshall MSA, TX	Y	46320 FQ	54060 AW	67250 TQ	TXBLS	10/01-12/01
Elementary and Secondary School	McAllen-Edinburg-Mission MSA, TX	Y	47200 FQ	60660 AW	74340 TQ	TXBLS	10/01-12/01
Elementary and Secondary School	Odessa-Midland MSA, TX	Y	42140 FQ	59760 AW	82700 TQ	TXBLS	10/01-12/01
Elementary and Secondary School	San Antonio MSA, TX	Y	49590 FQ	64220 AW	83740 TQ	TXBLS	10/01-12/01
Elementary and Secondary School	Tyler MSA, TX	Y	42110 FQ	56700 AW	71700 TQ	TXBLS	10/01-12/01
Elementary and Secondary School	Waco MSA, TX	Y	44370 FQ	56580 AW	71620 TQ	TXBLS	10/01-12/01
Elementary and Secondary School	Utah	Y	53120 FQ	66860 AW	83960 TQ	UTBLS	10/01-12/01
Elementary and Secondary School	Provo-Orem MSA, UT	Y	53820 FQ	69580 AW	89960 TQ	UTBLS	10/01-12/01
Elementary and Secondary School	Salt Lake City-Ogden MSA, UT	Y	55940 FQ	67730 AW	85020 TQ	UTBLS	10/01-12/01
Elementary and Secondary School	Vermont	Y	45840 FQ	61220 AW	81460 TQ	VTBLS	10/01-12/01
Elementary and Secondary School	Burlington MSA, VT	Y	46650 FQ	67550 AW	88910 TQ	VTBLS	10/01-12/01
Elementary and Secondary School	Virginia	Y	43550 FQ	65200 AW	91410 TQ	VABLS	10/01-12/01
Elementary and Secondary School	Lynchburg MSA, VA	Y	26420 FQ	55860 AW	81060 TQ	VABLS	10/01-12/01
Elementary and Secondary School	Norfolk-Virginia Beach-Newport News MSA, VA-NC	Y	40800 FQ	62220 AW	85870 TQ	VABLS	10/01-12/01
Elementary and Secondary School	Richmond-Petersburg MSA, VA	Y	45970 FQ	65210 AW	87040 TQ	VABLS	10/01-12/01
Elementary and Secondary School	Washington	Y	59640 FQ	76490 AW	95640 TQ	WABLS	10/01-12/01
Elementary and Secondary School	Bremerton PMSA, WA	Y	52500 FQ	74390 AW	90580 TQ	WABLS	10/01-12/01
Elementary and Secondary School	Olympia PMSA, WA	Y	56680 FQ	74050 AW	91970 TQ	WABLS	10/01-12/01
Elementary and Secondary School	Richland-Kennewick-Pasco MSA, WA	Y	61450 FQ	73390 AW	89960 TQ	WABLS	10/01-12/01
Elementary and Secondary School	Seattle-Bellevue-Everett PMSA, WA	Y	61510 FQ	81770 AW	107570 TQ	WABLS	10/01-12/01
Elementary and Secondary School	Spokane MSA, WA	Y	61770 FQ	75580 AW	93090 TQ	WABLS	10/01-12/01
Elementary and Secondary School	Tacoma PMSA, WA	Y	62760 FQ	79850 AW	95690 TQ	WABLS	10/01-12/01
Elementary and Secondary School	Yakima MSA, WA	Y	61420 FQ	73970 AW	89660 TQ	WABLS	10/01-12/01
Elementary and Secondary School	West Virginia	Y	42190 FQ	53370 AW	67570 TQ	WVBLS	10/01-12/01

AAW	Average annual wage	**AOH**	Average offered, high	**ASH**	Average starting, high	**H**	Hourly	**M**	Monthly	**S**	Special: hourly and annual
AE	Average entry wage	**AOL**	Average offered, low	**ASL**	Average starting, low	**HI**	Highest wage paid	**MTC**	Median total compensation	**TQ**	Third quartile wage
AEX	Average experienced wage	**APH**	Average pay, high range	**AW**	Average wage paid	**HR**	High end range	**MW**	Median wage paid	**W**	Weekly
AO	Average offered	**APL**	Average pay, low range	**FQ**	First quartile wage	**LR**	Low end range	**SQ**	Second quartile wage	**Y**	Yearly

Occupation/Type/Industry	Location	Per	Low	Mid	High	Source	Date
Education Administrator							
Elementary and Secondary School	Huntington-Ashland MSA, WV-KY-OH	Y	43930 FQ	55630 AW	71030 TQ	WVBLS	10/01-12/01
Elementary and Secondary School	Wisconsin	Y	56570 FQ	71890 AW	91440 TQ	WIBLS	10/01-12/01
Elementary and Secondary School	Appleton-Oshkosh-Neenah MSA, WI	Y	56570 FQ	70150 AW	89350 TQ	WIBLS	10/01-12/01
Elementary and Secondary School	Green Bay MSA, WI	Y	59220 FQ	83830 AW		WIBLS	10/01-12/01
Elementary and Secondary School	Madison MSA, WI	Y	53470 FQ	71840 AW	92860 TQ	WIBLS	10/01-12/01
Elementary and Secondary School	Milwaukee-Waukesha PMSA, WI	Y	56400 FQ	76400 AW	96390 TQ	WIBLS	10/01-12/01
Elementary and Secondary School	Racine PMSA, WI	Y	54840 FQ	70140 AW	90900 TQ	WIBLS	10/01-12/01
Elementary and Secondary School	Wyoming	Y	48220 FQ	57440 AW	70930 TQ	WYBLS	10/01-12/01
Elementary and Secondary School	Puerto Rico	Y	23820 FQ	29720 AW	35770 TQ	PRBLS	10/01-12/01
Elementary and Secondary School	Virgin Islands	Y	41300 FQ	62340 AW	114910 TQ	VIBLS	10/01-12/01
Elementary and Secondary School	Guam	Y	26360 FQ	46620 AW	104480 TQ	GUBLS	10/01-12/01
Postsecondary	Alabama	Y	31930 FQ	68540 AW	121860 TQ	ALBLS	10/01-12/01
Postsecondary	Birmingham MSA, AL	Y	34420 FQ	71190 AW	139590 TQ	ALBLS	10/01-12/01
Postsecondary	Huntsville MSA, AL	Y	30190 FQ	65220 AW	116650 TQ	ALBLS	10/01-12/01
Postsecondary	Mobile MSA, AL	Y	29260 FQ	71820 AW	134200 TQ	ALBLS	10/01-12/01
Postsecondary	Montgomery MSA, AL	Y	30590 FQ	71580 AW	116990 TQ	ALBLS	10/01-12/01
Postsecondary	Arizona	Y	40120 FQ	68940 AW	101090 TQ	AZBLS	10/01-12/01
Postsecondary	Phoenix-Mesa MSA, AZ	Y	37040 FQ	65880 AW	90830 TQ	AZBLS	10/01-12/01
Postsecondary	Arkansas	Y	37960 FQ	67010 AW	105270 TQ	ARBLS	10/01-12/01
Postsecondary	Little Rock-North Little Rock MSA, AR	Y	38010 FQ	71380 AW	115690 TQ	ARBLS	10/01-12/01
Postsecondary	California	Y	39360 FQ	74420 AW	113090 TQ	CABLS	10/01-12/01
Postsecondary	Fresno MSA, CA	Y	40870 FQ	71630 AW	104800 TQ	CABLS	10/01-12/01
Postsecondary	Los Angeles-Long Beach PMSA, CA	Y	47670 FQ	73870 AW	110900 TQ	CABLS	10/01-12/01
Postsecondary	Oakland PMSA, CA	Y	35420 FQ	71210 AW	111410 TQ	CABLS	10/01-12/01
Postsecondary	Orange County PMSA, CA	Y	41340 FQ	75780 AW	114670 TQ	CABLS	10/01-12/01
Postsecondary	Riverside-San Bernardino PMSA, CA	Y	37800 FQ	76660 AW	116890 TQ	CABLS	10/01-12/01
Postsecondary	Sacramento PMSA, CA	Y	46990 FQ	80310 AW	116310 TQ	CABLS	10/01-12/01
Postsecondary	Salinas MSA, CA	Y	44320 FQ	77360 AW	112120 TQ	CABLS	10/01-12/01
Postsecondary	San Diego MSA, CA	Y	29460 FQ	61470 AW	101360 TQ	CABLS	10/01-12/01
Postsecondary	San Francisco PMSA, CA	Y	57030 FQ	86350 AW	121310 TQ	CABLS	10/01-12/01
Postsecondary	San Jose PMSA, CA	Y	41300 FQ	71480 AW	110310 TQ	CABLS	10/01-12/01
Postsecondary	Santa Cruz-Watsonville PMSA, CA	Y	48210 FQ	85900 AW	138180 TQ	CABLS	10/01-12/01
Postsecondary	Ventura PMSA, CA	Y	34160 FQ	57180 AW	96530 TQ	CABLS	10/01-12/01
Postsecondary	Colorado	Y	35060 FQ	63880 AW	110000 TQ	COBLS	10/01-12/01
Postsecondary	Boulder-Longmont PMSA, CO	Y	37120 FQ	63650 AW	103010 TQ	COBLS	10/01-12/01
Postsecondary	Colorado Springs MSA, CO	Y	30830 FQ	52190 AW	90240 TQ	COBLS	10/01-12/01
Postsecondary	Denver PMSA, CO	Y	36510 FQ	68250 AW	119150 TQ	COBLS	10/01-12/01
Postsecondary	Fort Collins-Loveland MSA, CO	Y	36270 FQ	68080 AW	114760 TQ	COBLS	10/01-12/01
Postsecondary	Connecticut	Y	36480 FQ	72920 AW	130270 TQ	CTBLS	10/01-12/01
Postsecondary	Bridgeport PMSA, CT	Y	44640 FQ	75990 AW	123130 TQ	CTBLS	10/01-12/01
Postsecondary	New Haven-Meriden PMSA, CT	Y	34600 FQ	53690 AW	75480 TQ	CTBLS	10/01-12/01
Postsecondary	New London-Norwich MSA, CT-RI	Y	33630 FQ	71200 AW	116900 TQ	CTBLS	10/01-12/01
Postsecondary	Stamford-Norwalk PMSA, CT	Y	39640 FQ	80630 AW		CTBLS	10/01-12/01
Postsecondary	Delaware	Y	38450 FQ	71530 AW	119040 TQ	DEBLS	10/01-12/01
Postsecondary	Wilmington-Newark PMSA, DE-MD	Y	42800 FQ	76370 AW	134330 TQ	DEBLS	10/01-12/01
Postsecondary	District of Columbia	Y	27920 FQ	63800 AW	120120 TQ	DCBLS	10/01-12/01
Postsecondary	Washington PMSA, DC-MD-VA-WV	Y	29530 FQ	68410 AW	139000 TQ	DCBLS	10/01-12/01
Postsecondary	Florida	Y	35570 FQ	64760 AW	104980 TQ	FLBLS	10/01-12/01
Postsecondary	Daytona Beach MSA, FL	Y	41240 FQ	73630 AW	117630 TQ	FLBLS	10/01-12/01
Postsecondary	Fort Lauderdale PMSA, FL	Y	28960 FQ	58520 AW	82250 TQ	FLBLS	10/01-12/01
Postsecondary	Fort Myers-Cape Coral MSA, FL	Y	39840 FQ	66650 AW	111590 TQ	FLBLS	10/01-12/01
Postsecondary	Gainesville MSA, FL	Y	37960 FQ	60260 AW	84290 TQ	FLBLS	10/01-12/01
Postsecondary	Jacksonville MSA, FL	Y	34920 FQ	58700 AW	90700 TQ	FLBLS	10/01-12/01
Postsecondary	Lakeland-Winter Haven MSA, FL	Y	27130 FQ	65970 AW	104720 TQ	FLBLS	10/01-12/01
Postsecondary	Melbourne-Titusville-Palm Bay MSA, FL	Y	44980 FQ	73740 AW	106090 TQ	FLBLS	10/01-12/01
Postsecondary	Miami PMSA, FL	Y	35290 FQ	64310 AW	109740 TQ	FLBLS	10/01-12/01

AAW	Average annual wage	**AOH**	Average offered, high	**ASH**	Average starting, high	**H**	Hourly	**M**	Monthly	**S**	Special: hourly and annual
AE	Average entry wage	**AOL**	Average offered, low	**ASL**	Average starting, low	**HI**	Highest wage paid	**MTC**	Median total compensation	**TQ**	Third quartile wage
AEX	Average experienced wage	**APH**	Average pay, high range	**AW**	Average wage paid	**HR**	High end range	**MW**	Median wage paid	**W**	Weekly
AO	Average offered	**APL**	Average pay, low range	**FQ**	First quartile wage	**LR**	Low end range	**SQ**	Second quartile wage	**Y**	Yearly

Occupation/Type/Industry	Location	Per	Low	Mid	High	Source	Date
Education Administrator							
Postsecondary	Orlando MSA, FL	Y	37920 FQ	67620 AW	108570 TQ	FLBLS	10/01-12/01
Postsecondary	Pensacola MSA, FL	Y	31860 FQ	54980 AW	91780 TQ	FLBLS	10/01-12/01
Postsecondary	Sarasota-Bradenton MSA, FL	Y	39410 FQ	73870 AW	123550 TQ	FLBLS	10/01-12/01
Postsecondary	Tallahassee MSA, FL	Y	39410 FQ	69540 AW	128150 TQ	FLBLS	10/01-12/01
Postsecondary	Tampa-St. Petersburg-Clearwater MSA, FL	Y	38620 FQ	68100 AW	113020 TQ	FLBLS	10/01-12/01
Postsecondary	West Palm Beach-Boca Raton MSA, FL	Y	34530 FQ	58480 AW	87900 TQ	FLBLS	10/01-12/01
Postsecondary	Georgia	Y	38960 FQ	77570 AW	136980 TQ	GABLS	10/01-12/01
Postsecondary	Atlanta MSA, GA	Y	40410 FQ	76660 AW	134430 TQ	GABLS	10/01-12/01
Postsecondary	Augusta-Aiken MSA, GA-SC	Y	38350 FQ	95830 AW		GABLS	10/01-12/01
Postsecondary	Columbus MSA, GA-AL	Y	27460 FQ	57990 AW	104280 TQ	GABLS	10/01-12/01
Postsecondary	Macon MSA, GA	Y	34800 FQ	74880 AW	130230 TQ	GABLS	10/01-12/01
Postsecondary	Hawaii	Y	41310 FQ	78160 AW	124170 TQ	HIBLS	10/01-12/01
Postsecondary	Honolulu MSA, HI	Y	37470 FQ	78470 AW	132150 TQ	HIBLS	10/01-12/01
Postsecondary	Idaho	Y	35240 FQ	72560 AW	113000 TQ	IDBLS	10/01-12/01
Postsecondary	Boise City MSA, ID	Y	26610 FQ	60700 AW	112010 TQ	IDBLS	10/01-12/01
Postsecondary	Illinois	Y	20080 FQ	54130 AW	92510 TQ	ILBLS	10/01-12/01
Postsecondary	Chicago PMSA, IL	Y	19970 FQ	54180 AW	91860 TQ	ILBLS	10/01-12/01
Postsecondary	Peoria-Pekin MSA, IL	Y	15550 FQ	47850 AW	91840 TQ	ILBLS	10/01-12/01
Postsecondary	Rockford MSA, IL	Y	26080 FQ	51750 AW	91580 TQ	ILBLS	10/01-12/01
Postsecondary	Indiana	Y	28750 FQ	53060 AW	88070 TQ	INBLS	10/01-12/01
Postsecondary	Fort Wayne MSA, IN	Y	27820 FQ	45840 AW	75870 TQ	INBLS	10/01-12/01
Postsecondary	Gary PMSA, IN	Y	31470 FQ	61640 AW	104040 TQ	INBLS	10/01-12/01
Postsecondary	Indianapolis MSA, IN	Y	29500 FQ	54640 AW	91240 TQ	INBLS	10/01-12/01
Postsecondary	South Bend MSA, IN	Y	26240 FQ	48900 AW	75800 TQ	INBLS	10/01-12/01
Postsecondary	Iowa	Y	33320 FQ	67110 AW	118920 TQ	IABLS	10/01-12/01
Postsecondary	Davenport-Moline-Rock Island MSA, IA-IL	Y	27580 FQ	52750 AW	86430 TQ	IABLS	10/01-12/01
Postsecondary	Des Moines MSA, IA	Y	31990 FQ	65280 AW	109420 TQ	IABLS	10/01-12/01
Postsecondary	Kansas	Y	36040 FQ	64770 AW	106570 TQ	KSBLS	10/01-12/01
Postsecondary	Wichita MSA, KS	Y	31840 FQ	46070 AW	59500 TQ	KSBLS	10/01-12/01
Postsecondary	Kentucky	Y	37460 FQ	71120 AW	120960 TQ	KYBLS	10/01-12/01
Postsecondary	Louisiana	Y	29630 FQ	57360 AW	97590 TQ	LABLS	10/01-12/01
Postsecondary	Baton Rouge MSA, LA	Y	32070 FQ	66800 AW	114070 TQ	LABLS	10/01-12/01
Postsecondary	Lafayette MSA, LA	Y	29700 FQ	52930 AW	81130 TQ	LABLS	10/01-12/01
Postsecondary	New Orleans MSA, LA	Y	30720 FQ	55050 AW	96320 TQ	LABLS	10/01-12/01
Postsecondary	Shreveport-Bossier City MSA, LA	Y	29470 FQ	54090 AW	91300 TQ	LABLS	10/01-12/01
Postsecondary	Maine	Y	32210 FQ	56710 AW	92290 TQ	MEBLS	10/01-12/01
Postsecondary	Portland MSA, ME	Y	32080 FQ	54720 AW	90710 TQ	MEBLS	10/01-12/01
Postsecondary	Maryland	Y	34900 FQ	67490 AW	111220 TQ	MDBLS	10/01-12/01
Postsecondary	Baltimore PMSA, MD	Y	34930 FQ	64530 AW	104980 TQ	MDBLS	10/01-12/01
Postsecondary	Massachusetts	Y	38580 FQ	69760 AW	122670 TQ	MABLS	10/01-12/01
Postsecondary	Boston PMSA, MA-NH	Y	38840 FQ	72040 AW	135240 TQ	MABLS	10/01-12/01
Postsecondary	Brockton PMSA, MA	Y	37640 FQ	60440 AW	93450 TQ	MABLS	10/01-12/01
Postsecondary	Springfield MSA, MA	Y	38370 FQ	64050 AW	96330 TQ	MABLS	10/01-12/01
Postsecondary	Worcester PMSA, MA-CT	Y	35840 FQ	59600 AW	90260 TQ	MABLS	10/01-12/01
Postsecondary	Michigan	Y	41240 FQ	77710 AW	125190 TQ	MIBLS	10/01-12/01
Postsecondary	Ann Arbor PMSA, MI	Y	39710 FQ	70340 AW	114020 TQ	MIBLS	10/01-12/01
Postsecondary	Detroit PMSA, MI	Y	40840 FQ	72190 AW	103550 TQ	MIBLS	10/01-12/01
Postsecondary	Flint PMSA, MI	Y	44350 FQ	80870 AW	118860 TQ	MIBLS	10/01-12/01
Postsecondary	Grand Rapids-Muskegon-Holland MSA, MI	Y	38680 FQ	73930 AW	122860 TQ	MIBLS	10/01-12/01
Postsecondary	Kalamazoo-Battle Creek MSA, MI	Y	49340 FQ	82020 AW	120890 TQ	MIBLS	10/01-12/01
Postsecondary	Saginaw-Bay City-Midland MSA, MI	Y	42800 FQ	80010 AW	141910 TQ	MIBLS	10/01-12/01
Postsecondary	Minnesota	Y	35810 FQ	67490 AW	106750 TQ	MNBLS	10/01-12/01
Postsecondary	Duluth-Superior MSA, MN-WI	Y	33400 FQ	60960 AW	92310 TQ	MNBLS	10/01-12/01
Postsecondary	Minneapolis-St. Paul MSA, MN-WI	Y	36380 FQ	70670 AW	114860 TQ	MNBLS	10/01-12/01
Postsecondary	St. Cloud MSA, MN	Y	41370 FQ	69190 AW	104160 TQ	MNBLS	10/01-12/01
Postsecondary	Mississippi	Y	35680 FQ	69460 AW	110710 TQ	MSBLS	10/01-12/01
Postsecondary	Jackson MSA, MS	Y	36040 FQ	72270 AW	108660 TQ	MSBLS	10/01-12/01
Postsecondary	Missouri	Y	38850 FQ	66460 AW	95210 TQ	MOBLS	10/01-12/01
Postsecondary	Kansas City MSA, MO-KS	Y	40730 FQ	68210 AW	105310 TQ	MOBLS	10/01-12/01
Postsecondary	St. Louis MSA, MO-IL	Y	33960 FQ	62180 AW	85570 TQ	MOBLS	10/01-12/01
Postsecondary	Springfield MSA, MO	Y	31690 FQ	67380 AW	104030 TQ	MOBLS	10/01-12/01
Postsecondary	Montana	Y	34590 FQ	65200 AW	102650 TQ	MTBLS	10/01-12/01
Postsecondary	Billings MSA, MT	Y	42130 FQ	73590 AW	108530 TQ	MTBLS	10/01-12/01

AAW	Average annual wage	**AOH**	Average offered, high	**ASH**	Average starting, high	**H**	Hourly	**M**	Monthly	**S**	Special: hourly and annual
AE	Average entry wage	**AOL**	Average offered, low	**ASL**	Average starting, low	**HI**	Highest wage paid	**MTC**	Median total compensation	**TQ**	Third quartile wage
AEX	Average experienced wage	**APH**	Average pay, high range	**AW**	Average wage paid	**HR**	High end range	**MW**	Median wage paid	**W**	Weekly
AO	Average offered	**APL**	Average pay, low range	**FQ**	First quartile wage	**LR**	Low end range	**SQ**	Second quartile wage	**Y**	Yearly

Occupation/Type/Industry	Location	Per	Low	Mid	High	Source	Date
Education Administrator							
Postsecondary	Nebraska	Y	33490 FQ	71180 AW		NEBLS	10/01-12/01
Postsecondary	Lincoln MSA, NE	Y	37110 FQ	77630 AW	139390 TQ	NEBLS	10/01-12/01
Postsecondary	Omaha MSA, NE-IA	Y	34990 FQ	82580 AW		NEBLS	10/01-12/01
Postsecondary	Nevada	Y	39630 FQ	76750 AW	131480 TQ	NVBLS	10/01-12/01
Postsecondary	Las Vegas MSA, NV-AZ	Y	43410 FQ	74910 AW	126690 TQ	NVBLS	10/01-12/01
Postsecondary	New Hampshire	Y	32760 FQ	57780 AW	91830 TQ	NHBLS	10/01-12/01
Postsecondary	Manchester PMSA, NH	Y	38140 FQ	55030 AW	79730 TQ	NHBLS	10/01-12/01
Postsecondary	Portsmouth-Rochester PMSA, NH-ME	Y	36050 FQ	76140 AW	134190 TQ	NHBLS	10/01-12/01
Postsecondary	New Jersey	Y	38620 FQ	69850 AW	112220 TQ	NJBLS	10/01-12/01
Postsecondary	Bergen-Passaic PMSA, NJ	Y	38900 FQ	73570 AW	118100 TQ	NJBLS	10/01-12/01
Postsecondary	Jersey City PMSA, NJ	Y	47030 FQ	77220 AW	132260 TQ	NJBLS	10/01-12/01
Postsecondary	Middlesex-Somerset-Hunterdon PMSA, NJ	Y	38010 FQ	70190 AW	116990 TQ	NJBLS	10/01-12/01
Postsecondary	Monmouth-Ocean PMSA, NJ	Y	41110 FQ	70370 AW	119610 TQ	NJBLS	10/01-12/01
Postsecondary	Newark PMSA, NJ	Y	38460 FQ	68390 AW	107880 TQ	NJBLS	10/01-12/01
Postsecondary	Trenton PMSA, NJ	Y	33850 FQ	66180 AW	107650 TQ	NJBLS	10/01-12/01
Postsecondary	New Mexico	Y	31750 FQ	55470 AW	88340 TQ	NMBLS	10/01-12/01
Postsecondary	New York	Y	40990 FQ	73110 AW	114290 TQ	NYBLS	10/01-12/01
Postsecondary	Albany-Schenectady-Troy MSA, NY	Y	37140 FQ	68880 AW	128470 TQ	NYBLS	10/01-12/01
Postsecondary	Binghamton MSA, NY	Y	37700 FQ	68400 AW	128650 TQ	NYBLS	10/01-12/01
Postsecondary	Buffalo-Niagara Falls MSA, NY	Y	37050 FQ	65940 AW	101160 TQ	NYBLS	10/01-12/01
Postsecondary	Dutchess County PMSA, NY	Y	46730 FQ	71740 AW	109800 TQ	NYBLS	10/01-12/01
Postsecondary	Nassau-Suffolk PMSA, NY	Y	36400 FQ	73480 AW	119280 TQ	NYBLS	10/01-12/01
Postsecondary	New York PMSA, NY	Y	49240 FQ	78580 AW	116040 TQ	NYBLS	10/01-12/01
Postsecondary	Rochester MSA, NY	Y	39730 FQ	75560 AW	133970 TQ	NYBLS	10/01-12/01
Postsecondary	Syracuse MSA, NY	Y	41980 FQ	78280 AW	139400 TQ	NYBLS	10/01-12/01
Postsecondary	Utica-Rome MSA, NY	Y	43060 FQ	64890 AW	92640 TQ	NYBLS	10/01-12/01
Postsecondary	North Carolina	Y	33530 FQ	64240 AW	109970 TQ	NCBLS	10/01-12/01
Postsecondary	Asheville MSA, NC	Y	27810 FQ	49400 AW	71910 TQ	NCBLS	10/01-12/01
Postsecondary	Charlotte-Gastonia-Rock Hill MSA, NC-SC	Y	35090 FQ	57360 AW	89260 TQ	NCBLS	10/01-12/01
Postsecondary	Fayetteville MSA, NC	Y	27900 FQ	55700 AW	99710 TQ	NCBLS	10/01-12/01
Postsecondary	Greensboro-Winston-Salem-High Point MSA, NC	Y	29170 FQ	64380 AW	125460 TQ	NCBLS	10/01-12/01
Postsecondary	Hickory-Morganton-Lenoir MSA, NC	Y	37900 FQ	52960 AW	70270 TQ	NCBLS	10/01-12/01
Postsecondary	Raleigh-Durham-Chapel Hill MSA, NC	Y	38900 FQ	74230 AW	125850 TQ	NCBLS	10/01-12/01
Postsecondary	Wilmington MSA, NC	Y	42150 FQ	73660 AW	111170 TQ	NCBLS	10/01-12/01
Postsecondary	North Dakota	Y	26050 FQ	61280 AW	106110 TQ	NDBLS	10/01-12/01
Postsecondary	Fargo-Moorhead MSA, ND-MN	Y	34940 FQ	63570 AW	104760 TQ	NDBLS	10/01-12/01
Postsecondary	Ohio	Y	33770 FQ	64270 AW	110850 TQ	OHBLS	10/01-12/01
Postsecondary	Akron PMSA, OH	Y	37530 FQ	72720 AW	129560 TQ	OHBLS	10/01-12/01
Postsecondary	Cincinnati PMSA, OH-KY-IN	Y	39960 FQ	75570 AW	131780 TQ	OHBLS	10/01-12/01
Postsecondary	Cleveland-Lorain-Elyria PMSA, OH	Y	32750 FQ	61270 AW	114150 TQ	OHBLS	10/01-12/01
Postsecondary	Columbus MSA, OH	Y	31270 FQ	62600 AW	107980 TQ	OHBLS	10/01-12/01
Postsecondary	Dayton-Springfield MSA, OH	Y	34820 FQ	58550 AW	81310 TQ	OHBLS	10/01-12/01
Postsecondary	Toledo MSA, OH	Y	41250 FQ	77430 AW		OHBLS	10/01-12/01
Postsecondary	Oklahoma	Y	26370 FQ	52590 AW	84780 TQ	OKBLS	10/01-12/01
Postsecondary	Oklahoma City MSA, OK	Y	24770 FQ	49640 AW	85250 TQ	OKBLS	10/01-12/01
Postsecondary	Tulsa MSA, OK	Y	39350 FQ	63790 AW	92780 TQ	OKBLS	10/01-12/01
Postsecondary	Oregon	Y	42090 FQ	72690 AW	116750 TQ	ORBLS	10/01-12/01
Postsecondary	Eugene-Springfield MSA, OR	Y	38170 FQ	64700 AW	104380 TQ	ORBLS	10/01-12/01
Postsecondary	Medford-Ashland MSA, OR	Y	38770 FQ	55930 AW	81150 TQ	ORBLS	10/01-12/01
Postsecondary	Portland-Vancouver PMSA, OR-WA	Y	45760 FQ	76530 AW	125240 TQ	ORBLS	10/01-12/01
Postsecondary	Salem PMSA, OR	Y	33160 FQ	54350 AW	85070 TQ	ORBLS	10/01-12/01
Postsecondary	Pennsylvania	Y	29670 FQ	63470 AW	108590 TQ	PABLS	10/01-12/01
Postsecondary	Allentown-Bethlehem-Easton MSA, PA	Y	32890 FQ	55430 AW	81460 TQ	PABLS	10/01-12/01
Postsecondary	Erie MSA, PA	Y	33030 FQ	69250 AW	129780 TQ	PABLS	10/01-12/01
Postsecondary	Harrisburg-Lebanon-Carlisle MSA, PA	Y	33440 FQ	67260 AW	143040 TQ	PABLS	10/01-12/01
Postsecondary	Johnstown MSA, PA	Y	36850 FQ	68130 AW	103710 TQ	PABLS	10/01-12/01
Postsecondary	Lancaster MSA, PA	Y	38360 FQ	70210 AW	113780 TQ	PABLS	10/01-12/01
Postsecondary	Philadelphia PMSA, PA-NJ	Y	28440 FQ	63500 AW	97640 TQ	PABLS	10/01-12/01

AAW Average annual wage; **AE** Average entry wage; **AEX** Average experienced wage; **AO** Average offered; **AOH** Average offered, high; **AOL** Average offered, low; **APH** Average pay, high range; **APL** Average pay, low range; **ASH** Average starting, high; **ASL** Average starting, low; **AW** Average wage paid; **FQ** First quartile wage; **H** Hourly; **HI** Highest wage paid; **HR** High end range; **LR** Low end range; **M** Monthly; **MTC** Median total compensation; **MW** Median wage paid; **SQ** Second quartile wage; **S** Special: hourly and annual; **TQ** Third quartile wage; **W** Weekly; **Y** Yearly

Occupation/Type/Industry	Location	Per	Low	Mid	High	Source	Date
Education Administrator							
Postsecondary	Pittsburgh MSA, PA	Y	27540 FQ	56470 AW	102220 TQ	PABLS	10/01-12/01
Postsecondary	Reading MSA, PA	Y	32200 FQ	62130 AW	96080 TQ	PABLS	10/01-12/01
Postsecondary	Scranton-Wilkes-Barre-Hazleton MSA, PA	Y	32490 FQ	56660 AW	88860 TQ	PABLS	10/01-12/01
Postsecondary	Rhode Island	Y	40130 FQ	67220 AW	106500 TQ	RIBLS	10/01-12/01
Postsecondary	Providence-Fall River-Warwick MSA, RI-MA	Y	40330 FQ	67280 AW	106290 TQ	RIBLS	10/01-12/01
Postsecondary	South Carolina	Y	28990 FQ	52770 AW	88170 TQ	SCBLS	10/01-12/01
Postsecondary	Charleston-North Charleston MSA, SC	Y	31850 FQ	51630 AW	82580 TQ	SCBLS	10/01-12/01
Postsecondary	Columbia MSA, SC	Y	25350 FQ	54620 AW	105220 TQ	SCBLS	10/01-12/01
Postsecondary	Greenville-Spartanburg-Anderson MSA, SC	Y	29870 FQ	47440 AW	78100 TQ	SCBLS	10/01-12/01
Postsecondary	South Dakota	Y	45050 FQ	73250 AW	109160 TQ	SDBLS	10/01-12/01
Postsecondary	Tennessee	Y	33910 FQ	70720 AW	131740 TQ	TNBLS	10/01-12/01
Postsecondary	Chattanooga MSA, TN-GA	Y	39040 FQ	62640 AW	100550 TQ	TNBLS	10/01-12/01
Postsecondary	Clarksville-Hopkinsville MSA, TN-KY	Y	19890 FQ	31490 AW	60260 TQ	TNBLS	10/01-12/01
Postsecondary	Johnson City-Kingsport-Bristol MSA, TN-VA	Y	31760 FQ	56480 AW	104250 TQ	TNBLS	10/01-12/01
Postsecondary	Knoxville MSA, TN	Y	34950 FQ	79600 AW	144660 TQ	TNBLS	10/01-12/01
Postsecondary	Memphis MSA, TN-AR-MS	Y	40560 FQ	78290 AW		TNBLS	10/01-12/01
Postsecondary	Nashville MSA, TN	Y	46420 FQ	84680 AW		TNBLS	10/01-12/01
Postsecondary	Texas	Y	30370 FQ	69740 AW	136390 TQ	TXBLS	10/01-12/01
Postsecondary	Austin-San Marcos MSA, TX	Y	27520 FQ	68490 AW		TXBLS	10/01-12/01
Postsecondary	Corpus Christi MSA, TX	Y	35660 FQ	71690 AW	118700 TQ	TXBLS	10/01-12/01
Postsecondary	Dallas PMSA, TX	Y	42950 FQ	78720 AW	134700 TQ	TXBLS	10/01-12/01
Postsecondary	El Paso MSA, TX	Y	40870 FQ	85550 AW	144160 TQ	TXBLS	10/01-12/01
Postsecondary	Fort Worth-Arlington PMSA, TX	Y	40590 FQ	71210 AW	115390 TQ	TXBLS	10/01-12/01
Postsecondary	Houston PMSA, TX	Y	27050 FQ	57500 AW	104170 TQ	TXBLS	10/01-12/01
Postsecondary	Killeen-Temple MSA, TX	Y	39810 FQ	70640 AW	109940 TQ	TXBLS	10/01-12/01
Postsecondary	Longview-Marshall MSA, TX	Y	29530 FQ	56100 AW	95280 TQ	TXBLS	10/01-12/01
Postsecondary	Lubbock MSA, TX	Y	37490 FQ	69900 AW	115020 TQ	TXBLS	10/01-12/01
Postsecondary	Odessa-Midland MSA, TX	Y	36190 FQ	72040 AW	110810 TQ	TXBLS	10/01-12/01
Postsecondary	San Antonio MSA, TX	Y	34050 FQ	63150 AW	102350 TQ	TXBLS	10/01-12/01
Postsecondary	Tyler MSA, TX	Y	33950 FQ	64770 AW	107020 TQ	TXBLS	10/01-12/01
Postsecondary	Utah	Y	32540 FQ	58770 AW	95830 TQ	UTBLS	10/01-12/01
Postsecondary	Provo-Orem MSA, UT	Y	33640 FQ	54880 AW	82060 TQ	UTBLS	10/01-12/01
Postsecondary	Salt Lake City-Ogden MSA, UT	Y	31500 FQ	56620 AW	90140 TQ	UTBLS	10/01-12/01
Postsecondary	Vermont	Y	31320 FQ	62310 AW	116710 TQ	VTBLS	10/01-12/01
Postsecondary	Burlington MSA, VT	Y	30330 FQ	65870 AW		VTBLS	10/01-12/01
Postsecondary	Virginia	Y	34280 FQ	73040 AW	134300 TQ	VABLS	10/01-12/01
Postsecondary	Lynchburg MSA, VA	Y	37250 FQ	72430 AW	125880 TQ	VABLS	10/01-12/01
Postsecondary	Norfolk-Virginia Beach-Newport News MSA, VA-NC	Y	36690 FQ	70800 AW	122870 TQ	VABLS	10/01-12/01
Postsecondary	Richmond-Petersburg MSA, VA	Y	39320 FQ	82760 AW	145370 TQ	VABLS	10/01-12/01
Postsecondary	Roanoke MSA, VA	Y	24340 FQ	48450 AW	78700 TQ	VABLS	10/01-12/01
Postsecondary	Washington	Y	43890 FQ	70960 AW	113280 TQ	WABLS	10/01-12/01
Postsecondary	Olympia PMSA, WA	Y	45370 FQ	68540 AW	104580 TQ	WABLS	10/01-12/01
Postsecondary	Richland-Kennewick-Pasco MSA, WA	Y	44810 FQ	63970 AW	91890 TQ	WABLS	10/01-12/01
Postsecondary	Seattle-Bellevue-Everett PMSA, WA	Y	44440 FQ	70950 AW	114770 TQ	WABLS	10/01-12/01
Postsecondary	Spokane MSA, WA	Y	43020 FQ	74400 AW	115210 TQ	WABLS	10/01-12/01
Postsecondary	Tacoma PMSA, WA	Y	41790 FQ	65060 AW	95090 TQ	WABLS	10/01-12/01
Postsecondary	Yakima MSA, WA	Y	46910 FQ	69640 AW	113560 TQ	WABLS	10/01-12/01
Postsecondary	West Virginia	Y	31750 FQ	58970 AW	102070 TQ	WVBLS	10/01-12/01
Postsecondary	Huntington-Ashland MSA, WV-KY-OH	Y	32610 FQ	63760 AW	112730 TQ	WVBLS	10/01-12/01
Postsecondary	Wisconsin	Y	36480 FQ	61790 AW	96740 TQ	WIBLS	10/01-12/01
Postsecondary	Milwaukee-Waukesha PMSA, WI	Y	38340 FQ	63000 AW	97130 TQ	WIBLS	10/01-12/01
Postsecondary	Wyoming	Y	39440 FQ	67780 AW	112490 TQ	WYBLS	10/01-12/01
Postsecondary	Puerto Rico	Y	24410 FQ	45780 AW	73730 TQ	PRBLS	10/01-12/01
Preschool and Child Care Center/Program	Alabama	Y	19200 FQ	56710 AW	134100 TQ	ALBLS	10/01-12/01
Preschool and Child Care Center/Program	Birmingham MSA, AL	Y	22300 FQ	84700 AW	140210 TQ	ALBLS	10/01-12/01
Preschool and Child Care Center/Program	Montgomery MSA, AL	Y	20290 FQ	46200 AW	119730 TQ	ALBLS	10/01-12/01

AAW	Average annual wage	**AOH**	Average offered, high	**ASH**	Average starting, high	**H**	Hourly	**M**	Monthly	**S**	Special: hourly and annual
AE	Average entry wage	**AOL**	Average offered, low	**ASL**	Average starting, low	**HI**	Highest wage paid	**MTC**	Median total compensation	**TQ**	Third quartile wage
AEX	Average experienced wage	**APH**	Average pay, high range	**AW**	Average wage paid	**HR**	High end range	**MW**	Median wage paid	**W**	Weekly
AO	Average offered	**APL**	Average pay, low range	**FQ**	First quartile wage	**LR**	Low end range	**SQ**	Second quartile wage	**Y**	Yearly

Occupation/Type/Industry	Location	Per	Low	Mid	High	Source	Date
Education Administrator							
Preschool and Child Care Center/Program	Alaska	Y	22630 FQ	32460 AW	49420 TQ	AKBLS	10/01-12/01
Preschool and Child Care Center/Program	Anchorage MSA, AK	Y	22120 FQ	29820 AW	44960 TQ	AKBLS	10/01-12/01
Preschool and Child Care Center/Program	Arizona	Y	17140 FQ	36780 AW	60240 TQ	AZBLS	10/01-12/01
Preschool and Child Care Center/Program	Phoenix-Mesa MSA, AZ	Y	17310 FQ	35160 AW	64550 TQ	AZBLS	10/01-12/01
Preschool and Child Care Center/Program	Tucson MSA, AZ	Y	15780 FQ	32610 AW	56100 TQ	AZBLS	10/01-12/01
Preschool and Child Care Center/Program	Arkansas	Y	17600 FQ	31020 AW	42930 TQ	ARBLS	10/01-12/01
Preschool and Child Care Center/Program	Fayetteville-Springdale-Rogers MSA, AR	Y	17910 FQ	33710 AW	58080 TQ	ARBLS	10/01-12/01
Preschool and Child Care Center/Program	Fort Smith MSA, AR-OK	Y	12920 FQ	19870 AW	31990 TQ	ARBLS	10/01-12/01
Preschool and Child Care Center/Program	Little Rock-North Little Rock MSA, AR	Y	29160 FQ	32540 AW	36180 TQ	ARBLS	10/01-12/01
Preschool and Child Care Center/Program	California	Y	21860 FQ	39900 AW	65960 TQ	CABLS	10/01-12/01
Preschool and Child Care Center/Program	Bakersfield MSA, CA	Y	16800 FQ	38310 AW	73930 TQ	CABLS	10/01-12/01
Preschool and Child Care Center/Program	Fresno MSA, CA	Y	19090 FQ	38540 AW	55970 TQ	CABLS	10/01-12/01
Preschool and Child Care Center/Program	Los Angeles-Long Beach PMSA, CA	Y	23560 FQ	40170 AW	71080 TQ	CABLS	10/01-12/01
Preschool and Child Care Center/Program	Modesto MSA, CA	Y	25600 FQ	45800 AW	90650 TQ	CABLS	10/01-12/01
Preschool and Child Care Center/Program	Oakland PMSA, CA	Y	24910 FQ	47060 AW	70300 TQ	CABLS	10/01-12/01
Preschool and Child Care Center/Program	Orange County PMSA, CA	Y	26140 FQ	35680 AW	50660 TQ	CABLS	10/01-12/01
Preschool and Child Care Center/Program	Riverside-San Bernardino PMSA, CA	Y	20340 FQ	36490 AW	57300 TQ	CABLS	10/01-12/01
Preschool and Child Care Center/Program	Sacramento PMSA, CA	Y	16020 FQ	38720 AW	76380 TQ	CABLS	10/01-12/01
Preschool and Child Care Center/Program	Salinas MSA, CA	Y	28140 FQ	48030 AW	77020 TQ	CABLS	10/01-12/01
Preschool and Child Care Center/Program	San Diego MSA, CA	Y	19680 FQ	40710 AW	87820 TQ	CABLS	10/01-12/01
Preschool and Child Care Center/Program	San Francisco PMSA, CA	Y	18150 FQ	38200 AW	56650 TQ	CABLS	10/01-12/01
Preschool and Child Care Center/Program	San Jose PMSA, CA	Y	31270 FQ	42660 AW	56380 TQ	CABLS	10/01-12/01
Preschool and Child Care Center/Program	San Luis Obispo-Atascadero-Paso Robles MSA, CA	Y	27100 FQ	40510 AW	57420 TQ	CABLS	10/01-12/01
Preschool and Child Care Center/Program	Santa Barbara-Santa Maria-Lompoc MSA, CA	Y	21770 FQ	35890 AW	54560 TQ	CABLS	10/01-12/01
Preschool and Child Care Center/Program	Santa Cruz-Watsonville PMSA, CA	Y	17560 FQ	36730 AW	56600 TQ	CABLS	10/01-12/01
Preschool and Child Care Center/Program	Santa Rosa PMSA, CA	Y	29120 FQ	34460 AW	38160 TQ	CABLS	10/01-12/01
Preschool and Child Care Center/Program	Stockton-Lodi MSA, CA	Y	25770 FQ	41200 AW	57230 TQ	CABLS	10/01-12/01
Preschool and Child Care Center/Program	Vallejo-Fairfield-Napa PMSA, CA	Y	24710 FQ	32800 AW	40610 TQ	CABLS	10/01-12/01
Preschool and Child Care Center/Program	Ventura PMSA, CA	Y	16520 FQ	35780 AW	54440 TQ	CABLS	10/01-12/01
Preschool and Child Care Center/Program	Visalia-Tulare-Porterville MSA, CA	Y	20020 FQ	25800 AW	28960 TQ	CABLS	10/01-12/01
Preschool and Child Care Center/Program	Colorado	Y	24180 FQ	34320 AW	51200 TQ	COBLS	10/01-12/01
Preschool and Child Care Center/Program	Boulder-Longmont PMSA, CO	Y	25000 FQ	32600 AW	45940 TQ	COBLS	10/01-12/01
Preschool and Child Care Center/Program	Colorado Springs MSA, CO	Y	24750 FQ	38190 AW	56930 TQ	COBLS	10/01-12/01
Preschool and Child Care Center/Program	Denver PMSA, CO	Y	26390 FQ	35760 AW	52290 TQ	COBLS	10/01-12/01
Preschool and Child Care Center/Program	Fort Collins-Loveland MSA, CO	Y	23080 FQ	34480 AW	43810 TQ	COBLS	10/01-12/01
Preschool and Child Care Center/Program	Greeley PMSA, CO	Y	16620 FQ	28410 AW	47300 TQ	COBLS	10/01-12/01
Preschool and Child Care Center/Program	Connecticut	Y	24710 FQ	44230 AW	75020 TQ	CTBLS	10/01-12/01
Preschool and Child Care Center/Program	Bridgeport PMSA, CT	Y	23110 FQ	41630 AW	74170 TQ	CTBLS	10/01-12/01
Preschool and Child Care Center/Program	Hartford MSA, CT	Y	23530 FQ	39750 AW	74570 TQ	CTBLS	10/01-12/01
Preschool and Child Care Center/Program	New Haven-Meriden PMSA, CT	Y	27110 FQ	49720 AW	72340 TQ	CTBLS	10/01-12/01
Preschool and Child Care Center/Program	New London-Norwich MSA, CT-RI	Y	25330 FQ	46250 AW	87700 TQ	CTBLS	10/01-12/01
Preschool and Child Care Center/Program	Stamford-Norwalk PMSA, CT	Y	35840 FQ	54030 AW	73460 TQ	CTBLS	10/01-12/01
Preschool and Child Care Center/Program	Waterbury PMSA, CT	Y	28040 FQ	63430 AW	132420 TQ	CTBLS	10/01-12/01
Preschool and Child Care Center/Program	Delaware	Y	23950 FQ	33970 AW	47530 TQ	DEBLS	10/01-12/01
Preschool and Child Care Center/Program	Wilmington-Newark PMSA, DE-MD	Y	23890 FQ	33770 AW	46390 TQ	DEBLS	10/01-12/01
Preschool and Child Care Center/Program	District of Columbia	Y	21700 FQ	31780 AW	37590 TQ	DCBLS	10/01-12/01
Preschool and Child Care Center/Program	Washington PMSA, DC-MD-VA-WV	Y	22500 FQ	35040 AW	46740 TQ	DCBLS	10/01-12/01
Preschool and Child Care Center/Program	Florida	Y	21000 FQ	34540 AW	57980 TQ	FLBLS	10/01-12/01
Preschool and Child Care Center/Program	Daytona Beach MSA, FL	Y	19240 FQ	31390 AW	57690 TQ	FLBLS	10/01-12/01
Preschool and Child Care Center/Program	Fort Lauderdale PMSA, FL	Y	19700 FQ	33680 AW	60950 TQ	FLBLS	10/01-12/01
Preschool and Child Care Center/Program	Fort Myers-Cape Coral MSA, FL	Y	24740 FQ	31990 AW	39910 TQ	FLBLS	10/01-12/01
Preschool and Child Care Center/Program	Fort Pierce-Port St. Lucie MSA, FL	Y	20060 FQ	31830 AW	52570 TQ	FLBLS	10/01-12/01
Preschool and Child Care Center/Program	Gainesville MSA, FL	Y	22940 FQ	35570 AW	65420 TQ	FLBLS	10/01-12/01
Preschool and Child Care Center/Program	Jacksonville MSA, FL	Y	19620 FQ	31670 AW	50010 TQ	FLBLS	10/01-12/01

AAW	Average annual wage	AOH	Average offered, high	ASH	Average starting, high	H	Hourly	M	Monthly	S	Special: hourly and annual
AE	Average entry wage	AOL	Average offered, low	ASL	Average starting, low	HI	Highest wage paid	MTC	Median total compensation	TQ	Third quartile wage
AEX	Average experienced wage	APH	Average pay, high range	AW	Average wage paid	HR	High end range	MW	Median wage paid	W	Weekly
AO	Average offered	APL	Average pay, low range	FQ	First quartile wage	LR	Low end range	SQ	Second quartile wage	Y	Yearly

Occupation/Type/Industry	Location	Per	Low	Mid	High	Source	Date
Education Administrator							
Preschool and Child Care Center/Program	Lakeland-Winter Haven MSA, FL	Y	16470 FQ	42260 AW	100300 TQ	FLBLS	10/01-12/01
Preschool and Child Care Center/Program	Melbourne-Titusville-Palm Bay MSA, FL	Y	23860 FQ	39140 AW	70270 TQ	FLBLS	10/01-12/01
Preschool and Child Care Center/Program	Miami PMSA, FL	Y	19740 FQ	31910 AW	62160 TQ	FLBLS	10/01-12/01
Preschool and Child Care Center/Program	Ocala MSA, FL	Y	22960 FQ	35000 AW	63020 TQ	FLBLS	10/01-12/01
Preschool and Child Care Center/Program	Orlando MSA, FL	Y	25090 FQ	35770 AW	46190 TQ	FLBLS	10/01-12/01
Preschool and Child Care Center/Program	Pensacola MSA, FL	Y	16860 FQ	36530 AW	57970 TQ	FLBLS	10/01-12/01
Preschool and Child Care Center/Program	Sarasota-Bradenton MSA, FL	Y	18630 FQ	26730 AW	42560 TQ	FLBLS	10/01-12/01
Preschool and Child Care Center/Program	Tampa-St. Petersburg-Clearwater MSA, FL	Y	23930 FQ	32990 AW	51700 TQ	FLBLS	10/01-12/01
Preschool and Child Care Center/Program	West Palm Beach-Boca Raton MSA, FL	Y	22140 FQ	40170 AW	67000 TQ	FLBLS	10/01-12/01
Preschool and Child Care Center/Program	Georgia	Y	28980 FQ	42680 AW	65580 TQ	GABLS	10/01-12/01
Preschool and Child Care Center/Program	Atlanta MSA, GA	Y	31260 FQ	41260 AW	54970 TQ	GABLS	10/01-12/01
Preschool and Child Care Center/Program	Augusta-Aiken MSA, GA-SC	Y	15060 FQ	34950 AW	75120 TQ	GABLS	10/01-12/01
Preschool and Child Care Center/Program	Macon MSA, GA	Y	20540 FQ	31710 AW	39200 TQ	GABLS	10/01-12/01
Preschool and Child Care Center/Program	Hawaii	Y	27540 FQ	39650 AW	54540 TQ	HIBLS	10/01-12/01
Preschool and Child Care Center/Program	Honolulu MSA, HI	Y	30940 FQ	42420 AW	55440 TQ	HIBLS	10/01-12/01
Preschool and Child Care Center/Program	Idaho	Y	17410 FQ	44900 AW	89480 TQ	IDBLS	10/01-12/01
Preschool and Child Care Center/Program	Boise City MSA, ID	Y	15540 FQ	33540 AW	86960 TQ	IDBLS	10/01-12/01
Preschool and Child Care Center/Program	Illinois	Y	17330 FQ	34190 AW	66720 TQ	ILBLS	10/01-12/01
Preschool and Child Care Center/Program	Chicago PMSA, IL	Y	17440 FQ	33350 AW	66020 TQ	ILBLS	10/01-12/01
Preschool and Child Care Center/Program	Peoria-Pekin MSA, IL	Y	18020 FQ	37640 AW	60850 TQ	ILBLS	10/01-12/01
Preschool and Child Care Center/Program	Rockford MSA, IL	Y	21480 FQ	43700 AW	79180 TQ	ILBLS	10/01-12/01
Preschool and Child Care Center/Program	Indiana	Y	19570 FQ	34680 AW	68980 TQ	INBLS	10/01-12/01
Preschool and Child Care Center/Program	Fort Wayne MSA, IN	Y	21730 FQ	41420 AW	76980 TQ	INBLS	10/01-12/01
Preschool and Child Care Center/Program	Indianapolis MSA, IN	Y	19630 FQ	31100 AW	54910 TQ	INBLS	10/01-12/01
Preschool and Child Care Center/Program	Lafayette MSA, IN	Y	23480 FQ	29560 AW	41640 TQ	INBLS	10/01-12/01
Preschool and Child Care Center/Program	South Bend MSA, IN	Y	19010 FQ	30070 AW	54010 TQ	INBLS	10/01-12/01
Preschool and Child Care Center/Program	Iowa	Y	19210 FQ	35230 AW	64550 TQ	IABLS	10/01-12/01
Preschool and Child Care Center/Program	Cedar Rapids MSA, IA	Y	19420 FQ	39930 AW	70030 TQ	IABLS	10/01-12/01
Preschool and Child Care Center/Program	Davenport-Moline-Rock Island MSA, IA-IL	Y	18980 FQ	33020 AW	80590 TQ	IABLS	10/01-12/01
Preschool and Child Care Center/Program	Des Moines MSA, IA	Y	23390 FQ	35390 AW	51070 TQ	IABLS	10/01-12/01
Preschool and Child Care Center/Program	Kansas	Y	21180 FQ	38060 AW	67810 TQ	KSBLS	10/01-12/01
Preschool and Child Care Center/Program	Topeka MSA, KS	Y	24490 FQ	31990 AW	46420 TQ	KSBLS	10/01-12/01
Preschool and Child Care Center/Program	Wichita MSA, KS	Y	28260 FQ	45400 AW	72230 TQ	KSBLS	10/01-12/01
Preschool and Child Care Center/Program	Kentucky	Y	15960 FQ	29870 AW	53850 TQ	KYBLS	10/01-12/01
Preschool and Child Care Center/Program	Lexington MSA, KY	Y	16050 FQ	27780 AW	46950 TQ	KYBLS	10/01-12/01
Preschool and Child Care Center/Program	Louisville MSA, KY-IN	Y	17940 FQ	26570 AW	41840 TQ	KYBLS	10/01-12/01
Preschool and Child Care Center/Program	Louisiana	Y	17750 FQ	28360 AW	45740 TQ	LABLS	10/01-12/01
Preschool and Child Care Center/Program	Baton Rouge MSA, LA	Y	18640 FQ	25380 AW	45150 TQ	LABLS	10/01-12/01
Preschool and Child Care Center/Program	Lafayette MSA, LA	Y	15800 FQ	25550 AW	43700 TQ	LABLS	10/01-12/01
Preschool and Child Care Center/Program	New Orleans MSA, LA	Y	18870 FQ	29780 AW	46640 TQ	LABLS	10/01-12/01
Preschool and Child Care Center/Program	Shreveport-Bossier City MSA, LA	Y	20790 FQ	25870 AW	29660 TQ	LABLS	10/01-12/01
Preschool and Child Care Center/Program	Maine	Y	24480 FQ	36030 AW	54400 TQ	MEBLS	10/01-12/01
Preschool and Child Care Center/Program	Portland MSA, ME	Y	25180 FQ	38090 AW	72760 TQ	MEBLS	10/01-12/01
Preschool and Child Care Center/Program	Maryland	Y	19820 FQ	32150 AW	46550 TQ	MDBLS	10/01-12/01
Preschool and Child Care Center/Program	Baltimore PMSA, MD	Y	19020 FQ	28720 AW	44550 TQ	MDBLS	10/01-12/01
Preschool and Child Care Center/Program	Massachusetts	Y	24130 FQ	40060 AW	58430 TQ	MABLS	10/01-12/01
Preschool and Child Care Center/Program	Boston PMSA, MA-NH	Y	23060 FQ	41670 AW	64750 TQ	MABLS	10/01-12/01
Preschool and Child Care Center/Program	Brockton PMSA, MA	Y	26450 FQ	33630 AW	49730 TQ	MABLS	10/01-12/01
Preschool and Child Care Center/Program	Lawrence PMSA, MA-NH	Y	22440 FQ	37470 AW	57360 TQ	MABLS	10/01-12/01
Preschool and Child Care Center/Program	Lowell PMSA, MA-NH	Y	25550 FQ	35060 AW	48580 TQ	MABLS	10/01-12/01
Preschool and Child Care Center/Program	New Bedford PMSA, MA	Y	21690 FQ	42780 AW	87300 TQ	MABLS	10/01-12/01
Preschool and Child Care Center/Program	Springfield MSA, MA	Y	28170 FQ	39310 AW	55610 TQ	MABLS	10/01-12/01
Preschool and Child Care Center/Program	Worcester PMSA, MA-CT	Y	25240 FQ	38700 AW	56430 TQ	MABLS	10/01-12/01
Preschool and Child Care Center/Program	Michigan	Y	22050 FQ	40870 AW	77090 TQ	MIBLS	10/01-12/01
Preschool and Child Care Center/Program	Ann Arbor PMSA, MI	Y	25280 FQ	37900 AW	55910 TQ	MIBLS	10/01-12/01
Preschool and Child Care Center/Program	Detroit PMSA, MI	Y	25830 FQ	51580 AW	92520 TQ	MIBLS	10/01-12/01
Preschool and Child Care Center/Program	Flint PMSA, MI	Y	11870 FQ	28670 AW	55200 TQ	MIBLS	10/01-12/01
Preschool and Child Care Center/Program	Grand Rapids-Muskegon-Holland MSA, MI	Y	20030 FQ	35750 AW	72760 TQ	MIBLS	10/01-12/01
Preschool and Child Care Center/Program	Lansing-East Lansing MSA, MI	Y	25010 FQ	42690 AW	83030 TQ	MIBLS	10/01-12/01
Preschool and Child Care Center/Program	Saginaw-Bay City-Midland MSA, MI	Y	21040 FQ	37720 AW	72680 TQ	MIBLS	10/01-12/01
Preschool and Child Care Center/Program	Minnesota	Y	22680 FQ	33210 AW	46380 TQ	MNBLS	10/01-12/01
Preschool and Child Care Center/Program	Duluth-Superior MSA, MN-WI	Y	24570 FQ	39370 AW	57040 TQ	MNBLS	10/01-12/01

AAW	Average annual wage	**AOH**	Average offered, high	**ASH**	Average starting, high	**H**	Hourly	**M**	Monthly	**S**	Special: hourly and annual
AE	Average entry wage	**AOL**	Average offered, low	**ASL**	Average starting, low	**HI**	Highest wage paid	**MTC**	Median total compensation	**TQ**	Third quartile wage
AEX	Average experienced wage	**APH**	Average pay, high range	**AW**	Average wage paid	**HR**	High end range	**MW**	Median wage paid	**W**	Weekly
AO	Average offered	**APL**	Average pay, low range	**FQ**	First quartile wage	**LR**	Low end range	**SQ**	Second quartile wage	**Y**	Yearly

Occupation/Type/Industry	Location	Per	Low	Mid	High	Source	Date
Education Administrator							
Preschool and Child Care Center/Program	Minneapolis-St. Paul MSA, MN-WI	Y	23370 FQ	33380 AW	47620 TQ	MNBLS	10/01-12/01
Preschool and Child Care Center/Program	Mississippi	Y	16890 FQ	34420 AW	59740 TQ	MSBLS	10/01-12/01
Preschool and Child Care Center/Program	Biloxi-Gulfport-Pascagoula MSA, MS	Y	18790 FQ	27630 AW	38970 TQ	MSBLS	10/01-12/01
Preschool and Child Care Center/Program	Jackson MSA, MS	Y	14800 FQ	26430 AW	38400 TQ	MSBLS	10/01-12/01
Preschool and Child Care Center/Program	Missouri	Y	20810 FQ	36800 AW	55970 TQ	MOBLS	10/01-12/01
Preschool and Child Care Center/Program	Kansas City MSA, MO-KS	Y	21300 FQ	35250 AW	55380 TQ	MOBLS	10/01-12/01
Preschool and Child Care Center/Program	St. Louis MSA, MO-IL	Y	22140 FQ	40200 AW	66090 TQ	MOBLS	10/01-12/01
Preschool and Child Care Center/Program	Springfield MSA, MO	Y	13190 FQ	24510 AW	44570 TQ	MOBLS	10/01-12/01
Preschool and Child Care Center/Program	Montana	Y	16600 FQ	35280 AW	70260 TQ	MTBLS	10/01-12/01
Preschool and Child Care Center/Program	Nebraska	Y	14970 FQ	30570 AW	48000 TQ	NEBLS	10/01-12/01
Preschool and Child Care Center/Program	Lincoln MSA, NE	Y	16340 FQ	28860 AW	39820 TQ	NEBLS	10/01-12/01
Preschool and Child Care Center/Program	Omaha MSA, NE-IA	Y	14820 FQ	31370 AW	50800 TQ	NEBLS	10/01-12/01
Preschool and Child Care Center/Program	Nevada	Y	20160 FQ	35240 AW	64290 TQ	NVBLS	10/01-12/01
Preschool and Child Care Center/Program	Las Vegas MSA, NV-AZ	Y	20420 FQ	30880 AW	47120 TQ	NVBLS	10/01-12/01
Preschool and Child Care Center/Program	Reno MSA, NV	Y	16030 FQ	32100 AW	63440 TQ	NVBLS	10/01-12/01
Preschool and Child Care Center/Program	New Hampshire	Y	19720 FQ	28550 AW	42740 TQ	NHBLS	10/01-12/01
Preschool and Child Care Center/Program	Nashua PMSA, NH	Y	23150 FQ	32400 AW	43430 TQ	NHBLS	10/01-12/01
Preschool and Child Care Center/Program	New Jersey	Y	28190 FQ	53090 AW	92920 TQ	NJBLS	10/01-12/01
Preschool and Child Care Center/Program	Atlantic-Cape May PMSA, NJ	Y	28470 FQ	77940 AW	118900 TQ	NJBLS	10/01-12/01
Preschool and Child Care Center/Program	Bergen-Passaic PMSA, NJ	Y	33830 FQ	53320 AW	74230 TQ	NJBLS	10/01-12/01
Preschool and Child Care Center/Program	Jersey City PMSA, NJ	Y	25810 FQ	59200 AW	99930 TQ	NJBLS	10/01-12/01
Preschool and Child Care Center/Program	Middlesex-Somerset-Hunterdon PMSA, NJ	Y	24900 FQ	50530 AW	103180 TQ	NJBLS	10/01-12/01
Preschool and Child Care Center/Program	Monmouth-Ocean PMSA, NJ	Y	28670 FQ	55070 AW	110320 TQ	NJBLS	10/01-12/01
Preschool and Child Care Center/Program	Newark PMSA, NJ	Y	30510 FQ	54430 AW	86150 TQ	NJBLS	10/01-12/01
Preschool and Child Care Center/Program	Trenton PMSA, NJ	Y	29570 FQ	48870 AW	82870 TQ	NJBLS	10/01-12/01
Preschool and Child Care Center/Program	New Mexico	Y	18340 FQ	38240 AW	61110 TQ	NMBLS	10/01-12/01
Preschool and Child Care Center/Program	Albuquerque MSA, NM	Y	17530 FQ	28210 AW	41360 TQ	NMBLS	10/01-12/01
Preschool and Child Care Center/Program	Las Cruces MSA, NM	Y	18740 FQ	41940 AW	57280 TQ	NMBLS	10/01-12/01
Preschool and Child Care Center/Program	New York	Y	26730 FQ	51010 AW	88010 TQ	NYBLS	10/01-12/01
Preschool and Child Care Center/Program	Albany-Schenectady-Troy MSA, NY	Y	25480 FQ	38580 AW	62860 TQ	NYBLS	10/01-12/01
Preschool and Child Care Center/Program	Buffalo-Niagara Falls MSA, NY	Y	19760 FQ	42240 AW	82860 TQ	NYBLS	10/01-12/01
Preschool and Child Care Center/Program	Dutchess County PMSA, NY	Y	25270 FQ	42740 AW	59040 TQ	NYBLS	10/01-12/01
Preschool and Child Care Center/Program	Nassau-Suffolk PMSA, NY	Y	29390 FQ	47520 AW	82370 TQ	NYBLS	10/01-12/01
Preschool and Child Care Center/Program	New York PMSA, NY	Y	33700 FQ	59140 AW	96720 TQ	NYBLS	10/01-12/01
Preschool and Child Care Center/Program	Newburgh PMSA, NY-PA	Y	20250 FQ	36540 AW	56590 TQ	NYBLS	10/01-12/01
Preschool and Child Care Center/Program	Rochester MSA, NY	Y	28160 FQ	43740 AW	69760 TQ	NYBLS	10/01-12/01
Preschool and Child Care Center/Program	Syracuse MSA, NY	Y	24900 FQ	40200 AW	58590 TQ	NYBLS	10/01-12/01
Preschool and Child Care Center/Program	Utica-Rome MSA, NY	Y	25950 FQ	41430 AW	66530 TQ	NYBLS	10/01-12/01
Preschool and Child Care Center/Program	North Carolina	Y	16480 FQ	31030 AW	49460 TQ	NCBLS	10/01-12/01
Preschool and Child Care Center/Program	Asheville MSA, NC	Y	22810 FQ	35500 AW	56890 TQ	NCBLS	10/01-12/01
Preschool and Child Care Center/Program	Charlotte-Gastonia-Rock Hill MSA, NC-SC	Y	22510 FQ	38290 AW	68050 TQ	NCBLS	10/01-12/01
Preschool and Child Care Center/Program	Greensboro-Winston-Salem-High Point MSA, NC	Y	22970 FQ	33030 AW	50310 TQ	NCBLS	10/01-12/01
Preschool and Child Care Center/Program	Raleigh-Durham-Chapel Hill MSA, NC	Y	18540 FQ	31530 AW	46270 TQ	NCBLS	10/01-12/01
Preschool and Child Care Center/Program	North Dakota	Y	16750 FQ	29100 AW	44340 TQ	NDBLS	10/01-12/01
Preschool and Child Care Center/Program	Fargo-Moorhead MSA, ND-MN	Y	17680 FQ	26900 AW	39380 TQ	NDBLS	10/01-12/01
Preschool and Child Care Center/Program	Ohio	Y	19800 FQ	32690 AW	56060 TQ	OHBLS	10/01-12/01
Preschool and Child Care Center/Program	Akron PMSA, OH	Y	19650 FQ	30420 AW	42760 TQ	OHBLS	10/01-12/01
Preschool and Child Care Center/Program	Canton-Massillon MSA, OH	Y	18350 FQ	26820 AW	46700 TQ	OHBLS	10/01-12/01
Preschool and Child Care Center/Program	Cincinnati PMSA, OH-KY-IN	Y	14660 FQ	33410 AW	54830 TQ	OHBLS	10/01-12/01
Preschool and Child Care Center/Program	Cleveland-Lorain-Elyria PMSA, OH	Y	20470 FQ	30640 AW	44660 TQ	OHBLS	10/01-12/01
Preschool and Child Care Center/Program	Columbus MSA, OH	Y	19730 FQ	28530 AW	41400 TQ	OHBLS	10/01-12/01
Preschool and Child Care Center/Program	Dayton-Springfield MSA, OH	Y	20200 FQ	36060 AW	67330 TQ	OHBLS	10/01-12/01
Preschool and Child Care Center/Program	Hamilton-Middletown PMSA, OH	Y	17500 FQ	25630 AW	33840 TQ	OHBLS	10/01-12/01
Preschool and Child Care Center/Program	Toledo MSA, OH	Y	18170 FQ	29330 AW	44520 TQ	OHBLS	10/01-12/01
Preschool and Child Care Center/Program	Youngstown-Warren MSA, OH	Y	16760 FQ	32020 AW	54080 TQ	OHBLS	10/01-12/01
Preschool and Child Care Center/Program	Oklahoma	Y	15610 FQ	28830 AW	49390 TQ	OKBLS	10/01-12/01
Preschool and Child Care Center/Program	Oklahoma City MSA, OK	Y	15140 FQ	31390 AW	56210 TQ	OKBLS	10/01-12/01
Preschool and Child Care Center/Program	Tulsa MSA, OK	Y	15630 FQ	26410 AW	36720 TQ	OKBLS	10/01-12/01
Preschool and Child Care Center/Program	Oregon	Y	23490 FQ	37410 AW	63530 TQ	ORBLS	10/01-12/01
Preschool and Child Care Center/Program	Eugene-Springfield MSA, OR	Y	20300 FQ	34930 AW	45050 TQ	ORBLS	10/01-12/01

AAW	Average annual wage	**AOH**	Average offered, high	**ASH**	Average starting, high	**H**	Hourly	**M**	Monthly	**S**	Special: hourly and annual
AE	Average entry wage	**AOL**	Average offered, low	**ASL**	Average starting, low	**HI**	Highest wage paid	**MTC**	Median total compensation	**TQ**	Third quartile wage
AEX	Average experienced wage	**APH**	Average pay, high range	**AW**	Average wage paid	**HR**	High end range	**MW**	Median wage paid	**W**	Weekly
AO	Average offered	**APL**	Average pay, low range	**FQ**	First quartile wage	**LR**	Low end range	**SQ**	Second quartile wage	**Y**	Yearly

Occupation/Type/Industry	Location	Per	Low	Mid	High	Source	Date
Education Administrator							
Preschool and Child Care Center/Program	Portland-Vancouver PMSA, OR-WA	Y	23540 FQ	37910 AW	67800 TQ	ORBLS	10/01-12/01
Preschool and Child Care Center/Program	Salem PMSA, OR	Y	27310 FQ	39580 AW	58900 TQ	ORBLS	10/01-12/01
Preschool and Child Care Center/Program	Pennsylvania	Y	16230 FQ	33570 AW	56720 TQ	PABLS	10/01-12/01
Preschool and Child Care Center/Program	Allentown-Bethlehem-Easton MSA, PA	Y	24560 FQ	41770 AW	73910 TQ	PABLS	10/01-12/01
Preschool and Child Care Center/Program	Erie MSA, PA	Y	18650 FQ	29990 AW	51430 TQ	PABLS	10/01-12/01
Preschool and Child Care Center/Program	Harrisburg-Lebanon-Carlisle MSA, PA	Y	20030 FQ	43210 AW	81310 TQ	PABLS	10/01-12/01
Preschool and Child Care Center/Program	Johnstown MSA, PA	Y	21810 FQ	40190 AW	68870 TQ	PABLS	10/01-12/01
Preschool and Child Care Center/Program	Lancaster MSA, PA	Y	17720 FQ	25500 AW	32960 TQ	PABLS	10/01-12/01
Preschool and Child Care Center/Program	Philadelphia PMSA, PA-NJ	Y	15840 FQ	34700 AW	56230 TQ	PABLS	10/01-12/01
Preschool and Child Care Center/Program	Pittsburgh MSA, PA	Y	18300 FQ	28360 AW	43970 TQ	PABLS	10/01-12/01
Preschool and Child Care Center/Program	Reading MSA, PA	Y	14660 FQ	22370 AW	34860 TQ	PABLS	10/01-12/01
Preschool and Child Care Center/Program	Scranton-Wilkes-Barre-Hazleton MSA, PA	Y	19200 FQ	27740 AW	42300 TQ	PABLS	10/01-12/01
Preschool and Child Care Center/Program	York MSA, PA	Y	19480 FQ	32590 AW	44410 TQ	PABLS	10/01-12/01
Preschool and Child Care Center/Program	Rhode Island	Y	18890 FQ	38180 AW	64420 TQ	RIBLS	10/01-12/01
Preschool and Child Care Center/Program	Providence-Fall River-Warwick MSA, RI-MA	Y	22810 FQ	37170 AW	58090 TQ	RIBLS	10/01-12/01
Preschool and Child Care Center/Program	South Carolina	Y	17130 FQ	34590 AW	73890 TQ	SCBLS	10/01-12/01
Preschool and Child Care Center/Program	Charleston-North Charleston MSA, SC	Y	21470 FQ	29590 AW	40990 TQ	SCBLS	10/01-12/01
Preschool and Child Care Center/Program	Columbia MSA, SC	Y	25130 FQ	57350 AW	92510 TQ	SCBLS	10/01-12/01
Preschool and Child Care Center/Program	Greenville-Spartanburg-Anderson MSA, SC	Y	17280 FQ	32200 AW	52100 TQ	SCBLS	10/01-12/01
Preschool and Child Care Center/Program	South Dakota	Y	26140 FQ	38440 AW	52000 TQ	SDBLS	10/01-12/01
Preschool and Child Care Center/Program	Tennessee	Y	18070 FQ	29470 AW	49260 TQ	TNBLS	10/01-12/01
Preschool and Child Care Center/Program	Chattanooga MSA, TN-GA	Y	19260 FQ	32290 AW	50580 TQ	TNBLS	10/01-12/01
Preschool and Child Care Center/Program	Clarksville-Hopkinsville MSA, TN-KY	Y	14630 FQ	26370 AW	39650 TQ	TNBLS	10/01-12/01
Preschool and Child Care Center/Program	Johnson City-Kingsport-Bristol MSA, TN-VA	Y	11660 FQ	20250 AW	34840 TQ	TNBLS	10/01-12/01
Preschool and Child Care Center/Program	Knoxville MSA, TN	Y	20820 FQ	32510 AW	48750 TQ	TNBLS	10/01-12/01
Preschool and Child Care Center/Program	Memphis MSA, TN-AR-MS	Y	18920 FQ	31070 AW	49260 TQ	TNBLS	10/01-12/01
Preschool and Child Care Center/Program	Nashville MSA, TN	Y	18640 FQ	24980 AW	43310 TQ	TNBLS	10/01-12/01
Preschool and Child Care Center/Program	Texas	Y	15620 FQ	29800 AW	53000 TQ	TXBLS	10/01-12/01
Preschool and Child Care Center/Program	Amarillo MSA, TX	Y	16670 FQ	34800 AW	56620 TQ	TXBLS	10/01-12/01
Preschool and Child Care Center/Program	Austin-San Marcos MSA, TX	Y	19470 FQ	31240 AW	51390 TQ	TXBLS	10/01-12/01
Preschool and Child Care Center/Program	Beaumont-Port Arthur MSA, TX	Y	14640 FQ	22790 AW	46140 TQ	TXBLS	10/01-12/01
Preschool and Child Care Center/Program	Brazoria PMSA, TX	Y	11850 FQ	27170 AW	58730 TQ	TXBLS	10/01-12/01
Preschool and Child Care Center/Program	Brownsville-Harlingen-San Benito MSA, TX	Y	18270 FQ	23750 AW	42380 TQ	TXBLS	10/01-12/01
Preschool and Child Care Center/Program	Corpus Christi MSA, TX	Y	13850 FQ	40680 AW	68580 TQ	TXBLS	10/01-12/01
Preschool and Child Care Center/Program	Dallas PMSA, TX	Y	18690 FQ	31380 AW	48280 TQ	TXBLS	10/01-12/01
Preschool and Child Care Center/Program	El Paso MSA, TX	Y	14940 FQ	22490 AW	40490 TQ	TXBLS	10/01-12/01
Preschool and Child Care Center/Program	Fort Worth-Arlington PMSA, TX	Y	15570 FQ	28130 AW	58780 TQ	TXBLS	10/01-12/01
Preschool and Child Care Center/Program	Houston PMSA, TX	Y	17170 FQ	30870 AW	49270 TQ	TXBLS	10/01-12/01
Preschool and Child Care Center/Program	Killeen-Temple MSA, TX	Y	14090 FQ	21140 AW	30320 TQ	TXBLS	10/01-12/01
Preschool and Child Care Center/Program	Longview-Marshall MSA, TX	Y	15120 FQ	36580 AW	57920 TQ	TXBLS	10/01-12/01
Preschool and Child Care Center/Program	Lubbock MSA, TX	Y	15430 FQ	21420 AW	32870 TQ	TXBLS	10/01-12/01
Preschool and Child Care Center/Program	McAllen-Edinburg-Mission MSA, TX	Y	19120 FQ	32980 AW	56230 TQ	TXBLS	10/01-12/01
Preschool and Child Care Center/Program	Odessa-Midland MSA, TX	Y	14320 FQ	30020 AW	55340 TQ	TXBLS	10/01-12/01
Preschool and Child Care Center/Program	San Antonio MSA, TX	Y	14010 FQ	26960 AW	50050 TQ	TXBLS	10/01-12/01
Preschool and Child Care Center/Program	Waco MSA, TX	Y	16600 FQ	33490 AW	55850 TQ	TXBLS	10/01-12/01
Preschool and Child Care Center/Program	Utah	Y	19610 FQ	37460 AW	63980 TQ	UTBLS	10/01-12/01
Preschool and Child Care Center/Program	Salt Lake City-Ogden MSA, UT	Y	19200 FQ	34300 AW	58370 TQ	UTBLS	10/01-12/01
Preschool and Child Care Center/Program	Vermont	Y	23050 FQ	43420 AW	70610 TQ	VTBLS	10/01-12/01
Preschool and Child Care Center/Program	Virginia	Y	18880 FQ	32300 AW	55690 TQ	VABLS	10/01-12/01
Preschool and Child Care Center/Program	Lynchburg MSA, VA	Y	17900 FQ	29450 AW	61000 TQ	VABLS	10/01-12/01
Preschool and Child Care Center/Program	Norfolk-Virginia Beach-Newport News MSA, VA-NC	Y	17260 FQ	30140 AW	55160 TQ	VABLS	10/01-12/01
Preschool and Child Care Center/Program	Richmond-Petersburg MSA, VA	Y	19530 FQ	33030 AW	56220 TQ	VABLS	10/01-12/01
Preschool and Child Care Center/Program	Roanoke MSA, VA	Y	16290 FQ	24180 AW	33960 TQ	VABLS	10/01-12/01
Preschool and Child Care Center/Program	Washington	Y	31040 FQ	50150 AW	74380 TQ	WABLS	10/01-12/01

AAW	Average annual wage	**AOH**	Average offered, high	**ASH**	Average starting, high	**H**	Hourly	**M**	Monthly	**S**	Special: hourly and annual
AE	Average entry wage	**AOL**	Average offered, low	**ASL**	Average starting, low	**HI**	Highest wage paid	**MTC**	Median total compensation	**TQ**	Third quartile wage
AEX	Average experienced wage	**APH**	Average pay, high range	**AW**	Average wage paid	**HR**	High end range	**MW**	Median wage paid	**W**	Weekly
AO	Average offered	**APL**	Average pay, low range	**FQ**	First quartile wage	**LR**	Low end range	**SQ**	Second quartile wage	**Y**	Yearly

Occupation/Type/Industry	Location	Per	Low	Mid	High	Source	Date
Education Administrator							
Preschool and Child Care Center/Program	Richland-Kennewick-Pasco MSA, WA	Y	30380 FQ	41720 AW	72040 TQ	WABLS	10/01-12/01
Preschool and Child Care Center/Program	Seattle-Bellevue-Everett PMSA, WA	Y	32680 FQ	54090 AW	73650 TQ	WABLS	10/01-12/01
Preschool and Child Care Center/Program	Spokane MSA, WA	Y	29410 FQ	42150 AW	57660 TQ	WABLS	10/01-12/01
Preschool and Child Care Center/Program	Tacoma PMSA, WA	Y	29740 FQ	53910 AW	93180 TQ	WABLS	10/01-12/01
Preschool and Child Care Center/Program	West Virginia	Y	16600 FQ	29180 AW	50340 TQ	WVBLS	10/01-12/01
Preschool and Child Care Center/Program	Huntington-Ashland MSA, WV-KY-OH	Y	19920 FQ	32800 AW	54470 TQ	WVBLS	10/01-12/01
Preschool and Child Care Center/Program	Wisconsin	Y	22530 FQ	39220 AW	79680 TQ	WIBLS	10/01-12/01
Preschool and Child Care Center/Program	Appleton-Oshkosh-Neenah MSA, WI	Y	19930 FQ	30920 AW	42430 TQ	WIBLS	10/01-12/01
Preschool and Child Care Center/Program	Green Bay MSA, WI	Y	20760 FQ	38650 AW	81410 TQ	WIBLS	10/01-12/01
Preschool and Child Care Center/Program	Madison MSA, WI	Y	25390 FQ	39340 AW	70870 TQ	WIBLS	10/01-12/01
Preschool and Child Care Center/Program	Milwaukee-Waukesha PMSA, WI	Y	23780 FQ	38250 AW	67310 TQ	WIBLS	10/01-12/01
Preschool and Child Care Center/Program	Racine PMSA, WI	Y	16410 FQ	35040 AW	56040 TQ	WIBLS	10/01-12/01
Preschool and Child Care Center/Program	Wyoming	Y	23400 FQ	33840 AW	51030 TQ	WYBLS	10/01-12/01
Preschool and Child Care Center/Program	Puerto Rico	Y	21330 FQ	36720 AW	55600 TQ	PRBLS	10/01-12/01
Preschool and Child Care Center/Program	Guam	Y	19490 FQ	48970 AW	70280 TQ	GUBLS	10/01-12/01
Education Teacher							
Postsecondary	Alabama	Y	32170 FQ	50730 AW	73180 TQ	ALBLS	10/01-12/01
Postsecondary	Birmingham MSA, AL	Y	32100 FQ	52280 AW	81510 TQ	ALBLS	10/01-12/01
Postsecondary	Huntsville MSA, AL	Y	33920 FQ	52550 AW	75710 TQ	ALBLS	10/01-12/01
Postsecondary	Arkansas	Y	25240 FQ	48220 AW	77690 TQ	ARBLS	10/01-12/01
Postsecondary	California	Y	24400 FQ	56990 AW	91970 TQ	CABLS	10/01-12/01
Postsecondary	Los Angeles-Long Beach PMSA, CA	Y	21360 FQ	54880 AW	90050 TQ	CABLS	10/01-12/01
Postsecondary	Oakland PMSA, CA	Y	21840 FQ	52530 AW	89230 TQ	CABLS	10/01-12/01
Postsecondary	Riverside-San Bernardino PMSA, CA	Y	24530 FQ	49990 AW	75950 TQ	CABLS	10/01-12/01
Postsecondary	San Francisco PMSA, CA	Y	40020 FQ	67300 AW	98680 TQ	CABLS	10/01-12/01
Postsecondary	Colorado	Y	27320 FQ	48010 AW	76740 TQ	COBLS	10/01-12/01
Postsecondary	Denver PMSA, CO	Y	28370 FQ	49400 AW	79210 TQ	COBLS	10/01-12/01
Postsecondary	Connecticut	Y	37040 FQ	56430 AW	89530 TQ	CTBLS	10/01-12/01
Postsecondary	Hartford MSA, CT	Y	36890 FQ	56390 AW	90210 TQ	CTBLS	10/01-12/01
Postsecondary	Delaware	Y	24430 FQ	57580 AW	92230 TQ	DEBLS	10/01-12/01
Postsecondary	District of Columbia	Y	27630 FQ	50050 AW	80440 TQ	DCBLS	10/01-12/01
Postsecondary	Washington PMSA, DC-MD-VA-WV	Y	24220 FQ	52770 AW	90660 TQ	DCBLS	10/01-12/01
Postsecondary	Florida	Y	32350 FQ	59080 AW	93750 TQ	FLBLS	10/01-12/01
Postsecondary	Fort Lauderdale PMSA, FL	Y	37370 FQ	65370 AW	108620 TQ	FLBLS	10/01-12/01
Postsecondary	Fort Pierce-Port St. Lucie MSA, FL	Y	24380 FQ	44290 AW	60460 TQ	FLBLS	10/01-12/01
Postsecondary	Gainesville MSA, FL	Y	35530 FQ	66580 AW	113500 TQ	FLBLS	10/01-12/01
Postsecondary	Jacksonville MSA, FL	Y	34320 FQ	57510 AW	85680 TQ	FLBLS	10/01-12/01
Postsecondary	Miami PMSA, FL	Y	38890 FQ	64660 AW	107220 TQ	FLBLS	10/01-12/01
Postsecondary	Orlando MSA, FL	Y	26860 FQ	53200 AW	85670 TQ	FLBLS	10/01-12/01
Postsecondary	Pensacola MSA, FL	Y	37910 FQ	60330 AW	93110 TQ	FLBLS	10/01-12/01
Postsecondary	Tallahassee MSA, FL	Y	39020 FQ	62020 AW	91890 TQ	FLBLS	10/01-12/01
Postsecondary	Tampa-St. Petersburg-Clearwater MSA, FL	Y	34140 FQ	58630 AW	93030 TQ	FLBLS	10/01-12/01
Postsecondary	West Palm Beach-Boca Raton MSA, FL	Y	32110 FQ	56550 AW	89200 TQ	FLBLS	10/01-12/01
Postsecondary	Georgia	Y	30630 FQ	50220 AW	74560 TQ	GABLS	10/01-12/01
Postsecondary	Atlanta MSA, GA	Y	25760 FQ	43210 AW	67850 TQ	GABLS	10/01-12/01
Postsecondary	Hawaii	Y	33820 FQ	53210 AW	78430 TQ	HIBLS	10/01-12/01
Postsecondary	Honolulu MSA, HI	Y	33490 FQ	54560 AW	81010 TQ	HIBLS	10/01-12/01
Postsecondary	Idaho	Y	36420 FQ	49950 AW	62800 TQ	IDBLS	10/01-12/01
Postsecondary	Illinois	Y	24080 FQ	50730 AW	85840 TQ	ILBLS	10/01-12/01
Postsecondary	Chicago PMSA, IL	Y	23800 FQ	51580 AW	87920 TQ	ILBLS	10/01-12/01
Postsecondary	Springfield MSA, IL	Y	19460 FQ	50560 AW	87280 TQ	ILBLS	10/01-12/01
Postsecondary	Indiana	Y	26660 FQ	48660 AW	79400 TQ	INBLS	10/01-12/01
Postsecondary	Fort Wayne MSA, IN	Y	37410 FQ	47310 AW	59810 TQ	INBLS	10/01-12/01
Postsecondary	Iowa	Y	31390 FQ	82200 AW		IABLS	10/01-12/01
Postsecondary	Davenport-Moline-Rock Island MSA, IA-IL	Y	25730 FQ	51460 AW	100350 TQ	IABLS	10/01-12/01
Postsecondary	Des Moines MSA, IA	Y	30900 FQ	67130 AW		IABLS	10/01-12/01
Postsecondary	Kansas	Y	23550 FQ	42330 AW	68730 TQ	KSBLS	10/01-12/01
Postsecondary	Kentucky	Y	28150 FQ	50220 AW	79040 TQ	KYBLS	10/01-12/01
Postsecondary	Louisville MSA, KY-IN	Y	28770 FQ	51770 AW	83090 TQ	KYBLS	10/01-12/01

AAW Average annual wage; AE Average entry wage; AEX Average experienced wage; AO Average offered; AOH Average offered, high; AOL Average offered, low; APH Average pay, high range; APL Average pay, low range; ASH Average starting, high; ASL Average starting, low; AW Average wage paid; FQ First quartile wage; H Hourly; HI Highest wage paid; HR High end range; LR Low end range; M Monthly; MTC Median total compensation; MW Median wage paid; SQ Second quartile wage; S Special: hourly and annual; TQ Third quartile wage; W Weekly; Y Yearly

Occupation/Type/Industry	Location	Per	Low	Mid	High	Source	Date
Education Teacher							
Postsecondary	Louisiana	Y	12700 FQ	38190 AW	61090 TQ	LABLS	10/01-12/01
Postsecondary	New Orleans MSA, LA	Y	11940 FQ	36840 AW	65430 TQ	LABLS	10/01-12/01
Postsecondary	Maine	Y	26680 FQ	44540 AW	65520 TQ	MEBLS	10/01-12/01
Postsecondary	Maryland	Y	30060 FQ	55440 AW	89040 TQ	MDBLS	10/01-12/01
Postsecondary	Baltimore PMSA, MD	Y	29340 FQ	48090 AW	75670 TQ	MDBLS	10/01-12/01
Postsecondary	Massachusetts	Y	30750 FQ	49410 AW	72590 TQ	MABLS	10/01-12/01
Postsecondary	Boston PMSA, MA-NH	Y	29890 FQ	49780 AW	73750 TQ	MABLS	10/01-12/01
Postsecondary	Brockton PMSA, MA	Y	29140 FQ	44470 AW	61050 TQ	MABLS	10/01-12/01
Postsecondary	Springfield MSA, MA	Y	36750 FQ	49880 AW	68840 TQ	MABLS	10/01-12/01
Postsecondary	Worcester PMSA, MA-CT	Y	28970 FQ	49770 AW	78850 TQ	MABLS	10/01-12/01
Postsecondary	Michigan	Y	30470 FQ	54980 AW	87420 TQ	MIBLS	10/01-12/01
Postsecondary	Ann Arbor PMSA, MI	Y	26360 FQ	47390 AW	74680 TQ	MIBLS	10/01-12/01
Postsecondary	Detroit PMSA, MI	Y	25220 FQ	45460 AW	72680 TQ	MIBLS	10/01-12/01
Postsecondary	Minnesota	Y	35370 FQ	46490 AW	59820 TQ	MNBLS	10/01-12/01
Postsecondary	Duluth-Superior MSA, MN-WI	Y	27090 FQ	45020 AW	67970 TQ	MNBLS	10/01-12/01
Postsecondary	St. Cloud MSA, MN	Y	30040 FQ	42490 AW	54420 TQ	MNBLS	10/01-12/01
Postsecondary	Mississippi	Y	31960 FQ	47420 AW	68070 TQ	MSBLS	10/01-12/01
Postsecondary	Jackson MSA, MS	Y	13740 FQ	41790 AW	58140 TQ	MSBLS	10/01-12/01
Postsecondary	Missouri	Y	20860 FQ	41270 AW	65230 TQ	MOBLS	10/01-12/01
Postsecondary	Kansas City MSA, MO-KS	Y	29160 FQ	44100 AW	66240 TQ	MOBLS	10/01-12/01
Postsecondary	St. Louis MSA, MO-IL	Y	19890 FQ	33770 AW	52060 TQ	MOBLS	10/01-12/01
Postsecondary	Springfield MSA, MO	Y	26440 FQ	50540 AW	75540 TQ	MOBLS	10/01-12/01
Postsecondary	Montana	Y	22760 FQ	46730 AW	75160 TQ	MTBLS	10/01-12/01
Postsecondary	Nebraska	Y	20890 FQ	43500 AW	68730 TQ	NEBLS	10/01-12/01
Postsecondary	Lincoln MSA, NE	Y	38800 FQ	59540 AW	90850 TQ	NEBLS	10/01-12/01
Postsecondary	Omaha MSA, NE-IA	Y	34380 FQ	53820 AW	73910 TQ	NEBLS	10/01-12/01
Postsecondary	Nevada	Y	23210 FQ	41320 AW	71800 TQ	NVBLS	10/01-12/01
Postsecondary	Las Vegas MSA, NV-AZ	Y	23230 FQ	39510 AW	70900 TQ	NVBLS	10/01-12/01
Postsecondary	New Hampshire	Y	29720 FQ	45060 AW	65450 TQ	NHBLS	10/01-12/01
Postsecondary	Manchester PMSA, NH	Y	25970 FQ	33370 AW	42630 TQ	NHBLS	10/01-12/01
Postsecondary	New Jersey	Y	31610 FQ	56330 AW	89250 TQ	NJBLS	10/01-12/01
Postsecondary	Bergen-Passaic PMSA, NJ	Y	29140 FQ	53310 AW	87580 TQ	NJBLS	10/01-12/01
Postsecondary	Monmouth-Ocean PMSA, NJ	Y	37890 FQ	59970 AW	85540 TQ	NJBLS	10/01-12/01
Postsecondary	Newark PMSA, NJ	Y	30080 FQ	54960 AW	88560 TQ	NJBLS	10/01-12/01
Postsecondary	New Mexico	Y	28720 FQ	46280 AW	65640 TQ	NMBLS	10/01-12/01
Postsecondary	New York	Y	31830 FQ	49050 AW	76700 TQ	NYBLS	10/01-12/01
Postsecondary	New York PMSA, NY	Y	33150 FQ	49460 AW	76680 TQ	NYBLS	10/01-12/01
Postsecondary	North Carolina	Y	30540 FQ	47910 AW	72110 TQ	NCBLS	10/01-12/01
Postsecondary	Asheville MSA, NC	Y	32580 FQ	45800 AW	66800 TQ	NCBLS	10/01-12/01
Postsecondary	Charlotte-Gastonia-Rock Hill MSA, NC-SC	Y	30760 FQ	48770 AW	71370 TQ	NCBLS	10/01-12/01
Postsecondary	Fayetteville MSA, NC	Y	38370 FQ	53450 AW	73430 TQ	NCBLS	10/01-12/01
Postsecondary	Greensboro-Winston-Salem-High Point MSA, NC	Y	31180 FQ	48960 AW	73460 TQ	NCBLS	10/01-12/01
Postsecondary	Hickory-Morganton-Lenoir MSA, NC	Y	30610 FQ	36750 AW	45360 TQ	NCBLS	10/01-12/01
Postsecondary	Raleigh-Durham-Chapel Hill MSA, NC	Y	31440 FQ	51200 AW	80050 TQ	NCBLS	10/01-12/01
Postsecondary	North Dakota	Y	28010 FQ	44770 AW	64620 TQ	NDBLS	10/01-12/01
Postsecondary	Fargo-Moorhead MSA, ND-MN	Y	25350 FQ	45260 AW	68920 TQ	NDBLS	10/01-12/01
Postsecondary	Ohio	Y	26340 FQ	46500 AW	70560 TQ	OHBLS	10/01-12/01
Postsecondary	Cincinnati PMSA, OH-KY-IN	Y	29920 FQ	52590 AW	81080 TQ	OHBLS	10/01-12/01
Postsecondary	Cleveland-Lorain-Elyria PMSA, OH	Y	22100 FQ	44560 AW	71600 TQ	OHBLS	10/01-12/01
Postsecondary	Columbus MSA, OH	Y	25440 FQ	38680 AW	57220 TQ	OHBLS	10/01-12/01
Postsecondary	Dayton-Springfield MSA, OH	Y	28340 FQ	48210 AW	72210 TQ	OHBLS	10/01-12/01
Postsecondary	Toledo MSA, OH	Y	22760 FQ	46620 AW	69920 TQ	OHBLS	10/01-12/01
Postsecondary	Youngstown-Warren MSA, OH	Y	30520 FQ	52610 AW	78800 TQ	OHBLS	10/01-12/01
Postsecondary	Oklahoma	Y	26810 FQ	42100 AW	59160 TQ	OKBLS	10/01-12/01
Postsecondary	Oklahoma City MSA, OK	Y	26880 FQ	43130 AW	62880 TQ	OKBLS	10/01-12/01
Postsecondary	Oregon	Y	33140 FQ	54770 AW	83680 TQ	ORBLS	10/01-12/01
Postsecondary	Eugene-Springfield MSA, OR	Y	36780 FQ	55780 AW	87840 TQ	ORBLS	10/01-12/01
Postsecondary	Portland-Vancouver PMSA, OR-WA	Y	33400 FQ	55260 AW	82550 TQ	ORBLS	10/01-12/01
Postsecondary	Salem PMSA, OR	Y	32330 FQ	52260 AW	79020 TQ	ORBLS	10/01-12/01
Postsecondary	Pennsylvania	Y	28370 FQ	54050 AW	86380 TQ	PABLS	10/01-12/01
Postsecondary	Allentown-Bethlehem-Easton MSA, PA	Y	27000 FQ	43580 AW	64440 TQ	PABLS	10/01-12/01
Postsecondary	Harrisburg-Lebanon-Carlisle MSA, PA	Y	31720 FQ	60400 AW	89570 TQ	PABLS	10/01-12/01

AAW	Average annual wage	AOH	Average offered, high	ASH	Average starting, high	H	Hourly	M	Monthly	S	Special: hourly and annual
AE	Average entry wage	AOL	Average offered, low	ASL	Average starting, low	HI	Highest wage paid	MTC	Median total compensation	TQ	Third quartile wage
AEX	Average experienced wage	APH	Average pay, high range	AW	Average wage paid	HR	High end range	MW	Median wage paid	W	Weekly
AO	Average offered	APL	Average pay, low range	FQ	First quartile wage	LR	Low end range	SQ	Second quartile wage	Y	Yearly

Occupation/Type/Industry	Location	Per	Low	Mid	High	Source	Date
Education Teacher							
Postsecondary	Philadelphia PMSA, PA-NJ	Y	27320 FQ	53390 AW	86120 TQ	PABLS	10/01-12/01
Postsecondary	Pittsburgh MSA, PA	Y	26580 FQ	50500 AW	84930 TQ	PABLS	10/01-12/01
Postsecondary	Scranton-Wilkes-Barre-Hazleton MSA, PA	Y	34410 FQ	52540 AW	80120 TQ	PABLS	10/01-12/01
Postsecondary	Rhode Island	Y	29310 FQ	52380 AW	83370 TQ	RIBLS	10/01-12/01
Postsecondary	South Carolina	Y	24830 FQ	49080 AW	75780 TQ	SCBLS	10/01-12/01
Postsecondary	Charleston-North Charleston MSA, SC	Y	25810 FQ	43250 AW	68160 TQ	SCBLS	10/01-12/01
Postsecondary	Columbia MSA, SC	Y	19830 FQ	49160 AW	85330 TQ	SCBLS	10/01-12/01
Postsecondary	Greenville-Spartanburg-Anderson MSA, SC	Y	32360 FQ	49860 AW	71550 TQ	SCBLS	10/01-12/01
Postsecondary	South Dakota	Y	31170 FQ	45280 AW	62380 TQ	SDBLS	10/01-12/01
Postsecondary	Tennessee	Y	22390 FQ	46360 AW	71560 TQ	TNBLS	10/01-12/01
Postsecondary	Chattanooga MSA, TN-GA	Y	30260 FQ	45960 AW	58370 TQ	TNBLS	10/01-12/01
Postsecondary	Johnson City-Kingsport-Bristol MSA, TN-VA	Y	20580 FQ	36050 AW	54390 TQ	TNBLS	10/01-12/01
Postsecondary	Knoxville MSA, TN	Y	19370 FQ	50270 AW	83360 TQ	TNBLS	10/01-12/01
Postsecondary	Memphis MSA, TN-AR-MS	Y	28800 FQ	46420 AW	66740 TQ	TNBLS	10/01-12/01
Postsecondary	Nashville MSA, TN	Y	24560 FQ	51030 AW	80730 TQ	TNBLS	10/01-12/01
Postsecondary	Texas	Y	26540 FQ	49750 AW	75750 TQ	TXBLS	10/01-12/01
Postsecondary	Austin-San Marcos MSA, TX	Y	27120 FQ	50690 AW	75810 TQ	TXBLS	10/01-12/01
Postsecondary	Dallas PMSA, TX	Y	29650 FQ	53540 AW	82050 TQ	TXBLS	10/01-12/01
Postsecondary	Fort Worth-Arlington PMSA, TX	Y	24020 FQ	47280 AW	75800 TQ	TXBLS	10/01-12/01
Postsecondary	Houston PMSA, TX	Y	28690 FQ	50010 AW	72450 TQ	TXBLS	10/01-12/01
Postsecondary	San Antonio MSA, TX	Y	25640 FQ	45150 AW	68570 TQ	TXBLS	10/01-12/01
Postsecondary	Utah	Y	24060 FQ	50220 AW	78230 TQ	UTBLS	10/01-12/01
Postsecondary	Salt Lake City-Ogden MSA, UT	Y	23350 FQ	46740 AW	70120 TQ	UTBLS	10/01-12/01
Postsecondary	Vermont	Y	38660 FQ	50610 AW	60650 TQ	VTBLS	10/01-12/01
Postsecondary	Burlington MSA, VT	Y	42430 FQ	50960 AW	56550 TQ	VTBLS	10/01-12/01
Postsecondary	Virginia	Y	23440 FQ	51140 AW	86740 TQ	VABLS	10/01-12/01
Postsecondary	Norfolk-Virginia Beach-Newport News MSA, VA-NC	Y	26810 FQ	57100 AW	93030 TQ	VABLS	10/01-12/01
Postsecondary	Richmond-Petersburg MSA, VA	Y	13590 FQ	49190 AW	82170 TQ	VABLS	10/01-12/01
Postsecondary	Roanoke MSA, VA	Y	13880 FQ	48410 AW	79810 TQ	VABLS	10/01-12/01
Postsecondary	Washington	Y	29200 FQ	52600 AW	81310 TQ	WABLS	10/01-12/01
Postsecondary	Seattle-Bellevue-Everett PMSA, WA	Y	39410 FQ	60250 AW	92810 TQ	WABLS	10/01-12/01
Postsecondary	Tacoma PMSA, WA	Y	40730 FQ	58920 AW	87060 TQ	WABLS	10/01-12/01
Postsecondary	West Virginia	Y	33370 FQ	56280 AW	84180 TQ	WVBLS	10/01-12/01
Postsecondary	Wisconsin	Y	24630 FQ	44610 AW	70400 TQ	WIBLS	10/01-12/01
Postsecondary	Milwaukee-Waukesha PMSA, WI	Y	19480 FQ	39650 AW	67070 TQ	WIBLS	10/01-12/01
Postsecondary	Wyoming	Y	34040 FQ	52290 AW	76610 TQ	WYBLS	10/01-12/01
Postsecondary	Puerto Rico	Y	23830 FQ	34780 AW	50090 TQ	PRBLS	10/01-12/01
Educational, Vocational, and School Counselor	Alabama	Y	27100 FQ	41190 AW	55550 TQ	ALBLS	10/01-12/01
	Birmingham MSA, AL	Y	28290 FQ	41880 AW	57530 TQ	ALBLS	10/01-12/01
	Huntsville MSA, AL	Y	34320 FQ	44400 AW	56900 TQ	ALBLS	10/01-12/01
	Mobile MSA, AL	Y	26290 FQ	36290 AW	45270 TQ	ALBLS	10/01-12/01
	Montgomery MSA, AL	Y	26660 FQ	39600 AW	52440 TQ	ALBLS	10/01-12/01
	Alaska	Y	33090 FQ	49550 AW	68610 TQ	AKBLS	10/01-12/01
	Arizona	Y	23160 FQ	37220 AW	55040 TQ	AZBLS	10/01-12/01
	Phoenix-Mesa MSA, AZ	Y	23110 FQ	37380 AW	56490 TQ	AZBLS	10/01-12/01
	Tucson MSA, AZ	Y	22800 FQ	36810 AW	53730 TQ	AZBLS	10/01-12/01
	Arkansas	Y	28050 FQ	40550 AW	53890 TQ	ARBLS	10/01-12/01
	Fayetteville-Springdale-Rogers MSA, AR	Y	27240 FQ	40440 AW	54940 TQ	ARBLS	10/01-12/01
	Fort Smith MSA, AR-OK	Y	28130 FQ	41760 AW	54610 TQ	ARBLS	10/01-12/01
	Little Rock-North Little Rock MSA, AR	Y	27450 FQ	41950 AW	55870 TQ	ARBLS	10/01-12/01
	California	Y	20690 FQ	48860 AW	76950 TQ	CABLS	10/01-12/01
	Bakersfield MSA, CA	Y	29180 FQ	47900 AW	68350 TQ	CABLS	10/01-12/01
	Chico-Paradise MSA, CA	Y	19710 FQ	48190 AW	74320 TQ	CABLS	10/01-12/01
	Fresno MSA, CA	Y	20770 FQ	57330 AW	96020 TQ	CABLS	10/01-12/01
	Los Angeles-Long Beach PMSA, CA	Y	26410 FQ	54910 AW	81930 TQ	CABLS	10/01-12/01

AAW	Average annual wage	**AOH**	Average offered, high	**ASH**	Average starting, high	**H**	Hourly	**M**	Monthly	**S**	Special: hourly and annual
AE	Average entry wage	**AOL**	Average offered, low	**ASL**	Average starting, low	**HI**	Highest wage paid	**MTC**	Median total compensation	**TQ**	Third quartile wage
AEX	Average experienced wage	**APH**	Average pay, high range	**AW**	Average wage paid	**HR**	High end range	**MW**	Median wage paid	**W**	Weekly
AO	Average offered	**APL**	Average pay, low range	**FQ**	First quartile wage	**LR**	Low end range	**SQ**	Second quartile wage	**Y**	Yearly

Occupation/Type/Industry	Location	Per	Low	Mid	High	Source	Date
Educational, Vocational, and School Counselor	Merced MSA, CA	Y	16760 FQ	52440 AW	83870 TQ	CABLS	10/01-12/01
	Modesto MSA, CA	Y	23340 FQ	52120 AW	76020 TQ	CABLS	10/01-12/01
	Oakland PMSA, CA	Y	16190 FQ	43840 AW	76940 TQ	CABLS	10/01-12/01
	Orange County PMSA, CA	Y	18640 FQ	42480 AW	77790 TQ	CABLS	10/01-12/01
	Redding MSA, CA	Y	32550 FQ	51750 AW	71720 TQ	CABLS	10/01-12/01
	Riverside-San Bernardino PMSA, CA	Y	21190 FQ	51120 AW	76550 TQ	CABLS	10/01-12/01
	Sacramento PMSA, CA	Y	15560 FQ	39220 AW	74450 TQ	CABLS	10/01-12/01
	Salinas MSA, CA	Y	14680 FQ	40260 AW	70970 TQ	CABLS	10/01-12/01
	San Diego MSA, CA	Y	17700 FQ	45130 AW	73610 TQ	CABLS	10/01-12/01
	San Francisco PMSA, CA	Y	22380 FQ	44210 AW	71380 TQ	CABLS	10/01-12/01
	San Jose PMSA, CA	Y	30390 FQ	49740 AW	71740 TQ	CABLS	10/01-12/01
	San Luis Obispo-Atascadero-Paso Robles MSA, CA	Y	15350 FQ	34800 AW	69070 TQ	CABLS	10/01-12/01
	Santa Barbara-Santa Maria-Lompoc MSA, CA	Y	19700 FQ	34440 AW	56220 TQ	CABLS	10/01-12/01
	Santa Cruz-Watsonville PMSA, CA	Y	31960 FQ	53790 AW	73900 TQ	CABLS	10/01-12/01
	Santa Rosa PMSA, CA	Y	16860 FQ	43930 AW	73410 TQ	CABLS	10/01-12/01
	Stockton-Lodi MSA, CA	Y	22150 FQ	49750 AW	73350 TQ	CABLS	10/01-12/01
	Vallejo-Fairfield-Napa PMSA, CA	Y	21800 FQ	47960 AW	72950 TQ	CABLS	10/01-12/01
	Ventura PMSA, CA	Y	19970 FQ	50910 AW	79750 TQ	CABLS	10/01-12/01
	Visalia-Tulare-Porterville MSA, CA	Y	20750 FQ	36070 AW	69980 TQ	CABLS	10/01-12/01
	Colorado	Y	27620 FQ	44820 AW	67280 TQ	COBLS	10/01-12/01
	Boulder-Longmont PMSA, CO	Y	23100 FQ	46990 AW	74710 TQ	COBLS	10/01-12/01
	Colorado Springs MSA, CO	Y	31260 FQ	46890 AW	66920 TQ	COBLS	10/01-12/01
	Denver PMSA, CO	Y	30690 FQ	48860 AW	69400 TQ	COBLS	10/01-12/01
	Fort Collins-Loveland MSA, CO	Y	31470 FQ	47760 AW	69780 TQ	COBLS	10/01-12/01
	Greeley PMSA, CO	Y	21620 FQ	43580 AW	65870 TQ	COBLS	10/01-12/01
	Connecticut	Y	26720 FQ	50580 AW	72310 TQ	CTBLS	10/01-12/01
	Bridgeport PMSA, CT	Y	25370 FQ	48000 AW	70050 TQ	CTBLS	10/01-12/01
	Danbury PMSA, CT	Y	23270 FQ	44900 AW	79760 TQ	CTBLS	10/01-12/01
	Hartford MSA, CT	Y	26650 FQ	48990 AW	69980 TQ	CTBLS	10/01-12/01
	New Haven-Meriden PMSA, CT	Y	26890 FQ	51540 AW	72900 TQ	CTBLS	10/01-12/01
	New London-Norwich MSA, CT-RI	Y	28040 FQ	51600 AW	71730 TQ	CTBLS	10/01-12/01
	Stamford-Norwalk PMSA, CT	Y	37110 FQ	60310 AW	87610 TQ	CTBLS	10/01-12/01
	Waterbury PMSA, CT	Y	38820 FQ	55960 AW	73560 TQ	CTBLS	10/01-12/01
	Delaware	Y	28400 FQ	50290 AW	75640 TQ	DEBLS	10/01-12/01
	Wilmington-Newark PMSA, DE-MD	Y	29610 FQ	51560 AW	76320 TQ	DEBLS	10/01-12/01
	District of Columbia	Y	29880 FQ	45140 AW	66890 TQ	DCBLS	10/01-12/01
	Washington PMSA, DC-MD-VA-WV	Y	24780 FQ	46180 AW	70290 TQ	DCBLS	10/01-12/01
	Florida	Y	28050 FQ	45490 AW	67170 TQ	FLBLS	10/01-12/01
	Fort Myers-Cape Coral MSA, FL	Y	30750 FQ	46740 AW	68280 TQ	FLBLS	10/01-12/01
	Fort Pierce-Port St. Lucie MSA, FL	Y	23740 FQ	45540 AW	69270 TQ	FLBLS	10/01-12/01
	Gainesville MSA, FL	Y	26460 FQ	41320 AW	60930 TQ	FLBLS	10/01-12/01
	Jacksonville MSA, FL	Y	16750 FQ	39940 AW	69100 TQ	FLBLS	10/01-12/01
	Melbourne-Titusville-Palm Bay MSA, FL	Y	24700 FQ	33090 AW	42960 TQ	FLBLS	10/01-12/01
	Ocala MSA, FL	Y	22740 FQ	29800 AW	34890 TQ	FLBLS	10/01-12/01
	Orlando MSA, FL	Y	25020 FQ	40410 AW	58200 TQ	FLBLS	10/01-12/01
	Pensacola MSA, FL	Y	28810 FQ	51640 AW	70700 TQ	FLBLS	10/01-12/01
	Sarasota-Bradenton MSA, FL	Y	25690 FQ	42750 AW	66010 TQ	FLBLS	10/01-12/01
	Tallahassee MSA, FL	Y	20410 FQ	38000 AW	66690 TQ	FLBLS	10/01-12/01
	Tampa-St. Petersburg-Clearwater MSA, FL	Y	23640 FQ	45530 AW	67990 TQ	FLBLS	10/01-12/01
	Georgia	Y	31530 FQ	49210 AW	67040 TQ	GABLS	10/01-12/01
	Atlanta MSA, GA	Y	35310 FQ	52230 AW	68990 TQ	GABLS	10/01-12/01
	Augusta-Aiken MSA, GA-SC	Y	28930 FQ	47490 AW	67130 TQ	GABLS	10/01-12/01
	Columbus MSA, GA-AL	Y	38750 FQ	48490 AW	62790 TQ	GABLS	10/01-12/01
	Macon MSA, GA	Y	27120 FQ	47070 AW	61150 TQ	GABLS	10/01-12/01
	Savannah MSA, GA	Y	30490 FQ	43170 AW	58110 TQ	GABLS	10/01-12/01
	Hawaii	Y	26630 FQ	40580 AW	56610 TQ	HIBLS	10/01-12/01

AAW	Average annual wage	AOH	Average offered, high	ASH	Average starting, high	H	Hourly	M	Monthly	S	Special: hourly and annual
AE	Average entry wage	AOL	Average offered, low	ASL	Average starting, low	HI	Highest wage paid	MTC	Median total compensation	TQ	Third quartile wage
AEX	Average experienced wage	APH	Average pay, high range	AW	Average wage paid	HR	High end range	MW	Median wage paid	W	Weekly
AO	Average offered	APL	Average pay, low range	FQ	First quartile wage	LR	Low end range	SQ	Second quartile wage	Y	Yearly

Occupation/Type/Industry	Location	Per	Low	Mid	High	Source	Date
Educational, Vocational, and School Counselor	Honolulu MSA, HI	Y	26570 FQ	40810 AW	57330 TQ	HIBLS	10/01-12/01
	Idaho	Y	32720 FQ	42810 AW	54670 TQ	IDBLS	10/01-12/01
	Boise City MSA, ID	Y	36980 FQ	44780 AW	55880 TQ	IDBLS	10/01-12/01
	Illinois	Y	23230 FQ	47810 AW	84250 TQ	ILBLS	10/01-12/01
	Champaign-Urbana MSA, IL	Y	22400 FQ	39730 AW	55800 TQ	ILBLS	10/01-12/01
	Chicago PMSA, IL	Y	23560 FQ	52410 AW	90850 TQ	ILBLS	10/01-12/01
	Peoria-Pekin MSA, IL	Y	26390 FQ	52680 AW	77060 TQ	ILBLS	10/01-12/01
	Rockford MSA, IL	Y	29390 FQ	46520 AW	63760 TQ	ILBLS	10/01-12/01
	Springfield MSA, IL	Y	20950 FQ	35170 AW	56630 TQ	ILBLS	10/01-12/01
	Indiana	Y	25980 FQ	43040 AW	63970 TQ	INBLS	10/01-12/01
	Elkhart-Goshen MSA, IN	Y	30330 FQ	47270 AW	67880 TQ	INBLS	10/01-12/01
	Evansville-Henderson MSA, IN-KY	Y	22260 FQ	40860 AW	57550 TQ	INBLS	10/01-12/01
	Fort Wayne MSA, IN	Y	28940 FQ	47220 AW	65720 TQ	INBLS	10/01-12/01
	Gary PMSA, IN	Y	30600 FQ	46110 AW	65130 TQ	INBLS	10/01-12/01
	Indianapolis MSA, IN	Y	27440 FQ	45670 AW	68920 TQ	INBLS	10/01-12/01
	Lafayette MSA, IN	Y	32520 FQ	44600 AW	60250 TQ	INBLS	10/01-12/01
	South Bend MSA, IN	Y	26660 FQ	43300 AW	63550 TQ	INBLS	10/01-12/01
	Iowa	Y	25720 FQ	38720 AW	54400 TQ	IABLS	10/01-12/01
	Cedar Rapids MSA, IA	Y	26520 FQ	41140 AW	55460 TQ	IABLS	10/01-12/01
	Davenport-Moline-Rock Island MSA, IA-IL	Y	25590 FQ	45900 AW	68430 TQ	IABLS	10/01-12/01
	Des Moines MSA, IA	Y	29270 FQ	42380 AW	58760 TQ	IABLS	10/01-12/01
	Kansas	Y	26470 FQ	39850 AW	52930 TQ	KSBLS	10/01-12/01
	Topeka MSA, KS	Y	30700 FQ	40690 AW	52820 TQ	KSBLS	10/01-12/01
	Wichita MSA, KS	Y	31990 FQ	42640 AW	54030 TQ	KSBLS	10/01-12/01
	Kentucky	Y	27090 FQ	44520 AW	60330 TQ	KYBLS	10/01-12/01
	Lexington MSA, KY	Y	28110 FQ	40610 AW	55140 TQ	KYBLS	10/01-12/01
	Louisville MSA, KY-IN	Y	28550 FQ	50410 AW	74220 TQ	KYBLS	10/01-12/01
	Louisiana	Y	27380 FQ	40130 AW	55560 TQ	LABLS	10/01-12/01
	Baton Rouge MSA, LA	Y	30100 FQ	44520 AW	66180 TQ	LABLS	10/01-12/01
	Houma MSA, LA	Y	27380 FQ	38190 AW	47710 TQ	LABLS	10/01-12/01
	Lafayette MSA, LA	Y	29030 FQ	41350 AW	56260 TQ	LABLS	10/01-12/01
	New Orleans MSA, LA	Y	24800 FQ	37440 AW	49980 TQ	LABLS	10/01-12/01
	Maine	Y	28910 FQ	40860 AW	55230 TQ	MEBLS	10/01-12/01
	Portland MSA, ME	Y	21630 FQ	38910 AW	55440 TQ	MEBLS	10/01-12/01
	Maryland	Y	21480 FQ	43330 AW	75270 TQ	MDBLS	10/01-12/01
	Baltimore PMSA, MD	Y	23170 FQ	46420 AW	83670 TQ	MDBLS	10/01-12/01
	Massachusetts	Y	24990 FQ	45170 AW	66390 TQ	MABLS	10/01-12/01
	Boston PMSA, MA-NH	Y	29520 FQ	46980 AW	68480 TQ	MABLS	10/01-12/01
	Brockton PMSA, MA	Y	25920 FQ	45150 AW	67710 TQ	MABLS	10/01-12/01
	Lawrence PMSA, MA-NH	Y	20730 FQ	40300 AW	64170 TQ	MABLS	10/01-12/01
	Lowell PMSA, MA-NH	Y	37110 FQ	48970 AW	62000 TQ	MABLS	10/01-12/01
	New Bedford PMSA, MA	Y	19840 FQ	38710 AW	60290 TQ	MABLS	10/01-12/01
	Springfield MSA, MA	Y	27200 FQ	43230 AW	56930 TQ	MABLS	10/01-12/01
	Worcester PMSA, MA-CT	Y	24210 FQ	45720 AW	63260 TQ	MABLS	10/01-12/01
	Michigan	Y	26030 FQ	51330 AW	79930 TQ	MIBLS	10/01-12/01
	Ann Arbor PMSA, MI	Y	32110 FQ	52680 AW	70080 TQ	MIBLS	10/01-12/01
	Detroit PMSA, MI	Y	21000 FQ	54880 AW	88050 TQ	MIBLS	10/01-12/01
	Flint PMSA, MI	Y	27100 FQ	43650 AW	61170 TQ	MIBLS	10/01-12/01
	Grand Rapids-Muskegon-Holland MSA, MI	Y	34880 FQ	51340 AW	70150 TQ	MIBLS	10/01-12/01
	Kalamazoo-Battle Creek MSA, MI	Y	27420 FQ	47310 AW	67200 TQ	MIBLS	10/01-12/01
	Lansing-East Lansing MSA, MI	Y	31080 FQ	48490 AW	64750 TQ	MIBLS	10/01-12/01
	Saginaw-Bay City-Midland MSA, MI	Y	33740 FQ	60030 AW	93910 TQ	MIBLS	10/01-12/01
	Minnesota	Y	20860 FQ	37810 AW	60360 TQ	MNBLS	10/01-12/01
	Duluth-Superior MSA, MN-WI	Y	17300 FQ	40220 AW	61740 TQ	MNBLS	10/01-12/01
	Minneapolis-St. Paul MSA, MN-WI	Y	23610 FQ	39890 AW	63060 TQ	MNBLS	10/01-12/01
	St. Cloud MSA, MN	Y	29830 FQ	44070 AW	61080 TQ	MNBLS	10/01-12/01
	Mississippi	Y	25160 FQ	37380 AW	52730 TQ	MSBLS	10/01-12/01
	Biloxi-Gulfport-Pascagoula MSA, MS	Y	25690 FQ	40240 AW	55770 TQ	MSBLS	10/01-12/01
	Jackson MSA, MS	Y	23480 FQ	34760 AW	46630 TQ	MSBLS	10/01-12/01
	Missouri	Y	18630 FQ	39730 AW	61300 TQ	MOBLS	10/01-12/01
	Kansas City MSA, MO-KS	Y	27850 FQ	43190 AW	58280 TQ	MOBLS	10/01-12/01
	St. Louis MSA, MO-IL	Y	23110 FQ	46990 AW	69610 TQ	MOBLS	10/01-12/01
	Springfield MSA, MO	Y	17440 FQ	32590 AW	48340 TQ	MOBLS	10/01-12/01
	Montana	Y	17370 FQ	32320 AW	47190 TQ	MTBLS	10/01-12/01

AAW	Average annual wage	**AOH**	Average offered, high	**ASH**	Average starting, high	**H**	Hourly	**M**	Monthly	**S**	Special: hourly and annual
AE	Average entry wage	**AOL**	Average offered, low	**ASL**	Average starting, low	**HI**	Highest wage paid	**MTC**	Median total compensation	**TQ**	Third quartile wage
AEX	Average experienced wage	**APH**	Average pay, high range	**AW**	Average wage paid	**HR**	High end range	**MW**	Median wage paid	**W**	Weekly
AO	Average offered	**APL**	Average pay, low range	**FQ**	First quartile wage	**LR**	Low end range	**SQ**	Second quartile wage	**Y**	Yearly

Occupation/Type/Industry	Location	Per	Low	Mid	High	Source	Date
Educational, Vocational, and School Counselor	Billings MSA, MT	Y	20590 FQ	37560 AW	56670 TQ	MTBLS	10/01-12/01
	Nebraska	Y	19410 FQ	35960 AW	51040 TQ	NEBLS	10/01-12/01
	Lincoln MSA, NE	Y	19610 FQ	35810 AW	53110 TQ	NEBLS	10/01-12/01
	Omaha MSA, NE-IA	Y	20410 FQ	35160 AW	52840 TQ	NEBLS	10/01-12/01
	Nevada	Y	31840 FQ	45990 AW	58690 TQ	NVBLS	10/01-12/01
	New Hampshire	Y	28970 FQ	40220 AW	54530 TQ	NHBLS	10/01-12/01
	Manchester PMSA, NH	Y	32020 FQ	44890 AW	57830 TQ	NHBLS	10/01-12/01
	Nashua PMSA, NH	Y	29240 FQ	43650 AW	57150 TQ	NHBLS	10/01-12/01
	Portsmouth-Rochester PMSA, NH-ME	Y	30380 FQ	41520 AW	55340 TQ	NHBLS	10/01-12/01
	New Jersey	Y	33170 FQ	58180 AW	86830 TQ	NJBLS	10/01-12/01
	Atlantic-Cape May PMSA, NJ	Y	28180 FQ	57550 AW	83990 TQ	NJBLS	10/01-12/01
	Bergen-Passaic PMSA, NJ	Y	32920 FQ	58700 AW	89960 TQ	NJBLS	10/01-12/01
	Middlesex-Somerset-Hunterdon PMSA, NJ	Y	36990 FQ	57010 AW	84250 TQ	NJBLS	10/01-12/01
	Monmouth-Ocean PMSA, NJ	Y	31650 FQ	57710 AW	89470 TQ	NJBLS	10/01-12/01
	Newark PMSA, NJ	Y	31540 FQ	59440 AW	87570 TQ	NJBLS	10/01-12/01
	Trenton PMSA, NJ	Y	29760 FQ	51590 AW	73610 TQ	NJBLS	10/01-12/01
	New Mexico	Y	18810 FQ	36420 AW	53080 TQ	NMBLS	10/01-12/01
	Albuquerque MSA, NM	Y	15740 FQ	33520 AW	51390 TQ	NMBLS	10/01-12/01
	Las Cruces MSA, NM	Y	24900 FQ	37460 AW	54420 TQ	NMBLS	10/01-12/01
	New York	Y	26330 FQ	61670 AW	118620 TQ	NYBLS	10/01-12/01
	Albany-Schenectady-Troy MSA, NY	Y	32080 FQ	51080 AW	74050 TQ	NYBLS	10/01-12/01
	Binghamton MSA, NY	Y	25290 FQ	43560 AW	60150 TQ	NYBLS	10/01-12/01
	Buffalo-Niagara Falls MSA, NY	Y	20470 FQ	41550 AW	65040 TQ	NYBLS	10/01-12/01
	Dutchess County PMSA, NY	Y	20730 FQ	45600 AW	70850 TQ	NYBLS	10/01-12/01
	Nassau-Suffolk PMSA, NY	Y	34020 FQ	61760 AW	96720 TQ	NYBLS	10/01-12/01
	New York PMSA, NY	Y	27820 FQ	77710 AW	135770 TQ	NYBLS	10/01-12/01
	Newburgh PMSA, NY-PA	Y	37210 FQ	56530 AW	73870 TQ	NYBLS	10/01-12/01
	Rochester MSA, NY	Y	27520 FQ	47810 AW	73900 TQ	NYBLS	10/01-12/01
	Syracuse MSA, NY	Y	25940 FQ	43930 AW	60970 TQ	NYBLS	10/01-12/01
	Utica-Rome MSA, NY	Y	24390 FQ	41200 AW	64390 TQ	NYBLS	10/01-12/01
	North Carolina	Y	24590 FQ	39200 AW	55200 TQ	NCBLS	10/01-12/01
	Asheville MSA, NC	Y	20920 FQ	37510 AW	55440 TQ	NCBLS	10/01-12/01
	Charlotte-Gastonia-Rock Hill MSA, NC-SC	Y	27290 FQ	40640 AW	56220 TQ	NCBLS	10/01-12/01
	Fayetteville MSA, NC	Y	27140 FQ	38710 AW	50170 TQ	NCBLS	10/01-12/01
	Greensboro-Winston-Salem-High Point MSA, NC	Y	21010 FQ	36800 AW	54300 TQ	NCBLS	10/01-12/01
	Hickory-Morganton-Lenoir MSA, NC	Y	32010 FQ	41050 AW	50770 TQ	NCBLS	10/01-12/01
	Raleigh-Durham-Chapel Hill MSA, NC	Y	21960 FQ	43380 AW	58810 TQ	NCBLS	10/01-12/01
	Wilmington MSA, NC	Y	27510 FQ	40390 AW	54190 TQ	NCBLS	10/01-12/01
	North Dakota	Y	20910 FQ	34270 AW	45470 TQ	NDBLS	10/01-12/01
	Fargo-Moorhead MSA, ND-MN	Y	26770 FQ	37880 AW	50850 TQ	NDBLS	10/01-12/01
	Ohio	Y	28440 FQ	48430 AW	69050 TQ	OHBLS	10/01-12/01
	Akron PMSA, OH	Y	30960 FQ	47630 AW	62290 TQ	OHBLS	10/01-12/01
	Canton-Massillon MSA, OH	Y	27850 FQ	47460 AW	66300 TQ	OHBLS	10/01-12/01
	Cincinnati PMSA, OH-KY-IN	Y	27200 FQ	46630 AW	67250 TQ	OHBLS	10/01-12/01
	Cleveland-Lorain-Elyria PMSA, OH	Y	27940 FQ	50660 AW	72710 TQ	OHBLS	10/01-12/01
	Columbus MSA, OH	Y	29170 FQ	51840 AW	73480 TQ	OHBLS	10/01-12/01
	Dayton-Springfield MSA, OH	Y	30230 FQ	51310 AW	68960 TQ	OHBLS	10/01-12/01
	Hamilton-Middletown PMSA, OH	Y	27040 FQ	45810 AW	63460 TQ	OHBLS	10/01-12/01
	Mansfield MSA, OH	Y	13210 FQ	39070 AW	56730 TQ	OHBLS	10/01-12/01
	Toledo MSA, OH	Y	35010 FQ	50560 AW	67320 TQ	OHBLS	10/01-12/01
	Youngstown-Warren MSA, OH	Y	17250 FQ	39870 AW	58390 TQ	OHBLS	10/01-12/01
	Oklahoma	Y	21220 FQ	35340 AW	47850 TQ	OKBLS	10/01-12/01
	Oklahoma City MSA, OK	Y	23830 FQ	36170 AW	53130 TQ	OKBLS	10/01-12/01
	Tulsa MSA, OK	Y	18900 FQ	33700 AW	45640 TQ	OKBLS	10/01-12/01
	Oregon	Y	29920 FQ	46180 AW	62520 TQ	ORBLS	10/01-12/01
	Eugene-Springfield MSA, OR	Y	30580 FQ	46610 AW	60830 TQ	ORBLS	10/01-12/01
	Medford-Ashland MSA, OR	Y	21900 FQ	42530 AW	56180 TQ	ORBLS	10/01-12/01
	Portland-Vancouver PMSA, OR-WA	Y	29750 FQ	46590 AW	66630 TQ	ORBLS	10/01-12/01
	Salem PMSA, OR	Y	28950 FQ	44640 AW	57580 TQ	ORBLS	10/01-12/01

AAW	Average annual wage	AOH	Average offered, high	ASH	Average starting, high	H	Hourly	M	Monthly	S	Special: hourly and annual
AE	Average entry wage	AOL	Average offered, low	ASL	Average starting, low	HI	Highest wage paid	MTC	Median total compensation	TQ	Third quartile wage
AEX	Average experienced wage	APH	Average pay, high range	AW	Average wage paid	HR	High end range	MW	Median wage paid	W	Weekly
AO	Average offered	APL	Average pay, low range	FQ	First quartile wage	LR	Low end range	SQ	Second quartile wage	Y	Yearly

Occupation/Type/Industry	Location	Per	Low	Mid	High	Source	Date
Educational, Vocational, and School Counselor	Pennsylvania	Y	24710 FQ	43660 AW	68430 TQ	PABLS	10/01-12/01
	Allentown-Bethlehem-Easton MSA, PA	Y	21260 FQ	36920 AW	61620 TQ	PABLS	10/01-12/01
	Erie MSA, PA	Y	24650 FQ	41680 AW	68190 TQ	PABLS	10/01-12/01
	Harrisburg-Lebanon-Carlisle MSA, PA	Y	21220 FQ	43030 AW	68600 TQ	PABLS	10/01-12/01
	Johnstown MSA, PA	Y	29070 FQ	49820 AW	69750 TQ	PABLS	10/01-12/01
	Lancaster MSA, PA	Y	22470 FQ	44030 AW	63060 TQ	PABLS	10/01-12/01
	Philadelphia PMSA, PA-NJ	Y	26350 FQ	45740 AW	71940 TQ	PABLS	10/01-12/01
	Pittsburgh MSA, PA	Y	23950 FQ	43820 AW	69410 TQ	PABLS	10/01-12/01
	Reading MSA, PA	Y	36130 FQ	52220 AW	70180 TQ	PABLS	10/01-12/01
	Scranton-Wilkes-Barre-Hazleton MSA, PA	Y	21680 FQ	42300 AW	65860 TQ	PABLS	10/01-12/01
	York MSA, PA	Y	30840 FQ	50200 AW	70670 TQ	PABLS	10/01-12/01
	Rhode Island	Y	26500 FQ	51190 AW	71520 TQ	RIBLS	10/01-12/01
	Providence-Fall River-Warwick MSA, RI-MA	Y	25180 FQ	49960 AW	70940 TQ	RIBLS	10/01-12/01
	South Carolina	Y	22080 FQ	40340 AW	57830 TQ	SCBLS	10/01-12/01
	Charleston-North Charleston MSA, SC	Y	18020 FQ	37010 AW	53040 TQ	SCBLS	10/01-12/01
	Columbia MSA, SC	Y	27920 FQ	40900 AW	58780 TQ	SCBLS	10/01-12/01
	Greenville-Spartanburg-Anderson MSA, SC	Y	21100 FQ	35290 AW	53710 TQ	SCBLS	10/01-12/01
	Myrtle Beach MSA, SC	Y	28530 FQ	64590 AW	136750 TQ	SCBLS	10/01-12/01
	South Dakota	Y	24680 FQ	34900 AW	47610 TQ	SDBLS	10/01-12/01
	Sioux Falls MSA, SD	Y	28320 FQ	39800 AW	53380 TQ	SDBLS	10/01-12/01
	Tennessee	Y	19800 FQ	35540 AW	51990 TQ	TNBLS	10/01-12/01
	Chattanooga MSA, TN-GA	Y	19760 FQ	35460 AW	55440 TQ	TNBLS	10/01-12/01
	Clarksville-Hopkinsville MSA, TN-KY	Y	22130 FQ	40920 AW	58720 TQ	TNBLS	10/01-12/01
	Johnson City-Kingsport-Bristol MSA, TN-VA	Y	25150 FQ	37640 AW	53570 TQ	TNBLS	10/01-12/01
	Knoxville MSA, TN	Y	20260 FQ	36300 AW	52870 TQ	TNBLS	10/01-12/01
	Memphis MSA, TN-AR-MS	Y	22700 FQ	37640 AW	55890 TQ	TNBLS	10/01-12/01
	Nashville MSA, TN	Y	25350 FQ	36720 AW	48920 TQ	TNBLS	10/01-12/01
	Texas	Y	26430 FQ	44810 AW	61110 TQ	TXBLS	10/01-12/01
	Austin-San Marcos MSA, TX	Y	27050 FQ	43380 AW	57920 TQ	TXBLS	10/01-12/01
	Beaumont-Port Arthur MSA, TX	Y	35520 FQ	47100 AW	58340 TQ	TXBLS	10/01-12/01
	Brazoria PMSA, TX	Y	24320 FQ	43710 AW	57610 TQ	TXBLS	10/01-12/01
	Brownsville-Harlingen-San Benito MSA, TX	Y	31210 FQ	46110 AW	57690 TQ	TXBLS	10/01-12/01
	Corpus Christi MSA, TX	Y	25930 FQ	51170 AW	71250 TQ	TXBLS	10/01-12/01
	Dallas PMSA, TX	Y	34100 FQ	50240 AW	68850 TQ	TXBLS	10/01-12/01
	El Paso MSA, TX	Y	22260 FQ	39110 AW	56160 TQ	TXBLS	10/01-12/01
	Fort Worth-Arlington PMSA, TX	Y	36890 FQ	51620 AW	68940 TQ	TXBLS	10/01-12/01
	Galveston-Texas City PMSA, TX	Y	35610 FQ	47050 AW	58780 TQ	TXBLS	10/01-12/01
	Houston PMSA, TX	Y	24570 FQ	41070 AW	60030 TQ	TXBLS	10/01-12/01
	Killeen-Temple MSA, TX	Y	35990 FQ	51450 AW	71380 TQ	TXBLS	10/01-12/01
	Laredo MSA, TX	Y	37760 FQ	48990 AW	61980 TQ	TXBLS	10/01-12/01
	Longview-Marshall MSA, TX	Y	21040 FQ	36140 AW	51650 TQ	TXBLS	10/01-12/01
	Lubbock MSA, TX	Y	24020 FQ	42620 AW	55180 TQ	TXBLS	10/01-12/01
	McAllen-Edinburg-Mission MSA, TX	Y	30820 FQ	46610 AW	58660 TQ	TXBLS	10/01-12/01
	Odessa-Midland MSA, TX	Y	27630 FQ	43290 AW	56660 TQ	TXBLS	10/01-12/01
	San Antonio MSA, TX	Y	26750 FQ	46410 AW	64600 TQ	TXBLS	10/01-12/01
	Tyler MSA, TX	Y	25630 FQ	40550 AW	55040 TQ	TXBLS	10/01-12/01
	Waco MSA, TX	Y	31170 FQ	44010 AW	56410 TQ	TXBLS	10/01-12/01
	Utah	Y	19630 FQ	34340 AW	51330 TQ	UTBLS	10/01-12/01
	Provo-Orem MSA, UT	Y	16660 FQ	33630 AW	51890 TQ	UTBLS	10/01-12/01
	Salt Lake City-Ogden MSA, UT	Y	19450 FQ	33870 AW	50540 TQ	UTBLS	10/01-12/01
	Vermont	Y	28340 FQ	41470 AW	56980 TQ	VTBLS	10/01-12/01
	Burlington MSA, VT	Y	30910 FQ	44000 AW	58420 TQ	VTBLS	10/01-12/01
	Virginia	Y	27440 FQ	45260 AW	66270 TQ	VABLS	10/01-12/01
	Lynchburg MSA, VA	Y	26950 FQ	38820 AW	58960 TQ	VABLS	10/01-12/01
	Norfolk-Virginia Beach-Newport News MSA, VA-NC	Y	23150 FQ	39390 AW	55930 TQ	VABLS	10/01-12/01

AAW	Average annual wage	**AOH**	Average offered, high	**ASH**	Average starting, high	**H**	Hourly	**M**	Monthly	**S**	Special: hourly and annual
AE	Average entry wage	**AOL**	Average offered, low	**ASL**	Average starting, low	**HI**	Highest wage paid	**MTC**	Median total compensation	**TQ**	Third quartile wage
AEX	Average experienced wage	**APH**	Average pay, high range	**AW**	Average wage paid	**HR**	High end range	**MW**	Median wage paid	**W**	Weekly
AO	Average offered	**APL**	Average pay, low range	**FQ**	First quartile wage	**LR**	Low end range	**SQ**	Second quartile wage	**Y**	Yearly

Occupation/Type/Industry	Location	Per	Low	Mid	High	Source	Date
Educational, Vocational, and School Counselor	Richmond-Petersburg MSA, VA	Y	31610 FQ	46650 AW	64610 TQ	VABLS	10/01-12/01
	Roanoke MSA, VA	Y	26140 FQ	61100 AW		VABLS	10/01-12/01
	Washington	Y	28940 FQ	42100 AW	56400 TQ	WABLS	10/01-12/01
	Bremerton PMSA, WA	Y	18640 FQ	40420 AW	56140 TQ	WABLS	10/01-12/01
	Olympia PMSA, WA	Y	32290 FQ	45080 AW	57220 TQ	WABLS	10/01-12/01
	Richland-Kennewick-Pasco MSA, WA	Y	31670 FQ	44500 AW	57240 TQ	WABLS	10/01-12/01
	Seattle-Bellevue-Everett PMSA, WA	Y	29490 FQ	41860 AW	56220 TQ	WABLS	10/01-12/01
	Spokane MSA, WA	Y	31710 FQ	43320 AW	56490 TQ	WABLS	10/01-12/01
	Tacoma PMSA, WA	Y	26650 FQ	42640 AW	56980 TQ	WABLS	10/01-12/01
	Yakima MSA, WA	Y	28850 FQ	40930 AW	54760 TQ	WABLS	10/01-12/01
	West Virginia	Y	24260 FQ	36940 AW	48260 TQ	WVBLS	10/01-12/01
	Charleston MSA, WV	Y	26140 FQ	37390 AW	53200 TQ	WVBLS	10/01-12/01
	Huntington-Ashland MSA, WV-KY-OH	Y	26550 FQ	40920 AW	55830 TQ	WVBLS	10/01-12/01
	Wisconsin	Y	27130 FQ	43500 AW	63590 TQ	WIBLS	10/01-12/01
	Appleton-Oshkosh-Neenah MSA, WI	Y	24160 FQ	43620 AW	67590 TQ	WIBLS	10/01-12/01
	Green Bay MSA, WI	Y	29720 FQ	45190 AW	65380 TQ	WIBLS	10/01-12/01
	Madison MSA, WI	Y	28790 FQ	43900 AW	60760 TQ	WIBLS	10/01-12/01
	Milwaukee-Waukesha PMSA, WI	Y	25620 FQ	40900 AW	64690 TQ	WIBLS	10/01-12/01
	Racine PMSA, WI	Y	24720 FQ	46640 AW	67210 TQ	WIBLS	10/01-12/01
	Wyoming	Y	26780 FQ	37960 AW	51770 TQ	WYBLS	10/01-12/01
	Cheyenne MSA, WY	Y	29750 FQ	41210 AW	54970 TQ	WYBLS	10/01-12/01
	Puerto Rico	Y	19060 FQ	25470 AW	33310 TQ	PRBLS	10/01-12/01
	Virgin Islands	Y	35200 FQ	51360 AW	72840 TQ	VIBLS	10/01-12/01
	Guam	Y	24900 FQ	34530 AW	44220 TQ	GUBLS	10/01-12/01
Electric Motor, Power Tool, and Related Repairer	Alabama	H	9.81 FQ	14.73 AW	20.33 TQ	ALBLS	10/01-12/01
	Birmingham MSA, AL	H	9.29 FQ	14.73 AW	19.89 TQ	ALBLS	10/01-12/01
	Montgomery MSA, AL	H	10.53 FQ	14.16 AW	18.78 TQ	ALBLS	10/01-12/01
	Alaska	H	16.90 FQ	38.45 AW	57.07 TQ	AKBLS	10/01-12/01
	Anchorage MSA, AK	H	23.99 FQ	37.85 AW	56.36 TQ	AKBLS	10/01-12/01
	Arizona	H	8.81 FQ	16.58 AW	24.67 TQ	AZBLS	10/01-12/01
	Phoenix-Mesa MSA, AZ	H	8.96 FQ	17.44 AW	25.51 TQ	AZBLS	10/01-12/01
	Arkansas	H	8.44 FQ	13.30 AW	18.50 TQ	ARBLS	10/01-12/01
	Fort Smith MSA, AR-OK	H	8.23 FQ	13.10 AW	17.22 TQ	ARBLS	10/01-12/01
	Little Rock-North Little Rock MSA, AR	H	10.62 FQ	15.76 AW	20.62 TQ	ARBLS	10/01-12/01
	California	H	9.54 FQ	16.65 AW	26.74 TQ	CABLS	10/01-12/01
	Bakersfield MSA, CA	H	8.94 FQ	16.79 AW	24.94 TQ	CABLS	10/01-12/01
	Fresno MSA, CA	H	9.93 FQ	17.20 AW	27.27 TQ	CABLS	10/01-12/01
	Los Angeles-Long Beach PMSA, CA	H	9.47 FQ	16.65 AW	29.16 TQ	CABLS	10/01-12/01
	Modesto MSA, CA	H	8.88 FQ	16.69 AW	22.41 TQ	CABLS	10/01-12/01
	Oakland PMSA, CA	H	11.89 FQ	18.77 AW	27.30 TQ	CABLS	10/01-12/01
	Orange County PMSA, CA	H	9.16 FQ	14.23 AW	17.11 TQ	CABLS	10/01-12/01
	Riverside-San Bernardino PMSA, CA	H	13.54 FQ	16.03 AW	20.47 TQ	CABLS	10/01-12/01
	Sacramento PMSA, CA	H	9.00 FQ	15.37 AW	22.93 TQ	CABLS	10/01-12/01
	San Diego MSA, CA	H	11.08 FQ	17.41 AW	23.83 TQ	CABLS	10/01-12/01
	San Francisco PMSA, CA	H	11.46 FQ	17.73 AW	22.14 TQ	CABLS	10/01-12/01
	San Jose PMSA, CA	H	8.53 FQ	20.31 AW	31.64 TQ	CABLS	10/01-12/01
	Stockton-Lodi MSA, CA	H	14.68 FQ	20.35 AW	27.23 TQ	CABLS	10/01-12/01
	Colorado	H	9.11 FQ	12.64 AW	17.62 TQ	COBLS	10/01-12/01
	Colorado Springs MSA, CO	H	9.05 FQ	10.19 AW	11.04 TQ	COBLS	10/01-12/01
	Denver PMSA, CO	H	10.69 FQ	15.88 AW	22.08 TQ	COBLS	10/01-12/01
	Connecticut	H	11.03 FQ	15.89 AW	21.93 TQ	CTBLS	10/01-12/01
	Washington PMSA, DC-MD-VA-WV	H	13.24 FQ	20.31 AW	31.05 TQ	DCBLS	10/01-12/01
	Florida	H	8.69 FQ	13.61 AW	17.99 TQ	FLBLS	10/01-12/01
	Fort Lauderdale PMSA, FL	H	6.01 FQ	11.52 AW	17.55 TQ	FLBLS	10/01-12/01
	Fort Myers-Cape Coral MSA, FL	H	11.59 FQ	13.24 AW	15.90 TQ	FLBLS	10/01-12/01
	Jacksonville MSA, FL	H	7.77 FQ	13.80 AW	18.49 TQ	FLBLS	10/01-12/01
	Lakeland-Winter Haven MSA, FL	H	11.24 FQ	14.52 AW	17.79 TQ	FLBLS	10/01-12/01

AAW	Average annual wage	**AOH**	Average offered, high	**ASH**	Average starting, high	**H**	Hourly	**M**	Monthly	**S**	Special: hourly and annual
AE	Average entry wage	**AOL**	Average offered, low	**ASL**	Average starting, low	**HI**	Highest wage paid	**MTC**	Median total compensation	**TQ**	Third quartile wage
AEX	Average experienced wage	**APH**	Average pay, high range	**AW**	Average wage paid	**HR**	High end range	**MW**	Median wage paid	**W**	Weekly
AO	Average offered	**APL**	Average pay, low range	**FQ**	First quartile wage	**LR**	Low end range	**SQ**	Second quartile wage	**Y**	Yearly

Occupation/Type/Industry	Location	Per	Low	Mid	High	Source	Date
Electric Motor, Power Tool, and Related Repairer	Miami PMSA, FL	H	9.31 FQ	12.59 AW	16.27 TQ	FLBLS	10/01-12/01
	Orlando MSA, FL	H	8.49 FQ	12.80 AW	17.47 TQ	FLBLS	10/01-12/01
	Pensacola MSA, FL	H	8.07 FQ	12.68 AW	19.05 TQ	FLBLS	10/01-12/01
	Sarasota-Bradenton MSA, FL	H	7.83 FQ	11.23 AW	13.81 TQ	FLBLS	10/01-12/01
	Tallahassee MSA, FL	H	6.52 FQ	13.33 AW	18.51 TQ	FLBLS	10/01-12/01
	Tampa-St. Petersburg-Clearwater MSA, FL	H	9.77 FQ	13.83 AW	19.64 TQ	FLBLS	10/01-12/01
	West Palm Beach-Boca Raton MSA, FL	H	8.29 FQ	15.32 AW	22.29 TQ	FLBLS	10/01-12/01
	Georgia	H	10.61 FQ	16.54 AW	25.11 TQ	GABLS	10/01-12/01
	Atlanta MSA, GA	H	11.52 FQ	18.78 AW	26.52 TQ	GABLS	10/01-12/01
	Hawaii	H	9.53 FQ	15.71 AW	24.53 TQ	HIBLS	10/01-12/01
	Honolulu MSA, HI	H	10.86 FQ	16.64 AW	25.90 TQ	HIBLS	10/01-12/01
	Idaho	H	8.54 FQ	19.27 AW	35.17 TQ	IDBLS	10/01-12/01
	Illinois	H	11.03 FQ	18.49 AW	26.65 TQ	ILBLS	10/01-12/01
	Chicago PMSA, IL	H	12.97 FQ	21.07 AW	27.69 TQ	ILBLS	10/01-12/01
	Indiana	H	11.35 FQ	18.27 AW	29.66 TQ	INBLS	10/01-12/01
	Evansville-Henderson MSA, IN-KY	H	9.66 FQ	16.38 AW	22.75 TQ	INBLS	10/01-12/01
	Fort Wayne MSA, IN	H	11.69 FQ	17.36 AW	30.20 TQ	INBLS	10/01-12/01
	Gary PMSA, IN	H	11.24 FQ	19.90 AW	27.05 TQ	INBLS	10/01-12/01
	Indianapolis MSA, IN	H	12.39 FQ	19.61 AW	32.68 TQ	INBLS	10/01-12/01
	South Bend MSA, IN	H	12.06 FQ	16.38 AW	21.41 TQ	INBLS	10/01-12/01
	Iowa	H	7.95 FQ	14.29 AW	21.34 TQ	IABLS	10/01-12/01
	Des Moines MSA, IA	H	12.05 FQ	14.57 AW	17.63 TQ	IABLS	10/01-12/01
	Kansas	H	8.16 FQ	13.34 AW	20.77 TQ	KSBLS	10/01-12/01
	Wichita MSA, KS	H	10.12 FQ	15.92 AW	24.55 TQ	KSBLS	10/01-12/01
	Kentucky	H	8.99 FQ	16.17 AW	25.83 TQ	KYBLS	10/01-12/01
	Lexington MSA, KY	H	8.77 FQ	15.87 AW	21.50 TQ	KYBLS	10/01-12/01
	Louisville MSA, KY-IN	H	10.09 FQ	17.24 AW	27.32 TQ	KYBLS	10/01-12/01
	Louisiana	H	8.94 FQ	15.29 AW	22.15 TQ	LABLS	10/01-12/01
	Baton Rouge MSA, LA	H	11.51 FQ	16.98 AW	24.64 TQ	LABLS	10/01-12/01
	Houma MSA, LA	H	7.73 FQ	13.00 AW	17.52 TQ	LABLS	10/01-12/01
	New Orleans MSA, LA	H	11.25 FQ	15.41 AW	19.32 TQ	LABLS	10/01-12/01
	Shreveport-Bossier City MSA, LA	H	7.39 FQ	13.31 AW	17.53 TQ	LABLS	10/01-12/01
	Maine	H	11.42 FQ	16.91 AW	23.11 TQ	MEBLS	10/01-12/01
	Portland MSA, ME	H	11.99 FQ	16.54 AW	22.38 TQ	MEBLS	10/01-12/01
	Maryland	H	11.77 FQ	22.14 AW	30.63 TQ	MDBLS	10/01-12/01
	Baltimore PMSA, MD	H	15.60 FQ	20.87 AW	26.95 TQ	MDBLS	10/01-12/01
	Massachusetts	H	12.20 FQ	18.45 AW	23.72 TQ	MABLS	10/01-12/01
	Boston PMSA, MA-NH	H	12.66 FQ	18.99 AW	23.66 TQ	MABLS	10/01-12/01
	Lawrence PMSA, MA-NH	H	11.11 FQ	16.82 AW	23.38 TQ	MABLS	10/01-12/01
	Springfield MSA, MA	H	12.23 FQ	18.00 AW	24.81 TQ	MABLS	10/01-12/01
	Michigan	H	9.83 FQ	16.81 AW	25.82 TQ	MIBLS	10/01-12/01
	Detroit PMSA, MI	H	10.22 FQ	18.08 AW	26.81 TQ	MIBLS	10/01-12/01
	Flint PMSA, MI	H	9.17 FQ	20.61 AW	33.72 TQ	MIBLS	10/01-12/01
	Grand Rapids-Muskegon-Holland MSA, MI	H	11.68 FQ	17.00 AW	23.45 TQ	MIBLS	10/01-12/01
	Minnesota	H	7.56 FQ	18.30 AW	33.51 TQ	MNBLS	10/01-12/01
	Duluth-Superior MSA, MN-WI	H	7.91 FQ	14.55 AW	21.94 TQ	MNBLS	10/01-12/01
	Minneapolis-St. Paul MSA, MN-WI	H	13.59 FQ	23.67 AW	35.32 TQ	MNBLS	10/01-12/01
	St. Cloud MSA, MN	H	12.05 FQ	15.86 AW	20.98 TQ	MNBLS	10/01-12/01
	Mississippi	H	7.71 FQ	13.19 AW	19.40 TQ	MSBLS	10/01-12/01
	Jackson MSA, MS	H	11.94 FQ	14.68 AW	17.29 TQ	MSBLS	10/01-12/01
	Missouri	H	8.16 FQ	14.46 AW	22.05 TQ	MOBLS	10/01-12/01
	Kansas City MSA, MO-KS	H	9.17 FQ	15.66 AW	22.65 TQ	MOBLS	10/01-12/01
	St. Louis MSA, MO-IL	H	9.37 FQ	16.30 AW	25.19 TQ	MOBLS	10/01-12/01
	Montana	H	9.60 FQ	19.24 AW	27.71 TQ	MTBLS	10/01-12/01
	Billings MSA, MT	H	9.19 FQ	14.88 AW	31.30 TQ	MTBLS	10/01-12/01
	Nebraska	H	5.65 FQ	9.96 AW	17.44 TQ	NEBLS	10/01-12/01
	Nevada	H	8.74 FQ	16.00 AW	20.99 TQ	NVBLS	10/01-12/01
	Las Vegas MSA, NV-AZ	H	8.33 FQ	16.12 AW	21.02 TQ	NVBLS	10/01-12/01
	New Hampshire	H	9.45 FQ	14.74 AW	21.27 TQ	NHBLS	10/01-12/01
	New Jersey	H	8.24 FQ	14.42 AW	21.01 TQ	NJBLS	10/01-12/01
	Bergen-Passaic PMSA, NJ	H	7.47 FQ	12.32 AW	20.65 TQ	NJBLS	10/01-12/01
	Middlesex-Somerset-Hunterdon PMSA, NJ	H	13.34 FQ	18.82 AW	26.08 TQ	NJBLS	10/01-12/01
	Newark PMSA, NJ	H	10.41 FQ	15.08 AW	19.20 TQ	NJBLS	10/01-12/01
	New Mexico	H	7.59 FQ	15.51 AW	26.32 TQ	NMBLS	10/01-12/01

AAW	Average annual wage	**AOH**	Average offered, high	**ASH**	Average starting, high	**H**	Hourly	**M**	Monthly	**S**	Special: hourly and annual
AE	Average entry wage	**AOL**	Average offered, low	**ASL**	Average starting, low	**HI**	Highest wage paid	**MTC**	Median total compensation	**TQ**	Third quartile wage
AEX	Average experienced wage	**APH**	Average pay, high range	**AW**	Average wage paid	**HR**	High end range	**MW**	Median wage paid	**W**	Weekly
AO	Average offered	**APL**	Average pay, low range	**FQ**	First quartile wage	**LR**	Low end range	**SQ**	Second quartile wage	**Y**	Yearly

Occupation/Type/Industry	Location	Per	Low	Mid	High	Source	Date
Electric Motor, Power Tool, and Related Repairer	Albuquerque MSA, NM	H	7.61 FQ	14.61 AW	22.78 TQ	NMBLS	10/01-12/01
	New York	H	6.33 FQ	14.52 AW	26.08 TQ	NYBLS	10/01-12/01
	Albany-Schenectady-Troy MSA, NY	H	10.23 FQ	14.20 AW	18.94 TQ	NYBLS	10/01-12/01
	Buffalo-Niagara Falls MSA, NY	H	7.64 FQ	17.69 AW	27.79 TQ	NYBLS	10/01-12/01
	Nassau-Suffolk PMSA, NY	H	8.51 FQ	18.30 AW	27.58 TQ	NYBLS	10/01-12/01
	New York PMSA, NY	H	5.88 FQ	11.29 AW	25.00 TQ	NYBLS	10/01-12/01
	Rochester MSA, NY	H	7.35 FQ	14.42 AW	21.05 TQ	NYBLS	10/01-12/01
	Syracuse MSA, NY	H	11.04 FQ	18.86 AW	27.74 TQ	NYBLS	10/01-12/01
	North Carolina	H	10.49 FQ	14.92 AW	21.57 TQ	NCBLS	10/01-12/01
	Charlotte-Gastonia-Rock Hill MSA, NC-SC	H	10.98 FQ	16.19 AW	21.49 TQ	NCBLS	10/01-12/01
	Fayetteville MSA, NC	H	9.62 FQ	13.93 AW	18.60 TQ	NCBLS	10/01-12/01
	Greensboro-Winston-Salem-High Point MSA, NC	H	12.37 FQ	17.37 AW	24.38 TQ	NCBLS	10/01-12/01
	Hickory-Morganton-Lenoir MSA, NC	H	11.56 FQ	14.24 AW	19.01 TQ	NCBLS	10/01-12/01
	Raleigh-Durham-Chapel Hill MSA, NC	H	11.01 FQ	13.00 AW	16.82 TQ	NCBLS	10/01-12/01
	North Dakota	H	9.95 FQ	15.64 AW	25.00 TQ	NDBLS	10/01-12/01
	Ohio	H	9.91 FQ	16.91 AW	26.09 TQ	OHBLS	10/01-12/01
	Akron PMSA, OH	H	9.47 FQ	11.57 AW	14.16 TQ	OHBLS	10/01-12/01
	Cincinnati PMSA, OH-KY-IN	H	9.63 FQ	18.40 AW	27.09 TQ	OHBLS	10/01-12/01
	Cleveland-Lorain-Elyria PMSA, OH	H	10.26 FQ	17.68 AW	26.88 TQ	OHBLS	10/01-12/01
	Columbus MSA, OH	H	9.95 FQ	15.95 AW	21.93 TQ	OHBLS	10/01-12/01
	Dayton-Springfield MSA, OH	H	10.93 FQ	17.37 AW	26.04 TQ	OHBLS	10/01-12/01
	Toledo MSA, OH	H	8.95 FQ	16.98 AW	27.79 TQ	OHBLS	10/01-12/01
	Youngstown-Warren MSA, OH	H	9.63 FQ	16.40 AW	26.44 TQ	OHBLS	10/01-12/01
	Oklahoma	H	7.98 FQ	14.09 AW	22.84 TQ	OKBLS	10/01-12/01
	Oklahoma City MSA, OK	H	8.09 FQ	14.74 AW	24.81 TQ	OKBLS	10/01-12/01
	Tulsa MSA, OK	H	7.93 FQ	12.79 AW	19.73 TQ	OKBLS	10/01-12/01
	Oregon	H	8.59 FQ	13.79 AW	21.37 TQ	ORBLS	10/01-12/01
	Eugene-Springfield MSA, OR	H	8.84 FQ	13.29 AW	18.54 TQ	ORBLS	10/01-12/01
	Medford-Ashland MSA, OR	H	9.15 FQ	12.98 AW	19.21 TQ	ORBLS	10/01-12/01
	Portland-Vancouver PMSA, OR-WA	H	10.67 FQ	16.29 AW	24.01 TQ	ORBLS	10/01-12/01
	Pennsylvania	H	9.43 FQ	15.51 AW	21.49 TQ	PABLS	10/01-12/01
	Allentown-Bethlehem-Easton MSA, PA	H	10.87 FQ	16.41 AW	21.31 TQ	PABLS	10/01-12/01
	Erie MSA, PA	H	9.43 FQ	15.20 AW	21.61 TQ	PABLS	10/01-12/01
	Harrisburg-Lebanon-Carlisle MSA, PA	H	10.13 FQ	14.79 AW	20.09 TQ	PABLS	10/01-12/01
	Lancaster MSA, PA	H	11.70 FQ	15.13 AW	18.84 TQ	PABLS	10/01-12/01
	Philadelphia PMSA, PA-NJ	H	9.92 FQ	15.29 AW	20.80 TQ	PABLS	10/01-12/01
	Pittsburgh MSA, PA	H	9.04 FQ	15.33 AW	21.95 TQ	PABLS	10/01-12/01
	York MSA, PA	H	10.94 FQ	15.05 AW	20.67 TQ	PABLS	10/01-12/01
	Rhode Island	H	10.06 FQ	14.68 AW	19.38 TQ	RIBLS	10/01-12/01
	Providence-Fall River-Warwick MSA, RI-MA	H	9.68 FQ	14.61 AW	19.63 TQ	RIBLS	10/01-12/01
	South Carolina	H	8.44 FQ	12.16 AW	17.28 TQ	SCBLS	10/01-12/01
	Charleston-North Charleston MSA, SC	H	8.88 FQ	11.66 AW	15.95 TQ	SCBLS	10/01-12/01
	Greenville-Spartanburg-Anderson MSA, SC	H	7.78 FQ	11.61 AW	17.46 TQ	SCBLS	10/01-12/01
	Tennessee	H	9.32 FQ	16.09 AW	23.41 TQ	TNBLS	10/01-12/01
	Chattanooga MSA, TN-GA	H	11.00 FQ	14.15 AW	17.12 TQ	TNBLS	10/01-12/01
	Memphis MSA, TN-AR-MS	H	11.00 FQ	16.46 AW	21.67 TQ	TNBLS	10/01-12/01
	Nashville MSA, TN	H	9.75 FQ	18.01 AW	28.75 TQ	TNBLS	10/01-12/01
	Texas	H	8.71 FQ	14.80 AW	25.07 TQ	TXBLS	10/01-12/01
	Amarillo MSA, TX	H	7.56 FQ	11.57 AW	19.55 TQ	TXBLS	10/01-12/01
	Austin-San Marcos MSA, TX	H	8.66 FQ	12.00 AW	15.70 TQ	TXBLS	10/01-12/01
	Beaumont-Port Arthur MSA, TX	H	11.03 FQ	18.86 AW	27.09 TQ	TXBLS	10/01-12/01
	Brazoria PMSA, TX	H	8.75 FQ	15.02 AW	25.49 TQ	TXBLS	10/01-12/01
	Corpus Christi MSA, TX	H	8.14 FQ	13.27 AW	23.17 TQ	TXBLS	10/01-12/01
	Dallas PMSA, TX	H	11.82 FQ	17.39 AW	25.85 TQ	TXBLS	10/01-12/01
	El Paso MSA, TX	H	9.22 FQ	12.96 AW	18.03 TQ	TXBLS	10/01-12/01
	Fort Worth-Arlington PMSA, TX	H	7.91 FQ	13.34 AW	19.65 TQ	TXBLS	10/01-12/01

AAW	Average annual wage	**AOH**	Average offered, high	**ASH**	Average starting, high	**H**	Hourly	**M**	Monthly	**S**	Special: hourly and annual
AE	Average entry wage	**AOL**	Average offered, low	**ASL**	Average starting, low	**HI**	Highest wage paid	**MTC**	Median total compensation	**TQ**	Third quartile wage
AEX	Average experienced wage	**APH**	Average pay, high range	**AW**	Average wage paid	**HR**	High end range	**MW**	Median wage paid	**W**	Weekly
AO	Average offered	**APL**	Average pay, low range	**FQ**	First quartile wage	**LR**	Low end range	**SQ**	Second quartile wage	**Y**	Yearly

Occupation/Type/Industry	Location	Per	Low	Mid	High	Source	Date
Electric Motor, Power Tool, and Related Repairer	Houston PMSA, TX	H	8.83 FQ	15.77 AW	27.11 TQ	TXBLS	10/01-12/01
	Lubbock MSA, TX	H	7.86 FQ	11.15 AW	15.78 TQ	TXBLS	10/01-12/01
	San Antonio MSA, TX	H	8.73 FQ	10.92 AW	15.10 TQ	TXBLS	10/01-12/01
	Utah	H	8.45 FQ	16.77 AW	30.67 TQ	UTBLS	10/01-12/01
	Salt Lake City-Ogden MSA, UT	H	9.43 FQ	19.16 AW	33.12 TQ	UTBLS	10/01-12/01
	Vermont	H	11.60 FQ	17.74 AW	25.68 TQ	VTBLS	10/01-12/01
	Virginia	H	10.08 FQ	14.90 AW	20.53 TQ	VABLS	10/01-12/01
	Lynchburg MSA, VA	H	8.43 FQ	12.40 AW	20.53 TQ	VABLS	10/01-12/01
	Norfolk-Virginia Beach-Newport News MSA, VA-NC	H	10.05 FQ	14.82 AW	20.59 TQ	VABLS	10/01-12/01
	Richmond-Petersburg MSA, VA	H	10.21 FQ	16.10 AW	23.13 TQ	VABLS	10/01-12/01
	Washington	H	12.25 FQ	18.88 AW	26.26 TQ	WABLS	10/01-12/01
	Seattle-Bellevue-Everett PMSA, WA	H	13.01 FQ	18.75 AW	25.18 TQ	WABLS	10/01-12/01
	Spokane MSA, WA	H	10.16 FQ	14.29 AW	20.22 TQ	WABLS	10/01-12/01
	Tacoma PMSA, WA	H	14.36 FQ	19.15 AW	23.05 TQ	WABLS	10/01-12/01
	West Virginia	H	8.83 FQ	13.74 AW	18.44 TQ	WVBLS	10/01-12/01
	Huntington-Ashland MSA, WV-KY-OH	H	12.01 FQ	15.40 AW	20.01 TQ	WVBLS	10/01-12/01
	Wisconsin	H	11.13 FQ	19.12 AW	30.76 TQ	WIBLS	10/01-12/01
	Appleton-Oshkosh-Neenah MSA, WI	H	10.67 FQ	16.10 AW	21.40 TQ	WIBLS	10/01-12/01
	Green Bay MSA, WI	H	13.77 FQ	16.77 AW	20.56 TQ	WIBLS	10/01-12/01
	Milwaukee-Waukesha PMSA, WI	H	10.01 FQ	17.97 AW	25.95 TQ	WIBLS	10/01-12/01
	Wyoming	H	9.37 FQ	14.53 AW	21.12 TQ	WYBLS	10/01-12/01
	Puerto Rico	H	6.20 FQ	10.02 AW	15.53 TQ	PRBLS	10/01-12/01
Electrical and Electronic Engineering Technician	Alabama	Y	24730 FQ	42050 AW	57690 TQ	ALBLS	10/01-12/01
	Birmingham MSA, AL	Y	24270 FQ	41520 AW	56340 TQ	ALBLS	10/01-12/01
	Huntsville MSA, AL	Y	24270 FQ	40970 AW	63610 TQ	ALBLS	10/01-12/01
	Mobile MSA, AL	Y	28430 FQ	47420 AW	95180 TQ	ALBLS	10/01-12/01
	Montgomery MSA, AL	Y	24340 FQ	40340 AW	54620 TQ	ALBLS	10/01-12/01
	Alaska	Y	34160 FQ	57170 AW	86560 TQ	AKBLS	10/01-12/01
	Anchorage MSA, AK	Y	32680 FQ	52030 AW	70340 TQ	AKBLS	10/01-12/01
	Arizona	Y	26140 FQ	39340 AW	56950 TQ	AZBLS	10/01-12/01
	Phoenix-Mesa MSA, AZ	Y	26160 FQ	39370 AW	57290 TQ	AZBLS	10/01-12/01
	Tucson MSA, AZ	Y	25340 FQ	36990 AW	51270 TQ	AZBLS	10/01-12/01
	Arkansas	Y	23000 FQ	37340 AW	55950 TQ	ARBLS	10/01-12/01
	Fayetteville-Springdale-Rogers MSA, AR	Y	31350 FQ	43060 AW	53910 TQ	ARBLS	10/01-12/01
	Fort Smith MSA, AR-OK	Y	27300 FQ	35080 AW	51050 TQ	ARBLS	10/01-12/01
	Little Rock-North Little Rock MSA, AR	Y	23020 FQ	39040 AW	56620 TQ	ARBLS	10/01-12/01
	California	Y	28020 FQ	46470 AW	68060 TQ	CABLS	10/01-12/01
	Bakersfield MSA, CA	Y	36670 FQ	52370 AW	70780 TQ	CABLS	10/01-12/01
	Chico-Paradise MSA, CA	Y	23720 FQ	36720 AW	62660 TQ	CABLS	10/01-12/01
	Fresno MSA, CA	Y	29040 FQ	46280 AW	68070 TQ	CABLS	10/01-12/01
	Los Angeles-Long Beach PMSA, CA	Y	25360 FQ	45270 AW	69600 TQ	CABLS	10/01-12/01
	Modesto MSA, CA	Y	30520 FQ	41970 AW	62200 TQ	CABLS	10/01-12/01
	Oakland PMSA, CA	Y	31890 FQ	50890 AW	72110 TQ	CABLS	10/01-12/01
	Orange County PMSA, CA	Y	26470 FQ	43280 AW	60130 TQ	CABLS	10/01-12/01
	Redding MSA, CA	Y	18090 FQ	39830 AW	57970 TQ	CABLS	10/01-12/01
	Riverside-San Bernardino PMSA, CA	Y	25480 FQ	44360 AW	65980 TQ	CABLS	10/01-12/01
	Sacramento PMSA, CA	Y	25600 FQ	41320 AW	57540 TQ	CABLS	10/01-12/01
	Salinas MSA, CA	Y	16040 FQ	34220 AW	59040 TQ	CABLS	10/01-12/01
	San Diego MSA, CA	Y	27010 FQ	43530 AW	65070 TQ	CABLS	10/01-12/01
	San Francisco PMSA, CA	Y	33070 FQ	46930 AW	65580 TQ	CABLS	10/01-12/01
	San Jose PMSA, CA	Y	31170 FQ	49790 AW	69470 TQ	CABLS	10/01-12/01
	San Luis Obispo-Atascadero-Paso Robles MSA, CA	Y	22310 FQ	47540 AW	98650 TQ	CABLS	10/01-12/01
	Santa Barbara-Santa Maria-Lompoc MSA, CA	Y	28240 FQ	44770 AW	67330 TQ	CABLS	10/01-12/01
	Santa Cruz-Watsonville PMSA, CA	Y	28080 FQ	43630 AW	63460 TQ	CABLS	10/01-12/01

AAW Average annual wage; **AE** Average entry wage; **AEX** Average experienced wage; **AO** Average offered; **AOH** Average offered, high; **AOL** Average offered, low; **APH** Average pay, high range; **APL** Average pay, low range; **ASH** Average starting, high; **ASL** Average starting, low; **AW** Average wage paid; **FQ** First quartile wage; **H** Hourly; **HI** Highest wage paid; **HR** High end range; **LR** Low end range; **M** Monthly; **MTC** Median total compensation; **MW** Median wage paid; **SQ** Second quartile wage; **S** Special: hourly and annual; **TQ** Third quartile wage; **W** Weekly; **Y** Yearly

Occupation/Type/Industry	Location	Per	Low	Mid	High	Source	Date
Electrical and Electronic Engineering Technician	Santa Rosa PMSA, CA	Y	29640 FQ	41000 AW	55390 TQ	CABLS	10/01-12/01
	Stockton-Lodi MSA, CA	Y	31310 FQ	42830 AW	56020 TQ	CABLS	10/01-12/01
	Vallejo-Fairfield-Napa PMSA, CA	Y	31290 FQ	43750 AW	63130 TQ	CABLS	10/01-12/01
	Ventura PMSA, CA	Y	28070 FQ	49140 AW	70740 TQ	CABLS	10/01-12/01
	Visalia-Tulare-Porterville MSA, CA	Y	31210 FQ	43750 AW	55270 TQ	CABLS	10/01-12/01
	Colorado	Y	26310 FQ	48860 AW	81800 TQ	COBLS	10/01-12/01
	Boulder-Longmont PMSA, CO	Y	30870 FQ	58580 AW	93770 TQ	COBLS	10/01-12/01
	Colorado Springs MSA, CO	Y	25360 FQ	39910 AW	55080 TQ	COBLS	10/01-12/01
	Denver PMSA, CO	Y	24740 FQ	48940 AW	76300 TQ	COBLS	10/01-12/01
	Fort Collins-Loveland MSA, CO	Y	29820 FQ	42270 AW	57110 TQ	COBLS	10/01-12/01
	Connecticut	Y	29400 FQ	43630 AW	58260 TQ	CTBLS	10/01-12/01
	Bridgeport PMSA, CT	Y	30900 FQ	43020 AW	57070 TQ	CTBLS	10/01-12/01
	Danbury PMSA, CT	Y	29200 FQ	44210 AW	57300 TQ	CTBLS	10/01-12/01
	Hartford MSA, CT	Y	29620 FQ	43740 AW	59380 TQ	CTBLS	10/01-12/01
	New Haven-Meriden PMSA, CT	Y	26770 FQ	40410 AW	54640 TQ	CTBLS	10/01-12/01
	Stamford-Norwalk PMSA, CT	Y	29620 FQ	46140 AW	67920 TQ	CTBLS	10/01-12/01
	Waterbury PMSA, CT	Y	30490 FQ	48070 AW	70120 TQ	CTBLS	10/01-12/01
	Delaware	Y	32690 FQ	49650 AW	68460 TQ	DEBLS	10/01-12/01
	Wilmington-Newark PMSA, DE-MD	Y	33710 FQ	49510 AW	68290 TQ	DEBLS	10/01-12/01
	District of Columbia	Y	33770 FQ	50650 AW	69440 TQ	DCBLS	10/01-12/01
	Washington PMSA, DC-MD-VA-WV	Y	29580 FQ	46680 AW	67170 TQ	DCBLS	10/01-12/01
	Florida	Y	25720 FQ	37820 AW	54200 TQ	FLBLS	10/01-12/01
	Daytona Beach MSA, FL	Y	21370 FQ	33530 AW	49820 TQ	FLBLS	10/01-12/01
	Fort Lauderdale PMSA, FL	Y	25370 FQ	41550 AW	56630 TQ	FLBLS	10/01-12/01
	Fort Myers-Cape Coral MSA, FL	Y	22700 FQ	32280 AW	48600 TQ	FLBLS	10/01-12/01
	Fort Pierce-Port St. Lucie MSA, FL	Y	23520 FQ	39330 AW	49910 TQ	FLBLS	10/01-12/01
	Fort Walton Beach MSA, FL	Y	24590 FQ	40910 AW	56350 TQ	FLBLS	10/01-12/01
	Gainesville MSA, FL	Y	27460 FQ	42450 AW	55540 TQ	FLBLS	10/01-12/01
	Jacksonville MSA, FL	Y	29360 FQ	42510 AW	57490 TQ	FLBLS	10/01-12/01
	Lakeland-Winter Haven MSA, FL	Y	24800 FQ	38460 AW	53770 TQ	FLBLS	10/01-12/01
	Melbourne-Titusville-Palm Bay MSA, FL	Y	25470 FQ	31340 AW	37430 TQ	FLBLS	10/01-12/01
	Miami PMSA, FL	Y	29100 FQ	46010 AW	61260 TQ	FLBLS	10/01-12/01
	Naples MSA, FL	Y	19310 FQ	34440 AW	54050 TQ	FLBLS	10/01-12/01
	Ocala MSA, FL	Y	29380 FQ	37680 AW	52800 TQ	FLBLS	10/01-12/01
	Orlando MSA, FL	Y	27850 FQ	38990 AW	48010 TQ	FLBLS	10/01-12/01
	Pensacola MSA, FL	Y	23450 FQ	37390 AW	53700 TQ	FLBLS	10/01-12/01
	Sarasota-Bradenton MSA, FL	Y	26630 FQ	39730 AW	54400 TQ	FLBLS	10/01-12/01
	Tallahassee MSA, FL	Y	24340 FQ	36250 AW	52070 TQ	FLBLS	10/01-12/01
	Tampa-St. Petersburg-Clearwater MSA, FL	Y	26590 FQ	41510 AW	58250 TQ	FLBLS	10/01-12/01
	West Palm Beach-Boca Raton MSA, FL	Y	25910 FQ	40320 AW	55050 TQ	FLBLS	10/01-12/01
	Georgia	Y	30650 FQ	45520 AW	57820 TQ	GABLS	10/01-12/01
	Atlanta MSA, GA	Y	30790 FQ	45990 AW	58420 TQ	GABLS	10/01-12/01
	Augusta-Aiken MSA, GA-SC	Y	26080 FQ	43880 AW	63190 TQ	GABLS	10/01-12/01
	Columbus MSA, GA-AL	Y	25850 FQ	41710 AW	55570 TQ	GABLS	10/01-12/01
	Macon MSA, GA	Y	35700 FQ	45050 AW	54870 TQ	GABLS	10/01-12/01
	Savannah MSA, GA	Y	29470 FQ	42740 AW	55380 TQ	GABLS	10/01-12/01
	Hawaii	Y	32500 FQ	46630 AW	68090 TQ	HIBLS	10/01-12/01
	Honolulu MSA, HI	Y	32130 FQ	46330 AW	68720 TQ	HIBLS	10/01-12/01
	Idaho	Y	27160 FQ	41080 AW	54040 TQ	IDBLS	10/01-12/01
	Boise City MSA, ID	Y	27460 FQ	40770 AW	52580 TQ	IDBLS	10/01-12/01
	Illinois	Y	25860 FQ	40770 AW	57780 TQ	ILBLS	10/01-12/01
	Champaign-Urbana MSA, IL	Y	31250 FQ	43650 AW	58600 TQ	ILBLS	10/01-12/01
	Chicago PMSA, IL	Y	26260 FQ	41130 AW	57500 TQ	ILBLS	10/01-12/01
	Peoria-Pekin MSA, IL	Y	26850 FQ	40660 AW	55860 TQ	ILBLS	10/01-12/01
	Rockford MSA, IL	Y	21510 FQ	40260 AW	56270 TQ	ILBLS	10/01-12/01
	Springfield MSA, IL	Y	26390 FQ	45550 AW	64150 TQ	ILBLS	10/01-12/01
	Indiana	Y	25740 FQ	40400 AW	57410 TQ	INBLS	10/01-12/01
	Elkhart-Goshen MSA, IN	Y	26850 FQ	33530 AW	44090 TQ	INBLS	10/01-12/01

AAW	Average annual wage	AOH	Average offered, high	ASH	Average starting, high	H	Hourly	M	Monthly	S	Special: hourly and annual
AE	Average entry wage	AOL	Average offered, low	ASL	Average starting, low	HI	Highest wage paid	MTC	Median total compensation	TQ	Third quartile wage
AEX	Average experienced wage	APH	Average pay, high range	AW	Average wage paid	HR	High end range	MW	Median wage paid	W	Weekly
AO	Average offered	APL	Average pay, low range	FQ	First quartile wage	LR	Low end range	SQ	Second quartile wage	Y	Yearly

Occupation/Type/Industry	Location	Per	Low	Mid	High	Source	Date
Electrical and Electronic Engineering Technician	Evansville-Henderson MSA, IN-KY	Y	22500 FQ	41350 AW	61430 TQ	INBLS	10/01-12/01
	Fort Wayne MSA, IN	Y	26260 FQ	40260 AW	57390 TQ	INBLS	10/01-12/01
	Gary PMSA, IN	Y	28580 FQ	44520 AW	61590 TQ	INBLS	10/01-12/01
	Indianapolis MSA, IN	Y	25720 FQ	37120 AW	52140 TQ	INBLS	10/01-12/01
	Lafayette MSA, IN	Y	24090 FQ	36720 AW	52290 TQ	INBLS	10/01-12/01
	South Bend MSA, IN	Y	23440 FQ	40650 AW	58700 TQ	INBLS	10/01-12/01
	Iowa	Y	25120 FQ	38910 AW	55390 TQ	IABLS	10/01-12/01
	Davenport-Moline-Rock Island MSA, IA-IL	Y	24820 FQ	40840 AW	56160 TQ	IABLS	10/01-12/01
	Des Moines MSA, IA	Y	27380 FQ	46980 AW	62220 TQ	IABLS	10/01-12/01
	Kansas	Y	21540 FQ	39660 AW	63830 TQ	KSBLS	10/01-12/01
	Topeka MSA, KS	Y	28600 FQ	40820 AW	55030 TQ	KSBLS	10/01-12/01
	Wichita MSA, KS	Y	21040 FQ	39270 AW	55610 TQ	KSBLS	10/01-12/01
	Kentucky	Y	27160 FQ	43800 AW	58470 TQ	KYBLS	10/01-12/01
	Lexington MSA, KY	Y	25110 FQ	40290 AW	57730 TQ	KYBLS	10/01-12/01
	Louisville MSA, KY-IN	Y	28160 FQ	44680 AW	58040 TQ	KYBLS	10/01-12/01
	Louisiana	Y	26180 FQ	44240 AW	58250 TQ	LABLS	10/01-12/01
	Baton Rouge MSA, LA	Y	26160 FQ	41940 AW	56730 TQ	LABLS	10/01-12/01
	Houma MSA, LA	Y	19020 FQ	33160 AW	53040 TQ	LABLS	10/01-12/01
	Lafayette MSA, LA	Y	24950 FQ	41470 AW	56950 TQ	LABLS	10/01-12/01
	Lake Charles MSA, LA	Y	30210 FQ	48700 AW	64460 TQ	LABLS	10/01-12/01
	New Orleans MSA, LA	Y	28380 FQ	46980 AW	61100 TQ	LABLS	10/01-12/01
	Shreveport-Bossier City MSA, LA	Y	26500 FQ	42450 AW	55680 TQ	LABLS	10/01-12/01
	Maine	Y	29610 FQ	44530 AW	61990 TQ	MEBLS	10/01-12/01
	Portland MSA, ME	Y	28920 FQ	40230 AW	54110 TQ	MEBLS	10/01-12/01
	Maryland	Y	26060 FQ	42770 AW	61800 TQ	MDBLS	10/01-12/01
	Baltimore PMSA, MD	Y	25360 FQ	41740 AW	58520 TQ	MDBLS	10/01-12/01
	Massachusetts	Y	30660 FQ	46640 AW	65390 TQ	MABLS	10/01-12/01
	Boston PMSA, MA-NH	Y	30750 FQ	48160 AW	70100 TQ	MABLS	10/01-12/01
	Brockton PMSA, MA	Y	30940 FQ	42160 AW	54190 TQ	MABLS	10/01-12/01
	Lawrence PMSA, MA-NH	Y	31150 FQ	45030 AW	58530 TQ	MABLS	10/01-12/01
	Lowell PMSA, MA-NH	Y	33490 FQ	44860 AW	58340 TQ	MABLS	10/01-12/01
	New Bedford PMSA, MA	Y	25030 FQ	39250 AW	55900 TQ	MABLS	10/01-12/01
	Springfield MSA, MA	Y	27800 FQ	42220 AW	55930 TQ	MABLS	10/01-12/01
	Worcester PMSA, MA-CT	Y	30340 FQ	43880 AW	57860 TQ	MABLS	10/01-12/01
	Michigan	Y	28270 FQ	44150 AW	63440 TQ	MIBLS	10/01-12/01
	Ann Arbor PMSA, MI	Y	19180 FQ	36740 AW	57450 TQ	MIBLS	10/01-12/01
	Detroit PMSA, MI	Y	30470 FQ	47510 AW	71620 TQ	MIBLS	10/01-12/01
	Flint PMSA, MI	Y	28850 FQ	46660 AW	67770 TQ	MIBLS	10/01-12/01
	Grand Rapids-Muskegon-Holland MSA, MI	Y	27380 FQ	39270 AW	55380 TQ	MIBLS	10/01-12/01
	Kalamazoo-Battle Creek MSA, MI	Y	29330 FQ	46140 AW	58200 TQ	MIBLS	10/01-12/01
	Lansing-East Lansing MSA, MI	Y	31070 FQ	45860 AW	59830 TQ	MIBLS	10/01-12/01
	Saginaw-Bay City-Midland MSA, MI	Y	34580 FQ	48550 AW	64860 TQ	MIBLS	10/01-12/01
	Minnesota	Y	28370 FQ	42490 AW	57810 TQ	MNBLS	10/01-12/01
	Duluth-Superior MSA, MN-WI	Y	24840 FQ	41370 AW	57060 TQ	MNBLS	10/01-12/01
	Minneapolis-St. Paul MSA, MN-WI	Y	30760 FQ	44380 AW	59270 TQ	MNBLS	10/01-12/01
	St. Cloud MSA, MN	Y	22040 FQ	39490 AW	55170 TQ	MNBLS	10/01-12/01
	Mississippi	Y	27290 FQ	41030 AW	55720 TQ	MSBLS	10/01-12/01
	Biloxi-Gulfport-Pascagoula MSA, MS	Y	29670 FQ	41400 AW	57850 TQ	MSBLS	10/01-12/01
	Jackson MSA, MS	Y	27750 FQ	40260 AW	54040 TQ	MSBLS	10/01-12/01
	Missouri	Y	22110 FQ	40080 AW	57500 TQ	MOBLS	10/01-12/01
	Kansas City MSA, MO-KS	Y	23210 FQ	43590 AW	74740 TQ	MOBLS	10/01-12/01
	St. Louis MSA, MO-IL	Y	26220 FQ	41420 AW	57290 TQ	MOBLS	10/01-12/01
	Springfield MSA, MO	Y	24480 FQ	39000 AW	56090 TQ	MOBLS	10/01-12/01
	Montana	Y	26640 FQ	41650 AW	56280 TQ	MTBLS	10/01-12/01
	Billings MSA, MT	Y	28310 FQ	44170 AW	57660 TQ	MTBLS	10/01-12/01
	Nebraska	Y	23890 FQ	38910 AW	54400 TQ	NEBLS	10/01-12/01
	Lincoln MSA, NE	Y	24800 FQ	39020 AW	55120 TQ	NEBLS	10/01-12/01
	Omaha MSA, NE-IA	Y	23590 FQ	38940 AW	54120 TQ	NEBLS	10/01-12/01
	Nevada	Y	28830 FQ	43090 AW	58290 TQ	NVBLS	10/01-12/01
	Las Vegas MSA, NV-AZ	Y	33550 FQ	45680 AW	62380 TQ	NVBLS	10/01-12/01
	Reno MSA, NV	Y	24350 FQ	37500 AW	51880 TQ	NVBLS	10/01-12/01
	New Hampshire	Y	30320 FQ	43970 AW	57180 TQ	NHBLS	10/01-12/01
	Manchester PMSA, NH	Y	31140 FQ	45330 AW	59790 TQ	NHBLS	10/01-12/01

AAW Average annual wage **AOH** Average offered, high **ASH** Average starting, high **H** Hourly **M** Monthly **S** Special: hourly and annual
AE Average entry wage **AOL** Average offered, low **ASL** Average starting, low **HI** Highest wage paid **MTC** Median total compensation **TQ** Third quartile wage
AEX Average experienced wage **APH** Average pay, high range **AW** Average wage paid **HR** High end range **MW** Median wage paid **W** Weekly
AO Average offered **APL** Average pay, low range **FQ** First quartile wage **LR** Low end range **SQ** Second quartile wage **Y** Yearly

Occupation/Type/Industry	Location	Per	Low	Mid	High	Source	Date
Electrical and Electronic Engineering Technician	Nashua PMSA, NH	Y	29730 FQ	42790 AW	55340 TQ	NHBLS	10/01-12/01
	Portsmouth-Rochester PMSA, NH-ME	Y	29590 FQ	42360 AW	57810 TQ	NHBLS	10/01-12/01
	New Jersey	Y	30380 FQ	47630 AW	72280 TQ	NJBLS	10/01-12/01
	Atlantic-Cape May PMSA, NJ	Y	35900 FQ	47960 AW	64530 TQ	NJBLS	10/01-12/01
	Bergen-Passaic PMSA, NJ	Y	32670 FQ	54930 AW	83720 TQ	NJBLS	10/01-12/01
	Jersey City PMSA, NJ	Y	34060 FQ	49000 AW	71240 TQ	NJBLS	10/01-12/01
	Middlesex-Somerset-Hunterdon PMSA, NJ	Y	28840 FQ	46250 AW	71120 TQ	NJBLS	10/01-12/01
	Monmouth-Ocean PMSA, NJ	Y	29090 FQ	48110 AW	68800 TQ	NJBLS	10/01-12/01
	Newark PMSA, NJ	Y	30170 FQ	44280 AW	60290 TQ	NJBLS	10/01-12/01
	Trenton PMSA, NJ	Y	28490 FQ	37660 AW	48790 TQ	NJBLS	10/01-12/01
	New Mexico	Y	26680 FQ	43220 AW	60650 TQ	NMBLS	10/01-12/01
	Albuquerque MSA, NM	Y	26450 FQ	41600 AW	56870 TQ	NMBLS	10/01-12/01
	Las Cruces MSA, NM	Y	25480 FQ	41810 AW	58110 TQ	NMBLS	10/01-12/01
	New York	Y	25770 FQ	44330 AW	65210 TQ	NYBLS	10/01-12/01
	Albany-Schenectady-Troy MSA, NY	Y	25620 FQ	43620 AW	57200 TQ	NYBLS	10/01-12/01
	Binghamton MSA, NY	Y	22740 FQ	33720 AW	51270 TQ	NYBLS	10/01-12/01
	Buffalo-Niagara Falls MSA, NY	Y	23280 FQ	37720 AW	56080 TQ	NYBLS	10/01-12/01
	Dutchess County PMSA, NY	Y	26140 FQ	43330 AW	57130 TQ	NYBLS	10/01-12/01
	Nassau-Suffolk PMSA, NY	Y	25070 FQ	42120 AW	59450 TQ	NYBLS	10/01-12/01
	New York PMSA, NY	Y	31240 FQ	49650 AW	70170 TQ	NYBLS	10/01-12/01
	Newburgh PMSA, NY-PA	Y	31770 FQ	44380 AW	57990 TQ	NYBLS	10/01-12/01
	Rochester MSA, NY	Y	25770 FQ	42920 AW	61860 TQ	NYBLS	10/01-12/01
	Syracuse MSA, NY	Y	27030 FQ	46410 AW	68650 TQ	NYBLS	10/01-12/01
	Utica-Rome MSA, NY	Y	22460 FQ	36700 AW	61770 TQ	NYBLS	10/01-12/01
	North Carolina	Y	29640 FQ	45100 AW	62150 TQ	NCBLS	10/01-12/01
	Asheville MSA, NC	Y	26630 FQ	39840 AW	53930 TQ	NCBLS	10/01-12/01
	Charlotte-Gastonia-Rock Hill MSA, NC-SC	Y	29960 FQ	44890 AW	56470 TQ	NCBLS	10/01-12/01
	Fayetteville MSA, NC	Y	30410 FQ	41050 AW	53280 TQ	NCBLS	10/01-12/01
	Greensboro-Winston-Salem-High Point MSA, NC	Y	30030 FQ	40910 AW	54720 TQ	NCBLS	10/01-12/01
	Hickory-Morganton-Lenoir MSA, NC	Y	30970 FQ	41450 AW	53930 TQ	NCBLS	10/01-12/01
	Raleigh-Durham-Chapel Hill MSA, NC	Y	30790 FQ	50210 AW	82590 TQ	NCBLS	10/01-12/01
	Wilmington MSA, NC	Y	21360 FQ	42610 AW	67890 TQ	NCBLS	10/01-12/01
	North Dakota	Y	23710 FQ	36110 AW	53010 TQ	NDBLS	10/01-12/01
	Fargo-Moorhead MSA, ND-MN	Y	23450 FQ	34500 AW	47550 TQ	NDBLS	10/01-12/01
	Ohio	Y	26460 FQ	42060 AW	58020 TQ	OHBLS	10/01-12/01
	Akron PMSA, OH	Y	23230 FQ	39750 AW	56470 TQ	OHBLS	10/01-12/01
	Canton-Massillon MSA, OH	Y	23520 FQ	40240 AW	54780 TQ	OHBLS	10/01-12/01
	Cincinnati PMSA, OH-KY-IN	Y	27580 FQ	43800 AW	59710 TQ	OHBLS	10/01-12/01
	Cleveland-Lorain-Elyria PMSA, OH	Y	28050 FQ	43050 AW	59090 TQ	OHBLS	10/01-12/01
	Columbus MSA, OH	Y	28490 FQ	41930 AW	55950 TQ	OHBLS	10/01-12/01
	Dayton-Springfield MSA, OH	Y	27030 FQ	41680 AW	58680 TQ	OHBLS	10/01-12/01
	Hamilton-Middletown PMSA, OH	Y	25730 FQ	37670 AW	54620 TQ	OHBLS	10/01-12/01
	Mansfield MSA, OH	Y	24710 FQ	38580 AW	56240 TQ	OHBLS	10/01-12/01
	Toledo MSA, OH	Y	28630 FQ	46140 AW	76290 TQ	OHBLS	10/01-12/01
	Youngstown-Warren MSA, OH	Y	21540 FQ	35930 AW	53560 TQ	OHBLS	10/01-12/01
	Oklahoma	Y	26040 FQ	42780 AW	61280 TQ	OKBLS	10/01-12/01
	Oklahoma City MSA, OK	Y	28480 FQ	44180 AW	62640 TQ	OKBLS	10/01-12/01
	Tulsa MSA, OK	Y	22450 FQ	39170 AW	60710 TQ	OKBLS	10/01-12/01
	Oregon	Y	24610 FQ	38550 AW	53160 TQ	ORBLS	10/01-12/01
	Eugene-Springfield MSA, OR	Y	17370 FQ	42590 AW	60620 TQ	ORBLS	10/01-12/01
	Medford-Ashland MSA, OR	Y	24860 FQ	38080 AW	53600 TQ	ORBLS	10/01-12/01
	Portland-Vancouver PMSA, OR-WA	Y	25220 FQ	40140 AW	56150 TQ	ORBLS	10/01-12/01
	Salem PMSA, OR	Y	33380 FQ	45860 AW	57370 TQ	ORBLS	10/01-12/01
	Pennsylvania	Y	25380 FQ	41340 AW	57450 TQ	PABLS	10/01-12/01
	Erie MSA, PA	Y	26780 FQ	40760 AW	55740 TQ	PABLS	10/01-12/01
	Harrisburg-Lebanon-Carlisle MSA, PA	Y	25550 FQ	39520 AW	55510 TQ	PABLS	10/01-12/01
	Johnstown MSA, PA	Y	18830 FQ	35780 AW	53310 TQ	PABLS	10/01-12/01
	Lancaster MSA, PA	Y	18290 FQ	37490 AW	54240 TQ	PABLS	10/01-12/01

AAW Average annual wage	AOH Average offered, high	ASH Average starting, high	H Hourly	M Monthly	S Special: hourly and annual
AE Average entry wage	AOL Average offered, low	ASL Average starting, low	HI Highest wage paid	MTC Median total compensation	TQ Third quartile wage
AEX Average experienced wage	APH Average pay, high range	AW Average wage paid	HR High end range	MW Median wage paid	W Weekly
AO Average offered	APL Average pay, low range	FQ First quartile wage	LR Low end range	SQ Second quartile wage	Y Yearly

Occupation/Type/Industry	Location	Per	Low	Mid	High	Source	Date
Electrical and Electronic Engineering Technician	Philadelphia PMSA, PA-NJ	Y	28080 FQ	44940 AW	66380 TQ	PABLS	10/01-12/01
	Pittsburgh MSA, PA	Y	26490 FQ	41850 AW	57710 TQ	PABLS	10/01-12/01
	Reading MSA, PA	Y	23280 FQ	36230 AW	53060 TQ	PABLS	10/01-12/01
	Scranton-Wilkes-Barre-Hazleton MSA, PA	Y	29470 FQ	42810 AW	55690 TQ	PABLS	10/01-12/01
	York MSA, PA	Y	23410 FQ	40500 AW	57400 TQ	PABLS	10/01-12/01
	Rhode Island	Y	26330 FQ	40820 AW	59410 TQ	RIBLS	10/01-12/01
	Providence-Fall River-Warwick MSA, RI-MA	Y	26260 FQ	38450 AW	53200 TQ	RIBLS	10/01-12/01
	South Carolina	Y	29630 FQ	43870 AW	59880 TQ	SCBLS	10/01-12/01
	Charleston-North Charleston MSA, SC	Y	29750 FQ	43170 AW	61930 TQ	SCBLS	10/01-12/01
	Columbia MSA, SC	Y	33730 FQ	45490 AW	58560 TQ	SCBLS	10/01-12/01
	Greenville-Spartanburg-Anderson MSA, SC	Y	29460 FQ	45390 AW	63140 TQ	SCBLS	10/01-12/01
	South Dakota	Y	23110 FQ	34580 AW	49000 TQ	SDBLS	10/01-12/01
	Sioux Falls MSA, SD	Y	24910 FQ	38500 AW	54040 TQ	SDBLS	10/01-12/01
	Tennessee	Y	26120 FQ	43170 AW	58360 TQ	TNBLS	10/01-12/01
	Chattanooga MSA, TN-GA	Y	26690 FQ	41170 AW	53940 TQ	TNBLS	10/01-12/01
	Clarksville-Hopkinsville MSA, TN-KY	Y	36240 FQ	48180 AW	60030 TQ	TNBLS	10/01-12/01
	Johnson City-Kingsport-Bristol MSA, TN-VA	Y	27800 FQ	40100 AW	56110 TQ	TNBLS	10/01-12/01
	Knoxville MSA, TN	Y	24870 FQ	41840 AW	58060 TQ	TNBLS	10/01-12/01
	Memphis MSA, TN-AR-MS	Y	20750 FQ	37590 AW	55340 TQ	TNBLS	10/01-12/01
	Nashville MSA, TN	Y	32140 FQ	47580 AW	60150 TQ	TNBLS	10/01-12/01
	Texas	Y	25610 FQ	44710 AW	67290 TQ	TXBLS	10/01-12/01
	Amarillo MSA, TX	Y	33510 FQ	50960 AW	65980 TQ	TXBLS	10/01-12/01
	Austin-San Marcos MSA, TX	Y	30030 FQ	44790 AW	65510 TQ	TXBLS	10/01-12/01
	Beaumont-Port Arthur MSA, TX	Y	22670 FQ	45060 AW	73680 TQ	TXBLS	10/01-12/01
	Brazoria PMSA, TX	Y	14120 FQ	38380 AW	62980 TQ	TXBLS	10/01-12/01
	Brownsville-Harlingen-San Benito MSA, TX	Y	18190 FQ	51050 AW	88550 TQ	TXBLS	10/01-12/01
	Corpus Christi MSA, TX	Y	23230 FQ	43000 AW	65750 TQ	TXBLS	10/01-12/01
	Dallas PMSA, TX	Y	30030 FQ	48440 AW	75510 TQ	TXBLS	10/01-12/01
	El Paso MSA, TX	Y	24420 FQ	41560 AW	57040 TQ	TXBLS	10/01-12/01
	Fort Worth-Arlington PMSA, TX	Y	29440 FQ	49960 AW	79200 TQ	TXBLS	10/01-12/01
	Houston PMSA, TX	Y	20110 FQ	41080 AW	63290 TQ	TXBLS	10/01-12/01
	Killeen-Temple MSA, TX	Y	30210 FQ	38130 AW	51780 TQ	TXBLS	10/01-12/01
	Longview-Marshall MSA, TX	Y	24950 FQ	36440 AW	52970 TQ	TXBLS	10/01-12/01
	Lubbock MSA, TX	Y	24210 FQ	37560 AW	54730 TQ	TXBLS	10/01-12/01
	McAllen-Edinburg-Mission MSA, TX	Y	22730 FQ	42910 AW	60290 TQ	TXBLS	10/01-12/01
	Odessa-Midland MSA, TX	Y	27160 FQ	43420 AW	57720 TQ	TXBLS	10/01-12/01
	San Antonio MSA, TX	Y	20770 FQ	37460 AW	55430 TQ	TXBLS	10/01-12/01
	Waco MSA, TX	Y	24300 FQ	38010 AW	56060 TQ	TXBLS	10/01-12/01
	Utah	Y	13500 FQ	36440 AW	54820 TQ	UTBLS	10/01-12/01
	Salt Lake City-Ogden MSA, UT	Y	26540 FQ	43080 AW	56210 TQ	UTBLS	10/01-12/01
	Vermont	Y	30280 FQ	46970 AW	67870 TQ	VTBLS	10/01-12/01
	Burlington MSA, VT	Y	30420 FQ	49530 AW	69360 TQ	VTBLS	10/01-12/01
	Virginia	Y	28280 FQ	44970 AW	64740 TQ	VABLS	10/01-12/01
	Lynchburg MSA, VA	Y	25220 FQ	41400 AW	59620 TQ	VABLS	10/01-12/01
	Norfolk-Virginia Beach-Newport News MSA, VA-NC	Y	27700 FQ	44040 AW	64080 TQ	VABLS	10/01-12/01
	Richmond-Petersburg MSA, VA	Y	25780 FQ	41420 AW	56910 TQ	VABLS	10/01-12/01
	Roanoke MSA, VA	Y	22330 FQ	37370 AW	52900 TQ	VABLS	10/01-12/01
	Washington	Y	24350 FQ	44460 AW	60730 TQ	WABLS	10/01-12/01
	Bremerton PMSA, WA	Y	40050 FQ	52770 AW	68210 TQ	WABLS	10/01-12/01
	Richland-Kennewick-Pasco MSA, WA	Y	33320 FQ	46250 AW	56340 TQ	WABLS	10/01-12/01
	Seattle-Bellevue-Everett PMSA, WA	Y	31030 FQ	47380 AW	60660 TQ	WABLS	10/01-12/01
	Spokane MSA, WA	Y	27210 FQ	39280 AW	52540 TQ	WABLS	10/01-12/01
	Tacoma PMSA, WA	Y	31290 FQ	46120 AW	67630 TQ	WABLS	10/01-12/01
	Yakima MSA, WA	Y	27460 FQ	42000 AW	56720 TQ	WABLS	10/01-12/01
	West Virginia	Y	23200 FQ	41790 AW	57440 TQ	WVBLS	10/01-12/01

AAW Average annual wage; **AE** Average entry wage; **AEX** Average experienced wage; **AO** Average offered; **AOH** Average offered, high; **AOL** Average offered, low; **APH** Average pay, high range; **APL** Average pay, low range; **ASH** Average starting, high; **ASL** Average starting, low; **AW** Average wage paid; **FQ** First quartile wage; **H** Hourly; **HI** Highest wage paid; **HR** High end range; **LR** Low end range; **M** Monthly; **MTC** Median total compensation; **MW** Median wage paid; **SQ** Second quartile wage; **S** Special: hourly and annual; **TQ** Third quartile wage; **W** Weekly; **Y** Yearly

Occupation/Type/Industry	Location	Per	Low	Mid	High	Source	Date
Electrical and Electronic Engineering Technician	Charleston MSA, WV	Y	22260 FQ	38660 AW	56140 TQ	WVBLS	10/01-12/01
	Huntington-Ashland MSA, WV-KY-OH	Y	26430 FQ	43800 AW	58530 TQ	WVBLS	10/01-12/01
	Wisconsin	Y	27120 FQ	41670 AW	58800 TQ	WIBLS	10/01-12/01
	Appleton-Oshkosh-Neenah MSA, WI	Y	25480 FQ	41920 AW	63090 TQ	WIBLS	10/01-12/01
	Green Bay MSA, WI	Y	27590 FQ	41250 AW	56520 TQ	WIBLS	10/01-12/01
	Madison MSA, WI	Y	26620 FQ	39490 AW	55950 TQ	WIBLS	10/01-12/01
	Milwaukee-Waukesha PMSA, WI	Y	29620 FQ	43650 AW	60460 TQ	WIBLS	10/01-12/01
	Racine PMSA, WI	Y	24850 FQ	36930 AW	56360 TQ	WIBLS	10/01-12/01
	Wyoming	Y	24310 FQ	41110 AW	56500 TQ	WYBLS	10/01-12/01
	Cheyenne MSA, WY	Y	24510 FQ	37810 AW	47920 TQ	WYBLS	10/01-12/01
	Puerto Rico	Y	15220 FQ	26440 AW	38310 TQ	PRBLS	10/01-12/01
	Guam	Y	18660 FQ	39040 AW	62960 TQ	GUBLS	10/01-12/01
Electrical and Electronic Equipment Assembler	Alabama	H	6.19 FQ	9.13 AW	13.48 TQ	ALBLS	10/01-12/01
	Arizona	H	6.74 FQ	11.50 AW	18.05 TQ	AZBLS	10/01-12/01
	Arkansas	H	7.19 FQ	11.67 AW	16.95 TQ	ARBLS	10/01-12/01
	California	H	7.08 FQ	11.87 AW	18.12 TQ	CABLS	10/01-12/01
	Colorado	H	7.17 FQ	10.88 AW	15.22 TQ	COBLS	10/01-12/01
	Connecticut	H	7.51 FQ	11.43 AW	17.21 TQ	CTBLS	10/01-12/01
	Delaware	H	8.71 FQ	16.40 AW	25.53 TQ	DEBLS	10/01-12/01
	Florida	H	6.31 FQ	9.46 AW	13.39 TQ	FLBLS	10/01-12/01
	Georgia	H	7.82 FQ	10.84 AW	14.79 TQ	GABLS	10/01-12/01
	Idaho	H	7.41 FQ	10.02 AW	13.12 TQ	IDBLS	10/01-12/01
	Illinois	H	7.34 FQ	10.91 AW	14.75 TQ	ILBLS	10/01-12/01
	Indiana	H	7.50 FQ	10.38 AW	14.05 TQ	INBLS	10/01-12/01
	Iowa	H	8.37 FQ	12.96 AW	19.13 TQ	IABLS	10/01-12/01
	Kansas	H	7.04 FQ	11.02 AW	17.41 TQ	KSBLS	10/01-12/01
	Kentucky	H	8.70 FQ	11.43 AW	15.95 TQ	KYBLS	10/01-12/01
	Louisiana	H	6.96 FQ	11.86 AW	16.93 TQ	LABLS	10/01-12/01
	Maine	H	7.38 FQ	10.11 AW	13.63 TQ	MEBLS	10/01-12/01
	Maryland	H	8.63 FQ	12.03 AW	18.36 TQ	MDBLS	10/01-12/01
	Massachusetts	H	8.98 FQ	13.22 AW	17.68 TQ	MABLS	10/01-12/01
	Michigan	H	8.71 FQ	12.06 AW	16.49 TQ	MIBLS	10/01-12/01
	Minnesota	H	8.25 FQ	12.40 AW	17.31 TQ	MNBLS	10/01-12/01
	Mississippi	H	5.98 FQ	9.08 AW	14.01 TQ	MSBLS	10/01-12/01
	Missouri	H	7.65 FQ	10.99 AW	14.56 TQ	MOBLS	10/01-12/01
	Montana	H	6.53 FQ	9.93 AW	14.86 TQ	MTBLS	10/01-12/01
	Nebraska	H	6.38 FQ	10.09 AW	13.89 TQ	NEBLS	10/01-12/01
	Nevada	H	6.57 FQ	10.74 AW	16.44 TQ	NVBLS	10/01-12/01
	New Hampshire	H	8.78 FQ	11.78 AW	15.70 TQ	NHBLS	10/01-12/01
	New Jersey	H	7.32 FQ	11.92 AW	17.86 TQ	NJBLS	10/01-12/01
	New Mexico	H	7.47 FQ	9.98 AW	13.25 TQ	NMBLS	10/01-12/01
	New York	H	7.35 FQ	12.12 AW	19.72 TQ	NYBLS	10/01-12/01
	North Carolina	H	8.10 FQ	11.98 AW	16.78 TQ	NCBLS	10/01-12/01
	North Dakota	H	7.23 FQ	9.85 AW	13.33 TQ	NDBLS	10/01-12/01
	Ohio	H	7.57 FQ	11.22 AW	16.12 TQ	OHBLS	10/01-12/01
	Oklahoma	H	7.11 FQ	10.68 AW	14.12 TQ	OKBLS	10/01-12/01
	Oregon	H	8.27 FQ	11.27 AW	15.62 TQ	ORBLS	10/01-12/01
	Pennsylvania	H	7.51 FQ	12.19 AW	17.60 TQ	PABLS	10/01-12/01
	Rhode Island	H	8.20 FQ	10.83 AW	14.80 TQ	RIBLS	10/01-12/01
	South Carolina	H	8.07 FQ	12.60 AW	18.27 TQ	SCBLS	10/01-12/01
	South Dakota	H	6.71 FQ	9.45 AW	12.68 TQ	SDBLS	10/01-12/01
	Tennessee	H	8.00 FQ	11.18 AW	15.26 TQ	TNBLS	10/01-12/01
	Texas	H	7.40 FQ	11.26 AW	17.01 TQ	TXBLS	10/01-12/01
	Utah	H	7.49 FQ	10.57 AW	14.57 TQ	UTBLS	10/01-12/01
	Vermont	H	7.80 FQ	12.14 AW	16.35 TQ	VTBLS	10/01-12/01
	Virginia	H	6.80 FQ	11.02 AW	16.38 TQ	VABLS	10/01-12/01
	Washington	H	7.68 FQ	11.76 AW	18.02 TQ	WABLS	10/01-12/01
	West Virginia	H	7.35 FQ	10.97 AW	14.43 TQ	WVBLS	10/01-12/01
	Wisconsin	H	7.59 FQ	11.68 AW	17.76 TQ	WIBLS	10/01-12/01
	Wyoming	H	7.17 FQ	13.31 AW	16.51 TQ	WYBLS	10/01-12/01
	Puerto Rico	H	5.56 FQ	6.68 AW	8.52 TQ	PRBLS	10/01-12/01
Electrical and Electronics Drafter	Alabama	Y	23310 FQ	44990 AW	78730 TQ	ALBLS	10/01-12/01
	Birmingham MSA, AL	Y	29110 FQ	42040 AW	60570 TQ	ALBLS	10/01-12/01
	Huntsville MSA, AL	Y	23220 FQ	49120 AW	84690 TQ	ALBLS	10/01-12/01
	Alaska	Y	36620 FQ	52150 AW	73530 TQ	AKBLS	10/01-12/01

AAW	Average annual wage	**AOH**	Average offered, high	**ASH**	Average starting, high	**H**	Hourly	**M**	Monthly	**S**	Special: hourly and annual
AE	Average entry wage	**AOL**	Average offered, low	**ASL**	Average starting, low	**HI**	Highest wage paid	**MTC**	Median total compensation	**TQ**	Third quartile wage
AEX	Average experienced wage	**APH**	Average pay, high range	**AW**	Average wage paid	**HR**	High end range	**MW**	Median wage paid	**W**	Weekly
AO	Average offered	**APL**	Average pay, low range	**FQ**	First quartile wage	**LR**	Low end range	**SQ**	Second quartile wage	**Y**	Yearly

Occupation/Type/Industry	Location	Per	Low	Mid	High	Source	Date
Electrical and Electronics Drafter	Anchorage MSA, AK	Y	36820 FQ	52150 AW	74570 TQ	AKBLS	10/01-12/01
	Arizona	Y	20490 FQ	37800 AW	57720 TQ	AZBLS	10/01-12/01
	Phoenix-Mesa MSA, AZ	Y	20280 FQ	37760 AW	58770 TQ	AZBLS	10/01-12/01
	Tucson MSA, AZ	Y	24760 FQ	39690 AW	55680 TQ	AZBLS	10/01-12/01
	Arkansas	Y	21540 FQ	36140 AW	54730 TQ	ARBLS	10/01-12/01
	Little Rock-North Little Rock MSA, AR	Y	18650 FQ	33200 AW	45020 TQ	ARBLS	10/01-12/01
	California	Y	27800 FQ	49360 AW	85560 TQ	CABLS	10/01-12/01
	Fresno MSA, CA	Y	23320 FQ	31380 AW	42930 TQ	CABLS	10/01-12/01
	Los Angeles-Long Beach PMSA, CA	Y	22060 FQ	47800 AW	82630 TQ	CABLS	10/01-12/01
	Oakland PMSA, CA	Y	36230 FQ	61730 AW	102640 TQ	CABLS	10/01-12/01
	Orange County PMSA, CA	Y	27360 FQ	43460 AW	66360 TQ	CABLS	10/01-12/01
	Riverside-San Bernardino PMSA, CA	Y	23940 FQ	38210 AW	56680 TQ	CABLS	10/01-12/01
	Sacramento PMSA, CA	Y	31450 FQ	44140 AW	56640 TQ	CABLS	10/01-12/01
	San Diego MSA, CA	Y	25140 FQ	45800 AW	73800 TQ	CABLS	10/01-12/01
	San Francisco PMSA, CA	Y	28830 FQ	49810 AW	78630 TQ	CABLS	10/01-12/01
	San Jose PMSA, CA	Y	30360 FQ	53200 AW	101480 TQ	CABLS	10/01-12/01
	San Luis Obispo-Atascadero-Paso Robles MSA, CA	Y	21860 FQ	42040 AW	70330 TQ	CABLS	10/01-12/01
	Santa Barbara-Santa Maria-Lompoc MSA, CA	Y	30210 FQ	44130 AW	59410 TQ	CABLS	10/01-12/01
	Santa Rosa PMSA, CA	Y	30420 FQ	42360 AW	68410 TQ	CABLS	10/01-12/01
	Stockton-Lodi MSA, CA	Y	24990 FQ	46120 AW	70980 TQ	CABLS	10/01-12/01
	Ventura PMSA, CA	Y	30010 FQ	47860 AW	71420 TQ	CABLS	10/01-12/01
	Visalia-Tulare-Porterville MSA, CA	Y	20100 FQ	30670 AW	43690 TQ	CABLS	10/01-12/01
	Colorado	Y	25040 FQ	40630 AW	58340 TQ	COBLS	10/01-12/01
	Boulder-Longmont PMSA, CO	Y	24770 FQ	37820 AW	55290 TQ	COBLS	10/01-12/01
	Colorado Springs MSA, CO	Y	23530 FQ	36890 AW	55280 TQ	COBLS	10/01-12/01
	Denver PMSA, CO	Y	27280 FQ	44010 AW	61110 TQ	COBLS	10/01-12/01
	Fort Collins-Loveland MSA, CO	Y	27280 FQ	39790 AW	56050 TQ	COBLS	10/01-12/01
	Connecticut	Y	30140 FQ	43590 AW	60970 TQ	CTBLS	10/01-12/01
	Danbury PMSA, CT	Y	31340 FQ	44000 AW	59610 TQ	CTBLS	10/01-12/01
	Hartford MSA, CT	Y	32520 FQ	46210 AW	66110 TQ	CTBLS	10/01-12/01
	New Haven-Meriden PMSA, CT	Y	31550 FQ	44630 AW	58430 TQ	CTBLS	10/01-12/01
	Stamford-Norwalk PMSA, CT	Y	27990 FQ	44280 AW	61230 TQ	CTBLS	10/01-12/01
	Delaware	Y	25130 FQ	47220 AW	68930 TQ	DEBLS	10/01-12/01
	Wilmington-Newark PMSA, DE-MD	Y	25770 FQ	46660 AW	69400 TQ	DEBLS	10/01-12/01
	District of Columbia	Y	30220 FQ	41650 AW	57060 TQ	DCBLS	10/01-12/01
	Washington PMSA, DC-MD-VA-WV	Y	25560 FQ	40390 AW	56520 TQ	DCBLS	10/01-12/01
	Florida	Y	23690 FQ	38200 AW	58900 TQ	FLBLS	10/01-12/01
	Fort Lauderdale PMSA, FL	Y	28380 FQ	38940 AW	62980 TQ	FLBLS	10/01-12/01
	Fort Myers-Cape Coral MSA, FL	Y	26170 FQ	37280 AW	46920 TQ	FLBLS	10/01-12/01
	Fort Walton Beach MSA, FL	Y	19930 FQ	28670 AW	40990 TQ	FLBLS	10/01-12/01
	Jacksonville MSA, FL	Y	21470 FQ	36500 AW	62260 TQ	FLBLS	10/01-12/01
	Melbourne-Titusville-Palm Bay MSA, FL	Y	25140 FQ	40610 AW	62180 TQ	FLBLS	10/01-12/01
	Miami PMSA, FL	Y	23660 FQ	40210 AW	60290 TQ	FLBLS	10/01-12/01
	Orlando MSA, FL	Y	26550 FQ	39610 AW	64140 TQ	FLBLS	10/01-12/01
	Sarasota-Bradenton MSA, FL	Y	27670 FQ	37500 AW	52600 TQ	FLBLS	10/01-12/01
	Tampa-St. Petersburg-Clearwater MSA, FL	Y	24760 FQ	37540 AW	53370 TQ	FLBLS	10/01-12/01
	West Palm Beach-Boca Raton MSA, FL	Y	26100 FQ	40960 AW	57450 TQ	FLBLS	10/01-12/01
	Georgia	Y	26650 FQ	40510 AW	58850 TQ	GABLS	10/01-12/01
	Atlanta MSA, GA	Y	27250 FQ	39840 AW	57760 TQ	GABLS	10/01-12/01
	Macon MSA, GA	Y	25860 FQ	39590 AW	61500 TQ	GABLS	10/01-12/01
	Hawaii	Y	20740 FQ	33630 AW	52820 TQ	HIBLS	10/01-12/01
	Honolulu MSA, HI	Y	20420 FQ	31980 AW	53940 TQ	HIBLS	10/01-12/01
	Idaho	Y	22640 FQ	38880 AW	55520 TQ	IDBLS	10/01-12/01
	Boise City MSA, ID	Y	23670 FQ	37480 AW	51210 TQ	IDBLS	10/01-12/01
	Illinois	Y	21350 FQ	35690 AW	57430 TQ	ILBLS	10/01-12/01
	Chicago PMSA, IL	Y	20890 FQ	32960 AW	46190 TQ	ILBLS	10/01-12/01
	Peoria-Pekin MSA, IL	Y	25400 FQ	36590 AW	47520 TQ	ILBLS	10/01-12/01
	Springfield MSA, IL	Y	23350 FQ	35030 AW	53100 TQ	ILBLS	10/01-12/01

AAW	Average annual wage	**AOH**	Average offered, high	**ASH**	Average starting, high	**H**	Hourly	**M**	Monthly	**S**	Special: hourly and annual
AE	Average entry wage	**AOL**	Average offered, low	**ASL**	Average starting, low	**HI**	Highest wage paid	**MTC**	Median total compensation	**TQ**	Third quartile wage
AEX	Average experienced wage	**APH**	Average pay, high range	**AW**	Average wage paid	**HR**	High end range	**MW**	Median wage paid	**W**	Weekly
AO	Average offered	**APL**	Average pay, low range	**FQ**	First quartile wage	**LR**	Low end range	**SQ**	Second quartile wage	**Y**	Yearly

Occupation/Type/Industry	Location	Per	Low	Mid	High	Source	Date
Electrical and Electronics Drafter	Indiana	Y	21000 FQ	36750 AW	57020 TQ	INBLS	10/01-12/01
	Elkhart-Goshen MSA, IN	Y	27140 FQ	43060 AW	65440 TQ	INBLS	10/01-12/01
	Evansville-Henderson MSA, IN-KY	Y	27470 FQ	39310 AW	53690 TQ	INBLS	10/01-12/01
	Fort Wayne MSA, IN	Y	19240 FQ	32200 AW	53000 TQ	INBLS	10/01-12/01
	Gary PMSA, IN	Y	30090 FQ	53000 AW	82220 TQ	INBLS	10/01-12/01
	Indianapolis MSA, IN	Y	22880 FQ	37430 AW	55760 TQ	INBLS	10/01-12/01
	South Bend MSA, IN	Y	29210 FQ	36350 AW	47630 TQ	INBLS	10/01-12/01
	Iowa	Y	24330 FQ	36120 AW	47920 TQ	IABLS	10/01-12/01
	Davenport-Moline-Rock Island MSA, IA-IL	Y	17150 FQ	29820 AW	42590 TQ	IABLS	10/01-12/01
	Kansas	Y	25140 FQ	44880 AW	70060 TQ	KSBLS	10/01-12/01
	Topeka MSA, KS	Y	37020 FQ	46340 AW	59340 TQ	KSBLS	10/01-12/01
	Kentucky	Y	21990 FQ	35310 AW	51680 TQ	KYBLS	10/01-12/01
	Lexington MSA, KY	Y	21420 FQ	33550 AW	49940 TQ	KYBLS	10/01-12/01
	Louisville MSA, KY-IN	Y	21970 FQ	36840 AW	54480 TQ	KYBLS	10/01-12/01
	Louisiana	Y	28550 FQ	45530 AW	67100 TQ	LABLS	10/01-12/01
	Baton Rouge MSA, LA	Y	26980 FQ	50730 AW	75280 TQ	LABLS	10/01-12/01
	Lake Charles MSA, LA	Y	32150 FQ	51340 AW	77690 TQ	LABLS	10/01-12/01
	New Orleans MSA, LA	Y	30100 FQ	42710 AW	65900 TQ	LABLS	10/01-12/01
	Maine	Y	26550 FQ	38950 AW	55760 TQ	MEBLS	10/01-12/01
	Portland MSA, ME	Y	25700 FQ	37670 AW	52780 TQ	MEBLS	10/01-12/01
	Maryland	Y	28570 FQ	46450 AW	60350 TQ	MDBLS	10/01-12/01
	Baltimore PMSA, MD	Y	33110 FQ	50670 AW	60970 TQ	MDBLS	10/01-12/01
	Massachusetts	Y	31230 FQ	50330 AW	73380 TQ	MABLS	10/01-12/01
	Boston PMSA, MA-NH	Y	30210 FQ	49680 AW	73780 TQ	MABLS	10/01-12/01
	Lawrence PMSA, MA-NH	Y	26200 FQ	43080 AW	58950 TQ	MABLS	10/01-12/01
	Lowell PMSA, MA-NH	Y	36830 FQ	56490 AW	85450 TQ	MABLS	10/01-12/01
	Springfield MSA, MA	Y	29160 FQ	43010 AW	64050 TQ	MABLS	10/01-12/01
	Worcester PMSA, MA-CT	Y	33230 FQ	55120 AW	73940 TQ	MABLS	10/01-12/01
	Michigan	Y	25230 FQ	42270 AW	58800 TQ	MIBLS	10/01-12/01
	Ann Arbor PMSA, MI	Y	25350 FQ	41880 AW	57450 TQ	MIBLS	10/01-12/01
	Detroit PMSA, MI	Y	26290 FQ	42370 AW	57490 TQ	MIBLS	10/01-12/01
	Flint PMSA, MI	Y	27030 FQ	51190 AW	84030 TQ	MIBLS	10/01-12/01
	Grand Rapids-Muskegon-Holland MSA, MI	Y	23070 FQ	37640 AW	56110 TQ	MIBLS	10/01-12/01
	Minnesota	Y	29300 FQ	45300 AW	64720 TQ	MNBLS	10/01-12/01
	Minneapolis-St. Paul MSA, MN-WI	Y	30630 FQ	46770 AW	65940 TQ	MNBLS	10/01-12/01
	Mississippi	Y	23500 FQ	44760 AW	81640 TQ	MSBLS	10/01-12/01
	Biloxi-Gulfport-Pascagoula MSA, MS	Y	24800 FQ	40890 AW	63200 TQ	MSBLS	10/01-12/01
	Jackson MSA, MS	Y	21970 FQ	50890 AW	86040 TQ	MSBLS	10/01-12/01
	Missouri	Y	23830 FQ	39620 AW	55520 TQ	MOBLS	10/01-12/01
	Kansas City MSA, MO-KS	Y	25190 FQ	39820 AW	58370 TQ	MOBLS	10/01-12/01
	St. Louis MSA, MO-IL	Y	24960 FQ	40930 AW	55380 TQ	MOBLS	10/01-12/01
	Montana	Y	22480 FQ	38780 AW	55730 TQ	MTBLS	10/01-12/01
	Nebraska	Y	23770 FQ	37660 AW	55030 TQ	NEBLS	10/01-12/01
	Lincoln MSA, NE	Y	26230 FQ	39160 AW	60190 TQ	NEBLS	10/01-12/01
	Nevada	Y	25460 FQ	36780 AW	52650 TQ	NVBLS	10/01-12/01
	Las Vegas MSA, NV-AZ	Y	25900 FQ	37260 AW	54120 TQ	NVBLS	10/01-12/01
	Reno MSA, NV	Y	24650 FQ	36670 AW	53180 TQ	NVBLS	10/01-12/01
	New Hampshire	Y	27220 FQ	48840 AW	78710 TQ	NHBLS	10/01-12/01
	Manchester PMSA, NH	Y	31570 FQ	46660 AW	59140 TQ	NHBLS	10/01-12/01
	Portsmouth-Rochester PMSA, NH-ME	Y	40520 FQ	70240 AW	88600 TQ	NHBLS	10/01-12/01
	New Jersey	Y	31660 FQ	50320 AW	71610 TQ	NJBLS	10/01-12/01
	Bergen-Passaic PMSA, NJ	Y	23010 FQ	41510 AW	66520 TQ	NJBLS	10/01-12/01
	Middlesex-Somerset-Hunterdon PMSA, NJ	Y	29410 FQ	53400 AW	81090 TQ	NJBLS	10/01-12/01
	Monmouth-Ocean PMSA, NJ	Y	29390 FQ	43720 AW	61170 TQ	NJBLS	10/01-12/01
	Newark PMSA, NJ	Y	38360 FQ	51320 AW	69750 TQ	NJBLS	10/01-12/01
	New Mexico	Y	26010 FQ	45490 AW	66980 TQ	NMBLS	10/01-12/01
	Albuquerque MSA, NM	Y	28800 FQ	49690 AW	70250 TQ	NMBLS	10/01-12/01
	New York	Y	27290 FQ	48430 AW	75560 TQ	NYBLS	10/01-12/01
	Albany-Schenectady-Troy MSA, NY	Y	24710 FQ	38790 AW	63650 TQ	NYBLS	10/01-12/01
	Binghamton MSA, NY	Y	29240 FQ	47340 AW	68370 TQ	NYBLS	10/01-12/01
	Buffalo-Niagara Falls MSA, NY	Y	25800 FQ	43860 AW	61110 TQ	NYBLS	10/01-12/01
	Nassau-Suffolk PMSA, NY	Y	26340 FQ	45660 AW	71600 TQ	NYBLS	10/01-12/01
	New York PMSA, NY	Y	30140 FQ	53840 AW	84050 TQ	NYBLS	10/01-12/01

AAW	Average annual wage	**AOH**	Average offered, high	**ASH**	Average starting, high	**H**	Hourly	**M**	Monthly	**S**	Special: hourly and annual
AE	Average entry wage	**AOL**	Average offered, low	**ASL**	Average starting, low	**HI**	Highest wage paid	**MTC**	Median total compensation	**TQ**	Third quartile wage
AEX	Average experienced wage	**APH**	Average pay, high range	**AW**	Average wage paid	**HR**	High end range	**MW**	Median wage paid	**W**	Weekly
AO	Average offered	**APL**	Average pay, low range	**FQ**	First quartile wage	**LR**	Low end range	**SQ**	Second quartile wage	**Y**	Yearly

Occupation/Type/Industry	Location	Per	Low	Mid	High	Source	Date
Electrical and Electronics Drafter	Rochester MSA, NY	Y	21600 FQ	42220 AW	58340 TQ	NYBLS	10/01-12/01
	Syracuse MSA, NY	Y	29880 FQ	54410 AW	73980 TQ	NYBLS	10/01-12/01
	North Carolina	Y	28970 FQ	41940 AW	64640 TQ	NCBLS	10/01-12/01
	Charlotte-Gastonia-Rock Hill MSA, NC-SC	Y	28880 FQ	43580 AW	66880 TQ	NCBLS	10/01-12/01
	Greensboro-Winston-Salem-High Point MSA, NC	Y	28460 FQ	36790 AW	50220 TQ	NCBLS	10/01-12/01
	Raleigh-Durham-Chapel Hill MSA, NC	Y	31050 FQ	46120 AW	64970 TQ	NCBLS	10/01-12/01
	North Dakota	Y	26640 FQ	41160 AW	57350 TQ	NDBLS	10/01-12/01
	Ohio	Y	23470 FQ	39660 AW	58080 TQ	OHBLS	10/01-12/01
	Akron PMSA, OH	Y	29890 FQ	41180 AW	58210 TQ	OHBLS	10/01-12/01
	Canton-Massillon MSA, OH	Y	20900 FQ	35390 AW	52220 TQ	OHBLS	10/01-12/01
	Cincinnati PMSA, OH-KY-IN	Y	23800 FQ	36710 AW	55570 TQ	OHBLS	10/01-12/01
	Cleveland-Lorain-Elyria PMSA, OH	Y	26040 FQ	42870 AW	59410 TQ	OHBLS	10/01-12/01
	Columbus MSA, OH	Y	21860 FQ	42000 AW	65880 TQ	OHBLS	10/01-12/01
	Dayton-Springfield MSA, OH	Y	26600 FQ	38710 AW	51350 TQ	OHBLS	10/01-12/01
	Hamilton-Middletown PMSA, OH	Y	29740 FQ	49370 AW	74130 TQ	OHBLS	10/01-12/01
	Toledo MSA, OH	Y	23520 FQ	39580 AW	60890 TQ	OHBLS	10/01-12/01
	Youngstown-Warren MSA, OH	Y	20370 FQ	32070 AW	44570 TQ	OHBLS	10/01-12/01
	Oklahoma	Y	21570 FQ	38560 AW	60920 TQ	OKBLS	10/01-12/01
	Oklahoma City MSA, OK	Y	24520 FQ	36410 AW	53380 TQ	OKBLS	10/01-12/01
	Tulsa MSA, OK	Y	24810 FQ	44220 AW	68570 TQ	OKBLS	10/01-12/01
	Oregon	Y	25680 FQ	51780 AW	100930 TQ	ORBLS	10/01-12/01
	Portland-Vancouver PMSA, OR-WA	Y	25670 FQ	55210 AW	103540 TQ	ORBLS	10/01-12/01
	Pennsylvania	Y	24640 FQ	39900 AW	56370 TQ	PABLS	10/01-12/01
	Allentown-Bethlehem-Easton MSA, PA	Y	26760 FQ	39700 AW	54780 TQ	PABLS	10/01-12/01
	Philadelphia PMSA, PA-NJ	Y	26600 FQ	44400 AW	64040 TQ	PABLS	10/01-12/01
	Pittsburgh MSA, PA	Y	23640 FQ	39110 AW	56250 TQ	PABLS	10/01-12/01
	Reading MSA, PA	Y	24530 FQ	39520 AW	55060 TQ	PABLS	10/01-12/01
	Scranton-Wilkes-Barre-Hazleton MSA, PA	Y	23860 FQ	34620 AW	45810 TQ	PABLS	10/01-12/01
	York MSA, PA	Y	25760 FQ	38230 AW	53380 TQ	PABLS	10/01-12/01
	Rhode Island	Y	28420 FQ	39940 AW	55140 TQ	RIBLS	10/01-12/01
	Providence-Fall River-Warwick MSA, RI-MA	Y	29290 FQ	41070 AW	55130 TQ	RIBLS	10/01-12/01
	South Carolina	Y	28880 FQ	42070 AW	59820 TQ	SCBLS	10/01-12/01
	Charleston-North Charleston MSA, SC	Y	32130 FQ	41620 AW	52430 TQ	SCBLS	10/01-12/01
	Columbia MSA, SC	Y	29580 FQ	37110 AW	51090 TQ	SCBLS	10/01-12/01
	Greenville-Spartanburg-Anderson MSA, SC	Y	25390 FQ	44040 AW	70260 TQ	SCBLS	10/01-12/01
	South Dakota	Y	24630 FQ	32260 AW	41780 TQ	SDBLS	10/01-12/01
	Tennessee	Y	25460 FQ	43230 AW	70360 TQ	TNBLS	10/01-12/01
	Chattanooga MSA, TN-GA	Y	24970 FQ	35670 AW	45710 TQ	TNBLS	10/01-12/01
	Johnson City-Kingsport-Bristol MSA, TN-VA	Y	24960 FQ	30220 AW	41590 TQ	TNBLS	10/01-12/01
	Knoxville MSA, TN	Y	28420 FQ	67100 AW	112610 TQ	TNBLS	10/01-12/01
	Memphis MSA, TN-AR-MS	Y	25800 FQ	42190 AW	57140 TQ	TNBLS	10/01-12/01
	Nashville MSA, TN	Y	28060 FQ	39340 AW	54710 TQ	TNBLS	10/01-12/01
	Texas	Y	28090 FQ	42160 AW	66920 TQ	TXBLS	10/01-12/01
	Austin-San Marcos MSA, TX	Y	24620 FQ	41940 AW	67630 TQ	TXBLS	10/01-12/01
	Corpus Christi MSA, TX	Y	26650 FQ	36040 AW	44400 TQ	TXBLS	10/01-12/01
	Dallas PMSA, TX	Y	21830 FQ	41430 AW	58470 TQ	TXBLS	10/01-12/01
	El Paso MSA, TX	Y	30120 FQ	44020 AW	61620 TQ	TXBLS	10/01-12/01
	Fort Worth-Arlington PMSA, TX	Y	28700 FQ	32810 AW	38500 TQ	TXBLS	10/01-12/01
	Houston PMSA, TX	Y	32100 FQ	54060 AW	82640 TQ	TXBLS	10/01-12/01
	San Antonio MSA, TX	Y	32450 FQ	47490 AW	59060 TQ	TXBLS	10/01-12/01
	Waco MSA, TX	Y	27750 FQ	38140 AW	46250 TQ	TXBLS	10/01-12/01
	Utah	Y	21120 FQ	38090 AW	59300 TQ	UTBLS	10/01-12/01
	Salt Lake City-Ogden MSA, UT	Y	23990 FQ	41930 AW	63130 TQ	UTBLS	10/01-12/01
	Vermont	Y	27560 FQ	41760 AW	57720 TQ	VTBLS	10/01-12/01
	Virginia	Y	22460 FQ	38640 AW	56050 TQ	VABLS	10/01-12/01
	Norfolk-Virginia Beach-Newport News MSA, VA-NC	Y	21460 FQ	34160 AW	49050 TQ	VABLS	10/01-12/01

AAW	Average annual wage	**AOH**	Average offered, high	**ASH**	Average starting, high	**H**	Hourly	**M**	Monthly	**S**	Special: hourly and annual
AE	Average entry wage	**AOL**	Average offered, low	**ASL**	Average starting, low	**HI**	Highest wage paid	**MTC**	Median total compensation	**TQ**	Third quartile wage
AEX	Average experienced wage	**APH**	Average pay, high range	**AW**	Average wage paid	**HR**	High end range	**MW**	Median wage paid	**W**	Weekly
AO	Average offered	**APL**	Average pay, low range	**FQ**	First quartile wage	**LR**	Low end range	**SQ**	Second quartile wage	**Y**	Yearly

Occupation/Type/Industry	Location	Per	Low	Mid	High	Source	Date
Electrical and Electronics Drafter	Richmond-Petersburg MSA, VA	Y	14340 FQ	34160 AW	50400 TQ	VABLS	10/01-12/01
	Washington	Y	27410 FQ	44820 AW	64200 TQ	WABLS	10/01-12/01
	Richland-Kennewick-Pasco MSA, WA	Y	23370 FQ	46590 AW	67010 TQ	WABLS	10/01-12/01
	Seattle-Bellevue-Everett PMSA, WA	Y	29710 FQ	46320 AW	64550 TQ	WABLS	10/01-12/01
	Spokane MSA, WA	Y	24630 FQ	38970 AW	60610 TQ	WABLS	10/01-12/01
	Tacoma PMSA, WA	Y	24540 FQ	38770 AW	52830 TQ	WABLS	10/01-12/01
	West Virginia	Y	14330 FQ	34230 AW	55630 TQ	WVBLS	10/01-12/01
	Huntington-Ashland MSA, WV-KY-OH	Y	21310 FQ	34950 AW	52220 TQ	WVBLS	10/01-12/01
	Wisconsin	Y	28180 FQ	42450 AW	63490 TQ	WIBLS	10/01-12/01
	Appleton-Oshkosh-Neenah MSA, WI	Y	30160 FQ	40680 AW	54440 TQ	WIBLS	10/01-12/01
	Green Bay MSA, WI	Y	30320 FQ	45780 AW	68160 TQ	WIBLS	10/01-12/01
	Madison MSA, WI	Y	27130 FQ	43400 AW	68560 TQ	WIBLS	10/01-12/01
	Milwaukee-Waukesha PMSA, WI	Y	29240 FQ	43930 AW	65870 TQ	WIBLS	10/01-12/01
	Racine PMSA, WI	Y	28770 FQ	35980 AW	44540 TQ	WIBLS	10/01-12/01
	Puerto Rico	Y	13480 FQ	25460 AW	40740 TQ	PRBLS	10/01-12/01
Electrical and Electronics Engineer	United States	Y		45200-70800 AW		BE	1/01-1/02
Electrical and Electronics Installer and Repairer							
Transportation Equipment	Alabama	H	12.47 FQ	20.69 AW	28.12 TQ	ALBLS	10/01-12/01
Transportation Equipment	Arizona	H	13.65 FQ	22.29 AW	31.21 TQ	AZBLS	10/01-12/01
Transportation Equipment	Phoenix-Mesa MSA, AZ	H	13.38 FQ	22.20 AW	31.34 TQ	AZBLS	10/01-12/01
Transportation Equipment	California	H	10.71 FQ	19.23 AW	26.77 TQ	CABLS	10/01-12/01
Transportation Equipment	Bakersfield MSA, CA	H	13.71 FQ	18.54 AW	25.64 TQ	CABLS	10/01-12/01
Transportation Equipment	Oakland PMSA, CA	H	11.01 FQ	16.62 AW	22.68 TQ	CABLS	10/01-12/01
Transportation Equipment	Orange County PMSA, CA	H	8.12 FQ	16.54 AW	26.39 TQ	CABLS	10/01-12/01
Transportation Equipment	Redding MSA, CA	H	12.44 FQ	16.28 AW	20.60 TQ	CABLS	10/01-12/01
Transportation Equipment	Riverside-San Bernardino PMSA, CA	H	12.75 FQ	20.42 AW	28.24 TQ	CABLS	10/01-12/01
Transportation Equipment	San Diego MSA, CA	H	12.68 FQ	20.14 AW	26.20 TQ	CABLS	10/01-12/01
Transportation Equipment	San Francisco PMSA, CA	H	7.54 FQ	9.72 AW	13.43 TQ	CABLS	10/01-12/01
Transportation Equipment	San Jose PMSA, CA	H	17.68 FQ	21.31 AW	26.97 TQ	CABLS	10/01-12/01
Transportation Equipment	Colorado	H	10.25 FQ	18.35 AW	22.78 TQ	COBLS	10/01-12/01
Transportation Equipment	Denver PMSA, CO	H	9.80 FQ	16.60 AW	22.33 TQ	COBLS	10/01-12/01
Transportation Equipment	Connecticut	H	12.45 FQ	22.99 AW	28.93 TQ	CTBLS	10/01-12/01
Transportation Equipment	New London-Norwich MSA, CT-RI	H	13.72 FQ	23.14 AW	29.00 TQ	CTBLS	10/01-12/01
Transportation Equipment	Washington PMSA, DC-MD-VA-WV	H	10.99 FQ	21.92 AW	33.75 TQ	DCBLS	10/01-12/01
Transportation Equipment	Florida	H	10.02 FQ	15.26 AW	22.08 TQ	FLBLS	10/01-12/01
Transportation Equipment	Fort Lauderdale PMSA, FL	H	11.12 FQ	17.75 AW	25.44 TQ	FLBLS	10/01-12/01
Transportation Equipment	Jacksonville MSA, FL	H	9.53 FQ	13.54 AW	18.16 TQ	FLBLS	10/01-12/01
Transportation Equipment	Miami PMSA, FL	H	10.13 FQ	16.19 AW	22.76 TQ	FLBLS	10/01-12/01
Transportation Equipment	Orlando MSA, FL	H	9.62 FQ	13.68 AW	20.08 TQ	FLBLS	10/01-12/01
Transportation Equipment	Sarasota-Bradenton MSA, FL	H	9.21 FQ	12.65 AW	17.51 TQ	FLBLS	10/01-12/01
Transportation Equipment	Tampa-St. Petersburg-Clearwater MSA, FL	H	10.50 FQ	15.39 AW	20.34 TQ	FLBLS	10/01-12/01
Transportation Equipment	West Palm Beach-Boca Raton MSA, FL	H	13.19 FQ	17.98 AW	22.87 TQ	FLBLS	10/01-12/01
Transportation Equipment	Georgia	H	9.25 FQ	17.21 AW	26.32 TQ	GABLS	10/01-12/01
Transportation Equipment	Atlanta MSA, GA	H	7.93 FQ	15.50 AW	22.46 TQ	GABLS	10/01-12/01
Transportation Equipment	Hawaii	H	13.66 FQ	19.19 AW	25.94 TQ	HIBLS	10/01-12/01
Transportation Equipment	Honolulu MSA, HI	H	13.73 FQ	19.28 AW	25.96 TQ	HIBLS	10/01-12/01
Transportation Equipment	Illinois	H	12.47 FQ	19.54 AW	27.94 TQ	ILBLS	10/01-12/01
Transportation Equipment	Chicago PMSA, IL	H	12.09 FQ	20.42 AW	32.12 TQ	ILBLS	10/01-12/01
Transportation Equipment	Indiana	H	11.54 FQ	18.12 AW	24.29 TQ	INBLS	10/01-12/01
Transportation Equipment	Fort Wayne MSA, IN	H	9.68 FQ	13.96 AW	22.98 TQ	INBLS	10/01-12/01
Transportation Equipment	Iowa	H	9.73 FQ	16.11 AW	22.87 TQ	IABLS	10/01-12/01
Transportation Equipment	Des Moines MSA, IA	H	9.48 FQ	15.57 AW	23.48 TQ	IABLS	10/01-12/01
Transportation Equipment	Kentucky	H	10.53 FQ	17.05 AW	22.30 TQ	KYBLS	10/01-12/01
Transportation Equipment	Louisville MSA, KY-IN	H	8.89 FQ	14.24 AW	22.52 TQ	KYBLS	10/01-12/01
Transportation Equipment	Louisiana	H	9.30 FQ	16.34 AW	24.44 TQ	LABLS	10/01-12/01
Transportation Equipment	Baton Rouge MSA, LA	H	9.51 FQ	16.55 AW	26.30 TQ	LABLS	10/01-12/01

AAW Average annual wage **AE** Average entry wage **AEX** Average experienced wage **AO** Average offered **AOH** Average offered, high **AOL** Average offered, low **APH** Average pay, high range **APL** Average pay, low range **ASH** Average starting, high **ASL** Average starting, low **AW** Average wage paid **FQ** First quartile wage **H** Hourly **HI** Highest wage paid **HR** High end range **LR** Low end range **M** Monthly **MTC** Median total compensation **MW** Median wage paid **SQ** Second quartile wage **S** Special: hourly and annual **TQ** Third quartile wage **W** Weekly **Y** Yearly

Occupation/Type/Industry	Location	Per	Low	Mid	High	Source	Date
Electrical and Electronics Installer and Repairer							
Transportation Equipment	New Orleans MSA, LA	H	8.98 FQ	14.69 AW	20.74 TQ	LABLS	10/01-12/01
Transportation Equipment	Maine	H	11.62 FQ	15.27 AW	20.44 TQ	MEBLS	10/01-12/01
Transportation Equipment	Maryland	H	10.78 FQ	19.39 AW	28.06 TQ	MDBLS	10/01-12/01
Transportation Equipment	Baltimore PMSA, MD	H	9.55 FQ	15.37 AW	25.07 TQ	MDBLS	10/01-12/01
Transportation Equipment	Massachusetts	H	10.61 FQ	17.51 AW	24.71 TQ	MABLS	10/01-12/01
Transportation Equipment	Boston PMSA, MA-NH	H	9.68 FQ	15.78 AW	25.62 TQ	MABLS	10/01-12/01
Transportation Equipment	Michigan	H	12.22 FQ	18.27 AW	26.29 TQ	MIBLS	10/01-12/01
Transportation Equipment	Detroit PMSA, MI	H	11.44 FQ	19.96 AW	27.95 TQ	MIBLS	10/01-12/01
Transportation Equipment	Grand Rapids-Muskegon-Holland MSA, MI	H	10.75 FQ	16.09 AW	22.29 TQ	MIBLS	10/01-12/01
Transportation Equipment	Minnesota	H	14.51 FQ	21.31 AW	28.15 TQ	MNBLS	10/01-12/01
Transportation Equipment	Kansas City MSA, MO-KS	H	11.96 FQ	18.01 AW	23.39 TQ	MOBLS	10/01-12/01
Transportation Equipment	New Hampshire	H	10.52 FQ	16.48 AW	22.29 TQ	NHBLS	10/01-12/01
Transportation Equipment	Manchester PMSA, NH	H	11.86 FQ	17.71 AW	22.70 TQ	NHBLS	10/01-12/01
Transportation Equipment	New Jersey	H	13.98 FQ	21.31 AW	30.71 TQ	NJBLS	10/01-12/01
Transportation Equipment	New York	H	14.15 FQ	21.29 AW	26.52 TQ	NYBLS	10/01-12/01
Transportation Equipment	Nassau-Suffolk PMSA, NY	H	9.82 FQ	16.14 AW	23.83 TQ	NYBLS	10/01-12/01
Transportation Equipment	Rochester MSA, NY	H	21.73 FQ	23.64 AW	26.63 TQ	NYBLS	10/01-12/01
Transportation Equipment	North Dakota	H	10.04 FQ	20.22 AW	29.25 TQ	NDBLS	10/01-12/01
Transportation Equipment	Ohio	H	12.88 FQ	18.62 AW	24.76 TQ	OHBLS	10/01-12/01
Transportation Equipment	Cleveland-Lorain-Elyria PMSA, OH	H	11.17 FQ	16.02 AW	20.58 TQ	OHBLS	10/01-12/01
Transportation Equipment	Dayton-Springfield MSA, OH	H	11.79 FQ	16.18 AW	20.73 TQ	OHBLS	10/01-12/01
Transportation Equipment	Oklahoma	H	8.59 FQ	18.69 AW	26.16 TQ	OKBLS	10/01-12/01
Transportation Equipment	Oregon	H	11.58 FQ	19.89 AW	31.12 TQ	ORBLS	10/01-12/01
Transportation Equipment	Pennsylvania	H	11.87 FQ	18.47 AW	26.76 TQ	PABLS	10/01-12/01
Transportation Equipment	Philadelphia PMSA, PA-NJ	H	14.05 FQ	23.58 AW	33.65 TQ	PABLS	10/01-12/01
Transportation Equipment	Pittsburgh MSA, PA	H	10.95 FQ	16.52 AW	25.06 TQ	PABLS	10/01-12/01
Transportation Equipment	Rhode Island	H	6.68 FQ	10.49 AW	18.55 TQ	RIBLS	10/01-12/01
Transportation Equipment	Providence-Fall River-Warwick MSA, RI-MA	H	6.61 FQ	8.31 AW	9.02 TQ	RIBLS	10/01-12/01
Transportation Equipment	South Carolina	H	12.00 FQ	18.40 AW	24.20 TQ	SCBLS	10/01-12/01
Transportation Equipment	Tennessee	H	13.88 FQ	19.35 AW	25.71 TQ	TNBLS	10/01-12/01
Transportation Equipment	Nashville MSA, TN	H	14.73 FQ	21.28 AW	26.59 TQ	TNBLS	10/01-12/01
Transportation Equipment	Texas	H	9.33 FQ	15.19 AW	23.20 TQ	TXBLS	10/01-12/01
Transportation Equipment	Austin-San Marcos MSA, TX	H	9.25 FQ	11.83 AW	16.42 TQ	TXBLS	10/01-12/01
Transportation Equipment	Corpus Christi MSA, TX	H	10.17 FQ	14.69 AW	23.79 TQ	TXBLS	10/01-12/01
Transportation Equipment	Dallas PMSA, TX	H	9.63 FQ	17.13 AW	26.60 TQ	TXBLS	10/01-12/01
Transportation Equipment	Fort Worth-Arlington PMSA, TX	H	9.78 FQ	14.39 AW	20.88 TQ	TXBLS	10/01-12/01
Transportation Equipment	Houston PMSA, TX	H	9.01 FQ	11.80 AW	16.44 TQ	TXBLS	10/01-12/01
Transportation Equipment	San Antonio MSA, TX	H	8.97 FQ	12.74 AW	20.85 TQ	TXBLS	10/01-12/01
Transportation Equipment	Utah	H	8.79 FQ	15.30 AW	22.80 TQ	UTBLS	10/01-12/01
Transportation Equipment	Virginia	H	9.20 FQ	16.59 AW	26.64 TQ	VABLS	10/01-12/01
Transportation Equipment	Norfolk-Virginia Beach-Newport News MSA, VA-NC	H	10.78 FQ	17.43 AW	24.84 TQ	VABLS	10/01-12/01
Transportation Equipment	Washington	H	11.31 FQ	19.29 AW	27.59 TQ	WABLS	10/01-12/01
Transportation Equipment	Bremerton PMSA, WA	H	11.63 FQ	14.85 AW	18.32 TQ	WABLS	10/01-12/01
Transportation Equipment	Seattle-Bellevue-Everett PMSA, WA	H	13.43 FQ	20.72 AW	26.99 TQ	WABLS	10/01-12/01
Transportation Equipment	West Virginia	H	15.58 FQ	19.81 AW	24.89 TQ	WVBLS	10/01-12/01
Transportation Equipment	Wisconsin	H	10.74 FQ	17.34 AW	25.64 TQ	WIBLS	10/01-12/01
Transportation Equipment	Milwaukee-Waukesha PMSA, WI	H	14.38 FQ	19.76 AW	27.56 TQ	WIBLS	10/01-12/01
Transportation Equipment	Virgin Islands	H	9.80 FQ	12.89 AW	17.03 TQ	VIBLS	10/01-12/01
Electrical and Electronics Repairer							
Commercial and Industrial Equipment	Alabama	H	9.44 FQ	17.98 AW	26.91 TQ	ALBLS	10/01-12/01
Commercial and Industrial Equipment	Birmingham MSA, AL	H	14.58 FQ	22.71 AW	32.47 TQ	ALBLS	10/01-12/01
Commercial and Industrial Equipment	Mobile MSA, AL	H	8.06 FQ	15.08 AW	25.49 TQ	ALBLS	10/01-12/01
Commercial and Industrial Equipment	Montgomery MSA, AL	H	15.26 FQ	20.34 AW	26.60 TQ	ALBLS	10/01-12/01
Commercial and Industrial Equipment	Alaska	H	21.20 FQ	28.16 AW	34.23 TQ	AKBLS	10/01-12/01
Commercial and Industrial Equipment	Tucson MSA, AZ	H	11.65 FQ	17.59 AW	26.17 TQ	AZBLS	10/01-12/01
Commercial and Industrial Equipment	Arkansas	H	9.79 FQ	16.79 AW	25.89 TQ	ARBLS	10/01-12/01
Commercial and Industrial Equipment	Fort Smith MSA, AR-OK	H	10.52 FQ	15.63 AW	20.39 TQ	ARBLS	10/01-12/01
Commercial and Industrial Equipment	Little Rock-North Little Rock MSA, AR	H	9.17 FQ	15.10 AW	20.59 TQ	ARBLS	10/01-12/01
Commercial and Industrial Equipment	California	H	11.97 FQ	19.98 AW	27.65 TQ	CABLS	10/01-12/01

AAW	Average annual wage	**AOH**	Average offered, high	**ASH**	Average starting, high	**H**	Hourly	**M**	Monthly	**S**	Special: hourly and annual
AE	Average entry wage	**AOL**	Average offered, low	**ASL**	Average starting, low	**HI**	Highest wage paid	**MTC**	Median total compensation	**TQ**	Third quartile wage
AEX	Average experienced wage	**APH**	Average pay, high range	**AW**	Average wage paid	**HR**	High end range	**MW**	Median wage paid	**W**	Weekly
AO	Average offered	**APL**	Average pay, low range	**FQ**	First quartile wage	**LR**	Low end range	**SQ**	Second quartile wage	**Y**	Yearly

Occupation/Type/Industry	Location	Per	Low	Mid	High	Source	Date
Electrical and Electronics Repairer							
Commercial and Industrial Equipment	Bakersfield MSA, CA	H	13.90 FQ	21.84 AW	27.56 TQ	CABLS	10/01-12/01
Commercial and Industrial Equipment	Chico-Paradise MSA, CA	H	14.69 FQ	17.24 AW	20.05 TQ	CABLS	10/01-12/01
Commercial and Industrial Equipment	Fresno MSA, CA	H	10.40 FQ	17.10 AW	22.84 TQ	CABLS	10/01-12/01
Commercial and Industrial Equipment	Los Angeles-Long Beach PMSA, CA	H	13.99 FQ	21.29 AW	27.69 TQ	CABLS	10/01-12/01
Commercial and Industrial Equipment	Oakland PMSA, CA	H	12.93 FQ	20.10 AW	28.00 TQ	CABLS	10/01-12/01
Commercial and Industrial Equipment	Orange County PMSA, CA	H	12.39 FQ	19.66 AW	26.94 TQ	CABLS	10/01-12/01
Commercial and Industrial Equipment	Riverside-San Bernardino PMSA, CA	H	15.22 FQ	20.81 AW	26.10 TQ	CABLS	10/01-12/01
Commercial and Industrial Equipment	Sacramento PMSA, CA	H	8.34 FQ	16.27 AW	26.09 TQ	CABLS	10/01-12/01
Commercial and Industrial Equipment	San Diego MSA, CA	H	11.58 FQ	17.73 AW	26.73 TQ	CABLS	10/01-12/01
Commercial and Industrial Equipment	San Francisco PMSA, CA	H	13.35 FQ	21.71 AW	28.76 TQ	CABLS	10/01-12/01
Commercial and Industrial Equipment	San Jose PMSA, CA	H	11.81 FQ	21.73 AW	32.54 TQ	CABLS	10/01-12/01
Commercial and Industrial Equipment	Santa Barbara-Santa Maria-Lompoc MSA, CA	H	18.92 FQ	24.16 AW	31.43 TQ	CABLS	10/01-12/01
Commercial and Industrial Equipment	Santa Cruz-Watsonville PMSA, CA	H	12.00 FQ	17.92 AW	24.88 TQ	CABLS	10/01-12/01
Commercial and Industrial Equipment	Santa Rosa PMSA, CA	H	13.81 FQ	20.51 AW	28.05 TQ	CABLS	10/01-12/01
Commercial and Industrial Equipment	Stockton-Lodi MSA, CA	H	17.04 FQ	22.15 AW	27.08 TQ	CABLS	10/01-12/01
Commercial and Industrial Equipment	Ventura PMSA, CA	H	14.56 FQ	20.36 AW	29.28 TQ	CABLS	10/01-12/01
Commercial and Industrial Equipment	Colorado	H	13.48 FQ	21.61 AW	31.18 TQ	COBLS	10/01-12/01
Commercial and Industrial Equipment	Colorado Springs MSA, CO	H	15.27 FQ	20.81 AW	28.19 TQ	COBLS	10/01-12/01
Commercial and Industrial Equipment	Denver PMSA, CO	H	15.19 FQ	22.53 AW	30.75 TQ	COBLS	10/01-12/01
Commercial and Industrial Equipment	Fort Collins-Loveland MSA, CO	H	15.26 FQ	22.83 AW	32.98 TQ	COBLS	10/01-12/01
Commercial and Industrial Equipment	Connecticut	H	11.46 FQ	16.71 AW	23.80 TQ	CTBLS	10/01-12/01
Commercial and Industrial Equipment	Bridgeport PMSA, CT	H	11.46 FQ	15.11 AW	21.47 TQ	CTBLS	10/01-12/01
Commercial and Industrial Equipment	Hartford MSA, CT	H	11.02 FQ	17.89 AW	26.26 TQ	CTBLS	10/01-12/01
Commercial and Industrial Equipment	New Haven-Meriden PMSA, CT	H	10.25 FQ	15.60 AW	22.75 TQ	CTBLS	10/01-12/01
Commercial and Industrial Equipment	New London-Norwich MSA, CT-RI	H	15.64 FQ	19.58 AW	25.11 TQ	CTBLS	10/01-12/01
Commercial and Industrial Equipment	Waterbury PMSA, CT	H	14.44 FQ	16.06 AW	18.15 TQ	CTBLS	10/01-12/01
Commercial and Industrial Equipment	Delaware	H	17.23 FQ	22.30 AW	28.82 TQ	DEBLS	10/01-12/01
Commercial and Industrial Equipment	Wilmington-Newark PMSA, DE-MD	H	17.34 FQ	22.51 AW	29.35 TQ	DEBLS	10/01-12/01
Commercial and Industrial Equipment	District of Columbia	H	17.83 FQ	27.19 AW	34.48 TQ	DCBLS	10/01-12/01
Commercial and Industrial Equipment	Washington PMSA, DC-MD-VA-WV	H	12.61 FQ	20.09 AW	28.21 TQ	DCBLS	10/01-12/01
Commercial and Industrial Equipment	Florida	H	10.54 FQ	16.80 AW	24.54 TQ	FLBLS	10/01-12/01
Commercial and Industrial Equipment	Daytona Beach MSA, FL	H	10.89 FQ	14.52 AW	19.87 TQ	FLBLS	10/01-12/01
Commercial and Industrial Equipment	Fort Lauderdale PMSA, FL	H	12.05 FQ	18.78 AW	22.71 TQ	FLBLS	10/01-12/01
Commercial and Industrial Equipment	Fort Myers-Cape Coral MSA, FL	H	9.88 FQ	15.12 AW	21.81 TQ	FLBLS	10/01-12/01
Commercial and Industrial Equipment	Fort Pierce-Port St. Lucie MSA, FL	H	9.60 FQ	13.76 AW	19.03 TQ	FLBLS	10/01-12/01
Commercial and Industrial Equipment	Fort Walton Beach MSA, FL	H	15.77 FQ	20.76 AW	25.91 TQ	FLBLS	10/01-12/01
Commercial and Industrial Equipment	Jacksonville MSA, FL	H	12.17 FQ	17.64 AW	22.72 TQ	FLBLS	10/01-12/01
Commercial and Industrial Equipment	Lakeland-Winter Haven MSA, FL	H	12.09 FQ	17.78 AW	22.13 TQ	FLBLS	10/01-12/01
Commercial and Industrial Equipment	Melbourne-Titusville-Palm Bay MSA, FL	H	11.80 FQ	19.13 AW	26.46 TQ	FLBLS	10/01-12/01
Commercial and Industrial Equipment	Miami PMSA, FL	H	11.16 FQ	17.60 AW	27.89 TQ	FLBLS	10/01-12/01
Commercial and Industrial Equipment	Orlando MSA, FL	H	10.40 FQ	15.57 AW	28.20 TQ	FLBLS	10/01-12/01
Commercial and Industrial Equipment	Pensacola MSA, FL	H	11.97 FQ	17.63 AW	21.45 TQ	FLBLS	10/01-12/01
Commercial and Industrial Equipment	Sarasota-Bradenton MSA, FL	H	10.07 FQ	14.71 AW	18.38 TQ	FLBLS	10/01-12/01
Commercial and Industrial Equipment	Tampa-St. Petersburg-Clearwater MSA, FL	H	10.09 FQ	16.60 AW	25.29 TQ	FLBLS	10/01-12/01
Commercial and Industrial Equipment	West Palm Beach-Boca Raton MSA, FL	H	8.95 FQ	14.27 AW	21.61 TQ	FLBLS	10/01-12/01
Commercial and Industrial Equipment	Georgia	H	11.92 FQ	17.54 AW	22.86 TQ	GABLS	10/01-12/01
Commercial and Industrial Equipment	Atlanta MSA, GA	H	12.92 FQ	17.79 AW	22.72 TQ	GABLS	10/01-12/01
Commercial and Industrial Equipment	Columbus MSA, GA-AL	H	11.77 FQ	16.16 AW	20.58 TQ	GABLS	10/01-12/01
Commercial and Industrial Equipment	Macon MSA, GA	H	17.43 FQ	19.28 AW	21.28 TQ	GABLS	10/01-12/01
Commercial and Industrial Equipment	Savannah MSA, GA	H	15.57 FQ	19.83 AW	25.50 TQ	GABLS	10/01-12/01
Commercial and Industrial Equipment	Hawaii	H	15.46 FQ	22.91 AW	30.61 TQ	HIBLS	10/01-12/01
Commercial and Industrial Equipment	Honolulu MSA, HI	H	15.15 FQ	22.94 AW	31.95 TQ	HIBLS	10/01-12/01
Commercial and Industrial Equipment	Idaho	H	11.53 FQ	18.40 AW	25.55 TQ	IDBLS	10/01-12/01
Commercial and Industrial Equipment	Boise City MSA, ID	H	12.02 FQ	18.16 AW	25.47 TQ	IDBLS	10/01-12/01
Commercial and Industrial Equipment	Illinois	H	10.69 FQ	18.96 AW	27.40 TQ	ILBLS	10/01-12/01

AAW	Average annual wage	AOH	Average offered, high	ASH	Average starting, high	H	Hourly	M	Monthly	S	Special: hourly and annual
AE	Average entry wage	AOL	Average offered, low	ASL	Average starting, low	HI	Highest wage paid	MTC	Median total compensation	TQ	Third quartile wage
AEX	Average experienced wage	APH	Average pay, high range	AW	Average wage paid	HR	High end range	MW	Median wage paid	W	Weekly
AO	Average offered	APL	Average pay, low range	FQ	First quartile wage	LR	Low end range	SQ	Second quartile wage	Y	Yearly

Occupation/Type/Industry	Location	Per	Low	Mid	High	Source	Date
Electrical and Electronics Repairer							
Commercial and Industrial Equipment	Chicago PMSA, IL	H	10.98 FQ	20.11 AW	28.80 TQ	ILBLS	10/01-12/01
Commercial and Industrial Equipment	Peoria-Pekin MSA, IL	H	13.87 FQ	18.26 AW	25.71 TQ	ILBLS	10/01-12/01
Commercial and Industrial Equipment	Rockford MSA, IL	H	9.35 FQ	17.02 AW	21.91 TQ	ILBLS	10/01-12/01
Commercial and Industrial Equipment	Springfield MSA, IL	H	14.04 FQ	18.42 AW	25.31 TQ	ILBLS	10/01-12/01
Commercial and Industrial Equipment	Indiana	H	12.32 FQ	17.91 AW	25.03 TQ	INBLS	10/01-12/01
Commercial and Industrial Equipment	Evansville-Henderson MSA, IN-KY	H	12.02 FQ	16.79 AW	22.26 TQ	INBLS	10/01-12/01
Commercial and Industrial Equipment	Fort Wayne MSA, IN	H	11.26 FQ	19.94 AW	26.87 TQ	INBLS	10/01-12/01
Commercial and Industrial Equipment	Gary PMSA, IN	H	14.68 FQ	18.27 AW	23.01 TQ	INBLS	10/01-12/01
Commercial and Industrial Equipment	Indianapolis MSA, IN	H	12.32 FQ	17.96 AW	25.67 TQ	INBLS	10/01-12/01
Commercial and Industrial Equipment	Lafayette MSA, IN	H	12.05 FQ	17.94 AW	24.73 TQ	INBLS	10/01-12/01
Commercial and Industrial Equipment	Iowa	H	13.42 FQ	17.58 AW	22.23 TQ	IABLS	10/01-12/01
Commercial and Industrial Equipment	Davenport-Moline-Rock Island MSA, IA-IL	H	12.54 FQ	18.83 AW	26.14 TQ	IABLS	10/01-12/01
Commercial and Industrial Equipment	Des Moines MSA, IA	H	12.83 FQ	16.50 AW	20.55 TQ	IABLS	10/01-12/01
Commercial and Industrial Equipment	Kansas	H	12.59 FQ	19.53 AW	26.46 TQ	KSBLS	10/01-12/01
Commercial and Industrial Equipment	Topeka MSA, KS	H	14.62 FQ	18.71 AW	22.40 TQ	KSBLS	10/01-12/01
Commercial and Industrial Equipment	Wichita MSA, KS	H	12.59 FQ	20.06 AW	26.37 TQ	KSBLS	10/01-12/01
Commercial and Industrial Equipment	Kentucky	H	12.09 FQ	20.66 AW	27.97 TQ	KYBLS	10/01-12/01
Commercial and Industrial Equipment	Lexington MSA, KY	H	12.80 FQ	18.15 AW	24.81 TQ	KYBLS	10/01-12/01
Commercial and Industrial Equipment	Louisville MSA, KY-IN	H	9.89 FQ	18.34 AW	30.65 TQ	KYBLS	10/01-12/01
Commercial and Industrial Equipment	Louisiana	H	10.80 FQ	19.20 AW	26.44 TQ	LABLS	10/01-12/01
Commercial and Industrial Equipment	Baton Rouge MSA, LA	H	15.99 FQ	22.61 AW	27.23 TQ	LABLS	10/01-12/01
Commercial and Industrial Equipment	Houma MSA, LA	H	10.30 FQ	19.78 AW	28.75 TQ	LABLS	10/01-12/01
Commercial and Industrial Equipment	Lafayette MSA, LA	H	13.56 FQ	16.61 AW	21.90 TQ	LABLS	10/01-12/01
Commercial and Industrial Equipment	Lake Charles MSA, LA	H	20.26 FQ	23.79 AW	27.44 TQ	LABLS	10/01-12/01
Commercial and Industrial Equipment	New Orleans MSA, LA	H	9.97 FQ	17.68 AW	25.51 TQ	LABLS	10/01-12/01
Commercial and Industrial Equipment	Shreveport-Bossier City MSA, LA	H	17.65 FQ	21.14 AW	26.04 TQ	LABLS	10/01-12/01
Commercial and Industrial Equipment	Maine	H	12.93 FQ	18.86 AW	25.46 TQ	MEBLS	10/01-12/01
Commercial and Industrial Equipment	Portland MSA, ME	H	18.49 FQ	23.11 AW	31.99 TQ	MEBLS	10/01-12/01
Commercial and Industrial Equipment	Maryland	H	10.37 FQ	17.46 AW	24.40 TQ	MDBLS	10/01-12/01
Commercial and Industrial Equipment	Baltimore PMSA, MD	H	8.67 FQ	16.60 AW	23.01 TQ	MDBLS	10/01-12/01
Commercial and Industrial Equipment	Massachusetts	H	14.48 FQ	21.43 AW	30.51 TQ	MABLS	10/01-12/01
Commercial and Industrial Equipment	Boston PMSA, MA-NH	H	15.17 FQ	22.30 AW	31.29 TQ	MABLS	10/01-12/01
Commercial and Industrial Equipment	Brockton PMSA, MA	H	10.18 FQ	17.94 AW	27.21 TQ	MABLS	10/01-12/01
Commercial and Industrial Equipment	Lawrence PMSA, MA-NH	H	12.42 FQ	20.48 AW	31.25 TQ	MABLS	10/01-12/01
Commercial and Industrial Equipment	Lowell PMSA, MA-NH	H	14.84 FQ	21.35 AW	30.28 TQ	MABLS	10/01-12/01
Commercial and Industrial Equipment	Springfield MSA, MA	H	12.99 FQ	18.27 AW	25.55 TQ	MABLS	10/01-12/01
Commercial and Industrial Equipment	Worcester PMSA, MA-CT	H	9.87 FQ	17.85 AW	27.07 TQ	MABLS	10/01-12/01
Commercial and Industrial Equipment	Michigan	H	12.41 FQ	19.75 AW	27.21 TQ	MIBLS	10/01-12/01
Commercial and Industrial Equipment	Ann Arbor PMSA, MI	H	16.04 FQ	24.16 AW	39.17 TQ	MIBLS	10/01-12/01
Commercial and Industrial Equipment	Detroit PMSA, MI	H	12.19 FQ	18.93 AW	26.41 TQ	MIBLS	10/01-12/01
Commercial and Industrial Equipment	Grand Rapids-Muskegon-Holland MSA, MI	H	13.25 FQ	19.32 AW	25.52 TQ	MIBLS	10/01-12/01
Commercial and Industrial Equipment	Kalamazoo-Battle Creek MSA, MI	H	10.86 FQ	21.39 AW	28.95 TQ	MIBLS	10/01-12/01
Commercial and Industrial Equipment	Saginaw-Bay City-Midland MSA, MI	H	11.77 FQ	17.26 AW	25.00 TQ	MIBLS	10/01-12/01
Commercial and Industrial Equipment	Minnesota	H	12.54 FQ	19.29 AW	26.48 TQ	MNBLS	10/01-12/01
Commercial and Industrial Equipment	Duluth-Superior MSA, MN-WI	H	10.10 FQ	19.98 AW	25.77 TQ	MNBLS	10/01-12/01
Commercial and Industrial Equipment	Minneapolis-St. Paul MSA, MN-WI	H	12.86 FQ	19.55 AW	26.67 TQ	MNBLS	10/01-12/01
Commercial and Industrial Equipment	St. Cloud MSA, MN	H	10.70 FQ	15.57 AW	24.04 TQ	MNBLS	10/01-12/01
Commercial and Industrial Equipment	Mississippi	H	11.76 FQ	16.34 AW	20.83 TQ	MSBLS	10/01-12/01
Commercial and Industrial Equipment	Jackson MSA, MS	H	11.63 FQ	15.55 AW	20.64 TQ	MSBLS	10/01-12/01
Commercial and Industrial Equipment	Missouri	H	10.60 FQ	18.35 AW	25.85 TQ	MOBLS	10/01-12/01
Commercial and Industrial Equipment	Kansas City MSA, MO-KS	H	11.97 FQ	20.00 AW	26.82 TQ	MOBLS	10/01-12/01
Commercial and Industrial Equipment	St. Louis MSA, MO-IL	H	10.59 FQ	19.04 AW	26.27 TQ	MOBLS	10/01-12/01
Commercial and Industrial Equipment	Springfield MSA, MO	H	10.65 FQ	18.86 AW	26.01 TQ	MOBLS	10/01-12/01
Commercial and Industrial Equipment	Montana	H	12.18 FQ	20.25 AW	31.13 TQ	MTBLS	10/01-12/01
Commercial and Industrial Equipment	Billings MSA, MT	H	10.83 FQ	19.16 AW	32.31 TQ	MTBLS	10/01-12/01
Commercial and Industrial Equipment	Nebraska	H	11.44 FQ	19.45 AW	29.54 TQ	NEBLS	10/01-12/01
Commercial and Industrial Equipment	Lincoln MSA, NE	H	12.88 FQ	17.51 AW	21.45 TQ	NEBLS	10/01-12/01
Commercial and Industrial Equipment	Omaha MSA, NE-IA	H	11.54 FQ	21.19 AW	33.08 TQ	NEBLS	10/01-12/01
Commercial and Industrial Equipment	Nevada	H	12.33 FQ	18.83 AW	26.39 TQ	NVBLS	10/01-12/01
Commercial and Industrial Equipment	Las Vegas MSA, NV-AZ	H	12.22 FQ	18.77 AW	26.76 TQ	NVBLS	10/01-12/01
Commercial and Industrial Equipment	New Hampshire	H	11.95 FQ	17.93 AW	24.60 TQ	NHBLS	10/01-12/01
Commercial and Industrial Equipment	Manchester PMSA, NH	H	13.07 FQ	19.71 AW	27.16 TQ	NHBLS	10/01-12/01
Commercial and Industrial Equipment	Nashua PMSA, NH	H	8.89 FQ	14.89 AW	21.49 TQ	NHBLS	10/01-12/01

AAW	Average annual wage	**AOH**	Average offered, high	**ASH**	Average starting, high	**H**	Hourly	**M**	Monthly	**S**	Special: hourly and annual
AE	Average entry wage	**AOL**	Average offered, low	**ASL**	Average starting, low	**HI**	Highest wage paid	**MTC**	Median total compensation	**TQ**	Third quartile wage
AEX	Average experienced wage	**APH**	Average pay, high range	**AW**	Average wage paid	**HR**	High end range	**MW**	Median wage paid	**W**	Weekly
AO	Average offered	**APL**	Average pay, low range	**FQ**	First quartile wage	**LR**	Low end range	**SQ**	Second quartile wage	**Y**	Yearly

Occupation/Type/Industry	Location	Per	Low	Mid	High	Source	Date
Electrical and Electronics Repairer							
Commercial and Industrial Equipment	Portsmouth-Rochester PMSA, NH-ME	H	15.16 FQ	19.48 AW	24.95 TQ	NHBLS	10/01-12/01
Commercial and Industrial Equipment	New Jersey	H	13.94 FQ	20.84 AW	27.95 TQ	NJBLS	10/01-12/01
Commercial and Industrial Equipment	Atlantic-Cape May PMSA, NJ	H	15.13 FQ	19.07 AW	24.01 TQ	NJBLS	10/01-12/01
Commercial and Industrial Equipment	Bergen-Passaic PMSA, NJ	H	14.04 FQ	21.97 AW	27.90 TQ	NJBLS	10/01-12/01
Commercial and Industrial Equipment	Jersey City PMSA, NJ	H	13.90 FQ	20.52 AW	26.92 TQ	NJBLS	10/01-12/01
Commercial and Industrial Equipment	Middlesex-Somerset-Hunterdon PMSA, NJ	H	12.94 FQ	20.31 AW	27.75 TQ	NJBLS	10/01-12/01
Commercial and Industrial Equipment	Monmouth-Ocean PMSA, NJ	H	14.18 FQ	19.97 AW	26.64 TQ	NJBLS	10/01-12/01
Commercial and Industrial Equipment	Newark PMSA, NJ	H	14.71 FQ	21.37 AW	28.32 TQ	NJBLS	10/01-12/01
Commercial and Industrial Equipment	Trenton PMSA, NJ	H	9.75 FQ	17.20 AW	24.03 TQ	NJBLS	10/01-12/01
Commercial and Industrial Equipment	New Mexico	H	11.96 FQ	20.69 AW	30.08 TQ	NMBLS	10/01-12/01
Commercial and Industrial Equipment	Albuquerque MSA, NM	H	15.59 FQ	22.66 AW	30.43 TQ	NMBLS	10/01-12/01
Commercial and Industrial Equipment	Las Cruces MSA, NM	H	9.73 FQ	22.25 AW	33.10 TQ	NMBLS	10/01-12/01
Commercial and Industrial Equipment	New York	H	11.80 FQ	19.21 AW	26.87 TQ	NYBLS	10/01-12/01
Commercial and Industrial Equipment	Albany-Schenectady-Troy MSA, NY	H	11.50 FQ	18.78 AW	26.88 TQ	NYBLS	10/01-12/01
Commercial and Industrial Equipment	Binghamton MSA, NY	H	15.38 FQ	21.61 AW	27.18 TQ	NYBLS	10/01-12/01
Commercial and Industrial Equipment	Buffalo-Niagara Falls MSA, NY	H	8.10 FQ	16.96 AW	26.37 TQ	NYBLS	10/01-12/01
Commercial and Industrial Equipment	Nassau-Suffolk PMSA, NY	H	14.04 FQ	20.20 AW	30.40 TQ	NYBLS	10/01-12/01
Commercial and Industrial Equipment	New York PMSA, NY	H	12.10 FQ	19.33 AW	26.26 TQ	NYBLS	10/01-12/01
Commercial and Industrial Equipment	Newburgh PMSA, NY-PA	H	17.43 FQ	21.60 AW	26.78 TQ	NYBLS	10/01-12/01
Commercial and Industrial Equipment	Rochester MSA, NY	H	12.61 FQ	19.88 AW	27.26 TQ	NYBLS	10/01-12/01
Commercial and Industrial Equipment	Syracuse MSA, NY	H	12.03 FQ	18.88 AW	26.87 TQ	NYBLS	10/01-12/01
Commercial and Industrial Equipment	North Carolina	H	10.82 FQ	17.64 AW	25.22 TQ	NCBLS	10/01-12/01
Commercial and Industrial Equipment	Asheville MSA, NC	H	10.16 FQ	16.84 AW	24.65 TQ	NCBLS	10/01-12/01
Commercial and Industrial Equipment	Charlotte-Gastonia-Rock Hill MSA, NC-SC	H	12.02 FQ	18.69 AW	25.68 TQ	NCBLS	10/01-12/01
Commercial and Industrial Equipment	Fayetteville MSA, NC	H	9.99 FQ	16.82 AW	24.77 TQ	NCBLS	10/01-12/01
Commercial and Industrial Equipment	Greensboro-Winston-Salem-High Point MSA, NC	H	13.51 FQ	18.98 AW	26.30 TQ	NCBLS	10/01-12/01
Commercial and Industrial Equipment	Hickory-Morganton-Lenoir MSA, NC	H	8.54 FQ	16.58 AW	23.18 TQ	NCBLS	10/01-12/01
Commercial and Industrial Equipment	Raleigh-Durham-Chapel Hill MSA, NC	H	11.29 FQ	17.21 AW	24.47 TQ	NCBLS	10/01-12/01
Commercial and Industrial Equipment	Wilmington MSA, NC	H	7.92 FQ	16.94 AW	26.05 TQ	NCBLS	10/01-12/01
Commercial and Industrial Equipment	North Dakota	H	8.42 FQ	17.88 AW	28.04 TQ	NDBLS	10/01-12/01
Commercial and Industrial Equipment	Fargo-Moorhead MSA, ND-MN	H	11.89 FQ	18.87 AW	27.18 TQ	NDBLS	10/01-12/01
Commercial and Industrial Equipment	Ohio	H	10.25 FQ	16.94 AW	24.90 TQ	OHBLS	10/01-12/01
Commercial and Industrial Equipment	Akron PMSA, OH	H	11.57 FQ	16.43 AW	23.39 TQ	OHBLS	10/01-12/01
Commercial and Industrial Equipment	Cincinnati PMSA, OH-KY-IN	H	9.42 FQ	17.27 AW	27.12 TQ	OHBLS	10/01-12/01
Commercial and Industrial Equipment	Cleveland-Lorain-Elyria PMSA, OH	H	11.75 FQ	16.78 AW	22.21 TQ	OHBLS	10/01-12/01
Commercial and Industrial Equipment	Columbus MSA, OH	H	11.33 FQ	17.67 AW	25.18 TQ	OHBLS	10/01-12/01
Commercial and Industrial Equipment	Dayton-Springfield MSA, OH	H	9.91 FQ	17.35 AW	25.83 TQ	OHBLS	10/01-12/01
Commercial and Industrial Equipment	Toledo MSA, OH	H	9.69 FQ	17.77 AW	26.14 TQ	OHBLS	10/01-12/01
Commercial and Industrial Equipment	Youngstown-Warren MSA, OH	H	8.74 FQ	17.17 AW	24.94 TQ	OHBLS	10/01-12/01
Commercial and Industrial Equipment	Oklahoma	H	9.63 FQ	16.06 AW	23.35 TQ	OKBLS	10/01-12/01
Commercial and Industrial Equipment	Oklahoma City MSA, OK	H	9.33 FQ	16.07 AW	24.12 TQ	OKBLS	10/01-12/01
Commercial and Industrial Equipment	Tulsa MSA, OK	H	10.24 FQ	15.35 AW	21.52 TQ	OKBLS	10/01-12/01
Commercial and Industrial Equipment	Oregon	H	14.04 FQ	19.74 AW	25.75 TQ	ORBLS	10/01-12/01
Commercial and Industrial Equipment	Portland-Vancouver PMSA, OR-WA	H	15.00 FQ	20.86 AW	26.83 TQ	ORBLS	10/01-12/01
Commercial and Industrial Equipment	Salem PMSA, OR	H	15.19 FQ	19.97 AW	26.06 TQ	ORBLS	10/01-12/01
Commercial and Industrial Equipment	Pennsylvania	H	11.62 FQ	18.33 AW	25.41 TQ	PABLS	10/01-12/01
Commercial and Industrial Equipment	Allentown-Bethlehem-Easton MSA, PA	H	9.71 FQ	17.56 AW	23.15 TQ	PABLS	10/01-12/01
Commercial and Industrial Equipment	Erie MSA, PA	H	11.09 FQ	16.79 AW	22.11 TQ	PABLS	10/01-12/01
Commercial and Industrial Equipment	Harrisburg-Lebanon-Carlisle MSA, PA	H	15.46 FQ	20.06 AW	26.50 TQ	PABLS	10/01-12/01
Commercial and Industrial Equipment	Lancaster MSA, PA	H	11.97 FQ	16.83 AW	22.18 TQ	PABLS	10/01-12/01
Commercial and Industrial Equipment	Philadelphia PMSA, PA-NJ	H	12.38 FQ	19.50 AW	26.96 TQ	PABLS	10/01-12/01
Commercial and Industrial Equipment	Pittsburgh MSA, PA	H	11.33 FQ	19.28 AW	26.48 TQ	PABLS	10/01-12/01
Commercial and Industrial Equipment	Reading MSA, PA	H	8.35 FQ	14.85 AW	20.66 TQ	PABLS	10/01-12/01
Commercial and Industrial Equipment	Scranton-Wilkes-Barre-Hazleton MSA, PA	H	14.12 FQ	22.11 AW	34.28 TQ	PABLS	10/01-12/01
Commercial and Industrial Equipment	York MSA, PA	H	14.24 FQ	19.46 AW	26.33 TQ	PABLS	10/01-12/01
Commercial and Industrial Equipment	Rhode Island	H	12.88 FQ	19.17 AW	26.24 TQ	RIBLS	10/01-12/01

AAW Average annual wage; AE Average entry wage; AEX Average experienced wage; AO Average offered; AOH Average offered, high; AOL Average offered, low; APH Average pay, high range; APL Average pay, low range; ASH Average starting, high; ASL Average starting, low; AW Average wage paid; FQ First quartile wage; H Hourly; HI Highest wage paid; HR High end range; LR Low end range; M Monthly; MTC Median total compensation; MW Median wage paid; SQ Second quartile wage; S Special: hourly and annual; TQ Third quartile wage; W Weekly; Y Yearly

Electrical and Electronics Repairer

Occupation/Type/Industry	Location	Per	Low	Mid	High	Source	Date
Commercial and Industrial Equipment	Providence-Fall River-Warwick MSA, RI-MA	H	13.01 FQ	19.36 AW	25.90 TQ	RIBLS	10/01-12/01
Commercial and Industrial Equipment	South Carolina	H	11.78 FQ	19.28 AW	29.93 TQ	SCBLS	10/01-12/01
Commercial and Industrial Equipment	Charleston-North Charleston MSA, SC	H	11.71 FQ	15.99 AW	20.97 TQ	SCBLS	10/01-12/01
Commercial and Industrial Equipment	Columbia MSA, SC	H	8.66 FQ	15.64 AW	24.28 TQ	SCBLS	10/01-12/01
Commercial and Industrial Equipment	Greenville-Spartanburg-Anderson MSA, SC	H	15.08 FQ	20.66 AW	27.04 TQ	SCBLS	10/01-12/01
Commercial and Industrial Equipment	South Dakota	H	11.44 FQ	18.43 AW	30.32 TQ	SDBLS	10/01-12/01
Commercial and Industrial Equipment	Sioux Falls MSA, SD	H	11.60 FQ	16.38 AW	21.17 TQ	SDBLS	10/01-12/01
Commercial and Industrial Equipment	Tennessee	H	11.61 FQ	18.53 AW	23.50 TQ	TNBLS	10/01-12/01
Commercial and Industrial Equipment	Chattanooga MSA, TN-GA	H	9.62 FQ	15.80 AW	21.25 TQ	TNBLS	10/01-12/01
Commercial and Industrial Equipment	Johnson City-Kingsport-Bristol MSA, TN-VA	H	15.69 FQ	19.72 AW	22.70 TQ	TNBLS	10/01-12/01
Commercial and Industrial Equipment	Knoxville MSA, TN	H	11.62 FQ	18.28 AW	25.24 TQ	TNBLS	10/01-12/01
Commercial and Industrial Equipment	Memphis MSA, TN-AR-MS	H	11.69 FQ	17.87 AW	25.82 TQ	TNBLS	10/01-12/01
Commercial and Industrial Equipment	Nashville MSA, TN	H	11.48 FQ	20.15 AW	33.77 TQ	TNBLS	10/01-12/01
Commercial and Industrial Equipment	Texas	H	9.40 FQ	18.98 AW	29.85 TQ	TXBLS	10/01-12/01
Commercial and Industrial Equipment	Austin-San Marcos MSA, TX	H	11.97 FQ	21.17 AW	32.46 TQ	TXBLS	10/01-12/01
Commercial and Industrial Equipment	Brazoria PMSA, TX	H	11.87 FQ	21.82 AW	31.40 TQ	TXBLS	10/01-12/01
Commercial and Industrial Equipment	Corpus Christi MSA, TX	H	15.85 FQ	20.67 AW	26.40 TQ	TXBLS	10/01-12/01
Commercial and Industrial Equipment	Dallas PMSA, TX	H	9.18 FQ	18.10 AW	26.99 TQ	TXBLS	10/01-12/01
Commercial and Industrial Equipment	El Paso MSA, TX	H	8.15 FQ	15.15 AW	24.55 TQ	TXBLS	10/01-12/01
Commercial and Industrial Equipment	Fort Worth-Arlington PMSA, TX	H	12.44 FQ	20.10 AW	31.07 TQ	TXBLS	10/01-12/01
Commercial and Industrial Equipment	Houston PMSA, TX	H	7.36 FQ	18.20 AW	28.78 TQ	TXBLS	10/01-12/01
Commercial and Industrial Equipment	Longview-Marshall MSA, TX	H	12.66 FQ	22.57 AW	32.45 TQ	TXBLS	10/01-12/01
Commercial and Industrial Equipment	McAllen-Edinburg-Mission MSA, TX	H	9.33 FQ	14.54 AW	23.92 TQ	TXBLS	10/01-12/01
Commercial and Industrial Equipment	Odessa Midland MSA, TX	H	9.79 FQ	15.62 AW	23.77 TQ	TXBLS	10/01-12/01
Commercial and Industrial Equipment	San Antonio MSA, TX	H	9.44 FQ	17.29 AW	25.62 TQ	TXBLS	10/01-12/01
Commercial and Industrial Equipment	Tyler MSA, TX	H	10.28 FQ	19.14 AW	32.44 TQ	TXBLS	10/01-12/01
Commercial and Industrial Equipment	Utah	H	12.75 FQ	18.74 AW	25.51 TQ	UTBLS	10/01-12/01
Commercial and Industrial Equipment	Provo-Orem MSA, UT	H	8.58 FQ	14.80 AW	21.13 TQ	UTBLS	10/01-12/01
Commercial and Industrial Equipment	Salt Lake City-Ogden MSA, UT	H	13.93 FQ	19.40 AW	25.72 TQ	UTBLS	10/01-12/01
Commercial and Industrial Equipment	Vermont	H	17.17 FQ	21.68 AW	28.30 TQ	VTBLS	10/01-12/01
Commercial and Industrial Equipment	Burlington MSA, VT	H	16.63 FQ	23.97 AW	34.38 TQ	VTBLS	10/01-12/01
Commercial and Industrial Equipment	Virginia	H	12.50 FQ	19.06 AW	25.86 TQ	VABLS	10/01-12/01
Commercial and Industrial Equipment	Norfolk-Virginia Beach-Newport News MSA, VA-NC	H	12.01 FQ	18.04 AW	24.34 TQ	VABLS	10/01-12/01
Commercial and Industrial Equipment	Richmond-Petersburg MSA, VA	H	13.29 FQ	20.89 AW	27.07 TQ	VABLS	10/01-12/01
Commercial and Industrial Equipment	Roanoke MSA, VA	H	12.23 FQ	19.88 AW	27.06 TQ	VABLS	10/01-12/01
Commercial and Industrial Equipment	Washington	H	13.86 FQ	21.24 AW	28.11 TQ	WABLS	10/01-12/01
Commercial and Industrial Equipment	Bremerton PMSA, WA	H	12.87 FQ	20.21 AW	26.45 TQ	WABLS	10/01-12/01
Commercial and Industrial Equipment	Olympia PMSA, WA	H	14.89 FQ	18.58 AW	29.64 TQ	WABLS	10/01-12/01
Commercial and Industrial Equipment	Seattle-Bellevue-Everett PMSA, WA	H	14.32 FQ	22.01 AW	30.49 TQ	WABLS	10/01-12/01
Commercial and Industrial Equipment	Spokane MSA, WA	H	13.69 FQ	21.18 AW	30.37 TQ	WABLS	10/01-12/01
Commercial and Industrial Equipment	Tacoma PMSA, WA	H	18.59 FQ	22.90 AW	26.71 TQ	WABLS	10/01-12/01
Commercial and Industrial Equipment	West Virginia	H	11.81 FQ	19.59 AW	26.43 TQ	WVBLS	10/01-12/01
Commercial and Industrial Equipment	Wisconsin	H	11.85 FQ	17.73 AW	24.43 TQ	WIBLS	10/01-12/01
Commercial and Industrial Equipment	Appleton-Oshkosh-Neenah MSA, WI	H	12.05 FQ	17.80 AW	24.26 TQ	WIBLS	10/01-12/01
Commercial and Industrial Equipment	Green Bay MSA, WI	H	12.37 FQ	18.58 AW	25.10 TQ	WIBLS	10/01-12/01
Commercial and Industrial Equipment	Madison MSA, WI	H	14.22 FQ	18.09 AW	21.24 TQ	WIBLS	10/01-12/01
Commercial and Industrial Equipment	Milwaukee-Waukesha PMSA, WI	H	12.98 FQ	19.58 AW	26.04 TQ	WIBLS	10/01-12/01
Commercial and Industrial Equipment	Wyoming	H	17.64 FQ	24.17 AW	32.22 TQ	WYBLS	10/01-12/01
Commercial and Industrial Equipment	Cheyenne MSA, WY	H	18.78 FQ	24.28 AW	31.59 TQ	WYBLS	10/01-12/01
Commercial and Industrial Equipment	Puerto Rico	H	6.85 FQ	10.93 AW	16.11 TQ	PRBLS	10/01-12/01
Commercial and Industrial Equipment	Guam	H	9.83 FQ	14.03 AW	20.64 TQ	GUBLS	10/01-12/01
Powerhouse, Substation, and Relay	Alaska	H	24.47 FQ	30.26 AW	35.25 TQ	AKBLS	10/01-12/01
Powerhouse, Substation, and Relay	Arizona	H	19.60 FQ	25.82 AW	33.24 TQ	AZBLS	10/01-12/01
Powerhouse, Substation, and Relay	Phoenix-Mesa MSA, AZ	H	20.06 FQ	26.91 AW	34.79 TQ	AZBLS	10/01-12/01
Powerhouse, Substation, and Relay	Arkansas	H	14.28 FQ	19.83 AW	26.29 TQ	ARBLS	10/01-12/01
Powerhouse, Substation, and Relay	Little Rock-North Little Rock MSA, AR	H	13.12 FQ	17.88 AW	21.96 TQ	ARBLS	10/01-12/01

AAW	Average annual wage	AOH	Average offered, high	ASH	Average starting, high	H	Hourly	M	Monthly	S	Special: hourly and annual
AE	Average entry wage	AOL	Average offered, low	ASL	Average starting, low	HI	Highest wage paid	MTC	Median total compensation	TQ	Third quartile wage
AEX	Average experienced wage	APH	Average pay, high range	AW	Average wage paid	HR	High end range	MW	Median wage paid	W	Weekly
AO	Average offered	APL	Average pay, low range	FQ	First quartile wage	LR	Low end range	SQ	Second quartile wage	Y	Yearly

Occupation/Type/Industry	Location	Per	Low	Mid	High	Source	Date
Electrical and Electronics Repairer							
Powerhouse, Substation, and Relay	California	H	12.37 FQ	23.69 AW	33.85 TQ	CABLS	10/01-12/01
Powerhouse, Substation, and Relay	Oakland PMSA, CA	H	12.39 FQ	22.74 AW	33.52 TQ	CABLS	10/01-12/01
Powerhouse, Substation, and Relay	Orange County PMSA, CA	H	8.14 FQ	20.94 AW	34.52 TQ	CABLS	10/01-12/01
Powerhouse, Substation, and Relay	Riverside-San Bernardino PMSA, CA	H	13.42 FQ	23.82 AW	34.46 TQ	CABLS	10/01-12/01
Powerhouse, Substation, and Relay	San Francisco PMSA, CA	H	13.24 FQ	23.21 AW	32.02 TQ	CABLS	10/01-12/01
Powerhouse, Substation, and Relay	Ventura PMSA, CA	H	11.42 FQ	18.95 AW	29.08 TQ	CABLS	10/01-12/01
Powerhouse, Substation, and Relay	Colorado	H	16.04 FQ	23.32 AW	28.25 TQ	COBLS	10/01-12/01
Powerhouse, Substation, and Relay	Denver PMSA, CO	H	22.05 FQ	24.70 AW	28.17 TQ	COBLS	10/01-12/01
Powerhouse, Substation, and Relay	Greeley PMSA, CO	H	21.78 FQ	25.37 AW	29.61 TQ	COBLS	10/01-12/01
Powerhouse, Substation, and Relay	Connecticut	H	17.97 FQ	23.72 AW	29.08 TQ	CTBLS	10/01-12/01
Powerhouse, Substation, and Relay	Hartford MSA, CT	H	17.79 FQ	22.81 AW	28.83 TQ	CTBLS	10/01-12/01
Powerhouse, Substation, and Relay	New Haven-Meriden PMSA, CT	H	13.34 FQ	22.01 AW	28.86 TQ	CTBLS	10/01-12/01
Powerhouse, Substation, and Relay	New London-Norwich MSA, CT-RI	H	18.97 FQ	24.13 AW	28.81 TQ	CTBLS	10/01-12/01
Powerhouse, Substation, and Relay	Washington PMSA, DC-MD-VA-WV	H	20.40 FQ	24.88 AW	28.91 TQ	DCBLS	10/01-12/01
Powerhouse, Substation, and Relay	Florida	H	15.57 FQ	22.03 AW	27.47 TQ	FLBLS	10/01-12/01
Powerhouse, Substation, and Relay	Tampa-St. Petersburg-Clearwater MSA, FL	H	14.15 FQ	20.07 AW	24.59 TQ	FLBLS	10/01-12/01
Powerhouse, Substation, and Relay	Georgia	H	15.18 FQ	21.07 AW	26.94 TQ	GABLS	10/01-12/01
Powerhouse, Substation, and Relay	Atlanta MSA, GA	H	18.06 FQ	22.07 AW	27.17 TQ	GABLS	10/01-12/01
Powerhouse, Substation, and Relay	Hawaii	H	18.66 FQ	26.32 AW	33.89 TQ	HIBLS	10/01-12/01
Powerhouse, Substation, and Relay	Honolulu MSA, HI	H	6.85 FQ	26.92 AW	34.65 TQ	HIBLS	10/01-12/01
Powerhouse, Substation, and Relay	Idaho	H	10.06 FQ	18.99 AW	31.39 TQ	IDBLS	10/01-12/01
Powerhouse, Substation, and Relay	Boise City MSA, ID	H	12.85 FQ	20.66 AW	29.91 TQ	IDBLS	10/01-12/01
Powerhouse, Substation, and Relay	Illinois	H	6.92 FQ	19.76 AW	27.65 TQ	ILBLS	10/01-12/01
Powerhouse, Substation, and Relay	Chicago PMSA, IL	H	6.22 FQ	17.13 AW	27.09 TQ	ILBLS	10/01-12/01
Powerhouse, Substation, and Relay	Rockford MSA, IL	H	12.58 FQ	18.77 AW	25.63 TQ	ILBLS	10/01-12/01
Powerhouse, Substation, and Relay	Indiana	H	17.16 FQ	24.07 AW	29.01 TQ	INBLS	10/01-12/01
Powerhouse, Substation, and Relay	Evansville-Henderson MSA, IN-KY	H	18.44 FQ	23.10 AW	27.05 TQ	INBLS	10/01-12/01
Powerhouse, Substation, and Relay	Fort Wayne MSA, IN	H	10.92 FQ	18.25 AW	28.09 TQ	INBLS	10/01-12/01
Powerhouse, Substation, and Relay	Indianapolis MSA, IN	H	15.30 FQ	23.50 AW	29.01 TQ	INBLS	10/01-12/01
Powerhouse, Substation, and Relay	Iowa	H	18.24 FQ	22.73 AW	27.34 TQ	IABLS	10/01-12/01
Powerhouse, Substation, and Relay	Davenport-Moline-Rock Island MSA, IA-IL	H	15.17 FQ	21.40 AW	27.48 TQ	IABLS	10/01-12/01
Powerhouse, Substation, and Relay	Des Moines MSA, IA	H	18.63 FQ	22.72 AW	27.02 TQ	IABLS	10/01-12/01
Powerhouse, Substation, and Relay	Kansas	H	10.25 FQ	21.52 AW	27.85 TQ	KSBLS	10/01-12/01
Powerhouse, Substation, and Relay	Topeka MSA, KS	H	20.50 FQ	24.72 AW	28.56 TQ	KSBLS	10/01-12/01
Powerhouse, Substation, and Relay	Kentucky	H	13.14 FQ	20.68 AW	28.02 TQ	KYBLS	10/01-12/01
Powerhouse, Substation, and Relay	Lexington MSA, KY	H	14.02 FQ	19.73 AW	25.80 TQ	KYBLS	10/01-12/01
Powerhouse, Substation, and Relay	Louisville MSA, KY-IN	H	20.70 FQ	25.86 AW	32.55 TQ	KYBLS	10/01-12/01
Powerhouse, Substation, and Relay	Louisiana	H	14.06 FQ	22.43 AW	31.57 TQ	LABLS	10/01-12/01
Powerhouse, Substation, and Relay	Baton Rouge MSA, LA	H	12.51 FQ	19.91 AW	26.08 TQ	LABLS	10/01-12/01
Powerhouse, Substation, and Relay	Lafayette MSA, LA	H	13.99 FQ	17.93 AW	21.88 TQ	LABLS	10/01-12/01
Powerhouse, Substation, and Relay	Lake Charles MSA, LA	H	14.25 FQ	22.35 AW	29.28 TQ	LABLS	10/01-12/01
Powerhouse, Substation, and Relay	New Orleans MSA, LA	H	23.28 FQ	27.84 AW	33.89 TQ	LABLS	10/01-12/01
Powerhouse, Substation, and Relay	Maine	H	15.72 FQ	19.61 AW	22.57 TQ	MEBLS	10/01-12/01
Powerhouse, Substation, and Relay	Maryland	H	18.59 FQ	25.22 AW	32.47 TQ	MDBLS	10/01-12/01
Powerhouse, Substation, and Relay	Baltimore PMSA, MD	H	20.47 FQ	26.23 AW	33.15 TQ	MDBLS	10/01-12/01
Powerhouse, Substation, and Relay	Massachusetts	H	14.69 FQ	22.75 AW	29.51 TQ	MABLS	10/01-12/01
Powerhouse, Substation, and Relay	Boston PMSA, MA-NH	H	15.02 FQ	23.09 AW	30.03 TQ	MABLS	10/01-12/01
Powerhouse, Substation, and Relay	Worcester PMSA, MA-CT	H	13.88 FQ	23.64 AW	30.36 TQ	MABLS	10/01-12/01
Powerhouse, Substation, and Relay	Michigan	H	19.75 FQ	25.81 AW	33.01 TQ	MIBLS	10/01-12/01
Powerhouse, Substation, and Relay	Detroit PMSA, MI	H	20.60 FQ	26.61 AW	33.62 TQ	MIBLS	10/01-12/01
Powerhouse, Substation, and Relay	Minnesota	H	10.03 FQ	21.49 AW	28.21 TQ	MNBLS	10/01-12/01
Powerhouse, Substation, and Relay	Duluth-Superior MSA, MN-WI	H	21.57 FQ	24.37 AW	27.77 TQ	MNBLS	10/01-12/01
Powerhouse, Substation, and Relay	Minneapolis-St. Paul MSA, MN-WI	H	7.67 FQ	18.49 AW	30.18 TQ	MNBLS	10/01-12/01
Powerhouse, Substation, and Relay	Mississippi	H	17.06 FQ	21.46 AW	26.87 TQ	MSBLS	10/01-12/01
Powerhouse, Substation, and Relay	Missouri	H	16.92 FQ	23.48 AW	28.27 TQ	MOBLS	10/01-12/01
Powerhouse, Substation, and Relay	Kansas City MSA, MO-KS	H	19.76 FQ	24.02 AW	27.91 TQ	MOBLS	10/01-12/01
Powerhouse, Substation, and Relay	Nebraska	H	18.65 FQ	24.53 AW	32.74 TQ	NEBLS	10/01-12/01
Powerhouse, Substation, and Relay	Lincoln MSA, NE	H	18.61 FQ	23.72 AW	31.84 TQ	NEBLS	10/01-12/01
Powerhouse, Substation, and Relay	Nevada	H	17.47 FQ	26.73 AW	34.68 TQ	NVBLS	10/01-12/01
Powerhouse, Substation, and Relay	Las Vegas MSA, NV-AZ	H	15.43 FQ	24.98 AW	33.89 TQ	NVBLS	10/01-12/01
Powerhouse, Substation, and Relay	New Hampshire	H	19.10 FQ	23.21 AW	27.02 TQ	NHBLS	10/01-12/01
Powerhouse, Substation, and Relay	New Jersey	H	21.32 FQ	26.62 AW	33.48 TQ	NJBLS	10/01-12/01

AAW Average annual wage **AE** Average entry wage **AEX** Average experienced wage **AO** Average offered **AOH** Average offered, high **AOL** Average offered, low **APH** Average pay, high range **APL** Average pay, low range **ASH** Average starting, high **ASL** Average starting, low **AW** Average wage paid **FQ** First quartile wage **H** Hourly **HI** Highest wage paid **HR** High end range **LR** Low end range **M** Monthly **MTC** Median total compensation **MW** Median wage paid **SQ** Second quartile wage **S** Special: hourly and annual **TQ** Third quartile wage **W** Weekly **Y** Yearly

Occupation/Type/Industry	Location	Per	Low	Mid	High	Source	Date
Electrical and Electronics Repairer							
Powerhouse, Substation, and Relay	Atlantic-Cape May PMSA, NJ	H	21.27 FQ	26.47 AW	33.07 TQ	NJBLS	10/01-12/01
Powerhouse, Substation, and Relay	Middlesex-Somerset-Hunterdon PMSA, NJ	H	16.32 FQ	24.26 AW	32.62 TQ	NJBLS	10/01-12/01
Powerhouse, Substation, and Relay	Albany-Schenectady-Troy MSA, NY	H	25.49 FQ	30.09 AW	34.53 TQ	NYBLS	10/01-12/01
Powerhouse, Substation, and Relay	Nassau-Suffolk PMSA, NY	H	12.10 FQ	21.49 AW	29.15 TQ	NYBLS	10/01-12/01
Powerhouse, Substation, and Relay	Syracuse MSA, NY	H	19.51 FQ	27.44 AW	34.77 TQ	NYBLS	10/01-12/01
Powerhouse, Substation, and Relay	North Carolina	H	13.17 FQ	21.93 AW	31.51 TQ	NCBLS	10/01-12/01
Powerhouse, Substation, and Relay	Charlotte-Gastonia-Rock Hill MSA, NC-SC	H	14.52 FQ	23.18 AW	31.99 TQ	NCBLS	10/01-12/01
Powerhouse, Substation, and Relay	North Dakota	H	22.14 FQ	25.26 AW	29.39 TQ	NDBLS	10/01-12/01
Powerhouse, Substation, and Relay	Ohio	H	15.83 FQ	21.42 AW	27.32 TQ	OHBLS	10/01-12/01
Powerhouse, Substation, and Relay	Cincinnati PMSA, OH-KY-IN	H	15.88 FQ	20.88 AW	27.23 TQ	OHBLS	10/01-12/01
Powerhouse, Substation, and Relay	Cleveland-Lorain-Elyria PMSA, OH	H	11.15 FQ	20.16 AW	27.05 TQ	OHBLS	10/01-12/01
Powerhouse, Substation, and Relay	Columbus MSA, OH	H	18.09 FQ	22.97 AW	29.39 TQ	OHBLS	10/01-12/01
Powerhouse, Substation, and Relay	Oklahoma	H	13.00 FQ	21.80 AW	27.53 TQ	OKBLS	10/01-12/01
Powerhouse, Substation, and Relay	Oklahoma City MSA, OK	H	18.07 FQ	23.82 AW	28.20 TQ	OKBLS	10/01-12/01
Powerhouse, Substation, and Relay	Tulsa MSA, OK	H	18.72 FQ	23.10 AW	26.89 TQ	OKBLS	10/01-12/01
Powerhouse, Substation, and Relay	Oregon	H	22.51 FQ	28.50 AW	34.93 TQ	ORBLS	10/01-12/01
Powerhouse, Substation, and Relay	Portland-Vancouver PMSA, OR-WA	H	22.29 FQ	25.97 AW	32.75 TQ	ORBLS	10/01-12/01
Powerhouse, Substation, and Relay	Pennsylvania	H	19.60 FQ	25.76 AW	34.08 TQ	PABLS	10/01-12/01
Powerhouse, Substation, and Relay	Harrisburg-Lebanon-Carlisle MSA, PA	H	18.70 FQ	26.52 AW	40.41 TQ	PABLS	10/01-12/01
Powerhouse, Substation, and Relay	Philadelphia PMSA, PA-NJ	H	18.87 FQ	26.10 AW	33.29 TQ	PABLS	10/01-12/01
Powerhouse, Substation, and Relay	Pittsburgh MSA, PA	H	18.11 FQ	24.10 AW	28.72 TQ	PABLS	10/01-12/01
Powerhouse, Substation, and Relay	South Carolina	H	12.04 FQ	18.64 AW	26.97 TQ	SCBLS	10/01-12/01
Powerhouse, Substation, and Relay	South Dakota	H	15.40 FQ	23.44 AW	31.72 TQ	SDBLS	10/01-12/01
Powerhouse, Substation, and Relay	Tennessee	H	14.80 FQ	19.51 AW	27.73 TQ	TNBLS	10/01-12/01
Powerhouse, Substation, and Relay	Nashville MSA, TN	H	14.40 FQ	22.69 AW	31.45 TQ	TNBLS	10/01-12/01
Powerhouse, Substation, and Relay	Texas	H	14.46 FQ	21.69 AW	27.71 TQ	TXBLS	10/01-12/01
Powerhouse, Substation, and Relay	Austin-San Marcos MSA, TX	H	14.83 FQ	21.83 AW	30.85 TQ	TXBLS	10/01-12/01
Powerhouse, Substation, and Relay	Corpus Christi MSA, TX	H	19.20 FQ	23.84 AW	27.87 TQ	TXBLS	10/01-12/01
Powerhouse, Substation, and Relay	Dallas PMSA, TX	H	12.17 FQ	18.28 AW	23.36 TQ	TXBLS	10/01-12/01
Powerhouse, Substation, and Relay	Houston PMSA, TX	H	16.76 FQ	23.66 AW	28.05 TQ	TXBLS	10/01-12/01
Powerhouse, Substation, and Relay	Longview-Marshall MSA, TX	H	19.34 FQ	23.69 AW	27.52 TQ	TXBLS	10/01-12/01
Powerhouse, Substation, and Relay	San Antonio MSA, TX	H	11.55 FQ	15.96 AW	21.11 TQ	TXBLS	10/01-12/01
Powerhouse, Substation, and Relay	Utah	H	19.16 FQ	25.00 AW	32.16 TQ	UTBLS	10/01-12/01
Powerhouse, Substation, and Relay	Salt Lake City-Ogden MSA, UT	H	19.06 FQ	24.19 AW	28.91 TQ	UTBLS	10/01-12/01
Powerhouse, Substation, and Relay	Vermont	H	15.46 FQ	21.74 AW	26.84 TQ	VTBLS	10/01-12/01
Powerhouse, Substation, and Relay	Virginia	H	21.09 FQ	24.50 AW	28.17 TQ	VABLS	10/01-12/01
Powerhouse, Substation, and Relay	Norfolk-Virginia Beach-Newport News MSA, VA-NC	H	21.84 FQ	24.17 AW	27.43 TQ	VABLS	10/01-12/01
Powerhouse, Substation, and Relay	Washington	H	21.55 FQ	26.86 AW	34.72 TQ	WABLS	10/01-12/01
Powerhouse, Substation, and Relay	Richland-Kennewick-Pasco MSA, WA	H	23.16 FQ	27.39 AW	34.50 TQ	WABLS	10/01-12/01
Powerhouse, Substation, and Relay	West Virginia	H	19.94 FQ	23.85 AW	27.60 TQ	WVBLS	10/01-12/01
Powerhouse, Substation, and Relay	Charleston MSA, WV	H	22.05 FQ	24.37 AW	27.17 TQ	WVBLS	10/01-12/01
Powerhouse, Substation, and Relay	Wisconsin	H	17.37 FQ	25.54 AW	33.90 TQ	WIBLS	10/01-12/01
Powerhouse, Substation, and Relay	Milwaukee-Waukesha PMSA, WI	H	13.79 FQ	25.47 AW	34.48 TQ	WIBLS	10/01-12/01
Powerhouse, Substation, and Relay	Wyoming	H	18.94 FQ	24.58 AW	30.37 TQ	WYBLS	10/01-12/01
Powerhouse, Substation, and Relay	Puerto Rico	H	11.03 FQ	15.25 AW	22.54 TQ	PRBLS	10/01-12/01
Electrical Engineer	Alabama	Y	40580 FQ	63230 AW	87480 TQ	ALBLS	10/01-12/01
	Birmingham MSA, AL	Y	46890 FQ	63890 AW	81170 TQ	ALBLS	10/01-12/01
	Huntsville MSA, AL	Y	43520 FQ	65960 AW	88920 TQ	ALBLS	10/01-12/01
	Mobile MSA, AL	Y	44090 FQ	65150 AW	87130 TQ	ALBLS	10/01-12/01
	Montgomery MSA, AL	Y	25850 FQ	48840 AW	73090 TQ	ALBLS	10/01-12/01
	Alaska	Y	45220 FQ	72450 AW	96430 TQ	AKBLS	10/01-12/01
	Anchorage MSA, AK	Y	45210 FQ	73030 AW	98350 TQ	AKBLS	10/01-12/01
	Arizona	Y	45270 FQ	73840 AW	113190 TQ	AZBLS	10/01-12/01
	Phoenix-Mesa MSA, AZ	Y	46220 FQ	74320 AW	112970 TQ	AZBLS	10/01-12/01
	Tucson MSA, AZ	Y	36790 FQ	74310 AW	117350 TQ	AZBLS	10/01-12/01
	Arkansas	Y	42720 FQ	61660 AW	85090 TQ	ARBLS	10/01-12/01
	Fayetteville-Springdale-Rogers MSA, AR	Y	39360 FQ	62610 AW	90770 TQ	ARBLS	10/01-12/01

AAW	Average annual wage	**AOH**	Average offered, high	**ASH**	Average starting, high	**H**	Hourly	**M**	Monthly	**S**	Special: hourly and annual
AE	Average entry wage	**AOL**	Average offered, low	**ASL**	Average starting, low	**HI**	Highest wage paid	**MTC**	Median total compensation	**TQ**	Third quartile wage
AEX	Average experienced wage	**APH**	Average pay, high range	**AW**	Average wage paid	**HR**	High end range	**MW**	Median wage paid	**W**	Weekly
AO	Average offered	**APL**	Average pay, low range	**FQ**	First quartile wage	**LR**	Low end range	**SQ**	Second quartile wage	**Y**	Yearly

Occupation/Type/Industry	Location	Per	Low	Mid	High	Source	Date
Electrical Engineer	Little Rock-North Little Rock MSA, AR	Y	44110 FQ	58300 AW	80470 TQ	ARBLS	10/01-12/01
	California	Y	44610 FQ	74900 AW	113270 TQ	CABLS	10/01-12/01
	Bakersfield MSA, CA	Y	46800 FQ	67890 AW	89400 TQ	CABLS	10/01-12/01
	Fresno MSA, CA	Y	43260 FQ	57990 AW	74840 TQ	CABLS	10/01-12/01
	Los Angeles-Long Beach PMSA, CA	Y	45640 FQ	71330 AW	104360 TQ	CABLS	10/01-12/01
	Modesto MSA, CA	Y	46600 FQ	78410 AW	118870 TQ	CABLS	10/01-12/01
	Oakland PMSA, CA	Y	25780 FQ	70040 AW	113370 TQ	CABLS	10/01-12/01
	Orange County PMSA, CA	Y	43230 FQ	66630 AW	96040 TQ	CABLS	10/01-12/01
	Redding MSA, CA	Y	38190 FQ	65800 AW	107420 TQ	CABLS	10/01-12/01
	Riverside-San Bernardino PMSA, CA	Y	41980 FQ	64730 AW	89420 TQ	CABLS	10/01-12/01
	Sacramento PMSA, CA	Y	48260 FQ	75990 AW	138080 TQ	CABLS	10/01-12/01
	Salinas MSA, CA	Y	56850 FQ	66200 AW	79030 TQ	CABLS	10/01-12/01
	San Diego MSA, CA	Y	24150 FQ	63530 AW	104840 TQ	CABLS	10/01-12/01
	San Francisco PMSA, CA	Y	51100 FQ	75770 AW	105800 TQ	CABLS	10/01-12/01
	San Jose PMSA, CA	Y	56710 FQ	88320 AW	129700 TQ	CABLS	10/01-12/01
	San Luis Obispo-Atascadero-Paso Robles MSA, CA	Y	38250 FQ	53580 AW	76950 TQ	CABLS	10/01-12/01
	Santa Barbara-Santa Maria-Lompoc MSA, CA	Y	47600 FQ	69130 AW	102070 TQ	CABLS	10/01-12/01
	Santa Cruz-Watsonville PMSA, CA	Y	20390 FQ	53940 AW	111650 TQ	CABLS	10/01-12/01
	Santa Rosa PMSA, CA	Y	52820 FQ	74190 AW	95880 TQ	CABLS	10/01-12/01
	Stockton-Lodi MSA, CA	Y	48770 FQ	63530 AW	85380 TQ	CABLS	10/01-12/01
	Vallejo-Fairfield-Napa PMSA, CA	Y	50550 FQ	72860 AW	93120 TQ	CABLS	10/01-12/01
	Ventura PMSA, CA	Y	51870 FQ	78700 AW	116810 TQ	CABLS	10/01-12/01
	Visalia-Tulare-Porterville MSA, CA	Y	44740 FQ	64310 AW	84530 TQ	CABLS	10/01-12/01
	Colorado	Y	44950 FQ	66130 AW	91950 TQ	COBLS	10/01-12/01
	Boulder-Longmont PMSA, CO	Y	47690 FQ	64670 AW	90680 TQ	COBLS	10/01-12/01
	Colorado Springs MSA, CO	Y	42840 FQ	64960 AW	89670 TQ	COBLS	10/01-12/01
	Denver PMSA, CO	Y	43630 FQ	65880 AW	91340 TQ	COBLS	10/01-12/01
	Fort Collins-Loveland MSA, CO	Y	45120 FQ	71430 AW	102100 TQ	COBLS	10/01-12/01
	Connecticut	Y	44280 FQ	67140 AW	92680 TQ	CTBLS	10/01-12/01
	Bridgeport PMSA, CT	Y	46380 FQ	68880 AW	95180 TQ	CTBLS	10/01-12/01
	Danbury PMSA, CT	Y	47660 FQ	71490 AW	96920 TQ	CTBLS	10/01-12/01
	Hartford MSA, CT	Y	46900 FQ	66430 AW	88940 TQ	CTBLS	10/01-12/01
	New Haven-Meriden PMSA, CT	Y	47700 FQ	68430 AW	98820 TQ	CTBLS	10/01-12/01
	New London-Norwich MSA, CT-RI	Y	40540 FQ	63690 AW	88860 TQ	CTBLS	10/01-12/01
	Stamford-Norwalk PMSA, CT	Y	44760 FQ	73680 AW	100840 TQ	CTBLS	10/01-12/01
	Waterbury PMSA, CT	Y	39790 FQ	56710 AW	86330 TQ	CTBLS	10/01-12/01
	Delaware	Y	40430 FQ	62040 AW	88560 TQ	DEBLS	10/01-12/01
	Wilmington-Newark PMSA, DE-MD	Y	40170 FQ	61940 AW	88600 TQ	DEBLS	10/01-12/01
	District of Columbia	Y	53060 FQ	75390 AW	104280 TQ	DCBLS	10/01-12/01
	Washington PMSA, DC-MD-VA-WV	Y	49680 FQ	72570 AW	102480 TQ	DCBLS	10/01-12/01
	Florida	Y	42940 FQ	63550 AW	88860 TQ	FLBLS	10/01-12/01
	Daytona Beach MSA, FL	Y	46300 FQ	63190 AW	91190 TQ	FLBLS	10/01-12/01
	Fort Lauderdale PMSA, FL	Y	48270 FQ	64930 AW	86780 TQ	FLBLS	10/01-12/01
	Fort Myers-Cape Coral MSA, FL	Y	40160 FQ	60540 AW	89050 TQ	FLBLS	10/01-12/01
	Fort Walton Beach MSA, FL	Y	44520 FQ	67660 AW	89880 TQ	FLBLS	10/01-12/01
	Gainesville MSA, FL	Y	45920 FQ	61460 AW	81410 TQ	FLBLS	10/01-12/01
	Jacksonville MSA, FL	Y	41060 FQ	62460 AW	90160 TQ	FLBLS	10/01-12/01
	Lakeland-Winter Haven MSA, FL	Y	40850 FQ	60760 AW	87780 TQ	FLBLS	10/01-12/01
	Melbourne-Titusville-Palm Bay MSA, FL	Y	41650 FQ	61420 AW	85610 TQ	FLBLS	10/01-12/01
	Miami PMSA, FL	Y	42010 FQ	67010 AW	105120 TQ	FLBLS	10/01-12/01
	Naples MSA, FL	Y	57660 FQ	63100 AW	70580 TQ	FLBLS	10/01-12/01
	Ocala MSA, FL	Y	40470 FQ	59630 AW	78160 TQ	FLBLS	10/01-12/01
	Orlando MSA, FL	Y	41400 FQ	60570 AW	85070 TQ	FLBLS	10/01-12/01
	Pensacola MSA, FL	Y	47620 FQ	69040 AW	96180 TQ	FLBLS	10/01-12/01
	Sarasota-Bradenton MSA, FL	Y	41230 FQ	64730 AW	104840 TQ	FLBLS	10/01-12/01
	Tallahassee MSA, FL	Y	38290 FQ	63150 AW	88870 TQ	FLBLS	10/01-12/01

AAW	Average annual wage	**AOH**	Average offered, high	**ASH**	Average starting, high	**H**	Hourly	**M**	Monthly	**S**	Special: hourly and annual
AE	Average entry wage	**AOL**	Average offered, low	**ASL**	Average starting, low	**HI**	Highest wage paid	**MTC**	Median total compensation	**TQ**	Third quartile wage
AEX	Average experienced wage	**APH**	Average pay, high range	**AW**	Average wage paid	**HR**	High end range	**MW**	Median wage paid	**W**	Weekly
AO	Average offered	**APL**	Average pay, low range	**FQ**	First quartile wage	**LR**	Low end range	**SQ**	Second quartile wage	**Y**	Yearly

Occupation/Type/Industry	Location	Per	Low	Mid	High	Source	Date
Electrical Engineer	Tampa-St. Petersburg-Clearwater MSA, FL	Y	43320 FQ	65000 AW	90730 TQ	FLBLS	10/01-12/01
	West Palm Beach-Boca Raton MSA, FL	Y	33240 FQ	59570 AW	86430 TQ	FLBLS	10/01-12/01
	Georgia	Y	45930 FQ	64530 AW	89820 TQ	GABLS	10/01-12/01
	Atlanta MSA, GA	Y	46560 FQ	64820 AW	89650 TQ	GABLS	10/01-12/01
	Macon MSA, GA	Y	47080 FQ	60870 AW	79500 TQ	GABLS	10/01-12/01
	Savannah MSA, GA	Y	44850 FQ	65660 AW	94520 TQ	GABLS	10/01-12/01
	Hawaii	Y	45640 FQ	66570 AW	88610 TQ	HIBLS	10/01-12/01
	Honolulu MSA, HI	Y	45630 FQ	66340 AW	87650 TQ	HIBLS	10/01-12/01
	Idaho	Y	34170 FQ	65330 AW	89160 TQ	IDBLS	10/01-12/01
	Illinois	Y	35730 FQ	60800 AW	89070 TQ	ILBLS	10/01-12/01
	Champaign-Urbana MSA, IL	Y	39470 FQ	58160 AW	80120 TQ	ILBLS	10/01-12/01
	Chicago PMSA, IL	Y	34210 FQ	60800 AW	89290 TQ	ILBLS	10/01-12/01
	Peoria-Pekin MSA, IL	Y	38450 FQ	57230 AW	84820 TQ	ILBLS	10/01-12/01
	Rockford MSA, IL	Y	42390 FQ	61020 AW	86930 TQ	ILBLS	10/01-12/01
	Indiana	Y	38290 FQ	59000 AW	84230 TQ	INBLS	10/01-12/01
	Elkhart-Goshen MSA, IN	Y	38150 FQ	70900 AW		INBLS	10/01-12/01
	Evansville-Henderson MSA, IN-KY	Y	38680 FQ	57600 AW	80760 TQ	INBLS	10/01-12/01
	Fort Wayne MSA, IN	Y	45290 FQ	61010 AW	84120 TQ	INBLS	10/01-12/01
	Gary PMSA, IN	Y	34740 FQ	56220 AW	81810 TQ	INBLS	10/01-12/01
	Indianapolis MSA, IN	Y	37680 FQ	58970 AW	84920 TQ	INBLS	10/01-12/01
	Lafayette MSA, IN	Y	47550 FQ	61010 AW	81080 TQ	INBLS	10/01-12/01
	South Bend MSA, IN	Y	43520 FQ	55830 AW	75330 TQ	INBLS	10/01-12/01
	Iowa	Y	44790 FQ	62120 AW	88200 TQ	IABLS	10/01-12/01
	Davenport-Moline-Rock Island MSA, IA-IL	Y	40370 FQ	63010 AW	94470 TQ	IABLS	10/01-12/01
	Des Moines MSA, IA	Y	43390 FQ	59090 AW	74110 TQ	IABLS	10/01-12/01
	Kansas	Y	41650 FQ	61510 AW	90220 TQ	KSBLS	10/01-12/01
	Topeka MSA, KS	Y	40950 FQ	60880 AW	90420 TQ	KSBLS	10/01-12/01
	Wichita MSA, KS	Y	38950 FQ	59450 AW	99620 TQ	KSBLS	10/01-12/01
	Kentucky	Y	41660 FQ	61220 AW	84940 TQ	KYBLS	10/01-12/01
	Lexington MSA, KY	Y	39290 FQ	61700 AW	87820 TQ	KYBLS	10/01-12/01
	Louisville MSA, KY-IN	Y	42300 FQ	63800 AW	88140 TQ	KYBLS	10/01-12/01
	Louisiana	Y	45450 FQ	69140 AW	100760 TQ	LABLS	10/01-12/01
	Baton Rouge MSA, LA	Y	49380 FQ	76780 AW	109810 TQ	LABLS	10/01-12/01
	Lafayette MSA, LA	Y	45500 FQ	71700 AW	109430 TQ	LABLS	10/01-12/01
	Lake Charles MSA, LA	Y	45910 FQ	68480 AW	94330 TQ	LABLS	10/01-12/01
	New Orleans MSA, LA	Y	45400 FQ	67730 AW	92540 TQ	LABLS	10/01-12/01
	Shreveport-Bossier City MSA, LA	Y	26950 FQ	63340 AW	107310 TQ	LABLS	10/01-12/01
	Maine	Y	46120 FQ	63530 AW	88030 TQ	MEBLS	10/01-12/01
	Maryland	Y	44830 FQ	70290 AW	105540 TQ	MDBLS	10/01-12/01
	Baltimore PMSA, MD	Y	45070 FQ	73080 AW	113450 TQ	MDBLS	10/01-12/01
	Massachusetts	Y	49810 FQ	76250 AW	111130 TQ	MABLS	10/01-12/01
	Boston PMSA, MA-NH	Y	49650 FQ	77040 AW	114120 TQ	MABLS	10/01-12/01
	Brockton PMSA, MA	Y	46740 FQ	63990 AW	87130 TQ	MABLS	10/01-12/01
	Lawrence PMSA, MA-NH	Y	50470 FQ	78320 AW	114180 TQ	MABLS	10/01-12/01
	Lowell PMSA, MA-NH	Y	51310 FQ	76490 AW	98290 TQ	MABLS	10/01-12/01
	Springfield MSA, MA	Y	47030 FQ	75010 AW	110700 TQ	MABLS	10/01-12/01
	Worcester PMSA, MA-CT	Y	53790 FQ	74170 AW	98170 TQ	MABLS	10/01-12/01
	Michigan	Y	42840 FQ	65490 AW	91730 TQ	MIBLS	10/01-12/01
	Ann Arbor PMSA, MI	Y	50090 FQ	71780 AW	90850 TQ	MIBLS	10/01-12/01
	Detroit PMSA, MI	Y	47040 FQ	69020 AW	93730 TQ	MIBLS	10/01-12/01
	Flint PMSA, MI	Y	45200 FQ	65280 AW	90230 TQ	MIBLS	10/01-12/01
	Grand Rapids-Muskegon-Holland MSA, MI	Y	38810 FQ	57590 AW	84730 TQ	MIBLS	10/01-12/01
	Kalamazoo-Battle Creek MSA, MI	Y	45400 FQ	62870 AW	89230 TQ	MIBLS	10/01-12/01
	Lansing-East Lansing MSA, MI	Y	37130 FQ	59570 AW	86840 TQ	MIBLS	10/01-12/01
	Saginaw-Bay City-Midland MSA, MI	Y	40880 FQ	61030 AW	88140 TQ	MIBLS	10/01-12/01
	Minnesota	Y	46410 FQ	65340 AW	89470 TQ	MNBLS	10/01-12/01
	Duluth-Superior MSA, MN-WI	Y	42420 FQ	66010 AW	90220 TQ	MNBLS	10/01-12/01
	Minneapolis-St. Paul MSA, MN-WI	Y	47640 FQ	67470 AW	91270 TQ	MNBLS	10/01-12/01
	St. Cloud MSA, MN	Y	47070 FQ	58310 AW	76010 TQ	MNBLS	10/01-12/01
	Mississippi	Y	33450 FQ	51990 AW	76570 TQ	MSBLS	10/01-12/01
	Jackson MSA, MS	Y	37250 FQ	49330 AW	69370 TQ	MSBLS	10/01-12/01
	Missouri	Y	41680 FQ	61730 AW	86640 TQ	MOBLS	10/01-12/01
	Kansas City MSA, MO-KS	Y	44090 FQ	64820 AW	90780 TQ	MOBLS	10/01-12/01

AAW Average annual wage; **AE** Average entry wage; **AEX** Average experienced wage; **AO** Average offered; **AOH** Average offered, high; **AOL** Average offered, low; **APH** Average pay, high range; **APL** Average pay, low range; **ASH** Average starting, high; **ASL** Average starting, low; **AW** Average wage paid; **FQ** First quartile wage; **H** Hourly; **HI** Highest wage paid; **HR** High end range; **LR** Low end range; **M** Monthly; **MTC** Median total compensation; **MW** Median wage paid; **SQ** Second quartile wage; **S** Special: hourly and annual; **TQ** Third quartile wage; **W** Weekly; **Y** Yearly

Occupation/Type/Industry	Location	Per	Low	Mid	High	Source	Date
Electrical Engineer	St. Louis MSA, MO-IL	Y	43930 FQ	60680 AW	83390 TQ	MOBLS	10/01-12/01
	Springfield MSA, MO	Y	38460 FQ	57500 AW	84750 TQ	MOBLS	10/01-12/01
	Montana	Y	20670 FQ	53330 AW	77830 TQ	MTBLS	10/01-12/01
	Billings MSA, MT	Y	46260 FQ	65900 AW	95040 TQ	MTBLS	10/01-12/01
	Nebraska	Y	42200 FQ	63800 AW	90480 TQ	NEBLS	10/01-12/01
	Lincoln MSA, NE	Y	40780 FQ	59440 AW	84890 TQ	NEBLS	10/01-12/01
	Omaha MSA, NE-IA	Y	43050 FQ	63330 AW	88510 TQ	NEBLS	10/01-12/01
	Nevada	Y	42750 FQ	66000 AW	92640 TQ	NVBLS	10/01-12/01
	Las Vegas MSA, NV-AZ	Y	41210 FQ	68230 AW	93080 TQ	NVBLS	10/01-12/01
	Reno MSA, NV	Y	45380 FQ	66190 AW	93460 TQ	NVBLS	10/01-12/01
	New Hampshire	Y	48240 FQ	73850 AW	106340 TQ	NHBLS	10/01-12/01
	Manchester PMSA, NH	Y	50540 FQ	68610 AW	91010 TQ	NHBLS	10/01-12/01
	Portsmouth-Rochester PMSA, NH-ME	Y	45310 FQ	61820 AW	81360 TQ	NHBLS	10/01-12/01
	New Jersey	Y	46220 FQ	70180 AW	101340 TQ	NJBLS	10/01-12/01
	Atlantic-Cape May PMSA, NJ	Y	47070 FQ	68690 AW	97000 TQ	NJBLS	10/01-12/01
	Bergen-Passaic PMSA, NJ	Y	44740 FQ	61100 AW	86560 TQ	NJBLS	10/01-12/01
	Jersey City PMSA, NJ	Y	46640 FQ	73260 AW	109840 TQ	NJBLS	10/01-12/01
	Middlesex-Somerset-Hunterdon PMSA, NJ	Y	47800 FQ	78140 AW	110120 TQ	NJBLS	10/01-12/01
	Monmouth-Ocean PMSA, NJ	Y	46950 FQ	77300 AW	110820 TQ	NJBLS	10/01-12/01
	Newark PMSA, NJ	Y	46820 FQ	70580 AW	96820 TQ	NJBLS	10/01-12/01
	Trenton PMSA, NJ	Y	43200 FQ	63670 AW	90240 TQ	NJBLS	10/01-12/01
	New Mexico	Y	49960 FQ	75330 AW	107820 TQ	NMBLS	10/01-12/01
	Albuquerque MSA, NM	Y	51570 FQ	74260 AW	104120 TQ	NMBLS	10/01-12/01
	New York	Y	44830 FQ	69400 AW	98740 TQ	NYBLS	10/01-12/01
	Albany-Schenectady-Troy MSA, NY	Y	42000 FQ	60280 AW	82340 TQ	NYBLS	10/01-12/01
	Binghamton MSA, NY	Y	46180 FQ	65480 AW	92950 TQ	NYBLS	10/01-12/01
	Buffalo-Niagara Falls MSA, NY	Y	42830 FQ	59440 AW	82320 TQ	NYBLS	10/01-12/01
	Nassau-Suffolk PMSA, NY	Y	49290 FQ	75590 AW	103700 TQ	NYBLS	10/01-12/01
	New York PMSA, NY	Y	45760 FQ	73130 AW	109630 TQ	NYBLS	10/01-12/01
	Rochester MSA, NY	Y	40580 FQ	66970 AW	100230 TQ	NYBLS	10/01-12/01
	Syracuse MSA, NY	Y	45250 FQ	69860 AW	98950 TQ	NYBLS	10/01-12/01
	Utica-Rome MSA, NY	Y	46920 FQ	70920 AW	93880 TQ	NYBLS	10/01-12/01
	North Carolina	Y	45280 FQ	67530 AW	93330 TQ	NCBLS	10/01-12/01
	Asheville MSA, NC	Y	39430 FQ	57230 AW	72740 TQ	NCBLS	10/01-12/01
	Charlotte-Gastonia-Rock Hill MSA, NC-SC	Y	44260 FQ	63500 AW	89920 TQ	NCBLS	10/01-12/01
	Raleigh-Durham-Chapel Hill MSA, NC	Y	46520 FQ	68870 AW	97800 TQ	NCBLS	10/01-12/01
	Wilmington MSA, NC	Y	51830 FQ	68890 AW	87930 TQ	NCBLS	10/01-12/01
	North Dakota	Y	43040 FQ	61820 AW	88050 TQ	NDBLS	10/01-12/01
	Ohio	Y	41130 FQ	62780 AW	87930 TQ	OHBLS	10/01-12/01
	Akron PMSA, OH	Y	37930 FQ	59990 AW	86520 TQ	OHBLS	10/01-12/01
	Canton-Massillon MSA, OH	Y	37570 FQ	61380 AW	86610 TQ	OHBLS	10/01-12/01
	Cincinnati PMSA, OH-KY-IN	Y	40320 FQ	60010 AW	82830 TQ	OHBLS	10/01-12/01
	Cleveland-Lorain-Elyria PMSA, OH	Y	44640 FQ	65290 AW	90880 TQ	OHBLS	10/01-12/01
	Columbus MSA, OH	Y	41350 FQ	63680 AW	90570 TQ	OHBLS	10/01-12/01
	Dayton-Springfield MSA, OH	Y	45140 FQ	66150 AW	87630 TQ	OHBLS	10/01-12/01
	Hamilton-Middletown PMSA, OH	Y	37870 FQ	61160 AW	93840 TQ	OHBLS	10/01-12/01
	Mansfield MSA, OH	Y	39370 FQ	56960 AW	72920 TQ	OHBLS	10/01-12/01
	Toledo MSA, OH	Y	39110 FQ	61690 AW	92740 TQ	OHBLS	10/01-12/01
	Youngstown-Warren MSA, OH	Y	32910 FQ	53430 AW	77970 TQ	OHBLS	10/01-12/01
	Oklahoma	Y	32500 FQ	57980 AW	86070 TQ	OKBLS	10/01-12/01
	Oklahoma City MSA, OK	Y	38440 FQ	59770 AW	85370 TQ	OKBLS	10/01-12/01
	Tulsa MSA, OK	Y	42940 FQ	63340 AW	88920 TQ	OKBLS	10/01-12/01
	Oregon	Y	48830 FQ	68900 AW	92570 TQ	ORBLS	10/01-12/01
	Eugene-Springfield MSA, OR	Y	47490 FQ	68990 AW	92300 TQ	ORBLS	10/01-12/01
	Portland-Vancouver PMSA, OR-WA	Y	49410 FQ	69750 AW	92410 TQ	ORBLS	10/01-12/01
	Salem PMSA, OR	Y	49830 FQ	67750 AW	88940 TQ	ORBLS	10/01-12/01
	Pennsylvania	Y	42890 FQ	64700 AW	89830 TQ	PABLS	10/01-12/01
	Allentown-Bethlehem-Easton MSA, PA	Y	46590 FQ	70460 AW	96010 TQ	PABLS	10/01-12/01
	Erie MSA, PA	Y	38430 FQ	55290 AW	78550 TQ	PABLS	10/01-12/01
	Harrisburg-Lebanon-Carlisle MSA, PA	Y	39690 FQ	58990 AW	82640 TQ	PABLS	10/01-12/01
	Johnstown MSA, PA	Y	39350 FQ	61490 AW	83300 TQ	PABLS	10/01-12/01

AAW	Average annual wage	**AOH**	Average offered, high	**ASH**	Average starting, high	**H**	Hourly	**M**	Monthly	**S**	Special: hourly and annual
AE	Average entry wage	**AOL**	Average offered, low	**ASL**	Average starting, low	**HI**	Highest wage paid	**MTC**	Median total compensation	**TQ**	Third quartile wage
AEX	Average experienced wage	**APH**	Average pay, high range	**AW**	Average wage paid	**HR**	High end range	**MW**	Median wage paid	**W**	Weekly
AO	Average offered	**APL**	Average pay, low range	**FQ**	First quartile wage	**LR**	Low end range	**SQ**	Second quartile wage	**Y**	Yearly

Occupation/Type/Industry	Location	Per	Low	Mid	High	Source	Date
Electrical Engineer	Lancaster MSA, PA	Y	41190 FQ	59110 AW	74670 TQ	PABLS	10/01-12/01
	Philadelphia PMSA, PA-NJ	Y	44020 FQ	67580 AW	92990 TQ	PABLS	10/01-12/01
	Pittsburgh MSA, PA	Y	47660 FQ	66660 AW	90700 TQ	PABLS	10/01-12/01
	Reading MSA, PA	Y	40440 FQ	58180 AW	76990 TQ	PABLS	10/01-12/01
	Scranton-Wilkes-Barre-Hazleton MSA, PA	Y	40490 FQ	58560 AW	81980 TQ	PABLS	10/01-12/01
	York MSA, PA	Y	37060 FQ	56730 AW	81180 TQ	PABLS	10/01-12/01
	Rhode Island	Y	40450 FQ	57220 AW	79830 TQ	RIBLS	10/01-12/01
	Providence-Fall River-Warwick MSA, RI-MA	Y	41490 FQ	61320 AW	87490 TQ	RIBLS	10/01-12/01
	South Carolina	Y	41810 FQ	65680 AW	94860 TQ	SCBLS	10/01-12/01
	Charleston-North Charleston MSA, SC	Y	22540 FQ	53430 AW	79020 TQ	SCBLS	10/01-12/01
	Columbia MSA, SC	Y	46380 FQ	60620 AW	84650 TQ	SCBLS	10/01-12/01
	Greenville-Spartanburg-Anderson MSA, SC	Y	45140 FQ	65170 AW	91360 TQ	SCBLS	10/01-12/01
	South Dakota	Y	41890 FQ	57970 AW	77110 TQ	SDBLS	10/01-12/01
	Sioux Falls MSA, SD	Y	43180 FQ	58810 AW	74930 TQ	SDBLS	10/01-12/01
	Tennessee	Y	44640 FQ	62270 AW	87720 TQ	TNBLS	10/01-12/01
	Chattanooga MSA, TN-GA	Y	48650 FQ	69250 AW	90210 TQ	TNBLS	10/01-12/01
	Clarksville-Hopkinsville MSA, TN-KY	Y	46090 FQ	58310 AW	76150 TQ	TNBLS	10/01-12/01
	Johnson City-Kingsport-Bristol MSA, TN-VA	Y	38400 FQ	55860 AW	76510 TQ	TNBLS	10/01-12/01
	Knoxville MSA, TN	Y	46410 FQ	66650 AW	90570 TQ	TNBLS	10/01-12/01
	Memphis MSA, TN-AR-MS	Y	36570 FQ	62700 AW	92550 TQ	TNBLS	10/01-12/01
	Nashville MSA, TN	Y	40130 FQ	59380 AW	84500 TQ	TNBLS	10/01-12/01
	Texas	Y	49120 FQ	75000 AW	107340 TQ	TXBLS	10/01-12/01
	Austin-San Marcos MSA, TX	Y	53330 FQ	81380 AW	119960 TQ	TXBLS	10/01-12/01
	Beaumont-Port Arthur MSA, TX	Y	48970 FQ	66720 AW	93220 TQ	TXBLS	10/01-12/01
	Brazoria PMSA, TX	Y	50410 FQ	80940 AW	114920 TQ	TXBLS	10/01-12/01
	Corpus Christi MSA, TX	Y	41010 FQ	63780 AW	90940 TQ	TXBLS	10/01 12/01
	Dallas PMSA, TX	Y	49020 FQ	72760 AW	102190 TQ	TXBLS	10/01-12/01
	El Paso MSA, TX	Y	50720 FQ	67990 AW	90030 TQ	TXBLS	10/01-12/01
	Fort Worth-Arlington PMSA, TX	Y	46040 FQ	66670 AW	93700 TQ	TXBLS	10/01-12/01
	Galveston-Texas City PMSA, TX	Y	49960 FQ	74900 AW	109360 TQ	TXBLS	10/01-12/01
	Houston PMSA, TX	Y	49630 FQ	78030 AW	107960 TQ	TXBLS	10/01-12/01
	Killeen-Temple MSA, TX	Y	45790 FQ	62460 AW	87060 TQ	TXBLS	10/01-12/01
	Longview-Marshall MSA, TX	Y	49300 FQ	70920 AW	100710 TQ	TXBLS	10/01-12/01
	Lubbock MSA, TX	Y	43150 FQ	60060 AW	80300 TQ	TXBLS	10/01-12/01
	San Antonio MSA, TX	Y	46730 FQ	69770 AW	96750 TQ	TXBLS	10/01-12/01
	Tyler MSA, TX	Y	51180 FQ	72630 AW	98030 TQ	TXBLS	10/01-12/01
	Waco MSA, TX	Y	47660 FQ	67040 AW	88850 TQ	TXBLS	10/01-12/01
	Utah	Y	42530 FQ	65610 AW	92470 TQ	UTBLS	10/01-12/01
	Provo-Orem MSA, UT	Y	44920 FQ	60500 AW	76790 TQ	UTBLS	10/01-12/01
	Salt Lake City-Ogden MSA, UT	Y	44350 FQ	68010 AW	98400 TQ	UTBLS	10/01-12/01
	Vermont	Y	42520 FQ	66790 AW	96320 TQ	VTBLS	10/01-12/01
	Burlington MSA, VT	Y	43520 FQ	70570 AW	99250 TQ	VTBLS	10/01-12/01
	Virginia	Y	45730 FQ	68010 AW	94110 TQ	VABLS	10/01-12/01
	Lynchburg MSA, VA	Y	33950 FQ	51880 AW	77190 TQ	VABLS	10/01-12/01
	Norfolk-Virginia Beach-Newport News MSA, VA-NC	Y	40120 FQ	56010 AW	74470 TQ	VABLS	10/01-12/01
	Richmond-Petersburg MSA, VA	Y	43490 FQ	63320 AW	86200 TQ	VABLS	10/01-12/01
	Roanoke MSA, VA	Y	40690 FQ	67200 AW	97720 TQ	VABLS	10/01-12/01
	Washington	Y	48250 FQ	70650 AW	93860 TQ	WABLS	10/01-12/01
	Bremerton PMSA, WA	Y	41440 FQ	60110 AW	72630 TQ	WABLS	10/01-12/01
	Richland-Kennewick-Pasco MSA, WA	Y	58420 FQ	79060 AW	108490 TQ	WABLS	10/01-12/01
	Seattle-Bellevue-Everett PMSA, WA	Y	49890 FQ	71960 AW	94830 TQ	WABLS	10/01-12/01
	Spokane MSA, WA	Y	41020 FQ	58860 AW	82130 TQ	WABLS	10/01-12/01
	Tacoma PMSA, WA	Y	47550 FQ	68380 AW	90120 TQ	WABLS	10/01-12/01
	West Virginia	Y	37050 FQ	60100 AW	84290 TQ	WVBLS	10/01-12/01
	Huntington-Ashland MSA, WV-KY-OH	Y	42180 FQ	63800 AW	88560 TQ	WVBLS	10/01-12/01
	Wisconsin	Y	41810 FQ	63300 AW	89040 TQ	WIBLS	10/01-12/01

AAW Average annual wage **AE** Average entry wage **AEX** Average experienced wage **AO** Average offered **AOH** Average offered, high **AOL** Average offered, low **APH** Average pay, high range **APL** Average pay, low range **ASH** Average starting, high **ASL** Average starting, low **AW** Average wage paid **FQ** First quartile wage **H** Hourly **HI** Highest wage paid **HR** High end range **LR** Low end range **M** Monthly **MTC** Median total compensation **MW** Median wage paid **SQ** Second quartile wage **S** Special: hourly and annual **TQ** Third quartile wage **W** Weekly **Y** Yearly

Occupation/Type/Industry	Location	Per	Low	Mid	High	Source	Date
Electrical Engineer	Appleton-Oshkosh-Neenah MSA, WI	Y	43780 FQ	60070 AW	77850 TQ	WIBLS	10/01-12/01
	Green Bay MSA, WI	Y	39790 FQ	57880 AW	79240 TQ	WIBLS	10/01-12/01
	Madison MSA, WI	Y	43010 FQ	70970 AW	145190 TQ	WIBLS	10/01-12/01
	Milwaukee-Waukesha PMSA, WI	Y	45470 FQ	66290 AW	91530 TQ	WIBLS	10/01-12/01
	Racine PMSA, WI	Y	44810 FQ	62600 AW	81260 TQ	WIBLS	10/01-12/01
	Wyoming	Y	47160 FQ	63270 AW	90050 TQ	WYBLS	10/01-12/01
	Puerto Rico	Y	26670 FQ	41370 AW	61110 TQ	PRBLS	10/01-12/01
	Guam	Y	25830 FQ	44040 AW	72460 TQ	GUBLS	10/01-12/01
Electrical Power-Line Installer and Repairer	Alabama	H	13.79 FQ	20.53 AW	26.62 TQ	ALBLS	10/01-12/01
	Birmingham MSA, AL	H	14.89 FQ	21.57 AW	26.83 TQ	ALBLS	10/01-12/01
	Mobile MSA, AL	H	16.78 FQ	19.87 AW	22.67 TQ	ALBLS	10/01-12/01
	Alaska	H	17.07 FQ	29.37 AW	35.77 TQ	AKBLS	10/01-12/01
	Arizona	H	18.40 FQ	22.95 AW	29.10 TQ	AZBLS	10/01-12/01
	Phoenix-Mesa MSA, AZ	H	18.93 FQ	23.27 AW	29.23 TQ	AZBLS	10/01-12/01
	Arkansas	H	11.33 FQ	18.31 AW	25.73 TQ	ARBLS	10/01-12/01
	Fayetteville-Springdale-Rogers MSA, AR	H	11.68 FQ	20.38 AW	27.49 TQ	ARBLS	10/01-12/01
	Fort Smith MSA, AR-OK	H	12.50 FQ	20.12 AW	27.16 TQ	ARBLS	10/01-12/01
	Little Rock-North Little Rock MSA, AR	H	11.27 FQ	17.69 AW	24.75 TQ	ARBLS	10/01-12/01
	California	H	11.79 FQ	25.05 AW	33.77 TQ	CABLS	10/01-12/01
	Los Angeles-Long Beach PMSA, CA	H	22.00 FQ	26.87 AW	33.38 TQ	CABLS	10/01-12/01
	Riverside-San Bernardino PMSA, CA	H	9.92 FQ	22.08 AW	33.18 TQ	CABLS	10/01-12/01
	Sacramento PMSA, CA	H	23.47 FQ	28.27 AW	34.18 TQ	CABLS	10/01-12/01
	Vallejo-Fairfield-Napa PMSA, CA	H	9.11 FQ	17.69 AW	32.21 TQ	CABLS	10/01-12/01
	Colorado	H	6.65 FQ	19.67 AW	27.56 TQ	COBLS	10/01-12/01
	Denver PMSA, CO	H	6.28 FQ	17.60 AW	27.24 TQ	COBLS	10/01-12/01
	Connecticut	H	17.37 FQ	25.37 AW	33.26 TQ	CTBLS	10/01-12/01
	Hartford MSA, CT	H	17.02 FQ	25.74 AW	33.65 TQ	CTBLS	10/01-12/01
	New London-Norwich MSA, CT-RI	H	17.97 FQ	23.19 AW	28.19 TQ	CTBLS	10/01-12/01
	Stamford-Norwalk PMSA, CT	H	15.94 FQ	25.76 AW	33.78 TQ	CTBLS	10/01-12/01
	Delaware	H	19.86 FQ	26.90 AW	33.74 TQ	DEBLS	10/01-12/01
	Wilmington-Newark PMSA, DE-MD	H	20.94 FQ	27.25 AW	33.92 TQ	DEBLS	10/01-12/01
	Washington PMSA, DC-MD-VA-WV	H	16.61 FQ	22.51 AW	27.07 TQ	DCBLS	10/01-12/01
	Florida	H	12.01 FQ	19.64 AW	26.57 TQ	FLBLS	10/01-12/01
	Fort Lauderdale PMSA, FL	H	12.77 FQ	18.02 AW	22.62 TQ	FLBLS	10/01-12/01
	Fort Pierce-Port St. Lucie MSA, FL	H	13.18 FQ	20.93 AW	27.91 TQ	FLBLS	10/01-12/01
	Fort Walton Beach MSA, FL	H	16.27 FQ	22.69 AW	26.69 TQ	FLBLS	10/01-12/01
	Lakeland-Winter Haven MSA, FL	H	12.99 FQ	19.44 AW	26.30 TQ	FLBLS	10/01-12/01
	Ocala MSA, FL	H	9.64 FQ	17.68 AW	26.59 TQ	FLBLS	10/01-12/01
	Orlando MSA, FL	H	11.47 FQ	19.90 AW	27.64 TQ	FLBLS	10/01-12/01
	Pensacola MSA, FL	H	13.82 FQ	21.03 AW	26.55 TQ	FLBLS	10/01-12/01
	Sarasota-Bradenton MSA, FL	H	11.97 FQ	19.02 AW	26.34 TQ	FLBLS	10/01-12/01
	Tampa-St. Petersburg-Clearwater MSA, FL	H	9.88 FQ	18.60 AW	26.71 TQ	FLBLS	10/01-12/01
	West Palm Beach-Boca Raton MSA, FL	H	13.82 FQ	20.22 AW	26.45 TQ	FLBLS	10/01-12/01
	Georgia	H	12.90 FQ	19.65 AW	26.34 TQ	GABLS	10/01-12/01
	Atlanta MSA, GA	H	12.58 FQ	19.69 AW	26.58 TQ	GABLS	10/01-12/01
	Augusta-Aiken MSA, GA-SC	H	15.95 FQ	24.57 AW	34.56 TQ	GABLS	10/01-12/01
	Macon MSA, GA	H	12.62 FQ	19.51 AW	26.55 TQ	GABLS	10/01-12/01
	Hawaii	H	25.85 FQ	30.16 AW	34.64 TQ	HIBLS	10/01-12/01
	Idaho	H	17.56 FQ	24.63 AW	32.77 TQ	IDBLS	10/01-12/01
	Boise City MSA, ID	H	15.24 FQ	22.21 AW	30.95 TQ	IDBLS	10/01-12/01
	Illinois	H	10.53 FQ	22.15 AW	36.90 TQ	ILBLS	10/01-12/01
	Chicago PMSA, IL	H	9.11 FQ	26.62 AW	41.66 TQ	ILBLS	10/01-12/01
	Peoria-Pekin MSA, IL	H	14.90 FQ	26.69 AW	36.93 TQ	ILBLS	10/01-12/01
	Rockford MSA, IL	H	8.96 FQ	27.81 AW	42.94 TQ	ILBLS	10/01-12/01
	Springfield MSA, IL	H	21.87 FQ	25.60 AW	29.28 TQ	ILBLS	10/01-12/01
	Indiana	H	15.41 FQ	22.19 AW	28.24 TQ	INBLS	10/01-12/01

AAW Average annual wage **AOH** Average offered, high **ASH** Average starting, high **H** Hourly **M** Monthly **S** Special: hourly and annual
AE Average entry wage **AOL** Average offered, low **ASL** Average starting, low **HI** Highest wage paid **MTC** Median total compensation **TQ** Third quartile wage
AEX Average experienced wage **APH** Average pay, high range **AW** Average wage paid **HR** High end range **MW** Median wage paid **W** Weekly
AO Average offered **APL** Average pay, low range **FQ** First quartile wage **LR** Low end range **SQ** Second quartile wage **Y** Yearly

Occupation/Type/Industry	Location	Per	Low	Mid	High	Source	Date
Electrical Power-Line Installer and Repairer	Evansville-Henderson MSA, IN-KY	H	14.40 FQ	22.68 AW	27.24 TQ	INBLS	10/01-12/01
	Fort Wayne MSA, IN	H	18.61 FQ	22.54 AW	27.14 TQ	INBLS	10/01-12/01
	Gary PMSA, IN	H	19.56 FQ	24.94 AW	30.54 TQ	INBLS	10/01-12/01
	Indianapolis MSA, IN	H	14.54 FQ	19.15 AW	26.44 TQ	INBLS	10/01-12/01
	Lafayette MSA, IN	H	16.10 FQ	23.49 AW	33.41 TQ	INBLS	10/01-12/01
	Iowa	H	14.87 FQ	21.11 AW	27.17 TQ	IABLS	10/01-12/01
	Cedar Rapids MSA, IA	H	19.08 FQ	24.18 AW	28.23 TQ	IABLS	10/01-12/01
	Davenport-Moline-Rock Island MSA, IA-IL	H	10.26 FQ	21.49 AW	32.32 TQ	IABLS	10/01-12/01
	Des Moines MSA, IA	H	14.49 FQ	20.21 AW	26.64 TQ	IABLS	10/01-12/01
	Kansas	H	14.27 FQ	21.59 AW	27.79 TQ	KSBLS	10/01-12/01
	Topeka MSA, KS	H	22.17 FQ	25.21 AW	28.69 TQ	KSBLS	10/01-12/01
	Wichita MSA, KS	H	12.85 FQ	21.31 AW	27.36 TQ	KSBLS	10/01-12/01
	Kentucky	H	13.25 FQ	19.84 AW	26.06 TQ	KYBLS	10/01-12/01
	Lexington MSA, KY	H	14.19 FQ	19.47 AW	25.43 TQ	KYBLS	10/01-12/01
	Louisville MSA, KY-IN	H	17.42 FQ	21.81 AW	26.87 TQ	KYBLS	10/01-12/01
	Louisiana	H	11.86 FQ	19.11 AW	26.56 TQ	LABLS	10/01-12/01
	Baton Rouge MSA, LA	H	14.88 FQ	19.82 AW	26.13 TQ	LABLS	10/01-12/01
	Houma MSA, LA	H	10.76 FQ	17.84 AW	25.39 TQ	LABLS	10/01-12/01
	Lafayette MSA, LA	H	12.14 FQ	20.21 AW	26.77 TQ	LABLS	10/01-12/01
	Lake Charles MSA, LA	H	11.75 FQ	17.75 AW	27.39 TQ	LABLS	10/01-12/01
	Shreveport-Bossier City MSA, LA	H	11.13 FQ	20.23 AW	26.67 TQ	LABLS	10/01-12/01
	Maine	H	16.25 FQ	19.99 AW	24.15 TQ	MEBLS	10/01-12/01
	Maryland	H	18.12 FQ	23.82 AW	29.02 TQ	MDBLS	10/01-12/01
	Baltimore PMSA, MD	H	17.63 FQ	23.89 AW	29.66 TQ	MDBLS	10/01-12/01
	Massachusetts	H	17.12 FQ	27.97 AW	40.74 TQ	MABLS	10/01-12/01
	Boston PMSA, MA-NH	H	16.16 FQ	28.66 AW	41.41 TQ	MABLS	10/01-12/01
	Lowell PMSA, MA-NH	H	14.36 FQ	21.33 AW	28.25 TQ	MABLS	10/01-12/01
	Springfield MSA, MA	H	18.15 FQ	27.68 AW	35.43 TQ	MABLS	10/01-12/01
	Worcester PMSA, MA-CT	H	12.60 FQ	29.52 AW	44.84 TQ	MABLS	10/01-12/01
	Michigan	H	13.93 FQ	22.50 AW	31.27 TQ	MIBLS	10/01-12/01
	Ann Arbor PMSA, MI	H	14.57 FQ	24.50 AW	32.83 TQ	MIBLS	10/01-12/01
	Detroit PMSA, MI	H	11.76 FQ	21.40 AW	29.65 TQ	MIBLS	10/01-12/01
	Grand Rapids-Muskegon-Holland MSA, MI	H	16.72 FQ	23.66 AW	32.90 TQ	MIBLS	10/01-12/01
	Kalamazoo-Battle Creek MSA, MI	H	14.03 FQ	23.46 AW	33.71 TQ	MIBLS	10/01-12/01
	Lansing-East Lansing MSA, MI	H	16.39 FQ	26.34 AW	38.02 TQ	MIBLS	10/01-12/01
	Saginaw-Bay City-Midland MSA, MI	H	9.32 FQ	19.47 AW	28.80 TQ	MIBLS	10/01-12/01
	Minnesota	H	16.99 FQ	24.29 AW	31.56 TQ	MNBLS	10/01-12/01
	Duluth-Superior MSA, MN-WI	H	16.60 FQ	24.11 AW	29.66 TQ	MNBLS	10/01-12/01
	Minneapolis-St. Paul MSA, MN-WI	H	18.37 FQ	25.28 AW	32.72 TQ	MNBLS	10/01-12/01
	St. Cloud MSA, MN	H	11.97 FQ	21.15 AW	30.66 TQ	MNBLS	10/01-12/01
	Mississippi	H	11.25 FQ	16.93 AW	22.71 TQ	MSBLS	10/01-12/01
	Biloxi-Gulfport-Pascagoula MSA, MS	H	11.93 FQ	19.05 AW	26.61 TQ	MSBLS	10/01-12/01
	Jackson MSA, MS	H	13.70 FQ	18.28 AW	24.38 TQ	MSBLS	10/01-12/01
	Missouri	H	14.27 FQ	21.63 AW	28.68 TQ	MOBLS	10/01-12/01
	Kansas City MSA, MO-KS	H	14.42 FQ	22.34 AW	30.20 TQ	MOBLS	10/01-12/01
	St. Louis MSA, MO-IL	H	10.78 FQ	16.01 AW	27.46 TQ	MOBLS	10/01-12/01
	Springfield MSA, MO	H	10.21 FQ	16.47 AW	23.52 TQ	MOBLS	10/01-12/01
	Montana	H	17.91 FQ	23.24 AW	28.08 TQ	MTBLS	10/01-12/01
	Nebraska	H	14.93 FQ	21.75 AW	27.69 TQ	NEBLS	10/01-12/01
	Nevada	H	19.12 FQ	27.90 AW	35.01 TQ	NVBLS	10/01-12/01
	Las Vegas MSA, NV-AZ	H	17.44 FQ	28.29 AW	35.07 TQ	NVBLS	10/01-12/01
	New Hampshire	H	13.14 FQ	21.76 AW	28.10 TQ	NHBLS	10/01-12/01
	Manchester PMSA, NH	H	12.89 FQ	21.08 AW	28.11 TQ	NHBLS	10/01-12/01
	Portsmouth-Rochester PMSA, NH-ME	H	17.88 FQ	23.81 AW	28.19 TQ	NHBLS	10/01-12/01
	New Jersey	H	21.30 FQ	27.37 AW	34.14 TQ	NJBLS	10/01-12/01
	Atlantic-Cape May PMSA, NJ	H	20.34 FQ	27.57 AW	33.89 TQ	NJBLS	10/01-12/01
	Bergen-Passaic PMSA, NJ	H	19.92 FQ	25.72 AW	33.40 TQ	NJBLS	10/01-12/01
	Middlesex-Somerset-Hunterdon PMSA, NJ	H	22.13 FQ	27.76 AW	33.98 TQ	NJBLS	10/01-12/01
	Monmouth-Ocean PMSA, NJ	H	21.60 FQ	27.91 AW	34.51 TQ	NJBLS	10/01-12/01
	Newark PMSA, NJ	H	23.05 FQ	28.55 AW	35.04 TQ	NJBLS	10/01-12/01
	Trenton PMSA, NJ	H	18.53 FQ	25.27 AW	33.11 TQ	NJBLS	10/01-12/01

AAW Average annual wage **AOH** Average offered, high **ASH** Average starting, high **H** Hourly **M** Monthly **S** Special: hourly and annual
AE Average entry wage **AOL** Average offered, low **ASL** Average starting, low **HI** Highest wage paid **MTC** Median total compensation **TQ** Third quartile wage
AEX Average experienced wage **APH** Average pay, high range **AW** Average wage paid **HR** High end range **MW** Median wage paid **W** Weekly
AO Average offered **APL** Average pay, low range **FQ** First quartile wage **LR** Low end range **SQ** Second quartile wage **Y** Yearly

Occupation/Type/Industry	Location	Per	Low	Mid	High	Source	Date
Electrical Power-Line Installer and Repairer	New Mexico	H	10.91 FQ	18.36 AW	26.28 TQ	NMBLS	10/01-12/01
	Albuquerque MSA, NM	H	12.00 FQ	18.56 AW	26.75 TQ	NMBLS	10/01-12/01
	New York	H	20.46 FQ	28.67 AW	35.32 TQ	NYBLS	10/01-12/01
	Albany-Schenectady-Troy MSA, NY	H	20.90 FQ	28.49 AW	35.15 TQ	NYBLS	10/01-12/01
	Buffalo-Niagara Falls MSA, NY	H	14.48 FQ	24.78 AW	34.77 TQ	NYBLS	10/01-12/01
	Nassau-Suffolk PMSA, NY	H	17.17 FQ	26.22 AW	34.05 TQ	NYBLS	10/01-12/01
	New York PMSA, NY	H	23.19 FQ	29.08 AW	34.83 TQ	NYBLS	10/01-12/01
	Rochester MSA, NY	H	26.03 FQ	32.99 AW	40.89 TQ	NYBLS	10/01-12/01
	Syracuse MSA, NY	H	24.79 FQ	30.12 AW	35.28 TQ	NYBLS	10/01-12/01
	North Carolina	H	12.94 FQ	19.64 AW	26.94 TQ	NCBLS	10/01-12/01
	Charlotte-Gastonia-Rock Hill MSA, NC-SC	H	11.80 FQ	19.96 AW	27.60 TQ	NCBLS	10/01-12/01
	Greensboro-Winston-Salem-High Point MSA, NC	H	14.35 FQ	21.61 AW	27.53 TQ	NCBLS	10/01-12/01
	Hickory-Morganton-Lenoir MSA, NC	H	16.39 FQ	22.71 AW	28.23 TQ	NCBLS	10/01-12/01
	Raleigh-Durham-Chapel Hill MSA, NC	H	13.84 FQ	20.05 AW	26.72 TQ	NCBLS	10/01-12/01
	North Dakota	H	17.82 FQ	21.40 AW	27.04 TQ	NDBLS	10/01-12/01
	Fargo-Moorhead MSA, ND-MN	H	12.29 FQ	20.25 AW	26.96 TQ	NDBLS	10/01-12/01
	Ohio	H	14.27 FQ	21.88 AW	27.57 TQ	OHBLS	10/01-12/01
	Canton-Massillon MSA, OH	H	17.09 FQ	24.25 AW	28.63 TQ	OHBLS	10/01-12/01
	Cincinnati PMSA, OH-KY-IN	H	15.72 FQ	22.43 AW	27.61 TQ	OHBLS	10/01-12/01
	Cleveland-Lorain-Elyria PMSA, OH	H	15.47 FQ	22.25 AW	27.79 TQ	OHBLS	10/01-12/01
	Columbus MSA, OH	H	15.21 FQ	22.10 AW	27.90 TQ	OHBLS	10/01-12/01
	Dayton-Springfield MSA, OH	H	16.59 FQ	21.70 AW	26.41 TQ	OHBLS	10/01-12/01
	Toledo MSA, OH	H	13.71 FQ	22.34 AW	27.66 TQ	OHBLS	10/01-12/01
	Oklahoma	H	11.81 FQ	19.32 AW	26.68 TQ	OKBLS	10/01-12/01
	Oklahoma City MSA, OK	H	12.56 FQ	20.35 AW	26.97 TQ	OKBLS	10/01-12/01
	Tulsa MSA, OK	H	11.20 FQ	18.12 AW	27.08 TQ	OKBLS	10/01-12/01
	Oregon	H	21.75 FQ	26.91 AW	33.69 TQ	ORBLS	10/01-12/01
	Eugene-Springfield MSA, OR	H	23.81 FQ	27.87 AW	34.60 TQ	ORBLS	10/01-12/01
	Portland-Vancouver PMSA, OR-WA	H	19.77 FQ	26.75 AW	33.85 TQ	ORBLS	10/01-12/01
	Salem PMSA, OR	H	23.42 FQ	27.65 AW	34.38 TQ	ORBLS	10/01-12/01
	Pennsylvania	H	14.62 FQ	24.24 AW	35.17 TQ	PABLS	10/01-12/01
	Allentown-Bethlehem-Easton MSA, PA	H	19.36 FQ	26.23 AW	34.18 TQ	PABLS	10/01-12/01
	Harrisburg-Lebanon-Carlisle MSA, PA	H	23.75 FQ	30.76 AW	39.85 TQ	PABLS	10/01-12/01
	Johnstown MSA, PA	H	19.93 FQ	26.80 AW	37.32 TQ	PABLS	10/01-12/01
	Philadelphia PMSA, PA-NJ	H	12.71 FQ	21.26 AW	30.16 TQ	PABLS	10/01-12/01
	Pittsburgh MSA, PA	H	21.71 FQ	29.64 AW	41.30 TQ	PABLS	10/01-12/01
	Reading MSA, PA	H	21.43 FQ	25.57 AW	29.24 TQ	PABLS	10/01-12/01
	Scranton-Wilkes-Barre-Hazleton MSA, PA	H	19.62 FQ	26.82 AW	36.55 TQ	PABLS	10/01-12/01
	York MSA, PA	H	22.23 FQ	26.58 AW	34.45 TQ	PABLS	10/01-12/01
	Rhode Island	H	16.27 FQ	23.11 AW	28.45 TQ	RIBLS	10/01-12/01
	Providence-Fall River-Warwick MSA, RI-MA	H	14.70 FQ	22.90 AW	28.42 TQ	RIBLS	10/01-12/01
	South Carolina	H	11.30 FQ	18.03 AW	26.29 TQ	SCBLS	10/01-12/01
	Charleston-North Charleston MSA, SC	H	10.91 FQ	18.83 AW	26.37 TQ	SCBLS	10/01-12/01
	Columbia MSA, SC	H	11.24 FQ	18.42 AW	27.94 TQ	SCBLS	10/01-12/01
	Greenville-Spartanburg-Anderson MSA, SC	H	13.89 FQ	18.56 AW	24.25 TQ	SCBLS	10/01-12/01
	Myrtle Beach MSA, SC	H	12.31 FQ	18.35 AW	22.57 TQ	SCBLS	10/01-12/01
	South Dakota	H	14.25 FQ	19.56 AW	25.63 TQ	SDBLS	10/01-12/01
	Sioux Falls MSA, SD	H	15.21 FQ	21.56 AW	30.28 TQ	SDBLS	10/01-12/01
	Tennessee	H	12.27 FQ	18.97 AW	25.80 TQ	TNBLS	10/01-12/01
	Chattanooga MSA, TN-GA	H	11.65 FQ	18.07 AW	25.73 TQ	TNBLS	10/01-12/01
	Clarksville-Hopkinsville MSA, TN-KY	H	11.66 FQ	17.62 AW	24.62 TQ	TNBLS	10/01-12/01
	Johnson City-Kingsport-Bristol MSA, TN-VA	H	13.74 FQ	20.99 AW	27.07 TQ	TNBLS	10/01-12/01
	Memphis MSA, TN-AR-MS	H	11.30 FQ	17.64 AW	25.14 TQ	TNBLS	10/01-12/01
	Nashville MSA, TN	H	11.74 FQ	19.17 AW	26.37 TQ	TNBLS	10/01-12/01

AAW	Average annual wage	**AOH**	Average offered, high	**ASH**	Average starting, high	**H**	Hourly	**M**	Monthly	**S**	Special: hourly and annual
AE	Average entry wage	**AOL**	Average offered, low	**ASL**	Average starting, low	**HI**	Highest wage paid	**MTC**	Median total compensation	**TQ**	Third quartile wage
AEX	Average experienced wage	**APH**	Average pay, high range	**AW**	Average wage paid	**HR**	High end range	**MW**	Median wage paid	**W**	Weekly
AO	Average offered	**APL**	Average pay, low range	**FQ**	First quartile wage	**LR**	Low end range	**SQ**	Second quartile wage	**Y**	Yearly

Occupation/Type/Industry	Location	Per	Low	Mid	High	Source	Date
Electrical Power-Line Installer and Repairer	Texas	H	9.59 FQ	17.96 AW	25.96 TQ	TXBLS	10/01-12/01
	Austin-San Marcos MSA, TX	H	12.79 FQ	19.06 AW	25.89 TQ	TXBLS	10/01-12/01
	Beaumont-Port Arthur MSA, TX	H	16.22 FQ	21.51 AW	26.66 TQ	TXBLS	10/01-12/01
	Brazoria PMSA, TX	H	7.27 FQ	12.73 AW	23.79 TQ	TXBLS	10/01-12/01
	Brownsville-Harlingen-San Benito MSA, TX	H	7.74 FQ	15.08 AW	23.19 TQ	TXBLS	10/01-12/01
	Corpus Christi MSA, TX	H	10.54 FQ	18.57 AW	26.56 TQ	TXBLS	10/01-12/01
	Dallas PMSA, TX	H	8.33 FQ	15.97 AW	24.30 TQ	TXBLS	10/01-12/01
	El Paso MSA, TX	H	16.13 FQ	22.87 AW	27.94 TQ	TXBLS	10/01-12/01
	Fort Worth-Arlington PMSA, TX	H	11.74 FQ	16.30 AW	21.39 TQ	TXBLS	10/01-12/01
	Galveston-Texas City PMSA, TX	H	18.50 FQ	22.78 AW	27.28 TQ	TXBLS	10/01-12/01
	Houston PMSA, TX	H	16.66 FQ	22.10 AW	26.63 TQ	TXBLS	10/01-12/01
	Laredo MSA, TX	H	14.68 FQ	20.72 AW	26.96 TQ	TXBLS	10/01-12/01
	Longview-Marshall MSA, TX	H	14.23 FQ	20.67 AW	26.88 TQ	TXBLS	10/01-12/01
	McAllen-Edinburg-Mission MSA, TX	H	10.87 FQ	19.45 AW	26.10 TQ	TXBLS	10/01-12/01
	Waco MSA, TX	H	9.16 FQ	14.95 AW	21.20 TQ	TXBLS	10/01-12/01
	Utah	H	10.66 FQ	21.67 AW	30.09 TQ	UTBLS	10/01-12/01
	Salt Lake City-Ogden MSA, UT	H	11.32 FQ	22.57 AW	31.35 TQ	UTBLS	10/01-12/01
	Vermont	H	17.13 FQ	22.55 AW	27.43 TQ	VTBLS	10/01-12/01
	Burlington MSA, VT	H	19.12 FQ	23.40 AW	27.51 TQ	VTBLS	10/01-12/01
	Virginia	H	14.55 FQ	21.79 AW	27.11 TQ	VABLS	10/01-12/01
	Lynchburg MSA, VA	H	12.50 FQ	21.51 AW	27.47 TQ	VABLS	10/01-12/01
	Norfolk-Virginia Beach-Newport News MSA, VA-NC	H	16.22 FQ	22.67 AW	27.17 TQ	VABLS	10/01-12/01
	Richmond-Petersburg MSA, VA	H	15.11 FQ	22.06 AW	26.96 TQ	VABLS	10/01-12/01
	Roanoke MSA, VA	H	12.02 FQ	18.96 AW	26.84 TQ	VABLS	10/01-12/01
	Washington	H	20.16 FQ	26.08 AW	33.44 TQ	WABLS	10/01-12/01
	Richland-Kennewick-Pasco MSA, WA	H	20.28 FQ	25.81 AW	33.39 TQ	WABLS	10/01-12/01
	Seattle-Bellevue-Everett PMSA, WA	H	18.92 FQ	26.37 AW	35.18 TQ	WABLS	10/01-12/01
	West Virginia	H	16.90 FQ	22.87 AW	27.41 TQ	WVBLS	10/01-12/01
	Charleston MSA, WV	H	11.95 FQ	21.22 AW	31.43 TQ	WVBLS	10/01-12/01
	Huntington-Ashland MSA, WV-KY-OH	H	18.55 FQ	22.80 AW	26.66 TQ	WVBLS	10/01-12/01
	Wisconsin	H	17.03 FQ	22.21 AW	28.38 TQ	WIBLS	10/01-12/01
	Milwaukee-Waukesha PMSA, WI	H	18.78 FQ	25.84 AW	34.86 TQ	WIBLS	10/01-12/01
	Wyoming	H	10.11 FQ	18.47 AW	27.57 TQ	WYBLS	10/01-12/01
	Cheyenne MSA, WY	H	9.50 FQ	13.59 AW	20.77 TQ	WYBLS	10/01-12/01
Electrician	Alabama	H	10.09 FQ	16.30 AW	24.08 TQ	ALBLS	10/01-12/01
	Birmingham MSA, AL	H	9.78 FQ	16.25 AW	21.91 TQ	ALBLS	10/01-12/01
	Huntsville MSA, AL	H	11.77 FQ	18.69 AW	30.60 TQ	ALBLS	10/01-12/01
	Mobile MSA, AL	H	9.75 FQ	16.05 AW	25.55 TQ	ALBLS	10/01-12/01
	Montgomery MSA, AL	H	9.33 FQ	12.93 AW	16.92 TQ	ALBLS	10/01-12/01
	Alaska	H	14.03 FQ	24.86 AW	35.54 TQ	AKBLS	10/01-12/01
	Anchorage MSA, AK	H	15.51 FQ	27.64 AW	36.51 TQ	AKBLS	10/01-12/01
	Arizona	H	11.45 FQ	18.03 AW	26.28 TQ	AZBLS	10/01-12/01
	Phoenix-Mesa MSA, AZ	H	12.05 FQ	18.69 AW	26.75 TQ	AZBLS	10/01-12/01
	Tucson MSA, AZ	H	9.68 FQ	15.75 AW	21.47 TQ	AZBLS	10/01-12/01
	Arkansas	H	9.82 FQ	15.97 AW	22.93 TQ	ARBLS	10/01-12/01
	Fayetteville-Springdale-Rogers MSA, AR	H	9.43 FQ	13.78 AW	18.48 TQ	ARBLS	10/01-12/01
	Fort Smith MSA, AR-OK	H	8.85 FQ	15.49 AW	21.25 TQ	ARBLS	10/01-12/01
	Little Rock-North Little Rock MSA, AR	H	9.46 FQ	15.14 AW	20.53 TQ	ARBLS	10/01-12/01
	California	H	12.85 FQ	23.09 AW	36.61 TQ	CABLS	10/01-12/01
	Bakersfield MSA, CA	H	12.19 FQ	20.33 AW	29.49 TQ	CABLS	10/01-12/01
	Chico-Paradise MSA, CA	H	12.08 FQ	19.75 AW	29.17 TQ	CABLS	10/01-12/01
	Fresno MSA, CA	H	10.48 FQ	17.74 AW	27.21 TQ	CABLS	10/01-12/01
	Los Angeles-Long Beach PMSA, CA	H	12.00 FQ	19.78 AW	31.70 TQ	CABLS	10/01-12/01
	Merced MSA, CA	H	12.05 FQ	20.23 AW	28.25 TQ	CABLS	10/01-12/01

AAW Average annual wage; AE Average entry wage; AEX Average experienced wage; AO Average offered; AOH Average offered, high; AOL Average offered, low; APH Average pay, high range; APL Average pay, low range; ASH Average starting, high; ASL Average starting, low; AW Average wage paid; FQ First quartile wage; H Hourly; HI Highest wage paid; HR High end range; LR Low end range; M Monthly; MTC Median total compensation; MW Median wage paid; SQ Second quartile wage; S Special: hourly and annual; TQ Third quartile wage; W Weekly; Y Yearly

Occupation/Type/Industry	Location	Per	Low	Mid	High	Source	Date
Electrician	Modesto MSA, CA	H	12.46 FQ	19.62 AW	27.76 TQ	CABLS	10/01-12/01
	Oakland PMSA, CA	H	16.67 FQ	31.00 AW	44.62 TQ	CABLS	10/01-12/01
	Orange County PMSA, CA	H	15.75 FQ	22.93 AW	33.31 TQ	CABLS	10/01-12/01
	Redding MSA, CA	H	8.38 FQ	16.90 AW	30.53 TQ	CABLS	10/01-12/01
	Riverside-San Bernardino PMSA, CA	H	12.80 FQ	21.52 AW	32.42 TQ	CABLS	10/01-12/01
	Sacramento PMSA, CA	H	11.81 FQ	21.41 AW	32.23 TQ	CABLS	10/01-12/01
	Salinas MSA, CA	H	13.02 FQ	23.74 AW	33.19 TQ	CABLS	10/01-12/01
	San Diego MSA, CA	H	12.16 FQ	20.26 AW	31.11 TQ	CABLS	10/01-12/01
	San Francisco PMSA, CA	H	16.47 FQ	30.09 AW	44.55 TQ	CABLS	10/01-12/01
	San Jose PMSA, CA	H	15.72 FQ	26.73 AW	41.31 TQ	CABLS	10/01-12/01
	San Luis Obispo-Atascadero-Paso Robles MSA, CA	H	17.48 FQ	23.05 AW	27.31 TQ	CABLS	10/01-12/01
	Santa Barbara-Santa Maria-Lompoc MSA, CA	H	16.97 FQ	23.42 AW	32.27 TQ	CABLS	10/01-12/01
	Santa Cruz-Watsonville PMSA, CA	H	18.46 FQ	27.23 AW	39.95 TQ	CABLS	10/01-12/01
	Santa Rosa PMSA, CA	H	12.30 FQ	22.86 AW	37.21 TQ	CABLS	10/01-12/01
	Stockton-Lodi MSA, CA	H	13.78 FQ	21.76 AW	32.82 TQ	CABLS	10/01-12/01
	Vallejo-Fairfield-Napa PMSA, CA	H	20.38 FQ	34.08 AW	42.46 TQ	CABLS	10/01-12/01
	Ventura PMSA, CA	H	10.76 FQ	22.49 AW	33.23 TQ	CABLS	10/01-12/01
	Visalia-Tulare-Porterville MSA, CA	H	10.44 FQ	16.48 AW	25.91 TQ	CABLS	10/01-12/01
	Colorado	H	12.24 FQ	21.03 AW	28.67 TQ	COBLS	10/01-12/01
	Boulder-Longmont PMSA, CO	H	10.39 FQ	18.88 AW	26.89 TQ	COBLS	10/01-12/01
	Colorado Springs MSA, CO	H	11.05 FQ	18.83 AW	26.69 TQ	COBLS	10/01-12/01
	Denver PMSA, CO	H	14.73 FQ	23.20 AW	30.80 TQ	COBLS	10/01-12/01
	Fort Collins-Loveland MSA, CO	H	10.60 FQ	17.42 AW	25.01 TQ	COBLS	10/01-12/01
	Greeley PMSA, CO	H	11.46 FQ	20.18 AW	32.21 TQ	COBLS	10/01-12/01
	Connecticut	H	13.11 FQ	21.65 AW	30.86 TQ	CTBLS	10/01-12/01
	Bridgeport PMSA, CT	H	17.31 FQ	23.65 AW	32.07 TQ	CTBLS	10/01-12/01
	Danbury PMSA, CT	H	12.63 FQ	21.88 AW	33.07 TQ	CTBLS	10/01-12/01
	Hartford MSA, CT	H	11.40 FQ	20.90 AW	31.80 TQ	CTBLS	10/01-12/01
	New Haven-Meriden PMSA, CT	H	14.74 FQ	21.95 AW	27.67 TQ	CTBLS	10/01-12/01
	New London-Norwich MSA, CT-RI	H	14.03 FQ	19.04 AW	27.15 TQ	CTBLS	10/01-12/01
	Stamford-Norwalk PMSA, CT	H	16.48 FQ	23.32 AW	29.07 TQ	CTBLS	10/01-12/01
	Waterbury PMSA, CT	H	15.38 FQ	23.16 AW	32.45 TQ	CTBLS	10/01-12/01
	Delaware	H	11.98 FQ	20.63 AW	29.66 TQ	DEBLS	10/01-12/01
	Wilmington-Newark PMSA, DE-MD	H	13.14 FQ	22.32 AW	31.41 TQ	DEBLS	10/01-12/01
	District of Columbia	H	17.49 FQ	24.33 AW	33.00 TQ	DCBLS	10/01-12/01
	Washington PMSA, DC-MD-VA-WV	H	11.81 FQ	20.44 AW	28.76 TQ	DCBLS	10/01-12/01
	Florida	H	10.24 FQ	15.47 AW	21.42 TQ	FLBLS	10/01-12/01
	Daytona Beach MSA, FL	H	10.31 FQ	14.31 AW	18.20 TQ	FLBLS	10/01-12/01
	Fort Lauderdale PMSA, FL	H	11.42 FQ	16.51 AW	22.05 TQ	FLBLS	10/01-12/01
	Fort Myers-Cape Coral MSA, FL	H	10.56 FQ	14.31 AW	17.40 TQ	FLBLS	10/01-12/01
	Fort Pierce-Port St. Lucie MSA, FL	H	7.43 FQ	12.80 AW	17.79 TQ	FLBLS	10/01-12/01
	Fort Walton Beach MSA, FL	H	10.72 FQ	15.21 AW	22.13 TQ	FLBLS	10/01-12/01
	Gainesville MSA, FL	H	8.28 FQ	13.17 AW	17.65 TQ	FLBLS	10/01-12/01
	Jacksonville MSA, FL	H	11.70 FQ	16.55 AW	21.48 TQ	FLBLS	10/01-12/01
	Lakeland-Winter Haven MSA, FL	H	11.16 FQ	16.92 AW	22.07 TQ	FLBLS	10/01-12/01
	Melbourne-Titusville-Palm Bay MSA, FL	H	10.05 FQ	16.75 AW	25.08 TQ	FLBLS	10/01-12/01
	Miami PMSA, FL	H	9.70 FQ	16.14 AW	24.56 TQ	FLBLS	10/01-12/01
	Naples MSA, FL	H	10.81 FQ	15.21 AW	20.46 TQ	FLBLS	10/01-12/01
	Ocala MSA, FL	H	9.92 FQ	13.79 AW	17.06 TQ	FLBLS	10/01-12/01
	Orlando MSA, FL	H	9.81 FQ	15.75 AW	21.42 TQ	FLBLS	10/01-12/01
	Pensacola MSA, FL	H	9.24 FQ	13.18 AW	19.67 TQ	FLBLS	10/01-12/01
	Sarasota-Bradenton MSA, FL	H	9.46 FQ	13.45 AW	17.32 TQ	FLBLS	10/01-12/01
	Tallahassee MSA, FL	H	9.43 FQ	13.45 AW	16.95 TQ	FLBLS	10/01-12/01
	Tampa-St. Petersburg-Clearwater MSA, FL	H	11.24 FQ	14.75 AW	19.68 TQ	FLBLS	10/01-12/01
	West Palm Beach-Boca Raton MSA, FL	H	11.62 FQ	16.15 AW	21.34 TQ	FLBLS	10/01-12/01

AAW	Average annual wage	**AOH**	Average offered, high	**ASH**	Average starting, high	**H**	Hourly	**M**	Monthly	**S**	Special: hourly and annual
AE	Average entry wage	**AOL**	Average offered, low	**ASL**	Average starting, low	**HI**	Highest wage paid	**MTC**	Median total compensation	**TQ**	Third quartile wage
AEX	Average experienced wage	**APH**	Average pay, high range	**AW**	Average wage paid	**HR**	High end range	**MW**	Median wage paid	**W**	Weekly
AO	Average offered	**APL**	Average pay, low range	**FQ**	First quartile wage	**LR**	Low end range	**SQ**	Second quartile wage	**Y**	Yearly

Occupation/Type/Industry	Location	Per	Low	Mid	High	Source	Date
Electrician	Georgia	H	11.16 FQ	17.72 AW	26.60 TQ	GABLS	10/01-12/01
	Atlanta MSA, GA	H	11.66 FQ	18.93 AW	27.51 TQ	GABLS	10/01-12/01
	Augusta-Aiken MSA, GA-SC	H	12.79 FQ	18.52 AW	26.19 TQ	GABLS	10/01-12/01
	Columbus MSA, GA-AL	H	11.40 FQ	15.68 AW	20.91 TQ	GABLS	10/01-12/01
	Macon MSA, GA	H	7.60 FQ	16.21 AW	23.12 TQ	GABLS	10/01-12/01
	Savannah MSA, GA	H	9.64 FQ	16.44 AW	25.24 TQ	GABLS	10/01-12/01
	Hawaii	H	15.15 FQ	24.66 AW	34.41 TQ	HIBLS	10/01-12/01
	Honolulu MSA, HI	H	16.65 FQ	25.35 AW	34.33 TQ	HIBLS	10/01-12/01
	Idaho	H	11.40 FQ	18.49 AW	26.37 TQ	IDBLS	10/01-12/01
	Boise City MSA, ID	H	11.87 FQ	18.59 AW	26.64 TQ	IDBLS	10/01-12/01
	Illinois	H	12.20 FQ	23.31 AW	34.17 TQ	ILBLS	10/01-12/01
	Champaign-Urbana MSA, IL	H	13.05 FQ	27.54 AW	43.36 TQ	ILBLS	10/01-12/01
	Chicago PMSA, IL	H	12.09 FQ	23.60 AW	34.61 TQ	ILBLS	10/01-12/01
	Peoria-Pekin MSA, IL	H	18.34 FQ	23.86 AW	28.37 TQ	ILBLS	10/01-12/01
	Rockford MSA, IL	H	12.37 FQ	21.85 AW	34.37 TQ	ILBLS	10/01-12/01
	Springfield MSA, IL	H	11.37 FQ	20.60 AW	32.52 TQ	ILBLS	10/01-12/01
	Indiana	H	13.09 FQ	21.79 AW	30.75 TQ	INBLS	10/01-12/01
	Elkhart-Goshen MSA, IN	H	13.62 FQ	21.11 AW	29.79 TQ	INBLS	10/01-12/01
	Evansville-Henderson MSA, IN-KY	H	13.13 FQ	21.45 AW	28.18 TQ	INBLS	10/01-12/01
	Fort Wayne MSA, IN	H	13.31 FQ	21.10 AW	29.56 TQ	INBLS	10/01-12/01
	Gary PMSA, IN	H	16.23 FQ	24.16 AW	32.87 TQ	INBLS	10/01-12/01
	Indianapolis MSA, IN	H	13.47 FQ	22.27 AW	32.12 TQ	INBLS	10/01-12/01
	Lafayette MSA, IN	H	11.10 FQ	20.24 AW	30.74 TQ	INBLS	10/01-12/01
	South Bend MSA, IN	H	13.87 FQ	20.81 AW	27.45 TQ	INBLS	10/01-12/01
	Iowa	H	11.22 FQ	18.52 AW	26.73 TQ	IABLS	10/01-12/01
	Cedar Rapids MSA, IA	H	14.06 FQ	22.80 AW	28.86 TQ	IABLS	10/01-12/01
	Davenport-Moline-Rock Island MSA, IA-IL	H	12.34 FQ	20.37 AW	27.38 TQ	IABLS	10/01-12/01
	Des Moines MSA, IA	H	11.45 FQ	17.56 AW	25.20 TQ	IABLS	10/01-12/01
	Kansas	H	11.27 FQ	18.78 AW	28.06 TQ	KSBLS	10/01-12/01
	Topeka MSA, KS	H	13.58 FQ	19.02 AW	25.73 TQ	KSBLS	10/01-12/01
	Wichita MSA, KS	H	11.13 FQ	18.54 AW	26.60 TQ	KSBLS	10/01-12/01
	Kentucky	H	11.28 FQ	18.69 AW	26.90 TQ	KYBLS	10/01-12/01
	Lexington MSA, KY	H	11.02 FQ	18.12 AW	25.97 TQ	KYBLS	10/01-12/01
	Louisville MSA, KY-IN	H	11.77 FQ	19.91 AW	27.87 TQ	KYBLS	10/01-12/01
	Louisiana	H	9.91 FQ	16.43 AW	23.17 TQ	LABLS	10/01-12/01
	Baton Rouge MSA, LA	H	9.39 FQ	14.66 AW	20.25 TQ	LABLS	10/01-12/01
	Houma MSA, LA	H	10.00 FQ	17.46 AW	27.72 TQ	LABLS	10/01-12/01
	Lafayette MSA, LA	H	10.18 FQ	16.67 AW	23.01 TQ	LABLS	10/01-12/01
	Lake Charles MSA, LA	H	11.40 FQ	17.69 AW	25.74 TQ	LABLS	10/01-12/01
	New Orleans MSA, LA	H	10.30 FQ	16.93 AW	22.84 TQ	LABLS	10/01-12/01
	Shreveport-Bossier City MSA, LA	H	10.78 FQ	20.05 AW	31.00 TQ	LABLS	10/01-12/01
	Maine	H	12.03 FQ	17.74 AW	24.54 TQ	MEBLS	10/01-12/01
	Portland MSA, ME	H	12.27 FQ	18.29 AW	25.31 TQ	MEBLS	10/01-12/01
	Maryland	H	12.28 FQ	20.44 AW	29.89 TQ	MDBLS	10/01-12/01
	Baltimore PMSA, MD	H	12.22 FQ	20.62 AW	31.16 TQ	MDBLS	10/01-12/01
	Massachusetts	H	13.99 FQ	23.30 AW	34.43 TQ	MABLS	10/01-12/01
	Boston PMSA, MA-NH	H	14.19 FQ	23.81 AW	34.34 TQ	MABLS	10/01-12/01
	Brockton PMSA, MA	H	12.73 FQ	22.13 AW	29.62 TQ	MABLS	10/01-12/01
	Lawrence PMSA, MA-NH	H	13.03 FQ	20.23 AW	27.27 TQ	MABLS	10/01-12/01
	Lowell PMSA, MA-NH	H	15.86 FQ	22.88 AW	29.87 TQ	MABLS	10/01-12/01
	New Bedford PMSA, MA	H	13.41 FQ	20.00 AW	27.33 TQ	MABLS	10/01-12/01
	Springfield MSA, MA	H	12.82 FQ	19.60 AW	25.73 TQ	MABLS	10/01-12/01
	Worcester PMSA, MA-CT	H	14.59 FQ	28.00 AW	42.31 TQ	MABLS	10/01-12/01
	Michigan	H	14.14 FQ	24.48 AW	34.48 TQ	MIBLS	10/01-12/01
	Ann Arbor PMSA, MI	H	13.85 FQ	23.92 AW	33.58 TQ	MIBLS	10/01-12/01
	Detroit PMSA, MI	H	15.76 FQ	27.09 AW	35.68 TQ	MIBLS	10/01-12/01
	Flint PMSA, MI	H	15.62 FQ	27.32 AW	34.99 TQ	MIBLS	10/01-12/01
	Grand Rapids-Muskegon-Holland MSA, MI	H	14.05 FQ	20.12 AW	27.91 TQ	MIBLS	10/01-12/01
	Kalamazoo-Battle Creek MSA, MI	H	12.14 FQ	21.11 AW	30.65 TQ	MIBLS	10/01-12/01
	Lansing-East Lansing MSA, MI	H	14.20 FQ	23.35 AW	33.12 TQ	MIBLS	10/01-12/01
	Saginaw-Bay City-Midland MSA, MI	H	14.84 FQ	25.75 AW	34.34 TQ	MIBLS	10/01-12/01
	Minnesota	H	14.53 FQ	24.37 AW	33.34 TQ	MNBLS	10/01-12/01
	Duluth-Superior MSA, MN-WI	H	17.50 FQ	22.77 AW	28.13 TQ	MNBLS	10/01-12/01
	Minneapolis-St. Paul MSA, MN-WI	H	18.10 FQ	26.72 AW	34.04 TQ	MNBLS	10/01-12/01
	St. Cloud MSA, MN	H	13.26 FQ	21.01 AW	28.93 TQ	MNBLS	10/01-12/01

AAW Average annual wage; **AE** Average entry wage; **AEX** Average experienced wage; **AO** Average offered; **AOH** Average offered, high; **AOL** Average offered, low; **APH** Average pay, high range; **APL** Average pay, low range; **ASH** Average starting, high; **ASL** Average starting, low; **AW** Average wage paid; **FQ** First quartile wage; **H** Hourly; **HI** Highest wage paid; **HR** High end range; **LR** Low end range; **M** Monthly; **MTC** Median total compensation; **MW** Median wage paid; **SQ** Second quartile wage; **S** Special: hourly and annual; **TQ** Third quartile wage; **W** Weekly; **Y** Yearly

Occupation/Type/Industry	Location	Per	Low	Mid	High	Source	Date
Electrician	Mississippi	H	11.39 FQ	16.16 AW	21.74 TQ	MSBLS	10/01-12/01
	Biloxi-Gulfport-Pascagoula MSA, MS	H	11.54 FQ	15.81 AW	19.71 TQ	MSBLS	10/01-12/01
	Jackson MSA, MS	H	12.58 FQ	17.61 AW	21.88 TQ	MSBLS	10/01-12/01
	Missouri	H	11.70 FQ	22.22 AW	32.50 TQ	MOBLS	10/01-12/01
	Kansas City MSA, MO-KS	H	11.19 FQ	20.93 AW	30.56 TQ	MOBLS	10/01-12/01
	St. Louis MSA, MO-IL	H	14.86 FQ	25.94 AW	35.49 TQ	MOBLS	10/01-12/01
	Springfield MSA, MO	H	10.29 FQ	16.22 AW	22.17 TQ	MOBLS	10/01-12/01
	Montana	H	14.05 FQ	20.57 AW	26.87 TQ	MTBLS	10/01-12/01
	Billings MSA, MT	H	14.81 FQ	20.59 AW	26.60 TQ	MTBLS	10/01-12/01
	Nebraska	H	11.02 FQ	17.55 AW	25.61 TQ	NEBLS	10/01-12/01
	Lincoln MSA, NE	H	10.58 FQ	17.22 AW	22.24 TQ	NEBLS	10/01-12/01
	Omaha MSA, NE-IA	H	11.21 FQ	18.81 AW	26.79 TQ	NEBLS	10/01-12/01
	Nevada	H	14.00 FQ	22.36 AW	31.62 TQ	NVBLS	10/01-12/01
	Las Vegas MSA, NV-AZ	H	14.00 FQ	22.43 AW	31.79 TQ	NVBLS	10/01-12/01
	Reno MSA, NV	H	10.22 FQ	20.62 AW	31.23 TQ	NVBLS	10/01-12/01
	New Hampshire	H	12.01 FQ	18.10 AW	24.29 TQ	NHBLS	10/01-12/01
	Manchester PMSA, NH	H	12.06 FQ	17.91 AW	22.47 TQ	NHBLS	10/01-12/01
	Nashua PMSA, NH	H	14.36 FQ	20.04 AW	28.44 TQ	NHBLS	10/01-12/01
	Portsmouth-Rochester PMSA, NH-ME	H	13.24 FQ	19.12 AW	25.34 TQ	NHBLS	10/01-12/01
	New Jersey	H	13.86 FQ	25.20 AW	39.89 TQ	NJBLS	10/01-12/01
	Atlantic-Cape May PMSA, NJ	H	14.85 FQ	23.14 AW	33.16 TQ	NJBLS	10/01-12/01
	Bergen-Passaic PMSA, NJ	H	14.05 FQ	25.31 AW	39.67 TQ	NJBLS	10/01-12/01
	Jersey City PMSA, NJ	H	16.59 FQ	23.62 AW	33.87 TQ	NJBLS	10/01-12/01
	Middlesex-Somerset-Hunterdon PMSA, NJ	H	10.25 FQ	24.14 AW	40.74 TQ	NJBLS	10/01-12/01
	Monmouth-Ocean PMSA, NJ	H	10.88 FQ	23.91 AW	40.86 TQ	NJBLS	10/01-12/01
	Newark PMSA, NJ	H	16.49 FQ	28.86 AW	41.28 TQ	NJBLS	10/01-12/01
	Trenton PMSA, NJ	H	13.50 FQ	22.89 AW	33.92 TQ	NJBLS	10/01-12/01
	New Mexico	H	11.36 FQ	17.76 AW	24.64 TQ	NMBLS	10/01-12/01
	Albuquerque MSA, NM	H	12.20 FQ	17.85 AW	22.93 TQ	NMBLS	10/01-12/01
	Las Cruces MSA, NM	H	8.65 FQ	16.02 AW	24.76 TQ	NMBLS	10/01-12/01
	New York	H	12.17 FQ	27.76 AW	43.06 TQ	NYBLS	10/01-12/01
	Albany-Schenectady-Troy MSA, NY	H	14.04 FQ	21.90 AW	31.68 TQ	NYBLS	10/01-12/01
	Binghamton MSA, NY	H	10.35 FQ	16.09 AW	24.94 TQ	NYBLS	10/01-12/01
	Buffalo-Niagara Falls MSA, NY	H	13.88 FQ	22.90 AW	28.66 TQ	NYBLS	10/01-12/01
	Dutchess County PMSA, NY	H	13.29 FQ	25.41 AW	34.91 TQ	NYBLS	10/01-12/01
	Nassau-Suffolk PMSA, NY	H	16.16 FQ	32.78 AW	45.96 TQ	NYBLS	10/01-12/01
	New York PMSA, NY	H	12.16 FQ	30.35 AW	43.74 TQ	NYBLS	10/01-12/01
	Newburgh PMSA, NY-PA	H	14.71 FQ	26.05 AW	34.06 TQ	NYBLS	10/01-12/01
	Rochester MSA, NY	H	10.08 FQ	20.70 AW	30.87 TQ	NYBLS	10/01-12/01
	Syracuse MSA, NY	H	11.58 FQ	17.68 AW	25.15 TQ	NYBLS	10/01-12/01
	Utica-Rome MSA, NY	H	8.48 FQ	17.04 AW	25.69 TQ	NYBLS	10/01-12/01
	North Carolina	H	11.10 FQ	15.84 AW	22.21 TQ	NCBLS	10/01-12/01
	Asheville MSA, NC	H	10.06 FQ	14.78 AW	20.85 TQ	NCBLS	10/01-12/01
	Charlotte-Gastonia-Rock Hill MSA, NC-SC	H	11.40 FQ	15.90 AW	22.04 TQ	NCBLS	10/01-12/01
	Fayetteville MSA, NC	H	10.22 FQ	15.25 AW	21.10 TQ	NCBLS	10/01-12/01
	Greensboro-Winston-Salem-High Point MSA, NC	H	11.32 FQ	15.96 AW	22.52 TQ	NCBLS	10/01-12/01
	Hickory-Morganton-Lenoir MSA, NC	H	10.42 FQ	14.26 AW	18.13 TQ	NCBLS	10/01-12/01
	Raleigh-Durham-Chapel Hill MSA, NC	H	12.24 FQ	17.98 AW	25.29 TQ	NCBLS	10/01-12/01
	Wilmington MSA, NC	H	10.12 FQ	15.39 AW	21.39 TQ	NCBLS	10/01-12/01
	North Dakota	H	11.22 FQ	17.61 AW	25.84 TQ	NDBLS	10/01-12/01
	Fargo-Moorhead MSA, ND-MN	H	11.40 FQ	18.07 AW	26.37 TQ	NDBLS	10/01-12/01
	Ohio	H	11.76 FQ	20.90 AW	31.46 TQ	OHBLS	10/01-12/01
	Akron PMSA, OH	H	11.20 FQ	19.88 AW	29.15 TQ	OHBLS	10/01-12/01
	Canton-Massillon MSA, OH	H	13.26 FQ	19.28 AW	26.54 TQ	OHBLS	10/01-12/01
	Cincinnati PMSA, OH-KY-IN	H	11.16 FQ	19.13 AW	26.69 TQ	OHBLS	10/01-12/01
	Cleveland-Lorain-Elyria PMSA, OH	H	10.55 FQ	22.24 AW	34.11 TQ	OHBLS	10/01-12/01
	Columbus MSA, OH	H	12.31 FQ	19.39 AW	26.96 TQ	OHBLS	10/01-12/01
	Dayton-Springfield MSA, OH	H	12.64 FQ	22.56 AW	32.74 TQ	OHBLS	10/01-12/01
	Hamilton-Middletown PMSA, OH	H	11.47 FQ	19.08 AW	26.44 TQ	OHBLS	10/01-12/01
	Mansfield MSA, OH	H	10.05 FQ	21.60 AW	34.50 TQ	OHBLS	10/01-12/01

AAW Average annual wage **AOH** Average offered, high **ASH** Average starting, high **H** Hourly **M** Monthly **S** Special: hourly and annual
AE Average entry wage **AOL** Average offered, low **ASL** Average starting, low **HI** Highest wage paid **MTC** Median total compensation **TQ** Third quartile wage
AEX Average experienced wage **APH** Average pay, high range **AW** Average wage paid **HR** High end range **MW** Median wage paid **W** Weekly
AO Average offered **APL** Average pay, low range **FQ** First quartile wage **LR** Low end range **SQ** Second quartile wage **Y** Yearly

Occupation/Type/Industry	Location	Per	Low	Mid	High	Source	Date
Electrician	Toledo MSA, OH	H	14.48 FQ	24.66 AW	33.87 TQ	OHBLS	10/01-12/01
	Youngstown-Warren MSA, OH	H	12.06 FQ	22.98 AW	34.31 TQ	OHBLS	10/01-12/01
	Oklahoma	H	10.31 FQ	17.21 AW	24.63 TQ	OKBLS	10/01-12/01
	Oklahoma City MSA, OK	H	9.67 FQ	16.72 AW	24.44 TQ	OKBLS	10/01-12/01
	Tulsa MSA, OK	H	11.13 FQ	17.62 AW	25.12 TQ	OKBLS	10/01-12/01
	Oregon	H	15.82 FQ	25.34 AW	34.17 TQ	ORBLS	10/01-12/01
	Eugene-Springfield MSA, OR	H	14.40 FQ	22.47 AW	29.21 TQ	ORBLS	10/01-12/01
	Medford-Ashland MSA, OR	H	14.35 FQ	22.66 AW	28.61 TQ	ORBLS	10/01-12/01
	Portland-Vancouver PMSA, OR-WA	H	18.18 FQ	27.20 AW	34.90 TQ	ORBLS	10/01-12/01
	Salem PMSA, OR	H	14.82 FQ	24.07 AW	33.52 TQ	ORBLS	10/01-12/01
	Pennsylvania	H	11.95 FQ	20.96 AW	32.24 TQ	PABLS	10/01-12/01
	Allentown-Bethlehem-Easton MSA, PA	H	12.29 FQ	20.93 AW	28.26 TQ	PABLS	10/01-12/01
	Erie MSA, PA	H	8.72 FQ	20.10 AW	27.09 TQ	PABLS	10/01-12/01
	Harrisburg-Lebanon-Carlisle MSA, PA	H	11.96 FQ	18.86 AW	26.20 TQ	PABLS	10/01-12/01
	Johnstown MSA, PA	H	10.35 FQ	18.78 AW	28.36 TQ	PABLS	10/01-12/01
	Lancaster MSA, PA	H	11.91 FQ	18.35 AW	27.80 TQ	PABLS	10/01-12/01
	Philadelphia PMSA, PA-NJ	H	13.52 FQ	22.94 AW	35.73 TQ	PABLS	10/01-12/01
	Pittsburgh MSA, PA	H	11.78 FQ	20.74 AW	28.30 TQ	PABLS	10/01-12/01
	Reading MSA, PA	H	10.98 FQ	19.03 AW	27.80 TQ	PABLS	10/01-12/01
	Scranton-Wilkes-Barre-Hazleton MSA, PA	H	10.73 FQ	20.80 AW	31.54 TQ	PABLS	10/01-12/01
	York MSA, PA	H	12.01 FQ	17.38 AW	22.86 TQ	PABLS	10/01-12/01
	Rhode Island	H	13.33 FQ	19.34 AW	26.73 TQ	RIBLS	10/01-12/01
	Providence-Fall River-Warwick MSA, RI-MA	H	13.58 FQ	19.67 AW	27.12 TQ	RIBLS	10/01-12/01
	South Carolina	H	11.10 FQ	15.99 AW	21.55 TQ	SCBLS	10/01-12/01
	Charleston-North Charleston MSA, SC	H	11.40 FQ	16.68 AW	21.63 TQ	SCBLS	10/01-12/01
	Columbia MSA, SC	H	11.91 FQ	16.43 AW	21.33 TQ	SCBLS	10/01-12/01
	Greenville-Spartanburg-Anderson MSA, SC	H	10.59 FQ	15.16 AW	21.14 TQ	SCBLS	10/01-12/01
	Myrtle Beach MSA, SC	H	10.49 FQ	14.93 AW	19.36 TQ	SCBLS	10/01-12/01
	South Dakota	H	10.76 FQ	16.06 AW	22.14 TQ	SDBLS	10/01-12/01
	Sioux Falls MSA, SD	H	10.17 FQ	15.64 AW	21.24 TQ	SDBLS	10/01-12/01
	Tennessee	H	10.89 FQ	18.20 AW	26.40 TQ	TNBLS	10/01-12/01
	Chattanooga MSA, TN-GA	H	12.11 FQ	19.76 AW	27.79 TQ	TNBLS	10/01-12/01
	Clarksville-Hopkinsville MSA, TN-KY	H	8.88 FQ	17.60 AW	28.05 TQ	TNBLS	10/01-12/01
	Johnson City-Kingsport-Bristol MSA, TN-VA	H	11.24 FQ	15.90 AW	22.49 TQ	TNBLS	10/01-12/01
	Knoxville MSA, TN	H	10.41 FQ	17.42 AW	22.26 TQ	TNBLS	10/01-12/01
	Memphis MSA, TN-AR-MS	H	10.22 FQ	18.27 AW	26.37 TQ	TNBLS	10/01-12/01
	Nashville MSA, TN	H	11.17 FQ	17.77 AW	26.43 TQ	TNBLS	10/01-12/01
	Texas	H	11.04 FQ	17.52 AW	25.40 TQ	TXBLS	10/01-12/01
	Amarillo MSA, TX	H	11.27 FQ	18.82 AW	26.22 TQ	TXBLS	10/01-12/01
	Austin-San Marcos MSA, TX	H	12.61 FQ	19.68 AW	26.52 TQ	TXBLS	10/01-12/01
	Beaumont-Port Arthur MSA, TX	H	10.45 FQ	17.45 AW	25.47 TQ	TXBLS	10/01-12/01
	Brazoria PMSA, TX	H	11.65 FQ	17.96 AW	25.78 TQ	TXBLS	10/01-12/01
	Brownsville-Harlingen-San Benito MSA, TX	H	8.61 FQ	12.24 AW	18.38 TQ	TXBLS	10/01-12/01
	Corpus Christi MSA, TX	H	11.97 FQ	16.81 AW	22.75 TQ	TXBLS	10/01-12/01
	Dallas PMSA, TX	H	12.31 FQ	17.89 AW	24.08 TQ	TXBLS	10/01-12/01
	El Paso MSA, TX	H	10.99 FQ	15.40 AW	20.19 TQ	TXBLS	10/01-12/01
	Fort Worth-Arlington PMSA, TX	H	10.91 FQ	18.16 AW	28.88 TQ	TXBLS	10/01-12/01
	Galveston-Texas City PMSA, TX	H	10.95 FQ	18.31 AW	24.26 TQ	TXBLS	10/01-12/01
	Houston PMSA, TX	H	11.58 FQ	17.88 AW	26.02 TQ	TXBLS	10/01-12/01
	Killeen-Temple MSA, TX	H	9.11 FQ	15.15 AW	21.72 TQ	TXBLS	10/01-12/01
	Laredo MSA, TX	H	9.67 FQ	14.24 AW	19.91 TQ	TXBLS	10/01-12/01
	Longview-Marshall MSA, TX	H	10.83 FQ	16.54 AW	21.18 TQ	TXBLS	10/01-12/01
	Lubbock MSA, TX	H	8.18 FQ	15.84 AW	24.73 TQ	TXBLS	10/01-12/01
	McAllen-Edinburg-Mission MSA, TX	H	8.91 FQ	12.69 AW	18.00 TQ	TXBLS	10/01-12/01
	Odessa-Midland MSA, TX	H	10.23 FQ	16.27 AW	26.93 TQ	TXBLS	10/01-12/01
	San Antonio MSA, TX	H	9.53 FQ	17.20 AW	25.85 TQ	TXBLS	10/01-12/01
	Tyler MSA, TX	H	10.79 FQ	15.00 AW	21.65 TQ	TXBLS	10/01-12/01
	Waco MSA, TX	H	10.46 FQ	17.12 AW	22.52 TQ	TXBLS	10/01-12/01

AAW	Average annual wage	**AOH**	Average offered, high	**ASH**	Average starting, high	**H**	Hourly	**M**	Monthly	**S**	Special: hourly and annual
AE	Average entry wage	**AOL**	Average offered, low	**ASL**	Average starting, low	**HI**	Highest wage paid	**MTC**	Median total compensation	**TQ**	Third quartile wage
AEX	Average experienced wage	**APH**	Average pay, high range	**AW**	Average wage paid	**HR**	High end range	**MW**	Median wage paid	**W**	Weekly
AO	Average offered	**APL**	Average pay, low range	**FQ**	First quartile wage	**LR**	Low end range	**SQ**	Second quartile wage	**Y**	Yearly

Occupation/Type/Industry	Location	Per	Low	Mid	High	Source	Date
Electrician	Utah	H	11.78 FQ	18.64 AW	26.53 TQ	UTBLS	10/01-12/01
	Provo-Orem MSA, UT	H	8.09 FQ	15.50 AW	22.64 TQ	UTBLS	10/01-12/01
	Salt Lake City-Ogden MSA, UT	H	12.62 FQ	19.49 AW	26.98 TQ	UTBLS	10/01-12/01
	Vermont	H	10.73 FQ	16.01 AW	21.96 TQ	VTBLS	10/01-12/01
	Burlington MSA, VT	H	11.56 FQ	17.53 AW	22.48 TQ	VTBLS	10/01-12/01
	Virginia	H	10.78 FQ	17.84 AW	25.90 TQ	VABLS	10/01-12/01
	Lynchburg MSA, VA	H	9.78 FQ	14.74 AW	21.13 TQ	VABLS	10/01-12/01
	Norfolk-Virginia Beach-Newport News MSA, VA-NC	H	10.60 FQ	16.17 AW	21.36 TQ	VABLS	10/01-12/01
	Richmond-Petersburg MSA, VA	H	11.51 FQ	19.17 AW	25.66 TQ	VABLS	10/01-12/01
	Roanoke MSA, VA	H	10.16 FQ	14.33 AW	18.08 TQ	VABLS	10/01-12/01
	Washington	H	12.75 FQ	22.31 AW	33.00 TQ	WABLS	10/01-12/01
	Bremerton PMSA, WA	H	17.27 FQ	24.06 AW	32.31 TQ	WABLS	10/01-12/01
	Olympia PMSA, WA	H	10.24 FQ	21.65 AW	32.40 TQ	WABLS	10/01-12/01
	Richland-Kennewick-Pasco MSA, WA	H	13.30 FQ	23.09 AW	32.24 TQ	WABLS	10/01-12/01
	Seattle-Bellevue-Everett PMSA, WA	H	14.57 FQ	23.15 AW	33.75 TQ	WABLS	10/01-12/01
	Spokane MSA, WA	H	11.92 FQ	18.79 AW	26.69 TQ	WABLS	10/01-12/01
	Tacoma PMSA, WA	H	13.80 FQ	21.00 AW	29.70 TQ	WABLS	10/01-12/01
	Yakima MSA, WA	H	11.71 FQ	20.88 AW	32.42 TQ	WABLS	10/01-12/01
	West Virginia	H	10.17 FQ	17.98 AW	25.95 TQ	WVBLS	10/01-12/01
	Charleston MSA, WV	H	8.70 FQ	18.86 AW	26.90 TQ	WVBLS	10/01-12/01
	Huntington-Ashland MSA, WV-KY-OH	H	12.51 FQ	20.09 AW	28.64 TQ	WVBLS	10/01-12/01
	Wisconsin	H	11.97 FQ	21.39 AW	30.04 TQ	WIBLS	10/01-12/01
	Appleton-Oshkosh-Neenah MSA, WI	H	9.92 FQ	18.96 AW	27.94 TQ	WIBLS	10/01-12/01
	Green Bay MSA, WI	H	11.62 FQ	21.01 AW	29.96 TQ	WIBLS	10/01-12/01
	Madison MSA, WI	H	11.58 FQ	22.18 AW	30.40 TQ	WIBLS	10/01-12/01
	Milwaukee-Waukesha PMSA, WI	H	13.68 FQ	23.55 AW	33.91 TQ	WIBLS	10/01-12/01
	Racine PMSA, WI	H	13.16 FQ	22.51 AW	29.27 TQ	WIBLS	10/01-12/01
	Wyoming	H	11.93 FQ	18.63 AW	25.56 TQ	WYBLS	10/01-12/01
	Cheyenne MSA, WY	H	10.27 FQ	18.26 AW	23.85 TQ	WYBLS	10/01-12/01
	Puerto Rico	H	6.07 FQ	9.40 AW	14.52 TQ	PRBLS	10/01-12/01
	Virgin Islands	H	11.37 FQ	14.82 AW	18.45 TQ	VIBLS	10/01-12/01
	Guam	H	9.75 FQ	13.00 AW	17.23 TQ	GUBLS	10/01-12/01
Electro-Mechanical Technician	Alabama	Y	21190 FQ	39090 AW	66140 TQ	ALBLS	10/01-12/01
	Alaska	Y	43170 FQ	56670 AW	69440 TQ	AKBLS	10/01-12/01
	Arizona	Y	31050 FQ	43240 AW	57760 TQ	AZBLS	10/01-12/01
	Arkansas	Y	22440 FQ	41350 AW	64610 TQ	ARBLS	10/01-12/01
	California	Y	24510 FQ	39820 AW	57500 TQ	CABLS	10/01-12/01
	Colorado	Y	27590 FQ	40590 AW	53090 TQ	COBLS	10/01-12/01
	Connecticut	Y	21720 FQ	37150 AW	53040 TQ	CTBLS	10/01-12/01
	Delaware	Y	24880 FQ	37790 AW	50250 TQ	DEBLS	10/01-12/01
	District of Columbia	Y	30850 FQ	43300 AW	58030 TQ	DCBLS	10/01-12/01
	Florida	Y	20940 FQ	36210 AW	53640 TQ	FLBLS	10/01-12/01
	Georgia	Y	20560 FQ	32120 AW	44290 TQ	GABLS	10/01-12/01
	Hawaii	Y	35880 FQ	49590 AW	64540 TQ	HIBLS	10/01-12/01
	Idaho	Y	29250 FQ	44260 AW	66540 TQ	IDBLS	10/01-12/01
	Illinois	Y	29810 FQ	58720 AW	93090 TQ	ILBLS	10/01-12/01
	Indiana	Y	25330 FQ	36280 AW	47220 TQ	INBLS	10/01-12/01
	Iowa	Y	23620 FQ	42280 AW	59640 TQ	IABLS	10/01-12/01
	Kansas	Y	26170 FQ	40850 AW	57280 TQ	KSBLS	10/01-12/01
	Kentucky	Y	27160 FQ	36960 AW	45770 TQ	KYBLS	10/01-12/01
	Louisiana	Y	25130 FQ	46780 AW	68430 TQ	LABLS	10/01-12/01
	Maine	Y	28350 FQ	41260 AW	55830 TQ	MEBLS	10/01-12/01
	Maryland	Y	27400 FQ	38510 AW	56480 TQ	MDBLS	10/01-12/01
	Massachusetts	Y	23130 FQ	39170 AW	57670 TQ	MABLS	10/01-12/01
	Michigan	Y	25560 FQ	41000 AW	55800 TQ	MIBLS	10/01-12/01
	Minnesota	Y	29850 FQ	41240 AW	53900 TQ	MNBLS	10/01-12/01
	Mississippi	Y	27070 FQ	40540 AW	54700 TQ	MSBLS	10/01-12/01
	Missouri	Y	20580 FQ	38400 AW	60250 TQ	MOBLS	10/01-12/01
	Montana	Y	24580 FQ	37910 AW	52010 TQ	MTBLS	10/01-12/01
	Nebraska	Y	29250 FQ	35910 AW	45460 TQ	NEBLS	10/01-12/01
	Nevada	Y	22210 FQ	37620 AW	53330 TQ	NVBLS	10/01-12/01
	New Hampshire	Y	24680 FQ	36240 AW	51410 TQ	NHBLS	10/01-12/01
	New Jersey	Y	21730 FQ	36910 AW	54650 TQ	NJBLS	10/01-12/01

AAW Average annual wage **AE** Average entry wage **AEX** Average experienced wage **AO** Average offered **AOH** Average offered, high **AOL** Average offered, low **APH** Average pay, high range **APL** Average pay, low range **ASH** Average starting, high **ASL** Average starting, low **AW** Average wage paid **FQ** First quartile wage **H** Hourly **HI** Highest wage paid **HR** High end range **LR** Low end range **M** Monthly **MTC** Median total compensation **MW** Median wage paid **SQ** Second quartile wage **S** Special: hourly and annual **TQ** Third quartile wage **W** Weekly **Y** Yearly

Occupation/Type/Industry	Location	Per	Low	Mid	High	Source	Date
Electro-Mechanical Technician	New Mexico	Y	27340 FQ	45760 AW	67380 TQ	NMBLS	10/01-12/01
	New York	Y	24800 FQ	38270 AW	53920 TQ	NYBLS	10/01-12/01
	North Carolina	Y	28790 FQ	39720 AW	54110 TQ	NCBLS	10/01-12/01
	North Dakota	Y	21630 FQ	34580 AW	44800 TQ	NDBLS	10/01-12/01
	Ohio	Y	24020 FQ	36340 AW	53860 TQ	OHBLS	10/01-12/01
	Oklahoma	Y	28620 FQ	43620 AW	60550 TQ	OKBLS	10/01-12/01
	Oregon	Y	23080 FQ	38540 AW	54980 TQ	ORBLS	10/01-12/01
	Pennsylvania	Y	26060 FQ	38130 AW	51690 TQ	PABLS	10/01-12/01
	Rhode Island	Y	22330 FQ	37990 AW	71750 TQ	RIBLS	10/01-12/01
	South Carolina	Y	30510 FQ	45450 AW	74220 TQ	SCBLS	10/01-12/01
	South Dakota	Y	22660 FQ	35390 AW	59180 TQ	SDBLS	10/01-12/01
	Tennessee	Y	21620 FQ	35810 AW	49050 TQ	TNBLS	10/01-12/01
	Texas	Y	22740 FQ	38500 AW	55080 TQ	TXBLS	10/01-12/01
	Utah	Y	27740 FQ	39690 AW	52110 TQ	UTBLS	10/01-12/01
	Vermont	Y	30370 FQ	39780 AW	52000 TQ	VTBLS	10/01-12/01
	Virginia	Y	21570 FQ	37350 AW	54010 TQ	VABLS	10/01-12/01
	Washington	Y	30040 FQ	46590 AW	64380 TQ	WABLS	10/01-12/01
	West Virginia	Y	21020 FQ	36890 AW	54780 TQ	WVBLS	10/01-12/01
	Wisconsin	Y	26870 FQ	41610 AW	57830 TQ	WIBLS	10/01-12/01
	Puerto Rico	Y	16580 FQ	31280 AW	44330 TQ	PRBLS	10/01-12/01
Electromechanical Equipment Assembler	Alabama	H	7.85 FQ	11.84 AW	16.80 TQ	ALBLS	10/01-12/01
	Arizona	H	10.11 FQ	18.35 AW	26.16 TQ	AZBLS	10/01-12/01
	Arkansas	H	8.40 FQ	11.76 AW	17.29 TQ	ARBLS	10/01-12/01
	California	H	7.44 FQ	12.08 AW	17.43 TQ	CABLS	10/01-12/01
	Colorado	H	8.26 FQ	11.99 AW	16.47 TQ	COBLS	10/01-12/01
	Connecticut	H	9.15 FQ	14.67 AW	21.35 TQ	CTBLS	10/01-12/01
	Florida	H	6.82 FQ	10.61 AW	15.25 TQ	FLBLS	10/01-12/01
	Georgia	H	9.18 FQ	12.69 AW	16.36 TQ	GABLS	10/01-12/01
	Idaho	H	9.26 FQ	11.37 AW	14.26 TQ	IDBLS	10/01-12/01
	Illinois	H	7.68 FQ	12.71 AW	19.51 TQ	ILBLS	10/01-12/01
	Indiana	H	6.98 FQ	10.62 AW	15.73 TQ	INBLS	10/01-12/01
	Iowa	H	9.00 FQ	12.06 AW	17.14 TQ	IABLS	10/01-12/01
	Kansas	H	6.56 FQ	12.08 AW	19.64 TQ	KSBLS	10/01-12/01
	Kentucky	H	6.39 FQ	11.14 AW	16.61 TQ	KYBLS	10/01-12/01
	Louisiana	H	8.28 FQ	13.42 AW	19.96 TQ	LABLS	10/01-12/01
	Maine	H	7.55 FQ	11.31 AW	16.13 TQ	MEBLS	10/01-12/01
	Maryland	H	6.69 FQ	11.58 AW	17.41 TQ	MDBLS	10/01-12/01
	Massachusetts	H	9.63 FQ	14.09 AW	19.69 TQ	MABLS	10/01-12/01
	Michigan	H	9.77 FQ	14.03 AW	19.82 TQ	MIBLS	10/01-12/01
	Minnesota	H	9.81 FQ	13.06 AW	16.85 TQ	MNBLS	10/01-12/01
	Mississippi	H	6.18 FQ	8.66 AW	11.16 TQ	MSBLS	10/01-12/01
	Missouri	H	7.78 FQ	13.01 AW	22.93 TQ	MOBLS	10/01-12/01
	Montana	H	9.61 FQ	12.85 AW	16.46 TQ	MTBLS	10/01-12/01
	Nebraska	H	6.94 FQ	10.91 AW	14.11 TQ	NEBLS	10/01-12/01
	Nevada	H	8.68 FQ	11.51 AW	15.57 TQ	NVBLS	10/01-12/01
	New Hampshire	H	9.32 FQ	12.20 AW	15.85 TQ	NHBLS	10/01-12/01
	New Jersey	H	8.77 FQ	14.16 AW	21.40 TQ	NJBLS	10/01-12/01
	New Mexico	H	7.91 FQ	12.33 AW	17.88 TQ	NMBLS	10/01-12/01
	New York	H	7.49 FQ	11.94 AW	18.45 TQ	NYBLS	10/01-12/01
	North Carolina	H	8.07 FQ	11.21 AW	14.62 TQ	NCBLS	10/01-12/01
	Ohio	H	7.84 FQ	14.05 AW	20.61 TQ	OHBLS	10/01-12/01
	Oklahoma	H	8.32 FQ	10.67 AW	14.14 TQ	OKBLS	10/01-12/01
	Oregon	H	8.45 FQ	12.16 AW	16.55 TQ	ORBLS	10/01-12/01
	Pennsylvania	H	8.13 FQ	13.76 AW	20.27 TQ	PABLS	10/01-12/01
	Rhode Island	H	6.68 FQ	9.69 AW	14.39 TQ	RIBLS	10/01-12/01
	South Carolina	H	9.37 FQ	13.19 AW	16.84 TQ	SCBLS	10/01-12/01
	South Dakota	H	7.58 FQ	10.44 AW	14.43 TQ	SDBLS	10/01-12/01
	Tennessee	H	9.44 FQ	12.68 AW	16.21 TQ	TNBLS	10/01-12/01
	Texas	H	6.52 FQ	10.60 AW	15.77 TQ	TXBLS	10/01-12/01
	Utah	H	9.21 FQ	12.68 AW	17.91 TQ	UTBLS	10/01-12/01
	Vermont	H	7.83 FQ	11.59 AW	18.99 TQ	VTBLS	10/01-12/01
	Virginia	H	9.06 FQ	12.07 AW	17.37 TQ	VABLS	10/01-12/01
	Washington	H	9.03 FQ	14.63 AW	24.50 TQ	WABLS	10/01-12/01
	West Virginia	H	7.53 FQ	9.84 AW	12.93 TQ	WVBLS	10/01-12/01
	Wisconsin	H	7.80 FQ	11.70 AW	16.72 TQ	WIBLS	10/01-12/01
	Puerto Rico	H	5.85 FQ	8.18 AW	13.40 TQ	PRBLS	10/01-12/01
Electronic Commerce Specialist	United States	Y		59750-89500 AW		WW	1/00-1/01

AAW	Average annual wage	**AOH**	Average offered, high	**ASH**	Average starting, high	**H**	Hourly	**M**	Monthly	**S**	Special: hourly and annual
AE	Average entry wage	**AOL**	Average offered, low	**ASL**	Average starting, low	**HI**	Highest wage paid	**MTC**	Median total compensation	**TQ**	Third quartile wage
AEX	Average experienced wage	**APH**	Average pay, high range	**AW**	Average wage paid	**HR**	High end range	**MW**	Median wage paid	**W**	Weekly
AO	Average offered	**APL**	Average pay, low range	**FQ**	First quartile wage	**LR**	Low end range	**SQ**	Second quartile wage	**Y**	Yearly

Occupation/Type/Industry	Location	Per	Low	Mid	High	Source	Date
Electronic Equipment Installer and Repairer							
Motor Vehicle	Alabama	H	9.05 FQ	12.45 AW	17.70 TQ	ALBLS	10/01-12/01
Motor Vehicle	Alaska	H	8.96 FQ	12.86 AW	18.11 TQ	AKBLS	10/01-12/01
Motor Vehicle	Anchorage MSA, AK	H	8.99 FQ	12.49 AW	17.08 TQ	AKBLS	10/01-12/01
Motor Vehicle	Arizona	H	8.09 FQ	14.61 AW	19.34 TQ	AZBLS	10/01-12/01
Motor Vehicle	Arkansas	H	9.30 FQ	11.57 AW	16.23 TQ	ARBLS	10/01-12/01
Motor Vehicle	California	H	7.92 FQ	11.52 AW	16.63 TQ	CABLS	10/01-12/01
Motor Vehicle	Los Angeles-Long Beach PMSA, CA	H	7.05 FQ	11.90 AW	18.00 TQ	CABLS	10/01-12/01
Motor Vehicle	Oakland PMSA, CA	H	7.39 FQ	10.20 AW	12.78 TQ	CABLS	10/01-12/01
Motor Vehicle	Orange County PMSA, CA	H	6.73 FQ	10.21 AW	13.14 TQ	CABLS	10/01-12/01
Motor Vehicle	Riverside-San Bernardino PMSA, CA	H	9.24 FQ	12.80 AW	18.52 TQ	CABLS	10/01-12/01
Motor Vehicle	Sacramento PMSA, CA	H	9.31 FQ	11.63 AW	13.88 TQ	CABLS	10/01-12/01
Motor Vehicle	San Diego MSA, CA	H	9.10 FQ	15.46 AW	25.87 TQ	CABLS	10/01-12/01
Motor Vehicle	San Francisco PMSA, CA	H	9.06 FQ	12.11 AW	22.58 TQ	CABLS	10/01-12/01
Motor Vehicle	San Jose PMSA, CA	H	8.73 FQ	9.77 AW	10.60 TQ	CABLS	10/01-12/01
Motor Vehicle	Ventura PMSA, CA	H	6.97 FQ	11.42 AW	18.90 TQ	CABLS	10/01-12/01
Motor Vehicle	Colorado	H	8.38 FQ	12.50 AW	17.26 TQ	COBLS	10/01-12/01
Motor Vehicle	Denver PMSA, CO	H	11.17 FQ	13.53 AW	19.25 TQ	COBLS	10/01-12/01
Motor Vehicle	Connecticut	H	8.49 FQ	12.56 AW	16.50 TQ	CTBLS	10/01-12/01
Motor Vehicle	Hartford MSA, CT	H	9.22 FQ	12.96 AW	16.48 TQ	CTBLS	10/01-12/01
Motor Vehicle	Washington PMSA, DC-MD-VA-WV	H	9.61 FQ	15.37 AW	24.10 TQ	DCBLS	10/01-12/01
Motor Vehicle	Florida	H	9.01 FQ	12.61 AW	16.85 TQ	FLBLS	10/01-12/01
Motor Vehicle	Fort Lauderdale PMSA, FL	H	9.72 FQ	13.62 AW	17.56 TQ	FLBLS	10/01-12/01
Motor Vehicle	Jacksonville MSA, FL	H	8.25 FQ	10.37 AW	14.63 TQ	FLBLS	10/01-12/01
Motor Vehicle	Georgia	H	6.72 FQ	10.96 AW	15.81 TQ	GABLS	10/01-12/01
Motor Vehicle	Atlanta MSA, GA	H	9.54 FQ	13.17 AW	16.96 TQ	GABLS	10/01-12/01
Motor Vehicle	Hawaii	H	7.40 FQ	10.28 AW	14.72 TQ	HIBLS	10/01-12/01
Motor Vehicle	Idaho	H	9.33 FQ	13.11 AW	20.74 TQ	IDBLS	10/01-12/01
Motor Vehicle	Illinois	H	8.53 FQ	13.99 AW	21.45 TQ	ILBLS	10/01-12/01
Motor Vehicle	Chicago PMSA, IL	H	9.21 FQ	13.57 AW	22.78 TQ	ILBLS	10/01-12/01
Motor Vehicle	Indiana	H	9.39 FQ	13.44 AW	17.01 TQ	INBLS	10/01-12/01
Motor Vehicle	Fort Wayne MSA, IN	H	9.24 FQ	14.77 AW	22.06 TQ	INBLS	10/01-12/01
Motor Vehicle	Indianapolis MSA, IN	H	12.26 FQ	14.49 AW	16.58 TQ	INBLS	10/01-12/01
Motor Vehicle	Iowa	H	8.15 FQ	12.26 AW	16.78 TQ	IABLS	10/01-12/01
Motor Vehicle	Davenport-Moline-Rock Island MSA, IA-IL	H	7.25 FQ	10.90 AW	15.64 TQ	IABLS	10/01-12/01
Motor Vehicle	Des Moines MSA, IA	H	8.99 FQ	13.83 AW	18.17 TQ	IABLS	10/01-12/01
Motor Vehicle	Kansas	H	8.03 FQ	10.61 AW	14.43 TQ	KSBLS	10/01-12/01
Motor Vehicle	Kentucky	H	7.89 FQ	12.08 AW	16.75 TQ	KYBLS	10/01-12/01
Motor Vehicle	Louisville MSA, KY-IN	H	7.43 FQ	11.75 AW	17.80 TQ	KYBLS	10/01-12/01
Motor Vehicle	Louisiana	H	8.59 FQ	13.57 AW	18.87 TQ	LABLS	10/01-12/01
Motor Vehicle	Maryland	H	8.89 FQ	13.49 AW	19.86 TQ	MDBLS	10/01-12/01
Motor Vehicle	Massachusetts	H	9.28 FQ	13.63 AW	19.60 TQ	MABLS	10/01-12/01
Motor Vehicle	Boston PMSA, MA-NH	H	9.60 FQ	16.56 AW	26.19 TQ	MABLS	10/01-12/01
Motor Vehicle	Worcester PMSA, MA-CT	H	9.19 FQ	12.33 AW	16.09 TQ	MABLS	10/01-12/01
Motor Vehicle	Michigan	H	8.95 FQ	12.70 AW	17.06 TQ	MIBLS	10/01-12/01
Motor Vehicle	Detroit PMSA, MI	H	10.16 FQ	13.35 AW	18.54 TQ	MIBLS	10/01-12/01
Motor Vehicle	Grand Rapids-Muskegon-Holland MSA, MI	H	8.90 FQ	11.25 AW	14.74 TQ	MIBLS	10/01-12/01
Motor Vehicle	Minnesota	H	8.96 FQ	12.26 AW	17.95 TQ	MNBLS	10/01-12/01
Motor Vehicle	Minneapolis-St. Paul MSA, MN-WI	H	9.00 FQ	11.93 AW	16.34 TQ	MNBLS	10/01-12/01
Motor Vehicle	Mississippi	H	6.20 FQ	9.65 AW	15.36 TQ	MSBLS	10/01-12/01
Motor Vehicle	Missouri	H	7.81 FQ	14.66 AW	24.87 TQ	MOBLS	10/01-12/01
Motor Vehicle	Kansas City MSA, MO-KS	H	9.10 FQ	12.40 AW	19.18 TQ	MOBLS	10/01-12/01
Motor Vehicle	St. Louis MSA, MO-IL	H	6.23 FQ	12.94 AW	25.25 TQ	MOBLS	10/01-12/01
Motor Vehicle	Montana	H	8.96 FQ	10.24 AW	11.11 TQ	MTBLS	10/01-12/01
Motor Vehicle	Nevada	H	8.81 FQ	11.52 AW	16.60 TQ	NVBLS	10/01-12/01
Motor Vehicle	Las Vegas MSA, NV-AZ	H	8.99 FQ	11.69 AW	16.62 TQ	NVBLS	10/01-12/01
Motor Vehicle	New Hampshire	H	10.32 FQ	16.47 AW	26.23 TQ	NHBLS	10/01-12/01
Motor Vehicle	New Jersey	H	9.66 FQ	14.61 AW	20.64 TQ	NJBLS	10/01-12/01
Motor Vehicle	Bergen-Passaic PMSA, NJ	H	10.61 FQ	14.71 AW	19.86 TQ	NJBLS	10/01-12/01
Motor Vehicle	Middlesex-Somerset-Hunterdon PMSA, NJ	H	9.54 FQ	14.92 AW	21.58 TQ	NJBLS	10/01-12/01
Motor Vehicle	Newark PMSA, NJ	H	10.56 FQ	15.13 AW	20.52 TQ	NJBLS	10/01-12/01
Motor Vehicle	New York	H	8.79 FQ	14.95 AW	17.59 TQ	NYBLS	10/01-12/01
Motor Vehicle	Buffalo-Niagara Falls MSA, NY	H	7.81 FQ	12.72 AW	19.88 TQ	NYBLS	10/01-12/01

AAW	Average annual wage	AOH	Average offered, high	ASH	Average starting, high	H	Hourly	M	Monthly	S	Special: hourly and annual
AE	Average entry wage	AOL	Average offered, low	ASL	Average starting, low	HI	Highest wage paid	MTC	Median total compensation	TQ	Third quartile wage
AEX	Average experienced wage	APH	Average pay, high range	AW	Average wage paid	HR	High end range	MW	Median wage paid	W	Weekly
AO	Average offered	APL	Average pay, low range	FQ	First quartile wage	LR	Low end range	SQ	Second quartile wage	Y	Yearly

Occupation/Type/Industry	Location	Per	Low	Mid	High	Source	Date
Electronic Equipment Installer and Repairer							
Motor Vehicle	Nassau-Suffolk PMSA, NY	H	14.39 FQ	15.70 AW	17.31 TQ	NYBLS	10/01-12/01
Motor Vehicle	New York PMSA, NY	H	7.51 FQ	12.76 AW	25.20 TQ	NYBLS	10/01-12/01
Motor Vehicle	Rochester MSA, NY	H	11.83 FQ	19.64 AW	26.26 TQ	NYBLS	10/01-12/01
Motor Vehicle	North Carolina	H	10.62 FQ	16.30 AW	21.79 TQ	NCBLS	10/01-12/01
Motor Vehicle	North Dakota	H	9.11 FQ	12.68 AW	16.97 TQ	NDBLS	10/01-12/01
Motor Vehicle	Ohio	H	8.23 FQ	12.19 AW	18.37 TQ	OHBLS	10/01-12/01
Motor Vehicle	Cincinnati PMSA, OH-KY-IN	H	9.06 FQ	11.08 AW	14.05 TQ	OHBLS	10/01-12/01
Motor Vehicle	Cleveland-Lorain-Elyria PMSA, OH	H	8.32 FQ	13.50 AW	20.64 TQ	OHBLS	10/01-12/01
Motor Vehicle	Columbus MSA, OH	H	7.99 FQ	10.51 AW	13.75 TQ	OHBLS	10/01-12/01
Motor Vehicle	Oklahoma	H	6.90 FQ	13.21 AW	21.31 TQ	OKBLS	10/01-12/01
Motor Vehicle	Oklahoma City MSA, OK	H	8.32 FQ	15.96 AW	22.90 TQ	OKBLS	10/01-12/01
Motor Vehicle	Oregon	H	9.38 FQ	14.01 AW	20.78 TQ	ORBLS	10/01-12/01
Motor Vehicle	Portland-Vancouver PMSA, OR-WA	H	9.20 FQ	14.52 AW	21.26 TQ	ORBLS	10/01-12/01
Motor Vehicle	Salem PMSA, OR	H	12.60 FQ	17.44 AW	23.12 TQ	ORBLS	10/01-12/01
Motor Vehicle	Pennsylvania	H	7.38 FQ	12.03 AW	17.17 TQ	PABLS	10/01-12/01
Motor Vehicle	Philadelphia PMSA, PA-NJ	H	6.51 FQ	11.44 AW	16.41 TQ	PABLS	10/01-12/01
Motor Vehicle	South Carolina	H	7.60 FQ	11.00 AW	18.86 TQ	SCBLS	10/01-12/01
Motor Vehicle	South Dakota	H	9.09 FQ	10.34 AW	12.02 TQ	SDBLS	10/01-12/01
Motor Vehicle	Tennessee	H	7.42 FQ	10.57 AW	14.47 TQ	TNBLS	10/01-12/01
Motor Vehicle	Johnson City-Kingsport-Bristol MSA, TN-VA	H	7.36 FQ	9.39 AW	11.07 TQ	TNBLS	10/01-12/01
Motor Vehicle	Memphis MSA, TN-AR-MS	H	9.67 FQ	12.37 AW	15.81 TQ	TNBLS	10/01-12/01
Motor Vehicle	Texas	H	7.82 FQ	14.40 AW	25.96 TQ	TXBLS	10/01-12/01
Motor Vehicle	Dallas PMSA, TX	H	9.34 FQ	14.22 AW	21.85 TQ	TXBLS	10/01-12/01
Motor Vehicle	Houston PMSA, TX	H	10.14 FQ	14.48 AW	23.51 TQ	TXBLS	10/01-12/01
Motor Vehicle	San Antonio MSA, TX	H	6.43 FQ	10.32 AW	13.74 TQ	TXBLS	10/01-12/01
Motor Vehicle	Utah	H	8.97 FQ	12.58 AW	17.90 TQ	UTBLS	10/01-12/01
Motor Vehicle	Salt Lake City-Ogden MSA, UT	H	9.14 FQ	12.77 AW	18.28 TQ	UTBLS	10/01-12/01
Motor Vehicle	Virginia	H	8.60 FQ	15.19 AW	24.31 TQ	VABLS	10/01-12/01
Motor Vehicle	Richmond-Petersburg MSA, VA	H	7.07 FQ	13.62 AW	21.93 TQ	VABLS	10/01-12/01
Motor Vehicle	Washington	H	10.25 FQ	17.44 AW	24.49 TQ	WABLS	10/01-12/01
Motor Vehicle	Seattle-Bellevue-Everett PMSA, WA	H	12.84 FQ	18.36 AW	23.14 TQ	WABLS	10/01-12/01
Motor Vehicle	West Virginia	H	10.35 FQ	14.60 AW	21.21 TQ	WVBLS	10/01-12/01
Motor Vehicle	Wisconsin	H	9.43 FQ	12.65 AW	17.03 TQ	WIBLS	10/01-12/01
Motor Vehicle	Milwaukee-Waukesha PMSA, WI	H	9.54 FQ	12.55 AW	16.67 TQ	WIBLS	10/01-12/01
Motor Vehicle	Puerto Rico	H	6.00 FQ	9.32 AW	14.01 TQ	PRBLS	10/01-12/01
Electronic Home Entertainment Equipment Installer and Repairer	Alabama	H	7.41 FQ	13.36 AW	21.61 TQ	ALBLS	10/01-12/01
	Arizona	H	10.03 FQ	16.25 AW	22.31 TQ	AZBLS	10/01-12/01
	Arkansas	H	7.15 FQ	11.21 AW	16.80 TQ	ARBLS	10/01-12/01
	California	H	7.56 FQ	14.49 AW	21.43 TQ	CABLS	10/01-12/01
	Colorado	H	9.20 FQ	15.29 AW	22.10 TQ	COBLS	10/01-12/01
	Connecticut	H	9.18 FQ	15.67 AW	22.95 TQ	CTBLS	10/01-12/01
	Delaware	H	9.20 FQ	16.50 AW	22.66 TQ	DEBLS	10/01-12/01
	Florida	H	8.16 FQ	14.37 AW	23.57 TQ	FLBLS	10/01-12/01
	Georgia	H	9.09 FQ	13.45 AW	18.97 TQ	GABLS	10/01-12/01
	Hawaii	H	6.09 FQ	11.69 AW	20.81 TQ	HIBLS	10/01-12/01
	Idaho	H	7.80 FQ	12.93 AW	20.21 TQ	IDBLS	10/01-12/01
	Illinois	H	9.88 FQ	16.25 AW	22.29 TQ	ILBLS	10/01-12/01
	Indiana	H	8.11 FQ	13.26 AW	20.46 TQ	INBLS	10/01-12/01
	Iowa	H	8.98 FQ	12.96 AW	17.51 TQ	IABLS	10/01-12/01
	Kansas	H	8.07 FQ	13.17 AW	17.65 TQ	KSBLS	10/01-12/01
	Kentucky	H	7.38 FQ	12.27 AW	17.35 TQ	KYBLS	10/01-12/01
	Louisiana	H	6.72 FQ	12.49 AW	19.06 TQ	LABLS	10/01-12/01
	Maine	H	7.13 FQ	12.13 AW	18.80 TQ	MEBLS	10/01-12/01
	Maryland	H	9.49 FQ	15.35 AW	21.70 TQ	MDBLS	10/01-12/01
	Massachusetts	H	11.50 FQ	16.50 AW	21.42 TQ	MABLS	10/01-12/01
	Michigan	H	7.65 FQ	13.17 AW	21.47 TQ	MIBLS	10/01-12/01
	Minnesota	H	7.34 FQ	13.77 AW	24.34 TQ	MNBLS	10/01-12/01
	Mississippi	H	6.68 FQ	11.01 AW	16.44 TQ	MSBLS	10/01-12/01
	Missouri	H	8.05 FQ	13.43 AW	20.21 TQ	MOBLS	10/01-12/01

AAW Average annual wage **AE** Average entry wage **AEX** Average experienced wage **AO** Average offered **AOH** Average offered, high **AOL** Average offered, low **APH** Average pay, high range **APL** Average pay, low range **ASH** Average starting, high **ASL** Average starting, low **AW** Average wage paid **FQ** First quartile wage **H** Hourly **HI** Highest wage paid **HR** High end range **LR** Low end range **M** Monthly **MTC** Median total compensation **MW** Median wage paid **SQ** Second quartile wage **S** Special: hourly and annual **TQ** Third quartile wage **W** Weekly **Y** Yearly

Occupation/Type/Industry	Location	Per	Low	Mid	High	Source	Date
Electronic Home Entertainment Equipment Installer and Repairer	Montana	H	7.46 FQ	12.32 AW	17.85 TQ	MTBLS	10/01-12/01
	Nebraska	H	8.93 FQ	12.66 AW	16.93 TQ	NEBLS	10/01-12/01
	Nevada	H	10.81 FQ	16.18 AW	23.10 TQ	NVBLS	10/01-12/01
	New Hampshire	H	9.15 FQ	15.25 AW	21.57 TQ	NHBLS	10/01-12/01
	New Jersey	H	9.65 FQ	15.45 AW	22.19 TQ	NJBLS	10/01-12/01
	New Mexico	H	7.51 FQ	12.17 AW	17.48 TQ	NMBLS	10/01-12/01
	New York	H	6.33 FQ	13.33 AW	22.65 TQ	NYBLS	10/01-12/01
	North Carolina	H	8.04 FQ	12.50 AW	18.93 TQ	NCBLS	10/01-12/01
	North Dakota	H	7.61 FQ	12.12 AW	17.43 TQ	NDBLS	10/01-12/01
	Ohio	H	8.98 FQ	13.82 AW	20.66 TQ	OHBLS	10/01-12/01
	Oklahoma	H	7.18 FQ	12.06 AW	17.17 TQ	OKBLS	10/01-12/01
	Oregon	H	8.82 FQ	13.65 AW	20.78 TQ	ORBLS	10/01-12/01
	Pennsylvania	H	8.61 FQ	13.67 AW	20.85 TQ	PABLS	10/01-12/01
	Rhode Island	H	14.86 FQ	20.02 AW	30.74 TQ	RIBLS	10/01-12/01
	South Carolina	H	6.92 FQ	14.15 AW	31.93 TQ	SCBLS	10/01-12/01
	South Dakota	H	8.10 FQ	11.74 AW	16.85 TQ	SDBLS	10/01-12/01
	Tennessee	H	6.84 FQ	12.31 AW	19.21 TQ	TNBLS	10/01-12/01
	Texas	H	8.70 FQ	13.21 AW	19.30 TQ	TXBLS	10/01-12/01
	Utah	H	9.79 FQ	13.80 AW	21.09 TQ	UTBLS	10/01-12/01
	Vermont	H	9.19 FQ	13.47 AW	17.04 TQ	VTBLS	10/01-12/01
	Virginia	H	8.53 FQ	12.69 AW	19.30 TQ	VABLS	10/01-12/01
	Washington	H	9.93 FQ	16.18 AW	22.73 TQ	WABLS	10/01-12/01
	West Virginia	H	7.83 FQ	10.70 AW	13.49 TQ	WVBLS	10/01-12/01
	Wisconsin	H	8.17 FQ	12.65 AW	18.43 TQ	WIBLS	10/01-12/01
	Wyoming	H	7.18 FQ	14.05 AW	29.89 TQ	WYBLS	10/01-12/01
	Puerto Rico	H	6.18 FQ	10.84 AW	16.41 TQ	PRBLS	10/01-12/01
Electronics Engineer							
Except Computer	Alabama	Y	47550 FQ	71360 AW	93780 TQ	ALBLS	10/01-12/01
Except Computer	Birmingham MSA, AL	Y	46990 FQ	64320 AW	84380 TQ	ALBLS	10/01-12/01
Except Computer	Huntsville MSA, AL	Y	53990 FQ	75040 AW	96640 TQ	ALBLS	10/01-12/01
Except Computer	Alaska	Y	59160 FQ	71120 AW	89480 TQ	AKBLS	10/01-12/01
Except Computer	Anchorage MSA, AK	Y	59420 FQ	71060 AW	89760 TQ	AKBLS	10/01-12/01
Except Computer	Arizona	Y	47140 FQ	70910 AW	104680 TQ	AZBLS	10/01-12/01
Except Computer	Phoenix-Mesa MSA, AZ	Y	47060 FQ	70610 AW	104840 TQ	AZBLS	10/01-12/01
Except Computer	Tucson MSA, AZ	Y	45880 FQ	74280 AW	110160 TQ	AZBLS	10/01-12/01
Except Computer	Arkansas	Y	39300 FQ	58470 AW	84620 TQ	ARBLS	10/01-12/01
Except Computer	Fayetteville-Springdale-Rogers MSA, AR	Y	30560 FQ	48980 AW	58080 TQ	ARBLS	10/01-12/01
Except Computer	Little Rock-North Little Rock MSA, AR	Y	45720 FQ	60970 AW	84530 TQ	ARBLS	10/01-12/01
Except Computer	California	Y	47560 FQ	75110 AW	109540 TQ	CABLS	10/01-12/01
Except Computer	Bakersfield MSA, CA	Y	58430 FQ	81710 AW	113160 TQ	CABLS	10/01-12/01
Except Computer	Los Angeles-Long Beach PMSA, CA	Y	42640 FQ	74740 AW	113020 TQ	CABLS	10/01-12/01
Except Computer	Oakland PMSA, CA	Y	52730 FQ	74670 AW	103220 TQ	CABLS	10/01-12/01
Except Computer	Orange County PMSA, CA	Y	46470 FQ	72370 AW	98650 TQ	CABLS	10/01-12/01
Except Computer	Riverside-San Bernardino PMSA, CA	Y	49030 FQ	68390 AW	88710 TQ	CABLS	10/01-12/01
Except Computer	Sacramento PMSA, CA	Y	46680 FQ	65420 AW	90870 TQ	CABLS	10/01-12/01
Except Computer	Salinas MSA, CA	Y	47510 FQ	63200 AW	85750 TQ	CABLS	10/01-12/01
Except Computer	San Diego MSA, CA	Y	50910 FQ	75830 AW	106600 TQ	CABLS	10/01-12/01
Except Computer	San Francisco PMSA, CA	Y	49050 FQ	75960 AW	109960 TQ	CABLS	10/01-12/01
Except Computer	San Jose PMSA, CA	Y	46960 FQ	78580 AW	117600 TQ	CABLS	10/01-12/01
Except Computer	Santa Barbara-Santa Maria-Lompoc MSA, CA	Y	52630 FQ	85840 AW	128630 TQ	CABLS	10/01-12/01
Except Computer	Santa Cruz-Watsonville PMSA, CA	Y	45750 FQ	73160 AW	106370 TQ	CABLS	10/01-12/01
Except Computer	Santa Rosa PMSA, CA	Y	46900 FQ	76530 AW	113080 TQ	CABLS	10/01-12/01
Except Computer	Stockton-Lodi MSA, CA	Y	46370 FQ	57180 AW	75870 TQ	CABLS	10/01-12/01
Except Computer	Vallejo-Fairfield-Napa PMSA, CA	Y	42340 FQ	61770 AW	93200 TQ	CABLS	10/01-12/01
Except Computer	Ventura PMSA, CA	Y	50620 FQ	73900 AW	99870 TQ	CABLS	10/01-12/01
Except Computer	Visalia-Tulare-Porterville MSA, CA	Y	34910 FQ	55960 AW	79820 TQ	CABLS	10/01-12/01
Except Computer	Colorado	Y	47620 FQ	70470 AW	102190 TQ	COBLS	10/01-12/01
Except Computer	Boulder-Longmont PMSA, CO	Y	53490 FQ	83840 AW	123980 TQ	COBLS	10/01-12/01
Except Computer	Colorado Springs MSA, CO	Y	48930 FQ	70030 AW	97410 TQ	COBLS	10/01-12/01
Except Computer	Denver PMSA, CO	Y	45570 FQ	64390 AW	89060 TQ	COBLS	10/01-12/01

AAW	Average annual wage	AOH	Average offered, high	ASH	Average starting, high	H	Hourly	M	Monthly	S	Special: hourly and annual
AE	Average entry wage	AOL	Average offered, low	ASL	Average starting, low	HI	Highest wage paid	MTC	Median total compensation	TQ	Third quartile wage
AEX	Average experienced wage	APH	Average pay, high range	AW	Average wage paid	HR	High end range	MW	Median wage paid	W	Weekly
AO	Average offered	APL	Average pay, low range	FQ	First quartile wage	LR	Low end range	SQ	Second quartile wage	Y	Yearly

Occupation/Type/Industry	Location	Per	Low	Mid	High	Source	Date
Electronics Engineer							
Except Computer	Fort Collins-Loveland MSA, CO	Y	44180 FQ	64720 AW	85000 TQ	COBLS	10/01-12/01
Except Computer	Greeley PMSA, CO	Y	46240 FQ	67630 AW	93050 TQ	COBLS	10/01-12/01
Except Computer	Connecticut	Y	46640 FQ	69120 AW	98950 TQ	CTBLS	10/01-12/01
Except Computer	Bridgeport PMSA, CT	Y	43670 FQ	71570 AW	102380 TQ	CTBLS	10/01-12/01
Except Computer	Danbury PMSA, CT	Y	46640 FQ	68940 AW	103200 TQ	CTBLS	10/01-12/01
Except Computer	Hartford MSA, CT	Y	45940 FQ	63140 AW	87190 TQ	CTBLS	10/01-12/01
Except Computer	New Haven-Meriden PMSA, CT	Y	47200 FQ	71560 AW	104140 TQ	CTBLS	10/01-12/01
Except Computer	New London-Norwich MSA, CT-RI	Y	49970 FQ	76120 AW	108600 TQ	CTBLS	10/01-12/01
Except Computer	Stamford-Norwalk PMSA, CT	Y	42540 FQ	66130 AW	95970 TQ	CTBLS	10/01-12/01
Except Computer	Delaware	Y	39840 FQ	64470 AW	90160 TQ	DEBLS	10/01-12/01
Except Computer	Wilmington-Newark PMSA, DE-MD	Y	44750 FQ	66830 AW	90950 TQ	DEBLS	10/01-12/01
Except Computer	District of Columbia	Y	57600 FQ	84120 AW	111750 TQ	DCBLS	10/01-12/01
Except Computer	Washington PMSA, DC-MD-VA-WV	Y	51530 FQ	77330 AW	108870 TQ	DCBLS	10/01-12/01
Except Computer	Florida	Y	43360 FQ	64790 AW	89360 TQ	FLBLS	10/01-12/01
Except Computer	Daytona Beach MSA, FL	Y	40110 FQ	56300 AW	74450 TQ	FLBLS	10/01-12/01
Except Computer	Fort Lauderdale PMSA, FL	Y	38600 FQ	60080 AW	87820 TQ	FLBLS	10/01-12/01
Except Computer	Fort Walton Beach MSA, FL	Y	48030 FQ	66300 AW	87870 TQ	FLBLS	10/01-12/01
Except Computer	Jacksonville MSA, FL	Y	42580 FQ	60700 AW	79860 TQ	FLBLS	10/01-12/01
Except Computer	Lakeland-Winter Haven MSA, FL	Y	46370 FQ	61330 AW	76200 TQ	FLBLS	10/01-12/01
Except Computer	Melbourne-Titusville-Palm Bay MSA, FL	Y	47900 FQ	69050 AW	90900 TQ	FLBLS	10/01-12/01
Except Computer	Miami PMSA, FL	Y	43430 FQ	69290 AW	90430 TQ	FLBLS	10/01-12/01
Except Computer	Ocala MSA, FL	Y	47010 FQ	65630 AW	88590 TQ	FLBLS	10/01-12/01
Except Computer	Orlando MSA, FL	Y	47830 FQ	68030 AW	89410 TQ	FLBLS	10/01-12/01
Except Computer	Sarasota-Bradenton MSA, FL	Y	38160 FQ	57700 AW	76510 TQ	FLBLS	10/01-12/01
Except Computer	Tallahassee MSA, FL	Y	44060 FQ	64190 AW	95610 TQ	FLBLS	10/01-12/01
Except Computer	Tampa-St. Petersburg-Clearwater MSA, FL	Y	41660 FQ	66470 AW	92850 TQ	FLBLS	10/01-12/01
Except Computer	West Palm Beach-Boca Raton MSA, FL	Y	30560 FQ	58580 AW	77460 TQ	FLBLS	10/01-12/01
Except Computer	Georgia	Y	43070 FQ	66550 AW	95240 TQ	GABLS	10/01-12/01
Except Computer	Atlanta MSA, GA	Y	44460 FQ	68230 AW	97360 TQ	GABLS	10/01-12/01
Except Computer	Augusta-Aiken MSA, GA-SC	Y	45690 FQ	66510 AW	87300 TQ	GABLS	10/01-12/01
Except Computer	Macon MSA, GA	Y	45200 FQ	61690 AW	77620 TQ	GABLS	10/01-12/01
Except Computer	Savannah MSA, GA	Y	43270 FQ	74450 AW	111050 TQ	GABLS	10/01-12/01
Except Computer	Hawaii	Y	49360 FQ	69190 AW	89290 TQ	HIBLS	10/01-12/01
Except Computer	Honolulu MSA, HI	Y	48570 FQ	69290 AW	89530 TQ	HIBLS	10/01-12/01
Except Computer	Idaho	Y	33410 FQ	69660 AW		IDBLS	10/01-12/01
Except Computer	Boise City MSA, ID	Y	43580 FQ	66850 AW	94610 TQ	IDBLS	10/01-12/01
Except Computer	Illinois	Y	44560 FQ	64520 AW	90330 TQ	ILBLS	10/01-12/01
Except Computer	Chicago PMSA, IL	Y	44480 FQ	65270 AW	91070 TQ	ILBLS	10/01-12/01
Except Computer	Rockford MSA, IL	Y	45320 FQ	71280 AW	108260 TQ	ILBLS	10/01-12/01
Except Computer	Springfield MSA, IL	Y	49060 FQ	60890 AW	73670 TQ	ILBLS	10/01-12/01
Except Computer	Indiana	Y	35900 FQ	57360 AW	78890 TQ	INBLS	10/01-12/01
Except Computer	Elkhart-Goshen MSA, IN	Y	31260 FQ	44220 AW	68650 TQ	INBLS	10/01-12/01
Except Computer	Fort Wayne MSA, IN	Y	38530 FQ	54970 AW	72660 TQ	INBLS	10/01-12/01
Except Computer	Indianapolis MSA, IN	Y	33580 FQ	51600 AW	71550 TQ	INBLS	10/01-12/01
Except Computer	South Bend MSA, IN	Y	46470 FQ	69080 AW	102520 TQ	INBLS	10/01-12/01
Except Computer	Iowa	Y	36030 FQ	54580 AW	72850 TQ	IABLS	10/01-12/01
Except Computer	Davenport-Moline-Rock Island MSA, IA-IL	Y	31960 FQ	56680 AW	82720 TQ	IABLS	10/01-12/01
Except Computer	Des Moines MSA, IA	Y	46550 FQ	52380 AW	62120 TQ	IABLS	10/01-12/01
Except Computer	Kansas	Y	41130 FQ	61670 AW	86430 TQ	KSBLS	10/01-12/01
Except Computer	Topeka MSA, KS	Y	45100 FQ	62680 AW	87280 TQ	KSBLS	10/01-12/01
Except Computer	Wichita MSA, KS	Y	40950 FQ	61320 AW	86980 TQ	KSBLS	10/01-12/01
Except Computer	Kentucky	Y	39160 FQ	61120 AW	84440 TQ	KYBLS	10/01-12/01
Except Computer	Lexington MSA, KY	Y	40230 FQ	61830 AW	85920 TQ	KYBLS	10/01-12/01
Except Computer	Louisville MSA, KY-IN	Y	39850 FQ	60930 AW	83060 TQ	KYBLS	10/01-12/01
Except Computer	Louisiana	Y	37750 FQ	62680 AW	89260 TQ	LABLS	10/01-12/01
Except Computer	Lafayette MSA, LA	Y	35980 FQ	65810 AW	96840 TQ	LABLS	10/01-12/01
Except Computer	New Orleans MSA, LA	Y	44220 FQ	65580 AW	89450 TQ	LABLS	10/01-12/01
Except Computer	Maine	Y	21950 FQ	58270 AW	90870 TQ	MEBLS	10/01-12/01
Except Computer	Maryland	Y	51670 FQ	75380 AW	105150 TQ	MDBLS	10/01-12/01
Except Computer	Baltimore PMSA, MD	Y	50150 FQ	74050 AW	105310 TQ	MDBLS	10/01-12/01
Except Computer	Massachusetts	Y	50670 FQ	75710 AW	108380 TQ	MABLS	10/01-12/01

AAW Average annual wage; **AE** Average entry wage; **AEX** Average experienced wage; **AO** Average offered; **AOH** Average offered, high; **AOL** Average offered, low; **APH** Average pay, high range; **APL** Average pay, low range; **ASH** Average starting, high; **ASL** Average starting, low; **AW** Average wage paid; **FQ** First quartile wage; **H** Hourly; **HI** Highest wage paid; **HR** High end range; **LR** Low end range; **M** Monthly; **MTC** Median total compensation; **MW** Median wage paid; **SQ** Second quartile wage; **S** Special: hourly and annual; **TQ** Third quartile wage; **W** Weekly; **Y** Yearly

Occupation/Type/Industry	Location	Per	Low	Mid	High	Source	Date
Electronics Engineer							
Except Computer	Boston PMSA, MA-NH	Y	52320 FQ	77480 AW	110490 TQ	MABLS	10/01-12/01
Except Computer	Brockton PMSA, MA	Y	45730 FQ	67460 AW	102940 TQ	MABLS	10/01-12/01
Except Computer	Lawrence PMSA, MA-NH	Y	48870 FQ	72560 AW	102260 TQ	MABLS	10/01-12/01
Except Computer	Lowell PMSA, MA-NH	Y	54900 FQ	77290 AW	103340 TQ	MABLS	10/01-12/01
Except Computer	Springfield MSA, MA	Y	46330 FQ	71970 AW	102700 TQ	MABLS	10/01-12/01
Except Computer	Worcester PMSA, MA-CT	Y	51480 FQ	77540 AW	109200 TQ	MABLS	10/01-12/01
Except Computer	Michigan	Y	38830 FQ	66810 AW	109340 TQ	MIBLS	10/01-12/01
Except Computer	Ann Arbor PMSA, MI	Y	34880 FQ	63940 AW	93180 TQ	MIBLS	10/01-12/01
Except Computer	Detroit PMSA, MI	Y	38410 FQ	70170 AW	119410 TQ	MIBLS	10/01-12/01
Except Computer	Flint PMSA, MI	Y	46540 FQ	66720 AW	104390 TQ	MIBLS	10/01-12/01
Except Computer	Grand Rapids-Muskegon-Holland MSA, MI	Y	38730 FQ	58200 AW	86750 TQ	MIBLS	10/01-12/01
Except Computer	Saginaw-Bay City-Midland MSA, MI	Y	45840 FQ	66580 AW	104010 TQ	MIBLS	10/01-12/01
Except Computer	Minnesota	Y	47250 FQ	71390 AW	105230 TQ	MNBLS	10/01-12/01
Except Computer	Duluth-Superior MSA, MN-WI	Y	37420 FQ	54170 AW	71590 TQ	MNBLS	10/01-12/01
Except Computer	Minneapolis-St. Paul MSA, MN-WI	Y	47550 FQ	72960 AW	108570 TQ	MNBLS	10/01-12/01
Except Computer	Mississippi	Y	37980 FQ	58730 AW	86620 TQ	MSBLS	10/01-12/01
Except Computer	Biloxi-Gulfport-Pascagoula MSA, MS	Y	34810 FQ	55880 AW	82520 TQ	MSBLS	10/01-12/01
Except Computer	Jackson MSA, MS	Y	45490 FQ	76940 AW	111410 TQ	MSBLS	10/01-12/01
Except Computer	Missouri	Y	38650 FQ	60600 AW	86980 TQ	MOBLS	10/01-12/01
Except Computer	Kansas City MSA, MO-KS	Y	41810 FQ	61960 AW	86400 TQ	MOBLS	10/01-12/01
Except Computer	St. Louis MSA, MO-IL	Y	38370 FQ	61840 AW	87110 TQ	MOBLS	10/01-12/01
Except Computer	Springfield MSA, MO	Y	36260 FQ	51930 AW	67730 TQ	MOBLS	10/01-12/01
Except Computer	Nebraska	Y	40060 FQ	61960 AW	88260 TQ	NEBLS	10/01-12/01
Except Computer	Lincoln MSA, NE	Y	38310 FQ	56590 AW	79130 TQ	NEBLS	10/01-12/01
Except Computer	Omaha MSA, NE-IA	Y	33770 FQ	62400 AW	90040 TQ	NEBLS	10/01-12/01
Except Computer	Nevada	Y	42350 FQ	62500 AW	89110 TQ	NVBLS	10/01-12/01
Except Computer	New Hampshire	Y	46350 FQ	68650 AW	100690 TQ	NHBLS	10/01-12/01
Except Computer	Manchester PMSA, NH	Y	45370 FQ	75630 AW	115660 TQ	NHBLS	10/01-12/01
Except Computer	Nashua PMSA, NH	Y	46450 FQ	66490 AW	90650 TQ	NHBLS	10/01-12/01
Except Computer	Portsmouth-Rochester PMSA, NH-ME	Y	48740 FQ	66600 AW	92450 TQ	NHBLS	10/01-12/01
Except Computer	New Jersey	Y	49760 FQ	74860 AW	107220 TQ	NJBLS	10/01-12/01
Except Computer	Atlantic-Cape May PMSA, NJ	Y	69280 FQ	84320 AW	108470 TQ	NJBLS	10/01-12/01
Except Computer	Bergen-Passaic PMSA, NJ	Y	51660 FQ	80400 AW	114460 TQ	NJBLS	10/01-12/01
Except Computer	Middlesex-Somerset-Hunterdon PMSA, NJ	Y	46030 FQ	72580 AW	105640 TQ	NJBLS	10/01-12/01
Except Computer	Monmouth-Ocean PMSA, NJ	Y	60260 FQ	79590 AW	104930 TQ	NJBLS	10/01-12/01
Except Computer	Newark PMSA, NJ	Y	46710 FQ	69930 AW	107550 TQ	NJBLS	10/01-12/01
Except Computer	New Mexico	Y	48030 FQ	73040 AW	103570 TQ	NMBLS	10/01-12/01
Except Computer	Albuquerque MSA, NM	Y	49610 FQ	75570 AW	107440 TQ	NMBLS	10/01-12/01
Except Computer	Las Cruces MSA, NM	Y	54200 FQ	71330 AW	90640 TQ	NMBLS	10/01-12/01
Except Computer	New York	Y	45870 FQ	67340 AW	94050 TQ	NYBLS	10/01-12/01
Except Computer	Albany-Schenectady-Troy MSA, NY	Y	40950 FQ	64940 AW	97230 TQ	NYBLS	10/01-12/01
Except Computer	Binghamton MSA, NY	Y	48690 FQ	67700 AW	87530 TQ	NYBLS	10/01-12/01
Except Computer	Buffalo-Niagara Falls MSA, NY	Y	38340 FQ	58940 AW	86670 TQ	NYBLS	10/01-12/01
Except Computer	Nassau-Suffolk PMSA, NY	Y	49470 FQ	67500 AW	94380 TQ	NYBLS	10/01-12/01
Except Computer	New York PMSA, NY	Y	45620 FQ	70350 AW	106040 TQ	NYBLS	10/01-12/01
Except Computer	Rochester MSA, NY	Y	45850 FQ	65480 AW	93390 TQ	NYBLS	10/01-12/01
Except Computer	Syracuse MSA, NY	Y	40320 FQ	62100 AW	87730 TQ	NYBLS	10/01-12/01
Except Computer	Utica-Rome MSA, NY	Y	49380 FQ	73730 AW	98710 TQ	NYBLS	10/01-12/01
Except Computer	North Carolina	Y	42360 FQ	64800 AW	92040 TQ	NCBLS	10/01-12/01
Except Computer	Asheville MSA, NC	Y	37190 FQ	55060 AW	79380 TQ	NCBLS	10/01-12/01
Except Computer	Charlotte-Gastonia-Rock Hill MSA, NC-SC	Y	36980 FQ	60420 AW	87090 TQ	NCBLS	10/01-12/01
Except Computer	Fayetteville MSA, NC	Y	38810 FQ	51990 AW	67810 TQ	NCBLS	10/01-12/01
Except Computer	Hickory-Morganton-Lenoir MSA, NC	Y	47320 FQ	76250 AW	117540 TQ	NCBLS	10/01-12/01
Except Computer	Raleigh-Durham-Chapel Hill MSA, NC	Y	48040 FQ	70510 AW	96840 TQ	NCBLS	10/01-12/01
Except Computer	Wilmington MSA, NC	Y	43010 FQ	57360 AW	80440 TQ	NCBLS	10/01-12/01
Except Computer	North Dakota	Y	48680 FQ	62680 AW	84100 TQ	NDBLS	10/01-12/01
Except Computer	Ohio	Y	40120 FQ	64630 AW	89620 TQ	OHBLS	10/01-12/01
Except Computer	Akron PMSA, OH	Y	44920 FQ	73540 AW	107950 TQ	OHBLS	10/01-12/01
Except Computer	Canton-Massillon MSA, OH	Y	42030 FQ	64210 AW	87890 TQ	OHBLS	10/01-12/01
Except Computer	Cincinnati PMSA, OH-KY-IN	Y	41210 FQ	61400 AW	85550 TQ	OHBLS	10/01-12/01

AAW Average annual wage; **AE** Average entry wage; **AEX** Average experienced wage; **AO** Average offered; **AOH** Average offered, high; **AOL** Average offered, low; **APH** Average pay, high range; **APL** Average pay, low range; **ASH** Average starting, high; **ASL** Average starting, low; **AW** Average wage paid; **FQ** First quartile wage; **H** Hourly; **HI** Highest wage paid; **HR** High end range; **LR** Low end range; **M** Monthly; **MTC** Median total compensation; **MW** Median wage paid; **SQ** Second quartile wage; **S** Special: hourly and annual; **TQ** Third quartile wage; **W** Weekly; **Y** Yearly

Occupation/Type/Industry	Location	Per	Low	Mid	High	Source	Date
Electronics Engineer							
Except Computer	Cleveland-Lorain-Elyria PMSA, OH	Y	35530 FQ	62430 AW	89240 TQ	OHBLS	10/01-12/01
Except Computer	Columbus MSA, OH	Y	42840 FQ	59740 AW	81180 TQ	OHBLS	10/01-12/01
Except Computer	Dayton-Springfield MSA, OH	Y	49790 FQ	72200 AW	92290 TQ	OHBLS	10/01-12/01
Except Computer	Hamilton-Middletown PMSA, OH	Y	48660 FQ	69420 AW	94170 TQ	OHBLS	10/01-12/01
Except Computer	Toledo MSA, OH	Y	32240 FQ	50830 AW	70720 TQ	OHBLS	10/01-12/01
Except Computer	Youngstown-Warren MSA, OH	Y	38630 FQ	54680 AW	70480 TQ	OHBLS	10/01-12/01
Except Computer	Oklahoma	Y	39470 FQ	60130 AW	84900 TQ	OKBLS	10/01-12/01
Except Computer	Oklahoma City MSA, OK	Y	42420 FQ	61950 AW	85490 TQ	OKBLS	10/01-12/01
Except Computer	Tulsa MSA, OK	Y	34050 FQ	58890 AW	87000 TQ	OKBLS	10/01-12/01
Except Computer	Oregon	Y	43480 FQ	61630 AW	86080 TQ	ORBLS	10/01-12/01
Except Computer	Eugene-Springfield MSA, OR	Y	40960 FQ	62150 AW	87850 TQ	ORBLS	10/01-12/01
Except Computer	Portland-Vancouver PMSA, OR-WA	Y	45290 FQ	65000 AW	91960 TQ	ORBLS	10/01-12/01
Except Computer	Pennsylvania	Y	40570 FQ	60600 AW	86110 TQ	PABLS	10/01-12/01
Except Computer	Allentown-Bethlehem-Easton MSA, PA	Y	39490 FQ	54420 AW	73540 TQ	PABLS	10/01-12/01
Except Computer	Lancaster MSA, PA	Y	44830 FQ	57570 AW	71110 TQ	PABLS	10/01-12/01
Except Computer	Philadelphia PMSA, PA-NJ	Y	45580 FQ	66820 AW	91830 TQ	PABLS	10/01-12/01
Except Computer	Pittsburgh MSA, PA	Y	40450 FQ	61390 AW	87080 TQ	PABLS	10/01-12/01
Except Computer	Reading MSA, PA	Y	43980 FQ	61670 AW	86270 TQ	PABLS	10/01-12/01
Except Computer	Scranton-Wilkes-Barre-Hazleton MSA, PA	Y	38520 FQ	57410 AW	84590 TQ	PABLS	10/01-12/01
Except Computer	York MSA, PA	Y	42020 FQ	59010 AW	81990 TQ	PABLS	10/01-12/01
Except Computer	Rhode Island	Y	57930 FQ	75140 AW	99030 TQ	RIBLS	10/01-12/01
Except Computer	Providence-Fall River-Warwick MSA, RI-MA	Y	50210 FQ	70450 AW	91380 TQ	RIBLS	10/01-12/01
Except Computer	South Carolina	Y	47140 FQ	69770 AW	90880 TQ	SCBLS	10/01-12/01
Except Computer	Charleston-North Charleston MSA, SC	Y	52080 FQ	72290 AW	89960 TQ	SCBLS	10/01-12/01
Except Computer	Columbia MSA, SC	Y	46360 FQ	64300 AW	87250 TQ	SCBLS	10/01-12/01
Except Computer	Greenville-Spartanburg-Anderson MSA, SC	Y	32400 FQ	53520 AW	72770 TQ	SCBLS	10/01-12/01
Except Computer	South Dakota	Y	38370 FQ	55340 AW	76740 TQ	SDBLS	10/01-12/01
Except Computer	Sioux Falls MSA, SD	Y	37270 FQ	52170 AW	70300 TQ	SDBLS	10/01-12/01
Except Computer	Tennessee	Y	39510 FQ	68090 AW	98580 TQ	TNBLS	10/01-12/01
Except Computer	Knoxville MSA, TN	Y	41090 FQ	70290 AW	97070 TQ	TNBLS	10/01-12/01
Except Computer	Memphis MSA, TN-AR-MS	Y	28120 FQ	57870 AW	88320 TQ	TNBLS	10/01-12/01
Except Computer	Nashville MSA, TN	Y	40270 FQ	63780 AW	92000 TQ	TNBLS	10/01-12/01
Except Computer	Texas	Y	48710 FQ	72200 AW	103680 TQ	TXBLS	10/01-12/01
Except Computer	Austin-San Marcos MSA, TX	Y	46040 FQ	74360 AW	115660 TQ	TXBLS	10/01-12/01
Except Computer	Corpus Christi MSA, TX	Y	47230 FQ	58710 AW	71470 TQ	TXBLS	10/01-12/01
Except Computer	Dallas PMSA, TX	Y	50000 FQ	72230 AW	100980 TQ	TXBLS	10/01-12/01
Except Computer	El Paso MSA, TX	Y	43130 FQ	61890 AW	86810 TQ	TXBLS	10/01-12/01
Except Computer	Fort Worth-Arlington PMSA, TX	Y	51330 FQ	72790 AW	98520 TQ	TXBLS	10/01-12/01
Except Computer	Houston PMSA, TX	Y	48330 FQ	74210 AW	113330 TQ	TXBLS	10/01-12/01
Except Computer	Killeen-Temple MSA, TX	Y	38770 FQ	60260 AW	81720 TQ	TXBLS	10/01-12/01
Except Computer	Odessa-Midland MSA, TX	Y	38580 FQ	56450 AW	74370 TQ	TXBLS	10/01-12/01
Except Computer	San Antonio MSA, TX	Y	48240 FQ	68490 AW	88570 TQ	TXBLS	10/01-12/01
Except Computer	Waco MSA, TX	Y	52750 FQ	76390 AW	100840 TQ	TXBLS	10/01-12/01
Except Computer	Utah	Y	45740 FQ	62750 AW	79950 TQ	UTBLS	10/01-12/01
Except Computer	Salt Lake City-Ogden MSA, UT	Y	46670 FQ	63070 AW	79720 TQ	UTBLS	10/01-12/01
Except Computer	Virginia	Y	48160 FQ	74120 AW	105580 TQ	VABLS	10/01-12/01
Except Computer	Norfolk-Virginia Beach-Newport News MSA, VA-NC	Y	49310 FQ	70410 AW	90480 TQ	VABLS	10/01-12/01
Except Computer	Richmond-Petersburg MSA, VA	Y	40350 FQ	66510 AW	88530 TQ	VABLS	10/01-12/01
Except Computer	Roanoke MSA, VA	Y	48040 FQ	100580 AW		VABLS	10/01-12/01
Except Computer	Washington	Y	48770 FQ	64630 AW	88470 TQ	WABLS	10/01-12/01
Except Computer	Bremerton PMSA, WA	Y	53670 FQ	66630 AW	85540 TQ	WABLS	10/01-12/01
Except Computer	Richland-Kennewick-Pasco MSA, WA	Y	51300 FQ	71750 AW	91420 TQ	WABLS	10/01-12/01
Except Computer	Seattle-Bellevue-Everett PMSA, WA	Y	49260 FQ	63050 AW	85610 TQ	WABLS	10/01-12/01
Except Computer	Spokane MSA, WA	Y	31190 FQ	55590 AW	84550 TQ	WABLS	10/01-12/01
Except Computer	Tacoma PMSA, WA	Y	48890 FQ	69730 AW	92050 TQ	WABLS	10/01-12/01
Except Computer	West Virginia	Y	41840 FQ	59020 AW	84200 TQ	WVBLS	10/01-12/01

AAW	Average annual wage	AOH	Average offered, high	ASH	Average starting, high	H	Hourly	M	Monthly	S	Special: hourly and annual
AE	Average entry wage	AOL	Average offered, low	ASL	Average starting, low	HI	Highest wage paid	MTC	Median total compensation	TQ	Third quartile wage
AEX	Average experienced wage	APH	Average pay, high range	AW	Average wage paid	HR	High end range	MW	Median wage paid	W	Weekly
AO	Average offered	APL	Average pay, low range	FQ	First quartile wage	LR	Low end range	SQ	Second quartile wage	Y	Yearly

Occupation/Type/Industry	Location	Per	Low	Mid	High	Source	Date
Electronics Engineer							
Except Computer	Wisconsin	Y	33930 FQ	59120 AW	86390 TQ	WIBLS	10/01-12/01
Except Computer	Madison MSA, WI	Y	31650 FQ	53410 AW	75150 TQ	WIBLS	10/01-12/01
Except Computer	Milwaukee-Waukesha PMSA, WI	Y	31890 FQ	55470 AW	81520 TQ	WIBLS	10/01-12/01
Except Computer	Wyoming	Y	31830 FQ	49910 AW	71840 TQ	WYBLS	10/01-12/01
Except Computer	Puerto Rico	Y	32520 FQ	51010 AW	74020 TQ	PRBLS	10/01-12/01
Elementary School Teacher							
Except Special Education	Alabama	Y	30520 FQ	38830 AW	47930 TQ	ALBLS	10/01-12/01
Except Special Education	Birmingham MSA, AL	Y	32280 FQ	41940 AW	54300 TQ	ALBLS	10/01-12/01
Except Special Education	Huntsville MSA, AL	Y	31260 FQ	39760 AW	49590 TQ	ALBLS	10/01-12/01
Except Special Education	Montgomery MSA, AL	Y	17130 FQ	32600 AW	44220 TQ	ALBLS	10/01-12/01
Except Special Education	Alaska	Y	34240 FQ	48990 AW	66630 TQ	AKBLS	10/01-12/01
Except Special Education	Arizona	Y	23730 FQ	35880 AW	53010 TQ	AZBLS	10/01-12/01
Except Special Education	Phoenix-Mesa MSA, AZ	Y	23350 FQ	35120 AW	50630 TQ	AZBLS	10/01-12/01
Except Special Education	Tucson MSA, AZ	Y	25240 FQ	41280 AW	62420 TQ	AZBLS	10/01-12/01
Except Special Education	Arkansas	Y	24870 FQ	33730 AW	44520 TQ	ARBLS	10/01-12/01
Except Special Education	Fayetteville-Springdale-Rogers MSA, AR	Y	26120 FQ	35570 AW	47270 TQ	ARBLS	10/01-12/01
Except Special Education	Fort Smith MSA, AR-OK	Y	26150 FQ	34490 AW	44700 TQ	ARBLS	10/01-12/01
Except Special Education	Little Rock-North Little Rock MSA, AR	Y	24920 FQ	34730 AW	45900 TQ	ARBLS	10/01-12/01
Except Special Education	California	Y	31830 FQ	48140 AW	68380 TQ	CABLS	10/01-12/01
Except Special Education	Bakersfield MSA, CA	Y	34720 FQ	49250 AW	68320 TQ	CABLS	10/01-12/01
Except Special Education	Chico-Paradise MSA, CA	Y	25780 FQ	44650 AW	66030 TQ	CABLS	10/01-12/01
Except Special Education	Fresno MSA, CA	Y	31030 FQ	44570 AW	59210 TQ	CABLS	10/01-12/01
Except Special Education	Los Angeles-Long Beach PMSA, CA	Y	35720 FQ	48900 AW	67920 TQ	CABLS	10/01-12/01
Except Special Education	Merced MSA, CA	Y	23700 FQ	45330 AW	66380 TQ	CABLS	10/01-12/01
Except Special Education	Modesto MSA, CA	Y	27550 FQ	49800 AW	72130 TQ	CABLS	10/01-12/01
Except Special Education	Oakland PMSA, CA	Y	30570 FQ	49210 AW	72620 TQ	CABLS	10/01-12/01
Except Special Education	Orange County PMSA, CA	Y	32680 FQ	47580 AW	67560 TQ	CABLS	10/01-12/01
Except Special Education	Redding MSA, CA	Y	24170 FQ	41490 AW	57180 TQ	CABLS	10/01-12/01
Except Special Education	Riverside-San Bernardino PMSA, CA	Y	33110 FQ	49120 AW	69000 TQ	CABLS	10/01-12/01
Except Special Education	Sacramento PMSA, CA	Y	31210 FQ	47830 AW	68780 TQ	CABLS	10/01-12/01
Except Special Education	Salinas MSA, CA	Y	30510 FQ	47060 AW	67580 TQ	CABLS	10/01-12/01
Except Special Education	San Diego MSA, CA	Y	23950 FQ	48860 AW	73230 TQ	CABLS	10/01-12/01
Except Special Education	San Francisco PMSA, CA	Y	27830 FQ	45230 AW	64100 TQ	CABLS	10/01-12/01
Except Special Education	San Jose PMSA, CA	Y	32290 FQ	51620 AW	71870 TQ	CABLS	10/01-12/01
Except Special Education	San Luis Obispo-Atascadero-Paso Robles MSA, CA	Y	25140 FQ	41670 AW	60340 TQ	CABLS	10/01-12/01
Except Special Education	Santa Barbara-Santa Maria-Lompoc MSA, CA	Y	28160 FQ	46250 AW	65600 TQ	CABLS	10/01-12/01
Except Special Education	Santa Cruz-Watsonville PMSA, CA	Y	28000 FQ	45740 AW	67320 TQ	CABLS	10/01-12/01
Except Special Education	Santa Rosa PMSA, CA	Y	29750 FQ	46230 AW	64210 TQ	CABLS	10/01-12/01
Except Special Education	Stockton-Lodi MSA, CA	Y	26740 FQ	45300 AW	65250 TQ	CABLS	10/01-12/01
Except Special Education	Vallejo-Fairfield-Napa PMSA, CA	Y	30020 FQ	46200 AW	63370 TQ	CABLS	10/01-12/01
Except Special Education	Ventura PMSA, CA	Y	33380 FQ	52310 AW	73900 TQ	CABLS	10/01-12/01
Except Special Education	Visalia-Tulare-Porterville MSA, CA	Y	27470 FQ	46680 AW	66090 TQ	CABLS	10/01-12/01
Except Special Education	Colorado	Y	25500 FQ	37950 AW	54390 TQ	COBLS	10/01-12/01
Except Special Education	Boulder-Longmont PMSA, CO	Y	25870 FQ	42960 AW	69770 TQ	COBLS	10/01-12/01
Except Special Education	Colorado Springs MSA, CO	Y	24880 FQ	37590 AW	55070 TQ	COBLS	10/01-12/01
Except Special Education	Denver PMSA, CO	Y	25410 FQ	37350 AW	53390 TQ	COBLS	10/01-12/01
Except Special Education	Fort Collins-Loveland MSA, CO	Y	26440 FQ	42040 AW	60060 TQ	COBLS	10/01-12/01
Except Special Education	Greeley PMSA, CO	Y	25140 FQ	35840 AW	49940 TQ	COBLS	10/01-12/01
Except Special Education	Connecticut	Y	31720 FQ	51620 AW	71980 TQ	CTBLS	10/01-12/01
Except Special Education	Bridgeport PMSA, CT	Y	32260 FQ	53450 AW	71720 TQ	CTBLS	10/01-12/01
Except Special Education	Danbury PMSA, CT	Y	32130 FQ	53330 AW	77010 TQ	CTBLS	10/01-12/01
Except Special Education	Hartford MSA, CT	Y	30540 FQ	51050 AW	72180 TQ	CTBLS	10/01-12/01
Except Special Education	New Haven-Meriden PMSA, CT	Y	32200 FQ	53010 AW	72990 TQ	CTBLS	10/01-12/01
Except Special Education	New London-Norwich MSA, CT-RI	Y	31870 FQ	48750 AW	69210 TQ	CTBLS	10/01-12/01
Except Special Education	Stamford-Norwalk PMSA, CT	Y	37720 FQ	53410 AW	74250 TQ	CTBLS	10/01-12/01
Except Special Education	Waterbury PMSA, CT	Y	32200 FQ	50500 AW	70660 TQ	CTBLS	10/01-12/01
Except Special Education	Delaware	Y	30560 FQ	52760 AW	79000 TQ	DEBLS	10/01-12/01

AAW	Average annual wage	AOH	Average offered, high	ASH	Average starting, high	H	Hourly	M	Monthly	S	Special: hourly and annual
AE	Average entry wage	AOL	Average offered, low	ASL	Average starting, low	HI	Highest wage paid	MTC	Median total compensation	TQ	Third quartile wage
AEX	Average experienced wage	APH	Average pay, high range	AW	Average wage paid	HR	High end range	MW	Median wage paid	W	Weekly
AO	Average offered	APL	Average pay, low range	FQ	First quartile wage	LR	Low end range	SQ	Second quartile wage	Y	Yearly

Occupation/Type/Industry	Location	Per	Low	Mid	High	Source	Date
Elementary School Teacher							
Except Special Education	Wilmington-Newark PMSA, DE-MD	Y	30570 FQ	52230 AW	76140 TQ	DEBLS	10/01-12/01
Except Special Education	Washington PMSA, DC-MD-VA-WV	Y	23430 FQ	43450 AW	70520 TQ	DCBLS	10/01-12/01
Except Special Education	Florida	Y	26970 FQ	40760 AW	58320 TQ	FLBLS	10/01-12/01
Except Special Education	Fort Myers-Cape Coral MSA, FL	Y	21940 FQ	33880 AW	46890 TQ	FLBLS	10/01-12/01
Except Special Education	Jacksonville MSA, FL	Y	30170 FQ	45560 AW	69760 TQ	FLBLS	10/01-12/01
Except Special Education	Melbourne-Titusville-Palm Bay MSA, FL	Y	19470 FQ	28600 AW	37480 TQ	FLBLS	10/01-12/01
Except Special Education	Ocala MSA, FL	Y	25600 FQ	39860 AW	57460 TQ	FLBLS	10/01-12/01
Except Special Education	Orlando MSA, FL	Y	26140 FQ	37540 AW	53620 TQ	FLBLS	10/01-12/01
Except Special Education	Pensacola MSA, FL	Y	32220 FQ	46880 AW	66660 TQ	FLBLS	10/01-12/01
Except Special Education	Sarasota-Bradenton MSA, FL	Y	24520 FQ	36920 AW	51930 TQ	FLBLS	10/01-12/01
Except Special Education	Tampa-St. Petersburg-Clearwater MSA, FL	Y	30690 FQ	41630 AW	58400 TQ	FLBLS	10/01-12/01
Except Special Education	Georgia	Y	31650 FQ	44580 AW	60470 TQ	GABLS	10/01-12/01
Except Special Education	Atlanta MSA, GA	Y	32490 FQ	44840 AW	61130 TQ	GABLS	10/01-12/01
Except Special Education	Augusta-Aiken MSA, GA-SC	Y	30310 FQ	43610 AW	62040 TQ	GABLS	10/01-12/01
Except Special Education	Columbus MSA, GA-AL	Y	30560 FQ	42780 AW	56480 TQ	GABLS	10/01-12/01
Except Special Education	Macon MSA, GA	Y	29420 FQ	44240 AW	64420 TQ	GABLS	10/01-12/01
Except Special Education	Savannah MSA, GA	Y	30530 FQ	42940 AW	58580 TQ	GABLS	10/01-12/01
Except Special Education	Hawaii	Y	26820 FQ	39190 AW	55590 TQ	HIBLS	10/01-12/01
Except Special Education	Honolulu MSA, HI	Y	26310 FQ	38920 AW	55920 TQ	HIBLS	10/01-12/01
Except Special Education	Idaho	Y	33130 FQ	39580 AW	45490 TQ	IDBLS	10/01-12/01
Except Special Education	Boise City MSA, ID	Y	33430 FQ	39840 AW	45660 TQ	IDBLS	10/01-12/01
Except Special Education	Illinois	Y	24450 FQ	41060 AW	64720 TQ	ILBLS	10/01-12/01
Except Special Education	Champaign-Urbana MSA, IL	Y	24630 FQ	39230 AW	59190 TQ	ILBLS	10/01-12/01
Except Special Education	Chicago PMSA, IL	Y	25970 FQ	43610 AW	69650 TQ	ILBLS	10/01-12/01
Except Special Education	Peoria-Pekin MSA, IL	Y	18870 FQ	37280 AW	54790 TQ	ILBLS	10/01-12/01
Except Special Education	Rockford MSA, IL	Y	25980 FQ	42320 AW	60230 TQ	ILBLS	10/01-12/01
Except Special Education	Springfield MSA, IL	Y	20710 FQ	38950 AW	60870 TQ	ILBLS	10/01 12/01
Except Special Education	Indiana	Y	26860 FQ	42610 AW	58190 TQ	INBLS	10/01-12/01
Except Special Education	Elkhart-Goshen MSA, IN	Y	24160 FQ	33340 AW	52610 TQ	INBLS	10/01-12/01
Except Special Education	Evansville-Henderson MSA, IN-KY	Y	29290 FQ	43880 AW	57680 TQ	INBLS	10/01-12/01
Except Special Education	Fort Wayne MSA, IN	Y	27540 FQ	43510 AW	58710 TQ	INBLS	10/01-12/01
Except Special Education	Gary PMSA, IN	Y	23200 FQ	39450 AW	58410 TQ	INBLS	10/01-12/01
Except Special Education	Indianapolis MSA, IN	Y	28420 FQ	43490 AW	60750 TQ	INBLS	10/01-12/01
Except Special Education	Lafayette MSA, IN	Y	30890 FQ	45470 AW	59470 TQ	INBLS	10/01-12/01
Except Special Education	Iowa	Y	21980 FQ	33670 AW	47080 TQ	IABLS	10/01-12/01
Except Special Education	Cedar Rapids MSA, IA	Y	21770 FQ	32030 AW	44750 TQ	IABLS	10/01-12/01
Except Special Education	Davenport-Moline-Rock Island MSA, IA-IL	Y	25100 FQ	42910 AW	60370 TQ	IABLS	10/01-12/01
Except Special Education	Des Moines MSA, IA	Y	25070 FQ	37260 AW	52400 TQ	IABLS	10/01-12/01
Except Special Education	Kansas	Y	24680 FQ	34790 AW	45330 TQ	KSBLS	10/01-12/01
Except Special Education	Topeka MSA, KS	Y	23930 FQ	33770 AW	44410 TQ	KSBLS	10/01-12/01
Except Special Education	Wichita MSA, KS	Y	28120 FQ	36670 AW	47370 TQ	KSBLS	10/01-12/01
Except Special Education	Kentucky	Y	26210 FQ	38460 AW	52160 TQ	KYBLS	10/01-12/01
Except Special Education	Louisiana	Y	25060 FQ	33670 AW	44080 TQ	LABLS	10/01-12/01
Except Special Education	Baton Rouge MSA, LA	Y	26500 FQ	35050 AW	44840 TQ	LABLS	10/01-12/01
Except Special Education	Houma MSA, LA	Y	25420 FQ	32800 AW	42530 TQ	LABLS	10/01-12/01
Except Special Education	Lafayette MSA, LA	Y	26450 FQ	34800 AW	44190 TQ	LABLS	10/01-12/01
Except Special Education	New Orleans MSA, LA	Y	24980 FQ	35080 AW	45100 TQ	LABLS	10/01-12/01
Except Special Education	Maine	Y	25220 FQ	37520 AW	48710 TQ	MEBLS	10/01-12/01
Except Special Education	Portland MSA, ME	Y	30230 FQ	41800 AW	54720 TQ	MEBLS	10/01-12/01
Except Special Education	Maryland	Y	22770 FQ	42080 AW	63600 TQ	MDBLS	10/01-12/01
Except Special Education	Baltimore PMSA, MD	Y	29960 FQ	49070 AW	74110 TQ	MDBLS	10/01-12/01
Except Special Education	Massachusetts	Y	30820 FQ	47140 AW	62460 TQ	MABLS	10/01-12/01
Except Special Education	Boston PMSA, MA-NH	Y	31050 FQ	48150 AW	65940 TQ	MABLS	10/01-12/01
Except Special Education	Brockton PMSA, MA	Y	31410 FQ	47780 AW	63660 TQ	MABLS	10/01-12/01
Except Special Education	Lawrence PMSA, MA-NH	Y	29600 FQ	45600 AW	64730 TQ	MABLS	10/01-12/01
Except Special Education	Lowell PMSA, MA-NH	Y	30210 FQ	45770 AW	60700 TQ	MABLS	10/01-12/01
Except Special Education	New Bedford PMSA, MA	Y	29530 FQ	46720 AW	61120 TQ	MABLS	10/01-12/01
Except Special Education	Springfield MSA, MA	Y	30260 FQ	46170 AW	57650 TQ	MABLS	10/01-12/01
Except Special Education	Worcester PMSA, MA-CT	Y	32830 FQ	47090 AW	58820 TQ	MABLS	10/01-12/01
Except Special Education	Michigan	Y	29430 FQ	48560 AW	69980 TQ	MIBLS	10/01-12/01
Except Special Education	Ann Arbor PMSA, MI	Y	32230 FQ	50790 AW	70250 TQ	MIBLS	10/01-12/01
Except Special Education	Detroit PMSA, MI	Y	29950 FQ	50270 AW	73050 TQ	MIBLS	10/01-12/01
Except Special Education	Flint PMSA, MI	Y	22310 FQ	40120 AW	62650 TQ	MIBLS	10/01-12/01

AAW	Average annual wage	**AOH**	Average offered, high	**ASH**	Average starting, high	**H**	Hourly	**M**	Monthly	**S**	Special: hourly and annual
AE	Average entry wage	**AOL**	Average offered, low	**ASL**	Average starting, low	**HI**	Highest wage paid	**MTC**	Median total compensation	**TQ**	Third quartile wage
AEX	Average experienced wage	**APH**	Average pay, high range	**AW**	Average wage paid	**HR**	High end range	**MW**	Median wage paid	**W**	Weekly
AO	Average offered	**APL**	Average pay, low range	**FQ**	First quartile wage	**LR**	Low end range	**SQ**	Second quartile wage	**Y**	Yearly

Occupation/Type/Industry	Location	Per	Low	Mid	High	Source	Date
Elementary School Teacher							
Except Special Education	Grand Rapids-Muskegon-Holland MSA, MI	Y	30140 FQ	47970 AW	69800 TQ	MIBLS	10/01-12/01
Except Special Education	Kalamazoo-Battle Creek MSA, MI	Y	29470 FQ	48500 AW	74150 TQ	MIBLS	10/01-12/01
Except Special Education	Lansing-East Lansing MSA, MI	Y	32290 FQ	49500 AW	68180 TQ	MIBLS	10/01-12/01
Except Special Education	Saginaw-Bay City-Midland MSA, MI	Y	29060 FQ	48810 AW	71060 TQ	MIBLS	10/01-12/01
Except Special Education	Minnesota	Y	28180 FQ	42750 AW	59430 TQ	MNBLS	10/01-12/01
Except Special Education	Duluth-Superior MSA, MN-WI	Y	25610 FQ	41310 AW	55200 TQ	MNBLS	10/01-12/01
Except Special Education	Minneapolis-St. Paul MSA, MN-WI	Y	29550 FQ	45050 AW	64650 TQ	MNBLS	10/01-12/01
Except Special Education	St. Cloud MSA, MN	Y	30470 FQ	42440 AW	56070 TQ	MNBLS	10/01-12/01
Except Special Education	Mississippi	Y	22850 FQ	31110 AW	41940 TQ	MSBLS	10/01-12/01
Except Special Education	Biloxi-Gulfport-Pascagoula MSA, MS	Y	26160 FQ	33460 AW	43050 TQ	MSBLS	10/01-12/01
Except Special Education	Jackson MSA, MS	Y	24200 FQ	30720 AW	40090 TQ	MSBLS	10/01-12/01
Except Special Education	Missouri	Y	22030 FQ	35310 AW	53650 TQ	MOBLS	10/01-12/01
Except Special Education	Kansas City MSA, MO-KS	Y	23200 FQ	34710 AW	51100 TQ	MOBLS	10/01-12/01
Except Special Education	St. Louis MSA, MO-IL	Y	23370 FQ	40040 AW	58240 TQ	MOBLS	10/01-12/01
Except Special Education	Springfield MSA, MO	Y	21390 FQ	31350 AW	43540 TQ	MOBLS	10/01-12/01
Except Special Education	Montana	Y	20360 FQ	32900 AW	45250 TQ	MTBLS	10/01-12/01
Except Special Education	Billings MSA, MT	Y	23030 FQ	34830 AW	46330 TQ	MTBLS	10/01-12/01
Except Special Education	Nebraska	Y	24710 FQ	38040 AW	53280 TQ	NEBLS	10/01-12/01
Except Special Education	Lincoln MSA, NE	Y	24470 FQ	36000 AW	51830 TQ	NEBLS	10/01-12/01
Except Special Education	Omaha MSA, NE-IA	Y	28760 FQ	44770 AW	63110 TQ	NEBLS	10/01-12/01
Except Special Education	New Hampshire	Y	27170 FQ	39080 AW	52900 TQ	NHBLS	10/01-12/01
Except Special Education	Portsmouth-Rochester PMSA, NH-ME	Y	27840 FQ	40620 AW	54470 TQ	NHBLS	10/01-12/01
Except Special Education	New Jersey	Y	30350 FQ	49400 AW	73720 TQ	NJBLS	10/01-12/01
Except Special Education	Atlantic-Cape May PMSA, NJ	Y	31640 FQ	48290 AW	71550 TQ	NJBLS	10/01-12/01
Except Special Education	Bergen-Passaic PMSA, NJ	Y	31800 FQ	55180 AW	86190 TQ	NJBLS	10/01-12/01
Except Special Education	Jersey City PMSA, NJ	Y	31830 FQ	55650 AW	88490 TQ	NJBLS	10/01-12/01
Except Special Education	Middlesex-Somerset-Hunterdon PMSA, NJ	Y	31340 FQ	50070 AW	71570 TQ	NJBLS	10/01-12/01
Except Special Education	Monmouth-Ocean PMSA, NJ	Y	28870 FQ	45860 AW	68960 TQ	NJBLS	10/01-12/01
Except Special Education	Newark PMSA, NJ	Y	29430 FQ	47110 AW	70040 TQ	NJBLS	10/01-12/01
Except Special Education	Trenton PMSA, NJ	Y	31700 FQ	49660 AW	70440 TQ	NJBLS	10/01-12/01
Except Special Education	New Mexico	Y	26160 FQ	36250 AW	50450 TQ	NMBLS	10/01-12/01
Except Special Education	Las Cruces MSA, NM	Y	26150 FQ	34120 AW	44090 TQ	NMBLS	10/01-12/01
Except Special Education	New York	Y	30320 FQ	59220 AW	101020 TQ	NYBLS	10/01-12/01
Except Special Education	Albany-Schenectady-Troy MSA, NY	Y	26270 FQ	49560 AW	72590 TQ	NYBLS	10/01-12/01
Except Special Education	Binghamton MSA, NY	Y	15190 FQ	35430 AW	55430 TQ	NYBLS	10/01-12/01
Except Special Education	Buffalo-Niagara Falls MSA, NY	Y	21310 FQ	47920 AW	70760 TQ	NYBLS	10/01-12/01
Except Special Education	Dutchess County PMSA, NY	Y	29720 FQ	59940 AW	100470 TQ	NYBLS	10/01-12/01
Except Special Education	Nassau-Suffolk PMSA, NY	Y	30900 FQ	60180 AW	94810 TQ	NYBLS	10/01-12/01
Except Special Education	Newburgh PMSA, NY-PA	Y	32820 FQ	53400 AW	72350 TQ	NYBLS	10/01-12/01
Except Special Education	Rochester MSA, NY	Y	28440 FQ	46240 AW	74770 TQ	NYBLS	10/01-12/01
Except Special Education	Syracuse MSA, NY	Y	29760 FQ	45710 AW	64760 TQ	NYBLS	10/01-12/01
Except Special Education	Utica-Rome MSA, NY	Y	23620 FQ	48350 AW	80810 TQ	NYBLS	10/01-12/01
Except Special Education	North Carolina	Y	25910 FQ	37850 AW	52590 TQ	NCBLS	10/01-12/01
Except Special Education	Asheville MSA, NC	Y	26590 FQ	38470 AW	51520 TQ	NCBLS	10/01-12/01
Except Special Education	Charlotte-Gastonia-Rock Hill MSA, NC-SC	Y	27450 FQ	38850 AW	53750 TQ	NCBLS	10/01-12/01
Except Special Education	Fayetteville MSA, NC	Y	26490 FQ	36760 AW	48090 TQ	NCBLS	10/01-12/01
Except Special Education	Greensboro-Winston-Salem-High Point MSA, NC	Y	26850 FQ	39540 AW	54830 TQ	NCBLS	10/01-12/01
Except Special Education	Hickory-Morganton-Lenoir MSA, NC	Y	24410 FQ	35250 AW	47970 TQ	NCBLS	10/01-12/01
Except Special Education	Raleigh-Durham-Chapel Hill MSA, NC	Y	27880 FQ	40550 AW	55690 TQ	NCBLS	10/01-12/01
Except Special Education	Wilmington MSA, NC	Y	25030 FQ	36200 AW	47790 TQ	NCBLS	10/01-12/01
Except Special Education	North Dakota	Y	22800 FQ	32610 AW	44100 TQ	NDBLS	10/01-12/01
Except Special Education	Fargo-Moorhead MSA, ND-MN	Y	24740 FQ	37060 AW	51770 TQ	NDBLS	10/01-12/01
Except Special Education	Ohio	Y	26110 FQ	42610 AW	59880 TQ	OHBLS	10/01-12/01
Except Special Education	Akron PMSA, OH	Y	22840 FQ	42240 AW	59070 TQ	OHBLS	10/01-12/01
Except Special Education	Canton-Massillon MSA, OH	Y	25680 FQ	39910 AW	56030 TQ	OHBLS	10/01-12/01
Except Special Education	Cincinnati PMSA, OH-KY-IN	Y	27940 FQ	44160 AW	64560 TQ	OHBLS	10/01-12/01

AAW Average annual wage; AE Average entry wage; AEX Average experienced wage; AO Average offered; AOH Average offered, high; AOL Average offered, low; APH Average pay, high range; APL Average pay, low range; ASH Average starting, high; ASL Average starting, low; AW Average wage paid; FQ First quartile wage; H Hourly; HI Highest wage paid; HR High end range; LR Low end range; M Monthly; MTC Median total compensation; MW Median wage paid; SQ Second quartile wage; S Special: hourly and annual; TQ Third quartile wage; W Weekly; Y Yearly

Occupation/Type/Industry	Location	Per	Low	Mid	High	Source	Date
Elementary School Teacher							
Except Special Education	Cleveland-Lorain-Elyria PMSA, OH	Y	26900 FQ	46570 AW	67930 TQ	OHBLS	10/01-12/01
Except Special Education	Columbus MSA, OH	Y	30710 FQ	45080 AW	61890 TQ	OHBLS	10/01-12/01
Except Special Education	Dayton-Springfield MSA, OH	Y	26420 FQ	40700 AW	57250 TQ	OHBLS	10/01-12/01
Except Special Education	Hamilton-Middletown PMSA, OH	Y	29920 FQ	43810 AW	56420 TQ	OHBLS	10/01-12/01
Except Special Education	Mansfield MSA, OH	Y	25650 FQ	40860 AW	55590 TQ	OHBLS	10/01-12/01
Except Special Education	Toledo MSA, OH	Y	23750 FQ	40740 AW	57430 TQ	OHBLS	10/01-12/01
Except Special Education	Youngstown-Warren MSA, OH	Y	24530 FQ	39460 AW	54870 TQ	OHBLS	10/01-12/01
Except Special Education	Oklahoma	Y	22710 FQ	31920 AW	42400 TQ	OKBLS	10/01-12/01
Except Special Education	Oklahoma City MSA, OK	Y	21530 FQ	31980 AW	44220 TQ	OKBLS	10/01-12/01
Except Special Education	Tulsa MSA, OK	Y	25090 FQ	32510 AW	41920 TQ	OKBLS	10/01-12/01
Except Special Education	Oregon	Y	29960 FQ	42690 AW	58040 TQ	ORBLS	10/01-12/01
Except Special Education	Eugene-Springfield MSA, OR	Y	29620 FQ	42650 AW	55430 TQ	ORBLS	10/01-12/01
Except Special Education	Medford-Ashland MSA, OR	Y	29680 FQ	41450 AW	55170 TQ	ORBLS	10/01-12/01
Except Special Education	Portland-Vancouver PMSA, OR-WA	Y	30390 FQ	44040 AW	60880 TQ	ORBLS	10/01-12/01
Except Special Education	Salem PMSA, OR	Y	28560 FQ	41240 AW	56380 TQ	ORBLS	10/01-12/01
Except Special Education	Pennsylvania	Y	28590 FQ	49370 AW	73720 TQ	PABLS	10/01-12/01
Except Special Education	Allentown-Bethlehem-Easton MSA, PA	Y	27740 FQ	50070 AW	72890 TQ	PABLS	10/01-12/01
Except Special Education	Erie MSA, PA	Y	29830 FQ	43500 AW	58130 TQ	PABLS	10/01-12/01
Except Special Education	Harrisburg-Lebanon-Carlisle MSA, PA	Y	24700 FQ	44180 AW	61130 TQ	PABLS	10/01-12/01
Except Special Education	Johnstown MSA, PA	Y	19070 FQ	43080 AW	64070 TQ	PABLS	10/01-12/01
Except Special Education	Lancaster MSA, PA	Y	30530 FQ	46700 AW	64980 TQ	PABLS	10/01-12/01
Except Special Education	Philadelphia PMSA, PA-NJ	Y	31020 FQ	51650 AW	76390 TQ	PABLS	10/01-12/01
Except Special Education	Pittsburgh MSA, PA	Y	28060 FQ	50980 AW	76870 TQ	PABLS	10/01-12/01
Except Special Education	Reading MSA, PA	Y	30510 FQ	50340 AW	70160 TQ	PABLS	10/01-12/01
Except Special Education	Scranton-Wilkes-Barre-Hazleton MSA, PA	Y	21920 FQ	48770 AW	75130 TQ	PABLS	10/01-12/01
Except Special Education	York MSA, PA	Y	27490 FQ	47930 AW	71660 TQ	PABLS	10/01-12/01
Except Special Education	Rhode Island	Y	26020 FQ	48740 AW	68770 TQ	RIBLS	10/01-12/01
Except Special Education	Providence-Fall River-Warwick MSA, RI-MA	Y	26990 FQ	48650 AW	68170 TQ	RIBLS	10/01-12/01
Except Special Education	South Carolina	Y	25980 FQ	38170 AW	53760 TQ	SCBLS	10/01-12/01
Except Special Education	Charleston-North Charleston MSA, SC	Y	26110 FQ	35950 AW	46830 TQ	SCBLS	10/01-12/01
Except Special Education	Columbia MSA, SC	Y	27210 FQ	39330 AW	55890 TQ	SCBLS	10/01-12/01
Except Special Education	Greenville-Spartanburg-Anderson MSA, SC	Y	27260 FQ	40860 AW	55540 TQ	SCBLS	10/01-12/01
Except Special Education	South Dakota	Y	23140 FQ	32000 AW	43780 TQ	SDBLS	10/01-12/01
Except Special Education	Tennessee	Y	24720 FQ	35190 AW	46720 TQ	TNBLS	10/01-12/01
Except Special Education	Chattanooga MSA, TN-GA	Y	18350 FQ	30990 AW	47340 TQ	TNBLS	10/01-12/01
Except Special Education	Johnson City-Kingsport-Bristol MSA, TN-VA	Y	23350 FQ	34280 AW	45580 TQ	TNBLS	10/01-12/01
Except Special Education	Knoxville MSA, TN	Y	29430 FQ	38110 AW	51960 TQ	TNBLS	10/01-12/01
Except Special Education	Memphis MSA, TN-AR-MS	Y	27010 FQ	40410 AW	51350 TQ	TNBLS	10/01-12/01
Except Special Education	Nashville MSA, TN	Y	24060 FQ	33040 AW	45030 TQ	TNBLS	10/01-12/01
Except Special Education	Texas	Y	29700 FQ	39190 AW	52790 TQ	TXBLS	10/01-12/01
Except Special Education	Austin-San Marcos MSA, TX	Y	29850 FQ	37780 AW	50500 TQ	TXBLS	10/01-12/01
Except Special Education	Beaumont-Port Arthur MSA, TX	Y	28980 FQ	37870 AW	50170 TQ	TXBLS	10/01-12/01
Except Special Education	Brazoria PMSA, TX	Y	30990 FQ	40390 AW	53050 TQ	TXBLS	10/01-12/01
Except Special Education	Corpus Christi MSA, TX	Y	31440 FQ	44650 AW	56480 TQ	TXBLS	10/01-12/01
Except Special Education	Dallas PMSA, TX	Y	30180 FQ	40390 AW	55500 TQ	TXBLS	10/01-12/01
Except Special Education	El Paso MSA, TX	Y	29860 FQ	37380 AW	49130 TQ	TXBLS	10/01-12/01
Except Special Education	Fort Worth-Arlington PMSA, TX	Y	30680 FQ	40010 AW	53280 TQ	TXBLS	10/01-12/01
Except Special Education	Houston PMSA, TX	Y	30790 FQ	40280 AW	53800 TQ	TXBLS	10/01-12/01
Except Special Education	Killeen-Temple MSA, TX	Y	28060 FQ	43780 AW	64160 TQ	TXBLS	10/01-12/01
Except Special Education	Laredo MSA, TX	Y	29940 FQ	39430 AW	52800 TQ	TXBLS	10/01-12/01
Except Special Education	Longview-Marshall MSA, TX	Y	26040 FQ	35600 AW	44810 TQ	TXBLS	10/01-12/01
Except Special Education	McAllen-Edinburg-Mission MSA, TX	Y	29470 FQ	38590 AW	53090 TQ	TXBLS	10/01-12/01
Except Special Education	Odessa-Midland MSA, TX	Y	29150 FQ	35640 AW	45380 TQ	TXBLS	10/01-12/01
Except Special Education	San Antonio MSA, TX	Y	31450 FQ	41750 AW	55640 TQ	TXBLS	10/01-12/01
Except Special Education	Tyler MSA, TX	Y	25150 FQ	35890 AW	45480 TQ	TXBLS	10/01-12/01
Except Special Education	Waco MSA, TX	Y	25320 FQ	35390 AW	45320 TQ	TXBLS	10/01-12/01
Except Special Education	Utah	Y	25070 FQ	37380 AW	52100 TQ	UTBLS	10/01-12/01
Except Special Education	Provo-Orem MSA, UT	Y	21740 FQ	35540 AW	51910 TQ	UTBLS	10/01-12/01

AAW Average annual wage; **AE** Average entry wage; **AEX** Average experienced wage; **AO** Average offered; **AOH** Average offered, high; **AOL** Average offered, low; **APH** Average pay, high range; **APL** Average pay, low range; **ASH** Average starting, high; **ASL** Average starting, low; **AW** Average wage paid; **FQ** First quartile wage; **H** Hourly; **HI** Highest wage paid; **HR** High end range; **LR** Low end range; **M** Monthly; **MTC** Median total compensation; **MW** Median wage paid; **SQ** Second quartile wage; **S** Special: hourly and annual; **TQ** Third quartile wage; **W** Weekly; **Y** Yearly

Occupation/Type/Industry	Location	Per	Low	Mid	High	Source	Date
Elementary School Teacher							
Except Special Education	Salt Lake City-Ogden MSA, UT	Y	25220 FQ	38010 AW	54370 TQ	UTBLS	10/01-12/01
Except Special Education	Vermont	Y	26160 FQ	38970 AW	52950 TQ	VTBLS	10/01-12/01
Except Special Education	Burlington MSA, VT	Y	23190 FQ	41000 AW	58790 TQ	VTBLS	10/01-12/01
Except Special Education	Virginia	Y	25330 FQ	41400 AW	59330 TQ	VABLS	10/01-12/01
Except Special Education	Lynchburg MSA, VA	Y	27610 FQ	35790 AW	47660 TQ	VABLS	10/01-12/01
Except Special Education	Norfolk-Virginia Beach-Newport News MSA, VA-NC	Y	21430 FQ	35680 AW	50450 TQ	VABLS	10/01-12/01
Except Special Education	Richmond-Petersburg MSA, VA	Y	31120 FQ	42650 AW	55930 TQ	VABLS	10/01-12/01
Except Special Education	Washington	Y	28390 FQ	42730 AW	56440 TQ	WABLS	10/01-12/01
Except Special Education	Bremerton PMSA, WA	Y	28520 FQ	42580 AW	55240 TQ	WABLS	10/01-12/01
Except Special Education	Olympia PMSA, WA	Y	27350 FQ	43810 AW	56540 TQ	WABLS	10/01-12/01
Except Special Education	Richland-Kennewick-Pasco MSA, WA	Y	30960 FQ	44760 AW	57610 TQ	WABLS	10/01-12/01
Except Special Education	Seattle-Bellevue-Everett PMSA, WA	Y	28630 FQ	42480 AW	56490 TQ	WABLS	10/01-12/01
Except Special Education	Spokane MSA, WA	Y	24990 FQ	42660 AW	57050 TQ	WABLS	10/01-12/01
Except Special Education	Tacoma PMSA, WA	Y	28150 FQ	42430 AW	56640 TQ	WABLS	10/01-12/01
Except Special Education	Yakima MSA, WA	Y	27750 FQ	40980 AW	54590 TQ	WABLS	10/01-12/01
Except Special Education	West Virginia	Y	29240 FQ	36550 AW	44510 TQ	WVBLS	10/01-12/01
Except Special Education	Huntington-Ashland MSA, WV-KY-OH	Y	26290 FQ	36700 AW	46640 TQ	WVBLS	10/01-12/01
Except Special Education	Wisconsin	Y	26190 FQ	41850 AW	58240 TQ	WIBLS	10/01-12/01
Except Special Education	Appleton-Oshkosh-Neenah MSA, WI	Y	24270 FQ	38200 AW	51890 TQ	WIBLS	10/01-12/01
Except Special Education	Green Bay MSA, WI	Y	30100 FQ	41550 AW	56050 TQ	WIBLS	10/01-12/01
Except Special Education	Madison MSA, WI	Y	24660 FQ	38120 AW	56020 TQ	WIBLS	10/01-12/01
Except Special Education	Milwaukee-Waukesha PMSA, WI	Y	26840 FQ	45390 AW	64860 TQ	WIBLS	10/01-12/01
Except Special Education	Racine PMSA, WI	Y	28670 FQ	41720 AW	56160 TQ	WIBLS	10/01-12/01
Except Special Education	Wyoming	Y	25570 FQ	36270 AW	46400 TQ	WYBLS	10/01-12/01
Except Special Education	Puerto Rico	Y	19190 FQ	23090 AW	27770 TQ	PRBLS	10/01-12/01
Except Special Education	Virgin Islands	Y	22070 FQ	35770 AW	54410 TQ	VIBLS	10/01-12/01
Except Special Education	Guam	Y	21490 FQ	32940 AW	44130 TQ	GUBLS	10/01-12/01
Elevator Installer and Repairer	Alabama	H	17.00 FQ	24.70 AW	31.39 TQ	ALBLS	10/01-12/01
	Arizona	H	10.47 FQ	17.79 AW	27.48 TQ	AZBLS	10/01-12/01
	Arkansas	H	15.72 FQ	20.49 AW	26.31 TQ	ARBLS	10/01-12/01
	California	H	15.41 FQ	28.28 AW	44.57 TQ	CABLS	10/01-12/01
	Colorado	H	18.09 FQ	24.74 AW	33.32 TQ	COBLS	10/01-12/01
	Connecticut	H	19.30 FQ	28.32 AW	35.60 TQ	CTBLS	10/01-12/01
	District of Columbia	H	10.45 FQ	20.67 AW	32.26 TQ	DCBLS	10/01-12/01
	Florida	H	9.85 FQ	20.97 AW	31.71 TQ	FLBLS	10/01-12/01
	Georgia	H	8.39 FQ	15.68 AW	25.19 TQ	GABLS	10/01-12/01
	Illinois	H	17.93 FQ	27.44 AW	36.11 TQ	ILBLS	10/01-12/01
	Indiana	H	17.40 FQ	24.65 AW	33.68 TQ	INBLS	10/01-12/01
	Iowa	H	14.97 FQ	22.06 AW	27.80 TQ	IABLS	10/01-12/01
	Kansas	H	7.01 FQ	14.51 AW	21.60 TQ	KSBLS	10/01-12/01
	Kentucky	H	16.42 FQ	22.54 AW	28.26 TQ	KYBLS	10/01-12/01
	Louisiana	H	10.18 FQ	19.83 AW	26.70 TQ	LABLS	10/01-12/01
	Maine	H	11.89 FQ	20.96 AW	27.01 TQ	MEBLS	10/01-12/01
	Maryland	H	12.21 FQ	21.54 AW	31.30 TQ	MDBLS	10/01-12/01
	Massachusetts	H	19.67 FQ	30.32 AW	41.65 TQ	MABLS	10/01-12/01
	Michigan	H	18.32 FQ	26.91 AW	33.96 TQ	MIBLS	10/01-12/01
	Minnesota	H	19.13 FQ	26.25 AW	33.56 TQ	MNBLS	10/01-12/01
	Mississippi	H	15.64 FQ	21.29 AW	27.76 TQ	MSBLS	10/01-12/01
	Missouri	H	17.28 FQ	25.56 AW	33.07 TQ	MOBLS	10/01-12/01
	Nebraska	H	15.15 FQ	24.80 AW	36.88 TQ	NEBLS	10/01-12/01
	Nevada	H	22.42 FQ	27.83 AW	37.51 TQ	NVBLS	10/01-12/01
	New Jersey	H	16.79 FQ	27.36 AW	36.05 TQ	NJBLS	10/01-12/01
	New Mexico	H	17.21 FQ	24.21 AW	28.47 TQ	NMBLS	10/01-12/01
	New York	H	16.88 FQ	26.39 AW	34.87 TQ	NYBLS	10/01-12/01
	North Carolina	H	7.41 FQ	14.56 AW	26.00 TQ	NCBLS	10/01-12/01
	Ohio	H	12.19 FQ	22.34 AW	33.95 TQ	OHBLS	10/01-12/01
	Oklahoma	H	17.64 FQ	20.70 AW	26.57 TQ	OKBLS	10/01-12/01
	Pennsylvania	H	18.36 FQ	29.32 AW	41.50 TQ	PABLS	10/01-12/01
	South Carolina	H	10.88 FQ	17.15 AW	24.39 TQ	SCBLS	10/01-12/01
	Tennessee	H	12.04 FQ	19.09 AW	26.22 TQ	TNBLS	10/01-12/01
	Texas	H	13.36 FQ	21.91 AW	30.40 TQ	TXBLS	10/01-12/01
	Virginia	H	12.93 FQ	19.50 AW	27.10 TQ	VABLS	10/01-12/01

AAW Average annual wage; AE Average entry wage; AEX Average experienced wage; AO Average offered; AOH Average offered, high; AOL Average offered, low; APH Average pay, high range; APL Average pay, low range; ASH Average starting, high; ASL Average starting, low; AW Average wage paid; FQ First quartile wage; H Hourly; HI Highest wage paid; HR High end range; LR Low end range; M Monthly; MTC Median total compensation; MW Median wage paid; SQ Second quartile wage; S Special: hourly and annual; TQ Third quartile wage; W Weekly; Y Yearly

Occupation/Type/Industry	Location	Per	Low	Mid	High	Source	Date
Elevator Installer and Repairer	West Virginia	H	16.96 FQ	23.54 AW	29.93 TQ	WVBLS	10/01-12/01
	Wisconsin	H	16.60 FQ	24.68 AW	34.20 TQ	WIBLS	10/01-12/01
	Puerto Rico	H	6.30 FQ	9.96 AW	13.39 TQ	PRBLS	10/01-12/01
Eligibility Interviewer							
Government Program	Alabama	H	10.61 FQ	15.37 AW	20.56 TQ	ALBLS	10/01-12/01
Government Program	Alaska	H	14.29 FQ	18.35 AW	24.21 TQ	AKBLS	10/01-12/01
Government Program	Arizona	H	10.77 FQ	13.15 AW	16.59 TQ	AZBLS	10/01-12/01
Government Program	Arkansas	H	6.23 FQ	10.02 AW	14.10 TQ	ARBLS	10/01-12/01
Government Program	California	H	12.00 FQ	14.47 AW	17.92 TQ	CABLS	10/01-12/01
Government Program	Colorado	H	11.12 FQ	14.92 AW	20.30 TQ	COBLS	10/01-12/01
Government Program	Connecticut	H	16.09 FQ	22.05 AW	26.50 TQ	CTBLS	10/01-12/01
Government Program	District of Columbia	H	10.94 FQ	16.20 AW	23.96 TQ	DCBLS	10/01-12/01
Government Program	Florida	H	9.31 FQ	12.41 AW	16.20 TQ	FLBLS	10/01-12/01
Government Program	Georgia	H	9.22 FQ	13.14 AW	18.32 TQ	GABLS	10/01-12/01
Government Program	Hawaii	H	11.89 FQ	16.81 AW	23.21 TQ	HIBLS	10/01-12/01
Government Program	Idaho	H	9.43 FQ	13.36 AW	19.11 TQ	IDBLS	10/01-12/01
Government Program	Illinois	H	10.23 FQ	16.06 AW	26.57 TQ	ILBLS	10/01-12/01
Government Program	Indiana	H	8.51 FQ	12.13 AW	18.01 TQ	INBLS	10/01-12/01
Government Program	Iowa	H	13.92 FQ	17.55 AW	20.97 TQ	IABLS	10/01-12/01
Government Program	Kansas	H	11.37 FQ	14.73 AW	18.83 TQ	KSBLS	10/01-12/01
Government Program	Kentucky	H	10.32 FQ	16.10 AW	23.99 TQ	KYBLS	10/01-12/01
Government Program	Louisiana	H	8.53 FQ	12.93 AW	18.25 TQ	LABLS	10/01-12/01
Government Program	Maine	H	11.06 FQ	14.03 AW	16.66 TQ	MEBLS	10/01-12/01
Government Program	Maryland	H	10.94 FQ	14.25 AW	17.72 TQ	MDBLS	10/01-12/01
Government Program	Massachusetts	H	11.48 FQ	16.50 AW	21.47 TQ	MABLS	10/01-12/01
Government Program	Michigan	H	13.86 FQ	17.95 AW	21.05 TQ	MIBLS	10/01-12/01
Government Program	Minnesota	H	12.57 FQ	16.87 AW	21.77 TQ	MNBLS	10/01-12/01
Government Program	Mississippi	H	9.02 FQ	11.57 AW	15.10 TQ	MSBLS	10/01-12/01
Government Program	Montana	H	10.86 FQ	13.70 AW	16.52 TQ	MTBLS	10/01-12/01
Government Program	Nebraska	H	7.62 FQ	12.50 AW	19.41 TQ	NEBLS	10/01-12/01
Government Program	New Hampshire	H	9.61 FQ	12.56 AW	16.02 TQ	NHBLS	10/01-12/01
Government Program	New Jersey	H	10.81 FQ	17.31 AW	25.06 TQ	NJBLS	10/01-12/01
Government Program	New Mexico	H	7.95 FQ	11.91 AW	16.68 TQ	NMBLS	10/01-12/01
Government Program	New York	H	12.35 FQ	16.58 AW	22.18 TQ	NYBLS	10/01-12/01
Government Program	North Carolina	H	9.86 FQ	13.15 AW	16.84 TQ	NCBLS	10/01-12/01
Government Program	North Dakota	H	9.46 FQ	13.16 AW	17.77 TQ	NDBLS	10/01-12/01
Government Program	Ohio	H	11.88 FQ	15.94 AW	20.66 TQ	OHBLS	10/01-12/01
Government Program	Oklahoma	H	7.73 FQ	12.93 AW	18.83 TQ	OKBLS	10/01-12/01
Government Program	Oregon	H	10.03 FQ	13.69 AW	17.69 TQ	ORBLS	10/01-12/01
Government Program	Pennsylvania	H	13.41 FQ	19.40 AW	25.74 TQ	PABLS	10/01-12/01
Government Program	Rhode Island	H	17.18 FQ	20.50 AW	25.91 TQ	RIBLS	10/01-12/01
Government Program	South Carolina	H	9.30 FQ	13.56 AW	19.31 TQ	SCBLS	10/01-12/01
Government Program	South Dakota	H	8.11 FQ	11.06 AW	13.37 TQ	SDBLS	10/01-12/01
Government Program	Tennessee	H	8.64 FQ	12.52 AW	16.36 TQ	TNBLS	10/01-12/01
Government Program	Texas	H	8.97 FQ	13.71 AW	18.95 TQ	TXBLS	10/01-12/01
Government Program	Utah	H	9.08 FQ	12.50 AW	16.87 TQ	UTBLS	10/01-12/01
Government Program	Vermont	H	8.07 FQ	13.35 AW	18.87 TQ	VTBLS	10/01-12/01
Government Program	Virginia	H	10.56 FQ	14.37 AW	19.79 TQ	VABLS	10/01-12/01
Government Program	Washington	H	12.29 FQ	17.59 AW	21.39 TQ	WABLS	10/01-12/01
Government Program	West Virginia	H	9.11 FQ	11.76 AW	14.87 TQ	WVBLS	10/01-12/01
Government Program	Wisconsin	H	11.01 FQ	15.42 AW	21.27 TQ	WIBLS	10/01-12/01
Government Program	Wyoming	H	13.13 FQ	17.55 AW	21.29 TQ	WYBLS	10/01-12/01
Government Program	Puerto Rico	H	5.93 FQ	8.53 AW	11.26 TQ	PRBLS	10/01-12/01
Government Program	Guam	H	9.79 FQ	13.63 AW	16.47 TQ	GUBLS	10/01-12/01
Embalmer	United States	H		15.07 AW		DEATHBUS	2001
	Alabama	H	7.52 FQ	15.99 AW	24.92 TQ	ALBLS	10/01-12/01
	Arizona	H	10.86 FQ	14.56 AW	19.91 TQ	AZBLS	10/01-12/01
	Phoenix-Mesa MSA, AZ	H	11.22 FQ	15.19 AW	20.43 TQ	AZBLS	10/01-12/01
	Arkansas	H	8.32 FQ	14.66 AW	21.32 TQ	ARBLS	10/01-12/01
	California	H	12.07 FQ	17.37 AW	21.77 TQ	CABLS	10/01-12/01
	Los Angeles-Long Beach PMSA, CA	H	13.73 FQ	17.66 AW	20.97 TQ	CABLS	10/01-12/01
	Oakland PMSA, CA	H	12.11 FQ	17.51 AW	23.41 TQ	CABLS	10/01-12/01
	Orange County PMSA, CA	H	11.10 FQ	13.71 AW	19.17 TQ	CABLS	10/01-12/01
	Riverside-San Bernardino PMSA, CA	H	11.68 FQ	15.42 AW	20.12 TQ	CABLS	10/01-12/01
	San Francisco PMSA, CA	H	18.13 FQ	21.21 AW	25.74 TQ	CABLS	10/01-12/01
	San Jose PMSA, CA	H	14.01 FQ	19.35 AW	22.74 TQ	CABLS	10/01-12/01
	Colorado	H	8.90 FQ	13.06 AW	20.38 TQ	COBLS	10/01-12/01
	Connecticut	H		24.70 AW		DEATHBUS	2001
	Connecticut	H	12.84 FQ	30.12 AW		CTBLS	10/01-12/01

AAW	Average annual wage	AOH	Average offered, high	ASH	Average starting, high	H	Hourly	M	Monthly	S	Special: hourly and annual
AE	Average entry wage	AOL	Average offered, low	ASL	Average starting, low	HI	Highest wage paid	MTC	Median total compensation	TQ	Third quartile wage
AEX	Average experienced wage	APH	Average pay, high range	AW	Average wage paid	HR	High end range	MW	Median wage paid	W	Weekly
AO	Average offered	APL	Average pay, low range	FQ	First quartile wage	LR	Low end range	SQ	Second quartile wage	Y	Yearly

Occupation/Type/Industry	Location	Per	Low	Mid	High	Source	Date
Embalmer	Bridgeport PMSA, CT	H	13.13 FQ	39.45 AW		CTBLS	10/01-12/01
	Hartford MSA, CT	H	12.32 FQ	22.70 AW	30.80 TQ	CTBLS	10/01-12/01
	New Haven-Meriden PMSA, CT	H	19.81 FQ	38.71 AW	52.43 TQ	CTBLS	10/01-12/01
	Washington PMSA, DC-MD-VA-WV	H	6.26 FQ	16.01 AW	25.88 TQ	DCBLS	10/01-12/01
	Florida	H	5.73 FQ	12.91 AW	21.77 TQ	FLBLS	10/01-12/01
	Miami PMSA, FL	H	5.83 FQ	13.17 AW	21.81 TQ	FLBLS	10/01-12/01
	Orlando MSA, FL	H	5.74 FQ	13.18 AW	18.83 TQ	FLBLS	10/01-12/01
	Tampa-St. Petersburg-Clearwater MSA, FL	H	5.37 FQ	8.05 AW	15.18 TQ	FLBLS	10/01-12/01
	Georgia	H	11.76 FQ	18.06 AW	26.20 TQ	GABLS	10/01-12/01
	Atlanta MSA, GA	H	15.46 FQ	18.31 AW	21.03 TQ	GABLS	10/01-12/01
	Illinois	H	12.22 FQ	23.75 AW	40.93 TQ	ILBLS	10/01-12/01
	Indiana	H	10.83 FQ	17.44 AW	23.71 TQ	INBLS	10/01-12/01
	Iowa	H	12.38 FQ	19.76 AW	27.19 TQ	IABLS	10/01-12/01
	Kansas	H	8.98 FQ	13.87 AW	23.67 TQ	KSBLS	10/01-12/01
	Kentucky	H	9.96 FQ	16.54 AW	30.37 TQ	KYBLS	10/01-12/01
	Lexington MSA, KY	H	9.44 FQ	12.04 AW	15.90 TQ	KYBLS	10/01-12/01
	Louisville MSA, KY-IN	H	10.04 FQ	15.99 AW	24.50 TQ	KYBLS	10/01-12/01
	Louisiana	H	7.75 FQ	17.79 AW	27.31 TQ	LABLS	10/01-12/01
	New Orleans MSA, LA	H	7.63 FQ	21.19 AW	41.58 TQ	LABLS	10/01-12/01
	Maryland	H	10.17 FQ	20.27 AW	38.91 TQ	MDBLS	10/01-12/01
	Baltimore PMSA, MD	H	14.21 FQ	21.22 AW	39.78 TQ	MDBLS	10/01-12/01
	Massachusetts	H	9.02 FQ	16.84 AW	28.80 TQ	MABLS	10/01-12/01
	Boston PMSA, MA-NH	H	9.88 FQ	15.26 AW	19.43 TQ	MABLS	10/01-12/01
	Michigan	H	12.08 FQ	19.58 AW	23.94 TQ	MIBLS	10/01-12/01
	Detroit PMSA, MI	H	14.85 FQ	21.20 AW	22.22 TQ	MIBLS	10/01-12/01
	Grand Rapids-Muskegon-Holland MSA, MI	H	10.64 FQ	14.40 AW	18.33 TQ	MIBLS	10/01-12/01
	Mississippi	H	10.27 FQ	15.39 AW	20.41 TQ	MSBLS	10/01-12/01
	Missouri	H	8.08 FQ	14.60 AW	24.29 TQ	MOBLS	10/01-12/01
	Kansas City MSA, MO-KS	H	8.75 FQ	10.61 AW	13.24 TQ	MOBLS	10/01-12/01
	St. Louis MSA, MO-IL	H	7.42 FQ	14.65 AW	27.18 TQ	MOBLS	10/01-12/01
	Springfield MSA, MO	H	7.90 FQ	17.00 AW	26.49 TQ	MOBLS	10/01-12/01
	Montana	H	11.75 FQ	21.45 AW	31.67 TQ	MTBLS	10/01-12/01
	Nevada	H	6.82 FQ	14.72 AW	21.14 TQ	NVBLS	10/01-12/01
	Las Vegas MSA, NV-AZ	H	6.80 FQ	14.07 AW	20.59 TQ	NVBLS	10/01-12/01
	New Hampshire	H	12.19 FQ	18.44 AW	25.05 TQ	NHBLS	10/01-12/01
	New Jersey	H	5.92 FQ	15.19 AW	33.54 TQ	NJBLS	10/01-12/01
	New York	H	14.41 FQ	18.21 AW	25.96 TQ	NYBLS	10/01-12/01
	Albany-Schenectady-Troy MSA, NY	H	14.42 FQ	15.91 AW	17.49 TQ	NYBLS	10/01-12/01
	North Carolina	H	10.90 FQ	17.72 AW	27.30 TQ	NCBLS	10/01-12/01
	Greensboro-Winston-Salem-High Point MSA, NC	H	11.49 FQ	17.17 AW	21.89 TQ	NCBLS	10/01-12/01
	Hickory-Morganton-Lenoir MSA, NC	H	13.46 FQ	16.64 AW	21.10 TQ	NCBLS	10/01-12/01
	Raleigh-Durham-Chapel Hill MSA, NC	H	12.33 FQ	20.13 AW	33.43 TQ	NCBLS	10/01-12/01
	Ohio	H	6.65 FQ	13.37 AW	20.73 TQ	OHBLS	10/01-12/01
	Cincinnati PMSA, OH-KY-IN	H	6.42 FQ	14.20 AW	22.97 TQ	OHBLS	10/01-12/01
	Columbus MSA, OH	H	8.70 FQ	16.58 AW	24.65 TQ	OHBLS	10/01-12/01
	Oklahoma	H	9.13 FQ	11.77 AW	18.47 TQ	OKBLS	10/01-12/01
	Pennsylvania	H	6.99 FQ	19.48 AW	32.34 TQ	PABLS	10/01-12/01
	Providence-Fall River-Warwick MSA, RI-MA	H	9.52 FQ	18.23 AW	28.26 TQ	RIBLS	10/01-12/01
	South Carolina	H	7.62 FQ	15.11 AW	22.95 TQ	SCBLS	10/01-12/01
	Greenville-Spartanburg-Anderson MSA, SC	H	9.50 FQ	16.26 AW	26.37 TQ	SCBLS	10/01-12/01
	Tennessee	H	11.57 FQ	16.51 AW	24.63 TQ	TNBLS	10/01-12/01
	Johnson City-Kingsport-Bristol MSA, TN-VA	H	11.18 FQ	15.66 AW	24.16 TQ	TNBLS	10/01-12/01
	Texas	H	6.14 FQ	12.00 AW	20.21 TQ	TXBLS	10/01-12/01
	Dallas PMSA, TX	H	8.75 FQ	10.50 AW	13.96 TQ	TXBLS	10/01-12/01
	Fort Worth-Arlington PMSA, TX	H	5.68 FQ	10.81 AW	19.45 TQ	TXBLS	10/01-12/01
	Houston PMSA, TX	H	7.37 FQ	11.62 AW	18.70 TQ	TXBLS	10/01-12/01
	San Antonio MSA, TX	H	5.58 FQ	12.47 AW	21.35 TQ	TXBLS	10/01-12/01
	Virginia	H	8.26 FQ	15.90 AW	25.42 TQ	VABLS	10/01-12/01

AAW	Average annual wage	AOH	Average offered, high	ASH	Average starting, high	H	Hourly	M	Monthly	S	Special: hourly and annual
AE	Average entry wage	AOL	Average offered, low	ASL	Average starting, low	HI	Highest wage paid	MTC	Median total compensation	TQ	Third quartile wage
AEX	Average experienced wage	APH	Average pay, high range	AW	Average wage paid	HR	High end range	MW	Median wage paid	W	Weekly
AO	Average offered	APL	Average pay, low range	FQ	First quartile wage	LR	Low end range	SQ	Second quartile wage	Y	Yearly

Occupation/Type/Industry	Location	Per	Low	Mid	High	Source	Date
Embalmer	Norfolk-Virginia Beach-Newport News MSA, VA-NC	H	8.28 FQ	17.04 AW	24.90 TQ	VABLS	10/01-12/01
	Richmond-Petersburg MSA, VA	H	9.78 FQ	18.49 AW	26.96 TQ	VABLS	10/01-12/01
	Washington	H	14.85 FQ	19.96 AW	26.48 TQ	WABLS	10/01-12/01
	Seattle-Bellevue-Everett PMSA, WA	H	15.62 FQ	20.48 AW	26.18 TQ	WABLS	10/01-12/01
	Tacoma PMSA, WA	H	13.82 FQ	20.84 AW	32.20 TQ	WABLS	10/01-12/01
	West Virginia	H	13.69 FQ	18.25 AW	21.43 TQ	WVBLS	10/01-12/01
	Wisconsin	H	13.48 FQ	22.05 AW	27.96 TQ	WIBLS	10/01-12/01
	Wisconsin	H		15.74 AW		DEATHBUS	2001
	Puerto Rico	H	6.76 FQ	13.69 AW	20.81 TQ	PRBLS	10/01-12/01
Emergency Management Specialist	Alabama	Y	17290 FQ	33870 AW	53220 TQ	ALBLS	10/01-12/01
	Arizona	Y	29910 FQ	48790 AW	76460 TQ	AZBLS	10/01-12/01
	Arkansas	Y	12940 FQ	28780 AW	49230 TQ	ARBLS	10/01-12/01
	California	Y	35000 FQ	59490 AW	90150 TQ	CABLS	10/01-12/01
	Colorado	Y	27570 FQ	57580 AW	87110 TQ	COBLS	10/01-12/01
	Connecticut	Y	25300 FQ	49220 AW	77810 TQ	CTBLS	10/01-12/01
	District of Columbia	Y	32230 FQ	47720 AW	67310 TQ	DCBLS	10/01-12/01
	Florida	Y	27880 FQ	49820 AW	84840 TQ	FLBLS	10/01-12/01
	Georgia	Y	15370 FQ	38240 AW	66550 TQ	GABLS	10/01-12/01
	Hawaii	Y	35570 FQ	51520 AW	70880 TQ	HIBLS	10/01-12/01
	Idaho	Y	13160 FQ	41760 AW	73720 TQ	IDBLS	10/01-12/01
	Illinois	Y	20060 FQ	35960 AW	59790 TQ	ILBLS	10/01-12/01
	Indiana	Y	14440 FQ	35180 AW	57260 TQ	INBLS	10/01-12/01
	Iowa	Y	16900 FQ	36140 AW	62760 TQ	IABLS	10/01-12/01
	Kansas	Y	20960 FQ	34250 AW	48020 TQ	KSBLS	10/01-12/01
	Kentucky	Y	21140 FQ	39100 AW	59810 TQ	KYBLS	10/01-12/01
	Louisiana	Y	22740 FQ	42940 AW	74310 TQ	LABLS	10/01-12/01
	Maine	Y	23410 FQ	39840 AW	57110 TQ	MEBLS	10/01-12/01
	Maryland	Y	30810 FQ	53090 AW	77620 TQ	MDBLS	10/01-12/01
	Massachusetts	Y	28450 FQ	56580 AW	89710 TQ	MABLS	10/01-12/01
	Michigan	Y	24060 FQ	42150 AW	62650 TQ	MIBLS	10/01-12/01
	Minnesota	Y	27530 FQ	45820 AW	70780 TQ	MNBLS	10/01-12/01
	Mississippi	Y	18430 FQ	32730 AW	57170 TQ	MSBLS	10/01-12/01
	Missouri	Y	15410 FQ	38300 AW	62620 TQ	MOBLS	10/01-12/01
	Montana	Y	13750 FQ	30230 AW	53630 TQ	MTBLS	10/01-12/01
	Nebraska	Y	15040 FQ	38290 AW	66740 TQ	NEBLS	10/01-12/01
	Nevada	Y	34220 FQ	53300 AW	82360 TQ	NVBLS	10/01-12/01
	New Jersey	Y	31280 FQ	50350 AW	75460 TQ	NJBLS	10/01-12/01
	New Mexico	Y	24790 FQ	47270 AW	73790 TQ	NMBLS	10/01-12/01
	New York	Y	33180 FQ	61150 AW	105840 TQ	NYBLS	10/01-12/01
	North Carolina	Y	28950 FQ	43080 AW	66330 TQ	NCBLS	10/01-12/01
	North Dakota	Y	12420 FQ	31290 AW	59020 TQ	NDBLS	10/01-12/01
	Ohio	Y	25280 FQ	44040 AW	68190 TQ	OHBLS	10/01-12/01
	Oklahoma	Y	19380 FQ	32740 AW	48910 TQ	OKBLS	10/01-12/01
	Oregon	Y	29130 FQ	46210 AW	72130 TQ	ORBLS	10/01-12/01
	Pennsylvania	Y	21470 FQ	44770 AW	71320 TQ	PABLS	10/01-12/01
	Rhode Island	Y	25880 FQ	37700 AW	54570 TQ	RIBLS	10/01-12/01
	South Carolina	Y	23050 FQ	38890 AW	61030 TQ	SCBLS	10/01-12/01
	South Dakota	Y	21360 FQ	29830 AW	40250 TQ	SDBLS	10/01-12/01
	Tennessee	Y	22730 FQ	41580 AW	67790 TQ	TNBLS	10/01-12/01
	Texas	Y	21750 FQ	47450 AW	75190 TQ	TXBLS	10/01-12/01
	Utah	Y	31450 FQ	47620 AW	62990 TQ	UTBLS	10/01-12/01
	Virginia	Y	21340 FQ	47430 AW	73970 TQ	VABLS	10/01-12/01
	Washington	Y	27260 FQ	50630 AW	80360 TQ	WABLS	10/01-12/01
	West Virginia	Y	13340 FQ	28900 AW	48910 TQ	WVBLS	10/01-12/01
	Wisconsin	Y	23790 FQ	42490 AW	67320 TQ	WIBLS	10/01-12/01
	Wyoming	Y	14640 FQ	33860 AW	57190 TQ	WYBLS	10/01-12/01
	Puerto Rico	Y	14790 FQ	25270 AW	42530 TQ	PRBLS	10/01-12/01
Emergency Medical Technician and Paramedic	United States	Y		22460 MW		OOH3	1/99-1/00
	Alabama	Y	14600 FQ	21250 AW	29440 TQ	ALBLS	10/01-12/01
	Birmingham MSA, AL	Y	14390 FQ	21820 AW	35320 TQ	ALBLS	10/01-12/01
	Mobile MSA, AL	Y	15250 FQ	22930 AW	33610 TQ	ALBLS	10/01-12/01
	Montgomery MSA, AL	Y	16040 FQ	23080 AW	30010 TQ	ALBLS	10/01-12/01
	Alaska	Y	17400 FQ	32330 AW	54300 TQ	AKBLS	10/01-12/01
	Anchorage MSA, AK	Y	19010 FQ	35730 AW	55530 TQ	AKBLS	10/01-12/01

AAW	Average annual wage	**AOH**	Average offered, high	**ASH**	Average starting, high	**H**	Hourly	**M**	Monthly	**S**	Special: hourly and annual
AE	Average entry wage	**AOL**	Average offered, low	**ASL**	Average starting, low	**HI**	Highest wage paid	**MTC**	Median total compensation	**TQ**	Third quartile wage
AEX	Average experienced wage	**APH**	Average pay, high range	**AW**	Average wage paid	**HR**	High end range	**MW**	Median wage paid	**W**	Weekly
AO	Average offered	**APL**	Average pay, low range	**FQ**	First quartile wage	**LR**	Low end range	**SQ**	Second quartile wage	**Y**	Yearly

Occupation/Type/Industry	Location	Per	Low	Mid	High	Source	Date
Emergency Medical Technician and Paramedic	Arizona	Y	12840 FQ	22890 AW	38430 TQ	AZBLS	10/01-12/01
	Phoenix-Mesa MSA, AZ	Y	12750 FQ	21820 AW	36500 TQ	AZBLS	10/01-12/01
	Tucson MSA, AZ	Y	18180 FQ	27190 AW	42760 TQ	AZBLS	10/01-12/01
	Arkansas	Y	13840 FQ	21950 AW	32700 TQ	ARBLS	10/01-12/01
	Fayetteville-Springdale-Rogers MSA, AR	Y	17380 FQ	24310 AW	32540 TQ	ARBLS	10/01-12/01
	Fort Smith MSA, AR-OK	Y	15690 FQ	23280 AW	35190 TQ	ARBLS	10/01-12/01
	Little Rock-North Little Rock MSA, AR	Y	14850 FQ	22070 AW	32840 TQ	ARBLS	10/01-12/01
	California	Y	16340 FQ	29960 AW	51490 TQ	CABLS	10/01-12/01
	Los Angeles-Long Beach PMSA, CA	Y	16320 FQ	25670 AW	37920 TQ	CABLS	10/01-12/01
	Merced MSA, CA	Y	15950 FQ	25890 AW	37170 TQ	CABLS	10/01-12/01
	Modesto MSA, CA	Y	15890 FQ	22640 AW	33130 TQ	CABLS	10/01-12/01
	Oakland PMSA, CA	Y	15530 FQ	26760 AW	37940 TQ	CABLS	10/01-12/01
	Orange County PMSA, CA	Y	17980 FQ	36510 AW	68840 TQ	CABLS	10/01-12/01
	Riverside-San Bernardino PMSA, CA	Y	16150 FQ	28400 AW	46550 TQ	CABLS	10/01-12/01
	Sacramento PMSA, CA	Y	22100 FQ	32340 AW	45260 TQ	CABLS	10/01-12/01
	Salinas MSA, CA	Y	18670 FQ	43350 AW	76880 TQ	CABLS	10/01-12/01
	San Diego MSA, CA	Y	16980 FQ	30270 AW	53050 TQ	CABLS	10/01-12/01
	San Francisco PMSA, CA	Y	23370 FQ	46210 AW	82170 TQ	CABLS	10/01-12/01
	San Jose PMSA, CA	Y	17970 FQ	33800 AW	47120 TQ	CABLS	10/01-12/01
	San Luis Obispo-Atascadero-Paso Robles MSA, CA	Y	18740 FQ	35980 AW	55980 TQ	CABLS	10/01-12/01
	Santa Barbara-Santa Maria-Lompoc MSA, CA	Y	16790 FQ	28530 AW	37990 TQ	CABLS	10/01-12/01
	Santa Cruz-Watsonville PMSA, CA	Y	23580 FQ	30260 AW	36120 TQ	CABLS	10/01-12/01
	Santa Rosa PMSA, CA	Y	15790 FQ	34160 AW	54120 TQ	CABLS	10/01-12/01
	Stockton-Lodi MSA, CA	Y	15520 FQ	23350 AW	35840 TQ	CABLS	10/01-12/01
	Vallejo-Fairfield-Napa PMSA, CA	Y	18550 FQ	28450 AW	47560 TQ	CABLS	10/01-12/01
	Ventura PMSA, CA	Y	17990 FQ	29660 AW	45470 TQ	CABLS	10/01-12/01
	Visalia-Tulare-Porterville MSA, CA	Y	15880 FQ	24810 AW	35630 TQ	CABLS	10/01-12/01
	Colorado	Y	18820 FQ	28750 AW	45490 TQ	COBLS	10/01-12/01
	Boulder-Longmont PMSA, CO	Y	16620 FQ	24310 AW	33510 TQ	COBLS	10/01-12/01
	Denver PMSA, CO	Y	19280 FQ	30390 AW	50890 TQ	COBLS	10/01-12/01
	Fort Collins-Loveland MSA, CO	Y	19460 FQ	29010 AW	43260 TQ	COBLS	10/01-12/01
	Connecticut	Y	18820 FQ	29410 AW	40860 TQ	CTBLS	10/01-12/01
	Bridgeport PMSA, CT	Y	15100 FQ	30770 AW	44270 TQ	CTBLS	10/01-12/01
	Danbury PMSA, CT	Y	19750 FQ	29430 AW	37860 TQ	CTBLS	10/01-12/01
	Hartford MSA, CT	Y	19350 FQ	31670 AW	42630 TQ	CTBLS	10/01-12/01
	New Haven-Meriden PMSA, CT	Y	18540 FQ	26290 AW	35300 TQ	CTBLS	10/01-12/01
	New London-Norwich MSA, CT-RI	Y	16060 FQ	25450 AW	34900 TQ	CTBLS	10/01-12/01
	Stamford-Norwalk PMSA, CT	Y	24710 FQ	37590 AW	48200 TQ	CTBLS	10/01-12/01
	Delaware	Y	17200 FQ	28140 AW	42010 TQ	DEBLS	10/01-12/01
	Wilmington-Newark PMSA, DE-MD	Y	17340 FQ	26260 AW	37530 TQ	DEBLS	10/01-12/01
	District of Columbia	Y	18190 FQ	39840 AW	67990 TQ	DCBLS	10/01-12/01
	Washington PMSA, DC-MD-VA-WV	Y	18710 FQ	33560 AW	59180 TQ	DCBLS	10/01-12/01
	Florida	Y	16690 FQ	26460 AW	41320 TQ	FLBLS	10/01-12/01
	Daytona Beach MSA, FL	Y	15640 FQ	23550 AW	33170 TQ	FLBLS	10/01-12/01
	Fort Lauderdale PMSA, FL	Y	18490 FQ	30430 AW	45920 TQ	FLBLS	10/01-12/01
	Fort Pierce-Port St. Lucie MSA, FL	Y	19240 FQ	28260 AW	35880 TQ	FLBLS	10/01-12/01
	Jacksonville MSA, FL	Y	17110 FQ	25190 AW	37020 TQ	FLBLS	10/01-12/01
	Melbourne-Titusville-Palm Bay MSA, FL	Y	16740 FQ	26830 AW	40900 TQ	FLBLS	10/01-12/01
	Miami PMSA, FL	Y	15220 FQ	23130 AW	33780 TQ	FLBLS	10/01-12/01
	Orlando MSA, FL	Y	18160 FQ	26740 AW	37060 TQ	FLBLS	10/01-12/01
	Pensacola MSA, FL	Y	20580 FQ	25820 AW	30310 TQ	FLBLS	10/01-12/01
	Sarasota-Bradenton MSA, FL	Y	18200 FQ	36010 AW	46540 TQ	FLBLS	10/01-12/01
	Tallahassee MSA, FL	Y	17750 FQ	24740 AW	31230 TQ	FLBLS	10/01-12/01
	Tampa-St. Petersburg-Clearwater MSA, FL	Y	18830 FQ	29430 AW	44280 TQ	FLBLS	10/01-12/01

AAW	Average annual wage	AOH	Average offered, high	ASH	Average starting, high	H	Hourly	M	Monthly	S	Special: hourly and annual
AE	Average entry wage	AOL	Average offered, low	ASL	Average starting, low	HI	Highest wage paid	MTC	Median total compensation	TQ	Third quartile wage
AEX	Average experienced wage	APH	Average pay, high range	AW	Average wage paid	HR	High end range	MW	Median wage paid	W	Weekly
AO	Average offered	APL	Average pay, low range	FQ	First quartile wage	LR	Low end range	SQ	Second quartile wage	Y	Yearly

Occupation/Type/Industry	Location	Per	Low	Mid	High	Source	Date
Emergency Medical Technician and Paramedic	West Palm Beach-Boca Raton MSA, FL	Y	21180 FQ	31120 AW	45780 TQ	FLBLS	10/01-12/01
	Georgia	Y	15780 FQ	23340 AW	32600 TQ	GABLS	10/01-12/01
	Atlanta MSA, GA	Y	16250 FQ	23920 AW	33290 TQ	GABLS	10/01-12/01
	Augusta-Aiken MSA, GA-SC	Y	16430 FQ	26710 AW	34260 TQ	GABLS	10/01-12/01
	Columbus MSA, GA-AL	Y	16040 FQ	24660 AW	34790 TQ	GABLS	10/01-12/01
	Macon MSA, GA	Y	15720 FQ	23710 AW	33390 TQ	GABLS	10/01-12/01
	Hawaii	Y	16380 FQ	28320 AW	42520 TQ	HIBLS	10/01-12/01
	Honolulu MSA, HI	Y	17830 FQ	29660 AW	43100 TQ	HIBLS	10/01-12/01
	Idaho	Y	13850 FQ	24840 AW	40250 TQ	IDBLS	10/01-12/01
	Boise City MSA, ID	Y	23310 FQ	33700 AW	44460 TQ	IDBLS	10/01-12/01
	Illinois	Y	14980 FQ	27060 AW	48090 TQ	ILBLS	10/01-12/01
	Chicago PMSA, IL	Y	17980 FQ	30150 AW	51830 TQ	ILBLS	10/01-12/01
	Peoria-Pekin MSA, IL	Y	13660 FQ	26080 AW	52060 TQ	ILBLS	10/01-12/01
	Rockford MSA, IL	Y	13570 FQ	26400 AW	40100 TQ	ILBLS	10/01-12/01
	Springfield MSA, IL	Y	12850 FQ	20970 AW	36050 TQ	ILBLS	10/01-12/01
	Indiana	Y	14850 FQ	23690 AW	34910 TQ	INBLS	10/01-12/01
	Elkhart-Goshen MSA, IN	Y	12080 FQ	23280 AW	36050 TQ	INBLS	10/01-12/01
	Evansville-Henderson MSA, IN-KY	Y	16470 FQ	25720 AW	36090 TQ	INBLS	10/01-12/01
	Fort Wayne MSA, IN	Y	18350 FQ	25110 AW	34460 TQ	INBLS	10/01-12/01
	Gary PMSA, IN	Y	15570 FQ	24370 AW	36570 TQ	INBLS	10/01-12/01
	Indianapolis MSA, IN	Y	16270 FQ	24510 AW	35430 TQ	INBLS	10/01-12/01
	Lafayette MSA, IN	Y	16100 FQ	24790 AW	34180 TQ	INBLS	10/01-12/01
	South Bend MSA, IN	Y	18350 FQ	22170 AW	27790 TQ	INBLS	10/01-12/01
	Iowa	Y	12650 FQ	21440 AW	31690 TQ	IABLS	10/01-12/01
	Davenport-Moline-Rock Island MSA, IA-IL	Y	13890 FQ	29500 AW	54020 TQ	IABLS	10/01-12/01
	Des Moines MSA, IA	Y	13940 FQ	28620 AW	50050 TQ	IABLS	10/01-12/01
	Kansas	Y	12290 FQ	18640 AW	28310 TQ	KSBLS	10/01-12/01
	Wichita MSA, KS	Y	12830 FQ	20070 AW	31310 TQ	KSBLS	10/01-12/01
	Kentucky	Y	14320 FQ	20590 AW	28800 TQ	KYBLS	10/01-12/01
	Lexington MSA, KY	Y	15290 FQ	25230 AW	36040 TQ	KYBLS	10/01-12/01
	Louisville MSA, KY-IN	Y	15970 FQ	22880 AW	33090 TQ	KYBLS	10/01-12/01
	Louisiana	Y	14890 FQ	25120 AW	35630 TQ	LABLS	10/01-12/01
	Baton Rouge MSA, LA	Y	16000 FQ	27330 AW	49790 TQ	LABLS	10/01-12/01
	Houma MSA, LA	Y	16700 FQ	26090 AW	35620 TQ	LABLS	10/01-12/01
	New Orleans MSA, LA	Y	15640 FQ	24680 AW	34910 TQ	LABLS	10/01-12/01
	Shreveport-Bossier City MSA, LA	Y	16540 FQ	29000 AW	47110 TQ	LABLS	10/01-12/01
	Maine	Y	13870 FQ	22340 AW	33650 TQ	MEBLS	10/01-12/01
	Portland MSA, ME	Y	12240 FQ	21490 AW	33800 TQ	MEBLS	10/01-12/01
	Maryland	Y	18780 FQ	28250 AW	44150 TQ	MDBLS	10/01-12/01
	Baltimore PMSA, MD	Y	18520 FQ	26720 AW	45300 TQ	MDBLS	10/01-12/01
	Massachusetts	Y	19090 FQ	28740 AW	42980 TQ	MABLS	10/01-12/01
	Boston PMSA, MA-NH	Y	19640 FQ	29790 AW	44680 TQ	MABLS	10/01-12/01
	Brockton PMSA, MA	Y	18880 FQ	27720 AW	36720 TQ	MABLS	10/01-12/01
	Lawrence PMSA, MA-NH	Y	20010 FQ	29110 AW	39770 TQ	MABLS	10/01-12/01
	Lowell PMSA, MA-NH	Y	15090 FQ	31510 AW	47510 TQ	MABLS	10/01-12/01
	New Bedford PMSA, MA	Y	17290 FQ	25900 AW	35780 TQ	MABLS	10/01-12/01
	Springfield MSA, MA	Y	19640 FQ	27820 AW	40770 TQ	MABLS	10/01-12/01
	Worcester PMSA, MA-CT	Y	14440 FQ	25470 AW	35250 TQ	MABLS	10/01-12/01
	Michigan	Y	13710 FQ	25120 AW	37500 TQ	MIBLS	10/01-12/01
	Ann Arbor PMSA, MI	Y	14420 FQ	26540 AW	37620 TQ	MIBLS	10/01-12/01
	Detroit PMSA, MI	Y	14760 FQ	27890 AW	39990 TQ	MIBLS	10/01-12/01
	Flint PMSA, MI	Y	13360 FQ	20970 AW	32780 TQ	MIBLS	10/01-12/01
	Grand Rapids-Muskegon-Holland MSA, MI	Y	15210 FQ	23920 AW	34360 TQ	MIBLS	10/01-12/01
	Kalamazoo-Battle Creek MSA, MI	Y	13590 FQ	21020 AW	28860 TQ	MIBLS	10/01-12/01
	Lansing-East Lansing MSA, MI	Y	13140 FQ	28300 AW	51220 TQ	MIBLS	10/01-12/01
	Minnesota	Y	13430 FQ	26280 AW	43270 TQ	MNBLS	10/01-12/01
	Duluth-Superior MSA, MN-WI	Y	12900 FQ	22480 AW	32500 TQ	MNBLS	10/01-12/01
	Minneapolis-St. Paul MSA, MN-WI	Y	16000 FQ	31060 AW	50050 TQ	MNBLS	10/01-12/01
	Mississippi	Y	14240 FQ	23340 AW	34360 TQ	MSBLS	10/01-12/01
	Jackson MSA, MS	Y	15720 FQ	23530 AW	33120 TQ	MSBLS	10/01-12/01
	Missouri	Y	13450 FQ	24000 AW	38370 TQ	MOBLS	10/01-12/01
	Kansas City MSA, MO-KS	Y	17450 FQ	27200 AW	40730 TQ	MOBLS	10/01-12/01
	St. Louis MSA, MO-IL	Y	12420 FQ	25900 AW	53630 TQ	MOBLS	10/01-12/01
	Montana	Y	12910 FQ	20940 AW	30950 TQ	MTBLS	10/01-12/01

AAW	Average annual wage	**AOH**	Average offered, high	**ASH**	Average starting, high	**H**	Hourly	**M**	Monthly	**S**	Special: hourly and annual
AE	Average entry wage	**AOL**	Average offered, low	**ASL**	Average starting, low	**HI**	Highest wage paid	**MTC**	Median total compensation	**TQ**	Third quartile wage
AEX	Average experienced wage	**APH**	Average pay, high range	**AW**	Average wage paid	**HR**	High end range	**MW**	Median wage paid	**W**	Weekly
AO	Average offered	**APL**	Average pay, low range	**FQ**	First quartile wage	**LR**	Low end range	**SQ**	Second quartile wage	**Y**	Yearly

Occupation/Type/Industry	Location	Per	Low	Mid	High	Source	Date
Emergency Medical Technician and Paramedic	Nebraska	Y	12940 FQ	23340 AW	38180 TQ	NEBLS	10/01-12/01
	Lincoln MSA, NE	Y	15470 FQ	22510 AW	35020 TQ	NEBLS	10/01-12/01
	Omaha MSA, NE-IA	Y	16080 FQ	30070 AW	53890 TQ	NEBLS	10/01-12/01
	Nevada	Y	13890 FQ	26800 AW	40200 TQ	NVBLS	10/01-12/01
	Las Vegas MSA, NV-AZ	Y	14130 FQ	26280 AW	40430 TQ	NVBLS	10/01-12/01
	Reno MSA, NV	Y	21260 FQ	26900 AW	34010 TQ	NVBLS	10/01-12/01
	New Hampshire	Y	16550 FQ	24620 AW	37970 TQ	NHBLS	10/01-12/01
	Manchester PMSA, NH	Y	15680 FQ	20180 AW	25750 TQ	NHBLS	10/01-12/01
	Portsmouth-Rochester PMSA, NH-ME	Y	18660 FQ	27660 AW	41320 TQ	NHBLS	10/01-12/01
	New Jersey	Y	19270 FQ	29500 AW	44530 TQ	NJBLS	10/01-12/01
	Atlantic-Cape May PMSA, NJ	Y	17150 FQ	22590 AW	28820 TQ	NJBLS	10/01-12/01
	Bergen-Passaic PMSA, NJ	Y	19520 FQ	29170 AW	44250 TQ	NJBLS	10/01-12/01
	Jersey City PMSA, NJ	Y	14590 FQ	28500 AW	47010 TQ	NJBLS	10/01-12/01
	Middlesex-Somerset-Hunterdon PMSA, NJ	Y	20160 FQ	29740 AW	43380 TQ	NJBLS	10/01-12/01
	Monmouth-Ocean PMSA, NJ	Y	18990 FQ	28130 AW	45020 TQ	NJBLS	10/01-12/01
	Newark PMSA, NJ	Y	20620 FQ	31000 AW	45460 TQ	NJBLS	10/01-12/01
	New Mexico	Y	17510 FQ	26720 AW	37860 TQ	NMBLS	10/01-12/01
	Albuquerque MSA, NM	Y	23400 FQ	30160 AW	40670 TQ	NMBLS	10/01-12/01
	New York	Y	17830 FQ	29970 AW	46390 TQ	NYBLS	10/01-12/01
	Albany-Schenectady-Troy MSA, NY	Y	16280 FQ	28190 AW	44690 TQ	NYBLS	10/01-12/01
	Binghamton MSA, NY	Y	15240 FQ	27110 AW	45380 TQ	NYBLS	10/01-12/01
	Dutchess County PMSA, NY	Y	17120 FQ	24510 AW	34390 TQ	NYBLS	10/01-12/01
	Nassau-Suffolk PMSA, NY	Y	18650 FQ	35110 AW	56250 TQ	NYBLS	10/01-12/01
	New York PMSA, NY	Y	19120 FQ	32900 AW	49390 TQ	NYBLS	10/01-12/01
	Rochester MSA, NY	Y	17160 FQ	24450 AW	32760 TQ	NYBLS	10/01-12/01
	Syracuse MSA, NY	Y	16240 FQ	25600 AW	34290 TQ	NYBLS	10/01-12/01
	North Carolina	Y	17380 FQ	25240 AW	34450 TQ	NCBLS	10/01-12/01
	Charlotte-Gastonia-Rock Hill MSA, NC-SC	Y	15770 FQ	24440 AW	35010 TQ	NCBLS	10/01-12/01
	Fayetteville MSA, NC	Y	19910 FQ	27420 AW	35330 TQ	NCBLS	10/01-12/01
	Greensboro-Winston-Salem-High Point MSA, NC	Y	17680 FQ	25490 AW	34830 TQ	NCBLS	10/01-12/01
	Hickory-Morganton-Lenoir MSA, NC	Y	15550 FQ	24820 AW	36590 TQ	NCBLS	10/01-12/01
	Raleigh-Durham-Chapel Hill MSA, NC	Y	20720 FQ	28660 AW	37540 TQ	NCBLS	10/01-12/01
	North Dakota	Y	12170 FQ	18450 AW	28780 TQ	NDBLS	10/01-12/01
	Fargo-Moorhead MSA, ND-MN	Y	16060 FQ	24220 AW	35130 TQ	NDBLS	10/01-12/01
	Ohio	Y	15080 FQ	25190 AW	40220 TQ	OHBLS	10/01-12/01
	Akron PMSA, OH	Y	13520 FQ	23860 AW	38010 TQ	OHBLS	10/01-12/01
	Canton-Massillon MSA, OH	Y	19460 FQ	28010 AW	40890 TQ	OHBLS	10/01-12/01
	Cincinnati PMSA, OH-KY-IN	Y	16790 FQ	28620 AW	49400 TQ	OHBLS	10/01-12/01
	Cleveland-Lorain-Elyria PMSA, OH	Y	16680 FQ	28680 AW	43240 TQ	OHBLS	10/01-12/01
	Columbus MSA, OH	Y	15950 FQ	26670 AW	37650 TQ	OHBLS	10/01-12/01
	Dayton-Springfield MSA, OH	Y	16220 FQ	24120 AW	35230 TQ	OHBLS	10/01-12/01
	Hamilton-Middletown PMSA, OH	Y	13030 FQ	30940 AW	65460 TQ	OHBLS	10/01-12/01
	Mansfield MSA, OH	Y	13640 FQ	19780 AW	27640 TQ	OHBLS	10/01-12/01
	Toledo MSA, OH	Y	14320 FQ	23730 AW	34940 TQ	OHBLS	10/01-12/01
	Youngstown-Warren MSA, OH	Y	15300 FQ	20820 AW	29020 TQ	OHBLS	10/01-12/01
	Oklahoma	Y	12870 FQ	20110 AW	28190 TQ	OKBLS	10/01-12/01
	Oklahoma City MSA, OK	Y	13220 FQ	20950 AW	32570 TQ	OKBLS	10/01-12/01
	Tulsa MSA, OK	Y	13480 FQ	21510 AW	30480 TQ	OKBLS	10/01-12/01
	Oregon	Y	15460 FQ	31940 AW	48120 TQ	ORBLS	10/01-12/01
	Eugene-Springfield MSA, OR	Y	14780 FQ	24670 AW	42870 TQ	ORBLS	10/01-12/01
	Portland-Vancouver PMSA, OR-WA	Y	20440 FQ	37470 AW	55090 TQ	ORBLS	10/01-12/01
	Salem PMSA, OR	Y	17300 FQ	27630 AW	40400 TQ	ORBLS	10/01-12/01
	Pennsylvania	Y	15380 FQ	23610 AW	34500 TQ	PABLS	10/01-12/01
	Allentown-Bethlehem-Easton MSA, PA	Y	17750 FQ	24560 AW	31790 TQ	PABLS	10/01-12/01
	Erie MSA, PA	Y	16370 FQ	25110 AW	34830 TQ	PABLS	10/01-12/01
	Harrisburg-Lebanon-Carlisle MSA, PA	Y	15930 FQ	24870 AW	34460 TQ	PABLS	10/01-12/01
	Johnstown MSA, PA	Y	13210 FQ	17600 AW	22910 TQ	PABLS	10/01-12/01
	Lancaster MSA, PA	Y	18970 FQ	23540 AW	29150 TQ	PABLS	10/01-12/01

AAW	Average annual wage	**AOH**	Average offered, high	**ASH**	Average starting, high	**H**	Hourly	**M**	Monthly	**S**	Special: hourly and annual
AE	Average entry wage	**AOL**	Average offered, low	**ASL**	Average starting, low	**HI**	Highest wage paid	**MTC**	Median total compensation	**TQ**	Third quartile wage
AEX	Average experienced wage	**APH**	Average pay, high range	**AW**	Average wage paid	**HR**	High end range	**MW**	Median wage paid	**W**	Weekly
AO	Average offered	**APL**	Average pay, low range	**FQ**	First quartile wage	**LR**	Low end range	**SQ**	Second quartile wage	**Y**	Yearly

Occupation/Type/Industry	Location	Per	Low	Mid	High	Source	Date
Emergency Medical Technician and Paramedic	Philadelphia PMSA, PA-NJ	Y	17300 FQ	27010 AW	39660 TQ	PABLS	10/01-12/01
	Pittsburgh MSA, PA	Y	15960 FQ	23410 AW	34200 TQ	PABLS	10/01-12/01
	Reading MSA, PA	Y	12660 FQ	21340 AW	31150 TQ	PABLS	10/01-12/01
	Scranton-Wilkes-Barre-Hazleton MSA, PA	Y	14480 FQ	21140 AW	29410 TQ	PABLS	10/01-12/01
	York MSA, PA	Y	14880 FQ	19060 AW	25740 TQ	PABLS	10/01-12/01
	Rhode Island	Y	16400 FQ	23660 AW	33600 TQ	RIBLS	10/01-12/01
	Providence-Fall River-Warwick MSA, RI-MA	Y	17070 FQ	24080 AW	34070 TQ	RIBLS	10/01-12/01
	South Carolina	Y	15970 FQ	24360 AW	33820 TQ	SCBLS	10/01-12/01
	Charleston-North Charleston MSA, SC	Y	17130 FQ	23600 AW	32420 TQ	SCBLS	10/01-12/01
	Columbia MSA, SC	Y	16350 FQ	23240 AW	32180 TQ	SCBLS	10/01-12/01
	Greenville-Spartanburg-Anderson MSA, SC	Y	19160 FQ	27020 AW	37220 TQ	SCBLS	10/01-12/01
	South Dakota	Y	15720 FQ	20700 AW	27540 TQ	SDBLS	10/01-12/01
	Tennessee	Y	15610 FQ	24320 AW	38970 TQ	TNBLS	10/01-12/01
	Chattanooga MSA, TN-GA	Y	16800 FQ	23850 AW	33450 TQ	TNBLS	10/01-12/01
	Johnson City-Kingsport-Bristol MSA, TN-VA	Y	13410 FQ	22800 AW	34970 TQ	TNBLS	10/01-12/01
	Knoxville MSA, TN	Y	15400 FQ	22510 AW	31650 TQ	TNBLS	10/01-12/01
	Memphis MSA, TN-AR-MS	Y	16290 FQ	28840 AW	44640 TQ	TNBLS	10/01-12/01
	Nashville MSA, TN	Y	16900 FQ	26900 AW	43020 TQ	TNBLS	10/01-12/01
	Texas	Y	15150 FQ	23170 AW	33970 TQ	TXBLS	10/01-12/01
	Amarillo MSA, TX	Y	16290 FQ	24400 AW	33040 TQ	TXBLS	10/01-12/01
	Austin-San Marcos MSA, TX	Y	18180 FQ	30460 AW	44130 TQ	TXBLS	10/01-12/01
	Beaumont-Port Arthur MSA, TX	Y	14250 FQ	20940 AW	27600 TQ	TXBLS	10/01-12/01
	Brazoria PMSA, TX	Y	13000 FQ	21820 AW	31080 TQ	TXBLS	10/01-12/01
	Brownsville-Harlingen-San Benito MSA, TX	Y	15760 FQ	21210 AW	28020 TQ	TXBLS	10/01-12/01
	Corpus Christi MSA, TX	Y	13460 FQ	24200 AW	48160 TQ	TXBLS	10/01-12/01
	Dallas PMSA, TX	Y	15650 FQ	22390 AW	29500 TQ	TXBLS	10/01-12/01
	El Paso MSA, TX	Y	13880 FQ	24310 AW	35420 TQ	TXBLS	10/01-12/01
	Fort Worth-Arlington PMSA, TX	Y	18740 FQ	27940 AW	35930 TQ	TXBLS	10/01-12/01
	Galveston-Texas City PMSA, TX	Y	15270 FQ	19940 AW	25180 TQ	TXBLS	10/01-12/01
	Houston PMSA, TX	Y	15830 FQ	23230 AW	32410 TQ	TXBLS	10/01-12/01
	Killeen-Temple MSA, TX	Y	15010 FQ	20310 AW	27470 TQ	TXBLS	10/01-12/01
	Laredo MSA, TX	Y	18660 FQ	21240 AW	25310 TQ	TXBLS	10/01-12/01
	Longview-Marshall MSA, TX	Y	18130 FQ	22360 AW	28520 TQ	TXBLS	10/01-12/01
	Lubbock MSA, TX	Y	15210 FQ	21810 AW	29720 TQ	TXBLS	10/01-12/01
	McAllen-Edinburg-Mission MSA, TX	Y	15120 FQ	17900 AW	21930 TQ	TXBLS	10/01-12/01
	Odessa-Midland MSA, TX	Y	14120 FQ	21220 AW	29610 TQ	TXBLS	10/01-12/01
	San Antonio MSA, TX	Y	15500 FQ	23180 AW	32690 TQ	TXBLS	10/01-12/01
	Utah	Y	14020 FQ	20930 AW	27940 TQ	UTBLS	10/01-12/01
	Provo-Orem MSA, UT	Y	12180 FQ	16520 AW	23570 TQ	UTBLS	10/01-12/01
	Salt Lake City-Ogden MSA, UT	Y	18780 FQ	23800 AW	29650 TQ	UTBLS	10/01-12/01
	Vermont	Y	14700 FQ	21530 AW	30150 TQ	VTBLS	10/01-12/01
	Virginia	Y	15590 FQ	25890 AW	37770 TQ	VABLS	10/01-12/01
	Norfolk-Virginia Beach-Newport News MSA, VA-NC	Y	17170 FQ	28690 AW	42380 TQ	VABLS	10/01-12/01
	Richmond-Petersburg MSA, VA	Y	17470 FQ	25530 AW	34890 TQ	VABLS	10/01-12/01
	Washington	Y	16330 FQ	34940 AW	60720 TQ	WABLS	10/01-12/01
	Bremerton PMSA, WA	Y	28320 FQ	51930 AW	71690 TQ	WABLS	10/01-12/01
	Olympia PMSA, WA	Y	16240 FQ	42400 AW	62130 TQ	WABLS	10/01-12/01
	Richland-Kennewick-Pasco MSA, WA	Y	19490 FQ	24840 AW	30040 TQ	WABLS	10/01-12/01
	Seattle-Bellevue-Everett PMSA, WA	Y	15760 FQ	31740 AW	56690 TQ	WABLS	10/01-12/01
	Spokane MSA, WA	Y	19670 FQ	32520 AW	55490 TQ	WABLS	10/01-12/01
	Tacoma PMSA, WA	Y	17140 FQ	39110 AW	69070 TQ	WABLS	10/01-12/01
	West Virginia	Y	12040 FQ	18730 AW	27640 TQ	WVBLS	10/01-12/01
	Huntington-Ashland MSA, WV-KY-OH	Y	17700 FQ	21510 AW	25870 TQ	WVBLS	10/01-12/01
	Wisconsin	Y	12690 FQ	22870 AW	36780 TQ	WIBLS	10/01-12/01

AAW	Average annual wage	**AOH**	Average offered, high	**ASH**	Average starting, high	**H**	Hourly	**M**	Monthly	**S**	Special: hourly and annual
AE	Average entry wage	**AOL**	Average offered, low	**ASL**	Average starting, low	**HI**	Highest wage paid	**MTC**	Median total compensation	**TQ**	Third quartile wage
AEX	Average experienced wage	**APH**	Average pay, high range	**AW**	Average wage paid	**HR**	High end range	**MW**	Median wage paid	**W**	Weekly
AO	Average offered	**APL**	Average pay, low range	**FQ**	First quartile wage	**LR**	Low end range	**SQ**	Second quartile wage	**Y**	Yearly

Occupation/Type/Industry	Location	Per	Low	Mid	High	Source	Date
Emergency Medical Technician and Paramedic	Appleton-Oshkosh-Neenah MSA, WI	Y	15120 FQ	19870 AW	25190 TQ	WIBLS	10/01-12/01
	Green Bay MSA, WI	Y	13980 FQ	28640 AW	50960 TQ	WIBLS	10/01-12/01
	Madison MSA, WI	Y	16410 FQ	29600 AW	43680 TQ	WIBLS	10/01-12/01
	Milwaukee-Waukesha PMSA, WI	Y	15980 FQ	29560 AW	55920 TQ	WIBLS	10/01-12/01
	Racine PMSA, WI	Y	15890 FQ	34950 AW	58700 TQ	WIBLS	10/01-12/01
	Wyoming	Y	11940 FQ	18320 AW	27620 TQ	WYBLS	10/01-12/01
	Puerto Rico	Y	11840 FQ	16830 AW	24620 TQ	PRBLS	10/01-12/01
	Virgin Islands	Y	22520 FQ	32440 AW	42350 TQ	VIBLS	10/01-12/01
Hospitals	United States	Y		23590 MW		OOH3	1/99-1/00
Local and suburban transportation	United States	Y		20950 MW		OOH3	1/99-1/00
Local government	United States	Y		24800 MW		OOH3	1/99-1/00
Employment, Recruitment, and Placement Specialist	Alabama	Y	20640 FQ	38020 AW	59140 TQ	ALBLS	10/01-12/01
	Birmingham MSA, AL	Y	21010 FQ	40080 AW	62100 TQ	ALBLS	10/01-12/01
	Huntsville MSA, AL	Y	26770 FQ	40310 AW	62420 TQ	ALBLS	10/01-12/01
	Mobile MSA, AL	Y	20000 FQ	33340 AW	51910 TQ	ALBLS	10/01-12/01
	Montgomery MSA, AL	Y	19910 FQ	37710 AW	62350 TQ	ALBLS	10/01-12/01
	Alaska	Y	25450 FQ	42260 AW	66780 TQ	AKBLS	10/01-12/01
	Anchorage MSA, AK	Y	27550 FQ	44670 AW	68770 TQ	AKBLS	10/01-12/01
	Arizona	Y	22360 FQ	37680 AW	56770 TQ	AZBLS	10/01-12/01
	Phoenix-Mesa MSA, AZ	Y	22950 FQ	38950 AW	58290 TQ	AZBLS	10/01-12/01
	Tucson MSA, AZ	Y	19720 FQ	33520 AW	50880 TQ	AZBLS	10/01-12/01
	Arkansas	Y	18960 FQ	30630 AW	46070 TQ	ARBLS	10/01-12/01
	Fayetteville-Springdale-Rogers MSA, AR	Y	19080 FQ	29000 AW	42180 TQ	ARBLS	10/01-12/01
	Fort Smith MSA, AR-OK	Y	17850 FQ	27060 AW	41440 TQ	ARBLS	10/01-12/01
	Little Rock-North Little Rock MSA, AR	Y	19900 FQ	33560 AW	52190 TQ	ARBLS	10/01-12/01
	California	Y	26090 FQ	50970 AW	88360 TQ	CABLS	10/01-12/01
	Bakersfield MSA, CA	Y	26230 FQ	42240 AW	61990 TQ	CABLS	10/01-12/01
	Chico-Paradise MSA, CA	Y	24980 FQ	60090 AW	140850 TQ	CABLS	10/01-12/01
	Fresno MSA, CA	Y	18710 FQ	37800 AW	65990 TQ	CABLS	10/01-12/01
	Los Angeles-Long Beach PMSA, CA	Y	23820 FQ	47430 AW	79730 TQ	CABLS	10/01-12/01
	Merced MSA, CA	Y	23750 FQ	35730 AW	55390 TQ	CABLS	10/01-12/01
	Modesto MSA, CA	Y	24700 FQ	36360 AW	48590 TQ	CABLS	10/01-12/01
	Oakland PMSA, CA	Y	30500 FQ	49290 AW	71300 TQ	CABLS	10/01-12/01
	Orange County PMSA, CA	Y	25770 FQ	48920 AW	78280 TQ	CABLS	10/01-12/01
	Redding MSA, CA	Y	19000 FQ	43590 AW	70440 TQ	CABLS	10/01-12/01
	Riverside-San Bernardino PMSA, CA	Y	24600 FQ	37200 AW	53770 TQ	CABLS	10/01-12/01
	Sacramento PMSA, CA	Y	27820 FQ	40790 AW	59320 TQ	CABLS	10/01-12/01
	Salinas MSA, CA	Y	25270 FQ	45320 AW	68730 TQ	CABLS	10/01-12/01
	San Diego MSA, CA	Y	27960 FQ	51240 AW	85600 TQ	CABLS	10/01-12/01
	San Francisco PMSA, CA	Y	32480 FQ	69090 AW	138980 TQ	CABLS	10/01-12/01
	San Jose PMSA, CA	Y	33540 FQ	64650 AW	113410 TQ	CABLS	10/01-12/01
	San Luis Obispo-Atascadero-Paso Robles MSA, CA	Y	25730 FQ	38820 AW	57700 TQ	CABLS	10/01-12/01
	Santa Barbara-Santa Maria-Lompoc MSA, CA	Y	30700 FQ	49380 AW	75360 TQ	CABLS	10/01-12/01
	Santa Cruz-Watsonville PMSA, CA	Y	27490 FQ	52850 AW	88760 TQ	CABLS	10/01-12/01
	Santa Rosa PMSA, CA	Y	26730 FQ	58620 AW	111040 TQ	CABLS	10/01-12/01
	Stockton-Lodi MSA, CA	Y	25130 FQ	40970 AW	62330 TQ	CABLS	10/01-12/01
	Vallejo-Fairfield-Napa PMSA, CA	Y	23270 FQ	40180 AW	61230 TQ	CABLS	10/01-12/01
	Ventura PMSA, CA	Y	18630 FQ	59710 AW		CABLS	10/01-12/01
	Visalia-Tulare-Porterville MSA, CA	Y	21420 FQ	36650 AW	57080 TQ	CABLS	10/01-12/01
	Colorado	Y	25710 FQ	42080 AW	65000 TQ	COBLS	10/01-12/01
	Boulder-Longmont PMSA, CO	Y	29630 FQ	45910 AW	77630 TQ	COBLS	10/01-12/01
	Colorado Springs MSA, CO	Y	25690 FQ	41750 AW	71410 TQ	COBLS	10/01-12/01
	Denver PMSA, CO	Y	26250 FQ	42180 AW	64180 TQ	COBLS	10/01-12/01
	Fort Collins-Loveland MSA, CO	Y	27700 FQ	40670 AW	56150 TQ	COBLS	10/01-12/01
	Greeley PMSA, CO	Y	21360 FQ	38300 AW	56470 TQ	COBLS	10/01-12/01
	Connecticut	Y	26930 FQ	58900 AW	111740 TQ	CTBLS	10/01-12/01
	Bridgeport PMSA, CT	Y	28550 FQ	44990 AW	67250 TQ	CTBLS	10/01-12/01

AAW	Average annual wage	AOH	Average offered, high	ASH	Average starting, high	H	Hourly	M	Monthly	S	Special: hourly and annual
AE	Average entry wage	AOL	Average offered, low	ASL	Average starting, low	HI	Highest wage paid	MTC	Median total compensation	TQ	Third quartile wage
AEX	Average experienced wage	APH	Average pay, high range	AW	Average wage paid	HR	High end range	MW	Median wage paid	W	Weekly
AO	Average offered	APL	Average pay, low range	FQ	First quartile wage	LR	Low end range	SQ	Second quartile wage	Y	Yearly

Occupation/Type/Industry	Location	Per	Low	Mid	High	Source	Date
Employment, Recruitment, and Placement Specialist	Danbury PMSA, CT	Y	25570 FQ	51490 AW	92610 TQ	CTBLS	10/01-12/01
	Hartford MSA, CT	Y	27060 FQ	49550 AW	85540 TQ	CTBLS	10/01-12/01
	New Haven-Meriden PMSA, CT	Y	25030 FQ	47870 AW	73890 TQ	CTBLS	10/01-12/01
	New London-Norwich MSA, CT-RI	Y	16580 FQ	35860 AW	54020 TQ	CTBLS	10/01-12/01
	Stamford-Norwalk PMSA, CT	Y	35320 FQ	84500 AW		CTBLS	10/01-12/01
	Waterbury PMSA, CT	Y	19880 FQ	43650 AW	71780 TQ	CTBLS	10/01-12/01
	Delaware	Y	24820 FQ	36930 AW	55580 TQ	DEBLS	10/01-12/01
	Wilmington-Newark PMSA, DE-MD	Y	25030 FQ	36590 AW	56020 TQ	DEBLS	10/01-12/01
	District of Columbia	Y	24400 FQ	44320 AW	72720 TQ	DCBLS	10/01-12/01
	Washington PMSA, DC-MD-VA-WV	Y	25940 FQ	45710 AW	72330 TQ	DCBLS	10/01-12/01
	Florida	Y	22780 FQ	36990 AW	57840 TQ	FLBLS	10/01-12/01
	Daytona Beach MSA, FL	Y	20360 FQ	33410 AW	52520 TQ	FLBLS	10/01-12/01
	Fort Lauderdale PMSA, FL	Y	24740 FQ	35140 AW	56410 TQ	FLBLS	10/01-12/01
	Fort Myers-Cape Coral MSA, FL	Y	26170 FQ	39770 AW	56440 TQ	FLBLS	10/01-12/01
	Fort Pierce-Port St. Lucie MSA, FL	Y	15870 FQ	28060 AW	60540 TQ	FLBLS	10/01-12/01
	Fort Walton Beach MSA, FL	Y	20660 FQ	38320 AW	63670 TQ	FLBLS	10/01-12/01
	Gainesville MSA, FL	Y	19280 FQ	38260 AW	68570 TQ	FLBLS	10/01-12/01
	Jacksonville MSA, FL	Y	24430 FQ	42970 AW	59410 TQ	FLBLS	10/01-12/01
	Lakeland-Winter Haven MSA, FL	Y	23140 FQ	35790 AW	57480 TQ	FLBLS	10/01-12/01
	Melbourne-Titusville-Palm Bay MSA, FL	Y	24230 FQ	39480 AW	58080 TQ	FLBLS	10/01-12/01
	Miami PMSA, FL	Y	17190 FQ	33590 AW	55400 TQ	FLBLS	10/01-12/01
	Naples MSA, FL	Y	17430 FQ	35230 AW	56100 TQ	FLBLS	10/01-12/01
	Ocala MSA, FL	Y	22390 FQ	33870 AW	49440 TQ	FLBLS	10/01-12/01
	Orlando MSA, FL	Y	24090 FQ	35430 AW	52790 TQ	FLBLS	10/01-12/01
	Pensacola MSA, FL	Y	21970 FQ	38750 AW	67540 TQ	FLBLS	10/01-12/01
	Sarasota-Bradenton MSA, FL	Y	23360 FQ	34530 AW	55760 TQ	FLBLS	10/01-12/01
	Tallahassee MSA, FL	Y	23600 FQ	40530 AW	62180 TQ	FLBLS	10/01-12/01
	Tampa-St. Petersburg-Clearwater MSA, FL	Y	24210 FQ	39850 AW	62240 TQ	FLBLS	10/01-12/01
	West Palm Beach-Boca Raton MSA, FL	Y	25140 FQ	41550 AW	59570 TQ	FLBLS	10/01-12/01
	Georgia	Y	24650 FQ	40820 AW	61710 TQ	GABLS	10/01-12/01
	Atlanta MSA, GA	Y	25840 FQ	43510 AW	66280 TQ	GABLS	10/01-12/01
	Augusta-Aiken MSA, GA-SC	Y	24420 FQ	44100 AW	72050 TQ	GABLS	10/01-12/01
	Columbus MSA, GA-AL	Y	24040 FQ	37330 AW	56010 TQ	GABLS	10/01-12/01
	Macon MSA, GA	Y	24650 FQ	38620 AW	59480 TQ	GABLS	10/01-12/01
	Savannah MSA, GA	Y	23990 FQ	32980 AW	45770 TQ	GABLS	10/01-12/01
	Hawaii	Y	28170 FQ	41110 AW	59100 TQ	HIBLS	10/01-12/01
	Honolulu MSA, HI	Y	27950 FQ	42390 AW	63210 TQ	HIBLS	10/01-12/01
	Idaho	Y	19980 FQ	37140 AW	59450 TQ	IDBLS	10/01-12/01
	Boise City MSA, ID	Y	19980 FQ	34560 AW	55220 TQ	IDBLS	10/01-12/01
	Illinois	Y	22870 FQ	42890 AW	66960 TQ	ILBLS	10/01-12/01
	Champaign-Urbana MSA, IL	Y	19450 FQ	35840 AW	59780 TQ	ILBLS	10/01-12/01
	Chicago PMSA, IL	Y	24350 FQ	44530 AW	68730 TQ	ILBLS	10/01-12/01
	Peoria-Pekin MSA, IL	Y	21700 FQ	37960 AW	61730 TQ	ILBLS	10/01-12/01
	Rockford MSA, IL	Y	20980 FQ	34470 AW	50810 TQ	ILBLS	10/01-12/01
	Springfield MSA, IL	Y	28150 FQ	43910 AW	62780 TQ	ILBLS	10/01-12/01
	Indiana	Y	19830 FQ	36890 AW	59090 TQ	INBLS	10/01-12/01
	Elkhart-Goshen MSA, IN	Y	25250 FQ	35640 AW	52000 TQ	INBLS	10/01-12/01
	Evansville-Henderson MSA, IN-KY	Y	17540 FQ	41570 AW	71400 TQ	INBLS	10/01-12/01
	Fort Wayne MSA, IN	Y	23310 FQ	36640 AW	55490 TQ	INBLS	10/01-12/01
	Gary PMSA, IN	Y	22490 FQ	37270 AW	58880 TQ	INBLS	10/01-12/01
	Indianapolis MSA, IN	Y	18230 FQ	37980 AW	58230 TQ	INBLS	10/01-12/01
	Lafayette MSA, IN	Y	20140 FQ	32060 AW	54980 TQ	INBLS	10/01-12/01
	South Bend MSA, IN	Y	20950 FQ	33830 AW	51630 TQ	INBLS	10/01-12/01
	Iowa	Y	23510 FQ	41700 AW	61730 TQ	IABLS	10/01-12/01
	Cedar Rapids MSA, IA	Y	26320 FQ	62720 AW		IABLS	10/01-12/01
	Davenport-Moline-Rock Island MSA, IA-IL	Y	24910 FQ	43290 AW	80570 TQ	IABLS	10/01-12/01
	Des Moines MSA, IA	Y	26060 FQ	40960 AW	61000 TQ	IABLS	10/01-12/01
	Kansas	Y	24580 FQ	42970 AW	74810 TQ	KSBLS	10/01-12/01
	Topeka MSA, KS	Y	21980 FQ	37800 AW	59120 TQ	KSBLS	10/01-12/01

AAW	Average annual wage	AOH	Average offered, high	ASH	Average starting, high	H	Hourly	M	Monthly	S	Special: hourly and annual
AE	Average entry wage	AOL	Average offered, low	ASL	Average starting, low	HI	Highest wage paid	MTC	Median total compensation	TQ	Third quartile wage
AEX	Average experienced wage	APH	Average pay, high range	AW	Average wage paid	HR	High end range	MW	Median wage paid	W	Weekly
AO	Average offered	APL	Average pay, low range	FQ	First quartile wage	LR	Low end range	SQ	Second quartile wage	Y	Yearly

Occupation/Type/Industry	Location	Per	Low	Mid	High	Source	Date
Employment, Recruitment, and Placement Specialist	Wichita MSA, KS	Y	26640 FQ	46480 AW	88890 TQ	KSBLS	10/01-12/01
	Kentucky	Y	22290 FQ	35860 AW	50990 TQ	KYBLS	10/01-12/01
	Lexington MSA, KY	Y	24080 FQ	38050 AW	56060 TQ	KYBLS	10/01-12/01
	Louisville MSA, KY-IN	Y	23450 FQ	37700 AW	53380 TQ	KYBLS	10/01-12/01
	Louisiana	Y	17080 FQ	34080 AW	52590 TQ	LABLS	10/01-12/01
	Baton Rouge MSA, LA	Y	27020 FQ	35650 AW	51780 TQ	LABLS	10/01-12/01
	Houma MSA, LA	Y	16810 FQ	36330 AW	49470 TQ	LABLS	10/01-12/01
	Lafayette MSA, LA	Y	23140 FQ	32940 AW	48050 TQ	LABLS	10/01-12/01
	Lake Charles MSA, LA	Y	18060 FQ	36240 AW	58280 TQ	LABLS	10/01-12/01
	New Orleans MSA, LA	Y	15420 FQ	32890 AW	54370 TQ	LABLS	10/01-12/01
	Shreveport-Bossier City MSA, LA	Y	21080 FQ	33510 AW	46410 TQ	LABLS	10/01-12/01
	Maine	Y	24260 FQ	37610 AW	56660 TQ	MEBLS	10/01-12/01
	Portland MSA, ME	Y	27330 FQ	42950 AW	58680 TQ	MEBLS	10/01-12/01
	Maryland	Y	25370 FQ	42100 AW	65740 TQ	MDBLS	10/01-12/01
	Baltimore PMSA, MD	Y	24840 FQ	39500 AW	59430 TQ	MDBLS	10/01-12/01
	Massachusetts	Y	23480 FQ	49960 AW	86940 TQ	MABLS	10/01-12/01
	Boston PMSA, MA-NH	Y	27300 FQ	54630 AW	93390 TQ	MABLS	10/01-12/01
	Brockton PMSA, MA	Y	26330 FQ	47190 AW	71420 TQ	MABLS	10/01-12/01
	Lawrence PMSA, MA-NH	Y	28890 FQ	46540 AW	68010 TQ	MABLS	10/01-12/01
	Lowell PMSA, MA-NH	Y	27260 FQ	53830 AW	91480 TQ	MABLS	10/01-12/01
	Springfield MSA, MA	Y	19740 FQ	31960 AW	49860 TQ	MABLS	10/01-12/01
	Worcester PMSA, MA-CT	Y	21550 FQ	39140 AW	67650 TQ	MABLS	10/01-12/01
	Michigan	Y	26200 FQ	42180 AW	62560 TQ	MIBLS	10/01-12/01
	Ann Arbor PMSA, MI	Y	28870 FQ	44250 AW	65640 TQ	MIBLS	10/01-12/01
	Detroit PMSA, MI	Y	28840 FQ	43290 AW	63550 TQ	MIBLS	10/01-12/01
	Flint PMSA, MI	Y	29150 FQ	39910 AW	54980 TQ	MIBLS	10/01-12/01
	Grand Rapids-Muskegon-Holland MSA, MI	Y	25200 FQ	39680 AW	55750 TQ	MIBLS	10/01-12/01
	Kalamazoo-Battle Creek MSA, MI	Y	21020 FQ	41180 AW	66420 TQ	MIBLS	10/01-12/01
	Lansing-East Lansing MSA, MI	Y	26100 FQ	48980 AW	73330 TQ	MIBLS	10/01-12/01
	Saginaw-Bay City-Midland MSA, MI	Y	20180 FQ	37520 AW	54780 TQ	MIBLS	10/01-12/01
	Minnesota	Y	26300 FQ	50650 AW	77450 TQ	MNBLS	10/01-12/01
	Duluth-Superior MSA, MN-WI	Y	26690 FQ	40830 AW	61860 TQ	MNBLS	10/01-12/01
	Minneapolis-St. Paul MSA, MN-WI	Y	26460 FQ	52040 AW	82380 TQ	MNBLS	10/01-12/01
	St. Cloud MSA, MN	Y	24630 FQ	37460 AW	55720 TQ	MNBLS	10/01-12/01
	Mississippi	Y	22510 FQ	32000 AW	45850 TQ	MSBLS	10/01-12/01
	Biloxi-Gulfport-Pascagoula MSA, MS	Y	20230 FQ	31420 AW	46730 TQ	MSBLS	10/01-12/01
	Jackson MSA, MS	Y	23320 FQ	33700 AW	49840 TQ	MSBLS	10/01-12/01
	Missouri	Y	22370 FQ	37050 AW	56920 TQ	MOBLS	10/01-12/01
	Kansas City MSA, MO-KS	Y	24790 FQ	43570 AW	77120 TQ	MOBLS	10/01-12/01
	St. Louis MSA, MO-IL	Y	23110 FQ	37350 AW	57490 TQ	MOBLS	10/01-12/01
	Springfield MSA, MO	Y	20870 FQ	40450 AW	60870 TQ	MOBLS	10/01-12/01
	Montana	Y	22640 FQ	32630 AW	46320 TQ	MTBLS	10/01-12/01
	Billings MSA, MT	Y	20890 FQ	43350 AW	80410 TQ	MTBLS	10/01-12/01
	Nebraska	Y	23830 FQ	39290 AW	57770 TQ	NEBLS	10/01-12/01
	Lincoln MSA, NE	Y	23520 FQ	38170 AW	53390 TQ	NEBLS	10/01-12/01
	Omaha MSA, NE-IA	Y	24320 FQ	39850 AW	58530 TQ	NEBLS	10/01-12/01
	Nevada	Y	21060 FQ	34220 AW	51960 TQ	NVBLS	10/01-12/01
	Las Vegas MSA, NV-AZ	Y	23560 FQ	35220 AW	51590 TQ	NVBLS	10/01-12/01
	Reno MSA, NV	Y	19710 FQ	33200 AW	57570 TQ	NVBLS	10/01-12/01
	New Hampshire	Y	25420 FQ	50820 AW	81890 TQ	NHBLS	10/01-12/01
	Manchester PMSA, NH	Y	29480 FQ	54720 AW	72160 TQ	NHBLS	10/01-12/01
	Nashua PMSA, NH	Y	24420 FQ	42540 AW	69190 TQ	NHBLS	10/01-12/01
	Portsmouth-Rochester PMSA, NH-ME	Y	24930 FQ	40090 AW	63210 TQ	NHBLS	10/01-12/01
	New Jersey	Y	30280 FQ	54610 AW	93240 TQ	NJBLS	10/01-12/01
	Atlantic-Cape May PMSA, NJ	Y	20900 FQ	34840 AW	50100 TQ	NJBLS	10/01-12/01
	Bergen-Passaic PMSA, NJ	Y	29770 FQ	47520 AW	73270 TQ	NJBLS	10/01-12/01
	Jersey City PMSA, NJ	Y	25760 FQ	50660 AW	88570 TQ	NJBLS	10/01-12/01
	Middlesex-Somerset-Hunterdon PMSA, NJ	Y	31330 FQ	54940 AW	98690 TQ	NJBLS	10/01-12/01
	Monmouth-Ocean PMSA, NJ	Y	25120 FQ	62820 AW	127860 TQ	NJBLS	10/01-12/01
	Newark PMSA, NJ	Y	32880 FQ	62890 AW		NJBLS	10/01-12/01
	Trenton PMSA, NJ	Y	28660 FQ	48100 AW	71290 TQ	NJBLS	10/01-12/01
	New Mexico	Y	22790 FQ	38760 AW	65070 TQ	NMBLS	10/01-12/01
	Albuquerque MSA, NM	Y	25460 FQ	41950 AW	65880 TQ	NMBLS	10/01-12/01

AAW	Average annual wage	**AOH**	Average offered, high	**ASH**	Average starting, high	**H**	Hourly	**M**	Monthly	**S**	Special: hourly and annual
AE	Average entry wage	**AOL**	Average offered, low	**ASL**	Average starting, low	**HI**	Highest wage paid	**MTC**	Median total compensation	**TQ**	Third quartile wage
AEX	Average experienced wage	**APH**	Average pay, high range	**AW**	Average wage paid	**HR**	High end range	**MW**	Median wage paid	**W**	Weekly
AO	Average offered	**APL**	Average pay, low range	**FQ**	First quartile wage	**LR**	Low end range	**SQ**	Second quartile wage	**Y**	Yearly

Occupation/Type/Industry	Location	Per	Low	Mid	High	Source	Date
Employment, Recruitment, and Placement Specialist	Las Cruces MSA, NM	Y	22130 FQ	30440 AW	43930 TQ	NMBLS	10/01-12/01
	New York	Y	26040 FQ	58360 AW	110860 TQ	NYBLS	10/01-12/01
	Albany-Schenectady-Troy MSA, NY	Y	27240 FQ	52440 AW	89990 TQ	NYBLS	10/01-12/01
	Binghamton MSA, NY	Y	24720 FQ	35880 AW	53010 TQ	NYBLS	10/01-12/01
	Buffalo-Niagara Falls MSA, NY	Y	24190 FQ	39410 AW	58360 TQ	NYBLS	10/01-12/01
	Dutchess County PMSA, NY	Y	22040 FQ	46420 AW	89190 TQ	NYBLS	10/01-12/01
	Nassau-Suffolk PMSA, NY	Y	35180 FQ	62760 AW	87060 TQ	NYBLS	10/01-12/01
	New York PMSA, NY	Y	25340 FQ	64030 AW		NYBLS	10/01-12/01
	Newburgh PMSA, NY-PA	Y	26560 FQ	64460 AW		NYBLS	10/01-12/01
	Rochester MSA, NY	Y	25030 FQ	38500 AW	61860 TQ	NYBLS	10/01-12/01
	Syracuse MSA, NY	Y	22960 FQ	40190 AW	62440 TQ	NYBLS	10/01-12/01
	Utica-Rome MSA, NY	Y	20300 FQ	29240 AW	43140 TQ	NYBLS	10/01-12/01
	North Carolina	Y	24590 FQ	41550 AW	66380 TQ	NCBLS	10/01-12/01
	Asheville MSA, NC	Y	22240 FQ	36670 AW	60620 TQ	NCBLS	10/01-12/01
	Charlotte-Gastonia-Rock Hill MSA, NC-SC	Y	26120 FQ	40940 AW	59680 TQ	NCBLS	10/01-12/01
	Fayetteville MSA, NC	Y	19130 FQ	32190 AW	52520 TQ	NCBLS	10/01-12/01
	Greensboro-Winston-Salem-High Point MSA, NC	Y	24580 FQ	40020 AW	56500 TQ	NCBLS	10/01-12/01
	Hickory-Morganton-Lenoir MSA, NC	Y	19780 FQ	33930 AW	50720 TQ	NCBLS	10/01-12/01
	Raleigh-Durham-Chapel Hill MSA, NC	Y	28090 FQ	43770 AW	69590 TQ	NCBLS	10/01-12/01
	Wilmington MSA, NC	Y	25500 FQ	58790 AW		NCBLS	10/01-12/01
	North Dakota	Y	23580 FQ	34030 AW	47420 TQ	NDBLS	10/01-12/01
	Fargo-Moorhead MSA, ND-MN	Y	25070 FQ	35160 AW	47890 TQ	NDBLS	10/01-12/01
	Ohio	Y	23210 FQ	39660 AW	59990 TQ	OHBLS	10/01-12/01
	Akron PMSA, OH	Y	22010 FQ	37090 AW	55340 TQ	OHBLS	10/01-12/01
	Canton-Massillon MSA, OH	Y	20780 FQ	36200 AW	54750 TQ	OHBLS	10/01-12/01
	Cincinnati PMSA, OH-KY-IN	Y	24180 FQ	39180 AW	61950 TQ	OHBLS	10/01-12/01
	Cleveland-Lorain-Elyria PMSA, OH	Y	22030 FQ	40970 AW	61660 TQ	OHBLS	10/01-12/01
	Columbus MSA, OH	Y	24280 FQ	39660 AW	59110 TQ	OHBLS	10/01-12/01
	Dayton-Springfield MSA, OH	Y	22950 FQ	48640 AW	139160 TQ	OHBLS	10/01-12/01
	Hamilton-Middletown PMSA, OH	Y	21190 FQ	42250 AW	65620 TQ	OHBLS	10/01-12/01
	Mansfield MSA, OH	Y	23260 FQ	40220 AW	70260 TQ	OHBLS	10/01-12/01
	Toledo MSA, OH	Y	20530 FQ	35640 AW	55210 TQ	OHBLS	10/01-12/01
	Youngstown-Warren MSA, OH	Y	22290 FQ	38290 AW	68410 TQ	OHBLS	10/01-12/01
	Oklahoma	Y	19800 FQ	33710 AW	52550 TQ	OKBLS	10/01-12/01
	Oklahoma City MSA, OK	Y	19080 FQ	34460 AW	53430 TQ	OKBLS	10/01-12/01
	Tulsa MSA, OK	Y	22470 FQ	34160 AW	52890 TQ	OKBLS	10/01-12/01
	Oregon	Y	24030 FQ	37290 AW	57210 TQ	ORBLS	10/01-12/01
	Eugene-Springfield MSA, OR	Y	22160 FQ	33410 AW	48950 TQ	ORBLS	10/01-12/01
	Medford-Ashland MSA, OR	Y	24030 FQ	35190 AW	45180 TQ	ORBLS	10/01-12/01
	Portland-Vancouver PMSA, OR-WA	Y	24720 FQ	39320 AW	62860 TQ	ORBLS	10/01-12/01
	Salem PMSA, OR	Y	22200 FQ	33790 AW	50180 TQ	ORBLS	10/01-12/01
	Pennsylvania	Y	23550 FQ	48420 AW	87740 TQ	PABLS	10/01-12/01
	Allentown-Bethlehem-Easton MSA, PA	Y	24240 FQ	37690 AW	58560 TQ	PABLS	10/01-12/01
	Erie MSA, PA	Y	22570 FQ	37200 AW	54870 TQ	PABLS	10/01-12/01
	Johnstown MSA, PA	Y	24830 FQ	40290 AW	55830 TQ	PABLS	10/01-12/01
	Lancaster MSA, PA	Y	24690 FQ	40630 AW	59530 TQ	PABLS	10/01-12/01
	Philadelphia PMSA, PA-NJ	Y	25360 FQ	55660 AW	131060 TQ	PABLS	10/01-12/01
	Pittsburgh MSA, PA	Y	21510 FQ	39450 AW	66410 TQ	PABLS	10/01-12/01
	Reading MSA, PA	Y	24470 FQ	36310 AW	54380 TQ	PABLS	10/01-12/01
	Scranton-Wilkes-Barre-Hazleton MSA, PA	Y	19910 FQ	34850 AW	53390 TQ	PABLS	10/01-12/01
	York MSA, PA	Y	22760 FQ	47810 AW	92490 TQ	PABLS	10/01-12/01
	Rhode Island	Y	24120 FQ	41230 AW	63090 TQ	RIBLS	10/01-12/01
	Providence-Fall River-Warwick MSA, RI-MA	Y	22330 FQ	40220 AW	61920 TQ	RIBLS	10/01-12/01
	South Carolina	Y	22800 FQ	34670 AW	55410 TQ	SCBLS	10/01-12/01
	Charleston-North Charleston MSA, SC	Y	22110 FQ	30710 AW	43960 TQ	SCBLS	10/01-12/01
	Columbia MSA, SC	Y	23910 FQ	33180 AW	48900 TQ	SCBLS	10/01-12/01

AAW	Average annual wage	AOH	Average offered, high	ASH	Average starting, high	H	Hourly	M	Monthly	S	Special: hourly and annual
AE	Average entry wage	AOL	Average offered, low	ASL	Average starting, low	HI	Highest wage paid	MTC	Median total compensation	TQ	Third quartile wage
AEX	Average experienced wage	APH	Average pay, high range	AW	Average wage paid	HR	High end range	MW	Median wage paid	W	Weekly
AO	Average offered	APL	Average pay, low range	FQ	First quartile wage	LR	Low end range	SQ	Second quartile wage	Y	Yearly

Occupation/Type/Industry	Location	Per	Low	Mid	High	Source	Date
Employment, Recruitment, and Placement Specialist	Greenville-Spartanburg-Anderson MSA, SC	Y	20900 FQ	33390 AW	52760 TQ	SCBLS	10/01-12/01
	Myrtle Beach MSA, SC	Y	23080 FQ	32060 AW	43850 TQ	SCBLS	10/01-12/01
	South Dakota	Y	23820 FQ	34480 AW	49590 TQ	SDBLS	10/01-12/01
	Sioux Falls MSA, SD	Y	24090 FQ	37390 AW	55260 TQ	SDBLS	10/01-12/01
	Tennessee	Y	19580 FQ	35980 AW	63950 TQ	TNBLS	10/01-12/01
	Chattanooga MSA, TN-GA	Y	21680 FQ	45220 AW	86700 TQ	TNBLS	10/01-12/01
	Clarksville-Hopkinsville MSA, TN-KY	Y	16710 FQ	32540 AW	53290 TQ	TNBLS	10/01-12/01
	Johnson City-Kingsport-Bristol MSA, TN-VA	Y	18680 FQ	33910 AW	60600 TQ	TNBLS	10/01-12/01
	Knoxville MSA, TN	Y	22190 FQ	40380 AW	65510 TQ	TNBLS	10/01-12/01
	Memphis MSA, TN-AR-MS	Y	19750 FQ	31010 AW	54000 TQ	TNBLS	10/01-12/01
	Nashville MSA, TN	Y	18470 FQ	35390 AW	58390 TQ	TNBLS	10/01-12/01
	Texas	Y	21260 FQ	41610 AW	69750 TQ	TXBLS	10/01-12/01
	Amarillo MSA, TX	Y	20610 FQ	32610 AW	45770 TQ	TXBLS	10/01-12/01
	Austin-San Marcos MSA, TX	Y	19010 FQ	34940 AW	53740 TQ	TXBLS	10/01-12/01
	Beaumont-Port Arthur MSA, TX	Y	22710 FQ	38020 AW	60610 TQ	TXBLS	10/01-12/01
	Brazoria PMSA, TX	Y	28630 FQ	43140 AW	68850 TQ	TXBLS	10/01-12/01
	Brownsville-Harlingen-San Benito MSA, TX	Y	17340 FQ	34320 AW	53570 TQ	TXBLS	10/01-12/01
	Corpus Christi MSA, TX	Y	18800 FQ	31360 AW	45940 TQ	TXBLS	10/01-12/01
	Dallas PMSA, TX	Y	18440 FQ	45050 AW	77690 TQ	TXBLS	10/01-12/01
	El Paso MSA, TX	Y	21010 FQ	35390 AW	56070 TQ	TXBLS	10/01-12/01
	Fort Worth-Arlington PMSA, TX	Y	24180 FQ	42030 AW	70380 TQ	TXBLS	10/01-12/01
	Galveston-Texas City PMSA, TX	Y	25940 FQ	39550 AW	58480 TQ	TXBLS	10/01-12/01
	Houston PMSA, TX	Y	24920 FQ	48180 AW	83730 TQ	TXBLS	10/01-12/01
	Killeen-Temple MSA, TX	Y	23640 FQ	38120 AW	62110 TQ	TXBLS	10/01-12/01
	Laredo MSA, TX	Y	18580 FQ	27990 AW	50110 TQ	TXBLS	10/01-12/01
	Longview-Marshall MSA, TX	Y	18860 FQ	28970 AW	41910 TQ	TXBLS	10/01-12/01
	Lubbock MSA, TX	Y	19690 FQ	34050 AW	49320 TQ	TXBLS	10/01-12/01
	Odessa-Midland MSA, TX	Y	19620 FQ	33260 AW	47780 TQ	TXBLS	10/01-12/01
	San Antonio MSA, TX	Y	22640 FQ	38730 AW	59720 TQ	TXBLS	10/01-12/01
	Tyler MSA, TX	Y	19530 FQ	31980 AW	51380 TQ	TXBLS	10/01-12/01
	Waco MSA, TX	Y	19810 FQ	35350 AW	58020 TQ	TXBLS	10/01-12/01
	Utah	Y	21780 FQ	39370 AW	57420 TQ	UTBLS	10/01-12/01
	Provo-Orem MSA, UT	Y	27230 FQ	52090 AW	97100 TQ	UTBLS	10/01-12/01
	Salt Lake City-Ogden MSA, UT	Y	20270 FQ	36110 AW	53740 TQ	UTBLS	10/01-12/01
	Vermont	Y	26280 FQ	50600 AW	123210 TQ	VTBLS	10/01-12/01
	Burlington MSA, VT	Y	25160 FQ	55000 AW	133180 TQ	VTBLS	10/01-12/01
	Virginia	Y	25080 FQ	42090 AW	66320 TQ	VABLS	10/01-12/01
	Lynchburg MSA, VA	Y	12780 FQ	32820 AW	53410 TQ	VABLS	10/01-12/01
	Norfolk-Virginia Beach-Newport News MSA, VA-NC	Y	21980 FQ	35820 AW	53940 TQ	VABLS	10/01-12/01
	Richmond-Petersburg MSA, VA	Y	25580 FQ	41610 AW	59550 TQ	VABLS	10/01-12/01
	Roanoke MSA, VA	Y	25100 FQ	38200 AW	52810 TQ	VABLS	10/01-12/01
	Washington	Y	28560 FQ	55440 AW	109950 TQ	WABLS	10/01-12/01
	Bremerton PMSA, WA	Y	25890 FQ	58930 AW		WABLS	10/01-12/01
	Olympia PMSA, WA	Y	26750 FQ	43380 AW	64420 TQ	WABLS	10/01-12/01
	Richland-Kennewick-Pasco MSA, WA	Y	26800 FQ	39150 AW	56360 TQ	WABLS	10/01-12/01
	Seattle-Bellevue-Everett PMSA, WA	Y	31580 FQ	60620 AW	140470 TQ	WABLS	10/01-12/01
	Spokane MSA, WA	Y	24300 FQ	42080 AW	57040 TQ	WABLS	10/01-12/01
	Tacoma PMSA, WA	Y	26690 FQ	43810 AW	63440 TQ	WABLS	10/01-12/01
	West Virginia	Y	17900 FQ	31070 AW	50160 TQ	WVBLS	10/01-12/01
	Charleston MSA, WV	Y	17050 FQ	37260 AW	61790 TQ	WVBLS	10/01-12/01
	Huntington-Ashland MSA, WV-KY-OH	Y	17920 FQ	29440 AW	40940 TQ	WVBLS	10/01-12/01
	Wisconsin	Y	23360 FQ	37530 AW	55520 TQ	WIBLS	10/01-12/01
	Appleton-Oshkosh-Neenah MSA, WI	Y	20620 FQ	38900 AW	66340 TQ	WIBLS	10/01-12/01
	Green Bay MSA, WI	Y	23500 FQ	38270 AW	55540 TQ	WIBLS	10/01-12/01
	Madison MSA, WI	Y	22200 FQ	34490 AW	52080 TQ	WIBLS	10/01-12/01

AAW	Average annual wage	AOH	Average offered, high	ASH	Average starting, high	H	Hourly	M	Monthly	S	Special: hourly and annual
AE	Average entry wage	AOL	Average offered, low	ASL	Average starting, low	HI	Highest wage paid	MTC	Median total compensation	TQ	Third quartile wage
AEX	Average experienced wage	APH	Average pay, high range	AW	Average wage paid	HR	High end range	MW	Median wage paid	W	Weekly
AO	Average offered	APL	Average pay, low range	FQ	First quartile wage	LR	Low end range	SQ	Second quartile wage	Y	Yearly

Occupation/Type/Industry	Location	Per	Low	Mid	High	Source	Date
Employment, Recruitment, and Placement Specialist	Milwaukee-Waukesha PMSA, WI	Y	25040 FQ	39900 AW	57160 TQ	WIBLS	10/01-12/01
	Racine PMSA, WI	Y	23570 FQ	36360 AW	55280 TQ	WIBLS	10/01-12/01
	Wyoming	Y	21990 FQ	33250 AW	50080 TQ	WYBLS	10/01-12/01
	Puerto Rico	Y	14890 FQ	26250 AW	43600 TQ	PRBLS	10/01-12/01
	Virgin Islands	Y	21690 FQ	36810 AW	57230 TQ	VIBLS	10/01-12/01
	Guam	Y	24560 FQ	36080 AW	48020 TQ	GUBLS	10/01-12/01
Engine and Other Machine Assembler	Alabama	H	8.97 FQ	12.25 AW	17.00 TQ	ALBLS	10/01-12/01
	Arizona	H	7.43 FQ	10.41 AW	14.42 TQ	AZBLS	10/01-12/01
	Arkansas	H	8.93 FQ	12.68 AW	17.57 TQ	ARBLS	10/01-12/01
	California	H	8.34 FQ	13.16 AW	17.72 TQ	CABLS	10/01-12/01
	Colorado	H	6.90 FQ	10.65 AW	16.02 TQ	COBLS	10/01-12/01
	Connecticut	H	9.06 FQ	15.68 AW	21.54 TQ	CTBLS	10/01-12/01
	Florida	H	8.00 FQ	12.16 AW	17.95 TQ	FLBLS	10/01-12/01
	Georgia	H	8.07 FQ	11.23 AW	15.06 TQ	GABLS	10/01-12/01
	Idaho	H	9.62 FQ	12.86 AW	16.67 TQ	IDBLS	10/01-12/01
	Illinois	H	7.09 FQ	13.91 AW	21.46 TQ	ILBLS	10/01-12/01
	Indiana	H	10.57 FQ	17.38 AW	24.77 TQ	INBLS	10/01-12/01
	Iowa	H	6.23 FQ	14.80 AW	21.92 TQ	IABLS	10/01-12/01
	Kansas	H	9.57 FQ	13.62 AW	18.32 TQ	KSBLS	10/01-12/01
	Kentucky	H	7.78 FQ	10.49 AW	14.85 TQ	KYBLS	10/01-12/01
	Louisiana	H	9.61 FQ	18.22 AW	36.96 TQ	LABLS	10/01-12/01
	Maine	H	9.74 FQ	16.26 AW	23.09 TQ	MEBLS	10/01-12/01
	Massachusetts	H	10.36 FQ	16.48 AW	21.48 TQ	MABLS	10/01-12/01
	Michigan	H	11.66 FQ	18.83 AW	26.66 TQ	MIBLS	10/01-12/01
	Minnesota	H	10.07 FQ	14.65 AW	19.92 TQ	MNBLS	10/01-12/01
	Mississippi	H	5.90 FQ	8.58 AW	11.01 TQ	MSBLS	10/01-12/01
	Missouri	H	8.64 FQ	14.14 AW	24.57 TQ	MOBLS	10/01-12/01
	Nebraska	H	7.96 FQ	11.39 AW	16.16 TQ	NEBLS	10/01-12/01
	New Hampshire	H	12.75 FQ	17.34 AW	21.40 TQ	NHBLS	10/01-12/01
	New Jersey	H	8.24 FQ	15.44 AW	24.15 TQ	NJBLS	10/01-12/01
	New York	H	7.11 FQ	12.01 AW	18.06 TQ	NYBLS	10/01-12/01
	North Dakota	H	8.87 FQ	10.46 AW	13.05 TQ	NDBLS	10/01-12/01
	Ohio	H	11.02 FQ	17.38 AW	25.57 TQ	OHBLS	10/01-12/01
	Oregon	H	10.31 FQ	17.09 AW	23.58 TQ	ORBLS	10/01-12/01
	Pennsylvania	H	9.67 FQ	14.01 AW	18.88 TQ	PABLS	10/01-12/01
	Rhode Island	H	11.27 FQ	15.37 AW	21.00 TQ	RIBLS	10/01-12/01
	South Carolina	H	8.99 FQ	14.42 AW	21.23 TQ	SCBLS	10/01-12/01
	South Dakota	H	8.67 FQ	11.25 AW	13.70 TQ	SDBLS	10/01-12/01
	Tennessee	H	11.07 FQ	15.86 AW	24.59 TQ	TNBLS	10/01-12/01
	Texas	H	7.78 FQ	12.68 AW	18.17 TQ	TXBLS	10/01-12/01
	Utah	H	11.64 FQ	15.55 AW	22.03 TQ	UTBLS	10/01-12/01
	Washington	H	9.17 FQ	14.37 AW	20.34 TQ	WABLS	10/01-12/01
	West Virginia	H	8.32 FQ	10.05 AW	11.67 TQ	WVBLS	10/01-12/01
	Wisconsin	H	10.18 FQ	16.20 AW	22.24 TQ	WIBLS	10/01-12/01
	Puerto Rico	H	6.40 FQ	12.63 AW	24.67 TQ	PRBLS	10/01-12/01
Engineer	United States	Y		79000 MW		CSE	1/01-1/01
Aerospace	East North Central	Y		68796 MW		AWSTMS	1/00-1/01
Aerospace	East South Central	Y		60557 MW		AWSTMS	1/00-1/01
Aerospace	Middle Atlantic	Y		57737 MW		AWSTMS	1/00-1/01
Aerospace	Mountain	Y		60869 MW		AWSTMS	1/00-1/01
Aerospace	New England	Y		57379 MW		AWSTMS	1/00-1/01
Aerospace	Pacific	Y		64578 MW		AWSTMS	1/00-1/01
Aerospace	South Atlantic	Y		56334 MW		AWSTMS	1/00-1/01
Aerospace	West North Central	Y		55864 MW		AWSTMS	1/00-1/01
Aerospace	West South Central	Y		70558 MW		AWSTMS	1/00-1/01
Electronics and Information Technology	United States	Y		93100 AW		CE	1/01-1/02
Tugboat	Jacksonville, FL	Y		35000-50000 AEX		FLTU	2002
Engineering Manager	Alabama	Y	54530 FQ	82570 AW	113280 TQ	ALBLS	10/01-12/01
	Birmingham MSA, AL	Y	51750 FQ	77380 AW	110340 TQ	ALBLS	10/01-12/01
	Huntsville MSA, AL	Y	72650 FQ	90620 AW	114440 TQ	ALBLS	10/01-12/01
	Mobile MSA, AL	Y	52910 FQ	81090 AW	113870 TQ	ALBLS	10/01-12/01
	Montgomery MSA, AL	Y	50200 FQ	73910 AW	108400 TQ	ALBLS	10/01-12/01
	Alaska	Y	62000 FQ	92830 AW	143310 TQ	AKBLS	10/01-12/01
	Anchorage MSA, AK	Y	66310 FQ	97980 AW		AKBLS	10/01-12/01
	Arizona	Y	54020 FQ	83830 AW	126500 TQ	AZBLS	10/01-12/01

AAW Average annual wage; AE Average entry wage; AEX Average experienced wage; AO Average offered; AOH Average offered, high; AOL Average offered, low; APH Average pay, high range; APL Average pay, low range; ASH Average starting, high; ASL Average starting, low; AW Average wage paid; FQ First quartile wage; H Hourly; HI Highest wage paid; HR High end range; LR Low end range; M Monthly; MTC Median total compensation; MW Median wage paid; SQ Second quartile wage; S Special: hourly and annual; TQ Third quartile wage; W Weekly; Y Yearly

Occupation/Type/Industry	Location	Per	Low	Mid	High	Source	Date
Engineering Manager	Phoenix-Mesa MSA, AZ	Y	55640 FQ	85380 AW	128280 TQ	AZBLS	10/01-12/01
	Tucson MSA, AZ	Y	55920 FQ	81560 AW	134910 TQ	AZBLS	10/01-12/01
	Arkansas	Y	45580 FQ	71330 AW	100580 TQ	ARBLS	10/01-12/01
	Fayetteville-Springdale-Rogers MSA, AR	Y	38260 FQ	68010 AW	123520 TQ	ARBLS	10/01-12/01
	Fort Smith MSA, AR-OK	Y	41160 FQ	73640 AW	111290 TQ	ARBLS	10/01-12/01
	Little Rock-North Little Rock MSA, AR	Y	49330 FQ	73230 AW	103060 TQ	ARBLS	10/01-12/01
	California	Y	63910 FQ	101040 AW		CABLS	10/01-12/01
	Bakersfield MSA, CA	Y	56710 FQ	91960 AW		CABLS	10/01-12/01
	Chico-Paradise MSA, CA	Y	48830 FQ	66550 AW	85860 TQ	CABLS	10/01-12/01
	Fresno MSA, CA	Y	48550 FQ	76640 AW	118280 TQ	CABLS	10/01-12/01
	Los Angeles-Long Beach PMSA, CA	Y	58290 FQ	91250 AW	136260 TQ	CABLS	10/01-12/01
	Modesto MSA, CA	Y	48860 FQ	77300 AW	104420 TQ	CABLS	10/01-12/01
	Oakland PMSA, CA	Y	69850 FQ	105180 AW		CABLS	10/01-12/01
	Orange County PMSA, CA	Y	67560 FQ	102400 AW	145200 TQ	CABLS	10/01-12/01
	Redding MSA, CA	Y	53100 FQ	78350 AW	111090 TQ	CABLS	10/01-12/01
	Riverside-San Bernardino PMSA, CA	Y	58930 FQ	84370 AW	118840 TQ	CABLS	10/01-12/01
	Sacramento PMSA, CA	Y	61170 FQ	91650 AW	133470 TQ	CABLS	10/01-12/01
	Salinas MSA, CA	Y	54240 FQ	90410 AW		CABLS	10/01-12/01
	San Diego MSA, CA	Y	60760 FQ	94870 AW	140150 TQ	CABLS	10/01-12/01
	San Francisco PMSA, CA	Y	64920 FQ	104550 AW		CABLS	10/01-12/01
	San Jose PMSA, CA	Y	85720 FQ	119600 AW		CABLS	10/01-12/01
	San Luis Obispo-Atascadero-Paso Robles MSA, CA	Y	52990 FQ	83580 AW	123810 TQ	CABLS	10/01-12/01
	Santa Barbara-Santa Maria-Lompoc MSA, CA	Y	61710 FQ	93680 AW		CABLS	10/01-12/01
	Santa Cruz-Watsonville PMSA, CA	Y	68560 FQ	109570 AW		CABLS	10/01-12/01
	Santa Rosa PMSA, CA	Y	63830 FQ	95520 AW	142880 TQ	CABLS	10/01-12/01
	Stockton-Lodi MSA, CA	Y	51070 FQ	75390 AW	107040 TQ	CABLS	10/01-12/01
	Vallejo-Fairfield-Napa PMSA, CA	Y	61930 FQ	91990 AW	139170 TQ	CABLS	10/01-12/01
	Ventura PMSA, CA	Y	66230 FQ	94390 AW	139920 TQ	CABLS	10/01-12/01
	Visalia-Tulare-Porterville MSA, CA	Y	48640 FQ	74690 AW	94170 TQ	CABLS	10/01-12/01
	Colorado	Y	58040 FQ	91030 AW	136310 TQ	COBLS	10/01-12/01
	Boulder-Longmont PMSA, CO	Y	74870 FQ	104860 AW		COBLS	10/01-12/01
	Colorado Springs MSA, CO	Y	58450 FQ	93300 AW	137040 TQ	COBLS	10/01-12/01
	Denver PMSA, CO	Y	58220 FQ	88510 AW	128890 TQ	COBLS	10/01-12/01
	Fort Collins-Loveland MSA, CO	Y	57010 FQ	92020 AW	133830 TQ	COBLS	10/01-12/01
	Greeley PMSA, CO	Y	56910 FQ	81710 AW	113010 TQ	COBLS	10/01-12/01
	Connecticut	Y	62530 FQ	92460 AW	136630 TQ	CTBLS	10/01-12/01
	Bridgeport PMSA, CT	Y	64870 FQ	98010 AW	143080 TQ	CTBLS	10/01-12/01
	Danbury PMSA, CT	Y	56820 FQ	85350 AW	126070 TQ	CTBLS	10/01-12/01
	Hartford MSA, CT	Y	62670 FQ	91430 AW	131740 TQ	CTBLS	10/01-12/01
	New Haven-Meriden PMSA, CT	Y	61110 FQ	94120 AW	140990 TQ	CTBLS	10/01-12/01
	Stamford-Norwalk PMSA, CT	Y	67460 FQ	106370 AW		CTBLS	10/01-12/01
	Waterbury PMSA, CT	Y	64570 FQ	92750 AW	123200 TQ	CTBLS	10/01-12/01
	Delaware	Y	55690 FQ	86130 AW	128810 TQ	DEBLS	10/01-12/01
	Wilmington-Newark PMSA, DE-MD	Y	56440 FQ	86280 AW	124190 TQ	DEBLS	10/01-12/01
	District of Columbia	Y	74310 FQ	96090 AW	116190 TQ	DCBLS	10/01-12/01
	Washington PMSA, DC-MD-VA-WV	Y	65390 FQ	94470 AW	129570 TQ	DCBLS	10/01-12/01
	Florida	Y	54190 FQ	90140 AW		FLBLS	10/01-12/01
	Daytona Beach MSA, FL	Y	53530 FQ	79430 AW	115400 TQ	FLBLS	10/01-12/01
	Fort Lauderdale PMSA, FL	Y	61840 FQ	103290 AW		FLBLS	10/01-12/01
	Fort Myers-Cape Coral MSA, FL	Y	48930 FQ	68920 AW	97260 TQ	FLBLS	10/01-12/01
	Fort Pierce-Port St. Lucie MSA, FL	Y	51160 FQ	78300 AW	115220 TQ	FLBLS	10/01-12/01
	Fort Walton Beach MSA, FL	Y	63760 FQ	85400 AW	110940 TQ	FLBLS	10/01-12/01
	Gainesville MSA, FL	Y	59600 FQ	86820 AW		FLBLS	10/01-12/01
	Jacksonville MSA, FL	Y	53130 FQ	84530 AW	123000 TQ	FLBLS	10/01-12/01
	Lakeland-Winter Haven MSA, FL	Y	48250 FQ	85420 AW		FLBLS	10/01-12/01

AAW Average annual wage **AE** Average entry wage **AEX** Average experienced wage **AO** Average offered **AOH** Average offered, high **AOL** Average offered, low **APH** Average pay, high range **APL** Average pay, low range **ASH** Average starting, high **ASL** Average starting, low **AW** Average wage paid **FQ** First quartile wage **H** Hourly **HI** Highest wage paid **HR** High end range **LR** Low end range **M** Monthly **MTC** Median total compensation **MW** Median wage paid **SQ** Second quartile wage **S** Special: hourly and annual **TQ** Third quartile wage **W** Weekly **Y** Yearly

Occupation/Type/Industry	Location	Per	Low	Mid	High	Source	Date
Engineering Manager	Melbourne-Titusville-Palm Bay MSA, FL	Y	59050 FQ	91650 AW	136290 TQ	FLBLS	10/01-12/01
	Miami PMSA, FL	Y	54740 FQ	101630 AW		FLBLS	10/01-12/01
	Naples MSA, FL	Y	47250 FQ	91800 AW	138070 TQ	FLBLS	10/01-12/01
	Ocala MSA, FL	Y	37420 FQ	75170 AW	113280 TQ	FLBLS	10/01-12/01
	Orlando MSA, FL	Y	60790 FQ	91860 AW	142150 TQ	FLBLS	10/01-12/01
	Pensacola MSA, FL	Y	54270 FQ	81650 AW	117130 TQ	FLBLS	10/01-12/01
	Sarasota-Bradenton MSA, FL	Y	59510 FQ	89330 AW	143240 TQ	FLBLS	10/01-12/01
	Tallahassee MSA, FL	Y	53880 FQ	103300 AW		FLBLS	10/01-12/01
	Tampa-St. Petersburg-Clearwater MSA, FL	Y	52900 FQ	85570 AW	135890 TQ	FLBLS	10/01-12/01
	West Palm Beach-Boca Raton MSA, FL	Y	56970 FQ	92170 AW	143570 TQ	FLBLS	10/01-12/01
	Georgia	Y	53650 FQ	89200 AW		GABLS	10/01-12/01
	Atlanta MSA, GA	Y	55160 FQ	94350 AW		GABLS	10/01-12/01
	Augusta-Aiken MSA, GA-SC	Y	66000 FQ	91420 AW	119120 TQ	GABLS	10/01-12/01
	Columbus MSA, GA-AL	Y	49700 FQ	81970 AW	117370 TQ	GABLS	10/01-12/01
	Macon MSA, GA	Y	59800 FQ	78780 AW	103180 TQ	GABLS	10/01-12/01
	Savannah MSA, GA	Y	55540 FQ	74930 AW	107630 TQ	GABLS	10/01-12/01
	Hawaii	Y	57350 FQ	82720 AW	112090 TQ	HIBLS	10/01-12/01
	Honolulu MSA, HI	Y	59290 FQ	83870 AW	112740 TQ	HIBLS	10/01-12/01
	Idaho	Y	55460 FQ	83590 AW	118810 TQ	IDBLS	10/01-12/01
	Boise City MSA, ID	Y	53380 FQ	84490 AW	123980 TQ	IDBLS	10/01-12/01
	Illinois	Y	45130 FQ	80970 AW	121980 TQ	ILBLS	10/01-12/01
	Champaign-Urbana MSA, IL	Y	37130 FQ	72150 AW	112630 TQ	ILBLS	10/01-12/01
	Chicago PMSA, IL	Y	43910 FQ	82330 AW	122850 TQ	ILBLS	10/01-12/01
	Peoria-Pekin MSA, IL	Y	61130 FQ	108250 AW		ILBLS	10/01-12/01
	Rockford MSA, IL	Y	49300 FQ	73930 AW	97770 TQ	ILBLS	10/01-12/01
	Springfield MSA, IL	Y	49640 FQ	75570 AW	107570 TQ	ILBLS	10/01-12/01
	Indiana	Y	50250 FQ	75900 AW	108920 TQ	INBLS	10/01-12/01
	Elkhart-Goshen MSA, IN	Y	39010 FQ	62860 AW	90560 TQ	INBLS	10/01-12/01
	Evansville-Henderson MSA, IN-KY	Y	48570 FQ	70110 AW	93260 TQ	INBLS	10/01-12/01
	Fort Wayne MSA, IN	Y	48250 FQ	76230 AW	113530 TQ	INBLS	10/01-12/01
	Gary PMSA, IN	Y	50000 FQ	73550 AW	96550 TQ	INBLS	10/01-12/01
	Indianapolis MSA, IN	Y	53410 FQ	78270 AW	110770 TQ	INBLS	10/01-12/01
	Lafayette MSA, IN	Y	65740 FQ	86560 AW	119980 TQ	INBLS	10/01-12/01
	South Bend MSA, IN	Y	50210 FQ	76130 AW	109950 TQ	INBLS	10/01-12/01
	Iowa	Y	49400 FQ	76690 AW	111330 TQ	IABLS	10/01-12/01
	Davenport-Moline-Rock Island MSA, IA-IL	Y	45620 FQ	73320 AW	103640 TQ	IABLS	10/01-12/01
	Des Moines MSA, IA	Y	47960 FQ	72520 AW	103800 TQ	IABLS	10/01-12/01
	Kansas	Y	52540 FQ	82340 AW	119560 TQ	KSBLS	10/01-12/01
	Topeka MSA, KS	Y	50400 FQ	80320 AW	113980 TQ	KSBLS	10/01-12/01
	Wichita MSA, KS	Y	53770 FQ	79210 AW	112820 TQ	KSBLS	10/01-12/01
	Kentucky	Y	51240 FQ	76070 AW	107250 TQ	KYBLS	10/01-12/01
	Lexington MSA, KY	Y	51570 FQ	75250 AW	107410 TQ	KYBLS	10/01-12/01
	Louisville MSA, KY-IN	Y	55920 FQ	80630 AW	109940 TQ	KYBLS	10/01-12/01
	Louisiana	Y	50010 FQ	81180 AW	121640 TQ	LABLS	10/01-12/01
	Baton Rouge MSA, LA	Y	47580 FQ	77940 AW	119500 TQ	LABLS	10/01-12/01
	Houma MSA, LA	Y	44910 FQ	71730 AW	105940 TQ	LABLS	10/01-12/01
	Lafayette MSA, LA	Y	49520 FQ	72820 AW	108350 TQ	LABLS	10/01-12/01
	Lake Charles MSA, LA	Y	51840 FQ	82940 AW	115390 TQ	LABLS	10/01-12/01
	New Orleans MSA, LA	Y	57470 FQ	87150 AW	128280 TQ	LABLS	10/01-12/01
	Shreveport-Bossier City MSA, LA	Y	42520 FQ	76580 AW	119920 TQ	LABLS	10/01-12/01
	Maine	Y	49540 FQ	75360 AW	109180 TQ	MEBLS	10/01-12/01
	Portland MSA, ME	Y	47740 FQ	79580 AW	115120 TQ	MEBLS	10/01-12/01
	Maryland	Y	58510 FQ	87230 AW	116890 TQ	MDBLS	10/01-12/01
	Baltimore PMSA, MD	Y	58590 FQ	87150 AW	118670 TQ	MDBLS	10/01-12/01
	Massachusetts	Y	63790 FQ	98230 AW		MABLS	10/01-12/01
	Boston PMSA, MA-NH	Y	66860 FQ	100790 AW		MABLS	10/01-12/01
	Brockton PMSA, MA	Y	51540 FQ	90520 AW	134600 TQ	MABLS	10/01-12/01
	Lawrence PMSA, MA-NH	Y	70480 FQ	102300 AW		MABLS	10/01-12/01
	Lowell PMSA, MA-NH	Y	49190 FQ	91890 AW		MABLS	10/01-12/01
	New Bedford PMSA, MA	Y	55850 FQ	85000 AW	116000 TQ	MABLS	10/01-12/01
	Springfield MSA, MA	Y	50680 FQ	77410 AW	117640 TQ	MABLS	10/01-12/01
	Worcester PMSA, MA-CT	Y	62990 FQ	100190 AW		MABLS	10/01-12/01
	Michigan	Y	60690 FQ	91140 AW	134600 TQ	MIBLS	10/01-12/01
	Ann Arbor PMSA, MI	Y	59180 FQ	87550 AW	138920 TQ	MIBLS	10/01-12/01
	Detroit PMSA, MI	Y	65610 FQ	95820 AW	139930 TQ	MIBLS	10/01-12/01
	Flint PMSA, MI	Y	68670 FQ	96460 AW	139220 TQ	MIBLS	10/01-12/01

AAW	Average annual wage	AOH	Average offered, high	ASH	Average starting, high	H	Hourly	M	Monthly	S	Special: hourly and annual
AE	Average entry wage	AOL	Average offered, low	ASL	Average starting, low	HI	Highest wage paid	MTC	Median total compensation	TQ	Third quartile wage
AEX	Average experienced wage	APH	Average pay, high range	AW	Average wage paid	HR	High end range	MW	Median wage paid	W	Weekly
AO	Average offered	APL	Average pay, low range	FQ	First quartile wage	LR	Low end range	SQ	Second quartile wage	Y	Yearly

Occupation/Type/Industry	Location	Per	Low	Mid	High	Source	Date
Engineering Manager	Grand Rapids-Muskegon-Holland MSA, MI	Y	54020 FQ	80370 AW	113360 TQ	MIBLS	10/01-12/01
	Kalamazoo-Battle Creek MSA, MI	Y	60150 FQ	89330 AW	131500 TQ	MIBLS	10/01-12/01
	Lansing-East Lansing MSA, MI	Y	57400 FQ	90380 AW	126150 TQ	MIBLS	10/01-12/01
	Saginaw-Bay City-Midland MSA, MI	Y	61860 FQ	94880 AW	136850 TQ	MIBLS	10/01-12/01
	Minnesota	Y	60760 FQ	89030 AW	131580 TQ	MNBLS	10/01-12/01
	Duluth-Superior MSA, MN-WI	Y	57700 FQ	75190 AW	105240 TQ	MNBLS	10/01-12/01
	Minneapolis-St. Paul MSA, MN-WI	Y	61770 FQ	90660 AW	133530 TQ	MNBLS	10/01-12/01
	St. Cloud MSA, MN	Y	51270 FQ	68840 AW	92650 TQ	MNBLS	10/01-12/01
	Mississippi	Y	46110 FQ	71500 AW	105390 TQ	MSBLS	10/01-12/01
	Biloxi-Gulfport-Pascagoula MSA, MS	Y	48650 FQ	72450 AW	104940 TQ	MSBLS	10/01-12/01
	Jackson MSA, MS	Y	50380 FQ	82120 AW	137570 TQ	MSBLS	10/01-12/01
	Missouri	Y	49550 FQ	78900 AW	113500 TQ	MOBLS	10/01-12/01
	Kansas City MSA, MO-KS	Y	52870 FQ	87280 AW	131080 TQ	MOBLS	10/01-12/01
	St. Louis MSA, MO-IL	Y	50730 FQ	79080 AW	112070 TQ	MOBLS	10/01-12/01
	Springfield MSA, MO	Y	50120 FQ	77050 AW	113490 TQ	MOBLS	10/01-12/01
	Montana	Y	40170 FQ	69520 AW	110430 TQ	MTBLS	10/01-12/01
	Billings MSA, MT	Y	35210 FQ	70700 AW	101660 TQ	MTBLS	10/01-12/01
	Nebraska	Y	50070 FQ	78460 AW	112670 TQ	NEBLS	10/01-12/01
	Lincoln MSA, NE	Y	57540 FQ	81750 AW	115510 TQ	NEBLS	10/01-12/01
	Omaha MSA, NE-IA	Y	50270 FQ	79500 AW	111660 TQ	NEBLS	10/01-12/01
	Nevada	Y	55590 FQ	86470 AW	126610 TQ	NVBLS	10/01-12/01
	Las Vegas MSA, NV-AZ	Y	56310 FQ	88940 AW	130690 TQ	NVBLS	10/01-12/01
	Reno MSA, NV	Y	61460 FQ	86600 AW	118420 TQ	NVBLS	10/01-12/01
	New Hampshire	Y	55520 FQ	84420 AW	120680 TQ	NHBLS	10/01-12/01
	Manchester PMSA, NH	Y	48770 FQ	75180 AW	109840 TQ	NHBLS	10/01-12/01
	Nashua PMSA, NH	Y	60460 FQ	93050 AW	138340 TQ	NHBLS	10/01-12/01
	Portsmouth-Rochester PMSA, NH-ME	Y	61110 FQ	81860 AW	109400 TQ	NHBLS	10/01-12/01
	New Jersey	Y	67350 FQ	98360 AW	142080 TQ	NJBLS	10/01-12/01
	Atlantic-Cape May PMSA, NJ	Y	60810 FQ	97820 AW		NJBLS	10/01-12/01
	Bergen-Passaic PMSA, NJ	Y	72190 FQ	103720 AW		NJBLS	10/01-12/01
	Jersey City PMSA, NJ	Y	62530 FQ	92350 AW	143920 TQ	NJBLS	10/01-12/01
	Middlesex-Somerset-Hunterdon PMSA, NJ	Y	66920 FQ	95580 AW	136080 TQ	NJBLS	10/01-12/01
	Monmouth-Ocean PMSA, NJ	Y	69180 FQ	98450 AW	138050 TQ	NJBLS	10/01-12/01
	Newark PMSA, NJ	Y	68080 FQ	99100 AW	141840 TQ	NJBLS	10/01-12/01
	Trenton PMSA, NJ	Y	65250 FQ	103240 AW		NJBLS	10/01-12/01
	New Mexico	Y	51800 FQ	82960 AW	119290 TQ	NMBLS	10/01-12/01
	Albuquerque MSA, NM	Y	55720 FQ	87530 AW	123580 TQ	NMBLS	10/01-12/01
	Las Cruces MSA, NM	Y	59280 FQ	81690 AW	110240 TQ	NMBLS	10/01-12/01
	New York	Y	63320 FQ	96740 AW		NYBLS	10/01-12/01
	Albany-Schenectady-Troy MSA, NY	Y	59900 FQ	86400 AW	116970 TQ	NYBLS	10/01-12/01
	Binghamton MSA, NY	Y	71230 FQ	108280 AW	143240 TQ	NYBLS	10/01-12/01
	Buffalo-Niagara Falls MSA, NY	Y	56650 FQ	81930 AW	113910 TQ	NYBLS	10/01-12/01
	Nassau-Suffolk PMSA, NY	Y	68690 FQ	97700 AW	143170 TQ	NYBLS	10/01-12/01
	New York PMSA, NY	Y	66320 FQ	102960 AW		NYBLS	10/01-12/01
	Newburgh PMSA, NY-PA	Y	60040 FQ	84840 AW	127780 TQ	NYBLS	10/01-12/01
	Rochester MSA, NY	Y	64430 FQ	93090 AW	135010 TQ	NYBLS	10/01-12/01
	Syracuse MSA, NY	Y	63400 FQ	92270 AW	124060 TQ	NYBLS	10/01-12/01
	Utica-Rome MSA, NY	Y	54040 FQ	79270 AW	114290 TQ	NYBLS	10/01-12/01
	North Carolina	Y	52820 FQ	86190 AW	128720 TQ	NCBLS	10/01-12/01
	Asheville MSA, NC	Y	39710 FQ	68920 AW	93460 TQ	NCBLS	10/01-12/01
	Charlotte-Gastonia-Rock Hill MSA, NC-SC	Y	52760 FQ	84470 AW	118130 TQ	NCBLS	10/01-12/01
	Fayetteville MSA, NC	Y	55550 FQ	75800 AW	97500 TQ	NCBLS	10/01-12/01
	Greensboro-Winston-Salem-High Point MSA, NC	Y	53520 FQ	88090 AW	133320 TQ	NCBLS	10/01-12/01
	Hickory-Morganton-Lenoir MSA, NC	Y	41170 FQ	70880 AW	104390 TQ	NCBLS	10/01-12/01
	Raleigh-Durham-Chapel Hill MSA, NC	Y	61610 FQ	96580 AW	139340 TQ	NCBLS	10/01-12/01
	Wilmington MSA, NC	Y	61870 FQ	84780 AW	116810 TQ	NCBLS	10/01-12/01
	North Dakota	Y	41610 FQ	68180 AW	101920 TQ	NDBLS	10/01-12/01
	Fargo-Moorhead MSA, ND-MN	Y	40550 FQ	71220 AW	112660 TQ	NDBLS	10/01-12/01

AAW Average annual wage; **AE** Average entry wage; **AEX** Average experienced wage; **AO** Average offered; **AOH** Average offered, high; **AOL** Average offered, low; **APH** Average pay, high range; **APL** Average pay, low range; **ASH** Average starting, high; **ASL** Average starting, low; **AW** Average wage paid; **FQ** First quartile wage; **H** Hourly; **HI** Highest wage paid; **HR** High end range; **LR** Low end range; **M** Monthly; **MTC** Median total compensation; **MW** Median wage paid; **SQ** Second quartile wage; **S** Special: hourly and annual; **TQ** Third quartile wage; **W** Weekly; **Y** Yearly

Occupation/Type/Industry	Location	Per	Low	Mid	High	Source	Date
Engineering Manager	Ohio	Y	53920 FQ	81940 AW	114570 TQ	OHBLS	10/01-12/01
	Akron PMSA, OH	Y	52000 FQ	80420 AW	115560 TQ	OHBLS	10/01-12/01
	Canton-Massillon MSA, OH	Y	42140 FQ	74630 AW	117790 TQ	OHBLS	10/01-12/01
	Cincinnati PMSA, OH-KY-IN	Y	54810 FQ	86750 AW	128720 TQ	OHBLS	10/01-12/01
	Cleveland-Lorain-Elyria PMSA, OH	Y	60150 FQ	82510 AW	108960 TQ	OHBLS	10/01-12/01
	Columbus MSA, OH	Y	53370 FQ	80520 AW	114010 TQ	OHBLS	10/01-12/01
	Dayton-Springfield MSA, OH	Y	57960 FQ	85880 AW	114160 TQ	OHBLS	10/01-12/01
	Hamilton-Middletown PMSA, OH	Y	55650 FQ	75810 AW	108380 TQ	OHBLS	10/01-12/01
	Mansfield MSA, OH	Y	46390 FQ	70360 AW	110560 TQ	OHBLS	10/01-12/01
	Toledo MSA, OH	Y	55600 FQ	81410 AW	123160 TQ	OHBLS	10/01-12/01
	Youngstown-Warren MSA, OH	Y	46680 FQ	76020 AW	112470 TQ	OHBLS	10/01-12/01
	Oklahoma	Y	47180 FQ	77770 AW	113640 TQ	OKBLS	10/01-12/01
	Oklahoma City MSA, OK	Y	49230 FQ	76620 AW	110870 TQ	OKBLS	10/01-12/01
	Tulsa MSA, OK	Y	46750 FQ	79910 AW	114200 TQ	OKBLS	10/01-12/01
	Oregon	Y	59930 FQ	92640 AW	138270 TQ	ORBLS	10/01-12/01
	Eugene-Springfield MSA, OR	Y	53030 FQ	83960 AW	119210 TQ	ORBLS	10/01-12/01
	Portland-Vancouver PMSA, OR-WA	Y	60800 FQ	94100 AW	139690 TQ	ORBLS	10/01-12/01
	Salem PMSA, OR	Y	57830 FQ	85650 AW	119490 TQ	ORBLS	10/01-12/01
	Pennsylvania	Y	52330 FQ	80970 AW	114620 TQ	PABLS	10/01-12/01
	Allentown-Bethlehem-Easton MSA, PA	Y	53950 FQ	80360 AW	113510 TQ	PABLS	10/01-12/01
	Erie MSA, PA	Y	47210 FQ	69490 AW	93590 TQ	PABLS	10/01-12/01
	Harrisburg-Lebanon-Carlisle MSA, PA	Y	55610 FQ	80110 AW	113930 TQ	PABLS	10/01-12/01
	Johnstown MSA, PA	Y	41380 FQ	74670 AW	108940 TQ	PABLS	10/01-12/01
	Lancaster MSA, PA	Y	51490 FQ	77860 AW	112780 TQ	PABLS	10/01-12/01
	Philadelphia PMSA, PA-NJ	Y	61140 FQ	88420 AW	123700 TQ	PABLS	10/01-12/01
	Pittsburgh MSA, PA	Y	49890 FQ	82360 AW	114220 TQ	PABLS	10/01-12/01
	Reading MSA, PA	Y	50860 FQ	75460 AW	100810 TQ	PABLS	10/01-12/01
	Scranton-Wilkes-Barre-Hazleton MSA, PA	Y	46110 FQ	70700 AW	98310 TQ	PABLS	10/01-12/01
	York MSA, PA	Y	44710 FQ	71860 AW	101340 TQ	PABLS	10/01-12/01
	Rhode Island	Y	62880 FQ	90340 AW	130720 TQ	RIBLS	10/01-12/01
	Providence-Fall River-Warwick MSA, RI-MA	Y	62150 FQ	89750 AW	126600 TQ	RIBLS	10/01-12/01
	South Carolina	Y	49960 FQ	80100 AW	114790 TQ	SCBLS	10/01-12/01
	Charleston-North Charleston MSA, SC	Y	48860 FQ	74030 AW	105500 TQ	SCBLS	10/01-12/01
	Columbia MSA, SC	Y	48510 FQ	76360 AW	112200 TQ	SCBLS	10/01-12/01
	Greenville-Spartanburg-Anderson MSA, SC	Y	52770 FQ	81560 AW	120160 TQ	SCBLS	10/01-12/01
	Myrtle Beach MSA, SC	Y	53280 FQ	73880 AW	97810 TQ	SCBLS	10/01-12/01
	South Dakota	Y	53940 FQ	74930 AW	97760 TQ	SDBLS	10/01-12/01
	Sioux Falls MSA, SD	Y	60260 FQ	75010 AW	94970 TQ	SDBLS	10/01-12/01
	Tennessee	Y	46900 FQ	76690 AW	114780 TQ	TNBLS	10/01-12/01
	Chattanooga MSA, TN-GA	Y	47520 FQ	72280 AW	93020 TQ	TNBLS	10/01-12/01
	Clarksville-Hopkinsville MSA, TN-KY	Y	52220 FQ	71900 AW	94960 TQ	TNBLS	10/01-12/01
	Johnson City-Kingsport-Bristol MSA, TN-VA	Y	40610 FQ	69450 AW	94730 TQ	TNBLS	10/01-12/01
	Knoxville MSA, TN	Y	48900 FQ	81700 AW	119110 TQ	TNBLS	10/01-12/01
	Memphis MSA, TN-AR-MS	Y	48720 FQ	78270 AW	116810 TQ	TNBLS	10/01-12/01
	Nashville MSA, TN	Y	46750 FQ	78010 AW	119130 TQ	TNBLS	10/01-12/01
	Texas	Y	53000 FQ	88900 AW	136470 TQ	TXBLS	10/01-12/01
	Amarillo MSA, TX	Y	47880 FQ	78410 AW	109630 TQ	TXBLS	10/01-12/01
	Austin-San Marcos MSA, TX	Y	55820 FQ	95010 AW		TXBLS	10/01-12/01
	Beaumont-Port Arthur MSA, TX	Y	51580 FQ	86300 AW	134790 TQ	TXBLS	10/01-12/01
	Brazoria PMSA, TX	Y	52290 FQ	82940 AW	115200 TQ	TXBLS	10/01-12/01
	Brownsville-Harlingen-San Benito MSA, TX	Y	50010 FQ	79540 AW	119190 TQ	TXBLS	10/01-12/01
	Corpus Christi MSA, TX	Y	50840 FQ	94060 AW		TXBLS	10/01-12/01
	Dallas PMSA, TX	Y	54370 FQ	88660 AW	134540 TQ	TXBLS	10/01-12/01
	El Paso MSA, TX	Y	36150 FQ	75550 AW	115770 TQ	TXBLS	10/01-12/01
	Fort Worth-Arlington PMSA, TX	Y	55200 FQ	88210 AW	126300 TQ	TXBLS	10/01-12/01
	Galveston-Texas City PMSA, TX	Y	54610 FQ	84720 AW	119120 TQ	TXBLS	10/01-12/01
	Houston PMSA, TX	Y	55990 FQ	92040 AW	139800 TQ	TXBLS	10/01-12/01

AAW	Average annual wage	**AOH**	Average offered, high	**ASH**	Average starting, high	**H**	Hourly	**M**	Monthly	**S**	Special: hourly and annual
AE	Average entry wage	**AOL**	Average offered, low	**ASL**	Average starting, low	**HI**	Highest wage paid	**MTC**	Median total compensation	**TQ**	Third quartile wage
AEX	Average experienced wage	**APH**	Average pay, high range	**AW**	Average wage paid	**HR**	High end range	**MW**	Median wage paid	**W**	Weekly
AO	Average offered	**APL**	Average pay, low range	**FQ**	First quartile wage	**LR**	Low end range	**SQ**	Second quartile wage	**Y**	Yearly

Occupation/Type/Industry	Location	Per	Low	Mid	High	Source	Date
Engineering Manager	Killeen-Temple MSA, TX	Y	45530 FQ	76760 AW	117910 TQ	TXBLS	10/01-12/01
	Longview-Marshall MSA, TX	Y	42470 FQ	67520 AW	106560 TQ	TXBLS	10/01-12/01
	Lubbock MSA, TX	Y	45300 FQ	70890 AW	107170 TQ	TXBLS	10/01-12/01
	McAllen-Edinburg-Mission MSA, TX	Y	35100 FQ	66710 AW	91320 TQ	TXBLS	10/01-12/01
	Odessa-Midland MSA, TX	Y	47180 FQ	92140 AW		TXBLS	10/01-12/01
	San Antonio MSA, TX	Y	53700 FQ	80270 AW	114310 TQ	TXBLS	10/01-12/01
	Tyler MSA, TX	Y	54050 FQ	82860 AW	111260 TQ	TXBLS	10/01-12/01
	Waco MSA, TX	Y	52000 FQ	80660 AW	110480 TQ	TXBLS	10/01-12/01
	Utah	Y	49460 FQ	77520 AW	113360 TQ	UTBLS	10/01-12/01
	Provo-Orem MSA, UT	Y	49230 FQ	75370 AW	114060 TQ	UTBLS	10/01-12/01
	Salt Lake City-Ogden MSA, UT	Y	51840 FQ	79300 AW	115140 TQ	UTBLS	10/01-12/01
	Vermont	Y	67280 FQ	108880 AW		VTBLS	10/01-12/01
	Virginia	Y	59460 FQ	89030 AW	125830 TQ	VABLS	10/01-12/01
	Lynchburg MSA, VA	Y	55470 FQ	85170 AW	115420 TQ	VABLS	10/01-12/01
	Norfolk-Virginia Beach-Newport News MSA, VA-NC	Y	58060 FQ	80420 AW	109810 TQ	VABLS	10/01-12/01
	Richmond-Petersburg MSA, VA	Y	51690 FQ	75560 AW	109230 TQ	VABLS	10/01-12/01
	Roanoke MSA, VA	Y	51080 FQ	79200 AW	112600 TQ	VABLS	10/01-12/01
	Washington	Y	60670 FQ	92620 AW	132590 TQ	WABLS	10/01-12/01
	Bremerton PMSA, WA	Y	61590 FQ	78850 AW	100900 TQ	WABLS	10/01-12/01
	Olympia PMSA, WA	Y	61250 FQ	84280 AW	117280 TQ	WABLS	10/01-12/01
	Richland-Kennewick-Pasco MSA, WA	Y	75940 FQ	99320 AW	119110 TQ	WABLS	10/01-12/01
	Seattle-Bellevue-Everett PMSA, WA	Y	60460 FQ	95260 AW	137740 TQ	WABLS	10/01-12/01
	Spokane MSA, WA	Y	57820 FQ	81270 AW	110680 TQ	WABLS	10/01-12/01
	Tacoma PMSA, WA	Y	63010 FQ	82230 AW	108190 TQ	WABLS	10/01-12/01
	Yakima MSA, WA	Y	56380 FQ	77380 AW	109080 TQ	WABLS	10/01-12/01
	West Virginia	Y	41630 FQ	71970 AW	105190 TQ	WVBLS	10/01-12/01
	Charleston MSA, WV	Y	46010 FQ	75030 AW	108060 TQ	WVBLS	10/01-12/01
	Huntington-Ashland MSA, WV-KY-OH	Y	54680 FQ	76040 AW	97750 TQ	WVBLS	10/01-12/01
	Wisconsin	Y	52900 FQ	78200 AW	111410 TQ	WIBLS	10/01-12/01
	Appleton-Oshkosh-Neenah MSA, WI	Y	56030 FQ	80200 AW	117590 TQ	WIBLS	10/01-12/01
	Green Bay MSA, WI	Y	55170 FQ	75840 AW	105990 TQ	WIBLS	10/01-12/01
	Madison MSA, WI	Y	53540 FQ	75930 AW	106370 TQ	WIBLS	10/01-12/01
	Milwaukee-Waukesha PMSA, WI	Y	57270 FQ	80900 AW	112160 TQ	WIBLS	10/01-12/01
	Racine PMSA, WI	Y	47240 FQ	78530 AW	111510 TQ	WIBLS	10/01-12/01
	Wyoming	Y	46880 FQ	72420 AW	109640 TQ	WYBLS	10/01-12/01
	Cheyenne MSA, WY	Y	44890 FQ	64670 AW	86800 TQ	WYBLS	10/01-12/01
	Puerto Rico	Y	43140 FQ	75510 AW	110720 TQ	PRBLS	10/01-12/01
	Guam	Y	28370 FQ	65630 AW	114220 TQ	GUBLS	10/01-12/01
Engineering Teacher							
Postsecondary	Alabama	Y	41840 FQ	72620 AW	111630 TQ	ALBLS	10/01-12/01
Postsecondary	California	Y	40180 FQ	72000 AW	111730 TQ	CABLS	10/01-12/01
Postsecondary	Orange County PMSA, CA	Y	41540 FQ	76230 AW	112200 TQ	CABLS	10/01-12/01
Postsecondary	San Francisco PMSA, CA	Y	38870 FQ	48880 AW	70530 TQ	CABLS	10/01-12/01
Postsecondary	San Jose PMSA, CA	Y	51280 FQ	67870 AW	89070 TQ	CABLS	10/01-12/01
Postsecondary	Colorado	Y	34680 FQ	69410 AW	113810 TQ	COBLS	10/01-12/01
Postsecondary	Connecticut	Y	42270 FQ	86430 AW		CTBLS	10/01-12/01
Postsecondary	District of Columbia	Y	41700 FQ	69080 AW	108080 TQ	DCBLS	10/01-12/01
Postsecondary	Washington PMSA, DC-MD-VA-WV	Y	42940 FQ	74990 AW	116440 TQ	DCBLS	10/01-12/01
Postsecondary	Florida	Y	42310 FQ	73960 AW	117490 TQ	FLBLS	10/01-12/01
Postsecondary	Fort Lauderdale PMSA, FL	Y	37230 FQ	50920 AW	61110 TQ	FLBLS	10/01-12/01
Postsecondary	Gainesville MSA, FL	Y	49810 FQ	80140 AW	122650 TQ	FLBLS	10/01-12/01
Postsecondary	Jacksonville MSA, FL	Y	37100 FQ	68620 AW	102790 TQ	FLBLS	10/01-12/01
Postsecondary	Melbourne-Titusville-Palm Bay MSA, FL	Y	38470 FQ	60750 AW	87240 TQ	FLBLS	10/01-12/01
Postsecondary	Miami PMSA, FL	Y	46440 FQ	78460 AW	132790 TQ	FLBLS	10/01-12/01
Postsecondary	Orlando MSA, FL	Y	41270 FQ	74830 AW	123030 TQ	FLBLS	10/01-12/01
Postsecondary	Tallahassee MSA, FL	Y	45390 FQ	72120 AW	107970 TQ	FLBLS	10/01-12/01
Postsecondary	Tampa-St. Petersburg-Clearwater MSA, FL	Y	39640 FQ	71830 AW	112470 TQ	FLBLS	10/01-12/01
Postsecondary	West Palm Beach-Boca Raton MSA, FL	Y	46040 FQ	75970 AW	122230 TQ	FLBLS	10/01-12/01

AAW Average annual wage; **AE** Average entry wage; **AEX** Average experienced wage; **AO** Average offered; **AOH** Average offered, high; **AOL** Average offered, low; **APH** Average pay, high range; **APL** Average pay, low range; **ASH** Average starting, high; **ASL** Average starting, low; **AW** Average wage paid; **FQ** First quartile wage; **H** Hourly; **HI** Highest wage paid; **HR** High end range; **LR** Low end range; **M** Monthly; **MTC** Median total compensation; **MW** Median wage paid; **SQ** Second quartile wage; **S** Special: hourly and annual; **TQ** Third quartile wage; **W** Weekly; **Y** Yearly

Occupation/Type/Industry	Location	Per	Low	Mid	High	Source	Date
Engineering Teacher							
Postsecondary	Georgia	Y	42540 FQ	62960 AW	86010 TQ	GABLS	10/01-12/01
Postsecondary	Atlanta MSA, GA	Y	40320 FQ	68110 AW	126180 TQ	GABLS	10/01-12/01
Postsecondary	Hawaii	Y	49890 FQ	74530 AW	108150 TQ	HIBLS	10/01-12/01
Postsecondary	Honolulu MSA, HI	Y	49820 FQ	74460 AW	108320 TQ	HIBLS	10/01-12/01
Postsecondary	Illinois	Y	16370 FQ	65550 AW	97540 TQ	ILBLS	10/01-12/01
Postsecondary	Chicago PMSA, IL	Y	15010 FQ	66610 AW	97880 TQ	ILBLS	10/01-12/01
Postsecondary	Indiana	Y	22210 FQ	62370 AW	103850 TQ	INBLS	10/01-12/01
Postsecondary	Kansas	Y	36600 FQ	62430 AW	94510 TQ	KSBLS	10/01-12/01
Postsecondary	Kentucky	Y	39020 FQ	71230 AW	108410 TQ	KYBLS	10/01-12/01
Postsecondary	Louisiana	Y	13530 FQ	64630 AW	110300 TQ	LABLS	10/01-12/01
Postsecondary	Maine	Y	35640 FQ	62660 AW	88590 TQ	MEBLS	10/01-12/01
Postsecondary	Maryland	Y	40280 FQ	76640 AW	120280 TQ	MDBLS	10/01-12/01
Postsecondary	Baltimore PMSA, MD	Y	38280 FQ	69600 AW	111120 TQ	MDBLS	10/01-12/01
Postsecondary	Massachusetts	Y	44340 FQ	71950 AW	107170 TQ	MABLS	10/01-12/01
Postsecondary	Boston PMSA, MA-NH	Y	43080 FQ	72380 AW	109560 TQ	MABLS	10/01-12/01
Postsecondary	Michigan	Y	47300 FQ	74320 AW	112160 TQ	MIBLS	10/01-12/01
Postsecondary	Detroit PMSA, MI	Y	50320 FQ	76280 AW	113670 TQ	MIBLS	10/01-12/01
Postsecondary	Minnesota	Y	45450 FQ	78500 AW	117820 TQ	MNBLS	10/01-12/01
Postsecondary	Minneapolis-St. Paul MSA, MN-WI	Y	57170 FQ	88270 AW	127290 TQ	MNBLS	10/01-12/01
Postsecondary	Mississippi	Y	35730 FQ	59760 AW	84210 TQ	MSBLS	10/01-12/01
Postsecondary	Missouri	Y	36250 FQ	68700 AW	108000 TQ	MOBLS	10/01-12/01
Postsecondary	St. Louis MSA, MO-IL	Y	37660 FQ	69770 AW	108580 TQ	MOBLS	10/01-12/01
Postsecondary	Montana	Y	31170 FQ	57480 AW	85730 TQ	MTBLS	10/01-12/01
Postsecondary	Nebraska	Y	47250 FQ	71530 AW	104000 TQ	NEBLS	10/01-12/01
Postsecondary	Omaha MSA, NE-IA	Y	51390 FQ	69680 AW	89730 TQ	NEBLS	10/01-12/01
Postsecondary	New Hampshire	Y	44430 FQ	76780 AW	118880 TQ	NHBLS	10/01-12/01
Postsecondary	New Jersey	Y	43540 FQ	76340 AW	120810 TQ	NJBLS	10/01-12/01
Postsecondary	Newark PMSA, NJ	Y	21130 FQ	62380 AW	100560 TQ	NJBLS	10/01-12/01
Postsecondary	New Mexico	Y	41110 FQ	60050 AW	81870 TQ	NMBLS	10/01-12/01
Postsecondary	New York	Y	43680 FQ	79780 AW		NYBLS	10/01-12/01
Postsecondary	Nassau-Suffolk PMSA, NY	Y	53940 FQ	78060 AW	108120 TQ	NYBLS	10/01-12/01
Postsecondary	New York PMSA, NY	Y	49280 FQ	85820 AW		NYBLS	10/01-12/01
Postsecondary	North Carolina	Y	41270 FQ	64590 AW	94770 TQ	NCBLS	10/01-12/01
Postsecondary	Charlotte-Gastonia-Rock Hill MSA, NC-SC	Y	41360 FQ	64210 AW	92310 TQ	NCBLS	10/01-12/01
Postsecondary	Greensboro-Winston-Salem-High Point MSA, NC	Y	45530 FQ	60090 AW	75740 TQ	NCBLS	10/01-12/01
Postsecondary	Raleigh-Durham-Chapel Hill MSA, NC	Y	47230 FQ	72600 AW	107470 TQ	NCBLS	10/01-12/01
Postsecondary	North Dakota	Y	40220 FQ	58660 AW	80390 TQ	NDBLS	10/01-12/01
Postsecondary	Fargo-Moorhead MSA, ND-MN	Y	42530 FQ	60950 AW	85710 TQ	NDBLS	10/01-12/01
Postsecondary	Ohio	Y	21510 FQ	58670 AW	91980 TQ	OHBLS	10/01-12/01
Postsecondary	Dayton-Springfield MSA, OH	Y	16890 FQ	47610 AW	79090 TQ	OHBLS	10/01-12/01
Postsecondary	Toledo MSA, OH	Y	23070 FQ	61320 AW	108720 TQ	OHBLS	10/01-12/01
Postsecondary	Youngstown-Warren MSA, OH	Y	37650 FQ	60170 AW	87350 TQ	OHBLS	10/01-12/01
Postsecondary	Oklahoma	Y	33850 FQ	56590 AW	89070 TQ	OKBLS	10/01-12/01
Postsecondary	Oklahoma City MSA, OK	Y	38150 FQ	61110 AW	95980 TQ	OKBLS	10/01-12/01
Postsecondary	Oregon	Y	44620 FQ	84090 AW	124480 TQ	ORBLS	10/01-12/01
Postsecondary	Portland-Vancouver PMSA, OR-WA	Y	41520 FQ	80090 AW	121410 TQ	ORBLS	10/01-12/01
Postsecondary	Pennsylvania	Y	32970 FQ	75220 AW	120340 TQ	PABLS	10/01-12/01
Postsecondary	Harrisburg-Lebanon-Carlisle MSA, PA	Y	28220 FQ	75620 AW	107420 TQ	PABLS	10/01-12/01
Postsecondary	Philadelphia PMSA, PA-NJ	Y	34180 FQ	74850 AW	120180 TQ	PABLS	10/01-12/01
Postsecondary	Pittsburgh MSA, PA	Y	30660 FQ	69310 AW	109130 TQ	PABLS	10/01-12/01
Postsecondary	Scranton-Wilkes-Barre-Hazleton MSA, PA	Y	30010 FQ	47360 AW	73460 TQ	PABLS	10/01-12/01
Postsecondary	Rhode Island	Y	39570 FQ	70470 AW	102340 TQ	RIBLS	10/01-12/01
Postsecondary	Providence-Fall River-Warwick MSA, RI-MA	Y	39480 FQ	70290 AW	102290 TQ	RIBLS	10/01-12/01
Postsecondary	South Carolina	Y	36540 FQ	50480 AW	73760 TQ	SCBLS	10/01-12/01
Postsecondary	Columbia MSA, SC	Y	32530 FQ	53160 AW	83270 TQ	SCBLS	10/01-12/01
Postsecondary	South Dakota	Y	39330 FQ	61680 AW	85650 TQ	SDBLS	10/01-12/01
Postsecondary	Tennessee	Y	38420 FQ	66220 AW	104700 TQ	TNBLS	10/01-12/01
Postsecondary	Memphis MSA, TN-AR-MS	Y	37190 FQ	57860 AW	81380 TQ	TNBLS	10/01-12/01
Postsecondary	Nashville MSA, TN	Y	37770 FQ	69530 AW	122610 TQ	TNBLS	10/01-12/01
Postsecondary	Texas	Y	37690 FQ	68570 AW	107720 TQ	TXBLS	10/01-12/01
Postsecondary	Dallas PMSA, TX	Y	39230 FQ	74460 AW	128060 TQ	TXBLS	10/01-12/01

AAW Average annual wage; AE Average entry wage; AEX Average experienced wage; AO Average offered; AOH Average offered, high; AOL Average offered, low; APH Average pay, high range; APL Average pay, low range; ASH Average starting, high; ASL Average starting, low; AW Average wage paid; FQ First quartile wage; H Hourly; HI Highest wage paid; HR High end range; LR Low end range; M Monthly; MTC Median total compensation; MW Median wage paid; SQ Second quartile wage; S Special: hourly and annual; TQ Third quartile wage; W Weekly; Y Yearly

Occupation/Type/Industry	Location	Per	Low	Mid	High	Source	Date
Engineering Teacher							
Postsecondary	Fort Worth-Arlington PMSA, TX	Y	37100 FQ	67780 AW	98360 TQ	TXBLS	10/01-12/01
Postsecondary	Houston PMSA, TX	Y	39100 FQ	69680 AW	107940 TQ	TXBLS	10/01-12/01
Postsecondary	Utah	Y	40340 FQ	76120 AW	116770 TQ	UTBLS	10/01-12/01
Postsecondary	Vermont	Y	35970 FQ	65870 AW	109190 TQ	VTBLS	10/01-12/01
Postsecondary	Virginia	Y	30900 FQ	74380 AW	130240 TQ	VABLS	10/01-12/01
Postsecondary	Richmond-Petersburg MSA, VA	Y	22580 FQ	53530 AW	94070 TQ	VABLS	10/01-12/01
Postsecondary	Washington	Y	42320 FQ	85270 AW	138690 TQ	WABLS	10/01-12/01
Postsecondary	Seattle-Bellevue-Everett PMSA, WA	Y	55420 FQ	96300 AW		WABLS	10/01-12/01
Postsecondary	Wisconsin	Y	41200 FQ	73710 AW	113100 TQ	WIBLS	10/01-12/01
Postsecondary	Wyoming	Y	42690 FQ	75160 AW	108980 TQ	WYBLS	10/01-12/01
Postsecondary	Puerto Rico	Y	27430 FQ	44190 AW	73550 TQ	PRBLS	10/01-12/01
English Language and Literature Teacher							
Postsecondary	Alabama	Y	16090 FQ	38930 AW	65090 TQ	ALBLS	10/01-12/01
Postsecondary	Birmingham MSA, AL	Y	21960 FQ	41510 AW	63100 TQ	ALBLS	10/01-12/01
Postsecondary	Huntsville MSA, AL	Y	17380 FQ	41210 AW	61050 TQ	ALBLS	10/01-12/01
Postsecondary	Mobile MSA, AL	Y	12640 FQ	32320 AW	52990 TQ	ALBLS	10/01-12/01
Postsecondary	Montgomery MSA, AL	Y	15530 FQ	38250 AW	62990 TQ	ALBLS	10/01-12/01
Postsecondary	Arizona	Y	19470 FQ	41010 AW	71790 TQ	AZBLS	10/01-12/01
Postsecondary	Arkansas	Y	20460 FQ	38560 AW	65890 TQ	ARBLS	10/01-12/01
Postsecondary	California	Y	32150 FQ	63890 AW	104800 TQ	CABLS	10/01-12/01
Postsecondary	Fresno MSA, CA	Y	25660 FQ	50170 AW	80820 TQ	CABLS	10/01-12/01
Postsecondary	Los Angeles-Long Beach PMSA, CA	Y	35100 FQ	66940 AW	107150 TQ	CABLS	10/01-12/01
Postsecondary	Oakland PMSA, CA	Y	27710 FQ	58210 AW	95220 TQ	CABLS	10/01-12/01
Postsecondary	Orange County PMSA, CA	Y	27460 FQ	61140 AW	109380 TQ	CABLS	10/01-12/01
Postsecondary	Riverside-San Bernardino PMSA, CA	Y	28260 FQ	56560 AW	93850 TQ	CABLS	10/01-12/01
Postsecondary	San Diego MSA, CA	Y	21820 FQ	57320 AW	94570 TQ	CABLS	10/01-12/01
Postsecondary	San Francisco PMSA, CA	Y	48460 FQ	80150 AW	117000 TQ	CABLS	10/01-12/01
Postsecondary	San Jose PMSA, CA	Y	37880 FQ	62870 AW	91740 TQ	CABLS	10/01-12/01
Postsecondary	Colorado	Y	26870 FQ	47660 AW	77050 TQ	COBLS	10/01-12/01
Postsecondary	Boulder-Longmont PMSA, CO	Y	25510 FQ	37750 AW	50280 TQ	COBLS	10/01-12/01
Postsecondary	Colorado Springs MSA, CO	Y	26810 FQ	53610 AW	87710 TQ	COBLS	10/01-12/01
Postsecondary	Denver PMSA, CO	Y	29370 FQ	48050 AW	77860 TQ	COBLS	10/01-12/01
Postsecondary	Fort Collins-Loveland MSA, CO	Y	26830 FQ	48330 AW	75980 TQ	COBLS	10/01-12/01
Postsecondary	Connecticut	Y	32890 FQ	53460 AW	83730 TQ	CTBLS	10/01-12/01
Postsecondary	Bridgeport PMSA, CT	Y	38780 FQ	57700 AW	80380 TQ	CTBLS	10/01-12/01
Postsecondary	Hartford MSA, CT	Y	31550 FQ	60590 AW	93680 TQ	CTBLS	10/01-12/01
Postsecondary	New Haven-Meriden PMSA, CT	Y	33480 FQ	43800 AW	56460 TQ	CTBLS	10/01-12/01
Postsecondary	Delaware	Y	37600 FQ	57850 AW	91340 TQ	DEBLS	10/01-12/01
Postsecondary	Wilmington-Newark PMSA, DE-MD	Y	37610 FQ	59530 AW	96760 TQ	DEBLS	10/01-12/01
Postsecondary	District of Columbia	Y	30910 FQ	56490 AW	86440 TQ	DCBLS	10/01-12/01
Postsecondary	Washington PMSA, DC-MD-VA-WV	Y	24790 FQ	54410 AW	88200 TQ	DCBLS	10/01-12/01
Postsecondary	Florida	Y	25310 FQ	51130 AW	84220 TQ	FLBLS	10/01-12/01
Postsecondary	Fort Lauderdale PMSA, FL	Y	24630 FQ	50310 AW	80240 TQ	FLBLS	10/01-12/01
Postsecondary	Gainesville MSA, FL	Y	35650 FQ	61150 AW	90550 TQ	FLBLS	10/01-12/01
Postsecondary	Jacksonville MSA, FL	Y	29300 FQ	56350 AW	91650 TQ	FLBLS	10/01-12/01
Postsecondary	Miami PMSA, FL	Y	36030 FQ	57650 AW	93320 TQ	FLBLS	10/01-12/01
Postsecondary	Orlando MSA, FL	Y	21770 FQ	44760 AW	76420 TQ	FLBLS	10/01-12/01
Postsecondary	Tallahassee MSA, FL	Y	35620 FQ	61430 AW	97340 TQ	FLBLS	10/01-12/01
Postsecondary	Tampa-St. Petersburg-Clearwater MSA, FL	Y	30380 FQ	49490 AW	76870 TQ	FLBLS	10/01-12/01
Postsecondary	West Palm Beach-Boca Raton MSA, FL	Y	21020 FQ	49160 AW	84260 TQ	FLBLS	10/01-12/01
Postsecondary	Georgia	Y	30850 FQ	48280 AW	71920 TQ	GABLS	10/01-12/01
Postsecondary	Atlanta MSA, GA	Y	33900 FQ	53230 AW	76490 TQ	GABLS	10/01-12/01
Postsecondary	Savannah MSA, GA	Y	15270 FQ	40530 AW	59930 TQ	GABLS	10/01-12/01
Postsecondary	Hawaii	Y	31430 FQ	48810 AW	69960 TQ	HIBLS	10/01-12/01
Postsecondary	Honolulu MSA, HI	Y	30980 FQ	49420 AW	70880 TQ	HIBLS	10/01-12/01
Postsecondary	Idaho	Y	26300 FQ	46050 AW	58900 TQ	IDBLS	10/01-12/01
Postsecondary	Illinois	Y	19280 FQ	46020 AW	83430 TQ	ILBLS	10/01-12/01
Postsecondary	Champaign-Urbana MSA, IL	Y	13810 FQ	44270 AW	85200 TQ	ILBLS	10/01-12/01

AAW Average annual wage; **AE** Average entry wage; **AEX** Average experienced wage; **AO** Average offered; **AOH** Average offered, high; **AOL** Average offered, low; **APH** Average pay, high range; **APL** Average pay, low range; **ASH** Average starting, high; **ASL** Average starting, low; **AW** Average wage paid; **FQ** First quartile wage; **H** Hourly; **HI** Highest wage paid; **HR** High end range; **LR** Low end range; **M** Monthly; **MTC** Median total compensation; **MW** Median wage paid; **SQ** Second quartile wage; **S** Special: hourly and annual; **TQ** Third quartile wage; **W** Weekly; **Y** Yearly

Occupation/Type/Industry	Location	Per	Low	Mid	High	Source	Date
English Language and Literature Teacher							
Postsecondary	Chicago PMSA, IL	Y	18180 FQ	48390 AW	86490 TQ	ILBLS	10/01-12/01
Postsecondary	Rockford MSA, IL	Y	28660 FQ	45370 AW	68950 TQ	ILBLS	10/01-12/01
Postsecondary	Indiana	Y	19930 FQ	43110 AW	70830 TQ	INBLS	10/01-12/01
Postsecondary	Evansville-Henderson MSA, IN-KY	Y	20120 FQ	36550 AW	54420 TQ	INBLS	10/01-12/01
Postsecondary	Fort Wayne MSA, IN	Y	27100 FQ	43130 AW	62000 TQ	INBLS	10/01-12/01
Postsecondary	South Bend MSA, IN	Y	16260 FQ	41270 AW	63380 TQ	INBLS	10/01-12/01
Postsecondary	Iowa	Y	29630 FQ	54430 AW	86420 TQ	IABLS	10/01-12/01
Postsecondary	Cedar Rapids MSA, IA	Y	31290 FQ	43390 AW	63860 TQ	IABLS	10/01-12/01
Postsecondary	Davenport-Moline-Rock Island MSA, IA-IL	Y	31040 FQ	54210 AW	80730 TQ	IABLS	10/01-12/01
Postsecondary	Des Moines MSA, IA	Y	31410 FQ	48780 AW	69080 TQ	IABLS	10/01-12/01
Postsecondary	Kansas	Y	18430 FQ	34860 AW	56170 TQ	KSBLS	10/01-12/01
Postsecondary	Wichita MSA, KS	Y	23220 FQ	36930 AW	60830 TQ	KSBLS	10/01-12/01
Postsecondary	Kentucky	Y	23840 FQ	41940 AW	63570 TQ	KYBLS	10/01-12/01
Postsecondary	Lexington MSA, KY	Y	26040 FQ	43820 AW	73110 TQ	KYBLS	10/01-12/01
Postsecondary	Louisville MSA, KY-IN	Y	24480 FQ	42220 AW	62030 TQ	KYBLS	10/01-12/01
Postsecondary	Louisiana	Y	20860 FQ	39380 AW	60800 TQ	LABLS	10/01-12/01
Postsecondary	Lafayette MSA, LA	Y	24820 FQ	49540 AW	83950 TQ	LABLS	10/01-12/01
Postsecondary	New Orleans MSA, LA	Y	20680 FQ	39280 AW	58820 TQ	LABLS	10/01-12/01
Postsecondary	Maine	Y	31040 FQ	45240 AW	65970 TQ	MEBLS	10/01-12/01
Postsecondary	Portland MSA, ME	Y	31600 FQ	45520 AW	62040 TQ	MEBLS	10/01-12/01
Postsecondary	Maryland	Y	22970 FQ	51440 AW	89960 TQ	MDBLS	10/01-12/01
Postsecondary	Baltimore PMSA, MD	Y	27950 FQ	50270 AW	82080 TQ	MDBLS	10/01-12/01
Postsecondary	Massachusetts	Y	28160 FQ	50530 AW	80540 TQ	MABLS	10/01-12/01
Postsecondary	Boston PMSA, MA-NH	Y	26750 FQ	49410 AW	78330 TQ	MABLS	10/01-12/01
Postsecondary	Brockton PMSA, MA	Y	32060 FQ	49810 AW	71530 TQ	MABLS	10/01-12/01
Postsecondary	Springfield MSA, MA	Y	38630 FQ	60970 AW	101270 TQ	MABLS	10/01-12/01
Postsecondary	Worcester PMSA, MA-CT	Y	31950 FQ	56740 AW	93520 TQ	MABLS	10/01-12/01
Postsecondary	Michigan	Y	28520 FQ	54310 AW	83490 TQ	MIBLS	10/01-12/01
Postsecondary	Ann Arbor PMSA, MI	Y	31960 FQ	55050 AW	81200 TQ	MIBLS	10/01-12/01
Postsecondary	Detroit PMSA, MI	Y	26800 FQ	52880 AW	84450 TQ	MIBLS	10/01-12/01
Postsecondary	Grand Rapids-Muskegon-Holland MSA, MI	Y	29230 FQ	53680 AW	80620 TQ	MIBLS	10/01-12/01
Postsecondary	Minnesota	Y	30750 FQ	49530 AW	70060 TQ	MNBLS	10/01-12/01
Postsecondary	Duluth-Superior MSA, MN-WI	Y	28510 FQ	48860 AW	69310 TQ	MNBLS	10/01-12/01
Postsecondary	Minneapolis-St. Paul MSA, MN-WI	Y	33180 FQ	50590 AW	69380 TQ	MNBLS	10/01-12/01
Postsecondary	St. Cloud MSA, MN	Y	25860 FQ	40870 AW	57730 TQ	MNBLS	10/01-12/01
Postsecondary	Mississippi	Y	23100 FQ	42620 AW	59650 TQ	MSBLS	10/01-12/01
Postsecondary	Jackson MSA, MS	Y	14230 FQ	35320 AW	53640 TQ	MSBLS	10/01-12/01
Postsecondary	Missouri	Y	25330 FQ	42480 AW	64040 TQ	MOBLS	10/01-12/01
Postsecondary	Kansas City MSA, MO-KS	Y	24180 FQ	40910 AW	59680 TQ	MOBLS	10/01-12/01
Postsecondary	St. Louis MSA, MO-IL	Y	24710 FQ	40480 AW	62590 TQ	MOBLS	10/01-12/01
Postsecondary	Montana	Y	21030 FQ	39940 AW	60810 TQ	MTBLS	10/01-12/01
Postsecondary	Nebraska	Y	29670 FQ	48890 AW	71700 TQ	NEBLS	10/01-12/01
Postsecondary	Lincoln MSA, NE	Y	38420 FQ	56770 AW	84960 TQ	NEBLS	10/01-12/01
Postsecondary	Omaha MSA, NE-IA	Y	31500 FQ	43390 AW	56980 TQ	NEBLS	10/01-12/01
Postsecondary	Nevada	Y	26010 FQ	45610 AW	73930 TQ	NVBLS	10/01-12/01
Postsecondary	Las Vegas MSA, NV-AZ	Y	26340 FQ	44770 AW	70100 TQ	NVBLS	10/01-12/01
Postsecondary	New Hampshire	Y	32360 FQ	52870 AW	82740 TQ	NHBLS	10/01-12/01
Postsecondary	Manchester PMSA, NH	Y	32820 FQ	42140 AW	54100 TQ	NHBLS	10/01-12/01
Postsecondary	New Jersey	Y	29360 FQ	58970 AW	91860 TQ	NJBLS	10/01-12/01
Postsecondary	Bergen-Passaic PMSA, NJ	Y	31920 FQ	55280 AW	87290 TQ	NJBLS	10/01-12/01
Postsecondary	Jersey City PMSA, NJ	Y	33380 FQ	62520 AW	94960 TQ	NJBLS	10/01-12/01
Postsecondary	Monmouth-Ocean PMSA, NJ	Y	31560 FQ	58170 AW	87220 TQ	NJBLS	10/01-12/01
Postsecondary	Newark PMSA, NJ	Y	20650 FQ	56110 AW	90820 TQ	NJBLS	10/01-12/01
Postsecondary	New Mexico	Y	28790 FQ	44940 AW	63950 TQ	NMBLS	10/01-12/01
Postsecondary	New York	Y	32410 FQ	57690 AW	99030 TQ	NYBLS	10/01-12/01
Postsecondary	Albany-Schenectady-Troy MSA, NY	Y	36950 FQ	54010 AW	84190 TQ	NYBLS	10/01-12/01
Postsecondary	Buffalo-Niagara Falls MSA, NY	Y	25510 FQ	47310 AW	68910 TQ	NYBLS	10/01-12/01
Postsecondary	Dutchess County PMSA, NY	Y	35500 FQ	57250 AW	105720 TQ	NYBLS	10/01-12/01
Postsecondary	Nassau-Suffolk PMSA, NY	Y	31570 FQ	56790 AW	87780 TQ	NYBLS	10/01-12/01
Postsecondary	New York PMSA, NY	Y	35980 FQ	59720 AW	103600 TQ	NYBLS	10/01-12/01
Postsecondary	Rochester MSA, NY	Y	24590 FQ	46750 AW	74930 TQ	NYBLS	10/01-12/01
Postsecondary	Syracuse MSA, NY	Y	38840 FQ	70920 AW	109870 TQ	NYBLS	10/01-12/01
Postsecondary	Utica-Rome MSA, NY	Y	29050 FQ	55910 AW	83690 TQ	NYBLS	10/01-12/01
Postsecondary	North Carolina	Y	28180 FQ	45010 AW	64940 TQ	NCBLS	10/01-12/01

Occupation/Type/Industry	Location	Per	Low	Mid	High	Source	Date
English Language and Literature Teacher							
Postsecondary	Asheville MSA, NC	Y	29800 FQ	50390 AW	68900 TQ	NCBLS	10/01-12/01
Postsecondary	Charlotte-Gastonia-Rock Hill MSA, NC-SC	Y	27040 FQ	45520 AW	67880 TQ	NCBLS	10/01-12/01
Postsecondary	Fayetteville MSA, NC	Y	27380 FQ	45510 AW	58190 TQ	NCBLS	10/01-12/01
Postsecondary	Greensboro-Winston-Salem-High Point MSA, NC	Y	30740 FQ	46070 AW	66160 TQ	NCBLS	10/01-12/01
Postsecondary	Hickory-Morganton-Lenoir MSA, NC	Y	32490 FQ	39970 AW	46880 TQ	NCBLS	10/01-12/01
Postsecondary	Raleigh-Durham-Chapel Hill MSA, NC	Y	23320 FQ	43790 AW	69450 TQ	NCBLS	10/01-12/01
Postsecondary	Wilmington MSA, NC	Y	35110 FQ	51280 AW	73070 TQ	NCBLS	10/01-12/01
Postsecondary	North Dakota	Y	21130 FQ	35460 AW	53820 TQ	NDBLS	10/01-12/01
Postsecondary	Fargo-Moorhead MSA, ND-MN	Y	24480 FQ	42340 AW	65630 TQ	NDBLS	10/01-12/01
Postsecondary	Ohio	Y	24810 FQ	45020 AW	70010 TQ	OHBLS	10/01-12/01
Postsecondary	Canton-Massillon MSA, OH	Y	24190 FQ	46110 AW	68010 TQ	OHBLS	10/01-12/01
Postsecondary	Cincinnati PMSA, OH-KY-IN	Y	26100 FQ	44280 AW	71910 TQ	OHBLS	10/01-12/01
Postsecondary	Cleveland-Lorain-Elyria PMSA, OH	Y	29310 FQ	51000 AW	79630 TQ	OHBLS	10/01-12/01
Postsecondary	Columbus MSA, OH	Y	27740 FQ	47050 AW	70400 TQ	OHBLS	10/01-12/01
Postsecondary	Dayton-Springfield MSA, OH	Y	17910 FQ	38940 AW	63590 TQ	OHBLS	10/01-12/01
Postsecondary	Toledo MSA, OH	Y	29650 FQ	46530 AW	70680 TQ	OHBLS	10/01-12/01
Postsecondary	Oklahoma	Y	24790 FQ	38460 AW	56050 TQ	OKBLS	10/01-12/01
Postsecondary	Oklahoma City MSA, OK	Y	24950 FQ	38430 AW	58380 TQ	OKBLS	10/01-12/01
Postsecondary	Tulsa MSA, OK	Y	23080 FQ	39130 AW	61710 TQ	OKBLS	10/01-12/01
Postsecondary	Oregon	Y	32990 FQ	57660 AW	87120 TQ	ORBLS	10/01-12/01
Postsecondary	Eugene-Springfield MSA, OR	Y	32660 FQ	59330 AW	89260 TQ	ORBLS	10/01-12/01
Postsecondary	Portland-Vancouver PMSA, OR-WA	Y	30710 FQ	56290 AW	86950 TQ	ORBLS	10/01-12/01
Postsecondary	Pennsylvania	Y	26780 FQ	56470 AW	93020 TQ	PABLS	10/01-12/01
Postsecondary	Allentown-Bethlehem-Easton MSA, PA	Y	26340 FQ	42610 AW	68200 TQ	PABLS	10/01-12/01
Postsecondary	Harrisburg-Lebanon-Carlisle MSA, PA	Y	25520 FQ	53700 AW	88000 TQ	PABLS	10/01-12/01
Postsecondary	Johnstown MSA, PA	Y	30460 FQ	55870 AW	123280 TQ	PABLS	10/01-12/01
Postsecondary	Lancaster MSA, PA	Y	36030 FQ	57600 AW	86810 TQ	PABLS	10/01-12/01
Postsecondary	Philadelphia PMSA, PA-NJ	Y	27520 FQ	59680 AW	118080 TQ	PABLS	10/01-12/01
Postsecondary	Pittsburgh MSA, PA	Y	25160 FQ	51780 AW	87570 TQ	PABLS	10/01-12/01
Postsecondary	Reading MSA, PA	Y	28180 FQ	61860 AW	128880 TQ	PABLS	10/01-12/01
Postsecondary	Scranton-Wilkes-Barre-Hazleton MSA, PA	Y	31870 FQ	51170 AW	75560 TQ	PABLS	10/01-12/01
Postsecondary	Rhode Island	Y	38450 FQ	61570 AW	87220 TQ	RIBLS	10/01-12/01
Postsecondary	Providence-Fall River-Warwick MSA, RI-MA	Y	37770 FQ	61080 AW	87320 TQ	RIBLS	10/01-12/01
Postsecondary	South Carolina	Y	29230 FQ	42580 AW	58190 TQ	SCBLS	10/01-12/01
Postsecondary	Columbia MSA, SC	Y	24490 FQ	43330 AW	58500 TQ	SCBLS	10/01-12/01
Postsecondary	Greenville-Spartanburg-Anderson MSA, SC	Y	26680 FQ	40260 AW	55810 TQ	SCBLS	10/01-12/01
Postsecondary	South Dakota	Y	29190 FQ	41410 AW	56270 TQ	SDBLS	10/01-12/01
Postsecondary	Tennessee	Y	24350 FQ	42390 AW	63500 TQ	TNBLS	10/01-12/01
Postsecondary	Chattanooga MSA, TN-GA	Y	27790 FQ	41000 AW	56770 TQ	TNBLS	10/01-12/01
Postsecondary	Johnson City-Kingsport-Bristol MSA, TN-VA	Y	21030 FQ	36570 AW	56120 TQ	TNBLS	10/01-12/01
Postsecondary	Knoxville MSA, TN	Y	25230 FQ	42250 AW	66430 TQ	TNBLS	10/01-12/01
Postsecondary	Memphis MSA, TN-AR-MS	Y	26300 FQ	43390 AW	63000 TQ	TNBLS	10/01-12/01
Postsecondary	Nashville MSA, TN	Y	28520 FQ	47800 AW	71590 TQ	TNBLS	10/01-12/01
Postsecondary	Texas	Y	20800 FQ	46790 AW	73180 TQ	TXBLS	10/01-12/01
Postsecondary	Austin-San Marcos MSA, TX	Y	36370 FQ	55100 AW	73130 TQ	TXBLS	10/01-12/01
Postsecondary	Dallas PMSA, TX	Y	21300 FQ	55210 AW	118520 TQ	TXBLS	10/01-12/01
Postsecondary	Fort Worth-Arlington PMSA, TX	Y	19460 FQ	44380 AW	70540 TQ	TXBLS	10/01-12/01
Postsecondary	Houston PMSA, TX	Y	33620 FQ	53530 AW	90710 TQ	TXBLS	10/01-12/01
Postsecondary	Killeen-Temple MSA, TX	Y	31560 FQ	48860 AW	69060 TQ	TXBLS	10/01-12/01
Postsecondary	Longview-Marshall MSA, TX	Y	26460 FQ	41120 AW	57360 TQ	TXBLS	10/01-12/01
Postsecondary	McAllen-Edinburg-Mission MSA, TX	Y	28100 FQ	48460 AW	71410 TQ	TXBLS	10/01-12/01
Postsecondary	Odessa-Midland MSA, TX	Y	19690 FQ	39010 AW	55630 TQ	TXBLS	10/01-12/01
Postsecondary	San Antonio MSA, TX	Y	19090 FQ	44440 AW	73260 TQ	TXBLS	10/01-12/01
Postsecondary	Tyler MSA, TX	Y	30900 FQ	42330 AW	57510 TQ	TXBLS	10/01-12/01
Postsecondary	Utah	Y	33810 FQ	51050 AW	80510 TQ	UTBLS	10/01-12/01

AAW	Average annual wage	AOH	Average offered, high	ASH	Average starting, high	H	Hourly	M	Monthly	S	Special: hourly and annual
AE	Average entry wage	AOL	Average offered, low	ASL	Average starting, low	HI	Highest wage paid	MTC	Median total compensation	TQ	Third quartile wage
AEX	Average experienced wage	APH	Average pay, high range	AW	Average wage paid	HR	High end range	MW	Median wage paid	W	Weekly
AO	Average offered	APL	Average pay, low range	FQ	First quartile wage	LR	Low end range	SQ	Second quartile wage	Y	Yearly

Occupation/Type/Industry	Location	Per	Low	Mid	High	Source	Date
English Language and Literature Teacher							
Postsecondary	Salt Lake City-Ogden MSA, UT	Y	36390 FQ	51960 AW	82910 TQ	UTBLS	10/01-12/01
Postsecondary	Vermont	Y	35970 FQ	51010 AW	64240 TQ	VTBLS	10/01-12/01
Postsecondary	Burlington MSA, VT	Y	37510 FQ	52930 AW	71000 TQ	VTBLS	10/01-12/01
Postsecondary	Virginia	Y	26440 FQ	49990 AW	77130 TQ	VABLS	10/01-12/01
Postsecondary	Norfolk-Virginia Beach-Newport News MSA, VA-NC	Y	32080 FQ	49400 AW	71240 TQ	VABLS	10/01-12/01
Postsecondary	Richmond-Petersburg MSA, VA	Y	21850 FQ	43120 AW	68170 TQ	VABLS	10/01-12/01
Postsecondary	Roanoke MSA, VA	Y	31220 FQ	46180 AW	70050 TQ	VABLS	10/01-12/01
Postsecondary	Washington	Y	26200 FQ	48300 AW	79330 TQ	WABLS	10/01-12/01
Postsecondary	Seattle-Bellevue-Everett PMSA, WA	Y	29610 FQ	53240 AW	89820 TQ	WABLS	10/01-12/01
Postsecondary	Tacoma PMSA, WA	Y	29280 FQ	49310 AW	81460 TQ	WABLS	10/01-12/01
Postsecondary	West Virginia	Y	29620 FQ	49100 AW	72480 TQ	WVBLS	10/01-12/01
Postsecondary	Wisconsin	Y	25790 FQ	43210 AW	62770 TQ	WIBLS	10/01-12/01
Postsecondary	Green Bay MSA, WI	Y	26390 FQ	38450 AW	55150 TQ	WIBLS	10/01-12/01
Postsecondary	Milwaukee-Waukesha PMSA, WI	Y	20720 FQ	40260 AW	62200 TQ	WIBLS	10/01-12/01
Postsecondary	Wyoming	Y	31410 FQ	45220 AW	64160 TQ	WYBLS	10/01-12/01
Postsecondary	Puerto Rico	Y	28520 FQ	43500 AW	69360 TQ	PRBLS	10/01-12/01
Environmental Engineer	Alabama	Y	29170 FQ	53020 AW	81950 TQ	ALBLS	10/01-12/01
	Birmingham MSA, AL	Y	37820 FQ	58940 AW	86150 TQ	ALBLS	10/01-12/01
	Huntsville MSA, AL	Y	27020 FQ	50980 AW	83640 TQ	ALBLS	10/01-12/01
	Mobile MSA, AL	Y	28820 FQ	58970 AW	85350 TQ	ALBLS	10/01-12/01
	Montgomery MSA, AL	Y	35530 FQ	47880 AW	76310 TQ	ALBLS	10/01-12/01
	Alaska	Y	51090 FQ	77590 AW	113370 TQ	AKBLS	10/01-12/01
	Anchorage MSA, AK	Y	46960 FQ	72930 AW	102770 TQ	AKBLS	10/01-12/01
	Arizona	Y	41530 FQ	64420 AW	90560 TQ	AZBLS	10/01-12/01
	Phoenix-Mesa MSA, AZ	Y	42810 FQ	65810 AW	91720 TQ	AZBLS	10/01-12/01
	Tucson MSA, AZ	Y	37790 FQ	55380 AW	71270 TQ	AZBLS	10/01-12/01
	Arkansas	Y	36430 FQ	61700 AW	89040 TQ	ARBLS	10/01-12/01
	Fayetteville-Springdale-Rogers MSA, AR	Y	36660 FQ	70180 AW	95970 TQ	ARBLS	10/01-12/01
	Little Rock-North Little Rock MSA, AR	Y	38610 FQ	62750 AW	89310 TQ	ARBLS	10/01-12/01
	California	Y	39520 FQ	64650 AW	95510 TQ	CABLS	10/01-12/01
	Bakersfield MSA, CA	Y	52780 FQ	76080 AW	105540 TQ	CABLS	10/01-12/01
	Fresno MSA, CA	Y	36730 FQ	54790 AW	82820 TQ	CABLS	10/01-12/01
	Los Angeles-Long Beach PMSA, CA	Y	43360 FQ	71500 AW	105960 TQ	CABLS	10/01-12/01
	Oakland PMSA, CA	Y	38710 FQ	65350 AW	93310 TQ	CABLS	10/01-12/01
	Orange County PMSA, CA	Y	32880 FQ	54430 AW	77810 TQ	CABLS	10/01-12/01
	Redding MSA, CA	Y	38710 FQ	57280 AW	81750 TQ	CABLS	10/01-12/01
	Riverside-San Bernardino PMSA, CA	Y	39760 FQ	59820 AW	81970 TQ	CABLS	10/01-12/01
	Sacramento PMSA, CA	Y	41410 FQ	59520 AW	76870 TQ	CABLS	10/01-12/01
	San Diego MSA, CA	Y	47390 FQ	64170 AW	84810 TQ	CABLS	10/01-12/01
	San Francisco PMSA, CA	Y	44370 FQ	72790 AW	101060 TQ	CABLS	10/01-12/01
	San Jose PMSA, CA	Y	47660 FQ	82380 AW	137210 TQ	CABLS	10/01-12/01
	Santa Rosa PMSA, CA	Y	39600 FQ	56680 AW	75650 TQ	CABLS	10/01-12/01
	Vallejo-Fairfield-Napa PMSA, CA	Y	46350 FQ	66110 AW	95600 TQ	CABLS	10/01-12/01
	Ventura PMSA, CA	Y	40760 FQ	61860 AW	85100 TQ	CABLS	10/01-12/01
	Colorado	Y	36130 FQ	59910 AW	87250 TQ	COBLS	10/01-12/01
	Boulder-Longmont PMSA, CO	Y	38270 FQ	58430 AW	79530 TQ	COBLS	10/01-12/01
	Colorado Springs MSA, CO	Y	32710 FQ	47430 AW	56530 TQ	COBLS	10/01-12/01
	Denver PMSA, CO	Y	42090 FQ	65360 AW	88850 TQ	COBLS	10/01-12/01
	Fort Collins-Loveland MSA, CO	Y	30780 FQ	46230 AW	70530 TQ	COBLS	10/01-12/01
	Greeley PMSA, CO	Y	50110 FQ	72660 AW	97770 TQ	COBLS	10/01-12/01
	Connecticut	Y	39920 FQ	64610 AW	90270 TQ	CTBLS	10/01-12/01
	Bridgeport PMSA, CT	Y	45000 FQ	72770 AW	90960 TQ	CTBLS	10/01-12/01
	Hartford MSA, CT	Y	40460 FQ	63550 AW	88250 TQ	CTBLS	10/01-12/01
	New Haven-Meriden PMSA, CT	Y	35650 FQ	62880 AW	102670 TQ	CTBLS	10/01-12/01
	Stamford-Norwalk PMSA, CT	Y	38800 FQ	68660 AW	117930 TQ	CTBLS	10/01-12/01
	Delaware	Y	38650 FQ	52440 AW	79890 TQ	DEBLS	10/01-12/01

AAW	Average annual wage	AOH	Average offered, high	ASH	Average starting, high	H	Hourly	M	Monthly	S	Special: hourly and annual
AE	Average entry wage	AOL	Average offered, low	ASL	Average starting, low	HI	Highest wage paid	MTC	Median total compensation	TQ	Third quartile wage
AEX	Average experienced wage	APH	Average pay, high range	AW	Average wage paid	HR	High end range	MW	Median wage paid	W	Weekly
AO	Average offered	APL	Average pay, low range	FQ	First quartile wage	LR	Low end range	SQ	Second quartile wage	Y	Yearly

Occupation/Type/Industry	Location	Per	Low	Mid	High	Source	Date
Environmental Engineer	Wilmington-Newark PMSA, DE-MD	Y	38730 FQ	52140 AW	80020 TQ	DEBLS	10/01-12/01
	District of Columbia	Y	43800 FQ	68130 AW	98790 TQ	DCBLS	10/01-12/01
	Washington PMSA, DC-MD-VA-WV	Y	51820 FQ	69800 AW	88990 TQ	DCBLS	10/01-12/01
	Florida	Y	36840 FQ	66210 AW	105730 TQ	FLBLS	10/01-12/01
	Fort Lauderdale PMSA, FL	Y	41690 FQ	64940 AW	85970 TQ	FLBLS	10/01-12/01
	Fort Myers-Cape Coral MSA, FL	Y	25960 FQ	63060 AW	109000 TQ	FLBLS	10/01-12/01
	Fort Walton Beach MSA, FL	Y	47330 FQ	74240 AW	104210 TQ	FLBLS	10/01-12/01
	Gainesville MSA, FL	Y	34830 FQ	55530 AW	83620 TQ	FLBLS	10/01-12/01
	Jacksonville MSA, FL	Y	43020 FQ	65090 AW	94160 TQ	FLBLS	10/01-12/01
	Lakeland-Winter Haven MSA, FL	Y	37370 FQ	63240 AW	99010 TQ	FLBLS	10/01-12/01
	Melbourne-Titusville-Palm Bay MSA, FL	Y	33900 FQ	55000 AW	75260 TQ	FLBLS	10/01-12/01
	Miami PMSA, FL	Y	46480 FQ	60970 AW	83870 TQ	FLBLS	10/01-12/01
	Orlando MSA, FL	Y	36380 FQ	68040 AW	130880 TQ	FLBLS	10/01-12/01
	Pensacola MSA, FL	Y	35040 FQ	64820 AW	104500 TQ	FLBLS	10/01-12/01
	Sarasota-Bradenton MSA, FL	Y	40840 FQ	61610 AW	81930 TQ	FLBLS	10/01-12/01
	Tallahassee MSA, FL	Y	57930 FQ	89620 AW	131110 TQ	FLBLS	10/01-12/01
	Tampa-St. Petersburg-Clearwater MSA, FL	Y	39220 FQ	67630 AW	117150 TQ	FLBLS	10/01-12/01
	West Palm Beach-Boca Raton MSA, FL	Y	27830 FQ	56960 AW	107130 TQ	FLBLS	10/01-12/01
	Georgia	Y	37380 FQ	57770 AW	82300 TQ	GABLS	10/01-12/01
	Atlanta MSA, GA	Y	37270 FQ	57650 AW	81800 TQ	GABLS	10/01-12/01
	Augusta-Aiken MSA, GA-SC	Y	46370 FQ	69980 AW	95060 TQ	GABLS	10/01-12/01
	Macon MSA, GA	Y	46420 FQ	62790 AW	83400 TQ	GABLS	10/01-12/01
	Savannah MSA, GA	Y	38680 FQ	60550 AW	85970 TQ	GABLS	10/01-12/01
	Hawaii	Y	43130 FQ	70000 AW	88720 TQ	HIBLS	10/01-12/01
	Honolulu MSA, HI	Y	43960 FQ	71100 AW	88890 TQ	HIBLS	10/01-12/01
	Idaho	Y	40670 FQ	63110 AW	89490 TQ	IDBLS	10/01-12/01
	Illinois	Y	35200 FQ	59800 AW	87410 TQ	ILBLS	10/01-12/01
	Chicago PMSA, IL	Y	34170 FQ	62670 AW	89960 TQ	ILBLS	10/01-12/01
	Indiana	Y	29440 FQ	53580 AW	80820 TQ	INBLS	10/01-12/01
	Evansville-Henderson MSA, IN-KY	Y	28980 FQ	51700 AW	73640 TQ	INBLS	10/01-12/01
	Fort Wayne MSA, IN	Y	38180 FQ	54910 AW	72650 TQ	INBLS	10/01-12/01
	Gary PMSA, IN	Y	45550 FQ	67710 AW	88890 TQ	INBLS	10/01-12/01
	Indianapolis MSA, IN	Y	33440 FQ	52900 AW	72700 TQ	INBLS	10/01-12/01
	Iowa	Y	32560 FQ	49890 AW	70520 TQ	IABLS	10/01-12/01
	Davenport-Moline-Rock Island MSA, IA-IL	Y	29300 FQ	60790 AW	89410 TQ	IABLS	10/01-12/01
	Kansas	Y	34890 FQ	56720 AW	80020 TQ	KSBLS	10/01-12/01
	Wichita MSA, KS	Y	30870 FQ	44760 AW	67450 TQ	KSBLS	10/01-12/01
	Kentucky	Y	41260 FQ	59900 AW	81500 TQ	KYBLS	10/01-12/01
	Lexington MSA, KY	Y	48580 FQ	59500 AW	74890 TQ	KYBLS	10/01-12/01
	Louisville MSA, KY-IN	Y	40300 FQ	60060 AW	84100 TQ	KYBLS	10/01-12/01
	Louisiana	Y	35190 FQ	58400 AW	88560 TQ	LABLS	10/01-12/01
	Baton Rouge MSA, LA	Y	34410 FQ	54720 AW	82850 TQ	LABLS	10/01-12/01
	Lake Charles MSA, LA	Y	44000 FQ	68130 AW	89410 TQ	LABLS	10/01-12/01
	New Orleans MSA, LA	Y	34700 FQ	63610 AW	101620 TQ	LABLS	10/01-12/01
	Maine	Y	37150 FQ	56380 AW	79240 TQ	MEBLS	10/01-12/01
	Portland MSA, ME	Y	38050 FQ	57790 AW	77500 TQ	MEBLS	10/01-12/01
	Maryland	Y	41810 FQ	64990 AW	90210 TQ	MDBLS	10/01-12/01
	Baltimore PMSA, MD	Y	38690 FQ	59980 AW	85720 TQ	MDBLS	10/01-12/01
	Massachusetts	Y	38720 FQ	62000 AW	88030 TQ	MABLS	10/01-12/01
	Boston PMSA, MA-NH	Y	39060 FQ	62590 AW	87980 TQ	MABLS	10/01-12/01
	Brockton PMSA, MA	Y	43210 FQ	65320 AW	88790 TQ	MABLS	10/01-12/01
	Lawrence PMSA, MA-NH	Y	32760 FQ	50860 AW	80670 TQ	MABLS	10/01-12/01
	Lowell PMSA, MA-NH	Y	43540 FQ	71940 AW	106170 TQ	MABLS	10/01-12/01
	New Bedford PMSA, MA	Y	38810 FQ	59370 AW	86540 TQ	MABLS	10/01-12/01
	Springfield MSA, MA	Y	37260 FQ	60670 AW	85380 TQ	MABLS	10/01-12/01
	Michigan	Y	37840 FQ	57630 AW	82820 TQ	MIBLS	10/01-12/01
	Ann Arbor PMSA, MI	Y	34800 FQ	52820 AW	83060 TQ	MIBLS	10/01-12/01
	Detroit PMSA, MI	Y	35620 FQ	59410 AW	89050 TQ	MIBLS	10/01-12/01
	Grand Rapids-Muskegon-Holland MSA, MI	Y	37350 FQ	53800 AW	71260 TQ	MIBLS	10/01-12/01
	Saginaw-Bay City-Midland MSA, MI	Y	46300 FQ	64550 AW	90090 TQ	MIBLS	10/01-12/01
	Minnesota	Y	40080 FQ	63090 AW	90450 TQ	MNBLS	10/01-12/01

AAW	Average annual wage	**AOH**	Average offered, high	**ASH**	Average starting, high	**H**	Hourly	**M**	Monthly	**S**	Special: hourly and annual
AE	Average entry wage	**AOL**	Average offered, low	**ASL**	Average starting, low	**HI**	Highest wage paid	**MTC**	Median total compensation	**TQ**	Third quartile wage
AEX	Average experienced wage	**APH**	Average pay, high range	**AW**	Average wage paid	**HR**	High end range	**MW**	Median wage paid	**W**	Weekly
AO	Average offered	**APL**	Average pay, low range	**FQ**	First quartile wage	**LR**	Low end range	**SQ**	Second quartile wage	**Y**	Yearly

Occupation/Type/Industry	Location	Per	Low	Mid	High	Source	Date
Environmental Engineer	Minneapolis-St. Paul MSA, MN-WI	Y	41000 FQ	64760 AW	92650 TQ	MNBLS	10/01-12/01
	Mississippi	Y	30210 FQ	53660 AW	81170 TQ	MSBLS	10/01-12/01
	Biloxi-Gulfport-Pascagoula MSA, MS	Y	23340 FQ	52060 AW	77040 TQ	MSBLS	10/01-12/01
	Jackson MSA, MS	Y	30530 FQ	52540 AW	76790 TQ	MSBLS	10/01-12/01
	Missouri	Y	36580 FQ	58440 AW	95140 TQ	MOBLS	10/01-12/01
	Kansas City MSA, MO-KS	Y	42650 FQ	62400 AW	86150 TQ	MOBLS	10/01-12/01
	St. Louis MSA, MO-IL	Y	32830 FQ	62290 AW	103130 TQ	MOBLS	10/01-12/01
	Montana	Y	32070 FQ	49950 AW	71820 TQ	MTBLS	10/01-12/01
	Billings MSA, MT	Y	33650 FQ	60730 AW	100190 TQ	MTBLS	10/01-12/01
	Nebraska	Y	43080 FQ	66080 AW	89650 TQ	NEBLS	10/01-12/01
	Lincoln MSA, NE	Y	35990 FQ	50950 AW	68420 TQ	NEBLS	10/01-12/01
	Omaha MSA, NE-IA	Y	42560 FQ	62550 AW	86880 TQ	NEBLS	10/01-12/01
	Nevada	Y	44120 FQ	65500 AW	90580 TQ	NVBLS	10/01-12/01
	New Hampshire	Y	37010 FQ	57730 AW	80840 TQ	NHBLS	10/01-12/01
	Manchester PMSA, NH	Y	46640 FQ	66680 AW	98080 TQ	NHBLS	10/01-12/01
	Portsmouth-Rochester PMSA, NH-ME	Y	35730 FQ	56900 AW	81840 TQ	NHBLS	10/01-12/01
	New Jersey	Y	37400 FQ	64610 AW	100830 TQ	NJBLS	10/01-12/01
	Atlantic-Cape May PMSA, NJ	Y	41150 FQ	68400 AW	107220 TQ	NJBLS	10/01-12/01
	Bergen-Passaic PMSA, NJ	Y	36610 FQ	64350 AW	95300 TQ	NJBLS	10/01-12/01
	Jersey City PMSA, NJ	Y	53520 FQ	64980 AW	74400 TQ	NJBLS	10/01-12/01
	Middlesex-Somerset-Hunterdon PMSA, NJ	Y	35440 FQ	64700 AW	112770 TQ	NJBLS	10/01-12/01
	Monmouth-Ocean PMSA, NJ	Y	33240 FQ	57940 AW	85210 TQ	NJBLS	10/01-12/01
	Newark PMSA, NJ	Y	40860 FQ	70590 AW	112390 TQ	NJBLS	10/01-12/01
	New Mexico	Y	39130 FQ	67250 AW	106410 TQ	NMBLS	10/01-12/01
	Albuquerque MSA, NM	Y	39810 FQ	65680 AW	94700 TQ	NMBLS	10/01-12/01
	Las Cruces MSA, NM	Y	33230 FQ	50580 AW	69590 TQ	NMBLS	10/01-12/01
	New York	Y	41930 FQ	65970 AW	94280 TQ	NYBLS	10/01-12/01
	Albany-Schenectady-Troy MSA, NY	Y	45160 FQ	62200 AW	84360 TQ	NYBLS	10/01-12/01
	Binghamton MSA, NY	Y	49040 FQ	71050 AW	97260 TQ	NYBLS	10/01-12/01
	Buffalo-Niagara Falls MSA, NY	Y	33200 FQ	59160 AW	81050 TQ	NYBLS	10/01-12/01
	Nassau-Suffolk PMSA, NY	Y	36180 FQ	71410 AW	119880 TQ	NYBLS	10/01-12/01
	New York PMSA, NY	Y	42770 FQ	65250 AW	89420 TQ	NYBLS	10/01-12/01
	Newburgh PMSA, NY-PA	Y	38040 FQ	58850 AW	84460 TQ	NYBLS	10/01-12/01
	Rochester MSA, NY	Y	48820 FQ	71140 AW	96950 TQ	NYBLS	10/01-12/01
	Syracuse MSA, NY	Y	36800 FQ	53000 AW	73330 TQ	NYBLS	10/01-12/01
	Utica-Rome MSA, NY	Y	39000 FQ	55810 AW	71060 TQ	NYBLS	10/01-12/01
	North Carolina	Y	39580 FQ	59490 AW	87070 TQ	NCBLS	10/01-12/01
	Asheville MSA, NC	Y	37370 FQ	48040 AW	63780 TQ	NCBLS	10/01-12/01
	Charlotte-Gastonia-Rock Hill MSA, NC-SC	Y	36870 FQ	59260 AW	90010 TQ	NCBLS	10/01-12/01
	Fayetteville MSA, NC	Y	39210 FQ	53000 AW	70940 TQ	NCBLS	10/01-12/01
	Greensboro-Winston-Salem-High Point MSA, NC	Y	38790 FQ	58240 AW	85490 TQ	NCBLS	10/01-12/01
	Raleigh-Durham-Chapel Hill MSA, NC	Y	41080 FQ	61760 AW	88990 TQ	NCBLS	10/01-12/01
	Wilmington MSA, NC	Y	40810 FQ	64330 AW	88830 TQ	NCBLS	10/01-12/01
	North Dakota	Y	35360 FQ	49270 AW	71530 TQ	NDBLS	10/01-12/01
	Ohio	Y	39480 FQ	62810 AW	92060 TQ	OHBLS	10/01-12/01
	Akron PMSA, OH	Y	38730 FQ	57970 AW	82270 TQ	OHBLS	10/01-12/01
	Canton-Massillon MSA, OH	Y	31280 FQ	48930 AW	76020 TQ	OHBLS	10/01-12/01
	Cincinnati PMSA, OH-KY-IN	Y	36880 FQ	62190 AW	91220 TQ	OHBLS	10/01-12/01
	Cleveland-Lorain-Elyria PMSA, OH	Y	39300 FQ	61720 AW	88340 TQ	OHBLS	10/01-12/01
	Columbus MSA, OH	Y	39850 FQ	55370 AW	75820 TQ	OHBLS	10/01-12/01
	Dayton-Springfield MSA, OH	Y	41760 FQ	73250 AW	116080 TQ	OHBLS	10/01-12/01
	Toledo MSA, OH	Y	45470 FQ	56440 AW	73950 TQ	OHBLS	10/01-12/01
	Youngstown-Warren MSA, OH	Y	41770 FQ	62870 AW	86620 TQ	OHBLS	10/01-12/01
	Oklahoma	Y	35690 FQ	56270 AW	82740 TQ	OKBLS	10/01-12/01
	Oklahoma City MSA, OK	Y	38970 FQ	60690 AW	87410 TQ	OKBLS	10/01-12/01
	Tulsa MSA, OK	Y	36770 FQ	53480 AW	75370 TQ	OKBLS	10/01-12/01
	Oregon	Y	48120 FQ	67540 AW	90190 TQ	ORBLS	10/01-12/01
	Portland-Vancouver PMSA, OR-WA	Y	48300 FQ	71000 AW	97270 TQ	ORBLS	10/01-12/01
	Pennsylvania	Y	34590 FQ	60740 AW	89070 TQ	PABLS	10/01-12/01
	Allentown-Bethlehem-Easton MSA, PA	Y	37030 FQ	57800 AW	90180 TQ	PABLS	10/01-12/01

Occupation/Type/Industry	Location	Per	Low	Mid	High	Source	Date
Environmental Engineer	Harrisburg-Lebanon-Carlisle MSA, PA	Y	30290 FQ	55030 AW	84720 TQ	PABLS	10/01-12/01
	Philadelphia PMSA, PA-NJ	Y	38490 FQ	63080 AW	92610 TQ	PABLS	10/01-12/01
	Pittsburgh MSA, PA	Y	40750 FQ	65350 AW	92050 TQ	PABLS	10/01-12/01
	Reading MSA, PA	Y	33030 FQ	59110 AW	92670 TQ	PABLS	10/01-12/01
	Rhode Island	Y	41070 FQ	61690 AW	87650 TQ	RIBLS	10/01-12/01
	Providence-Fall River-Warwick MSA, RI-MA	Y	40670 FQ	60910 AW	86890 TQ	RIBLS	10/01-12/01
	South Carolina	Y	33720 FQ	53420 AW	82690 TQ	SCBLS	10/01-12/01
	Charleston-North Charleston MSA, SC	Y	34050 FQ	57370 AW	72680 TQ	SCBLS	10/01-12/01
	Columbia MSA, SC	Y	32160 FQ	43830 AW	56350 TQ	SCBLS	10/01-12/01
	Greenville-Spartanburg-Anderson MSA, SC	Y	37370 FQ	55730 AW	84410 TQ	SCBLS	10/01-12/01
	South Dakota	Y	36100 FQ	53440 AW	69910 TQ	SDBLS	10/01-12/01
	Tennessee	Y	34160 FQ	60230 AW	88440 TQ	TNBLS	10/01-12/01
	Chattanooga MSA, TN-GA	Y	38620 FQ	57130 AW	83390 TQ	TNBLS	10/01-12/01
	Johnson City-Kingsport-Bristol MSA, TN-VA	Y	37840 FQ	51050 AW	65820 TQ	TNBLS	10/01-12/01
	Knoxville MSA, TN	Y	35610 FQ	64240 AW	89300 TQ	TNBLS	10/01-12/01
	Memphis MSA, TN-AR-MS	Y	23270 FQ	48780 AW	77200 TQ	TNBLS	10/01-12/01
	Nashville MSA, TN	Y	35980 FQ	55260 AW	76130 TQ	TNBLS	10/01-12/01
	Texas	Y	37890 FQ	63850 AW	96180 TQ	TXBLS	10/01-12/01
	Austin-San Marcos MSA, TX	Y	47580 FQ	65690 AW	88290 TQ	TXBLS	10/01-12/01
	Beaumont-Port Arthur MSA, TX	Y	48040 FQ	67660 AW	99810 TQ	TXBLS	10/01-12/01
	Brazoria PMSA, TX	Y	44790 FQ	72260 AW	120330 TQ	TXBLS	10/01-12/01
	Corpus Christi MSA, TX	Y	44980 FQ	70610 AW	108080 TQ	TXBLS	10/01-12/01
	Dallas PMSA, TX	Y	36000 FQ	56810 AW	86380 TQ	TXBLS	10/01-12/01
	El Paso MSA, TX	Y	32390 FQ	52150 AW	75380 TQ	TXBLS	10/01-12/01
	Fort Worth-Arlington PMSA, TX	Y	27720 FQ	58980 AW	96460 TQ	TXBLS	10/01-12/01
	Galveston-Texas City PMSA, TX	Y	48220 FQ	68880 AW	90020 TQ	TXBLS	10/01-12/01
	Houston PMSA, TX	Y	45000 FQ	71910 AW	109200 TQ	TXBLS	10/01-12/01
	Odessa-Midland MSA, TX	Y	28190 FQ	63960 AW	96710 TQ	TXBLS	10/01-12/01
	San Antonio MSA, TX	Y	43750 FQ	62540 AW	85830 TQ	TXBLS	10/01-12/01
	Utah	Y	39820 FQ	57450 AW	82750 TQ	UTBLS	10/01-12/01
	Salt Lake City-Ogden MSA, UT	Y	40620 FQ	57720 AW	83370 TQ	UTBLS	10/01-12/01
	Vermont	Y	39360 FQ	58530 AW	85020 TQ	VTBLS	10/01-12/01
	Virginia	Y	42770 FQ	67000 AW	89260 TQ	VABLS	10/01-12/01
	Lynchburg MSA, VA	Y	78350 FQ	84070 AW	96290 TQ	VABLS	10/01-12/01
	Norfolk-Virginia Beach-Newport News MSA, VA-NC	Y	39230 FQ	58200 AW	80880 TQ	VABLS	10/01-12/01
	Richmond-Petersburg MSA, VA	Y	37800 FQ	54020 AW	72070 TQ	VABLS	10/01-12/01
	Roanoke MSA, VA	Y	36790 FQ	50090 AW	69270 TQ	VABLS	10/01-12/01
	Washington	Y	46500 FQ	67560 AW	93160 TQ	WABLS	10/01-12/01
	Bremerton PMSA, WA	Y	47960 FQ	63750 AW	82510 TQ	WABLS	10/01-12/01
	Olympia PMSA, WA	Y	48600 FQ	59850 AW	71260 TQ	WABLS	10/01-12/01
	Richland-Kennewick-Pasco MSA, WA	Y	52800 FQ	73580 AW	97260 TQ	WABLS	10/01-12/01
	Seattle-Bellevue-Everett PMSA, WA	Y	42290 FQ	67140 AW	96820 TQ	WABLS	10/01-12/01
	Spokane MSA, WA	Y	49300 FQ	65730 AW	86130 TQ	WABLS	10/01-12/01
	Tacoma PMSA, WA	Y	53110 FQ	71340 AW	101880 TQ	WABLS	10/01-12/01
	West Virginia	Y	33340 FQ	56090 AW	84480 TQ	WVBLS	10/01-12/01
	Charleston MSA, WV	Y	38260 FQ	56280 AW	90710 TQ	WVBLS	10/01-12/01
	Wisconsin	Y	41140 FQ	61040 AW	84310 TQ	WIBLS	10/01-12/01
	Appleton-Oshkosh-Neenah MSA, WI	Y	39910 FQ	57670 AW	72410 TQ	WIBLS	10/01-12/01
	Green Bay MSA, WI	Y	42220 FQ	56980 AW	72470 TQ	WIBLS	10/01-12/01
	Madison MSA, WI	Y	44880 FQ	65550 AW	89860 TQ	WIBLS	10/01-12/01
	Milwaukee-Waukesha PMSA, WI	Y	41010 FQ	61220 AW	86600 TQ	WIBLS	10/01-12/01
	Wyoming	Y	38860 FQ	61280 AW	88830 TQ	WYBLS	10/01-12/01
	Puerto Rico	Y	28260 FQ	51450 AW	76740 TQ	PRBLS	10/01-12/01
Environmental Engineering Technician	Alabama	Y	17530 FQ	32230 AW	54720 TQ	ALBLS	10/01-12/01

AAW Average annual wage; AE Average entry wage; AEX Average experienced wage; AO Average offered; AOH Average offered, high; AOL Average offered, low; APH Average pay, high range; APL Average pay, low range; ASH Average starting, high; ASL Average starting, low; AW Average wage paid; FQ First quartile wage; H Hourly; HI Highest wage paid; HR High end range; LR Low end range; M Monthly; MTC Median total compensation; MW Median wage paid; SQ Second quartile wage; S Special: hourly and annual; TQ Third quartile wage; W Weekly; Y Yearly

Occupation/Type/Industry	Location	Per	Low	Mid	High	Source	Date
Environmental Engineering Technician	Birmingham MSA, AL	Y	18830 FQ	29440 AW	46260 TQ	ALBLS	10/01-12/01
	Alaska	Y	31360 FQ	41780 AW	54870 TQ	AKBLS	10/01-12/01
	Arizona	Y	25450 FQ	37600 AW	53460 TQ	AZBLS	10/01-12/01
	Phoenix-Mesa MSA, AZ	Y	25700 FQ	38790 AW	54280 TQ	AZBLS	10/01-12/01
	Tucson MSA, AZ	Y	25370 FQ	33030 AW	41480 TQ	AZBLS	10/01-12/01
	Arkansas	Y	21520 FQ	36740 AW	52180 TQ	ARBLS	10/01-12/01
	Fayetteville-Springdale-Rogers MSA, AR	Y	20640 FQ	32090 AW	49010 TQ	ARBLS	10/01-12/01
	Little Rock-North Little Rock MSA, AR	Y	20730 FQ	33050 AW	46870 TQ	ARBLS	10/01-12/01
	California	Y	26130 FQ	42930 AW	64070 TQ	CABLS	10/01-12/01
	Bakersfield MSA, CA	Y	20920 FQ	33700 AW	45920 TQ	CABLS	10/01-12/01
	Los Angeles-Long Beach PMSA, CA	Y	31570 FQ	48920 AW	67280 TQ	CABLS	10/01-12/01
	Oakland PMSA, CA	Y	30770 FQ	46340 AW	66310 TQ	CABLS	10/01-12/01
	Orange County PMSA, CA	Y	24510 FQ	39740 AW	54560 TQ	CABLS	10/01-12/01
	Riverside-San Bernardino PMSA, CA	Y	27730 FQ	43290 AW	70370 TQ	CABLS	10/01-12/01
	Sacramento PMSA, CA	Y	24000 FQ	35210 AW	45740 TQ	CABLS	10/01-12/01
	Salinas MSA, CA	Y	29530 FQ	43350 AW	57730 TQ	CABLS	10/01-12/01
	San Diego MSA, CA	Y	20170 FQ	36610 AW	55710 TQ	CABLS	10/01-12/01
	San Francisco PMSA, CA	Y	25920 FQ	43070 AW	57450 TQ	CABLS	10/01-12/01
	San Jose PMSA, CA	Y	29730 FQ	41590 AW	57270 TQ	CABLS	10/01-12/01
	Santa Rosa PMSA, CA	Y	29390 FQ	41260 AW	55670 TQ	CABLS	10/01-12/01
	Ventura PMSA, CA	Y	20730 FQ	40920 AW	70390 TQ	CABLS	10/01-12/01
	Colorado	Y	24640 FQ	37910 AW	61180 TQ	COBLS	10/01-12/01
	Colorado Springs MSA, CO	Y	23950 FQ	29990 AW	37200 TQ	COBLS	10/01-12/01
	Denver PMSA, CO	Y	31340 FQ	47290 AW	69900 TQ	COBLS	10/01-12/01
	Fort Collins-Loveland MSA, CO	Y	24200 FQ	32120 AW	46160 TQ	COBLS	10/01-12/01
	Connecticut	Y	26000 FQ	42720 AW	66070 TQ	CTBLS	10/01-12/01
	Hartford MSA, CT	Y	25420 FQ	40590 AW	63990 TQ	CTBLS	10/01-12/01
	Delaware	Y	23820 FQ	33650 AW	49530 TQ	DEBLS	10/01-12/01
	Washington PMSA, DC-MD-VA-WV	Y	23950 FQ	35070 AW	46260 TQ	DCBLS	10/01-12/01
	Florida	Y	20790 FQ	33340 AW	48200 TQ	FLBLS	10/01-12/01
	Fort Lauderdale PMSA, FL	Y	20310 FQ	32990 AW	54250 TQ	FLBLS	10/01-12/01
	Fort Myers-Cape Coral MSA, FL	Y	20600 FQ	30620 AW	42900 TQ	FLBLS	10/01-12/01
	Fort Walton Beach MSA, FL	Y	14390 FQ	22320 AW	30530 TQ	FLBLS	10/01-12/01
	Gainesville MSA, FL	Y	23340 FQ	44590 AW	68660 TQ	FLBLS	10/01-12/01
	Jacksonville MSA, FL	Y	22200 FQ	32960 AW	53340 TQ	FLBLS	10/01-12/01
	Lakeland-Winter Haven MSA, FL	Y	20170 FQ	37950 AW	53830 TQ	FLBLS	10/01-12/01
	Miami PMSA, FL	Y	19770 FQ	30950 AW	43400 TQ	FLBLS	10/01-12/01
	Orlando MSA, FL	Y	25060 FQ	31310 AW	37830 TQ	FLBLS	10/01-12/01
	Sarasota-Bradenton MSA, FL	Y	17520 FQ	24960 AW	36180 TQ	FLBLS	10/01-12/01
	Tampa-St. Petersburg-Clearwater MSA, FL	Y	24320 FQ	34540 AW	50250 TQ	FLBLS	10/01-12/01
	West Palm Beach-Boca Raton MSA, FL	Y	21270 FQ	35710 AW	47240 TQ	FLBLS	10/01-12/01
	Georgia	Y	21430 FQ	41450 AW	60790 TQ	GABLS	10/01-12/01
	Atlanta MSA, GA	Y	20470 FQ	41430 AW	60790 TQ	GABLS	10/01-12/01
	Hawaii	Y	27990 FQ	39660 AW	58470 TQ	HIBLS	10/01-12/01
	Honolulu MSA, HI	Y	27620 FQ	40220 AW	59120 TQ	HIBLS	10/01-12/01
	Idaho	Y	27840 FQ	38560 AW	51050 TQ	IDBLS	10/01-12/01
	Boise City MSA, ID	Y	27720 FQ	39960 AW	53380 TQ	IDBLS	10/01-12/01
	Illinois	Y	21750 FQ	38930 AW	61580 TQ	ILBLS	10/01-12/01
	Chicago PMSA, IL	Y	25230 FQ	42010 AW	67100 TQ	ILBLS	10/01-12/01
	Springfield MSA, IL	Y	19480 FQ	31010 AW	44290 TQ	ILBLS	10/01-12/01
	Indiana	Y	21620 FQ	36920 AW	51870 TQ	INBLS	10/01-12/01
	Gary PMSA, IN	Y	22410 FQ	36860 AW	47800 TQ	INBLS	10/01-12/01
	Indianapolis MSA, IN	Y	24490 FQ	39570 AW	60610 TQ	INBLS	10/01-12/01
	Iowa	Y	19880 FQ	36130 AW	48510 TQ	IABLS	10/01-12/01
	Kansas	Y	26160 FQ	41460 AW	62670 TQ	KSBLS	10/01-12/01
	Kentucky	Y	20500 FQ	35340 AW	52330 TQ	KYBLS	10/01-12/01
	Louisiana	Y	21900 FQ	37120 AW	59290 TQ	LABLS	10/01-12/01
	Baton Rouge MSA, LA	Y	24080 FQ	39590 AW	63240 TQ	LABLS	10/01-12/01
	Lake Charles MSA, LA	Y	22590 FQ	33690 AW	52270 TQ	LABLS	10/01-12/01
	New Orleans MSA, LA	Y	23510 FQ	39530 AW	64840 TQ	LABLS	10/01-12/01

AAW Average annual wage **AE** Average entry wage **AEX** Average experienced wage **AO** Average offered **AOH** Average offered, high **AOL** Average offered, low **APH** Average pay, high range **APL** Average pay, low range **ASH** Average starting, high **ASL** Average starting, low **AW** Average wage paid **FQ** First quartile wage **H** Hourly **HI** Highest wage paid **HR** High end range **LR** Low end range **M** Monthly **MTC** Median total compensation **MW** Median wage paid **SQ** Second quartile wage **S** Special: hourly and annual **TQ** Third quartile wage **W** Weekly **Y** Yearly

Occupation/Type/Industry	Location	Per	Low	Mid	High	Source	Date
Environmental Engineering Technician	Shreveport-Bossier City MSA, LA	Y	18490 FQ	29500 AW	43880 TQ	LABLS	10/01-12/01
	Maine	Y	27940 FQ	36360 AW	51340 TQ	MEBLS	10/01-12/01
	Maryland	Y	26260 FQ	40020 AW	53890 TQ	MDBLS	10/01-12/01
	Baltimore PMSA, MD	Y	26000 FQ	40430 AW	55900 TQ	MDBLS	10/01-12/01
	Massachusetts	Y	26100 FQ	39930 AW	56530 TQ	MABLS	10/01-12/01
	Boston PMSA, MA-NH	Y	28390 FQ	43000 AW	58680 TQ	MABLS	10/01-12/01
	Michigan	Y	26760 FQ	51790 AW	70590 TQ	MIBLS	10/01-12/01
	Detroit PMSA, MI	Y	29930 FQ	56820 AW	70510 TQ	MIBLS	10/01-12/01
	Grand Rapids-Muskegon-Holland MSA, MI	Y	24280 FQ	40660 AW	70800 TQ	MIBLS	10/01-12/01
	Saginaw-Bay City-Midland MSA, MI	Y	29580 FQ	53340 AW	71690 TQ	MIBLS	10/01-12/01
	Minnesota	Y	27510 FQ	40720 AW	56090 TQ	MNBLS	10/01-12/01
	Minneapolis-St. Paul MSA, MN-WI	Y	26050 FQ	39720 AW	55490 TQ	MNBLS	10/01-12/01
	Mississippi	Y	22200 FQ	36570 AW	52980 TQ	MSBLS	10/01-12/01
	Missouri	Y	21500 FQ	38080 AW	70760 TQ	MOBLS	10/01-12/01
	Kansas City MSA, MO-KS	Y	22010 FQ	29080 AW	39100 TQ	MOBLS	10/01-12/01
	St. Louis MSA, MO-IL	Y	21390 FQ	39700 AW	70420 TQ	MOBLS	10/01-12/01
	Montana	Y	21960 FQ	30600 AW	42290 TQ	MTBLS	10/01-12/01
	Nebraska	Y	19020 FQ	36250 AW	54800 TQ	NEBLS	10/01-12/01
	Nevada	Y	31870 FQ	46790 AW	63910 TQ	NVBLS	10/01-12/01
	Las Vegas MSA, NV-AZ	Y	27860 FQ	44160 AW	60120 TQ	NVBLS	10/01-12/01
	New Hampshire	Y	27120 FQ	37500 AW	51920 TQ	NHBLS	10/01-12/01
	Manchester PMSA, NH	Y	25980 FQ	38270 AW	53720 TQ	NHBLS	10/01-12/01
	Nashua PMSA, NH	Y	30490 FQ	38670 AW	51530 TQ	NHBLS	10/01-12/01
	New Jersey	Y	29010 FQ	45770 AW	68340 TQ	NJBLS	10/01-12/01
	Bergen-Passaic PMSA, NJ	Y	28180 FQ	44550 AW	69190 TQ	NJBLS	10/01-12/01
	Middlesex-Somerset-Hunterdon PMSA, NJ	Y	32650 FQ	51160 AW	69890 TQ	NJBLS	10/01-12/01
	Monmouth-Ocean PMSA, NJ	Y	26380 FQ	35340 AW	51250 TQ	NJBLS	10/01-12/01
	Newark PMSA, NJ	Y	25600 FQ	48490 AW	78070 TQ	NJBLS	10/01-12/01
	New Mexico	Y	18550 FQ	33400 AW	54630 TQ	NMBLS	10/01-12/01
	Albuquerque MSA, NM	Y	19660 FQ	36900 AW	56740 TQ	NMBLS	10/01-12/01
	New York	Y	25620 FQ	39830 AW	60120 TQ	NYBLS	10/01-12/01
	Albany-Schenectady-Troy MSA, NY	Y	33580 FQ	42670 AW	50300 TQ	NYBLS	10/01-12/01
	Binghamton MSA, NY	Y	12130 FQ	29450 AW	43880 TQ	NYBLS	10/01-12/01
	Buffalo-Niagara Falls MSA, NY	Y	28830 FQ	35220 AW	44220 TQ	NYBLS	10/01-12/01
	Nassau-Suffolk PMSA, NY	Y	29300 FQ	42850 AW	54720 TQ	NYBLS	10/01-12/01
	New York PMSA, NY	Y	24570 FQ	39550 AW	67230 TQ	NYBLS	10/01-12/01
	Rochester MSA, NY	Y	27020 FQ	40690 AW	53450 TQ	NYBLS	10/01-12/01
	Syracuse MSA, NY	Y	21960 FQ	38970 AW	63640 TQ	NYBLS	10/01-12/01
	North Carolina	Y	22230 FQ	37570 AW	51980 TQ	NCBLS	10/01-12/01
	Charlotte-Gastonia-Rock Hill MSA, NC-SC	Y	20980 FQ	35790 AW	44470 TQ	NCBLS	10/01-12/01
	Greensboro-Winston-Salem-High Point MSA, NC	Y	29870 FQ	38420 AW	44570 TQ	NCBLS	10/01-12/01
	Raleigh-Durham-Chapel Hill MSA, NC	Y	23680 FQ	38560 AW	55080 TQ	NCBLS	10/01-12/01
	Wilmington MSA, NC	Y	26970 FQ	42530 AW	54770 TQ	NCBLS	10/01-12/01
	Ohio	Y	22270 FQ	34210 AW	48450 TQ	OHBLS	10/01-12/01
	Cincinnati PMSA, OH-KY-IN	Y	22590 FQ	35870 AW	48130 TQ	OHBLS	10/01-12/01
	Cleveland-Lorain-Elyria PMSA, OH	Y	24720 FQ	34210 AW	45140 TQ	OHBLS	10/01-12/01
	Columbus MSA, OH	Y	24240 FQ	32850 AW	46700 TQ	OHBLS	10/01-12/01
	Dayton-Springfield MSA, OH	Y	23770 FQ	38900 AW	53650 TQ	OHBLS	10/01-12/01
	Hamilton-Middletown PMSA, OH	Y	19920 FQ	30420 AW	36390 TQ	OHBLS	10/01-12/01
	Toledo MSA, OH	Y	19750 FQ	31580 AW	47090 TQ	OHBLS	10/01-12/01
	Oklahoma	Y	20060 FQ	33410 AW	50660 TQ	OKBLS	10/01-12/01
	Oklahoma City MSA, OK	Y	18690 FQ	31630 AW	47610 TQ	OKBLS	10/01-12/01
	Tulsa MSA, OK	Y	21130 FQ	33840 AW	49740 TQ	OKBLS	10/01-12/01
	Oregon	Y	29150 FQ	41960 AW	57420 TQ	ORBLS	10/01-12/01
	Portland-Vancouver PMSA, OR-WA	Y	29180 FQ	42770 AW	58550 TQ	ORBLS	10/01-12/01
	Pennsylvania	Y	20820 FQ	35000 AW	60160 TQ	PABLS	10/01-12/01
	Allentown-Bethlehem-Easton MSA, PA	Y	24790 FQ	45110 AW	70320 TQ	PABLS	10/01-12/01

AAW	Average annual wage	**AOH**	Average offered, high	**ASH**	Average starting, high	**H**	Hourly	**M**	Monthly	**S**	Special: hourly and annual
AE	Average entry wage	**AOL**	Average offered, low	**ASL**	Average starting, low	**HI**	Highest wage paid	**MTC**	Median total compensation	**TQ**	Third quartile wage
AEX	Average experienced wage	**APH**	Average pay, high range	**AW**	Average wage paid	**HR**	High end range	**MW**	Median wage paid	**W**	Weekly
AO	Average offered	**APL**	Average pay, low range	**FQ**	First quartile wage	**LR**	Low end range	**SQ**	Second quartile wage	**Y**	Yearly

Occupation/Type/Industry	Location	Per	Low	Mid	High	Source	Date
Environmental Engineering Technician	Harrisburg-Lebanon-Carlisle MSA, PA	Y	23280 FQ	33170 AW	45110 TQ	PABLS	10/01-12/01
	Philadelphia PMSA, PA-NJ	Y	21700 FQ	37970 AW	64670 TQ	PABLS	10/01-12/01
	Pittsburgh MSA, PA	Y	24490 FQ	43490 AW	68170 TQ	PABLS	10/01-12/01
	Reading MSA, PA	Y	20500 FQ	30210 AW	48970 TQ	PABLS	10/01-12/01
	Rhode Island	Y	26260 FQ	37930 AW	45330 TQ	RIBLS	10/01-12/01
	Providence-Fall River-Warwick MSA, RI-MA	Y	28010 FQ	39570 AW	47040 TQ	RIBLS	10/01-12/01
	South Carolina	Y	25710 FQ	47980 AW	81010 TQ	SCBLS	10/01-12/01
	Charleston-North Charleston MSA, SC	Y	22180 FQ	43820 AW	63960 TQ	SCBLS	10/01-12/01
	Greenville-Spartanburg-Anderson MSA, SC	Y	23610 FQ	31660 AW	42030 TQ	SCBLS	10/01-12/01
	Tennessee	Y	23420 FQ	38160 AW	53950 TQ	TNBLS	10/01-12/01
	Johnson City-Kingsport-Bristol MSA, TN-VA	Y	20540 FQ	30180 AW	41240 TQ	TNBLS	10/01-12/01
	Knoxville MSA, TN	Y	23740 FQ	37480 AW	59490 TQ	TNBLS	10/01-12/01
	Nashville MSA, TN	Y	23250 FQ	38260 AW	56890 TQ	TNBLS	10/01-12/01
	Texas	Y	19100 FQ	35150 AW	56570 TQ	TXBLS	10/01-12/01
	Austin-San Marcos MSA, TX	Y	24500 FQ	32510 AW	42520 TQ	TXBLS	10/01-12/01
	Dallas PMSA, TX	Y	26210 FQ	45930 AW	68960 TQ	TXBLS	10/01-12/01
	El Paso MSA, TX	Y	16270 FQ	25970 AW	47240 TQ	TXBLS	10/01-12/01
	Houston PMSA, TX	Y	18810 FQ	32210 AW	46750 TQ	TXBLS	10/01-12/01
	San Antonio MSA, TX	Y	19900 FQ	33130 AW	54760 TQ	TXBLS	10/01-12/01
	Utah	Y	22520 FQ	36340 AW	53790 TQ	UTBLS	10/01-12/01
	Salt Lake City-Ogden MSA, UT	Y	22250 FQ	36110 AW	54110 TQ	UTBLS	10/01-12/01
	Virginia	Y	22230 FQ	34830 AW	52720 TQ	VABLS	10/01-12/01
	Norfolk-Virginia Beach-Newport News MSA, VA-NC	Y	23090 FQ	34980 AW	43610 TQ	VABLS	10/01-12/01
	Richmond-Petersburg MSA, VA	Y	23740 FQ	39240 AW	65420 TQ	VABLS	10/01-12/01
	Washington	Y	28820 FQ	45760 AW	74220 TQ	WABLS	10/01-12/01
	Richland-Kennewick-Pasco MSA, WA	Y	31640 FQ	57080 AW	87650 TQ	WABLS	10/01-12/01
	Seattle-Bellevue-Everett PMSA, WA	Y	27110 FQ	39040 AW	51850 TQ	WABLS	10/01-12/01
	West Virginia	Y	21070 FQ	35790 AW	52160 TQ	WVBLS	10/01-12/01
	Wisconsin	Y	25720 FQ	40580 AW	62970 TQ	WIBLS	10/01-12/01
	Green Bay MSA, WI	Y	30960 FQ	43970 AW	68020 TQ	WIBLS	10/01-12/01
	Madison MSA, WI	Y	25020 FQ	38880 AW	55760 TQ	WIBLS	10/01-12/01
	Milwaukee-Waukesha PMSA, WI	Y	28350 FQ	44120 AW	65950 TQ	WIBLS	10/01-12/01
	Puerto Rico	Y	12410 FQ	27090 AW	43700 TQ	PRBLS	10/01-12/01
Environmental Manager	Midwest	Y		50000 AW		SAFEDIR	2001
	Northeast	Y		88000 AW		SAFEDIR	2001
	South	Y		55000 AW		SAFEDIR	2001
Environmental Science and Protection Technician, Including Health	Alabama	Y	19030 FQ	40670 AW	71730 TQ	ALBLS	10/01-12/01
	Birmingham MSA, AL	Y	18990 FQ	33210 AW	62110 TQ	ALBLS	10/01-12/01
	Mobile MSA, AL	Y	19760 FQ	27620 AW	29060 TQ	ALBLS	10/01-12/01
	Alaska	Y	30470 FQ	39900 AW	53650 TQ	AKBLS	10/01-12/01
	Anchorage MSA, AK	Y	31720 FQ	41020 AW	56730 TQ	AKBLS	10/01-12/01
	Arizona	Y	30240 FQ	44940 AW	62690 TQ	AZBLS	10/01-12/01
	Phoenix-Mesa MSA, AZ	Y	30830 FQ	48420 AW	68840 TQ	AZBLS	10/01-12/01
	Arkansas	Y	19700 FQ	28700 AW	37440 TQ	ARBLS	10/01-12/01
	Little Rock-North Little Rock MSA, AR	Y	18670 FQ	25920 AW	41840 TQ	ARBLS	10/01-12/01
	California	Y	23400 FQ	41070 AW	65610 TQ	CABLS	10/01-12/01
	Fresno MSA, CA	Y	15490 FQ	29800 AW	51830 TQ	CABLS	10/01-12/01
	Los Angeles-Long Beach PMSA, CA	Y	25320 FQ	41980 AW	64960 TQ	CABLS	10/01-12/01
	Oakland PMSA, CA	Y	36050 FQ	54120 AW	75770 TQ	CABLS	10/01-12/01
	Orange County PMSA, CA	Y	21130 FQ	36920 AW	63850 TQ	CABLS	10/01-12/01
	Riverside-San Bernardino PMSA, CA	Y	21720 FQ	35550 AW	50960 TQ	CABLS	10/01-12/01
	Sacramento PMSA, CA	Y	23870 FQ	33590 AW	47080 TQ	CABLS	10/01-12/01

AAW Average annual wage; **AE** Average entry wage; **AEX** Average experienced wage; **AO** Average offered; **AOH** Average offered, high; **AOL** Average offered, low; **APH** Average pay, high range; **APL** Average pay, low range; **ASH** Average starting, high; **ASL** Average starting, low; **AW** Average wage paid; **FQ** First quartile wage; **H** Hourly; **HI** Highest wage paid; **HR** High end range; **LR** Low end range; **M** Monthly; **MTC** Median total compensation; **MW** Median wage paid; **SQ** Second quartile wage; **S** Special: hourly and annual; **TQ** Third quartile wage; **W** Weekly; **Y** Yearly

Occupation/Type/Industry	Location	Per	Low	Mid	High	Source	Date
Environmental Science and Protection Technician, Including Health	San Diego MSA, CA	Y	23720 FQ	37260 AW	48100 TQ	CABLS	10/01-12/01
	San Francisco PMSA, CA	Y	24910 FQ	42280 AW	68930 TQ	CABLS	10/01-12/01
	San Jose PMSA, CA	Y	34110 FQ	55850 AW	89440 TQ	CABLS	10/01-12/01
	San Luis Obispo-Atascadero-Paso Robles MSA, CA	Y	25260 FQ	49550 AW	79130 TQ	CABLS	10/01-12/01
	Stockton-Lodi MSA, CA	Y	19380 FQ	25080 AW	32390 TQ	CABLS	10/01-12/01
	Ventura PMSA, CA	Y	24420 FQ	42570 AW	65000 TQ	CABLS	10/01-12/01
	Colorado	Y	29370 FQ	43890 AW	60310 TQ	COBLS	10/01-12/01
	Colorado Springs MSA, CO	Y	29150 FQ	38450 AW	53000 TQ	COBLS	10/01-12/01
	Denver PMSA, CO	Y	30270 FQ	46640 AW	65380 TQ	COBLS	10/01-12/01
	Connecticut	Y	27460 FQ	41660 AW	58010 TQ	CTBLS	10/01-12/01
	Bridgeport PMSA, CT	Y	28530 FQ	43090 AW	77960 TQ	CTBLS	10/01-12/01
	Hartford MSA, CT	Y	27640 FQ	41020 AW	58490 TQ	CTBLS	10/01-12/01
	Delaware	Y	25630 FQ	44540 AW	63320 TQ	DEBLS	10/01-12/01
	Wilmington-Newark PMSA, DE-MD	Y	28460 FQ	43820 AW	58280 TQ	DEBLS	10/01-12/01
	District of Columbia	Y	19270 FQ	35250 AW	53060 TQ	DCBLS	10/01-12/01
	Washington PMSA, DC-MD-VA-WV	Y	21970 FQ	36230 AW	56930 TQ	DCBLS	10/01-12/01
	Florida	Y	19710 FQ	32330 AW	46120 TQ	FLBLS	10/01-12/01
	Daytona Beach MSA, FL	Y	18440 FQ	28040 AW	39480 TQ	FLBLS	10/01-12/01
	Fort Lauderdale PMSA, FL	Y	20230 FQ	31180 AW	44550 TQ	FLBLS	10/01-12/01
	Fort Myers-Cape Coral MSA, FL	Y	22450 FQ	30780 AW	42630 TQ	FLBLS	10/01-12/01
	Fort Pierce-Port St. Lucie MSA, FL	Y	17780 FQ	28300 AW	41020 TQ	FLBLS	10/01-12/01
	Fort Walton Beach MSA, FL	Y	17560 FQ	25510 AW	34600 TQ	FLBLS	10/01-12/01
	Gainesville MSA, FL	Y	21290 FQ	33140 AW	48660 TQ	FLBLS	10/01-12/01
	Jacksonville MSA, FL	Y	19050 FQ	28780 AW	36570 TQ	FLBLS	10/01-12/01
	Lakeland-Winter Haven MSA, FL	Y	21990 FQ	36830 AW	52360 TQ	FLBLS	10/01-12/01
	Melbourne-Titusville-Palm Bay MSA, FL	Y	16430 FQ	33210 AW	46870 TQ	FLBLS	10/01-12/01
	Miami PMSA, FL	Y	26510 FQ	36000 AW	52380 TQ	FLBLS	10/01-12/01
	Orlando MSA, FL	Y	22600 FQ	30430 AW	35890 TQ	FLBLS	10/01-12/01
	Pensacola MSA, FL	Y	21740 FQ	33560 AW	43960 TQ	FLBLS	10/01-12/01
	Sarasota-Bradenton MSA, FL	Y	24130 FQ	32190 AW	42300 TQ	FLBLS	10/01-12/01
	Tallahassee MSA, FL	Y	17880 FQ	28590 AW	43310 TQ	FLBLS	10/01-12/01
	Tampa-St. Petersburg-Clearwater MSA, FL	Y	21540 FQ	35340 AW	61450 TQ	FLBLS	10/01-12/01
	West Palm Beach-Boca Raton MSA, FL	Y	25950 FQ	35870 AW	48270 TQ	FLBLS	10/01-12/01
	Georgia	Y	16590 FQ	35190 AW	66070 TQ	GABLS	10/01-12/01
	Atlanta MSA, GA	Y	23220 FQ	43730 AW	75490 TQ	GABLS	10/01-12/01
	Savannah MSA, GA	Y	14960 FQ	21850 AW	34090 TQ	GABLS	10/01-12/01
	Hawaii	Y	23340 FQ	31200 AW	47170 TQ	HIBLS	10/01-12/01
	Honolulu MSA, HI	Y	22990 FQ	30440 AW	50250 TQ	HIBLS	10/01-12/01
	Idaho	Y	26110 FQ	44490 AW	58050 TQ	IDBLS	10/01-12/01
	Boise City MSA, ID	Y	24430 FQ	39420 AW	56260 TQ	IDBLS	10/01-12/01
	Illinois	Y	19180 FQ	36460 AW	54770 TQ	ILBLS	10/01-12/01
	Chicago PMSA, IL	Y	19140 FQ	33930 AW	53200 TQ	ILBLS	10/01-12/01
	Peoria-Pekin MSA, IL	Y	27440 FQ	40410 AW	54490 TQ	ILBLS	10/01-12/01
	Indiana	Y	19640 FQ	33600 AW	53650 TQ	INBLS	10/01-12/01
	Evansville-Henderson MSA, IN-KY	Y	20550 FQ	32130 AW	48350 TQ	INBLS	10/01-12/01
	Fort Wayne MSA, IN	Y	21940 FQ	34470 AW	52490 TQ	INBLS	10/01-12/01
	Indianapolis MSA, IN	Y	23630 FQ	35700 AW	56270 TQ	INBLS	10/01-12/01
	Lafayette MSA, IN	Y	27400 FQ	39540 AW	50330 TQ	INBLS	10/01-12/01
	South Bend MSA, IN	Y	11520 FQ	21680 AW	32520 TQ	INBLS	10/01-12/01
	Iowa	Y	20820 FQ	39510 AW	54320 TQ	IABLS	10/01-12/01
	Davenport-Moline-Rock Island MSA, IA-IL	Y	21920 FQ	34930 AW	51760 TQ	IABLS	10/01-12/01
	Kansas	Y	25320 FQ	37550 AW	54280 TQ	KSBLS	10/01-12/01
	Topeka MSA, KS	Y	24580 FQ	34350 AW	47310 TQ	KSBLS	10/01-12/01
	Wichita MSA, KS	Y	26140 FQ	39970 AW	56060 TQ	KSBLS	10/01-12/01
	Kentucky	Y	21530 FQ	37950 AW	56890 TQ	KYBLS	10/01-12/01
	Lexington MSA, KY	Y	20590 FQ	32280 AW	49410 TQ	KYBLS	10/01-12/01
	Louisville MSA, KY-IN	Y	19200 FQ	33380 AW	53210 TQ	KYBLS	10/01-12/01
	Louisiana	Y	18780 FQ	36200 AW	57170 TQ	LABLS	10/01-12/01
	Baton Rouge MSA, LA	Y	21920 FQ	34110 AW	51510 TQ	LABLS	10/01-12/01

AAW Average annual wage; AE Average entry wage; AEX Average experienced wage; AO Average offered; AOH Average offered, high; AOL Average offered, low; APH Average pay, high range; APL Average pay, low range; ASH Average starting, high; ASL Average starting, low; AW Average wage paid; FQ First quartile wage; H Hourly; HI Highest wage paid; HR High end range; LR Low end range; M Monthly; MTC Median total compensation; MW Median wage paid; SQ Second quartile wage; S Special: hourly and annual; TQ Third quartile wage; W Weekly; Y Yearly

Occupation/Type/Industry	Location	Per	Low	Mid	High	Source	Date
Environmental Science and Protection Technician, Including Health	New Orleans MSA, LA	Y	17670 FQ	37010 AW	56310 TQ	LABLS	10/01-12/01
	Maine	Y	19300 FQ	27310 AW	37820 TQ	MEBLS	10/01-12/01
	Portland MSA, ME	Y	19980 FQ	27750 AW	37940 TQ	MEBLS	10/01-12/01
	Maryland	Y	26430 FQ	38910 AW	53340 TQ	MDBLS	10/01-12/01
	Baltimore PMSA, MD	Y	28190 FQ	40350 AW	53670 TQ	MDBLS	10/01-12/01
	Massachusetts	Y	26100 FQ	39290 AW	56850 TQ	MABLS	10/01-12/01
	Boston PMSA, MA-NH	Y	29220 FQ	42160 AW	58190 TQ	MABLS	10/01-12/01
	Lowell PMSA, MA-NH	Y	21620 FQ	42280 AW	81560 TQ	MABLS	10/01-12/01
	New Bedford PMSA, MA	Y	24940 FQ	34320 AW	53340 TQ	MABLS	10/01-12/01
	Springfield MSA, MA	Y	24470 FQ	34630 AW	49750 TQ	MABLS	10/01-12/01
	Michigan	Y	24090 FQ	36410 AW	51040 TQ	MIBLS	10/01-12/01
	Ann Arbor PMSA, MI	Y	22740 FQ	28240 AW	38400 TQ	MIBLS	10/01-12/01
	Detroit PMSA, MI	Y	25730 FQ	40390 AW	58730 TQ	MIBLS	10/01-12/01
	Grand Rapids-Muskegon-Holland MSA, MI	Y	28670 FQ	38000 AW	52910 TQ	MIBLS	10/01-12/01
	Lansing-East Lansing MSA, MI	Y	17390 FQ	35520 AW	55010 TQ	MIBLS	10/01-12/01
	Minnesota	Y	24860 FQ	38440 AW	57250 TQ	MNBLS	10/01-12/01
	Duluth-Superior MSA, MN-WI	Y	25930 FQ	39730 AW	57100 TQ	MNBLS	10/01-12/01
	Minneapolis-St. Paul MSA, MN-WI	Y	23970 FQ	39380 AW	58960 TQ	MNBLS	10/01-12/01
	Mississippi	Y	20200 FQ	36070 AW	55350 TQ	MSBLS	10/01-12/01
	Jackson MSA, MS	Y	21920 FQ	35410 AW	48020 TQ	MSBLS	10/01-12/01
	Missouri	Y	23450 FQ	36780 AW	55140 TQ	MOBLS	10/01-12/01
	Kansas City MSA, MO-KS	Y	28640 FQ	44360 AW	58340 TQ	MOBLS	10/01-12/01
	St. Louis MSA, MO-IL	Y	23760 FQ	39270 AW	55550 TQ	MOBLS	10/01-12/01
	Montana	Y	20150 FQ	27960 AW	36610 TQ	MTBLS	10/01-12/01
	Nebraska	Y	15790 FQ	27430 AW	39130 TQ	NEBLS	10/01-12/01
	Omaha MSA, NE-IA	Y	24290 FQ	31170 AW	44260 TQ	NEBLS	10/01-12/01
	Nevada	Y	20590 FQ	42440 AW	60200 TQ	NVBLS	10/01-12/01
	Las Vegas MSA, NV-AZ	Y	17300 FQ	37200 AW	55540 TQ	NVBLS	10/01-12/01
	New Hampshire	Y	23630 FQ	34170 AW	49380 TQ	NHBLS	10/01-12/01
	New Jersey	Y	28630 FQ	41580 AW	58020 TQ	NJBLS	10/01-12/01
	Middlesex-Somerset-Hunterdon PMSA, NJ	Y	26640 FQ	42200 AW	59980 TQ	NJBLS	10/01-12/01
	Monmouth-Ocean PMSA, NJ	Y	31140 FQ	47150 AW	69640 TQ	NJBLS	10/01-12/01
	Newark PMSA, NJ	Y	30840 FQ	39560 AW	52040 TQ	NJBLS	10/01-12/01
	Trenton PMSA, NJ	Y	32230 FQ	47810 AW	72790 TQ	NJBLS	10/01-12/01
	New Mexico	Y	20740 FQ	31000 AW	44110 TQ	NMBLS	10/01-12/01
	New York	Y	20180 FQ	32570 AW	48360 TQ	NYBLS	10/01-12/01
	Albany-Schenectady-Troy MSA, NY	Y	19810 FQ	26830 AW	45440 TQ	NYBLS	10/01-12/01
	Binghamton MSA, NY	Y	16520 FQ	28090 AW	41650 TQ	NYBLS	10/01-12/01
	Buffalo-Niagara Falls MSA, NY	Y	23150 FQ	36770 AW	53210 TQ	NYBLS	10/01-12/01
	Nassau-Suffolk PMSA, NY	Y	24920 FQ	35560 AW	47240 TQ	NYBLS	10/01-12/01
	New York PMSA, NY	Y	21520 FQ	33800 AW	49200 TQ	NYBLS	10/01-12/01
	Newburgh PMSA, NY-PA	Y	19380 FQ	30850 AW	48410 TQ	NYBLS	10/01-12/01
	Rochester MSA, NY	Y	22050 FQ	32850 AW	51730 TQ	NYBLS	10/01-12/01
	Syracuse MSA, NY	Y	19690 FQ	28460 AW	43340 TQ	NYBLS	10/01-12/01
	Utica-Rome MSA, NY	Y	18360 FQ	32120 AW	53900 TQ	NYBLS	10/01-12/01
	North Carolina	Y	23150 FQ	34790 AW	48420 TQ	NCBLS	10/01-12/01
	Asheville MSA, NC	Y	29080 FQ	35790 AW	44650 TQ	NCBLS	10/01-12/01
	Charlotte-Gastonia-Rock Hill MSA, NC-SC	Y	25010 FQ	35800 AW	51960 TQ	NCBLS	10/01-12/01
	Fayetteville MSA, NC	Y	27640 FQ	35750 AW	43600 TQ	NCBLS	10/01-12/01
	Greensboro-Winston-Salem-High Point MSA, NC	Y	23840 FQ	35730 AW	49640 TQ	NCBLS	10/01-12/01
	Raleigh-Durham-Chapel Hill MSA, NC	Y	19980 FQ	32220 AW	45960 TQ	NCBLS	10/01-12/01
	Wilmington MSA, NC	Y	30010 FQ	43500 AW	56450 TQ	NCBLS	10/01-12/01
	Ohio	Y	21810 FQ	37470 AW	54800 TQ	OHBLS	10/01-12/01
	Akron PMSA, OH	Y	22100 FQ	40810 AW	55100 TQ	OHBLS	10/01-12/01
	Cincinnati PMSA, OH-KY-IN	Y	22750 FQ	36290 AW	53030 TQ	OHBLS	10/01-12/01
	Cleveland-Lorain-Elyria PMSA, OH	Y	27260 FQ	40140 AW	55070 TQ	OHBLS	10/01-12/01
	Columbus MSA, OH	Y	19270 FQ	28460 AW	48480 TQ	OHBLS	10/01-12/01
	Dayton-Springfield MSA, OH	Y	21060 FQ	36630 AW	53400 TQ	OHBLS	10/01-12/01
	Hamilton-Middletown PMSA, OH	Y	24190 FQ	37610 AW	46040 TQ	OHBLS	10/01-12/01
	Youngstown-Warren MSA, OH	Y	24950 FQ	33230 AW	43520 TQ	OHBLS	10/01-12/01

AAW Average annual wage; **AE** Average entry wage; **AEX** Average experienced wage; **AO** Average offered; **AOH** Average offered, high; **AOL** Average offered, low; **APH** Average pay, high range; **APL** Average pay, low range; **ASH** Average starting, high; **ASL** Average starting, low; **AW** Average wage paid; **FQ** First quartile wage; **H** Hourly; **HI** Highest wage paid; **HR** High end range; **LR** Low end range; **M** Monthly; **MTC** Median total compensation; **MW** Median wage paid; **SQ** Second quartile wage; **S** Special: hourly and annual; **TQ** Third quartile wage; **W** Weekly; **Y** Yearly

Occupation/Type/Industry	Location	Per	Low	Mid	High	Source	Date
Environmental Science and Protection Technician, Including Health	Oklahoma	Y	20370 FQ	32570 AW	45320 TQ	OKBLS	10/01-12/01
	Tulsa MSA, OK	Y	20440 FQ	33340 AW	51330 TQ	OKBLS	10/01-12/01
	Oregon	Y	28450 FQ	36140 AW	50810 TQ	ORBLS	10/01-12/01
	Portland-Vancouver PMSA, OR-WA	Y	29580 FQ	42110 AW	55910 TQ	ORBLS	10/01-12/01
	Pennsylvania	Y	21580 FQ	37870 AW	56080 TQ	PABLS	10/01-12/01
	Harrisburg-Lebanon-Carlisle MSA, PA	Y	22710 FQ	40370 AW	57270 TQ	PABLS	10/01-12/01
	Philadelphia PMSA, PA-NJ	Y	21620 FQ	37490 AW	54780 TQ	PABLS	10/01-12/01
	Pittsburgh MSA, PA	Y	22910 FQ	35480 AW	52260 TQ	PABLS	10/01-12/01
	Reading MSA, PA	Y	20680 FQ	31320 AW	45090 TQ	PABLS	10/01-12/01
	Rhode Island	Y	19770 FQ	34780 AW	52470 TQ	RIBLS	10/01-12/01
	Providence-Fall River-Warwick MSA, RI-MA	Y	21740 FQ	37370 AW	54660 TQ	RIBLS	10/01-12/01
	South Carolina	Y	25700 FQ	40960 AW	58320 TQ	SCBLS	10/01-12/01
	Charleston-North Charleston MSA, SC	Y	25220 FQ	40930 AW	67420 TQ	SCBLS	10/01-12/01
	Greenville-Spartanburg-Anderson MSA, SC	Y	27320 FQ	43920 AW	58840 TQ	SCBLS	10/01-12/01
	South Dakota	Y	19710 FQ	26520 AW	33490 TQ	SDBLS	10/01-12/01
	Tennessee	Y	21980 FQ	36880 AW	52510 TQ	TNBLS	10/01-12/01
	Johnson City-Kingsport-Bristol MSA, TN-VA	Y	19770 FQ	33570 AW	47080 TQ	TNBLS	10/01-12/01
	Memphis MSA, TN-AR-MS	Y	20920 FQ	34360 AW	52840 TQ	TNBLS	10/01-12/01
	Nashville MSA, TN	Y	16750 FQ	28720 AW	37050 TQ	TNBLS	10/01-12/01
	Texas	Y	18740 FQ	36570 AW	58280 TQ	TXBLS	10/01-12/01
	Amarillo MSA, TX	Y	20160 FQ	30910 AW	44050 TQ	TXBLS	10/01-12/01
	Austin-San Marcos MSA, TX	Y	17810 FQ	34920 AW	51760 TQ	TXBLS	10/01-12/01
	Beaumont-Port Arthur MSA, TX	Y	25710 FQ	37280 AW	59310 TQ	TXBLS	10/01-12/01
	Corpus Christi MSA, TX	Y	25970 FQ	43710 AW	66500 TQ	TXBLS	10/01-12/01
	Dallas PMSA, TX	Y	27390 FQ	36650 AW	50940 TQ	TXBLS	10/01-12/01
	El Paso MSA, TX	Y	15370 FQ	26810 AW	41150 TQ	TXBLS	10/01-12/01
	Fort Worth-Arlington PMSA, TX	Y	28720 FQ	37010 AW	51030 TQ	TXBLS	10/01-12/01
	Galveston-Texas City PMSA, TX	Y	23970 FQ	34610 AW	47530 TQ	TXBLS	10/01-12/01
	Houston PMSA, TX	Y	23640 FQ	41090 AW	65380 TQ	TXBLS	10/01-12/01
	Longview-Marshall MSA, TX	Y	14200 FQ	30390 AW	56110 TQ	TXBLS	10/01-12/01
	Lubbock MSA, TX	Y	13150 FQ	22370 AW	39360 TQ	TXBLS	10/01-12/01
	San Antonio MSA, TX	Y	25520 FQ	34580 AW	44620 TQ	TXBLS	10/01-12/01
	Utah	Y	18620 FQ	37760 AW	53720 TQ	UTBLS	10/01-12/01
	Salt Lake City-Ogden MSA, UT	Y	17160 FQ	37710 AW	53410 TQ	UTBLS	10/01-12/01
	Vermont	Y	21140 FQ	29060 AW	40560 TQ	VTBLS	10/01-12/01
	Virginia	Y	19300 FQ	32930 AW	48250 TQ	VABLS	10/01-12/01
	Norfolk-Virginia Beach-Newport News MSA, VA-NC	Y	19420 FQ	30080 AW	43040 TQ	VABLS	10/01-12/01
	Richmond-Petersburg MSA, VA	Y	22020 FQ	34010 AW	45950 TQ	VABLS	10/01-12/01
	Washington	Y	27450 FQ	41560 AW	57040 TQ	WABLS	10/01-12/01
	Richland-Kennewick-Pasco MSA, WA	Y	31110 FQ	43280 AW	56480 TQ	WABLS	10/01-12/01
	Seattle-Bellevue-Everett PMSA, WA	Y	26870 FQ	42590 AW	58930 TQ	WABLS	10/01-12/01
	Spokane MSA, WA	Y	27810 FQ	39650 AW	53810 TQ	WABLS	10/01-12/01
	Tacoma PMSA, WA	Y	29490 FQ	43630 AW	56420 TQ	WABLS	10/01-12/01
	West Virginia	Y	12340 FQ	27870 AW	52840 TQ	WVBLS	10/01-12/01
	Charleston MSA, WV	Y	18850 FQ	36630 AW	64270 TQ	WVBLS	10/01-12/01
	Wisconsin	Y	24910 FQ	38480 AW	57310 TQ	WIBLS	10/01-12/01
	Madison MSA, WI	Y	29180 FQ	34600 AW	43280 TQ	WIBLS	10/01-12/01
	Milwaukee-Waukesha PMSA, WI	Y	23880 FQ	41070 AW	66050 TQ	WIBLS	10/01-12/01
	Wyoming	Y	13870 FQ	26890 AW	43580 TQ	WYBLS	10/01-12/01
	Puerto Rico	Y	13440 FQ	30180 AW	50590 TQ	PRBLS	10/01-12/01
Environmental Science Teacher							
Postsecondary	California	Y	36810 FQ	70310 AW	106190 TQ	CABLS	10/01-12/01
Postsecondary	Connecticut	Y	32670 FQ	60560 AW	95800 TQ	CTBLS	10/01-12/01

AAW	Average annual wage	**AOH**	Average offered, high	**ASH**	Average starting, high	**H**	Hourly	**M**	Monthly	**S**	Special: hourly and annual		
AE	Average entry wage	**AOL**	Average offered, low	**ASL**	Average starting, low	**HI**	Highest wage paid	**MTC**	Median total compensation	**TQ**	Third quartile wage		
AEX	Average experienced wage	**APH**	Average pay, high range	**AW**	Average wage paid	**HR**	High end range	**MW**	Median wage paid	**W**	Weekly		
AO	Average offered	**APL**	Average pay, low range	**FQ**	First quartile wage	**LR**	Low end range	**SQ**	Second quartile wage	**Y**	Yearly		

Occupation/Type/Industry	Location	Per	Low	Mid	High	Source	Date
Environmental Science Teacher							
Postsecondary	District of Columbia	Y	32060 FQ	61760 AW	97480 TQ	DCBLS	10/01-12/01
Postsecondary	Florida	Y	33960 FQ	67150 AW	115290 TQ	FLBLS	10/01-12/01
Postsecondary	Georgia	Y	42330 FQ	64530 AW	93210 TQ	GABLS	10/01-12/01
Postsecondary	Illinois	Y	30080 FQ	52940 AW	87700 TQ	ILBLS	10/01-12/01
Postsecondary	Iowa	Y	40480 FQ	59340 AW	97150 TQ	IABLS	10/01-12/01
Postsecondary	Louisiana	Y	27970 FQ	58840 AW	98140 TQ	LABLS	10/01-12/01
Postsecondary	Maryland	Y	44790 FQ	71790 AW	113740 TQ	MDBLS	10/01-12/01
Postsecondary	Massachusetts	Y	40430 FQ	57800 AW	79030 TQ	MABLS	10/01-12/01
Postsecondary	Michigan	Y	33670 FQ	62190 AW	92140 TQ	MIBLS	10/01-12/01
Postsecondary	Minnesota	Y	37580 FQ	66010 AW	106400 TQ	MNBLS	10/01-12/01
Postsecondary	Missouri	Y	25540 FQ	55190 AW	99260 TQ	MOBLS	10/01-12/01
Postsecondary	New Hampshire	Y	34230 FQ	63750 AW	112870 TQ	NHBLS	10/01-12/01
Postsecondary	New Jersey	Y	38610 FQ	67860 AW	97970 TQ	NJBLS	10/01-12/01
Postsecondary	New York	Y	45110 FQ	70150 AW	100740 TQ	NYBLS	10/01-12/01
Postsecondary	North Carolina	Y	36520 FQ	63820 AW	111420 TQ	NCBLS	10/01-12/01
Postsecondary	Ohio	Y	38910 FQ	62450 AW	91620 TQ	OHBLS	10/01-12/01
Postsecondary	Oklahoma	Y	28090 FQ	57500 AW	97650 TQ	OKBLS	10/01-12/01
Postsecondary	Oregon	Y	46120 FQ	74730 AW	97940 TQ	ORBLS	10/01-12/01
Postsecondary	Pennsylvania	Y	28770 FQ	58170 AW	92830 TQ	PABLS	10/01-12/01
Postsecondary	Tennessee	Y	36830 FQ	59920 AW	90900 TQ	TNBLS	10/01-12/01
Postsecondary	Texas	Y	30340 FQ	62630 AW	112610 TQ	TXBLS	10/01-12/01
Postsecondary	Utah	Y	33240 FQ	67270 AW	114900 TQ	UTBLS	10/01-12/01
Postsecondary	Virginia	Y	26040 FQ	60230 AW	94220 TQ	VABLS	10/01-12/01
Postsecondary	Washington	Y	34940 FQ	58220 AW	90150 TQ	WABLS	10/01-12/01
Postsecondary	Wisconsin	Y	33460 FQ	59360 AW	89680 TQ	WIBLS	10/01-12/01
Environmental Scientist and Specialist, Including Health	Alabama	Y	27980 FQ	43310 AW	64780 TQ	ALBLS	10/01-12/01
	Birmingham MSA, AL	Y	31960 FQ	54660 AW	84350 TQ	ALBLS	10/01-12/01
	Huntsville MSA, AL	Y	26590 FQ	48270 AW	77450 TQ	ALBLS	10/01-12/01
	Mobile MSA, AL	Y	26800 FQ	36660 AW	50320 TQ	ALBLS	10/01-12/01
	Alaska	Y	38350 FQ	56820 AW	79230 TQ	AKBLS	10/01-12/01
	Anchorage MSA, AK	Y	39150 FQ	58420 AW	81510 TQ	AKBLS	10/01-12/01
	Arizona	Y	31020 FQ	49990 AW	73630 TQ	AZBLS	10/01-12/01
	Phoenix-Mesa MSA, AZ	Y	31210 FQ	50950 AW	74700 TQ	AZBLS	10/01-12/01
	Tucson MSA, AZ	Y	30790 FQ	48000 AW	66760 TQ	AZBLS	10/01-12/01
	Arkansas	Y	29660 FQ	46140 AW	69380 TQ	ARBLS	10/01-12/01
	Little Rock-North Little Rock MSA, AR	Y	32620 FQ	49430 AW	71410 TQ	ARBLS	10/01-12/01
	California	Y	39090 FQ	60650 AW	88240 TQ	CABLS	10/01-12/01
	Bakersfield MSA, CA	Y	45400 FQ	69850 AW	96200 TQ	CABLS	10/01-12/01
	Chico-Paradise MSA, CA	Y	31130 FQ	40770 AW	54870 TQ	CABLS	10/01-12/01
	Fresno MSA, CA	Y	32610 FQ	52290 AW	73280 TQ	CABLS	10/01-12/01
	Los Angeles-Long Beach PMSA, CA	Y	37410 FQ	65270 AW	93360 TQ	CABLS	10/01-12/01
	Oakland PMSA, CA	Y	44400 FQ	66010 AW	100100 TQ	CABLS	10/01-12/01
	Orange County PMSA, CA	Y	43170 FQ	59870 AW	81300 TQ	CABLS	10/01-12/01
	Riverside-San Bernardino PMSA, CA	Y	39010 FQ	53870 AW	71690 TQ	CABLS	10/01-12/01
	Sacramento PMSA, CA	Y	40520 FQ	58400 AW	71950 TQ	CABLS	10/01-12/01
	San Diego MSA, CA	Y	39500 FQ	55990 AW	76680 TQ	CABLS	10/01-12/01
	San Francisco PMSA, CA	Y	41590 FQ	66910 AW	93250 TQ	CABLS	10/01-12/01
	San Jose PMSA, CA	Y	42130 FQ	61810 AW	93790 TQ	CABLS	10/01-12/01
	San Luis Obispo-Atascadero-Paso Robles MSA, CA	Y	42880 FQ	72480 AW	117710 TQ	CABLS	10/01-12/01
	Santa Barbara-Santa Maria-Lompoc MSA, CA	Y	45750 FQ	58400 AW	71310 TQ	CABLS	10/01-12/01
	Santa Cruz-Watsonville PMSA, CA	Y	27070 FQ	47010 AW	64810 TQ	CABLS	10/01-12/01
	Vallejo-Fairfield-Napa PMSA, CA	Y	33370 FQ	50390 AW	62470 TQ	CABLS	10/01-12/01
	Ventura PMSA, CA	Y	39260 FQ	64430 AW	93960 TQ	CABLS	10/01-12/01
	Colorado	Y	36640 FQ	59200 AW	86480 TQ	COBLS	10/01-12/01
	Boulder-Longmont PMSA, CO	Y	34040 FQ	50260 AW	66040 TQ	COBLS	10/01-12/01
	Denver PMSA, CO	Y	37020 FQ	61560 AW	88030 TQ	COBLS	10/01-12/01
	Greeley PMSA, CO	Y	31840 FQ	45010 AW	65120 TQ	COBLS	10/01-12/01
	Connecticut	Y	32110 FQ	52170 AW	72680 TQ	CTBLS	10/01-12/01
	Bridgeport PMSA, CT	Y	32300 FQ	51130 AW	73530 TQ	CTBLS	10/01-12/01
	Hartford MSA, CT	Y	32130 FQ	51770 AW	70970 TQ	CTBLS	10/01-12/01
	New Haven-Meriden PMSA, CT	Y	31980 FQ	49840 AW	71600 TQ	CTBLS	10/01-12/01

AAW Average annual wage **AOH** Average offered, high **ASH** Average starting, high **H** Hourly **M** Monthly **S** Special: hourly and annual
AE Average entry wage **AOL** Average offered, low **ASL** Average starting, low **HI** Highest wage paid **MTC** Median total compensation **TQ** Third quartile wage
AEX Average experienced wage **APH** Average pay, high range **AW** Average wage paid **HR** High end range **MW** Median wage paid **W** Weekly
AO Average offered **APL** Average pay, low range **FQ** First quartile wage **LR** Low end range **SQ** Second quartile wage **Y** Yearly

Occupation/Type/Industry	Location	Per	Low	Mid	High	Source	Date
Environmental Scientist and Specialist, Including Health	Delaware	Y	30920 FQ	42550 AW	55710 TQ	DEBLS	10/01-12/01
	Wilmington-Newark PMSA, DE-MD	Y	30450 FQ	42060 AW	55110 TQ	DEBLS	10/01-12/01
	District of Columbia	Y	38600 FQ	69210 AW	101320 TQ	DCBLS	10/01-12/01
	Washington PMSA, DC-MD-VA-WV	Y	33390 FQ	63910 AW	99890 TQ	DCBLS	10/01-12/01
	Florida	Y	29810 FQ	51370 AW	85120 TQ	FLBLS	10/01-12/01
	Daytona Beach MSA, FL	Y	27010 FQ	38080 AW	54900 TQ	FLBLS	10/01-12/01
	Fort Lauderdale PMSA, FL	Y	30860 FQ	47650 AW	70920 TQ	FLBLS	10/01-12/01
	Fort Myers-Cape Coral MSA, FL	Y	30020 FQ	49600 AW	87340 TQ	FLBLS	10/01-12/01
	Fort Pierce-Port St. Lucie MSA, FL	Y	30160 FQ	57340 AW	84090 TQ	FLBLS	10/01-12/01
	Fort Walton Beach MSA, FL	Y	33180 FQ	54980 AW	70030 TQ	FLBLS	10/01-12/01
	Gainesville MSA, FL	Y	27200 FQ	42400 AW	59620 TQ	FLBLS	10/01-12/01
	Jacksonville MSA, FL	Y	31120 FQ	55200 AW	97200 TQ	FLBLS	10/01-12/01
	Lakeland-Winter Haven MSA, FL	Y	28790 FQ	38570 AW	54990 TQ	FLBLS	10/01-12/01
	Melbourne-Titusville-Palm Bay MSA, FL	Y	31340 FQ	43300 AW	55440 TQ	FLBLS	10/01-12/01
	Miami PMSA, FL	Y	28550 FQ	44730 AW	69970 TQ	FLBLS	10/01-12/01
	Naples MSA, FL	Y	29320 FQ	43470 AW	78870 TQ	FLBLS	10/01-12/01
	Orlando MSA, FL	Y	28320 FQ	48720 AW	75910 TQ	FLBLS	10/01-12/01
	Pensacola MSA, FL	Y	30800 FQ	62640 AW	100140 TQ	FLBLS	10/01-12/01
	Sarasota-Bradenton MSA, FL	Y	29700 FQ	40740 AW	53700 TQ	FLBLS	10/01-12/01
	Tallahassee MSA, FL	Y	35340 FQ	73130 AW	118220 TQ	FLBLS	10/01-12/01
	Tampa-St. Petersburg-Clearwater MSA, FL	Y	30270 FQ	49320 AW	79600 TQ	FLBLS	10/01-12/01
	West Palm Beach-Boca Raton MSA, FL	Y	30690 FQ	50180 AW	80070 TQ	FLBLS	10/01-12/01
	Georgia	Y	32250 FQ	48950 AW	71820 TQ	GABLS	10/01-12/01
	Atlanta MSA, GA	Y	33050 FQ	49710 AW	73170 TQ	GABLS	10/01-12/01
	Augusta-Aiken MSA, GA-SC	Y	27510 FQ	53480 AW	82370 TQ	GABLS	10/01-12/01
	Macon MSA, GA	Y	36930 FQ	47400 AW	61460 TQ	GABLS	10/01-12/01
	Savannah MSA, GA	Y	28260 FQ	45500 AW	68310 TQ	GABLS	10/01-12/01
	Hawaii	Y	32560 FQ	52210 AW	78400 TQ	HIBLS	10/01-12/01
	Honolulu MSA, HI	Y	32800 FQ	53800 AW	82580 TQ	HIBLS	10/01-12/01
	Idaho	Y	37980 FQ	55660 AW	82200 TQ	IDBLS	10/01-12/01
	Boise City MSA, ID	Y	38010 FQ	49270 AW	64820 TQ	IDBLS	10/01-12/01
	Illinois	Y	20340 FQ	51890 AW	83230 TQ	ILBLS	10/01-12/01
	Chicago PMSA, IL	Y	20060 FQ	52830 AW	83630 TQ	ILBLS	10/01-12/01
	Springfield MSA, IL	Y	18300 FQ	35800 AW	60270 TQ	ILBLS	10/01-12/01
	Indiana	Y	28630 FQ	42460 AW	60670 TQ	INBLS	10/01-12/01
	Fort Wayne MSA, IN	Y	28310 FQ	41220 AW	56090 TQ	INBLS	10/01-12/01
	Gary PMSA, IN	Y	27150 FQ	46700 AW	77760 TQ	INBLS	10/01-12/01
	Indianapolis MSA, IN	Y	29060 FQ	42430 AW	60630 TQ	INBLS	10/01-12/01
	South Bend MSA, IN	Y	28370 FQ	38160 AW	50570 TQ	INBLS	10/01-12/01
	Iowa	Y	26930 FQ	46840 AW	71500 TQ	IABLS	10/01-12/01
	Davenport-Moline-Rock Island MSA, IA-IL	Y	36030 FQ	62470 AW	89690 TQ	IABLS	10/01-12/01
	Des Moines MSA, IA	Y	26740 FQ	43790 AW	66930 TQ	IABLS	10/01-12/01
	Kansas	Y	30580 FQ	46930 AW	66090 TQ	KSBLS	10/01-12/01
	Topeka MSA, KS	Y	36720 FQ	46330 AW	56240 TQ	KSBLS	10/01-12/01
	Wichita MSA, KS	Y	36740 FQ	44890 AW	60740 TQ	KSBLS	10/01-12/01
	Kentucky	Y	29600 FQ	44540 AW	62070 TQ	KYBLS	10/01-12/01
	Lexington MSA, KY	Y	26550 FQ	44130 AW	67340 TQ	KYBLS	10/01-12/01
	Louisville MSA, KY-IN	Y	27350 FQ	41750 AW	57860 TQ	KYBLS	10/01-12/01
	Louisiana	Y	17170 FQ	40760 AW	65040 TQ	LABLS	10/01-12/01
	Baton Rouge MSA, LA	Y	22860 FQ	37660 AW	56030 TQ	LABLS	10/01-12/01
	Lafayette MSA, LA	Y	22170 FQ	38570 AW	54020 TQ	LABLS	10/01-12/01
	Lake Charles MSA, LA	Y	36210 FQ	57050 AW	86170 TQ	LABLS	10/01-12/01
	New Orleans MSA, LA	Y	12270 FQ	35460 AW	61360 TQ	LABLS	10/01-12/01
	Shreveport-Bossier City MSA, LA	Y	25520 FQ	42170 AW	56240 TQ	LABLS	10/01-12/01
	Maine	Y	30360 FQ	41260 AW	53800 TQ	MEBLS	10/01-12/01
	Portland MSA, ME	Y	27640 FQ	39420 AW	55080 TQ	MEBLS	10/01-12/01
	Maryland	Y	30470 FQ	48740 AW	74000 TQ	MDBLS	10/01-12/01
	Baltimore PMSA, MD	Y	30530 FQ	46480 AW	69250 TQ	MDBLS	10/01-12/01
	Massachusetts	Y	35050 FQ	54810 AW	76150 TQ	MABLS	10/01-12/01
	Boston PMSA, MA-NH	Y	38870 FQ	57760 AW	81380 TQ	MABLS	10/01-12/01
	Lawrence PMSA, MA-NH	Y	29330 FQ	45130 AW	62600 TQ	MABLS	10/01-12/01

Occupation/Type/Industry	Location	Per	Low	Mid	High	Source	Date
Environmental Scientist and Specialist, Including Health	Lowell PMSA, MA-NH	Y	29220 FQ	54180 AW	78680 TQ	MABLS	10/01-12/01
	Springfield MSA, MA	Y	31320 FQ	49910 AW	70330 TQ	MABLS	10/01-12/01
	Michigan	Y	32140 FQ	49630 AW	69930 TQ	MIBLS	10/01-12/01
	Ann Arbor PMSA, MI	Y	26960 FQ	47690 AW	81950 TQ	MIBLS	10/01-12/01
	Detroit PMSA, MI	Y	32110 FQ	46170 AW	64340 TQ	MIBLS	10/01-12/01
	Grand Rapids-Muskegon-Holland MSA, MI	Y	34560 FQ	61510 AW	123870 TQ	MIBLS	10/01-12/01
	Kalamazoo-Battle Creek MSA, MI	Y	36800 FQ	49310 AW	66570 TQ	MIBLS	10/01-12/01
	Saginaw-Bay City-Midland MSA, MI	Y	32600 FQ	56300 AW	88650 TQ	MIBLS	10/01-12/01
	Minnesota	Y	34630 FQ	50820 AW	68700 TQ	MNBLS	10/01-12/01
	Duluth-Superior MSA, MN-WI	Y	35120 FQ	50760 AW	66630 TQ	MNBLS	10/01-12/01
	Minneapolis-St. Paul MSA, MN-WI	Y	34550 FQ	51800 AW	69770 TQ	MNBLS	10/01-12/01
	Mississippi	Y	23520 FQ	35480 AW	52000 TQ	MSBLS	10/01-12/01
	Biloxi-Gulfport-Pascagoula MSA, MS	Y	22750 FQ	40380 AW	55270 TQ	MSBLS	10/01-12/01
	Jackson MSA, MS	Y	24210 FQ	35950 AW	52960 TQ	MSBLS	10/01-12/01
	Kansas City MSA, MO-KS	Y	27450 FQ	46680 AW	72350 TQ	MOBLS	10/01-12/01
	St. Louis MSA, MO-IL	Y	31480 FQ	47810 AW	78960 TQ	MOBLS	10/01-12/01
	Montana	Y	31510 FQ	48120 AW	86470 TQ	MTBLS	10/01-12/01
	Nebraska	Y	22190 FQ	34490 AW	50800 TQ	NEBLS	10/01-12/01
	Lincoln MSA, NE	Y	29670 FQ	40340 AW	53390 TQ	NEBLS	10/01-12/01
	Omaha MSA, NE-IA	Y	22380 FQ	33040 AW	49130 TQ	NEBLS	10/01-12/01
	Nevada	Y	37860 FQ	52330 AW	70620 TQ	NVBLS	10/01-12/01
	Las Vegas MSA, NV-AZ	Y	36950 FQ	54940 AW	73890 TQ	NVBLS	10/01-12/01
	Reno MSA, NV	Y	36920 FQ	46720 AW	62840 TQ	NVBLS	10/01-12/01
	New Hampshire	Y	31760 FQ	44030 AW	57760 TQ	NHBLS	10/01-12/01
	New Jersey	Y	33050 FQ	57970 AW	85370 TQ	NJBLS	10/01-12/01
	Atlantic-Cape May PMSA, NJ	Y	32030 FQ	51020 AW	70620 TQ	NJBLS	10/01-12/01
	Bergen-Passaic PMSA, NJ	Y	31810 FQ	52070 AW	79280 TQ	NJBLS	10/01-12/01
	Middlesex-Somerset-Hunterdon PMSA, NJ	Y	35910 FQ	68610 AW		NJBLS	10/01-12/01
	Monmouth-Ocean PMSA, NJ	Y	32310 FQ	53730 AW	72670 TQ	NJBLS	10/01-12/01
	Newark PMSA, NJ	Y	34690 FQ	63330 AW	93570 TQ	NJBLS	10/01-12/01
	New Mexico	Y	27040 FQ	46310 AW	75910 TQ	NMBLS	10/01-12/01
	Albuquerque MSA, NM	Y	34000 FQ	49150 AW	74630 TQ	NMBLS	10/01-12/01
	Las Cruces MSA, NM	Y	19380 FQ	35320 AW	61880 TQ	NMBLS	10/01-12/01
	New York	Y	32260 FQ	52440 AW	73870 TQ	NYBLS	10/01-12/01
	Albany-Schenectady-Troy MSA, NY	Y	37990 FQ	55800 AW	80760 TQ	NYBLS	10/01-12/01
	Buffalo-Niagara Falls MSA, NY	Y	34900 FQ	53250 AW	72180 TQ	NYBLS	10/01-12/01
	Dutchess County PMSA, NY	Y	35790 FQ	53910 AW	72760 TQ	NYBLS	10/01-12/01
	Nassau-Suffolk PMSA, NY	Y	30790 FQ	46580 AW	68390 TQ	NYBLS	10/01-12/01
	New York PMSA, NY	Y	35230 FQ	60170 AW	86740 TQ	NYBLS	10/01-12/01
	Rochester MSA, NY	Y	26910 FQ	43620 AW	65340 TQ	NYBLS	10/01-12/01
	Syracuse MSA, NY	Y	23830 FQ	40050 AW	58910 TQ	NYBLS	10/01-12/01
	Utica-Rome MSA, NY	Y	45420 FQ	50690 AW	56520 TQ	NYBLS	10/01-12/01
	North Carolina	Y	30160 FQ	48380 AW	77000 TQ	NCBLS	10/01-12/01
	Asheville MSA, NC	Y	30080 FQ	36500 AW	44700 TQ	NCBLS	10/01-12/01
	Charlotte-Gastonia-Rock Hill MSA, NC-SC	Y	31970 FQ	52820 AW	80730 TQ	NCBLS	10/01-12/01
	Fayetteville MSA, NC	Y	28800 FQ	39460 AW	54020 TQ	NCBLS	10/01-12/01
	Greensboro-Winston-Salem-High Point MSA, NC	Y	31320 FQ	53460 AW	93770 TQ	NCBLS	10/01-12/01
	Raleigh-Durham-Chapel Hill MSA, NC	Y	32450 FQ	52340 AW	84090 TQ	NCBLS	10/01-12/01
	Wilmington MSA, NC	Y	27290 FQ	42840 AW	63240 TQ	NCBLS	10/01-12/01
	North Dakota	Y	24090 FQ	34390 AW	51940 TQ	NDBLS	10/01-12/01
	Ohio	Y	25990 FQ	47850 AW	69230 TQ	OHBLS	10/01-12/01
	Canton-Massillon MSA, OH	Y	27520 FQ	39010 AW	57740 TQ	OHBLS	10/01-12/01
	Cincinnati PMSA, OH-KY-IN	Y	33300 FQ	52840 AW	80710 TQ	OHBLS	10/01-12/01
	Cleveland-Lorain-Elyria PMSA, OH	Y	19270 FQ	40520 AW	66020 TQ	OHBLS	10/01-12/01
	Dayton-Springfield MSA, OH	Y	34070 FQ	51540 AW	68770 TQ	OHBLS	10/01-12/01
	Toledo MSA, OH	Y	19690 FQ	37620 AW	64950 TQ	OHBLS	10/01-12/01
	Youngstown-Warren MSA, OH	Y	27040 FQ	39210 AW	55560 TQ	OHBLS	10/01-12/01
	Oklahoma	Y	28060 FQ	48330 AW	84780 TQ	OKBLS	10/01-12/01
	Oklahoma City MSA, OK	Y	30530 FQ	45850 AW	67350 TQ	OKBLS	10/01-12/01

AAW	Average annual wage	AOH	Average offered, high	ASH	Average starting, high	H	Hourly	M	Monthly	S	Special: hourly and annual
AE	Average entry wage	AOL	Average offered, low	ASL	Average starting, low	HI	Highest wage paid	MTC	Median total compensation	TQ	Third quartile wage
AEX	Average experienced wage	APH	Average pay, high range	AW	Average wage paid	HR	High end range	MW	Median wage paid	W	Weekly
AO	Average offered	APL	Average pay, low range	FQ	First quartile wage	LR	Low end range	SQ	Second quartile wage	Y	Yearly

Occupation/Type/Industry	Location	Per	Low	Mid	High	Source	Date
Environmental Scientist and Specialist, Including Health	Tulsa MSA, OK	Y	27600 FQ	50960 AW	97510 TQ	OKBLS	10/01-12/01
	Oregon	Y	31900 FQ	50900 AW	71290 TQ	ORBLS	10/01-12/01
	Portland-Vancouver PMSA, OR-WA	Y	31290 FQ	50850 AW	72220 TQ	ORBLS	10/01-12/01
	Pennsylvania	Y	27870 FQ	49350 AW	79350 TQ	PABLS	10/01-12/01
	Philadelphia PMSA, PA-NJ	Y	28260 FQ	50840 AW	79190 TQ	PABLS	10/01-12/01
	Pittsburgh MSA, PA	Y	26950 FQ	44360 AW	69660 TQ	PABLS	10/01-12/01
	Reading MSA, PA	Y	31570 FQ	47120 AW	69430 TQ	PABLS	10/01-12/01
	Rhode Island	Y	32100 FQ	52020 AW	73360 TQ	RIBLS	10/01-12/01
	Providence-Fall River-Warwick MSA, RI-MA	Y	31720 FQ	52610 AW	74720 TQ	RIBLS	10/01-12/01
	South Carolina	Y	24330 FQ	46290 AW	76950 TQ	SCBLS	10/01-12/01
	Charleston-North Charleston MSA, SC	Y	25600 FQ	46280 AW	63920 TQ	SCBLS	10/01-12/01
	Columbia MSA, SC	Y	23280 FQ	35430 AW	60570 TQ	SCBLS	10/01-12/01
	Greenville-Spartanburg-Anderson MSA, SC	Y	26740 FQ	49890 AW	80610 TQ	SCBLS	10/01-12/01
	South Dakota	Y	28500 FQ	42570 AW	57910 TQ	SDBLS	10/01-12/01
	Tennessee	Y	24840 FQ	42940 AW	67690 TQ	TNBLS	10/01-12/01
	Chattanooga MSA, TN-GA	Y	27140 FQ	39710 AW	54030 TQ	TNBLS	10/01-12/01
	Johnson City-Kingsport-Bristol MSA, TN-VA	Y	24320 FQ	42900 AW	67440 TQ	TNBLS	10/01-12/01
	Knoxville MSA, TN	Y	22290 FQ	41540 AW	69030 TQ	TNBLS	10/01-12/01
	Memphis MSA, TN-AR-MS	Y	26490 FQ	46520 AW	74740 TQ	TNBLS	10/01-12/01
	Nashville MSA, TN	Y	26370 FQ	41400 AW	58000 TQ	TNBLS	10/01-12/01
	Texas	Y	26720 FQ	46290 AW	76750 TQ	TXBLS	10/01-12/01
	Austin-San Marcos MSA, TX	Y	27060 FQ	45290 AW	67860 TQ	TXBLS	10/01-12/01
	Beaumont-Port Arthur MSA, TX	Y	27000 FQ	41230 AW	73540 TQ	TXBLS	10/01-12/01
	Brownsville-Harlingen-San Benito MSA, TX	Y	19730 FQ	31090 AW	51070 TQ	TXBLS	10/01-12/01
	Corpus Christi MSA, TX	Y	31520 FQ	54420 AW	87590 TQ	TXBLS	10/01-12/01
	Dallas PMSA, TX	Y	27380 FQ	44680 AW	68880 TQ	TXBLS	10/01-12/01
	El Paso MSA, TX	Y	24140 FQ	41030 AW	66560 TQ	TXBLS	10/01-12/01
	Fort Worth-Arlington PMSA, TX	Y	27550 FQ	37570 AW	47850 TQ	TXBLS	10/01-12/01
	Galveston-Texas City PMSA, TX	Y	29600 FQ	52120 AW	84580 TQ	TXBLS	10/01-12/01
	Houston PMSA, TX	Y	28850 FQ	61250 AW	106790 TQ	TXBLS	10/01-12/01
	Odessa-Midland MSA, TX	Y	28990 FQ	63750 AW	104660 TQ	TXBLS	10/01-12/01
	San Antonio MSA, TX	Y	29430 FQ	46280 AW	67100 TQ	TXBLS	10/01-12/01
	Utah	Y	31850 FQ	46990 AW	61430 TQ	UTBLS	10/01-12/01
	Provo-Orem MSA, UT	Y	32040 FQ	43500 AW	58790 TQ	UTBLS	10/01-12/01
	Salt Lake City-Ogden MSA, UT	Y	35620 FQ	47850 AW	57950 TQ	UTBLS	10/01-12/01
	Vermont	Y	25720 FQ	43480 AW	67260 TQ	VTBLS	10/01-12/01
	Burlington MSA, VT	Y	23200 FQ	42270 AW	79120 TQ	VTBLS	10/01-12/01
	Virginia	Y	29500 FQ	52870 AW	88320 TQ	VABLS	10/01-12/01
	Lynchburg MSA, VA	Y	25160 FQ	39760 AW	65200 TQ	VABLS	10/01-12/01
	Norfolk-Virginia Beach-Newport News MSA, VA-NC	Y	28820 FQ	43990 AW	64950 TQ	VABLS	10/01-12/01
	Richmond-Petersburg MSA, VA	Y	30860 FQ	44840 AW	65570 TQ	VABLS	10/01-12/01
	Roanoke MSA, VA	Y	29160 FQ	41000 AW	54580 TQ	VABLS	10/01-12/01
	Washington	Y	34500 FQ	55390 AW	82170 TQ	WABLS	10/01-12/01
	Bremerton PMSA, WA	Y	39460 FQ	53490 AW	69970 TQ	WABLS	10/01-12/01
	Olympia PMSA, WA	Y	36070 FQ	49060 AW	63420 TQ	WABLS	10/01-12/01
	Richland-Kennewick-Pasco MSA, WA	Y	42530 FQ	65540 AW	95640 TQ	WABLS	10/01-12/01
	Seattle-Bellevue-Everett PMSA, WA	Y	30550 FQ	56260 AW	85430 TQ	WABLS	10/01-12/01
	Spokane MSA, WA	Y	31560 FQ	46740 AW	58910 TQ	WABLS	10/01-12/01
	Tacoma PMSA, WA	Y	38140 FQ	53210 AW	72850 TQ	WABLS	10/01-12/01
	West Virginia	Y	26360 FQ	41460 AW	58690 TQ	WVBLS	10/01-12/01
	Charleston MSA, WV	Y	26250 FQ	38830 AW	53560 TQ	WVBLS	10/01-12/01
	Wisconsin	Y	29190 FQ	45360 AW	64280 TQ	WIBLS	10/01-12/01
	Appleton-Oshkosh-Neenah MSA, WI	Y	32280 FQ	47470 AW	63530 TQ	WIBLS	10/01-12/01
	Green Bay MSA, WI	Y	31500 FQ	47900 AW	69990 TQ	WIBLS	10/01-12/01
	Madison MSA, WI	Y	35590 FQ	48680 AW	67620 TQ	WIBLS	10/01-12/01

AAW Average annual wage **AOH** Average offered, high **ASH** Average starting, high **H** Hourly **M** Monthly **S** Special: hourly and annual
AE Average entry wage **AOL** Average offered, low **ASL** Average starting, low **HI** Highest wage paid **MTC** Median total compensation **TQ** Third quartile wage
AEX Average experienced wage **APH** Average pay, high range **AW** Average wage paid **HR** High end range **MW** Median wage paid **W** Weekly
AO Average offered **APL** Average pay, low range **FQ** First quartile wage **LR** Low end range **SQ** Second quartile wage **Y** Yearly

Occupation/Type/Industry	Location	Per	Low	Mid	High	Source	Date
Environmental Scientist and Specialist, Including Health	Milwaukee-Waukesha PMSA, WI	Y	30470 FQ	45800 AW	66430 TQ	WIBLS	10/01-12/01
	Wyoming	Y	27040 FQ	51870 AW	80120 TQ	WYBLS	10/01-12/01
	Puerto Rico	Y	14520 FQ	26820 AW	48030 TQ	PRBLS	10/01-12/01
	Virgin Islands	Y	24200 FQ	32100 AW	48930 TQ	VIBLS	10/01-12/01
	Guam	Y	25390 FQ	48690 AW	83210 TQ	GUBLS	10/01-12/01
Environmental Technology Professional	San Diego, CA	Y		45429 AW		SDBJ1	1/99-1/00
Epidemiologist	California	Y	45720 FQ	57600 AW	72300 TQ	CABLS	10/01-12/01
	Los Angeles-Long Beach PMSA, CA	Y	45810 FQ	53710 AW	67170 TQ	CABLS	10/01-12/01
	Oakland PMSA, CA	Y	40230 FQ	65470 AW	106090 TQ	CABLS	10/01-12/01
	San Jose PMSA, CA	Y	73650 FQ	95060 AW	135160 TQ	CABLS	10/01-12/01
	District of Columbia	Y	36400 FQ	60700 AW	86640 TQ	DCBLS	10/01-12/01
	Washington PMSA, DC-MD-VA-WV	Y	40240 FQ	69790 AW	100750 TQ	DCBLS	10/01-12/01
	Florida	Y	40080 FQ	54920 AW	72010 TQ	FLBLS	10/01-12/01
	Georgia	Y	36290 FQ	53260 AW	77220 TQ	GABLS	10/01-12/01
	Atlanta MSA, GA	Y	36230 FQ	54480 AW	83620 TQ	GABLS	10/01-12/01
	Hawaii	Y	30800 FQ	42450 AW	54790 TQ	HIBLS	10/01-12/01
	Honolulu MSA, HI	Y	30850 FQ	43300 AW	58100 TQ	HIBLS	10/01-12/01
	Idaho	Y	36940 FQ	54120 AW	71870 TQ	IDBLS	10/01-12/01
	Illinois	Y	33950 FQ	48780 AW	65530 TQ	ILBLS	10/01-12/01
	Chicago PMSA, IL	Y	35060 FQ	48940 AW	65430 TQ	ILBLS	10/01-12/01
	Louisiana	Y	25420 FQ	37610 AW	52500 TQ	LABLS	10/01-12/01
	New Orleans MSA, LA	Y	28750 FQ	38280 AW	52890 TQ	LABLS	10/01-12/01
	Maryland	Y	39280 FQ	65610 AW	107540 TQ	MDBLS	10/01-12/01
	Baltimore PMSA, MD	Y	39220 FQ	64950 AW	107700 TQ	MDBLS	10/01-12/01
	Massachusetts	Y	38940 FQ	55490 AW	75230 TQ	MABLS	10/01-12/01
	Boston PMSA, MA-NH	Y	39050 FQ	54570 AW	73080 TQ	MABLS	10/01-12/01
	Michigan	Y	37880 FQ	51520 AW	66570 TQ	MIBLS	10/01-12/01
	Minnesota	Y	41330 FQ	59880 AW	84490 TQ	MNBLS	10/01-12/01
	Minneapolis-St. Paul MSA, MN-WI	Y	40980 FQ	60110 AW	85720 TQ	MNBLS	10/01-12/01
	Mississippi	Y	21100 FQ	27490 AW	35940 TQ	MSBLS	10/01-12/01
	New Jersey	Y	40170 FQ	63370 AW	100500 TQ	NJBLS	10/01-12/01
	New York	Y	30170 FQ	60540 AW	103530 TQ	NYBLS	10/01-12/01
	North Carolina	Y	29900 FQ	54390 AW	89140 TQ	NCBLS	10/01-12/01
	Raleigh-Durham-Chapel Hill MSA, NC	Y	34350 FQ	58970 AW	92320 TQ	NCBLS	10/01-12/01
	Oregon	Y	40340 FQ	59410 AW	111310 TQ	ORBLS	10/01-12/01
	Pennsylvania	Y	27950 FQ	49920 AW	71270 TQ	PABLS	10/01-12/01
	Tennessee	Y	36240 FQ	62500 AW	101090 TQ	TNBLS	10/01-12/01
	Nashville MSA, TN	Y	37010 FQ	64880 AW	107260 TQ	TNBLS	10/01-12/01
	Texas	Y	31300 FQ	50230 AW	69950 TQ	TXBLS	10/01-12/01
	Houston PMSA, TX	Y	27820 FQ	47890 AW	69970 TQ	TXBLS	10/01-12/01
	Utah	Y	33580 FQ	51110 AW	73970 TQ	UTBLS	10/01-12/01
	Virginia	Y	40990 FQ	76590 AW	110620 TQ	VABLS	10/01-12/01
	Washington	Y	45460 FQ	69350 AW	108140 TQ	WABLS	10/01-12/01
	Wisconsin	Y	34480 FQ	49550 AW	67720 TQ	WIBLS	10/01-12/01
	Puerto Rico	Y	23450 FQ	28340 AW	36560 TQ	PRBLS	10/01-12/01
Etcher and Engraver	Alabama	H	7.85 FQ	10.77 AW	13.83 TQ	ALBLS	10/01-12/01
	Arizona	H	6.91 FQ	12.35 AW	23.46 TQ	AZBLS	10/01-12/01
	Arkansas	H	6.97 FQ	11.43 AW	16.99 TQ	ARBLS	10/01-12/01
	California	H	7.41 FQ	11.89 AW	18.38 TQ	CABLS	10/01-12/01
	Colorado	H	7.04 FQ	10.76 AW	16.64 TQ	COBLS	10/01-12/01
	Florida	H	6.91 FQ	9.64 AW	13.88 TQ	FLBLS	10/01-12/01
	Georgia	H	8.46 FQ	11.20 AW	15.72 TQ	GABLS	10/01-12/01
	Hawaii	H	6.89 FQ	8.89 AW	11.98 TQ	HIBLS	10/01-12/01
	Idaho	H	8.74 FQ	9.63 AW	10.85 TQ	IDBLS	10/01-12/01
	Illinois	H	7.42 FQ	17.73 AW	34.30 TQ	ILBLS	10/01-12/01
	Indiana	H	6.26 FQ	10.44 AW	16.55 TQ	INBLS	10/01-12/01
	Iowa	H	7.65 FQ	12.06 AW	17.66 TQ	IABLS	10/01-12/01
	Kansas	H	5.95 FQ	9.53 AW	18.29 TQ	KSBLS	10/01-12/01
	Kentucky	H	6.52 FQ	12.91 AW	21.43 TQ	KYBLS	10/01-12/01
	Louisiana	H	5.61 FQ	7.19 AW	10.06 TQ	LABLS	10/01-12/01
	Maine	H	8.89 FQ	10.08 AW	11.90 TQ	MEBLS	10/01-12/01
	Maryland	H	7.62 FQ	12.61 AW	19.44 TQ	MDBLS	10/01-12/01

AAW	Average annual wage	**AOH**	Average offered, high	**ASH**	Average starting, high	**H**	Hourly	**M**	Monthly	**S**	Special: hourly and annual
AE	Average entry wage	**AOL**	Average offered, low	**ASL**	Average starting, low	**HI**	Highest wage paid	**MTC**	Median total compensation	**TQ**	Third quartile wage
AEX	Average experienced wage	**APH**	Average pay, high range	**AW**	Average wage paid	**HR**	High end range	**MW**	Median wage paid	**W**	Weekly
AO	Average offered	**APL**	Average pay, low range	**FQ**	First quartile wage	**LR**	Low end range	**SQ**	Second quartile wage	**Y**	Yearly

Occupation/Type/Industry	Location	Per	Low	Mid	High	Source	Date
Etcher and Engraver	Massachusetts	H	7.78 FQ	11.70 AW	17.66 TQ	MABLS	10/01-12/01
	Michigan	H	7.43 FQ	14.13 AW	24.72 TQ	MIBLS	10/01-12/01
	Minnesota	H	6.39 FQ	12.36 AW	17.53 TQ	MNBLS	10/01-12/01
	Mississippi	H	7.70 FQ	10.32 AW	13.17 TQ	MSBLS	10/01-12/01
	Missouri	H	7.80 FQ	11.01 AW	15.38 TQ	MOBLS	10/01-12/01
	New Jersey	H	6.74 FQ	14.39 AW	29.75 TQ	NJBLS	10/01-12/01
	New York	H	7.51 FQ	12.67 AW	19.32 TQ	NYBLS	10/01-12/01
	North Carolina	H	7.88 FQ	11.23 AW	15.80 TQ	NCBLS	10/01-12/01
	North Dakota	H	5.96 FQ	8.56 AW	10.85 TQ	NDBLS	10/01-12/01
	Ohio	H	7.48 FQ	12.26 AW	18.13 TQ	OHBLS	10/01-12/01
	Oklahoma	H	6.29 FQ	9.71 AW	15.31 TQ	OKBLS	10/01-12/01
	Oregon	H	7.51 FQ	12.00 AW	20.46 TQ	ORBLS	10/01-12/01
	Pennsylvania	H	7.60 FQ	11.00 AW	15.39 TQ	PABLS	10/01-12/01
	Rhode Island	H	6.74 FQ	12.74 AW	20.77 TQ	RIBLS	10/01-12/01
	South Carolina	H	7.31 FQ	11.80 AW	16.91 TQ	SCBLS	10/01-12/01
	South Dakota	H	7.54 FQ	10.01 AW	13.17 TQ	SDBLS	10/01-12/01
	Tennessee	H	8.07 FQ	11.86 AW	17.18 TQ	TNBLS	10/01-12/01
	Texas	H	6.47 FQ	11.24 AW	16.36 TQ	TXBLS	10/01-12/01
	Utah	H	8.80 FQ	11.01 AW	13.47 TQ	UTBLS	10/01-12/01
	Virginia	H	8.69 FQ	14.34 AW	23.99 TQ	VABLS	10/01-12/01
	Washington	H	7.88 FQ	15.78 AW	26.56 TQ	WABLS	10/01-12/01
	Wisconsin	H	8.20 FQ	13.72 AW	21.60 TQ	WIBLS	10/01-12/01
Excavating and Loading Machine and Dragline Operator	Alabama	H	9.25 FQ	14.91 AW	23.40 TQ	ALBLS	10/01-12/01
	Birmingham MSA, AL	H	10.81 FQ	17.06 AW	28.18 TQ	ALBLS	10/01-12/01
	Huntsville MSA, AL	H	8.99 FQ	11.94 AW	14.47 TQ	ALBLS	10/01-12/01
	Mobile MSA, AL	H	9.38 FQ	12.53 AW	17.17 TQ	ALBLS	10/01-12/01
	Montgomery MSA, AL	H	7.71 FQ	10.95 AW	18.39 TQ	ALBLS	10/01-12/01
	Alaska	H	11.91 FQ	22.00 AW	37.06 TQ	AKBLS	10/01-12/01
	Anchorage MSA, AK	H	10.52 FQ	16.90 AW	24.90 TQ	AKBLS	10/01-12/01
	Arizona	H	10.81 FQ	18.56 AW	27.70 TQ	AZBLS	10/01-12/01
	Phoenix-Mesa MSA, AZ	H	10.89 FQ	19.48 AW	28.22 TQ	AZBLS	10/01-12/01
	Arkansas	H	7.85 FQ	11.43 AW	15.98 TQ	ARBLS	10/01-12/01
	Fayetteville-Springdale-Rogers MSA, AR	H	10.07 FQ	13.13 AW	16.62 TQ	ARBLS	10/01-12/01
	Fort Smith MSA, AR-OK	H	6.26 FQ	11.53 AW	16.15 TQ	ARBLS	10/01-12/01
	Little Rock-North Little Rock MSA, AR	H	9.33 FQ	12.05 AW	16.08 TQ	ARBLS	10/01-12/01
	California	H	13.20 FQ	22.16 AW	32.36 TQ	CABLS	10/01-12/01
	Bakersfield MSA, CA	H	12.31 FQ	15.95 AW	20.26 TQ	CABLS	10/01-12/01
	Fresno MSA, CA	H	11.35 FQ	14.04 AW	19.16 TQ	CABLS	10/01-12/01
	Los Angeles-Long Beach PMSA, CA	H	13.08 FQ	21.78 AW	29.22 TQ	CABLS	10/01-12/01
	Modesto MSA, CA	H	15.54 FQ	26.03 AW	35.01 TQ	CABLS	10/01-12/01
	Oakland PMSA, CA	H	15.34 FQ	22.58 AW	27.89 TQ	CABLS	10/01-12/01
	Orange County PMSA, CA	H	11.97 FQ	17.25 AW	26.23 TQ	CABLS	10/01-12/01
	Redding MSA, CA	H	16.61 FQ	26.64 AW	34.42 TQ	CABLS	10/01-12/01
	Riverside-San Bernardino PMSA, CA	H	16.47 FQ	22.92 AW	32.94 TQ	CABLS	10/01-12/01
	Sacramento PMSA, CA	H	15.28 FQ	18.36 AW	21.37 TQ	CABLS	10/01-12/01
	San Diego MSA, CA	H	12.18 FQ	22.52 AW	33.67 TQ	CABLS	10/01-12/01
	San Jose PMSA, CA	H	14.58 FQ	23.31 AW	32.70 TQ	CABLS	10/01-12/01
	Santa Barbara-Santa Maria-Lompoc MSA, CA	H	8.19 FQ	14.87 AW	22.68 TQ	CABLS	10/01-12/01
	Santa Rosa PMSA, CA	H	15.50 FQ	21.94 AW	27.59 TQ	CABLS	10/01-12/01
	Stockton-Lodi MSA, CA	H	14.84 FQ	27.53 AW	34.70 TQ	CABLS	10/01-12/01
	Vallejo-Fairfield-Napa PMSA, CA	H	16.71 FQ	25.22 AW	39.91 TQ	CABLS	10/01-12/01
	Ventura PMSA, CA	H	15.86 FQ	25.81 AW	33.35 TQ	CABLS	10/01-12/01
	Visalia-Tulare-Porterville MSA, CA	H	10.02 FQ	15.31 AW	20.76 TQ	CABLS	10/01-12/01
	Colorado	H	12.71 FQ	16.78 AW	21.19 TQ	COBLS	10/01-12/01
	Colorado Springs MSA, CO	H	12.01 FQ	15.47 AW	19.51 TQ	COBLS	10/01-12/01
	Denver PMSA, CO	H	14.32 FQ	17.53 AW	21.05 TQ	COBLS	10/01-12/01
	Fort Collins-Loveland MSA, CO	H	12.78 FQ	16.13 AW	20.62 TQ	COBLS	10/01-12/01
	Greeley PMSA, CO	H	10.08 FQ	15.11 AW	19.04 TQ	COBLS	10/01-12/01
	Connecticut	H	13.61 FQ	17.92 AW	24.13 TQ	CTBLS	10/01-12/01
	Bridgeport PMSA, CT	H	17.94 FQ	21.20 AW	25.94 TQ	CTBLS	10/01-12/01
	Hartford MSA, CT	H	13.74 FQ	16.98 AW	23.22 TQ	CTBLS	10/01-12/01
	Stamford-Norwalk PMSA, CT	H	15.88 FQ	19.80 AW	23.01 TQ	CTBLS	10/01-12/01

AAW	Average annual wage	AOH	Average offered, high	ASH	Average starting, high	H	Hourly	M	Monthly	S	Special: hourly and annual
AE	Average entry wage	AOL	Average offered, low	ASL	Average starting, low	HI	Highest wage paid	MTC	Median total compensation	TQ	Third quartile wage
AEX	Average experienced wage	APH	Average pay, high range	AW	Average wage paid	HR	High end range	MW	Median wage paid	W	Weekly
AO	Average offered	APL	Average pay, low range	FQ	First quartile wage	LR	Low end range	SQ	Second quartile wage	Y	Yearly

Occupation/Type/Industry	Location	Per	Low	Mid	High	Source	Date
Excavating and Loading Machine and Dragline Operator	Delaware	H	13.51 FQ	16.84 AW	21.17 TQ	DEBLS	10/01-12/01
	Wilmington-Newark PMSA, DE-MD	H	11.28 FQ	15.68 AW	20.81 TQ	DEBLS	10/01-12/01
	Washington PMSA, DC-MD-VA-WV	H	10.14 FQ	14.17 AW	19.19 TQ	DCBLS	10/01-12/01
	Florida	H	9.24 FQ	13.09 AW	17.75 TQ	FLBLS	10/01-12/01
	Daytona Beach MSA, FL	H	9.51 FQ	15.53 AW	24.07 TQ	FLBLS	10/01-12/01
	Fort Lauderdale PMSA, FL	H	11.62 FQ	15.11 AW	20.55 TQ	FLBLS	10/01-12/01
	Fort Myers-Cape Coral MSA, FL	H	9.45 FQ	12.49 AW	15.69 TQ	FLBLS	10/01-12/01
	Fort Pierce-Port St. Lucie MSA, FL	H	9.44 FQ	12.61 AW	16.91 TQ	FLBLS	10/01-12/01
	Jacksonville MSA, FL	H	9.22 FQ	11.70 AW	13.93 TQ	FLBLS	10/01-12/01
	Lakeland-Winter Haven MSA, FL	H	11.03 FQ	14.40 AW	18.11 TQ	FLBLS	10/01-12/01
	Miami PMSA, FL	H	9.66 FQ	14.89 AW	24.92 TQ	FLBLS	10/01-12/01
	Naples MSA, FL	H	12.53 FQ	16.28 AW	22.68 TQ	FLBLS	10/01-12/01
	Ocala MSA, FL	H	8.53 FQ	12.20 AW	19.14 TQ	FLBLS	10/01-12/01
	Orlando MSA, FL	H	9.53 FQ	12.57 AW	16.24 TQ	FLBLS	10/01-12/01
	Pensacola MSA, FL	H	8.36 FQ	11.82 AW	16.50 TQ	FLBLS	10/01-12/01
	Sarasota-Bradenton MSA, FL	H	9.19 FQ	11.83 AW	15.11 TQ	FLBLS	10/01-12/01
	Tampa-St. Petersburg-Clearwater MSA, FL	H	8.94 FQ	11.79 AW	15.99 TQ	FLBLS	10/01-12/01
	West Palm Beach-Boca Raton MSA, FL	H	9.01 FQ	13.05 AW	17.60 TQ	FLBLS	10/01-12/01
	Georgia	H	9.45 FQ	16.04 AW	28.26 TQ	GABLS	10/01-12/01
	Atlanta MSA, GA	H	10.75 FQ	19.45 AW	31.80 TQ	GABLS	10/01-12/01
	Augusta-Aiken MSA, GA-SC	H	9.44 FQ	13.67 AW	21.04 TQ	GABLS	10/01-12/01
	Columbus MSA, GA-AL	H	7.69 FQ	11.36 AW	15.73 TQ	GABLS	10/01-12/01
	Macon MSA, GA	H	9.45 FQ	12.97 AW	16.90 TQ	GABLS	10/01-12/01
	Savannah MSA, GA	H	9.24 FQ	12.38 AW	15.78 TQ	GABLS	10/01-12/01
	Hawaii	H	13.59 FQ	26.75 AW	41.08 TQ	HIBLS	10/01-12/01
	Honolulu MSA, HI	H	23.26 FQ	33.06 AW	51.49 TQ	HIBLS	10/01-12/01
	Idaho	H	10.64 FQ	14.48 AW	18.77 TQ	IDBLS	10/01-12/01
	Boise City MSA, ID	H	9.71 FQ	14.11 AW	19.72 TQ	IDBLS	10/01-12/01
	Illinois	H	15.53 FQ	23.68 AW	28.32 TQ	ILBLS	10/01-12/01
	Chicago PMSA, IL	H	13.24 FQ	24.27 AW	33.32 TQ	ILBLS	10/01-12/01
	Peoria-Pekin MSA, IL	H	14.37 FQ	24.03 AW	33.07 TQ	ILBLS	10/01-12/01
	Springfield MSA, IL	H	18.30 FQ	23.10 AW	28.00 TQ	ILBLS	10/01-12/01
	Indiana	H	11.94 FQ	17.35 AW	23.23 TQ	INBLS	10/01-12/01
	Evansville-Henderson MSA, IN-KY	H	14.15 FQ	19.36 AW	26.95 TQ	INBLS	10/01-12/01
	Fort Wayne MSA, IN	H	11.95 FQ	17.59 AW	26.38 TQ	INBLS	10/01-12/01
	Indianapolis MSA, IN	H	14.78 FQ	19.18 AW	22.25 TQ	INBLS	10/01-12/01
	Lafayette MSA, IN	H	13.95 FQ	16.61 AW	20.41 TQ	INBLS	10/01-12/01
	Iowa	H	9.98 FQ	15.46 AW	23.27 TQ	IABLS	10/01-12/01
	Cedar Rapids MSA, IA	H	10.98 FQ	16.23 AW	22.14 TQ	IABLS	10/01-12/01
	Davenport-Moline-Rock Island MSA, IA-IL	H	13.85 FQ	16.05 AW	20.63 TQ	IABLS	10/01-12/01
	Des Moines MSA, IA	H	10.68 FQ	18.90 AW	26.25 TQ	IABLS	10/01-12/01
	Kansas	H	9.27 FQ	13.78 AW	20.45 TQ	KSBLS	10/01-12/01
	Wichita MSA, KS	H	9.02 FQ	11.86 AW	16.80 TQ	KSBLS	10/01-12/01
	Kentucky	H	9.68 FQ	13.99 AW	20.74 TQ	KYBLS	10/01-12/01
	Lexington MSA, KY	H	12.05 FQ	20.18 AW	28.08 TQ	KYBLS	10/01-12/01
	Louisville MSA, KY-IN	H	9.73 FQ	14.18 AW	19.20 TQ	KYBLS	10/01-12/01
	Louisiana	H	8.83 FQ	13.66 AW	21.57 TQ	LABLS	10/01-12/01
	Baton Rouge MSA, LA	H	8.00 FQ	13.62 AW	23.12 TQ	LABLS	10/01-12/01
	Lafayette MSA, LA	H	8.66 FQ	15.86 AW	25.72 TQ	LABLS	10/01-12/01
	Lake Charles MSA, LA	H	9.98 FQ	15.39 AW	25.95 TQ	LABLS	10/01-12/01
	New Orleans MSA, LA	H	8.41 FQ	12.43 AW	16.48 TQ	LABLS	10/01-12/01
	Maine	H	9.91 FQ	13.72 AW	17.95 TQ	MEBLS	10/01-12/01
	Portland MSA, ME	H	10.16 FQ	14.12 AW	17.72 TQ	MEBLS	10/01-12/01
	Maryland	H	11.23 FQ	15.03 AW	20.14 TQ	MDBLS	10/01-12/01
	Baltimore PMSA, MD	H	11.71 FQ	15.95 AW	20.65 TQ	MDBLS	10/01-12/01
	Massachusetts	H	15.46 FQ	21.99 AW	32.86 TQ	MABLS	10/01-12/01
	Boston PMSA, MA-NH	H	17.73 FQ	22.98 AW	36.89 TQ	MABLS	10/01-12/01
	Brockton PMSA, MA	H	16.36 FQ	23.03 AW	32.22 TQ	MABLS	10/01-12/01
	Lawrence PMSA, MA-NH	H	10.59 FQ	16.73 AW	21.68 TQ	MABLS	10/01-12/01
	Lowell PMSA, MA-NH	H	13.20 FQ	20.27 AW	28.88 TQ	MABLS	10/01-12/01
	New Bedford PMSA, MA	H	15.45 FQ	20.26 AW	25.32 TQ	MABLS	10/01-12/01
	Springfield MSA, MA	H	11.46 FQ	19.64 AW	27.35 TQ	MABLS	10/01-12/01

AAW Average annual wage **AE** Average entry wage **AEX** Average experienced wage **AO** Average offered **AOH** Average offered, high **AOL** Average offered, low **APH** Average pay, high range **APL** Average pay, low range **ASH** Average starting, high **ASL** Average starting, low **AW** Average wage paid **FQ** First quartile wage **H** Hourly **HI** Highest wage paid **HR** High end range **LR** Low end range **M** Monthly **MTC** Median total compensation **MW** Median wage paid **SQ** Second quartile wage **S** Special: hourly and annual **TQ** Third quartile wage **W** Weekly **Y** Yearly

Occupation/Type/Industry	Location	Per	Low	Mid	High	Source	Date
Excavating and Loading Machine and Dragline Operator	Worcester PMSA, MA-CT	H	14.03 FQ	19.40 AW	24.95 TQ	MABLS	10/01-12/01
	Michigan	H	11.11 FQ	17.39 AW	26.84 TQ	MIBLS	10/01-12/01
	Ann Arbor PMSA, MI	H	11.53 FQ	14.47 AW	20.71 TQ	MIBLS	10/01-12/01
	Detroit PMSA, MI	H	13.10 FQ	22.02 AW	31.37 TQ	MIBLS	10/01-12/01
	Flint PMSA, MI	H	11.93 FQ	17.77 AW	21.36 TQ	MIBLS	10/01-12/01
	Grand Rapids-Muskegon-Holland MSA, MI	H	11.61 FQ	16.63 AW	25.91 TQ	MIBLS	10/01-12/01
	Kalamazoo-Battle Creek MSA, MI	H	9.19 FQ	12.30 AW	19.62 TQ	MIBLS	10/01-12/01
	Lansing-East Lansing MSA, MI	H	12.09 FQ	18.32 AW	26.20 TQ	MIBLS	10/01-12/01
	Saginaw-Bay City-Midland MSA, MI	H	10.01 FQ	18.88 AW	26.74 TQ	MIBLS	10/01-12/01
	Minnesota	H	11.32 FQ	17.47 AW	24.86 TQ	MNBLS	10/01-12/01
	Duluth-Superior MSA, MN-WI	H	15.43 FQ	19.63 AW	25.70 TQ	MNBLS	10/01-12/01
	Minneapolis-St. Paul MSA, MN-WI	H	11.82 FQ	18.08 AW	25.46 TQ	MNBLS	10/01-12/01
	St. Cloud MSA, MN	H	12.03 FQ	15.32 AW	18.06 TQ	MNBLS	10/01-12/01
	Mississippi	H	9.16 FQ	12.60 AW	17.58 TQ	MSBLS	10/01-12/01
	Biloxi-Gulfport-Pascagoula MSA, MS	H	9.03 FQ	11.08 AW	13.20 TQ	MSBLS	10/01-12/01
	Missouri	H	9.43 FQ	15.09 AW	20.99 TQ	MOBLS	10/01-12/01
	Kansas City MSA, MO-KS	H	12.89 FQ	17.08 AW	21.41 TQ	MOBLS	10/01-12/01
	St. Louis MSA, MO-IL	H	11.75 FQ	18.16 AW	26.77 TQ	MOBLS	10/01-12/01
	Springfield MSA, MO	H	9.28 FQ	13.51 AW	20.27 TQ	MOBLS	10/01-12/01
	Montana	H	14.06 FQ	17.34 AW	23.35 TQ	MTBLS	10/01-12/01
	Nebraska	H	10.43 FQ	15.29 AW	20.37 TQ	NEBLS	10/01-12/01
	Lincoln MSA, NE	H	12.55 FQ	15.15 AW	17.27 TQ	NEBLS	10/01-12/01
	Omaha MSA, NE-IA	H	11.09 FQ	15.87 AW	20.66 TQ	NEBLS	10/01-12/01
	Nevada	H	14.51 FQ	19.69 AW	25.91 TQ	NVBLS	10/01-12/01
	Las Vegas MSA, NV-AZ	H	14.58 FQ	19.76 AW	26.05 TQ	NVBLS	10/01-12/01
	New Hampshire	H	11.98 FQ	16.44 AW	22.14 TQ	NHBLS	10/01-12/01
	Manchester PMSA, NH	H	14.31 FQ	17.03 AW	20.91 TQ	NHBLS	10/01-12/01
	Nashua PMSA, NH	H	14.02 FQ	17.65 AW	22.77 TQ	NHBLS	10/01-12/01
	Portsmouth-Rochester PMSA, NH-ME	H	13.36 FQ	18.49 AW	24.50 TQ	NHBLS	10/01-12/01
	New Jersey	H	12.20 FQ	20.39 AW	32.02 TQ	NJBLS	10/01-12/01
	Bergen-Passaic PMSA, NJ	H	13.45 FQ	22.02 AW	33.57 TQ	NJBLS	10/01-12/01
	Jersey City PMSA, NJ	H	11.24 FQ	16.46 AW	26.57 TQ	NJBLS	10/01-12/01
	Middlesex-Somerset-Hunterdon PMSA, NJ	H	14.08 FQ	20.90 AW	29.68 TQ	NJBLS	10/01-12/01
	Monmouth-Ocean PMSA, NJ	H	11.45 FQ	17.20 AW	22.27 TQ	NJBLS	10/01-12/01
	Newark PMSA, NJ	H	11.80 FQ	19.17 AW	28.80 TQ	NJBLS	10/01-12/01
	New Mexico	H	9.72 FQ	17.28 AW	27.81 TQ	NMBLS	10/01-12/01
	Albuquerque MSA, NM	H	11.39 FQ	19.01 AW	26.90 TQ	NMBLS	10/01-12/01
	Las Cruces MSA, NM	H	5.94 FQ	12.07 AW	19.85 TQ	NMBLS	10/01-12/01
	New York	H	10.22 FQ	17.12 AW	27.30 TQ	NYBLS	10/01-12/01
	Albany-Schenectady-Troy MSA, NY	H	9.92 FQ	18.12 AW	27.10 TQ	NYBLS	10/01-12/01
	Buffalo-Niagara Falls MSA, NY	H	10.17 FQ	18.66 AW	27.23 TQ	NYBLS	10/01-12/01
	Dutchess County PMSA, NY	H	14.35 FQ	17.16 AW	21.66 TQ	NYBLS	10/01-12/01
	Nassau-Suffolk PMSA, NY	H	9.31 FQ	14.80 AW	22.20 TQ	NYBLS	10/01-12/01
	New York PMSA, NY	H	17.19 FQ	26.27 AW	41.49 TQ	NYBLS	10/01-12/01
	Rochester MSA, NY	H	11.52 FQ	18.92 AW	32.39 TQ	NYBLS	10/01-12/01
	Utica-Rome MSA, NY	H	12.15 FQ	16.40 AW	20.52 TQ	NYBLS	10/01-12/01
	North Carolina	H	9.78 FQ	14.36 AW	19.04 TQ	NCBLS	10/01-12/01
	Asheville MSA, NC	H	7.67 FQ	12.87 AW	23.38 TQ	NCBLS	10/01-12/01
	Charlotte-Gastonia-Rock Hill MSA, NC-SC	H	11.74 FQ	15.07 AW	18.11 TQ	NCBLS	10/01-12/01
	Greensboro-Winston-Salem-High Point MSA, NC	H	10.44 FQ	13.94 AW	17.48 TQ	NCBLS	10/01-12/01
	Hickory-Morganton-Lenoir MSA, NC	H	10.26 FQ	15.09 AW	24.36 TQ	NCBLS	10/01-12/01
	Raleigh-Durham-Chapel Hill MSA, NC	H	11.20 FQ	15.56 AW	20.53 TQ	NCBLS	10/01-12/01
	Wilmington MSA, NC	H	11.18 FQ	16.00 AW	20.81 TQ	NCBLS	10/01-12/01
	North Dakota	H	14.09 FQ	19.28 AW	27.14 TQ	NDBLS	10/01-12/01
	Fargo-Moorhead MSA, ND-MN	H	14.30 FQ	16.37 AW	20.06 TQ	NDBLS	10/01-12/01
	Ohio	H	10.03 FQ	18.61 AW	30.86 TQ	OHBLS	10/01-12/01
	Canton-Massillon MSA, OH	H	9.73 FQ	19.98 AW	26.96 TQ	OHBLS	10/01-12/01

AAW Average annual wage	**AOH** Average offered, high	**ASH** Average starting, high	**H** Hourly	**M** Monthly	**S** Special: hourly and annual
AE Average entry wage	**AOL** Average offered, low	**ASL** Average starting, low	**HI** Highest wage paid	**MTC** Median total compensation	**TQ** Third quartile wage
AEX Average experienced wage	**APH** Average pay, high range	**AW** Average wage paid	**HR** High end range	**MW** Median wage paid	**W** Weekly
AO Average offered	**APL** Average pay, low range	**FQ** First quartile wage	**LR** Low end range	**SQ** Second quartile wage	**Y** Yearly

Occupation/Type/Industry	Location	Per	Low	Mid	High	Source	Date
Excavating and Loading Machine and Dragline Operator	Cincinnati PMSA, OH-KY-IN	H	12.78 FQ	17.43 AW	21.11 TQ	OHBLS	10/01-12/01
	Cleveland-Lorain-Elyria PMSA, OH	H	14.70 FQ	18.89 AW	23.37 TQ	OHBLS	10/01-12/01
	Columbus MSA, OH	H	13.24 FQ	20.44 AW	35.68 TQ	OHBLS	10/01-12/01
	Dayton-Springfield MSA, OH	H	21.43 FQ	28.92 AW	34.84 TQ	OHBLS	10/01-12/01
	Hamilton-Middletown PMSA, OH	H	14.33 FQ	16.77 AW	20.76 TQ	OHBLS	10/01-12/01
	Youngstown-Warren MSA, OH	H	9.26 FQ	13.88 AW	20.20 TQ	OHBLS	10/01-12/01
	Oklahoma	H	9.16 FQ	12.53 AW	16.86 TQ	OKBLS	10/01-12/01
	Oklahoma City MSA, OK	H	9.32 FQ	12.36 AW	16.73 TQ	OKBLS	10/01-12/01
	Tulsa MSA, OK	H	10.34 FQ	13.89 AW	18.46 TQ	OKBLS	10/01-12/01
	Oregon	H	11.84 FQ	17.97 AW	25.64 TQ	ORBLS	10/01-12/01
	Eugene-Springfield MSA, OR	H	11.80 FQ	16.97 AW	23.49 TQ	ORBLS	10/01-12/01
	Portland-Vancouver PMSA, OR-WA	H	15.60 FQ	21.15 AW	27.53 TQ	ORBLS	10/01-12/01
	Salem PMSA, OR	H	13.46 FQ	18.79 AW	26.86 TQ	ORBLS	10/01-12/01
	Pennsylvania	H	9.74 FQ	15.55 AW	21.82 TQ	PABLS	10/01-12/01
	Allentown-Bethlehem-Easton MSA, PA	H	12.84 FQ	17.01 AW	21.55 TQ	PABLS	10/01-12/01
	Harrisburg-Lebanon-Carlisle MSA, PA	H	10.96 FQ	15.77 AW	25.55 TQ	PABLS	10/01-12/01
	Johnstown MSA, PA	H	10.25 FQ	13.82 AW	17.55 TQ	PABLS	10/01-12/01
	Philadelphia PMSA, PA-NJ	H	9.09 FQ	20.53 AW	32.52 TQ	PABLS	10/01-12/01
	Pittsburgh MSA, PA	H	12.47 FQ	17.22 AW	21.30 TQ	PABLS	10/01-12/01
	Reading MSA, PA	H	11.31 FQ	17.48 AW	24.50 TQ	PABLS	10/01-12/01
	Scranton-Wilkes-Barre-Hazleton MSA, PA	H	12.09 FQ	17.63 AW	21.90 TQ	PABLS	10/01-12/01
	York MSA, PA	H	12.19 FQ	16.47 AW	21.27 TQ	PABLS	10/01-12/01
	Rhode Island	H	13.50 FQ	18.96 AW	23.12 TQ	RIBLS	10/01-12/01
	Providence-Fall River-Warwick MSA, RI-MA	H	14.00 FQ	19.12 AW	23.43 TQ	RIBLS	10/01-12/01
	South Carolina	H	9.41 FQ	13.58 AW	19.33 TQ	SCBLS	10/01-12/01
	Charleston-North Charleston MSA, SC	H	9.92 FQ	14.04 AW	20.31 TQ	SCBLS	10/01-12/01
	Columbia MSA, SC	H	8.77 FQ	13.66 AW	17.91 TQ	SCBLS	10/01-12/01
	Greenville-Spartanburg-Anderson MSA, SC	H	10.96 FQ	15.76 AW	20.98 TQ	SCBLS	10/01-12/01
	Myrtle Beach MSA, SC	H	9.23 FQ	10.95 AW	13.58 TQ	SCBLS	10/01-12/01
	South Dakota	H	10.86 FQ	13.45 AW	16.94 TQ	SDBLS	10/01-12/01
	Sioux Falls MSA, SD	H	11.28 FQ	13.54 AW	16.82 TQ	SDBLS	10/01-12/01
	Tennessee	H	9.35 FQ	13.12 AW	17.10 TQ	TNBLS	10/01-12/01
	Chattanooga MSA, TN-GA	H	11.41 FQ	13.80 AW	16.81 TQ	TNBLS	10/01-12/01
	Clarksville-Hopkinsville MSA, TN-KY	H	9.19 FQ	12.98 AW	18.04 TQ	TNBLS	10/01-12/01
	Johnson City-Kingsport-Bristol MSA, TN-VA	H	8.15 FQ	11.20 AW	13.34 TQ	TNBLS	10/01-12/01
	Knoxville MSA, TN	H	9.32 FQ	11.75 AW	14.99 TQ	TNBLS	10/01-12/01
	Memphis MSA, TN-AR-MS	H	9.52 FQ	13.52 AW	18.25 TQ	TNBLS	10/01-12/01
	Nashville MSA, TN	H	10.93 FQ	14.82 AW	20.72 TQ	TNBLS	10/01-12/01
	Texas	H	9.38 FQ	13.96 AW	22.25 TQ	TXBLS	10/01-12/01
	Amarillo MSA, TX	H	7.31 FQ	8.72 AW	10.68 TQ	TXBLS	10/01-12/01
	Austin-San Marcos MSA, TX	H	10.86 FQ	16.84 AW	25.76 TQ	TXBLS	10/01-12/01
	Beaumont-Port Arthur MSA, TX	H	9.57 FQ	12.58 AW	16.34 TQ	TXBLS	10/01-12/01
	Brazoria PMSA, TX	H	11.55 FQ	14.97 AW	17.81 TQ	TXBLS	10/01-12/01
	Corpus Christi MSA, TX	H	7.54 FQ	11.72 AW	21.98 TQ	TXBLS	10/01-12/01
	Dallas PMSA, TX	H	9.68 FQ	14.04 AW	20.06 TQ	TXBLS	10/01-12/01
	Fort Worth-Arlington PMSA, TX	H	10.80 FQ	14.39 AW	20.51 TQ	TXBLS	10/01-12/01
	Galveston-Texas City PMSA, TX	H	9.77 FQ	13.84 AW	17.79 TQ	TXBLS	10/01-12/01
	Houston PMSA, TX	H	10.60 FQ	13.69 AW	17.34 TQ	TXBLS	10/01-12/01
	Laredo MSA, TX	H	8.85 FQ	11.18 AW	13.44 TQ	TXBLS	10/01-12/01
	Longview-Marshall MSA, TX	H	9.60 FQ	14.97 AW	26.01 TQ	TXBLS	10/01-12/01
	McAllen-Edinburg-Mission MSA, TX	H	7.86 FQ	10.16 AW	12.91 TQ	TXBLS	10/01-12/01
	Odessa-Midland MSA, TX	H	9.66 FQ	12.49 AW	17.53 TQ	TXBLS	10/01-12/01
	San Antonio MSA, TX	H	9.16 FQ	12.24 AW	16.59 TQ	TXBLS	10/01-12/01
	Waco MSA, TX	H	9.16 FQ	11.34 AW	13.79 TQ	TXBLS	10/01-12/01
	Utah	H	10.83 FQ	15.90 AW	21.66 TQ	UTBLS	10/01-12/01
	Provo-Orem MSA, UT	H	12.34 FQ	16.72 AW	21.17 TQ	UTBLS	10/01-12/01

AAW Average annual wage **AE** Average entry wage **AEX** Average experienced wage **AO** Average offered **AOH** Average offered, high **AOL** Average offered, low **APH** Average pay, high range **APL** Average pay, low range **ASH** Average starting, high **ASL** Average starting, low **AW** Average wage paid **FQ** First quartile wage **H** Hourly **HI** Highest wage paid **HR** High end range **LR** Low end range **M** Monthly **MTC** Median total compensation **MW** Median wage paid **SQ** Second quartile wage **S** Special: hourly and annual **TQ** Third quartile wage **W** Weekly **Y** Yearly

Occupation/Type/Industry	Location	Per	Low	Mid	High	Source	Date
Excavating and Loading Machine and Dragline Operator	Salt Lake City-Ogden MSA, UT	H	9.96 FQ	15.21 AW	21.31 TQ	UTBLS	10/01-12/01
	Vermont	H	8.79 FQ	12.54 AW	16.78 TQ	VTBLS	10/01-12/01
	Burlington MSA, VT	H	7.00 FQ	10.64 AW	16.23 TQ	VTBLS	10/01-12/01
	Virginia	H	9.21 FQ	13.26 AW	18.70 TQ	VABLS	10/01-12/01
	Lynchburg MSA, VA	H	9.80 FQ	15.71 AW	21.44 TQ	VABLS	10/01-12/01
	Norfolk-Virginia Beach-Newport News MSA, VA-NC	H	10.37 FQ	14.23 AW	18.61 TQ	VABLS	10/01-12/01
	Richmond-Petersburg MSA, VA	H	8.56 FQ	12.69 AW	16.80 TQ	VABLS	10/01-12/01
	Roanoke MSA, VA	H	9.41 FQ	11.90 AW	16.11 TQ	VABLS	10/01-12/01
	Washington	H	14.39 FQ	21.28 AW	27.91 TQ	WABLS	10/01-12/01
	Bremerton PMSA, WA	H	9.79 FQ	16.65 AW	21.98 TQ	WABLS	10/01-12/01
	Seattle-Bellevue-Everett PMSA, WA	H	14.92 FQ	21.09 AW	29.21 TQ	WABLS	10/01-12/01
	Tacoma PMSA, WA	H	16.46 FQ	23.79 AW	27.85 TQ	WABLS	10/01-12/01
	West Virginia	H	9.74 FQ	16.42 AW	22.54 TQ	WVBLS	10/01-12/01
	Charleston MSA, WV	H	9.34 FQ	14.96 AW	20.42 TQ	WVBLS	10/01-12/01
	Huntington-Ashland MSA, WV-KY-OH	H	8.74 FQ	17.11 AW	27.46 TQ	WVBLS	10/01-12/01
	Wisconsin	H	12.44 FQ	19.13 AW	28.90 TQ	WIBLS	10/01-12/01
	Appleton-Oshkosh-Neenah MSA, WI	H	15.18 FQ	18.67 AW	22.62 TQ	WIBLS	10/01-12/01
	Green Bay MSA, WI	H	13.71 FQ	18.71 AW	29.67 TQ	WIBLS	10/01-12/01
	Madison MSA, WI	H	14.66 FQ	18.71 AW	22.77 TQ	WIBLS	10/01-12/01
	Milwaukee-Waukesha PMSA, WI	H	15.34 FQ	21.22 AW	28.96 TQ	WIBLS	10/01-12/01
	Racine PMSA, WI	H	27.83 FQ	31.10 AW	36.22 TQ	WIBLS	10/01-12/01
	Wyoming	H	12.06 FQ	20.04 AW	27.59 TQ	WYBLS	10/01-12/01
	Puerto Rico	H	6.09 FQ	8.85 AW	11.40 TQ	PRBLS	10/01-12/01
	Guam	H	9.33 FQ	11.70 AW	14.27 TQ	GUBLS	10/01-12/01
Executive Secretary and Administrative Assistant	Alabama	H	9.31 FQ	14.15 AW	20.11 TQ	ALBLS	10/01-12/01
	Birmingham MSA, AL	H	10.56 FQ	15.65 AW	21.16 TQ	ALBLS	10/01-12/01
	Huntsville MSA, AL	H	9.72 FQ	14.25 AW	19.69 TQ	ALBLS	10/01-12/01
	Mobile MSA, AL	H	8.89 FQ	13.22 AW	19.55 TQ	ALBLS	10/01-12/01
	Montgomery MSA, AL	H	9.57 FQ	15.04 AW	22.78 TQ	ALBLS	10/01-12/01
	Alaska	H	12.15 FQ	18.28 AW	26.43 TQ	AKBLS	10/01-12/01
	Anchorage MSA, AK	H	11.81 FQ	17.80 AW	26.50 TQ	AKBLS	10/01-12/01
	Arizona	H	10.25 FQ	14.99 AW	20.95 TQ	AZBLS	10/01-12/01
	Phoenix-Mesa MSA, AZ	H	10.76 FQ	15.43 AW	21.29 TQ	AZBLS	10/01-12/01
	Tucson MSA, AZ	H	9.78 FQ	13.87 AW	18.36 TQ	AZBLS	10/01-12/01
	Arkansas	H	9.56 FQ	13.84 AW	19.08 TQ	ARBLS	10/01-12/01
	Fayetteville-Springdale-Rogers MSA, AR	H	9.66 FQ	13.54 AW	18.16 TQ	ARBLS	10/01-12/01
	Fort Smith MSA, AR-OK	H	9.44 FQ	13.89 AW	20.29 TQ	ARBLS	10/01-12/01
	Little Rock-North Little Rock MSA, AR	H	9.84 FQ	14.27 AW	19.90 TQ	ARBLS	10/01-12/01
	California	H	11.74 FQ	18.24 AW	26.25 TQ	CABLS	10/01-12/01
	Bakersfield MSA, CA	H	9.69 FQ	15.46 AW	22.04 TQ	CABLS	10/01-12/01
	Chico-Paradise MSA, CA	H	9.49 FQ	14.12 AW	20.17 TQ	CABLS	10/01-12/01
	Fresno MSA, CA	H	10.93 FQ	16.41 AW	22.34 TQ	CABLS	10/01-12/01
	Los Angeles-Long Beach PMSA, CA	H	11.81 FQ	17.70 AW	25.46 TQ	CABLS	10/01-12/01
	Merced MSA, CA	H	9.79 FQ	14.31 AW	20.38 TQ	CABLS	10/01-12/01
	Modesto MSA, CA	H	10.57 FQ	15.41 AW	20.91 TQ	CABLS	10/01-12/01
	Oakland PMSA, CA	H	12.95 FQ	19.73 AW	27.96 TQ	CABLS	10/01-12/01
	Orange County PMSA, CA	H	12.11 FQ	18.48 AW	25.76 TQ	CABLS	10/01-12/01
	Redding MSA, CA	H	9.44 FQ	14.71 AW	21.51 TQ	CABLS	10/01-12/01
	Riverside-San Bernardino PMSA, CA	H	10.90 FQ	15.73 AW	21.59 TQ	CABLS	10/01-12/01
	Sacramento PMSA, CA	H	10.54 FQ	18.02 AW	25.28 TQ	CABLS	10/01-12/01
	Salinas MSA, CA	H	11.82 FQ	17.40 AW	23.99 TQ	CABLS	10/01-12/01
	San Diego MSA, CA	H	11.23 FQ	17.53 AW	25.10 TQ	CABLS	10/01-12/01
	San Francisco PMSA, CA	H	13.99 FQ	20.41 AW	28.96 TQ	CABLS	10/01-12/01
	San Jose PMSA, CA	H	14.57 FQ	21.66 AW	30.27 TQ	CABLS	10/01-12/01
	San Luis Obispo-Atascadero-Paso Robles MSA, CA	H	10.09 FQ	15.50 AW	21.76 TQ	CABLS	10/01-12/01

AAW	Average annual wage	AOH	Average offered, high	ASH	Average starting, high	H	Hourly	M	Monthly	S	Special: hourly and annual
AE	Average entry wage	AOL	Average offered, low	ASL	Average starting, low	HI	Highest wage paid	MTC	Median total compensation	TQ	Third quartile wage
AEX	Average experienced wage	APH	Average pay, high range	AW	Average wage paid	HR	High end range	MW	Median wage paid	W	Weekly
AO	Average offered	APL	Average pay, low range	FQ	First quartile wage	LR	Low end range	SQ	Second quartile wage	Y	Yearly

Occupation/Type/Industry	Location	Per	Low	Mid	High	Source	Date
Executive Secretary and Administrative Assistant							
	Santa Barbara-Santa Maria-Lompoc MSA, CA	H	11.73 FQ	17.35 AW	23.99 TQ	CABLS	10/01-12/01
	Santa Cruz-Watsonville PMSA, CA	H	11.16 FQ	18.41 AW	26.22 TQ	CABLS	10/01-12/01
	Santa Rosa PMSA, CA	H	12.03 FQ	17.67 AW	24.71 TQ	CABLS	10/01-12/01
	Stockton-Lodi MSA, CA	H	10.82 FQ	16.96 AW	24.77 TQ	CABLS	10/01-12/01
	Vallejo-Fairfield-Napa PMSA, CA	H	9.61 FQ	16.18 AW	23.13 TQ	CABLS	10/01-12/01
	Ventura PMSA, CA	H	11.65 FQ	18.46 AW	27.19 TQ	CABLS	10/01-12/01
	Visalia-Tulare-Porterville MSA, CA	H	10.01 FQ	15.71 AW	21.56 TQ	CABLS	10/01-12/01
	Colorado	H	11.91 FQ	17.28 AW	23.25 TQ	COBLS	10/01-12/01
	Boulder-Longmont PMSA, CO	H	13.14 FQ	18.14 AW	24.56 TQ	COBLS	10/01-12/01
	Colorado Springs MSA, CO	H	11.75 FQ	16.55 AW	22.07 TQ	COBLS	10/01-12/01
	Denver PMSA, CO	H	12.27 FQ	17.71 AW	23.72 TQ	COBLS	10/01-12/01
	Fort Collins-Loveland MSA, CO	H	10.10 FQ	14.84 AW	20.91 TQ	COBLS	10/01-12/01
	Greeley PMSA, CO	H	11.18 FQ	15.80 AW	22.11 TQ	COBLS	10/01-12/01
	Connecticut	H	12.94 FQ	18.96 AW	26.25 TQ	CTBLS	10/01-12/01
	Bridgeport PMSA, CT	H	12.16 FQ	17.87 AW	24.54 TQ	CTBLS	10/01-12/01
	Danbury PMSA, CT	H	11.79 FQ	18.12 AW	25.48 TQ	CTBLS	10/01-12/01
	Hartford MSA, CT	H	13.18 FQ	18.59 AW	25.47 TQ	CTBLS	10/01-12/01
	New Haven-Meriden PMSA, CT	H	12.94 FQ	18.16 AW	24.68 TQ	CTBLS	10/01-12/01
	New London-Norwich MSA, CT-RI	H	11.98 FQ	17.31 AW	22.89 TQ	CTBLS	10/01-12/01
	Stamford-Norwalk PMSA, CT	H	14.41 FQ	21.81 AW	31.74 TQ	CTBLS	10/01-12/01
	Waterbury PMSA, CT	H	11.98 FQ	17.81 AW	25.00 TQ	CTBLS	10/01-12/01
	Delaware	H	11.01 FQ	16.33 AW	22.66 TQ	DEBLS	10/01-12/01
	Wilmington-Newark PMSA, DE-MD	H	11.43 FQ	16.82 AW	23.31 TQ	DEBLS	10/01-12/01
	District of Columbia	H	12.57 FQ	18.61 AW	27.02 TQ	DCBLS	10/01-12/01
	Washington PMSA, DC-MD-VA-WV	H	12.68 FQ	18.49 AW	26.02 TQ	DCBLS	10/01-12/01
	Florida	H	10.31 FQ	15.60 AW	22.13 TQ	FLBLS	10/01-12/01
	Daytona Beach MSA, FL	H	9.94 FQ	14.85 AW	21.07 TQ	FLBLS	10/01-12/01
	Fort Lauderdale PMSA, FL	H	11.09 FQ	18.00 AW	26.83 TQ	FLBLS	10/01-12/01
	Fort Myers-Cape Coral MSA, FL	H	10.69 FQ	14.96 AW	20.55 TQ	FLBLS	10/01-12/01
	Fort Pierce-Port St. Lucie MSA, FL	H	10.37 FQ	14.81 AW	20.76 TQ	FLBLS	10/01-12/01
	Fort Walton Beach MSA, FL	H	9.35 FQ	14.96 AW	24.41 TQ	FLBLS	10/01-12/01
	Gainesville MSA, FL	H	9.76 FQ	14.31 AW	20.62 TQ	FLBLS	10/01-12/01
	Jacksonville MSA, FL	H	9.94 FQ	14.49 AW	19.96 TQ	FLBLS	10/01-12/01
	Lakeland-Winter Haven MSA, FL	H	9.65 FQ	14.72 AW	21.58 TQ	FLBLS	10/01-12/01
	Melbourne-Titusville-Palm Bay MSA, FL	H	9.48 FQ	19.38 AW	48.94 TQ	FLBLS	10/01-12/01
	Miami PMSA, FL	H	10.50 FQ	15.85 AW	22.57 TQ	FLBLS	10/01-12/01
	Naples MSA, FL	H	11.09 FQ	15.93 AW	23.21 TQ	FLBLS	10/01-12/01
	Ocala MSA, FL	H	9.19 FQ	13.83 AW	20.32 TQ	FLBLS	10/01-12/01
	Orlando MSA, FL	H	10.47 FQ	14.87 AW	20.43 TQ	FLBLS	10/01-12/01
	Pensacola MSA, FL	H	8.91 FQ	13.86 AW	20.31 TQ	FLBLS	10/01-12/01
	Sarasota-Bradenton MSA, FL	H	9.54 FQ	14.13 AW	19.65 TQ	FLBLS	10/01-12/01
	Tallahassee MSA, FL	H	10.50 FQ	17.05 AW	29.53 TQ	FLBLS	10/01-12/01
	Tampa-St. Petersburg-Clearwater MSA, FL	H	10.90 FQ	15.15 AW	21.19 TQ	FLBLS	10/01-12/01
	West Palm Beach-Boca Raton MSA, FL	H	11.16 FQ	16.28 AW	23.43 TQ	FLBLS	10/01-12/01
	Georgia	H	10.17 FQ	15.72 AW	21.72 TQ	GABLS	10/01-12/01
	Atlanta MSA, GA	H	11.42 FQ	16.72 AW	22.53 TQ	GABLS	10/01-12/01
	Augusta-Aiken MSA, GA-SC	H	9.28 FQ	14.49 AW	22.55 TQ	GABLS	10/01-12/01
	Columbus MSA, GA-AL	H	8.99 FQ	13.10 AW	17.54 TQ	GABLS	10/01-12/01
	Macon MSA, GA	H	9.14 FQ	13.07 AW	17.93 TQ	GABLS	10/01-12/01
	Savannah MSA, GA	H	9.54 FQ	13.95 AW	19.16 TQ	GABLS	10/01-12/01
	Hawaii	H	11.77 FQ	17.87 AW	25.30 TQ	HIBLS	10/01-12/01
	Honolulu MSA, HI	H	11.71 FQ	18.03 AW	25.47 TQ	HIBLS	10/01-12/01
	Idaho	H	9.41 FQ	13.81 AW	19.45 TQ	IDBLS	10/01-12/01
	Boise City MSA, ID	H	9.72 FQ	13.92 AW	19.09 TQ	IDBLS	10/01-12/01
	Illinois	H	9.75 FQ	15.54 AW	22.15 TQ	ILBLS	10/01-12/01
	Champaign-Urbana MSA, IL	H	8.60 FQ	14.10 AW	21.09 TQ	ILBLS	10/01-12/01

AAW Average annual wage; AE Average entry wage; AEX Average experienced wage; AO Average offered; AOH Average offered, high; AOL Average offered, low; APH Average pay, high range; APL Average pay, low range; ASH Average starting, high; ASL Average starting, low; AW Average wage paid; FQ First quartile wage; H Hourly; HI Highest wage paid; HR High end range; LR Low end range; M Monthly; MTC Median total compensation; MW Median wage paid; SQ Second quartile wage; S Special: hourly and annual; TQ Third quartile wage; W Weekly; Y Yearly

Occupation/Type/Industry	Location	Per	Low	Mid	High	Source	Date
Executive Secretary and Administrative Assistant	Chicago PMSA, IL	H	10.52 FQ	15.95 AW	22.40 TQ	ILBLS	10/01-12/01
	Peoria-Pekin MSA, IL	H	9.19 FQ	13.99 AW	19.37 TQ	ILBLS	10/01-12/01
	Rockford MSA, IL	H	9.43 FQ	14.01 AW	19.67 TQ	ILBLS	10/01-12/01
	Indiana	H	9.85 FQ	15.13 AW	21.32 TQ	INBLS	10/01-12/01
	Elkhart-Goshen MSA, IN	H	9.65 FQ	14.75 AW	20.16 TQ	INBLS	10/01-12/01
	Evansville-Henderson MSA, IN-KY	H	9.50 FQ	14.39 AW	19.49 TQ	INBLS	10/01-12/01
	Fort Wayne MSA, IN	H	9.60 FQ	14.68 AW	21.01 TQ	INBLS	10/01-12/01
	Gary PMSA, IN	H	9.09 FQ	13.84 AW	19.31 TQ	INBLS	10/01-12/01
	Indianapolis MSA, IN	H	10.86 FQ	16.54 AW	26.50 TQ	INBLS	10/01-12/01
	Lafayette MSA, IN	H	9.93 FQ	14.97 AW	21.28 TQ	INBLS	10/01-12/01
	South Bend MSA, IN	H	10.12 FQ	14.35 AW	19.14 TQ	INBLS	10/01-12/01
	Iowa	H	9.34 FQ	14.02 AW	19.86 TQ	IABLS	10/01-12/01
	Cedar Rapids MSA, IA	H	9.69 FQ	14.31 AW	20.29 TQ	IABLS	10/01-12/01
	Davenport-Moline-Rock Island MSA, IA-IL	H	8.60 FQ	13.10 AW	18.39 TQ	IABLS	10/01-12/01
	Des Moines MSA, IA	H	10.70 FQ	15.33 AW	20.83 TQ	IABLS	10/01-12/01
	Kansas	H	10.33 FQ	14.72 AW	20.39 TQ	KSBLS	10/01-12/01
	Topeka MSA, KS	H	9.41 FQ	12.82 AW	16.67 TQ	KSBLS	10/01-12/01
	Wichita MSA, KS	H	11.34 FQ	15.76 AW	21.45 TQ	KSBLS	10/01-12/01
	Kentucky	H	9.52 FQ	14.41 AW	20.59 TQ	KYBLS	10/01-12/01
	Lexington MSA, KY	H	10.17 FQ	14.43 AW	19.27 TQ	KYBLS	10/01-12/01
	Louisville MSA, KY-IN	H	10.09 FQ	14.82 AW	20.60 TQ	KYBLS	10/01-12/01
	Louisiana	H	8.93 FQ	13.77 AW	19.62 TQ	LABLS	10/01-12/01
	Baton Rouge MSA, LA	H	9.93 FQ	14.76 AW	20.18 TQ	LABLS	10/01-12/01
	Houma MSA, LA	H	9.50 FQ	15.37 AW	23.85 TQ	LABLS	10/01-12/01
	Lafayette MSA, LA	H	8.21 FQ	13.27 AW	19.00 TQ	LABLS	10/01-12/01
	Lake Charles MSA, LA	H	9.23 FQ	13.91 AW	19.85 TQ	LABLS	10/01-12/01
	New Orleans MSA, LA	H	8.72 FQ	13.64 AW	19.52 TQ	LABLS	10/01-12/01
	Shreveport-Bossier City MSA, LA	H	9.27 FQ	13.23 AW	18.63 TQ	LABLS	10/01-12/01
	Maine	H	9.84 FQ	14.15 AW	19.84 TQ	MEBLS	10/01-12/01
	Portland MSA, ME	H	9.79 FQ	14.25 AW	19.94 TQ	MEBLS	10/01-12/01
	Maryland	H	13.63 FQ	17.60 AW	23.02 TQ	MDBLS	10/01-12/01
	Baltimore PMSA, MD	H	13.76 FQ	17.37 AW	22.03 TQ	MDBLS	10/01-12/01
	Massachusetts	H	12.36 FQ	18.21 AW	25.33 TQ	MABLS	10/01-12/01
	Boston PMSA, MA-NH	H	13.39 FQ	18.87 AW	25.88 TQ	MABLS	10/01-12/01
	Brockton PMSA, MA	H	11.03 FQ	17.02 AW	23.13 TQ	MABLS	10/01-12/01
	Lawrence PMSA, MA-NH	H	11.69 FQ	17.00 AW	23.40 TQ	MABLS	10/01-12/01
	Lowell PMSA, MA-NH	H	12.15 FQ	18.02 AW	25.14 TQ	MABLS	10/01-12/01
	New Bedford PMSA, MA	H	9.50 FQ	14.67 AW	20.42 TQ	MABLS	10/01-12/01
	Springfield MSA, MA	H	10.82 FQ	16.70 AW	23.53 TQ	MABLS	10/01-12/01
	Worcester PMSA, MA-CT	H	11.49 FQ	16.96 AW	24.46 TQ	MABLS	10/01-12/01
	Michigan	H	11.31 FQ	16.84 AW	23.37 TQ	MIBLS	10/01-12/01
	Ann Arbor PMSA, MI	H	10.49 FQ	16.37 AW	22.37 TQ	MIBLS	10/01-12/01
	Detroit PMSA, MI	H	12.21 FQ	17.79 AW	25.03 TQ	MIBLS	10/01-12/01
	Flint PMSA, MI	H	9.62 FQ	15.69 AW	22.67 TQ	MIBLS	10/01-12/01
	Grand Rapids-Muskegon-Holland MSA, MI	H	11.17 FQ	15.66 AW	21.33 TQ	MIBLS	10/01-12/01
	Kalamazoo-Battle Creek MSA, MI	H	10.89 FQ	16.07 AW	22.09 TQ	MIBLS	10/01-12/01
	Lansing-East Lansing MSA, MI	H	11.88 FQ	17.90 AW	23.45 TQ	MIBLS	10/01-12/01
	Saginaw-Bay City-Midland MSA, MI	H	9.71 FQ	15.39 AW	21.90 TQ	MIBLS	10/01-12/01
	Minnesota	H	11.95 FQ	16.65 AW	22.05 TQ	MNBLS	10/01-12/01
	Duluth-Superior MSA, MN-WI	H	9.61 FQ	14.69 AW	21.52 TQ	MNBLS	10/01-12/01
	Minneapolis-St. Paul MSA, MN-WI	H	12.54 FQ	17.10 AW	22.34 TQ	MNBLS	10/01-12/01
	St. Cloud MSA, MN	H	10.33 FQ	14.30 AW	18.48 TQ	MNBLS	10/01-12/01
	Mississippi	H	8.41 FQ	13.21 AW	18.86 TQ	MSBLS	10/01-12/01
	Biloxi-Gulfport-Pascagoula MSA, MS	H	8.05 FQ	12.85 AW	18.92 TQ	MSBLS	10/01-12/01
	Jackson MSA, MS	H	8.31 FQ	13.30 AW	18.60 TQ	MSBLS	10/01-12/01
	Missouri	H	9.65 FQ	14.89 AW	21.02 TQ	MOBLS	10/01-12/01
	Kansas City MSA, MO-KS	H	11.15 FQ	15.69 AW	21.24 TQ	MOBLS	10/01-12/01
	St. Louis MSA, MO-IL	H	10.20 FQ	15.80 AW	22.19 TQ	MOBLS	10/01-12/01
	Springfield MSA, MO	H	8.63 FQ	12.89 AW	18.05 TQ	MOBLS	10/01-12/01
	Montana	H	8.20 FQ	13.17 AW	19.47 TQ	MTBLS	10/01-12/01
	Billings MSA, MT	H	8.63 FQ	12.70 AW	17.07 TQ	MTBLS	10/01-12/01
	Nebraska	H	9.53 FQ	13.79 AW	19.00 TQ	NEBLS	10/01-12/01
	Lincoln MSA, NE	H	9.66 FQ	13.75 AW	18.97 TQ	NEBLS	10/01-12/01

AAW Average annual wage; **AE** Average entry wage; **AEX** Average experienced wage; **AO** Average offered; **AOH** Average offered, high; **AOL** Average offered, low; **APH** Average pay, high range; **APL** Average pay, low range; **ASH** Average starting, high; **ASL** Average starting, low; **AW** Average wage paid; **FQ** First quartile wage; **H** Hourly; **HI** Highest wage paid; **HR** High end range; **LR** Low end range; **M** Monthly; **MTC** Median total compensation; **MW** Median wage paid; **SQ** Second quartile wage; **S** Special: hourly and annual; **TQ** Third quartile wage; **W** Weekly; **Y** Yearly

Occupation/Type/Industry	Location	Per	Low	Mid	High	Source	Date
Executive Secretary and Administrative Assistant	Omaha MSA, NE-IA	H	10.01 FQ	14.24 AW	19.45 TQ	NEBLS	10/01-12/01
	Nevada	H	9.80 FQ	16.26 AW	23.41 TQ	NVBLS	10/01-12/01
	Las Vegas MSA, NV-AZ	H	9.48 FQ	15.89 AW	22.54 TQ	NVBLS	10/01-12/01
	Reno MSA, NV	H	10.98 FQ	17.06 AW	24.65 TQ	NVBLS	10/01-12/01
	New Hampshire	H	10.34 FQ	15.16 AW	21.15 TQ	NHBLS	10/01-12/01
	Manchester PMSA, NH	H	10.59 FQ	15.91 AW	21.77 TQ	NHBLS	10/01-12/01
	Nashua PMSA, NH	H	11.18 FQ	16.12 AW	22.12 TQ	NHBLS	10/01-12/01
	Portsmouth-Rochester PMSA, NH-ME	H	10.22 FQ	14.56 AW	19.66 TQ	NHBLS	10/01-12/01
	New Jersey	H	13.27 FQ	19.50 AW	26.98 TQ	NJBLS	10/01-12/01
	Atlantic-Cape May PMSA, NJ	H	12.02 FQ	18.05 AW	26.38 TQ	NJBLS	10/01-12/01
	Bergen-Passaic PMSA, NJ	H	13.82 FQ	20.01 AW	27.38 TQ	NJBLS	10/01-12/01
	Jersey City PMSA, NJ	H	13.50 FQ	19.35 AW	26.54 TQ	NJBLS	10/01-12/01
	Middlesex-Somerset-Hunterdon PMSA, NJ	H	14.24 FQ	20.19 AW	27.43 TQ	NJBLS	10/01-12/01
	Monmouth-Ocean PMSA, NJ	H	12.55 FQ	18.19 AW	25.06 TQ	NJBLS	10/01-12/01
	Newark PMSA, NJ	H	13.59 FQ	19.99 AW	27.46 TQ	NJBLS	10/01-12/01
	Trenton PMSA, NJ	H	12.56 FQ	19.36 AW	27.05 TQ	NJBLS	10/01-12/01
	New Mexico	H	9.19 FQ	14.01 AW	19.98 TQ	NMBLS	10/01-12/01
	Albuquerque MSA, NM	H	9.36 FQ	13.58 AW	18.46 TQ	NMBLS	10/01-12/01
	Las Cruces MSA, NM	H	8.16 FQ	12.61 AW	17.62 TQ	NMBLS	10/01-12/01
	New York	H	11.20 FQ	18.74 AW	28.06 TQ	NYBLS	10/01-12/01
	Albany-Schenectady-Troy MSA, NY	H	10.35 FQ	16.50 AW	24.46 TQ	NYBLS	10/01-12/01
	Binghamton MSA, NY	H	8.95 FQ	13.84 AW	20.11 TQ	NYBLS	10/01-12/01
	Buffalo-Niagara Falls MSA, NY	H	9.08 FQ	15.13 AW	22.34 TQ	NYBLS	10/01-12/01
	Dutchess County PMSA, NY	H	9.60 FQ	15.67 AW	22.16 TQ	NYBLS	10/01-12/01
	Nassau-Suffolk PMSA, NY	H	10.40 FQ	17.83 AW	26.50 TQ	NYBLS	10/01-12/01
	New York PMSA, NY	H	12.92 FQ	20.39 AW	30.24 TQ	NYBLS	10/01-12/01
	Newburgh PMSA, NY-PA	H	10.05 FQ	15.50 AW	21.81 TQ	NYBLS	10/01-12/01
	Rochester MSA, NY	H	9.56 FQ	14.85 AW	20.99 TQ	NYBLS	10/01-12/01
	Syracuse MSA, NY	H	9.58 FQ	14.69 AW	21.05 TQ	NYBLS	10/01-12/01
	Utica-Rome MSA, NY	H	9.04 FQ	14.12 AW	20.61 TQ	NYBLS	10/01-12/01
	North Carolina	H	10.13 FQ	14.85 AW	20.74 TQ	NCBLS	10/01-12/01
	Asheville MSA, NC	H	9.73 FQ	14.11 AW	19.49 TQ	NCBLS	10/01-12/01
	Charlotte-Gastonia-Rock Hill MSA, NC-SC	H	11.16 FQ	15.38 AW	20.87 TQ	NCBLS	10/01-12/01
	Fayetteville MSA, NC	H	8.46 FQ	12.93 AW	17.60 TQ	NCBLS	10/01-12/01
	Greensboro-Winston-Salem-High Point MSA, NC	H	10.49 FQ	14.87 AW	20.32 TQ	NCBLS	10/01-12/01
	Hickory-Morganton-Lenoir MSA, NC	H	10.15 FQ	14.20 AW	19.35 TQ	NCBLS	10/01-12/01
	Raleigh-Durham-Chapel Hill MSA, NC	H	11.32 FQ	15.96 AW	22.00 TQ	NCBLS	10/01-12/01
	Wilmington MSA, NC	H	9.55 FQ	13.83 AW	19.04 TQ	NCBLS	10/01-12/01
	North Dakota	H	8.80 FQ	12.49 AW	17.97 TQ	NDBLS	10/01-12/01
	Fargo-Moorhead MSA, ND-MN	H	9.32 FQ	13.77 AW	20.55 TQ	NDBLS	10/01-12/01
	Ohio	H	9.81 FQ	15.44 AW	21.79 TQ	OHBLS	10/01-12/01
	Akron PMSA, OH	H	10.10 FQ	14.78 AW	20.76 TQ	OHBLS	10/01-12/01
	Canton-Massillon MSA, OH	H	9.48 FQ	13.90 AW	20.04 TQ	OHBLS	10/01-12/01
	Cincinnati PMSA, OH-KY-IN	H	10.08 FQ	15.70 AW	22.21 TQ	OHBLS	10/01-12/01
	Cleveland-Lorain-Elyria PMSA, OH	H	10.07 FQ	15.58 AW	21.54 TQ	OHBLS	10/01-12/01
	Columbus MSA, OH	H	10.96 FQ	17.38 AW	25.12 TQ	OHBLS	10/01-12/01
	Dayton-Springfield MSA, OH	H	9.54 FQ	14.44 AW	20.40 TQ	OHBLS	10/01-12/01
	Hamilton-Middletown PMSA, OH	H	9.59 FQ	14.50 AW	21.14 TQ	OHBLS	10/01-12/01
	Mansfield MSA, OH	H	9.21 FQ	13.66 AW	20.07 TQ	OHBLS	10/01-12/01
	Toledo MSA, OH	H	9.91 FQ	14.99 AW	20.84 TQ	OHBLS	10/01-12/01
	Youngstown-Warren MSA, OH	H	7.65 FQ	13.83 AW	21.03 TQ	OHBLS	10/01-12/01
	Oklahoma	H	8.69 FQ	13.43 AW	19.54 TQ	OKBLS	10/01-12/01
	Oklahoma City MSA, OK	H	8.86 FQ	13.48 AW	19.51 TQ	OKBLS	10/01-12/01
	Tulsa MSA, OK	H	9.18 FQ	14.18 AW	20.48 TQ	OKBLS	10/01-12/01
	Oregon	H	11.05 FQ	15.97 AW	21.40 TQ	ORBLS	10/01-12/01
	Eugene-Springfield MSA, OR	H	11.10 FQ	15.23 AW	20.39 TQ	ORBLS	10/01-12/01
	Medford-Ashland MSA, OR	H	9.68 FQ	14.33 AW	19.18 TQ	ORBLS	10/01-12/01
	Portland-Vancouver PMSA, OR-WA	H	11.70 FQ	16.74 AW	22.09 TQ	ORBLS	10/01-12/01
	Salem PMSA, OR	H	10.41 FQ	14.86 AW	19.97 TQ	ORBLS	10/01-12/01

AAW Average annual wage **AE** Average entry wage **AEX** Average experienced wage **AO** Average offered **AOH** Average offered, high **AOL** Average offered, low **APH** Average pay, high range **APL** Average pay, low range **ASH** Average starting, high **ASL** Average starting, low **AW** Average wage paid **FQ** First quartile wage **H** Hourly **HI** Highest wage paid **HR** High end range **LR** Low end range **M** Monthly **MTC** Median total compensation **MW** Median wage paid **SQ** Second quartile wage **S** Special: hourly and annual **TQ** Third quartile wage **W** Weekly **Y** Yearly

Occupation/Type/Industry	Location	Per	Low	Mid	High	Source	Date
Executive Secretary and Administrative Assistant	Pennsylvania	H	9.77 FQ	15.12 AW	21.51 TQ	PABLS	10/01-12/01
	Allentown-Bethlehem-Easton MSA, PA	H	9.88 FQ	14.08 AW	19.19 TQ	PABLS	10/01-12/01
	Erie MSA, PA	H	9.11 FQ	13.74 AW	19.90 TQ	PABLS	10/01-12/01
	Harrisburg-Lebanon-Carlisle MSA, PA	H	9.97 FQ	14.83 AW	20.59 TQ	PABLS	10/01-12/01
	Johnstown MSA, PA	H	7.54 FQ	11.87 AW	16.86 TQ	PABLS	10/01-12/01
	Lancaster MSA, PA	H	9.54 FQ	14.05 AW	19.78 TQ	PABLS	10/01-12/01
	Philadelphia PMSA, PA-NJ	H	10.84 FQ	16.47 AW	23.45 TQ	PABLS	10/01-12/01
	Pittsburgh MSA, PA	H	9.96 FQ	14.83 AW	20.57 TQ	PABLS	10/01-12/01
	Reading MSA, PA	H	9.41 FQ	14.17 AW	20.10 TQ	PABLS	10/01-12/01
	Scranton-Wilkes-Barre-Hazleton MSA, PA	H	9.07 FQ	13.46 AW	19.38 TQ	PABLS	10/01-12/01
	York MSA, PA	H	8.54 FQ	13.90 AW	19.81 TQ	PABLS	10/01-12/01
	Rhode Island	H	11.46 FQ	17.08 AW	24.59 TQ	RIBLS	10/01-12/01
	Providence-Fall River-Warwick MSA, RI-MA	H	11.45 FQ	17.34 AW	25.06 TQ	RIBLS	10/01-12/01
	South Carolina	H	9.43 FQ	14.36 AW	20.44 TQ	SCBLS	10/01-12/01
	Charleston-North Charleston MSA, SC	H	9.44 FQ	13.89 AW	19.74 TQ	SCBLS	10/01-12/01
	Columbia MSA, SC	H	10.03 FQ	15.30 AW	21.10 TQ	SCBLS	10/01-12/01
	Greenville-Spartanburg-Anderson MSA, SC	H	9.38 FQ	14.52 AW	20.53 TQ	SCBLS	10/01-12/01
	Myrtle Beach MSA, SC	H	8.86 FQ	13.29 AW	17.88 TQ	SCBLS	10/01-12/01
	South Dakota	H	9.65 FQ	12.67 AW	16.37 TQ	SDBLS	10/01-12/01
	Sioux Falls MSA, SD	H	10.00 FQ	13.15 AW	16.75 TQ	SDBLS	10/01-12/01
	Tennessee	H	9.41 FQ	14.22 AW	20.18 TQ	TNBLS	10/01-12/01
	Chattanooga MSA, TN-GA	H	9.23 FQ	13.85 AW	19.90 TQ	TNBLS	10/01-12/01
	Clarksville-Hopkinsville MSA, TN-KY	H	8.56 FQ	11.32 AW	15.92 TQ	TNBLS	10/01-12/01
	Johnson City-Kingsport-Bristol MSA, TN-VA	H	8.72 FQ	12.68 AW	17.55 TQ	TNBLS	10/01-12/01
	Knoxville MSA, TN	H	9.48 FQ	14.33 AW	19.99 TQ	TNBLS	10/01-12/01
	Memphis MSA, TN-AR-MS	H	10.11 FQ	15.12 AW	21.39 TQ	TNBLS	10/01-12/01
	Nashville MSA, TN	H	10.08 FQ	14.75 AW	20.46 TQ	TNBLS	10/01-12/01
	Texas	H	9.82 FQ	15.46 AW	21.91 TQ	TXBLS	10/01-12/01
	Amarillo MSA, TX	H	8.63 FQ	13.40 AW	18.67 TQ	TXBLS	10/01-12/01
	Austin-San Marcos MSA, TX	H	9.97 FQ	14.20 AW	19.79 TQ	TXBLS	10/01-12/01
	Beaumont-Port Arthur MSA, TX	H	9.21 FQ	14.25 AW	20.84 TQ	TXBLS	10/01-12/01
	Brazoria PMSA, TX	H	9.27 FQ	14.79 AW	22.64 TQ	TXBLS	10/01-12/01
	Brownsville-Harlingen-San Benito MSA, TX	H	8.41 FQ	14.07 AW	21.84 TQ	TXBLS	10/01-12/01
	Corpus Christi MSA, TX	H	8.13 FQ	13.94 AW	20.25 TQ	TXBLS	10/01-12/01
	Dallas PMSA, TX	H	11.43 FQ	17.05 AW	23.23 TQ	TXBLS	10/01-12/01
	El Paso MSA, TX	H	8.69 FQ	14.63 AW	20.17 TQ	TXBLS	10/01-12/01
	Fort Worth-Arlington PMSA, TX	H	10.00 FQ	15.68 AW	22.02 TQ	TXBLS	10/01-12/01
	Galveston-Texas City PMSA, TX	H	9.65 FQ	14.90 AW	21.08 TQ	TXBLS	10/01-12/01
	Houston PMSA, TX	H	11.12 FQ	16.81 AW	23.11 TQ	TXBLS	10/01-12/01
	Killeen-Temple MSA, TX	H	9.37 FQ	13.06 AW	17.10 TQ	TXBLS	10/01-12/01
	Laredo MSA, TX	H	8.51 FQ	13.75 AW	19.71 TQ	TXBLS	10/01-12/01
	Longview-Marshall MSA, TX	H	9.29 FQ	13.59 AW	18.20 TQ	TXBLS	10/01-12/01
	Lubbock MSA, TX	H	9.42 FQ	13.80 AW	18.32 TQ	TXBLS	10/01-12/01
	McAllen-Edinburg-Mission MSA, TX	H	8.70 FQ	13.33 AW	18.46 TQ	TXBLS	10/01-12/01
	Odessa-Midland MSA, TX	H	9.01 FQ	13.85 AW	19.74 TQ	TXBLS	10/01-12/01
	San Antonio MSA, TX	H	8.86 FQ	13.91 AW	20.46 TQ	TXBLS	10/01-12/01
	Tyler MSA, TX	H	9.47 FQ	13.46 AW	17.96 TQ	TXBLS	10/01-12/01
	Waco MSA, TX	H	8.09 FQ	13.00 AW	19.15 TQ	TXBLS	10/01-12/01
	Utah	H	10.20 FQ	14.89 AW	19.91 TQ	UTBLS	10/01-12/01
	Provo-Orem MSA, UT	H	9.56 FQ	14.25 AW	19.27 TQ	UTBLS	10/01-12/01
	Salt Lake City-Ogden MSA, UT	H	10.41 FQ	14.64 AW	19.81 TQ	UTBLS	10/01-12/01
	Vermont	H	11.40 FQ	15.69 AW	20.68 TQ	VTBLS	10/01-12/01
	Burlington MSA, VT	H	12.08 FQ	16.48 AW	21.08 TQ	VTBLS	10/01-12/01
	Virginia	H	10.43 FQ	16.33 AW	23.38 TQ	VABLS	10/01-12/01
	Lynchburg MSA, VA	H	9.55 FQ	13.71 AW	18.30 TQ	VABLS	10/01-12/01

AAW	Average annual wage	**AOH**	Average offered, high	**ASH**	Average starting, high	**H**	Hourly	**M**	Monthly	**S**	Special: hourly and annual
AE	Average entry wage	**AOL**	Average offered, low	**ASL**	Average starting, low	**HI**	Highest wage paid	**MTC**	Median total compensation	**TQ**	Third quartile wage
AEX	Average experienced wage	**APH**	Average pay, high range	**AW**	Average wage paid	**HR**	High end range	**MW**	Median wage paid	**W**	Weekly
AO	Average offered	**APL**	Average pay, low range	**FQ**	First quartile wage	**LR**	Low end range	**SQ**	Second quartile wage	**Y**	Yearly

Occupation/Type/Industry	Location	Per	Low	Mid	High	Source	Date
Executive Secretary and Administrative Assistant	Norfolk-Virginia Beach-Newport News MSA, VA-NC	H	8.74 FQ	14.20 AW	20.39 TQ	VABLS	10/01-12/01
	Richmond-Petersburg MSA, VA	H	10.77 FQ	15.30 AW	20.89 TQ	VABLS	10/01-12/01
	Roanoke MSA, VA	H	10.18 FQ	14.85 AW	20.98 TQ	VABLS	10/01-12/01
	Washington	H	12.29 FQ	18.25 AW	25.45 TQ	WABLS	10/01-12/01
	Bremerton PMSA, WA	H	10.98 FQ	16.58 AW	22.57 TQ	WABLS	10/01-12/01
	Olympia PMSA, WA	H	12.28 FQ	18.63 AW	26.09 TQ	WABLS	10/01-12/01
	Richland-Kennewick-Pasco MSA, WA	H	12.83 FQ	18.15 AW	24.55 TQ	WABLS	10/01-12/01
	Seattle-Bellevue-Everett PMSA, WA	H	12.91 FQ	18.86 AW	26.16 TQ	WABLS	10/01-12/01
	Spokane MSA, WA	H	11.48 FQ	15.95 AW	21.39 TQ	WABLS	10/01-12/01
	Tacoma PMSA, WA	H	11.64 FQ	17.73 AW	24.89 TQ	WABLS	10/01-12/01
	Yakima MSA, WA	H	10.82 FQ	16.81 AW	22.14 TQ	WABLS	10/01-12/01
	West Virginia	H	8.57 FQ	13.18 AW	18.99 TQ	WVBLS	10/01-12/01
	Charleston MSA, WV	H	9.16 FQ	14.27 AW	20.53 TQ	WVBLS	10/01-12/01
	Huntington-Ashland MSA, WV-KY-OH	H	7.98 FQ	12.66 AW	18.13 TQ	WVBLS	10/01-12/01
	Wisconsin	H	9.15 FQ	14.18 AW	20.34 TQ	WIBLS	10/01-12/01
	Appleton-Oshkosh-Neenah MSA, WI	H	7.60 FQ	12.62 AW	18.68 TQ	WIBLS	10/01-12/01
	Green Bay MSA, WI	H	9.64 FQ	13.98 AW	20.15 TQ	WIBLS	10/01-12/01
	Madison MSA, WI	H	10.84 FQ	15.69 AW	21.06 TQ	WIBLS	10/01-12/01
	Milwaukee-Waukesha PMSA, WI	H	10.40 FQ	15.41 AW	21.27 TQ	WIBLS	10/01-12/01
	Racine PMSA, WI	H	9.23 FQ	15.48 AW	24.03 TQ	WIBLS	10/01-12/01
	Wyoming	H	9.01 FQ	13.27 AW	18.94 TQ	WYBLS	10/01-12/01
	Cheyenne MSA, WY	H	8.00 FQ	12.81 AW	18.71 TQ	WYBLS	10/01-12/01
	Puerto Rico	H	7.03 FQ	10.26 AW	14.99 TQ	PRBLS	10/01-12/01
	Virgin Islands	H	10.30 FQ	13.82 AW	17.77 TQ	VIBLS	10/01-12/01
	Guam	H	7.78 FQ	13.76 AW	20.65 TQ	GUBLS	10/01-12/01
Explosives Worker, Ordnance Handling Expert, and Blaster	Alabama	H	14.13 FQ	17.81 AW	22.94 TQ	ALBLS	10/01-12/01
	Alaska	H	13.92 FQ	21.91 AW	27.59 TQ	AKBLS	10/01-12/01
	Arizona	H	16.71 FQ	18.70 AW	21.09 TQ	AZBLS	10/01-12/01
	Arkansas	H	9.59 FQ	13.79 AW	17.96 TQ	ARBLS	10/01-12/01
	California	H	13.83 FQ	19.02 AW	25.64 TQ	CABLS	10/01-12/01
	Colorado	H	10.45 FQ	18.28 AW	24.28 TQ	COBLS	10/01-12/01
	Connecticut	H	14.52 FQ	17.28 AW	21.50 TQ	CTBLS	10/01-12/01
	Florida	H	9.93 FQ	16.15 AW	21.27 TQ	FLBLS	10/01-12/01
	Georgia	H	14.04 FQ	16.21 AW	19.67 TQ	GABLS	10/01-12/01
	Illinois	H	9.02 FQ	17.75 AW	29.50 TQ	ILBLS	10/01-12/01
	Indiana	H	13.57 FQ	16.41 AW	20.54 TQ	INBLS	10/01-12/01
	Iowa	H	10.68 FQ	16.52 AW	24.14 TQ	IABLS	10/01-12/01
	Kansas	H	9.81 FQ	12.79 AW	16.19 TQ	KSBLS	10/01-12/01
	Kentucky	H	11.50 FQ	14.56 AW	18.61 TQ	KYBLS	10/01-12/01
	Louisiana	H	10.96 FQ	15.17 AW	20.44 TQ	LABLS	10/01-12/01
	Maryland	H	15.35 FQ	18.94 AW	21.24 TQ	MDBLS	10/01-12/01
	Massachusetts	H	18.20 FQ	21.89 AW	28.00 TQ	MABLS	10/01-12/01
	Missouri	H	9.88 FQ	15.27 AW	20.97 TQ	MOBLS	10/01-12/01
	Montana	H	16.83 FQ	26.24 AW	33.38 TQ	MTBLS	10/01-12/01
	Nevada	H	16.94 FQ	18.97 AW	21.81 TQ	NVBLS	10/01-12/01
	New Hampshire	H	14.91 FQ	22.72 AW	30.70 TQ	NHBLS	10/01-12/01
	New Jersey	H	16.56 FQ	19.84 AW	25.77 TQ	NJBLS	10/01-12/01
	New Mexico	H	13.92 FQ	24.87 AW	33.70 TQ	NMBLS	10/01-12/01
	New York	H	14.31 FQ	20.42 AW	34.90 TQ	NYBLS	10/01-12/01
	North Carolina	H	11.18 FQ	15.80 AW	21.17 TQ	NCBLS	10/01-12/01
	Ohio	H	12.19 FQ	17.34 AW	26.38 TQ	OHBLS	10/01-12/01
	Oklahoma	H	11.23 FQ	14.66 AW	19.90 TQ	OKBLS	10/01-12/01
	Oregon	H	13.79 FQ	17.85 AW	21.66 TQ	ORBLS	10/01-12/01
	Pennsylvania	H	11.84 FQ	17.13 AW	22.04 TQ	PABLS	10/01-12/01
	Tennessee	H	8.01 FQ	13.58 AW	20.61 TQ	TNBLS	10/01-12/01
	Texas	H	8.04 FQ	14.49 AW	20.94 TQ	TXBLS	10/01-12/01
	Utah	H	14.65 FQ	18.57 AW	21.49 TQ	UTBLS	10/01-12/01
	Vermont	H	9.87 FQ	14.51 AW	18.01 TQ	VTBLS	10/01-12/01
	Virginia	H	12.37 FQ	17.41 AW	22.26 TQ	VABLS	10/01-12/01
	Washington	H	14.22 FQ	19.96 AW	26.90 TQ	WABLS	10/01-12/01
	West Virginia	H	9.64 FQ	13.90 AW	19.92 TQ	WVBLS	10/01-12/01

Occupation/Type/Industry	Location	Per	Low	Mid	High	Source	Date
Explosives Worker, Ordnance Handling Expert, and Blaster	Wisconsin	H	13.55 FQ	17.82 AW	24.46 TQ	WIBLS	10/01-12/01
Export Clerk	United States	Y		29500 AW		WT	6/01-6/02
	North Central	Y		28300 AW		WT	6/01-6/02
	Northeast	Y		31600 AW		WT	6/01-6/02
	South Central	Y		27600 AW		WT	6/01-6/02
	Southeast	Y		26300 AW		WT	6/01-6/02
	West	Y		32300 AW		WT	6/01-6/02
Extruding and Drawing Machine Setter, Operator, and Tender							
Metals and Plastics	Alabama	H	8.02 FQ	12.20 AW	16.63 TQ	ALBLS	10/01-12/01
Metals and Plastics	Birmingham MSA, AL	H	8.97 FQ	11.42 AW	13.88 TQ	ALBLS	10/01-12/01
Metals and Plastics	Huntsville MSA, AL	H	7.58 FQ	10.57 AW	13.53 TQ	ALBLS	10/01-12/01
Metals and Plastics	Montgomery MSA, AL	H	7.47 FQ	10.84 AW	13.42 TQ	ALBLS	10/01-12/01
Metals and Plastics	Arizona	H	7.40 FQ	11.52 AW	16.45 TQ	AZBLS	10/01-12/01
Metals and Plastics	Phoenix-Mesa MSA, AZ	H	7.89 FQ	12.21 AW	16.77 TQ	AZBLS	10/01-12/01
Metals and Plastics	Tucson MSA, AZ	H	6.26 FQ	9.14 AW	14.41 TQ	AZBLS	10/01-12/01
Metals and Plastics	Arkansas	H	8.44 FQ	12.80 AW	16.58 TQ	ARBLS	10/01-12/01
Metals and Plastics	Fayetteville-Springdale-Rogers MSA, AR	H	8.82 FQ	13.28 AW	17.12 TQ	ARBLS	10/01-12/01
Metals and Plastics	Fort Smith MSA, AR-OK	H	7.71 FQ	12.86 AW	16.50 TQ	ARBLS	10/01-12/01
Metals and Plastics	California	H	6.66 FQ	11.31 AW	17.15 TQ	CABLS	10/01-12/01
Metals and Plastics	Bakersfield MSA, CA	H	7.93 FQ	12.01 AW	17.54 TQ	CABLS	10/01-12/01
Metals and Plastics	Fresno MSA, CA	H	6.43 FQ	10.61 AW	16.81 TQ	CABLS	10/01-12/01
Metals and Plastics	Los Angeles-Long Beach PMSA, CA	H	6.50 FQ	9.79 AW	14.55 TQ	CABLS	10/01-12/01
Metals and Plastics	Oakland PMSA, CA	H	9.01 FQ	18.03 AW	25.90 TQ	CABLS	10/01-12/01
Metals and Plastics	Orange County PMSA, CA	H	7.47 FQ	13.01 AW	19.62 TQ	CABLS	10/01-12/01
Metals and Plastics	Riverside-San Bernardino PMSA, CA	H	7.88 FQ	12.14 AW	17.10 TQ	CABLS	10/01-12/01
Metals and Plastics	Sacramento PMSA, CA	H	6.36 FQ	7.84 AW	11.26 TQ	CABLS	10/01-12/01
Metals and Plastics	San Diego MSA, CA	H	7.74 FQ	11.70 AW	16.12 TQ	CABLS	10/01-12/01
Metals and Plastics	San Francisco PMSA, CA	H	6.48 FQ	11.53 AW	19.32 TQ	CABLS	10/01-12/01
Metals and Plastics	San Jose PMSA, CA	H	7.96 FQ	12.04 AW	16.98 TQ	CABLS	10/01-12/01
Metals and Plastics	Santa Barbara-Santa Maria-Lompoc MSA, CA	H	6.94 FQ	13.72 AW	17.34 TQ	CABLS	10/01-12/01
Metals and Plastics	Stockton-Lodi MSA, CA	H	7.53 FQ	10.93 AW	15.67 TQ	CABLS	10/01-12/01
Metals and Plastics	Ventura PMSA, CA	H	7.29 FQ	10.36 AW	15.75 TQ	CABLS	10/01-12/01
Metals and Plastics	Visalia-Tulare-Porterville MSA, CA	H	7.05 FQ	12.68 AW	17.57 TQ	CABLS	10/01-12/01
Metals and Plastics	Colorado	H	8.34 FQ	12.23 AW	16.41 TQ	COBLS	10/01-12/01
Metals and Plastics	Denver PMSA, CO	H	8.32 FQ	13.51 AW	17.07 TQ	COBLS	10/01-12/01
Metals and Plastics	Connecticut	H	7.75 FQ	13.10 AW	19.14 TQ	CTBLS	10/01-12/01
Metals and Plastics	Bridgeport PMSA, CT	H	7.20 FQ	14.09 AW	20.88 TQ	CTBLS	10/01-12/01
Metals and Plastics	Hartford MSA, CT	H	9.05 FQ	15.45 AW	22.13 TQ	CTBLS	10/01-12/01
Metals and Plastics	New Haven-Meriden PMSA, CT	H	7.55 FQ	12.29 AW	17.28 TQ	CTBLS	10/01-12/01
Metals and Plastics	New London-Norwich MSA, CT-RI	H	10.53 FQ	14.37 AW	17.16 TQ	CTBLS	10/01-12/01
Metals and Plastics	Waterbury PMSA, CT	H	8.76 FQ	12.86 AW	17.54 TQ	CTBLS	10/01-12/01
Metals and Plastics	Delaware	H	9.05 FQ	13.38 AW	17.33 TQ	DEBLS	10/01-12/01
Metals and Plastics	Wilmington-Newark PMSA, DE-MD	H	8.94 FQ	13.21 AW	17.14 TQ	DEBLS	10/01-12/01
Metals and Plastics	Washington PMSA, DC-MD-VA-WV	H	8.05 FQ	11.37 AW	15.69 TQ	DCBLS	10/01-12/01
Metals and Plastics	Florida	H	7.33 FQ	11.01 AW	16.20 TQ	FLBLS	10/01-12/01
Metals and Plastics	Daytona Beach MSA, FL	H	7.68 FQ	12.20 AW	17.20 TQ	FLBLS	10/01-12/01
Metals and Plastics	Fort Lauderdale PMSA, FL	H	7.65 FQ	10.62 AW	13.79 TQ	FLBLS	10/01-12/01
Metals and Plastics	Jacksonville MSA, FL	H	7.29 FQ	11.99 AW	20.19 TQ	FLBLS	10/01-12/01
Metals and Plastics	Lakeland-Winter Haven MSA, FL	H	7.75 FQ	10.43 AW	13.48 TQ	FLBLS	10/01-12/01
Metals and Plastics	Miami PMSA, FL	H	7.22 FQ	9.78 AW	12.98 TQ	FLBLS	10/01-12/01
Metals and Plastics	Ocala MSA, FL	H	7.31 FQ	10.19 AW	13.03 TQ	FLBLS	10/01-12/01
Metals and Plastics	Orlando MSA, FL	H	7.55 FQ	10.30 AW	14.09 TQ	FLBLS	10/01-12/01
Metals and Plastics	Sarasota-Bradenton MSA, FL	H	6.98 FQ	9.48 AW	13.42 TQ	FLBLS	10/01-12/01
Metals and Plastics	Tampa-St. Petersburg-Clearwater MSA, FL	H	7.59 FQ	11.36 AW	13.91 TQ	FLBLS	10/01-12/01
Metals and Plastics	West Palm Beach-Boca Raton MSA, FL	H	6.15 FQ	10.56 AW	16.36 TQ	FLBLS	10/01-12/01
Metals and Plastics	Georgia	H	7.94 FQ	12.18 AW	16.83 TQ	GABLS	10/01-12/01

AAW	Average annual wage	AOH	Average offered, high	ASH	Average starting, high	H	Hourly	M	Monthly	S	Special: hourly and annual
AE	Average entry wage	AOL	Average offered, low	ASL	Average starting, low	HI	Highest wage paid	MTC	Median total compensation	TQ	Third quartile wage
AEX	Average experienced wage	APH	Average pay, high range	AW	Average wage paid	HR	High end range	MW	Median wage paid	W	Weekly
AO	Average offered	APL	Average pay, low range	FQ	First quartile wage	LR	Low end range	SQ	Second quartile wage	Y	Yearly

Occupation/Type/Industry	Location	Per	Low	Mid	High	Source	Date
Extruding and Drawing Machine Setter, Operator, and Tender							
Metals and Plastics	Atlanta MSA, GA	H	9.46 FQ	13.68 AW	18.74 TQ	GABLS	10/01-12/01
Metals and Plastics	Augusta-Aiken MSA, GA-SC	H	7.24 FQ	9.51 AW	13.01 TQ	GABLS	10/01-12/01
Metals and Plastics	Macon MSA, GA	H	5.97 FQ	11.12 AW	14.08 TQ	GABLS	10/01-12/01
Metals and Plastics	Idaho	H	6.33 FQ	10.19 AW	14.19 TQ	IDBLS	10/01-12/01
Metals and Plastics	Illinois	H	7.03 FQ	12.43 AW	17.93 TQ	ILBLS	10/01-12/01
Metals and Plastics	Chicago PMSA, IL	H	7.73 FQ	13.38 AW	21.16 TQ	ILBLS	10/01-12/01
Metals and Plastics	Peoria-Pekin MSA, IL	H	5.39 FQ	7.08 AW	9.63 TQ	ILBLS	10/01-12/01
Metals and Plastics	Rockford MSA, IL	H	9.13 FQ	13.16 AW	17.27 TQ	ILBLS	10/01-12/01
Metals and Plastics	Indiana	H	9.01 FQ	13.05 AW	16.94 TQ	INBLS	10/01-12/01
Metals and Plastics	Elkhart-Goshen MSA, IN	H	7.61 FQ	11.29 AW	14.34 TQ	INBLS	10/01-12/01
Metals and Plastics	Evansville-Henderson MSA, IN-KY	H	8.18 FQ	12.31 AW	16.61 TQ	INBLS	10/01-12/01
Metals and Plastics	Fort Wayne MSA, IN	H	9.72 FQ	13.69 AW	17.20 TQ	INBLS	10/01-12/01
Metals and Plastics	Gary PMSA, IN	H	10.01 FQ	14.73 AW	23.63 TQ	INBLS	10/01-12/01
Metals and Plastics	Indianapolis MSA, IN	H	9.96 FQ	13.49 AW	16.85 TQ	INBLS	10/01-12/01
Metals and Plastics	Lafayette MSA, IN	H	9.50 FQ	12.13 AW	14.55 TQ	INBLS	10/01-12/01
Metals and Plastics	South Bend MSA, IN	H	7.97 FQ	12.47 AW	16.94 TQ	INBLS	10/01-12/01
Metals and Plastics	Iowa	H	8.67 FQ	12.69 AW	17.97 TQ	IABLS	10/01-12/01
Metals and Plastics	Davenport-Moline-Rock Island MSA, IA-IL	H	6.56 FQ	10.63 AW	15.31 TQ	IABLS	10/01-12/01
Metals and Plastics	Kansas	H	9.40 FQ	13.52 AW	22.96 TQ	KSBLS	10/01-12/01
Metals and Plastics	Wichita MSA, KS	H	10.49 FQ	20.25 AW	27.56 TQ	KSBLS	10/01-12/01
Metals and Plastics	Kentucky	H	8.87 FQ	12.76 AW	17.28 TQ	KYBLS	10/01-12/01
Metals and Plastics	Lexington MSA, KY	H	7.95 FQ	12.14 AW	17.33 TQ	KYBLS	10/01-12/01
Metals and Plastics	Louisville MSA, KY-IN	H	8.08 FQ	12.53 AW	16.77 TQ	KYBLS	10/01-12/01
Metals and Plastics	Louisiana	H	7.60 FQ	11.75 AW	16.55 TQ	LABLS	10/01-12/01
Metals and Plastics	Baton Rouge MSA, LA	H	7.93 FQ	13.22 AW	17.23 TQ	LABLS	10/01-12/01
Metals and Plastics	Lafayette MSA, LA	H	5.80 FQ	9.58 AW	15.15 TQ	LABLS	10/01-12/01
Metals and Plastics	New Orleans MSA, LA	H	8.05 FQ	10.51 AW	13.51 TQ	LABLS	10/01-12/01
Metals and Plastics	Maine	H	8.50 FQ	12.74 AW	16.88 TQ	MEBLS	10/01-12/01
Metals and Plastics	Maryland	H	9.43 FQ	12.01 AW	15.62 TQ	MDBLS	10/01-12/01
Metals and Plastics	Baltimore PMSA, MD	H	9.38 FQ	11.71 AW	14.86 TQ	MDBLS	10/01-12/01
Metals and Plastics	Massachusetts	H	8.11 FQ	13.96 AW	20.69 TQ	MABLS	10/01-12/01
Metals and Plastics	Boston PMSA, MA-NH	H	8.35 FQ	14.06 AW	19.55 TQ	MABLS	10/01-12/01
Metals and Plastics	Brockton PMSA, MA	H	7.97 FQ	10.71 AW	13.79 TQ	MABLS	10/01-12/01
Metals and Plastics	Lawrence PMSA, MA-NH	H	8.05 FQ	11.88 AW	18.29 TQ	MABLS	10/01-12/01
Metals and Plastics	Lowell PMSA, MA-NH	H	8.07 FQ	12.04 AW	16.36 TQ	MABLS	10/01-12/01
Metals and Plastics	New Bedford PMSA, MA	H	10.17 FQ	13.75 AW	17.31 TQ	MABLS	10/01-12/01
Metals and Plastics	Springfield MSA, MA	H	7.11 FQ	12.08 AW	17.85 TQ	MABLS	10/01-12/01
Metals and Plastics	Worcester PMSA, MA-CT	H	9.07 FQ	17.62 AW	32.25 TQ	MABLS	10/01-12/01
Metals and Plastics	Michigan	H	8.60 FQ	12.65 AW	17.99 TQ	MIBLS	10/01-12/01
Metals and Plastics	Ann Arbor PMSA, MI	H	8.43 FQ	14.87 AW	21.66 TQ	MIBLS	10/01-12/01
Metals and Plastics	Detroit PMSA, MI	H	8.47 FQ	12.14 AW	18.38 TQ	MIBLS	10/01-12/01
Metals and Plastics	Flint PMSA, MI	H	9.45 FQ	15.35 AW	26.00 TQ	MIBLS	10/01-12/01
Metals and Plastics	Grand Rapids-Muskegon-Holland MSA, MI	H	9.03 FQ	12.38 AW	16.60 TQ	MIBLS	10/01-12/01
Metals and Plastics	Kalamazoo-Battle Creek MSA, MI	H	8.00 FQ	12.17 AW	16.67 TQ	MIBLS	10/01-12/01
Metals and Plastics	Minnesota	H	9.21 FQ	14.09 AW	20.47 TQ	MNBLS	10/01-12/01
Metals and Plastics	Duluth-Superior MSA, MN-WI	H	9.71 FQ	12.08 AW	13.89 TQ	MNBLS	10/01-12/01
Metals and Plastics	Minneapolis-St. Paul MSA, MN-WI	H	9.15 FQ	14.42 AW	21.20 TQ	MNBLS	10/01-12/01
Metals and Plastics	Mississippi	H	8.65 FQ	11.14 AW	13.60 TQ	MSBLS	10/01-12/01
Metals and Plastics	Jackson MSA, MS	H	7.81 FQ	11.01 AW	13.39 TQ	MSBLS	10/01-12/01
Metals and Plastics	Missouri	H	7.34 FQ	12.05 AW	15.67 TQ	MOBLS	10/01-12/01
Metals and Plastics	Kansas City MSA, MO-KS	H	9.78 FQ	12.96 AW	17.39 TQ	MOBLS	10/01-12/01
Metals and Plastics	St. Louis MSA, MO-IL	H	7.12 FQ	11.65 AW	16.39 TQ	MOBLS	10/01-12/01
Metals and Plastics	Springfield MSA, MO	H	10.93 FQ	13.11 AW	16.46 TQ	MOBLS	10/01-12/01
Metals and Plastics	Nebraska	H	8.32 FQ	12.41 AW	18.11 TQ	NEBLS	10/01-12/01
Metals and Plastics	Omaha MSA, NE-IA	H	9.80 FQ	13.56 AW	17.15 TQ	NEBLS	10/01-12/01
Metals and Plastics	Nevada	H	8.40 FQ	12.39 AW	16.62 TQ	NVBLS	10/01-12/01
Metals and Plastics	Las Vegas MSA, NV-AZ	H	8.08 FQ	10.83 AW	14.19 TQ	NVBLS	10/01-12/01
Metals and Plastics	Reno MSA, NV	H	8.23 FQ	13.31 AW	17.80 TQ	NVBLS	10/01-12/01
Metals and Plastics	New Hampshire	H	9.44 FQ	12.64 AW	16.56 TQ	NHBLS	10/01-12/01
Metals and Plastics	Manchester PMSA, NH	H	9.83 FQ	11.95 AW	14.03 TQ	NHBLS	10/01-12/01
Metals and Plastics	Nashua PMSA, NH	H	9.53 FQ	12.22 AW	15.82 TQ	NHBLS	10/01-12/01
Metals and Plastics	New Jersey	H	7.75 FQ	13.19 AW	18.62 TQ	NJBLS	10/01-12/01
Metals and Plastics	Bergen-Passaic PMSA, NJ	H	7.34 FQ	12.44 AW	16.81 TQ	NJBLS	10/01-12/01
Metals and Plastics	Jersey City PMSA, NJ	H	6.43 FQ	14.20 AW	31.67 TQ	NJBLS	10/01-12/01

AAW	Average annual wage	AOH	Average offered, high	ASH	Average starting, high	H	Hourly	M	Monthly	S	Special: hourly and annual
AE	Average entry wage	AOL	Average offered, low	ASL	Average starting, low	HI	Highest wage paid	MTC	Median total compensation	TQ	Third quartile wage
AEX	Average experienced wage	APH	Average pay, high range	AW	Average wage paid	HR	High end range	MW	Median wage paid	W	Weekly
AO	Average offered	APL	Average pay, low range	FQ	First quartile wage	LR	Low end range	SQ	Second quartile wage	Y	Yearly

Occupation/Type/Industry	Location	Per	Low	Mid	High	Source	Date
Extruding and Drawing Machine Setter, Operator, and Tender							
Metals and Plastics	Middlesex-Somerset-Hunterdon PMSA, NJ	H	9.09 FQ	12.94 AW	17.84 TQ	NJBLS	10/01-12/01
Metals and Plastics	Monmouth-Ocean PMSA, NJ	H	11.60 FQ	14.90 AW	17.48 TQ	NJBLS	10/01-12/01
Metals and Plastics	Newark PMSA, NJ	H	7.37 FQ	12.88 AW	18.37 TQ	NJBLS	10/01-12/01
Metals and Plastics	Trenton PMSA, NJ	H	7.10 FQ	11.75 AW	17.07 TQ	NJBLS	10/01-12/01
Metals and Plastics	New Mexico	H	6.46 FQ	13.78 AW	26.92 TQ	NMBLS	10/01-12/01
Metals and Plastics	New York	H	8.23 FQ	11.61 AW	16.40 TQ	NYBLS	10/01-12/01
Metals and Plastics	Albany-Schenectady-Troy MSA, NY	H	8.83 FQ	12.52 AW	18.60 TQ	NYBLS	10/01-12/01
Metals and Plastics	Binghamton MSA, NY	H	7.97 FQ	10.93 AW	13.87 TQ	NYBLS	10/01-12/01
Metals and Plastics	Buffalo-Niagara Falls MSA, NY	H	8.44 FQ	10.41 AW	13.40 TQ	NYBLS	10/01-12/01
Metals and Plastics	Nassau-Suffolk PMSA, NY	H	7.44 FQ	10.75 AW	15.55 TQ	NYBLS	10/01-12/01
Metals and Plastics	New York PMSA, NY	H	9.05 FQ	12.74 AW	17.61 TQ	NYBLS	10/01-12/01
Metals and Plastics	Rochester MSA, NY	H	8.30 FQ	12.30 AW	17.45 TQ	NYBLS	10/01-12/01
Metals and Plastics	Syracuse MSA, NY	H	8.61 FQ	10.49 AW	13.97 TQ	NYBLS	10/01-12/01
Metals and Plastics	Utica-Rome MSA, NY	H	8.22 FQ	11.46 AW	13.78 TQ	NYBLS	10/01-12/01
Metals and Plastics	North Carolina	H	7.47 FQ	11.36 AW	16.26 TQ	NCBLS	10/01-12/01
Metals and Plastics	Charlotte-Gastonia-Rock Hill MSA, NC-SC	H	7.49 FQ	11.53 AW	16.33 TQ	NCBLS	10/01-12/01
Metals and Plastics	Greensboro-Winston-Salem-High Point MSA, NC	H	7.14 FQ	11.79 AW	16.17 TQ	NCBLS	10/01-12/01
Metals and Plastics	Hickory-Morganton-Lenoir MSA, NC	H	11.79 FQ	14.35 AW	16.84 TQ	NCBLS	10/01-12/01
Metals and Plastics	Raleigh-Durham-Chapel Hill MSA, NC	H	8.11 FQ	11.30 AW	14.66 TQ	NCBLS	10/01-12/01
Metals and Plastics	Ohio	H	7.96 FQ	12.53 AW	17.31 TQ	OHBLS	10/01-12/01
Metals and Plastics	Akron PMSA, OH	H	7.46 FQ	11.03 AW	17.00 TQ	OHBLS	10/01-12/01
Metals and Plastics	Cincinnati PMSA, OH-KY-IN	H	9.03 FQ	13.43 AW	17.89 TQ	OHBLS	10/01-12/01
Metals and Plastics	Cleveland-Lorain-Elyria PMSA, OH	H	7.57 FQ	12.55 AW	16.91 TQ	OHBLS	10/01-12/01
Metals and Plastics	Columbus MSA, OH	H	9.37 FQ	13.96 AW	19.06 TQ	OHBLS	10/01-12/01
Metals and Plastics	Dayton-Springfield MSA, OH	H	8.16 FQ	12.36 AW	16.53 TQ	OHBLS	10/01-12/01
Metals and Plastics	Hamilton-Middletown PMSA, OH	H	9.53 FQ	13.61 AW	19.11 TQ	OHBLS	10/01-12/01
Metals and Plastics	Mansfield MSA, OH	H	8.13 FQ	10.70 AW	13.82 TQ	OHBLS	10/01-12/01
Metals and Plastics	Toledo MSA, OH	H	9.56 FQ	13.21 AW	18.41 TQ	OHBLS	10/01-12/01
Metals and Plastics	Youngstown-Warren MSA, OH	H	7.96 FQ	13.22 AW	20.17 TQ	OHBLS	10/01-12/01
Metals and Plastics	Oklahoma	H	7.32 FQ	11.66 AW	17.32 TQ	OKBLS	10/01-12/01
Metals and Plastics	Oklahoma City MSA, OK	H	7.31 FQ	10.63 AW	14.84 TQ	OKBLS	10/01-12/01
Metals and Plastics	Tulsa MSA, OK	H	7.22 FQ	11.68 AW	16.97 TQ	OKBLS	10/01-12/01
Metals and Plastics	Oregon	H	8.53 FQ	12.63 AW	19.05 TQ	ORBLS	10/01-12/01
Metals and Plastics	Portland-Vancouver PMSA, OR-WA	H	8.04 FQ	12.37 AW	19.43 TQ	ORBLS	10/01-12/01
Metals and Plastics	Pennsylvania	H	8.43 FQ	13.74 AW	19.82 TQ	PABLS	10/01-12/01
Metals and Plastics	Erie MSA, PA	H	7.22 FQ	11.29 AW	16.82 TQ	PABLS	10/01-12/01
Metals and Plastics	Harrisburg-Lebanon-Carlisle MSA, PA	H	7.03 FQ	10.47 AW	14.73 TQ	PABLS	10/01-12/01
Metals and Plastics	Lancaster MSA, PA	H	11.60 FQ	15.07 AW	18.68 TQ	PABLS	10/01-12/01
Metals and Plastics	Philadelphia PMSA, PA-NJ	H	11.23 FQ	15.62 AW	20.56 TQ	PABLS	10/01-12/01
Metals and Plastics	Pittsburgh MSA, PA	H	8.15 FQ	15.42 AW	22.89 TQ	PABLS	10/01-12/01
Metals and Plastics	Reading MSA, PA	H	10.18 FQ	15.65 AW	20.92 TQ	PABLS	10/01-12/01
Metals and Plastics	Scranton-Wilkes-Barre-Hazleton MSA, PA	H	7.51 FQ	11.64 AW	16.47 TQ	PABLS	10/01-12/01
Metals and Plastics	York MSA, PA	H	9.81 FQ	13.22 AW	17.71 TQ	PABLS	10/01-12/01
Metals and Plastics	Rhode Island	H	7.47 FQ	11.76 AW	16.46 TQ	RIBLS	10/01-12/01
Metals and Plastics	Providence-Fall River-Warwick MSA, RI-MA	H	7.69 FQ	12.01 AW	16.45 TQ	RIBLS	10/01-12/01
Metals and Plastics	South Carolina	H	9.92 FQ	15.08 AW	21.39 TQ	SCBLS	10/01-12/01
Metals and Plastics	Charleston-North Charleston MSA, SC	H	10.54 FQ	13.26 AW	16.85 TQ	SCBLS	10/01-12/01
Metals and Plastics	Columbia MSA, SC	H	10.68 FQ	14.82 AW	20.38 TQ	SCBLS	10/01-12/01
Metals and Plastics	Greenville-Spartanburg-Anderson MSA, SC	H	11.01 FQ	16.32 AW	21.42 TQ	SCBLS	10/01-12/01
Metals and Plastics	South Dakota	H	8.21 FQ	10.98 AW	15.07 TQ	SDBLS	10/01-12/01
Metals and Plastics	Sioux Falls MSA, SD	H	7.51 FQ	9.67 AW	13.16 TQ	SDBLS	10/01-12/01
Metals and Plastics	Tennessee	H	8.57 FQ	12.05 AW	16.22 TQ	TNBLS	10/01-12/01
Metals and Plastics	Chattanooga MSA, TN-GA	H	8.94 FQ	11.43 AW	14.15 TQ	TNBLS	10/01-12/01
Metals and Plastics	Knoxville MSA, TN	H	7.73 FQ	10.87 AW	15.58 TQ	TNBLS	10/01-12/01
Metals and Plastics	Memphis MSA, TN-AR-MS	H	8.70 FQ	12.05 AW	16.30 TQ	TNBLS	10/01-12/01

AAW	Average annual wage	AOH	Average offered, high	ASH	Average starting, high	H	Hourly	M	Monthly	S	Special: hourly and annual
AE	Average entry wage	AOL	Average offered, low	ASL	Average starting, low	HI	Highest wage paid	MTC	Median total compensation	TQ	Third quartile wage
AEX	Average experienced wage	APH	Average pay, high range	AW	Average wage paid	HR	High end range	MW	Median wage paid	W	Weekly
AO	Average offered	APL	Average pay, low range	FQ	First quartile wage	LR	Low end range	SQ	Second quartile wage	Y	Yearly

Occupation/Type/Industry	Location	Per	Low	Mid	High	Source	Date
Extruding and Drawing Machine Setter, Operator, and Tender							
Metals and Plastics	Nashville MSA, TN	H	9.47 FQ	13.20 AW	16.66 TQ	TNBLS	10/01-12/01
Metals and Plastics	Texas	H	7.57 FQ	11.60 AW	16.55 TQ	TXBLS	10/01-12/01
Metals and Plastics	Austin-San Marcos MSA, TX	H	7.30 FQ	11.02 AW	16.78 TQ	TXBLS	10/01-12/01
Metals and Plastics	Dallas PMSA, TX	H	7.60 FQ	11.06 AW	14.51 TQ	TXBLS	10/01-12/01
Metals and Plastics	El Paso MSA, TX	H	8.56 FQ	11.39 AW	16.32 TQ	TXBLS	10/01-12/01
Metals and Plastics	Fort Worth-Arlington PMSA, TX	H	8.53 FQ	10.62 AW	13.81 TQ	TXBLS	10/01-12/01
Metals and Plastics	Houston PMSA, TX	H	8.67 FQ	14.35 AW	28.89 TQ	TXBLS	10/01-12/01
Metals and Plastics	Longview-Marshall MSA, TX	H	10.94 FQ	13.07 AW	16.55 TQ	TXBLS	10/01-12/01
Metals and Plastics	San Antonio MSA, TX	H	5.99 FQ	10.15 AW	16.45 TQ	TXBLS	10/01-12/01
Metals and Plastics	Waco MSA, TX	H	8.37 FQ	12.52 AW	16.42 TQ	TXBLS	10/01-12/01
Metals and Plastics	Utah	H	9.17 FQ	12.19 AW	15.96 TQ	UTBLS	10/01-12/01
Metals and Plastics	Salt Lake City-Ogden MSA, UT	H	9.27 FQ	12.39 AW	16.46 TQ	UTBLS	10/01-12/01
Metals and Plastics	Vermont	H	8.89 FQ	13.13 AW	16.97 TQ	VTBLS	10/01-12/01
Metals and Plastics	Virginia	H	8.63 FQ	12.43 AW	17.49 TQ	VABLS	10/01-12/01
Metals and Plastics	Norfolk-Virginia Beach-Newport News MSA, VA-NC	H	7.64 FQ	11.22 AW	14.02 TQ	VABLS	10/01-12/01
Metals and Plastics	Richmond-Petersburg MSA, VA	H	9.56 FQ	17.02 AW	24.96 TQ	VABLS	10/01-12/01
Metals and Plastics	Roanoke MSA, VA	H	9.38 FQ	11.94 AW	15.02 TQ	VABLS	10/01-12/01
Metals and Plastics	Washington	H	8.16 FQ	12.98 AW	19.28 TQ	WABLS	10/01-12/01
Metals and Plastics	Seattle-Bellevue-Everett PMSA, WA	H	8.29 FQ	12.65 AW	18.75 TQ	WABLS	10/01-12/01
Metals and Plastics	Tacoma PMSA, WA	H	8.02 FQ	12.09 AW	17.21 TQ	WABLS	10/01-12/01
Metals and Plastics	Yakima MSA, WA	H	8.73 FQ	13.71 AW	17.22 TQ	WABLS	10/01-12/01
Metals and Plastics	West Virginia	H	8.68 FQ	11.99 AW	16.83 TQ	WVBLS	10/01-12/01
Metals and Plastics	Huntington-Ashland MSA, WV-KY-OH	H	9.51 FQ	14.44 AW	16.93 TQ	WVBLS	10/01-12/01
Metals and Plastics	Wisconsin	H	8.60 FQ	12.77 AW	16.98 TQ	WIBLS	10/01-12/01
Metals and Plastics	Appleton-Oshkosh-Neenah MSA, WI	H	9.99 FQ	13.01 AW	16.63 TQ	WIBLS	10/01-12/01
Metals and Plastics	Green Bay MSA, WI	H	6.44 FQ	10.13 AW	15.65 TQ	WIBLS	10/01-12/01
Metals and Plastics	Madison MSA, WI	H	9.47 FQ	13.70 AW	17.72 TQ	WIBLS	10/01-12/01
Metals and Plastics	Milwaukee-Waukesha PMSA, WI	H	8.54 FQ	13.17 AW	17.62 TQ	WIBLS	10/01-12/01
Metals and Plastics	Puerto Rico	H	5.58 FQ	7.59 AW	12.20 TQ	PRBLS	10/01-12/01
Extruding and Forming Machine Setter, Operator, and Tender							
Synthetic and Glass Fiber	Alabama	H	8.66 FQ	11.88 AW	15.26 TQ	ALBLS	10/01-12/01
Synthetic and Glass Fiber	Arizona	H	6.49 FQ	10.29 AW	14.37 TQ	AZBLS	10/01-12/01
Synthetic and Glass Fiber	California	H	6.91 FQ	9.57 AW	13.60 TQ	CABLS	10/01-12/01
Synthetic and Glass Fiber	Los Angeles-Long Beach PMSA, CA	H	6.86 FQ	8.85 AW	11.93 TQ	CABLS	10/01-12/01
Synthetic and Glass Fiber	Riverside-San Bernardino PMSA, CA	H	7.04 FQ	9.53 AW	13.75 TQ	CABLS	10/01-12/01
Synthetic and Glass Fiber	Delaware	H	11.11 FQ	15.72 AW	20.02 TQ	DEBLS	10/01-12/01
Synthetic and Glass Fiber	Wilmington-Newark PMSA, DE-MD	H	11.19 FQ	15.76 AW	20.29 TQ	DEBLS	10/01-12/01
Synthetic and Glass Fiber	Jacksonville MSA, FL	H	6.84 FQ	8.66 AW	10.71 TQ	FLBLS	10/01-12/01
Synthetic and Glass Fiber	Georgia	H	8.59 FQ	12.41 AW	16.70 TQ	GABLS	10/01-12/01
Synthetic and Glass Fiber	Atlanta MSA, GA	H	6.63 FQ	13.12 AW	20.13 TQ	GABLS	10/01-12/01
Synthetic and Glass Fiber	Augusta-Aiken MSA, GA-SC	H	10.24 FQ	13.87 AW	16.71 TQ	GABLS	10/01-12/01
Synthetic and Glass Fiber	Illinois	H	8.23 FQ	11.96 AW	16.98 TQ	ILBLS	10/01-12/01
Synthetic and Glass Fiber	Chicago PMSA, IL	H	7.72 FQ	11.90 AW	18.92 TQ	ILBLS	10/01-12/01
Synthetic and Glass Fiber	Fort Wayne MSA, IN	H	7.83 FQ	11.51 AW	14.69 TQ	INBLS	10/01-12/01
Synthetic and Glass Fiber	Iowa	H	8.07 FQ	15.28 AW	22.00 TQ	IABLS	10/01-12/01
Synthetic and Glass Fiber	Kansas	H	10.77 FQ	13.12 AW	16.34 TQ	KSBLS	10/01-12/01
Synthetic and Glass Fiber	Wichita MSA, KS	H	10.81 FQ	12.72 AW	15.84 TQ	KSBLS	10/01-12/01
Synthetic and Glass Fiber	Kentucky	H	7.65 FQ	12.42 AW	17.29 TQ	KYBLS	10/01-12/01
Synthetic and Glass Fiber	Louisiana	H	6.46 FQ	12.00 AW	20.79 TQ	LABLS	10/01-12/01
Synthetic and Glass Fiber	Maine	H	9.10 FQ	11.54 AW	13.45 TQ	MEBLS	10/01-12/01
Synthetic and Glass Fiber	Massachusetts	H	9.83 FQ	13.39 AW	17.22 TQ	MABLS	10/01-12/01
Synthetic and Glass Fiber	Boston PMSA, MA-NH	H	9.58 FQ	13.38 AW	17.36 TQ	MABLS	10/01-12/01
Synthetic and Glass Fiber	Worcester PMSA, MA-CT	H	10.88 FQ	13.26 AW	16.30 TQ	MABLS	10/01-12/01
Synthetic and Glass Fiber	Michigan	H	11.45 FQ	14.96 AW	19.65 TQ	MIBLS	10/01-12/01
Synthetic and Glass Fiber	Minnesota	H	7.59 FQ	12.18 AW	16.41 TQ	MNBLS	10/01-12/01

AAW	Average annual wage	AOH	Average offered, high	ASH	Average starting, high	H	Hourly	M	Monthly	S	Special: hourly and annual
AE	Average entry wage	AOL	Average offered, low	ASL	Average starting, low	HI	Highest wage paid	MTC	Median total compensation	TQ	Third quartile wage
AEX	Average experienced wage	APH	Average pay, high range	AW	Average wage paid	HR	High end range	MW	Median wage paid	W	Weekly
AO	Average offered	APL	Average pay, low range	FQ	First quartile wage	LR	Low end range	SQ	Second quartile wage	Y	Yearly

Occupation/Type/Industry	Location	Per	Low	Mid	High	Source	Date
Extruding and Forming Machine Setter, Operator, and Tender							
Synthetic and Glass Fiber	Minneapolis-St. Paul MSA, MN-WI	H	7.59 FQ	12.18 AW	16.41 TQ	MNBLS	10/01-12/01
Synthetic and Glass Fiber	Mississippi	H	8.23 FQ	11.89 AW	16.34 TQ	MSBLS	10/01-12/01
Synthetic and Glass Fiber	Missouri	H	7.83 FQ	9.45 AW	11.10 TQ	MOBLS	10/01-12/01
Synthetic and Glass Fiber	Nebraska	H	7.53 FQ	10.98 AW	18.05 TQ	NEBLS	10/01-12/01
Synthetic and Glass Fiber	New Hampshire	H	9.42 FQ	12.48 AW	16.12 TQ	NHBLS	10/01-12/01
Synthetic and Glass Fiber	New Jersey	H	6.05 FQ	10.91 AW	16.20 TQ	NJBLS	10/01-12/01
Synthetic and Glass Fiber	Bergen-Passaic PMSA, NJ	H	5.79 FQ	9.66 AW	14.81 TQ	NJBLS	10/01-12/01
Synthetic and Glass Fiber	Jersey City PMSA, NJ	H	5.75 FQ	9.67 AW	13.95 TQ	NJBLS	10/01-12/01
Synthetic and Glass Fiber	Middlesex-Somerset-Hunterdon PMSA, NJ	H	5.98 FQ	9.71 AW	14.81 TQ	NJBLS	10/01-12/01
Synthetic and Glass Fiber	New Mexico	H	7.39 FQ	12.50 AW	16.64 TQ	NMBLS	10/01-12/01
Synthetic and Glass Fiber	Albuquerque MSA, NM	H	11.40 FQ	14.61 AW	18.02 TQ	NMBLS	10/01-12/01
Synthetic and Glass Fiber	New York	H	9.29 FQ	14.14 AW	17.74 TQ	NYBLS	10/01-12/01
Synthetic and Glass Fiber	New York PMSA, NY	H	7.88 FQ	13.23 AW	17.46 TQ	NYBLS	10/01-12/01
Synthetic and Glass Fiber	Rochester MSA, NY	H	13.78 FQ	15.91 AW	18.55 TQ	NYBLS	10/01-12/01
Synthetic and Glass Fiber	North Carolina	H	9.16 FQ	13.88 AW	18.22 TQ	NCBLS	10/01-12/01
Synthetic and Glass Fiber	Charlotte-Gastonia-Rock Hill MSA, NC-SC	H	9.34 FQ	13.32 AW	17.08 TQ	NCBLS	10/01-12/01
Synthetic and Glass Fiber	Hickory-Morganton-Lenoir MSA, NC	H	9.74 FQ	12.97 AW	16.86 TQ	NCBLS	10/01-12/01
Synthetic and Glass Fiber	Raleigh-Durham-Chapel Hill MSA, NC	H	9.29 FQ	12.98 AW	17.50 TQ	NCBLS	10/01-12/01
Synthetic and Glass Fiber	Ohio	H	11.33 FQ	13.27 AW	16.70 TQ	OHBLS	10/01-12/01
Synthetic and Glass Fiber	Cleveland-Lorain-Elyria PMSA, OH	H	11.51 FQ	14.39 AW	19.26 TQ	OHBLS	10/01-12/01
Synthetic and Glass Fiber	Columbus MSA, OH	H	11.74 FQ	12.80 AW	14.15 TQ	OHBLS	10/01-12/01
Synthetic and Glass Fiber	Oklahoma	H	7.25 FQ	11.39 AW	15.91 TQ	OKBLS	10/01-12/01
Synthetic and Glass Fiber	Tulsa MSA, OK	H	9.34 FQ	12.09 AW	14.18 TQ	OKBLS	10/01-12/01
Synthetic and Glass Fiber	Pennsylvania	H	9.48 FQ	15.25 AW	20.99 TQ	PABLS	10/01-12/01
Synthetic and Glass Fiber	Allentown-Bethlehem-Easton MSA, PA	H	10.80 FQ	13.82 AW	19.53 TQ	PABLS	10/01-12/01
Synthetic and Glass Fiber	Philadelphia PMSA, PA-NJ	H	9.87 FQ	13.63 AW	18.31 TQ	PABLS	10/01-12/01
Synthetic and Glass Fiber	Pittsburgh MSA, PA	H	8.39 FQ	15.40 AW	20.78 TQ	PABLS	10/01-12/01
Synthetic and Glass Fiber	Scranton-Wilkes-Barre-Hazleton MSA, PA	H	8.97 FQ	13.78 AW	18.41 TQ	PABLS	10/01-12/01
Synthetic and Glass Fiber	Rhode Island	H	9.86 FQ	12.33 AW	15.69 TQ	RIBLS	10/01-12/01
Synthetic and Glass Fiber	Providence-Fall River-Warwick MSA, RI-MA	H	10.30 FQ	12.93 AW	16.52 TQ	RIBLS	10/01-12/01
Synthetic and Glass Fiber	South Carolina	H	9.47 FQ	13.40 AW	16.98 TQ	SCBLS	10/01-12/01
Synthetic and Glass Fiber	Charleston-North Charleston MSA, SC	H	11.36 FQ	14.14 AW	17.10 TQ	SCBLS	10/01-12/01
Synthetic and Glass Fiber	Greenville-Spartanburg-Anderson MSA, SC	H	9.58 FQ	13.61 AW	17.12 TQ	SCBLS	10/01-12/01
Synthetic and Glass Fiber	Tennessee	H	10.07 FQ	14.64 AW	17.96 TQ	TNBLS	10/01-12/01
Synthetic and Glass Fiber	Johnson City-Kingsport-Bristol MSA, TN-VA	H	9.86 FQ	14.65 AW	17.65 TQ	TNBLS	10/01-12/01
Synthetic and Glass Fiber	Memphis MSA, TN-AR-MS	H	9.34 FQ	11.79 AW	16.26 TQ	TNBLS	10/01-12/01
Synthetic and Glass Fiber	Texas	H	5.94 FQ	8.69 AW	12.20 TQ	TXBLS	10/01-12/01
Synthetic and Glass Fiber	Utah	H	7.75 FQ	11.14 AW	15.74 TQ	UTBLS	10/01-12/01
Synthetic and Glass Fiber	Salt Lake City-Ogden MSA, UT	H	7.73 FQ	11.01 AW	15.58 TQ	UTBLS	10/01-12/01
Synthetic and Glass Fiber	Virginia	H	8.78 FQ	13.72 AW	20.13 TQ	VABLS	10/01-12/01
Synthetic and Glass Fiber	Richmond-Petersburg MSA, VA	H	9.82 FQ	13.04 AW	17.36 TQ	VABLS	10/01-12/01
Synthetic and Glass Fiber	Washington	H	7.70 FQ	10.90 AW	15.55 TQ	WABLS	10/01-12/01
Synthetic and Glass Fiber	West Virginia	H	9.60 FQ	14.45 AW	18.02 TQ	WVBLS	10/01-12/01
Synthetic and Glass Fiber	Wisconsin	H	9.74 FQ	15.66 AW	25.84 TQ	WIBLS	10/01-12/01
Synthetic and Glass Fiber	Appleton-Oshkosh-Neenah MSA, WI	H	11.75 FQ	14.52 AW	17.62 TQ	WIBLS	10/01-12/01
Extruding, Forming, Pressing, and Compacting Machine Setter, Operator, and Tender	Alabama	H	8.77 FQ	13.29 AW	20.64 TQ	ALBLS	10/01-12/01
	Birmingham MSA, AL	H	7.97 FQ	10.91 AW	13.79 TQ	ALBLS	10/01-12/01
	Montgomery MSA, AL	H	7.64 FQ	12.39 AW	17.63 TQ	ALBLS	10/01-12/01
	Arizona	H	7.56 FQ	12.32 AW	20.46 TQ	AZBLS	10/01-12/01
	Phoenix-Mesa MSA, AZ	H	8.00 FQ	11.06 AW	15.29 TQ	AZBLS	10/01-12/01
	Tucson MSA, AZ	H	5.70 FQ	8.54 AW	10.90 TQ	AZBLS	10/01-12/01

AAW	Average annual wage	AOH	Average offered, high	ASH	Average starting, high	H	Hourly	M	Monthly	S	Special: hourly and annual
AE	Average entry wage	AOL	Average offered, low	ASL	Average starting, low	HI	Highest wage paid	MTC	Median total compensation	TQ	Third quartile wage
AEX	Average experienced wage	APH	Average pay, high range	AW	Average wage paid	HR	High end range	MW	Median wage paid	W	Weekly
AO	Average offered	APL	Average pay, low range	FQ	First quartile wage	LR	Low end range	SQ	Second quartile wage	Y	Yearly

Occupation/Type/Industry	Location	Per	Low	Mid	High	Source	Date
Extruding, Forming, Pressing, and Compacting Machine Setter, Operator, and Tender	Arkansas	H	9.23 FQ	13.24 AW	20.41 TQ	ARBLS	10/01-12/01
	Fort Smith MSA, AR-OK	H	9.30 FQ	11.96 AW	16.44 TQ	ARBLS	10/01-12/01
	Little Rock-North Little Rock MSA, AR	H	9.07 FQ	11.36 AW	13.53 TQ	ARBLS	10/01-12/01
	California	H	7.02 FQ	11.39 AW	18.02 TQ	CABLS	10/01-12/01
	Fresno MSA, CA	H	8.01 FQ	13.64 AW	20.75 TQ	CABLS	10/01-12/01
	Los Angeles-Long Beach PMSA, CA	H	6.83 FQ	11.60 AW	19.06 TQ	CABLS	10/01-12/01
	Modesto MSA, CA	H	9.72 FQ	12.75 AW	16.08 TQ	CABLS	10/01-12/01
	Oakland PMSA, CA	H	7.40 FQ	12.98 AW	21.53 TQ	CABLS	10/01-12/01
	Orange County PMSA, CA	H	6.83 FQ	9.37 AW	12.91 TQ	CABLS	10/01-12/01
	Riverside-San Bernardino PMSA, CA	H	7.30 FQ	10.38 AW	15.23 TQ	CABLS	10/01-12/01
	Sacramento PMSA, CA	H	6.53 FQ	10.98 AW	16.65 TQ	CABLS	10/01-12/01
	San Diego MSA, CA	H	7.33 FQ	10.52 AW	16.48 TQ	CABLS	10/01-12/01
	San Francisco PMSA, CA	H	6.92 FQ	14.05 AW	21.07 TQ	CABLS	10/01-12/01
	Santa Barbara-Santa Maria-Lompoc MSA, CA	H	7.28 FQ	10.35 AW	14.75 TQ	CABLS	10/01-12/01
	Santa Rosa PMSA, CA	H	9.22 FQ	13.48 AW	18.62 TQ	CABLS	10/01-12/01
	Vallejo-Fairfield-Napa PMSA, CA	H	8.27 FQ	13.71 AW	19.36 TQ	CABLS	10/01-12/01
	Ventura PMSA, CA	H	7.37 FQ	11.16 AW	17.08 TQ	CABLS	10/01-12/01
	Visalia-Tulare-Porterville MSA, CA	H	7.52 FQ	9.45 AW	11.04 TQ	CABLS	10/01-12/01
	Colorado	H	8.28 FQ	12.26 AW	17.52 TQ	COBLS	10/01-12/01
	Colorado Springs MSA, CO	H	7.65 FQ	11.59 AW	16.48 TQ	COBLS	10/01-12/01
	Denver PMSA, CO	H	9.74 FQ	13.83 AW	19.06 TQ	COBLS	10/01-12/01
	Greeley PMSA, CO	H	6.10 FQ	10.55 AW	15.92 TQ	COBLS	10/01-12/01
	Connecticut	H	8.90 FQ	11.68 AW	16.70 TQ	CTBLS	10/01-12/01
	Bridgeport PMSA, CT	H	9.48 FQ	12.95 AW	16.98 TQ	CTBLS	10/01-12/01
	Danbury PMSA, CT	H	8.80 FQ	13.74 AW	24.01 TQ	CTBLS	10/01-12/01
	Hartford MSA, CT	H	9.39 FQ	13.68 AW	18.40 TQ	CTBLS	10/01-12/01
	New Haven-Meriden PMSA, CT	H	8.47 FQ	11.30 AW	16.96 TQ	CTBLS	10/01-12/01
	New London-Norwich MSA, CT-RI	H	9.22 FQ	10.42 AW	11.83 TQ	CTBLS	10/01-12/01
	Washington PMSA, DC-MD-VA-WV	H	9.21 FQ	13.45 AW	17.24 TQ	DCBLS	10/01-12/01
	Florida	H	8.44 FQ	12.20 AW	16.83 TQ	FLBLS	10/01-12/01
	Fort Lauderdale PMSA, FL	H	7.49 FQ	11.42 AW	15.02 TQ	FLBLS	10/01-12/01
	Fort Myers-Cape Coral MSA, FL	H	9.26 FQ	11.86 AW	14.84 TQ	FLBLS	10/01-12/01
	Jacksonville MSA, FL	H	8.74 FQ	14.87 AW	26.28 TQ	FLBLS	10/01-12/01
	Lakeland-Winter Haven MSA, FL	H	8.25 FQ	10.74 AW	13.96 TQ	FLBLS	10/01-12/01
	Miami PMSA, FL	H	7.52 FQ	11.80 AW	15.55 TQ	FLBLS	10/01-12/01
	Orlando MSA, FL	H	8.49 FQ	11.20 AW	14.00 TQ	FLBLS	10/01-12/01
	Tampa-St. Petersburg-Clearwater MSA, FL	H	9.14 FQ	13.70 AW	17.45 TQ	FLBLS	10/01-12/01
	Georgia	H	7.90 FQ	12.23 AW	16.80 TQ	GABLS	10/01-12/01
	Atlanta MSA, GA	H	9.49 FQ	13.32 AW	17.00 TQ	GABLS	10/01-12/01
	Augusta-Aiken MSA, GA-SC	H	8.34 FQ	13.39 AW	18.22 TQ	GABLS	10/01-12/01
	Columbus MSA, GA-AL	H	8.82 FQ	12.11 AW	16.96 TQ	GABLS	10/01-12/01
	Macon MSA, GA	H	7.37 FQ	9.58 AW	13.34 TQ	GABLS	10/01-12/01
	Hawaii	H	6.74 FQ	12.24 AW	22.79 TQ	HIBLS	10/01-12/01
	Honolulu MSA, HI	H	6.48 FQ	12.17 AW	23.68 TQ	HIBLS	10/01-12/01
	Idaho	H	8.62 FQ	11.08 AW	13.66 TQ	IDBLS	10/01-12/01
	Boise City MSA, ID	H	9.17 FQ	11.35 AW	13.34 TQ	IDBLS	10/01-12/01
	Illinois	H	9.67 FQ	14.97 AW	22.38 TQ	ILBLS	10/01-12/01
	Chicago PMSA, IL	H	9.63 FQ	14.83 AW	23.28 TQ	ILBLS	10/01-12/01
	Rockford MSA, IL	H	11.90 FQ	19.89 AW	32.84 TQ	ILBLS	10/01-12/01
	Indiana	H	8.88 FQ	12.30 AW	17.49 TQ	INBLS	10/01-12/01
	Elkhart-Goshen MSA, IN	H	7.90 FQ	13.24 AW	19.89 TQ	INBLS	10/01-12/01
	Evansville-Henderson MSA, IN-KY	H	9.27 FQ	11.67 AW	14.21 TQ	INBLS	10/01-12/01
	Fort Wayne MSA, IN	H	9.14 FQ	13.15 AW	19.93 TQ	INBLS	10/01-12/01
	Gary PMSA, IN	H	7.98 FQ	15.72 AW	23.07 TQ	INBLS	10/01-12/01
	Lafayette MSA, IN	H	6.45 FQ	11.27 AW	13.68 TQ	INBLS	10/01-12/01
	Iowa	H	10.06 FQ	14.74 AW	21.93 TQ	IABLS	10/01-12/01
	Des Moines MSA, IA	H	9.68 FQ	12.82 AW	18.56 TQ	IABLS	10/01-12/01

AAW	Average annual wage	AOH	Average offered, high	ASH	Average starting, high	H	Hourly	M	Monthly	S	Special: hourly and annual
AE	Average entry wage	AOL	Average offered, low	ASL	Average starting, low	HI	Highest wage paid	MTC	Median total compensation	TQ	Third quartile wage
AEX	Average experienced wage	APH	Average pay, high range	AW	Average wage paid	HR	High end range	MW	Median wage paid	W	Weekly
AO	Average offered	APL	Average pay, low range	FQ	First quartile wage	LR	Low end range	SQ	Second quartile wage	Y	Yearly

Occupation/Type/Industry	Location	Per	Low	Mid	High	Source	Date
Extruding, Forming, Pressing, and Compacting Machine Setter, Operator, and Tender	Kansas	H	9.14 FQ	13.23 AW	19.61 TQ	KSBLS	10/01-12/01
	Kentucky	H	8.77 FQ	12.76 AW	18.56 TQ	KYBLS	10/01-12/01
	Lexington MSA, KY	H	9.77 FQ	14.68 AW	22.22 TQ	KYBLS	10/01-12/01
	Louisville MSA, KY-IN	H	9.79 FQ	16.01 AW	26.76 TQ	KYBLS	10/01-12/01
	Louisiana	H	8.08 FQ	12.90 AW	20.34 TQ	LABLS	10/01-12/01
	Lafayette MSA, LA	H	6.31 FQ	11.84 AW	19.82 TQ	LABLS	10/01-12/01
	New Orleans MSA, LA	H	7.54 FQ	11.31 AW	19.12 TQ	LABLS	10/01-12/01
	Maine	H	8.90 FQ	15.12 AW	22.51 TQ	MEBLS	10/01-12/01
	Maryland	H	8.86 FQ	13.60 AW	20.31 TQ	MDBLS	10/01-12/01
	Baltimore PMSA, MD	H	9.02 FQ	13.71 AW	20.56 TQ	MDBLS	10/01-12/01
	Massachusetts	H	8.65 FQ	13.21 AW	19.39 TQ	MABLS	10/01-12/01
	Boston PMSA, MA-NH	H	8.47 FQ	13.47 AW	19.63 TQ	MABLS	10/01-12/01
	Brockton PMSA, MA	H	9.33 FQ	12.91 AW	17.56 TQ	MABLS	10/01-12/01
	Lawrence PMSA, MA-NH	H	8.12 FQ	11.78 AW	17.30 TQ	MABLS	10/01-12/01
	New Bedford PMSA, MA	H	8.92 FQ	14.12 AW	20.58 TQ	MABLS	10/01-12/01
	Springfield MSA, MA	H	11.13 FQ	13.89 AW	16.80 TQ	MABLS	10/01-12/01
	Worcester PMSA, MA-CT	H	9.66 FQ	13.79 AW	18.68 TQ	MABLS	10/01-12/01
	Michigan	H	8.34 FQ	13.01 AW	20.52 TQ	MIBLS	10/01-12/01
	Ann Arbor PMSA, MI	H	11.00 FQ	13.76 AW	19.90 TQ	MIBLS	10/01-12/01
	Detroit PMSA, MI	H	7.92 FQ	11.27 AW	16.31 TQ	MIBLS	10/01-12/01
	Grand Rapids-Muskegon-Holland MSA, MI	H	8.21 FQ	12.84 AW	17.60 TQ	MIBLS	10/01-12/01
	Kalamazoo-Battle Creek MSA, MI	H	10.26 FQ	13.66 AW	17.28 TQ	MIBLS	10/01-12/01
	Saginaw-Bay City-Midland MSA, MI	H	7.48 FQ	12.14 AW	16.62 TQ	MIBLS	10/01-12/01
	Minnesota	H	8.83 FQ	14.25 AW	20.04 TQ	MNBLS	10/01-12/01
	Minneapolis-St. Paul MSA, MN-WI	H	9.90 FQ	15.05 AW	20.29 TQ	MNBLS	10/01-12/01
	Mississippi	H	8.48 FQ	11.45 AW	15.41 TQ	MSBLS	10/01-12/01
	Jackson MSA, MS	H	7.42 FQ	9.51 AW	12.28 TQ	MSBLS	10/01-12/01
	Missouri	H	8.04 FQ	12.84 AW	17.56 TQ	MOBLS	10/01-12/01
	Kansas City MSA, MO-KS	H	8.57 FQ	14.27 AW	20.05 TQ	MOBLS	10/01-12/01
	St. Louis MSA, MO-IL	H	9.38 FQ	13.66 AW	17.97 TQ	MOBLS	10/01-12/01
	Montana	H	7.03 FQ	11.74 AW	20.60 TQ	MTBLS	10/01-12/01
	Billings MSA, MT	H	6.54 FQ	8.29 AW	10.77 TQ	MTBLS	10/01-12/01
	Nebraska	H	9.49 FQ	13.57 AW	17.17 TQ	NEBLS	10/01-12/01
	Lincoln MSA, NE	H	9.76 FQ	14.83 AW	20.70 TQ	NEBLS	10/01-12/01
	Omaha MSA, NE-IA	H	8.23 FQ	10.99 AW	15.46 TQ	NEBLS	10/01-12/01
	Nevada	H	9.65 FQ	13.68 AW	17.93 TQ	NVBLS	10/01-12/01
	Las Vegas MSA, NV-AZ	H	9.52 FQ	13.84 AW	18.56 TQ	NVBLS	10/01-12/01
	Reno MSA, NV	H	9.40 FQ	12.61 AW	18.64 TQ	NVBLS	10/01-12/01
	New Hampshire	H	9.00 FQ	12.16 AW	16.50 TQ	NHBLS	10/01-12/01
	Nashua PMSA, NH	H	9.38 FQ	12.50 AW	16.30 TQ	NHBLS	10/01-12/01
	Portsmouth-Rochester PMSA, NH-ME	H	10.26 FQ	14.83 AW	20.09 TQ	NHBLS	10/01-12/01
	New Jersey	H	8.17 FQ	13.48 AW	20.28 TQ	NJBLS	10/01-12/01
	Bergen-Passaic PMSA, NJ	H	6.98 FQ	11.22 AW	15.99 TQ	NJBLS	10/01-12/01
	Jersey City PMSA, NJ	H	7.66 FQ	11.33 AW	16.09 TQ	NJBLS	10/01-12/01
	Middlesex-Somerset-Hunterdon PMSA, NJ	H	8.04 FQ	13.08 AW	18.08 TQ	NJBLS	10/01-12/01
	Monmouth-Ocean PMSA, NJ	H	8.41 FQ	13.26 AW	20.07 TQ	NJBLS	10/01-12/01
	Newark PMSA, NJ	H	7.87 FQ	12.29 AW	17.27 TQ	NJBLS	10/01-12/01
	Trenton PMSA, NJ	H	8.12 FQ	12.49 AW	17.53 TQ	NJBLS	10/01-12/01
	New York	H	6.52 FQ	11.84 AW	18.11 TQ	NYBLS	10/01-12/01
	Albany-Schenectady-Troy MSA, NY	H	7.58 FQ	12.20 AW	16.93 TQ	NYBLS	10/01-12/01
	Buffalo-Niagara Falls MSA, NY	H	10.65 FQ	14.68 AW	20.82 TQ	NYBLS	10/01-12/01
	Nassau-Suffolk PMSA, NY	H	7.02 FQ	10.35 AW	16.58 TQ	NYBLS	10/01-12/01
	New York PMSA, NY	H	5.66 FQ	9.44 AW	13.30 TQ	NYBLS	10/01-12/01
	Rochester MSA, NY	H	7.86 FQ	13.31 AW	20.01 TQ	NYBLS	10/01-12/01
	Syracuse MSA, NY	H	9.59 FQ	13.64 AW	17.89 TQ	NYBLS	10/01-12/01
	North Carolina	H	9.28 FQ	15.05 AW	24.39 TQ	NCBLS	10/01-12/01
	Greensboro-Winston-Salem-High Point MSA, NC	H	11.26 FQ	20.03 AW	26.97 TQ	NCBLS	10/01-12/01
	Hickory-Morganton-Lenoir MSA, NC	H	8.24 FQ	13.25 AW	16.90 TQ	NCBLS	10/01-12/01
	Raleigh-Durham-Chapel Hill MSA, NC	H	9.76 FQ	12.78 AW	16.50 TQ	NCBLS	10/01-12/01

AAW	Average annual wage	**AOH**	Average offered, high	**ASH**	Average starting, high	**H**	Hourly	**M**	Monthly	**S**	Special: hourly and annual
AE	Average entry wage	**AOL**	Average offered, low	**ASL**	Average starting, low	**HI**	Highest wage paid	**MTC**	Median total compensation	**TQ**	Third quartile wage
AEX	Average experienced wage	**APH**	Average pay, high range	**AW**	Average wage paid	**HR**	High end range	**MW**	Median wage paid	**W**	Weekly
AO	Average offered	**APL**	Average pay, low range	**FQ**	First quartile wage	**LR**	Low end range	**SQ**	Second quartile wage	**Y**	Yearly

Occupation/Type/Industry	Location	Per	Low	Mid	High	Source	Date
Extruding, Forming, Pressing, and Compacting Machine Setter, Operator, and Tender	North Dakota	H	9.17 FQ	13.22 AW	18.47 TQ	NDBLS	10/01-12/01
	Ohio	H	9.12 FQ	14.13 AW	22.06 TQ	OHBLS	10/01-12/01
	Akron PMSA, OH	H	9.73 FQ	14.97 AW	21.17 TQ	OHBLS	10/01-12/01
	Canton-Massillon MSA, OH	H	9.46 FQ	11.82 AW	13.88 TQ	OHBLS	10/01-12/01
	Cincinnati PMSA, OH-KY-IN	H	8.57 FQ	12.72 AW	18.41 TQ	OHBLS	10/01-12/01
	Cleveland-Lorain-Elyria PMSA, OH	H	7.86 FQ	13.37 AW	21.10 TQ	OHBLS	10/01-12/01
	Columbus MSA, OH	H	11.54 FQ	14.45 AW	17.36 TQ	OHBLS	10/01-12/01
	Hamilton-Middletown PMSA, OH	H	8.17 FQ	13.99 AW	20.62 TQ	OHBLS	10/01-12/01
	Mansfield MSA, OH	H	11.46 FQ	18.59 AW	26.78 TQ	OHBLS	10/01-12/01
	Toledo MSA, OH	H	9.74 FQ	12.02 AW	15.24 TQ	OHBLS	10/01-12/01
	Youngstown-Warren MSA, OH	H	7.16 FQ	13.12 AW	17.09 TQ	OHBLS	10/01-12/01
	Oklahoma	H	7.48 FQ	11.51 AW	18.69 TQ	OKBLS	10/01-12/01
	Oklahoma City MSA, OK	H	7.64 FQ	10.72 AW	13.88 TQ	OKBLS	10/01-12/01
	Tulsa MSA, OK	H	7.85 FQ	11.75 AW	16.85 TQ	OKBLS	10/01-12/01
	Oregon	H	8.41 FQ	13.39 AW	17.75 TQ	ORBLS	10/01-12/01
	Eugene-Springfield MSA, OR	H	10.11 FQ	14.15 AW	17.11 TQ	ORBLS	10/01-12/01
	Medford-Ashland MSA, OR	H	9.40 FQ	14.96 AW	20.28 TQ	ORBLS	10/01-12/01
	Portland-Vancouver PMSA, OR-WA	H	8.09 FQ	13.36 AW	19.81 TQ	ORBLS	10/01-12/01
	Salem PMSA, OR	H	7.22 FQ	10.57 AW	16.51 TQ	ORBLS	10/01-12/01
	Pennsylvania	H	8.22 FQ	13.72 AW	20.33 TQ	PABLS	10/01-12/01
	Allentown-Bethlehem-Easton MSA, PA	H	9.73 FQ	13.66 AW	16.65 TQ	PABLS	10/01-12/01
	Erie MSA, PA	H	5.84 FQ	8.07 AW	11.91 TQ	PABLS	10/01-12/01
	Harrisburg-Lebanon-Carlisle MSA, PA	H	6.12 FQ	11.50 AW	17.23 TQ	PABLS	10/01-12/01
	Lancaster MSA, PA	H	8.57 FQ	13.79 AW	23.73 TQ	PABLS	10/01-12/01
	Philadelphia PMSA, PA-NJ	H	8.66 FQ	14.19 AW	20.61 TQ	PABLS	10/01-12/01
	Pittsburgh MSA, PA	H	8.63 FQ	12.77 AW	16.65 TQ	PABLS	10/01-12/01
	Reading MSA, PA	H	10.11 FQ	14.56 AW	17.73 TQ	PABLS	10/01-12/01
	Scranton-Wilkes-Barre-Hazleton MSA, PA	H	8.26 FQ	13.69 AW	20.53 TQ	PABLS	10/01-12/01
	York MSA, PA	H	10.06 FQ	15.68 AW	21.54 TQ	PABLS	10/01-12/01
	Rhode Island	H	8.34 FQ	13.26 AW	20.00 TQ	RIBLS	10/01-12/01
	Providence-Fall River-Warwick MSA, RI-MA	H	7.88 FQ	12.29 AW	19.43 TQ	RIBLS	10/01-12/01
	South Carolina	H	9.21 FQ	13.99 AW	20.73 TQ	SCBLS	10/01-12/01
	Charleston-North Charleston MSA, SC	H	8.44 FQ	13.47 AW	28.41 TQ	SCBLS	10/01-12/01
	Columbia MSA, SC	H	9.21 FQ	12.91 AW	19.04 TQ	SCBLS	10/01-12/01
	Greenville-Spartanburg-Anderson MSA, SC	H	13.48 FQ	17.91 AW	21.65 TQ	SCBLS	10/01-12/01
	South Dakota	H	9.63 FQ	12.65 AW	16.00 TQ	SDBLS	10/01-12/01
	Sioux Falls MSA, SD	H	10.37 FQ	12.58 AW	15.63 TQ	SDBLS	10/01-12/01
	Tennessee	H	8.76 FQ	12.09 AW	16.05 TQ	TNBLS	10/01-12/01
	Chattanooga MSA, TN-GA	H	8.76 FQ	10.66 AW	13.00 TQ	TNBLS	10/01-12/01
	Clarksville-Hopkinsville MSA, TN-KY	H	7.62 FQ	10.43 AW	14.92 TQ	TNBLS	10/01-12/01
	Johnson City-Kingsport-Bristol MSA, TN-VA	H	7.53 FQ	10.96 AW	13.93 TQ	TNBLS	10/01-12/01
	Knoxville MSA, TN	H	10.88 FQ	13.87 AW	16.78 TQ	TNBLS	10/01-12/01
	Memphis MSA, TN-AR-MS	H	7.65 FQ	13.20 AW	17.32 TQ	TNBLS	10/01-12/01
	Nashville MSA, TN	H	7.88 FQ	11.87 AW	19.84 TQ	TNBLS	10/01-12/01
	Texas	H	7.22 FQ	11.42 AW	16.60 TQ	TXBLS	10/01-12/01
	Austin-San Marcos MSA, TX	H	7.09 FQ	10.98 AW	16.88 TQ	TXBLS	10/01-12/01
	Dallas PMSA, TX	H	7.18 FQ	10.24 AW	14.07 TQ	TXBLS	10/01-12/01
	Fort Worth-Arlington PMSA, TX	H	7.51 FQ	10.28 AW	14.42 TQ	TXBLS	10/01-12/01
	Houston PMSA, TX	H	6.88 FQ	10.40 AW	15.70 TQ	TXBLS	10/01-12/01
	McAllen-Edinburg-Mission MSA, TX	H	6.29 FQ	8.81 AW	13.04 TQ	TXBLS	10/01-12/01
	San Antonio MSA, TX	H	7.22 FQ	9.85 AW	13.76 TQ	TXBLS	10/01-12/01
	Waco MSA, TX	H	6.63 FQ	9.65 AW	14.66 TQ	TXBLS	10/01-12/01
	Utah	H	7.30 FQ	10.70 AW	14.27 TQ	UTBLS	10/01-12/01
	Provo-Orem MSA, UT	H	7.51 FQ	10.81 AW	15.70 TQ	UTBLS	10/01-12/01
	Salt Lake City-Ogden MSA, UT	H	7.80 FQ	11.43 AW	14.36 TQ	UTBLS	10/01-12/01
	Vermont	H	8.75 FQ	12.52 AW	16.36 TQ	VTBLS	10/01-12/01

AAW	Average annual wage	**AOH**	Average offered, high	**ASH**	Average starting, high	**H**	Hourly	**M**	Monthly	**S**	Special: hourly and annual
AE	Average entry wage	**AOL**	Average offered, low	**ASL**	Average starting, low	**HI**	Highest wage paid	**MTC**	Median total compensation	**TQ**	Third quartile wage
AEX	Average experienced wage	**APH**	Average pay, high range	**AW**	Average wage paid	**HR**	High end range	**MW**	Median wage paid	**W**	Weekly
AO	Average offered	**APL**	Average pay, low range	**FQ**	First quartile wage	**LR**	Low end range	**SQ**	Second quartile wage	**Y**	Yearly

Occupation/Type/Industry	Location	Per	Low	Mid	High	Source	Date
Extruding, Forming, Pressing, and Compacting Machine Setter, Operator, and Tender	Burlington MSA, VT	H	7.59 FQ	10.56 AW	13.58 TQ	VTBLS	10/01-12/01
	Virginia	H	8.02 FQ	12.53 AW	17.37 TQ	VABLS	10/01-12/01
	Norfolk-Virginia Beach-Newport News MSA, VA-NC	H	7.33 FQ	14.10 AW	21.13 TQ	VABLS	10/01-12/01
	Richmond-Petersburg MSA, VA	H	9.53 FQ	14.69 AW	20.17 TQ	VABLS	10/01-12/01
	Washington	H	8.85 FQ	13.54 AW	20.98 TQ	WABLS	10/01-12/01
	Seattle-Bellevue-Everett PMSA, WA	H	8.97 FQ	12.74 AW	19.36 TQ	WABLS	10/01-12/01
	Spokane MSA, WA	H	8.60 FQ	12.87 AW	16.54 TQ	WABLS	10/01-12/01
	West Virginia	H	6.60 FQ	13.20 AW	18.71 TQ	WVBLS	10/01-12/01
	Charleston MSA, WV	H	8.47 FQ	10.35 AW	12.99 TQ	WVBLS	10/01-12/01
	Huntington-Ashland MSA, WV-KY-OH	H	5.82 FQ	8.99 AW	13.42 TQ	WVBLS	10/01-12/01
	Wisconsin	H	9.42 FQ	14.95 AW	20.82 TQ	WIBLS	10/01-12/01
	Green Bay MSA, WI	H	9.74 FQ	12.94 AW	17.24 TQ	WIBLS	10/01-12/01
	Madison MSA, WI	H	9.41 FQ	13.08 AW	19.52 TQ	WIBLS	10/01-12/01
	Milwaukee-Waukesha PMSA, WI	H	6.62 FQ	12.87 AW	19.88 TQ	WIBLS	10/01-12/01
	Puerto Rico	H	5.73 FQ	9.23 AW	13.76 TQ	PRBLS	10/01-12/01
Fabric and Apparel Patternmaker	Alabama	H	7.45 FQ	9.70 AW	13.08 TQ	ALBLS	10/01-12/01
	California	H	7.21 FQ	17.74 AW	27.79 TQ	CABLS	10/01-12/01
	Colorado	H	9.15 FQ	14.69 AW	22.19 TQ	COBLS	10/01-12/01
	Connecticut	H	7.71 FQ	14.96 AW	27.44 TQ	CTBLS	10/01-12/01
	Florida	H	6.32 FQ	11.90 AW	18.20 TQ	FLBLS	10/01-12/01
	Georgia	H	7.48 FQ	11.25 AW	18.46 TQ	GABLS	10/01-12/01
	Hawaii	H	7.27 FQ	11.53 AW	16.85 TQ	HIBLS	10/01-12/01
	Illinois	H	7.95 FQ	12.43 AW	18.92 TQ	ILBLS	10/01-12/01
	Indiana	H	7.51 FQ	10.55 AW	14.67 TQ	INBLS	10/01-12/01
	Iowa	H	7.75 FQ	11.54 AW	16.11 TQ	IABLS	10/01-12/01
	Kansas	H	7.49 FQ	11.81 AW	18.87 TQ	KSBLS	10/01-12/01
	Kentucky	H	7.48 FQ	12.04 AW	15.02 TQ	KYBLS	10/01-12/01
	Maine	H	7.38 FQ	12.33 AW	20.14 TQ	MEBLS	10/01-12/01
	Maryland	H	8.52 FQ	13.26 AW	21.36 TQ	MDBLS	10/01-12/01
	Massachusetts	H	7.00 FQ	12.64 AW	20.33 TQ	MABLS	10/01-12/01
	Michigan	H	10.04 FQ	18.76 AW	27.33 TQ	MIBLS	10/01-12/01
	Minnesota	H	7.72 FQ	10.93 AW	15.45 TQ	MNBLS	10/01-12/01
	Mississippi	H	7.51 FQ	10.76 AW	13.87 TQ	MSBLS	10/01-12/01
	Missouri	H	7.48 FQ	12.35 AW	18.55 TQ	MOBLS	10/01-12/01
	New Jersey	H	8.84 FQ	18.30 AW	34.68 TQ	NJBLS	10/01-12/01
	New York	H	6.77 FQ	19.34 AW	41.05 TQ	NYBLS	10/01-12/01
	North Carolina	H	7.88 FQ	12.97 AW	19.48 TQ	NCBLS	10/01-12/01
	Ohio	H	7.59 FQ	9.73 AW	12.55 TQ	OHBLS	10/01-12/01
	Oklahoma	H	5.94 FQ	9.11 AW	14.12 TQ	OKBLS	10/01-12/01
	Oregon	H	9.25 FQ	17.48 AW	26.46 TQ	ORBLS	10/01-12/01
	Pennsylvania	H	7.99 FQ	16.23 AW	31.52 TQ	PABLS	10/01-12/01
	South Carolina	H	8.27 FQ	11.60 AW	16.01 TQ	SCBLS	10/01-12/01
	Tennessee	H	7.27 FQ	10.42 AW	15.25 TQ	TNBLS	10/01-12/01
	Texas	H	7.01 FQ	11.46 AW	18.58 TQ	TXBLS	10/01-12/01
	Vermont	H	7.28 FQ	10.95 AW	16.19 TQ	VTBLS	10/01-12/01
	Virginia	H	7.40 FQ	12.44 AW	17.78 TQ	VABLS	10/01-12/01
	Washington	H	7.06 FQ	12.11 AW	19.13 TQ	WABLS	10/01-12/01
	Wisconsin	H	9.37 FQ	11.74 AW	14.17 TQ	WIBLS	10/01-12/01
	Puerto Rico	H	5.69 FQ	9.72 AW	14.77 TQ	PRBLS	10/01-12/01
Fabric Mender							
Except Garment	California	H	7.03 FQ	12.86 AW	20.80 TQ	CABLS	10/01-12/01
Except Garment	Los Angeles-Long Beach PMSA, CA	H	6.71 FQ	8.27 AW	9.40 TQ	CABLS	10/01-12/01
Except Garment	Colorado	H	6.60 FQ	12.58 AW	16.87 TQ	COBLS	10/01-12/01
Except Garment	Florida	H	8.97 FQ	16.60 AW	21.46 TQ	FLBLS	10/01-12/01
Except Garment	Georgia	H	7.41 FQ	9.92 AW	14.75 TQ	GABLS	10/01-12/01
Except Garment	Atlanta MSA, GA	H	6.05 FQ	9.16 AW	13.47 TQ	GABLS	10/01-12/01
Except Garment	Illinois	H	7.52 FQ	15.89 AW	21.98 TQ	ILBLS	10/01-12/01
Except Garment	Louisiana	H	6.14 FQ	11.93 AW	21.09 TQ	LABLS	10/01-12/01
Except Garment	Maine	H	10.67 FQ	16.60 AW	21.07 TQ	MEBLS	10/01-12/01
Except Garment	Mississippi	H	5.87 FQ	10.25 AW	18.74 TQ	MSBLS	10/01-12/01
Except Garment	New Hampshire	H	9.18 FQ	10.86 AW	11.59 TQ	NHBLS	10/01-12/01

AAW Average annual wage; AE Average entry wage; AEX Average experienced wage; AO Average offered; AOH Average offered, high; AOL Average offered, low; APH Average pay, high range; APL Average pay, low range; ASH Average starting, high; ASL Average starting, low; AW Average wage paid; FQ First quartile wage; H Hourly; HI Highest wage paid; HR High end range; LR Low end range; M Monthly; MTC Median total compensation; MW Median wage paid; SQ Second quartile wage; S Special: hourly and annual; TQ Third quartile wage; W Weekly; Y Yearly

Occupation/Type/Industry	Location	Per	Low	Mid	High	Source	Date
Fabric Mender							
Except Garment	New York	H	6.68 FQ	12.21 AW	19.87 TQ	NYBLS	10/01-12/01
Except Garment	New York PMSA, NY	H	6.06 FQ	8.62 AW	11.34 TQ	NYBLS	10/01-12/01
Except Garment	North Carolina	H	6.08 FQ	10.13 AW	14.56 TQ	NCBLS	10/01-12/01
Except Garment	Ohio	H	8.89 FQ	16.83 AW	22.14 TQ	OHBLS	10/01-12/01
Except Garment	Cleveland-Lorain-Elyria PMSA, OH	H	18.52 FQ	20.06 AW	22.68 TQ	OHBLS	10/01-12/01
Except Garment	Oklahoma	H	8.44 FQ	14.55 AW	20.37 TQ	OKBLS	10/01-12/01
Except Garment	Pennsylvania	H	6.76 FQ	11.77 AW	19.21 TQ	PABLS	10/01-12/01
Except Garment	South Carolina	H	6.79 FQ	12.22 AW	17.91 TQ	SCBLS	10/01-12/01
Except Garment	Texas	H	7.32 FQ	11.12 AW	19.28 TQ	TXBLS	10/01-12/01
Except Garment	Houston PMSA, TX	H	7.22 FQ	8.56 AW	8.83 TQ	TXBLS	10/01-12/01
Except Garment	Virginia	H	9.40 FQ	14.84 AW	20.43 TQ	VABLS	10/01-12/01
Except Garment	Washington	H	9.63 FQ	20.61 AW	26.26 TQ	WABLS	10/01-12/01
Faculty Member							
Community College	United States	Y		43637 AW		MSW	1/99-1/00
Community College	North Carolina	Y		36205 AW		MSW	1/99-1/00
Faller	Alabama	H	8.07 FQ	13.25 AW	19.19 TQ	ALBLS	10/01-12/01
	Alaska	H	14.62 FQ	29.29 AW	42.75 TQ	AKBLS	10/01-12/01
	Arizona	H	5.93 FQ	7.57 AW	10.34 TQ	AZBLS	10/01-12/01
	Arkansas	H	6.03 FQ	8.99 AW	12.55 TQ	ARBLS	10/01-12/01
	California	H	12.34 FQ	30.21 AW	43.15 TQ	CABLS	10/01-12/01
	Florida	H	6.73 FQ	12.79 AW	22.80 TQ	FLBLS	10/01-12/01
	Georgia	H	7.45 FQ	10.09 AW	14.06 TQ	GABLS	10/01-12/01
	Idaho	H	6.27 FQ	18.97 AW	32.17 TQ	IDBLS	10/01-12/01
	Indiana	H	8.16 FQ	13.22 AW	17.31 TQ	INBLS	10/01-12/01
	Kentucky	H	7.92 FQ	10.68 AW	13.38 TQ	KYBLS	10/01-12/01
	Louisiana	H	6.39 FQ	12.29 AW	16.71 TQ	LABLS	10/01-12/01
	Maine	H	6.73 FQ	17.31 AW	38.67 TQ	MEBLS	10/01-12/01
	Maryland	H	6.41 FQ	12.45 AW	16.40 TQ	MDBLS	10/01-12/01
	Michigan	H	9.46 FQ	11.87 AW	16.35 TQ	MIBLS	10/01-12/01
	Minnesota	H	8.34 FQ	12.90 AW	19.09 TQ	MNBLS	10/01-12/01
	Mississippi	H	7.29 FQ	10.11 AW	13.90 TQ	MSBLS	10/01-12/01
	Missouri	H	7.08 FQ	10.16 AW	14.18 TQ	MOBLS	10/01-12/01
	Montana	H	8.70 FQ	22.06 AW	36.46 TQ	MTBLS	10/01-12/01
	New Hampshire	H	14.82 FQ	16.22 AW	18.03 TQ	NHBLS	10/01-12/01
	New Jersey	H	9.59 FQ	15.81 AW	22.69 TQ	NJBLS	10/01-12/01
	New York	H	6.32 FQ	14.01 AW	31.44 TQ	NYBLS	10/01-12/01
	North Carolina	H	8.82 FQ	11.39 AW	13.94 TQ	NCBLS	10/01-12/01
	Ohio	H	9.45 FQ	11.55 AW	13.87 TQ	OHBLS	10/01-12/01
	Oregon	H	15.86 FQ	22.47 AW	29.34 TQ	ORBLS	10/01-12/01
	Pennsylvania	H	5.78 FQ	9.90 AW	16.91 TQ	PABLS	10/01-12/01
	South Carolina	H	6.97 FQ	11.17 AW	14.66 TQ	SCBLS	10/01-12/01
	Tennessee	H	8.44 FQ	10.35 AW	13.39 TQ	TNBLS	10/01-12/01
	Texas	H	10.43 FQ	15.58 AW	21.03 TQ	TXBLS	10/01-12/01
	Vermont	H	6.39 FQ	8.33 AW	12.06 TQ	VTBLS	10/01-12/01
	Virginia	H	6.23 FQ	11.35 AW	16.16 TQ	VABLS	10/01-12/01
	Washington	H	16.85 FQ	23.87 AW	30.76 TQ	WABLS	10/01-12/01
	West Virginia	H	5.99 FQ	9.80 AW	15.49 TQ	WVBLS	10/01-12/01
	Wisconsin	H	7.46 FQ	12.99 AW	26.39 TQ	WIBLS	10/01-12/01
Family and General Practitioner	Alabama	Y	81170 FQ	114150 AW		ALBLS	10/01-12/01
	Birmingham MSA, AL	Y	94900 FQ	118900 AW		ALBLS	10/01-12/01
	Huntsville MSA, AL	Y	77070 FQ	92820 AW	136770 TQ	ALBLS	10/01-12/01
	Mobile MSA, AL	Y	91790 FQ	117300 AW	144460 TQ	ALBLS	10/01-12/01
	Montgomery MSA, AL	Y	91530 FQ	104540 AW		ALBLS	10/01-12/01
	Alaska	Y	68470 FQ	114550 AW		AKBLS	10/01-12/01
	Anchorage MSA, AK	Y	64070 FQ	115610 AW		AKBLS	10/01-12/01
	Arizona	Y	85210 FQ	122140 AW		AZBLS	10/01-12/01
	Phoenix-Mesa MSA, AZ	Y	44060 FQ	114980 AW		AZBLS	10/01-12/01
	Tucson MSA, AZ	Y	101740 FQ	132630 AW		AZBLS	10/01-12/01
	Arkansas	Y	85880 FQ	121620 AW		ARBLS	10/01-12/01
	Fayetteville-Springdale-Rogers MSA, AR	Y	90680 FQ	120640 AW		ARBLS	10/01-12/01
	Fort Smith MSA, AR-OK	Y	121080 FQ	140330 AW		ARBLS	10/01-12/01
	Little Rock-North Little Rock MSA, AR	Y	80120 FQ	101330 AW	137030 TQ	ARBLS	10/01-12/01
	California	Y	33540 FQ	85610 AW		CABLS	10/01-12/01
	Bakersfield MSA, CA	Y	33390 FQ	98220 AW		CABLS	10/01-12/01
	Fresno MSA, CA	Y	72060 FQ	109390 AW		CABLS	10/01-12/01

AAW	Average annual wage	AOH	Average offered, high	ASH	Average starting, high	H	Hourly	M	Monthly	S	Special: hourly and annual
AE	Average entry wage	AOL	Average offered, low	ASL	Average starting, low	HI	Highest wage paid	MTC	Median total compensation	TQ	Third quartile wage
AEX	Average experienced wage	APH	Average pay, high range	AW	Average wage paid	HR	High end range	MW	Median wage paid	W	Weekly
AO	Average offered	APL	Average pay, low range	FQ	First quartile wage	LR	Low end range	SQ	Second quartile wage	Y	Yearly

Occupation/Type/Industry	Location	Per	Low	Mid	High	Source	Date
Family and General Practitioner	Los Angeles-Long Beach PMSA, CA	Y	32040 FQ	67410 AW	121250 TQ	CABLS	10/01-12/01
	Merced MSA, CA	Y	91740 FQ	115470 AW		CABLS	10/01-12/01
	Oakland PMSA, CA	Y	66530 FQ	110440 AW		CABLS	10/01-12/01
	Orange County PMSA, CA	Y	66550 FQ	114800 AW	145340 TQ	CABLS	10/01-12/01
	Redding MSA, CA	Y	57400 FQ	112920 AW		CABLS	10/01-12/01
	Riverside-San Bernardino PMSA, CA	Y	41830 FQ	111530 AW		CABLS	10/01-12/01
	Sacramento PMSA, CA	Y	61830 FQ	95390 AW	123140 TQ	CABLS	10/01-12/01
	Salinas MSA, CA	Y	86960 FQ	117000 AW		CABLS	10/01-12/01
	San Diego MSA, CA	Y	72640 FQ	101550 AW	144400 TQ	CABLS	10/01-12/01
	San Francisco PMSA, CA	Y	92950 FQ	116370 AW		CABLS	10/01-12/01
	San Jose PMSA, CA	Y	37980 FQ	78850 AW	139570 TQ	CABLS	10/01-12/01
	Santa Cruz-Watsonville PMSA, CA	Y	94580 FQ	119980 AW		CABLS	10/01-12/01
	Santa Rosa PMSA, CA	Y	96250 FQ	119170 AW	142840 TQ	CABLS	10/01-12/01
	Stockton-Lodi MSA, CA	Y	43100 FQ	106340 AW		CABLS	10/01-12/01
	Vallejo-Fairfield-Napa PMSA, CA	Y	42470 FQ	102690 AW		CABLS	10/01-12/01
	Ventura PMSA, CA	Y	84000 FQ	127950 AW		CABLS	10/01-12/01
	Visalia-Tulare-Porterville MSA, CA	Y	106280 FQ	128620 AW		CABLS	10/01-12/01
	Colorado	Y	72350 FQ	106690 AW		COBLS	10/01-12/01
	Boulder-Longmont PMSA, CO	Y	101290 FQ	121770 AW		COBLS	10/01-12/01
	Colorado Springs MSA, CO	Y	91250 FQ	105850 AW	139270 TQ	COBLS	10/01-12/01
	Denver PMSA, CO	Y	53950 FQ	97520 AW	139250 TQ	COBLS	10/01-12/01
	Fort Collins-Loveland MSA, CO	Y	89820 FQ	127090 AW		COBLS	10/01-12/01
	Connecticut	Y	83100 FQ	117060 AW		CTBLS	10/01-12/01
	Bridgeport PMSA, CT	Y	71830 FQ	91170 AW	116530 TQ	CTBLS	10/01-12/01
	Hartford MSA, CT	Y	83950 FQ	116510 AW		CTBLS	10/01-12/01
	New Haven-Meriden PMSA, CT	Y	76550 FQ	102600 AW		CTBLS	10/01-12/01
	New London-Norwich MSA, CT-RI	Y	105250 FQ	133940 AW		CTBLS	10/01-12/01
	Stamford-Norwalk PMSA, CT	Y	96730 FQ	127480 AW		CTBLS	10/01-12/01
	Delaware	Y	59790 FQ	89780 AW		DEBLS	10/01-12/01
	Wilmington-Newark PMSA, DE-MD	Y	60370 FQ	87830 AW		DEBLS	10/01-12/01
	District of Columbia	Y	33510 FQ	74670 AW		DCBLS	10/01-12/01
	Washington PMSA, DC-MD-VA-WV	Y	38400 FQ	91650 AW		DCBLS	10/01-12/01
	Florida	Y	56590 FQ	118120 AW		FLBLS	10/01-12/01
	Fort Lauderdale PMSA, FL	Y	76810 FQ	131020 AW		FLBLS	10/01-12/01
	Fort Pierce-Port St. Lucie MSA, FL	Y	102540 FQ	133730 AW		FLBLS	10/01-12/01
	Gainesville MSA, FL	Y	91170 FQ	116600 AW		FLBLS	10/01-12/01
	Jacksonville MSA, FL	Y	40740 FQ	109530 AW		FLBLS	10/01-12/01
	Lakeland-Winter Haven MSA, FL	Y	94790 FQ	124170 AW		FLBLS	10/01-12/01
	Melbourne-Titusville-Palm Bay MSA, FL	Y	97910 FQ	133000 AW		FLBLS	10/01-12/01
	Miami PMSA, FL	Y	44450 FQ	115530 AW		FLBLS	10/01-12/01
	Naples MSA, FL	Y	98290 FQ	119830 AW		FLBLS	10/01-12/01
	Orlando MSA, FL	Y	92740 FQ	105180 AW		FLBLS	10/01-12/01
	Pensacola MSA, FL	Y	97370 FQ	133570 AW		FLBLS	10/01-12/01
	Sarasota-Bradenton MSA, FL	Y	110120 FQ	132230 AW		FLBLS	10/01-12/01
	Tampa-St. Petersburg-Clearwater MSA, FL	Y	92100 FQ	119590 AW		FLBLS	10/01-12/01
	West Palm Beach-Boca Raton MSA, FL	Y	92340 FQ	129730 AW		FLBLS	10/01-12/01
	Georgia	Y	77510 FQ	118730 AW		GABLS	10/01-12/01
	Atlanta MSA, GA	Y	77240 FQ	117130 AW		GABLS	10/01-12/01
	Augusta-Aiken MSA, GA-SC	Y	47350 FQ	96710 AW		GABLS	10/01-12/01
	Columbus MSA, GA-AL	Y	99840 FQ	131310 AW		GABLS	10/01-12/01
	Macon MSA, GA	Y	89100 FQ	125180 AW		GABLS	10/01-12/01
	Savannah MSA, GA	Y	29880 FQ	86090 AW		GABLS	10/01-12/01
	Hawaii	Y	43830 FQ	114640 AW		HIBLS	10/01-12/01
	Honolulu MSA, HI	Y	41440 FQ	115060 AW		HIBLS	10/01-12/01
	Idaho	Y	40280 FQ	103270 AW		IDBLS	10/01-12/01
	Boise City MSA, ID	Y	34600 FQ	97190 AW		IDBLS	10/01-12/01
	Illinois	Y	53060 FQ	116360 AW		ILBLS	10/01-12/01

AAW	Average annual wage	AOH	Average offered, high	ASH	Average starting, high	H	Hourly	M	Monthly	S	Special: hourly and annual
AE	Average entry wage	AOL	Average offered, low	ASL	Average starting, low	HI	Highest wage paid	MTC	Median total compensation	TQ	Third quartile wage
AEX	Average experienced wage	APH	Average pay, high range	AW	Average wage paid	HR	High end range	MW	Median wage paid	W	Weekly
AO	Average offered	APL	Average pay, low range	FQ	First quartile wage	LR	Low end range	SQ	Second quartile wage	Y	Yearly

Occupation/Type/Industry	Location	Per	Low	Mid	High	Source	Date
Family and General Practitioner	Peoria-Pekin MSA, IL	Y	117110 FQ	138460 AW		ILBLS	10/01-12/01
	Springfield MSA, IL	Y	50820 FQ	101690 AW		ILBLS	10/01-12/01
	Indiana	Y	84510 FQ	122640 AW		INBLS	10/01-12/01
	Evansville-Henderson MSA, IN-KY	Y	95340 FQ	122780 AW		INBLS	10/01-12/01
	Fort Wayne MSA, IN	Y	95720 FQ	124980 AW		INBLS	10/01-12/01
	Gary PMSA, IN	Y	83850 FQ	127040 AW		INBLS	10/01-12/01
	Indianapolis MSA, IN	Y	80970 FQ	120900 AW		INBLS	10/01-12/01
	South Bend MSA, IN	Y	72820 FQ	111460 AW		INBLS	10/01-12/01
	Iowa	Y	46050 FQ	117860 AW		IABLS	10/01-12/01
	Cedar Rapids MSA, IA	Y	113230 FQ	136230 AW		IABLS	10/01-12/01
	Davenport-Moline-Rock Island MSA, IA-IL	Y	41490 FQ	121820 AW		IABLS	10/01-12/01
	Des Moines MSA, IA	Y	40580 FQ	107040 AW		IABLS	10/01-12/01
	Kansas	Y	87040 FQ	121050 AW		KSBLS	10/01-12/01
	Topeka MSA, KS	Y	35950 FQ	108720 AW		KSBLS	10/01-12/01
	Wichita MSA, KS	Y	85170 FQ	122980 AW		KSBLS	10/01-12/01
	Kentucky	Y	88080 FQ	120160 AW		KYBLS	10/01-12/01
	Lexington MSA, KY	Y	82740 FQ	104290 AW		KYBLS	10/01-12/01
	Louisville MSA, KY-IN	Y	41080 FQ	103710 AW		KYBLS	10/01-12/01
	Louisiana	Y	38710 FQ	111920 AW		LABLS	10/01-12/01
	Baton Rouge MSA, LA	Y	36070 FQ	108100 AW		LABLS	10/01-12/01
	Houma MSA, LA	Y	124660 FQ	138170 AW		LABLS	10/01-12/01
	Lafayette MSA, LA	Y	117490 FQ	135000 AW		LABLS	10/01-12/01
	New Orleans MSA, LA	Y	34500 FQ	100430 AW		LABLS	10/01-12/01
	Shreveport-Bossier City MSA, LA	Y	93790 FQ	124750 AW		LABLS	10/01-12/01
	Maine	Y	69370 FQ	108830 AW		MEBLS	10/01-12/01
	Portland MSA, ME	Y	66800 FQ	104150 AW		MEBLS	10/01-12/01
	Maryland	Y	45280 FQ	100130 AW		MDBLS	10/01-12/01
	Baltimore PMSA, MD	Y	38660 FQ	93070 AW		MDBLS	10/01-12/01
	Massachusetts	Y	47050 FQ	112530 AW		MABLS	10/01-12/01
	Boston PMSA, MA-NH	Y	48020 FQ	106410 AW		MABLS	10/01-12/01
	Lawrence PMSA, MA-NH	Y	95090 FQ	122750 AW		MABLS	10/01-12/01
	Lowell PMSA, MA-NH	Y	103480 FQ	129580 AW		MABLS	10/01-12/01
	New Bedford PMSA, MA	Y	96820 FQ	123110 AW		MABLS	10/01-12/01
	Springfield MSA, MA	Y	108140 FQ	138040 AW		MABLS	10/01-12/01
	Worcester PMSA, MA-CT	Y	41180 FQ	92270 AW		MABLS	10/01-12/01
	Michigan	Y	76550 FQ	118490 AW		MIBLS	10/01-12/01
	Ann Arbor PMSA, MI	Y	91810 FQ	116190 AW		MIBLS	10/01-12/01
	Detroit PMSA, MI	Y	36950 FQ	105350 AW		MIBLS	10/01-12/01
	Grand Rapids-Muskegon-Holland MSA, MI	Y	107920 FQ	134730 AW		MIBLS	10/01-12/01
	Kalamazoo-Battle Creek MSA, MI	Y	98900 FQ	125120 AW		MIBLS	10/01-12/01
	Lansing-East Lansing MSA, MI	Y	120310 FQ	132640 AW		MIBLS	10/01-12/01
	Saginaw-Bay City-Midland MSA, MI	Y	60510 FQ	107110 AW		MIBLS	10/01-12/01
	Minnesota	Y	94930 FQ	126440 AW		MNBLS	10/01-12/01
	Duluth-Superior MSA, MN-WI	Y	97160 FQ	126730 AW		MNBLS	10/01-12/01
	Minneapolis-St. Paul MSA, MN-WI	Y	95020 FQ	126420 AW		MNBLS	10/01-12/01
	Mississippi	Y	49540 FQ	103540 AW		MSBLS	10/01-12/01
	Biloxi-Gulfport-Pascagoula MSA, MS	Y	79440 FQ	106880 AW		MSBLS	10/01-12/01
	Jackson MSA, MS	Y	38130 FQ	84960 AW	145600 TQ	MSBLS	10/01-12/01
	Missouri	Y	57360 FQ	101260 AW		MOBLS	10/01-12/01
	Kansas City MSA, MO-KS	Y	55430 FQ	111540 AW		MOBLS	10/01-12/01
	Springfield MSA, MO	Y	91860 FQ	122140 AW		MOBLS	10/01-12/01
	Montana	Y	91410 FQ	120310 AW		MTBLS	10/01-12/01
	Billings MSA, MT	Y	121930 FQ	136730 AW		MTBLS	10/01-12/01
	Nebraska	Y	79190 FQ	123850 AW		NEBLS	10/01-12/01
	Lincoln MSA, NE	Y	103890 FQ	133370 AW		NEBLS	10/01-12/01
	Omaha MSA, NE-IA	Y	66410 FQ	115370 AW		NEBLS	10/01-12/01
	Nevada	Y	99580 FQ	130250 AW		NVBLS	10/01-12/01
	Las Vegas MSA, NV-AZ	Y	98930 FQ	132300 AW		NVBLS	10/01-12/01
	Reno MSA, NV	Y	94780 FQ	114120 AW		NVBLS	10/01-12/01
	New Hampshire	Y	76980 FQ	118400 AW		NHBLS	10/01-12/01
	Manchester PMSA, NH	Y	47840 FQ	107900 AW		NHBLS	10/01-12/01
	New Jersey	Y	46810 FQ	108590 AW		NJBLS	10/01-12/01
	Atlantic-Cape May PMSA, NJ	Y	92510 FQ	123760 AW		NJBLS	10/01-12/01
	Bergen-Passaic PMSA, NJ	Y	44350 FQ	116380 AW		NJBLS	10/01-12/01

Occupation/Type/Industry	Location	Per	Low	Mid	High	Source	Date
Family and General Practitioner	Jersey City PMSA, NJ	Y	36670 FQ	66070 AW		NJBLS	10/01-12/01
	Middlesex-Somerset-Hunterdon PMSA, NJ	Y	43640 FQ	101700 AW		NJBLS	10/01-12/01
	Monmouth-Ocean PMSA, NJ	Y	67580 FQ	116970 AW		NJBLS	10/01-12/01
	Newark PMSA, NJ	Y	85840 FQ	107830 AW		NJBLS	10/01-12/01
	Trenton PMSA, NJ	Y	73620 FQ	125320 AW		NJBLS	10/01-12/01
	New Mexico	Y	77270 FQ	112790 AW		NMBLS	10/01-12/01
	Albuquerque MSA, NM	Y	80510 FQ	113280 AW		NMBLS	10/01-12/01
	Las Cruces MSA, NM	Y	37320 FQ	84440 AW		NMBLS	10/01-12/01
	New York	Y	41100 FQ	97710 AW		NYBLS	10/01-12/01
	Albany-Schenectady-Troy MSA, NY	Y	92870 FQ	120510 AW		NYBLS	10/01-12/01
	Buffalo-Niagara Falls MSA, NY	Y	38010 FQ	91640 AW		NYBLS	10/01-12/01
	Dutchess County PMSA, NY	Y	95530 FQ	117640 AW		NYBLS	10/01-12/01
	Nassau-Suffolk PMSA, NY	Y	64550 FQ	113540 AW		NYBLS	10/01-12/01
	New York PMSA, NY	Y	38710 FQ	81470 AW	139880 TQ	NYBLS	10/01-12/01
	Newburgh PMSA, NY-PA	Y	96140 FQ	126520 AW		NYBLS	10/01-12/01
	Rochester MSA, NY	Y	92400 FQ	107480 AW	143670 TQ	NYBLS	10/01-12/01
	Syracuse MSA, NY	Y	39630 FQ	91080 AW	136730 TQ	NYBLS	10/01-12/01
	North Carolina	Y	73320 FQ	119120 AW		NCBLS	10/01-12/01
	Charlotte-Gastonia-Rock Hill MSA, NC-SC	Y	97490 FQ	125580 AW		NCBLS	10/01-12/01
	Fayetteville MSA, NC	Y	95230 FQ	119570 AW		NCBLS	10/01-12/01
	Greensboro-Winston-Salem-High Point MSA, NC	Y	73290 FQ	115320 AW		NCBLS	10/01-12/01
	Hickory-Morganton-Lenoir MSA, NC	Y	103610 FQ	129310 AW		NCBLS	10/01-12/01
	Raleigh-Durham-Chapel Hill MSA, NC	Y	75930 FQ	113870 AW		NCBLS	10/01-12/01
	Wilmington MSA, NC	Y	84320 FQ	123270 AW		NCBLS	10/01-12/01
	North Dakota	Y	83490 FQ	123220 AW		NDBLS	10/01-12/01
	Fargo-Moorhead MSA, ND-MN	Y	88130 FQ	125270 AW		NDBLS	10/01-12/01
	Ohio	Y	75050 FQ	117890 AW		OHBLS	10/01-12/01
	Akron PMSA, OH	Y	100880 FQ	127380 AW		OHBLS	10/01-12/01
	Canton-Massillon MSA, OH	Y	72240 FQ	115870 AW		OHBLS	10/01-12/01
	Cincinnati PMSA, OH-KY-IN	Y	81180 FQ	119000 AW		OHBLS	10/01-12/01
	Cleveland-Lorain-Elyria PMSA, OH	Y	41420 FQ	102490 AW		OHBLS	10/01-12/01
	Columbus MSA, OH	Y	99400 FQ	124910 AW		OHBLS	10/01-12/01
	Dayton-Springfield MSA, OH	Y	100570 FQ	130370 AW		OHBLS	10/01-12/01
	Hamilton-Middletown PMSA, OH	Y	115980 FQ	128000 AW		OHBLS	10/01-12/01
	Toledo MSA, OH	Y	76520 FQ	105290 AW		OHBLS	10/01-12/01
	Youngstown-Warren MSA, OH	Y	97930 FQ	126080 AW		OHBLS	10/01-12/01
	Oklahoma	Y	80850 FQ	122240 AW		OKBLS	10/01-12/01
	Oklahoma City MSA, OK	Y	91020 FQ	129640 AW		OKBLS	10/01-12/01
	Tulsa MSA, OK	Y	75460 FQ	109060 AW		OKBLS	10/01-12/01
	Oregon	Y	90200 FQ	109650 AW		ORBLS	10/01-12/01
	Eugene-Springfield MSA, OR	Y	95650 FQ	112040 AW	143520 TQ	ORBLS	10/01-12/01
	Medford-Ashland MSA, OR	Y	91130 FQ	108020 AW		ORBLS	10/01-12/01
	Portland-Vancouver PMSA, OR-WA	Y	88950 FQ	105910 AW	138970 TQ	ORBLS	10/01-12/01
	Salem PMSA, OR	Y	83870 FQ	119030 AW		ORBLS	10/01-12/01
	Pennsylvania	Y	42480 FQ	111020 AW		PABLS	10/01-12/01
	Allentown-Bethlehem-Easton MSA, PA	Y	81340 FQ	124350 AW		PABLS	10/01-12/01
	Erie MSA, PA	Y	114140 FQ	135680 AW		PABLS	10/01-12/01
	Harrisburg-Lebanon-Carlisle MSA, PA	Y	84270 FQ	109170 AW		PABLS	10/01-12/01
	Lancaster MSA, PA	Y	93840 FQ	124700 AW		PABLS	10/01-12/01
	Philadelphia PMSA, PA-NJ	Y	65160 FQ	116340 AW		PABLS	10/01-12/01
	Pittsburgh MSA, PA	Y	40030 FQ	95370 AW		PABLS	10/01-12/01
	York MSA, PA	Y	28300 FQ	92210 AW		PABLS	10/01-12/01
	Rhode Island	Y	83010 FQ	123510 AW		RIBLS	10/01-12/01
	Providence-Fall River-Warwick MSA, RI-MA	Y	82400 FQ	122120 AW		RIBLS	10/01-12/01
	South Carolina	Y	41900 FQ	109770 AW		SCBLS	10/01-12/01
	Charleston-North Charleston MSA, SC	Y	90200 FQ	110390 AW		SCBLS	10/01-12/01
	Columbia MSA, SC	Y	92980 FQ	108620 AW		SCBLS	10/01-12/01

AAW Average annual wage; AE Average entry wage; AEX Average experienced wage; AO Average offered; AOH Average offered, high; AOL Average offered, low; APH Average pay, high range; APL Average pay, low range; ASH Average starting, high; ASL Average starting, low; AW Average wage paid; FQ First quartile wage; H Hourly; HI Highest wage paid; HR High end range; LR Low end range; M Monthly; MTC Median total compensation; MW Median wage paid; SQ Second quartile wage; S Special: hourly and annual; TQ Third quartile wage; W Weekly; Y Yearly

Occupation/Type/Industry	Location	Per	Low	Mid	High	Source	Date
Family and General Practitioner	Myrtle Beach MSA, SC	Y	56450 FQ	128210 AW		SCBLS	10/01-12/01
	South Dakota	Y	40290 FQ	94400 AW		SDBLS	10/01-12/01
	Sioux Falls MSA, SD	Y	36110 FQ	67130 AW	133890 TQ	SDBLS	10/01-12/01
	Tennessee	Y	58210 FQ	101730 AW		TNBLS	10/01-12/01
	Clarksville-Hopkinsville MSA, TN-KY	Y	85970 FQ	123670 AW		TNBLS	10/01-12/01
	Johnson City-Kingsport-Bristol MSA, TN-VA	Y	84370 FQ	113920 AW		TNBLS	10/01-12/01
	Knoxville MSA, TN	Y	78730 FQ	123040 AW		TNBLS	10/01-12/01
	Memphis MSA, TN-AR-MS	Y	53500 FQ	81280 AW		TNBLS	10/01-12/01
	Nashville MSA, TN	Y	77210 FQ	101150 AW	144000 TQ	TNBLS	10/01-12/01
	Texas	Y	44340 FQ	109440 AW		TXBLS	10/01-12/01
	Amarillo MSA, TX	Y	94300 FQ	116930 AW		TXBLS	10/01-12/01
	Austin-San Marcos MSA, TX	Y	26410 FQ	77950 AW		TXBLS	10/01-12/01
	Brownsville-Harlingen-San Benito MSA, TX	Y	72660 FQ	108290 AW		TXBLS	10/01-12/01
	Corpus Christi MSA, TX	Y	15910 FQ	110120 AW		TXBLS	10/01-12/01
	Dallas PMSA, TX	Y	60840 FQ	109150 AW		TXBLS	10/01-12/01
	El Paso MSA, TX	Y	53960 FQ	103910 AW		TXBLS	10/01-12/01
	Fort Worth-Arlington PMSA, TX	Y	84510 FQ	130360 AW		TXBLS	10/01-12/01
	Houston PMSA, TX	Y	95570 FQ	127120 AW		TXBLS	10/01-12/01
	Laredo MSA, TX	Y	53020 FQ	111600 AW		TXBLS	10/01-12/01
	Longview-Marshall MSA, TX	Y	93500 FQ	106570 AW		TXBLS	10/01-12/01
	San Antonio MSA, TX	Y	80680 FQ	121490 AW		TXBLS	10/01-12/01
	Tyler MSA, TX	Y	49870 FQ	110130 AW		TXBLS	10/01-12/01
	Waco MSA, TX	Y	59570 FQ	113410 AW		TXBLS	10/01-12/01
	Utah	Y	61170 FQ	117780 AW		UTBLS	10/01-12/01
	Provo-Orem MSA, UT	Y	54850 FQ	121310 AW		UTBLS	10/01-12/01
	Salt Lake City-Ogden MSA, UT	Y	70820 FQ	118140 AW		UTBLS	10/01-12/01
	Vermont	Y	59740 FQ	104780 AW		VTBLS	10/01-12/01
	Burlington MSA, VT	Y	42210 FQ	85710 AW	136660 TQ	VTBLS	10/01-12/01
	Virginia	Y	56250 FQ	104650 AW		VABLS	10/01-12/01
	Norfolk-Virginia Beach-Newport News MSA, VA-NC	Y	51480 FQ	118230 AW		VABLS	10/01-12/01
	Richmond-Petersburg MSA, VA	Y	72800 FQ	93160 AW		VABLS	10/01-12/01
	Roanoke MSA, VA	Y	37580 FQ	92310 AW	139690 TQ	VABLS	10/01-12/01
	Washington	Y	92090 FQ	123550 AW		WABLS	10/01-12/01
	Bremerton PMSA, WA	Y	86960 FQ	107730 AW	139980 TQ	WABLS	10/01-12/01
	Olympia PMSA, WA	Y	41420 FQ	114730 AW		WABLS	10/01-12/01
	Seattle-Bellevue-Everett PMSA, WA	Y	95570 FQ	127370 AW		WABLS	10/01-12/01
	Spokane MSA, WA	Y	101860 FQ	126430 AW		WABLS	10/01-12/01
	Tacoma PMSA, WA	Y	83800 FQ	109840 AW		WABLS	10/01-12/01
	Yakima MSA, WA	Y	36130 FQ	87420 AW		WABLS	10/01-12/01
	West Virginia	Y	82380 FQ	117660 AW		WVBLS	10/01-12/01
	Charleston MSA, WV	Y	61720 FQ	98400 AW		WVBLS	10/01-12/01
	Huntington-Ashland MSA, WV-KY-OH	Y	43990 FQ	108730 AW		WVBLS	10/01-12/01
	Wisconsin	Y	76690 FQ	119440 AW		WIBLS	10/01-12/01
	Appleton-Oshkosh-Neenah MSA, WI	Y	118670 FQ	134150 AW		WIBLS	10/01-12/01
	Green Bay MSA, WI	Y	95250 FQ	122880 AW		WIBLS	10/01-12/01
	Madison MSA, WI	Y	39660 FQ	103550 AW		WIBLS	10/01-12/01
	Milwaukee-Waukesha PMSA, WI	Y	97140 FQ	120360 AW		WIBLS	10/01-12/01
	Wyoming	Y	74300 FQ	112120 AW		WYBLS	10/01-12/01
	Cheyenne MSA, WY	Y	32220 FQ	96530 AW	137610 TQ	WYBLS	10/01-12/01
	Puerto Rico	Y	34360 FQ	65270 AW	108400 TQ	PRBLS	10/01-12/01
	Guam	Y	99050 FQ	130130 AW		GUBLS	10/01-12/01
Farm and Home Management Advisor	Alabama	Y	25590 FQ	43370 AW	62610 TQ	ALBLS	10/01-12/01
	Arkansas	Y	13320 FQ	27930 AW	48100 TQ	ARBLS	10/01-12/01
	California	Y	24820 FQ	44690 AW	67350 TQ	CABLS	10/01-12/01
	Colorado	Y	22570 FQ	37870 AW	57340 TQ	COBLS	10/01-12/01
	Florida	Y	16130 FQ	39610 AW	73330 TQ	FLBLS	10/01-12/01
	Georgia	Y	12050 FQ	20330 AW	33640 TQ	GABLS	10/01-12/01
	Hawaii	Y	42510 FQ	57160 AW	77590 TQ	HIBLS	10/01-12/01

AAW	Average annual wage	AOH	Average offered, high	ASH	Average starting, high	H	Hourly	M	Monthly	S	Special: hourly and annual
AE	Average entry wage	AOL	Average offered, low	ASL	Average starting, low	HI	Highest wage paid	MTC	Median total compensation	TQ	Third quartile wage
AEX	Average experienced wage	APH	Average pay, high range	AW	Average wage paid	HR	High end range	MW	Median wage paid	W	Weekly
AO	Average offered	APL	Average pay, low range	FQ	First quartile wage	LR	Low end range	SQ	Second quartile wage	Y	Yearly

Occupation/Type/Industry	Location	Per	Low	Mid	High	Source	Date
Farm and Home Management Advisor	Idaho	Y	13980 FQ	31460 AW	50250 TQ	IDBLS	10/01-12/01
	Illinois	Y	14310 FQ	37710 AW	62020 TQ	ILBLS	10/01-12/01
	Indiana	Y	19580 FQ	40370 AW	64350 TQ	INBLS	10/01-12/01
	Kansas	Y	18660 FQ	36960 AW	51360 TQ	KSBLS	10/01-12/01
	Kentucky	Y	26720 FQ	48300 AW	74460 TQ	KYBLS	10/01-12/01
	Louisiana	Y	27510 FQ	39010 AW	54880 TQ	LABLS	10/01-12/01
	Maine	Y	32800 FQ	51960 AW	70020 TQ	MEBLS	10/01-12/01
	Maryland	Y	23910 FQ	34780 AW	58540 TQ	MDBLS	10/01-12/01
	Minnesota	Y	33580 FQ	46460 AW	57330 TQ	MNBLS	10/01-12/01
	Mississippi	Y	12030 FQ	22250 AW	41550 TQ	MSBLS	10/01-12/01
	Missouri	Y	14760 FQ	37110 AW	60940 TQ	MOBLS	10/01-12/01
	Montana	Y	12210 FQ	20960 AW	33280 TQ	MTBLS	10/01-12/01
	Nebraska	Y	28210 FQ	47800 AW	71820 TQ	NEBLS	10/01-12/01
	New Jersey	Y	12200 FQ	30040 AW	52050 TQ	NJBLS	10/01-12/01
	New Mexico	Y	26230 FQ	43810 AW	65880 TQ	NMBLS	10/01-12/01
	New York	Y	23140 FQ	35580 AW	49780 TQ	NYBLS	10/01-12/01
	North Dakota	Y	22680 FQ	37250 AW	55240 TQ	NDBLS	10/01-12/01
	Oklahoma	Y	28910 FQ	42050 AW	54120 TQ	OKBLS	10/01-12/01
	Oregon	Y	26880 FQ	48800 AW	71760 TQ	ORBLS	10/01-12/01
	Pennsylvania	Y	23310 FQ	43130 AW	64850 TQ	PABLS	10/01-12/01
	South Carolina	Y	22810 FQ	34890 AW	49940 TQ	SCBLS	10/01-12/01
	South Dakota	Y	21300 FQ	39500 AW	63680 TQ	SDBLS	10/01-12/01
	Tennessee	Y	22370 FQ	39310 AW	60630 TQ	TNBLS	10/01-12/01
	Texas	Y	13270 FQ	33910 AW	65000 TQ	TXBLS	10/01-12/01
	Virginia	Y	32380 FQ	47420 AW	60370 TQ	VABLS	10/01-12/01
	Washington	Y	33290 FQ	50150 AW	71440 TQ	WABLS	10/01-12/01
	West Virginia	Y	13560 FQ	27560 AW	50730 TQ	WVBLS	10/01-12/01
	Wisconsin	Y	19590 FQ	48800 AW	118560 TQ	WIBLS	10/01-12/01
	Wyoming	Y	26360 FQ	40660 AW	56140 TQ	WYBLS	10/01-12/01
	Puerto Rico	Y	16270 FQ	26120 AW	48090 TQ	PRBLS	10/01-12/01
Farm Equipment Mechanic	Alabama	H	7.81 FQ	12.35 AW	17.71 TQ	ALBLS	10/01-12/01
	Arizona	H	10.05 FQ	15.68 AW	20.75 TQ	AZBLS	10/01-12/01
	Arkansas	H	8.68 FQ	12.13 AW	16.85 TQ	ARBLS	10/01-12/01
	California	H	8.71 FQ	14.63 AW	21.35 TQ	CABLS	10/01-12/01
	Colorado	H	8.41 FQ	13.04 AW	18.53 TQ	COBLS	10/01-12/01
	Connecticut	H	9.35 FQ	15.34 AW	21.85 TQ	CTBLS	10/01-12/01
	Delaware	H	10.09 FQ	14.03 AW	17.21 TQ	DEBLS	10/01-12/01
	Florida	H	8.65 FQ	13.71 AW	19.96 TQ	FLBLS	10/01-12/01
	Georgia	H	7.93 FQ	12.55 AW	17.53 TQ	GABLS	10/01-12/01
	Hawaii	H	12.52 FQ	17.31 AW	21.80 TQ	HIBLS	10/01-12/01
	Idaho	H	10.32 FQ	14.18 AW	17.54 TQ	IDBLS	10/01-12/01
	Illinois	H	8.79 FQ	12.80 AW	17.35 TQ	ILBLS	10/01-12/01
	Indiana	H	8.41 FQ	13.09 AW	17.45 TQ	INBLS	10/01-12/01
	Iowa	H	9.26 FQ	12.65 AW	16.83 TQ	IABLS	10/01-12/01
	Kansas	H	7.96 FQ	11.98 AW	17.78 TQ	KSBLS	10/01-12/01
	Kentucky	H	7.47 FQ	11.83 AW	16.60 TQ	KYBLS	10/01-12/01
	Louisiana	H	8.39 FQ	12.51 AW	17.54 TQ	LABLS	10/01-12/01
	Maine	H	6.47 FQ	9.59 AW	13.01 TQ	MEBLS	10/01-12/01
	Maryland	H	9.42 FQ	14.75 AW	20.95 TQ	MDBLS	10/01-12/01
	Massachusetts	H	8.94 FQ	11.64 AW	15.75 TQ	MABLS	10/01-12/01
	Michigan	H	8.66 FQ	15.37 AW	24.69 TQ	MIBLS	10/01-12/01
	Minnesota	H	9.81 FQ	14.17 AW	20.58 TQ	MNBLS	10/01-12/01
	Mississippi	H	7.31 FQ	11.94 AW	18.03 TQ	MSBLS	10/01-12/01
	Missouri	H	8.24 FQ	12.57 AW	17.26 TQ	MOBLS	10/01-12/01
	Montana	H	9.24 FQ	12.70 AW	16.82 TQ	MTBLS	10/01-12/01
	Nebraska	H	8.11 FQ	12.56 AW	17.35 TQ	NEBLS	10/01-12/01
	Nevada	H	11.85 FQ	16.25 AW	21.25 TQ	NVBLS	10/01-12/01
	New Hampshire	H	9.58 FQ	13.83 AW	18.19 TQ	NHBLS	10/01-12/01
	New Jersey	H	9.90 FQ	15.22 AW	20.91 TQ	NJBLS	10/01-12/01
	New Mexico	H	7.74 FQ	12.80 AW	19.11 TQ	NMBLS	10/01-12/01
	New York	H	7.81 FQ	12.87 AW	18.72 TQ	NYBLS	10/01-12/01
	North Carolina	H	8.38 FQ	13.01 AW	17.80 TQ	NCBLS	10/01-12/01
	North Dakota	H	9.38 FQ	12.92 AW	16.82 TQ	NDBLS	10/01-12/01
	Ohio	H	8.64 FQ	12.94 AW	18.19 TQ	OHBLS	10/01-12/01
	Oklahoma	H	6.75 FQ	10.47 AW	16.57 TQ	OKBLS	10/01-12/01
	Oregon	H	10.86 FQ	14.56 AW	17.34 TQ	ORBLS	10/01-12/01
	Pennsylvania	H	6.58 FQ	11.77 AW	19.34 TQ	PABLS	10/01-12/01
	South Carolina	H	8.64 FQ	12.72 AW	16.80 TQ	SCBLS	10/01-12/01
	South Dakota	H	9.02 FQ	12.38 AW	17.12 TQ	SDBLS	10/01-12/01
	Tennessee	H	8.51 FQ	12.02 AW	14.58 TQ	TNBLS	10/01-12/01

AAW Average annual wage; **AE** Average entry wage; **AEX** Average experienced wage; **AO** Average offered; **AOH** Average offered, high; **AOL** Average offered, low; **APH** Average pay, high range; **APL** Average pay, low range; **ASH** Average starting, high; **ASL** Average starting, low; **AW** Average wage paid; **FQ** First quartile wage; **H** Hourly; **HI** Highest wage paid; **HR** High end range; **LR** Low end range; **M** Monthly; **MTC** Median total compensation; **MW** Median wage paid; **SQ** Second quartile wage; **S** Special: hourly and annual; **TQ** Third quartile wage; **W** Weekly; **Y** Yearly

Occupation/Type/Industry	Location	Per	Low	Mid	High	Source	Date
Farm Equipment Mechanic	Texas	H	7.07 FQ	12.94 AW	19.76 TQ	TXBLS	10/01-12/01
	Utah	H	11.30 FQ	12.92 AW	15.84 TQ	UTBLS	10/01-12/01
	Vermont	H	9.47 FQ	13.97 AW	20.12 TQ	VTBLS	10/01-12/01
	Virginia	H	8.79 FQ	12.72 AW	17.33 TQ	VABLS	10/01-12/01
	Washington	H	10.79 FQ	14.70 AW	19.38 TQ	WABLS	10/01-12/01
	West Virginia	H	7.49 FQ	9.44 AW	11.16 TQ	WVBLS	10/01-12/01
	Wisconsin	H	8.73 FQ	12.85 AW	17.42 TQ	WIBLS	10/01-12/01
	Wyoming	H	8.84 FQ	12.92 AW	17.70 TQ	WYBLS	10/01-12/01
Farm Labor Contractor	California	H	6.40 FQ	9.72 AW	12.31 TQ	CABLS	10/01-12/01
	Florida	H	5.59 FQ	7.94 AW	12.57 TQ	FLBLS	10/01-12/01
	Georgia	H	5.53 FQ	8.84 AW	15.02 TQ	GABLS	10/01-12/01
	Illinois	H	6.40 FQ	12.05 AW	22.07 TQ	ILBLS	10/01-12/01
	Iowa	H	5.93 FQ	8.54 AW	11.02 TQ	IABLS	10/01-12/01
	Mississippi	H	7.38 FQ	8.87 AW	11.28 TQ	MSBLS	10/01-12/01
	Ohio	H	21.52 FQ	25.16 AW	44.27 TQ	OHBLS	10/01-12/01
	South Carolina	H	17.24 FQ	19.88 AW	25.89 TQ	SCBLS	10/01-12/01
	Texas	H	6.05 FQ	8.12 AW	10.56 TQ	TXBLS	10/01-12/01
	Washington	H	6.77 FQ	7.72 AW	6.99 TQ	WABLS	10/01-12/01
Farm, Ranch, and Other Agricultural Manager	Alabama	Y	28200 FQ	49390 AW	84570 TQ	ALBLS	10/01-12/01
	Arizona	Y	20760 FQ	53480 AW	86650 TQ	AZBLS	10/01-12/01
	Arkansas	Y	29820 FQ	41110 AW	65230 TQ	ARBLS	10/01-12/01
	California	Y	26950 FQ	56660 AW	93260 TQ	CABLS	10/01-12/01
	Colorado	Y	30090 FQ	41970 AW	55650 TQ	COBLS	10/01-12/01
	Connecticut	Y	31170 FQ	61120 AW	90070 TQ	CTBLS	10/01-12/01
	Florida	Y	24400 FQ	41190 AW	65320 TQ	FLBLS	10/01-12/01
	Georgia	Y	35390 FQ	46590 AW	67510 TQ	GABLS	10/01-12/01
	Idaho	Y	22680 FQ	48820 AW	83310 TQ	IDBLS	10/01-12/01
	Illinois	Y	23270 FQ	46880 AW	78690 TQ	ILBLS	10/01-12/01
	Indiana	Y	20820 FQ	39770 AW	68680 TQ	INBLS	10/01-12/01
	Iowa	Y	29700 FQ	50050 AW	76250 TQ	IABLS	10/01-12/01
	Kansas	Y	20620 FQ	41670 AW	63940 TQ	KSBLS	10/01-12/01
	Kentucky	Y	27000 FQ	51410 AW	85900 TQ	KYBLS	10/01-12/01
	Louisiana	Y	21960 FQ	41390 AW	58540 TQ	LABLS	10/01-12/01
	Maryland	Y	12340 FQ	31480 AW	69730 TQ	MDBLS	10/01-12/01
	Massachusetts	Y	19400 FQ	43190 AW	94050 TQ	MABLS	10/01-12/01
	Michigan	Y	16010 FQ	43980 AW	144370 TQ	MIBLS	10/01-12/01
	Minnesota	Y	21290 FQ	51800 AW	90220 TQ	MNBLS	10/01-12/01
	Missouri	Y	23260 FQ	36350 AW	49710 TQ	MOBLS	10/01-12/01
	Nebraska	Y	27970 FQ	50840 AW	81500 TQ	NEBLS	10/01-12/01
	Nevada	Y	36580 FQ	57330 AW	91780 TQ	NVBLS	10/01-12/01
	New Mexico	Y	20850 FQ	33670 AW	43760 TQ	NMBLS	10/01-12/01
	New York	Y	26120 FQ	51260 AW	90980 TQ	NYBLS	10/01-12/01
	North Carolina	Y	19040 FQ	51540 AW	106790 TQ	NCBLS	10/01-12/01
	Ohio	Y	23080 FQ	44520 AW	79930 TQ	OHBLS	10/01-12/01
	Oklahoma	Y	24120 FQ	40420 AW	66030 TQ	OKBLS	10/01-12/01
	Oregon	Y	28770 FQ	50430 AW	88190 TQ	ORBLS	10/01-12/01
	Pennsylvania	Y	36410 FQ	53460 AW	71230 TQ	PABLS	10/01-12/01
	South Carolina	Y	20300 FQ	51660 AW	125770 TQ	SCBLS	10/01-12/01
	Tennessee	Y	22970 FQ	40050 AW	54990 TQ	TNBLS	10/01-12/01
	Texas	Y	20840 FQ	41040 AW	68930 TQ	TXBLS	10/01-12/01
	Utah	Y	29950 FQ	49070 AW	71990 TQ	UTBLS	10/01-12/01
	Virginia	Y	27280 FQ	42990 AW	69630 TQ	VABLS	10/01-12/01
	Washington	Y	32560 FQ	58560 AW	102780 TQ	WABLS	10/01-12/01
	Wisconsin	Y	17870 FQ	48110 AW	108960 TQ	WIBLS	10/01-12/01
Farmworker							
Farm and Ranch Animal	Alabama	H	5.70 FQ	8.37 AW	12.13 TQ	ALBLS	10/01-12/01
Farm and Ranch Animal	Arizona	H	5.84 FQ	8.05 AW	11.86 TQ	AZBLS	10/01-12/01
Farm and Ranch Animal	Arkansas	H	5.99 FQ	8.86 AW	12.54 TQ	ARBLS	10/01-12/01
Farm and Ranch Animal	California	H	6.40 FQ	7.92 AW	10.65 TQ	CABLS	10/01-12/01
Farm and Ranch Animal	Colorado	H	5.81 FQ	8.71 AW	13.40 TQ	COBLS	10/01-12/01
Farm and Ranch Animal	Connecticut	H	7.57 FQ	11.15 AW	15.51 TQ	CTBLS	10/01-12/01
Farm and Ranch Animal	Florida	H	5.70 FQ	7.24 AW	10.24 TQ	FLBLS	10/01-12/01
Farm and Ranch Animal	Georgia	H	5.97 FQ	8.93 AW	14.15 TQ	GABLS	10/01-12/01
Farm and Ranch Animal	Hawaii	H	5.80 FQ	7.93 AW	10.66 TQ	HIBLS	10/01-12/01
Farm and Ranch Animal	Idaho	H	5.62 FQ	7.54 AW	10.64 TQ	IDBLS	10/01-12/01
Farm and Ranch Animal	Illinois	H	5.88 FQ	7.53 AW	9.66 TQ	ILBLS	10/01-12/01
Farm and Ranch Animal	Indiana	H	5.84 FQ	8.56 AW	12.17 TQ	INBLS	10/01-12/01
Farm and Ranch Animal	Iowa	H	6.39 FQ	9.40 AW	13.20 TQ	IABLS	10/01-12/01

AAW Average annual wage; **AE** Average entry wage; **AEX** Average experienced wage; **AO** Average offered; **AOH** Average offered, high; **AOL** Average offered, low; **APH** Average pay, high range; **APL** Average pay, low range; **ASH** Average starting, high; **ASL** Average starting, low; **AW** Average wage paid; **FQ** First quartile wage; **H** Hourly; **HI** Highest wage paid; **HR** High end range; **LR** Low end range; **M** Monthly; **MTC** Median total compensation; **MW** Median wage paid; **SQ** Second quartile wage; **S** Special: hourly and annual; **TQ** Third quartile wage; **W** Weekly; **Y** Yearly

Occupation/Type/Industry	Location	Per	Low	Mid	High	Source	Date
Farmworker							
Farm and Ranch Animal	Kansas	H	5.84 FQ	7.74 AW	10.44 TQ	KSBLS	10/01-12/01
Farm and Ranch Animal	Kentucky	H	7.07 FQ	8.87 AW	11.64 TQ	KYBLS	10/01-12/01
Farm and Ranch Animal	Louisiana	H	5.74 FQ	8.23 AW	12.01 TQ	LABLS	10/01-12/01
Farm and Ranch Animal	Maine	H	6.72 FQ	9.13 AW	12.57 TQ	MEBLS	10/01-12/01
Farm and Ranch Animal	Maryland	H	6.78 FQ	9.82 AW	13.96 TQ	MDBLS	10/01-12/01
Farm and Ranch Animal	Massachusetts	H	7.37 FQ	8.68 AW	10.90 TQ	MABLS	10/01-12/01
Farm and Ranch Animal	Michigan	H	5.80 FQ	8.94 AW	14.94 TQ	MIBLS	10/01-12/01
Farm and Ranch Animal	Minnesota	H	5.86 FQ	9.46 AW	14.02 TQ	MNBLS	10/01-12/01
Farm and Ranch Animal	Mississippi	H	5.58 FQ	7.42 AW	11.22 TQ	MSBLS	10/01-12/01
Farm and Ranch Animal	Missouri	H	6.99 FQ	10.11 AW	15.33 TQ	MOBLS	10/01-12/01
Farm and Ranch Animal	Montana	H	5.68 FQ	7.85 AW	11.64 TQ	MTBLS	10/01-12/01
Farm and Ranch Animal	Nebraska	H	5.89 FQ	8.02 AW	11.42 TQ	NEBLS	10/01-12/01
Farm and Ranch Animal	Nevada	H	6.13 FQ	9.58 AW	14.15 TQ	NVBLS	10/01-12/01
Farm and Ranch Animal	New Hampshire	H	5.85 FQ	8.35 AW	12.25 TQ	NHBLS	10/01-12/01
Farm and Ranch Animal	New Jersey	H	6.53 FQ	9.76 AW	12.85 TQ	NJBLS	10/01-12/01
Farm and Ranch Animal	New Mexico	H	5.73 FQ	8.68 AW	13.00 TQ	NMBLS	10/01-12/01
Farm and Ranch Animal	New York	H	5.90 FQ	8.65 AW	12.28 TQ	NYBLS	10/01-12/01
Farm and Ranch Animal	North Carolina	H	6.24 FQ	9.29 AW	13.37 TQ	NCBLS	10/01-12/01
Farm and Ranch Animal	Ohio	H	5.87 FQ	8.53 AW	11.79 TQ	OHBLS	10/01-12/01
Farm and Ranch Animal	Oklahoma	H	5.74 FQ	7.72 AW	10.75 TQ	OKBLS	10/01-12/01
Farm and Ranch Animal	Oregon	H	6.82 FQ	9.12 AW	12.21 TQ	ORBLS	10/01-12/01
Farm and Ranch Animal	Pennsylvania	H	5.98 FQ	9.33 AW	13.89 TQ	PABLS	10/01-12/01
Farm and Ranch Animal	South Carolina	H	7.25 FQ	9.45 AW	12.57 TQ	SCBLS	10/01-12/01
Farm and Ranch Animal	South Dakota	H	6.15 FQ	9.11 AW	12.80 TQ	SDBLS	10/01-12/01
Farm and Ranch Animal	Tennessee	H	5.80 FQ	8.58 AW	13.43 TQ	TNBLS	10/01-12/01
Farm and Ranch Animal	Texas	H	5.62 FQ	8.13 AW	12.33 TQ	TXBLS	10/01-12/01
Farm and Ranch Animal	Utah	H	6.07 FQ	9.10 AW	13.52 TQ	UTBLS	10/01-12/01
Farm and Ranch Animal	Vermont	H	7.71 FQ	12.46 AW	16.69 TQ	VTBLS	10/01-12/01
Farm and Ranch Animal	Virginia	H	6.30 FQ	9.47 AW	15.45 TQ	VABLS	10/01-12/01
Farm and Ranch Animal	Washington	H	7.08 FQ	9.87 AW	14.35 TQ	WABLS	10/01-12/01
Farm and Ranch Animal	West Virginia	H	5.63 FQ	7.22 AW	10.16 TQ	WVBLS	10/01-12/01
Farm and Ranch Animal	Wisconsin	H	6.26 FQ	9.34 AW	13.34 TQ	WIBLS	10/01-12/01
Farm and Ranch Animal	Wyoming	H	5.84 FQ	8.84 AW	15.06 TQ	WYBLS	10/01-12/01
Farm and Ranch Animal	Puerto Rico	H	5.49 FQ	6.67 AW	8.34 TQ	PRBLS	10/01-12/01
Farmworker and Laborer							
Crop, Nursery, and Greenhouse	Alabama	H	5.81 FQ	8.00 AW	10.62 TQ	ALBLS	10/01-12/01
Crop, Nursery, and Greenhouse	Alaska	H	8.62 FQ	10.78 AW	13.61 TQ	AKBLS	10/01-12/01
Crop, Nursery, and Greenhouse	Arizona	H	5.61 FQ	6.70 AW	8.29 TQ	AZBLS	10/01-12/01
Crop, Nursery, and Greenhouse	Arkansas	H	5.76 FQ	6.95 AW	9.54 TQ	ARBLS	10/01-12/01
Crop, Nursery, and Greenhouse	California	H	6.39 FQ	7.51 AW	8.89 TQ	CABLS	10/01-12/01
Crop, Nursery, and Greenhouse	Colorado	H	5.98 FQ	8.90 AW	12.64 TQ	COBLS	10/01-12/01
Crop, Nursery, and Greenhouse	Connecticut	H	6.57 FQ	9.05 AW	12.74 TQ	CTBLS	10/01-12/01
Crop, Nursery, and Greenhouse	Delaware	H	7.05 FQ	10.51 AW	14.51 TQ	DEBLS	10/01-12/01
Crop, Nursery, and Greenhouse	Florida	H	5.61 FQ	7.20 AW	9.68 TQ	FLBLS	10/01-12/01
Crop, Nursery, and Greenhouse	Georgia	H	5.63 FQ	7.29 AW	10.24 TQ	GABLS	10/01-12/01
Crop, Nursery, and Greenhouse	Hawaii	H	5.79 FQ	8.13 AW	11.51 TQ	HIBLS	10/01-12/01
Crop, Nursery, and Greenhouse	Idaho	H	5.64 FQ	7.15 AW	10.36 TQ	IDBLS	10/01-12/01
Crop, Nursery, and Greenhouse	Illinois	H	5.98 FQ	9.46 AW	14.91 TQ	ILBLS	10/01-12/01
Crop, Nursery, and Greenhouse	Indiana	H	6.50 FQ	8.98 AW	11.01 TQ	INBLS	10/01-12/01
Crop, Nursery, and Greenhouse	Iowa	H	5.77 FQ	8.48 AW	11.89 TQ	IABLS	10/01-12/01
Crop, Nursery, and Greenhouse	Kansas	H	5.88 FQ	8.35 AW	12.09 TQ	KSBLS	10/01-12/01
Crop, Nursery, and Greenhouse	Kentucky	H	5.94 FQ	8.59 AW	11.62 TQ	KYBLS	10/01-12/01
Crop, Nursery, and Greenhouse	Louisiana	H	5.59 FQ	7.49 AW	10.50 TQ	LABLS	10/01-12/01
Crop, Nursery, and Greenhouse	Maryland	H	6.87 FQ	9.08 AW	12.82 TQ	MDBLS	10/01-12/01
Crop, Nursery, and Greenhouse	Massachusetts	H	7.26 FQ	10.25 AW	14.39 TQ	MABLS	10/01-12/01
Crop, Nursery, and Greenhouse	Michigan	H	6.03 FQ	9.01 AW	12.33 TQ	MIBLS	10/01-12/01
Crop, Nursery, and Greenhouse	Minnesota	H	6.46 FQ	9.29 AW	12.85 TQ	MNBLS	10/01-12/01
Crop, Nursery, and Greenhouse	Mississippi	H	5.41 FQ	6.84 AW	9.37 TQ	MSBLS	10/01-12/01
Crop, Nursery, and Greenhouse	Missouri	H	5.80 FQ	8.45 AW	12.81 TQ	MOBLS	10/01-12/01
Crop, Nursery, and Greenhouse	Montana	H	6.06 FQ	8.70 AW	14.47 TQ	MTBLS	10/01-12/01
Crop, Nursery, and Greenhouse	Nebraska	H	6.08 FQ	9.29 AW	15.36 TQ	NEBLS	10/01-12/01
Crop, Nursery, and Greenhouse	Nevada	H	5.85 FQ	8.11 AW	11.56 TQ	NVBLS	10/01-12/01
Crop, Nursery, and Greenhouse	New Hampshire	H	7.10 FQ	9.87 AW	13.86 TQ	NHBLS	10/01-12/01
Crop, Nursery, and Greenhouse	New Jersey	H	5.72 FQ	8.45 AW	11.44 TQ	NJBLS	10/01-12/01
Crop, Nursery, and Greenhouse	New Mexico	H	5.49 FQ	6.16 AW	6.98 TQ	NMBLS	10/01-12/01
Crop, Nursery, and Greenhouse	New York	H	6.42 FQ	8.96 AW	12.69 TQ	NYBLS	10/01-12/01
Crop, Nursery, and Greenhouse	North Carolina	H	5.69 FQ	7.17 AW	10.50 TQ	NCBLS	10/01-12/01
Crop, Nursery, and Greenhouse	North Dakota	H	5.85 FQ	7.50 AW	10.91 TQ	NDBLS	10/01-12/01
Crop, Nursery, and Greenhouse	Ohio	H	6.86 FQ	10.00 AW	15.76 TQ	OHBLS	10/01-12/01
Crop, Nursery, and Greenhouse	Oklahoma	H	5.50 FQ	7.01 AW	9.25 TQ	OKBLS	10/01-12/01
Crop, Nursery, and Greenhouse	Oregon	H	6.61 FQ	7.83 AW	10.28 TQ	ORBLS	10/01-12/01

AAW	Average annual wage	**AOH**	Average offered, high	**ASH**	Average starting, high	**H**	Hourly	**M**	Monthly	**S**	Special: hourly and annual
AE	Average entry wage	**AOL**	Average offered, low	**ASL**	Average starting, low	**HI**	Highest wage paid	**MTC**	Median total compensation	**TQ**	Third quartile wage
AEX	Average experienced wage	**APH**	Average pay, high range	**AW**	Average wage paid	**HR**	High end range	**MW**	Median wage paid	**W**	Weekly
AO	Average offered	**APL**	Average pay, low range	**FQ**	First quartile wage	**LR**	Low end range	**SQ**	Second quartile wage	**Y**	Yearly

Occupation/Type/Industry	Location	Per	Low	Mid	High	Source	Date
Farmworker and Laborer							
Crop, Nursery, and Greenhouse	Pennsylvania	H	5.85 FQ	8.62 AW	12.11 TQ	PABLS	10/01-12/01
Crop, Nursery, and Greenhouse	Rhode Island	H	6.96 FQ	10.41 AW	17.47 TQ	RIBLS	10/01-12/01
Crop, Nursery, and Greenhouse	South Carolina	H	5.79 FQ	8.29 AW	12.00 TQ	SCBLS	10/01-12/01
Crop, Nursery, and Greenhouse	South Dakota	H	6.30 FQ	8.01 AW	10.21 TQ	SDBLS	10/01-12/01
Crop, Nursery, and Greenhouse	Tennessee	H	5.66 FQ	7.98 AW	10.78 TQ	TNBLS	10/01-12/01
Crop, Nursery, and Greenhouse	Texas	H	5.56 FQ	6.90 AW	9.93 TQ	TXBLS	10/01-12/01
Crop, Nursery, and Greenhouse	Utah	H	5.81 FQ	6.91 AW	9.02 TQ	UTBLS	10/01-12/01
Crop, Nursery, and Greenhouse	Vermont	H	6.52 FQ	8.37 AW	10.69 TQ	VTBLS	10/01-12/01
Crop, Nursery, and Greenhouse	Virginia	H	5.84 FQ	8.31 AW	11.48 TQ	VABLS	10/01-12/01
Crop, Nursery, and Greenhouse	Washington	H	6.84 FQ	8.61 AW	12.19 TQ	WABLS	10/01-12/01
Crop, Nursery, and Greenhouse	West Virginia	H	5.66 FQ	8.14 AW	11.48 TQ	WVBLS	10/01-12/01
Crop, Nursery, and Greenhouse	Wisconsin	H	6.11 FQ	8.65 AW	11.93 TQ	WIBLS	10/01-12/01
Crop, Nursery, and Greenhouse	Wyoming	H	6.20 FQ	10.23 AW	12.25 TQ	WYBLS	10/01-12/01
Crop, Nursery, and Greenhouse	Puerto Rico	H	5.61 FQ	7.71 AW	11.45 TQ	PRBLS	10/01-12/01
Fashion Buyer	United States	Y	25000-30000 AE			COSGIRL2	1/01-1/02
Fashion Designer	United States	Y	25000-30000 AE			COSGIRL2	1/01-1/02
	Alabama	Y	23930 FQ	42680 AW	72730 TQ	ALBLS	10/01-12/01
	Arizona	Y	21540 FQ	37850 AW	64070 TQ	AZBLS	10/01-12/01
	Phoenix-Mesa MSA, AZ	Y	21090 FQ	37580 AW	67100 TQ	AZBLS	10/01-12/01
	California	Y	27790 FQ	57130 AW	100490 TQ	CABLS	10/01-12/01
	Los Angeles-Long Beach PMSA, CA	Y	32450 FQ	58350 AW	98390 TQ	CABLS	10/01-12/01
	Orange County PMSA, CA	Y	25760 FQ	59070 AW	109830 TQ	CABLS	10/01-12/01
	San Diego MSA, CA	Y	24630 FQ	50680 AW	99990 TQ	CABLS	10/01-12/01
	San Francisco PMSA, CA	Y	34590 FQ	60950 AW	104120 TQ	CABLS	10/01-12/01
	Santa Rosa PMSA, CA	Y	22310 FQ	53810 AW	111250 TQ	CABLS	10/01-12/01
	Colorado	Y	19360 FQ	39080 AW	65690 TQ	COBLS	10/01-12/01
	Boulder-Longmont PMSA, CO	Y	28780 FQ	45740 AW	66760 TQ	COBLS	10/01-12/01
	Connecticut	Y	17210 FQ	55010 AW	124270 TQ	CTBLS	10/01-12/01
	Washington PMSA, DC-MD-VA-WV	Y	20050 FQ	48650 AW	91470 TQ	DCBLS	10/01-12/01
	Florida	Y	17270 FQ	42180 AW	71720 TQ	FLBLS	10/01-12/01
	Miami PMSA, FL	Y	14670 FQ	44700 AW	78450 TQ	FLBLS	10/01-12/01
	Georgia	Y	32030 FQ	60580 AW	116630 TQ	GABLS	10/01-12/01
	Atlanta MSA, GA	Y	36830 FQ	64090 AW	128780 TQ	GABLS	10/01-12/01
	Illinois	Y	19010 FQ	44090 AW	85420 TQ	ILBLS	10/01-12/01
	Chicago PMSA, IL	Y	20020 FQ	43260 AW	80970 TQ	ILBLS	10/01-12/01
	Indiana	Y	17120 FQ	35570 AW	81790 TQ	INBLS	10/01-12/01
	Iowa	Y	17030 FQ	27120 AW	36050 TQ	IABLS	10/01-12/01
	Des Moines MSA, IA	Y	19160 FQ	23440 AW	28360 TQ	IABLS	10/01-12/01
	Kentucky	Y	14440 FQ	20610 AW	34090 TQ	KYBLS	10/01-12/01
	Massachusetts	Y	27900 FQ	48780 AW	82830 TQ	MABLS	10/01-12/01
	Boston PMSA, MA-NH	Y	30150 FQ	49930 AW	82550 TQ	MABLS	10/01-12/01
	Michigan	Y	18750 FQ	37050 AW	59360 TQ	MIBLS	10/01-12/01
	Minnesota	Y	20300 FQ	30890 AW	44220 TQ	MNBLS	10/01-12/01
	Missouri	Y	16320 FQ	36010 AW	68580 TQ	MOBLS	10/01-12/01
	New Jersey	Y	27750 FQ	69910 AW	119680 TQ	NJBLS	10/01-12/01
	Bergen-Passaic PMSA, NJ	Y	23720 FQ	49600 AW	91970 TQ	NJBLS	10/01-12/01
	Middlesex-Somerset-Hunterdon PMSA, NJ	Y	73170 FQ	102090 AW	122020 TQ	NJBLS	10/01-12/01
	New York	Y	34930 FQ	69050 AW	118020 TQ	NYBLS	10/01-12/01
	Nassau-Suffolk PMSA, NY	Y	25450 FQ	52350 AW	88380 TQ	NYBLS	10/01-12/01
	New York PMSA, NY	Y	36060 FQ	69990 AW	119090 TQ	NYBLS	10/01-12/01
	North Carolina	Y	21240 FQ	43610 AW	79960 TQ	NCBLS	10/01-12/01
	Greensboro-Winston-Salem-High Point MSA, NC	Y	20830 FQ	44040 AW	81980 TQ	NCBLS	10/01-12/01
	Ohio	Y	19490 FQ	48000 AW	93610 TQ	OHBLS	10/01-12/01
	Columbus MSA, OH	Y	29350 FQ	76870 AW	139330 TQ	OHBLS	10/01-12/01
	Oklahoma	Y	12810 FQ	25790 AW	38140 TQ	OKBLS	10/01-12/01
	Oregon	Y	30410 FQ	48050 AW	74670 TQ	ORBLS	10/01-12/01
	Portland-Vancouver PMSA, OR-WA	Y	30160 FQ	47960 AW	75640 TQ	ORBLS	10/01-12/01
	Pennsylvania	Y	18480 FQ	40470 AW	74960 TQ	PABLS	10/01-12/01
	Philadelphia PMSA, PA-NJ	Y	21260 FQ	42240 AW	75780 TQ	PABLS	10/01-12/01
	Providence-Fall River-Warwick MSA, RI-MA	Y	20010 FQ	47370 AW	84820 TQ	RIBLS	10/01-12/01
	South Carolina	Y	20250 FQ	40490 AW	74270 TQ	SCBLS	10/01-12/01
	Tennessee	Y	20260 FQ	56340 AW	110840 TQ	TNBLS	10/01-12/01

AAW Average annual wage; **AE** Average entry wage; **AEX** Average experienced wage; **AO** Average offered; **AOH** Average offered, high; **AOL** Average offered, low; **APH** Average pay, high range; **APL** Average pay, low range; **ASH** Average starting, high; **ASL** Average starting, low; **AW** Average wage paid; **FQ** First quartile wage; **H** Hourly; **HI** Highest wage paid; **HR** High end range; **LR** Low end range; **M** Monthly; **MTC** Median total compensation; **MW** Median wage paid; **SQ** Second quartile wage; **S** Special: hourly and annual; **TQ** Third quartile wage; **W** Weekly; **Y** Yearly

Occupation/Type/Industry	Location	Per	Low	Mid	High	Source	Date
Fashion Designer	Memphis MSA, TN-AR-MS	Y	31310 FQ	64100 AW	119500 TQ	TNBLS	10/01-12/01
	Texas	Y	16280 FQ	32900 AW	55300 TQ	TXBLS	10/01-12/01
	Dallas PMSA, TX	Y	24630 FQ	38470 AW	57310 TQ	TXBLS	10/01-12/01
	Virginia	Y	20810 FQ	41810 AW	87180 TQ	VABLS	10/01-12/01
	Washington	Y	23010 FQ	47990 AW	75800 TQ	WABLS	10/01-12/01
	Seattle-Bellevue-Everett PMSA, WA	Y	23250 FQ	48690 AW	77650 TQ	WABLS	10/01-12/01
	Wisconsin	Y	20950 FQ	43500 AW	81010 TQ	WIBLS	10/01-12/01
	Puerto Rico	Y	14300 FQ	29270 AW	70750 TQ	PRBLS	10/01-12/01
FBI Agent	United States	Y	36621 AE		57345 AEX	OOH2	1/99-1/00
FBI Supervisor							
GS-14	United States	Y		67765 AW		OOH2	1/99-1/00
GS-15	United States	Y		79710 AW		OOH2	1/99-1/00
Fence Erector	Alabama	H	6.52 FQ	8.80 AW	11.11 TQ	ALBLS	10/01-12/01
	Arizona	H	7.23 FQ	10.40 AW	17.11 TQ	AZBLS	10/01-12/01
	Arkansas	H	6.95 FQ	9.50 AW	13.51 TQ	ARBLS	10/01-12/01
	California	H	6.48 FQ	12.14 AW	21.79 TQ	CABLS	10/01-12/01
	Colorado	H	8.95 FQ	12.76 AW	16.92 TQ	COBLS	10/01-12/01
	Connecticut	H	10.44 FQ	14.81 AW	20.29 TQ	CTBLS	10/01-12/01
	Florida	H	6.39 FQ	10.48 AW	15.90 TQ	FLBLS	10/01-12/01
	Georgia	H	5.95 FQ	10.89 AW	17.59 TQ	GABLS	10/01-12/01
	Hawaii	H	7.50 FQ	10.55 AW	13.96 TQ	HIBLS	10/01-12/01
	Idaho	H	8.96 FQ	13.14 AW	18.77 TQ	IDBLS	10/01-12/01
	Illinois	H	8.95 FQ	14.18 AW	22.81 TQ	ILBLS	10/01-12/01
	Indiana	H	8.51 FQ	10.74 AW	15.23 TQ	INBLS	10/01-12/01
	Iowa	H	7.21 FQ	9.92 AW	14.35 TQ	IABLS	10/01-12/01
	Kansas	H	7.70 FQ	9.95 AW	12.73 TQ	KSBLS	10/01-12/01
	Kentucky	H	8.01 FQ	12.49 AW	16.32 TQ	KYBLS	10/01-12/01
	Louisiana	H	7.50 FQ	10.83 AW	15.85 TQ	LABLS	10/01-12/01
	Maryland	H	8.44 FQ	12.05 AW	16.33 TQ	MDBLS	10/01-12/01
	Massachusetts	H	13.07 FQ	17.23 AW	22.85 TQ	MABLS	10/01-12/01
	Michigan	H	9.23 FQ	15.12 AW	23.24 TQ	MIBLS	10/01-12/01
	Minnesota	H	8.70 FQ	12.66 AW	17.02 TQ	MNBLS	10/01-12/01
	Mississippi	H	6.76 FQ	10.80 AW	15.84 TQ	MSBLS	10/01-12/01
	Missouri	H	7.59 FQ	12.11 AW	20.20 TQ	MOBLS	10/01-12/01
	Montana	H	7.69 FQ	10.46 AW	15.04 TQ	MTBLS	10/01-12/01
	Nebraska	H	6.96 FQ	10.51 AW	14.03 TQ	NEBLS	10/01-12/01
	Nevada	H	10.33 FQ	14.20 AW	19.74 TQ	NVBLS	10/01-12/01
	New Jersey	H	7.54 FQ	16.44 AW	26.47 TQ	NJBLS	10/01-12/01
	New Mexico	H	6.35 FQ	10.55 AW	14.75 TQ	NMBLS	10/01-12/01
	New York	H	7.23 FQ	10.99 AW	17.46 TQ	NYBLS	10/01-12/01
	North Carolina	H	7.10 FQ	10.05 AW	14.17 TQ	NCBLS	10/01-12/01
	North Dakota	H	8.30 FQ	12.50 AW	16.90 TQ	NDBLS	10/01-12/01
	Ohio	H	7.73 FQ	12.10 AW	16.45 TQ	OHBLS	10/01-12/01
	Oklahoma	H	7.14 FQ	11.09 AW	17.04 TQ	OKBLS	10/01-12/01
	Oregon	H	8.20 FQ	11.96 AW	16.58 TQ	ORBLS	10/01-12/01
	Pennsylvania	H	8.90 FQ	13.09 AW	27.70 TQ	PABLS	10/01-12/01
	South Carolina	H	6.17 FQ	8.76 AW	11.18 TQ	SCBLS	10/01-12/01
	Tennessee	H	7.36 FQ	9.71 AW	12.85 TQ	TNBLS	10/01-12/01
	Texas	H	6.50 FQ	9.16 AW	13.53 TQ	TXBLS	10/01-12/01
	Utah	H	8.66 FQ	10.58 AW	13.63 TQ	UTBLS	10/01-12/01
	Vermont	H	9.00 FQ	11.53 AW	16.89 TQ	VTBLS	10/01-12/01
	Virginia	H	7.18 FQ	11.05 AW	16.36 TQ	VABLS	10/01-12/01
	Washington	H	8.12 FQ	13.10 AW	18.90 TQ	WABLS	10/01-12/01
	West Virginia	H	6.74 FQ	10.72 AW	15.89 TQ	WVBLS	10/01-12/01
	Wisconsin	H	12.67 FQ	18.30 AW	21.76 TQ	WIBLS	10/01-12/01
	Wyoming	H	7.48 FQ	10.50 AW	14.05 TQ	WYBLS	10/01-12/01
Fiberglass Laminator and Fabricator	Alabama	H	6.80 FQ	10.93 AW	19.19 TQ	ALBLS	10/01-12/01
	Arkansas	H	7.52 FQ	10.29 AW	13.59 TQ	ARBLS	10/01-12/01
	California	H	7.02 FQ	12.48 AW	20.28 TQ	CABLS	10/01-12/01
	Fresno MSA, CA	H	8.62 FQ	13.82 AW	20.79 TQ	CABLS	10/01-12/01
	Los Angeles-Long Beach PMSA, CA	H	7.05 FQ	10.87 AW	14.97 TQ	CABLS	10/01-12/01
	Oakland PMSA, CA	H	10.22 FQ	17.83 AW	22.48 TQ	CABLS	10/01-12/01
	Orange County PMSA, CA	H	6.60 FQ	9.89 AW	13.82 TQ	CABLS	10/01-12/01
	Riverside-San Bernardino PMSA, CA	H	6.70 FQ	11.91 AW	29.58 TQ	CABLS	10/01-12/01

AAW	Average annual wage	**AOH**	Average offered, high	**ASH**	Average starting, high	**H**	Hourly	**M**	Monthly	**S**	Special: hourly and annual
AE	Average entry wage	**AOL**	Average offered, low	**ASL**	Average starting, low	**HI**	Highest wage paid	**MTC**	Median total compensation	**TQ**	Third quartile wage
AEX	Average experienced wage	**APH**	Average pay, high range	**AW**	Average wage paid	**HR**	High end range	**MW**	Median wage paid	**W**	Weekly
AO	Average offered	**APL**	Average pay, low range	**FQ**	First quartile wage	**LR**	Low end range	**SQ**	Second quartile wage	**Y**	Yearly

Occupation/Type/Industry	Location	Per	Low	Mid	High	Source	Date
Fiberglass Laminator and Fabricator	Sacramento PMSA, CA	H	9.63 FQ	16.03 AW	28.53 TQ	CABLS	10/01-12/01
	San Diego MSA, CA	H	9.81 FQ	16.56 AW	21.76 TQ	CABLS	10/01-12/01
	Colorado	H	7.64 FQ	11.08 AW	14.63 TQ	COBLS	10/01-12/01
	Denver PMSA, CO	H	7.87 FQ	11.08 AW	13.48 TQ	COBLS	10/01-12/01
	Connecticut	H	6.71 FQ	11.69 AW	17.55 TQ	CTBLS	10/01-12/01
	New Haven-Meriden PMSA, CT	H	6.56 FQ	10.59 AW	17.55 TQ	CTBLS	10/01-12/01
	Delaware	H	7.45 FQ	8.99 AW	12.18 TQ	DEBLS	10/01-12/01
	Washington PMSA, DC-MD-VA-WV	H	6.10 FQ	10.82 AW	16.03 TQ	DCBLS	10/01-12/01
	Florida	H	7.89 FQ	11.60 AW	16.44 TQ	FLBLS	10/01-12/01
	Daytona Beach MSA, FL	H	8.26 FQ	11.37 AW	14.89 TQ	FLBLS	10/01-12/01
	Fort Lauderdale PMSA, FL	H	9.22 FQ	13.99 AW	19.71 TQ	FLBLS	10/01-12/01
	Fort Myers-Cape Coral MSA, FL	H	10.77 FQ	15.00 AW	19.66 TQ	FLBLS	10/01-12/01
	Fort Pierce-Port St. Lucie MSA, FL	H	8.88 FQ	14.01 AW	20.77 TQ	FLBLS	10/01-12/01
	Gainesville MSA, FL	H	7.86 FQ	10.88 AW	13.47 TQ	FLBLS	10/01-12/01
	Melbourne-Titusville-Palm Bay MSA, FL	H	9.05 FQ	13.03 AW	16.47 TQ	FLBLS	10/01-12/01
	Miami PMSA, FL	H	7.44 FQ	9.55 AW	12.94 TQ	FLBLS	10/01-12/01
	Orlando MSA, FL	H	7.82 FQ	10.65 AW	13.92 TQ	FLBLS	10/01-12/01
	Pensacola MSA, FL	H	7.66 FQ	11.03 AW	16.61 TQ	FLBLS	10/01-12/01
	Sarasota-Bradenton MSA, FL	H	9.31 FQ	11.59 AW	15.17 TQ	FLBLS	10/01-12/01
	Tampa-St. Petersburg-Clearwater MSA, FL	H	8.48 FQ	11.22 AW	14.62 TQ	FLBLS	10/01-12/01
	West Palm Beach-Boca Raton MSA, FL	H	9.64 FQ	13.39 AW	17.39 TQ	FLBLS	10/01-12/01
	Georgia	H	7.68 FQ	11.05 AW	16.09 TQ	GABLS	10/01-12/01
	Atlanta MSA, GA	H	7.53 FQ	10.15 AW	15.68 TQ	GABLS	10/01-12/01
	Augusta-Aiken MSA, GA-SC	H	8.94 FQ	11.23 AW	13.29 TQ	GABLS	10/01-12/01
	Hawaii	H	7.80 FQ	12.85 AW	19.77 TQ	HIBLS	10/01-12/01
	Illinois	H	6.59 FQ	9.75 AW	13.80 TQ	ILBLS	10/01-12/01
	Peoria-Pekin MSA, IL	H	9.71 FQ	16.80 AW	25.79 TQ	ILBLS	10/01-12/01
	Indiana	H	7.79 FQ	12.07 AW	17.66 TQ	INBLS	10/01-12/01
	Elkhart-Goshen MSA, IN	H	8.87 FQ	13.17 AW	19.59 TQ	INBLS	10/01-12/01
	Gary PMSA, IN	H	7.92 FQ	12.40 AW	17.21 TQ	INBLS	10/01-12/01
	Indianapolis MSA, IN	H	8.75 FQ	13.07 AW	18.06 TQ	INBLS	10/01-12/01
	Davenport-Moline-Rock Island MSA, IA-IL	H	6.28 FQ	14.81 AW	21.92 TQ	IABLS	10/01-12/01
	Kentucky	H	7.61 FQ	10.99 AW	13.99 TQ	KYBLS	10/01-12/01
	Louisiana	H	7.38 FQ	11.12 AW	15.05 TQ	LABLS	10/01-12/01
	New Orleans MSA, LA	H	7.68 FQ	11.19 AW	14.54 TQ	LABLS	10/01-12/01
	Maine	H	8.93 FQ	12.52 AW	17.58 TQ	MEBLS	10/01-12/01
	Portland MSA, ME	H	9.03 FQ	13.54 AW	20.31 TQ	MEBLS	10/01-12/01
	Maryland	H	8.26 FQ	13.21 AW	19.88 TQ	MDBLS	10/01-12/01
	Boston PMSA, MA-NH	H	9.53 FQ	11.89 AW	16.09 TQ	MABLS	10/01-12/01
	Lowell PMSA, MA-NH	H	8.82 FQ	12.58 AW	17.70 TQ	MABLS	10/01-12/01
	Michigan	H	10.03 FQ	15.40 AW	24.09 TQ	MIBLS	10/01-12/01
	Detroit PMSA, MI	H	9.33 FQ	17.40 AW	27.19 TQ	MIBLS	10/01-12/01
	Grand Rapids-Muskegon-Holland MSA, MI	H	10.24 FQ	14.57 AW	19.81 TQ	MIBLS	10/01-12/01
	Minnesota	H	8.07 FQ	10.89 AW	14.55 TQ	MNBLS	10/01-12/01
	Minneapolis-St. Paul MSA, MN-WI	H	7.47 FQ	11.09 AW	15.53 TQ	MNBLS	10/01-12/01
	Missouri	H	7.43 FQ	12.83 AW	19.05 TQ	MOBLS	10/01-12/01
	Nebraska	H	7.83 FQ	10.83 AW	14.66 TQ	NEBLS	10/01-12/01
	Nevada	H	8.58 FQ	13.67 AW	22.36 TQ	NVBLS	10/01-12/01
	Las Vegas MSA, NV-AZ	H	7.90 FQ	13.48 AW	22.91 TQ	NVBLS	10/01-12/01
	New Jersey	H	9.08 FQ	12.29 AW	16.26 TQ	NJBLS	10/01-12/01
	Atlantic-Cape May PMSA, NJ	H	8.03 FQ	11.39 AW	16.16 TQ	NJBLS	10/01-12/01
	Bergen-Passaic PMSA, NJ	H	12.72 FQ	18.19 AW	22.01 TQ	NJBLS	10/01-12/01
	Middlesex-Somerset-Hunterdon PMSA, NJ	H	11.67 FQ	14.16 AW	17.10 TQ	NJBLS	10/01-12/01
	Monmouth-Ocean PMSA, NJ	H	8.40 FQ	13.74 AW	23.09 TQ	NJBLS	10/01-12/01
	New York	H	8.46 FQ	13.33 AW	19.44 TQ	NYBLS	10/01-12/01
	Buffalo-Niagara Falls MSA, NY	H	8.83 FQ	10.95 AW	14.23 TQ	NYBLS	10/01-12/01
	Nassau-Suffolk PMSA, NY	H	7.73 FQ	14.34 AW	20.74 TQ	NYBLS	10/01-12/01
	New York PMSA, NY	H	8.05 FQ	12.32 AW	16.94 TQ	NYBLS	10/01-12/01
	Syracuse MSA, NY	H	8.71 FQ	12.78 AW	16.47 TQ	NYBLS	10/01-12/01

AAW Average annual wage; **AE** Average entry wage; **AEX** Average experienced wage; **AO** Average offered; **AOH** Average offered, high; **AOL** Average offered, low; **APH** Average pay, high range; **APL** Average pay, low range; **ASH** Average starting, high; **ASL** Average starting, low; **AW** Average wage paid; **FQ** First quartile wage; **H** Hourly; **HI** Highest wage paid; **HR** High end range; **LR** Low end range; **M** Monthly; **MTC** Median total compensation; **MW** Median wage paid; **SQ** Second quartile wage; **S** Special: hourly and annual; **TQ** Third quartile wage; **W** Weekly; **Y** Yearly

Occupation/Type/Industry	Location	Per	Low	Mid	High	Source	Date
Fiberglass Laminator and Fabricator	North Carolina	H	8.77 FQ	12.78 AW	16.49 TQ	NCBLS	10/01-12/01
	Charlotte-Gastonia-Rock Hill MSA, NC-SC	H	7.37 FQ	12.92 AW	17.12 TQ	NCBLS	10/01-12/01
	Greensboro-Winston-Salem-High Point MSA, NC	H	8.52 FQ	16.01 AW	27.36 TQ	NCBLS	10/01-12/01
	North Dakota	H	8.74 FQ	12.94 AW	19.13 TQ	NDBLS	10/01-12/01
	Fargo-Moorhead MSA, ND-MN	H	9.20 FQ	13.80 AW	20.61 TQ	NDBLS	10/01-12/01
	Ohio	H	8.28 FQ	11.66 AW	15.62 TQ	OHBLS	10/01-12/01
	Canton-Massillon MSA, OH	H	7.86 FQ	11.18 AW	14.40 TQ	OHBLS	10/01-12/01
	Cleveland-Lorain-Elyria PMSA, OH	H	9.56 FQ	12.28 AW	16.13 TQ	OHBLS	10/01-12/01
	Oklahoma	H	7.67 FQ	14.51 AW	26.49 TQ	OKBLS	10/01-12/01
	Tulsa MSA, OK	H	8.15 FQ	16.19 AW	27.16 TQ	OKBLS	10/01-12/01
	Oregon	H	7.84 FQ	11.26 AW	15.42 TQ	ORBLS	10/01-12/01
	Eugene-Springfield MSA, OR	H	9.60 FQ	12.49 AW	16.24 TQ	ORBLS	10/01-12/01
	Portland-Vancouver PMSA, OR-WA	H	7.80 FQ	12.65 AW	18.49 TQ	ORBLS	10/01-12/01
	Salem PMSA, OR	H	7.26 FQ	9.93 AW	16.18 TQ	ORBLS	10/01-12/01
	Pittsburgh MSA, PA	H	7.73 FQ	11.85 AW	16.13 TQ	PABLS	10/01-12/01
	Rhode Island	H	9.74 FQ	14.36 AW	21.03 TQ	RIBLS	10/01-12/01
	Providence-Fall River-Warwick MSA, RI-MA	H	10.47 FQ	15.25 AW	23.03 TQ	RIBLS	10/01-12/01
	South Carolina	H	8.00 FQ	12.91 AW	20.91 TQ	SCBLS	10/01-12/01
	Columbia MSA, SC	H	7.98 FQ	10.83 AW	14.82 TQ	SCBLS	10/01-12/01
	Greenville-Spartanburg-Anderson MSA, SC	H	8.01 FQ	15.90 AW	22.10 TQ	SCBLS	10/01-12/01
	Tennessee	H	7.47 FQ	11.80 AW	16.60 TQ	TNBLS	10/01-12/01
	Chattanooga MSA, TN-GA	H	7.43 FQ	10.94 AW	13.88 TQ	TNBLS	10/01-12/01
	Johnson City-Kingsport-Bristol MSA, TN-VA	H	8.12 FQ	11.12 AW	14.03 TQ	TNBLS	10/01-12/01
	Knoxville MSA, TN	H	8.51 FQ	10.78 AW	13.03 TQ	TNBLS	10/01-12/01
	Nashville MSA, TN	H	6.55 FQ	12.95 AW	23.84 TQ	TNBLS	10/01-12/01
	Texas	H	7.14 FQ	11.61 AW	18.70 TQ	TXBLS	10/01-12/01
	Austin-San Marcos MSA, TX	H	7.46 FQ	9.89 AW	13.27 TQ	TXBLS	10/01-12/01
	Beaumont-Port Arthur MSA, TX	H	6.96 FQ	8.08 AW	9.35 TQ	TXBLS	10/01-12/01
	Brazoria PMSA, TX	H	8.64 FQ	12.47 AW	17.81 TQ	TXBLS	10/01-12/01
	Dallas PMSA, TX	H	7.64 FQ	11.11 AW	14.38 TQ	TXBLS	10/01-12/01
	Galveston-Texas City PMSA, TX	H	6.14 FQ	11.71 AW	19.19 TQ	TXBLS	10/01-12/01
	Houston PMSA, TX	H	8.11 FQ	11.67 AW	15.84 TQ	TXBLS	10/01-12/01
	San Antonio MSA, TX	H	7.42 FQ	11.40 AW	16.99 TQ	TXBLS	10/01-12/01
	Utah	H	7.70 FQ	11.94 AW	20.19 TQ	UTBLS	10/01-12/01
	Salt Lake City-Ogden MSA, UT	H	7.64 FQ	11.74 AW	20.73 TQ	UTBLS	10/01-12/01
	Virginia	H	7.92 FQ	11.81 AW	15.35 TQ	VABLS	10/01-12/01
	Washington	H	9.25 FQ	13.84 AW	17.90 TQ	WABLS	10/01-12/01
	Seattle-Bellevue-Everett PMSA, WA	H	9.05 FQ	13.98 AW	19.96 TQ	WABLS	10/01-12/01
	Tacoma PMSA, WA	H	10.12 FQ	14.61 AW	20.07 TQ	WABLS	10/01-12/01
	West Virginia	H	5.86 FQ	9.15 AW	13.79 TQ	WVBLS	10/01-12/01
	Wisconsin	H	7.81 FQ	12.13 AW	16.70 TQ	WIBLS	10/01-12/01
	Appleton-Oshkosh-Neenah MSA, WI	H	7.20 FQ	10.25 AW	14.40 TQ	WIBLS	10/01-12/01
	Milwaukee-Waukesha PMSA, WI	H	7.68 FQ	13.75 AW	18.88 TQ	WIBLS	10/01-12/01
	Wyoming	H	7.86 FQ	9.93 AW	11.65 TQ	WYBLS	10/01-12/01
File Clerk	Alabama	H	5.90 FQ	8.55 AW	12.31 TQ	ALBLS	10/01-12/01
	Birmingham MSA, AL	H	5.90 FQ	8.76 AW	12.34 TQ	ALBLS	10/01-12/01
	Huntsville MSA, AL	H	6.68 FQ	10.05 AW	13.79 TQ	ALBLS	10/01-12/01
	Mobile MSA, AL	H	6.10 FQ	8.82 AW	12.77 TQ	ALBLS	10/01-12/01
	Montgomery MSA, AL	H	5.83 FQ	7.89 AW	11.46 TQ	ALBLS	10/01-12/01
	Alaska	H	7.64 FQ	11.09 AW	16.14 TQ	AKBLS	10/01-12/01
	Anchorage MSA, AK	H	7.83 FQ	11.97 AW	16.79 TQ	AKBLS	10/01-12/01
	Arizona	H	6.09 FQ	9.04 AW	12.90 TQ	AZBLS	10/01-12/01
	Phoenix-Mesa MSA, AZ	H	6.39 FQ	9.47 AW	13.18 TQ	AZBLS	10/01-12/01
	Tucson MSA, AZ	H	5.80 FQ	8.00 AW	11.58 TQ	AZBLS	10/01-12/01
	Arkansas	H	5.84 FQ	8.15 AW	11.24 TQ	ARBLS	10/01-12/01

AAW Average annual wage; AE Average entry wage; AEX Average experienced wage; AO Average offered; AOH Average offered, high; AOL Average offered, low; APH Average pay, high range; APL Average pay, low range; ASH Average starting, high; ASL Average starting, low; AW Average wage paid; FQ First quartile wage; H Hourly; HI Highest wage paid; HR High end range; LR Low end range; M Monthly; MTC Median total compensation; MW Median wage paid; SQ Second quartile wage; S Special: hourly and annual; TQ Third quartile wage; W Weekly; Y Yearly

Occupation/Type/Industry	Location	Per	Low	Mid	High	Source	Date
File Clerk	Fayetteville-Springdale-Rogers MSA, AR	H	6.19 FQ	8.03 AW	10.32 TQ	ARBLS	10/01-12/01
	Fort Smith MSA, AR-OK	H	6.05 FQ	8.53 AW	11.56 TQ	ARBLS	10/01-12/01
	Little Rock-North Little Rock MSA, AR	H	5.75 FQ	8.85 AW	14.45 TQ	ARBLS	10/01-12/01
	California	H	6.99 FQ	10.79 AW	15.88 TQ	CABLS	10/01-12/01
	Bakersfield MSA, CA	H	6.75 FQ	9.81 AW	13.42 TQ	CABLS	10/01-12/01
	Chico-Paradise MSA, CA	H	7.05 FQ	9.06 AW	10.90 TQ	CABLS	10/01-12/01
	Fresno MSA, CA	H	6.48 FQ	7.97 AW	10.66 TQ	CABLS	10/01-12/01
	Los Angeles-Long Beach PMSA, CA	H	6.94 FQ	10.64 AW	15.67 TQ	CABLS	10/01-12/01
	Merced MSA, CA	H	6.80 FQ	13.31 AW	26.38 TQ	CABLS	10/01-12/01
	Modesto MSA, CA	H	6.45 FQ	8.29 AW	11.12 TQ	CABLS	10/01-12/01
	Oakland PMSA, CA	H	7.75 FQ	12.68 AW	17.43 TQ	CABLS	10/01-12/01
	Orange County PMSA, CA	H	6.96 FQ	10.69 AW	16.04 TQ	CABLS	10/01-12/01
	Redding MSA, CA	H	6.57 FQ	8.50 AW	10.65 TQ	CABLS	10/01-12/01
	Riverside-San Bernardino PMSA, CA	H	6.93 FQ	10.58 AW	14.54 TQ	CABLS	10/01-12/01
	Sacramento PMSA, CA	H	7.16 FQ	10.56 AW	15.55 TQ	CABLS	10/01-12/01
	Salinas MSA, CA	H	6.71 FQ	9.17 AW	12.49 TQ	CABLS	10/01-12/01
	San Diego MSA, CA	H	7.07 FQ	9.78 AW	13.57 TQ	CABLS	10/01-12/01
	San Francisco PMSA, CA	H	8.96 FQ	12.98 AW	16.77 TQ	CABLS	10/01-12/01
	San Jose PMSA, CA	H	9.25 FQ	13.14 AW	17.12 TQ	CABLS	10/01-12/01
	San Luis Obispo-Atascadero-Paso Robles MSA, CA	H	6.42 FQ	8.48 AW	13.05 TQ	CABLS	10/01-12/01
	Santa Barbara-Santa Maria-Lompoc MSA, CA	H	7.04 FQ	9.57 AW	12.75 TQ	CABLS	10/01-12/01
	Santa Cruz-Watsonville PMSA, CA	H	6.65 FQ	10.27 AW	14.99 TQ	CABLS	10/01-12/01
	Santa Rosa PMSA, CA	H	7.18 FQ	10.12 AW	15.75 TQ	CABLS	10/01-12/01
	Stockton-Lodi MSA, CA	H	7.15 FQ	10.81 AW	16.97 TQ	CABLS	10/01-12/01
	Vallejo-Fairfield-Napa PMSA, CA	H	7.43 FQ	11.40 AW	17.37 TQ	CABLS	10/01-12/01
	Ventura PMSA, CA	H	6.89 FQ	9.50 AW	13.10 TQ	CABLS	10/01-12/01
	Visalia-Tulare-Porterville MSA, CA	H	6.57 FQ	8.73 AW	11.42 TQ	CABLS	10/01-12/01
	Colorado	H	6.74 FQ	10.09 AW	13.78 TQ	COBLS	10/01-12/01
	Boulder-Longmont PMSA, CO	H	7.05 FQ	9.56 AW	12.73 TQ	COBLS	10/01-12/01
	Colorado Springs MSA, CO	H	7.42 FQ	9.81 AW	12.73 TQ	COBLS	10/01-12/01
	Denver PMSA, CO	H	7.47 FQ	10.72 AW	14.50 TQ	COBLS	10/01-12/01
	Fort Collins-Loveland MSA, CO	H	7.38 FQ	9.26 AW	11.57 TQ	COBLS	10/01-12/01
	Greeley PMSA, CO	H	6.07 FQ	9.97 AW	13.36 TQ	COBLS	10/01-12/01
	Connecticut	H	7.12 FQ	10.60 AW	15.10 TQ	CTBLS	10/01-12/01
	Bridgeport PMSA, CT	H	7.99 FQ	11.09 AW	15.93 TQ	CTBLS	10/01-12/01
	Danbury PMSA, CT	H	7.15 FQ	10.50 AW	14.05 TQ	CTBLS	10/01-12/01
	Hartford MSA, CT	H	7.45 FQ	10.73 AW	14.67 TQ	CTBLS	10/01-12/01
	New Haven-Meriden PMSA, CT	H	6.90 FQ	10.03 AW	14.05 TQ	CTBLS	10/01-12/01
	New London-Norwich MSA, CT-RI	H	7.07 FQ	10.63 AW	15.67 TQ	CTBLS	10/01-12/01
	Stamford-Norwalk PMSA, CT	H	6.84 FQ	10.77 AW	16.82 TQ	CTBLS	10/01-12/01
	Waterbury PMSA, CT	H	7.06 FQ	11.21 AW	15.26 TQ	CTBLS	10/01-12/01
	Delaware	H	7.21 FQ	10.17 AW	13.53 TQ	DEBLS	10/01-12/01
	Wilmington-Newark PMSA, DE-MD	H	7.29 FQ	10.52 AW	13.90 TQ	DEBLS	10/01-12/01
	District of Columbia	H	7.84 FQ	11.87 AW	16.90 TQ	DCBLS	10/01-12/01
	Washington PMSA, DC-MD-VA-WV	H	6.27 FQ	11.09 AW	16.50 TQ	DCBLS	10/01-12/01
	Florida	H	6.43 FQ	9.56 AW	13.26 TQ	FLBLS	10/01-12/01
	Daytona Beach MSA, FL	H	6.28 FQ	8.97 AW	12.16 TQ	FLBLS	10/01-12/01
	Fort Lauderdale PMSA, FL	H	6.98 FQ	10.36 AW	14.49 TQ	FLBLS	10/01-12/01
	Fort Myers-Cape Coral MSA, FL	H	6.23 FQ	8.59 AW	11.11 TQ	FLBLS	10/01-12/01
	Fort Pierce-Port St. Lucie MSA, FL	H	7.14 FQ	9.06 AW	11.51 TQ	FLBLS	10/01-12/01
	Fort Walton Beach MSA, FL	H	6.19 FQ	9.08 AW	12.65 TQ	FLBLS	10/01-12/01
	Gainesville MSA, FL	H	6.68 FQ	8.70 AW	11.84 TQ	FLBLS	10/01-12/01
	Jacksonville MSA, FL	H	7.05 FQ	9.34 AW	12.60 TQ	FLBLS	10/01-12/01
	Lakeland-Winter Haven MSA, FL	H	6.41 FQ	8.88 AW	12.15 TQ	FLBLS	10/01-12/01

AAW Average annual wage	**AOH** Average offered, high	**ASH** Average starting, high	**H** Hourly	**M** Monthly	**S** Special: hourly and annual
AE Average entry wage	**AOL** Average offered, low	**ASL** Average starting, low	**HI** Highest wage paid	**MTC** Median total compensation	**TQ** Third quartile wage
AEX Average experienced wage	**APH** Average pay, high range	**AW** Average wage paid	**HR** High end range	**MW** Median wage paid	**W** Weekly
AO Average offered	**APL** Average pay, low range	**FQ** First quartile wage	**LR** Low end range	**SQ** Second quartile wage	**Y** Yearly

Occupation/Type/Industry	Location	Per	Low	Mid	High	Source	Date
File Clerk	Melbourne-Titusville-Palm Bay MSA, FL	H	7.01 FQ	9.70 AW	13.24 TQ	FLBLS	10/01-12/01
	Miami PMSA, FL	H	6.14 FQ	9.07 AW	12.34 TQ	FLBLS	10/01-12/01
	Naples MSA, FL	H	6.81 FQ	10.08 AW	13.21 TQ	FLBLS	10/01-12/01
	Ocala MSA, FL	H	5.84 FQ	8.79 AW	11.89 TQ	FLBLS	10/01-12/01
	Orlando MSA, FL	H	7.23 FQ	10.19 AW	14.06 TQ	FLBLS	10/01-12/01
	Pensacola MSA, FL	H	6.08 FQ	7.82 AW	10.08 TQ	FLBLS	10/01-12/01
	Sarasota-Bradenton MSA, FL	H	5.93 FQ	8.20 AW	10.75 TQ	FLBLS	10/01-12/01
	Tallahassee MSA, FL	H	7.14 FQ	14.29 AW	25.80 TQ	FLBLS	10/01-12/01
	Tampa-St. Petersburg-Clearwater MSA, FL	H	6.14 FQ	8.87 AW	12.30 TQ	FLBLS	10/01-12/01
	West Palm Beach-Boca Raton MSA, FL	H	7.37 FQ	10.66 AW	14.62 TQ	FLBLS	10/01-12/01
	Georgia	H	6.25 FQ	9.42 AW	13.22 TQ	GABLS	10/01-12/01
	Atlanta MSA, GA	H	6.85 FQ	9.99 AW	13.80 TQ	GABLS	10/01-12/01
	Augusta-Aiken MSA, GA-SC	H	6.75 FQ	8.64 AW	11.30 TQ	GABLS	10/01-12/01
	Columbus MSA, GA-AL	H	5.85 FQ	7.90 AW	10.62 TQ	GABLS	10/01-12/01
	Macon MSA, GA	H	6.15 FQ	8.60 AW	11.43 TQ	GABLS	10/01-12/01
	Savannah MSA, GA	H	5.79 FQ	8.23 AW	11.19 TQ	GABLS	10/01-12/01
	Hawaii	H	6.77 FQ	9.87 AW	13.66 TQ	HIBLS	10/01-12/01
	Honolulu MSA, HI	H	7.21 FQ	10.11 AW	13.81 TQ	HIBLS	10/01-12/01
	Idaho	H	6.16 FQ	8.90 AW	12.45 TQ	IDBLS	10/01-12/01
	Boise City MSA, ID	H	7.17 FQ	9.82 AW	13.49 TQ	IDBLS	10/01-12/01
	Illinois	H	6.99 FQ	10.36 AW	14.93 TQ	ILBLS	10/01-12/01
	Champaign-Urbana MSA, IL	H	6.51 FQ	9.39 AW	13.27 TQ	ILBLS	10/01-12/01
	Chicago PMSA, IL	H	7.45 FQ	10.81 AW	15.51 TQ	ILBLS	10/01-12/01
	Peoria-Pekin MSA, IL	H	6.54 FQ	8.79 AW	12.10 TQ	ILBLS	10/01-12/01
	Rockford MSA, IL	H	6.83 FQ	8.97 AW	11.40 TQ	ILBLS	10/01-12/01
	Springfield MSA, IL	H	6.37 FQ	9.29 AW	12.52 TQ	ILBLS	10/01-12/01
	Indiana	H	6.60 FQ	9.24 AW	12.51 TQ	INBLS	10/01-12/01
	Elkhart-Goshen MSA, IN	H	6.75 FQ	9.09 AW	13.26 TQ	INBLS	10/01-12/01
	Evansville-Henderson MSA, IN-KY	H	6.20 FQ	8.09 AW	10.75 TQ	INBLS	10/01-12/01
	Fort Wayne MSA, IN	H	6.77 FQ	9.50 AW	13.11 TQ	INBLS	10/01-12/01
	Gary PMSA, IN	H	6.23 FQ	9.27 AW	12.95 TQ	INBLS	10/01-12/01
	Indianapolis MSA, IN	H	7.61 FQ	10.16 AW	13.46 TQ	INBLS	10/01-12/01
	Lafayette MSA, IN	H	6.13 FQ	8.65 AW	10.87 TQ	INBLS	10/01-12/01
	South Bend MSA, IN	H	6.71 FQ	9.03 AW	11.21 TQ	INBLS	10/01-12/01
	Iowa	H	6.38 FQ	9.34 AW	12.95 TQ	IABLS	10/01-12/01
	Cedar Rapids MSA, IA	H	7.44 FQ	9.85 AW	13.04 TQ	IABLS	10/01-12/01
	Davenport-Moline-Rock Island MSA, IA-IL	H	6.21 FQ	9.84 AW	13.82 TQ	IABLS	10/01-12/01
	Des Moines MSA, IA	H	7.44 FQ	9.79 AW	12.82 TQ	IABLS	10/01-12/01
	Kansas	H	5.96 FQ	9.10 AW	13.12 TQ	KSBLS	10/01-12/01
	Topeka MSA, KS	H	6.46 FQ	9.79 AW	15.11 TQ	KSBLS	10/01-12/01
	Wichita MSA, KS	H	6.76 FQ	8.87 AW	11.89 TQ	KSBLS	10/01-12/01
	Kentucky	H	6.40 FQ	8.86 AW	11.80 TQ	KYBLS	10/01-12/01
	Lexington MSA, KY	H	6.10 FQ	9.33 AW	13.12 TQ	KYBLS	10/01-12/01
	Louisville MSA, KY-IN	H	7.14 FQ	9.06 AW	11.31 TQ	KYBLS	10/01-12/01
	Louisiana	H	5.84 FQ	7.93 AW	10.60 TQ	LABLS	10/01-12/01
	Baton Rouge MSA, LA	H	6.09 FQ	8.14 AW	10.68 TQ	LABLS	10/01-12/01
	Houma MSA, LA	H	5.73 FQ	7.63 AW	10.81 TQ	LABLS	10/01-12/01
	Lafayette MSA, LA	H	6.26 FQ	7.96 AW	10.31 TQ	LABLS	10/01-12/01
	Lake Charles MSA, LA	H	5.59 FQ	6.83 AW	9.63 TQ	LABLS	10/01-12/01
	New Orleans MSA, LA	H	6.55 FQ	8.73 AW	11.66 TQ	LABLS	10/01-12/01
	Shreveport-Bossier City MSA, LA	H	5.68 FQ	8.01 AW	11.95 TQ	LABLS	10/01-12/01
	Maine	H	6.56 FQ	8.73 AW	11.21 TQ	MEBLS	10/01-12/01
	Portland MSA, ME	H	7.42 FQ	9.62 AW	12.90 TQ	MEBLS	10/01-12/01
	Maryland	H	6.09 FQ	10.61 AW	15.87 TQ	MDBLS	10/01-12/01
	Baltimore PMSA, MD	H	7.59 FQ	10.98 AW	15.23 TQ	MDBLS	10/01-12/01
	Massachusetts	H	7.46 FQ	11.17 AW	16.04 TQ	MABLS	10/01-12/01
	Boston PMSA, MA-NH	H	7.70 FQ	11.46 AW	16.45 TQ	MABLS	10/01-12/01
	Brockton PMSA, MA	H	7.26 FQ	10.42 AW	14.33 TQ	MABLS	10/01-12/01
	Lawrence PMSA, MA-NH	H	7.05 FQ	10.57 AW	14.89 TQ	MABLS	10/01-12/01
	Lowell PMSA, MA-NH	H	7.35 FQ	9.95 AW	14.46 TQ	MABLS	10/01-12/01
	New Bedford PMSA, MA	H	7.11 FQ	9.95 AW	13.24 TQ	MABLS	10/01-12/01
	Springfield MSA, MA	H	7.22 FQ	9.97 AW	13.76 TQ	MABLS	10/01-12/01
	Worcester PMSA, MA-CT	H	7.62 FQ	12.33 AW	16.84 TQ	MABLS	10/01-12/01
	Michigan	H	6.14 FQ	9.74 AW	13.97 TQ	MIBLS	10/01-12/01
	Ann Arbor PMSA, MI	H	6.40 FQ	11.03 AW	18.77 TQ	MIBLS	10/01-12/01
	Detroit PMSA, MI	H	6.00 FQ	9.84 AW	14.07 TQ	MIBLS	10/01-12/01

AAW Average annual wage **AE** Average entry wage **AEX** Average experienced wage **AO** Average offered **AOH** Average offered, high **AOL** Average offered, low **APH** Average pay, high range **APL** Average pay, low range **ASH** Average starting, high **ASL** Average starting, low **AW** Average wage paid **FQ** First quartile wage **H** Hourly **HI** Highest wage paid **HR** High end range **LR** Low end range **M** Monthly **MTC** Median total compensation **MW** Median wage paid **SQ** Second quartile wage **S** Special: hourly and annual **TQ** Third quartile wage **W** Weekly **Y** Yearly

Occupation/Type/Industry	Location	Per	Low	Mid	High	Source	Date
File Clerk	Flint PMSA, MI	H	5.81 FQ	7.86 AW	10.55 TQ	MIBLS	10/01-12/01
	Grand Rapids-Muskegon-Holland MSA, MI	H	7.61 FQ	10.48 AW	13.49 TQ	MIBLS	10/01-12/01
	Kalamazoo-Battle Creek MSA, MI	H	6.15 FQ	9.60 AW	13.86 TQ	MIBLS	10/01-12/01
	Lansing-East Lansing MSA, MI	H	6.97 FQ	10.31 AW	15.76 TQ	MIBLS	10/01-12/01
	Saginaw-Bay City-Midland MSA, MI	H	6.04 FQ	8.84 AW	12.91 TQ	MIBLS	10/01-12/01
	Minnesota	H	7.81 FQ	10.36 AW	13.52 TQ	MNBLS	10/01-12/01
	Duluth-Superior MSA, MN-WI	H	6.14 FQ	8.01 AW	10.22 TQ	MNBLS	10/01-12/01
	Minneapolis-St. Paul MSA, MN-WI	H	8.65 FQ	10.67 AW	13.78 TQ	MNBLS	10/01-12/01
	St. Cloud MSA, MN	H	7.47 FQ	9.76 AW	12.78 TQ	MNBLS	10/01-12/01
	Mississippi	H	5.86 FQ	7.86 AW	10.57 TQ	MSBLS	10/01-12/01
	Biloxi-Gulfport-Pascagoula MSA, MS	H	5.73 FQ	7.36 AW	9.66 TQ	MSBLS	10/01-12/01
	Jackson MSA, MS	H	6.06 FQ	8.47 AW	11.21 TQ	MSBLS	10/01-12/01
	Missouri	H	6.54 FQ	9.73 AW	13.71 TQ	MOBLS	10/01-12/01
	Kansas City MSA, MO-KS	H	7.43 FQ	10.62 AW	13.87 TQ	MOBLS	10/01-12/01
	St. Louis MSA, MO-IL	H	6.73 FQ	10.09 AW	14.99 TQ	MOBLS	10/01-12/01
	Springfield MSA, MO	H	5.84 FQ	7.99 AW	11.48 TQ	MOBLS	10/01-12/01
	Montana	H	5.68 FQ	7.58 AW	10.36 TQ	MTBLS	10/01-12/01
	Billings MSA, MT	H	6.08 FQ	8.57 AW	11.55 TQ	MTBLS	10/01-12/01
	Nebraska	H	6.93 FQ	9.53 AW	12.80 TQ	NEBLS	10/01-12/01
	Omaha MSA, NE-IA	H	7.18 FQ	9.76 AW	13.12 TQ	NEBLS	10/01-12/01
	Nevada	H	7.12 FQ	9.85 AW	12.76 TQ	NVBLS	10/01-12/01
	Las Vegas MSA, NV-AZ	H	7.33 FQ	9.89 AW	12.78 TQ	NVBLS	10/01-12/01
	Reno MSA, NV	H	6.41 FQ	9.74 AW	13.38 TQ	NVBLS	10/01-12/01
	New Hampshire	H	6.13 FQ	9.21 AW	12.33 TQ	NHBLS	10/01-12/01
	Manchester PMSA, NH	H	7.58 FQ	10.11 AW	12.92 TQ	NHBLS	10/01-12/01
	Nashua PMSA, NH	H	6.99 FQ	10.34 AW	14.97 TQ	NHBLS	10/01-12/01
	Portsmouth-Rochester PMSA, NH-ME	H	5.71 FQ	8.02 AW	11.47 TQ	NHBLS	10/01-12/01
	New Jersey	H	7.04 FQ	10.65 AW	15.37 TQ	NJBLS	10/01-12/01
	Atlantic-Cape May PMSA, NJ	H	6.36 FQ	9.57 AW	13.68 TQ	NJBLS	10/01-12/01
	Bergen-Passaic PMSA, NJ	H	6.39 FQ	10.25 AW	14.89 TQ	NJBLS	10/01-12/01
	Jersey City PMSA, NJ	H	6.92 FQ	9.48 AW	13.72 TQ	NJBLS	10/01-12/01
	Middlesex-Somerset-Hunterdon PMSA, NJ	H	7.70 FQ	12.11 AW	19.04 TQ	NJBLS	10/01-12/01
	Monmouth-Ocean PMSA, NJ	H	6.98 FQ	10.12 AW	14.41 TQ	NJBLS	10/01-12/01
	Newark PMSA, NJ	H	7.18 FQ	11.00 AW	14.20 TQ	NJBLS	10/01-12/01
	Trenton PMSA, NJ	H	7.38 FQ	11.81 AW	17.93 TQ	NJBLS	10/01-12/01
	New Mexico	H	6.10 FQ	8.44 AW	10.94 TQ	NMBLS	10/01-12/01
	Albuquerque MSA, NM	H	6.74 FQ	8.88 AW	11.12 TQ	NMBLS	10/01-12/01
	Las Cruces MSA, NM	H	5.40 FQ	6.47 AW	8.37 TQ	NMBLS	10/01-12/01
	New York	H	7.09 FQ	10.91 AW	16.01 TQ	NYBLS	10/01-12/01
	Albany-Schenectady-Troy MSA, NY	H	7.31 FQ	10.90 AW	15.95 TQ	NYBLS	10/01-12/01
	Binghamton MSA, NY	H	7.04 FQ	9.02 AW	12.78 TQ	NYBLS	10/01-12/01
	Buffalo-Niagara Falls MSA, NY	H	6.66 FQ	10.10 AW	15.71 TQ	NYBLS	10/01-12/01
	Dutchess County PMSA, NY	H	7.29 FQ	9.84 AW	13.16 TQ	NYBLS	10/01-12/01
	Nassau-Suffolk PMSA, NY	H	6.59 FQ	10.61 AW	15.79 TQ	NYBLS	10/01-12/01
	New York PMSA, NY	H	7.40 FQ	11.53 AW	16.47 TQ	NYBLS	10/01-12/01
	Newburgh PMSA, NY-PA	H	7.25 FQ	9.76 AW	13.39 TQ	NYBLS	10/01-12/01
	Rochester MSA, NY	H	7.04 FQ	9.52 AW	13.39 TQ	NYBLS	10/01-12/01
	Syracuse MSA, NY	H	5.98 FQ	9.11 AW	12.08 TQ	NYBLS	10/01-12/01
	Utica-Rome MSA, NY	H	6.65 FQ	9.11 AW	12.96 TQ	NYBLS	10/01-12/01
	North Carolina	H	6.29 FQ	9.39 AW	13.01 TQ	NCBLS	10/01-12/01
	Asheville MSA, NC	H	7.10 FQ	8.91 AW	11.08 TQ	NCBLS	10/01-12/01
	Charlotte-Gastonia-Rock Hill MSA, NC-SC	H	6.62 FQ	9.72 AW	13.28 TQ	NCBLS	10/01-12/01
	Fayetteville MSA, NC	H	6.27 FQ	9.24 AW	13.02 TQ	NCBLS	10/01-12/01
	Greensboro-Winston-Salem-High Point MSA, NC	H	7.37 FQ	10.15 AW	13.67 TQ	NCBLS	10/01-12/01
	Hickory-Morganton-Lenoir MSA, NC	H	7.24 FQ	8.98 AW	11.07 TQ	NCBLS	10/01-12/01
	Raleigh-Durham-Chapel Hill MSA, NC	H	7.90 FQ	10.57 AW	13.70 TQ	NCBLS	10/01-12/01
	Wilmington MSA, NC	H	6.24 FQ	9.02 AW	12.95 TQ	NCBLS	10/01-12/01
	North Dakota	H	6.15 FQ	8.64 AW	11.79 TQ	NDBLS	10/01-12/01

AAW Average annual wage; **AE** Average entry wage; **AEX** Average experienced wage; **AO** Average offered; **AOH** Average offered, high; **AOL** Average offered, low; **APH** Average pay, high range; **APL** Average pay, low range; **ASH** Average starting, high; **ASL** Average starting, low; **AW** Average wage paid; **FQ** First quartile wage; **H** Hourly; **HI** Highest wage paid; **HR** High end range; **LR** Low end range; **M** Monthly; **MTC** Median total compensation; **MW** Median wage paid; **SQ** Second quartile wage; **S** Special: hourly and annual; **TQ** Third quartile wage; **W** Weekly; **Y** Yearly

Occupation/Type/Industry	Location	Per	Low	Mid	High	Source	Date
File Clerk	Fargo-Moorhead MSA, ND-MN	H	6.80 FQ	9.56 AW	12.75 TQ	NDBLS	10/01-12/01
	Ohio	H	6.40 FQ	9.63 AW	13.68 TQ	OHBLS	10/01-12/01
	Akron PMSA, OH	H	6.23 FQ	9.19 AW	13.01 TQ	OHBLS	10/01-12/01
	Canton-Massillon MSA, OH	H	6.16 FQ	8.77 AW	12.34 TQ	OHBLS	10/01-12/01
	Cincinnati PMSA, OH-KY-IN	H	7.12 FQ	10.33 AW	14.93 TQ	OHBLS	10/01-12/01
	Cleveland-Lorain-Elyria PMSA, OH	H	6.17 FQ	9.62 AW	13.40 TQ	OHBLS	10/01-12/01
	Columbus MSA, OH	H	7.04 FQ	10.14 AW	13.82 TQ	OHBLS	10/01-12/01
	Dayton-Springfield MSA, OH	H	6.18 FQ	9.49 AW	13.57 TQ	OHBLS	10/01-12/01
	Mansfield MSA, OH	H	7.09 FQ	10.88 AW	16.07 TQ	OHBLS	10/01-12/01
	Toledo MSA, OH	H	6.14 FQ	8.61 AW	11.71 TQ	OHBLS	10/01-12/01
	Youngstown-Warren MSA, OH	H	6.00 FQ	8.29 AW	11.22 TQ	OHBLS	10/01-12/01
	Oklahoma	H	6.06 FQ	9.31 AW	13.96 TQ	OKBLS	10/01-12/01
	Oklahoma City MSA, OK	H	6.32 FQ	10.17 AW	15.84 TQ	OKBLS	10/01-12/01
	Tulsa MSA, OK	H	6.27 FQ	9.25 AW	13.32 TQ	OKBLS	10/01-12/01
	Oregon	H	7.05 FQ	9.96 AW	13.87 TQ	ORBLS	10/01-12/01
	Eugene-Springfield MSA, OR	H	7.48 FQ	9.95 AW	13.35 TQ	ORBLS	10/01-12/01
	Medford-Ashland MSA, OR	H	7.09 FQ	9.89 AW	15.85 TQ	ORBLS	10/01-12/01
	Portland-Vancouver PMSA, OR-WA	H	7.14 FQ	10.27 AW	13.98 TQ	ORBLS	10/01-12/01
	Salem PMSA, OR	H	7.16 FQ	9.25 AW	11.43 TQ	ORBLS	10/01-12/01
	Pennsylvania	H	6.19 FQ	9.26 AW	12.98 TQ	PABLS	10/01-12/01
	Allentown-Bethlehem-Easton MSA, PA	H	6.53 FQ	9.25 AW	12.47 TQ	PABLS	10/01-12/01
	Erie MSA, PA	H	6.29 FQ	8.46 AW	11.39 TQ	PABLS	10/01-12/01
	Harrisburg-Lebanon-Carlisle MSA, PA	H	7.35 FQ	9.87 AW	12.49 TQ	PABLS	10/01-12/01
	Johnstown MSA, PA	H	6.19 FQ	9.12 AW	12.08 TQ	PABLS	10/01-12/01
	Lancaster MSA, PA	H	6.43 FQ	10.76 AW	13.15 TQ	PABLS	10/01-12/01
	Philadelphia PMSA, PA-NJ	H	6.17 FQ	9.31 AW	13.11 TQ	PABLS	10/01-12/01
	Pittsburgh MSA, PA	H	6.47 FQ	9.47 AW	13.01 TQ	PABLS	10/01-12/01
	Reading MSA, PA	H	6.45 FQ	8.95 AW	12.54 TQ	PABLS	10/01-12/01
	Scranton-Wilkes-Barre-Hazleton MSA, PA	H	6.67 FQ	8.80 AW	11.46 TQ	PABLS	10/01-12/01
	York MSA, PA	H	6.77 FQ	9.30 AW	13.08 TQ	PABLS	10/01-12/01
	Rhode Island	H	7.37 FQ	10.82 AW	15.79 TQ	RIBLS	10/01-12/01
	Providence-Fall River-Warwick MSA, RI-MA	H	7.33 FQ	10.74 AW	15.62 TQ	RIBLS	10/01-12/01
	South Carolina	H	6.22 FQ	9.15 AW	12.64 TQ	SCBLS	10/01-12/01
	Charleston-North Charleston MSA, SC	H	6.06 FQ	8.26 AW	10.72 TQ	SCBLS	10/01-12/01
	Columbia MSA, SC	H	6.51 FQ	9.38 AW	12.97 TQ	SCBLS	10/01-12/01
	Greenville-Spartanburg-Anderson MSA, SC	H	6.54 FQ	9.38 AW	12.67 TQ	SCBLS	10/01-12/01
	Myrtle Beach MSA, SC	H	7.58 FQ	9.63 AW	12.39 TQ	SCBLS	10/01-12/01
	South Dakota	H	7.06 FQ	8.70 AW	11.23 TQ	SDBLS	10/01-12/01
	Sioux Falls MSA, SD	H	7.36 FQ	8.97 AW	11.65 TQ	SDBLS	10/01-12/01
	Tennessee	H	6.30 FQ	8.90 AW	12.28 TQ	TNBLS	10/01-12/01
	Chattanooga MSA, TN-GA	H	7.33 FQ	9.57 AW	13.00 TQ	TNBLS	10/01-12/01
	Clarksville-Hopkinsville MSA, TN-KY	H	5.66 FQ	7.32 AW	9.83 TQ	TNBLS	10/01-12/01
	Johnson City-Kingsport-Bristol MSA, TN-VA	H	6.06 FQ	9.14 AW	13.30 TQ	TNBLS	10/01-12/01
	Knoxville MSA, TN	H	6.33 FQ	8.55 AW	11.40 TQ	TNBLS	10/01-12/01
	Memphis MSA, TN-AR-MS	H	6.25 FQ	8.85 AW	11.91 TQ	TNBLS	10/01-12/01
	Nashville MSA, TN	H	6.76 FQ	9.90 AW	13.65 TQ	TNBLS	10/01-12/01
	Texas	H	6.26 FQ	9.52 AW	13.87 TQ	TXBLS	10/01-12/01
	Amarillo MSA, TX	H	6.15 FQ	8.44 AW	11.03 TQ	TXBLS	10/01-12/01
	Austin-San Marcos MSA, TX	H	7.03 FQ	10.09 AW	14.53 TQ	TXBLS	10/01-12/01
	Beaumont-Port Arthur MSA, TX	H	5.51 FQ	7.30 AW	10.66 TQ	TXBLS	10/01-12/01
	Brazoria PMSA, TX	H	5.83 FQ	8.38 AW	13.15 TQ	TXBLS	10/01-12/01
	Brownsville-Harlingen-San Benito MSA, TX	H	5.83 FQ	7.57 AW	10.45 TQ	TXBLS	10/01-12/01
	Corpus Christi MSA, TX	H	6.24 FQ	9.61 AW	15.15 TQ	TXBLS	10/01-12/01
	Dallas PMSA, TX	H	7.19 FQ	10.46 AW	14.58 TQ	TXBLS	10/01-12/01
	El Paso MSA, TX	H	5.85 FQ	8.16 AW	11.10 TQ	TXBLS	10/01-12/01
	Fort Worth-Arlington PMSA, TX	H	6.71 FQ	9.88 AW	14.39 TQ	TXBLS	10/01-12/01
	Galveston-Texas City PMSA, TX	H	6.18 FQ	8.99 AW	12.38 TQ	TXBLS	10/01-12/01

AAW	Average annual wage	**AOH**	Average offered, high	**ASH**	Average starting, high	**H**	Hourly	**M**	Monthly	**S**	Special: hourly and annual
AE	Average entry wage	**AOL**	Average offered, low	**ASL**	Average starting, low	**HI**	Highest wage paid	**MTC**	Median total compensation	**TQ**	Third quartile wage
AEX	Average experienced wage	**APH**	Average pay, high range	**AW**	Average wage paid	**HR**	High end range	**MW**	Median wage paid	**W**	Weekly
AO	Average offered	**APL**	Average pay, low range	**FQ**	First quartile wage	**LR**	Low end range	**SQ**	Second quartile wage	**Y**	Yearly

Occupation/Type/Industry	Location	Per	Low	Mid	High	Source	Date
File Clerk	Houston PMSA, TX	H	7.07 FQ	10.15 AW	14.84 TQ	TXBLS	10/01-12/01
	Killeen-Temple MSA, TX	H	6.06 FQ	9.02 AW	13.32 TQ	TXBLS	10/01-12/01
	Laredo MSA, TX	H	5.78 FQ	7.51 AW	10.85 TQ	TXBLS	10/01-12/01
	Longview-Marshall MSA, TX	H	5.83 FQ	7.98 AW	11.32 TQ	TXBLS	10/01-12/01
	Lubbock MSA, TX	H	5.57 FQ	7.57 AW	10.45 TQ	TXBLS	10/01-12/01
	McAllen-Edinburg-Mission MSA, TX	H	6.08 FQ	8.33 AW	11.08 TQ	TXBLS	10/01-12/01
	Odessa-Midland MSA, TX	H	6.14 FQ	8.84 AW	12.86 TQ	TXBLS	10/01-12/01
	San Antonio MSA, TX	H	6.01 FQ	8.76 AW	12.52 TQ	TXBLS	10/01-12/01
	Tyler MSA, TX	H	6.24 FQ	8.90 AW	12.24 TQ	TXBLS	10/01-12/01
	Waco MSA, TX	H	5.98 FQ	9.18 AW	13.53 TQ	TXBLS	10/01-12/01
	Utah	H	6.61 FQ	9.59 AW	13.33 TQ	UTBLS	10/01-12/01
	Provo-Orem MSA, UT	H	6.46 FQ	8.82 AW	11.96 TQ	UTBLS	10/01-12/01
	Salt Lake City-Ogden MSA, UT	H	7.15 FQ	10.00 AW	13.57 TQ	UTBLS	10/01-12/01
	Vermont	H	7.16 FQ	9.57 AW	12.41 TQ	VTBLS	10/01-12/01
	Burlington MSA, VT	H	7.28 FQ	9.88 AW	12.84 TQ	VTBLS	10/01-12/01
	Virginia	H	6.57 FQ	10.10 AW	14.38 TQ	VABLS	10/01-12/01
	Lynchburg MSA, VA	H	6.13 FQ	9.12 AW	12.46 TQ	VABLS	10/01-12/01
	Norfolk-Virginia Beach-Newport News MSA, VA-NC	H	6.39 FQ	8.91 AW	11.57 TQ	VABLS	10/01-12/01
	Richmond-Petersburg MSA, VA	H	6.28 FQ	9.19 AW	12.90 TQ	VABLS	10/01-12/01
	Roanoke MSA, VA	H	7.01 FQ	9.48 AW	13.57 TQ	VABLS	10/01-12/01
	Washington	H	7.20 FQ	10.41 AW	14.47 TQ	WABLS	10/01-12/01
	Bremerton PMSA, WA	H	7.04 FQ	8.79 AW	11.25 TQ	WABLS	10/01-12/01
	Olympia PMSA, WA	H	7.52 FQ	9.25 AW	11.22 TQ	WABLS	10/01-12/01
	Richland-Kennewick-Pasco MSA, WA	H	6.97 FQ	9.96 AW	17.67 TQ	WABLS	10/01-12/01
	Seattle-Bellevue-Everett PMSA, WA	H	7.86 FQ	11.33 AW	16.03 TQ	WABLS	10/01-12/01
	Spokane MSA, WA	H	7.01 FQ	8.47 AW	10.49 TQ	WABLS	10/01-12/01
	Tacoma PMSA, WA	H	7.09 FQ	10.25 AW	13.60 TQ	WABLS	10/01-12/01
	Yakima MSA, WA	H	6.97 FQ	10.02 AW	15.59 TQ	WABLS	10/01-12/01
	West Virginia	H	5.79 FQ	8.49 AW	12.95 TQ	WVBLS	10/01-12/01
	Charleston MSA, WV	H	5.87 FQ	8.69 AW	12.47 TQ	WVBLS	10/01-12/01
	Huntington-Ashland MSA, WV-KY-OH	H	5.91 FQ	8.85 AW	13.28 TQ	WVBLS	10/01-12/01
	Wisconsin	H	6.83 FQ	9.65 AW	13.18 TQ	WIBLS	10/01-12/01
	Appleton-Oshkosh-Neenah MSA, WI	H	7.38 FQ	9.97 AW	13.14 TQ	WIBLS	10/01-12/01
	Green Bay MSA, WI	H	7.62 FQ	10.34 AW	15.76 TQ	WIBLS	10/01-12/01
	Madison MSA, WI	H	6.44 FQ	9.43 AW	13.47 TQ	WIBLS	10/01-12/01
	Milwaukee-Waukesha PMSA, WI	H	7.40 FQ	10.20 AW	13.56 TQ	WIBLS	10/01-12/01
	Racine PMSA, WI	H	6.34 FQ	9.48 AW	13.10 TQ	WIBLS	10/01-12/01
	Wyoming	H	5.76 FQ	8.27 AW	12.61 TQ	WYBLS	10/01-12/01
	Cheyenne MSA, WY	H	5.69 FQ	8.20 AW	13.50 TQ	WYBLS	10/01-12/01
	Puerto Rico	H	5.69 FQ	7.28 AW	10.12 TQ	PRBLS	10/01-12/01
	Virgin Islands	H	5.86 FQ	7.76 AW	9.92 TQ	VIBLS	10/01-12/01
	Guam	H	5.79 FQ	8.44 AW	11.65 TQ	GUBLS	10/01-12/01
Financial Analyst	Alabama	Y	29410 FQ	46710 AW	70020 TQ	ALBLS	10/01-12/01
	Birmingham MSA, AL	Y	29260 FQ	45700 AW	69970 TQ	ALBLS	10/01-12/01
	Huntsville MSA, AL	Y	32640 FQ	47980 AW	63920 TQ	ALBLS	10/01-12/01
	Mobile MSA, AL	Y	27320 FQ	50400 AW	95580 TQ	ALBLS	10/01-12/01
	Montgomery MSA, AL	Y	33210 FQ	49910 AW	64300 TQ	ALBLS	10/01-12/01
	Alaska	Y	37320 FQ	57820 AW	80440 TQ	AKBLS	10/01-12/01
	Anchorage MSA, AK	Y	41740 FQ	57560 AW	72860 TQ	AKBLS	10/01-12/01
	Arizona	Y	27250 FQ	50710 AW	75660 TQ	AZBLS	10/01-12/01
	Phoenix-Mesa MSA, AZ	Y	26260 FQ	50230 AW	76230 TQ	AZBLS	10/01-12/01
	Tucson MSA, AZ	Y	33140 FQ	53770 AW	73750 TQ	AZBLS	10/01-12/01
	Arkansas	Y	28560 FQ	52750 AW	85930 TQ	ARBLS	10/01-12/01
	Fayetteville-Springdale-Rogers MSA, AR	Y	29210 FQ	64690 AW	111600 TQ	ARBLS	10/01-12/01
	Little Rock-North Little Rock MSA, AR	Y	28460 FQ	48410 AW	73490 TQ	ARBLS	10/01-12/01
	California	Y	38720 FQ	66060 AW	103630 TQ	CABLS	10/01-12/01
	Bakersfield MSA, CA	Y	32950 FQ	57620 AW	88540 TQ	CABLS	10/01-12/01
	Fresno MSA, CA	Y	29940 FQ	58530 AW	97530 TQ	CABLS	10/01-12/01
	Los Angeles-Long Beach PMSA, CA	Y	38590 FQ	65830 AW	107520 TQ	CABLS	10/01-12/01

AAW	Average annual wage	AOH	Average offered, high	ASH	Average starting, high	H	Hourly	M	Monthly	S	Special: hourly and annual
AE	Average entry wage	AOL	Average offered, low	ASL	Average starting, low	HI	Highest wage paid	MTC	Median total compensation	TQ	Third quartile wage
AEX	Average experienced wage	APH	Average pay, high range	AW	Average wage paid	HR	High end range	MW	Median wage paid	W	Weekly
AO	Average offered	APL	Average pay, low range	FQ	First quartile wage	LR	Low end range	SQ	Second quartile wage	Y	Yearly

Occupation/Type/Industry	Location	Per	Low	Mid	High	Source	Date
Financial Analyst	Oakland PMSA, CA	Y	39640 FQ	63710 AW	89120 TQ	CABLS	10/01-12/01
	Orange County PMSA, CA	Y	39290 FQ	63610 AW	100640 TQ	CABLS	10/01-12/01
	Riverside-San Bernardino PMSA, CA	Y	29060 FQ	49390 AW	82340 TQ	CABLS	10/01-12/01
	Sacramento PMSA, CA	Y	38600 FQ	59530 AW	85380 TQ	CABLS	10/01-12/01
	Salinas MSA, CA	Y	37100 FQ	59470 AW	83710 TQ	CABLS	10/01-12/01
	San Diego MSA, CA	Y	36250 FQ	62730 AW	112190 TQ	CABLS	10/01-12/01
	San Francisco PMSA, CA	Y	42760 FQ	71860 AW	114870 TQ	CABLS	10/01-12/01
	San Jose PMSA, CA	Y	46290 FQ	76150 AW	132950 TQ	CABLS	10/01-12/01
	Santa Barbara-Santa Maria-Lompoc MSA, CA	Y	36960 FQ	62770 AW	94270 TQ	CABLS	10/01-12/01
	Santa Cruz-Watsonville PMSA, CA	Y	29540 FQ	57760 AW	92690 TQ	CABLS	10/01-12/01
	Santa Rosa PMSA, CA	Y	42760 FQ	67410 AW	99780 TQ	CABLS	10/01-12/01
	Vallejo-Fairfield-Napa PMSA, CA	Y	46900 FQ	64310 AW	85480 TQ	CABLS	10/01-12/01
	Ventura PMSA, CA	Y	39350 FQ	58580 AW	79720 TQ	CABLS	10/01-12/01
	Colorado	Y	35050 FQ	62360 AW	109270 TQ	COBLS	10/01-12/01
	Boulder-Longmont PMSA, CO	Y	37120 FQ	64300 AW	105490 TQ	COBLS	10/01-12/01
	Colorado Springs MSA, CO	Y	37150 FQ	64320 AW	90780 TQ	COBLS	10/01-12/01
	Denver PMSA, CO	Y	34280 FQ	61890 AW	121950 TQ	COBLS	10/01-12/01
	Fort Collins-Loveland MSA, CO	Y	49110 FQ	67280 AW	93660 TQ	COBLS	10/01-12/01
	Greeley PMSA, CO	Y	40350 FQ	67630 AW	123770 TQ	COBLS	10/01-12/01
	Connecticut	Y	36800 FQ	72120 AW		CTBLS	10/01-12/01
	Bridgeport PMSA, CT	Y	39210 FQ	66630 AW	117640 TQ	CTBLS	10/01-12/01
	Danbury PMSA, CT	Y	39920 FQ	70290 AW		CTBLS	10/01-12/01
	Hartford MSA, CT	Y	33000 FQ	53700 AW	78040 TQ	CTBLS	10/01-12/01
	New Haven-Meriden PMSA, CT	Y	38060 FQ	62520 AW	108520 TQ	CTBLS	10/01-12/01
	New London-Norwich MSA, CT-RI	Y	40410 FQ	61180 AW	92960 TQ	CTBLS	10/01-12/01
	Stamford-Norwalk PMSA, CT	Y	41400 FQ	93020 AW		CTBLS	10/01-12/01
	Waterbury PMSA, CT	Y	35140 FQ	68880 AW	102520 TQ	CTBLS	10/01-12/01
	Delaware	Y	30870 FQ	60290 AW	109130 TQ	DEBLS	10/01-12/01
	Wilmington-Newark PMSA, DE-MD	Y	30600 FQ	57220 AW	96120 TQ	DEBLS	10/01-12/01
	District of Columbia	Y	42620 FQ	68610 AW	107560 TQ	DCBLS	10/01-12/01
	Washington PMSA, DC-MD-VA-WV	Y	38710 FQ	62520 AW	94210 TQ	DCBLS	10/01-12/01
	Florida	Y	29460 FQ	52660 AW	85940 TQ	FLBLS	10/01-12/01
	Fort Lauderdale PMSA, FL	Y	27520 FQ	58140 AW	92480 TQ	FLBLS	10/01-12/01
	Fort Myers-Cape Coral MSA, FL	Y	32880 FQ	58140 AW	87320 TQ	FLBLS	10/01-12/01
	Fort Pierce-Port St. Lucie MSA, FL	Y	30040 FQ	45250 AW	58200 TQ	FLBLS	10/01-12/01
	Gainesville MSA, FL	Y	32580 FQ	48310 AW	68420 TQ	FLBLS	10/01-12/01
	Jacksonville MSA, FL	Y	29940 FQ	51320 AW	81770 TQ	FLBLS	10/01-12/01
	Lakeland-Winter Haven MSA, FL	Y	23280 FQ	42290 AW	61550 TQ	FLBLS	10/01-12/01
	Melbourne-Titusville-Palm Bay MSA, FL	Y	32490 FQ	51220 AW	77390 TQ	FLBLS	10/01-12/01
	Miami PMSA, FL	Y	32030 FQ	55040 AW	85780 TQ	FLBLS	10/01-12/01
	Orlando MSA, FL	Y	31300 FQ	52450 AW	87180 TQ	FLBLS	10/01-12/01
	Pensacola MSA, FL	Y	34600 FQ	54220 AW	79500 TQ	FLBLS	10/01-12/01
	Sarasota-Bradenton MSA, FL	Y	31570 FQ	53110 AW	83250 TQ	FLBLS	10/01-12/01
	Tallahassee MSA, FL	Y	28350 FQ	63630 AW	110350 TQ	FLBLS	10/01-12/01
	Tampa-St. Petersburg-Clearwater MSA, FL	Y	26600 FQ	46850 AW	77060 TQ	FLBLS	10/01-12/01
	West Palm Beach-Boca Raton MSA, FL	Y	30400 FQ	53290 AW	95250 TQ	FLBLS	10/01-12/01
	Georgia	Y	33150 FQ	58910 AW	94530 TQ	GABLS	10/01-12/01
	Atlanta MSA, GA	Y	34160 FQ	61160 AW	99020 TQ	GABLS	10/01-12/01
	Augusta-Aiken MSA, GA-SC	Y	25430 FQ	51950 AW	74320 TQ	GABLS	10/01-12/01
	Columbus MSA, GA-AL	Y	30390 FQ	47130 AW	66920 TQ	GABLS	10/01-12/01
	Macon MSA, GA	Y	35670 FQ	59160 AW	87980 TQ	GABLS	10/01-12/01
	Savannah MSA, GA	Y	36800 FQ	47830 AW	70390 TQ	GABLS	10/01-12/01
	Hawaii	Y	33680 FQ	54520 AW	77410 TQ	HIBLS	10/01-12/01
	Honolulu MSA, HI	Y	33790 FQ	53820 AW	76640 TQ	HIBLS	10/01-12/01
	Idaho	Y	28830 FQ	64090 AW		IDBLS	10/01-12/01
	Boise City MSA, ID	Y	27450 FQ	67180 AW		IDBLS	10/01-12/01
	Illinois	Y	30000 FQ	58960 AW	103460 TQ	ILBLS	10/01-12/01

AAW	Average annual wage	**AOH**	Average offered, high	**ASH**	Average starting, high	**H**	Hourly	**M**	Monthly	**S**	Special: hourly and annual
AE	Average entry wage	**AOL**	Average offered, low	**ASL**	Average starting, low	**HI**	Highest wage paid	**MTC**	Median total compensation	**TQ**	Third quartile wage
AEX	Average experienced wage	**APH**	Average pay, high range	**AW**	Average wage paid	**HR**	High end range	**MW**	Median wage paid	**W**	Weekly
AO	Average offered	**APL**	Average pay, low range	**FQ**	First quartile wage	**LR**	Low end range	**SQ**	Second quartile wage	**Y**	Yearly

Occupation/Type/Industry	Location	Per	Low	Mid	High	Source	Date
Financial Analyst	Champaign-Urbana MSA, IL	Y	20150 FQ	50570 AW	81870 TQ	ILBLS	10/01-12/01
	Chicago PMSA, IL	Y	29910 FQ	59180 AW	105100 TQ	ILBLS	10/01-12/01
	Peoria-Pekin MSA, IL	Y	21000 FQ	58620 AW	127080 TQ	ILBLS	10/01-12/01
	Rockford MSA, IL	Y	28220 FQ	64210 AW	116670 TQ	ILBLS	10/01-12/01
	Springfield MSA, IL	Y	28350 FQ	54760 AW	83800 TQ	ILBLS	10/01-12/01
	Indiana	Y	32590 FQ	59390 AW	90930 TQ	INBLS	10/01-12/01
	Evansville-Henderson MSA, IN-KY	Y	31790 FQ	54060 AW	78430 TQ	INBLS	10/01-12/01
	Fort Wayne MSA, IN	Y	31420 FQ	56410 AW	87070 TQ	INBLS	10/01-12/01
	Gary PMSA, IN	Y	35170 FQ	54390 AW	71190 TQ	INBLS	10/01-12/01
	Indianapolis MSA, IN	Y	37000 FQ	63230 AW	100300 TQ	INBLS	10/01-12/01
	South Bend MSA, IN	Y	30220 FQ	53400 AW	78330 TQ	INBLS	10/01-12/01
	Iowa	Y	29170 FQ	48790 AW	75330 TQ	IABLS	10/01-12/01
	Davenport-Moline-Rock Island MSA, IA-IL	Y	25700 FQ	53750 AW	88010 TQ	IABLS	10/01-12/01
	Des Moines MSA, IA	Y	31010 FQ	49750 AW	75270 TQ	IABLS	10/01-12/01
	Kansas	Y	29580 FQ	47080 AW	69570 TQ	KSBLS	10/01-12/01
	Topeka MSA, KS	Y	34390 FQ	49220 AW	70430 TQ	KSBLS	10/01-12/01
	Wichita MSA, KS	Y	33280 FQ	51420 AW	79950 TQ	KSBLS	10/01-12/01
	Kentucky	Y	30670 FQ	52150 AW	82590 TQ	KYBLS	10/01-12/01
	Louisville MSA, KY-IN	Y	30170 FQ	52530 AW	86600 TQ	KYBLS	10/01-12/01
	Louisiana	Y	25280 FQ	52230 AW	87990 TQ	LABLS	10/01-12/01
	Baton Rouge MSA, LA	Y	23910 FQ	45950 AW	73350 TQ	LABLS	10/01-12/01
	Lafayette MSA, LA	Y	36860 FQ	57660 AW	71580 TQ	LABLS	10/01-12/01
	Lake Charles MSA, LA	Y	34280 FQ	70090 AW	110570 TQ	LABLS	10/01-12/01
	New Orleans MSA, LA	Y	31830 FQ	60180 AW	96320 TQ	LABLS	10/01-12/01
	Shreveport-Bossier City MSA, LA	Y	33150 FQ	51060 AW	80450 TQ	LABLS	10/01-12/01
	Maine	Y	27170 FQ	51800 AW	79760 TQ	MEBLS	10/01-12/01
	Portland MSA, ME	Y	26840 FQ	48040 AW	76930 TQ	MEBLS	10/01-12/01
	Maryland	Y	38430 FQ	51700 AW	69840 TQ	MDBLS	10/01-12/01
	Baltimore PMSA, MD	Y	38930 FQ	50640 AW	61250 TQ	MDBLS	10/01-12/01
	Massachusetts	Y	36790 FQ	66760 AW	123410 TQ	MABLS	10/01-12/01
	Boston PMSA, MA-NH	Y	36460 FQ	67340 AW	131130 TQ	MABLS	10/01-12/01
	Brockton PMSA, MA	Y	40740 FQ	62640 AW	86690 TQ	MABLS	10/01-12/01
	Lawrence PMSA, MA-NH	Y	39930 FQ	64450 AW	93360 TQ	MABLS	10/01-12/01
	Lowell PMSA, MA-NH	Y	33130 FQ	60350 AW	87930 TQ	MABLS	10/01-12/01
	Worcester PMSA, MA-CT	Y	34770 FQ	65430 AW	107790 TQ	MABLS	10/01-12/01
	Michigan	Y	36370 FQ	63320 AW	102600 TQ	MIBLS	10/01-12/01
	Ann Arbor PMSA, MI	Y	32400 FQ	50320 AW	69740 TQ	MIBLS	10/01-12/01
	Detroit PMSA, MI	Y	39330 FQ	68410 AW	109600 TQ	MIBLS	10/01-12/01
	Flint PMSA, MI	Y	39800 FQ	57170 AW	73020 TQ	MIBLS	10/01-12/01
	Grand Rapids-Muskegon-Holland MSA, MI	Y	30560 FQ	61380 AW	110700 TQ	MIBLS	10/01-12/01
	Kalamazoo-Battle Creek MSA, MI	Y	27680 FQ	45850 AW	72810 TQ	MIBLS	10/01-12/01
	Saginaw-Bay City-Midland MSA, MI	Y	33600 FQ	55930 AW	80740 TQ	MIBLS	10/01-12/01
	Minnesota	Y	37590 FQ	63540 AW	105790 TQ	MNBLS	10/01-12/01
	Duluth-Superior MSA, MN-WI	Y	38820 FQ	61170 AW	88210 TQ	MNBLS	10/01-12/01
	Minneapolis-St. Paul MSA, MN-WI	Y	37450 FQ	64070 AW	111580 TQ	MNBLS	10/01-12/01
	St. Cloud MSA, MN	Y	35450 FQ	62400 AW	95110 TQ	MNBLS	10/01-12/01
	Biloxi-Gulfport-Pascagoula MSA, MS	Y	29390 FQ	51730 AW	86410 TQ	MSBLS	10/01-12/01
	Missouri	Y	28370 FQ	54720 AW	91000 TQ	MOBLS	10/01-12/01
	Kansas City MSA, MO-KS	Y	30290 FQ	51400 AW	78800 TQ	MOBLS	10/01-12/01
	St. Louis MSA, MO-IL	Y	27900 FQ	53550 AW	88200 TQ	MOBLS	10/01-12/01
	Springfield MSA, MO	Y	30230 FQ	48010 AW	83020 TQ	MOBLS	10/01-12/01
	Montana	Y	26930 FQ	40330 AW	60750 TQ	MTBLS	10/01-12/01
	Nebraska	Y	25140 FQ	50240 AW	83760 TQ	NEBLS	10/01-12/01
	Lincoln MSA, NE	Y	13750 FQ	38520 AW	59080 TQ	NEBLS	10/01-12/01
	Omaha MSA, NE-IA	Y	26120 FQ	50180 AW	81050 TQ	NEBLS	10/01-12/01
	Nevada	Y	26650 FQ	48320 AW	79200 TQ	NVBLS	10/01-12/01
	Las Vegas MSA, NV-AZ	Y	27310 FQ	52350 AW	86130 TQ	NVBLS	10/01-12/01
	Reno MSA, NV	Y	25990 FQ	40930 AW	60850 TQ	NVBLS	10/01-12/01
	New Hampshire	Y	33070 FQ	60110 AW	105660 TQ	NHBLS	10/01-12/01
	Manchester PMSA, NH	Y	32870 FQ	55660 AW	106050 TQ	NHBLS	10/01-12/01
	Nashua PMSA, NH	Y	38240 FQ	65560 AW	105420 TQ	NHBLS	10/01-12/01
	Portsmouth-Rochester PMSA, NH-ME	Y	35020 FQ	67150 AW	115330 TQ	NHBLS	10/01-12/01
	New Jersey	Y	38800 FQ	65000 AW	101370 TQ	NJBLS	10/01-12/01

AAW Average annual wage · AE Average entry wage · AEX Average experienced wage · AO Average offered · AOH Average offered, high · AOL Average offered, low · APH Average pay, high range · APL Average pay, low range · ASH Average starting, high · ASL Average starting, low · AW Average wage paid · FQ First quartile wage · H Hourly · HI Highest wage paid · HR High end range · LR Low end range · M Monthly · MTC Median total compensation · MW Median wage paid · SQ Second quartile wage · S Special: hourly and annual · TQ Third quartile wage · W Weekly · Y Yearly

Occupation/Type/Industry	Location	Per	Low	Mid	High	Source	Date
Financial Analyst	Atlantic-Cape May PMSA, NJ	Y	31550 FQ	50040 AW	70140 TQ	NJBLS	10/01-12/01
	Bergen-Passaic PMSA, NJ	Y	39330 FQ	62650 AW	91520 TQ	NJBLS	10/01-12/01
	Jersey City PMSA, NJ	Y	39740 FQ	67550 AW	107660 TQ	NJBLS	10/01-12/01
	Middlesex-Somerset-Hunterdon PMSA, NJ	Y	42790 FQ	65450 AW	90670 TQ	NJBLS	10/01-12/01
	Monmouth-Ocean PMSA, NJ	Y	36140 FQ	65580 AW	111600 TQ	NJBLS	10/01-12/01
	Newark PMSA, NJ	Y	36890 FQ	65940 AW	110480 TQ	NJBLS	10/01-12/01
	Trenton PMSA, NJ	Y	37500 FQ	58730 AW	90750 TQ	NJBLS	10/01-12/01
	New Mexico	Y	26330 FQ	47670 AW	72900 TQ	NMBLS	10/01-12/01
	Albuquerque MSA, NM	Y	28370 FQ	49890 AW	74450 TQ	NMBLS	10/01-12/01
	New York	Y	41780 FQ	79970 AW		NYBLS	10/01-12/01
	Albany-Schenectady-Troy MSA, NY	Y	32200 FQ	59440 AW	98300 TQ	NYBLS	10/01-12/01
	Binghamton MSA, NY	Y	36640 FQ	60450 AW	92480 TQ	NYBLS	10/01-12/01
	Buffalo-Niagara Falls MSA, NY	Y	31840 FQ	53430 AW	81180 TQ	NYBLS	10/01-12/01
	Nassau-Suffolk PMSA, NY	Y	33150 FQ	57440 AW	88480 TQ	NYBLS	10/01-12/01
	New York PMSA, NY	Y	45090 FQ	85500 AW		NYBLS	10/01-12/01
	Newburgh PMSA, NY-PA	Y	40410 FQ	65200 AW	92030 TQ	NYBLS	10/01-12/01
	Rochester MSA, NY	Y	37530 FQ	58850 AW	89930 TQ	NYBLS	10/01-12/01
	Syracuse MSA, NY	Y	31350 FQ	52610 AW	77020 TQ	NYBLS	10/01-12/01
	North Carolina	Y	31980 FQ	61020 AW	110300 TQ	NCBLS	10/01-12/01
	Asheville MSA, NC	Y	35920 FQ	59310 AW	89890 TQ	NCBLS	10/01-12/01
	Charlotte-Gastonia-Rock Hill MSA, NC-SC	Y	30730 FQ	64400 AW	128680 TQ	NCBLS	10/01-12/01
	Greensboro-Winston-Salem-High Point MSA, NC	Y	31200 FQ	49720 AW	74620 TQ	NCBLS	10/01-12/01
	Hickory-Morganton-Lenoir MSA, NC	Y	33990 FQ	57790 AW	89060 TQ	NCBLS	10/01-12/01
	Raleigh-Durham-Chapel Hill MSA, NC	Y	36870 FQ	64880 AW	106040 TQ	NCBLS	10/01-12/01
	Wilmington MSA, NC	Y	35240 FQ	46180 AW	61750 TQ	NCBLS	10/01-12/01
	North Dakota	Y	34680 FQ	49530 AW	71340 TQ	NDBLS	10/01-12/01
	Fargo-Moorhead MSA, ND-MN	Y	37550 FQ	52590 AW	73610 TQ	NDBLS	10/01-12/01
	Ohio	Y	32170 FQ	53940 AW	84320 TQ	OHBLS	10/01-12/01
	Akron PMSA, OH	Y	29730 FQ	53280 AW	89230 TQ	OHBLS	10/01-12/01
	Cincinnati PMSA, OH-KY-IN	Y	30870 FQ	52660 AW	82110 TQ	OHBLS	10/01-12/01
	Cleveland-Lorain-Elyria PMSA, OH	Y	32130 FQ	55620 AW	87400 TQ	OHBLS	10/01-12/01
	Columbus MSA, OH	Y	33550 FQ	51630 AW	76210 TQ	OHBLS	10/01-12/01
	Dayton-Springfield MSA, OH	Y	33700 FQ	51270 AW	80250 TQ	OHBLS	10/01-12/01
	Hamilton-Middletown PMSA, OH	Y	32440 FQ	51230 AW	74880 TQ	OHBLS	10/01-12/01
	Toledo MSA, OH	Y	32910 FQ	55120 AW		OHBLS	10/01-12/01
	Oklahoma	Y	26580 FQ	49370 AW	85690 TQ	OKBLS	10/01-12/01
	Oklahoma City MSA, OK	Y	16690 FQ	41120 AW	57750 TQ	OKBLS	10/01-12/01
	Tulsa MSA, OK	Y	29250 FQ	48280 AW	70240 TQ	OKBLS	10/01-12/01
	Oregon	Y	36420 FQ	65020 AW	113020 TQ	ORBLS	10/01-12/01
	Eugene-Springfield MSA, OR	Y	33000 FQ	54370 AW	81520 TQ	ORBLS	10/01-12/01
	Medford-Ashland MSA, OR	Y	28060 FQ	71430 AW		ORBLS	10/01-12/01
	Portland-Vancouver PMSA, OR-WA	Y	36630 FQ	65490 AW	113940 TQ	ORBLS	10/01-12/01
	Pennsylvania	Y	26220 FQ	52900 AW	90050 TQ	PABLS	10/01-12/01
	Allentown-Bethlehem-Easton MSA, PA	Y	32160 FQ	51020 AW	75110 TQ	PABLS	10/01-12/01
	Erie MSA, PA	Y	28670 FQ	46810 AW	71830 TQ	PABLS	10/01-12/01
	Harrisburg-Lebanon-Carlisle MSA, PA	Y	32100 FQ	53260 AW	78880 TQ	PABLS	10/01-12/01
	Lancaster MSA, PA	Y	31020 FQ	48550 AW	78240 TQ	PABLS	10/01-12/01
	Philadelphia PMSA, PA-NJ	Y	23920 FQ	54680 AW	95030 TQ	PABLS	10/01-12/01
	Pittsburgh MSA, PA	Y	28110 FQ	56540 AW	104600 TQ	PABLS	10/01-12/01
	Reading MSA, PA	Y	26340 FQ	48900 AW	81640 TQ	PABLS	10/01-12/01
	Scranton-Wilkes-Barre-Hazleton MSA, PA	Y	23640 FQ	37190 AW	56270 TQ	PABLS	10/01-12/01
	York MSA, PA	Y	29800 FQ	53160 AW	87440 TQ	PABLS	10/01-12/01
	Rhode Island	Y	36210 FQ	52480 AW	74070 TQ	RIBLS	10/01-12/01
	Providence-Fall River-Warwick MSA, RI-MA	Y	36440 FQ	52970 AW	74990 TQ	RIBLS	10/01-12/01
	South Carolina	Y	27410 FQ	43630 AW	61400 TQ	SCBLS	10/01-12/01
	Charleston-North Charleston MSA, SC	Y	24650 FQ	45570 AW	68040 TQ	SCBLS	10/01-12/01

AAW	Average annual wage	**AOH**	Average offered, high	**ASH**	Average starting, high	**H**	Hourly	**M**	Monthly	**S**	Special: hourly and annual
AE	Average entry wage	**AOL**	Average offered, low	**ASL**	Average starting, low	**HI**	Highest wage paid	**MTC**	Median total compensation	**TQ**	Third quartile wage
AEX	Average experienced wage	**APH**	Average pay, high range	**AW**	Average wage paid	**HR**	High end range	**MW**	Median wage paid	**W**	Weekly
AO	Average offered	**APL**	Average pay, low range	**FQ**	First quartile wage	**LR**	Low end range	**SQ**	Second quartile wage	**Y**	Yearly

Occupation/Type/Industry	Location	Per	Low	Mid	High	Source	Date
Financial Analyst	Columbia MSA, SC	Y	26590 FQ	42550 AW	58280 TQ	SCBLS	10/01-12/01
	Greenville-Spartanburg-Anderson MSA, SC	Y	29060 FQ	42960 AW	58210 TQ	SCBLS	10/01-12/01
	Myrtle Beach MSA, SC	Y	34110 FQ	43540 AW	56070 TQ	SCBLS	10/01-12/01
	South Dakota	Y	29440 FQ	44450 AW	64820 TQ	SDBLS	10/01-12/01
	Sioux Falls MSA, SD	Y	30880 FQ	44310 AW	62250 TQ	SDBLS	10/01-12/01
	Tennessee	Y	29880 FQ	56000 AW	93400 TQ	TNBLS	10/01-12/01
	Chattanooga MSA, TN-GA	Y	29130 FQ	50690 AW	79870 TQ	TNBLS	10/01-12/01
	Johnson City-Kingsport-Bristol MSA, TN-VA	Y	28920 FQ	52880 AW	85600 TQ	TNBLS	10/01-12/01
	Knoxville MSA, TN	Y	31440 FQ	48730 AW	69360 TQ	TNBLS	10/01-12/01
	Memphis MSA, TN-AR-MS	Y	30690 FQ	61650 AW		TNBLS	10/01-12/01
	Nashville MSA, TN	Y	27560 FQ	53040 AW	82870 TQ	TNBLS	10/01-12/01
	Texas	Y	31760 FQ	59590 AW	93740 TQ	TXBLS	10/01-12/01
	Amarillo MSA, TX	Y	11540 FQ	32030 AW	58960 TQ	TXBLS	10/01-12/01
	Austin-San Marcos MSA, TX	Y	39340 FQ	60490 AW	83290 TQ	TXBLS	10/01-12/01
	Beaumont-Port Arthur MSA, TX	Y	18860 FQ	53510 AW	87250 TQ	TXBLS	10/01-12/01
	Brownsville-Harlingen-San Benito MSA, TX	Y	30100 FQ	54890 AW	88830 TQ	TXBLS	10/01-12/01
	Corpus Christi MSA, TX	Y	31310 FQ	56130 AW	87790 TQ	TXBLS	10/01-12/01
	Dallas PMSA, TX	Y	33260 FQ	60900 AW	95140 TQ	TXBLS	10/01-12/01
	El Paso MSA, TX	Y	32850 FQ	59180 AW	93430 TQ	TXBLS	10/01-12/01
	Fort Worth-Arlington PMSA, TX	Y	33000 FQ	58870 AW	89080 TQ	TXBLS	10/01-12/01
	Houston PMSA, TX	Y	31210 FQ	60070 AW	95780 TQ	TXBLS	10/01-12/01
	Longview-Marshall MSA, TX	Y	31130 FQ	66350 AW	142210 TQ	TXBLS	10/01-12/01
	Lubbock MSA, TX	Y	31930 FQ	65760 AW	94650 TQ	TXBLS	10/01-12/01
	San Antonio MSA, TX	Y	28610 FQ	58190 AW	93040 TQ	TXBLS	10/01-12/01
	Tyler MSA, TX	Y	25090 FQ	49120 AW	86900 TQ	TXBLS	10/01-12/01
	Waco MSA, TX	Y	25100 FQ	47620 AW	76360 TQ	TXBLS	10/01-12/01
	Utah	Y	32630 FQ	69160 AW		UTBLS	10/01-12/01
	Provo-Orem MSA, UT	Y	33450 FQ	59560 AW	116740 TQ	UTBLS	10/01-12/01
	Salt Lake City-Ogden MSA, UT	Y	32900 FQ	69620 AW		UTBLS	10/01-12/01
	Vermont	Y	37220 FQ	64490 AW	99100 TQ	VTBLS	10/01-12/01
	Burlington MSA, VT	Y	39440 FQ	59980 AW	86320 TQ	VTBLS	10/01-12/01
	Virginia	Y	37640 FQ	60230 AW	91140 TQ	VABLS	10/01-12/01
	Lynchburg MSA, VA	Y	33780 FQ	52010 AW	71100 TQ	VABLS	10/01-12/01
	Norfolk-Virginia Beach-Newport News MSA, VA-NC	Y	32640 FQ	53800 AW	85030 TQ	VABLS	10/01-12/01
	Richmond-Petersburg MSA, VA	Y	36730 FQ	57800 AW	84050 TQ	VABLS	10/01-12/01
	Roanoke MSA, VA	Y	36900 FQ	58720 AW	92440 TQ	VABLS	10/01-12/01
	Washington	Y	38770 FQ	71830 AW		WABLS	10/01-12/01
	Olympia PMSA, WA	Y	39930 FQ	60860 AW	86120 TQ	WABLS	10/01-12/01
	Seattle-Bellevue-Everett PMSA, WA	Y	39270 FQ	75210 AW		WABLS	10/01-12/01
	Spokane MSA, WA	Y	37190 FQ	58680 AW	88880 TQ	WABLS	10/01-12/01
	Tacoma PMSA, WA	Y	38800 FQ	62630 AW	105430 TQ	WABLS	10/01-12/01
	West Virginia	Y	31060 FQ	58160 AW	101220 TQ	WVBLS	10/01-12/01
	Charleston MSA, WV	Y	29240 FQ	48980 AW	78860 TQ	WVBLS	10/01-12/01
	Huntington-Ashland MSA, WV-KY-OH	Y	27630 FQ	48000 AW	78680 TQ	WVBLS	10/01-12/01
	Wisconsin	Y	33020 FQ	60590 AW	100460 TQ	WIBLS	10/01-12/01
	Appleton-Oshkosh-Neenah MSA, WI	Y	27910 FQ	59030 AW		WIBLS	10/01-12/01
	Green Bay MSA, WI	Y	28690 FQ	49860 AW	65920 TQ	WIBLS	10/01-12/01
	Madison MSA, WI	Y	35640 FQ	63260 AW	116750 TQ	WIBLS	10/01-12/01
	Milwaukee-Waukesha PMSA, WI	Y	35920 FQ	63330 AW	101940 TQ	WIBLS	10/01-12/01
	Racine PMSA, WI	Y	24260 FQ	46610 AW	75630 TQ	WIBLS	10/01-12/01
	Wyoming	Y	28860 FQ	53890 AW	85500 TQ	WYBLS	10/01-12/01
	Puerto Rico	Y	23510 FQ	41780 AW	60770 TQ	PRBLS	10/01-12/01
Financial Examiner	Alabama	Y	30390 FQ	54720 AW	87070 TQ	ALBLS	10/01-12/01
	Arizona	Y	28630 FQ	56230 AW	89410 TQ	AZBLS	10/01-12/01
	Arkansas	Y	27280 FQ	52190 AW	84510 TQ	ARBLS	10/01-12/01
	California	Y	35110 FQ	62620 AW	100160 TQ	CABLS	10/01-12/01
	Colorado	Y	32590 FQ	60350 AW	87730 TQ	COBLS	10/01-12/01
	Connecticut	Y	31390 FQ	62230 AW	92890 TQ	CTBLS	10/01-12/01
	Delaware	Y	25830 FQ	53990 AW	95090 TQ	DEBLS	10/01-12/01

AAW Average annual wage; AE Average entry wage; AEX Average experienced wage; AO Average offered; AOH Average offered, high; AOL Average offered, low; APH Average pay, high range; APL Average pay, low range; ASH Average starting, high; ASL Average starting, low; AW Average wage paid; FQ First quartile wage; H Hourly; HI Highest wage paid; HR High end range; LR Low end range; M Monthly; MTC Median total compensation; MW Median wage paid; SQ Second quartile wage; S Special: hourly and annual; TQ Third quartile wage; W Weekly; Y Yearly

Occupation/Type/Industry	Location	Per	Low	Mid	High	Source	Date
Financial Examiner	District of Columbia	Y	49150 FQ	85840 AW	126490 TQ	DCBLS	10/01-12/01
	Florida	Y	27660 FQ	53770 AW	85780 TQ	FLBLS	10/01-12/01
	Georgia	Y	30670 FQ	56590 AW	96710 TQ	GABLS	10/01-12/01
	Hawaii	Y	39270 FQ	59980 AW	86220 TQ	HIBLS	10/01-12/01
	Idaho	Y	31480 FQ	44970 AW	58740 TQ	IDBLS	10/01-12/01
	Illinois	Y	33000 FQ	59970 AW	90730 TQ	ILBLS	10/01-12/01
	Indiana	Y	29590 FQ	53700 AW	87770 TQ	INBLS	10/01-12/01
	Iowa	Y	29570 FQ	50280 AW	77680 TQ	IABLS	10/01-12/01
	Kansas	Y	32940 FQ	57270 AW	86890 TQ	KSBLS	10/01-12/01
	Kentucky	Y	23650 FQ	43880 AW	78600 TQ	KYBLS	10/01-12/01
	Louisiana	Y	27490 FQ	50250 AW	78660 TQ	LABLS	10/01-12/01
	Maine	Y	32720 FQ	51300 AW	81120 TQ	MEBLS	10/01-12/01
	Maryland	Y	29890 FQ	48680 AW	77850 TQ	MDBLS	10/01-12/01
	Massachusetts	Y	41810 FQ	86990 AW		MABLS	10/01-12/01
	Michigan	Y	29790 FQ	67210 AW	127970 TQ	MIBLS	10/01-12/01
	Minnesota	Y	33660 FQ	62100 AW	93750 TQ	MNBLS	10/01-12/01
	Mississippi	Y	23240 FQ	46400 AW	79160 TQ	MSBLS	10/01-12/01
	Missouri	Y	34170 FQ	63430 AW	103120 TQ	MOBLS	10/01-12/01
	Montana	Y	28830 FQ	48010 AW	79640 TQ	MTBLS	10/01-12/01
	Nebraska	Y	27780 FQ	51900 AW	79450 TQ	NEBLS	10/01-12/01
	Nevada	Y	36700 FQ	47080 AW	66740 TQ	NVBLS	10/01-12/01
	New Hampshire	Y	30460 FQ	52040 AW	79730 TQ	NHBLS	10/01-12/01
	New Jersey	Y	37200 FQ	69810 AW	133400 TQ	NJBLS	10/01-12/01
	New Mexico	Y	22820 FQ	50450 AW	86650 TQ	NMBLS	10/01-12/01
	New York	Y	35340 FQ	68270 AW	127430 TQ	NYBLS	10/01-12/01
	North Carolina	Y	31910 FQ	59250 AW	96300 TQ	NCBLS	10/01-12/01
	North Dakota	Y	31840 FQ	50950 AW	82160 TQ	NDBLS	10/01-12/01
	Ohio	Y	31120 FQ	57510 AW	87720 TQ	OHBLS	10/01-12/01
	Oklahoma	Y	24860 FQ	55620 AW	87140 TQ	OKBLS	10/01-12/01
	Oregon	Y	34270 FQ	58240 AW	89330 TQ	ORBLS	10/01-12/01
	Pennsylvania	Y	31130 FQ	57820 AW	88960 TQ	PABLS	10/01-12/01
	Rhode Island	Y	31880 FQ	49590 AW	75080 TQ	RIBLS	10/01-12/01
	South Carolina	Y	21990 FQ	41090 AW	68820 TQ	SCBLS	10/01-12/01
	South Dakota	Y	26390 FQ	52110 AW	81700 TQ	SDBLS	10/01-12/01
	Tennessee	Y	29490 FQ	56110 AW	90580 TQ	TNBLS	10/01-12/01
	Texas	Y	27280 FQ	53320 AW	85540 TQ	TXBLS	10/01-12/01
	Utah	Y	25880 FQ	46430 AW	75300 TQ	UTBLS	10/01-12/01
	Vermont	Y	37510 FQ	50480 AW	67540 TQ	VTBLS	10/01-12/01
	Virginia	Y	32050 FQ	58490 AW	90170 TQ	VABLS	10/01-12/01
	Washington	Y	35670 FQ	59030 AW	90450 TQ	WABLS	10/01-12/01
	West Virginia	Y	20500 FQ	48580 AW	80900 TQ	WVBLS	10/01-12/01
	Wisconsin	Y	30100 FQ	56010 AW	89510 TQ	WIBLS	10/01-12/01
	Puerto Rico	Y	22830 FQ	40190 AW	67400 TQ	PRBLS	10/01-12/01
Financial Manager	Alabama	Y	32130 FQ	61940 AW	100480 TQ	ALBLS	10/01-12/01
	Birmingham MSA, AL	Y	35100 FQ	65620 AW	118960 TQ	ALBLS	10/01-12/01
	Huntsville MSA, AL	Y	30970 FQ	62540 AW	92230 TQ	ALBLS	10/01-12/01
	Mobile MSA, AL	Y	28030 FQ	62200 AW	109450 TQ	ALBLS	10/01-12/01
	Montgomery MSA, AL	Y	36370 FQ	68000 AW	120480 TQ	ALBLS	10/01-12/01
	Alaska	Y	38970 FQ	68160 AW	113340 TQ	AKBLS	10/01-12/01
	Anchorage MSA, AK	Y	41280 FQ	71200 AW	130940 TQ	AKBLS	10/01-12/01
	Arizona	Y	36420 FQ	68820 AW	113740 TQ	AZBLS	10/01-12/01
	Phoenix-Mesa MSA, AZ	Y	39230 FQ	71310 AW	116520 TQ	AZBLS	10/01-12/01
	Tucson MSA, AZ	Y	30410 FQ	62990 AW	109280 TQ	AZBLS	10/01-12/01
	Arkansas	Y	29020 FQ	56140 AW	92180 TQ	ARBLS	10/01-12/01
	Fayetteville-Springdale-Rogers MSA, AR	Y	27680 FQ	55960 AW	90960 TQ	ARBLS	10/01-12/01
	Fort Smith MSA, AR-OK	Y	29610 FQ	58980 AW	96330 TQ	ARBLS	10/01-12/01
	Little Rock-North Little Rock MSA, AR	Y	30900 FQ	57580 AW	94220 TQ	ARBLS	10/01-12/01
	California	Y	46310 FQ	85200 AW		CABLS	10/01-12/01
	Bakersfield MSA, CA	Y	35930 FQ	69430 AW	128050 TQ	CABLS	10/01-12/01
	Chico-Paradise MSA, CA	Y	29800 FQ	56620 AW	89750 TQ	CABLS	10/01-12/01
	Fresno MSA, CA	Y	38990 FQ	65930 AW	107280 TQ	CABLS	10/01-12/01
	Los Angeles-Long Beach PMSA, CA	Y	48380 FQ	87420 AW		CABLS	10/01-12/01
	Merced MSA, CA	Y	35590 FQ	62650 AW	98530 TQ	CABLS	10/01-12/01
	Modesto MSA, CA	Y	40080 FQ	68560 AW	106790 TQ	CABLS	10/01-12/01
	Oakland PMSA, CA	Y	53260 FQ	88240 AW	140170 TQ	CABLS	10/01-12/01
	Orange County PMSA, CA	Y	52710 FQ	88430 AW	136730 TQ	CABLS	10/01-12/01
	Redding MSA, CA	Y	33460 FQ	52890 AW	86120 TQ	CABLS	10/01-12/01
	Riverside-San Bernardino PMSA, CA	Y	36250 FQ	71280 AW	116500 TQ	CABLS	10/01-12/01

AAW	Average annual wage	AOH	Average offered, high	ASH	Average starting, high	H	Hourly	M	Monthly	S	Special: hourly and annual
AE	Average entry wage	AOL	Average offered, low	ASL	Average starting, low	HI	Highest wage paid	MTC	Median total compensation	TQ	Third quartile wage
AEX	Average experienced wage	APH	Average pay, high range	AW	Average wage paid	HR	High end range	MW	Median wage paid	W	Weekly
AO	Average offered	APL	Average pay, low range	FQ	First quartile wage	LR	Low end range	SQ	Second quartile wage	Y	Yearly

Occupation/Type/Industry	Location	Per	Low	Mid	High	Source	Date
Financial Manager	Sacramento PMSA, CA	Y	40990 FQ	70560 AW	110980 TQ	CABLS	10/01-12/01
	Salinas MSA, CA	Y	42460 FQ	80330 AW	138950 TQ	CABLS	10/01-12/01
	San Diego MSA, CA	Y	42640 FQ	78860 AW	139760 TQ	CABLS	10/01-12/01
	San Francisco PMSA, CA	Y	52380 FQ	96310 AW		CABLS	10/01-12/01
	San Jose PMSA, CA	Y	59870 FQ	100670 AW		CABLS	10/01-12/01
	San Luis Obispo-Atascadero-Paso Robles MSA, CA	Y	38000 FQ	63040 AW	99070 TQ	CABLS	10/01-12/01
	Santa Barbara-Santa Maria-Lompoc MSA, CA	Y	42270 FQ	72840 AW	134280 TQ	CABLS	10/01-12/01
	Santa Cruz-Watsonville PMSA, CA	Y	41370 FQ	76400 AW	131220 TQ	CABLS	10/01-12/01
	Santa Rosa PMSA, CA	Y	42470 FQ	78000 AW	141430 TQ	CABLS	10/01-12/01
	Stockton-Lodi MSA, CA	Y	40170 FQ	70730 AW	111770 TQ	CABLS	10/01-12/01
	Vallejo-Fairfield-Napa PMSA, CA	Y	48040 FQ	87160 AW	112930 TQ	CABLS	10/01-12/01
	Ventura PMSA, CA	Y	43120 FQ	81540 AW		CABLS	10/01-12/01
	Visalia-Tulare-Porterville MSA, CA	Y	42920 FQ	70120 AW	119340 TQ	CABLS	10/01-12/01
	Colorado	Y	41840 FQ	76630 AW	131700 TQ	COBLS	10/01-12/01
	Boulder-Longmont PMSA, CO	Y	45800 FQ	80420 AW	123550 TQ	COBLS	10/01-12/01
	Colorado Springs MSA, CO	Y	39570 FQ	71390 AW	119090 TQ	COBLS	10/01-12/01
	Denver PMSA, CO	Y	45270 FQ	80880 AW	144350 TQ	COBLS	10/01-12/01
	Fort Collins-Loveland MSA, CO	Y	41980 FQ	71620 AW	112270 TQ	COBLS	10/01-12/01
	Greeley PMSA, CO	Y	34830 FQ	61890 AW	99310 TQ	COBLS	10/01-12/01
	Connecticut	Y	48300 FQ	89520 AW		CTBLS	10/01-12/01
	Bridgeport PMSA, CT	Y	47080 FQ	83740 AW	140920 TQ	CTBLS	10/01-12/01
	Danbury PMSA, CT	Y	38060 FQ	78160 AW	140630 TQ	CTBLS	10/01-12/01
	Hartford MSA, CT	Y	53620 FQ	91710 AW		CTBLS	10/01-12/01
	New Haven-Meriden PMSA, CT	Y	43460 FQ	71690 AW	110440 TQ	CTBLS	10/01-12/01
	New London-Norwich MSA, CT-RI	Y	40040 FQ	76000 AW	127360 TQ	CTBLS	10/01-12/01
	Stamford-Norwalk PMSA, CT	Y	59340 FQ	106270 AW		CTBLS	10/01-12/01
	Waterbury PMSA, CT	Y	47070 FQ	80450 AW	138040 TQ	CTBLS	10/01-12/01
	Delaware	Y	33650 FQ	66900 AW	112760 TQ	DEBLS	10/01-12/01
	Wilmington-Newark PMSA, DE-MD	Y	36770 FQ	67900 AW	113970 TQ	DEBLS	10/01-12/01
	District of Columbia	Y	46970 FQ	81240 AW	113710 TQ	DCBLS	10/01-12/01
	Washington PMSA, DC-MD-VA-WV	Y	44370 FQ	80100 AW	119660 TQ	DCBLS	10/01-12/01
	Florida	Y	37120 FQ	70830 AW	123020 TQ	FLBLS	10/01-12/01
	Daytona Beach MSA, FL	Y	30390 FQ	59930 AW	98640 TQ	FLBLS	10/01-12/01
	Fort Lauderdale PMSA, FL	Y	38160 FQ	71240 AW	117340 TQ	FLBLS	10/01-12/01
	Fort Myers-Cape Coral MSA, FL	Y	35430 FQ	62310 AW	97600 TQ	FLBLS	10/01-12/01
	Fort Pierce-Port St. Lucie MSA, FL	Y	36930 FQ	59820 AW	90570 TQ	FLBLS	10/01-12/01
	Fort Walton Beach MSA, FL	Y	35750 FQ	63160 AW	94040 TQ	FLBLS	10/01-12/01
	Gainesville MSA, FL	Y	32110 FQ	68980 AW	117290 TQ	FLBLS	10/01-12/01
	Jacksonville MSA, FL	Y	41520 FQ	75280 AW	125160 TQ	FLBLS	10/01-12/01
	Lakeland-Winter Haven MSA, FL	Y	35370 FQ	67140 AW	110110 TQ	FLBLS	10/01-12/01
	Melbourne-Titusville-Palm Bay MSA, FL	Y	36620 FQ	67690 AW	115140 TQ	FLBLS	10/01-12/01
	Miami PMSA, FL	Y	40740 FQ	79390 AW		FLBLS	10/01-12/01
	Naples MSA, FL	Y	38580 FQ	69690 AW	124530 TQ	FLBLS	10/01-12/01
	Ocala MSA, FL	Y	28060 FQ	63200 AW	117050 TQ	FLBLS	10/01-12/01
	Orlando MSA, FL	Y	36880 FQ	68930 AW	118430 TQ	FLBLS	10/01-12/01
	Pensacola MSA, FL	Y	32620 FQ	59570 AW	93390 TQ	FLBLS	10/01-12/01
	Sarasota-Bradenton MSA, FL	Y	36170 FQ	72860 AW	136600 TQ	FLBLS	10/01-12/01
	Tallahassee MSA, FL	Y	36810 FQ	73780 AW	144100 TQ	FLBLS	10/01-12/01
	Tampa-St. Petersburg-Clearwater MSA, FL	Y	37230 FQ	68870 AW	114370 TQ	FLBLS	10/01-12/01
	West Palm Beach-Boca Raton MSA, FL	Y	38960 FQ	73350 AW	129820 TQ	FLBLS	10/01-12/01
	Georgia	Y	39770 FQ	73180 AW	127540 TQ	GABLS	10/01-12/01
	Atlanta MSA, GA	Y	42360 FQ	77490 AW	135710 TQ	GABLS	10/01-12/01
	Augusta-Aiken MSA, GA-SC	Y	34890 FQ	62360 AW	98560 TQ	GABLS	10/01-12/01
	Columbus MSA, GA-AL	Y	36970 FQ	62280 AW	93570 TQ	GABLS	10/01-12/01
	Macon MSA, GA	Y	32870 FQ	60380 AW	93230 TQ	GABLS	10/01-12/01
	Savannah MSA, GA	Y	38330 FQ	62810 AW	89530 TQ	GABLS	10/01-12/01

AAW	Average annual wage	**AOH**	Average offered, high	**ASH**	Average starting, high	**H**	Hourly	**M**	Monthly	**S**	Special: hourly and annual
AE	Average entry wage	**AOL**	Average offered, low	**ASL**	Average starting, low	**HI**	Highest wage paid	**MTC**	Median total compensation	**TQ**	Third quartile wage
AEX	Average experienced wage	**APH**	Average pay, high range	**AW**	Average wage paid	**HR**	High end range	**MW**	Median wage paid	**W**	Weekly
AO	Average offered	**APL**	Average pay, low range	**FQ**	First quartile wage	**LR**	Low end range	**SQ**	Second quartile wage	**Y**	Yearly

Occupation/Type/Industry	Location	Per	Low	Mid	High	Source	Date
Financial Manager	Hawaii	Y	42230 FQ	67270 AW	104430 TQ	HIBLS	10/01-12/01
	Honolulu MSA, HI	Y	42360 FQ	68040 AW	103960 TQ	HIBLS	10/01-12/01
	Idaho	Y	28010 FQ	58030 AW	97680 TQ	IDBLS	10/01-12/01
	Boise City MSA, ID	Y	32110 FQ	63870 AW	106770 TQ	IDBLS	10/01-12/01
	Illinois	Y	39360 FQ	74660 AW	123940 TQ	ILBLS	10/01-12/01
	Champaign-Urbana MSA, IL	Y	31300 FQ	62170 AW	101280 TQ	ILBLS	10/01-12/01
	Chicago PMSA, IL	Y	43390 FQ	78440 AW	130510 TQ	ILBLS	10/01-12/01
	Peoria-Pekin MSA, IL	Y	24830 FQ	56770 AW	103320 TQ	ILBLS	10/01-12/01
	Rockford MSA, IL	Y	37600 FQ	64830 AW	96050 TQ	ILBLS	10/01-12/01
	Springfield MSA, IL	Y	33510 FQ	65450 AW	97650 TQ	ILBLS	10/01-12/01
	Indiana	Y	37410 FQ	67640 AW	109480 TQ	INBLS	10/01-12/01
	Elkhart-Goshen MSA, IN	Y	38770 FQ	67810 AW	110460 TQ	INBLS	10/01-12/01
	Evansville-Henderson MSA, IN-KY	Y	34550 FQ	58390 AW	92820 TQ	INBLS	10/01-12/01
	Fort Wayne MSA, IN	Y	35110 FQ	62450 AW	101380 TQ	INBLS	10/01-12/01
	Gary PMSA, IN	Y	38360 FQ	64450 AW	98750 TQ	INBLS	10/01-12/01
	Indianapolis MSA, IN	Y	41970 FQ	73970 AW	117700 TQ	INBLS	10/01-12/01
	Lafayette MSA, IN	Y	31740 FQ	67690 AW	107450 TQ	INBLS	10/01-12/01
	South Bend MSA, IN	Y	33770 FQ	68620 AW	132650 TQ	INBLS	10/01-12/01
	Iowa	Y	31740 FQ	63090 AW	105410 TQ	IABLS	10/01-12/01
	Cedar Rapids MSA, IA	Y	40210 FQ	71950 AW	114150 TQ	IABLS	10/01-12/01
	Davenport-Moline-Rock Island MSA, IA-IL	Y	31650 FQ	62310 AW	102570 TQ	IABLS	10/01-12/01
	Des Moines MSA, IA	Y	36030 FQ	70400 AW	115600 TQ	IABLS	10/01-12/01
	Kansas	Y	33540 FQ	65080 AW	108170 TQ	KSBLS	10/01-12/01
	Topeka MSA, KS	Y	36390 FQ	62900 AW	100930 TQ	KSBLS	10/01-12/01
	Wichita MSA, KS	Y	37140 FQ	64110 AW	97510 TQ	KSBLS	10/01-12/01
	Kentucky	Y	29180 FQ	58240 AW	95580 TQ	KYBLS	10/01-12/01
	Lexington MSA, KY	Y	34720 FQ	62020 AW	96380 TQ	KYBLS	10/01-12/01
	Louisville MSA, KY-IN	Y	33780 FQ	63050 AW	105470 TQ	KYBLS	10/01-12/01
	Louisiana	Y	29830 FQ	56530 AW	91630 TQ	LABLS	10/01-12/01
	Baton Rouge MSA, LA	Y	32740 FQ	57310 AW	87300 TQ	LABLS	10/01-12/01
	Houma MSA, LA	Y	31460 FQ	53050 AW	92460 TQ	LABLS	10/01-12/01
	Lafayette MSA, LA	Y	29080 FQ	56230 AW	91310 TQ	LABLS	10/01-12/01
	Lake Charles MSA, LA	Y	33840 FQ	68510 AW	126240 TQ	LABLS	10/01-12/01
	New Orleans MSA, LA	Y	30340 FQ	58160 AW	96640 TQ	LABLS	10/01-12/01
	Shreveport-Bossier City MSA, LA	Y	28130 FQ	54600 AW	88650 TQ	LABLS	10/01-12/01
	Maine	Y	32880 FQ	59810 AW	96060 TQ	MEBLS	10/01-12/01
	Portland MSA, ME	Y	36830 FQ	64620 AW	105250 TQ	MEBLS	10/01-12/01
	Maryland	Y	34990 FQ	69320 AW	118600 TQ	MDBLS	10/01-12/01
	Baltimore PMSA, MD	Y	33000 FQ	68050 AW	121040 TQ	MDBLS	10/01-12/01
	Massachusetts	Y	42090 FQ	83980 AW		MABLS	10/01-12/01
	Boston PMSA, MA-NH	Y	46600 FQ	89690 AW		MABLS	10/01-12/01
	Brockton PMSA, MA	Y	30320 FQ	61220 AW	100000 TQ	MABLS	10/01-12/01
	Lawrence PMSA, MA-NH	Y	39230 FQ	72420 AW	120450 TQ	MABLS	10/01-12/01
	Lowell PMSA, MA-NH	Y	43470 FQ	75630 AW	124470 TQ	MABLS	10/01-12/01
	New Bedford PMSA, MA	Y	33520 FQ	55340 AW	87160 TQ	MABLS	10/01-12/01
	Springfield MSA, MA	Y	35360 FQ	70370 AW	115580 TQ	MABLS	10/01-12/01
	Worcester PMSA, MA-CT	Y	33990 FQ	65990 AW	110020 TQ	MABLS	10/01-12/01
	Michigan	Y	45370 FQ	81660 AW		MIBLS	10/01-12/01
	Ann Arbor PMSA, MI	Y	42240 FQ	78140 AW	122730 TQ	MIBLS	10/01-12/01
	Detroit PMSA, MI	Y	52950 FQ	88750 AW		MIBLS	10/01-12/01
	Flint PMSA, MI	Y	41140 FQ	76920 AW	134850 TQ	MIBLS	10/01-12/01
	Grand Rapids-Muskegon-Holland MSA, MI	Y	41880 FQ	71410 AW	111710 TQ	MIBLS	10/01-12/01
	Kalamazoo-Battle Creek MSA, MI	Y	41980 FQ	75650 AW		MIBLS	10/01-12/01
	Lansing-East Lansing MSA, MI	Y	48300 FQ	78640 AW	133250 TQ	MIBLS	10/01-12/01
	Saginaw-Bay City-Midland MSA, MI	Y	39350 FQ	80110 AW		MIBLS	10/01-12/01
	Minnesota	Y	50840 FQ	85310 AW		MNBLS	10/01-12/01
	Duluth-Superior MSA, MN-WI	Y	39060 FQ	70560 AW	111330 TQ	MNBLS	10/01-12/01
	Minneapolis-St. Paul MSA, MN-WI	Y	54980 FQ	88550 AW		MNBLS	10/01-12/01
	St. Cloud MSA, MN	Y	43840 FQ	79860 AW	129740 TQ	MNBLS	10/01-12/01
	Mississippi	Y	29160 FQ	56040 AW	91120 TQ	MSBLS	10/01-12/01
	Biloxi-Gulfport-Pascagoula MSA, MS	Y	31430 FQ	56230 AW	90650 TQ	MSBLS	10/01-12/01
	Jackson MSA, MS	Y	36120 FQ	61440 AW	103500 TQ	MSBLS	10/01-12/01
	Missouri	Y	33500 FQ	65290 AW	107690 TQ	MOBLS	10/01-12/01
	Kansas City MSA, MO-KS	Y	36680 FQ	69480 AW	115630 TQ	MOBLS	10/01-12/01

AAW	Average annual wage	**AOH**	Average offered, high	**ASH**	Average starting, high	**H**	Hourly	**M**	Monthly	**S**	Special: hourly and annual
AE	Average entry wage	**AOL**	Average offered, low	**ASL**	Average starting, low	**HI**	Highest wage paid	**MTC**	Median total compensation	**TQ**	Third quartile wage
AEX	Average experienced wage	**APH**	Average pay, high range	**AW**	Average wage paid	**HR**	High end range	**MW**	Median wage paid	**W**	Weekly
AO	Average offered	**APL**	Average pay, low range	**FQ**	First quartile wage	**LR**	Low end range	**SQ**	Second quartile wage	**Y**	Yearly

Occupation/Type/Industry	Location	Per	Low	Mid	High	Source	Date
Financial Manager	St. Louis MSA, MO-IL	Y	38330 FQ	68940 AW	114030 TQ	MOBLS	10/01-12/01
	Springfield MSA, MO	Y	26780 FQ	56910 AW	92270 TQ	MOBLS	10/01-12/01
	Montana	Y	24930 FQ	49480 AW	81940 TQ	MTBLS	10/01-12/01
	Billings MSA, MT	Y	24390 FQ	53980 AW	91070 TQ	MTBLS	10/01-12/01
	Nebraska	Y	34150 FQ	64200 AW	108410 TQ	NEBLS	10/01-12/01
	Lincoln MSA, NE	Y	38270 FQ	61550 AW	96200 TQ	NEBLS	10/01-12/01
	Omaha MSA, NE-IA	Y	35580 FQ	67170 AW	117530 TQ	NEBLS	10/01-12/01
	Nevada	Y	33790 FQ	70020 AW	123040 TQ	NVBLS	10/01-12/01
	Las Vegas MSA, NV-AZ	Y	32850 FQ	70070 AW	123090 TQ	NVBLS	10/01-12/01
	Reno MSA, NV	Y	38430 FQ	72430 AW	130700 TQ	NVBLS	10/01-12/01
	New Hampshire	Y	36550 FQ	65780 AW	108340 TQ	NHBLS	10/01-12/01
	Manchester PMSA, NH	Y	39710 FQ	69870 AW	121980 TQ	NHBLS	10/01-12/01
	Nashua PMSA, NH	Y	41410 FQ	71460 AW	111300 TQ	NHBLS	10/01-12/01
	Portsmouth-Rochester PMSA, NH-ME	Y	36090 FQ	65450 AW	109060 TQ	NHBLS	10/01-12/01
	New Jersey	Y	41630 FQ	86720 AW		NJBLS	10/01-12/01
	Atlantic-Cape May PMSA, NJ	Y	44980 FQ	75290 AW	120360 TQ	NJBLS	10/01-12/01
	Bergen-Passaic PMSA, NJ	Y	43390 FQ	89450 AW		NJBLS	10/01-12/01
	Jersey City PMSA, NJ	Y	36550 FQ	89800 AW		NJBLS	10/01-12/01
	Middlesex-Somerset-Hunterdon PMSA, NJ	Y	52400 FQ	92200 AW		NJBLS	10/01-12/01
	Monmouth-Ocean PMSA, NJ	Y	38860 FQ	79040 AW		NJBLS	10/01-12/01
	Newark PMSA, NJ	Y	44420 FQ	90210 AW		NJBLS	10/01-12/01
	Trenton PMSA, NJ	Y	43870 FQ	83870 AW	144870 TQ	NJBLS	10/01-12/01
	New Mexico	Y	30340 FQ	57190 AW	92940 TQ	NMBLS	10/01-12/01
	Albuquerque MSA, NM	Y	32910 FQ	61480 AW	99740 TQ	NMBLS	10/01-12/01
	Las Cruces MSA, NM	Y	25770 FQ	50330 AW	82160 TQ	NMBLS	10/01-12/01
	New York	Y	54630 FQ	101240 AW		NYBLS	10/01-12/01
	Albany-Schenectady-Troy MSA, NY	Y	47910 FQ	78570 AW	116720 TQ	NYBLS	10/01-12/01
	Binghamton MSA, NY	Y	41750 FQ	71030 AW	113490 TQ	NYBLS	10/01-12/01
	Buffalo-Niagara Falls MSA, NY	Y	42240 FQ	75450 AW	130360 TQ	NYBLS	10/01-12/01
	Dutchess County PMSA, NY	Y	48830 FQ	85340 AW		NYBLS	10/01-12/01
	Nassau-Suffolk PMSA, NY	Y	49760 FQ	93790 AW		NYBLS	10/01-12/01
	New York PMSA, NY	Y	62100 FQ	107720 AW		NYBLS	10/01-12/01
	Newburgh PMSA, NY-PA	Y	42460 FQ	73930 AW	136720 TQ	NYBLS	10/01-12/01
	Rochester MSA, NY	Y	46410 FQ	81170 AW	140510 TQ	NYBLS	10/01-12/01
	Syracuse MSA, NY	Y	46570 FQ	76580 AW	122320 TQ	NYBLS	10/01-12/01
	Utica-Rome MSA, NY	Y	39310 FQ	70940 AW	117180 TQ	NYBLS	10/01-12/01
	North Carolina	Y	37620 FQ	71730 AW	128490 TQ	NCBLS	10/01-12/01
	Asheville MSA, NC	Y	32710 FQ	61520 AW	98200 TQ	NCBLS	10/01-12/01
	Charlotte-Gastonia-Rock Hill MSA, NC-SC	Y	42720 FQ	79830 AW		NCBLS	10/01-12/01
	Fayetteville MSA, NC	Y	31410 FQ	60210 AW	93620 TQ	NCBLS	10/01-12/01
	Greensboro-Winston-Salem-High Point MSA, NC	Y	38670 FQ	73290 AW	127060 TQ	NCBLS	10/01-12/01
	Hickory-Morganton-Lenoir MSA, NC	Y	31330 FQ	63100 AW	118960 TQ	NCBLS	10/01-12/01
	Raleigh-Durham-Chapel Hill MSA, NC	Y	39010 FQ	71750 AW	118330 TQ	NCBLS	10/01-12/01
	Wilmington MSA, NC	Y	29910 FQ	58740 AW	92050 TQ	NCBLS	10/01-12/01
	North Dakota	Y	28750 FQ	53560 AW	83550 TQ	NDBLS	10/01-12/01
	Fargo-Moorhead MSA, ND-MN	Y	32220 FQ	61490 AW	110080 TQ	NDBLS	10/01-12/01
	Ohio	Y	38380 FQ	70720 AW	117670 TQ	OHBLS	10/01-12/01
	Akron PMSA, OH	Y	36850 FQ	68860 AW	110370 TQ	OHBLS	10/01-12/01
	Canton-Massillon MSA, OH	Y	32530 FQ	62730 AW	100960 TQ	OHBLS	10/01-12/01
	Cincinnati PMSA, OH-KY-IN	Y	37980 FQ	70470 AW	121850 TQ	OHBLS	10/01-12/01
	Cleveland-Lorain-Elyria PMSA, OH	Y	42990 FQ	77410 AW	132360 TQ	OHBLS	10/01-12/01
	Columbus MSA, OH	Y	42190 FQ	74850 AW	127410 TQ	OHBLS	10/01-12/01
	Dayton-Springfield MSA, OH	Y	38050 FQ	69600 AW	109460 TQ	OHBLS	10/01-12/01
	Hamilton-Middletown PMSA, OH	Y	37390 FQ	67510 AW	105350 TQ	OHBLS	10/01-12/01
	Mansfield MSA, OH	Y	34020 FQ	59540 AW	89090 TQ	OHBLS	10/01-12/01
	Toledo MSA, OH	Y	40430 FQ	67120 AW	103960 TQ	OHBLS	10/01-12/01
	Youngstown-Warren MSA, OH	Y	32130 FQ	64930 AW	119580 TQ	OHBLS	10/01-12/01
	Oklahoma	Y	28300 FQ	58790 AW	96480 TQ	OKBLS	10/01-12/01
	Oklahoma City MSA, OK	Y	30160 FQ	59210 AW	92530 TQ	OKBLS	10/01-12/01
	Tulsa MSA, OK	Y	28780 FQ	64400 AW	109440 TQ	OKBLS	10/01-12/01
	Oregon	Y	39760 FQ	70380 AW	113220 TQ	ORBLS	10/01-12/01

AAW Average annual wage; **AE** Average entry wage; **AEX** Average experienced wage; **AO** Average offered; **AOH** Average offered, high; **AOL** Average offered, low; **APH** Average pay, high range; **APL** Average pay, low range; **ASH** Average starting, high; **ASL** Average starting, low; **AW** Average wage paid; **FQ** First quartile wage; **H** Hourly; **HI** Highest wage paid; **HR** High end range; **LR** Low end range; **M** Monthly; **MTC** Median total compensation; **MW** Median wage paid; **SQ** Second quartile wage; **S** Special: hourly and annual; **TQ** Third quartile wage; **W** Weekly; **Y** Yearly

Occupation/Type/Industry	Location	Per	Low	Mid	High	Source	Date
Financial Manager	Eugene-Springfield MSA, OR	Y	40010 FQ	65540 AW	102960 TQ	ORBLS	10/01-12/01
	Medford-Ashland MSA, OR	Y	37260 FQ	60490 AW	91360 TQ	ORBLS	10/01-12/01
	Portland-Vancouver PMSA, OR-WA	Y	43220 FQ	76470 AW	124590 TQ	ORBLS	10/01-12/01
	Salem PMSA, OR	Y	37230 FQ	63250 AW	94270 TQ	ORBLS	10/01-12/01
	Pennsylvania	Y	30000 FQ	61480 AW	106860 TQ	PABLS	10/01-12/01
	Allentown-Bethlehem-Easton MSA, PA	Y	30100 FQ	58100 AW	96360 TQ	PABLS	10/01-12/01
	Erie MSA, PA	Y	32290 FQ	60390 AW	94490 TQ	PABLS	10/01-12/01
	Harrisburg-Lebanon-Carlisle MSA, PA	Y	37310 FQ	66130 AW	111030 TQ	PABLS	10/01-12/01
	Johnstown MSA, PA	Y	29620 FQ	54640 AW	84800 TQ	PABLS	10/01-12/01
	Lancaster MSA, PA	Y	27410 FQ	58850 AW	98440 TQ	PABLS	10/01-12/01
	Philadelphia PMSA, PA-NJ	Y	32410 FQ	69600 AW	122680 TQ	PABLS	10/01-12/01
	Pittsburgh MSA, PA	Y	33120 FQ	58610 AW	94080 TQ	PABLS	10/01-12/01
	Reading MSA, PA	Y	21950 FQ	48440 AW	86850 TQ	PABLS	10/01-12/01
	Scranton-Wilkes-Barre-Hazleton MSA, PA	Y	30510 FQ	50700 AW	79830 TQ	PABLS	10/01-12/01
	York MSA, PA	Y	32580 FQ	63260 AW	104060 TQ	PABLS	10/01-12/01
	Rhode Island	Y	56090 FQ	89960 AW		RIBLS	10/01-12/01
	Providence-Fall River-Warwick MSA, RI-MA	Y	45670 FQ	84500 AW		RIBLS	10/01-12/01
	South Carolina	Y	31520 FQ	58370 AW	92550 TQ	SCBLS	10/01-12/01
	Charleston-North Charleston MSA, SC	Y	32050 FQ	55440 AW	88400 TQ	SCBLS	10/01-12/01
	Columbia MSA, SC	Y	32600 FQ	58680 AW	90030 TQ	SCBLS	10/01-12/01
	Greenville-Spartanburg-Anderson MSA, SC	Y	36240 FQ	64530 AW	102630 TQ	SCBLS	10/01-12/01
	Myrtle Beach MSA, SC	Y	23190 FQ	50260 AW	85930 TQ	SCBLS	10/01-12/01
	South Dakota	Y	47060 FQ	69950 AW	101820 TQ	SDBLS	10/01-12/01
	Sioux Falls MSA, SD	Y	47600 FQ	74950 AW	113220 TQ	SDBLS	10/01-12/01
	Tennessee	Y	29220 FQ	58560 AW	98940 TQ	TNBLS	10/01-12/01
	Chattanooga MSA, TN-GA	Y	25910 FQ	51850 AW	84250 TQ	TNBLS	10/01-12/01
	Clarksville-Hopkinsville MSA, TN-KY	Y	28990 FQ	53150 AW	87440 TQ	TNBLS	10/01-12/01
	Johnson City-Kingsport-Bristol MSA, TN-VA	Y	26840 FQ	54190 AW	89890 TQ	TNBLS	10/01-12/01
	Knoxville MSA, TN	Y	27020 FQ	55770 AW	95790 TQ	TNBLS	10/01-12/01
	Memphis MSA, TN-AR-MS	Y	32920 FQ	64940 AW	114400 TQ	TNBLS	10/01-12/01
	Nashville MSA, TN	Y	30780 FQ	61840 AW	101020 TQ	TNBLS	10/01-12/01
	Texas	Y	36390 FQ	72310 AW	123350 TQ	TXBLS	10/01-12/01
	Amarillo MSA, TX	Y	31750 FQ	60360 AW	96070 TQ	TXBLS	10/01-12/01
	Austin-San Marcos MSA, TX	Y	41590 FQ	74600 AW	128980 TQ	TXBLS	10/01-12/01
	Beaumont-Port Arthur MSA, TX	Y	35270 FQ	67340 AW	125020 TQ	TXBLS	10/01-12/01
	Brazoria PMSA, TX	Y	29750 FQ	58630 AW	90960 TQ	TXBLS	10/01-12/01
	Brownsville-Harlingen-San Benito MSA, TX	Y	28480 FQ	60230 AW	90380 TQ	TXBLS	10/01-12/01
	Corpus Christi MSA, TX	Y	27170 FQ	59450 AW	95360 TQ	TXBLS	10/01-12/01
	Dallas PMSA, TX	Y	40760 FQ	81760 AW	140150 TQ	TXBLS	10/01-12/01
	El Paso MSA, TX	Y	33650 FQ	64310 AW	109830 TQ	TXBLS	10/01-12/01
	Fort Worth-Arlington PMSA, TX	Y	39830 FQ	72570 AW	114530 TQ	TXBLS	10/01-12/01
	Galveston-Texas City PMSA, TX	Y	14750 FQ	53810 AW	102810 TQ	TXBLS	10/01-12/01
	Houston PMSA, TX	Y	41460 FQ	75750 AW	128410 TQ	TXBLS	10/01-12/01
	Killeen-Temple MSA, TX	Y	30430 FQ	57360 AW	89840 TQ	TXBLS	10/01-12/01
	Laredo MSA, TX	Y	34920 FQ	73180 AW	139790 TQ	TXBLS	10/01-12/01
	Longview-Marshall MSA, TX	Y	32750 FQ	63360 AW	102960 TQ	TXBLS	10/01-12/01
	Lubbock MSA, TX	Y	22780 FQ	53600 AW	89820 TQ	TXBLS	10/01-12/01
	McAllen-Edinburg-Mission MSA, TX	Y	31790 FQ	60270 AW	93270 TQ	TXBLS	10/01-12/01
	Odessa-Midland MSA, TX	Y	28790 FQ	64350 AW	108650 TQ	TXBLS	10/01-12/01
	San Antonio MSA, TX	Y	32970 FQ	67430 AW	111160 TQ	TXBLS	10/01-12/01
	Tyler MSA, TX	Y	28970 FQ	63550 AW	107420 TQ	TXBLS	10/01-12/01
	Waco MSA, TX	Y	22630 FQ	55120 AW	105720 TQ	TXBLS	10/01-12/01
	Utah	Y	25780 FQ	60290 AW	102880 TQ	UTBLS	10/01-12/01
	Provo-Orem MSA, UT	Y	28430 FQ	59920 AW	94080 TQ	UTBLS	10/01-12/01
	Salt Lake City-Ogden MSA, UT	Y	25390 FQ	60730 AW	105050 TQ	UTBLS	10/01-12/01
	Vermont	Y	48880 FQ	78540 AW	127370 TQ	VTBLS	10/01-12/01
	Burlington MSA, VT	Y	44220 FQ	78070 AW	129360 TQ	VTBLS	10/01-12/01

AAW Average annual wage **AE** Average entry wage **AEX** Average experienced wage **AO** Average offered **AOH** Average offered, high **AOL** Average offered, low **APH** Average pay, high range **APL** Average pay, low range **ASH** Average starting, high **ASL** Average starting, low **AW** Average wage paid **FQ** First quartile wage **H** Hourly **HI** Highest wage paid **HR** High end range **LR** Low end range **M** Monthly **MTC** Median total compensation **MW** Median wage paid **SQ** Second quartile wage **S** Special: hourly and annual **TQ** Third quartile wage **W** Weekly **Y** Yearly

Occupation/Type/Industry	Location	Per	Low	Mid	High	Source	Date
Financial Manager	Virginia	Y	42250 FQ	77220 AW	117790 TQ	VABLS	10/01-12/01
	Lynchburg MSA, VA	Y	29540 FQ	65890 AW	111340 TQ	VABLS	10/01-12/01
	Norfolk-Virginia Beach-Newport News MSA, VA-NC	Y	40060 FQ	68240 AW	99340 TQ	VABLS	10/01-12/01
	Richmond-Petersburg MSA, VA	Y	44890 FQ	75860 AW	114700 TQ	VABLS	10/01-12/01
	Roanoke MSA, VA	Y	39340 FQ	72210 AW	114550 TQ	VABLS	10/01-12/01
	Washington	Y	45690 FQ	78760 AW	131400 TQ	WABLS	10/01-12/01
	Bremerton PMSA, WA	Y	42440 FQ	72610 AW	110100 TQ	WABLS	10/01-12/01
	Olympia PMSA, WA	Y	44440 FQ	67610 AW	101390 TQ	WABLS	10/01-12/01
	Richland-Kennewick-Pasco MSA, WA	Y	43190 FQ	75040 AW	113940 TQ	WABLS	10/01-12/01
	Seattle-Bellevue-Everett PMSA, WA	Y	49410 FQ	84670 AW	142640 TQ	WABLS	10/01-12/01
	Spokane MSA, WA	Y	42200 FQ	70810 AW	109240 TQ	WABLS	10/01-12/01
	Tacoma PMSA, WA	Y	42280 FQ	70810 AW	113720 TQ	WABLS	10/01-12/01
	Yakima MSA, WA	Y	40470 FQ	62450 AW	89400 TQ	WABLS	10/01-12/01
	West Virginia	Y	29710 FQ	55280 AW	89410 TQ	WVBLS	10/01-12/01
	Charleston MSA, WV	Y	32110 FQ	60880 AW	105420 TQ	WVBLS	10/01-12/01
	Huntington-Ashland MSA, WV-KY-OH	Y	29200 FQ	55020 AW	88510 TQ	WVBLS	10/01-12/01
	Wisconsin	Y	33130 FQ	65790 AW	111620 TQ	WIBLS	10/01-12/01
	Appleton-Oshkosh-Neenah MSA, WI	Y	35190 FQ	63930 AW	96290 TQ	WIBLS	10/01-12/01
	Green Bay MSA, WI	Y	34930 FQ	74340 AW	136350 TQ	WIBLS	10/01-12/01
	Madison MSA, WI	Y	36980 FQ	64380 AW	99420 TQ	WIBLS	10/01-12/01
	Milwaukee-Waukesha PMSA, WI	Y	34340 FQ	71730 AW	123550 TQ	WIBLS	10/01-12/01
	Racine PMSA, WI	Y	38940 FQ	67660 AW	112890 TQ	WIBLS	10/01-12/01
	Wyoming	Y	27700 FQ	55870 AW	95540 TQ	WYBLS	10/01-12/01
	Cheyenne MSA, WY	Y	33750 FQ	51160 AW	71560 TQ	WYBLS	10/01-12/01
	Puerto Rico	Y	25090 FQ	50540 AW	86120 TQ	PRBLS	10/01-12/01
	Virgin Islands	Y	37350 FQ	58970 AW	88210 TQ	VIBLS	10/01-12/01
	Guam	Y	30210 FQ	54730 AW	87750 TQ	GUBLS	10/01-12/01
Financial Services Professional	San Diego, CA	Y		57321 AW		SDBJ1	1/99-1/00
Fine Artist, Including Painter, Sculptor, and Illustrator	Alabama	Y	19280 FQ	29380 AW	45280 TQ	ALBLS	10/01-12/01
	Arizona	Y	21390 FQ	42520 AW	70940 TQ	AZBLS	10/01-12/01
	Phoenix-Mesa MSA, AZ	Y	21690 FQ	41980 AW	70150 TQ	AZBLS	10/01-12/01
	Arkansas	Y	18160 FQ	25940 AW	42820 TQ	ARBLS	10/01-12/01
	California	Y	21370 FQ	42260 AW	63790 TQ	CABLS	10/01-12/01
	Los Angeles-Long Beach PMSA, CA	Y	17730 FQ	38610 AW	59320 TQ	CABLS	10/01-12/01
	Oakland PMSA, CA	Y	30300 FQ	44930 AW	60810 TQ	CABLS	10/01-12/01
	Orange County PMSA, CA	Y	36900 FQ	52390 AW	72100 TQ	CABLS	10/01-12/01
	San Diego MSA, CA	Y	28090 FQ	40370 AW	58630 TQ	CABLS	10/01-12/01
	San Francisco PMSA, CA	Y	24820 FQ	47890 AW	84480 TQ	CABLS	10/01-12/01
	San Jose PMSA, CA	Y	13840 FQ	44140 AW	70360 TQ	CABLS	10/01-12/01
	Colorado	Y	14630 FQ	29140 AW	51080 TQ	COBLS	10/01-12/01
	Denver PMSA, CO	Y	14590 FQ	27470 AW	52320 TQ	COBLS	10/01-12/01
	Connecticut	Y	21060 FQ	38460 AW	71840 TQ	CTBLS	10/01-12/01
	Hartford MSA, CT	Y	23110 FQ	32670 AW	46840 TQ	CTBLS	10/01-12/01
	Delaware	Y	23500 FQ	31200 AW	41760 TQ	DEBLS	10/01-12/01
	District of Columbia	Y	22540 FQ	45910 AW	68030 TQ	DCBLS	10/01-12/01
	Washington PMSA, DC-MD-VA-WV	Y	23420 FQ	41290 AW	65410 TQ	DCBLS	10/01-12/01
	Florida	Y	18650 FQ	45840 AW	93380 TQ	FLBLS	10/01-12/01
	Fort Lauderdale PMSA, FL	Y	12770 FQ	33880 AW	71740 TQ	FLBLS	10/01-12/01
	Jacksonville MSA, FL	Y	20950 FQ	31780 AW	42360 TQ	FLBLS	10/01-12/01
	Miami PMSA, FL	Y	29340 FQ	73170 AW		FLBLS	10/01-12/01
	Orlando MSA, FL	Y	25810 FQ	43580 AW	55850 TQ	FLBLS	10/01-12/01
	Tallahassee MSA, FL	Y	24700 FQ	31850 AW	43810 TQ	FLBLS	10/01-12/01
	Tampa-St. Petersburg-Clearwater MSA, FL	Y	20860 FQ	51040 AW		FLBLS	10/01-12/01
	West Palm Beach-Boca Raton MSA, FL	Y	14250 FQ	32820 AW	52990 TQ	FLBLS	10/01-12/01
	Georgia	Y	22020 FQ	59680 AW		GABLS	10/01-12/01
	Hawaii	Y	15560 FQ	35500 AW	56810 TQ	HIBLS	10/01-12/01
	Honolulu MSA, HI	Y	14510 FQ	36330 AW	61610 TQ	HIBLS	10/01-12/01

AAW	Average annual wage	AOH	Average offered, high	ASH	Average starting, high	H	Hourly	M	Monthly	S	Special: hourly and annual
AE	Average entry wage	AOL	Average offered, low	ASL	Average starting, low	HI	Highest wage paid	MTC	Median total compensation	TQ	Third quartile wage
AEX	Average experienced wage	APH	Average pay, high range	AW	Average wage paid	HR	High end range	MW	Median wage paid	W	Weekly
AO	Average offered	APL	Average pay, low range	FQ	First quartile wage	LR	Low end range	SQ	Second quartile wage	Y	Yearly

Occupation/Type/Industry	Location	Per	Low	Mid	High	Source	Date
Fine Artist, Including Painter, Sculptor, and Illustrator	Illinois	Y	17590 FQ	31340 AW	48250 TQ	ILBLS	10/01-12/01
	Chicago PMSA, IL	Y	17840 FQ	31410 AW	48050 TQ	ILBLS	10/01-12/01
	Indiana	Y	12300 FQ	35690 AW	83260 TQ	INBLS	10/01-12/01
	Indianapolis MSA, IN	Y	21160 FQ	48210 AW	88890 TQ	INBLS	10/01-12/01
	Iowa	Y	19560 FQ	29600 AW	44750 TQ	IABLS	10/01-12/01
	Kansas	Y	14450 FQ	31880 AW	55700 TQ	KSBLS	10/01-12/01
	Kentucky	Y	17520 FQ	30450 AW	47530 TQ	KYBLS	10/01-12/01
	Lexington MSA, KY	Y	20370 FQ	27490 AW	38750 TQ	KYBLS	10/01-12/01
	Louisiana	Y	12850 FQ	21600 AW	34910 TQ	LABLS	10/01-12/01
	New Orleans MSA, LA	Y	13010 FQ	19230 AW	27460 TQ	LABLS	10/01-12/01
	Maryland	Y	23260 FQ	37930 AW	53970 TQ	MDBLS	10/01-12/01
	Baltimore PMSA, MD	Y	16240 FQ	42030 AW	55800 TQ	MDBLS	10/01-12/01
	Massachusetts	Y	14780 FQ	34340 AW	52260 TQ	MABLS	10/01-12/01
	Boston PMSA, MA-NH	Y	14560 FQ	33200 AW	49900 TQ	MABLS	10/01-12/01
	Michigan	Y	16840 FQ	34270 AW	60950 TQ	MIBLS	10/01-12/01
	Detroit PMSA, MI	Y	20610 FQ	47890 AW	68930 TQ	MIBLS	10/01-12/01
	Grand Rapids-Muskegon-Holland MSA, MI	Y	13780 FQ	27700 AW	56020 TQ	MIBLS	10/01-12/01
	Minnesota	Y	21580 FQ	40660 AW	59410 TQ	MNBLS	10/01-12/01
	Minneapolis-St. Paul MSA, MN-WI	Y	26300 FQ	43670 AW	62490 TQ	MNBLS	10/01-12/01
	Mississippi	Y	12750 FQ	27270 AW	43970 TQ	MSBLS	10/01-12/01
	Missouri	Y	13050 FQ	29660 AW	48210 TQ	MOBLS	10/01-12/01
	Kansas City MSA, MO-KS	Y	12290 FQ	23820 AW	42470 TQ	MOBLS	10/01-12/01
	St. Louis MSA, MO-IL	Y	23190 FQ	38540 AW	58420 TQ	MOBLS	10/01-12/01
	Nebraska	Y	14950 FQ	24150 AW	35710 TQ	NEBLS	10/01-12/01
	Omaha MSA, NE-IA	Y	13030 FQ	32880 AW	64170 TQ	NEBLS	10/01-12/01
	Nevada	Y	21140 FQ	39770 AW	63670 TQ	NVBLS	10/01-12/01
	New Hampshire	Y	24400 FQ	34300 AW	49810 TQ	NHBLS	10/01-12/01
	New Jersey	Y	15310 FQ	37040 AW	70950 TQ	NJBLS	10/01-12/01
	Bergen-Passaic PMSA, NJ	Y	13700 FQ	24820 AW	39270 TQ	NJBLS	10/01-12/01
	Jersey City PMSA, NJ	Y	28850 FQ	56250 AW	89190 TQ	NJBLS	10/01-12/01
	Newark PMSA, NJ	Y	20540 FQ	43820 AW	72530 TQ	NJBLS	10/01-12/01
	New Mexico	Y	19650 FQ	40500 AW	73240 TQ	NMBLS	10/01-12/01
	New York	Y	14460 FQ	44950 AW	110280 TQ	NYBLS	10/01-12/01
	Nassau-Suffolk PMSA, NY	Y	37840 FQ	72000 AW	141800 TQ	NYBLS	10/01-12/01
	New York PMSA, NY	Y	13870 FQ	42810 AW	135110 TQ	NYBLS	10/01-12/01
	North Carolina	Y	22980 FQ	35220 AW	50590 TQ	NCBLS	10/01-12/01
	Charlotte-Gastonia-Rock Hill MSA, NC-SC	Y	17700 FQ	34020 AW	47550 TQ	NCBLS	10/01-12/01
	Raleigh-Durham-Chapel Hill MSA, NC	Y	26730 FQ	36890 AW	52320 TQ	NCBLS	10/01-12/01
	Ohio	Y	18760 FQ	34650 AW	53930 TQ	OHBLS	10/01-12/01
	Akron PMSA, OH	Y	15330 FQ	39170 AW	57760 TQ	OHBLS	10/01-12/01
	Cincinnati PMSA, OH-KY-IN	Y	23010 FQ	39950 AW	58340 TQ	OHBLS	10/01-12/01
	Cleveland-Lorain-Elyria PMSA, OH	Y	12980 FQ	31760 AW	45280 TQ	OHBLS	10/01-12/01
	Columbus MSA, OH	Y	19330 FQ	29620 AW	48220 TQ	OHBLS	10/01-12/01
	Dayton-Springfield MSA, OH	Y	23490 FQ	37670 AW	52500 TQ	OHBLS	10/01-12/01
	Oklahoma	Y	18540 FQ	37510 AW	55840 TQ	OKBLS	10/01-12/01
	Oregon	Y	19810 FQ	35670 AW	54100 TQ	ORBLS	10/01-12/01
	Portland-Vancouver PMSA, OR-WA	Y	20540 FQ	36000 AW	52700 TQ	ORBLS	10/01-12/01
	Pennsylvania	Y	14900 FQ	42240 AW	77900 TQ	PABLS	10/01-12/01
	Philadelphia PMSA, PA-NJ	Y	22260 FQ	50580 AW		PABLS	10/01-12/01
	Pittsburgh MSA, PA	Y	12810 FQ	34940 AW	78460 TQ	PABLS	10/01-12/01
	Rhode Island	Y	18700 FQ	37390 AW	64430 TQ	RIBLS	10/01-12/01
	Providence-Fall River-Warwick MSA, RI-MA	Y	18470 FQ	36510 AW	64920 TQ	RIBLS	10/01-12/01
	South Carolina	Y	19480 FQ	47790 AW		SCBLS	10/01-12/01
	Tennessee	Y	24050 FQ	37630 AW	57820 TQ	TNBLS	10/01-12/01
	Texas	Y	18580 FQ	36760 AW	54910 TQ	TXBLS	10/01-12/01
	Dallas PMSA, TX	Y	29650 FQ	36970 AW	49360 TQ	TXBLS	10/01-12/01
	Houston PMSA, TX	Y	23380 FQ	35460 AW	46710 TQ	TXBLS	10/01-12/01
	Utah	Y	18930 FQ	30390 AW	49760 TQ	UTBLS	10/01-12/01
	Provo-Orem MSA, UT	Y	18960 FQ	37090 AW	56550 TQ	UTBLS	10/01-12/01
	Salt Lake City-Ogden MSA, UT	Y	18960 FQ	29050 AW	40520 TQ	UTBLS	10/01-12/01
	Vermont	Y	16280 FQ	30040 AW	51830 TQ	VTBLS	10/01-12/01
	Virginia	Y	12060 FQ	32720 AW	58830 TQ	VABLS	10/01-12/01

AAW Average annual wage; **AE** Average entry wage; **AEX** Average experienced wage; **AO** Average offered; **AOH** Average offered, high; **AOL** Average offered, low; **APH** Average pay, high range; **APL** Average pay, low range; **ASH** Average starting, high; **ASL** Average starting, low; **AW** Average wage paid; **FQ** First quartile wage; **H** Hourly; **HI** Highest wage paid; **HR** High end range; **LR** Low end range; **M** Monthly; **MTC** Median total compensation; **MW** Median wage paid; **SQ** Second quartile wage; **S** Special: hourly and annual; **TQ** Third quartile wage; **W** Weekly; **Y** Yearly

Occupation/Type/Industry	Location	Per	Low	Mid	High	Source	Date
Fine Artist, Including Painter, Sculptor, and Illustrator	Norfolk-Virginia Beach-Newport News MSA, VA-NC	Y	12930 FQ	36560 AW	56660 TQ	VABLS	10/01-12/01
	Richmond-Petersburg MSA, VA	Y	11460 FQ	16940 AW	36770 TQ	VABLS	10/01-12/01
	Washington	Y	22650 FQ	37830 AW	54080 TQ	WABLS	10/01-12/01
	Seattle-Bellevue-Everett PMSA, WA	Y	22960 FQ	39590 AW	55260 TQ	WABLS	10/01-12/01
	Spokane MSA, WA	Y	31090 FQ	38020 AW	50860 TQ	WABLS	10/01-12/01
	Wisconsin	Y	19560 FQ	33300 AW	51630 TQ	WIBLS	10/01-12/01
	Madison MSA, WI	Y	19400 FQ	29780 AW	44120 TQ	WIBLS	10/01-12/01
	Milwaukee-Waukesha PMSA, WI	Y	20650 FQ	31720 AW	45040 TQ	WIBLS	10/01-12/01
Fire and Crash Rescue Worker							
Airport	United States	Y	16000 ASL		48000 ASH	AEAC	1/99-1/99
Fire Fighter	Alabama	Y	22390 FQ	32360 AW	43800 TQ	ALBLS	10/01-12/01
	Birmingham MSA, AL	Y	28310 FQ	37980 AW	51500 TQ	ALBLS	10/01-12/01
	Alaska	Y	18480 FQ	26540 AW	39310 TQ	AKBLS	10/01-12/01
	Arizona	Y	12990 FQ	32630 AW	55600 TQ	AZBLS	10/01-12/01
	Phoenix-Mesa MSA, AZ	Y	25710 FQ	42860 AW	58330 TQ	AZBLS	10/01-12/01
	Tucson MSA, AZ	Y	12780 FQ	24440 AW	36310 TQ	AZBLS	10/01-12/01
	Arkansas	Y	15540 FQ	27810 AW	42670 TQ	ARBLS	10/01-12/01
	Fayetteville-Springdale-Rogers MSA, AR	Y	14470 FQ	18160 AW	22480 TQ	ARBLS	10/01-12/01
	Little Rock-North Little Rock MSA, AR	Y	18080 FQ	32680 AW	45030 TQ	ARBLS	10/01-12/01
	California	Y	25070 FQ	48050 AW	73200 TQ	CABLS	10/01-12/01
	Bakersfield MSA, CA	Y	25370 FQ	36760 AW	46770 TQ	CABLS	10/01-12/01
	Chico-Paradise MSA, CA	Y	23610 FQ	35630 AW	55270 TQ	CABLS	10/01-12/01
	Fresno MSA, CA	Y	26550 FQ	44090 AW	60070 TQ	CABLS	10/01-12/01
	Los Angeles-Long Beach PMSA, CA	Y	39830 FQ	56320 AW	73890 TQ	CABLS	10/01-12/01
	Merced MSA, CA	Y	28340 FQ	41540 AW	48330 TQ	CABLS	10/01-12/01
	Modesto MSA, CA	Y	31880 FQ	39850 AW	48130 TQ	CABLS	10/01-12/01
	Oakland PMSA, CA	Y	45710 FQ	67100 AW	90210 TQ	CABLS	10/01-12/01
	Orange County PMSA, CA	Y	39700 FQ	55440 AW	70740 TQ	CABLS	10/01-12/01
	Redding MSA, CA	Y	18880 FQ	29430 AW	59330 TQ	CABLS	10/01-12/01
	Riverside-San Bernardino PMSA, CA	Y	17340 FQ	38350 AW	62440 TQ	CABLS	10/01-12/01
	Sacramento PMSA, CA	Y	26380 FQ	40270 AW	54480 TQ	CABLS	10/01-12/01
	Salinas MSA, CA	Y	21010 FQ	38320 AW	66170 TQ	CABLS	10/01-12/01
	San Diego MSA, CA	Y	29620 FQ	45630 AW	59240 TQ	CABLS	10/01-12/01
	San Francisco PMSA, CA	Y	33370 FQ	58200 AW	86030 TQ	CABLS	10/01-12/01
	San Jose PMSA, CA	Y	26220 FQ	55310 AW	81750 TQ	CABLS	10/01-12/01
	San Luis Obispo-Atascadero-Paso Robles MSA, CA	Y	23600 FQ	36850 AW	56430 TQ	CABLS	10/01-12/01
	Santa Barbara-Santa Maria-Lompoc MSA, CA	Y	30220 FQ	49340 AW	71360 TQ	CABLS	10/01-12/01
	Santa Cruz-Watsonville PMSA, CA	Y	24370 FQ	48930 AW	75580 TQ	CABLS	10/01-12/01
	Santa Rosa PMSA, CA	Y	13750 FQ	29500 AW	45170 TQ	CABLS	10/01-12/01
	Stockton-Lodi MSA, CA	Y	15270 FQ	31660 AW	52270 TQ	CABLS	10/01-12/01
	Vallejo-Fairfield-Napa PMSA, CA	Y	24990 FQ	57170 AW	91110 TQ	CABLS	10/01-12/01
	Ventura PMSA, CA	Y	32030 FQ	48130 AW	78100 TQ	CABLS	10/01-12/01
	Visalia-Tulare-Porterville MSA, CA	Y	24360 FQ	35520 AW	46260 TQ	CABLS	10/01-12/01
	Colorado	Y	27690 FQ	43230 AW	57780 TQ	COBLS	10/01-12/01
	Colorado Springs MSA, CO	Y	23090 FQ	39990 AW	57000 TQ	COBLS	10/01-12/01
	Denver PMSA, CO	Y	34760 FQ	46940 AW	58290 TQ	COBLS	10/01-12/01
	Connecticut	Y	31360 FQ	45660 AW	58060 TQ	CTBLS	10/01-12/01
	Bridgeport PMSA, CT	Y	38500 FQ	47190 AW	58290 TQ	CTBLS	10/01-12/01
	Hartford MSA, CT	Y	20700 FQ	43160 AW	57600 TQ	CTBLS	10/01-12/01
	New Haven-Meriden PMSA, CT	Y	40650 FQ	50540 AW	58630 TQ	CTBLS	10/01-12/01
	New London-Norwich MSA, CT-RI	Y	22770 FQ	35710 AW	45760 TQ	CTBLS	10/01-12/01
	Stamford-Norwalk PMSA, CT	Y	44190 FQ	52610 AW	59950 TQ	CTBLS	10/01-12/01
	Delaware	Y	25300 FQ	36770 AW	46480 TQ	DEBLS	10/01-12/01

AAW	Average annual wage	**AOH**	Average offered, high	**ASH**	Average starting, high	**H**	Hourly	**M**	Monthly	**S**	Special: hourly and annual
AE	Average entry wage	**AOL**	Average offered, low	**ASL**	Average starting, low	**HI**	Highest wage paid	**MTC**	Median total compensation	**TQ**	Third quartile wage
AEX	Average experienced wage	**APH**	Average pay, high range	**AW**	Average wage paid	**HR**	High end range	**MW**	Median wage paid	**W**	Weekly
AO	Average offered	**APL**	Average pay, low range	**FQ**	First quartile wage	**LR**	Low end range	**SQ**	Second quartile wage	**Y**	Yearly

Occupation/Type/Industry	Location	Per	Low	Mid	High	Source	Date
Fire Fighter	Washington PMSA, DC-MD-VA-WV	Y	25450 FQ	41530 AW	61530 TQ	DCBLS	10/01-12/01
	Florida	Y	16660 FQ	32460 AW	49900 TQ	FLBLS	10/01-12/01
	Daytona Beach MSA, FL	Y	19210 FQ	29980 AW	45510 TQ	FLBLS	10/01-12/01
	Fort Lauderdale PMSA, FL	Y	26910 FQ	40480 AW	54980 TQ	FLBLS	10/01-12/01
	Fort Myers-Cape Coral MSA, FL	Y	26520 FQ	38660 AW	55440 TQ	FLBLS	10/01-12/01
	Fort Walton Beach MSA, FL	Y	20220 FQ	28880 AW	40240 TQ	FLBLS	10/01-12/01
	Lakeland-Winter Haven MSA, FL	Y	18170 FQ	26190 AW	40310 TQ	FLBLS	10/01-12/01
	Melbourne-Titusville-Palm Bay MSA, FL	Y	21600 FQ	29400 AW	37720 TQ	FLBLS	10/01-12/01
	Miami PMSA, FL	Y	35100 FQ	50670 AW	67230 TQ	FLBLS	10/01-12/01
	Naples MSA, FL	Y	22540 FQ	33750 AW	47320 TQ	FLBLS	10/01-12/01
	Pensacola MSA, FL	Y	19920 FQ	27370 AW	35240 TQ	FLBLS	10/01-12/01
	Sarasota-Bradenton MSA, FL	Y	19300 FQ	34200 AW	44980 TQ	FLBLS	10/01-12/01
	Tallahassee MSA, FL	Y	20430 FQ	31010 AW	45390 TQ	FLBLS	10/01-12/01
	Tampa-St. Petersburg-Clearwater MSA, FL	Y	18380 FQ	33160 AW	44460 TQ	FLBLS	10/01-12/01
	Georgia	Y	17530 FQ	29920 AW	44100 TQ	GABLS	10/01-12/01
	Atlanta MSA, GA	Y	19930 FQ	33620 AW	46670 TQ	GABLS	10/01-12/01
	Macon MSA, GA	Y	19280 FQ	27920 AW	36870 TQ	GABLS	10/01-12/01
	Savannah MSA, GA	Y	25520 FQ	34620 AW	45260 TQ	GABLS	10/01-12/01
	Hawaii	Y	28710 FQ	34850 AW	43560 TQ	HIBLS	10/01-12/01
	Honolulu MSA, HI	Y	29200 FQ	35770 AW	44170 TQ	HIBLS	10/01-12/01
	Idaho	Y	12380 FQ	23130 AW	42100 TQ	IDBLS	10/01-12/01
	Illinois	Y	12570 FQ	34670 AW	58020 TQ	ILBLS	10/01-12/01
	Champaign-Urbana MSA, IL	Y	11630 FQ	21100 AW	47860 TQ	ILBLS	10/01-12/01
	Chicago PMSA, IL	Y	22220 FQ	41980 AW	61620 TQ	ILBLS	10/01-12/01
	Peoria-Pekin MSA, IL	Y	14130 FQ	37290 AW	62990 TQ	ILBLS	10/01-12/01
	Indiana	Y	20370 FQ	33080 AW	44680 TQ	INBLS	10/01-12/01
	Elkhart-Goshen MSA, IN	Y	11490 FQ	14660 AW	17170 TQ	INBLS	10/01-12/01
	Evansville-Henderson MSA, IN-KY	Y	18570 FQ	24630 AW	34790 TQ	INBLS	10/01-12/01
	Fort Wayne MSA, IN	Y	23100 FQ	26060 AW	30650 TQ	INBLS	10/01-12/01
	Gary PMSA, IN	Y	20290 FQ	32000 AW	43160 TQ	INBLS	10/01-12/01
	Indianapolis MSA, IN	Y	28480 FQ	38770 AW	47100 TQ	INBLS	10/01-12/01
	Lafayette MSA, IN	Y	29420 FQ	36770 AW	45980 TQ	INBLS	10/01-12/01
	Iowa	Y	12880 FQ	30390 AW	44980 TQ	IABLS	10/01-12/01
	Davenport-Moline-Rock Island MSA, IA-IL	Y	23440 FQ	39300 AW	55350 TQ	IABLS	10/01-12/01
	Des Moines MSA, IA	Y	13180 FQ	33500 AW	52350 TQ	IABLS	10/01-12/01
	Kansas	Y	12690 FQ	24220 AW	36360 TQ	KSBLS	10/01-12/01
	Topeka MSA, KS	Y	12360 FQ	23470 AW	35620 TQ	KSBLS	10/01-12/01
	Wichita MSA, KS	Y	21070 FQ	29880 AW	36980 TQ	KSBLS	10/01-12/01
	Kentucky	Y	16080 FQ	24590 AW	35000 TQ	KYBLS	10/01-12/01
	Lexington MSA, KY	Y	16010 FQ	21970 AW	32400 TQ	KYBLS	10/01-12/01
	Louisville MSA, KY-IN	Y	18430 FQ	30130 AW	44930 TQ	KYBLS	10/01-12/01
	Louisiana	Y	14980 FQ	27190 AW	47260 TQ	LABLS	10/01-12/01
	Baton Rouge MSA, LA	Y	14400 FQ	21930 AW	35590 TQ	LABLS	10/01-12/01
	Lake Charles MSA, LA	Y	16390 FQ	28620 AW	48830 TQ	LABLS	10/01-12/01
	New Orleans MSA, LA	Y	16330 FQ	27710 AW	45180 TQ	LABLS	10/01-12/01
	Maine	Y	13820 FQ	26150 AW	37160 TQ	MEBLS	10/01-12/01
	Portland MSA, ME	Y	12750 FQ	26830 AW	36990 TQ	MEBLS	10/01-12/01
	Maryland	Y	28310 FQ	40170 AW	55270 TQ	MDBLS	10/01-12/01
	Baltimore PMSA, MD	Y	29110 FQ	38870 AW	52070 TQ	MDBLS	10/01-12/01
	Massachusetts	Y	21160 FQ	38120 AW	55040 TQ	MABLS	10/01-12/01
	Boston PMSA, MA-NH	Y	24640 FQ	39660 AW	55480 TQ	MABLS	10/01-12/01
	Brockton PMSA, MA	Y	25210 FQ	38930 AW	53480 TQ	MABLS	10/01-12/01
	Lawrence PMSA, MA-NH	Y	19950 FQ	33070 AW	46780 TQ	MABLS	10/01-12/01
	Lowell PMSA, MA-NH	Y	36980 FQ	47020 AW	57450 TQ	MABLS	10/01-12/01
	New Bedford PMSA, MA	Y	14340 FQ	25850 AW	35720 TQ	MABLS	10/01-12/01
	Springfield MSA, MA	Y	29270 FQ	36280 AW	45840 TQ	MABLS	10/01-12/01
	Worcester PMSA, MA-CT	Y	14260 FQ	33960 AW	55730 TQ	MABLS	10/01-12/01
	Michigan	Y	17500 FQ	33380 AW	50590 TQ	MIBLS	10/01-12/01
	Ann Arbor PMSA, MI	Y	33480 FQ	48310 AW	59180 TQ	MIBLS	10/01-12/01
	Detroit PMSA, MI	Y	17870 FQ	35780 AW	53910 TQ	MIBLS	10/01-12/01
	Flint PMSA, MI	Y	20970 FQ	28180 AW	39710 TQ	MIBLS	10/01-12/01
	Grand Rapids-Muskegon-Holland MSA, MI	Y	25160 FQ	35320 AW	53580 TQ	MIBLS	10/01-12/01
	Kalamazoo-Battle Creek MSA, MI	Y	26450 FQ	34560 AW	44760 TQ	MIBLS	10/01-12/01

AAW Average annual wage; **AE** Average entry wage; **AEX** Average experienced wage; **AO** Average offered; **AOH** Average offered, high; **AOL** Average offered, low; **APH** Average pay, high range; **APL** Average pay, low range; **ASH** Average starting, high; **ASL** Average starting, low; **AW** Average wage paid; **FQ** First quartile wage; **H** Hourly; **HI** Highest wage paid; **HR** High end range; **LR** Low end range; **M** Monthly; **MTC** Median total compensation; **MW** Median wage paid; **SQ** Second quartile wage; **S** Special: hourly and annual; **TQ** Third quartile wage; **W** Weekly; **Y** Yearly

Occupation/Type/Industry	Location	Per	Low	Mid	High	Source	Date
Fire Fighter	Saginaw-Bay City-Midland MSA, MI	Y	13620 FQ	33820 AW	47220 TQ	MIBLS	10/01-12/01
	Minnesota	Y	12920 FQ	25660 AW	42320 TQ	MNBLS	10/01-12/01
	Duluth-Superior MSA, MN-WI	Y	14770 FQ	32420 AW	44510 TQ	MNBLS	10/01-12/01
	Minneapolis-St. Paul MSA, MN-WI	Y	13560 FQ	26000 AW	48720 TQ	MNBLS	10/01-12/01
	St. Cloud MSA, MN	Y	14270 FQ	29640 AW	43210 TQ	MNBLS	10/01-12/01
	Mississippi	Y	14450 FQ	25840 AW	35340 TQ	MSBLS	10/01-12/01
	Biloxi-Gulfport-Pascagoula MSA, MS	Y	20390 FQ	29130 AW	35490 TQ	MSBLS	10/01-12/01
	Jackson MSA, MS	Y	20400 FQ	29440 AW	37130 TQ	MSBLS	10/01-12/01
	Missouri	Y	14290 FQ	43600 AW	70640 TQ	MOBLS	10/01-12/01
	Kansas City MSA, MO-KS	Y	19320 FQ	37670 AW	60160 TQ	MOBLS	10/01-12/01
	St. Louis MSA, MO-IL	Y	13070 FQ	43740 AW	70580 TQ	MOBLS	10/01-12/01
	Montana	Y	11790 FQ	25080 AW	43960 TQ	MTBLS	10/01-12/01
	Nebraska	Y	24190 FQ	37670 AW	56200 TQ	NEBLS	10/01-12/01
	Nevada	Y	24560 FQ	37250 AW	52420 TQ	NVBLS	10/01-12/01
	Las Vegas MSA, NV-AZ	Y	14930 FQ	35850 AW	52040 TQ	NVBLS	10/01-12/01
	New Hampshire	Y	18920 FQ	32880 AW	45160 TQ	NHBLS	10/01-12/01
	Nashua PMSA, NH	Y	20420 FQ	33240 AW	44750 TQ	NHBLS	10/01-12/01
	Portsmouth-Rochester PMSA, NH-ME	Y	13370 FQ	29910 AW	43140 TQ	NHBLS	10/01-12/01
	New Jersey	Y	32190 FQ	54030 AW	73430 TQ	NJBLS	10/01-12/01
	Bergen-Passaic PMSA, NJ	Y	35570 FQ	61200 AW	84160 TQ	NJBLS	10/01-12/01
	Middlesex-Somerset-Hunterdon PMSA, NJ	Y	30140 FQ	53030 AW	75780 TQ	NJBLS	10/01-12/01
	Monmouth-Ocean PMSA, NJ	Y	29780 FQ	41500 AW	60270 TQ	NJBLS	10/01-12/01
	Newark PMSA, NJ	Y	40930 FQ	59240 AW	73850 TQ	NJBLS	10/01-12/01
	Trenton PMSA, NJ	Y	36650 FQ	44960 AW	61820 TQ	NJBLS	10/01-12/01
	New Mexico	Y	17820 FQ	26400 AW	35830 TQ	NMBLS	10/01-12/01
	Albuquerque MSA, NM	Y	17230 FQ	26300 AW	33490 TQ	NMBLS	10/01-12/01
	Las Cruces MSA, NM	Y	20950 FQ	28150 AW	36060 TQ	NMBLS	10/01-12/01
	New York	Y	31920 FQ	47620 AW	60530 TQ	NYBLS	10/01-12/01
	Albany-Schenectady-Troy MSA, NY	Y	29830 FQ	38050 AW	46060 TQ	NYBLS	10/01-12/01
	Nassau-Suffolk PMSA, NY	Y	31080 FQ	46220 AW	60290 TQ	NYBLS	10/01-12/01
	Rochester MSA, NY	Y	23150 FQ	41600 AW	54870 TQ	NYBLS	10/01-12/01
	North Carolina	Y	15520 FQ	27980 AW	40770 TQ	NCBLS	10/01-12/01
	Asheville MSA, NC	Y	12490 FQ	18750 AW	26810 TQ	NCBLS	10/01-12/01
	Charlotte-Gastonia-Rock Hill MSA, NC-SC	Y	23370 FQ	34120 AW	44800 TQ	NCBLS	10/01-12/01
	Fayetteville MSA, NC	Y	13140 FQ	27430 AW	39860 TQ	NCBLS	10/01-12/01
	Greensboro-Winston-Salem-High Point MSA, NC	Y	16990 FQ	28930 AW	41320 TQ	NCBLS	10/01-12/01
	Hickory-Morganton-Lenoir MSA, NC	Y	23370 FQ	28160 AW	34930 TQ	NCBLS	10/01-12/01
	Raleigh-Durham-Chapel Hill MSA, NC	Y	24570 FQ	31880 AW	41820 TQ	NCBLS	10/01-12/01
	Wilmington MSA, NC	Y	20750 FQ	25690 AW	29170 TQ	NCBLS	10/01-12/01
	North Dakota	Y	26960 FQ	35830 AW	44390 TQ	NDBLS	10/01-12/01
	Ohio	Y	13750 FQ	29800 AW	45920 TQ	OHBLS	10/01-12/01
	Akron PMSA, OH	Y	20100 FQ	34140 AW	46320 TQ	OHBLS	10/01-12/01
	Canton-Massillon MSA, OH	Y	20690 FQ	35700 AW	46360 TQ	OHBLS	10/01-12/01
	Cincinnati PMSA, OH-KY-IN	Y	15850 FQ	30200 AW	45370 TQ	OHBLS	10/01-12/01
	Cleveland-Lorain-Elyria PMSA, OH	Y	16400 FQ	35660 AW	48680 TQ	OHBLS	10/01-12/01
	Columbus MSA, OH	Y	12240 FQ	24640 AW	44960 TQ	OHBLS	10/01-12/01
	Dayton-Springfield MSA, OH	Y	15810 FQ	28910 AW	44090 TQ	OHBLS	10/01-12/01
	Hamilton-Middletown PMSA, OH	Y	19830 FQ	26260 AW	35990 TQ	OHBLS	10/01-12/01
	Mansfield MSA, OH	Y	16610 FQ	30480 AW	43480 TQ	OHBLS	10/01-12/01
	Toledo MSA, OH	Y	20150 FQ	31310 AW	46200 TQ	OHBLS	10/01-12/01
	Youngstown-Warren MSA, OH	Y	19980 FQ	31230 AW	44940 TQ	OHBLS	10/01-12/01
	Oklahoma	Y	15830 FQ	32330 AW	49740 TQ	OKBLS	10/01-12/01
	Tulsa MSA, OK	Y	30840 FQ	34550 AW	38600 TQ	OKBLS	10/01-12/01
	Oregon	Y	14230 FQ	34790 AW	54970 TQ	ORBLS	10/01-12/01
	Eugene-Springfield MSA, OR	Y	19720 FQ	33920 AW	43920 TQ	ORBLS	10/01-12/01
	Portland-Vancouver PMSA, OR-WA	Y	30160 FQ	43900 AW	60370 TQ	ORBLS	10/01-12/01
	Salem PMSA, OR	Y	22130 FQ	38240 AW	52520 TQ	ORBLS	10/01-12/01
	Pennsylvania	Y	27700 FQ	41510 AW	55760 TQ	PABLS	10/01-12/01

AAW	Average annual wage	AOH	Average offered, high	ASH	Average starting, high	H	Hourly	M	Monthly	S	Special: hourly and annual
AE	Average entry wage	AOL	Average offered, low	ASL	Average starting, low	HI	Highest wage paid	MTC	Median total compensation	TQ	Third quartile wage
AEX	Average experienced wage	APH	Average pay, high range	AW	Average wage paid	HR	High end range	MW	Median wage paid	W	Weekly
AO	Average offered	APL	Average pay, low range	FQ	First quartile wage	LR	Low end range	SQ	Second quartile wage	Y	Yearly

Occupation/Type/Industry	Location	Per	Low	Mid	High	Source	Date
Fire Fighter	Allentown-Bethlehem-Easton MSA, PA	Y	12680 FQ	33090 AW	44900 TQ	PABLS	10/01-12/01
	Harrisburg-Lebanon-Carlisle MSA, PA	Y	29470 FQ	39040 AW	54470 TQ	PABLS	10/01-12/01
	Scranton-Wilkes-Barre-Hazleton MSA, PA	Y	14860 FQ	35430 AW	53150 TQ	PABLS	10/01-12/01
	York MSA, PA	Y	29780 FQ	40230 AW	57240 TQ	PABLS	10/01-12/01
	Rhode Island	Y	32370 FQ	41010 AW	48640 TQ	RIBLS	10/01-12/01
	Providence-Fall River-Warwick MSA, RI-MA	Y	32000 FQ	41130 AW	50690 TQ	RIBLS	10/01-12/01
	South Carolina	Y	18820 FQ	26680 AW	35850 TQ	SCBLS	10/01-12/01
	Charleston-North Charleston MSA, SC	Y	19290 FQ	26420 AW	36480 TQ	SCBLS	10/01-12/01
	Columbia MSA, SC	Y	23570 FQ	27490 AW	34170 TQ	SCBLS	10/01-12/01
	Greenville-Spartanburg-Anderson MSA, SC	Y	19630 FQ	26780 AW	35480 TQ	SCBLS	10/01-12/01
	South Dakota	Y	12810 FQ	28200 AW	41320 TQ	SDBLS	10/01-12/01
	Tennessee	Y	16170 FQ	30460 AW	44680 TQ	TNBLS	10/01-12/01
	Chattanooga MSA, TN-GA	Y	15890 FQ	31980 AW	45730 TQ	TNBLS	10/01-12/01
	Clarksville-Hopkinsville MSA, TN-KY	Y	24260 FQ	30380 AW	35330 TQ	TNBLS	10/01-12/01
	Johnson City-Kingsport-Bristol MSA, TN-VA	Y	12670 FQ	24310 AW	39670 TQ	TNBLS	10/01-12/01
	Memphis MSA, TN-AR-MS	Y	25870 FQ	38100 AW	46690 TQ	TNBLS	10/01-12/01
	Nashville MSA, TN	Y	24840 FQ	31910 AW	41720 TQ	TNBLS	10/01-12/01
	Texas	Y	23410 FQ	36060 AW	49180 TQ	TXBLS	10/01-12/01
	Austin-San Marcos MSA, TX	Y	20160 FQ	33410 AW	51520 TQ	TXBLS	10/01-12/01
	Brownsville-Harlingen-San Benito MSA, TX	Y	20850 FQ	29500 AW	41240 TQ	TXBLS	10/01-12/01
	Corpus Christi MSA, TX	Y	17390 FQ	37040 AW	46590 TQ	TXBLS	10/01-12/01
	Dallas PMSA, TX	Y	26680 FQ	40400 AW	55150 TQ	TXBLS	10/01-12/01
	El Paso MSA, TX	Y	14930 FQ	29540 AW	45970 TQ	TXBLS	10/01-12/01
	Fort Worth-Arlington PMSA, TX	Y	28180 FQ	38730 AW	47350 TQ	TXBLS	10/01-12/01
	Galveston-Texas City PMSA, TX	Y	20800 FQ	31950 AW	44230 TQ	TXBLS	10/01-12/01
	Houston PMSA, TX	Y	31430 FQ	41940 AW	53200 TQ	TXBLS	10/01-12/01
	Killeen-Temple MSA, TX	Y	23250 FQ	28200 AW	38330 TQ	TXBLS	10/01-12/01
	McAllen-Edinburg-Mission MSA, TX	Y	15080 FQ	23350 AW	31890 TQ	TXBLS	10/01-12/01
	Utah	Y	14970 FQ	26950 AW	42600 TQ	UTBLS	10/01-12/01
	Provo-Orem MSA, UT	Y	12440 FQ	18340 AW	28980 TQ	UTBLS	10/01-12/01
	Salt Lake City-Ogden MSA, UT	Y	17020 FQ	30270 AW	47170 TQ	UTBLS	10/01-12/01
	Vermont	Y	16880 FQ	28090 AW	39410 TQ	VTBLS	10/01-12/01
	Burlington MSA, VT	Y	22010 FQ	30390 AW	41940 TQ	VTBLS	10/01-12/01
	Virginia	Y	21690 FQ	34470 AW	47600 TQ	VABLS	10/01-12/01
	Norfolk-Virginia Beach-Newport News MSA, VA-NC	Y	20930 FQ	30480 AW	38010 TQ	VABLS	10/01-12/01
	Richmond-Petersburg MSA, VA	Y	23160 FQ	34590 AW	45900 TQ	VABLS	10/01-12/01
	Roanoke MSA, VA	Y	25480 FQ	32760 AW	42560 TQ	VABLS	10/01-12/01
	Washington	Y	15950 FQ	40160 AW	58900 TQ	WABLS	10/01-12/01
	Bremerton PMSA, WA	Y	25500 FQ	36060 AW	54430 TQ	WABLS	10/01-12/01
	Olympia PMSA, WA	Y	15460 FQ	41470 AW	56110 TQ	WABLS	10/01-12/01
	Richland-Kennewick-Pasco MSA, WA	Y	29450 FQ	41730 AW	57700 TQ	WABLS	10/01-12/01
	Seattle-Bellevue-Everett PMSA, WA	Y	15010 FQ	43800 AW	60190 TQ	WABLS	10/01-12/01
	Spokane MSA, WA	Y	16530 FQ	39670 AW	61920 TQ	WABLS	10/01-12/01
	Tacoma PMSA, WA	Y	29430 FQ	47320 AW	66870 TQ	WABLS	10/01-12/01
	Yakima MSA, WA	Y	14450 FQ	39090 AW	57360 TQ	WABLS	10/01-12/01
	West Virginia	Y	22550 FQ	29950 AW	36880 TQ	WVBLS	10/01-12/01
	Huntington-Ashland MSA, WV-KY-OH	Y	18260 FQ	26430 AW	37870 TQ	WVBLS	10/01-12/01
	Wisconsin	Y	13970 FQ	32560 AW	55300 TQ	WIBLS	10/01-12/01
	Appleton-Oshkosh-Neenah MSA, WI	Y	19660 FQ	32400 AW	51140 TQ	WIBLS	10/01-12/01
	Green Bay MSA, WI	Y	19900 FQ	35720 AW	47740 TQ	WIBLS	10/01-12/01
	Madison MSA, WI	Y	13910 FQ	23100 AW	40100 TQ	WIBLS	10/01-12/01

AAW Average annual wage **AOH** Average offered, high **ASH** Average starting, high **H** Hourly **M** Monthly **S** Special: hourly and annual
AE Average entry wage **AOL** Average offered, low **ASL** Average starting, low **HI** Highest wage paid **MTC** Median total compensation **TQ** Third quartile wage
AEX Average experienced wage **APH** Average pay, high range **AW** Average wage paid **HR** High end range **MW** Median wage paid **W** Weekly
AO Average offered **APL** Average pay, low range **FQ** First quartile wage **LR** Low end range **SQ** Second quartile wage **Y** Yearly

Occupation/Type/Industry	Location	Per	Low	Mid	High	Source	Date
Fire Fighter	Milwaukee-Waukesha PMSA, WI	Y	15100 FQ	42380 AW	59900 TQ	WIBLS	10/01-12/01
	Wyoming	Y	12790 FQ	29240 AW	47250 TQ	WYBLS	10/01-12/01
	Cheyenne MSA, WY	Y	24500 FQ	30880 AW	36170 TQ	WYBLS	10/01-12/01
	Puerto Rico	Y	14430 FQ	17460 AW	21490 TQ	PRBLS	10/01-12/01
	Virgin Islands	Y	18610 FQ	23310 AW	30270 TQ	VIBLS	10/01-12/01
Fire Inspector and Investigator	Alabama	Y	26010 FQ	37120 AW	46500 TQ	ALBLS	10/01-12/01
	Alaska	Y	52100 FQ	65550 AW	82780 TQ	AKBLS	10/01-12/01
	Arizona	Y	30580 FQ	45950 AW	70000 TQ	AZBLS	10/01-12/01
	Phoenix-Mesa MSA, AZ	Y	30520 FQ	45730 AW	71360 TQ	AZBLS	10/01-12/01
	Tucson MSA, AZ	Y	32030 FQ	50560 AW	70120 TQ	AZBLS	10/01-12/01
	California	Y	42500 FQ	61720 AW	88370 TQ	CABLS	10/01-12/01
	Los Angeles-Long Beach PMSA, CA	Y	42760 FQ	60090 AW	77080 TQ	CABLS	10/01-12/01
	Modesto MSA, CA	Y	31270 FQ	45340 AW	58110 TQ	CABLS	10/01-12/01
	Oakland PMSA, CA	Y	47220 FQ	68400 AW	100540 TQ	CABLS	10/01-12/01
	Orange County PMSA, CA	Y	46820 FQ	51760 AW	58700 TQ	CABLS	10/01-12/01
	Riverside-San Bernardino PMSA, CA	Y	45570 FQ	62000 AW	82000 TQ	CABLS	10/01-12/01
	Sacramento PMSA, CA	Y	38840 FQ	52120 AW	67380 TQ	CABLS	10/01-12/01
	San Diego MSA, CA	Y	42580 FQ	52030 AW	61130 TQ	CABLS	10/01-12/01
	San Jose PMSA, CA	Y	62500 FQ	85690 AW	110260 TQ	CABLS	10/01-12/01
	Colorado	Y	20510 FQ	46060 AW	72180 TQ	COBLS	10/01-12/01
	Denver PMSA, CO	Y	20240 FQ	45060 AW	72170 TQ	COBLS	10/01-12/01
	Connecticut	Y	20830 FQ	43900 AW	65350 TQ	CTBLS	10/01-12/01
	Bridgeport PMSA, CT	Y	14420 FQ	43360 AW	62760 TQ	CTBLS	10/01-12/01
	Hartford MSA, CT	Y	20990 FQ	45400 AW	64440 TQ	CTBLS	10/01-12/01
	New Haven-Meriden PMSA, CT	Y	18690 FQ	38820 AW	58330 TQ	CTBLS	10/01-12/01
	New London-Norwich MSA, CT-RI	Y	26420 FQ	40170 AW	55540 TQ	CTBLS	10/01-12/01
	Stamford-Norwalk PMSA, CT	Y	38900 FQ	57130 AW	74360 TQ	CTBLS	10/01-12/01
	Washington PMSA, DC-MD-VA-WV	Y	41770 FQ	58620 AW	74530 TQ	DCBLS	10/01-12/01
	Florida	Y	31130 FQ	47920 AW	72720 TQ	FLBLS	10/01-12/01
	Fort Lauderdale PMSA, FL	Y	34640 FQ	51950 AW	70580 TQ	FLBLS	10/01-12/01
	Miami PMSA, FL	Y	42040 FQ	62440 AW	88510 TQ	FLBLS	10/01-12/01
	Orlando MSA, FL	Y	28270 FQ	43810 AW	66200 TQ	FLBLS	10/01-12/01
	Tampa-St. Petersburg-Clearwater MSA, FL	Y	31860 FQ	49330 AW	70850 TQ	FLBLS	10/01-12/01
	Georgia	Y	26290 FQ	38080 AW	53810 TQ	GABLS	10/01-12/01
	Atlanta MSA, GA	Y	27200 FQ	41530 AW	57450 TQ	GABLS	10/01-12/01
	Illinois	Y	37830 FQ	49060 AW	64750 TQ	ILBLS	10/01-12/01
	Indiana	Y	11950 FQ	30180 AW	49460 TQ	INBLS	10/01-12/01
	Gary PMSA, IN	Y	12220 FQ	32720 AW	52810 TQ	INBLS	10/01-12/01
	Indianapolis MSA, IN	Y	11470 FQ	25600 AW	47310 TQ	INBLS	10/01-12/01
	Iowa	Y	31180 FQ	47940 AW	70670 TQ	IABLS	10/01-12/01
	Kansas	Y	26810 FQ	41250 AW	55930 TQ	KSBLS	10/01-12/01
	Kentucky	Y	24770 FQ	35410 AW	46610 TQ	KYBLS	10/01-12/01
	Louisiana	Y	18530 FQ	24580 AW	32790 TQ	LABLS	10/01-12/01
	Baton Rouge MSA, LA	Y	18690 FQ	26050 AW	38640 TQ	LABLS	10/01-12/01
	Lafayette MSA, LA	Y	24650 FQ	27850 AW	31310 TQ	LABLS	10/01-12/01
	New Orleans MSA, LA	Y	15950 FQ	22390 AW	32410 TQ	LABLS	10/01-12/01
	Maine	Y	25470 FQ	33600 AW	42610 TQ	MEBLS	10/01-12/01
	Maryland	Y	36170 FQ	53560 AW	69270 TQ	MDBLS	10/01-12/01
	Massachusetts	Y	28690 FQ	44480 AW	65490 TQ	MABLS	10/01-12/01
	Boston PMSA, MA-NH	Y	31660 FQ	48620 AW	68370 TQ	MABLS	10/01-12/01
	Michigan	Y	33240 FQ	48100 AW	64820 TQ	MIBLS	10/01-12/01
	Detroit PMSA, MI	Y	36690 FQ	50890 AW	67870 TQ	MIBLS	10/01-12/01
	Minnesota	Y	29010 FQ	45030 AW	58010 TQ	MNBLS	10/01-12/01
	Minneapolis-St. Paul MSA, MN-WI	Y	37000 FQ	47060 AW	59710 TQ	MNBLS	10/01-12/01
	Mississippi	Y	26060 FQ	43060 AW	58480 TQ	MSBLS	10/01-12/01
	Missouri	Y	29130 FQ	47980 AW	72630 TQ	MOBLS	10/01-12/01
	St. Louis MSA, MO-IL	Y	38890 FQ	58660 AW	83310 TQ	MOBLS	10/01-12/01
	Montana	Y	27580 FQ	37990 AW	45910 TQ	MTBLS	10/01-12/01
	Nebraska	Y	29810 FQ	39620 AW	53690 TQ	NEBLS	10/01-12/01
	Nevada	Y	34970 FQ	52820 AW	70880 TQ	NVBLS	10/01-12/01
	Las Vegas MSA, NV-AZ	Y	30800 FQ	54370 AW	71560 TQ	NVBLS	10/01-12/01
	New Hampshire	Y	24860 FQ	38460 AW	53640 TQ	NHBLS	10/01-12/01
	New Jersey	Y	26750 FQ	44950 AW	68730 TQ	NJBLS	10/01-12/01
	Bergen-Passaic PMSA, NJ	Y	24320 FQ	42020 AW	73830 TQ	NJBLS	10/01-12/01

AAW	Average annual wage	**AOH**	Average offered, high	**ASH**	Average starting, high	**H**	Hourly	**M**	Monthly	**S**	Special: hourly and annual
AE	Average entry wage	**AOL**	Average offered, low	**ASL**	Average starting, low	**HI**	Highest wage paid	**MTC**	Median total compensation	**TQ**	Third quartile wage
AEX	Average experienced wage	**APH**	Average pay, high range	**AW**	Average wage paid	**HR**	High end range	**MW**	Median wage paid	**W**	Weekly
AO	Average offered	**APL**	Average pay, low range	**FQ**	First quartile wage	**LR**	Low end range	**SQ**	Second quartile wage	**Y**	Yearly

Occupation/Type/Industry	Location	Per	Low	Mid	High	Source	Date
Fire Inspector and Investigator	Middlesex-Somerset-Hunterdon PMSA, NJ	Y	30550 FQ	39610 AW	57860 TQ	NJBLS	10/01-12/01
	Newark PMSA, NJ	Y	30010 FQ	47720 AW	69900 TQ	NJBLS	10/01-12/01
	Trenton PMSA, NJ	Y	33880 FQ	47670 AW	65360 TQ	NJBLS	10/01-12/01
	New Mexico	Y	24520 FQ	37210 AW	47660 TQ	NMBLS	10/01-12/01
	Albuquerque MSA, NM	Y	27110 FQ	40320 AW	48670 TQ	NMBLS	10/01-12/01
	New York	Y	23350 FQ	41650 AW	65510 TQ	NYBLS	10/01-12/01
	Albany-Schenectady-Troy MSA, NY	Y	38370 FQ	51880 AW	71740 TQ	NYBLS	10/01-12/01
	Buffalo-Niagara Falls MSA, NY	Y	35550 FQ	43080 AW	52980 TQ	NYBLS	10/01-12/01
	New York PMSA, NY	Y	21850 FQ	38760 AW	64040 TQ	NYBLS	10/01-12/01
	Rochester MSA, NY	Y	24410 FQ	35890 AW	45630 TQ	NYBLS	10/01-12/01
	North Carolina	Y	25280 FQ	36610 AW	49990 TQ	NCBLS	10/01-12/01
	Charlotte-Gastonia-Rock Hill MSA, NC-SC	Y	30640 FQ	43710 AW	64260 TQ	NCBLS	10/01-12/01
	Greensboro-Winston-Salem-High Point MSA, NC	Y	28110 FQ	36340 AW	46180 TQ	NCBLS	10/01-12/01
	Raleigh-Durham-Chapel Hill MSA, NC	Y	23720 FQ	34440 AW	47560 TQ	NCBLS	10/01-12/01
	Ohio	Y	31380 FQ	48420 AW	65390 TQ	OHBLS	10/01-12/01
	Cleveland-Lorain-Elyria PMSA, OH	Y	30810 FQ	46470 AW	62240 TQ	OHBLS	10/01-12/01
	Columbus MSA, OH	Y	41070 FQ	57080 AW	74200 TQ	OHBLS	10/01-12/01
	Dayton-Springfield MSA, OH	Y	26290 FQ	61820 AW	90810 TQ	OHBLS	10/01-12/01
	Oklahoma	Y	22450 FQ	38980 AW	60930 TQ	OKBLS	10/01-12/01
	Oklahoma City MSA, OK	Y	28590 FQ	48720 AW	71000 TQ	OKBLS	10/01-12/01
	Oregon	Y	31140 FQ	51610 AW	70290 TQ	ORBLS	10/01-12/01
	Pennsylvania	Y	28370 FQ	44440 AW	62280 TQ	PABLS	10/01-12/01
	Philadelphia PMSA, PA-NJ	Y	32320 FQ	45570 AW	62760 TQ	PABLS	10/01-12/01
	Rhode Island	Y	34560 FQ	42780 AW	52310 TQ	RIBLS	10/01-12/01
	Providence-Fall River-Warwick MSA, RI-MA	Y	34080 FQ	42520 AW	51950 TQ	RIBLS	10/01-12/01
	South Carolina	Y	22810 FQ	31150 AW	41770 TQ	SCBLS	10/01-12/01
	Greenville-Spartanburg-Anderson MSA, SC	Y	21990 FQ	29800 AW	34960 TQ	SCBLS	10/01-12/01
	Tennessee	Y	24210 FQ	39580 AW	55780 TQ	TNBLS	10/01-12/01
	Memphis MSA, TN-AR-MS	Y	22430 FQ	45590 AW	59780 TQ	TNBLS	10/01-12/01
	Nashville MSA, TN	Y	30980 FQ	40950 AW	47670 TQ	TNBLS	10/01-12/01
	Texas	Y	30090 FQ	42790 AW	58930 TQ	TXBLS	10/01-12/01
	Dallas PMSA, TX	Y	36520 FQ	52230 AW	69290 TQ	TXBLS	10/01-12/01
	Fort Worth-Arlington PMSA, TX	Y	35100 FQ	49980 AW	67690 TQ	TXBLS	10/01-12/01
	Houston PMSA, TX	Y	29470 FQ	44120 AW	58920 TQ	TXBLS	10/01-12/01
	Utah	Y	28690 FQ	43250 AW	58440 TQ	UTBLS	10/01-12/01
	Salt Lake City-Ogden MSA, UT	Y	33310 FQ	45900 AW	59440 TQ	UTBLS	10/01-12/01
	Vermont	Y	31220 FQ	41390 AW	53560 TQ	VTBLS	10/01-12/01
	Virginia	Y	29940 FQ	42980 AW	63420 TQ	VABLS	10/01-12/01
	Norfolk-Virginia Beach-Newport News MSA, VA-NC	Y	32130 FQ	44370 AW	62350 TQ	VABLS	10/01-12/01
	Washington	Y	41740 FQ	57680 AW	72730 TQ	WABLS	10/01-12/01
	Seattle-Bellevue-Everett PMSA, WA	Y	49450 FQ	61660 AW	73800 TQ	WABLS	10/01-12/01
	West Virginia	Y	22960 FQ	29690 AW	36530 TQ	WVBLS	10/01-12/01
	Wisconsin	Y	12150 FQ	33510 AW	56990 TQ	WIBLS	10/01-12/01
	Appleton-Oshkosh-Neenah MSA, WI	Y	12290 FQ	30060 AW	53670 TQ	WIBLS	10/01-12/01
	Milwaukee-Waukesha PMSA, WI	Y	41430 FQ	52820 AW	67280 TQ	WIBLS	10/01-12/01
	Puerto Rico	Y	14320 FQ	20980 AW	32580 TQ	PRBLS	10/01-12/01
Firewall Specialist							
Internet and E-Commerce	United States	Y		59750-82750 AW		IW	1/00-1/01
First-Line Supervisor/Manager							
Construction Trade and Extraction Workers	Alabama	H	12.77 FQ	20.63 AW	29.95 TQ	ALBLS	10/01-12/01
Construction Trade and Extraction Workers	Birmingham MSA, AL	H	15.52 FQ	22.65 AW	29.80 TQ	ALBLS	10/01-12/01
Construction Trade and Extraction Workers	Huntsville MSA, AL	H	12.17 FQ	18.20 AW	26.03 TQ	ALBLS	10/01-12/01
Construction Trade and Extraction Workers	Mobile MSA, AL	H	14.10 FQ	22.44 AW	34.66 TQ	ALBLS	10/01-12/01
Construction Trade and Extraction Workers	Montgomery MSA, AL	H	11.22 FQ	20.95 AW	33.03 TQ	ALBLS	10/01-12/01

AAW Average annual wage; AE Average entry wage; AEX Average experienced wage; AO Average offered; AOH Average offered, high; AOL Average offered, low; APH Average pay, high range; APL Average pay, low range; ASH Average starting, high; ASL Average starting, low; AW Average wage paid; FQ First quartile wage; H Hourly; HI Highest wage paid; HR High end range; LR Low end range; M Monthly; MTC Median total compensation; MW Median wage paid; SQ Second quartile wage; S Special: hourly and annual; TQ Third quartile wage; W Weekly; Y Yearly

Occupation/Type/Industry	Location	Per	Low	Mid	High	Source	Date
First-Line Supervisor/Manager							
Construction Trade and Extraction Workers	Alaska	H	20.76 FQ	32.18 AW	48.90 TQ	AKBLS	10/01-12/01
Construction Trade and Extraction Workers	Anchorage MSA, AK	H	21.49 FQ	33.26 AW	46.17 TQ	AKBLS	10/01-12/01
Construction Trade and Extraction Workers	Arizona	H	14.76 FQ	22.63 AW	32.67 TQ	AZBLS	10/01-12/01
Construction Trade and Extraction Workers	Phoenix-Mesa MSA, AZ	H	15.08 FQ	23.35 AW	33.39 TQ	AZBLS	10/01-12/01
Construction Trade and Extraction Workers	Tucson MSA, AZ	H	14.61 FQ	21.62 AW	30.31 TQ	AZBLS	10/01-12/01
Construction Trade and Extraction Workers	Arkansas	H	12.03 FQ	18.31 AW	26.00 TQ	ARBLS	10/01-12/01
Construction Trade and Extraction Workers	Fayetteville-Springdale-Rogers MSA, AR	H	13.58 FQ	19.69 AW	27.36 TQ	ARBLS	10/01-12/01
Construction Trade and Extraction Workers	Fort Smith MSA, AR-OK	H	13.40 FQ	19.69 AW	26.72 TQ	ARBLS	10/01-12/01
Construction Trade and Extraction Workers	Little Rock-North Little Rock MSA, AR	H	13.68 FQ	18.53 AW	25.32 TQ	ARBLS	10/01-12/01
Construction Trade and Extraction Workers	California	H	18.34 FQ	28.51 AW	41.12 TQ	CABLS	10/01-12/01
Construction Trade and Extraction Workers	Bakersfield MSA, CA	H	15.05 FQ	26.05 AW	38.41 TQ	CABLS	10/01-12/01
Construction Trade and Extraction Workers	Chico-Paradise MSA, CA	H	15.91 FQ	25.25 AW	35.69 TQ	CABLS	10/01-12/01
Construction Trade and Extraction Workers	Fresno MSA, CA	H	14.84 FQ	25.40 AW	34.39 TQ	CABLS	10/01-12/01
Construction Trade and Extraction Workers	Los Angeles-Long Beach PMSA, CA	H	16.03 FQ	28.25 AW	43.09 TQ	CABLS	10/01-12/01
Construction Trade and Extraction Workers	Merced MSA, CA	H	16.87 FQ	24.40 AW	33.87 TQ	CABLS	10/01-12/01
Construction Trade and Extraction Workers	Modesto MSA, CA	H	17.54 FQ	24.88 AW	35.25 TQ	CABLS	10/01-12/01
Construction Trade and Extraction Workers	Oakland PMSA, CA	H	22.00 FQ	31.49 AW	43.97 TQ	CABLS	10/01-12/01
Construction Trade and Extraction Workers	Orange County PMSA, CA	H	19.85 FQ	28.59 AW	39.05 TQ	CABLS	10/01-12/01
Construction Trade and Extraction Workers	Redding MSA, CA	H	15.10 FQ	24.63 AW	34.34 TQ	CABLS	10/01-12/01
Construction Trade and Extraction Workers	Riverside-San Bernardino PMSA, CA	H	17.94 FQ	26.97 AW	37.02 TQ	CABLS	10/01-12/01
Construction Trade and Extraction Workers	Sacramento PMSA, CA	H	19.67 FQ	27.75 AW	36.80 TQ	CABLS	10/01-12/01
Construction Trade and Extraction Workers	Salinas MSA, CA	H	21.65 FQ	31.01 AW	42.77 TQ	CABLS	10/01-12/01
Construction Trade and Extraction Workers	San Diego MSA, CA	H	19.93 FQ	29.10 AW	39.71 TQ	CABLS	10/01-12/01
Construction Trade and Extraction Workers	San Francisco PMSA, CA	H	19.62 FQ	31.13 AW	45.12 TQ	CABLS	10/01-12/01
Construction Trade and Extraction Workers	San Jose PMSA, CA	H	22.01 FQ	33.27 AW	44.19 TQ	CABLS	10/01-12/01
Construction Trade and Extraction Workers	San Luis Obispo-Atascadero-Paso Robles MSA, CA	H	19.03 FQ	26.78 AW	34.37 TQ	CABLS	10/01-12/01
Construction Trade and Extraction Workers	Santa Barbara-Santa Maria-Lompoc MSA, CA	H	18.24 FQ	28.68 AW	41.91 TQ	CABLS	10/01-12/01
Construction Trade and Extraction Workers	Santa Cruz-Watsonville PMSA, CA	H	17.81 FQ	28.55 AW	38.07 TQ	CABLS	10/01-12/01
Construction Trade and Extraction Workers	Santa Rosa PMSA, CA	H	21.00 FQ	29.94 AW	42.41 TQ	CABLS	10/01-12/01
Construction Trade and Extraction Workers	Stockton-Lodi MSA, CA	H	18.41 FQ	26.02 AW	37.45 TQ	CABLS	10/01-12/01
Construction Trade and Extraction Workers	Vallejo-Fairfield-Napa PMSA, CA	H	22.34 FQ	30.55 AW	41.13 TQ	CABLS	10/01-12/01
Construction Trade and Extraction Workers	Ventura PMSA, CA	H	17.92 FQ	28.48 AW	40.00 TQ	CABLS	10/01-12/01
Construction Trade and Extraction Workers	Visalia-Tulare-Porterville MSA, CA	H	15.58 FQ	22.48 AW	31.54 TQ	CABLS	10/01-12/01
Construction Trade and Extraction Workers	Colorado	H	15.72 FQ	24.81 AW	35.36 TQ	COBLS	10/01-12/01
Construction Trade and Extraction Workers	Boulder-Longmont PMSA, CO	H	14.40 FQ	22.78 AW	31.00 TQ	COBLS	10/01-12/01
Construction Trade and Extraction Workers	Colorado Springs MSA, CO	H	13.60 FQ	21.62 AW	29.73 TQ	COBLS	10/01-12/01
Construction Trade and Extraction Workers	Denver PMSA, CO	H	16.13 FQ	25.81 AW	36.80 TQ	COBLS	10/01-12/01
Construction Trade and Extraction Workers	Fort Collins-Loveland MSA, CO	H	16.43 FQ	24.01 AW	33.59 TQ	COBLS	10/01-12/01
Construction Trade and Extraction Workers	Greeley PMSA, CO	H	16.12 FQ	25.07 AW	36.09 TQ	COBLS	10/01-12/01
Construction Trade and Extraction Workers	Connecticut	H	18.36 FQ	27.27 AW	38.04 TQ	CTBLS	10/01-12/01
Construction Trade and Extraction Workers	Bridgeport PMSA, CT	H	19.15 FQ	26.73 AW	37.61 TQ	CTBLS	10/01-12/01
Construction Trade and Extraction Workers	Danbury PMSA, CT	H	16.61 FQ	25.61 AW	38.93 TQ	CTBLS	10/01-12/01
Construction Trade and Extraction Workers	Hartford MSA, CT	H	17.68 FQ	25.43 AW	33.70 TQ	CTBLS	10/01-12/01
Construction Trade and Extraction Workers	New Haven-Meriden PMSA, CT	H	21.45 FQ	30.94 AW	43.18 TQ	CTBLS	10/01-12/01
Construction Trade and Extraction Workers	New London-Norwich MSA, CT-RI	H	17.66 FQ	27.99 AW	41.34 TQ	CTBLS	10/01-12/01
Construction Trade and Extraction Workers	Stamford-Norwalk PMSA, CT	H	17.58 FQ	28.39 AW	38.69 TQ	CTBLS	10/01-12/01
Construction Trade and Extraction Workers	Waterbury PMSA, CT	H	18.60 FQ	28.50 AW	44.32 TQ	CTBLS	10/01-12/01
Construction Trade and Extraction Workers	Delaware	H	15.30 FQ	22.59 AW	31.46 TQ	DEBLS	10/01-12/01
Construction Trade and Extraction Workers	Wilmington-Newark PMSA, DE-MD	H	15.89 FQ	22.91 AW	31.28 TQ	DEBLS	10/01-12/01
Construction Trade and Extraction Workers	District of Columbia	H	17.18 FQ	26.94 AW	36.45 TQ	DCBLS	10/01-12/01
Construction Trade and Extraction Workers	Washington PMSA, DC-MD-VA-WV	H	15.97 FQ	24.97 AW	34.29 TQ	DCBLS	10/01-12/01
Construction Trade and Extraction Workers	Florida	H	12.81 FQ	20.62 AW	30.00 TQ	FLBLS	10/01-12/01
Construction Trade and Extraction Workers	Daytona Beach MSA, FL	H	12.11 FQ	17.44 AW	24.21 TQ	FLBLS	10/01-12/01
Construction Trade and Extraction Workers	Fort Lauderdale PMSA, FL	H	14.24 FQ	22.47 AW	32.61 TQ	FLBLS	10/01-12/01
Construction Trade and Extraction Workers	Fort Myers-Cape Coral MSA, FL	H	12.81 FQ	21.56 AW	30.57 TQ	FLBLS	10/01-12/01

AAW Average annual wage; AE Average entry wage; AEX Average experienced wage; AO Average offered; AOH Average offered, high; AOL Average offered, low; APH Average pay, high range; APL Average pay, low range; ASH Average starting, high; ASL Average starting, low; AW Average wage paid; FQ First quartile wage; H Hourly; HI Highest wage paid; HR High end range; LR Low end range; M Monthly; MTC Median total compensation; MW Median wage paid; SQ Second quartile wage; S Special: hourly and annual; TQ Third quartile wage; W Weekly; Y Yearly

Occupation/Type/Industry	Location	Per	Low	Mid	High	Source	Date
First-Line Supervisor/Manager							
Construction Trade and Extraction Workers	Fort Pierce-Port St. Lucie MSA, FL	H	11.70 FQ	18.89 AW	26.96 TQ	FLBLS	10/01-12/01
Construction Trade and Extraction Workers	Fort Walton Beach MSA, FL	H	11.95 FQ	18.89 AW	25.67 TQ	FLBLS	10/01-12/01
Construction Trade and Extraction Workers	Gainesville MSA, FL	H	11.55 FQ	17.61 AW	24.89 TQ	FLBLS	10/01-12/01
Construction Trade and Extraction Workers	Jacksonville MSA, FL	H	13.84 FQ	20.86 AW	28.81 TQ	FLBLS	10/01-12/01
Construction Trade and Extraction Workers	Lakeland-Winter Haven MSA, FL	H	13.33 FQ	19.81 AW	27.38 TQ	FLBLS	10/01-12/01
Construction Trade and Extraction Workers	Melbourne-Titusville-Palm Bay MSA, FL	H	14.03 FQ	20.04 AW	27.27 TQ	FLBLS	10/01-12/01
Construction Trade and Extraction Workers	Miami PMSA, FL	H	12.23 FQ	20.93 AW	32.76 TQ	FLBLS	10/01-12/01
Construction Trade and Extraction Workers	Naples MSA, FL	H	14.24 FQ	22.65 AW	33.19 TQ	FLBLS	10/01-12/01
Construction Trade and Extraction Workers	Ocala MSA, FL	H	11.55 FQ	20.34 AW	35.53 TQ	FLBLS	10/01-12/01
Construction Trade and Extraction Workers	Orlando MSA, FL	H	13.73 FQ	21.37 AW	31.89 TQ	FLBLS	10/01-12/01
Construction Trade and Extraction Workers	Pensacola MSA, FL	H	12.15 FQ	18.35 AW	26.05 TQ	FLBLS	10/01-12/01
Construction Trade and Extraction Workers	Sarasota-Bradenton MSA, FL	H	12.79 FQ	21.49 AW	31.90 TQ	FLBLS	10/01-12/01
Construction Trade and Extraction Workers	Tallahassee MSA, FL	H	12.97 FQ	19.18 AW	26.73 TQ	FLBLS	10/01-12/01
Construction Trade and Extraction Workers	Tampa-St. Petersburg-Clearwater MSA, FL	H	13.35 FQ	20.42 AW	29.93 TQ	FLBLS	10/01-12/01
Construction Trade and Extraction Workers	West Palm Beach-Boca Raton MSA, FL	H	11.83 FQ	20.13 AW	28.54 TQ	FLBLS	10/01-12/01
Construction Trade and Extraction Workers	Georgia	H	14.16 FQ	21.65 AW	31.52 TQ	GABLS	10/01-12/01
Construction Trade and Extraction Workers	Atlanta MSA, GA	H	15.73 FQ	23.22 AW	33.55 TQ	GABLS	10/01-12/01
Construction Trade and Extraction Workers	Augusta-Aiken MSA, GA-SC	H	13.11 FQ	23.60 AW	42.18 TQ	GABLS	10/01-12/01
Construction Trade and Extraction Workers	Columbus MSA, GA-AL	H	12.64 FQ	19.06 AW	26.76 TQ	GABLS	10/01-12/01
Construction Trade and Extraction Workers	Macon MSA, GA	H	10.72 FQ	19.62 AW	27.13 TQ	GABLS	10/01-12/01
Construction Trade and Extraction Workers	Savannah MSA, GA	H	14.25 FQ	20.72 AW	28.53 TQ	GABLS	10/01-12/01
Construction Trade and Extraction Workers	Hawaii	H	18.99 FQ	28.38 AW	40.30 TQ	HIBLS	10/01-12/01
Construction Trade and Extraction Workers	Honolulu MSA, HI	H	19.09 FQ	28.48 AW	40.78 TQ	HIBLS	10/01-12/01
Construction Trade and Extraction Workers	Idaho	H	13.26 FQ	20.57 AW	28.55 TQ	IDBLS	10/01-12/01
Construction Trade and Extraction Workers	Boise City MSA, ID	H	14.78 FQ	22.02 AW	30.93 TQ	IDBLS	10/01-12/01
Construction Trade and Extraction Workers	Illinois	H	6.17 FQ	23.23 AW	36.13 TQ	ILBLS	10/01-12/01
Construction Trade and Extraction Workers	Champaign-Urbana MSA, IL	H	16.92 FQ	29.41 AW		ILBLS	10/01-12/01
Construction Trade and Extraction Workers	Chicago PMSA, IL	H	5.82 FQ	22.68 AW	37.76 TQ	ILBLS	10/01-12/01
Construction Trade and Extraction Workers	Peoria-Pekin MSA, IL	H	16.57 FQ	26.30 AW	35.91 TQ	ILBLS	10/01-12/01
Construction Trade and Extraction Workers	Rockford MSA, IL	H	15.07 FQ	27.48 AW	35.29 TQ	ILBLS	10/01-12/01
Construction Trade and Extraction Workers	Springfield MSA, IL	H	16.60 FQ	23.26 AW	32.58 TQ	ILBLS	10/01-12/01
Construction Trade and Extraction Workers	Indiana	H	13.22 FQ	22.48 AW	33.17 TQ	INBLS	10/01-12/01
Construction Trade and Extraction Workers	Elkhart-Goshen MSA, IN	H	14.36 FQ	20.05 AW	28.85 TQ	INBLS	10/01-12/01
Construction Trade and Extraction Workers	Evansville-Henderson MSA, IN-KY	H	15.03 FQ	22.76 AW	33.65 TQ	INBLS	10/01-12/01
Construction Trade and Extraction Workers	Fort Wayne MSA, IN	H	15.24 FQ	23.01 AW	33.36 TQ	INBLS	10/01-12/01
Construction Trade and Extraction Workers	Gary PMSA, IN	H	14.98 FQ	25.28 AW	35.53 TQ	INBLS	10/01-12/01
Construction Trade and Extraction Workers	Indianapolis MSA, IN	H	12.77 FQ	22.25 AW	32.62 TQ	INBLS	10/01-12/01
Construction Trade and Extraction Workers	Lafayette MSA, IN	H	12.28 FQ	19.41 AW	30.35 TQ	INBLS	10/01-12/01
Construction Trade and Extraction Workers	South Bend MSA, IN	H	18.08 FQ	29.71 AW	52.09 TQ	INBLS	10/01-12/01
Construction Trade and Extraction Workers	Iowa	H	11.53 FQ	20.13 AW	30.35 TQ	IABLS	10/01-12/01
Construction Trade and Extraction Workers	Cedar Rapids MSA, IA	H	14.26 FQ	24.30 AW	35.16 TQ	IABLS	10/01-12/01
Construction Trade and Extraction Workers	Davenport-Moline-Rock Island MSA, IA-IL	H	17.24 FQ	25.07 AW	33.65 TQ	IABLS	10/01-12/01
Construction Trade and Extraction Workers	Des Moines MSA, IA	H	9.48 FQ	20.78 AW	31.62 TQ	IABLS	10/01-12/01
Construction Trade and Extraction Workers	Kansas	H	13.72 FQ	21.25 AW	30.98 TQ	KSBLS	10/01-12/01
Construction Trade and Extraction Workers	Topeka MSA, KS	H	14.63 FQ	20.68 AW	27.37 TQ	KSBLS	10/01-12/01
Construction Trade and Extraction Workers	Wichita MSA, KS	H	15.41 FQ	22.06 AW	29.20 TQ	KSBLS	10/01-12/01
Construction Trade and Extraction Workers	Kentucky	H	12.95 FQ	21.25 AW	31.43 TQ	KYBLS	10/01-12/01
Construction Trade and Extraction Workers	Lexington MSA, KY	H	14.16 FQ	20.01 AW	27.97 TQ	KYBLS	10/01-12/01
Construction Trade and Extraction Workers	Louisville MSA, KY-IN	H	13.90 FQ	22.12 AW	30.81 TQ	KYBLS	10/01-12/01
Construction Trade and Extraction Workers	Louisiana	H	12.29 FQ	19.61 AW	28.81 TQ	LABLS	10/01-12/01
Construction Trade and Extraction Workers	Baton Rouge MSA, LA	H	12.75 FQ	19.20 AW	26.56 TQ	LABLS	10/01-12/01
Construction Trade and Extraction Workers	Houma MSA, LA	H	12.28 FQ	19.16 AW	26.55 TQ	LABLS	10/01-12/01
Construction Trade and Extraction Workers	Lafayette MSA, LA	H	12.55 FQ	19.00 AW	28.03 TQ	LABLS	10/01-12/01
Construction Trade and Extraction Workers	Lake Charles MSA, LA	H	11.05 FQ	21.25 AW	32.44 TQ	LABLS	10/01-12/01
Construction Trade and Extraction Workers	New Orleans MSA, LA	H	14.07 FQ	22.11 AW	35.42 TQ	LABLS	10/01-12/01
Construction Trade and Extraction Workers	Shreveport-Bossier City MSA, LA	H	11.68 FQ	15.56 AW	22.62 TQ	LABLS	10/01-12/01
Construction Trade and Extraction Workers	Maine	H	12.77 FQ	20.03 AW	28.16 TQ	MEBLS	10/01-12/01
Construction Trade and Extraction Workers	Portland MSA, ME	H	15.85 FQ	24.19 AW	35.88 TQ	MEBLS	10/01-12/01
Construction Trade and Extraction Workers	Maryland	H	15.96 FQ	23.25 AW	32.38 TQ	MDBLS	10/01-12/01
Construction Trade and Extraction Workers	Baltimore PMSA, MD	H	15.66 FQ	22.57 AW	30.65 TQ	MDBLS	10/01-12/01
Construction Trade and Extraction Workers	Massachusetts	H	17.68 FQ	27.16 AW	39.24 TQ	MABLS	10/01-12/01
Construction Trade and Extraction Workers	Boston PMSA, MA-NH	H	20.08 FQ	29.06 AW	41.20 TQ	MABLS	10/01-12/01
Construction Trade and Extraction Workers	Brockton PMSA, MA	H	17.39 FQ	27.61 AW	41.67 TQ	MABLS	10/01-12/01

AAW	Average annual wage	AOH	Average offered, high	ASH	Average starting, high	H	Hourly	M	Monthly	S	Special: hourly and annual
AE	Average entry wage	AOL	Average offered, low	ASL	Average starting, low	HI	Highest wage paid	MTC	Median total compensation	TQ	Third quartile wage
AEX	Average experienced wage	APH	Average pay, high range	AW	Average wage paid	HR	High end range	MW	Median wage paid	W	Weekly
AO	Average offered	APL	Average pay, low range	FQ	First quartile wage	LR	Low end range	SQ	Second quartile wage	Y	Yearly

Occupation/Type/Industry	Location	Per	Low	Mid	High	Source	Date
First-Line Supervisor/Manager							
Construction Trade and Extraction Workers	Lawrence PMSA, MA-NH	H	18.25 FQ	26.31 AW	37.48 TQ	MABLS	10/01-12/01
Construction Trade and Extraction Workers	Lowell PMSA, MA-NH	H	18.26 FQ	24.50 AW	32.90 TQ	MABLS	10/01-12/01
Construction Trade and Extraction Workers	New Bedford PMSA, MA	H	14.23 FQ	22.69 AW	34.81 TQ	MABLS	10/01-12/01
Construction Trade and Extraction Workers	Springfield MSA, MA	H	15.41 FQ	23.10 AW	32.63 TQ	MABLS	10/01-12/01
Construction Trade and Extraction Workers	Worcester PMSA, MA-CT	H	16.46 FQ	26.00 AW	35.83 TQ	MABLS	10/01-12/01
Construction Trade and Extraction Workers	Michigan	H	16.71 FQ	27.56 AW	42.48 TQ	MIBLS	10/01-12/01
Construction Trade and Extraction Workers	Ann Arbor PMSA, MI	H	16.37 FQ	30.29 AW	48.21 TQ	MIBLS	10/01-12/01
Construction Trade and Extraction Workers	Detroit PMSA, MI	H	18.29 FQ	29.65 AW	44.62 TQ	MIBLS	10/01-12/01
Construction Trade and Extraction Workers	Flint PMSA, MI	H	18.96 FQ	29.86 AW	44.80 TQ	MIBLS	10/01-12/01
Construction Trade and Extraction Workers	Grand Rapids-Muskegon-Holland MSA, MI	H	16.71 FQ	26.97 AW	43.73 TQ	MIBLS	10/01-12/01
Construction Trade and Extraction Workers	Kalamazoo-Battle Creek MSA, MI	H	16.81 FQ	27.22 AW	36.11 TQ	MIBLS	10/01-12/01
Construction Trade and Extraction Workers	Lansing-East Lansing MSA, MI	H	17.96 FQ	25.67 AW	34.53 TQ	MIBLS	10/01-12/01
Construction Trade and Extraction Workers	Saginaw-Bay City-Midland MSA, MI	H	16.73 FQ	26.34 AW	38.76 TQ	MIBLS	10/01-12/01
Construction Trade and Extraction Workers	Minnesota	H	16.22 FQ	25.68 AW	35.25 TQ	MNBLS	10/01-12/01
Construction Trade and Extraction Workers	Duluth-Superior MSA, MN-WI	H	15.40 FQ	23.92 AW	32.91 TQ	MNBLS	10/01-12/01
Construction Trade and Extraction Workers	Minneapolis-St. Paul MSA, MN-WI	H	18.03 FQ	27.59 AW	36.82 TQ	MNBLS	10/01-12/01
Construction Trade and Extraction Workers	St. Cloud MSA, MN	H	13.36 FQ	22.63 AW	33.35 TQ	MNBLS	10/01-12/01
Construction Trade and Extraction Workers	Mississippi	H	12.17 FQ	19.60 AW	28.44 TQ	MSBLS	10/01-12/01
Construction Trade and Extraction Workers	Biloxi-Gulfport-Pascagoula MSA, MS	H	13.30 FQ	19.48 AW	27.16 TQ	MSBLS	10/01-12/01
Construction Trade and Extraction Workers	Jackson MSA, MS	H	12.78 FQ	21.46 AW	29.20 TQ	MSBLS	10/01-12/01
Construction Trade and Extraction Workers	Missouri	H	14.44 FQ	22.92 AW	33.35 TQ	MOBLS	10/01-12/01
Construction Trade and Extraction Workers	Kansas City MSA, MO-KS	H	15.59 FQ	24.40 AW	33.95 TQ	MOBLS	10/01-12/01
Construction Trade and Extraction Workers	St. Louis MSA, MO-IL	H	16.96 FQ	25.59 AW	35.03 TQ	MOBLS	10/01-12/01
Construction Trade and Extraction Workers	Springfield MSA, MO	H	14.18 FQ	21.20 AW	29.45 TQ	MOBLS	10/01-12/01
Construction Trade and Extraction Workers	Montana	H	12.65 FQ	19.79 AW	27.88 TQ	MTBLS	10/01-12/01
Construction Trade and Extraction Workers	Billings MSA, MT	H	15.52 FQ	21.10 AW	27.46 TQ	MTBLS	10/01-12/01
Construction Trade and Extraction Workers	Nebraska	H	13.37 FQ	20.81 AW	29.03 TQ	NEBLS	10/01-12/01
Construction Trade and Extraction Workers	Lincoln MSA, NE	H	14.17 FQ	20.89 AW	27.78 TQ	NEBLS	10/01-12/01
Construction Trade and Extraction Workers	Omaha MSA, NE-IA	H	15.69 FQ	22.49 AW	30.13 TQ	NEBLS	10/01-12/01
Construction Trade and Extraction Workers	Nevada	H	15.92 FQ	24.90 AW	34.95 TQ	NVBLS	10/01-12/01
Construction Trade and Extraction Workers	Las Vegas MSA, NV-AZ	H	15.32 FQ	24.20 AW	34.41 TQ	NVBLS	10/01-12/01
Construction Trade and Extraction Workers	Reno MSA, NV	H	16.55 FQ	25.00 AW	34.56 TQ	NVBLS	10/01-12/01
Construction Trade and Extraction Workers	New Hampshire	H	13.66 FQ	20.66 AW	29.95 TQ	NHBLS	10/01-12/01
Construction Trade and Extraction Workers	Manchester PMSA, NH	H	15.01 FQ	22.90 AW	32.61 TQ	NHBLS	10/01-12/01
Construction Trade and Extraction Workers	Nashua PMSA, NH	H	14.57 FQ	20.85 AW	28.61 TQ	NHBLS	10/01-12/01
Construction Trade and Extraction Workers	Portsmouth-Rochester PMSA, NH-ME	H	14.80 FQ	20.58 AW	26.94 TQ	NHBLS	10/01-12/01
Construction Trade and Extraction Workers	New Jersey	H	18.06 FQ	29.99 AW	43.72 TQ	NJBLS	10/01-12/01
Construction Trade and Extraction Workers	Atlantic-Cape May PMSA, NJ	H	19.67 FQ	30.89 AW	43.28 TQ	NJBLS	10/01-12/01
Construction Trade and Extraction Workers	Bergen-Passaic PMSA, NJ	H	19.01 FQ	32.97 AW	45.14 TQ	NJBLS	10/01-12/01
Construction Trade and Extraction Workers	Jersey City PMSA, NJ	H	20.63 FQ	31.36 AW	47.45 TQ	NJBLS	10/01-12/01
Construction Trade and Extraction Workers	Middlesex-Somerset-Hunterdon PMSA, NJ	H	15.16 FQ	27.36 AW	42.00 TQ	NJBLS	10/01-12/01
Construction Trade and Extraction Workers	Monmouth-Ocean PMSA, NJ	H	17.90 FQ	28.91 AW	40.90 TQ	NJBLS	10/01-12/01
Construction Trade and Extraction Workers	Newark PMSA, NJ	H	20.50 FQ	31.81 AW	47.95 TQ	NJBLS	10/01-12/01
Construction Trade and Extraction Workers	Trenton PMSA, NJ	H	18.73 FQ	28.39 AW	41.39 TQ	NJBLS	10/01-12/01
Construction Trade and Extraction Workers	New Mexico	H	12.75 FQ	21.35 AW	32.08 TQ	NMBLS	10/01-12/01
Construction Trade and Extraction Workers	Albuquerque MSA, NM	H	13.22 FQ	20.72 AW	29.73 TQ	NMBLS	10/01-12/01
Construction Trade and Extraction Workers	Las Cruces MSA, NM	H	12.66 FQ	18.30 AW	25.78 TQ	NMBLS	10/01-12/01
Construction Trade and Extraction Workers	New York	H	15.65 FQ	28.99 AW	46.05 TQ	NYBLS	10/01-12/01
Construction Trade and Extraction Workers	Albany-Schenectady-Troy MSA, NY	H	15.40 FQ	24.03 AW	35.19 TQ	NYBLS	10/01-12/01
Construction Trade and Extraction Workers	Binghamton MSA, NY	H	14.40 FQ	21.71 AW	30.01 TQ	NYBLS	10/01-12/01
Construction Trade and Extraction Workers	Buffalo-Niagara Falls MSA, NY	H	12.38 FQ	22.82 AW	33.63 TQ	NYBLS	10/01-12/01
Construction Trade and Extraction Workers	Dutchess County PMSA, NY	H	12.80 FQ	21.41 AW	34.26 TQ	NYBLS	10/01-12/01
Construction Trade and Extraction Workers	Nassau-Suffolk PMSA, NY	H	16.69 FQ	30.40 AW	49.33 TQ	NYBLS	10/01-12/01
Construction Trade and Extraction Workers	New York PMSA, NY	H	19.71 FQ	34.17 AW	52.75 TQ	NYBLS	10/01-12/01
Construction Trade and Extraction Workers	Newburgh PMSA, NY-PA	H	15.67 FQ	26.38 AW	36.55 TQ	NYBLS	10/01-12/01
Construction Trade and Extraction Workers	Rochester MSA, NY	H	13.44 FQ	24.64 AW	38.90 TQ	NYBLS	10/01-12/01
Construction Trade and Extraction Workers	Syracuse MSA, NY	H	15.13 FQ	23.90 AW	36.92 TQ	NYBLS	10/01-12/01
Construction Trade and Extraction Workers	Utica-Rome MSA, NY	H	12.03 FQ	21.17 AW	32.04 TQ	NYBLS	10/01-12/01
Construction Trade and Extraction Workers	North Carolina	H	13.12 FQ	20.59 AW	29.13 TQ	NCBLS	10/01-12/01
Construction Trade and Extraction Workers	Asheville MSA, NC	H	13.02 FQ	20.04 AW	27.29 TQ	NCBLS	10/01-12/01
Construction Trade and Extraction Workers	Charlotte-Gastonia-Rock Hill MSA, NC-SC	H	14.58 FQ	23.72 AW	38.15 TQ	NCBLS	10/01-12/01

AAW	Average annual wage	**AOH**	Average offered, high	**ASH**	Average starting, high	**H**	Hourly	**M**	Monthly	**S**	Special: hourly and annual
AE	Average entry wage	**AOL**	Average offered, low	**ASL**	Average starting, low	**HI**	Highest wage paid	**MTC**	Median total compensation	**TQ**	Third quartile wage
AEX	Average experienced wage	**APH**	Average pay, high range	**AW**	Average wage paid	**HR**	High end range	**MW**	Median wage paid	**W**	Weekly
AO	Average offered	**APL**	Average pay, low range	**FQ**	First quartile wage	**LR**	Low end range	**SQ**	Second quartile wage	**Y**	Yearly

Occupation/Type/Industry	Location	Per	Low	Mid	High	Source	Date
First-Line Supervisor/Manager							
Construction Trade and Extraction Workers	Fayetteville MSA, NC	H	11.41 FQ	17.90 AW	25.75 TQ	NCBLS	10/01-12/01
Construction Trade and Extraction Workers	Greensboro-Winston-Salem-High Point MSA, NC	H	12.53 FQ	19.65 AW	27.60 TQ	NCBLS	10/01-12/01
Construction Trade and Extraction Workers	Hickory-Morganton-Lenoir MSA, NC	H	13.31 FQ	18.98 AW	26.75 TQ	NCBLS	10/01-12/01
Construction Trade and Extraction Workers	Raleigh-Durham-Chapel Hill MSA, NC	H	12.19 FQ	20.04 AW	28.28 TQ	NCBLS	10/01-12/01
Construction Trade and Extraction Workers	Wilmington MSA, NC	H	13.55 FQ	19.06 AW	26.81 TQ	NCBLS	10/01-12/01
Construction Trade and Extraction Workers	North Dakota	H	13.93 FQ	19.92 AW	27.65 TQ	NDBLS	10/01-12/01
Construction Trade and Extraction Workers	Fargo-Moorhead MSA, ND-MN	H	14.48 FQ	20.86 AW	28.29 TQ	NDBLS	10/01-12/01
Construction Trade and Extraction Workers	Ohio	H	14.88 FQ	23.93 AW	34.01 TQ	OHBLS	10/01-12/01
Construction Trade and Extraction Workers	Akron PMSA, OH	H	15.25 FQ	27.06 AW	50.49 TQ	OHBLS	10/01-12/01
Construction Trade and Extraction Workers	Canton-Massillon MSA, OH	H	11.97 FQ	21.10 AW	30.10 TQ	OHBLS	10/01-12/01
Construction Trade and Extraction Workers	Cincinnati PMSA, OH-KY-IN	H	15.88 FQ	23.09 AW	32.55 TQ	OHBLS	10/01-12/01
Construction Trade and Extraction Workers	Cleveland-Lorain-Elyria PMSA, OH	H	15.84 FQ	24.86 AW	34.19 TQ	OHBLS	10/01-12/01
Construction Trade and Extraction Workers	Columbus MSA, OH	H	16.19 FQ	25.81 AW	35.22 TQ	OHBLS	10/01-12/01
Construction Trade and Extraction Workers	Dayton-Springfield MSA, OH	H	15.25 FQ	21.67 AW	28.69 TQ	OHBLS	10/01-12/01
Construction Trade and Extraction Workers	Hamilton-Middletown PMSA, OH	H	15.26 FQ	23.62 AW	33.08 TQ	OHBLS	10/01-12/01
Construction Trade and Extraction Workers	Mansfield MSA, OH	H	15.10 FQ	21.67 AW	28.14 TQ	OHBLS	10/01-12/01
Construction Trade and Extraction Workers	Toledo MSA, OH	H	14.25 FQ	25.77 AW	37.77 TQ	OHBLS	10/01-12/01
Construction Trade and Extraction Workers	Youngstown-Warren MSA, OH	H	15.80 FQ	22.82 AW	30.32 TQ	OHBLS	10/01-12/01
Construction Trade and Extraction Workers	Oklahoma	H	12.22 FQ	20.62 AW	29.69 TQ	OKBLS	10/01-12/01
Construction Trade and Extraction Workers	Oklahoma City MSA, OK	H	13.32 FQ	21.59 AW	31.09 TQ	OKBLS	10/01-12/01
Construction Trade and Extraction Workers	Tulsa MSA, OK	H	12.91 FQ	20.81 AW	28.52 TQ	OKBLS	10/01-12/01
Construction Trade and Extraction Workers	Oregon	H	16.44 FQ	26.57 AW	38.29 TQ	ORBLS	10/01-12/01
Construction Trade and Extraction Workers	Eugene-Springfield MSA, OR	H	16.59 FQ	25.37 AW	35.85 TQ	ORBLS	10/01-12/01
Construction Trade and Extraction Workers	Medford-Ashland MSA, OR	H	15.61 FQ	23.71 AW	39.22 TQ	ORBLS	10/01-12/01
Construction Trade and Extraction Workers	Portland-Vancouver PMSA, OR-WA	H	18.41 FQ	28.00 AW	40.21 TQ	ORBLS	10/01-12/01
Construction Trade and Extraction Workers	Salem PMSA, OR	H	16.79 FQ	26.70 AW	38.45 TQ	ORBLS	10/01-12/01
Construction Trade and Extraction Workers	Pennsylvania	H	14.57 FQ	23.76 AW	35.54 TQ	PABLS	10/01-12/01
Construction Trade and Extraction Workers	Allentown-Bethlehem-Easton MSA, PA	H	14.83 FQ	24.03 AW	34.13 TQ	PABLS	10/01-12/01
Construction Trade and Extraction Workers	Erie MSA, PA	H	13.49 FQ	20.46 AW	27.89 TQ	PABLS	10/01-12/01
Construction Trade and Extraction Workers	Harrisburg-Lebanon-Carlisle MSA, PA	H	16.08 FQ	23.45 AW	31.96 TQ	PABLS	10/01-12/01
Construction Trade and Extraction Workers	Johnstown MSA, PA	H	13.06 FQ	20.43 AW	29.38 TQ	PABLS	10/01-12/01
Construction Trade and Extraction Workers	Lancaster MSA, PA	H	14.69 FQ	21.28 AW	28.87 TQ	PABLS	10/01-12/01
Construction Trade and Extraction Workers	Philadelphia PMSA, PA-NJ	H	17.72 FQ	27.39 AW	42.85 TQ	PABLS	10/01-12/01
Construction Trade and Extraction Workers	Pittsburgh MSA, PA	H	14.09 FQ	23.43 AW	34.82 TQ	PABLS	10/01-12/01
Construction Trade and Extraction Workers	Reading MSA, PA	H	15.87 FQ	21.78 AW	32.12 TQ	PABLS	10/01-12/01
Construction Trade and Extraction Workers	Scranton-Wilkes-Barre-Hazleton MSA, PA	H	13.74 FQ	20.49 AW	30.70 TQ	PABLS	10/01-12/01
Construction Trade and Extraction Workers	York MSA, PA	H	14.80 FQ	22.95 AW	34.89 TQ	PABLS	10/01-12/01
Construction Trade and Extraction Workers	Rhode Island	H	17.02 FQ	25.84 AW	35.34 TQ	RIBLS	10/01-12/01
Construction Trade and Extraction Workers	Providence-Fall River-Warwick MSA, RI-MA	H	16.78 FQ	25.40 AW	34.45 TQ	RIBLS	10/01-12/01
Construction Trade and Extraction Workers	South Carolina	H	12.54 FQ	20.53 AW	30.63 TQ	SCBLS	10/01-12/01
Construction Trade and Extraction Workers	Charleston-North Charleston MSA, SC	H	14.27 FQ	20.60 AW	27.84 TQ	SCBLS	10/01-12/01
Construction Trade and Extraction Workers	Columbia MSA, SC	H	11.44 FQ	18.86 AW	26.55 TQ	SCBLS	10/01-12/01
Construction Trade and Extraction Workers	Greenville-Spartanburg-Anderson MSA, SC	H	12.10 FQ	18.71 AW	26.13 TQ	SCBLS	10/01-12/01
Construction Trade and Extraction Workers	Myrtle Beach MSA, SC	H	12.25 FQ	18.92 AW	28.42 TQ	SCBLS	10/01-12/01
Construction Trade and Extraction Workers	South Dakota	H	14.37 FQ	19.09 AW	25.89 TQ	SDBLS	10/01-12/01
Construction Trade and Extraction Workers	Sioux Falls MSA, SD	H	15.06 FQ	20.56 AW	27.85 TQ	SDBLS	10/01-12/01
Construction Trade and Extraction Workers	Tennessee	H	12.80 FQ	19.95 AW	28.09 TQ	TNBLS	10/01-12/01
Construction Trade and Extraction Workers	Chattanooga MSA, TN-GA	H	13.85 FQ	19.13 AW	26.25 TQ	TNBLS	10/01-12/01
Construction Trade and Extraction Workers	Clarksville-Hopkinsville MSA, TN-KY	H	12.54 FQ	19.04 AW	27.02 TQ	TNBLS	10/01-12/01
Construction Trade and Extraction Workers	Johnson City-Kingsport-Bristol MSA, TN-VA	H	11.23 FQ	16.34 AW	23.04 TQ	TNBLS	10/01-12/01
Construction Trade and Extraction Workers	Knoxville MSA, TN	H	12.90 FQ	19.44 AW	28.19 TQ	TNBLS	10/01-12/01
Construction Trade and Extraction Workers	Memphis MSA, TN-AR-MS	H	14.58 FQ	21.58 AW	29.55 TQ	TNBLS	10/01-12/01
Construction Trade and Extraction Workers	Nashville MSA, TN	H	14.41 FQ	22.30 AW	31.71 TQ	TNBLS	10/01-12/01
Construction Trade and Extraction Workers	Texas	H	13.16 FQ	21.62 AW	32.28 TQ	TXBLS	10/01-12/01
Construction Trade and Extraction Workers	Amarillo MSA, TX	H	11.61 FQ	19.19 AW	27.92 TQ	TXBLS	10/01-12/01
Construction Trade and Extraction Workers	Austin-San Marcos MSA, TX	H	12.87 FQ	21.40 AW	31.64 TQ	TXBLS	10/01-12/01

AAW Average annual wage; AE Average entry wage; AEX Average experienced wage; AO Average offered; AOH Average offered, high; AOL Average offered, low; APH Average pay, high range; APL Average pay, low range; ASH Average starting, high; ASL Average starting, low; AW Average wage paid; FQ First quartile wage; H Hourly; HI Highest wage paid; HR High end range; LR Low end range; M Monthly; MTC Median total compensation; MW Median wage paid; SQ Second quartile wage; S Special: hourly and annual; TQ Third quartile wage; W Weekly; Y Yearly

Occupation/Type/Industry	Location	Per	Low	Mid	High	Source	Date
First-Line Supervisor/Manager							
Construction Trade and Extraction Workers	Beaumont-Port Arthur MSA, TX	H	14.62 FQ	20.40 AW	27.35 TQ	TXBLS	10/01-12/01
Construction Trade and Extraction Workers	Brazoria PMSA, TX	H	13.78 FQ	21.49 AW	31.25 TQ	TXBLS	10/01-12/01
Construction Trade and Extraction Workers	Brownsville-Harlingen-San Benito MSA, TX	H	9.36 FQ	14.85 AW	21.77 TQ	TXBLS	10/01-12/01
Construction Trade and Extraction Workers	Corpus Christi MSA, TX	H	12.38 FQ	19.79 AW	29.70 TQ	TXBLS	10/01-12/01
Construction Trade and Extraction Workers	Dallas PMSA, TX	H	14.24 FQ	23.12 AW	33.24 TQ	TXBLS	10/01-12/01
Construction Trade and Extraction Workers	El Paso MSA, TX	H	11.63 FQ	19.80 AW	32.05 TQ	TXBLS	10/01-12/01
Construction Trade and Extraction Workers	Fort Worth-Arlington PMSA, TX	H	14.64 FQ	21.76 AW	31.05 TQ	TXBLS	10/01-12/01
Construction Trade and Extraction Workers	Galveston-Texas City PMSA, TX	H	13.50 FQ	21.15 AW	29.76 TQ	TXBLS	10/01-12/01
Construction Trade and Extraction Workers	Houston PMSA, TX	H	13.92 FQ	22.54 AW	33.61 TQ	TXBLS	10/01-12/01
Construction Trade and Extraction Workers	Killeen-Temple MSA, TX	H	12.29 FQ	18.84 AW	26.55 TQ	TXBLS	10/01-12/01
Construction Trade and Extraction Workers	Laredo MSA, TX	H	10.67 FQ	18.96 AW	30.82 TQ	TXBLS	10/01-12/01
Construction Trade and Extraction Workers	Longview-Marshall MSA, TX	H	12.19 FQ	19.66 AW	29.37 TQ	TXBLS	10/01-12/01
Construction Trade and Extraction Workers	Lubbock MSA, TX	H	12.74 FQ	19.37 AW	26.94 TQ	TXBLS	10/01-12/01
Construction Trade and Extraction Workers	McAllen-Edinburg-Mission MSA, TX	H	10.06 FQ	16.77 AW	25.80 TQ	TXBLS	10/01-12/01
Construction Trade and Extraction Workers	Odessa-Midland MSA, TX	H	14.31 FQ	22.24 AW	32.30 TQ	TXBLS	10/01-12/01
Construction Trade and Extraction Workers	San Antonio MSA, TX	H	11.93 FQ	19.84 AW	31.16 TQ	TXBLS	10/01-12/01
Construction Trade and Extraction Workers	Tyler MSA, TX	H	13.05 FQ	22.11 AW	35.36 TQ	TXBLS	10/01-12/01
Construction Trade and Extraction Workers	Waco MSA, TX	H	12.91 FQ	19.80 AW	28.14 TQ	TXBLS	10/01-12/01
Construction Trade and Extraction Workers	Utah	H	14.12 FQ	20.63 AW	29.12 TQ	UTBLS	10/01-12/01
Construction Trade and Extraction Workers	Provo-Orem MSA, UT	H	14.49 FQ	21.50 AW	31.19 TQ	UTBLS	10/01-12/01
Construction Trade and Extraction Workers	Salt Lake City-Ogden MSA, UT	H	14.14 FQ	20.89 AW	28.01 TQ	UTBLS	10/01-12/01
Construction Trade and Extraction Workers	Vermont	H	15.39 FQ	22.58 AW	31.99 TQ	VTBLS	10/01-12/01
Construction Trade and Extraction Workers	Burlington MSA, VT	H	16.89 FQ	24.11 AW	33.59 TQ	VTBLS	10/01-12/01
Construction Trade and Extraction Workers	Virginia	H	13.94 FQ	22.63 AW	33.66 TQ	VABLS	10/01-12/01
Construction Trade and Extraction Workers	Lynchburg MSA, VA	H	13.97 FQ	19.27 AW	26.43 TQ	VABLS	10/01-12/01
Construction Trade and Extraction Workers	Norfolk-Virginia Beach-Newport News MSA, VA-NC	H	13.28 FQ	20.97 AW	31.19 TQ	VABLS	10/01-12/01
Construction Trade and Extraction Workers	Richmond-Petersburg MSA, VA	H	15.08 FQ	23.19 AW	36.62 TQ	VABLS	10/01-12/01
Construction Trade and Extraction Workers	Roanoke MSA, VA	H	12.60 FQ	18.88 AW	25.60 TQ	VABLS	10/01-12/01
Construction Trade and Extraction Workers	Washington	H	19.31 FQ	28.68 AW	40.65 TQ	WABLS	10/01-12/01
Construction Trade and Extraction Workers	Bremerton PMSA, WA	H	21.23 FQ	27.86 AW	34.07 TQ	WABLS	10/01-12/01
Construction Trade and Extraction Workers	Olympia PMSA, WA	H	18.24 FQ	26.37 AW	40.28 TQ	WABLS	10/01-12/01
Construction Trade and Extraction Workers	Richland-Kennewick-Pasco MSA, WA	H	20.25 FQ	27.76 AW	34.59 TQ	WABLS	10/01-12/01
Construction Trade and Extraction Workers	Seattle-Bellevue-Everett PMSA, WA	H	21.30 FQ	31.02 AW	43.94 TQ	WABLS	10/01-12/01
Construction Trade and Extraction Workers	Spokane MSA, WA	H	17.80 FQ	24.05 AW	32.56 TQ	WABLS	10/01-12/01
Construction Trade and Extraction Workers	Tacoma PMSA, WA	H	19.95 FQ	28.91 AW	39.21 TQ	WABLS	10/01-12/01
Construction Trade and Extraction Workers	Yakima MSA, WA	H	17.67 FQ	25.03 AW	34.20 TQ	WABLS	10/01-12/01
Construction Trade and Extraction Workers	West Virginia	H	12.53 FQ	22.39 AW	34.27 TQ	WVBLS	10/01-12/01
Construction Trade and Extraction Workers	Charleston MSA, WV	H	11.78 FQ	20.54 AW	30.67 TQ	WVBLS	10/01-12/01
Construction Trade and Extraction Workers	Huntington-Ashland MSA, WV-KY-OH	H	13.71 FQ	22.08 AW	32.82 TQ	WVBLS	10/01-12/01
Construction Trade and Extraction Workers	Wisconsin	H	15.89 FQ	25.60 AW	35.25 TQ	WIBLS	10/01-12/01
Construction Trade and Extraction Workers	Appleton-Oshkosh-Neenah MSA, WI	H	18.39 FQ	24.80 AW	31.25 TQ	WIBLS	10/01-12/01
Construction Trade and Extraction Workers	Green Bay MSA, WI	H	17.11 FQ	24.12 AW	33.14 TQ	WIBLS	10/01-12/01
Construction Trade and Extraction Workers	Madison MSA, WI	H	19.99 FQ	28.48 AW	40.64 TQ	WIBLS	10/01-12/01
Construction Trade and Extraction Workers	Milwaukee-Waukesha PMSA, WI	H	15.78 FQ	27.12 AW	35.36 TQ	WIBLS	10/01-12/01
Construction Trade and Extraction Workers	Racine PMSA, WI	H	14.74 FQ	23.47 AW	33.58 TQ	WIBLS	10/01-12/01
Construction Trade and Extraction Workers	Wyoming	H	13.59 FQ	22.98 AW	35.39 TQ	WYBLS	10/01-12/01
Construction Trade and Extraction Workers	Cheyenne MSA, WY	H	14.82 FQ	20.50 AW	29.27 TQ	WYBLS	10/01-12/01
Construction Trade and Extraction Workers	Puerto Rico	H	7.08 FQ	10.98 AW	16.17 TQ	PRBLS	10/01-12/01
Construction Trade and Extraction Workers	Virgin Islands	H	14.47 FQ	19.73 AW	26.14 TQ	VIBLS	10/01-12/01
Construction Trade and Extraction Workers	Guam	H	11.93 FQ	17.42 AW	25.42 TQ	GUBLS	10/01-12/01
Correctional Officers	Alabama	Y	23870 FQ	38500 AW	52560 TQ	ALBLS	10/01-12/01
Correctional Officers	Alaska	Y	57720 FQ	66670 AW	83990 TQ	AKBLS	10/01-12/01
Correctional Officers	Arizona	Y	29210 FQ	39130 AW	55150 TQ	AZBLS	10/01-12/01
Correctional Officers	Phoenix-Mesa MSA, AZ	Y	29080 FQ	37890 AW	53640 TQ	AZBLS	10/01-12/01
Correctional Officers	Arkansas	Y	26960 FQ	43120 AW	60990 TQ	ARBLS	10/01-12/01
Correctional Officers	California	Y	46820 FQ	61440 AW	75320 TQ	CABLS	10/01-12/01
Correctional Officers	Bakersfield MSA, CA	Y	44930 FQ	60260 AW	71680 TQ	CABLS	10/01-12/01

AAW	Average annual wage	AOH	Average offered, high	ASH	Average starting, high	H	Hourly	M	Monthly	S	Special: hourly and annual
AE	Average entry wage	AOL	Average offered, low	ASL	Average starting, low	HI	Highest wage paid	MTC	Median total compensation	TQ	Third quartile wage
AEX	Average experienced wage	APH	Average pay, high range	AW	Average wage paid	HR	High end range	MW	Median wage paid	W	Weekly
AO	Average offered	APL	Average pay, low range	FQ	First quartile wage	LR	Low end range	SQ	Second quartile wage	Y	Yearly

Occupation/Type/Industry	Location	Per	Low	Mid	High	Source	Date
First-Line Supervisor/Manager							
Correctional Officers	Los Angeles-Long Beach PMSA, CA	Y	48040 FQ	60990 AW	73590 TQ	CABLS	10/01-12/01
Correctional Officers	Riverside-San Bernardino PMSA, CA	Y	47450 FQ	60610 AW	71750 TQ	CABLS	10/01-12/01
Correctional Officers	Sacramento PMSA, CA	Y	57100 FQ	65670 AW	82770 TQ	CABLS	10/01-12/01
Correctional Officers	San Diego MSA, CA	Y	38730 FQ	52930 AW	71690 TQ	CABLS	10/01-12/01
Correctional Officers	San Francisco PMSA, CA	Y	40550 FQ	60400 AW	76730 TQ	CABLS	10/01-12/01
Correctional Officers	Colorado	Y	40330 FQ	50880 AW	65530 TQ	COBLS	10/01-12/01
Correctional Officers	Denver PMSA, CO	Y	45160 FQ	52380 AW	65580 TQ	COBLS	10/01-12/01
Correctional Officers	Connecticut	Y	46360 FQ	57870 AW	70710 TQ	CTBLS	10/01-12/01
Correctional Officers	Washington PMSA, DC-MD-VA-WV	Y	25430 FQ	43490 AW	72010 TQ	DCBLS	10/01-12/01
Correctional Officers	Florida	Y	32630 FQ	45420 AW	58950 TQ	FLBLS	10/01-12/01
Correctional Officers	Daytona Beach MSA, FL	Y	29990 FQ	41130 AW	54610 TQ	FLBLS	10/01-12/01
Correctional Officers	Fort Lauderdale PMSA, FL	Y	36350 FQ	51190 AW	70280 TQ	FLBLS	10/01-12/01
Correctional Officers	Lakeland-Winter Haven MSA, FL	Y	33630 FQ	46530 AW	63420 TQ	FLBLS	10/01-12/01
Correctional Officers	Melbourne-Titusville-Palm Bay MSA, FL	Y	23660 FQ	39430 AW	55940 TQ	FLBLS	10/01-12/01
Correctional Officers	Miami PMSA, FL	Y	37570 FQ	46600 AW	57520 TQ	FLBLS	10/01-12/01
Correctional Officers	Orlando MSA, FL	Y	35540 FQ	51080 AW	69990 TQ	FLBLS	10/01-12/01
Correctional Officers	Pensacola MSA, FL	Y	30140 FQ	41390 AW	54420 TQ	FLBLS	10/01-12/01
Correctional Officers	Tallahassee MSA, FL	Y	37390 FQ	46950 AW	55490 TQ	FLBLS	10/01-12/01
Correctional Officers	West Palm Beach-Boca Raton MSA, FL	Y	37590 FQ	59120 AW	82210 TQ	FLBLS	10/01-12/01
Correctional Officers	Georgia	Y	24520 FQ	36080 AW	52430 TQ	GABLS	10/01-12/01
Correctional Officers	Atlanta MSA, GA	Y	25480 FQ	39710 AW	56520 TQ	GABLS	10/01-12/01
Correctional Officers	Augusta-Aiken MSA, GA-SC	Y	27420 FQ	44510 AW	61110 TQ	GABLS	10/01-12/01
Correctional Officers	Macon MSA, GA	Y	28710 FQ	35620 AW	43350 TQ	GABLS	10/01-12/01
Correctional Officers	Hawaii	Y	39530 FQ	51650 AW	66310 TQ	HIBLS	10/01-12/01
Correctional Officers	Honolulu MSA, HI	Y	37660 FQ	51030 AW	65500 TQ	HIBLS	10/01-12/01
Correctional Officers	Illinois	Y	39960 FQ	52420 AW	67720 TQ	ILBLS	10/01-12/01
Correctional Officers	Chicago PMSA, IL	Y	38530 FQ	53810 AW	70100 TQ	ILBLS	10/01-12/01
Correctional Officers	Iowa	Y	35910 FQ	48040 AW	63300 TQ	IABLS	10/01-12/01
Correctional Officers	Davenport-Moline-Rock Island MSA, IA-IL	Y	36260 FQ	47060 AW	56810 TQ	IABLS	10/01-12/01
Correctional Officers	Kansas	Y	26460 FQ	42200 AW	55140 TQ	KSBLS	10/01-12/01
Correctional Officers	Kentucky	Y	24240 FQ	36570 AW	52010 TQ	KYBLS	10/01-12/01
Correctional Officers	Lexington MSA, KY	Y	31050 FQ	40330 AW	52190 TQ	KYBLS	10/01-12/01
Correctional Officers	Louisiana	Y	25350 FQ	37040 AW	51420 TQ	LABLS	10/01-12/01
Correctional Officers	Baton Rouge MSA, LA	Y	26300 FQ	36840 AW	45230 TQ	LABLS	10/01-12/01
Correctional Officers	New Orleans MSA, LA	Y	22820 FQ	37230 AW	57650 TQ	LABLS	10/01-12/01
Correctional Officers	Maine	Y	29580 FQ	39540 AW	50570 TQ	MEBLS	10/01-12/01
Correctional Officers	Massachusetts	Y	31670 FQ	51010 AW	72320 TQ	MABLS	10/01-12/01
Correctional Officers	Michigan	Y	43290 FQ	50160 AW	56370 TQ	MIBLS	10/01-12/01
Correctional Officers	Minnesota	Y	30450 FQ	49930 AW	71470 TQ	MNBLS	10/01-12/01
Correctional Officers	Mississippi	Y	23170 FQ	31360 AW	43340 TQ	MSBLS	10/01-12/01
Correctional Officers	Jackson MSA, MS	Y	23120 FQ	28230 AW	35330 TQ	MSBLS	10/01-12/01
Correctional Officers	Kansas City MSA, MO-KS	Y	27970 FQ	44560 AW	55370 TQ	MOBLS	10/01-12/01
Correctional Officers	St. Louis MSA, MO-IL	Y	38800 FQ	53510 AW	70950 TQ	MOBLS	10/01-12/01
Correctional Officers	Nebraska	Y	29410 FQ	36680 AW	47070 TQ	NEBLS	10/01-12/01
Correctional Officers	Omaha MSA, NE-IA	Y	29710 FQ	38540 AW	48070 TQ	NEBLS	10/01-12/01
Correctional Officers	Nevada	Y	39060 FQ	53480 AW	71640 TQ	NVBLS	10/01-12/01
Correctional Officers	New Hampshire	Y	35820 FQ	41530 AW	51560 TQ	NHBLS	10/01-12/01
Correctional Officers	New Jersey	Y	37040 FQ	59400 AW	81600 TQ	NJBLS	10/01-12/01
Correctional Officers	Bergen-Passaic PMSA, NJ	Y	71920 FQ	78230 AW	93570 TQ	NJBLS	10/01-12/01
Correctional Officers	Monmouth-Ocean PMSA, NJ	Y	44750 FQ	62270 AW	85590 TQ	NJBLS	10/01-12/01
Correctional Officers	Newark PMSA, NJ	Y	31730 FQ	48630 AW	70460 TQ	NJBLS	10/01-12/01
Correctional Officers	Trenton PMSA, NJ	Y	49180 FQ	65100 AW	82270 TQ	NJBLS	10/01-12/01
Correctional Officers	New Mexico	Y	24120 FQ	31300 AW	39870 TQ	NMBLS	10/01-12/01
Correctional Officers	Albany-Schenectady-Troy MSA, NY	Y	35610 FQ	56450 AW	74940 TQ	NYBLS	10/01-12/01
Correctional Officers	Newburgh PMSA, NY-PA	Y	41040 FQ	51270 AW	64750 TQ	NYBLS	10/01-12/01
Correctional Officers	Rochester MSA, NY	Y	37700 FQ	57670 AW	74250 TQ	NYBLS	10/01-12/01
Correctional Officers	North Carolina	Y	26310 FQ	37530 AW	53010 TQ	NCBLS	10/01-12/01
Correctional Officers	Ohio	Y	36120 FQ	45030 AW	55680 TQ	OHBLS	10/01-12/01
Correctional Officers	Columbus MSA, OH	Y	36890 FQ	45380 AW	55280 TQ	OHBLS	10/01-12/01
Correctional Officers	Toledo MSA, OH	Y	31250 FQ	44060 AW	61950 TQ	OHBLS	10/01-12/01
Correctional Officers	Youngstown-Warren MSA, OH	Y	25000 FQ	39810 AW	53690 TQ	OHBLS	10/01-12/01
Correctional Officers	Oklahoma	Y	23240 FQ	35170 AW	51750 TQ	OKBLS	10/01-12/01
Correctional Officers	Tulsa MSA, OK	Y	19510 FQ	29490 AW	44550 TQ	OKBLS	10/01-12/01

AAW Average annual wage; AE Average entry wage; AEX Average experienced wage; AO Average offered; AOH Average offered, high; AOL Average offered, low; APH Average pay, high range; APL Average pay, low range; ASH Average starting, high; ASL Average starting, low; AW Average wage paid; FQ First quartile wage; H Hourly; HI Highest wage paid; HR High end range; LR Low end range; M Monthly; MTC Median total compensation; MW Median wage paid; SQ Second quartile wage; S Special: hourly and annual; TQ Third quartile wage; W Weekly; Y Yearly

Occupation/Type/Industry	Location	Per	Low	Mid	High	Source	Date
First-Line Supervisor/Manager							
Correctional Officers	Oregon	Y	37080 FQ	47930 AW	65460 TQ	ORBLS	10/01-12/01
Correctional Officers	Portland-Vancouver PMSA, OR-WA	Y	36490 FQ	50770 AW	70300 TQ	ORBLS	10/01-12/01
Correctional Officers	Pennsylvania	Y	27640 FQ	50240 AW	81940 TQ	PABLS	10/01-12/01
Correctional Officers	Philadelphia PMSA, PA-NJ	Y	35790 FQ	52990 AW	70570 TQ	PABLS	10/01-12/01
Correctional Officers	Pittsburgh MSA, PA	Y	21850 FQ	43860 AW	79110 TQ	PABLS	10/01-12/01
Correctional Officers	South Carolina	Y	31500 FQ	50820 AW	69840 TQ	SCBLS	10/01-12/01
Correctional Officers	Tennessee	Y	20340 FQ	33650 AW	53310 TQ	TNBLS	10/01-12/01
Correctional Officers	Memphis MSA, TN-AR-MS	Y	22330 FQ	36010 AW	54290 TQ	TNBLS	10/01-12/01
Correctional Officers	Texas	Y	28270 FQ	33580 AW	45910 TQ	TXBLS	10/01-12/01
Correctional Officers	Austin-San Marcos MSA, TX	Y	23530 FQ	38440 AW	63890 TQ	TXBLS	10/01-12/01
Correctional Officers	Dallas PMSA, TX	Y	26010 FQ	39230 AW	56840 TQ	TXBLS	10/01-12/01
Correctional Officers	El Paso MSA, TX	Y	29200 FQ	40040 AW	54320 TQ	TXBLS	10/01-12/01
Correctional Officers	Utah	Y	35760 FQ	44320 AW	55080 TQ	UTBLS	10/01-12/01
Correctional Officers	Salt Lake City-Ogden MSA, UT	Y	36160 FQ	45470 AW	55730 TQ	UTBLS	10/01-12/01
Correctional Officers	Vermont	Y	35170 FQ	42480 AW	53640 TQ	VTBLS	10/01-12/01
Correctional Officers	Virginia	Y	29480 FQ	37930 AW	49160 TQ	VABLS	10/01-12/01
Correctional Officers	Norfolk-Virginia Beach-Newport News MSA, VA-NC	Y	29340 FQ	35340 AW	44940 TQ	VABLS	10/01-12/01
Correctional Officers	Richmond-Petersburg MSA, VA	Y	29900 FQ	39010 AW	51060 TQ	VABLS	10/01-12/01
Correctional Officers	Washington	Y	36720 FQ	45790 AW	58320 TQ	WABLS	10/01-12/01
Correctional Officers	Seattle-Bellevue-Everett PMSA, WA	Y	37020 FQ	47930 AW	65760 TQ	WABLS	10/01-12/01
Correctional Officers	West Virginia	Y	26780 FQ	38910 AW	54710 TQ	WVBLS	10/01-12/01
Correctional Officers	Wisconsin	Y	30850 FQ	45210 AW	56500 TQ	WIBLS	10/01-12/01
Correctional Officers	Milwaukee-Waukesha PMSA, WI	Y	17800 FQ	35450 AW	54020 TQ	WIBLS	10/01-12/01
Correctional Officers	Wyoming	Y	31330 FQ	41160 AW	55000 TQ	WYBLS	10/01-12/01
Correctional Officers	Puerto Rico	Y	20450 FQ	35590 AW	55380 TQ	PRBLS	10/01-12/01
Farming, Fishing, and Forestry Workers	Alabama	H	10.31 FQ	16.88 AW	27.15 TQ	ALBLS	10/01-12/01
Farming, Fishing, and Forestry Workers	Alaska	H	16.07 FQ	25.81 AW	35.57 TQ	AKBLS	10/01-12/01
Farming, Fishing, and Forestry Workers	Arizona	H	10.08 FQ	16.43 AW	27.41 TQ	AZBLS	10/01-12/01
Farming, Fishing, and Forestry Workers	Arkansas	H	10.12 FQ	16.84 AW	26.58 TQ	ARBLS	10/01-12/01
Farming, Fishing, and Forestry Workers	California	H	8.19 FQ	16.71 AW	28.21 TQ	CABLS	10/01-12/01
Farming, Fishing, and Forestry Workers	Colorado	H	11.20 FQ	19.58 AW	29.89 TQ	COBLS	10/01-12/01
Farming, Fishing, and Forestry Workers	Connecticut	H	11.42 FQ	20.24 AW	29.70 TQ	CTBLS	10/01-12/01
Farming, Fishing, and Forestry Workers	Delaware	H	13.46 FQ	19.80 AW	25.69 TQ	DEBLS	10/01-12/01
Farming, Fishing, and Forestry Workers	Florida	H	9.05 FQ	15.66 AW	24.06 TQ	FLBLS	10/01-12/01
Farming, Fishing, and Forestry Workers	Georgia	H	11.81 FQ	17.66 AW	25.50 TQ	GABLS	10/01-12/01
Farming, Fishing, and Forestry Workers	Hawaii	H	8.88 FQ	16.03 AW	25.08 TQ	HIBLS	10/01-12/01
Farming, Fishing, and Forestry Workers	Idaho	H	9.07 FQ	17.31 AW	25.91 TQ	IDBLS	10/01-12/01
Farming, Fishing, and Forestry Workers	Illinois	H	5.98 FQ	14.35 AW	23.35 TQ	ILBLS	10/01-12/01
Farming, Fishing, and Forestry Workers	Indiana	H	11.24 FQ	17.78 AW	26.43 TQ	INBLS	10/01-12/01
Farming, Fishing, and Forestry Workers	Iowa	H	10.86 FQ	21.16 AW	34.41 TQ	IABLS	10/01-12/01
Farming, Fishing, and Forestry Workers	Kansas	H	11.99 FQ	17.80 AW	26.24 TQ	KSBLS	10/01-12/01
Farming, Fishing, and Forestry Workers	Kentucky	H	9.98 FQ	15.62 AW	23.99 TQ	KYBLS	10/01-12/01
Farming, Fishing, and Forestry Workers	Louisiana	H	9.38 FQ	16.51 AW	24.74 TQ	LABLS	10/01-12/01
Farming, Fishing, and Forestry Workers	Maine	H	9.48 FQ	16.41 AW	24.67 TQ	MEBLS	10/01-12/01
Farming, Fishing, and Forestry Workers	Maryland	H	12.66 FQ	19.25 AW	28.90 TQ	MDBLS	10/01-12/01
Farming, Fishing, and Forestry Workers	Massachusetts	H	12.18 FQ	19.25 AW	31.85 TQ	MABLS	10/01-12/01
Farming, Fishing, and Forestry Workers	Michigan	H	9.29 FQ	20.19 AW	32.39 TQ	MIBLS	10/01-12/01
Farming, Fishing, and Forestry Workers	Minnesota	H	10.82 FQ	19.34 AW	27.66 TQ	MNBLS	10/01-12/01
Farming, Fishing, and Forestry Workers	Mississippi	H	9.65 FQ	15.57 AW	22.85 TQ	MSBLS	10/01-12/01
Farming, Fishing, and Forestry Workers	Missouri	H	9.70 FQ	15.86 AW	23.76 TQ	MOBLS	10/01-12/01
Farming, Fishing, and Forestry Workers	Montana	H	9.37 FQ	16.98 AW	24.44 TQ	MTBLS	10/01-12/01
Farming, Fishing, and Forestry Workers	Nebraska	H	10.88 FQ	15.73 AW	21.75 TQ	NEBLS	10/01-12/01
Farming, Fishing, and Forestry Workers	Nevada	H	13.35 FQ	19.61 AW	26.16 TQ	NVBLS	10/01-12/01
Farming, Fishing, and Forestry Workers	New Hampshire	H	11.63 FQ	18.40 AW	27.04 TQ	NHBLS	10/01-12/01
Farming, Fishing, and Forestry Workers	New Jersey	H	11.96 FQ	17.82 AW	26.32 TQ	NJBLS	10/01-12/01
Farming, Fishing, and Forestry Workers	New Mexico	H	7.29 FQ	10.70 AW	16.41 TQ	NMBLS	10/01-12/01
Farming, Fishing, and Forestry Workers	New York	H	11.61 FQ	17.06 AW	26.62 TQ	NYBLS	10/01-12/01
Farming, Fishing, and Forestry Workers	North Carolina	H	10.49 FQ	21.96 AW	38.49 TQ	NCBLS	10/01-12/01
Farming, Fishing, and Forestry Workers	Ohio	H	11.49 FQ	17.35 AW	24.99 TQ	OHBLS	10/01-12/01
Farming, Fishing, and Forestry Workers	Oklahoma	H	8.51 FQ	15.96 AW	24.24 TQ	OKBLS	10/01-12/01
Farming, Fishing, and Forestry Workers	Oregon	H	12.13 FQ	20.40 AW	32.87 TQ	ORBLS	10/01-12/01
Farming, Fishing, and Forestry Workers	Pennsylvania	H	10.95 FQ	19.87 AW	30.12 TQ	PABLS	10/01-12/01
Farming, Fishing, and Forestry Workers	South Carolina	H	11.89 FQ	20.00 AW	29.80 TQ	SCBLS	10/01-12/01
Farming, Fishing, and Forestry Workers	South Dakota	H	11.70 FQ	16.93 AW	22.04 TQ	SDBLS	10/01-12/01

AAW Average annual wage; AE Average entry wage; AEX Average experienced wage; AO Average offered; AOH Average offered, high; AOL Average offered, low; APH Average pay, high range; APL Average pay, low range; ASH Average starting, high; ASL Average starting, low; AW Average wage paid; FQ First quartile wage; H Hourly; HI Highest wage paid; HR High end range; LR Low end range; M Monthly; MTC Median total compensation; MW Median wage paid; SQ Second quartile wage; S Special: hourly and annual; TQ Third quartile wage; W Weekly; Y Yearly

Occupation/Type/Industry	Location	Per	Low	Mid	High	Source	Date
First-Line Supervisor/Manager							
Farming, Fishing, and Forestry Workers	Tennessee	H	8.91 FQ	15.87 AW	25.82 TQ	TNBLS	10/01-12/01
Farming, Fishing, and Forestry Workers	Texas	H	10.81 FQ	16.10 AW	21.83 TQ	TXBLS	10/01-12/01
Farming, Fishing, and Forestry Workers	Utah	H	11.94 FQ	17.56 AW	23.42 TQ	UTBLS	10/01-12/01
Farming, Fishing, and Forestry Workers	Vermont	H	17.63 FQ	21.61 AW	24.23 TQ	VTBLS	10/01-12/01
Farming, Fishing, and Forestry Workers	Virginia	H	8.33 FQ	17.04 AW	28.70 TQ	VABLS	10/01-12/01
Farming, Fishing, and Forestry Workers	Washington	H	9.88 FQ	19.77 AW	32.83 TQ	WABLS	10/01-12/01
Farming, Fishing, and Forestry Workers	West Virginia	H	8.57 FQ	18.59 AW	28.74 TQ	WVBLS	10/01-12/01
Farming, Fishing, and Forestry Workers	Wisconsin	H	9.75 FQ	18.25 AW	28.51 TQ	WIBLS	10/01-12/01
Farming, Fishing, and Forestry Workers	Wyoming	H	11.71 FQ	16.41 AW	21.85 TQ	WYBLS	10/01-12/01
Farming, Fishing, and Forestry Workers	Puerto Rico	H	5.95 FQ	10.61 AW	16.79 TQ	PRBLS	10/01-12/01
Fire Fighting and Prevention Workers	Alabama	Y	32170 FQ	45190 AW	61410 TQ	ALBLS	10/01-12/01
Fire Fighting and Prevention Workers	Birmingham MSA, AL	Y	39010 FQ	51640 AW	74880 TQ	ALBLS	10/01-12/01
Fire Fighting and Prevention Workers	Alaska	Y	38120 FQ	57700 AW	78630 TQ	AKBLS	10/01-12/01
Fire Fighting and Prevention Workers	Arizona	Y	35960 FQ	57260 AW	75270 TQ	AZBLS	10/01-12/01
Fire Fighting and Prevention Workers	Phoenix-Mesa MSA, AZ	Y	44950 FQ	62160 AW	76140 TQ	AZBLS	10/01-12/01
Fire Fighting and Prevention Workers	Tucson MSA, AZ	Y	36420 FQ	55700 AW	74070 TQ	AZBLS	10/01-12/01
Fire Fighting and Prevention Workers	Arkansas	Y	24510 FQ	38210 AW	55490 TQ	ARBLS	10/01-12/01
Fire Fighting and Prevention Workers	Little Rock-North Little Rock MSA, AR	Y	29880 FQ	43950 AW	59010 TQ	ARBLS	10/01-12/01
Fire Fighting and Prevention Workers	California	Y	46650 FQ	69060 AW	96430 TQ	CABLS	10/01-12/01
Fire Fighting and Prevention Workers	Bakersfield MSA, CA	Y	38410 FQ	51030 AW	70640 TQ	CABLS	10/01-12/01
Fire Fighting and Prevention Workers	Chico-Paradise MSA, CA	Y	44000 FQ	51140 AW	57270 TQ	CABLS	10/01-12/01
Fire Fighting and Prevention Workers	Fresno MSA, CA	Y	47920 FQ	62640 AW	76850 TQ	CABLS	10/01-12/01
Fire Fighting and Prevention Workers	Los Angeles-Long Beach PMSA, CA	Y	59900 FQ	80440 AW	96590 TQ	CABLS	10/01-12/01
Fire Fighting and Prevention Workers	Merced MSA, CA	Y	48920 FQ	55600 AW	68960 TQ	CABLS	10/01-12/01
Fire Fighting and Prevention Workers	Modesto MSA, CA	Y	47470 FQ	58100 AW	78720 TQ	CABLS	10/01-12/01
Fire Fighting and Prevention Workers	Oakland PMSA, CA	Y	50290 FQ	87270 AW	121150 TQ	CABLS	10/01-12/01
Fire Fighting and Prevention Workers	Orange County PMSA, CA	Y	57240 FQ	69830 AW	87630 TQ	CABLS	10/01-12/01
Fire Fighting and Prevention Workers	Redding MSA, CA	Y	24900 FQ	42370 AW	58870 TQ	CABLS	10/01-12/01
Fire Fighting and Prevention Workers	Riverside-San Bernardino PMSA, CA	Y	47580 FQ	62460 AW	82440 TQ	CABLS	10/01-12/01
Fire Fighting and Prevention Workers	Sacramento PMSA, CA	Y	48770 FQ	62510 AW	81150 TQ	CABLS	10/01-12/01
Fire Fighting and Prevention Workers	Salinas MSA, CA	Y	45130 FQ	52040 AW	64260 TQ	CABLS	10/01-12/01
Fire Fighting and Prevention Workers	San Diego MSA, CA	Y	46670 FQ	73590 AW	96160 TQ	CABLS	10/01-12/01
Fire Fighting and Prevention Workers	San Francisco PMSA, CA	Y	42960 FQ	74350 AW	127900 TQ	CABLS	10/01-12/01
Fire Fighting and Prevention Workers	San Jose PMSA, CA	Y	52070 FQ	82290 AW	107370 TQ	CABLS	10/01-12/01
Fire Fighting and Prevention Workers	San Luis Obispo-Atascadero-Paso Robles MSA, CA	Y	48130 FQ	58700 AW	74310 TQ	CABLS	10/01-12/01
Fire Fighting and Prevention Workers	Santa Barbara-Santa Maria-Lompoc MSA, CA	Y	52040 FQ	78980 AW	97880 TQ	CABLS	10/01-12/01
Fire Fighting and Prevention Workers	Santa Cruz-Watsonville PMSA, CA	Y	47780 FQ	72010 AW	107000 TQ	CABLS	10/01-12/01
Fire Fighting and Prevention Workers	Santa Rosa PMSA, CA	Y	23160 FQ	67110 AW	92900 TQ	CABLS	10/01-12/01
Fire Fighting and Prevention Workers	Vallejo-Fairfield-Napa PMSA, CA	Y	47400 FQ	69040 AW	120070 TQ	CABLS	10/01-12/01
Fire Fighting and Prevention Workers	Visalia-Tulare-Porterville MSA, CA	Y	33650 FQ	45030 AW	56260 TQ	CABLS	10/01-12/01
Fire Fighting and Prevention Workers	Colorado	Y	40120 FQ	61410 AW	80380 TQ	COBLS	10/01-12/01
Fire Fighting and Prevention Workers	Denver PMSA, CO	Y	52950 FQ	66560 AW	84180 TQ	COBLS	10/01-12/01
Fire Fighting and Prevention Workers	Connecticut	Y	47950 FQ	62330 AW	84850 TQ	CTBLS	10/01-12/01
Fire Fighting and Prevention Workers	Bridgeport PMSA, CT	Y	43390 FQ	62740 AW	76200 TQ	CTBLS	10/01-12/01
Fire Fighting and Prevention Workers	Hartford MSA, CT	Y	48780 FQ	63230 AW	93960 TQ	CTBLS	10/01-12/01
Fire Fighting and Prevention Workers	New Haven-Meriden PMSA, CT	Y	47360 FQ	58660 AW	75980 TQ	CTBLS	10/01-12/01
Fire Fighting and Prevention Workers	New London-Norwich MSA, CT-RI	Y	40500 FQ	51250 AW	66400 TQ	CTBLS	10/01-12/01
Fire Fighting and Prevention Workers	Stamford-Norwalk PMSA, CT	Y	51700 FQ	67040 AW	88900 TQ	CTBLS	10/01-12/01
Fire Fighting and Prevention Workers	Delaware	Y	37710 FQ	49700 AW	64740 TQ	DEBLS	10/01-12/01
Fire Fighting and Prevention Workers	Wilmington-Newark PMSA, DE-MD	Y	38230 FQ	50920 AW	65760 TQ	DEBLS	10/01-12/01
Fire Fighting and Prevention Workers	Washington PMSA, DC-MD-VA-WV	Y	40240 FQ	69250 AW	93180 TQ	DCBLS	10/01-12/01
Fire Fighting and Prevention Workers	Florida	Y	33700 FQ	50500 AW	70410 TQ	FLBLS	10/01-12/01
Fire Fighting and Prevention Workers	Daytona Beach MSA, FL	Y	27190 FQ	43750 AW	59440 TQ	FLBLS	10/01-12/01
Fire Fighting and Prevention Workers	Fort Lauderdale PMSA, FL	Y	49240 FQ	64160 AW	82610 TQ	FLBLS	10/01-12/01
Fire Fighting and Prevention Workers	Fort Myers-Cape Coral MSA, FL	Y	36710 FQ	51780 AW	68950 TQ	FLBLS	10/01-12/01
Fire Fighting and Prevention Workers	Fort Walton Beach MSA, FL	Y	32480 FQ	42720 AW	54320 TQ	FLBLS	10/01-12/01
Fire Fighting and Prevention Workers	Melbourne-Titusville-Palm Bay MSA, FL	Y	29910 FQ	45420 AW	61900 TQ	FLBLS	10/01-12/01

AAW	Average annual wage	AOH	Average offered, high	ASH	Average starting, high	H	Hourly	M	Monthly	S	Special: hourly and annual
AE	Average entry wage	AOL	Average offered, low	ASL	Average starting, low	HI	Highest wage paid	MTC	Median total compensation	TQ	Third quartile wage
AEX	Average experienced wage	APH	Average pay, high range	AW	Average wage paid	HR	High end range	MW	Median wage paid	W	Weekly
AO	Average offered	APL	Average pay, low range	FQ	First quartile wage	LR	Low end range	SQ	Second quartile wage	Y	Yearly

Occupation/Type/Industry	Location	Per	Low	Mid	High	Source	Date
First-Line Supervisor/Manager							
Fire Fighting and Prevention Workers	Miami PMSA, FL	Y	48040 FQ	65000 AW	91820 TQ	FLBLS	10/01-12/01
Fire Fighting and Prevention Workers	Naples MSA, FL	Y	29110 FQ	51360 AW	83100 TQ	FLBLS	10/01-12/01
Fire Fighting and Prevention Workers	Orlando MSA, FL	Y	33080 FQ	45470 AW	64350 TQ	FLBLS	10/01-12/01
Fire Fighting and Prevention Workers	Pensacola MSA, FL	Y	29500 FQ	38160 AW	53560 TQ	FLBLS	10/01-12/01
Fire Fighting and Prevention Workers	Sarasota-Bradenton MSA, FL	Y	32920 FQ	46850 AW	60680 TQ	FLBLS	10/01-12/01
Fire Fighting and Prevention Workers	Tampa-St. Petersburg-Clearwater MSA, FL	Y	31500 FQ	46260 AW	59150 TQ	FLBLS	10/01-12/01
Fire Fighting and Prevention Workers	Georgia	Y	30200 FQ	45720 AW	64050 TQ	GABLS	10/01-12/01
Fire Fighting and Prevention Workers	Atlanta MSA, GA	Y	33370 FQ	50500 AW	68770 TQ	GABLS	10/01-12/01
Fire Fighting and Prevention Workers	Augusta-Aiken MSA, GA-SC	Y	35250 FQ	52200 AW	82140 TQ	GABLS	10/01-12/01
Fire Fighting and Prevention Workers	Macon MSA, GA	Y	13240 FQ	37020 AW	47590 TQ	GABLS	10/01-12/01
Fire Fighting and Prevention Workers	Savannah MSA, GA	Y	39250 FQ	48980 AW	60140 TQ	GABLS	10/01-12/01
Fire Fighting and Prevention Workers	Hawaii	Y	40770 FQ	51010 AW	64520 TQ	HIBLS	10/01-12/01
Fire Fighting and Prevention Workers	Honolulu MSA, HI	Y	41950 FQ	51590 AW	65300 TQ	HIBLS	10/01-12/01
Fire Fighting and Prevention Workers	Idaho	Y	13320 FQ	49490 AW	83390 TQ	IDBLS	10/01-12/01
Fire Fighting and Prevention Workers	Boise City MSA, ID	Y	31850 FQ	65700 AW	128710 TQ	IDBLS	10/01-12/01
Fire Fighting and Prevention Workers	Illinois	Y	30220 FQ	54650 AW	80510 TQ	ILBLS	10/01-12/01
Fire Fighting and Prevention Workers	Champaign-Urbana MSA, IL	Y	27590 FQ	55250 AW	82030 TQ	ILBLS	10/01-12/01
Fire Fighting and Prevention Workers	Chicago PMSA, IL	Y	32420 FQ	58510 AW	83870 TQ	ILBLS	10/01-12/01
Fire Fighting and Prevention Workers	Peoria-Pekin MSA, IL	Y	29850 FQ	52170 AW	73010 TQ	ILBLS	10/01-12/01
Fire Fighting and Prevention Workers	Springfield MSA, IL	Y	35800 FQ	58430 AW	83680 TQ	ILBLS	10/01-12/01
Fire Fighting and Prevention Workers	Indiana	Y	23370 FQ	42860 AW	57850 TQ	INBLS	10/01-12/01
Fire Fighting and Prevention Workers	Gary PMSA, IN	Y	12450 FQ	37800 AW	56460 TQ	INBLS	10/01-12/01
Fire Fighting and Prevention Workers	Indianapolis MSA, IN	Y	35530 FQ	50400 AW	59910 TQ	INBLS	10/01-12/01
Fire Fighting and Prevention Workers	Iowa	Y	13410 FQ	39670 AW	59460 TQ	IABLS	10/01-12/01
Fire Fighting and Prevention Workers	Kansas	Y	24340 FQ	38840 AW	58820 TQ	KSBLS	10/01-12/01
Fire Fighting and Prevention Workers	Topeka MSA, KS	Y	23960 FQ	30150 AW	42910 TQ	KSBLS	10/01-12/01
Fire Fighting and Prevention Workers	Kentucky	Y	22440 FQ	39140 AW	58920 TQ	KYBLS	10/01-12/01
Fire Fighting and Prevention Workers	Louisville MSA, KY-IN	Y	35790 FQ	51290 AW	65910 TQ	KYBLS	10/01-12/01
Fire Fighting and Prevention Workers	Louisiana	Y	26360 FQ	38680 AW	55920 TQ	LABLS	10/01-12/01
Fire Fighting and Prevention Workers	Baton Rouge MSA, LA	Y	27450 FQ	37380 AW	51080 TQ	LABLS	10/01-12/01
Fire Fighting and Prevention Workers	Lake Charles MSA, LA	Y	21630 FQ	36090 AW	56690 TQ	LABLS	10/01-12/01
Fire Fighting and Prevention Workers	New Orleans MSA, LA	Y	26320 FQ	38340 AW	55470 TQ	LABLS	10/01-12/01
Fire Fighting and Prevention Workers	Shreveport-Bossier City MSA, LA	Y	42510 FQ	55110 AW	70780 TQ	LABLS	10/01-12/01
Fire Fighting and Prevention Workers	Maine	Y	24360 FQ	39480 AW	51890 TQ	MEBLS	10/01-12/01
Fire Fighting and Prevention Workers	Maryland	Y	36340 FQ	55400 AW	80640 TQ	MDBLS	10/01-12/01
Fire Fighting and Prevention Workers	Baltimore PMSA, MD	Y	30400 FQ	51390 AW	74420 TQ	MDBLS	10/01-12/01
Fire Fighting and Prevention Workers	Massachusetts	Y	39210 FQ	54300 AW	77570 TQ	MABLS	10/01-12/01
Fire Fighting and Prevention Workers	Boston PMSA, MA-NH	Y	39850 FQ	55740 AW	83660 TQ	MABLS	10/01-12/01
Fire Fighting and Prevention Workers	Brockton PMSA, MA	Y	40840 FQ	55600 AW	76600 TQ	MABLS	10/01-12/01
Fire Fighting and Prevention Workers	Lawrence PMSA, MA-NH	Y	37080 FQ	47430 AW	65900 TQ	MABLS	10/01-12/01
Fire Fighting and Prevention Workers	Lowell PMSA, MA-NH	Y	44010 FQ	56500 AW	73500 TQ	MABLS	10/01-12/01
Fire Fighting and Prevention Workers	Springfield MSA, MA	Y	44300 FQ	54590 AW	69100 TQ	MABLS	10/01-12/01
Fire Fighting and Prevention Workers	Worcester PMSA, MA-CT	Y	14280 FQ	41810 AW	67740 TQ	MABLS	10/01-12/01
Fire Fighting and Prevention Workers	Michigan	Y	37050 FQ	52260 AW	70230 TQ	MIBLS	10/01-12/01
Fire Fighting and Prevention Workers	Ann Arbor PMSA, MI	Y	48570 FQ	54360 AW	62620 TQ	MIBLS	10/01-12/01
Fire Fighting and Prevention Workers	Detroit PMSA, MI	Y	46500 FQ	57330 AW	72730 TQ	MIBLS	10/01-12/01
Fire Fighting and Prevention Workers	Kalamazoo-Battle Creek MSA, MI	Y	30320 FQ	39210 AW	52760 TQ	MIBLS	10/01-12/01
Fire Fighting and Prevention Workers	Minnesota	Y	25410 FQ	52710 AW	71510 TQ	MNBLS	10/01-12/01
Fire Fighting and Prevention Workers	Duluth-Superior MSA, MN-WI	Y	46910 FQ	55060 AW	69050 TQ	MNBLS	10/01-12/01
Fire Fighting and Prevention Workers	Minneapolis-St. Paul MSA, MN-WI	Y	14920 FQ	51150 AW	73280 TQ	MNBLS	10/01-12/01
Fire Fighting and Prevention Workers	Mississippi	Y	24240 FQ	41010 AW	68750 TQ	MSBLS	10/01-12/01
Fire Fighting and Prevention Workers	Biloxi-Gulfport-Pascagoula MSA, MS	Y	31930 FQ	41800 AW	53990 TQ	MSBLS	10/01-12/01
Fire Fighting and Prevention Workers	Jackson MSA, MS	Y	31790 FQ	54810 AW	74460 TQ	MSBLS	10/01-12/01
Fire Fighting and Prevention Workers	Missouri	Y	22240 FQ	52710 AW	79440 TQ	MOBLS	10/01-12/01
Fire Fighting and Prevention Workers	Kansas City MSA, MO-KS	Y	37730 FQ	56590 AW	80340 TQ	MOBLS	10/01-12/01
Fire Fighting and Prevention Workers	St. Louis MSA, MO-IL	Y	35950 FQ	60070 AW	83550 TQ	MOBLS	10/01-12/01
Fire Fighting and Prevention Workers	Springfield MSA, MO	Y	13110 FQ	49670 AW	82030 TQ	MOBLS	10/01-12/01
Fire Fighting and Prevention Workers	Montana	Y	11640 FQ	26140 AW	53090 TQ	MTBLS	10/01-12/01
Fire Fighting and Prevention Workers	Nevada	Y	39160 FQ	57690 AW	87140 TQ	NVBLS	10/01-12/01
Fire Fighting and Prevention Workers	Las Vegas MSA, NV-AZ	Y	46530 FQ	61530 AW	88830 TQ	NVBLS	10/01-12/01
Fire Fighting and Prevention Workers	New Hampshire	Y	36850 FQ	46150 AW	58440 TQ	NHBLS	10/01-12/01
Fire Fighting and Prevention Workers	Portsmouth-Rochester PMSA, NH-ME	Y	37880 FQ	47300 AW	59780 TQ	NHBLS	10/01-12/01
Fire Fighting and Prevention Workers	New Jersey	Y	45990 FQ	71360 AW	97240 TQ	NJBLS	10/01-12/01
Fire Fighting and Prevention Workers	Atlantic-Cape May PMSA, NJ	Y	49480 FQ	63430 AW	76090 TQ	NJBLS	10/01-12/01
Fire Fighting and Prevention Workers	Bergen-Passaic PMSA, NJ	Y	40410 FQ	69110 AW	93990 TQ	NJBLS	10/01-12/01

AAW Average annual wage; AE Average entry wage; AEX Average experienced wage; AO Average offered; AOH Average offered, high; AOL Average offered, low; APH Average pay, high range; APL Average pay, low range; ASH Average starting, high; ASL Average starting, low; AW Average wage paid; FQ First quartile wage; H Hourly; HI Highest wage paid; HR High end range; LR Low end range; M Monthly; MTC Median total compensation; MW Median wage paid; SQ Second quartile wage; S Special: hourly and annual; TQ Third quartile wage; W Weekly; Y Yearly

Occupation/Type/Industry	Location	Per	Low	Mid	High	Source	Date
First-Line Supervisor/Manager							
Fire Fighting and Prevention Workers	Middlesex-Somerset-Hunterdon PMSA, NJ	Y	47850 FQ	84520 AW	123600 TQ	NJBLS	10/01-12/01
Fire Fighting and Prevention Workers	Monmouth-Ocean PMSA, NJ	Y	36470 FQ	53660 AW	73570 TQ	NJBLS	10/01-12/01
Fire Fighting and Prevention Workers	Newark PMSA, NJ	Y	60490 FQ	78760 AW	105100 TQ	NJBLS	10/01-12/01
Fire Fighting and Prevention Workers	Trenton PMSA, NJ	Y	26110 FQ	60280 AW	86030 TQ	NJBLS	10/01-12/01
Fire Fighting and Prevention Workers	New Mexico	Y	22740 FQ	38630 AW	57050 TQ	NMBLS	10/01-12/01
Fire Fighting and Prevention Workers	Albuquerque MSA, NM	Y	31410 FQ	45200 AW	62350 TQ	NMBLS	10/01-12/01
Fire Fighting and Prevention Workers	New York	Y	49560 FQ	69410 AW	93220 TQ	NYBLS	10/01-12/01
Fire Fighting and Prevention Workers	Albany-Schenectady-Troy MSA, NY	Y	38520 FQ	48660 AW	66310 TQ	NYBLS	10/01-12/01
Fire Fighting and Prevention Workers	Nassau-Suffolk PMSA, NY	Y	40110 FQ	61370 AW	78420 TQ	NYBLS	10/01-12/01
Fire Fighting and Prevention Workers	Newburgh PMSA, NY-PA	Y	39360 FQ	52900 AW	69600 TQ	NYBLS	10/01-12/01
Fire Fighting and Prevention Workers	Rochester MSA, NY	Y	48440 FQ	60890 AW	73300 TQ	NYBLS	10/01-12/01
Fire Fighting and Prevention Workers	North Carolina	Y	31920 FQ	47480 AW	67770 TQ	NCBLS	10/01-12/01
Fire Fighting and Prevention Workers	Charlotte-Gastonia-Rock Hill MSA, NC-SC	Y	37720 FQ	55410 AW	71940 TQ	NCBLS	10/01-12/01
Fire Fighting and Prevention Workers	Greensboro-Winston-Salem-High Point MSA, NC	Y	31560 FQ	45640 AW	61200 TQ	NCBLS	10/01-12/01
Fire Fighting and Prevention Workers	North Dakota	Y	38880 FQ	47980 AW	59320 TQ	NDBLS	10/01-12/01
Fire Fighting and Prevention Workers	Ohio	Y	28920 FQ	50180 AW	69270 TQ	OHBLS	10/01-12/01
Fire Fighting and Prevention Workers	Akron PMSA, OH	Y	40170 FQ	50890 AW	59920 TQ	OHBLS	10/01-12/01
Fire Fighting and Prevention Workers	Cincinnati PMSA, OH-KY-IN	Y	31930 FQ	50200 AW	71090 TQ	OHBLS	10/01-12/01
Fire Fighting and Prevention Workers	Cleveland-Lorain-Elyria PMSA, OH	Y	43400 FQ	55350 AW	71520 TQ	OHBLS	10/01-12/01
Fire Fighting and Prevention Workers	Dayton-Springfield MSA, OH	Y	24570 FQ	52860 AW	109160 TQ	OHBLS	10/01-12/01
Fire Fighting and Prevention Workers	Hamilton-Middletown PMSA, OH	Y	27110 FQ	44510 AW	61000 TQ	OHBLS	10/01-12/01
Fire Fighting and Prevention Workers	Mansfield MSA, OH	Y	12470 FQ	33940 AW	57440 TQ	OHBLS	10/01-12/01
Fire Fighting and Prevention Workers	Toledo MSA, OH	Y	21480 FQ	42490 AW	67810 TQ	OHBLS	10/01-12/01
Fire Fighting and Prevention Workers	Youngstown-Warren MSA, OH	Y	30870 FQ	39430 AW	56790 TQ	OHBLS	10/01-12/01
Fire Fighting and Prevention Workers	Oklahoma	Y	27310 FQ	38200 AW	56930 TQ	OKBLS	10/01-12/01
Fire Fighting and Prevention Workers	Oklahoma City MSA, OK	Y	30920 FQ	46890 AW	69620 TQ	OKBLS	10/01-12/01
Fire Fighting and Prevention Workers	Tulsa MSA, OK	Y	26710 FQ	40370 AW	58780 TQ	OKBLS	10/01-12/01
Fire Fighting and Prevention Workers	Oregon	Y	37260 FQ	53970 AW	71580 TQ	ORBLS	10/01-12/01
Fire Fighting and Prevention Workers	Portland-Vancouver PMSA, OR-WA	Y	46500 FQ	60060 AW	76060 TQ	ORBLS	10/01-12/01
Fire Fighting and Prevention Workers	Pennsylvania	Y	38560 FQ	55890 AW	77180 TQ	PABLS	10/01-12/01
Fire Fighting and Prevention Workers	Scranton-Wilkes-Barre-Hazleton MSA, PA	Y	14360 FQ	42030 AW	56030 TQ	PABLS	10/01-12/01
Fire Fighting and Prevention Workers	Rhode Island	Y	39600 FQ	50710 AW	66730 TQ	RIBLS	10/01-12/01
Fire Fighting and Prevention Workers	Providence-Fall River-Warwick MSA, RI-MA	Y	39440 FQ	50450 AW	66580 TQ	RIBLS	10/01-12/01
Fire Fighting and Prevention Workers	South Carolina	Y	29980 FQ	41260 AW	58180 TQ	SCBLS	10/01-12/01
Fire Fighting and Prevention Workers	Charleston-North Charleston MSA, SC	Y	30280 FQ	39320 AW	54080 TQ	SCBLS	10/01-12/01
Fire Fighting and Prevention Workers	Columbia MSA, SC	Y	35360 FQ	46890 AW	61300 TQ	SCBLS	10/01-12/01
Fire Fighting and Prevention Workers	Greenville-Spartanburg-Anderson MSA, SC	Y	33050 FQ	41630 AW	59330 TQ	SCBLS	10/01-12/01
Fire Fighting and Prevention Workers	South Dakota	Y	36010 FQ	48110 AW	63370 TQ	SDBLS	10/01-12/01
Fire Fighting and Prevention Workers	Tennessee	Y	33000 FQ	48740 AW	61200 TQ	TNBLS	10/01-12/01
Fire Fighting and Prevention Workers	Clarksville-Hopkinsville MSA, TN-KY	Y	28110 FQ	40750 AW	55660 TQ	TNBLS	10/01-12/01
Fire Fighting and Prevention Workers	Johnson City-Kingsport-Bristol MSA, TN-VA	Y	30640 FQ	43460 AW	58290 TQ	TNBLS	10/01-12/01
Fire Fighting and Prevention Workers	Knoxville MSA, TN	Y	35010 FQ	44960 AW	56920 TQ	TNBLS	10/01-12/01
Fire Fighting and Prevention Workers	Nashville MSA, TN	Y	39090 FQ	49480 AW	60620 TQ	TNBLS	10/01-12/01
Fire Fighting and Prevention Workers	Texas	Y	36760 FQ	51230 AW	70470 TQ	TXBLS	10/01-12/01
Fire Fighting and Prevention Workers	Austin-San Marcos MSA, TX	Y	37670 FQ	53510 AW	70490 TQ	TXBLS	10/01-12/01
Fire Fighting and Prevention Workers	Beaumont-Port Arthur MSA, TX	Y	30520 FQ	45580 AW	64610 TQ	TXBLS	10/01-12/01
Fire Fighting and Prevention Workers	Brownsville-Harlingen-San Benito MSA, TX	Y	24420 FQ	37870 AW	54440 TQ	TXBLS	10/01-12/01
Fire Fighting and Prevention Workers	Dallas PMSA, TX	Y	39850 FQ	55910 AW	73530 TQ	TXBLS	10/01-12/01
Fire Fighting and Prevention Workers	El Paso MSA, TX	Y	32750 FQ	40610 AW	47040 TQ	TXBLS	10/01-12/01
Fire Fighting and Prevention Workers	Fort Worth-Arlington PMSA, TX	Y	44280 FQ	55840 AW	70750 TQ	TXBLS	10/01-12/01
Fire Fighting and Prevention Workers	Houston PMSA, TX	Y	46700 FQ	58450 AW	76100 TQ	TXBLS	10/01-12/01
Fire Fighting and Prevention Workers	Killeen-Temple MSA, TX	Y	27220 FQ	40850 AW	53890 TQ	TXBLS	10/01-12/01
Fire Fighting and Prevention Workers	McAllen-Edinburg-Mission MSA, TX	Y	29950 FQ	38790 AW	51670 TQ	TXBLS	10/01-12/01
Fire Fighting and Prevention Workers	Utah	Y	34740 FQ	51190 AW	72880 TQ	UTBLS	10/01-12/01

AAW	Average annual wage	AOH	Average offered, high	ASH	Average starting, high	H	Hourly	M	Monthly	S	Special: hourly and annual
AE	Average entry wage	AOL	Average offered, low	ASL	Average starting, low	HI	Highest wage paid	MTC	Median total compensation	TQ	Third quartile wage
AEX	Average experienced wage	APH	Average pay, high range	AW	Average wage paid	HR	High end range	MW	Median wage paid	W	Weekly
AO	Average offered	APL	Average pay, low range	FQ	First quartile wage	LR	Low end range	SQ	Second quartile wage	Y	Yearly

Occupation/Type/Industry	Location	Per	Low	Mid	High	Source	Date
First-Line Supervisor/Manager							
Fire Fighting and Prevention Workers	Salt Lake City-Ogden MSA, UT	Y	36450 FQ	53430 AW	73950 TQ	UTBLS	10/01-12/01
Fire Fighting and Prevention Workers	Virginia	Y	35070 FQ	54610 AW	85060 TQ	VABLS	10/01-12/01
Fire Fighting and Prevention Workers	Norfolk-Virginia Beach-Newport News MSA, VA-NC	Y	34100 FQ	46480 AW	61730 TQ	VABLS	10/01-12/01
Fire Fighting and Prevention Workers	Richmond-Petersburg MSA, VA	Y	36080 FQ	47960 AW	64140 TQ	VABLS	10/01-12/01
Fire Fighting and Prevention Workers	Washington	Y	45910 FQ	63350 AW	85770 TQ	WABLS	10/01-12/01
Fire Fighting and Prevention Workers	Bremerton PMSA, WA	Y	36230 FQ	53120 AW	74480 TQ	WABLS	10/01-12/01
Fire Fighting and Prevention Workers	Olympia PMSA, WA	Y	58720 FQ	68930 AW	85440 TQ	WABLS	10/01-12/01
Fire Fighting and Prevention Workers	Richland-Kennewick-Pasco MSA, WA	Y	43920 FQ	60000 AW	82570 TQ	WABLS	10/01-12/01
Fire Fighting and Prevention Workers	Seattle-Bellevue-Everett PMSA, WA	Y	54080 FQ	70090 AW	93010 TQ	WABLS	10/01-12/01
Fire Fighting and Prevention Workers	Tacoma PMSA, WA	Y	43710 FQ	60240 AW	85900 TQ	WABLS	10/01-12/01
Fire Fighting and Prevention Workers	Yakima MSA, WA	Y	37070 FQ	48330 AW	67290 TQ	WABLS	10/01-12/01
Fire Fighting and Prevention Workers	West Virginia	Y	30580 FQ	40460 AW	55900 TQ	WVBLS	10/01-12/01
Fire Fighting and Prevention Workers	Charleston MSA, WV	Y	32520 FQ	44330 AW	64580 TQ	WVBLS	10/01-12/01
Fire Fighting and Prevention Workers	Huntington-Ashland MSA, WV-KY-OH	Y	19800 FQ	32810 AW	44430 TQ	WVBLS	10/01-12/01
Fire Fighting and Prevention Workers	Wisconsin	Y	17940 FQ	50510 AW	71760 TQ	WIBLS	10/01-12/01
Fire Fighting and Prevention Workers	Appleton-Oshkosh-Neenah MSA, WI	Y	47860 FQ	54790 AW	66130 TQ	WIBLS	10/01-12/01
Fire Fighting and Prevention Workers	Green Bay MSA, WI	Y	39870 FQ	48960 AW	58970 TQ	WIBLS	10/01-12/01
Fire Fighting and Prevention Workers	Wyoming	Y	37220 FQ	49530 AW	66110 TQ	WYBLS	10/01-12/01
Fire Fighting and Prevention Workers	Puerto Rico	Y	18380 FQ	24870 AW	32190 TQ	PRBLS	10/01-12/01
Food Preparation and Serving Workers	Alabama	H	6.99 FQ	10.49 AW	15.37 TQ	ALBLS	10/01-12/01
Food Preparation and Serving Workers	Birmingham MSA, AL	H	7.67 FQ	10.39 AW	13.70 TQ	ALBLS	10/01-12/01
Food Preparation and Serving Workers	Huntsville MSA, AL	H	7.64 FQ	12.47 AW	19.28 TQ	ALBLS	10/01-12/01
Food Preparation and Serving Workers	Mobile MSA, AL	H	7.58 FQ	12.10 AW	18.35 TQ	ALBLS	10/01-12/01
Food Preparation and Serving Workers	Montgomery MSA, AL	H	7.53 FQ	10.55 AW	13.99 TQ	ALBLS	10/01-12/01
Food Preparation and Serving Workers	Alaska	H	8.85 FQ	16.03 AW	25.08 TQ	AKBLS	10/01-12/01
Food Preparation and Serving Workers	Anchorage MSA, AK	H	8.18 FQ	14.19 AW	21.81 TQ	AKBLS	10/01-12/01
Food Preparation and Serving Workers	Arizona	H	7.55 FQ	11.39 AW	16.07 TQ	AZBLS	10/01-12/01
Food Preparation and Serving Workers	Phoenix-Mesa MSA, AZ	H	7.63 FQ	11.51 AW	16.15 TQ	AZBLS	10/01-12/01
Food Preparation and Serving Workers	Tucson MSA, AZ	H	7.78 FQ	11.61 AW	16.30 TQ	AZBLS	10/01-12/01
Food Preparation and Serving Workers	Arkansas	H	6.99 FQ	10.52 AW	14.51 TQ	ARBLS	10/01-12/01
Food Preparation and Serving Workers	Fayetteville-Springdale-Rogers MSA, AR	H	7.06 FQ	10.90 AW	15.16 TQ	ARBLS	10/01-12/01
Food Preparation and Serving Workers	Fort Smith MSA, AR-OK	H	6.80 FQ	10.40 AW	14.24 TQ	ARBLS	10/01-12/01
Food Preparation and Serving Workers	Little Rock-North Little Rock MSA, AR	H	7.68 FQ	11.94 AW	16.94 TQ	ARBLS	10/01-12/01
Food Preparation and Serving Workers	California	H	7.84 FQ	13.02 AW	19.99 TQ	CABLS	10/01-12/01
Food Preparation and Serving Workers	Bakersfield MSA, CA	H	7.78 FQ	11.54 AW	16.39 TQ	CABLS	10/01-12/01
Food Preparation and Serving Workers	Chico-Paradise MSA, CA	H	7.47 FQ	11.63 AW	17.15 TQ	CABLS	10/01-12/01
Food Preparation and Serving Workers	Fresno MSA, CA	H	7.83 FQ	12.67 AW	18.89 TQ	CABLS	10/01-12/01
Food Preparation and Serving Workers	Los Angeles-Long Beach PMSA, CA	H	7.65 FQ	12.88 AW	20.18 TQ	CABLS	10/01-12/01
Food Preparation and Serving Workers	Merced MSA, CA	H	7.51 FQ	11.50 AW	17.56 TQ	CABLS	10/01-12/01
Food Preparation and Serving Workers	Modesto MSA, CA	H	7.80 FQ	12.06 AW	16.80 TQ	CABLS	10/01-12/01
Food Preparation and Serving Workers	Oakland PMSA, CA	H	8.71 FQ	13.92 AW	21.24 TQ	CABLS	10/01-12/01
Food Preparation and Serving Workers	Orange County PMSA, CA	H	8.16 FQ	13.47 AW	20.51 TQ	CABLS	10/01-12/01
Food Preparation and Serving Workers	Redding MSA, CA	H	6.81 FQ	11.27 AW	17.67 TQ	CABLS	10/01-12/01
Food Preparation and Serving Workers	Riverside-San Bernardino PMSA, CA	H	7.74 FQ	12.28 AW	17.59 TQ	CABLS	10/01-12/01
Food Preparation and Serving Workers	Sacramento PMSA, CA	H	7.61 FQ	12.57 AW	18.16 TQ	CABLS	10/01-12/01
Food Preparation and Serving Workers	Salinas MSA, CA	H	7.61 FQ	12.49 AW	19.70 TQ	CABLS	10/01-12/01
Food Preparation and Serving Workers	San Diego MSA, CA	H	7.63 FQ	12.36 AW	19.43 TQ	CABLS	10/01-12/01
Food Preparation and Serving Workers	San Francisco PMSA, CA	H	10.34 FQ	17.20 AW	25.05 TQ	CABLS	10/01-12/01
Food Preparation and Serving Workers	San Jose PMSA, CA	H	9.00 FQ	13.74 AW	20.56 TQ	CABLS	10/01-12/01
Food Preparation and Serving Workers	San Luis Obispo-Atascadero-Paso Robles MSA, CA	H	7.65 FQ	12.71 AW	20.51 TQ	CABLS	10/01-12/01
Food Preparation and Serving Workers	Santa Barbara-Santa Maria-Lompoc MSA, CA	H	8.40 FQ	13.21 AW	17.26 TQ	CABLS	10/01-12/01
Food Preparation and Serving Workers	Santa Cruz-Watsonville PMSA, CA	H	8.46 FQ	12.38 AW	17.58 TQ	CABLS	10/01-12/01
Food Preparation and Serving Workers	Santa Rosa PMSA, CA	H	8.60 FQ	13.22 AW	18.51 TQ	CABLS	10/01-12/01
Food Preparation and Serving Workers	Stockton-Lodi MSA, CA	H	8.06 FQ	12.33 AW	17.36 TQ	CABLS	10/01-12/01
Food Preparation and Serving Workers	Vallejo-Fairfield-Napa PMSA, CA	H	8.01 FQ	12.89 AW	18.02 TQ	CABLS	10/01-12/01

AAW	Average annual wage	AOH	Average offered, high	ASH	Average starting, high	H	Hourly	M	Monthly	S	Special: hourly and annual
AE	Average entry wage	AOL	Average offered, low	ASL	Average starting, low	HI	Highest wage paid	MTC	Median total compensation	TQ	Third quartile wage
AEX	Average experienced wage	APH	Average pay, high range	AW	Average wage paid	HR	High end range	MW	Median wage paid	W	Weekly
AO	Average offered	APL	Average pay, low range	FQ	First quartile wage	LR	Low end range	SQ	Second quartile wage	Y	Yearly

Occupation/Type/Industry	Location	Per	Low	Mid	High	Source	Date
First-Line Supervisor/Manager							
Food Preparation and Serving Workers	Ventura PMSA, CA	H	7.96 FQ	11.89 AW	17.59 TQ	CABLS	10/01-12/01
Food Preparation and Serving Workers	Visalia-Tulare-Porterville MSA, CA	H	7.12 FQ	11.81 AW	15.11 TQ	CABLS	10/01-12/01
Food Preparation and Serving Workers	Colorado	H	7.05 FQ	13.23 AW	19.95 TQ	COBLS	10/01-12/01
Food Preparation and Serving Workers	Boulder-Longmont PMSA, CO	H	8.93 FQ	13.61 AW	19.38 TQ	COBLS	10/01-12/01
Food Preparation and Serving Workers	Colorado Springs MSA, CO	H	5.92 FQ	11.42 AW	17.51 TQ	COBLS	10/01-12/01
Food Preparation and Serving Workers	Denver PMSA, CO	H	6.63 FQ	13.85 AW	20.37 TQ	COBLS	10/01-12/01
Food Preparation and Serving Workers	Fort Collins-Loveland MSA, CO	H	7.62 FQ	10.74 AW	15.36 TQ	COBLS	10/01-12/01
Food Preparation and Serving Workers	Greeley PMSA, CO	H	9.41 FQ	13.80 AW	18.99 TQ	COBLS	10/01-12/01
Food Preparation and Serving Workers	Connecticut	H	8.73 FQ	14.99 AW	22.82 TQ	CTBLS	10/01-12/01
Food Preparation and Serving Workers	Bridgeport PMSA, CT	H	10.03 FQ	17.29 AW	25.25 TQ	CTBLS	10/01-12/01
Food Preparation and Serving Workers	Danbury PMSA, CT	H	10.73 FQ	14.72 AW	20.87 TQ	CTBLS	10/01-12/01
Food Preparation and Serving Workers	Hartford MSA, CT	H	8.15 FQ	14.05 AW	22.30 TQ	CTBLS	10/01-12/01
Food Preparation and Serving Workers	New Haven-Meriden PMSA, CT	H	10.80 FQ	15.68 AW	21.09 TQ	CTBLS	10/01-12/01
Food Preparation and Serving Workers	New London-Norwich MSA, CT-RI	H	8.48 FQ	14.57 AW	22.38 TQ	CTBLS	10/01-12/01
Food Preparation and Serving Workers	Stamford-Norwalk PMSA, CT	H	8.30 FQ	15.44 AW	26.31 TQ	CTBLS	10/01-12/01
Food Preparation and Serving Workers	Waterbury PMSA, CT	H	10.31 FQ	16.11 AW	25.31 TQ	CTBLS	10/01-12/01
Food Preparation and Serving Workers	Delaware	H	8.54 FQ	13.89 AW	20.11 TQ	DEBLS	10/01-12/01
Food Preparation and Serving Workers	Wilmington-Newark PMSA, DE-MD	H	9.53 FQ	14.89 AW	20.70 TQ	DEBLS	10/01-12/01
Food Preparation and Serving Workers	District of Columbia	H	10.11 FQ	15.10 AW	21.40 TQ	DCBLS	10/01-12/01
Food Preparation and Serving Workers	Washington PMSA, DC-MD-VA-WV	H	8.80 FQ	13.21 AW	20.00 TQ	DCBLS	10/01-12/01
Food Preparation and Serving Workers	Florida	H	7.73 FQ	12.72 AW	19.43 TQ	FLBLS	10/01-12/01
Food Preparation and Serving Workers	Daytona Beach MSA, FL	H	7.78 FQ	12.14 AW	16.86 TQ	FLBLS	10/01-12/01
Food Preparation and Serving Workers	Fort Lauderdale PMSA, FL	H	7.63 FQ	13.80 AW	20.10 TQ	FLBLS	10/01-12/01
Food Preparation and Serving Workers	Fort Myers-Cape Coral MSA, FL	H	7.80 FQ	13.19 AW	19.76 TQ	FLBLS	10/01-12/01
Food Preparation and Serving Workers	Fort Pierce-Port St. Lucie MSA, FL	H	7.85 FQ	12.25 AW	17.35 TQ	FLBLS	10/01-12/01
Food Preparation and Serving Workers	Fort Walton Beach MSA, FL	H	7.74 FQ	11.15 AW	15.80 TQ	FLBLS	10/01-12/01
Food Preparation and Serving Workers	Gainesville MSA, FL	H	7.43 FQ	11.09 AW	16.44 TQ	FLBLS	10/01-12/01
Food Preparation and Serving Workers	Jacksonville MSA, FL	H	7.71 FQ	12.84 AW	19.72 TQ	FLBLS	10/01-12/01
Food Preparation and Serving Workers	Lakeland-Winter Haven MSA, FL	H	7.58 FQ	11.87 AW	17.35 TQ	FLBLS	10/01-12/01
Food Preparation and Serving Workers	Melbourne-Titusville-Palm Bay MSA, FL	H	7.51 FQ	11.66 AW	16.55 TQ	FLBLS	10/01-12/01
Food Preparation and Serving Workers	Miami PMSA, FL	H	7.62 FQ	14.33 AW	21.37 TQ	FLBLS	10/01-12/01
Food Preparation and Serving Workers	Naples MSA, FL	H	9.54 FQ	15.34 AW	21.46 TQ	FLBLS	10/01-12/01
Food Preparation and Serving Workers	Ocala MSA, FL	H	7.32 FQ	10.68 AW	15.88 TQ	FLBLS	10/01-12/01
Food Preparation and Serving Workers	Orlando MSA, FL	H	7.95 FQ	13.05 AW	20.11 TQ	FLBLS	10/01-12/01
Food Preparation and Serving Workers	Pensacola MSA, FL	H	7.43 FQ	11.73 AW	16.70 TQ	FLBLS	10/01-12/01
Food Preparation and Serving Workers	Sarasota-Bradenton MSA, FL	H	8.23 FQ	12.14 AW	17.01 TQ	FLBLS	10/01-12/01
Food Preparation and Serving Workers	Tallahassee MSA, FL	H	7.51 FQ	11.17 AW	16.15 TQ	FLBLS	10/01-12/01
Food Preparation and Serving Workers	Tampa-St. Petersburg-Clearwater MSA, FL	H	7.83 FQ	12.40 AW	18.32 TQ	FLBLS	10/01-12/01
Food Preparation and Serving Workers	West Palm Beach-Boca Raton MSA, FL	H	8.93 FQ	12.49 AW	16.55 TQ	FLBLS	10/01-12/01
Food Preparation and Serving Workers	Georgia	H	8.08 FQ	13.31 AW	19.82 TQ	GABLS	10/01-12/01
Food Preparation and Serving Workers	Atlanta MSA, GA	H	9.17 FQ	14.60 AW	20.45 TQ	GABLS	10/01-12/01
Food Preparation and Serving Workers	Augusta-Aiken MSA, GA-SC	H	7.57 FQ	11.17 AW	15.15 TQ	GABLS	10/01-12/01
Food Preparation and Serving Workers	Columbus MSA, GA-AL	H	8.13 FQ	11.10 AW	14.01 TQ	GABLS	10/01-12/01
Food Preparation and Serving Workers	Macon MSA, GA	H	9.65 FQ	12.17 AW	14.37 TQ	GABLS	10/01-12/01
Food Preparation and Serving Workers	Savannah MSA, GA	H	8.90 FQ	12.55 AW	18.01 TQ	GABLS	10/01-12/01
Food Preparation and Serving Workers	Hawaii	H	8.16 FQ	14.14 AW	21.13 TQ	HIBLS	10/01-12/01
Food Preparation and Serving Workers	Honolulu MSA, HI	H	7.90 FQ	13.47 AW	20.23 TQ	HIBLS	10/01-12/01
Food Preparation and Serving Workers	Idaho	H	6.11 FQ	9.55 AW	13.83 TQ	IDBLS	10/01-12/01
Food Preparation and Serving Workers	Boise City MSA, ID	H	7.40 FQ	10.59 AW	15.15 TQ	IDBLS	10/01-12/01
Food Preparation and Serving Workers	Illinois	H	7.63 FQ	12.34 AW	19.06 TQ	ILBLS	10/01-12/01
Food Preparation and Serving Workers	Champaign-Urbana MSA, IL	H	6.18 FQ	9.40 AW	12.93 TQ	ILBLS	10/01-12/01
Food Preparation and Serving Workers	Chicago PMSA, IL	H	8.81 FQ	12.69 AW	19.01 TQ	ILBLS	10/01-12/01
Food Preparation and Serving Workers	Peoria-Pekin MSA, IL	H	7.60 FQ	11.90 AW	16.24 TQ	ILBLS	10/01-12/01
Food Preparation and Serving Workers	Rockford MSA, IL	H	5.87 FQ	9.78 AW	15.77 TQ	ILBLS	10/01-12/01
Food Preparation and Serving Workers	Springfield MSA, IL	H	7.49 FQ	13.11 AW	20.86 TQ	ILBLS	10/01-12/01
Food Preparation and Serving Workers	Indiana	H	7.70 FQ	11.48 AW	16.53 TQ	INBLS	10/01-12/01
Food Preparation and Serving Workers	Elkhart-Goshen MSA, IN	H	6.83 FQ	11.06 AW	16.23 TQ	INBLS	10/01-12/01
Food Preparation and Serving Workers	Evansville-Henderson MSA, IN-KY	H	8.03 FQ	12.36 AW	18.99 TQ	INBLS	10/01-12/01

AAW	Average annual wage	AOH	Average offered, high	ASH	Average starting, high	H	Hourly	M	Monthly	S	Special: hourly and annual
AE	Average entry wage	AOL	Average offered, low	ASL	Average starting, low	HI	Highest wage paid	MTC	Median total compensation	TQ	Third quartile wage
AEX	Average experienced wage	APH	Average pay, high range	AW	Average wage paid	HR	High end range	MW	Median wage paid	W	Weekly
AO	Average offered	APL	Average pay, low range	FQ	First quartile wage	LR	Low end range	SQ	Second quartile wage	Y	Yearly

Occupation/Type/Industry	Location	Per	Low	Mid	High	Source	Date
First-Line Supervisor/Manager							
Food Preparation and Serving Workers	Fort Wayne MSA, IN	H	8.92 FQ	11.79 AW	16.23 TQ	INBLS	10/01-12/01
Food Preparation and Serving Workers	Gary PMSA, IN	H	7.15 FQ	11.71 AW	17.64 TQ	INBLS	10/01-12/01
Food Preparation and Serving Workers	Indianapolis MSA, IN	H	8.87 FQ	12.21 AW	16.66 TQ	INBLS	10/01-12/01
Food Preparation and Serving Workers	Lafayette MSA, IN	H	7.69 FQ	11.69 AW	18.37 TQ	INBLS	10/01-12/01
Food Preparation and Serving Workers	South Bend MSA, IN	H	7.09 FQ	11.32 AW	17.40 TQ	INBLS	10/01-12/01
Food Preparation and Serving Workers	Iowa	H	7.47 FQ	11.28 AW	16.60 TQ	IABLS	10/01-12/01
Food Preparation and Serving Workers	Cedar Rapids MSA, IA	H	9.11 FQ	12.92 AW	19.75 TQ	IABLS	10/01-12/01
Food Preparation and Serving Workers	Davenport-Moline-Rock Island MSA, IA-IL	H	7.42 FQ	11.19 AW	16.23 TQ	IABLS	10/01-12/01
Food Preparation and Serving Workers	Des Moines MSA, IA	H	8.25 FQ	13.43 AW	24.18 TQ	IABLS	10/01-12/01
Food Preparation and Serving Workers	Kansas	H	6.58 FQ	10.76 AW	16.21 TQ	KSBLS	10/01-12/01
Food Preparation and Serving Workers	Topeka MSA, KS	H	7.36 FQ	10.39 AW	13.43 TQ	KSBLS	10/01-12/01
Food Preparation and Serving Workers	Wichita MSA, KS	H	7.95 FQ	11.66 AW	16.23 TQ	KSBLS	10/01-12/01
Food Preparation and Serving Workers	Kentucky	H	6.97 FQ	10.34 AW	15.45 TQ	KYBLS	10/01-12/01
Food Preparation and Serving Workers	Lexington MSA, KY	H	6.90 FQ	10.79 AW	15.77 TQ	KYBLS	10/01-12/01
Food Preparation and Serving Workers	Louisville MSA, KY-IN	H	7.14 FQ	11.12 AW	16.89 TQ	KYBLS	10/01-12/01
Food Preparation and Serving Workers	Louisiana	H	7.06 FQ	11.16 AW	16.30 TQ	LABLS	10/01-12/01
Food Preparation and Serving Workers	Baton Rouge MSA, LA	H	7.56 FQ	11.39 AW	15.92 TQ	LABLS	10/01-12/01
Food Preparation and Serving Workers	Houma MSA, LA	H	6.51 FQ	10.15 AW	15.66 TQ	LABLS	10/01-12/01
Food Preparation and Serving Workers	Lafayette MSA, LA	H	8.75 FQ	12.90 AW	18.59 TQ	LABLS	10/01-12/01
Food Preparation and Serving Workers	Lake Charles MSA, LA	H	7.13 FQ	9.91 AW	13.38 TQ	LABLS	10/01-12/01
Food Preparation and Serving Workers	New Orleans MSA, LA	H	7.95 FQ	11.07 AW	15.76 TQ	LABLS	10/01-12/01
Food Preparation and Serving Workers	Shreveport-Bossier City MSA, LA	H	6.74 FQ	13.99 AW	31.14 TQ	LABLS	10/01-12/01
Food Preparation and Serving Workers	Maine	H	7.26 FQ	10.64 AW	15.09 TQ	MEBLS	10/01-12/01
Food Preparation and Serving Workers	Portland MSA, ME	H	7.45 FQ	10.36 AW	14.70 TQ	MEBLS	10/01-12/01
Food Preparation and Serving Workers	Maryland	H	8.39 FQ	12.87 AW	19.00 TQ	MDBLS	10/01-12/01
Food Preparation and Serving Workers	Baltimore PMSA, MD	H	8.36 FQ	12.85 AW	17.64 TQ	MDBLS	10/01-12/01
Food Preparation and Serving Workers	Massachusetts	H	9.04 FQ	25.16 AW		MABLS	10/01-12/01
Food Preparation and Serving Workers	Boston PMSA, MA-NH	H	9.21 FQ	32.94 AW		MABLS	10/01-12/01
Food Preparation and Serving Workers	Brockton PMSA, MA	H	9.03 FQ	11.47 AW	14.38 TQ	MABLS	10/01-12/01
Food Preparation and Serving Workers	Lawrence PMSA, MA-NH	H	9.05 FQ	17.34 AW	24.82 TQ	MABLS	10/01 12/01
Food Preparation and Serving Workers	Lowell PMSA, MA-NH	H	7.73 FQ	16.24 AW	30.80 TQ	MABLS	10/01-12/01
Food Preparation and Serving Workers	New Bedford PMSA, MA	H	8.72 FQ	12.84 AW	16.92 TQ	MABLS	10/01-12/01
Food Preparation and Serving Workers	Springfield MSA, MA	H	9.19 FQ	13.95 AW	19.94 TQ	MABLS	10/01-12/01
Food Preparation and Serving Workers	Worcester PMSA, MA-CT	H	10.20 FQ	13.60 AW	17.42 TQ	MABLS	10/01-12/01
Food Preparation and Serving Workers	Michigan	H	7.84 FQ	12.88 AW	19.31 TQ	MIBLS	10/01-12/01
Food Preparation and Serving Workers	Ann Arbor PMSA, MI	H	8.43 FQ	12.31 AW	18.64 TQ	MIBLS	10/01-12/01
Food Preparation and Serving Workers	Detroit PMSA, MI	H	8.17 FQ	13.71 AW	20.00 TQ	MIBLS	10/01-12/01
Food Preparation and Serving Workers	Flint PMSA, MI	H	7.26 FQ	11.53 AW	17.20 TQ	MIBLS	10/01-12/01
Food Preparation and Serving Workers	Grand Rapids-Muskegon-Holland MSA, MI	H	7.93 FQ	12.68 AW	18.82 TQ	MIBLS	10/01-12/01
Food Preparation and Serving Workers	Kalamazoo-Battle Creek MSA, MI	H	7.60 FQ	12.49 AW	19.86 TQ	MIBLS	10/01-12/01
Food Preparation and Serving Workers	Lansing-East Lansing MSA, MI	H	8.67 FQ	11.95 AW	17.84 TQ	MIBLS	10/01-12/01
Food Preparation and Serving Workers	Saginaw-Bay City-Midland MSA, MI	H	8.58 FQ	13.63 AW	19.66 TQ	MIBLS	10/01-12/01
Food Preparation and Serving Workers	Minnesota	H	7.51 FQ	11.96 AW	17.14 TQ	MNBLS	10/01-12/01
Food Preparation and Serving Workers	Duluth-Superior MSA, MN-WI	H	6.92 FQ	10.62 AW	15.48 TQ	MNBLS	10/01-12/01
Food Preparation and Serving Workers	Minneapolis-St. Paul MSA, MN-WI	H	8.66 FQ	13.01 AW	17.50 TQ	MNBLS	10/01-12/01
Food Preparation and Serving Workers	St. Cloud MSA, MN	H	7.55 FQ	10.11 AW	15.15 TQ	MNBLS	10/01-12/01
Food Preparation and Serving Workers	Mississippi	H	6.58 FQ	9.92 AW	13.27 TQ	MSBLS	10/01-12/01
Food Preparation and Serving Workers	Biloxi-Gulfport-Pascagoula MSA, MS	H	6.07 FQ	9.64 AW	13.46 TQ	MSBLS	10/01-12/01
Food Preparation and Serving Workers	Jackson MSA, MS	H	7.94 FQ	10.66 AW	13.86 TQ	MSBLS	10/01-12/01
Food Preparation and Serving Workers	Missouri	H	6.76 FQ	10.84 AW	15.91 TQ	MOBLS	10/01-12/01
Food Preparation and Serving Workers	Kansas City MSA, MO-KS	H	6.99 FQ	12.07 AW	16.79 TQ	MOBLS	10/01-12/01
Food Preparation and Serving Workers	St. Louis MSA, MO-IL	H	8.10 FQ	12.23 AW	18.12 TQ	MOBLS	10/01-12/01
Food Preparation and Serving Workers	Springfield MSA, MO	H	7.06 FQ	10.37 AW	16.04 TQ	MOBLS	10/01-12/01
Food Preparation and Serving Workers	Montana	H	7.14 FQ	9.77 AW	13.33 TQ	MTBLS	10/01-12/01
Food Preparation and Serving Workers	Billings MSA, MT	H	6.32 FQ	8.86 AW	12.03 TQ	MTBLS	10/01-12/01
Food Preparation and Serving Workers	Nebraska	H	6.94 FQ	11.13 AW	16.34 TQ	NEBLS	10/01-12/01
Food Preparation and Serving Workers	Lincoln MSA, NE	H	6.54 FQ	11.30 AW	17.15 TQ	NEBLS	10/01-12/01
Food Preparation and Serving Workers	Omaha MSA, NE-IA	H	7.65 FQ	11.52 AW	16.59 TQ	NEBLS	10/01-12/01
Food Preparation and Serving Workers	Nevada	H	7.57 FQ	12.67 AW	18.28 TQ	NVBLS	10/01-12/01
Food Preparation and Serving Workers	Las Vegas MSA, NV-AZ	H	7.99 FQ	12.91 AW	17.85 TQ	NVBLS	10/01-12/01
Food Preparation and Serving Workers	Reno MSA, NV	H	6.78 FQ	11.91 AW	18.76 TQ	NVBLS	10/01-12/01
Food Preparation and Serving Workers	New Hampshire	H	7.20 FQ	11.92 AW	17.35 TQ	NHBLS	10/01-12/01
Food Preparation and Serving Workers	Manchester PMSA, NH	H	6.03 FQ	10.48 AW	14.64 TQ	NHBLS	10/01-12/01
Food Preparation and Serving Workers	Nashua PMSA, NH	H	8.05 FQ	11.06 AW	14.95 TQ	NHBLS	10/01-12/01

AAW	Average annual wage	**AOH**	Average offered, high	**ASH**	Average starting, high	**H**	Hourly	**M**	Monthly	**S**	Special: hourly and annual
AE	Average entry wage	**AOL**	Average offered, low	**ASL**	Average starting, low	**HI**	Highest wage paid	**MTC**	Median total compensation	**TQ**	Third quartile wage
AEX	Average experienced wage	**APH**	Average pay, high range	**AW**	Average wage paid	**HR**	High end range	**MW**	Median wage paid	**W**	Weekly
AO	Average offered	**APL**	Average pay, low range	**FQ**	First quartile wage	**LR**	Low end range	**SQ**	Second quartile wage	**Y**	Yearly

Occupation/Type/Industry	Location	Per	Low	Mid	High	Source	Date
First-Line Supervisor/Manager							
Food Preparation and Serving Workers	Portsmouth-Rochester PMSA, NH-ME	H	9.21 FQ	13.23 AW	18.16 TQ	NHBLS	10/01-12/01
Food Preparation and Serving Workers	New Jersey	H	8.10 FQ	14.93 AW	22.25 TQ	NJBLS	10/01-12/01
Food Preparation and Serving Workers	Atlantic-Cape May PMSA, NJ	H	9.49 FQ	15.86 AW	23.95 TQ	NJBLS	10/01-12/01
Food Preparation and Serving Workers	Bergen-Passaic PMSA, NJ	H	10.78 FQ	15.92 AW	23.36 TQ	NJBLS	10/01-12/01
Food Preparation and Serving Workers	Jersey City PMSA, NJ	H	9.50 FQ	16.45 AW	25.33 TQ	NJBLS	10/01-12/01
Food Preparation and Serving Workers	Middlesex-Somerset-Hunterdon PMSA, NJ	H	9.05 FQ	15.44 AW	23.41 TQ	NJBLS	10/01-12/01
Food Preparation and Serving Workers	Monmouth-Ocean PMSA, NJ	H	10.30 FQ	16.58 AW	21.50 TQ	NJBLS	10/01-12/01
Food Preparation and Serving Workers	Newark PMSA, NJ	H	8.46 FQ	14.51 AW	22.74 TQ	NJBLS	10/01-12/01
Food Preparation and Serving Workers	Trenton PMSA, NJ	H	9.71 FQ	15.36 AW	24.37 TQ	NJBLS	10/01-12/01
Food Preparation and Serving Workers	New Mexico	H	6.25 FQ	9.72 AW	13.97 TQ	NMBLS	10/01-12/01
Food Preparation and Serving Workers	Albuquerque MSA, NM	H	6.51 FQ	10.56 AW	14.91 TQ	NMBLS	10/01-12/01
Food Preparation and Serving Workers	Las Cruces MSA, NM	H	5.95 FQ	8.63 AW	13.00 TQ	NMBLS	10/01-12/01
Food Preparation and Serving Workers	New York	H	7.06 FQ	13.27 AW	21.14 TQ	NYBLS	10/01-12/01
Food Preparation and Serving Workers	Albany-Schenectady-Troy MSA, NY	H	7.88 FQ	11.81 AW	18.37 TQ	NYBLS	10/01-12/01
Food Preparation and Serving Workers	Binghamton MSA, NY	H	7.77 FQ	14.10 AW	20.62 TQ	NYBLS	10/01-12/01
Food Preparation and Serving Workers	Buffalo-Niagara Falls MSA, NY	H	7.23 FQ	12.14 AW	19.78 TQ	NYBLS	10/01-12/01
Food Preparation and Serving Workers	Dutchess County PMSA, NY	H	6.23 FQ	11.35 AW	18.14 TQ	NYBLS	10/01-12/01
Food Preparation and Serving Workers	Nassau-Suffolk PMSA, NY	H	7.78 FQ	13.24 AW	20.47 TQ	NYBLS	10/01-12/01
Food Preparation and Serving Workers	New York PMSA, NY	H	6.90 FQ	14.20 AW	22.98 TQ	NYBLS	10/01-12/01
Food Preparation and Serving Workers	Newburgh PMSA, NY-PA	H	8.30 FQ	13.85 AW	16.95 TQ	NYBLS	10/01-12/01
Food Preparation and Serving Workers	Rochester MSA, NY	H	7.84 FQ	12.66 AW	17.89 TQ	NYBLS	10/01-12/01
Food Preparation and Serving Workers	Syracuse MSA, NY	H	6.61 FQ	12.95 AW	20.80 TQ	NYBLS	10/01-12/01
Food Preparation and Serving Workers	Utica-Rome MSA, NY	H	6.12 FQ	10.98 AW	18.24 TQ	NYBLS	10/01-12/01
Food Preparation and Serving Workers	North Carolina	H	7.81 FQ	12.30 AW	17.35 TQ	NCBLS	10/01-12/01
Food Preparation and Serving Workers	Asheville MSA, NC	H	8.23 FQ	12.62 AW	16.71 TQ	NCBLS	10/01-12/01
Food Preparation and Serving Workers	Charlotte-Gastonia-Rock Hill MSA, NC-SC	H	7.71 FQ	13.10 AW	19.67 TQ	NCBLS	10/01-12/01
Food Preparation and Serving Workers	Fayetteville MSA, NC	H	7.61 FQ	11.29 AW	16.82 TQ	NCBLS	10/01-12/01
Food Preparation and Serving Workers	Greensboro-Winston-Salem-High Point MSA, NC	H	9.19 FQ	13.34 AW	18.13 TQ	NCBLS	10/01-12/01
Food Preparation and Serving Workers	Hickory-Morganton-Lenoir MSA, NC	H	7.93 FQ	11.39 AW	15.83 TQ	NCBLS	10/01-12/01
Food Preparation and Serving Workers	Raleigh-Durham-Chapel Hill MSA, NC	H	8.69 FQ	12.22 AW	17.09 TQ	NCBLS	10/01-12/01
Food Preparation and Serving Workers	Wilmington MSA, NC	H	6.22 FQ	12.01 AW	16.61 TQ	NCBLS	10/01-12/01
Food Preparation and Serving Workers	North Dakota	H	7.14 FQ	10.16 AW	15.01 TQ	NDBLS	10/01-12/01
Food Preparation and Serving Workers	Fargo-Moorhead MSA, ND-MN	H	7.16 FQ	10.21 AW	15.26 TQ	NDBLS	10/01-12/01
Food Preparation and Serving Workers	Ohio	H	6.55 FQ	10.95 AW	16.32 TQ	OHBLS	10/01-12/01
Food Preparation and Serving Workers	Akron PMSA, OH	H	7.30 FQ	10.29 AW	14.69 TQ	OHBLS	10/01-12/01
Food Preparation and Serving Workers	Canton-Massillon MSA, OH	H	5.68 FQ	10.17 AW	16.31 TQ	OHBLS	10/01-12/01
Food Preparation and Serving Workers	Cincinnati PMSA, OH-KY-IN	H	5.81 FQ	10.76 AW	16.68 TQ	OHBLS	10/01-12/01
Food Preparation and Serving Workers	Cleveland-Lorain-Elyria PMSA, OH	H	5.94 FQ	11.53 AW	16.66 TQ	OHBLS	10/01-12/01
Food Preparation and Serving Workers	Columbus MSA, OH	H	7.49 FQ	11.87 AW	16.93 TQ	OHBLS	10/01-12/01
Food Preparation and Serving Workers	Dayton-Springfield MSA, OH	H	7.57 FQ	10.93 AW	15.57 TQ	OHBLS	10/01-12/01
Food Preparation and Serving Workers	Hamilton-Middletown PMSA, OH	H	7.72 FQ	11.51 AW	16.52 TQ	OHBLS	10/01-12/01
Food Preparation and Serving Workers	Mansfield MSA, OH	H	6.76 FQ	10.17 AW	14.15 TQ	OHBLS	10/01-12/01
Food Preparation and Serving Workers	Toledo MSA, OH	H	7.68 FQ	12.48 AW	17.74 TQ	OHBLS	10/01-12/01
Food Preparation and Serving Workers	Youngstown-Warren MSA, OH	H	6.85 FQ	9.76 AW	13.98 TQ	OHBLS	10/01-12/01
Food Preparation and Serving Workers	Oklahoma	H	6.32 FQ	9.71 AW	13.65 TQ	OKBLS	10/01-12/01
Food Preparation and Serving Workers	Oklahoma City MSA, OK	H	6.39 FQ	10.18 AW	14.01 TQ	OKBLS	10/01-12/01
Food Preparation and Serving Workers	Tulsa MSA, OK	H	7.46 FQ	10.31 AW	14.42 TQ	OKBLS	10/01-12/01
Food Preparation and Serving Workers	Oregon	H	8.93 FQ	12.65 AW	17.15 TQ	ORBLS	10/01-12/01
Food Preparation and Serving Workers	Eugene-Springfield MSA, OR	H	7.96 FQ	11.05 AW	15.19 TQ	ORBLS	10/01-12/01
Food Preparation and Serving Workers	Medford-Ashland MSA, OR	H	7.36 FQ	11.39 AW	16.81 TQ	ORBLS	10/01-12/01
Food Preparation and Serving Workers	Portland-Vancouver PMSA, OR-WA	H	9.59 FQ	12.73 AW	17.05 TQ	ORBLS	10/01-12/01
Food Preparation and Serving Workers	Salem PMSA, OR	H	8.95 FQ	12.68 AW	17.86 TQ	ORBLS	10/01-12/01
Food Preparation and Serving Workers	Pennsylvania	H	7.24 FQ	12.61 AW	20.02 TQ	PABLS	10/01-12/01
Food Preparation and Serving Workers	Allentown-Bethlehem-Easton MSA, PA	H	7.58 FQ	12.13 AW	16.12 TQ	PABLS	10/01-12/01
Food Preparation and Serving Workers	Erie MSA, PA	H	7.51 FQ	11.57 AW	16.45 TQ	PABLS	10/01-12/01
Food Preparation and Serving Workers	Harrisburg-Lebanon-Carlisle MSA, PA	H	8.11 FQ	12.37 AW	16.91 TQ	PABLS	10/01-12/01
Food Preparation and Serving Workers	Johnstown MSA, PA	H	6.47 FQ	9.71 AW	14.38 TQ	PABLS	10/01-12/01

AAW	Average annual wage	AOH	Average offered, high	ASH	Average starting, high	H	Hourly	M	Monthly	S	Special: hourly and annual
AE	Average entry wage	AOL	Average offered, low	ASL	Average starting, low	HI	Highest wage paid	MTC	Median total compensation	TQ	Third quartile wage
AEX	Average experienced wage	APH	Average pay, high range	AW	Average wage paid	HR	High end range	MW	Median wage paid	W	Weekly
AO	Average offered	APL	Average pay, low range	FQ	First quartile wage	LR	Low end range	SQ	Second quartile wage	Y	Yearly

Occupation/Type/Industry	Location	Per	Low	Mid	High	Source	Date
First-Line Supervisor/Manager							
Food Preparation and Serving Workers	Lancaster MSA, PA	H	8.67 FQ	19.23 AW	62.71 TQ	PABLS	10/01-12/01
Food Preparation and Serving Workers	Philadelphia PMSA, PA-NJ	H	6.93 FQ	13.07 AW	20.75 TQ	PABLS	10/01-12/01
Food Preparation and Serving Workers	Pittsburgh MSA, PA	H	6.71 FQ	13.31 AW	24.06 TQ	PABLS	10/01-12/01
Food Preparation and Serving Workers	Reading MSA, PA	H	8.83 FQ	12.58 AW	17.03 TQ	PABLS	10/01-12/01
Food Preparation and Serving Workers	Scranton-Wilkes-Barre-Hazleton MSA, PA	H	6.59 FQ	11.32 AW	18.34 TQ	PABLS	10/01-12/01
Food Preparation and Serving Workers	York MSA, PA	H	7.79 FQ	12.10 AW	18.41 TQ	PABLS	10/01-12/01
Food Preparation and Serving Workers	Rhode Island	H	7.63 FQ	13.66 AW	20.85 TQ	RIBLS	10/01-12/01
Food Preparation and Serving Workers	Providence-Fall River-Warwick MSA, RI-MA	H	7.57 FQ	13.73 AW	21.19 TQ	RIBLS	10/01-12/01
Food Preparation and Serving Workers	South Carolina	H	6.90 FQ	10.68 AW	14.80 TQ	SCBLS	10/01-12/01
Food Preparation and Serving Workers	Charleston-North Charleston MSA, SC	H	8.62 FQ	11.08 AW	13.66 TQ	SCBLS	10/01-12/01
Food Preparation and Serving Workers	Columbia MSA, SC	H	6.39 FQ	10.55 AW	14.98 TQ	SCBLS	10/01-12/01
Food Preparation and Serving Workers	Greenville-Spartanburg-Anderson MSA, SC	H	7.65 FQ	11.09 AW	16.39 TQ	SCBLS	10/01-12/01
Food Preparation and Serving Workers	Myrtle Beach MSA, SC	H	6.43 FQ	11.27 AW	15.91 TQ	SCBLS	10/01-12/01
Food Preparation and Serving Workers	South Dakota	H	8.89 FQ	11.19 AW	14.01 TQ	SDBLS	10/01-12/01
Food Preparation and Serving Workers	Sioux Falls MSA, SD	H	9.57 FQ	11.79 AW	13.85 TQ	SDBLS	10/01-12/01
Food Preparation and Serving Workers	Tennessee	H	7.40 FQ	11.31 AW	16.63 TQ	TNBLS	10/01-12/01
Food Preparation and Serving Workers	Chattanooga MSA, TN-GA	H	7.39 FQ	11.28 AW	16.60 TQ	TNBLS	10/01-12/01
Food Preparation and Serving Workers	Clarksville-Hopkinsville MSA, TN-KY	H	6.70 FQ	9.56 AW	14.22 TQ	TNBLS	10/01-12/01
Food Preparation and Serving Workers	Johnson City-Kingsport-Bristol MSA, TN-VA	H	7.32 FQ	10.77 AW	15.02 TQ	TNBLS	10/01-12/01
Food Preparation and Serving Workers	Knoxville MSA, TN	H	8.61 FQ	11.76 AW	17.10 TQ	TNBLS	10/01-12/01
Food Preparation and Serving Workers	Memphis MSA, TN-AR-MS	H	7.58 FQ	11.43 AW	16.90 TQ	TNBLS	10/01-12/01
Food Preparation and Serving Workers	Nashville MSA, TN	H	7.46 FQ	11.93 AW	16.84 TQ	TNBLS	10/01-12/01
Food Preparation and Serving Workers	Texas	H	6.19 FQ	10.10 AW	15.24 TQ	TXBLS	10/01-12/01
Food Preparation and Serving Workers	Amarillo MSA, TX	H	6.17 FQ	9.33 AW	13.82 TQ	TXBLS	10/01-12/01
Food Preparation and Serving Workers	Austin-San Marcos MSA, TX	H	5.99 FQ	10.48 AW	15.69 TQ	TXBLS	10/01-12/01
Food Preparation and Serving Workers	Beaumont-Port Arthur MSA, TX	H	6.33 FQ	9.07 AW	13.56 TQ	TXBLS	10/01-12/01
Food Preparation and Serving Workers	Brazoria PMSA, TX	H	6.17 FQ	9.23 AW	14.46 TQ	TXBLS	10/01-12/01
Food Preparation and Serving Workers	Brownsville-Harlingen-San Benito MSA, TX	H	6.23 FQ	8.83 AW	12.68 TQ	TXBLS	10/01-12/01
Food Preparation and Serving Workers	Corpus Christi MSA, TX	H	6.38 FQ	8.83 AW	11.49 TQ	TXBLS	10/01-12/01
Food Preparation and Serving Workers	Dallas PMSA, TX	H	7.54 FQ	11.12 AW	16.97 TQ	TXBLS	10/01-12/01
Food Preparation and Serving Workers	El Paso MSA, TX	H	5.64 FQ	10.31 AW	16.94 TQ	TXBLS	10/01-12/01
Food Preparation and Serving Workers	Fort Worth-Arlington PMSA, TX	H	6.00 FQ	10.14 AW	15.74 TQ	TXBLS	10/01-12/01
Food Preparation and Serving Workers	Galveston-Texas City PMSA, TX	H	6.03 FQ	10.10 AW	15.74 TQ	TXBLS	10/01-12/01
Food Preparation and Serving Workers	Houston PMSA, TX	H	6.39 FQ	10.23 AW	14.62 TQ	TXBLS	10/01-12/01
Food Preparation and Serving Workers	Killeen-Temple MSA, TX	H	6.50 FQ	9.75 AW	15.50 TQ	TXBLS	10/01-12/01
Food Preparation and Serving Workers	Laredo MSA, TX	H	6.47 FQ	11.19 AW	19.68 TQ	TXBLS	10/01-12/01
Food Preparation and Serving Workers	Longview-Marshall MSA, TX	H	5.96 FQ	9.95 AW	15.05 TQ	TXBLS	10/01-12/01
Food Preparation and Serving Workers	Lubbock MSA, TX	H	6.61 FQ	11.32 AW	16.87 TQ	TXBLS	10/01-12/01
Food Preparation and Serving Workers	McAllen-Edinburg-Mission MSA, TX	H	6.45 FQ	8.91 AW	12.36 TQ	TXBLS	10/01-12/01
Food Preparation and Serving Workers	Odessa-Midland MSA, TX	H	5.77 FQ	8.32 AW	12.04 TQ	TXBLS	10/01-12/01
Food Preparation and Serving Workers	San Antonio MSA, TX	H	7.29 FQ	10.76 AW	16.18 TQ	TXBLS	10/01-12/01
Food Preparation and Serving Workers	Tyler MSA, TX	H	5.81 FQ	8.67 AW	12.06 TQ	TXBLS	10/01-12/01
Food Preparation and Serving Workers	Waco MSA, TX	H	7.02 FQ	9.57 AW	13.06 TQ	TXBLS	10/01-12/01
Food Preparation and Serving Workers	Utah	H	8.27 FQ	11.82 AW	15.45 TQ	UTBLS	10/01-12/01
Food Preparation and Serving Workers	Provo-Orem MSA, UT	H	8.41 FQ	11.35 AW	14.03 TQ	UTBLS	10/01-12/01
Food Preparation and Serving Workers	Salt Lake City-Ogden MSA, UT	H	9.08 FQ	12.07 AW	15.53 TQ	UTBLS	10/01-12/01
Food Preparation and Serving Workers	Vermont	H	9.66 FQ	14.59 AW	20.44 TQ	VTBLS	10/01-12/01
Food Preparation and Serving Workers	Burlington MSA, VT	H	9.79 FQ	15.23 AW	20.72 TQ	VTBLS	10/01-12/01
Food Preparation and Serving Workers	Virginia	H	7.47 FQ	11.90 AW	17.79 TQ	VABLS	10/01-12/01
Food Preparation and Serving Workers	Lynchburg MSA, VA	H	7.47 FQ	10.49 AW	15.43 TQ	VABLS	10/01-12/01
Food Preparation and Serving Workers	Norfolk-Virginia Beach-Newport News MSA, VA-NC	H	7.07 FQ	10.54 AW	15.35 TQ	VABLS	10/01-12/01
Food Preparation and Serving Workers	Richmond-Petersburg MSA, VA	H	8.92 FQ	14.03 AW	20.13 TQ	VABLS	10/01-12/01
Food Preparation and Serving Workers	Roanoke MSA, VA	H	8.86 FQ	12.32 AW	14.79 TQ	VABLS	10/01-12/01
Food Preparation and Serving Workers	Washington	H	10.22 FQ	15.98 AW	22.56 TQ	WABLS	10/01-12/01
Food Preparation and Serving Workers	Bremerton PMSA, WA	H	7.06 FQ	13.60 AW	18.22 TQ	WABLS	10/01-12/01
Food Preparation and Serving Workers	Olympia PMSA, WA	H	9.23 FQ	15.21 AW	21.40 TQ	WABLS	10/01-12/01

AAW	Average annual wage	AOH	Average offered, high	ASH	Average starting, high	H	Hourly	M	Monthly	S	Special: hourly and annual
AE	Average entry wage	AOL	Average offered, low	ASL	Average starting, low	HI	Highest wage paid	MTC	Median total compensation	TQ	Third quartile wage
AEX	Average experienced wage	APH	Average pay, high range	AW	Average wage paid	HR	High end range	MW	Median wage paid	W	Weekly
AO	Average offered	APL	Average pay, low range	FQ	First quartile wage	LR	Low end range	SQ	Second quartile wage	Y	Yearly

Occupation/Type/Industry	Location	Per	Low	Mid	High	Source	Date
First-Line Supervisor/Manager							
Food Preparation and Serving Workers	Richland-Kennewick-Pasco MSA, WA	H	8.29 FQ	13.46 AW	20.36 TQ	WABLS	10/01-12/01
Food Preparation and Serving Workers	Seattle-Bellevue-Everett PMSA, WA	H	11.88 FQ	17.51 AW	23.90 TQ	WABLS	10/01-12/01
Food Preparation and Serving Workers	Spokane MSA, WA	H	9.72 FQ	13.98 AW	20.68 TQ	WABLS	10/01-12/01
Food Preparation and Serving Workers	Tacoma PMSA, WA	H	9.79 FQ	14.34 AW	19.73 TQ	WABLS	10/01-12/01
Food Preparation and Serving Workers	Yakima MSA, WA	H	9.35 FQ	13.69 AW	18.29 TQ	WABLS	10/01-12/01
Food Preparation and Serving Workers	West Virginia	H	6.42 FQ	9.18 AW	12.42 TQ	WVBLS	10/01-12/01
Food Preparation and Serving Workers	Charleston MSA, WV	H	5.87 FQ	8.75 AW	13.09 TQ	WVBLS	10/01-12/01
Food Preparation and Serving Workers	Huntington-Ashland MSA, WV-KY-OH	H	6.45 FQ	9.37 AW	13.73 TQ	WVBLS	10/01-12/01
Food Preparation and Serving Workers	Wisconsin	H	7.60 FQ	12.06 AW	17.78 TQ	WIBLS	10/01-12/01
Food Preparation and Serving Workers	Appleton-Oshkosh-Neenah MSA, WI	H	7.93 FQ	11.39 AW	16.46 TQ	WIBLS	10/01-12/01
Food Preparation and Serving Workers	Green Bay MSA, WI	H	8.60 FQ	15.03 AW	21.85 TQ	WIBLS	10/01-12/01
Food Preparation and Serving Workers	Madison MSA, WI	H	7.57 FQ	12.76 AW	19.87 TQ	WIBLS	10/01-12/01
Food Preparation and Serving Workers	Milwaukee-Waukesha PMSA, WI	H	9.35 FQ	13.49 AW	19.33 TQ	WIBLS	10/01-12/01
Food Preparation and Serving Workers	Racine PMSA, WI	H	9.39 FQ	12.78 AW	17.36 TQ	WIBLS	10/01-12/01
Food Preparation and Serving Workers	Wyoming	H	7.04 FQ	10.41 AW	15.76 TQ	WYBLS	10/01-12/01
Food Preparation and Serving Workers	Cheyenne MSA, WY	H	7.11 FQ	9.69 AW	13.87 TQ	WYBLS	10/01-12/01
Food Preparation and Serving Workers	Puerto Rico	H	5.70 FQ	8.52 AW	12.62 TQ	PRBLS	10/01-12/01
Food Preparation and Serving Workers	Virgin Islands	H	9.02 FQ	11.45 AW	14.72 TQ	VIBLS	10/01-12/01
Food Preparation and Serving Workers	Guam	H	6.30 FQ	9.55 AW	14.97 TQ	GUBLS	10/01-12/01
Helpers, Laborers, and Material Movers	Alabama	H	9.36 FQ	16.44 AW	24.79 TQ	ALBLS	10/01-12/01
Helpers, Laborers, and Material Movers	Birmingham MSA, AL	H	11.48 FQ	17.12 AW	25.12 TQ	ALBLS	10/01-12/01
Helpers, Laborers, and Material Movers	Huntsville MSA, AL	H	9.66 FQ	16.18 AW	25.32 TQ	ALBLS	10/01-12/01
Helpers, Laborers, and Material Movers	Mobile MSA, AL	H	11.27 FQ	17.22 AW	24.73 TQ	ALBLS	10/01-12/01
Helpers, Laborers, and Material Movers	Montgomery MSA, AL	H	11.74 FQ	17.15 AW	25.86 TQ	ALBLS	10/01-12/01
Helpers, Laborers, and Material Movers	Alaska	H	11.70 FQ	19.93 AW	32.99 TQ	AKBLS	10/01-12/01
Helpers, Laborers, and Material Movers	Anchorage MSA, AK	H	11.62 FQ	19.12 AW	32.42 TQ	AKBLS	10/01-12/01
Helpers, Laborers, and Material Movers	Arizona	H	9.80 FQ	17.54 AW	28.26 TQ	AZBLS	10/01-12/01
Helpers, Laborers, and Material Movers	Phoenix-Mesa MSA, AZ	H	9.79 FQ	17.76 AW	29.09 TQ	AZBLS	10/01-12/01
Helpers, Laborers, and Material Movers	Tucson MSA, AZ	H	10.31 FQ	17.18 AW	22.95 TQ	AZBLS	10/01-12/01
Helpers, Laborers, and Material Movers	Arkansas	H	9.31 FQ	15.94 AW	24.56 TQ	ARBLS	10/01-12/01
Helpers, Laborers, and Material Movers	Fayetteville-Springdale-Rogers MSA, AR	H	7.86 FQ	14.88 AW	24.56 TQ	ARBLS	10/01-12/01
Helpers, Laborers, and Material Movers	Fort Smith MSA, AR-OK	H	9.40 FQ	15.47 AW	24.96 TQ	ARBLS	10/01-12/01
Helpers, Laborers, and Material Movers	Little Rock-North Little Rock MSA, AR	H	10.15 FQ	16.91 AW	23.18 TQ	ARBLS	10/01-12/01
Helpers, Laborers, and Material Movers	California	H	12.08 FQ	20.14 AW	29.42 TQ	CABLS	10/01-12/01
Helpers, Laborers, and Material Movers	Bakersfield MSA, CA	H	13.63 FQ	20.61 AW	27.81 TQ	CABLS	10/01-12/01
Helpers, Laborers, and Material Movers	Chico-Paradise MSA, CA	H	8.94 FQ	18.78 AW	31.39 TQ	CABLS	10/01-12/01
Helpers, Laborers, and Material Movers	Fresno MSA, CA	H	12.27 FQ	19.45 AW	28.56 TQ	CABLS	10/01-12/01
Helpers, Laborers, and Material Movers	Los Angeles-Long Beach PMSA, CA	H	11.40 FQ	19.51 AW	29.64 TQ	CABLS	10/01-12/01
Helpers, Laborers, and Material Movers	Merced MSA, CA	H	11.85 FQ	18.57 AW	26.64 TQ	CABLS	10/01-12/01
Helpers, Laborers, and Material Movers	Modesto MSA, CA	H	11.35 FQ	17.96 AW	25.42 TQ	CABLS	10/01-12/01
Helpers, Laborers, and Material Movers	Oakland PMSA, CA	H	15.18 FQ	23.78 AW	33.95 TQ	CABLS	10/01-12/01
Helpers, Laborers, and Material Movers	Orange County PMSA, CA	H	12.32 FQ	20.09 AW	28.51 TQ	CABLS	10/01-12/01
Helpers, Laborers, and Material Movers	Redding MSA, CA	H	9.92 FQ	15.10 AW	19.47 TQ	CABLS	10/01-12/01
Helpers, Laborers, and Material Movers	Riverside-San Bernardino PMSA, CA	H	12.20 FQ	20.29 AW	27.90 TQ	CABLS	10/01-12/01
Helpers, Laborers, and Material Movers	Sacramento PMSA, CA	H	13.43 FQ	20.25 AW	27.77 TQ	CABLS	10/01-12/01
Helpers, Laborers, and Material Movers	Salinas MSA, CA	H	12.85 FQ	21.35 AW	32.77 TQ	CABLS	10/01-12/01
Helpers, Laborers, and Material Movers	San Diego MSA, CA	H	11.90 FQ	18.27 AW	26.53 TQ	CABLS	10/01-12/01
Helpers, Laborers, and Material Movers	San Francisco PMSA, CA	H	12.63 FQ	20.45 AW	30.20 TQ	CABLS	10/01-12/01
Helpers, Laborers, and Material Movers	San Jose PMSA, CA	H	12.91 FQ	21.62 AW	29.37 TQ	CABLS	10/01-12/01
Helpers, Laborers, and Material Movers	San Luis Obispo-Atascadero-Paso Robles MSA, CA	H	14.75 FQ	19.85 AW	26.75 TQ	CABLS	10/01-12/01
Helpers, Laborers, and Material Movers	Santa Barbara-Santa Maria-Lompoc MSA, CA	H	12.11 FQ	20.51 AW	28.76 TQ	CABLS	10/01-12/01
Helpers, Laborers, and Material Movers	Santa Cruz-Watsonville PMSA, CA	H	11.51 FQ	20.93 AW	34.69 TQ	CABLS	10/01-12/01
Helpers, Laborers, and Material Movers	Santa Rosa PMSA, CA	H	8.97 FQ	17.12 AW	27.04 TQ	CABLS	10/01-12/01
Helpers, Laborers, and Material Movers	Stockton-Lodi MSA, CA	H	12.30 FQ	20.86 AW	28.94 TQ	CABLS	10/01-12/01
Helpers, Laborers, and Material Movers	Vallejo-Fairfield-Napa PMSA, CA	H	12.71 FQ	20.88 AW	29.79 TQ	CABLS	10/01-12/01
Helpers, Laborers, and Material Movers	Ventura PMSA, CA	H	11.70 FQ	20.46 AW	27.61 TQ	CABLS	10/01-12/01
Helpers, Laborers, and Material Movers	Visalia-Tulare-Porterville MSA, CA	H	12.07 FQ	18.97 AW	26.77 TQ	CABLS	10/01-12/01

AAW	Average annual wage	**AOH**	Average offered, high	**ASH**	Average starting, high	**H**	Hourly	**M**	Monthly	**S**	Special: hourly and annual
AE	Average entry wage	**AOL**	Average offered, low	**ASL**	Average starting, low	**HI**	Highest wage paid	**MTC**	Median total compensation	**TQ**	Third quartile wage
AEX	Average experienced wage	**APH**	Average pay, high range	**AW**	Average wage paid	**HR**	High end range	**MW**	Median wage paid	**W**	Weekly
AO	Average offered	**APL**	Average pay, low range	**FQ**	First quartile wage	**LR**	Low end range	**SQ**	Second quartile wage	**Y**	Yearly

Occupation/Type/Industry	Location	Per	Low	Mid	High	Source	Date
First-Line Supervisor/Manager							
Helpers, Laborers, and Material Movers	Colorado	H	10.40 FQ	18.63 AW	28.19 TQ	COBLS	10/01-12/01
Helpers, Laborers, and Material Movers	Boulder-Longmont PMSA, CO	H	11.05 FQ	17.23 AW	24.62 TQ	COBLS	10/01-12/01
Helpers, Laborers, and Material Movers	Colorado Springs MSA, CO	H	9.94 FQ	22.97 AW	50.24 TQ	COBLS	10/01-12/01
Helpers, Laborers, and Material Movers	Denver PMSA, CO	H	11.73 FQ	19.23 AW	28.28 TQ	COBLS	10/01-12/01
Helpers, Laborers, and Material Movers	Fort Collins-Loveland MSA, CO	H	10.30 FQ	16.39 AW	24.40 TQ	COBLS	10/01-12/01
Helpers, Laborers, and Material Movers	Greeley PMSA, CO	H	12.47 FQ	18.46 AW	23.60 TQ	COBLS	10/01-12/01
Helpers, Laborers, and Material Movers	Connecticut	H	13.39 FQ	20.33 AW	28.27 TQ	CTBLS	10/01-12/01
Helpers, Laborers, and Material Movers	Bridgeport PMSA, CT	H	12.49 FQ	20.16 AW	30.44 TQ	CTBLS	10/01-12/01
Helpers, Laborers, and Material Movers	Danbury PMSA, CT	H	13.75 FQ	19.32 AW	27.34 TQ	CTBLS	10/01-12/01
Helpers, Laborers, and Material Movers	Hartford MSA, CT	H	13.26 FQ	19.61 AW	27.20 TQ	CTBLS	10/01-12/01
Helpers, Laborers, and Material Movers	New Haven-Meriden PMSA, CT	H	14.13 FQ	21.57 AW	31.28 TQ	CTBLS	10/01-12/01
Helpers, Laborers, and Material Movers	New London-Norwich MSA, CT-RI	H	10.97 FQ	19.66 AW	30.91 TQ	CTBLS	10/01-12/01
Helpers, Laborers, and Material Movers	Stamford-Norwalk PMSA, CT	H	13.59 FQ	20.77 AW	27.91 TQ	CTBLS	10/01-12/01
Helpers, Laborers, and Material Movers	Waterbury PMSA, CT	H	16.44 FQ	23.18 AW	31.18 TQ	CTBLS	10/01-12/01
Helpers, Laborers, and Material Movers	Delaware	H	11.60 FQ	18.97 AW	28.02 TQ	DEBLS	10/01-12/01
Helpers, Laborers, and Material Movers	Wilmington-Newark PMSA, DE-MD	H	11.22 FQ	19.47 AW	29.77 TQ	DEBLS	10/01-12/01
Helpers, Laborers, and Material Movers	District of Columbia	H	11.75 FQ	16.87 AW	23.83 TQ	DCBLS	10/01-12/01
Helpers, Laborers, and Material Movers	Washington PMSA, DC-MD-VA-WV	H	12.21 FQ	18.47 AW	26.39 TQ	DCBLS	10/01-12/01
Helpers, Laborers, and Material Movers	Florida	H	10.44 FQ	17.79 AW	27.20 TQ	FLBLS	10/01-12/01
Helpers, Laborers, and Material Movers	Daytona Beach MSA, FL	H	9.62 FQ	15.02 AW	21.04 TQ	FLBLS	10/01-12/01
Helpers, Laborers, and Material Movers	Fort Lauderdale PMSA, FL	H	11.76 FQ	17.96 AW	26.00 TQ	FLBLS	10/01-12/01
Helpers, Laborers, and Material Movers	Fort Myers-Cape Coral MSA, FL	H	8.79 FQ	13.56 AW	19.98 TQ	FLBLS	10/01-12/01
Helpers, Laborers, and Material Movers	Fort Pierce-Port St. Lucie MSA, FL	H	10.31 FQ	15.78 AW	23.96 TQ	FLBLS	10/01-12/01
Helpers, Laborers, and Material Movers	Fort Walton Beach MSA, FL	H	8.70 FQ	12.54 AW	18.48 TQ	FLBLS	10/01-12/01
Helpers, Laborers, and Material Movers	Gainesville MSA, FL	H	11.32 FQ	17.35 AW	24.04 TQ	FLBLS	10/01-12/01
Helpers, Laborers, and Material Movers	Jacksonville MSA, FL	H	11.17 FQ	18.38 AW	27.18 TQ	FLBLS	10/01-12/01
Helpers, Laborers, and Material Movers	Lakeland-Winter Haven MSA, FL	H	9.94 FQ	15.60 AW	22.21 TQ	FLBLS	10/01-12/01
Helpers, Laborers, and Material Movers	Melbourne-Titusville-Palm Bay MSA, FL	H	10.84 FQ	18.16 AW	29.13 TQ	FLBLS	10/01-12/01
Helpers, Laborers, and Material Movers	Miami PMSA, FL	H	10.30 FQ	17.43 AW	26.26 TQ	FLBLS	10/01-12/01
Helpers, Laborers, and Material Movers	Naples MSA, FL	H	11.84 FQ	16.57 AW	24.86 TQ	FLBLS	10/01-12/01
Helpers, Laborers, and Material Movers	Ocala MSA, FL	H	9.55 FQ	17.81 AW	30.65 TQ	FLBLS	10/01-12/01
Helpers, Laborers, and Material Movers	Orlando MSA, FL	H	10.50 FQ	17.04 AW	24.95 TQ	FLBLS	10/01-12/01
Helpers, Laborers, and Material Movers	Pensacola MSA, FL	H	10.10 FQ	14.63 AW	20.87 TQ	FLBLS	10/01-12/01
Helpers, Laborers, and Material Movers	Sarasota-Bradenton MSA, FL	H	8.18 FQ	17.08 AW	27.51 TQ	FLBLS	10/01-12/01
Helpers, Laborers, and Material Movers	Tallahassee MSA, FL	H	10.58 FQ	15.17 AW	21.19 TQ	FLBLS	10/01-12/01
Helpers, Laborers, and Material Movers	Tampa-St. Petersburg-Clearwater MSA, FL	H	11.28 FQ	20.47 AW	36.62 TQ	FLBLS	10/01-12/01
Helpers, Laborers, and Material Movers	West Palm Beach-Boca Raton MSA, FL	H	11.48 FQ	17.61 AW	25.95 TQ	FLBLS	10/01-12/01
Helpers, Laborers, and Material Movers	Georgia	H	10.42 FQ	17.61 AW	26.26 TQ	GABLS	10/01-12/01
Helpers, Laborers, and Material Movers	Atlanta MSA, GA	H	13.08 FQ	19.78 AW	27.88 TQ	GABLS	10/01-12/01
Helpers, Laborers, and Material Movers	Augusta-Aiken MSA, GA-SC	H	9.53 FQ	14.87 AW	21.84 TQ	GABLS	10/01-12/01
Helpers, Laborers, and Material Movers	Columbus MSA, GA-AL	H	9.58 FQ	16.18 AW	23.39 TQ	GABLS	10/01-12/01
Helpers, Laborers, and Material Movers	Macon MSA, GA	H	11.24 FQ	16.88 AW	24.60 TQ	GABLS	10/01-12/01
Helpers, Laborers, and Material Movers	Savannah MSA, GA	H	12.11 FQ	17.36 AW	23.76 TQ	GABLS	10/01-12/01
Helpers, Laborers, and Material Movers	Hawaii	H	9.25 FQ	17.36 AW	26.93 TQ	HIBLS	10/01-12/01
Helpers, Laborers, and Material Movers	Honolulu MSA, HI	H	8.62 FQ	17.80 AW	28.81 TQ	HIBLS	10/01-12/01
Helpers, Laborers, and Material Movers	Idaho	H	10.42 FQ	16.26 AW	22.77 TQ	IDBLS	10/01-12/01
Helpers, Laborers, and Material Movers	Boise City MSA, ID	H	11.33 FQ	17.14 AW	24.42 TQ	IDBLS	10/01-12/01
Helpers, Laborers, and Material Movers	Illinois	H	10.55 FQ	18.87 AW	28.72 TQ	ILBLS	10/01-12/01
Helpers, Laborers, and Material Movers	Champaign-Urbana MSA, IL	H	11.63 FQ	17.94 AW	26.38 TQ	ILBLS	10/01-12/01
Helpers, Laborers, and Material Movers	Chicago PMSA, IL	H	10.75 FQ	19.79 AW	31.02 TQ	ILBLS	10/01-12/01
Helpers, Laborers, and Material Movers	Peoria-Pekin MSA, IL	H	10.25 FQ	16.27 AW	22.32 TQ	ILBLS	10/01-12/01
Helpers, Laborers, and Material Movers	Rockford MSA, IL	H	9.59 FQ	15.75 AW	25.24 TQ	ILBLS	10/01-12/01
Helpers, Laborers, and Material Movers	Springfield MSA, IL	H	11.28 FQ	16.53 AW	21.45 TQ	ILBLS	10/01-12/01
Helpers, Laborers, and Material Movers	Indiana	H	10.92 FQ	17.71 AW	26.12 TQ	INBLS	10/01-12/01
Helpers, Laborers, and Material Movers	Elkhart-Goshen MSA, IN	H	10.62 FQ	18.13 AW	25.75 TQ	INBLS	10/01-12/01
Helpers, Laborers, and Material Movers	Evansville-Henderson MSA, IN-KY	H	11.03 FQ	15.86 AW	22.67 TQ	INBLS	10/01-12/01
Helpers, Laborers, and Material Movers	Fort Wayne MSA, IN	H	11.13 FQ	17.67 AW	27.76 TQ	INBLS	10/01-12/01
Helpers, Laborers, and Material Movers	Gary PMSA, IN	H	11.59 FQ	18.92 AW	26.65 TQ	INBLS	10/01-12/01
Helpers, Laborers, and Material Movers	Indianapolis MSA, IN	H	11.97 FQ	17.90 AW	25.54 TQ	INBLS	10/01-12/01

AAW	Average annual wage	**AOH**	Average offered, high	**ASH**	Average starting, high	**H**	Hourly	**M**	Monthly	**S**	Special: hourly and annual
AE	Average entry wage	**AOL**	Average offered, low	**ASL**	Average starting, low	**HI**	Highest wage paid	**MTC**	Median total compensation	**TQ**	Third quartile wage
AEX	Average experienced wage	**APH**	Average pay, high range	**AW**	Average wage paid	**HR**	High end range	**MW**	Median wage paid	**W**	Weekly
AO	Average offered	**APL**	Average pay, low range	**FQ**	First quartile wage	**LR**	Low end range	**SQ**	Second quartile wage	**Y**	Yearly

Occupation/Type/Industry	Location	Per	Low	Mid	High	Source	Date
First-Line Supervisor/Manager							
Helpers, Laborers, and Material Movers	Lafayette MSA, IN	H	11.78 FQ	20.01 AW	29.56 TQ	INBLS	10/01-12/01
Helpers, Laborers, and Material Movers	South Bend MSA, IN	H	13.26 FQ	22.96 AW	32.10 TQ	INBLS	10/01-12/01
Helpers, Laborers, and Material Movers	Iowa	H	9.04 FQ	16.85 AW	25.32 TQ	IABLS	10/01-12/01
Helpers, Laborers, and Material Movers	Cedar Rapids MSA, IA	H	13.40 FQ	18.56 AW	26.02 TQ	IABLS	10/01-12/01
Helpers, Laborers, and Material Movers	Davenport-Moline-Rock Island MSA, IA-IL	H	9.01 FQ	16.30 AW	23.50 TQ	IABLS	10/01-12/01
Helpers, Laborers, and Material Movers	Des Moines MSA, IA	H	10.22 FQ	17.13 AW	25.26 TQ	IABLS	10/01-12/01
Helpers, Laborers, and Material Movers	Kansas	H	10.75 FQ	17.49 AW	26.06 TQ	KSBLS	10/01-12/01
Helpers, Laborers, and Material Movers	Topeka MSA, KS	H	12.04 FQ	18.50 AW	26.07 TQ	KSBLS	10/01-12/01
Helpers, Laborers, and Material Movers	Wichita MSA, KS	H	11.76 FQ	17.78 AW	25.55 TQ	KSBLS	10/01-12/01
Helpers, Laborers, and Material Movers	Kentucky	H	9.66 FQ	17.60 AW	29.04 TQ	KYBLS	10/01-12/01
Helpers, Laborers, and Material Movers	Lexington MSA, KY	H	9.19 FQ	17.92 AW	39.14 TQ	KYBLS	10/01-12/01
Helpers, Laborers, and Material Movers	Louisville MSA, KY-IN	H	11.03 FQ	18.15 AW	28.06 TQ	KYBLS	10/01-12/01
Helpers, Laborers, and Material Movers	Louisiana	H	10.05 FQ	17.37 AW	27.14 TQ	LABLS	10/01-12/01
Helpers, Laborers, and Material Movers	Baton Rouge MSA, LA	H	10.27 FQ	16.60 AW	21.45 TQ	LABLS	10/01-12/01
Helpers, Laborers, and Material Movers	Houma MSA, LA	H	9.05 FQ	14.61 AW	25.07 TQ	LABLS	10/01-12/01
Helpers, Laborers, and Material Movers	Lafayette MSA, LA	H	10.02 FQ	18.35 AW	29.32 TQ	LABLS	10/01-12/01
Helpers, Laborers, and Material Movers	Lake Charles MSA, LA	H	9.88 FQ	21.08 AW	35.75 TQ	LABLS	10/01-12/01
Helpers, Laborers, and Material Movers	New Orleans MSA, LA	H	10.70 FQ	16.91 AW	24.09 TQ	LABLS	10/01-12/01
Helpers, Laborers, and Material Movers	Shreveport-Bossier City MSA, LA	H	11.27 FQ	14.97 AW	20.87 TQ	LABLS	10/01-12/01
Helpers, Laborers, and Material Movers	Maine	H	10.99 FQ	16.34 AW	23.97 TQ	MEBLS	10/01-12/01
Helpers, Laborers, and Material Movers	Portland MSA, ME	H	11.91 FQ	18.04 AW	26.63 TQ	MEBLS	10/01-12/01
Helpers, Laborers, and Material Movers	Maryland	H	11.89 FQ	18.87 AW	27.53 TQ	MDBLS	10/01-12/01
Helpers, Laborers, and Material Movers	Baltimore PMSA, MD	H	11.75 FQ	18.60 AW	26.79 TQ	MDBLS	10/01-12/01
Helpers, Laborers, and Material Movers	Massachusetts	H	12.82 FQ	19.67 AW	27.19 TQ	MABLS	10/01-12/01
Helpers, Laborers, and Material Movers	Boston PMSA, MA-NH	H	12.97 FQ	19.80 AW	26.78 TQ	MABLS	10/01-12/01
Helpers, Laborers, and Material Movers	Brockton PMSA, MA	H	12.40 FQ	19.41 AW	27.76 TQ	MABLS	10/01-12/01
Helpers, Laborers, and Material Movers	Lawrence PMSA, MA-NH	H	15.00 FQ	21.38 AW	30.43 TQ	MABLS	10/01-12/01
Helpers, Laborers, and Material Movers	Lowell PMSA, MA-NH	H	14.16 FQ	18.01 AW	24.34 TQ	MABLS	10/01-12/01
Helpers, Laborers, and Material Movers	New Bedford PMSA, MA	H	14.28 FQ	20.12 AW	26.85 TQ	MABLS	10/01-12/01
Helpers, Laborers, and Material Movers	Springfield MSA, MA	H	12.17 FQ	20.10 AW	31.12 TQ	MABLS	10/01-12/01
Helpers, Laborers, and Material Movers	Worcester PMSA, MA-CT	H	11.60 FQ	18.58 AW	26.59 TQ	MABLS	10/01-12/01
Helpers, Laborers, and Material Movers	Michigan	H	12.63 FQ	22.16 AW	33.57 TQ	MIBLS	10/01-12/01
Helpers, Laborers, and Material Movers	Ann Arbor PMSA, MI	H	11.50 FQ	21.89 AW	33.22 TQ	MIBLS	10/01-12/01
Helpers, Laborers, and Material Movers	Detroit PMSA, MI	H	13.23 FQ	22.13 AW	33.43 TQ	MIBLS	10/01-12/01
Helpers, Laborers, and Material Movers	Flint PMSA, MI	H	10.83 FQ	20.91 AW	32.16 TQ	MIBLS	10/01-12/01
Helpers, Laborers, and Material Movers	Grand Rapids-Muskegon-Holland MSA, MI	H	15.28 FQ	27.05 AW	41.68 TQ	MIBLS	10/01-12/01
Helpers, Laborers, and Material Movers	Kalamazoo-Battle Creek MSA, MI	H	12.43 FQ	20.76 AW	31.43 TQ	MIBLS	10/01-12/01
Helpers, Laborers, and Material Movers	Lansing-East Lansing MSA, MI	H	10.79 FQ	18.78 AW	30.04 TQ	MIBLS	10/01-12/01
Helpers, Laborers, and Material Movers	Saginaw-Bay City-Midland MSA, MI	H	11.72 FQ	20.75 AW	31.33 TQ	MIBLS	10/01-12/01
Helpers, Laborers, and Material Movers	Minnesota	H	11.06 FQ	19.25 AW	28.85 TQ	MNBLS	10/01-12/01
Helpers, Laborers, and Material Movers	Duluth-Superior MSA, MN-WI	H	11.40 FQ	19.68 AW	31.02 TQ	MNBLS	10/01-12/01
Helpers, Laborers, and Material Movers	Minneapolis-St. Paul MSA, MN-WI	H	11.33 FQ	20.09 AW	31.52 TQ	MNBLS	10/01-12/01
Helpers, Laborers, and Material Movers	St. Cloud MSA, MN	H	10.99 FQ	16.58 AW	24.42 TQ	MNBLS	10/01-12/01
Helpers, Laborers, and Material Movers	Mississippi	H	9.84 FQ	15.92 AW	24.19 TQ	MSBLS	10/01-12/01
Helpers, Laborers, and Material Movers	Biloxi-Gulfport-Pascagoula MSA, MS	H	10.79 FQ	19.29 AW	26.50 TQ	MSBLS	10/01-12/01
Helpers, Laborers, and Material Movers	Jackson MSA, MS	H	9.08 FQ	13.97 AW	18.95 TQ	MSBLS	10/01-12/01
Helpers, Laborers, and Material Movers	Missouri	H	8.77 FQ	15.99 AW	25.21 TQ	MOBLS	10/01-12/01
Helpers, Laborers, and Material Movers	Kansas City MSA, MO-KS	H	10.60 FQ	18.23 AW	27.20 TQ	MOBLS	10/01-12/01
Helpers, Laborers, and Material Movers	St. Louis MSA, MO-IL	H	8.96 FQ	17.63 AW	26.46 TQ	MOBLS	10/01-12/01
Helpers, Laborers, and Material Movers	Springfield MSA, MO	H	8.17 FQ	15.82 AW	25.48 TQ	MOBLS	10/01-12/01
Helpers, Laborers, and Material Movers	Montana	H	9.27 FQ	14.48 AW	21.96 TQ	MTBLS	10/01-12/01
Helpers, Laborers, and Material Movers	Billings MSA, MT	H	9.32 FQ	14.33 AW	22.03 TQ	MTBLS	10/01-12/01
Helpers, Laborers, and Material Movers	Nebraska	H	8.51 FQ	15.26 AW	23.33 TQ	NEBLS	10/01-12/01
Helpers, Laborers, and Material Movers	Lincoln MSA, NE	H	11.28 FQ	17.24 AW	22.21 TQ	NEBLS	10/01-12/01
Helpers, Laborers, and Material Movers	Omaha MSA, NE-IA	H	11.32 FQ	17.66 AW	25.70 TQ	NEBLS	10/01-12/01
Helpers, Laborers, and Material Movers	Nevada	H	11.07 FQ	16.55 AW	23.46 TQ	NVBLS	10/01-12/01
Helpers, Laborers, and Material Movers	Las Vegas MSA, NV-AZ	H	11.79 FQ	16.64 AW	23.49 TQ	NVBLS	10/01-12/01
Helpers, Laborers, and Material Movers	Reno MSA, NV	H	7.64 FQ	15.76 AW	23.88 TQ	NVBLS	10/01-12/01
Helpers, Laborers, and Material Movers	New Hampshire	H	11.25 FQ	16.69 AW	23.04 TQ	NHBLS	10/01-12/01
Helpers, Laborers, and Material Movers	Manchester PMSA, NH	H	11.01 FQ	16.88 AW	24.67 TQ	NHBLS	10/01-12/01
Helpers, Laborers, and Material Movers	Nashua PMSA, NH	H	10.84 FQ	15.93 AW	23.36 TQ	NHBLS	10/01-12/01
Helpers, Laborers, and Material Movers	Portsmouth-Rochester PMSA, NH-ME	H	9.77 FQ	15.78 AW	22.18 TQ	NHBLS	10/01-12/01
Helpers, Laborers, and Material Movers	New Jersey	H	11.94 FQ	20.92 AW	30.94 TQ	NJBLS	10/01-12/01

AAW	Average annual wage	AOH	Average offered, high	ASH	Average starting, high	H	Hourly	M	Monthly	S	Special: hourly and annual
AE	Average entry wage	AOL	Average offered, low	ASL	Average starting, low	HI	Highest wage paid	MTC	Median total compensation	TQ	Third quartile wage
AEX	Average experienced wage	APH	Average pay, high range	AW	Average wage paid	HR	High end range	MW	Median wage paid	W	Weekly
AO	Average offered	APL	Average pay, low range	FQ	First quartile wage	LR	Low end range	SQ	Second quartile wage	Y	Yearly

Occupation/Type/Industry	Location	Per	Low	Mid	High	Source	Date
First-Line Supervisor/Manager							
Helpers, Laborers, and Material Movers	Atlantic-Cape May PMSA, NJ	H	8.55 FQ	17.62 AW	28.45 TQ	NJBLS	10/01-12/01
Helpers, Laborers, and Material Movers	Bergen-Passaic PMSA, NJ	H	10.02 FQ	21.76 AW	32.39 TQ	NJBLS	10/01-12/01
Helpers, Laborers, and Material Movers	Jersey City PMSA, NJ	H	12.42 FQ	20.99 AW	35.19 TQ	NJBLS	10/01-12/01
Helpers, Laborers, and Material Movers	Middlesex-Somerset-Hunterdon PMSA, NJ	H	12.17 FQ	21.43 AW	31.54 TQ	NJBLS	10/01-12/01
Helpers, Laborers, and Material Movers	Monmouth-Ocean PMSA, NJ	H	11.02 FQ	18.99 AW	28.47 TQ	NJBLS	10/01-12/01
Helpers, Laborers, and Material Movers	Newark PMSA, NJ	H	12.48 FQ	20.62 AW	28.63 TQ	NJBLS	10/01-12/01
Helpers, Laborers, and Material Movers	Trenton PMSA, NJ	H	13.27 FQ	20.72 AW	30.87 TQ	NJBLS	10/01-12/01
Helpers, Laborers, and Material Movers	New Mexico	H	8.66 FQ	15.21 AW	24.31 TQ	NMBLS	10/01-12/01
Helpers, Laborers, and Material Movers	Albuquerque MSA, NM	H	9.00 FQ	15.84 AW	24.94 TQ	NMBLS	10/01-12/01
Helpers, Laborers, and Material Movers	Las Cruces MSA, NM	H	6.39 FQ	13.08 AW	20.14 TQ	NMBLS	10/01-12/01
Helpers, Laborers, and Material Movers	New York	H	10.20 FQ	19.33 AW	29.31 TQ	NYBLS	10/01-12/01
Helpers, Laborers, and Material Movers	Albany-Schenectady-Troy MSA, NY	H	9.08 FQ	16.75 AW	25.75 TQ	NYBLS	10/01-12/01
Helpers, Laborers, and Material Movers	Binghamton MSA, NY	H	12.23 FQ	19.47 AW	26.81 TQ	NYBLS	10/01-12/01
Helpers, Laborers, and Material Movers	Buffalo-Niagara Falls MSA, NY	H	7.80 FQ	18.57 AW	31.03 TQ	NYBLS	10/01-12/01
Helpers, Laborers, and Material Movers	Dutchess County PMSA, NY	H	13.51 FQ	20.57 AW	32.90 TQ	NYBLS	10/01-12/01
Helpers, Laborers, and Material Movers	Nassau-Suffolk PMSA, NY	H	8.77 FQ	18.58 AW	28.21 TQ	NYBLS	10/01-12/01
Helpers, Laborers, and Material Movers	New York PMSA, NY	H	11.78 FQ	20.91 AW	31.79 TQ	NYBLS	10/01-12/01
Helpers, Laborers, and Material Movers	Newburgh PMSA, NY-PA	H	11.24 FQ	18.30 AW	26.56 TQ	NYBLS	10/01-12/01
Helpers, Laborers, and Material Movers	Rochester MSA, NY	H	11.32 FQ	18.12 AW	26.86 TQ	NYBLS	10/01-12/01
Helpers, Laborers, and Material Movers	Syracuse MSA, NY	H	11.60 FQ	20.22 AW	29.39 TQ	NYBLS	10/01-12/01
Helpers, Laborers, and Material Movers	Utica-Rome MSA, NY	H	10.92 FQ	18.02 AW	26.20 TQ	NYBLS	10/01-12/01
Helpers, Laborers, and Material Movers	North Carolina	H	10.87 FQ	17.58 AW	26.16 TQ	NCBLS	10/01-12/01
Helpers, Laborers, and Material Movers	Asheville MSA, NC	H	10.84 FQ	18.11 AW	26.35 TQ	NCBLS	10/01-12/01
Helpers, Laborers, and Material Movers	Charlotte-Gastonia-Rock Hill MSA, NC-SC	H	11.73 FQ	18.07 AW	25.70 TQ	NCBLS	10/01-12/01
Helpers, Laborers, and Material Movers	Fayetteville MSA, NC	H	12.40 FQ	16.40 AW	23.52 TQ	NCBLS	10/01-12/01
Helpers, Laborers, and Material Movers	Greensboro-Winston-Salem-High Point MSA, NC	H	11.33 FQ	18.70 AW	28.34 TQ	NCBLS	10/01-12/01
Helpers, Laborers, and Material Movers	Hickory-Morganton-Lenoir MSA, NC	H	10.87 FQ	15.95 AW	22.40 TQ	NCBLS	10/01-12/01
Helpers, Laborers, and Material Movers	Raleigh-Durham-Chapel Hill MSA, NC	H	11.40 FQ	17.81 AW	28.23 TQ	NCBLS	10/01-12/01
Helpers, Laborers, and Material Movers	Wilmington MSA, NC	H	8.28 FQ	15.00 AW	22.06 TQ	NCBLS	10/01-12/01
Helpers, Laborers, and Material Movers	North Dakota	H	8.39 FQ	14.62 AW	22.80 TQ	NDBLS	10/01-12/01
Helpers, Laborers, and Material Movers	Fargo-Moorhead MSA, ND-MN	H	8.83 FQ	15.28 AW	25.91 TQ	NDBLS	10/01-12/01
Helpers, Laborers, and Material Movers	Ohio	H	10.07 FQ	17.58 AW	26.91 TQ	OHBLS	10/01-12/01
Helpers, Laborers, and Material Movers	Akron PMSA, OH	H	11.55 FQ	18.48 AW	27.11 TQ	OHBLS	10/01-12/01
Helpers, Laborers, and Material Movers	Canton-Massillon MSA, OH	H	9.85 FQ	17.70 AW	27.67 TQ	OHBLS	10/01-12/01
Helpers, Laborers, and Material Movers	Cincinnati PMSA, OH-KY-IN	H	9.81 FQ	17.44 AW	27.37 TQ	OHBLS	10/01-12/01
Helpers, Laborers, and Material Movers	Cleveland-Lorain-Elyria PMSA, OH	H	10.03 FQ	18.22 AW	28.22 TQ	OHBLS	10/01-12/01
Helpers, Laborers, and Material Movers	Columbus MSA, OH	H	10.24 FQ	16.96 AW	25.59 TQ	OHBLS	10/01-12/01
Helpers, Laborers, and Material Movers	Dayton-Springfield MSA, OH	H	9.86 FQ	17.79 AW	27.79 TQ	OHBLS	10/01-12/01
Helpers, Laborers, and Material Movers	Hamilton-Middletown PMSA, OH	H	9.75 FQ	18.19 AW	30.09 TQ	OHBLS	10/01-12/01
Helpers, Laborers, and Material Movers	Mansfield MSA, OH	H	9.11 FQ	17.22 AW	30.43 TQ	OHBLS	10/01-12/01
Helpers, Laborers, and Material Movers	Toledo MSA, OH	H	10.23 FQ	17.65 AW	26.20 TQ	OHBLS	10/01-12/01
Helpers, Laborers, and Material Movers	Youngstown-Warren MSA, OH	H	9.88 FQ	18.96 AW	28.25 TQ	OHBLS	10/01-12/01
Helpers, Laborers, and Material Movers	Oklahoma	H	8.25 FQ	16.59 AW	26.59 TQ	OKBLS	10/01-12/01
Helpers, Laborers, and Material Movers	Oklahoma City MSA, OK	H	7.35 FQ	16.45 AW	26.95 TQ	OKBLS	10/01-12/01
Helpers, Laborers, and Material Movers	Tulsa MSA, OK	H	10.10 FQ	17.50 AW	27.38 TQ	OKBLS	10/01-12/01
Helpers, Laborers, and Material Movers	Oregon	H	11.02 FQ	17.63 AW	26.65 TQ	ORBLS	10/01-12/01
Helpers, Laborers, and Material Movers	Eugene-Springfield MSA, OR	H	10.02 FQ	18.74 AW	27.92 TQ	ORBLS	10/01-12/01
Helpers, Laborers, and Material Movers	Medford-Ashland MSA, OR	H	10.71 FQ	14.76 AW	23.63 TQ	ORBLS	10/01-12/01
Helpers, Laborers, and Material Movers	Portland-Vancouver PMSA, OR-WA	H	11.35 FQ	18.03 AW	26.94 TQ	ORBLS	10/01-12/01
Helpers, Laborers, and Material Movers	Salem PMSA, OR	H	10.64 FQ	18.28 AW	31.93 TQ	ORBLS	10/01-12/01
Helpers, Laborers, and Material Movers	Pennsylvania	H	10.98 FQ	18.24 AW	26.53 TQ	PABLS	10/01-12/01
Helpers, Laborers, and Material Movers	Allentown-Bethlehem-Easton MSA, PA	H	10.15 FQ	18.74 AW	28.69 TQ	PABLS	10/01-12/01
Helpers, Laborers, and Material Movers	Erie MSA, PA	H	10.62 FQ	18.04 AW	26.10 TQ	PABLS	10/01-12/01
Helpers, Laborers, and Material Movers	Harrisburg-Lebanon-Carlisle MSA, PA	H	12.23 FQ	18.55 AW	26.05 TQ	PABLS	10/01-12/01
Helpers, Laborers, and Material Movers	Johnstown MSA, PA	H	10.06 FQ	16.14 AW	21.70 TQ	PABLS	10/01-12/01
Helpers, Laborers, and Material Movers	Lancaster MSA, PA	H	13.07 FQ	19.62 AW	27.17 TQ	PABLS	10/01-12/01
Helpers, Laborers, and Material Movers	Philadelphia PMSA, PA-NJ	H	12.57 FQ	19.84 AW	28.01 TQ	PABLS	10/01-12/01
Helpers, Laborers, and Material Movers	Pittsburgh MSA, PA	H	10.61 FQ	18.34 AW	27.05 TQ	PABLS	10/01-12/01

AAW	Average annual wage	**AOH**	Average offered, high	**ASH**	Average starting, high	**H**	Hourly	**M**	Monthly	**S**	Special: hourly and annual
AE	Average entry wage	**AOL**	Average offered, low	**ASL**	Average starting, low	**HI**	Highest wage paid	**MTC**	Median total compensation	**TQ**	Third quartile wage
AEX	Average experienced wage	**APH**	Average pay, high range	**AW**	Average wage paid	**HR**	High end range	**MW**	Median wage paid	**W**	Weekly
AO	Average offered	**APL**	Average pay, low range	**FQ**	First quartile wage	**LR**	Low end range	**SQ**	Second quartile wage	**Y**	Yearly

Occupation/Type/Industry	Location	Per	Low	Mid	High	Source	Date
First-Line Supervisor/Manager							
Helpers, Laborers, and Material Movers	Reading MSA, PA	H	9.82 FQ	17.20 AW	26.68 TQ	PABLS	10/01-12/01
Helpers, Laborers, and Material Movers	Scranton-Wilkes-Barre-Hazleton MSA, PA	H	10.18 FQ	17.19 AW	25.01 TQ	PABLS	10/01-12/01
Helpers, Laborers, and Material Movers	York MSA, PA	H	10.05 FQ	16.53 AW	24.49 TQ	PABLS	10/01-12/01
Helpers, Laborers, and Material Movers	Rhode Island	H	10.31 FQ	20.28 AW	39.14 TQ	RIBLS	10/01-12/01
Helpers, Laborers, and Material Movers	Providence-Fall River-Warwick MSA, RI-MA	H	10.55 FQ	20.08 AW	37.74 TQ	RIBLS	10/01-12/01
Helpers, Laborers, and Material Movers	South Carolina	H	9.90 FQ	16.40 AW	25.06 TQ	SCBLS	10/01-12/01
Helpers, Laborers, and Material Movers	Charleston-North Charleston MSA, SC	H	9.54 FQ	14.98 AW	21.98 TQ	SCBLS	10/01-12/01
Helpers, Laborers, and Material Movers	Columbia MSA, SC	H	10.26 FQ	17.49 AW	25.87 TQ	SCBLS	10/01-12/01
Helpers, Laborers, and Material Movers	Greenville-Spartanburg-Anderson MSA, SC	H	10.89 FQ	16.65 AW	25.31 TQ	SCBLS	10/01-12/01
Helpers, Laborers, and Material Movers	Myrtle Beach MSA, SC	H	9.75 FQ	14.44 AW	20.66 TQ	SCBLS	10/01-12/01
Helpers, Laborers, and Material Movers	South Dakota	H	11.51 FQ	16.84 AW	22.13 TQ	SDBLS	10/01-12/01
Helpers, Laborers, and Material Movers	Sioux Falls MSA, SD	H	11.19 FQ	16.57 AW	22.94 TQ	SDBLS	10/01-12/01
Helpers, Laborers, and Material Movers	Tennessee	H	11.66 FQ	19.39 AW	27.21 TQ	TNBLS	10/01-12/01
Helpers, Laborers, and Material Movers	Chattanooga MSA, TN-GA	H	8.82 FQ	19.08 AW	25.96 TQ	TNBLS	10/01-12/01
Helpers, Laborers, and Material Movers	Clarksville-Hopkinsville MSA, TN-KY	H	10.67 FQ	16.71 AW	23.48 TQ	TNBLS	10/01-12/01
Helpers, Laborers, and Material Movers	Johnson City-Kingsport-Bristol MSA, TN-VA	H	10.93 FQ	16.80 AW	23.08 TQ	TNBLS	10/01-12/01
Helpers, Laborers, and Material Movers	Knoxville MSA, TN	H	11.85 FQ	19.06 AW	27.67 TQ	TNBLS	10/01-12/01
Helpers, Laborers, and Material Movers	Memphis MSA, TN-AR-MS	H	12.77 FQ	19.70 AW	27.49 TQ	TNBLS	10/01-12/01
Helpers, Laborers, and Material Movers	Nashville MSA, TN	H	12.00 FQ	19.95 AW	28.01 TQ	TNBLS	10/01-12/01
Helpers, Laborers, and Material Movers	Texas	H	9.50 FQ	17.12 AW	26.16 TQ	TXBLS	10/01-12/01
Helpers, Laborers, and Material Movers	Amarillo MSA, TX	H	8.50 FQ	15.14 AW	23.71 TQ	TXBLS	10/01-12/01
Helpers, Laborers, and Material Movers	Austin-San Marcos MSA, TX	H	8.24 FQ	16.00 AW	24.99 TQ	TXBLS	10/01-12/01
Helpers, Laborers, and Material Movers	Beaumont-Port Arthur MSA, TX	H	10.63 FQ	17.32 AW	27.42 TQ	TXBLS	10/01-12/01
Helpers, Laborers, and Material Movers	Brazoria PMSA, TX	H	9.63 FQ	17.16 AW	25.91 TQ	TXBLS	10/01-12/01
Helpers, Laborers, and Material Movers	Brownsville-Harlingen-San Benito MSA, TX	H	7.79 FQ	14.64 AW	23.50 TQ	TXBLS	10/01-12/01
Helpers, Laborers, and Material Movers	Corpus Christi MSA, TX	H	8.47 FQ	15.00 AW	22.69 TQ	TXBLS	10/01-12/01
Helpers, Laborers, and Material Movers	Dallas PMSA, TX	H	10.67 FQ	18.37 AW	26.70 TQ	TXBLS	10/01-12/01
Helpers, Laborers, and Material Movers	El Paso MSA, TX	H	9.02 FQ	15.53 AW	24.32 TQ	TXBLS	10/01-12/01
Helpers, Laborers, and Material Movers	Fort Worth-Arlington PMSA, TX	H	11.74 FQ	18.54 AW	26.32 TQ	TXBLS	10/01-12/01
Helpers, Laborers, and Material Movers	Galveston-Texas City PMSA, TX	H	9.30 FQ	14.66 AW	22.51 TQ	TXBLS	10/01-12/01
Helpers, Laborers, and Material Movers	Houston PMSA, TX	H	9.15 FQ	17.40 AW	27.41 TQ	TXBLS	10/01-12/01
Helpers, Laborers, and Material Movers	Killeen-Temple MSA, TX	H	10.05 FQ	16.99 AW	22.29 TQ	TXBLS	10/01-12/01
Helpers, Laborers, and Material Movers	Laredo MSA, TX	H	8.84 FQ	17.19 AW	28.43 TQ	TXBLS	10/01-12/01
Helpers, Laborers, and Material Movers	Longview-Marshall MSA, TX	H	9.26 FQ	15.47 AW	23.92 TQ	TXBLS	10/01-12/01
Helpers, Laborers, and Material Movers	Lubbock MSA, TX	H	10.78 FQ	16.54 AW	23.78 TQ	TXBLS	10/01-12/01
Helpers, Laborers, and Material Movers	McAllen-Edinburg-Mission MSA, TX	H	7.74 FQ	15.17 AW	23.35 TQ	TXBLS	10/01-12/01
Helpers, Laborers, and Material Movers	Odessa-Midland MSA, TX	H	8.80 FQ	17.70 AW	26.72 TQ	TXBLS	10/01-12/01
Helpers, Laborers, and Material Movers	San Antonio MSA, TX	H	9.34 FQ	16.25 AW	23.77 TQ	TXBLS	10/01-12/01
Helpers, Laborers, and Material Movers	Tyler MSA, TX	H	11.30 FQ	17.19 AW	23.33 TQ	TXBLS	10/01-12/01
Helpers, Laborers, and Material Movers	Waco MSA, TX	H	10.00 FQ	16.78 AW	24.99 TQ	TXBLS	10/01-12/01
Helpers, Laborers, and Material Movers	Utah	H	11.29 FQ	17.02 AW	25.24 TQ	UTBLS	10/01-12/01
Helpers, Laborers, and Material Movers	Provo-Orem MSA, UT	H	11.23 FQ	16.06 AW	22.00 TQ	UTBLS	10/01-12/01
Helpers, Laborers, and Material Movers	Salt Lake City-Ogden MSA, UT	H	11.41 FQ	17.00 AW	24.44 TQ	UTBLS	10/01-12/01
Helpers, Laborers, and Material Movers	Vermont	H	12.82 FQ	22.72 AW	35.56 TQ	VTBLS	10/01-12/01
Helpers, Laborers, and Material Movers	Burlington MSA, VT	H	11.67 FQ	21.23 AW	32.15 TQ	VTBLS	10/01-12/01
Helpers, Laborers, and Material Movers	Virginia	H	11.19 FQ	17.47 AW	25.27 TQ	VABLS	10/01-12/01
Helpers, Laborers, and Material Movers	Lynchburg MSA, VA	H	11.67 FQ	18.06 AW	25.87 TQ	VABLS	10/01-12/01
Helpers, Laborers, and Material Movers	Norfolk-Virginia Beach-Newport News MSA, VA-NC	H	11.43 FQ	18.50 AW	26.80 TQ	VABLS	10/01-12/01
Helpers, Laborers, and Material Movers	Richmond-Petersburg MSA, VA	H	10.92 FQ	17.54 AW	25.19 TQ	VABLS	10/01-12/01
Helpers, Laborers, and Material Movers	Roanoke MSA, VA	H	10.34 FQ	16.95 AW	25.15 TQ	VABLS	10/01-12/01
Helpers, Laborers, and Material Movers	Washington	H	12.64 FQ	19.80 AW	28.87 TQ	WABLS	10/01-12/01
Helpers, Laborers, and Material Movers	Bremerton PMSA, WA	H	12.64 FQ	18.01 AW	25.64 TQ	WABLS	10/01-12/01
Helpers, Laborers, and Material Movers	Olympia PMSA, WA	H	14.17 FQ	20.76 AW	28.62 TQ	WABLS	10/01-12/01
Helpers, Laborers, and Material Movers	Richland-Kennewick-Pasco MSA, WA	H	11.87 FQ	18.25 AW	25.40 TQ	WABLS	10/01-12/01

AAW Average annual wage **AOH** Average offered, high **ASH** Average starting, high **H** Hourly **M** Monthly **S** Special: hourly and annual
AE Average entry wage **AOL** Average offered, low **ASL** Average starting, low **HI** Highest wage paid **MTC** Median total compensation **TQ** Third quartile wage
AEX Average experienced wage **APH** Average pay, high range **AW** Average wage paid **HR** High end range **MW** Median wage paid **W** Weekly
AO Average offered **APL** Average pay, low range **FQ** First quartile wage **LR** Low end range **SQ** Second quartile wage **Y** Yearly

Occupation/Type/Industry	Location	Per	Low	Mid	High	Source	Date
First-Line Supervisor/Manager							
Helpers, Laborers, and Material Movers	Seattle-Bellevue-Everett PMSA, WA	H	12.87 FQ	19.84 AW	28.56 TQ	WABLS	10/01-12/01
Helpers, Laborers, and Material Movers	Spokane MSA, WA	H	12.75 FQ	18.46 AW	26.06 TQ	WABLS	10/01-12/01
Helpers, Laborers, and Material Movers	Tacoma PMSA, WA	H	12.67 FQ	20.52 AW	31.37 TQ	WABLS	10/01-12/01
Helpers, Laborers, and Material Movers	Yakima MSA, WA	H	10.39 FQ	17.41 AW	26.30 TQ	WABLS	10/01-12/01
Helpers, Laborers, and Material Movers	West Virginia	H	9.64 FQ	18.21 AW	30.04 TQ	WVBLS	10/01-12/01
Helpers, Laborers, and Material Movers	Charleston MSA, WV	H	12.51 FQ	21.14 AW	33.01 TQ	WVBLS	10/01-12/01
Helpers, Laborers, and Material Movers	Huntington-Ashland MSA, WV-KY-OH	H	8.84 FQ	14.89 AW	24.49 TQ	WVBLS	10/01-12/01
Helpers, Laborers, and Material Movers	Wisconsin	H	11.15 FQ	18.51 AW	26.95 TQ	WIBLS	10/01-12/01
Helpers, Laborers, and Material Movers	Appleton-Oshkosh-Neenah MSA, WI	H	12.12 FQ	17.94 AW	27.26 TQ	WIBLS	10/01-12/01
Helpers, Laborers, and Material Movers	Green Bay MSA, WI	H	10.23 FQ	20.22 AW	31.67 TQ	WIBLS	10/01-12/01
Helpers, Laborers, and Material Movers	Madison MSA, WI	H	9.36 FQ	16.66 AW	25.83 TQ	WIBLS	10/01-12/01
Helpers, Laborers, and Material Movers	Milwaukee-Waukesha PMSA, WI	H	11.71 FQ	18.23 AW	26.55 TQ	WIBLS	10/01-12/01
Helpers, Laborers, and Material Movers	Racine PMSA, WI	H	12.44 FQ	20.05 AW	27.92 TQ	WIBLS	10/01-12/01
Helpers, Laborers, and Material Movers	Wyoming	H	7.83 FQ	16.07 AW	27.00 TQ	WYBLS	10/01-12/01
Helpers, Laborers, and Material Movers	Cheyenne MSA, WY	H	11.66 FQ	17.58 AW	24.96 TQ	WYBLS	10/01-12/01
Helpers, Laborers, and Material Movers	Puerto Rico	H	5.93 FQ	10.67 AW	18.91 TQ	PRBLS	10/01-12/01
Helpers, Laborers, and Material Movers	Guam	H	9.22 FQ	14.03 AW	20.27 TQ	GUBLS	10/01-12/01
Housekeeping and Janitorial Workers	Alabama	H	7.41 FQ	11.76 AW	17.04 TQ	ALBLS	10/01-12/01
Housekeeping and Janitorial Workers	Alaska	H	9.58 FQ	17.37 AW	26.30 TQ	AKBLS	10/01-12/01
Housekeeping and Janitorial Workers	Arizona	H	7.94 FQ	13.41 AW	20.51 TQ	AZBLS	10/01-12/01
Housekeeping and Janitorial Workers	Arkansas	H	7.19 FQ	11.05 AW	16.62 TQ	ARBLS	10/01-12/01
Housekeeping and Janitorial Workers	California	H	9.09 FQ	16.38 AW	25.47 TQ	CABLS	10/01-12/01
Housekeeping and Janitorial Workers	Colorado	H	9.04 FQ	14.24 AW	21.95 TQ	COBLS	10/01-12/01
Housekeeping and Janitorial Workers	Connecticut	H	9.40 FQ	17.12 AW	26.63 TQ	CTBLS	10/01-12/01
Housekeeping and Janitorial Workers	Delaware	H	8.89 FQ	13.71 AW	19.21 TQ	DEBLS	10/01-12/01
Housekeeping and Janitorial Workers	District of Columbia	H	7.14 FQ	11.68 AW	18.81 TQ	DCBLS	10/01-12/01
Housekeeping and Janitorial Workers	Florida	H	8.11 FQ	12.74 AW	19.51 TQ	FLBLS	10/01-12/01
Housekeeping and Janitorial Workers	Georgia	H	8.29 FQ	12.55 AW	17.54 TQ	GABLS	10/01-12/01
Housekeeping and Janitorial Workers	Hawaii	H	8.33 FQ	14.81 AW	20.54 TQ	HIBLS	10/01-12/01
Housekeeping and Janitorial Workers	Idaho	H	7.50 FQ	12.54 AW	19.87 TQ	IDBLS	10/01-12/01
Housekeeping and Janitorial Workers	Illinois	H	7.75 FQ	15.54 AW	24.85 TQ	ILBLS	10/01-12/01
Housekeeping and Janitorial Workers	Indiana	H	8.83 FQ	13.75 AW	19.81 TQ	INBLS	10/01-12/01
Housekeeping and Janitorial Workers	Iowa	H	7.60 FQ	12.76 AW	18.89 TQ	IABLS	10/01-12/01
Housekeeping and Janitorial Workers	Kansas	H	7.82 FQ	12.89 AW	20.25 TQ	KSBLS	10/01-12/01
Housekeeping and Janitorial Workers	Kentucky	H	7.74 FQ	11.90 AW	16.84 TQ	KYBLS	10/01-12/01
Housekeeping and Janitorial Workers	Louisiana	H	7.03 FQ	10.88 AW	16.20 TQ	LABLS	10/01-12/01
Housekeeping and Janitorial Workers	Maine	H	8.71 FQ	12.81 AW	19.10 TQ	MEBLS	10/01-12/01
Housekeeping and Janitorial Workers	Maryland	H	7.93 FQ	14.59 AW	23.17 TQ	MDBLS	10/01-12/01
Housekeeping and Janitorial Workers	Massachusetts	H	10.95 FQ	16.43 AW	22.82 TQ	MABLS	10/01-12/01
Housekeeping and Janitorial Workers	Michigan	H	9.07 FQ	15.71 AW	22.24 TQ	MIBLS	10/01-12/01
Housekeeping and Janitorial Workers	Minnesota	H	8.71 FQ	14.12 AW	20.96 TQ	MNBLS	10/01-12/01
Housekeeping and Janitorial Workers	Mississippi	H	7.09 FQ	10.88 AW	16.42 TQ	MSBLS	10/01-12/01
Housekeeping and Janitorial Workers	Missouri	H	7.54 FQ	13.13 AW	20.40 TQ	MOBLS	10/01-12/01
Housekeeping and Janitorial Workers	Montana	H	7.33 FQ	11.24 AW	15.71 TQ	MTBLS	10/01-12/01
Housekeeping and Janitorial Workers	Nebraska	H	8.05 FQ	12.44 AW	17.36 TQ	NEBLS	10/01-12/01
Housekeeping and Janitorial Workers	Nevada	H	9.15 FQ	13.25 AW	17.48 TQ	NVBLS	10/01-12/01
Housekeeping and Janitorial Workers	New Hampshire	H	9.59 FQ	14.73 AW	21.16 TQ	NHBLS	10/01-12/01
Housekeeping and Janitorial Workers	New Jersey	H	9.99 FQ	16.66 AW	25.27 TQ	NJBLS	10/01-12/01
Housekeeping and Janitorial Workers	New Mexico	H	7.32 FQ	12.63 AW	21.39 TQ	NMBLS	10/01-12/01
Housekeeping and Janitorial Workers	New York	H	9.89 FQ	17.84 AW	26.86 TQ	NYBLS	10/01-12/01
Housekeeping and Janitorial Workers	North Carolina	H	7.86 FQ	12.44 AW	18.22 TQ	NCBLS	10/01-12/01
Housekeeping and Janitorial Workers	North Dakota	H	7.57 FQ	11.47 AW	16.66 TQ	NDBLS	10/01-12/01
Housekeeping and Janitorial Workers	Ohio	H	8.60 FQ	14.19 AW	21.37 TQ	OHBLS	10/01-12/01
Housekeeping and Janitorial Workers	Oklahoma	H	7.05 FQ	11.52 AW	17.32 TQ	OKBLS	10/01-12/01
Housekeeping and Janitorial Workers	Oregon	H	8.80 FQ	13.90 AW	20.54 TQ	ORBLS	10/01-12/01
Housekeeping and Janitorial Workers	Pennsylvania	H	9.12 FQ	14.67 AW	21.71 TQ	PABLS	10/01-12/01
Housekeeping and Janitorial Workers	Rhode Island	H	9.56 FQ	16.23 AW	24.28 TQ	RIBLS	10/01-12/01
Housekeeping and Janitorial Workers	South Carolina	H	7.90 FQ	12.03 AW	17.48 TQ	SCBLS	10/01-12/01
Housekeeping and Janitorial Workers	South Dakota	H	8.97 FQ	12.70 AW	17.09 TQ	SDBLS	10/01-12/01
Housekeeping and Janitorial Workers	Tennessee	H	7.08 FQ	12.00 AW	19.00 TQ	TNBLS	10/01-12/01
Housekeeping and Janitorial Workers	Texas	H	7.26 FQ	12.14 AW	20.01 TQ	TXBLS	10/01-12/01
Housekeeping and Janitorial Workers	Utah	H	8.50 FQ	13.44 AW	19.55 TQ	UTBLS	10/01-12/01
Housekeeping and Janitorial Workers	Vermont	H	9.92 FQ	15.56 AW	21.73 TQ	VTBLS	10/01-12/01
Housekeeping and Janitorial Workers	Virginia	H	8.38 FQ	13.43 AW	19.84 TQ	VABLS	10/01-12/01
Housekeeping and Janitorial Workers	Washington	H	9.79 FQ	15.74 AW	22.75 TQ	WABLS	10/01-12/01
Housekeeping and Janitorial Workers	West Virginia	H	6.98 FQ	11.09 AW	16.75 TQ	WVBLS	10/01-12/01
Housekeeping and Janitorial Workers	Wisconsin	H	8.15 FQ	13.63 AW	20.34 TQ	WIBLS	10/01-12/01

AAW Average annual wage; AE Average entry wage; AEX Average experienced wage; AO Average offered; AOH Average offered, high; AOL Average offered, low; APH Average pay, high range; APL Average pay, low range; ASH Average starting, high; ASL Average starting, low; AW Average wage paid; FQ First quartile wage; H Hourly; HI Highest wage paid; HR High end range; LR Low end range; M Monthly; MTC Median total compensation; MW Median wage paid; SQ Second quartile wage; S Special: hourly and annual; TQ Third quartile wage; W Weekly; Y Yearly

Occupation/Type/Industry	Location	Per	Low	Mid	High	Source	Date
First-Line Supervisor/Manager							
Housekeeping and Janitorial Workers	Wyoming	H	8.28 FQ	12.15 AW	17.25 TQ	WYBLS	10/01-12/01
Housekeeping and Janitorial Workers	Puerto Rico	H	5.94 FQ	9.00 AW	13.22 TQ	PRBLS	10/01-12/01
Housekeeping and Janitorial Workers	Virgin Islands	H	9.55 FQ	12.26 AW	15.76 TQ	VIBLS	10/01-12/01
Housekeeping and Janitorial Workers	Guam	H	7.05 FQ	11.72 AW	20.17 TQ	GUBLS	10/01-12/01
Landscaping, Lawn, Grounds	Alabama	H	9.04 FQ	14.90 AW	21.06 TQ	ALBLS	10/01-12/01
Landscaping, Lawn, Grounds	Alaska	H	13.46 FQ	21.09 AW	31.06 TQ	AKBLS	10/01-12/01
Landscaping, Lawn, Grounds	Arizona	H	8.59 FQ	14.11 AW	21.69 TQ	AZBLS	10/01-12/01
Landscaping, Lawn, Grounds	Arkansas	H	9.36 FQ	14.08 AW	22.75 TQ	ARBLS	10/01-12/01
Landscaping, Lawn, Grounds	California	H	10.15 FQ	17.72 AW	26.79 TQ	CABLS	10/01-12/01
Landscaping, Lawn, Grounds	Colorado	H	11.87 FQ	17.93 AW	24.99 TQ	COBLS	10/01-12/01
Landscaping, Lawn, Grounds	Connecticut	H	13.11 FQ	22.43 AW	34.49 TQ	CTBLS	10/01-12/01
Landscaping, Lawn, Grounds	Delaware	H	9.11 FQ	15.04 AW	21.70 TQ	DEBLS	10/01-12/01
Landscaping, Lawn, Grounds	District of Columbia	H	8.13 FQ	15.22 AW	24.55 TQ	DCBLS	10/01-12/01
Landscaping, Lawn, Grounds	Florida	H	8.97 FQ	15.34 AW	22.84 TQ	FLBLS	10/01-12/01
Landscaping, Lawn, Grounds	Georgia	H	10.57 FQ	16.45 AW	26.40 TQ	GABLS	10/01-12/01
Landscaping, Lawn, Grounds	Hawaii	H	11.20 FQ	17.36 AW	25.23 TQ	HIBLS	10/01-12/01
Landscaping, Lawn, Grounds	Idaho	H	8.99 FQ	14.95 AW	21.59 TQ	IDBLS	10/01-12/01
Landscaping, Lawn, Grounds	Illinois	H	8.83 FQ	15.43 AW	22.69 TQ	ILBLS	10/01-12/01
Landscaping, Lawn, Grounds	Indiana	H	9.86 FQ	16.14 AW	24.54 TQ	INBLS	10/01-12/01
Landscaping, Lawn, Grounds	Iowa	H	7.77 FQ	13.80 AW	20.57 TQ	IABLS	10/01-12/01
Landscaping, Lawn, Grounds	Kansas	H	10.30 FQ	15.98 AW	24.04 TQ	KSBLS	10/01-12/01
Landscaping, Lawn, Grounds	Kentucky	H	9.45 FQ	15.20 AW	21.83 TQ	KYBLS	10/01-12/01
Landscaping, Lawn, Grounds	Louisiana	H	8.99 FQ	13.71 AW	21.13 TQ	LABLS	10/01-12/01
Landscaping, Lawn, Grounds	Maine	H	9.61 FQ	14.03 AW	19.61 TQ	MEBLS	10/01-12/01
Landscaping, Lawn, Grounds	Maryland	H	10.19 FQ	15.95 AW	23.55 TQ	MDBLS	10/01-12/01
Landscaping, Lawn, Grounds	Massachusetts	H	13.73 FQ	21.05 AW	27.77 TQ	MABLS	10/01-12/01
Landscaping, Lawn, Grounds	Michigan	H	9.57 FQ	17.98 AW	27.46 TQ	MIBLS	10/01-12/01
Landscaping, Lawn, Grounds	Minnesota	H	10.53 FQ	18.88 AW	31.74 TQ	MNBLS	10/01-12/01
Landscaping, Lawn, Grounds	Mississippi	H	8.32 FQ	14.36 AW	20.37 TQ	MSBLS	10/01-12/01
Landscaping, Lawn, Grounds	Missouri	H	9.77 FQ	15.97 AW	22.61 TQ	MOBLS	10/01-12/01
Landscaping, Lawn, Grounds	Montana	H	8.14 FQ	14.30 AW	22.70 TQ	MTBLS	10/01-12/01
Landscaping, Lawn, Grounds	Nebraska	H	10.22 FQ	16.74 AW	21.35 TQ	NEBLS	10/01-12/01
Landscaping, Lawn, Grounds	Nevada	H	9.96 FQ	18.04 AW	28.03 TQ	NVBLS	10/01-12/01
Landscaping, Lawn, Grounds	New Hampshire	H	10.81 FQ	16.33 AW	24.14 TQ	NHBLS	10/01-12/01
Landscaping, Lawn, Grounds	New Jersey	H	12.13 FQ	19.94 AW	29.04 TQ	NJBLS	10/01-12/01
Landscaping, Lawn, Grounds	New Mexico	H	7.72 FQ	12.42 AW	17.50 TQ	NMBLS	10/01-12/01
Landscaping, Lawn, Grounds	New York	H	11.40 FQ	21.64 AW	34.94 TQ	NYBLS	10/01-12/01
Landscaping, Lawn, Grounds	North Carolina	H	10.05 FQ	16.24 AW	23.12 TQ	NCBLS	10/01-12/01
Landscaping, Lawn, Grounds	North Dakota	H	8.27 FQ	15.11 AW	24.85 TQ	NDBLS	10/01-12/01
Landscaping, Lawn, Grounds	Ohio	H	9.57 FQ	16.24 AW	24.09 TQ	OHBLS	10/01-12/01
Landscaping, Lawn, Grounds	Oklahoma	H	7.29 FQ	12.24 AW	17.98 TQ	OKBLS	10/01-12/01
Landscaping, Lawn, Grounds	Oregon	H	11.43 FQ	19.49 AW	28.19 TQ	ORBLS	10/01-12/01
Landscaping, Lawn, Grounds	Pennsylvania	H	9.97 FQ	16.40 AW	24.54 TQ	PABLS	10/01-12/01
Landscaping, Lawn, Grounds	Rhode Island	H	13.31 FQ	25.25 AW	60.14 TQ	RIBLS	10/01-12/01
Landscaping, Lawn, Grounds	South Carolina	H	9.04 FQ	14.33 AW	20.81 TQ	SCBLS	10/01-12/01
Landscaping, Lawn, Grounds	South Dakota	H	9.79 FQ	13.35 AW	18.16 TQ	SDBLS	10/01-12/01
Landscaping, Lawn, Grounds	Tennessee	H	9.10 FQ	13.21 AW	20.18 TQ	TNBLS	10/01-12/01
Landscaping, Lawn, Grounds	Texas	H	8.36 FQ	14.06 AW	21.72 TQ	TXBLS	10/01-12/01
Landscaping, Lawn, Grounds	Utah	H	9.87 FQ	14.90 AW	21.91 TQ	UTBLS	10/01-12/01
Landscaping, Lawn, Grounds	Vermont	H	10.65 FQ	17.71 AW	26.89 TQ	VTBLS	10/01-12/01
Landscaping, Lawn, Grounds	Virginia	H	10.28 FQ	18.10 AW	33.93 TQ	VABLS	10/01-12/01
Landscaping, Lawn, Grounds	Washington	H	12.68 FQ	21.05 AW	32.01 TQ	WABLS	10/01-12/01
Landscaping, Lawn, Grounds	West Virginia	H	6.64 FQ	11.60 AW	18.53 TQ	WVBLS	10/01-12/01
Landscaping, Lawn, Grounds	Wisconsin	H	9.09 FQ	17.00 AW	26.35 TQ	WIBLS	10/01-12/01
Landscaping, Lawn, Grounds	Wyoming	H	8.34 FQ	15.96 AW	22.68 TQ	WYBLS	10/01-12/01
Landscaping, Lawn, Grounds	Puerto Rico	H	6.05 FQ	10.18 AW	16.29 TQ	PRBLS	10/01-12/01
Landscaping, Lawn, Grounds	Virgin Islands	H	11.26 FQ	14.64 AW	20.15 TQ	VIBLS	10/01-12/01
Landscaping, Lawn, Grounds	Guam	H	6.86 FQ	11.54 AW	17.01 TQ	GUBLS	10/01-12/01
Mechanics, Installers, and Repairers	Alabama	H	12.07 FQ	20.54 AW	31.68 TQ	ALBLS	10/01-12/01
Mechanics, Installers, and Repairers	Birmingham MSA, AL	H	12.86 FQ	21.44 AW	32.68 TQ	ALBLS	10/01-12/01
Mechanics, Installers, and Repairers	Huntsville MSA, AL	H	11.55 FQ	19.22 AW	31.64 TQ	ALBLS	10/01-12/01
Mechanics, Installers, and Repairers	Mobile MSA, AL	H	11.70 FQ	19.35 AW	28.32 TQ	ALBLS	10/01-12/01
Mechanics, Installers, and Repairers	Montgomery MSA, AL	H	11.71 FQ	19.42 AW	29.59 TQ	ALBLS	10/01-12/01
Mechanics, Installers, and Repairers	Alaska	H	18.44 FQ	30.52 AW	43.00 TQ	AKBLS	10/01-12/01
Mechanics, Installers, and Repairers	Anchorage MSA, AK	H	17.80 FQ	28.52 AW	41.09 TQ	AKBLS	10/01-12/01
Mechanics, Installers, and Repairers	Arizona	H	13.20 FQ	23.12 AW	34.35 TQ	AZBLS	10/01-12/01
Mechanics, Installers, and Repairers	Phoenix-Mesa MSA, AZ	H	13.51 FQ	24.01 AW	35.64 TQ	AZBLS	10/01-12/01
Mechanics, Installers, and Repairers	Tucson MSA, AZ	H	12.78 FQ	21.09 AW	29.87 TQ	AZBLS	10/01-12/01
Mechanics, Installers, and Repairers	Arkansas	H	11.73 FQ	19.60 AW	28.78 TQ	ARBLS	10/01-12/01
Mechanics, Installers, and Repairers	Fayetteville-Springdale-Rogers MSA, AR	H	11.85 FQ	19.03 AW	27.17 TQ	ARBLS	10/01-12/01

AAW	Average annual wage	**AOH**	Average offered, high	**ASH**	Average starting, high	**H**	Hourly	**M**	Monthly	**S**	Special: hourly and annual
AE	Average entry wage	**AOL**	Average offered, low	**ASL**	Average starting, low	**HI**	Highest wage paid	**MTC**	Median total compensation	**TQ**	Third quartile wage
AEX	Average experienced wage	**APH**	Average pay, high range	**AW**	Average wage paid	**HR**	High end range	**MW**	Median wage paid	**W**	Weekly
AO	Average offered	**APL**	Average pay, low range	**FQ**	First quartile wage	**LR**	Low end range	**SQ**	Second quartile wage	**Y**	Yearly

Occupation/Type/Industry	Location	Per	Low	Mid	High	Source	Date
First-Line Supervisor/Manager							
Mechanics, Installers, and Repairers	Fort Smith MSA, AR-OK	H	11.66 FQ	18.80 AW	27.83 TQ	ARBLS	10/01-12/01
Mechanics, Installers, and Repairers	Little Rock-North Little Rock MSA, AR	H	13.91 FQ	21.82 AW	31.37 TQ	ARBLS	10/01-12/01
Mechanics, Installers, and Repairers	California	H	15.33 FQ	26.13 AW	38.16 TQ	CABLS	10/01-12/01
Mechanics, Installers, and Repairers	Bakersfield MSA, CA	H	13.80 FQ	24.32 AW	35.66 TQ	CABLS	10/01-12/01
Mechanics, Installers, and Repairers	Chico-Paradise MSA, CA	H	14.74 FQ	21.71 AW	31.50 TQ	CABLS	10/01-12/01
Mechanics, Installers, and Repairers	Fresno MSA, CA	H	13.98 FQ	24.31 AW	35.93 TQ	CABLS	10/01-12/01
Mechanics, Installers, and Repairers	Los Angeles-Long Beach PMSA, CA	H	15.20 FQ	26.19 AW	37.88 TQ	CABLS	10/01-12/01
Mechanics, Installers, and Repairers	Merced MSA, CA	H	11.43 FQ	21.57 AW	33.82 TQ	CABLS	10/01-12/01
Mechanics, Installers, and Repairers	Modesto MSA, CA	H	15.41 FQ	23.78 AW	34.11 TQ	CABLS	10/01-12/01
Mechanics, Installers, and Repairers	Oakland PMSA, CA	H	20.13 FQ	29.90 AW	41.99 TQ	CABLS	10/01-12/01
Mechanics, Installers, and Repairers	Orange County PMSA, CA	H	16.65 FQ	27.15 AW	40.82 TQ	CABLS	10/01-12/01
Mechanics, Installers, and Repairers	Redding MSA, CA	H	15.71 FQ	23.12 AW	32.95 TQ	CABLS	10/01-12/01
Mechanics, Installers, and Repairers	Riverside-San Bernardino PMSA, CA	H	14.73 FQ	22.79 AW	34.26 TQ	CABLS	10/01-12/01
Mechanics, Installers, and Repairers	Sacramento PMSA, CA	H	17.51 FQ	27.04 AW	40.51 TQ	CABLS	10/01-12/01
Mechanics, Installers, and Repairers	Salinas MSA, CA	H	14.26 FQ	25.24 AW	39.27 TQ	CABLS	10/01-12/01
Mechanics, Installers, and Repairers	San Diego MSA, CA	H	15.35 FQ	26.24 AW	35.63 TQ	CABLS	10/01-12/01
Mechanics, Installers, and Repairers	San Francisco PMSA, CA	H	21.15 FQ	29.87 AW	39.12 TQ	CABLS	10/01-12/01
Mechanics, Installers, and Repairers	San Jose PMSA, CA	H	15.52 FQ	29.53 AW	52.72 TQ	CABLS	10/01-12/01
Mechanics, Installers, and Repairers	San Luis Obispo-Atascadero-Paso Robles MSA, CA	H	13.48 FQ	23.66 AW	35.85 TQ	CABLS	10/01-12/01
Mechanics, Installers, and Repairers	Santa Barbara-Santa Maria-Lompoc MSA, CA	H	14.33 FQ	23.46 AW	33.11 TQ	CABLS	10/01-12/01
Mechanics, Installers, and Repairers	Santa Cruz-Watsonville PMSA, CA	H	15.97 FQ	23.69 AW	33.12 TQ	CABLS	10/01-12/01
Mechanics, Installers, and Repairers	Santa Rosa PMSA, CA	H	15.70 FQ	27.22 AW	40.66 TQ	CABLS	10/01-12/01
Mechanics, Installers, and Repairers	Stockton-Lodi MSA, CA	H	14.50 FQ	23.19 AW	33.40 TQ	CABLS	10/01-12/01
Mechanics, Installers, and Repairers	Vallejo-Fairfield-Napa PMSA, CA	H	16.82 FQ	26.08 AW	37.72 TQ	CABLS	10/01-12/01
Mechanics, Installers, and Repairers	Ventura PMSA, CA	H	11.92 FQ	23.67 AW	36.35 TQ	CABLS	10/01-12/01
Mechanics, Installers, and Repairers	Visalia-Tulare-Porterville MSA, CA	H	12.52 FQ	22.07 AW	31.40 TQ	CABLS	10/01-12/01
Mechanics, Installers, and Repairers	Colorado	H	15.05 FQ	24.10 AW	34.26 TQ	COBLS	10/01-12/01
Mechanics, Installers, and Repairers	Boulder-Longmont PMSA, CO	H	16.76 FQ	25.81 AW	38.37 TQ	COBLS	10/01-12/01
Mechanics, Installers, and Repairers	Colorado Springs MSA, CO	H	15.13 FQ	22.55 AW	32.50 TQ	COBLS	10/01-12/01
Mechanics, Installers, and Repairers	Denver PMSA, CO	H	16.06 FQ	25.54 AW	35.26 TQ	COBLS	10/01-12/01
Mechanics, Installers, and Repairers	Fort Collins-Loveland MSA, CO	H	8.82 FQ	19.72 AW	28.17 TQ	COBLS	10/01-12/01
Mechanics, Installers, and Repairers	Greeley PMSA, CO	H	15.05 FQ	22.47 AW	31.96 TQ	COBLS	10/01-12/01
Mechanics, Installers, and Repairers	Connecticut	H	15.59 FQ	26.98 AW	39.99 TQ	CTBLS	10/01-12/01
Mechanics, Installers, and Repairers	Bridgeport PMSA, CT	H	17.18 FQ	26.21 AW	37.65 TQ	CTBLS	10/01-12/01
Mechanics, Installers, and Repairers	Danbury PMSA, CT	H	16.71 FQ	26.85 AW	35.73 TQ	CTBLS	10/01-12/01
Mechanics, Installers, and Repairers	Hartford MSA, CT	H	15.57 FQ	27.20 AW	40.78 TQ	CTBLS	10/01-12/01
Mechanics, Installers, and Repairers	New Haven-Meriden PMSA, CT	H	12.74 FQ	25.28 AW	37.86 TQ	CTBLS	10/01-12/01
Mechanics, Installers, and Repairers	New London-Norwich MSA, CT-RI	H	17.97 FQ	28.39 AW	42.21 TQ	CTBLS	10/01-12/01
Mechanics, Installers, and Repairers	Stamford-Norwalk PMSA, CT	H	19.45 FQ	30.02 AW	43.85 TQ	CTBLS	10/01-12/01
Mechanics, Installers, and Repairers	Waterbury PMSA, CT	H	16.55 FQ	25.18 AW	34.87 TQ	CTBLS	10/01-12/01
Mechanics, Installers, and Repairers	Delaware	H	13.66 FQ	23.60 AW	34.72 TQ	DEBLS	10/01-12/01
Mechanics, Installers, and Repairers	Wilmington-Newark PMSA, DE-MD	H	14.00 FQ	24.59 AW	36.17 TQ	DEBLS	10/01-12/01
Mechanics, Installers, and Repairers	District of Columbia	H	16.54 FQ	25.01 AW	34.27 TQ	DCBLS	10/01-12/01
Mechanics, Installers, and Repairers	Washington PMSA, DC-MD-VA-WV	H	15.15 FQ	26.04 AW	40.11 TQ	DCBLS	10/01-12/01
Mechanics, Installers, and Repairers	Florida	H	13.34 FQ	22.11 AW	33.52 TQ	FLBLS	10/01-12/01
Mechanics, Installers, and Repairers	Daytona Beach MSA, FL	H	12.29 FQ	18.52 AW	26.72 TQ	FLBLS	10/01-12/01
Mechanics, Installers, and Repairers	Fort Lauderdale PMSA, FL	H	15.57 FQ	24.33 AW	36.59 TQ	FLBLS	10/01-12/01
Mechanics, Installers, and Repairers	Fort Myers-Cape Coral MSA, FL	H	12.21 FQ	21.43 AW	32.77 TQ	FLBLS	10/01-12/01
Mechanics, Installers, and Repairers	Fort Pierce-Port St. Lucie MSA, FL	H	13.19 FQ	21.37 AW	32.09 TQ	FLBLS	10/01-12/01
Mechanics, Installers, and Repairers	Fort Walton Beach MSA, FL	H	11.51 FQ	21.87 AW	34.37 TQ	FLBLS	10/01-12/01
Mechanics, Installers, and Repairers	Gainesville MSA, FL	H	12.55 FQ	21.14 AW	36.92 TQ	FLBLS	10/01-12/01
Mechanics, Installers, and Repairers	Jacksonville MSA, FL	H	13.58 FQ	21.56 AW	32.29 TQ	FLBLS	10/01-12/01
Mechanics, Installers, and Repairers	Lakeland-Winter Haven MSA, FL	H	11.83 FQ	20.97 AW	32.77 TQ	FLBLS	10/01-12/01
Mechanics, Installers, and Repairers	Melbourne-Titusville-Palm Bay MSA, FL	H	12.19 FQ	21.47 AW	31.54 TQ	FLBLS	10/01-12/01

AAW Average annual wage	AOH Average offered, high	ASH Average starting, high	H Hourly	M Monthly	S Special: hourly and annual
AE Average entry wage	AOL Average offered, low	ASL Average starting, low	HI Highest wage paid	MTC Median total compensation	TQ Third quartile wage
AEX Average experienced wage	APH Average pay, high range	AW Average wage paid	HR High end range	MW Median wage paid	W Weekly
AO Average offered	APL Average pay, low range	FQ First quartile wage	LR Low end range	SQ Second quartile wage	Y Yearly

Occupation/Type/Industry	Location	Per	Low	Mid	High	Source	Date
First-Line Supervisor/Manager							
Mechanics, Installers, and Repairers	Miami PMSA, FL	H	13.26 FQ	22.06 AW	34.19 TQ	FLBLS	10/01-12/01
Mechanics, Installers, and Repairers	Naples MSA, FL	H	12.50 FQ	21.12 AW	30.95 TQ	FLBLS	10/01-12/01
Mechanics, Installers, and Repairers	Ocala MSA, FL	H	11.76 FQ	19.43 AW	30.71 TQ	FLBLS	10/01-12/01
Mechanics, Installers, and Repairers	Orlando MSA, FL	H	14.23 FQ	22.03 AW	32.53 TQ	FLBLS	10/01-12/01
Mechanics, Installers, and Repairers	Pensacola MSA, FL	H	13.43 FQ	20.90 AW	32.34 TQ	FLBLS	10/01-12/01
Mechanics, Installers, and Repairers	Sarasota-Bradenton MSA, FL	H	12.69 FQ	21.64 AW	33.88 TQ	FLBLS	10/01-12/01
Mechanics, Installers, and Repairers	Tallahassee MSA, FL	H	13.32 FQ	25.17 AW		FLBLS	10/01-12/01
Mechanics, Installers, and Repairers	Tampa-St. Petersburg-Clearwater MSA, FL	H	13.33 FQ	21.83 AW	32.03 TQ	FLBLS	10/01-12/01
Mechanics, Installers, and Repairers	West Palm Beach-Boca Raton MSA, FL	H	15.45 FQ	24.34 AW	38.11 TQ	FLBLS	10/01-12/01
Mechanics, Installers, and Repairers	Georgia	H	14.28 FQ	22.65 AW	33.46 TQ	GABLS	10/01-12/01
Mechanics, Installers, and Repairers	Atlanta MSA, GA	H	14.82 FQ	23.53 AW	34.75 TQ	GABLS	10/01-12/01
Mechanics, Installers, and Repairers	Augusta-Aiken MSA, GA-SC	H	14.31 FQ	23.00 AW	35.52 TQ	GABLS	10/01-12/01
Mechanics, Installers, and Repairers	Columbus MSA, GA-AL	H	11.22 FQ	20.05 AW	30.91 TQ	GABLS	10/01-12/01
Mechanics, Installers, and Repairers	Macon MSA, GA	H	15.47 FQ	21.95 AW	27.56 TQ	GABLS	10/01-12/01
Mechanics, Installers, and Repairers	Savannah MSA, GA	H	13.79 FQ	21.11 AW	29.46 TQ	GABLS	10/01-12/01
Mechanics, Installers, and Repairers	Hawaii	H	12.43 FQ	23.94 AW	35.36 TQ	HIBLS	10/01-12/01
Mechanics, Installers, and Repairers	Honolulu MSA, HI	H	12.08 FQ	24.43 AW	36.39 TQ	HIBLS	10/01-12/01
Mechanics, Installers, and Repairers	Idaho	H	13.38 FQ	20.78 AW	31.29 TQ	IDBLS	10/01-12/01
Mechanics, Installers, and Repairers	Boise City MSA, ID	H	13.83 FQ	20.84 AW	30.72 TQ	IDBLS	10/01-12/01
Mechanics, Installers, and Repairers	Illinois	H	12.52 FQ	22.67 AW	34.74 TQ	ILBLS	10/01-12/01
Mechanics, Installers, and Repairers	Champaign-Urbana MSA, IL	H	12.40 FQ	20.88 AW	29.96 TQ	ILBLS	10/01-12/01
Mechanics, Installers, and Repairers	Chicago PMSA, IL	H	13.01 FQ	23.26 AW	35.79 TQ	ILBLS	10/01-12/01
Mechanics, Installers, and Repairers	Peoria-Pekin MSA, IL	H	11.78 FQ	22.20 AW	32.20 TQ	ILBLS	10/01-12/01
Mechanics, Installers, and Repairers	Rockford MSA, IL	H	7.20 FQ	21.50 AW	35.72 TQ	ILBLS	10/01-12/01
Mechanics, Installers, and Repairers	Springfield MSA, IL	H	12.41 FQ	22.68 AW	34.62 TQ	ILBLS	10/01-12/01
Mechanics, Installers, and Repairers	Indiana	H	12.45 FQ	22.52 AW	34.28 TQ	INBLS	10/01-12/01
Mechanics, Installers, and Repairers	Elkhart-Goshen MSA, IN	H	14.38 FQ	21.22 AW	29.03 TQ	INBLS	10/01-12/01
Mechanics, Installers, and Repairers	Evansville-Henderson MSA, IN-KY	H	13.73 FQ	22.67 AW	33.86 TQ	INBLS	10/01-12/01
Mechanics, Installers, and Repairers	Fort Wayne MSA, IN	H	9.94 FQ	20.72 AW	33.28 TQ	INBLS	10/01-12/01
Mechanics, Installers, and Repairers	Gary PMSA, IN	H	15.63 FQ	24.49 AW	34.45 TQ	INBLS	10/01-12/01
Mechanics, Installers, and Repairers	Indianapolis MSA, IN	H	12.16 FQ	23.64 AW	40.64 TQ	INBLS	10/01-12/01
Mechanics, Installers, and Repairers	Lafayette MSA, IN	H	12.87 FQ	22.31 AW	33.53 TQ	INBLS	10/01-12/01
Mechanics, Installers, and Repairers	South Bend MSA, IN	H	13.57 FQ	23.40 AW	33.45 TQ	INBLS	10/01-12/01
Mechanics, Installers, and Repairers	Iowa	H	11.89 FQ	20.23 AW	29.27 TQ	IABLS	10/01-12/01
Mechanics, Installers, and Repairers	Cedar Rapids MSA, IA	H	14.03 FQ	22.52 AW	33.45 TQ	IABLS	10/01-12/01
Mechanics, Installers, and Repairers	Davenport-Moline-Rock Island MSA, IA-IL	H	12.81 FQ	21.79 AW	33.27 TQ	IABLS	10/01-12/01
Mechanics, Installers, and Repairers	Des Moines MSA, IA	H	13.06 FQ	23.47 AW	33.99 TQ	IABLS	10/01-12/01
Mechanics, Installers, and Repairers	Kansas	H	13.53 FQ	22.26 AW	32.97 TQ	KSBLS	10/01-12/01
Mechanics, Installers, and Repairers	Topeka MSA, KS	H	13.93 FQ	21.31 AW	30.59 TQ	KSBLS	10/01-12/01
Mechanics, Installers, and Repairers	Wichita MSA, KS	H	14.17 FQ	23.06 AW	33.73 TQ	KSBLS	10/01-12/01
Mechanics, Installers, and Repairers	Kentucky	H	12.22 FQ	20.96 AW	32.07 TQ	KYBLS	10/01-12/01
Mechanics, Installers, and Repairers	Lexington MSA, KY	H	11.48 FQ	20.94 AW	32.60 TQ	KYBLS	10/01-12/01
Mechanics, Installers, and Repairers	Louisville MSA, KY-IN	H	13.67 FQ	22.06 AW	32.50 TQ	KYBLS	10/01-12/01
Mechanics, Installers, and Repairers	Louisiana	H	12.41 FQ	21.81 AW	33.40 TQ	LABLS	10/01-12/01
Mechanics, Installers, and Repairers	Baton Rouge MSA, LA	H	12.90 FQ	21.68 AW	34.65 TQ	LABLS	10/01-12/01
Mechanics, Installers, and Repairers	Houma MSA, LA	H	11.54 FQ	20.26 AW	28.28 TQ	LABLS	10/01-12/01
Mechanics, Installers, and Repairers	Lafayette MSA, LA	H	14.95 FQ	22.08 AW	29.23 TQ	LABLS	10/01-12/01
Mechanics, Installers, and Repairers	Lake Charles MSA, LA	H	12.00 FQ	23.27 AW	35.56 TQ	LABLS	10/01-12/01
Mechanics, Installers, and Repairers	New Orleans MSA, LA	H	14.26 FQ	23.16 AW	35.89 TQ	LABLS	10/01-12/01
Mechanics, Installers, and Repairers	Shreveport-Bossier City MSA, LA	H	9.50 FQ	18.67 AW	28.98 TQ	LABLS	10/01-12/01
Mechanics, Installers, and Repairers	Maine	H	13.71 FQ	22.09 AW	33.12 TQ	MEBLS	10/01-12/01
Mechanics, Installers, and Repairers	Portland MSA, ME	H	14.77 FQ	22.41 AW	32.47 TQ	MEBLS	10/01-12/01
Mechanics, Installers, and Repairers	Maryland	H	13.22 FQ	21.97 AW	33.02 TQ	MDBLS	10/01-12/01
Mechanics, Installers, and Repairers	Baltimore PMSA, MD	H	12.30 FQ	20.99 AW	31.24 TQ	MDBLS	10/01-12/01
Mechanics, Installers, and Repairers	Massachusetts	H	15.91 FQ	25.63 AW	37.49 TQ	MABLS	10/01-12/01
Mechanics, Installers, and Repairers	Boston PMSA, MA-NH	H	16.08 FQ	26.65 AW	39.29 TQ	MABLS	10/01-12/01
Mechanics, Installers, and Repairers	Brockton PMSA, MA	H	17.34 FQ	24.75 AW	33.18 TQ	MABLS	10/01-12/01
Mechanics, Installers, and Repairers	Lawrence PMSA, MA-NH	H	16.53 FQ	26.24 AW	38.50 TQ	MABLS	10/01-12/01
Mechanics, Installers, and Repairers	Lowell PMSA, MA-NH	H	18.13 FQ	26.10 AW	34.86 TQ	MABLS	10/01-12/01
Mechanics, Installers, and Repairers	New Bedford PMSA, MA	H	14.15 FQ	21.99 AW	32.67 TQ	MABLS	10/01-12/01
Mechanics, Installers, and Repairers	Springfield MSA, MA	H	15.68 FQ	23.91 AW	35.60 TQ	MABLS	10/01-12/01
Mechanics, Installers, and Repairers	Worcester PMSA, MA-CT	H	15.80 FQ	22.56 AW	34.74 TQ	MABLS	10/01-12/01
Mechanics, Installers, and Repairers	Michigan	H	14.35 FQ	25.24 AW	37.20 TQ	MIBLS	10/01-12/01
Mechanics, Installers, and Repairers	Ann Arbor PMSA, MI	H	14.78 FQ	25.68 AW	35.19 TQ	MIBLS	10/01-12/01
Mechanics, Installers, and Repairers	Detroit PMSA, MI	H	14.93 FQ	26.56 AW	39.48 TQ	MIBLS	10/01-12/01
Mechanics, Installers, and Repairers	Flint PMSA, MI	H	15.42 FQ	26.23 AW	37.84 TQ	MIBLS	10/01-12/01

AAW	Average annual wage	**AOH**	Average offered, high	**ASH**	Average starting, high	**H**	Hourly	**M**	Monthly	**S**	Special: hourly and annual
AE	Average entry wage	**AOL**	Average offered, low	**ASL**	Average starting, low	**HI**	Highest wage paid	**MTC**	Median total compensation	**TQ**	Third quartile wage
AEX	Average experienced wage	**APH**	Average pay, high range	**AW**	Average wage paid	**HR**	High end range	**MW**	Median wage paid	**W**	Weekly
AO	Average offered	**APL**	Average pay, low range	**FQ**	First quartile wage	**LR**	Low end range	**SQ**	Second quartile wage	**Y**	Yearly

Occupation/Type/Industry	Location	Per	Low	Mid	High	Source	Date
First-Line Supervisor/Manager							
Mechanics, Installers, and Repairers	Grand Rapids-Muskegon-Holland MSA, MI	H	14.95 FQ	25.46 AW	36.07 TQ	MIBLS	10/01-12/01
Mechanics, Installers, and Repairers	Kalamazoo-Battle Creek MSA, MI	H	15.79 FQ	25.77 AW	37.94 TQ	MIBLS	10/01-12/01
Mechanics, Installers, and Repairers	Lansing-East Lansing MSA, MI	H	13.94 FQ	24.58 AW	35.93 TQ	MIBLS	10/01-12/01
Mechanics, Installers, and Repairers	Saginaw-Bay City-Midland MSA, MI	H	12.39 FQ	24.08 AW	35.10 TQ	MIBLS	10/01-12/01
Mechanics, Installers, and Repairers	Minnesota	H	14.54 FQ	23.47 AW	33.62 TQ	MNBLS	10/01-12/01
Mechanics, Installers, and Repairers	Duluth-Superior MSA, MN-WI	H	14.46 FQ	22.80 AW	32.38 TQ	MNBLS	10/01-12/01
Mechanics, Installers, and Repairers	Minneapolis-St. Paul MSA, MN-WI	H	15.25 FQ	23.51 AW	33.29 TQ	MNBLS	10/01-12/01
Mechanics, Installers, and Repairers	St. Cloud MSA, MN	H	14.21 FQ	20.55 AW	27.36 TQ	MNBLS	10/01-12/01
Mechanics, Installers, and Repairers	Mississippi	H	11.95 FQ	19.67 AW	28.90 TQ	MSBLS	10/01-12/01
Mechanics, Installers, and Repairers	Biloxi-Gulfport-Pascagoula MSA, MS	H	13.08 FQ	21.01 AW	29.14 TQ	MSBLS	10/01-12/01
Mechanics, Installers, and Repairers	Jackson MSA, MS	H	11.94 FQ	18.84 AW	27.17 TQ	MSBLS	10/01-12/01
Mechanics, Installers, and Repairers	Missouri	H	12.01 FQ	21.50 AW	32.74 TQ	MOBLS	10/01-12/01
Mechanics, Installers, and Repairers	Kansas City MSA, MO-KS	H	14.20 FQ	23.63 AW	34.12 TQ	MOBLS	10/01-12/01
Mechanics, Installers, and Repairers	St. Louis MSA, MO-IL	H	13.30 FQ	22.79 AW	33.72 TQ	MOBLS	10/01-12/01
Mechanics, Installers, and Repairers	Springfield MSA, MO	H	10.73 FQ	19.99 AW	28.03 TQ	MOBLS	10/01-12/01
Mechanics, Installers, and Repairers	Montana	H	12.40 FQ	20.82 AW	30.86 TQ	MTBLS	10/01-12/01
Mechanics, Installers, and Repairers	Billings MSA, MT	H	14.35 FQ	21.33 AW	32.57 TQ	MTBLS	10/01-12/01
Mechanics, Installers, and Repairers	Nebraska	H	11.56 FQ	21.27 AW	32.59 TQ	NEBLS	10/01-12/01
Mechanics, Installers, and Repairers	Lincoln MSA, NE	H	12.37 FQ	20.66 AW	29.39 TQ	NEBLS	10/01-12/01
Mechanics, Installers, and Repairers	Omaha MSA, NE-IA	H	13.30 FQ	22.69 AW	33.53 TQ	NEBLS	10/01-12/01
Mechanics, Installers, and Repairers	Nevada	H	14.21 FQ	23.28 AW	33.91 TQ	NVBLS	10/01-12/01
Mechanics, Installers, and Repairers	Las Vegas MSA, NV-AZ	H	14.05 FQ	22.95 AW	33.87 TQ	NVBLS	10/01-12/01
Mechanics, Installers, and Repairers	Reno MSA, NV	H	14.29 FQ	23.12 AW	32.90 TQ	NVBLS	10/01-12/01
Mechanics, Installers, and Repairers	New Hampshire	H	14.15 FQ	22.70 AW	33.03 TQ	NHBLS	10/01-12/01
Mechanics, Installers, and Repairers	Manchester PMSA, NH	H	15.97 FQ	24.89 AW	34.13 TQ	NHBLS	10/01-12/01
Mechanics, Installers, and Repairers	Nashua PMSA, NH	H	14.40 FQ	23.14 AW	34.45 TQ	NHBLS	10/01-12/01
Mechanics, Installers, and Repairers	Portsmouth-Rochester PMSA, NH-ME	H	16.07 FQ	24.12 AW	33.69 TQ	NHBLS	10/01-12/01
Mechanics, Installers, and Repairers	New Jersey	H	17.83 FQ	27.50 AW	38.65 TQ	NJBLS	10/01-12/01
Mechanics, Installers, and Repairers	Atlantic-Cape May PMSA, NJ	H	16.49 FQ	25.09 AW	36.50 TQ	NJBLS	10/01-12/01
Mechanics, Installers, and Repairers	Bergen-Passaic PMSA, NJ	H	18.78 FQ	29.14 AW	41.79 TQ	NJBLS	10/01-12/01
Mechanics, Installers, and Repairers	Jersey City PMSA, NJ	H	17.68 FQ	25.60 AW	35.29 TQ	NJBLS	10/01-12/01
Mechanics, Installers, and Repairers	Middlesex-Somerset-Hunterdon PMSA, NJ	H	18.12 FQ	27.70 AW	39.71 TQ	NJBLS	10/01-12/01
Mechanics, Installers, and Repairers	Monmouth-Ocean PMSA, NJ	H	16.95 FQ	27.82 AW	36.04 TQ	NJBLS	10/01-12/01
Mechanics, Installers, and Repairers	Newark PMSA, NJ	H	18.68 FQ	28.33 AW	40.76 TQ	NJBLS	10/01-12/01
Mechanics, Installers, and Repairers	Trenton PMSA, NJ	H	17.19 FQ	25.82 AW	34.44 TQ	NJBLS	10/01-12/01
Mechanics, Installers, and Repairers	New Mexico	H	11.86 FQ	22.30 AW	38.27 TQ	NMBLS	10/01-12/01
Mechanics, Installers, and Repairers	Albuquerque MSA, NM	H	14.30 FQ	25.25 AW	41.55 TQ	NMBLS	10/01-12/01
Mechanics, Installers, and Repairers	Las Cruces MSA, NM	H	10.91 FQ	18.33 AW	23.10 TQ	NMBLS	10/01-12/01
Mechanics, Installers, and Repairers	New York	H	14.54 FQ	25.94 AW	39.68 TQ	NYBLS	10/01-12/01
Mechanics, Installers, and Repairers	Albany-Schenectady-Troy MSA, NY	H	12.35 FQ	22.06 AW	32.96 TQ	NYBLS	10/01-12/01
Mechanics, Installers, and Repairers	Binghamton MSA, NY	H	14.11 FQ	21.42 AW	32.96 TQ	NYBLS	10/01-12/01
Mechanics, Installers, and Repairers	Buffalo-Niagara Falls MSA, NY	H	11.73 FQ	22.81 AW	34.04 TQ	NYBLS	10/01-12/01
Mechanics, Installers, and Repairers	Dutchess County PMSA, NY	H	17.50 FQ	23.73 AW	33.41 TQ	NYBLS	10/01-12/01
Mechanics, Installers, and Repairers	Nassau-Suffolk PMSA, NY	H	16.26 FQ	28.90 AW	43.88 TQ	NYBLS	10/01-12/01
Mechanics, Installers, and Repairers	New York PMSA, NY	H	15.55 FQ	28.26 AW	41.43 TQ	NYBLS	10/01-12/01
Mechanics, Installers, and Repairers	Newburgh PMSA, NY-PA	H	14.18 FQ	24.42 AW	34.84 TQ	NYBLS	10/01-12/01
Mechanics, Installers, and Repairers	Rochester MSA, NY	H	12.24 FQ	23.05 AW	34.30 TQ	NYBLS	10/01-12/01
Mechanics, Installers, and Repairers	Syracuse MSA, NY	H	13.17 FQ	23.82 AW	36.97 TQ	NYBLS	10/01-12/01
Mechanics, Installers, and Repairers	Utica-Rome MSA, NY	H	13.61 FQ	21.20 AW	31.17 TQ	NYBLS	10/01-12/01
Mechanics, Installers, and Repairers	North Carolina	H	13.96 FQ	22.88 AW	33.98 TQ	NCBLS	10/01-12/01
Mechanics, Installers, and Repairers	Asheville MSA, NC	H	13.33 FQ	21.70 AW	30.53 TQ	NCBLS	10/01-12/01
Mechanics, Installers, and Repairers	Charlotte-Gastonia-Rock Hill MSA, NC-SC	H	14.37 FQ	23.19 AW	34.64 TQ	NCBLS	10/01-12/01
Mechanics, Installers, and Repairers	Fayetteville MSA, NC	H	12.76 FQ	20.96 AW	31.06 TQ	NCBLS	10/01-12/01
Mechanics, Installers, and Repairers	Greensboro-Winston-Salem-High Point MSA, NC	H	15.28 FQ	24.35 AW	34.62 TQ	NCBLS	10/01-12/01
Mechanics, Installers, and Repairers	Hickory-Morganton-Lenoir MSA, NC	H	13.46 FQ	21.05 AW	31.70 TQ	NCBLS	10/01-12/01
Mechanics, Installers, and Repairers	Raleigh-Durham-Chapel Hill MSA, NC	H	14.12 FQ	26.04 AW	45.08 TQ	NCBLS	10/01-12/01
Mechanics, Installers, and Repairers	Wilmington MSA, NC	H	11.97 FQ	20.39 AW	34.28 TQ	NCBLS	10/01-12/01
Mechanics, Installers, and Repairers	North Dakota	H	11.94 FQ	20.78 AW	31.72 TQ	NDBLS	10/01-12/01

AAW	Average annual wage	AOH	Average offered, high	ASH	Average starting, high	H	Hourly	M	Monthly	S	Special: hourly and annual
AE	Average entry wage	AOL	Average offered, low	ASL	Average starting, low	HI	Highest wage paid	MTC	Median total compensation	TQ	Third quartile wage
AEX	Average experienced wage	APH	Average pay, high range	AW	Average wage paid	HR	High end range	MW	Median wage paid	W	Weekly
AO	Average offered	APL	Average pay, low range	FQ	First quartile wage	LR	Low end range	SQ	Second quartile wage	Y	Yearly

Occupation/Type/Industry	Location	Per	Low	Mid	High	Source	Date
First-Line Supervisor/Manager							
Mechanics, Installers, and Repairers	Fargo-Moorhead MSA, ND-MN	H	10.69 FQ	19.55 AW	28.93 TQ	NDBLS	10/01-12/01
Mechanics, Installers, and Repairers	Ohio	H	12.80 FQ	22.60 AW	33.94 TQ	OHBLS	10/01-12/01
Mechanics, Installers, and Repairers	Akron PMSA, OH	H	14.55 FQ	22.55 AW	31.72 TQ	OHBLS	10/01-12/01
Mechanics, Installers, and Repairers	Canton-Massillon MSA, OH	H	13.76 FQ	21.72 AW	32.77 TQ	OHBLS	10/01-12/01
Mechanics, Installers, and Repairers	Cincinnati PMSA, OH-KY-IN	H	12.58 FQ	23.21 AW	34.49 TQ	OHBLS	10/01-12/01
Mechanics, Installers, and Repairers	Cleveland-Lorain-Elyria PMSA, OH	H	12.26 FQ	22.94 AW	36.03 TQ	OHBLS	10/01-12/01
Mechanics, Installers, and Repairers	Columbus MSA, OH	H	13.32 FQ	22.67 AW	33.60 TQ	OHBLS	10/01-12/01
Mechanics, Installers, and Repairers	Dayton-Springfield MSA, OH	H	13.96 FQ	23.00 AW	33.87 TQ	OHBLS	10/01-12/01
Mechanics, Installers, and Repairers	Hamilton-Middletown PMSA, OH	H	14.23 FQ	22.42 AW	31.54 TQ	OHBLS	10/01-12/01
Mechanics, Installers, and Repairers	Mansfield MSA, OH	H	13.03 FQ	21.12 AW	30.76 TQ	OHBLS	10/01-12/01
Mechanics, Installers, and Repairers	Toledo MSA, OH	H	14.91 FQ	23.47 AW	35.26 TQ	OHBLS	10/01-12/01
Mechanics, Installers, and Repairers	Youngstown-Warren MSA, OH	H	12.62 FQ	22.75 AW	34.12 TQ	OHBLS	10/01-12/01
Mechanics, Installers, and Repairers	Oklahoma	H	11.88 FQ	21.05 AW	32.05 TQ	OKBLS	10/01-12/01
Mechanics, Installers, and Repairers	Oklahoma City MSA, OK	H	11.96 FQ	21.18 AW	31.84 TQ	OKBLS	10/01-12/01
Mechanics, Installers, and Repairers	Tulsa MSA, OK	H	13.77 FQ	22.94 AW	34.20 TQ	OKBLS	10/01-12/01
Mechanics, Installers, and Repairers	Oregon	H	15.47 FQ	24.94 AW	36.49 TQ	ORBLS	10/01-12/01
Mechanics, Installers, and Repairers	Eugene-Springfield MSA, OR	H	17.48 FQ	27.20 AW	40.78 TQ	ORBLS	10/01-12/01
Mechanics, Installers, and Repairers	Medford-Ashland MSA, OR	H	14.58 FQ	23.90 AW	37.25 TQ	ORBLS	10/01-12/01
Mechanics, Installers, and Repairers	Portland-Vancouver PMSA, OR-WA	H	16.57 FQ	25.47 AW	36.02 TQ	ORBLS	10/01-12/01
Mechanics, Installers, and Repairers	Salem PMSA, OR	H	14.15 FQ	23.80 AW	35.80 TQ	ORBLS	10/01-12/01
Mechanics, Installers, and Repairers	Pennsylvania	H	14.16 FQ	23.15 AW	33.81 TQ	PABLS	10/01-12/01
Mechanics, Installers, and Repairers	Allentown-Bethlehem-Easton MSA, PA	H	14.86 FQ	23.11 AW	33.04 TQ	PABLS	10/01-12/01
Mechanics, Installers, and Repairers	Erie MSA, PA	H	14.73 FQ	22.40 AW	32.64 TQ	PABLS	10/01-12/01
Mechanics, Installers, and Repairers	Harrisburg-Lebanon-Carlisle MSA, PA	H	14.07 FQ	22.39 AW	33.26 TQ	PABLS	10/01-12/01
Mechanics, Installers, and Repairers	Johnstown MSA, PA	H	10.86 FQ	18.58 AW	27.97 TQ	PABLS	10/01-12/01
Mechanics, Installers, and Repairers	Lancaster MSA, PA	H	13.15 FQ	21.71 AW	32.41 TQ	PABLS	10/01-12/01
Mechanics, Installers, and Repairers	Philadelphia PMSA, PA-NJ	H	16.66 FQ	25.00 AW	34.50 TQ	PABLS	10/01-12/01
Mechanics, Installers, and Repairers	Pittsburgh MSA, PA	H	14.13 FQ	23.01 AW	33.71 TQ	PABLS	10/01-12/01
Mechanics, Installers, and Repairers	Reading MSA, PA	H	16.55 FQ	23.75 AW	34.12 TQ	PABLS	10/01-12/01
Mechanics, Installers, and Repairers	Scranton-Wilkes-Barre-Hazleton MSA, PA	H	12.46 FQ	23.17 AW	35.17 TQ	PABLS	10/01-12/01
Mechanics, Installers, and Repairers	York MSA, PA	H	14.19 FQ	23.06 AW	34.49 TQ	PABLS	10/01-12/01
Mechanics, Installers, and Repairers	Rhode Island	H	14.35 FQ	23.93 AW	36.23 TQ	RIBLS	10/01-12/01
Mechanics, Installers, and Repairers	Providence-Fall River-Warwick MSA, RI-MA	H	14.30 FQ	23.97 AW	35.88 TQ	RIBLS	10/01-12/01
Mechanics, Installers, and Repairers	South Carolina	H	12.60 FQ	21.63 AW	33.48 TQ	SCBLS	10/01-12/01
Mechanics, Installers, and Repairers	Charleston-North Charleston MSA, SC	H	14.19 FQ	22.37 AW	33.40 TQ	SCBLS	10/01-12/01
Mechanics, Installers, and Repairers	Columbia MSA, SC	H	13.85 FQ	22.34 AW	33.80 TQ	SCBLS	10/01-12/01
Mechanics, Installers, and Repairers	Greenville-Spartanburg-Anderson MSA, SC	H	11.80 FQ	20.29 AW	31.51 TQ	SCBLS	10/01-12/01
Mechanics, Installers, and Repairers	Myrtle Beach MSA, SC	H	12.22 FQ	20.00 AW	29.81 TQ	SCBLS	10/01-12/01
Mechanics, Installers, and Repairers	South Dakota	H	13.93 FQ	21.26 AW	28.75 TQ	SDBLS	10/01-12/01
Mechanics, Installers, and Repairers	Sioux Falls MSA, SD	H	15.20 FQ	21.72 AW	28.28 TQ	SDBLS	10/01-12/01
Mechanics, Installers, and Repairers	Tennessee	H	12.03 FQ	20.24 AW	30.42 TQ	TNBLS	10/01-12/01
Mechanics, Installers, and Repairers	Chattanooga MSA, TN-GA	H	12.18 FQ	20.40 AW	28.55 TQ	TNBLS	10/01-12/01
Mechanics, Installers, and Repairers	Clarksville-Hopkinsville MSA, TN-KY	H	13.21 FQ	20.99 AW	31.11 TQ	TNBLS	10/01-12/01
Mechanics, Installers, and Repairers	Johnson City-Kingsport-Bristol MSA, TN-VA	H	11.12 FQ	19.08 AW	30.28 TQ	TNBLS	10/01-12/01
Mechanics, Installers, and Repairers	Knoxville MSA, TN	H	12.30 FQ	20.00 AW	29.14 TQ	TNBLS	10/01-12/01
Mechanics, Installers, and Repairers	Memphis MSA, TN-AR-MS	H	12.23 FQ	19.87 AW	28.75 TQ	TNBLS	10/01-12/01
Mechanics, Installers, and Repairers	Nashville MSA, TN	H	12.70 FQ	20.57 AW	30.97 TQ	TNBLS	10/01-12/01
Mechanics, Installers, and Repairers	Texas	H	12.54 FQ	21.71 AW	33.46 TQ	TXBLS	10/01-12/01
Mechanics, Installers, and Repairers	Amarillo MSA, TX	H	11.54 FQ	20.67 AW	34.22 TQ	TXBLS	10/01-12/01
Mechanics, Installers, and Repairers	Austin-San Marcos MSA, TX	H	11.63 FQ	22.80 AW	34.43 TQ	TXBLS	10/01-12/01
Mechanics, Installers, and Repairers	Beaumont-Port Arthur MSA, TX	H	13.27 FQ	21.68 AW	35.09 TQ	TXBLS	10/01-12/01
Mechanics, Installers, and Repairers	Brazoria PMSA, TX	H	13.91 FQ	21.89 AW	34.07 TQ	TXBLS	10/01-12/01
Mechanics, Installers, and Repairers	Brownsville-Harlingen-San Benito MSA, TX	H	10.57 FQ	18.41 AW	27.44 TQ	TXBLS	10/01-12/01
Mechanics, Installers, and Repairers	Corpus Christi MSA, TX	H	11.58 FQ	20.83 AW	32.25 TQ	TXBLS	10/01-12/01
Mechanics, Installers, and Repairers	Dallas PMSA, TX	H	13.66 FQ	23.30 AW	35.39 TQ	TXBLS	10/01-12/01
Mechanics, Installers, and Repairers	El Paso MSA, TX	H	10.86 FQ	18.44 AW	28.95 TQ	TXBLS	10/01-12/01

AAW Average annual wage **AE** Average entry wage **AEX** Average experienced wage **AO** Average offered **AOH** Average offered, high **AOL** Average offered, low **APH** Average pay, high range **APL** Average pay, low range **ASH** Average starting, high **ASL** Average starting, low **AW** Average wage paid **FQ** First quartile wage **H** Hourly **HI** Highest wage paid **HR** High end range **LR** Low end range **M** Monthly **MTC** Median total compensation **MW** Median wage paid **SQ** Second quartile wage **S** Special: hourly and annual **TQ** Third quartile wage **W** Weekly **Y** Yearly

Occupation/Type/Industry	Location	Per	Low	Mid	High	Source	Date
First-Line Supervisor/Manager							
Mechanics, Installers, and Repairers	Fort Worth-Arlington PMSA, TX	H	13.99 FQ	22.07 AW	31.78 TQ	TXBLS	10/01-12/01
Mechanics, Installers, and Repairers	Galveston-Texas City PMSA, TX	H	12.64 FQ	22.45 AW	33.08 TQ	TXBLS	10/01-12/01
Mechanics, Installers, and Repairers	Houston PMSA, TX	H	12.99 FQ	22.25 AW	34.77 TQ	TXBLS	10/01-12/01
Mechanics, Installers, and Repairers	Killeen-Temple MSA, TX	H	11.44 FQ	19.87 AW	27.25 TQ	TXBLS	10/01-12/01
Mechanics, Installers, and Repairers	Laredo MSA, TX	H	10.90 FQ	17.55 AW	27.05 TQ	TXBLS	10/01-12/01
Mechanics, Installers, and Repairers	Longview-Marshall MSA, TX	H	12.72 FQ	20.13 AW	31.24 TQ	TXBLS	10/01-12/01
Mechanics, Installers, and Repairers	Lubbock MSA, TX	H	11.20 FQ	19.67 AW	30.31 TQ	TXBLS	10/01-12/01
Mechanics, Installers, and Repairers	McAllen-Edinburg-Mission MSA, TX	H	9.85 FQ	17.81 AW	27.04 TQ	TXBLS	10/01-12/01
Mechanics, Installers, and Repairers	Odessa-Midland MSA, TX	H	12.48 FQ	21.49 AW	33.81 TQ	TXBLS	10/01-12/01
Mechanics, Installers, and Repairers	San Antonio MSA, TX	H	13.56 FQ	21.24 AW	31.68 TQ	TXBLS	10/01-12/01
Mechanics, Installers, and Repairers	Tyler MSA, TX	H	11.87 FQ	21.86 AW	33.30 TQ	TXBLS	10/01-12/01
Mechanics, Installers, and Repairers	Waco MSA, TX	H	12.20 FQ	20.54 AW	31.46 TQ	TXBLS	10/01-12/01
Mechanics, Installers, and Repairers	Utah	H	11.14 FQ	20.93 AW	31.70 TQ	UTBLS	10/01-12/01
Mechanics, Installers, and Repairers	Provo-Orem MSA, UT	H	5.87 FQ	16.15 AW	28.32 TQ	UTBLS	10/01-12/01
Mechanics, Installers, and Repairers	Salt Lake City-Ogden MSA, UT	H	12.74 FQ	21.91 AW	32.06 TQ	UTBLS	10/01-12/01
Mechanics, Installers, and Repairers	Vermont	H	14.97 FQ	22.93 AW	32.91 TQ	VTBLS	10/01-12/01
Mechanics, Installers, and Repairers	Burlington MSA, VT	H	16.01 FQ	23.70 AW	33.42 TQ	VTBLS	10/01-12/01
Mechanics, Installers, and Repairers	Virginia	H	14.32 FQ	23.94 AW	36.56 TQ	VABLS	10/01-12/01
Mechanics, Installers, and Repairers	Lynchburg MSA, VA	H	14.24 FQ	22.11 AW	34.17 TQ	VABLS	10/01-12/01
Mechanics, Installers, and Repairers	Norfolk-Virginia Beach-Newport News MSA, VA-NC	H	14.31 FQ	21.97 AW	31.24 TQ	VABLS	10/01-12/01
Mechanics, Installers, and Repairers	Richmond-Petersburg MSA, VA	H	14.66 FQ	23.48 AW	35.65 TQ	VABLS	10/01-12/01
Mechanics, Installers, and Repairers	Roanoke MSA, VA	H	13.47 FQ	21.03 AW	28.45 TQ	VABLS	10/01-12/01
Mechanics, Installers, and Repairers	Washington	H	15.96 FQ	25.43 AW	36.10 TQ	WABLS	10/01-12/01
Mechanics, Installers, and Repairers	Bremerton PMSA, WA	H	21.32 FQ	27.42 AW	33.69 TQ	WABLS	10/01-12/01
Mechanics, Installers, and Repairers	Olympia PMSA, WA	H	16.41 FQ	25.28 AW	36.45 TQ	WABLS	10/01-12/01
Mechanics, Installers, and Repairers	Richland-Kennewick-Pasco MSA, WA	H	16.43 FQ	25.08 AW	34.00 TQ	WABLS	10/01-12/01
Mechanics, Installers, and Repairers	Seattle-Bellevue-Everett PMSA, WA	H	15.58 FQ	25.57 AW	36.97 TQ	WABLS	10/01-12/01
Mechanics, Installers, and Repairers	Spokane MSA, WA	H	15.58 FQ	23.20 AW	32.37 TQ	WABLS	10/01-12/01
Mechanics, Installers, and Repairers	Tacoma PMSA, WA	H	17.19 FQ	25.92 AW	35.09 TQ	WABLS	10/01-12/01
Mechanics, Installers, and Repairers	Yakima MSA, WA	H	14.33 FQ	21.68 AW	30.42 TQ	WABLS	10/01-12/01
Mechanics, Installers, and Repairers	West Virginia	H	11.42 FQ	21.88 AW	34.57 TQ	WVBLS	10/01-12/01
Mechanics, Installers, and Repairers	Charleston MSA, WV	H	12.63 FQ	23.07 AW	33.88 TQ	WVBLS	10/01-12/01
Mechanics, Installers, and Repairers	Huntington-Ashland MSA, WV-KY-OH	H	11.65 FQ	20.47 AW	31.82 TQ	WVBLS	10/01-12/01
Mechanics, Installers, and Repairers	Wisconsin	H	14.74 FQ	24.75 AW	35.54 TQ	WIBLS	10/01-12/01
Mechanics, Installers, and Repairers	Appleton-Oshkosh-Neenah MSA, WI	H	14.83 FQ	25.48 AW	35.57 TQ	WIBLS	10/01-12/01
Mechanics, Installers, and Repairers	Green Bay MSA, WI	H	15.21 FQ	23.81 AW	35.35 TQ	WIBLS	10/01-12/01
Mechanics, Installers, and Repairers	Madison MSA, WI	H	14.88 FQ	24.23 AW	33.31 TQ	WIBLS	10/01-12/01
Mechanics, Installers, and Repairers	Milwaukee-Waukesha PMSA, WI	H	16.00 FQ	27.56 AW	40.16 TQ	WIBLS	10/01-12/01
Mechanics, Installers, and Repairers	Racine PMSA, WI	H	17.06 FQ	24.39 AW	34.29 TQ	WIBLS	10/01-12/01
Mechanics, Installers, and Repairers	Wyoming	H	11.90 FQ	22.92 AW	34.29 TQ	WYBLS	10/01-12/01
Mechanics, Installers, and Repairers	Cheyenne MSA, WY	H	10.92 FQ	20.43 AW	29.21 TQ	WYBLS	10/01-12/01
Mechanics, Installers, and Repairers	Puerto Rico	H	8.16 FQ	16.11 AW	26.60 TQ	PRBLS	10/01-12/01
Mechanics, Installers, and Repairers	Virgin Islands	H	12.72 FQ	18.37 AW	25.82 TQ	VIBLS	10/01-12/01
Mechanics, Installers, and Repairers	Guam	H	10.31 FQ	18.56 AW	27.75 TQ	GUBLS	10/01-12/01
Non-Retail Sales Workers	Alabama	Y	23080 FQ	51790 AW	88790 TQ	ALBLS	10/01-12/01
Non-Retail Sales Workers	Birmingham MSA, AL	Y	24810 FQ	57270 AW	94490 TQ	ALBLS	10/01-12/01
Non-Retail Sales Workers	Huntsville MSA, AL	Y	19870 FQ	45780 AW	98530 TQ	ALBLS	10/01-12/01
Non-Retail Sales Workers	Mobile MSA, AL	Y	20230 FQ	43640 AW	67470 TQ	ALBLS	10/01-12/01
Non-Retail Sales Workers	Montgomery MSA, AL	Y	28220 FQ	55540 AW	94980 TQ	ALBLS	10/01-12/01
Non-Retail Sales Workers	Alaska	Y	18440 FQ	46670 AW	80700 TQ	AKBLS	10/01-12/01
Non-Retail Sales Workers	Anchorage MSA, AK	Y	20870 FQ	50930 AW	84150 TQ	AKBLS	10/01-12/01
Non-Retail Sales Workers	Arizona	Y	21850 FQ	48230 AW	83730 TQ	AZBLS	10/01-12/01
Non-Retail Sales Workers	Phoenix-Mesa MSA, AZ	Y	22240 FQ	48890 AW	84870 TQ	AZBLS	10/01-12/01
Non-Retail Sales Workers	Tucson MSA, AZ	Y	20300 FQ	45190 AW	80940 TQ	AZBLS	10/01-12/01
Non-Retail Sales Workers	Arkansas	Y	15390 FQ	41150 AW	73950 TQ	ARBLS	10/01-12/01
Non-Retail Sales Workers	Fayetteville-Springdale-Rogers MSA, AR	Y	13050 FQ	34160 AW	69710 TQ	ARBLS	10/01-12/01
Non-Retail Sales Workers	Fort Smith MSA, AR-OK	Y	23280 FQ	45220 AW	78630 TQ	ARBLS	10/01-12/01

AAW Average annual wage **AE** Average entry wage **AEX** Average experienced wage **AO** Average offered **AOH** Average offered, high **AOL** Average offered, low **APH** Average pay, high range **APL** Average pay, low range **ASH** Average starting, high **ASL** Average starting, low **AW** Average wage paid **FQ** First quartile wage **H** Hourly **HI** Highest wage paid **HR** High end range **LR** Low end range **M** Monthly **MTC** Median total compensation **MW** Median wage paid **SQ** Second quartile wage **S** Special: hourly and annual **TQ** Third quartile wage **W** Weekly **Y** Yearly

Occupation/Type/Industry	Location	Per	Low	Mid	High	Source	Date
First-Line Supervisor/Manager							
Non-Retail Sales Workers	Little Rock-North Little Rock MSA, AR	Y	15250 FQ	41090 AW	72780 TQ	ARBLS	10/01-12/01
Non-Retail Sales Workers	California	Y	29520 FQ	62920 AW	113090 TQ	CABLS	10/01-12/01
Non-Retail Sales Workers	Bakersfield MSA, CA	Y	36560 FQ	60220 AW	100280 TQ	CABLS	10/01-12/01
Non-Retail Sales Workers	Chico-Paradise MSA, CA	Y	24470 FQ	46580 AW	73170 TQ	CABLS	10/01-12/01
Non-Retail Sales Workers	Fresno MSA, CA	Y	33060 FQ	62080 AW	106020 TQ	CABLS	10/01-12/01
Non-Retail Sales Workers	Los Angeles-Long Beach PMSA, CA	Y	28680 FQ	60200 AW	109330 TQ	CABLS	10/01-12/01
Non-Retail Sales Workers	Merced MSA, CA	Y	24000 FQ	38850 AW	60040 TQ	CABLS	10/01-12/01
Non-Retail Sales Workers	Modesto MSA, CA	Y	32070 FQ	53980 AW	85760 TQ	CABLS	10/01-12/01
Non-Retail Sales Workers	Oakland PMSA, CA	Y	36220 FQ	74240 AW	128550 TQ	CABLS	10/01-12/01
Non-Retail Sales Workers	Orange County PMSA, CA	Y	30930 FQ	71390 AW	130640 TQ	CABLS	10/01-12/01
Non-Retail Sales Workers	Redding MSA, CA	Y	28580 FQ	40590 AW	62900 TQ	CABLS	10/01-12/01
Non-Retail Sales Workers	Riverside-San Bernardino PMSA, CA	Y	29130 FQ	52030 AW	95750 TQ	CABLS	10/01-12/01
Non-Retail Sales Workers	Sacramento PMSA, CA	Y	27280 FQ	51910 AW	89550 TQ	CABLS	10/01-12/01
Non-Retail Sales Workers	Salinas MSA, CA	Y	32470 FQ	62090 AW	106260 TQ	CABLS	10/01-12/01
Non-Retail Sales Workers	San Diego MSA, CA	Y	28140 FQ	57070 AW	106330 TQ	CABLS	10/01-12/01
Non-Retail Sales Workers	San Francisco PMSA, CA	Y	32730 FQ	68030 AW	117690 TQ	CABLS	10/01-12/01
Non-Retail Sales Workers	San Jose PMSA, CA	Y	36920 FQ	73070 AW	120210 TQ	CABLS	10/01-12/01
Non-Retail Sales Workers	San Luis Obispo-Atascadero-Paso Robles MSA, CA	Y	25560 FQ	53810 AW	91770 TQ	CABLS	10/01-12/01
Non-Retail Sales Workers	Santa Barbara-Santa Maria-Lompoc MSA, CA	Y	32310 FQ	67300 AW		CABLS	10/01-12/01
Non-Retail Sales Workers	Santa Cruz-Watsonville PMSA, CA	Y	31410 FQ	57150 AW	87720 TQ	CABLS	10/01-12/01
Non-Retail Sales Workers	Santa Rosa PMSA, CA	Y	28680 FQ	56130 AW	92760 TQ	CABLS	10/01-12/01
Non-Retail Sales Workers	Stockton-Lodi MSA, CA	Y	35400 FQ	61340 AW	94210 TQ	CABLS	10/01-12/01
Non-Retail Sales Workers	Vallejo-Fairfield-Napa PMSA, CA	Y	28520 FQ	53380 AW	85240 TQ	CABLS	10/01-12/01
Non-Retail Sales Workers	Ventura PMSA, CA	Y	27580 FQ	57410 AW	109500 TQ	CABLS	10/01-12/01
Non-Retail Sales Workers	Visalia-Tulare-Porterville MSA, CA	Y	29460 FQ	54140 AW	93100 TQ	CABLS	10/01-12/01
Non-Retail Sales Workers	Colorado	Y	28640 FQ	57870 AW	97600 TQ	COBLS	10/01-12/01
Non-Retail Sales Workers	Boulder-Longmont PMSA, CO	Y	29280 FQ	58370 AW	96410 TQ	COBLS	10/01-12/01
Non-Retail Sales Workers	Colorado Springs MSA, CO	Y	25160 FQ	52350 AW	98980 TQ	COBLS	10/01-12/01
Non-Retail Sales Workers	Denver PMSA, CO	Y	31850 FQ	60500 AW	97870 TQ	COBLS	10/01-12/01
Non-Retail Sales Workers	Fort Collins-Loveland MSA, CO	Y	25990 FQ	56710 AW	117120 TQ	COBLS	10/01-12/01
Non-Retail Sales Workers	Greeley PMSA, CO	Y	26860 FQ	55730 AW	140750 TQ	COBLS	10/01-12/01
Non-Retail Sales Workers	Connecticut	Y	31450 FQ	67000 AW	117750 TQ	CTBLS	10/01-12/01
Non-Retail Sales Workers	Bridgeport PMSA, CT	Y	36170 FQ	69480 AW	122650 TQ	CTBLS	10/01-12/01
Non-Retail Sales Workers	Danbury PMSA, CT	Y	30560 FQ	58460 AW	91970 TQ	CTBLS	10/01-12/01
Non-Retail Sales Workers	Hartford MSA, CT	Y	29270 FQ	61930 AW	101320 TQ	CTBLS	10/01-12/01
Non-Retail Sales Workers	New Haven-Meriden PMSA, CT	Y	34470 FQ	76520 AW		CTBLS	10/01-12/01
Non-Retail Sales Workers	New London-Norwich MSA, CT-RI	Y	29840 FQ	57380 AW	101270 TQ	CTBLS	10/01-12/01
Non-Retail Sales Workers	Stamford-Norwalk PMSA, CT	Y	38460 FQ	78710 AW		CTBLS	10/01-12/01
Non-Retail Sales Workers	Waterbury PMSA, CT	Y	36920 FQ	67860 AW	144620 TQ	CTBLS	10/01-12/01
Non-Retail Sales Workers	Delaware	Y	27760 FQ	55610 AW	90430 TQ	DEBLS	10/01-12/01
Non-Retail Sales Workers	Wilmington-Newark PMSA, DE-MD	Y	26320 FQ	56220 AW	93240 TQ	DEBLS	10/01-12/01
Non-Retail Sales Workers	District of Columbia	Y	23140 FQ	46700 AW	87090 TQ	DCBLS	10/01-12/01
Non-Retail Sales Workers	Washington PMSA, DC-MD-VA-WV	Y	23140 FQ	57170 AW	115050 TQ	DCBLS	10/01-12/01
Non-Retail Sales Workers	Florida	Y	24540 FQ	53460 AW	98510 TQ	FLBLS	10/01-12/01
Non-Retail Sales Workers	Daytona Beach MSA, FL	Y	22080 FQ	50180 AW	103490 TQ	FLBLS	10/01-12/01
Non-Retail Sales Workers	Fort Lauderdale PMSA, FL	Y	26770 FQ	57440 AW	101520 TQ	FLBLS	10/01-12/01
Non-Retail Sales Workers	Fort Myers-Cape Coral MSA, FL	Y	22330 FQ	48070 AW	88480 TQ	FLBLS	10/01-12/01
Non-Retail Sales Workers	Fort Pierce-Port St. Lucie MSA, FL	Y	24160 FQ	49260 AW	80380 TQ	FLBLS	10/01-12/01
Non-Retail Sales Workers	Fort Walton Beach MSA, FL	Y	16260 FQ	41240 AW	79030 TQ	FLBLS	10/01-12/01
Non-Retail Sales Workers	Gainesville MSA, FL	Y	19050 FQ	43740 AW	88940 TQ	FLBLS	10/01-12/01
Non-Retail Sales Workers	Jacksonville MSA, FL	Y	29650 FQ	60250 AW	142250 TQ	FLBLS	10/01-12/01
Non-Retail Sales Workers	Lakeland-Winter Haven MSA, FL	Y	24650 FQ	44460 AW	72060 TQ	FLBLS	10/01-12/01
Non-Retail Sales Workers	Melbourne-Titusville-Palm Bay MSA, FL	Y	24300 FQ	52070 AW	101340 TQ	FLBLS	10/01-12/01
Non-Retail Sales Workers	Miami PMSA, FL	Y	27480 FQ	54430 AW	99840 TQ	FLBLS	10/01-12/01

AAW	Average annual wage	AOH	Average offered, high	ASH	Average starting, high	H	Hourly	M	Monthly	S	Special: hourly and annual
AE	Average entry wage	AOL	Average offered, low	ASL	Average starting, low	HI	Highest wage paid	MTC	Median total compensation	TQ	Third quartile wage
AEX	Average experienced wage	APH	Average pay, high range	AW	Average wage paid	HR	High end range	MW	Median wage paid	W	Weekly
AO	Average offered	APL	Average pay, low range	FQ	First quartile wage	LR	Low end range	SQ	Second quartile wage	Y	Yearly

Occupation/Type/Industry	Location	Per	Low	Mid	High	Source	Date
First-Line Supervisor/Manager							
Non-Retail Sales Workers	Naples MSA, FL	Y	21370 FQ	62380 AW		FLBLS	10/01-12/01
Non-Retail Sales Workers	Ocala MSA, FL	Y	20900 FQ	46900 AW	76030 TQ	FLBLS	10/01-12/01
Non-Retail Sales Workers	Orlando MSA, FL	Y	25130 FQ	52660 AW	90600 TQ	FLBLS	10/01-12/01
Non-Retail Sales Workers	Pensacola MSA, FL	Y	16610 FQ	41660 AW	85140 TQ	FLBLS	10/01-12/01
Non-Retail Sales Workers	Sarasota-Bradenton MSA, FL	Y	20160 FQ	49150 AW	90390 TQ	FLBLS	10/01-12/01
Non-Retail Sales Workers	Tallahassee MSA, FL	Y	21660 FQ	47550 AW	96270 TQ	FLBLS	10/01-12/01
Non-Retail Sales Workers	Tampa-St. Petersburg-Clearwater MSA, FL	Y	24720 FQ	54760 AW	100910 TQ	FLBLS	10/01-12/01
Non-Retail Sales Workers	West Palm Beach-Boca Raton MSA, FL	Y	25840 FQ	53150 AW	100740 TQ	FLBLS	10/01-12/01
Non-Retail Sales Workers	Georgia	Y	23210 FQ	52950 AW	92430 TQ	GABLS	10/01-12/01
Non-Retail Sales Workers	Atlanta MSA, GA	Y	23080 FQ	51640 AW	89430 TQ	GABLS	10/01-12/01
Non-Retail Sales Workers	Augusta-Aiken MSA, GA-SC	Y	20670 FQ	41100 AW	85170 TQ	GABLS	10/01-12/01
Non-Retail Sales Workers	Columbus MSA, GA-AL	Y	22150 FQ	49490 AW	87040 TQ	GABLS	10/01-12/01
Non-Retail Sales Workers	Macon MSA, GA	Y	23610 FQ	39950 AW	62200 TQ	GABLS	10/01-12/01
Non-Retail Sales Workers	Savannah MSA, GA	Y	24070 FQ	50120 AW	97780 TQ	GABLS	10/01-12/01
Non-Retail Sales Workers	Hawaii	Y	23510 FQ	44740 AW	70340 TQ	HIBLS	10/01-12/01
Non-Retail Sales Workers	Honolulu MSA, HI	Y	25410 FQ	47550 AW	74300 TQ	HIBLS	10/01-12/01
Non-Retail Sales Workers	Idaho	Y	24380 FQ	44120 AW	69770 TQ	IDBLS	10/01-12/01
Non-Retail Sales Workers	Boise City MSA, ID	Y	25680 FQ	49050 AW	77090 TQ	IDBLS	10/01-12/01
Non-Retail Sales Workers	Illinois	Y	22720 FQ	52440 AW	90390 TQ	ILBLS	10/01-12/01
Non-Retail Sales Workers	Champaign-Urbana MSA, IL	Y	23110 FQ	45470 AW	79840 TQ	ILBLS	10/01-12/01
Non-Retail Sales Workers	Chicago PMSA, IL	Y	26810 FQ	55340 AW	92740 TQ	ILBLS	10/01-12/01
Non-Retail Sales Workers	Peoria-Pekin MSA, IL	Y	15470 FQ	31200 AW	61170 TQ	ILBLS	10/01-12/01
Non-Retail Sales Workers	Rockford MSA, IL	Y	19380 FQ	44360 AW	69520 TQ	ILBLS	10/01-12/01
Non-Retail Sales Workers	Springfield MSA, IL	Y	20180 FQ	39610 AW	71890 TQ	ILBLS	10/01-12/01
Non-Retail Sales Workers	Indiana	Y	25320 FQ	58860 AW	111180 TQ	INBLS	10/01-12/01
Non-Retail Sales Workers	Elkhart-Goshen MSA, IN	Y	31150 FQ	64890 AW	112660 TQ	INBLS	10/01-12/01
Non-Retail Sales Workers	Evansville-Henderson MSA, IN-KY	Y	26590 FQ	57890 AW	105180 TQ	INBLS	10/01-12/01
Non-Retail Sales Workers	Fort Wayne MSA, IN	Y	31030 FQ	60640 AW	103490 TQ	INBLS	10/01-12/01
Non-Retail Sales Workers	Gary PMSA, IN	Y	21180 FQ	49090 AW	85340 TQ	INBLS	10/01-12/01
Non-Retail Sales Workers	Indianapolis MSA, IN	Y	25160 FQ	59330 AW	116880 TQ	INBLS	10/01-12/01
Non-Retail Sales Workers	Lafayette MSA, IN	Y	36350 FQ	65900 AW	113220 TQ	INBLS	10/01-12/01
Non-Retail Sales Workers	South Bend MSA, IN	Y	27520 FQ	56760 AW	101710 TQ	INBLS	10/01-12/01
Non-Retail Sales Workers	Iowa	Y	12820 FQ	40040 AW	79540 TQ	IABLS	10/01-12/01
Non-Retail Sales Workers	Cedar Rapids MSA, IA	Y	29300 FQ	56290 AW	105710 TQ	IABLS	10/01-12/01
Non-Retail Sales Workers	Davenport-Moline-Rock Island MSA, IA-IL	Y	23590 FQ	44870 AW	69320 TQ	IABLS	10/01-12/01
Non-Retail Sales Workers	Des Moines MSA, IA	Y	27610 FQ	55400 AW	88820 TQ	IABLS	10/01-12/01
Non-Retail Sales Workers	Kansas	Y	23650 FQ	54030 AW	89250 TQ	KSBLS	10/01-12/01
Non-Retail Sales Workers	Topeka MSA, KS	Y	20650 FQ	46260 AW	85560 TQ	KSBLS	10/01-12/01
Non-Retail Sales Workers	Wichita MSA, KS	Y	24520 FQ	52790 AW	92470 TQ	KSBLS	10/01-12/01
Non-Retail Sales Workers	Kentucky	Y	23500 FQ	49440 AW	90830 TQ	KYBLS	10/01-12/01
Non-Retail Sales Workers	Lexington MSA, KY	Y	23770 FQ	55450 AW	91790 TQ	KYBLS	10/01-12/01
Non-Retail Sales Workers	Louisville MSA, KY-IN	Y	23530 FQ	52850 AW	100760 TQ	KYBLS	10/01-12/01
Non-Retail Sales Workers	Louisiana	Y	19410 FQ	44910 AW	77550 TQ	LABLS	10/01-12/01
Non-Retail Sales Workers	Baton Rouge MSA, LA	Y	26120 FQ	55020 AW	88600 TQ	LABLS	10/01-12/01
Non-Retail Sales Workers	Houma MSA, LA	Y	21970 FQ	40670 AW	57740 TQ	LABLS	10/01-12/01
Non-Retail Sales Workers	Lafayette MSA, LA	Y	18780 FQ	42430 AW	76320 TQ	LABLS	10/01-12/01
Non-Retail Sales Workers	Lake Charles MSA, LA	Y	16270 FQ	38420 AW	80390 TQ	LABLS	10/01-12/01
Non-Retail Sales Workers	New Orleans MSA, LA	Y	17620 FQ	46310 AW	81750 TQ	LABLS	10/01-12/01
Non-Retail Sales Workers	Shreveport-Bossier City MSA, LA	Y	20580 FQ	36310 AW	57810 TQ	LABLS	10/01-12/01
Non-Retail Sales Workers	Maine	Y	25270 FQ	43960 AW	66370 TQ	MEBLS	10/01-12/01
Non-Retail Sales Workers	Portland MSA, ME	Y	25030 FQ	42830 AW	61510 TQ	MEBLS	10/01-12/01
Non-Retail Sales Workers	Maryland	Y	23090 FQ	52130 AW	97500 TQ	MDBLS	10/01-12/01
Non-Retail Sales Workers	Baltimore PMSA, MD	Y	24720 FQ	49760 AW	83600 TQ	MDBLS	10/01-12/01
Non-Retail Sales Workers	Massachusetts	Y	29040 FQ	63860 AW	110290 TQ	MABLS	10/01-12/01
Non-Retail Sales Workers	Boston PMSA, MA-NH	Y	34190 FQ	71130 AW	116130 TQ	MABLS	10/01-12/01
Non-Retail Sales Workers	Brockton PMSA, MA	Y	35960 FQ	61080 AW	92260 TQ	MABLS	10/01-12/01
Non-Retail Sales Workers	Lawrence PMSA, MA-NH	Y	33710 FQ	67600 AW	108110 TQ	MABLS	10/01-12/01
Non-Retail Sales Workers	Lowell PMSA, MA-NH	Y	30870 FQ	55790 AW	88850 TQ	MABLS	10/01-12/01
Non-Retail Sales Workers	Springfield MSA, MA	Y	23750 FQ	55430 AW	93190 TQ	MABLS	10/01-12/01
Non-Retail Sales Workers	Worcester PMSA, MA-CT	Y	34980 FQ	59530 AW	93110 TQ	MABLS	10/01-12/01
Non-Retail Sales Workers	Michigan	Y	31080 FQ	68550 AW	134420 TQ	MIBLS	10/01-12/01
Non-Retail Sales Workers	Ann Arbor PMSA, MI	Y	36760 FQ	75160 AW		MIBLS	10/01-12/01
Non-Retail Sales Workers	Detroit PMSA, MI	Y	35270 FQ	73590 AW	142090 TQ	MIBLS	10/01-12/01
Non-Retail Sales Workers	Flint PMSA, MI	Y	25940 FQ	56630 AW	113070 TQ	MIBLS	10/01-12/01
Non-Retail Sales Workers	Grand Rapids-Muskegon-Holland MSA, MI	Y	30580 FQ	66890 AW		MIBLS	10/01-12/01

AAW	Average annual wage	AOH	Average offered, high	ASH	Average starting, high	H	Hourly	M	Monthly	S	Special: hourly and annual
AE	Average entry wage	AOL	Average offered, low	ASL	Average starting, low	HI	Highest wage paid	MTC	Median total compensation	TQ	Third quartile wage
AEX	Average experienced wage	APH	Average pay, high range	AW	Average wage paid	HR	High end range	MW	Median wage paid	W	Weekly
AO	Average offered	APL	Average pay, low range	FQ	First quartile wage	LR	Low end range	SQ	Second quartile wage	Y	Yearly

Occupation/Type/Industry	Location	Per	Low	Mid	High	Source	Date
First-Line Supervisor/Manager							
Non-Retail Sales Workers	Kalamazoo-Battle Creek MSA, MI	Y	30700 FQ	57400 AW	94090 TQ	MIBLS	10/01-12/01
Non-Retail Sales Workers	Lansing-East Lansing MSA, MI	Y	25910 FQ	55240 AW	90360 TQ	MIBLS	10/01-12/01
Non-Retail Sales Workers	Saginaw-Bay City-Midland MSA, MI	Y	28620 FQ	63660 AW	106770 TQ	MIBLS	10/01-12/01
Non-Retail Sales Workers	Minnesota	Y	35790 FQ	65540 AW	109100 TQ	MNBLS	10/01-12/01
Non-Retail Sales Workers	Duluth-Superior MSA, MN-WI	Y	24490 FQ	45640 AW	71930 TQ	MNBLS	10/01-12/01
Non-Retail Sales Workers	Minneapolis-St. Paul MSA, MN-WI	Y	39620 FQ	68120 AW	109350 TQ	MNBLS	10/01-12/01
Non-Retail Sales Workers	St. Cloud MSA, MN	Y	12030 FQ	31410 AW	70260 TQ	MNBLS	10/01-12/01
Non-Retail Sales Workers	Mississippi	Y	21100 FQ	47090 AW	86750 TQ	MSBLS	10/01-12/01
Non-Retail Sales Workers	Biloxi-Gulfport-Pascagoula MSA, MS	Y	19840 FQ	40190 AW	64260 TQ	MSBLS	10/01-12/01
Non-Retail Sales Workers	Jackson MSA, MS	Y	28690 FQ	63100 AW	117530 TQ	MSBLS	10/01-12/01
Non-Retail Sales Workers	Missouri	Y	22820 FQ	47360 AW	86760 TQ	MOBLS	10/01-12/01
Non-Retail Sales Workers	Kansas City MSA, MO-KS	Y	21810 FQ	51550 AW	88150 TQ	MOBLS	10/01-12/01
Non-Retail Sales Workers	St. Louis MSA, MO-IL	Y	25370 FQ	49320 AW	89210 TQ	MOBLS	10/01-12/01
Non-Retail Sales Workers	Springfield MSA, MO	Y	24750 FQ	53290 AW	102880 TQ	MOBLS	10/01-12/01
Non-Retail Sales Workers	Montana	Y	20570 FQ	40520 AW	64490 TQ	MTBLS	10/01-12/01
Non-Retail Sales Workers	Billings MSA, MT	Y	18970 FQ	38140 AW	63620 TQ	MTBLS	10/01-12/01
Non-Retail Sales Workers	Nebraska	Y	23530 FQ	47320 AW	78000 TQ	NEBLS	10/01-12/01
Non-Retail Sales Workers	Lincoln MSA, NE	Y	21380 FQ	40780 AW	59180 TQ	NEBLS	10/01-12/01
Non-Retail Sales Workers	Omaha MSA, NE-IA	Y	28090 FQ	51540 AW	86670 TQ	NEBLS	10/01-12/01
Non-Retail Sales Workers	Nevada	Y	17180 FQ	45190 AW	84230 TQ	NVBLS	10/01-12/01
Non-Retail Sales Workers	Las Vegas MSA, NV-AZ	Y	17680 FQ	46560 AW	88340 TQ	NVBLS	10/01-12/01
Non-Retail Sales Workers	Reno MSA, NV	Y	15800 FQ	41530 AW	73070 TQ	NVBLS	10/01-12/01
Non-Retail Sales Workers	New Hampshire	Y	32300 FQ	73650 AW	136550 TQ	NHBLS	10/01-12/01
Non-Retail Sales Workers	Manchester PMSA, NH	Y	31210 FQ	63910 AW	107020 TQ	NHBLS	10/01-12/01
Non-Retail Sales Workers	Nashua PMSA, NH	Y	34820 FQ	62770 AW	99250 TQ	NHBLS	10/01-12/01
Non-Retail Sales Workers	Portsmouth-Rochester PMSA, NH-ME	Y	32210 FQ	54780 AW	91660 TQ	NHBLS	10/01-12/01
Non-Retail Sales Workers	New Jersey	Y	38870 FQ	80230 AW	143230 TQ	NJBLS	10/01-12/01
Non-Retail Sales Workers	Atlantic-Cape May PMSA, NJ	Y	27150 FQ	50090 AW	93240 TQ	NJBLS	10/01-12/01
Non-Retail Sales Workers	Bergen-Passaic PMSA, NJ	Y	44650 FQ	87470 AW		NJBLS	10/01-12/01
Non-Retail Sales Workers	Jersey City PMSA, NJ	Y	41790 FQ	76230 AW	136590 TQ	NJBLS	10/01-12/01
Non-Retail Sales Workers	Middlesex-Somerset-Hunterdon PMSA, NJ	Y	39290 FQ	81750 AW	138690 TQ	NJBLS	10/01-12/01
Non-Retail Sales Workers	Monmouth-Ocean PMSA, NJ	Y	32580 FQ	71090 AW	143420 TQ	NJBLS	10/01-12/01
Non-Retail Sales Workers	Newark PMSA, NJ	Y	46990 FQ	86970 AW	142350 TQ	NJBLS	10/01-12/01
Non-Retail Sales Workers	Trenton PMSA, NJ	Y	33310 FQ	68940 AW	123470 TQ	NJBLS	10/01-12/01
Non-Retail Sales Workers	New Mexico	Y	20650 FQ	42610 AW	67020 TQ	NMBLS	10/01-12/01
Non-Retail Sales Workers	Albuquerque MSA, NM	Y	22950 FQ	45150 AW	68810 TQ	NMBLS	10/01-12/01
Non-Retail Sales Workers	Las Cruces MSA, NM	Y	17500 FQ	27960 AW	45970 TQ	NMBLS	10/01-12/01
Non-Retail Sales Workers	New York	Y	38380 FQ	86040 AW		NYBLS	10/01-12/01
Non-Retail Sales Workers	Albany-Schenectady-Troy MSA, NY	Y	31990 FQ	68370 AW	116600 TQ	NYBLS	10/01-12/01
Non-Retail Sales Workers	Binghamton MSA, NY	Y	27730 FQ	56980 AW	108100 TQ	NYBLS	10/01-12/01
Non-Retail Sales Workers	Buffalo-Niagara Falls MSA, NY	Y	32810 FQ	67820 AW	130930 TQ	NYBLS	10/01-12/01
Non-Retail Sales Workers	Dutchess County PMSA, NY	Y	23780 FQ	69230 AW		NYBLS	10/01-12/01
Non-Retail Sales Workers	Nassau-Suffolk PMSA, NY	Y	44180 FQ	98990 AW		NYBLS	10/01-12/01
Non-Retail Sales Workers	New York PMSA, NY	Y	45890 FQ	93940 AW		NYBLS	10/01-12/01
Non-Retail Sales Workers	Newburgh PMSA, NY-PA	Y	30700 FQ	63250 AW	122830 TQ	NYBLS	10/01-12/01
Non-Retail Sales Workers	Rochester MSA, NY	Y	29900 FQ	64500 AW	112250 TQ	NYBLS	10/01-12/01
Non-Retail Sales Workers	Syracuse MSA, NY	Y	31280 FQ	70220 AW	132310 TQ	NYBLS	10/01-12/01
Non-Retail Sales Workers	Utica-Rome MSA, NY	Y	31140 FQ	65980 AW	124590 TQ	NYBLS	10/01-12/01
Non-Retail Sales Workers	North Carolina	Y	24060 FQ	51090 AW	94920 TQ	NCBLS	10/01-12/01
Non-Retail Sales Workers	Asheville MSA, NC	Y	22650 FQ	54880 AW	87450 TQ	NCBLS	10/01-12/01
Non-Retail Sales Workers	Charlotte-Gastonia-Rock Hill MSA, NC-SC	Y	25530 FQ	52220 AW	101360 TQ	NCBLS	10/01-12/01
Non-Retail Sales Workers	Fayetteville MSA, NC	Y	23160 FQ	38730 AW	59440 TQ	NCBLS	10/01-12/01
Non-Retail Sales Workers	Greensboro-Winston-Salem-High Point MSA, NC	Y	28030 FQ	56160 AW	102010 TQ	NCBLS	10/01-12/01
Non-Retail Sales Workers	Hickory-Morganton-Lenoir MSA, NC	Y	16300 FQ	38200 AW	73990 TQ	NCBLS	10/01-12/01
Non-Retail Sales Workers	Raleigh-Durham-Chapel Hill MSA, NC	Y	28030 FQ	56480 AW	106480 TQ	NCBLS	10/01-12/01
Non-Retail Sales Workers	Wilmington MSA, NC	Y	22780 FQ	55490 AW		NCBLS	10/01-12/01
Non-Retail Sales Workers	North Dakota	Y	20640 FQ	37080 AW	62130 TQ	NDBLS	10/01-12/01
Non-Retail Sales Workers	Fargo-Moorhead MSA, ND-MN	Y	22740 FQ	44310 AW	90750 TQ	NDBLS	10/01-12/01

AAW Average annual wage; AE Average entry wage; AEX Average experienced wage; AO Average offered; AOH Average offered, high; AOL Average offered, low; APH Average pay, high range; APL Average pay, low range; ASH Average starting, high; ASL Average starting, low; AW Average wage paid; FQ First quartile wage; H Hourly; HI Highest wage paid; HR High end range; LR Low end range; M Monthly; MTC Median total compensation; MW Median wage paid; SQ Second quartile wage; S Special: hourly and annual; TQ Third quartile wage; W Weekly; Y Yearly

Occupation/Type/Industry	Location	Per	Low	Mid	High	Source	Date
First-Line Supervisor/Manager							
Non-Retail Sales Workers	Ohio	Y	28880 FQ	60090 AW	105690 TQ	OHBLS	10/01-12/01
Non-Retail Sales Workers	Akron PMSA, OH	Y	34140 FQ	69440 AW	128400 TQ	OHBLS	10/01-12/01
Non-Retail Sales Workers	Canton-Massillon MSA, OH	Y	24880 FQ	52830 AW	107650 TQ	OHBLS	10/01-12/01
Non-Retail Sales Workers	Cincinnati PMSA, OH-KY-IN	Y	21530 FQ	60070 AW	117030 TQ	OHBLS	10/01-12/01
Non-Retail Sales Workers	Cleveland-Lorain-Elyria PMSA, OH	Y	32920 FQ	59880 AW	101850 TQ	OHBLS	10/01-12/01
Non-Retail Sales Workers	Columbus MSA, OH	Y	30230 FQ	58780 AW	92520 TQ	OHBLS	10/01-12/01
Non-Retail Sales Workers	Dayton-Springfield MSA, OH	Y	32110 FQ	67090 AW	123350 TQ	OHBLS	10/01-12/01
Non-Retail Sales Workers	Hamilton-Middletown PMSA, OH	Y	30020 FQ	68680 AW	135110 TQ	OHBLS	10/01-12/01
Non-Retail Sales Workers	Mansfield MSA, OH	Y	24150 FQ	46650 AW	80120 TQ	OHBLS	10/01-12/01
Non-Retail Sales Workers	Toledo MSA, OH	Y	29980 FQ	55290 AW	96900 TQ	OHBLS	10/01-12/01
Non-Retail Sales Workers	Youngstown-Warren MSA, OH	Y	23320 FQ	52800 AW	89690 TQ	OHBLS	10/01-12/01
Non-Retail Sales Workers	Oklahoma	Y	20690 FQ	42460 AW	73120 TQ	OKBLS	10/01-12/01
Non-Retail Sales Workers	Oklahoma City MSA, OK	Y	21420 FQ	41960 AW	74370 TQ	OKBLS	10/01-12/01
Non-Retail Sales Workers	Tulsa MSA, OK	Y	25850 FQ	49020 AW	85540 TQ	OKBLS	10/01-12/01
Non-Retail Sales Workers	Oregon	Y	28340 FQ	59390 AW	105930 TQ	ORBLS	10/01-12/01
Non-Retail Sales Workers	Eugene-Springfield MSA, OR	Y	26550 FQ	53900 AW	93850 TQ	ORBLS	10/01-12/01
Non-Retail Sales Workers	Medford-Ashland MSA, OR	Y	25210 FQ	50330 AW	75030 TQ	ORBLS	10/01-12/01
Non-Retail Sales Workers	Portland-Vancouver PMSA, OR-WA	Y	30490 FQ	62560 AW	111770 TQ	ORBLS	10/01-12/01
Non-Retail Sales Workers	Salem PMSA, OR	Y	28070 FQ	55010 AW	76210 TQ	ORBLS	10/01-12/01
Non-Retail Sales Workers	Pennsylvania	Y	26660 FQ	56600 AW	93070 TQ	PABLS	10/01-12/01
Non-Retail Sales Workers	Allentown-Bethlehem-Easton MSA, PA	Y	27040 FQ	54080 AW	90520 TQ	PABLS	10/01-12/01
Non-Retail Sales Workers	Erie MSA, PA	Y	21040 FQ	47810 AW	79410 TQ	PABLS	10/01-12/01
Non-Retail Sales Workers	Harrisburg-Lebanon-Carlisle MSA, PA	Y	27210 FQ	58820 AW	111980 TQ	PABLS	10/01-12/01
Non-Retail Sales Workers	Johnstown MSA, PA	Y	30120 FQ	62200 AW		PABLS	10/01-12/01
Non-Retail Sales Workers	Lancaster MSA, PA	Y	27270 FQ	54260 AW	83710 TQ	PABLS	10/01-12/01
Non-Retail Sales Workers	Philadelphia PMSA, PA-NJ	Y	30890 FQ	63930 AW	116000 TQ	PABLS	10/01-12/01
Non-Retail Sales Workers	Pittsburgh MSA, PA	Y	24170 FQ	51960 AW	88540 TQ	PABLS	10/01-12/01
Non-Retail Sales Workers	Reading MSA, PA	Y	30130 FQ	52520 AW	88380 TQ	PABLS	10/01-12/01
Non-Retail Sales Workers	Scranton-Wilkes-Barre-Hazleton MSA, PA	Y	22040 FQ	51820 AW	86050 TQ	PABLS	10/01-12/01
Non-Retail Sales Workers	York MSA, PA	Y	24090 FQ	53670 AW	93300 TQ	PABLS	10/01-12/01
Non-Retail Sales Workers	Rhode Island	Y	32740 FQ	66600 AW	125430 TQ	RIBLS	10/01-12/01
Non-Retail Sales Workers	Providence-Fall River-Warwick MSA, RI-MA	Y	30840 FQ	63180 AW	118730 TQ	RIBLS	10/01-12/01
Non-Retail Sales Workers	South Carolina	Y	22440 FQ	47350 AW	84540 TQ	SCBLS	10/01-12/01
Non-Retail Sales Workers	Charleston-North Charleston MSA, SC	Y	21420 FQ	42050 AW	66140 TQ	SCBLS	10/01-12/01
Non-Retail Sales Workers	Columbia MSA, SC	Y	22160 FQ	43850 AW	72280 TQ	SCBLS	10/01-12/01
Non-Retail Sales Workers	Greenville-Spartanburg-Anderson MSA, SC	Y	22070 FQ	50600 AW	91780 TQ	SCBLS	10/01-12/01
Non-Retail Sales Workers	Myrtle Beach MSA, SC	Y	25320 FQ	41820 AW	57240 TQ	SCBLS	10/01-12/01
Non-Retail Sales Workers	South Dakota	Y	28040 FQ	55790 AW	98990 TQ	SDBLS	10/01-12/01
Non-Retail Sales Workers	Sioux Falls MSA, SD	Y	34770 FQ	61060 AW	96560 TQ	SDBLS	10/01-12/01
Non-Retail Sales Workers	Tennessee	Y	19790 FQ	43340 AW	76790 TQ	TNBLS	10/01-12/01
Non-Retail Sales Workers	Chattanooga MSA, TN-GA	Y	20540 FQ	44970 AW	83160 TQ	TNBLS	10/01-12/01
Non-Retail Sales Workers	Clarksville-Hopkinsville MSA, TN-KY	Y	18340 FQ	37170 AW	57510 TQ	TNBLS	10/01-12/01
Non-Retail Sales Workers	Johnson City-Kingsport-Bristol MSA, TN-VA	Y	13120 FQ	35060 AW	56630 TQ	TNBLS	10/01-12/01
Non-Retail Sales Workers	Knoxville MSA, TN	Y	20370 FQ	36530 AW	65990 TQ	TNBLS	10/01-12/01
Non-Retail Sales Workers	Memphis MSA, TN-AR-MS	Y	21770 FQ	47570 AW	82000 TQ	TNBLS	10/01-12/01
Non-Retail Sales Workers	Nashville MSA, TN	Y	24400 FQ	47040 AW	77270 TQ	TNBLS	10/01-12/01
Non-Retail Sales Workers	Texas	Y	20770 FQ	50050 AW	92440 TQ	TXBLS	10/01-12/01
Non-Retail Sales Workers	Amarillo MSA, TX	Y	24420 FQ	42000 AW	65960 TQ	TXBLS	10/01-12/01
Non-Retail Sales Workers	Austin-San Marcos MSA, TX	Y	22750 FQ	53550 AW	106250 TQ	TXBLS	10/01-12/01
Non-Retail Sales Workers	Beaumont-Port Arthur MSA, TX	Y	24650 FQ	47960 AW	74920 TQ	TXBLS	10/01-12/01
Non-Retail Sales Workers	Brazoria PMSA, TX	Y	13990 FQ	36130 AW	66340 TQ	TXBLS	10/01-12/01
Non-Retail Sales Workers	Brownsville-Harlingen-San Benito MSA, TX	Y	23300 FQ	49350 AW	91410 TQ	TXBLS	10/01-12/01
Non-Retail Sales Workers	Corpus Christi MSA, TX	Y	19190 FQ	41290 AW	64760 TQ	TXBLS	10/01-12/01
Non-Retail Sales Workers	Dallas PMSA, TX	Y	20240 FQ	51710 AW	96420 TQ	TXBLS	10/01-12/01
Non-Retail Sales Workers	Fort Worth-Arlington PMSA, TX	Y	15230 FQ	48420 AW	104760 TQ	TXBLS	10/01-12/01
Non-Retail Sales Workers	Galveston-Texas City PMSA, TX	Y	22160 FQ	42870 AW	76520 TQ	TXBLS	10/01-12/01

AAW	Average annual wage	AOH	Average offered, high	ASH	Average starting, high	H	Hourly	M	Monthly	S	Special: hourly and annual
AE	Average entry wage	AOL	Average offered, low	ASL	Average starting, low	HI	Highest wage paid	MTC	Median total compensation	TQ	Third quartile wage
AEX	Average experienced wage	APH	Average pay, high range	AW	Average wage paid	HR	High end range	MW	Median wage paid	W	Weekly
AO	Average offered	APL	Average pay, low range	FQ	First quartile wage	LR	Low end range	SQ	Second quartile wage	Y	Yearly

Occupation/Type/Industry	Location	Per	Low	Mid	High	Source	Date
First-Line Supervisor/Manager							
Non-Retail Sales Workers	Houston PMSA, TX	Y	27130 FQ	54480 AW	87270 TQ	TXBLS	10/01-12/01
Non-Retail Sales Workers	Killeen-Temple MSA, TX	Y	19860 FQ	46200 AW	88430 TQ	TXBLS	10/01-12/01
Non-Retail Sales Workers	Laredo MSA, TX	Y	26140 FQ	47750 AW	82200 TQ	TXBLS	10/01-12/01
Non-Retail Sales Workers	Longview-Marshall MSA, TX	Y	20040 FQ	41000 AW	68530 TQ	TXBLS	10/01-12/01
Non-Retail Sales Workers	Lubbock MSA, TX	Y	24980 FQ	49610 AW	82760 TQ	TXBLS	10/01-12/01
Non-Retail Sales Workers	McAllen-Edinburg-Mission MSA, TX	Y	17990 FQ	44800 AW	86840 TQ	TXBLS	10/01-12/01
Non-Retail Sales Workers	Odessa-Midland MSA, TX	Y	13990 FQ	46800 AW	86090 TQ	TXBLS	10/01-12/01
Non-Retail Sales Workers	San Antonio MSA, TX	Y	23400 FQ	46220 AW	86800 TQ	TXBLS	10/01-12/01
Non-Retail Sales Workers	Tyler MSA, TX	Y	17450 FQ	39780 AW	63550 TQ	TXBLS	10/01-12/01
Non-Retail Sales Workers	Waco MSA, TX	Y	21810 FQ	52290 AW	124750 TQ	TXBLS	10/01-12/01
Non-Retail Sales Workers	Utah	Y	22600 FQ	45190 AW	78310 TQ	UTBLS	10/01-12/01
Non-Retail Sales Workers	Provo-Orem MSA, UT	Y	21240 FQ	37400 AW	61320 TQ	UTBLS	10/01-12/01
Non-Retail Sales Workers	Salt Lake City-Ogden MSA, UT	Y	23810 FQ	48210 AW	83310 TQ	UTBLS	10/01-12/01
Non-Retail Sales Workers	Vermont	Y	34240 FQ	67560 AW	105370 TQ	VTBLS	10/01-12/01
Non-Retail Sales Workers	Burlington MSA, VT	Y	34710 FQ	67880 AW	120380 TQ	VTBLS	10/01-12/01
Non-Retail Sales Workers	Virginia	Y	20610 FQ	56310 AW	112800 TQ	VABLS	10/01-12/01
Non-Retail Sales Workers	Lynchburg MSA, VA	Y	22560 FQ	52870 AW	92180 TQ	VABLS	10/01-12/01
Non-Retail Sales Workers	Norfolk-Virginia Beach-Newport News MSA, VA-NC	Y	18200 FQ	48620 AW	83680 TQ	VABLS	10/01-12/01
Non-Retail Sales Workers	Richmond-Petersburg MSA, VA	Y	25530 FQ	56790 AW	103390 TQ	VABLS	10/01-12/01
Non-Retail Sales Workers	Roanoke MSA, VA	Y	22050 FQ	66630 AW	140430 TQ	VABLS	10/01-12/01
Non-Retail Sales Workers	Washington	Y	35280 FQ	68720 AW	110940 TQ	WABLS	10/01-12/01
Non-Retail Sales Workers	Bremerton PMSA, WA	Y	32290 FQ	63760 AW	139600 TQ	WABLS	10/01-12/01
Non-Retail Sales Workers	Olympia PMSA, WA	Y	26340 FQ	49160 AW	73180 TQ	WABLS	10/01-12/01
Non-Retail Sales Workers	Richland-Kennewick-Pasco MSA, WA	Y	26520 FQ	50130 AW	72650 TQ	WABLS	10/01-12/01
Non-Retail Sales Workers	Seattle-Bellevue-Everett PMSA, WA	Y	39040 FQ	72030 AW	111170 TQ	WABLS	10/01-12/01
Non-Retail Sales Workers	Spokane MSA, WA	Y	32650 FQ	69210 AW		WABLS	10/01-12/01
Non-Retail Sales Workers	Tacoma PMSA, WA	Y	35170 FQ	61270 AW	96950 TQ	WABLS	10/01-12/01
Non-Retail Sales Workers	Yakima MSA, WA	Y	35140 FQ	83870 AW		WABLS	10/01-12/01
Non-Retail Sales Workers	West Virginia	Y	21280 FQ	42980 AW	71360 TQ	WVBLS	10/01-12/01
Non-Retail Sales Workers	Charleston MSA, WV	Y	25040 FQ	41480 AW	64950 TQ	WVBLS	10/01-12/01
Non-Retail Sales Workers	Huntington-Ashland MSA, WV-KY-OH	Y	24540 FQ	49590 AW	85570 TQ	WVBLS	10/01-12/01
Non-Retail Sales Workers	Wisconsin	Y	27040 FQ	59110 AW	108860 TQ	WIBLS	10/01-12/01
Non-Retail Sales Workers	Appleton-Oshkosh-Neenah MSA, WI	Y	27420 FQ	53770 AW	87080 TQ	WIBLS	10/01-12/01
Non-Retail Sales Workers	Green Bay MSA, WI	Y	31340 FQ	51480 AW	82900 TQ	WIBLS	10/01-12/01
Non-Retail Sales Workers	Madison MSA, WI	Y	26550 FQ	55280 AW	92640 TQ	WIBLS	10/01-12/01
Non-Retail Sales Workers	Milwaukee-Waukesha PMSA, WI	Y	32270 FQ	68780 AW	125480 TQ	WIBLS	10/01-12/01
Non-Retail Sales Workers	Racine PMSA, WI	Y	25760 FQ	60630 AW	124200 TQ	WIBLS	10/01-12/01
Non-Retail Sales Workers	Wyoming	Y	16710 FQ	35070 AW	56250 TQ	WYBLS	10/01-12/01
Non-Retail Sales Workers	Puerto Rico	Y	17300 FQ	37840 AW	68180 TQ	PRBLS	10/01-12/01
Non-Retail Sales Workers	Virgin Islands	Y	24140 FQ	34860 AW	44840 TQ	VIBLS	10/01-12/01
Non-Retail Sales Workers	Guam	Y	22930 FQ	35450 AW	53880 TQ	GUBLS	10/01-12/01
Office and Administrative Support Workers	Alabama	H	9.37 FQ	17.43 AW	27.63 TQ	ALBLS	10/01-12/01
Office and Administrative Support Workers	Alaska	H	12.29 FQ	20.52 AW	29.79 TQ	AKBLS	10/01-12/01
Office and Administrative Support Workers	Arizona	H	11.57 FQ	19.35 AW	28.46 TQ	AZBLS	10/01-12/01
Office and Administrative Support Workers	Arkansas	H	8.66 FQ	14.96 AW	22.98 TQ	ARBLS	10/01-12/01
Office and Administrative Support Workers	California	H	12.97 FQ	22.10 AW	33.27 TQ	CABLS	10/01-12/01
Office and Administrative Support Workers	Colorado	H	12.26 FQ	20.47 AW	31.17 TQ	COBLS	10/01-12/01
Office and Administrative Support Workers	Connecticut	H	13.99 FQ	21.95 AW	31.89 TQ	CTBLS	10/01-12/01
Office and Administrative Support Workers	Delaware	H	10.43 FQ	19.29 AW	28.54 TQ	DEBLS	10/01-12/01
Office and Administrative Support Workers	District of Columbia	H	13.35 FQ	28.20 AW	51.21 TQ	DCBLS	10/01-12/01
Office and Administrative Support Workers	Florida	H	10.89 FQ	18.36 AW	27.46 TQ	FLBLS	10/01-12/01
Office and Administrative Support Workers	Georgia	H	11.32 FQ	18.77 AW	27.91 TQ	GABLS	10/01-12/01
Office and Administrative Support Workers	Hawaii	H	12.27 FQ	19.96 AW	29.73 TQ	HIBLS	10/01-12/01
Office and Administrative Support Workers	Idaho	H	9.17 FQ	16.12 AW	25.63 TQ	IDBLS	10/01-12/01
Office and Administrative Support Workers	Illinois	H	10.96 FQ	19.30 AW	29.19 TQ	ILBLS	10/01-12/01
Office and Administrative Support Workers	Indiana	H	10.25 FQ	17.62 AW	26.57 TQ	INBLS	10/01-12/01
Office and Administrative Support Workers	Iowa	H	9.44 FQ	16.78 AW	26.19 TQ	IABLS	10/01-12/01
Office and Administrative Support Workers	Kansas	H	10.27 FQ	17.53 AW	26.68 TQ	KSBLS	10/01-12/01
Office and Administrative Support Workers	Kentucky	H	9.99 FQ	16.93 AW	25.94 TQ	KYBLS	10/01-12/01
Office and Administrative Support Workers	Louisiana	H	9.29 FQ	17.57 AW	28.92 TQ	LABLS	10/01-12/01
Office and Administrative Support Workers	Maine	H	10.17 FQ	16.25 AW	24.08 TQ	MEBLS	10/01-12/01

AAW	Average annual wage	AOH	Average offered, high	ASH	Average starting, high	H	Hourly	M	Monthly	S	Special: hourly and annual
AE	Average entry wage	AOL	Average offered, low	ASL	Average starting, low	HI	Highest wage paid	MTC	Median total compensation	TQ	Third quartile wage
AEX	Average experienced wage	APH	Average pay, high range	AW	Average wage paid	HR	High end range	MW	Median wage paid	W	Weekly
AO	Average offered	APL	Average pay, low range	FQ	First quartile wage	LR	Low end range	SQ	Second quartile wage	Y	Yearly

Occupation/Type/Industry	Location	Per	Low	Mid	High	Source	Date
First-Line Supervisor/Manager							
Office and Administrative Support Workers	Maryland	H	11.74 FQ	19.97 AW	30.13 TQ	MDBLS	10/01-12/01
Office and Administrative Support Workers	Massachusetts	H	13.57 FQ	22.08 AW	32.92 TQ	MABLS	10/01-12/01
Office and Administrative Support Workers	Michigan	H	11.22 FQ	20.03 AW	30.88 TQ	MIBLS	10/01-12/01
Office and Administrative Support Workers	Minnesota	H	11.88 FQ	19.60 AW	28.12 TQ	MNBLS	10/01-12/01
Office and Administrative Support Workers	Mississippi	H	9.14 FQ	15.73 AW	24.41 TQ	MSBLS	10/01-12/01
Office and Administrative Support Workers	Missouri	H	9.61 FQ	17.37 AW	27.18 TQ	MOBLS	10/01-12/01
Office and Administrative Support Workers	Montana	H	8.80 FQ	14.84 AW	22.40 TQ	MTBLS	10/01-12/01
Office and Administrative Support Workers	Nebraska	H	10.02 FQ	16.90 AW	26.00 TQ	NEBLS	10/01-12/01
Office and Administrative Support Workers	Nevada	H	11.47 FQ	17.90 AW	26.36 TQ	NVBLS	10/01-12/01
Office and Administrative Support Workers	New Hampshire	H	11.28 FQ	17.97 AW	26.54 TQ	NHBLS	10/01-12/01
Office and Administrative Support Workers	New Jersey	H	13.85 FQ	22.80 AW	33.94 TQ	NJBLS	10/01-12/01
Office and Administrative Support Workers	New Mexico	H	9.17 FQ	15.82 AW	24.03 TQ	NMBLS	10/01-12/01
Office and Administrative Support Workers	New York	H	12.45 FQ	22.78 AW	35.88 TQ	NYBLS	10/01-12/01
Office and Administrative Support Workers	North Carolina	H	10.71 FQ	18.92 AW	28.84 TQ	NCBLS	10/01-12/01
Office and Administrative Support Workers	North Dakota	H	8.92 FQ	15.14 AW	22.68 TQ	NDBLS	10/01-12/01
Office and Administrative Support Workers	Ohio	H	10.99 FQ	18.22 AW	26.78 TQ	OHBLS	10/01-12/01
Office and Administrative Support Workers	Oklahoma	H	9.25 FQ	17.04 AW	26.75 TQ	OKBLS	10/01-12/01
Office and Administrative Support Workers	Oregon	H	11.59 FQ	18.52 AW	26.80 TQ	ORBLS	10/01-12/01
Office and Administrative Support Workers	Pennsylvania	H	10.65 FQ	18.78 AW	29.19 TQ	PABLS	10/01-12/01
Office and Administrative Support Workers	Rhode Island	H	13.24 FQ	20.14 AW	28.64 TQ	RIBLS	10/01-12/01
Office and Administrative Support Workers	South Carolina	H	10.07 FQ	16.94 AW	25.50 TQ	SCBLS	10/01-12/01
Office and Administrative Support Workers	South Dakota	H	11.65 FQ	17.35 AW	24.63 TQ	SDBLS	10/01-12/01
Office and Administrative Support Workers	Tennessee	H	9.72 FQ	17.22 AW	26.63 TQ	TNBLS	10/01-12/01
Office and Administrative Support Workers	Texas	H	10.32 FQ	19.02 AW	29.30 TQ	TXBLS	10/01-12/01
Office and Administrative Support Workers	Utah	H	10.26 FQ	17.20 AW	26.16 TQ	UTBLS	10/01-12/01
Office and Administrative Support Workers	Vermont	H	13.40 FQ	20.49 AW	28.20 TQ	VTBLS	10/01-12/01
Office and Administrative Support Workers	Virginia	H	11.17 FQ	19.78 AW	31.38 TQ	VABLS	10/01-12/01
Office and Administrative Support Workers	Washington	H	13.18 FQ	21.25 AW	31.74 TQ	WABLS	10/01-12/01
Office and Administrative Support Workers	West Virginia	H	8.93 FQ	15.52 AW	25.00 TQ	WVBLS	10/01-12/01
Office and Administrative Support Workers	Wisconsin	H	10.97 FQ	19.54 AW	30.83 TQ	WIBLS	10/01-12/01
Office and Administrative Support Workers	Wyoming	H	9.37 FQ	16.13 AW	25.12 TQ	WYBLS	10/01-12/01
Office and Administrative Support Workers	Puerto Rico	H	8.12 FQ	13.82 AW	21.43 TQ	PRBLS	10/01-12/01
Office and Administrative Support Workers	Virgin Islands	H	11.65 FQ	15.88 AW	21.14 TQ	VIBLS	10/01-12/01
Office and Administrative Support Workers	Guam	H	8.26 FQ	15.03 AW	23.12 TQ	GUBLS	10/01-12/01
Personal Service Workers	Alabama	H	7.37 FQ	12.42 AW	20.24 TQ	ALBLS	10/01-12/01
Personal Service Workers	Alaska	H	9.68 FQ	16.78 AW	25.06 TQ	AKBLS	10/01-12/01
Personal Service Workers	Arizona	H	9.35 FQ	14.60 AW	22.15 TQ	AZBLS	10/01-12/01
Personal Service Workers	Arkansas	H	8.08 FQ	11.75 AW	17.01 TQ	ARBLS	10/01-12/01
Personal Service Workers	California	H	8.83 FQ	16.61 AW	26.67 TQ	CABLS	10/01-12/01
Personal Service Workers	Colorado	H	8.04 FQ	13.36 AW	22.61 TQ	COBLS	10/01-12/01
Personal Service Workers	Connecticut	H	10.96 FQ	19.96 AW	30.79 TQ	CTBLS	10/01-12/01
Personal Service Workers	Delaware	H	6.50 FQ	13.69 AW	22.70 TQ	DEBLS	10/01-12/01
Personal Service Workers	District of Columbia	H	10.03 FQ	17.08 AW	26.16 TQ	DCBLS	10/01-12/01
Personal Service Workers	Florida	H	8.53 FQ	15.06 AW	24.43 TQ	FLBLS	10/01-12/01
Personal Service Workers	Georgia	H	7.94 FQ	15.47 AW	24.63 TQ	GABLS	10/01-12/01
Personal Service Workers	Hawaii	H	9.49 FQ	15.70 AW	23.03 TQ	HIBLS	10/01-12/01
Personal Service Workers	Idaho	H	5.96 FQ	11.23 AW	18.55 TQ	IDBLS	10/01-12/01
Personal Service Workers	Illinois	H	6.02 FQ	13.50 AW	23.81 TQ	ILBLS	10/01-12/01
Personal Service Workers	Indiana	H	8.66 FQ	15.64 AW	23.33 TQ	INBLS	10/01-12/01
Personal Service Workers	Iowa	H	8.00 FQ	13.45 AW	19.94 TQ	IABLS	10/01-12/01
Personal Service Workers	Kansas	H	8.78 FQ	12.96 AW	18.37 TQ	KSBLS	10/01-12/01
Personal Service Workers	Kentucky	H	8.03 FQ	13.91 AW	23.30 TQ	KYBLS	10/01-12/01
Personal Service Workers	Louisiana	H	7.25 FQ	11.68 AW	16.93 TQ	LABLS	10/01-12/01
Personal Service Workers	Maine	H	9.06 FQ	12.43 AW	18.56 TQ	MEBLS	10/01-12/01
Personal Service Workers	Maryland	H	9.05 FQ	14.48 AW	22.19 TQ	MDBLS	10/01-12/01
Personal Service Workers	Massachusetts	H	10.76 FQ	15.58 AW	22.91 TQ	MABLS	10/01-12/01
Personal Service Workers	Michigan	H	6.96 FQ	15.26 AW	24.40 TQ	MIBLS	10/01-12/01
Personal Service Workers	Minnesota	H	9.52 FQ	14.69 AW	21.77 TQ	MNBLS	10/01-12/01
Personal Service Workers	Mississippi	H	8.51 FQ	13.46 AW	22.86 TQ	MSBLS	10/01-12/01
Personal Service Workers	Missouri	H	7.60 FQ	13.02 AW	18.64 TQ	MOBLS	10/01-12/01
Personal Service Workers	Montana	H	6.41 FQ	9.83 AW	17.45 TQ	MTBLS	10/01-12/01
Personal Service Workers	Nebraska	H	7.51 FQ	14.68 AW	25.10 TQ	NEBLS	10/01-12/01
Personal Service Workers	Nevada	H	8.52 FQ	14.56 AW	23.66 TQ	NVBLS	10/01-12/01
Personal Service Workers	New Hampshire	H	9.03 FQ	13.29 AW	20.33 TQ	NHBLS	10/01-12/01
Personal Service Workers	New Jersey	H	9.93 FQ	17.07 AW	26.11 TQ	NJBLS	10/01-12/01
Personal Service Workers	New Mexico	H	7.78 FQ	13.53 AW	21.03 TQ	NMBLS	10/01-12/01
Personal Service Workers	New York	H	9.39 FQ	15.80 AW	24.81 TQ	NYBLS	10/01-12/01
Personal Service Workers	North Carolina	H	8.29 FQ	15.56 AW	26.19 TQ	NCBLS	10/01-12/01
Personal Service Workers	North Dakota	H	6.69 FQ	11.08 AW	16.48 TQ	NDBLS	10/01-12/01
Personal Service Workers	Ohio	H	8.41 FQ	14.02 AW	21.28 TQ	OHBLS	10/01-12/01
Personal Service Workers	Oklahoma	H	7.16 FQ	11.92 AW	18.59 TQ	OKBLS	10/01-12/01

AAW	Average annual wage	**AOH**	Average offered, high	**ASH**	Average starting, high	**H**	Hourly	**M**	Monthly	**S**	Special: hourly and annual
AE	Average entry wage	**AOL**	Average offered, low	**ASL**	Average starting, low	**HI**	Highest wage paid	**MTC**	Median total compensation	**TQ**	Third quartile wage
AEX	Average experienced wage	**APH**	Average pay, high range	**AW**	Average wage paid	**HR**	High end range	**MW**	Median wage paid	**W**	Weekly
AO	Average offered	**APL**	Average pay, low range	**FQ**	First quartile wage	**LR**	Low end range	**SQ**	Second quartile wage	**Y**	Yearly

Occupation/Type/Industry	Location	Per	Low	Mid	High	Source	Date
First-Line Supervisor/Manager							
Personal Service Workers	Oregon	H	9.17 FQ	15.32 AW	23.24 TQ	ORBLS	10/01-12/01
Personal Service Workers	Pennsylvania	H	7.16 FQ	14.19 AW	24.49 TQ	PABLS	10/01-12/01
Personal Service Workers	Rhode Island	H	9.44 FQ	15.67 AW	22.31 TQ	RIBLS	10/01-12/01
Personal Service Workers	South Carolina	H	9.74 FQ	18.29 AW	33.19 TQ	SCBLS	10/01-12/01
Personal Service Workers	South Dakota	H	9.42 FQ	13.99 AW	20.25 TQ	SDBLS	10/01-12/01
Personal Service Workers	Tennessee	H	7.02 FQ	13.20 AW	20.80 TQ	TNBLS	10/01-12/01
Personal Service Workers	Texas	H	7.66 FQ	13.78 AW	22.25 TQ	TXBLS	10/01-12/01
Personal Service Workers	Utah	H	7.88 FQ	13.46 AW	20.39 TQ	UTBLS	10/01-12/01
Personal Service Workers	Vermont	H	10.94 FQ	17.89 AW	26.20 TQ	VTBLS	10/01-12/01
Personal Service Workers	Virginia	H	9.35 FQ	17.58 AW	27.29 TQ	VABLS	10/01-12/01
Personal Service Workers	Washington	H	10.86 FQ	17.90 AW	27.51 TQ	WABLS	10/01-12/01
Personal Service Workers	West Virginia	H	6.43 FQ	11.41 AW	19.41 TQ	WVBLS	10/01-12/01
Personal Service Workers	Wisconsin	H	9.04 FQ	14.91 AW	23.15 TQ	WIBLS	10/01-12/01
Personal Service Workers	Wyoming	H	7.69 FQ	12.44 AW	19.63 TQ	WYBLS	10/01-12/01
Personal Service Workers	Puerto Rico	H	7.33 FQ	12.11 AW	17.32 TQ	PRBLS	10/01-12/01
Personal Service Workers	Virgin Islands	H	10.02 FQ	13.23 AW	16.79 TQ	VIBLS	10/01-12/01
Personal Service Workers	Guam	H	9.84 FQ	15.84 AW	24.84 TQ	GUBLS	10/01-12/01
Police and Detectives	Alabama	Y	27110 FQ	43700 AW	61270 TQ	ALBLS	10/01-12/01
Police and Detectives	Birmingham MSA, AL	Y	25140 FQ	39370 AW	60540 TQ	ALBLS	10/01-12/01
Police and Detectives	Huntsville MSA, AL	Y	24240 FQ	34340 AW	50710 TQ	ALBLS	10/01-12/01
Police and Detectives	Mobile MSA, AL	Y	31150 FQ	45440 AW	60740 TQ	ALBLS	10/01-12/01
Police and Detectives	Montgomery MSA, AL	Y	45160 FQ	55150 AW	78100 TQ	ALBLS	10/01-12/01
Police and Detectives	Alaska	Y	49170 FQ	69290 AW	90210 TQ	AKBLS	10/01-12/01
Police and Detectives	Arizona	Y	40860 FQ	61570 AW	82230 TQ	AZBLS	10/01-12/01
Police and Detectives	Phoenix-Mesa MSA, AZ	Y	47720 FQ	66590 AW	86240 TQ	AZBLS	10/01-12/01
Police and Detectives	Tucson MSA, AZ	Y	38090 FQ	58490 AW	84640 TQ	AZBLS	10/01-12/01
Police and Detectives	Arkansas	Y	25950 FQ	41820 AW	62430 TQ	ARBLS	10/01-12/01
Police and Detectives	Fayetteville-Springdale-Rogers MSA, AR	Y	28270 FQ	38990 AW	47800 TQ	ARBLS	10/01-12/01
Police and Detectives	Little Rock-North Little Rock MSA, AR	Y	31540 FQ	51740 AW	75410 TQ	ARBLS	10/01-12/01
Police and Detectives	California	Y	58360 FQ	78490 AW	103570 TQ	CABLS	10/01-12/01
Police and Detectives	Bakersfield MSA, CA	Y	51310 FQ	67270 AW	88970 TQ	CABLS	10/01-12/01
Police and Detectives	Chico-Paradise MSA, CA	Y	40750 FQ	60160 AW	87100 TQ	CABLS	10/01-12/01
Police and Detectives	Fresno MSA, CA	Y	46400 FQ	71180 AW	90980 TQ	CABLS	10/01-12/01
Police and Detectives	Los Angeles-Long Beach PMSA, CA	Y	63150 FQ	79540 AW	103710 TQ	CABLS	10/01-12/01
Police and Detectives	Merced MSA, CA	Y	50920 FQ	63910 AW	83430 TQ	CABLS	10/01-12/01
Police and Detectives	Modesto MSA, CA	Y	49910 FQ	65560 AW	85780 TQ	CABLS	10/01-12/01
Police and Detectives	Oakland PMSA, CA	Y	62310 FQ	88260 AW	120790 TQ	CABLS	10/01-12/01
Police and Detectives	Orange County PMSA, CA	Y	69360 FQ	91080 AW	119790 TQ	CABLS	10/01-12/01
Police and Detectives	Redding MSA, CA	Y	63530 FQ	79250 AW	97480 TQ	CABLS	10/01-12/01
Police and Detectives	Riverside-San Bernardino PMSA, CA	Y	58120 FQ	75770 AW	96960 TQ	CABLS	10/01-12/01
Police and Detectives	Sacramento PMSA, CA	Y	64350 FQ	81500 AW	97370 TQ	CABLS	10/01-12/01
Police and Detectives	Salinas MSA, CA	Y	36330 FQ	64070 AW	98530 TQ	CABLS	10/01-12/01
Police and Detectives	San Diego MSA, CA	Y	63550 FQ	79500 AW	95510 TQ	CABLS	10/01-12/01
Police and Detectives	San Francisco PMSA, CA	Y	64660 FQ	90050 AW	116410 TQ	CABLS	10/01-12/01
Police and Detectives	San Jose PMSA, CA	Y	62220 FQ	79940 AW	103700 TQ	CABLS	10/01-12/01
Police and Detectives	San Luis Obispo-Atascadero-Paso Robles MSA, CA	Y	51520 FQ	67480 AW	89040 TQ	CABLS	10/01-12/01
Police and Detectives	Santa Barbara-Santa Maria-Lompoc MSA, CA	Y	61060 FQ	78370 AW	104410 TQ	CABLS	10/01-12/01
Police and Detectives	Santa Cruz-Watsonville PMSA, CA	Y	63020 FQ	80230 AW	102960 TQ	CABLS	10/01-12/01
Police and Detectives	Santa Rosa PMSA, CA	Y	57860 FQ	76800 AW	96070 TQ	CABLS	10/01-12/01
Police and Detectives	Stockton-Lodi MSA, CA	Y	48300 FQ	62570 AW	87880 TQ	CABLS	10/01-12/01
Police and Detectives	Vallejo-Fairfield-Napa PMSA, CA	Y	64200 FQ	83450 AW	109730 TQ	CABLS	10/01-12/01
Police and Detectives	Ventura PMSA, CA	Y	56000 FQ	79100 AW	105520 TQ	CABLS	10/01-12/01
Police and Detectives	Visalia-Tulare-Porterville MSA, CA	Y	41940 FQ	70960 AW	97580 TQ	CABLS	10/01-12/01
Police and Detectives	Colorado	Y	45130 FQ	63680 AW	86250 TQ	COBLS	10/01-12/01
Police and Detectives	Boulder-Longmont PMSA, CO	Y	47590 FQ	66950 AW	89740 TQ	COBLS	10/01-12/01
Police and Detectives	Colorado Springs MSA, CO	Y	49580 FQ	60160 AW	74980 TQ	COBLS	10/01-12/01
Police and Detectives	Denver PMSA, CO	Y	52170 FQ	69710 AW	89910 TQ	COBLS	10/01-12/01
Police and Detectives	Fort Collins-Loveland MSA, CO	Y	42020 FQ	62380 AW	84310 TQ	COBLS	10/01-12/01
Police and Detectives	Greeley PMSA, CO	Y	38690 FQ	52470 AW	70740 TQ	COBLS	10/01-12/01
Police and Detectives	Connecticut	Y	46770 FQ	61110 AW	77160 TQ	CTBLS	10/01-12/01
Police and Detectives	Bridgeport PMSA, CT	Y	51580 FQ	64590 AW	76190 TQ	CTBLS	10/01-12/01

AAW	Average annual wage	**AOH**	Average offered, high	**ASH**	Average starting, high	**H**	Hourly	**M**	Monthly	**S**	Special: hourly and annual
AE	Average entry wage	**AOL**	Average offered, low	**ASL**	Average starting, low	**HI**	Highest wage paid	**MTC**	Median total compensation	**TQ**	Third quartile wage
AEX	Average experienced wage	**APH**	Average pay, high range	**AW**	Average wage paid	**HR**	High end range	**MW**	Median wage paid	**W**	Weekly
AO	Average offered	**APL**	Average pay, low range	**FQ**	First quartile wage	**LR**	Low end range	**SQ**	Second quartile wage	**Y**	Yearly

Occupation/Type/Industry	Location	Per	Low	Mid	High	Source	Date
First-Line Supervisor/Manager							
Police and Detectives	Danbury PMSA, CT	Y	44290 FQ	59350 AW	75250 TQ	CTBLS	10/01-12/01
Police and Detectives	Hartford MSA, CT	Y	50180 FQ	63010 AW	78230 TQ	CTBLS	10/01-12/01
Police and Detectives	New Haven-Meriden PMSA, CT	Y	49650 FQ	61410 AW	77440 TQ	CTBLS	10/01-12/01
Police and Detectives	New London-Norwich MSA, CT-RI	Y	48830 FQ	55900 AW	67450 TQ	CTBLS	10/01-12/01
Police and Detectives	Stamford-Norwalk PMSA, CT	Y	31160 FQ	58840 AW	85850 TQ	CTBLS	10/01-12/01
Police and Detectives	Delaware	Y	50250 FQ	66740 AW	87320 TQ	DEBLS	10/01-12/01
Police and Detectives	Wilmington-Newark PMSA, DE-MD	Y	36670 FQ	58710 AW	82810 TQ	DEBLS	10/01-12/01
Police and Detectives	District of Columbia	Y	51470 FQ	80760 AW	108910 TQ	DCBLS	10/01-12/01
Police and Detectives	Washington PMSA, DC-MD-VA-WV	Y	47900 FQ	75830 AW	105510 TQ	DCBLS	10/01-12/01
Police and Detectives	Florida	Y	39550 FQ	64110 AW	94410 TQ	FLBLS	10/01-12/01
Police and Detectives	Daytona Beach MSA, FL	Y	35510 FQ	53040 AW	73990 TQ	FLBLS	10/01-12/01
Police and Detectives	Fort Lauderdale PMSA, FL	Y	45760 FQ	69200 AW	92210 TQ	FLBLS	10/01-12/01
Police and Detectives	Fort Myers-Cape Coral MSA, FL	Y	41650 FQ	58870 AW	76070 TQ	FLBLS	10/01-12/01
Police and Detectives	Fort Pierce-Port St. Lucie MSA, FL	Y	41440 FQ	57830 AW	75610 TQ	FLBLS	10/01-12/01
Police and Detectives	Gainesville MSA, FL	Y	43210 FQ	61230 AW	80790 TQ	FLBLS	10/01-12/01
Police and Detectives	Jacksonville MSA, FL	Y	41350 FQ	63500 AW	90600 TQ	FLBLS	10/01-12/01
Police and Detectives	Lakeland-Winter Haven MSA, FL	Y	37390 FQ	55260 AW	73670 TQ	FLBLS	10/01-12/01
Police and Detectives	Melbourne-Titusville-Palm Bay MSA, FL	Y	40730 FQ	55610 AW	72190 TQ	FLBLS	10/01-12/01
Police and Detectives	Miami PMSA, FL	Y	56730 FQ	79210 AW	108340 TQ	FLBLS	10/01-12/01
Police and Detectives	Ocala MSA, FL	Y	43640 FQ	63750 AW	89430 TQ	FLBLS	10/01-12/01
Police and Detectives	Orlando MSA, FL	Y	40670 FQ	62710 AW	89370 TQ	FLBLS	10/01-12/01
Police and Detectives	Pensacola MSA, FL	Y	33370 FQ	57220 AW	97930 TQ	FLBLS	10/01-12/01
Police and Detectives	Sarasota-Bradenton MSA, FL	Y	44370 FQ	61140 AW	77000 TQ	FLBLS	10/01-12/01
Police and Detectives	Tallahassee MSA, FL	Y	37500 FQ	60310 AW	105700 TQ	FLBLS	10/01-12/01
Police and Detectives	Tampa-St. Petersburg-Clearwater MSA, FL	Y	39890 FQ	62630 AW	91220 TQ	FLBLS	10/01-12/01
Police and Detectives	West Palm Beach-Boca Raton MSA, FL	Y	52070 FQ	74290 AW	123960 TQ	FLBLS	10/01-12/01
Police and Detectives	Georgia	Y	30710 FQ	47690 AW	70040 TQ	GABLS	10/01-12/01
Police and Detectives	Atlanta MSA, GA	Y	35060 FQ	52580 AW	72960 TQ	GABLS	10/01-12/01
Police and Detectives	Augusta-Aiken MSA, GA-SC	Y	26210 FQ	39430 AW	57410 TQ	GABLS	10/01-12/01
Police and Detectives	Columbus MSA, GA-AL	Y	29350 FQ	43620 AW	63060 TQ	GABLS	10/01-12/01
Police and Detectives	Macon MSA, GA	Y	31030 FQ	42990 AW	59760 TQ	GABLS	10/01-12/01
Police and Detectives	Savannah MSA, GA	Y	26700 FQ	44820 AW	67580 TQ	GABLS	10/01-12/01
Police and Detectives	Hawaii	Y	45430 FQ	54860 AW	69090 TQ	HIBLS	10/01-12/01
Police and Detectives	Idaho	Y	31100 FQ	46340 AW	64820 TQ	IDBLS	10/01-12/01
Police and Detectives	Boise City MSA, ID	Y	31220 FQ	50050 AW	79830 TQ	IDBLS	10/01-12/01
Police and Detectives	Illinois	Y	39060 FQ	58480 AW	83480 TQ	ILBLS	10/01-12/01
Police and Detectives	Champaign-Urbana MSA, IL	Y	41460 FQ	54780 AW	71290 TQ	ILBLS	10/01-12/01
Police and Detectives	Chicago PMSA, IL	Y	39590 FQ	59600 AW	84250 TQ	ILBLS	10/01-12/01
Police and Detectives	Peoria-Pekin MSA, IL	Y	28550 FQ	57180 AW	74440 TQ	ILBLS	10/01-12/01
Police and Detectives	Rockford MSA, IL	Y	40450 FQ	59890 AW	81900 TQ	ILBLS	10/01-12/01
Police and Detectives	Indiana	Y	32650 FQ	47170 AW	58610 TQ	INBLS	10/01-12/01
Police and Detectives	Elkhart-Goshen MSA, IN	Y	37740 FQ	46930 AW	57260 TQ	INBLS	10/01-12/01
Police and Detectives	Evansville-Henderson MSA, IN-KY	Y	34100 FQ	46880 AW	56870 TQ	INBLS	10/01-12/01
Police and Detectives	Fort Wayne MSA, IN	Y	38430 FQ	45890 AW	54920 TQ	INBLS	10/01-12/01
Police and Detectives	Gary PMSA, IN	Y	38700 FQ	50520 AW	64890 TQ	INBLS	10/01-12/01
Police and Detectives	Indianapolis MSA, IN	Y	33800 FQ	48220 AW	58900 TQ	INBLS	10/01-12/01
Police and Detectives	Lafayette MSA, IN	Y	31250 FQ	43610 AW	60350 TQ	INBLS	10/01-12/01
Police and Detectives	South Bend MSA, IN	Y	38830 FQ	53840 AW	87970 TQ	INBLS	10/01-12/01
Police and Detectives	Iowa	Y	28170 FQ	46470 AW	70320 TQ	IABLS	10/01-12/01
Police and Detectives	Davenport-Moline-Rock Island MSA, IA-IL	Y	31280 FQ	48830 AW	74280 TQ	IABLS	10/01-12/01
Police and Detectives	Des Moines MSA, IA	Y	36830 FQ	59410 AW	85350 TQ	IABLS	10/01-12/01
Police and Detectives	Kansas	Y	29970 FQ	48030 AW	67610 TQ	KSBLS	10/01-12/01
Police and Detectives	Topeka MSA, KS	Y	38760 FQ	51220 AW	65730 TQ	KSBLS	10/01-12/01
Police and Detectives	Wichita MSA, KS	Y	36200 FQ	45950 AW	57040 TQ	KSBLS	10/01-12/01
Police and Detectives	Kentucky	Y	30700 FQ	47440 AW	69700 TQ	KYBLS	10/01-12/01
Police and Detectives	Lexington MSA, KY	Y	34290 FQ	47700 AW	62290 TQ	KYBLS	10/01-12/01
Police and Detectives	Louisville MSA, KY-IN	Y	35210 FQ	52940 AW	81110 TQ	KYBLS	10/01-12/01
Police and Detectives	Louisiana	Y	24510 FQ	41270 AW	70130 TQ	LABLS	10/01-12/01
Police and Detectives	Baton Rouge MSA, LA	Y	31290 FQ	43610 AW	57030 TQ	LABLS	10/01-12/01

AAW	Average annual wage	**AOH**	Average offered, high	**ASH**	Average starting, high	**H**	Hourly	**M**	Monthly	**S**	Special: hourly and annual
AE	Average entry wage	**AOL**	Average offered, low	**ASL**	Average starting, low	**HI**	Highest wage paid	**MTC**	Median total compensation	**TQ**	Third quartile wage
AEX	Average experienced wage	**APH**	Average pay, high range	**AW**	Average wage paid	**HR**	High end range	**MW**	Median wage paid	**W**	Weekly
AO	Average offered	**APL**	Average pay, low range	**FQ**	First quartile wage	**LR**	Low end range	**SQ**	Second quartile wage	**Y**	Yearly

Occupation/Type/Industry	Location	Per	Low	Mid	High	Source	Date
First-Line Supervisor/Manager							
Police and Detectives	Lake Charles MSA, LA	Y	22770 FQ	31170 AW	40810 TQ	LABLS	10/01-12/01
Police and Detectives	New Orleans MSA, LA	Y	25510 FQ	43070 AW	78930 TQ	LABLS	10/01-12/01
Police and Detectives	Shreveport-Bossier City MSA, LA	Y	18630 FQ	41580 AW	69820 TQ	LABLS	10/01-12/01
Police and Detectives	Maine	Y	32640 FQ	44320 AW	58080 TQ	MEBLS	10/01-12/01
Police and Detectives	Portland MSA, ME	Y	35840 FQ	47620 AW	68480 TQ	MEBLS	10/01-12/01
Police and Detectives	Maryland	Y	39540 FQ	57990 AW	84240 TQ	MDBLS	10/01-12/01
Police and Detectives	Baltimore PMSA, MD	Y	41020 FQ	56650 AW	79390 TQ	MDBLS	10/01-12/01
Police and Detectives	Massachusetts	Y	45000 FQ	63990 AW	86490 TQ	MABLS	10/01-12/01
Police and Detectives	Boston PMSA, MA-NH	Y	44810 FQ	64260 AW	86440 TQ	MABLS	10/01-12/01
Police and Detectives	Brockton PMSA, MA	Y	44390 FQ	62600 AW	85820 TQ	MABLS	10/01-12/01
Police and Detectives	Lawrence PMSA, MA-NH	Y	44110 FQ	60780 AW	84310 TQ	MABLS	10/01-12/01
Police and Detectives	Lowell PMSA, MA-NH	Y	46840 FQ	63300 AW	87520 TQ	MABLS	10/01-12/01
Police and Detectives	New Bedford PMSA, MA	Y	46540 FQ	71210 AW	92470 TQ	MABLS	10/01-12/01
Police and Detectives	Springfield MSA, MA	Y	43620 FQ	63750 AW	89010 TQ	MABLS	10/01-12/01
Police and Detectives	Worcester PMSA, MA-CT	Y	47090 FQ	64180 AW	86920 TQ	MABLS	10/01-12/01
Police and Detectives	Michigan	Y	42900 FQ	58130 AW	73200 TQ	MIBLS	10/01-12/01
Police and Detectives	Ann Arbor PMSA, MI	Y	38810 FQ	57810 AW	73360 TQ	MIBLS	10/01-12/01
Police and Detectives	Detroit PMSA, MI	Y	49580 FQ	62550 AW	76380 TQ	MIBLS	10/01-12/01
Police and Detectives	Grand Rapids-Muskegon-Holland MSA, MI	Y	46890 FQ	55600 AW	69210 TQ	MIBLS	10/01-12/01
Police and Detectives	Kalamazoo-Battle Creek MSA, MI	Y	39740 FQ	55310 AW	72720 TQ	MIBLS	10/01-12/01
Police and Detectives	Lansing-East Lansing MSA, MI	Y	48870 FQ	57820 AW	70330 TQ	MIBLS	10/01-12/01
Police and Detectives	Saginaw-Bay City-Midland MSA, MI	Y	43090 FQ	54300 AW	68310 TQ	MIBLS	10/01-12/01
Police and Detectives	Minnesota	Y	41200 FQ	57960 AW	74260 TQ	MNBLS	10/01-12/01
Police and Detectives	Duluth-Superior MSA, MN-WI	Y	47360 FQ	56260 AW	71030 TQ	MNBLS	10/01-12/01
Police and Detectives	Minneapolis-St. Paul MSA, MN-WI	Y	49970 FQ	63560 AW	78180 TQ	MNBLS	10/01-12/01
Police and Detectives	St. Cloud MSA, MN	Y	45910 FQ	55350 AW	68770 TQ	MNBLS	10/01-12/01
Police and Detectives	Mississippi	Y	22910 FQ	40780 AW	65180 TQ	MSBLS	10/01-12/01
Police and Detectives	Biloxi-Gulfport-Pascagoula MSA, MS	Y	32300 FQ	46610 AW	69350 TQ	MSBLS	10/01-12/01
Police and Detectives	Jackson MSA, MS	Y	32660 FQ	54590 AW	75760 TQ	MSBLS	10/01-12/01
Police and Detectives	Missouri	Y	25980 FQ	47010 AW	70240 TQ	MOBLS	10/01-12/01
Police and Detectives	Kansas City MSA, MO-KS	Y	29770 FQ	54530 AW	77810 TQ	MOBLS	10/01-12/01
Police and Detectives	St. Louis MSA, MO-IL	Y	29330 FQ	46040 AW	71770 TQ	MOBLS	10/01-12/01
Police and Detectives	Springfield MSA, MO	Y	34360 FQ	43570 AW	47770 TQ	MOBLS	10/01-12/01
Police and Detectives	Montana	Y	22040 FQ	39560 AW	63810 TQ	MTBLS	10/01-12/01
Police and Detectives	Billings MSA, MT	Y	39340 FQ	55960 AW	77190 TQ	MTBLS	10/01-12/01
Police and Detectives	Nebraska	Y	29160 FQ	47630 AW	71560 TQ	NEBLS	10/01-12/01
Police and Detectives	Lincoln MSA, NE	Y	39820 FQ	59160 AW	85610 TQ	NEBLS	10/01-12/01
Police and Detectives	Omaha MSA, NE-IA	Y	38570 FQ	54310 AW	75560 TQ	NEBLS	10/01-12/01
Police and Detectives	Nevada	Y	50400 FQ	67530 AW	87810 TQ	NVBLS	10/01-12/01
Police and Detectives	Las Vegas MSA, NV-AZ	Y	50190 FQ	68930 AW	90650 TQ	NVBLS	10/01-12/01
Police and Detectives	Reno MSA, NV	Y	50490 FQ	65810 AW	85720 TQ	NVBLS	10/01-12/01
Police and Detectives	New Hampshire	Y	34500 FQ	50540 AW	70220 TQ	NHBLS	10/01-12/01
Police and Detectives	Nashua PMSA, NH	Y	45260 FQ	61670 AW	73580 TQ	NHBLS	10/01-12/01
Police and Detectives	Portsmouth-Rochester PMSA, NH-ME	Y	38230 FQ	53180 AW	71560 TQ	NHBLS	10/01-12/01
Police and Detectives	New Jersey	Y	58180 FQ	78670 AW	105310 TQ	NJBLS	10/01-12/01
Police and Detectives	Atlantic-Cape May PMSA, NJ	Y	57010 FQ	69340 AW	86530 TQ	NJBLS	10/01-12/01
Police and Detectives	Bergen-Passaic PMSA, NJ	Y	74550 FQ	89490 AW	114840 TQ	NJBLS	10/01-12/01
Police and Detectives	Jersey City PMSA, NJ	Y	61660 FQ	82500 AW	112900 TQ	NJBLS	10/01-12/01
Police and Detectives	Middlesex-Somerset-Hunterdon PMSA, NJ	Y	60860 FQ	80720 AW	102390 TQ	NJBLS	10/01-12/01
Police and Detectives	Monmouth-Ocean PMSA, NJ	Y	40910 FQ	81420 AW	113960 TQ	NJBLS	10/01-12/01
Police and Detectives	Newark PMSA, NJ	Y	45730 FQ	73970 AW	99030 TQ	NJBLS	10/01-12/01
Police and Detectives	New Mexico	Y	30660 FQ	46220 AW	66490 TQ	NMBLS	10/01-12/01
Police and Detectives	Albuquerque MSA, NM	Y	31320 FQ	47660 AW	70880 TQ	NMBLS	10/01-12/01
Police and Detectives	Las Cruces MSA, NM	Y	38810 FQ	51790 AW	70070 TQ	NMBLS	10/01-12/01
Police and Detectives	New York	Y	49860 FQ	70640 AW	95520 TQ	NYBLS	10/01-12/01
Police and Detectives	Albany-Schenectady-Troy MSA, NY	Y	48570 FQ	63680 AW	81370 TQ	NYBLS	10/01-12/01
Police and Detectives	Binghamton MSA, NY	Y	33400 FQ	57320 AW	100890 TQ	NYBLS	10/01-12/01
Police and Detectives	Buffalo-Niagara Falls MSA, NY	Y	47050 FQ	59840 AW	77040 TQ	NYBLS	10/01-12/01
Police and Detectives	Dutchess County PMSA, NY	Y	49370 FQ	60920 AW	74260 TQ	NYBLS	10/01-12/01
Police and Detectives	Nassau-Suffolk PMSA, NY	Y	69320 FQ	92890 AW	118370 TQ	NYBLS	10/01-12/01
Police and Detectives	Newburgh PMSA, NY-PA	Y	42460 FQ	57940 AW	76250 TQ	NYBLS	10/01-12/01

AAW Average annual wage **AE** Average entry wage **AEX** Average experienced wage **AO** Average offered **AOH** Average offered, high **AOL** Average offered, low **APH** Average pay, high range **APL** Average pay, low range **ASH** Average starting, high **ASL** Average starting, low **AW** Average wage paid **FQ** First quartile wage **H** Hourly **HI** Highest wage paid **HR** High end range **LR** Low end range **M** Monthly **MTC** Median total compensation **MW** Median wage paid **SQ** Second quartile wage **S** Special: hourly and annual **TQ** Third quartile wage **W** Weekly **Y** Yearly

Occupation/Type/Industry	Location	Per	Low	Mid	High	Source	Date
First-Line Supervisor/Manager							
Police and Detectives	Rochester MSA, NY	Y	41590 FQ	56420 AW	75780 TQ	NYBLS	10/01-12/01
Police and Detectives	Syracuse MSA, NY	Y	28530 FQ	49290 AW	68870 TQ	NYBLS	10/01-12/01
Police and Detectives	Utica-Rome MSA, NY	Y	28160 FQ	41450 AW	57410 TQ	NYBLS	10/01-12/01
Police and Detectives	North Carolina	Y	29440 FQ	44830 AW	66720 TQ	NCBLS	10/01-12/01
Police and Detectives	Charlotte-Gastonia-Rock Hill MSA, NC-SC	Y	31310 FQ	50450 AW	72060 TQ	NCBLS	10/01-12/01
Police and Detectives	Greensboro-Winston-Salem-High Point MSA, NC	Y	33500 FQ	50040 AW	70140 TQ	NCBLS	10/01-12/01
Police and Detectives	Hickory-Morganton-Lenoir MSA, NC	Y	29640 FQ	39570 AW	53610 TQ	NCBLS	10/01-12/01
Police and Detectives	Raleigh-Durham-Chapel Hill MSA, NC	Y	27550 FQ	48070 AW	69570 TQ	NCBLS	10/01-12/01
Police and Detectives	Wilmington MSA, NC	Y	29670 FQ	41390 AW	55580 TQ	NCBLS	10/01-12/01
Police and Detectives	North Dakota	Y	32850 FQ	47440 AW	66240 TQ	NDBLS	10/01-12/01
Police and Detectives	Fargo-Moorhead MSA, ND-MN	Y	39270 FQ	53940 AW	76880 TQ	NDBLS	10/01-12/01
Police and Detectives	Ohio	Y	38150 FQ	54480 AW	73700 TQ	OHBLS	10/01-12/01
Police and Detectives	Akron PMSA, OH	Y	42560 FQ	60980 AW	89730 TQ	OHBLS	10/01-12/01
Police and Detectives	Canton-Massillon MSA, OH	Y	27900 FQ	55310 AW	75560 TQ	OHBLS	10/01-12/01
Police and Detectives	Cincinnati PMSA, OH-KY-IN	Y	40510 FQ	56310 AW	74300 TQ	OHBLS	10/01-12/01
Police and Detectives	Cleveland-Lorain-Elyria PMSA, OH	Y	47640 FQ	57530 AW	72660 TQ	OHBLS	10/01-12/01
Police and Detectives	Columbus MSA, OH	Y	33670 FQ	55520 AW	78230 TQ	OHBLS	10/01-12/01
Police and Detectives	Dayton-Springfield MSA, OH	Y	37370 FQ	55660 AW	73940 TQ	OHBLS	10/01-12/01
Police and Detectives	Hamilton-Middletown PMSA, OH	Y	44210 FQ	57050 AW	72880 TQ	OHBLS	10/01-12/01
Police and Detectives	Mansfield MSA, OH	Y	31130 FQ	44050 AW	58440 TQ	OHBLS	10/01-12/01
Police and Detectives	Toledo MSA, OH	Y	39020 FQ	50750 AW	70400 TQ	OHBLS	10/01-12/01
Police and Detectives	Youngstown-Warren MSA, OH	Y	30610 FQ	45850 AW	64160 TQ	OHBLS	10/01-12/01
Police and Detectives	Oklahoma	Y	20460 FQ	39340 AW	60480 TQ	OKBLS	10/01-12/01
Police and Detectives	Oklahoma City MSA, OK	Y	29840 FQ	51320 AW	75260 TQ	OKBLS	10/01-12/01
Police and Detectives	Tulsa MSA, OK	Y	18690 FQ	40120 AW	55630 TQ	OKBLS	10/01-12/01
Police and Detectives	Oregon	Y	44340 FQ	62290 AW	82400 TQ	ORBLS	10/01-12/01
Police and Detectives	Eugene-Springfield MSA, OR	Y	48800 FQ	62970 AW	83470 TQ	ORBLS	10/01-12/01
Police and Detectives	Medford-Ashland MSA, OR	Y	41030 FQ	53640 AW	73020 TQ	ORBLS	10/01-12/01
Police and Detectives	Portland-Vancouver PMSA, OR-WA	Y	57460 FQ	67300 AW	85170 TQ	ORBLS	10/01-12/01
Police and Detectives	Salem PMSA, OR	Y	51570 FQ	65910 AW	84520 TQ	ORBLS	10/01-12/01
Police and Detectives	Pennsylvania	Y	37130 FQ	61400 AW	87840 TQ	PABLS	10/01-12/01
Police and Detectives	Allentown-Bethlehem-Easton MSA, PA	Y	37940 FQ	57690 AW	75720 TQ	PABLS	10/01-12/01
Police and Detectives	Harrisburg-Lebanon-Carlisle MSA, PA	Y	59750 FQ	77530 AW	95460 TQ	PABLS	10/01-12/01
Police and Detectives	Johnstown MSA, PA	Y	28000 FQ	46240 AW	83610 TQ	PABLS	10/01-12/01
Police and Detectives	Lancaster MSA, PA	Y	46010 FQ	64520 AW	92110 TQ	PABLS	10/01-12/01
Police and Detectives	Philadelphia PMSA, PA-NJ	Y	54800 FQ	69890 AW	90190 TQ	PABLS	10/01-12/01
Police and Detectives	Pittsburgh MSA, PA	Y	35900 FQ	60470 AW	87970 TQ	PABLS	10/01-12/01
Police and Detectives	Reading MSA, PA	Y	39440 FQ	50200 AW	61700 TQ	PABLS	10/01-12/01
Police and Detectives	Scranton-Wilkes-Barre-Hazleton MSA, PA	Y	34520 FQ	55440 AW	84560 TQ	PABLS	10/01-12/01
Police and Detectives	York MSA, PA	Y	46980 FQ	55850 AW	69860 TQ	PABLS	10/01-12/01
Police and Detectives	Rhode Island	Y	45150 FQ	58380 AW	74290 TQ	RIBLS	10/01-12/01
Police and Detectives	Providence-Fall River-Warwick MSA, RI-MA	Y	45180 FQ	58710 AW	75130 TQ	RIBLS	10/01-12/01
Police and Detectives	South Carolina	Y	24880 FQ	38980 AW	56030 TQ	SCBLS	10/01-12/01
Police and Detectives	Charleston-North Charleston MSA, SC	Y	26640 FQ	45490 AW	65960 TQ	SCBLS	10/01-12/01
Police and Detectives	Columbia MSA, SC	Y	28090 FQ	41190 AW	57490 TQ	SCBLS	10/01-12/01
Police and Detectives	Greenville-Spartanburg-Anderson MSA, SC	Y	26730 FQ	38960 AW	53260 TQ	SCBLS	10/01-12/01
Police and Detectives	South Dakota	Y	31370 FQ	44070 AW	63710 TQ	SDBLS	10/01-12/01
Police and Detectives	Sioux Falls MSA, SD	Y	33980 FQ	53260 AW	83570 TQ	SDBLS	10/01-12/01
Police and Detectives	Tennessee	Y	30800 FQ	47560 AW	61110 TQ	TNBLS	10/01-12/01
Police and Detectives	Chattanooga MSA, TN-GA	Y	29240 FQ	46370 AW	69730 TQ	TNBLS	10/01-12/01
Police and Detectives	Clarksville-Hopkinsville MSA, TN-KY	Y	30530 FQ	41850 AW	56100 TQ	TNBLS	10/01-12/01
Police and Detectives	Johnson City-Kingsport-Bristol MSA, TN-VA	Y	29850 FQ	42690 AW	56790 TQ	TNBLS	10/01-12/01
Police and Detectives	Knoxville MSA, TN	Y	32640 FQ	45460 AW	60340 TQ	TNBLS	10/01-12/01
Police and Detectives	Memphis MSA, TN-AR-MS	Y	28660 FQ	50410 AW	64480 TQ	TNBLS	10/01-12/01
Police and Detectives	Texas	Y	35800 FQ	56320 AW	80580 TQ	TXBLS	10/01-12/01

AAW	Average annual wage	**AOH**	Average offered, high	**ASH**	Average starting, high	**H**	Hourly	**M**	Monthly	**S**	Special: hourly and annual
AE	Average entry wage	**AOL**	Average offered, low	**ASL**	Average starting, low	**HI**	Highest wage paid	**MTC**	Median total compensation	**TQ**	Third quartile wage
AEX	Average experienced wage	**APH**	Average pay, high range	**AW**	Average wage paid	**HR**	High end range	**MW**	Median wage paid	**W**	Weekly
AO	Average offered	**APL**	Average pay, low range	**FQ**	First quartile wage	**LR**	Low end range	**SQ**	Second quartile wage	**Y**	Yearly

Occupation/Type/Industry	Location	Per	Low	Mid	High	Source	Date
First-Line Supervisor/Manager							
Police and Detectives	Austin-San Marcos MSA, TX	Y	49680 FQ	66230 AW	87810 TQ	TXBLS	10/01-12/01
Police and Detectives	Beaumont-Port Arthur MSA, TX	Y	27100 FQ	44160 AW	61220 TQ	TXBLS	10/01-12/01
Police and Detectives	Brazoria PMSA, TX	Y	27840 FQ	44440 AW	58270 TQ	TXBLS	10/01-12/01
Police and Detectives	Brownsville-Harlingen-San Benito MSA, TX	Y	32210 FQ	56880 AW	77140 TQ	TXBLS	10/01-12/01
Police and Detectives	Corpus Christi MSA, TX	Y	33160 FQ	58000 AW	76140 TQ	TXBLS	10/01-12/01
Police and Detectives	Dallas PMSA, TX	Y	36950 FQ	59960 AW	82580 TQ	TXBLS	10/01-12/01
Police and Detectives	El Paso MSA, TX	Y	39440 FQ	53020 AW	82460 TQ	TXBLS	10/01-12/01
Police and Detectives	Fort Worth-Arlington PMSA, TX	Y	44610 FQ	60420 AW	78490 TQ	TXBLS	10/01-12/01
Police and Detectives	Galveston-Texas City PMSA, TX	Y	37780 FQ	58810 AW	88000 TQ	TXBLS	10/01-12/01
Police and Detectives	Houston PMSA, TX	Y	40410 FQ	64170 AW	92690 TQ	TXBLS	10/01-12/01
Police and Detectives	Killeen-Temple MSA, TX	Y	25610 FQ	40120 AW	62720 TQ	TXBLS	10/01-12/01
Police and Detectives	Longview-Marshall MSA, TX	Y	21970 FQ	43960 AW	68760 TQ	TXBLS	10/01-12/01
Police and Detectives	McAllen-Edinburg-Mission MSA, TX	Y	29420 FQ	50750 AW	79130 TQ	TXBLS	10/01-12/01
Police and Detectives	Odessa-Midland MSA, TX	Y	38580 FQ	50120 AW	68960 TQ	TXBLS	10/01-12/01
Police and Detectives	San Antonio MSA, TX	Y	38390 FQ	59590 AW	89100 TQ	TXBLS	10/01-12/01
Police and Detectives	Tyler MSA, TX	Y	39350 FQ	48850 AW	64630 TQ	TXBLS	10/01-12/01
Police and Detectives	Waco MSA, TX	Y	22880 FQ	44530 AW	67190 TQ	TXBLS	10/01-12/01
Police and Detectives	Utah	Y	40350 FQ	53840 AW	69880 TQ	UTBLS	10/01-12/01
Police and Detectives	Provo-Orem MSA, UT	Y	40710 FQ	51580 AW	60900 TQ	UTBLS	10/01-12/01
Police and Detectives	Salt Lake City-Ogden MSA, UT	Y	42250 FQ	56200 AW	72110 TQ	UTBLS	10/01-12/01
Police and Detectives	Vermont	Y	34400 FQ	51560 AW	72100 TQ	VTBLS	10/01-12/01
Police and Detectives	Burlington MSA, VT	Y	38890 FQ	60260 AW	88410 TQ	VTBLS	10/01-12/01
Police and Detectives	Virginia	Y	36640 FQ	59850 AW	90140 TQ	VABLS	10/01-12/01
Police and Detectives	Lynchburg MSA, VA	Y	32940 FQ	51500 AW	77460 TQ	VABLS	10/01-12/01
Police and Detectives	Norfolk-Virginia Beach-Newport News MSA, VA-NC	Y	35830 FQ	52740 AW	74160 TQ	VABLS	10/01-12/01
Police and Detectives	Richmond-Petersburg MSA, VA	Y	39270 FQ	59210 AW	84580 TQ	VABLS	10/01-12/01
Police and Detectives	Roanoke MSA, VA	Y	38720 FQ	52330 AW	70610 TQ	VABLS	10/01-12/01
Police and Detectives	Washington	Y	49230 FQ	65590 AW	85850 TQ	WABLS	10/01-12/01
Police and Detectives	Bremerton PMSA, WA	Y	32850 FQ	57890 AW	80910 TQ	WABLS	10/01-12/01
Police and Detectives	Olympia PMSA, WA	Y	52750 FQ	67110 AW	85840 TQ	WABLS	10/01-12/01
Police and Detectives	Richland-Kennewick-Pasco MSA, WA	Y	58990 FQ	71230 AW	97960 TQ	WABLS	10/01-12/01
Police and Detectives	Seattle-Bellevue-Everett PMSA, WA	Y	57470 FQ	70210 AW	89110 TQ	WABLS	10/01-12/01
Police and Detectives	Tacoma PMSA, WA	Y	26460 FQ	59580 AW	85990 TQ	WABLS	10/01-12/01
Police and Detectives	Yakima MSA, WA	Y	47020 FQ	61990 AW	85570 TQ	WABLS	10/01-12/01
Police and Detectives	West Virginia	Y	23280 FQ	41570 AW	67210 TQ	WVBLS	10/01-12/01
Police and Detectives	Charleston MSA, WV	Y	31890 FQ	53280 AW	85070 TQ	WVBLS	10/01-12/01
Police and Detectives	Huntington-Ashland MSA, WV-KY-OH	Y	19250 FQ	37070 AW	56810 TQ	WVBLS	10/01-12/01
Police and Detectives	Wisconsin	Y	39420 FQ	55080 AW	73580 TQ	WIBLS	10/01-12/01
Police and Detectives	Appleton-Oshkosh-Neenah MSA, WI	Y	37340 FQ	54970 AW	72130 TQ	WIBLS	10/01-12/01
Police and Detectives	Green Bay MSA, WI	Y	39610 FQ	48010 AW	59400 TQ	WIBLS	10/01-12/01
Police and Detectives	Madison MSA, WI	Y	45620 FQ	63780 AW	84820 TQ	WIBLS	10/01-12/01
Police and Detectives	Milwaukee-Waukesha PMSA, WI	Y	48850 FQ	62460 AW	79860 TQ	WIBLS	10/01-12/01
Police and Detectives	Racine PMSA, WI	Y	37080 FQ	58420 AW	74440 TQ	WIBLS	10/01-12/01
Police and Detectives	Wyoming	Y	30580 FQ	44430 AW	59070 TQ	WYBLS	10/01-12/01
Police and Detectives	Cheyenne MSA, WY	Y	38400 FQ	48190 AW	66530 TQ	WYBLS	10/01-12/01
Police and Detectives	Puerto Rico	Y	19880 FQ	25790 AW	29260 TQ	PRBLS	10/01-12/01
Production and Operating Workers	Alabama	H	11.10 FQ	19.87 AW	30.81 TQ	ALBLS	10/01-12/01
Production and Operating Workers	Birmingham MSA, AL	H	12.89 FQ	21.92 AW	33.42 TQ	ALBLS	10/01-12/01
Production and Operating Workers	Huntsville MSA, AL	H	11.78 FQ	21.71 AW	35.01 TQ	ALBLS	10/01-12/01
Production and Operating Workers	Mobile MSA, AL	H	11.44 FQ	21.35 AW	32.05 TQ	ALBLS	10/01-12/01
Production and Operating Workers	Montgomery MSA, AL	H	10.62 FQ	17.97 AW	27.47 TQ	ALBLS	10/01-12/01
Production and Operating Workers	Alaska	H	12.52 FQ	28.82 AW	48.30 TQ	AKBLS	10/01-12/01
Production and Operating Workers	Anchorage MSA, AK	H	15.37 FQ	26.42 AW	43.62 TQ	AKBLS	10/01-12/01
Production and Operating Workers	Arizona	H	11.83 FQ	20.51 AW	32.24 TQ	AZBLS	10/01-12/01
Production and Operating Workers	Phoenix-Mesa MSA, AZ	H	12.25 FQ	21.07 AW	33.00 TQ	AZBLS	10/01-12/01
Production and Operating Workers	Tucson MSA, AZ	H	10.96 FQ	18.22 AW	27.69 TQ	AZBLS	10/01-12/01
Production and Operating Workers	Arkansas	H	10.11 FQ	17.93 AW	27.77 TQ	ARBLS	10/01-12/01

AAW Average annual wage **AOH** Average offered, high **ASH** Average starting, high **H** Hourly **M** Monthly **S** Special: hourly and annual
AE Average entry wage **AOL** Average offered, low **ASL** Average starting, low **HI** Highest wage paid **MTC** Median total compensation **TQ** Third quartile wage
AEX Average experienced wage **APH** Average pay, high range **AW** Average wage paid **HR** High end range **MW** Median wage paid **W** Weekly
AO Average offered **APL** Average pay, low range **FQ** First quartile wage **LR** Low end range **SQ** Second quartile wage **Y** Yearly

Occupation/Type/Industry	Location	Per	Low	Mid	High	Source	Date
First-Line Supervisor/Manager							
Production and Operating Workers	Fayetteville-Springdale-Rogers MSA, AR	H	10.05 FQ	16.26 AW	24.37 TQ	ARBLS	10/01-12/01
Production and Operating Workers	Fort Smith MSA, AR-OK	H	9.96 FQ	16.69 AW	25.56 TQ	ARBLS	10/01-12/01
Production and Operating Workers	Little Rock-North Little Rock MSA, AR	H	11.88 FQ	19.50 AW	28.43 TQ	ARBLS	10/01-12/01
Production and Operating Workers	California	H	11.93 FQ	22.59 AW	35.59 TQ	CABLS	10/01-12/01
Production and Operating Workers	Bakersfield MSA, CA	H	11.89 FQ	23.56 AW	38.44 TQ	CABLS	10/01-12/01
Production and Operating Workers	Chico-Paradise MSA, CA	H	12.59 FQ	20.70 AW	31.06 TQ	CABLS	10/01-12/01
Production and Operating Workers	Fresno MSA, CA	H	11.77 FQ	19.08 AW	29.40 TQ	CABLS	10/01-12/01
Production and Operating Workers	Los Angeles-Long Beach PMSA, CA	H	10.99 FQ	21.20 AW	34.06 TQ	CABLS	10/01-12/01
Production and Operating Workers	Merced MSA, CA	H	12.83 FQ	19.94 AW	28.47 TQ	CABLS	10/01-12/01
Production and Operating Workers	Modesto MSA, CA	H	11.93 FQ	20.43 AW	32.38 TQ	CABLS	10/01-12/01
Production and Operating Workers	Oakland PMSA, CA	H	15.09 FQ	26.16 AW	39.75 TQ	CABLS	10/01-12/01
Production and Operating Workers	Orange County PMSA, CA	H	12.26 FQ	22.38 AW	34.48 TQ	CABLS	10/01-12/01
Production and Operating Workers	Redding MSA, CA	H	10.95 FQ	20.55 AW	32.70 TQ	CABLS	10/01-12/01
Production and Operating Workers	Riverside-San Bernardino PMSA, CA	H	11.92 FQ	20.84 AW	32.20 TQ	CABLS	10/01-12/01
Production and Operating Workers	Sacramento PMSA, CA	H	12.31 FQ	21.54 AW	32.08 TQ	CABLS	10/01-12/01
Production and Operating Workers	Salinas MSA, CA	H	10.53 FQ	21.82 AW	34.30 TQ	CABLS	10/01-12/01
Production and Operating Workers	San Diego MSA, CA	H	11.43 FQ	22.71 AW	35.72 TQ	CABLS	10/01-12/01
Production and Operating Workers	San Francisco PMSA, CA	H	13.66 FQ	27.35 AW	42.53 TQ	CABLS	10/01-12/01
Production and Operating Workers	San Jose PMSA, CA	H	16.72 FQ	28.38 AW	43.88 TQ	CABLS	10/01-12/01
Production and Operating Workers	San Luis Obispo-Atascadero-Paso Robles MSA, CA	H	13.33 FQ	21.63 AW	33.39 TQ	CABLS	10/01-12/01
Production and Operating Workers	Santa Barbara-Santa Maria-Lompoc MSA, CA	H	12.34 FQ	22.53 AW	35.33 TQ	CABLS	10/01-12/01
Production and Operating Workers	Santa Cruz-Watsonville PMSA, CA	H	11.51 FQ	22.52 AW	35.87 TQ	CABLS	10/01-12/01
Production and Operating Workers	Santa Rosa PMSA, CA	H	12.69 FQ	22.51 AW	33.46 TQ	CABLS	10/01-12/01
Production and Operating Workers	Stockton-Lodi MSA, CA	H	12.01 FQ	21.53 AW	33.92 TQ	CABLS	10/01-12/01
Production and Operating Workers	Vallejo-Fairfield-Napa PMSA, CA	H	14.01 FQ	23.38 AW	38.31 TQ	CABLS	10/01-12/01
Production and Operating Workers	Ventura PMSA, CA	H	12.74 FQ	23.19 AW	35.02 TQ	CABLS	10/01-12/01
Production and Operating Workers	Visalia-Tulare-Porterville MSA, CA	H	11.26 FQ	18.56 AW	26.72 TQ	CABLS	10/01-12/01
Production and Operating Workers	Colorado	H	12.94 FQ	21.64 AW	32.48 TQ	COBLS	10/01-12/01
Production and Operating Workers	Boulder-Longmont PMSA, CO	H	14.22 FQ	23.46 AW	34.86 TQ	COBLS	10/01-12/01
Production and Operating Workers	Colorado Springs MSA, CO	H	12.99 FQ	21.42 AW	31.86 TQ	COBLS	10/01-12/01
Production and Operating Workers	Denver PMSA, CO	H	13.12 FQ	21.53 AW	32.26 TQ	COBLS	10/01-12/01
Production and Operating Workers	Fort Collins-Loveland MSA, CO	H	13.67 FQ	23.28 AW	34.64 TQ	COBLS	10/01-12/01
Production and Operating Workers	Greeley PMSA, CO	H	14.01 FQ	20.64 AW	28.83 TQ	COBLS	10/01-12/01
Production and Operating Workers	Connecticut	H	15.00 FQ	25.41 AW	38.20 TQ	CTBLS	10/01-12/01
Production and Operating Workers	Bridgeport PMSA, CT	H	15.69 FQ	25.70 AW	37.06 TQ	CTBLS	10/01-12/01
Production and Operating Workers	Danbury PMSA, CT	H	14.89 FQ	25.07 AW	36.54 TQ	CTBLS	10/01-12/01
Production and Operating Workers	Hartford MSA, CT	H	14.92 FQ	24.64 AW	35.69 TQ	CTBLS	10/01-12/01
Production and Operating Workers	New Haven-Meriden PMSA, CT	H	14.32 FQ	24.94 AW	37.43 TQ	CTBLS	10/01-12/01
Production and Operating Workers	New London-Norwich MSA, CT-RI	H	17.17 FQ	27.31 AW	40.77 TQ	CTBLS	10/01-12/01
Production and Operating Workers	Stamford-Norwalk PMSA, CT	H	16.03 FQ	29.10 AW	52.21 TQ	CTBLS	10/01-12/01
Production and Operating Workers	Waterbury PMSA, CT	H	15.08 FQ	24.91 AW	39.37 TQ	CTBLS	10/01-12/01
Production and Operating Workers	Delaware	H	12.85 FQ	24.02 AW	37.51 TQ	DEBLS	10/01-12/01
Production and Operating Workers	Wilmington-Newark PMSA, DE-MD	H	14.36 FQ	25.67 AW	39.21 TQ	DEBLS	10/01-12/01
Production and Operating Workers	District of Columbia	H	7.67 FQ	21.46 AW	35.57 TQ	DCBLS	10/01-12/01
Production and Operating Workers	Washington PMSA, DC-MD-VA-WV	H	12.26 FQ	22.51 AW	34.36 TQ	DCBLS	10/01-12/01
Production and Operating Workers	Florida	H	11.24 FQ	20.05 AW	32.29 TQ	FLBLS	10/01-12/01
Production and Operating Workers	Daytona Beach MSA, FL	H	10.92 FQ	18.40 AW	29.12 TQ	FLBLS	10/01-12/01
Production and Operating Workers	Fort Lauderdale PMSA, FL	H	10.25 FQ	19.62 AW	32.35 TQ	FLBLS	10/01-12/01
Production and Operating Workers	Fort Myers-Cape Coral MSA, FL	H	11.70 FQ	19.54 AW	30.93 TQ	FLBLS	10/01-12/01
Production and Operating Workers	Fort Pierce-Port St. Lucie MSA, FL	H	13.02 FQ	23.18 AW	36.29 TQ	FLBLS	10/01-12/01
Production and Operating Workers	Fort Walton Beach MSA, FL	H	11.01 FQ	19.91 AW	31.34 TQ	FLBLS	10/01-12/01
Production and Operating Workers	Gainesville MSA, FL	H	9.08 FQ	17.95 AW	29.11 TQ	FLBLS	10/01-12/01
Production and Operating Workers	Jacksonville MSA, FL	H	11.84 FQ	20.01 AW	30.12 TQ	FLBLS	10/01-12/01
Production and Operating Workers	Lakeland-Winter Haven MSA, FL	H	11.96 FQ	20.18 AW	30.14 TQ	FLBLS	10/01-12/01

AAW	Average annual wage	AOH	Average offered, high	ASH	Average starting, high	H	Hourly	M	Monthly	S	Special: hourly and annual
AE	Average entry wage	AOL	Average offered, low	ASL	Average starting, low	HI	Highest wage paid	MTC	Median total compensation	TQ	Third quartile wage
AEX	Average experienced wage	APH	Average pay, high range	AW	Average wage paid	HR	High end range	MW	Median wage paid	W	Weekly
AO	Average offered	APL	Average pay, low range	FQ	First quartile wage	LR	Low end range	SQ	Second quartile wage	Y	Yearly

Occupation/Type/Industry	Location	Per	Low	Mid	High	Source	Date
First-Line Supervisor/Manager							
Production and Operating Workers	Melbourne-Titusville-Palm Bay MSA, FL	H	10.97 FQ	19.24 AW	30.63 TQ	FLBLS	10/01-12/01
Production and Operating Workers	Miami PMSA, FL	H	11.28 FQ	22.91 AW	39.10 TQ	FLBLS	10/01-12/01
Production and Operating Workers	Naples MSA, FL	H	10.90 FQ	19.07 AW	28.79 TQ	FLBLS	10/01-12/01
Production and Operating Workers	Ocala MSA, FL	H	11.15 FQ	18.21 AW	27.30 TQ	FLBLS	10/01-12/01
Production and Operating Workers	Orlando MSA, FL	H	11.71 FQ	20.04 AW	32.98 TQ	FLBLS	10/01-12/01
Production and Operating Workers	Pensacola MSA, FL	H	10.86 FQ	20.60 AW	34.63 TQ	FLBLS	10/01-12/01
Production and Operating Workers	Sarasota-Bradenton MSA, FL	H	10.97 FQ	18.84 AW	30.00 TQ	FLBLS	10/01-12/01
Production and Operating Workers	Tallahassee MSA, FL	H	10.73 FQ	17.59 AW	25.96 TQ	FLBLS	10/01-12/01
Production and Operating Workers	Tampa-St. Petersburg-Clearwater MSA, FL	H	11.59 FQ	19.05 AW	29.05 TQ	FLBLS	10/01-12/01
Production and Operating Workers	West Palm Beach-Boca Raton MSA, FL	H	11.84 FQ	21.47 AW	33.57 TQ	FLBLS	10/01-12/01
Production and Operating Workers	Georgia	H	12.25 FQ	20.65 AW	31.05 TQ	GABLS	10/01-12/01
Production and Operating Workers	Atlanta MSA, GA	H	13.40 FQ	21.75 AW	32.40 TQ	GABLS	10/01-12/01
Production and Operating Workers	Augusta-Aiken MSA, GA-SC	H	13.46 FQ	23.41 AW	34.63 TQ	GABLS	10/01-12/01
Production and Operating Workers	Columbus MSA, GA-AL	H	12.62 FQ	20.83 AW	27.96 TQ	GABLS	10/01-12/01
Production and Operating Workers	Macon MSA, GA	H	12.44 FQ	21.09 AW	28.66 TQ	GABLS	10/01-12/01
Production and Operating Workers	Savannah MSA, GA	H	13.92 FQ	21.90 AW	31.33 TQ	GABLS	10/01-12/01
Production and Operating Workers	Hawaii	H	10.53 FQ	21.54 AW	34.86 TQ	HIBLS	10/01-12/01
Production and Operating Workers	Honolulu MSA, HI	H	10.70 FQ	21.74 AW	34.57 TQ	HIBLS	10/01-12/01
Production and Operating Workers	Idaho	H	10.65 FQ	18.90 AW	27.41 TQ	IDBLS	10/01-12/01
Production and Operating Workers	Boise City MSA, ID	H	12.55 FQ	19.68 AW	27.01 TQ	IDBLS	10/01-12/01
Production and Operating Workers	Illinois	H	11.08 FQ	20.79 AW	32.40 TQ	ILBLS	10/01-12/01
Production and Operating Workers	Champaign-Urbana MSA, IL	H	10.04 FQ	17.34 AW	27.40 TQ	ILBLS	10/01-12/01
Production and Operating Workers	Chicago PMSA, IL	H	11.05 FQ	21.10 AW	32.85 TQ	ILBLS	10/01-12/01
Production and Operating Workers	Peoria-Pekin MSA, IL	H	12.51 FQ	23.63 AW	40.49 TQ	ILBLS	10/01-12/01
Production and Operating Workers	Rockford MSA, IL	H	12.26 FQ	21.29 AW	32.08 TQ	ILBLS	10/01-12/01
Production and Operating Workers	Springfield MSA, IL	H	11.72 FQ	18.91 AW	27.52 TQ	ILBLS	10/01-12/01
Production and Operating Workers	Indiana	H	12.49 FQ	20.93 AW	31.21 TQ	INBLS	10/01-12/01
Production and Operating Workers	Elkhart-Goshen MSA, IN	H	12.11 FQ	19.19 AW	26.79 TQ	INBLS	10/01-12/01
Production and Operating Workers	Evansville-Henderson MSA, IN-KY	H	12.51 FQ	19.68 AW	27.75 TQ	INBLS	10/01-12/01
Production and Operating Workers	Fort Wayne MSA, IN	H	13.20 FQ	21.05 AW	30.90 TQ	INBLS	10/01-12/01
Production and Operating Workers	Gary PMSA, IN	H	14.41 FQ	24.07 AW	34.37 TQ	INBLS	10/01-12/01
Production and Operating Workers	Indianapolis MSA, IN	H	13.21 FQ	21.41 AW	31.37 TQ	INBLS	10/01-12/01
Production and Operating Workers	Lafayette MSA, IN	H	14.07 FQ	23.84 AW	36.00 TQ	INBLS	10/01-12/01
Production and Operating Workers	South Bend MSA, IN	H	12.25 FQ	22.47 AW	36.39 TQ	INBLS	10/01-12/01
Production and Operating Workers	Iowa	H	11.07 FQ	20.10 AW	31.47 TQ	IABLS	10/01-12/01
Production and Operating Workers	Cedar Rapids MSA, IA	H	12.81 FQ	21.02 AW	30.56 TQ	IABLS	10/01-12/01
Production and Operating Workers	Davenport-Moline-Rock Island MSA, IA-IL	H	11.47 FQ	19.56 AW	31.13 TQ	IABLS	10/01-12/01
Production and Operating Workers	Des Moines MSA, IA	H	8.88 FQ	20.33 AW	31.80 TQ	IABLS	10/01-12/01
Production and Operating Workers	Kansas	H	12.70 FQ	21.53 AW	31.83 TQ	KSBLS	10/01-12/01
Production and Operating Workers	Topeka MSA, KS	H	12.28 FQ	19.60 AW	27.40 TQ	KSBLS	10/01-12/01
Production and Operating Workers	Wichita MSA, KS	H	14.49 FQ	24.60 AW	34.64 TQ	KSBLS	10/01-12/01
Production and Operating Workers	Kentucky	H	11.66 FQ	20.17 AW	31.43 TQ	KYBLS	10/01-12/01
Production and Operating Workers	Lexington MSA, KY	H	13.10 FQ	21.35 AW	31.46 TQ	KYBLS	10/01-12/01
Production and Operating Workers	Louisville MSA, KY-IN	H	12.69 FQ	21.18 AW	32.64 TQ	KYBLS	10/01-12/01
Production and Operating Workers	Louisiana	H	11.18 FQ	22.54 AW	37.11 TQ	LABLS	10/01-12/01
Production and Operating Workers	Baton Rouge MSA, LA	H	11.82 FQ	24.75 AW	39.93 TQ	LABLS	10/01-12/01
Production and Operating Workers	Houma MSA, LA	H	11.13 FQ	20.39 AW	35.18 TQ	LABLS	10/01-12/01
Production and Operating Workers	Lafayette MSA, LA	H	9.22 FQ	18.51 AW	32.24 TQ	LABLS	10/01-12/01
Production and Operating Workers	Lake Charles MSA, LA	H	12.35 FQ	24.83 AW	37.18 TQ	LABLS	10/01-12/01
Production and Operating Workers	New Orleans MSA, LA	H	12.80 FQ	23.50 AW	39.06 TQ	LABLS	10/01-12/01
Production and Operating Workers	Shreveport-Bossier City MSA, LA	H	10.58 FQ	19.44 AW	31.54 TQ	LABLS	10/01-12/01
Production and Operating Workers	Maine	H	11.66 FQ	20.52 AW	32.21 TQ	MEBLS	10/01-12/01
Production and Operating Workers	Portland MSA, ME	H	12.56 FQ	20.10 AW	28.88 TQ	MEBLS	10/01-12/01
Production and Operating Workers	Maryland	H	12.77 FQ	21.89 AW	32.61 TQ	MDBLS	10/01-12/01
Production and Operating Workers	Baltimore PMSA, MD	H	12.47 FQ	21.57 AW	31.96 TQ	MDBLS	10/01-12/01
Production and Operating Workers	Massachusetts	H	14.07 FQ	22.88 AW	33.63 TQ	MABLS	10/01-12/01
Production and Operating Workers	Boston PMSA, MA-NH	H	14.35 FQ	23.28 AW	34.02 TQ	MABLS	10/01-12/01
Production and Operating Workers	Brockton PMSA, MA	H	14.09 FQ	21.38 AW	31.34 TQ	MABLS	10/01-12/01
Production and Operating Workers	Lawrence PMSA, MA-NH	H	15.50 FQ	25.09 AW	37.98 TQ	MABLS	10/01-12/01
Production and Operating Workers	Lowell PMSA, MA-NH	H	14.49 FQ	22.77 AW	32.58 TQ	MABLS	10/01-12/01
Production and Operating Workers	New Bedford PMSA, MA	H	12.19 FQ	20.49 AW	28.75 TQ	MABLS	10/01-12/01
Production and Operating Workers	Springfield MSA, MA	H	14.29 FQ	22.09 AW	32.37 TQ	MABLS	10/01-12/01
Production and Operating Workers	Worcester PMSA, MA-CT	H	14.91 FQ	22.72 AW	31.83 TQ	MABLS	10/01-12/01
Production and Operating Workers	Michigan	H	14.14 FQ	25.20 AW	39.24 TQ	MIBLS	10/01-12/01
Production and Operating Workers	Ann Arbor PMSA, MI	H	14.41 FQ	25.30 AW	38.94 TQ	MIBLS	10/01-12/01

AAW Average annual wage
AE Average entry wage
AEX Average experienced wage
AO Average offered
AOH Average offered, high
AOL Average offered, low
APH Average pay, high range
APL Average pay, low range
ASH Average starting, high
ASL Average starting, low
AW Average wage paid
FQ First quartile wage
H Hourly
HI Highest wage paid
HR High end range
LR Low end range
M Monthly
MTC Median total compensation
MW Median wage paid
SQ Second quartile wage
S Special: hourly and annual
TQ Third quartile wage
W Weekly
Y Yearly

Occupation/Type/Industry	Location	Per	Low	Mid	High	Source	Date
First-Line Supervisor/Manager							
Production and Operating Workers	Detroit PMSA, MI	H	15.06 FQ	27.71 AW	42.66 TQ	MIBLS	10/01-12/01
Production and Operating Workers	Flint PMSA, MI	H	15.56 FQ	27.80 AW	37.05 TQ	MIBLS	10/01-12/01
Production and Operating Workers	Grand Rapids-Muskegon-Holland MSA, MI	H	13.93 FQ	22.93 AW	35.54 TQ	MIBLS	10/01-12/01
Production and Operating Workers	Kalamazoo-Battle Creek MSA, MI	H	13.43 FQ	22.74 AW	35.83 TQ	MIBLS	10/01-12/01
Production and Operating Workers	Lansing-East Lansing MSA, MI	H	13.40 FQ	24.13 AW	36.50 TQ	MIBLS	10/01-12/01
Production and Operating Workers	Saginaw-Bay City-Midland MSA, MI	H	13.95 FQ	24.31 AW	34.47 TQ	MIBLS	10/01-12/01
Production and Operating Workers	Minnesota	H	13.08 FQ	21.42 AW	31.87 TQ	MNBLS	10/01-12/01
Production and Operating Workers	Duluth-Superior MSA, MN-WI	H	11.79 FQ	21.23 AW	31.01 TQ	MNBLS	10/01-12/01
Production and Operating Workers	Minneapolis-St. Paul MSA, MN-WI	H	14.64 FQ	22.97 AW	33.40 TQ	MNBLS	10/01-12/01
Production and Operating Workers	St. Cloud MSA, MN	H	11.69 FQ	19.01 AW	26.99 TQ	MNBLS	10/01-12/01
Production and Operating Workers	Mississippi	H	10.51 FQ	17.46 AW	26.55 TQ	MSBLS	10/01-12/01
Production and Operating Workers	Biloxi-Gulfport-Pascagoula MSA, MS	H	11.15 FQ	21.19 AW	33.00 TQ	MSBLS	10/01-12/01
Production and Operating Workers	Jackson MSA, MS	H	10.35 FQ	17.25 AW	25.89 TQ	MSBLS	10/01-12/01
Production and Operating Workers	Missouri	H	10.94 FQ	20.11 AW	32.13 TQ	MOBLS	10/01-12/01
Production and Operating Workers	Kansas City MSA, MO-KS	H	12.95 FQ	23.14 AW	34.58 TQ	MOBLS	10/01-12/01
Production and Operating Workers	St. Louis MSA, MO-IL	H	12.29 FQ	22.08 AW	34.39 TQ	MOBLS	10/01-12/01
Production and Operating Workers	Springfield MSA, MO	H	11.19 FQ	16.50 AW	24.59 TQ	MOBLS	10/01-12/01
Production and Operating Workers	Montana	H	9.25 FQ	17.66 AW	27.38 TQ	MTBLS	10/01-12/01
Production and Operating Workers	Billings MSA, MT	H	8.35 FQ	18.03 AW	28.61 TQ	MTBLS	10/01-12/01
Production and Operating Workers	Nebraska	H	11.84 FQ	19.34 AW	28.83 TQ	NEBLS	10/01-12/01
Production and Operating Workers	Lincoln MSA, NE	H	13.12 FQ	20.37 AW	30.64 TQ	NEBLS	10/01-12/01
Production and Operating Workers	Omaha MSA, NE-IA	H	12.87 FQ	21.27 AW	31.80 TQ	NEBLS	10/01-12/01
Production and Operating Workers	Nevada	H	11.28 FQ	20.86 AW	33.33 TQ	NVBLS	10/01-12/01
Production and Operating Workers	Las Vegas MSA, NV-AZ	H	10.88 FQ	20.74 AW	33.29 TQ	NVBLS	10/01-12/01
Production and Operating Workers	Reno MSA, NV	H	11.26 FQ	19.85 AW	31.18 TQ	NVBLS	10/01-12/01
Production and Operating Workers	New Hampshire	H	13.15 FQ	20.54 AW	29.48 TQ	NHBLS	10/01-12/01
Production and Operating Workers	Manchester PMSA, NH	H	13.50 FQ	20.35 AW	31.03 TQ	NHBLS	10/01-12/01
Production and Operating Workers	Nashua PMSA, NH	H	14.31 FQ	22.46 AW	32.76 TQ	NHBLS	10/01-12/01
Production and Operating Workers	Portsmouth-Rochester PMSA, NH-ME	H	13.73 FQ	19.97 AW	27.10 TQ	NHBLS	10/01-12/01
Production and Operating Workers	New Jersey	H	14.64 FQ	24.90 AW	37.04 TQ	NJBLS	10/01-12/01
Production and Operating Workers	Atlantic-Cape May PMSA, NJ	H	12.20 FQ	23.09 AW	33.62 TQ	NJBLS	10/01-12/01
Production and Operating Workers	Bergen-Passaic PMSA, NJ	H	14.93 FQ	25.98 AW	39.21 TQ	NJBLS	10/01-12/01
Production and Operating Workers	Jersey City PMSA, NJ	H	13.02 FQ	22.80 AW	35.11 TQ	NJBLS	10/01-12/01
Production and Operating Workers	Middlesex-Somerset-Hunterdon PMSA, NJ	H	15.61 FQ	24.99 AW	36.09 TQ	NJBLS	10/01-12/01
Production and Operating Workers	Monmouth-Ocean PMSA, NJ	H	13.97 FQ	24.67 AW	40.42 TQ	NJBLS	10/01-12/01
Production and Operating Workers	Newark PMSA, NJ	H	14.85 FQ	24.95 AW	36.68 TQ	NJBLS	10/01-12/01
Production and Operating Workers	Trenton PMSA, NJ	H	15.58 FQ	22.97 AW	32.04 TQ	NJBLS	10/01-12/01
Production and Operating Workers	New Mexico	H	8.89 FQ	19.66 AW	32.83 TQ	NMBLS	10/01-12/01
Production and Operating Workers	Albuquerque MSA, NM	H	7.78 FQ	20.10 AW	34.31 TQ	NMBLS	10/01-12/01
Production and Operating Workers	Las Cruces MSA, NM	H	8.71 FQ	17.66 AW	28.43 TQ	NMBLS	10/01-12/01
Production and Operating Workers	New York	H	12.04 FQ	23.08 AW	37.16 TQ	NYBLS	10/01-12/01
Production and Operating Workers	Albany-Schenectady-Troy MSA, NY	H	12.00 FQ	21.69 AW	34.12 TQ	NYBLS	10/01-12/01
Production and Operating Workers	Binghamton MSA, NY	H	10.88 FQ	19.58 AW	30.52 TQ	NYBLS	10/01-12/01
Production and Operating Workers	Buffalo-Niagara Falls MSA, NY	H	12.99 FQ	22.53 AW	34.14 TQ	NYBLS	10/01-12/01
Production and Operating Workers	Dutchess County PMSA, NY	H	14.56 FQ	23.62 AW	36.56 TQ	NYBLS	10/01-12/01
Production and Operating Workers	Nassau-Suffolk PMSA, NY	H	12.08 FQ	24.46 AW	39.02 TQ	NYBLS	10/01-12/01
Production and Operating Workers	New York PMSA, NY	H	11.90 FQ	25.09 AW	41.85 TQ	NYBLS	10/01-12/01
Production and Operating Workers	Newburgh PMSA, NY-PA	H	11.71 FQ	21.19 AW	32.77 TQ	NYBLS	10/01-12/01
Production and Operating Workers	Rochester MSA, NY	H	13.70 FQ	23.16 AW	34.55 TQ	NYBLS	10/01-12/01
Production and Operating Workers	Syracuse MSA, NY	H	12.99 FQ	22.27 AW	34.25 TQ	NYBLS	10/01-12/01
Production and Operating Workers	Utica-Rome MSA, NY	H	9.82 FQ	17.61 AW	26.68 TQ	NYBLS	10/01-12/01
Production and Operating Workers	North Carolina	H	11.84 FQ	19.96 AW	30.30 TQ	NCBLS	10/01-12/01
Production and Operating Workers	Asheville MSA, NC	H	10.68 FQ	17.97 AW	26.96 TQ	NCBLS	10/01-12/01
Production and Operating Workers	Charlotte-Gastonia-Rock Hill MSA, NC-SC	H	12.37 FQ	20.78 AW	31.10 TQ	NCBLS	10/01-12/01
Production and Operating Workers	Fayetteville MSA, NC	H	10.20 FQ	18.39 AW	30.47 TQ	NCBLS	10/01-12/01
Production and Operating Workers	Greensboro-Winston-Salem-High Point MSA, NC	H	11.90 FQ	19.48 AW	28.50 TQ	NCBLS	10/01-12/01
Production and Operating Workers	Hickory-Morganton-Lenoir MSA, NC	H	11.69 FQ	17.76 AW	25.03 TQ	NCBLS	10/01-12/01
Production and Operating Workers	Raleigh-Durham-Chapel Hill MSA, NC	H	11.77 FQ	22.87 AW	37.92 TQ	NCBLS	10/01-12/01

AAW	Average annual wage	AOH	Average offered, high	ASH	Average starting, high	H	Hourly	M	Monthly	S	Special: hourly and annual
AE	Average entry wage	AOL	Average offered, low	ASL	Average starting, low	HI	Highest wage paid	MTC	Median total compensation	TQ	Third quartile wage
AEX	Average experienced wage	APH	Average pay, high range	AW	Average wage paid	HR	High end range	MW	Median wage paid	W	Weekly
AO	Average offered	APL	Average pay, low range	FQ	First quartile wage	LR	Low end range	SQ	Second quartile wage	Y	Yearly

Occupation/Type/Industry	Location	Per	Low	Mid	High	Source	Date
First-Line Supervisor/Manager							
Production and Operating Workers	Wilmington MSA, NC	H	13.15 FQ	21.42 AW	34.28 TQ	NCBLS	10/01-12/01
Production and Operating Workers	North Dakota	H	9.60 FQ	18.52 AW	30.94 TQ	NDBLS	10/01-12/01
Production and Operating Workers	Fargo-Moorhead MSA, ND-MN	H	8.21 FQ	15.69 AW	23.03 TQ	NDBLS	10/01-12/01
Production and Operating Workers	Ohio	H	12.76 FQ	21.61 AW	32.75 TQ	OHBLS	10/01-12/01
Production and Operating Workers	Akron PMSA, OH	H	12.78 FQ	21.47 AW	33.51 TQ	OHBLS	10/01-12/01
Production and Operating Workers	Canton-Massillon MSA, OH	H	11.66 FQ	19.68 AW	28.55 TQ	OHBLS	10/01-12/01
Production and Operating Workers	Cincinnati PMSA, OH-KY-IN	H	13.87 FQ	22.03 AW	32.15 TQ	OHBLS	10/01-12/01
Production and Operating Workers	Cleveland-Lorain-Elyria PMSA, OH	H	14.06 FQ	22.92 AW	34.28 TQ	OHBLS	10/01-12/01
Production and Operating Workers	Columbus MSA, OH	H	12.86 FQ	21.45 AW	31.42 TQ	OHBLS	10/01-12/01
Production and Operating Workers	Dayton-Springfield MSA, OH	H	12.88 FQ	23.43 AW	34.04 TQ	OHBLS	10/01-12/01
Production and Operating Workers	Hamilton-Middletown PMSA, OH	H	10.54 FQ	21.13 AW	30.78 TQ	OHBLS	10/01-12/01
Production and Operating Workers	Mansfield MSA, OH	H	10.44 FQ	18.43 AW	27.74 TQ	OHBLS	10/01-12/01
Production and Operating Workers	Toledo MSA, OH	H	12.73 FQ	22.14 AW	34.48 TQ	OHBLS	10/01-12/01
Production and Operating Workers	Youngstown-Warren MSA, OH	H	11.89 FQ	21.50 AW	33.60 TQ	OHBLS	10/01-12/01
Production and Operating Workers	Oklahoma	H	10.88 FQ	19.59 AW	30.32 TQ	OKBLS	10/01-12/01
Production and Operating Workers	Oklahoma City MSA, OK	H	10.67 FQ	19.94 AW	31.11 TQ	OKBLS	10/01-12/01
Production and Operating Workers	Tulsa MSA, OK	H	13.26 FQ	21.09 AW	31.75 TQ	OKBLS	10/01-12/01
Production and Operating Workers	Oregon	H	12.76 FQ	21.76 AW	32.54 TQ	ORBLS	10/01-12/01
Production and Operating Workers	Eugene-Springfield MSA, OR	H	12.04 FQ	20.18 AW	31.54 TQ	ORBLS	10/01-12/01
Production and Operating Workers	Medford-Ashland MSA, OR	H	12.61 FQ	20.26 AW	27.64 TQ	ORBLS	10/01-12/01
Production and Operating Workers	Portland-Vancouver PMSA, OR-WA	H	13.78 FQ	23.28 AW	34.63 TQ	ORBLS	10/01-12/01
Production and Operating Workers	Salem PMSA, OR	H	12.03 FQ	19.95 AW	30.76 TQ	ORBLS	10/01-12/01
Production and Operating Workers	Pennsylvania	H	12.69 FQ	21.29 AW	31.84 TQ	PABLS	10/01-12/01
Production and Operating Workers	Allentown-Bethlehem-Easton MSA, PA	H	13.34 FQ	20.81 AW	31.30 TQ	PABLS	10/01-12/01
Production and Operating Workers	Erie MSA, PA	H	11.39 FQ	18.61 AW	26.62 TQ	PABLS	10/01-12/01
Production and Operating Workers	Harrisburg-Lebanon-Carlisle MSA, PA	H	12.59 FQ	22.12 AW	35.73 TQ	PABLS	10/01-12/01
Production and Operating Workers	Johnstown MSA, PA	H	10.15 FQ	17.60 AW	26.42 TQ	PABLS	10/01-12/01
Production and Operating Workers	Lancaster MSA, PA	H	12.91 FQ	20.40 AW	28.61 TQ	PABLS	10/01-12/01
Production and Operating Workers	Philadelphia PMSA, PA-NJ	H	14.07 FQ	24.05 AW	36.05 TQ	PABLS	10/01-12/01
Production and Operating Workers	Pittsburgh MSA, PA	H	13.65 FQ	22.07 AW	32.41 TQ	PABLS	10/01-12/01
Production and Operating Workers	Reading MSA, PA	H	12.83 FQ	20.59 AW	28.52 TQ	PABLS	10/01-12/01
Production and Operating Workers	Scranton-Wilkes-Barre-Hazleton MSA, PA	H	12.10 FQ	19.98 AW	29.42 TQ	PABLS	10/01-12/01
Production and Operating Workers	York MSA, PA	H	12.93 FQ	20.36 AW	29.02 TQ	PABLS	10/01-12/01
Production and Operating Workers	Rhode Island	H	12.69 FQ	22.34 AW	33.53 TQ	RIBLS	10/01-12/01
Production and Operating Workers	Providence-Fall River-Warwick MSA, RI-MA	H	12.82 FQ	22.11 AW	33.30 TQ	RIBLS	10/01-12/01
Production and Operating Workers	South Carolina	H	12.25 FQ	20.77 AW	31.61 TQ	SCBLS	10/01-12/01
Production and Operating Workers	Charleston-North Charleston MSA, SC	H	11.37 FQ	20.61 AW	32.99 TQ	SCBLS	10/01-12/01
Production and Operating Workers	Columbia MSA, SC	H	12.12 FQ	20.90 AW	30.51 TQ	SCBLS	10/01-12/01
Production and Operating Workers	Greenville-Spartanburg-Anderson MSA, SC	H	13.46 FQ	21.88 AW	32.51 TQ	SCBLS	10/01-12/01
Production and Operating Workers	Myrtle Beach MSA, SC	H	8.92 FQ	17.80 AW	29.53 TQ	SCBLS	10/01-12/01
Production and Operating Workers	South Dakota	H	12.76 FQ	18.63 AW	25.84 TQ	SDBLS	10/01-12/01
Production and Operating Workers	Sioux Falls MSA, SD	H	13.69 FQ	18.99 AW	25.87 TQ	SDBLS	10/01-12/01
Production and Operating Workers	Tennessee	H	11.27 FQ	19.29 AW	29.06 TQ	TNBLS	10/01-12/01
Production and Operating Workers	Chattanooga MSA, TN-GA	H	12.64 FQ	19.67 AW	28.13 TQ	TNBLS	10/01-12/01
Production and Operating Workers	Clarksville-Hopkinsville MSA, TN-KY	H	11.76 FQ	19.29 AW	26.27 TQ	TNBLS	10/01-12/01
Production and Operating Workers	Johnson City-Kingsport-Bristol MSA, TN-VA	H	11.84 FQ	20.88 AW	31.66 TQ	TNBLS	10/01-12/01
Production and Operating Workers	Knoxville MSA, TN	H	13.10 FQ	20.87 AW	30.29 TQ	TNBLS	10/01-12/01
Production and Operating Workers	Memphis MSA, TN-AR-MS	H	9.93 FQ	18.75 AW	29.22 TQ	TNBLS	10/01-12/01
Production and Operating Workers	Nashville MSA, TN	H	12.09 FQ	19.61 AW	29.37 TQ	TNBLS	10/01-12/01
Production and Operating Workers	Texas	H	10.86 FQ	20.71 AW	33.59 TQ	TXBLS	10/01-12/01
Production and Operating Workers	Amarillo MSA, TX	H	10.93 FQ	19.13 AW	29.32 TQ	TXBLS	10/01-12/01
Production and Operating Workers	Austin-San Marcos MSA, TX	H	10.48 FQ	20.85 AW	33.34 TQ	TXBLS	10/01-12/01
Production and Operating Workers	Beaumont-Port Arthur MSA, TX	H	13.42 FQ	24.76 AW	36.90 TQ	TXBLS	10/01-12/01
Production and Operating Workers	Brazoria PMSA, TX	H	13.58 FQ	23.76 AW	38.34 TQ	TXBLS	10/01-12/01
Production and Operating Workers	Brownsville-Harlingen-San Benito MSA, TX	H	8.75 FQ	15.57 AW	22.19 TQ	TXBLS	10/01-12/01
Production and Operating Workers	Corpus Christi MSA, TX	H	9.91 FQ	20.26 AW	33.67 TQ	TXBLS	10/01-12/01
Production and Operating Workers	Dallas PMSA, TX	H	10.88 FQ	21.96 AW	36.39 TQ	TXBLS	10/01-12/01

AAW	Average annual wage	**AOH**	Average offered, high	**ASH**	Average starting, high	**H**	Hourly	**M**	Monthly	**S**	Special: hourly and annual
AE	Average entry wage	**AOL**	Average offered, low	**ASL**	Average starting, low	**HI**	Highest wage paid	**MTC**	Median total compensation	**TQ**	Third quartile wage
AEX	Average experienced wage	**APH**	Average pay, high range	**AW**	Average wage paid	**HR**	High end range	**MW**	Median wage paid	**W**	Weekly
AO	Average offered	**APL**	Average pay, low range	**FQ**	First quartile wage	**LR**	Low end range	**SQ**	Second quartile wage	**Y**	Yearly

Occupation/Type/Industry	Location	Per	Low	Mid	High	Source	Date
First-Line Supervisor/Manager							
Production and Operating Workers	El Paso MSA, TX	H	9.14 FQ	16.70 AW	26.33 TQ	TXBLS	10/01-12/01
Production and Operating Workers	Fort Worth-Arlington PMSA, TX	H	12.04 FQ	21.19 AW	32.46 TQ	TXBLS	10/01-12/01
Production and Operating Workers	Galveston-Texas City PMSA, TX	H	12.11 FQ	22.04 AW	34.78 TQ	TXBLS	10/01-12/01
Production and Operating Workers	Houston PMSA, TX	H	12.40 FQ	22.86 AW	35.91 TQ	TXBLS	10/01-12/01
Production and Operating Workers	Killeen-Temple MSA, TX	H	10.39 FQ	16.55 AW	25.24 TQ	TXBLS	10/01-12/01
Production and Operating Workers	Laredo MSA, TX	H	8.04 FQ	16.48 AW	26.58 TQ	TXBLS	10/01-12/01
Production and Operating Workers	Longview-Marshall MSA, TX	H	11.56 FQ	17.38 AW	24.05 TQ	TXBLS	10/01-12/01
Production and Operating Workers	Lubbock MSA, TX	H	9.38 FQ	16.33 AW	22.85 TQ	TXBLS	10/01-12/01
Production and Operating Workers	McAllen-Edinburg-Mission MSA, TX	H	7.53 FQ	14.10 AW	22.79 TQ	TXBLS	10/01-12/01
Production and Operating Workers	Odessa-Midland MSA, TX	H	12.41 FQ	21.81 AW	34.92 TQ	TXBLS	10/01-12/01
Production and Operating Workers	San Antonio MSA, TX	H	10.25 FQ	17.43 AW	26.18 TQ	TXBLS	10/01-12/01
Production and Operating Workers	Tyler MSA, TX	H	11.01 FQ	18.31 AW	26.87 TQ	TXBLS	10/01-12/01
Production and Operating Workers	Waco MSA, TX	H	7.88 FQ	16.70 AW	26.12 TQ	TXBLS	10/01-12/01
Production and Operating Workers	Utah	H	11.16 FQ	19.23 AW	28.89 TQ	UTBLS	10/01-12/01
Production and Operating Workers	Provo-Orem MSA, UT	H	10.88 FQ	18.55 AW	27.33 TQ	UTBLS	10/01-12/01
Production and Operating Workers	Salt Lake City-Ogden MSA, UT	H	12.04 FQ	19.55 AW	28.73 TQ	UTBLS	10/01-12/01
Production and Operating Workers	Vermont	H	14.43 FQ	22.23 AW	31.79 TQ	VTBLS	10/01-12/01
Production and Operating Workers	Burlington MSA, VT	H	14.80 FQ	22.72 AW	32.10 TQ	VTBLS	10/01-12/01
Production and Operating Workers	Virginia	H	11.88 FQ	21.00 AW	32.44 TQ	VABLS	10/01-12/01
Production and Operating Workers	Lynchburg MSA, VA	H	11.77 FQ	20.46 AW	33.54 TQ	VABLS	10/01-12/01
Production and Operating Workers	Norfolk-Virginia Beach-Newport News MSA, VA-NC	H	12.63 FQ	22.00 AW	31.58 TQ	VABLS	10/01-12/01
Production and Operating Workers	Richmond-Petersburg MSA, VA	H	14.05 FQ	24.22 AW	36.17 TQ	VABLS	10/01-12/01
Production and Operating Workers	Roanoke MSA, VA	H	11.72 FQ	19.86 AW	28.47 TQ	VABLS	10/01-12/01
Production and Operating Workers	Washington	H	14.31 FQ	23.73 AW	35.30 TQ	WABLS	10/01-12/01
Production and Operating Workers	Bremerton PMSA, WA	H	18.06 FQ	27.81 AW	34.27 TQ	WABLS	10/01-12/01
Production and Operating Workers	Olympia PMSA, WA	H	10.99 FQ	19.56 AW	29.21 TQ	WABLS	10/01-12/01
Production and Operating Workers	Richland-Kennewick-Pasco MSA, WA	H	14.58 FQ	22.22 AW	33.60 TQ	WABLS	10/01-12/01
Production and Operating Workers	Seattle-Bellevue-Everett PMSA, WA	H	15.31 FQ	24.98 AW	36.63 TQ	WABLS	10/01-12/01
Production and Operating Workers	Spokane MSA, WA	H	12.37 FQ	19.77 AW	28.78 TQ	WABLS	10/01-12/01
Production and Operating Workers	Tacoma PMSA, WA	H	14.32 FQ	22.45 AW	33.08 TQ	WABLS	10/01-12/01
Production and Operating Workers	Yakima MSA, WA	H	14.79 FQ	22.22 AW	31.77 TQ	WABLS	10/01-12/01
Production and Operating Workers	West Virginia	H	11.24 FQ	21.99 AW	35.85 TQ	WVBLS	10/01-12/01
Production and Operating Workers	Charleston MSA, WV	H	11.15 FQ	23.89 AW	36.56 TQ	WVBLS	10/01-12/01
Production and Operating Workers	Huntington-Ashland MSA, WV-KY-OH	H	12.37 FQ	23.64 AW	38.42 TQ	WVBLS	10/01-12/01
Production and Operating Workers	Wisconsin	H	13.09 FQ	22.29 AW	33.72 TQ	WIBLS	10/01-12/01
Production and Operating Workers	Appleton-Oshkosh-Neenah MSA, WI	H	12.87 FQ	23.03 AW	36.68 TQ	WIBLS	10/01-12/01
Production and Operating Workers	Green Bay MSA, WI	H	14.07 FQ	22.22 AW	33.84 TQ	WIBLS	10/01-12/01
Production and Operating Workers	Madison MSA, WI	H	14.70 FQ	21.69 AW	31.37 TQ	WIBLS	10/01-12/01
Production and Operating Workers	Milwaukee-Waukesha PMSA, WI	H	14.73 FQ	25.67 AW	39.47 TQ	WIBLS	10/01-12/01
Production and Operating Workers	Racine PMSA, WI	H	11.76 FQ	20.74 AW	30.53 TQ	WIBLS	10/01-12/01
Production and Operating Workers	Wyoming	H	11.41 FQ	23.13 AW	36.30 TQ	WYBLS	10/01-12/01
Production and Operating Workers	Cheyenne MSA, WY	H	9.08 FQ	17.01 AW	28.19 TQ	WYBLS	10/01-12/01
Production and Operating Workers	Puerto Rico	H	7.67 FQ	16.02 AW	26.82 TQ	PRBLS	10/01-12/01
Production and Operating Workers	Virgin Islands	H	13.45 FQ	27.08 AW	41.59 TQ	VIBLS	10/01-12/01
Production and Operating Workers	Guam	H	6.94 FQ	16.72 AW	26.11 TQ	GUBLS	10/01-12/01
Retail Sales Workers	Alabama	Y	15770 FQ	28070 AW	45300 TQ	ALBLS	10/01-12/01
Retail Sales Workers	Birmingham MSA, AL	Y	17870 FQ	30040 AW	47420 TQ	ALBLS	10/01-12/01
Retail Sales Workers	Huntsville MSA, AL	Y	15410 FQ	29190 AW	56250 TQ	ALBLS	10/01-12/01
Retail Sales Workers	Mobile MSA, AL	Y	15840 FQ	28590 AW	48650 TQ	ALBLS	10/01-12/01
Retail Sales Workers	Montgomery MSA, AL	Y	15910 FQ	28000 AW	44590 TQ	ALBLS	10/01-12/01
Retail Sales Workers	Alaska	Y	18760 FQ	34420 AW	55050 TQ	AKBLS	10/01-12/01
Retail Sales Workers	Anchorage MSA, AK	Y	18450 FQ	37040 AW	60010 TQ	AKBLS	10/01-12/01
Retail Sales Workers	Arizona	Y	17820 FQ	33150 AW	52940 TQ	AZBLS	10/01-12/01
Retail Sales Workers	Phoenix-Mesa MSA, AZ	Y	19120 FQ	33990 AW	53630 TQ	AZBLS	10/01-12/01
Retail Sales Workers	Tucson MSA, AZ	Y	16820 FQ	35230 AW	56090 TQ	AZBLS	10/01-12/01
Retail Sales Workers	Arkansas	Y	15180 FQ	26200 AW	41860 TQ	ARBLS	10/01-12/01
Retail Sales Workers	Fayetteville-Springdale-Rogers MSA, AR	Y	15910 FQ	27750 AW	44170 TQ	ARBLS	10/01-12/01
Retail Sales Workers	Fort Smith MSA, AR-OK	Y	15520 FQ	27260 AW	41300 TQ	ARBLS	10/01-12/01

AAW Average annual wage; AE Average entry wage; AEX Average experienced wage; AO Average offered; AOH Average offered, high; AOL Average offered, low; APH Average pay, high range; APL Average pay, low range; ASH Average starting, high; ASL Average starting, low; AW Average wage paid; FQ First quartile wage; H Hourly; HI Highest wage paid; HR High end range; LR Low end range; M Monthly; MTC Median total compensation; MW Median wage paid; SQ Second quartile wage; S Special: hourly and annual; TQ Third quartile wage; W Weekly; Y Yearly

Occupation/Type/Industry	Location	Per	Low	Mid	High	Source	Date
First-Line Supervisor/Manager							
Retail Sales Workers	Little Rock-North Little Rock MSA, AR	Y	15890 FQ	28820 AW	45160 TQ	ARBLS	10/01-12/01
Retail Sales Workers	California	Y	19600 FQ	37370 AW	59640 TQ	CABLS	10/01-12/01
Retail Sales Workers	Bakersfield MSA, CA	Y	18740 FQ	34760 AW	59070 TQ	CABLS	10/01-12/01
Retail Sales Workers	Chico-Paradise MSA, CA	Y	17550 FQ	31480 AW	48420 TQ	CABLS	10/01-12/01
Retail Sales Workers	Fresno MSA, CA	Y	18970 FQ	34910 AW	55390 TQ	CABLS	10/01-12/01
Retail Sales Workers	Los Angeles-Long Beach PMSA, CA	Y	19150 FQ	37140 AW	57800 TQ	CABLS	10/01-12/01
Retail Sales Workers	Merced MSA, CA	Y	19540 FQ	32330 AW	47350 TQ	CABLS	10/01-12/01
Retail Sales Workers	Modesto MSA, CA	Y	18720 FQ	34360 AW	56230 TQ	CABLS	10/01-12/01
Retail Sales Workers	Oakland PMSA, CA	Y	20260 FQ	39230 AW	67580 TQ	CABLS	10/01-12/01
Retail Sales Workers	Orange County PMSA, CA	Y	20070 FQ	39080 AW	59480 TQ	CABLS	10/01-12/01
Retail Sales Workers	Redding MSA, CA	Y	18640 FQ	32180 AW	51880 TQ	CABLS	10/01-12/01
Retail Sales Workers	Riverside-San Bernardino PMSA, CA	Y	19910 FQ	37540 AW	59810 TQ	CABLS	10/01-12/01
Retail Sales Workers	Sacramento PMSA, CA	Y	19120 FQ	35810 AW	61400 TQ	CABLS	10/01-12/01
Retail Sales Workers	Salinas MSA, CA	Y	20270 FQ	36970 AW	60750 TQ	CABLS	10/01-12/01
Retail Sales Workers	San Diego MSA, CA	Y	19560 FQ	37110 AW	57340 TQ	CABLS	10/01-12/01
Retail Sales Workers	San Francisco PMSA, CA	Y	22770 FQ	40540 AW	65700 TQ	CABLS	10/01-12/01
Retail Sales Workers	San Jose PMSA, CA	Y	21890 FQ	41510 AW	72690 TQ	CABLS	10/01-12/01
Retail Sales Workers	San Luis Obispo-Atascadero-Paso Robles MSA, CA	Y	17760 FQ	33690 AW	51730 TQ	CABLS	10/01-12/01
Retail Sales Workers	Santa Barbara-Santa Maria-Lompoc MSA, CA	Y	19210 FQ	35330 AW	55140 TQ	CABLS	10/01-12/01
Retail Sales Workers	Santa Cruz-Watsonville PMSA, CA	Y	19970 FQ	36770 AW	57560 TQ	CABLS	10/01-12/01
Retail Sales Workers	Santa Rosa PMSA, CA	Y	20740 FQ	36270 AW	54650 TQ	CABLS	10/01-12/01
Retail Sales Workers	Stockton-Lodi MSA, CA	Y	16960 FQ	35050 AW	62910 TQ	CABLS	10/01-12/01
Retail Sales Workers	Vallejo-Fairfield-Napa PMSA, CA	Y	19240 FQ	37330 AW	67600 TQ	CABLS	10/01-12/01
Retail Sales Workers	Ventura PMSA, CA	Y	19690 FQ	38320 AW	62110 TQ	CABLS	10/01-12/01
Retail Sales Workers	Visalia-Tulare-Porterville MSA, CA	Y	17730 FQ	32850 AW	52460 TQ	CABLS	10/01-12/01
Retail Sales Workers	Colorado	Y	20140 FQ	36850 AW	58600 TQ	COBLS	10/01-12/01
Retail Sales Workers	Boulder-Longmont PMSA, CO	Y	21710 FQ	35070 AW	56840 TQ	COBLS	10/01-12/01
Retail Sales Workers	Colorado Springs MSA, CO	Y	18800 FQ	34010 AW	58010 TQ	COBLS	10/01-12/01
Retail Sales Workers	Denver PMSA, CO	Y	21800 FQ	40440 AW	65650 TQ	COBLS	10/01-12/01
Retail Sales Workers	Fort Collins-Loveland MSA, CO	Y	20780 FQ	35750 AW	58020 TQ	COBLS	10/01-12/01
Retail Sales Workers	Greeley PMSA, CO	Y	19620 FQ	36130 AW	62830 TQ	COBLS	10/01-12/01
Retail Sales Workers	Connecticut	Y	20410 FQ	38140 AW	58950 TQ	CTBLS	10/01-12/01
Retail Sales Workers	Bridgeport PMSA, CT	Y	21260 FQ	42030 AW	65400 TQ	CTBLS	10/01-12/01
Retail Sales Workers	Danbury PMSA, CT	Y	20980 FQ	37890 AW	56790 TQ	CTBLS	10/01-12/01
Retail Sales Workers	Hartford MSA, CT	Y	19760 FQ	36190 AW	57450 TQ	CTBLS	10/01-12/01
Retail Sales Workers	New Haven-Meriden PMSA, CT	Y	20940 FQ	37650 AW	56450 TQ	CTBLS	10/01-12/01
Retail Sales Workers	New London-Norwich MSA, CT-RI	Y	19100 FQ	35430 AW	58070 TQ	CTBLS	10/01-12/01
Retail Sales Workers	Stamford-Norwalk PMSA, CT	Y	23240 FQ	42690 AW	66460 TQ	CTBLS	10/01-12/01
Retail Sales Workers	Waterbury PMSA, CT	Y	19930 FQ	38800 AW	61140 TQ	CTBLS	10/01-12/01
Retail Sales Workers	Delaware	Y	17870 FQ	32560 AW	49800 TQ	DEBLS	10/01-12/01
Retail Sales Workers	Wilmington-Newark PMSA, DE-MD	Y	18700 FQ	33700 AW	52640 TQ	DEBLS	10/01-12/01
Retail Sales Workers	District of Columbia	Y	18940 FQ	35920 AW	54190 TQ	DCBLS	10/01-12/01
Retail Sales Workers	Washington PMSA, DC-MD-VA-WV	Y	19220 FQ	34090 AW	53170 TQ	DCBLS	10/01-12/01
Retail Sales Workers	Florida	Y	18820 FQ	36170 AW	61970 TQ	FLBLS	10/01-12/01
Retail Sales Workers	Daytona Beach MSA, FL	Y	18330 FQ	33850 AW	55610 TQ	FLBLS	10/01-12/01
Retail Sales Workers	Fort Lauderdale PMSA, FL	Y	18860 FQ	37510 AW	65810 TQ	FLBLS	10/01-12/01
Retail Sales Workers	Fort Myers-Cape Coral MSA, FL	Y	18650 FQ	34090 AW	55160 TQ	FLBLS	10/01-12/01
Retail Sales Workers	Fort Pierce-Port St. Lucie MSA, FL	Y	18710 FQ	34750 AW	55790 TQ	FLBLS	10/01-12/01
Retail Sales Workers	Fort Walton Beach MSA, FL	Y	17600 FQ	30630 AW	45330 TQ	FLBLS	10/01-12/01
Retail Sales Workers	Gainesville MSA, FL	Y	17360 FQ	33140 AW	55630 TQ	FLBLS	10/01-12/01
Retail Sales Workers	Jacksonville MSA, FL	Y	18990 FQ	35220 AW	57680 TQ	FLBLS	10/01-12/01
Retail Sales Workers	Lakeland-Winter Haven MSA, FL	Y	17950 FQ	34170 AW	56270 TQ	FLBLS	10/01-12/01
Retail Sales Workers	Melbourne-Titusville-Palm Bay MSA, FL	Y	17990 FQ	34100 AW	56470 TQ	FLBLS	10/01-12/01
Retail Sales Workers	Miami PMSA, FL	Y	18920 FQ	36520 AW	64680 TQ	FLBLS	10/01-12/01

AAW	Average annual wage	**AOH**	Average offered, high	**ASH**	Average starting, high	**H**	Hourly	**M**	Monthly	**S**	Special: hourly and annual
AE	Average entry wage	**AOL**	Average offered, low	**ASL**	Average starting, low	**HI**	Highest wage paid	**MTC**	Median total compensation	**TQ**	Third quartile wage
AEX	Average experienced wage	**APH**	Average pay, high range	**AW**	Average wage paid	**HR**	High end range	**MW**	Median wage paid	**W**	Weekly
AO	Average offered	**APL**	Average pay, low range	**FQ**	First quartile wage	**LR**	Low end range	**SQ**	Second quartile wage	**Y**	Yearly

Occupation/Type/Industry	Location	Per	Low	Mid	High	Source	Date
First-Line Supervisor/Manager							
Retail Sales Workers	Naples MSA, FL	Y	20140 FQ	39100 AW	71140 TQ	FLBLS	10/01-12/01
Retail Sales Workers	Ocala MSA, FL	Y	18170 FQ	34230 AW	56190 TQ	FLBLS	10/01-12/01
Retail Sales Workers	Orlando MSA, FL	Y	18810 FQ	34340 AW	56530 TQ	FLBLS	10/01-12/01
Retail Sales Workers	Pensacola MSA, FL	Y	17210 FQ	32030 AW	55840 TQ	FLBLS	10/01-12/01
Retail Sales Workers	Sarasota-Bradenton MSA, FL	Y	20000 FQ	34360 AW	55860 TQ	FLBLS	10/01-12/01
Retail Sales Workers	Tallahassee MSA, FL	Y	16920 FQ	29800 AW	46910 TQ	FLBLS	10/01-12/01
Retail Sales Workers	Tampa-St. Petersburg-Clearwater MSA, FL	Y	19730 FQ	41820 AW	91820 TQ	FLBLS	10/01-12/01
Retail Sales Workers	West Palm Beach-Boca Raton MSA, FL	Y	20160 FQ	38210 AW	64780 TQ	FLBLS	10/01-12/01
Retail Sales Workers	Georgia	Y	17600 FQ	29980 AW	45520 TQ	GABLS	10/01-12/01
Retail Sales Workers	Atlanta MSA, GA	Y	17880 FQ	31580 AW	50820 TQ	GABLS	10/01-12/01
Retail Sales Workers	Augusta-Aiken MSA, GA-SC	Y	18680 FQ	30110 AW	44210 TQ	GABLS	10/01-12/01
Retail Sales Workers	Columbus MSA, GA-AL	Y	16930 FQ	27760 AW	40880 TQ	GABLS	10/01-12/01
Retail Sales Workers	Macon MSA, GA	Y	17180 FQ	31180 AW	56800 TQ	GABLS	10/01-12/01
Retail Sales Workers	Savannah MSA, GA	Y	18860 FQ	28030 AW	40410 TQ	GABLS	10/01-12/01
Retail Sales Workers	Hawaii	Y	19140 FQ	33570 AW	53620 TQ	HIBLS	10/01-12/01
Retail Sales Workers	Honolulu MSA, HI	Y	19150 FQ	33730 AW	54180 TQ	HIBLS	10/01-12/01
Retail Sales Workers	Idaho	Y	15750 FQ	28340 AW	45310 TQ	IDBLS	10/01-12/01
Retail Sales Workers	Boise City MSA, ID	Y	16090 FQ	29680 AW	44800 TQ	IDBLS	10/01-12/01
Retail Sales Workers	Illinois	Y	17070 FQ	33970 AW	56490 TQ	ILBLS	10/01-12/01
Retail Sales Workers	Champaign-Urbana MSA, IL	Y	16520 FQ	29640 AW	45050 TQ	ILBLS	10/01-12/01
Retail Sales Workers	Chicago PMSA, IL	Y	18850 FQ	36530 AW	59900 TQ	ILBLS	10/01-12/01
Retail Sales Workers	Peoria-Pekin MSA, IL	Y	16250 FQ	35910 AW	66380 TQ	ILBLS	10/01-12/01
Retail Sales Workers	Rockford MSA, IL	Y	17450 FQ	33320 AW	53420 TQ	ILBLS	10/01-12/01
Retail Sales Workers	Springfield MSA, IL	Y	16550 FQ	29520 AW	44960 TQ	ILBLS	10/01-12/01
Retail Sales Workers	Indiana	Y	17180 FQ	31350 AW	51140 TQ	INBLS	10/01-12/01
Retail Sales Workers	Elkhart-Goshen MSA, IN	Y	16930 FQ	33160 AW	53250 TQ	INBLS	10/01-12/01
Retail Sales Workers	Evansville-Henderson MSA, IN-KY	Y	15890 FQ	34300 AW	66500 TQ	INBLS	10/01-12/01
Retail Sales Workers	Fort Wayne MSA, IN	Y	16770 FQ	30150 AW	45880 TQ	INBLS	10/01-12/01
Retail Sales Workers	Gary PMSA, IN	Y	18780 FQ	31880 AW	51830 TQ	INBLS	10/01-12/01
Retail Sales Workers	Indianapolis MSA, IN	Y	18770 FQ	33630 AW	53970 TQ	INBLS	10/01-12/01
Retail Sales Workers	Lafayette MSA, IN	Y	17090 FQ	30500 AW	44050 TQ	INBLS	10/01-12/01
Retail Sales Workers	South Bend MSA, IN	Y	16670 FQ	33460 AW	56560 TQ	INBLS	10/01-12/01
Retail Sales Workers	Iowa	Y	16140 FQ	30360 AW	48190 TQ	IABLS	10/01-12/01
Retail Sales Workers	Cedar Rapids MSA, IA	Y	17960 FQ	31850 AW	52200 TQ	IABLS	10/01-12/01
Retail Sales Workers	Davenport-Moline-Rock Island MSA, IA-IL	Y	14340 FQ	30970 AW	52820 TQ	IABLS	10/01-12/01
Retail Sales Workers	Des Moines MSA, IA	Y	18640 FQ	33580 AW	53550 TQ	IABLS	10/01-12/01
Retail Sales Workers	Kansas	Y	15320 FQ	27680 AW	43670 TQ	KSBLS	10/01-12/01
Retail Sales Workers	Topeka MSA, KS	Y	16940 FQ	28050 AW	44060 TQ	KSBLS	10/01-12/01
Retail Sales Workers	Wichita MSA, KS	Y	16180 FQ	28070 AW	44680 TQ	KSBLS	10/01-12/01
Retail Sales Workers	Kentucky	Y	16010 FQ	27790 AW	43510 TQ	KYBLS	10/01-12/01
Retail Sales Workers	Lexington MSA, KY	Y	15760 FQ	29450 AW	45650 TQ	KYBLS	10/01-12/01
Retail Sales Workers	Louisville MSA, KY-IN	Y	17550 FQ	30440 AW	49570 TQ	KYBLS	10/01-12/01
Retail Sales Workers	Louisiana	Y	16720 FQ	29320 AW	45130 TQ	LABLS	10/01-12/01
Retail Sales Workers	Baton Rouge MSA, LA	Y	18490 FQ	30240 AW	44600 TQ	LABLS	10/01-12/01
Retail Sales Workers	Houma MSA, LA	Y	15690 FQ	26520 AW	42720 TQ	LABLS	10/01-12/01
Retail Sales Workers	Lafayette MSA, LA	Y	16610 FQ	30660 AW	49210 TQ	LABLS	10/01-12/01
Retail Sales Workers	Lake Charles MSA, LA	Y	15540 FQ	28900 AW	44160 TQ	LABLS	10/01-12/01
Retail Sales Workers	New Orleans MSA, LA	Y	16910 FQ	29910 AW	47310 TQ	LABLS	10/01-12/01
Retail Sales Workers	Shreveport-Bossier City MSA, LA	Y	16380 FQ	29410 AW	45000 TQ	LABLS	10/01-12/01
Retail Sales Workers	Maine	Y	17550 FQ	29960 AW	44460 TQ	MEBLS	10/01-12/01
Retail Sales Workers	Portland MSA, ME	Y	19430 FQ	31710 AW	45270 TQ	MEBLS	10/01-12/01
Retail Sales Workers	Maryland	Y	18900 FQ	32630 AW	50360 TQ	MDBLS	10/01-12/01
Retail Sales Workers	Baltimore PMSA, MD	Y	18980 FQ	32560 AW	48910 TQ	MDBLS	10/01-12/01
Retail Sales Workers	Massachusetts	Y	19450 FQ	34820 AW	54760 TQ	MABLS	10/01-12/01
Retail Sales Workers	Boston PMSA, MA-NH	Y	20160 FQ	36440 AW	57020 TQ	MABLS	10/01-12/01
Retail Sales Workers	Brockton PMSA, MA	Y	18550 FQ	35020 AW	56510 TQ	MABLS	10/01-12/01
Retail Sales Workers	Lawrence PMSA, MA-NH	Y	19120 FQ	31880 AW	46920 TQ	MABLS	10/01-12/01
Retail Sales Workers	Lowell PMSA, MA-NH	Y	19300 FQ	34940 AW	55850 TQ	MABLS	10/01-12/01
Retail Sales Workers	New Bedford PMSA, MA	Y	17760 FQ	33260 AW	58580 TQ	MABLS	10/01-12/01
Retail Sales Workers	Springfield MSA, MA	Y	18090 FQ	30550 AW	45360 TQ	MABLS	10/01-12/01
Retail Sales Workers	Worcester PMSA, MA-CT	Y	18240 FQ	33980 AW	52230 TQ	MABLS	10/01-12/01
Retail Sales Workers	Michigan	Y	18010 FQ	34610 AW	56660 TQ	MIBLS	10/01-12/01
Retail Sales Workers	Ann Arbor PMSA, MI	Y	18970 FQ	36550 AW	59730 TQ	MIBLS	10/01-12/01
Retail Sales Workers	Detroit PMSA, MI	Y	19060 FQ	36630 AW	59450 TQ	MIBLS	10/01-12/01
Retail Sales Workers	Flint PMSA, MI	Y	19920 FQ	34260 AW	53240 TQ	MIBLS	10/01-12/01

AAW Average annual wage; **AE** Average entry wage; **AEX** Average experienced wage; **AO** Average offered; **AOH** Average offered, high; **AOL** Average offered, low; **APH** Average pay, high range; **APL** Average pay, low range; **ASH** Average starting, high; **ASL** Average starting, low; **AW** Average wage paid; **FQ** First quartile wage; **H** Hourly; **HI** Highest wage paid; **HR** High end range; **LR** Low end range; **M** Monthly; **MTC** Median total compensation; **MW** Median wage paid; **SQ** Second quartile wage; **S** Special: hourly and annual; **TQ** Third quartile wage; **W** Weekly; **Y** Yearly

Occupation/Type/Industry	Location	Per	Low	Mid	High	Source	Date
First-Line Supervisor/Manager							
Retail Sales Workers	Grand Rapids-Muskegon-Holland MSA, MI	Y	17110 FQ	34840 AW	64150 TQ	MIBLS	10/01-12/01
Retail Sales Workers	Kalamazoo-Battle Creek MSA, MI	Y	18810 FQ	32070 AW	47890 TQ	MIBLS	10/01-12/01
Retail Sales Workers	Lansing-East Lansing MSA, MI	Y	19050 FQ	34880 AW	55230 TQ	MIBLS	10/01-12/01
Retail Sales Workers	Saginaw-Bay City-Midland MSA, MI	Y	18250 FQ	33090 AW	55530 TQ	MIBLS	10/01-12/01
Retail Sales Workers	Minnesota	Y	18920 FQ	33650 AW	54390 TQ	MNBLS	10/01-12/01
Retail Sales Workers	Duluth-Superior MSA, MN-WI	Y	16420 FQ	29730 AW	44870 TQ	MNBLS	10/01-12/01
Retail Sales Workers	Minneapolis-St. Paul MSA, MN-WI	Y	20060 FQ	36280 AW	59580 TQ	MNBLS	10/01-12/01
Retail Sales Workers	St. Cloud MSA, MN	Y	19760 FQ	33230 AW	52970 TQ	MNBLS	10/01-12/01
Retail Sales Workers	Mississippi	Y	15940 FQ	27350 AW	42740 TQ	MSBLS	10/01-12/01
Retail Sales Workers	Biloxi-Gulfport-Pascagoula MSA, MS	Y	16250 FQ	27190 AW	40570 TQ	MSBLS	10/01-12/01
Retail Sales Workers	Jackson MSA, MS	Y	18550 FQ	31290 AW	49230 TQ	MSBLS	10/01-12/01
Retail Sales Workers	Missouri	Y	15810 FQ	29540 AW	45730 TQ	MOBLS	10/01-12/01
Retail Sales Workers	Kansas City MSA, MO-KS	Y	18310 FQ	32510 AW	50760 TQ	MOBLS	10/01-12/01
Retail Sales Workers	St. Louis MSA, MO-IL	Y	16370 FQ	31410 AW	48610 TQ	MOBLS	10/01-12/01
Retail Sales Workers	Springfield MSA, MO	Y	15610 FQ	30220 AW	45760 TQ	MOBLS	10/01-12/01
Retail Sales Workers	Montana	Y	15370 FQ	27920 AW	47120 TQ	MTBLS	10/01-12/01
Retail Sales Workers	Billings MSA, MT	Y	15460 FQ	31560 AW	57710 TQ	MTBLS	10/01-12/01
Retail Sales Workers	Nebraska	Y	16000 FQ	31730 AW	50720 TQ	NEBLS	10/01-12/01
Retail Sales Workers	Lincoln MSA, NE	Y	15090 FQ	32470 AW	51870 TQ	NEBLS	10/01-12/01
Retail Sales Workers	Omaha MSA, NE-IA	Y	18040 FQ	34500 AW	55560 TQ	NEBLS	10/01-12/01
Retail Sales Workers	Nevada	Y	18590 FQ	33450 AW	55770 TQ	NVBLS	10/01-12/01
Retail Sales Workers	Las Vegas MSA, NV-AZ	Y	18080 FQ	32740 AW	55530 TQ	NVBLS	10/01-12/01
Retail Sales Workers	Reno MSA, NV	Y	19490 FQ	35670 AW	56080 TQ	NVBLS	10/01-12/01
Retail Sales Workers	New Hampshire	Y	17890 FQ	30700 AW	47710 TQ	NHBLS	10/01-12/01
Retail Sales Workers	Manchester PMSA, NH	Y	18190 FQ	32690 AW	53430 TQ	NHBLS	10/01-12/01
Retail Sales Workers	Nashua PMSA, NH	Y	19720 FQ	33270 AW	48690 TQ	NHBLS	10/01-12/01
Retail Sales Workers	Portsmouth-Rochester PMSA, NH-ME	Y	18220 FQ	30330 AW	49410 TQ	NHBLS	10/01-12/01
Retail Sales Workers	New Jersey	Y	21240 FQ	39750 AW	64000 TQ	NJBLS	10/01-12/01
Retail Sales Workers	Atlantic-Cape May PMSA, NJ	Y	19780 FQ	35150 AW	56920 TQ	NJBLS	10/01-12/01
Retail Sales Workers	Bergen-Passaic PMSA, NJ	Y	23050 FQ	43230 AW	75100 TQ	NJBLS	10/01-12/01
Retail Sales Workers	Jersey City PMSA, NJ	Y	20860 FQ	37910 AW	65170 TQ	NJBLS	10/01-12/01
Retail Sales Workers	Middlesex-Somerset-Hunterdon PMSA, NJ	Y	20650 FQ	37920 AW	61840 TQ	NJBLS	10/01-12/01
Retail Sales Workers	Monmouth-Ocean PMSA, NJ	Y	22110 FQ	39510 AW	57650 TQ	NJBLS	10/01-12/01
Retail Sales Workers	Newark PMSA, NJ	Y	22300 FQ	41580 AW	66000 TQ	NJBLS	10/01-12/01
Retail Sales Workers	Trenton PMSA, NJ	Y	20370 FQ	42470 AW	76530 TQ	NJBLS	10/01-12/01
Retail Sales Workers	New Mexico	Y	15900 FQ	29620 AW	48430 TQ	NMBLS	10/01-12/01
Retail Sales Workers	Albuquerque MSA, NM	Y	18080 FQ	31880 AW	51070 TQ	NMBLS	10/01-12/01
Retail Sales Workers	Las Cruces MSA, NM	Y	15090 FQ	28380 AW	43720 TQ	NMBLS	10/01-12/01
Retail Sales Workers	New York	Y	18290 FQ	36730 AW	63250 TQ	NYBLS	10/01-12/01
Retail Sales Workers	Albany-Schenectady-Troy MSA, NY	Y	18540 FQ	32900 AW	54260 TQ	NYBLS	10/01-12/01
Retail Sales Workers	Binghamton MSA, NY	Y	16030 FQ	30260 AW	47800 TQ	NYBLS	10/01-12/01
Retail Sales Workers	Buffalo-Niagara Falls MSA, NY	Y	17660 FQ	30700 AW	48180 TQ	NYBLS	10/01-12/01
Retail Sales Workers	Dutchess County PMSA, NY	Y	17110 FQ	33450 AW	53060 TQ	NYBLS	10/01-12/01
Retail Sales Workers	Nassau-Suffolk PMSA, NY	Y	18990 FQ	38900 AW	68470 TQ	NYBLS	10/01-12/01
Retail Sales Workers	New York PMSA, NY	Y	19310 FQ	40420 AW	70750 TQ	NYBLS	10/01-12/01
Retail Sales Workers	Newburgh PMSA, NY-PA	Y	19280 FQ	35400 AW	54870 TQ	NYBLS	10/01-12/01
Retail Sales Workers	Rochester MSA, NY	Y	16750 FQ	34550 AW	65550 TQ	NYBLS	10/01-12/01
Retail Sales Workers	Syracuse MSA, NY	Y	16840 FQ	32320 AW	54230 TQ	NYBLS	10/01-12/01
Retail Sales Workers	Utica-Rome MSA, NY	Y	18130 FQ	30860 AW	46920 TQ	NYBLS	10/01-12/01
Retail Sales Workers	North Carolina	Y	17820 FQ	30330 AW	45990 TQ	NCBLS	10/01-12/01
Retail Sales Workers	Asheville MSA, NC	Y	17630 FQ	30110 AW	48200 TQ	NCBLS	10/01-12/01
Retail Sales Workers	Charlotte-Gastonia-Rock Hill MSA, NC-SC	Y	18570 FQ	31330 AW	46580 TQ	NCBLS	10/01-12/01
Retail Sales Workers	Fayetteville MSA, NC	Y	16570 FQ	27910 AW	39920 TQ	NCBLS	10/01-12/01
Retail Sales Workers	Greensboro-Winston-Salem-High Point MSA, NC	Y	18400 FQ	32500 AW	51360 TQ	NCBLS	10/01-12/01
Retail Sales Workers	Hickory-Morganton-Lenoir MSA, NC	Y	16590 FQ	31550 AW	54660 TQ	NCBLS	10/01-12/01
Retail Sales Workers	Raleigh-Durham-Chapel Hill MSA, NC	Y	19130 FQ	32090 AW	45520 TQ	NCBLS	10/01-12/01
Retail Sales Workers	Wilmington MSA, NC	Y	18590 FQ	30790 AW	48610 TQ	NCBLS	10/01-12/01
Retail Sales Workers	North Dakota	Y	15870 FQ	28510 AW	45610 TQ	NDBLS	10/01-12/01

AAW	Average annual wage	AOH	Average offered, high	ASH	Average starting, high	H	Hourly	M	Monthly	S	Special: hourly and annual
AE	Average entry wage	AOL	Average offered, low	ASL	Average starting, low	HI	Highest wage paid	MTC	Median total compensation	TQ	Third quartile wage
AEX	Average experienced wage	APH	Average pay, high range	AW	Average wage paid	HR	High end range	MW	Median wage paid	W	Weekly
AO	Average offered	APL	Average pay, low range	FQ	First quartile wage	LR	Low end range	SQ	Second quartile wage	Y	Yearly

First-Line Supervisor/Manager

Occupation/Type/Industry	Location	Per	Low	Mid	High	Source	Date
Retail Sales Workers	Fargo-Moorhead MSA, ND-MN	Y	16830 FQ	31190 AW	47870 TQ	NDBLS	10/01-12/01
Retail Sales Workers	Ohio	Y	17140 FQ	31130 AW	49140 TQ	OHBLS	10/01-12/01
Retail Sales Workers	Akron PMSA, OH	Y	16800 FQ	31680 AW	51690 TQ	OHBLS	10/01-12/01
Retail Sales Workers	Canton-Massillon MSA, OH	Y	16260 FQ	27560 AW	41270 TQ	OHBLS	10/01-12/01
Retail Sales Workers	Cincinnati PMSA, OH-KY-IN	Y	17070 FQ	32340 AW	53780 TQ	OHBLS	10/01-12/01
Retail Sales Workers	Cleveland-Lorain-Elyria PMSA, OH	Y	17630 FQ	33420 AW	55150 TQ	OHBLS	10/01-12/01
Retail Sales Workers	Columbus MSA, OH	Y	19400 FQ	32610 AW	47130 TQ	OHBLS	10/01-12/01
Retail Sales Workers	Dayton-Springfield MSA, OH	Y	17630 FQ	30140 AW	47120 TQ	OHBLS	10/01-12/01
Retail Sales Workers	Hamilton-Middletown PMSA, OH	Y	16870 FQ	29920 AW	49720 TQ	OHBLS	10/01-12/01
Retail Sales Workers	Mansfield MSA, OH	Y	15430 FQ	27970 AW	42370 TQ	OHBLS	10/01-12/01
Retail Sales Workers	Toledo MSA, OH	Y	17500 FQ	31320 AW	51990 TQ	OHBLS	10/01-12/01
Retail Sales Workers	Youngstown-Warren MSA, OH	Y	18080 FQ	30430 AW	44600 TQ	OHBLS	10/01-12/01
Retail Sales Workers	Oklahoma	Y	15520 FQ	28010 AW	44640 TQ	OKBLS	10/01-12/01
Retail Sales Workers	Oklahoma City MSA, OK	Y	15700 FQ	28760 AW	45850 TQ	OKBLS	10/01-12/01
Retail Sales Workers	Tulsa MSA, OK	Y	16570 FQ	31890 AW	52240 TQ	OKBLS	10/01-12/01
Retail Sales Workers	Oregon	Y	19660 FQ	36480 AW	57910 TQ	ORBLS	10/01-12/01
Retail Sales Workers	Eugene-Springfield MSA, OR	Y	19480 FQ	37620 AW	60730 TQ	ORBLS	10/01-12/01
Retail Sales Workers	Medford-Ashland MSA, OR	Y	19420 FQ	33930 AW	53720 TQ	ORBLS	10/01-12/01
Retail Sales Workers	Portland-Vancouver PMSA, OR-WA	Y	20560 FQ	38630 AW	64600 TQ	ORBLS	10/01-12/01
Retail Sales Workers	Salem PMSA, OR	Y	19680 FQ	36100 AW	57560 TQ	ORBLS	10/01-12/01
Retail Sales Workers	Pennsylvania	Y	18380 FQ	31960 AW	49150 TQ	PABLS	10/01-12/01
Retail Sales Workers	Allentown-Bethlehem-Easton MSA, PA	Y	19350 FQ	32800 AW	48150 TQ	PABLS	10/01-12/01
Retail Sales Workers	Erie MSA, PA	Y	17690 FQ	28940 AW	44620 TQ	PABLS	10/01-12/01
Retail Sales Workers	Harrisburg-Lebanon-Carlisle MSA, PA	Y	19220 FQ	30220 AW	43750 TQ	PABLS	10/01-12/01
Retail Sales Workers	Johnstown MSA, PA	Y	16960 FQ	28140 AW	41450 TQ	PABLS	10/01-12/01
Retail Sales Workers	Lancaster MSA, PA	Y	19210 FQ	33350 AW	55280 TQ	PABLS	10/01-12/01
Retail Sales Workers	Philadelphia PMSA, PA-NJ	Y	20110 FQ	35550 AW	55160 TQ	PABLS	10/01-12/01
Retail Sales Workers	Pittsburgh MSA, PA	Y	17340 FQ	30700 AW	47670 TQ	PABLS	10/01-12/01
Retail Sales Workers	Reading MSA, PA	Y	19160 FQ	32240 AW	49070 TQ	PABLS	10/01-12/01
Retail Sales Workers	Scranton-Wilkes-Barre-Hazleton MSA, PA	Y	18460 FQ	29060 AW	42670 TQ	PABLS	10/01-12/01
Retail Sales Workers	York MSA, PA	Y	19540 FQ	32400 AW	46850 TQ	PABLS	10/01-12/01
Retail Sales Workers	Rhode Island	Y	18940 FQ	35660 AW	58620 TQ	RIBLS	10/01-12/01
Retail Sales Workers	Providence-Fall River-Warwick MSA, RI-MA	Y	18940 FQ	34740 AW	55280 TQ	RIBLS	10/01-12/01
Retail Sales Workers	South Carolina	Y	18500 FQ	31100 AW	46750 TQ	SCBLS	10/01-12/01
Retail Sales Workers	Charleston-North Charleston MSA, SC	Y	18570 FQ	32080 AW	49240 TQ	SCBLS	10/01-12/01
Retail Sales Workers	Columbia MSA, SC	Y	18070 FQ	34050 AW	53070 TQ	SCBLS	10/01-12/01
First-Line Sales Workers	Greenville-Spartanburg-Anderson MSA, SC	Y	18230 FQ	30640 AW	47150 TQ	SCBLS	10/01-12/01
Retail Sales Workers	Myrtle Beach MSA, SC	Y	20360 FQ	31630 AW	43730 TQ	SCBLS	10/01-12/01
Retail Sales Workers	South Dakota	Y	20810 FQ	32750 AW	46050 TQ	SDBLS	10/01-12/01
Retail Sales Workers	Sioux Falls MSA, SD	Y	20700 FQ	32800 AW	47210 TQ	SDBLS	10/01-12/01
Retail Sales Workers	Tennessee	Y	16580 FQ	29410 AW	46410 TQ	TNBLS	10/01-12/01
Retail Sales Workers	Chattanooga MSA, TN-GA	Y	16450 FQ	28940 AW	46010 TQ	TNBLS	10/01-12/01
Retail Sales Workers	Clarksville-Hopkinsville MSA, TN-KY	Y	15780 FQ	27930 AW	49940 TQ	TNBLS	10/01-12/01
Retail Sales Workers	Johnson City-Kingsport-Bristol MSA, TN-VA	Y	16270 FQ	28620 AW	44220 TQ	TNBLS	10/01-12/01
Retail Sales Workers	Knoxville MSA, TN	Y	16420 FQ	27950 AW	42740 TQ	TNBLS	10/01-12/01
Retail Sales Workers	Memphis MSA, TN-AR-MS	Y	17880 FQ	30650 AW	45210 TQ	TNBLS	10/01-12/01
Retail Sales Workers	Nashville MSA, TN	Y	17310 FQ	30940 AW	53380 TQ	TNBLS	10/01-12/01
Retail Sales Workers	Texas	Y	15910 FQ	30710 AW	48350 TQ	TXBLS	10/01-12/01
Retail Sales Workers	Amarillo MSA, TX	Y	14970 FQ	28060 AW	45750 TQ	TXBLS	10/01-12/01
Retail Sales Workers	Austin-San Marcos MSA, TX	Y	17110 FQ	30600 AW	46350 TQ	TXBLS	10/01-12/01
Retail Sales Workers	Beaumont-Port Arthur MSA, TX	Y	13100 FQ	27810 AW	44660 TQ	TXBLS	10/01-12/01
Retail Sales Workers	Brazoria PMSA, TX	Y	14300 FQ	27450 AW	40840 TQ	TXBLS	10/01-12/01
Retail Sales Workers	Brownsville-Harlingen-San Benito MSA, TX	Y	13360 FQ	26970 AW	46330 TQ	TXBLS	10/01-12/01
Retail Sales Workers	Corpus Christi MSA, TX	Y	16130 FQ	30960 AW	50140 TQ	TXBLS	10/01-12/01
Retail Sales Workers	Dallas PMSA, TX	Y	16280 FQ	32620 AW	53260 TQ	TXBLS	10/01-12/01
Retail Sales Workers	El Paso MSA, TX	Y	15080 FQ	29500 AW	48410 TQ	TXBLS	10/01-12/01

AAW	Average annual wage	AOH	Average offered, high	ASH	Average starting, high	H	Hourly	M	Monthly	S	Special: hourly and annual
AE	Average entry wage	AOL	Average offered, low	ASL	Average starting, low	HI	Highest wage paid	MTC	Median total compensation	TQ	Third quartile wage
AEX	Average experienced wage	APH	Average pay, high range	AW	Average wage paid	HR	High end range	MW	Median wage paid	W	Weekly
AO	Average offered	APL	Average pay, low range	FQ	First quartile wage	LR	Low end range	SQ	Second quartile wage	Y	Yearly

Occupation/Type/Industry	Location	Per	Low	Mid	High	Source	Date
First-Line Supervisor/Manager							
Retail Sales Workers	Fort Worth-Arlington PMSA, TX	Y	17740 FQ	32230 AW	52110 TQ	TXBLS	10/01-12/01
Retail Sales Workers	Galveston-Texas City PMSA, TX	Y	18310 FQ	29420 AW	42750 TQ	TXBLS	10/01-12/01
Retail Sales Workers	Houston PMSA, TX	Y	16810 FQ	32040 AW	47450 TQ	TXBLS	10/01-12/01
Retail Sales Workers	Killeen-Temple MSA, TX	Y	15700 FQ	27500 AW	41040 TQ	TXBLS	10/01-12/01
Retail Sales Workers	Laredo MSA, TX	Y	13990 FQ	25700 AW	39720 TQ	TXBLS	10/01-12/01
Retail Sales Workers	Longview-Marshall MSA, TX	Y	14740 FQ	28270 AW	43200 TQ	TXBLS	10/01-12/01
Retail Sales Workers	Lubbock MSA, TX	Y	14750 FQ	30570 AW	53290 TQ	TXBLS	10/01-12/01
Retail Sales Workers	McAllen-Edinburg-Mission MSA, TX	Y	13220 FQ	26530 AW	47440 TQ	TXBLS	10/01-12/01
Retail Sales Workers	Odessa-Midland MSA, TX	Y	16270 FQ	31000 AW	55600 TQ	TXBLS	10/01-12/01
Retail Sales Workers	San Antonio MSA, TX	Y	17600 FQ	32060 AW	45970 TQ	TXBLS	10/01-12/01
Retail Sales Workers	Tyler MSA, TX	Y	16350 FQ	28930 AW	44370 TQ	TXBLS	10/01-12/01
Retail Sales Workers	Waco MSA, TX	Y	14950 FQ	31080 AW	47140 TQ	TXBLS	10/01-12/01
Retail Sales Workers	Utah	Y	17620 FQ	30670 AW	47040 TQ	UTBLS	10/01-12/01
Retail Sales Workers	Provo-Orem MSA, UT	Y	16430 FQ	28440 AW	44150 TQ	UTBLS	10/01-12/01
Retail Sales Workers	Salt Lake City-Ogden MSA, UT	Y	18760 FQ	32100 AW	49520 TQ	UTBLS	10/01-12/01
Retail Sales Workers	Vermont	Y	20240 FQ	36600 AW	57290 TQ	VTBLS	10/01-12/01
Retail Sales Workers	Burlington MSA, VT	Y	22970 FQ	40510 AW	67990 TQ	VTBLS	10/01-12/01
Retail Sales Workers	Virginia	Y	17500 FQ	31040 AW	49280 TQ	VABLS	10/01-12/01
Retail Sales Workers	Lynchburg MSA, VA	Y	15970 FQ	25690 AW	36630 TQ	VABLS	10/01-12/01
Retail Sales Workers	Norfolk-Virginia Beach-Newport News MSA, VA-NC	Y	16800 FQ	29900 AW	44920 TQ	VABLS	10/01-12/01
Retail Sales Workers	Richmond-Petersburg MSA, VA	Y	18110 FQ	32390 AW	50070 TQ	VABLS	10/01-12/01
Retail Sales Workers	Roanoke MSA, VA	Y	19350 FQ	30370 AW	45130 TQ	VABLS	10/01-12/01
Retail Sales Workers	Washington	Y	21400 FQ	40150 AW	62820 TQ	WABLS	10/01-12/01
Retail Sales Workers	Bremerton PMSA, WA	Y	18830 FQ	32960 AW	52400 TQ	WABLS	10/01-12/01
Retail Sales Workers	Olympia PMSA, WA	Y	21390 FQ	37690 AW	60730 TQ	WABLS	10/01-12/01
Retail Sales Workers	Richland-Kennewick-Pasco MSA, WA	Y	19960 FQ	33890 AW	53820 TQ	WABLS	10/01-12/01
Retail Sales Workers	Seattle-Bellevue-Everett PMSA, WA	Y	23440 FQ	43420 AW	71710 TQ	WABLS	10/01-12/01
Retail Sales Workers	Spokane MSA, WA	Y	20610 FQ	37340 AW	58240 TQ	WABLS	10/01-12/01
Retail Sales Workers	Tacoma PMSA, WA	Y	20790 FQ	40000 AW	67240 TQ	WABLS	10/01-12/01
Retail Sales Workers	Yakima MSA, WA	Y	19820 FQ	36720 AW	56320 TQ	WABLS	10/01-12/01
Retail Sales Workers	West Virginia	Y	14910 FQ	25140 AW	40010 TQ	WVBLS	10/01-12/01
Retail Sales Workers	Charleston MSA, WV	Y	15530 FQ	26860 AW	42640 TQ	WVBLS	10/01-12/01
Retail Sales Workers	Huntington-Ashland MSA, WV-KY-OH	Y	15150 FQ	25100 AW	39940 TQ	WVBLS	10/01-12/01
Retail Sales Workers	Wisconsin	Y	18490 FQ	34290 AW	57040 TQ	WIBLS	10/01-12/01
Retail Sales Workers	Appleton-Oshkosh-Neenah MSA, WI	Y	19160 FQ	35260 AW	59860 TQ	WIBLS	10/01-12/01
Retail Sales Workers	Green Bay MSA, WI	Y	20840 FQ	39120 AW	67100 TQ	WIBLS	10/01-12/01
Retail Sales Workers	Madison MSA, WI	Y	19550 FQ	35320 AW	61670 TQ	WIBLS	10/01-12/01
Retail Sales Workers	Milwaukee-Waukesha PMSA, WI	Y	19620 FQ	37590 AW	66800 TQ	WIBLS	10/01-12/01
Retail Sales Workers	Racine PMSA, WI	Y	18540 FQ	33130 AW	55920 TQ	WIBLS	10/01-12/01
Retail Sales Workers	Wyoming	Y	15140 FQ	28140 AW	45130 TQ	WYBLS	10/01-12/01
Retail Sales Workers	Cheyenne MSA, WY	Y	15980 FQ	29620 AW	45550 TQ	WYBLS	10/01-12/01
Retail Sales Workers	Puerto Rico	Y	13210 FQ	23350 AW	37660 TQ	PRBLS	10/01-12/01
Retail Sales Workers	Virgin Islands	Y	20140 FQ	28810 AW	40970 TQ	VIBLS	10/01-12/01
Retail Sales Workers	Guam	Y	14990 FQ	26750 AW	44140 TQ	GUBLS	10/01-12/01
Transportation, Movers, Drivers	Alabama	H	10.89 FQ	19.05 AW	28.33 TQ	ALBLS	10/01-12/01
Transportation, Movers, Drivers	Birmingham MSA, AL	H	12.29 FQ	21.47 AW	31.39 TQ	ALBLS	10/01-12/01
Transportation, Movers, Drivers	Huntsville MSA, AL	H	10.57 FQ	19.78 AW	32.91 TQ	ALBLS	10/01-12/01
Transportation, Movers, Drivers	Mobile MSA, AL	H	10.66 FQ	18.63 AW	27.66 TQ	ALBLS	10/01-12/01
Transportation, Movers, Drivers	Montgomery MSA, AL	H	11.26 FQ	19.29 AW	28.47 TQ	ALBLS	10/01-12/01
Transportation, Movers, Drivers	Alaska	H	15.74 FQ	27.37 AW	47.80 TQ	AKBLS	10/01-12/01
Transportation, Movers, Drivers	Anchorage MSA, AK	H	15.76 FQ	27.54 AW	49.24 TQ	AKBLS	10/01-12/01
Transportation, Movers, Drivers	Arizona	H	10.28 FQ	19.62 AW	32.24 TQ	AZBLS	10/01-12/01
Transportation, Movers, Drivers	Phoenix-Mesa MSA, AZ	H	10.47 FQ	19.70 AW	32.23 TQ	AZBLS	10/01-12/01
Transportation, Movers, Drivers	Tucson MSA, AZ	H	10.28 FQ	20.33 AW	33.02 TQ	AZBLS	10/01-12/01
Transportation, Movers, Drivers	Arkansas	H	11.53 FQ	20.32 AW	29.99 TQ	ARBLS	10/01-12/01
Transportation, Movers, Drivers	Fayetteville-Springdale-Rogers MSA, AR	H	11.97 FQ	19.11 AW	27.94 TQ	ARBLS	10/01-12/01
Transportation, Movers, Drivers	Fort Smith MSA, AR-OK	H	13.20 FQ	22.99 AW	31.91 TQ	ARBLS	10/01-12/01

AAW Average annual wage; AE Average entry wage; AEX Average experienced wage; AO Average offered; AOH Average offered, high; AOL Average offered, low; APH Average pay, high range; APL Average pay, low range; ASH Average starting, high; ASL Average starting, low; AW Average wage paid; FQ First quartile wage; H Hourly; HI Highest wage paid; HR High end range; LR Low end range; M Monthly; MTC Median total compensation; MW Median wage paid; SQ Second quartile wage; S Special: hourly and annual; TQ Third quartile wage; W Weekly; Y Yearly

Occupation/Type/Industry	Location	Per	Low	Mid	High	Source	Date
First-Line Supervisor/Manager							
Transportation, Movers, Drivers	Little Rock-North Little Rock MSA, AR	H	13.01 FQ	20.99 AW	32.43 TQ	ARBLS	10/01-12/01
Transportation, Movers, Drivers	California	H	11.41 FQ	22.73 AW	35.53 TQ	CABLS	10/01-12/01
Transportation, Movers, Drivers	Bakersfield MSA, CA	H	12.51 FQ	20.77 AW	28.78 TQ	CABLS	10/01-12/01
Transportation, Movers, Drivers	Chico-Paradise MSA, CA	H	11.95 FQ	19.11 AW	27.17 TQ	CABLS	10/01-12/01
Transportation, Movers, Drivers	Fresno MSA, CA	H	11.34 FQ	19.55 AW	28.97 TQ	CABLS	10/01-12/01
Transportation, Movers, Drivers	Los Angeles-Long Beach PMSA, CA	H	10.66 FQ	23.34 AW	37.64 TQ	CABLS	10/01-12/01
Transportation, Movers, Drivers	Merced MSA, CA	H	12.68 FQ	22.80 AW	36.65 TQ	CABLS	10/01-12/01
Transportation, Movers, Drivers	Modesto MSA, CA	H	12.62 FQ	21.47 AW	30.36 TQ	CABLS	10/01-12/01
Transportation, Movers, Drivers	Oakland PMSA, CA	H	14.08 FQ	26.73 AW	41.45 TQ	CABLS	10/01-12/01
Transportation, Movers, Drivers	Orange County PMSA, CA	H	11.28 FQ	20.02 AW	31.43 TQ	CABLS	10/01-12/01
Transportation, Movers, Drivers	Redding MSA, CA	H	13.25 FQ	22.34 AW	37.72 TQ	CABLS	10/01-12/01
Transportation, Movers, Drivers	Riverside-San Bernardino PMSA, CA	H	14.64 FQ	23.71 AW	34.33 TQ	CABLS	10/01-12/01
Transportation, Movers, Drivers	Sacramento PMSA, CA	H	13.28 FQ	24.49 AW	35.23 TQ	CABLS	10/01-12/01
Transportation, Movers, Drivers	Salinas MSA, CA	H	11.70 FQ	20.60 AW	29.36 TQ	CABLS	10/01-12/01
Transportation, Movers, Drivers	San Diego MSA, CA	H	9.82 FQ	18.64 AW	31.72 TQ	CABLS	10/01-12/01
Transportation, Movers, Drivers	San Francisco PMSA, CA	H	13.69 FQ	23.63 AW	37.66 TQ	CABLS	10/01-12/01
Transportation, Movers, Drivers	San Jose PMSA, CA	H	14.11 FQ	24.34 AW	36.78 TQ	CABLS	10/01-12/01
Transportation, Movers, Drivers	San Luis Obispo-Atascadero-Paso Robles MSA, CA	H	12.60 FQ	21.42 AW	33.11 TQ	CABLS	10/01-12/01
Transportation, Movers, Drivers	Santa Barbara-Santa Maria-Lompoc MSA, CA	H	11.31 FQ	21.58 AW	35.31 TQ	CABLS	10/01-12/01
Transportation, Movers, Drivers	Santa Cruz-Watsonville PMSA, CA	H	12.88 FQ	21.17 AW	30.73 TQ	CABLS	10/01-12/01
Transportation, Movers, Drivers	Santa Rosa PMSA, CA	H	8.74 FQ	21.08 AW	32.99 TQ	CABLS	10/01-12/01
Transportation, Movers, Drivers	Stockton-Lodi MSA, CA	H	15.11 FQ	24.20 AW	33.95 TQ	CABLS	10/01-12/01
Transportation, Movers, Drivers	Vallejo-Fairfield-Napa PMSA, CA	H	14.91 FQ	26.63 AW	42.29 TQ	CABLS	10/01-12/01
Transportation, Movers, Drivers	Ventura PMSA, CA	H	13.70 FQ	24.27 AW	39.21 TQ	CABLS	10/01-12/01
Transportation, Movers, Drivers	Visalia-Tulare-Porterville MSA, CA	H	9.91 FQ	17.58 AW	26.46 TQ	CABLS	10/01-12/01
Transportation, Movers, Drivers	Colorado	H	12.44 FQ	21.99 AW	32.56 TQ	COBLS	10/01-12/01
Transportation, Movers, Drivers	Boulder-Longmont PMSA, CO	H	13.79 FQ	28.89 AW	60.52 TQ	COBLS	10/01-12/01
Transportation, Movers, Drivers	Colorado Springs MSA, CO	H	13.22 FQ	21.32 AW	28.04 TQ	COBLS	10/01-12/01
Transportation, Movers, Drivers	Denver PMSA, CO	H	12.39 FQ	22.62 AW	33.33 TQ	COBLS	10/01-12/01
Transportation, Movers, Drivers	Fort Collins-Loveland MSA, CO	H	7.83 FQ	16.23 AW	22.16 TQ	COBLS	10/01-12/01
Transportation, Movers, Drivers	Greeley PMSA, CO	H	13.68 FQ	21.69 AW	30.28 TQ	COBLS	10/01-12/01
Transportation, Movers, Drivers	Connecticut	H	14.24 FQ	24.28 AW	36.93 TQ	CTBLS	10/01-12/01
Transportation, Movers, Drivers	Bridgeport PMSA, CT	H	15.04 FQ	24.72 AW	40.14 TQ	CTBLS	10/01-12/01
Transportation, Movers, Drivers	Danbury PMSA, CT	H	12.73 FQ	25.20 AW	36.65 TQ	CTBLS	10/01-12/01
Transportation, Movers, Drivers	Hartford MSA, CT	H	14.48 FQ	24.47 AW	37.45 TQ	CTBLS	10/01-12/01
Transportation, Movers, Drivers	New Haven-Meriden PMSA, CT	H	11.95 FQ	22.90 AW	37.07 TQ	CTBLS	10/01-12/01
Transportation, Movers, Drivers	New London-Norwich MSA, CT-RI	H	14.17 FQ	22.67 AW	32.55 TQ	CTBLS	10/01-12/01
Transportation, Movers, Drivers	Stamford-Norwalk PMSA, CT	H	15.43 FQ	26.20 AW	42.65 TQ	CTBLS	10/01-12/01
Transportation, Movers, Drivers	Waterbury PMSA, CT	H	13.83 FQ	23.71 AW	33.72 TQ	CTBLS	10/01-12/01
Transportation, Movers, Drivers	Delaware	H	12.99 FQ	20.71 AW	30.88 TQ	DEBLS	10/01-12/01
Transportation, Movers, Drivers	Wilmington-Newark PMSA, DE-MD	H	13.38 FQ	20.20 AW	27.80 TQ	DEBLS	10/01-12/01
Transportation, Movers, Drivers	District of Columbia	H	7.73 FQ	19.46 AW	48.24 TQ	DCBLS	10/01-12/01
Transportation, Movers, Drivers	Washington PMSA, DC-MD-VA-WV	H	8.67 FQ	21.94 AW	42.63 TQ	DCBLS	10/01-12/01
Transportation, Movers, Drivers	Florida	H	10.10 FQ	19.67 AW	29.62 TQ	FLBLS	10/01-12/01
Transportation, Movers, Drivers	Daytona Beach MSA, FL	H	10.51 FQ	20.14 AW	28.82 TQ	FLBLS	10/01-12/01
Transportation, Movers, Drivers	Fort Lauderdale PMSA, FL	H	11.34 FQ	20.04 AW	29.08 TQ	FLBLS	10/01-12/01
Transportation, Movers, Drivers	Fort Myers-Cape Coral MSA, FL	H	11.67 FQ	19.14 AW	29.07 TQ	FLBLS	10/01-12/01
Transportation, Movers, Drivers	Fort Pierce-Port St. Lucie MSA, FL	H	11.50 FQ	18.71 AW	26.20 TQ	FLBLS	10/01-12/01
Transportation, Movers, Drivers	Fort Walton Beach MSA, FL	H	9.26 FQ	19.99 AW	36.10 TQ	FLBLS	10/01-12/01
Transportation, Movers, Drivers	Gainesville MSA, FL	H	9.75 FQ	21.45 AW	36.22 TQ	FLBLS	10/01-12/01
Transportation, Movers, Drivers	Jacksonville MSA, FL	H	12.66 FQ	22.75 AW	34.61 TQ	FLBLS	10/01-12/01
Transportation, Movers, Drivers	Lakeland-Winter Haven MSA, FL	H	12.68 FQ	19.67 AW	27.64 TQ	FLBLS	10/01-12/01
Transportation, Movers, Drivers	Melbourne-Titusville-Palm Bay MSA, FL	H	10.68 FQ	19.03 AW	27.78 TQ	FLBLS	10/01-12/01
Transportation, Movers, Drivers	Miami PMSA, FL	H	8.08 FQ	20.06 AW	34.18 TQ	FLBLS	10/01-12/01

AAW	Average annual wage	**AOH**	Average offered, high	**ASH**	Average starting, high	**H**	Hourly	**M**	Monthly	**S**	Special: hourly and annual
AE	Average entry wage	**AOL**	Average offered, low	**ASL**	Average starting, low	**HI**	Highest wage paid	**MTC**	Median total compensation	**TQ**	Third quartile wage
AEX	Average experienced wage	**APH**	Average pay, high range	**AW**	Average wage paid	**HR**	High end range	**MW**	Median wage paid	**W**	Weekly
AO	Average offered	**APL**	Average pay, low range	**FQ**	First quartile wage	**LR**	Low end range	**SQ**	Second quartile wage	**Y**	Yearly

Occupation/Type/Industry	Location	Per	Low	Mid	High	Source	Date
First-Line Supervisor/Manager							
Transportation, Movers, Drivers	Naples MSA, FL	H	10.84 FQ	18.63 AW	29.44 TQ	FLBLS	10/01-12/01
Transportation, Movers, Drivers	Ocala MSA, FL	H	11.67 FQ	18.04 AW	25.65 TQ	FLBLS	10/01-12/01
Transportation, Movers, Drivers	Orlando MSA, FL	H	9.96 FQ	18.72 AW	27.65 TQ	FLBLS	10/01-12/01
Transportation, Movers, Drivers	Pensacola MSA, FL	H	9.71 FQ	20.18 AW	33.74 TQ	FLBLS	10/01-12/01
Transportation, Movers, Drivers	Sarasota-Bradenton MSA, FL	H	9.55 FQ	19.50 AW	29.61 TQ	FLBLS	10/01-12/01
Transportation, Movers, Drivers	Tallahassee MSA, FL	H	11.22 FQ	18.28 AW	30.42 TQ	FLBLS	10/01-12/01
Transportation, Movers, Drivers	Tampa-St. Petersburg-Clearwater MSA, FL	H	11.06 FQ	19.34 AW	26.96 TQ	FLBLS	10/01-12/01
Transportation, Movers, Drivers	West Palm Beach-Boca Raton MSA, FL	H	10.51 FQ	18.71 AW	27.25 TQ	FLBLS	10/01-12/01
Transportation, Movers, Drivers	Georgia	H	12.99 FQ	22.70 AW	34.86 TQ	GABLS	10/01-12/01
Transportation, Movers, Drivers	Atlanta MSA, GA	H	15.40 FQ	26.32 AW	42.70 TQ	GABLS	10/01-12/01
Transportation, Movers, Drivers	Augusta-Aiken MSA, GA-SC	H	11.14 FQ	18.54 AW	28.71 TQ	GABLS	10/01-12/01
Transportation, Movers, Drivers	Columbus MSA, GA-AL	H	13.60 FQ	19.76 AW	26.55 TQ	GABLS	10/01-12/01
Transportation, Movers, Drivers	Macon MSA, GA	H	12.53 FQ	22.24 AW	34.56 TQ	GABLS	10/01-12/01
Transportation, Movers, Drivers	Savannah MSA, GA	H	13.90 FQ	20.23 AW	28.30 TQ	GABLS	10/01-12/01
Transportation, Movers, Drivers	Hawaii	H	10.00 FQ	21.21 AW	34.72 TQ	HIBLS	10/01-12/01
Transportation, Movers, Drivers	Honolulu MSA, HI	H	9.73 FQ	20.97 AW	34.58 TQ	HIBLS	10/01-12/01
Transportation, Movers, Drivers	Idaho	H	9.86 FQ	17.54 AW	28.03 TQ	IDBLS	10/01-12/01
Transportation, Movers, Drivers	Boise City MSA, ID	H	10.61 FQ	17.95 AW	27.13 TQ	IDBLS	10/01-12/01
Transportation, Movers, Drivers	Illinois	H	11.20 FQ	22.39 AW	33.71 TQ	ILBLS	10/01-12/01
Transportation, Movers, Drivers	Champaign-Urbana MSA, IL	H	11.93 FQ	21.25 AW	27.05 TQ	ILBLS	10/01-12/01
Transportation, Movers, Drivers	Chicago PMSA, IL	H	12.12 FQ	23.64 AW	34.49 TQ	ILBLS	10/01-12/01
Transportation, Movers, Drivers	Peoria-Pekin MSA, IL	H	9.01 FQ	19.50 AW	35.48 TQ	ILBLS	10/01-12/01
Transportation, Movers, Drivers	Rockford MSA, IL	H	11.30 FQ	19.13 AW	28.75 TQ	ILBLS	10/01-12/01
Transportation, Movers, Drivers	Springfield MSA, IL	H	9.77 FQ	20.76 AW	36.37 TQ	ILBLS	10/01-12/01
Transportation, Movers, Drivers	Indiana	H	11.86 FQ	20.68 AW	30.23 TQ	INBLS	10/01-12/01
Transportation, Movers, Drivers	Elkhart-Goshen MSA, IN	H	13.83 FQ	19.97 AW	27.28 TQ	INBLS	10/01-12/01
Transportation, Movers, Drivers	Evansville-Henderson MSA, IN-KY	H	11.50 FQ	19.05 AW	27.34 TQ	INBLS	10/01-12/01
Transportation, Movers, Drivers	Fort Wayne MSA, IN	H	13.13 FQ	19.93 AW	29.63 TQ	INBLS	10/01-12/01
Transportation, Movers, Drivers	Gary PMSA, IN	H	11.41 FQ	21.62 AW	29.27 TQ	INBLS	10/01-12/01
Transportation, Movers, Drivers	Indianapolis MSA, IN	H	11.57 FQ	21.01 AW	29.76 TQ	INBLS	10/01-12/01
Transportation, Movers, Drivers	Lafayette MSA, IN	H	11.33 FQ	24.38 AW	35.74 TQ	INBLS	10/01-12/01
Transportation, Movers, Drivers	South Bend MSA, IN	H	13.77 FQ	21.88 AW	31.85 TQ	INBLS	10/01-12/01
Transportation, Movers, Drivers	Iowa	H	11.86 FQ	19.16 AW	27.17 TQ	IABLS	10/01-12/01
Transportation, Movers, Drivers	Cedar Rapids MSA, IA	H	14.21 FQ	18.88 AW	26.42 TQ	IABLS	10/01-12/01
Transportation, Movers, Drivers	Davenport-Moline-Rock Island MSA, IA-IL	H	12.19 FQ	20.85 AW	33.65 TQ	IABLS	10/01-12/01
Transportation, Movers, Drivers	Des Moines MSA, IA	H	11.77 FQ	19.98 AW	27.75 TQ	IABLS	10/01-12/01
Transportation, Movers, Drivers	Kansas	H	11.52 FQ	21.04 AW	33.52 TQ	KSBLS	10/01-12/01
Transportation, Movers, Drivers	Topeka MSA, KS	H	13.82 FQ	22.29 AW	33.38 TQ	KSBLS	10/01-12/01
Transportation, Movers, Drivers	Wichita MSA, KS	H	11.25 FQ	20.69 AW	38.02 TQ	KSBLS	10/01-12/01
Transportation, Movers, Drivers	Kentucky	H	11.32 FQ	19.15 AW	28.54 TQ	KYBLS	10/01-12/01
Transportation, Movers, Drivers	Lexington MSA, KY	H	11.38 FQ	17.87 AW	26.65 TQ	KYBLS	10/01-12/01
Transportation, Movers, Drivers	Louisville MSA, KY-IN	H	13.11 FQ	20.45 AW	31.81 TQ	KYBLS	10/01-12/01
Transportation, Movers, Drivers	Louisiana	H	11.52 FQ	20.02 AW	30.06 TQ	LABLS	10/01-12/01
Transportation, Movers, Drivers	Baton Rouge MSA, LA	H	11.51 FQ	18.49 AW	27.43 TQ	LABLS	10/01-12/01
Transportation, Movers, Drivers	Houma MSA, LA	H	11.68 FQ	21.31 AW	31.13 TQ	LABLS	10/01-12/01
Transportation, Movers, Drivers	Lafayette MSA, LA	H	13.63 FQ	21.43 AW	29.00 TQ	LABLS	10/01-12/01
Transportation, Movers, Drivers	Lake Charles MSA, LA	H	12.50 FQ	18.21 AW	25.01 TQ	LABLS	10/01-12/01
Transportation, Movers, Drivers	New Orleans MSA, LA	H	11.91 FQ	19.57 AW	29.01 TQ	LABLS	10/01-12/01
Transportation, Movers, Drivers	Shreveport-Bossier City MSA, LA	H	12.10 FQ	23.16 AW	35.79 TQ	LABLS	10/01-12/01
Transportation, Movers, Drivers	Maine	H	11.68 FQ	18.60 AW	27.04 TQ	MEBLS	10/01-12/01
Transportation, Movers, Drivers	Portland MSA, ME	H	11.13 FQ	18.65 AW	26.68 TQ	MEBLS	10/01-12/01
Transportation, Movers, Drivers	Maryland	H	10.00 FQ	20.07 AW	29.12 TQ	MDBLS	10/01-12/01
Transportation, Movers, Drivers	Baltimore PMSA, MD	H	11.19 FQ	20.32 AW	28.54 TQ	MDBLS	10/01-12/01
Transportation, Movers, Drivers	Massachusetts	H	12.76 FQ	21.76 AW	31.76 TQ	MABLS	10/01-12/01
Transportation, Movers, Drivers	Boston PMSA, MA-NH	H	12.97 FQ	22.70 AW	33.07 TQ	MABLS	10/01-12/01
Transportation, Movers, Drivers	Brockton PMSA, MA	H	15.12 FQ	22.26 AW	32.00 TQ	MABLS	10/01-12/01
Transportation, Movers, Drivers	Lawrence PMSA, MA-NH	H	12.36 FQ	19.50 AW	26.83 TQ	MABLS	10/01-12/01
Transportation, Movers, Drivers	Lowell PMSA, MA-NH	H	14.57 FQ	23.53 AW	33.58 TQ	MABLS	10/01-12/01
Transportation, Movers, Drivers	New Bedford PMSA, MA	H	12.24 FQ	19.57 AW	31.01 TQ	MABLS	10/01-12/01
Transportation, Movers, Drivers	Springfield MSA, MA	H	10.75 FQ	18.68 AW	26.90 TQ	MABLS	10/01-12/01
Transportation, Movers, Drivers	Worcester PMSA, MA-CT	H	12.69 FQ	20.63 AW	31.30 TQ	MABLS	10/01-12/01
Transportation, Movers, Drivers	Michigan	H	12.75 FQ	22.71 AW	33.77 TQ	MIBLS	10/01-12/01
Transportation, Movers, Drivers	Ann Arbor PMSA, MI	H	14.06 FQ	25.63 AW	37.98 TQ	MIBLS	10/01-12/01
Transportation, Movers, Drivers	Detroit PMSA, MI	H	13.81 FQ	23.86 AW	34.31 TQ	MIBLS	10/01-12/01
Transportation, Movers, Drivers	Flint PMSA, MI	H	13.96 FQ	23.58 AW	32.70 TQ	MIBLS	10/01-12/01

AAW	Average annual wage	**AOH**	Average offered, high	**ASH**	Average starting, high	**H**	Hourly	**M**	Monthly	**S**	Special: hourly and annual
AE	Average entry wage	**AOL**	Average offered, low	**ASL**	Average starting, low	**HI**	Highest wage paid	**MTC**	Median total compensation	**TQ**	Third quartile wage
AEX	Average experienced wage	**APH**	Average pay, high range	**AW**	Average wage paid	**HR**	High end range	**MW**	Median wage paid	**W**	Weekly
AO	Average offered	**APL**	Average pay, low range	**FQ**	First quartile wage	**LR**	Low end range	**SQ**	Second quartile wage	**Y**	Yearly

Occupation/Type/Industry	Location	Per	Low	Mid	High	Source	Date
First-Line Supervisor/Manager							
Transportation, Movers, Drivers	Grand Rapids-Muskegon-Holland MSA, MI	H	14.61 FQ	21.99 AW	33.43 TQ	MIBLS	10/01-12/01
Transportation, Movers, Drivers	Kalamazoo-Battle Creek MSA, MI	H	12.85 FQ	23.41 AW	34.47 TQ	MIBLS	10/01-12/01
Transportation, Movers, Drivers	Lansing-East Lansing MSA, MI	H	11.77 FQ	21.41 AW	34.29 TQ	MIBLS	10/01-12/01
Transportation, Movers, Drivers	Saginaw-Bay City-Midland MSA, MI	H	11.87 FQ	21.66 AW	33.04 TQ	MIBLS	10/01-12/01
Transportation, Movers, Drivers	Minnesota	H	10.97 FQ	19.81 AW	28.30 TQ	MNBLS	10/01-12/01
Transportation, Movers, Drivers	Duluth-Superior MSA, MN-WI	H	11.73 FQ	19.68 AW	27.74 TQ	MNBLS	10/01-12/01
Transportation, Movers, Drivers	Minneapolis-St. Paul MSA, MN-WI	H	12.64 FQ	21.15 AW	29.65 TQ	MNBLS	10/01-12/01
Transportation, Movers, Drivers	St. Cloud MSA, MN	H	11.12 FQ	19.67 AW	27.80 TQ	MNBLS	10/01-12/01
Transportation, Movers, Drivers	Mississippi	H	9.71 FQ	17.00 AW	27.60 TQ	MSBLS	10/01-12/01
Transportation, Movers, Drivers	Biloxi-Gulfport-Pascagoula MSA, MS	H	11.27 FQ	20.67 AW	38.97 TQ	MSBLS	10/01-12/01
Transportation, Movers, Drivers	Jackson MSA, MS	H	12.21 FQ	20.16 AW	28.22 TQ	MSBLS	10/01-12/01
Transportation, Movers, Drivers	Missouri	H	9.72 FQ	19.78 AW	31.61 TQ	MOBLS	10/01-12/01
Transportation, Movers, Drivers	Kansas City MSA, MO-KS	H	13.20 FQ	23.24 AW	39.84 TQ	MOBLS	10/01-12/01
Transportation, Movers, Drivers	St. Louis MSA, MO-IL	H	9.73 FQ	20.64 AW	31.93 TQ	MOBLS	10/01-12/01
Transportation, Movers, Drivers	Springfield MSA, MO	H	11.17 FQ	19.60 AW	31.08 TQ	MOBLS	10/01-12/01
Transportation, Movers, Drivers	Montana	H	10.11 FQ	20.19 AW	33.77 TQ	MTBLS	10/01-12/01
Transportation, Movers, Drivers	Billings MSA, MT	H	9.83 FQ	19.18 AW	33.66 TQ	MTBLS	10/01-12/01
Transportation, Movers, Drivers	Nebraska	H	11.40 FQ	19.57 AW	31.99 TQ	NEBLS	10/01-12/01
Transportation, Movers, Drivers	Lincoln MSA, NE	H	10.07 FQ	16.59 AW	26.11 TQ	NEBLS	10/01-12/01
Transportation, Movers, Drivers	Omaha MSA, NE-IA	H	13.44 FQ	20.16 AW	29.42 TQ	NEBLS	10/01-12/01
Transportation, Movers, Drivers	Nevada	H	10.89 FQ	19.12 AW	28.18 TQ	NVBLS	10/01-12/01
Transportation, Movers, Drivers	Las Vegas MSA, NV-AZ	H	10.11 FQ	19.22 AW	28.87 TQ	NVBLS	10/01-12/01
Transportation, Movers, Drivers	Reno MSA, NV	H	11.90 FQ	18.66 AW	27.92 TQ	NVBLS	10/01-12/01
Transportation, Movers, Drivers	New Hampshire	H	12.67 FQ	23.95 AW	40.89 TQ	NHBLS	10/01-12/01
Transportation, Movers, Drivers	Manchester PMSA, NH	H	13.16 FQ	24.67 AW	39.12 TQ	NHBLS	10/01-12/01
Transportation, Movers, Drivers	Nashua PMSA, NH	H	16.24 FQ	36.65 AW	65.88 TQ	NHBLS	10/01-12/01
Transportation, Movers, Drivers	Portsmouth-Rochester PMSA, NH-ME	H	12.99 FQ	19.45 AW	29.09 TQ	NHBLS	10/01-12/01
Transportation, Movers, Drivers	New Jersey	H	12.78 FQ	23.18 AW	34.40 TQ	NJBLS	10/01-12/01
Transportation, Movers, Drivers	Atlantic-Cape May PMSA, NJ	H	11.61 FQ	18.49 AW	26.81 TQ	NJBLS	10/01-12/01
Transportation, Movers, Drivers	Bergen-Passaic PMSA, NJ	H	11.56 FQ	21.97 AW	34.77 TQ	NJBLS	10/01-12/01
Transportation, Movers, Drivers	Jersey City PMSA, NJ	H	14.83 FQ	24.01 AW	35.71 TQ	NJBLS	10/01-12/01
Transportation, Movers, Drivers	Middlesex-Somerset-Hunterdon PMSA, NJ	H	13.46 FQ	23.38 AW	33.63 TQ	NJBLS	10/01-12/01
Transportation, Movers, Drivers	Monmouth-Ocean PMSA, NJ	H	12.83 FQ	22.58 AW	31.88 TQ	NJBLS	10/01-12/01
Transportation, Movers, Drivers	Newark PMSA, NJ	H	12.27 FQ	24.42 AW	36.99 TQ	NJBLS	10/01-12/01
Transportation, Movers, Drivers	Trenton PMSA, NJ	H	13.14 FQ	22.84 AW	33.50 TQ	NJBLS	10/01-12/01
Transportation, Movers, Drivers	New Mexico	H	10.66 FQ	20.90 AW	33.71 TQ	NMBLS	10/01-12/01
Transportation, Movers, Drivers	Albuquerque MSA, NM	H	10.48 FQ	22.63 AW	46.34 TQ	NMBLS	10/01-12/01
Transportation, Movers, Drivers	Las Cruces MSA, NM	H	11.78 FQ	14.08 AW	16.78 TQ	NMBLS	10/01-12/01
Transportation, Movers, Drivers	New York	H	12.64 FQ	23.12 AW	37.01 TQ	NYBLS	10/01-12/01
Transportation, Movers, Drivers	Albany-Schenectady-Troy MSA, NY	H	11.55 FQ	20.54 AW	30.12 TQ	NYBLS	10/01-12/01
Transportation, Movers, Drivers	Binghamton MSA, NY	H	11.30 FQ	20.17 AW	29.45 TQ	NYBLS	10/01-12/01
Transportation, Movers, Drivers	Buffalo-Niagara Falls MSA, NY	H	11.58 FQ	21.95 AW	34.46 TQ	NYBLS	10/01-12/01
Transportation, Movers, Drivers	Dutchess County PMSA, NY	H	14.48 FQ	21.89 AW	32.07 TQ	NYBLS	10/01-12/01
Transportation, Movers, Drivers	Nassau-Suffolk PMSA, NY	H	13.84 FQ	25.49 AW	43.34 TQ	NYBLS	10/01-12/01
Transportation, Movers, Drivers	New York PMSA, NY	H	12.94 FQ	23.69 AW	38.65 TQ	NYBLS	10/01-12/01
Transportation, Movers, Drivers	Newburgh PMSA, NY-PA	H	15.39 FQ	22.75 AW	32.73 TQ	NYBLS	10/01-12/01
Transportation, Movers, Drivers	Rochester MSA, NY	H	11.66 FQ	19.77 AW	28.12 TQ	NYBLS	10/01-12/01
Transportation, Movers, Drivers	Syracuse MSA, NY	H	12.73 FQ	20.23 AW	30.27 TQ	NYBLS	10/01-12/01
Transportation, Movers, Drivers	Utica-Rome MSA, NY	H	11.67 FQ	20.94 AW	31.10 TQ	NYBLS	10/01-12/01
Transportation, Movers, Drivers	North Carolina	H	12.19 FQ	19.21 AW	27.20 TQ	NCBLS	10/01-12/01
Transportation, Movers, Drivers	Asheville MSA, NC	H	13.29 FQ	18.65 AW	25.19 TQ	NCBLS	10/01-12/01
Transportation, Movers, Drivers	Charlotte-Gastonia-Rock Hill MSA, NC-SC	H	12.86 FQ	21.06 AW	29.00 TQ	NCBLS	10/01-12/01
Transportation, Movers, Drivers	Fayetteville MSA, NC	H	11.48 FQ	18.41 AW	30.45 TQ	NCBLS	10/01-12/01
Transportation, Movers, Drivers	Greensboro-Winston-Salem-High Point MSA, NC	H	12.13 FQ	18.84 AW	26.15 TQ	NCBLS	10/01-12/01
Transportation, Movers, Drivers	Hickory-Morganton-Lenoir MSA, NC	H	11.91 FQ	19.45 AW	29.45 TQ	NCBLS	10/01-12/01
Transportation, Movers, Drivers	Raleigh-Durham-Chapel Hill MSA, NC	H	13.51 FQ	19.91 AW	31.17 TQ	NCBLS	10/01-12/01
Transportation, Movers, Drivers	Wilmington MSA, NC	H	12.46 FQ	19.09 AW	28.22 TQ	NCBLS	10/01-12/01
Transportation, Movers, Drivers	North Dakota	H	11.45 FQ	19.33 AW	28.17 TQ	NDBLS	10/01-12/01

AAW	Average annual wage	AOH	Average offered, high	ASH	Average starting, high	H	Hourly	M	Monthly	S	Special: hourly and annual
AE	Average entry wage	AOL	Average offered, low	ASL	Average starting, low	HI	Highest wage paid	MTC	Median total compensation	TQ	Third quartile wage
AEX	Average experienced wage	APH	Average pay, high range	AW	Average wage paid	HR	High end range	MW	Median wage paid	W	Weekly
AO	Average offered	APL	Average pay, low range	FQ	First quartile wage	LR	Low end range	SQ	Second quartile wage	Y	Yearly

Occupation/Type/Industry	Location	Per	Low	Mid	High	Source	Date
First-Line Supervisor/Manager							
Transportation, Movers, Drivers	Fargo-Moorhead MSA, ND-MN	H	11.08 FQ	19.26 AW	27.05 TQ	NDBLS	10/01-12/01
Transportation, Movers, Drivers	Ohio	H	12.19 FQ	20.31 AW	30.05 TQ	OHBLS	10/01-12/01
Transportation, Movers, Drivers	Akron PMSA, OH	H	9.66 FQ	21.55 AW	45.63 TQ	OHBLS	10/01-12/01
Transportation, Movers, Drivers	Canton-Massillon MSA, OH	H	12.50 FQ	19.63 AW	32.04 TQ	OHBLS	10/01-12/01
Transportation, Movers, Drivers	Cincinnati PMSA, OH-KY-IN	H	13.18 FQ	20.60 AW	29.09 TQ	OHBLS	10/01-12/01
Transportation, Movers, Drivers	Cleveland-Lorain-Elyria PMSA, OH	H	13.64 FQ	21.54 AW	33.39 TQ	OHBLS	10/01-12/01
Transportation, Movers, Drivers	Columbus MSA, OH	H	13.58 FQ	19.05 AW	26.56 TQ	OHBLS	10/01-12/01
Transportation, Movers, Drivers	Dayton-Springfield MSA, OH	H	11.69 FQ	22.11 AW	33.99 TQ	OHBLS	10/01-12/01
Transportation, Movers, Drivers	Hamilton-Middletown PMSA, OH	H	14.32 FQ	19.74 AW	27.63 TQ	OHBLS	10/01-12/01
Transportation, Movers, Drivers	Mansfield MSA, OH	H	11.11 FQ	18.13 AW	26.62 TQ	OHBLS	10/01-12/01
Transportation, Movers, Drivers	Toledo MSA, OH	H	11.94 FQ	21.73 AW	32.69 TQ	OHBLS	10/01-12/01
Transportation, Movers, Drivers	Youngstown-Warren MSA, OH	H	10.67 FQ	20.54 AW	32.61 TQ	OHBLS	10/01-12/01
Transportation, Movers, Drivers	Oklahoma	H	9.75 FQ	19.95 AW	31.03 TQ	OKBLS	10/01-12/01
Transportation, Movers, Drivers	Oklahoma City MSA, OK	H	13.15 FQ	21.90 AW	33.92 TQ	OKBLS	10/01-12/01
Transportation, Movers, Drivers	Tulsa MSA, OK	H	11.36 FQ	21.16 AW	32.10 TQ	OKBLS	10/01-12/01
Transportation, Movers, Drivers	Oregon	H	12.16 FQ	22.81 AW	38.46 TQ	ORBLS	10/01-12/01
Transportation, Movers, Drivers	Eugene-Springfield MSA, OR	H	9.64 FQ	19.58 AW	27.91 TQ	ORBLS	10/01-12/01
Transportation, Movers, Drivers	Medford-Ashland MSA, OR	H	9.57 FQ	19.18 AW	33.91 TQ	ORBLS	10/01-12/01
Transportation, Movers, Drivers	Portland-Vancouver PMSA, OR-WA	H	13.59 FQ	25.32 AW	41.41 TQ	ORBLS	10/01-12/01
Transportation, Movers, Drivers	Salem PMSA, OR	H	11.77 FQ	19.55 AW	27.61 TQ	ORBLS	10/01-12/01
Transportation, Movers, Drivers	Pennsylvania	H	11.66 FQ	20.59 AW	31.21 TQ	PABLS	10/01-12/01
Transportation, Movers, Drivers	Allentown-Bethlehem-Easton MSA, PA	H	15.49 FQ	21.55 AW	29.45 TQ	PABLS	10/01-12/01
Transportation, Movers, Drivers	Erie MSA, PA	H	9.35 FQ	18.73 AW	28.53 TQ	PABLS	10/01-12/01
Transportation, Movers, Drivers	Harrisburg-Lebanon-Carlisle MSA, PA	H	13.97 FQ	21.34 AW	30.70 TQ	PABLS	10/01-12/01
Transportation, Movers, Drivers	Johnstown MSA, PA	H	9.84 FQ	18.96 AW	30.91 TQ	PABLS	10/01-12/01
Transportation, Movers, Drivers	Lancaster MSA, PA	H	13.70 FQ	20.32 AW	27.48 TQ	PABLS	10/01-12/01
Transportation, Movers, Drivers	Philadelphia PMSA, PA-NJ	H	13.42 FQ	23.08 AW	33.60 TQ	PABLS	10/01-12/01
Transportation, Movers, Drivers	Pittsburgh MSA, PA	H	11.11 FQ	17.88 AW	28.31 TQ	PABLS	10/01-12/01
Transportation, Movers, Drivers	Reading MSA, PA	H	12.30 FQ	18.80 AW	26.45 TQ	PABLS	10/01-12/01
Transportation, Movers, Drivers	Scranton-Wilkes-Barre-Hazleton MSA, PA	H	8.63 FQ	18.36 AW	27.91 TQ	PABLS	10/01-12/01
Transportation, Movers, Drivers	York MSA, PA	H	12.79 FQ	20.37 AW	28.75 TQ	PABLS	10/01-12/01
Transportation, Movers, Drivers	Rhode Island	H	13.58 FQ	21.54 AW	31.99 TQ	RIBLS	10/01-12/01
Transportation, Movers, Drivers	Providence-Fall River-Warwick MSA, RI-MA	H	13.62 FQ	21.71 AW	32.04 TQ	RIBLS	10/01-12/01
Transportation, Movers, Drivers	South Carolina	H	12.39 FQ	21.93 AW	33.84 TQ	SCBLS	10/01-12/01
Transportation, Movers, Drivers	Charleston-North Charleston MSA, SC	H	13.17 FQ	22.64 AW	34.44 TQ	SCBLS	10/01-12/01
Transportation, Movers, Drivers	Columbia MSA, SC	H	13.48 FQ	25.21 AW	34.54 TQ	SCBLS	10/01-12/01
Transportation, Movers, Drivers	Greenville-Spartanburg-Anderson MSA, SC	H	13.55 FQ	22.63 AW	35.32 TQ	SCBLS	10/01-12/01
Transportation, Movers, Drivers	Myrtle Beach MSA, SC	H	11.33 FQ	20.84 AW	32.98 TQ	SCBLS	10/01-12/01
Transportation, Movers, Drivers	South Dakota	H	12.86 FQ	20.38 AW	27.17 TQ	SDBLS	10/01-12/01
Transportation, Movers, Drivers	Sioux Falls MSA, SD	H	12.43 FQ	20.18 AW	27.70 TQ	SDBLS	10/01-12/01
Transportation, Movers, Drivers	Tennessee	H	11.24 FQ	20.62 AW	30.16 TQ	TNBLS	10/01-12/01
Transportation, Movers, Drivers	Chattanooga MSA, TN-GA	H	15.40 FQ	22.06 AW	30.06 TQ	TNBLS	10/01-12/01
Transportation, Movers, Drivers	Clarksville-Hopkinsville MSA, TN-KY	H	11.45 FQ	18.15 AW	27.35 TQ	TNBLS	10/01-12/01
Transportation, Movers, Drivers	Johnson City-Kingsport-Bristol MSA, TN-VA	H	10.40 FQ	17.22 AW	25.68 TQ	TNBLS	10/01-12/01
Transportation, Movers, Drivers	Knoxville MSA, TN	H	12.04 FQ	20.28 AW	28.08 TQ	TNBLS	10/01-12/01
Transportation, Movers, Drivers	Memphis MSA, TN-AR-MS	H	11.09 FQ	22.94 AW	34.35 TQ	TNBLS	10/01-12/01
Transportation, Movers, Drivers	Nashville MSA, TN	H	7.45 FQ	17.13 AW	28.00 TQ	TNBLS	10/01-12/01
Transportation, Movers, Drivers	Texas	H	10.36 FQ	20.22 AW	32.03 TQ	TXBLS	10/01-12/01
Transportation, Movers, Drivers	Amarillo MSA, TX	H	9.73 FQ	16.73 AW	25.92 TQ	TXBLS	10/01-12/01
Transportation, Movers, Drivers	Austin-San Marcos MSA, TX	H	9.42 FQ	15.39 AW	24.34 TQ	TXBLS	10/01-12/01
Transportation, Movers, Drivers	Beaumont-Port Arthur MSA, TX	H	11.89 FQ	20.16 AW	31.51 TQ	TXBLS	10/01-12/01
Transportation, Movers, Drivers	Brazoria PMSA, TX	H	14.30 FQ	19.34 AW	25.61 TQ	TXBLS	10/01-12/01
Transportation, Movers, Drivers	Brownsville-Harlingen-San Benito MSA, TX	H	9.25 FQ	15.63 AW	23.38 TQ	TXBLS	10/01-12/01
Transportation, Movers, Drivers	Corpus Christi MSA, TX	H	8.69 FQ	18.69 AW	32.05 TQ	TXBLS	10/01-12/01
Transportation, Movers, Drivers	Dallas PMSA, TX	H	11.32 FQ	20.05 AW	30.40 TQ	TXBLS	10/01-12/01
Transportation, Movers, Drivers	El Paso MSA, TX	H	9.18 FQ	16.44 AW	26.10 TQ	TXBLS	10/01-12/01

AAW	Average annual wage	**AOH**	Average offered, high	**ASH**	Average starting, high	**H**	Hourly	**M**	Monthly	**S**	Special: hourly and annual
AE	Average entry wage	**AOL**	Average offered, low	**ASL**	Average starting, low	**HI**	Highest wage paid	**MTC**	Median total compensation	**TQ**	Third quartile wage
AEX	Average experienced wage	**APH**	Average pay, high range	**AW**	Average wage paid	**HR**	High end range	**MW**	Median wage paid	**W**	Weekly
AO	Average offered	**APL**	Average pay, low range	**FQ**	First quartile wage	**LR**	Low end range	**SQ**	Second quartile wage	**Y**	Yearly

Occupation/Type/Industry	Location	Per	Low	Mid	High	Source	Date
First-Line Supervisor/Manager							
Transportation, Movers, Drivers	Fort Worth-Arlington PMSA, TX	H	13.36 FQ	24.57 AW	45.32 TQ	TXBLS	10/01-12/01
Transportation, Movers, Drivers	Galveston-Texas City PMSA, TX	H	9.95 FQ	21.56 AW	33.68 TQ	TXBLS	10/01-12/01
Transportation, Movers, Drivers	Houston PMSA, TX	H	12.69 FQ	23.32 AW	38.27 TQ	TXBLS	10/01-12/01
Transportation, Movers, Drivers	Killeen-Temple MSA, TX	H	12.54 FQ	21.01 AW	33.80 TQ	TXBLS	10/01-12/01
Transportation, Movers, Drivers	Laredo MSA, TX	H	9.84 FQ	21.08 AW	31.73 TQ	TXBLS	10/01-12/01
Transportation, Movers, Drivers	Longview-Marshall MSA, TX	H	10.39 FQ	20.06 AW	33.23 TQ	TXBLS	10/01-12/01
Transportation, Movers, Drivers	Lubbock MSA, TX	H	9.91 FQ	16.73 AW	25.68 TQ	TXBLS	10/01-12/01
Transportation, Movers, Drivers	McAllen-Edinburg-Mission MSA, TX	H	6.27 FQ	15.20 AW	25.70 TQ	TXBLS	10/01-12/01
Transportation, Movers, Drivers	Odessa-Midland MSA, TX	H	6.40 FQ	14.98 AW	26.07 TQ	TXBLS	10/01-12/01
Transportation, Movers, Drivers	San Antonio MSA, TX	H	10.51 FQ	18.12 AW	28.65 TQ	TXBLS	10/01-12/01
Transportation, Movers, Drivers	Tyler MSA, TX	H	11.51 FQ	17.72 AW	27.18 TQ	TXBLS	10/01-12/01
Transportation, Movers, Drivers	Waco MSA, TX	H	10.52 FQ	18.35 AW	26.88 TQ	TXBLS	10/01-12/01
Transportation, Movers, Drivers	Utah	H	10.29 FQ	19.17 AW	31.30 TQ	UTBLS	10/01-12/01
Transportation, Movers, Drivers	Provo-Orem MSA, UT	H	13.07 FQ	18.54 AW	27.26 TQ	UTBLS	10/01-12/01
Transportation, Movers, Drivers	Salt Lake City-Ogden MSA, UT	H	10.27 FQ	19.40 AW	32.42 TQ	UTBLS	10/01-12/01
Transportation, Movers, Drivers	Vermont	H	13.83 FQ	25.00 AW	38.64 TQ	VTBLS	10/01-12/01
Transportation, Movers, Drivers	Burlington MSA, VT	H	15.52 FQ	23.56 AW	35.38 TQ	VTBLS	10/01-12/01
Transportation, Movers, Drivers	Virginia	H	10.89 FQ	20.95 AW	33.53 TQ	VABLS	10/01-12/01
Transportation, Movers, Drivers	Lynchburg MSA, VA	H	10.12 FQ	19.34 AW	31.50 TQ	VABLS	10/01-12/01
Transportation, Movers, Drivers	Norfolk-Virginia Beach-Newport News MSA, VA-NC	H	12.50 FQ	21.92 AW	35.48 TQ	VABLS	10/01-12/01
Transportation, Movers, Drivers	Richmond-Petersburg MSA, VA	H	9.23 FQ	18.24 AW	28.67 TQ	VABLS	10/01-12/01
Transportation, Movers, Drivers	Roanoke MSA, VA	H	10.46 FQ	18.12 AW	27.02 TQ	VABLS	10/01-12/01
Transportation, Movers, Drivers	Washington	H	14.87 FQ	25.75 AW	39.70 TQ	WABLS	10/01-12/01
Transportation, Movers, Drivers	Bremerton PMSA, WA	H	16.85 FQ	26.09 AW	37.45 TQ	WABLS	10/01-12/01
Transportation, Movers, Drivers	Olympia PMSA, WA	H	14.88 FQ	24.57 AW	38.84 TQ	WABLS	10/01-12/01
Transportation, Movers, Drivers	Richland-Kennewick-Pasco MSA, WA	H	13.77 FQ	21.36 AW	28.68 TQ	WABLS	10/01-12/01
Transportation, Movers, Drivers	Seattle-Bellevue-Everett PMSA, WA	H	15.72 FQ	26.93 AW	41.50 TQ	WABLS	10/01-12/01
Transportation, Movers, Drivers	Spokane MSA, WA	H	12.03 FQ	21.82 AW	35.43 TQ	WABLS	10/01-12/01
Transportation, Movers, Drivers	Tacoma PMSA, WA	H	17.13 FQ	26.92 AW	39.88 TQ	WABLS	10/01-12/01
Transportation, Movers, Drivers	Yakima MSA, WA	H	12.85 FQ	20.65 AW	29.04 TQ	WABLS	10/01-12/01
Transportation, Movers, Drivers	West Virginia	H	11.22 FQ	17.99 AW	30.94 TQ	WVBLS	10/01-12/01
Transportation, Movers, Drivers	Charleston MSA, WV	H	10.26 FQ	18.19 AW	32.20 TQ	WVBLS	10/01-12/01
Transportation, Movers, Drivers	Huntington-Ashland MSA, WV-KY-OH	H	9.19 FQ	18.74 AW	31.30 TQ	WVBLS	10/01-12/01
Transportation, Movers, Drivers	Wisconsin	H	12.86 FQ	21.34 AW	31.28 TQ	WIBLS	10/01-12/01
Transportation, Movers, Drivers	Appleton-Oshkosh-Neenah MSA, WI	H	14.19 FQ	19.87 AW	29.48 TQ	WIBLS	10/01-12/01
Transportation, Movers, Drivers	Green Bay MSA, WI	H	14.42 FQ	22.47 AW	29.40 TQ	WIBLS	10/01-12/01
Transportation, Movers, Drivers	Madison MSA, WI	H	13.39 FQ	21.33 AW	28.95 TQ	WIBLS	10/01-12/01
Transportation, Movers, Drivers	Milwaukee-Waukesha PMSA, WI	H	12.53 FQ	21.20 AW	31.02 TQ	WIBLS	10/01-12/01
Transportation, Movers, Drivers	Racine PMSA, WI	H	8.49 FQ	18.71 AW	27.95 TQ	WIBLS	10/01-12/01
Transportation, Movers, Drivers	Wyoming	H	11.09 FQ	23.29 AW	35.97 TQ	WYBLS	10/01-12/01
Transportation, Movers, Drivers	Cheyenne MSA, WY	H	6.50 FQ	16.68 AW	31.81 TQ	WYBLS	10/01-12/01
Transportation, Movers, Drivers	Puerto Rico	H	6.75 FQ	12.59 AW	21.73 TQ	PRBLS	10/01-12/01
Transportation, Movers, Drivers	Virgin Islands	H	11.18 FQ	18.01 AW	25.45 TQ	VIBLS	10/01-12/01
Transportation, Movers, Drivers	Guam	H	9.45 FQ	16.77 AW	27.34 TQ	GUBLS	10/01-12/01
First Mate							
Tugboat	Jacksonville, FL	Y		50000 AEX		FLTU	2002
Fish and Game Warden	Arizona	Y	25530 FQ	38440 AW	51560 TQ	AZBLS	10/01-12/01
	Arkansas	Y	18190 FQ	29430 AW	46290 TQ	ARBLS	10/01-12/01
	California	Y	39140 FQ	49160 AW	63950 TQ	CABLS	10/01-12/01
	Colorado	Y	33190 FQ	45610 AW	55580 TQ	COBLS	10/01-12/01
	Connecticut	Y	29010 FQ	40260 AW	53550 TQ	CTBLS	10/01-12/01
	Georgia	Y	23040 FQ	26910 AW	33080 TQ	GABLS	10/01-12/01
	Hawaii	Y	32450 FQ	42090 AW	53560 TQ	HIBLS	10/01-12/01
	Idaho	Y	35740 FQ	43710 AW	56220 TQ	IDBLS	10/01-12/01
	Illinois	Y	20910 FQ	36670 AW	47640 TQ	ILBLS	10/01-12/01
	Iowa	Y	33900 FQ	45360 AW	54880 TQ	IABLS	10/01-12/01
	Louisiana	Y	25650 FQ	37280 AW	53050 TQ	LABLS	10/01-12/01
	Maine	Y	29040 FQ	36070 AW	43350 TQ	MEBLS	10/01-12/01

AAW Average annual wage; AE Average entry wage; AEX Average experienced wage; AO Average offered; AOH Average offered, high; AOL Average offered, low; APH Average pay, high range; APL Average pay, low range; ASH Average starting, high; ASL Average starting, low; AW Average wage paid; FQ First quartile wage; H Hourly; HI Highest wage paid; HR High end range; LR Low end range; M Monthly; MTC Median total compensation; MW Median wage paid; SQ Second quartile wage; S Special: hourly and annual; TQ Third quartile wage; W Weekly; Y Yearly

Occupation/Type/Industry	Location	Per	Low	Mid	High	Source	Date
Fish and Game Warden	Massachusetts	Y	19060 FQ	39830 AW	54740 TQ	MABLS	10/01-12/01
	Michigan	Y	38390 FQ	48840 AW	58970 TQ	MIBLS	10/01-12/01
	Mississippi	Y	18680 FQ	29910 AW	42710 TQ	MSBLS	10/01-12/01
	Nebraska	Y	32080 FQ	40250 AW	48310 TQ	NEBLS	10/01-12/01
	Nevada	Y	36830 FQ	47530 AW	55810 TQ	NVBLS	10/01-12/01
	New Mexico	Y	23800 FQ	34410 AW	47530 TQ	NMBLS	10/01-12/01
	New York	Y	32470 FQ	52530 AW	70120 TQ	NYBLS	10/01-12/01
	North Carolina	Y	23920 FQ	36830 AW	52810 TQ	NCBLS	10/01-12/01
	Ohio	Y	32170 FQ	43020 AW	54410 TQ	OHBLS	10/01-12/01
	Oklahoma	Y	22800 FQ	31510 AW	42740 TQ	OKBLS	10/01-12/01
	South Dakota	Y	28730 FQ	35130 AW	44040 TQ	SDBLS	10/01-12/01
	Tennessee	Y	25490 FQ	37610 AW	52910 TQ	TNBLS	10/01-12/01
	Texas	Y	35850 FQ	44690 AW	55170 TQ	TXBLS	10/01-12/01
	Utah	Y	24970 FQ	35520 AW	50400 TQ	UTBLS	10/01-12/01
	Vermont	Y	26480 FQ	38680 AW	52240 TQ	VTBLS	10/01-12/01
	Virginia	Y	26930 FQ	36960 AW	51480 TQ	VABLS	10/01-12/01
	Washington	Y	33210 FQ	46390 AW	56350 TQ	WABLS	10/01-12/01
	Wisconsin	Y	29890 FQ	41450 AW	54150 TQ	WIBLS	10/01-12/01
	Wyoming	Y	27380 FQ	39580 AW	51360 TQ	WYBLS	10/01-12/01
Fitness Trainer and Aerobics Instructor	United States	Y		18500-25760 AW		FREEP1	1/00-1/00
	Alabama	H	5.84 FQ	11.75 AW	20.31 TQ	ALBLS	10/01-12/01
	Alaska	H	7.87 FQ	15.07 AW	21.66 TQ	AKBLS	10/01-12/01
	Arizona	H	6.90 FQ	12.46 AW	23.23 TQ	AZBLS	10/01-12/01
	Arkansas	H	6.13 FQ	10.01 AW	15.34 TQ	ARBLS	10/01-12/01
	California	H	6.59 FQ	17.26 AW	32.90 TQ	CABLS	10/01-12/01
	Colorado	H	7.69 FQ	15.05 AW	25.97 TQ	COBLS	10/01-12/01
	Connecticut	H	8.41 FQ	18.14 AW	37.31 TQ	CTBLS	10/01-12/01
	Delaware	H	7.18 FQ	12.19 AW	19.70 TQ	DEBLS	10/01-12/01
	District of Columbia	H	7.30 FQ	16.46 AW	39.56 TQ	DCBLS	10/01-12/01
	Florida	H	6.08 FQ	12.54 AW	22.98 TQ	FLBLS	10/01-12/01
	Georgia	H	6.87 FQ	19.26 AW	39.09 TQ	GABLS	10/01-12/01
	Hawaii	H	7.28 FQ	14.13 AW	24.50 TQ	HIBLS	10/01-12/01
	Idaho	H	6.97 FQ	13.88 AW	18.56 TQ	IDBLS	10/01-12/01
	Illinois	H	6.64 FQ	15.79 AW	29.71 TQ	ILBLS	10/01-12/01
	Indiana	H	6.12 FQ	12.87 AW	24.41 TQ	INBLS	10/01-12/01
	Iowa	H	5.74 FQ	9.06 AW	13.90 TQ	IABLS	10/01-12/01
	Kansas	H	5.87 FQ	10.98 AW	20.03 TQ	KSBLS	10/01-12/01
	Kentucky	H	5.97 FQ	10.67 AW	17.13 TQ	KYBLS	10/01-12/01
	Louisiana	H	5.66 FQ	9.64 AW	15.91 TQ	LABLS	10/01-12/01
	Maine	H	6.41 FQ	11.41 AW	17.34 TQ	MEBLS	10/01-12/01
	Maryland	H	6.26 FQ	12.66 AW	22.38 TQ	MDBLS	10/01-12/01
	Massachusetts	H	7.13 FQ	14.32 AW	26.37 TQ	MABLS	10/01-12/01
	Michigan	H	6.51 FQ	12.57 AW	21.05 TQ	MIBLS	10/01-12/01
	Minnesota	H	6.64 FQ	12.42 AW	20.81 TQ	MNBLS	10/01-12/01
	Mississippi	H	6.17 FQ	10.00 AW	15.28 TQ	MSBLS	10/01-12/01
	Missouri	H	5.85 FQ	10.31 AW	17.59 TQ	MOBLS	10/01-12/01
	Montana	H	5.89 FQ	9.42 AW	13.48 TQ	MTBLS	10/01-12/01
	Nebraska	H	6.19 FQ	12.59 AW	21.05 TQ	NEBLS	10/01-12/01
	Nevada	H	5.94 FQ	12.24 AW	20.64 TQ	NVBLS	10/01-12/01
	New Hampshire	H	7.37 FQ	12.16 AW	17.63 TQ	NHBLS	10/01-12/01
	New Jersey	H	7.27 FQ	12.06 AW	21.36 TQ	NJBLS	10/01-12/01
	New Mexico	H	6.82 FQ	14.05 AW	22.04 TQ	NMBLS	10/01-12/01
	New York	H	6.99 FQ	19.27 AW	37.68 TQ	NYBLS	10/01-12/01
	North Carolina	H	6.44 FQ	11.77 AW	19.19 TQ	NCBLS	10/01-12/01
	North Dakota	H	5.71 FQ	8.58 AW	12.75 TQ	NDBLS	10/01-12/01
	Ohio	H	6.22 FQ	11.18 AW	18.73 TQ	OHBLS	10/01-12/01
	Oklahoma	H	5.91 FQ	10.49 AW	17.07 TQ	OKBLS	10/01-12/01
	Oregon	H	7.85 FQ	15.56 AW	26.37 TQ	ORBLS	10/01-12/01
	Pennsylvania	H	6.01 FQ	10.66 AW	16.88 TQ	PABLS	10/01-12/01
	Rhode Island	H	6.84 FQ	10.18 AW	17.39 TQ	RIBLS	10/01-12/01
	South Carolina	H	6.42 FQ	12.39 AW	19.73 TQ	SCBLS	10/01-12/01
	South Dakota	H	6.37 FQ	9.67 AW	14.11 TQ	SDBLS	10/01-12/01
	Tennessee	H	5.99 FQ	10.74 AW	19.21 TQ	TNBLS	10/01-12/01
	Texas	H	6.74 FQ	14.75 AW	25.04 TQ	TXBLS	10/01-12/01
	Utah	H	8.02 FQ	17.13 AW	25.90 TQ	UTBLS	10/01-12/01
	Vermont	H	7.35 FQ	13.31 AW	17.89 TQ	VTBLS	10/01-12/01
	Virginia	H	6.97 FQ	14.89 AW	29.23 TQ	VABLS	10/01-12/01
	Washington	H	7.47 FQ	15.76 AW	28.69 TQ	WABLS	10/01-12/01
	West Virginia	H	6.04 FQ	9.93 AW	15.48 TQ	WVBLS	10/01-12/01

AAW Average annual wage · **AE** Average entry wage · **AEX** Average experienced wage · **AO** Average offered · **AOH** Average offered, high · **AOL** Average offered, low · **APH** Average pay, high range · **APL** Average pay, low range · **ASH** Average starting, high · **ASL** Average starting, low · **AW** Average wage paid · **FQ** First quartile wage · **H** Hourly · **HI** Highest wage paid · **HR** High end range · **LR** Low end range · **M** Monthly · **MTC** Median total compensation · **MW** Median wage paid · **SQ** Second quartile wage · **S** Special: hourly and annual · **TQ** Third quartile wage · **W** Weekly · **Y** Yearly

Occupation/Type/Industry	Location	Per	Low	Mid	High	Source	Date
Fitness Trainer and Aerobics Instructor	Wisconsin	H	6.17 FQ	10.66 AW	17.35 TQ	WIBLS	10/01-12/01
	Wyoming	H	6.14 FQ	10.58 AW	17.36 TQ	WYBLS	10/01-12/01
	Puerto Rico	H	5.92 FQ	8.63 AW	11.16 TQ	PRBLS	10/01-12/01
Flight Attendant	United States	Y		38820 MW		OOH	2002
	Alaska	Y	17360 FQ	33670 AW	50860 TQ	AKBLS	10/01-12/01
	Anchorage MSA, AK	Y	17270 FQ	33920 AW	51970 TQ	AKBLS	10/01-12/01
	Los Angeles-Long Beach PMSA, CA	Y	21380 FQ	50130 AW	107890 TQ	CABLS	10/01-12/01
	Connecticut	Y	46470 FQ	50860 AW	57770 TQ	CTBLS	10/01-12/01
	Washington PMSA, DC-MD-VA-WV	Y	31270 FQ	57860 AW	89830 TQ	DCBLS	10/01-12/01
	Florida	Y	27590 FQ	47270 AW	71840 TQ	FLBLS	10/01-12/01
	Miami PMSA, FL	Y	28900 FQ	49260 AW	72700 TQ	FLBLS	10/01-12/01
	Georgia	Y	39210 FQ	45980 AW	56340 TQ	GABLS	10/01-12/01
	Atlanta MSA, GA	Y	39210 FQ	45980 AW	56340 TQ	GABLS	10/01-12/01
	Hawaii	Y	25300 FQ	67420 AW	94170 TQ	HIBLS	10/01-12/01
	Honolulu MSA, HI	Y	25900 FQ	67920 AW	94230 TQ	HIBLS	10/01-12/01
	Illinois	Y	17020 FQ	35420 AW	57780 TQ	ILBLS	10/01-12/01
	Chicago PMSA, IL	Y	17020 FQ	35420 AW	57760 TQ	ILBLS	10/01-12/01
	Indiana	Y	16100 FQ	23390 AW	40590 TQ	INBLS	10/01-12/01
	Kentucky	Y	18600 FQ	45010 AW	84470 TQ	KYBLS	10/01-12/01
	Louisiana	Y	16150 FQ	50550 AW	101720 TQ	LABLS	10/01-12/01
	Massachusetts	Y	24800 FQ	54000 AW	96410 TQ	MABLS	10/01-12/01
	Boston PMSA, MA-NH	Y	24800 FQ	54000 AW	96410 TQ	MABLS	10/01-12/01
	Kansas City MSA, MO-KS	Y	22010 FQ	41010 AW	65110 TQ	MOBLS	10/01-12/01
	Nevada	Y	15380 FQ	27060 AW	43350 TQ	NVBLS	10/01-12/01
	Las Vegas MSA, NV-AZ	Y	15350 FQ	26460 AW	41890 TQ	NVBLS	10/01-12/01
	New York	Y	17100 FQ	34840 AW	56920 TQ	NYBLS	10/01-12/01
	New York PMSA, NY	Y	17060 FQ	34960 AW	57010 TQ	NYBLS	10/01-12/01
	Raleigh-Durham-Chapel Hill MSA, NC	Y	14840 FQ	42160 AW	86520 TQ	NCBLS	10/01-12/01
	Oregon	Y	17370 FQ	50750 AW	99120 TQ	ORBLS	10/01-12/01
	Portland-Vancouver PMSA, OR-WA	Y	17370 FQ	50750 AW	99120 TQ	ORBLS	10/01-12/01
	Texas	Y	21970 FQ	68470 AW	124190 TQ	TXBLS	10/01-12/01
	San Antonio MSA, TX	Y	16760 FQ	31020 AW	45300 TQ	TXBLS	10/01-12/01
	Virginia	Y	27500 FQ	56800 AW	88580 TQ	VABLS	10/01-12/01
	Washington	Y	33710 FQ	71910 AW	93740 TQ	WABLS	10/01-12/01
	Seattle-Bellevue-Everett PMSA, WA	Y	33720 FQ	71930 AW	93740 TQ	WABLS	10/01-12/01
	Wisconsin	Y	27020 FQ	55540 AW	99360 TQ	WIBLS	10/01-12/01
Flight Dispatcher							
Airlines	United States	Y	75000 ASL		100000 ASH	AEAC	1/99-1/99
Flight Physician							
Airport	United States	Y	65000 ASL		90000 ASH	AEAC	1/99-1/99
Floor Layer							
Except Carpet, Wood, and Hard Tile	Alabama	H	8.74 FQ	12.05 AW	14.79 TQ	ALBLS	10/01-12/01
Except Carpet, Wood, and Hard Tile	Alaska	H	14.15 FQ	22.65 AW	27.53 TQ	AKBLS	10/01-12/01
Except Carpet, Wood, and Hard Tile	Arizona	H	6.69 FQ	13.28 AW	23.22 TQ	AZBLS	10/01-12/01
Except Carpet, Wood, and Hard Tile	Arkansas	H	9.10 FQ	12.90 AW	20.70 TQ	ARBLS	10/01-12/01
Except Carpet, Wood, and Hard Tile	California	H	9.97 FQ	18.60 AW	29.58 TQ	CABLS	10/01-12/01
Except Carpet, Wood, and Hard Tile	Colorado	H	10.08 FQ	17.39 AW	27.63 TQ	COBLS	10/01-12/01
Except Carpet, Wood, and Hard Tile	Connecticut	H	12.41 FQ	19.08 AW	26.20 TQ	CTBLS	10/01-12/01
Except Carpet, Wood, and Hard Tile	Delaware	H	10.09 FQ	13.45 AW	17.30 TQ	DEBLS	10/01-12/01
Except Carpet, Wood, and Hard Tile	Florida	H	7.75 FQ	15.91 AW	30.99 TQ	FLBLS	10/01-12/01
Except Carpet, Wood, and Hard Tile	Georgia	H	8.51 FQ	12.28 AW	16.42 TQ	GABLS	10/01-12/01
Except Carpet, Wood, and Hard Tile	Hawaii	H	8.95 FQ	18.22 AW	38.44 TQ	HIBLS	10/01-12/01
Except Carpet, Wood, and Hard Tile	Idaho	H	8.84 FQ	12.80 AW	17.41 TQ	IDBLS	10/01-12/01
Except Carpet, Wood, and Hard Tile	Illinois	H	12.16 FQ	21.05 AW	31.28 TQ	ILBLS	10/01-12/01
Except Carpet, Wood, and Hard Tile	Indiana	H	6.35 FQ	11.72 AW	18.34 TQ	INBLS	10/01-12/01
Except Carpet, Wood, and Hard Tile	Iowa	H	6.14 FQ	12.36 AW	20.52 TQ	IABLS	10/01-12/01
Except Carpet, Wood, and Hard Tile	Kansas	H	9.34 FQ	15.20 AW	24.64 TQ	KSBLS	10/01-12/01
Except Carpet, Wood, and Hard Tile	Kentucky	H	9.82 FQ	19.74 AW	33.21 TQ	KYBLS	10/01-12/01
Except Carpet, Wood, and Hard Tile	Louisiana	H	7.98 FQ	11.42 AW	16.36 TQ	LABLS	10/01-12/01
Except Carpet, Wood, and Hard Tile	Maryland	H	11.04 FQ	14.71 AW	19.41 TQ	MDBLS	10/01-12/01
Except Carpet, Wood, and Hard Tile	Massachusetts	H	15.04 FQ	19.74 AW	27.07 TQ	MABLS	10/01-12/01
Except Carpet, Wood, and Hard Tile	Michigan	H	9.02 FQ	14.06 AW	23.88 TQ	MIBLS	10/01-12/01
Except Carpet, Wood, and Hard Tile	Minnesota	H	12.05 FQ	19.42 AW	26.53 TQ	MNBLS	10/01-12/01

AAW	Average annual wage	**AOH**	Average offered, high	**ASH**	Average starting, high	**H**	Hourly	**M**	Monthly	**S**	Special: hourly and annual
AE	Average entry wage	**AOL**	Average offered, low	**ASL**	Average starting, low	**HI**	Highest wage paid	**MTC**	Median total compensation	**TQ**	Third quartile wage
AEX	Average experienced wage	**APH**	Average pay, high range	**AW**	Average wage paid	**HR**	High end range	**MW**	Median wage paid	**W**	Weekly
AO	Average offered	**APL**	Average pay, low range	**FQ**	First quartile wage	**LR**	Low end range	**SQ**	Second quartile wage	**Y**	Yearly

Occupation/Type/Industry	Location	Per	Low	Mid	High	Source	Date
Floor Layer							
Except Carpet, Wood, and Hard Tile	Mississippi	H	8.42 FQ	11.66 AW	16.24 TQ	MSBLS	10/01-12/01
Except Carpet, Wood, and Hard Tile	Missouri	H	9.93 FQ	16.70 AW	25.79 TQ	MOBLS	10/01-12/01
Except Carpet, Wood, and Hard Tile	Nebraska	H	13.99 FQ	24.71 AW	41.35 TQ	NEBLS	10/01-12/01
Except Carpet, Wood, and Hard Tile	Nevada	H	15.07 FQ	20.40 AW	26.34 TQ	NVBLS	10/01-12/01
Except Carpet, Wood, and Hard Tile	New Jersey	H	10.57 FQ	24.89 AW	40.08 TQ	NJBLS	10/01-12/01
Except Carpet, Wood, and Hard Tile	New York	H	7.21 FQ	11.90 AW	19.56 TQ	NYBLS	10/01-12/01
Except Carpet, Wood, and Hard Tile	North Carolina	H	9.11 FQ	13.18 AW	16.84 TQ	NCBLS	10/01-12/01
Except Carpet, Wood, and Hard Tile	Ohio	H	11.34 FQ	18.05 AW	24.79 TQ	OHBLS	10/01-12/01
Except Carpet, Wood, and Hard Tile	Oklahoma	H	8.52 FQ	13.75 AW	21.59 TQ	OKBLS	10/01-12/01
Except Carpet, Wood, and Hard Tile	Oregon	H	6.71 FQ	14.49 AW	23.16 TQ	ORBLS	10/01-12/01
Except Carpet, Wood, and Hard Tile	Pennsylvania	H	6.61 FQ	16.07 AW	30.75 TQ	PABLS	10/01-12/01
Except Carpet, Wood, and Hard Tile	South Carolina	H	9.46 FQ	13.03 AW	16.71 TQ	SCBLS	10/01-12/01
Except Carpet, Wood, and Hard Tile	Tennessee	H	8.89 FQ	16.12 AW	23.42 TQ	TNBLS	10/01-12/01
Except Carpet, Wood, and Hard Tile	Texas	H	8.76 FQ	12.10 AW	17.31 TQ	TXBLS	10/01-12/01
Except Carpet, Wood, and Hard Tile	Vermont	H	9.61 FQ	13.20 AW	18.95 TQ	VTBLS	10/01-12/01
Except Carpet, Wood, and Hard Tile	Virginia	H	9.67 FQ	14.86 AW	23.17 TQ	VABLS	10/01-12/01
Except Carpet, Wood, and Hard Tile	Washington	H	10.87 FQ	16.99 AW	24.19 TQ	WABLS	10/01-12/01
Except Carpet, Wood, and Hard Tile	Wisconsin	H	10.73 FQ	18.13 AW	26.05 TQ	WIBLS	10/01-12/01
Except Carpet, Wood, and Hard Tile	Wyoming	H	9.09 FQ	14.10 AW	21.52 TQ	WYBLS	10/01-12/01
Floor Sander and Finisher	Alabama	H	5.92 FQ	13.31 AW	20.62 TQ	ALBLS	10/01-12/01
	California	H	10.80 FQ	18.73 AW	29.59 TQ	CABLS	10/01-12/01
	Los Angeles-Long Beach PMSA, CA	H	11.32 FQ	16.81 AW	25.11 TQ	CABLS	10/01-12/01
	San Francisco PMSA, CA	H	18.41 FQ	28.98 AW	38.74 TQ	CABLS	10/01-12/01
	Colorado	H	9.86 FQ	15.87 AW	21.65 TQ	COBLS	10/01-12/01
	Denver PMSA, CO	H	11.19 FQ	17.41 AW	22.06 TQ	COBLS	10/01-12/01
	Connecticut	H	8.99 FQ	13.43 AW	20.87 TQ	CTBLS	10/01-12/01
	Hartford MSA, CT	H	8.85 FQ	12.03 AW	17.32 TQ	CTBLS	10/01-12/01
	Washington PMSA, DC-MD-VA-WV	H	9.40 FQ	15.06 AW	21.64 TQ	DCBLS	10/01-12/01
	Florida	H	7.34 FQ	12.14 AW	16.91 TQ	FLBLS	10/01-12/01
	Miami PMSA, FL	H	9.56 FQ	12.96 AW	16.35 TQ	FLBLS	10/01-12/01
	Georgia	H	9.20 FQ	11.11 AW	13.31 TQ	GABLS	10/01-12/01
	Illinois	H	8.79 FQ	12.31 AW	21.62 TQ	ILBLS	10/01-12/01
	Chicago PMSA, IL	H	8.79 FQ	12.20 AW	22.33 TQ	ILBLS	10/01-12/01
	Indiana	H	9.60 FQ	14.55 AW	20.87 TQ	INBLS	10/01-12/01
	Iowa	H	7.70 FQ	12.02 AW	19.28 TQ	IABLS	10/01-12/01
	Kansas	H	7.57 FQ	11.55 AW	16.77 TQ	KSBLS	10/01-12/01
	Kentucky	H	6.21 FQ	12.13 AW	21.45 TQ	KYBLS	10/01-12/01
	Louisiana	H	8.75 FQ	12.11 AW	16.54 TQ	LABLS	10/01-12/01
	New Orleans MSA, LA	H	8.97 FQ	12.10 AW	16.86 TQ	LABLS	10/01-12/01
	Maryland	H	8.92 FQ	16.28 AW	25.51 TQ	MDBLS	10/01-12/01
	Baltimore PMSA, MD	H	11.23 FQ	18.99 AW	27.26 TQ	MDBLS	10/01-12/01
	Massachusetts	H	9.84 FQ	15.53 AW	25.42 TQ	MABLS	10/01-12/01
	Boston PMSA, MA-NH	H	9.73 FQ	14.37 AW	23.23 TQ	MABLS	10/01-12/01
	Michigan	H	8.75 FQ	13.41 AW	21.08 TQ	MIBLS	10/01-12/01
	Minnesota	H	9.11 FQ	13.92 AW	20.17 TQ	MNBLS	10/01-12/01
	Minneapolis-St. Paul MSA, MN-WI	H	9.06 FQ	13.86 AW	20.39 TQ	MNBLS	10/01-12/01
	Mississippi	H	9.10 FQ	13.03 AW	17.54 TQ	MSBLS	10/01-12/01
	Missouri	H	10.44 FQ	15.41 AW	25.11 TQ	MOBLS	10/01-12/01
	Kansas City MSA, MO-KS	H	10.78 FQ	14.82 AW	21.49 TQ	MOBLS	10/01-12/01
	St. Louis MSA, MO-IL	H	9.79 FQ	15.86 AW	26.08 TQ	MOBLS	10/01-12/01
	Nebraska	H	9.18 FQ	11.82 AW	16.03 TQ	NEBLS	10/01-12/01
	Nevada	H	13.85 FQ	15.09 AW	16.65 TQ	NVBLS	10/01-12/01
	Las Vegas MSA, NV-AZ	H	13.85 FQ	15.09 AW	16.65 TQ	NVBLS	10/01-12/01
	New Jersey	H	11.42 FQ	15.51 AW	19.25 TQ	NJBLS	10/01-12/01
	Bergen-Passaic PMSA, NJ	H	10.52 FQ	14.72 AW	18.20 TQ	NJBLS	10/01-12/01
	New York	H	10.00 FQ	13.01 AW	16.55 TQ	NYBLS	10/01-12/01
	Syracuse MSA, NY	H	7.96 FQ	11.64 AW	14.36 TQ	NYBLS	10/01-12/01
	North Carolina	H	8.16 FQ	12.20 AW	15.69 TQ	NCBLS	10/01-12/01
	Charlotte-Gastonia-Rock Hill MSA, NC-SC	H	9.61 FQ	15.42 AW	18.29 TQ	NCBLS	10/01-12/01
	Wilmington MSA, NC	H	7.94 FQ	10.77 AW	13.78 TQ	NCBLS	10/01-12/01
	Ohio	H	8.97 FQ	11.86 AW	15.65 TQ	OHBLS	10/01-12/01
	Cincinnati PMSA, OH-KY-IN	H	9.36 FQ	13.49 AW	18.81 TQ	OHBLS	10/01-12/01
	Columbus MSA, OH	H	9.01 FQ	11.79 AW	15.23 TQ	OHBLS	10/01-12/01
	Oklahoma	H	9.40 FQ	13.28 AW	17.48 TQ	OKBLS	10/01-12/01
	Tulsa MSA, OK	H	10.12 FQ	14.18 AW	19.59 TQ	OKBLS	10/01-12/01
	Oregon	H	9.63 FQ	13.30 AW	18.33 TQ	ORBLS	10/01-12/01
	Pennsylvania	H	7.73 FQ	11.85 AW	17.33 TQ	PABLS	10/01-12/01

AAW Average annual wage; AE Average entry wage; AEX Average experienced wage; AO Average offered; AOH Average offered, high; AOL Average offered, low; APH Average pay, high range; APL Average pay, low range; ASH Average starting, high; ASL Average starting, low; AW Average wage paid; FQ First quartile wage; H Hourly; HI Highest wage paid; HR High end range; LR Low end range; M Monthly; MTC Median total compensation; MW Median wage paid; SQ Second quartile wage; S Special: hourly and annual; TQ Third quartile wage; W Weekly; Y Yearly

Occupation/Type/Industry	Location	Per	Low	Mid	High	Source	Date
Floor Sander and Finisher	Philadelphia PMSA, PA-NJ	H	10.09 FQ	17.02 AW	29.57 TQ	PABLS	10/01-12/01
	Rhode Island	H	11.54 FQ	14.18 AW	20.31 TQ	RIBLS	10/01-12/01
	South Carolina	H	8.13 FQ	11.90 AW	15.17 TQ	SCBLS	10/01-12/01
	Charleston-North Charleston MSA, SC	H	8.60 FQ	11.87 AW	13.88 TQ	SCBLS	10/01-12/01
	Tennessee	H	8.17 FQ	10.66 AW	14.31 TQ	TNBLS	10/01-12/01
	Memphis MSA, TN-AR-MS	H	8.73 FQ	9.83 AW	11.37 TQ	TNBLS	10/01-12/01
	Texas	H	7.65 FQ	11.29 AW	15.64 TQ	TXBLS	10/01-12/01
	Dallas PMSA, TX	H	8.27 FQ	11.45 AW	15.91 TQ	TXBLS	10/01-12/01
	Houston PMSA, TX	H	7.61 FQ	11.68 AW	16.38 TQ	TXBLS	10/01-12/01
	Utah	H	10.15 FQ	14.13 AW	16.81 TQ	UTBLS	10/01-12/01
	Salt Lake City-Ogden MSA, UT	H	10.01 FQ	14.15 AW	16.77 TQ	UTBLS	10/01-12/01
	Vermont	H	10.17 FQ	12.52 AW	15.32 TQ	VTBLS	10/01-12/01
	Virginia	H	9.12 FQ	12.98 AW	17.86 TQ	VABLS	10/01-12/01
	Richmond-Petersburg MSA, VA	H	9.13 FQ	12.01 AW	16.57 TQ	VABLS	10/01-12/01
	Washington	H	9.60 FQ	12.91 AW	19.05 TQ	WABLS	10/01-12/01
	Seattle-Bellevue-Everett PMSA, WA	H	9.84 FQ	13.29 AW	19.27 TQ	WABLS	10/01-12/01
	Wisconsin	H	9.63 FQ	14.00 AW	17.99 TQ	WIBLS	10/01-12/01
	Green Bay MSA, WI	H	9.38 FQ	13.58 AW	17.22 TQ	WIBLS	10/01-12/01
Floral Designer	Alabama	Y	12360 FQ	16530 AW	21800 TQ	ALBLS	10/01-12/01
	Alaska	Y	16340 FQ	22020 AW	28910 TQ	AKBLS	10/01-12/01
	Arizona	Y	14870 FQ	20680 AW	27520 TQ	AZBLS	10/01-12/01
	Arkansas	Y	12640 FQ	17410 AW	23180 TQ	ARBLS	10/01-12/01
	California	Y	15090 FQ	23430 AW	35100 TQ	CABLS	10/01-12/01
	Colorado	Y	16070 FQ	22650 AW	33940 TQ	COBLS	10/01-12/01
	Connecticut	Y	17590 FQ	24690 AW	33220 TQ	CTBLS	10/01-12/01
	Delaware	Y	15390 FQ	21370 AW	28660 TQ	DEBLS	10/01-12/01
	District of Columbia	Y	20000 FQ	27890 AW	38000 TQ	DCBLS	10/01-12/01
	Florida	Y	14790 FQ	20350 AW	26740 TQ	FLBLS	10/01-12/01
	Georgia	Y	11740 FQ	16240 AW	23600 TQ	GABLS	10/01-12/01
	Hawaii	Y	12480 FQ	20910 AW	28500 TQ	HIBLS	10/01-12/01
	Idaho	Y	11790 FQ	16380 AW	22550 TQ	IDBLS	10/01-12/01
	Illinois	Y	14100 FQ	21060 AW	29850 TQ	ILBLS	10/01-12/01
	Indiana	Y	13670 FQ	18410 AW	25520 TQ	INBLS	10/01-12/01
	Iowa	Y	12630 FQ	18740 AW	27560 TQ	IABLS	10/01-12/01
	Kansas	Y	13140 FQ	19070 AW	26600 TQ	KSBLS	10/01-12/01
	Kentucky	Y	12470 FQ	17050 AW	22680 TQ	KYBLS	10/01-12/01
	Louisiana	Y	12010 FQ	16600 AW	22920 TQ	LABLS	10/01-12/01
	Maine	Y	12500 FQ	20590 AW	29040 TQ	MEBLS	10/01-12/01
	Maryland	Y	14480 FQ	21320 AW	29950 TQ	MDBLS	10/01-12/01
	Massachusetts	Y	16170 FQ	25040 AW	35270 TQ	MABLS	10/01-12/01
	Michigan	Y	13410 FQ	20100 AW	26960 TQ	MIBLS	10/01-12/01
	Minnesota	Y	13100 FQ	21330 AW	31210 TQ	MNBLS	10/01-12/01
	Mississippi	Y	12450 FQ	17180 AW	22770 TQ	MSBLS	10/01-12/01
	Missouri	Y	13110 FQ	19360 AW	27260 TQ	MOBLS	10/01-12/01
	Montana	Y	12010 FQ	15960 AW	20880 TQ	MTBLS	10/01-12/01
	Nebraska	Y	12880 FQ	17030 AW	22810 TQ	NEBLS	10/01-12/01
	Nevada	Y	16480 FQ	22940 AW	29720 TQ	NVBLS	10/01-12/01
	New Hampshire	Y	16150 FQ	22610 AW	31410 TQ	NHBLS	10/01-12/01
	New Jersey	Y	14860 FQ	25570 AW	44110 TQ	NJBLS	10/01-12/01
	New Mexico	Y	12380 FQ	17590 AW	22880 TQ	NMBLS	10/01-12/01
	New York	Y	13230 FQ	27020 AW	45050 TQ	NYBLS	10/01-12/01
	North Carolina	Y	13070 FQ	18700 AW	26380 TQ	NCBLS	10/01-12/01
	North Dakota	Y	12630 FQ	16660 AW	21640 TQ	NDBLS	10/01-12/01
	Ohio	Y	12590 FQ	18960 AW	27550 TQ	OHBLS	10/01-12/01
	Oklahoma	Y	14530 FQ	19210 AW	26040 TQ	OKBLS	10/01-12/01
	Oregon	Y	15540 FQ	20680 AW	27300 TQ	ORBLS	10/01-12/01
	Pennsylvania	Y	12430 FQ	18860 AW	27880 TQ	PABLS	10/01-12/01
	Rhode Island	Y	15180 FQ	24550 AW	36730 TQ	RIBLS	10/01-12/01
	South Carolina	Y	12640 FQ	19810 AW	29410 TQ	SCBLS	10/01-12/01
	South Dakota	Y	11960 FQ	15750 AW	21340 TQ	SDBLS	10/01-12/01
	Tennessee	Y	13290 FQ	19360 AW	25420 TQ	TNBLS	10/01-12/01
	Texas	Y	12500 FQ	18110 AW	24670 TQ	TXBLS	10/01-12/01
	Utah	Y	13000 FQ	18860 AW	24040 TQ	UTBLS	10/01-12/01
	Vermont	Y	15980 FQ	22470 AW	32710 TQ	VTBLS	10/01-12/01
	Virginia	Y	13400 FQ	19970 AW	31020 TQ	VABLS	10/01-12/01
	Washington	Y	14790 FQ	22150 AW	31730 TQ	WABLS	10/01-12/01
	West Virginia	Y	11930 FQ	16150 AW	22080 TQ	WVBLS	10/01-12/01
	Wisconsin	Y	12770 FQ	19130 AW	26500 TQ	WIBLS	10/01-12/01

AAW Average annual wage **AE** Average entry wage **AEX** Average experienced wage **AO** Average offered **AOH** Average offered, high **AOL** Average offered, low **APH** Average pay, high range **APL** Average pay, low range **ASH** Average starting, high **ASL** Average starting, low **AW** Average wage paid **FQ** First quartile wage **H** Hourly **HI** Highest wage paid **HR** High end range **LR** Low end range **M** Monthly **MTC** Median total compensation **MW** Median wage paid **SQ** Second quartile wage **S** Special: hourly and annual **TQ** Third quartile wage **W** Weekly **Y** Yearly

Occupation/Type/Industry	Location	Per	Low	Mid	High	Source	Date
Floral Designer	Wyoming	Y	11950 FQ	15760 AW	20470 TQ	WYBLS	10/01-12/01
	Puerto Rico	Y	11800 FQ	14510 AW	19400 TQ	PRBLS	10/01-12/01
	Guam	Y	11880 FQ	15270 AW	21450 TQ	GUBLS	10/01-12/01
Food and Beverage Manager							
Golf Course	St. Louis, MO	Y		54100 AW		SLBJ	1/00-1/01
Food and Tobacco Roasting, Baking, and Drying Machine Operator and Tender	Alabama	H	6.30 FQ	10.26 AW	13.30 TQ	ALBLS	10/01-12/01
	Arkansas	H	7.67 FQ	10.59 AW	15.32 TQ	ARBLS	10/01-12/01
	Fayetteville-Springdale-Rogers MSA, AR	H	8.86 FQ	9.76 AW	10.83 TQ	ARBLS	10/01-12/01
	Little Rock-North Little Rock MSA, AR	H	9.30 FQ	13.23 AW	18.06 TQ	ARBLS	10/01-12/01
	California	H	6.92 FQ	13.39 AW	20.91 TQ	CABLS	10/01-12/01
	Fresno MSA, CA	H	7.20 FQ	12.90 AW	21.11 TQ	CABLS	10/01-12/01
	Los Angeles-Long Beach PMSA, CA	H	7.01 FQ	15.05 AW	21.21 TQ	CABLS	10/01-12/01
	Merced MSA, CA	H	6.62 FQ	9.11 AW	14.87 TQ	CABLS	10/01-12/01
	Modesto MSA, CA	H	6.49 FQ	10.70 AW	19.49 TQ	CABLS	10/01-12/01
	Oakland PMSA, CA	H	7.13 FQ	13.87 AW	21.90 TQ	CABLS	10/01-12/01
	Orange County PMSA, CA	H	6.41 FQ	8.83 AW	13.12 TQ	CABLS	10/01-12/01
	Riverside-San Bernardino PMSA, CA	H	7.89 FQ	15.44 AW	20.80 TQ	CABLS	10/01-12/01
	San Diego MSA, CA	H	6.69 FQ	10.31 AW	17.82 TQ	CABLS	10/01-12/01
	San Francisco PMSA, CA	H	11.71 FQ	17.32 AW	21.62 TQ	CABLS	10/01-12/01
	San Jose PMSA, CA	H	7.68 FQ	12.12 AW	18.06 TQ	CABLS	10/01-12/01
	Visalia-Tulare-Porterville MSA, CA	H	7.42 FQ	15.78 AW	21.32 TQ	CABLS	10/01-12/01
	Colorado	H	7.32 FQ	12.01 AW	16.79 TQ	COBLS	10/01-12/01
	Denver PMSA, CO	H	8.32 FQ	13.53 AW	17.10 TQ	COBLS	10/01-12/01
	Connecticut	H	8.10 FQ	13.00 AW	18.87 TQ	CTBLS	10/01-12/01
	Washington PMSA, DC-MD-VA-WV	H	7.78 FQ	11.05 AW	15.47 TQ	DCBLS	10/01-12/01
	Florida	H	7.17 FQ	11.26 AW	14.38 TQ	FLBLS	10/01-12/01
	Lakeland-Winter Haven MSA, FL	H	10.38 FQ	12.30 AW	14.35 TQ	FLBLS	10/01-12/01
	Miami PMSA, FL	H	9.23 FQ	11.52 AW	13.69 TQ	FLBLS	10/01-12/01
	Georgia	H	7.04 FQ	9.96 AW	15.48 TQ	GABLS	10/01-12/01
	Idaho	H	9.08 FQ	11.28 AW	15.72 TQ	IDBLS	10/01-12/01
	Illinois	H	9.17 FQ	12.86 AW	16.67 TQ	ILBLS	10/01-12/01
	Chicago PMSA, IL	H	9.40 FQ	12.88 AW	16.76 TQ	ILBLS	10/01-12/01
	Indiana	H	8.63 FQ	13.35 AW	18.24 TQ	INBLS	10/01-12/01
	Indianapolis MSA, IN	H	8.57 FQ	14.12 AW	19.78 TQ	INBLS	10/01-12/01
	Iowa	H	7.92 FQ	11.72 AW	16.37 TQ	IABLS	10/01-12/01
	Kansas	H	6.88 FQ	11.71 AW	16.14 TQ	KSBLS	10/01-12/01
	Kentucky	H	7.61 FQ	11.53 AW	16.08 TQ	KYBLS	10/01-12/01
	Louisville MSA, KY-IN	H	7.57 FQ	12.38 AW	16.78 TQ	KYBLS	10/01-12/01
	Louisiana	H	5.92 FQ	9.80 AW	13.94 TQ	LABLS	10/01-12/01
	New Orleans MSA, LA	H	7.29 FQ	11.67 AW	15.79 TQ	LABLS	10/01-12/01
	Maine	H	7.34 FQ	10.84 AW	15.50 TQ	MEBLS	10/01-12/01
	Maryland	H	10.09 FQ	12.75 AW	15.83 TQ	MDBLS	10/01-12/01
	Baltimore PMSA, MD	H	11.11 FQ	12.94 AW	15.77 TQ	MDBLS	10/01-12/01
	Massachusetts	H	6.90 FQ	11.96 AW	17.82 TQ	MABLS	10/01-12/01
	Boston PMSA, MA-NH	H	6.80 FQ	12.11 AW	18.12 TQ	MABLS	10/01-12/01
	Michigan	H	6.24 FQ	14.93 AW	27.15 TQ	MIBLS	10/01-12/01
	Detroit PMSA, MI	H	8.63 FQ	12.20 AW	16.19 TQ	MIBLS	10/01-12/01
	Grand Rapids-Muskegon-Holland MSA, MI	H	8.69 FQ	12.16 AW	16.51 TQ	MIBLS	10/01-12/01
	Minnesota	H	9.59 FQ	13.41 AW	17.30 TQ	MNBLS	10/01-12/01
	Mississippi	H	7.34 FQ	8.35 AW	10.09 TQ	MSBLS	10/01-12/01
	Missouri	H	8.15 FQ	12.58 AW	16.95 TQ	MOBLS	10/01-12/01
	Kansas City MSA, MO-KS	H	6.88 FQ	12.31 AW	20.85 TQ	MOBLS	10/01-12/01
	St. Louis MSA, MO-IL	H	8.74 FQ	13.13 AW	16.51 TQ	MOBLS	10/01-12/01
	Nebraska	H	8.83 FQ	14.81 AW	25.09 TQ	NEBLS	10/01-12/01
	New Jersey	H	6.40 FQ	10.93 AW	16.97 TQ	NJBLS	10/01-12/01
	Atlantic-Cape May PMSA, NJ	H	5.83 FQ	8.86 AW	13.92 TQ	NJBLS	10/01-12/01
	Bergen-Passaic PMSA, NJ	H	6.20 FQ	11.32 AW	18.56 TQ	NJBLS	10/01-12/01
	Newark PMSA, NJ	H	7.24 FQ	10.90 AW	16.93 TQ	NJBLS	10/01-12/01
	New Mexico	H	6.02 FQ	9.20 AW	14.28 TQ	NMBLS	10/01-12/01
	New York	H	6.96 FQ	10.59 AW	15.99 TQ	NYBLS	10/01-12/01

AAW	Average annual wage	AOH	Average offered, high	ASH	Average starting, high	H	Hourly	M	Monthly	S	Special: hourly and annual
AE	Average entry wage	AOL	Average offered, low	ASL	Average starting, low	HI	Highest wage paid	MTC	Median total compensation	TQ	Third quartile wage
AEX	Average experienced wage	APH	Average pay, high range	AW	Average wage paid	HR	High end range	MW	Median wage paid	W	Weekly
AO	Average offered	APL	Average pay, low range	FQ	First quartile wage	LR	Low end range	SQ	Second quartile wage	Y	Yearly

Occupation/Type/Industry	Location	Per	Low	Mid	High	Source	Date
Food and Tobacco Roasting, Baking, and Drying Machine Operator and Tender	Albany-Schenectady-Troy MSA, NY	H	10.85 FQ	13.64 AW	17.34 TQ	NYBLS	10/01-12/01
	Buffalo-Niagara Falls MSA, NY	H	7.52 FQ	11.91 AW	18.81 TQ	NYBLS	10/01-12/01
	Nassau-Suffolk PMSA, NY	H	7.52 FQ	9.56 AW	13.24 TQ	NYBLS	10/01-12/01
	New York PMSA, NY	H	6.93 FQ	10.67 AW	16.11 TQ	NYBLS	10/01-12/01
	Rochester MSA, NY	H	6.96 FQ	8.85 AW	12.87 TQ	NYBLS	10/01-12/01
	North Carolina	H	6.12 FQ	13.21 AW	26.01 TQ	NCBLS	10/01-12/01
	Charlotte-Gastonia-Rock Hill MSA, NC-SC	H	7.80 FQ	12.17 AW	16.36 TQ	NCBLS	10/01-12/01
	Greensboro-Winston-Salem-High Point MSA, NC	H	17.83 FQ	23.17 AW	27.50 TQ	NCBLS	10/01-12/01
	North Dakota	H	9.09 FQ	13.02 AW	20.41 TQ	NDBLS	10/01-12/01
	Ohio	H	9.78 FQ	14.10 AW	19.02 TQ	OHBLS	10/01-12/01
	Oklahoma	H	7.50 FQ	10.35 AW	13.54 TQ	OKBLS	10/01-12/01
	Tulsa MSA, OK	H	9.16 FQ	12.40 AW	16.40 TQ	OKBLS	10/01-12/01
	Oregon	H	8.89 FQ	12.99 AW	18.94 TQ	ORBLS	10/01-12/01
	Portland-Vancouver PMSA, OR-WA	H	9.69 FQ	14.68 AW	19.14 TQ	ORBLS	10/01-12/01
	Pennsylvania	H	7.48 FQ	11.29 AW	15.78 TQ	PABLS	10/01-12/01
	Harrisburg-Lebanon-Carlisle MSA, PA	H	9.36 FQ	12.35 AW	16.50 TQ	PABLS	10/01-12/01
	Lancaster MSA, PA	H	7.53 FQ	10.08 AW	15.13 TQ	PABLS	10/01-12/01
	Philadelphia PMSA, PA-NJ	H	8.23 FQ	12.21 AW	16.52 TQ	PABLS	10/01-12/01
	Pittsburgh MSA, PA	H	6.11 FQ	9.17 AW	12.49 TQ	PABLS	10/01-12/01
	Reading MSA, PA	H	9.30 FQ	12.97 AW	17.25 TQ	PABLS	10/01-12/01
	Scranton-Wilkes-Barre-Hazleton MSA, PA	H	8.34 FQ	11.44 AW	13.29 TQ	PABLS	10/01-12/01
	York MSA, PA	H	5.70 FQ	10.42 AW	14.27 TQ	PABLS	10/01-12/01
	South Carolina	H	7.56 FQ	10.41 AW	14.58 TQ	SCBLS	10/01-12/01
	South Dakota	H	7.79 FQ	10.95 AW	15.05 TQ	SDBLS	10/01-12/01
	Tennessee	H	6.40 FQ	11.03 AW	14.65 TQ	TNBLS	10/01-12/01
	Texas	H	7.27 FQ	10.49 AW	14.73 TQ	TXBLS	10/01-12/01
	San Antonio MSA, TX	H	8.54 FQ	12.26 AW	16.74 TQ	TXBLS	10/01-12/01
	Utah	H	6.82 FQ	8.90 AW	11.31 TQ	UTBLS	10/01-12/01
	Virginia	H	6.15 FQ	10.70 AW	16.28 TQ	VABLS	10/01-12/01
	Washington	H	6.74 FQ	10.26 AW	17.12 TQ	WABLS	10/01-12/01
	Seattle-Bellevue-Everett PMSA, WA	H	6.74 FQ	9.65 AW	18.09 TQ	WABLS	10/01-12/01
	Wisconsin	H	9.09 FQ	12.66 AW	18.66 TQ	WIBLS	10/01-12/01
Food Batchmaker	Alabama	H	6.45 FQ	9.69 AW	13.94 TQ	ALBLS	10/01-12/01
	Birmingham MSA, AL	H	8.84 FQ	11.51 AW	16.06 TQ	ALBLS	10/01-12/01
	Mobile MSA, AL	H	5.61 FQ	6.89 AW	9.12 TQ	ALBLS	10/01-12/01
	Alaska	H	7.15 FQ	8.93 AW	12.57 TQ	AKBLS	10/01-12/01
	Arizona	H	6.76 FQ	10.92 AW	15.13 TQ	AZBLS	10/01-12/01
	Phoenix-Mesa MSA, AZ	H	7.19 FQ	11.17 AW	15.30 TQ	AZBLS	10/01-12/01
	Arkansas	H	7.16 FQ	10.35 AW	14.46 TQ	ARBLS	10/01-12/01
	Fayetteville-Springdale-Rogers MSA, AR	H	7.73 FQ	10.15 AW	13.43 TQ	ARBLS	10/01-12/01
	Fort Smith MSA, AR-OK	H	7.20 FQ	11.24 AW	16.53 TQ	ARBLS	10/01-12/01
	Little Rock-North Little Rock MSA, AR	H	7.24 FQ	9.33 AW	10.97 TQ	ARBLS	10/01-12/01
	California	H	6.65 FQ	10.93 AW	17.95 TQ	CABLS	10/01-12/01
	Fresno MSA, CA	H	7.94 FQ	14.13 AW	21.61 TQ	CABLS	10/01-12/01
	Los Angeles-Long Beach PMSA, CA	H	6.48 FQ	9.87 AW	17.53 TQ	CABLS	10/01-12/01
	Merced MSA, CA	H	6.66 FQ	12.19 AW	17.53 TQ	CABLS	10/01-12/01
	Modesto MSA, CA	H	7.22 FQ	11.82 AW	16.54 TQ	CABLS	10/01-12/01
	Oakland PMSA, CA	H	7.83 FQ	14.08 AW	21.44 TQ	CABLS	10/01-12/01
	Orange County PMSA, CA	H	6.60 FQ	9.76 AW	13.94 TQ	CABLS	10/01-12/01
	Riverside-San Bernardino PMSA, CA	H	6.74 FQ	11.19 AW	18.81 TQ	CABLS	10/01-12/01
	Sacramento PMSA, CA	H	6.93 FQ	11.09 AW	16.77 TQ	CABLS	10/01-12/01
	Salinas MSA, CA	H	6.68 FQ	9.02 AW	10.52 TQ	CABLS	10/01-12/01
	San Diego MSA, CA	H	6.51 FQ	8.43 AW	11.97 TQ	CABLS	10/01-12/01
	San Francisco PMSA, CA	H	7.41 FQ	11.38 AW	16.80 TQ	CABLS	10/01-12/01
	San Jose PMSA, CA	H	7.72 FQ	12.54 AW	18.24 TQ	CABLS	10/01-12/01
	Santa Barbara-Santa Maria-Lompoc MSA, CA	H	8.00 FQ	9.26 AW	10.50 TQ	CABLS	10/01-12/01

AAW	Average annual wage	AOH	Average offered, high	ASH	Average starting, high	H	Hourly	M	Monthly	S	Special: hourly and annual
AE	Average entry wage	AOL	Average offered, low	ASL	Average starting, low	HI	Highest wage paid	MTC	Median total compensation	TQ	Third quartile wage
AEX	Average experienced wage	APH	Average pay, high range	AW	Average wage paid	HR	High end range	MW	Median wage paid	W	Weekly
AO	Average offered	APL	Average pay, low range	FQ	First quartile wage	LR	Low end range	SQ	Second quartile wage	Y	Yearly

Occupation/Type/Industry	Location	Per	Low	Mid	High	Source	Date
Food Batchmaker	Santa Cruz-Watsonville PMSA, CA	H	7.63 FQ	11.18 AW	19.63 TQ	CABLS	10/01-12/01
	Santa Rosa PMSA, CA	H	9.66 FQ	14.61 AW	17.55 TQ	CABLS	10/01-12/01
	Stockton-Lodi MSA, CA	H	7.07 FQ	13.77 AW	23.59 TQ	CABLS	10/01-12/01
	Ventura PMSA, CA	H	6.77 FQ	10.04 AW	16.63 TQ	CABLS	10/01-12/01
	Visalia-Tulare-Porterville MSA, CA	H	6.92 FQ	10.99 AW	16.49 TQ	CABLS	10/01-12/01
	Colorado	H	6.23 FQ	10.67 AW	16.21 TQ	COBLS	10/01-12/01
	Denver PMSA, CO	H	6.30 FQ	11.02 AW	16.34 TQ	COBLS	10/01-12/01
	Connecticut	H	7.31 FQ	11.79 AW	16.82 TQ	CTBLS	10/01-12/01
	Hartford MSA, CT	H	7.50 FQ	11.95 AW	16.70 TQ	CTBLS	10/01-12/01
	New Haven-Meriden PMSA, CT	H	6.99 FQ	10.72 AW	15.24 TQ	CTBLS	10/01-12/01
	Delaware	H	8.24 FQ	11.41 AW	15.74 TQ	DEBLS	10/01-12/01
	Washington PMSA, DC-MD-VA-WV	H	6.65 FQ	9.72 AW	14.35 TQ	DCBLS	10/01-12/01
	Florida	H	6.19 FQ	9.86 AW	15.18 TQ	FLBLS	10/01-12/01
	Fort Lauderdale PMSA, FL	H	5.73 FQ	8.75 AW	11.59 TQ	FLBLS	10/01-12/01
	Lakeland-Winter Haven MSA, FL	H	9.60 FQ	12.88 AW	16.07 TQ	FLBLS	10/01-12/01
	Miami PMSA, FL	H	5.87 FQ	8.17 AW	12.44 TQ	FLBLS	10/01-12/01
	Orlando MSA, FL	H	5.83 FQ	9.70 AW	15.94 TQ	FLBLS	10/01-12/01
	Sarasota-Bradenton MSA, FL	H	7.53 FQ	10.18 AW	15.57 TQ	FLBLS	10/01-12/01
	Tampa-St. Petersburg-Clearwater MSA, FL	H	7.19 FQ	10.20 AW	15.42 TQ	FLBLS	10/01-12/01
	Georgia	H	7.24 FQ	11.17 AW	16.83 TQ	GABLS	10/01-12/01
	Atlanta MSA, GA	H	7.49 FQ	11.17 AW	16.51 TQ	GABLS	10/01-12/01
	Columbus MSA, GA-AL	H	7.43 FQ	16.53 AW	26.07 TQ	GABLS	10/01-12/01
	Hawaii	H	5.96 FQ	8.41 AW	11.51 TQ	HIBLS	10/01-12/01
	Honolulu MSA, HI	H	5.93 FQ	8.19 AW	10.92 TQ	HIBLS	10/01-12/01
	Idaho	H	8.62 FQ	11.11 AW	14.39 TQ	IDBLS	10/01-12/01
	Boise City MSA, ID	H	8.64 FQ	11.37 AW	13.84 TQ	IDBLS	10/01-12/01
	Illinois	H	7.30 FQ	11.10 AW	17.07 TQ	ILBLS	10/01-12/01
	Chicago PMSA, IL	H	7.43 FQ	11.16 AW	17.17 TQ	ILBLS	10/01-12/01
	Rockford MSA, IL	H	7.80 FQ	12.32 AW	18.86 TQ	ILBLS	10/01-12/01
	Indiana	H	6.68 FQ	11.24 AW	16.35 TQ	INBLS	10/01-12/01
	Elkhart-Goshen MSA, IN	H	6.43 FQ	11.05 AW	16.65 TQ	INBLS	10/01-12/01
	Evansville-Henderson MSA, IN-KY	H	8.25 FQ	12.29 AW	16.63 TQ	INBLS	10/01-12/01
	Fort Wayne MSA, IN	H	8.90 FQ	12.07 AW	16.41 TQ	INBLS	10/01-12/01
	Gary PMSA, IN	H	5.88 FQ	8.07 AW	12.29 TQ	INBLS	10/01-12/01
	Indianapolis MSA, IN	H	7.34 FQ	10.81 AW	15.69 TQ	INBLS	10/01-12/01
	Iowa	H	8.79 FQ	12.47 AW	16.98 TQ	IABLS	10/01-12/01
	Davenport-Moline-Rock Island MSA, IA-IL	H	7.21 FQ	10.87 AW	16.41 TQ	IABLS	10/01-12/01
	Des Moines MSA, IA	H	9.10 FQ	12.71 AW	16.60 TQ	IABLS	10/01-12/01
	Kansas	H	6.97 FQ	10.64 AW	16.50 TQ	KSBLS	10/01-12/01
	Topeka MSA, KS	H	14.13 FQ	16.85 AW	20.48 TQ	KSBLS	10/01-12/01
	Wichita MSA, KS	H	10.54 FQ	14.22 AW	17.61 TQ	KSBLS	10/01-12/01
	Kentucky	H	6.50 FQ	12.37 AW	18.03 TQ	KYBLS	10/01-12/01
	Louisville MSA, KY-IN	H	9.28 FQ	12.37 AW	16.04 TQ	KYBLS	10/01-12/01
	Louisiana	H	6.20 FQ	10.75 AW	17.79 TQ	LABLS	10/01-12/01
	Lafayette MSA, LA	H	7.35 FQ	10.39 AW	13.84 TQ	LABLS	10/01-12/01
	Maine	H	6.53 FQ	11.72 AW	16.69 TQ	MEBLS	10/01-12/01
	Maryland	H	7.13 FQ	10.85 AW	16.03 TQ	MDBLS	10/01-12/01
	Baltimore PMSA, MD	H	7.38 FQ	11.43 AW	16.66 TQ	MDBLS	10/01-12/01
	Massachusetts	H	8.24 FQ	12.47 AW	16.61 TQ	MABLS	10/01-12/01
	Boston PMSA, MA-NH	H	8.67 FQ	12.73 AW	16.85 TQ	MABLS	10/01-12/01
	Brockton PMSA, MA	H	8.63 FQ	12.83 AW	16.64 TQ	MABLS	10/01-12/01
	Springfield MSA, MA	H	9.71 FQ	13.51 AW	16.51 TQ	MABLS	10/01-12/01
	Worcester PMSA, MA-CT	H	8.36 FQ	13.06 AW	16.84 TQ	MABLS	10/01-12/01
	Michigan	H	7.00 FQ	11.54 AW	17.13 TQ	MIBLS	10/01-12/01
	Detroit PMSA, MI	H	7.52 FQ	11.57 AW	16.53 TQ	MIBLS	10/01-12/01
	Flint PMSA, MI	H	6.93 FQ	14.47 AW	24.67 TQ	MIBLS	10/01-12/01
	Grand Rapids-Muskegon-Holland MSA, MI	H	7.32 FQ	11.36 AW	16.60 TQ	MIBLS	10/01-12/01
	Kalamazoo-Battle Creek MSA, MI	H	7.30 FQ	14.21 AW	26.10 TQ	MIBLS	10/01-12/01
	Lansing-East Lansing MSA, MI	H	7.22 FQ	10.11 AW	16.71 TQ	MIBLS	10/01-12/01
	Saginaw-Bay City-Midland MSA, MI	H	5.40 FQ	8.40 AW	15.38 TQ	MIBLS	10/01-12/01
	Minnesota	H	7.93 FQ	12.47 AW	17.26 TQ	MNBLS	10/01-12/01

AAW	Average annual wage	AOH	Average offered, high	ASH	Average starting, high	H	Hourly	M	Monthly	S	Special: hourly and annual
AE	Average entry wage	AOL	Average offered, low	ASL	Average starting, low	HI	Highest wage paid	MTC	Median total compensation	TQ	Third quartile wage
AEX	Average experienced wage	APH	Average pay, high range	AW	Average wage paid	HR	High end range	MW	Median wage paid	W	Weekly
AO	Average offered	APL	Average pay, low range	FQ	First quartile wage	LR	Low end range	SQ	Second quartile wage	Y	Yearly

Occupation/Type/Industry	Location	Per	Low	Mid	High	Source	Date
Food Batchmaker	Minneapolis-St. Paul MSA, MN-WI	H	8.47 FQ	12.77 AW	17.44 TQ	MNBLS	10/01-12/01
	Mississippi	H	5.87 FQ	9.15 AW	14.97 TQ	MSBLS	10/01-12/01
	Missouri	H	8.11 FQ	11.82 AW	16.20 TQ	MOBLS	10/01-12/01
	Kansas City MSA, MO-KS	H	7.46 FQ	10.11 AW	13.29 TQ	MOBLS	10/01-12/01
	St. Louis MSA, MO-IL	H	7.87 FQ	12.76 AW	17.86 TQ	MOBLS	10/01-12/01
	Springfield MSA, MO	H	7.17 FQ	12.56 AW	17.55 TQ	MOBLS	10/01-12/01
	Montana	H	5.64 FQ	7.30 AW	11.63 TQ	MTBLS	10/01-12/01
	Nebraska	H	6.64 FQ	12.07 AW	17.78 TQ	NEBLS	10/01-12/01
	Lincoln MSA, NE	H	5.54 FQ	8.50 AW	14.95 TQ	NEBLS	10/01-12/01
	Omaha MSA, NE-IA	H	6.28 FQ	13.04 AW	23.00 TQ	NEBLS	10/01-12/01
	Nevada	H	6.01 FQ	10.89 AW	16.33 TQ	NVBLS	10/01-12/01
	Las Vegas MSA, NV-AZ	H	6.86 FQ	13.05 AW	16.63 TQ	NVBLS	10/01-12/01
	Reno MSA, NV	H	6.04 FQ	11.40 AW	16.38 TQ	NVBLS	10/01-12/01
	New Hampshire	H	6.51 FQ	12.80 AW	22.78 TQ	NHBLS	10/01-12/01
	Manchester PMSA, NH	H	8.90 FQ	11.75 AW	16.38 TQ	NHBLS	10/01-12/01
	Portsmouth-Rochester PMSA, NH-ME	H	5.94 FQ	9.54 AW	14.69 TQ	NHBLS	10/01-12/01
	New Jersey	H	6.13 FQ	10.95 AW	19.06 TQ	NJBLS	10/01-12/01
	Bergen-Passaic PMSA, NJ	H	6.10 FQ	9.44 AW	14.89 TQ	NJBLS	10/01-12/01
	Jersey City PMSA, NJ	H	5.79 FQ	8.41 AW	14.26 TQ	NJBLS	10/01-12/01
	Middlesex-Somerset-Hunterdon PMSA, NJ	H	9.56 FQ	18.84 AW	30.57 TQ	NJBLS	10/01-12/01
	Monmouth-Ocean PMSA, NJ	H	5.44 FQ	7.86 AW	11.78 TQ	NJBLS	10/01-12/01
	Newark PMSA, NJ	H	6.26 FQ	9.77 AW	14.82 TQ	NJBLS	10/01-12/01
	Trenton PMSA, NJ	H	7.22 FQ	10.23 AW	14.11 TQ	NJBLS	10/01-12/01
	New Mexico	H	5.67 FQ	10.10 AW	20.75 TQ	NMBLS	10/01-12/01
	Albuquerque MSA, NM	H	5.67 FQ	11.65 AW	23.01 TQ	NMBLS	10/01-12/01
	Las Cruces MSA, NM	H	5.79 FQ	6.73 AW	8.49 TQ	NMBLS	10/01-12/01
	New York	H	5.83 FQ	9.43 AW	14.85 TQ	NYBLS	10/01-12/01
	Albany-Schenectady-Troy MSA, NY	H	5.73 FQ	9.57 AW	16.26 TQ	NYBLS	10/01-12/01
	Binghamton MSA, NY	H	5.88 FQ	10.94 AW	16.77 TQ	NYBLS	10/01-12/01
	Buffalo-Niagara Falls MSA, NY	H	5.69 FQ	9.41 AW	17.28 TQ	NYBLS	10/01-12/01
	Dutchess County PMSA, NY	H	5.82 FQ	8.34 AW	13.76 TQ	NYBLS	10/01-12/01
	Nassau-Suffolk PMSA, NY	H	6.14 FQ	9.05 AW	13.37 TQ	NYBLS	10/01-12/01
	New York PMSA, NY	H	6.14 FQ	9.80 AW	13.83 TQ	NYBLS	10/01-12/01
	Newburgh PMSA, NY-PA	H	5.63 FQ	8.95 AW	15.75 TQ	NYBLS	10/01-12/01
	Rochester MSA, NY	H	5.69 FQ	9.57 AW	16.20 TQ	NYBLS	10/01-12/01
	Syracuse MSA, NY	H	5.59 FQ	8.96 AW	14.86 TQ	NYBLS	10/01-12/01
	Utica-Rome MSA, NY	H	5.71 FQ	8.14 AW	13.06 TQ	NYBLS	10/01-12/01
	North Carolina	H	7.13 FQ	10.17 AW	14.22 TQ	NCBLS	10/01-12/01
	Asheville MSA, NC	H	8.95 FQ	12.73 AW	16.48 TQ	NCBLS	10/01-12/01
	Charlotte-Gastonia-Rock Hill MSA, NC-SC	H	7.63 FQ	9.69 AW	12.98 TQ	NCBLS	10/01-12/01
	Greensboro-Winston-Salem-High Point MSA, NC	H	7.80 FQ	11.63 AW	16.29 TQ	NCBLS	10/01-12/01
	Hickory-Morganton-Lenoir MSA, NC	H	5.94 FQ	8.73 AW	12.85 TQ	NCBLS	10/01-12/01
	Raleigh-Durham-Chapel Hill MSA, NC	H	6.81 FQ	8.28 AW	10.68 TQ	NCBLS	10/01-12/01
	North Dakota	H	6.28 FQ	8.79 AW	12.17 TQ	NDBLS	10/01-12/01
	Fargo-Moorhead MSA, ND-MN	H	5.84 FQ	8.35 AW	12.05 TQ	NDBLS	10/01-12/01
	Ohio	H	6.62 FQ	11.47 AW	17.03 TQ	OHBLS	10/01-12/01
	Canton-Massillon MSA, OH	H	9.20 FQ	13.35 AW	16.82 TQ	OHBLS	10/01-12/01
	Cincinnati PMSA, OH-KY-IN	H	9.80 FQ	14.63 AW	19.72 TQ	OHBLS	10/01-12/01
	Cleveland-Lorain-Elyria PMSA, OH	H	7.64 FQ	11.52 AW	17.17 TQ	OHBLS	10/01-12/01
	Columbus MSA, OH	H	7.56 FQ	11.46 AW	16.96 TQ	OHBLS	10/01-12/01
	Dayton-Springfield MSA, OH	H	5.46 FQ	7.55 AW	10.74 TQ	OHBLS	10/01-12/01
	Toledo MSA, OH	H	6.20 FQ	9.68 AW	15.38 TQ	OHBLS	10/01-12/01
	Oklahoma	H	6.02 FQ	9.61 AW	13.40 TQ	OKBLS	10/01-12/01
	Oklahoma City MSA, OK	H	6.01 FQ	9.39 AW	13.31 TQ	OKBLS	10/01-12/01
	Tulsa MSA, OK	H	6.02 FQ	10.34 AW	15.69 TQ	OKBLS	10/01-12/01
	Oregon	H	7.41 FQ	10.16 AW	14.17 TQ	ORBLS	10/01-12/01
	Eugene-Springfield MSA, OR	H	7.49 FQ	9.34 AW	11.96 TQ	ORBLS	10/01-12/01
	Medford-Ashland MSA, OR	H	7.23 FQ	8.50 AW	11.51 TQ	ORBLS	10/01-12/01
	Portland-Vancouver PMSA, OR-WA	H	7.67 FQ	10.61 AW	15.51 TQ	ORBLS	10/01-12/01
	Salem PMSA, OR	H	7.36 FQ	10.66 AW	14.34 TQ	ORBLS	10/01-12/01

AAW Average annual wage; **AE** Average entry wage; **AEX** Average experienced wage; **AO** Average offered; **AOH** Average offered, high; **AOL** Average offered, low; **APH** Average pay, high range; **APL** Average pay, low range; **ASH** Average starting, high; **ASL** Average starting, low; **AW** Average wage paid; **FQ** First quartile wage; **H** Hourly; **HI** Highest wage paid; **HR** High end range; **LR** Low end range; **M** Monthly; **MTC** Median total compensation; **MW** Median wage paid; **SQ** Second quartile wage; **S** Special: hourly and annual; **TQ** Third quartile wage; **W** Weekly; **Y** Yearly

Occupation/Type/Industry	Location	Per	Low	Mid	High	Source	Date
Food Batchmaker	Pennsylvania	H	7.34 FQ	12.25 AW	17.63 TQ	PABLS	10/01-12/01
	Allentown-Bethlehem-Easton MSA, PA	H	9.12 FQ	16.38 AW	20.77 TQ	PABLS	10/01-12/01
	Erie MSA, PA	H	7.35 FQ	9.63 AW	12.14 TQ	PABLS	10/01-12/01
	Harrisburg-Lebanon-Carlisle MSA, PA	H	8.21 FQ	14.08 AW	20.26 TQ	PABLS	10/01-12/01
	Johnstown MSA, PA	H	7.37 FQ	10.36 AW	14.77 TQ	PABLS	10/01-12/01
	Lancaster MSA, PA	H	6.81 FQ	11.67 AW	16.80 TQ	PABLS	10/01-12/01
	Philadelphia PMSA, PA-NJ	H	8.10 FQ	12.54 AW	17.96 TQ	PABLS	10/01-12/01
	Pittsburgh MSA, PA	H	5.79 FQ	8.65 AW	13.69 TQ	PABLS	10/01-12/01
	Reading MSA, PA	H	6.16 FQ	10.39 AW	15.77 TQ	PABLS	10/01-12/01
	Scranton-Wilkes-Barre-Hazleton MSA, PA	H	7.21 FQ	10.63 AW	13.37 TQ	PABLS	10/01-12/01
	York MSA, PA	H	8.64 FQ	11.39 AW	14.17 TQ	PABLS	10/01-12/01
	Rhode Island	H	7.29 FQ	10.94 AW	15.97 TQ	RIBLS	10/01-12/01
	Providence-Fall River-Warwick MSA, RI-MA	H	7.32 FQ	11.06 AW	16.04 TQ	RIBLS	10/01-12/01
	South Carolina	H	7.26 FQ	11.48 AW	16.27 TQ	SCBLS	10/01-12/01
	Greenville-Spartanburg-Anderson MSA, SC	H	7.41 FQ	13.41 AW	16.76 TQ	SCBLS	10/01-12/01
	South Dakota	H	6.25 FQ	9.49 AW	12.54 TQ	SDBLS	10/01-12/01
	Tennessee	H	8.87 FQ	13.78 AW	17.89 TQ	TNBLS	10/01-12/01
	Chattanooga MSA, TN-GA	H	8.12 FQ	14.08 AW	19.55 TQ	TNBLS	10/01-12/01
	Johnson City-Kingsport-Bristol MSA, TN-VA	H	5.95 FQ	11.46 AW	15.80 TQ	TNBLS	10/01-12/01
	Texas	H	5.93 FQ	9.09 AW	14.43 TQ	TXBLS	10/01-12/01
	Amarillo MSA, TX	H	6.76 FQ	9.04 AW	12.89 TQ	TXBLS	10/01-12/01
	Austin-San Marcos MSA, TX	H	6.09 FQ	8.20 AW	10.26 TQ	TXBLS	10/01-12/01
	Corpus Christi MSA, TX	H	5.86 FQ	8.51 AW	13.34 TQ	TXBLS	10/01-12/01
	Dallas PMSA, TX	H	5.86 FQ	9.64 AW	15.60 TQ	TXBLS	10/01-12/01
	El Paso MSA, TX	H	5.72 FQ	6.60 AW	7.90 TQ	TXBLS	10/01-12/01
	Fort Worth-Arlington PMSA, TX	H	6.47 FQ	8.80 AW	12.09 TQ	TXBLS	10/01-12/01
	Houston PMSA, TX	H	5.71 FQ	8.69 AW	13.81 TQ	TXBLS	10/01-12/01
	Laredo MSA, TX	H	6.46 FQ	9.64 AW	15.46 TQ	TXBLS	10/01-12/01
	McAllen-Edinburg-Mission MSA, TX	H	5.78 FQ	8.61 AW	13.32 TQ	TXBLS	10/01-12/01
	San Antonio MSA, TX	H	5.85 FQ	8.33 AW	13.09 TQ	TXBLS	10/01-12/01
	Waco MSA, TX	H	5.82 FQ	8.43 AW	13.39 TQ	TXBLS	10/01-12/01
	Utah	H	6.56 FQ	10.43 AW	15.86 TQ	UTBLS	10/01-12/01
	Provo-Orem MSA, UT	H	6.54 FQ	8.55 AW	10.72 TQ	UTBLS	10/01-12/01
	Salt Lake City-Ogden MSA, UT	H	6.21 FQ	9.35 AW	14.63 TQ	UTBLS	10/01-12/01
	Vermont	H	7.61 FQ	11.94 AW	16.49 TQ	VTBLS	10/01-12/01
	Virginia	H	6.43 FQ	10.06 AW	14.79 TQ	VABLS	10/01-12/01
	Lynchburg MSA, VA	H	6.78 FQ	10.85 AW	15.47 TQ	VABLS	10/01-12/01
	Norfolk-Virginia Beach-Newport News MSA, VA-NC	H	6.49 FQ	9.70 AW	13.13 TQ	VABLS	10/01-12/01
	Richmond-Petersburg MSA, VA	H	6.18 FQ	10.90 AW	15.19 TQ	VABLS	10/01-12/01
	Washington	H	7.15 FQ	11.32 AW	16.79 TQ	WABLS	10/01-12/01
	Seattle-Bellevue-Everett PMSA, WA	H	6.94 FQ	11.54 AW	17.49 TQ	WABLS	10/01-12/01
	Spokane MSA, WA	H	7.31 FQ	9.92 AW	13.68 TQ	WABLS	10/01-12/01
	Tacoma PMSA, WA	H	9.06 FQ	13.01 AW	18.74 TQ	WABLS	10/01-12/01
	Yakima MSA, WA	H	11.48 FQ	13.75 AW	17.23 TQ	WABLS	10/01-12/01
	Wisconsin	H	8.29 FQ	12.07 AW	16.30 TQ	WIBLS	10/01-12/01
	Appleton-Oshkosh-Neenah MSA, WI	H	10.98 FQ	13.91 AW	16.73 TQ	WIBLS	10/01-12/01
	Green Bay MSA, WI	H	7.55 FQ	11.92 AW	16.22 TQ	WIBLS	10/01-12/01
	Madison MSA, WI	H	7.46 FQ	11.47 AW	16.29 TQ	WIBLS	10/01-12/01
	Milwaukee-Waukesha PMSA, WI	H	8.82 FQ	11.96 AW	16.77 TQ	WIBLS	10/01-12/01
	Puerto Rico	H	5.41 FQ	6.93 AW	10.54 TQ	PRBLS	10/01-12/01
Food Cooking Machine Operator and Tender	Alabama	H	6.49 FQ	8.66 AW	11.46 TQ	ALBLS	10/01-12/01
	Arizona	H	5.76 FQ	9.87 AW	18.73 TQ	AZBLS	10/01-12/01
	Arkansas	H	7.33 FQ	9.60 AW	12.15 TQ	ARBLS	10/01-12/01
	California	H	6.94 FQ	11.32 AW	18.11 TQ	CABLS	10/01-12/01
	Colorado	H	7.22 FQ	10.15 AW	15.11 TQ	COBLS	10/01-12/01

AAW Average annual wage; AE Average entry wage; AEX Average experienced wage; AO Average offered; AOH Average offered, high; AOL Average offered, low; APH Average pay, high range; APL Average pay, low range; ASH Average starting, high; ASL Average starting, low; AW Average wage paid; FQ First quartile wage; H Hourly; HI Highest wage paid; HR High end range; LR Low end range; M Monthly; MTC Median total compensation; MW Median wage paid; SQ Second quartile wage; S Special: hourly and annual; TQ Third quartile wage; W Weekly; Y Yearly

Occupation/Type/Industry	Location	Per	Low	Mid	High	Source	Date
Food Cooking Machine Operator and Tender	Connecticut	H	7.70 FQ	11.48 AW	15.89 TQ	CTBLS	10/01-12/01
	Delaware	H	7.24 FQ	9.99 AW	14.19 TQ	DEBLS	10/01-12/01
	Florida	H	6.00 FQ	9.00 AW	13.65 TQ	FLBLS	10/01-12/01
	Georgia	H	7.10 FQ	8.53 AW	11.04 TQ	GABLS	10/01-12/01
	Hawaii	H	5.83 FQ	9.01 AW	14.95 TQ	HIBLS	10/01-12/01
	Idaho	H	6.57 FQ	10.65 AW	14.98 TQ	IDBLS	10/01-12/01
	Illinois	H	7.94 FQ	12.45 AW	18.82 TQ	ILBLS	10/01-12/01
	Indiana	H	6.35 FQ	9.87 AW	13.59 TQ	INBLS	10/01-12/01
	Iowa	H	7.96 FQ	12.58 AW	19.75 TQ	IABLS	10/01-12/01
	Kansas	H	8.31 FQ	12.11 AW	16.42 TQ	KSBLS	10/01-12/01
	Kentucky	H	8.87 FQ	10.93 AW	13.51 TQ	KYBLS	10/01-12/01
	Louisiana	H	5.93 FQ	8.93 AW	12.66 TQ	LABLS	10/01-12/01
	Maine	H	7.16 FQ	11.53 AW	16.83 TQ	MEBLS	10/01-12/01
	Maryland	H	7.21 FQ	11.09 AW	16.12 TQ	MDBLS	10/01-12/01
	Massachusetts	H	7.19 FQ	10.82 AW	16.01 TQ	MABLS	10/01-12/01
	Michigan	H	7.91 FQ	12.62 AW	17.17 TQ	MIBLS	10/01-12/01
	Minnesota	H	9.03 FQ	12.84 AW	18.50 TQ	MNBLS	10/01-12/01
	Mississippi	H	6.03 FQ	8.00 AW	10.35 TQ	MSBLS	10/01-12/01
	Missouri	H	7.23 FQ	11.15 AW	15.71 TQ	MOBLS	10/01-12/01
	Montana	H	6.29 FQ	9.74 AW	15.45 TQ	MTBLS	10/01-12/01
	Nebraska	H	6.55 FQ	13.71 AW	24.85 TQ	NEBLS	10/01-12/01
	Nevada	H	5.87 FQ	9.98 AW	17.55 TQ	NVBLS	10/01-12/01
	New Hampshire	H	5.95 FQ	8.03 AW	11.04 TQ	NHBLS	10/01-12/01
	New Jersey	H	6.33 FQ	10.82 AW	16.39 TQ	NJBLS	10/01-12/01
	New Mexico	H	5.59 FQ	6.94 AW	9.58 TQ	NMBLS	10/01-12/01
	New York	H	5.88 FQ	9.96 AW	15.73 TQ	NYBLS	10/01-12/01
	North Carolina	H	5.85 FQ	9.53 AW	14.77 TQ	NCBLS	10/01-12/01
	North Dakota	H	7.41 FQ	9.84 AW	12.83 TQ	NDBLS	10/01-12/01
	Ohio	H	7.92 FQ	11.13 AW	15.34 TQ	OHBLS	10/01-12/01
	Oklahoma	H	6.69 FQ	9.22 AW	11.43 TQ	OKBLS	10/01-12/01
	Oregon	H	8.09 FQ	12.00 AW	17.25 TQ	ORBLS	10/01-12/01
	Pennsylvania	H	7.65 FQ	11.99 AW	16.41 TQ	PABLS	10/01-12/01
	South Dakota	H	7.70 FQ	10.63 AW	14.11 TQ	SDBLS	10/01-12/01
	Tennessee	H	6.51 FQ	11.05 AW	14.71 TQ	TNBLS	10/01-12/01
	Texas	H	6.25 FQ	10.59 AW	16.05 TQ	TXBLS	10/01-12/01
	Utah	H	7.58 FQ	11.09 AW	13.31 TQ	UTBLS	10/01-12/01
	Vermont	H	6.75 FQ	11.11 AW	16.68 TQ	VTBLS	10/01-12/01
	Virginia	H	6.16 FQ	8.75 AW	11.13 TQ	VABLS	10/01-12/01
	Washington	H	7.56 FQ	11.75 AW	16.29 TQ	WABLS	10/01-12/01
	West Virginia	H	5.72 FQ	8.03 AW	10.69 TQ	WVBLS	10/01-12/01
	Wisconsin	H	9.94 FQ	15.02 AW	23.25 TQ	WIBLS	10/01-12/01
	Puerto Rico	H	5.48 FQ	8.12 AW	12.87 TQ	PRBLS	10/01-12/01
Food Preparation and Serving Worker							
Including Fast Food	Alabama	H	5.49 FQ	6.32 AW	7.60 TQ	ALBLS	10/01-12/01
Including Fast Food	Alaska	H	6.32 FQ	8.14 AW	10.93 TQ	AKBLS	10/01-12/01
Including Fast Food	Arizona	H	5.49 FQ	6.61 AW	8.33 TQ	AZBLS	10/01-12/01
Including Fast Food	Arkansas	H	5.55 FQ	6.40 AW	7.74 TQ	ARBLS	10/01-12/01
Including Fast Food	California	H	6.41 FQ	7.71 AW	9.76 TQ	CABLS	10/01-12/01
Including Fast Food	Colorado	H	5.77 FQ	7.50 AW	9.80 TQ	COBLS	10/01-12/01
Including Fast Food	Connecticut	H	6.73 FQ	8.66 AW	11.08 TQ	CTBLS	10/01-12/01
Including Fast Food	Delaware	H	6.50 FQ	7.91 AW	10.25 TQ	DEBLS	10/01-12/01
Including Fast Food	District of Columbia	H	6.69 FQ	8.48 AW	11.19 TQ	DCBLS	10/01-12/01
Including Fast Food	Florida	H	5.56 FQ	6.71 AW	8.62 TQ	FLBLS	10/01-12/01
Including Fast Food	Georgia	H	5.49 FQ	6.82 AW	8.72 TQ	GABLS	10/01-12/01
Including Fast Food	Hawaii	H	5.67 FQ	6.85 AW	8.56 TQ	HIBLS	10/01-12/01
Including Fast Food	Idaho	H	5.61 FQ	6.62 AW	8.24 TQ	IDBLS	10/01-12/01
Including Fast Food	Illinois	H	5.53 FQ	6.80 AW	8.53 TQ	ILBLS	10/01-12/01
Including Fast Food	Indiana	H	5.62 FQ	6.78 AW	8.38 TQ	INBLS	10/01-12/01
Including Fast Food	Iowa	H	5.59 FQ	6.77 AW	8.51 TQ	IABLS	10/01-12/01
Including Fast Food	Kansas	H	5.66 FQ	7.09 AW	8.91 TQ	KSBLS	10/01-12/01
Including Fast Food	Kentucky	H	5.58 FQ	6.66 AW	8.38 TQ	KYBLS	10/01-12/01
Including Fast Food	Louisiana	H	5.49 FQ	6.61 AW	8.29 TQ	LABLS	10/01-12/01
Including Fast Food	Maine	H	5.62 FQ	7.19 AW	9.52 TQ	MEBLS	10/01-12/01
Including Fast Food	Maryland	H	5.57 FQ	7.11 AW	9.38 TQ	MDBLS	10/01-12/01
Including Fast Food	Massachusetts	H	6.93 FQ	8.38 AW	10.50 TQ	MABLS	10/01-12/01
Including Fast Food	Michigan	H	5.65 FQ	7.32 AW	9.91 TQ	MIBLS	10/01-12/01
Including Fast Food	Minnesota	H	5.65 FQ	7.30 AW	9.50 TQ	MNBLS	10/01-12/01
Including Fast Food	Mississippi	H	5.62 FQ	6.53 AW	8.11 TQ	MSBLS	10/01-12/01
Including Fast Food	Missouri	H	5.66 FQ	7.15 AW	9.26 TQ	MOBLS	10/01-12/01

AAW	Average annual wage	AOH	Average offered, high	ASH	Average starting, high	H	Hourly	M	Monthly	S	Special: hourly and annual
AE	Average entry wage	AOL	Average offered, low	ASL	Average starting, low	HI	Highest wage paid	MTC	Median total compensation	TQ	Third quartile wage
AEX	Average experienced wage	APH	Average pay, high range	AW	Average wage paid	HR	High end range	MW	Median wage paid	W	Weekly
AO	Average offered	APL	Average pay, low range	FQ	First quartile wage	LR	Low end range	SQ	Second quartile wage	Y	Yearly

Occupation/Type/Industry	Location	Per	Low	Mid	High	Source	Date
Food Preparation and Serving Worker							
Including Fast Food	Montana	H	5.72 FQ	6.96 AW	8.56 TQ	MTBLS	10/01-12/01
Including Fast Food	Nebraska	H	5.66 FQ	7.16 AW	8.87 TQ	NEBLS	10/01-12/01
Including Fast Food	Nevada	H	5.72 FQ	7.80 AW	10.86 TQ	NVBLS	10/01-12/01
Including Fast Food	New Hampshire	H	6.06 FQ	8.10 AW	10.75 TQ	NHBLS	10/01-12/01
Including Fast Food	New Jersey	H	5.62 FQ	7.60 AW	10.42 TQ	NJBLS	10/01-12/01
Including Fast Food	New Mexico	H	5.59 FQ	6.80 AW	9.21 TQ	NMBLS	10/01-12/01
Including Fast Food	New York	H	5.57 FQ	7.15 AW	9.49 TQ	NYBLS	10/01-12/01
Including Fast Food	North Carolina	H	5.57 FQ	6.95 AW	9.00 TQ	NCBLS	10/01-12/01
Including Fast Food	North Dakota	H	5.46 FQ	6.52 AW	8.17 TQ	NDBLS	10/01-12/01
Including Fast Food	Ohio	H	5.61 FQ	6.92 AW	8.69 TQ	OHBLS	10/01-12/01
Including Fast Food	Oklahoma	H	5.53 FQ	6.57 AW	8.21 TQ	OKBLS	10/01-12/01
Including Fast Food	Oregon	H	6.83 FQ	7.94 AW	9.39 TQ	ORBLS	10/01-12/01
Including Fast Food	Pennsylvania	H	5.62 FQ	7.08 AW	9.08 TQ	PABLS	10/01-12/01
Including Fast Food	Rhode Island	H	6.41 FQ	7.41 AW	8.78 TQ	RIBLS	10/01-12/01
Including Fast Food	South Carolina	H	5.63 FQ	7.10 AW	9.24 TQ	SCBLS	10/01-12/01
Including Fast Food	South Dakota	H	5.75 FQ	7.58 AW	10.21 TQ	SDBLS	10/01-12/01
Including Fast Food	Tennessee	H	5.66 FQ	6.68 AW	8.33 TQ	TNBLS	10/01-12/01
Including Fast Food	Texas	H	5.48 FQ	6.51 AW	8.14 TQ	TXBLS	10/01-12/01
Including Fast Food	Utah	H	5.56 FQ	6.94 AW	8.92 TQ	UTBLS	10/01-12/01
Including Fast Food	Vermont	H	6.44 FQ	7.79 AW	9.84 TQ	VTBLS	10/01-12/01
Including Fast Food	Virginia	H	5.68 FQ	7.30 AW	9.65 TQ	VABLS	10/01-12/01
Including Fast Food	Washington	H	6.80 FQ	8.10 AW	10.32 TQ	WABLS	10/01-12/01
Including Fast Food	West Virginia	H	5.54 FQ	6.59 AW	8.11 TQ	WVBLS	10/01-12/01
Including Fast Food	Wisconsin	H	5.76 FQ	7.56 AW	10.04 TQ	WIBLS	10/01-12/01
Including Fast Food	Wyoming	H	5.53 FQ	6.43 AW	7.89 TQ	WYBLS	10/01-12/01
Including Fast Food	Puerto Rico	H	5.52 FQ	6.13 AW	6.96 TQ	PRBLS	10/01-12/01
Including Fast Food	Virgin Islands	H	5.64 FQ	6.72 AW	8.58 TQ	VIBLS	10/01-12/01
Including Fast Food	Guam	H	5.69 FQ	7.02 AW	8.73 TQ	GUBLS	10/01-12/01
Food Preparation Worker	Alabama	H	5.65 FQ	7.01 AW	8.97 TQ	ALBLS	10/01-12/01
	Alaska	H	6.11 FQ	10.30 AW	16.17 TQ	AKBLS	10/01-12/01
	Arizona	H	5.59 FQ	7.15 AW	9.04 TQ	AZBLS	10/01-12/01
	Arkansas	H	5.64 FQ	7.15 AW	9.09 TQ	ARBLS	10/01-12/01
	California	H	6.74 FQ	8.83 AW	12.33 TQ	CABLS	10/01-12/01
	Colorado	H	6.37 FQ	8.74 AW	12.45 TQ	COBLS	10/01-12/01
	Connecticut	H	7.07 FQ	9.75 AW	13.19 TQ	CTBLS	10/01-12/01
	Delaware	H	6.67 FQ	8.50 AW	11.27 TQ	DEBLS	10/01-12/01
	District of Columbia	H	7.37 FQ	10.45 AW	14.01 TQ	DCBLS	10/01-12/01
	Florida	H	5.84 FQ	7.87 AW	10.66 TQ	FLBLS	10/01-12/01
	Georgia	H	5.71 FQ	7.90 AW	10.85 TQ	GABLS	10/01-12/01
	Hawaii	H	6.90 FQ	10.37 AW	14.24 TQ	HIBLS	10/01-12/01
	Idaho	H	5.89 FQ	7.81 AW	10.45 TQ	IDBLS	10/01-12/01
	Illinois	H	5.60 FQ	7.12 AW	9.48 TQ	ILBLS	10/01-12/01
	Indiana	H	5.92 FQ	7.70 AW	9.49 TQ	INBLS	10/01-12/01
	Iowa	H	5.74 FQ	7.54 AW	10.14 TQ	IABLS	10/01-12/01
	Kansas	H	5.80 FQ	7.42 AW	9.48 TQ	KSBLS	10/01-12/01
	Kentucky	H	5.79 FQ	7.87 AW	10.61 TQ	KYBLS	10/01-12/01
	Louisiana	H	5.53 FQ	6.67 AW	8.33 TQ	LABLS	10/01-12/01
	Maine	H	5.95 FQ	8.14 AW	10.67 TQ	MEBLS	10/01-12/01
	Maryland	H	5.88 FQ	8.77 AW	12.54 TQ	MDBLS	10/01-12/01
	Massachusetts	H	7.09 FQ	9.32 AW	12.29 TQ	MABLS	10/01-12/01
	Michigan	H	5.81 FQ	8.58 AW	12.13 TQ	MIBLS	10/01-12/01
	Minnesota	H	6.14 FQ	9.00 AW	12.81 TQ	MNBLS	10/01-12/01
	Mississippi	H	5.53 FQ	6.48 AW	8.11 TQ	MSBLS	10/01-12/01
	Missouri	H	5.77 FQ	7.74 AW	10.39 TQ	MOBLS	10/01-12/01
	Montana	H	5.71 FQ	7.23 AW	9.26 TQ	MTBLS	10/01-12/01
	Nebraska	H	5.83 FQ	7.71 AW	10.10 TQ	NEBLS	10/01-12/01
	Nevada	H	6.03 FQ	9.35 AW	13.07 TQ	NVBLS	10/01-12/01
	New Hampshire	H	6.47 FQ	8.69 AW	11.16 TQ	NHBLS	10/01-12/01
	New Jersey	H	5.86 FQ	8.82 AW	12.84 TQ	NJBLS	10/01-12/01
	New Mexico	H	5.71 FQ	7.26 AW	9.73 TQ	NMBLS	10/01-12/01
	New York	H	5.86 FQ	8.75 AW	12.61 TQ	NYBLS	10/01-12/01
	North Carolina	H	5.64 FQ	7.34 AW	9.91 TQ	NCBLS	10/01-12/01
	North Dakota	H	5.87 FQ	8.97 AW	13.84 TQ	NDBLS	10/01-12/01
	Ohio	H	5.77 FQ	7.99 AW	10.97 TQ	OHBLS	10/01-12/01
	Oklahoma	H	5.60 FQ	6.88 AW	8.69 TQ	OKBLS	10/01-12/01
	Oregon	H	6.65 FQ	8.30 AW	11.19 TQ	ORBLS	10/01-12/01
	Pennsylvania	H	5.71 FQ	7.89 AW	11.00 TQ	PABLS	10/01-12/01
	Rhode Island	H	6.70 FQ	9.22 AW	13.43 TQ	RIBLS	10/01-12/01
	South Carolina	H	5.70 FQ	7.37 AW	9.75 TQ	SCBLS	10/01-12/01

AAW	Average annual wage	**AOH**	Average offered, high	**ASH**	Average starting, high	**H**	Hourly	**M**	Monthly	**S**	Special: hourly and annual
AE	Average entry wage	**AOL**	Average offered, low	**ASL**	Average starting, low	**HI**	Highest wage paid	**MTC**	Median total compensation	**TQ**	Third quartile wage
AEX	Average experienced wage	**APH**	Average pay, high range	**AW**	Average wage paid	**HR**	High end range	**MW**	Median wage paid	**W**	Weekly
AO	Average offered	**APL**	Average pay, low range	**FQ**	First quartile wage	**LR**	Low end range	**SQ**	Second quartile wage	**Y**	Yearly

Occupation/Type/Industry	Location	Per	Low	Mid	High	Source	Date
Food Preparation Worker	South Dakota	H	5.70 FQ	7.24 AW	8.97 TQ	SDBLS	10/01-12/01
	Tennessee	H	5.72 FQ	7.92 AW	11.21 TQ	TNBLS	10/01-12/01
	Texas	H	5.67 FQ	7.36 AW	9.92 TQ	TXBLS	10/01-12/01
	Utah	H	5.83 FQ	7.88 AW	10.49 TQ	UTBLS	10/01-12/01
	Vermont	H	6.49 FQ	8.03 AW	10.34 TQ	VTBLS	10/01-12/01
	Virginia	H	5.69 FQ	7.40 AW	9.84 TQ	VABLS	10/01-12/01
	Washington	H	6.98 FQ	8.84 AW	11.56 TQ	WABLS	10/01-12/01
	West Virginia	H	5.66 FQ	7.15 AW	9.63 TQ	WVBLS	10/01-12/01
	Wisconsin	H	6.18 FQ	8.16 AW	10.66 TQ	WIBLS	10/01-12/01
	Wyoming	H	5.64 FQ	7.38 AW	10.13 TQ	WYBLS	10/01-12/01
	Puerto Rico	H	5.40 FQ	6.01 AW	6.78 TQ	PRBLS	10/01-12/01
	Virgin Islands	H	5.45 FQ	6.71 AW	8.59 TQ	VIBLS	10/01-12/01
	Guam	H	5.65 FQ	7.21 AW	10.43 TQ	GUBLS	10/01-12/01
Food Server							
Nonrestaurant	Alabama	H	5.56 FQ	6.99 AW	8.74 TQ	ALBLS	10/01-12/01
Nonrestaurant	Alaska	H	6.15 FQ	8.72 AW	13.40 TQ	AKBLS	10/01-12/01
Nonrestaurant	Arizona	H	5.53 FQ	6.94 AW	8.75 TQ	AZBLS	10/01-12/01
Nonrestaurant	Arkansas	H	5.50 FQ	6.55 AW	8.34 TQ	ARBLS	10/01-12/01
Nonrestaurant	California	H	6.50 FQ	8.90 AW	12.95 TQ	CABLS	10/01-12/01
Nonrestaurant	Colorado	H	5.93 FQ	8.96 AW	12.78 TQ	COBLS	10/01-12/01
Nonrestaurant	Connecticut	H	7.05 FQ	9.90 AW	13.46 TQ	CTBLS	10/01-12/01
Nonrestaurant	Delaware	H	6.83 FQ	9.43 AW	13.34 TQ	DEBLS	10/01-12/01
Nonrestaurant	District of Columbia	H	6.88 FQ	9.71 AW	13.59 TQ	DCBLS	10/01-12/01
Nonrestaurant	Florida	H	5.66 FQ	7.31 AW	10.03 TQ	FLBLS	10/01-12/01
Nonrestaurant	Georgia	H	5.67 FQ	7.90 AW	11.09 TQ	GABLS	10/01-12/01
Nonrestaurant	Hawaii	H	6.06 FQ	10.84 AW	16.83 TQ	HIBLS	10/01-12/01
Nonrestaurant	Idaho	H	5.60 FQ	6.76 AW	8.75 TQ	IDBLS	10/01-12/01
Nonrestaurant	Illinois	H	6.05 FQ	9.71 AW	14.28 TQ	ILBLS	10/01-12/01
Nonrestaurant	Indiana	H	5.67 FQ	7.63 AW	10.56 TQ	INBLS	10/01-12/01
Nonrestaurant	Iowa	H	5.76 FQ	7.49 AW	10.16 TQ	IABLS	10/01-12/01
Nonrestaurant	Kansas	H	5.68 FQ	6.86 AW	8.71 TQ	KSBLS	10/01-12/01
Nonrestaurant	Kentucky	H	5.68 FQ	7.42 AW	9.90 TQ	KYBLS	10/01-12/01
Nonrestaurant	Louisiana	H	5.58 FQ	6.59 AW	8.20 TQ	LABLS	10/01-12/01
Nonrestaurant	Maine	H	5.91 FQ	7.87 AW	10.25 TQ	MEBLS	10/01-12/01
Nonrestaurant	Maryland	H	5.92 FQ	7.95 AW	10.71 TQ	MDBLS	10/01-12/01
Nonrestaurant	Massachusetts	H	6.97 FQ	9.82 AW	14.87 TQ	MABLS	10/01-12/01
Nonrestaurant	Michigan	H	6.01 FQ	8.48 AW	11.35 TQ	MIBLS	10/01-12/01
Nonrestaurant	Minnesota	H	5.77 FQ	8.14 AW	11.13 TQ	MNBLS	10/01-12/01
Nonrestaurant	Mississippi	H	5.48 FQ	6.29 AW	7.46 TQ	MSBLS	10/01-12/01
Nonrestaurant	Missouri	H	5.69 FQ	7.61 AW	10.36 TQ	MOBLS	10/01-12/01
Nonrestaurant	Montana	H	5.69 FQ	6.84 AW	8.84 TQ	MTBLS	10/01-12/01
Nonrestaurant	Nebraska	H	5.82 FQ	7.43 AW	9.24 TQ	NEBLS	10/01-12/01
Nonrestaurant	Nevada	H	5.97 FQ	8.89 AW	12.04 TQ	NVBLS	10/01-12/01
Nonrestaurant	New Hampshire	H	6.01 FQ	8.08 AW	10.96 TQ	NHBLS	10/01-12/01
Nonrestaurant	New Jersey	H	6.12 FQ	9.38 AW	13.93 TQ	NJBLS	10/01-12/01
Nonrestaurant	New Mexico	H	5.62 FQ	6.97 AW	9.67 TQ	NMBLS	10/01-12/01
Nonrestaurant	New York	H	6.25 FQ	10.67 AW	15.26 TQ	NYBLS	10/01-12/01
Nonrestaurant	North Carolina	H	5.72 FQ	7.59 AW	10.05 TQ	NCBLS	10/01-12/01
Nonrestaurant	North Dakota	H	5.81 FQ	7.57 AW	10.01 TQ	NDBLS	10/01-12/01
Nonrestaurant	Ohio	H	5.71 FQ	7.73 AW	10.62 TQ	OHBLS	10/01-12/01
Nonrestaurant	Oklahoma	H	5.50 FQ	6.88 AW	9.45 TQ	OKBLS	10/01-12/01
Nonrestaurant	Oregon	H	6.84 FQ	8.50 AW	11.03 TQ	ORBLS	10/01-12/01
Nonrestaurant	Pennsylvania	H	5.70 FQ	7.89 AW	10.83 TQ	PABLS	10/01-12/01
Nonrestaurant	Rhode Island	H	6.54 FQ	9.00 AW	12.85 TQ	RIBLS	10/01-12/01
Nonrestaurant	South Carolina	H	5.65 FQ	7.04 AW	9.70 TQ	SCBLS	10/01-12/01
Nonrestaurant	South Dakota	H	6.26 FQ	7.66 AW	8.94 TQ	SDBLS	10/01-12/01
Nonrestaurant	Tennessee	H	5.76 FQ	7.74 AW	10.67 TQ	TNBLS	10/01-12/01
Nonrestaurant	Texas	H	5.51 FQ	6.60 AW	8.48 TQ	TXBLS	10/01-12/01
Nonrestaurant	Utah	H	5.82 FQ	7.46 AW	9.49 TQ	UTBLS	10/01-12/01
Nonrestaurant	Vermont	H	6.42 FQ	7.77 AW	9.76 TQ	VTBLS	10/01-12/01
Nonrestaurant	Virginia	H	5.85 FQ	7.64 AW	10.21 TQ	VABLS	10/01-12/01
Nonrestaurant	Washington	H	6.82 FQ	8.50 AW	11.45 TQ	WABLS	10/01-12/01
Nonrestaurant	West Virginia	H	5.64 FQ	7.18 AW	9.84 TQ	WVBLS	10/01-12/01
Nonrestaurant	Wisconsin	H	6.30 FQ	8.51 AW	11.01 TQ	WIBLS	10/01-12/01
Nonrestaurant	Wyoming	H	5.65 FQ	6.53 AW	8.11 TQ	WYBLS	10/01-12/01
Nonrestaurant	Puerto Rico	H	5.60 FQ	6.82 AW	8.79 TQ	PRBLS	10/01-12/01
Nonrestaurant	Virgin Islands	H	5.82 FQ	7.52 AW	9.68 TQ	VIBLS	10/01-12/01
Food Service Manager	Alabama	Y	17910 FQ	31000 AW	49080 TQ	ALBLS	10/01-12/01
	Birmingham MSA, AL	Y	21220 FQ	33870 AW	51180 TQ	ALBLS	10/01-12/01
	Huntsville MSA, AL	Y	18390 FQ	32250 AW	51640 TQ	ALBLS	10/01-12/01
	Mobile MSA, AL	Y	19680 FQ	36460 AW	56110 TQ	ALBLS	10/01-12/01

AAW	Average annual wage	**AOH**	Average offered, high	**ASH**	Average starting, high	**H**	Hourly	**M**	Monthly	**S**	Special: hourly and annual
AE	Average entry wage	**AOL**	Average offered, low	**ASL**	Average starting, low	**HI**	Highest wage paid	**MTC**	Median total compensation	**TQ**	Third quartile wage
AEX	Average experienced wage	**APH**	Average pay, high range	**AW**	Average wage paid	**HR**	High end range	**MW**	Median wage paid	**W**	Weekly
AO	Average offered	**APL**	Average pay, low range	**FQ**	First quartile wage	**LR**	Low end range	**SQ**	Second quartile wage	**Y**	Yearly

Occupation/Type/Industry	Location	Per	Low	Mid	High	Source	Date
Food Service Manager	Montgomery MSA, AL	Y	19190 FQ	31520 AW	52320 TQ	ALBLS	10/01-12/01
	Alaska	Y	15220 FQ	34820 AW	54380 TQ	AKBLS	10/01-12/01
	Anchorage MSA, AK	Y	15320 FQ	35640 AW	53970 TQ	AKBLS	10/01-12/01
	Arizona	Y	22710 FQ	33240 AW	48360 TQ	AZBLS	10/01-12/01
	Phoenix-Mesa MSA, AZ	Y	23750 FQ	34050 AW	48350 TQ	AZBLS	10/01-12/01
	Tucson MSA, AZ	Y	22190 FQ	36620 AW	54790 TQ	AZBLS	10/01-12/01
	Arkansas	Y	20430 FQ	36640 AW	56130 TQ	ARBLS	10/01-12/01
	Fayetteville-Springdale-Rogers MSA, AR	Y	29150 FQ	36030 AW	47330 TQ	ARBLS	10/01-12/01
	Fort Smith MSA, AR-OK	Y	17630 FQ	30720 AW	53160 TQ	ARBLS	10/01-12/01
	Little Rock-North Little Rock MSA, AR	Y	21210 FQ	46390 AW	78560 TQ	ARBLS	10/01-12/01
	California	Y	28710 FQ	59680 AW	107940 TQ	CABLS	10/01-12/01
	Bakersfield MSA, CA	Y	23190 FQ	33320 AW	43410 TQ	CABLS	10/01-12/01
	Chico-Paradise MSA, CA	Y	24670 FQ	39700 AW	56710 TQ	CABLS	10/01-12/01
	Fresno MSA, CA	Y	27550 FQ	40570 AW	52800 TQ	CABLS	10/01-12/01
	Merced MSA, CA	Y	19620 FQ	34800 AW	53150 TQ	CABLS	10/01-12/01
	Modesto MSA, CA	Y	23940 FQ	36500 AW	55790 TQ	CABLS	10/01-12/01
	Oakland PMSA, CA	Y	23960 FQ	43070 AW	69030 TQ	CABLS	10/01-12/01
	Orange County PMSA, CA	Y	28050 FQ	42010 AW	65170 TQ	CABLS	10/01-12/01
	Redding MSA, CA	Y	24190 FQ	34800 AW	51620 TQ	CABLS	10/01-12/01
	Riverside-San Bernardino PMSA, CA	Y	25570 FQ	35730 AW	52260 TQ	CABLS	10/01-12/01
	Sacramento PMSA, CA	Y	25710 FQ	41350 AW	74750 TQ	CABLS	10/01-12/01
	Salinas MSA, CA	Y	26340 FQ	42870 AW	66090 TQ	CABLS	10/01-12/01
	San Diego MSA, CA	Y	29140 FQ	40270 AW	61080 TQ	CABLS	10/01-12/01
	San Francisco PMSA, CA	Y	29520 FQ	45800 AW	68040 TQ	CABLS	10/01-12/01
	San Jose PMSA, CA	Y	25160 FQ	45140 AW	68820 TQ	CABLS	10/01-12/01
	San Luis Obispo-Atascadero-Paso Robles MSA, CA	Y	20440 FQ	32150 AW	43630 TQ	CABLS	10/01-12/01
	Santa Barbara-Santa Maria-Lompoc MSA, CA	Y	25620 FQ	39080 AW	57350 TQ	CABLS	10/01-12/01
	Santa Cruz-Watsonville PMSA, CA	Y	28390 FQ	41320 AW	60480 TQ	CABLS	10/01-12/01
	Santa Rosa PMSA, CA	Y	29500 FQ	40440 AW	55270 TQ	CABLS	10/01-12/01
	Stockton-Lodi MSA, CA	Y	27250 FQ	44220 AW	68980 TQ	CABLS	10/01-12/01
	Vallejo-Fairfield-Napa PMSA, CA	Y	27820 FQ	43190 AW	68380 TQ	CABLS	10/01-12/01
	Ventura PMSA, CA	Y	29630 FQ	41300 AW	58440 TQ	CABLS	10/01-12/01
	Visalia-Tulare-Porterville MSA, CA	Y	22630 FQ	33970 AW	49290 TQ	CABLS	10/01-12/01
	Colorado	Y	23390 FQ	43890 AW	78030 TQ	COBLS	10/01-12/01
	Boulder-Longmont PMSA, CO	Y	20310 FQ	40150 AW	79710 TQ	COBLS	10/01-12/01
	Colorado Springs MSA, CO	Y	24690 FQ	41770 AW	68190 TQ	COBLS	10/01-12/01
	Denver PMSA, CO	Y	29350 FQ	44500 AW	78300 TQ	COBLS	10/01-12/01
	Fort Collins-Loveland MSA, CO	Y	25220 FQ	69860 AW	143040 TQ	COBLS	10/01-12/01
	Greeley PMSA, CO	Y	18910 FQ	32800 AW	65340 TQ	COBLS	10/01-12/01
	Connecticut	Y	26800 FQ	44840 AW	65490 TQ	CTBLS	10/01-12/01
	Bridgeport PMSA, CT	Y	16730 FQ	34440 AW	53790 TQ	CTBLS	10/01-12/01
	Danbury PMSA, CT	Y	28060 FQ	50980 AW	84540 TQ	CTBLS	10/01-12/01
	Hartford MSA, CT	Y	34240 FQ	46670 AW	64760 TQ	CTBLS	10/01-12/01
	New Haven-Meriden PMSA, CT	Y	25970 FQ	42510 AW	57520 TQ	CTBLS	10/01-12/01
	New London-Norwich MSA, CT-RI	Y	28550 FQ	45400 AW	65150 TQ	CTBLS	10/01-12/01
	Stamford-Norwalk PMSA, CT	Y	37470 FQ	54750 AW	74780 TQ	CTBLS	10/01-12/01
	Waterbury PMSA, CT	Y	28340 FQ	46610 AW	70220 TQ	CTBLS	10/01-12/01
	Delaware	Y	19860 FQ	33590 AW	51380 TQ	DEBLS	10/01-12/01
	Wilmington-Newark PMSA, DE-MD	Y	20170 FQ	35510 AW	56030 TQ	DEBLS	10/01-12/01
	District of Columbia	Y	25500 FQ	40330 AW	56730 TQ	DCBLS	10/01-12/01
	Washington PMSA, DC-MD-VA-WV	Y	24000 FQ	39470 AW	56260 TQ	DCBLS	10/01-12/01
	Florida	Y	24730 FQ	41770 AW	73270 TQ	FLBLS	10/01-12/01
	Daytona Beach MSA, FL	Y	26480 FQ	37530 AW	49560 TQ	FLBLS	10/01-12/01
	Fort Lauderdale PMSA, FL	Y	24500 FQ	38280 AW	54860 TQ	FLBLS	10/01-12/01
	Fort Myers-Cape Coral MSA, FL	Y	21300 FQ	34630 AW	47530 TQ	FLBLS	10/01-12/01
	Fort Pierce-Port St. Lucie MSA, FL	Y	28040 FQ	43340 AW	77330 TQ	FLBLS	10/01-12/01
	Fort Walton Beach MSA, FL	Y	23700 FQ	35790 AW	48040 TQ	FLBLS	10/01-12/01

AAW	Average annual wage	**AOH**	Average offered, high	**ASH**	Average starting, high	**H**	Hourly	**M**	Monthly	**S**	Special: hourly and annual
AE	Average entry wage	**AOL**	Average offered, low	**ASL**	Average starting, low	**HI**	Highest wage paid	**MTC**	Median total compensation	**TQ**	Third quartile wage
AEX	Average experienced wage	**APH**	Average pay, high range	**AW**	Average wage paid	**HR**	High end range	**MW**	Median wage paid	**W**	Weekly
AO	Average offered	**APL**	Average pay, low range	**FQ**	First quartile wage	**LR**	Low end range	**SQ**	Second quartile wage	**Y**	Yearly

Occupation/Type/Industry	Location	Per	Low	Mid	High	Source	Date
Food Service Manager	Gainesville MSA, FL	Y	24130 FQ	38480 AW	56740 TQ	FLBLS	10/01-12/01
	Jacksonville MSA, FL	Y	27750 FQ	43740 AW	69400 TQ	FLBLS	10/01-12/01
	Lakeland-Winter Haven MSA, FL	Y	29280 FQ	45180 AW	59890 TQ	FLBLS	10/01-12/01
	Melbourne-Titusville-Palm Bay MSA, FL	Y	24990 FQ	41390 AW	69220 TQ	FLBLS	10/01-12/01
	Miami PMSA, FL	Y	27690 FQ	52000 AW	90280 TQ	FLBLS	10/01-12/01
	Naples MSA, FL	Y	24040 FQ	39350 AW	56140 TQ	FLBLS	10/01-12/01
	Ocala MSA, FL	Y	23020 FQ	36290 AW	46270 TQ	FLBLS	10/01-12/01
	Orlando MSA, FL	Y	27520 FQ	45980 AW	85610 TQ	FLBLS	10/01-12/01
	Pensacola MSA, FL	Y	22740 FQ	35640 AW	46800 TQ	FLBLS	10/01-12/01
	Sarasota-Bradenton MSA, FL	Y	26430 FQ	36010 AW	51470 TQ	FLBLS	10/01-12/01
	Tallahassee MSA, FL	Y	24860 FQ	34810 AW	44820 TQ	FLBLS	10/01-12/01
	Tampa-St. Petersburg-Clearwater MSA, FL	Y	20590 FQ	36390 AW	51280 TQ	FLBLS	10/01-12/01
	West Palm Beach-Boca Raton MSA, FL	Y	23990 FQ	43630 AW	68370 TQ	FLBLS	10/01-12/01
	Georgia	Y	23790 FQ	36290 AW	52230 TQ	GABLS	10/01-12/01
	Atlanta MSA, GA	Y	25110 FQ	39340 AW	53880 TQ	GABLS	10/01-12/01
	Augusta-Aiken MSA, GA-SC	Y	16690 FQ	31130 AW	50850 TQ	GABLS	10/01-12/01
	Columbus MSA, GA-AL	Y	21650 FQ	35260 AW	53040 TQ	GABLS	10/01-12/01
	Macon MSA, GA	Y	23890 FQ	32640 AW	41600 TQ	GABLS	10/01-12/01
	Savannah MSA, GA	Y	19070 FQ	33230 AW	45730 TQ	GABLS	10/01-12/01
	Hawaii	Y	29200 FQ	42840 AW	72220 TQ	HIBLS	10/01-12/01
	Honolulu MSA, HI	Y	28400 FQ	41440 AW	74440 TQ	HIBLS	10/01-12/01
	Idaho	Y	14470 FQ	28040 AW	41080 TQ	IDBLS	10/01-12/01
	Boise City MSA, ID	Y	21350 FQ	32260 AW	50570 TQ	IDBLS	10/01-12/01
	Illinois	Y	15430 FQ	31860 AW	51640 TQ	ILBLS	10/01-12/01
	Champaign-Urbana MSA, IL	Y	17400 FQ	29500 AW	42260 TQ	ILBLS	10/01-12/01
	Chicago PMSA, IL	Y	16750 FQ	34260 AW	53570 TQ	ILBLS	10/01-12/01
	Peoria-Pekin MSA, IL	Y	13820 FQ	30720 AW	50340 TQ	ILBLS	10/01-12/01
	Rockford MSA, IL	Y	15930 FQ	28240 AW	45260 TQ	ILBLS	10/01-12/01
	Springfield MSA, IL	Y	15710 FQ	29600 AW	47850 TQ	ILBLS	10/01-12/01
	Indiana	Y	20950 FQ	35310 AW	53240 TQ	INBLS	10/01-12/01
	Elkhart-Goshen MSA, IN	Y	17450 FQ	32270 AW	45180 TQ	INBLS	10/01-12/01
	Evansville-Henderson MSA, IN-KY	Y	20020 FQ	29930 AW	46250 TQ	INBLS	10/01-12/01
	Fort Wayne MSA, IN	Y	26830 FQ	36700 AW	48390 TQ	INBLS	10/01-12/01
	Gary PMSA, IN	Y	20770 FQ	32390 AW	47020 TQ	INBLS	10/01-12/01
	Indianapolis MSA, IN	Y	30450 FQ	42310 AW	55690 TQ	INBLS	10/01-12/01
	Lafayette MSA, IN	Y	26530 FQ	37610 AW	51710 TQ	INBLS	10/01-12/01
	South Bend MSA, IN	Y	19040 FQ	31700 AW	63280 TQ	INBLS	10/01-12/01
	Iowa	Y	19110 FQ	31030 AW	44690 TQ	IABLS	10/01-12/01
	Cedar Rapids MSA, IA	Y	18040 FQ	29280 AW	37530 TQ	IABLS	10/01-12/01
	Davenport-Moline-Rock Island MSA, IA-IL	Y	15390 FQ	28540 AW	44630 TQ	IABLS	10/01-12/01
	Des Moines MSA, IA	Y	26450 FQ	39250 AW	64170 TQ	IABLS	10/01-12/01
	Kansas	Y	23780 FQ	31810 AW	44270 TQ	KSBLS	10/01-12/01
	Topeka MSA, KS	Y	24570 FQ	32550 AW	38030 TQ	KSBLS	10/01-12/01
	Wichita MSA, KS	Y	25370 FQ	32560 AW	41970 TQ	KSBLS	10/01-12/01
	Kentucky	Y	19110 FQ	30880 AW	45750 TQ	KYBLS	10/01-12/01
	Lexington MSA, KY	Y	17360 FQ	29520 AW	42690 TQ	KYBLS	10/01-12/01
	Louisville MSA, KY-IN	Y	23090 FQ	34640 AW	50090 TQ	KYBLS	10/01-12/01
	Louisiana	Y	19800 FQ	37630 AW	55720 TQ	LABLS	10/01-12/01
	Baton Rouge MSA, LA	Y	23540 FQ	41070 AW	54740 TQ	LABLS	10/01-12/01
	Houma MSA, LA	Y	21670 FQ	31840 AW	42840 TQ	LABLS	10/01-12/01
	Lafayette MSA, LA	Y	16510 FQ	38050 AW	92340 TQ	LABLS	10/01-12/01
	Lake Charles MSA, LA	Y	18370 FQ	32840 AW	55880 TQ	LABLS	10/01-12/01
	New Orleans MSA, LA	Y	23790 FQ	38380 AW	64330 TQ	LABLS	10/01-12/01
	Shreveport-Bossier City MSA, LA	Y	18280 FQ	36440 AW	60620 TQ	LABLS	10/01-12/01
	Maine	Y	19290 FQ	34560 AW	54910 TQ	MEBLS	10/01-12/01
	Portland MSA, ME	Y	18760 FQ	31050 AW	44940 TQ	MEBLS	10/01-12/01
	Maryland	Y	23980 FQ	39300 AW	56890 TQ	MDBLS	10/01-12/01
	Baltimore PMSA, MD	Y	26040 FQ	42750 AW	62210 TQ	MDBLS	10/01-12/01
	Massachusetts	Y	23510 FQ	39270 AW	55190 TQ	MABLS	10/01-12/01
	Boston PMSA, MA-NH	Y	27460 FQ	42070 AW	56100 TQ	MABLS	10/01-12/01
	Brockton PMSA, MA	Y	29690 FQ	39570 AW	52800 TQ	MABLS	10/01-12/01
	Lawrence PMSA, MA-NH	Y	21990 FQ	36340 AW	52490 TQ	MABLS	10/01-12/01
	Lowell PMSA, MA-NH	Y	25590 FQ	37670 AW	54850 TQ	MABLS	10/01-12/01
	New Bedford PMSA, MA	Y	26460 FQ	33150 AW	40720 TQ	MABLS	10/01-12/01
	Springfield MSA, MA	Y	19880 FQ	33780 AW	53050 TQ	MABLS	10/01-12/01

AAW Average annual wage; **AE** Average entry wage; **AEX** Average experienced wage; **AO** Average offered; **AOH** Average offered, high; **AOL** Average offered, low; **APH** Average pay, high range; **APL** Average pay, low range; **ASH** Average starting, high; **ASL** Average starting, low; **AW** Average wage paid; **FQ** First quartile wage; **H** Hourly; **HI** Highest wage paid; **HR** High end range; **LR** Low end range; **M** Monthly; **MTC** Median total compensation; **MW** Median wage paid; **SQ** Second quartile wage; **S** Special: hourly and annual; **TQ** Third quartile wage; **W** Weekly; **Y** Yearly

Occupation/Type/Industry	Location	Per	Low	Mid	High	Source	Date
Food Service Manager	Worcester PMSA, MA-CT	Y	24460 FQ	39350 AW	58090 TQ	MABLS	10/01-12/01
	Michigan	Y	23330 FQ	39720 AW	61050 TQ	MIBLS	10/01-12/01
	Ann Arbor PMSA, MI	Y	18940 FQ	32150 AW	53100 TQ	MIBLS	10/01-12/01
	Detroit PMSA, MI	Y	27450 FQ	45500 AW	65260 TQ	MIBLS	10/01-12/01
	Flint PMSA, MI	Y	23180 FQ	30870 AW	50370 TQ	MIBLS	10/01-12/01
	Grand Rapids-Muskegon-Holland MSA, MI	Y	25820 FQ	40720 AW	58050 TQ	MIBLS	10/01-12/01
	Kalamazoo-Battle Creek MSA, MI	Y	24960 FQ	37640 AW	56990 TQ	MIBLS	10/01-12/01
	Lansing-East Lansing MSA, MI	Y	23400 FQ	33570 AW	46340 TQ	MIBLS	10/01-12/01
	Saginaw-Bay City-Midland MSA, MI	Y	28330 FQ	44260 AW	71510 TQ	MIBLS	10/01-12/01
	Minnesota	Y	21840 FQ	38770 AW	61720 TQ	MNBLS	10/01-12/01
	Duluth-Superior MSA, MN-WI	Y	15820 FQ	30230 AW	44320 TQ	MNBLS	10/01-12/01
	Minneapolis-St. Paul MSA, MN-WI	Y	23770 FQ	42610 AW	70300 TQ	MNBLS	10/01-12/01
	St. Cloud MSA, MN	Y	22440 FQ	31210 AW	45000 TQ	MNBLS	10/01-12/01
	Mississippi	Y	13370 FQ	28450 AW	47300 TQ	MSBLS	10/01-12/01
	Biloxi-Gulfport-Pascagoula MSA, MS	Y	19140 FQ	31230 AW	46520 TQ	MSBLS	10/01-12/01
	Jackson MSA, MS	Y	17280 FQ	36440 AW	67010 TQ	MSBLS	10/01-12/01
	Missouri	Y	19350 FQ	34290 AW	53600 TQ	MOBLS	10/01-12/01
	Kansas City MSA, MO-KS	Y	21700 FQ	35600 AW	55740 TQ	MOBLS	10/01-12/01
	St. Louis MSA, MO-IL	Y	17090 FQ	36490 AW	56740 TQ	MOBLS	10/01-12/01
	Springfield MSA, MO	Y	20530 FQ	32520 AW	51980 TQ	MOBLS	10/01-12/01
	Montana	Y	16350 FQ	26020 AW	36550 TQ	MTBLS	10/01-12/01
	Billings MSA, MT	Y	15780 FQ	23010 AW	35580 TQ	MTBLS	10/01-12/01
	Nebraska	Y	19630 FQ	30480 AW	44550 TQ	NEBLS	10/01-12/01
	Lincoln MSA, NE	Y	22590 FQ	29120 AW	41310 TQ	NEBLS	10/01-12/01
	Omaha MSA, NE-IA	Y	19760 FQ	33300 AW	50700 TQ	NEBLS	10/01-12/01
	Nevada	Y	25310 FQ	43010 AW	63830 TQ	NVBLS	10/01-12/01
	Las Vegas MSA, NV-AZ	Y	26860 FQ	44800 AW	71590 TQ	NVBLS	10/01-12/01
	Reno MSA, NV	Y	24480 FQ	37010 AW	48420 TQ	NVBLS	10/01-12/01
	New Hampshire	Y	21120 FQ	32610 AW	46200 TQ	NHBLS	10/01-12/01
	Manchester PMSA, NH	Y	24800 FQ	35550 AW	46960 TQ	NHBLS	10/01-12/01
	Nashua PMSA, NH	Y	20040 FQ	32870 AW	48260 TQ	NHBLS	10/01-12/01
	Portsmouth-Rochester PMSA, NH-ME	Y	24330 FQ	37100 AW	56360 TQ	NHBLS	10/01-12/01
	New Jersey	Y	26870 FQ	52340 AW	86080 TQ	NJBLS	10/01-12/01
	Atlantic-Cape May PMSA, NJ	Y	23570 FQ	38760 AW	62740 TQ	NJBLS	10/01-12/01
	Bergen-Passaic PMSA, NJ	Y	37050 FQ	54880 AW	72480 TQ	NJBLS	10/01-12/01
	Jersey City PMSA, NJ	Y	31620 FQ	64070 AW		NJBLS	10/01-12/01
	Middlesex-Somerset-Hunterdon PMSA, NJ	Y	33330 FQ	47670 AW	65330 TQ	NJBLS	10/01-12/01
	Monmouth-Ocean PMSA, NJ	Y	26320 FQ	58010 AW		NJBLS	10/01-12/01
	Newark PMSA, NJ	Y	26590 FQ	53290 AW	84330 TQ	NJBLS	10/01-12/01
	Trenton PMSA, NJ	Y	31900 FQ	55200 AW	100130 TQ	NJBLS	10/01-12/01
	New Mexico	Y	16540 FQ	30420 AW	45580 TQ	NMBLS	10/01-12/01
	Albuquerque MSA, NM	Y	16920 FQ	34460 AW	53430 TQ	NMBLS	10/01-12/01
	Las Cruces MSA, NM	Y	13220 FQ	28360 AW	54180 TQ	NMBLS	10/01-12/01
	New York	Y	25190 FQ	42730 AW	71030 TQ	NYBLS	10/01-12/01
	Albany-Schenectady-Troy MSA, NY	Y	24880 FQ	37450 AW	55300 TQ	NYBLS	10/01-12/01
	Binghamton MSA, NY	Y	21310 FQ	36210 AW	65280 TQ	NYBLS	10/01-12/01
	Buffalo-Niagara Falls MSA, NY	Y	24690 FQ	34410 AW	44550 TQ	NYBLS	10/01-12/01
	Dutchess County PMSA, NY	Y	27880 FQ	43650 AW	63980 TQ	NYBLS	10/01-12/01
	Nassau-Suffolk PMSA, NY	Y	29850 FQ	46020 AW	75500 TQ	NYBLS	10/01-12/01
	New York PMSA, NY	Y	25140 FQ	47010 AW	80840 TQ	NYBLS	10/01-12/01
	Newburgh PMSA, NY-PA	Y	25130 FQ	40340 AW	63120 TQ	NYBLS	10/01-12/01
	Rochester MSA, NY	Y	24940 FQ	36210 AW	51060 TQ	NYBLS	10/01-12/01
	Syracuse MSA, NY	Y	23880 FQ	37630 AW	55730 TQ	NYBLS	10/01-12/01
	Utica-Rome MSA, NY	Y	21560 FQ	35710 AW	55990 TQ	NYBLS	10/01-12/01
	North Carolina	Y	19860 FQ	33770 AW	50410 TQ	NCBLS	10/01-12/01
	Asheville MSA, NC	Y	20740 FQ	32100 AW	44900 TQ	NCBLS	10/01-12/01
	Charlotte-Gastonia-Rock Hill MSA, NC-SC	Y	22150 FQ	33510 AW	45010 TQ	NCBLS	10/01-12/01
	Fayetteville MSA, NC	Y	25670 FQ	37500 AW	52080 TQ	NCBLS	10/01-12/01
	Greensboro-Winston-Salem-High Point MSA, NC	Y	22020 FQ	36710 AW	53080 TQ	NCBLS	10/01-12/01
	Hickory-Morganton-Lenoir MSA, NC	Y	16700 FQ	31080 AW	45360 TQ	NCBLS	10/01-12/01

AAW	Average annual wage	AOH	Average offered, high	ASH	Average starting, high	H	Hourly	M	Monthly	S	Special: hourly and annual
AE	Average entry wage	AOL	Average offered, low	ASL	Average starting, low	HI	Highest wage paid	MTC	Median total compensation	TQ	Third quartile wage
AEX	Average experienced wage	APH	Average pay, high range	AW	Average wage paid	HR	High end range	MW	Median wage paid	W	Weekly
AO	Average offered	APL	Average pay, low range	FQ	First quartile wage	LR	Low end range	SQ	Second quartile wage	Y	Yearly

Occupation/Type/Industry	Location	Per	Low	Mid	High	Source	Date
Food Service Manager	Raleigh-Durham-Chapel Hill MSA, NC	Y	20700 FQ	36360 AW	55720 TQ	NCBLS	10/01-12/01
	Wilmington MSA, NC	Y	19960 FQ	31910 AW	47750 TQ	NCBLS	10/01-12/01
	North Dakota	Y	19270 FQ	29740 AW	45890 TQ	NDBLS	10/01-12/01
	Fargo-Moorhead MSA, ND-MN	Y	20020 FQ	32560 AW	51310 TQ	NDBLS	10/01-12/01
	Ohio	Y	19680 FQ	33890 AW	48960 TQ	OHBLS	10/01-12/01
	Akron PMSA, OH	Y	20420 FQ	33970 AW	53970 TQ	OHBLS	10/01-12/01
	Canton-Massillon MSA, OH	Y	16160 FQ	29260 AW	45230 TQ	OHBLS	10/01-12/01
	Cincinnati PMSA, OH-KY-IN	Y	20480 FQ	35220 AW	50390 TQ	OHBLS	10/01-12/01
	Cleveland-Lorain-Elyria PMSA, OH	Y	20070 FQ	40670 AW	71440 TQ	OHBLS	10/01-12/01
	Columbus MSA, OH	Y	22970 FQ	34880 AW	45850 TQ	OHBLS	10/01-12/01
	Dayton-Springfield MSA, OH	Y	22620 FQ	33120 AW	45520 TQ	OHBLS	10/01-12/01
	Hamilton-Middletown PMSA, OH	Y	20310 FQ	33460 AW	48890 TQ	OHBLS	10/01-12/01
	Mansfield MSA, OH	Y	19830 FQ	27100 AW	39250 TQ	OHBLS	10/01-12/01
	Toledo MSA, OH	Y	19700 FQ	32370 AW	45820 TQ	OHBLS	10/01-12/01
	Youngstown-Warren MSA, OH	Y	16570 FQ	28580 AW	42890 TQ	OHBLS	10/01-12/01
	Oklahoma	Y	16500 FQ	29230 AW	43220 TQ	OKBLS	10/01-12/01
	Oklahoma City MSA, OK	Y	20740 FQ	31510 AW	43580 TQ	OKBLS	10/01-12/01
	Tulsa MSA, OK	Y	23250 FQ	31500 AW	43090 TQ	OKBLS	10/01-12/01
	Oregon	Y	24300 FQ	38940 AW	56790 TQ	ORBLS	10/01-12/01
	Eugene-Springfield MSA, OR	Y	23520 FQ	34360 AW	45710 TQ	ORBLS	10/01-12/01
	Medford-Ashland MSA, OR	Y	19130 FQ	30660 AW	38280 TQ	ORBLS	10/01-12/01
	Portland-Vancouver PMSA, OR-WA	Y	27210 FQ	46970 AW	78280 TQ	ORBLS	10/01-12/01
	Salem PMSA, OR	Y	24610 FQ	35960 AW	48190 TQ	ORBLS	10/01-12/01
	Pennsylvania	Y	18550 FQ	35850 AW	59230 TQ	PABLS	10/01-12/01
	Allentown-Bethlehem-Easton MSA, PA	Y	14550 FQ	39540 AW	80300 TQ	PABLS	10/01-12/01
	Erie MSA, PA	Y	17450 FQ	29100 AW	36480 TQ	PABLS	10/01-12/01
	Harrisburg-Lebanon-Carlisle MSA, PA	Y	19680 FQ	35710 AW	57560 TQ	PABLS	10/01-12/01
	Johnstown MSA, PA	Y	15370 FQ	29290 AW	53570 TQ	PABLS	10/01-12/01
	Lancaster MSA, PA	Y	21490 FQ	33540 AW	50050 TQ	PABLS	10/01-12/01
	Philadelphia PMSA, PA-NJ	Y	21060 FQ	43640 AW	71310 TQ	PABLS	10/01-12/01
	Pittsburgh MSA, PA	Y	23780 FQ	38170 AW	73330 TQ	PABLS	10/01-12/01
	Reading MSA, PA	Y	19260 FQ	34080 AW	52630 TQ	PABLS	10/01-12/01
	Scranton-Wilkes-Barre-Hazleton MSA, PA	Y	20020 FQ	31800 AW	49090 TQ	PABLS	10/01-12/01
	York MSA, PA	Y	23450 FQ	32360 AW	47440 TQ	PABLS	10/01-12/01
	Rhode Island	Y	30500 FQ	49950 AW	74950 TQ	RIBLS	10/01-12/01
	Providence-Fall River-Warwick MSA, RI-MA	Y	22800 FQ	44680 AW	72920 TQ	RIBLS	10/01-12/01
	South Carolina	Y	19120 FQ	30370 AW	42780 TQ	SCBLS	10/01-12/01
	Charleston-North Charleston MSA, SC	Y	23810 FQ	31760 AW	42520 TQ	SCBLS	10/01-12/01
	Columbia MSA, SC	Y	19780 FQ	28520 AW	40340 TQ	SCBLS	10/01-12/01
	Greenville-Spartanburg-Anderson MSA, SC	Y	17990 FQ	28380 AW	39380 TQ	SCBLS	10/01-12/01
	Myrtle Beach MSA, SC	Y	20590 FQ	32840 AW	44950 TQ	SCBLS	10/01-12/01
	South Dakota	Y	30070 FQ	36410 AW	45230 TQ	SDBLS	10/01-12/01
	Sioux Falls MSA, SD	Y	30430 FQ	35790 AW	44560 TQ	SDBLS	10/01-12/01
	Tennessee	Y	16550 FQ	31010 AW	46170 TQ	TNBLS	10/01-12/01
	Chattanooga MSA, TN-GA	Y	16350 FQ	33260 AW	45820 TQ	TNBLS	10/01-12/01
	Clarksville-Hopkinsville MSA, TN-KY	Y	12370 FQ	23110 AW	43010 TQ	TNBLS	10/01-12/01
	Johnson City-Kingsport-Bristol MSA, TN-VA	Y	16620 FQ	29750 AW	43530 TQ	TNBLS	10/01-12/01
	Knoxville MSA, TN	Y	17430 FQ	34870 AW	51840 TQ	TNBLS	10/01-12/01
	Memphis MSA, TN-AR-MS	Y	19630 FQ	33050 AW	47500 TQ	TNBLS	10/01-12/01
	Nashville MSA, TN	Y	20690 FQ	33210 AW	48440 TQ	TNBLS	10/01-12/01
	Texas	Y	18970 FQ	31920 AW	48870 TQ	TXBLS	10/01-12/01
	Amarillo MSA, TX	Y	16720 FQ	31220 AW	46220 TQ	TXBLS	10/01-12/01
	Austin-San Marcos MSA, TX	Y	20780 FQ	33060 AW	44730 TQ	TXBLS	10/01-12/01
	Beaumont-Port Arthur MSA, TX	Y	19400 FQ	31670 AW	49570 TQ	TXBLS	10/01-12/01
	Brazoria PMSA, TX	Y	15730 FQ	27600 AW	43510 TQ	TXBLS	10/01-12/01
	Brownsville-Harlingen-San Benito MSA, TX	Y	16270 FQ	26230 AW	36940 TQ	TXBLS	10/01-12/01
	Corpus Christi MSA, TX	Y	14850 FQ	22850 AW	34150 TQ	TXBLS	10/01-12/01

AAW Average annual wage; **AE** Average entry wage; **AEX** Average experienced wage; **AO** Average offered; **AOH** Average offered, high; **AOL** Average offered, low; **APH** Average pay, high range; **APL** Average pay, low range; **ASH** Average starting, high; **ASL** Average starting, low; **AW** Average wage paid; **FQ** First quartile wage; **H** Hourly; **HI** Highest wage paid; **HR** High end range; **LR** Low end range; **M** Monthly; **MTC** Median total compensation; **MW** Median wage paid; **SQ** Second quartile wage; **S** Special: hourly and annual; **TQ** Third quartile wage; **W** Weekly; **Y** Yearly

Occupation/Type/Industry	Location	Per	Low	Mid	High	Source	Date
Food Service Manager	Dallas PMSA, TX	Y	21450 FQ	36350 AW	57120 TQ	TXBLS	10/01-12/01
	El Paso MSA, TX	Y	17310 FQ	32490 AW	45120 TQ	TXBLS	10/01-12/01
	Fort Worth-Arlington PMSA, TX	Y	19190 FQ	34650 AW	61300 TQ	TXBLS	10/01-12/01
	Galveston-Texas City PMSA, TX	Y	16810 FQ	30480 AW	46750 TQ	TXBLS	10/01-12/01
	Houston PMSA, TX	Y	20010 FQ	30580 AW	42060 TQ	TXBLS	10/01-12/01
	Killeen-Temple MSA, TX	Y	16350 FQ	31400 AW	45500 TQ	TXBLS	10/01-12/01
	Laredo MSA, TX	Y	15790 FQ	26070 AW	43010 TQ	TXBLS	10/01-12/01
	Longview-Marshall MSA, TX	Y	18560 FQ	30170 AW	45920 TQ	TXBLS	10/01-12/01
	Lubbock MSA, TX	Y	19780 FQ	31900 AW	49830 TQ	TXBLS	10/01-12/01
	McAllen-Edinburg-Mission MSA, TX	Y	19340 FQ	30620 AW	47740 TQ	TXBLS	10/01-12/01
	Odessa-Midland MSA, TX	Y	20040 FQ	30650 AW	44560 TQ	TXBLS	10/01-12/01
	San Antonio MSA, TX	Y	19080 FQ	30440 AW	45610 TQ	TXBLS	10/01-12/01
	Tyler MSA, TX	Y	19190 FQ	30840 AW	44660 TQ	TXBLS	10/01-12/01
	Waco MSA, TX	Y	17740 FQ	28770 AW	43840 TQ	TXBLS	10/01-12/01
	Utah	Y	19030 FQ	31120 AW	45020 TQ	UTBLS	10/01-12/01
	Provo-Orem MSA, UT	Y	18630 FQ	30940 AW	45680 TQ	UTBLS	10/01-12/01
	Salt Lake City-Ogden MSA, UT	Y	20290 FQ	32900 AW	45650 TQ	UTBLS	10/01-12/01
	Vermont	Y	25240 FQ	45170 AW	68630 TQ	VTBLS	10/01-12/01
	Burlington MSA, VT	Y	20310 FQ	41750 AW	73860 TQ	VTBLS	10/01-12/01
	Virginia	Y	20810 FQ	37460 AW	55440 TQ	VABLS	10/01-12/01
	Lynchburg MSA, VA	Y	18000 FQ	38400 AW	60770 TQ	VABLS	10/01-12/01
	Norfolk-Virginia Beach-Newport News MSA, VA-NC	Y	15950 FQ	31490 AW	47520 TQ	VABLS	10/01-12/01
	Richmond-Petersburg MSA, VA	Y	25430 FQ	42980 AW	57150 TQ	VABLS	10/01-12/01
	Roanoke MSA, VA	Y	17800 FQ	31030 AW	48020 TQ	VABLS	10/01-12/01
	Washington	Y	30170 FQ	52900 AW	90020 TQ	WABLS	10/01-12/01
	Bremerton PMSA, WA	Y	36860 FQ	57110 AW	86290 TQ	WABLS	10/01-12/01
	Olympia PMSA, WA	Y	31330 FQ	68110 AW	109280 TQ	WABLS	10/01-12/01
	Seattle-Bellevue-Everett PMSA, WA	Y	31720 FQ	51730 AW	72440 TQ	WABLS	10/01-12/01
	Spokane MSA, WA	Y	29720 FQ	53900 AW	86360 TQ	WABLS	10/01-12/01
	Tacoma PMSA, WA	Y	28300 FQ	44570 AW	56590 TQ	WABLS	10/01-12/01
	Yakima MSA, WA	Y	31250 FQ	45770 AW	78310 TQ	WABLS	10/01-12/01
	West Virginia	Y	19520 FQ	32240 AW	44670 TQ	WVBLS	10/01-12/01
	Charleston MSA, WV	Y	18010 FQ	31340 AW	44990 TQ	WVBLS	10/01-12/01
	Huntington-Ashland MSA, WV-KY-OH	Y	16930 FQ	28940 AW	43660 TQ	WVBLS	10/01-12/01
	Wisconsin	Y	20680 FQ	33020 AW	48910 TQ	WIBLS	10/01-12/01
	Appleton-Oshkosh-Neenah MSA, WI	Y	23690 FQ	33750 AW	45130 TQ	WIBLS	10/01-12/01
	Green Bay MSA, WI	Y	23490 FQ	34180 AW	47820 TQ	WIBLS	10/01-12/01
	Madison MSA, WI	Y	21650 FQ	35340 AW	48700 TQ	WIBLS	10/01-12/01
	Milwaukee-Waukesha PMSA, WI	Y	23570 FQ	36620 AW	54860 TQ	WIBLS	10/01-12/01
	Racine PMSA, WI	Y	24160 FQ	34190 AW	49110 TQ	WIBLS	10/01-12/01
	Wyoming	Y	16770 FQ	30470 AW	46160 TQ	WYBLS	10/01-12/01
	Cheyenne MSA, WY	Y	21100 FQ	33880 AW	47250 TQ	WYBLS	10/01-12/01
	Puerto Rico	Y	22790 FQ	38880 AW	54100 TQ	PRBLS	10/01-12/01
	Virgin Islands	Y	24700 FQ	35250 AW	52830 TQ	VIBLS	10/01-12/01
	Guam	Y	18410 FQ	31320 AW	45370 TQ	GUBLS	10/01-12/01
Food Services Worker	United States	H		12.09 AW		TRAIN	1/01-1/02
College	United States	H		11.83 AW		TRAIN	1/01-1/02
Hospital	United States	H		12.17 AW		TRAIN	1/01-1/02
Military	United States	H		12.90 AW		TRAIN	1/01-1/02
Nursing Home	United States	H		9.05 AW		TRAIN	1/01-1/02
School	United States	H		11.94 AW		TRAIN	1/01-1/02
Foreign Language and Literature Teacher							
Postsecondary	Alabama	Y	25010 FQ	43170 AW	67350 TQ	ALBLS	10/01-12/01
Postsecondary	Arkansas	Y	22930 FQ	47420 AW	75750 TQ	ARBLS	10/01-12/01
Postsecondary	California	Y	35410 FQ	61320 AW	96590 TQ	CABLS	10/01-12/01
Postsecondary	Los Angeles-Long Beach PMSA, CA	Y	33590 FQ	57620 AW	90830 TQ	CABLS	10/01-12/01
Postsecondary	Oakland PMSA, CA	Y	31060 FQ	55420 AW	89680 TQ	CABLS	10/01-12/01

AAW	Average annual wage	AOH	Average offered, high	ASH	Average starting, high	H	Hourly	M	Monthly	S	Special: hourly and annual
AE	Average entry wage	AOL	Average offered, low	ASL	Average starting, low	HI	Highest wage paid	MTC	Median total compensation	TQ	Third quartile wage
AEX	Average experienced wage	APH	Average pay, high range	AW	Average wage paid	HR	High end range	MW	Median wage paid	W	Weekly
AO	Average offered	APL	Average pay, low range	FQ	First quartile wage	LR	Low end range	SQ	Second quartile wage	Y	Yearly

Occupation/Type/Industry	Location	Per	Low	Mid	High	Source	Date
Foreign Language and Literature Teacher							
Postsecondary	Orange County PMSA, CA	Y	31240 FQ	57050 AW	94380 TQ	CABLS	10/01-12/01
Postsecondary	Riverside-San Bernardino PMSA, CA	Y	35150 FQ	57010 AW	90100 TQ	CABLS	10/01-12/01
Postsecondary	San Francisco PMSA, CA	Y	38690 FQ	63000 AW	104240 TQ	CABLS	10/01-12/01
Postsecondary	San Jose PMSA, CA	Y	45370 FQ	60960 AW	76020 TQ	CABLS	10/01-12/01
Postsecondary	Colorado	Y	25960 FQ	43210 AW	68710 TQ	COBLS	10/01-12/01
Postsecondary	Denver PMSA, CO	Y	25490 FQ	39200 AW	64330 TQ	COBLS	10/01-12/01
Postsecondary	Connecticut	Y	25280 FQ	54430 AW	89930 TQ	CTBLS	10/01-12/01
Postsecondary	Hartford MSA, CT	Y	36670 FQ	61190 AW	94230 TQ	CTBLS	10/01-12/01
Postsecondary	Delaware	Y	30670 FQ	50830 AW	76800 TQ	DEBLS	10/01-12/01
Postsecondary	District of Columbia	Y	31910 FQ	53900 AW	79470 TQ	DCBLS	10/01-12/01
Postsecondary	Washington PMSA, DC-MD-VA-WV	Y	28700 FQ	48830 AW	74920 TQ	DCBLS	10/01-12/01
Postsecondary	Florida	Y	25830 FQ	51890 AW	85440 TQ	FLBLS	10/01-12/01
Postsecondary	Fort Lauderdale PMSA, FL	Y	13880 FQ	30100 AW	47100 TQ	FLBLS	10/01-12/01
Postsecondary	Gainesville MSA, FL	Y	32270 FQ	59730 AW	100700 TQ	FLBLS	10/01-12/01
Postsecondary	Miami PMSA, FL	Y	39110 FQ	57490 AW	83880 TQ	FLBLS	10/01-12/01
Postsecondary	Orlando MSA, FL	Y	24070 FQ	45520 AW	76070 TQ	FLBLS	10/01-12/01
Postsecondary	Tallahassee MSA, FL	Y	37810 FQ	59970 AW	90970 TQ	FLBLS	10/01-12/01
Postsecondary	Tampa-St. Petersburg-Clearwater MSA, FL	Y	29970 FQ	49960 AW	72730 TQ	FLBLS	10/01-12/01
Postsecondary	West Palm Beach-Boca Raton MSA, FL	Y	28420 FQ	56950 AW	125130 TQ	FLBLS	10/01-12/01
Postsecondary	Georgia	Y	21290 FQ	45260 AW	67370 TQ	GABLS	10/01-12/01
Postsecondary	Atlanta MSA, GA	Y	20140 FQ	42930 AW	67880 TQ	GABLS	10/01-12/01
Postsecondary	Hawaii	Y	31400 FQ	48270 AW	74400 TQ	HIBLS	10/01-12/01
Postsecondary	Honolulu MSA, HI	Y	31390 FQ	48750 AW	75430 TQ	HIBLS	10/01-12/01
Postsecondary	Idaho	Y	23050 FQ	40500 AW	59570 TQ	IDBLS	10/01-12/01
Postsecondary	Illinois	Y	24510 FQ	50690 AW	88330 TQ	ILBLS	10/01-12/01
Postsecondary	Champaign-Urbana MSA, IL	Y	21910 FQ	56270 AW	91020 TQ	ILBLS	10/01-12/01
Postsecondary	Chicago PMSA, IL	Y	26420 FQ	51270 AW	89790 TQ	ILBLS	10/01-12/01
Postsecondary	Indiana	Y	30350 FQ	49200 AW	71960 TQ	INBLS	10/01-12/01
Postsecondary	Fort Wayne MSA, IN	Y	40160 FQ	49240 AW	59400 TQ	INBLS	10/01-12/01
Postsecondary	Indianapolis MSA, IN	Y	29420 FQ	47840 AW	69590 TQ	INBLS	10/01-12/01
Postsecondary	Iowa	Y	30460 FQ	55590 AW	80530 TQ	IABLS	10/01-12/01
Postsecondary	Kansas	Y	18500 FQ	32750 AW	58990 TQ	KSBLS	10/01-12/01
Postsecondary	Kentucky	Y	28720 FQ	48980 AW	73690 TQ	KYBLS	10/01-12/01
Postsecondary	Louisiana	Y	24470 FQ	45680 AW	69850 TQ	LABLS	10/01-12/01
Postsecondary	New Orleans MSA, LA	Y	17400 FQ	45350 AW	71160 TQ	LABLS	10/01-12/01
Postsecondary	Maine	Y	31960 FQ	47550 AW	64070 TQ	MEBLS	10/01-12/01
Postsecondary	Maryland	Y	22830 FQ	48700 AW	76310 TQ	MDBLS	10/01-12/01
Postsecondary	Baltimore PMSA, MD	Y	21660 FQ	45320 AW	74220 TQ	MDBLS	10/01-12/01
Postsecondary	Massachusetts	Y	31840 FQ	52920 AW	83720 TQ	MABLS	10/01-12/01
Postsecondary	Boston PMSA, MA-NH	Y	31140 FQ	51470 AW	82690 TQ	MABLS	10/01-12/01
Postsecondary	Springfield MSA, MA	Y	39860 FQ	65620 AW	105180 TQ	MABLS	10/01-12/01
Postsecondary	Worcester PMSA, MA-CT	Y	37460 FQ	58390 AW	79460 TQ	MABLS	10/01-12/01
Postsecondary	Michigan	Y	28500 FQ	49720 AW	78690 TQ	MIBLS	10/01-12/01
Postsecondary	Ann Arbor PMSA, MI	Y	25710 FQ	46920 AW	73350 TQ	MIBLS	10/01-12/01
Postsecondary	Detroit PMSA, MI	Y	26310 FQ	45580 AW	87930 TQ	MIBLS	10/01-12/01
Postsecondary	Minnesota	Y	32310 FQ	51040 AW	75460 TQ	MNBLS	10/01-12/01
Postsecondary	Minneapolis-St. Paul MSA, MN-WI	Y	32930 FQ	54260 AW	88660 TQ	MNBLS	10/01-12/01
Postsecondary	St. Cloud MSA, MN	Y	31060 FQ	47260 AW	60420 TQ	MNBLS	10/01-12/01
Postsecondary	Mississippi	Y	23900 FQ	40260 AW	57830 TQ	MSBLS	10/01-12/01
Postsecondary	Missouri	Y	26810 FQ	43340 AW	60730 TQ	MOBLS	10/01-12/01
Postsecondary	Kansas City MSA, MO-KS	Y	22920 FQ	33970 AW	55680 TQ	MOBLS	10/01-12/01
Postsecondary	St. Louis MSA, MO-IL	Y	26660 FQ	44630 AW	66510 TQ	MOBLS	10/01-12/01
Postsecondary	Montana	Y	23860 FQ	52990 AW	80900 TQ	MTBLS	10/01-12/01
Postsecondary	Nebraska	Y	30090 FQ	44840 AW	65550 TQ	NEBLS	10/01-12/01
Postsecondary	Nevada	Y	23400 FQ	38970 AW	59660 TQ	NVBLS	10/01-12/01
Postsecondary	Las Vegas MSA, NV-AZ	Y	23040 FQ	37910 AW	51330 TQ	NVBLS	10/01-12/01
Postsecondary	New Hampshire	Y	33660 FQ	58960 AW	96510 TQ	NHBLS	10/01-12/01
Postsecondary	Manchester PMSA, NH	Y	30470 FQ	41220 AW	54580 TQ	NHBLS	10/01-12/01
Postsecondary	New Jersey	Y	26090 FQ	56150 AW	91360 TQ	NJBLS	10/01-12/01
Postsecondary	Jersey City PMSA, NJ	Y	39190 FQ	66110 AW	100800 TQ	NJBLS	10/01-12/01
Postsecondary	Middlesex-Somerset-Hunterdon PMSA, NJ	Y	26120 FQ	61200 AW	99080 TQ	NJBLS	10/01-12/01
Postsecondary	Newark PMSA, NJ	Y	33760 FQ	59440 AW	94510 TQ	NJBLS	10/01-12/01
Postsecondary	New Mexico	Y	22630 FQ	39190 AW	59520 TQ	NMBLS	10/01-12/01
Postsecondary	New York	Y	26780 FQ	59770 AW	108870 TQ	NYBLS	10/01-12/01

AAW Average annual wage; **AE** Average entry wage; **AEX** Average experienced wage; **AO** Average offered; **AOH** Average offered, high; **AOL** Average offered, low; **APH** Average pay, high range; **APL** Average pay, low range; **ASH** Average starting, high; **ASL** Average starting, low; **AW** Average wage paid; **FQ** First quartile wage; **H** Hourly; **HI** Highest wage paid; **HR** High end range; **LR** Low end range; **M** Monthly; **MTC** Median total compensation; **MW** Median wage paid; **SQ** Second quartile wage; **S** Special: hourly and annual; **TQ** Third quartile wage; **W** Weekly; **Y** Yearly

Occupation/Type/Industry	Location	Per	Low	Mid	High	Source	Date
Foreign Language and Literature Teacher							
Postsecondary	Albany-Schenectady-Troy MSA, NY	Y	38700 FQ	58310 AW	99840 TQ	NYBLS	10/01-12/01
Postsecondary	New York PMSA, NY	Y	22020 FQ	63790 AW	118880 TQ	NYBLS	10/01-12/01
Postsecondary	North Carolina	Y	27250 FQ	45100 AW	68980 TQ	NCBLS	10/01-12/01
Postsecondary	Asheville MSA, NC	Y	29560 FQ	45770 AW	66380 TQ	NCBLS	10/01-12/01
Postsecondary	Charlotte-Gastonia-Rock Hill MSA, NC-SC	Y	27440 FQ	53990 AW	87840 TQ	NCBLS	10/01-12/01
Postsecondary	Fayetteville MSA, NC	Y	39100 FQ	49020 AW	60880 TQ	NCBLS	10/01-12/01
Postsecondary	Greensboro-Winston-Salem-High Point MSA, NC	Y	28740 FQ	44170 AW	58370 TQ	NCBLS	10/01-12/01
Postsecondary	Raleigh-Durham-Chapel Hill MSA, NC	Y	26160 FQ	43950 AW	67940 TQ	NCBLS	10/01-12/01
Postsecondary	Wilmington MSA, NC	Y	26230 FQ	43080 AW	63790 TQ	NCBLS	10/01-12/01
Postsecondary	North Dakota	Y	22870 FQ	36430 AW	48610 TQ	NDBLS	10/01-12/01
Postsecondary	Fargo-Moorhead MSA, ND-MN	Y	28180 FQ	44290 AW	57590 TQ	NDBLS	10/01-12/01
Postsecondary	Ohio	Y	26830 FQ	46920 AW	72560 TQ	OHBLS	10/01-12/01
Postsecondary	Cincinnati PMSA, OH-KY-IN	Y	28670 FQ	49620 AW	83950 TQ	OHBLS	10/01-12/01
Postsecondary	Cleveland-Lorain-Elyria PMSA, OH	Y	30860 FQ	52220 AW	76420 TQ	OHBLS	10/01-12/01
Postsecondary	Columbus MSA, OH	Y	25980 FQ	44540 AW	68530 TQ	OHBLS	10/01-12/01
Postsecondary	Dayton-Springfield MSA, OH	Y	24810 FQ	45480 AW	70330 TQ	OHBLS	10/01-12/01
Postsecondary	Toledo MSA, OH	Y	25740 FQ	44490 AW	57410 TQ	OHBLS	10/01-12/01
Postsecondary	Youngstown-Warren MSA, OH	Y	26290 FQ	42970 AW	64400 TQ	OHBLS	10/01-12/01
Postsecondary	Oklahoma	Y	25310 FQ	37980 AW	56490 TQ	OKBLS	10/01-12/01
Postsecondary	Oklahoma City MSA, OK	Y	25780 FQ	39440 AW	58950 TQ	OKBLS	10/01-12/01
Postsecondary	Oregon	Y	31020 FQ	51210 AW	78490 TQ	ORBLS	10/01-12/01
Postsecondary	Eugene-Springfield MSA, OR	Y	34850 FQ	52160 AW	81830 TQ	ORBLS	10/01-12/01
Postsecondary	Portland-Vancouver PMSA, OR-WA	Y	30440 FQ	50340 AW	75920 TQ	ORBLS	10/01-12/01
Postsecondary	Pennsylvania	Y	28320 FQ	56030 AW	89640 TQ	PABLS	10/01-12/01
Postsecondary	Allentown-Bethlehem-Easton MSA, PA	Y	30380 FQ	49850 AW	83430 TQ	PABLS	10/01-12/01
Postsecondary	Harrisburg-Lebanon-Carlisle MSA, PA	Y	31880 FQ	55160 AW	85170 TQ	PABLS	10/01-12/01
Postsecondary	Philadelphia PMSA, PA-NJ	Y	25360 FQ	55840 AW	91100 TQ	PABLS	10/01-12/01
Postsecondary	Pittsburgh MSA, PA	Y	28750 FQ	56200 AW	89200 TQ	PABLS	10/01-12/01
Postsecondary	Reading MSA, PA	Y	25580 FQ	51320 AW	83300 TQ	PABLS	10/01-12/01
Postsecondary	Scranton-Wilkes-Barre-Hazleton MSA, PA	Y	24400 FQ	52610 AW	75550 TQ	PABLS	10/01-12/01
Postsecondary	Rhode Island	Y	32070 FQ	53760 AW	85100 TQ	RIBLS	10/01-12/01
Postsecondary	South Carolina	Y	19020 FQ	39220 AW	63120 TQ	SCBLS	10/01-12/01
Postsecondary	Charleston-North Charleston MSA, SC	Y	18480 FQ	31810 AW	57430 TQ	SCBLS	10/01-12/01
Postsecondary	Greenville-Spartanburg-Anderson MSA, SC	Y	33560 FQ	48610 AW	70580 TQ	SCBLS	10/01-12/01
Postsecondary	South Dakota	Y	29020 FQ	42370 AW	59070 TQ	SDBLS	10/01-12/01
Postsecondary	Tennessee	Y	24880 FQ	43400 AW	72270 TQ	TNBLS	10/01-12/01
Postsecondary	Knoxville MSA, TN	Y	24670 FQ	39290 AW	60080 TQ	TNBLS	10/01-12/01
Postsecondary	Memphis MSA, TN-AR-MS	Y	25840 FQ	44180 AW	71280 TQ	TNBLS	10/01-12/01
Postsecondary	Nashville MSA, TN	Y	26330 FQ	48360 AW	85630 TQ	TNBLS	10/01-12/01
Postsecondary	Texas	Y	21140 FQ	46300 AW	69910 TQ	TXBLS	10/01-12/01
Postsecondary	Dallas PMSA, TX	Y	20320 FQ	49340 AW	73190 TQ	TXBLS	10/01-12/01
Postsecondary	Fort Worth-Arlington PMSA, TX	Y	17620 FQ	43790 AW	70050 TQ	TXBLS	10/01-12/01
Postsecondary	Houston PMSA, TX	Y	25940 FQ	50670 AW	83880 TQ	TXBLS	10/01-12/01
Postsecondary	McAllen-Edinburg-Mission MSA, TX	Y	21250 FQ	48110 AW	73440 TQ	TXBLS	10/01-12/01
Postsecondary	San Antonio MSA, TX	Y	20840 FQ	45300 AW	72500 TQ	TXBLS	10/01-12/01
Postsecondary	Utah	Y	34220 FQ	55480 AW	89320 TQ	UTBLS	10/01-12/01
Postsecondary	Vermont	Y	28910 FQ	52440 AW	85400 TQ	VTBLS	10/01-12/01
Postsecondary	Burlington MSA, VT	Y	27970 FQ	52440 AW	85990 TQ	VTBLS	10/01-12/01
Postsecondary	Virginia	Y	28370 FQ	47410 AW	74660 TQ	VABLS	10/01-12/01
Postsecondary	Norfolk-Virginia Beach-Newport News MSA, VA-NC	Y	30760 FQ	52190 AW	83840 TQ	VABLS	10/01-12/01
Postsecondary	Richmond-Petersburg MSA, VA	Y	24620 FQ	44940 AW	67880 TQ	VABLS	10/01-12/01
Postsecondary	Washington	Y	27420 FQ	47030 AW	73420 TQ	WABLS	10/01-12/01

AAW	Average annual wage	**AOH**	Average offered, high	**ASH**	Average starting, high	**H**	Hourly	**M**	Monthly	**S**	Special: hourly and annual
AE	Average entry wage	**AOL**	Average offered, low	**ASL**	Average starting, low	**HI**	Highest wage paid	**MTC**	Median total compensation	**TQ**	Third quartile wage
AEX	Average experienced wage	**APH**	Average pay, high range	**AW**	Average wage paid	**HR**	High end range	**MW**	Median wage paid	**W**	Weekly
AO	Average offered	**APL**	Average pay, low range	**FQ**	First quartile wage	**LR**	Low end range	**SQ**	Second quartile wage	**Y**	Yearly

Occupation/Type/Industry	Location	Per	Low	Mid	High	Source	Date
Foreign Language and Literature Teacher							
Postsecondary	Seattle-Bellevue-Everett PMSA, WA	Y	30260 FQ	51800 AW	83340 TQ	WABLS	10/01-12/01
Postsecondary	Tacoma PMSA, WA	Y	29580 FQ	47600 AW	72530 TQ	WABLS	10/01-12/01
Postsecondary	West Virginia	Y	29480 FQ	51300 AW	83180 TQ	WVBLS	10/01-12/01
Postsecondary	Wisconsin	Y	26660 FQ	46040 AW	71370 TQ	WIBLS	10/01-12/01
Postsecondary	Puerto Rico	Y	29980 FQ	44680 AW	69100 TQ	PRBLS	10/01-12/01
Forensic Accountant	Florida	H		175-300 AW		SFLSS	2001
Forensic Science Technician	Alabama	Y	28160 FQ	40540 AW	60930 TQ	ALBLS	10/01-12/01
	Birmingham MSA, AL	Y	29720 FQ	41970 AW	70810 TQ	ALBLS	10/01-12/01
	Arizona	Y	25000 FQ	44980 AW	68640 TQ	AZBLS	10/01-12/01
	Phoenix-Mesa MSA, AZ	Y	29160 FQ	47920 AW	70210 TQ	AZBLS	10/01-12/01
	California	Y	28230 FQ	44160 AW	65570 TQ	CABLS	10/01-12/01
	Oakland PMSA, CA	Y	27630 FQ	50220 AW	81570 TQ	CABLS	10/01-12/01
	Sacramento PMSA, CA	Y	31620 FQ	43630 AW	63020 TQ	CABLS	10/01-12/01
	Colorado	Y	33220 FQ	44750 AW	56830 TQ	COBLS	10/01-12/01
	Denver PMSA, CO	Y	33280 FQ	44460 AW	56280 TQ	COBLS	10/01-12/01
	Connecticut	Y	35340 FQ	56340 AW	81280 TQ	CTBLS	10/01-12/01
	Washington PMSA, DC-MD-VA-WV	Y	34220 FQ	55570 AW	80610 TQ	DCBLS	10/01-12/01
	Florida	Y	23630 FQ	36000 AW	51990 TQ	FLBLS	10/01-12/01
	Fort Lauderdale PMSA, FL	Y	28500 FQ	33800 AW	42090 TQ	FLBLS	10/01-12/01
	Miami PMSA, FL	Y	25540 FQ	36910 AW	55650 TQ	FLBLS	10/01-12/01
	Orlando MSA, FL	Y	23210 FQ	35450 AW	53450 TQ	FLBLS	10/01-12/01
	Pensacola MSA, FL	Y	22810 FQ	37560 AW	54080 TQ	FLBLS	10/01-12/01
	Tallahassee MSA, FL	Y	26590 FQ	40940 AW	62830 TQ	FLBLS	10/01-12/01
	Tampa-St. Petersburg-Clearwater MSA, FL	Y	27920 FQ	40040 AW	51670 TQ	FLBLS	10/01-12/01
	West Palm Beach-Boca Raton MSA, FL	Y	24230 FQ	34690 AW	51530 TQ	FLBLS	10/01-12/01
	Georgia	Y	18570 FQ	28180 AW	40630 TQ	GABLS	10/01-12/01
	Atlanta MSA, GA	Y	20160 FQ	32050 AW	46730 TQ	GABLS	10/01-12/01
	Hawaii	Y	29840 FQ	40440 AW	54600 TQ	HIBLS	10/01-12/01
	Illinois	Y	24960 FQ	45560 AW	67180 TQ	ILBLS	10/01-12/01
	Chicago PMSA, IL	Y	25790 FQ	44360 AW	65650 TQ	ILBLS	10/01-12/01
	Indiana	Y	24510 FQ	41430 AW	61100 TQ	INBLS	10/01-12/01
	Maryland	Y	30520 FQ	41810 AW	55340 TQ	MDBLS	10/01-12/01
	Baltimore PMSA, MD	Y	30000 FQ	38500 AW	45550 TQ	MDBLS	10/01-12/01
	Michigan	Y	30090 FQ	47070 AW	60520 TQ	MIBLS	10/01-12/01
	Detroit PMSA, MI	Y	27400 FQ	45010 AW	60440 TQ	MIBLS	10/01-12/01
	Mississippi	Y	25540 FQ	39510 AW	55300 TQ	MSBLS	10/01-12/01
	St. Louis MSA, MO-IL	Y	24100 FQ	44190 AW	66760 TQ	MOBLS	10/01-12/01
	Nebraska	Y	20860 FQ	35330 AW	49920 TQ	NEBLS	10/01-12/01
	Nevada	Y	27990 FQ	45360 AW	69950 TQ	NVBLS	10/01-12/01
	New Mexico	Y	18890 FQ	35840 AW	53440 TQ	NMBLS	10/01-12/01
	New York	Y	31650 FQ	48780 AW	68450 TQ	NYBLS	10/01-12/01
	North Carolina	Y	22220 FQ	32870 AW	48960 TQ	NCBLS	10/01-12/01
	Raleigh-Durham-Chapel Hill MSA, NC	Y	21250 FQ	31820 AW	49870 TQ	NCBLS	10/01-12/01
	Ohio	Y	29320 FQ	38100 AW	54370 TQ	OHBLS	10/01-12/01
	Cleveland-Lorain-Elyria PMSA, OH	Y	28800 FQ	37040 AW	54010 TQ	OHBLS	10/01-12/01
	Oklahoma	Y	22170 FQ	29290 AW	37590 TQ	OKBLS	10/01-12/01
	Oregon	Y	33890 FQ	47600 AW	62980 TQ	ORBLS	10/01-12/01
	Pennsylvania	Y	25090 FQ	44260 AW	77100 TQ	PABLS	10/01-12/01
	Tennessee	Y	23070 FQ	32860 AW	47770 TQ	TNBLS	10/01-12/01
	Texas	Y	24610 FQ	40130 AW	54870 TQ	TXBLS	10/01-12/01
	Dallas PMSA, TX	Y	28670 FQ	41800 AW	56050 TQ	TXBLS	10/01-12/01
	Houston PMSA, TX	Y	35960 FQ	58840 AW	116310 TQ	TXBLS	10/01-12/01
	Utah	Y	25710 FQ	35160 AW	47670 TQ	UTBLS	10/01-12/01
	Salt Lake City-Ogden MSA, UT	Y	25600 FQ	35120 AW	47480 TQ	UTBLS	10/01-12/01
	Virginia	Y	28240 FQ	40960 AW	63020 TQ	VABLS	10/01-12/01
	Washington	Y	32180 FQ	46070 AW	58850 TQ	WABLS	10/01-12/01
	Olympia PMSA, WA	Y	26270 FQ	38400 AW	52350 TQ	WABLS	10/01-12/01
	Tacoma PMSA, WA	Y	40510 FQ	51350 AW	65020 TQ	WABLS	10/01-12/01
Forest and Conservation Technician	Alabama	Y	18290 FQ	28040 AW	40320 TQ	ALBLS	10/01-12/01

AAW	Average annual wage	**AOH**	Average offered, high	**ASH**	Average starting, high	**H**	Hourly	**M**	Monthly	**S**	Special: hourly and annual
AE	Average entry wage	**AOL**	Average offered, low	**ASL**	Average starting, low	**HI**	Highest wage paid	**MTC**	Median total compensation	**TQ**	Third quartile wage
AEX	Average experienced wage	**APH**	Average pay, high range	**AW**	Average wage paid	**HR**	High end range	**MW**	Median wage paid	**W**	Weekly
AO	Average offered	**APL**	Average pay, low range	**FQ**	First quartile wage	**LR**	Low end range	**SQ**	Second quartile wage	**Y**	Yearly

Occupation/Type/Industry	Location	Per	Low	Mid	High	Source	Date
Forest and Conservation Technician	Alaska	Y	26440 FQ	38350 AW	52180 TQ	AKBLS	10/01-12/01
	Arizona	Y	18610 FQ	27210 AW	38770 TQ	AZBLS	10/01-12/01
	Arkansas	Y	21860 FQ	29610 AW	38830 TQ	ARBLS	10/01-12/01
	California	Y	22910 FQ	33040 AW	45870 TQ	CABLS	10/01-12/01
	Colorado	Y	19990 FQ	30900 AW	44580 TQ	COBLS	10/01-12/01
	Florida	Y	21920 FQ	31410 AW	43230 TQ	FLBLS	10/01-12/01
	Georgia	Y	18610 FQ	30280 AW	43190 TQ	GABLS	10/01-12/01
	Hawaii	Y	24080 FQ	32030 AW	42290 TQ	HIBLS	10/01-12/01
	Idaho	Y	22450 FQ	33650 AW	48620 TQ	IDBLS	10/01-12/01
	Illinois	Y	21820 FQ	31810 AW	42230 TQ	ILBLS	10/01-12/01
	Indiana	Y	20580 FQ	31340 AW	42710 TQ	INBLS	10/01-12/01
	Iowa	Y	18650 FQ	29830 AW	40580 TQ	IABLS	10/01-12/01
	Kansas	Y	18010 FQ	29470 AW	41620 TQ	KSBLS	10/01-12/01
	Kentucky	Y	18390 FQ	25120 AW	35420 TQ	KYBLS	10/01-12/01
	Louisiana	Y	21870 FQ	36640 AW	56230 TQ	LABLS	10/01-12/01
	Maine	Y	19350 FQ	26330 AW	36990 TQ	MEBLS	10/01-12/01
	Michigan	Y	24000 FQ	34970 AW	44780 TQ	MIBLS	10/01-12/01
	Minnesota	Y	19770 FQ	31770 AW	43160 TQ	MNBLS	10/01-12/01
	Mississippi	Y	19140 FQ	29660 AW	41680 TQ	MSBLS	10/01-12/01
	Missouri	Y	19670 FQ	30880 AW	43390 TQ	MOBLS	10/01-12/01
	Montana	Y	19360 FQ	31180 AW	46510 TQ	MTBLS	10/01-12/01
	Nebraska	Y	19240 FQ	30000 AW	41400 TQ	NEBLS	10/01-12/01
	Nevada	Y	22960 FQ	30240 AW	41620 TQ	NVBLS	10/01-12/01
	New Hampshire	Y	19270 FQ	27790 AW	41150 TQ	NHBLS	10/01-12/01
	New Mexico	Y	19670 FQ	29160 AW	42170 TQ	NMBLS	10/01-12/01
	New York	Y	24980 FQ	35290 AW	47110 TQ	NYBLS	10/01-12/01
	North Carolina	Y	22250 FQ	31630 AW	42970 TQ	NCBLS	10/01-12/01
	North Dakota	Y	18660 FQ	26610 AW	35090 TQ	NDBLS	10/01-12/01
	Ohio	Y	20670 FQ	30930 AW	43490 TQ	OHBLS	10/01-12/01
	Oklahoma	Y	19720 FQ	29760 AW	41440 TQ	OKBLS	10/01-12/01
	Oregon	Y	23730 FQ	36840 AW	52100 TQ	ORBLS	10/01-12/01
	Pennsylvania	Y	11640 FQ	45800 AW	107990 TQ	PABLS	10/01-12/01
	South Carolina	Y	19410 FQ	28600 AW	38740 TQ	SCBLS	10/01-12/01
	South Dakota	Y	19080 FQ	26180 AW	35510 TQ	SDBLS	10/01-12/01
	Tennessee	Y	19050 FQ	28370 AW	39470 TQ	TNBLS	10/01-12/01
	Texas	Y	18840 FQ	28300 AW	41780 TQ	TXBLS	10/01-12/01
	Utah	Y	18750 FQ	26640 AW	39790 TQ	UTBLS	10/01-12/01
	Vermont	Y	22830 FQ	35000 AW	50040 TQ	VTBLS	10/01-12/01
	Virginia	Y	17720 FQ	29500 AW	43330 TQ	VABLS	10/01-12/01
	Washington	Y	23870 FQ	35160 AW	48510 TQ	WABLS	10/01-12/01
	West Virginia	Y	22860 FQ	36400 AW	56730 TQ	WVBLS	10/01-12/01
	Wisconsin	Y	20190 FQ	31400 AW	42310 TQ	WIBLS	10/01-12/01
	Wyoming	Y	20390 FQ	28980 AW	41440 TQ	WYBLS	10/01-12/01
	Puerto Rico	Y	18430 FQ	31180 AW	42640 TQ	PRBLS	10/01-12/01
Forest and Conservation Worker	Alabama	H	8.05 FQ	12.13 AW	14.56 TQ	ALBLS	10/01-12/01
	Arizona	H	7.01 FQ	14.13 AW	20.52 TQ	AZBLS	10/01-12/01
	Arkansas	H	8.27 FQ	11.89 AW	18.14 TQ	ARBLS	10/01-12/01
	California	H	6.39 FQ	9.46 AW	12.95 TQ	CABLS	10/01-12/01
	Colorado	H	8.26 FQ	15.08 AW	21.03 TQ	COBLS	10/01-12/01
	Delaware	H	10.41 FQ	13.46 AW	17.12 TQ	DEBLS	10/01-12/01
	Florida	H	7.17 FQ	9.82 AW	15.87 TQ	FLBLS	10/01-12/01
	Georgia	H	6.16 FQ	10.52 AW	17.44 TQ	GABLS	10/01-12/01
	Hawaii	H	9.58 FQ	11.32 AW	13.09 TQ	HIBLS	10/01-12/01
	Idaho	H	9.85 FQ	13.97 AW	16.58 TQ	IDBLS	10/01-12/01
	Illinois	H	5.87 FQ	9.64 AW	16.18 TQ	ILBLS	10/01-12/01
	Iowa	H	7.14 FQ	10.73 AW	16.01 TQ	IABLS	10/01-12/01
	Louisiana	H	7.66 FQ	11.26 AW	14.58 TQ	LABLS	10/01-12/01
	Michigan	H	5.44 FQ	11.43 AW	20.70 TQ	MIBLS	10/01-12/01
	Minnesota	H	12.21 FQ	16.96 AW	22.07 TQ	MNBLS	10/01-12/01
	Missouri	H	8.40 FQ	14.44 AW	20.39 TQ	MOBLS	10/01-12/01
	Montana	H	5.71 FQ	10.87 AW	19.01 TQ	MTBLS	10/01-12/01
	New Hampshire	H	7.29 FQ	9.72 AW	12.53 TQ	NHBLS	10/01-12/01
	New Mexico	H	9.08 FQ	11.41 AW	14.10 TQ	NMBLS	10/01-12/01
	New York	H	11.44 FQ	15.32 AW	20.74 TQ	NYBLS	10/01-12/01
	Ohio	H	6.03 FQ	8.44 AW	12.43 TQ	OHBLS	10/01-12/01
	Pennsylvania	H	7.45 FQ	15.68 AW	25.22 TQ	PABLS	10/01-12/01
	South Carolina	H	6.97 FQ	8.42 AW	10.59 TQ	SCBLS	10/01-12/01
	South Dakota	H	5.84 FQ	10.38 AW	16.13 TQ	SDBLS	10/01-12/01
	Tennessee	H	6.39 FQ	9.76 AW	13.89 TQ	TNBLS	10/01-12/01
	Texas	H	6.57 FQ	9.57 AW	13.99 TQ	TXBLS	10/01-12/01

AAW	Average annual wage	**AOH**	Average offered, high	**ASH**	Average starting, high	**H**	Hourly	**M**	Monthly	**S**	Special: hourly and annual
AE	Average entry wage	**AOL**	Average offered, low	**ASL**	Average starting, low	**HI**	Highest wage paid	**MTC**	Median total compensation	**TQ**	Third quartile wage
AEX	Average experienced wage	**APH**	Average pay, high range	**AW**	Average wage paid	**HR**	High end range	**MW**	Median wage paid	**W**	Weekly
AO	Average offered	**APL**	Average pay, low range	**FQ**	First quartile wage	**LR**	Low end range	**SQ**	Second quartile wage	**Y**	Yearly

Occupation/Type/Industry	Location	Per	Low	Mid	High	Source	Date
Forest and Conservation Worker	Virginia	H	6.95 FQ	9.30 AW	12.95 TQ	VABLS	10/01-12/01
	Washington	H	6.73 FQ	9.12 AW	14.29 TQ	WABLS	10/01-12/01
	Wisconsin	H	7.28 FQ	15.00 AW	19.84 TQ	WIBLS	10/01-12/01
	Wyoming	H	8.79 FQ	10.83 AW	15.58 TQ	WYBLS	10/01-12/01
Forest Fire Inspector and Prevention Specialist	California	Y	25020 FQ	44590 AW	66590 TQ	CABLS	10/01-12/01
	Georgia	Y	24060 FQ	34380 AW	43930 TQ	GABLS	10/01-12/01
	Maine	Y	29290 FQ	37390 AW	44010 TQ	MEBLS	10/01-12/01
	New York	Y	33740 FQ	43370 AW	55380 TQ	NYBLS	10/01-12/01
	Oregon	Y	20630 FQ	36130 AW	67270 TQ	ORBLS	10/01-12/01
	Pennsylvania	Y	31750 FQ	44410 AW	55350 TQ	PABLS	10/01-12/01
	South Carolina	Y	23320 FQ	26290 AW	29620 TQ	SCBLS	10/01-12/01
Forester	Alabama	Y	24860 FQ	52300 AW	74470 TQ	ALBLS	10/01-12/01
	Alaska	Y	40890 FQ	56520 AW	75490 TQ	AKBLS	10/01-12/01
	Arizona	Y	26990 FQ	42370 AW	56530 TQ	AZBLS	10/01-12/01
	Arkansas	Y	22160 FQ	43670 AW	65470 TQ	ARBLS	10/01-12/01
	California	Y	27280 FQ	53660 AW	83620 TQ	CABLS	10/01-12/01
	Colorado	Y	36660 FQ	50090 AW	69110 TQ	COBLS	10/01-12/01
	Florida	Y	29560 FQ	40620 AW	57590 TQ	FLBLS	10/01-12/01
	Georgia	Y	29320 FQ	47940 AW	76200 TQ	GABLS	10/01-12/01
	Idaho	Y	37360 FQ	47980 AW	62990 TQ	IDBLS	10/01-12/01
	Illinois	Y	36330 FQ	51550 AW	69020 TQ	ILBLS	10/01-12/01
	Indiana	Y	28750 FQ	42760 AW	64640 TQ	INBLS	10/01-12/01
	Iowa	Y	21540 FQ	41970 AW	57140 TQ	IABLS	10/01-12/01
	Louisiana	Y	31560 FQ	51290 AW	80240 TQ	LABLS	10/01-12/01
	Maine	Y	28550 FQ	43120 AW	56770 TQ	MEBLS	10/01-12/01
	Michigan	Y	34610 FQ	47680 AW	62700 TQ	MIBLS	10/01-12/01
	Minnesota	Y	30070 FQ	46810 AW	65940 TQ	MNBLS	10/01-12/01
	Mississippi	Y	27480 FQ	41770 AW	56610 TQ	MSBLS	10/01-12/01
	Montana	Y	35380 FQ	49890 AW	68590 TQ	MTBLS	10/01-12/01
	Nebraska	Y	30090 FQ	45790 AW	68940 TQ	NEBLS	10/01-12/01
	Nevada	Y	35830 FQ	46650 AW	55900 TQ	NVBLS	10/01-12/01
	New Hampshire	Y	31710 FQ	48510 AW	70830 TQ	NHBLS	10/01-12/01
	New Mexico	Y	28490 FQ	48840 AW	75150 TQ	NMBLS	10/01-12/01
	New York	Y	27460 FQ	44490 AW	65810 TQ	NYBLS	10/01-12/01
	North Carolina	Y	31850 FQ	48410 AW	69370 TQ	NCBLS	10/01-12/01
	North Dakota	Y	25340 FQ	39260 AW	56130 TQ	NDBLS	10/01-12/01
	Ohio	Y	25300 FQ	46500 AW	69530 TQ	OHBLS	10/01-12/01
	Oklahoma	Y	27990 FQ	43180 AW	57510 TQ	OKBLS	10/01-12/01
	Oregon	Y	38930 FQ	52990 AW	71230 TQ	ORBLS	10/01-12/01
	Pennsylvania	Y	26940 FQ	45610 AW	70440 TQ	PABLS	10/01-12/01
	South Carolina	Y	24980 FQ	47350 AW	81050 TQ	SCBLS	10/01-12/01
	South Dakota	Y	25940 FQ	39060 AW	54420 TQ	SDBLS	10/01-12/01
	Tennessee	Y	22830 FQ	34360 AW	53350 TQ	TNBLS	10/01-12/01
	Texas	Y	22860 FQ	39700 AW	58260 TQ	TXBLS	10/01-12/01
	Utah	Y	26340 FQ	40510 AW	56580 TQ	UTBLS	10/01-12/01
	Vermont	Y	28620 FQ	44040 AW	55790 TQ	VTBLS	10/01-12/01
	Virginia	Y	31660 FQ	47090 AW	63560 TQ	VABLS	10/01-12/01
	Washington	Y	36770 FQ	48700 AW	60280 TQ	WABLS	10/01-12/01
	West Virginia	Y	23250 FQ	40290 AW	60800 TQ	WVBLS	10/01-12/01
	Wisconsin	Y	20020 FQ	39570 AW	57910 TQ	WIBLS	10/01-12/01
	Wyoming	Y	36530 FQ	47270 AW	56680 TQ	WYBLS	10/01-12/01
Forestry and Conservation Science Teacher							
Postsecondary	California	Y	39210 FQ	62420 AW	99180 TQ	CABLS	10/01-12/01
Postsecondary	Florida	Y	52510 FQ	77070 AW	113940 TQ	FLBLS	10/01-12/01
Postsecondary	Maine	Y	37700 FQ	53740 AW	71370 TQ	MEBLS	10/01-12/01
Postsecondary	Minnesota	Y	16640 FQ	55710 AW	101020 TQ	MNBLS	10/01-12/01
Postsecondary	New Jersey	Y	42050 FQ	57920 AW	79160 TQ	NJBLS	10/01-12/01
Postsecondary	North Carolina	Y	45970 FQ	68730 AW	100180 TQ	NCBLS	10/01-12/01
Postsecondary	Ohio	Y	36610 FQ	58270 AW	90940 TQ	OHBLS	10/01-12/01
Postsecondary	Oregon	Y	43250 FQ	65980 AW	90460 TQ	ORBLS	10/01-12/01
Postsecondary	Pennsylvania	Y	31190 FQ	65140 AW	102840 TQ	PABLS	10/01-12/01
Postsecondary	South Carolina	Y	37760 FQ	53690 AW	85440 TQ	SCBLS	10/01-12/01
Postsecondary	Texas	Y	35820 FQ	65990 AW	103280 TQ	TXBLS	10/01-12/01
Postsecondary	Virginia	Y	51280 FQ	79020 AW	114730 TQ	VABLS	10/01-12/01
Postsecondary	Washington	Y	51910 FQ	84130 AW	118760 TQ	WABLS	10/01-12/01

AAW	Average annual wage	**AOH**	Average offered, high	**ASH**	Average starting, high	**H**	Hourly	**M**	Monthly	**S**	Special: hourly and annual
AE	Average entry wage	**AOL**	Average offered, low	**ASL**	Average starting, low	**HI**	Highest wage paid	**MTC**	Median total compensation	**TQ**	Third quartile wage
AEX	Average experienced wage	**APH**	Average pay, high range	**AW**	Average wage paid	**HR**	High end range	**MW**	Median wage paid	**W**	Weekly
AO	Average offered	**APL**	Average pay, low range	**FQ**	First quartile wage	**LR**	Low end range	**SQ**	Second quartile wage	**Y**	Yearly

Occupation/Type/Industry	Location	Per	Low	Mid	High	Source	Date
Forging Machine Setter, Operator, and Tender							
Metals and Plastics	Alabama	H	6.68 FQ	16.38 AW	27.42 TQ	ALBLS	10/01-12/01
Metals and Plastics	Birmingham MSA, AL	H	7.93 FQ	14.71 AW	24.71 TQ	ALBLS	10/01-12/01
Metals and Plastics	Arizona	H	7.74 FQ	12.81 AW	20.80 TQ	AZBLS	10/01-12/01
Metals and Plastics	Phoenix-Mesa MSA, AZ	H	8.80 FQ	12.81 AW	17.27 TQ	AZBLS	10/01-12/01
Metals and Plastics	Tucson MSA, AZ	H	6.45 FQ	13.12 AW	23.60 TQ	AZBLS	10/01-12/01
Metals and Plastics	Arkansas	H	7.34 FQ	11.93 AW	15.46 TQ	ARBLS	10/01-12/01
Metals and Plastics	Fayetteville-Springdale-Rogers MSA, AR	H	9.22 FQ	12.69 AW	15.84 TQ	ARBLS	10/01-12/01
Metals and Plastics	Little Rock-North Little Rock MSA, AR	H	8.87 FQ	12.45 AW	15.98 TQ	ARBLS	10/01-12/01
Metals and Plastics	California	H	7.04 FQ	12.30 AW	19.30 TQ	CABLS	10/01-12/01
Metals and Plastics	Fresno MSA, CA	H	8.18 FQ	12.03 AW	16.12 TQ	CABLS	10/01-12/01
Metals and Plastics	Los Angeles-Long Beach PMSA, CA	H	6.84 FQ	13.00 AW	20.76 TQ	CABLS	10/01-12/01
Metals and Plastics	Oakland PMSA, CA	H	6.67 FQ	12.15 AW	19.99 TQ	CABLS	10/01-12/01
Metals and Plastics	Orange County PMSA, CA	H	6.99 FQ	12.00 AW	19.33 TQ	CABLS	10/01-12/01
Metals and Plastics	Riverside-San Bernardino PMSA, CA	H	7.40 FQ	11.44 AW	16.66 TQ	CABLS	10/01-12/01
Metals and Plastics	San Diego MSA, CA	H	7.19 FQ	11.60 AW	16.40 TQ	CABLS	10/01-12/01
Metals and Plastics	San Francisco PMSA, CA	H	6.75 FQ	11.11 AW	18.21 TQ	CABLS	10/01-12/01
Metals and Plastics	San Jose PMSA, CA	H	8.72 FQ	12.85 AW	16.38 TQ	CABLS	10/01-12/01
Metals and Plastics	Santa Rosa PMSA, CA	H	8.52 FQ	13.20 AW	19.71 TQ	CABLS	10/01-12/01
Metals and Plastics	Ventura PMSA, CA	H	7.08 FQ	13.48 AW	21.66 TQ	CABLS	10/01-12/01
Metals and Plastics	Colorado	H	5.93 FQ	10.74 AW	17.14 TQ	COBLS	10/01-12/01
Metals and Plastics	Colorado Springs MSA, CO	H	6.19 FQ	12.12 AW	19.19 TQ	COBLS	10/01-12/01
Metals and Plastics	Connecticut	H	8.22 FQ	13.38 AW	17.63 TQ	CTBLS	10/01-12/01
Metals and Plastics	Hartford MSA, CT	H	8.01 FQ	13.44 AW	17.61 TQ	CTBLS	10/01-12/01
Metals and Plastics	New Haven-Meriden PMSA, CT	H	9.43 FQ	16.58 AW	25.40 TQ	CTBLS	10/01-12/01
Metals and Plastics	Florida	H	7.85 FQ	11.53 AW	16.65 TQ	FLBLS	10/01-12/01
Metals and Plastics	Jacksonville MSA, FL	H	8.27 FQ	11.25 AW	14.85 TQ	FLBLS	10/01-12/01
Metals and Plastics	Miami PMSA, FL	H	7.40 FQ	10.37 AW	13.29 TQ	FLBLS	10/01-12/01
Metals and Plastics	Orlando MSA, FL	H	8.94 FQ	11.96 AW	16.90 TQ	FLBLS	10/01-12/01
Metals and Plastics	Georgia	H	6.28 FQ	9.94 AW	14.55 TQ	GABLS	10/01-12/01
Metals and Plastics	Atlanta MSA, GA	H	6.09 FQ	9.50 AW	13.99 TQ	GABLS	10/01-12/01
Metals and Plastics	Savannah MSA, GA	H	5.98 FQ	8.15 AW	10.98 TQ	GABLS	10/01-12/01
Metals and Plastics	Illinois	H	8.42 FQ	13.11 AW	17.44 TQ	ILBLS	10/01-12/01
Metals and Plastics	Chicago PMSA, IL	H	9.09 FQ	13.22 AW	17.34 TQ	ILBLS	10/01-12/01
Metals and Plastics	Peoria-Pekin MSA, IL	H	5.98 FQ	11.70 AW	25.50 TQ	ILBLS	10/01-12/01
Metals and Plastics	Rockford MSA, IL	H	8.95 FQ	14.71 AW	19.53 TQ	ILBLS	10/01-12/01
Metals and Plastics	Indiana	H	8.44 FQ	13.96 AW	21.73 TQ	INBLS	10/01-12/01
Metals and Plastics	Elkhart-Goshen MSA, IN	H	9.71 FQ	15.22 AW	24.36 TQ	INBLS	10/01-12/01
Metals and Plastics	Evansville-Henderson MSA, IN-KY	H	7.54 FQ	11.05 AW	16.31 TQ	INBLS	10/01-12/01
Metals and Plastics	Fort Wayne MSA, IN	H	8.11 FQ	12.31 AW	15.99 TQ	INBLS	10/01-12/01
Metals and Plastics	Gary PMSA, IN	H	6.16 FQ	12.45 AW	23.93 TQ	INBLS	10/01-12/01
Metals and Plastics	Indianapolis MSA, IN	H	7.51 FQ	15.46 AW	25.88 TQ	INBLS	10/01-12/01
Metals and Plastics	South Bend MSA, IN	H	8.08 FQ	12.85 AW	16.54 TQ	INBLS	10/01-12/01
Metals and Plastics	Iowa	H	10.78 FQ	13.76 AW	17.85 TQ	IABLS	10/01-12/01
Metals and Plastics	Davenport-Moline-Rock Island MSA, IA-IL	H	8.87 FQ	11.13 AW	13.49 TQ	IABLS	10/01-12/01
Metals and Plastics	Kansas	H	7.22 FQ	12.34 AW	19.03 TQ	KSBLS	10/01-12/01
Metals and Plastics	Wichita MSA, KS	H	8.08 FQ	15.59 AW	25.62 TQ	KSBLS	10/01-12/01
Metals and Plastics	Kentucky	H	7.42 FQ	11.51 AW	15.45 TQ	KYBLS	10/01-12/01
Metals and Plastics	Lexington MSA, KY	H	6.79 FQ	11.00 AW	14.37 TQ	KYBLS	10/01-12/01
Metals and Plastics	Louisville MSA, KY-IN	H	8.93 FQ	11.80 AW	15.73 TQ	KYBLS	10/01-12/01
Metals and Plastics	Louisiana	H	6.28 FQ	10.04 AW	15.25 TQ	LABLS	10/01-12/01
Metals and Plastics	Shreveport-Bossier City MSA, LA	H	7.37 FQ	11.92 AW	16.27 TQ	LABLS	10/01-12/01
Metals and Plastics	Maine	H	5.87 FQ	8.88 AW	13.10 TQ	MEBLS	10/01-12/01
Metals and Plastics	Maryland	H	6.95 FQ	11.82 AW	19.22 TQ	MDBLS	10/01-12/01
Metals and Plastics	Baltimore PMSA, MD	H	7.80 FQ	12.81 AW	19.76 TQ	MDBLS	10/01-12/01
Metals and Plastics	Massachusetts	H	9.14 FQ	17.49 AW	26.90 TQ	MABLS	10/01-12/01
Metals and Plastics	Boston PMSA, MA-NH	H	9.71 FQ	18.69 AW	27.54 TQ	MABLS	10/01-12/01
Metals and Plastics	Springfield MSA, MA	H	11.81 FQ	18.78 AW	27.17 TQ	MABLS	10/01-12/01
Metals and Plastics	Worcester PMSA, MA-CT	H	10.55 FQ	17.80 AW	23.00 TQ	MABLS	10/01-12/01
Metals and Plastics	Michigan	H	8.91 FQ	17.39 AW	26.89 TQ	MIBLS	10/01-12/01
Metals and Plastics	Ann Arbor PMSA, MI	H	7.77 FQ	17.09 AW	26.92 TQ	MIBLS	10/01-12/01
Metals and Plastics	Detroit PMSA, MI	H	9.25 FQ	17.47 AW	26.95 TQ	MIBLS	10/01-12/01

AAW	Average annual wage	**AOH**	Average offered, high	**ASH**	Average starting, high	**H**	Hourly	**M**	Monthly	**S**	Special: hourly and annual
AE	Average entry wage	**AOL**	Average offered, low	**ASL**	Average starting, low	**HI**	Highest wage paid	**MTC**	Median total compensation	**TQ**	Third quartile wage
AEX	Average experienced wage	**APH**	Average pay, high range	**AW**	Average wage paid	**HR**	High end range	**MW**	Median wage paid	**W**	Weekly
AO	Average offered	**APL**	Average pay, low range	**FQ**	First quartile wage	**LR**	Low end range	**SQ**	Second quartile wage	**Y**	Yearly

Occupation/Type/Industry	Location	Per	Low	Mid	High	Source	Date
Forging Machine Setter, Operator, and Tender							
Metals and Plastics	Grand Rapids-Muskegon-Holland MSA, MI	H	8.08 FQ	15.17 AW	26.30 TQ	MIBLS	10/01-12/01
Metals and Plastics	Kalamazoo-Battle Creek MSA, MI	H	10.58 FQ	14.63 AW	21.13 TQ	MIBLS	10/01-12/01
Metals and Plastics	Lansing-East Lansing MSA, MI	H	10.45 FQ	19.16 AW	26.38 TQ	MIBLS	10/01-12/01
Metals and Plastics	Minnesota	H	7.45 FQ	11.26 AW	16.34 TQ	MNBLS	10/01-12/01
Metals and Plastics	Minneapolis-St. Paul MSA, MN-WI	H	7.39 FQ	10.11 AW	13.70 TQ	MNBLS	10/01-12/01
Metals and Plastics	Mississippi	H	6.51 FQ	10.32 AW	13.57 TQ	MSBLS	10/01-12/01
Metals and Plastics	Jackson MSA, MS	H	5.82 FQ	7.74 AW	10.20 TQ	MSBLS	10/01-12/01
Metals and Plastics	Missouri	H	8.32 FQ	12.94 AW	17.25 TQ	MOBLS	10/01-12/01
Metals and Plastics	Kansas City MSA, MO-KS	H	9.21 FQ	12.14 AW	16.11 TQ	MOBLS	10/01-12/01
Metals and Plastics	St. Louis MSA, MO-IL	H	7.39 FQ	15.08 AW	25.51 TQ	MOBLS	10/01-12/01
Metals and Plastics	Springfield MSA, MO	H	13.03 FQ	15.21 AW	17.21 TQ	MOBLS	10/01-12/01
Metals and Plastics	Montana	H	6.32 FQ	9.58 AW	13.50 TQ	MTBLS	10/01-12/01
Metals and Plastics	Nebraska	H	9.48 FQ	13.07 AW	16.21 TQ	NEBLS	10/01-12/01
Metals and Plastics	New Hampshire	H	8.56 FQ	15.25 AW	19.92 TQ	NHBLS	10/01-12/01
Metals and Plastics	New Jersey	H	6.34 FQ	10.72 AW	16.73 TQ	NJBLS	10/01-12/01
Metals and Plastics	Bergen-Passaic PMSA, NJ	H	6.33 FQ	10.97 AW	17.24 TQ	NJBLS	10/01-12/01
Metals and Plastics	Newark PMSA, NJ	H	6.95 FQ	11.63 AW	16.75 TQ	NJBLS	10/01-12/01
Metals and Plastics	New York	H	8.98 FQ	18.36 AW	27.83 TQ	NYBLS	10/01-12/01
Metals and Plastics	Albany-Schenectady-Troy MSA, NY	H	10.42 FQ	16.16 AW	25.75 TQ	NYBLS	10/01-12/01
Metals and Plastics	Nassau-Suffolk PMSA, NY	H	10.65 FQ	13.87 AW	19.87 TQ	NYBLS	10/01-12/01
Metals and Plastics	New York PMSA, NY	H	6.64 FQ	10.26 AW	14.39 TQ	NYBLS	10/01-12/01
Metals and Plastics	Rochester MSA, NY	H	6.77 FQ	12.18 AW	18.24 TQ	NYBLS	10/01-12/01
Metals and Plastics	Syracuse MSA, NY	H	16.39 FQ	24.23 AW	28.44 TQ	NYBLS	10/01-12/01
Metals and Plastics	North Carolina	H	5.97 FQ	10.63 AW	16.65 TQ	NCBLS	10/01-12/01
Metals and Plastics	Charlotte-Gastonia-Rock Hill MSA, NC-SC	H	7.75 FQ	12.10 AW	17.12 TQ	NCBLS	10/01-12/01
Metals and Plastics	Greensboro-Winston-Salem-High Point MSA, NC	H	6.13 FQ	12.51 AW	20.79 TQ	NCBLS	10/01-12/01
Metals and Plastics	Ohio	H	8.73 FQ	14.30 AW	23.00 TQ	OHBLS	10/01-12/01
Metals and Plastics	Cincinnati PMSA, OH-KY-IN	H	8.39 FQ	14.52 AW	20.81 TQ	OHBLS	10/01-12/01
Metals and Plastics	Cleveland-Lorain-Elyria PMSA, OH	H	10.47 FQ	16.17 AW	22.14 TQ	OHBLS	10/01-12/01
Metals and Plastics	Columbus MSA, OH	H	6.03 FQ	10.68 AW	14.98 TQ	OHBLS	10/01-12/01
Metals and Plastics	Dayton-Springfield MSA, OH	H	7.04 FQ	10.89 AW	14.72 TQ	OHBLS	10/01-12/01
Metals and Plastics	Toledo MSA, OH	H	9.53 FQ	17.42 AW	28.00 TQ	OHBLS	10/01-12/01
Metals and Plastics	Youngstown-Warren MSA, OH	H	9.16 FQ	13.83 AW	25.67 TQ	OHBLS	10/01-12/01
Metals and Plastics	Oklahoma	H	7.05 FQ	10.58 AW	16.31 TQ	OKBLS	10/01-12/01
Metals and Plastics	Tulsa MSA, OK	H	7.88 FQ	13.03 AW	17.41 TQ	OKBLS	10/01-12/01
Metals and Plastics	Oregon	H	9.14 FQ	15.43 AW	23.90 TQ	ORBLS	10/01-12/01
Metals and Plastics	Portland-Vancouver PMSA, OR-WA	H	9.21 FQ	15.37 AW	23.72 TQ	ORBLS	10/01-12/01
Metals and Plastics	Pennsylvania	H	7.43 FQ	12.29 AW	17.50 TQ	PABLS	10/01-12/01
Metals and Plastics	Allentown-Bethlehem-Easton MSA, PA	H	9.36 FQ	12.12 AW	16.50 TQ	PABLS	10/01-12/01
Metals and Plastics	Harrisburg-Lebanon-Carlisle MSA, PA	H	6.50 FQ	9.35 AW	13.32 TQ	PABLS	10/01-12/01
Metals and Plastics	Lancaster MSA, PA	H	11.26 FQ	13.83 AW	17.13 TQ	PABLS	10/01-12/01
Metals and Plastics	Philadelphia PMSA, PA-NJ	H	7.02 FQ	12.80 AW	19.49 TQ	PABLS	10/01-12/01
Metals and Plastics	Pittsburgh MSA, PA	H	9.16 FQ	13.87 AW	18.13 TQ	PABLS	10/01-12/01
Metals and Plastics	Scranton-Wilkes-Barre-Hazleton MSA, PA	H	7.70 FQ	11.99 AW	15.95 TQ	PABLS	10/01-12/01
Metals and Plastics	York MSA, PA	H	6.20 FQ	9.57 AW	14.57 TQ	PABLS	10/01-12/01
Metals and Plastics	Rhode Island	H	7.29 FQ	9.85 AW	13.90 TQ	RIBLS	10/01-12/01
Metals and Plastics	Providence-Fall River-Warwick MSA, RI-MA	H	7.29 FQ	9.52 AW	12.95 TQ	RIBLS	10/01-12/01
Metals and Plastics	South Carolina	H	8.57 FQ	11.29 AW	14.65 TQ	SCBLS	10/01-12/01
Metals and Plastics	Columbia MSA, SC	H	7.65 FQ	10.49 AW	13.34 TQ	SCBLS	10/01-12/01
Metals and Plastics	Greenville-Spartanburg-Anderson MSA, SC	H	8.28 FQ	11.54 AW	14.54 TQ	SCBLS	10/01-12/01
Metals and Plastics	South Dakota	H	9.48 FQ	13.19 AW	18.99 TQ	SDBLS	10/01-12/01
Metals and Plastics	Sioux Falls MSA, SD	H	9.72 FQ	15.48 AW	20.67 TQ	SDBLS	10/01-12/01
Metals and Plastics	Tennessee	H	7.77 FQ	11.31 AW	14.87 TQ	TNBLS	10/01-12/01
Metals and Plastics	Memphis MSA, TN-AR-MS	H	10.85 FQ	11.86 AW	13.29 TQ	TNBLS	10/01-12/01
Metals and Plastics	Nashville MSA, TN	H	6.92 FQ	12.35 AW	20.62 TQ	TNBLS	10/01-12/01
Metals and Plastics	Texas	H	7.05 FQ	10.89 AW	15.52 TQ	TXBLS	10/01-12/01

AAW Average annual wage; AE Average entry wage; AEX Average experienced wage; AO Average offered; AOH Average offered, high; AOL Average offered, low; APH Average pay, high range; APL Average pay, low range; ASH Average starting, high; ASL Average starting, low; AW Average wage paid; FQ First quartile wage; H Hourly; HI Highest wage paid; HR High end range; LR Low end range; M Monthly; MTC Median total compensation; MW Median wage paid; SQ Second quartile wage; S Special: hourly and annual; TQ Third quartile wage; W Weekly; Y Yearly

Occupation/Type/Industry	Location	Per	Low	Mid	High	Source	Date
Forging Machine Setter, Operator, and Tender							
Metals and Plastics	Beaumont-Port Arthur MSA, TX	H	7.10 FQ	10.53 AW	15.20 TQ	TXBLS	10/01-12/01
Metals and Plastics	Dallas PMSA, TX	H	6.18 FQ	9.94 AW	14.42 TQ	TXBLS	10/01-12/01
Metals and Plastics	Fort Worth-Arlington PMSA, TX	H	7.91 FQ	11.17 AW	16.07 TQ	TXBLS	10/01-12/01
Metals and Plastics	Houston PMSA, TX	H	7.97 FQ	11.35 AW	15.44 TQ	TXBLS	10/01-12/01
Metals and Plastics	Utah	H	9.18 FQ	12.72 AW	17.80 TQ	UTBLS	10/01-12/01
Metals and Plastics	Provo-Orem MSA, UT	H	9.97 FQ	15.41 AW	22.93 TQ	UTBLS	10/01-12/01
Metals and Plastics	Salt Lake City-Ogden MSA, UT	H	9.14 FQ	12.16 AW	17.16 TQ	UTBLS	10/01-12/01
Metals and Plastics	Virginia	H	6.58 FQ	10.06 AW	14.04 TQ	VABLS	10/01-12/01
Metals and Plastics	Norfolk-Virginia Beach-Newport News MSA, VA-NC	H	6.63 FQ	9.33 AW	13.64 TQ	VABLS	10/01-12/01
Metals and Plastics	Richmond-Petersburg MSA, VA	H	6.31 FQ	13.93 AW	26.96 TQ	VABLS	10/01-12/01
Metals and Plastics	Washington	H	9.13 FQ	13.07 AW	17.47 TQ	WABLS	10/01-12/01
Metals and Plastics	Seattle-Bellevue-Everett PMSA, WA	H	11.21 FQ	15.05 AW	19.39 TQ	WABLS	10/01-12/01
Metals and Plastics	West Virginia	H	8.94 FQ	10.64 AW	13.08 TQ	WVBLS	10/01-12/01
Metals and Plastics	Huntington-Ashland MSA, WV-KY-OH	H	7.35 FQ	11.18 AW	16.73 TQ	WVBLS	10/01-12/01
Metals and Plastics	Wisconsin	H	8.12 FQ	13.52 AW	22.60 TQ	WIBLS	10/01-12/01
Metals and Plastics	Appleton-Oshkosh-Neenah MSA, WI	H	10.44 FQ	13.99 AW	17.35 TQ	WIBLS	10/01-12/01
Metals and Plastics	Madison MSA, WI	H	8.49 FQ	14.14 AW	17.65 TQ	WIBLS	10/01-12/01
Metals and Plastics	Milwaukee-Waukesha PMSA, WI	H	7.31 FQ	13.93 AW	24.19 TQ	WIBLS	10/01-12/01
Metals and Plastics	Racine PMSA, WI	H	7.49 FQ	11.83 AW	17.50 TQ	WIBLS	10/01-12/01
Foundry Mold and Coremaker	Alabama	H	7.92 FQ	11.82 AW	16.22 TQ	ALBLS	10/01-12/01
	Birmingham MSA, AL	H	8.10 FQ	12.04 AW	16.50 TQ	ALBLS	10/01-12/01
	Arizona	H	8.28 FQ	12.37 AW	16.50 TQ	AZBLS	10/01-12/01
	Phoenix-Mesa MSA, AZ	H	8.43 FQ	12.78 AW	17.55 TQ	AZBLS	10/01-12/01
	Arkansas	H	9.30 FQ	13.22 AW	16.40 TQ	ARBLS	10/01-12/01
	California	H	6.85 FQ	10.55 AW	15.44 TQ	CABLS	10/01-12/01
	Los Angeles-Long Beach PMSA, CA	H	6.74 FQ	9.87 AW	13.40 TQ	CABLS	10/01-12/01
	Oakland PMSA, CA	H	7.84 FQ	14.78 AW	19.07 TQ	CABLS	10/01-12/01
	Orange County PMSA, CA	H	7.48 FQ	12.83 AW	23.66 TQ	CABLS	10/01-12/01
	Riverside-San Bernardino PMSA, CA	H	6.85 FQ	10.17 AW	14.98 TQ	CABLS	10/01-12/01
	Ventura PMSA, CA	H	6.71 FQ	9.52 AW	12.54 TQ	CABLS	10/01-12/01
	Colorado	H	8.84 FQ	12.11 AW	16.62 TQ	COBLS	10/01-12/01
	Colorado Springs MSA, CO	H	7.57 FQ	12.33 AW	19.84 TQ	COBLS	10/01-12/01
	Denver PMSA, CO	H	9.37 FQ	12.38 AW	15.47 TQ	COBLS	10/01-12/01
	Connecticut	H	8.81 FQ	11.85 AW	15.17 TQ	CTBLS	10/01-12/01
	Hartford MSA, CT	H	8.55 FQ	11.38 AW	13.96 TQ	CTBLS	10/01-12/01
	Florida	H	7.34 FQ	10.42 AW	14.99 TQ	FLBLS	10/01-12/01
	Tampa-St. Petersburg-Clearwater MSA, FL	H	7.13 FQ	11.17 AW	18.30 TQ	FLBLS	10/01-12/01
	Georgia	H	9.47 FQ	13.48 AW	17.57 TQ	GABLS	10/01-12/01
	Atlanta MSA, GA	H	8.62 FQ	12.10 AW	14.87 TQ	GABLS	10/01-12/01
	Illinois	H	9.31 FQ	13.61 AW	20.43 TQ	ILBLS	10/01-12/01
	Chicago PMSA, IL	H	9.38 FQ	13.40 AW	19.60 TQ	ILBLS	10/01-12/01
	Peoria-Pekin MSA, IL	H	12.02 FQ	17.71 AW	22.51 TQ	ILBLS	10/01-12/01
	Rockford MSA, IL	H	8.25 FQ	11.32 AW	15.10 TQ	ILBLS	10/01-12/01
	Indiana	H	9.86 FQ	13.90 AW	19.24 TQ	INBLS	10/01-12/01
	South Bend MSA, IN	H	11.24 FQ	17.36 AW	24.68 TQ	INBLS	10/01-12/01
	Iowa	H	9.27 FQ	12.33 AW	15.04 TQ	IABLS	10/01-12/01
	Davenport-Moline-Rock Island MSA, IA-IL	H	7.33 FQ	9.70 AW	14.85 TQ	IABLS	10/01-12/01
	Kansas	H	8.13 FQ	11.00 AW	14.27 TQ	KSBLS	10/01-12/01
	Louisiana	H	7.19 FQ	12.34 AW	17.92 TQ	LABLS	10/01-12/01
	Maryland	H	8.37 FQ	14.21 AW	21.38 TQ	MDBLS	10/01-12/01
	Baltimore PMSA, MD	H	8.27 FQ	14.26 AW	21.47 TQ	MDBLS	10/01-12/01
	Massachusetts	H	9.70 FQ	14.96 AW	22.81 TQ	MABLS	10/01-12/01
	Boston PMSA, MA-NH	H	9.62 FQ	14.14 AW	20.75 TQ	MABLS	10/01-12/01
	Brockton PMSA, MA	H	11.22 FQ	17.55 AW	25.64 TQ	MABLS	10/01-12/01
	Springfield MSA, MA	H	9.39 FQ	17.97 AW	27.88 TQ	MABLS	10/01-12/01

AAW Average annual wage **AOH** Average offered, high **ASH** Average starting, high **H** Hourly **M** Monthly **S** Special: hourly and annual
AE Average entry wage **AOL** Average offered, low **ASL** Average starting, low **HI** Highest wage paid **MTC** Median total compensation **TQ** Third quartile wage
AEX Average experienced wage **APH** Average pay, high range **AW** Average wage paid **HR** High end range **MW** Median wage paid **W** Weekly
AO Average offered **APL** Average pay, low range **FQ** First quartile wage **LR** Low end range **SQ** Second quartile wage **Y** Yearly

Occupation/Type/Industry	Location	Per	Low	Mid	High	Source	Date
Foundry Mold and Coremaker	Michigan	H	8.90 FQ	14.24 AW	20.98 TQ	MIBLS	10/01-12/01
	Ann Arbor PMSA, MI	H	10.52 FQ	14.10 AW	18.00 TQ	MIBLS	10/01-12/01
	Detroit PMSA, MI	H	8.84 FQ	14.12 AW	20.47 TQ	MIBLS	10/01-12/01
	Minnesota	H	10.50 FQ	15.29 AW	20.68 TQ	MNBLS	10/01-12/01
	Minneapolis-St. Paul MSA, MN-WI	H	11.07 FQ	16.13 AW	21.62 TQ	MNBLS	10/01-12/01
	Mississippi	H	8.66 FQ	11.29 AW	14.32 TQ	MSBLS	10/01-12/01
	Missouri	H	7.65 FQ	11.38 AW	14.46 TQ	MOBLS	10/01-12/01
	St. Louis MSA, MO-IL	H	9.30 FQ	12.64 AW	16.65 TQ	MOBLS	10/01-12/01
	Nebraska	H	9.79 FQ	14.06 AW	20.02 TQ	NEBLS	10/01-12/01
	Nevada	H	10.02 FQ	12.05 AW	14.14 TQ	NVBLS	10/01-12/01
	Las Vegas MSA, NV-AZ	H	10.06 FQ	12.08 AW	14.14 TQ	NVBLS	10/01-12/01
	New Hampshire	H	9.33 FQ	13.94 AW	23.71 TQ	NHBLS	10/01-12/01
	Nashua PMSA, NH	H	10.74 FQ	15.34 AW	25.20 TQ	NHBLS	10/01-12/01
	New Jersey	H	9.78 FQ	13.32 AW	17.35 TQ	NJBLS	10/01-12/01
	Newark PMSA, NJ	H	9.81 FQ	13.70 AW	17.63 TQ	NJBLS	10/01-12/01
	New Mexico	H	8.56 FQ	10.01 AW	12.51 TQ	NMBLS	10/01-12/01
	New York	H	7.03 FQ	14.49 AW	26.33 TQ	NYBLS	10/01-12/01
	Buffalo-Niagara Falls MSA, NY	H	8.41 FQ	12.18 AW	16.99 TQ	NYBLS	10/01-12/01
	New York PMSA, NY	H	6.50 FQ	12.44 AW	24.68 TQ	NYBLS	10/01-12/01
	Rochester MSA, NY	H	6.98 FQ	12.50 AW	20.50 TQ	NYBLS	10/01-12/01
	Syracuse MSA, NY	H	7.57 FQ	12.27 AW	19.96 TQ	NYBLS	10/01-12/01
	North Carolina	H	9.72 FQ	14.81 AW	21.33 TQ	NCBLS	10/01-12/01
	Charlotte-Gastonia-Rock Hill MSA, NC-SC	H	8.39 FQ	15.15 AW	21.13 TQ	NCBLS	10/01-12/01
	Ohio	H	9.63 FQ	15.74 AW	26.29 TQ	OHBLS	10/01-12/01
	Akron PMSA, OH	H	9.75 FQ	12.21 AW	14.56 TQ	OHBLS	10/01-12/01
	Canton-Massillon MSA, OH	H	8.76 FQ	13.53 AW	17.87 TQ	OHBLS	10/01-12/01
	Cincinnati PMSA, OH-KY-IN	H	9.63 FQ	13.56 AW	17.38 TQ	OHBLS	10/01-12/01
	Cleveland-Lorain-Elyria PMSA, OH	H	9.09 FQ	15.12 AW	23.93 TQ	OHBLS	10/01-12/01
	Columbus MSA, OH	H	10.53 FQ	18.96 AW	27.98 TQ	OHBLS	10/01-12/01
	Dayton-Springfield MSA, OH	H	8.21 FQ	13.36 AW	17.84 TQ	OHBLS	10/01-12/01
	Mansfield MSA, OH	H	9.48 FQ	12.01 AW	15.16 TQ	OHBLS	10/01-12/01
	Toledo MSA, OH	H	7.98 FQ	14.45 AW	27.76 TQ	OHBLS	10/01-12/01
	Youngstown-Warren MSA, OH	H	9.55 FQ	12.72 AW	19.10 TQ	OHBLS	10/01-12/01
	Oklahoma	H	7.72 FQ	10.99 AW	14.54 TQ	OKBLS	10/01-12/01
	Oklahoma City MSA, OK	H	7.63 FQ	10.88 AW	16.47 TQ	OKBLS	10/01-12/01
	Tulsa MSA, OK	H	8.37 FQ	11.22 AW	14.00 TQ	OKBLS	10/01-12/01
	Oregon	H	9.21 FQ	13.85 AW	19.38 TQ	ORBLS	10/01-12/01
	Eugene-Springfield MSA, OR	H	7.82 FQ	10.68 AW	13.68 TQ	ORBLS	10/01-12/01
	Portland-Vancouver PMSA, OR-WA	H	9.42 FQ	14.57 AW	20.40 TQ	ORBLS	10/01-12/01
	Pennsylvania	H	9.24 FQ	12.92 AW	17.95 TQ	PABLS	10/01-12/01
	Allentown-Bethlehem-Easton MSA, PA	H	8.32 FQ	13.02 AW	17.45 TQ	PABLS	10/01-12/01
	Erie MSA, PA	H	9.34 FQ	12.05 AW	14.32 TQ	PABLS	10/01-12/01
	Johnstown MSA, PA	H	11.10 FQ	12.16 AW	13.41 TQ	PABLS	10/01-12/01
	Philadelphia PMSA, PA-NJ	H	9.50 FQ	15.21 AW	21.83 TQ	PABLS	10/01-12/01
	Pittsburgh MSA, PA	H	8.18 FQ	12.62 AW	18.06 TQ	PABLS	10/01-12/01
	Reading MSA, PA	H	8.09 FQ	12.98 AW	20.27 TQ	PABLS	10/01-12/01
	York MSA, PA	H	9.20 FQ	12.46 AW	18.96 TQ	PABLS	10/01-12/01
	Rhode Island	H	6.60 FQ	12.58 AW	21.72 TQ	RIBLS	10/01-12/01
	Providence-Fall River-Warwick MSA, RI-MA	H	6.65 FQ	12.81 AW	21.32 TQ	RIBLS	10/01-12/01
	South Carolina	H	9.18 FQ	12.12 AW	14.72 TQ	SCBLS	10/01-12/01
	Tennessee	H	9.71 FQ	12.57 AW	15.95 TQ	TNBLS	10/01-12/01
	Knoxville MSA, TN	H	9.43 FQ	11.21 AW	13.92 TQ	TNBLS	10/01-12/01
	Memphis MSA, TN-AR-MS	H	8.26 FQ	11.52 AW	15.73 TQ	TNBLS	10/01-12/01
	Texas	H	6.06 FQ	10.20 AW	13.63 TQ	TXBLS	10/01-12/01
	Dallas PMSA, TX	H	8.55 FQ	13.25 AW	21.20 TQ	TXBLS	10/01-12/01
	Fort Worth-Arlington PMSA, TX	H	6.30 FQ	11.08 AW	13.75 TQ	TXBLS	10/01-12/01
	Houston PMSA, TX	H	6.21 FQ	10.84 AW	13.71 TQ	TXBLS	10/01-12/01
	Utah	H	7.90 FQ	11.44 AW	15.98 TQ	UTBLS	10/01-12/01
	Provo-Orem MSA, UT	H	7.72 FQ	12.06 AW	18.41 TQ	UTBLS	10/01-12/01
	Vermont	H	9.56 FQ	14.98 AW	24.90 TQ	VTBLS	10/01-12/01
	Burlington MSA, VT	H	9.46 FQ	13.12 AW	20.91 TQ	VTBLS	10/01-12/01
	Virginia	H	7.92 FQ	11.05 AW	15.96 TQ	VABLS	10/01-12/01
	Washington	H	9.38 FQ	13.12 AW	17.36 TQ	WABLS	10/01-12/01

AAW Average annual wage; AE Average entry wage; AEX Average experienced wage; AO Average offered; AOH Average offered, high; AOL Average offered, low; APH Average pay, high range; APL Average pay, low range; ASH Average starting, high; ASL Average starting, low; AW Average wage paid; FQ First quartile wage; H Hourly; HI Highest wage paid; HR High end range; LR Low end range; M Monthly; MTC Median total compensation; MW Median wage paid; SQ Second quartile wage; S Special: hourly and annual; TQ Third quartile wage; W Weekly; Y Yearly

Occupation/Type/Industry	Location	Per	Low	Mid	High	Source	Date
Foundry Mold and Coremaker	Seattle-Bellevue-Everett PMSA, WA	H	10.78 FQ	14.21 AW	17.57 TQ	WABLS	10/01-12/01
	Tacoma PMSA, WA	H	8.83 FQ	13.19 AW	17.83 TQ	WABLS	10/01-12/01
	West Virginia	H	9.57 FQ	14.65 AW	18.33 TQ	WVBLS	10/01-12/01
	Wisconsin	H	8.73 FQ	12.33 AW	16.54 TQ	WIBLS	10/01-12/01
	Appleton-Oshkosh-Neenah MSA, WI	H	9.40 FQ	11.99 AW	14.48 TQ	WIBLS	10/01-12/01
	Milwaukee-Waukesha PMSA, WI	H	8.78 FQ	12.85 AW	17.38 TQ	WIBLS	10/01-12/01
	Racine PMSA, WI	H	8.56 FQ	13.03 AW	19.56 TQ	WIBLS	10/01-12/01
Fundraiser							
Non-Profit Organization, Men	United States	Y		77978 Y		NONPROF	2001
Non-Profit Organization, Women	United States	Y		53593 Y		NONPROF	2001
Funeral Attendant	United States	H		8.88 AW		DEATHBUS	2001
	Alabama	H	5.62 FQ	7.76 AW	11.51 TQ	ALBLS	10/01-12/01
	Arizona	H	6.77 FQ	9.02 AW	12.77 TQ	AZBLS	10/01-12/01
	Arkansas	H	5.62 FQ	7.08 AW	8.75 TQ	ARBLS	10/01-12/01
	California	H	8.22 FQ	11.38 AW	16.72 TQ	CABLS	10/01-12/01
	Colorado	H	7.38 FQ	10.36 AW	13.86 TQ	COBLS	10/01-12/01
	Connecticut	H	7.00 FQ	10.08 AW	12.77 TQ	CTBLS	10/01-12/01
	Delaware	H	6.92 FQ	13.39 AW	18.10 TQ	DEBLS	10/01-12/01
	Florida	H	5.77 FQ	8.01 AW	11.31 TQ	FLBLS	10/01-12/01
	Georgia	H	5.78 FQ	7.98 AW	11.26 TQ	GABLS	10/01-12/01
	Hawaii	H	5.82 FQ	8.25 AW	11.02 TQ	HIBLS	10/01-12/01
	Idaho	H		10.98 AW		DEATHBUS	2001
	Idaho	H	7.25 FQ	10.66 AW	16.04 TQ	IDBLS	10/01-12/01
	Illinois	H	6.38 FQ	9.51 AW	14.84 TQ	ILBLS	10/01-12/01
	Indiana	H	5.81 FQ	8.38 AW	10.97 TQ	INBLS	10/01-12/01
	Iowa	H	5.61 FQ	7.48 AW	10.03 TQ	IABLS	10/01-12/01
	Kansas	H	5.64 FQ	8.32 AW	13.52 TQ	KSBLS	10/01-12/01
	Kentucky	H	5.67 FQ	7.53 AW	9.76 TQ	KYBLS	10/01-12/01
	Louisiana	H	5.66 FQ	7.97 AW	12.69 TQ	LABLS	10/01-12/01
	Maine	H	6.43 FQ	9.96 AW	13.78 TQ	MEBLS	10/01-12/01
	Maryland	H	7.86 FQ	11.18 AW	15.94 TQ	MDBLS	10/01-12/01
	Massachusetts	H	6.89 FQ	9.19 AW	11.46 TQ	MABLS	10/01-12/01
	Michigan	H	7.10 FQ	9.86 AW	13.77 TQ	MIBLS	10/01-12/01
	Minnesota	H	6.03 FQ	12.65 AW	25.96 TQ	MNBLS	10/01-12/01
	Mississippi	H	5.77 FQ	9.29 AW	13.23 TQ	MSBLS	10/01-12/01
	Missouri	H	6.03 FQ	8.45 AW	10.89 TQ	MOBLS	10/01-12/01
	Montana	H	6.45 FQ	8.66 AW	10.57 TQ	MTBLS	10/01-12/01
	Nebraska	H	5.86 FQ	8.36 AW	10.88 TQ	NEBLS	10/01-12/01
	Nevada	H	6.73 FQ	9.85 AW	14.73 TQ	NVBLS	10/01-12/01
	New Jersey	H	6.86 FQ	11.13 AW	13.93 TQ	NJBLS	10/01-12/01
	New Mexico	H	6.03 FQ	8.11 AW	10.48 TQ	NMBLS	10/01-12/01
	New York	H	5.88 FQ	8.79 AW	11.28 TQ	NYBLS	10/01-12/01
	North Carolina	H	6.14 FQ	10.36 AW	15.91 TQ	NCBLS	10/01-12/01
	North Dakota	H	5.55 FQ	7.15 AW	10.30 TQ	NDBLS	10/01-12/01
	Ohio	H	5.86 FQ	9.29 AW	15.10 TQ	OHBLS	10/01-12/01
	Oklahoma	H	6.00 FQ	8.11 AW	10.64 TQ	OKBLS	10/01-12/01
	Oregon	H	8.52 FQ	11.76 AW	19.52 TQ	ORBLS	10/01-12/01
	Pennsylvania	H	5.68 FQ	8.24 AW	11.82 TQ	PABLS	10/01-12/01
	Rhode Island	H	6.97 FQ	10.35 AW	13.35 TQ	RIBLS	10/01-12/01
	Rhode Island	H		11.74 AW		DEATHBUS	2001
	South Carolina	H	5.78 FQ	8.37 AW	12.42 TQ	SCBLS	10/01-12/01
	South Dakota	H	6.15 FQ	8.28 AW	10.54 TQ	SDBLS	10/01-12/01
	Tennessee	H	6.08 FQ	8.16 AW	10.38 TQ	TNBLS	10/01-12/01
	Texas	H	5.77 FQ	9.81 AW	16.65 TQ	TXBLS	10/01-12/01
	Utah	H	7.12 FQ	14.98 AW	21.40 TQ	UTBLS	10/01-12/01
	Vermont	H		10.05 AW		DEATHBUS	2001
	Vermont	H	7.00 FQ	11.98 AW	16.95 TQ	VTBLS	10/01-12/01
	Virginia	H	6.54 FQ	9.03 AW	12.26 TQ	VABLS	10/01-12/01
	Washington	H	7.43 FQ	11.60 AW	17.58 TQ	WABLS	10/01-12/01
	Washington	H		13.32 AW		DEATHBUS	2001
	West Virginia	H	6.03 FQ	8.75 AW	11.92 TQ	WVBLS	10/01-12/01
	Wisconsin	H	7.17 FQ	10.06 AW	15.01 TQ	WIBLS	10/01-12/01
	Wyoming	H	7.39 FQ	10.73 AW	14.05 TQ	WYBLS	10/01-12/01
	Puerto Rico	H	5.67 FQ	6.83 AW	8.56 TQ	PRBLS	10/01-12/01
Funeral Director	United States	H		20.61 AW		DEATHBUS	2001
	Alabama	Y	20080 FQ	35230 AW	57090 TQ	ALBLS	10/01-12/01
	Birmingham MSA, AL	Y	17990 FQ	28790 AW	42380 TQ	ALBLS	10/01-12/01

AAW	Average annual wage	**AOH**	Average offered, high	**ASH**	Average starting, high	**H**	Hourly	**M**	Monthly	**S**	Special: hourly and annual
AE	Average entry wage	**AOL**	Average offered, low	**ASL**	Average starting, low	**HI**	Highest wage paid	**MTC**	Median total compensation	**TQ**	Third quartile wage
AEX	Average experienced wage	**APH**	Average pay, high range	**AW**	Average wage paid	**HR**	High end range	**MW**	Median wage paid	**W**	Weekly
AO	Average offered	**APL**	Average pay, low range	**FQ**	First quartile wage	**LR**	Low end range	**SQ**	Second quartile wage	**Y**	Yearly

Occupation/Type/Industry	Location	Per	Low	Mid	High	Source	Date
Funeral Director	Huntsville MSA, AL	Y	23140 FQ	36670 AW	44470 TQ	ALBLS	10/01-12/01
	Mobile MSA, AL	Y	19840 FQ	33280 AW	52830 TQ	ALBLS	10/01-12/01
	Arizona	Y	27420 FQ	39530 AW	55830 TQ	AZBLS	10/01-12/01
	Phoenix-Mesa MSA, AZ	Y	27480 FQ	40520 AW	55630 TQ	AZBLS	10/01-12/01
	Tucson MSA, AZ	Y	27460 FQ	38920 AW	56210 TQ	AZBLS	10/01-12/01
	Arkansas	Y	15110 FQ	24380 AW	38850 TQ	ARBLS	10/01-12/01
	Little Rock-North Little Rock MSA, AR	Y	21290 FQ	34680 AW	49510 TQ	ARBLS	10/01-12/01
	California	Y	28360 FQ	53470 AW	91670 TQ	CABLS	10/01-12/01
	Bakersfield MSA, CA	Y	18150 FQ	51230 AW		CABLS	10/01-12/01
	Fresno MSA, CA	Y	32480 FQ	64080 AW	115080 TQ	CABLS	10/01-12/01
	Los Angeles-Long Beach PMSA, CA	Y	33610 FQ	69750 AW		CABLS	10/01-12/01
	Oakland PMSA, CA	Y	23640 FQ	43640 AW	81900 TQ	CABLS	10/01-12/01
	Orange County PMSA, CA	Y	29270 FQ	36890 AW	46270 TQ	CABLS	10/01-12/01
	Riverside-San Bernardino PMSA, CA	Y	30340 FQ	45300 AW	68990 TQ	CABLS	10/01-12/01
	Sacramento PMSA, CA	Y	24140 FQ	32220 AW	43620 TQ	CABLS	10/01-12/01
	San Diego MSA, CA	Y	17530 FQ	40430 AW	62350 TQ	CABLS	10/01-12/01
	San Francisco PMSA, CA	Y	31750 FQ	45910 AW	63650 TQ	CABLS	10/01-12/01
	Colorado	Y	25180 FQ	39200 AW	76890 TQ	COBLS	10/01-12/01
	Denver PMSA, CO	Y	25250 FQ	34360 AW	45550 TQ	COBLS	10/01-12/01
	Connecticut	Y	30750 FQ	77520 AW	145410 TQ	CTBLS	10/01-12/01
	Hartford MSA, CT	Y	28770 FQ	59980 AW	90360 TQ	CTBLS	10/01-12/01
	New Haven-Meriden PMSA, CT	Y	46560 FQ	115700 AW		CTBLS	10/01-12/01
	Delaware	Y	37890 FQ	60700 AW	86930 TQ	DEBLS	10/01-12/01
	Wilmington-Newark PMSA, DE-MD	Y	21810 FQ	62470 AW	89820 TQ	DEBLS	10/01-12/01
	District of Columbia	Y	27320 FQ	50600 AW		DCBLS	10/01-12/01
	Washington PMSA, DC-MD-VA-WV	Y	29340 FQ	47710 AW	71010 TQ	DCBLS	10/01-12/01
	Florida	Y	25590 FQ	44300 AW	66320 TQ	FLBLS	10/01-12/01
	Daytona Beach MSA, FL	Y	25500 FQ	43090 AW	47380 TQ	FLBLS	10/01-12/01
	Fort Lauderdale PMSA, FL	Y	18700 FQ	31470 AW	49580 TQ	FLBLS	10/01-12/01
	Jacksonville MSA, FL	Y	30230 FQ	48260 AW	69730 TQ	FLBLS	10/01-12/01
	Melbourne-Titusville-Palm Bay MSA, FL	Y	28070 FQ	60510 AW	105630 TQ	FLBLS	10/01-12/01
	Miami PMSA, FL	Y	24900 FQ	41510 AW	60240 TQ	FLBLS	10/01-12/01
	Orlando MSA, FL	Y	29830 FQ	45510 AW	60600 TQ	FLBLS	10/01-12/01
	Pensacola MSA, FL	Y	24620 FQ	39150 AW	59780 TQ	FLBLS	10/01-12/01
	Sarasota-Bradenton MSA, FL	Y	26990 FQ	32980 AW	41760 TQ	FLBLS	10/01-12/01
	Tampa-St. Petersburg-Clearwater MSA, FL	Y	26310 FQ	44370 AW	66330 TQ	FLBLS	10/01-12/01
	Georgia	Y	23630 FQ	36750 AW	46700 TQ	GABLS	10/01-12/01
	Atlanta MSA, GA	Y	25210 FQ	38250 AW	48930 TQ	GABLS	10/01-12/01
	Augusta-Aiken MSA, GA-SC	Y	23280 FQ	35360 AW	52240 TQ	GABLS	10/01-12/01
	Macon MSA, GA	Y	21040 FQ	42050 AW	80000 TQ	GABLS	10/01-12/01
	Savannah MSA, GA	Y	15200 FQ	26820 AW	51390 TQ	GABLS	10/01-12/01
	Hawaii	Y	20580 FQ	39180 AW	56050 TQ	HIBLS	10/01-12/01
	Idaho	Y	36770 FQ	45580 AW	64800 TQ	IDBLS	10/01-12/01
	Illinois	Y	17020 FQ	47690 AW	73120 TQ	ILBLS	10/01-12/01
	Chicago PMSA, IL	Y	30910 FQ	53100 AW	74970 TQ	ILBLS	10/01-12/01
	Peoria-Pekin MSA, IL	Y	34790 FQ	46470 AW	58680 TQ	ILBLS	10/01-12/01
	Rockford MSA, IL	Y	33830 FQ	78330 AW		ILBLS	10/01-12/01
	Indiana	Y	21890 FQ	62680 AW		INBLS	10/01-12/01
	Evansville-Henderson MSA, IN-KY	Y	24830 FQ	36460 AW	53380 TQ	INBLS	10/01-12/01
	Gary PMSA, IN	Y	27030 FQ	55350 AW	114440 TQ	INBLS	10/01-12/01
	Indianapolis MSA, IN	Y	22590 FQ	57940 AW	88950 TQ	INBLS	10/01-12/01
	Iowa	Y	25030 FQ	44570 AW	75660 TQ	IABLS	10/01-12/01
	Des Moines MSA, IA	Y	28120 FQ	41750 AW	56870 TQ	IABLS	10/01-12/01
	Kansas	Y	26010 FQ	40150 AW	56800 TQ	KSBLS	10/01-12/01
	Kentucky	Y	19660 FQ	37900 AW	65660 TQ	KYBLS	10/01-12/01
	Louisville MSA, KY-IN	Y	19980 FQ	39720 AW	67350 TQ	KYBLS	10/01-12/01
	Louisiana	Y	13650 FQ	35820 AW	62430 TQ	LABLS	10/01-12/01
	Houma MSA, LA	Y	18590 FQ	33950 AW	46440 TQ	LABLS	10/01-12/01
	Lake Charles MSA, LA	Y	25010 FQ	36200 AW	46620 TQ	LABLS	10/01-12/01
	New Orleans MSA, LA	Y	13800 FQ	46500 AW	71230 TQ	LABLS	10/01-12/01
	Shreveport-Bossier City MSA, LA	Y	23560 FQ	32530 AW	43700 TQ	LABLS	10/01-12/01
	Maine	Y	20220 FQ	51240 AW	85450 TQ	MEBLS	10/01-12/01

AAW	Average annual wage	**AOH**	Average offered, high	**ASH**	Average starting, high	**H**	Hourly	**M**	Monthly	**S**	Special: hourly and annual
AE	Average entry wage	**AOL**	Average offered, low	**ASL**	Average starting, low	**HI**	Highest wage paid	**MTC**	Median total compensation	**TQ**	Third quartile wage
AEX	Average experienced wage	**APH**	Average pay, high range	**AW**	Average wage paid	**HR**	High end range	**MW**	Median wage paid	**W**	Weekly
AO	Average offered	**APL**	Average pay, low range	**FQ**	First quartile wage	**LR**	Low end range	**SQ**	Second quartile wage	**Y**	Yearly

Occupation/Type/Industry	Location	Per	Low	Mid	High	Source	Date
Funeral Director	Maryland	Y	24870 FQ	41510 AW	60370 TQ	MDBLS	10/01-12/01
	Baltimore PMSA, MD	Y	24160 FQ	40020 AW	58270 TQ	MDBLS	10/01-12/01
	Massachusetts	Y	39980 FQ	64200 AW	90590 TQ	MABLS	10/01-12/01
	Boston PMSA, MA-NH	Y	43170 FQ	61250 AW	87090 TQ	MABLS	10/01-12/01
	Springfield MSA, MA	Y	49190 FQ	67280 AW	92600 TQ	MABLS	10/01-12/01
	Michigan	Y	30550 FQ	51760 AW	94090 TQ	MIBLS	10/01-12/01
	Detroit PMSA, MI	Y	30620 FQ	49980 AW	94410 TQ	MIBLS	10/01-12/01
	Grand Rapids-Muskegon-Holland MSA, MI	Y	31760 FQ	58340 AW	116380 TQ	MIBLS	10/01-12/01
	Kalamazoo-Battle Creek MSA, MI	Y	32020 FQ	48300 AW	68620 TQ	MIBLS	10/01-12/01
	Lansing-East Lansing MSA, MI	Y	33860 FQ	64160 AW	120000 TQ	MIBLS	10/01-12/01
	Saginaw-Bay City-Midland MSA, MI	Y	36750 FQ	69380 AW		MIBLS	10/01-12/01
	Minnesota	Y	31400 FQ	52450 AW	84550 TQ	MNBLS	10/01-12/01
	Duluth-Superior MSA, MN-WI	Y	31810 FQ	43850 AW	54400 TQ	MNBLS	10/01-12/01
	Minneapolis-St. Paul MSA, MN-WI	Y	35490 FQ	55780 AW	86890 TQ	MNBLS	10/01-12/01
	St. Cloud MSA, MN	Y	31860 FQ	55480 AW	109700 TQ	MNBLS	10/01-12/01
	Mississippi	Y	18530 FQ	32310 AW	44370 TQ	MSBLS	10/01-12/01
	Missouri	Y	18280 FQ	40390 AW	78000 TQ	MOBLS	10/01-12/01
	Kansas City MSA, MO-KS	Y	18550 FQ	30800 AW	45850 TQ	MOBLS	10/01-12/01
	St. Louis MSA, MO-IL	Y	17460 FQ	39180 AW	57030 TQ	MOBLS	10/01-12/01
	Montana	Y	29130 FQ	40010 AW	60860 TQ	MTBLS	10/01-12/01
	Nebraska	Y	29250 FQ	47440 AW	71620 TQ	NEBLS	10/01-12/01
	Omaha MSA, NE-IA	Y	30810 FQ	50430 AW	92570 TQ	NEBLS	10/01-12/01
	Nevada	Y	26140 FQ	38660 AW	46270 TQ	NVBLS	10/01-12/01
	Las Vegas MSA, NV-AZ	Y	24920 FQ	37890 AW	45850 TQ	NVBLS	10/01-12/01
	New Hampshire	Y	26620 FQ	54190 AW	106430 TQ	NHBLS	10/01-12/01
	Portsmouth-Rochester PMSA, NH-ME	Y	24020 FQ	39670 AW	87920 TQ	NHBLS	10/01-12/01
	New Jersey	Y	34680 FQ	64510 AW	116510 TQ	NJBLS	10/01-12/01
	Bergen-Passaic PMSA, NJ	Y	37350 FQ	65300 AW	107810 TQ	NJBLS	10/01-12/01
	Jersey City PMSA, NJ	Y	38760 FQ	72420 AW	137600 TQ	NJBLS	10/01-12/01
	Middlesex-Somerset-Hunterdon PMSA, NJ	Y	29680 FQ	47490 AW	95280 TQ	NJBLS	10/01-12/01
	Monmouth-Ocean PMSA, NJ	Y	39080 FQ	63120 AW	102920 TQ	NJBLS	10/01-12/01
	Newark PMSA, NJ	Y	39520 FQ	70670 AW	134870 TQ	NJBLS	10/01-12/01
	New Mexico	Y	23760 FQ	39250 AW	56240 TQ	NMBLS	10/01-12/01
	New York	Y	32500 FQ	62890 AW	117450 TQ	NYBLS	10/01-12/01
	Albany-Schenectady-Troy MSA, NY	Y	36290 FQ	42660 AW	53720 TQ	NYBLS	10/01-12/01
	Binghamton MSA, NY	Y	16800 FQ	37250 AW	57240 TQ	NYBLS	10/01-12/01
	Buffalo-Niagara Falls MSA, NY	Y	43700 FQ	61940 AW	108370 TQ	NYBLS	10/01-12/01
	Dutchess County PMSA, NY	Y	48210 FQ	60720 AW	95020 TQ	NYBLS	10/01-12/01
	Nassau-Suffolk PMSA, NY	Y	36260 FQ	52660 AW	71480 TQ	NYBLS	10/01-12/01
	New York PMSA, NY	Y	39550 FQ	78510 AW		NYBLS	10/01-12/01
	Rochester MSA, NY	Y	41730 FQ	73030 AW	92830 TQ	NYBLS	10/01-12/01
	Utica-Rome MSA, NY	Y	29510 FQ	41420 AW	54460 TQ	NYBLS	10/01-12/01
	North Carolina	Y	25190 FQ	51840 AW	84250 TQ	NCBLS	10/01-12/01
	Charlotte-Gastonia-Rock Hill MSA, NC-SC	Y	17490 FQ	37700 AW	65750 TQ	NCBLS	10/01-12/01
	Greensboro-Winston-Salem-High Point MSA, NC	Y	39550 FQ	54810 AW	72090 TQ	NCBLS	10/01-12/01
	Hickory-Morganton-Lenoir MSA, NC	Y	20750 FQ	58020 AW	113330 TQ	NCBLS	10/01-12/01
	Raleigh-Durham-Chapel Hill MSA, NC	Y	26530 FQ	50320 AW	70470 TQ	NCBLS	10/01-12/01
	North Dakota	Y	20890 FQ	43880 AW	67820 TQ	NDBLS	10/01-12/01
	Ohio	Y	25460 FQ	53720 AW	89920 TQ	OHBLS	10/01-12/01
	Akron PMSA, OH	Y	32330 FQ	56650 AW	88370 TQ	OHBLS	10/01-12/01
	Cincinnati PMSA, OH-KY-IN	Y	21780 FQ	41310 AW	57310 TQ	OHBLS	10/01-12/01
	Cleveland-Lorain-Elyria PMSA, OH	Y	31080 FQ	44550 AW	57980 TQ	OHBLS	10/01-12/01
	Dayton-Springfield MSA, OH	Y	35990 FQ	67730 AW	92610 TQ	OHBLS	10/01-12/01
	Mansfield MSA, OH	Y	26540 FQ	50160 AW	70990 TQ	OHBLS	10/01-12/01
	Toledo MSA, OH	Y	34770 FQ	64340 AW		OHBLS	10/01-12/01
	Youngstown-Warren MSA, OH	Y	29540 FQ	43200 AW	56330 TQ	OHBLS	10/01-12/01
	Oklahoma	Y	17770 FQ	40470 AW	57430 TQ	OKBLS	10/01-12/01
	Oklahoma City MSA, OK	Y	26050 FQ	45690 AW	69880 TQ	OKBLS	10/01-12/01
	Tulsa MSA, OK	Y	38980 FQ	47100 AW	56510 TQ	OKBLS	10/01-12/01

AAW	Average annual wage	**AOH**	Average offered, high	**ASH**	Average starting, high	**H**	Hourly	**M**	Monthly	**S**	Special: hourly and annual
AE	Average entry wage	**AOL**	Average offered, low	**ASL**	Average starting, low	**HI**	Highest wage paid	**MTC**	Median total compensation	**TQ**	Third quartile wage
AEX	Average experienced wage	**APH**	Average pay, high range	**AW**	Average wage paid	**HR**	High end range	**MW**	Median wage paid	**W**	Weekly
AO	Average offered	**APL**	Average pay, low range	**FQ**	First quartile wage	**LR**	Low end range	**SQ**	Second quartile wage	**Y**	Yearly

Occupation/Type/Industry	Location	Per	Low	Mid	High	Source	Date
Funeral Director	Oregon	Y	31300 FQ	50760 AW	73690 TQ	ORBLS	10/01-12/01
	Portland-Vancouver PMSA, OR-WA	Y	27640 FQ	47500 AW	68470 TQ	ORBLS	10/01-12/01
	Salem PMSA, OR	Y	32340 FQ	47480 AW	66750 TQ	ORBLS	10/01-12/01
	Pennsylvania	Y	17650 FQ	45840 AW	72060 TQ	PABLS	10/01-12/01
	Allentown-Bethlehem-Easton MSA, PA	Y	33470 FQ	71280 AW	103820 TQ	PABLS	10/01-12/01
	Harrisburg-Lebanon-Carlisle MSA, PA	Y	31040 FQ	38530 AW	44360 TQ	PABLS	10/01-12/01
	Lancaster MSA, PA	Y	31210 FQ	51110 AW	78260 TQ	PABLS	10/01-12/01
	Philadelphia PMSA, PA-NJ	Y	14810 FQ	46870 AW	85810 TQ	PABLS	10/01-12/01
	Pittsburgh MSA, PA	Y	16110 FQ	40430 AW	56370 TQ	PABLS	10/01-12/01
	Reading MSA, PA	Y	17630 FQ	41810 AW	64790 TQ	PABLS	10/01-12/01
	Scranton-Wilkes-Barre-Hazleton MSA, PA	Y	20700 FQ	36270 AW	54400 TQ	PABLS	10/01-12/01
	York MSA, PA	Y	36170 FQ	51010 AW	82850 TQ	PABLS	10/01-12/01
	Rhode Island	Y	29690 FQ	45230 AW	66780 TQ	RIBLS	10/01-12/01
	Providence-Fall River-Warwick MSA, RI-MA	Y	33510 FQ	51440 AW	85590 TQ	RIBLS	10/01-12/01
	South Carolina	Y	24270 FQ	38320 AW	54990 TQ	SCBLS	10/01-12/01
	Charleston-North Charleston MSA, SC	Y	27360 FQ	35180 AW	51820 TQ	SCBLS	10/01-12/01
	Columbia MSA, SC	Y	27960 FQ	38530 AW	56620 TQ	SCBLS	10/01-12/01
	Greenville-Spartanburg-Anderson MSA, SC	Y	27280 FQ	40900 AW	58950 TQ	SCBLS	10/01-12/01
	South Dakota	Y	31880 FQ	42910 AW	55000 TQ	SDBLS	10/01-12/01
	Tennessee	Y	20630 FQ	43050 AW	74550 TQ	TNBLS	10/01-12/01
	Chattanooga MSA, TN-GA	Y	13110 FQ	32630 AW	57350 TQ	TNBLS	10/01-12/01
	Clarksville-Hopkinsville MSA, TN-KY	Y	20240 FQ	32230 AW	48570 TQ	TNBLS	10/01-12/01
	Johnson City-Kingsport-Bristol MSA, TN-VA	Y	20050 FQ	32260 AW	57750 TQ	TNBLS	10/01-12/01
	Knoxville MSA, TN	Y	24460 FQ	47160 AW	71310 TQ	TNBLS	10/01-12/01
	Nashville MSA, TN	Y	13410 FQ	35210 AW	56680 TQ	TNBLS	10/01-12/01
	Texas	Y	22240 FQ	40970 AW	58590 TQ	TXBLS	10/01-12/01
	Austin-San Marcos MSA, TX	Y	25970 FQ	38360 AW	54280 TQ	TXBLS	10/01-12/01
	Beaumont-Port Arthur MSA, TX	Y	31430 FQ	50080 AW	68310 TQ	TXBLS	10/01-12/01
	Dallas PMSA, TX	Y	19300 FQ	35220 AW	54540 TQ	TXBLS	10/01-12/01
	Fort Worth-Arlington PMSA, TX	Y	30350 FQ	43650 AW	57710 TQ	TXBLS	10/01-12/01
	Houston PMSA, TX	Y	28250 FQ	45390 AW	60750 TQ	TXBLS	10/01-12/01
	McAllen-Edinburg-Mission MSA, TX	Y	20700 FQ	33040 AW	43790 TQ	TXBLS	10/01-12/01
	San Antonio MSA, TX	Y	25250 FQ	49140 AW	83480 TQ	TXBLS	10/01-12/01
	Waco MSA, TX	Y	20220 FQ	38070 AW	65160 TQ	TXBLS	10/01-12/01
	Utah	Y	36720 FQ	55230 AW	83830 TQ	UTBLS	10/01-12/01
	Salt Lake City-Ogden MSA, UT	Y	39130 FQ	60330 AW	86500 TQ	UTBLS	10/01-12/01
	Vermont	Y	30570 FQ	40760 AW	56330 TQ	VTBLS	10/01-12/01
	Virginia	Y	29510 FQ	51780 AW	85520 TQ	VABLS	10/01-12/01
	Norfolk-Virginia Beach-Newport News MSA, VA-NC	Y	14420 FQ	44550 AW	64060 TQ	VABLS	10/01-12/01
	Richmond-Petersburg MSA, VA	Y	49040 FQ	73570 AW	135280 TQ	VABLS	10/01-12/01
	Washington	Y	34290 FQ	56630 AW	77440 TQ	WABLS	10/01-12/01
	West Virginia	Y	30670 FQ	43120 AW	55350 TQ	WVBLS	10/01-12/01
	Charleston MSA, WV	Y	19560 FQ	34130 AW	45840 TQ	WVBLS	10/01-12/01
	Huntington-Ashland MSA, WV-KY-OH	Y	20290 FQ	42010 AW	61980 TQ	WVBLS	10/01-12/01
	Wisconsin	Y	31190 FQ	56930 AW	84040 TQ	WIBLS	10/01-12/01
	Appleton-Oshkosh-Neenah MSA, WI	Y	31750 FQ	50910 AW	101570 TQ	WIBLS	10/01-12/01
	Milwaukee-Waukesha PMSA, WI	Y	38910 FQ	63330 AW	75760 TQ	WIBLS	10/01-12/01
	Wyoming	Y	27580 FQ	43970 AW	68180 TQ	WYBLS	10/01-12/01
	Puerto Rico	Y	16710 FQ	31140 AW	55060 TQ	PRBLS	10/01-12/01
Furnace, Kiln, Oven, Drier, and Kettle Operator and Tender	Alabama	H	8.55 FQ	15.09 AW	21.97 TQ	ALBLS	10/01-12/01
	Birmingham MSA, AL	H	6.84 FQ	16.64 AW	25.41 TQ	ALBLS	10/01-12/01

AAW	Average annual wage	AOH	Average offered, high	ASH	Average starting, high	H	Hourly	M	Monthly	S	Special: hourly and annual
AE	Average entry wage	AOL	Average offered, low	ASL	Average starting, low	HI	Highest wage paid	MTC	Median total compensation	TQ	Third quartile wage
AEX	Average experienced wage	APH	Average pay, high range	AW	Average wage paid	HR	High end range	MW	Median wage paid	W	Weekly
AO	Average offered	APL	Average pay, low range	FQ	First quartile wage	LR	Low end range	SQ	Second quartile wage	Y	Yearly

Occupation/Type/Industry	Location	Per	Low	Mid	High	Source	Date
Furnace, Kiln, Oven, Drier, and Kettle Operator and Tender	Mobile MSA, AL	H	8.95 FQ	13.04 AW	18.51 TQ	ALBLS	10/01-12/01
	Montgomery MSA, AL	H	6.55 FQ	11.32 AW	17.95 TQ	ALBLS	10/01-12/01
	Arizona	H	7.83 FQ	11.25 AW	17.84 TQ	AZBLS	10/01-12/01
	Phoenix-Mesa MSA, AZ	H	7.97 FQ	10.95 AW	15.80 TQ	AZBLS	10/01-12/01
	Arkansas	H	7.37 FQ	12.57 AW	17.47 TQ	ARBLS	10/01-12/01
	Little Rock-North Little Rock MSA, AR	H	9.73 FQ	11.78 AW	13.58 TQ	ARBLS	10/01-12/01
	California	H	7.02 FQ	12.23 AW	17.81 TQ	CABLS	10/01-12/01
	Los Angeles-Long Beach PMSA, CA	H	6.66 FQ	11.72 AW	17.77 TQ	CABLS	10/01-12/01
	Oakland PMSA, CA	H	9.16 FQ	14.86 AW	20.48 TQ	CABLS	10/01-12/01
	Orange County PMSA, CA	H	7.99 FQ	10.93 AW	13.51 TQ	CABLS	10/01-12/01
	Riverside-San Bernardino PMSA, CA	H	6.68 FQ	13.41 AW	20.96 TQ	CABLS	10/01-12/01
	Sacramento PMSA, CA	H	12.70 FQ	15.09 AW	17.52 TQ	CABLS	10/01-12/01
	San Diego MSA, CA	H	7.85 FQ	10.77 AW	15.22 TQ	CABLS	10/01-12/01
	San Francisco PMSA, CA	H	12.78 FQ	15.66 AW	17.92 TQ	CABLS	10/01-12/01
	San Jose PMSA, CA	H	8.50 FQ	13.57 AW	20.27 TQ	CABLS	10/01-12/01
	Stockton-Lodi MSA, CA	H	7.86 FQ	12.44 AW	17.46 TQ	CABLS	10/01-12/01
	Colorado	H	9.39 FQ	13.41 AW	18.82 TQ	COBLS	10/01-12/01
	Connecticut	H	9.47 FQ	14.03 AW	20.19 TQ	CTBLS	10/01-12/01
	Hartford MSA, CT	H	9.78 FQ	14.69 AW	23.87 TQ	CTBLS	10/01-12/01
	New Haven-Meriden PMSA, CT	H	9.14 FQ	12.81 AW	16.51 TQ	CTBLS	10/01-12/01
	Delaware	H	10.32 FQ	14.26 AW	16.96 TQ	DEBLS	10/01-12/01
	Wilmington-Newark PMSA, DE-MD	H	10.38 FQ	14.27 AW	17.30 TQ	DEBLS	10/01-12/01
	Washington PMSA, DC-MD-VA-WV	H	8.41 FQ	12.67 AW	17.54 TQ	DCBLS	10/01-12/01
	Florida	H	7.50 FQ	12.30 AW	18.33 TQ	FLBLS	10/01-12/01
	Jacksonville MSA, FL	H	9.36 FQ	13.34 AW	17.53 TQ	FLBLS	10/01-12/01
	Lakeland-Winter Haven MSA, FL	H	6.59 FQ	12.97 AW	24.42 TQ	FLBLS	10/01-12/01
	Miami PMSA, FL	H	6.32 FQ	9.53 AW	13.32 TQ	FLBLS	10/01-12/01
	Tampa-St. Petersburg-Clearwater MSA, FL	H	6.31 FQ	11.12 AW	16.60 TQ	FLBLS	10/01-12/01
	Georgia	H	7.09 FQ	11.65 AW	18.61 TQ	GABLS	10/01-12/01
	Atlanta MSA, GA	H	9.01 FQ	12.72 AW	19.51 TQ	GABLS	10/01-12/01
	Augusta-Aiken MSA, GA-SC	H	12.12 FQ	16.97 AW	24.04 TQ	GABLS	10/01-12/01
	Columbus MSA, GA-AL	H	8.96 FQ	13.93 AW	19.64 TQ	GABLS	10/01-12/01
	Macon MSA, GA	H	9.93 FQ	15.93 AW	21.32 TQ	GABLS	10/01-12/01
	Savannah MSA, GA	H	12.07 FQ	17.77 AW	24.99 TQ	GABLS	10/01-12/01
	Idaho	H	12.32 FQ	16.12 AW	21.13 TQ	IDBLS	10/01-12/01
	Illinois	H	8.22 FQ	13.66 AW	19.56 TQ	ILBLS	10/01-12/01
	Rockford MSA, IL	H	8.50 FQ	14.01 AW	22.16 TQ	ILBLS	10/01-12/01
	Indiana	H	8.97 FQ	16.12 AW	23.13 TQ	INBLS	10/01-12/01
	Elkhart-Goshen MSA, IN	H	6.54 FQ	10.99 AW	13.72 TQ	INBLS	10/01-12/01
	Fort Wayne MSA, IN	H	15.30 FQ	19.15 AW	22.19 TQ	INBLS	10/01-12/01
	Gary PMSA, IN	H	15.76 FQ	19.70 AW	24.57 TQ	INBLS	10/01-12/01
	Indianapolis MSA, IN	H	9.85 FQ	16.71 AW	25.08 TQ	INBLS	10/01-12/01
	Iowa	H	8.96 FQ	13.50 AW	18.82 TQ	IABLS	10/01-12/01
	Des Moines MSA, IA	H	8.97 FQ	13.25 AW	18.53 TQ	IABLS	10/01-12/01
	Kansas	H	9.68 FQ	14.21 AW	19.57 TQ	KSBLS	10/01-12/01
	Kentucky	H	9.11 FQ	15.52 AW	23.07 TQ	KYBLS	10/01-12/01
	Louisville MSA, KY-IN	H	8.10 FQ	14.78 AW	24.76 TQ	KYBLS	10/01-12/01
	Louisiana	H	7.37 FQ	12.96 AW	20.29 TQ	LABLS	10/01-12/01
	Baton Rouge MSA, LA	H	8.55 FQ	17.04 AW	25.69 TQ	LABLS	10/01-12/01
	Lafayette MSA, LA	H	5.60 FQ	8.74 AW	13.39 TQ	LABLS	10/01-12/01
	New Orleans MSA, LA	H	6.90 FQ	13.01 AW	21.35 TQ	LABLS	10/01-12/01
	Maine	H	9.94 FQ	14.93 AW	25.02 TQ	MEBLS	10/01-12/01
	Maryland	H	10.88 FQ	15.37 AW	20.51 TQ	MDBLS	10/01-12/01
	Baltimore PMSA, MD	H	12.00 FQ	15.98 AW	20.84 TQ	MDBLS	10/01-12/01
	Massachusetts	H	9.68 FQ	13.52 AW	18.00 TQ	MABLS	10/01-12/01
	Boston PMSA, MA-NH	H	9.58 FQ	13.50 AW	17.87 TQ	MABLS	10/01-12/01
	Worcester PMSA, MA-CT	H	9.58 FQ	13.36 AW	16.86 TQ	MABLS	10/01-12/01
	Michigan	H	11.34 FQ	17.08 AW	25.62 TQ	MIBLS	10/01-12/01
	Detroit PMSA, MI	H	13.56 FQ	20.59 AW	26.56 TQ	MIBLS	10/01-12/01
	Grand Rapids-Muskegon-Holland MSA, MI	H	11.83 FQ	15.59 AW	20.20 TQ	MIBLS	10/01-12/01
	Minnesota	H	12.43 FQ	18.14 AW	23.89 TQ	MNBLS	10/01-12/01
	Duluth-Superior MSA, MN-WI	H	15.61 FQ	19.45 AW	22.30 TQ	MNBLS	10/01-12/01

AAW	Average annual wage	**AOH**	Average offered, high	**ASH**	Average starting, high	**H**	Hourly	**M**	Monthly	**S**	Special: hourly and annual
AE	Average entry wage	**AOL**	Average offered, low	**ASL**	Average starting, low	**HI**	Highest wage paid	**MTC**	Median total compensation	**TQ**	Third quartile wage
AEX	Average experienced wage	**APH**	Average pay, high range	**AW**	Average wage paid	**HR**	High end range	**MW**	Median wage paid	**W**	Weekly
AO	Average offered	**APL**	Average pay, low range	**FQ**	First quartile wage	**LR**	Low end range	**SQ**	Second quartile wage	**Y**	Yearly

Occupation/Type/Industry	Location	Per	Low	Mid	High	Source	Date
Furnace, Kiln, Oven, Drier, and Kettle Operator and Tender	Mississippi	H	8.80 FQ	12.59 AW	18.97 TQ	MSBLS	10/01-12/01
	Jackson MSA, MS	H	7.34 FQ	9.50 AW	12.14 TQ	MSBLS	10/01-12/01
	Missouri	H	8.60 FQ	12.48 AW	16.92 TQ	MOBLS	10/01-12/01
	Kansas City MSA, MO-KS	H	9.45 FQ	13.24 AW	19.95 TQ	MOBLS	10/01-12/01
	St. Louis MSA, MO-IL	H	9.00 FQ	13.73 AW	17.95 TQ	MOBLS	10/01-12/01
	Montana	H	10.53 FQ	13.38 AW	16.43 TQ	MTBLS	10/01-12/01
	Omaha MSA, NE-IA	H	11.52 FQ	16.78 AW	23.37 TQ	NEBLS	10/01-12/01
	Nevada	H	14.83 FQ	18.77 AW	22.12 TQ	NVBLS	10/01-12/01
	Las Vegas MSA, NV-AZ	H	11.29 FQ	17.50 AW	21.82 TQ	NVBLS	10/01-12/01
	New Hampshire	H	10.10 FQ	14.60 AW	20.74 TQ	NHBLS	10/01-12/01
	New Jersey	H	6.13 FQ	13.00 AW	18.61 TQ	NJBLS	10/01-12/01
	Bergen-Passaic PMSA, NJ	H	5.71 FQ	9.34 AW	13.05 TQ	NJBLS	10/01-12/01
	Middlesex-Somerset-Hunterdon PMSA, NJ	H	6.34 FQ	14.27 AW	20.24 TQ	NJBLS	10/01-12/01
	Newark PMSA, NJ	H	5.76 FQ	11.97 AW	17.90 TQ	NJBLS	10/01-12/01
	New Mexico	H	7.42 FQ	11.40 AW	22.30 TQ	NMBLS	10/01-12/01
	Albuquerque MSA, NM	H	7.63 FQ	12.30 AW	25.01 TQ	NMBLS	10/01-12/01
	New York	H	10.28 FQ	16.03 AW	21.58 TQ	NYBLS	10/01-12/01
	Albany-Schenectady-Troy MSA, NY	H	14.10 FQ	17.99 AW	21.66 TQ	NYBLS	10/01-12/01
	Buffalo-Niagara Falls MSA, NY	H	8.36 FQ	13.37 AW	19.53 TQ	NYBLS	10/01-12/01
	New York PMSA, NY	H	7.65 FQ	11.40 AW	16.81 TQ	NYBLS	10/01-12/01
	Rochester MSA, NY	H	11.63 FQ	18.15 AW	22.45 TQ	NYBLS	10/01-12/01
	Syracuse MSA, NY	H	11.79 FQ	14.56 AW	18.36 TQ	NYBLS	10/01-12/01
	North Carolina	H	8.66 FQ	12.24 AW	16.81 TQ	NCBLS	10/01-12/01
	Charlotte-Gastonia-Rock Hill MSA, NC-SC	H	8.60 FQ	13.00 AW	21.05 TQ	NCBLS	10/01-12/01
	Greensboro-Winston-Salem-High Point MSA, NC	H	8.83 FQ	11.03 AW	14.12 TQ	NCBLS	10/01-12/01
	Raleigh-Durham-Chapel Hill MSA, NC	H	7.79 FQ	11.19 AW	15.54 TQ	NCBLS	10/01-12/01
	North Dakota	H	8.20 FQ	12.52 AW	19.46 TQ	NDBLS	10/01-12/01
	Ohio	H	10.19 FQ	14.67 AW	18.73 TQ	OHBLS	10/01-12/01
	Canton-Massillon MSA, OH	H	10.72 FQ	13.60 AW	16.87 TQ	OHBLS	10/01-12/01
	Cincinnati PMSA, OH-KY-IN	H	10.37 FQ	13.63 AW	17.03 TQ	OHBLS	10/01-12/01
	Cleveland-Lorain-Elyria PMSA, OH	H	10.92 FQ	14.94 AW	21.08 TQ	OHBLS	10/01-12/01
	Columbus MSA, OH	H	10.30 FQ	14.67 AW	17.59 TQ	OHBLS	10/01-12/01
	Dayton-Springfield MSA, OH	H	10.72 FQ	15.17 AW	18.71 TQ	OHBLS	10/01-12/01
	Hamilton-Middletown PMSA, OH	H	6.70 FQ	13.06 AW	17.63 TQ	OHBLS	10/01-12/01
	Mansfield MSA, OH	H	13.16 FQ	16.56 AW	20.46 TQ	OHBLS	10/01-12/01
	Toledo MSA, OH	H	12.80 FQ	15.47 AW	18.22 TQ	OHBLS	10/01-12/01
	Youngstown-Warren MSA, OH	H	6.15 FQ	12.73 AW	20.66 TQ	OHBLS	10/01-12/01
	Oklahoma	H	9.08 FQ	15.21 AW	20.80 TQ	OKBLS	10/01-12/01
	Tulsa MSA, OK	H	9.75 FQ	14.88 AW	20.45 TQ	OKBLS	10/01-12/01
	Oregon	H	10.34 FQ	14.89 AW	19.64 TQ	ORBLS	10/01-12/01
	Eugene-Springfield MSA, OR	H	9.48 FQ	14.15 AW	17.57 TQ	ORBLS	10/01-12/01
	Medford-Ashland MSA, OR	H	11.56 FQ	14.33 AW	17.16 TQ	ORBLS	10/01-12/01
	Portland-Vancouver PMSA, OR-WA	H	9.02 FQ	15.04 AW	21.98 TQ	ORBLS	10/01-12/01
	Pennsylvania	H	9.57 FQ	13.86 AW	19.02 TQ	PABLS	10/01-12/01
	Allentown-Bethlehem-Easton MSA, PA	H	10.31 FQ	15.53 AW	20.83 TQ	PABLS	10/01-12/01
	Harrisburg-Lebanon-Carlisle MSA, PA	H	10.97 FQ	15.57 AW	20.77 TQ	PABLS	10/01-12/01
	Philadelphia PMSA, PA-NJ	H	11.03 FQ	13.26 AW	16.55 TQ	PABLS	10/01-12/01
	Pittsburgh MSA, PA	H	9.51 FQ	13.76 AW	18.34 TQ	PABLS	10/01-12/01
	Reading MSA, PA	H	9.81 FQ	14.69 AW	20.43 TQ	PABLS	10/01-12/01
	Scranton-Wilkes-Barre-Hazleton MSA, PA	H	11.24 FQ	16.29 AW	21.18 TQ	PABLS	10/01-12/01
	York MSA, PA	H	11.35 FQ	14.57 AW	17.93 TQ	PABLS	10/01-12/01
	Rhode Island	H	8.73 FQ	13.74 AW	17.24 TQ	RIBLS	10/01-12/01
	Providence-Fall River-Warwick MSA, RI-MA	H	8.57 FQ	13.18 AW	16.84 TQ	RIBLS	10/01-12/01
	South Carolina	H	7.70 FQ	13.80 AW	20.84 TQ	SCBLS	10/01-12/01
	Charleston-North Charleston MSA, SC	H	8.72 FQ	16.48 AW	21.22 TQ	SCBLS	10/01-12/01
	Columbia MSA, SC	H	11.40 FQ	14.34 AW	19.48 TQ	SCBLS	10/01-12/01

Occupation/Type/Industry	Location	Per	Low	Mid	High	Source	Date
Furnace, Kiln, Oven, Drier, and Kettle Operator and Tender	Greenville-Spartanburg-Anderson MSA, SC	H	9.23 FQ	14.83 AW	21.23 TQ	SCBLS	10/01-12/01
	Tennessee	H	9.11 FQ	12.24 AW	16.00 TQ	TNBLS	10/01-12/01
	Chattanooga MSA, TN-GA	H	8.81 FQ	12.59 AW	19.69 TQ	TNBLS	10/01-12/01
	Clarksville-Hopkinsville MSA, TN-KY	H	7.86 FQ	11.07 AW	13.48 TQ	TNBLS	10/01-12/01
	Johnson City-Kingsport-Bristol MSA, TN-VA	H	10.34 FQ	13.06 AW	16.25 TQ	TNBLS	10/01-12/01
	Memphis MSA, TN-AR-MS	H	7.03 FQ	9.87 AW	12.89 TQ	TNBLS	10/01-12/01
	Texas	H	7.29 FQ	12.52 AW	20.83 TQ	TXBLS	10/01-12/01
	Austin-San Marcos MSA, TX	H	6.49 FQ	11.05 AW	18.05 TQ	TXBLS	10/01-12/01
	Dallas PMSA, TX	H	8.38 FQ	13.15 AW	20.83 TQ	TXBLS	10/01-12/01
	Fort Worth-Arlington PMSA, TX	H	7.24 FQ	10.95 AW	16.91 TQ	TXBLS	10/01-12/01
	Houston PMSA, TX	H	5.73 FQ	13.54 AW	26.06 TQ	TXBLS	10/01-12/01
	Longview-Marshall MSA, TX	H	6.06 FQ	7.74 AW	9.04 TQ	TXBLS	10/01-12/01
	San Antonio MSA, TX	H	7.37 FQ	11.99 AW	18.59 TQ	TXBLS	10/01-12/01
	Utah	H	8.90 FQ	14.59 AW	21.35 TQ	UTBLS	10/01-12/01
	Vermont	H	8.99 FQ	11.70 AW	14.99 TQ	VTBLS	10/01-12/01
	Virginia	H	8.49 FQ	13.10 AW	18.98 TQ	VABLS	10/01-12/01
	Lynchburg MSA, VA	H	8.04 FQ	11.90 AW	14.51 TQ	VABLS	10/01-12/01
	Washington	H	9.70 FQ	15.25 AW	21.04 TQ	WABLS	10/01-12/01
	Seattle-Bellevue-Everett PMSA, WA	H	8.67 FQ	13.85 AW	20.71 TQ	WABLS	10/01-12/01
	Tacoma PMSA, WA	H	11.48 FQ	15.82 AW	21.09 TQ	WABLS	10/01-12/01
	West Virginia	H	7.64 FQ	11.75 AW	17.47 TQ	WVBLS	10/01-12/01
	Huntington-Ashland MSA, WV-KY-OH	H	8.61 FQ	11.58 AW	15.13 TQ	WVBLS	10/01-12/01
	Wisconsin	H	9.47 FQ	13.67 AW	19.48 TQ	WIBLS	10/01-12/01
	Appleton-Oshkosh-Neenah MSA, WI	H	11.32 FQ	16.10 AW	22.01 TQ	WIBLS	10/01-12/01
	Milwaukee-Waukesha PMSA, WI	H	9.92 FQ	14.27 AW	19.92 TQ	WIBLS	10/01-12/01
	Wyoming	H	11.52 FQ	18.78 AW	26.06 TQ	WYBLS	10/01-12/01
	Puerto Rico	H	7.02 FQ	10.48 AW	13.73 TQ	PRBLS	10/01-12/01
Furniture Finisher	Alabama	H	7.36 FQ	9.76 AW	12.57 TQ	ALBLS	10/01-12/01
	Arizona	H	6.94 FQ	11.51 AW	17.19 TQ	AZBLS	10/01-12/01
	Arkansas	H	6.90 FQ	9.91 AW	14.91 TQ	ARBLS	10/01-12/01
	California	H	6.73 FQ	10.68 AW	16.72 TQ	CABLS	10/01-12/01
	Colorado	H	8.63 FQ	13.80 AW	18.94 TQ	COBLS	10/01-12/01
	Connecticut	H	10.67 FQ	15.43 AW	21.09 TQ	CTBLS	10/01-12/01
	Florida	H	7.43 FQ	11.50 AW	16.47 TQ	FLBLS	10/01-12/01
	Georgia	H	7.47 FQ	11.63 AW	16.38 TQ	GABLS	10/01-12/01
	Hawaii	H	6.97 FQ	10.08 AW	14.83 TQ	HIBLS	10/01-12/01
	Idaho	H	7.10 FQ	10.06 AW	13.98 TQ	IDBLS	10/01-12/01
	Illinois	H	7.20 FQ	12.13 AW	19.63 TQ	ILBLS	10/01-12/01
	Indiana	H	8.60 FQ	11.84 AW	15.80 TQ	INBLS	10/01-12/01
	Iowa	H	6.05 FQ	8.77 AW	12.17 TQ	IABLS	10/01-12/01
	Kansas	H	8.47 FQ	12.61 AW	17.42 TQ	KSBLS	10/01-12/01
	Kentucky	H	7.60 FQ	10.73 AW	15.18 TQ	KYBLS	10/01-12/01
	Louisiana	H	5.92 FQ	9.96 AW	13.75 TQ	LABLS	10/01-12/01
	Maine	H	7.29 FQ	10.31 AW	14.54 TQ	MEBLS	10/01-12/01
	Maryland	H	8.49 FQ	13.07 AW	18.31 TQ	MDBLS	10/01-12/01
	Massachusetts	H	7.25 FQ	12.05 AW	18.53 TQ	MABLS	10/01-12/01
	Michigan	H	9.01 FQ	13.90 AW	19.40 TQ	MIBLS	10/01-12/01
	Minnesota	H	9.30 FQ	13.63 AW	20.61 TQ	MNBLS	10/01-12/01
	Mississippi	H	7.36 FQ	9.65 AW	12.91 TQ	MSBLS	10/01-12/01
	Missouri	H	7.32 FQ	10.57 AW	15.83 TQ	MOBLS	10/01-12/01
	Montana	H	6.75 FQ	10.30 AW	14.68 TQ	MTBLS	10/01-12/01
	Nebraska	H	7.28 FQ	10.98 AW	15.16 TQ	NEBLS	10/01-12/01
	Nevada	H	6.45 FQ	10.52 AW	16.15 TQ	NVBLS	10/01-12/01
	New Hampshire	H	8.83 FQ	15.31 AW	21.73 TQ	NHBLS	10/01-12/01
	New Jersey	H	8.29 FQ	13.71 AW	20.68 TQ	NJBLS	10/01-12/01
	New Mexico	H	7.43 FQ	10.50 AW	14.48 TQ	NMBLS	10/01-12/01
	New York	H	6.73 FQ	11.95 AW	17.95 TQ	NYBLS	10/01-12/01
	North Carolina	H	7.84 FQ	10.72 AW	13.85 TQ	NCBLS	10/01-12/01
	Ohio	H	8.00 FQ	12.00 AW	16.24 TQ	OHBLS	10/01-12/01
	Oklahoma	H	7.50 FQ	11.13 AW	15.77 TQ	OKBLS	10/01-12/01
	Oregon	H	6.94 FQ	10.75 AW	14.96 TQ	ORBLS	10/01-12/01
	Pennsylvania	H	7.43 FQ	11.99 AW	16.94 TQ	PABLS	10/01-12/01

AAW	Average annual wage	**AOH**	Average offered, high	**ASH**	Average starting, high	**H**	Hourly	**M**	Monthly	**S**	Special: hourly and annual
AE	Average entry wage	**AOL**	Average offered, low	**ASL**	Average starting, low	**HI**	Highest wage paid	**MTC**	Median total compensation	**TQ**	Third quartile wage
AEX	Average experienced wage	**APH**	Average pay, high range	**AW**	Average wage paid	**HR**	High end range	**MW**	Median wage paid	**W**	Weekly
AO	Average offered	**APL**	Average pay, low range	**FQ**	First quartile wage	**LR**	Low end range	**SQ**	Second quartile wage	**Y**	Yearly

Occupation/Type/Industry	Location	Per	Low	Mid	High	Source	Date
Furniture Finisher	Rhode Island	H	7.66 FQ	12.76 AW	19.59 TQ	RIBLS	10/01-12/01
	South Carolina	H	7.24 FQ	10.26 AW	15.41 TQ	SCBLS	10/01-12/01
	Tennessee	H	7.13 FQ	10.31 AW	13.62 TQ	TNBLS	10/01-12/01
	Texas	H	6.88 FQ	10.75 AW	16.03 TQ	TXBLS	10/01-12/01
	Utah	H	7.82 FQ	12.64 AW	18.97 TQ	UTBLS	10/01-12/01
	Vermont	H	7.84 FQ	10.93 AW	14.53 TQ	VTBLS	10/01-12/01
	Virginia	H	7.38 FQ	11.44 AW	16.75 TQ	VABLS	10/01-12/01
	Washington	H	8.94 FQ	13.03 AW	18.25 TQ	WABLS	10/01-12/01
	West Virginia	H	7.22 FQ	9.53 AW	11.42 TQ	WVBLS	10/01-12/01
	Wisconsin	H	7.57 FQ	10.56 AW	14.76 TQ	WIBLS	10/01-12/01
	Puerto Rico	H	5.38 FQ	6.60 AW	8.02 TQ	PRBLS	10/01-12/01
Gaming and Sports Book Writer and Runner	Alaska	H	8.96 FQ	11.72 AW	19.54 TQ	AKBLS	10/01-12/01
	Arizona	H	7.12 FQ	9.36 AW	12.41 TQ	AZBLS	10/01-12/01
	California	H	6.58 FQ	8.52 AW	10.44 TQ	CABLS	10/01-12/01
	Colorado	H	6.81 FQ	8.26 AW	10.57 TQ	COBLS	10/01-12/01
	Florida	H	6.03 FQ	9.07 AW	12.75 TQ	FLBLS	10/01-12/01
	Illinois	H	6.29 FQ	11.25 AW	19.35 TQ	ILBLS	10/01-12/01
	Iowa	H	5.63 FQ	8.20 AW	11.37 TQ	IABLS	10/01-12/01
	Louisiana	H	7.40 FQ	9.25 AW	10.91 TQ	LABLS	10/01-12/01
	Maryland	H	5.85 FQ	10.23 AW	16.72 TQ	MDBLS	10/01-12/01
	Massachusetts	H	6.83 FQ	9.48 AW	16.13 TQ	MABLS	10/01-12/01
	Minnesota	H	5.84 FQ	8.36 AW	11.07 TQ	MNBLS	10/01-12/01
	Mississippi	H	5.79 FQ	7.78 AW	10.56 TQ	MSBLS	10/01-12/01
	Montana	H	5.72 FQ	6.95 AW	8.39 TQ	MTBLS	10/01-12/01
	Nebraska	H	5.91 FQ	8.00 AW	10.50 TQ	NEBLS	10/01-12/01
	Nevada	H	6.77 FQ	9.07 AW	11.56 TQ	NVBLS	10/01-12/01
	New Hampshire	H	7.84 FQ	12.96 AW	17.00 TQ	NHBLS	10/01-12/01
	New Jersey	H	7.25 FQ	9.50 AW	12.22 TQ	NJBLS	10/01-12/01
	New York	H	8.71 FQ	14.89 AW	19.77 TQ	NYBLS	10/01-12/01
	North Dakota	H	5.68 FQ	7.36 AW	9.70 TQ	NDBLS	10/01-12/01
	Oregon	H	6.90 FQ	8.44 AW	10.39 TQ	ORBLS	10/01-12/01
	Pennsylvania	H	5.86 FQ	7.24 AW	8.87 TQ	PABLS	10/01-12/01
	South Dakota	H	6.96 FQ	8.21 AW	10.36 TQ	SDBLS	10/01-12/01
	Texas	H	5.77 FQ	10.35 AW	19.10 TQ	TXBLS	10/01-12/01
	Washington	H	6.85 FQ	8.63 AW	13.54 TQ	WABLS	10/01-12/01
Gaming Cage Worker	Arizona	H	8.34 FQ	10.45 AW	13.34 TQ	AZBLS	10/01-12/01
	California	H	8.24 FQ	11.26 AW	15.95 TQ	CABLS	10/01-12/01
	Colorado	H	9.66 FQ	12.56 AW	16.10 TQ	COBLS	10/01-12/01
	Florida	H	7.93 FQ	10.89 AW	14.18 TQ	FLBLS	10/01-12/01
	Idaho	H	6.08 FQ	10.11 AW	16.04 TQ	IDBLS	10/01-12/01
	Illinois	H	8.45 FQ	10.92 AW	13.52 TQ	ILBLS	10/01-12/01
	Indiana	H	8.95 FQ	10.36 AW	12.99 TQ	INBLS	10/01-12/01
	Iowa	H	7.77 FQ	9.80 AW	12.20 TQ	IABLS	10/01-12/01
	Kansas	H	7.52 FQ	10.18 AW	13.84 TQ	KSBLS	10/01-12/01
	Louisiana	H	7.14 FQ	9.49 AW	12.09 TQ	LABLS	10/01-12/01
	Michigan	H	7.48 FQ	10.04 AW	12.90 TQ	MIBLS	10/01-12/01
	Mississippi	H	7.46 FQ	10.13 AW	13.71 TQ	MSBLS	10/01-12/01
	Missouri	H	7.64 FQ	10.36 AW	13.39 TQ	MOBLS	10/01-12/01
	Nevada	H	7.72 FQ	11.36 AW	15.59 TQ	NVBLS	10/01-12/01
	New Hampshire	H	7.53 FQ	10.15 AW	13.32 TQ	NHBLS	10/01-12/01
	New Jersey	H	8.45 FQ	11.14 AW	14.71 TQ	NJBLS	10/01-12/01
	New Mexico	H	7.45 FQ	8.98 AW	11.17 TQ	NMBLS	10/01-12/01
	New York	H	7.81 FQ	11.06 AW	14.58 TQ	NYBLS	10/01-12/01
	Ohio	H	7.57 FQ	12.25 AW	17.18 TQ	OHBLS	10/01-12/01
	South Dakota	H	6.94 FQ	8.56 AW	10.89 TQ	SDBLS	10/01-12/01
	Tennessee	H	7.11 FQ	9.68 AW	13.49 TQ	TNBLS	10/01-12/01
	Washington	H	7.76 FQ	9.90 AW	13.07 TQ	WABLS	10/01-12/01
	West Virginia	H	8.55 FQ	10.16 AW	13.03 TQ	WVBLS	10/01-12/01
	Wisconsin	H	7.50 FQ	10.59 AW	13.42 TQ	WIBLS	10/01-12/01
	Puerto Rico	H	5.98 FQ	7.57 AW	8.79 TQ	PRBLS	10/01-12/01
Gaming Change Person and Booth Cashier	Arizona	Y	15940 FQ	21370 AW	27480 TQ	AZBLS	10/01-12/01
	California	Y	13610 FQ	19340 AW	27020 TQ	CABLS	10/01-12/01
	Colorado	Y	14600 FQ	22020 AW	28780 TQ	COBLS	10/01-12/01
	Florida	Y	13260 FQ	19350 AW	26600 TQ	FLBLS	10/01-12/01
	Georgia	Y	12400 FQ	18220 AW	23870 TQ	GABLS	10/01-12/01
	Illinois	Y	15490 FQ	21940 AW	30410 TQ	ILBLS	10/01-12/01
	Indiana	Y	14440 FQ	19560 AW	25580 TQ	INBLS	10/01-12/01

AAW	Average annual wage	**AOH**	Average offered, high	**ASH**	Average starting, high	**H**	Hourly	**M**	Monthly	**S**	Special: hourly and annual
AE	Average entry wage	**AOL**	Average offered, low	**ASL**	Average starting, low	**HI**	Highest wage paid	**MTC**	Median total compensation	**TQ**	Third quartile wage
AEX	Average experienced wage	**APH**	Average pay, high range	**AW**	Average wage paid	**HR**	High end range	**MW**	Median wage paid	**W**	Weekly
AO	Average offered	**APL**	Average pay, low range	**FQ**	First quartile wage	**LR**	Low end range	**SQ**	Second quartile wage	**Y**	Yearly

Occupation/Type/Industry	Location	Per	Low	Mid	High	Source	Date
Gaming Change Person and Booth Cashier	Iowa	Y	15150 FQ	19370 AW	23890 TQ	IABLS	10/01-12/01
	Louisiana	Y	14600 FQ	18070 AW	22650 TQ	LABLS	10/01-12/01
	Maine	Y	11910 FQ	14820 AW	21220 TQ	MEBLS	10/01-12/01
	Maryland	Y	12500 FQ	18470 AW	23590 TQ	MDBLS	10/01-12/01
	Michigan	Y	14480 FQ	18670 AW	22350 TQ	MIBLS	10/01-12/01
	Minnesota	Y	12330 FQ	18390 AW	24330 TQ	MNBLS	10/01-12/01
	Mississippi	Y	14280 FQ	19030 AW	25420 TQ	MSBLS	10/01-12/01
	Missouri	Y	14630 FQ	19390 AW	26600 TQ	MOBLS	10/01-12/01
	Montana	Y	11640 FQ	14120 AW	17410 TQ	MTBLS	10/01-12/01
	Nevada	Y	12650 FQ	18970 AW	26170 TQ	NVBLS	10/01-12/01
	New Jersey	Y	15720 FQ	20960 AW	27240 TQ	NJBLS	10/01-12/01
	New Mexico	Y	13100 FQ	17010 AW	21680 TQ	NMBLS	10/01-12/01
	New York	Y	12230 FQ	18150 AW	25670 TQ	NYBLS	10/01-12/01
	Oklahoma	Y	11840 FQ	14700 AW	17800 TQ	OKBLS	10/01-12/01
	Oregon	Y	16430 FQ	25150 AW	35980 TQ	ORBLS	10/01-12/01
	South Carolina	Y	11580 FQ	16770 AW	27370 TQ	SCBLS	10/01-12/01
	South Dakota	Y	12890 FQ	16050 AW	18630 TQ	SDBLS	10/01-12/01
	Tennessee	Y	14620 FQ	21030 AW	27340 TQ	TNBLS	10/01-12/01
	Texas	Y	12520 FQ	26200 AW	53680 TQ	TXBLS	10/01-12/01
	Washington	Y	15000 FQ	21620 AW	34380 TQ	WABLS	10/01-12/01
	West Virginia	Y	14200 FQ	18090 AW	25280 TQ	WVBLS	10/01-12/01
	Wisconsin	Y	12390 FQ	18410 AW	26530 TQ	WIBLS	10/01-12/01
	Puerto Rico	Y	11600 FQ	15300 AW	21020 TQ	PRBLS	10/01-12/01
Gaming Dealer	Arizona	H	5.56 FQ	8.37 AW	13.07 TQ	AZBLS	10/01-12/01
	California	H	6.39 FQ	10.31 AW	19.77 TQ	CABLS	10/01-12/01
	Colorado	H	5.51 FQ	8.70 AW	22.88 TQ	COBLS	10/01-12/01
	Florida	H	5.72 FQ	7.16 AW	8.69 TQ	FLBLS	10/01-12/01
	Georgia	H	5.74 FQ	8.07 AW	13.34 TQ	GABLS	10/01-12/01
	Illinois	H	5.60 FQ	6.98 AW	8.68 TQ	ILBLS	10/01-12/01
	Indiana	H	5.50 FQ	7.06 AW	8.47 TQ	INBLS	10/01-12/01
	Iowa	H	5.57 FQ	6.88 AW	8.35 TQ	IABLS	10/01-12/01
	Louisiana	H	5.58 FQ	6.96 AW	8.24 TQ	LABLS	10/01-12/01
	Michigan	H	5.49 FQ	8.35 AW	16.22 TQ	MIBLS	10/01-12/01
	Minnesota	H	5.80 FQ	10.16 AW	14.04 TQ	MNBLS	10/01-12/01
	Mississippi	H	5.55 FQ	7.36 AW	10.50 TQ	MSBLS	10/01-12/01
	Missouri	H	5.73 FQ	9.97 AW	16.38 TQ	MOBLS	10/01-12/01
	Nevada	H	5.50 FQ	6.34 AW	7.07 TQ	NVBLS	10/01-12/01
	New Jersey	H	5.57 FQ	8.34 AW	18.50 TQ	NJBLS	10/01-12/01
	New Mexico	H	5.48 FQ	7.15 AW	9.05 TQ	NMBLS	10/01-12/01
	New York	H	5.66 FQ	6.95 AW	8.54 TQ	NYBLS	10/01-12/01
	North Dakota	H	5.54 FQ	7.44 AW	11.72 TQ	NDBLS	10/01-12/01
	Ohio	H	5.53 FQ	10.07 AW	16.26 TQ	OHBLS	10/01-12/01
	Pennsylvania	H	5.83 FQ	7.53 AW	11.70 TQ	PABLS	10/01-12/01
	South Dakota	H	5.70 FQ	7.41 AW	9.56 TQ	SDBLS	10/01-12/01
	Washington	H	6.74 FQ	7.49 AW	9.31 TQ	WABLS	10/01-12/01
	Wisconsin	H	5.82 FQ	10.00 AW	23.00 TQ	WIBLS	10/01-12/01
	Puerto Rico	H	5.62 FQ	7.10 AW	9.18 TQ	PRBLS	10/01-12/01
Gaming Manager	California	Y	44250 FQ	76970 AW		CABLS	10/01-12/01
	Colorado	Y	34450 FQ	55920 AW	83600 TQ	COBLS	10/01-12/01
	Florida	Y	26410 FQ	55040 AW	99570 TQ	FLBLS	10/01-12/01
	Illinois	Y	25410 FQ	52400 AW	88060 TQ	ILBLS	10/01-12/01
	Indiana	Y	35140 FQ	58130 AW	88960 TQ	INBLS	10/01-12/01
	Iowa	Y	28700 FQ	51770 AW	83070 TQ	IABLS	10/01-12/01
	Louisiana	Y	24900 FQ	49860 AW	82700 TQ	LABLS	10/01-12/01
	Michigan	Y	32840 FQ	52900 AW	93990 TQ	MIBLS	10/01-12/01
	Minnesota	Y	27550 FQ	53190 AW	80790 TQ	MNBLS	10/01-12/01
	Mississippi	Y	37410 FQ	67550 AW	114450 TQ	MSBLS	10/01-12/01
	Missouri	Y	44160 FQ	63290 AW	102240 TQ	MOBLS	10/01-12/01
	Nevada	Y	37560 FQ	64950 AW	110330 TQ	NVBLS	10/01-12/01
	New Jersey	Y	45150 FQ	66600 AW	97240 TQ	NJBLS	10/01-12/01
	New York	Y	28480 FQ	52620 AW	78040 TQ	NYBLS	10/01-12/01
	Oklahoma	Y	19220 FQ	32950 AW	50450 TQ	OKBLS	10/01-12/01
	South Carolina	Y	19410 FQ	30910 AW	47990 TQ	SCBLS	10/01-12/01
	Texas	Y	38090 FQ	54820 AW	82920 TQ	TXBLS	10/01-12/01
	Washington	Y	31220 FQ	64940 AW		WABLS	10/01-12/01
	Wisconsin	Y	28120 FQ	46640 AW	73820 TQ	WIBLS	10/01-12/01
	Puerto Rico	Y	33020 FQ	54540 AW	86770 TQ	PRBLS	10/01-12/01
Gaming Supervisor	Arizona	H	11.82 FQ	18.55 AW	26.35 TQ	AZBLS	10/01-12/01

AAW	Average annual wage	AOH	Average offered, high	ASH	Average starting, high	H	Hourly	M	Monthly	S	Special: hourly and annual
AE	Average entry wage	AOL	Average offered, low	ASL	Average starting, low	HI	Highest wage paid	MTC	Median total compensation	TQ	Third quartile wage
AEX	Average experienced wage	APH	Average pay, high range	AW	Average wage paid	HR	High end range	MW	Median wage paid	W	Weekly
AO	Average offered	APL	Average pay, low range	FQ	First quartile wage	LR	Low end range	SQ	Second quartile wage	Y	Yearly

Occupation/Type/Industry	Location	Per	Low	Mid	High	Source	Date
Gaming Supervisor	California	H	9.89 FQ	16.71 AW	26.65 TQ	CABLS	10/01-12/01
	Colorado	H	12.75 FQ	19.09 AW	26.52 TQ	COBLS	10/01-12/01
	Florida	H	10.94 FQ	19.88 AW	28.11 TQ	FLBLS	10/01-12/01
	Georgia	H	10.51 FQ	16.88 AW	24.01 TQ	GABLS	10/01-12/01
	Illinois	H	13.24 FQ	29.04 AW		ILBLS	10/01-12/01
	Indiana	H	13.98 FQ	19.45 AW	25.40 TQ	INBLS	10/01-12/01
	Iowa	H	11.32 FQ	16.64 AW	21.91 TQ	IABLS	10/01-12/01
	Kansas	H	11.48 FQ	17.69 AW	24.96 TQ	KSBLS	10/01-12/01
	Louisiana	H	13.70 FQ	18.52 AW	27.77 TQ	LABLS	10/01-12/01
	Maryland	H	7.29 FQ	10.34 AW	19.09 TQ	MDBLS	10/01-12/01
	Massachusetts	H	10.95 FQ	18.59 AW	26.02 TQ	MABLS	10/01-12/01
	Michigan	H	11.81 FQ	17.31 AW	24.46 TQ	MIBLS	10/01-12/01
	Minnesota	H	6.45 FQ	11.90 AW	19.49 TQ	MNBLS	10/01-12/01
	Mississippi	H	12.04 FQ	18.98 AW	26.11 TQ	MSBLS	10/01-12/01
	Missouri	H	14.44 FQ	19.14 AW	24.51 TQ	MOBLS	10/01-12/01
	Montana	H	9.34 FQ	13.95 AW	22.59 TQ	MTBLS	10/01-12/01
	Nevada	H	11.28 FQ	19.29 AW	27.13 TQ	NVBLS	10/01-12/01
	New Jersey	H	16.44 FQ	22.71 AW	28.22 TQ	NJBLS	10/01-12/01
	New York	H	12.24 FQ	20.09 AW	29.11 TQ	NYBLS	10/01-12/01
	North Dakota	H	7.63 FQ	12.32 AW	17.38 TQ	NDBLS	10/01-12/01
	Ohio	H	10.33 FQ	16.72 AW	24.71 TQ	OHBLS	10/01-12/01
	Oklahoma	H	6.51 FQ	10.51 AW	14.57 TQ	OKBLS	10/01-12/01
	Oregon	H	9.93 FQ	15.90 AW	21.50 TQ	ORBLS	10/01-12/01
	South Carolina	H	7.43 FQ	10.82 AW	13.94 TQ	SCBLS	10/01-12/01
	South Dakota	H	10.70 FQ	13.55 AW	17.57 TQ	SDBLS	10/01-12/01
	Texas	H	6.96 FQ	15.55 AW	26.20 TQ	TXBLS	10/01-12/01
	Washington	H	13.54 FQ	18.83 AW	24.51 TQ	WABLS	10/01-12/01
	West Virginia	H	11.32 FQ	18.55 AW	26.82 TQ	WVBLS	10/01-12/01
	Puerto Rico	H	8.89 FQ	11.70 AW	16.21 TQ	PRBLS	10/01-12/01
Gaming Surveillance Officer and Gaming Investigator	Arizona	Y	19830 FQ	26370 AW	36220 TQ	AZBLS	10/01-12/01
	California	Y	17740 FQ	24730 AW	33540 TQ	CABLS	10/01-12/01
	Colorado	Y	19020 FQ	24490 AW	32440 TQ	COBLS	10/01-12/01
	Florida	Y	13510 FQ	25980 AW	37500 TQ	FLBLS	10/01-12/01
	Illinois	Y	16020 FQ	21050 AW	24360 TQ	ILBLS	10/01-12/01
	Indiana	Y	19690 FQ	29040 AW	38850 TQ	INBLS	10/01-12/01
	Iowa	Y	17510 FQ	23300 AW	30240 TQ	IABLS	10/01-12/01
	Louisiana	Y	15770 FQ	21960 AW	30370 TQ	LABLS	10/01-12/01
	Michigan	Y	18440 FQ	28120 AW	39090 TQ	MIBLS	10/01-12/01
	Minnesota	Y	16050 FQ	24730 AW	34950 TQ	MNBLS	10/01-12/01
	Mississippi	Y	16560 FQ	24810 AW	35590 TQ	MSBLS	10/01-12/01
	Missouri	Y	18670 FQ	27730 AW	36080 TQ	MOBLS	10/01-12/01
	Nevada	Y	21030 FQ	31290 AW	42750 TQ	NVBLS	10/01-12/01
	New Jersey	Y	20250 FQ	30240 AW	41960 TQ	NJBLS	10/01-12/01
	New Mexico	Y	15440 FQ	21920 AW	29890 TQ	NMBLS	10/01-12/01
	New York	Y	15760 FQ	25510 AW	36450 TQ	NYBLS	10/01-12/01
	Oklahoma	Y	14390 FQ	19570 AW	23930 TQ	OKBLS	10/01-12/01
	Oregon	Y	16560 FQ	24430 AW	32450 TQ	ORBLS	10/01-12/01
	South Dakota	Y	15220 FQ	18820 AW	24640 TQ	SDBLS	10/01-12/01
	Texas	Y	12510 FQ	20980 AW	34580 TQ	TXBLS	10/01-12/01
	Washington	Y	19680 FQ	27370 AW	37550 TQ	WABLS	10/01-12/01
	West Virginia	Y	15690 FQ	23590 AW	34600 TQ	WVBLS	10/01-12/01
	Puerto Rico	Y	12220 FQ	16500 AW	22160 TQ	PRBLS	10/01-12/01
Gaming Surveillance Officer and Investigator	United States	Y		21220 MW		OOH12	1999-2000
Miscellaneous Amusement and Recreation Services	United States	Y		20650 MW		OOH12	1999-2000
Gas Compressor and Gas Pumping Station Operator	Alabama	H	16.71 FQ	23.12 AW	28.49 TQ	ALBLS	10/01-12/01
	Arkansas	H	18.54 FQ	22.97 AW	27.60 TQ	ARBLS	10/01-12/01
	California	H	14.73 FQ	21.95 AW	28.16 TQ	CABLS	10/01-12/01
	Riverside-San Bernardino PMSA, CA	H	17.93 FQ	22.54 AW	28.03 TQ	CABLS	10/01-12/01
	Colorado	H	17.99 FQ	23.08 AW	29.25 TQ	COBLS	10/01-12/01
	Connecticut	H	15.34 FQ	21.41 AW	27.44 TQ	CTBLS	10/01-12/01
	District of Columbia	H	7.23 FQ	8.77 AW	12.44 TQ	DCBLS	10/01-12/01
	Washington PMSA, DC-MD-VA-WV	H	7.39 FQ	13.57 AW	22.58 TQ	DCBLS	10/01-12/01
	Florida	H	15.98 FQ	23.77 AW	28.91 TQ	FLBLS	10/01-12/01

AAW	Average annual wage	AOH	Average offered, high	ASH	Average starting, high	H	Hourly	M	Monthly	S	Special: hourly and annual
AE	Average entry wage	AOL	Average offered, low	ASL	Average starting, low	HI	Highest wage paid	MTC	Median total compensation	TQ	Third quartile wage
AEX	Average experienced wage	APH	Average pay, high range	AW	Average wage paid	HR	High end range	MW	Median wage paid	W	Weekly
AO	Average offered	APL	Average pay, low range	FQ	First quartile wage	LR	Low end range	SQ	Second quartile wage	Y	Yearly

Occupation/Type/Industry	Location	Per	Low	Mid	High	Source	Date
Gas Compressor and Gas Pumping Station Operator	Illinois	H	9.94 FQ	16.83 AW	25.59 TQ	ILBLS	10/01-12/01
	Chicago PMSA, IL	H	9.63 FQ	17.53 AW	24.42 TQ	ILBLS	10/01-12/01
	Indiana	H	9.77 FQ	17.39 AW	25.01 TQ	INBLS	10/01-12/01
	Iowa	H	11.25 FQ	20.68 AW	27.92 TQ	IABLS	10/01-12/01
	Kansas	H	18.54 FQ	22.58 AW	27.20 TQ	KSBLS	10/01-12/01
	Louisiana	H	15.29 FQ	20.47 AW	26.92 TQ	LABLS	10/01-12/01
	Massachusetts	H	13.62 FQ	22.74 AW	29.16 TQ	MABLS	10/01-12/01
	Michigan	H	17.60 FQ	21.57 AW	27.26 TQ	MIBLS	10/01-12/01
	Detroit PMSA, MI	H	17.30 FQ	19.05 AW	21.16 TQ	MIBLS	10/01-12/01
	Minnesota	H	16.64 FQ	22.21 AW	27.93 TQ	MNBLS	10/01-12/01
	Minneapolis-St. Paul MSA, MN-WI	H	15.78 FQ	21.53 AW	26.85 TQ	MNBLS	10/01-12/01
	Mississippi	H	14.51 FQ	21.03 AW	27.82 TQ	MSBLS	10/01-12/01
	Missouri	H	15.56 FQ	21.46 AW	26.99 TQ	MOBLS	10/01-12/01
	St. Louis MSA, MO-IL	H	9.12 FQ	16.16 AW	24.64 TQ	MOBLS	10/01-12/01
	Montana	H	17.69 FQ	20.50 AW	23.12 TQ	MTBLS	10/01-12/01
	New Jersey	H	14.67 FQ	16.96 AW	20.32 TQ	NJBLS	10/01-12/01
	New York	H	6.30 FQ	17.07 AW	26.55 TQ	NYBLS	10/01-12/01
	Ohio	H	12.26 FQ	18.91 AW	27.08 TQ	OHBLS	10/01-12/01
	Oklahoma	H	10.54 FQ	20.16 AW	26.77 TQ	OKBLS	10/01-12/01
	Oregon	H	18.35 FQ	22.28 AW	27.23 TQ	ORBLS	10/01-12/01
	Pennsylvania	H	10.58 FQ	20.13 AW	27.96 TQ	PABLS	10/01-12/01
	South Carolina	H	9.37 FQ	12.66 AW	17.19 TQ	SCBLS	10/01-12/01
	Tennessee	H	11.82 FQ	16.76 AW	22.07 TQ	TNBLS	10/01-12/01
	Memphis MSA, TN-AR-MS	H	15.03 FQ	20.53 AW	26.58 TQ	TNBLS	10/01-12/01
	Texas	H	15.35 FQ	21.98 AW	31.15 TQ	TXBLS	10/01-12/01
	Corpus Christi MSA, TX	H	17.96 FQ	23.42 AW	31.24 TQ	TXBLS	10/01-12/01
	Houston PMSA, TX	H	14.13 FQ	23.20 AW	33.94 TQ	TXBLS	10/01-12/01
	Longview-Marshall MSA, TX	H	17.49 FQ	21.23 AW	26.75 TQ	TXBLS	10/01-12/01
	Utah	H	10.03 FQ	17.87 AW	26.68 TQ	UTBLS	10/01-12/01
	Virginia	H	16.19 FQ	21.28 AW	27.19 TQ	VABLS	10/01-12/01
	Washington	H	7.78 FQ	15.76 AW	27.57 TQ	WABLS	10/01-12/01
	Seattle-Bellevue-Everett PMSA, WA	H	10.34 FQ	20.55 AW	29.75 TQ	WABLS	10/01-12/01
	West Virginia	H	17.76 FQ	21.92 AW	28.15 TQ	WVBLS	10/01-12/01
	Charleston MSA, WV	H	16.46 FQ	19.40 AW	22.05 TQ	WVBLS	10/01-12/01
	Wyoming	H	15.50 FQ	21.44 AW	27.77 TQ	WYBLS	10/01-12/01
Gas Plant Operator	Alabama	H	12.23 FQ	19.26 AW	27.81 TQ	ALBLS	10/01-12/01
	Arizona	H	18.06 FQ	24.48 AW	30.40 TQ	AZBLS	10/01-12/01
	Arkansas	H	14.02 FQ	21.49 AW	27.93 TQ	ARBLS	10/01-12/01
	California	H	19.55 FQ	27.33 AW	34.90 TQ	CABLS	10/01-12/01
	Colorado	H	14.78 FQ	21.45 AW	29.47 TQ	COBLS	10/01-12/01
	Connecticut	H	18.12 FQ	24.98 AW	33.25 TQ	CTBLS	10/01-12/01
	Florida	H	12.25 FQ	21.13 AW	32.70 TQ	FLBLS	10/01-12/01
	Georgia	H	14.61 FQ	19.02 AW	25.26 TQ	GABLS	10/01-12/01
	Illinois	H	15.24 FQ	24.79 AW	35.39 TQ	ILBLS	10/01-12/01
	Indiana	H	17.20 FQ	22.74 AW	28.92 TQ	INBLS	10/01-12/01
	Iowa	H	17.29 FQ	22.94 AW	28.72 TQ	IABLS	10/01-12/01
	Kansas	H	17.27 FQ	21.80 AW	27.73 TQ	KSBLS	10/01-12/01
	Kentucky	H	14.85 FQ	19.98 AW	27.03 TQ	KYBLS	10/01-12/01
	Louisiana	H	11.93 FQ	20.57 AW	26.76 TQ	LABLS	10/01-12/01
	Maryland	H	16.80 FQ	27.10 AW	36.25 TQ	MDBLS	10/01-12/01
	Massachusetts	H	20.78 FQ	26.73 AW	33.39 TQ	MABLS	10/01-12/01
	Michigan	H	15.31 FQ	21.98 AW	29.16 TQ	MIBLS	10/01-12/01
	Minnesota	H	17.05 FQ	22.18 AW	28.20 TQ	MNBLS	10/01-12/01
	Mississippi	H	15.45 FQ	21.86 AW	28.47 TQ	MSBLS	10/01-12/01
	Missouri	H	18.35 FQ	23.93 AW	31.64 TQ	MOBLS	10/01-12/01
	Nebraska	H	11.34 FQ	19.35 AW	27.37 TQ	NEBLS	10/01-12/01
	New Jersey	H	17.42 FQ	21.92 AW	26.38 TQ	NJBLS	10/01-12/01
	New Mexico	H	12.29 FQ	19.02 AW	26.24 TQ	NMBLS	10/01-12/01
	New York	H	18.05 FQ	25.96 AW	34.10 TQ	NYBLS	10/01-12/01
	North Carolina	H	14.65 FQ	19.09 AW	25.38 TQ	NCBLS	10/01-12/01
	Ohio	H	17.92 FQ	22.75 AW	27.18 TQ	OHBLS	10/01-12/01
	Oklahoma	H	8.06 FQ	18.21 AW	26.39 TQ	OKBLS	10/01-12/01
	Pennsylvania	H	17.94 FQ	22.14 AW	27.26 TQ	PABLS	10/01-12/01
	South Carolina	H	14.03 FQ	21.13 AW	27.99 TQ	SCBLS	10/01-12/01
	Tennessee	H	14.06 FQ	20.66 AW	26.75 TQ	TNBLS	10/01-12/01
	Texas	H	17.15 FQ	22.30 AW	27.98 TQ	TXBLS	10/01-12/01
	Utah	H	14.65 FQ	20.58 AW	26.91 TQ	UTBLS	10/01-12/01
	Virginia	H	15.52 FQ	21.92 AW	27.96 TQ	VABLS	10/01-12/01

AAW	Average annual wage	AOH	Average offered, high	ASH	Average starting, high	H	Hourly	M	Monthly	S	Special: hourly and annual
AE	Average entry wage	AOL	Average offered, low	ASL	Average starting, low	HI	Highest wage paid	MTC	Median total compensation	TQ	Third quartile wage
AEX	Average experienced wage	APH	Average pay, high range	AW	Average wage paid	HR	High end range	MW	Median wage paid	W	Weekly
AO	Average offered	APL	Average pay, low range	FQ	First quartile wage	LR	Low end range	SQ	Second quartile wage	Y	Yearly

Occupation/Type/Industry	Location	Per	Low	Mid	High	Source	Date
Gas Plant Operator	Washington	H	18.90 FQ	22.91 AW	28.01 TQ	WABLS	10/01-12/01
	West Virginia	H	16.68 FQ	21.93 AW	27.56 TQ	WVBLS	10/01-12/01
	Wisconsin	H	15.63 FQ	25.60 AW	35.03 TQ	WIBLS	10/01-12/01
	Wyoming	H	15.75 FQ	21.91 AW	30.36 TQ	WYBLS	10/01-12/01
	Puerto Rico	H	6.08 FQ	12.09 AW	20.24 TQ	PRBLS	10/01-12/01
General and Operations Manager	Alabama	Y	25430 FQ	64170 AW	126580 TQ	ALBLS	10/01-12/01
	Birmingham MSA, AL	Y	30340 FQ	72920 AW		ALBLS	10/01-12/01
	Huntsville MSA, AL	Y	27210 FQ	69650 AW	132060 TQ	ALBLS	10/01-12/01
	Mobile MSA, AL	Y	26830 FQ	67650 AW	140850 TQ	ALBLS	10/01-12/01
	Montgomery MSA, AL	Y	27500 FQ	65630 AW	121550 TQ	ALBLS	10/01-12/01
	Alaska	Y	29040 FQ	66450 AW	119950 TQ	AKBLS	10/01-12/01
	Anchorage MSA, AK	Y	30150 FQ	70730 AW	139110 TQ	AKBLS	10/01-12/01
	Arizona	Y	33290 FQ	73180 AW	135620 TQ	AZBLS	10/01-12/01
	Phoenix-Mesa MSA, AZ	Y	35730 FQ	76540 AW	139250 TQ	AZBLS	10/01-12/01
	Tucson MSA, AZ	Y	30380 FQ	68020 AW	133290 TQ	AZBLS	10/01-12/01
	Arkansas	Y	28880 FQ	64800 AW	124070 TQ	ARBLS	10/01-12/01
	Fayetteville-Springdale-Rogers MSA, AR	Y	25520 FQ	62070 AW	122510 TQ	ARBLS	10/01-12/01
	Fort Smith MSA, AR-OK	Y	28450 FQ	63080 AW	120730 TQ	ARBLS	10/01-12/01
	Little Rock-North Little Rock MSA, AR	Y	35160 FQ	73820 AW		ARBLS	10/01-12/01
	California	Y	40910 FQ	88280 AW		CABLS	10/01-12/01
	Bakersfield MSA, CA	Y	35050 FQ	71530 AW	129660 TQ	CABLS	10/01-12/01
	Chico-Paradise MSA, CA	Y	33680 FQ	70040 AW	136820 TQ	CABLS	10/01-12/01
	Fresno MSA, CA	Y	38700 FQ	75640 AW		CABLS	10/01-12/01
	Los Angeles-Long Beach PMSA, CA	Y	42380 FQ	90580 AW		CABLS	10/01-12/01
	Merced MSA, CA	Y	33410 FQ	71840 AW		CABLS	10/01-12/01
	Modesto MSA, CA	Y	38320 FQ	77960 AW	144930 TQ	CABLS	10/01-12/01
	Oakland PMSA, CA	Y	43360 FQ	89530 AW		CABLS	10/01-12/01
	Orange County PMSA, CA	Y	43530 FQ	92870 AW		CABLS	10/01-12/01
	Redding MSA, CA	Y	32380 FQ	65270 AW	114800 TQ	CABLS	10/01-12/01
	Riverside-San Bernardino PMSA, CA	Y	38510 FQ	80140 AW		CABLS	10/01-12/01
	Sacramento PMSA, CA	Y	39330 FQ	78980 AW		CABLS	10/01-12/01
	Salinas MSA, CA	Y	37440 FQ	80920 AW		CABLS	10/01-12/01
	San Diego MSA, CA	Y	39410 FQ	86250 AW		CABLS	10/01-12/01
	San Francisco PMSA, CA	Y	44760 FQ	98190 AW		CABLS	10/01-12/01
	San Jose PMSA, CA	Y	49050 FQ	103990 AW		CABLS	10/01-12/01
	San Luis Obispo-Atascadero-Paso Robles MSA, CA	Y	35780 FQ	72340 AW		CABLS	10/01-12/01
	Santa Barbara-Santa Maria-Lompoc MSA, CA	Y	37510 FQ	79360 AW		CABLS	10/01-12/01
	Santa Cruz-Watsonville PMSA, CA	Y	38710 FQ	85390 AW		CABLS	10/01-12/01
	Santa Rosa PMSA, CA	Y	39440 FQ	81240 AW		CABLS	10/01-12/01
	Stockton-Lodi MSA, CA	Y	32010 FQ	74520 AW		CABLS	10/01-12/01
	Vallejo-Fairfield-Napa PMSA, CA	Y	38070 FQ	79230 AW		CABLS	10/01-12/01
	Ventura PMSA, CA	Y	41320 FQ	87600 AW		CABLS	10/01-12/01
	Visalia-Tulare-Porterville MSA, CA	Y	36340 FQ	73160 AW	124460 TQ	CABLS	10/01-12/01
	Colorado	Y	35300 FQ	79280 AW		COBLS	10/01-12/01
	Boulder-Longmont PMSA, CO	Y	39720 FQ	89560 AW		COBLS	10/01-12/01
	Colorado Springs MSA, CO	Y	34560 FQ	73430 AW		COBLS	10/01-12/01
	Denver PMSA, CO	Y	38630 FQ	85100 AW		COBLS	10/01-12/01
	Fort Collins-Loveland MSA, CO	Y	36480 FQ	77670 AW		COBLS	10/01-12/01
	Greeley PMSA, CO	Y	30940 FQ	70430 AW	140060 TQ	COBLS	10/01-12/01
	Connecticut	Y	45650 FQ	96380 AW		CTBLS	10/01-12/01
	Bridgeport PMSA, CT	Y	39140 FQ	89690 AW		CTBLS	10/01-12/01
	Danbury PMSA, CT	Y	39630 FQ	87380 AW		CTBLS	10/01-12/01
	Hartford MSA, CT	Y	48740 FQ	96310 AW		CTBLS	10/01-12/01
	New Haven-Meriden PMSA, CT	Y	46350 FQ	92160 AW		CTBLS	10/01-12/01
	New London-Norwich MSA, CT-RI	Y	40230 FQ	93050 AW		CTBLS	10/01-12/01
	Stamford-Norwalk PMSA, CT	Y	50450 FQ	109460 AW		CTBLS	10/01-12/01
	Waterbury PMSA, CT	Y	42320 FQ	90530 AW		CTBLS	10/01-12/01
	Delaware	Y	30240 FQ	68920 AW	139530 TQ	DEBLS	10/01-12/01
	Wilmington-Newark PMSA, DE-MD	Y	30860 FQ	71410 AW	144810 TQ	DEBLS	10/01-12/01

AAW	Average annual wage	**AOH**	Average offered, high	**ASH**	Average starting, high	**H**	Hourly	**M**	Monthly	**S**	Special: hourly and annual
AE	Average entry wage	**AOL**	Average offered, low	**ASL**	Average starting, low	**HI**	Highest wage paid	**MTC**	Median total compensation	**TQ**	Third quartile wage
AEX	Average experienced wage	**APH**	Average pay, high range	**AW**	Average wage paid	**HR**	High end range	**MW**	Median wage paid	**W**	Weekly
AO	Average offered	**APL**	Average pay, low range	**FQ**	First quartile wage	**LR**	Low end range	**SQ**	Second quartile wage	**Y**	Yearly

Occupation/Type/Industry	Location	Per	Low	Mid	High	Source	Date
General and Operations Manager	District of Columbia	Y	36270 FQ	72940 AW	138230 TQ	DCBLS	10/01-12/01
	Washington PMSA, DC-MD-VA-WV	Y	35290 FQ	79710 AW		DCBLS	10/01-12/01
	Florida	Y	28690 FQ	68620 AW		FLBLS	10/01-12/01
	Daytona Beach MSA, FL	Y	23760 FQ	58670 AW	118970 TQ	FLBLS	10/01-12/01
	Fort Lauderdale PMSA, FL	Y	30520 FQ	73890 AW		FLBLS	10/01-12/01
	Fort Myers-Cape Coral MSA, FL	Y	30830 FQ	64790 AW	130300 TQ	FLBLS	10/01-12/01
	Fort Pierce-Port St. Lucie MSA, FL	Y	28150 FQ	63020 AW	118370 TQ	FLBLS	10/01-12/01
	Fort Walton Beach MSA, FL	Y	25190 FQ	60420 AW	122930 TQ	FLBLS	10/01-12/01
	Gainesville MSA, FL	Y	25600 FQ	58430 AW	107810 TQ	FLBLS	10/01-12/01
	Jacksonville MSA, FL	Y	30370 FQ	71610 AW		FLBLS	10/01-12/01
	Lakeland-Winter Haven MSA, FL	Y	27230 FQ	66000 AW	133360 TQ	FLBLS	10/01-12/01
	Melbourne-Titusville-Palm Bay MSA, FL	Y	26420 FQ	63280 AW	115410 TQ	FLBLS	10/01-12/01
	Miami PMSA, FL	Y	28180 FQ	70310 AW		FLBLS	10/01-12/01
	Naples MSA, FL	Y	32370 FQ	71550 AW		FLBLS	10/01-12/01
	Ocala MSA, FL	Y	25830 FQ	57630 AW	110920 TQ	FLBLS	10/01-12/01
	Orlando MSA, FL	Y	28760 FQ	68200 AW	141320 TQ	FLBLS	10/01-12/01
	Pensacola MSA, FL	Y	27940 FQ	57490 AW	105240 TQ	FLBLS	10/01-12/01
	Sarasota-Bradenton MSA, FL	Y	27490 FQ	67980 AW	140840 TQ	FLBLS	10/01-12/01
	Tallahassee MSA, FL	Y	26030 FQ	66870 AW		FLBLS	10/01-12/01
	Tampa-St. Petersburg-Clearwater MSA, FL	Y	30440 FQ	70210 AW		FLBLS	10/01-12/01
	West Palm Beach-Boca Raton MSA, FL	Y	31320 FQ	76550 AW		FLBLS	10/01-12/01
	Georgia	Y	36190 FQ	71600 AW	139800 TQ	GABLS	10/01-12/01
	Atlanta MSA, GA	Y	38070 FQ	77190 AW		GABLS	10/01-12/01
	Augusta-Aiken MSA, GA-SC	Y	32350 FQ	63490 AW	116690 TQ	GABLS	10/01-12/01
	Columbus MSA, GA-AL	Y	32550 FQ	62090 AW	102730 TQ	GABLS	10/01-12/01
	Macon MSA, GA	Y	34900 FQ	62410 AW	107830 TQ	GABLS	10/01-12/01
	Savannah MSA, GA	Y	34480 FQ	63750 AW	115140 TQ	GABLS	10/01-12/01
	Hawaii	Y	35910 FQ	72530 AW	133400 TQ	HIBLS	10/01-12/01
	Honolulu MSA, HI	Y	37330 FQ	74480 AW	136940 TQ	HIBLS	10/01-12/01
	Idaho	Y	24480 FQ	54120 AW	93370 TQ	IDBLS	10/01-12/01
	Boise City MSA, ID	Y	29510 FQ	58200 AW	98220 TQ	IDBLS	10/01-12/01
	Illinois	Y	27620 FQ	68110 AW	141840 TQ	ILBLS	10/01-12/01
	Champaign-Urbana MSA, IL	Y	25170 FQ	57500 AW	103860 TQ	ILBLS	10/01-12/01
	Chicago PMSA, IL	Y	32770 FQ	74970 AW		ILBLS	10/01-12/01
	Peoria-Pekin MSA, IL	Y	28440 FQ	65380 AW	122960 TQ	ILBLS	10/01-12/01
	Rockford MSA, IL	Y	27190 FQ	60620 AW	115080 TQ	ILBLS	10/01-12/01
	Springfield MSA, IL	Y	29490 FQ	57750 AW	102590 TQ	ILBLS	10/01-12/01
	Indiana	Y	33460 FQ	71910 AW	137750 TQ	INBLS	10/01-12/01
	Elkhart-Goshen MSA, IN	Y	33350 FQ	69790 AW	122650 TQ	INBLS	10/01-12/01
	Evansville-Henderson MSA, IN-KY	Y	31140 FQ	64500 AW	128380 TQ	INBLS	10/01-12/01
	Fort Wayne MSA, IN	Y	32550 FQ	70540 AW	141050 TQ	INBLS	10/01-12/01
	Gary PMSA, IN	Y	31980 FQ	68490 AW	123840 TQ	INBLS	10/01-12/01
	Indianapolis MSA, IN	Y	38890 FQ	79560 AW		INBLS	10/01-12/01
	Lafayette MSA, IN	Y	32720 FQ	70030 AW		INBLS	10/01-12/01
	South Bend MSA, IN	Y	33840 FQ	76260 AW		INBLS	10/01-12/01
	Iowa	Y	25770 FQ	62140 AW	121250 TQ	IABLS	10/01-12/01
	Cedar Rapids MSA, IA	Y	35090 FQ	75630 AW	141570 TQ	IABLS	10/01-12/01
	Davenport-Moline-Rock Island MSA, IA-IL	Y	22430 FQ	56110 AW	108070 TQ	IABLS	10/01-12/01
	Des Moines MSA, IA	Y	32430 FQ	73880 AW		IABLS	10/01-12/01
	Kansas	Y	29540 FQ	65500 AW	129060 TQ	KSBLS	10/01-12/01
	Topeka MSA, KS	Y	31860 FQ	61260 AW	109400 TQ	KSBLS	10/01-12/01
	Wichita MSA, KS	Y	31540 FQ	67380 AW	129600 TQ	KSBLS	10/01-12/01
	Kentucky	Y	27440 FQ	60330 AW	113710 TQ	KYBLS	10/01-12/01
	Lexington MSA, KY	Y	28240 FQ	63890 AW	141070 TQ	KYBLS	10/01-12/01
	Louisville MSA, KY-IN	Y	29530 FQ	65940 AW	126040 TQ	KYBLS	10/01-12/01
	Louisiana	Y	27850 FQ	61880 AW	119950 TQ	LABLS	10/01-12/01
	Baton Rouge MSA, LA	Y	30290 FQ	62500 AW	118210 TQ	LABLS	10/01-12/01
	Houma MSA, LA	Y	27300 FQ	60800 AW	110490 TQ	LABLS	10/01-12/01
	Lafayette MSA, LA	Y	26220 FQ	62370 AW	118360 TQ	LABLS	10/01-12/01
	Lake Charles MSA, LA	Y	27270 FQ	57710 AW	106740 TQ	LABLS	10/01-12/01
	New Orleans MSA, LA	Y	29300 FQ	65250 AW	135480 TQ	LABLS	10/01-12/01
	Shreveport-Bossier City MSA, LA	Y	25770 FQ	59910 AW	120390 TQ	LABLS	10/01-12/01

Occupation/Type/Industry	Location	Per	Low	Mid	High	Source	Date
General and Operations Manager	Maine	Y	27440 FQ	58200 AW	106070 TQ	MEBLS	10/01-12/01
	Portland MSA, ME	Y	31050 FQ	65830 AW	118390 TQ	MEBLS	10/01-12/01
	Maryland	Y	31610 FQ	70820 AW	144560 TQ	MDBLS	10/01-12/01
	Baltimore PMSA, MD	Y	31830 FQ	67830 AW	141480 TQ	MDBLS	10/01-12/01
	Massachusetts	Y	40090 FQ	84300 AW		MABLS	10/01-12/01
	Boston PMSA, MA-NH	Y	44130 FQ	90280 AW		MABLS	10/01-12/01
	Brockton PMSA, MA	Y	39870 FQ	76450 AW		MABLS	10/01-12/01
	Lawrence PMSA, MA-NH	Y	36620 FQ	81520 AW		MABLS	10/01-12/01
	Lowell PMSA, MA-NH	Y	40420 FQ	85420 AW		MABLS	10/01-12/01
	New Bedford PMSA, MA	Y	30460 FQ	64540 AW	118340 TQ	MABLS	10/01-12/01
	Springfield MSA, MA	Y	33970 FQ	70190 AW	136410 TQ	MABLS	10/01-12/01
	Worcester PMSA, MA-CT	Y	39010 FQ	80580 AW		MABLS	10/01-12/01
	Michigan	Y	41200 FQ	85230 AW		MIBLS	10/01-12/01
	Ann Arbor PMSA, MI	Y	37330 FQ	83180 AW		MIBLS	10/01-12/01
	Detroit PMSA, MI	Y	45250 FQ	92560 AW		MIBLS	10/01-12/01
	Flint PMSA, MI	Y	35680 FQ	75680 AW		MIBLS	10/01-12/01
	Grand Rapids-Muskegon-Holland MSA, MI	Y	41860 FQ	82160 AW		MIBLS	10/01-12/01
	Kalamazoo-Battle Creek MSA, MI	Y	37270 FQ	79740 AW		MIBLS	10/01-12/01
	Lansing-East Lansing MSA, MI	Y	47290 FQ	81580 AW	137770 TQ	MIBLS	10/01-12/01
	Saginaw-Bay City-Midland MSA, MI	Y	38770 FQ	83530 AW		MIBLS	10/01-12/01
	Minnesota	Y	32590 FQ	75060 AW		MNBLS	10/01-12/01
	Duluth-Superior MSA, MN-WI	Y	28640 FQ	57760 AW	99090 TQ	MNBLS	10/01-12/01
	Minneapolis-St. Paul MSA, MN-WI	Y	37620 FQ	82750 AW		MNBLS	10/01-12/01
	St. Cloud MSA, MN	Y	28380 FQ	61060 AW	118760 TQ	MNBLS	10/01-12/01
	Mississippi	Y	25530 FQ	58480 AW	114100 TQ	MSBLS	10/01-12/01
	Biloxi-Gulfport-Pascagoula MSA, MS	Y	22000 FQ	54240 AW	103120 TQ	MSBLS	10/01-12/01
	Jackson MSA, MS	Y	30030 FQ	63060 AW	124120 TQ	MSBLS	10/01-12/01
	Missouri	Y	29810 FQ	65060 AW	130300 TQ	MOBLS	10/01-12/01
	Kansas City MSA, MO-KS	Y	33810 FQ	73780 AW		MOBLS	10/01-12/01
	St. Louis MSA, MO-IL	Y	30240 FQ	68970 AW	145080 TQ	MOBLS	10/01-12/01
	Springfield MSA, MO	Y	27410 FQ	57310 AW	102480 TQ	MOBLS	10/01-12/01
	Montana	Y	19680 FQ	46210 AW	83500 TQ	MTBLS	10/01-12/01
	Billings MSA, MT	Y	22460 FQ	49540 AW	91320 TQ	MTBLS	10/01-12/01
	Nebraska	Y	25570 FQ	61780 AW	119440 TQ	NEBLS	10/01-12/01
	Lincoln MSA, NE	Y	27750 FQ	64740 AW	127580 TQ	NEBLS	10/01-12/01
	Omaha MSA, NE-IA	Y	28320 FQ	69130 AW	138310 TQ	NEBLS	10/01-12/01
	Nevada	Y	34670 FQ	77300 AW		NVBLS	10/01-12/01
	Las Vegas MSA, NV-AZ	Y	33330 FQ	75530 AW		NVBLS	10/01-12/01
	Reno MSA, NV	Y	39360 FQ	81920 AW		NVBLS	10/01-12/01
	New Hampshire	Y	30270 FQ	69060 AW	143130 TQ	NHBLS	10/01-12/01
	Manchester PMSA, NH	Y	29210 FQ	70380 AW	137330 TQ	NHBLS	10/01-12/01
	Nashua PMSA, NH	Y	36790 FQ	79060 AW		NHBLS	10/01-12/01
	Portsmouth-Rochester PMSA, NH-ME	Y	30490 FQ	69900 AW	141250 TQ	NHBLS	10/01-12/01
	New Jersey	Y	46560 FQ	99290 AW		NJBLS	10/01-12/01
	Atlantic-Cape May PMSA, NJ	Y	32250 FQ	82970 AW		NJBLS	10/01-12/01
	Bergen-Passaic PMSA, NJ	Y	49270 FQ	103910 AW		NJBLS	10/01-12/01
	Jersey City PMSA, NJ	Y	46260 FQ	97500 AW		NJBLS	10/01-12/01
	Middlesex-Somerset-Hunterdon PMSA, NJ	Y	45590 FQ	100820 AW		NJBLS	10/01-12/01
	Monmouth-Ocean PMSA, NJ	Y	41430 FQ	92480 AW		NJBLS	10/01-12/01
	Newark PMSA, NJ	Y	53210 FQ	105240 AW		NJBLS	10/01-12/01
	Trenton PMSA, NJ	Y	50570 FQ	98480 AW		NJBLS	10/01-12/01
	New Mexico	Y	26360 FQ	59800 AW	111120 TQ	NMBLS	10/01-12/01
	Albuquerque MSA, NM	Y	30100 FQ	66070 AW	124760 TQ	NMBLS	10/01-12/01
	Las Cruces MSA, NM	Y	23920 FQ	52270 AW	92960 TQ	NMBLS	10/01-12/01
	New York	Y	47530 FQ	98140 AW		NYBLS	10/01-12/01
	Albany-Schenectady-Troy MSA, NY	Y	42070 FQ	83460 AW		NYBLS	10/01-12/01
	Binghamton MSA, NY	Y	34940 FQ	75840 AW	140920 TQ	NYBLS	10/01-12/01
	Buffalo-Niagara Falls MSA, NY	Y	36890 FQ	81380 AW		NYBLS	10/01-12/01
	Dutchess County PMSA, NY	Y	49860 FQ	85010 AW		NYBLS	10/01-12/01
	Nassau-Suffolk PMSA, NY	Y	50270 FQ	99880 AW		NYBLS	10/01-12/01
	New York PMSA, NY	Y	53520 FQ	106950 AW		NYBLS	10/01-12/01
	Newburgh PMSA, NY-PA	Y	39720 FQ	80770 AW		NYBLS	10/01-12/01
	Rochester MSA, NY	Y	43130 FQ	88690 AW		NYBLS	10/01-12/01

AAW	Average annual wage	AOH	Average offered, high	ASH	Average starting, high	H	Hourly	M	Monthly	S	Special: hourly and annual
AE	Average entry wage	AOL	Average offered, low	ASL	Average starting, low	HI	Highest wage paid	MTC	Median total compensation	TQ	Third quartile wage
AEX	Average experienced wage	APH	Average pay, high range	AW	Average wage paid	HR	High end range	MW	Median wage paid	W	Weekly
AO	Average offered	APL	Average pay, low range	FQ	First quartile wage	LR	Low end range	SQ	Second quartile wage	Y	Yearly

Occupation/Type/Industry	Location	Per	Low	Mid	High	Source	Date
General and Operations Manager	Syracuse MSA, NY	Y	42590 FQ	84960 AW		NYBLS	10/01-12/01
	Utica-Rome MSA, NY	Y	39160 FQ	76190 AW	142730 TQ	NYBLS	10/01-12/01
	North Carolina	Y	29920 FQ	68980 AW		NCBLS	10/01-12/01
	Asheville MSA, NC	Y	27970 FQ	61230 AW	128210 TQ	NCBLS	10/01-12/01
	Charlotte-Gastonia-Rock Hill MSA, NC-SC	Y	31150 FQ	74560 AW		NCBLS	10/01-12/01
	Fayetteville MSA, NC	Y	27800 FQ	59700 AW	115650 TQ	NCBLS	10/01-12/01
	Greensboro-Winston-Salem-High Point MSA, NC	Y	30350 FQ	69410 AW	145100 TQ	NCBLS	10/01-12/01
	Hickory-Morganton-Lenoir MSA, NC	Y	28240 FQ	66920 AW		NCBLS	10/01-12/01
	Raleigh-Durham-Chapel Hill MSA, NC	Y	31590 FQ	74130 AW		NCBLS	10/01-12/01
	Wilmington MSA, NC	Y	27580 FQ	61060 AW	114420 TQ	NCBLS	10/01-12/01
	North Dakota	Y	26620 FQ	57450 AW	104120 TQ	NDBLS	10/01-12/01
	Fargo-Moorhead MSA, ND-MN	Y	30900 FQ	65050 AW	129570 TQ	NDBLS	10/01-12/01
	Ohio	Y	30890 FQ	70040 AW	144990 TQ	OHBLS	10/01-12/01
	Akron PMSA, OH	Y	35490 FQ	75610 AW		OHBLS	10/01-12/01
	Canton-Massillon MSA, OH	Y	29090 FQ	62730 AW	123790 TQ	OHBLS	10/01-12/01
	Cincinnati PMSA, OH-KY-IN	Y	31580 FQ	72260 AW		OHBLS	10/01-12/01
	Cleveland-Lorain-Elyria PMSA, OH	Y	30780 FQ	73350 AW		OHBLS	10/01-12/01
	Columbus MSA, OH	Y	34380 FQ	72690 AW		OHBLS	10/01-12/01
	Dayton-Springfield MSA, OH	Y	31160 FQ	68820 AW	132180 TQ	OHBLS	10/01-12/01
	Hamilton-Middletown PMSA, OH	Y	29590 FQ	68360 AW	143980 TQ	OHBLS	10/01-12/01
	Mansfield MSA, OH	Y	27520 FQ	62230 AW	139590 TQ	OHBLS	10/01-12/01
	Toledo MSA, OH	Y	31890 FQ	72000 AW		OHBLS	10/01-12/01
	Youngstown-Warren MSA, OH	Y	27050 FQ	65980 AW	134760 TQ	OHBLS	10/01-12/01
	Oklahoma	Y	24180 FQ	57540 AW	111480 TQ	OKBLS	10/01-12/01
	Oklahoma City MSA, OK	Y	25770 FQ	59610 AW	113790 TQ	OKBLS	10/01-12/01
	Tulsa MSA, OK	Y	26330 FQ	65850 AW	136180 TQ	OKBLS	10/01-12/01
	Oregon	Y	36860 FQ	78110 AW		ORBLS	10/01-12/01
	Eugene-Springfield MSA, OR	Y	32990 FQ	71930 AW	140820 TQ	ORBLS	10/01-12/01
	Medford-Ashland MSA, OR	Y	26780 FQ	66330 AW	144380 TQ	ORBLS	10/01-12/01
	Portland-Vancouver PMSA, OR-WA	Y	40470 FQ	84470 AW		ORBLS	10/01-12/01
	Salem PMSA, OR	Y	36030 FQ	69500 AW	120170 TQ	ORBLS	10/01-12/01
	Pennsylvania	Y	31630 FQ	72010 AW	143390 TQ	PABLS	10/01-12/01
	Allentown-Bethlehem-Easton MSA, PA	Y	21790 FQ	66530 AW	132260 TQ	PABLS	10/01-12/01
	Erie MSA, PA	Y	27980 FQ	62790 AW	129020 TQ	PABLS	10/01-12/01
	Harrisburg-Lebanon-Carlisle MSA, PA	Y	31170 FQ	68380 AW	128870 TQ	PABLS	10/01-12/01
	Johnstown MSA, PA	Y	27920 FQ	60290 AW	110320 TQ	PABLS	10/01-12/01
	Lancaster MSA, PA	Y	34820 FQ	68760 AW	128220 TQ	PABLS	10/01-12/01
	Philadelphia PMSA, PA-NJ	Y	38500 FQ	83780 AW		PABLS	10/01-12/01
	Pittsburgh MSA, PA	Y	31460 FQ	71030 AW	135350 TQ	PABLS	10/01-12/01
	Reading MSA, PA	Y	30260 FQ	69660 AW		PABLS	10/01-12/01
	Scranton-Wilkes-Barre-Hazleton MSA, PA	Y	29630 FQ	62520 AW	114950 TQ	PABLS	10/01-12/01
	York MSA, PA	Y	31320 FQ	63850 AW	116050 TQ	PABLS	10/01-12/01
	Rhode Island	Y	41180 FQ	85400 AW		RIBLS	10/01-12/01
	Providence-Fall River-Warwick MSA, RI-MA	Y	37500 FQ	78730 AW		RIBLS	10/01-12/01
	South Carolina	Y	28040 FQ	60640 AW	112610 TQ	SCBLS	10/01-12/01
	Charleston-North Charleston MSA, SC	Y	26540 FQ	59340 AW	109850 TQ	SCBLS	10/01-12/01
	Columbia MSA, SC	Y	30770 FQ	62570 AW	110740 TQ	SCBLS	10/01-12/01
	Greenville-Spartanburg-Anderson MSA, SC	Y	29630 FQ	65070 AW	132130 TQ	SCBLS	10/01-12/01
	Myrtle Beach MSA, SC	Y	23490 FQ	52210 AW	97330 TQ	SCBLS	10/01-12/01
	South Dakota	Y	50300 FQ	79510 AW	133190 TQ	SDBLS	10/01-12/01
	Sioux Falls MSA, SD	Y	51500 FQ	85190 AW		SDBLS	10/01-12/01
	Tennessee	Y	26230 FQ	63350 AW	128560 TQ	TNBLS	10/01-12/01
	Chattanooga MSA, TN-GA	Y	28620 FQ	62930 AW	125290 TQ	TNBLS	10/01-12/01
	Clarksville-Hopkinsville MSA, TN-KY	Y	21590 FQ	53490 AW	104040 TQ	TNBLS	10/01-12/01
	Johnson City-Kingsport-Bristol MSA, TN-VA	Y	23770 FQ	56320 AW	109180 TQ	TNBLS	10/01-12/01
	Knoxville MSA, TN	Y	24710 FQ	61520 AW	117790 TQ	TNBLS	10/01-12/01

AAW	Average annual wage	**AOH**	Average offered, high	**ASH**	Average starting, high	**H**	Hourly	**M**	Monthly	**S**	Special: hourly and annual
AE	Average entry wage	**AOL**	Average offered, low	**ASL**	Average starting, low	**HI**	Highest wage paid	**MTC**	Median total compensation	**TQ**	Third quartile wage
AEX	Average experienced wage	**APH**	Average pay, high range	**AW**	Average wage paid	**HR**	High end range	**MW**	Median wage paid	**W**	Weekly
AO	Average offered	**APL**	Average pay, low range	**FQ**	First quartile wage	**LR**	Low end range	**SQ**	Second quartile wage	**Y**	Yearly

Occupation/Type/Industry	Location	Per	Low	Mid	High	Source	Date
General and Operations Manager	Memphis MSA, TN-AR-MS	Y	30810 FQ	68470 AW		TNBLS	10/01-12/01
	Nashville MSA, TN	Y	31940 FQ	70400 AW	144000 TQ	TNBLS	10/01-12/01
	Texas	Y	26960 FQ	68070 AW	141690 TQ	TXBLS	10/01-12/01
	Amarillo MSA, TX	Y	24780 FQ	56270 AW	106800 TQ	TXBLS	10/01-12/01
	Austin-San Marcos MSA, TX	Y	29700 FQ	70530 AW	144220 TQ	TXBLS	10/01-12/01
	Beaumont-Port Arthur MSA, TX	Y	25100 FQ	61790 AW	136990 TQ	TXBLS	10/01-12/01
	Brazoria PMSA, TX	Y	28110 FQ	64460 AW	117630 TQ	TXBLS	10/01-12/01
	Brownsville-Harlingen-San Benito MSA, TX	Y	22060 FQ	54660 AW	113770 TQ	TXBLS	10/01-12/01
	Corpus Christi MSA, TX	Y	25740 FQ	61090 AW	118580 TQ	TXBLS	10/01-12/01
	Dallas PMSA, TX	Y	30850 FQ	77510 AW		TXBLS	10/01-12/01
	El Paso MSA, TX	Y	23140 FQ	60140 AW	117690 TQ	TXBLS	10/01-12/01
	Fort Worth-Arlington PMSA, TX	Y	28690 FQ	66000 AW	121040 TQ	TXBLS	10/01-12/01
	Galveston-Texas City PMSA, TX	Y	23140 FQ	57830 AW	108940 TQ	TXBLS	10/01-12/01
	Houston PMSA, TX	Y	26700 FQ	72610 AW		TXBLS	10/01-12/01
	Killeen-Temple MSA, TX	Y	24030 FQ	55640 AW	99790 TQ	TXBLS	10/01-12/01
	Laredo MSA, TX	Y	24740 FQ	55020 AW	104430 TQ	TXBLS	10/01-12/01
	Longview-Marshall MSA, TX	Y	27190 FQ	58920 AW	102820 TQ	TXBLS	10/01-12/01
	Lubbock MSA, TX	Y	22210 FQ	55010 AW	101610 TQ	TXBLS	10/01-12/01
	McAllen-Edinburg-Mission MSA, TX	Y	20290 FQ	53200 AW	101950 TQ	TXBLS	10/01-12/01
	Odessa-Midland MSA, TX	Y	27370 FQ	62460 AW	105070 TQ	TXBLS	10/01-12/01
	San Antonio MSA, TX	Y	28740 FQ	66110 AW	140910 TQ	TXBLS	10/01-12/01
	Tyler MSA, TX	Y	26050 FQ	63800 AW	130770 TQ	TXBLS	10/01-12/01
	Waco MSA, TX	Y	25390 FQ	67550 AW	142490 TQ	TXBLS	10/01-12/01
	Utah	Y	27170 FQ	63150 AW	124470 TQ	UTBLS	10/01-12/01
	Provo-Orem MSA, UT	Y	28730 FQ	60490 AW	120720 TQ	UTBLS	10/01-12/01
	Salt Lake City-Ogden MSA, UT	Y	28730 FQ	66740 AW	133930 TQ	UTBLS	10/01-12/01
	Vermont	Y	43830 FQ	87550 AW		VTBLS	10/01-12/01
	Burlington MSA, VT	Y	45500 FQ	92050 AW		VTBLS	10/01-12/01
	Virginia	Y	31600 FQ	75020 AW		VABLS	10/01-12/01
	Lynchburg MSA, VA	Y	28650 FQ	61750 AW	116020 TQ	VABLS	10/01-12/01
	Norfolk-Virginia Beach-Newport News MSA, VA-NC	Y	28190 FQ	65850 AW	132410 TQ	VABLS	10/01-12/01
	Richmond-Petersburg MSA, VA	Y	32940 FQ	76030 AW	144990 TQ	VABLS	10/01-12/01
	Roanoke MSA, VA	Y	30570 FQ	66100 AW	131640 TQ	VABLS	10/01-12/01
	Washington	Y	43960 FQ	91790 AW		WABLS	10/01-12/01
	Bremerton PMSA, WA	Y	36090 FQ	77230 AW	141920 TQ	WABLS	10/01-12/01
	Olympia PMSA, WA	Y	46540 FQ	83230 AW	135840 TQ	WABLS	10/01-12/01
	Richland-Kennewick-Pasco MSA, WA	Y	43170 FQ	90730 AW		WABLS	10/01-12/01
	Seattle-Bellevue-Everett PMSA, WA	Y	46610 FQ	98060 AW		WABLS	10/01-12/01
	Spokane MSA, WA	Y	40910 FQ	87250 AW		WABLS	10/01-12/01
	Tacoma PMSA, WA	Y	45500 FQ	89070 AW		WABLS	10/01-12/01
	Yakima MSA, WA	Y	41910 FQ	78110 AW	142220 TQ	WABLS	10/01-12/01
	West Virginia	Y	23290 FQ	54790 AW	103400 TQ	WVBLS	10/01-12/01
	Charleston MSA, WV	Y	29900 FQ	61750 AW	108780 TQ	WVBLS	10/01-12/01
	Huntington-Ashland MSA, WV-KY-OH	Y	23470 FQ	53880 AW	104440 TQ	WVBLS	10/01-12/01
	Wisconsin	Y	30220 FQ	72180 AW	145100 TQ	WIBLS	10/01-12/01
	Appleton-Oshkosh-Neenah MSA, WI	Y	30820 FQ	69660 AW	136860 TQ	WIBLS	10/01-12/01
	Green Bay MSA, WI	Y	30700 FQ	72870 AW		WIBLS	10/01-12/01
	Madison MSA, WI	Y	31820 FQ	76410 AW		WIBLS	10/01-12/01
	Milwaukee-Waukesha PMSA, WI	Y	36570 FQ	81970 AW		WIBLS	10/01-12/01
	Racine PMSA, WI	Y	30300 FQ	69750 AW	138700 TQ	WIBLS	10/01-12/01
	Wyoming	Y	26490 FQ	58620 AW	104390 TQ	WYBLS	10/01-12/01
	Cheyenne MSA, WY	Y	27020 FQ	58910 AW	110730 TQ	WYBLS	10/01-12/01
	Puerto Rico	Y	31470 FQ	70160 AW	132120 TQ	PRBLS	10/01-12/01
	Virgin Islands	Y	37220 FQ	66300 AW	111040 TQ	VIBLS	10/01-12/01
	Guam	Y	22400 FQ	49770 AW	88200 TQ	GUBLS	10/01-12/01
General Information Systems Technician	United States	Y		30962 AW		ACC	1/99-1/00

AAW	Average annual wage	**AOH**	Average offered, high	**ASH**	Average starting, high	**H**	Hourly	**M**	Monthly	**S**	Special: hourly and annual
AE	Average entry wage	**AOL**	Average offered, low	**ASL**	Average starting, low	**HI**	Highest wage paid	**MTC**	Median total compensation	**TQ**	Third quartile wage
AEX	Average experienced wage	**APH**	Average pay, high range	**AW**	Average wage paid	**HR**	High end range	**MW**	Median wage paid	**W**	Weekly
AO	Average offered	**APL**	Average pay, low range	**FQ**	First quartile wage	**LR**	Low end range	**SQ**	Second quartile wage	**Y**	Yearly

Occupation/Type/Industry	Location	Per	Low	Mid	High	Source	Date
General Manager							
Environment	United States	Y		69002 AW		SAFEDIR	2001
Environment	Midwest	Y		60833 AW		SAFEDIR	2001
Environment	Northeast	Y		100000 AW		SAFEDIR	2001
Environment	South	Y		72000 AW		SAFEDIR	2001
Environment	West	Y		52510 AW		SAFEDIR	2001
General Office Worker	United States	Y		28600 AW		USATOD4	1/00-1/01
General Schedule Employee G-1							
Federal Government	United States	Y	16528 AE			OPM13	2003
Federal Government	Huntsville MSA, AL	Y	16595 AE			OPM13	2003
Federal Government	Los Angeles-Riverside-Orange County CMSA, CA	Y	17656 AE			OPM13	2003
Federal Government	Sacramento-Yolo CMSA, CA	Y	17038 AE			OPM13	2003
Federal Government	San Diego MSA, CA	Y	17146 AE			OPM13	2003
Federal Government	San Francisco-Oakland-San Jose CMSA, CA	Y	18111 AE			OPM13	2003
Federal Government	Denver-Boulder-Greeley CMSA, CO	Y	17244 AE			OPM13	2003
Federal Government	Hartford MSA, CT	Y	17361 AE			OPM13	2003
Federal Government	Washington-Baltimore CMSA, DC-MD-VA-WV	Y	16961 AE			OPM13	2003
Federal Government	Miami-Fort Lauderdale CMSA, FL	Y	17108 AE			OPM13	2003
Federal Government	Orlando MSA, FL	Y	16533 AE			OPM13	2003
Federal Government	Atlanta MSA, GA	Y	16696 AE			OPM13	2003
Federal Government	Chicago-Gary-Kenosha CMSA, IL-IN-WI	Y	17432 AE			OPM13	2003
Federal Government	Indianapolis MSA, IN	Y	16560 AE			OPM13	2003
Federal Government	Boston-Worcester-Lawrence CMSA, MA-NH-ME-CT-RI	Y	17279 AE			OPM13	2003
Federal Government	Detroit-Ann Arbor-Flint CMSA, MI	Y	17452 AE			OPM13	2003
Federal Government	Minneapolis-St. Paul MSA, MN-WI	Y	16973 AE			OPM13	2003
Federal Government	Kansas City MSA, MO-KS	Y	16626 AE			OPM13	2003
Federal Government	St. Louis MSA, MO-IL	Y	16580 AE			OPM13	2003
Federal Government	New York-Northern New Jersey-Long Island CMSA, NY-NJ-CT-PA	Y	17531 AE			OPM13	2003
Federal Government	Cincinnati-Hamilton CMSA, OH-KY-IN	Y	17053 AE			OPM13	2003
Federal Government	Cleveland-Akron CMSA, OH	Y	16786 AE			OPM13	2003
Federal Government	Columbus MSA, OH	Y	16842 AE			OPM13	2003
Federal Government	Dayton-Springfield MSA, OH	Y	16678 AE			OPM13	2003
Federal Government	Portland-Salem CMSA, OR-WA	Y	16985 AE			OPM13	2003
Federal Government	Philadelphia-Wilmington-Atlantic City CMSA, PA-NJ-DE-MD	Y	17056 AE			OPM13	2003
Federal Government	Pittsburgh MSA, PA	Y	16662 AE			OPM13	2003
Federal Government	Dallas-Fort Worth CMSA, TX	Y	16872 AE			OPM13	2003
Federal Government	Houston-Galveston-Brazoria CMSA, TX	Y	18045 AE			OPM13	2003
Federal Government	Richmond-Petersburg MSA, VA	Y	16685 AE			OPM13	2003
Federal Government	Seattle-Tacoma-Bremerton CMSA, WA	Y	17005 AE			OPM13	2003
Federal Government	Milwaukee-Racine CMSA, WI	Y	16743 AE			OPM13	2003
Geographer	California	Y	35550 FQ	49250 AW	69250 TQ	CABLS	10/01-12/01
	Washington PMSA, DC-MD-VA-WV	Y	39380 FQ	60300 AW	85410 TQ	DCBLS	10/01-12/01
	Maryland	Y	38640 FQ	55480 AW	70890 TQ	MDBLS	10/01-12/01
	Oregon	Y	31650 FQ	44140 AW	68280 TQ	ORBLS	10/01-12/01
	Texas	Y	22130 FQ	39890 AW	58910 TQ	TXBLS	10/01-12/01
	Utah	Y	28470 FQ	47430 AW	67690 TQ	UTBLS	10/01-12/01
	Virginia	Y	32520 FQ	60990 AW	96190 TQ	VABLS	10/01-12/01
	Washington	Y	32960 FQ	49520 AW	70160 TQ	WABLS	10/01-12/01
Geography Teacher							
Postsecondary	California	Y	38240 FQ	66070 AW	97270 TQ	CABLS	10/01-12/01

AAW Average annual wage	**AOH** Average offered, high	**ASH** Average starting, high	**H** Hourly	**M** Monthly	**S** Special: hourly and annual
AE Average entry wage	**AOL** Average offered, low	**ASL** Average starting, low	**HI** Highest wage paid	**MTC** Median total compensation	**TQ** Third quartile wage
AEX Average experienced wage	**APH** Average pay, high range	**AW** Average wage paid	**HR** High end range	**MW** Median wage paid	**W** Weekly
AO Average offered	**APL** Average pay, low range	**FQ** First quartile wage	**LR** Low end range	**SQ** Second quartile wage	**Y** Yearly

Occupation/Type/Industry	Location	Per	Low	Mid	High	Source	Date
Geography Teacher							
Postsecondary	San Francisco PMSA, CA	Y	42060 FQ	66520 AW	91880 TQ	CABLS	10/01-12/01
Postsecondary	Colorado	Y	32720 FQ	54040 AW	85830 TQ	COBLS	10/01-12/01
Postsecondary	Denver PMSA, CO	Y	32590 FQ	57130 AW	89270 TQ	COBLS	10/01-12/01
Postsecondary	District of Columbia	Y	35770 FQ	55090 AW	80860 TQ	DCBLS	10/01-12/01
Postsecondary	Washington PMSA, DC-MD-VA-WV	Y	29280 FQ	58870 AW	95590 TQ	DCBLS	10/01-12/01
Postsecondary	Florida	Y	36650 FQ	62150 AW	95430 TQ	FLBLS	10/01-12/01
Postsecondary	Gainesville MSA, FL	Y	36080 FQ	67280 AW	97850 TQ	FLBLS	10/01-12/01
Postsecondary	Tallahassee MSA, FL	Y	42110 FQ	60460 AW	88230 TQ	FLBLS	10/01-12/01
Postsecondary	Tampa-St. Petersburg-Clearwater MSA, FL	Y	26720 FQ	54930 AW	96650 TQ	FLBLS	10/01-12/01
Postsecondary	Georgia	Y	41800 FQ	60160 AW	85050 TQ	GABLS	10/01-12/01
Postsecondary	Hawaii	Y	38260 FQ	61900 AW	88830 TQ	HIBLS	10/01-12/01
Postsecondary	Honolulu MSA, HI	Y	39480 FQ	63790 AW	90460 TQ	HIBLS	10/01-12/01
Postsecondary	Illinois	Y	29230 FQ	61290 AW	90960 TQ	ILBLS	10/01-12/01
Postsecondary	Chicago PMSA, IL	Y	30070 FQ	63540 AW	91650 TQ	ILBLS	10/01-12/01
Postsecondary	Indiana	Y	30720 FQ	56260 AW	88700 TQ	INBLS	10/01-12/01
Postsecondary	Iowa	Y	36080 FQ	62970 AW	89990 TQ	IABLS	10/01-12/01
Postsecondary	Kansas	Y	37850 FQ	62450 AW	89240 TQ	KSBLS	10/01-12/01
Postsecondary	Kentucky	Y	37430 FQ	57980 AW	90150 TQ	KYBLS	10/01-12/01
Postsecondary	Maryland	Y	37430 FQ	70350 AW	125330 TQ	MDBLS	10/01-12/01
Postsecondary	Baltimore PMSA, MD	Y	39020 FQ	73900 AW	127110 TQ	MDBLS	10/01-12/01
Postsecondary	Massachusetts	Y	36770 FQ	57620 AW	87420 TQ	MABLS	10/01-12/01
Postsecondary	Boston PMSA, MA-NH	Y	35910 FQ	56810 AW	85170 TQ	MABLS	10/01-12/01
Postsecondary	Michigan	Y	37290 FQ	61900 AW	95700 TQ	MIBLS	10/01-12/01
Postsecondary	Minnesota	Y	34000 FQ	55090 AW	84740 TQ	MNBLS	10/01-12/01
Postsecondary	Minneapolis-St. Paul MSA, MN-WI	Y	38930 FQ	59760 AW	92550 TQ	MNBLS	10/01-12/01
Postsecondary	Missouri	Y	32670 FQ	53200 AW	77790 TQ	MOBLS	10/01-12/01
Postsecondary	St. Louis MSA, MO-IL	Y	28290 FQ	54130 AW	86520 TQ	MOBLS	10/01-12/01
Postsecondary	Nebraska	Y	31930 FQ	47950 AW	65350 TQ	NEBLS	10/01-12/01
Postsecondary	Nevada	Y	25100 FQ	53750 AW	83960 TQ	NVBLS	10/01-12/01
Postsecondary	New Jersey	Y	35160 FQ	63420 AW	99770 TQ	NJBLS	10/01-12/01
Postsecondary	New York	Y	36230 FQ	63570 AW	96410 TQ	NYBLS	10/01-12/01
Postsecondary	North Carolina	Y	34010 FQ	53720 AW	85100 TQ	NCBLS	10/01-12/01
Postsecondary	Ohio	Y	35420 FQ	58720 AW	88400 TQ	OHBLS	10/01-12/01
Postsecondary	Oklahoma	Y	24760 FQ	45930 AW	79690 TQ	OKBLS	10/01-12/01
Postsecondary	Oregon	Y	31470 FQ	66800 AW	93240 TQ	ORBLS	10/01-12/01
Postsecondary	Pennsylvania	Y	34050 FQ	61440 AW	90580 TQ	PABLS	10/01-12/01
Postsecondary	Philadelphia PMSA, PA-NJ	Y	35850 FQ	61680 AW	90110 TQ	PABLS	10/01-12/01
Postsecondary	Pittsburgh MSA, PA	Y	35530 FQ	58270 AW	85950 TQ	PABLS	10/01-12/01
Postsecondary	Scranton-Wilkes-Barre-Hazleton MSA, PA	Y	23350 FQ	56240 AW	84470 TQ	PABLS	10/01-12/01
Postsecondary	South Carolina	Y	26050 FQ	44310 AW	71720 TQ	SCBLS	10/01-12/01
Postsecondary	Tennessee	Y	36210 FQ	53660 AW	73690 TQ	TNBLS	10/01-12/01
Postsecondary	Nashville MSA, TN	Y	38930 FQ	51730 AW	70020 TQ	TNBLS	10/01-12/01
Postsecondary	Texas	Y	27170 FQ	51420 AW	76180 TQ	TXBLS	10/01-12/01
Postsecondary	Virginia	Y	29890 FQ	59720 AW	97250 TQ	VABLS	10/01-12/01
Postsecondary	Washington	Y	31320 FQ	53390 AW	84960 TQ	WABLS	10/01-12/01
Postsecondary	Seattle-Bellevue-Everett PMSA, WA	Y	37320 FQ	65220 AW	92610 TQ	WABLS	10/01-12/01
Postsecondary	West Virginia	Y	37430 FQ	58170 AW	85990 TQ	WVBLS	10/01-12/01
Postsecondary	Wisconsin	Y	33690 FQ	50550 AW	73720 TQ	WIBLS	10/01-12/01
Geological and Petroleum Technician							
	Alabama	Y	29330 FQ	39830 AW	60720 TQ	ALBLS	10/01-12/01
	Alaska	Y	34680 FQ	52340 AW	69950 TQ	AKBLS	10/01-12/01
	Arizona	Y	18460 FQ	41890 AW	61100 TQ	AZBLS	10/01-12/01
	Arkansas	Y	18100 FQ	34000 AW	48030 TQ	ARBLS	10/01-12/01
	California	Y	25050 FQ	42640 AW	61700 TQ	CABLS	10/01-12/01
	Colorado	Y	20090 FQ	34830 AW	58550 TQ	COBLS	10/01-12/01
	Delaware	Y	13540 FQ	29260 AW	60020 TQ	DEBLS	10/01-12/01
	Florida	Y	18500 FQ	27550 AW	38780 TQ	FLBLS	10/01-12/01
	Georgia	Y	21680 FQ	33290 AW	43220 TQ	GABLS	10/01-12/01
	Idaho	Y	23200 FQ	40680 AW	55750 TQ	IDBLS	10/01-12/01
	Illinois	Y	28140 FQ	43950 AW	61940 TQ	ILBLS	10/01-12/01
	Kansas	Y	29880 FQ	50260 AW	69230 TQ	KSBLS	10/01-12/01
	Louisiana	Y	25620 FQ	48400 AW	71230 TQ	LABLS	10/01-12/01
	Maine	Y	33580 FQ	50560 AW	71860 TQ	MEBLS	10/01-12/01
	Massachusetts	Y	24980 FQ	38980 AW	55530 TQ	MABLS	10/01-12/01
	Michigan	Y	24330 FQ	47750 AW	69270 TQ	MIBLS	10/01-12/01

AAW	Average annual wage	AOH	Average offered, high	ASH	Average starting, high	H	Hourly	M	Monthly	S	Special: hourly and annual
AE	Average entry wage	AOL	Average offered, low	ASL	Average starting, low	HI	Highest wage paid	MTC	Median total compensation	TQ	Third quartile wage
AEX	Average experienced wage	APH	Average pay, high range	AW	Average wage paid	HR	High end range	MW	Median wage paid	W	Weekly
AO	Average offered	APL	Average pay, low range	FQ	First quartile wage	LR	Low end range	SQ	Second quartile wage	Y	Yearly

Occupation/Type/Industry	Location	Per	Low	Mid	High	Source	Date
Geological and Petroleum Technician	Montana	Y	29850 FQ	35320 AW	43590 TQ	MTBLS	10/01-12/01
	Nebraska	Y	19370 FQ	31740 AW	47870 TQ	NEBLS	10/01-12/01
	Nevada	Y	20900 FQ	32560 AW	44630 TQ	NVBLS	10/01-12/01
	New Jersey	Y	29700 FQ	33300 AW	36420 TQ	NJBLS	10/01-12/01
	New Mexico	Y	15890 FQ	32210 AW	55680 TQ	NMBLS	10/01-12/01
	New York	Y	29950 FQ	48050 AW	71310 TQ	NYBLS	10/01-12/01
	Ohio	Y	19890 FQ	34890 AW	55150 TQ	OHBLS	10/01-12/01
	Oklahoma	Y	22880 FQ	38990 AW	59150 TQ	OKBLS	10/01-12/01
	Oregon	Y	14580 FQ	32420 AW	55200 TQ	ORBLS	10/01-12/01
	Pennsylvania	Y	26130 FQ	40680 AW	55820 TQ	PABLS	10/01-12/01
	South Carolina	Y	19720 FQ	31740 AW	46570 TQ	SCBLS	10/01-12/01
	Texas	Y	15390 FQ	41770 AW	67350 TQ	TXBLS	10/01-12/01
	Utah	Y	28790 FQ	50350 AW	83390 TQ	UTBLS	10/01-12/01
	Virginia	Y	30340 FQ	40750 AW	60580 TQ	VABLS	10/01-12/01
	Washington	Y	15410 FQ	32550 AW	48690 TQ	WABLS	10/01-12/01
	West Virginia	Y	17730 FQ	34440 AW	55140 TQ	WVBLS	10/01-12/01
	Wyoming	Y	35610 FQ	40730 AW	44680 TQ	WYBLS	10/01-12/01
	Puerto Rico	Y	14920 FQ	20280 AW	29310 TQ	PRBLS	10/01-12/01
Geoscientist							
Except Hydrologist and Geographer	Alabama	Y	37240 FQ	50340 AW	76470 TQ	ALBLS	10/01-12/01
Except Hydrologist and Geographer	Alaska	Y	41550 FQ	81530 AW	127540 TQ	AKBLS	10/01-12/01
Except Hydrologist and Geographer	Arizona	Y	29820 FQ	52840 AW	86520 TQ	AZBLS	10/01-12/01
Except Hydrologist and Geographer	Arkansas	Y	29310 FQ	53730 AW	87740 TQ	ARBLS	10/01-12/01
Except Hydrologist and Geographer	California	Y	36040 FQ	64140 AW	101520 TQ	CABLS	10/01-12/01
Except Hydrologist and Geographer	Colorado	Y	34850 FQ	69960 AW	112400 TQ	COBLS	10/01-12/01
Except Hydrologist and Geographer	Connecticut	Y	31300 FQ	57310 AW	103890 TQ	CTBLS	10/01-12/01
Except Hydrologist and Geographer	Delaware	Y	42590 FQ	81550 AW	131820 TQ	DEBLS	10/01-12/01
Except Hydrologist and Geographer	Florida	Y	36070 FQ	64600 AW	106990 TQ	FLBLS	10/01-12/01
Except Hydrologist and Geographer	Georgia	Y	31670 FQ	50660 AW	72720 TQ	GABLS	10/01-12/01
Except Hydrologist and Geographer	Hawaii	Y	37780 FQ	66310 AW	105300 TQ	HIBLS	10/01-12/01
Except Hydrologist and Geographer	Idaho	Y	39670 FQ	54030 AW	70910 TQ	IDBLS	10/01-12/01
Except Hydrologist and Geographer	Illinois	Y	28260 FQ	55800 AW	76630 TQ	ILBLS	10/01-12/01
Except Hydrologist and Geographer	Indiana	Y	32840 FQ	47090 AW	68740 TQ	INBLS	10/01-12/01
Except Hydrologist and Geographer	Iowa	Y	31270 FQ	47520 AW	65620 TQ	IABLS	10/01-12/01
Except Hydrologist and Geographer	Kansas	Y	37600 FQ	51290 AW	68160 TQ	KSBLS	10/01-12/01
Except Hydrologist and Geographer	Kentucky	Y	29730 FQ	43200 AW	64320 TQ	KYBLS	10/01-12/01
Except Hydrologist and Geographer	Louisiana	Y	42310 FQ	80340 AW	122440 TQ	LABLS	10/01-12/01
Except Hydrologist and Geographer	Maine	Y	35260 FQ	46430 AW	63040 TQ	MEBLS	10/01-12/01
Except Hydrologist and Geographer	Maryland	Y	40490 FQ	70000 AW	106650 TQ	MDBLS	10/01-12/01
Except Hydrologist and Geographer	Massachusetts	Y	32130 FQ	48930 AW	75510 TQ	MABLS	10/01-12/01
Except Hydrologist and Geographer	Michigan	Y	30530 FQ	51010 AW	71630 TQ	MIBLS	10/01-12/01
Except Hydrologist and Geographer	Minnesota	Y	33810 FQ	61960 AW	87500 TQ	MNBLS	10/01-12/01
Except Hydrologist and Geographer	Mississippi	Y	39320 FQ	61220 AW	90710 TQ	MSBLS	10/01-12/01
Except Hydrologist and Geographer	Missouri	Y	30300 FQ	45180 AW	67270 TQ	MOBLS	10/01-12/01
Except Hydrologist and Geographer	Montana	Y	32220 FQ	70720 AW	134980 TQ	MTBLS	10/01-12/01
Except Hydrologist and Geographer	Nebraska	Y	23480 FQ	47630 AW	75960 TQ	NEBLS	10/01-12/01
Except Hydrologist and Geographer	Nevada	Y	40280 FQ	63120 AW	89060 TQ	NVBLS	10/01-12/01
Except Hydrologist and Geographer	New Hampshire	Y	34030 FQ	56970 AW	89100 TQ	NHBLS	10/01-12/01
Except Hydrologist and Geographer	New Jersey	Y	36080 FQ	55820 AW	79130 TQ	NJBLS	10/01-12/01
Except Hydrologist and Geographer	New Mexico	Y	37520 FQ	71060 AW	111960 TQ	NMBLS	10/01-12/01
Except Hydrologist and Geographer	New York	Y	27790 FQ	53680 AW	77900 TQ	NYBLS	10/01-12/01
Except Hydrologist and Geographer	North Carolina	Y	37280 FQ	50600 AW	58520 TQ	NCBLS	10/01-12/01
Except Hydrologist and Geographer	Ohio	Y	31130 FQ	53830 AW	73960 TQ	OHBLS	10/01-12/01
Except Hydrologist and Geographer	Oklahoma	Y	44540 FQ	84410 AW	122750 TQ	OKBLS	10/01-12/01
Except Hydrologist and Geographer	Oregon	Y	37260 FQ	54510 AW	78620 TQ	ORBLS	10/01-12/01
Except Hydrologist and Geographer	Pennsylvania	Y	31320 FQ	56240 AW	79620 TQ	PABLS	10/01-12/01
Except Hydrologist and Geographer	South Dakota	Y	36740 FQ	49420 AW	64280 TQ	SDBLS	10/01-12/01
Except Hydrologist and Geographer	Tennessee	Y	29790 FQ	43690 AW	65760 TQ	TNBLS	10/01-12/01
Except Hydrologist and Geographer	Texas	Y	31430 FQ	76800 AW	133340 TQ	TXBLS	10/01-12/01
Except Hydrologist and Geographer	Utah	Y	36520 FQ	54130 AW	74160 TQ	UTBLS	10/01-12/01
Except Hydrologist and Geographer	Vermont	Y	31180 FQ	53530 AW	88220 TQ	VTBLS	10/01-12/01
Except Hydrologist and Geographer	Virginia	Y	35720 FQ	71110 AW	111560 TQ	VABLS	10/01-12/01
Except Hydrologist and Geographer	Washington	Y	40480 FQ	62940 AW	95240 TQ	WABLS	10/01-12/01
Except Hydrologist and Geographer	West Virginia	Y	26460 FQ	47660 AW	79700 TQ	WVBLS	10/01-12/01
Except Hydrologist and Geographer	Wisconsin	Y	30290 FQ	46750 AW	71770 TQ	WIBLS	10/01-12/01
Except Hydrologist and Geographer	Wyoming	Y	39260 FQ	63700 AW	93990 TQ	WYBLS	10/01-12/01
Glazier	Alabama	H	8.38 FQ	12.63 AW	16.91 TQ	ALBLS	10/01-12/01
	Birmingham MSA, AL	H	11.04 FQ	14.52 AW	17.41 TQ	ALBLS	10/01-12/01
	Huntsville MSA, AL	H	8.07 FQ	12.07 AW	16.86 TQ	ALBLS	10/01-12/01

AAW	Average annual wage	**AOH**	Average offered, high	**ASH**	Average starting, high	**H**	Hourly	**M**	Monthly	**S**	Special: hourly and annual
AE	Average entry wage	**AOL**	Average offered, low	**ASL**	Average starting, low	**HI**	Highest wage paid	**MTC**	Median total compensation	**TQ**	Third quartile wage
AEX	Average experienced wage	**APH**	Average pay, high range	**AW**	Average wage paid	**HR**	High end range	**MW**	Median wage paid	**W**	Weekly
AO	Average offered	**APL**	Average pay, low range	**FQ**	First quartile wage	**LR**	Low end range	**SQ**	Second quartile wage	**Y**	Yearly

Occupation/Type/Industry	Location	Per	Low	Mid	High	Source	Date
Glazier	Mobile MSA, AL	H	9.69 FQ	12.67 AW	16.15 TQ	ALBLS	10/01-12/01
	Montgomery MSA, AL	H	10.45 FQ	13.83 AW	16.91 TQ	ALBLS	10/01-12/01
	Alaska	H	19.47 FQ	23.81 AW	27.75 TQ	AKBLS	10/01-12/01
	Anchorage MSA, AK	H	22.38 FQ	24.22 AW	27.76 TQ	AKBLS	10/01-12/01
	Arizona	H	8.29 FQ	12.87 AW	19.46 TQ	AZBLS	10/01-12/01
	Phoenix-Mesa MSA, AZ	H	8.98 FQ	13.72 AW	20.03 TQ	AZBLS	10/01-12/01
	Tucson MSA, AZ	H	7.83 FQ	12.25 AW	17.98 TQ	AZBLS	10/01-12/01
	Arkansas	H	5.70 FQ	8.93 AW	14.02 TQ	ARBLS	10/01-12/01
	Fayetteville-Springdale-Rogers MSA, AR	H	9.37 FQ	11.63 AW	14.87 TQ	ARBLS	10/01-12/01
	California	H	9.82 FQ	19.42 AW	32.19 TQ	CABLS	10/01-12/01
	Chico-Paradise MSA, CA	H	8.51 FQ	12.95 AW	17.51 TQ	CABLS	10/01-12/01
	Fresno MSA, CA	H	7.59 FQ	15.79 AW	27.58 TQ	CABLS	10/01-12/01
	Los Angeles-Long Beach PMSA, CA	H	9.94 FQ	18.30 AW	30.34 TQ	CABLS	10/01-12/01
	Modesto MSA, CA	H	10.36 FQ	14.64 AW	18.67 TQ	CABLS	10/01-12/01
	Oakland PMSA, CA	H	10.78 FQ	23.28 AW	34.38 TQ	CABLS	10/01-12/01
	Orange County PMSA, CA	H	11.69 FQ	19.19 AW	30.58 TQ	CABLS	10/01-12/01
	Redding MSA, CA	H	9.41 FQ	13.00 AW	17.22 TQ	CABLS	10/01-12/01
	Riverside-San Bernardino PMSA, CA	H	9.10 FQ	18.01 AW	31.30 TQ	CABLS	10/01-12/01
	Sacramento PMSA, CA	H	7.10 FQ	17.33 AW	26.95 TQ	CABLS	10/01-12/01
	Salinas MSA, CA	H	13.23 FQ	22.37 AW	31.79 TQ	CABLS	10/01-12/01
	San Diego MSA, CA	H	10.26 FQ	19.41 AW	27.64 TQ	CABLS	10/01-12/01
	San Francisco PMSA, CA	H	14.81 FQ	24.80 AW	35.16 TQ	CABLS	10/01-12/01
	San Jose PMSA, CA	H	10.08 FQ	20.15 AW	33.62 TQ	CABLS	10/01-12/01
	Santa Barbara-Santa Maria-Lompoc MSA, CA	H	8.12 FQ	16.59 AW	27.31 TQ	CABLS	10/01-12/01
	Santa Cruz-Watsonville PMSA, CA	H	10.85 FQ	15.82 AW	22.21 TQ	CABLS	10/01-12/01
	Santa Rosa PMSA, CA	H	12.37 FQ	18.94 AW	25.16 TQ	CABLS	10/01-12/01
	Stockton-Lodi MSA, CA	H	9.75 FQ	14.94 AW	20.80 TQ	CABLS	10/01-12/01
	Vallejo-Fairfield-Napa PMSA, CA	H	9.10 FQ	14.40 AW	20.98 TQ	CABLS	10/01-12/01
	Ventura PMSA, CA	H	11.56 FQ	18.32 AW	22.78 TQ	CABLS	10/01-12/01
	Visalia-Tulare-Porterville MSA, CA	H	7.66 FQ	12.81 AW	18.29 TQ	CABLS	10/01-12/01
	Colorado	H	10.60 FQ	19.00 AW	26.48 TQ	COBLS	10/01-12/01
	Boulder-Longmont PMSA, CO	H	9.63 FQ	14.16 AW	20.66 TQ	COBLS	10/01-12/01
	Colorado Springs MSA, CO	H	8.87 FQ	13.63 AW	17.66 TQ	COBLS	10/01-12/01
	Denver PMSA, CO	H	15.06 FQ	21.17 AW	26.90 TQ	COBLS	10/01-12/01
	Fort Collins-Loveland MSA, CO	H	8.23 FQ	13.58 AW	20.57 TQ	COBLS	10/01-12/01
	Connecticut	H	12.04 FQ	19.33 AW	27.85 TQ	CTBLS	10/01-12/01
	Bridgeport PMSA, CT	H	14.85 FQ	20.64 AW	26.96 TQ	CTBLS	10/01-12/01
	Danbury PMSA, CT	H	10.50 FQ	14.88 AW	19.25 TQ	CTBLS	10/01-12/01
	Hartford MSA, CT	H	12.04 FQ	18.67 AW	37.47 TQ	CTBLS	10/01-12/01
	New Haven-Meriden PMSA, CT	H	17.62 FQ	23.59 AW	28.54 TQ	CTBLS	10/01-12/01
	Stamford-Norwalk PMSA, CT	H	10.28 FQ	21.31 AW	33.20 TQ	CTBLS	10/01-12/01
	Delaware	H	8.62 FQ	12.11 AW	16.10 TQ	DEBLS	10/01-12/01
	Wilmington-Newark PMSA, DE-MD	H	8.52 FQ	12.78 AW	17.72 TQ	DEBLS	10/01-12/01
	District of Columbia	H	7.53 FQ	17.10 AW	26.81 TQ	DCBLS	10/01-12/01
	Washington PMSA, DC-MD-VA-WV	H	10.17 FQ	17.64 AW	26.34 TQ	DCBLS	10/01-12/01
	Florida	H	5.86 FQ	10.79 AW	16.79 TQ	FLBLS	10/01-12/01
	Daytona Beach MSA, FL	H	8.16 FQ	10.64 AW	13.76 TQ	FLBLS	10/01-12/01
	Fort Lauderdale PMSA, FL	H	9.49 FQ	13.67 AW	19.80 TQ	FLBLS	10/01-12/01
	Fort Myers-Cape Coral MSA, FL	H	9.07 FQ	13.56 AW	17.30 TQ	FLBLS	10/01-12/01
	Fort Pierce-Port St. Lucie MSA, FL	H	8.01 FQ	11.00 AW	13.99 TQ	FLBLS	10/01-12/01
	Fort Walton Beach MSA, FL	H	8.26 FQ	11.20 AW	15.56 TQ	FLBLS	10/01-12/01
	Jacksonville MSA, FL	H	7.98 FQ	12.29 AW	16.46 TQ	FLBLS	10/01-12/01
	Lakeland-Winter Haven MSA, FL	H	8.76 FQ	13.87 AW	18.88 TQ	FLBLS	10/01-12/01
	Melbourne-Titusville-Palm Bay MSA, FL	H	8.71 FQ	12.22 AW	16.67 TQ	FLBLS	10/01-12/01
	Miami PMSA, FL	H	6.28 FQ	11.67 AW	16.75 TQ	FLBLS	10/01-12/01
	Orlando MSA, FL	H	9.11 FQ	12.67 AW	16.57 TQ	FLBLS	10/01-12/01
	Pensacola MSA, FL	H	7.86 FQ	10.98 AW	14.23 TQ	FLBLS	10/01-12/01

AAW	Average annual wage	AOH	Average offered, high	ASH	Average starting, high	H	Hourly	M	Monthly	S	Special: hourly and annual
AE	Average entry wage	AOL	Average offered, low	ASL	Average starting, low	HI	Highest wage paid	MTC	Median total compensation	TQ	Third quartile wage
AEX	Average experienced wage	APH	Average pay, high range	AW	Average wage paid	HR	High end range	MW	Median wage paid	W	Weekly
AO	Average offered	APL	Average pay, low range	FQ	First quartile wage	LR	Low end range	SQ	Second quartile wage	Y	Yearly

Occupation/Type/Industry	Location	Per	Low	Mid	High	Source	Date
Glazier	Sarasota-Bradenton MSA, FL	H	9.24 FQ	11.72 AW	15.67 TQ	FLBLS	10/01-12/01
	Tallahassee MSA, FL	H	8.55 FQ	13.30 AW	16.94 TQ	FLBLS	10/01-12/01
	Tampa-St. Petersburg-Clearwater MSA, FL	H	5.54 FQ	7.19 AW	12.08 TQ	FLBLS	10/01-12/01
	West Palm Beach-Boca Raton MSA, FL	H	6.84 FQ	14.08 AW	20.63 TQ	FLBLS	10/01-12/01
	Georgia	H	8.83 FQ	14.94 AW	21.81 TQ	GABLS	10/01-12/01
	Atlanta MSA, GA	H	10.93 FQ	15.94 AW	22.37 TQ	GABLS	10/01-12/01
	Macon MSA, GA	H	10.32 FQ	15.09 AW	19.68 TQ	GABLS	10/01-12/01
	Savannah MSA, GA	H	7.86 FQ	18.20 AW	22.65 TQ	GABLS	10/01-12/01
	Hawaii	H	11.26 FQ	23.11 AW	28.56 TQ	HIBLS	10/01-12/01
	Honolulu MSA, HI	H	23.47 FQ	25.26 AW	28.75 TQ	HIBLS	10/01-12/01
	Idaho	H	9.25 FQ	13.57 AW	17.77 TQ	IDBLS	10/01-12/01
	Boise City MSA, ID	H	9.38 FQ	14.15 AW	18.32 TQ	IDBLS	10/01-12/01
	Illinois	H	15.85 FQ	26.42 AW	33.54 TQ	ILBLS	10/01-12/01
	Chicago PMSA, IL	H	18.97 FQ	28.12 AW	33.71 TQ	ILBLS	10/01-12/01
	Springfield MSA, IL	H	9.51 FQ	14.23 AW	17.47 TQ	ILBLS	10/01-12/01
	Indiana	H	10.33 FQ	15.45 AW	23.72 TQ	INBLS	10/01-12/01
	Evansville-Henderson MSA, IN-KY	H	8.93 FQ	16.45 AW	24.22 TQ	INBLS	10/01-12/01
	Gary PMSA, IN	H	7.43 FQ	11.91 AW	16.42 TQ	INBLS	10/01-12/01
	Indianapolis MSA, IN	H	11.16 FQ	15.01 AW	23.20 TQ	INBLS	10/01-12/01
	Lafayette MSA, IN	H	9.23 FQ	17.37 AW	26.92 TQ	INBLS	10/01-12/01
	South Bend MSA, IN	H	13.76 FQ	15.89 AW	19.61 TQ	INBLS	10/01-12/01
	Iowa	H	8.28 FQ	15.61 AW	21.74 TQ	IABLS	10/01-12/01
	Davenport-Moline-Rock Island MSA, IA-IL	H	11.99 FQ	18.43 AW	24.16 TQ	IABLS	10/01-12/01
	Des Moines MSA, IA	H	12.05 FQ	17.97 AW	22.21 TQ	IABLS	10/01-12/01
	Kansas	H	8.38 FQ	15.53 AW	24.29 TQ	KSBLS	10/01-12/01
	Wichita MSA, KS	H	9.49 FQ	13.33 AW	18.29 TQ	KSBLS	10/01-12/01
	Kentucky	H	9.13 FQ	12.71 AW	17.63 TQ	KYBLS	10/01-12/01
	Louisville MSA, KY-IN	H	9.75 FQ	13.17 AW	17.96 TQ	KYBLS	10/01-12/01
	Louisiana	H	8.92 FQ	14.16 AW	17.56 TQ	LABLS	10/01-12/01
	Baton Rouge MSA, LA	H	11.01 FQ	14.96 AW	17.27 TQ	LABLS	10/01-12/01
	Lafayette MSA, LA	H	7.64 FQ	11.08 AW	15.64 TQ	LABLS	10/01-12/01
	New Orleans MSA, LA	H	8.66 FQ	13.79 AW	17.18 TQ	LABLS	10/01-12/01
	Maine	H	9.78 FQ	12.82 AW	15.94 TQ	MEBLS	10/01-12/01
	Maryland	H	9.79 FQ	16.20 AW	23.90 TQ	MDBLS	10/01-12/01
	Baltimore PMSA, MD	H	9.63 FQ	15.07 AW	21.69 TQ	MDBLS	10/01-12/01
	Massachusetts	H	12.61 FQ	20.10 AW	31.16 TQ	MABLS	10/01-12/01
	Boston PMSA, MA-NH	H	13.72 FQ	23.54 AW	33.30 TQ	MABLS	10/01-12/01
	Brockton PMSA, MA	H	17.61 FQ	21.62 AW	26.90 TQ	MABLS	10/01-12/01
	Lawrence PMSA, MA-NH	H	9.94 FQ	16.37 AW	25.28 TQ	MABLS	10/01-12/01
	Springfield MSA, MA	H	12.95 FQ	15.60 AW	17.57 TQ	MABLS	10/01-12/01
	Michigan	H	10.64 FQ	16.73 AW	23.79 TQ	MIBLS	10/01-12/01
	Ann Arbor PMSA, MI	H	15.61 FQ	21.05 AW	26.21 TQ	MIBLS	10/01-12/01
	Detroit PMSA, MI	H	11.29 FQ	17.77 AW	25.22 TQ	MIBLS	10/01-12/01
	Flint PMSA, MI	H	12.90 FQ	17.98 AW	21.99 TQ	MIBLS	10/01-12/01
	Grand Rapids-Muskegon-Holland MSA, MI	H	9.75 FQ	14.68 AW	21.21 TQ	MIBLS	10/01-12/01
	Kalamazoo-Battle Creek MSA, MI	H	9.60 FQ	14.73 AW	20.86 TQ	MIBLS	10/01-12/01
	Lansing-East Lansing MSA, MI	H	11.72 FQ	15.35 AW	21.82 TQ	MIBLS	10/01-12/01
	Minnesota	H	10.22 FQ	17.80 AW	27.14 TQ	MNBLS	10/01-12/01
	Minneapolis-St. Paul MSA, MN-WI	H	10.88 FQ	20.40 AW	30.38 TQ	MNBLS	10/01-12/01
	Mississippi	H	8.44 FQ	12.08 AW	16.69 TQ	MSBLS	10/01-12/01
	Jackson MSA, MS	H	7.91 FQ	13.45 AW	19.46 TQ	MSBLS	10/01-12/01
	Missouri	H	9.58 FQ	19.24 AW	31.05 TQ	MOBLS	10/01-12/01
	Kansas City MSA, MO-KS	H	11.23 FQ	18.72 AW	30.72 TQ	MOBLS	10/01-12/01
	St. Louis MSA, MO-IL	H	11.19 FQ	22.25 AW	31.81 TQ	MOBLS	10/01-12/01
	Montana	H	9.67 FQ	13.62 AW	17.92 TQ	MTBLS	10/01-12/01
	Billings MSA, MT	H	11.27 FQ	13.73 AW	17.21 TQ	MTBLS	10/01-12/01
	Nebraska	H	9.38 FQ	15.72 AW	24.14 TQ	NEBLS	10/01-12/01
	Omaha MSA, NE-IA	H	11.33 FQ	17.90 AW	26.81 TQ	NEBLS	10/01-12/01
	Nevada	H	10.25 FQ	16.12 AW	24.76 TQ	NVBLS	10/01-12/01
	Las Vegas MSA, NV-AZ	H	10.06 FQ	16.41 AW	25.19 TQ	NVBLS	10/01-12/01
	Reno MSA, NV	H	10.03 FQ	15.58 AW	23.29 TQ	NVBLS	10/01-12/01
	New Hampshire	H	10.92 FQ	15.56 AW	21.15 TQ	NHBLS	10/01-12/01
	New Jersey	H	8.22 FQ	18.56 AW	32.48 TQ	NJBLS	10/01-12/01
	Atlantic-Cape May PMSA, NJ	H	10.69 FQ	19.91 AW	28.36 TQ	NJBLS	10/01-12/01
	Bergen-Passaic PMSA, NJ	H	9.99 FQ	14.37 AW	17.41 TQ	NJBLS	10/01-12/01

AAW	Average annual wage	AOH	Average offered, high	ASH	Average starting, high	H	Hourly	M	Monthly	S	Special: hourly and annual
AE	Average entry wage	AOL	Average offered, low	ASL	Average starting, low	HI	Highest wage paid	MTC	Median total compensation	TQ	Third quartile wage
AEX	Average experienced wage	APH	Average pay, high range	AW	Average wage paid	HR	High end range	MW	Median wage paid	W	Weekly
AO	Average offered	APL	Average pay, low range	FQ	First quartile wage	LR	Low end range	SQ	Second quartile wage	Y	Yearly

Occupation/Type/Industry	Location	Per	Low	Mid	High	Source	Date
Glazier	Jersey City PMSA, NJ	H	9.75 FQ	22.48 AW	32.28 TQ	NJBLS	10/01-12/01
	Monmouth-Ocean PMSA, NJ	H	7.21 FQ	8.91 AW	8.81 TQ	NJBLS	10/01-12/01
	Newark PMSA, NJ	H	8.98 FQ	21.31 AW	33.65 TQ	NJBLS	10/01-12/01
	New Mexico	H	7.62 FQ	12.17 AW	19.05 TQ	NMBLS	10/01-12/01
	Albuquerque MSA, NM	H	8.74 FQ	14.98 AW	21.01 TQ	NMBLS	10/01-12/01
	Las Cruces MSA, NM	H	6.87 FQ	12.49 AW	20.36 TQ	NMBLS	10/01-12/01
	New York	H	9.30 FQ	15.93 AW	25.47 TQ	NYBLS	10/01-12/01
	Albany-Schenectady-Troy MSA, NY	H	11.08 FQ	15.81 AW	20.23 TQ	NYBLS	10/01-12/01
	Nassau-Suffolk PMSA, NY	H	8.85 FQ	17.23 AW	37.76 TQ	NYBLS	10/01-12/01
	New York PMSA, NY	H	9.14 FQ	14.84 AW	23.75 TQ	NYBLS	10/01-12/01
	Newburgh PMSA, NY-PA	H	9.98 FQ	17.51 AW	24.13 TQ	NYBLS	10/01-12/01
	Rochester MSA, NY	H	11.98 FQ	19.66 AW	32.32 TQ	NYBLS	10/01-12/01
	Utica-Rome MSA, NY	H	9.73 FQ	15.65 AW	31.99 TQ	NYBLS	10/01-12/01
	North Carolina	H	8.01 FQ	12.64 AW	18.09 TQ	NCBLS	10/01-12/01
	Charlotte-Gastonia-Rock Hill MSA, NC-SC	H	9.31 FQ	14.27 AW	20.21 TQ	NCBLS	10/01-12/01
	Greensboro-Winston-Salem-High Point MSA, NC	H	6.39 FQ	12.28 AW	17.33 TQ	NCBLS	10/01-12/01
	Hickory-Morganton-Lenoir MSA, NC	H	7.97 FQ	11.27 AW	15.49 TQ	NCBLS	10/01-12/01
	Raleigh-Durham-Chapel Hill MSA, NC	H	8.44 FQ	13.22 AW	20.27 TQ	NCBLS	10/01-12/01
	North Dakota	H	9.42 FQ	12.72 AW	16.73 TQ	NDBLS	10/01-12/01
	Ohio	H	10.11 FQ	15.38 AW	21.76 TQ	OHBLS	10/01-12/01
	Akron PMSA, OH	H	11.82 FQ	16.62 AW	21.52 TQ	OHBLS	10/01-12/01
	Canton-Massillon MSA, OH	H	11.62 FQ	15.00 AW	19.23 TQ	OHBLS	10/01-12/01
	Cincinnati PMSA, OH-KY-IN	H	10.09 FQ	16.50 AW	22.52 TQ	OHBLS	10/01-12/01
	Cleveland-Lorain-Elyria PMSA, OH	H	11.61 FQ	16.24 AW	21.72 TQ	OHBLS	10/01-12/01
	Dayton-Springfield MSA, OH	H	9.43 FQ	14.40 AW	20.09 TQ	OHBLS	10/01-12/01
	Toledo MSA, OH	H	7.93 FQ	13.90 AW	20.82 TQ	OHBLS	10/01-12/01
	Youngstown-Warren MSA, OH	H	11.48 FQ	13.65 AW	16.48 TQ	OHBLS	10/01-12/01
	Oklahoma	H	7.86 FQ	11.56 AW	16.07 TQ	OKBLS	10/01-12/01
	Oklahoma City MSA, OK	H	8.55 FQ	12.33 AW	16.72 TQ	OKBLS	10/01-12/01
	Tulsa MSA, OK	H	8.82 FQ	11.88 AW	16.04 TQ	OKBLS	10/01-12/01
	Oregon	H	10.90 FQ	18.10 AW	27.23 TQ	ORBLS	10/01-12/01
	Medford-Ashland MSA, OR	H	9.55 FQ	12.89 AW	16.42 TQ	ORBLS	10/01-12/01
	Portland-Vancouver PMSA, OR-WA	H	13.77 FQ	21.48 AW	28.26 TQ	ORBLS	10/01-12/01
	Salem PMSA, OR	H	8.70 FQ	12.71 AW	19.16 TQ	ORBLS	10/01-12/01
	Pennsylvania	H	9.79 FQ	15.79 AW	26.53 TQ	PABLS	10/01-12/01
	Erie MSA, PA	H	11.03 FQ	18.96 AW	28.05 TQ	PABLS	10/01-12/01
	Harrisburg-Lebanon-Carlisle MSA, PA	H	9.96 FQ	17.67 AW	31.17 TQ	PABLS	10/01-12/01
	Johnstown MSA, PA	H	9.53 FQ	16.25 AW	20.72 TQ	PABLS	10/01-12/01
	Philadelphia PMSA, PA-NJ	H	10.53 FQ	20.42 AW	33.62 TQ	PABLS	10/01-12/01
	Pittsburgh MSA, PA	H	11.07 FQ	15.27 AW	25.66 TQ	PABLS	10/01-12/01
	Scranton-Wilkes-Barre-Hazleton MSA, PA	H	8.85 FQ	12.12 AW	16.65 TQ	PABLS	10/01-12/01
	York MSA, PA	H	9.35 FQ	11.36 AW	14.28 TQ	PABLS	10/01-12/01
	Rhode Island	H	9.74 FQ	16.71 AW	26.14 TQ	RIBLS	10/01-12/01
	Providence-Fall River-Warwick MSA, RI-MA	H	9.76 FQ	16.62 AW	24.56 TQ	RIBLS	10/01-12/01
	South Carolina	H	8.63 FQ	13.40 AW	18.27 TQ	SCBLS	10/01-12/01
	Charleston-North Charleston MSA, SC	H	9.03 FQ	12.78 AW	17.16 TQ	SCBLS	10/01-12/01
	Columbia MSA, SC	H	10.66 FQ	13.61 AW	17.10 TQ	SCBLS	10/01-12/01
	Greenville-Spartanburg-Anderson MSA, SC	H	8.71 FQ	14.78 AW	24.27 TQ	SCBLS	10/01-12/01
	Myrtle Beach MSA, SC	H	8.54 FQ	13.30 AW	19.00 TQ	SCBLS	10/01-12/01
	South Dakota	H	9.41 FQ	13.27 AW	17.27 TQ	SDBLS	10/01-12/01
	Sioux Falls MSA, SD	H	11.10 FQ	14.39 AW	17.62 TQ	SDBLS	10/01-12/01
	Tennessee	H	8.82 FQ	12.89 AW	16.89 TQ	TNBLS	10/01-12/01
	Chattanooga MSA, TN-GA	H	8.32 FQ	13.09 AW	17.43 TQ	TNBLS	10/01-12/01
	Clarksville-Hopkinsville MSA, TN-KY	H	9.44 FQ	13.40 AW	17.27 TQ	TNBLS	10/01-12/01
	Johnson City-Kingsport-Bristol MSA, TN-VA	H	7.10 FQ	10.26 AW	15.20 TQ	TNBLS	10/01-12/01
	Knoxville MSA, TN	H	9.14 FQ	12.28 AW	16.59 TQ	TNBLS	10/01-12/01
	Memphis MSA, TN-AR-MS	H	9.25 FQ	13.98 AW	18.32 TQ	TNBLS	10/01-12/01
	Nashville MSA, TN	H	9.47 FQ	13.30 AW	16.51 TQ	TNBLS	10/01-12/01

AAW	Average annual wage	**AOH**	Average offered, high	**ASH**	Average starting, high	**H**	Hourly	**M**	Monthly	**S**	Special: hourly and annual
AE	Average entry wage	**AOL**	Average offered, low	**ASL**	Average starting, low	**HI**	Highest wage paid	**MTC**	Median total compensation	**TQ**	Third quartile wage
AEX	Average experienced wage	**APH**	Average pay, high range	**AW**	Average wage paid	**HR**	High end range	**MW**	Median wage paid	**W**	Weekly
AO	Average offered	**APL**	Average pay, low range	**FQ**	First quartile wage	**LR**	Low end range	**SQ**	Second quartile wage	**Y**	Yearly

Occupation/Type/Industry	Location	Per	Low	Mid	High	Source	Date
Glazier	Texas	H	8.05 FQ	12.86 AW	18.05 TQ	TXBLS	10/01-12/01
	Amarillo MSA, TX	H	8.69 FQ	11.41 AW	13.97 TQ	TXBLS	10/01-12/01
	Austin-San Marcos MSA, TX	H	7.75 FQ	12.27 AW	17.15 TQ	TXBLS	10/01-12/01
	Corpus Christi MSA, TX	H	7.79 FQ	11.28 AW	14.99 TQ	TXBLS	10/01-12/01
	Dallas PMSA, TX	H	9.45 FQ	14.09 AW	19.19 TQ	TXBLS	10/01-12/01
	El Paso MSA, TX	H	7.16 FQ	8.99 AW	11.69 TQ	TXBLS	10/01-12/01
	Fort Worth-Arlington PMSA, TX	H	9.46 FQ	14.53 AW	20.60 TQ	TXBLS	10/01-12/01
	Galveston-Texas City PMSA, TX	H	8.72 FQ	14.42 AW	20.64 TQ	TXBLS	10/01-12/01
	Houston PMSA, TX	H	10.37 FQ	15.29 AW	19.82 TQ	TXBLS	10/01-12/01
	Longview-Marshall MSA, TX	H	8.68 FQ	12.12 AW	16.77 TQ	TXBLS	10/01-12/01
	Lubbock MSA, TX	H	7.61 FQ	10.73 AW	16.23 TQ	TXBLS	10/01-12/01
	Odessa-Midland MSA, TX	H	9.41 FQ	11.39 AW	14.01 TQ	TXBLS	10/01-12/01
	San Antonio MSA, TX	H	8.04 FQ	13.07 AW	17.93 TQ	TXBLS	10/01-12/01
	Tyler MSA, TX	H	9.55 FQ	12.83 AW	18.34 TQ	TXBLS	10/01-12/01
	Waco MSA, TX	H	8.93 FQ	11.40 AW	14.91 TQ	TXBLS	10/01-12/01
	Utah	H	9.37 FQ	15.43 AW	20.77 TQ	UTBLS	10/01-12/01
	Provo-Orem MSA, UT	H	11.61 FQ	15.75 AW	21.11 TQ	UTBLS	10/01-12/01
	Salt Lake City-Ogden MSA, UT	H	9.19 FQ	15.58 AW	20.79 TQ	UTBLS	10/01-12/01
	Vermont	H	8.99 FQ	13.14 AW	17.04 TQ	VTBLS	10/01-12/01
	Burlington MSA, VT	H	8.35 FQ	12.62 AW	16.65 TQ	VTBLS	10/01-12/01
	Virginia	H	8.67 FQ	14.27 AW	20.87 TQ	VABLS	10/01-12/01
	Norfolk-Virginia Beach-Newport News MSA, VA-NC	H	9.39 FQ	13.81 AW	17.58 TQ	VABLS	10/01-12/01
	Richmond-Petersburg MSA, VA	H	9.73 FQ	13.76 AW	17.57 TQ	VABLS	10/01-12/01
	Washington	H	11.29 FQ	20.01 AW	31.60 TQ	WABLS	10/01-12/01
	Bremerton PMSA, WA	H	8.58 FQ	18.94 AW	27.99 TQ	WABLS	10/01-12/01
	Olympia PMSA, WA	H	10.20 FQ	14.80 AW	20.56 TQ	WABLS	10/01-12/01
	Richland-Kennewick-Pasco MSA, WA	H	11.58 FQ	14.43 AW	17.20 TQ	WABLS	10/01-12/01
	Seattle-Bellevue-Everett PMSA, WA	H	11.98 FQ	22.62 AW	33.33 TQ	WABLS	10/01-12/01
	Spokane MSA, WA	H	11.83 FQ	18.17 AW	26.19 TQ	WABLS	10/01-12/01
	Tacoma PMSA, WA	H	10.37 FQ	18.63 AW	28.99 TQ	WABLS	10/01-12/01
	Yakima MSA, WA	H	9.66 FQ	12.40 AW	16.26 TQ	WABLS	10/01-12/01
	West Virginia	H	6.24 FQ	11.76 AW	20.61 TQ	WVBLS	10/01-12/01
	Wisconsin	H	7.88 FQ	16.72 AW	27.22 TQ	WIBLS	10/01-12/01
	Appleton-Oshkosh-Neenah MSA, WI	H	9.57 FQ	15.89 AW	24.84 TQ	WIBLS	10/01-12/01
	Madison MSA, WI	H	11.99 FQ	20.85 AW	34.78 TQ	WIBLS	10/01-12/01
	Milwaukee-Waukesha PMSA, WI	H	9.83 FQ	20.13 AW	27.51 TQ	WIBLS	10/01-12/01
	Wyoming	H	8.12 FQ	11.35 AW	14.58 TQ	WYBLS	10/01-12/01
	Puerto Rico	H	5.63 FQ	6.36 AW	7.52 TQ	PRBLS	10/01-12/01
Golf Course Grounds Superintendent	St. Louis, MO	Y		81200 AW		SLBJ	1/00-1/01
Golf Pro	St. Louis, MO	Y		66200 AW		SLBJ	1/00-1/01
Governor	Alabama	Y		94654 AW		USATOD2	1/99-1/99
	Alaska	Y		81648 AW		USATOD2	1/99-1/99
	Arizona	Y		95000 AW		USATOD2	1/99-1/99
	Arkansas	Y		68448 AW		USATOD2	1/99-1/99
	California	Y		165000 AW		USATOD2	1/99-1/99
	Colorado	Y		90000 AW		USATOD2	1/99-1/99
	Connecticut	Y		78000 AW		USATOD2	1/99-1/99
	Delaware	Y		107000 AW		USATOD2	1/99-1/99
	Florida	Y		117240 AW		USATOD2	1/99-1/99
	Georgia	Y		122998 AW		USATOD2	1/99-1/99
	Hawaii	Y		94780 AW		USATOD2	1/99-1/99
	Idaho	Y		95500 AW		USATOD2	1/99-1/99
	Illinois	Y		140200 AW		USATOD2	1/99-1/99
	Indiana	Y		77200 AW		USATOD2	1/99-1/99
	Iowa	Y		104352 AW		USATOD2	1/99-1/99
	Kansas	Y		91742 AW		USATOD2	1/99-1/99
	Kentucky	Y		97068 AW		USATOD2	1/99-1/99
	Louisiana	Y		95000 AW		USATOD2	1/99-1/99

AAW Average annual wage **AOH** Average offered, high **ASH** Average starting, high **H** Hourly **M** Monthly **S** Special: hourly and annual
AE Average entry wage **AOL** Average offered, low **ASL** Average starting, low **HI** Highest wage paid **MTC** Median total compensation **TQ** Third quartile wage
AEX Average experienced wage **APH** Average pay, high range **AW** Average wage paid **HR** High end range **MW** Median wage paid **W** Weekly
AO Average offered **APL** Average pay, low range **FQ** First quartile wage **LR** Low end range **SQ** Second quartile wage **Y** Yearly

Occupation/Type/Industry	Location	Per	Low	Mid	High	Source	Date
Governor	Maine	Y		70000 AW		USATOD2	1/99-1/99
	Maryland	Y		120000 AW		USATOD2	1/99-1/99
	Massachusetts	Y		135000 AW		USATOD2	1/99-1/99
	Michigan	Y		151245 AW		USATOD2	1/99-1/99
	Minnesota	Y		120303 AW		USATOD2	1/99-1/99
	Mississippi	Y		101800 AW		USATOD2	1/99-1/99
	Missouri	Y		112755 AW		USATOD2	1/99-1/99
	Montana	Y		83672 AW		USATOD2	1/99-1/99
	Nebraska	Y		65000 AW		USATOD2	1/99-1/99
	Nevada	Y		117000 AW		USATOD2	1/99-1/99
	New Hampshire	Y		93263 AW		USATOD2	1/99-1/99
	New Jersey	Y		130000 AW		USATOD2	1/99-1/99
	New Mexico	Y		90000 AW		USATOD2	1/99-1/99
	New York	Y		179000 AW		USATOD2	1/99-1/99
	North Carolina	Y		107132 AW		USATOD2	1/99-1/99
	North Dakota	Y		76884 AW		USATOD2	1/99-1/99
	Ohio	Y		119225 AW		USATOD2	1/99-1/99
	Oklahoma	Y		101040 AW		USATOD2	1/99-1/99
	Oregon	Y		88300 AW		USATOD2	1/99-1/99
	Pennsylvania	Y		135559 AW		USATOD2	1/99-1/99
	Rhode Island	Y		95000 AW		USATOD2	1/99-1/99
	South Carolina	Y		106078 AW		USATOD2	1/99-1/99
	South Dakota	Y		89898 AW		USATOD2	1/99-1/99
	Tennessee	Y		85000 AW		USATOD2	1/99-1/99
	Texas	Y		115345 AW		USATOD2	1/99-1/99
	Utah	Y		93000 AW		USATOD2	1/99-1/99
	Vermont	Y		99632 AW		USATOD2	1/99-1/99
	Virginia	Y		110000 AW		USATOD2	1/99-1/99
	Washington	Y		132000 AW		USATOD2	1/99-1/99
	West Virginia	Y		99000 AW		USATOD2	1/99-1/99
	Wisconsin	Y		115699 AW		USATOD2	1/99-1/99
	Wyoming	Y		95000 AW		USATOD2	1/99-1/99
Grader and Sorter							
Agricultural Product	Alabama	H	5.86 FQ	7.78 AW	10.11 TQ	ALBLS	10/01-12/01
Agricultural Product	Alaska	H	6.52 FQ	11.83 AW	17.34 TQ	AKBLS	10/01-12/01
Agricultural Product	Arizona	H	5.62 FQ	8.80 AW	10.96 TQ	AZBLS	10/01-12/01
Agricultural Product	Arkansas	H	7.06 FQ	9.28 AW	11.29 TQ	ARBLS	10/01-12/01
Agricultural Product	California	H	6.38 FQ	7.54 AW	9.56 TQ	CABLS	10/01-12/01
Agricultural Product	Colorado	H	5.68 FQ	7.91 AW	11.12 TQ	COBLS	10/01-12/01
Agricultural Product	Delaware	H	6.67 FQ	9.26 AW	14.20 TQ	DEBLS	10/01-12/01
Agricultural Product	Florida	H	5.63 FQ	7.44 AW	10.44 TQ	FLBLS	10/01-12/01
Agricultural Product	Georgia	H	5.69 FQ	6.94 AW	9.33 TQ	GABLS	10/01-12/01
Agricultural Product	Idaho	H	5.59 FQ	6.93 AW	9.69 TQ	IDBLS	10/01-12/01
Agricultural Product	Illinois	H	7.04 FQ	9.65 AW	13.03 TQ	ILBLS	10/01-12/01
Agricultural Product	Indiana	H	6.12 FQ	10.44 AW	16.40 TQ	INBLS	10/01-12/01
Agricultural Product	Iowa	H	7.39 FQ	10.56 AW	15.32 TQ	IABLS	10/01-12/01
Agricultural Product	Kansas	H	7.48 FQ	11.21 AW	16.81 TQ	KSBLS	10/01-12/01
Agricultural Product	Kentucky	H	6.34 FQ	8.61 AW	12.68 TQ	KYBLS	10/01-12/01
Agricultural Product	Louisiana	H	5.70 FQ	7.44 AW	10.45 TQ	LABLS	10/01-12/01
Agricultural Product	Maine	H	5.89 FQ	8.72 AW	12.54 TQ	MEBLS	10/01-12/01
Agricultural Product	Maryland	H	5.59 FQ	7.64 AW	10.75 TQ	MDBLS	10/01-12/01
Agricultural Product	Massachusetts	H	7.02 FQ	10.31 AW	18.20 TQ	MABLS	10/01-12/01
Agricultural Product	Michigan	H	5.71 FQ	8.11 AW	12.76 TQ	MIBLS	10/01-12/01
Agricultural Product	Minnesota	H	7.03 FQ	10.16 AW	15.73 TQ	MNBLS	10/01-12/01
Agricultural Product	Mississippi	H	5.90 FQ	8.68 AW	12.57 TQ	MSBLS	10/01-12/01
Agricultural Product	Missouri	H	5.72 FQ	8.15 AW	11.32 TQ	MOBLS	10/01-12/01
Agricultural Product	Montana	H	6.74 FQ	9.36 AW	12.31 TQ	MTBLS	10/01-12/01
Agricultural Product	Nebraska	H	6.16 FQ	9.56 AW	12.86 TQ	NEBLS	10/01-12/01
Agricultural Product	New Hampshire	H	8.60 FQ	11.91 AW	18.13 TQ	NHBLS	10/01-12/01
Agricultural Product	New Jersey	H	5.73 FQ	8.35 AW	11.80 TQ	NJBLS	10/01-12/01
Agricultural Product	New Mexico	H	5.49 FQ	6.13 AW	6.91 TQ	NMBLS	10/01-12/01
Agricultural Product	New York	H	5.78 FQ	8.86 AW	12.75 TQ	NYBLS	10/01-12/01
Agricultural Product	North Carolina	H	5.53 FQ	8.11 AW	13.59 TQ	NCBLS	10/01-12/01
Agricultural Product	North Dakota	H	8.28 FQ	10.63 AW	14.04 TQ	NDBLS	10/01-12/01
Agricultural Product	Ohio	H	6.44 FQ	10.06 AW	16.11 TQ	OHBLS	10/01-12/01
Agricultural Product	Oklahoma	H	6.49 FQ	10.08 AW	13.89 TQ	OKBLS	10/01-12/01
Agricultural Product	Oregon	H	6.81 FQ	8.46 AW	10.79 TQ	ORBLS	10/01-12/01
Agricultural Product	Pennsylvania	H	6.25 FQ	9.39 AW	13.12 TQ	PABLS	10/01-12/01
Agricultural Product	Rhode Island	H	7.06 FQ	9.30 AW	15.76 TQ	RIBLS	10/01-12/01
Agricultural Product	South Carolina	H	7.14 FQ	9.36 AW	15.00 TQ	SCBLS	10/01-12/01
Agricultural Product	South Dakota	H	7.18 FQ	9.37 AW	12.28 TQ	SDBLS	10/01-12/01
Agricultural Product	Tennessee	H	6.24 FQ	9.39 AW	13.28 TQ	TNBLS	10/01-12/01

AAW Average annual wage **AE** Average entry wage **AEX** Average experienced wage **AO** Average offered **AOH** Average offered, high **AOL** Average offered, low **APH** Average pay, high range **APL** Average pay, low range **ASH** Average starting, high **ASL** Average starting, low **AW** Average wage paid **FQ** First quartile wage **H** Hourly **HI** Highest wage paid **HR** High end range **LR** Low end range **M** Monthly **MTC** Median total compensation **MW** Median wage paid **SQ** Second quartile wage **S** Special: hourly and annual **TQ** Third quartile wage **W** Weekly **Y** Yearly

Occupation/Type/Industry	Location	Per	Low	Mid	High	Source	Date
Grader and Sorter							
Agricultural Product	Texas	H	5.62 FQ	8.12 AW	11.21 TQ	TXBLS	10/01-12/01
Agricultural Product	Utah	H	7.07 FQ	9.14 AW	12.52 TQ	UTBLS	10/01-12/01
Agricultural Product	Vermont	H	6.62 FQ	8.91 AW	12.50 TQ	VTBLS	10/01-12/01
Agricultural Product	Virginia	H	6.04 FQ	8.13 AW	10.58 TQ	VABLS	10/01-12/01
Agricultural Product	Washington	H	6.86 FQ	8.41 AW	10.74 TQ	WABLS	10/01-12/01
Agricultural Product	West Virginia	H	7.38 FQ	9.93 AW	13.42 TQ	WVBLS	10/01-12/01
Agricultural Product	Wisconsin	H	5.99 FQ	9.21 AW	13.53 TQ	WIBLS	10/01-12/01
Agricultural Product	Puerto Rico	H	5.71 FQ	7.30 AW	9.96 TQ	PRBLS	10/01-12/01
Graduate Teaching Assistant	Alabama	Y	12780 FQ	23980 AW	35380 TQ	ALBLS	10/01-12/01
	California	Y	22750 FQ	34500 AW	45930 TQ	CABLS	10/01-12/01
	Colorado	Y	12070 FQ	21630 AW	35090 TQ	COBLS	10/01-12/01
	District of Columbia	Y	14970 FQ	27970 AW	41020 TQ	DCBLS	10/01-12/01
	Florida	Y	11990 FQ	14250 AW	15170 TQ	FLBLS	10/01-12/01
	Georgia	Y	12150 FQ	20620 AW	35260 TQ	GABLS	10/01-12/01
	Hawaii	Y	23880 FQ	28730 AW	34880 TQ	HIBLS	10/01-12/01
	Illinois	Y	12030 FQ	15270 AW	21880 TQ	ILBLS	10/01-12/01
	Indiana	Y	12970 FQ	28670 AW	44620 TQ	INBLS	10/01-12/01
	Kansas	Y	14050 FQ	29400 AW	49620 TQ	KSBLS	10/01-12/01
	Louisiana	Y	11420 FQ	16440 AW	28800 TQ	LABLS	10/01-12/01
	Maine	Y	11140 FQ	13600 AW	17170 TQ	MEBLS	10/01-12/01
	Maryland	Y	16520 FQ	23100 AW	35460 TQ	MDBLS	10/01-12/01
	Massachusetts	Y	14730 FQ	31780 AW	54360 TQ	MABLS	10/01-12/01
	Michigan	Y	12060 FQ	24370 AW	41010 TQ	MIBLS	10/01-12/01
	Minnesota	Y	18880 FQ	21690 AW	23080 TQ	MNBLS	10/01-12/01
	Mississippi	Y	18770 FQ	31780 AW	55170 TQ	MSBLS	10/01-12/01
	Missouri	Y	12330 FQ	20470 AW	34100 TQ	MOBLS	10/01-12/01
	Montana	Y	12830 FQ	28050 AW	43680 TQ	MTBLS	10/01-12/01
	Nebraska	Y	15460 FQ	30800 AW	52460 TQ	NEBLS	10/01-12/01
	New Hampshire	Y	11480 FQ	12730 AW	14260 TQ	NHBLS	10/01-12/01
	New Jersey	Y	12350 FQ	19350 AW	27600 TQ	NJBLS	10/01-12/01
	New York	Y	12760 FQ	22230 AW	34230 TQ	NYBLS	10/01-12/01
	North Carolina	Y	11730 FQ	19610 AW	34040 TQ	NCBLS	10/01-12/01
	North Dakota	Y	23460 FQ	28150 AW	35470 TQ	NDBLS	10/01-12/01
	Ohio	Y	11970 FQ	23900 AW	42630 TQ	OHBLS	10/01-12/01
	Oklahoma	Y	13120 FQ	17500 AW	26340 TQ	OKBLS	10/01-12/01
	Oregon	Y	20670 FQ	28690 AW	40240 TQ	ORBLS	10/01-12/01
	Pennsylvania	Y	12200 FQ	20080 AW	34270 TQ	PABLS	10/01-12/01
	Rhode Island	Y	14090 FQ	20000 AW	23700 TQ	RIBLS	10/01-12/01
	South Carolina	Y	23600 FQ	26340 AW	29100 TQ	SCBLS	10/01-12/01
	South Dakota	Y	19030 FQ	22910 AW	31210 TQ	SDBLS	10/01-12/01
	Tennessee	Y	12460 FQ	20260 AW	27700 TQ	TNBLS	10/01-12/01
	Texas	Y	13400 FQ	25020 AW	37220 TQ	TXBLS	10/01-12/01
	Utah	Y	12350 FQ	20820 AW	35180 TQ	UTBLS	10/01-12/01
	Vermont	Y	13530 FQ	23300 AW	36820 TQ	VTBLS	10/01-12/01
	Virginia	Y	12150 FQ	17990 AW	29660 TQ	VABLS	10/01-12/01
	Washington	Y	23840 FQ	35540 AW	46200 TQ	WABLS	10/01-12/01
	West Virginia	Y	12100 FQ	17880 AW	32970 TQ	WVBLS	10/01-12/01
	Puerto Rico	Y	17950 FQ	25840 AW	35910 TQ	PRBLS	10/01-12/01
Graphic Designer	Alabama	Y	20910 FQ	37600 AW	57310 TQ	ALBLS	10/01-12/01
	Alaska	Y	17100 FQ	32530 AW	51640 TQ	AKBLS	10/01-12/01
	Arizona	Y	22730 FQ	37370 AW	54880 TQ	AZBLS	10/01-12/01
	Arkansas	Y	16430 FQ	27650 AW	40430 TQ	ARBLS	10/01-12/01
	California	Y	24220 FQ	44840 AW	71370 TQ	CABLS	10/01-12/01
	Colorado	Y	22050 FQ	36440 AW	53080 TQ	COBLS	10/01-12/01
	Connecticut	Y	25420 FQ	42770 AW	65580 TQ	CTBLS	10/01-12/01
	Delaware	Y	22130 FQ	35070 AW	55920 TQ	DEBLS	10/01-12/01
	District of Columbia	Y	28820 FQ	43300 AW	67430 TQ	DCBLS	10/01-12/01
	Florida	Y	18800 FQ	34520 AW	49450 TQ	FLBLS	10/01-12/01
	Georgia	Y	24240 FQ	37850 AW	55470 TQ	GABLS	10/01-12/01
	Hawaii	Y	19230 FQ	33530 AW	55680 TQ	HIBLS	10/01-12/01
	Idaho	Y	19520 FQ	29890 AW	41940 TQ	IDBLS	10/01-12/01
	Illinois	Y	23430 FQ	43200 AW	73040 TQ	ILBLS	10/01-12/01
	Indiana	Y	19940 FQ	32620 AW	46200 TQ	INBLS	10/01-12/01
	Iowa	Y	18770 FQ	30330 AW	44990 TQ	IABLS	10/01-12/01
	Kansas	Y	19160 FQ	31780 AW	46250 TQ	KSBLS	10/01-12/01
	Kentucky	Y	19050 FQ	31460 AW	46850 TQ	KYBLS	10/01-12/01
	Louisiana	Y	18440 FQ	29860 AW	48110 TQ	LABLS	10/01-12/01
	Maine	Y	22230 FQ	35600 AW	52230 TQ	MEBLS	10/01-12/01
	Maryland	Y	23080 FQ	41290 AW	60010 TQ	MDBLS	10/01-12/01
	Massachusetts	Y	27060 FQ	52420 AW	91900 TQ	MABLS	10/01-12/01

AAW	Average annual wage	AOH	Average offered, high	ASH	Average starting, high	H	Hourly	M	Monthly	S	Special: hourly and annual
AE	Average entry wage	AOL	Average offered, low	ASL	Average starting, low	HI	Highest wage paid	MTC	Median total compensation	TQ	Third quartile wage
AEX	Average experienced wage	APH	Average pay, high range	AW	Average wage paid	HR	High end range	MW	Median wage paid	W	Weekly
AO	Average offered	APL	Average pay, low range	FQ	First quartile wage	LR	Low end range	SQ	Second quartile wage	Y	Yearly

Occupation/Type/Industry	Location	Per	Low	Mid	High	Source	Date
Graphic Designer	Michigan	Y	24710 FQ	42660 AW	66700 TQ	MIBLS	10/01-12/01
	Minnesota	Y	22690 FQ	37830 AW	54690 TQ	MNBLS	10/01-12/01
	Mississippi	Y	18440 FQ	29700 AW	43140 TQ	MSBLS	10/01-12/01
	Missouri	Y	20310 FQ	34970 AW	53690 TQ	MOBLS	10/01-12/01
	Montana	Y	18960 FQ	28470 AW	39800 TQ	MTBLS	10/01-12/01
	Nebraska	Y	19480 FQ	32140 AW	44890 TQ	NEBLS	10/01-12/01
	Nevada	Y	22070 FQ	42150 AW	57970 TQ	NVBLS	10/01-12/01
	New Hampshire	Y	21310 FQ	34470 AW	53500 TQ	NHBLS	10/01-12/01
	New Jersey	Y	24700 FQ	41280 AW	63010 TQ	NJBLS	10/01-12/01
	New Mexico	Y	18970 FQ	34540 AW	56640 TQ	NMBLS	10/01-12/01
	New York	Y	25030 FQ	48240 AW	80200 TQ	NYBLS	10/01-12/01
	North Carolina	Y	20980 FQ	36760 AW	55870 TQ	NCBLS	10/01-12/01
	North Dakota	Y	14300 FQ	27110 AW	41130 TQ	NDBLS	10/01-12/01
	Ohio	Y	20670 FQ	35720 AW	54330 TQ	OHBLS	10/01-12/01
	Oklahoma	Y	16590 FQ	29820 AW	44980 TQ	OKBLS	10/01-12/01
	Oregon	Y	20560 FQ	36050 AW	53410 TQ	ORBLS	10/01-12/01
	Pennsylvania	Y	21570 FQ	37660 AW	57290 TQ	PABLS	10/01-12/01
	Rhode Island	Y	22840 FQ	39510 AW	59570 TQ	RIBLS	10/01-12/01
	South Carolina	Y	20970 FQ	33010 AW	47700 TQ	SCBLS	10/01-12/01
	South Dakota	Y	19680 FQ	28150 AW	41980 TQ	SDBLS	10/01-12/01
	Tennessee	Y	16870 FQ	33270 AW	52090 TQ	TNBLS	10/01-12/01
	Texas	Y	18670 FQ	36980 AW	56150 TQ	TXBLS	10/01-12/01
	Utah	Y	20570 FQ	34690 AW	50260 TQ	UTBLS	10/01-12/01
	Vermont	Y	23800 FQ	33910 AW	46090 TQ	VTBLS	10/01-12/01
	Virginia	Y	21520 FQ	37640 AW	55830 TQ	VABLS	10/01-12/01
	Washington	Y	23440 FQ	43640 AW	66130 TQ	WABLS	10/01-12/01
	West Virginia	Y	18680 FQ	28640 AW	43150 TQ	WVBLS	10/01-12/01
	Wisconsin	Y	21670 FQ	36710 AW	55530 TQ	WIBLS	10/01-12/01
	Wyoming	Y	16520 FQ	29150 AW	46570 TQ	WYBLS	10/01-12/01
	Puerto Rico	Y	12660 FQ	22090 AW	35680 TQ	PRBLS	10/01-12/01
	Guam	Y	18920 FQ	27480 AW	37840 TQ	GUBLS	10/01-12/01
Grinding and Polishing Worker							
Hand	Alabama	H	7.75 FQ	11.13 AW	16.02 TQ	ALBLS	10/01-12/01
Hand	Arizona	H	6.81 FQ	9.58 AW	12.17 TQ	AZBLS	10/01-12/01
Hand	Arkansas	H	7.33 FQ	9.85 AW	12.93 TQ	ARBLS	10/01-12/01
Hand	California	H	6.93 FQ	10.29 AW	15.49 TQ	CABLS	10/01-12/01
Hand	Colorado	H	8.02 FQ	12.23 AW	18.84 TQ	COBLS	10/01-12/01
Hand	Connecticut	H	8.55 FQ	12.06 AW	15.80 TQ	CTBLS	10/01-12/01
Hand	Florida	H	7.32 FQ	10.35 AW	14.25 TQ	FLBLS	10/01-12/01
Hand	Georgia	H	7.44 FQ	10.63 AW	14.06 TQ	GABLS	10/01-12/01
Hand	Hawaii	H	7.84 FQ	14.19 AW	26.68 TQ	HIBLS	10/01-12/01
Hand	Idaho	H	6.10 FQ	9.62 AW	15.16 TQ	IDBLS	10/01-12/01
Hand	Illinois	H	7.74 FQ	14.50 AW	25.91 TQ	ILBLS	10/01-12/01
Hand	Indiana	H	8.43 FQ	13.00 AW	19.66 TQ	INBLS	10/01-12/01
Hand	Iowa	H	6.93 FQ	10.55 AW	13.56 TQ	IABLS	10/01-12/01
Hand	Kansas	H	7.81 FQ	11.20 AW	15.40 TQ	KSBLS	10/01-12/01
Hand	Kentucky	H	7.47 FQ	10.88 AW	14.07 TQ	KYBLS	10/01-12/01
Hand	Louisiana	H	7.10 FQ	9.98 AW	15.29 TQ	LABLS	10/01-12/01
Hand	Maine	H	6.61 FQ	9.66 AW	13.17 TQ	MEBLS	10/01-12/01
Hand	Maryland	H	7.25 FQ	11.87 AW	16.72 TQ	MDBLS	10/01-12/01
Hand	Massachusetts	H	9.16 FQ	13.17 AW	18.08 TQ	MABLS	10/01-12/01
Hand	Michigan	H	9.56 FQ	16.30 AW	25.88 TQ	MIBLS	10/01-12/01
Hand	Minnesota	H	8.05 FQ	12.53 AW	17.49 TQ	MNBLS	10/01-12/01
Hand	Mississippi	H	8.27 FQ	10.98 AW	15.09 TQ	MSBLS	10/01-12/01
Hand	Missouri	H	7.16 FQ	14.31 AW	25.38 TQ	MOBLS	10/01-12/01
Hand	Montana	H	6.30 FQ	11.14 AW	17.37 TQ	MTBLS	10/01-12/01
Hand	Nevada	H	6.68 FQ	9.85 AW	14.24 TQ	NVBLS	10/01-12/01
Hand	New Hampshire	H	9.51 FQ	14.07 AW	18.63 TQ	NHBLS	10/01-12/01
Hand	New Jersey	H	9.22 FQ	14.96 AW	22.79 TQ	NJBLS	10/01-12/01
Hand	New Mexico	H	6.66 FQ	9.91 AW	14.95 TQ	NMBLS	10/01-12/01
Hand	New York	H	7.55 FQ	11.88 AW	16.96 TQ	NYBLS	10/01-12/01
Hand	North Carolina	H	7.75 FQ	11.41 AW	15.92 TQ	NCBLS	10/01-12/01
Hand	North Dakota	H	7.97 FQ	11.54 AW	17.70 TQ	NDBLS	10/01-12/01
Hand	Ohio	H	8.56 FQ	13.80 AW	23.43 TQ	OHBLS	10/01-12/01
Hand	Oklahoma	H	7.20 FQ	10.93 AW	16.65 TQ	OKBLS	10/01-12/01
Hand	Oregon	H	7.13 FQ	10.63 AW	14.90 TQ	ORBLS	10/01-12/01
Hand	Pennsylvania	H	7.78 FQ	12.05 AW	16.91 TQ	PABLS	10/01-12/01
Hand	Rhode Island	H	7.16 FQ	11.13 AW	15.45 TQ	RIBLS	10/01-12/01
Hand	South Carolina	H	8.28 FQ	13.48 AW	20.42 TQ	SCBLS	10/01-12/01
Hand	South Dakota	H	6.86 FQ	9.64 AW	13.29 TQ	SDBLS	10/01-12/01
Hand	Tennessee	H	7.09 FQ	10.59 AW	14.95 TQ	TNBLS	10/01-12/01
Hand	Texas	H	6.75 FQ	9.55 AW	13.61 TQ	TXBLS	10/01-12/01

AAW	Average annual wage	**AOH**	Average offered, high	**ASH**	Average starting, high	**H**	Hourly	**M**	Monthly	**S**	Special: hourly and annual
AE	Average entry wage	**AOL**	Average offered, low	**ASL**	Average starting, low	**HI**	Highest wage paid	**MTC**	Median total compensation	**TQ**	Third quartile wage
AEX	Average experienced wage	**APH**	Average pay, high range	**AW**	Average wage paid	**HR**	High end range	**MW**	Median wage paid	**W**	Weekly
AO	Average offered	**APL**	Average pay, low range	**FQ**	First quartile wage	**LR**	Low end range	**SQ**	Second quartile wage	**Y**	Yearly

Occupation/Type/Industry	Location	Per	Low	Mid	High	Source	Date
Grinding and Polishing Worker							
Hand	Utah	H	7.42 FQ	10.38 AW	13.64 TQ	UTBLS	10/01-12/01
Hand	Vermont	H	7.60 FQ	10.75 AW	15.13 TQ	VTBLS	10/01-12/01
Hand	Virginia	H	8.02 FQ	11.31 AW	16.70 TQ	VABLS	10/01-12/01
Hand	Washington	H	9.06 FQ	13.54 AW	17.79 TQ	WABLS	10/01-12/01
Hand	West Virginia	H	7.21 FQ	10.22 AW	14.86 TQ	WVBLS	10/01-12/01
Hand	Wisconsin	H	8.62 FQ	12.89 AW	18.56 TQ	WIBLS	10/01-12/01
Hand	Puerto Rico	H	5.50 FQ	7.83 AW	13.11 TQ	PRBLS	10/01-12/01
Grinding, Lapping, Polishing, and Buffing Machine Tool Setter, Operator, and Tender							
Metals and Plastics	Alabama	H	7.12 FQ	13.35 AW	25.92 TQ	ALBLS	10/01-12/01
Metals and Plastics	Birmingham MSA, AL	H	7.17 FQ	12.98 AW	23.00 TQ	ALBLS	10/01-12/01
Metals and Plastics	Mobile MSA, AL	H	7.31 FQ	11.28 AW	16.95 TQ	ALBLS	10/01-12/01
Metals and Plastics	Arizona	H	6.54 FQ	10.94 AW	15.88 TQ	AZBLS	10/01-12/01
Metals and Plastics	Phoenix-Mesa MSA, AZ	H	6.27 FQ	10.91 AW	16.78 TQ	AZBLS	10/01-12/01
Metals and Plastics	Tucson MSA, AZ	H	8.57 FQ	11.67 AW	13.87 TQ	AZBLS	10/01-12/01
Metals and Plastics	Arkansas	H	7.54 FQ	11.62 AW	16.39 TQ	ARBLS	10/01-12/01
Metals and Plastics	Fayetteville-Springdale-Rogers MSA, AR	H	8.91 FQ	11.41 AW	14.03 TQ	ARBLS	10/01-12/01
Metals and Plastics	Fort Smith MSA, AR-OK	H	7.72 FQ	11.41 AW	16.02 TQ	ARBLS	10/01-12/01
Metals and Plastics	Little Rock-North Little Rock MSA, AR	H	7.60 FQ	11.07 AW	15.50 TQ	ARBLS	10/01-12/01
Metals and Plastics	California	H	7.05 FQ	11.06 AW	17.34 TQ	CABLS	10/01-12/01
Metals and Plastics	Bakersfield MSA, CA	H	7.69 FQ	10.69 AW	16.14 TQ	CABLS	10/01-12/01
Metals and Plastics	Fresno MSA, CA	H	6.84 FQ	9.68 AW	14.08 TQ	CABLS	10/01-12/01
Metals and Plastics	Los Angeles-Long Beach PMSA, CA	H	6.97 FQ	10.77 AW	17.54 TQ	CABLS	10/01-12/01
Metals and Plastics	Modesto MSA, CA	H	8.08 FQ	10.82 AW	13.69 TQ	CABLS	10/01-12/01
Metals and Plastics	Oakland PMSA, CA	H	9.17 FQ	13.48 AW	19.84 TQ	CABLS	10/01-12/01
Metals and Plastics	Orange County PMSA, CA	H	6.83 FQ	9.91 AW	14.40 TQ	CABLS	10/01-12/01
Metals and Plastics	Riverside-San Bernardino PMSA, CA	H	7.24 FQ	10.42 AW	15.54 TQ	CABLS	10/01-12/01
Metals and Plastics	Sacramento PMSA, CA	H	9.28 FQ	13.75 AW	20.04 TQ	CABLS	10/01-12/01
Metals and Plastics	San Diego MSA, CA	H	7.68 FQ	11.67 AW	16.50 TQ	CABLS	10/01-12/01
Metals and Plastics	San Francisco PMSA, CA	H	8.27 FQ	13.02 AW	19.07 TQ	CABLS	10/01-12/01
Metals and Plastics	San Jose PMSA, CA	H	7.01 FQ	14.01 AW	23.98 TQ	CABLS	10/01-12/01
Metals and Plastics	San Luis Obispo-Atascadero-Paso Robles MSA, CA	H	6.67 FQ	9.83 AW	15.16 TQ	CABLS	10/01-12/01
Metals and Plastics	Santa Barbara-Santa Maria-Lompoc MSA, CA	H	7.73 FQ	11.16 AW	16.64 TQ	CABLS	10/01-12/01
Metals and Plastics	Santa Cruz-Watsonville PMSA, CA	H	7.24 FQ	10.16 AW	13.79 TQ	CABLS	10/01-12/01
Metals and Plastics	Santa Rosa PMSA, CA	H	7.97 FQ	12.21 AW	17.20 TQ	CABLS	10/01-12/01
Metals and Plastics	Stockton-Lodi MSA, CA	H	8.26 FQ	11.61 AW	14.01 TQ	CABLS	10/01-12/01
Metals and Plastics	Ventura PMSA, CA	H	6.82 FQ	10.16 AW	14.11 TQ	CABLS	10/01-12/01
Metals and Plastics	Visalia-Tulare-Porterville MSA, CA	H	7.45 FQ	10.66 AW	14.48 TQ	CABLS	10/01-12/01
Metals and Plastics	Colorado	H	8.77 FQ	11.79 AW	16.28 TQ	COBLS	10/01-12/01
Metals and Plastics	Boulder-Longmont PMSA, CO	H	8.54 FQ	14.09 AW	24.58 TQ	COBLS	10/01-12/01
Metals and Plastics	Colorado Springs MSA, CO	H	7.87 FQ	12.08 AW	17.20 TQ	COBLS	10/01-12/01
Metals and Plastics	Denver PMSA, CO	H	8.99 FQ	11.75 AW	15.86 TQ	COBLS	10/01-12/01
Metals and Plastics	Fort Collins-Loveland MSA, CO	H	7.33 FQ	10.72 AW	18.84 TQ	COBLS	10/01-12/01
Metals and Plastics	Connecticut	H	10.35 FQ	14.95 AW	20.34 TQ	CTBLS	10/01-12/01
Metals and Plastics	Bridgeport PMSA, CT	H	8.83 FQ	14.04 AW	20.34 TQ	CTBLS	10/01-12/01
Metals and Plastics	Danbury PMSA, CT	H	9.84 FQ	13.52 AW	16.98 TQ	CTBLS	10/01-12/01
Metals and Plastics	Hartford MSA, CT	H	11.22 FQ	15.42 AW	20.77 TQ	CTBLS	10/01-12/01
Metals and Plastics	New Haven-Meriden PMSA, CT	H	9.87 FQ	14.26 AW	17.87 TQ	CTBLS	10/01-12/01
Metals and Plastics	Stamford-Norwalk PMSA, CT	H	7.35 FQ	10.75 AW	16.45 TQ	CTBLS	10/01-12/01
Metals and Plastics	Waterbury PMSA, CT	H	10.12 FQ	14.33 AW	19.83 TQ	CTBLS	10/01-12/01
Metals and Plastics	Delaware	H	10.13 FQ	17.44 AW	31.75 TQ	DEBLS	10/01-12/01
Metals and Plastics	Wilmington-Newark PMSA, DE-MD	H	10.20 FQ	20.52 AW	32.87 TQ	DEBLS	10/01-12/01
Metals and Plastics	Washington PMSA, DC-MD-VA-WV	H	7.81 FQ	11.86 AW	17.59 TQ	DCBLS	10/01-12/01
Metals and Plastics	Florida	H	7.49 FQ	11.34 AW	16.46 TQ	FLBLS	10/01-12/01
Metals and Plastics	Fort Lauderdale PMSA, FL	H	7.58 FQ	12.38 AW	20.06 TQ	FLBLS	10/01-12/01
Metals and Plastics	Gainesville MSA, FL	H	7.82 FQ	10.35 AW	13.55 TQ	FLBLS	10/01-12/01
Metals and Plastics	Jacksonville MSA, FL	H	7.59 FQ	10.89 AW	18.11 TQ	FLBLS	10/01-12/01

AAW	Average annual wage	AOH	Average offered, high	ASH	Average starting, high	H	Hourly	M	Monthly	S	Special: hourly and annual
AE	Average entry wage	AOL	Average offered, low	ASL	Average starting, low	HI	Highest wage paid	MTC	Median total compensation	TQ	Third quartile wage
AEX	Average experienced wage	APH	Average pay, high range	AW	Average wage paid	HR	High end range	MW	Median wage paid	W	Weekly
AO	Average offered	APL	Average pay, low range	FQ	First quartile wage	LR	Low end range	SQ	Second quartile wage	Y	Yearly

Occupation/Type/Industry	Location	Per	Low	Mid	High	Source	Date
Grinding, Lapping, Polishing, and Buffing Machine Tool Setter, Operator, and Tender							
Metals and Plastics	Miami PMSA, FL	H	6.51 FQ	10.05 AW	14.69 TQ	FLBLS	10/01-12/01
Metals and Plastics	Orlando MSA, FL	H	8.38 FQ	11.07 AW	15.69 TQ	FLBLS	10/01-12/01
Metals and Plastics	Sarasota-Bradenton MSA, FL	H	8.06 FQ	11.78 AW	15.72 TQ	FLBLS	10/01-12/01
Metals and Plastics	Tampa-St. Petersburg-Clearwater MSA, FL	H	7.54 FQ	11.31 AW	17.56 TQ	FLBLS	10/01-12/01
Metals and Plastics	West Palm Beach-Boca Raton MSA, FL	H	8.67 FQ	14.21 AW	18.31 TQ	FLBLS	10/01-12/01
Metals and Plastics	Georgia	H	7.24 FQ	11.72 AW	16.89 TQ	GABLS	10/01-12/01
Metals and Plastics	Atlanta MSA, GA	H	7.54 FQ	12.03 AW	17.63 TQ	GABLS	10/01-12/01
Metals and Plastics	Columbus MSA, GA-AL	H	9.05 FQ	11.56 AW	14.23 TQ	GABLS	10/01-12/01
Metals and Plastics	Savannah MSA, GA	H	7.73 FQ	9.61 AW	11.01 TQ	GABLS	10/01-12/01
Metals and Plastics	Hawaii	H	7.87 FQ	12.04 AW	17.65 TQ	HIBLS	10/01-12/01
Metals and Plastics	Honolulu MSA, HI	H	7.82 FQ	11.92 AW	17.72 TQ	HIBLS	10/01-12/01
Metals and Plastics	Idaho	H	7.89 FQ	11.75 AW	16.52 TQ	IDBLS	10/01-12/01
Metals and Plastics	Boise City MSA, ID	H	9.22 FQ	12.65 AW	16.79 TQ	IDBLS	10/01-12/01
Metals and Plastics	Illinois	H	8.31 FQ	13.92 AW	20.45 TQ	ILBLS	10/01-12/01
Metals and Plastics	Champaign-Urbana MSA, IL	H	8.74 FQ	11.63 AW	15.81 TQ	ILBLS	10/01-12/01
Metals and Plastics	Chicago PMSA, IL	H	8.27 FQ	13.87 AW	20.02 TQ	ILBLS	10/01-12/01
Metals and Plastics	Peoria-Pekin MSA, IL	H	9.65 FQ	18.40 AW	25.98 TQ	ILBLS	10/01-12/01
Metals and Plastics	Rockford MSA, IL	H	9.44 FQ	15.06 AW	21.17 TQ	ILBLS	10/01-12/01
Metals and Plastics	Indiana	H	9.28 FQ	14.94 AW	23.70 TQ	INBLS	10/01-12/01
Metals and Plastics	Elkhart-Goshen MSA, IN	H	9.14 FQ	14.91 AW	24.55 TQ	INBLS	10/01-12/01
Metals and Plastics	Evansville-Henderson MSA, IN-KY	H	8.68 FQ	11.82 AW	14.16 TQ	INBLS	10/01-12/01
Metals and Plastics	Fort Wayne MSA, IN	H	9.66 FQ	13.52 AW	18.26 TQ	INBLS	10/01-12/01
Metals and Plastics	Gary PMSA, IN	H	11.49 FQ	19.60 AW	26.76 TQ	INBLS	10/01-12/01
Metals and Plastics	Indianapolis MSA, IN	H	7.92 FQ	15.48 AW	26.36 TQ	INBLS	10/01-12/01
Metals and Plastics	South Bend MSA, IN	H	9.21 FQ	12.05 AW	16.30 TQ	INBLS	10/01-12/01
Metals and Plastics	Iowa	H	9.27 FQ	12.69 AW	16.86 TQ	IABLS	10/01-12/01
Metals and Plastics	Cedar Rapids MSA, IA	H	15.11 FQ	18.61 AW	21.85 TQ	IABLS	10/01-12/01
Metals and Plastics	Davenport-Moline-Rock Island MSA, IA-IL	H	8.84 FQ	12.25 AW	17.10 TQ	IABLS	10/01-12/01
Metals and Plastics	Kansas	H	8.31 FQ	13.92 AW	23.57 TQ	KSBLS	10/01-12/01
Metals and Plastics	Wichita MSA, KS	H	9.43 FQ	16.48 AW	25.95 TQ	KSBLS	10/01-12/01
Metals and Plastics	Kentucky	H	8.52 FQ	11.76 AW	16.27 TQ	KYBLS	10/01-12/01
Metals and Plastics	Lexington MSA, KY	H	9.22 FQ	11.18 AW	13.77 TQ	KYBLS	10/01-12/01
Metals and Plastics	Louisville MSA, KY-IN	H	7.64 FQ	11.48 AW	16.35 TQ	KYBLS	10/01-12/01
Metals and Plastics	Louisiana	H	6.50 FQ	10.39 AW	15.66 TQ	LABLS	10/01-12/01
Metals and Plastics	Baton Rouge MSA, LA	H	6.66 FQ	10.48 AW	15.62 TQ	LABLS	10/01-12/01
Metals and Plastics	New Orleans MSA, LA	H	8.85 FQ	10.72 AW	13.24 TQ	LABLS	10/01-12/01
Metals and Plastics	Shreveport-Bossier City MSA, LA	H	6.06 FQ	8.00 AW	10.78 TQ	LABLS	10/01-12/01
Metals and Plastics	Maine	H	8.84 FQ	13.95 AW	20.86 TQ	MEBLS	10/01-12/01
Metals and Plastics	Portland MSA, ME	H	8.85 FQ	12.24 AW	16.77 TQ	MEBLS	10/01-12/01
Metals and Plastics	Maryland	H	9.21 FQ	14.01 AW	21.56 TQ	MDBLS	10/01-12/01
Metals and Plastics	Baltimore PMSA, MD	H	9.97 FQ	14.31 AW	20.63 TQ	MDBLS	10/01-12/01
Metals and Plastics	Massachusetts	H	9.47 FQ	14.26 AW	20.93 TQ	MABLS	10/01-12/01
Metals and Plastics	Boston PMSA, MA-NH	H	9.58 FQ	14.23 AW	21.97 TQ	MABLS	10/01-12/01
Metals and Plastics	Brockton PMSA, MA	H	9.06 FQ	13.49 AW	18.49 TQ	MABLS	10/01-12/01
Metals and Plastics	Lawrence PMSA, MA-NH	H	9.17 FQ	14.18 AW	21.01 TQ	MABLS	10/01-12/01
Metals and Plastics	Lowell PMSA, MA-NH	H	10.60 FQ	14.20 AW	20.69 TQ	MABLS	10/01-12/01
Metals and Plastics	New Bedford PMSA, MA	H	8.40 FQ	13.87 AW	20.09 TQ	MABLS	10/01-12/01
Metals and Plastics	Springfield MSA, MA	H	9.77 FQ	13.88 AW	17.83 TQ	MABLS	10/01-12/01
Metals and Plastics	Worcester PMSA, MA-CT	H	10.45 FQ	15.25 AW	21.11 TQ	MABLS	10/01-12/01
Metals and Plastics	Michigan	H	9.56 FQ	15.87 AW	24.89 TQ	MIBLS	10/01-12/01
Metals and Plastics	Detroit PMSA, MI	H	10.28 FQ	17.08 AW	25.36 TQ	MIBLS	10/01-12/01
Metals and Plastics	Grand Rapids-Muskegon-Holland MSA, MI	H	8.58 FQ	13.63 AW	17.58 TQ	MIBLS	10/01-12/01
Metals and Plastics	Kalamazoo-Battle Creek MSA, MI	H	9.44 FQ	12.92 AW	16.94 TQ	MIBLS	10/01-12/01
Metals and Plastics	Lansing-East Lansing MSA, MI	H	9.22 FQ	13.31 AW	17.49 TQ	MIBLS	10/01-12/01
Metals and Plastics	Saginaw-Bay City-Midland MSA, MI	H	7.88 FQ	16.71 AW	30.43 TQ	MIBLS	10/01-12/01
Metals and Plastics	Minnesota	H	9.72 FQ	14.33 AW	20.18 TQ	MNBLS	10/01-12/01
Metals and Plastics	Duluth-Superior MSA, MN-WI	H	7.54 FQ	11.22 AW	14.23 TQ	MNBLS	10/01-12/01
Metals and Plastics	Minneapolis-St. Paul MSA, MN-WI	H	10.57 FQ	15.20 AW	20.82 TQ	MNBLS	10/01-12/01
Metals and Plastics	St. Cloud MSA, MN	H	9.43 FQ	12.92 AW	16.74 TQ	MNBLS	10/01-12/01
Metals and Plastics	Mississippi	H	7.32 FQ	10.19 AW	14.34 TQ	MSBLS	10/01-12/01

AAW	Average annual wage	AOH	Average offered, high	ASH	Average starting, high	H	Hourly	M	Monthly	S	Special: hourly and annual
AE	Average entry wage	AOL	Average offered, low	ASL	Average starting, low	HI	Highest wage paid	MTC	Median total compensation	TQ	Third quartile wage
AEX	Average experienced wage	APH	Average pay, high range	AW	Average wage paid	HR	High end range	MW	Median wage paid	W	Weekly
AO	Average offered	APL	Average pay, low range	FQ	First quartile wage	LR	Low end range	SQ	Second quartile wage	Y	Yearly

Occupation/Type/Industry	Location	Per	Low	Mid	High	Source	Date
Grinding, Lapping, Polishing, and Buffing Machine Tool Setter, Operator, and Tender							
Metals and Plastics	Biloxi-Gulfport-Pascagoula MSA, MS	H	7.63 FQ	13.33 AW	17.32 TQ	MSBLS	10/01-12/01
Metals and Plastics	Jackson MSA, MS	H	7.49 FQ	9.70 AW	12.57 TQ	MSBLS	10/01-12/01
Metals and Plastics	Missouri	H	8.11 FQ	12.08 AW	17.08 TQ	MOBLS	10/01-12/01
Metals and Plastics	Kansas City MSA, MO-KS	H	8.77 FQ	13.55 AW	18.66 TQ	MOBLS	10/01-12/01
Metals and Plastics	St. Louis MSA, MO-IL	H	7.91 FQ	12.52 AW	18.58 TQ	MOBLS	10/01-12/01
Metals and Plastics	Springfield MSA, MO	H	10.25 FQ	13.52 AW	17.12 TQ	MOBLS	10/01-12/01
Metals and Plastics	Montana	H	8.92 FQ	12.95 AW	16.44 TQ	MTBLS	10/01-12/01
Metals and Plastics	Nebraska	H	8.46 FQ	11.52 AW	14.42 TQ	NEBLS	10/01-12/01
Metals and Plastics	Lincoln MSA, NE	H	9.73 FQ	13.12 AW	17.29 TQ	NEBLS	10/01-12/01
Metals and Plastics	Omaha MSA, NE-IA	H	9.25 FQ	12.75 AW	19.58 TQ	NEBLS	10/01-12/01
Metals and Plastics	Nevada	H	7.45 FQ	11.03 AW	14.43 TQ	NVBLS	10/01-12/01
Metals and Plastics	Las Vegas MSA, NV-AZ	H	8.18 FQ	11.43 AW	14.41 TQ	NVBLS	10/01-12/01
Metals and Plastics	Reno MSA, NV	H	7.66 FQ	11.21 AW	15.16 TQ	NVBLS	10/01-12/01
Metals and Plastics	New Hampshire	H	8.95 FQ	12.36 AW	16.69 TQ	NHBLS	10/01-12/01
Metals and Plastics	Manchester PMSA, NH	H	9.04 FQ	12.09 AW	17.20 TQ	NHBLS	10/01-12/01
Metals and Plastics	Nashua PMSA, NH	H	8.87 FQ	11.95 AW	15.98 TQ	NHBLS	10/01-12/01
Metals and Plastics	Portsmouth-Rochester PMSA, NH-ME	H	9.56 FQ	12.74 AW	16.55 TQ	NHBLS	10/01-12/01
Metals and Plastics	New Jersey	H	8.24 FQ	13.28 AW	18.72 TQ	NJBLS	10/01-12/01
Metals and Plastics	Bergen-Passaic PMSA, NJ	H	9.12 FQ	14.04 AW	19.48 TQ	NJBLS	10/01-12/01
Metals and Plastics	Middlesex-Somerset-Hunterdon PMSA, NJ	H	7.70 FQ	11.10 AW	15.73 TQ	NJBLS	10/01-12/01
Metals and Plastics	Newark PMSA, NJ	H	9.02 FQ	14.21 AW	18.07 TQ	NJBLS	10/01-12/01
Metals and Plastics	New Mexico	H	7.13 FQ	10.25 AW	15.21 TQ	NMBLS	10/01-12/01
Metals and Plastics	Albuquerque MSA, NM	H	7.44 FQ	11.35 AW	16.42 TQ	NMBLS	10/01-12/01
Metals and Plastics	New York	H	7.98 FQ	12.61 AW	18.20 TQ	NYBLS	10/01-12/01
Metals and Plastics	Albany-Schenectady-Troy MSA, NY	H	7.93 FQ	12.12 AW	20.00 TQ	NYBLS	10/01-12/01
Metals and Plastics	Buffalo-Niagara Falls MSA, NY	H	8.17 FQ	15.17 AW	25.64 TQ	NYBLS	10/01-12/01
Metals and Plastics	Dutchess County PMSA, NY	H	8.91 FQ	12.45 AW	18.14 TQ	NYBLS	10/01-12/01
Metals and Plastics	Nassau-Suffolk PMSA, NY	H	6.53 FQ	11.60 AW	17.48 TQ	NYBLS	10/01-12/01
Metals and Plastics	New York PMSA, NY	H	8.11 FQ	11.96 AW	16.72 TQ	NYBLS	10/01-12/01
Metals and Plastics	Rochester MSA, NY	H	8.69 FQ	12.46 AW	19.29 TQ	NYBLS	10/01-12/01
Metals and Plastics	Syracuse MSA, NY	H	7.50 FQ	11.55 AW	16.65 TQ	NYBLS	10/01-12/01
Metals and Plastics	Utica-Rome MSA, NY	H	9.86 FQ	12.92 AW	16.36 TQ	NYBLS	10/01-12/01
Metals and Plastics	North Carolina	H	8.23 FQ	13.11 AW	20.33 TQ	NCBLS	10/01-12/01
Metals and Plastics	Asheville MSA, NC	H	7.48 FQ	10.11 AW	14.50 TQ	NCBLS	10/01-12/01
Metals and Plastics	Charlotte-Gastonia-Rock Hill MSA, NC-SC	H	10.84 FQ	15.71 AW	20.99 TQ	NCBLS	10/01-12/01
Metals and Plastics	Greensboro-Winston-Salem-High Point MSA, NC	H	7.32 FQ	11.20 AW	16.55 TQ	NCBLS	10/01-12/01
Metals and Plastics	Hickory-Morganton-Lenoir MSA, NC	H	9.24 FQ	12.66 AW	19.43 TQ	NCBLS	10/01-12/01
Metals and Plastics	Raleigh-Durham-Chapel Hill MSA, NC	H	7.36 FQ	9.70 AW	13.87 TQ	NCBLS	10/01-12/01
Metals and Plastics	North Dakota	H	7.30 FQ	9.54 AW	11.07 TQ	NDBLS	10/01-12/01
Metals and Plastics	Ohio	H	8.99 FQ	13.88 AW	18.93 TQ	OHBLS	10/01-12/01
Metals and Plastics	Akron PMSA, OH	H	8.78 FQ	12.73 AW	17.24 TQ	OHBLS	10/01-12/01
Metals and Plastics	Canton-Massillon MSA, OH	H	10.39 FQ	14.30 AW	18.07 TQ	OHBLS	10/01-12/01
Metals and Plastics	Cincinnati PMSA, OH-KY-IN	H	9.61 FQ	13.67 AW	17.44 TQ	OHBLS	10/01-12/01
Metals and Plastics	Cleveland-Lorain-Elyria PMSA, OH	H	9.14 FQ	14.10 AW	17.84 TQ	OHBLS	10/01-12/01
Metals and Plastics	Columbus MSA, OH	H	9.01 FQ	11.80 AW	15.86 TQ	OHBLS	10/01-12/01
Metals and Plastics	Dayton-Springfield MSA, OH	H	10.05 FQ	15.67 AW	21.27 TQ	OHBLS	10/01-12/01
Metals and Plastics	Hamilton-Middletown PMSA, OH	H	10.01 FQ	14.86 AW	20.64 TQ	OHBLS	10/01-12/01
Metals and Plastics	Mansfield MSA, OH	H	9.42 FQ	11.63 AW	15.84 TQ	OHBLS	10/01-12/01
Metals and Plastics	Toledo MSA, OH	H	9.62 FQ	16.68 AW	31.05 TQ	OHBLS	10/01-12/01
Metals and Plastics	Youngstown-Warren MSA, OH	H	7.97 FQ	13.72 AW	30.60 TQ	OHBLS	10/01-12/01
Metals and Plastics	Oklahoma	H	7.61 FQ	12.53 AW	18.03 TQ	OKBLS	10/01-12/01
Metals and Plastics	Oklahoma City MSA, OK	H	7.37 FQ	9.82 AW	13.43 TQ	OKBLS	10/01-12/01
Metals and Plastics	Tulsa MSA, OK	H	7.53 FQ	11.84 AW	17.18 TQ	OKBLS	10/01-12/01
Metals and Plastics	Oregon	H	9.39 FQ	13.65 AW	20.16 TQ	ORBLS	10/01-12/01
Metals and Plastics	Eugene-Springfield MSA, OR	H	8.90 FQ	11.67 AW	16.75 TQ	ORBLS	10/01-12/01
Metals and Plastics	Portland-Vancouver PMSA, OR-WA	H	9.38 FQ	13.47 AW	19.24 TQ	ORBLS	10/01-12/01
Metals and Plastics	Pennsylvania	H	9.07 FQ	13.32 AW	18.24 TQ	PABLS	10/01-12/01

AAW	Average annual wage	AOH	Average offered, high	ASH	Average starting, high	H	Hourly	M	Monthly	S	Special: hourly and annual
AE	Average entry wage	AOL	Average offered, low	ASL	Average starting, low	HI	Highest wage paid	MTC	Median total compensation	TQ	Third quartile wage
AEX	Average experienced wage	APH	Average pay, high range	AW	Average wage paid	HR	High end range	MW	Median wage paid	W	Weekly
AO	Average offered	APL	Average pay, low range	FQ	First quartile wage	LR	Low end range	SQ	Second quartile wage	Y	Yearly

Occupation/Type/Industry	Location	Per	Low	Mid	High	Source	Date
Grinding, Lapping, Polishing, and Buffing Machine Tool Setter, Operator, and Tender							
Metals and Plastics	Allentown-Bethlehem-Easton MSA, PA	H	9.07 FQ	13.02 AW	17.18 TQ	PABLS	10/01-12/01
Metals and Plastics	Erie MSA, PA	H	8.43 FQ	11.63 AW	16.56 TQ	PABLS	10/01-12/01
Metals and Plastics	Harrisburg-Lebanon-Carlisle MSA, PA	H	10.44 FQ	13.66 AW	17.20 TQ	PABLS	10/01-12/01
Metals and Plastics	Lancaster MSA, PA	H	8.92 FQ	12.32 AW	16.81 TQ	PABLS	10/01-12/01
Metals and Plastics	Philadelphia PMSA, PA-NJ	H	9.25 FQ	14.54 AW	20.70 TQ	PABLS	10/01-12/01
Metals and Plastics	Pittsburgh MSA, PA	H	9.53 FQ	13.81 AW	18.58 TQ	PABLS	10/01-12/01
Metals and Plastics	Reading MSA, PA	H	9.53 FQ	13.22 AW	18.11 TQ	PABLS	10/01-12/01
Metals and Plastics	Scranton-Wilkes-Barre-Hazleton MSA, PA	H	7.27 FQ	10.96 AW	15.57 TQ	PABLS	10/01-12/01
Metals and Plastics	York MSA, PA	H	7.13 FQ	12.90 AW	17.55 TQ	PABLS	10/01-12/01
Metals and Plastics	Rhode Island	H	7.49 FQ	11.27 AW	16.61 TQ	RIBLS	10/01-12/01
Metals and Plastics	Providence-Fall River-Warwick MSA, RI-MA	H	7.54 FQ	11.35 AW	16.47 TQ	RIBLS	10/01-12/01
Metals and Plastics	South Carolina	H	9.22 FQ	13.28 AW	16.99 TQ	SCBLS	10/01-12/01
Metals and Plastics	Charleston-North Charleston MSA, SC	H	7.64 FQ	10.54 AW	13.33 TQ	SCBLS	10/01-12/01
Metals and Plastics	Columbia MSA, SC	H	9.08 FQ	11.92 AW	13.91 TQ	SCBLS	10/01-12/01
Metals and Plastics	South Dakota	H	7.14 FQ	10.33 AW	13.76 TQ	SDBLS	10/01-12/01
Metals and Plastics	Sioux Falls MSA, SD	H	9.35 FQ	12.12 AW	17.04 TQ	SDBLS	10/01-12/01
Metals and Plastics	Tennessee	H	8.17 FQ	11.50 AW	15.82 TQ	TNBLS	10/01-12/01
Metals and Plastics	Chattanooga MSA, TN-GA	H	8.96 FQ	11.63 AW	13.74 TQ	TNBLS	10/01-12/01
Metals and Plastics	Clarksville-Hopkinsville MSA, TN-KY	H	8.16 FQ	12.10 AW	16.36 TQ	TNBLS	10/01-12/01
Metals and Plastics	Johnson City-Kingsport-Bristol MSA, TN-VA	H	8.84 FQ	13.02 AW	16.93 TQ	TNBLS	10/01-12/01
Metals and Plastics	Knoxville MSA, TN	H	8.42 FQ	12.13 AW	17.49 TQ	TNBLS	10/01-12/01
Metals and Plastics	Memphis MSA, TN-AR-MS	H	7.90 FQ	10.84 AW	13.96 TQ	TNBLS	10/01-12/01
Metals and Plastics	Nashville MSA, TN	H	9.10 FQ	12.80 AW	19.85 TQ	TNBLS	10/01-12/01
Metals and Plastics	Texas	H	6.54 FQ	11.04 AW	16.79 TQ	TXBLS	10/01-12/01
Metals and Plastics	Austin-San Marcos MSA, TX	H	7.79 FQ	10.80 AW	14.68 TQ	TXBLS	10/01-12/01
Metals and Plastics	Beaumont-Port Arthur MSA, TX	H	6.48 FQ	8.28 AW	11.72 TQ	TXBLS	10/01-12/01
Metals and Plastics	Brownsville-Harlingen-San Benito MSA, TX	H	5.57 FQ	8.97 AW	14.66 TQ	TXBLS	10/01-12/01
Metals and Plastics	Dallas PMSA, TX	H	6.75 FQ	10.65 AW	16.94 TQ	TXBLS	10/01-12/01
Metals and Plastics	El Paso MSA, TX	H	8.01 FQ	11.92 AW	15.86 TQ	TXBLS	10/01-12/01
Metals and Plastics	Fort Worth-Arlington PMSA, TX	H	7.07 FQ	13.02 AW	25.94 TQ	TXBLS	10/01-12/01
Metals and Plastics	Houston PMSA, TX	H	6.88 FQ	11.81 AW	20.31 TQ	TXBLS	10/01-12/01
Metals and Plastics	Killeen-Temple MSA, TX	H	7.33 FQ	10.27 AW	14.52 TQ	TXBLS	10/01-12/01
Metals and Plastics	Lubbock MSA, TX	H	6.89 FQ	9.60 AW	12.81 TQ	TXBLS	10/01-12/01
Metals and Plastics	Odessa-Midland MSA, TX	H	7.33 FQ	10.49 AW	16.01 TQ	TXBLS	10/01-12/01
Metals and Plastics	San Antonio MSA, TX	H	7.50 FQ	10.84 AW	14.78 TQ	TXBLS	10/01-12/01
Metals and Plastics	Tyler MSA, TX	H	7.00 FQ	9.03 AW	11.14 TQ	TXBLS	10/01-12/01
Metals and Plastics	Utah	H	7.26 FQ	10.50 AW	13.62 TQ	UTBLS	10/01-12/01
Metals and Plastics	Salt Lake City-Ogden MSA, UT	H	6.99 FQ	10.23 AW	13.79 TQ	UTBLS	10/01-12/01
Metals and Plastics	Vermont	H	7.74 FQ	10.80 AW	14.91 TQ	VTBLS	10/01-12/01
Metals and Plastics	Burlington MSA, VT	H	8.43 FQ	11.37 AW	15.13 TQ	VTBLS	10/01-12/01
Metals and Plastics	Virginia	H	8.25 FQ	11.58 AW	15.67 TQ	VABLS	10/01-12/01
Metals and Plastics	Norfolk-Virginia Beach-Newport News MSA, VA-NC	H	7.39 FQ	10.35 AW	13.96 TQ	VABLS	10/01-12/01
Metals and Plastics	Richmond-Petersburg MSA, VA	H	8.76 FQ	12.81 AW	17.54 TQ	VABLS	10/01-12/01
Metals and Plastics	Roanoke MSA, VA	H	8.18 FQ	10.35 AW	13.03 TQ	VABLS	10/01-12/01
Metals and Plastics	Washington	H	8.64 FQ	12.47 AW	18.06 TQ	WABLS	10/01-12/01
Metals and Plastics	Seattle-Bellevue-Everett PMSA, WA	H	9.18 FQ	13.41 AW	20.83 TQ	WABLS	10/01-12/01
Metals and Plastics	Spokane MSA, WA	H	8.46 FQ	10.65 AW	13.48 TQ	WABLS	10/01-12/01
Metals and Plastics	Tacoma PMSA, WA	H	8.51 FQ	13.06 AW	18.69 TQ	WABLS	10/01-12/01
Metals and Plastics	West Virginia	H	7.27 FQ	12.68 AW	21.17 TQ	WVBLS	10/01-12/01
Metals and Plastics	Huntington-Ashland MSA, WV-KY-OH	H	8.39 FQ	13.38 AW	17.39 TQ	WVBLS	10/01-12/01
Metals and Plastics	Wisconsin	H	9.16 FQ	13.67 AW	20.10 TQ	WIBLS	10/01-12/01
Metals and Plastics	Appleton-Oshkosh-Neenah MSA, WI	H	8.01 FQ	16.51 AW	27.21 TQ	WIBLS	10/01-12/01

AAW Average annual wage; **AE** Average entry wage; **AEX** Average experienced wage; **AO** Average offered; **AOH** Average offered, high; **AOL** Average offered, low; **APH** Average pay, high range; **APL** Average pay, low range; **ASH** Average starting, high; **ASL** Average starting, low; **AW** Average wage paid; **FQ** First quartile wage; **H** Hourly; **HI** Highest wage paid; **HR** High end range; **LR** Low end range; **M** Monthly; **MTC** Median total compensation; **MW** Median wage paid; **SQ** Second quartile wage; **S** Special: hourly and annual; **TQ** Third quartile wage; **W** Weekly; **Y** Yearly

Occupation/Type/Industry	Location	Per	Low	Mid	High	Source	Date
Grinding, Lapping, Polishing, and Buffing Machine Tool Setter, Operator, and Tender							
Metals and Plastics	Green Bay MSA, WI	H	10.78 FQ	14.70 AW	20.10 TQ	WIBLS	10/01-12/01
Metals and Plastics	Madison MSA, WI	H	9.71 FQ	13.03 AW	16.63 TQ	WIBLS	10/01-12/01
Metals and Plastics	Milwaukee-Waukesha PMSA, WI	H	9.13 FQ	12.65 AW	17.84 TQ	WIBLS	10/01-12/01
Metals and Plastics	Racine PMSA, WI	H	9.14 FQ	14.64 AW	19.67 TQ	WIBLS	10/01-12/01
Metals and Plastics	Wyoming	H	7.43 FQ	8.58 AW	10.48 TQ	WYBLS	10/01-12/01
Metals and Plastics	Puerto Rico	H	5.96 FQ	8.15 AW	10.79 TQ	PRBLS	10/01-12/01
Hairdresser, Hairstylist, and Cosmetologist	Alabama	H	5.85 FQ	8.90 AW	13.16 TQ	ALBLS	10/01-12/01
	Birmingham MSA, AL	H	5.93 FQ	10.07 AW	14.33 TQ	ALBLS	10/01-12/01
	Huntsville MSA, AL	H	5.81 FQ	8.68 AW	12.58 TQ	ALBLS	10/01-12/01
	Mobile MSA, AL	H	5.85 FQ	7.31 AW	8.77 TQ	ALBLS	10/01-12/01
	Montgomery MSA, AL	H	5.88 FQ	9.96 AW	16.30 TQ	ALBLS	10/01-12/01
	Alaska	H	6.50 FQ	13.14 AW	22.35 TQ	AKBLS	10/01-12/01
	Anchorage MSA, AK	H	7.09 FQ	13.96 AW	21.29 TQ	AKBLS	10/01-12/01
	Arizona	H	5.77 FQ	8.51 AW	12.14 TQ	AZBLS	10/01-12/01
	Phoenix-Mesa MSA, AZ	H	5.80 FQ	8.65 AW	11.64 TQ	AZBLS	10/01-12/01
	Tucson MSA, AZ	H	5.68 FQ	8.06 AW	13.14 TQ	AZBLS	10/01-12/01
	Arkansas	H	5.83 FQ	8.53 AW	12.91 TQ	ARBLS	10/01-12/01
	Fayetteville-Springdale-Rogers MSA, AR	H	5.91 FQ	9.32 AW	13.27 TQ	ARBLS	10/01-12/01
	Fort Smith MSA, AR-OK	H	5.95 FQ	8.00 AW	11.04 TQ	ARBLS	10/01-12/01
	Little Rock-North Little Rock MSA, AR	H	5.72 FQ	8.72 AW	18.20 TQ	ARBLS	10/01-12/01
	California	H	6.53 FQ	9.86 AW	15.78 TQ	CABLS	10/01-12/01
	Bakersfield MSA, CA	H	7.42 FQ	9.53 AW	12.34 TQ	CABLS	10/01-12/01
	Chico-Paradise MSA, CA	H	6.86 FQ	8.03 AW	9.58 TQ	CABLS	10/01-12/01
	Fresno MSA, CA	H	6.76 FQ	10.33 AW	14.33 TQ	CABLS	10/01-12/01
	Los Angeles-Long Beach PMSA, CA	H	6.39 FQ	9.04 AW	14.23 TQ	CABLS	10/01-12/01
	Merced MSA, CA	H	6.55 FQ	8.40 AW	11.30 TQ	CABLS	10/01-12/01
	Modesto MSA, CA	H	6.64 FQ	9.44 AW	13.29 TQ	CABLS	10/01-12/01
	Oakland PMSA, CA	H	6.67 FQ	9.85 AW	13.94 TQ	CABLS	10/01-12/01
	Orange County PMSA, CA	H	6.67 FQ	9.47 AW	14.86 TQ	CABLS	10/01-12/01
	Redding MSA, CA	H	6.96 FQ	8.33 AW	11.18 TQ	CABLS	10/01-12/01
	Riverside-San Bernardino PMSA, CA	H	6.70 FQ	9.56 AW	13.22 TQ	CABLS	10/01-12/01
	Sacramento PMSA, CA	H	7.33 FQ	9.07 AW	11.10 TQ	CABLS	10/01-12/01
	Salinas MSA, CA	H	7.34 FQ	12.54 AW	19.12 TQ	CABLS	10/01-12/01
	San Diego MSA, CA	H	6.93 FQ	10.27 AW	17.02 TQ	CABLS	10/01-12/01
	San Francisco PMSA, CA	H	6.66 FQ	14.02 AW	24.11 TQ	CABLS	10/01-12/01
	San Jose PMSA, CA	H	6.91 FQ	11.56 AW	17.34 TQ	CABLS	10/01-12/01
	San Luis Obispo-Atascadero-Paso Robles MSA, CA	H	6.82 FQ	12.23 AW	20.59 TQ	CABLS	10/01-12/01
	Santa Barbara-Santa Maria-Lompoc MSA, CA	H	7.01 FQ	10.19 AW	13.85 TQ	CABLS	10/01-12/01
	Santa Cruz-Watsonville PMSA, CA	H	6.56 FQ	9.15 AW	11.76 TQ	CABLS	10/01-12/01
	Santa Rosa PMSA, CA	H	7.19 FQ	9.52 AW	11.86 TQ	CABLS	10/01-12/01
	Stockton-Lodi MSA, CA	H	6.60 FQ	9.14 AW	11.49 TQ	CABLS	10/01-12/01
	Vallejo-Fairfield-Napa PMSA, CA	H	6.66 FQ	8.85 AW	12.23 TQ	CABLS	10/01-12/01
	Ventura PMSA, CA	H	6.60 FQ	10.35 AW	16.72 TQ	CABLS	10/01-12/01
	Visalia-Tulare-Porterville MSA, CA	H	6.62 FQ	8.11 AW	10.06 TQ	CABLS	10/01-12/01
	Colorado	H	6.94 FQ	10.52 AW	13.92 TQ	COBLS	10/01-12/01
	Boulder-Longmont PMSA, CO	H	7.59 FQ	11.56 AW	14.01 TQ	COBLS	10/01-12/01
	Colorado Springs MSA, CO	H	7.27 FQ	10.31 AW	13.39 TQ	COBLS	10/01-12/01
	Denver PMSA, CO	H	7.80 FQ	10.52 AW	13.42 TQ	COBLS	10/01-12/01
	Fort Collins-Loveland MSA, CO	H	7.16 FQ	12.77 AW	20.02 TQ	COBLS	10/01-12/01
	Greeley PMSA, CO	H	5.85 FQ	7.86 AW	11.72 TQ	COBLS	10/01-12/01
	Connecticut	H	6.65 FQ	11.59 AW	18.60 TQ	CTBLS	10/01-12/01
	Bridgeport PMSA, CT	H	6.71 FQ	9.51 AW	13.02 TQ	CTBLS	10/01-12/01
	Danbury PMSA, CT	H	6.91 FQ	12.16 AW	22.65 TQ	CTBLS	10/01-12/01
	Hartford MSA, CT	H	6.89 FQ	12.90 AW	22.14 TQ	CTBLS	10/01-12/01

AAW	Average annual wage	AOH	Average offered, high	ASH	Average starting, high	H	Hourly	M	Monthly	S	Special: hourly and annual
AE	Average entry wage	AOL	Average offered, low	ASL	Average starting, low	HI	Highest wage paid	MTC	Median total compensation	TQ	Third quartile wage
AEX	Average experienced wage	APH	Average pay, high range	AW	Average wage paid	HR	High end range	MW	Median wage paid	W	Weekly
AO	Average offered	APL	Average pay, low range	FQ	First quartile wage	LR	Low end range	SQ	Second quartile wage	Y	Yearly

Occupation/Type/Industry	Location	Per	Low	Mid	High	Source	Date
Hairdresser, Hairstylist, and Cosmetologist	New Haven-Meriden PMSA, CT	H	6.53 FQ	10.58 AW	15.93 TQ	CTBLS	10/01-12/01
	New London-Norwich MSA, CT-RI	H	6.57 FQ	9.29 AW	14.35 TQ	CTBLS	10/01-12/01
	Stamford-Norwalk PMSA, CT	H	6.99 FQ	15.58 AW	25.48 TQ	CTBLS	10/01-12/01
	Waterbury PMSA, CT	H	6.50 FQ	8.34 AW	13.25 TQ	CTBLS	10/01-12/01
	Delaware	H	6.39 FQ	10.32 AW	16.86 TQ	DEBLS	10/01-12/01
	Wilmington-Newark PMSA, DE-MD	H	6.38 FQ	10.63 AW	17.25 TQ	DEBLS	10/01-12/01
	District of Columbia	H	10.48 FQ	17.13 AW	30.47 TQ	DCBLS	10/01-12/01
	Washington PMSA, DC-MD-VA-WV	H	5.93 FQ	12.88 AW	23.72 TQ	DCBLS	10/01-12/01
	Florida	H	5.96 FQ	10.29 AW	16.92 TQ	FLBLS	10/01-12/01
	Daytona Beach MSA, FL	H	5.73 FQ	7.32 AW	10.48 TQ	FLBLS	10/01-12/01
	Fort Lauderdale PMSA, FL	H	5.67 FQ	8.68 AW	15.09 TQ	FLBLS	10/01-12/01
	Fort Myers-Cape Coral MSA, FL	H	5.80 FQ	9.76 AW	16.09 TQ	FLBLS	10/01-12/01
	Fort Pierce-Port St. Lucie MSA, FL	H	5.80 FQ	10.20 AW	17.61 TQ	FLBLS	10/01-12/01
	Fort Walton Beach MSA, FL	H	5.60 FQ	8.31 AW	13.17 TQ	FLBLS	10/01-12/01
	Gainesville MSA, FL	H	6.77 FQ	10.13 AW	22.81 TQ	FLBLS	10/01-12/01
	Jacksonville MSA, FL	H	6.54 FQ	9.83 AW	15.22 TQ	FLBLS	10/01-12/01
	Lakeland-Winter Haven MSA, FL	H	5.74 FQ	8.47 AW	13.46 TQ	FLBLS	10/01-12/01
	Melbourne-Titusville-Palm Bay MSA, FL	H	5.72 FQ	8.27 AW	12.35 TQ	FLBLS	10/01-12/01
	Miami PMSA, FL	H	5.91 FQ	10.07 AW	16.47 TQ	FLBLS	10/01-12/01
	Naples MSA, FL	H	6.07 FQ	11.51 AW	19.49 TQ	FLBLS	10/01-12/01
	Ocala MSA, FL	H	5.94 FQ	8.63 AW	12.46 TQ	FLBLS	10/01-12/01
	Orlando MSA, FL	H	6.40 FQ	12.65 AW	20.95 TQ	FLBLS	10/01-12/01
	Pensacola MSA, FL	H	5.96 FQ	8.72 AW	12.86 TQ	FLBLS	10/01-12/01
	Sarasota-Bradenton MSA, FL	H	5.75 FQ	9.94 AW	16.48 TQ	FLBLS	10/01-12/01
	Tallahassee MSA, FL	H	6.00 FQ	12.82 AW	20.57 TQ	FLBLS	10/01-12/01
	Tampa-St. Petersburg-Clearwater MSA, FL	H	6.32 FQ	11.28 AW	17.51 TQ	FLBLS	10/01-12/01
	West Palm Beach-Boca Raton MSA, FL	H	5.96 FQ	9.93 AW	13.68 TQ	FLBLS	10/01-12/01
	Georgia	H	6.24 FQ	11.04 AW	18.43 TQ	GABLS	10/01-12/01
	Atlanta MSA, GA	H	6.84 FQ	11.98 AW	22.86 TQ	GABLS	10/01-12/01
	Augusta-Aiken MSA, GA-SC	H	6.15 FQ	9.41 AW	13.01 TQ	GABLS	10/01-12/01
	Columbus MSA, GA-AL	H	6.02 FQ	9.21 AW	13.32 TQ	GABLS	10/01-12/01
	Macon MSA, GA	H	5.84 FQ	8.23 AW	12.04 TQ	GABLS	10/01-12/01
	Savannah MSA, GA	H	5.69 FQ	7.79 AW	11.71 TQ	GABLS	10/01-12/01
	Hawaii	H	6.24 FQ	12.14 AW	21.49 TQ	HIBLS	10/01-12/01
	Honolulu MSA, HI	H	6.18 FQ	12.65 AW	25.66 TQ	HIBLS	10/01-12/01
	Idaho	H	5.71 FQ	7.55 AW	9.68 TQ	IDBLS	10/01-12/01
	Boise City MSA, ID	H	5.93 FQ	7.48 AW	9.06 TQ	IDBLS	10/01-12/01
	Illinois	H	6.39 FQ	11.22 AW	18.74 TQ	ILBLS	10/01-12/01
	Champaign-Urbana MSA, IL	H	6.62 FQ	13.04 AW	21.23 TQ	ILBLS	10/01-12/01
	Chicago PMSA, IL	H	6.64 FQ	11.61 AW	19.10 TQ	ILBLS	10/01-12/01
	Peoria-Pekin MSA, IL	H	6.11 FQ	10.80 AW	17.60 TQ	ILBLS	10/01-12/01
	Rockford MSA, IL	H	7.47 FQ	14.20 AW	21.41 TQ	ILBLS	10/01-12/01
	Springfield MSA, IL	H	6.11 FQ	12.70 AW	21.15 TQ	ILBLS	10/01-12/01
	Indiana	H	6.15 FQ	9.70 AW	14.99 TQ	INBLS	10/01-12/01
	Elkhart-Goshen MSA, IN	H	6.04 FQ	9.10 AW	13.31 TQ	INBLS	10/01-12/01
	Evansville-Henderson MSA, IN-KY	H	5.92 FQ	8.60 AW	12.65 TQ	INBLS	10/01-12/01
	Fort Wayne MSA, IN	H	6.37 FQ	10.67 AW	16.38 TQ	INBLS	10/01-12/01
	Gary PMSA, IN	H	5.90 FQ	8.58 AW	11.47 TQ	INBLS	10/01-12/01
	Indianapolis MSA, IN	H	6.56 FQ	10.35 AW	16.63 TQ	INBLS	10/01-12/01
	Lafayette MSA, IN	H	5.75 FQ	9.19 AW	14.91 TQ	INBLS	10/01-12/01
	South Bend MSA, IN	H	6.24 FQ	10.32 AW	15.08 TQ	INBLS	10/01-12/01
	Iowa	H	6.05 FQ	10.27 AW	16.27 TQ	IABLS	10/01-12/01
	Cedar Rapids MSA, IA	H	6.05 FQ	10.13 AW	16.24 TQ	IABLS	10/01-12/01
	Davenport-Moline-Rock Island MSA, IA-IL	H	6.25 FQ	9.17 AW	12.65 TQ	IABLS	10/01-12/01
	Des Moines MSA, IA	H	7.63 FQ	12.76 AW	20.79 TQ	IABLS	10/01-12/01
	Kansas	H	6.05 FQ	10.67 AW	16.03 TQ	KSBLS	10/01-12/01
	Topeka MSA, KS	H	5.70 FQ	8.75 AW	13.14 TQ	KSBLS	10/01-12/01
	Wichita MSA, KS	H	6.10 FQ	10.37 AW	13.94 TQ	KSBLS	10/01-12/01
	Kentucky	H	6.42 FQ	11.06 AW	16.45 TQ	KYBLS	10/01-12/01

AAW Average annual wage; AE Average entry wage; AEX Average experienced wage; AO Average offered; AOH Average offered, high; AOL Average offered, low; APH Average pay, high range; APL Average pay, low range; ASH Average starting, high; ASL Average starting, low; AW Average wage paid; FQ First quartile wage; H Hourly; HI Highest wage paid; HR High end range; LR Low end range; M Monthly; MTC Median total compensation; MW Median wage paid; SQ Second quartile wage; S Special: hourly and annual; TQ Third quartile wage; W Weekly; Y Yearly

Occupation/Type/Industry	Location	Per	Low	Mid	High	Source	Date
Hairdresser, Hairstylist, and Cosmetologist	Lexington MSA, KY	H	6.01 FQ	11.71 AW	23.76 TQ	KYBLS	10/01-12/01
	Louisville MSA, KY-IN	H	7.02 FQ	12.76 AW	17.79 TQ	KYBLS	10/01-12/01
	Louisiana	H	5.81 FQ	8.87 AW	13.60 TQ	LABLS	10/01-12/01
	Baton Rouge MSA, LA	H	5.96 FQ	8.61 AW	12.58 TQ	LABLS	10/01-12/01
	Houma MSA, LA	H	5.85 FQ	8.97 AW	12.01 TQ	LABLS	10/01-12/01
	Lafayette MSA, LA	H	5.74 FQ	8.63 AW	12.80 TQ	LABLS	10/01-12/01
	Lake Charles MSA, LA	H	5.88 FQ	8.25 AW	11.09 TQ	LABLS	10/01-12/01
	New Orleans MSA, LA	H	5.73 FQ	9.03 AW	13.89 TQ	LABLS	10/01-12/01
	Shreveport-Bossier City MSA, LA	H	5.81 FQ	8.29 AW	11.57 TQ	LABLS	10/01-12/01
	Maine	H	6.09 FQ	9.25 AW	13.87 TQ	MEBLS	10/01-12/01
	Portland MSA, ME	H	6.11 FQ	8.63 AW	12.66 TQ	MEBLS	10/01-12/01
	Maryland	H	6.10 FQ	9.99 AW	16.62 TQ	MDBLS	10/01-12/01
	Baltimore PMSA, MD	H	6.09 FQ	9.48 AW	15.61 TQ	MDBLS	10/01-12/01
	Massachusetts	H	6.93 FQ	11.30 AW	19.22 TQ	MABLS	10/01-12/01
	Boston PMSA, MA-NH	H	6.97 FQ	11.46 AW	19.28 TQ	MABLS	10/01-12/01
	Brockton PMSA, MA	H	6.82 FQ	9.46 AW	16.15 TQ	MABLS	10/01-12/01
	Lawrence PMSA, MA-NH	H	6.93 FQ	11.34 AW	17.08 TQ	MABLS	10/01-12/01
	Lowell PMSA, MA-NH	H	6.99 FQ	10.46 AW	14.27 TQ	MABLS	10/01-12/01
	New Bedford PMSA, MA	H	7.33 FQ	13.15 AW	25.16 TQ	MABLS	10/01-12/01
	Springfield MSA, MA	H	6.88 FQ	13.80 AW	25.23 TQ	MABLS	10/01-12/01
	Worcester PMSA, MA-CT	H	7.10 FQ	10.97 AW	19.61 TQ	MABLS	10/01-12/01
	Michigan	H	5.85 FQ	9.60 AW	14.25 TQ	MIBLS	10/01-12/01
	Ann Arbor PMSA, MI	H	6.59 FQ	11.56 AW	19.96 TQ	MIBLS	10/01-12/01
	Detroit PMSA, MI	H	5.73 FQ	9.52 AW	14.24 TQ	MIBLS	10/01-12/01
	Flint PMSA, MI	H	6.10 FQ	9.33 AW	14.45 TQ	MIBLS	10/01-12/01
	Grand Rapids-Muskegon-Holland MSA, MI	H	6.32 FQ	10.24 AW	15.46 TQ	MIBLS	10/01-12/01
	Kalamazoo-Battle Creek MSA, MI	H	5.76 FQ	8.92 AW	13.21 TQ	MIBLS	10/01-12/01
	Lansing-East Lansing MSA, MI	H	5.69 FQ	8.57 AW	13.78 TQ	MIBLS	10/01-12/01
	Saginaw-Bay City-Midland MSA, MI	H	6.15 FQ	9.42 AW	12.11 TQ	MIBLS	10/01-12/01
	Minnesota	H	6.70 FQ	11.02 AW	16.40 TQ	MNBLS	10/01-12/01
	Duluth-Superior MSA, MN-WI	H	5.68 FQ	8.40 AW	11.52 TQ	MNBLS	10/01-12/01
	Minneapolis-St. Paul MSA, MN-WI	H	7.14 FQ	11.59 AW	17.21 TQ	MNBLS	10/01-12/01
	St. Cloud MSA, MN	H	7.57 FQ	10.40 AW	13.68 TQ	MNBLS	10/01-12/01
	Mississippi	H	6.04 FQ	9.50 AW	13.82 TQ	MSBLS	10/01-12/01
	Biloxi-Gulfport-Pascagoula MSA, MS	H	6.45 FQ	8.32 AW	10.39 TQ	MSBLS	10/01-12/01
	Jackson MSA, MS	H	7.16 FQ	10.73 AW	14.46 TQ	MSBLS	10/01-12/01
	Missouri	H	6.09 FQ	9.93 AW	14.69 TQ	MOBLS	10/01-12/01
	Kansas City MSA, MO-KS	H	6.45 FQ	11.56 AW	16.42 TQ	MOBLS	10/01-12/01
	St. Louis MSA, MO-IL	H	6.19 FQ	10.15 AW	15.33 TQ	MOBLS	10/01-12/01
	Springfield MSA, MO	H	5.84 FQ	9.02 AW	13.34 TQ	MOBLS	10/01-12/01
	Montana	H	5.93 FQ	8.75 AW	13.37 TQ	MTBLS	10/01-12/01
	Billings MSA, MT	H	5.87 FQ	8.95 AW	14.42 TQ	MTBLS	10/01-12/01
	Nebraska	H	6.24 FQ	10.76 AW	17.27 TQ	NEBLS	10/01-12/01
	Lincoln MSA, NE	H	6.23 FQ	10.94 AW	16.66 TQ	NEBLS	10/01-12/01
	Omaha MSA, NE-IA	H	7.51 FQ	12.14 AW	20.34 TQ	NEBLS	10/01-12/01
	Nevada	H	5.75 FQ	9.18 AW	14.80 TQ	NVBLS	10/01-12/01
	Las Vegas MSA, NV-AZ	H	5.78 FQ	9.41 AW	15.62 TQ	NVBLS	10/01-12/01
	Reno MSA, NV	H	5.61 FQ	8.25 AW	12.62 TQ	NVBLS	10/01-12/01
	New Hampshire	H	6.22 FQ	10.13 AW	16.54 TQ	NHBLS	10/01-12/01
	Manchester PMSA, NH	H	6.42 FQ	11.25 AW	18.91 TQ	NHBLS	10/01-12/01
	Nashua PMSA, NH	H	6.73 FQ	10.11 AW	14.44 TQ	NHBLS	10/01-12/01
	Portsmouth-Rochester PMSA, NH-ME	H	6.33 FQ	11.53 AW	19.69 TQ	NHBLS	10/01-12/01
	New Jersey	H	6.10 FQ	10.07 AW	15.67 TQ	NJBLS	10/01-12/01
	Atlantic-Cape May PMSA, NJ	H	6.22 FQ	10.19 AW	16.08 TQ	NJBLS	10/01-12/01
	Bergen-Passaic PMSA, NJ	H	5.81 FQ	8.62 AW	11.94 TQ	NJBLS	10/01-12/01
	Jersey City PMSA, NJ	H	5.95 FQ	9.26 AW	15.15 TQ	NJBLS	10/01-12/01
	Middlesex-Somerset-Hunterdon PMSA, NJ	H	6.01 FQ	10.45 AW	17.18 TQ	NJBLS	10/01-12/01
	Monmouth-Ocean PMSA, NJ	H	6.75 FQ	9.47 AW	12.67 TQ	NJBLS	10/01-12/01
	Newark PMSA, NJ	H	7.24 FQ	11.22 AW	17.06 TQ	NJBLS	10/01-12/01
	Trenton PMSA, NJ	H	8.68 FQ	13.96 AW	23.33 TQ	NJBLS	10/01-12/01
	New Mexico	H	5.92 FQ	8.21 AW	11.78 TQ	NMBLS	10/01-12/01
	Albuquerque MSA, NM	H	5.89 FQ	8.37 AW	12.32 TQ	NMBLS	10/01-12/01
	Las Cruces MSA, NM	H	5.91 FQ	8.00 AW	12.77 TQ	NMBLS	10/01-12/01

AAW	Average annual wage	AOH	Average offered, high	ASH	Average starting, high	H	Hourly	M	Monthly	S	Special: hourly and annual
AE	Average entry wage	AOL	Average offered, low	ASL	Average starting, low	HI	Highest wage paid	MTC	Median total compensation	TQ	Third quartile wage
AEX	Average experienced wage	APH	Average pay, high range	AW	Average wage paid	HR	High end range	MW	Median wage paid	W	Weekly
AO	Average offered	APL	Average pay, low range	FQ	First quartile wage	LR	Low end range	SQ	Second quartile wage	Y	Yearly

Occupation/Type/Industry	Location	Per	Low	Mid	High	Source	Date
Hairdresser, Hairstylist, and Cosmetologist	New York	H	5.81 FQ	9.90 AW	14.12 TQ	NYBLS	10/01-12/01
	Albany-Schenectady-Troy MSA, NY	H	5.75 FQ	8.78 AW	12.82 TQ	NYBLS	10/01-12/01
	Binghamton MSA, NY	H	5.79 FQ	8.43 AW	13.44 TQ	NYBLS	10/01-12/01
	Buffalo-Niagara Falls MSA, NY	H	5.69 FQ	7.43 AW	10.68 TQ	NYBLS	10/01-12/01
	Dutchess County PMSA, NY	H	5.67 FQ	8.16 AW	13.40 TQ	NYBLS	10/01-12/01
	Nassau-Suffolk PMSA, NY	H	5.48 FQ	8.41 AW	13.87 TQ	NYBLS	10/01-12/01
	New York PMSA, NY	H	6.39 FQ	11.22 AW	14.35 TQ	NYBLS	10/01-12/01
	Newburgh PMSA, NY-PA	H	5.85 FQ	8.33 AW	13.82 TQ	NYBLS	10/01-12/01
	Rochester MSA, NY	H	5.85 FQ	9.69 AW	16.66 TQ	NYBLS	10/01-12/01
	Syracuse MSA, NY	H	6.10 FQ	11.60 AW	20.46 TQ	NYBLS	10/01-12/01
	Utica-Rome MSA, NY	H	5.76 FQ	8.01 AW	10.75 TQ	NYBLS	10/01-12/01
	North Carolina	H	6.19 FQ	11.05 AW	17.39 TQ	NCBLS	10/01-12/01
	Asheville MSA, NC	H	6.13 FQ	11.03 AW	20.73 TQ	NCBLS	10/01-12/01
	Charlotte-Gastonia-Rock Hill MSA, NC-SC	H	7.40 FQ	12.13 AW	21.74 TQ	NCBLS	10/01-12/01
	Fayetteville MSA, NC	H	5.86 FQ	8.62 AW	12.96 TQ	NCBLS	10/01-12/01
	Greensboro-Winston-Salem-High Point MSA, NC	H	5.90 FQ	12.22 AW	21.96 TQ	NCBLS	10/01-12/01
	Hickory-Morganton-Lenoir MSA, NC	H	5.84 FQ	7.98 AW	11.11 TQ	NCBLS	10/01-12/01
	Raleigh-Durham-Chapel Hill MSA, NC	H	6.23 FQ	12.34 AW	17.32 TQ	NCBLS	10/01-12/01
	Wilmington MSA, NC	H	6.16 FQ	8.93 AW	12.91 TQ	NCBLS	10/01-12/01
	North Dakota	H	5.91 FQ	9.23 AW	14.01 TQ	NDBLS	10/01-12/01
	Fargo-Moorhead MSA, ND-MN	H	6.07 FQ	10.39 AW	15.49 TQ	NDBLS	10/01-12/01
	Ohio	H	5.82 FQ	9.67 AW	15.29 TQ	OHBLS	10/01-12/01
	Akron PMSA, OH	H	6.15 FQ	9.98 AW	16.38 TQ	OHBLS	10/01-12/01
	Canton-Massillon MSA, OH	H	5.78 FQ	8.14 AW	11.07 TQ	OHBLS	10/01-12/01
	Cincinnati PMSA, OH-KY-IN	H	6.22 FQ	11.60 AW	16.86 TQ	OHBLS	10/01-12/01
	Cleveland-Lorain-Elyria PMSA, OH	H	5.63 FQ	8.22 AW	13.50 TQ	OHBLS	10/01-12/01
	Columbus MSA, OH	H	6.04 FQ	12.18 AW	23.51 TQ	OHBLS	10/01-12/01
	Dayton-Springfield MSA, OH	H	5.89 FQ	9.56 AW	13.93 TQ	OHBLS	10/01-12/01
	Hamilton-Middletown PMSA, OH	H	5.56 FQ	8.02 AW	13.01 TQ	OHBLS	10/01-12/01
	Mansfield MSA, OH	H	5.89 FQ	8.51 AW	13.06 TQ	OHBLS	10/01-12/01
	Toledo MSA, OH	H	6.94 FQ	10.56 AW	17.55 TQ	OHBLS	10/01-12/01
	Youngstown-Warren MSA, OH	H	5.78 FQ	8.91 AW	12.76 TQ	OHBLS	10/01-12/01
	Oklahoma	H	6.10 FQ	8.95 AW	13.01 TQ	OKBLS	10/01-12/01
	Oklahoma City MSA, OK	H	6.18 FQ	8.29 AW	10.84 TQ	OKBLS	10/01-12/01
	Tulsa MSA, OK	H	6.48 FQ	10.50 AW	16.48 TQ	OKBLS	10/01-12/01
	Oregon	H	7.18 FQ	11.34 AW	16.98 TQ	ORBLS	10/01-12/01
	Eugene-Springfield MSA, OR	H	7.17 FQ	10.68 AW	16.52 TQ	ORBLS	10/01-12/01
	Medford-Ashland MSA, OR	H	7.15 FQ	9.78 AW	13.95 TQ	ORBLS	10/01-12/01
	Portland-Vancouver PMSA, OR-WA	H	7.39 FQ	11.83 AW	18.05 TQ	ORBLS	10/01-12/01
	Salem PMSA, OR	H	6.84 FQ	10.27 AW	15.89 TQ	ORBLS	10/01-12/01
	Pennsylvania	H	5.83 FQ	9.26 AW	13.97 TQ	PABLS	10/01-12/01
	Allentown-Bethlehem-Easton MSA, PA	H	5.77 FQ	9.14 AW	13.46 TQ	PABLS	10/01-12/01
	Erie MSA, PA	H	5.73 FQ	7.32 AW	9.55 TQ	PABLS	10/01-12/01
	Harrisburg-Lebanon-Carlisle MSA, PA	H	6.04 FQ	10.01 AW	16.05 TQ	PABLS	10/01-12/01
	Johnstown MSA, PA	H	5.99 FQ	10.07 AW	18.07 TQ	PABLS	10/01-12/01
	Lancaster MSA, PA	H	5.77 FQ	9.12 AW	15.08 TQ	PABLS	10/01-12/01
	Philadelphia PMSA, PA-NJ	H	5.84 FQ	9.77 AW	15.55 TQ	PABLS	10/01-12/01
	Pittsburgh MSA, PA	H	5.97 FQ	9.29 AW	13.62 TQ	PABLS	10/01-12/01
	Reading MSA, PA	H	5.72 FQ	8.44 AW	12.18 TQ	PABLS	10/01-12/01
	Scranton-Wilkes-Barre-Hazleton MSA, PA	H	5.71 FQ	7.15 AW	9.34 TQ	PABLS	10/01-12/01
	York MSA, PA	H	5.86 FQ	9.48 AW	18.94 TQ	PABLS	10/01-12/01
	Rhode Island	H	6.83 FQ	10.45 AW	15.65 TQ	RIBLS	10/01-12/01
	Providence-Fall River-Warwick MSA, RI-MA	H	6.84 FQ	10.01 AW	14.30 TQ	RIBLS	10/01-12/01
	South Carolina	H	5.88 FQ	9.81 AW	16.59 TQ	SCBLS	10/01-12/01
	Charleston-North Charleston MSA, SC	H	5.92 FQ	12.52 AW	19.25 TQ	SCBLS	10/01-12/01
	Columbia MSA, SC	H	5.82 FQ	9.05 AW	14.24 TQ	SCBLS	10/01-12/01

AAW	Average annual wage	**AOH**	Average offered, high	**ASH**	Average starting, high	**H**	Hourly	**M**	Monthly	**S**	Special: hourly and annual
AE	Average entry wage	**AOL**	Average offered, low	**ASL**	Average starting, low	**HI**	Highest wage paid	**MTC**	Median total compensation	**TQ**	Third quartile wage
AEX	Average experienced wage	**APH**	Average pay, high range	**AW**	Average wage paid	**HR**	High end range	**MW**	Median wage paid	**W**	Weekly
AO	Average offered	**APL**	Average pay, low range	**FQ**	First quartile wage	**LR**	Low end range	**SQ**	Second quartile wage	**Y**	Yearly

Occupation/Type/Industry	Location	Per	Low	Mid	High	Source	Date
Hairdresser, Hairstylist, and Cosmetologist	Greenville-Spartanburg-Anderson MSA, SC	H	5.89 FQ	9.52 AW	16.37 TQ	SCBLS	10/01-12/01
	Myrtle Beach MSA, SC	H	6.03 FQ	9.11 AW	13.38 TQ	SCBLS	10/01-12/01
	South Dakota	H	8.69 FQ	11.18 AW	14.74 TQ	SDBLS	10/01-12/01
	Sioux Falls MSA, SD	H	9.43 FQ	12.74 AW	16.69 TQ	SDBLS	10/01-12/01
	Tennessee	H	6.05 FQ	10.77 AW	17.29 TQ	TNBLS	10/01-12/01
	Chattanooga MSA, TN-GA	H	6.20 FQ	10.32 AW	16.10 TQ	TNBLS	10/01-12/01
	Clarksville-Hopkinsville MSA, TN-KY	H	6.87 FQ	9.39 AW	13.20 TQ	TNBLS	10/01-12/01
	Johnson City-Kingsport-Bristol MSA, TN-VA	H	5.86 FQ	9.88 AW	16.09 TQ	TNBLS	10/01-12/01
	Knoxville MSA, TN	H	6.71 FQ	11.48 AW	17.36 TQ	TNBLS	10/01-12/01
	Memphis MSA, TN-AR-MS	H	6.52 FQ	12.25 AW	20.47 TQ	TNBLS	10/01-12/01
	Nashville MSA, TN	H	5.79 FQ	10.44 AW	17.09 TQ	TNBLS	10/01-12/01
	Texas	H	5.96 FQ	10.35 AW	17.12 TQ	TXBLS	10/01-12/01
	Amarillo MSA, TX	H	5.95 FQ	8.42 AW	12.12 TQ	TXBLS	10/01-12/01
	Austin-San Marcos MSA, TX	H	6.59 FQ	11.33 AW	17.07 TQ	TXBLS	10/01-12/01
	Beaumont-Port Arthur MSA, TX	H	5.63 FQ	7.13 AW	9.77 TQ	TXBLS	10/01-12/01
	Brazoria PMSA, TX	H	5.96 FQ	9.68 AW	16.32 TQ	TXBLS	10/01-12/01
	Brownsville-Harlingen-San Benito MSA, TX	H	5.63 FQ	6.67 AW	8.53 TQ	TXBLS	10/01-12/01
	Corpus Christi MSA, TX	H	5.83 FQ	9.03 AW	13.61 TQ	TXBLS	10/01-12/01
	Dallas PMSA, TX	H	5.83 FQ	9.90 AW	16.19 TQ	TXBLS	10/01-12/01
	El Paso MSA, TX	H	5.57 FQ	8.20 AW	15.94 TQ	TXBLS	10/01-12/01
	Fort Worth-Arlington PMSA, TX	H	6.41 FQ	10.82 AW	16.66 TQ	TXBLS	10/01-12/01
	Galveston-Texas City PMSA, TX	H	5.74 FQ	7.99 AW	12.59 TQ	TXBLS	10/01-12/01
	Houston PMSA, TX	H	6.36 FQ	12.85 AW	21.30 TQ	TXBLS	10/01-12/01
	Killeen-Temple MSA, TX	H	5.75 FQ	9.18 AW	13.81 TQ	TXBLS	10/01-12/01
	Laredo MSA, TX	H	5.64 FQ	7.23 AW	10.34 TQ	TXBLS	10/01-12/01
	Longview-Marshall MSA, TX	H	5.88 FQ	7.97 AW	10.39 TQ	TXBLS	10/01-12/01
	Lubbock MSA, TX	H	6.23 FQ	8.87 AW	11.46 TQ	TXBLS	10/01-12/01
	McAllen-Edinburg-Mission MSA, TX	H	5.74 FQ	7.69 AW	10.63 TQ	TXBLS	10/01-12/01
	Odessa-Midland MSA, TX	H	6.05 FQ	8.79 AW	10.96 TQ	TXBLS	10/01-12/01
	San Antonio MSA, TX	H	7.15 FQ	11.94 AW	23.23 TQ	TXBLS	10/01-12/01
	Tyler MSA, TX	H	5.71 FQ	7.74 AW	10.36 TQ	TXBLS	10/01-12/01
	Waco MSA, TX	H	6.68 FQ	8.92 AW	10.61 TQ	TXBLS	10/01-12/01
	Utah	H	6.77 FQ	10.00 AW	13.37 TQ	UTBLS	10/01-12/01
	Provo-Orem MSA, UT	H	7.30 FQ	10.08 AW	13.36 TQ	UTBLS	10/01-12/01
	Salt Lake City-Ogden MSA, UT	H	6.79 FQ	10.14 AW	13.38 TQ	UTBLS	10/01-12/01
	Vermont	H	6.88 FQ	10.18 AW	13.84 TQ	VTBLS	10/01-12/01
	Burlington MSA, VT	H	7.45 FQ	10.52 AW	14.11 TQ	VTBLS	10/01-12/01
	Virginia	H	5.95 FQ	11.48 AW	19.39 TQ	VABLS	10/01-12/01
	Lynchburg MSA, VA	H	5.87 FQ	9.30 AW	13.97 TQ	VABLS	10/01-12/01
	Norfolk-Virginia Beach-Newport News MSA, VA-NC	H	6.55 FQ	10.54 AW	14.12 TQ	VABLS	10/01-12/01
	Richmond-Petersburg MSA, VA	H	6.32 FQ	10.61 AW	15.70 TQ	VABLS	10/01-12/01
	Roanoke MSA, VA	H	6.08 FQ	9.79 AW	14.35 TQ	VABLS	10/01-12/01
	Washington	H	7.32 FQ	14.03 AW	23.13 TQ	WABLS	10/01-12/01
	Bremerton PMSA, WA	H	7.80 FQ	10.31 AW	12.83 TQ	WABLS	10/01-12/01
	Olympia PMSA, WA	H	7.22 FQ	9.88 AW	13.51 TQ	WABLS	10/01-12/01
	Richland-Kennewick-Pasco MSA, WA	H	6.86 FQ	10.04 AW	15.86 TQ	WABLS	10/01-12/01
	Seattle-Bellevue-Everett PMSA, WA	H	8.84 FQ	17.97 AW	27.12 TQ	WABLS	10/01-12/01
	Spokane MSA, WA	H	7.55 FQ	10.94 AW	17.04 TQ	WABLS	10/01-12/01
	Tacoma PMSA, WA	H	7.37 FQ	10.78 AW	14.43 TQ	WABLS	10/01-12/01
	Yakima MSA, WA	H	6.88 FQ	9.88 AW	13.87 TQ	WABLS	10/01-12/01
	West Virginia	H	5.76 FQ	8.38 AW	13.18 TQ	WVBLS	10/01-12/01
	Charleston MSA, WV	H	5.88 FQ	9.24 AW	13.70 TQ	WVBLS	10/01-12/01
	Huntington-Ashland MSA, WV-KY-OH	H	5.88 FQ	8.75 AW	14.24 TQ	WVBLS	10/01-12/01
	Wisconsin	H	6.28 FQ	10.73 AW	16.44 TQ	WIBLS	10/01-12/01
	Appleton-Oshkosh-Neenah MSA, WI	H	7.38 FQ	10.12 AW	13.45 TQ	WIBLS	10/01-12/01

AAW Average annual wage; AE Average entry wage; AEX Average experienced wage; AO Average offered; AOH Average offered, high; AOL Average offered, low; APH Average pay, high range; APL Average pay, low range; ASH Average starting, high; ASL Average starting, low; AW Average wage paid; FQ First quartile wage; H Hourly; HI Highest wage paid; HR High end range; LR Low end range; M Monthly; MTC Median total compensation; MW Median wage paid; SQ Second quartile wage; S Special: hourly and annual; TQ Third quartile wage; W Weekly; Y Yearly

Occupation/Type/Industry	Location	Per	Low	Mid	High	Source	Date
Hairdresser, Hairstylist, and Cosmetologist	Green Bay MSA, WI	H	7.48 FQ	11.05 AW	14.58 TQ	WIBLS	10/01-12/01
	Madison MSA, WI	H	8.47 FQ	12.84 AW	18.86 TQ	WIBLS	10/01-12/01
	Milwaukee-Waukesha PMSA, WI	H	6.16 FQ	11.82 AW	20.18 TQ	WIBLS	10/01-12/01
	Racine PMSA, WI	H	6.03 FQ	10.49 AW	15.96 TQ	WIBLS	10/01-12/01
	Wyoming	H	5.70 FQ	7.91 AW	12.45 TQ	WYBLS	10/01-12/01
	Cheyenne MSA, WY	H	6.26 FQ	8.76 AW	13.42 TQ	WYBLS	10/01-12/01
	Puerto Rico	H	5.67 FQ	7.95 AW	11.87 TQ	PRBLS	10/01-12/01
	Guam	H	5.64 FQ	10.47 AW	24.36 TQ	GUBLS	10/01-12/01
Hazardous Materials Removal Worker	Alabama	H	9.26 FQ	13.75 AW	21.79 TQ	ALBLS	10/01-12/01
	Birmingham MSA, AL	H	9.31 FQ	11.73 AW	13.92 TQ	ALBLS	10/01-12/01
	Huntsville MSA, AL	H	11.58 FQ	17.14 AW	28.51 TQ	ALBLS	10/01-12/01
	Alaska	H	15.68 FQ	23.58 AW	29.13 TQ	AKBLS	10/01-12/01
	Anchorage MSA, AK	H	11.91 FQ	16.49 AW	21.34 TQ	AKBLS	10/01-12/01
	Arizona	H	11.77 FQ	16.54 AW	28.82 TQ	AZBLS	10/01-12/01
	Phoenix-Mesa MSA, AZ	H	12.09 FQ	16.66 AW	29.04 TQ	AZBLS	10/01-12/01
	Arkansas	H	10.21 FQ	15.42 AW	20.65 TQ	ARBLS	10/01-12/01
	Little Rock-North Little Rock MSA, AR	H	8.70 FQ	15.69 AW	22.28 TQ	ARBLS	10/01-12/01
	California	H	9.90 FQ	15.63 AW	24.16 TQ	CABLS	10/01-12/01
	Fresno MSA, CA	H	6.55 FQ	13.12 AW	21.40 TQ	CABLS	10/01-12/01
	Los Angeles-Long Beach PMSA, CA	H	10.17 FQ	16.34 AW	26.06 TQ	CABLS	10/01-12/01
	Oakland PMSA, CA	H	8.79 FQ	14.99 AW	23.66 TQ	CABLS	10/01-12/01
	Orange County PMSA, CA	H	11.25 FQ	14.49 AW	17.87 TQ	CABLS	10/01-12/01
	Riverside-San Bernardino PMSA, CA	H	10.08 FQ	17.01 AW	25.44 TQ	CABLS	10/01-12/01
	Sacramento PMSA, CA	H	9.62 FQ	15.30 AW	21.91 TQ	CABLS	10/01-12/01
	San Diego MSA, CA	H	12.00 FQ	18.83 AW	25.77 TQ	CABLS	10/01-12/01
	San Francisco PMSA, CA	H	12.77 FQ	19.69 AW	27.76 TQ	CABLS	10/01-12/01
	San Jose PMSA, CA	H	11.64 FQ	16.30 AW	24.63 TQ	CABLS	10/01-12/01
	Santa Barbara-Santa Maria-Lompoc MSA, CA	H	17.06 FQ	19.90 AW	25.25 TQ	CABLS	10/01-12/01
	Stockton-Lodi MSA, CA	H	11.72 FQ	15.73 AW	23.29 TQ	CABLS	10/01-12/01
	Colorado Springs MSA, CO	H	6.32 FQ	13.25 AW	17.64 TQ	COBLS	10/01-12/01
	Connecticut	H	7.60 FQ	14.13 AW	20.49 TQ	CTBLS	10/01-12/01
	Bridgeport PMSA, CT	H	8.55 FQ	15.21 AW	20.82 TQ	CTBLS	10/01-12/01
	Hartford MSA, CT	H	6.73 FQ	13.41 AW	17.96 TQ	CTBLS	10/01-12/01
	New Haven-Meriden PMSA, CT	H	7.71 FQ	13.44 AW	21.18 TQ	CTBLS	10/01-12/01
	New London-Norwich MSA, CT-RI	H	12.30 FQ	18.14 AW	25.75 TQ	CTBLS	10/01-12/01
	Delaware	H	12.18 FQ	15.86 AW	18.28 TQ	DEBLS	10/01-12/01
	Wilmington-Newark PMSA, DE-MD	H	13.90 FQ	16.20 AW	18.17 TQ	DEBLS	10/01-12/01
	Washington PMSA, DC-MD-VA-WV	H	11.22 FQ	16.49 AW	26.06 TQ	DCBLS	10/01-12/01
	Florida	H	7.96 FQ	13.06 AW	20.56 TQ	FLBLS	10/01-12/01
	Jacksonville MSA, FL	H	7.85 FQ	10.82 AW	14.88 TQ	FLBLS	10/01-12/01
	Melbourne-Titusville-Palm Bay MSA, FL	H	7.86 FQ	12.88 AW	20.70 TQ	FLBLS	10/01-12/01
	Miami PMSA, FL	H	9.42 FQ	17.03 AW	30.58 TQ	FLBLS	10/01-12/01
	Orlando MSA, FL	H	7.96 FQ	13.73 AW	18.78 TQ	FLBLS	10/01-12/01
	Tampa-St. Petersburg-Clearwater MSA, FL	H	8.09 FQ	12.54 AW	20.41 TQ	FLBLS	10/01-12/01
	Georgia	H	10.65 FQ	14.68 AW	21.12 TQ	GABLS	10/01-12/01
	Atlanta MSA, GA	H	10.61 FQ	14.91 AW	21.40 TQ	GABLS	10/01-12/01
	Savannah MSA, GA	H	10.01 FQ	11.75 AW	13.22 TQ	GABLS	10/01-12/01
	Hawaii	H	10.79 FQ	15.88 AW	22.06 TQ	HIBLS	10/01-12/01
	Honolulu MSA, HI	H	10.96 FQ	16.13 AW	22.45 TQ	HIBLS	10/01-12/01
	Illinois	H	11.60 FQ	17.49 AW	27.08 TQ	ILBLS	10/01-12/01
	Chicago PMSA, IL	H	15.80 FQ	23.64 AW	28.05 TQ	ILBLS	10/01-12/01
	Indiana	H	9.45 FQ	16.20 AW	24.94 TQ	INBLS	10/01-12/01
	Fort Wayne MSA, IN	H	11.88 FQ	17.96 AW	25.18 TQ	INBLS	10/01-12/01
	Gary PMSA, IN	H	7.78 FQ	13.25 AW	23.43 TQ	INBLS	10/01-12/01
	Iowa	H	7.71 FQ	10.79 AW	14.01 TQ	IABLS	10/01-12/01
	Cedar Rapids MSA, IA	H	9.24 FQ	12.79 AW	23.72 TQ	IABLS	10/01-12/01
	Kansas	H	10.82 FQ	15.30 AW	20.18 TQ	KSBLS	10/01-12/01
	Wichita MSA, KS	H	9.29 FQ	11.68 AW	14.78 TQ	KSBLS	10/01-12/01

AAW	Average annual wage	**AOH**	Average offered, high	**ASH**	Average starting, high	**H**	Hourly	**M**	Monthly	**S**	Special: hourly and annual
AE	Average entry wage	**AOL**	Average offered, low	**ASL**	Average starting, low	**HI**	Highest wage paid	**MTC**	Median total compensation	**TQ**	Third quartile wage
AEX	Average experienced wage	**APH**	Average pay, high range	**AW**	Average wage paid	**HR**	High end range	**MW**	Median wage paid	**W**	Weekly
AO	Average offered	**APL**	Average pay, low range	**FQ**	First quartile wage	**LR**	Low end range	**SQ**	Second quartile wage	**Y**	Yearly

Occupation/Type/Industry	Location	Per	Low	Mid	High	Source	Date
Hazardous Materials Removal Worker	Kentucky	H	8.50 FQ	13.91 AW	18.25 TQ	KYBLS	10/01-12/01
	Louisville MSA, KY-IN	H	11.63 FQ	15.15 AW	17.66 TQ	KYBLS	10/01-12/01
	Louisiana	H	6.44 FQ	13.49 AW	21.35 TQ	LABLS	10/01-12/01
	Baton Rouge MSA, LA	H	9.53 FQ	14.57 AW	22.38 TQ	LABLS	10/01-12/01
	New Orleans MSA, LA	H	7.21 FQ	14.08 AW	21.26 TQ	LABLS	10/01-12/01
	Maine	H	9.70 FQ	13.08 AW	16.60 TQ	MEBLS	10/01-12/01
	Portland MSA, ME	H	8.86 FQ	13.51 AW	16.94 TQ	MEBLS	10/01-12/01
	Maryland	H	10.08 FQ	14.89 AW	24.61 TQ	MDBLS	10/01-12/01
	Baltimore PMSA, MD	H	9.71 FQ	12.73 AW	16.87 TQ	MDBLS	10/01-12/01
	Massachusetts	H	11.91 FQ	17.03 AW	25.27 TQ	MABLS	10/01-12/01
	Boston PMSA, MA-NH	H	11.92 FQ	17.57 AW	25.83 TQ	MABLS	10/01-12/01
	Lawrence PMSA, MA-NH	H	12.15 FQ	16.19 AW	23.06 TQ	MABLS	10/01-12/01
	Springfield MSA, MA	H	12.21 FQ	17.59 AW	25.45 TQ	MABLS	10/01-12/01
	Michigan	H	12.05 FQ	19.82 AW	26.74 TQ	MIBLS	10/01-12/01
	Detroit PMSA, MI	H	12.64 FQ	20.08 AW	26.71 TQ	MIBLS	10/01-12/01
	Grand Rapids-Muskegon-Holland MSA, MI	H	10.28 FQ	19.00 AW	28.10 TQ	MIBLS	10/01-12/01
	Lansing-East Lansing MSA, MI	H	7.99 FQ	16.39 AW	22.93 TQ	MIBLS	10/01-12/01
	Minnesota	H	12.05 FQ	19.77 AW	26.30 TQ	MNBLS	10/01-12/01
	Duluth-Superior MSA, MN-WI	H	10.35 FQ	13.85 AW	22.79 TQ	MNBLS	10/01-12/01
	Minneapolis-St. Paul MSA, MN-WI	H	17.16 FQ	21.19 AW	26.57 TQ	MNBLS	10/01-12/01
	Mississippi	H	8.16 FQ	13.24 AW	23.48 TQ	MSBLS	10/01-12/01
	Jackson MSA, MS	H	9.64 FQ	16.19 AW	25.95 TQ	MSBLS	10/01-12/01
	Missouri	H	12.14 FQ	20.21 AW	28.17 TQ	MOBLS	10/01-12/01
	Kansas City MSA, MO-KS	H	11.84 FQ	17.89 AW	26.35 TQ	MOBLS	10/01-12/01
	St. Louis MSA, MO-IL	H	12.38 FQ	20.14 AW	28.10 TQ	MOBLS	10/01-12/01
	Montana	H	11.92 FQ	16.32 AW	24.35 TQ	MTBLS	10/01-12/01
	Nebraska	H	9.82 FQ	12.95 AW	16.84 TQ	NEBLS	10/01-12/01
	Nevada	H	11.86 FQ	17.14 AW	24.06 TQ	NVBLS	10/01-12/01
	Las Vegas MSA, NV-AZ	H	11.59 FQ	17.48 AW	24.67 TQ	NVBLS	10/01-12/01
	New Jersey	H	12.13 FQ	20.78 AW	27.61 TQ	NJBLS	10/01-12/01
	Bergen-Passaic PMSA, NJ	H	13.50 FQ	21.99 AW	26.55 TQ	NJBLS	10/01-12/01
	Middlesex-Somerset-Hunterdon PMSA, NJ	H	10.69 FQ	18.82 AW	27.32 TQ	NJBLS	10/01-12/01
	Monmouth-Ocean PMSA, NJ	H	12.62 FQ	22.15 AW	33.27 TQ	NJBLS	10/01-12/01
	Newark PMSA, NJ	H	10.51 FQ	19.37 AW	27.65 TQ	NJBLS	10/01-12/01
	New Mexico	H	10.15 FQ	15.24 AW	20.99 TQ	NMBLS	10/01-12/01
	New York	H	11.48 FQ	19.88 AW	26.45 TQ	NYBLS	10/01-12/01
	Albany-Schenectady-Troy MSA, NY	H	9.27 FQ	13.84 AW	21.05 TQ	NYBLS	10/01-12/01
	Buffalo-Niagara Falls MSA, NY	H	15.73 FQ	22.62 AW	26.70 TQ	NYBLS	10/01-12/01
	Nassau-Suffolk PMSA, NY	H	8.90 FQ	18.90 AW	26.32 TQ	NYBLS	10/01-12/01
	New York PMSA, NY	H	17.74 FQ	21.97 AW	26.85 TQ	NYBLS	10/01-12/01
	Rochester MSA, NY	H	11.46 FQ	15.56 AW	21.33 TQ	NYBLS	10/01-12/01
	North Carolina	H	9.35 FQ	12.70 AW	17.83 TQ	NCBLS	10/01-12/01
	Charlotte-Gastonia-Rock Hill MSA, NC-SC	H	9.53 FQ	17.49 AW	28.39 TQ	NCBLS	10/01-12/01
	Fayetteville MSA, NC	H	9.47 FQ	12.06 AW	16.69 TQ	NCBLS	10/01-12/01
	Greensboro-Winston-Salem-High Point MSA, NC	H	8.72 FQ	10.87 AW	13.96 TQ	NCBLS	10/01-12/01
	Wilmington MSA, NC	H	9.33 FQ	12.31 AW	15.64 TQ	NCBLS	10/01-12/01
	North Dakota	H	13.32 FQ	20.41 AW	30.54 TQ	NDBLS	10/01-12/01
	Ohio	H	11.09 FQ	15.79 AW	21.15 TQ	OHBLS	10/01-12/01
	Cincinnati PMSA, OH-KY-IN	H	10.06 FQ	14.19 AW	18.44 TQ	OHBLS	10/01-12/01
	Cleveland-Lorain-Elyria PMSA, OH	H	12.61 FQ	18.32 AW	21.82 TQ	OHBLS	10/01-12/01
	Columbus MSA, OH	H	11.93 FQ	15.31 AW	20.01 TQ	OHBLS	10/01-12/01
	Dayton-Springfield MSA, OH	H	9.31 FQ	14.76 AW	18.66 TQ	OHBLS	10/01-12/01
	Toledo MSA, OH	H	10.08 FQ	16.13 AW	21.99 TQ	OHBLS	10/01-12/01
	Oklahoma	H	10.20 FQ	13.12 AW	16.59 TQ	OKBLS	10/01-12/01
	Oklahoma City MSA, OK	H	11.48 FQ	12.81 AW	14.05 TQ	OKBLS	10/01-12/01
	Tulsa MSA, OK	H	9.51 FQ	11.98 AW	14.44 TQ	OKBLS	10/01-12/01
	Oregon	H	11.43 FQ	16.88 AW	26.97 TQ	ORBLS	10/01-12/01
	Portland-Vancouver PMSA, OR-WA	H	10.51 FQ	16.76 AW	27.58 TQ	ORBLS	10/01-12/01
	Pennsylvania	H	10.17 FQ	18.33 AW	27.54 TQ	PABLS	10/01-12/01
	Philadelphia PMSA, PA-NJ	H	9.13 FQ	20.16 AW	27.74 TQ	PABLS	10/01-12/01
	Rhode Island	H	11.20 FQ	15.26 AW	20.23 TQ	RIBLS	10/01-12/01
	South Carolina	H	10.23 FQ	16.92 AW	25.25 TQ	SCBLS	10/01-12/01

Occupation/Type/Industry	Location	Per	Low	Mid	High	Source	Date
Hazardous Materials Removal Worker							
	Charleston-North Charleston MSA, SC	H	9.76 FQ	11.60 AW	13.59 TQ	SCBLS	10/01-12/01
	Columbia MSA, SC	H	9.47 FQ	11.11 AW	13.61 TQ	SCBLS	10/01-12/01
	Tennessee	H	10.05 FQ	13.98 AW	20.01 TQ	TNBLS	10/01-12/01
	Knoxville MSA, TN	H	10.83 FQ	13.16 AW	16.46 TQ	TNBLS	10/01-12/01
	Nashville MSA, TN	H	9.47 FQ	12.06 AW	14.85 TQ	TNBLS	10/01-12/01
	Texas	H	9.99 FQ	14.66 AW	23.38 TQ	TXBLS	10/01-12/01
	Austin-San Marcos MSA, TX	H	10.96 FQ	16.14 AW	24.92 TQ	TXBLS	10/01-12/01
	Beaumont-Port Arthur MSA, TX	H	11.38 FQ	12.92 AW	14.71 TQ	TXBLS	10/01-12/01
	Corpus Christi MSA, TX	H	9.99 FQ	13.68 AW	18.30 TQ	TXBLS	10/01-12/01
	Dallas PMSA, TX	H	11.06 FQ	14.55 AW	23.04 TQ	TXBLS	10/01-12/01
	Houston PMSA, TX	H	10.12 FQ	13.17 AW	16.90 TQ	TXBLS	10/01-12/01
	Longview-Marshall MSA, TX	H	8.99 FQ	11.04 AW	13.45 TQ	TXBLS	10/01-12/01
	Utah	H	11.64 FQ	15.81 AW	22.07 TQ	UTBLS	10/01-12/01
	Salt Lake City-Ogden MSA, UT	H	11.28 FQ	13.60 AW	16.97 TQ	UTBLS	10/01-12/01
	Virginia	H	9.98 FQ	13.18 AW	16.79 TQ	VABLS	10/01-12/01
	Norfolk-Virginia Beach-Newport News MSA, VA-NC	H	9.89 FQ	13.14 AW	16.81 TQ	VABLS	10/01-12/01
	Richmond-Petersburg MSA, VA	H	9.67 FQ	12.21 AW	15.15 TQ	VABLS	10/01-12/01
	Washington	H	11.89 FQ	20.23 AW	27.31 TQ	WABLS	10/01-12/01
	Richland-Kennewick-Pasco MSA, WA	H	18.00 FQ	24.09 AW	30.42 TQ	WABLS	10/01-12/01
	Seattle-Bellevue-Everett PMSA, WA	H	12.20 FQ	19.79 AW	27.51 TQ	WABLS	10/01-12/01
	Spokane MSA, WA	H	14.05 FQ	16.95 AW	21.18 TQ	WABLS	10/01-12/01
	Tacoma PMSA, WA	H	12.66 FQ	18.48 AW	26.64 TQ	WABLS	10/01-12/01
	West Virginia	H	9.87 FQ	15.08 AW	17.99 TQ	WVBLS	10/01-12/01
	Charleston MSA, WV	H	9.47 FQ	15.00 AW	22.91 TQ	WVBLS	10/01-12/01
	Huntington-Ashland MSA, WV-KY-OH	H	13.88 FQ	15.15 AW	16.70 TQ	WVBLS	10/01-12/01
	Wisconsin	H	10.25 FQ	15.13 AW	21.00 TQ	WIBLS	10/01-12/01
	Milwaukee-Waukesha PMSA, WI	H	10.13 FQ	15.66 AW	21.56 TQ	WIBLS	10/01-12/01
	Puerto Rico	H	6.17 FQ	7.84 AW	9.69 TQ	PRBLS	10/01-12/01
Head Coach							
Men's Team, Big 10 School	United States	Y		133495 AW		KRTNS	1/01-1/02
Men's Team, College	Fort Wayne, IN	Y		16567 AW		KRTNS	1/01-1/02
Men's Team, Division-I School	Indiana	Y		53497 AW		KRTNS	1/01-1/02
Women's Team, Big 10 School	United States	Y		60695 AW		KRTNS	1/01-1/02
Women's Team, College	Fort Wayne, IN	Y		13325 AW		KRTNS	1/01-1/02
Women's Team, Division-I School	Indiana	Y		37302 AW		KRTNS	1/01-1/02
Health and Hygiene Manager							
Environment	United States	Y		81500 AW		SAFEDIR	2001
Environment	Midwest	Y		85000 AW		SAFEDIR	2001
Environment	Northeast	Y		92250 AW		SAFEDIR	2001
Health and Safety Engineer							
Except Mining	Alabama	Y	38800 FQ	55670 AW	76050 TQ	ALBLS	10/01-12/01
Except Mining	Alaska	Y	46780 FQ	85790 AW	123400 TQ	AKBLS	10/01-12/01
Except Mining	Arizona	Y	36640 FQ	58940 AW	86550 TQ	AZBLS	10/01-12/01
Except Mining	Arkansas	Y	28690 FQ	51510 AW	90550 TQ	ARBLS	10/01-12/01
Except Mining	California	Y	32260 FQ	57470 AW	85880 TQ	CABLS	10/01-12/01
Except Mining	Colorado	Y	40310 FQ	63670 AW	95300 TQ	COBLS	10/01-12/01
Except Mining	Connecticut	Y	38930 FQ	60820 AW	90840 TQ	CTBLS	10/01-12/01
Except Mining	Delaware	Y	42780 FQ	61170 AW	85190 TQ	DEBLS	10/01-12/01
Except Mining	District of Columbia	Y	48190 FQ	73290 AW	104000 TQ	DCBLS	10/01-12/01
Except Mining	Florida	Y	35790 FQ	55040 AW	77970 TQ	FLBLS	10/01-12/01
Except Mining	Georgia	Y	45020 FQ	60610 AW	81480 TQ	GABLS	10/01-12/01
Except Mining	Hawaii	Y	35940 FQ	55120 AW	79430 TQ	HIBLS	10/01-12/01
Except Mining	Illinois	Y	37130 FQ	56660 AW	78150 TQ	ILBLS	10/01-12/01
Except Mining	Indiana	Y	38610 FQ	55390 AW	75480 TQ	INBLS	10/01-12/01
Except Mining	Iowa	Y	30540 FQ	45890 AW	67070 TQ	IABLS	10/01-12/01
Except Mining	Kansas	Y	42940 FQ	57930 AW	76040 TQ	KSBLS	10/01-12/01
Except Mining	Kentucky	Y	35580 FQ	50410 AW	69820 TQ	KYBLS	10/01-12/01
Except Mining	Louisiana	Y	34510 FQ	58670 AW	75780 TQ	LABLS	10/01-12/01

AAW	Average annual wage	AOH	Average offered, high	ASH	Average starting, high	H	Hourly	M	Monthly	S	Special: hourly and annual
AE	Average entry wage	AOL	Average offered, low	ASL	Average starting, low	HI	Highest wage paid	MTC	Median total compensation	TQ	Third quartile wage
AEX	Average experienced wage	APH	Average pay, high range	AW	Average wage paid	HR	High end range	MW	Median wage paid	W	Weekly
AO	Average offered	APL	Average pay, low range	FQ	First quartile wage	LR	Low end range	SQ	Second quartile wage	Y	Yearly

Occupation/Type/Industry	Location	Per	Low	Mid	High	Source	Date
Health and Safety Engineer							
Except Mining	Maine	Y	32930 FQ	52090 AW	76260 TQ	MEBLS	10/01-12/01
Except Mining	Maryland	Y	43010 FQ	66370 AW	90470 TQ	MDBLS	10/01-12/01
Except Mining	Massachusetts	Y	42010 FQ	68990 AW	108450 TQ	MABLS	10/01-12/01
Except Mining	Michigan	Y	42100 FQ	62770 AW	86750 TQ	MIBLS	10/01-12/01
Except Mining	Minnesota	Y	38100 FQ	61340 AW	86230 TQ	MNBLS	10/01-12/01
Except Mining	Mississippi	Y	33670 FQ	54020 AW	74030 TQ	MSBLS	10/01-12/01
Except Mining	Missouri	Y	36650 FQ	58020 AW	83620 TQ	MOBLS	10/01-12/01
Except Mining	Montana	Y	31080 FQ	54360 AW	80460 TQ	MTBLS	10/01-12/01
Except Mining	Nebraska	Y	43450 FQ	58700 AW	76630 TQ	NEBLS	10/01-12/01
Except Mining	Nevada	Y	35980 FQ	52660 AW	72370 TQ	NVBLS	10/01-12/01
Except Mining	New Hampshire	Y	38820 FQ	58240 AW	84290 TQ	NHBLS	10/01-12/01
Except Mining	New Jersey	Y	47480 FQ	67840 AW	95810 TQ	NJBLS	10/01-12/01
Except Mining	New Mexico	Y	35630 FQ	53040 AW	80920 TQ	NMBLS	10/01-12/01
Except Mining	New York	Y	41980 FQ	63250 AW	88690 TQ	NYBLS	10/01-12/01
Except Mining	North Carolina	Y	34990 FQ	56670 AW	84970 TQ	NCBLS	10/01-12/01
Except Mining	North Dakota	Y	46700 FQ	59750 AW	77110 TQ	NDBLS	10/01-12/01
Except Mining	Ohio	Y	36970 FQ	55820 AW	80440 TQ	OHBLS	10/01-12/01
Except Mining	Oklahoma	Y	30650 FQ	53400 AW	82650 TQ	OKBLS	10/01-12/01
Except Mining	Oregon	Y	37230 FQ	56600 AW	76780 TQ	ORBLS	10/01-12/01
Except Mining	Pennsylvania	Y	30110 FQ	54000 AW	80840 TQ	PABLS	10/01-12/01
Except Mining	Rhode Island	Y	43170 FQ	58030 AW	78100 TQ	RIBLS	10/01-12/01
Except Mining	South Carolina	Y	41200 FQ	69750 AW	93160 TQ	SCBLS	10/01-12/01
Except Mining	South Dakota	Y	35200 FQ	49090 AW	58530 TQ	SDBLS	10/01-12/01
Except Mining	Tennessee	Y	37910 FQ	57370 AW	88170 TQ	TNBLS	10/01-12/01
Except Mining	Texas	Y	36330 FQ	58890 AW	86980 TQ	TXBLS	10/01-12/01
Except Mining	Utah	Y	45440 FQ	62050 AW	85970 TQ	UTBLS	10/01-12/01
Except Mining	Vermont	Y	38510 FQ	59390 AW	107970 TQ	VTBLS	10/01-12/01
Except Mining	Virginia	Y	37550 FQ	56680 AW	84240 TQ	VABLS	10/01-12/01
Except Mining	Washington	Y	45040 FQ	63290 AW	85820 TQ	WABLS	10/01-12/01
Except Mining	West Virginia	Y	32930 FQ	53810 AW	76460 TQ	WVBLS	10/01-12/01
Except Mining	Wisconsin	Y	36860 FQ	54120 AW	73980 TQ	WIBLS	10/01-12/01
Except Mining	Wyoming	Y	32810 FQ	55870 AW	83190 TQ	WYBLS	10/01-12/01
Except Mining	Puerto Rico	Y	32170 FQ	55850 AW	82530 TQ	PRBLS	10/01-12/01
Health Educator	Alabama	Y	14940 FQ	31780 AW	53970 TQ	ALBLS	10/01-12/01
	Alaska	Y	23970 FQ	36990 AW	55430 TQ	AKBLS	10/01-12/01
	Arizona	Y	21720 FQ	37530 AW	65490 TQ	AZBLS	10/01-12/01
	Arkansas	Y	23240 FQ	38890 AW	59050 TQ	ARBLS	10/01-12/01
	California	Y	23180 FQ	40900 AW	67400 TQ	CABLS	10/01-12/01
	Colorado	Y	21880 FQ	39850 AW	58410 TQ	COBLS	10/01-12/01
	Connecticut	Y	20870 FQ	40910 AW	70430 TQ	CTBLS	10/01-12/01
	District of Columbia	Y	28340 FQ	60670 AW	89410 TQ	DCBLS	10/01-12/01
	Florida	Y	21960 FQ	34850 AW	51700 TQ	FLBLS	10/01-12/01
	Georgia	Y	22510 FQ	41180 AW	67620 TQ	GABLS	10/01-12/01
	Hawaii	Y	21710 FQ	36210 AW	63270 TQ	HIBLS	10/01-12/01
	Idaho	Y	20750 FQ	40850 AW	58550 TQ	IDBLS	10/01-12/01
	Illinois	Y	17940 FQ	35030 AW	56230 TQ	ILBLS	10/01-12/01
	Indiana	Y	18220 FQ	32230 AW	49840 TQ	INBLS	10/01-12/01
	Iowa	Y	20400 FQ	35680 AW	55590 TQ	IABLS	10/01-12/01
	Kansas	Y	20610 FQ	33220 AW	48120 TQ	KSBLS	10/01-12/01
	Kentucky	Y	20000 FQ	33430 AW	53180 TQ	KYBLS	10/01-12/01
	Louisiana	Y	14670 FQ	29110 AW	52260 TQ	LABLS	10/01-12/01
	Maine	Y	19520 FQ	47020 AW	104080 TQ	MEBLS	10/01-12/01
	Maryland	Y	29630 FQ	57420 AW	90170 TQ	MDBLS	10/01-12/01
	Massachusetts	Y	21810 FQ	39980 AW	67870 TQ	MABLS	10/01-12/01
	Michigan	Y	27710 FQ	42710 AW	57700 TQ	MIBLS	10/01-12/01
	Minnesota	Y	24930 FQ	39980 AW	61470 TQ	MNBLS	10/01-12/01
	Mississippi	Y	23420 FQ	35080 AW	53430 TQ	MSBLS	10/01-12/01
	Missouri	Y	21900 FQ	32550 AW	50030 TQ	MOBLS	10/01-12/01
	Montana	Y	16860 FQ	32170 AW	45870 TQ	MTBLS	10/01-12/01
	Nebraska	Y	20850 FQ	36210 AW	49640 TQ	NEBLS	10/01-12/01
	Nevada	Y	14650 FQ	39240 AW	57710 TQ	NVBLS	10/01-12/01
	New Hampshire	Y	18060 FQ	34490 AW	54430 TQ	NHBLS	10/01-12/01
	New Jersey	Y	26330 FQ	46180 AW	68500 TQ	NJBLS	10/01-12/01
	New Mexico	Y	18710 FQ	32830 AW	49640 TQ	NMBLS	10/01-12/01
	New York	Y	21770 FQ	38640 AW	59360 TQ	NYBLS	10/01-12/01
	North Carolina	Y	22350 FQ	35510 AW	52210 TQ	NCBLS	10/01-12/01
	Ohio	Y	22530 FQ	36520 AW	53540 TQ	OHBLS	10/01-12/01
	Oklahoma	Y	16960 FQ	25920 AW	40410 TQ	OKBLS	10/01-12/01
	Oregon	Y	18220 FQ	30500 AW	51660 TQ	ORBLS	10/01-12/01
	Pennsylvania	Y	21710 FQ	38460 AW	54900 TQ	PABLS	10/01-12/01
	Rhode Island	Y	28750 FQ	52670 AW	71790 TQ	RIBLS	10/01-12/01

AAW	Average annual wage	**AOH**	Average offered, high	**ASH**	Average starting, high	**H**	Hourly	**M**	Monthly	**S**	Special: hourly and annual
AE	Average entry wage	**AOL**	Average offered, low	**ASL**	Average starting, low	**HI**	Highest wage paid	**MTC**	Median total compensation	**TQ**	Third quartile wage
AEX	Average experienced wage	**APH**	Average pay, high range	**AW**	Average wage paid	**HR**	High end range	**MW**	Median wage paid	**W**	Weekly
AO	Average offered	**APL**	Average pay, low range	**FQ**	First quartile wage	**LR**	Low end range	**SQ**	Second quartile wage	**Y**	Yearly

Occupation/Type/Industry	Location	Per	Low	Mid	High	Source	Date
Health Educator	South Carolina	Y	24360 FQ	41240 AW	60420 TQ	SCBLS	10/01-12/01
	South Dakota	Y	19340 FQ	35080 AW	56520 TQ	SDBLS	10/01-12/01
	Tennessee	Y	19320 FQ	32130 AW	54600 TQ	TNBLS	10/01-12/01
	Texas	Y	21250 FQ	33480 AW	49280 TQ	TXBLS	10/01-12/01
	Utah	Y	24880 FQ	38940 AW	60370 TQ	UTBLS	10/01-12/01
	Vermont	Y	26130 FQ	38450 AW	55020 TQ	VTBLS	10/01-12/01
	Virginia	Y	20440 FQ	36180 AW	54230 TQ	VABLS	10/01-12/01
	Washington	Y	29440 FQ	41350 AW	54250 TQ	WABLS	10/01-12/01
	West Virginia	Y	17820 FQ	30320 AW	47970 TQ	WVBLS	10/01-12/01
	Wisconsin	Y	17710 FQ	34070 AW	54610 TQ	WIBLS	10/01-12/01
	Wyoming	Y	19650 FQ	29560 AW	42610 TQ	WYBLS	10/01-12/01
	Puerto Rico	Y	15010 FQ	20510 AW	27550 TQ	PRBLS	10/01-12/01
Health Specialties Teacher							
Postsecondary	Alabama	Y	32830 FQ	71140 AW	126800 TQ	ALBLS	10/01-12/01
Postsecondary	Arizona	Y	22150 FQ	46210 AW	85430 TQ	AZBLS	10/01-12/01
Postsecondary	Arkansas	Y	22490 FQ	39400 AW	60940 TQ	ARBLS	10/01-12/01
Postsecondary	California	Y	40910 FQ	76230 AW	136560 TQ	CABLS	10/01-12/01
Postsecondary	Colorado	Y	17320 FQ	60430 AW	127870 TQ	COBLS	10/01-12/01
Postsecondary	Delaware	Y	36590 FQ	51100 AW	75530 TQ	DEBLS	10/01-12/01
Postsecondary	District of Columbia	Y	32730 FQ	71020 AW	122590 TQ	DCBLS	10/01-12/01
Postsecondary	Florida	Y	37250 FQ	87020 AW		FLBLS	10/01-12/01
Postsecondary	Georgia	Y	32410 FQ	67050 AW	111600 TQ	GABLS	10/01-12/01
Postsecondary	Hawaii	Y	40810 FQ	77500 AW	116010 TQ	HIBLS	10/01-12/01
Postsecondary	Indiana	Y	30320 FQ	69320 AW	131640 TQ	INBLS	10/01-12/01
Postsecondary	Iowa	Y	34440 FQ	78570 AW		IABLS	10/01-12/01
Postsecondary	Kansas	Y	19040 FQ	54580 AW	104380 TQ	KSBLS	10/01-12/01
Postsecondary	Kentucky	Y	36180 FQ	70380 AW	131060 TQ	KYBLS	10/01-12/01
Postsecondary	Louisiana	Y	31590 FQ	58460 AW	84520 TQ	LABLS	10/01-12/01
Postsecondary	Maine	Y	27310 FQ	44490 AW	59550 TQ	MEBLS	10/01-12/01
Postsecondary	Maryland	Y	40060 FQ	90410 AW		MDBLS	10/01-12/01
Postsecondary	Massachusetts	Y	37630 FQ	79170 AW		MABLS	10/01-12/01
Postsecondary	Michigan	Y	39400 FQ	74500 AW	120500 TQ	MIBLS	10/01-12/01
Postsecondary	Minnesota	Y	35900 FQ	63100 AW	103390 TQ	MNBLS	10/01-12/01
Postsecondary	Mississippi	Y	35910 FQ	66130 AW	107280 TQ	MSBLS	10/01-12/01
Postsecondary	Missouri	Y	32890 FQ	53140 AW	75210 TQ	MOBLS	10/01-12/01
Postsecondary	Montana	Y	27440 FQ	57580 AW	103670 TQ	MTBLS	10/01-12/01
Postsecondary	Nebraska	Y	32220 FQ	71640 AW	114730 TQ	NEBLS	10/01-12/01
Postsecondary	New Jersey	Y	38540 FQ	67060 AW	112170 TQ	NJBLS	10/01-12/01
Postsecondary	New Mexico	Y	27580 FQ	46330 AW	72040 TQ	NMBLS	10/01-12/01
Postsecondary	New York	Y	40220 FQ	73930 AW	122800 TQ	NYBLS	10/01-12/01
Postsecondary	North Carolina	Y	32960 FQ	55900 AW	95020 TQ	NCBLS	10/01-12/01
Postsecondary	North Dakota	Y	20480 FQ	52850 AW	85620 TQ	NDBLS	10/01-12/01
Postsecondary	Ohio	Y	29680 FQ	64100 AW	119950 TQ	OHBLS	10/01-12/01
Postsecondary	Oklahoma	Y	33120 FQ	44520 AW	59580 TQ	OKBLS	10/01-12/01
Postsecondary	Pennsylvania	Y	29520 FQ	53430 AW	88370 TQ	PABLS	10/01-12/01
Postsecondary	Rhode Island	Y	39020 FQ	64150 AW	92930 TQ	RIBLS	10/01-12/01
Postsecondary	South Carolina	Y	24400 FQ	44650 AW	67830 TQ	SCBLS	10/01-12/01
Postsecondary	South Dakota	Y	31690 FQ	53310 AW	75940 TQ	SDBLS	10/01-12/01
Postsecondary	Tennessee	Y	42450 FQ	82010 AW		TNBLS	10/01-12/01
Postsecondary	Texas	Y	31580 FQ	62580 AW	121690 TQ	TXBLS	10/01-12/01
Postsecondary	Utah	Y	29260 FQ	45840 AW	73430 TQ	UTBLS	10/01-12/01
Postsecondary	Vermont	Y	31390 FQ	58810 AW	104950 TQ	VTBLS	10/01-12/01
Postsecondary	Virginia	Y	34110 FQ	68250 AW	117980 TQ	VABLS	10/01-12/01
Postsecondary	Washington	Y	39490 FQ	78760 AW	133130 TQ	WABLS	10/01-12/01
Postsecondary	Wyoming	Y	31810 FQ	63710 AW	111760 TQ	WYBLS	10/01-12/01
Postsecondary	Puerto Rico	Y	22010 FQ	45630 AW	96290 TQ	PRBLS	10/01-12/01
Heat Treating Equipment Setter, Operator, and Tender							
Metals and Plastics	Alabama	H	9.28 FQ	13.70 AW	17.76 TQ	ALBLS	10/01-12/01
Metals and Plastics	Birmingham MSA, AL	H	9.90 FQ	14.37 AW	19.18 TQ	ALBLS	10/01-12/01
Metals and Plastics	Arizona	H	8.00 FQ	11.92 AW	18.31 TQ	AZBLS	10/01-12/01
Metals and Plastics	Phoenix-Mesa MSA, AZ	H	7.92 FQ	11.63 AW	17.91 TQ	AZBLS	10/01-12/01
Metals and Plastics	Arkansas	H	7.20 FQ	11.16 AW	14.05 TQ	ARBLS	10/01-12/01
Metals and Plastics	California	H	7.64 FQ	12.64 AW	19.48 TQ	CABLS	10/01-12/01
Metals and Plastics	Los Angeles-Long Beach PMSA, CA	H	7.66 FQ	12.64 AW	19.27 TQ	CABLS	10/01-12/01
Metals and Plastics	Oakland PMSA, CA	H	10.33 FQ	15.44 AW	22.20 TQ	CABLS	10/01-12/01
Metals and Plastics	Orange County PMSA, CA	H	7.45 FQ	11.23 AW	16.87 TQ	CABLS	10/01-12/01
Metals and Plastics	Riverside-San Bernardino PMSA, CA	H	7.61 FQ	11.20 AW	16.20 TQ	CABLS	10/01-12/01

AAW	Average annual wage	AOH	Average offered, high	ASH	Average starting, high	H	Hourly	M	Monthly	S	Special: hourly and annual
AE	Average entry wage	AOL	Average offered, low	ASL	Average starting, low	HI	Highest wage paid	MTC	Median total compensation	TQ	Third quartile wage
AEX	Average experienced wage	APH	Average pay, high range	AW	Average wage paid	HR	High end range	MW	Median wage paid	W	Weekly
AO	Average offered	APL	Average pay, low range	FQ	First quartile wage	LR	Low end range	SQ	Second quartile wage	Y	Yearly

Occupation/Type/Industry	Location	Per	Low	Mid	High	Source	Date
Heat Treating Equipment Setter, Operator, and Tender							
Metals and Plastics	San Diego MSA, CA	H	10.14 FQ	14.56 AW	19.15 TQ	CABLS	10/01-12/01
Metals and Plastics	San Francisco PMSA, CA	H	8.03 FQ	17.77 AW	30.06 TQ	CABLS	10/01-12/01
Metals and Plastics	San Jose PMSA, CA	H	10.60 FQ	18.27 AW	24.83 TQ	CABLS	10/01-12/01
Metals and Plastics	Colorado	H	9.72 FQ	14.71 AW	20.44 TQ	COBLS	10/01-12/01
Metals and Plastics	Denver PMSA, CO	H	9.07 FQ	14.89 AW	20.49 TQ	COBLS	10/01-12/01
Metals and Plastics	Connecticut	H	9.52 FQ	14.88 AW	20.49 TQ	CTBLS	10/01-12/01
Metals and Plastics	Bridgeport PMSA, CT	H	9.79 FQ	14.43 AW	19.36 TQ	CTBLS	10/01-12/01
Metals and Plastics	Hartford MSA, CT	H	9.43 FQ	15.13 AW	20.73 TQ	CTBLS	10/01-12/01
Metals and Plastics	New Haven-Meriden PMSA, CT	H	8.78 FQ	13.65 AW	19.84 TQ	CTBLS	10/01-12/01
Metals and Plastics	Waterbury PMSA, CT	H	9.20 FQ	14.32 AW	20.50 TQ	CTBLS	10/01-12/01
Metals and Plastics	Delaware	H	9.51 FQ	14.64 AW	24.23 TQ	DEBLS	10/01-12/01
Metals and Plastics	Washington PMSA, DC-MD-VA-WV	H	8.42 FQ	14.39 AW	26.63 TQ	DCBLS	10/01-12/01
Metals and Plastics	Florida	H	7.34 FQ	11.71 AW	16.76 TQ	FLBLS	10/01-12/01
Metals and Plastics	Orlando MSA, FL	H	8.81 FQ	13.66 AW	17.41 TQ	FLBLS	10/01-12/01
Metals and Plastics	Tampa-St. Petersburg-Clearwater MSA, FL	H	7.62 FQ	10.76 AW	15.18 TQ	FLBLS	10/01-12/01
Metals and Plastics	Georgia	H	9.35 FQ	12.32 AW	16.54 TQ	GABLS	10/01-12/01
Metals and Plastics	Atlanta MSA, GA	H	9.74 FQ	12.76 AW	16.52 TQ	GABLS	10/01-12/01
Metals and Plastics	Illinois	H	8.79 FQ	12.90 AW	19.87 TQ	ILBLS	10/01-12/01
Metals and Plastics	Chicago PMSA, IL	H	8.86 FQ	12.61 AW	19.60 TQ	ILBLS	10/01-12/01
Metals and Plastics	Peoria-Pekin MSA, IL	H	12.40 FQ	21.36 AW	27.97 TQ	ILBLS	10/01-12/01
Metals and Plastics	Rockford MSA, IL	H	8.97 FQ	13.34 AW	19.35 TQ	ILBLS	10/01-12/01
Metals and Plastics	Indiana	H	9.52 FQ	15.74 AW	24.84 TQ	INBLS	10/01-12/01
Metals and Plastics	Elkhart-Goshen MSA, IN	H	10.83 FQ	14.61 AW	19.33 TQ	INBLS	10/01-12/01
Metals and Plastics	Evansville-Henderson MSA, IN-KY	H	10.48 FQ	13.59 AW	17.18 TQ	INBLS	10/01-12/01
Metals and Plastics	Fort Wayne MSA, IN	H	9.33 FQ	12.47 AW	19.41 TQ	INBLS	10/01-12/01
Metals and Plastics	Gary PMSA, IN	H	13.45 FQ	19.50 AW	25.86 TQ	INBLS	10/01-12/01
Metals and Plastics	Indianapolis MSA, IN	H	9.50 FQ	17.30 AW	26.74 TQ	INBLS	10/01-12/01
Metals and Plastics	South Bend MSA, IN	H	9.23 FQ	13.45 AW	20.59 TQ	INBLS	10/01-12/01
Metals and Plastics	Iowa	H	9.54 FQ	15.43 AW	20.65 TQ	IABLS	10/01-12/01
Metals and Plastics	Davenport-Moline-Rock Island MSA, IA-IL	H	9.37 FQ	13.82 AW	17.52 TQ	IABLS	10/01-12/01
Metals and Plastics	Kansas	H	5.94 FQ	12.25 AW	21.18 TQ	KSBLS	10/01-12/01
Metals and Plastics	Wichita MSA, KS	H	9.59 FQ	15.79 AW	24.40 TQ	KSBLS	10/01-12/01
Metals and Plastics	Kentucky	H	9.81 FQ	13.31 AW	16.96 TQ	KYBLS	10/01-12/01
Metals and Plastics	Lexington MSA, KY	H	9.07 FQ	12.21 AW	16.40 TQ	KYBLS	10/01-12/01
Metals and Plastics	Louisville MSA, KY-IN	H	11.28 FQ	15.32 AW	19.44 TQ	KYBLS	10/01-12/01
Metals and Plastics	Louisiana	H	8.57 FQ	12.40 AW	16.76 TQ	LABLS	10/01-12/01
Metals and Plastics	Baton Rouge MSA, LA	H	8.72 FQ	12.49 AW	16.81 TQ	LABLS	10/01-12/01
Metals and Plastics	Maine	H	10.46 FQ	12.95 AW	16.27 TQ	MEBLS	10/01-12/01
Metals and Plastics	Maryland	H	9.54 FQ	14.89 AW	22.57 TQ	MDBLS	10/01-12/01
Metals and Plastics	Baltimore PMSA, MD	H	9.67 FQ	15.12 AW	22.19 TQ	MDBLS	10/01-12/01
Metals and Plastics	Massachusetts	H	9.56 FQ	13.85 AW	19.21 TQ	MABLS	10/01-12/01
Metals and Plastics	Boston PMSA, MA-NH	H	9.44 FQ	13.29 AW	18.99 TQ	MABLS	10/01-12/01
Metals and Plastics	Springfield MSA, MA	H	11.23 FQ	14.83 AW	17.72 TQ	MABLS	10/01-12/01
Metals and Plastics	Worcester PMSA, MA-CT	H	9.90 FQ	14.91 AW	20.95 TQ	MABLS	10/01-12/01
Metals and Plastics	Michigan	H	9.37 FQ	15.58 AW	23.81 TQ	MIBLS	10/01-12/01
Metals and Plastics	Ann Arbor PMSA, MI	H	13.89 FQ	19.46 AW	31.17 TQ	MIBLS	10/01-12/01
Metals and Plastics	Detroit PMSA, MI	H	10.31 FQ	16.02 AW	22.58 TQ	MIBLS	10/01-12/01
Metals and Plastics	Grand Rapids-Muskegon-Holland MSA, MI	H	9.52 FQ	16.51 AW	26.64 TQ	MIBLS	10/01-12/01
Metals and Plastics	Kalamazoo-Battle Creek MSA, MI	H	6.53 FQ	10.46 AW	13.70 TQ	MIBLS	10/01-12/01
Metals and Plastics	Saginaw-Bay City-Midland MSA, MI	H	7.83 FQ	13.55 AW	24.52 TQ	MIBLS	10/01-12/01
Metals and Plastics	Minnesota	H	10.55 FQ	15.55 AW	21.49 TQ	MNBLS	10/01-12/01
Metals and Plastics	Minneapolis-St. Paul MSA, MN-WI	H	10.36 FQ	15.60 AW	21.76 TQ	MNBLS	10/01-12/01
Metals and Plastics	Mississippi	H	9.29 FQ	11.57 AW	13.71 TQ	MSBLS	10/01-12/01
Metals and Plastics	Missouri	H	7.77 FQ	13.87 AW	21.26 TQ	MOBLS	10/01-12/01
Metals and Plastics	Kansas City MSA, MO-KS	H	7.79 FQ	15.28 AW	23.61 TQ	MOBLS	10/01-12/01
Metals and Plastics	St. Louis MSA, MO-IL	H	9.27 FQ	15.45 AW	22.05 TQ	MOBLS	10/01-12/01
Metals and Plastics	Nebraska	H	6.48 FQ	13.58 AW	20.89 TQ	NEBLS	10/01-12/01
Metals and Plastics	Nevada	H	9.01 FQ	13.12 AW	19.77 TQ	NVBLS	10/01-12/01
Metals and Plastics	New Hampshire	H	10.85 FQ	14.80 AW	20.39 TQ	NHBLS	10/01-12/01
Metals and Plastics	New Jersey	H	8.01 FQ	12.63 AW	17.35 TQ	NJBLS	10/01-12/01
Metals and Plastics	Bergen-Passaic PMSA, NJ	H	7.46 FQ	10.72 AW	16.18 TQ	NJBLS	10/01-12/01

AAW	Average annual wage	**AOH**	Average offered, high	**ASH**	Average starting, high	**H**	Hourly	**M**	Monthly	**S**	Special: hourly and annual
AE	Average entry wage	**AOL**	Average offered, low	**ASL**	Average starting, low	**HI**	Highest wage paid	**MTC**	Median total compensation	**TQ**	Third quartile wage
AEX	Average experienced wage	**APH**	Average pay, high range	**AW**	Average wage paid	**HR**	High end range	**MW**	Median wage paid	**W**	Weekly
AO	Average offered	**APL**	Average pay, low range	**FQ**	First quartile wage	**LR**	Low end range	**SQ**	Second quartile wage	**Y**	Yearly

Occupation/Type/Industry	Location	Per	Low	Mid	High	Source	Date
Heat Treating Equipment Setter, Operator, and Tender							
Metals and Plastics	Jersey City PMSA, NJ	H	10.17 FQ	13.35 AW	17.12 TQ	NJBLS	10/01-12/01
Metals and Plastics	Middlesex-Somerset-Hunterdon PMSA, NJ	H	8.58 FQ	13.20 AW	18.98 TQ	NJBLS	10/01-12/01
Metals and Plastics	Newark PMSA, NJ	H	10.70 FQ	13.34 AW	16.69 TQ	NJBLS	10/01-12/01
Metals and Plastics	New York	H	9.38 FQ	14.85 AW	22.97 TQ	NYBLS	10/01-12/01
Metals and Plastics	Buffalo-Niagara Falls MSA, NY	H	10.40 FQ	18.63 AW	27.77 TQ	NYBLS	10/01-12/01
Metals and Plastics	Nassau-Suffolk PMSA, NY	H	8.87 FQ	13.82 AW	23.38 TQ	NYBLS	10/01-12/01
Metals and Plastics	New York PMSA, NY	H	9.37 FQ	14.64 AW	23.99 TQ	NYBLS	10/01-12/01
Metals and Plastics	Rochester MSA, NY	H	9.20 FQ	13.01 AW	17.09 TQ	NYBLS	10/01-12/01
Metals and Plastics	Utica-Rome MSA, NY	H	8.93 FQ	13.13 AW	17.25 TQ	NYBLS	10/01-12/01
Metals and Plastics	North Carolina	H	7.95 FQ	13.43 AW	19.72 TQ	NCBLS	10/01-12/01
Metals and Plastics	Charlotte-Gastonia-Rock Hill MSA, NC-SC	H	6.80 FQ	14.24 AW	20.81 TQ	NCBLS	10/01-12/01
Metals and Plastics	Greensboro-Winston-Salem-High Point MSA, NC	H	8.14 FQ	12.90 AW	18.31 TQ	NCBLS	10/01-12/01
Metals and Plastics	Hickory-Morganton-Lenoir MSA, NC	H	9.25 FQ	13.15 AW	16.94 TQ	NCBLS	10/01-12/01
Metals and Plastics	Raleigh-Durham-Chapel Hill MSA, NC	H	12.07 FQ	14.35 AW	16.53 TQ	NCBLS	10/01-12/01
Metals and Plastics	Ohio	H	9.63 FQ	14.95 AW	23.89 TQ	OHBLS	10/01-12/01
Metals and Plastics	Akron PMSA, OH	H	9.44 FQ	16.12 AW	26.21 TQ	OHBLS	10/01-12/01
Metals and Plastics	Canton-Massillon MSA, OH	H	9.77 FQ	13.62 AW	18.09 TQ	OHBLS	10/01-12/01
Metals and Plastics	Cincinnati PMSA, OH-KY-IN	H	9.66 FQ	14.59 AW	20.07 TQ	OHBLS	10/01-12/01
Metals and Plastics	Cleveland-Lorain-Elyria PMSA, OH	H	9.47 FQ	13.68 AW	17.99 TQ	OHBLS	10/01-12/01
Metals and Plastics	Columbus MSA, OH	H	9.34 FQ	12.92 AW	17.45 TQ	OHBLS	10/01-12/01
Metals and Plastics	Dayton-Springfield MSA, OH	H	10.61 FQ	19.17 AW	27.18 TQ	OHBLS	10/01-12/01
Metals and Plastics	Hamilton-Middletown PMSA, OH	H	9.36 FQ	13.06 AW	16.99 TQ	OHBLS	10/01-12/01
Metals and Plastics	Mansfield MSA, OH	H	11.23 FQ	14.37 AW	29.17 TQ	OHBLS	10/01-12/01
Metals and Plastics	Toledo MSA, OH	H	8.76 FQ	11.97 AW	16.22 TQ	OHBLS	10/01-12/01
Metals and Plastics	Youngstown-Warren MSA, OH	H	9.32 FQ	15.01 AW	28.82 TQ	OHBLS	10/01-12/01
Metals and Plastics	Oklahoma	H	8.35 FQ	14.70 AW	24.57 TQ	OKBLS	10/01-12/01
Metals and Plastics	Oklahoma City MSA, OK	H	9.36 FQ	15.48 AW	22.95 TQ	OKBLS	10/01-12/01
Metals and Plastics	Tulsa MSA, OK	H	8.32 FQ	14.47 AW	25.80 TQ	OKBLS	10/01-12/01
Metals and Plastics	Oregon	H	10.53 FQ	15.45 AW	21.90 TQ	ORBLS	10/01-12/01
Metals and Plastics	Portland-Vancouver PMSA, OR-WA	H	9.01 FQ	14.64 AW	21.46 TQ	ORBLS	10/01-12/01
Metals and Plastics	Pennsylvania	H	8.78 FQ	14.19 AW	20.22 TQ	PABLS	10/01-12/01
Metals and Plastics	Allentown-Bethlehem-Easton MSA, PA	H	10.07 FQ	13.63 AW	16.97 TQ	PABLS	10/01-12/01
Metals and Plastics	Erie MSA, PA	H	8.95 FQ	13.53 AW	19.84 TQ	PABLS	10/01-12/01
Metals and Plastics	Harrisburg-Lebanon-Carlisle MSA, PA	H	12.21 FQ	17.09 AW	23.53 TQ	PABLS	10/01-12/01
Metals and Plastics	Johnstown MSA, PA	H	11.01 FQ	15.25 AW	20.60 TQ	PABLS	10/01-12/01
Metals and Plastics	Lancaster MSA, PA	H	11.64 FQ	15.16 AW	18.85 TQ	PABLS	10/01-12/01
Metals and Plastics	Philadelphia PMSA, PA-NJ	H	6.94 FQ	13.79 AW	20.57 TQ	PABLS	10/01-12/01
Metals and Plastics	Pittsburgh MSA, PA	H	9.65 FQ	15.05 AW	20.98 TQ	PABLS	10/01-12/01
Metals and Plastics	Reading MSA, PA	H	9.43 FQ	13.92 AW	19.00 TQ	PABLS	10/01-12/01
Metals and Plastics	York MSA, PA	H	9.28 FQ	15.36 AW	21.32 TQ	PABLS	10/01-12/01
Metals and Plastics	Rhode Island	H	8.38 FQ	12.64 AW	18.96 TQ	RIBLS	10/01-12/01
Metals and Plastics	Providence-Fall River-Warwick MSA, RI-MA	H	8.43 FQ	12.48 AW	18.51 TQ	RIBLS	10/01-12/01
Metals and Plastics	South Carolina	H	11.17 FQ	13.16 AW	16.47 TQ	SCBLS	10/01-12/01
Metals and Plastics	Columbia MSA, SC	H	9.77 FQ	13.67 AW	19.33 TQ	SCBLS	10/01-12/01
Metals and Plastics	Tennessee	H	8.59 FQ	11.83 AW	16.21 TQ	TNBLS	10/01-12/01
Metals and Plastics	Johnson City-Kingsport-Bristol MSA, TN-VA	H	9.56 FQ	13.49 AW	16.88 TQ	TNBLS	10/01-12/01
Metals and Plastics	Memphis MSA, TN-AR-MS	H	7.74 FQ	11.10 AW	14.92 TQ	TNBLS	10/01-12/01
Metals and Plastics	Nashville MSA, TN	H	9.35 FQ	13.20 AW	20.67 TQ	TNBLS	10/01-12/01
Metals and Plastics	Texas	H	8.39 FQ	12.59 AW	17.02 TQ	TXBLS	10/01-12/01
Metals and Plastics	Austin-San Marcos MSA, TX	H	8.59 FQ	12.60 AW	17.33 TQ	TXBLS	10/01-12/01
Metals and Plastics	Dallas PMSA, TX	H	8.01 FQ	12.17 AW	16.81 TQ	TXBLS	10/01-12/01
Metals and Plastics	Fort Worth-Arlington PMSA, TX	H	8.31 FQ	14.49 AW	24.56 TQ	TXBLS	10/01-12/01
Metals and Plastics	Houston PMSA, TX	H	7.87 FQ	11.86 AW	16.53 TQ	TXBLS	10/01-12/01
Metals and Plastics	San Antonio MSA, TX	H	8.70 FQ	13.41 AW	17.20 TQ	TXBLS	10/01-12/01
Metals and Plastics	Utah	H	8.68 FQ	12.62 AW	17.73 TQ	UTBLS	10/01-12/01

AAW	Average annual wage	AOH	Average offered, high	ASH	Average starting, high	H	Hourly	M	Monthly	S	Special: hourly and annual
AE	Average entry wage	AOL	Average offered, low	ASL	Average starting, low	HI	Highest wage paid	MTC	Median total compensation	TQ	Third quartile wage
AEX	Average experienced wage	APH	Average pay, high range	AW	Average wage paid	HR	High end range	MW	Median wage paid	W	Weekly
AO	Average offered	APL	Average pay, low range	FQ	First quartile wage	LR	Low end range	SQ	Second quartile wage	Y	Yearly

Occupation/Type/Industry	Location	Per	Low	Mid	High	Source	Date
Heat Treating Equipment Setter, Operator, and Tender							
Metals and Plastics	Salt Lake City-Ogden MSA, UT	H	8.83 FQ	12.72 AW	17.76 TQ	UTBLS	10/01-12/01
Metals and Plastics	Vermont	H	9.63 FQ	14.76 AW	21.01 TQ	VTBLS	10/01-12/01
Metals and Plastics	Virginia	H	8.92 FQ	12.86 AW	17.79 TQ	VABLS	10/01-12/01
Metals and Plastics	Lynchburg MSA, VA	H	8.85 FQ	11.08 AW	14.59 TQ	VABLS	10/01-12/01
Metals and Plastics	Norfolk-Virginia Beach-Newport News MSA, VA-NC	H	11.08 FQ	14.77 AW	17.57 TQ	VABLS	10/01-12/01
Metals and Plastics	Richmond-Petersburg MSA, VA	H	11.41 FQ	16.68 AW	23.50 TQ	VABLS	10/01-12/01
Metals and Plastics	Washington	H	8.61 FQ	13.66 AW	19.78 TQ	WABLS	10/01-12/01
Metals and Plastics	Seattle-Bellevue-Everett PMSA, WA	H	11.75 FQ	15.78 AW	20.80 TQ	WABLS	10/01-12/01
Metals and Plastics	West Virginia	H	10.37 FQ	16.17 AW	20.77 TQ	WVBLS	10/01-12/01
Metals and Plastics	Huntington-Ashland MSA, WV-KY-OH	H	7.06 FQ	13.28 AW	19.75 TQ	WVBLS	10/01-12/01
Metals and Plastics	Wisconsin	H	9.97 FQ	14.32 AW	19.55 TQ	WIBLS	10/01-12/01
Metals and Plastics	Appleton-Oshkosh-Neenah MSA, WI	H	9.76 FQ	13.91 AW	18.40 TQ	WIBLS	10/01-12/01
Metals and Plastics	Milwaukee-Waukesha PMSA, WI	H	10.27 FQ	14.67 AW	20.22 TQ	WIBLS	10/01-12/01
Metals and Plastics	Racine PMSA, WI	H	9.64 FQ	14.82 AW	20.44 TQ	WIBLS	10/01-12/01
Metals and Plastics	Puerto Rico	H	6.14 FQ	9.52 AW	13.05 TQ	PRBLS	10/01-12/01
Heating, Air Conditioning, and Refrigeration Mechanic and Installer	Alabama	H	8.63 FQ	14.15 AW	21.00 TQ	ALBLS	10/01-12/01
	Birmingham MSA, AL	H	8.80 FQ	15.93 AW	21.45 TQ	ALBLS	10/01-12/01
	Huntsville MSA, AL	H	8.89 FQ	12.95 AW	20.29 TQ	ALBLS	10/01-12/01
	Mobile MSA, AL	H	8.90 FQ	12.75 AW	17.64 TQ	ALBLS	10/01-12/01
	Montgomery MSA, AL	H	7.63 FQ	13.62 AW	20.85 TQ	ALBLS	10/01-12/01
	Alaska	H	14.00 FQ	22.43 AW	31.11 TQ	AKBLS	10/01-12/01
	Anchorage MSA, AK	H	10.39 FQ	21.58 AW	31.22 TQ	AKBLS	10/01-12/01
	Arizona	H	10.33 FQ	16.51 AW	23.46 TQ	AZBLS	10/01-12/01
	Phoenix-Mesa MSA, AZ	H	10.30 FQ	16.69 AW	24.00 TQ	AZBLS	10/01-12/01
	Tucson MSA, AZ	H	10.91 FQ	16.51 AW	22.44 TQ	AZBLS	10/01-12/01
	Arkansas	H	9.48 FQ	14.47 AW	20.85 TQ	ARBLS	10/01-12/01
	Fayetteville-Springdale-Rogers MSA, AR	H	10.76 FQ	14.78 AW	20.55 TQ	ARBLS	10/01-12/01
	Fort Smith MSA, AR-OK	H	9.60 FQ	14.38 AW	20.75 TQ	ARBLS	10/01-12/01
	Little Rock-North Little Rock MSA, AR	H	9.79 FQ	16.12 AW	22.68 TQ	ARBLS	10/01-12/01
	California	H	11.08 FQ	19.45 AW	28.56 TQ	CABLS	10/01-12/01
	Bakersfield MSA, CA	H	12.49 FQ	19.44 AW	26.96 TQ	CABLS	10/01-12/01
	Chico-Paradise MSA, CA	H	8.47 FQ	16.94 AW	24.40 TQ	CABLS	10/01-12/01
	Fresno MSA, CA	H	11.15 FQ	18.77 AW	25.87 TQ	CABLS	10/01-12/01
	Los Angeles-Long Beach PMSA, CA	H	11.20 FQ	20.13 AW	29.42 TQ	CABLS	10/01-12/01
	Merced MSA, CA	H	9.54 FQ	15.37 AW	22.62 TQ	CABLS	10/01-12/01
	Modesto MSA, CA	H	12.94 FQ	19.81 AW	27.20 TQ	CABLS	10/01-12/01
	Oakland PMSA, CA	H	7.80 FQ	16.64 AW	28.10 TQ	CABLS	10/01-12/01
	Orange County PMSA, CA	H	12.27 FQ	20.92 AW	32.00 TQ	CABLS	10/01-12/01
	Redding MSA, CA	H	9.74 FQ	20.46 AW	40.39 TQ	CABLS	10/01-12/01
	Riverside-San Bernardino PMSA, CA	H	11.02 FQ	17.65 AW	25.68 TQ	CABLS	10/01-12/01
	Sacramento PMSA, CA	H	13.67 FQ	20.85 AW	30.93 TQ	CABLS	10/01-12/01
	Salinas MSA, CA	H	12.72 FQ	21.95 AW	34.02 TQ	CABLS	10/01-12/01
	San Diego MSA, CA	H	10.96 FQ	18.21 AW	25.84 TQ	CABLS	10/01-12/01
	San Francisco PMSA, CA	H	12.62 FQ	20.70 AW	27.62 TQ	CABLS	10/01-12/01
	San Jose PMSA, CA	H	14.95 FQ	24.27 AW	39.56 TQ	CABLS	10/01-12/01
	San Luis Obispo-Atascadero-Paso Robles MSA, CA	H	12.48 FQ	25.52 AW	36.15 TQ	CABLS	10/01-12/01
	Santa Barbara-Santa Maria-Lompoc MSA, CA	H	17.37 FQ	20.04 AW	24.60 TQ	CABLS	10/01-12/01
	Santa Cruz-Watsonville PMSA, CA	H	13.35 FQ	20.18 AW	27.00 TQ	CABLS	10/01-12/01
	Santa Rosa PMSA, CA	H	13.56 FQ	20.29 AW	28.08 TQ	CABLS	10/01-12/01
	Stockton-Lodi MSA, CA	H	11.90 FQ	17.50 AW	22.96 TQ	CABLS	10/01-12/01

AAW	Average annual wage	AOH	Average offered, high	ASH	Average starting, high	H	Hourly	M	Monthly	S	Special: hourly and annual
AE	Average entry wage	AOL	Average offered, low	ASL	Average starting, low	HI	Highest wage paid	MTC	Median total compensation	TQ	Third quartile wage
AEX	Average experienced wage	APH	Average pay, high range	AW	Average wage paid	HR	High end range	MW	Median wage paid	W	Weekly
AO	Average offered	APL	Average pay, low range	FQ	First quartile wage	LR	Low end range	SQ	Second quartile wage	Y	Yearly

Occupation/Type/Industry	Location	Per	Low	Mid	High	Source	Date
Heating, Air Conditioning, and Refrigeration Mechanic and Installer	Vallejo-Fairfield-Napa PMSA, CA	H	11.70 FQ	19.56 AW	26.36 TQ	CABLS	10/01-12/01
	Ventura PMSA, CA	H	13.16 FQ	20.72 AW	27.24 TQ	CABLS	10/01-12/01
	Visalia-Tulare-Porterville MSA, CA	H	10.98 FQ	18.49 AW	26.98 TQ	CABLS	10/01-12/01
	Colorado	H	10.36 FQ	15.96 AW	21.96 TQ	COBLS	10/01-12/01
	Boulder-Longmont PMSA, CO	H	10.79 FQ	18.11 AW	26.57 TQ	COBLS	10/01-12/01
	Colorado Springs MSA, CO	H	9.99 FQ	14.73 AW	20.62 TQ	COBLS	10/01-12/01
	Denver PMSA, CO	H	10.43 FQ	16.11 AW	21.79 TQ	COBLS	10/01-12/01
	Fort Collins-Loveland MSA, CO	H	10.55 FQ	15.56 AW	22.13 TQ	COBLS	10/01-12/01
	Greeley PMSA, CO	H	9.52 FQ	14.05 AW	19.66 TQ	COBLS	10/01-12/01
	Connecticut	H	13.75 FQ	20.17 AW	27.11 TQ	CTBLS	10/01-12/01
	Bridgeport PMSA, CT	H	14.90 FQ	23.25 AW	33.91 TQ	CTBLS	10/01-12/01
	Danbury PMSA, CT	H	14.37 FQ	18.25 AW	22.04 TQ	CTBLS	10/01-12/01
	Hartford MSA, CT	H	13.51 FQ	20.28 AW	28.58 TQ	CTBLS	10/01-12/01
	New Haven-Meriden PMSA, CT	H	15.83 FQ	21.86 AW	29.88 TQ	CTBLS	10/01-12/01
	New London-Norwich MSA, CT-RI	H	14.29 FQ	17.77 AW	23.10 TQ	CTBLS	10/01-12/01
	Stamford-Norwalk PMSA, CT	H	12.75 FQ	18.36 AW	25.15 TQ	CTBLS	10/01-12/01
	Waterbury PMSA, CT	H	11.38 FQ	16.84 AW	24.87 TQ	CTBLS	10/01-12/01
	Delaware	H	11.74 FQ	16.06 AW	21.94 TQ	DEBLS	10/01-12/01
	Wilmington-Newark PMSA, DE-MD	H	12.09 FQ	16.23 AW	22.02 TQ	DEBLS	10/01-12/01
	District of Columbia	H	13.38 FQ	19.65 AW	26.26 TQ	DCBLS	10/01-12/01
	Washington PMSA, DC-MD-VA-WV	H	11.68 FQ	19.25 AW	28.01 TQ	DCBLS	10/01-12/01
	Florida	H	9.48 FQ	14.35 AW	20.39 TQ	FLBLS	10/01-12/01
	Daytona Beach MSA, FL	H	10.28 FQ	13.44 AW	16.98 TQ	FLBLS	10/01-12/01
	Fort Lauderdale PMSA, FL	H	9.62 FQ	15.81 AW	21.43 TQ	FLBLS	10/01-12/01
	Fort Myers-Cape Coral MSA, FL	H	9.73 FQ	13.53 AW	17.34 TQ	FLBLS	10/01-12/01
	Fort Pierce-Port St. Lucie MSA, FL	H	9.30 FQ	13.83 AW	19.34 TQ	FLBLS	10/01-12/01
	Fort Walton Beach MSA, FL	H	9.88 FQ	15.49 AW	24.06 TQ	FLBLS	10/01-12/01
	Gainesville MSA, FL	H	10.12 FQ	14.53 AW	19.26 TQ	FLBLS	10/01-12/01
	Jacksonville MSA, FL	H	9.02 FQ	14.24 AW	20.56 TQ	FLBLS	10/01-12/01
	Lakeland-Winter Haven MSA, FL	H	9.85 FQ	15.28 AW	24.08 TQ	FLBLS	10/01-12/01
	Melbourne-Titusville-Palm Bay MSA, FL	H	9.31 FQ	15.42 AW	21.18 TQ	FLBLS	10/01-12/01
	Miami PMSA, FL	H	9.96 FQ	15.28 AW	21.45 TQ	FLBLS	10/01-12/01
	Naples MSA, FL	H	11.46 FQ	16.39 AW	21.05 TQ	FLBLS	10/01-12/01
	Ocala MSA, FL	H	8.47 FQ	12.50 AW	16.73 TQ	FLBLS	10/01-12/01
	Orlando MSA, FL	H	9.97 FQ	13.69 AW	18.31 TQ	FLBLS	10/01-12/01
	Pensacola MSA, FL	H	9.18 FQ	14.43 AW	20.76 TQ	FLBLS	10/01-12/01
	Sarasota-Bradenton MSA, FL	H	5.88 FQ	12.06 AW	16.88 TQ	FLBLS	10/01-12/01
	Tallahassee MSA, FL	H	8.55 FQ	11.99 AW	16.85 TQ	FLBLS	10/01-12/01
	Tampa-St. Petersburg-Clearwater MSA, FL	H	9.74 FQ	14.62 AW	20.42 TQ	FLBLS	10/01-12/01
	West Palm Beach-Boca Raton MSA, FL	H	9.69 FQ	14.55 AW	21.20 TQ	FLBLS	10/01-12/01
	Georgia	H	10.92 FQ	17.84 AW	26.69 TQ	GABLS	10/01-12/01
	Atlanta MSA, GA	H	11.69 FQ	19.86 AW	27.89 TQ	GABLS	10/01-12/01
	Augusta-Aiken MSA, GA-SC	H	9.81 FQ	14.85 AW	22.17 TQ	GABLS	10/01-12/01
	Columbus MSA, GA-AL	H	9.09 FQ	12.59 AW	16.87 TQ	GABLS	10/01-12/01
	Macon MSA, GA	H	9.74 FQ	14.86 AW	20.20 TQ	GABLS	10/01-12/01
	Savannah MSA, GA	H	11.69 FQ	16.67 AW	25.65 TQ	GABLS	10/01-12/01
	Hawaii	H	13.05 FQ	21.78 AW	32.10 TQ	HIBLS	10/01-12/01
	Honolulu MSA, HI	H	12.72 FQ	22.34 AW	32.82 TQ	HIBLS	10/01-12/01
	Idaho	H	9.96 FQ	15.25 AW	20.99 TQ	IDBLS	10/01-12/01
	Boise City MSA, ID	H	12.21 FQ	18.12 AW	22.71 TQ	IDBLS	10/01-12/01
	Illinois	H	11.93 FQ	21.27 AW	34.12 TQ	ILBLS	10/01-12/01
	Chicago PMSA, IL	H	14.15 FQ	23.92 AW	36.01 TQ	ILBLS	10/01-12/01
	Peoria-Pekin MSA, IL	H	12.95 FQ	19.90 AW	28.22 TQ	ILBLS	10/01-12/01
	Rockford MSA, IL	H	14.73 FQ	22.99 AW	34.96 TQ	ILBLS	10/01-12/01
	Springfield MSA, IL	H	12.14 FQ	23.48 AW	34.57 TQ	ILBLS	10/01-12/01
	Indiana	H	11.61 FQ	17.72 AW	25.49 TQ	INBLS	10/01-12/01
	Elkhart-Goshen MSA, IN	H	10.98 FQ	17.43 AW	27.15 TQ	INBLS	10/01-12/01

AAW	Average annual wage	**AOH**	Average offered, high	**ASH**	Average starting, high	**H**	Hourly	**M**	Monthly	**S**	Special: hourly and annual
AE	Average entry wage	**AOL**	Average offered, low	**ASL**	Average starting, low	**HI**	Highest wage paid	**MTC**	Median total compensation	**TQ**	Third quartile wage
AEX	Average experienced wage	**APH**	Average pay, high range	**AW**	Average wage paid	**HR**	High end range	**MW**	Median wage paid	**W**	Weekly
AO	Average offered	**APL**	Average pay, low range	**FQ**	First quartile wage	**LR**	Low end range	**SQ**	Second quartile wage	**Y**	Yearly

Occupation/Type/Industry	Location	Per	Low	Mid	High	Source	Date
Heating, Air Conditioning, and Refrigeration Mechanic and Installer	Evansville-Henderson MSA, IN-KY	H	11.51 FQ	16.59 AW	24.16 TQ	INBLS	10/01-12/01
	Fort Wayne MSA, IN	H	11.44 FQ	15.62 AW	20.61 TQ	INBLS	10/01-12/01
	Gary PMSA, IN	H	12.47 FQ	18.31 AW	25.51 TQ	INBLS	10/01-12/01
	Indianapolis MSA, IN	H	13.53 FQ	19.65 AW	26.51 TQ	INBLS	10/01-12/01
	Lafayette MSA, IN	H	11.26 FQ	16.67 AW	21.53 TQ	INBLS	10/01-12/01
	South Bend MSA, IN	H	12.07 FQ	18.46 AW	25.85 TQ	INBLS	10/01-12/01
	Iowa	H	11.41 FQ	18.60 AW	27.95 TQ	IABLS	10/01-12/01
	Cedar Rapids MSA, IA	H	14.71 FQ	23.45 AW	32.14 TQ	IABLS	10/01-12/01
	Davenport-Moline-Rock Island MSA, IA-IL	H	9.48 FQ	15.35 AW	21.58 TQ	IABLS	10/01-12/01
	Des Moines MSA, IA	H	12.10 FQ	17.61 AW	26.16 TQ	IABLS	10/01-12/01
	Kansas	H	11.15 FQ	17.12 AW	26.65 TQ	KSBLS	10/01-12/01
	Topeka MSA, KS	H	11.59 FQ	16.58 AW	22.59 TQ	KSBLS	10/01-12/01
	Wichita MSA, KS	H	12.10 FQ	18.14 AW	27.54 TQ	KSBLS	10/01-12/01
	Kentucky	H	8.63 FQ	13.96 AW	21.08 TQ	KYBLS	10/01-12/01
	Lexington MSA, KY	H	13.46 FQ	18.14 AW	21.48 TQ	KYBLS	10/01-12/01
	Louisville MSA, KY-IN	H	10.12 FQ	16.38 AW	24.51 TQ	KYBLS	10/01-12/01
	Louisiana	H	7.64 FQ	12.99 AW	19.96 TQ	LABLS	10/01-12/01
	Baton Rouge MSA, LA	H	10.25 FQ	15.02 AW	20.60 TQ	LABLS	10/01-12/01
	Houma MSA, LA	H	8.01 FQ	13.64 AW	19.24 TQ	LABLS	10/01-12/01
	Lafayette MSA, LA	H	8.14 FQ	13.91 AW	20.98 TQ	LABLS	10/01-12/01
	Lake Charles MSA, LA	H	10.15 FQ	15.44 AW	21.75 TQ	LABLS	10/01-12/01
	New Orleans MSA, LA	H	7.67 FQ	12.15 AW	19.22 TQ	LABLS	10/01-12/01
	Shreveport-Bossier City MSA, LA	H	8.75 FQ	13.41 AW	21.00 TQ	LABLS	10/01-12/01
	Maine	H	9.79 FQ	15.47 AW	21.12 TQ	MEBLS	10/01-12/01
	Portland MSA, ME	H	12.15 FQ	17.16 AW	21.75 TQ	MEBLS	10/01-12/01
	Maryland	H	10.14 FQ	16.75 AW	23.90 TQ	MDBLS	10/01-12/01
	Baltimore PMSA, MD	H	8.87 FQ	15.84 AW	23.28 TQ	MDBLS	10/01-12/01
	Massachusetts	H	14.52 FQ	20.30 AW	27.10 TQ	MABLS	10/01-12/01
	Boston PMSA, MA-NH	H	15.88 FQ	21.20 AW	27.54 TQ	MABLS	10/01-12/01
	Brockton PMSA, MA	H	13.62 FQ	19.24 AW	26.40 TQ	MABLS	10/01-12/01
	Lawrence PMSA, MA-NH	H	10.63 FQ	17.53 AW	25.19 TQ	MABLS	10/01-12/01
	Lowell PMSA, MA-NH	H	10.14 FQ	16.12 AW	22.93 TQ	MABLS	10/01-12/01
	New Bedford PMSA, MA	H	12.65 FQ	19.20 AW	27.33 TQ	MABLS	10/01-12/01
	Springfield MSA, MA	H	9.57 FQ	15.88 AW	23.00 TQ	MABLS	10/01-12/01
	Worcester PMSA, MA-CT	H	14.41 FQ	18.55 AW	26.45 TQ	MABLS	10/01-12/01
	Michigan	H	11.89 FQ	18.56 AW	27.30 TQ	MIBLS	10/01-12/01
	Ann Arbor PMSA, MI	H	13.12 FQ	22.02 AW	30.81 TQ	MIBLS	10/01-12/01
	Detroit PMSA, MI	H	13.68 FQ	18.71 AW	27.02 TQ	MIBLS	10/01-12/01
	Flint PMSA, MI	H	11.48 FQ	17.24 AW	28.35 TQ	MIBLS	10/01-12/01
	Grand Rapids-Muskegon-Holland MSA, MI	H	12.69 FQ	20.60 AW	29.83 TQ	MIBLS	10/01-12/01
	Kalamazoo-Battle Creek MSA, MI	H	13.14 FQ	20.09 AW	27.71 TQ	MIBLS	10/01-12/01
	Lansing-East Lansing MSA, MI	H	10.81 FQ	20.07 AW	31.35 TQ	MIBLS	10/01-12/01
	Saginaw-Bay City-Midland MSA, MI	H	8.10 FQ	15.46 AW	26.62 TQ	MIBLS	10/01-12/01
	Minnesota	H	12.01 FQ	18.97 AW	26.82 TQ	MNBLS	10/01-12/01
	Duluth-Superior MSA, MN-WI	H	7.16 FQ	16.44 AW	24.07 TQ	MNBLS	10/01-12/01
	Minneapolis-St. Paul MSA, MN-WI	H	11.58 FQ	18.84 AW	26.64 TQ	MNBLS	10/01-12/01
	St. Cloud MSA, MN	H	11.54 FQ	20.53 AW	27.67 TQ	MNBLS	10/01-12/01
	Mississippi	H	8.16 FQ	13.48 AW	19.81 TQ	MSBLS	10/01-12/01
	Biloxi-Gulfport-Pascagoula MSA, MS	H	9.75 FQ	14.79 AW	18.93 TQ	MSBLS	10/01-12/01
	Jackson MSA, MS	H	10.94 FQ	16.80 AW	22.79 TQ	MSBLS	10/01-12/01
	Missouri	H	10.75 FQ	18.48 AW	27.77 TQ	MOBLS	10/01-12/01
	Kansas City MSA, MO-KS	H	11.42 FQ	17.35 AW	27.77 TQ	MOBLS	10/01-12/01
	St. Louis MSA, MO-IL	H	12.36 FQ	20.38 AW	28.95 TQ	MOBLS	10/01-12/01
	Springfield MSA, MO	H	9.98 FQ	13.87 AW	18.05 TQ	MOBLS	10/01-12/01
	Montana	H	9.44 FQ	16.04 AW	23.88 TQ	MTBLS	10/01-12/01
	Billings MSA, MT	H	10.50 FQ	16.09 AW	25.71 TQ	MTBLS	10/01-12/01
	Nebraska	H	10.23 FQ	16.84 AW	23.45 TQ	NEBLS	10/01-12/01
	Lincoln MSA, NE	H	10.89 FQ	18.15 AW	23.16 TQ	NEBLS	10/01-12/01
	Omaha MSA, NE-IA	H	12.03 FQ	17.93 AW	26.63 TQ	NEBLS	10/01-12/01
	Nevada	H	11.33 FQ	17.04 AW	24.24 TQ	NVBLS	10/01-12/01
	Las Vegas MSA, NV-AZ	H	11.29 FQ	16.64 AW	23.10 TQ	NVBLS	10/01-12/01
	Reno MSA, NV	H	13.83 FQ	19.46 AW	26.24 TQ	NVBLS	10/01-12/01

AAW Average annual wage **AE** Average entry wage **AEX** Average experienced wage **AO** Average offered **AOH** Average offered, high **AOL** Average offered, low **APH** Average pay, high range **APL** Average pay, low range **ASH** Average starting, high **ASL** Average starting, low **AW** Average wage paid **FQ** First quartile wage **H** Hourly **HI** Highest wage paid **HR** High end range **LR** Low end range **M** Monthly **MTC** Median total compensation **MW** Median wage paid **SQ** Second quartile wage **S** Special: hourly and annual **TQ** Third quartile wage **W** Weekly **Y** Yearly

Occupation/Type/Industry	Location	Per	Low	Mid	High	Source	Date
Heating, Air Conditioning, and Refrigeration Mechanic and Installer	New Hampshire	H	11.31 FQ	16.72 AW	21.51 TQ	NHBLS	10/01-12/01
	Manchester PMSA, NH	H	13.88 FQ	18.17 AW	24.46 TQ	NHBLS	10/01-12/01
	Nashua PMSA, NH	H	14.53 FQ	18.84 AW	25.57 TQ	NHBLS	10/01-12/01
	Portsmouth-Rochester PMSA, NH-ME	H	13.05 FQ	17.38 AW	21.39 TQ	NHBLS	10/01-12/01
	New Jersey	H	12.13 FQ	19.38 AW	27.77 TQ	NJBLS	10/01-12/01
	Atlantic-Cape May PMSA, NJ	H	11.89 FQ	18.90 AW	25.76 TQ	NJBLS	10/01-12/01
	Bergen-Passaic PMSA, NJ	H	11.02 FQ	20.89 AW	31.98 TQ	NJBLS	10/01-12/01
	Jersey City PMSA, NJ	H	14.16 FQ	20.11 AW	27.20 TQ	NJBLS	10/01-12/01
	Middlesex-Somerset-Hunterdon PMSA, NJ	H	13.47 FQ	20.51 AW	27.04 TQ	NJBLS	10/01-12/01
	Monmouth-Ocean PMSA, NJ	H	9.90 FQ	16.71 AW	23.52 TQ	NJBLS	10/01-12/01
	Newark PMSA, NJ	H	14.47 FQ	20.41 AW	28.44 TQ	NJBLS	10/01-12/01
	Trenton PMSA, NJ	H	12.76 FQ	18.52 AW	25.88 TQ	NJBLS	10/01-12/01
	New Mexico	H	9.67 FQ	14.45 AW	20.03 TQ	NMBLS	10/01-12/01
	Albuquerque MSA, NM	H	10.75 FQ	15.35 AW	20.84 TQ	NMBLS	10/01-12/01
	Las Cruces MSA, NM	H	8.53 FQ	14.20 AW	19.98 TQ	NMBLS	10/01-12/01
	New York	H	9.87 FQ	18.55 AW	27.39 TQ	NYBLS	10/01-12/01
	Albany-Schenectady-Troy MSA, NY	H	9.63 FQ	15.23 AW	22.15 TQ	NYBLS	10/01-12/01
	Binghamton MSA, NY	H	13.53 FQ	19.70 AW	26.17 TQ	NYBLS	10/01-12/01
	Buffalo-Niagara Falls MSA, NY	H	13.55 FQ	15.99 AW	20.26 TQ	NYBLS	10/01-12/01
	Dutchess County PMSA, NY	H	12.74 FQ	17.00 AW	21.58 TQ	NYBLS	10/01-12/01
	Nassau-Suffolk PMSA, NY	H	9.62 FQ	18.78 AW	27.78 TQ	NYBLS	10/01-12/01
	New York PMSA, NY	H	9.59 FQ	20.83 AW	30.72 TQ	NYBLS	10/01-12/01
	Newburgh PMSA, NY-PA	H	9.51 FQ	16.93 AW	22.88 TQ	NYBLS	10/01-12/01
	Rochester MSA, NY	H	9.90 FQ	16.75 AW	22.36 TQ	NYBLS	10/01-12/01
	Syracuse MSA, NY	H	11.70 FQ	17.49 AW	25.30 TQ	NYBLS	10/01-12/01
	Utica-Rome MSA, NY	H	10.51 FQ	15.51 AW	21.42 TQ	NYBLS	10/01-12/01
	North Carolina	H	9.33 FQ	15.08 AW	21.33 TQ	NCBLS	10/01-12/01
	Asheville MSA, NC	H	9.70 FQ	14.34 AW	19.30 TQ	NCBLS	10/01-12/01
	Charlotte-Gastonia-Rock Hill MSA, NC-SC	H	8.21 FQ	16.02 AW	22.94 TQ	NCBLS	10/01-12/01
	Fayetteville MSA, NC	H	9.55 FQ	14.37 AW	20.45 TQ	NCBLS	10/01-12/01
	Greensboro-Winston-Salem-High Point MSA, NC	H	10.16 FQ	16.76 AW	22.85 TQ	NCBLS	10/01-12/01
	Hickory-Morganton-Lenoir MSA, NC	H	9.31 FQ	13.44 AW	17.72 TQ	NCBLS	10/01-12/01
	Raleigh-Durham-Chapel Hill MSA, NC	H	9.88 FQ	15.78 AW	21.27 TQ	NCBLS	10/01-12/01
	Wilmington MSA, NC	H	10.72 FQ	15.72 AW	20.86 TQ	NCBLS	10/01-12/01
	North Dakota	H	9.72 FQ	15.49 AW	21.98 TQ	NDBLS	10/01-12/01
	Fargo-Moorhead MSA, ND-MN	H	12.46 FQ	18.73 AW	26.52 TQ	NDBLS	10/01-12/01
	Ohio	H	9.77 FQ	15.97 AW	23.09 TQ	OHBLS	10/01-12/01
	Akron PMSA, OH	H	9.71 FQ	15.84 AW	22.93 TQ	OHBLS	10/01-12/01
	Canton-Massillon MSA, OH	H	10.37 FQ	17.14 AW	23.17 TQ	OHBLS	10/01-12/01
	Cincinnati PMSA, OH-KY-IN	H	10.64 FQ	16.41 AW	22.99 TQ	OHBLS	10/01-12/01
	Cleveland-Lorain-Elyria PMSA, OH	H	10.34 FQ	17.65 AW	26.95 TQ	OHBLS	10/01-12/01
	Columbus MSA, OH	H	9.19 FQ	14.19 AW	21.69 TQ	OHBLS	10/01-12/01
	Dayton-Springfield MSA, OH	H	11.40 FQ	16.18 AW	22.29 TQ	OHBLS	10/01-12/01
	Hamilton-Middletown PMSA, OH	H	10.03 FQ	16.13 AW	22.36 TQ	OHBLS	10/01-12/01
	Mansfield MSA, OH	H	8.00 FQ	13.85 AW	22.16 TQ	OHBLS	10/01-12/01
	Toledo MSA, OH	H	14.19 FQ	18.25 AW	21.46 TQ	OHBLS	10/01-12/01
	Youngstown-Warren MSA, OH	H	11.60 FQ	17.08 AW	26.40 TQ	OHBLS	10/01-12/01
	Oklahoma	H	8.87 FQ	14.47 AW	21.08 TQ	OKBLS	10/01-12/01
	Oklahoma City MSA, OK	H	9.07 FQ	15.03 AW	21.43 TQ	OKBLS	10/01-12/01
	Tulsa MSA, OK	H	9.68 FQ	15.28 AW	21.43 TQ	OKBLS	10/01-12/01
	Oregon	H	10.55 FQ	18.56 AW	27.28 TQ	ORBLS	10/01-12/01
	Eugene-Springfield MSA, OR	H	9.86 FQ	15.20 AW	22.92 TQ	ORBLS	10/01-12/01
	Medford-Ashland MSA, OR	H	9.86 FQ	14.87 AW	21.03 TQ	ORBLS	10/01-12/01
	Portland-Vancouver PMSA, OR-WA	H	12.07 FQ	20.58 AW	31.52 TQ	ORBLS	10/01-12/01
	Salem PMSA, OR	H	9.42 FQ	14.96 AW	22.76 TQ	ORBLS	10/01-12/01
	Pennsylvania	H	11.08 FQ	18.48 AW	27.34 TQ	PABLS	10/01-12/01
	Allentown-Bethlehem-Easton MSA, PA	H	11.85 FQ	15.89 AW	21.30 TQ	PABLS	10/01-12/01

AAW	Average annual wage	**AOH**	Average offered, high	**ASH**	Average starting, high	**H**	Hourly	**M**	Monthly	**S**	Special: hourly and annual
AE	Average entry wage	**AOL**	Average offered, low	**ASL**	Average starting, low	**HI**	Highest wage paid	**MTC**	Median total compensation	**TQ**	Third quartile wage
AEX	Average experienced wage	**APH**	Average pay, high range	**AW**	Average wage paid	**HR**	High end range	**MW**	Median wage paid	**W**	Weekly
AO	Average offered	**APL**	Average pay, low range	**FQ**	First quartile wage	**LR**	Low end range	**SQ**	Second quartile wage	**Y**	Yearly

Occupation/Type/Industry	Location	Per	Low	Mid	High	Source	Date
Heating, Air Conditioning, and Refrigeration Mechanic and Installer	Erie MSA, PA	H	9.07 FQ	12.18 AW	17.31 TQ	PABLS	10/01-12/01
	Harrisburg-Lebanon-Carlisle MSA, PA	H	10.11 FQ	15.73 AW	22.91 TQ	PABLS	10/01-12/01
	Johnstown MSA, PA	H	8.67 FQ	13.11 AW	17.32 TQ	PABLS	10/01-12/01
	Lancaster MSA, PA	H	11.81 FQ	16.11 AW	21.38 TQ	PABLS	10/01-12/01
	Philadelphia PMSA, PA-NJ	H	13.03 FQ	21.13 AW	33.15 TQ	PABLS	10/01-12/01
	Pittsburgh MSA, PA	H	10.94 FQ	17.24 AW	25.18 TQ	PABLS	10/01-12/01
	Reading MSA, PA	H	10.87 FQ	16.70 AW	22.35 TQ	PABLS	10/01-12/01
	Scranton-Wilkes-Barre-Hazleton MSA, PA	H	9.62 FQ	15.71 AW	22.72 TQ	PABLS	10/01-12/01
	York MSA, PA	H	11.76 FQ	18.32 AW	26.72 TQ	PABLS	10/01-12/01
	Rhode Island	H	12.48 FQ	18.73 AW	29.37 TQ	RIBLS	10/01-12/01
	Providence-Fall River-Warwick MSA, RI-MA	H	13.02 FQ	19.32 AW	29.07 TQ	RIBLS	10/01-12/01
	South Carolina	H	9.31 FQ	14.23 AW	20.16 TQ	SCBLS	10/01-12/01
	Charleston-North Charleston MSA, SC	H	10.96 FQ	15.10 AW	20.31 TQ	SCBLS	10/01-12/01
	Columbia MSA, SC	H	9.21 FQ	12.96 AW	17.67 TQ	SCBLS	10/01-12/01
	Greenville-Spartanburg-Anderson MSA, SC	H	10.22 FQ	14.64 AW	20.28 TQ	SCBLS	10/01-12/01
	Myrtle Beach MSA, SC	H	7.98 FQ	12.09 AW	16.98 TQ	SCBLS	10/01-12/01
	South Dakota	H	10.57 FQ	15.00 AW	20.83 TQ	SDBLS	10/01-12/01
	Sioux Falls MSA, SD	H	11.10 FQ	15.58 AW	20.85 TQ	SDBLS	10/01-12/01
	Tennessee	H	9.59 FQ	15.96 AW	25.23 TQ	TNBLS	10/01-12/01
	Chattanooga MSA, TN-GA	H	10.80 FQ	15.95 AW	22.05 TQ	TNBLS	10/01-12/01
	Clarksville-Hopkinsville MSA, TN-KY	H	10.42 FQ	17.06 AW	25.15 TQ	TNBLS	10/01-12/01
	Johnson City-Kingsport-Bristol MSA, TN-VA	H	7.77 FQ	13.63 AW	18.39 TQ	TNBLS	10/01-12/01
	Knoxville MSA, TN	H	8.98 FQ	13.95 AW	20.63 TQ	TNBLS	10/01-12/01
	Memphis MSA, TN-AR-MS	H	10.96 FQ	18.05 AW	28.72 TQ	TNBLS	10/01-12/01
	Nashville MSA, TN	H	9.81 FQ	17.08 AW	27.17 TQ	TNBLS	10/01-12/01
	Texas	H	9.71 FQ	15.67 AW	22.35 TQ	TXBLS	10/01-12/01
	Amarillo MSA, TX	H	9.70 FQ	14.29 AW	19.65 TQ	TXBLS	10/01-12/01
	Austin-San Marcos MSA, TX	H	10.40 FQ	17.13 AW	28.19 TQ	TXBLS	10/01-12/01
	Beaumont-Port Arthur MSA, TX	H	11.59 FQ	16.02 AW	20.34 TQ	TXBLS	10/01-12/01
	Brazoria PMSA, TX	H	10.12 FQ	14.22 AW	20.50 TQ	TXBLS	10/01-12/01
	Brownsville-Harlingen-San Benito MSA, TX	H	7.10 FQ	12.02 AW	19.02 TQ	TXBLS	10/01-12/01
	Corpus Christi MSA, TX	H	9.54 FQ	14.94 AW	20.83 TQ	TXBLS	10/01-12/01
	Dallas PMSA, TX	H	10.37 FQ	16.29 AW	21.75 TQ	TXBLS	10/01-12/01
	El Paso MSA, TX	H	7.24 FQ	13.02 AW	20.10 TQ	TXBLS	10/01-12/01
	Fort Worth-Arlington PMSA, TX	H	11.54 FQ	15.57 AW	20.79 TQ	TXBLS	10/01-12/01
	Galveston-Texas City PMSA, TX	H	9.69 FQ	14.32 AW	19.66 TQ	TXBLS	10/01-12/01
	Houston PMSA, TX	H	10.85 FQ	16.51 AW	24.04 TQ	TXBLS	10/01-12/01
	Killeen-Temple MSA, TX	H	9.61 FQ	14.68 AW	20.94 TQ	TXBLS	10/01-12/01
	Laredo MSA, TX	H	6.84 FQ	10.71 AW	15.01 TQ	TXBLS	10/01-12/01
	Longview-Marshall MSA, TX	H	7.80 FQ	12.77 AW	20.39 TQ	TXBLS	10/01-12/01
	Lubbock MSA, TX	H	11.44 FQ	15.40 AW	20.43 TQ	TXBLS	10/01-12/01
	McAllen-Edinburg-Mission MSA, TX	H	7.54 FQ	12.33 AW	19.26 TQ	TXBLS	10/01-12/01
	Odessa-Midland MSA, TX	H	10.50 FQ	14.87 AW	20.41 TQ	TXBLS	10/01-12/01
	San Antonio MSA, TX	H	10.18 FQ	17.84 AW	25.64 TQ	TXBLS	10/01-12/01
	Tyler MSA, TX	H	7.90 FQ	11.63 AW	18.41 TQ	TXBLS	10/01-12/01
	Waco MSA, TX	H	9.20 FQ	14.75 AW	21.37 TQ	TXBLS	10/01-12/01
	Utah	H	10.62 FQ	16.25 AW	23.21 TQ	UTBLS	10/01-12/01
	Provo-Orem MSA, UT	H	11.34 FQ	16.40 AW	22.10 TQ	UTBLS	10/01-12/01
	Salt Lake City-Ogden MSA, UT	H	11.30 FQ	17.21 AW	25.47 TQ	UTBLS	10/01-12/01
	Vermont	H	11.17 FQ	16.13 AW	21.48 TQ	VTBLS	10/01-12/01
	Burlington MSA, VT	H	13.21 FQ	17.80 AW	22.35 TQ	VTBLS	10/01-12/01
	Virginia	H	10.61 FQ	17.79 AW	26.85 TQ	VABLS	10/01-12/01
	Lynchburg MSA, VA	H	11.34 FQ	15.95 AW	21.12 TQ	VABLS	10/01-12/01
	Norfolk-Virginia Beach-Newport News MSA, VA-NC	H	11.08 FQ	16.02 AW	21.13 TQ	VABLS	10/01-12/01

AAW	Average annual wage	AOH	Average offered, high	ASH	Average starting, high	H	Hourly	M	Monthly	S	Special: hourly and annual
AE	Average entry wage	AOL	Average offered, low	ASL	Average starting, low	HI	Highest wage paid	MTC	Median total compensation	TQ	Third quartile wage
AEX	Average experienced wage	APH	Average pay, high range	AW	Average wage paid	HR	High end range	MW	Median wage paid	W	Weekly
AO	Average offered	APL	Average pay, low range	FQ	First quartile wage	LR	Low end range	SQ	Second quartile wage	Y	Yearly

Occupation/Type/Industry	Location	Per	Low	Mid	High	Source	Date
Heating, Air Conditioning, and Refrigeration Mechanic and Installer	Richmond-Petersburg MSA, VA	H	11.46 FQ	17.39 AW	24.45 TQ	VABLS	10/01-12/01
	Roanoke MSA, VA	H	8.95 FQ	13.78 AW	18.26 TQ	VABLS	10/01-12/01
	Washington	H	9.94 FQ	18.23 AW	26.97 TQ	WABLS	10/01-12/01
	Bremerton PMSA, WA	H	17.56 FQ	21.84 AW	26.59 TQ	WABLS	10/01-12/01
	Olympia PMSA, WA	H	18.58 FQ	21.00 AW	22.99 TQ	WABLS	10/01-12/01
	Richland-Kennewick-Pasco MSA, WA	H	12.65 FQ	16.77 AW	21.44 TQ	WABLS	10/01-12/01
	Seattle-Bellevue-Everett PMSA, WA	H	15.78 FQ	23.63 AW	33.11 TQ	WABLS	10/01-12/01
	Spokane MSA, WA	H	8.99 FQ	12.86 AW	19.09 TQ	WABLS	10/01-12/01
	Tacoma PMSA, WA	H	13.09 FQ	18.98 AW	25.55 TQ	WABLS	10/01-12/01
	Yakima MSA, WA	H	12.50 FQ	16.47 AW	21.24 TQ	WABLS	10/01-12/01
	West Virginia	H	8.82 FQ	15.24 AW	21.90 TQ	WVBLS	10/01-12/01
	Charleston MSA, WV	H	11.64 FQ	18.10 AW	29.00 TQ	WVBLS	10/01-12/01
	Huntington-Ashland MSA, WV-KY-OH	H	7.77 FQ	12.77 AW	19.41 TQ	WVBLS	10/01-12/01
	Wisconsin	H	10.78 FQ	17.82 AW	28.14 TQ	WIBLS	10/01-12/01
	Appleton-Oshkosh-Neenah MSA, WI	H	11.71 FQ	17.45 AW	25.96 TQ	WIBLS	10/01-12/01
	Green Bay MSA, WI	H	11.07 FQ	16.30 AW	25.65 TQ	WIBLS	10/01-12/01
	Madison MSA, WI	H	11.60 FQ	17.58 AW	25.90 TQ	WIBLS	10/01-12/01
	Milwaukee-Waukesha PMSA, WI	H	12.25 FQ	20.71 AW	32.37 TQ	WIBLS	10/01-12/01
	Racine PMSA, WI	H	12.29 FQ	22.59 AW	34.97 TQ	WIBLS	10/01-12/01
	Wyoming	H	11.28 FQ	16.43 AW	22.99 TQ	WYBLS	10/01-12/01
	Puerto Rico	H	5.82 FQ	8.78 AW	13.07 TQ	PRBLS	10/01-12/01
	Virgin Islands	H	10.40 FQ	13.95 AW	17.70 TQ	VIBLS	10/01-12/01
	Guam	H	9.41 FQ	13.52 AW	18.26 TQ	GUBLS	10/01-12/01
Helicopter Pilot	United States	Y	29000 ASL		57000 ASH	AEAC	1/99-1/99
Help Desk and Information Technology Support Professional							
Information Technology	United States	Y	35450 AOL			IOMA5	1/01-1/02
Helper							
Mason, Tile and Marble Setter	Alabama	H	8.29 FQ	10.42 AW	13.10 TQ	ALBLS	10/01-12/01
Mason, Tile and Marble Setter	Arizona	H	5.85 FQ	8.74 AW	13.17 TQ	AZBLS	10/01-12/01
Mason, Tile and Marble Setter	Arkansas	H	7.61 FQ	9.49 AW	11.31 TQ	ARBLS	10/01-12/01
Mason, Tile and Marble Setter	California	H	8.28 FQ	12.73 AW	18.93 TQ	CABLS	10/01-12/01
Mason, Tile and Marble Setter	Colorado	H	9.54 FQ	13.17 AW	16.98 TQ	COBLS	10/01-12/01
Mason, Tile and Marble Setter	Connecticut	H	13.39 FQ	18.14 AW	21.87 TQ	CTBLS	10/01-12/01
Mason, Tile and Marble Setter	Delaware	H	9.20 FQ	10.94 AW	13.15 TQ	DEBLS	10/01-12/01
Mason, Tile and Marble Setter	Florida	H	7.20 FQ	10.14 AW	13.37 TQ	FLBLS	10/01-12/01
Mason, Tile and Marble Setter	Georgia	H	7.87 FQ	10.96 AW	14.92 TQ	GABLS	10/01-12/01
Mason, Tile and Marble Setter	Hawaii	H	9.70 FQ	16.14 AW	23.77 TQ	HIBLS	10/01-12/01
Mason, Tile and Marble Setter	Idaho	H	9.34 FQ	12.65 AW	16.42 TQ	IDBLS	10/01-12/01
Mason, Tile and Marble Setter	Illinois	H	12.72 FQ	21.40 AW	27.20 TQ	ILBLS	10/01-12/01
Mason, Tile and Marble Setter	Indiana	H	7.94 FQ	13.12 AW	19.09 TQ	INBLS	10/01-12/01
Mason, Tile and Marble Setter	Iowa	H	8.07 FQ	13.62 AW	20.37 TQ	IABLS	10/01-12/01
Mason, Tile and Marble Setter	Kansas	H	7.40 FQ	11.47 AW	16.44 TQ	KSBLS	10/01-12/01
Mason, Tile and Marble Setter	Kentucky	H	7.57 FQ	12.31 AW	18.31 TQ	KYBLS	10/01-12/01
Mason, Tile and Marble Setter	Louisiana	H	7.53 FQ	10.75 AW	14.40 TQ	LABLS	10/01-12/01
Mason, Tile and Marble Setter	Maine	H	8.05 FQ	11.39 AW	14.59 TQ	MEBLS	10/01-12/01
Mason, Tile and Marble Setter	Maryland	H	9.04 FQ	11.62 AW	15.45 TQ	MDBLS	10/01-12/01
Mason, Tile and Marble Setter	Massachusetts	H	11.96 FQ	18.75 AW	26.20 TQ	MABLS	10/01-12/01
Mason, Tile and Marble Setter	Michigan	H	9.58 FQ	15.19 AW	22.51 TQ	MIBLS	10/01-12/01
Mason, Tile and Marble Setter	Minnesota	H	11.02 FQ	19.42 AW	27.10 TQ	MNBLS	10/01-12/01
Mason, Tile and Marble Setter	Mississippi	H	6.32 FQ	9.35 AW	12.52 TQ	MSBLS	10/01-12/01
Mason, Tile and Marble Setter	Missouri	H	9.98 FQ	16.66 AW	25.25 TQ	MOBLS	10/01-12/01
Mason, Tile and Marble Setter	Montana	H	7.57 FQ	12.72 AW	17.46 TQ	MTBLS	10/01-12/01
Mason, Tile and Marble Setter	Nebraska	H	8.68 FQ	11.88 AW	14.56 TQ	NEBLS	10/01-12/01
Mason, Tile and Marble Setter	Nevada	H	9.27 FQ	13.21 AW	22.76 TQ	NVBLS	10/01-12/01
Mason, Tile and Marble Setter	New Hampshire	H	9.60 FQ	13.60 AW	17.42 TQ	NHBLS	10/01-12/01
Mason, Tile and Marble Setter	New Jersey	H	8.03 FQ	16.17 AW	25.87 TQ	NJBLS	10/01-12/01
Mason, Tile and Marble Setter	New Mexico	H	7.57 FQ	10.11 AW	13.31 TQ	NMBLS	10/01-12/01
Mason, Tile and Marble Setter	New York	H	6.07 FQ	16.09 AW	27.02 TQ	NYBLS	10/01-12/01

AAW	Average annual wage	**AOH**	Average offered, high	**ASH**	Average starting, high	**H**	Hourly	**M**	Monthly	**S**	Special: hourly and annual
AE	Average entry wage	**AOL**	Average offered, low	**ASL**	Average starting, low	**HI**	Highest wage paid	**MTC**	Median total compensation	**TQ**	Third quartile wage
AEX	Average experienced wage	**APH**	Average pay, high range	**AW**	Average wage paid	**HR**	High end range	**MW**	Median wage paid	**W**	Weekly
AO	Average offered	**APL**	Average pay, low range	**FQ**	First quartile wage	**LR**	Low end range	**SQ**	Second quartile wage	**Y**	Yearly

Occupation/Type/Industry	Location	Per	Low	Mid	High	Source	Date
Helper							
Mason, Tile and Marble Setter	North Carolina	H	8.16 FQ	10.25 AW	13.08 TQ	NCBLS	10/01-12/01
Mason, Tile and Marble Setter	North Dakota	H	7.73 FQ	10.20 AW	13.98 TQ	NDBLS	10/01-12/01
Mason, Tile and Marble Setter	Ohio	H	8.42 FQ	13.23 AW	19.18 TQ	OHBLS	10/01-12/01
Mason, Tile and Marble Setter	Oklahoma	H	8.32 FQ	10.35 AW	13.20 TQ	OKBLS	10/01-12/01
Mason, Tile and Marble Setter	Oregon	H	7.36 FQ	13.51 AW	23.20 TQ	ORBLS	10/01-12/01
Mason, Tile and Marble Setter	Pennsylvania	H	8.57 FQ	13.73 AW	22.09 TQ	PABLS	10/01-12/01
Mason, Tile and Marble Setter	Rhode Island	H	11.86 FQ	15.57 AW	22.20 TQ	RIBLS	10/01-12/01
Mason, Tile and Marble Setter	South Carolina	H	8.48 FQ	10.80 AW	13.44 TQ	SCBLS	10/01-12/01
Mason, Tile and Marble Setter	South Dakota	H	8.83 FQ	11.18 AW	14.26 TQ	SDBLS	10/01-12/01
Mason, Tile and Marble Setter	Tennessee	H	8.75 FQ	10.61 AW	13.31 TQ	TNBLS	10/01-12/01
Mason, Tile and Marble Setter	Texas	H	7.39 FQ	10.29 AW	13.77 TQ	TXBLS	10/01-12/01
Mason, Tile and Marble Setter	Utah	H	7.68 FQ	11.12 AW	16.42 TQ	UTBLS	10/01-12/01
Mason, Tile and Marble Setter	Vermont	H	9.21 FQ	11.68 AW	14.49 TQ	VTBLS	10/01-12/01
Mason, Tile and Marble Setter	Virginia	H	8.51 FQ	10.66 AW	13.21 TQ	VABLS	10/01-12/01
Mason, Tile and Marble Setter	Washington	H	8.00 FQ	15.87 AW	26.31 TQ	WABLS	10/01-12/01
Mason, Tile and Marble Setter	West Virginia	H	7.46 FQ	11.58 AW	24.60 TQ	WVBLS	10/01-12/01
Mason, Tile and Marble Setter	Wisconsin	H	9.98 FQ	14.69 AW	21.65 TQ	WIBLS	10/01-12/01
Mason, Tile and Marble Setter	Wyoming	H	7.66 FQ	10.84 AW	16.29 TQ	WYBLS	10/01-12/01
Mason, Tile and Marble Setter	Puerto Rico	H	5.51 FQ	6.46 AW	7.88 TQ	PRBLS	10/01-12/01
Mason, Tile and Marble Setter	Virgin Islands	H	7.25 FQ	9.02 AW	10.81 TQ	VIBLS	10/01-12/01
Carpenter	Alabama	H	6.84 FQ	9.07 AW	12.06 TQ	ALBLS	10/01-12/01
Carpenter	Alaska	H	9.81 FQ	14.66 AW	20.29 TQ	AKBLS	10/01-12/01
Carpenter	Arizona	H	6.02 FQ	8.93 AW	12.27 TQ	AZBLS	10/01-12/01
Carpenter	Arkansas	H	6.42 FQ	9.29 AW	12.54 TQ	ARBLS	10/01-12/01
Carpenter	California	H	7.51 FQ	11.83 AW	16.92 TQ	CABLS	10/01-12/01
Carpenter	Colorado	H	6.51 FQ	10.54 AW	14.26 TQ	COBLS	10/01-12/01
Carpenter	Connecticut	H	9.00 FQ	12.70 AW	16.80 TQ	CTBLS	10/01-12/01
Carpenter	Delaware	H	7.85 FQ	10.09 AW	12.31 TQ	DEBLS	10/01-12/01
Carpenter	District of Columbia	H	9.10 FQ	12.54 AW	16.66 TQ	DCBLS	10/01-12/01
Carpenter	Florida	H	7.53 FQ	10.80 AW	13.97 TQ	FLBLS	10/01-12/01
Carpenter	Georgia	H	7.60 FQ	10.71 AW	14.45 TQ	GABLS	10/01-12/01
Carpenter	Hawaii	H	9.58 FQ	13.64 AW	19.88 TQ	HIBLS	10/01-12/01
Carpenter	Idaho	H	7.50 FQ	10.11 AW	14.17 TQ	IDBLS	10/01-12/01
Carpenter	Illinois	H	7.85 FQ	12.03 AW	21.65 TQ	ILBLS	10/01-12/01
Carpenter	Indiana	H	7.09 FQ	10.97 AW	16.09 TQ	INBLS	10/01-12/01
Carpenter	Iowa	H	6.58 FQ	9.44 AW	13.20 TQ	IABLS	10/01-12/01
Carpenter	Kansas	H	7.12 FQ	10.11 AW	13.17 TQ	KSBLS	10/01-12/01
Carpenter	Kentucky	H	6.14 FQ	9.45 AW	13.81 TQ	KYBLS	10/01-12/01
Carpenter	Louisiana	H	6.39 FQ	10.14 AW	14.20 TQ	LABLS	10/01-12/01
Carpenter	Maine	H	7.24 FQ	9.45 AW	12.61 TQ	MEBLS	10/01-12/01
Carpenter	Maryland	H	8.20 FQ	11.75 AW	15.58 TQ	MDBLS	10/01-12/01
Carpenter	Massachusetts	H	9.47 FQ	13.46 AW	18.12 TQ	MABLS	10/01-12/01
Carpenter	Michigan	H	8.05 FQ	12.08 AW	19.09 TQ	MIBLS	10/01-12/01
Carpenter	Minnesota	H	8.79 FQ	12.07 AW	16.31 TQ	MNBLS	10/01-12/01
Carpenter	Mississippi	H	6.87 FQ	9.28 AW	12.15 TQ	MSBLS	10/01-12/01
Carpenter	Missouri	H	7.94 FQ	11.48 AW	17.06 TQ	MOBLS	10/01-12/01
Carpenter	Montana	H	7.61 FQ	10.71 AW	14.54 TQ	MTBLS	10/01-12/01
Carpenter	Nebraska	H	6.35 FQ	9.84 AW	13.19 TQ	NEBLS	10/01-12/01
Carpenter	Nevada	H	7.25 FQ	11.69 AW	17.14 TQ	NVBLS	10/01-12/01
Carpenter	New Hampshire	H	9.11 FQ	10.99 AW	13.90 TQ	NHBLS	10/01-12/01
Carpenter	New Jersey	H	7.69 FQ	12.89 AW	20.61 TQ	NJBLS	10/01-12/01
Carpenter	New Mexico	H	7.36 FQ	10.64 AW	15.97 TQ	NMBLS	10/01-12/01
Carpenter	New York	H	7.38 FQ	11.50 AW	16.48 TQ	NYBLS	10/01-12/01
Carpenter	North Carolina	H	7.39 FQ	9.89 AW	12.92 TQ	NCBLS	10/01-12/01
Carpenter	North Dakota	H	7.55 FQ	10.04 AW	13.22 TQ	NDBLS	10/01-12/01
Carpenter	Ohio	H	7.01 FQ	10.31 AW	13.94 TQ	OHBLS	10/01-12/01
Carpenter	Oklahoma	H	6.78 FQ	10.20 AW	14.75 TQ	OKBLS	10/01-12/01
Carpenter	Oregon	H	7.40 FQ	10.80 AW	16.03 TQ	ORBLS	10/01-12/01
Carpenter	Pennsylvania	H	6.90 FQ	10.31 AW	14.59 TQ	PABLS	10/01-12/01
Carpenter	Rhode Island	H	10.54 FQ	14.12 AW	17.31 TQ	RIBLS	10/01-12/01
Carpenter	South Carolina	H	6.69 FQ	9.56 AW	12.89 TQ	SCBLS	10/01-12/01
Carpenter	South Dakota	H	6.02 FQ	8.40 AW	10.95 TQ	SDBLS	10/01-12/01
Carpenter	Tennessee	H	7.55 FQ	10.02 AW	13.05 TQ	TNBLS	10/01-12/01
Carpenter	Texas	H	7.17 FQ	9.85 AW	12.94 TQ	TXBLS	10/01-12/01
Carpenter	Utah	H	6.19 FQ	8.28 AW	10.59 TQ	UTBLS	10/01-12/01
Carpenter	Vermont	H	8.45 FQ	10.88 AW	13.63 TQ	VTBLS	10/01-12/01
Carpenter	Virginia	H	6.80 FQ	9.68 AW	13.02 TQ	VABLS	10/01-12/01
Carpenter	Washington	H	7.79 FQ	11.15 AW	15.84 TQ	WABLS	10/01-12/01
Carpenter	West Virginia	H	6.05 FQ	8.72 AW	10.87 TQ	WVBLS	10/01-12/01
Carpenter	Wisconsin	H	7.74 FQ	11.14 AW	14.38 TQ	WIBLS	10/01-12/01
Carpenter	Wyoming	H	8.38 FQ	11.52 AW	16.30 TQ	WYBLS	10/01-12/01

AAW Average annual wage **AE** Average entry wage **AEX** Average experienced wage **AO** Average offered **AOH** Average offered, high **AOL** Average offered, low **APH** Average pay, high range **APL** Average pay, low range **ASH** Average starting, high **ASL** Average starting, low **AW** Average wage paid **FQ** First quartile wage **H** Hourly **HI** Highest wage paid **HR** High end range **LR** Low end range **M** Monthly **MTC** Median total compensation **MW** Median wage paid **SQ** Second quartile wage **S** Special: hourly and annual **TQ** Third quartile wage **W** Weekly **Y** Yearly

Occupation/Type/Industry	Location	Per	Low	Mid	High	Source	Date
Helper							
Carpenter	Puerto Rico	H	5.52 FQ	6.24 AW	7.07 TQ	PRBLS	10/01-12/01
Carpenter	Virgin Islands	H	8.13 FQ	10.14 AW	12.81 TQ	VIBLS	10/01-12/01
Electrician	Alabama	H	7.12 FQ	9.70 AW	13.86 TQ	ALBLS	10/01-12/01
Electrician	Alaska	H	9.48 FQ	17.39 AW	23.57 TQ	AKBLS	10/01-12/01
Electrician	Arizona	H	6.21 FQ	9.14 AW	12.91 TQ	AZBLS	10/01-12/01
Electrician	Arkansas	H	7.34 FQ	9.51 AW	12.68 TQ	ARBLS	10/01-12/01
Electrician	California	H	7.99 FQ	12.47 AW	17.56 TQ	CABLS	10/01-12/01
Electrician	Colorado	H	8.64 FQ	14.20 AW	20.43 TQ	COBLS	10/01-12/01
Electrician	Connecticut	H	8.91 FQ	12.92 AW	18.44 TQ	CTBLS	10/01-12/01
Electrician	Delaware	H	7.60 FQ	11.12 AW	15.84 TQ	DEBLS	10/01-12/01
Electrician	District of Columbia	H	9.51 FQ	17.20 AW	22.49 TQ	DCBLS	10/01-12/01
Electrician	Florida	H	7.45 FQ	9.96 AW	13.20 TQ	FLBLS	10/01-12/01
Electrician	Georgia	H	7.65 FQ	10.35 AW	13.50 TQ	GABLS	10/01-12/01
Electrician	Hawaii	H	9.89 FQ	14.06 AW	18.25 TQ	HIBLS	10/01-12/01
Electrician	Idaho	H	6.60 FQ	12.43 AW	16.57 TQ	IDBLS	10/01-12/01
Electrician	Illinois	H	7.75 FQ	13.62 AW	19.66 TQ	ILBLS	10/01-12/01
Electrician	Indiana	H	7.75 FQ	11.52 AW	16.80 TQ	INBLS	10/01-12/01
Electrician	Iowa	H	7.50 FQ	11.42 AW	15.98 TQ	IABLS	10/01-12/01
Electrician	Kansas	H	7.29 FQ	10.06 AW	13.53 TQ	KSBLS	10/01-12/01
Electrician	Kentucky	H	7.18 FQ	10.04 AW	13.66 TQ	KYBLS	10/01-12/01
Electrician	Louisiana	H	7.38 FQ	10.41 AW	13.92 TQ	LABLS	10/01-12/01
Electrician	Maine	H	9.30 FQ	11.63 AW	14.08 TQ	MEBLS	10/01-12/01
Electrician	Maryland	H	8.51 FQ	11.58 AW	15.82 TQ	MDBLS	10/01-12/01
Electrician	Massachusetts	H	9.33 FQ	14.94 AW	22.16 TQ	MABLS	10/01-12/01
Electrician	Michigan	H	6.67 FQ	12.14 AW	16.70 TQ	MIBLS	10/01-12/01
Electrician	Minnesota	H	8.25 FQ	13.11 AW	19.01 TQ	MNBLS	10/01-12/01
Electrician	Mississippi	H	6.76 FQ	9.90 AW	13.86 TQ	MSBLS	10/01-12/01
Electrician	Missouri	H	7.64 FQ	11.98 AW	17.27 TQ	MOBLS	10/01-12/01
Electrician	Montana	H	8.41 FQ	11.73 AW	14.78 TQ	MTBLS	10/01-12/01
Electrician	Nebraska	H	7.67 FQ	10.75 AW	15.04 TQ	NEBLS	10/01-12/01
Electrician	Nevada	H	7.98 FQ	12.52 AW	18.53 TQ	NVBLS	10/01 12/01
Electrician	New Hampshire	H	5.66 FQ	9.46 AW	15.46 TQ	NHBLS	10/01-12/01
Electrician	New Jersey	H	6.74 FQ	12.16 AW	18.54 TQ	NJBLS	10/01-12/01
Electrician	New Mexico	H	7.27 FQ	10.57 AW	15.30 TQ	NMBLS	10/01-12/01
Electrician	New York	H	7.45 FQ	13.78 AW	20.80 TQ	NYBLS	10/01-12/01
Electrician	North Carolina	H	7.73 FQ	10.57 AW	13.66 TQ	NCBLS	10/01-12/01
Electrician	North Dakota	H	6.26 FQ	11.31 AW	16.59 TQ	NDBLS	10/01-12/01
Electrician	Ohio	H	7.37 FQ	10.60 AW	15.04 TQ	OHBLS	10/01-12/01
Electrician	Oklahoma	H	7.85 FQ	11.01 AW	15.03 TQ	OKBLS	10/01-12/01
Electrician	Oregon	H	8.43 FQ	13.87 AW	19.29 TQ	ORBLS	10/01-12/01
Electrician	Pennsylvania	H	8.30 FQ	11.80 AW	17.61 TQ	PABLS	10/01-12/01
Electrician	Rhode Island	H	8.78 FQ	10.75 AW	14.02 TQ	RIBLS	10/01-12/01
Electrician	South Carolina	H	7.30 FQ	10.80 AW	16.28 TQ	SCBLS	10/01-12/01
Electrician	South Dakota	H	6.80 FQ	8.82 AW	12.10 TQ	SDBLS	10/01-12/01
Electrician	Tennessee	H	7.91 FQ	10.81 AW	14.53 TQ	TNBLS	10/01-12/01
Electrician	Texas	H	7.54 FQ	10.88 AW	15.42 TQ	TXBLS	10/01-12/01
Electrician	Utah	H	7.46 FQ	11.36 AW	16.85 TQ	UTBLS	10/01-12/01
Electrician	Vermont	H	8.49 FQ	10.58 AW	13.25 TQ	VTBLS	10/01-12/01
Electrician	Virginia	H	7.62 FQ	10.97 AW	15.02 TQ	VABLS	10/01-12/01
Electrician	Washington	H	9.27 FQ	14.26 AW	23.59 TQ	WABLS	10/01-12/01
Electrician	West Virginia	H	6.39 FQ	10.23 AW	15.47 TQ	WVBLS	10/01-12/01
Electrician	Wisconsin	H	8.63 FQ	12.01 AW	17.54 TQ	WIBLS	10/01-12/01
Electrician	Wyoming	H	6.92 FQ	10.89 AW	16.24 TQ	WYBLS	10/01-12/01
Electrician	Puerto Rico	H	5.58 FQ	6.83 AW	8.60 TQ	PRBLS	10/01-12/01
Electrician	Virgin Islands	H	7.90 FQ	10.00 AW	12.74 TQ	VIBLS	10/01-12/01
Electrician	Guam	H	6.54 FQ	9.21 AW	11.30 TQ	GUBLS	10/01-12/01
Extraction Worker	Alabama	H	7.09 FQ	11.42 AW	17.59 TQ	ALBLS	10/01-12/01
Extraction Worker	Alaska	H	13.44 FQ	21.50 AW	32.99 TQ	AKBLS	10/01-12/01
Extraction Worker	Arizona	H	8.81 FQ	12.11 AW	16.30 TQ	AZBLS	10/01-12/01
Extraction Worker	Arkansas	H	7.44 FQ	10.50 AW	13.91 TQ	ARBLS	10/01-12/01
Extraction Worker	California	H	7.86 FQ	12.27 AW	17.03 TQ	CABLS	10/01-12/01
Extraction Worker	Colorado	H	9.17 FQ	13.98 AW	20.49 TQ	COBLS	10/01-12/01
Extraction Worker	Connecticut	H	7.63 FQ	10.90 AW	18.82 TQ	CTBLS	10/01-12/01
Extraction Worker	Florida	H	6.96 FQ	9.30 AW	11.59 TQ	FLBLS	10/01-12/01
Extraction Worker	Georgia	H	7.18 FQ	11.38 AW	16.24 TQ	GABLS	10/01-12/01
Extraction Worker	Hawaii	H	12.45 FQ	28.76 AW	41.92 TQ	HIBLS	10/01-12/01
Extraction Worker	Idaho	H	6.32 FQ	9.57 AW	12.35 TQ	IDBLS	10/01-12/01
Extraction Worker	Illinois	H	7.87 FQ	11.75 AW	18.26 TQ	ILBLS	10/01-12/01
Extraction Worker	Indiana	H	7.68 FQ	12.38 AW	18.15 TQ	INBLS	10/01-12/01
Extraction Worker	Iowa	H	9.06 FQ	16.00 AW	26.02 TQ	IABLS	10/01-12/01
Extraction Worker	Kansas	H	7.51 FQ	10.37 AW	15.02 TQ	KSBLS	10/01-12/01

AAW	Average annual wage	AOH	Average offered, high	ASH	Average starting, high	H	Hourly	M	Monthly	S	Special: hourly and annual
AE	Average entry wage	AOL	Average offered, low	ASL	Average starting, low	HI	Highest wage paid	MTC	Median total compensation	TQ	Third quartile wage
AEX	Average experienced wage	APH	Average pay, high range	AW	Average wage paid	HR	High end range	MW	Median wage paid	W	Weekly
AO	Average offered	APL	Average pay, low range	FQ	First quartile wage	LR	Low end range	SQ	Second quartile wage	Y	Yearly

Occupation/Type/Industry	Location	Per	Low	Mid	High	Source	Date
Helper							
Extraction Worker	Kentucky	H	8.86 FQ	13.70 AW	19.21 TQ	KYBLS	10/01-12/01
Extraction Worker	Louisiana	H	7.50 FQ	10.31 AW	13.36 TQ	LABLS	10/01-12/01
Extraction Worker	Maine	H	7.46 FQ	8.70 AW	10.55 TQ	MEBLS	10/01-12/01
Extraction Worker	Maryland	H	8.21 FQ	12.61 AW	16.21 TQ	MDBLS	10/01-12/01
Extraction Worker	Massachusetts	H	12.43 FQ	16.91 AW	21.55 TQ	MABLS	10/01-12/01
Extraction Worker	Michigan	H	8.98 FQ	12.05 AW	15.47 TQ	MIBLS	10/01-12/01
Extraction Worker	Minnesota	H	7.91 FQ	10.83 AW	13.72 TQ	MNBLS	10/01-12/01
Extraction Worker	Mississippi	H	7.87 FQ	12.10 AW	16.20 TQ	MSBLS	10/01-12/01
Extraction Worker	Montana	H	8.16 FQ	11.38 AW	14.99 TQ	MTBLS	10/01-12/01
Extraction Worker	Nebraska	H	6.41 FQ	10.46 AW	15.75 TQ	NEBLS	10/01-12/01
Extraction Worker	Nevada	H	7.63 FQ	12.69 AW	17.40 TQ	NVBLS	10/01-12/01
Extraction Worker	New Jersey	H	9.88 FQ	15.47 AW	21.26 TQ	NJBLS	10/01-12/01
Extraction Worker	New Mexico	H	8.40 FQ	11.78 AW	15.90 TQ	NMBLS	10/01-12/01
Extraction Worker	New York	H	7.63 FQ	12.59 AW	18.96 TQ	NYBLS	10/01-12/01
Extraction Worker	North Carolina	H	6.99 FQ	9.52 AW	11.64 TQ	NCBLS	10/01-12/01
Extraction Worker	North Dakota	H	11.27 FQ	16.62 AW	26.52 TQ	NDBLS	10/01-12/01
Extraction Worker	Ohio	H	9.44 FQ	14.38 AW	25.84 TQ	OHBLS	10/01-12/01
Extraction Worker	Oklahoma	H	9.13 FQ	12.34 AW	16.73 TQ	OKBLS	10/01-12/01
Extraction Worker	Oregon	H	7.79 FQ	11.17 AW	15.60 TQ	ORBLS	10/01-12/01
Extraction Worker	Pennsylvania	H	8.55 FQ	13.92 AW	19.94 TQ	PABLS	10/01-12/01
Extraction Worker	South Carolina	H	6.83 FQ	9.30 AW	11.50 TQ	SCBLS	10/01-12/01
Extraction Worker	South Dakota	H	5.69 FQ	8.71 AW	14.57 TQ	SDBLS	10/01-12/01
Extraction Worker	Tennessee	H	8.78 FQ	11.54 AW	13.80 TQ	TNBLS	10/01-12/01
Extraction Worker	Texas	H	7.43 FQ	11.65 AW	16.24 TQ	TXBLS	10/01-12/01
Extraction Worker	Utah	H	9.69 FQ	14.31 AW	19.48 TQ	UTBLS	10/01-12/01
Extraction Worker	Vermont	H	7.90 FQ	12.01 AW	17.79 TQ	VTBLS	10/01-12/01
Extraction Worker	Virginia	H	8.02 FQ	13.53 AW	19.58 TQ	VABLS	10/01-12/01
Extraction Worker	Washington	H	9.88 FQ	14.48 AW	21.58 TQ	WABLS	10/01-12/01
Extraction Worker	West Virginia	H	7.45 FQ	12.57 AW	20.31 TQ	WVBLS	10/01-12/01
Extraction Worker	Wisconsin	H	8.22 FQ	12.11 AW	15.75 TQ	WIBLS	10/01-12/01
Extraction Worker	Wyoming	H	9.65 FQ	14.55 AW	18.73 TQ	WYBLS	10/01-12/01
Extraction Worker	Puerto Rico	H	5.64 FQ	7.27 AW	10.39 TQ	PRBLS	10/01-12/01
Installation and Repair Worker	Alabama	H	6.87 FQ	10.64 AW	16.08 TQ	ALBLS	10/01-12/01
Installation and Repair Worker	Birmingham MSA, AL	H	6.43 FQ	11.35 AW	16.76 TQ	ALBLS	10/01-12/01
Installation and Repair Worker	Huntsville MSA, AL	H	6.92 FQ	10.19 AW	13.55 TQ	ALBLS	10/01-12/01
Installation and Repair Worker	Mobile MSA, AL	H	7.47 FQ	9.84 AW	13.06 TQ	ALBLS	10/01-12/01
Installation and Repair Worker	Montgomery MSA, AL	H	6.96 FQ	9.27 AW	13.06 TQ	ALBLS	10/01-12/01
Installation and Repair Worker	Alaska	H	7.23 FQ	12.73 AW	21.16 TQ	AKBLS	10/01-12/01
Installation and Repair Worker	Anchorage MSA, AK	H	7.36 FQ	11.21 AW	19.53 TQ	AKBLS	10/01-12/01
Installation and Repair Worker	Arizona	H	6.25 FQ	9.99 AW	15.72 TQ	AZBLS	10/01-12/01
Installation and Repair Worker	Phoenix-Mesa MSA, AZ	H	7.07 FQ	10.52 AW	16.54 TQ	AZBLS	10/01-12/01
Installation and Repair Worker	Tucson MSA, AZ	H	5.67 FQ	8.73 AW	13.78 TQ	AZBLS	10/01-12/01
Installation and Repair Worker	Arkansas	H	5.98 FQ	8.85 AW	12.06 TQ	ARBLS	10/01-12/01
Installation and Repair Worker	Fayetteville-Springdale-Rogers MSA, AR	H	6.30 FQ	9.15 AW	11.39 TQ	ARBLS	10/01-12/01
Installation and Repair Worker	Fort Smith MSA, AR-OK	H	6.87 FQ	9.54 AW	15.53 TQ	ARBLS	10/01-12/01
Installation and Repair Worker	Little Rock-North Little Rock MSA, AR	H	6.27 FQ	8.97 AW	12.60 TQ	ARBLS	10/01-12/01
Installation and Repair Worker	California	H	6.77 FQ	11.57 AW	19.17 TQ	CABLS	10/01-12/01
Installation and Repair Worker	Bakersfield MSA, CA	H	6.82 FQ	10.48 AW	18.95 TQ	CABLS	10/01-12/01
Installation and Repair Worker	Chico-Paradise MSA, CA	H	7.57 FQ	10.89 AW	16.34 TQ	CABLS	10/01-12/01
Installation and Repair Worker	Fresno MSA, CA	H	6.39 FQ	10.39 AW	18.24 TQ	CABLS	10/01-12/01
Installation and Repair Worker	Los Angeles-Long Beach PMSA, CA	H	6.58 FQ	12.42 AW	23.84 TQ	CABLS	10/01-12/01
Installation and Repair Worker	Merced MSA, CA	H	6.50 FQ	10.84 AW	16.65 TQ	CABLS	10/01-12/01
Installation and Repair Worker	Modesto MSA, CA	H	7.00 FQ	11.77 AW	16.71 TQ	CABLS	10/01-12/01
Installation and Repair Worker	Oakland PMSA, CA	H	8.50 FQ	12.80 AW	18.54 TQ	CABLS	10/01-12/01
Installation and Repair Worker	Orange County PMSA, CA	H	6.55 FQ	11.00 AW	17.24 TQ	CABLS	10/01-12/01
Installation and Repair Worker	Redding MSA, CA	H	7.16 FQ	10.99 AW	15.93 TQ	CABLS	10/01-12/01
Installation and Repair Worker	Riverside-San Bernardino PMSA, CA	H	7.00 FQ	10.08 AW	14.35 TQ	CABLS	10/01-12/01
Installation and Repair Worker	Sacramento PMSA, CA	H	7.04 FQ	10.95 AW	15.15 TQ	CABLS	10/01-12/01
Installation and Repair Worker	Salinas MSA, CA	H	7.08 FQ	12.01 AW	17.54 TQ	CABLS	10/01-12/01
Installation and Repair Worker	San Diego MSA, CA	H	6.85 FQ	10.50 AW	16.16 TQ	CABLS	10/01-12/01
Installation and Repair Worker	San Francisco PMSA, CA	H	7.94 FQ	13.32 AW	21.18 TQ	CABLS	10/01-12/01
Installation and Repair Worker	San Jose PMSA, CA	H	7.11 FQ	11.25 AW	17.76 TQ	CABLS	10/01-12/01
Installation and Repair Worker	San Luis Obispo-Atascadero-Paso Robles MSA, CA	H	7.15 FQ	10.34 AW	15.59 TQ	CABLS	10/01-12/01
Installation and Repair Worker	Santa Barbara-Santa Maria-Lompoc MSA, CA	H	7.61 FQ	11.67 AW	16.60 TQ	CABLS	10/01-12/01
Installation and Repair Worker	Santa Rosa PMSA, CA	H	7.09 FQ	10.57 AW	14.74 TQ	CABLS	10/01-12/01

AAW	Average annual wage	**AOH**	Average offered, high	**ASH**	Average starting, high	**H**	Hourly	**M**	Monthly	**S**	Special: hourly and annual
AE	Average entry wage	**AOL**	Average offered, low	**ASL**	Average starting, low	**HI**	Highest wage paid	**MTC**	Median total compensation	**TQ**	Third quartile wage
AEX	Average experienced wage	**APH**	Average pay, high range	**AW**	Average wage paid	**HR**	High end range	**MW**	Median wage paid	**W**	Weekly
AO	Average offered	**APL**	Average pay, low range	**FQ**	First quartile wage	**LR**	Low end range	**SQ**	Second quartile wage	**Y**	Yearly

Occupation/Type/Industry	Location	Per	Low	Mid	High	Source	Date
Helper							
Installation and Repair Worker	Stockton-Lodi MSA, CA	H	6.78 FQ	10.75 AW	16.42 TQ	CABLS	10/01-12/01
Installation and Repair Worker	Vallejo-Fairfield-Napa PMSA, CA	H	9.04 FQ	15.97 AW	25.33 TQ	CABLS	10/01-12/01
Installation and Repair Worker	Ventura PMSA, CA	H	7.20 FQ	10.16 AW	15.15 TQ	CABLS	10/01-12/01
Installation and Repair Worker	Visalia-Tulare-Porterville MSA, CA	H	7.06 FQ	10.45 AW	14.02 TQ	CABLS	10/01-12/01
Installation and Repair Worker	Colorado	H	7.52 FQ	12.18 AW	18.90 TQ	COBLS	10/01-12/01
Installation and Repair Worker	Boulder-Longmont PMSA, CO	H	7.46 FQ	12.55 AW	19.73 TQ	COBLS	10/01-12/01
Installation and Repair Worker	Colorado Springs MSA, CO	H	6.87 FQ	12.31 AW	20.11 TQ	COBLS	10/01-12/01
Installation and Repair Worker	Denver PMSA, CO	H	8.44 FQ	12.75 AW	19.09 TQ	COBLS	10/01-12/01
Installation and Repair Worker	Fort Collins-Loveland MSA, CO	H	7.00 FQ	12.47 AW	19.86 TQ	COBLS	10/01-12/01
Installation and Repair Worker	Greeley PMSA, CO	H	7.35 FQ	9.68 AW	15.97 TQ	COBLS	10/01-12/01
Installation and Repair Worker	Connecticut	H	8.23 FQ	12.25 AW	17.68 TQ	CTBLS	10/01-12/01
Installation and Repair Worker	Bridgeport PMSA, CT	H	7.56 FQ	12.34 AW	21.19 TQ	CTBLS	10/01-12/01
Installation and Repair Worker	Danbury PMSA, CT	H	8.86 FQ	13.44 AW	20.90 TQ	CTBLS	10/01-12/01
Installation and Repair Worker	Hartford MSA, CT	H	7.81 FQ	11.45 AW	15.47 TQ	CTBLS	10/01-12/01
Installation and Repair Worker	New Haven-Meriden PMSA, CT	H	7.67 FQ	12.60 AW	17.65 TQ	CTBLS	10/01-12/01
Installation and Repair Worker	New London-Norwich MSA, CT-RI	H	8.96 FQ	13.37 AW	19.57 TQ	CTBLS	10/01-12/01
Installation and Repair Worker	Stamford-Norwalk PMSA, CT	H	8.89 FQ	12.10 AW	18.09 TQ	CTBLS	10/01-12/01
Installation and Repair Worker	Waterbury PMSA, CT	H	9.33 FQ	12.63 AW	19.60 TQ	CTBLS	10/01-12/01
Installation and Repair Worker	Delaware	H	7.26 FQ	11.75 AW	18.11 TQ	DEBLS	10/01-12/01
Installation and Repair Worker	Wilmington-Newark PMSA, DE-MD	H	7.79 FQ	11.81 AW	17.44 TQ	DEBLS	10/01-12/01
Installation and Repair Worker	District of Columbia	H	8.16 FQ	15.83 AW	22.53 TQ	DCBLS	10/01-12/01
Installation and Repair Worker	Washington PMSA, DC-MD-VA-WV	H	6.76 FQ	11.02 AW	16.16 TQ	DCBLS	10/01-12/01
Installation and Repair Worker	Florida	H	6.70 FQ	9.66 AW	13.99 TQ	FLBLS	10/01-12/01
Installation and Repair Worker	Daytona Beach MSA, FL	H	7.17 FQ	9.40 AW	12.22 TQ	FLBLS	10/01-12/01
Installation and Repair Worker	Fort Lauderdale PMSA, FL	H	6.38 FQ	10.56 AW	16.29 TQ	FLBLS	10/01-12/01
Installation and Repair Worker	Fort Myers-Cape Coral MSA, FL	H	7.12 FQ	9.50 AW	12.54 TQ	FLBLS	10/01-12/01
Installation and Repair Worker	Fort Pierce-Port St. Lucie MSA, FL	H	7.19 FQ	8.83 AW	11.34 TQ	FLBLS	10/01-12/01
Installation and Repair Worker	Fort Walton Beach MSA, FL	H	6.25 FQ	8.09 AW	10.78 TQ	FLBLS	10/01-12/01
Installation and Repair Worker	Gainesville MSA, FL	H	7.49 FQ	9.78 AW	12.83 TQ	FLBLS	10/01-12/01
Installation and Repair Worker	Jacksonville MSA, FL	H	6.42 FQ	9.88 AW	14.10 TQ	FLBLS	10/01-12/01
Installation and Repair Worker	Lakeland-Winter Haven MSA, FL	H	6.08 FQ	9.07 AW	13.76 TQ	FLBLS	10/01-12/01
Installation and Repair Worker	Melbourne-Titusville-Palm Bay MSA, FL	H	7.10 FQ	10.09 AW	14.25 TQ	FLBLS	10/01-12/01
Installation and Repair Worker	Miami PMSA, FL	H	6.94 FQ	9.05 AW	12.73 TQ	FLBLS	10/01-12/01
Installation and Repair Worker	Naples MSA, FL	H	7.88 FQ	10.95 AW	14.12 TQ	FLBLS	10/01-12/01
Installation and Repair Worker	Ocala MSA, FL	H	6.74 FQ	9.27 AW	13.08 TQ	FLBLS	10/01-12/01
Installation and Repair Worker	Orlando MSA, FL	H	7.51 FQ	11.67 AW	16.67 TQ	FLBLS	10/01-12/01
Installation and Repair Worker	Pensacola MSA, FL	H	5.60 FQ	7.85 AW	11.05 TQ	FLBLS	10/01-12/01
Installation and Repair Worker	Sarasota-Bradenton MSA, FL	H	6.69 FQ	10.06 AW	14.43 TQ	FLBLS	10/01-12/01
Installation and Repair Worker	Tallahassee MSA, FL	H	6.94 FQ	9.68 AW	13.72 TQ	FLBLS	10/01-12/01
Installation and Repair Worker	Tampa-St. Petersburg-Clearwater MSA, FL	H	6.02 FQ	8.99 AW	12.83 TQ	FLBLS	10/01-12/01
Installation and Repair Worker	West Palm Beach-Boca Raton MSA, FL	H	7.55 FQ	9.30 AW	10.63 TQ	FLBLS	10/01-12/01
Installation and Repair Worker	Georgia	H	6.80 FQ	10.47 AW	15.86 TQ	GABLS	10/01-12/01
Installation and Repair Worker	Atlanta MSA, GA	H	7.19 FQ	10.99 AW	16.63 TQ	GABLS	10/01-12/01
Installation and Repair Worker	Augusta-Aiken MSA, GA-SC	H	6.74 FQ	11.88 AW	23.36 TQ	GABLS	10/01-12/01
Installation and Repair Worker	Columbus MSA, GA-AL	H	5.94 FQ	10.27 AW	18.19 TQ	GABLS	10/01-12/01
Installation and Repair Worker	Macon MSA, GA	H	6.03 FQ	9.64 AW	15.91 TQ	GABLS	10/01-12/01
Installation and Repair Worker	Savannah MSA, GA	H	6.89 FQ	10.47 AW	15.43 TQ	GABLS	10/01-12/01
Installation and Repair Worker	Hawaii	H	7.02 FQ	10.60 AW	16.12 TQ	HIBLS	10/01-12/01
Installation and Repair Worker	Honolulu MSA, HI	H	7.06 FQ	10.13 AW	16.47 TQ	HIBLS	10/01-12/01
Installation and Repair Worker	Idaho	H	7.25 FQ	10.91 AW	15.55 TQ	IDBLS	10/01-12/01
Installation and Repair Worker	Boise City MSA, ID	H	7.83 FQ	10.94 AW	14.31 TQ	IDBLS	10/01-12/01
Installation and Repair Worker	Illinois	H	6.34 FQ	11.77 AW	18.47 TQ	ILBLS	10/01-12/01
Installation and Repair Worker	Champaign-Urbana MSA, IL	H	6.79 FQ	10.63 AW	16.29 TQ	ILBLS	10/01-12/01
Installation and Repair Worker	Chicago PMSA, IL	H	6.25 FQ	11.93 AW	19.50 TQ	ILBLS	10/01-12/01
Installation and Repair Worker	Peoria-Pekin MSA, IL	H	8.33 FQ	12.73 AW	19.13 TQ	ILBLS	10/01-12/01
Installation and Repair Worker	Rockford MSA, IL	H	5.89 FQ	11.01 AW	18.29 TQ	ILBLS	10/01-12/01
Installation and Repair Worker	Springfield MSA, IL	H	8.17 FQ	10.68 AW	13.34 TQ	ILBLS	10/01-12/01
Installation and Repair Worker	Indiana	H	6.77 FQ	11.43 AW	18.43 TQ	INBLS	10/01-12/01

AAW	Average annual wage	**AOH**	Average offered, high	**ASH**	Average starting, high	**H**	Hourly	**M**	Monthly	**S**	Special: hourly and annual
AE	Average entry wage	**AOL**	Average offered, low	**ASL**	Average starting, low	**HI**	Highest wage paid	**MTC**	Median total compensation	**TQ**	Third quartile wage
AEX	Average experienced wage	**APH**	Average pay, high range	**AW**	Average wage paid	**HR**	High end range	**MW**	Median wage paid	**W**	Weekly
AO	Average offered	**APL**	Average pay, low range	**FQ**	First quartile wage	**LR**	Low end range	**SQ**	Second quartile wage	**Y**	Yearly

Occupation/Type/Industry	Location	Per	Low	Mid	High	Source	Date
Helper							
Installation and Repair Worker	Elkhart-Goshen MSA, IN	H	6.47 FQ	13.73 AW	21.04 TQ	INBLS	10/01-12/01
Installation and Repair Worker	Evansville-Henderson MSA, IN-KY	H	6.13 FQ	12.02 AW	19.54 TQ	INBLS	10/01-12/01
Installation and Repair Worker	Fort Wayne MSA, IN	H	7.63 FQ	12.01 AW	16.42 TQ	INBLS	10/01-12/01
Installation and Repair Worker	Gary PMSA, IN	H	5.89 FQ	11.14 AW	20.32 TQ	INBLS	10/01-12/01
Installation and Repair Worker	Indianapolis MSA, IN	H	7.15 FQ	11.59 AW	17.09 TQ	INBLS	10/01-12/01
Installation and Repair Worker	Lafayette MSA, IN	H	6.93 FQ	9.63 AW	14.46 TQ	INBLS	10/01-12/01
Installation and Repair Worker	South Bend MSA, IN	H	6.85 FQ	9.84 AW	15.95 TQ	INBLS	10/01-12/01
Installation and Repair Worker	Iowa	H	7.13 FQ	12.00 AW	17.52 TQ	IABLS	10/01-12/01
Installation and Repair Worker	Cedar Rapids MSA, IA	H	7.63 FQ	13.27 AW	21.17 TQ	IABLS	10/01-12/01
Installation and Repair Worker	Davenport-Moline-Rock Island MSA, IA-IL	H	6.41 FQ	11.75 AW	17.90 TQ	IABLS	10/01-12/01
Installation and Repair Worker	Kansas	H	7.38 FQ	11.10 AW	15.88 TQ	KSBLS	10/01-12/01
Installation and Repair Worker	Topeka MSA, KS	H	7.79 FQ	11.13 AW	13.84 TQ	KSBLS	10/01-12/01
Installation and Repair Worker	Wichita MSA, KS	H	7.74 FQ	11.35 AW	14.14 TQ	KSBLS	10/01-12/01
Installation and Repair Worker	Kentucky	H	6.61 FQ	11.27 AW	18.61 TQ	KYBLS	10/01-12/01
Installation and Repair Worker	Lexington MSA, KY	H	6.70 FQ	11.25 AW	15.74 TQ	KYBLS	10/01-12/01
Installation and Repair Worker	Louisville MSA, KY-IN	H	6.58 FQ	9.92 AW	16.38 TQ	KYBLS	10/01-12/01
Installation and Repair Worker	Louisiana	H	6.52 FQ	9.92 AW	14.13 TQ	LABLS	10/01-12/01
Installation and Repair Worker	Baton Rouge MSA, LA	H	6.67 FQ	9.60 AW	13.20 TQ	LABLS	10/01-12/01
Installation and Repair Worker	Houma MSA, LA	H	6.97 FQ	10.29 AW	14.52 TQ	LABLS	10/01-12/01
Installation and Repair Worker	Lafayette MSA, LA	H	6.78 FQ	9.82 AW	13.41 TQ	LABLS	10/01-12/01
Installation and Repair Worker	Lake Charles MSA, LA	H	7.22 FQ	9.92 AW	13.46 TQ	LABLS	10/01-12/01
Installation and Repair Worker	New Orleans MSA, LA	H	6.31 FQ	10.50 AW	15.76 TQ	LABLS	10/01-12/01
Installation and Repair Worker	Shreveport-Bossier City MSA, LA	H	6.54 FQ	9.05 AW	12.86 TQ	LABLS	10/01-12/01
Installation and Repair Worker	Maine	H	6.88 FQ	12.51 AW	18.72 TQ	MEBLS	10/01-12/01
Installation and Repair Worker	Portland MSA, ME	H	6.28 FQ	12.18 AW	17.65 TQ	MEBLS	10/01-12/01
Installation and Repair Worker	Maryland	H	7.38 FQ	10.68 AW	14.69 TQ	MDBLS	10/01-12/01
Installation and Repair Worker	Baltimore PMSA, MD	H	7.54 FQ	10.86 AW	15.20 TQ	MDBLS	10/01-12/01
Installation and Repair Worker	Massachusetts	H	7.68 FQ	12.73 AW	18.74 TQ	MABLS	10/01-12/01
Installation and Repair Worker	Boston PMSA, MA-NH	H	7.48 FQ	12.30 AW	18.31 TQ	MABLS	10/01-12/01
Installation and Repair Worker	Brockton PMSA, MA	H	7.67 FQ	12.47 AW	17.91 TQ	MABLS	10/01-12/01
Installation and Repair Worker	Lawrence PMSA, MA-NH	H	8.06 FQ	13.25 AW	20.78 TQ	MABLS	10/01-12/01
Installation and Repair Worker	Lowell PMSA, MA-NH	H	7.69 FQ	14.89 AW	22.19 TQ	MABLS	10/01-12/01
Installation and Repair Worker	New Bedford PMSA, MA	H	7.84 FQ	12.46 AW	20.52 TQ	MABLS	10/01-12/01
Installation and Repair Worker	Springfield MSA, MA	H	7.58 FQ	12.55 AW	18.52 TQ	MABLS	10/01-12/01
Installation and Repair Worker	Worcester PMSA, MA-CT	H	8.14 FQ	13.57 AW	17.40 TQ	MABLS	10/01-12/01
Installation and Repair Worker	Michigan	H	7.60 FQ	12.41 AW	18.06 TQ	MIBLS	10/01-12/01
Installation and Repair Worker	Ann Arbor PMSA, MI	H	7.98 FQ	11.76 AW	17.09 TQ	MIBLS	10/01-12/01
Installation and Repair Worker	Detroit PMSA, MI	H	8.00 FQ	12.79 AW	17.76 TQ	MIBLS	10/01-12/01
Installation and Repair Worker	Flint PMSA, MI	H	7.76 FQ	12.95 AW	19.12 TQ	MIBLS	10/01-12/01
Installation and Repair Worker	Grand Rapids-Muskegon-Holland MSA, MI	H	7.54 FQ	12.43 AW	18.57 TQ	MIBLS	10/01-12/01
Installation and Repair Worker	Kalamazoo-Battle Creek MSA, MI	H	8.25 FQ	13.88 AW	20.84 TQ	MIBLS	10/01-12/01
Installation and Repair Worker	Lansing-East Lansing MSA, MI	H	8.58 FQ	12.75 AW	17.60 TQ	MIBLS	10/01-12/01
Installation and Repair Worker	Saginaw-Bay City-Midland MSA, MI	H	6.54 FQ	11.05 AW	17.26 TQ	MIBLS	10/01-12/01
Installation and Repair Worker	Minnesota	H	7.15 FQ	12.22 AW	19.05 TQ	MNBLS	10/01-12/01
Installation and Repair Worker	Duluth-Superior MSA, MN-WI	H	7.35 FQ	15.11 AW	21.99 TQ	MNBLS	10/01-12/01
Installation and Repair Worker	Minneapolis-St. Paul MSA, MN-WI	H	7.21 FQ	12.12 AW	19.37 TQ	MNBLS	10/01-12/01
Installation and Repair Worker	St. Cloud MSA, MN	H	6.34 FQ	11.65 AW	20.29 TQ	MNBLS	10/01-12/01
Installation and Repair Worker	Mississippi	H	6.63 FQ	10.71 AW	16.51 TQ	MSBLS	10/01-12/01
Installation and Repair Worker	Jackson MSA, MS	H	6.97 FQ	9.33 AW	11.62 TQ	MSBLS	10/01-12/01
Installation and Repair Worker	Missouri	H	6.91 FQ	11.69 AW	18.24 TQ	MOBLS	10/01-12/01
Installation and Repair Worker	Kansas City MSA, MO-KS	H	7.63 FQ	12.48 AW	19.99 TQ	MOBLS	10/01-12/01
Installation and Repair Worker	St. Louis MSA, MO-IL	H	7.07 FQ	11.75 AW	17.51 TQ	MOBLS	10/01-12/01
Installation and Repair Worker	Springfield MSA, MO	H	6.51 FQ	10.77 AW	16.14 TQ	MOBLS	10/01-12/01
Installation and Repair Worker	Montana	H	6.62 FQ	12.00 AW	22.00 TQ	MTBLS	10/01-12/01
Installation and Repair Worker	Billings MSA, MT	H	5.97 FQ	10.60 AW	21.24 TQ	MTBLS	10/01-12/01
Installation and Repair Worker	Nebraska	H	6.30 FQ	11.01 AW	16.45 TQ	NEBLS	10/01-12/01
Installation and Repair Worker	Lincoln MSA, NE	H	7.45 FQ	11.47 AW	17.26 TQ	NEBLS	10/01-12/01
Installation and Repair Worker	Omaha MSA, NE-IA	H	8.51 FQ	12.62 AW	18.22 TQ	NEBLS	10/01-12/01
Installation and Repair Worker	Nevada	H	7.19 FQ	12.29 AW	19.28 TQ	NVBLS	10/01-12/01
Installation and Repair Worker	Las Vegas MSA, NV-AZ	H	6.83 FQ	11.26 AW	17.59 TQ	NVBLS	10/01-12/01
Installation and Repair Worker	Reno MSA, NV	H	8.53 FQ	14.12 AW	19.97 TQ	NVBLS	10/01-12/01
Installation and Repair Worker	New Hampshire	H	7.78 FQ	11.79 AW	16.76 TQ	NHBLS	10/01-12/01
Installation and Repair Worker	Manchester PMSA, NH	H	7.67 FQ	12.34 AW	18.13 TQ	NHBLS	10/01-12/01

AAW	Average annual wage	**AOH**	Average offered, high	**ASH**	Average starting, high	**H**	Hourly	**M**	Monthly	**S**	Special: hourly and annual
AE	Average entry wage	**AOL**	Average offered, low	**ASL**	Average starting, low	**HI**	Highest wage paid	**MTC**	Median total compensation	**TQ**	Third quartile wage
AEX	Average experienced wage	**APH**	Average pay, high range	**AW**	Average wage paid	**HR**	High end range	**MW**	Median wage paid	**W**	Weekly
AO	Average offered	**APL**	Average pay, low range	**FQ**	First quartile wage	**LR**	Low end range	**SQ**	Second quartile wage	**Y**	Yearly

Occupation/Type/Industry	Location	Per	Low	Mid	High	Source	Date
Helper							
Installation and Repair Worker	Portsmouth-Rochester PMSA, NH-ME	H	7.72 FQ	11.13 AW	15.99 TQ	NHBLS	10/01-12/01
Installation and Repair Worker	New Jersey	H	6.28 FQ	11.02 AW	17.49 TQ	NJBLS	10/01-12/01
Installation and Repair Worker	Atlantic-Cape May PMSA, NJ	H	6.00 FQ	11.10 AW	18.97 TQ	NJBLS	10/01-12/01
Installation and Repair Worker	Bergen-Passaic PMSA, NJ	H	7.16 FQ	10.86 AW	15.27 TQ	NJBLS	10/01-12/01
Installation and Repair Worker	Jersey City PMSA, NJ	H	7.74 FQ	12.44 AW	19.38 TQ	NJBLS	10/01-12/01
Installation and Repair Worker	Middlesex-Somerset-Hunterdon PMSA, NJ	H	5.66 FQ	11.36 AW	22.07 TQ	NJBLS	10/01-12/01
Installation and Repair Worker	Monmouth-Ocean PMSA, NJ	H	5.76 FQ	10.00 AW	17.89 TQ	NJBLS	10/01-12/01
Installation and Repair Worker	Newark PMSA, NJ	H	7.08 FQ	10.75 AW	15.74 TQ	NJBLS	10/01-12/01
Installation and Repair Worker	Trenton PMSA, NJ	H	8.21 FQ	13.72 AW	21.09 TQ	NJBLS	10/01-12/01
Installation and Repair Worker	New Mexico	H	6.46 FQ	11.04 AW	17.23 TQ	NMBLS	10/01-12/01
Installation and Repair Worker	Albuquerque MSA, NM	H	7.93 FQ	11.81 AW	17.04 TQ	NMBLS	10/01-12/01
Installation and Repair Worker	Las Cruces MSA, NM	H	6.20 FQ	9.74 AW	15.57 TQ	NMBLS	10/01-12/01
Installation and Repair Worker	New York	H	7.00 FQ	12.97 AW	20.12 TQ	NYBLS	10/01-12/01
Installation and Repair Worker	Albany-Schenectady-Troy MSA, NY	H	8.60 FQ	11.78 AW	16.14 TQ	NYBLS	10/01-12/01
Installation and Repair Worker	Binghamton MSA, NY	H	7.75 FQ	11.95 AW	15.77 TQ	NYBLS	10/01-12/01
Installation and Repair Worker	Buffalo-Niagara Falls MSA, NY	H	6.50 FQ	13.52 AW	21.60 TQ	NYBLS	10/01-12/01
Installation and Repair Worker	Dutchess County PMSA, NY	H	7.01 FQ	12.41 AW	19.76 TQ	NYBLS	10/01-12/01
Installation and Repair Worker	Nassau-Suffolk PMSA, NY	H	6.46 FQ	11.27 AW	17.81 TQ	NYBLS	10/01-12/01
Installation and Repair Worker	New York PMSA, NY	H	7.97 FQ	14.48 AW	21.37 TQ	NYBLS	10/01-12/01
Installation and Repair Worker	Newburgh PMSA, NY-PA	H	6.81 FQ	11.86 AW	16.67 TQ	NYBLS	10/01-12/01
Installation and Repair Worker	Rochester MSA, NY	H	7.09 FQ	11.95 AW	17.45 TQ	NYBLS	10/01-12/01
Installation and Repair Worker	Syracuse MSA, NY	H	7.84 FQ	12.92 AW	17.47 TQ	NYBLS	10/01-12/01
Installation and Repair Worker	Utica-Rome MSA, NY	H	7.12 FQ	11.59 AW	16.32 TQ	NYBLS	10/01-12/01
Installation and Repair Worker	North Carolina	H	7.18 FQ	10.86 AW	15.68 TQ	NCBLS	10/01-12/01
Installation and Repair Worker	Asheville MSA, NC	H	7.36 FQ	11.50 AW	17.40 TQ	NCBLS	10/01-12/01
Installation and Repair Worker	Charlotte-Gastonia-Rock Hill MSA, NC-SC	H	6.57 FQ	10.89 AW	15.98 TQ	NCBLS	10/01-12/01
Installation and Repair Worker	Fayetteville MSA, NC	H	7.42 FQ	10.07 AW	13.95 TQ	NCBLS	10/01-12/01
Installation and Repair Worker	Greensboro-Winston-Salem-High Point MSA, NC	H	7.62 FQ	11.63 AW	16.83 TQ	NCBLS	10/01-12/01
Installation and Repair Worker	Hickory-Morganton-Lenoir MSA, NC	H	7.63 FQ	10.41 AW	13.68 TQ	NCBLS	10/01-12/01
Installation and Repair Worker	Raleigh-Durham-Chapel Hill MSA, NC	H	8.02 FQ	11.17 AW	15.83 TQ	NCBLS	10/01-12/01
Installation and Repair Worker	Wilmington MSA, NC	H	8.17 FQ	12.27 AW	18.76 TQ	NCBLS	10/01-12/01
Installation and Repair Worker	North Dakota	H	6.30 FQ	10.28 AW	16.18 TQ	NDBLS	10/01-12/01
Installation and Repair Worker	Fargo-Moorhead MSA, ND-MN	H	9.23 FQ	12.27 AW	17.39 TQ	NDBLS	10/01-12/01
Installation and Repair Worker	Ohio	H	7.26 FQ	11.52 AW	17.47 TQ	OHBLS	10/01-12/01
Installation and Repair Worker	Akron PMSA, OH	H	6.17 FQ	10.43 AW	16.01 TQ	OHBLS	10/01-12/01
Installation and Repair Worker	Canton-Massillon MSA, OH	H	6.82 FQ	10.72 AW	16.55 TQ	OHBLS	10/01-12/01
Installation and Repair Worker	Cincinnati PMSA, OH-KY-IN	H	7.33 FQ	11.40 AW	17.15 TQ	OHBLS	10/01-12/01
Installation and Repair Worker	Cleveland-Lorain-Elyria PMSA, OH	H	7.65 FQ	12.79 AW	19.40 TQ	OHBLS	10/01-12/01
Installation and Repair Worker	Columbus MSA, OH	H	7.51 FQ	11.20 AW	16.58 TQ	OHBLS	10/01-12/01
Installation and Repair Worker	Dayton-Springfield MSA, OH	H	7.23 FQ	12.44 AW	20.03 TQ	OHBLS	10/01-12/01
Installation and Repair Worker	Hamilton-Middletown PMSA, OH	H	6.84 FQ	15.69 AW	21.56 TQ	OHBLS	10/01-12/01
Installation and Repair Worker	Mansfield MSA, OH	H	7.01 FQ	10.50 AW	14.65 TQ	OHBLS	10/01-12/01
Installation and Repair Worker	Toledo MSA, OH	H	7.29 FQ	10.14 AW	15.40 TQ	OHBLS	10/01-12/01
Installation and Repair Worker	Youngstown-Warren MSA, OH	H	6.78 FQ	11.27 AW	17.28 TQ	OHBLS	10/01-12/01
Installation and Repair Worker	Oklahoma	H	6.15 FQ	10.74 AW	17.96 TQ	OKBLS	10/01-12/01
Installation and Repair Worker	Oklahoma City MSA, OK	H	6.09 FQ	11.06 AW	19.55 TQ	OKBLS	10/01-12/01
Installation and Repair Worker	Tulsa MSA, OK	H	7.01 FQ	11.88 AW	22.36 TQ	OKBLS	10/01-12/01
Installation and Repair Worker	Oregon	H	7.28 FQ	11.10 AW	16.40 TQ	ORBLS	10/01-12/01
Installation and Repair Worker	Eugene-Springfield MSA, OR	H	7.61 FQ	10.37 AW	15.42 TQ	ORBLS	10/01-12/01
Installation and Repair Worker	Medford-Ashland MSA, OR	H	7.28 FQ	10.94 AW	16.29 TQ	ORBLS	10/01-12/01
Installation and Repair Worker	Portland-Vancouver PMSA, OR-WA	H	8.58 FQ	11.75 AW	16.88 TQ	ORBLS	10/01-12/01
Installation and Repair Worker	Salem PMSA, OR	H	7.35 FQ	10.33 AW	14.24 TQ	ORBLS	10/01-12/01
Installation and Repair Worker	Pennsylvania	H	6.75 FQ	12.46 AW	20.83 TQ	PABLS	10/01-12/01
Installation and Repair Worker	Allentown-Bethlehem-Easton MSA, PA	H	7.84 FQ	12.85 AW	20.59 TQ	PABLS	10/01-12/01
Installation and Repair Worker	Erie MSA, PA	H	7.09 FQ	12.04 AW	19.09 TQ	PABLS	10/01-12/01
Installation and Repair Worker	Harrisburg-Lebanon-Carlisle MSA, PA	H	5.75 FQ	10.10 AW	16.23 TQ	PABLS	10/01-12/01
Installation and Repair Worker	Johnstown MSA, PA	H	6.02 FQ	10.24 AW	16.15 TQ	PABLS	10/01-12/01

AAW	Average annual wage	AOH	Average offered, high	ASH	Average starting, high	H	Hourly	M	Monthly	S	Special: hourly and annual
AE	Average entry wage	AOL	Average offered, low	ASL	Average starting, low	HI	Highest wage paid	MTC	Median total compensation	TQ	Third quartile wage
AEX	Average experienced wage	APH	Average pay, high range	AW	Average wage paid	HR	High end range	MW	Median wage paid	W	Weekly
AO	Average offered	APL	Average pay, low range	FQ	First quartile wage	LR	Low end range	SQ	Second quartile wage	Y	Yearly

Occupation/Type/Industry	Location	Per	Low	Mid	High	Source	Date
Helper							
Installation and Repair Worker	Lancaster MSA, PA	H	6.10 FQ	10.82 AW	17.64 TQ	PABLS	10/01-12/01
Installation and Repair Worker	Philadelphia PMSA, PA-NJ	H	7.18 FQ	13.16 AW	23.14 TQ	PABLS	10/01-12/01
Installation and Repair Worker	Pittsburgh MSA, PA	H	7.24 FQ	12.18 AW	18.28 TQ	PABLS	10/01-12/01
Installation and Repair Worker	Reading MSA, PA	H	6.16 FQ	10.64 AW	17.52 TQ	PABLS	10/01-12/01
Installation and Repair Worker	Scranton-Wilkes-Barre-Hazleton MSA, PA	H	8.43 FQ	13.93 AW	20.77 TQ	PABLS	10/01-12/01
Installation and Repair Worker	York MSA, PA	H	9.17 FQ	15.63 AW	24.28 TQ	PABLS	10/01-12/01
Installation and Repair Worker	Rhode Island	H	7.39 FQ	11.79 AW	18.96 TQ	RIBLS	10/01-12/01
Installation and Repair Worker	Providence-Fall River-Warwick MSA, RI-MA	H	7.40 FQ	11.63 AW	18.70 TQ	RIBLS	10/01-12/01
Installation and Repair Worker	South Carolina	H	7.21 FQ	10.29 AW	14.32 TQ	SCBLS	10/01-12/01
Installation and Repair Worker	Charleston-North Charleston MSA, SC	H	7.14 FQ	10.45 AW	14.94 TQ	SCBLS	10/01-12/01
Installation and Repair Worker	Columbia MSA, SC	H	7.60 FQ	10.47 AW	13.79 TQ	SCBLS	10/01-12/01
Installation and Repair Worker	Greenville-Spartanburg-Anderson MSA, SC	H	7.71 FQ	9.87 AW	11.61 TQ	SCBLS	10/01-12/01
Installation and Repair Worker	Myrtle Beach MSA, SC	H	6.75 FQ	11.28 AW	18.91 TQ	SCBLS	10/01-12/01
Installation and Repair Worker	South Dakota	H	6.05 FQ	8.29 AW	10.97 TQ	SDBLS	10/01-12/01
Installation and Repair Worker	Sioux Falls MSA, SD	H	6.26 FQ	8.63 AW	10.96 TQ	SDBLS	10/01-12/01
Installation and Repair Worker	Tennessee	H	7.15 FQ	11.47 AW	17.00 TQ	TNBLS	10/01-12/01
Installation and Repair Worker	Chattanooga MSA, TN-GA	H	6.08 FQ	9.85 AW	14.47 TQ	TNBLS	10/01-12/01
Installation and Repair Worker	Clarksville-Hopkinsville MSA, TN-KY	H	6.49 FQ	10.31 AW	15.86 TQ	TNBLS	10/01-12/01
Installation and Repair Worker	Johnson City-Kingsport-Bristol MSA, TN-VA	H	6.40 FQ	9.02 AW	12.47 TQ	TNBLS	10/01-12/01
Installation and Repair Worker	Knoxville MSA, TN	H	7.88 FQ	11.08 AW	15.08 TQ	TNBLS	10/01-12/01
Installation and Repair Worker	Memphis MSA, TN-AR-MS	H	7.51 FQ	11.55 AW	16.96 TQ	TNBLS	10/01-12/01
Installation and Repair Worker	Nashville MSA, TN	H	7.79 FQ	12.30 AW	17.59 TQ	TNBLS	10/01-12/01
Installation and Repair Worker	Texas	H	6.25 FQ	9.93 AW	14.94 TQ	TXBLS	10/01-12/01
Installation and Repair Worker	Amarillo MSA, TX	H	7.86 FQ	9.68 AW	11.06 TQ	TXBLS	10/01-12/01
Installation and Repair Worker	Austin-San Marcos MSA, TX	H	5.89 FQ	9.85 AW	14.56 TQ	TXBLS	10/01-12/01
Installation and Repair Worker	Beaumont-Port Arthur MSA, TX	H	6.06 FQ	9.48 AW	13.91 TQ	TXBLS	10/01-12/01
Installation and Repair Worker	Brazoria PMSA, TX	H	6.18 FQ	9.92 AW	14.04 TQ	TXBLS	10/01-12/01
Installation and Repair Worker	Brownsville-Harlingen-San Benito MSA, TX	H	5.68 FQ	7.24 AW	9.54 TQ	TXBLS	10/01-12/01
Installation and Repair Worker	Corpus Christi MSA, TX	H	5.93 FQ	8.98 AW	12.52 TQ	TXBLS	10/01-12/01
Installation and Repair Worker	Dallas PMSA, TX	H	6.25 FQ	9.87 AW	14.00 TQ	TXBLS	10/01-12/01
Installation and Repair Worker	El Paso MSA, TX	H	6.20 FQ	8.75 AW	11.47 TQ	TXBLS	10/01-12/01
Installation and Repair Worker	Fort Worth-Arlington PMSA, TX	H	6.95 FQ	10.75 AW	15.64 TQ	TXBLS	10/01-12/01
Installation and Repair Worker	Galveston-Texas City PMSA, TX	H	7.50 FQ	9.93 AW	13.29 TQ	TXBLS	10/01-12/01
Installation and Repair Worker	Houston PMSA, TX	H	7.02 FQ	10.75 AW	16.34 TQ	TXBLS	10/01-12/01
Installation and Repair Worker	Killeen-Temple MSA, TX	H	5.98 FQ	10.38 AW	16.17 TQ	TXBLS	10/01-12/01
Installation and Repair Worker	Laredo MSA, TX	H	5.92 FQ	8.36 AW	11.34 TQ	TXBLS	10/01-12/01
Installation and Repair Worker	Longview-Marshall MSA, TX	H	6.30 FQ	9.07 AW	11.48 TQ	TXBLS	10/01-12/01
Installation and Repair Worker	Lubbock MSA, TX	H	5.73 FQ	8.50 AW	11.98 TQ	TXBLS	10/01-12/01
Installation and Repair Worker	McAllen-Edinburg-Mission MSA, TX	H	5.71 FQ	8.02 AW	12.55 TQ	TXBLS	10/01-12/01
Installation and Repair Worker	Odessa-Midland MSA, TX	H	6.78 FQ	8.97 AW	11.77 TQ	TXBLS	10/01-12/01
Installation and Repair Worker	San Antonio MSA, TX	H	6.27 FQ	10.42 AW	16.16 TQ	TXBLS	10/01-12/01
Installation and Repair Worker	Tyler MSA, TX	H	5.83 FQ	8.35 AW	12.62 TQ	TXBLS	10/01-12/01
Installation and Repair Worker	Waco MSA, TX	H	6.15 FQ	9.59 AW	14.27 TQ	TXBLS	10/01-12/01
Installation and Repair Worker	Utah	H	6.30 FQ	10.31 AW	16.16 TQ	UTBLS	10/01-12/01
Installation and Repair Worker	Provo-Orem MSA, UT	H	6.26 FQ	8.84 AW	13.20 TQ	UTBLS	10/01-12/01
Installation and Repair Worker	Salt Lake City-Ogden MSA, UT	H	6.46 FQ	10.71 AW	16.70 TQ	UTBLS	10/01-12/01
Installation and Repair Worker	Vermont	H	6.79 FQ	9.22 AW	12.08 TQ	VTBLS	10/01-12/01
Installation and Repair Worker	Burlington MSA, VT	H	6.67 FQ	9.33 AW	12.60 TQ	VTBLS	10/01-12/01
Installation and Repair Worker	Virginia	H	6.45 FQ	10.07 AW	14.50 TQ	VABLS	10/01-12/01
Installation and Repair Worker	Lynchburg MSA, VA	H	6.12 FQ	8.90 AW	12.09 TQ	VABLS	10/01-12/01
Installation and Repair Worker	Norfolk-Virginia Beach-Newport News MSA, VA-NC	H	6.92 FQ	9.77 AW	13.60 TQ	VABLS	10/01-12/01
Installation and Repair Worker	Richmond-Petersburg MSA, VA	H	6.16 FQ	9.13 AW	12.24 TQ	VABLS	10/01-12/01
Installation and Repair Worker	Roanoke MSA, VA	H	7.50 FQ	11.70 AW	17.48 TQ	VABLS	10/01-12/01
Installation and Repair Worker	Washington	H	7.27 FQ	12.59 AW	20.48 TQ	WABLS	10/01-12/01
Installation and Repair Worker	Bremerton PMSA, WA	H	7.01 FQ	11.97 AW	23.26 TQ	WABLS	10/01-12/01
Installation and Repair Worker	Olympia PMSA, WA	H	8.35 FQ	12.50 AW	17.71 TQ	WABLS	10/01-12/01

AAW Average annual wage **AE** Average entry wage **AEX** Average experienced wage **AO** Average offered **AOH** Average offered, high **AOL** Average offered, low **APH** Average pay, high range **APL** Average pay, low range **ASH** Average starting, high **ASL** Average starting, low **AW** Average wage paid **FQ** First quartile wage **H** Hourly **HI** Highest wage paid **HR** High end range **LR** Low end range **M** Monthly **MTC** Median total compensation **MW** Median wage paid **SQ** Second quartile wage **S** Special: hourly and annual **TQ** Third quartile wage **W** Weekly **Y** Yearly

Occupation/Type/Industry	Location	Per	Low	Mid	High	Source	Date
Helper							
Installation and Repair Worker	Richland-Kennewick-Pasco MSA, WA	H	7.39 FQ	11.20 AW	16.10 TQ	WABLS	10/01-12/01
Installation and Repair Worker	Seattle-Bellevue-Everett PMSA, WA	H	8.37 FQ	14.48 AW	22.65 TQ	WABLS	10/01-12/01
Installation and Repair Worker	Spokane MSA, WA	H	7.01 FQ	9.74 AW	13.53 TQ	WABLS	10/01-12/01
Installation and Repair Worker	Tacoma PMSA, WA	H	7.66 FQ	11.35 AW	16.65 TQ	WABLS	10/01-12/01
Installation and Repair Worker	Yakima MSA, WA	H	7.31 FQ	12.37 AW	18.71 TQ	WABLS	10/01-12/01
Installation and Repair Worker	West Virginia	H	6.44 FQ	10.96 AW	22.00 TQ	WVBLS	10/01-12/01
Installation and Repair Worker	Charleston MSA, WV	H	8.72 FQ	17.92 AW	27.90 TQ	WVBLS	10/01-12/01
Installation and Repair Worker	Huntington-Ashland MSA, WV-KY-OH	H	7.21 FQ	11.66 AW	19.85 TQ	WVBLS	10/01-12/01
Installation and Repair Worker	Wisconsin	H	6.58 FQ	11.23 AW	17.07 TQ	WIBLS	10/01-12/01
Installation and Repair Worker	Appleton-Oshkosh-Neenah MSA, WI	H	5.97 FQ	11.56 AW	17.19 TQ	WIBLS	10/01-12/01
Installation and Repair Worker	Green Bay MSA, WI	H	7.67 FQ	12.43 AW	21.06 TQ	WIBLS	10/01-12/01
Installation and Repair Worker	Madison MSA, WI	H	6.19 FQ	11.09 AW	16.83 TQ	WIBLS	10/01-12/01
Installation and Repair Worker	Milwaukee-Waukesha PMSA, WI	H	6.90 FQ	11.10 AW	16.59 TQ	WIBLS	10/01-12/01
Installation and Repair Worker	Racine PMSA, WI	H	7.15 FQ	10.59 AW	18.23 TQ	WIBLS	10/01-12/01
Installation and Repair Worker	Wyoming	H	7.23 FQ	13.03 AW	20.30 TQ	WYBLS	10/01-12/01
Installation and Repair Worker	Cheyenne MSA, WY	H	6.01 FQ	9.00 AW	14.28 TQ	WYBLS	10/01-12/01
Installation and Repair Worker	Puerto Rico	H	5.63 FQ	7.65 AW	12.66 TQ	PRBLS	10/01-12/01
Installation and Repair Worker	Virgin Islands	H	6.37 FQ	8.83 AW	11.21 TQ	VIBLS	10/01-12/01
Installation and Repair Worker	Guam	H	6.49 FQ	8.45 AW	11.10 TQ	GUBLS	10/01-12/01
Painter, Paperhanger, Plasterer	Alabama	H	7.02 FQ	10.09 AW	15.95 TQ	ALBLS	10/01-12/01
Painter, Paperhanger, Plasterer	Alaska	H	10.29 FQ	14.54 AW	24.37 TQ	AKBLS	10/01-12/01
Painter, Paperhanger, Plasterer	Arizona	H	6.15 FQ	9.17 AW	12.90 TQ	AZBLS	10/01-12/01
Painter, Paperhanger, Plasterer	Arkansas	H	6.59 FQ	9.36 AW	13.91 TQ	ARBLS	10/01-12/01
Painter, Paperhanger, Plasterer	California	H	6.96 FQ	10.20 AW	15.97 TQ	CABLS	10/01-12/01
Painter, Paperhanger, Plasterer	Colorado	H	6.78 FQ	9.73 AW	13.26 TQ	COBLS	10/01-12/01
Painter, Paperhanger, Plasterer	Connecticut	H	10.98 FQ	14.47 AW	19.35 TQ	CTBLS	10/01-12/01
Painter, Paperhanger, Plasterer	Delaware	H	8.15 FQ	13.09 AW	16.49 TQ	DEBLS	10/01-12/01
Painter, Paperhanger, Plasterer	Florida	H	6.83 FQ	9.19 AW	12.35 TQ	FLBLS	10/01-12/01
Painter, Paperhanger, Plasterer	Georgia	H	7.05 FQ	10.03 AW	13.14 TQ	GABLS	10/01-12/01
Painter, Paperhanger, Plasterer	Hawaii	H	7.09 FQ	9.97 AW	13.54 TQ	HIBLS	10/01-12/01
Painter, Paperhanger, Plasterer	Idaho	H	6.65 FQ	8.45 AW	10.84 TQ	IDBLS	10/01-12/01
Painter, Paperhanger, Plasterer	Illinois	H	10.03 FQ	21.65 AW	27.59 TQ	ILBLS	10/01-12/01
Painter, Paperhanger, Plasterer	Indiana	H	7.20 FQ	10.04 AW	13.82 TQ	INBLS	10/01-12/01
Painter, Paperhanger, Plasterer	Iowa	H	7.38 FQ	10.20 AW	14.90 TQ	IABLS	10/01-12/01
Painter, Paperhanger, Plasterer	Kansas	H	8.18 FQ	10.70 AW	13.91 TQ	KSBLS	10/01-12/01
Painter, Paperhanger, Plasterer	Kentucky	H	5.87 FQ	9.26 AW	12.94 TQ	KYBLS	10/01-12/01
Painter, Paperhanger, Plasterer	Louisiana	H	5.94 FQ	9.79 AW	14.81 TQ	LABLS	10/01-12/01
Painter, Paperhanger, Plasterer	Maine	H	6.45 FQ	10.26 AW	13.76 TQ	MEBLS	10/01-12/01
Painter, Paperhanger, Plasterer	Maryland	H	7.63 FQ	10.73 AW	13.94 TQ	MDBLS	10/01-12/01
Painter, Paperhanger, Plasterer	Massachusetts	H	8.90 FQ	12.47 AW	21.04 TQ	MABLS	10/01-12/01
Painter, Paperhanger, Plasterer	Michigan	H	8.08 FQ	13.08 AW	24.29 TQ	MIBLS	10/01-12/01
Painter, Paperhanger, Plasterer	Minnesota	H	7.23 FQ	14.75 AW	24.80 TQ	MNBLS	10/01-12/01
Painter, Paperhanger, Plasterer	Mississippi	H	6.02 FQ	8.32 AW	11.92 TQ	MSBLS	10/01-12/01
Painter, Paperhanger, Plasterer	Missouri	H	7.71 FQ	11.82 AW	17.64 TQ	MOBLS	10/01-12/01
Painter, Paperhanger, Plasterer	Montana	H	6.15 FQ	9.17 AW	11.42 TQ	MTBLS	10/01-12/01
Painter, Paperhanger, Plasterer	Nebraska	H	7.00 FQ	9.69 AW	13.18 TQ	NEBLS	10/01-12/01
Painter, Paperhanger, Plasterer	Nevada	H	7.19 FQ	10.19 AW	15.36 TQ	NVBLS	10/01-12/01
Painter, Paperhanger, Plasterer	New Hampshire	H	5.72 FQ	9.59 AW	16.13 TQ	NHBLS	10/01-12/01
Painter, Paperhanger, Plasterer	New Jersey	H	8.57 FQ	15.04 AW	21.70 TQ	NJBLS	10/01-12/01
Painter, Paperhanger, Plasterer	New Mexico	H	6.56 FQ	9.03 AW	12.45 TQ	NMBLS	10/01-12/01
Painter, Paperhanger, Plasterer	New York	H	6.80 FQ	10.92 AW	18.28 TQ	NYBLS	10/01-12/01
Painter, Paperhanger, Plasterer	North Carolina	H	7.13 FQ	9.25 AW	11.97 TQ	NCBLS	10/01-12/01
Painter, Paperhanger, Plasterer	North Dakota	H	7.91 FQ	10.13 AW	12.73 TQ	NDBLS	10/01-12/01
Painter, Paperhanger, Plasterer	Ohio	H	7.73 FQ	11.89 AW	18.09 TQ	OHBLS	10/01-12/01
Painter, Paperhanger, Plasterer	Oklahoma	H	6.06 FQ	8.18 AW	11.11 TQ	OKBLS	10/01-12/01
Painter, Paperhanger, Plasterer	Oregon	H	7.52 FQ	10.37 AW	14.20 TQ	ORBLS	10/01-12/01
Painter, Paperhanger, Plasterer	Pennsylvania	H	7.15 FQ	10.91 AW	16.17 TQ	PABLS	10/01-12/01
Painter, Paperhanger, Plasterer	Rhode Island	H	7.06 FQ	10.64 AW	14.53 TQ	RIBLS	10/01-12/01
Painter, Paperhanger, Plasterer	South Carolina	H	7.36 FQ	9.19 AW	11.68 TQ	SCBLS	10/01-12/01
Painter, Paperhanger, Plasterer	South Dakota	H	6.66 FQ	8.10 AW	10.31 TQ	SDBLS	10/01-12/01
Painter, Paperhanger, Plasterer	Tennessee	H	7.05 FQ	10.14 AW	17.19 TQ	TNBLS	10/01-12/01
Painter, Paperhanger, Plasterer	Texas	H	6.90 FQ	8.77 AW	10.95 TQ	TXBLS	10/01-12/01
Painter, Paperhanger, Plasterer	Utah	H	7.10 FQ	9.20 AW	12.27 TQ	UTBLS	10/01-12/01
Painter, Paperhanger, Plasterer	Vermont	H	7.56 FQ	9.62 AW	12.10 TQ	VTBLS	10/01-12/01
Painter, Paperhanger, Plasterer	Virginia	H	6.64 FQ	8.83 AW	11.56 TQ	VABLS	10/01-12/01
Painter, Paperhanger, Plasterer	Washington	H	7.92 FQ	11.36 AW	15.48 TQ	WABLS	10/01-12/01

AAW	Average annual wage	AOH	Average offered, high	ASH	Average starting, high	H	Hourly	M	Monthly	S	Special: hourly and annual
AE	Average entry wage	AOL	Average offered, low	ASL	Average starting, low	HI	Highest wage paid	MTC	Median total compensation	TQ	Third quartile wage
AEX	Average experienced wage	APH	Average pay, high range	AW	Average wage paid	HR	High end range	MW	Median wage paid	W	Weekly
AO	Average offered	APL	Average pay, low range	FQ	First quartile wage	LR	Low end range	SQ	Second quartile wage	Y	Yearly

Occupation/Type/Industry	Location	Per	Low	Mid	High	Source	Date
Helper							
Painter, Paperhanger, Plasterer	West Virginia	H	6.89 FQ	9.30 AW	12.81 TQ	WVBLS	10/01-12/01
Painter, Paperhanger, Plasterer	Wisconsin	H	8.26 FQ	11.51 AW	14.50 TQ	WIBLS	10/01-12/01
Painter, Paperhanger, Plasterer	Wyoming	H	6.06 FQ	8.83 AW	11.40 TQ	WYBLS	10/01-12/01
Painter, Paperhanger, Plasterer	Puerto Rico	H	5.55 FQ	6.21 AW	6.96 TQ	PRBLS	10/01-12/01
Pipelayer, Plumber, Pipefitter, and Steamfitter	Alabama	H	7.42 FQ	10.07 AW	13.49 TQ	ALBLS	10/01-12/01
Pipelayer, Plumber, Pipefitter, and Steamfitter	Arizona	H	6.85 FQ	9.99 AW	14.90 TQ	AZBLS	10/01-12/01
Pipelayer, Plumber, Pipefitter, and Steamfitter	Arkansas	H	7.22 FQ	9.52 AW	12.15 TQ	ARBLS	10/01-12/01
Pipelayer, Plumber, Pipefitter, and Steamfitter	California	H	8.20 FQ	12.47 AW	17.60 TQ	CABLS	10/01-12/01
Pipelayer, Plumber, Pipefitter, and Steamfitter	Colorado	H	9.75 FQ	13.44 AW	17.86 TQ	COBLS	10/01-12/01
Pipelayer, Plumber, Pipefitter, and Steamfitter	Connecticut	H	7.74 FQ	11.89 AW	17.23 TQ	CTBLS	10/01-12/01
Pipelayer, Plumber, Pipefitter, and Steamfitter	Delaware	H	7.06 FQ	9.46 AW	11.48 TQ	DEBLS	10/01-12/01
Pipelayer, Plumber, Pipefitter, and Steamfitter	District of Columbia	H	7.59 FQ	9.91 AW	12.15 TQ	DCBLS	10/01-12/01
Pipelayer, Plumber, Pipefitter, and Steamfitter	Florida	H	7.28 FQ	10.07 AW	13.40 TQ	FLBLS	10/01-12/01
Pipelayer, Plumber, Pipefitter, and Steamfitter	Georgia	H	8.22 FQ	10.99 AW	13.89 TQ	GABLS	10/01-12/01
Pipelayer, Plumber, Pipefitter, and Steamfitter	Hawaii	H	9.13 FQ	10.80 AW	13.36 TQ	HIBLS	10/01-12/01
Pipelayer, Plumber, Pipefitter, and Steamfitter	Idaho	H	8.27 FQ	12.43 AW	17.48 TQ	IDBLS	10/01-12/01
Pipelayer, Plumber, Pipefitter, and Steamfitter	Illinois	H	7.69 FQ	15.78 AW	24.35 TQ	ILBLS	10/01-12/01
Pipelayer, Plumber, Pipefitter, and Steamfitter	Indiana	H	6.39 FQ	10.81 AW	15.31 TQ	INBLS	10/01-12/01
Pipelayer, Plumber, Pipefitter, and Steamfitter	Iowa	H	7.37 FQ	10.44 AW	14.19 TQ	IABLS	10/01-12/01
Pipelayer, Plumber, Pipefitter, and Steamfitter	Kansas	H	7.78 FQ	10.67 AW	15.00 TQ	KSBLS	10/01-12/01
Pipelayer, Plumber, Pipefitter, and Steamfitter	Kentucky	H	8.00 FQ	10.74 AW	14.98 TQ	KYBLS	10/01-12/01
Pipelayer, Plumber, Pipefitter, and Steamfitter	Louisiana	H	7.31 FQ	9.87 AW	13.47 TQ	LABLS	10/01-12/01
Pipelayer, Plumber, Pipefitter, and Steamfitter	Maine	H	7.67 FQ	9.81 AW	13.23 TQ	MEBLS	10/01-12/01
Pipelayer, Plumber, Pipefitter, and Steamfitter	Maryland	H	8.73 FQ	12.05 AW	16.64 TQ	MDBLS	10/01-12/01
Pipelayer, Plumber, Pipefitter, and Steamfitter	Massachusetts	H	9.75 FQ	13.46 AW	18.75 TQ	MABLS	10/01-12/01
Pipelayer, Plumber, Pipefitter, and Steamfitter	Michigan	H	8.08 FQ	12.07 AW	17.22 TQ	MIBLS	10/01-12/01
Pipelayer, Plumber, Pipefitter, and Steamfitter	Minnesota	H	9.54 FQ	13.72 AW	19.32 TQ	MNBLS	10/01-12/01
Pipelayer, Plumber, Pipefitter, and Steamfitter	Mississippi	H	6.83 FQ	9.62 AW	13.34 TQ	MSBLS	10/01-12/01
Pipelayer, Plumber, Pipefitter, and Steamfitter	Missouri	H	7.76 FQ	12.52 AW	18.39 TQ	MOBLS	10/01-12/01
Pipelayer, Plumber, Pipefitter, and Steamfitter	Montana	H	9.08 FQ	11.35 AW	16.10 TQ	MTBLS	10/01-12/01
Pipelayer, Plumber, Pipefitter, and Steamfitter	Nebraska	H	7.19 FQ	10.99 AW	15.54 TQ	NEBLS	10/01-12/01
Pipelayer, Plumber, Pipefitter, and Steamfitter	Nevada	H	8.35 FQ	11.42 AW	15.55 TQ	NVBLS	10/01-12/01
Pipelayer, Plumber, Pipefitter, and Steamfitter	New Hampshire	H	9.73 FQ	13.37 AW	17.97 TQ	NHBLS	10/01-12/01
Pipelayer, Plumber, Pipefitter, and Steamfitter	New Jersey	H	7.61 FQ	12.95 AW	19.10 TQ	NJBLS	10/01-12/01
Pipelayer, Plumber, Pipefitter, and Steamfitter	New Mexico	H	6.53 FQ	9.29 AW	13.00 TQ	NMBLS	10/01-12/01
Pipelayer, Plumber, Pipefitter, and Steamfitter	New York	H	8.47 FQ	13.88 AW	25.54 TQ	NYBLS	10/01-12/01
Pipelayer, Plumber, Pipefitter, and Steamfitter	North Carolina	H	8.17 FQ	10.68 AW	13.85 TQ	NCBLS	10/01-12/01

AAW	Average annual wage	**AOH**	Average offered, high	**ASH**	Average starting, high	**H**	Hourly	**M**	Monthly	**S**	Special: hourly and annual
AE	Average entry wage	**AOL**	Average offered, low	**ASL**	Average starting, low	**HI**	Highest wage paid	**MTC**	Median total compensation	**TQ**	Third quartile wage
AEX	Average experienced wage	**APH**	Average pay, high range	**AW**	Average wage paid	**HR**	High end range	**MW**	Median wage paid	**W**	Weekly
AO	Average offered	**APL**	Average pay, low range	**FQ**	First quartile wage	**LR**	Low end range	**SQ**	Second quartile wage	**Y**	Yearly

Occupation/Type/Industry	Location	Per	Low	Mid	High	Source	Date
Helper							
Pipelayer, Plumber, Pipefitter, and Steamfitter	North Dakota	H	5.75 FQ	8.24 AW	13.02 TQ	NDBLS	10/01-12/01
Pipelayer, Plumber, Pipefitter, and Steamfitter	Ohio	H	8.86 FQ	11.66 AW	16.08 TQ	OHBLS	10/01-12/01
Pipelayer, Plumber, Pipefitter, and Steamfitter	Oklahoma	H	7.19 FQ	10.37 AW	13.71 TQ	OKBLS	10/01-12/01
Pipelayer, Plumber, Pipefitter, and Steamfitter	Oregon	H	9.06 FQ	11.97 AW	16.31 TQ	ORBLS	10/01-12/01
Pipelayer, Plumber, Pipefitter, and Steamfitter	Pennsylvania	H	5.87 FQ	11.33 AW	18.71 TQ	PABLS	10/01-12/01
Pipelayer, Plumber, Pipefitter, and Steamfitter	Rhode Island	H	7.85 FQ	13.32 AW	22.91 TQ	RIBLS	10/01-12/01
Pipelayer, Plumber, Pipefitter, and Steamfitter	South Carolina	H	6.89 FQ	10.19 AW	14.20 TQ	SCBLS	10/01-12/01
Pipelayer, Plumber, Pipefitter, and Steamfitter	South Dakota	H	7.46 FQ	9.53 AW	12.29 TQ	SDBLS	10/01-12/01
Pipelayer, Plumber, Pipefitter, and Steamfitter	Tennessee	H	8.73 FQ	10.74 AW	13.71 TQ	TNBLS	10/01-12/01
Pipelayer, Plumber, Pipefitter, and Steamfitter	Texas	H	7.21 FQ	10.21 AW	13.87 TQ	TXBLS	10/01-12/01
Pipelayer, Plumber, Pipefitter, and Steamfitter	Utah	H	6.28 FQ	9.46 AW	14.22 TQ	UTBLS	10/01-12/01
Pipelayer, Plumber, Pipefitter, and Steamfitter	Vermont	H	8.85 FQ	11.58 AW	16.77 TQ	VTBLS	10/01-12/01
Pipelayer, Plumber, Pipefitter, and Steamfitter	Virginia	H	6.99 FQ	9.71 AW	12.96 TQ	VABLS	10/01-12/01
Pipelayer, Plumber, Pipefitter, and Steamfitter	Washington	H	8.30 FQ	12.66 AW	17.35 TQ	WABLS	10/01-12/01
Pipelayer, Plumber, Pipefitter, and Steamfitter	West Virginia	H	7.21 FQ	10.93 AW	18.31 TQ	WVBLS	10/01-12/01
Pipelayer, Plumber, Pipefitter, and Steamfitter	Wisconsin	H	7.26 FQ	10.13 AW	16.37 TQ	WIBLS	10/01-12/01
Pipelayer, Plumber, Pipefitter, and Steamfitter	Wyoming	H	6.20 FQ	11.08 AW	16.16 TQ	WYBLS	10/01-12/01
Pipelayer, Plumber, Pipefitter, and Steamfitter	Puerto Rico	H	5.61 FQ	7.29 AW	11.12 TQ	PRBLS	10/01-12/01
Pipelayer, Plumber, Pipefitter, and Steamfitter	Guam	H	5.92 FQ	7.60 AW	9.96 TQ	GUBLS	10/01-12/01
Production Worker	Alabama	H	6.05 FQ	9.74 AW	16.12 TQ	ALBLS	10/01-12/01
Production Worker	Alaska	H	9.15 FQ	14.42 AW	22.66 TQ	AKBLS	10/01-12/01
Production Worker	Arizona	H	5.71 FQ	8.06 AW	10.96 TQ	AZBLS	10/01-12/01
Production Worker	Arkansas	H	6.08 FQ	9.26 AW	12.86 TQ	ARBLS	10/01-12/01
Production Worker	California	H	6.55 FQ	9.46 AW	14.40 TQ	CABLS	10/01-12/01
Production Worker	Colorado	H	6.05 FQ	9.28 AW	13.29 TQ	COBLS	10/01-12/01
Production Worker	Connecticut	H	7.34 FQ	10.76 AW	15.03 TQ	CTBLS	10/01-12/01
Production Worker	Delaware	H	6.46 FQ	9.65 AW	17.07 TQ	DEBLS	10/01-12/01
Production Worker	District of Columbia	H	6.91 FQ	9.83 AW	15.56 TQ	DCBLS	10/01-12/01
Production Worker	Florida	H	5.98 FQ	8.68 AW	12.52 TQ	FLBLS	10/01-12/01
Production Worker	Georgia	H	6.27 FQ	9.00 AW	12.64 TQ	GABLS	10/01-12/01
Production Worker	Hawaii	H	6.90 FQ	8.90 AW	13.11 TQ	HIBLS	10/01-12/01
Production Worker	Idaho	H	6.04 FQ	8.76 AW	12.95 TQ	IDBLS	10/01-12/01
Production Worker	Illinois	H	5.96 FQ	8.92 AW	12.99 TQ	ILBLS	10/01-12/01
Production Worker	Indiana	H	7.01 FQ	10.21 AW	14.58 TQ	INBLS	10/01-12/01
Production Worker	Iowa	H	7.36 FQ	10.73 AW	15.05 TQ	IABLS	10/01-12/01
Production Worker	Kansas	H	6.81 FQ	10.17 AW	14.26 TQ	KSBLS	10/01-12/01
Production Worker	Kentucky	H	7.20 FQ	11.71 AW	19.02 TQ	KYBLS	10/01-12/01
Production Worker	Louisiana	H	5.92 FQ	9.59 AW	14.71 TQ	LABLS	10/01-12/01
Production Worker	Maine	H	6.90 FQ	10.41 AW	15.21 TQ	MEBLS	10/01-12/01
Production Worker	Maryland	H	7.35 FQ	11.30 AW	16.45 TQ	MDBLS	10/01-12/01
Production Worker	Massachusetts	H	7.48 FQ	10.77 AW	15.27 TQ	MABLS	10/01-12/01
Production Worker	Michigan	H	6.79 FQ	10.72 AW	16.62 TQ	MIBLS	10/01-12/01
Production Worker	Minnesota	H	7.36 FQ	10.93 AW	16.23 TQ	MNBLS	10/01-12/01
Production Worker	Mississippi	H	6.31 FQ	9.39 AW	12.67 TQ	MSBLS	10/01-12/01
Production Worker	Missouri	H	6.64 FQ	10.00 AW	14.79 TQ	MOBLS	10/01-12/01
Production Worker	Montana	H	5.98 FQ	9.59 AW	13.96 TQ	MTBLS	10/01-12/01
Production Worker	Nebraska	H	7.46 FQ	10.60 AW	14.31 TQ	NEBLS	10/01-12/01
Production Worker	Nevada	H	6.87 FQ	10.06 AW	14.51 TQ	NVBLS	10/01-12/01
Production Worker	New Hampshire	H	6.44 FQ	10.12 AW	14.17 TQ	NHBLS	10/01-12/01
Production Worker	New Jersey	H	6.25 FQ	9.99 AW	14.78 TQ	NJBLS	10/01-12/01
Production Worker	New Mexico	H	6.11 FQ	8.71 AW	11.87 TQ	NMBLS	10/01-12/01
Production Worker	New York	H	6.64 FQ	10.18 AW	13.92 TQ	NYBLS	10/01-12/01

AAW	Average annual wage	AOH	Average offered, high	ASH	Average starting, high	H	Hourly	M	Monthly	S	Special: hourly and annual
AE	Average entry wage	AOL	Average offered, low	ASL	Average starting, low	HI	Highest wage paid	MTC	Median total compensation	TQ	Third quartile wage
AEX	Average experienced wage	APH	Average pay, high range	AW	Average wage paid	HR	High end range	MW	Median wage paid	W	Weekly
AO	Average offered	APL	Average pay, low range	FQ	First quartile wage	LR	Low end range	SQ	Second quartile wage	Y	Yearly

Occupation/Type/Industry	Location	Per	Low	Mid	High	Source	Date
Helper							
Production Worker	North Carolina	H	6.76 FQ	9.80 AW	13.62 TQ	NCBLS	10/01-12/01
Production Worker	North Dakota	H	7.12 FQ	9.28 AW	12.65 TQ	NDBLS	10/01-12/01
Production Worker	Ohio	H	7.12 FQ	10.89 AW	16.14 TQ	OHBLS	10/01-12/01
Production Worker	Oklahoma	H	6.17 FQ	9.20 AW	13.74 TQ	OKBLS	10/01-12/01
Production Worker	Oregon	H	7.16 FQ	10.03 AW	15.27 TQ	ORBLS	10/01-12/01
Production Worker	Pennsylvania	H	6.70 FQ	10.46 AW	15.44 TQ	PABLS	10/01-12/01
Production Worker	Rhode Island	H	6.64 FQ	8.73 AW	12.61 TQ	RIBLS	10/01-12/01
Production Worker	South Carolina	H	6.88 FQ	9.53 AW	13.43 TQ	SCBLS	10/01-12/01
Production Worker	South Dakota	H	7.11 FQ	8.19 AW	9.65 TQ	SDBLS	10/01-12/01
Production Worker	Tennessee	H	6.54 FQ	9.84 AW	14.47 TQ	TNBLS	10/01-12/01
Production Worker	Texas	H	6.09 FQ	8.81 AW	12.47 TQ	TXBLS	10/01-12/01
Production Worker	Utah	H	6.29 FQ	9.14 AW	12.79 TQ	UTBLS	10/01-12/01
Production Worker	Vermont	H	7.62 FQ	10.80 AW	14.47 TQ	VTBLS	10/01-12/01
Production Worker	Virginia	H	7.00 FQ	10.18 AW	13.89 TQ	VABLS	10/01-12/01
Production Worker	Washington	H	7.53 FQ	10.97 AW	16.21 TQ	WABLS	10/01-12/01
Production Worker	West Virginia	H	6.51 FQ	10.97 AW	17.67 TQ	WVBLS	10/01-12/01
Production Worker	Wisconsin	H	7.27 FQ	10.77 AW	15.30 TQ	WIBLS	10/01-12/01
Production Worker	Wyoming	H	5.88 FQ	8.72 AW	13.10 TQ	WYBLS	10/01-12/01
Production Worker	Puerto Rico	H	5.76 FQ	8.15 AW	11.66 TQ	PRBLS	10/01-12/01
Production Worker	Guam	H	5.78 FQ	8.23 AW	11.83 TQ	GUBLS	10/01-12/01
Roofer	Alabama	H	6.73 FQ	8.32 AW	10.71 TQ	ALBLS	10/01-12/01
Roofer	Arizona	H	5.79 FQ	7.39 AW	9.61 TQ	AZBLS	10/01-12/01
Roofer	Arkansas	H	7.20 FQ	8.84 AW	10.87 TQ	ARBLS	10/01-12/01
Roofer	California	H	7.46 FQ	10.32 AW	14.10 TQ	CABLS	10/01-12/01
Roofer	Colorado	H	6.90 FQ	9.80 AW	12.78 TQ	COBLS	10/01-12/01
Roofer	Connecticut	H	9.02 FQ	13.03 AW	18.31 TQ	CTBLS	10/01-12/01
Roofer	Delaware	H	8.31 FQ	10.98 AW	13.85 TQ	DEBLS	10/01-12/01
Roofer	Florida	H	7.08 FQ	9.11 AW	11.65 TQ	FLBLS	10/01-12/01
Roofer	Georgia	H	7.44 FQ	9.45 AW	12.04 TQ	GABLS	10/01-12/01
Roofer	Idaho	H	7.21 FQ	8.67 AW	10.83 TQ	IDBLS	10/01-12/01
Roofer	Illinois	H	7.45 FQ	12.87 AW	19.45 TQ	ILBLS	10/01-12/01
Roofer	Indiana	H	6.91 FQ	9.86 AW	13.26 TQ	INBLS	10/01-12/01
Roofer	Iowa	H	6.48 FQ	9.96 AW	14.55 TQ	IABLS	10/01-12/01
Roofer	Kansas	H	6.64 FQ	8.79 AW	11.64 TQ	KSBLS	10/01-12/01
Roofer	Kentucky	H	6.36 FQ	9.64 AW	12.68 TQ	KYBLS	10/01-12/01
Roofer	Louisiana	H	6.24 FQ	8.35 AW	11.16 TQ	LABLS	10/01-12/01
Roofer	Maine	H	7.46 FQ	9.34 AW	11.24 TQ	MEBLS	10/01-12/01
Roofer	Maryland	H	7.76 FQ	10.26 AW	13.28 TQ	MDBLS	10/01-12/01
Roofer	Massachusetts	H	7.85 FQ	12.67 AW	16.73 TQ	MABLS	10/01-12/01
Roofer	Michigan	H	8.42 FQ	11.72 AW	16.25 TQ	MIBLS	10/01-12/01
Roofer	Minnesota	H	8.03 FQ	12.73 AW	18.37 TQ	MNBLS	10/01-12/01
Roofer	Mississippi	H	6.14 FQ	8.41 AW	11.69 TQ	MSBLS	10/01-12/01
Roofer	Missouri	H	7.98 FQ	10.84 AW	14.81 TQ	MOBLS	10/01-12/01
Roofer	Nebraska	H	7.31 FQ	9.41 AW	12.13 TQ	NEBLS	10/01-12/01
Roofer	Nevada	H	9.00 FQ	11.94 AW	15.32 TQ	NVBLS	10/01-12/01
Roofer	New Hampshire	H	7.70 FQ	10.46 AW	13.31 TQ	NHBLS	10/01-12/01
Roofer	New Jersey	H	7.97 FQ	12.21 AW	17.86 TQ	NJBLS	10/01-12/01
Roofer	New Mexico	H	6.68 FQ	8.99 AW	13.00 TQ	NMBLS	10/01-12/01
Roofer	New York	H	6.54 FQ	13.64 AW	24.21 TQ	NYBLS	10/01-12/01
Roofer	North Carolina	H	7.50 FQ	9.64 AW	12.18 TQ	NCBLS	10/01-12/01
Roofer	North Dakota	H	7.81 FQ	9.68 AW	11.59 TQ	NDBLS	10/01-12/01
Roofer	Ohio	H	8.04 FQ	11.41 AW	16.13 TQ	OHBLS	10/01-12/01
Roofer	Oklahoma	H	6.57 FQ	10.51 AW	16.28 TQ	OKBLS	10/01-12/01
Roofer	Oregon	H	7.57 FQ	10.51 AW	15.77 TQ	ORBLS	10/01-12/01
Roofer	Pennsylvania	H	7.03 FQ	9.62 AW	13.26 TQ	PABLS	10/01-12/01
Roofer	South Carolina	H	7.15 FQ	9.15 AW	12.60 TQ	SCBLS	10/01-12/01
Roofer	South Dakota	H	5.97 FQ	8.06 AW	10.64 TQ	SDBLS	10/01-12/01
Roofer	Tennessee	H	7.69 FQ	11.31 AW	13.22 TQ	TNBLS	10/01-12/01
Roofer	Texas	H	7.02 FQ	9.12 AW	11.62 TQ	TXBLS	10/01-12/01
Roofer	Utah	H	7.42 FQ	9.49 AW	11.29 TQ	UTBLS	10/01-12/01
Roofer	Vermont	H	6.98 FQ	8.74 AW	10.91 TQ	VTBLS	10/01-12/01
Roofer	Virginia	H	6.83 FQ	9.28 AW	11.75 TQ	VABLS	10/01-12/01
Roofer	Washington	H	7.97 FQ	10.85 AW	15.16 TQ	WABLS	10/01-12/01
Roofer	West Virginia	H	6.32 FQ	8.46 AW	10.79 TQ	WVBLS	10/01-12/01
Roofer	Wisconsin	H	8.92 FQ	11.31 AW	14.14 TQ	WIBLS	10/01-12/01
Roofer	Wyoming	H	7.23 FQ	8.94 AW	10.67 TQ	WYBLS	10/01-12/01
Roofer	Puerto Rico	H	5.53 FQ	6.67 AW	9.26 TQ	PRBLS	10/01-12/01
Highway Maintenance Worker	Alabama	H	6.63 FQ	10.05 AW	14.35 TQ	ALBLS	10/01-12/01
	Huntsville MSA, AL	H	8.46 FQ	12.69 AW	16.80 TQ	ALBLS	10/01-12/01
	Mobile MSA, AL	H	7.45 FQ	10.33 AW	14.34 TQ	ALBLS	10/01-12/01
	Montgomery MSA, AL	H	7.31 FQ	10.81 AW	15.22 TQ	ALBLS	10/01-12/01

AAW Average annual wage **AE** Average entry wage **AEX** Average experienced wage **AO** Average offered **AOH** Average offered, high **AOL** Average offered, low **APH** Average pay, high range **APL** Average pay, low range **ASH** Average starting, high **ASL** Average starting, low **AW** Average wage paid **FQ** First quartile wage **H** Hourly **HI** Highest wage paid **HR** High end range **LR** Low end range **M** Monthly **MTC** Median total compensation **MW** Median wage paid **SQ** Second quartile wage **S** Special: hourly and annual **TQ** Third quartile wage **W** Weekly **Y** Yearly

Occupation/Type/Industry	Location	Per	Low	Mid	High	Source	Date
Highway Maintenance Worker	Alaska	H	12.33 FQ	21.02 AW	26.96 TQ	AKBLS	10/01-12/01
	Anchorage MSA, AK	H	11.40 FQ	20.29 AW	26.54 TQ	AKBLS	10/01-12/01
	Arizona	H	9.24 FQ	12.70 AW	16.96 TQ	AZBLS	10/01-12/01
	Phoenix-Mesa MSA, AZ	H	9.94 FQ	13.80 AW	17.82 TQ	AZBLS	10/01-12/01
	Arkansas	H	6.93 FQ	10.22 AW	14.35 TQ	ARBLS	10/01-12/01
	Fayetteville-Springdale-Rogers MSA, AR	H	8.90 FQ	11.52 AW	15.51 TQ	ARBLS	10/01-12/01
	Fort Smith MSA, AR-OK	H	6.48 FQ	10.93 AW	16.07 TQ	ARBLS	10/01-12/01
	Little Rock-North Little Rock MSA, AR	H	7.41 FQ	10.63 AW	15.25 TQ	ARBLS	10/01-12/01
	California	H	9.24 FQ	17.46 AW	25.55 TQ	CABLS	10/01-12/01
	Bakersfield MSA, CA	H	12.35 FQ	16.27 AW	22.96 TQ	CABLS	10/01-12/01
	Chico-Paradise MSA, CA	H	10.40 FQ	14.57 AW	19.60 TQ	CABLS	10/01-12/01
	Los Angeles-Long Beach PMSA, CA	H	13.77 FQ	19.15 AW	26.38 TQ	CABLS	10/01-12/01
	Merced MSA, CA	H	14.88 FQ	16.84 AW	19.67 TQ	CABLS	10/01-12/01
	Oakland PMSA, CA	H	14.99 FQ	20.35 AW	27.50 TQ	CABLS	10/01-12/01
	Orange County PMSA, CA	H	7.08 FQ	12.07 AW	21.41 TQ	CABLS	10/01-12/01
	Redding MSA, CA	H	13.41 FQ	25.58 AW	33.41 TQ	CABLS	10/01-12/01
	Riverside-San Bernardino PMSA, CA	H	14.91 FQ	21.20 AW	27.24 TQ	CABLS	10/01-12/01
	Sacramento PMSA, CA	H	14.12 FQ	17.97 AW	21.98 TQ	CABLS	10/01-12/01
	San Diego MSA, CA	H	11.37 FQ	16.46 AW	21.40 TQ	CABLS	10/01-12/01
	San Francisco PMSA, CA	H	6.74 FQ	20.32 AW	28.01 TQ	CABLS	10/01-12/01
	San Jose PMSA, CA	H	12.30 FQ	18.05 AW	25.21 TQ	CABLS	10/01-12/01
	San Luis Obispo-Atascadero-Paso Robles MSA, CA	H	10.81 FQ	15.62 AW	19.99 TQ	CABLS	10/01-12/01
	Santa Barbara-Santa Maria-Lompoc MSA, CA	H	12.96 FQ	18.24 AW	24.69 TQ	CABLS	10/01-12/01
	Stockton-Lodi MSA, CA	H	13.06 FQ	20.62 AW	32.34 TQ	CABLS	10/01-12/01
	Vallejo-Fairfield-Napa PMSA, CA	H	12.29 FQ	18.14 AW	22.11 TQ	CABLS	10/01-12/01
	Ventura PMSA, CA	H	9.32 FQ	16.61 AW	23.44 TQ	CABLS	10/01-12/01
	Visalia-Tulare-Porterville MSA, CA	H	14.28 FQ	16.83 AW	21.07 TQ	CABLS	10/01-12/01
	Colorado	H	11.31 FQ	15.89 AW	20.72 TQ	COBLS	10/01-12/01
	Boulder-Longmont PMSA, CO	H	11.47 FQ	16.02 AW	21.20 TQ	COBLS	10/01-12/01
	Colorado Springs MSA, CO	H	12.15 FQ	15.92 AW	20.47 TQ	COBLS	10/01-12/01
	Denver PMSA, CO	H	12.09 FQ	16.52 AW	20.91 TQ	COBLS	10/01-12/01
	Fort Collins-Loveland MSA, CO	H	11.91 FQ	17.58 AW	23.19 TQ	COBLS	10/01-12/01
	Greeley PMSA, CO	H	12.20 FQ	16.47 AW	20.65 TQ	COBLS	10/01-12/01
	Connecticut	H	14.40 FQ	18.47 AW	23.64 TQ	CTBLS	10/01-12/01
	Bridgeport PMSA, CT	H	15.49 FQ	19.88 AW	25.37 TQ	CTBLS	10/01-12/01
	Danbury PMSA, CT	H	15.07 FQ	18.77 AW	22.56 TQ	CTBLS	10/01-12/01
	Hartford MSA, CT	H	13.62 FQ	18.20 AW	24.08 TQ	CTBLS	10/01-12/01
	New Haven-Meriden PMSA, CT	H	15.09 FQ	19.10 AW	23.38 TQ	CTBLS	10/01-12/01
	New London-Norwich MSA, CT-RI	H	14.69 FQ	17.74 AW	22.19 TQ	CTBLS	10/01-12/01
	Stamford-Norwalk PMSA, CT	H	15.46 FQ	20.06 AW	25.40 TQ	CTBLS	10/01-12/01
	Waterbury PMSA, CT	H	14.99 FQ	18.93 AW	22.78 TQ	CTBLS	10/01-12/01
	Delaware	H	9.04 FQ	12.99 AW	17.69 TQ	DEBLS	10/01-12/01
	Wilmington-Newark PMSA, DE-MD	H	10.76 FQ	13.75 AW	17.76 TQ	DEBLS	10/01-12/01
	Washington PMSA, DC-MD-VA-WV	H	9.88 FQ	15.06 AW	20.71 TQ	DCBLS	10/01-12/01
	Florida	H	6.14 FQ	10.38 AW	14.05 TQ	FLBLS	10/01-12/01
	Daytona Beach MSA, FL	H	7.37 FQ	9.49 AW	12.25 TQ	FLBLS	10/01-12/01
	Fort Pierce-Port St. Lucie MSA, FL	H	7.53 FQ	10.28 AW	13.71 TQ	FLBLS	10/01-12/01
	Jacksonville MSA, FL	H	6.15 FQ	11.62 AW	16.18 TQ	FLBLS	10/01-12/01
	Lakeland-Winter Haven MSA, FL	H	7.77 FQ	10.61 AW	14.15 TQ	FLBLS	10/01-12/01
	Melbourne-Titusville-Palm Bay MSA, FL	H	8.37 FQ	11.35 AW	14.10 TQ	FLBLS	10/01-12/01
	Miami PMSA, FL	H	8.40 FQ	11.89 AW	15.59 TQ	FLBLS	10/01-12/01
	Ocala MSA, FL	H	7.30 FQ	10.19 AW	14.88 TQ	FLBLS	10/01-12/01
	Orlando MSA, FL	H	7.45 FQ	11.06 AW	15.56 TQ	FLBLS	10/01-12/01
	Sarasota-Bradenton MSA, FL	H	5.70 FQ	9.40 AW	13.16 TQ	FLBLS	10/01-12/01
	Tallahassee MSA, FL	H	6.00 FQ	8.11 AW	11.23 TQ	FLBLS	10/01-12/01

AAW	Average annual wage	**AOH**	Average offered, high	**ASH**	Average starting, high	**H**	Hourly	**M**	Monthly	**S**	Special: hourly and annual
AE	Average entry wage	**AOL**	Average offered, low	**ASL**	Average starting, low	**HI**	Highest wage paid	**MTC**	Median total compensation	**TQ**	Third quartile wage
AEX	Average experienced wage	**APH**	Average pay, high range	**AW**	Average wage paid	**HR**	High end range	**MW**	Median wage paid	**W**	Weekly
AO	Average offered	**APL**	Average pay, low range	**FQ**	First quartile wage	**LR**	Low end range	**SQ**	Second quartile wage	**Y**	Yearly

Occupation/Type/Industry	Location	Per	Low	Mid	High	Source	Date
Highway Maintenance Worker	Tampa-St. Petersburg-Clearwater MSA, FL	H	5.43 FQ	7.81 AW	11.04 TQ	FLBLS	10/01-12/01
	West Palm Beach-Boca Raton MSA, FL	H	5.90 FQ	11.37 AW	16.53 TQ	FLBLS	10/01-12/01
	Georgia	H	7.39 FQ	9.86 AW	13.08 TQ	GABLS	10/01-12/01
	Atlanta MSA, GA	H	7.63 FQ	10.41 AW	14.44 TQ	GABLS	10/01-12/01
	Augusta-Aiken MSA, GA-SC	H	7.57 FQ	10.05 AW	11.66 TQ	GABLS	10/01-12/01
	Macon MSA, GA	H	7.39 FQ	9.80 AW	12.01 TQ	GABLS	10/01-12/01
	Savannah MSA, GA	H	7.52 FQ	9.19 AW	11.15 TQ	GABLS	10/01-12/01
	Idaho	H	11.21 FQ	15.30 AW	20.68 TQ	IDBLS	10/01-12/01
	Boise City MSA, ID	H	11.67 FQ	13.87 AW	18.27 TQ	IDBLS	10/01-12/01
	Illinois	H	10.48 FQ	17.95 AW	25.05 TQ	ILBLS	10/01-12/01
	Champaign-Urbana MSA, IL	H	8.66 FQ	15.11 AW	22.66 TQ	ILBLS	10/01-12/01
	Chicago PMSA, IL	H	11.59 FQ	18.42 AW	25.03 TQ	ILBLS	10/01-12/01
	Peoria-Pekin MSA, IL	H	12.54 FQ	18.87 AW	25.40 TQ	ILBLS	10/01-12/01
	Rockford MSA, IL	H	7.57 FQ	16.11 AW	23.66 TQ	ILBLS	10/01-12/01
	Springfield MSA, IL	H	5.78 FQ	16.76 AW	25.59 TQ	ILBLS	10/01-12/01
	Indiana	H	9.03 FQ	11.82 AW	15.36 TQ	INBLS	10/01-12/01
	Elkhart-Goshen MSA, IN	H	9.00 FQ	11.61 AW	15.23 TQ	INBLS	10/01-12/01
	Evansville-Henderson MSA, IN-KY	H	8.39 FQ	10.68 AW	13.47 TQ	INBLS	10/01-12/01
	Fort Wayne MSA, IN	H	9.46 FQ	13.22 AW	18.04 TQ	INBLS	10/01-12/01
	Gary PMSA, IN	H	8.52 FQ	12.85 AW	17.46 TQ	INBLS	10/01-12/01
	Indianapolis MSA, IN	H	9.52 FQ	12.44 AW	15.31 TQ	INBLS	10/01-12/01
	Lafayette MSA, IN	H	8.85 FQ	11.07 AW	13.40 TQ	INBLS	10/01-12/01
	South Bend MSA, IN	H	9.07 FQ	12.22 AW	16.49 TQ	INBLS	10/01-12/01
	Iowa	H	11.59 FQ	14.34 AW	17.54 TQ	IABLS	10/01-12/01
	Davenport-Moline-Rock Island MSA, IA-IL	H	9.66 FQ	17.68 AW	24.89 TQ	IABLS	10/01-12/01
	Des Moines MSA, IA	H	12.54 FQ	15.63 AW	19.70 TQ	IABLS	10/01-12/01
	Kansas	H	8.54 FQ	11.16 AW	14.65 TQ	KSBLS	10/01-12/01
	Topeka MSA, KS	H	8.51 FQ	12.65 AW	16.48 TQ	KSBLS	10/01-12/01
	Wichita MSA, KS	H	8.62 FQ	10.40 AW	12.94 TQ	KSBLS	10/01-12/01
	Kentucky	H	7.56 FQ	10.14 AW	13.63 TQ	KYBLS	10/01-12/01
	Lexington MSA, KY	H	7.76 FQ	10.25 AW	13.06 TQ	KYBLS	10/01-12/01
	Louisville MSA, KY-IN	H	8.10 FQ	11.36 AW	16.04 TQ	KYBLS	10/01-12/01
	Louisiana	H	6.11 FQ	9.31 AW	14.24 TQ	LABLS	10/01-12/01
	Baton Rouge MSA, LA	H	6.10 FQ	9.03 AW	13.77 TQ	LABLS	10/01-12/01
	Lafayette MSA, LA	H	6.09 FQ	8.93 AW	14.78 TQ	LABLS	10/01-12/01
	Lake Charles MSA, LA	H	8.35 FQ	13.10 AW	19.51 TQ	LABLS	10/01-12/01
	New Orleans MSA, LA	H	6.37 FQ	10.59 AW	15.97 TQ	LABLS	10/01-12/01
	Shreveport-Bossier City MSA, LA	H	6.73 FQ	9.80 AW	13.83 TQ	LABLS	10/01-12/01
	Maine	H	9.04 FQ	12.21 AW	15.95 TQ	MEBLS	10/01-12/01
	Portland MSA, ME	H	10.00 FQ	13.01 AW	16.53 TQ	MEBLS	10/01-12/01
	Maryland	H	7.43 FQ	11.29 AW	16.34 TQ	MDBLS	10/01-12/01
	Baltimore PMSA, MD	H	7.24 FQ	10.22 AW	14.00 TQ	MDBLS	10/01-12/01
	Massachusetts	H	11.80 FQ	16.55 AW	21.90 TQ	MABLS	10/01-12/01
	Boston PMSA, MA-NH	H	11.07 FQ	16.77 AW	22.63 TQ	MABLS	10/01-12/01
	Brockton PMSA, MA	H	12.20 FQ	16.69 AW	21.63 TQ	MABLS	10/01-12/01
	Lawrence PMSA, MA-NH	H	9.09 FQ	17.10 AW	31.88 TQ	MABLS	10/01-12/01
	Lowell PMSA, MA-NH	H	12.08 FQ	15.59 AW	20.83 TQ	MABLS	10/01-12/01
	New Bedford PMSA, MA	H	11.86 FQ	14.29 AW	17.21 TQ	MABLS	10/01-12/01
	Springfield MSA, MA	H	11.83 FQ	16.21 AW	21.30 TQ	MABLS	10/01-12/01
	Worcester PMSA, MA-CT	H	12.75 FQ	16.88 AW	21.60 TQ	MABLS	10/01-12/01
	Michigan	H	12.23 FQ	15.90 AW	20.39 TQ	MIBLS	10/01-12/01
	Ann Arbor PMSA, MI	H	12.15 FQ	15.46 AW	19.20 TQ	MIBLS	10/01-12/01
	Detroit PMSA, MI	H	11.82 FQ	16.86 AW	21.74 TQ	MIBLS	10/01-12/01
	Grand Rapids-Muskegon-Holland MSA, MI	H	10.55 FQ	15.33 AW	20.27 TQ	MIBLS	10/01-12/01
	Kalamazoo-Battle Creek MSA, MI	H	12.16 FQ	15.21 AW	18.21 TQ	MIBLS	10/01-12/01
	Lansing-East Lansing MSA, MI	H	14.06 FQ	17.37 AW	21.61 TQ	MIBLS	10/01-12/01
	Saginaw-Bay City-Midland MSA, MI	H	13.09 FQ	15.99 AW	18.32 TQ	MIBLS	10/01-12/01
	Minnesota	H	11.49 FQ	16.07 AW	20.71 TQ	MNBLS	10/01-12/01
	Duluth-Superior MSA, MN-WI	H	12.65 FQ	16.28 AW	20.60 TQ	MNBLS	10/01-12/01
	Minneapolis-St. Paul MSA, MN-WI	H	14.18 FQ	17.98 AW	21.33 TQ	MNBLS	10/01-12/01
	St. Cloud MSA, MN	H	12.55 FQ	16.54 AW	20.66 TQ	MNBLS	10/01-12/01
	Mississippi	H	6.52 FQ	9.07 AW	11.53 TQ	MSBLS	10/01-12/01

AAW Average annual wage **AE** Average entry wage **AEX** Average experienced wage **AO** Average offered **AOH** Average offered, high **AOL** Average offered, low **APH** Average pay, high range **APL** Average pay, low range **ASH** Average starting, high **ASL** Average starting, low **AW** Average wage paid **FQ** First quartile wage **H** Hourly **HI** Highest wage paid **HR** High end range **LR** Low end range **M** Monthly **MTC** Median total compensation **MW** Median wage paid **SQ** Second quartile wage **S** Special: hourly and annual **TQ** Third quartile wage **W** Weekly **Y** Yearly

Occupation/Type/Industry	Location	Per	Low	Mid	High	Source	Date
Highway Maintenance Worker	Biloxi-Gulfport-Pascagoula MSA, MS	H	6.01 FQ	8.64 AW	11.03 TQ	MSBLS	10/01-12/01
	Jackson MSA, MS	H	7.43 FQ	9.30 AW	12.82 TQ	MSBLS	10/01-12/01
	Missouri	H	7.82 FQ	10.76 AW	13.96 TQ	MOBLS	10/01-12/01
	Kansas City MSA, MO-KS	H	7.77 FQ	11.21 AW	15.87 TQ	MOBLS	10/01-12/01
	St. Louis MSA, MO-IL	H	8.62 FQ	14.09 AW	22.42 TQ	MOBLS	10/01-12/01
	Springfield MSA, MO	H	7.70 FQ	9.93 AW	12.89 TQ	MOBLS	10/01-12/01
	Montana	H	10.35 FQ	13.40 AW	16.82 TQ	MTBLS	10/01-12/01
	Nebraska	H	9.34 FQ	11.96 AW	15.49 TQ	NEBLS	10/01-12/01
	Omaha MSA, NE-IA	H	11.48 FQ	14.29 AW	16.95 TQ	NEBLS	10/01-12/01
	Nevada	H	10.91 FQ	15.62 AW	20.67 TQ	NVBLS	10/01-12/01
	Las Vegas MSA, NV-AZ	H	8.83 FQ	13.34 AW	19.34 TQ	NVBLS	10/01-12/01
	New Hampshire	H	9.16 FQ	12.15 AW	16.48 TQ	NHBLS	10/01-12/01
	Manchester PMSA, NH	H	9.32 FQ	12.07 AW	16.80 TQ	NHBLS	10/01-12/01
	Nashua PMSA, NH	H	9.44 FQ	13.39 AW	17.15 TQ	NHBLS	10/01-12/01
	Portsmouth-Rochester PMSA, NH-ME	H	9.26 FQ	14.02 AW	18.74 TQ	NHBLS	10/01-12/01
	New Jersey	H	11.30 FQ	17.57 AW	25.87 TQ	NJBLS	10/01-12/01
	Atlantic-Cape May PMSA, NJ	H	11.00 FQ	15.17 AW	20.91 TQ	NJBLS	10/01-12/01
	Bergen-Passaic PMSA, NJ	H	10.33 FQ	19.91 AW	28.49 TQ	NJBLS	10/01-12/01
	Jersey City PMSA, NJ	H	10.05 FQ	16.58 AW	24.45 TQ	NJBLS	10/01-12/01
	Middlesex-Somerset-Hunterdon PMSA, NJ	H	11.96 FQ	18.15 AW	25.94 TQ	NJBLS	10/01-12/01
	Monmouth-Ocean PMSA, NJ	H	10.09 FQ	16.26 AW	24.18 TQ	NJBLS	10/01-12/01
	Newark PMSA, NJ	H	12.07 FQ	18.40 AW	25.80 TQ	NJBLS	10/01-12/01
	Trenton PMSA, NJ	H	11.04 FQ	15.42 AW	20.69 TQ	NJBLS	10/01-12/01
	New Mexico	H	7.81 FQ	11.08 AW	15.10 TQ	NMBLS	10/01-12/01
	Albuquerque MSA, NM	H	9.36 FQ	12.48 AW	16.50 TQ	NMBLS	10/01-12/01
	Las Cruces MSA, NM	H	6.59 FQ	9.30 AW	12.74 TQ	NMBLS	10/01-12/01
	New York	H	9.77 FQ	14.19 AW	19.53 TQ	NYBLS	10/01-12/01
	Albany-Schenectady-Troy MSA, NY	H	10.77 FQ	13.69 AW	17.42 TQ	NYBLS	10/01-12/01
	Binghamton MSA, NY	H	10.75 FQ	12.60 AW	15.56 TQ	NYBLS	10/01-12/01
	Buffalo-Niagara Falls MSA, NY	H	11.95 FQ	15.44 AW	19.75 TQ	NYBLS	10/01-12/01
	Dutchess County PMSA, NY	H	8.27 FQ	13.93 AW	20.58 TQ	NYBLS	10/01-12/01
	Nassau-Suffolk PMSA, NY	H	9.04 FQ	15.10 AW	21.91 TQ	NYBLS	10/01-12/01
	New York PMSA, NY	H	11.48 FQ	17.90 AW	24.72 TQ	NYBLS	10/01-12/01
	Newburgh PMSA, NY-PA	H	10.84 FQ	14.96 AW	20.23 TQ	NYBLS	10/01-12/01
	Rochester MSA, NY	H	10.16 FQ	14.96 AW	20.61 TQ	NYBLS	10/01-12/01
	Syracuse MSA, NY	H	10.16 FQ	15.09 AW	22.12 TQ	NYBLS	10/01-12/01
	Utica-Rome MSA, NY	H	9.55 FQ	12.64 AW	16.05 TQ	NYBLS	10/01-12/01
	North Carolina	H	7.47 FQ	10.24 AW	13.69 TQ	NCBLS	10/01-12/01
	Asheville MSA, NC	H	8.81 FQ	10.45 AW	13.29 TQ	NCBLS	10/01-12/01
	Charlotte-Gastonia-Rock Hill MSA, NC-SC	H	7.48 FQ	10.46 AW	14.42 TQ	NCBLS	10/01-12/01
	Greensboro-Winston-Salem-High Point MSA, NC	H	7.77 FQ	11.10 AW	16.23 TQ	NCBLS	10/01-12/01
	Hickory-Morganton-Lenoir MSA, NC	H	8.70 FQ	10.23 AW	12.50 TQ	NCBLS	10/01-12/01
	Raleigh-Durham-Chapel Hill MSA, NC	H	8.04 FQ	11.81 AW	16.77 TQ	NCBLS	10/01-12/01
	Wilmington MSA, NC	H	7.42 FQ	12.27 AW	17.63 TQ	NCBLS	10/01-12/01
	North Dakota	H	9.33 FQ	11.94 AW	15.22 TQ	NDBLS	10/01-12/01
	Fargo-Moorhead MSA, ND-MN	H	11.52 FQ	15.34 AW	19.87 TQ	NDBLS	10/01-12/01
	Ohio	H	9.95 FQ	14.40 AW	18.90 TQ	OHBLS	10/01-12/01
	Akron PMSA, OH	H	10.96 FQ	13.47 AW	16.92 TQ	OHBLS	10/01-12/01
	Canton-Massillon MSA, OH	H	10.86 FQ	14.22 AW	18.04 TQ	OHBLS	10/01-12/01
	Cincinnati PMSA, OH-KY-IN	H	9.09 FQ	14.75 AW	20.98 TQ	OHBLS	10/01-12/01
	Cleveland-Lorain-Elyria PMSA, OH	H	11.05 FQ	15.44 AW	19.88 TQ	OHBLS	10/01-12/01
	Columbus MSA, OH	H	9.39 FQ	13.07 AW	17.19 TQ	OHBLS	10/01-12/01
	Dayton-Springfield MSA, OH	H	9.74 FQ	14.74 AW	19.84 TQ	OHBLS	10/01-12/01
	Hamilton-Middletown PMSA, OH	H	10.89 FQ	15.47 AW	21.13 TQ	OHBLS	10/01-12/01
	Mansfield MSA, OH	H	9.99 FQ	14.14 AW	17.54 TQ	OHBLS	10/01-12/01
	Toledo MSA, OH	H	11.12 FQ	15.20 AW	18.30 TQ	OHBLS	10/01-12/01
	Youngstown-Warren MSA, OH	H	9.98 FQ	15.33 AW	21.09 TQ	OHBLS	10/01-12/01
	Oklahoma	H	7.41 FQ	9.79 AW	12.87 TQ	OKBLS	10/01-12/01
	Oklahoma City MSA, OK	H	7.35 FQ	9.95 AW	13.38 TQ	OKBLS	10/01-12/01
	Tulsa MSA, OK	H	7.41 FQ	9.96 AW	13.37 TQ	OKBLS	10/01-12/01

AAW Average annual wage; **AE** Average entry wage; **AEX** Average experienced wage; **AO** Average offered; **AOH** Average offered, high; **AOL** Average offered, low; **APH** Average pay, high range; **APL** Average pay, low range; **ASH** Average starting, high; **ASL** Average starting, low; **AW** Average wage paid; **FQ** First quartile wage; **H** Hourly; **HI** Highest wage paid; **HR** High end range; **LR** Low end range; **M** Monthly; **MTC** Median total compensation; **MW** Median wage paid; **SQ** Second quartile wage; **S** Special: hourly and annual; **TQ** Third quartile wage; **W** Weekly; **Y** Yearly

Occupation/Type/Industry	Location	Per	Low	Mid	High	Source	Date
Highway Maintenance Worker	Oregon	H	12.03 FQ	15.54 AW	19.80 TQ	ORBLS	10/01-12/01
	Eugene-Springfield MSA, OR	H	11.79 FQ	16.35 AW	21.19 TQ	ORBLS	10/01-12/01
	Medford-Ashland MSA, OR	H	11.11 FQ	15.49 AW	22.67 TQ	ORBLS	10/01-12/01
	Portland-Vancouver PMSA, OR-WA	H	12.72 FQ	16.60 AW	21.28 TQ	ORBLS	10/01-12/01
	Pennsylvania	H	9.27 FQ	14.76 AW	22.38 TQ	PABLS	10/01-12/01
	Allentown-Bethlehem-Easton MSA, PA	H	7.66 FQ	13.06 AW	19.27 TQ	PABLS	10/01-12/01
	Erie MSA, PA	H	8.97 FQ	13.58 AW	23.90 TQ	PABLS	10/01-12/01
	Harrisburg-Lebanon-Carlisle MSA, PA	H	12.66 FQ	20.01 AW	27.22 TQ	PABLS	10/01-12/01
	Johnstown MSA, PA	H	7.33 FQ	13.05 AW	22.72 TQ	PABLS	10/01-12/01
	Lancaster MSA, PA	H	9.52 FQ	14.07 AW	21.08 TQ	PABLS	10/01-12/01
	Philadelphia PMSA, PA-NJ	H	11.17 FQ	17.21 AW	24.77 TQ	PABLS	10/01-12/01
	Pittsburgh MSA, PA	H	9.57 FQ	13.57 AW	18.70 TQ	PABLS	10/01-12/01
	Reading MSA, PA	H	9.61 FQ	15.22 AW	20.65 TQ	PABLS	10/01-12/01
	Scranton-Wilkes-Barre-Hazleton MSA, PA	H	8.58 FQ	13.95 AW	19.01 TQ	PABLS	10/01-12/01
	York MSA, PA	H	12.06 FQ	15.28 AW	19.25 TQ	PABLS	10/01-12/01
	Rhode Island	H	14.37 FQ	17.69 AW	22.00 TQ	RIBLS	10/01-12/01
	Providence-Fall River-Warwick MSA, RI-MA	H	14.69 FQ	17.96 AW	22.11 TQ	RIBLS	10/01-12/01
	South Carolina	H	7.37 FQ	12.55 AW	21.71 TQ	SCBLS	10/01-12/01
	Greenville-Spartanburg-Anderson MSA, SC	H	8.01 FQ	11.58 AW	14.55 TQ	SCBLS	10/01-12/01
	South Dakota	H	7.67 FQ	10.76 AW	14.25 TQ	SDBLS	10/01-12/01
	Sioux Falls MSA, SD	H	7.98 FQ	11.80 AW	16.81 TQ	SDBLS	10/01-12/01
	Tennessee	H	7.62 FQ	10.93 AW	14.27 TQ	TNBLS	10/01-12/01
	Chattanooga MSA, TN-GA	H	7.53 FQ	9.66 AW	12.78 TQ	TNBLS	10/01-12/01
	Clarksville-Hopkinsville MSA, TN-KY	H	8.47 FQ	10.34 AW	13.33 TQ	TNBLS	10/01-12/01
	Johnson City-Kingsport-Bristol MSA, TN-VA	H	7.90 FQ	11.47 AW	16.11 TQ	TNBLS	10/01-12/01
	Knoxville MSA, TN	H	7.10 FQ	11.17 AW	15.10 TQ	TNBLS	10/01-12/01
	Memphis MSA, TN-AR-MS	H	8.26 FQ	11.90 AW	14.22 TQ	TNBLS	10/01-12/01
	Nashville MSA, TN	H	7.72 FQ	11.37 AW	14.62 TQ	TNBLS	10/01-12/01
	Texas	H	7.72 FQ	11.86 AW	17.30 TQ	TXBLS	10/01-12/01
	Austin-San Marcos MSA, TX	H	9.90 FQ	13.40 AW	17.70 TQ	TXBLS	10/01-12/01
	Beaumont-Port Arthur MSA, TX	H	8.32 FQ	16.36 AW	25.06 TQ	TXBLS	10/01-12/01
	Brazoria PMSA, TX	H	7.52 FQ	9.21 AW	13.21 TQ	TXBLS	10/01-12/01
	Brownsville-Harlingen-San Benito MSA, TX	H	5.74 FQ	7.84 AW	10.55 TQ	TXBLS	10/01-12/01
	Corpus Christi MSA, TX	H	7.36 FQ	12.62 AW	19.81 TQ	TXBLS	10/01-12/01
	Dallas PMSA, TX	H	9.47 FQ	13.00 AW	16.87 TQ	TXBLS	10/01-12/01
	El Paso MSA, TX	H	7.61 FQ	9.79 AW	14.02 TQ	TXBLS	10/01-12/01
	Fort Worth-Arlington PMSA, TX	H	8.46 FQ	11.73 AW	16.02 TQ	TXBLS	10/01-12/01
	Galveston-Texas City PMSA, TX	H	9.33 FQ	14.62 AW	22.87 TQ	TXBLS	10/01-12/01
	Houston PMSA, TX	H	7.48 FQ	10.42 AW	14.11 TQ	TXBLS	10/01-12/01
	Killeen-Temple MSA, TX	H	7.98 FQ	11.86 AW	18.16 TQ	TXBLS	10/01-12/01
	Longview-Marshall MSA, TX	H	7.69 FQ	12.20 AW	18.00 TQ	TXBLS	10/01-12/01
	Lubbock MSA, TX	H	10.10 FQ	14.35 AW	19.44 TQ	TXBLS	10/01-12/01
	McAllen-Edinburg-Mission MSA, TX	H	6.20 FQ	8.78 AW	11.82 TQ	TXBLS	10/01-12/01
	San Antonio MSA, TX	H	8.19 FQ	12.00 AW	18.12 TQ	TXBLS	10/01-12/01
	Waco MSA, TX	H	5.73 FQ	8.56 AW	11.50 TQ	TXBLS	10/01-12/01
	Utah	H	10.77 FQ	15.41 AW	21.28 TQ	UTBLS	10/01-12/01
	Provo-Orem MSA, UT	H	9.41 FQ	13.62 AW	18.03 TQ	UTBLS	10/01-12/01
	Salt Lake City-Ogden MSA, UT	H	10.99 FQ	16.79 AW	22.02 TQ	UTBLS	10/01-12/01
	Vermont	H	9.94 FQ	12.85 AW	16.49 TQ	VTBLS	10/01-12/01
	Burlington MSA, VT	H	9.83 FQ	13.26 AW	17.47 TQ	VTBLS	10/01-12/01
	Virginia	H	8.83 FQ	12.91 AW	16.58 TQ	VABLS	10/01-12/01
	Lynchburg MSA, VA	H	9.60 FQ	12.82 AW	16.22 TQ	VABLS	10/01-12/01
	Norfolk-Virginia Beach-Newport News MSA, VA-NC	H	8.30 FQ	12.11 AW	16.07 TQ	VABLS	10/01-12/01
	Richmond-Petersburg MSA, VA	H	9.12 FQ	12.35 AW	15.99 TQ	VABLS	10/01-12/01
	Washington	H	14.20 FQ	17.77 AW	21.40 TQ	WABLS	10/01-12/01

AAW Average annual wage **AE** Average entry wage **AEX** Average experienced wage **AO** Average offered **AOH** Average offered, high **AOL** Average offered, low **APH** Average pay, high range **APL** Average pay, low range **ASH** Average starting, high **ASL** Average starting, low **AW** Average wage paid **FQ** First quartile wage **H** Hourly **HI** Highest wage paid **HR** High end range **LR** Low end range **M** Monthly **MTC** Median total compensation **MW** Median wage paid **SQ** Second quartile wage **S** Special: hourly and annual **TQ** Third quartile wage **W** Weekly **Y** Yearly

Occupation/Type/Industry	Location	Per	Low	Mid	High	Source	Date
Highway Maintenance Worker	Bremerton PMSA, WA	H	16.96 FQ	19.84 AW	22.90 TQ	WABLS	10/01-12/01
	Olympia PMSA, WA	H	14.70 FQ	18.80 AW	23.97 TQ	WABLS	10/01-12/01
	Richland-Kennewick-Pasco MSA, WA	H	14.57 FQ	18.80 AW	24.45 TQ	WABLS	10/01-12/01
	Seattle-Bellevue-Everett PMSA, WA	H	14.81 FQ	18.86 AW	22.92 TQ	WABLS	10/01-12/01
	Tacoma PMSA, WA	H	14.74 FQ	18.07 AW	21.38 TQ	WABLS	10/01-12/01
	Yakima MSA, WA	H	14.76 FQ	18.01 AW	21.58 TQ	WABLS	10/01-12/01
	West Virginia	H	6.93 FQ	9.79 AW	12.60 TQ	WVBLS	10/01-12/01
	Charleston MSA, WV	H	6.64 FQ	10.09 AW	15.11 TQ	WVBLS	10/01-12/01
	Huntington-Ashland MSA, WV-KY-OH	H	7.65 FQ	10.84 AW	14.95 TQ	WVBLS	10/01-12/01
	Wisconsin	H	9.29 FQ	15.03 AW	20.48 TQ	WIBLS	10/01-12/01
	Appleton-Oshkosh-Neenah MSA, WI	H	9.04 FQ	14.33 AW	19.05 TQ	WIBLS	10/01-12/01
	Green Bay MSA, WI	H	13.56 FQ	15.69 AW	18.04 TQ	WIBLS	10/01-12/01
	Madison MSA, WI	H	9.59 FQ	14.03 AW	18.22 TQ	WIBLS	10/01-12/01
	Milwaukee-Waukesha PMSA, WI	H	13.49 FQ	18.31 AW	23.40 TQ	WIBLS	10/01-12/01
	Racine PMSA, WI	H	12.38 FQ	17.17 AW	21.49 TQ	WIBLS	10/01-12/01
	Wyoming	H	9.73 FQ	12.96 AW	16.47 TQ	WYBLS	10/01-12/01
	Puerto Rico	H	5.52 FQ	8.59 AW	16.14 TQ	PRBLS	10/01-12/01
Historian	California	Y	43920 FQ	58650 AW	75250 TQ	CABLS	10/01-12/01
	Colorado	Y	27660 FQ	49990 AW	74480 TQ	COBLS	10/01-12/01
	District of Columbia	Y	37810 FQ	57160 AW	85320 TQ	DCBLS	10/01-12/01
	Washington PMSA, DC-MD-VA-WV	Y	37830 FQ	59260 AW	88290 TQ	DCBLS	10/01-12/01
	Georgia	Y	30870 FQ	45010 AW	64830 TQ	GABLS	10/01-12/01
	Atlanta MSA, GA	Y	30340 FQ	43860 AW	63720 TQ	GABLS	10/01-12/01
	Maryland	Y	22930 FQ	52460 AW	81800 TQ	MDBLS	10/01-12/01
	Massachusetts	Y	28110 FQ	52240 AW	73600 TQ	MABLS	10/01-12/01
	Minnesota	Y	29350 FQ	44300 AW	68170 TQ	MNBLS	10/01-12/01
	Minneapolis-St. Paul MSA, MN-WI	Y	29300 FQ	44110 AW	68320 TQ	MNBLS	10/01-12/01
	Mississippi	Y	13290 FQ	26450 AW	43780 TQ	MSBLS	10/01-12/01
	Montana	Y	26060 FQ	36220 AW	47530 TQ	MTBLS	10/01-12/01
	New York	Y	12530 FQ	26150 AW	46300 TQ	NYBLS	10/01-12/01
	Rochester MSA, NY	Y	11970 FQ	23220 AW	39720 TQ	NYBLS	10/01-12/01
	Pennsylvania	Y	31470 FQ	45910 AW	62940 TQ	PABLS	10/01-12/01
	South Carolina	Y	32980 FQ	45180 AW	56970 TQ	SCBLS	10/01-12/01
	Tennessee	Y	22870 FQ	29030 AW	39100 TQ	TNBLS	10/01-12/01
	Texas	Y	21410 FQ	36390 AW	58420 TQ	TXBLS	10/01-12/01
	Houston PMSA, TX	Y	25630 FQ	37800 AW	56070 TQ	TXBLS	10/01-12/01
	Virginia	Y	28340 FQ	59200 AW	96290 TQ	VABLS	10/01-12/01
	Richmond-Petersburg MSA, VA	Y	25760 FQ	49390 AW	90360 TQ	VABLS	10/01-12/01
	Wisconsin	Y	22490 FQ	38100 AW	65530 TQ	WIBLS	10/01-12/01
	Madison MSA, WI	Y	22550 FQ	37960 AW	66750 TQ	WIBLS	10/01-12/01
	Wyoming	Y	25740 FQ	39310 AW	52720 TQ	WYBLS	10/01-12/01
History Teacher							
Postsecondary	Alabama	Y	15490 FQ	42920 AW	74980 TQ	ALBLS	10/01-12/01
Postsecondary	Birmingham MSA, AL	Y	18360 FQ	45800 AW	77440 TQ	ALBLS	10/01-12/01
Postsecondary	Huntsville MSA, AL	Y	15680 FQ	44490 AW	72460 TQ	ALBLS	10/01-12/01
Postsecondary	Montgomery MSA, AL	Y	17440 FQ	40770 AW	58430 TQ	ALBLS	10/01-12/01
Postsecondary	Arizona	Y	28890 FQ	42020 AW	65670 TQ	AZBLS	10/01-12/01
Postsecondary	Arkansas	Y	19490 FQ	42080 AW	74030 TQ	ARBLS	10/01-12/01
Postsecondary	California	Y	38190 FQ	64370 AW	95890 TQ	CABLS	10/01-12/01
Postsecondary	Los Angeles-Long Beach PMSA, CA	Y	39950 FQ	65780 AW	98790 TQ	CABLS	10/01-12/01
Postsecondary	Riverside-San Bernardino PMSA, CA	Y	37200 FQ	57880 AW	87620 TQ	CABLS	10/01-12/01
Postsecondary	San Diego MSA, CA	Y	36290 FQ	64080 AW	95340 TQ	CABLS	10/01-12/01
Postsecondary	San Francisco PMSA, CA	Y	47180 FQ	73450 AW	108970 TQ	CABLS	10/01-12/01
Postsecondary	San Jose PMSA, CA	Y	47880 FQ	68890 AW	90300 TQ	CABLS	10/01-12/01
Postsecondary	Colorado	Y	31470 FQ	51860 AW	79830 TQ	COBLS	10/01-12/01
Postsecondary	Denver PMSA, CO	Y	31600 FQ	52330 AW	79640 TQ	COBLS	10/01-12/01
Postsecondary	Connecticut	Y	35910 FQ	64870 AW	101740 TQ	CTBLS	10/01-12/01
Postsecondary	Hartford MSA, CT	Y	38190 FQ	67940 AW	105910 TQ	CTBLS	10/01-12/01
Postsecondary	Delaware	Y	18090 FQ	59580 AW	94370 TQ	DEBLS	10/01-12/01
Postsecondary	Wilmington-Newark PMSA, DE-MD	Y	17660 FQ	59870 AW	97260 TQ	DEBLS	10/01-12/01

AAW Average annual wage **AE** Average entry wage **AEX** Average experienced wage **AO** Average offered **AOH** Average offered, high **AOL** Average offered, low **APH** Average pay, high range **APL** Average pay, low range **ASH** Average starting, high **ASL** Average starting, low **AW** Average wage paid **FQ** First quartile wage **H** Hourly **HI** Highest wage paid **HR** High end range **LR** Low end range **M** Monthly **MTC** Median total compensation **MW** Median wage paid **SQ** Second quartile wage **S** Special: hourly and annual **TQ** Third quartile wage **W** Weekly **Y** Yearly

Occupation/Type/Industry	Location	Per	Low	Mid	High	Source	Date
History Teacher							
Postsecondary	District of Columbia	Y	36590 FQ	56980 AW	88180 TQ	DCBLS	10/01-12/01
Postsecondary	Washington PMSA, DC-MD-VA-WV	Y	33380 FQ	57320 AW	88970 TQ	DCBLS	10/01-12/01
Postsecondary	Florida	Y	37170 FQ	61100 AW	95020 TQ	FLBLS	10/01-12/01
Postsecondary	Fort Lauderdale PMSA, FL	Y	37270 FQ	65120 AW	96720 TQ	FLBLS	10/01-12/01
Postsecondary	Gainesville MSA, FL	Y	40330 FQ	66700 AW	101810 TQ	FLBLS	10/01-12/01
Postsecondary	Miami PMSA, FL	Y	38370 FQ	61640 AW	101560 TQ	FLBLS	10/01-12/01
Postsecondary	Orlando MSA, FL	Y	27860 FQ	55660 AW	89940 TQ	FLBLS	10/01-12/01
Postsecondary	Tallahassee MSA, FL	Y	41040 FQ	66300 AW	107240 TQ	FLBLS	10/01-12/01
Postsecondary	Tampa-St. Petersburg-Clearwater MSA, FL	Y	37010 FQ	60450 AW	87620 TQ	FLBLS	10/01-12/01
Postsecondary	West Palm Beach-Boca Raton MSA, FL	Y	38090 FQ	58500 AW	89820 TQ	FLBLS	10/01-12/01
Postsecondary	Georgia	Y	36530 FQ	54510 AW	81820 TQ	GABLS	10/01-12/01
Postsecondary	Atlanta MSA, GA	Y	38580 FQ	59050 AW	88180 TQ	GABLS	10/01-12/01
Postsecondary	Hawaii	Y	36350 FQ	53380 AW	80240 TQ	HIBLS	10/01-12/01
Postsecondary	Honolulu MSA, HI	Y	36340 FQ	53980 AW	82180 TQ	HIBLS	10/01-12/01
Postsecondary	Idaho	Y	36700 FQ	50360 AW	61220 TQ	IDBLS	10/01-12/01
Postsecondary	Illinois	Y	28770 FQ	62060 AW	109100 TQ	ILBLS	10/01-12/01
Postsecondary	Champaign-Urbana MSA, IL	Y	28950 FQ	63160 AW	111950 TQ	ILBLS	10/01-12/01
Postsecondary	Chicago PMSA, IL	Y	30970 FQ	66080 AW	113040 TQ	ILBLS	10/01-12/01
Postsecondary	Indiana	Y	31500 FQ	51820 AW	80420 TQ	INBLS	10/01-12/01
Postsecondary	South Bend MSA, IN	Y	35590 FQ	48490 AW	71490 TQ	INBLS	10/01-12/01
Postsecondary	Iowa	Y	31150 FQ	49920 AW	72150 TQ	IABLS	10/01-12/01
Postsecondary	Des Moines MSA, IA	Y	30580 FQ	41820 AW	60040 TQ	IABLS	10/01-12/01
Postsecondary	Kansas	Y	22490 FQ	37360 AW	63970 TQ	KSBLS	10/01-12/01
Postsecondary	Kentucky	Y	24150 FQ	49720 AW	80180 TQ	KYBLS	10/01-12/01
Postsecondary	Louisiana	Y	26360 FQ	46570 AW	71400 TQ	LABLS	10/01-12/01
Postsecondary	New Orleans MSA, LA	Y	18250 FQ	46820 AW	74350 TQ	LABLS	10/01-12/01
Postsecondary	Maine	Y	35390 FQ	50970 AW	68930 TQ	MEBLS	10/01-12/01
Postsecondary	Maryland	Y	29870 FQ	57130 AW	90940 TQ	MDBLS	10/01-12/01
Postsecondary	Baltimore PMSA, MD	Y	30740 FQ	55130 AW	89010 TQ	MDBLS	10/01-12/01
Postsecondary	Massachusetts	Y	37410 FQ	58090 AW	90530 TQ	MABLS	10/01-12/01
Postsecondary	Boston PMSA, MA-NH	Y	36840 FQ	55890 AW	84920 TQ	MABLS	10/01-12/01
Postsecondary	Springfield MSA, MA	Y	38000 FQ	71490 AW	117980 TQ	MABLS	10/01-12/01
Postsecondary	Worcester PMSA, MA-CT	Y	38890 FQ	66300 AW	103540 TQ	MABLS	10/01-12/01
Postsecondary	Michigan	Y	33020 FQ	55230 AW	85220 TQ	MIBLS	10/01-12/01
Postsecondary	Ann Arbor PMSA, MI	Y	31010 FQ	54710 AW	87750 TQ	MIBLS	10/01-12/01
Postsecondary	Detroit PMSA, MI	Y	28560 FQ	47930 AW	73780 TQ	MIBLS	10/01-12/01
Postsecondary	Minnesota	Y	35840 FQ	56270 AW	81380 TQ	MNBLS	10/01-12/01
Postsecondary	Minneapolis-St. Paul MSA, MN-WI	Y	38770 FQ	60470 AW	92730 TQ	MNBLS	10/01-12/01
Postsecondary	Mississippi	Y	31010 FQ	46720 AW	62870 TQ	MSBLS	10/01-12/01
Postsecondary	Jackson MSA, MS	Y	14940 FQ	35500 AW	53270 TQ	MSBLS	10/01-12/01
Postsecondary	Missouri	Y	25240 FQ	44750 AW	69200 TQ	MOBLS	10/01-12/01
Postsecondary	Kansas City MSA, MO-KS	Y	27070 FQ	44630 AW	61980 TQ	MOBLS	10/01-12/01
Postsecondary	St. Louis MSA, MO-IL	Y	23960 FQ	44080 AW	77120 TQ	MOBLS	10/01-12/01
Postsecondary	Springfield MSA, MO	Y	37490 FQ	54570 AW	84920 TQ	MOBLS	10/01-12/01
Postsecondary	Montana	Y	23300 FQ	57500 AW	111220 TQ	MTBLS	10/01-12/01
Postsecondary	Nebraska	Y	32410 FQ	50230 AW	71620 TQ	NEBLS	10/01-12/01
Postsecondary	Lincoln MSA, NE	Y	37680 FQ	59860 AW	89960 TQ	NEBLS	10/01-12/01
Postsecondary	Nevada	Y	24780 FQ	49240 AW	82640 TQ	NVBLS	10/01-12/01
Postsecondary	Las Vegas MSA, NV-AZ	Y	25040 FQ	47990 AW	78580 TQ	NVBLS	10/01-12/01
Postsecondary	New Hampshire	Y	39190 FQ	60580 AW	97070 TQ	NHBLS	10/01-12/01
Postsecondary	New Jersey	Y	22960 FQ	60720 AW	90630 TQ	NJBLS	10/01-12/01
Postsecondary	Jersey City PMSA, NJ	Y	33160 FQ	58560 AW	89880 TQ	NJBLS	10/01-12/01
Postsecondary	Newark PMSA, NJ	Y	20890 FQ	55810 AW	88920 TQ	NJBLS	10/01-12/01
Postsecondary	New Mexico	Y	22350 FQ	39660 AW	56950 TQ	NMBLS	10/01-12/01
Postsecondary	New York	Y	36460 FQ	62770 AW	105750 TQ	NYBLS	10/01-12/01
Postsecondary	Albany-Schenectady-Troy MSA, NY	Y	39370 FQ	65260 AW	106390 TQ	NYBLS	10/01-12/01
Postsecondary	Dutchess County PMSA, NY	Y	36880 FQ	60200 AW	112020 TQ	NYBLS	10/01-12/01
Postsecondary	Nassau-Suffolk PMSA, NY	Y	37270 FQ	64920 AW	110500 TQ	NYBLS	10/01-12/01
Postsecondary	New York PMSA, NY	Y	37520 FQ	62010 AW	105640 TQ	NYBLS	10/01-12/01
Postsecondary	Rochester MSA, NY	Y	24220 FQ	52910 AW	87360 TQ	NYBLS	10/01-12/01
Postsecondary	North Carolina	Y	31810 FQ	48080 AW	70640 TQ	NCBLS	10/01-12/01
Postsecondary	Asheville MSA, NC	Y	39580 FQ	52130 AW	74440 TQ	NCBLS	10/01-12/01
Postsecondary	Charlotte-Gastonia-Rock Hill MSA, NC-SC	Y	31610 FQ	53690 AW	86270 TQ	NCBLS	10/01-12/01
Postsecondary	Fayetteville MSA, NC	Y	34460 FQ	49740 AW	59660 TQ	NCBLS	10/01-12/01

AAW	Average annual wage	**AOH**	Average offered, high	**ASH**	Average starting, high	**H**	Hourly	**M**	Monthly	**S**	Special: hourly and annual
AE	Average entry wage	**AOL**	Average offered, low	**ASL**	Average starting, low	**HI**	Highest wage paid	**MTC**	Median total compensation	**TQ**	Third quartile wage
AEX	Average experienced wage	**APH**	Average pay, high range	**AW**	Average wage paid	**HR**	High end range	**MW**	Median wage paid	**W**	Weekly
AO	Average offered	**APL**	Average pay, low range	**FQ**	First quartile wage	**LR**	Low end range	**SQ**	Second quartile wage	**Y**	Yearly

Occupation/Type/Industry	Location	Per	Low	Mid	High	Source	Date
History Teacher							
Postsecondary	Greensboro-Winston-Salem-High Point MSA, NC	Y	31210 FQ	46030 AW	65850 TQ	NCBLS	10/01-12/01
Postsecondary	Hickory-Morganton-Lenoir MSA, NC	Y	32010 FQ	39090 AW	46660 TQ	NCBLS	10/01-12/01
Postsecondary	Raleigh-Durham-Chapel Hill MSA, NC	Y	31360 FQ	48640 AW	73050 TQ	NCBLS	10/01-12/01
Postsecondary	Wilmington MSA, NC	Y	33360 FQ	52070 AW	80470 TQ	NCBLS	10/01-12/01
Postsecondary	North Dakota	Y	21420 FQ	41110 AW	61600 TQ	NDBLS	10/01-12/01
Postsecondary	Ohio	Y	27240 FQ	48530 AW	76240 TQ	OHBLS	10/01-12/01
Postsecondary	Cincinnati PMSA, OH-KY-IN	Y	32610 FQ	52290 AW	79520 TQ	OHBLS	10/01-12/01
Postsecondary	Cleveland-Lorain-Elyria PMSA, OH	Y	27110 FQ	50400 AW	79300 TQ	OHBLS	10/01-12/01
Postsecondary	Columbus MSA, OH	Y	28510 FQ	46960 AW	73800 TQ	OHBLS	10/01-12/01
Postsecondary	Dayton-Springfield MSA, OH	Y	17690 FQ	45500 AW	73670 TQ	OHBLS	10/01-12/01
Postsecondary	Toledo MSA, OH	Y	28080 FQ	50300 AW	81490 TQ	OHBLS	10/01-12/01
Postsecondary	Youngstown-Warren MSA, OH	Y	37870 FQ	57610 AW	87500 TQ	OHBLS	10/01-12/01
Postsecondary	Oklahoma	Y	24160 FQ	43640 AW	67410 TQ	OKBLS	10/01-12/01
Postsecondary	Oklahoma City MSA, OK	Y	26670 FQ	47630 AW	69010 TQ	OKBLS	10/01-12/01
Postsecondary	Oregon	Y	31850 FQ	61590 AW	88510 TQ	ORBLS	10/01-12/01
Postsecondary	Portland-Vancouver PMSA, OR-WA	Y	23700 FQ	53540 AW	85280 TQ	ORBLS	10/01-12/01
Postsecondary	Pennsylvania	Y	28620 FQ	55650 AW	86130 TQ	PABLS	10/01-12/01
Postsecondary	Allentown-Bethlehem-Easton MSA, PA	Y	30990 FQ	52350 AW	77380 TQ	PABLS	10/01-12/01
Postsecondary	Lancaster MSA, PA	Y	41570 FQ	59890 AW	90090 TQ	PABLS	10/01-12/01
Postsecondary	Philadelphia PMSA, PA-NJ	Y	27270 FQ	54550 AW	86690 TQ	PABLS	10/01-12/01
Postsecondary	Pittsburgh MSA, PA	Y	26130 FQ	54900 AW	87060 TQ	PABLS	10/01-12/01
Postsecondary	Scranton-Wilkes-Barre-Hazleton MSA, PA	Y	32430 FQ	53820 AW	78430 TQ	PABLS	10/01-12/01
Postsecondary	Rhode Island	Y	35790 FQ	58390 AW	91230 TQ	RIBLS	10/01-12/01
Postsecondary	South Carolina	Y	28910 FQ	44960 AW	69490 TQ	SCBLS	10/01-12/01
Postsecondary	Charleston-North Charleston MSA, SC	Y	30690 FQ	42200 AW	61340 TQ	SCBLS	10/01-12/01
Postsecondary	Greenville-Spartanburg-Anderson MSA, SC	Y	29880 FQ	46820 AW	71850 TQ	SCBLS	10/01-12/01
Postsecondary	South Dakota	Y	27330 FQ	44520 AW	65130 TQ	SDBLS	10/01-12/01
Postsecondary	Tennessee	Y	30510 FQ	46940 AW	67050 TQ	TNBLS	10/01-12/01
Postsecondary	Johnson City-Kingsport-Bristol MSA, TN-VA	Y	23260 FQ	44270 AW	59830 TQ	TNBLS	10/01-12/01
Postsecondary	Knoxville MSA, TN	Y	27070 FQ	44180 AW	65480 TQ	TNBLS	10/01-12/01
Postsecondary	Memphis MSA, TN-AR-MS	Y	33550 FQ	49430 AW	69900 TQ	TNBLS	10/01-12/01
Postsecondary	Nashville MSA, TN	Y	36460 FQ	50590 AW	70100 TQ	TNBLS	10/01-12/01
Postsecondary	Texas	Y	30350 FQ	55600 AW	88330 TQ	TXBLS	10/01-12/01
Postsecondary	Austin-San Marcos MSA, TX	Y	42310 FQ	59120 AW	75460 TQ	TXBLS	10/01-12/01
Postsecondary	Dallas PMSA, TX	Y	29830 FQ	63220 AW	134400 TQ	TXBLS	10/01-12/01
Postsecondary	El Paso MSA, TX	Y	24550 FQ	49300 AW	76750 TQ	TXBLS	10/01-12/01
Postsecondary	Fort Worth-Arlington PMSA, TX	Y	36960 FQ	61010 AW	92150 TQ	TXBLS	10/01-12/01
Postsecondary	Houston PMSA, TX	Y	38820 FQ	62830 AW	103340 TQ	TXBLS	10/01-12/01
Postsecondary	San Antonio MSA, TX	Y	30850 FQ	55110 AW	89080 TQ	TXBLS	10/01-12/01
Postsecondary	Utah	Y	40170 FQ	62780 AW	95890 TQ	UTBLS	10/01-12/01
Postsecondary	Vermont	Y	34600 FQ	48530 AW	64650 TQ	VTBLS	10/01-12/01
Postsecondary	Burlington MSA, VT	Y	35080 FQ	49910 AW	70930 TQ	VTBLS	10/01-12/01
Postsecondary	Virginia	Y	27750 FQ	56190 AW	89500 TQ	VABLS	10/01-12/01
Postsecondary	Norfolk-Virginia Beach-Newport News MSA, VA-NC	Y	38870 FQ	62820 AW	97600 TQ	VABLS	10/01-12/01
Postsecondary	Richmond-Petersburg MSA, VA	Y	18220 FQ	47130 AW	85610 TQ	VABLS	10/01-12/01
Postsecondary	Washington	Y	29190 FQ	52240 AW	83950 TQ	WABLS	10/01-12/01
Postsecondary	Seattle-Bellevue-Everett PMSA, WA	Y	31560 FQ	58140 AW	92750 TQ	WABLS	10/01-12/01
Postsecondary	Tacoma PMSA, WA	Y	32460 FQ	57220 AW	91550 TQ	WABLS	10/01-12/01
Postsecondary	West Virginia	Y	33920 FQ	53900 AW	76130 TQ	WVBLS	10/01-12/01
Postsecondary	Wisconsin	Y	26470 FQ	49610 AW	76130 TQ	WIBLS	10/01-12/01
Postsecondary	Milwaukee-Waukesha PMSA, WI	Y	21230 FQ	44030 AW	68490 TQ	WIBLS	10/01-12/01
Postsecondary	Wyoming	Y	36170 FQ	52150 AW	71440 TQ	WYBLS	10/01-12/01
Postsecondary	Puerto Rico	Y	27140 FQ	41600 AW	58570 TQ	PRBLS	10/01-12/01
Hoist and Winch Operator	Alabama	H	8.20 FQ	13.33 AW	20.95 TQ	ALBLS	10/01-12/01
	Arizona	H	9.26 FQ	14.41 AW	21.27 TQ	AZBLS	10/01-12/01

AAW Average annual wage	AOH Average offered, high	ASH Average starting, high	H Hourly	M Monthly	S Special: hourly and annual
AE Average entry wage	AOL Average offered, low	ASL Average starting, low	HI Highest wage paid	MTC Median total compensation	TQ Third quartile wage
AEX Average experienced wage	APH Average pay, high range	AW Average wage paid	HR High end range	MW Median wage paid	W Weekly
AO Average offered	APL Average pay, low range	FQ First quartile wage	LR Low end range	SQ Second quartile wage	Y Yearly

Occupation/Type/Industry	Location	Per	Low	Mid	High	Source	Date
Hoist and Winch Operator	Arkansas	H	7.42 FQ	10.96 AW	16.34 TQ	ARBLS	10/01-12/01
	California	H	12.53 FQ	24.52 AW	40.85 TQ	CABLS	10/01-12/01
	Los Angeles-Long Beach PMSA, CA	H	12.39 FQ	28.37 AW	42.79 TQ	CABLS	10/01-12/01
	Oakland PMSA, CA	H	15.17 FQ	29.41 AW	42.40 TQ	CABLS	10/01-12/01
	Riverside-San Bernardino PMSA, CA	H	10.29 FQ	15.54 AW	22.65 TQ	CABLS	10/01-12/01
	Colorado	H	11.06 FQ	16.48 AW	25.71 TQ	COBLS	10/01-12/01
	Connecticut	H	8.13 FQ	16.86 AW	28.19 TQ	CTBLS	10/01-12/01
	Delaware	H	15.04 FQ	21.35 AW	31.25 TQ	DEBLS	10/01-12/01
	Florida	H	10.56 FQ	18.46 AW	32.45 TQ	FLBLS	10/01-12/01
	Fort Lauderdale PMSA, FL	H	11.82 FQ	18.23 AW	25.91 TQ	FLBLS	10/01-12/01
	Fort Myers-Cape Coral MSA, FL	H	11.01 FQ	12.02 AW	13.27 TQ	FLBLS	10/01-12/01
	Jacksonville MSA, FL	H	13.00 FQ	16.34 AW	17.54 TQ	FLBLS	10/01-12/01
	Naples MSA, FL	H	14.31 FQ	15.56 AW	17.27 TQ	FLBLS	10/01-12/01
	Orlando MSA, FL	H	17.19 FQ	25.82 AW	41.23 TQ	FLBLS	10/01-12/01
	Tampa-St. Petersburg-Clearwater MSA, FL	H	12.42 FQ	21.05 AW	34.89 TQ	FLBLS	10/01-12/01
	Georgia	H	9.55 FQ	15.69 AW	23.20 TQ	GABLS	10/01-12/01
	Atlanta MSA, GA	H	10.18 FQ	18.20 AW	26.64 TQ	GABLS	10/01-12/01
	Savannah MSA, GA	H	13.80 FQ	16.71 AW	20.41 TQ	GABLS	10/01-12/01
	Idaho	H	8.42 FQ	16.23 AW	25.92 TQ	IDBLS	10/01-12/01
	Illinois	H	5.87 FQ	14.71 AW	24.29 TQ	ILBLS	10/01-12/01
	Chicago PMSA, IL	H	5.86 FQ	14.63 AW	24.38 TQ	ILBLS	10/01-12/01
	Indiana	H	9.65 FQ	17.51 AW	28.62 TQ	INBLS	10/01-12/01
	Fort Wayne MSA, IN	H	9.44 FQ	14.10 AW	17.16 TQ	INBLS	10/01-12/01
	Gary PMSA, IN	H	17.02 FQ	24.96 AW	32.75 TQ	INBLS	10/01-12/01
	Indianapolis MSA, IN	H	9.11 FQ	14.60 AW	25.30 TQ	INBLS	10/01-12/01
	Iowa	H	9.61 FQ	13.63 AW	19.10 TQ	IABLS	10/01-12/01
	Kansas	H	10.75 FQ	17.46 AW	30.23 TQ	KSBLS	10/01-12/01
	Kentucky	H	9.89 FQ	15.00 AW	21.48 TQ	KYBLS	10/01-12/01
	Louisville MSA, KY-IN	H	10.00 FQ	15.29 AW	20.92 TQ	KYBLS	10/01-12/01
	Louisiana	H	9.61 FQ	14.28 AW	19.41 TQ	LABLS	10/01-12/01
	New Orleans MSA, LA	H	10.00 FQ	14.29 AW	18.03 TQ	LABLS	10/01-12/01
	Maryland	H	11.45 FQ	17.23 AW	27.46 TQ	MDBLS	10/01-12/01
	Massachusetts	H	13.61 FQ	22.75 AW	38.26 TQ	MABLS	10/01-12/01
	Boston PMSA, MA-NH	H	14.95 FQ	23.24 AW	36.68 TQ	MABLS	10/01-12/01
	Michigan	H	9.50 FQ	15.82 AW	23.29 TQ	MIBLS	10/01-12/01
	Detroit PMSA, MI	H	9.17 FQ	16.75 AW	25.62 TQ	MIBLS	10/01-12/01
	Grand Rapids-Muskegon-Holland MSA, MI	H	9.84 FQ	14.98 AW	21.56 TQ	MIBLS	10/01-12/01
	Minnesota	H	9.31 FQ	17.70 AW	31.37 TQ	MNBLS	10/01-12/01
	Minneapolis-St. Paul MSA, MN-WI	H	14.78 FQ	24.20 AW	36.22 TQ	MNBLS	10/01-12/01
	Mississippi	H	8.53 FQ	12.10 AW	19.81 TQ	MSBLS	10/01-12/01
	Biloxi-Gulfport-Pascagoula MSA, MS	H	9.46 FQ	16.67 AW	22.27 TQ	MSBLS	10/01-12/01
	Missouri	H	9.14 FQ	13.22 AW	20.13 TQ	MOBLS	10/01-12/01
	Kansas City MSA, MO-KS	H	10.12 FQ	18.41 AW	31.07 TQ	MOBLS	10/01-12/01
	St. Louis MSA, MO-IL	H	10.98 FQ	15.48 AW	24.82 TQ	MOBLS	10/01-12/01
	New Jersey	H	7.31 FQ	17.27 AW	32.00 TQ	NJBLS	10/01-12/01
	Middlesex-Somerset-Hunterdon PMSA, NJ	H	7.10 FQ	17.69 AW	32.80 TQ	NJBLS	10/01-12/01
	New York	H	9.00 FQ	16.29 AW	26.43 TQ	NYBLS	10/01-12/01
	North Carolina	H	7.63 FQ	11.81 AW	16.13 TQ	NCBLS	10/01-12/01
	Ohio	H	11.45 FQ	19.62 AW	27.26 TQ	OHBLS	10/01-12/01
	Cincinnati PMSA, OH-KY-IN	H	12.41 FQ	18.24 AW	25.11 TQ	OHBLS	10/01-12/01
	Cleveland-Lorain-Elyria PMSA, OH	H	14.36 FQ	20.66 AW	27.26 TQ	OHBLS	10/01-12/01
	Columbus MSA, OH	H	13.14 FQ	19.55 AW	25.91 TQ	OHBLS	10/01-12/01
	Oklahoma	H	8.45 FQ	13.99 AW	21.78 TQ	OKBLS	10/01-12/01
	Tulsa MSA, OK	H	11.99 FQ	15.88 AW	25.76 TQ	OKBLS	10/01-12/01
	Oregon	H	11.24 FQ	17.47 AW	29.29 TQ	ORBLS	10/01-12/01
	Eugene-Springfield MSA, OR	H	14.11 FQ	15.50 AW	17.32 TQ	ORBLS	10/01-12/01
	Portland-Vancouver PMSA, OR-WA	H	11.28 FQ	19.33 AW	32.32 TQ	ORBLS	10/01-12/01
	Pennsylvania	H	10.61 FQ	15.86 AW	29.62 TQ	PABLS	10/01-12/01
	Philadelphia PMSA, PA-NJ	H	9.68 FQ	19.62 AW	34.29 TQ	PABLS	10/01-12/01
	South Carolina	H	8.90 FQ	12.04 AW	15.92 TQ	SCBLS	10/01-12/01
	South Dakota	H	10.50 FQ	15.04 AW	20.65 TQ	SDBLS	10/01-12/01
	Tennessee	H	9.15 FQ	12.69 AW	18.11 TQ	TNBLS	10/01-12/01

AAW Average annual wage; **AE** Average entry wage; **AEX** Average experienced wage; **AO** Average offered; **AOH** Average offered, high; **AOL** Average offered, low; **APH** Average pay, high range; **APL** Average pay, low range; **ASH** Average starting, high; **ASL** Average starting, low; **AW** Average wage paid; **FQ** First quartile wage; **H** Hourly; **HI** Highest wage paid; **HR** High end range; **LR** Low end range; **M** Monthly; **MTC** Median total compensation; **MW** Median wage paid; **SQ** Second quartile wage; **S** Special: hourly and annual; **TQ** Third quartile wage; **W** Weekly; **Y** Yearly

Occupation/Type/Industry	Location	Per	Low	Mid	High	Source	Date
Hoist and Winch Operator	Nashville MSA, TN	H	9.22 FQ	12.24 AW	17.18 TQ	TNBLS	10/01-12/01
	Texas	H	9.32 FQ	16.29 AW	26.25 TQ	TXBLS	10/01-12/01
	Dallas PMSA, TX	H	9.26 FQ	14.45 AW	21.36 TQ	TXBLS	10/01-12/01
	Houston PMSA, TX	H	11.45 FQ	18.66 AW	32.15 TQ	TXBLS	10/01-12/01
	Virginia	H	9.19 FQ	15.20 AW	21.83 TQ	VABLS	10/01-12/01
	Norfolk-Virginia Beach-Newport News MSA, VA-NC	H	8.42 FQ	13.13 AW	24.26 TQ	VABLS	10/01-12/01
	Washington	H	9.93 FQ	20.71 AW	33.93 TQ	WABLS	10/01-12/01
	Seattle-Bellevue-Everett PMSA, WA	H	10.81 FQ	21.77 AW	33.66 TQ	WABLS	10/01-12/01
	Tacoma PMSA, WA	H	12.24 FQ	23.61 AW	35.20 TQ	WABLS	10/01-12/01
	West Virginia	H	10.54 FQ	20.12 AW	34.17 TQ	WVBLS	10/01-12/01
	Wisconsin	H	8.73 FQ	12.76 AW	19.88 TQ	WIBLS	10/01-12/01
	Puerto Rico	H	5.81 FQ	9.09 AW	14.27 TQ	PRBLS	10/01-12/01
Home Appliance Repairer	Alabama	H	7.83 FQ	15.40 AW	22.55 TQ	ALBLS	10/01-12/01
	Alaska	H	7.30 FQ	14.12 AW	22.11 TQ	AKBLS	10/01-12/01
	Arizona	H	9.37 FQ	14.92 AW	21.29 TQ	AZBLS	10/01-12/01
	Arkansas	H	7.45 FQ	12.14 AW	17.01 TQ	ARBLS	10/01-12/01
	California	H	9.21 FQ	16.69 AW	27.66 TQ	CABLS	10/01-12/01
	Colorado	H	8.38 FQ	15.06 AW	23.90 TQ	COBLS	10/01-12/01
	Connecticut	H	10.09 FQ	18.24 AW	26.47 TQ	CTBLS	10/01-12/01
	Delaware	H	7.90 FQ	13.96 AW	20.82 TQ	DEBLS	10/01-12/01
	Florida	H	8.51 FQ	13.51 AW	19.65 TQ	FLBLS	10/01-12/01
	Georgia	H	9.35 FQ	20.29 AW	49.55 TQ	GABLS	10/01-12/01
	Hawaii	H	9.71 FQ	16.12 AW	22.66 TQ	HIBLS	10/01-12/01
	Idaho	H	8.41 FQ	12.08 AW	19.25 TQ	IDBLS	10/01-12/01
	Illinois	H	6.42 FQ	14.83 AW	21.44 TQ	ILBLS	10/01-12/01
	Indiana	H	9.07 FQ	15.78 AW	23.20 TQ	INBLS	10/01-12/01
	Iowa	H	7.87 FQ	15.62 AW	32.88 TQ	IABLS	10/01-12/01
	Kansas	H	8.94 FQ	14.20 AW	20.38 TQ	KSBLS	10/01-12/01
	Kentucky	H	7.58 FQ	13.38 AW	20.06 TQ	KYBLS	10/01-12/01
	Louisiana	H	7.74 FQ	13.12 AW	19.14 TQ	LABLS	10/01-12/01
	Maine	H	10.34 FQ	14.17 AW	20.07 TQ	MEBLS	10/01-12/01
	Maryland	H	9.91 FQ	17.52 AW	26.26 TQ	MDBLS	10/01-12/01
	Massachusetts	H	11.30 FQ	16.83 AW	25.37 TQ	MABLS	10/01-12/01
	Michigan	H	9.34 FQ	14.55 AW	21.03 TQ	MIBLS	10/01-12/01
	Minnesota	H	7.31 FQ	15.73 AW	22.75 TQ	MNBLS	10/01-12/01
	Mississippi	H	6.23 FQ	10.38 AW	15.38 TQ	MSBLS	10/01-12/01
	Missouri	H	7.82 FQ	13.77 AW	23.19 TQ	MOBLS	10/01-12/01
	Montana	H	8.37 FQ	12.64 AW	17.51 TQ	MTBLS	10/01-12/01
	Nebraska	H	6.73 FQ	14.70 AW	21.52 TQ	NEBLS	10/01-12/01
	Nevada	H	7.47 FQ	13.08 AW	20.02 TQ	NVBLS	10/01-12/01
	New Hampshire	H	9.38 FQ	15.09 AW	23.50 TQ	NHBLS	10/01-12/01
	New Jersey	H	12.73 FQ	19.70 AW	26.40 TQ	NJBLS	10/01-12/01
	New Mexico	H	7.12 FQ	11.46 AW	16.78 TQ	NMBLS	10/01-12/01
	New York	H	8.08 FQ	14.73 AW	22.28 TQ	NYBLS	10/01-12/01
	North Carolina	H	7.33 FQ	12.98 AW	19.75 TQ	NCBLS	10/01-12/01
	North Dakota	H	8.05 FQ	14.26 AW	21.68 TQ	NDBLS	10/01-12/01
	Ohio	H	9.19 FQ	14.31 AW	21.40 TQ	OHBLS	10/01-12/01
	Oklahoma	H	7.78 FQ	13.22 AW	20.49 TQ	OKBLS	10/01-12/01
	Oregon	H	8.27 FQ	14.28 AW	20.71 TQ	ORBLS	10/01-12/01
	Pennsylvania	H	8.51 FQ	14.55 AW	21.52 TQ	PABLS	10/01-12/01
	Rhode Island	H	11.54 FQ	15.60 AW	20.20 TQ	RIBLS	10/01-12/01
	South Carolina	H	8.54 FQ	14.32 AW	21.34 TQ	SCBLS	10/01-12/01
	South Dakota	H	8.37 FQ	14.18 AW	21.98 TQ	SDBLS	10/01-12/01
	Tennessee	H	8.38 FQ	12.89 AW	19.11 TQ	TNBLS	10/01-12/01
	Texas	H	8.38 FQ	13.13 AW	19.62 TQ	TXBLS	10/01-12/01
	Utah	H	9.98 FQ	14.68 AW	20.86 TQ	UTBLS	10/01-12/01
	Vermont	H	8.25 FQ	13.52 AW	18.33 TQ	VTBLS	10/01-12/01
	Virginia	H	9.06 FQ	16.34 AW	28.30 TQ	VABLS	10/01-12/01
	Washington	H	10.02 FQ	17.91 AW	25.47 TQ	WABLS	10/01-12/01
	West Virginia	H	7.27 FQ	11.84 AW	19.94 TQ	WVBLS	10/01-12/01
	Wisconsin	H	9.19 FQ	14.08 AW	20.52 TQ	WIBLS	10/01-12/01
	Wyoming	H	8.77 FQ	15.57 AW	22.44 TQ	WYBLS	10/01-12/01
	Puerto Rico	H	7.85 FQ	12.88 AW	19.06 TQ	PRBLS	10/01-12/01
Home Economics Teacher							
Postsecondary	Arizona	Y	24040 FQ	35940 AW	60740 TQ	AZBLS	10/01-12/01
Postsecondary	California	Y	32830 FQ	64050 AW	108100 TQ	CABLS	10/01-12/01
Postsecondary	Colorado	Y	29400 FQ	45280 AW	72450 TQ	COBLS	10/01-12/01
Postsecondary	Florida	Y	13220 FQ	56280 AW	101750 TQ	FLBLS	10/01-12/01

AAW	Average annual wage	**AOH**	Average offered, high	**ASH**	Average starting, high	**H**	Hourly	**M**	Monthly	**S**	Special: hourly and annual
AE	Average entry wage	**AOL**	Average offered, low	**ASL**	Average starting, low	**HI**	Highest wage paid	**MTC**	Median total compensation	**TQ**	Third quartile wage
AEX	Average experienced wage	**APH**	Average pay, high range	**AW**	Average wage paid	**HR**	High end range	**MW**	Median wage paid	**W**	Weekly
AO	Average offered	**APL**	Average pay, low range	**FQ**	First quartile wage	**LR**	Low end range	**SQ**	Second quartile wage	**Y**	Yearly

Occupation/Type/Industry	Location	Per	Low	Mid	High	Source	Date
Home Economics Teacher							
Postsecondary	Georgia	Y	37790 FQ	61280 AW	89900 TQ	GABLS	10/01-12/01
Postsecondary	Illinois	Y	15010 FQ	40980 AW	71010 TQ	ILBLS	10/01-12/01
Postsecondary	Indiana	Y	27940 FQ	51440 AW	86210 TQ	INBLS	10/01-12/01
Postsecondary	Kansas	Y	22720 FQ	44730 AW	67880 TQ	KSBLS	10/01-12/01
Postsecondary	Kentucky	Y	29700 FQ	48160 AW	71780 TQ	KYBLS	10/01-12/01
Postsecondary	Louisiana	Y	16530 FQ	38090 AW	60420 TQ	LABLS	10/01-12/01
Postsecondary	Massachusetts	Y	27840 FQ	57200 AW	98280 TQ	MABLS	10/01-12/01
Postsecondary	Michigan	Y	36090 FQ	62860 AW	93480 TQ	MIBLS	10/01-12/01
Postsecondary	Minnesota	Y	28940 FQ	53370 AW	82900 TQ	MNBLS	10/01-12/01
Postsecondary	Mississippi	Y	31330 FQ	42290 AW	56130 TQ	MSBLS	10/01-12/01
Postsecondary	Missouri	Y	22230 FQ	50610 AW	83880 TQ	MOBLS	10/01-12/01
Postsecondary	Nebraska	Y	30960 FQ	53170 AW	85650 TQ	NEBLS	10/01-12/01
Postsecondary	New Jersey	Y	30620 FQ	62080 AW	103000 TQ	NJBLS	10/01-12/01
Postsecondary	New York	Y	25160 FQ	49100 AW	84490 TQ	NYBLS	10/01-12/01
Postsecondary	North Carolina	Y	35130 FQ	50080 AW	71580 TQ	NCBLS	10/01-12/01
Postsecondary	Ohio	Y	20670 FQ	40900 AW	56650 TQ	OHBLS	10/01-12/01
Postsecondary	Oklahoma	Y	17590 FQ	34130 AW	49420 TQ	OKBLS	10/01-12/01
Postsecondary	Oregon	Y	14680 FQ	35580 AW	56880 TQ	ORBLS	10/01-12/01
Postsecondary	Pennsylvania	Y	24860 FQ	51870 AW	82930 TQ	PABLS	10/01-12/01
Postsecondary	South Carolina	Y	12580 FQ	45370 AW	79360 TQ	SCBLS	10/01-12/01
Postsecondary	South Dakota	Y	31340 FQ	43870 AW	62560 TQ	SDBLS	10/01-12/01
Postsecondary	Tennessee	Y	35190 FQ	65700 AW	120130 TQ	TNBLS	10/01-12/01
Postsecondary	Texas	Y	30770 FQ	52160 AW	79790 TQ	TXBLS	10/01-12/01
Postsecondary	Utah	Y	37850 FQ	55510 AW	84120 TQ	UTBLS	10/01-12/01
Postsecondary	Washington	Y	26590 FQ	46510 AW	69790 TQ	WABLS	10/01-12/01
Postsecondary	Wisconsin	Y	25720 FQ	47110 AW	74290 TQ	WIBLS	10/01-12/01
Home Health Aide	United States	Y			18490 HI	FREEP1	1/00-1/00
	Alabama	H	5.71 FQ	7.76 AW	10.44 TQ	ALBLS	10/01-12/01
	Alaska	H	9.01 FQ	11.66 AW	15.01 TQ	AKBLS	10/01-12/01
	Arizona	H	6.41 FQ	8.46 AW	10.66 TQ	AZBLS	10/01-12/01
	Arkansas	H	5.75 FQ	7.20 AW	9.01 TQ	ARBLS	10/01-12/01
	California	H	6.86 FQ	9.45 AW	13.44 TQ	CABLS	10/01-12/01
	Colorado	H	7.23 FQ	11.26 AW	16.91 TQ	COBLS	10/01-12/01
	Connecticut	H	9.03 FQ	11.53 AW	14.05 TQ	CTBLS	10/01-12/01
	Delaware	H	7.07 FQ	9.18 AW	10.96 TQ	DEBLS	10/01-12/01
	District of Columbia	H	7.27 FQ	9.28 AW	11.00 TQ	DCBLS	10/01-12/01
	Florida	H	6.70 FQ	8.69 AW	10.90 TQ	FLBLS	10/01-12/01
	Georgia	H	5.97 FQ	8.03 AW	10.51 TQ	GABLS	10/01-12/01
	Hawaii	H	5.96 FQ	8.16 AW	10.71 TQ	HIBLS	10/01-12/01
	Idaho	H	6.06 FQ	7.89 AW	10.22 TQ	IDBLS	10/01-12/01
	Illinois	H	5.82 FQ	8.36 AW	10.92 TQ	ILBLS	10/01-12/01
	Indiana	H	6.97 FQ	8.92 AW	11.07 TQ	INBLS	10/01-12/01
	Iowa	H	6.90 FQ	8.50 AW	10.56 TQ	IABLS	10/01-12/01
	Kansas	H	6.35 FQ	8.62 AW	11.02 TQ	KSBLS	10/01-12/01
	Kentucky	H	6.15 FQ	8.28 AW	10.99 TQ	KYBLS	10/01-12/01
	Louisiana	H	5.65 FQ	8.18 AW	12.45 TQ	LABLS	10/01-12/01
	Maine	H	7.05 FQ	8.94 AW	11.38 TQ	MEBLS	10/01-12/01
	Maryland	H	7.10 FQ	8.65 AW	10.77 TQ	MDBLS	10/01-12/01
	Massachusetts	H	8.47 FQ	10.52 AW	13.28 TQ	MABLS	10/01-12/01
	Michigan	H	7.09 FQ	9.01 AW	11.24 TQ	MIBLS	10/01-12/01
	Minnesota	H	7.47 FQ	9.62 AW	11.95 TQ	MNBLS	10/01-12/01
	Mississippi	H	6.04 FQ	8.54 AW	12.64 TQ	MSBLS	10/01-12/01
	Missouri	H	6.31 FQ	8.07 AW	10.20 TQ	MOBLS	10/01-12/01
	Montana	H	6.55 FQ	8.32 AW	11.11 TQ	MTBLS	10/01-12/01
	Nebraska	H	6.39 FQ	9.32 AW	11.85 TQ	NEBLS	10/01-12/01
	Nevada	H	6.61 FQ	9.59 AW	15.28 TQ	NVBLS	10/01-12/01
	New Hampshire	H	8.00 FQ	10.37 AW	13.17 TQ	NHBLS	10/01-12/01
	New Jersey	H	7.49 FQ	9.43 AW	11.21 TQ	NJBLS	10/01-12/01
	New Mexico	H	6.51 FQ	8.26 AW	10.47 TQ	NMBLS	10/01-12/01
	New York	H	6.40 FQ	9.04 AW	13.57 TQ	NYBLS	10/01-12/01
	North Carolina	H	6.42 FQ	8.18 AW	10.42 TQ	NCBLS	10/01-12/01
	North Dakota	H	6.32 FQ	7.82 AW	9.50 TQ	NDBLS	10/01-12/01
	Ohio	H	7.05 FQ	8.78 AW	10.92 TQ	OHBLS	10/01-12/01
	Oklahoma	H	5.82 FQ	7.94 AW	10.71 TQ	OKBLS	10/01-12/01
	Oregon	H	7.42 FQ	9.09 AW	11.26 TQ	ORBLS	10/01-12/01
	Pennsylvania	H	6.74 FQ	8.84 AW	11.02 TQ	PABLS	10/01-12/01
	Rhode Island	H	8.51 FQ	11.27 AW	15.74 TQ	RIBLS	10/01-12/01
	South Carolina	H	7.02 FQ	8.40 AW	10.40 TQ	SCBLS	10/01-12/01
	South Dakota	H	6.50 FQ	8.14 AW	10.22 TQ	SDBLS	10/01-12/01
	Tennessee	H	6.57 FQ	8.20 AW	10.39 TQ	TNBLS	10/01-12/01
	Texas	H	5.72 FQ	8.48 AW	17.09 TQ	TXBLS	10/01-12/01

AAW Average annual wage **AE** Average entry wage **AEX** Average experienced wage **AO** Average offered **AOH** Average offered, high **AOL** Average offered, low **APH** Average pay, high range **APL** Average pay, low range **ASH** Average starting, high **ASL** Average starting, low **AW** Average wage paid **FQ** First quartile wage **H** Hourly **HI** Highest wage paid **HR** High end range **LR** Low end range **M** Monthly **MTC** Median total compensation **MW** Median wage paid **SQ** Second quartile wage **S** Special: hourly and annual **TQ** Third quartile wage **W** Weekly **Y** Yearly

Occupation/Type/Industry	Location	Per	Low	Mid	High	Source	Date
Home Health Aide	Utah	H	6.62 FQ	9.44 AW	13.11 TQ	UTBLS	10/01-12/01
	Vermont	H	7.08 FQ	8.55 AW	10.77 TQ	VTBLS	10/01-12/01
	Virginia	H	6.13 FQ	8.20 AW	10.48 TQ	VABLS	10/01-12/01
	Washington	H	7.22 FQ	8.95 AW	11.05 TQ	WABLS	10/01-12/01
	West Virginia	H	5.63 FQ	6.72 AW	8.42 TQ	WVBLS	10/01-12/01
	Wisconsin	H	7.40 FQ	9.14 AW	11.26 TQ	WIBLS	10/01-12/01
	Wyoming	H	6.21 FQ	8.06 AW	10.32 TQ	WYBLS	10/01-12/01
	Puerto Rico	H	5.35 FQ	6.03 AW	6.73 TQ	PRBLS	10/01-12/01
	Virgin Islands	H	5.75 FQ	8.89 AW	13.15 TQ	VIBLS	10/01-12/01
	Guam	H	5.62 FQ	7.64 AW	11.51 TQ	GUBLS	10/01-12/01
Hospice Administrator	United States	Y		59850 MW		HMA	1/99-1/00
Host and Hostess							
Restaurant, Lounge, and Coffee Shop	Alabama	H	5.60 FQ	6.90 AW	8.66 TQ	ALBLS	10/01-12/01
Restaurant, Lounge, and Coffee Shop	Birmingham MSA, AL	H	5.74 FQ	7.47 AW	10.55 TQ	ALBLS	10/01-12/01
Restaurant, Lounge, and Coffee Shop	Huntsville MSA, AL	H	5.70 FQ	6.94 AW	8.55 TQ	ALBLS	10/01-12/01
Restaurant, Lounge, and Coffee Shop	Mobile MSA, AL	H	5.64 FQ	6.82 AW	8.60 TQ	ALBLS	10/01-12/01
Restaurant, Lounge, and Coffee Shop	Montgomery MSA, AL	H	5.45 FQ	6.33 AW	7.85 TQ	ALBLS	10/01-12/01
Restaurant, Lounge, and Coffee Shop	Alaska	H	6.17 FQ	8.18 AW	11.08 TQ	AKBLS	10/01-12/01
Restaurant, Lounge, and Coffee Shop	Anchorage MSA, AK	H	6.17 FQ	8.03 AW	10.90 TQ	AKBLS	10/01-12/01
Restaurant, Lounge, and Coffee Shop	Arizona	H	5.70 FQ	7.32 AW	9.54 TQ	AZBLS	10/01-12/01
Restaurant, Lounge, and Coffee Shop	Phoenix-Mesa MSA, AZ	H	5.77 FQ	7.49 AW	9.74 TQ	AZBLS	10/01-12/01
Restaurant, Lounge, and Coffee Shop	Tucson MSA, AZ	H	5.56 FQ	7.08 AW	9.50 TQ	AZBLS	10/01-12/01
Restaurant, Lounge, and Coffee Shop	Arkansas	H	5.68 FQ	6.99 AW	8.68 TQ	ARBLS	10/01-12/01
Restaurant, Lounge, and Coffee Shop	Fayetteville-Springdale-Rogers MSA, AR	H	5.91 FQ	7.32 AW	8.81 TQ	ARBLS	10/01-12/01
Restaurant, Lounge, and Coffee Shop	Fort Smith MSA, AR-OK	H	5.42 FQ	6.43 AW	8.11 TQ	ARBLS	10/01-12/01
Restaurant, Lounge, and Coffee Shop	Little Rock-North Little Rock MSA, AR	H	6.02 FQ	7.61 AW	9.42 TQ	ARBLS	10/01-12/01
Restaurant, Lounge, and Coffee Shop	California	H	6.45 FQ	7.79 AW	9.50 TQ	CABLS	10/01-12/01
Restaurant, Lounge, and Coffee Shop	Bakersfield MSA, CA	H	6.38 FQ	7.10 AW	8.22 TQ	CABLS	10/01-12/01
Restaurant, Lounge, and Coffee Shop	Chico-Paradise MSA, CA	H	6.46 FQ	7.48 AW	8.39 TQ	CABLS	10/01-12/01
Restaurant, Lounge, and Coffee Shop	Fresno MSA, CA	H	6.37 FQ	7.08 AW	8.27 TQ	CABLS	10/01-12/01
Restaurant, Lounge, and Coffee Shop	Los Angeles-Long Beach PMSA, CA	H	6.49 FQ	7.71 AW	8.69 TQ	CABLS	10/01-12/01
Restaurant, Lounge, and Coffee Shop	Merced MSA, CA	H	6.36 FQ	7.03 AW	8.35 TQ	CABLS	10/01-12/01
Restaurant, Lounge, and Coffee Shop	Modesto MSA, CA	H	6.38 FQ	7.14 AW	8.35 TQ	CABLS	10/01-12/01
Restaurant, Lounge, and Coffee Shop	Oakland PMSA, CA	H	6.65 FQ	8.15 AW	9.78 TQ	CABLS	10/01-12/01
Restaurant, Lounge, and Coffee Shop	Orange County PMSA, CA	H	6.39 FQ	7.71 AW	10.02 TQ	CABLS	10/01-12/01
Restaurant, Lounge, and Coffee Shop	Redding MSA, CA	H	6.35 FQ	7.04 AW	8.27 TQ	CABLS	10/01-12/01
Restaurant, Lounge, and Coffee Shop	Riverside-San Bernardino PMSA, CA	H	6.39 FQ	7.22 AW	8.33 TQ	CABLS	10/01-12/01
Restaurant, Lounge, and Coffee Shop	Sacramento PMSA, CA	H	6.40 FQ	8.02 AW	11.35 TQ	CABLS	10/01-12/01
Restaurant, Lounge, and Coffee Shop	Salinas MSA, CA	H	6.54 FQ	8.84 AW	14.26 TQ	CABLS	10/01-12/01
Restaurant, Lounge, and Coffee Shop	San Diego MSA, CA	H	6.62 FQ	7.99 AW	9.93 TQ	CABLS	10/01-12/01
Restaurant, Lounge, and Coffee Shop	San Francisco PMSA, CA	H	6.81 FQ	8.62 AW	11.08 TQ	CABLS	10/01-12/01
Restaurant, Lounge, and Coffee Shop	San Jose PMSA, CA	H	6.63 FQ	9.11 AW	13.13 TQ	CABLS	10/01-12/01
Restaurant, Lounge, and Coffee Shop	San Luis Obispo-Atascadero-Paso Robles MSA, CA	H	6.56 FQ	8.23 AW	10.68 TQ	CABLS	10/01-12/01
Restaurant, Lounge, and Coffee Shop	Santa Barbara-Santa Maria-Lompoc MSA, CA	H	6.38 FQ	8.06 AW	12.23 TQ	CABLS	10/01-12/01
Restaurant, Lounge, and Coffee Shop	Santa Cruz-Watsonville PMSA, CA	H	6.50 FQ	8.38 AW	10.02 TQ	CABLS	10/01-12/01
Restaurant, Lounge, and Coffee Shop	Santa Rosa PMSA, CA	H	6.42 FQ	7.60 AW	9.46 TQ	CABLS	10/01-12/01
Restaurant, Lounge, and Coffee Shop	Stockton-Lodi MSA, CA	H	6.34 FQ	7.03 AW	8.23 TQ	CABLS	10/01-12/01
Restaurant, Lounge, and Coffee Shop	Vallejo-Fairfield-Napa PMSA, CA	H	6.39 FQ	7.57 AW	9.54 TQ	CABLS	10/01-12/01
Restaurant, Lounge, and Coffee Shop	Ventura PMSA, CA	H	6.37 FQ	7.26 AW	8.61 TQ	CABLS	10/01-12/01
Restaurant, Lounge, and Coffee Shop	Visalia-Tulare-Porterville MSA, CA	H	6.34 FQ	6.84 AW	7.53 TQ	CABLS	10/01-12/01
Restaurant, Lounge, and Coffee Shop	Colorado	H	5.74 FQ	7.73 AW	10.14 TQ	COBLS	10/01-12/01
Restaurant, Lounge, and Coffee Shop	Boulder-Longmont PMSA, CO	H	6.34 FQ	7.83 AW	9.09 TQ	COBLS	10/01-12/01
Restaurant, Lounge, and Coffee Shop	Colorado Springs MSA, CO	H	5.85 FQ	7.65 AW	9.82 TQ	COBLS	10/01-12/01
Restaurant, Lounge, and Coffee Shop	Denver PMSA, CO	H	5.74 FQ	7.92 AW	10.74 TQ	COBLS	10/01-12/01
Restaurant, Lounge, and Coffee Shop	Fort Collins-Loveland MSA, CO	H	5.45 FQ	6.63 AW	8.43 TQ	COBLS	10/01-12/01
Restaurant, Lounge, and Coffee Shop	Greeley PMSA, CO	H	5.62 FQ	6.59 AW	8.19 TQ	COBLS	10/01-12/01
Restaurant, Lounge, and Coffee Shop	Connecticut	H	6.59 FQ	8.71 AW	12.29 TQ	CTBLS	10/01-12/01
Restaurant, Lounge, and Coffee Shop	Bridgeport PMSA, CT	H	6.83 FQ	9.37 AW	14.22 TQ	CTBLS	10/01-12/01
Restaurant, Lounge, and Coffee Shop	Danbury PMSA, CT	H	6.59 FQ	8.56 AW	10.71 TQ	CTBLS	10/01-12/01
Restaurant, Lounge, and Coffee Shop	Hartford MSA, CT	H	6.53 FQ	7.96 AW	10.33 TQ	CTBLS	10/01-12/01

AAW	Average annual wage	**AOH**	Average offered, high	**ASH**	Average starting, high	**H**	Hourly	**M**	Monthly	**S**	Special: hourly and annual
AE	Average entry wage	**AOL**	Average offered, low	**ASL**	Average starting, low	**HI**	Highest wage paid	**MTC**	Median total compensation	**TQ**	Third quartile wage
AEX	Average experienced wage	**APH**	Average pay, high range	**AW**	Average wage paid	**HR**	High end range	**MW**	Median wage paid	**W**	Weekly
AO	Average offered	**APL**	Average pay, low range	**FQ**	First quartile wage	**LR**	Low end range	**SQ**	Second quartile wage	**Y**	Yearly

Occupation/Type/Industry	Location	Per	Low	Mid	High	Source	Date
Host and Hostess							
Restaurant, Lounge, and Coffee Shop	New Haven-Meriden PMSA, CT	H	6.60 FQ	8.58 AW	11.51 TQ	CTBLS	10/01-12/01
Restaurant, Lounge, and Coffee Shop	New London-Norwich MSA, CT-RI	H	6.73 FQ	9.16 AW	13.03 TQ	CTBLS	10/01-12/01
Restaurant, Lounge, and Coffee Shop	Stamford-Norwalk PMSA, CT	H	7.31 FQ	11.67 AW	19.28 TQ	CTBLS	10/01-12/01
Restaurant, Lounge, and Coffee Shop	Waterbury PMSA, CT	H	6.62 FQ	8.39 AW	10.64 TQ	CTBLS	10/01-12/01
Restaurant, Lounge, and Coffee Shop	Delaware	H	6.62 FQ	8.16 AW	10.48 TQ	DEBLS	10/01-12/01
Restaurant, Lounge, and Coffee Shop	Wilmington-Newark PMSA, DE-MD	H	6.64 FQ	8.24 AW	10.66 TQ	DEBLS	10/01-12/01
Restaurant, Lounge, and Coffee Shop	District of Columbia	H	7.83 FQ	10.58 AW	13.41 TQ	DCBLS	10/01-12/01
Restaurant, Lounge, and Coffee Shop	Washington PMSA, DC-MD-VA-WV	H	6.05 FQ	8.57 AW	11.09 TQ	DCBLS	10/01-12/01
Restaurant, Lounge, and Coffee Shop	Florida	H	5.73 FQ	7.42 AW	10.08 TQ	FLBLS	10/01-12/01
Restaurant, Lounge, and Coffee Shop	Daytona Beach MSA, FL	H	5.78 FQ	6.99 AW	8.73 TQ	FLBLS	10/01-12/01
Restaurant, Lounge, and Coffee Shop	Fort Lauderdale PMSA, FL	H	5.75 FQ	7.08 AW	8.97 TQ	FLBLS	10/01-12/01
Restaurant, Lounge, and Coffee Shop	Fort Myers-Cape Coral MSA, FL	H	5.81 FQ	7.64 AW	10.22 TQ	FLBLS	10/01-12/01
Restaurant, Lounge, and Coffee Shop	Fort Pierce-Port St. Lucie MSA, FL	H	5.68 FQ	7.36 AW	10.14 TQ	FLBLS	10/01-12/01
Restaurant, Lounge, and Coffee Shop	Fort Walton Beach MSA, FL	H	5.60 FQ	6.65 AW	8.45 TQ	FLBLS	10/01-12/01
Restaurant, Lounge, and Coffee Shop	Gainesville MSA, FL	H	5.56 FQ	6.50 AW	8.16 TQ	FLBLS	10/01-12/01
Restaurant, Lounge, and Coffee Shop	Jacksonville MSA, FL	H	5.84 FQ	7.41 AW	8.87 TQ	FLBLS	10/01-12/01
Restaurant, Lounge, and Coffee Shop	Lakeland-Winter Haven MSA, FL	H	5.65 FQ	6.90 AW	8.43 TQ	FLBLS	10/01-12/01
Restaurant, Lounge, and Coffee Shop	Melbourne-Titusville-Palm Bay MSA, FL	H	5.65 FQ	6.94 AW	8.91 TQ	FLBLS	10/01-12/01
Restaurant, Lounge, and Coffee Shop	Miami PMSA, FL	H	5.60 FQ	7.01 AW	9.49 TQ	FLBLS	10/01-12/01
Restaurant, Lounge, and Coffee Shop	Naples MSA, FL	H	6.13 FQ	8.98 AW	11.83 TQ	FLBLS	10/01-12/01
Restaurant, Lounge, and Coffee Shop	Ocala MSA, FL	H	5.79 FQ	6.91 AW	8.65 TQ	FLBLS	10/01-12/01
Restaurant, Lounge, and Coffee Shop	Orlando MSA, FL	H	5.85 FQ	8.04 AW	11.67 TQ	FLBLS	10/01-12/01
Restaurant, Lounge, and Coffee Shop	Pensacola MSA, FL	H	5.69 FQ	7.09 AW	9.22 TQ	FLBLS	10/01-12/01
Restaurant, Lounge, and Coffee Shop	Sarasota-Bradenton MSA, FL	H	5.83 FQ	7.61 AW	9.15 TQ	FLBLS	10/01-12/01
Restaurant, Lounge, and Coffee Shop	Tallahassee MSA, FL	H	5.57 FQ	6.58 AW	8.26 TQ	FLBLS	10/01-12/01
Restaurant, Lounge, and Coffee Shop	Tampa-St. Petersburg-Clearwater MSA, FL	H	5.87 FQ	7.54 AW	9.84 TQ	FLBLS	10/01-12/01
Restaurant, Lounge, and Coffee Shop	West Palm Beach-Boca Raton MSA, FL	H	5.71 FQ	7.73 AW	10.52 TQ	FLBLS	10/01-12/01
Restaurant, Lounge, and Coffee Shop	Georgia	H	5.52 FQ	7.00 AW	8.85 TQ	GABLS	10/01-12/01
Restaurant, Lounge, and Coffee Shop	Atlanta MSA, GA	H	5.46 FQ	7.00 AW	9.08 TQ	GABLS	10/01-12/01
Restaurant, Lounge, and Coffee Shop	Augusta-Aiken MSA, GA-SC	H	5.61 FQ	6.95 AW	9.14 TQ	GABLS	10/01-12/01
Restaurant, Lounge, and Coffee Shop	Columbus MSA, GA-AL	H	5.65 FQ	6.54 AW	8.13 TQ	GABLS	10/01-12/01
Restaurant, Lounge, and Coffee Shop	Macon MSA, GA	H	5.78 FQ	6.93 AW	8.30 TQ	GABLS	10/01-12/01
Restaurant, Lounge, and Coffee Shop	Savannah MSA, GA	H	6.03 FQ	7.63 AW	8.88 TQ	GABLS	10/01-12/01
Restaurant, Lounge, and Coffee Shop	Hawaii	H	6.29 FQ	9.61 AW	14.05 TQ	HIBLS	10/01-12/01
Restaurant, Lounge, and Coffee Shop	Honolulu MSA, HI	H	6.33 FQ	9.60 AW	14.68 TQ	HIBLS	10/01-12/01
Restaurant, Lounge, and Coffee Shop	Idaho	H	5.66 FQ	6.87 AW	8.67 TQ	IDBLS	10/01-12/01
Restaurant, Lounge, and Coffee Shop	Boise City MSA, ID	H	5.74 FQ	7.27 AW	9.07 TQ	IDBLS	10/01-12/01
Restaurant, Lounge, and Coffee Shop	Illinois	H	5.72 FQ	7.74 AW	10.15 TQ	ILBLS	10/01-12/01
Restaurant, Lounge, and Coffee Shop	Champaign-Urbana MSA, IL	H	5.79 FQ	7.93 AW	10.15 TQ	ILBLS	10/01-12/01
Restaurant, Lounge, and Coffee Shop	Chicago PMSA, IL	H	5.91 FQ	8.11 AW	10.43 TQ	ILBLS	10/01-12/01
Restaurant, Lounge, and Coffee Shop	Peoria-Pekin MSA, IL	H	5.39 FQ	6.29 AW	7.89 TQ	ILBLS	10/01-12/01
Restaurant, Lounge, and Coffee Shop	Rockford MSA, IL	H	5.72 FQ	7.12 AW	8.94 TQ	ILBLS	10/01-12/01
Restaurant, Lounge, and Coffee Shop	Springfield MSA, IL	H	5.61 FQ	7.06 AW	8.80 TQ	ILBLS	10/01-12/01
Restaurant, Lounge, and Coffee Shop	Indiana	H	5.69 FQ	7.34 AW	9.79 TQ	INBLS	10/01-12/01
Restaurant, Lounge, and Coffee Shop	Elkhart-Goshen MSA, IN	H	5.64 FQ	7.63 AW	10.14 TQ	INBLS	10/01-12/01
Restaurant, Lounge, and Coffee Shop	Evansville-Henderson MSA, IN-KY	H	5.80 FQ	7.50 AW	9.94 TQ	INBLS	10/01-12/01
Restaurant, Lounge, and Coffee Shop	Fort Wayne MSA, IN	H	5.72 FQ	7.13 AW	8.78 TQ	INBLS	10/01-12/01
Restaurant, Lounge, and Coffee Shop	Gary PMSA, IN	H	5.69 FQ	6.86 AW	8.35 TQ	INBLS	10/01-12/01
Restaurant, Lounge, and Coffee Shop	Indianapolis MSA, IN	H	5.66 FQ	7.59 AW	10.29 TQ	INBLS	10/01-12/01
Restaurant, Lounge, and Coffee Shop	Lafayette MSA, IN	H	5.72 FQ	7.29 AW	9.66 TQ	INBLS	10/01-12/01
Restaurant, Lounge, and Coffee Shop	South Bend MSA, IN	H	5.92 FQ	7.71 AW	10.02 TQ	INBLS	10/01-12/01
Restaurant, Lounge, and Coffee Shop	Iowa	H	5.66 FQ	7.13 AW	9.40 TQ	IABLS	10/01-12/01
Restaurant, Lounge, and Coffee Shop	Cedar Rapids MSA, IA	H	5.67 FQ	6.60 AW	8.20 TQ	IABLS	10/01-12/01
Restaurant, Lounge, and Coffee Shop	Davenport-Moline-Rock Island MSA, IA-IL	H	5.86 FQ	7.35 AW	8.88 TQ	IABLS	10/01-12/01
Restaurant, Lounge, and Coffee Shop	Des Moines MSA, IA	H	6.11 FQ	8.05 AW	10.42 TQ	IABLS	10/01-12/01
Restaurant, Lounge, and Coffee Shop	Kansas	H	5.74 FQ	7.10 AW	8.88 TQ	KSBLS	10/01-12/01
Restaurant, Lounge, and Coffee Shop	Topeka MSA, KS	H	5.72 FQ	6.57 AW	8.07 TQ	KSBLS	10/01-12/01
Restaurant, Lounge, and Coffee Shop	Wichita MSA, KS	H	5.65 FQ	6.46 AW	7.91 TQ	KSBLS	10/01-12/01
Restaurant, Lounge, and Coffee Shop	Kentucky	H	5.76 FQ	7.21 AW	8.84 TQ	KYBLS	10/01-12/01

AAW	Average annual wage	AOH	Average offered, high	ASH	Average starting, high	H	Hourly	M	Monthly	S	Special: hourly and annual
AE	Average entry wage	AOL	Average offered, low	ASL	Average starting, low	HI	Highest wage paid	MTC	Median total compensation	TQ	Third quartile wage
AEX	Average experienced wage	APH	Average pay, high range	AW	Average wage paid	HR	High end range	MW	Median wage paid	W	Weekly
AO	Average offered	APL	Average pay, low range	FQ	First quartile wage	LR	Low end range	SQ	Second quartile wage	Y	Yearly

Occupation/Type/Industry	Location	Per	Low	Mid	High	Source	Date
Host and Hostess							
Restaurant, Lounge, and Coffee Shop	Lexington MSA, KY	H	5.83 FQ	7.25 AW	8.82 TQ	KYBLS	10/01-12/01
Restaurant, Lounge, and Coffee Shop	Louisville MSA, KY-IN	H	5.84 FQ	7.59 AW	9.57 TQ	KYBLS	10/01-12/01
Restaurant, Lounge, and Coffee Shop	Louisiana	H	5.61 FQ	6.83 AW	8.63 TQ	LABLS	10/01-12/01
Restaurant, Lounge, and Coffee Shop	Baton Rouge MSA, LA	H	5.63 FQ	6.85 AW	8.92 TQ	LABLS	10/01-12/01
Restaurant, Lounge, and Coffee Shop	Houma MSA, LA	H	5.53 FQ	6.38 AW	7.97 TQ	LABLS	10/01-12/01
Restaurant, Lounge, and Coffee Shop	Lafayette MSA, LA	H	5.70 FQ	6.77 AW	8.22 TQ	LABLS	10/01-12/01
Restaurant, Lounge, and Coffee Shop	Lake Charles MSA, LA	H	5.72 FQ	7.19 AW	8.77 TQ	LABLS	10/01-12/01
Restaurant, Lounge, and Coffee Shop	New Orleans MSA, LA	H	5.60 FQ	6.97 AW	8.78 TQ	LABLS	10/01-12/01
Restaurant, Lounge, and Coffee Shop	Shreveport-Bossier City MSA, LA	H	5.58 FQ	6.60 AW	8.22 TQ	LABLS	10/01-12/01
Restaurant, Lounge, and Coffee Shop	Maine	H	5.77 FQ	7.61 AW	10.33 TQ	MEBLS	10/01-12/01
Restaurant, Lounge, and Coffee Shop	Portland MSA, ME	H	5.88 FQ	8.23 AW	11.76 TQ	MEBLS	10/01-12/01
Restaurant, Lounge, and Coffee Shop	Maryland	H	5.63 FQ	7.45 AW	10.17 TQ	MDBLS	10/01-12/01
Restaurant, Lounge, and Coffee Shop	Baltimore PMSA, MD	H	5.57 FQ	7.36 AW	10.22 TQ	MDBLS	10/01-12/01
Restaurant, Lounge, and Coffee Shop	Massachusetts	H	6.97 FQ	8.80 AW	11.38 TQ	MABLS	10/01-12/01
Restaurant, Lounge, and Coffee Shop	Boston PMSA, MA-NH	H	6.95 FQ	8.70 AW	11.53 TQ	MABLS	10/01-12/01
Restaurant, Lounge, and Coffee Shop	Brockton PMSA, MA	H	7.44 FQ	8.98 AW	10.55 TQ	MABLS	10/01-12/01
Restaurant, Lounge, and Coffee Shop	Lawrence PMSA, MA-NH	H	6.78 FQ	8.29 AW	10.49 TQ	MABLS	10/01-12/01
Restaurant, Lounge, and Coffee Shop	Lowell PMSA, MA-NH	H	7.12 FQ	9.14 AW	11.92 TQ	MABLS	10/01-12/01
Restaurant, Lounge, and Coffee Shop	New Bedford PMSA, MA	H	6.81 FQ	7.78 AW	9.14 TQ	MABLS	10/01-12/01
Restaurant, Lounge, and Coffee Shop	Springfield MSA, MA	H	6.95 FQ	8.87 AW	11.94 TQ	MABLS	10/01-12/01
Restaurant, Lounge, and Coffee Shop	Worcester PMSA, MA-CT	H	7.28 FQ	8.89 AW	10.95 TQ	MABLS	10/01-12/01
Restaurant, Lounge, and Coffee Shop	Michigan	H	5.58 FQ	7.11 AW	9.46 TQ	MIBLS	10/01-12/01
Restaurant, Lounge, and Coffee Shop	Ann Arbor PMSA, MI	H	5.78 FQ	7.82 AW	10.24 TQ	MIBLS	10/01-12/01
Restaurant, Lounge, and Coffee Shop	Detroit PMSA, MI	H	5.49 FQ	6.97 AW	9.24 TQ	MIBLS	10/01-12/01
Restaurant, Lounge, and Coffee Shop	Flint PMSA, MI	H	5.57 FQ	7.53 AW	11.52 TQ	MIBLS	10/01-12/01
Restaurant, Lounge, and Coffee Shop	Grand Rapids-Muskegon-Holland MSA, MI	H	5.78 FQ	7.32 AW	9.86 TQ	MIBLS	10/01-12/01
Restaurant, Lounge, and Coffee Shop	Kalamazoo-Battle Creek MSA, MI	H	5.62 FQ	7.15 AW	8.94 TQ	MIBLS	10/01-12/01
Restaurant, Lounge, and Coffee Shop	Lansing-East Lansing MSA, MI	H	5.59 FQ	7.07 AW	9.29 TQ	MIBLS	10/01-12/01
Restaurant, Lounge, and Coffee Shop	Saginaw-Bay City-Midland MSA, MI	H	5.64 FQ	6.56 AW	8.24 TQ	MIBLS	10/01-12/01
Restaurant, Lounge, and Coffee Shop	Minnesota	H	5.96 FQ	7.98 AW	10.51 TQ	MNBLS	10/01-12/01
Restaurant, Lounge, and Coffee Shop	Duluth-Superior MSA, MN-WI	H	5.51 FQ	6.25 AW	7.13 TQ	MNBLS	10/01-12/01
Restaurant, Lounge, and Coffee Shop	Minneapolis-St. Paul MSA, MN-WI	H	6.49 FQ	8.38 AW	10.74 TQ	MNBLS	10/01-12/01
Restaurant, Lounge, and Coffee Shop	St. Cloud MSA, MN	H	5.74 FQ	6.87 AW	8.76 TQ	MNBLS	10/01-12/01
Restaurant, Lounge, and Coffee Shop	Mississippi	H	5.49 FQ	6.72 AW	8.51 TQ	MSBLS	10/01-12/01
Restaurant, Lounge, and Coffee Shop	Biloxi-Gulfport-Pascagoula MSA, MS	H	5.50 FQ	6.83 AW	8.79 TQ	MSBLS	10/01-12/01
Restaurant, Lounge, and Coffee Shop	Jackson MSA, MS	H	5.64 FQ	6.79 AW	8.84 TQ	MSBLS	10/01-12/01
Restaurant, Lounge, and Coffee Shop	Missouri	H	5.66 FQ	7.48 AW	10.43 TQ	MOBLS	10/01-12/01
Restaurant, Lounge, and Coffee Shop	Kansas City MSA, MO-KS	H	5.88 FQ	8.10 AW	11.33 TQ	MOBLS	10/01-12/01
Restaurant, Lounge, and Coffee Shop	St. Louis MSA, MO-IL	H	5.58 FQ	7.24 AW	9.55 TQ	MOBLS	10/01-12/01
Restaurant, Lounge, and Coffee Shop	Springfield MSA, MO	H	5.70 FQ	6.45 AW	7.26 TQ	MOBLS	10/01-12/01
Restaurant, Lounge, and Coffee Shop	Montana	H	5.74 FQ	7.09 AW	8.80 TQ	MTBLS	10/01-12/01
Restaurant, Lounge, and Coffee Shop	Billings MSA, MT	H	5.88 FQ	7.03 AW	8.24 TQ	MTBLS	10/01-12/01
Restaurant, Lounge, and Coffee Shop	Nebraska	H	5.70 FQ	6.97 AW	8.73 TQ	NEBLS	10/01-12/01
Restaurant, Lounge, and Coffee Shop	Lincoln MSA, NE	H	5.75 FQ	7.17 AW	8.80 TQ	NEBLS	10/01-12/01
Restaurant, Lounge, and Coffee Shop	Omaha MSA, NE-IA	H	5.81 FQ	7.28 AW	8.96 TQ	NEBLS	10/01-12/01
Restaurant, Lounge, and Coffee Shop	Nevada	H	6.27 FQ	9.54 AW	13.30 TQ	NVBLS	10/01-12/01
Restaurant, Lounge, and Coffee Shop	Las Vegas MSA, NV-AZ	H	6.80 FQ	10.19 AW	13.50 TQ	NVBLS	10/01-12/01
Restaurant, Lounge, and Coffee Shop	Reno MSA, NV	H	5.98 FQ	7.82 AW	10.09 TQ	NVBLS	10/01-12/01
Restaurant, Lounge, and Coffee Shop	New Hampshire	H	6.54 FQ	8.45 AW	10.79 TQ	NHBLS	10/01-12/01
Restaurant, Lounge, and Coffee Shop	Manchester PMSA, NH	H	6.30 FQ	8.72 AW	11.11 TQ	NHBLS	10/01-12/01
Restaurant, Lounge, and Coffee Shop	Nashua PMSA, NH	H	6.14 FQ	8.18 AW	11.12 TQ	NHBLS	10/01-12/01
Restaurant, Lounge, and Coffee Shop	Portsmouth-Rochester PMSA, NH-ME	H	6.32 FQ	8.82 AW	11.63 TQ	NHBLS	10/01-12/01
Restaurant, Lounge, and Coffee Shop	New Jersey	H	5.86 FQ	8.24 AW	11.35 TQ	NJBLS	10/01-12/01
Restaurant, Lounge, and Coffee Shop	Atlantic-Cape May PMSA, NJ	H	6.50 FQ	9.58 AW	13.07 TQ	NJBLS	10/01-12/01
Restaurant, Lounge, and Coffee Shop	Bergen-Passaic PMSA, NJ	H	5.69 FQ	7.40 AW	9.28 TQ	NJBLS	10/01-12/01
Restaurant, Lounge, and Coffee Shop	Jersey City PMSA, NJ	H	5.94 FQ	8.36 AW	11.50 TQ	NJBLS	10/01-12/01
Restaurant, Lounge, and Coffee Shop	Middlesex-Somerset-Hunterdon PMSA, NJ	H	5.97 FQ	8.86 AW	12.59 TQ	NJBLS	10/01-12/01
Restaurant, Lounge, and Coffee Shop	Monmouth-Ocean PMSA, NJ	H	5.65 FQ	7.21 AW	9.82 TQ	NJBLS	10/01-12/01
Restaurant, Lounge, and Coffee Shop	Newark PMSA, NJ	H	6.18 FQ	8.91 AW	11.29 TQ	NJBLS	10/01-12/01
Restaurant, Lounge, and Coffee Shop	Trenton PMSA, NJ	H	5.88 FQ	8.05 AW	11.21 TQ	NJBLS	10/01-12/01
Restaurant, Lounge, and Coffee Shop	New Mexico	H	5.53 FQ	6.58 AW	8.34 TQ	NMBLS	10/01-12/01
Restaurant, Lounge, and Coffee Shop	Albuquerque MSA, NM	H	5.65 FQ	6.56 AW	8.21 TQ	NMBLS	10/01-12/01
Restaurant, Lounge, and Coffee Shop	Las Cruces MSA, NM	H	5.63 FQ	6.30 AW	7.22 TQ	NMBLS	10/01-12/01

AAW	Average annual wage	AOH	Average offered, high	ASH	Average starting, high	H	Hourly	M	Monthly	S	Special: hourly and annual
AE	Average entry wage	AOL	Average offered, low	ASL	Average starting, low	HI	Highest wage paid	MTC	Median total compensation	TQ	Third quartile wage
AEX	Average experienced wage	APH	Average pay, high range	AW	Average wage paid	HR	High end range	MW	Median wage paid	W	Weekly
AO	Average offered	APL	Average pay, low range	FQ	First quartile wage	LR	Low end range	SQ	Second quartile wage	Y	Yearly

Host and Hostess

Occupation/Type/Industry	Location	Per	Low	Mid	High	Source	Date
Restaurant, Lounge, and Coffee Shop	New York	H	5.82 FQ	9.29 AW	15.20 TQ	NYBLS	10/01-12/01
Restaurant, Lounge, and Coffee Shop	Albany-Schenectady-Troy MSA, NY	H	5.70 FQ	7.42 AW	9.56 TQ	NYBLS	10/01-12/01
Restaurant, Lounge, and Coffee Shop	Binghamton MSA, NY	H	5.69 FQ	6.97 AW	9.28 TQ	NYBLS	10/01-12/01
Restaurant, Lounge, and Coffee Shop	Buffalo-Niagara Falls MSA, NY	H	5.45 FQ	6.51 AW	8.17 TQ	NYBLS	10/01-12/01
Restaurant, Lounge, and Coffee Shop	Dutchess County PMSA, NY	H	6.11 FQ	8.85 AW	14.02 TQ	NYBLS	10/01-12/01
Restaurant, Lounge, and Coffee Shop	Nassau-Suffolk PMSA, NY	H	6.00 FQ	9.27 AW	15.59 TQ	NYBLS	10/01-12/01
Restaurant, Lounge, and Coffee Shop	New York PMSA, NY	H	8.37 FQ	11.46 AW	16.68 TQ	NYBLS	10/01-12/01
Restaurant, Lounge, and Coffee Shop	Newburgh PMSA, NY-PA	H	5.81 FQ	7.99 AW	10.54 TQ	NYBLS	10/01-12/01
Restaurant, Lounge, and Coffee Shop	Rochester MSA, NY	H	5.62 FQ	7.48 AW	9.97 TQ	NYBLS	10/01-12/01
Restaurant, Lounge, and Coffee Shop	Syracuse MSA, NY	H	5.45 FQ	6.62 AW	8.39 TQ	NYBLS	10/01-12/01
Restaurant, Lounge, and Coffee Shop	Utica-Rome MSA, NY	H	5.57 FQ	6.37 AW	7.26 TQ	NYBLS	10/01-12/01
Restaurant, Lounge, and Coffee Shop	North Carolina	H	5.65 FQ	7.13 AW	8.81 TQ	NCBLS	10/01-12/01
Restaurant, Lounge, and Coffee Shop	Asheville MSA, NC	H	5.82 FQ	7.12 AW	8.73 TQ	NCBLS	10/01-12/01
Restaurant, Lounge, and Coffee Shop	Charlotte-Gastonia-Rock Hill MSA, NC-SC	H	6.04 FQ	7.75 AW	9.10 TQ	NCBLS	10/01-12/01
Restaurant, Lounge, and Coffee Shop	Fayetteville MSA, NC	H	5.79 FQ	7.51 AW	10.99 TQ	NCBLS	10/01-12/01
Restaurant, Lounge, and Coffee Shop	Greensboro-Winston-Salem-High Point MSA, NC	H	5.48 FQ	6.31 AW	7.54 TQ	NCBLS	10/01-12/01
Restaurant, Lounge, and Coffee Shop	Hickory-Morganton-Lenoir MSA, NC	H	5.54 FQ	6.84 AW	8.74 TQ	NCBLS	10/01-12/01
Restaurant, Lounge, and Coffee Shop	Raleigh-Durham-Chapel Hill MSA, NC	H	5.77 FQ	7.25 AW	8.66 TQ	NCBLS	10/01-12/01
Restaurant, Lounge, and Coffee Shop	Wilmington MSA, NC	H	5.64 FQ	6.68 AW	8.06 TQ	NCBLS	10/01-12/01
Restaurant, Lounge, and Coffee Shop	North Dakota	H	5.60 FQ	6.59 AW	8.41 TQ	NDBLS	10/01-12/01
Restaurant, Lounge, and Coffee Shop	Fargo-Moorhead MSA, ND-MN	H	5.62 FQ	6.48 AW	7.66 TQ	NDBLS	10/01-12/01
Restaurant, Lounge, and Coffee Shop	Ohio	H	5.65 FQ	7.20 AW	9.28 TQ	OHBLS	10/01-12/01
Restaurant, Lounge, and Coffee Shop	Akron PMSA, OH	H	5.52 FQ	7.00 AW	9.36 TQ	OHBLS	10/01-12/01
Restaurant, Lounge, and Coffee Shop	Canton-Massillon MSA, OH	H	5.65 FQ	6.75 AW	8.31 TQ	OHBLS	10/01-12/01
Restaurant, Lounge, and Coffee Shop	Cincinnati PMSA, OH-KY-IN	H	5.78 FQ	7.37 AW	9.51 TQ	OHBLS	10/01-12/01
Restaurant, Lounge, and Coffee Shop	Cleveland-Lorain-Elyria PMSA, OH	H	5.62 FQ	7.38 AW	9.71 TQ	OHBLS	10/01-12/01
Restaurant, Lounge, and Coffee Shop	Columbus MSA, OH	H	5.82 FQ	7.48 AW	9.51 TQ	OHBLS	10/01-12/01
Restaurant, Lounge, and Coffee Shop	Dayton-Springfield MSA, OH	H	5.69 FQ	7.42 AW	9.95 TQ	OHBLS	10/01-12/01
Restaurant, Lounge, and Coffee Shop	Hamilton-Middletown PMSA, OH	H	5.78 FQ	7.28 AW	8.96 TQ	OHBLS	10/01-12/01
Restaurant, Lounge, and Coffee Shop	Mansfield MSA, OH	H	5.63 FQ	6.73 AW	8.29 TQ	OHBLS	10/01-12/01
Restaurant, Lounge, and Coffee Shop	Toledo MSA, OH	H	5.77 FQ	7.18 AW	8.72 TQ	OHBLS	10/01-12/01
Restaurant, Lounge, and Coffee Shop	Youngstown-Warren MSA, OH	H	5.70 FQ	6.90 AW	8.49 TQ	OHBLS	10/01-12/01
Restaurant, Lounge, and Coffee Shop	Oklahoma	H	5.57 FQ	6.75 AW	8.62 TQ	OKBLS	10/01-12/01
Restaurant, Lounge, and Coffee Shop	Oklahoma City MSA, OK	H	5.67 FQ	7.13 AW	9.27 TQ	OKBLS	10/01-12/01
Restaurant, Lounge, and Coffee Shop	Tulsa MSA, OK	H	5.59 FQ	6.62 AW	8.13 TQ	OKBLS	10/01-12/01
Restaurant, Lounge, and Coffee Shop	Oregon	H	6.75 FQ	7.56 AW	8.76 TQ	ORBLS	10/01-12/01
Restaurant, Lounge, and Coffee Shop	Eugene-Springfield MSA, OR	H	7.01 FQ	7.83 AW	8.91 TQ	ORBLS	10/01-12/01
Restaurant, Lounge, and Coffee Shop	Medford-Ashland MSA, OR	H	6.88 FQ	7.81 AW	8.93 TQ	ORBLS	10/01-12/01
Restaurant, Lounge, and Coffee Shop	Portland-Vancouver PMSA, OR-WA	H	6.73 FQ	7.38 AW	8.48 TQ	ORBLS	10/01-12/01
Restaurant, Lounge, and Coffee Shop	Salem PMSA, OR	H	6.62 FQ	7.28 AW	8.58 TQ	ORBLS	10/01-12/01
Restaurant, Lounge, and Coffee Shop	Pennsylvania	H	5.68 FQ	7.23 AW	9.40 TQ	PABLS	10/01-12/01
Restaurant, Lounge, and Coffee Shop	Allentown-Bethlehem-Easton MSA, PA	H	5.67 FQ	6.99 AW	8.59 TQ	PABLS	10/01-12/01
Restaurant, Lounge, and Coffee Shop	Erie MSA, PA	H	5.54 FQ	6.94 AW	8.52 TQ	PABLS	10/01-12/01
Restaurant, Lounge, and Coffee Shop	Harrisburg-Lebanon-Carlisle MSA, PA	H	5.80 FQ	7.49 AW	9.09 TQ	PABLS	10/01-12/01
Restaurant, Lounge, and Coffee Shop	Johnstown MSA, PA	H	5.70 FQ	6.51 AW	7.98 TQ	PABLS	10/01-12/01
Restaurant, Lounge, and Coffee Shop	Lancaster MSA, PA	H	5.59 FQ	7.31 AW	9.79 TQ	PABLS	10/01-12/01
Restaurant, Lounge, and Coffee Shop	Philadelphia PMSA, PA-NJ	H	5.80 FQ	7.94 AW	10.73 TQ	PABLS	10/01-12/01
Restaurant, Lounge, and Coffee Shop	Pittsburgh MSA, PA	H	5.67 FQ	6.82 AW	8.48 TQ	PABLS	10/01-12/01
Restaurant, Lounge, and Coffee Shop	Reading MSA, PA	H	5.80 FQ	7.42 AW	10.16 TQ	PABLS	10/01-12/01
Restaurant, Lounge, and Coffee Shop	Scranton-Wilkes-Barre-Hazleton MSA, PA	H	5.77 FQ	7.42 AW	10.25 TQ	PABLS	10/01-12/01
Restaurant, Lounge, and Coffee Shop	York MSA, PA	H	5.74 FQ	7.20 AW	8.81 TQ	PABLS	10/01-12/01
Restaurant, Lounge, and Coffee Shop	Rhode Island	H	6.66 FQ	8.25 AW	10.55 TQ	RIBLS	10/01-12/01
Restaurant, Lounge, and Coffee Shop	Providence-Fall River-Warwick MSA, RI-MA	H	6.71 FQ	8.20 AW	10.50 TQ	RIBLS	10/01-12/01
Restaurant, Lounge, and Coffee Shop	South Carolina	H	5.65 FQ	7.23 AW	10.14 TQ	SCBLS	10/01-12/01
Restaurant, Lounge, and Coffee Shop	Charleston-North Charleston MSA, SC	H	5.52 FQ	6.36 AW	7.89 TQ	SCBLS	10/01-12/01
Restaurant, Lounge, and Coffee Shop	Columbia MSA, SC	H	5.62 FQ	6.67 AW	8.44 TQ	SCBLS	10/01-12/01

AAW	Average annual wage	AOH	Average offered, high	ASH	Average starting, high	H	Hourly	M	Monthly	S	Special: hourly and annual
AE	Average entry wage	AOL	Average offered, low	ASL	Average starting, low	HI	Highest wage paid	MTC	Median total compensation	TQ	Third quartile wage
AEX	Average experienced wage	APH	Average pay, high range	AW	Average wage paid	HR	High end range	MW	Median wage paid	W	Weekly
AO	Average offered	APL	Average pay, low range	FQ	First quartile wage	LR	Low end range	SQ	Second quartile wage	Y	Yearly

Occupation/Type/Industry	Location	Per	Low	Mid	High	Source	Date
Host and Hostess							
Restaurant, Lounge, and Coffee Shop	Greenville-Spartanburg-Anderson MSA, SC	H	5.79 FQ	7.85 AW	10.65 TQ	SCBLS	10/01-12/01
Restaurant, Lounge, and Coffee Shop	Myrtle Beach MSA, SC	H	5.65 FQ	7.20 AW	9.17 TQ	SCBLS	10/01-12/01
Restaurant, Lounge, and Coffee Shop	South Dakota	H	5.61 FQ	6.80 AW	8.56 TQ	SDBLS	10/01-12/01
Restaurant, Lounge, and Coffee Shop	Sioux Falls MSA, SD	H	5.87 FQ	7.37 AW	8.87 TQ	SDBLS	10/01-12/01
Restaurant, Lounge, and Coffee Shop	Tennessee	H	5.72 FQ	7.30 AW	9.14 TQ	TNBLS	10/01-12/01
Restaurant, Lounge, and Coffee Shop	Chattanooga MSA, TN-GA	H	5.58 FQ	7.01 AW	8.69 TQ	TNBLS	10/01-12/01
Restaurant, Lounge, and Coffee Shop	Clarksville-Hopkinsville MSA, TN-KY	H	5.85 FQ	7.21 AW	8.77 TQ	TNBLS	10/01-12/01
Restaurant, Lounge, and Coffee Shop	Johnson City-Kingsport-Bristol MSA, TN-VA	H	5.58 FQ	6.53 AW	8.28 TQ	TNBLS	10/01-12/01
Restaurant, Lounge, and Coffee Shop	Knoxville MSA, TN	H	5.74 FQ	6.99 AW	8.77 TQ	TNBLS	10/01-12/01
Restaurant, Lounge, and Coffee Shop	Memphis MSA, TN-AR-MS	H	5.71 FQ	6.99 AW	9.00 TQ	TNBLS	10/01-12/01
Restaurant, Lounge, and Coffee Shop	Nashville MSA, TN	H	6.05 FQ	8.41 AW	11.57 TQ	TNBLS	10/01-12/01
Restaurant, Lounge, and Coffee Shop	Texas	H	5.61 FQ	7.09 AW	9.02 TQ	TXBLS	10/01-12/01
Restaurant, Lounge, and Coffee Shop	Amarillo MSA, TX	H	5.66 FQ	6.59 AW	8.13 TQ	TXBLS	10/01-12/01
Restaurant, Lounge, and Coffee Shop	Austin-San Marcos MSA, TX	H	5.73 FQ	7.01 AW	8.57 TQ	TXBLS	10/01-12/01
Restaurant, Lounge, and Coffee Shop	Beaumont-Port Arthur MSA, TX	H	5.68 FQ	7.02 AW	8.77 TQ	TXBLS	10/01-12/01
Restaurant, Lounge, and Coffee Shop	Brazoria PMSA, TX	H	5.62 FQ	6.53 AW	8.11 TQ	TXBLS	10/01-12/01
Restaurant, Lounge, and Coffee Shop	Brownsville-Harlingen-San Benito MSA, TX	H	5.61 FQ	6.61 AW	8.44 TQ	TXBLS	10/01-12/01
Restaurant, Lounge, and Coffee Shop	Corpus Christi MSA, TX	H	5.58 FQ	6.82 AW	8.68 TQ	TXBLS	10/01-12/01
Restaurant, Lounge, and Coffee Shop	Dallas PMSA, TX	H	5.58 FQ	7.24 AW	10.40 TQ	TXBLS	10/01-12/01
Restaurant, Lounge, and Coffee Shop	El Paso MSA, TX	H	5.52 FQ	6.39 AW	7.61 TQ	TXBLS	10/01-12/01
Restaurant, Lounge, and Coffee Shop	Fort Worth-Arlington PMSA, TX	H	5.68 FQ	7.11 AW	8.99 TQ	TXBLS	10/01-12/01
Restaurant, Lounge, and Coffee Shop	Galveston-Texas City PMSA, TX	H	5.61 FQ	7.17 AW	8.82 TQ	TXBLS	10/01-12/01
Restaurant, Lounge, and Coffee Shop	Houston PMSA, TX	H	5.55 FQ	7.39 AW	10.53 TQ	TXBLS	10/01-12/01
Restaurant, Lounge, and Coffee Shop	Killeen-Temple MSA, TX	H	5.62 FQ	6.53 AW	7.89 TQ	TXBLS	10/01-12/01
Restaurant, Lounge, and Coffee Shop	Laredo MSA, TX	H	5.47 FQ	6.01 AW	6.83 TQ	TXBLS	10/01-12/01
Restaurant, Lounge, and Coffee Shop	Longview-Marshall MSA, TX	H	5.61 FQ	6.53 AW	7.99 TQ	TXBLS	10/01-12/01
Restaurant, Lounge, and Coffee Shop	Lubbock MSA, TX	H	5.59 FQ	6.46 AW	7.75 TQ	TXBLS	10/01-12/01
Restaurant, Lounge, and Coffee Shop	McAllen-Edinburg-Mission MSA, TX	H	5.52 FQ	6.26 AW	7.36 TQ	TXBLS	10/01-12/01
Restaurant, Lounge, and Coffee Shop	Odessa-Midland MSA, TX	H	5.61 FQ	6.74 AW	8.49 TQ	TXBLS	10/01-12/01
Restaurant, Lounge, and Coffee Shop	San Antonio MSA, TX	H	5.71 FQ	7.27 AW	9.04 TQ	TXBLS	10/01-12/01
Restaurant, Lounge, and Coffee Shop	Tyler MSA, TX	H	5.64 FQ	6.65 AW	8.37 TQ	TXBLS	10/01-12/01
Restaurant, Lounge, and Coffee Shop	Waco MSA, TX	H	5.76 FQ	6.81 AW	8.30 TQ	TXBLS	10/01-12/01
Restaurant, Lounge, and Coffee Shop	Utah	H	5.72 FQ	7.21 AW	8.87 TQ	UTBLS	10/01-12/01
Restaurant, Lounge, and Coffee Shop	Provo-Orem MSA, UT	H	5.89 FQ	7.38 AW	9.20 TQ	UTBLS	10/01-12/01
Restaurant, Lounge, and Coffee Shop	Salt Lake City-Ogden MSA, UT	H	5.75 FQ	7.30 AW	9.01 TQ	UTBLS	10/01-12/01
Restaurant, Lounge, and Coffee Shop	Vermont	H	6.45 FQ	8.07 AW	10.86 TQ	VTBLS	10/01-12/01
Restaurant, Lounge, and Coffee Shop	Burlington MSA, VT	H	6.35 FQ	7.45 AW	9.12 TQ	VTBLS	10/01-12/01
Restaurant, Lounge, and Coffee Shop	Virginia	H	5.70 FQ	7.34 AW	9.72 TQ	VABLS	10/01-12/01
Restaurant, Lounge, and Coffee Shop	Lynchburg MSA, VA	H	5.67 FQ	6.76 AW	8.73 TQ	VABLS	10/01-12/01
Restaurant, Lounge, and Coffee Shop	Norfolk-Virginia Beach-Newport News MSA, VA-NC	H	5.65 FQ	7.10 AW	9.41 TQ	VABLS	10/01-12/01
Restaurant, Lounge, and Coffee Shop	Richmond-Petersburg MSA, VA	H	5.75 FQ	6.96 AW	8.57 TQ	VABLS	10/01-12/01
Restaurant, Lounge, and Coffee Shop	Roanoke MSA, VA	H	5.71 FQ	7.00 AW	8.57 TQ	VABLS	10/01-12/01
Restaurant, Lounge, and Coffee Shop	Washington	H	6.74 FQ	7.99 AW	10.10 TQ	WABLS	10/01-12/01
Restaurant, Lounge, and Coffee Shop	Bremerton PMSA, WA	H	6.82 FQ	7.56 AW	8.72 TQ	WABLS	10/01-12/01
Restaurant, Lounge, and Coffee Shop	Olympia PMSA, WA	H	6.89 FQ	7.80 AW	9.08 TQ	WABLS	10/01-12/01
Restaurant, Lounge, and Coffee Shop	Richland-Kennewick-Pasco MSA, WA	H	6.98 FQ	9.44 AW	12.83 TQ	WABLS	10/01-12/01
Restaurant, Lounge, and Coffee Shop	Seattle-Bellevue-Everett PMSA, WA	H	7.03 FQ	8.71 AW	10.46 TQ	WABLS	10/01-12/01
Restaurant, Lounge, and Coffee Shop	Spokane MSA, WA	H	6.78 FQ	7.53 AW	9.01 TQ	WABLS	10/01-12/01
Restaurant, Lounge, and Coffee Shop	Tacoma PMSA, WA	H	6.84 FQ	7.82 AW	9.49 TQ	WABLS	10/01-12/01
Restaurant, Lounge, and Coffee Shop	Yakima MSA, WA	H	6.76 FQ	7.28 AW	8.33 TQ	WABLS	10/01-12/01
Restaurant, Lounge, and Coffee Shop	West Virginia	H	5.59 FQ	6.41 AW	7.70 TQ	WVBLS	10/01-12/01
Restaurant, Lounge, and Coffee Shop	Charleston MSA, WV	H	5.49 FQ	6.33 AW	7.78 TQ	WVBLS	10/01-12/01
Restaurant, Lounge, and Coffee Shop	Huntington-Ashland MSA, WV-KY-OH	H	5.52 FQ	6.42 AW	7.86 TQ	WVBLS	10/01-12/01
Restaurant, Lounge, and Coffee Shop	Wisconsin	H	5.83 FQ	7.78 AW	10.32 TQ	WIBLS	10/01-12/01
Restaurant, Lounge, and Coffee Shop	Appleton-Oshkosh-Neenah MSA, WI	H	6.66 FQ	8.35 AW	10.65 TQ	WIBLS	10/01-12/01

AAW	Average annual wage	AOH	Average offered, high	ASH	Average starting, high	H	Hourly	M	Monthly	S	Special: hourly and annual
AE	Average entry wage	AOL	Average offered, low	ASL	Average starting, low	HI	Highest wage paid	MTC	Median total compensation	TQ	Third quartile wage
AEX	Average experienced wage	APH	Average pay, high range	AW	Average wage paid	HR	High end range	MW	Median wage paid	W	Weekly
AO	Average offered	APL	Average pay, low range	FQ	First quartile wage	LR	Low end range	SQ	Second quartile wage	Y	Yearly

Occupation/Type/Industry	Location	Per	Low	Mid	High	Source	Date
Host and Hostess							
Restaurant, Lounge, and Coffee Shop	Green Bay MSA, WI	H	5.95 FQ	8.06 AW	10.53 TQ	WIBLS	10/01-12/01
Restaurant, Lounge, and Coffee Shop	Madison MSA, WI	H	6.16 FQ	7.89 AW	9.97 TQ	WIBLS	10/01-12/01
Restaurant, Lounge, and Coffee Shop	Milwaukee-Waukesha PMSA, WI	H	6.27 FQ	8.18 AW	11.30 TQ	WIBLS	10/01-12/01
Restaurant, Lounge, and Coffee Shop	Racine PMSA, WI	H	5.56 FQ	7.29 AW	9.76 TQ	WIBLS	10/01-12/01
Restaurant, Lounge, and Coffee Shop	Wyoming	H	5.58 FQ	7.06 AW	9.32 TQ	WYBLS	10/01-12/01
Restaurant, Lounge, and Coffee Shop	Cheyenne MSA, WY	H	5.67 FQ	6.86 AW	8.55 TQ	WYBLS	10/01-12/01
Restaurant, Lounge, and Coffee Shop	Puerto Rico	H	5.67 FQ	6.71 AW	8.54 TQ	PRBLS	10/01-12/01
Restaurant, Lounge, and Coffee Shop	Virgin Islands	H	6.05 FQ	7.92 AW	10.08 TQ	VIBLS	10/01-12/01
Restaurant, Lounge, and Coffee Shop	Guam	H	5.54 FQ	7.16 AW	9.71 TQ	GUBLS	10/01-12/01
Hotel, Motel, and Resort Desk Clerk	Alabama	H	5.62 FQ	7.01 AW	8.94 TQ	ALBLS	10/01-12/01
	Birmingham MSA, AL	H	5.65 FQ	7.19 AW	9.00 TQ	ALBLS	10/01-12/01
	Huntsville MSA, AL	H	5.65 FQ	6.50 AW	8.06 TQ	ALBLS	10/01-12/01
	Mobile MSA, AL	H	5.65 FQ	7.35 AW	9.85 TQ	ALBLS	10/01-12/01
	Montgomery MSA, AL	H	5.82 FQ	7.26 AW	8.47 TQ	ALBLS	10/01-12/01
	Alaska	H	7.27 FQ	9.33 AW	11.89 TQ	AKBLS	10/01-12/01
	Anchorage MSA, AK	H	7.08 FQ	9.20 AW	11.86 TQ	AKBLS	10/01-12/01
	Arizona	H	5.77 FQ	7.63 AW	10.09 TQ	AZBLS	10/01-12/01
	Phoenix-Mesa MSA, AZ	H	5.79 FQ	7.88 AW	10.35 TQ	AZBLS	10/01-12/01
	Tucson MSA, AZ	H	5.91 FQ	8.03 AW	10.75 TQ	AZBLS	10/01-12/01
	Arkansas	H	5.70 FQ	6.95 AW	8.65 TQ	ARBLS	10/01-12/01
	Fayetteville-Springdale-Rogers MSA, AR	H	5.95 FQ	7.37 AW	8.85 TQ	ARBLS	10/01-12/01
	Fort Smith MSA, AR-OK	H	5.66 FQ	6.63 AW	8.19 TQ	ARBLS	10/01-12/01
	Little Rock-North Little Rock MSA, AR	H	5.70 FQ	7.35 AW	9.07 TQ	ARBLS	10/01-12/01
	California	H	6.87 FQ	9.41 AW	12.81 TQ	CABLS	10/01-12/01
	Bakersfield MSA, CA	H	6.43 FQ	7.61 AW	8.96 TQ	CABLS	10/01-12/01
	Chico-Paradise MSA, CA	H	6.67 FQ	7.69 AW	8.87 TQ	CABLS	10/01-12/01
	Fresno MSA, CA	H	6.65 FQ	8.02 AW	9.66 TQ	CABLS	10/01-12/01
	Los Angeles-Long Beach PMSA, CA	H	7.25 FQ	9.57 AW	12.36 TQ	CABLS	10/01-12/01
	Merced MSA, CA	H	6.44 FQ	7.45 AW	8.76 TQ	CABLS	10/01-12/01
	Modesto MSA, CA	H	6.54 FQ	7.57 AW	8.56 TQ	CABLS	10/01-12/01
	Oakland PMSA, CA	H	6.64 FQ	8.85 AW	10.93 TQ	CABLS	10/01-12/01
	Orange County PMSA, CA	H	7.20 FQ	9.10 AW	10.93 TQ	CABLS	10/01-12/01
	Redding MSA, CA	H	6.46 FQ	7.67 AW	9.08 TQ	CABLS	10/01-12/01
	Riverside-San Bernardino PMSA, CA	H	6.81 FQ	9.16 AW	12.68 TQ	CABLS	10/01-12/01
	Sacramento PMSA, CA	H	6.68 FQ	8.56 AW	10.95 TQ	CABLS	10/01-12/01
	Salinas MSA, CA	H	6.80 FQ	9.75 AW	12.92 TQ	CABLS	10/01-12/01
	San Diego MSA, CA	H	6.96 FQ	9.71 AW	12.50 TQ	CABLS	10/01-12/01
	San Francisco PMSA, CA	H	8.70 FQ	12.37 AW	16.67 TQ	CABLS	10/01-12/01
	San Jose PMSA, CA	H	7.14 FQ	9.90 AW	13.32 TQ	CABLS	10/01-12/01
	San Luis Obispo-Atascadero-Paso Robles MSA, CA	H	7.16 FQ	8.51 AW	10.44 TQ	CABLS	10/01-12/01
	Santa Barbara-Santa Maria-Lompoc MSA, CA	H	6.85 FQ	9.27 AW	12.51 TQ	CABLS	10/01-12/01
	Santa Cruz-Watsonville PMSA, CA	H	6.40 FQ	8.74 AW	11.46 TQ	CABLS	10/01-12/01
	Santa Rosa PMSA, CA	H	6.70 FQ	9.40 AW	12.19 TQ	CABLS	10/01-12/01
	Stockton-Lodi MSA, CA	H	6.44 FQ	7.39 AW	8.62 TQ	CABLS	10/01-12/01
	Vallejo-Fairfield-Napa PMSA, CA	H	6.87 FQ	8.50 AW	10.95 TQ	CABLS	10/01-12/01
	Ventura PMSA, CA	H	7.17 FQ	8.29 AW	10.12 TQ	CABLS	10/01-12/01
	Visalia-Tulare-Porterville MSA, CA	H	6.41 FQ	7.82 AW	10.45 TQ	CABLS	10/01-12/01
	Colorado	H	6.56 FQ	9.04 AW	11.12 TQ	COBLS	10/01-12/01
	Boulder-Longmont PMSA, CO	H	7.07 FQ	8.72 AW	10.96 TQ	COBLS	10/01-12/01
	Colorado Springs MSA, CO	H	7.18 FQ	8.44 AW	10.30 TQ	COBLS	10/01-12/01
	Denver PMSA, CO	H	7.66 FQ	9.44 AW	11.08 TQ	COBLS	10/01-12/01
	Fort Collins-Loveland MSA, CO	H	5.43 FQ	7.22 AW	10.33 TQ	COBLS	10/01-12/01
	Greeley PMSA, CO	H	5.95 FQ	7.78 AW	9.86 TQ	COBLS	10/01-12/01
	Connecticut	H	7.64 FQ	9.58 AW	11.63 TQ	CTBLS	10/01-12/01
	Bridgeport PMSA, CT	H	7.20 FQ	9.15 AW	11.14 TQ	CTBLS	10/01-12/01
	Danbury PMSA, CT	H	8.29 FQ	10.44 AW	13.56 TQ	CTBLS	10/01-12/01
	Hartford MSA, CT	H	7.70 FQ	9.39 AW	11.33 TQ	CTBLS	10/01-12/01

AAW	Average annual wage	**AOH**	Average offered, high	**ASH**	Average starting, high	**H**	Hourly	**M**	Monthly	**S**	Special: hourly and annual
AE	Average entry wage	**AOL**	Average offered, low	**ASL**	Average starting, low	**HI**	Highest wage paid	**MTC**	Median total compensation	**TQ**	Third quartile wage
AEX	Average experienced wage	**APH**	Average pay, high range	**AW**	Average wage paid	**HR**	High end range	**MW**	Median wage paid	**W**	Weekly
AO	Average offered	**APL**	Average pay, low range	**FQ**	First quartile wage	**LR**	Low end range	**SQ**	Second quartile wage	**Y**	Yearly

Occupation/Type/Industry	Location	Per	Low	Mid	High	Source	Date
Hotel, Motel, and Resort Desk Clerk	New Haven-Meriden PMSA, CT	H	7.65 FQ	9.02 AW	10.91 TQ	CTBLS	10/01-12/01
	New London-Norwich MSA, CT-RI	H	7.58 FQ	9.74 AW	12.19 TQ	CTBLS	10/01-12/01
	Stamford-Norwalk PMSA, CT	H	7.83 FQ	10.25 AW	12.97 TQ	CTBLS	10/01-12/01
	Waterbury PMSA, CT	H	7.46 FQ	9.48 AW	11.21 TQ	CTBLS	10/01-12/01
	Delaware	H	7.19 FQ	8.79 AW	11.06 TQ	DEBLS	10/01-12/01
	Wilmington-Newark PMSA, DE-MD	H	7.22 FQ	9.00 AW	11.58 TQ	DEBLS	10/01-12/01
	District of Columbia	H	7.50 FQ	11.06 AW	14.24 TQ	DCBLS	10/01-12/01
	Washington PMSA, DC-MD-VA-WV	H	6.79 FQ	9.14 AW	12.55 TQ	DCBLS	10/01-12/01
	Florida	H	6.13 FQ	8.24 AW	10.63 TQ	FLBLS	10/01-12/01
	Daytona Beach MSA, FL	H	5.97 FQ	7.84 AW	10.00 TQ	FLBLS	10/01-12/01
	Fort Lauderdale PMSA, FL	H	6.99 FQ	8.87 AW	11.07 TQ	FLBLS	10/01-12/01
	Fort Myers-Cape Coral MSA, FL	H	6.89 FQ	8.45 AW	10.64 TQ	FLBLS	10/01-12/01
	Fort Pierce-Port St. Lucie MSA, FL	H	6.98 FQ	8.57 AW	10.56 TQ	FLBLS	10/01-12/01
	Fort Walton Beach MSA, FL	H	5.77 FQ	7.35 AW	9.24 TQ	FLBLS	10/01-12/01
	Gainesville MSA, FL	H	5.77 FQ	7.37 AW	9.47 TQ	FLBLS	10/01-12/01
	Jacksonville MSA, FL	H	6.10 FQ	8.22 AW	10.30 TQ	FLBLS	10/01-12/01
	Lakeland-Winter Haven MSA, FL	H	7.45 FQ	10.01 AW	13.17 TQ	FLBLS	10/01-12/01
	Melbourne-Titusville-Palm Bay MSA, FL	H	5.80 FQ	7.48 AW	9.58 TQ	FLBLS	10/01-12/01
	Miami PMSA, FL	H	5.92 FQ	8.13 AW	10.61 TQ	FLBLS	10/01-12/01
	Naples MSA, FL	H	8.29 FQ	10.15 AW	13.01 TQ	FLBLS	10/01-12/01
	Ocala MSA, FL	H	5.84 FQ	7.03 AW	8.65 TQ	FLBLS	10/01-12/01
	Orlando MSA, FL	H	6.56 FQ	8.36 AW	10.61 TQ	FLBLS	10/01-12/01
	Pensacola MSA, FL	H	5.70 FQ	7.20 AW	9.50 TQ	FLBLS	10/01-12/01
	Sarasota-Bradenton MSA, FL	H	7.16 FQ	8.67 AW	11.23 TQ	FLBLS	10/01-12/01
	Tallahassee MSA, FL	H	5.62 FQ	7.24 AW	8.95 TQ	FLBLS	10/01-12/01
	Tampa-St. Petersburg-Clearwater MSA, FL	H	5.94 FQ	7.71 AW	9.77 TQ	FLBLS	10/01-12/01
	West Palm Beach-Boca Raton MSA, FL	H	6.77 FQ	8.77 AW	11.29 TQ	FLBLS	10/01-12/01
	Georgia	H	6.14 FQ	8.53 AW	11.42 TQ	GABLS	10/01-12/01
	Atlanta MSA, GA	H	7.18 FQ	9.24 AW	12.28 TQ	GABLS	10/01-12/01
	Augusta-Aiken MSA, GA-SC	H	6.27 FQ	8.14 AW	10.53 TQ	GABLS	10/01-12/01
	Columbus MSA, GA-AL	H	5.58 FQ	7.06 AW	8.49 TQ	GABLS	10/01-12/01
	Macon MSA, GA	H	5.94 FQ	8.10 AW	10.82 TQ	GABLS	10/01-12/01
	Savannah MSA, GA	H	5.83 FQ	8.41 AW	11.04 TQ	GABLS	10/01-12/01
	Hawaii	H	8.88 FQ	13.54 AW	17.05 TQ	HIBLS	10/01-12/01
	Honolulu MSA, HI	H	8.33 FQ	13.16 AW	17.14 TQ	HIBLS	10/01-12/01
	Idaho	H	5.81 FQ	7.33 AW	8.86 TQ	IDBLS	10/01-12/01
	Boise City MSA, ID	H	5.94 FQ	7.52 AW	8.85 TQ	IDBLS	10/01-12/01
	Illinois	H	6.05 FQ	8.57 AW	11.11 TQ	ILBLS	10/01-12/01
	Champaign-Urbana MSA, IL	H	5.67 FQ	7.50 AW	10.36 TQ	ILBLS	10/01-12/01
	Chicago PMSA, IL	H	7.37 FQ	9.56 AW	12.12 TQ	ILBLS	10/01-12/01
	Peoria-Pekin MSA, IL	H	6.71 FQ	7.93 AW	9.19 TQ	ILBLS	10/01-12/01
	Rockford MSA, IL	H	5.81 FQ	7.74 AW	10.13 TQ	ILBLS	10/01-12/01
	Springfield MSA, IL	H	6.99 FQ	8.36 AW	10.44 TQ	ILBLS	10/01-12/01
	Indiana	H	5.95 FQ	7.61 AW	9.18 TQ	INBLS	10/01-12/01
	Elkhart-Goshen MSA, IN	H	6.16 FQ	7.73 AW	9.34 TQ	INBLS	10/01-12/01
	Evansville-Henderson MSA, IN-KY	H	5.93 FQ	7.25 AW	8.82 TQ	INBLS	10/01-12/01
	Fort Wayne MSA, IN	H	5.62 FQ	7.36 AW	9.03 TQ	INBLS	10/01-12/01
	Gary PMSA, IN	H	6.10 FQ	7.66 AW	9.27 TQ	INBLS	10/01-12/01
	Indianapolis MSA, IN	H	7.04 FQ	8.36 AW	10.28 TQ	INBLS	10/01-12/01
	Lafayette MSA, IN	H	5.96 FQ	7.36 AW	8.63 TQ	INBLS	10/01-12/01
	South Bend MSA, IN	H	6.01 FQ	7.52 AW	8.85 TQ	INBLS	10/01-12/01
	Iowa	H	5.90 FQ	7.65 AW	9.72 TQ	IABLS	10/01-12/01
	Cedar Rapids MSA, IA	H	6.05 FQ	8.16 AW	10.76 TQ	IABLS	10/01-12/01
	Davenport-Moline-Rock Island MSA, IA-IL	H	5.80 FQ	7.35 AW	8.85 TQ	IABLS	10/01-12/01
	Des Moines MSA, IA	H	7.24 FQ	8.69 AW	10.60 TQ	IABLS	10/01-12/01
	Kansas	H	5.84 FQ	7.39 AW	9.11 TQ	KSBLS	10/01-12/01
	Topeka MSA, KS	H	5.91 FQ	7.54 AW	9.74 TQ	KSBLS	10/01-12/01
	Wichita MSA, KS	H	6.78 FQ	7.99 AW	9.22 TQ	KSBLS	10/01-12/01
	Kentucky	H	5.94 FQ	7.48 AW	8.98 TQ	KYBLS	10/01-12/01

AAW Average annual wage **AOH** Average offered, high **ASH** Average starting, high **H** Hourly **M** Monthly **S** Special: hourly and annual
AE Average entry wage **AOL** Average offered, low **ASL** Average starting, low **HI** Highest wage paid **MTC** Median total compensation **TQ** Third quartile wage
AEX Average experienced wage **APH** Average pay, high range **AW** Average wage paid **HR** High end range **MW** Median wage paid **W** Weekly
AO Average offered **APL** Average pay, low range **FQ** First quartile wage **LR** Low end range **SQ** Second quartile wage **Y** Yearly

Occupation/Type/Industry	Location	Per	Low	Mid	High	Source	Date
Hotel, Motel, and Resort Desk Clerk	Lexington MSA, KY	H	6.25 FQ	7.62 AW	8.77 TQ	KYBLS	10/01-12/01
	Louisville MSA, KY-IN	H	6.26 FQ	7.98 AW	10.00 TQ	KYBLS	10/01-12/01
	Louisiana	H	5.73 FQ	7.29 AW	9.15 TQ	LABLS	10/01-12/01
	Baton Rouge MSA, LA	H	5.66 FQ	7.05 AW	8.93 TQ	LABLS	10/01-12/01
	Houma MSA, LA	H	5.62 FQ	6.34 AW	7.42 TQ	LABLS	10/01-12/01
	Lafayette MSA, LA	H	5.64 FQ	7.16 AW	8.81 TQ	LABLS	10/01-12/01
	Lake Charles MSA, LA	H	5.82 FQ	6.98 AW	8.48 TQ	LABLS	10/01-12/01
	New Orleans MSA, LA	H	5.94 FQ	7.81 AW	9.75 TQ	LABLS	10/01-12/01
	Shreveport-Bossier City MSA, LA	H	5.85 FQ	7.53 AW	9.87 TQ	LABLS	10/01-12/01
	Maine	H	5.93 FQ	8.54 AW	11.38 TQ	MEBLS	10/01-12/01
	Portland MSA, ME	H	7.35 FQ	9.36 AW	12.71 TQ	MEBLS	10/01-12/01
	Maryland	H	6.31 FQ	8.28 AW	10.62 TQ	MDBLS	10/01-12/01
	Baltimore PMSA, MD	H	6.81 FQ	8.28 AW	10.47 TQ	MDBLS	10/01-12/01
	Massachusetts	H	7.56 FQ	10.21 AW	13.49 TQ	MABLS	10/01-12/01
	Boston PMSA, MA-NH	H	7.76 FQ	10.75 AW	14.53 TQ	MABLS	10/01-12/01
	Brockton PMSA, MA	H	7.39 FQ	9.44 AW	12.26 TQ	MABLS	10/01-12/01
	Lawrence PMSA, MA-NH	H	8.16 FQ	9.76 AW	11.81 TQ	MABLS	10/01-12/01
	Lowell PMSA, MA-NH	H	7.81 FQ	10.08 AW	12.90 TQ	MABLS	10/01-12/01
	Springfield MSA, MA	H	7.33 FQ	9.77 AW	12.96 TQ	MABLS	10/01-12/01
	Worcester PMSA, MA-CT	H	7.18 FQ	9.32 AW	12.56 TQ	MABLS	10/01-12/01
	Michigan	H	6.10 FQ	8.10 AW	10.31 TQ	MIBLS	10/01-12/01
	Ann Arbor PMSA, MI	H	6.81 FQ	8.59 AW	10.68 TQ	MIBLS	10/01-12/01
	Detroit PMSA, MI	H	6.54 FQ	8.42 AW	10.47 TQ	MIBLS	10/01-12/01
	Flint PMSA, MI	H	6.98 FQ	8.26 AW	10.21 TQ	MIBLS	10/01-12/01
	Grand Rapids-Muskegon-Holland MSA, MI	H	6.49 FQ	8.18 AW	10.05 TQ	MIBLS	10/01-12/01
	Kalamazoo-Battle Creek MSA, MI	H	6.18 FQ	8.22 AW	10.57 TQ	MIBLS	10/01-12/01
	Lansing-East Lansing MSA, MI	H	6.36 FQ	7.85 AW	9.61 TQ	MIBLS	10/01-12/01
	Saginaw-Bay City-Midland MSA, MI	H	5.81 FQ	7.55 AW	9.81 TQ	MIBLS	10/01-12/01
	Minnesota	H	6.26 FQ	8.29 AW	10.64 TQ	MNBLS	10/01-12/01
	Duluth-Superior MSA, MN-WI	H	5.77 FQ	6.98 AW	8.74 TQ	MNBLS	10/01-12/01
	Minneapolis-St. Paul MSA, MN-WI	H	6.86 FQ	9.10 AW	11.64 TQ	MNBLS	10/01-12/01
	St. Cloud MSA, MN	H	6.13 FQ	7.62 AW	8.99 TQ	MNBLS	10/01-12/01
	Mississippi	H	5.63 FQ	7.20 AW	8.79 TQ	MSBLS	10/01-12/01
	Biloxi-Gulfport-Pascagoula MSA, MS	H	6.04 FQ	7.67 AW	9.06 TQ	MSBLS	10/01-12/01
	Jackson MSA, MS	H	6.23 FQ	7.85 AW	9.13 TQ	MSBLS	10/01-12/01
	Missouri	H	5.78 FQ	7.69 AW	10.21 TQ	MOBLS	10/01-12/01
	Kansas City MSA, MO-KS	H	6.37 FQ	8.26 AW	10.67 TQ	MOBLS	10/01-12/01
	St. Louis MSA, MO-IL	H	6.26 FQ	8.35 AW	10.71 TQ	MOBLS	10/01-12/01
	Springfield MSA, MO	H	5.72 FQ	7.28 AW	8.81 TQ	MOBLS	10/01-12/01
	Montana	H	5.61 FQ	6.98 AW	9.02 TQ	MTBLS	10/01-12/01
	Billings MSA, MT	H	5.61 FQ	7.25 AW	9.65 TQ	MTBLS	10/01-12/01
	Nebraska	H	5.95 FQ	7.74 AW	10.02 TQ	NEBLS	10/01-12/01
	Lincoln MSA, NE	H	6.78 FQ	8.25 AW	10.08 TQ	NEBLS	10/01-12/01
	Omaha MSA, NE-IA	H	6.63 FQ	8.75 AW	11.03 TQ	NEBLS	10/01-12/01
	Nevada	H	7.21 FQ	11.08 AW	15.76 TQ	NVBLS	10/01-12/01
	Las Vegas MSA, NV-AZ	H	7.46 FQ	11.57 AW	16.05 TQ	NVBLS	10/01-12/01
	Reno MSA, NV	H	7.04 FQ	9.34 AW	12.49 TQ	NVBLS	10/01-12/01
	New Hampshire	H	7.28 FQ	9.13 AW	11.06 TQ	NHBLS	10/01-12/01
	Manchester PMSA, NH	H	7.43 FQ	9.15 AW	11.15 TQ	NHBLS	10/01-12/01
	Nashua PMSA, NH	H	7.42 FQ	8.91 AW	10.91 TQ	NHBLS	10/01-12/01
	Portsmouth-Rochester PMSA, NH-ME	H	7.43 FQ	9.30 AW	11.46 TQ	NHBLS	10/01-12/01
	New Jersey	H	7.45 FQ	9.72 AW	12.72 TQ	NJBLS	10/01-12/01
	Atlantic-Cape May PMSA, NJ	H	7.33 FQ	9.71 AW	13.28 TQ	NJBLS	10/01-12/01
	Bergen-Passaic PMSA, NJ	H	7.63 FQ	9.54 AW	11.76 TQ	NJBLS	10/01-12/01
	Jersey City PMSA, NJ	H	6.67 FQ	9.69 AW	12.34 TQ	NJBLS	10/01-12/01
	Middlesex-Somerset-Hunterdon PMSA, NJ	H	8.32 FQ	10.04 AW	12.23 TQ	NJBLS	10/01-12/01
	Monmouth-Ocean PMSA, NJ	H	7.67 FQ	10.04 AW	13.12 TQ	NJBLS	10/01-12/01
	Newark PMSA, NJ	H	7.76 FQ	10.33 AW	13.73 TQ	NJBLS	10/01-12/01
	Trenton PMSA, NJ	H	8.41 FQ	10.02 AW	12.51 TQ	NJBLS	10/01-12/01
	New Mexico	H	5.66 FQ	7.28 AW	9.77 TQ	NMBLS	10/01-12/01
	Albuquerque MSA, NM	H	5.85 FQ	7.45 AW	8.86 TQ	NMBLS	10/01-12/01
	Las Cruces MSA, NM	H	5.52 FQ	6.19 AW	7.15 TQ	NMBLS	10/01-12/01
	New York	H	6.62 FQ	11.31 AW	18.17 TQ	NYBLS	10/01-12/01

AAW Average annual wage; **AE** Average entry wage; **AEX** Average experienced wage; **AO** Average offered; **AOH** Average offered, high; **AOL** Average offered, low; **APH** Average pay, high range; **APL** Average pay, low range; **ASH** Average starting, high; **ASL** Average starting, low; **AW** Average wage paid; **FQ** First quartile wage; **H** Hourly; **HI** Highest wage paid; **HR** High end range; **LR** Low end range; **M** Monthly; **MTC** Median total compensation; **MW** Median wage paid; **SQ** Second quartile wage; **S** Special: hourly and annual; **TQ** Third quartile wage; **W** Weekly; **Y** Yearly

Occupation/Type/Industry	Location	Per	Low	Mid	High	Source	Date
Hotel, Motel, and Resort Desk Clerk	Albany-Schenectady-Troy MSA, NY	H	7.05 FQ	8.35 AW	10.29 TQ	NYBLS	10/01-12/01
	Binghamton MSA, NY	H	6.33 FQ	7.77 AW	9.01 TQ	NYBLS	10/01-12/01
	Buffalo-Niagara Falls MSA, NY	H	6.03 FQ	7.57 AW	9.02 TQ	NYBLS	10/01-12/01
	Dutchess County PMSA, NY	H	6.34 FQ	8.22 AW	10.36 TQ	NYBLS	10/01-12/01
	Nassau-Suffolk PMSA, NY	H	7.48 FQ	9.43 AW	12.50 TQ	NYBLS	10/01-12/01
	New York PMSA, NY	H	10.40 FQ	15.51 AW	20.37 TQ	NYBLS	10/01-12/01
	Newburgh PMSA, NY-PA	H	7.14 FQ	8.25 AW	10.02 TQ	NYBLS	10/01-12/01
	Rochester MSA, NY	H	6.44 FQ	8.32 AW	10.66 TQ	NYBLS	10/01-12/01
	Syracuse MSA, NY	H	5.73 FQ	7.89 AW	11.89 TQ	NYBLS	10/01-12/01
	Utica-Rome MSA, NY	H	7.41 FQ	10.71 AW	16.87 TQ	NYBLS	10/01-12/01
	North Carolina	H	6.14 FQ	8.12 AW	10.47 TQ	NCBLS	10/01-12/01
	Asheville MSA, NC	H	7.13 FQ	8.12 AW	9.65 TQ	NCBLS	10/01-12/01
	Charlotte-Gastonia-Rock Hill MSA, NC-SC	H	7.22 FQ	8.90 AW	10.88 TQ	NCBLS	10/01-12/01
	Fayetteville MSA, NC	H	6.13 FQ	7.46 AW	8.67 TQ	NCBLS	10/01-12/01
	Greensboro-Winston-Salem-High Point MSA, NC	H	6.44 FQ	7.85 AW	9.39 TQ	NCBLS	10/01-12/01
	Hickory-Morganton-Lenoir MSA, NC	H	5.98 FQ	7.71 AW	8.97 TQ	NCBLS	10/01-12/01
	Raleigh-Durham-Chapel Hill MSA, NC	H	7.45 FQ	8.95 AW	10.99 TQ	NCBLS	10/01-12/01
	Wilmington MSA, NC	H	6.23 FQ	8.32 AW	10.68 TQ	NCBLS	10/01-12/01
	North Dakota	H	5.71 FQ	7.11 AW	8.55 TQ	NDBLS	10/01-12/01
	Fargo-Moorhead MSA, ND-MN	H	6.71 FQ	8.06 AW	8.89 TQ	NDBLS	10/01-12/01
	Ohio	H	5.90 FQ	7.79 AW	10.09 TQ	OHBLS	10/01-12/01
	Akron PMSA, OH	H	5.89 FQ	7.67 AW	10.01 TQ	OHBLS	10/01-12/01
	Canton-Massillon MSA, OH	H	6.13 FQ	7.80 AW	9.52 TQ	OHBLS	10/01-12/01
	Cincinnati PMSA, OH-KY-IN	H	6.77 FQ	8.27 AW	10.36 TQ	OHBLS	10/01-12/01
	Cleveland-Lorain-Elyria PMSA, OH	H	6.90 FQ	8.46 AW	10.50 TQ	OHBLS	10/01-12/01
	Columbus MSA, OH	H	5.95 FQ	7.92 AW	10.20 TQ	OHBLS	10/01-12/01
	Dayton-Springfield MSA, OH	H	6.97 FQ	8.33 AW	10.36 TQ	OHBLS	10/01-12/01
	Hamilton-Middletown PMSA, OH	H	5.64 FQ	7.52 AW	10.30 TQ	OHBLS	10/01-12/01
	Mansfield MSA, OH	H	5.74 FQ	7.27 AW	8.79 TQ	OHBLS	10/01-12/01
	Toledo MSA, OH	H	5.78 FQ	7.42 AW	9.19 TQ	OHBLS	10/01-12/01
	Youngstown-Warren MSA, OH	H	5.49 FQ	6.78 AW	8.60 TQ	OHBLS	10/01-12/01
	Oklahoma	H	5.75 FQ	7.23 AW	8.81 TQ	OKBLS	10/01-12/01
	Oklahoma City MSA, OK	H	6.19 FQ	7.68 AW	9.19 TQ	OKBLS	10/01-12/01
	Tulsa MSA, OK	H	6.00 FQ	7.54 AW	8.88 TQ	OKBLS	10/01-12/01
	Oregon	H	7.21 FQ	8.43 AW	10.28 TQ	ORBLS	10/01-12/01
	Eugene-Springfield MSA, OR	H	6.74 FQ	8.12 AW	10.37 TQ	ORBLS	10/01-12/01
	Medford-Ashland MSA, OR	H	7.42 FQ	8.61 AW	10.60 TQ	ORBLS	10/01-12/01
	Portland-Vancouver PMSA, OR-WA	H	7.26 FQ	8.51 AW	10.36 TQ	ORBLS	10/01-12/01
	Salem PMSA, OR	H	7.25 FQ	8.37 AW	9.95 TQ	ORBLS	10/01-12/01
	Pennsylvania	H	6.07 FQ	8.33 AW	10.89 TQ	PABLS	10/01-12/01
	Allentown-Bethlehem-Easton MSA, PA	H	6.18 FQ	8.00 AW	10.07 TQ	PABLS	10/01-12/01
	Erie MSA, PA	H	6.15 FQ	7.33 AW	8.46 TQ	PABLS	10/01-12/01
	Harrisburg-Lebanon-Carlisle MSA, PA	H	6.16 FQ	8.00 AW	10.40 TQ	PABLS	10/01-12/01
	Johnstown MSA, PA	H	5.55 FQ	6.90 AW	8.94 TQ	PABLS	10/01-12/01
	Lancaster MSA, PA	H	7.18 FQ	8.80 AW	11.10 TQ	PABLS	10/01-12/01
	Philadelphia PMSA, PA-NJ	H	7.17 FQ	9.42 AW	12.45 TQ	PABLS	10/01-12/01
	Pittsburgh MSA, PA	H	5.64 FQ	7.24 AW	9.63 TQ	PABLS	10/01-12/01
	Reading MSA, PA	H	5.75 FQ	7.46 AW	8.85 TQ	PABLS	10/01-12/01
	Scranton-Wilkes-Barre-Hazleton MSA, PA	H	6.85 FQ	8.33 AW	10.37 TQ	PABLS	10/01-12/01
	York MSA, PA	H	7.15 FQ	8.76 AW	10.69 TQ	PABLS	10/01-12/01
	Rhode Island	H	7.14 FQ	9.30 AW	11.99 TQ	RIBLS	10/01-12/01
	Providence-Fall River-Warwick MSA, RI-MA	H	6.92 FQ	8.79 AW	11.51 TQ	RIBLS	10/01-12/01
	South Carolina	H	6.51 FQ	8.42 AW	10.52 TQ	SCBLS	10/01-12/01
	Charleston-North Charleston MSA, SC	H	6.26 FQ	8.57 AW	10.61 TQ	SCBLS	10/01-12/01
	Columbia MSA, SC	H	6.89 FQ	8.66 AW	10.57 TQ	SCBLS	10/01-12/01

AAW	Average annual wage	**AOH**	Average offered, high	**ASH**	Average starting, high	**H**	Hourly	**M**	Monthly	**S**	Special: hourly and annual
AE	Average entry wage	**AOL**	Average offered, low	**ASL**	Average starting, low	**HI**	Highest wage paid	**MTC**	Median total compensation	**TQ**	Third quartile wage
AEX	Average experienced wage	**APH**	Average pay, high range	**AW**	Average wage paid	**HR**	High end range	**MW**	Median wage paid	**W**	Weekly
AO	Average offered	**APL**	Average pay, low range	**FQ**	First quartile wage	**LR**	Low end range	**SQ**	Second quartile wage	**Y**	Yearly

Occupation/Type/Industry	Location	Per	Low	Mid	High	Source	Date
Hotel, Motel, and Resort Desk Clerk	Greenville-Spartanburg-Anderson MSA, SC	H	6.84 FQ	8.60 AW	10.58 TQ	SCBLS	10/01-12/01
	Myrtle Beach MSA, SC	H	7.12 FQ	8.58 AW	10.53 TQ	SCBLS	10/01-12/01
	South Dakota	H	5.98 FQ	7.58 AW	9.22 TQ	SDBLS	10/01-12/01
	Sioux Falls MSA, SD	H	6.42 FQ	8.16 AW	10.23 TQ	SDBLS	10/01-12/01
	Tennessee	H	6.41 FQ	8.04 AW	9.95 TQ	TNBLS	10/01-12/01
	Chattanooga MSA, TN-GA	H	6.37 FQ	8.06 AW	10.21 TQ	TNBLS	10/01-12/01
	Clarksville-Hopkinsville MSA, TN-KY	H	5.74 FQ	6.76 AW	8.33 TQ	TNBLS	10/01-12/01
	Johnson City-Kingsport-Bristol MSA, TN-VA	H	5.69 FQ	6.79 AW	8.57 TQ	TNBLS	10/01-12/01
	Knoxville MSA, TN	H	7.22 FQ	8.36 AW	10.22 TQ	TNBLS	10/01-12/01
	Memphis MSA, TN-AR-MS	H	6.31 FQ	7.92 AW	9.18 TQ	TNBLS	10/01-12/01
	Nashville MSA, TN	H	7.15 FQ	8.47 AW	10.38 TQ	TNBLS	10/01-12/01
	Texas	H	5.71 FQ	7.44 AW	9.85 TQ	TXBLS	10/01-12/01
	Amarillo MSA, TX	H	5.73 FQ	6.88 AW	8.59 TQ	TXBLS	10/01-12/01
	Austin-San Marcos MSA, TX	H	6.36 FQ	8.27 AW	10.48 TQ	TXBLS	10/01-12/01
	Beaumont-Port Arthur MSA, TX	H	5.63 FQ	6.98 AW	9.15 TQ	TXBLS	10/01-12/01
	Brazoria PMSA, TX	H	5.54 FQ	7.01 AW	9.51 TQ	TXBLS	10/01-12/01
	Brownsville-Harlingen-San Benito MSA, TX	H	5.70 FQ	6.80 AW	8.49 TQ	TXBLS	10/01-12/01
	Corpus Christi MSA, TX	H	5.68 FQ	7.09 AW	8.96 TQ	TXBLS	10/01-12/01
	Dallas PMSA, TX	H	6.78 FQ	8.18 AW	10.29 TQ	TXBLS	10/01-12/01
	El Paso MSA, TX	H	5.72 FQ	7.24 AW	10.22 TQ	TXBLS	10/01-12/01
	Fort Worth-Arlington PMSA, TX	H	5.70 FQ	7.72 AW	10.43 TQ	TXBLS	10/01-12/01
	Galveston-Texas City PMSA, TX	H	5.81 FQ	7.58 AW	9.74 TQ	TXBLS	10/01-12/01
	Houston PMSA, TX	H	5.55 FQ	7.36 AW	9.89 TQ	TXBLS	10/01-12/01
	Killeen-Temple MSA, TX	H	5.71 FQ	7.20 AW	8.99 TQ	TXBLS	10/01-12/01
	Laredo MSA, TX	H	5.73 FQ	6.91 AW	8.42 TQ	TXBLS	10/01-12/01
	Longview-Marshall MSA, TX	H	5.61 FQ	6.83 AW	8.66 TQ	TXBLS	10/01-12/01
	Lubbock MSA, TX	H	5.71 FQ	7.15 AW	9.28 TQ	TXBLS	10/01-12/01
	McAllen-Edinburg-Mission MSA, TX	H	5.57 FQ	6.38 AW	7.68 TQ	TXBLS	10/01-12/01
	Odessa-Midland MSA, TX	H	5.63 FQ	6.78 AW	8.57 TQ	TXBLS	10/01-12/01
	San Antonio MSA, TX	H	5.77 FQ	7.68 AW	10.14 TQ	TXBLS	10/01-12/01
	Tyler MSA, TX	H	5.64 FQ	7.23 AW	9.54 TQ	TXBLS	10/01-12/01
	Waco MSA, TX	H	5.76 FQ	7.25 AW	8.83 TQ	TXBLS	10/01-12/01
	Utah	H	6.60 FQ	8.35 AW	10.37 TQ	UTBLS	10/01-12/01
	Provo-Orem MSA, UT	H	6.56 FQ	8.14 AW	11.37 TQ	UTBLS	10/01-12/01
	Salt Lake City-Ogden MSA, UT	H	7.06 FQ	8.74 AW	10.36 TQ	UTBLS	10/01-12/01
	Vermont	H	7.36 FQ	9.25 AW	11.19 TQ	VTBLS	10/01-12/01
	Burlington MSA, VT	H	7.51 FQ	9.41 AW	12.52 TQ	VTBLS	10/01-12/01
	Virginia	H	6.04 FQ	7.95 AW	10.32 TQ	VABLS	10/01-12/01
	Lynchburg MSA, VA	H	5.88 FQ	8.11 AW	10.71 TQ	VABLS	10/01-12/01
	Norfolk-Virginia Beach-Newport News MSA, VA-NC	H	6.32 FQ	8.10 AW	10.42 TQ	VABLS	10/01-12/01
	Richmond-Petersburg MSA, VA	H	5.99 FQ	7.73 AW	10.02 TQ	VABLS	10/01-12/01
	Roanoke MSA, VA	H	5.85 FQ	7.36 AW	8.75 TQ	VABLS	10/01-12/01
	Washington	H	7.10 FQ	9.02 AW	11.86 TQ	WABLS	10/01-12/01
	Bremerton PMSA, WA	H	7.19 FQ	8.39 AW	10.45 TQ	WABLS	10/01-12/01
	Olympia PMSA, WA	H	7.45 FQ	9.16 AW	11.43 TQ	WABLS	10/01-12/01
	Richland-Kennewick-Pasco MSA, WA	H	7.04 FQ	8.28 AW	9.21 TQ	WABLS	10/01-12/01
	Seattle-Bellevue-Everett PMSA, WA	H	7.57 FQ	9.89 AW	13.06 TQ	WABLS	10/01-12/01
	Spokane MSA, WA	H	6.89 FQ	7.99 AW	9.76 TQ	WABLS	10/01-12/01
	Tacoma PMSA, WA	H	6.95 FQ	8.52 AW	10.69 TQ	WABLS	10/01-12/01
	Yakima MSA, WA	H	6.98 FQ	9.00 AW	12.83 TQ	WABLS	10/01-12/01
	West Virginia	H	5.55 FQ	6.59 AW	8.34 TQ	WVBLS	10/01-12/01
	Charleston MSA, WV	H	5.55 FQ	6.63 AW	8.19 TQ	WVBLS	10/01-12/01
	Huntington-Ashland MSA, WV-KY-OH	H	5.53 FQ	6.60 AW	8.50 TQ	WVBLS	10/01-12/01
	Wisconsin	H	6.50 FQ	8.20 AW	10.35 TQ	WIBLS	10/01-12/01
	Appleton-Oshkosh-Neenah MSA, WI	H	6.93 FQ	8.32 AW	10.17 TQ	WIBLS	10/01-12/01

AAW Average annual wage **AE** Average entry wage **AEX** Average experienced wage **AO** Average offered **AOH** Average offered, high **AOL** Average offered, low **APH** Average pay, high range **APL** Average pay, low range **ASH** Average starting, high **ASL** Average starting, low **AW** Average wage paid **FQ** First quartile wage **H** Hourly **HI** Highest wage paid **HR** High end range **LR** Low end range **M** Monthly **MTC** Median total compensation **MW** Median wage paid **SQ** Second quartile wage **S** Special: hourly and annual **TQ** Third quartile wage **W** Weekly **Y** Yearly

Occupation/Type/Industry	Location	Per	Low	Mid	High	Source	Date
Hotel, Motel, and Resort Desk Clerk	Green Bay MSA, WI	H	7.09 FQ	8.43 AW	10.38 TQ	WIBLS	10/01-12/01
	Madison MSA, WI	H	7.23 FQ	8.52 AW	10.41 TQ	WIBLS	10/01-12/01
	Milwaukee-Waukesha PMSA, WI	H	7.41 FQ	8.71 AW	11.04 TQ	WIBLS	10/01-12/01
	Racine PMSA, WI	H	5.92 FQ	7.84 AW	10.32 TQ	WIBLS	10/01-12/01
	Wyoming	H	5.80 FQ	7.66 AW	10.88 TQ	WYBLS	10/01-12/01
	Cheyenne MSA, WY	H	5.71 FQ	6.86 AW	8.51 TQ	WYBLS	10/01-12/01
	Puerto Rico	H	5.51 FQ	6.88 AW	8.73 TQ	PRBLS	10/01-12/01
	Virgin Islands	H	6.96 FQ	8.58 AW	10.85 TQ	VIBLS	10/01-12/01
	Guam	H	5.62 FQ	7.62 AW	10.38 TQ	GUBLS	10/01-12/01
Human Resources Assistant							
Except Payroll and Timekeeping	Alabama	H	8.81 FQ	12.89 AW	17.59 TQ	ALBLS	10/01-12/01
Except Payroll and Timekeeping	Alaska	H	12.24 FQ	16.74 AW	22.73 TQ	AKBLS	10/01-12/01
Except Payroll and Timekeeping	Arizona	H	8.70 FQ	13.28 AW	18.23 TQ	AZBLS	10/01-12/01
Except Payroll and Timekeeping	Arkansas	H	7.55 FQ	10.96 AW	15.42 TQ	ARBLS	10/01-12/01
Except Payroll and Timekeeping	California	H	11.03 FQ	16.95 AW	24.06 TQ	CABLS	10/01-12/01
Except Payroll and Timekeeping	Colorado	H	10.17 FQ	15.20 AW	20.64 TQ	COBLS	10/01-12/01
Except Payroll and Timekeeping	Connecticut	H	11.02 FQ	16.60 AW	22.55 TQ	CTBLS	10/01-12/01
Except Payroll and Timekeeping	Delaware	H	10.39 FQ	15.08 AW	21.25 TQ	DEBLS	10/01-12/01
Except Payroll and Timekeeping	District of Columbia	H	12.04 FQ	16.80 AW	21.37 TQ	DCBLS	10/01-12/01
Except Payroll and Timekeeping	Florida	H	9.25 FQ	13.32 AW	17.75 TQ	FLBLS	10/01-12/01
Except Payroll and Timekeeping	Georgia	H	9.45 FQ	13.96 AW	19.23 TQ	GABLS	10/01-12/01
Except Payroll and Timekeeping	Hawaii	H	10.52 FQ	14.66 AW	19.78 TQ	HIBLS	10/01-12/01
Except Payroll and Timekeeping	Idaho	H	8.95 FQ	12.54 AW	16.74 TQ	IDBLS	10/01-12/01
Except Payroll and Timekeeping	Illinois	H	9.85 FQ	14.53 AW	20.27 TQ	ILBLS	10/01-12/01
Except Payroll and Timekeeping	Indiana	H	9.29 FQ	13.52 AW	18.25 TQ	INBLS	10/01-12/01
Except Payroll and Timekeeping	Iowa	H	9.32 FQ	13.74 AW	18.74 TQ	IABLS	10/01-12/01
Except Payroll and Timekeeping	Kansas	H	9.32 FQ	13.37 AW	17.76 TQ	KSBLS	10/01-12/01
Except Payroll and Timekeeping	Kentucky	H	9.22 FQ	13.06 AW	17.44 TQ	KYBLS	10/01-12/01
Except Payroll and Timekeeping	Louisiana	H	8.55 FQ	13.20 AW	18.78 TQ	LABLS	10/01-12/01
Except Payroll and Timekeeping	Maine	H	9.67 FQ	13.54 AW	17.60 TQ	MEBLS	10/01-12/01
Except Payroll and Timekeeping	Maryland	H	10.72 FQ	15.22 AW	20.50 TQ	MDBLS	10/01-12/01
Except Payroll and Timekeeping	Massachusetts	H	11.23 FQ	16.29 AW	22.19 TQ	MABLS	10/01-12/01
Except Payroll and Timekeeping	Michigan	H	10.21 FQ	14.76 AW	20.28 TQ	MIBLS	10/01-12/01
Except Payroll and Timekeeping	Minnesota	H	10.87 FQ	15.00 AW	19.98 TQ	MNBLS	10/01-12/01
Except Payroll and Timekeeping	Mississippi	H	8.45 FQ	12.43 AW	16.98 TQ	MSBLS	10/01-12/01
Except Payroll and Timekeeping	Missouri	H	9.70 FQ	14.03 AW	18.72 TQ	MOBLS	10/01-12/01
Except Payroll and Timekeeping	Montana	H	8.18 FQ	12.55 AW	17.69 TQ	MTBLS	10/01-12/01
Except Payroll and Timekeeping	Nebraska	H	9.02 FQ	13.24 AW	18.55 TQ	NEBLS	10/01-12/01
Except Payroll and Timekeeping	Nevada	H	9.35 FQ	13.65 AW	19.23 TQ	NVBLS	10/01-12/01
Except Payroll and Timekeeping	New Hampshire	H	9.48 FQ	13.71 AW	18.48 TQ	NHBLS	10/01-12/01
Except Payroll and Timekeeping	New Jersey	H	11.25 FQ	16.65 AW	22.38 TQ	NJBLS	10/01-12/01
Except Payroll and Timekeeping	New Mexico	H	8.32 FQ	12.88 AW	18.32 TQ	NMBLS	10/01-12/01
Except Payroll and Timekeeping	New York	H	9.61 FQ	16.01 AW	22.98 TQ	NYBLS	10/01-12/01
Except Payroll and Timekeeping	North Carolina	H	9.67 FQ	13.99 AW	18.47 TQ	NCBLS	10/01-12/01
Except Payroll and Timekeeping	North Dakota	H	9.07 FQ	13.43 AW	19.58 TQ	NDBLS	10/01-12/01
Except Payroll and Timekeeping	Ohio	H	9.79 FQ	14.11 AW	19.22 TQ	OHBLS	10/01-12/01
Except Payroll and Timekeeping	Oklahoma	H	8.33 FQ	12.58 AW	17.29 TQ	OKBLS	10/01-12/01
Except Payroll and Timekeeping	Oregon	H	9.77 FQ	14.43 AW	19.96 TQ	ORBLS	10/01-12/01
Except Payroll and Timekeeping	Pennsylvania	H	9.43 FQ	14.72 AW	21.20 TQ	PABLS	10/01-12/01
Except Payroll and Timekeeping	Rhode Island	H	10.09 FQ	14.39 AW	19.11 TQ	RIBLS	10/01-12/01
Except Payroll and Timekeeping	South Carolina	H	7.81 FQ	12.06 AW	16.88 TQ	SCBLS	10/01-12/01
Except Payroll and Timekeeping	South Dakota	H	8.65 FQ	11.34 AW	14.80 TQ	SDBLS	10/01-12/01
Except Payroll and Timekeeping	Tennessee	H	9.42 FQ	13.91 AW	18.95 TQ	TNBLS	10/01-12/01
Except Payroll and Timekeeping	Texas	H	9.76 FQ	14.30 AW	19.72 TQ	TXBLS	10/01-12/01
Except Payroll and Timekeeping	Utah	H	9.64 FQ	14.12 AW	19.64 TQ	UTBLS	10/01-12/01
Except Payroll and Timekeeping	Vermont	H	10.27 FQ	13.90 AW	17.71 TQ	VTBLS	10/01-12/01
Except Payroll and Timekeeping	Virginia	H	10.08 FQ	15.02 AW	20.58 TQ	VABLS	10/01-12/01
Except Payroll and Timekeeping	Washington	H	11.16 FQ	15.53 AW	20.68 TQ	WABLS	10/01-12/01
Except Payroll and Timekeeping	West Virginia	H	8.01 FQ	13.22 AW	19.06 TQ	WVBLS	10/01-12/01
Except Payroll and Timekeeping	Wisconsin	H	10.15 FQ	14.97 AW	20.99 TQ	WIBLS	10/01-12/01
Except Payroll and Timekeeping	Wyoming	H	8.25 FQ	13.03 AW	19.14 TQ	WYBLS	10/01-12/01
Except Payroll and Timekeeping	Puerto Rico	H	6.16 FQ	9.86 AW	15.19 TQ	PRBLS	10/01-12/01
Except Payroll and Timekeeping	Virgin Islands	H	8.66 FQ	11.13 AW	14.33 TQ	VIBLS	10/01-12/01
Except Payroll and Timekeeping	Guam	H	7.02 FQ	11.58 AW	15.00 TQ	GUBLS	10/01-12/01
Human Resources Manager	Alabama	Y	29300 FQ	54940 AW	86830 TQ	ALBLS	10/01-12/01
	Birmingham MSA, AL	Y	30840 FQ	58380 AW	90410 TQ	ALBLS	10/01-12/01
	Huntsville MSA, AL	Y	32820 FQ	60980 AW	92390 TQ	ALBLS	10/01-12/01
	Mobile MSA, AL	Y	29240 FQ	52120 AW	77610 TQ	ALBLS	10/01-12/01

AAW	Average annual wage	AOH	Average offered, high	ASH	Average starting, high	H	Hourly	M	Monthly	S	Special: hourly and annual
AE	Average entry wage	AOL	Average offered, low	ASL	Average starting, low	HI	Highest wage paid	MTC	Median total compensation	TQ	Third quartile wage
AEX	Average experienced wage	APH	Average pay, high range	AW	Average wage paid	HR	High end range	MW	Median wage paid	W	Weekly
AO	Average offered	APL	Average pay, low range	FQ	First quartile wage	LR	Low end range	SQ	Second quartile wage	Y	Yearly

Occupation/Type/Industry	Location	Per	Low	Mid	High	Source	Date
Human Resources Manager	Montgomery MSA, AL	Y	29080 FQ	51620 AW	77380 TQ	ALBLS	10/01-12/01
	Alaska	Y	41000 FQ	67910 AW	97260 TQ	AKBLS	10/01-12/01
	Anchorage MSA, AK	Y	40290 FQ	69610 AW	117040 TQ	AKBLS	10/01-12/01
	Arizona	Y	32960 FQ	58200 AW	93410 TQ	AZBLS	10/01-12/01
	Phoenix-Mesa MSA, AZ	Y	33820 FQ	60000 AW	96830 TQ	AZBLS	10/01-12/01
	Tucson MSA, AZ	Y	30410 FQ	52240 AW	84030 TQ	AZBLS	10/01-12/01
	Arkansas	Y	31100 FQ	60260 AW	98670 TQ	ARBLS	10/01-12/01
	Fayetteville-Springdale-Rogers MSA, AR	Y	24990 FQ	47900 AW	76890 TQ	ARBLS	10/01-12/01
	Fort Smith MSA, AR-OK	Y	31380 FQ	54470 AW	84270 TQ	ARBLS	10/01-12/01
	Little Rock-North Little Rock MSA, AR	Y	38970 FQ	71430 AW	113480 TQ	ARBLS	10/01-12/01
	California	Y	39440 FQ	73420 AW	113770 TQ	CABLS	10/01-12/01
	Bakersfield MSA, CA	Y	31840 FQ	59400 AW	95410 TQ	CABLS	10/01-12/01
	Chico-Paradise MSA, CA	Y	32850 FQ	52030 AW	73080 TQ	CABLS	10/01-12/01
	Fresno MSA, CA	Y	33560 FQ	57080 AW	86320 TQ	CABLS	10/01-12/01
	Los Angeles-Long Beach PMSA, CA	Y	38870 FQ	68650 AW	110530 TQ	CABLS	10/01-12/01
	Merced MSA, CA	Y	36820 FQ	63060 AW	98940 TQ	CABLS	10/01-12/01
	Modesto MSA, CA	Y	33060 FQ	59620 AW	93160 TQ	CABLS	10/01-12/01
	Oakland PMSA, CA	Y	41480 FQ	75380 AW	122040 TQ	CABLS	10/01-12/01
	Orange County PMSA, CA	Y	46820 FQ	81940 AW	112430 TQ	CABLS	10/01-12/01
	Redding MSA, CA	Y	25710 FQ	42220 AW	63660 TQ	CABLS	10/01-12/01
	Riverside-San Bernardino PMSA, CA	Y	32540 FQ	60170 AW	102620 TQ	CABLS	10/01-12/01
	Sacramento PMSA, CA	Y	35430 FQ	64930 AW	104700 TQ	CABLS	10/01-12/01
	Salinas MSA, CA	Y	36070 FQ	65030 AW	101950 TQ	CABLS	10/01-12/01
	San Diego MSA, CA	Y	38670 FQ	64920 AW	96180 TQ	CABLS	10/01-12/01
	San Francisco PMSA, CA	Y	45400 FQ	81500 AW	133180 TQ	CABLS	10/01-12/01
	San Jose PMSA, CA	Y	47180 FQ	87430 AW	140130 TQ	CABLS	10/01-12/01
	San Luis Obispo-Atascadero-Paso Robles MSA, CA	Y	33730 FQ	66240 AW	105360 TQ	CABLS	10/01-12/01
	Santa Barbara-Santa Maria-Lompoc MSA, CA	Y	33120 FQ	61510 AW	93770 TQ	CABLS	10/01-12/01
	Santa Cruz-Watsonville PMSA, CA	Y	29860 FQ	65010 AW	96390 TQ	CABLS	10/01-12/01
	Santa Rosa PMSA, CA	Y	36820 FQ	66180 AW	117920 TQ	CABLS	10/01-12/01
	Stockton-Lodi MSA, CA	Y	29970 FQ	58600 AW	90310 TQ	CABLS	10/01-12/01
	Vallejo-Fairfield-Napa PMSA, CA	Y	58300 FQ	92430 AW	112600 TQ	CABLS	10/01-12/01
	Ventura PMSA, CA	Y	40750 FQ	71820 AW	115310 TQ	CABLS	10/01-12/01
	Visalia-Tulare-Porterville MSA, CA	Y	38310 FQ	60590 AW	90730 TQ	CABLS	10/01-12/01
	Colorado	Y	38950 FQ	68800 AW	109210 TQ	COBLS	10/01-12/01
	Boulder-Longmont PMSA, CO	Y	47390 FQ	74650 AW	117170 TQ	COBLS	10/01-12/01
	Colorado Springs MSA, CO	Y	37250 FQ	65890 AW	97520 TQ	COBLS	10/01-12/01
	Denver PMSA, CO	Y	40200 FQ	71140 AW	112110 TQ	COBLS	10/01-12/01
	Fort Collins-Loveland MSA, CO	Y	37810 FQ	62060 AW	90160 TQ	COBLS	10/01-12/01
	Greeley PMSA, CO	Y	33490 FQ	57910 AW	88990 TQ	COBLS	10/01-12/01
	Connecticut	Y	39750 FQ	77100 AW		CTBLS	10/01-12/01
	Bridgeport PMSA, CT	Y	41700 FQ	76020 AW	142790 TQ	CTBLS	10/01-12/01
	Danbury PMSA, CT	Y	43050 FQ	76790 AW	134910 TQ	CTBLS	10/01-12/01
	Hartford MSA, CT	Y	39550 FQ	73230 AW	127070 TQ	CTBLS	10/01-12/01
	New Haven-Meriden PMSA, CT	Y	35820 FQ	67270 AW	103640 TQ	CTBLS	10/01-12/01
	New London-Norwich MSA, CT-RI	Y	36650 FQ	71110 AW	124410 TQ	CTBLS	10/01-12/01
	Stamford-Norwalk PMSA, CT	Y	48480 FQ	98030 AW		CTBLS	10/01-12/01
	Waterbury PMSA, CT	Y	37330 FQ	68040 AW	107840 TQ	CTBLS	10/01-12/01
	Delaware	Y	36320 FQ	65010 AW	108220 TQ	DEBLS	10/01-12/01
	Wilmington-Newark PMSA, DE-MD	Y	38660 FQ	66200 AW	109920 TQ	DEBLS	10/01-12/01
	District of Columbia	Y	41660 FQ	70020 AW	105420 TQ	DCBLS	10/01-12/01
	Washington PMSA, DC-MD-VA-WV	Y	41900 FQ	73200 AW	110080 TQ	DCBLS	10/01-12/01
	Florida	Y	32420 FQ	60210 AW	96160 TQ	FLBLS	10/01-12/01
	Daytona Beach MSA, FL	Y	24520 FQ	48410 AW	79060 TQ	FLBLS	10/01-12/01
	Fort Lauderdale PMSA, FL	Y	34730 FQ	63010 AW	98850 TQ	FLBLS	10/01-12/01
	Fort Myers-Cape Coral MSA, FL	Y	31510 FQ	49870 AW	75170 TQ	FLBLS	10/01-12/01

AAW	Average annual wage	AOH	Average offered, high	ASH	Average starting, high	H	Hourly	M	Monthly	S	Special: hourly and annual
AE	Average entry wage	AOL	Average offered, low	ASL	Average starting, low	HI	Highest wage paid	MTC	Median total compensation	TQ	Third quartile wage
AEX	Average experienced wage	APH	Average pay, high range	AW	Average wage paid	HR	High end range	MW	Median wage paid	W	Weekly
AO	Average offered	APL	Average pay, low range	FQ	First quartile wage	LR	Low end range	SQ	Second quartile wage	Y	Yearly

Occupation/Type/Industry	Location	Per	Low	Mid	High	Source	Date
Human Resources Manager	Fort Pierce-Port St. Lucie MSA, FL	Y	22420 FQ	47100 AW	81580 TQ	FLBLS	10/01-12/01
	Fort Walton Beach MSA, FL	Y	28470 FQ	52760 AW	77680 TQ	FLBLS	10/01-12/01
	Gainesville MSA, FL	Y	31770 FQ	57150 AW	87860 TQ	FLBLS	10/01-12/01
	Jacksonville MSA, FL	Y	38920 FQ	65880 AW	112400 TQ	FLBLS	10/01-12/01
	Lakeland-Winter Haven MSA, FL	Y	27200 FQ	54310 AW	92390 TQ	FLBLS	10/01-12/01
	Melbourne-Titusville-Palm Bay MSA, FL	Y	32600 FQ	60330 AW	93170 TQ	FLBLS	10/01-12/01
	Miami PMSA, FL	Y	32230 FQ	61930 AW	102200 TQ	FLBLS	10/01-12/01
	Naples MSA, FL	Y	32380 FQ	54520 AW	88630 TQ	FLBLS	10/01-12/01
	Ocala MSA, FL	Y	28050 FQ	56140 AW	78600 TQ	FLBLS	10/01-12/01
	Orlando MSA, FL	Y	34790 FQ	58590 AW	92050 TQ	FLBLS	10/01-12/01
	Pensacola MSA, FL	Y	24810 FQ	52400 AW	87060 TQ	FLBLS	10/01-12/01
	Sarasota-Bradenton MSA, FL	Y	32210 FQ	54660 AW	86110 TQ	FLBLS	10/01-12/01
	Tallahassee MSA, FL	Y	37030 FQ	63460 AW	103710 TQ	FLBLS	10/01-12/01
	Tampa-St. Petersburg-Clearwater MSA, FL	Y	31920 FQ	61320 AW	101140 TQ	FLBLS	10/01-12/01
	West Palm Beach-Boca Raton MSA, FL	Y	35380 FQ	68470 AW	122110 TQ	FLBLS	10/01-12/01
	Georgia	Y	35000 FQ	62770 AW	99470 TQ	GABLS	10/01-12/01
	Atlanta MSA, GA	Y	36480 FQ	65330 AW	104610 TQ	GABLS	10/01-12/01
	Augusta-Aiken MSA, GA-SC	Y	35630 FQ	68540 AW	104560 TQ	GABLS	10/01-12/01
	Columbus MSA, GA-AL	Y	33390 FQ	56850 AW	85190 TQ	GABLS	10/01-12/01
	Macon MSA, GA	Y	33200 FQ	58280 AW	90190 TQ	GABLS	10/01-12/01
	Savannah MSA, GA	Y	33790 FQ	59010 AW	95180 TQ	GABLS	10/01-12/01
	Hawaii	Y	38750 FQ	61420 AW	91390 TQ	HIBLS	10/01-12/01
	Honolulu MSA, HI	Y	39050 FQ	61980 AW	91040 TQ	HIBLS	10/01-12/01
	Idaho	Y	24610 FQ	55700 AW	91950 TQ	IDBLS	10/01-12/01
	Boise City MSA, ID	Y	27450 FQ	58290 AW	92420 TQ	IDBLS	10/01-12/01
	Illinois	Y	33530 FQ	69550 AW	115100 TQ	ILBLS	10/01-12/01
	Champaign-Urbana MSA, IL	Y	31500 FQ	62370 AW	115500 TQ	ILBLS	10/01-12/01
	Chicago PMSA, IL	Y	35200 FQ	72330 AW	116640 TQ	ILBLS	10/01-12/01
	Peoria-Pekin MSA, IL	Y	31120 FQ	62420 AW	96290 TQ	ILBLS	10/01-12/01
	Rockford MSA, IL	Y	31510 FQ	57690 AW	88140 TQ	ILBLS	10/01-12/01
	Springfield MSA, IL	Y	28640 FQ	46780 AW	70060 TQ	ILBLS	10/01-12/01
	Indiana	Y	29730 FQ	56570 AW	90080 TQ	INBLS	10/01-12/01
	Elkhart-Goshen MSA, IN	Y	26020 FQ	50850 AW	86190 TQ	INBLS	10/01-12/01
	Evansville-Henderson MSA, IN-KY	Y	26650 FQ	51860 AW	88480 TQ	INBLS	10/01-12/01
	Fort Wayne MSA, IN	Y	26190 FQ	50180 AW	80990 TQ	INBLS	10/01-12/01
	Gary PMSA, IN	Y	27220 FQ	54570 AW	87180 TQ	INBLS	10/01-12/01
	Indianapolis MSA, IN	Y	37000 FQ	61740 AW	94260 TQ	INBLS	10/01-12/01
	Lafayette MSA, IN	Y	32220 FQ	57080 AW	93570 TQ	INBLS	10/01-12/01
	South Bend MSA, IN	Y	29430 FQ	54200 AW	76700 TQ	INBLS	10/01-12/01
	Iowa	Y	30260 FQ	55760 AW	88670 TQ	IABLS	10/01-12/01
	Cedar Rapids MSA, IA	Y	35690 FQ	68180 AW	110730 TQ	IABLS	10/01-12/01
	Davenport-Moline-Rock Island MSA, IA-IL	Y	29590 FQ	56490 AW	90720 TQ	IABLS	10/01-12/01
	Des Moines MSA, IA	Y	33400 FQ	59260 AW	90090 TQ	IABLS	10/01-12/01
	Kansas	Y	33040 FQ	62610 AW	103490 TQ	KSBLS	10/01-12/01
	Topeka MSA, KS	Y	33640 FQ	66690 AW	111480 TQ	KSBLS	10/01-12/01
	Wichita MSA, KS	Y	34690 FQ	62940 AW	100000 TQ	KSBLS	10/01-12/01
	Kentucky	Y	28880 FQ	55990 AW	87930 TQ	KYBLS	10/01-12/01
	Lexington MSA, KY	Y	27860 FQ	58660 AW	92910 TQ	KYBLS	10/01-12/01
	Louisville MSA, KY-IN	Y	29070 FQ	58120 AW	89930 TQ	KYBLS	10/01-12/01
	Louisiana	Y	29470 FQ	52220 AW	83860 TQ	LABLS	10/01-12/01
	Baton Rouge MSA, LA	Y	31420 FQ	52660 AW	82900 TQ	LABLS	10/01-12/01
	Houma MSA, LA	Y	29920 FQ	50740 AW	71240 TQ	LABLS	10/01-12/01
	Lafayette MSA, LA	Y	30490 FQ	55970 AW	94800 TQ	LABLS	10/01-12/01
	Lake Charles MSA, LA	Y	28730 FQ	55000 AW	89570 TQ	LABLS	10/01-12/01
	New Orleans MSA, LA	Y	28740 FQ	53070 AW	86130 TQ	LABLS	10/01-12/01
	Shreveport-Bossier City MSA, LA	Y	26910 FQ	47540 AW	73090 TQ	LABLS	10/01-12/01
	Maine	Y	31660 FQ	55070 AW	86590 TQ	MEBLS	10/01-12/01
	Portland MSA, ME	Y	35690 FQ	59700 AW	92720 TQ	MEBLS	10/01-12/01
	Maryland	Y	39690 FQ	68310 AW	106210 TQ	MDBLS	10/01-12/01
	Baltimore PMSA, MD	Y	40080 FQ	68270 AW	106270 TQ	MDBLS	10/01-12/01
	Massachusetts	Y	39840 FQ	71510 AW	115220 TQ	MABLS	10/01-12/01
	Boston PMSA, MA-NH	Y	42280 FQ	75170 AW	120390 TQ	MABLS	10/01-12/01
	Brockton PMSA, MA	Y	35080 FQ	62690 AW	97770 TQ	MABLS	10/01-12/01
	Lowell PMSA, MA-NH	Y	44060 FQ	63140 AW	92570 TQ	MABLS	10/01-12/01

AAW Average annual wage · AE Average entry wage · AEX Average experienced wage · AO Average offered · AOH Average offered, high · AOL Average offered, low · APH Average pay, high range · APL Average pay, low range · ASH Average starting, high · ASL Average starting, low · AW Average wage paid · FQ First quartile wage · H Hourly · HI Highest wage paid · HR High end range · LR Low end range · M Monthly · MTC Median total compensation · MW Median wage paid · SQ Second quartile wage · S Special: hourly and annual · TQ Third quartile wage · W Weekly · Y Yearly

Occupation/Type/Industry	Location	Per	Low	Mid	High	Source	Date
Human Resources Manager	New Bedford PMSA, MA	Y	35900 FQ	57790 AW	89920 TQ	MABLS	10/01-12/01
	Springfield MSA, MA	Y	31150 FQ	59220 AW	91820 TQ	MABLS	10/01-12/01
	Worcester PMSA, MA-CT	Y	36330 FQ	64810 AW	100260 TQ	MABLS	10/01-12/01
	Michigan	Y	42710 FQ	78460 AW	121490 TQ	MIBLS	10/01-12/01
	Ann Arbor PMSA, MI	Y	39680 FQ	73430 AW	112450 TQ	MIBLS	10/01-12/01
	Detroit PMSA, MI	Y	46270 FQ	83870 AW	129290 TQ	MIBLS	10/01-12/01
	Flint PMSA, MI	Y	44010 FQ	79860 AW	122210 TQ	MIBLS	10/01-12/01
	Grand Rapids-Muskegon-Holland MSA, MI	Y	40560 FQ	71350 AW	108750 TQ	MIBLS	10/01-12/01
	Kalamazoo-Battle Creek MSA, MI	Y	37150 FQ	77420 AW	131100 TQ	MIBLS	10/01-12/01
	Lansing-East Lansing MSA, MI	Y	36550 FQ	66750 AW	101650 TQ	MIBLS	10/01-12/01
	Saginaw-Bay City-Midland MSA, MI	Y	43060 FQ	76300 AW	113960 TQ	MIBLS	10/01-12/01
	Minnesota	Y	45550 FQ	74730 AW	114430 TQ	MNBLS	10/01-12/01
	Duluth-Superior MSA, MN-WI	Y	38180 FQ	63990 AW	95570 TQ	MNBLS	10/01-12/01
	Minneapolis-St. Paul MSA, MN-WI	Y	47700 FQ	76560 AW	116260 TQ	MNBLS	10/01-12/01
	St. Cloud MSA, MN	Y	38570 FQ	65850 AW	94280 TQ	MNBLS	10/01-12/01
	Mississippi	Y	28770 FQ	50660 AW	77670 TQ	MSBLS	10/01-12/01
	Biloxi-Gulfport-Pascagoula MSA, MS	Y	28480 FQ	54550 AW	83720 TQ	MSBLS	10/01-12/01
	Jackson MSA, MS	Y	31360 FQ	53390 AW	83620 TQ	MSBLS	10/01-12/01
	Missouri	Y	32180 FQ	60030 AW	97160 TQ	MOBLS	10/01-12/01
	Kansas City MSA, MO-KS	Y	34160 FQ	63720 AW	106900 TQ	MOBLS	10/01-12/01
	St. Louis MSA, MO-IL	Y	33110 FQ	63820 AW	103120 TQ	MOBLS	10/01-12/01
	Springfield MSA, MO	Y	23570 FQ	52190 AW	82610 TQ	MOBLS	10/01-12/01
	Montana	Y	26340 FQ	45690 AW	69800 TQ	MTBLS	10/01-12/01
	Billings MSA, MT	Y	23650 FQ	46680 AW	76310 TQ	MTBLS	10/01-12/01
	Nebraska	Y	31200 FQ	60780 AW	96640 TQ	NEBLS	10/01-12/01
	Lincoln MSA, NE	Y	34750 FQ	59840 AW	87920 TQ	NEBLS	10/01-12/01
	Omaha MSA, NE-IA	Y	31600 FQ	61800 AW	96320 TQ	NEBLS	10/01-12/01
	Nevada	Y	33670 FQ	60350 AW	94040 TQ	NVBLS	10/01-12/01
	Las Vegas MSA, NV-AZ	Y	31720 FQ	58800 AW	91450 TQ	NVBLS	10/01-12/01
	Reno MSA, NV	Y	35620 FQ	63050 AW	103200 TQ	NVBLS	10/01-12/01
	New Hampshire	Y	32230 FQ	55620 AW	85610 TQ	NHBLS	10/01-12/01
	Manchester PMSA, NH	Y	32640 FQ	53510 AW	84620 TQ	NHBLS	10/01-12/01
	Nashua PMSA, NH	Y	35510 FQ	62950 AW	90530 TQ	NHBLS	10/01-12/01
	Portsmouth-Rochester PMSA, NH-ME	Y	29700 FQ	53280 AW	85590 TQ	NHBLS	10/01-12/01
	New Jersey	Y	49840 FQ	83710 AW	128720 TQ	NJBLS	10/01-12/01
	Atlantic-Cape May PMSA, NJ	Y	38500 FQ	67010 AW	101930 TQ	NJBLS	10/01-12/01
	Bergen-Passaic PMSA, NJ	Y	47470 FQ	80710 AW	123290 TQ	NJBLS	10/01-12/01
	Jersey City PMSA, NJ	Y	42380 FQ	79120 AW	130940 TQ	NJBLS	10/01-12/01
	Middlesex-Somerset-Hunterdon PMSA, NJ	Y	49660 FQ	79690 AW	122250 TQ	NJBLS	10/01-12/01
	Newark PMSA, NJ	Y	55290 FQ	90540 AW	132910 TQ	NJBLS	10/01-12/01
	Trenton PMSA, NJ	Y	53390 FQ	76990 AW	104410 TQ	NJBLS	10/01-12/01
	New Mexico	Y	26340 FQ	51050 AW	83880 TQ	NMBLS	10/01-12/01
	Albuquerque MSA, NM	Y	29920 FQ	55470 AW	88500 TQ	NMBLS	10/01-12/01
	Las Cruces MSA, NM	Y	22630 FQ	48590 AW	82450 TQ	NMBLS	10/01-12/01
	New York	Y	43880 FQ	79790 AW	132390 TQ	NYBLS	10/01-12/01
	Albany-Schenectady-Troy MSA, NY	Y	37680 FQ	67550 AW	101730 TQ	NYBLS	10/01-12/01
	Binghamton MSA, NY	Y	38310 FQ	65460 AW	109930 TQ	NYBLS	10/01-12/01
	Buffalo-Niagara Falls MSA, NY	Y	39390 FQ	68590 AW	108930 TQ	NYBLS	10/01-12/01
	Dutchess County PMSA, NY	Y	36200 FQ	73540 AW	127700 TQ	NYBLS	10/01-12/01
	Nassau-Suffolk PMSA, NY	Y	44890 FQ	78140 AW	119260 TQ	NYBLS	10/01-12/01
	New York PMSA, NY	Y	50210 FQ	86300 AW	145480 TQ	NYBLS	10/01-12/01
	Newburgh PMSA, NY-PA	Y	36320 FQ	68320 AW	110900 TQ	NYBLS	10/01-12/01
	Rochester MSA, NY	Y	40430 FQ	71480 AW	113820 TQ	NYBLS	10/01-12/01
	Syracuse MSA, NY	Y	37700 FQ	65140 AW	100150 TQ	NYBLS	10/01-12/01
	Utica-Rome MSA, NY	Y	31030 FQ	57930 AW	92560 TQ	NYBLS	10/01-12/01
	North Carolina	Y	33350 FQ	63440 AW	104710 TQ	NCBLS	10/01-12/01
	Asheville MSA, NC	Y	25960 FQ	49930 AW	81650 TQ	NCBLS	10/01-12/01
	Charlotte-Gastonia-Rock Hill MSA, NC-SC	Y	35970 FQ	70050 AW	124750 TQ	NCBLS	10/01-12/01
	Fayetteville MSA, NC	Y	29450 FQ	51900 AW	80910 TQ	NCBLS	10/01-12/01
	Greensboro-Winston-Salem-High Point MSA, NC	Y	34920 FQ	64260 AW	108100 TQ	NCBLS	10/01-12/01

AAW	Average annual wage	**AOH**	Average offered, high	**ASH**	Average starting, high	**H**	Hourly	**M**	Monthly	**S**	Special: hourly and annual
AE	Average entry wage	**AOL**	Average offered, low	**ASL**	Average starting, low	**HI**	Highest wage paid	**MTC**	Median total compensation	**TQ**	Third quartile wage
AEX	Average experienced wage	**APH**	Average pay, high range	**AW**	Average wage paid	**HR**	High end range	**MW**	Median wage paid	**W**	Weekly
AO	Average offered	**APL**	Average pay, low range	**FQ**	First quartile wage	**LR**	Low end range	**SQ**	Second quartile wage	**Y**	Yearly

Occupation/Type/Industry	Location	Per	Low	Mid	High	Source	Date
Human Resources Manager	Hickory-Morganton-Lenoir MSA, NC	Y	30030 FQ	50640 AW	84090 TQ	NCBLS	10/01-12/01
	Raleigh-Durham-Chapel Hill MSA, NC	Y	37940 FQ	69310 AW	111700 TQ	NCBLS	10/01-12/01
	Wilmington MSA, NC	Y	28620 FQ	56020 AW	89200 TQ	NCBLS	10/01-12/01
	North Dakota	Y	27030 FQ	47230 AW	78830 TQ	NDBLS	10/01-12/01
	Fargo-Moorhead MSA, ND-MN	Y	28540 FQ	51910 AW	94330 TQ	NDBLS	10/01-12/01
	Ohio	Y	32540 FQ	61150 AW	97090 TQ	OHBLS	10/01-12/01
	Akron PMSA, OH	Y	34100 FQ	64510 AW	103920 TQ	OHBLS	10/01-12/01
	Canton-Massillon MSA, OH	Y	25510 FQ	54900 AW	91990 TQ	OHBLS	10/01-12/01
	Cincinnati PMSA, OH-KY-IN	Y	32300 FQ	60810 AW	99020 TQ	OHBLS	10/01-12/01
	Cleveland-Lorain-Elyria PMSA, OH	Y	36980 FQ	67000 AW	109450 TQ	OHBLS	10/01-12/01
	Columbus MSA, OH	Y	34030 FQ	61040 AW	93690 TQ	OHBLS	10/01-12/01
	Dayton-Springfield MSA, OH	Y	33250 FQ	64980 AW	105640 TQ	OHBLS	10/01-12/01
	Hamilton-Middletown PMSA, OH	Y	33110 FQ	59540 AW	94750 TQ	OHBLS	10/01-12/01
	Mansfield MSA, OH	Y	30740 FQ	57780 AW	104610 TQ	OHBLS	10/01-12/01
	Toledo MSA, OH	Y	30290 FQ	57270 AW	90050 TQ	OHBLS	10/01-12/01
	Youngstown-Warren MSA, OH	Y	29350 FQ	54910 AW	91230 TQ	OHBLS	10/01-12/01
	Oklahoma	Y	28590 FQ	51910 AW	79610 TQ	OKBLS	10/01-12/01
	Oklahoma City MSA, OK	Y	30470 FQ	52670 AW	81400 TQ	OKBLS	10/01-12/01
	Tulsa MSA, OK	Y	30330 FQ	54280 AW	81510 TQ	OKBLS	10/01-12/01
	Oregon	Y	35190 FQ	63440 AW	100290 TQ	ORBLS	10/01-12/01
	Eugene-Springfield MSA, OR	Y	36510 FQ	62660 AW	97340 TQ	ORBLS	10/01-12/01
	Medford-Ashland MSA, OR	Y	30700 FQ	53990 AW	91350 TQ	ORBLS	10/01-12/01
	Portland-Vancouver PMSA, OR-WA	Y	38100 FQ	66430 AW	104320 TQ	ORBLS	10/01-12/01
	Salem PMSA, OR	Y	34240 FQ	56250 AW	87050 TQ	ORBLS	10/01-12/01
	Pennsylvania	Y	33580 FQ	62520 AW	97540 TQ	PABLS	10/01-12/01
	Allentown-Bethlehem-Easton MSA, PA	Y	37610 FQ	70330 AW	112530 TQ	PABLS	10/01-12/01
	Erie MSA, PA	Y	32760 FQ	58880 AW	94240 TQ	PABLS	10/01-12/01
	Harrisburg-Lebanon-Carlisle MSA, PA	Y	35280 FQ	62940 AW	103550 TQ	PABLS	10/01-12/01
	Johnstown MSA, PA	Y	23210 FQ	50570 AW	79130 TQ	PABLS	10/01-12/01
	Lancaster MSA, PA	Y	33300 FQ	60380 AW	92660 TQ	PABLS	10/01-12/01
	Philadelphia PMSA, PA-NJ	Y	39080 FQ	67230 AW	104090 TQ	PABLS	10/01-12/01
	Pittsburgh MSA, PA	Y	27120 FQ	58160 AW	93050 TQ	PABLS	10/01-12/01
	Reading MSA, PA	Y	36140 FQ	59380 AW	95520 TQ	PABLS	10/01-12/01
	Scranton-Wilkes-Barre-Hazleton MSA, PA	Y	25890 FQ	49360 AW	79890 TQ	PABLS	10/01-12/01
	York MSA, PA	Y	31920 FQ	56800 AW	93600 TQ	PABLS	10/01-12/01
	Rhode Island	Y	31400 FQ	63630 AW	107280 TQ	RIBLS	10/01-12/01
	Providence-Fall River-Warwick MSA, RI-MA	Y	31770 FQ	63250 AW	106740 TQ	RIBLS	10/01-12/01
	South Carolina	Y	30050 FQ	54660 AW	86750 TQ	SCBLS	10/01-12/01
	Charleston-North Charleston MSA, SC	Y	30410 FQ	50990 AW	74540 TQ	SCBLS	10/01-12/01
	Columbia MSA, SC	Y	34370 FQ	54200 AW	78140 TQ	SCBLS	10/01-12/01
	Greenville-Spartanburg-Anderson MSA, SC	Y	30450 FQ	56120 AW	88140 TQ	SCBLS	10/01-12/01
	Myrtle Beach MSA, SC	Y	25570 FQ	47390 AW	75160 TQ	SCBLS	10/01-12/01
	South Dakota	Y	41840 FQ	62330 AW	88970 TQ	SDBLS	10/01-12/01
	Sioux Falls MSA, SD	Y	45350 FQ	65720 AW	90180 TQ	SDBLS	10/01-12/01
	Tennessee	Y	29700 FQ	55440 AW	90470 TQ	TNBLS	10/01-12/01
	Chattanooga MSA, TN-GA	Y	29360 FQ	52110 AW	82320 TQ	TNBLS	10/01-12/01
	Clarksville-Hopkinsville MSA, TN-KY	Y	15000 FQ	47890 AW	81000 TQ	TNBLS	10/01-12/01
	Johnson City-Kingsport-Bristol MSA, TN-VA	Y	27750 FQ	55110 AW	89600 TQ	TNBLS	10/01-12/01
	Knoxville MSA, TN	Y	30410 FQ	54960 AW	87540 TQ	TNBLS	10/01-12/01
	Memphis MSA, TN-AR-MS	Y	33490 FQ	59060 AW	95230 TQ	TNBLS	10/01-12/01
	Nashville MSA, TN	Y	31520 FQ	57780 AW	94530 TQ	TNBLS	10/01-12/01
	Texas	Y	32540 FQ	62960 AW	101910 TQ	TXBLS	10/01-12/01
	Amarillo MSA, TX	Y	24220 FQ	52350 AW	87600 TQ	TXBLS	10/01-12/01
	Austin-San Marcos MSA, TX	Y	38730 FQ	66730 AW	113320 TQ	TXBLS	10/01-12/01
	Beaumont-Port Arthur MSA, TX	Y	29170 FQ	57570 AW	98590 TQ	TXBLS	10/01-12/01
	Brazoria PMSA, TX	Y	41760 FQ	71960 AW	107710 TQ	TXBLS	10/01-12/01

AAW	Average annual wage	**AOH**	Average offered, high	**ASH**	Average starting, high	**H**	Hourly	**M**	Monthly	**S**	Special: hourly and annual
AE	Average entry wage	**AOL**	Average offered, low	**ASL**	Average starting, low	**HI**	Highest wage paid	**MTC**	Median total compensation	**TQ**	Third quartile wage
AEX	Average experienced wage	**APH**	Average pay, high range	**AW**	Average wage paid	**HR**	High end range	**MW**	Median wage paid	**W**	Weekly
AO	Average offered	**APL**	Average pay, low range	**FQ**	First quartile wage	**LR**	Low end range	**SQ**	Second quartile wage	**Y**	Yearly

Occupation/Type/Industry	Location	Per	Low	Mid	High	Source	Date
Human Resources Manager	Brownsville-Harlingen-San Benito MSA, TX	Y	27420 FQ	53640 AW	100610 TQ	TXBLS	10/01-12/01
	Corpus Christi MSA, TX	Y	29440 FQ	58960 AW	97750 TQ	TXBLS	10/01-12/01
	Dallas PMSA, TX	Y	38290 FQ	69120 AW	110790 TQ	TXBLS	10/01-12/01
	El Paso MSA, TX	Y	28060 FQ	52260 AW	86470 TQ	TXBLS	10/01-12/01
	Fort Worth-Arlington PMSA, TX	Y	31230 FQ	60340 AW	93350 TQ	TXBLS	10/01-12/01
	Galveston-Texas City PMSA, TX	Y	27440 FQ	58000 AW	98060 TQ	TXBLS	10/01-12/01
	Houston PMSA, TX	Y	35920 FQ	64530 AW	105260 TQ	TXBLS	10/01-12/01
	Killeen-Temple MSA, TX	Y	29830 FQ	54330 AW	85150 TQ	TXBLS	10/01-12/01
	Laredo MSA, TX	Y	25950 FQ	48890 AW	72850 TQ	TXBLS	10/01-12/01
	Longview-Marshall MSA, TX	Y	32190 FQ	52370 AW	73610 TQ	TXBLS	10/01-12/01
	Lubbock MSA, TX	Y	26010 FQ	51030 AW	83200 TQ	TXBLS	10/01-12/01
	McAllen-Edinburg-Mission MSA, TX	Y	25250 FQ	50670 AW	75270 TQ	TXBLS	10/01-12/01
	Odessa-Midland MSA, TX	Y	23460 FQ	52060 AW	95650 TQ	TXBLS	10/01-12/01
	San Antonio MSA, TX	Y	26960 FQ	57230 AW	92960 TQ	TXBLS	10/01-12/01
	Tyler MSA, TX	Y	29810 FQ	53950 AW	85990 TQ	TXBLS	10/01-12/01
	Waco MSA, TX	Y	24800 FQ	47300 AW	78910 TQ	TXBLS	10/01-12/01
	Utah	Y	30200 FQ	56450 AW	87890 TQ	UTBLS	10/01-12/01
	Provo-Orem MSA, UT	Y	30700 FQ	56050 AW	81930 TQ	UTBLS	10/01-12/01
	Salt Lake City-Ogden MSA, UT	Y	30790 FQ	56790 AW	88270 TQ	UTBLS	10/01-12/01
	Vermont	Y	38850 FQ	61730 AW	90770 TQ	VTBLS	10/01-12/01
	Burlington MSA, VT	Y	40790 FQ	66310 AW	100770 TQ	VTBLS	10/01-12/01
	Virginia	Y	40100 FQ	72550 AW	111070 TQ	VABLS	10/01-12/01
	Lynchburg MSA, VA	Y	37210 FQ	67110 AW	104520 TQ	VABLS	10/01-12/01
	Norfolk-Virginia Beach-Newport News MSA, VA-NC	Y	36560 FQ	67920 AW	104090 TQ	VABLS	10/01-12/01
	Richmond-Petersburg MSA, VA	Y	35840 FQ	65870 AW	99540 TQ	VABLS	10/01-12/01
	Roanoke MSA, VA	Y	35450 FQ	68220 AW	108180 TQ	VABLS	10/01-12/01
	Washington	Y	44210 FQ	72080 AW	107180 TQ	WABLS	10/01-12/01
	Bremerton PMSA, WA	Y	47780 FQ	73680 AW	103430 TQ	WABLS	10/01-12/01
	Olympia PMSA, WA	Y	45720 FQ	68940 AW	102590 TQ	WABLS	10/01-12/01
	Richland-Kennewick-Pasco MSA, WA	Y	50850 FQ	78600 AW	117010 TQ	WABLS	10/01-12/01
	Seattle-Bellevue-Everett PMSA, WA	Y	45960 FQ	74010 AW	109540 TQ	WABLS	10/01-12/01
	Spokane MSA, WA	Y	42410 FQ	64260 AW	91260 TQ	WABLS	10/01-12/01
	Tacoma PMSA, WA	Y	36410 FQ	69400 AW	106180 TQ	WABLS	10/01-12/01
	Yakima MSA, WA	Y	36970 FQ	63430 AW	98480 TQ	WABLS	10/01-12/01
	West Virginia	Y	27750 FQ	52160 AW	88110 TQ	WVBLS	10/01-12/01
	Charleston MSA, WV	Y	30880 FQ	56290 AW	97360 TQ	WVBLS	10/01-12/01
	Huntington-Ashland MSA, WV-KY-OH	Y	24980 FQ	46860 AW	77620 TQ	WVBLS	10/01-12/01
	Wisconsin	Y	32050 FQ	57600 AW	88620 TQ	WIBLS	10/01-12/01
	Appleton-Oshkosh-Neenah MSA, WI	Y	30520 FQ	56030 AW	87990 TQ	WIBLS	10/01-12/01
	Green Bay MSA, WI	Y	38700 FQ	64230 AW	93600 TQ	WIBLS	10/01-12/01
	Madison MSA, WI	Y	35390 FQ	58140 AW	86180 TQ	WIBLS	10/01-12/01
	Milwaukee-Waukesha PMSA, WI	Y	37310 FQ	62280 AW	92900 TQ	WIBLS	10/01-12/01
	Racine PMSA, WI	Y	39810 FQ	56170 AW	73050 TQ	WIBLS	10/01-12/01
	Wyoming	Y	26560 FQ	53790 AW	88120 TQ	WYBLS	10/01-12/01
	Cheyenne MSA, WY	Y	32870 FQ	52470 AW	70020 TQ	WYBLS	10/01-12/01
	Puerto Rico	Y	26170 FQ	50200 AW	84460 TQ	PRBLS	10/01-12/01
	Virgin Islands	Y	31160 FQ	48200 AW	71990 TQ	VIBLS	10/01-12/01
	Guam	Y	22390 FQ	45900 AW	73790 TQ	GUBLS	10/01-12/01
Environment	United States	Y		48909 AW		SAFEDIR	2001
Environment	Midwest	Y		55143 AW		SAFEDIR	2001
Environment	Northeast	Y		53000 AW		SAFEDIR	2001
Environment	South	Y		44444 AW		SAFEDIR	2001
Environment	West	Y		55567 AW		SAFEDIR	2001
Hydrologist	Alaska	Y	41120 FQ	61180 AW	86440 TQ	AKBLS	10/01-12/01
	Arizona	Y	34820 FQ	53340 AW	80150 TQ	AZBLS	10/01-12/01
	California	Y	42760 FQ	71280 AW	109730 TQ	CABLS	10/01-12/01
	Colorado	Y	43500 FQ	64280 AW	90250 TQ	COBLS	10/01-12/01
	Connecticut	Y	38240 FQ	53610 AW	71350 TQ	CTBLS	10/01-12/01
	Delaware	Y	38160 FQ	56030 AW	80440 TQ	DEBLS	10/01-12/01

AAW	Average annual wage	**AOH**	Average offered, high	**ASH**	Average starting, high	**H**	Hourly	**M**	Monthly	**S**	Special: hourly and annual
AE	Average entry wage	**AOL**	Average offered, low	**ASL**	Average starting, low	**HI**	Highest wage paid	**MTC**	Median total compensation	**TQ**	Third quartile wage
AEX	Average experienced wage	**APH**	Average pay, high range	**AW**	Average wage paid	**HR**	High end range	**MW**	Median wage paid	**W**	Weekly
AO	Average offered	**APL**	Average pay, low range	**FQ**	First quartile wage	**LR**	Low end range	**SQ**	Second quartile wage	**Y**	Yearly

Occupation/Type/Industry	Location	Per	Low	Mid	High	Source	Date
Hydrologist	Florida	Y	34200 FQ	53390 AW	70810 TQ	FLBLS	10/01-12/01
	Georgia	Y	44700 FQ	66780 AW	93120 TQ	GABLS	10/01-12/01
	Hawaii	Y	39030 FQ	54970 AW	71410 TQ	HIBLS	10/01-12/01
	Idaho	Y	39830 FQ	56970 AW	81840 TQ	IDBLS	10/01-12/01
	Illinois	Y	43070 FQ	63780 AW	89130 TQ	ILBLS	10/01-12/01
	Indiana	Y	46010 FQ	60580 AW	82900 TQ	INBLS	10/01-12/01
	Louisiana	Y	30180 FQ	52270 AW	81980 TQ	LABLS	10/01-12/01
	Maine	Y	37440 FQ	45860 AW	63250 TQ	MEBLS	10/01-12/01
	Maryland	Y	39980 FQ	62440 AW	91640 TQ	MDBLS	10/01-12/01
	Massachusetts	Y	41590 FQ	61200 AW	82310 TQ	MABLS	10/01-12/01
	Michigan	Y	38430 FQ	59990 AW	84360 TQ	MIBLS	10/01-12/01
	Minnesota	Y	38260 FQ	56030 AW	72430 TQ	MNBLS	10/01-12/01
	Missouri	Y	38160 FQ	58770 AW	80470 TQ	MOBLS	10/01-12/01
	Montana	Y	33770 FQ	51770 AW	69840 TQ	MTBLS	10/01-12/01
	Nebraska	Y	35930 FQ	46440 AW	67170 TQ	NEBLS	10/01-12/01
	Nevada	Y	42450 FQ	61860 AW	85820 TQ	NVBLS	10/01-12/01
	New Hampshire	Y	42130 FQ	54780 AW	68300 TQ	NHBLS	10/01-12/01
	New Jersey	Y	35830 FQ	58400 AW	76390 TQ	NJBLS	10/01-12/01
	New Mexico	Y	35660 FQ	52670 AW	79840 TQ	NMBLS	10/01-12/01
	New York	Y	32870 FQ	56010 AW	87460 TQ	NYBLS	10/01-12/01
	North Carolina	Y	37160 FQ	49730 AW	71220 TQ	NCBLS	10/01-12/01
	Ohio	Y	28420 FQ	51480 AW	74540 TQ	OHBLS	10/01-12/01
	Oklahoma	Y	37270 FQ	55550 AW	80280 TQ	OKBLS	10/01-12/01
	Oregon	Y	40130 FQ	56850 AW	75100 TQ	ORBLS	10/01-12/01
	Pennsylvania	Y	38930 FQ	59970 AW	83990 TQ	PABLS	10/01-12/01
	South Carolina	Y	25890 FQ	43100 AW	59090 TQ	SCBLS	10/01-12/01
	South Dakota	Y	35670 FQ	48310 AW	66960 TQ	SDBLS	10/01-12/01
	Tennessee	Y	47330 FQ	58000 AW	70610 TQ	TNBLS	10/01-12/01
	Texas	Y	37410 FQ	54680 AW	76870 TQ	TXBLS	10/01-12/01
	Utah	Y	38110 FQ	61040 AW	89140 TQ	UTBLS	10/01-12/01
	Vermont	Y	25670 FQ	48860 AW	80130 TQ	VTBLS	10/01-12/01
	Virginia	Y	39710 FQ	71570 AW	109390 TQ	VABLS	10/01-12/01
	Washington	Y	39920 FQ	60500 AW	86860 TQ	WABLS	10/01-12/01
	Wisconsin	Y	32540 FQ	51820 AW	75530 TQ	WIBLS	10/01-12/01
	Wyoming	Y	42600 FQ	55910 AW	69990 TQ	WYBLS	10/01-12/01
Illustrator							
Free Lance	United States	Y	15000-20000 AE	35000-45000 AW	200000 HI	COSGIRL1	1/01-1/02
Industrial Engineer	Alabama	Y	35670 FQ	57950 AW	86470 TQ	ALBLS	10/01-12/01
	Birmingham MSA, AL	Y	38770 FQ	66850 AW	102380 TQ	ALBLS	10/01-12/01
	Huntsville MSA, AL	Y	39740 FQ	62670 AW	91460 TQ	ALBLS	10/01-12/01
	Mobile MSA, AL	Y	36070 FQ	58060 AW	83230 TQ	ALBLS	10/01-12/01
	Montgomery MSA, AL	Y	33090 FQ	52400 AW	76550 TQ	ALBLS	10/01-12/01
	Alaska	Y	52910 FQ	75740 AW	106870 TQ	AKBLS	10/01-12/01
	Anchorage MSA, AK	Y	53630 FQ	70690 AW	102080 TQ	AKBLS	10/01-12/01
	Arizona	Y	34760 FQ	59070 AW	87260 TQ	AZBLS	10/01-12/01
	Phoenix-Mesa MSA, AZ	Y	33540 FQ	55780 AW	85210 TQ	AZBLS	10/01-12/01
	Tucson MSA, AZ	Y	48060 FQ	66690 AW	90560 TQ	AZBLS	10/01-12/01
	Arkansas	Y	36860 FQ	54270 AW	74290 TQ	ARBLS	10/01-12/01
	Fayetteville-Springdale-Rogers MSA, AR	Y	25070 FQ	48570 AW	71070 TQ	ARBLS	10/01-12/01
	Fort Smith MSA, AR-OK	Y	35060 FQ	54480 AW	75720 TQ	ARBLS	10/01-12/01
	Little Rock-North Little Rock MSA, AR	Y	35730 FQ	54620 AW	76010 TQ	ARBLS	10/01-12/01
	California	Y	41820 FQ	68090 AW	98660 TQ	CABLS	10/01-12/01
	Bakersfield MSA, CA	Y	49710 FQ	69480 AW	93720 TQ	CABLS	10/01-12/01
	Fresno MSA, CA	Y	33180 FQ	54920 AW	75350 TQ	CABLS	10/01-12/01
	Los Angeles-Long Beach PMSA, CA	Y	41080 FQ	64430 AW	89160 TQ	CABLS	10/01-12/01
	Modesto MSA, CA	Y	35790 FQ	57690 AW	82740 TQ	CABLS	10/01-12/01
	Oakland PMSA, CA	Y	48030 FQ	71080 AW	101090 TQ	CABLS	10/01-12/01
	Orange County PMSA, CA	Y	42470 FQ	63780 AW	88780 TQ	CABLS	10/01-12/01
	Riverside-San Bernardino PMSA, CA	Y	40700 FQ	61980 AW	87240 TQ	CABLS	10/01-12/01
	Sacramento PMSA, CA	Y	45870 FQ	67040 AW	91600 TQ	CABLS	10/01-12/01
	San Diego MSA, CA	Y	36980 FQ	60880 AW	87330 TQ	CABLS	10/01-12/01
	San Francisco PMSA, CA	Y	44840 FQ	72500 AW	105160 TQ	CABLS	10/01-12/01
	San Jose PMSA, CA	Y	51260 FQ	79890 AW	117520 TQ	CABLS	10/01-12/01
	San Luis Obispo-Atascadero-Paso Robles MSA, CA	Y	33790 FQ	63770 AW	92560 TQ	CABLS	10/01-12/01

AAW	Average annual wage	**AOH**	Average offered, high	**ASH**	Average starting, high	**H**	Hourly	**M**	Monthly	**S**	Special: hourly and annual
AE	Average entry wage	**AOL**	Average offered, low	**ASL**	Average starting, low	**HI**	Highest wage paid	**MTC**	Median total compensation	**TQ**	Third quartile wage
AEX	Average experienced wage	**APH**	Average pay, high range	**AW**	Average wage paid	**HR**	High end range	**MW**	Median wage paid	**W**	Weekly
AO	Average offered	**APL**	Average pay, low range	**FQ**	First quartile wage	**LR**	Low end range	**SQ**	Second quartile wage	**Y**	Yearly

Occupation/Type/Industry	Location	Per	Low	Mid	High	Source	Date
Industrial Engineer	Santa Barbara-Santa Maria-Lompoc MSA, CA	Y	43690 FQ	66110 AW	92100 TQ	CABLS	10/01-12/01
	Santa Cruz-Watsonville PMSA, CA	Y	45410 FQ	66860 AW	106570 TQ	CABLS	10/01-12/01
	Santa Rosa PMSA, CA	Y	40020 FQ	69440 AW	98430 TQ	CABLS	10/01-12/01
	Stockton-Lodi MSA, CA	Y	14990 FQ	41800 AW	76180 TQ	CABLS	10/01-12/01
	Vallejo-Fairfield-Napa PMSA, CA	Y	44490 FQ	67870 AW	88000 TQ	CABLS	10/01-12/01
	Ventura PMSA, CA	Y	43310 FQ	60350 AW	80620 TQ	CABLS	10/01-12/01
	Colorado	Y	43110 FQ	65570 AW	91600 TQ	COBLS	10/01-12/01
	Boulder-Longmont PMSA, CO	Y	43510 FQ	68140 AW	101250 TQ	COBLS	10/01-12/01
	Colorado Springs MSA, CO	Y	43560 FQ	66140 AW	91840 TQ	COBLS	10/01-12/01
	Denver PMSA, CO	Y	43400 FQ	62680 AW	86040 TQ	COBLS	10/01-12/01
	Fort Collins-Loveland MSA, CO	Y	42730 FQ	70310 AW	93900 TQ	COBLS	10/01-12/01
	Connecticut	Y	41740 FQ	62960 AW	89920 TQ	CTBLS	10/01-12/01
	Bridgeport PMSA, CT	Y	44970 FQ	70300 AW	97930 TQ	CTBLS	10/01-12/01
	Danbury PMSA, CT	Y	45240 FQ	68000 AW	99100 TQ	CTBLS	10/01-12/01
	Hartford MSA, CT	Y	40050 FQ	59020 AW	77630 TQ	CTBLS	10/01-12/01
	New Haven-Meriden PMSA, CT	Y	39540 FQ	56320 AW	76700 TQ	CTBLS	10/01-12/01
	New London-Norwich MSA, CT-RI	Y	48870 FQ	68560 AW	92790 TQ	CTBLS	10/01-12/01
	Stamford-Norwalk PMSA, CT	Y	48480 FQ	72150 AW	102690 TQ	CTBLS	10/01-12/01
	Waterbury PMSA, CT	Y	43650 FQ	59490 AW	76690 TQ	CTBLS	10/01-12/01
	Delaware	Y	34720 FQ	61930 AW	89360 TQ	DEBLS	10/01-12/01
	Wilmington-Newark PMSA, DE-MD	Y	40120 FQ	63630 AW	89720 TQ	DEBLS	10/01-12/01
	District of Columbia	Y	45280 FQ	67540 AW	91210 TQ	DCBLS	10/01-12/01
	Washington PMSA, DC-MD-VA-WV	Y	33340 FQ	62200 AW	90060 TQ	DCBLS	10/01-12/01
	Florida	Y	39050 FQ	60010 AW	87080 TQ	FLBLS	10/01-12/01
	Daytona Beach MSA, FL	Y	37650 FQ	56330 AW	77700 TQ	FLBLS	10/01-12/01
	Fort Lauderdale PMSA, FL	Y	40270 FQ	58390 AW	87250 TQ	FLBLS	10/01-12/01
	Fort Myers-Cape Coral MSA, FL	Y	35260 FQ	48420 AW	69440 TQ	FLBLS	10/01-12/01
	Fort Pierce-Port St. Lucie MSA, FL	Y	29350 FQ	44620 AW	67640 TQ	FLBLS	10/01-12/01
	Fort Walton Beach MSA, FL	Y	35920 FQ	49020 AW	69670 TQ	FLBLS	10/01-12/01
	Jacksonville MSA, FL	Y	40960 FQ	60090 AW	87090 TQ	FLBLS	10/01-12/01
	Lakeland-Winter Haven MSA, FL	Y	41100 FQ	58940 AW	88070 TQ	FLBLS	10/01-12/01
	Melbourne-Titusville-Palm Bay MSA, FL	Y	41480 FQ	57130 AW	75320 TQ	FLBLS	10/01-12/01
	Miami PMSA, FL	Y	39380 FQ	60190 AW	81270 TQ	FLBLS	10/01-12/01
	Ocala MSA, FL	Y	40460 FQ	59520 AW	81780 TQ	FLBLS	10/01-12/01
	Orlando MSA, FL	Y	34250 FQ	60160 AW	88340 TQ	FLBLS	10/01-12/01
	Sarasota-Bradenton MSA, FL	Y	38700 FQ	58180 AW	88580 TQ	FLBLS	10/01-12/01
	Tallahassee MSA, FL	Y	30560 FQ	47490 AW	66820 TQ	FLBLS	10/01-12/01
	Tampa-St. Petersburg-Clearwater MSA, FL	Y	40220 FQ	60480 AW	86950 TQ	FLBLS	10/01-12/01
	West Palm Beach-Boca Raton MSA, FL	Y	41900 FQ	66240 AW	93920 TQ	FLBLS	10/01-12/01
	Georgia	Y	44440 FQ	60780 AW	74800 TQ	GABLS	10/01-12/01
	Atlanta MSA, GA	Y	48030 FQ	62660 AW	75590 TQ	GABLS	10/01-12/01
	Columbus MSA, GA-AL	Y	34720 FQ	51410 AW	70760 TQ	GABLS	10/01-12/01
	Macon MSA, GA	Y	40150 FQ	57050 AW	70960 TQ	GABLS	10/01-12/01
	Savannah MSA, GA	Y	40110 FQ	50390 AW	58260 TQ	GABLS	10/01-12/01
	Hawaii	Y	50250 FQ	67310 AW	86830 TQ	HIBLS	10/01-12/01
	Honolulu MSA, HI	Y	50300 FQ	68080 AW	87080 TQ	HIBLS	10/01-12/01
	Illinois	Y	40120 FQ	60460 AW	84850 TQ	ILBLS	10/01-12/01
	Champaign-Urbana MSA, IL	Y	34080 FQ	51190 AW	70350 TQ	ILBLS	10/01-12/01
	Chicago PMSA, IL	Y	41480 FQ	61960 AW	85990 TQ	ILBLS	10/01-12/01
	Peoria-Pekin MSA, IL	Y	51730 FQ	71130 AW	90360 TQ	ILBLS	10/01-12/01
	Rockford MSA, IL	Y	34720 FQ	52880 AW	71140 TQ	ILBLS	10/01-12/01
	Springfield MSA, IL	Y	42630 FQ	54820 AW	71500 TQ	ILBLS	10/01-12/01
	Indiana	Y	37560 FQ	55630 AW	75600 TQ	INBLS	10/01-12/01
	Elkhart-Goshen MSA, IN	Y	34620 FQ	52220 AW	70390 TQ	INBLS	10/01-12/01
	Evansville-Henderson MSA, IN-KY	Y	26580 FQ	46270 AW	72370 TQ	INBLS	10/01-12/01
	Fort Wayne MSA, IN	Y	34320 FQ	51460 AW	71560 TQ	INBLS	10/01-12/01
	Gary PMSA, IN	Y	43280 FQ	59500 AW	79870 TQ	INBLS	10/01-12/01

AAW Average annual wage **AE** Average entry wage **AEX** Average experienced wage **AO** Average offered **AOH** Average offered, high **AOL** Average offered, low **APH** Average pay, high range **APL** Average pay, low range **ASH** Average starting, high **ASL** Average starting, low **AW** Average wage paid **FQ** First quartile wage **H** Hourly **HI** Highest wage paid **HR** High end range **LR** Low end range **M** Monthly **MTC** Median total compensation **MW** Median wage paid **SQ** Second quartile wage **S** Special: hourly and annual **TQ** Third quartile wage **W** Weekly **Y** Yearly

Occupation/Type/Industry	Location	Per	Low	Mid	High	Source	Date
Industrial Engineer	Indianapolis MSA, IN	Y	40660 FQ	58640 AW	80700 TQ	INBLS	10/01-12/01
	Lafayette MSA, IN	Y	38800 FQ	53430 AW	71480 TQ	INBLS	10/01-12/01
	South Bend MSA, IN	Y	38450 FQ	56600 AW	76820 TQ	INBLS	10/01-12/01
	Iowa	Y	35510 FQ	52520 AW	71510 TQ	IABLS	10/01-12/01
	Davenport-Moline-Rock Island MSA, IA-IL	Y	37600 FQ	54970 AW	74410 TQ	IABLS	10/01-12/01
	Des Moines MSA, IA	Y	31440 FQ	54130 AW	76350 TQ	IABLS	10/01-12/01
	Kansas	Y	39050 FQ	54440 AW	74220 TQ	KSBLS	10/01-12/01
	Topeka MSA, KS	Y	43560 FQ	60740 AW	82270 TQ	KSBLS	10/01-12/01
	Wichita MSA, KS	Y	42860 FQ	54850 AW	72500 TQ	KSBLS	10/01-12/01
	Kentucky	Y	39170 FQ	58340 AW	82780 TQ	KYBLS	10/01-12/01
	Lexington MSA, KY	Y	42350 FQ	61710 AW	88270 TQ	KYBLS	10/01-12/01
	Louisiana	Y	41200 FQ	66730 AW	102850 TQ	LABLS	10/01-12/01
	Baton Rouge MSA, LA	Y	42410 FQ	67780 AW	94350 TQ	LABLS	10/01-12/01
	Lake Charles MSA, LA	Y	47660 FQ	73540 AW	106500 TQ	LABLS	10/01-12/01
	New Orleans MSA, LA	Y	43920 FQ	71610 AW	112810 TQ	LABLS	10/01-12/01
	Shreveport-Bossier City MSA, LA	Y	44030 FQ	61200 AW	89890 TQ	LABLS	10/01-12/01
	Maine	Y	37750 FQ	58430 AW	83660 TQ	MEBLS	10/01-12/01
	Portland MSA, ME	Y	34510 FQ	49120 AW	67810 TQ	MEBLS	10/01-12/01
	Maryland	Y	36120 FQ	61090 AW	89410 TQ	MDBLS	10/01-12/01
	Baltimore PMSA, MD	Y	34950 FQ	62610 AW	90870 TQ	MDBLS	10/01-12/01
	Massachusetts	Y	43480 FQ	65170 AW	91340 TQ	MABLS	10/01-12/01
	Boston PMSA, MA-NH	Y	43210 FQ	65820 AW	92150 TQ	MABLS	10/01-12/01
	Brockton PMSA, MA	Y	43180 FQ	59380 AW	80890 TQ	MABLS	10/01-12/01
	Lawrence PMSA, MA-NH	Y	48140 FQ	67970 AW	96890 TQ	MABLS	10/01-12/01
	Lowell PMSA, MA-NH	Y	42910 FQ	64310 AW	87240 TQ	MABLS	10/01-12/01
	New Bedford PMSA, MA	Y	38410 FQ	55920 AW	71950 TQ	MABLS	10/01-12/01
	Springfield MSA, MA	Y	39710 FQ	59990 AW	86110 TQ	MABLS	10/01-12/01
	Worcester PMSA, MA-CT	Y	41650 FQ	61830 AW	90310 TQ	MABLS	10/01-12/01
	Michigan	Y	44080 FQ	64680 AW	88860 TQ	MIBLS	10/01-12/01
	Ann Arbor PMSA, MI	Y	48170 FQ	65320 AW	86110 TQ	MIBLS	10/01-12/01
	Detroit PMSA, MI	Y	48030 FQ	68270 AW	92340 TQ	MIBLS	10/01-12/01
	Flint PMSA, MI	Y	50730 FQ	67650 AW	88250 TQ	MIBLS	10/01-12/01
	Grand Rapids-Muskegon-Holland MSA, MI	Y	40670 FQ	58210 AW	77810 TQ	MIBLS	10/01-12/01
	Kalamazoo-Battle Creek MSA, MI	Y	37300 FQ	53300 AW	71240 TQ	MIBLS	10/01-12/01
	Minnesota	Y	42630 FQ	65390 AW	94400 TQ	MNBLS	10/01-12/01
	Duluth-Superior MSA, MN-WI	Y	37060 FQ	51970 AW	72290 TQ	MNBLS	10/01-12/01
	Minneapolis-St. Paul MSA, MN-WI	Y	46550 FQ	68390 AW	96470 TQ	MNBLS	10/01-12/01
	St. Cloud MSA, MN	Y	31510 FQ	45860 AW	70600 TQ	MNBLS	10/01-12/01
	Mississippi	Y	32180 FQ	48700 AW	68800 TQ	MSBLS	10/01-12/01
	Biloxi-Gulfport-Pascagoula MSA, MS	Y	33590 FQ	51740 AW	70540 TQ	MSBLS	10/01-12/01
	Jackson MSA, MS	Y	35900 FQ	50290 AW	69580 TQ	MSBLS	10/01-12/01
	Missouri	Y	38860 FQ	58280 AW	83840 TQ	MOBLS	10/01-12/01
	Kansas City MSA, MO-KS	Y	41040 FQ	58890 AW	80770 TQ	MOBLS	10/01-12/01
	St. Louis MSA, MO-IL	Y	40890 FQ	60400 AW	85650 TQ	MOBLS	10/01-12/01
	Springfield MSA, MO	Y	31610 FQ	54800 AW	80270 TQ	MOBLS	10/01-12/01
	Montana	Y	32370 FQ	52870 AW	75330 TQ	MTBLS	10/01-12/01
	Nebraska	Y	38610 FQ	55110 AW	75630 TQ	NEBLS	10/01-12/01
	Lincoln MSA, NE	Y	39190 FQ	54430 AW	72630 TQ	NEBLS	10/01-12/01
	Omaha MSA, NE-IA	Y	40690 FQ	59410 AW	82700 TQ	NEBLS	10/01-12/01
	Nevada	Y	37930 FQ	59890 AW	88190 TQ	NVBLS	10/01-12/01
	Las Vegas MSA, NV-AZ	Y	36550 FQ	60890 AW	89490 TQ	NVBLS	10/01-12/01
	Reno MSA, NV	Y	40320 FQ	57080 AW	78150 TQ	NVBLS	10/01-12/01
	New Hampshire	Y	43350 FQ	61160 AW	83950 TQ	NHBLS	10/01-12/01
	Manchester PMSA, NH	Y	45470 FQ	58820 AW	79770 TQ	NHBLS	10/01-12/01
	Nashua PMSA, NH	Y	48380 FQ	67600 AW	93020 TQ	NHBLS	10/01-12/01
	Portsmouth-Rochester PMSA, NH-ME	Y	44750 FQ	58440 AW	74930 TQ	NHBLS	10/01-12/01
	New Jersey	Y	44360 FQ	66130 AW	93940 TQ	NJBLS	10/01-12/01
	Bergen-Passaic PMSA, NJ	Y	43380 FQ	64830 AW	88740 TQ	NJBLS	10/01-12/01
	Jersey City PMSA, NJ	Y	43920 FQ	63650 AW	88800 TQ	NJBLS	10/01-12/01
	Middlesex-Somerset-Hunterdon PMSA, NJ	Y	42500 FQ	71640 AW	109510 TQ	NJBLS	10/01-12/01
	Monmouth-Ocean PMSA, NJ	Y	41940 FQ	59880 AW	82780 TQ	NJBLS	10/01-12/01
	Newark PMSA, NJ	Y	45420 FQ	64660 AW	92650 TQ	NJBLS	10/01-12/01
	Trenton PMSA, NJ	Y	47040 FQ	66520 AW	100730 TQ	NJBLS	10/01-12/01
	New Mexico	Y	40760 FQ	62040 AW	89250 TQ	NMBLS	10/01-12/01

Occupation/Type/Industry	Location	Per	Low	Mid	High	Source	Date
Industrial Engineer	Albuquerque MSA, NM	Y	41810 FQ	60980 AW	85740 TQ	NMBLS	10/01-12/01
	New York	Y	37900 FQ	59890 AW	86790 TQ	NYBLS	10/01-12/01
	Albany-Schenectady-Troy MSA, NY	Y	39830 FQ	60830 AW	86880 TQ	NYBLS	10/01-12/01
	Binghamton MSA, NY	Y	35670 FQ	54160 AW	81620 TQ	NYBLS	10/01-12/01
	Buffalo-Niagara Falls MSA, NY	Y	31380 FQ	53280 AW	74270 TQ	NYBLS	10/01-12/01
	Nassau-Suffolk PMSA, NY	Y	41690 FQ	62710 AW	88250 TQ	NYBLS	10/01-12/01
	New York PMSA, NY	Y	38740 FQ	62320 AW	88560 TQ	NYBLS	10/01-12/01
	Newburgh PMSA, NY-PA	Y	35320 FQ	55640 AW	102970 TQ	NYBLS	10/01-12/01
	Rochester MSA, NY	Y	41210 FQ	62650 AW	88370 TQ	NYBLS	10/01-12/01
	Syracuse MSA, NY	Y	40290 FQ	56840 AW	73520 TQ	NYBLS	10/01-12/01
	Utica-Rome MSA, NY	Y	32100 FQ	44580 AW	60510 TQ	NYBLS	10/01-12/01
	North Carolina	Y	37650 FQ	58640 AW	84750 TQ	NCBLS	10/01-12/01
	Asheville MSA, NC	Y	39060 FQ	53360 AW	71210 TQ	NCBLS	10/01-12/01
	Charlotte-Gastonia-Rock Hill MSA, NC-SC	Y	38810 FQ	58330 AW	79890 TQ	NCBLS	10/01-12/01
	Fayetteville MSA, NC	Y	41830 FQ	71260 AW	88440 TQ	NCBLS	10/01-12/01
	Greensboro-Winston-Salem-High Point MSA, NC	Y	36010 FQ	58560 AW	85810 TQ	NCBLS	10/01-12/01
	Hickory-Morganton-Lenoir MSA, NC	Y	32440 FQ	51430 AW	73700 TQ	NCBLS	10/01-12/01
	Raleigh-Durham-Chapel Hill MSA, NC	Y	44770 FQ	65820 AW	94580 TQ	NCBLS	10/01-12/01
	Wilmington MSA, NC	Y	34590 FQ	66510 AW	93260 TQ	NCBLS	10/01-12/01
	North Dakota	Y	26440 FQ	48820 AW	68170 TQ	NDBLS	10/01-12/01
	Fargo-Moorhead MSA, ND-MN	Y	38600 FQ	57320 AW	84380 TQ	NDBLS	10/01-12/01
	Ohio	Y	39950 FQ	59810 AW	83920 TQ	OHBLS	10/01-12/01
	Akron PMSA, OH	Y	41170 FQ	61360 AW	84630 TQ	OHBLS	10/01-12/01
	Canton-Massillon MSA, OH	Y	41030 FQ	61580 AW	86680 TQ	OHBLS	10/01-12/01
	Cincinnati PMSA, OH-KY-IN	Y	40530 FQ	59520 AW	81290 TQ	OHBLS	10/01-12/01
	Cleveland-Lorain-Elyria PMSA, OH	Y	42200 FQ	61760 AW	86300 TQ	OHBLS	10/01-12/01
	Columbus MSA, OH	Y	43940 FQ	60340 AW	81070 TQ	OHBLS	10/01-12/01
	Dayton-Springfield MSA, OH	Y	45080 FQ	63960 AW	86300 TQ	OHBLS	10/01-12/01
	Hamilton-Middletown PMSA, OH	Y	37640 FQ	59440 AW	84580 TQ	OHBLS	10/01-12/01
	Mansfield MSA, OH	Y	33210 FQ	51820 AW	80390 TQ	OHBLS	10/01-12/01
	Toledo MSA, OH	Y	38000 FQ	58350 AW	85570 TQ	OHBLS	10/01-12/01
	Youngstown-Warren MSA, OH	Y	47860 FQ	64780 AW	86940 TQ	OHBLS	10/01-12/01
	Oklahoma	Y	37820 FQ	59290 AW	86130 TQ	OKBLS	10/01-12/01
	Oklahoma City MSA, OK	Y	34330 FQ	59770 AW	89480 TQ	OKBLS	10/01-12/01
	Tulsa MSA, OK	Y	39550 FQ	58240 AW	82250 TQ	OKBLS	10/01-12/01
	Oregon	Y	43160 FQ	63050 AW	89580 TQ	ORBLS	10/01-12/01
	Eugene-Springfield MSA, OR	Y	39830 FQ	67200 AW	102330 TQ	ORBLS	10/01-12/01
	Portland-Vancouver PMSA, OR-WA	Y	44370 FQ	63590 AW	89950 TQ	ORBLS	10/01-12/01
	Pennsylvania	Y	38150 FQ	58560 AW	84300 TQ	PABLS	10/01-12/01
	Allentown-Bethlehem-Easton MSA, PA	Y	31990 FQ	51040 AW	73020 TQ	PABLS	10/01-12/01
	Erie MSA, PA	Y	32900 FQ	45700 AW	60640 TQ	PABLS	10/01-12/01
	Harrisburg-Lebanon-Carlisle MSA, PA	Y	41330 FQ	59620 AW	82740 TQ	PABLS	10/01-12/01
	Johnstown MSA, PA	Y	31850 FQ	52910 AW	71020 TQ	PABLS	10/01-12/01
	Lancaster MSA, PA	Y	37300 FQ	56860 AW	82080 TQ	PABLS	10/01-12/01
	Philadelphia PMSA, PA-NJ	Y	43320 FQ	64410 AW	90790 TQ	PABLS	10/01-12/01
	Pittsburgh MSA, PA	Y	39520 FQ	60640 AW	85670 TQ	PABLS	10/01-12/01
	Reading MSA, PA	Y	37780 FQ	56670 AW	76430 TQ	PABLS	10/01-12/01
	Scranton-Wilkes-Barre-Hazleton MSA, PA	Y	37040 FQ	51750 AW	73200 TQ	PABLS	10/01-12/01
	York MSA, PA	Y	40500 FQ	56890 AW	75840 TQ	PABLS	10/01-12/01
	Rhode Island	Y	44560 FQ	64280 AW	89190 TQ	RIBLS	10/01-12/01
	Providence-Fall River-Warwick MSA, RI-MA	Y	44620 FQ	64520 AW	89040 TQ	RIBLS	10/01-12/01
	South Carolina	Y	40200 FQ	65450 AW	91980 TQ	SCBLS	10/01-12/01
	Charleston-North Charleston MSA, SC	Y	45980 FQ	62820 AW	84620 TQ	SCBLS	10/01-12/01
	Columbia MSA, SC	Y	31590 FQ	48670 AW	71540 TQ	SCBLS	10/01-12/01
	Greenville-Spartanburg-Anderson MSA, SC	Y	42890 FQ	67770 AW	91310 TQ	SCBLS	10/01-12/01
	South Dakota	Y	39750 FQ	56420 AW	77500 TQ	SDBLS	10/01-12/01

AAW	Average annual wage	**AOH**	Average offered, high	**ASH**	Average starting, high	**H**	Hourly	**M**	Monthly	**S**	Special: hourly and annual
AE	Average entry wage	**AOL**	Average offered, low	**ASL**	Average starting, low	**HI**	Highest wage paid	**MTC**	Median total compensation	**TQ**	Third quartile wage
AEX	Average experienced wage	**APH**	Average pay, high range	**AW**	Average wage paid	**HR**	High end range	**MW**	Median wage paid	**W**	Weekly
AO	Average offered	**APL**	Average pay, low range	**FQ**	First quartile wage	**LR**	Low end range	**SQ**	Second quartile wage	**Y**	Yearly

Occupation/Type/Industry	Location	Per	Low	Mid	High	Source	Date
Industrial Engineer	Sioux Falls MSA, SD	Y	39100 FQ	49900 AW	62430 TQ	SDBLS	10/01-12/01
	Tennessee	Y	36780 FQ	54400 AW	74780 TQ	TNBLS	10/01-12/01
	Chattanooga MSA, TN-GA	Y	38060 FQ	53480 AW	74320 TQ	TNBLS	10/01-12/01
	Clarksville-Hopkinsville MSA, TN-KY	Y	38630 FQ	50580 AW	67460 TQ	TNBLS	10/01-12/01
	Johnson City-Kingsport-Bristol MSA, TN-VA	Y	36210 FQ	52610 AW	71370 TQ	TNBLS	10/01-12/01
	Knoxville MSA, TN	Y	42010 FQ	58910 AW	83160 TQ	TNBLS	10/01-12/01
	Memphis MSA, TN-AR-MS	Y	36890 FQ	54830 AW	72420 TQ	TNBLS	10/01-12/01
	Nashville MSA, TN	Y	34910 FQ	55710 AW	79200 TQ	TNBLS	10/01-12/01
	Texas	Y	42620 FQ	65510 AW	94360 TQ	TXBLS	10/01-12/01
	Amarillo MSA, TX	Y	26120 FQ	55070 AW	87820 TQ	TXBLS	10/01-12/01
	Austin-San Marcos MSA, TX	Y	37070 FQ	64950 AW	93780 TQ	TXBLS	10/01-12/01
	Beaumont-Port Arthur MSA, TX	Y	46690 FQ	69170 AW	91830 TQ	TXBLS	10/01-12/01
	Brazoria PMSA, TX	Y	44470 FQ	74050 AW	121720 TQ	TXBLS	10/01-12/01
	Brownsville-Harlingen-San Benito MSA, TX	Y	40280 FQ	58440 AW	86150 TQ	TXBLS	10/01-12/01
	Corpus Christi MSA, TX	Y	39390 FQ	59790 AW	80700 TQ	TXBLS	10/01-12/01
	Dallas PMSA, TX	Y	46670 FQ	67750 AW	94660 TQ	TXBLS	10/01-12/01
	El Paso MSA, TX	Y	39030 FQ	55850 AW	79830 TQ	TXBLS	10/01-12/01
	Fort Worth-Arlington PMSA, TX	Y	41070 FQ	61010 AW	87550 TQ	TXBLS	10/01-12/01
	Galveston-Texas City PMSA, TX	Y	46900 FQ	63300 AW	88490 TQ	TXBLS	10/01-12/01
	Houston PMSA, TX	Y	45050 FQ	67310 AW	101350 TQ	TXBLS	10/01-12/01
	Killeen-Temple MSA, TX	Y	22510 FQ	52690 AW	74900 TQ	TXBLS	10/01-12/01
	Longview-Marshall MSA, TX	Y	39290 FQ	54670 AW	76670 TQ	TXBLS	10/01-12/01
	Lubbock MSA, TX	Y	32780 FQ	50200 AW	72040 TQ	TXBLS	10/01-12/01
	Odessa-Midland MSA, TX	Y	53700 FQ	80530 AW	113860 TQ	TXBLS	10/01-12/01
	San Antonio MSA, TX	Y	33810 FQ	53490 AW	75200 TQ	TXBLS	10/01-12/01
	Waco MSA, TX	Y	46460 FQ	60920 AW	78670 TQ	TXBLS	10/01-12/01
	Utah	Y	36370 FQ	56700 AW	79600 TQ	UTBLS	10/01-12/01
	Provo-Orem MSA, UT	Y	36250 FQ	54110 AW	74250 TQ	UTBLS	10/01-12/01
	Salt Lake City-Ogden MSA, UT	Y	38740 FQ	57760 AW	80150 TQ	UTBLS	10/01-12/01
	Vermont	Y	38500 FQ	58860 AW	80720 TQ	VTBLS	10/01-12/01
	Burlington MSA, VT	Y	42890 FQ	62350 AW	86930 TQ	VTBLS	10/01-12/01
	Virginia	Y	34350 FQ	58470 AW	87540 TQ	VABLS	10/01-12/01
	Lynchburg MSA, VA	Y	32130 FQ	53410 AW	75960 TQ	VABLS	10/01-12/01
	Norfolk-Virginia Beach-Newport News MSA, VA-NC	Y	41950 FQ	59460 AW	81450 TQ	VABLS	10/01-12/01
	Richmond-Petersburg MSA, VA	Y	36990 FQ	60450 AW	91280 TQ	VABLS	10/01-12/01
	Roanoke MSA, VA	Y	39150 FQ	50910 AW	67150 TQ	VABLS	10/01-12/01
	Washington	Y	46630 FQ	66760 AW	92130 TQ	WABLS	10/01-12/01
	Bremerton PMSA, WA	Y	48290 FQ	63110 AW	84650 TQ	WABLS	10/01-12/01
	Richland-Kennewick-Pasco MSA, WA	Y	50970 FQ	77870 AW	110030 TQ	WABLS	10/01-12/01
	Seattle-Bellevue-Everett PMSA, WA	Y	46760 FQ	66040 AW	89140 TQ	WABLS	10/01-12/01
	Spokane MSA, WA	Y	33880 FQ	52620 AW	72780 TQ	WABLS	10/01-12/01
	Tacoma PMSA, WA	Y	37840 FQ	56500 AW	76380 TQ	WABLS	10/01-12/01
	Yakima MSA, WA	Y	50580 FQ	63620 AW	77530 TQ	WABLS	10/01-12/01
	West Virginia	Y	26940 FQ	56960 AW	82650 TQ	WVBLS	10/01-12/01
	Charleston MSA, WV	Y	44490 FQ	62970 AW	87110 TQ	WVBLS	10/01-12/01
	Huntington-Ashland MSA, WV-KY-OH	Y	35390 FQ	58360 AW	84320 TQ	WVBLS	10/01-12/01
	Wisconsin	Y	37760 FQ	57850 AW	79850 TQ	WIBLS	10/01-12/01
	Appleton-Oshkosh-Neenah MSA, WI	Y	40920 FQ	56860 AW	77140 TQ	WIBLS	10/01-12/01
	Green Bay MSA, WI	Y	42000 FQ	62300 AW	86530 TQ	WIBLS	10/01-12/01
	Madison MSA, WI	Y	28200 FQ	53150 AW	77210 TQ	WIBLS	10/01-12/01
	Milwaukee-Waukesha PMSA, WI	Y	42690 FQ	62170 AW	84220 TQ	WIBLS	10/01-12/01
	Racine PMSA, WI	Y	31890 FQ	48870 AW	72690 TQ	WIBLS	10/01-12/01
	Wyoming	Y	41430 FQ	60870 AW	86420 TQ	WYBLS	10/01-12/01
	Puerto Rico	Y	32410 FQ	52600 AW	78820 TQ	PRBLS	10/01-12/01
Industrial Engineering Technician	Alabama	Y	22730 FQ	36500 AW	53370 TQ	ALBLS	10/01-12/01
	Birmingham MSA, AL	Y	28530 FQ	40990 AW	55740 TQ	ALBLS	10/01-12/01
	Huntsville MSA, AL	Y	30680 FQ	46870 AW	71400 TQ	ALBLS	10/01-12/01

AAW	Average annual wage	AOH	Average offered, high	ASH	Average starting, high	H	Hourly	M	Monthly	S	Special: hourly and annual
AE	Average entry wage	AOL	Average offered, low	ASL	Average starting, low	HI	Highest wage paid	MTC	Median total compensation	TQ	Third quartile wage
AEX	Average experienced wage	APH	Average pay, high range	AW	Average wage paid	HR	High end range	MW	Median wage paid	W	Weekly
AO	Average offered	APL	Average pay, low range	FQ	First quartile wage	LR	Low end range	SQ	Second quartile wage	Y	Yearly

Occupation/Type/Industry	Location	Per	Low	Mid	High	Source	Date
Industrial Engineering Technician	Montgomery MSA, AL	Y	23000 FQ	29380 AW	38520 TQ	ALBLS	10/01-12/01
	Arizona	Y	28350 FQ	45220 AW	70340 TQ	AZBLS	10/01-12/01
	Phoenix-Mesa MSA, AZ	Y	28160 FQ	45560 AW	70980 TQ	AZBLS	10/01-12/01
	Tucson MSA, AZ	Y	30520 FQ	41720 AW	56620 TQ	AZBLS	10/01-12/01
	Arkansas	Y	24840 FQ	36810 AW	50960 TQ	ARBLS	10/01-12/01
	Fayetteville-Springdale-Rogers MSA, AR	Y	25320 FQ	34540 AW	49300 TQ	ARBLS	10/01-12/01
	Fort Smith MSA, AR-OK	Y	26980 FQ	37340 AW	44120 TQ	ARBLS	10/01-12/01
	Little Rock-North Little Rock MSA, AR	Y	25330 FQ	34770 AW	43820 TQ	ARBLS	10/01-12/01
	California	Y	29280 FQ	47340 AW	71440 TQ	CABLS	10/01-12/01
	Fresno MSA, CA	Y	26390 FQ	46970 AW	72300 TQ	CABLS	10/01-12/01
	Los Angeles-Long Beach PMSA, CA	Y	28200 FQ	47400 AW	74000 TQ	CABLS	10/01-12/01
	Oakland PMSA, CA	Y	29340 FQ	49940 AW	97030 TQ	CABLS	10/01-12/01
	Orange County PMSA, CA	Y	29480 FQ	45100 AW	71050 TQ	CABLS	10/01-12/01
	Riverside-San Bernardino PMSA, CA	Y	26110 FQ	44560 AW	65740 TQ	CABLS	10/01-12/01
	San Diego MSA, CA	Y	27640 FQ	43080 AW	64030 TQ	CABLS	10/01-12/01
	San Francisco PMSA, CA	Y	26980 FQ	44110 AW	68280 TQ	CABLS	10/01-12/01
	San Jose PMSA, CA	Y	30720 FQ	47870 AW	68550 TQ	CABLS	10/01-12/01
	Santa Barbara-Santa Maria-Lompoc MSA, CA	Y	28850 FQ	47710 AW	70030 TQ	CABLS	10/01-12/01
	Santa Rosa PMSA, CA	Y	35420 FQ	48430 AW	68520 TQ	CABLS	10/01-12/01
	Vallejo-Fairfield-Napa PMSA, CA	Y	26630 FQ	54280 AW	87850 TQ	CABLS	10/01-12/01
	Ventura PMSA, CA	Y	32000 FQ	58420 AW	89800 TQ	CABLS	10/01-12/01
	Colorado	Y	26830 FQ	42580 AW	60220 TQ	COBLS	10/01-12/01
	Boulder-Longmont PMSA, CO	Y	32390 FQ	45990 AW	60960 TQ	COBLS	10/01-12/01
	Denver PMSA, CO	Y	25100 FQ	39900 AW	65750 TQ	COBLS	10/01-12/01
	Fort Collins-Loveland MSA, CO	Y	23320 FQ	36770 AW	51900 TQ	COBLS	10/01-12/01
	Connecticut	Y	28940 FQ	48000 AW	74910 TQ	CTBLS	10/01-12/01
	Bridgeport PMSA, CT	Y	28390 FQ	44240 AW	68030 TQ	CTBLS	10/01-12/01
	Danbury PMSA, CT	Y	33350 FQ	48820 AW	70840 TQ	CTBLS	10/01-12/01
	Hartford MSA, CT	Y	28950 FQ	53470 AW	84960 TQ	CTBLS	10/01-12/01
	New Haven-Meriden PMSA, CT	Y	27620 FQ	42600 AW	65060 TQ	CTBLS	10/01-12/01
	Stamford-Norwalk PMSA, CT	Y	29600 FQ	43140 AW	58580 TQ	CTBLS	10/01-12/01
	Delaware	Y	22570 FQ	41250 AW	61330 TQ	DEBLS	10/01-12/01
	Wilmington-Newark PMSA, DE-MD	Y	22320 FQ	42460 AW	66430 TQ	DEBLS	10/01-12/01
	Washington PMSA, DC-MD-VA-WV	Y	31500 FQ	62530 AW	92750 TQ	DCBLS	10/01-12/01
	Florida	Y	24390 FQ	38820 AW	59600 TQ	FLBLS	10/01-12/01
	Daytona Beach MSA, FL	Y	23350 FQ	33330 AW	44140 TQ	FLBLS	10/01-12/01
	Fort Lauderdale PMSA, FL	Y	26730 FQ	48750 AW	85290 TQ	FLBLS	10/01-12/01
	Fort Walton Beach MSA, FL	Y	21270 FQ	35880 AW	55230 TQ	FLBLS	10/01-12/01
	Jacksonville MSA, FL	Y	29780 FQ	41150 AW	54990 TQ	FLBLS	10/01-12/01
	Lakeland-Winter Haven MSA, FL	Y	24390 FQ	36170 AW	51490 TQ	FLBLS	10/01-12/01
	Melbourne-Titusville-Palm Bay MSA, FL	Y	24310 FQ	34520 AW	48500 TQ	FLBLS	10/01-12/01
	Miami PMSA, FL	Y	24490 FQ	37200 AW	51450 TQ	FLBLS	10/01-12/01
	Ocala MSA, FL	Y	25920 FQ	34340 AW	43660 TQ	FLBLS	10/01-12/01
	Orlando MSA, FL	Y	26200 FQ	45800 AW	67780 TQ	FLBLS	10/01-12/01
	Tampa-St. Petersburg-Clearwater MSA, FL	Y	22390 FQ	32860 AW	45130 TQ	FLBLS	10/01-12/01
	West Palm Beach-Boca Raton MSA, FL	Y	25260 FQ	45680 AW	67890 TQ	FLBLS	10/01-12/01
	Georgia	Y	25680 FQ	39620 AW	56040 TQ	GABLS	10/01-12/01
	Atlanta MSA, GA	Y	26380 FQ	41420 AW	61500 TQ	GABLS	10/01-12/01
	Macon MSA, GA	Y	36340 FQ	46100 AW	55190 TQ	GABLS	10/01-12/01
	Savannah MSA, GA	Y	24110 FQ	33780 AW	47020 TQ	GABLS	10/01-12/01
	Idaho	Y	23680 FQ	42870 AW	83780 TQ	IDBLS	10/01-12/01
	Boise City MSA, ID	Y	23130 FQ	40700 AW	70790 TQ	IDBLS	10/01-12/01
	Illinois	Y	24410 FQ	41900 AW	59960 TQ	ILBLS	10/01-12/01
	Chicago PMSA, IL	Y	23590 FQ	41260 AW	58710 TQ	ILBLS	10/01-12/01
	Peoria-Pekin MSA, IL	Y	39000 FQ	55030 AW	70720 TQ	ILBLS	10/01-12/01
	Rockford MSA, IL	Y	28740 FQ	42790 AW	59250 TQ	ILBLS	10/01-12/01
	Indiana	Y	28290 FQ	42450 AW	65700 TQ	INBLS	10/01-12/01
	Elkhart-Goshen MSA, IN	Y	25140 FQ	34320 AW	48210 TQ	INBLS	10/01-12/01

AAW	Average annual wage	**AOH**	Average offered, high	**ASH**	Average starting, high	**H**	Hourly	**M**	Monthly	**S**	Special: hourly and annual
AE	Average entry wage	**AOL**	Average offered, low	**ASL**	Average starting, low	**HI**	Highest wage paid	**MTC**	Median total compensation	**TQ**	Third quartile wage
AEX	Average experienced wage	**APH**	Average pay, high range	**AW**	Average wage paid	**HR**	High end range	**MW**	Median wage paid	**W**	Weekly
AO	Average offered	**APL**	Average pay, low range	**FQ**	First quartile wage	**LR**	Low end range	**SQ**	Second quartile wage	**Y**	Yearly

Occupation/Type/Industry	Location	Per	Low	Mid	High	Source	Date
Industrial Engineering Technician	Evansville-Henderson MSA, IN-KY	Y	31400 FQ	40850 AW	54910 TQ	INBLS	10/01-12/01
	Fort Wayne MSA, IN	Y	30000 FQ	47140 AW	73240 TQ	INBLS	10/01-12/01
	Indianapolis MSA, IN	Y	30360 FQ	45470 AW	71280 TQ	INBLS	10/01-12/01
	South Bend MSA, IN	Y	29550 FQ	53120 AW	76550 TQ	INBLS	10/01-12/01
	Iowa	Y	25440 FQ	41350 AW	59910 TQ	IABLS	10/01-12/01
	Davenport-Moline-Rock Island MSA, IA-IL	Y	28880 FQ	44550 AW	61110 TQ	IABLS	10/01-12/01
	Des Moines MSA, IA	Y	23830 FQ	45330 AW	72590 TQ	IABLS	10/01-12/01
	Kansas	Y	30680 FQ	46060 AW	66740 TQ	KSBLS	10/01-12/01
	Kentucky	Y	23880 FQ	39940 AW	57090 TQ	KYBLS	10/01-12/01
	Lexington MSA, KY	Y	30230 FQ	42210 AW	55550 TQ	KYBLS	10/01-12/01
	Louisville MSA, KY-IN	Y	24480 FQ	41690 AW	63490 TQ	KYBLS	10/01-12/01
	Louisiana	Y	22800 FQ	49220 AW	81990 TQ	LABLS	10/01-12/01
	Baton Rouge MSA, LA	Y	19240 FQ	37770 AW	64670 TQ	LABLS	10/01-12/01
	Houma MSA, LA	Y	21990 FQ	38900 AW	66790 TQ	LABLS	10/01-12/01
	New Orleans MSA, LA	Y	41380 FQ	64420 AW	91620 TQ	LABLS	10/01-12/01
	Maine	Y	25180 FQ	37070 AW	50910 TQ	MEBLS	10/01-12/01
	Portland MSA, ME	Y	25660 FQ	33300 AW	42680 TQ	MEBLS	10/01-12/01
	Maryland	Y	24800 FQ	36740 AW	54800 TQ	MDBLS	10/01-12/01
	Baltimore PMSA, MD	Y	24580 FQ	35110 AW	51910 TQ	MDBLS	10/01-12/01
	Massachusetts	Y	29440 FQ	48270 AW	73660 TQ	MABLS	10/01-12/01
	Boston PMSA, MA-NH	Y	28890 FQ	49310 AW	76580 TQ	MABLS	10/01-12/01
	Lawrence PMSA, MA-NH	Y	30020 FQ	41870 AW	56990 TQ	MABLS	10/01-12/01
	Lowell PMSA, MA-NH	Y	29140 FQ	52910 AW	88680 TQ	MABLS	10/01-12/01
	New Bedford PMSA, MA	Y	28210 FQ	39480 AW	51490 TQ	MABLS	10/01-12/01
	Springfield MSA, MA	Y	26240 FQ	40350 AW	57820 TQ	MABLS	10/01-12/01
	Worcester PMSA, MA-CT	Y	31420 FQ	43760 AW	56610 TQ	MABLS	10/01-12/01
	Michigan	Y	28080 FQ	49990 AW	83610 TQ	MIBLS	10/01-12/01
	Ann Arbor PMSA, MI	Y	31950 FQ	44640 AW	67610 TQ	MIBLS	10/01-12/01
	Detroit PMSA, MI	Y	30620 FQ	55780 AW	89400 TQ	MIBLS	10/01-12/01
	Flint PMSA, MI	Y	57500 FQ	72370 AW	92190 TQ	MIBLS	10/01-12/01
	Grand Rapids-Muskegon-Holland MSA, MI	Y	25850 FQ	36890 AW	50390 TQ	MIBLS	10/01-12/01
	Kalamazoo-Battle Creek MSA, MI	Y	26830 FQ	41740 AW	69440 TQ	MIBLS	10/01-12/01
	Saginaw-Bay City-Midland MSA, MI	Y	28480 FQ	51810 AW	88010 TQ	MIBLS	10/01-12/01
	Minnesota	Y	30760 FQ	46800 AW	69090 TQ	MNBLS	10/01-12/01
	Minneapolis-St. Paul MSA, MN-WI	Y	33150 FQ	48990 AW	71080 TQ	MNBLS	10/01-12/01
	Mississippi	Y	21950 FQ	33530 AW	46020 TQ	MSBLS	10/01-12/01
	Biloxi-Gulfport-Pascagoula MSA, MS	Y	25470 FQ	37260 AW	47080 TQ	MSBLS	10/01-12/01
	Missouri	Y	23620 FQ	37810 AW	58120 TQ	MOBLS	10/01-12/01
	Kansas City MSA, MO-KS	Y	29520 FQ	46500 AW	78030 TQ	MOBLS	10/01-12/01
	St. Louis MSA, MO-IL	Y	24830 FQ	42260 AW	61710 TQ	MOBLS	10/01-12/01
	Nebraska	Y	24750 FQ	37480 AW	53510 TQ	NEBLS	10/01-12/01
	Omaha MSA, NE-IA	Y	23740 FQ	38140 AW	63040 TQ	NEBLS	10/01-12/01
	New Hampshire	Y	26950 FQ	36240 AW	45910 TQ	NHBLS	10/01-12/01
	Manchester PMSA, NH	Y	26390 FQ	35650 AW	44480 TQ	NHBLS	10/01-12/01
	Nashua PMSA, NH	Y	28430 FQ	34820 AW	43720 TQ	NHBLS	10/01-12/01
	Portsmouth-Rochester PMSA, NH-ME	Y	26190 FQ	39920 AW	61560 TQ	NHBLS	10/01-12/01
	New Jersey	Y	29640 FQ	46310 AW	74400 TQ	NJBLS	10/01-12/01
	Bergen-Passaic PMSA, NJ	Y	30280 FQ	48070 AW	80680 TQ	NJBLS	10/01-12/01
	Middlesex-Somerset-Hunterdon PMSA, NJ	Y	30130 FQ	45650 AW	70450 TQ	NJBLS	10/01-12/01
	Newark PMSA, NJ	Y	28570 FQ	46160 AW	76960 TQ	NJBLS	10/01-12/01
	Trenton PMSA, NJ	Y	31260 FQ	50680 AW	85370 TQ	NJBLS	10/01-12/01
	New Mexico	Y	28110 FQ	39570 AW	55260 TQ	NMBLS	10/01-12/01
	Albuquerque MSA, NM	Y	29630 FQ	41090 AW	56300 TQ	NMBLS	10/01-12/01
	New York	Y	26220 FQ	45560 AW	70870 TQ	NYBLS	10/01-12/01
	Albany-Schenectady-Troy MSA, NY	Y	28670 FQ	57010 AW	93490 TQ	NYBLS	10/01-12/01
	Binghamton MSA, NY	Y	23410 FQ	34800 AW	52560 TQ	NYBLS	10/01-12/01
	Buffalo-Niagara Falls MSA, NY	Y	24110 FQ	37060 AW	54770 TQ	NYBLS	10/01-12/01
	Nassau-Suffolk PMSA, NY	Y	23850 FQ	42240 AW	58510 TQ	NYBLS	10/01-12/01
	New York PMSA, NY	Y	29190 FQ	48110 AW	72890 TQ	NYBLS	10/01-12/01
	Rochester MSA, NY	Y	32910 FQ	49060 AW	69430 TQ	NYBLS	10/01-12/01
	Syracuse MSA, NY	Y	23490 FQ	40030 AW	57870 TQ	NYBLS	10/01-12/01

AAW	Average annual wage	**AOH**	Average offered, high	**ASH**	Average starting, high	**H**	Hourly	**M**	Monthly	**S**	Special: hourly and annual
AE	Average entry wage	**AOL**	Average offered, low	**ASL**	Average starting, low	**HI**	Highest wage paid	**MTC**	Median total compensation	**TQ**	Third quartile wage
AEX	Average experienced wage	**APH**	Average pay, high range	**AW**	Average wage paid	**HR**	High end range	**MW**	Median wage paid	**W**	Weekly
AO	Average offered	**APL**	Average pay, low range	**FQ**	First quartile wage	**LR**	Low end range	**SQ**	Second quartile wage	**Y**	Yearly

Occupation/Type/Industry	Location	Per	Low	Mid	High	Source	Date
Industrial Engineering Technician	North Carolina	Y	24790 FQ	43210 AW	70410 TQ	NCBLS	10/01-12/01
	Charlotte-Gastonia-Rock Hill MSA, NC-SC	Y	25020 FQ	42190 AW	68890 TQ	NCBLS	10/01-12/01
	Greensboro-Winston-Salem-High Point MSA, NC	Y	24650 FQ	37450 AW	54810 TQ	NCBLS	10/01-12/01
	Hickory-Morganton-Lenoir MSA, NC	Y	23380 FQ	34910 AW	46080 TQ	NCBLS	10/01-12/01
	North Dakota	Y	26110 FQ	34820 AW	45820 TQ	NDBLS	10/01-12/01
	Fargo-Moorhead MSA, ND-MN	Y	25170 FQ	32020 AW	40300 TQ	NDBLS	10/01-12/01
	Ohio	Y	26270 FQ	40270 AW	57380 TQ	OHBLS	10/01-12/01
	Akron PMSA, OH	Y	26990 FQ	41670 AW	57130 TQ	OHBLS	10/01-12/01
	Canton-Massillon MSA, OH	Y	28190 FQ	40490 AW	56170 TQ	OHBLS	10/01-12/01
	Cincinnati PMSA, OH-KY-IN	Y	25580 FQ	43680 AW	69980 TQ	OHBLS	10/01-12/01
	Cleveland-Lorain-Elyria PMSA, OH	Y	28730 FQ	40540 AW	55930 TQ	OHBLS	10/01-12/01
	Columbus MSA, OH	Y	25990 FQ	40280 AW	56740 TQ	OHBLS	10/01-12/01
	Dayton-Springfield MSA, OH	Y	28930 FQ	41840 AW	58150 TQ	OHBLS	10/01-12/01
	Hamilton-Middletown PMSA, OH	Y	30520 FQ	43520 AW	62720 TQ	OHBLS	10/01-12/01
	Mansfield MSA, OH	Y	24570 FQ	38100 AW	56570 TQ	OHBLS	10/01-12/01
	Toledo MSA, OH	Y	25460 FQ	40090 AW	57090 TQ	OHBLS	10/01-12/01
	Youngstown-Warren MSA, OH	Y	16530 FQ	37020 AW	58290 TQ	OHBLS	10/01-12/01
	Oklahoma	Y	21650 FQ	39300 AW	55250 TQ	OKBLS	10/01-12/01
	Oklahoma City MSA, OK	Y	29010 FQ	43320 AW	55600 TQ	OKBLS	10/01-12/01
	Tulsa MSA, OK	Y	19220 FQ	32190 AW	52970 TQ	OKBLS	10/01-12/01
	Pennsylvania	Y	29540 FQ	51220 AW	80890 TQ	PABLS	10/01-12/01
	Allentown-Bethlehem-Easton MSA, PA	Y	30750 FQ	56240 AW	85510 TQ	PABLS	10/01-12/01
	Erie MSA, PA	Y	20090 FQ	42410 AW	67310 TQ	PABLS	10/01-12/01
	Lancaster MSA, PA	Y	29930 FQ	37240 AW	51170 TQ	PABLS	10/01-12/01
	Philadelphia PMSA, PA-NJ	Y	33810 FQ	55480 AW	83410 TQ	PABLS	10/01-12/01
	Pittsburgh MSA, PA	Y	30560 FQ	58590 AW	91410 TQ	PABLS	10/01-12/01
	Reading MSA, PA	Y	28310 FQ	44100 AW	69340 TQ	PABLS	10/01-12/01
	Scranton-Wilkes-Barre-Hazleton MSA, PA	Y	23460 FQ	37710 AW	56380 TQ	PABLS	10/01-12/01
	York MSA, PA	Y	28850 FQ	43570 AW	58600 TQ	PABLS	10/01-12/01
	Rhode Island	Y	29280 FQ	37460 AW	47000 TQ	RIBLS	10/01-12/01
	Providence-Fall River-Warwick MSA, RI-MA	Y	29800 FQ	38590 AW	49720 TQ	RIBLS	10/01-12/01
	South Carolina	Y	28860 FQ	45120 AW	60750 TQ	SCBLS	10/01-12/01
	Columbia MSA, SC	Y	25950 FQ	38330 AW	54450 TQ	SCBLS	10/01-12/01
	Greenville-Spartanburg-Anderson MSA, SC	Y	32640 FQ	48310 AW	65150 TQ	SCBLS	10/01-12/01
	South Dakota	Y	24350 FQ	34190 AW	44140 TQ	SDBLS	10/01-12/01
	Tennessee	Y	25320 FQ	40860 AW	58630 TQ	TNBLS	10/01-12/01
	Chattanooga MSA, TN-GA	Y	28720 FQ	37910 AW	51970 TQ	TNBLS	10/01-12/01
	Johnson City-Kingsport-Bristol MSA, TN-VA	Y	23720 FQ	34720 AW	47880 TQ	TNBLS	10/01-12/01
	Knoxville MSA, TN	Y	28300 FQ	43310 AW	73690 TQ	TNBLS	10/01-12/01
	Memphis MSA, TN-AR-MS	Y	24860 FQ	41750 AW	70180 TQ	TNBLS	10/01-12/01
	Nashville MSA, TN	Y	25970 FQ	36320 AW	46530 TQ	TNBLS	10/01-12/01
	Texas	Y	28510 FQ	46740 AW	76460 TQ	TXBLS	10/01-12/01
	Beaumont-Port Arthur MSA, TX	Y	28500 FQ	49490 AW	87160 TQ	TXBLS	10/01-12/01
	Brazoria PMSA, TX	Y	29490 FQ	47070 AW	70580 TQ	TXBLS	10/01-12/01
	Corpus Christi MSA, TX	Y	33640 FQ	52820 AW	72990 TQ	TXBLS	10/01-12/01
	Dallas PMSA, TX	Y	31570 FQ	58570 AW	93520 TQ	TXBLS	10/01-12/01
	El Paso MSA, TX	Y	23300 FQ	36460 AW	57060 TQ	TXBLS	10/01-12/01
	Houston PMSA, TX	Y	26970 FQ	51000 AW	76510 TQ	TXBLS	10/01-12/01
	San Antonio MSA, TX	Y	27040 FQ	39340 AW	50690 TQ	TXBLS	10/01-12/01
	Utah	Y	23610 FQ	39600 AW	55430 TQ	UTBLS	10/01-12/01
	Salt Lake City-Ogden MSA, UT	Y	25580 FQ	41060 AW	55700 TQ	UTBLS	10/01-12/01
	Burlington MSA, VT	Y	25380 FQ	41930 AW	61170 TQ	VTBLS	10/01-12/01
	Virginia	Y	27300 FQ	49450 AW	84310 TQ	VABLS	10/01-12/01
	Norfolk-Virginia Beach-Newport News MSA, VA-NC	Y	29380 FQ	44390 AW	65890 TQ	VABLS	10/01-12/01
	Richmond-Petersburg MSA, VA	Y	28500 FQ	39760 AW	56070 TQ	VABLS	10/01-12/01
	Roanoke MSA, VA	Y	26220 FQ	37120 AW	53660 TQ	VABLS	10/01-12/01

AAW Average annual wage **AOH** Average offered, high **ASH** Average starting, high **H** Hourly **M** Monthly **S** Special: hourly and annual
AE Average entry wage **AOL** Average offered, low **ASL** Average starting, low **HI** Highest wage paid **MTC** Median total compensation **TQ** Third quartile wage
AEX Average experienced wage **APH** Average pay, high range **AW** Average wage paid **HR** High end range **MW** Median wage paid **W** Weekly
AO Average offered **APL** Average pay, low range **FQ** First quartile wage **LR** Low end range **SQ** Second quartile wage **Y** Yearly

Occupation/Type/Industry	Location	Per	Low	Mid	High	Source	Date
Industrial Engineering Technician	Washington	Y	33830 FQ	51740 AW	71070 TQ	WABLS	10/01-12/01
	Seattle-Bellevue-Everett PMSA, WA	Y	37990 FQ	53000 AW	70190 TQ	WABLS	10/01-12/01
	Spokane MSA, WA	Y	27220 FQ	38550 AW	56090 TQ	WABLS	10/01-12/01
	Tacoma PMSA, WA	Y	33920 FQ	58290 AW	88880 TQ	WABLS	10/01-12/01
	Yakima MSA, WA	Y	37080 FQ	52420 AW	70550 TQ	WABLS	10/01-12/01
	West Virginia	Y	24470 FQ	40290 AW	64740 TQ	WVBLS	10/01-12/01
	Charleston MSA, WV	Y	26710 FQ	50430 AW	70650 TQ	WVBLS	10/01-12/01
	Wisconsin	Y	29250 FQ	42660 AW	58510 TQ	WIBLS	10/01-12/01
	Appleton-Oshkosh-Neenah MSA, WI	Y	34640 FQ	47410 AW	59830 TQ	WIBLS	10/01-12/01
	Green Bay MSA, WI	Y	25040 FQ	37610 AW	49660 TQ	WIBLS	10/01-12/01
	Madison MSA, WI	Y	32040 FQ	45930 AW	63700 TQ	WIBLS	10/01-12/01
	Milwaukee-Waukesha PMSA, WI	Y	30730 FQ	44240 AW	63130 TQ	WIBLS	10/01-12/01
	Racine PMSA, WI	Y	30120 FQ	43090 AW	61590 TQ	WIBLS	10/01-12/01
	Puerto Rico	Y	16570 FQ	27750 AW	42370 TQ	PRBLS	10/01-12/01
Industrial Machinery Mechanic	Alabama	H	10.02 FQ	15.40 AW	23.69 TQ	ALBLS	10/01-12/01
	Birmingham MSA, AL	H	10.02 FQ	17.97 AW	26.52 TQ	ALBLS	10/01-12/01
	Huntsville MSA, AL	H	9.49 FQ	19.57 AW	28.04 TQ	ALBLS	10/01-12/01
	Mobile MSA, AL	H	11.08 FQ	16.50 AW	22.52 TQ	ALBLS	10/01-12/01
	Montgomery MSA, AL	H	10.93 FQ	15.15 AW	19.92 TQ	ALBLS	10/01-12/01
	Alaska	H	14.77 FQ	24.81 AW	35.33 TQ	AKBLS	10/01-12/01
	Anchorage MSA, AK	H	17.36 FQ	25.47 AW	36.86 TQ	AKBLS	10/01-12/01
	Arizona	H	12.42 FQ	18.28 AW	24.45 TQ	AZBLS	10/01-12/01
	Phoenix-Mesa MSA, AZ	H	12.31 FQ	18.62 AW	25.34 TQ	AZBLS	10/01-12/01
	Tucson MSA, AZ	H	12.61 FQ	17.01 AW	21.74 TQ	AZBLS	10/01-12/01
	Arkansas	H	11.07 FQ	16.82 AW	26.15 TQ	ARBLS	10/01-12/01
	Fayetteville-Springdale-Rogers MSA, AR	H	11.52 FQ	14.63 AW	19.10 TQ	ARBLS	10/01-12/01
	Fort Smith MSA, AR-OK	H	9.61 FQ	13.97 AW	18.01 TQ	ARBLS	10/01-12/01
	Little Rock-North Little Rock MSA, AR	H	11.11 FQ	16.41 AW	23.70 TQ	ARBLS	10/01-12/01
	California	H	13.00 FQ	20.50 AW	27.33 TQ	CABLS	10/01-12/01
	Bakersfield MSA, CA	H	10.89 FQ	22.80 AW	33.40 TQ	CABLS	10/01-12/01
	Chico-Paradise MSA, CA	H	12.54 FQ	18.20 AW	22.44 TQ	CABLS	10/01-12/01
	Fresno MSA, CA	H	13.12 FQ	18.69 AW	24.67 TQ	CABLS	10/01-12/01
	Los Angeles-Long Beach PMSA, CA	H	12.46 FQ	20.35 AW	27.05 TQ	CABLS	10/01-12/01
	Merced MSA, CA	H	11.63 FQ	17.19 AW	22.38 TQ	CABLS	10/01-12/01
	Modesto MSA, CA	H	12.78 FQ	19.05 AW	25.78 TQ	CABLS	10/01-12/01
	Oakland PMSA, CA	H	18.35 FQ	23.27 AW	27.81 TQ	CABLS	10/01-12/01
	Orange County PMSA, CA	H	12.92 FQ	21.13 AW	28.17 TQ	CABLS	10/01-12/01
	Riverside-San Bernardino PMSA, CA	H	14.26 FQ	21.67 AW	30.10 TQ	CABLS	10/01-12/01
	Sacramento PMSA, CA	H	14.31 FQ	20.16 AW	26.41 TQ	CABLS	10/01-12/01
	Salinas MSA, CA	H	13.91 FQ	21.94 AW	28.48 TQ	CABLS	10/01-12/01
	San Diego MSA, CA	H	12.03 FQ	18.24 AW	25.71 TQ	CABLS	10/01-12/01
	San Francisco PMSA, CA	H	14.25 FQ	20.68 AW	26.85 TQ	CABLS	10/01-12/01
	San Jose PMSA, CA	H	12.92 FQ	20.98 AW	27.75 TQ	CABLS	10/01-12/01
	San Luis Obispo-Atascadero-Paso Robles MSA, CA	H	9.86 FQ	19.90 AW	26.96 TQ	CABLS	10/01-12/01
	Santa Barbara-Santa Maria-Lompoc MSA, CA	H	19.20 FQ	23.74 AW	27.72 TQ	CABLS	10/01-12/01
	Santa Rosa PMSA, CA	H	12.23 FQ	19.17 AW	25.94 TQ	CABLS	10/01-12/01
	Stockton-Lodi MSA, CA	H	16.90 FQ	20.19 AW	23.51 TQ	CABLS	10/01-12/01
	Vallejo-Fairfield-Napa PMSA, CA	H	15.36 FQ	20.79 AW	26.85 TQ	CABLS	10/01-12/01
	Ventura PMSA, CA	H	11.94 FQ	20.29 AW	27.93 TQ	CABLS	10/01-12/01
	Visalia-Tulare-Porterville MSA, CA	H	9.59 FQ	15.86 AW	23.44 TQ	CABLS	10/01-12/01
	Colorado	H	11.90 FQ	18.96 AW	26.66 TQ	COBLS	10/01-12/01
	Boulder-Longmont PMSA, CO	H	10.82 FQ	19.28 AW	27.13 TQ	COBLS	10/01-12/01
	Denver PMSA, CO	H	12.75 FQ	18.82 AW	25.90 TQ	COBLS	10/01-12/01
	Fort Collins-Loveland MSA, CO	H	8.86 FQ	17.57 AW	25.70 TQ	COBLS	10/01-12/01
	Greeley PMSA, CO	H	10.13 FQ	18.01 AW	26.51 TQ	COBLS	10/01-12/01
	Connecticut	H	13.04 FQ	19.86 AW	27.55 TQ	CTBLS	10/01-12/01
	Bridgeport PMSA, CT	H	14.86 FQ	20.05 AW	25.93 TQ	CTBLS	10/01-12/01
	Danbury PMSA, CT	H	17.97 FQ	22.88 AW	28.23 TQ	CTBLS	10/01-12/01
	Hartford MSA, CT	H	12.02 FQ	18.70 AW	26.84 TQ	CTBLS	10/01-12/01

AAW Average annual wage; **AE** Average entry wage; **AEX** Average experienced wage; **AO** Average offered; **AOH** Average offered, high; **AOL** Average offered, low; **APH** Average pay, high range; **APL** Average pay, low range; **ASH** Average starting, high; **ASL** Average starting, low; **AW** Average wage paid; **FQ** First quartile wage; **H** Hourly; **HI** Highest wage paid; **HR** High end range; **LR** Low end range; **M** Monthly; **MTC** Median total compensation; **MW** Median wage paid; **SQ** Second quartile wage; **S** Special: hourly and annual; **TQ** Third quartile wage; **W** Weekly; **Y** Yearly

Occupation/Type/Industry	Location	Per	Low	Mid	High	Source	Date
Industrial Machinery Mechanic	New Haven-Meriden PMSA, CT	H	14.57 FQ	21.59 AW	28.14 TQ	CTBLS	10/01-12/01
	New London-Norwich MSA, CT-RI	H	14.32 FQ	20.78 AW	27.11 TQ	CTBLS	10/01-12/01
	Stamford-Norwalk PMSA, CT	H	14.99 FQ	19.65 AW	25.73 TQ	CTBLS	10/01-12/01
	Waterbury PMSA, CT	H	13.11 FQ	18.54 AW	24.78 TQ	CTBLS	10/01-12/01
	Delaware	H	13.24 FQ	21.01 AW	28.03 TQ	DEBLS	10/01-12/01
	Wilmington-Newark PMSA, DE-MD	H	15.88 FQ	22.88 AW	28.46 TQ	DEBLS	10/01-12/01
	District of Columbia	H	15.93 FQ	21.76 AW	28.73 TQ	DCBLS	10/01-12/01
	Washington PMSA, DC-MD-VA-WV	H	13.23 FQ	20.33 AW	28.28 TQ	DCBLS	10/01-12/01
	Florida	H	10.97 FQ	16.64 AW	24.78 TQ	FLBLS	10/01-12/01
	Daytona Beach MSA, FL	H	11.10 FQ	16.99 AW	24.93 TQ	FLBLS	10/01-12/01
	Fort Lauderdale PMSA, FL	H	11.53 FQ	19.22 AW	27.36 TQ	FLBLS	10/01-12/01
	Fort Myers-Cape Coral MSA, FL	H	10.33 FQ	14.69 AW	21.38 TQ	FLBLS	10/01-12/01
	Fort Pierce-Port St. Lucie MSA, FL	H	13.02 FQ	17.11 AW	21.30 TQ	FLBLS	10/01-12/01
	Gainesville MSA, FL	H	10.46 FQ	12.90 AW	15.74 TQ	FLBLS	10/01-12/01
	Jacksonville MSA, FL	H	10.09 FQ	14.14 AW	18.94 TQ	FLBLS	10/01-12/01
	Lakeland-Winter Haven MSA, FL	H	12.93 FQ	18.69 AW	26.84 TQ	FLBLS	10/01-12/01
	Melbourne-Titusville-Palm Bay MSA, FL	H	13.51 FQ	19.39 AW	25.68 TQ	FLBLS	10/01-12/01
	Miami PMSA, FL	H	10.63 FQ	15.36 AW	20.83 TQ	FLBLS	10/01-12/01
	Ocala MSA, FL	H	9.49 FQ	13.11 AW	17.54 TQ	FLBLS	10/01-12/01
	Orlando MSA, FL	H	10.47 FQ	15.90 AW	22.53 TQ	FLBLS	10/01-12/01
	Sarasota-Bradenton MSA, FL	H	11.22 FQ	17.44 AW	26.80 TQ	FLBLS	10/01-12/01
	Tallahassee MSA, FL	H	9.59 FQ	12.37 AW	16.00 TQ	FLBLS	10/01-12/01
	Tampa-St. Petersburg-Clearwater MSA, FL	H	11.63 FQ	17.02 AW	23.86 TQ	FLBLS	10/01-12/01
	West Palm Beach-Boca Raton MSA, FL	H	12.64 FQ	19.31 AW	26.93 TQ	FLBLS	10/01-12/01
	Georgia	H	11.55 FQ	16.62 AW	23.70 TQ	GABLS	10/01-12/01
	Atlanta MSA, GA	H	11.81 FQ	17.31 AW	23.40 TQ	GABLS	10/01-12/01
	Augusta-Aiken MSA, GA-SC	H	11.69 FQ	17.80 AW	25.61 TQ	GABLS	10/01-12/01
	Columbus MSA, GA-AL	H	9.82 FQ	14.49 AW	20.72 TQ	GABLS	10/01-12/01
	Macon MSA, GA	H	14.19 FQ	18.36 AW	21.88 TQ	GABLS	10/01-12/01
	Savannah MSA, GA	H	14.39 FQ	19.28 AW	25.81 TQ	GABLS	10/01-12/01
	Hawaii	H	13.89 FQ	18.90 AW	27.81 TQ	HIBLS	10/01-12/01
	Honolulu MSA, HI	H	13.80 FQ	19.08 AW	28.45 TQ	HIBLS	10/01-12/01
	Illinois	H	11.60 FQ	18.03 AW	25.56 TQ	ILBLS	10/01-12/01
	Champaign-Urbana MSA, IL	H	10.77 FQ	15.76 AW	21.64 TQ	ILBLS	10/01-12/01
	Chicago PMSA, IL	H	11.40 FQ	17.59 AW	25.15 TQ	ILBLS	10/01-12/01
	Peoria-Pekin MSA, IL	H	13.97 FQ	18.11 AW	23.69 TQ	ILBLS	10/01-12/01
	Rockford MSA, IL	H	14.99 FQ	19.32 AW	23.32 TQ	ILBLS	10/01-12/01
	Springfield MSA, IL	H	12.56 FQ	21.06 AW	30.00 TQ	ILBLS	10/01-12/01
	Indiana	H	13.53 FQ	20.49 AW	30.92 TQ	INBLS	10/01-12/01
	Elkhart-Goshen MSA, IN	H	12.63 FQ	18.42 AW	24.80 TQ	INBLS	10/01-12/01
	Evansville-Henderson MSA, IN-KY	H	11.20 FQ	18.45 AW	26.78 TQ	INBLS	10/01-12/01
	Fort Wayne MSA, IN	H	13.68 FQ	17.07 AW	21.86 TQ	INBLS	10/01-12/01
	Indianapolis MSA, IN	H	14.52 FQ	23.44 AW	34.22 TQ	INBLS	10/01-12/01
	Lafayette MSA, IN	H	18.41 FQ	20.19 AW	22.64 TQ	INBLS	10/01-12/01
	South Bend MSA, IN	H	13.59 FQ	17.14 AW	24.45 TQ	INBLS	10/01-12/01
	Iowa	H	9.37 FQ	14.75 AW	21.12 TQ	IABLS	10/01-12/01
	Cedar Rapids MSA, IA	H	13.26 FQ	18.77 AW	25.39 TQ	IABLS	10/01-12/01
	Davenport-Moline-Rock Island MSA, IA-IL	H	11.53 FQ	18.95 AW	26.19 TQ	IABLS	10/01-12/01
	Des Moines MSA, IA	H	10.79 FQ	14.80 AW	18.89 TQ	IABLS	10/01-12/01
	Kansas	H	11.56 FQ	18.06 AW	25.92 TQ	KSBLS	10/01-12/01
	Topeka MSA, KS	H	11.59 FQ	17.06 AW	22.20 TQ	KSBLS	10/01-12/01
	Wichita MSA, KS	H	10.02 FQ	19.21 AW	26.70 TQ	KSBLS	10/01-12/01
	Kentucky	H	12.24 FQ	17.96 AW	25.06 TQ	KYBLS	10/01-12/01
	Lexington MSA, KY	H	13.98 FQ	17.41 AW	21.25 TQ	KYBLS	10/01-12/01
	Louisville MSA, KY-IN	H	13.62 FQ	19.82 AW	26.66 TQ	KYBLS	10/01-12/01
	Louisiana	H	12.09 FQ	18.88 AW	26.22 TQ	LABLS	10/01-12/01
	Baton Rouge MSA, LA	H	14.93 FQ	19.68 AW	24.01 TQ	LABLS	10/01-12/01
	Houma MSA, LA	H	12.22 FQ	17.97 AW	24.14 TQ	LABLS	10/01-12/01
	Lafayette MSA, LA	H	10.30 FQ	17.17 AW	26.04 TQ	LABLS	10/01-12/01
	Lake Charles MSA, LA	H	12.86 FQ	19.42 AW	26.34 TQ	LABLS	10/01-12/01

AAW Average annual wage **AOH** Average offered, high **ASH** Average starting, high **H** Hourly **M** Monthly **S** Special: hourly and annual
AE Average entry wage **AOL** Average offered, low **ASL** Average starting, low **HI** Highest wage paid **MTC** Median total compensation **TQ** Third quartile wage
AEX Average experienced wage **APH** Average pay, high range **AW** Average wage paid **HR** High end range **MW** Median wage paid **W** Weekly
AO Average offered **APL** Average pay, low range **FQ** First quartile wage **LR** Low end range **SQ** Second quartile wage **Y** Yearly

Occupation/Type/Industry	Location	Per	Low	Mid	High	Source	Date
Industrial Machinery Mechanic	New Orleans MSA, LA	H	12.11 FQ	17.30 AW	24.40 TQ	LABLS	10/01-12/01
	Shreveport-Bossier City MSA, LA	H	10.44 FQ	18.59 AW	26.89 TQ	LABLS	10/01-12/01
	Maine	H	11.56 FQ	17.88 AW	26.06 TQ	MEBLS	10/01-12/01
	Portland MSA, ME	H	11.35 FQ	15.42 AW	20.75 TQ	MEBLS	10/01-12/01
	Maryland	H	11.89 FQ	18.21 AW	25.91 TQ	MDBLS	10/01-12/01
	Baltimore PMSA, MD	H	11.97 FQ	18.19 AW	25.52 TQ	MDBLS	10/01-12/01
	Massachusetts	H	12.54 FQ	18.78 AW	26.28 TQ	MABLS	10/01-12/01
	Boston PMSA, MA-NH	H	12.77 FQ	19.78 AW	26.77 TQ	MABLS	10/01-12/01
	Brockton PMSA, MA	H	11.85 FQ	17.43 AW	24.21 TQ	MABLS	10/01-12/01
	Lawrence PMSA, MA-NH	H	14.91 FQ	19.66 AW	25.70 TQ	MABLS	10/01-12/01
	Lowell PMSA, MA-NH	H	13.72 FQ	20.94 AW	29.41 TQ	MABLS	10/01-12/01
	New Bedford PMSA, MA	H	11.42 FQ	16.33 AW	24.28 TQ	MABLS	10/01-12/01
	Springfield MSA, MA	H	12.62 FQ	16.94 AW	24.53 TQ	MABLS	10/01-12/01
	Worcester PMSA, MA-CT	H	13.87 FQ	18.59 AW	24.78 TQ	MABLS	10/01-12/01
	Michigan	H	14.38 FQ	24.23 AW	34.19 TQ	MIBLS	10/01-12/01
	Detroit PMSA, MI	H	15.11 FQ	24.79 AW	34.53 TQ	MIBLS	10/01-12/01
	Grand Rapids-Muskegon-Holland MSA, MI	H	14.73 FQ	22.95 AW	32.53 TQ	MIBLS	10/01-12/01
	Kalamazoo-Battle Creek MSA, MI	H	15.45 FQ	22.09 AW	29.11 TQ	MIBLS	10/01-12/01
	Saginaw-Bay City-Midland MSA, MI	H	18.28 FQ	28.71 AW	35.20 TQ	MIBLS	10/01-12/01
	Minnesota	H	14.09 FQ	20.21 AW	26.98 TQ	MNBLS	10/01-12/01
	Duluth-Superior MSA, MN-WI	H	13.62 FQ	20.00 AW	29.50 TQ	MNBLS	10/01-12/01
	Minneapolis-St. Paul MSA, MN-WI	H	15.29 FQ	21.09 AW	27.21 TQ	MNBLS	10/01-12/01
	Mississippi	H	9.74 FQ	17.04 AW	25.73 TQ	MSBLS	10/01-12/01
	Jackson MSA, MS	H	7.75 FQ	13.55 AW	20.63 TQ	MSBLS	10/01-12/01
	Missouri	H	12.53 FQ	18.52 AW	25.45 TQ	MOBLS	10/01-12/01
	Kansas City MSA, MO-KS	H	14.15 FQ	20.49 AW	27.99 TQ	MOBLS	10/01-12/01
	St. Louis MSA, MO-IL	H	14.12 FQ	19.83 AW	26.96 TQ	MOBLS	10/01-12/01
	Springfield MSA, MO	H	13.75 FQ	17.59 AW	21.69 TQ	MOBLS	10/01-12/01
	Montana	H	12.27 FQ	17.42 AW	26.36 TQ	MTBLS	10/01-12/01
	Billings MSA, MT	H	12.66 FQ	21.03 AW	34.03 TQ	MTBLS	10/01-12/01
	Nebraska	H	11.17 FQ	15.73 AW	22.05 TQ	NEBLS	10/01-12/01
	Lincoln MSA, NE	H	12.70 FQ	16.79 AW	21.17 TQ	NEBLS	10/01-12/01
	Omaha MSA, NE-IA	H	11.33 FQ	16.99 AW	24.26 TQ	NEBLS	10/01-12/01
	Nevada	H	13.96 FQ	21.33 AW	28.06 TQ	NVBLS	10/01-12/01
	Las Vegas MSA, NV-AZ	H	14.24 FQ	21.07 AW	27.56 TQ	NVBLS	10/01-12/01
	Reno MSA, NV	H	12.47 FQ	22.85 AW	35.00 TQ	NVBLS	10/01-12/01
	New Hampshire	H	13.55 FQ	18.02 AW	23.64 TQ	NHBLS	10/01-12/01
	Manchester PMSA, NH	H	14.15 FQ	17.73 AW	21.86 TQ	NHBLS	10/01-12/01
	Nashua PMSA, NH	H	14.56 FQ	20.92 AW	27.22 TQ	NHBLS	10/01-12/01
	Portsmouth-Rochester PMSA, NH-ME	H	14.92 FQ	19.54 AW	24.86 TQ	NHBLS	10/01-12/01
	New Jersey	H	13.47 FQ	19.87 AW	27.55 TQ	NJBLS	10/01-12/01
	Atlantic-Cape May PMSA, NJ	H	12.47 FQ	16.81 AW	20.99 TQ	NJBLS	10/01-12/01
	Bergen-Passaic PMSA, NJ	H	12.98 FQ	19.72 AW	27.97 TQ	NJBLS	10/01-12/01
	Jersey City PMSA, NJ	H	14.23 FQ	20.37 AW	27.14 TQ	NJBLS	10/01-12/01
	Middlesex-Somerset-Hunterdon PMSA, NJ	H	13.03 FQ	19.37 AW	26.23 TQ	NJBLS	10/01-12/01
	Monmouth-Ocean PMSA, NJ	H	12.94 FQ	20.33 AW	27.29 TQ	NJBLS	10/01-12/01
	Newark PMSA, NJ	H	14.06 FQ	20.80 AW	29.53 TQ	NJBLS	10/01-12/01
	Trenton PMSA, NJ	H	13.54 FQ	19.81 AW	26.85 TQ	NJBLS	10/01-12/01
	New Mexico	H	13.43 FQ	20.97 AW	31.00 TQ	NMBLS	10/01-12/01
	Albuquerque MSA, NM	H	16.06 FQ	25.31 AW	33.40 TQ	NMBLS	10/01-12/01
	New York	H	12.35 FQ	20.10 AW	29.95 TQ	NYBLS	10/01-12/01
	Albany-Schenectady-Troy MSA, NY	H	12.25 FQ	19.62 AW	30.29 TQ	NYBLS	10/01-12/01
	Binghamton MSA, NY	H	13.66 FQ	19.45 AW	30.62 TQ	NYBLS	10/01-12/01
	Buffalo-Niagara Falls MSA, NY	H	14.10 FQ	21.65 AW	29.36 TQ	NYBLS	10/01-12/01
	Dutchess County PMSA, NY	H	14.06 FQ	18.88 AW	24.66 TQ	NYBLS	10/01-12/01
	Nassau-Suffolk PMSA, NY	H	14.08 FQ	21.90 AW	31.53 TQ	NYBLS	10/01-12/01
	New York PMSA, NY	H	11.92 FQ	21.39 AW	31.74 TQ	NYBLS	10/01-12/01
	Newburgh PMSA, NY-PA	H	11.81 FQ	18.94 AW	31.53 TQ	NYBLS	10/01-12/01
	Rochester MSA, NY	H	12.14 FQ	17.38 AW	25.08 TQ	NYBLS	10/01-12/01
	Syracuse MSA, NY	H	13.28 FQ	19.50 AW	27.14 TQ	NYBLS	10/01-12/01
	Utica-Rome MSA, NY	H	9.98 FQ	16.17 AW	30.61 TQ	NYBLS	10/01-12/01
	North Carolina	H	10.94 FQ	16.47 AW	25.30 TQ	NCBLS	10/01-12/01
	Asheville MSA, NC	H	11.53 FQ	14.74 AW	20.31 TQ	NCBLS	10/01-12/01

AAW	Average annual wage	**AOH**	Average offered, high	**ASH**	Average starting, high	**H**	Hourly	**M**	Monthly	**S**	Special: hourly and annual
AE	Average entry wage	**AOL**	Average offered, low	**ASL**	Average starting, low	**HI**	Highest wage paid	**MTC**	Median total compensation	**TQ**	Third quartile wage
AEX	Average experienced wage	**APH**	Average pay, high range	**AW**	Average wage paid	**HR**	High end range	**MW**	Median wage paid	**W**	Weekly
AO	Average offered	**APL**	Average pay, low range	**FQ**	First quartile wage	**LR**	Low end range	**SQ**	Second quartile wage	**Y**	Yearly

Occupation/Type/Industry	Location	Per	Low	Mid	High	Source	Date
Industrial Machinery Mechanic	Charlotte-Gastonia-Rock Hill MSA, NC-SC	H	11.20 FQ	17.20 AW	26.42 TQ	NCBLS	10/01-12/01
	Fayetteville MSA, NC	H	12.16 FQ	18.80 AW	26.50 TQ	NCBLS	10/01-12/01
	Greensboro-Winston-Salem-High Point MSA, NC	H	11.50 FQ	19.51 AW	27.15 TQ	NCBLS	10/01-12/01
	Hickory-Morganton-Lenoir MSA, NC	H	9.88 FQ	13.63 AW	18.86 TQ	NCBLS	10/01-12/01
	Raleigh-Durham-Chapel Hill MSA, NC	H	11.89 FQ	18.21 AW	26.00 TQ	NCBLS	10/01-12/01
	Wilmington MSA, NC	H	14.26 FQ	21.00 AW	27.08 TQ	NCBLS	10/01-12/01
	North Dakota	H	11.53 FQ	18.16 AW	25.32 TQ	NDBLS	10/01-12/01
	Fargo-Moorhead MSA, ND-MN	H	10.30 FQ	14.37 AW	18.28 TQ	NDBLS	10/01-12/01
	Ohio	H	13.50 FQ	21.03 AW	32.41 TQ	OHBLS	10/01-12/01
	Akron PMSA, OH	H	13.20 FQ	18.16 AW	24.64 TQ	OHBLS	10/01-12/01
	Canton-Massillon MSA, OH	H	12.60 FQ	18.44 AW	29.94 TQ	OHBLS	10/01-12/01
	Cincinnati PMSA, OH-KY-IN	H	14.14 FQ	20.28 AW	27.77 TQ	OHBLS	10/01-12/01
	Cleveland-Lorain-Elyria PMSA, OH	H	13.94 FQ	21.77 AW	33.74 TQ	OHBLS	10/01-12/01
	Columbus MSA, OH	H	11.51 FQ	17.54 AW	24.71 TQ	OHBLS	10/01-12/01
	Dayton-Springfield MSA, OH	H	12.40 FQ	23.09 AW	33.90 TQ	OHBLS	10/01-12/01
	Hamilton-Middletown PMSA, OH	H	12.70 FQ	17.91 AW	24.87 TQ	OHBLS	10/01-12/01
	Toledo MSA, OH	H	15.50 FQ	25.72 AW	35.48 TQ	OHBLS	10/01-12/01
	Youngstown-Warren MSA, OH	H	16.49 FQ	29.40 AW	35.56 TQ	OHBLS	10/01-12/01
	Oklahoma	H	10.35 FQ	15.82 AW	21.47 TQ	OKBLS	10/01-12/01
	Oklahoma City MSA, OK	H	10.91 FQ	16.25 AW	22.76 TQ	OKBLS	10/01-12/01
	Tulsa MSA, OK	H	10.68 FQ	16.09 AW	21.54 TQ	OKBLS	10/01-12/01
	Oregon	H	13.11 FQ	19.02 AW	26.17 TQ	ORBLS	10/01-12/01
	Eugene-Springfield MSA, OR	H	12.37 FQ	17.22 AW	21.68 TQ	ORBLS	10/01-12/01
	Medford-Ashland MSA, OR	H	14.20 FQ	18.53 AW	25.79 TQ	ORBLS	10/01-12/01
	Portland-Vancouver PMSA, OR-WA	H	15.09 FQ	21.02 AW	27.09 TQ	ORBLS	10/01-12/01
	Salem PMSA, OR	H	11.80 FQ	16.90 AW	22.66 TQ	ORBLS	10/01-12/01
	Pennsylvania	H	12.24 FQ	18.37 AW	26.02 TQ	PABLS	10/01-12/01
	Allentown-Bethlehem-Easton MSA, PA	H	10.38 FQ	16.23 AW	22.26 TQ	PABLS	10/01-12/01
	Erie MSA, PA	H	11.06 FQ	15.82 AW	20.98 TQ	PABLS	10/01-12/01
	Harrisburg-Lebanon-Carlisle MSA, PA	H	12.72 FQ	18.00 AW	24.46 TQ	PABLS	10/01-12/01
	Johnstown MSA, PA	H	9.45 FQ	15.95 AW	25.73 TQ	PABLS	10/01-12/01
	Lancaster MSA, PA	H	13.79 FQ	17.55 AW	21.35 TQ	PABLS	10/01-12/01
	Philadelphia PMSA, PA-NJ	H	13.77 FQ	19.38 AW	26.06 TQ	PABLS	10/01-12/01
	Pittsburgh MSA, PA	H	12.49 FQ	18.66 AW	26.94 TQ	PABLS	10/01-12/01
	Reading MSA, PA	H	12.44 FQ	17.12 AW	21.58 TQ	PABLS	10/01-12/01
	Scranton-Wilkes-Barre-Hazleton MSA, PA	H	10.24 FQ	16.73 AW	23.64 TQ	PABLS	10/01-12/01
	York MSA, PA	H	12.40 FQ	18.83 AW	29.23 TQ	PABLS	10/01-12/01
	Rhode Island	H	10.60 FQ	15.01 AW	20.37 TQ	RIBLS	10/01-12/01
	Providence-Fall River-Warwick MSA, RI-MA	H	11.08 FQ	15.24 AW	20.64 TQ	RIBLS	10/01-12/01
	South Carolina	H	11.80 FQ	17.50 AW	25.11 TQ	SCBLS	10/01-12/01
	Greenville-Spartanburg-Anderson MSA, SC	H	12.69 FQ	18.30 AW	25.41 TQ	SCBLS	10/01-12/01
	Myrtle Beach MSA, SC	H	8.63 FQ	13.76 AW	18.18 TQ	SCBLS	10/01-12/01
	South Dakota	H	11.40 FQ	14.61 AW	19.10 TQ	SDBLS	10/01-12/01
	Sioux Falls MSA, SD	H	11.56 FQ	14.88 AW	19.43 TQ	SDBLS	10/01-12/01
	Tennessee	H	11.91 FQ	17.14 AW	24.57 TQ	TNBLS	10/01-12/01
	Chattanooga MSA, TN-GA	H	11.67 FQ	16.27 AW	24.24 TQ	TNBLS	10/01-12/01
	Clarksville-Hopkinsville MSA, TN-KY	H	11.76 FQ	17.85 AW	21.38 TQ	TNBLS	10/01-12/01
	Johnson City-Kingsport-Bristol MSA, TN-VA	H	12.95 FQ	16.41 AW	20.11 TQ	TNBLS	10/01-12/01
	Knoxville MSA, TN	H	11.42 FQ	14.20 AW	19.60 TQ	TNBLS	10/01-12/01
	Memphis MSA, TN-AR-MS	H	13.87 FQ	19.14 AW	26.62 TQ	TNBLS	10/01-12/01
	Nashville MSA, TN	H	13.81 FQ	18.00 AW	22.12 TQ	TNBLS	10/01-12/01
	Texas	H	11.03 FQ	18.52 AW	26.69 TQ	TXBLS	10/01-12/01
	Amarillo MSA, TX	H	9.08 FQ	14.16 AW	21.62 TQ	TXBLS	10/01-12/01
	Austin-San Marcos MSA, TX	H	11.38 FQ	17.53 AW	25.35 TQ	TXBLS	10/01-12/01
	Beaumont-Port Arthur MSA, TX	H	17.20 FQ	23.91 AW	28.13 TQ	TXBLS	10/01-12/01
	Brazoria PMSA, TX	H	11.01 FQ	21.88 AW	28.37 TQ	TXBLS	10/01-12/01

AAW	Average annual wage	**AOH**	Average offered, high	**ASH**	Average starting, high	**H**	Hourly	**M**	Monthly	**S**	Special: hourly and annual
AE	Average entry wage	**AOL**	Average offered, low	**ASL**	Average starting, low	**HI**	Highest wage paid	**MTC**	Median total compensation	**TQ**	Third quartile wage
AEX	Average experienced wage	**APH**	Average pay, high range	**AW**	Average wage paid	**HR**	High end range	**MW**	Median wage paid	**W**	Weekly
AO	Average offered	**APL**	Average pay, low range	**FQ**	First quartile wage	**LR**	Low end range	**SQ**	Second quartile wage	**Y**	Yearly

Occupation/Type/Industry	Location	Per	Low	Mid	High	Source	Date
Industrial Machinery Mechanic	Brownsville-Harlingen-San Benito MSA, TX	H	9.02 FQ	13.99 AW	20.24 TQ	TXBLS	10/01-12/01
	Corpus Christi MSA, TX	H	10.04 FQ	17.76 AW	25.97 TQ	TXBLS	10/01-12/01
	Dallas PMSA, TX	H	11.92 FQ	17.60 AW	24.52 TQ	TXBLS	10/01-12/01
	El Paso MSA, TX	H	9.14 FQ	14.11 AW	20.72 TQ	TXBLS	10/01-12/01
	Fort Worth-Arlington PMSA, TX	H	11.18 FQ	17.73 AW	24.93 TQ	TXBLS	10/01-12/01
	Galveston-Texas City PMSA, TX	H	11.56 FQ	21.93 AW	28.04 TQ	TXBLS	10/01-12/01
	Houston PMSA, TX	H	11.85 FQ	19.81 AW	27.39 TQ	TXBLS	10/01-12/01
	Laredo MSA, TX	H	9.15 FQ	16.15 AW	22.12 TQ	TXBLS	10/01-12/01
	Longview-Marshall MSA, TX	H	9.59 FQ	15.22 AW	21.27 TQ	TXBLS	10/01-12/01
	Lubbock MSA, TX	H	8.16 FQ	15.67 AW	22.09 TQ	TXBLS	10/01-12/01
	McAllen-Edinburg-Mission MSA, TX	H	7.83 FQ	13.09 AW	21.23 TQ	TXBLS	10/01-12/01
	Odessa-Midland MSA, TX	H	9.33 FQ	17.62 AW	26.94 TQ	TXBLS	10/01-12/01
	San Antonio MSA, TX	H	11.28 FQ	15.65 AW	20.84 TQ	TXBLS	10/01-12/01
	Tyler MSA, TX	H	12.53 FQ	18.41 AW	24.60 TQ	TXBLS	10/01-12/01
	Waco MSA, TX	H	10.03 FQ	15.51 AW	20.76 TQ	TXBLS	10/01-12/01
	Utah	H	13.82 FQ	19.87 AW	26.92 TQ	UTBLS	10/01-12/01
	Provo-Orem MSA, UT	H	15.78 FQ	18.60 AW	21.25 TQ	UTBLS	10/01-12/01
	Salt Lake City-Ogden MSA, UT	H	13.69 FQ	19.81 AW	26.70 TQ	UTBLS	10/01-12/01
	Vermont	H	11.89 FQ	17.57 AW	25.39 TQ	VTBLS	10/01-12/01
	Burlington MSA, VT	H	12.72 FQ	17.75 AW	23.50 TQ	VTBLS	10/01-12/01
	Virginia	H	11.55 FQ	17.07 AW	24.67 TQ	VABLS	10/01-12/01
	Lynchburg MSA, VA	H	12.46 FQ	18.00 AW	25.34 TQ	VABLS	10/01-12/01
	Norfolk-Virginia Beach-Newport News MSA, VA-NC	H	12.42 FQ	16.41 AW	20.37 TQ	VABLS	10/01-12/01
	Richmond-Petersburg MSA, VA	H	13.91 FQ	20.09 AW	27.71 TQ	VABLS	10/01-12/01
	Roanoke MSA, VA	H	9.71 FQ	16.35 AW	22.62 TQ	VABLS	10/01-12/01
	Washington	H	14.39 FQ	20.33 AW	27.13 TQ	WABLS	10/01-12/01
	Bremerton PMSA, WA	H	11.84 FQ	18.14 AW	26.05 TQ	WABLS	10/01-12/01
	Olympia PMSA, WA	H	14.06 FQ	17.80 AW	21.44 TQ	WABLS	10/01-12/01
	Richland-Kennewick-Pasco MSA, WA	H	14.15 FQ	17.52 AW	24.73 TQ	WABLS	10/01-12/01
	Seattle-Bellevue-Everett PMSA, WA	H	15.39 FQ	21.24 AW	28.04 TQ	WABLS	10/01-12/01
	Spokane MSA, WA	H	13.17 FQ	18.33 AW	22.54 TQ	WABLS	10/01-12/01
	Tacoma PMSA, WA	H	15.68 FQ	21.61 AW	27.90 TQ	WABLS	10/01-12/01
	Yakima MSA, WA	H	14.41 FQ	17.89 AW	21.42 TQ	WABLS	10/01-12/01
	West Virginia	H	11.49 FQ	18.42 AW	24.10 TQ	WVBLS	10/01-12/01
	Charleston MSA, WV	H	14.47 FQ	20.66 AW	27.68 TQ	WVBLS	10/01-12/01
	Wisconsin	H	12.90 FQ	20.18 AW	28.77 TQ	WIBLS	10/01-12/01
	Appleton-Oshkosh-Neenah MSA, WI	H	16.52 FQ	21.25 AW	26.84 TQ	WIBLS	10/01-12/01
	Madison MSA, WI	H	14.22 FQ	19.90 AW	28.05 TQ	WIBLS	10/01-12/01
	Milwaukee-Waukesha PMSA, WI	H	11.85 FQ	21.78 AW	31.73 TQ	WIBLS	10/01-12/01
	Racine PMSA, WI	H	14.14 FQ	20.83 AW	27.93 TQ	WIBLS	10/01-12/01
	Wyoming	H	14.87 FQ	22.05 AW	27.57 TQ	WYBLS	10/01-12/01
	Puerto Rico	H	7.84 FQ	12.82 AW	17.77 TQ	PRBLS	10/01-12/01
	Virgin Islands	H	12.48 FQ	15.94 AW	20.52 TQ	VIBLS	10/01-12/01
Industrial-Organizational Psychologist	California	Y	41440 FQ	74070 AW	135370 TQ	CABLS	10/01-12/01
	Los Angeles-Long Beach PMSA, CA	Y	38720 FQ	62370 AW	77140 TQ	CABLS	10/01-12/01
	District of Columbia	Y	39150 FQ	69910 AW	115560 TQ	DCBLS	10/01-12/01
	Washington PMSA, DC-MD-VA-WV	Y	40420 FQ	70070 AW	111220 TQ	DCBLS	10/01-12/01
	Florida	Y	43820 FQ	66090 AW	87780 TQ	FLBLS	10/01-12/01
	West Palm Beach-Boca Raton MSA, FL	Y	58050 FQ	64390 AW	71280 TQ	FLBLS	10/01-12/01
	Michigan	Y	56250 FQ	82300 AW	116040 TQ	MIBLS	10/01-12/01
	Minneapolis-St. Paul MSA, MN-WI	Y	48270 FQ	76540 AW	114670 TQ	MNBLS	10/01-12/01
	New York	Y	31380 FQ	60830 AW	88240 TQ	NYBLS	10/01-12/01
	Texas	Y	43500 FQ	71190 AW	128640 TQ	TXBLS	10/01-12/01
	Virginia	Y	32640 FQ	61720 AW	94320 TQ	VABLS	10/01-12/01

AAW Average annual wage; **AE** Average entry wage; **AEX** Average experienced wage; **AO** Average offered; **AOH** Average offered, high; **AOL** Average offered, low; **APH** Average pay, high range; **APL** Average pay, low range; **ASH** Average starting, high; **ASL** Average starting, low; **AW** Average wage paid; **FQ** First quartile wage; **H** Hourly; **HI** Highest wage paid; **HR** High end range; **LR** Low end range; **M** Monthly; **MTC** Median total compensation; **MW** Median wage paid; **SQ** Second quartile wage; **S** Special: hourly and annual; **TQ** Third quartile wage; **W** Weekly; **Y** Yearly

Occupation/Type/Industry	Location	Per	Low	Mid	High	Source	Date
Industrial Production Manager	Alabama	Y	33490 FQ	60530 AW	94260 TQ	ALBLS	10/01-12/01
	Birmingham MSA, AL	Y	37250 FQ	60720 AW	89700 TQ	ALBLS	10/01-12/01
	Huntsville MSA, AL	Y	37150 FQ	66450 AW	108120 TQ	ALBLS	10/01-12/01
	Mobile MSA, AL	Y	38620 FQ	65650 AW	96060 TQ	ALBLS	10/01-12/01
	Montgomery MSA, AL	Y	28740 FQ	55340 AW	87280 TQ	ALBLS	10/01-12/01
	Alaska	Y	33120 FQ	61730 AW	112160 TQ	AKBLS	10/01-12/01
	Anchorage MSA, AK	Y	39280 FQ	68060 AW	128850 TQ	AKBLS	10/01-12/01
	Arizona	Y	39210 FQ	70050 AW	108090 TQ	AZBLS	10/01-12/01
	Phoenix-Mesa MSA, AZ	Y	41650 FQ	71200 AW	107790 TQ	AZBLS	10/01-12/01
	Tucson MSA, AZ	Y	39670 FQ	73730 AW	119110 TQ	AZBLS	10/01-12/01
	Arkansas	Y	34750 FQ	61540 AW	96580 TQ	ARBLS	10/01-12/01
	Fayetteville-Springdale-Rogers MSA, AR	Y	34070 FQ	68460 AW	111420 TQ	ARBLS	10/01-12/01
	Fort Smith MSA, AR-OK	Y	36620 FQ	57160 AW	90980 TQ	ARBLS	10/01-12/01
	Little Rock-North Little Rock MSA, AR	Y	35580 FQ	62790 AW	94820 TQ	ARBLS	10/01-12/01
	California	Y	41650 FQ	75030 AW	119030 TQ	CABLS	10/01-12/01
	Bakersfield MSA, CA	Y	37850 FQ	77220 AW	117880 TQ	CABLS	10/01-12/01
	Chico-Paradise MSA, CA	Y	26630 FQ	47720 AW	77070 TQ	CABLS	10/01-12/01
	Fresno MSA, CA	Y	44080 FQ	64430 AW	88370 TQ	CABLS	10/01-12/01
	Los Angeles-Long Beach PMSA, CA	Y	40280 FQ	70090 AW	108880 TQ	CABLS	10/01-12/01
	Merced MSA, CA	Y	42310 FQ	65260 AW	91780 TQ	CABLS	10/01-12/01
	Modesto MSA, CA	Y	39610 FQ	63920 AW	90230 TQ	CABLS	10/01-12/01
	Oakland PMSA, CA	Y	50090 FQ	86060 AW	137520 TQ	CABLS	10/01-12/01
	Orange County PMSA, CA	Y	45230 FQ	74920 AW	115240 TQ	CABLS	10/01-12/01
	Riverside-San Bernardino PMSA, CA	Y	37730 FQ	65760 AW	104710 TQ	CABLS	10/01-12/01
	Sacramento PMSA, CA	Y	38290 FQ	70600 AW	109060 TQ	CABLS	10/01-12/01
	Salinas MSA, CA	Y	37340 FQ	72200 AW	112710 TQ	CABLS	10/01-12/01
	San Diego MSA, CA	Y	37150 FQ	70720 AW	112330 TQ	CABLS	10/01-12/01
	San Francisco PMSA, CA	Y	42120 FQ	74430 AW	118850 TQ	CABLS	10/01-12/01
	San Jose PMSA, CA	Y	58680 FQ	95910 AW		CABLS	10/01-12/01
	San Luis Obispo-Atascadero-Paso Robles MSA, CA	Y	38740 FQ	68140 AW	106230 TQ	CABLS	10/01-12/01
	Santa Barbara-Santa Maria-Lompoc MSA, CA	Y	44390 FQ	75830 AW	118150 TQ	CABLS	10/01-12/01
	Santa Cruz-Watsonville PMSA, CA	Y	47930 FQ	78710 AW	136310 TQ	CABLS	10/01-12/01
	Santa Rosa PMSA, CA	Y	39750 FQ	79940 AW		CABLS	10/01-12/01
	Stockton-Lodi MSA, CA	Y	38410 FQ	62590 AW	90150 TQ	CABLS	10/01-12/01
	Vallejo-Fairfield-Napa PMSA, CA	Y	43700 FQ	80580 AW		CABLS	10/01-12/01
	Ventura PMSA, CA	Y	41570 FQ	73720 AW	110450 TQ	CABLS	10/01-12/01
	Visalia-Tulare-Porterville MSA, CA	Y	32920 FQ	61700 AW	95190 TQ	CABLS	10/01-12/01
	Colorado	Y	38210 FQ	68660 AW	111780 TQ	COBLS	10/01-12/01
	Boulder-Longmont PMSA, CO	Y	49630 FQ	84190 AW	134620 TQ	COBLS	10/01-12/01
	Colorado Springs MSA, CO	Y	36710 FQ	73990 AW	119030 TQ	COBLS	10/01-12/01
	Denver PMSA, CO	Y	38060 FQ	65910 AW	104040 TQ	COBLS	10/01-12/01
	Fort Collins-Loveland MSA, CO	Y	39220 FQ	69610 AW	113050 TQ	COBLS	10/01-12/01
	Greeley PMSA, CO	Y	40640 FQ	59290 AW	84740 TQ	COBLS	10/01-12/01
	Connecticut	Y	47660 FQ	80380 AW	133220 TQ	CTBLS	10/01-12/01
	Bridgeport PMSA, CT	Y	43570 FQ	75840 AW	133000 TQ	CTBLS	10/01-12/01
	Danbury PMSA, CT	Y	49300 FQ	75500 AW	114680 TQ	CTBLS	10/01-12/01
	Hartford MSA, CT	Y	49510 FQ	80710 AW	137930 TQ	CTBLS	10/01-12/01
	New Haven-Meriden PMSA, CT	Y	43390 FQ	76660 AW	125480 TQ	CTBLS	10/01-12/01
	New London-Norwich MSA, CT-RI	Y	57790 FQ	86500 AW	118750 TQ	CTBLS	10/01-12/01
	Stamford-Norwalk PMSA, CT	Y	51690 FQ	97260 AW		CTBLS	10/01-12/01
	Waterbury PMSA, CT	Y	49700 FQ	77500 AW	118550 TQ	CTBLS	10/01-12/01
	Delaware	Y	42490 FQ	77530 AW	123090 TQ	DEBLS	10/01-12/01
	Wilmington-Newark PMSA, DE-MD	Y	44870 FQ	81620 AW	133110 TQ	DEBLS	10/01-12/01
	District of Columbia	Y	40670 FQ	60490 AW	84760 TQ	DCBLS	10/01-12/01
	Washington PMSA, DC-MD-VA-WV	Y	40380 FQ	69740 AW	109070 TQ	DCBLS	10/01-12/01
	Florida	Y	36690 FQ	66060 AW	109220 TQ	FLBLS	10/01-12/01
	Daytona Beach MSA, FL	Y	33040 FQ	58810 AW	87720 TQ	FLBLS	10/01-12/01
	Fort Lauderdale PMSA, FL	Y	38330 FQ	67140 AW	110080 TQ	FLBLS	10/01-12/01

AAW	Average annual wage	**AOH**	Average offered, high	**ASH**	Average starting, high	**H**	Hourly	**M**	Monthly	**S**	Special: hourly and annual
AE	Average entry wage	**AOL**	Average offered, low	**ASL**	Average starting, low	**HI**	Highest wage paid	**MTC**	Median total compensation	**TQ**	Third quartile wage
AEX	Average experienced wage	**APH**	Average pay, high range	**AW**	Average wage paid	**HR**	High end range	**MW**	Median wage paid	**W**	Weekly
AO	Average offered	**APL**	Average pay, low range	**FQ**	First quartile wage	**LR**	Low end range	**SQ**	Second quartile wage	**Y**	Yearly

Occupation/Type/Industry	Location	Per	Low	Mid	High	Source	Date
Industrial Production Manager	Fort Myers-Cape Coral MSA, FL	Y	22800 FQ	68620 AW		FLBLS	10/01-12/01
	Fort Pierce-Port St. Lucie MSA, FL	Y	30010 FQ	66540 AW	134860 TQ	FLBLS	10/01-12/01
	Gainesville MSA, FL	Y	30860 FQ	65320 AW	99490 TQ	FLBLS	10/01-12/01
	Jacksonville MSA, FL	Y	34600 FQ	61530 AW	102120 TQ	FLBLS	10/01-12/01
	Lakeland-Winter Haven MSA, FL	Y	38430 FQ	62760 AW	96170 TQ	FLBLS	10/01-12/01
	Melbourne-Titusville-Palm Bay MSA, FL	Y	36650 FQ	62970 AW	100630 TQ	FLBLS	10/01-12/01
	Miami PMSA, FL	Y	32860 FQ	65700 AW	98740 TQ	FLBLS	10/01-12/01
	Ocala MSA, FL	Y	37490 FQ	60210 AW	98300 TQ	FLBLS	10/01-12/01
	Orlando MSA, FL	Y	38840 FQ	67380 AW	116020 TQ	FLBLS	10/01-12/01
	Pensacola MSA, FL	Y	30680 FQ	67510 AW	115260 TQ	FLBLS	10/01-12/01
	Sarasota-Bradenton MSA, FL	Y	37070 FQ	67190 AW	117250 TQ	FLBLS	10/01-12/01
	Tallahassee MSA, FL	Y	32930 FQ	60900 AW	108520 TQ	FLBLS	10/01-12/01
	Tampa-St. Petersburg-Clearwater MSA, FL	Y	38770 FQ	66850 AW	108630 TQ	FLBLS	10/01-12/01
	West Palm Beach-Boca Raton MSA, FL	Y	37890 FQ	78380 AW		FLBLS	10/01-12/01
	Georgia	Y	36610 FQ	61340 AW	93920 TQ	GABLS	10/01-12/01
	Atlanta MSA, GA	Y	37660 FQ	64390 AW	102620 TQ	GABLS	10/01-12/01
	Augusta-Aiken MSA, GA-SC	Y	38770 FQ	71790 AW	103170 TQ	GABLS	10/01-12/01
	Columbus MSA, GA-AL	Y	40450 FQ	58750 AW	83500 TQ	GABLS	10/01-12/01
	Macon MSA, GA	Y	38860 FQ	63900 AW	94330 TQ	GABLS	10/01-12/01
	Savannah MSA, GA	Y	38050 FQ	62520 AW	88610 TQ	GABLS	10/01-12/01
	Hawaii	Y	33390 FQ	58640 AW	95300 TQ	HIBLS	10/01-12/01
	Honolulu MSA, HI	Y	33900 FQ	59370 AW	96160 TQ	HIBLS	10/01-12/01
	Idaho	Y	28550 FQ	57150 AW	95850 TQ	IDBLS	10/01-12/01
	Boise City MSA, ID	Y	36680 FQ	63610 AW	103180 TQ	IDBLS	10/01-12/01
	Illinois	Y	37610 FQ	67790 AW	109240 TQ	ILBLS	10/01-12/01
	Champaign-Urbana MSA, IL	Y	32690 FQ	57390 AW	98110 TQ	ILBLS	10/01-12/01
	Chicago PMSA, IL	Y	39800 FQ	69120 AW	109240 TQ	ILBLS	10/01-12/01
	Rockford MSA, IL	Y	41110 FQ	66200 AW	93420 TQ	ILBLS	10/01-12/01
	Indiana	Y	38270 FQ	64190 AW	93390 TQ	INBLS	10/01-12/01
	Elkhart-Goshen MSA, IN	Y	35870 FQ	58890 AW	85510 TQ	INBLS	10/01-12/01
	Evansville-Henderson MSA, IN-KY	Y	36410 FQ	58690 AW	85730 TQ	INBLS	10/01-12/01
	Fort Wayne MSA, IN	Y	38400 FQ	60500 AW	89080 TQ	INBLS	10/01-12/01
	Gary PMSA, IN	Y	48260 FQ	73540 AW	106990 TQ	INBLS	10/01-12/01
	Indianapolis MSA, IN	Y	40150 FQ	65450 AW	94870 TQ	INBLS	10/01-12/01
	Lafayette MSA, IN	Y	50220 FQ	74000 AW	107900 TQ	INBLS	10/01-12/01
	South Bend MSA, IN	Y	37190 FQ	57670 AW	80520 TQ	INBLS	10/01-12/01
	Iowa	Y	33540 FQ	61150 AW	95660 TQ	IABLS	10/01-12/01
	Cedar Rapids MSA, IA	Y	47430 FQ	73440 AW	107590 TQ	IABLS	10/01-12/01
	Davenport-Moline-Rock Island MSA, IA-IL	Y	33040 FQ	60340 AW	94190 TQ	IABLS	10/01-12/01
	Des Moines MSA, IA	Y	31660 FQ	60610 AW	92030 TQ	IABLS	10/01-12/01
	Kansas	Y	38260 FQ	68490 AW	108280 TQ	KSBLS	10/01-12/01
	Topeka MSA, KS	Y	39200 FQ	64380 AW	94100 TQ	KSBLS	10/01-12/01
	Wichita MSA, KS	Y	50200 FQ	79770 AW	114850 TQ	KSBLS	10/01-12/01
	Kentucky	Y	32790 FQ	62870 AW	99780 TQ	KYBLS	10/01-12/01
	Lexington MSA, KY	Y	40750 FQ	70490 AW	106930 TQ	KYBLS	10/01-12/01
	Louisville MSA, KY-IN	Y	35860 FQ	64390 AW	102080 TQ	KYBLS	10/01-12/01
	Louisiana	Y	34390 FQ	66310 AW	113870 TQ	LABLS	10/01-12/01
	Baton Rouge MSA, LA	Y	39040 FQ	70470 AW	111710 TQ	LABLS	10/01-12/01
	Houma MSA, LA	Y	35610 FQ	66050 AW	113910 TQ	LABLS	10/01-12/01
	Lafayette MSA, LA	Y	31520 FQ	51810 AW	81810 TQ	LABLS	10/01-12/01
	Lake Charles MSA, LA	Y	35770 FQ	74670 AW	114400 TQ	LABLS	10/01-12/01
	New Orleans MSA, LA	Y	38190 FQ	70840 AW	126480 TQ	LABLS	10/01-12/01
	Shreveport-Bossier City MSA, LA	Y	27280 FQ	54250 AW	88910 TQ	LABLS	10/01-12/01
	Maine	Y	31580 FQ	60610 AW	97990 TQ	MEBLS	10/01-12/01
	Portland MSA, ME	Y	31870 FQ	53060 AW	84130 TQ	MEBLS	10/01-12/01
	Maryland	Y	39030 FQ	67800 AW	106130 TQ	MDBLS	10/01-12/01
	Baltimore PMSA, MD	Y	39350 FQ	70560 AW	109660 TQ	MDBLS	10/01-12/01
	Massachusetts	Y	42990 FQ	73780 AW	113970 TQ	MABLS	10/01-12/01
	Boston PMSA, MA-NH	Y	47820 FQ	78500 AW	118770 TQ	MABLS	10/01-12/01
	Brockton PMSA, MA	Y	38870 FQ	64740 AW	101180 TQ	MABLS	10/01-12/01
	Lawrence PMSA, MA-NH	Y	40310 FQ	69280 AW	111100 TQ	MABLS	10/01-12/01
	Lowell PMSA, MA-NH	Y	37510 FQ	67660 AW	105460 TQ	MABLS	10/01-12/01
	New Bedford PMSA, MA	Y	47630 FQ	70660 AW	94340 TQ	MABLS	10/01-12/01

AAW	Average annual wage	AOH	Average offered, high	ASH	Average starting, high	H	Hourly	M	Monthly	S	Special: hourly and annual
AE	Average entry wage	AOL	Average offered, low	ASL	Average starting, low	HI	Highest wage paid	MTC	Median total compensation	TQ	Third quartile wage
AEX	Average experienced wage	APH	Average pay, high range	AW	Average wage paid	HR	High end range	MW	Median wage paid	W	Weekly
AO	Average offered	APL	Average pay, low range	FQ	First quartile wage	LR	Low end range	SQ	Second quartile wage	Y	Yearly

Occupation/Type/Industry	Location	Per	Low	Mid	High	Source	Date
Industrial Production Manager	Springfield MSA, MA	Y	39840 FQ	64310 AW	99840 TQ	MABLS	10/01-12/01
	Worcester PMSA, MA-CT	Y	39540 FQ	71350 AW	112920 TQ	MABLS	10/01-12/01
	Michigan	Y	45430 FQ	79750 AW	131020 TQ	MIBLS	10/01-12/01
	Ann Arbor PMSA, MI	Y	52360 FQ	81650 AW	118400 TQ	MIBLS	10/01-12/01
	Detroit PMSA, MI	Y	50030 FQ	85810 AW	138380 TQ	MIBLS	10/01-12/01
	Flint PMSA, MI	Y	63260 FQ	88740 AW	138390 TQ	MIBLS	10/01-12/01
	Grand Rapids-Muskegon-Holland MSA, MI	Y	45310 FQ	75400 AW	132790 TQ	MIBLS	10/01-12/01
	Kalamazoo-Battle Creek MSA, MI	Y	40800 FQ	77980 AW	131010 TQ	MIBLS	10/01-12/01
	Lansing-East Lansing MSA, MI	Y	45110 FQ	77140 AW	128070 TQ	MIBLS	10/01-12/01
	Saginaw-Bay City-Midland MSA, MI	Y	45380 FQ	78290 AW	117840 TQ	MIBLS	10/01-12/01
	Minnesota	Y	43120 FQ	72950 AW	116640 TQ	MNBLS	10/01-12/01
	Duluth-Superior MSA, MN-WI	Y	35300 FQ	64570 AW	99300 TQ	MNBLS	10/01-12/01
	Minneapolis-St. Paul MSA, MN-WI	Y	47590 FQ	77890 AW	121620 TQ	MNBLS	10/01-12/01
	St. Cloud MSA, MN	Y	33320 FQ	54140 AW	72630 TQ	MNBLS	10/01-12/01
	Mississippi	Y	32990 FQ	61150 AW	93370 TQ	MSBLS	10/01-12/01
	Jackson MSA, MS	Y	32420 FQ	54340 AW	80470 TQ	MSBLS	10/01-12/01
	Missouri	Y	31910 FQ	62620 AW	97580 TQ	MOBLS	10/01-12/01
	Kansas City MSA, MO-KS	Y	37080 FQ	68920 AW	110190 TQ	MOBLS	10/01-12/01
	St. Louis MSA, MO-IL	Y	37910 FQ	67680 AW	105730 TQ	MOBLS	10/01-12/01
	Springfield MSA, MO	Y	28300 FQ	49780 AW	84720 TQ	MOBLS	10/01-12/01
	Montana	Y	26610 FQ	48540 AW	75610 TQ	MTBLS	10/01-12/01
	Billings MSA, MT	Y	28830 FQ	56620 AW	122780 TQ	MTBLS	10/01-12/01
	Nebraska	Y	34480 FQ	60810 AW	94290 TQ	NEBLS	10/01-12/01
	Lincoln MSA, NE	Y	37030 FQ	63550 AW	99040 TQ	NEBLS	10/01-12/01
	Omaha MSA, NE-IA	Y	36700 FQ	64680 AW	97050 TQ	NEBLS	10/01-12/01
	Nevada	Y	38530 FQ	64560 AW	96600 TQ	NVBLS	10/01-12/01
	Las Vegas MSA, NV-AZ	Y	37530 FQ	63620 AW	95430 TQ	NVBLS	10/01-12/01
	Reno MSA, NV	Y	37430 FQ	65390 AW	96490 TQ	NVBLS	10/01-12/01
	New Hampshire	Y	37680 FQ	68560 AW	108890 TQ	NHBLS	10/01-12/01
	Manchester PMSA, NH	Y	40830 FQ	71130 AW	120600 TQ	NHBLS	10/01-12/01
	Nashua PMSA, NH	Y	46080 FQ	77140 AW	123060 TQ	NHBLS	10/01-12/01
	Portsmouth-Rochester PMSA, NH-ME	Y	41320 FQ	69660 AW	104490 TQ	NHBLS	10/01-12/01
	New Jersey	Y	50650 FQ	84340 AW	137910 TQ	NJBLS	10/01-12/01
	Atlantic-Cape May PMSA, NJ	Y	50140 FQ	77200 AW	121830 TQ	NJBLS	10/01-12/01
	Bergen-Passaic PMSA, NJ	Y	52050 FQ	87510 AW		NJBLS	10/01-12/01
	Jersey City PMSA, NJ	Y	55160 FQ	89640 AW	142550 TQ	NJBLS	10/01-12/01
	Middlesex-Somerset-Hunterdon PMSA, NJ	Y	51370 FQ	83340 AW	122090 TQ	NJBLS	10/01-12/01
	Monmouth-Ocean PMSA, NJ	Y	47650 FQ	87980 AW		NJBLS	10/01-12/01
	Newark PMSA, NJ	Y	50880 FQ	86690 AW	141500 TQ	NJBLS	10/01-12/01
	Trenton PMSA, NJ	Y	50900 FQ	78260 AW	126400 TQ	NJBLS	10/01-12/01
	New Mexico	Y	33350 FQ	66670 AW	109060 TQ	NMBLS	10/01-12/01
	Albuquerque MSA, NM	Y	36970 FQ	73230 AW	112340 TQ	NMBLS	10/01-12/01
	Las Cruces MSA, NM	Y	29200 FQ	49460 AW	72000 TQ	NMBLS	10/01-12/01
	New York	Y	42230 FQ	78230 AW	141030 TQ	NYBLS	10/01-12/01
	Albany-Schenectady-Troy MSA, NY	Y	42440 FQ	71890 AW	111650 TQ	NYBLS	10/01-12/01
	Binghamton MSA, NY	Y	35120 FQ	66540 AW	102260 TQ	NYBLS	10/01-12/01
	Buffalo-Niagara Falls MSA, NY	Y	42270 FQ	73040 AW	112240 TQ	NYBLS	10/01-12/01
	Dutchess County PMSA, NY	Y	47180 FQ	81810 AW	128080 TQ	NYBLS	10/01-12/01
	Nassau-Suffolk PMSA, NY	Y	49240 FQ	80810 AW	144840 TQ	NYBLS	10/01-12/01
	New York PMSA, NY	Y	40740 FQ	88620 AW		NYBLS	10/01-12/01
	Newburgh PMSA, NY-PA	Y	45400 FQ	73930 AW	116090 TQ	NYBLS	10/01-12/01
	Rochester MSA, NY	Y	43260 FQ	73960 AW	110770 TQ	NYBLS	10/01-12/01
	Syracuse MSA, NY	Y	41140 FQ	66770 AW	93830 TQ	NYBLS	10/01-12/01
	Utica-Rome MSA, NY	Y	32840 FQ	55570 AW	82810 TQ	NYBLS	10/01-12/01
	North Carolina	Y	35220 FQ	64280 AW	105030 TQ	NCBLS	10/01-12/01
	Asheville MSA, NC	Y	36770 FQ	59160 AW	88790 TQ	NCBLS	10/01-12/01
	Charlotte-Gastonia-Rock Hill MSA, NC-SC	Y	39300 FQ	67110 AW	101180 TQ	NCBLS	10/01-12/01
	Fayetteville MSA, NC	Y	36870 FQ	55840 AW	85770 TQ	NCBLS	10/01-12/01
	Greensboro-Winston-Salem-High Point MSA, NC	Y	35460 FQ	63830 AW	106320 TQ	NCBLS	10/01-12/01
	Hickory-Morganton-Lenoir MSA, NC	Y	35110 FQ	56520 AW	87280 TQ	NCBLS	10/01-12/01

AAW	Average annual wage	**AOH**	Average offered, high	**ASH**	Average starting, high	**H**	Hourly	**M**	Monthly	**S**	Special: hourly and annual
AE	Average entry wage	**AOL**	Average offered, low	**ASL**	Average starting, low	**HI**	Highest wage paid	**MTC**	Median total compensation	**TQ**	Third quartile wage
AEX	Average experienced wage	**APH**	Average pay, high range	**AW**	Average wage paid	**HR**	High end range	**MW**	Median wage paid	**W**	Weekly
AO	Average offered	**APL**	Average pay, low range	**FQ**	First quartile wage	**LR**	Low end range	**SQ**	Second quartile wage	**Y**	Yearly

Occupation/Type/Industry	Location	Per	Low	Mid	High	Source	Date
Industrial Production Manager	Raleigh-Durham-Chapel Hill MSA, NC	Y	44730 FQ	82460 AW	130400 TQ	NCBLS	10/01-12/01
	Wilmington MSA, NC	Y	34470 FQ	67040 AW	97850 TQ	NCBLS	10/01-12/01
	North Dakota	Y	28810 FQ	49560 AW	81870 TQ	NDBLS	10/01-12/01
	Fargo-Moorhead MSA, ND-MN	Y	32560 FQ	56090 AW	94440 TQ	NDBLS	10/01-12/01
	Ohio	Y	38740 FQ	65660 AW	99660 TQ	OHBLS	10/01-12/01
	Akron PMSA, OH	Y	39850 FQ	65560 AW	100840 TQ	OHBLS	10/01-12/01
	Canton-Massillon MSA, OH	Y	37140 FQ	61070 AW	103020 TQ	OHBLS	10/01-12/01
	Cincinnati PMSA, OH-KY-IN	Y	40880 FQ	67610 AW	100110 TQ	OHBLS	10/01-12/01
	Cleveland-Lorain-Elyria PMSA, OH	Y	38480 FQ	64180 AW	98470 TQ	OHBLS	10/01-12/01
	Columbus MSA, OH	Y	40010 FQ	66210 AW	96970 TQ	OHBLS	10/01-12/01
	Dayton-Springfield MSA, OH	Y	39370 FQ	68660 AW	107370 TQ	OHBLS	10/01-12/01
	Hamilton-Middletown PMSA, OH	Y	43560 FQ	66770 AW	95790 TQ	OHBLS	10/01-12/01
	Mansfield MSA, OH	Y	41080 FQ	71110 AW	108150 TQ	OHBLS	10/01-12/01
	Toledo MSA, OH	Y	38170 FQ	66960 AW	104940 TQ	OHBLS	10/01-12/01
	Youngstown-Warren MSA, OH	Y	35910 FQ	68550 AW	99740 TQ	OHBLS	10/01-12/01
	Oklahoma	Y	31280 FQ	57360 AW	89900 TQ	OKBLS	10/01-12/01
	Oklahoma City MSA, OK	Y	29490 FQ	55150 AW	87980 TQ	OKBLS	10/01-12/01
	Tulsa MSA, OK	Y	34580 FQ	61190 AW	96540 TQ	OKBLS	10/01-12/01
	Oregon	Y	40660 FQ	69960 AW	109980 TQ	ORBLS	10/01-12/01
	Eugene-Springfield MSA, OR	Y	36800 FQ	65320 AW	110460 TQ	ORBLS	10/01-12/01
	Medford-Ashland MSA, OR	Y	33920 FQ	57590 AW	85630 TQ	ORBLS	10/01-12/01
	Portland-Vancouver PMSA, OR-WA	Y	41790 FQ	72050 AW	112790 TQ	ORBLS	10/01-12/01
	Salem PMSA, OR	Y	44090 FQ	73250 AW	118060 TQ	ORBLS	10/01-12/01
	Pennsylvania	Y	35270 FQ	63480 AW	96600 TQ	PABLS	10/01-12/01
	Allentown-Bethlehem-Easton MSA, PA	Y	37950 FQ	70760 AW	115560 TQ	PABLS	10/01-12/01
	Erie MSA, PA	Y	32460 FQ	54750 AW	80100 TQ	PABLS	10/01-12/01
	Harrisburg-Lebanon-Carlisle MSA, PA	Y	38800 FQ	71080 AW	113810 TQ	PABLS	10/01-12/01
	Johnstown MSA, PA	Y	24710 FQ	46920 AW	71250 TQ	PABLS	10/01-12/01
	Lancaster MSA, PA	Y	34870 FQ	65090 AW	101820 TQ	PABLS	10/01-12/01
	Philadelphia PMSA, PA-NJ	Y	40650 FQ	70660 AW	109320 TQ	PABLS	10/01-12/01
	Pittsburgh MSA, PA	Y	38820 FQ	62950 AW	91550 TQ	PABLS	10/01-12/01
	Reading MSA, PA	Y	39360 FQ	61550 AW	95570 TQ	PABLS	10/01-12/01
	Scranton-Wilkes-Barre-Hazleton MSA, PA	Y	35860 FQ	61910 AW	96990 TQ	PABLS	10/01-12/01
	York MSA, PA	Y	37000 FQ	66390 AW	100590 TQ	PABLS	10/01-12/01
	Rhode Island	Y	47630 FQ	78460 AW	122670 TQ	RIBLS	10/01-12/01
	Providence-Fall River-Warwick MSA, RI-MA	Y	44470 FQ	75910 AW	118170 TQ	RIBLS	10/01-12/01
	South Carolina	Y	32000 FQ	60070 AW	92310 TQ	SCBLS	10/01-12/01
	Charleston-North Charleston MSA, SC	Y	37150 FQ	62930 AW	97710 TQ	SCBLS	10/01-12/01
	Columbia MSA, SC	Y	32660 FQ	61110 AW	101660 TQ	SCBLS	10/01-12/01
	Greenville-Spartanburg-Anderson MSA, SC	Y	34200 FQ	59000 AW	88310 TQ	SCBLS	10/01-12/01
	Myrtle Beach MSA, SC	Y	28050 FQ	47890 AW	70540 TQ	SCBLS	10/01-12/01
	South Dakota	Y	44490 FQ	63810 AW	88890 TQ	SDBLS	10/01-12/01
	Sioux Falls MSA, SD	Y	47210 FQ	61370 AW	82220 TQ	SDBLS	10/01-12/01
	Tennessee	Y	31530 FQ	57680 AW	90240 TQ	TNBLS	10/01-12/01
	Chattanooga MSA, TN-GA	Y	38080 FQ	60100 AW	86670 TQ	TNBLS	10/01-12/01
	Clarksville-Hopkinsville MSA, TN-KY	Y	36200 FQ	57910 AW	87050 TQ	TNBLS	10/01-12/01
	Johnson City-Kingsport-Bristol MSA, TN-VA	Y	31270 FQ	59560 AW	90400 TQ	TNBLS	10/01-12/01
	Knoxville MSA, TN	Y	31670 FQ	59630 AW	90000 TQ	TNBLS	10/01-12/01
	Memphis MSA, TN-AR-MS	Y	30920 FQ	54900 AW	88390 TQ	TNBLS	10/01-12/01
	Nashville MSA, TN	Y	32930 FQ	59770 AW	93410 TQ	TNBLS	10/01-12/01
	Texas	Y	34650 FQ	67310 AW	110530 TQ	TXBLS	10/01-12/01
	Amarillo MSA, TX	Y	27380 FQ	60040 AW	102910 TQ	TXBLS	10/01-12/01
	Austin-San Marcos MSA, TX	Y	37470 FQ	69410 AW	106580 TQ	TXBLS	10/01-12/01
	Beaumont-Port Arthur MSA, TX	Y	33540 FQ	70210 AW	109020 TQ	TXBLS	10/01-12/01
	Brazoria PMSA, TX	Y	46560 FQ	68900 AW	97460 TQ	TXBLS	10/01-12/01
	Brownsville-Harlingen-San Benito MSA, TX	Y	30630 FQ	51360 AW	87140 TQ	TXBLS	10/01-12/01
	Corpus Christi MSA, TX	Y	28100 FQ	53230 AW	93190 TQ	TXBLS	10/01-12/01

AAW Average annual wage; AE Average entry wage; AEX Average experienced wage; AO Average offered; AOH Average offered, high; AOL Average offered, low; APH Average pay, high range; APL Average pay, low range; ASH Average starting, high; ASL Average starting, low; AW Average wage paid; FQ First quartile wage; H Hourly; HI Highest wage paid; HR High end range; LR Low end range; M Monthly; MTC Median total compensation; MW Median wage paid; SQ Second quartile wage; S Special: hourly and annual; TQ Third quartile wage; W Weekly; Y Yearly

Occupation/Type/Industry	Location	Per	Low	Mid	High	Source	Date
Industrial Production Manager	Dallas PMSA, TX	Y	36920 FQ	71940 AW	112930 TQ	TXBLS	10/01-12/01
	El Paso MSA, TX	Y	30170 FQ	53350 AW	84530 TQ	TXBLS	10/01-12/01
	Fort Worth-Arlington PMSA, TX	Y	36060 FQ	67090 AW	106150 TQ	TXBLS	10/01-12/01
	Galveston-Texas City PMSA, TX	Y	33560 FQ	64360 AW	93650 TQ	TXBLS	10/01-12/01
	Houston PMSA, TX	Y	39430 FQ	74330 AW	131710 TQ	TXBLS	10/01-12/01
	Killeen-Temple MSA, TX	Y	33820 FQ	60250 AW	85030 TQ	TXBLS	10/01-12/01
	Longview-Marshall MSA, TX	Y	33860 FQ	56310 AW	84440 TQ	TXBLS	10/01-12/01
	Lubbock MSA, TX	Y	33650 FQ	55160 AW	85530 TQ	TXBLS	10/01-12/01
	McAllen-Edinburg-Mission MSA, TX	Y	23580 FQ	52180 AW	81450 TQ	TXBLS	10/01-12/01
	Odessa-Midland MSA, TX	Y	32380 FQ	68250 AW	128530 TQ	TXBLS	10/01-12/01
	San Antonio MSA, TX	Y	28620 FQ	54580 AW	87550 TQ	TXBLS	10/01-12/01
	Tyler MSA, TX	Y	29950 FQ	53160 AW	82250 TQ	TXBLS	10/01-12/01
	Waco MSA, TX	Y	20820 FQ	50310 AW	86310 TQ	TXBLS	10/01-12/01
	Utah	Y	34780 FQ	61870 AW	96890 TQ	UTBLS	10/01-12/01
	Provo-Orem MSA, UT	Y	35700 FQ	61510 AW	92160 TQ	UTBLS	10/01-12/01
	Salt Lake City-Ogden MSA, UT	Y	36030 FQ	61010 AW	96420 TQ	UTBLS	10/01-12/01
	Vermont	Y	50580 FQ	80170 AW	127440 TQ	VTBLS	10/01-12/01
	Burlington MSA, VT	Y	55330 FQ	82520 AW	126010 TQ	VTBLS	10/01-12/01
	Virginia	Y	36550 FQ	65400 AW	99770 TQ	VABLS	10/01-12/01
	Lynchburg MSA, VA	Y	35410 FQ	61890 AW	94120 TQ	VABLS	10/01-12/01
	Norfolk-Virginia Beach-Newport News MSA, VA-NC	Y	36880 FQ	64440 AW	96300 TQ	VABLS	10/01-12/01
	Richmond-Petersburg MSA, VA	Y	40990 FQ	71690 AW	105460 TQ	VABLS	10/01-12/01
	Roanoke MSA, VA	Y	32570 FQ	57190 AW	83580 TQ	VABLS	10/01-12/01
	Washington	Y	44540 FQ	74170 AW	112200 TQ	WABLS	10/01-12/01
	Olympia PMSA, WA	Y	29700 FQ	63330 AW	101690 TQ	WABLS	10/01-12/01
	Richland-Kennewick-Pasco MSA, WA	Y	42040 FQ	71220 AW	101020 TQ	WABLS	10/01-12/01
	Seattle-Bellevue-Everett PMSA, WA	Y	47460 FQ	76520 AW	112970 TQ	WABLS	10/01-12/01
	Spokane MSA, WA	Y	40380 FQ	68060 AW	102910 TQ	WABLS	10/01-12/01
	Tacoma PMSA, WA	Y	41660 FQ	66700 AW	94930 TQ	WABLS	10/01-12/01
	Yakima MSA, WA	Y	35530 FQ	72340 AW	118520 TQ	WABLS	10/01-12/01
	West Virginia	Y	28620 FQ	55000 AW	88770 TQ	WVBLS	10/01-12/01
	Charleston MSA, WV	Y	31170 FQ	57210 AW	92800 TQ	WVBLS	10/01-12/01
	Huntington-Ashland MSA, WV-KY-OH	Y	36040 FQ	63020 AW	103710 TQ	WVBLS	10/01-12/01
	Wisconsin	Y	37820 FQ	63050 AW	92200 TQ	WIBLS	10/01-12/01
	Appleton-Oshkosh-Neenah MSA, WI	Y	38060 FQ	63870 AW	95480 TQ	WIBLS	10/01-12/01
	Green Bay MSA, WI	Y	38050 FQ	62020 AW	87070 TQ	WIBLS	10/01-12/01
	Madison MSA, WI	Y	38110 FQ	64250 AW	96720 TQ	WIBLS	10/01-12/01
	Milwaukee-Waukesha PMSA, WI	Y	41940 FQ	67050 AW	94250 TQ	WIBLS	10/01-12/01
	Racine PMSA, WI	Y	46530 FQ	67020 AW	93510 TQ	WIBLS	10/01-12/01
	Wyoming	Y	24890 FQ	62580 AW	103150 TQ	WYBLS	10/01-12/01
	Puerto Rico	Y	32250 FQ	71150 AW	113560 TQ	PRBLS	10/01-12/01
Industrial Truck and Tractor Operator	Alabama	H	8.01 FQ	12.06 AW	17.94 TQ	ALBLS	10/01-12/01
	Birmingham MSA, AL	H	8.79 FQ	13.02 AW	17.89 TQ	ALBLS	10/01-12/01
	Huntsville MSA, AL	H	7.55 FQ	13.10 AW	20.79 TQ	ALBLS	10/01-12/01
	Mobile MSA, AL	H	7.45 FQ	11.36 AW	16.36 TQ	ALBLS	10/01-12/01
	Montgomery MSA, AL	H	7.45 FQ	10.02 AW	12.91 TQ	ALBLS	10/01-12/01
	Alaska	H	10.45 FQ	16.57 AW	28.83 TQ	AKBLS	10/01-12/01
	Anchorage MSA, AK	H	10.79 FQ	16.86 AW	31.27 TQ	AKBLS	10/01-12/01
	Arizona	H	7.90 FQ	11.90 AW	16.96 TQ	AZBLS	10/01-12/01
	Phoenix-Mesa MSA, AZ	H	8.06 FQ	11.98 AW	16.91 TQ	AZBLS	10/01-12/01
	Tucson MSA, AZ	H	7.35 FQ	11.14 AW	16.33 TQ	AZBLS	10/01-12/01
	Arkansas	H	7.86 FQ	11.16 AW	15.43 TQ	ARBLS	10/01-12/01
	Fayetteville-Springdale-Rogers MSA, AR	H	8.67 FQ	11.53 AW	15.73 TQ	ARBLS	10/01-12/01
	Fort Smith MSA, AR-OK	H	8.00 FQ	11.78 AW	15.90 TQ	ARBLS	10/01-12/01
	Little Rock-North Little Rock MSA, AR	H	7.65 FQ	10.73 AW	15.41 TQ	ARBLS	10/01-12/01
	California	H	7.90 FQ	13.82 AW	21.32 TQ	CABLS	10/01-12/01

AAW	Average annual wage	**AOH**	Average offered, high	**ASH**	Average starting, high	**H**	Hourly	**M**	Monthly	**S**	Special: hourly and annual
AE	Average entry wage	**AOL**	Average offered, low	**ASL**	Average starting, low	**HI**	Highest wage paid	**MTC**	Median total compensation	**TQ**	Third quartile wage
AEX	Average experienced wage	**APH**	Average pay, high range	**AW**	Average wage paid	**HR**	High end range	**MW**	Median wage paid	**W**	Weekly
AO	Average offered	**APL**	Average pay, low range	**FQ**	First quartile wage	**LR**	Low end range	**SQ**	Second quartile wage	**Y**	Yearly

Occupation/Type/Industry	Location	Per	Low	Mid	High	Source	Date
Industrial Truck and Tractor Operator	Bakersfield MSA, CA	H	7.36 FQ	11.12 AW	16.92 TQ	CABLS	10/01-12/01
	Chico-Paradise MSA, CA	H	8.15 FQ	12.75 AW	17.23 TQ	CABLS	10/01-12/01
	Fresno MSA, CA	H	6.79 FQ	11.18 AW	16.87 TQ	CABLS	10/01-12/01
	Los Angeles-Long Beach PMSA, CA	H	7.61 FQ	13.65 AW	24.30 TQ	CABLS	10/01-12/01
	Merced MSA, CA	H	7.81 FQ	12.93 AW	19.04 TQ	CABLS	10/01-12/01
	Modesto MSA, CA	H	7.73 FQ	12.96 AW	17.87 TQ	CABLS	10/01-12/01
	Oakland PMSA, CA	H	8.52 FQ	15.91 AW	23.32 TQ	CABLS	10/01-12/01
	Orange County PMSA, CA	H	8.16 FQ	13.72 AW	20.45 TQ	CABLS	10/01-12/01
	Redding MSA, CA	H	9.26 FQ	15.56 AW	20.88 TQ	CABLS	10/01-12/01
	Riverside-San Bernardino PMSA, CA	H	8.59 FQ	13.11 AW	18.89 TQ	CABLS	10/01-12/01
	Sacramento PMSA, CA	H	8.93 FQ	14.58 AW	24.06 TQ	CABLS	10/01-12/01
	Salinas MSA, CA	H	8.76 FQ	13.93 AW	20.67 TQ	CABLS	10/01-12/01
	San Diego MSA, CA	H	8.33 FQ	13.93 AW	21.10 TQ	CABLS	10/01-12/01
	San Francisco PMSA, CA	H	10.05 FQ	16.75 AW	25.41 TQ	CABLS	10/01-12/01
	San Jose PMSA, CA	H	9.03 FQ	14.52 AW	20.14 TQ	CABLS	10/01-12/01
	San Luis Obispo-Atascadero-Paso Robles MSA, CA	H	8.29 FQ	12.74 AW	19.33 TQ	CABLS	10/01-12/01
	Santa Barbara-Santa Maria-Lompoc MSA, CA	H	7.81 FQ	13.56 AW	20.20 TQ	CABLS	10/01-12/01
	Santa Cruz-Watsonville PMSA, CA	H	9.12 FQ	13.47 AW	18.00 TQ	CABLS	10/01-12/01
	Santa Rosa PMSA, CA	H	9.45 FQ	13.44 AW	18.98 TQ	CABLS	10/01-12/01
	Stockton-Lodi MSA, CA	H	8.94 FQ	14.43 AW	20.91 TQ	CABLS	10/01-12/01
	Vallejo-Fairfield-Napa PMSA, CA	H	7.91 FQ	13.78 AW	20.79 TQ	CABLS	10/01-12/01
	Ventura PMSA, CA	H	8.72 FQ	15.18 AW	26.90 TQ	CABLS	10/01-12/01
	Visalia-Tulare-Porterville MSA, CA	H	7.07 FQ	11.10 AW	16.53 TQ	CABLS	10/01-12/01
	Colorado	H	8.98 FQ	12.62 AW	17.05 TQ	COBLS	10/01-12/01
	Boulder-Longmont PMSA, CO	H	8.72 FQ	12.54 AW	16.84 TQ	COBLS	10/01-12/01
	Colorado Springs MSA, CO	H	9.01 FQ	11.86 AW	16.17 TQ	COBLS	10/01-12/01
	Denver PMSA, CO	H	9.52 FQ	13.37 AW	17.48 TQ	COBLS	10/01-12/01
	Fort Collins-Loveland MSA, CO	H	8.73 FQ	12.23 AW	16.35 TQ	COBLS	10/01-12/01
	Greeley PMSA, CO	H	7.53 FQ	11.92 AW	17.61 TQ	COBLS	10/01-12/01
	Connecticut	H	9.54 FQ	14.11 AW	18.98 TQ	CTBLS	10/01-12/01
	Bridgeport PMSA, CT	H	9.60 FQ	13.91 AW	20.54 TQ	CTBLS	10/01-12/01
	Danbury PMSA, CT	H	9.15 FQ	12.99 AW	17.47 TQ	CTBLS	10/01-12/01
	Hartford MSA, CT	H	9.21 FQ	14.44 AW	21.02 TQ	CTBLS	10/01-12/01
	New Haven-Meriden PMSA, CT	H	10.30 FQ	14.23 AW	17.31 TQ	CTBLS	10/01-12/01
	New London-Norwich MSA, CT-RI	H	9.53 FQ	13.43 AW	18.25 TQ	CTBLS	10/01-12/01
	Stamford-Norwalk PMSA, CT	H	11.05 FQ	14.77 AW	17.82 TQ	CTBLS	10/01-12/01
	Waterbury PMSA, CT	H	9.49 FQ	13.84 AW	19.62 TQ	CTBLS	10/01-12/01
	Delaware	H	8.34 FQ	13.74 AW	20.40 TQ	DEBLS	10/01-12/01
	Wilmington-Newark PMSA, DE-MD	H	9.19 FQ	15.14 AW	21.57 TQ	DEBLS	10/01-12/01
	District of Columbia	H	9.25 FQ	14.71 AW	20.51 TQ	DCBLS	10/01-12/01
	Washington PMSA, DC-MD-VA-WV	H	9.47 FQ	14.36 AW	21.42 TQ	DCBLS	10/01-12/01
	Florida	H	7.70 FQ	11.47 AW	16.73 TQ	FLBLS	10/01-12/01
	Daytona Beach MSA, FL	H	8.12 FQ	11.11 AW	15.24 TQ	FLBLS	10/01-12/01
	Fort Lauderdale PMSA, FL	H	8.31 FQ	11.63 AW	16.49 TQ	FLBLS	10/01-12/01
	Fort Myers-Cape Coral MSA, FL	H	8.29 FQ	11.68 AW	16.33 TQ	FLBLS	10/01-12/01
	Fort Pierce-Port St. Lucie MSA, FL	H	7.89 FQ	10.96 AW	14.33 TQ	FLBLS	10/01-12/01
	Gainesville MSA, FL	H	7.82 FQ	10.42 AW	13.02 TQ	FLBLS	10/01-12/01
	Jacksonville MSA, FL	H	8.07 FQ	12.68 AW	17.90 TQ	FLBLS	10/01-12/01
	Lakeland-Winter Haven MSA, FL	H	7.43 FQ	10.99 AW	16.37 TQ	FLBLS	10/01-12/01
	Melbourne-Titusville-Palm Bay MSA, FL	H	8.54 FQ	10.98 AW	13.82 TQ	FLBLS	10/01-12/01
	Miami PMSA, FL	H	6.56 FQ	10.39 AW	16.04 TQ	FLBLS	10/01-12/01
	Naples MSA, FL	H	8.43 FQ	11.61 AW	15.80 TQ	FLBLS	10/01-12/01
	Ocala MSA, FL	H	8.08 FQ	12.75 AW	19.59 TQ	FLBLS	10/01-12/01
	Orlando MSA, FL	H	8.52 FQ	11.71 AW	16.25 TQ	FLBLS	10/01-12/01
	Pensacola MSA, FL	H	7.83 FQ	10.72 AW	14.70 TQ	FLBLS	10/01-12/01

AAW	Average annual wage	**AOH**	Average offered, high	**ASH**	Average starting, high	**H**	Hourly	**M**	Monthly	**S**	Special: hourly and annual
AE	Average entry wage	**AOL**	Average offered, low	**ASL**	Average starting, low	**HI**	Highest wage paid	**MTC**	Median total compensation	**TQ**	Third quartile wage
AEX	Average experienced wage	**APH**	Average pay, high range	**AW**	Average wage paid	**HR**	High end range	**MW**	Median wage paid	**W**	Weekly
AO	Average offered	**APL**	Average pay, low range	**FQ**	First quartile wage	**LR**	Low end range	**SQ**	Second quartile wage	**Y**	Yearly

Occupation/Type/Industry	Location	Per	Low	Mid	High	Source	Date
Industrial Truck and Tractor Operator	Sarasota-Bradenton MSA, FL	H	8.06 FQ	11.82 AW	16.99 TQ	FLBLS	10/01-12/01
	Tallahassee MSA, FL	H	7.60 FQ	11.44 AW	15.67 TQ	FLBLS	10/01-12/01
	Tampa-St. Petersburg-Clearwater MSA, FL	H	8.20 FQ	11.74 AW	16.85 TQ	FLBLS	10/01-12/01
	West Palm Beach-Boca Raton MSA, FL	H	7.68 FQ	11.34 AW	16.77 TQ	FLBLS	10/01-12/01
	Georgia	H	8.30 FQ	11.70 AW	16.38 TQ	GABLS	10/01-12/01
	Atlanta MSA, GA	H	8.79 FQ	12.00 AW	16.72 TQ	GABLS	10/01-12/01
	Augusta-Aiken MSA, GA-SC	H	8.08 FQ	11.42 AW	15.82 TQ	GABLS	10/01-12/01
	Columbus MSA, GA-AL	H	7.75 FQ	10.98 AW	13.76 TQ	GABLS	10/01-12/01
	Macon MSA, GA	H	7.97 FQ	12.28 AW	19.64 TQ	GABLS	10/01-12/01
	Savannah MSA, GA	H	8.72 FQ	13.79 AW	24.66 TQ	GABLS	10/01-12/01
	Hawaii	H	8.72 FQ	14.81 AW	26.20 TQ	HIBLS	10/01-12/01
	Honolulu MSA, HI	H	8.82 FQ	15.41 AW	28.64 TQ	HIBLS	10/01-12/01
	Idaho	H	7.86 FQ	11.66 AW	15.82 TQ	IDBLS	10/01-12/01
	Boise City MSA, ID	H	7.74 FQ	11.34 AW	15.06 TQ	IDBLS	10/01-12/01
	Illinois	H	9.18 FQ	13.80 AW	20.55 TQ	ILBLS	10/01-12/01
	Champaign-Urbana MSA, IL	H	9.38 FQ	13.19 AW	20.21 TQ	ILBLS	10/01-12/01
	Chicago PMSA, IL	H	9.30 FQ	14.30 AW	21.37 TQ	ILBLS	10/01-12/01
	Peoria-Pekin MSA, IL	H	9.21 FQ	12.35 AW	18.04 TQ	ILBLS	10/01-12/01
	Rockford MSA, IL	H	9.55 FQ	13.85 AW	18.23 TQ	ILBLS	10/01-12/01
	Springfield MSA, IL	H	8.71 FQ	13.04 AW	16.51 TQ	ILBLS	10/01-12/01
	Indiana	H	9.16 FQ	13.39 AW	19.76 TQ	INBLS	10/01-12/01
	Elkhart-Goshen MSA, IN	H	9.47 FQ	12.50 AW	16.06 TQ	INBLS	10/01-12/01
	Evansville-Henderson MSA, IN-KY	H	9.43 FQ	13.68 AW	18.78 TQ	INBLS	10/01-12/01
	Fort Wayne MSA, IN	H	9.28 FQ	13.40 AW	19.71 TQ	INBLS	10/01-12/01
	Gary PMSA, IN	H	10.52 FQ	15.59 AW	21.40 TQ	INBLS	10/01-12/01
	Indianapolis MSA, IN	H	9.43 FQ	13.89 AW	21.95 TQ	INBLS	10/01-12/01
	Lafayette MSA, IN	H	10.15 FQ	14.85 AW	20.58 TQ	INBLS	10/01-12/01
	South Bend MSA, IN	H	9.25 FQ	12.17 AW	16.10 TQ	INBLS	10/01-12/01
	Iowa	H	8.58 FQ	12.48 AW	17.44 TQ	IABLS	10/01-12/01
	Cedar Rapids MSA, IA	H	9.59 FQ	14.01 AW	19.58 TQ	IABLS	10/01-12/01
	Davenport-Moline-Rock Island MSA, IA-IL	H	8.12 FQ	12.47 AW	18.11 TQ	IABLS	10/01-12/01
	Des Moines MSA, IA	H	8.13 FQ	11.89 AW	16.57 TQ	IABLS	10/01-12/01
	Kansas	H	8.64 FQ	12.08 AW	16.35 TQ	KSBLS	10/01-12/01
	Topeka MSA, KS	H	9.88 FQ	13.09 AW	17.08 TQ	KSBLS	10/01-12/01
	Wichita MSA, KS	H	8.71 FQ	12.22 AW	17.09 TQ	KSBLS	10/01-12/01
	Kentucky	H	8.66 FQ	12.30 AW	17.02 TQ	KYBLS	10/01-12/01
	Lexington MSA, KY	H	8.74 FQ	12.35 AW	17.60 TQ	KYBLS	10/01-12/01
	Louisville MSA, KY-IN	H	8.98 FQ	12.59 AW	18.05 TQ	KYBLS	10/01-12/01
	Louisiana	H	7.52 FQ	11.47 AW	16.52 TQ	LABLS	10/01-12/01
	Baton Rouge MSA, LA	H	7.76 FQ	11.76 AW	16.98 TQ	LABLS	10/01-12/01
	Houma MSA, LA	H	8.55 FQ	15.73 AW	21.32 TQ	LABLS	10/01-12/01
	Lafayette MSA, LA	H	7.43 FQ	10.06 AW	13.28 TQ	LABLS	10/01-12/01
	Lake Charles MSA, LA	H	7.67 FQ	11.46 AW	18.20 TQ	LABLS	10/01-12/01
	New Orleans MSA, LA	H	7.71 FQ	11.95 AW	16.47 TQ	LABLS	10/01-12/01
	Shreveport-Bossier City MSA, LA	H	7.65 FQ	11.58 AW	16.38 TQ	LABLS	10/01-12/01
	Maine	H	8.55 FQ	12.23 AW	17.45 TQ	MEBLS	10/01-12/01
	Portland MSA, ME	H	9.07 FQ	12.73 AW	16.84 TQ	MEBLS	10/01-12/01
	Maryland	H	9.12 FQ	13.90 AW	20.67 TQ	MDBLS	10/01-12/01
	Baltimore PMSA, MD	H	9.19 FQ	14.13 AW	21.89 TQ	MDBLS	10/01-12/01
	Massachusetts	H	9.63 FQ	13.92 AW	19.31 TQ	MABLS	10/01-12/01
	Boston PMSA, MA-NH	H	9.69 FQ	13.92 AW	19.15 TQ	MABLS	10/01-12/01
	Brockton PMSA, MA	H	9.28 FQ	14.11 AW	21.10 TQ	MABLS	10/01-12/01
	Lawrence PMSA, MA-NH	H	9.55 FQ	12.74 AW	16.54 TQ	MABLS	10/01-12/01
	Lowell PMSA, MA-NH	H	10.27 FQ	13.61 AW	17.12 TQ	MABLS	10/01-12/01
	New Bedford PMSA, MA	H	8.85 FQ	13.26 AW	18.33 TQ	MABLS	10/01-12/01
	Springfield MSA, MA	H	9.22 FQ	13.37 AW	18.88 TQ	MABLS	10/01-12/01
	Worcester PMSA, MA-CT	H	9.93 FQ	15.78 AW	26.77 TQ	MABLS	10/01-12/01
	Michigan	H	9.72 FQ	16.90 AW	26.60 TQ	MIBLS	10/01-12/01
	Ann Arbor PMSA, MI	H	9.88 FQ	18.23 AW	27.20 TQ	MIBLS	10/01-12/01
	Detroit PMSA, MI	H	10.53 FQ	18.73 AW	27.11 TQ	MIBLS	10/01-12/01
	Flint PMSA, MI	H	11.04 FQ	22.34 AW	28.02 TQ	MIBLS	10/01-12/01
	Grand Rapids-Muskegon-Holland MSA, MI	H	9.85 FQ	14.15 AW	22.80 TQ	MIBLS	10/01-12/01
	Kalamazoo-Battle Creek MSA, MI	H	9.13 FQ	14.40 AW	25.30 TQ	MIBLS	10/01-12/01
	Lansing-East Lansing MSA, MI	H	9.52 FQ	17.71 AW	26.47 TQ	MIBLS	10/01-12/01

AAW Average annual wage **AOH** Average offered, high **ASH** Average starting, high **H** Hourly **M** Monthly **S** Special: hourly and annual
AE Average entry wage **AOL** Average offered, low **ASL** Average starting, low **HI** Highest wage paid **MTC** Median total compensation **TQ** Third quartile wage
AEX Average experienced wage **APH** Average pay, high range **AW** Average wage paid **HR** High end range **MW** Median wage paid **W** Weekly
AO Average offered **APL** Average pay, low range **FQ** First quartile wage **LR** Low end range **SQ** Second quartile wage **Y** Yearly

Occupation/Type/Industry	Location	Per	Low	Mid	High	Source	Date
Industrial Truck and Tractor Operator	Saginaw-Bay City-Midland MSA, MI	H	9.47 FQ	17.96 AW	26.55 TQ	MIBLS	10/01-12/01
	Minnesota	H	9.93 FQ	14.25 AW	19.31 TQ	MNBLS	10/01-12/01
	Duluth-Superior MSA, MN-WI	H	9.68 FQ	15.32 AW	21.02 TQ	MNBLS	10/01-12/01
	Minneapolis-St. Paul MSA, MN-WI	H	10.97 FQ	15.17 AW	20.15 TQ	MNBLS	10/01-12/01
	St. Cloud MSA, MN	H	9.16 FQ	12.65 AW	17.16 TQ	MNBLS	10/01-12/01
	Mississippi	H	7.79 FQ	10.92 AW	14.05 TQ	MSBLS	10/01-12/01
	Biloxi-Gulfport-Pascagoula MSA, MS	H	7.52 FQ	11.90 AW	19.10 TQ	MSBLS	10/01-12/01
	Jackson MSA, MS	H	7.96 FQ	10.92 AW	14.53 TQ	MSBLS	10/01-12/01
	Missouri	H	7.83 FQ	12.11 AW	17.41 TQ	MOBLS	10/01-12/01
	Kansas City MSA, MO-KS	H	9.39 FQ	13.08 AW	18.26 TQ	MOBLS	10/01-12/01
	St. Louis MSA, MO-IL	H	8.49 FQ	13.19 AW	19.56 TQ	MOBLS	10/01-12/01
	Springfield MSA, MO	H	8.20 FQ	11.44 AW	14.82 TQ	MOBLS	10/01-12/01
	Montana	H	7.45 FQ	11.92 AW	16.73 TQ	MTBLS	10/01-12/01
	Billings MSA, MT	H	8.13 FQ	11.60 AW	16.33 TQ	MTBLS	10/01-12/01
	Nebraska	H	9.18 FQ	12.43 AW	16.59 TQ	NEBLS	10/01-12/01
	Lincoln MSA, NE	H	9.58 FQ	12.23 AW	14.97 TQ	NEBLS	10/01-12/01
	Omaha MSA, NE-IA	H	9.21 FQ	12.66 AW	16.99 TQ	NEBLS	10/01-12/01
	Nevada	H	8.27 FQ	14.20 AW	21.32 TQ	NVBLS	10/01-12/01
	Las Vegas MSA, NV-AZ	H	9.45 FQ	14.94 AW	21.05 TQ	NVBLS	10/01-12/01
	Reno MSA, NV	H	7.68 FQ	13.42 AW	24.43 TQ	NVBLS	10/01-12/01
	New Hampshire	H	8.65 FQ	12.29 AW	16.49 TQ	NHBLS	10/01-12/01
	Manchester PMSA, NH	H	10.08 FQ	13.87 AW	16.94 TQ	NHBLS	10/01-12/01
	Nashua PMSA, NH	H	9.68 FQ	12.93 AW	16.84 TQ	NHBLS	10/01-12/01
	Portsmouth-Rochester PMSA, NH-ME	H	9.37 FQ	12.71 AW	16.33 TQ	NHBLS	10/01-12/01
	New Jersey	H	8.92 FQ	13.78 AW	20.26 TQ	NJBLS	10/01-12/01
	Atlantic-Cape May PMSA, NJ	H	8.86 FQ	12.79 AW	18.42 TQ	NJBLS	10/01-12/01
	Bergen-Passaic PMSA, NJ	H	8.71 FQ	13.75 AW	19.75 TQ	NJBLS	10/01-12/01
	Jersey City PMSA, NJ	H	8.73 FQ	13.37 AW	20.11 TQ	NJBLS	10/01-12/01
	Middlesex-Somerset-Hunterdon PMSA, NJ	H	8.73 FQ	14.23 AW	21.28 TQ	NJBLS	10/01-12/01
	Monmouth-Ocean PMSA, NJ	H	9.03 FQ	13.86 AW	22.29 TQ	NJBLS	10/01-12/01
	Newark PMSA, NJ	H	8.93 FQ	13.72 AW	20.43 TQ	NJBLS	10/01-12/01
	Trenton PMSA, NJ	H	9.14 FQ	14.18 AW	20.28 TQ	NJBLS	10/01-12/01
	New Mexico	H	7.51 FQ	11.49 AW	15.82 TQ	NMBLS	10/01-12/01
	Albuquerque MSA, NM	H	8.26 FQ	11.99 AW	15.72 TQ	NMBLS	10/01-12/01
	Las Cruces MSA, NM	H	6.92 FQ	10.15 AW	13.89 TQ	NMBLS	10/01-12/01
	New York	H	8.86 FQ	14.06 AW	21.04 TQ	NYBLS	10/01-12/01
	Albany-Schenectady-Troy MSA, NY	H	9.04 FQ	13.69 AW	20.08 TQ	NYBLS	10/01-12/01
	Binghamton MSA, NY	H	9.39 FQ	12.84 AW	16.57 TQ	NYBLS	10/01-12/01
	Buffalo-Niagara Falls MSA, NY	H	9.08 FQ	15.71 AW	25.05 TQ	NYBLS	10/01-12/01
	Dutchess County PMSA, NY	H	9.24 FQ	14.30 AW	23.37 TQ	NYBLS	10/01-12/01
	Nassau-Suffolk PMSA, NY	H	9.53 FQ	15.05 AW	20.80 TQ	NYBLS	10/01-12/01
	New York PMSA, NY	H	8.63 FQ	13.86 AW	20.97 TQ	NYBLS	10/01-12/01
	Newburgh PMSA, NY-PA	H	10.80 FQ	17.28 AW	22.16 TQ	NYBLS	10/01-12/01
	Rochester MSA, NY	H	9.01 FQ	13.32 AW	18.77 TQ	NYBLS	10/01-12/01
	Syracuse MSA, NY	H	8.72 FQ	14.72 AW	24.86 TQ	NYBLS	10/01-12/01
	Utica-Rome MSA, NY	H	7.25 FQ	11.15 AW	15.15 TQ	NYBLS	10/01-12/01
	North Carolina	H	8.42 FQ	11.97 AW	16.91 TQ	NCBLS	10/01-12/01
	Asheville MSA, NC	H	7.98 FQ	11.79 AW	15.93 TQ	NCBLS	10/01-12/01
	Charlotte-Gastonia-Rock Hill MSA, NC-SC	H	9.25 FQ	13.39 AW	19.22 TQ	NCBLS	10/01-12/01
	Fayetteville MSA, NC	H	7.22 FQ	10.09 AW	13.93 TQ	NCBLS	10/01-12/01
	Greensboro-Winston-Salem-High Point MSA, NC	H	8.99 FQ	12.54 AW	18.61 TQ	NCBLS	10/01-12/01
	Hickory-Morganton-Lenoir MSA, NC	H	8.91 FQ	11.51 AW	15.27 TQ	NCBLS	10/01-12/01
	Raleigh-Durham-Chapel Hill MSA, NC	H	8.88 FQ	11.18 AW	14.19 TQ	NCBLS	10/01-12/01
	Wilmington MSA, NC	H	8.13 FQ	13.60 AW	17.33 TQ	NCBLS	10/01-12/01
	North Dakota	H	7.74 FQ	11.55 AW	16.13 TQ	NDBLS	10/01-12/01
	Fargo-Moorhead MSA, ND-MN	H	7.79 FQ	11.42 AW	15.87 TQ	NDBLS	10/01-12/01
	Ohio	H	9.22 FQ	13.70 AW	20.30 TQ	OHBLS	10/01-12/01
	Akron PMSA, OH	H	9.47 FQ	14.11 AW	19.91 TQ	OHBLS	10/01-12/01
	Canton-Massillon MSA, OH	H	9.54 FQ	14.64 AW	21.53 TQ	OHBLS	10/01-12/01

AAW	Average annual wage	**AOH**	Average offered, high	**ASH**	Average starting, high	**H**	Hourly	**M**	Monthly	**S**	Special: hourly and annual
AE	Average entry wage	**AOL**	Average offered, low	**ASL**	Average starting, low	**HI**	Highest wage paid	**MTC**	Median total compensation	**TQ**	Third quartile wage
AEX	Average experienced wage	**APH**	Average pay, high range	**AW**	Average wage paid	**HR**	High end range	**MW**	Median wage paid	**W**	Weekly
AO	Average offered	**APL**	Average pay, low range	**FQ**	First quartile wage	**LR**	Low end range	**SQ**	Second quartile wage	**Y**	Yearly

Occupation/Type/Industry	Location	Per	Low	Mid	High	Source	Date
Industrial Truck and Tractor Operator	Cincinnati PMSA, OH-KY-IN	H	9.40 FQ	12.97 AW	17.49 TQ	OHBLS	10/01-12/01
	Cleveland-Lorain-Elyria PMSA, OH	H	9.22 FQ	14.25 AW	22.25 TQ	OHBLS	10/01-12/01
	Columbus MSA, OH	H	9.45 FQ	12.65 AW	16.54 TQ	OHBLS	10/01-12/01
	Dayton-Springfield MSA, OH	H	8.86 FQ	13.89 AW	21.77 TQ	OHBLS	10/01-12/01
	Hamilton-Middletown PMSA, OH	H	9.21 FQ	12.85 AW	16.85 TQ	OHBLS	10/01-12/01
	Mansfield MSA, OH	H	8.86 FQ	16.58 AW	27.48 TQ	OHBLS	10/01-12/01
	Toledo MSA, OH	H	9.65 FQ	15.45 AW	24.49 TQ	OHBLS	10/01-12/01
	Youngstown-Warren MSA, OH	H	8.56 FQ	16.13 AW	26.73 TQ	OHBLS	10/01-12/01
	Oklahoma	H	7.82 FQ	11.58 AW	16.70 TQ	OKBLS	10/01-12/01
	Oklahoma City MSA, OK	H	7.88 FQ	11.25 AW	14.52 TQ	OKBLS	10/01-12/01
	Tulsa MSA, OK	H	8.10 FQ	12.01 AW	16.90 TQ	OKBLS	10/01-12/01
	Oregon	H	8.73 FQ	13.14 AW	17.62 TQ	ORBLS	10/01-12/01
	Eugene-Springfield MSA, OR	H	9.06 FQ	12.50 AW	16.50 TQ	ORBLS	10/01-12/01
	Medford-Ashland MSA, OR	H	9.16 FQ	12.20 AW	15.99 TQ	ORBLS	10/01-12/01
	Portland-Vancouver PMSA, OR-WA	H	9.46 FQ	14.24 AW	19.60 TQ	ORBLS	10/01-12/01
	Salem PMSA, OR	H	7.74 FQ	11.40 AW	16.01 TQ	ORBLS	10/01-12/01
	Pennsylvania	H	9.05 FQ	13.34 AW	18.65 TQ	PABLS	10/01-12/01
	Allentown-Bethlehem-Easton MSA, PA	H	9.53 FQ	12.56 AW	16.37 TQ	PABLS	10/01-12/01
	Erie MSA, PA	H	9.20 FQ	12.88 AW	17.12 TQ	PABLS	10/01-12/01
	Harrisburg-Lebanon-Carlisle MSA, PA	H	9.34 FQ	13.34 AW	19.08 TQ	PABLS	10/01-12/01
	Johnstown MSA, PA	H	8.58 FQ	11.48 AW	15.17 TQ	PABLS	10/01-12/01
	Lancaster MSA, PA	H	10.02 FQ	13.41 AW	17.11 TQ	PABLS	10/01-12/01
	Philadelphia PMSA, PA-NJ	H	9.31 FQ	14.04 AW	20.16 TQ	PABLS	10/01-12/01
	Pittsburgh MSA, PA	H	8.97 FQ	14.60 AW	20.83 TQ	PABLS	10/01-12/01
	Reading MSA, PA	H	9.34 FQ	12.75 AW	16.43 TQ	PABLS	10/01-12/01
	Scranton-Wilkes-Barre-Hazleton MSA, PA	H	8.12 FQ	12.52 AW	17.06 TQ	PABLS	10/01-12/01
	York MSA, PA	H	9.36 FQ	12.37 AW	15.99 TQ	PABLS	10/01-12/01
	Rhode Island	H	8.77 FQ	12.26 AW	16.29 TQ	RIBLS	10/01-12/01
	Providence-Fall River-Warwick MSA, RI-MA	H	9.01 FQ	12.74 AW	16.67 TQ	RIBLS	10/01-12/01
	South Carolina	H	8.64 FQ	11.64 AW	15.48 TQ	SCBLS	10/01-12/01
	Charleston-North Charleston MSA, SC	H	8.14 FQ	11.15 AW	14.33 TQ	SCBLS	10/01-12/01
	Columbia MSA, SC	H	8.84 FQ	12.01 AW	16.21 TQ	SCBLS	10/01-12/01
	Greenville-Spartanburg-Anderson MSA, SC	H	9.08 FQ	12.23 AW	16.31 TQ	SCBLS	10/01-12/01
	Myrtle Beach MSA, SC	H	8.34 FQ	11.34 AW	14.20 TQ	SCBLS	10/01-12/01
	South Dakota	H	8.95 FQ	11.73 AW	15.24 TQ	SDBLS	10/01-12/01
	Sioux Falls MSA, SD	H	9.61 FQ	12.40 AW	15.89 TQ	SDBLS	10/01-12/01
	Tennessee	H	8.83 FQ	12.15 AW	16.66 TQ	TNBLS	10/01-12/01
	Chattanooga MSA, TN-GA	H	9.21 FQ	12.26 AW	16.43 TQ	TNBLS	10/01-12/01
	Clarksville-Hopkinsville MSA, TN-KY	H	7.95 FQ	11.60 AW	16.13 TQ	TNBLS	10/01-12/01
	Johnson City-Kingsport-Bristol MSA, TN-VA	H	8.63 FQ	11.40 AW	14.46 TQ	TNBLS	10/01-12/01
	Knoxville MSA, TN	H	8.39 FQ	12.13 AW	16.65 TQ	TNBLS	10/01-12/01
	Memphis MSA, TN-AR-MS	H	9.14 FQ	11.85 AW	16.27 TQ	TNBLS	10/01-12/01
	Nashville MSA, TN	H	9.37 FQ	13.20 AW	17.63 TQ	TNBLS	10/01-12/01
	Texas	H	7.49 FQ	11.05 AW	15.41 TQ	TXBLS	10/01-12/01
	Amarillo MSA, TX	H	7.91 FQ	11.37 AW	16.09 TQ	TXBLS	10/01-12/01
	Austin-San Marcos MSA, TX	H	7.56 FQ	10.80 AW	14.27 TQ	TXBLS	10/01-12/01
	Beaumont-Port Arthur MSA, TX	H	7.71 FQ	11.72 AW	16.08 TQ	TXBLS	10/01-12/01
	Brazoria PMSA, TX	H	8.27 FQ	11.56 AW	15.55 TQ	TXBLS	10/01-12/01
	Brownsville-Harlingen-San Benito MSA, TX	H	5.98 FQ	8.03 AW	10.62 TQ	TXBLS	10/01-12/01
	Corpus Christi MSA, TX	H	7.18 FQ	9.92 AW	13.52 TQ	TXBLS	10/01-12/01
	Dallas PMSA, TX	H	8.35 FQ	11.47 AW	15.25 TQ	TXBLS	10/01-12/01
	El Paso MSA, TX	H	6.44 FQ	9.04 AW	11.68 TQ	TXBLS	10/01-12/01
	Fort Worth-Arlington PMSA, TX	H	8.32 FQ	11.21 AW	15.50 TQ	TXBLS	10/01-12/01
	Galveston-Texas City PMSA, TX	H	8.82 FQ	11.84 AW	15.78 TQ	TXBLS	10/01-12/01
	Houston PMSA, TX	H	7.84 FQ	11.20 AW	16.07 TQ	TXBLS	10/01-12/01
	Killeen-Temple MSA, TX	H	7.00 FQ	10.76 AW	14.62 TQ	TXBLS	10/01-12/01

AAW	Average annual wage	**AOH**	Average offered, high	**ASH**	Average starting, high	**H**	Hourly	**M**	Monthly	**S**	Special: hourly and annual
AE	Average entry wage	**AOL**	Average offered, low	**ASL**	Average starting, low	**HI**	Highest wage paid	**MTC**	Median total compensation	**TQ**	Third quartile wage
AEX	Average experienced wage	**APH**	Average pay, high range	**AW**	Average wage paid	**HR**	High end range	**MW**	Median wage paid	**W**	Weekly
AO	Average offered	**APL**	Average pay, low range	**FQ**	First quartile wage	**LR**	Low end range	**SQ**	Second quartile wage	**Y**	Yearly

Occupation/Type/Industry	Location	Per	Low	Mid	High	Source	Date
Industrial Truck and Tractor Operator	Laredo MSA, TX	H	5.83 FQ	7.96 AW	10.92 TQ	TXBLS	10/01-12/01
	Longview-Marshall MSA, TX	H	7.60 FQ	10.39 AW	13.37 TQ	TXBLS	10/01-12/01
	Lubbock MSA, TX	H	6.81 FQ	9.88 AW	13.32 TQ	TXBLS	10/01-12/01
	McAllen-Edinburg-Mission MSA, TX	H	5.70 FQ	8.06 AW	11.07 TQ	TXBLS	10/01-12/01
	Odessa-Midland MSA, TX	H	7.28 FQ	13.20 AW	20.41 TQ	TXBLS	10/01-12/01
	San Antonio MSA, TX	H	7.66 FQ	10.83 AW	14.16 TQ	TXBLS	10/01-12/01
	Tyler MSA, TX	H	7.65 FQ	11.39 AW	16.40 TQ	TXBLS	10/01-12/01
	Waco MSA, TX	H	8.67 FQ	11.12 AW	14.05 TQ	TXBLS	10/01-12/01
	Utah	H	8.70 FQ	11.86 AW	16.00 TQ	UTBLS	10/01-12/01
	Provo-Orem MSA, UT	H	9.01 FQ	12.79 AW	17.09 TQ	UTBLS	10/01-12/01
	Salt Lake City-Ogden MSA, UT	H	8.67 FQ	11.77 AW	15.92 TQ	UTBLS	10/01-12/01
	Vermont	H	9.19 FQ	14.05 AW	22.64 TQ	VTBLS	10/01-12/01
	Burlington MSA, VT	H	9.76 FQ	12.68 AW	16.29 TQ	VTBLS	10/01-12/01
	Virginia	H	8.64 FQ	12.61 AW	17.60 TQ	VABLS	10/01-12/01
	Lynchburg MSA, VA	H	8.92 FQ	12.60 AW	17.12 TQ	VABLS	10/01-12/01
	Norfolk-Virginia Beach-Newport News MSA, VA-NC	H	8.66 FQ	13.08 AW	18.06 TQ	VABLS	10/01-12/01
	Richmond-Petersburg MSA, VA	H	8.87 FQ	13.11 AW	19.07 TQ	VABLS	10/01-12/01
	Roanoke MSA, VA	H	8.91 FQ	11.76 AW	14.26 TQ	VABLS	10/01-12/01
	Washington	H	9.19 FQ	14.26 AW	20.41 TQ	WABLS	10/01-12/01
	Bremerton PMSA, WA	H	9.30 FQ	13.33 AW	17.31 TQ	WABLS	10/01-12/01
	Olympia PMSA, WA	H	9.24 FQ	12.57 AW	16.81 TQ	WABLS	10/01-12/01
	Richland-Kennewick-Pasco MSA, WA	H	8.41 FQ	11.87 AW	15.16 TQ	WABLS	10/01-12/01
	Seattle-Bellevue-Everett PMSA, WA	H	9.90 FQ	15.12 AW	21.05 TQ	WABLS	10/01-12/01
	Spokane MSA, WA	H	9.04 FQ	12.99 AW	18.68 TQ	WABLS	10/01-12/01
	Tacoma PMSA, WA	H	10.59 FQ	16.31 AW	25.01 TQ	WABLS	10/01-12/01
	Yakima MSA, WA	H	8.06 FQ	11.48 AW	15.84 TQ	WABLS	10/01-12/01
	West Virginia	H	8.02 FQ	13.82 AW	22.42 TQ	WVBLS	10/01-12/01
	Charleston MSA, WV	H	8.42 FQ	13.55 AW	22.02 TQ	WVBLS	10/01-12/01
	Huntington-Ashland MSA, WV-KY-OH	H	6.52 FQ	11.66 AW	17.69 TQ	WVBLS	10/01-12/01
	Wisconsin	H	9.49 FQ	13.41 AW	18.32 TQ	WIBLS	10/01-12/01
	Appleton-Oshkosh-Neenah MSA, WI	H	9.78 FQ	14.44 AW	19.61 TQ	WIBLS	10/01-12/01
	Green Bay MSA, WI	H	9.66 FQ	14.11 AW	20.38 TQ	WIBLS	10/01-12/01
	Madison MSA, WI	H	9.04 FQ	13.30 AW	18.53 TQ	WIBLS	10/01-12/01
	Milwaukee-Waukesha PMSA, WI	H	9.49 FQ	14.13 AW	21.12 TQ	WIBLS	10/01-12/01
	Racine PMSA, WI	H	8.65 FQ	11.41 AW	14.14 TQ	WIBLS	10/01-12/01
	Wyoming	H	9.16 FQ	16.56 AW	25.52 TQ	WYBLS	10/01-12/01
	Cheyenne MSA, WY	H	7.66 FQ	10.93 AW	14.95 TQ	WYBLS	10/01-12/01
	Puerto Rico	H	5.72 FQ	8.39 AW	12.59 TQ	PRBLS	10/01-12/01
	Virgin Islands	H	8.11 FQ	12.23 AW	17.27 TQ	VIBLS	10/01-12/01
	Guam	H	7.13 FQ	10.32 AW	14.33 TQ	GUBLS	10/01-12/01
Information Technologist	United States	Y		49258 AW		ACC	1/99-1/00
	San Jose, CA	Y		85150 AW		ITNA	1/99-1/00
	Seattle, WA	Y		129300 AW		ITNA	1/99-1/00
County Government	United States	Y		46452 AW		ACC	1/99-1/00
County Government	Midwest	Y		42442 AW		ACC	1/99-1/00
County Government	South	Y		48294 AW		ACC	1/99-1/00
Health	Middle Atlantic	Y		101458 AW		USWIRE	1/01-1/02
Health	New England	Y		100076 AW		USWIRE	1/01-1/02
Health	Pacific	Y		97960 AW		USWIRE	1/01-1/02
Municipal Government	United States	Y		47759 AW		ACC	1/99-1/00
Information Technology Business Analyst	United States	Y		65063 AW		INFO4	1/00-1/01
Information Technology Employee G-5							
Federal Government	Los Angeles-Riverside-Orange County CMSA, CA	Y	33991 AE			OPM11	2003
Federal Government	San Diego MSA, CA	Y	32819 AE			OPM9	2003

AAW Average annual wage; AE Average entry wage; AEX Average experienced wage; AO Average offered; AOH Average offered, high; AOL Average offered, low; APH Average pay, high range; APL Average pay, low range; ASH Average starting, high; ASL Average starting, low; AW Average wage paid; FQ First quartile wage; H Hourly; HI Highest wage paid; HR High end range; LR Low end range; M Monthly; MTC Median total compensation; MW Median wage paid; SQ Second quartile wage; S Special: hourly and annual; TQ Third quartile wage; W Weekly; Y Yearly

Occupation/Type/Industry	Location	Per	Low	Mid	High	Source	Date
Information Technology Employee G-5							
Federal Government	San Francisco-Oakland-San Jose CMSA, CA	Y	34929 AE			OPM12	2003
Federal Government	Detroit-Ann Arbor-Flint CMSA, MI	Y	33522 AE			OPM10	2003
Federal Government	Milwaukee-Racine CMSA, WI	Y	32350 AE			OPM8	2003
Information Technology Employee G-7							
Federal Government	Miami-Fort Lauderdale CMSA, FL	Y	39200 AE			OPM9	2003
Federal Government	Atlanta MSA, GA	Y	38619 AE			OPM8	2003
Federal Government	Chicago-Gary-Kenosha CMSA, IL-IN-WI	Y	40071 AE			OPM10	2003
Federal Government	New York-Northern New Jersey-Long Island CMSA, NY-NJ-CT-PA	Y	40652 AE			OPM11	2003
Information Technology Employee G-9							
Federal Government	Sacramento-Yolo CMSA, CA	Y	46175 AE			OPM9	2003
Federal Government	Hartford MSA, CT	Y	47240 AE			OPM10	2003
Federal Government	Dayton-Springfield MSA, OH	Y	46175 AE			OPM8	2003
Information Technology Employee G-11							
Federal Government	Boston-Worcester-Lawrence CMSA, MA-NH-ME-CT-RI	Y	52860 AE			OPM10	2003
Federal Government	Philadelphia-Wilmington-Atlantic City CMSA, PA-NJ-DE-MD	Y	51571 AE			OPM9	2003
Federal Government	Richmond-Petersburg MSA, VA	Y	50712 AE			OPM8	2003
Information Technology Employee G-12							
Federal Government	Denver-Boulder-Greeley CMSA, CO	Y	60779 AE			OPM10	2003
Federal Government	Columbus MSA, OH	Y	59234 AE			OPM9	2003
Federal Government	Pittsburgh MSA, PA	Y	58204 AE			OPM8	2003
Information Technology Employee G-13							
Federal Government	Kansas City MSA, MO-KS	Y	63089 AE			OPM8	2003
Federal Government	Cincinnati-Hamilton CMSA, OH-KY-IN	Y	64314 AE			OPM9	2003
Information Technology Professional G-5							
Federal Government	San Diego MSA, CA	Y	32819 AE			OPM	2003
Information Technology Professional G-7							
Federal Government	Miami-Fort Lauderdale CMSA, FL	Y	39200 AE			OPM	2003
Information Technology Professional G-9							
Federal Government	Sacramento-Yolo CMSA, CA	Y	46175 AE			OPM	2003
Information Technology Professional G-11							
Federal Government	Philadelphia-Wilmington-Atlantic City MSA, PA-NJ-DE-MD	Y	51571 AE			OPM	2003
Information Technology Professional G-12							
Federal Government	Columbus MSA, OH	Y	59234 AE			OPM	2003

AAW	Average annual wage	AOH	Average offered, high	ASH	Average starting, high	H	Hourly	M	Monthly	S	Special: hourly and annual
AE	Average entry wage	AOL	Average offered, low	ASL	Average starting, low	HI	Highest wage paid	MTC	Median total compensation	TQ	Third quartile wage
AEX	Average experienced wage	APH	Average pay, high range	AW	Average wage paid	HR	High end range	MW	Median wage paid	W	Weekly
AO	Average offered	APL	Average pay, low range	FQ	First quartile wage	LR	Low end range	SQ	Second quartile wage	Y	Yearly

Occupation/Type/Industry	Location	Per	Low	Mid	High	Source	Date
Information Technology Professional G-13							
Federal Government	Cincinnati-Hamilton MSA, OH-KY-IN	Y	64314 AE			OPM	2003
Inspector, Tester, Sorter, Sampler, and Weigher	Alabama	H	7.10 FQ	12.63 AW	21.13 TQ	ALBLS	10/01-12/01
	Alaska	H	7.65 FQ	20.89 AW	38.79 TQ	AKBLS	10/01-12/01
	Arizona	H	7.42 FQ	13.47 AW	21.38 TQ	AZBLS	10/01-12/01
	Arkansas	H	7.51 FQ	11.70 AW	17.43 TQ	ARBLS	10/01-12/01
	California	H	6.83 FQ	13.39 AW	22.80 TQ	CABLS	10/01-12/01
	Colorado	H	8.30 FQ	13.75 AW	20.95 TQ	COBLS	10/01-12/01
	Connecticut	H	8.87 FQ	15.48 AW	23.02 TQ	CTBLS	10/01-12/01
	Delaware	H	9.49 FQ	16.00 AW	24.90 TQ	DEBLS	10/01-12/01
	District of Columbia	H	12.74 FQ	20.74 AW	29.79 TQ	DCBLS	10/01-12/01
	Florida	H	7.26 FQ	12.56 AW	20.45 TQ	FLBLS	10/01-12/01
	Georgia	H	7.64 FQ	12.25 AW	19.04 TQ	GABLS	10/01-12/01
	Hawaii	H	6.68 FQ	18.59 AW	31.20 TQ	HIBLS	10/01-12/01
	Idaho	H	7.21 FQ	13.52 AW	22.23 TQ	IDBLS	10/01-12/01
	Illinois	H	7.77 FQ	13.61 AW	21.57 TQ	ILBLS	10/01-12/01
	Indiana	H	8.64 FQ	14.85 AW	23.74 TQ	INBLS	10/01-12/01
	Iowa	H	8.93 FQ	14.56 AW	20.96 TQ	IABLS	10/01-12/01
	Kansas	H	9.07 FQ	15.30 AW	23.05 TQ	KSBLS	10/01-12/01
	Kentucky	H	7.91 FQ	13.82 AW	22.45 TQ	KYBLS	10/01-12/01
	Louisiana	H	7.61 FQ	15.75 AW	25.39 TQ	LABLS	10/01-12/01
	Maine	H	7.33 FQ	12.94 AW	20.42 TQ	MEBLS	10/01-12/01
	Maryland	H	7.54 FQ	14.34 AW	22.97 TQ	MDBLS	10/01-12/01
	Massachusetts	H	8.78 FQ	15.38 AW	23.05 TQ	MABLS	10/01-12/01
	Michigan	H	8.82 FQ	17.65 AW	27.29 TQ	MIBLS	10/01-12/01
	Minnesota	H	9.70 FQ	15.15 AW	22.34 TQ	MNBLS	10/01-12/01
	Mississippi	H	7.35 FQ	12.69 AW	20.38 TQ	MSBLS	10/01-12/01
	Missouri	H	8.47 FQ	15.07 AW	25.89 TQ	MOBLS	10/01-12/01
	Montana	H	6.39 FQ	14.04 AW	24.11 TQ	MTBLS	10/01-12/01
	Nebraska	H	8.66 FQ	13.23 AW	20.42 TQ	NEBLS	10/01-12/01
	Nevada	H	7.50 FQ	13.77 AW	21.10 TQ	NVBLS	10/01-12/01
	New Hampshire	H	9.03 FQ	13.70 AW	19.97 TQ	NHBLS	10/01-12/01
	New Jersey	H	8.57 FQ	15.35 AW	24.73 TQ	NJBLS	10/01-12/01
	New Mexico	H	5.72 FQ	12.05 AW	20.30 TQ	NMBLS	10/01-12/01
	New York	H	7.30 FQ	13.97 AW	24.24 TQ	NYBLS	10/01-12/01
	North Carolina	H	7.52 FQ	11.64 AW	16.95 TQ	NCBLS	10/01-12/01
	North Dakota	H	7.23 FQ	12.64 AW	22.42 TQ	NDBLS	10/01-12/01
	Ohio	H	8.63 FQ	15.15 AW	24.34 TQ	OHBLS	10/01-12/01
	Oklahoma	H	8.13 FQ	15.09 AW	21.92 TQ	OKBLS	10/01-12/01
	Oregon	H	8.56 FQ	14.24 AW	21.14 TQ	ORBLS	10/01-12/01
	Pennsylvania	H	8.37 FQ	14.20 AW	21.44 TQ	PABLS	10/01-12/01
	Rhode Island	H	7.46 FQ	12.29 AW	17.69 TQ	RIBLS	10/01-12/01
	South Carolina	H	7.78 FQ	12.93 AW	19.88 TQ	SCBLS	10/01-12/01
	South Dakota	H	7.89 FQ	11.73 AW	16.05 TQ	SDBLS	10/01-12/01
	Tennessee	H	7.91 FQ	12.67 AW	19.25 TQ	TNBLS	10/01-12/01
	Texas	H	7.00 FQ	13.87 AW	22.33 TQ	TXBLS	10/01-12/01
	Utah	H	7.96 FQ	14.05 AW	23.01 TQ	UTBLS	10/01-12/01
	Vermont	H	8.95 FQ	14.01 AW	20.21 TQ	VTBLS	10/01-12/01
	Virginia	H	8.10 FQ	14.15 AW	23.96 TQ	VABLS	10/01-12/01
	Washington	H	7.70 FQ	14.65 AW	24.14 TQ	WABLS	10/01-12/01
	West Virginia	H	6.51 FQ	13.81 AW	21.50 TQ	WVBLS	10/01-12/01
	Wisconsin	H	8.10 FQ	13.95 AW	21.29 TQ	WIBLS	10/01-12/01
	Wyoming	H	8.40 FQ	14.90 AW	22.08 TQ	WYBLS	10/01-12/01
	Puerto Rico	H	5.91 FQ	9.95 AW	15.98 TQ	PRBLS	10/01-12/01
	Virgin Islands	H	9.72 FQ	13.82 AW	16.88 TQ	VIBLS	10/01-12/01
	Guam	H	5.84 FQ	11.46 AW	18.35 TQ	GUBLS	10/01-12/01
Instructional Coordinator	Alabama	Y	25080 FQ	46050 AW	68500 TQ	ALBLS	10/01-12/01
	Alaska	Y	29170 FQ	47980 AW	73860 TQ	AKBLS	10/01-12/01
	Arizona	Y	24000 FQ	40710 AW	61070 TQ	AZBLS	10/01-12/01
	Arkansas	Y	19780 FQ	40740 AW	63090 TQ	ARBLS	10/01-12/01
	California	Y	27920 FQ	56090 AW	84810 TQ	CABLS	10/01-12/01
	Colorado	Y	23990 FQ	50570 AW	102450 TQ	COBLS	10/01-12/01
	Connecticut	Y	32000 FQ	56900 AW	87900 TQ	CTBLS	10/01-12/01
	Delaware	Y	25150 FQ	46720 AW	81920 TQ	DEBLS	10/01-12/01
	District of Columbia	Y	27990 FQ	47400 AW	79670 TQ	DCBLS	10/01-12/01
	Florida	Y	27370 FQ	49580 AW	81310 TQ	FLBLS	10/01-12/01
	Georgia	Y	25390 FQ	44790 AW	69120 TQ	GABLS	10/01-12/01

AAW Average annual wage	**AOH** Average offered, high	**ASH** Average starting, high	**H** Hourly	**M** Monthly	**S** Special: hourly and annual
AE Average entry wage	**AOL** Average offered, low	**ASL** Average starting, low	**HI** Highest wage paid	**MTC** Median total compensation	**TQ** Third quartile wage
AEX Average experienced wage	**APH** Average pay, high range	**AW** Average wage paid	**HR** High end range	**MW** Median wage paid	**W** Weekly
AO Average offered	**APL** Average pay, low range	**FQ** First quartile wage	**LR** Low end range	**SQ** Second quartile wage	**Y** Yearly

Occupation/Type/Industry	Location	Per	Low	Mid	High	Source	Date
Instructional Coordinator	Hawaii	Y	27030 FQ	44170 AW	71200 TQ	HIBLS	10/01-12/01
	Idaho	Y	18540 FQ	31920 AW	51510 TQ	IDBLS	10/01-12/01
	Illinois	Y	24020 FQ	46400 AW	78400 TQ	ILBLS	10/01-12/01
	Indiana	Y	23510 FQ	50340 AW	81800 TQ	INBLS	10/01-12/01
	Iowa	Y	21410 FQ	41880 AW	61220 TQ	IABLS	10/01-12/01
	Kansas	Y	25940 FQ	48230 AW	69370 TQ	KSBLS	10/01-12/01
	Kentucky	Y	26800 FQ	45800 AW	69370 TQ	KYBLS	10/01-12/01
	Louisiana	Y	21870 FQ	38910 AW	55960 TQ	LABLS	10/01-12/01
	Maine	Y	30470 FQ	45280 AW	62810 TQ	MEBLS	10/01-12/01
	Maryland	Y	25240 FQ	43250 AW	71270 TQ	MDBLS	10/01-12/01
	Massachusetts	Y	28050 FQ	54180 AW	80880 TQ	MABLS	10/01-12/01
	Michigan	Y	31470 FQ	54560 AW	83460 TQ	MIBLS	10/01-12/01
	Minnesota	Y	30380 FQ	49070 AW	69930 TQ	MNBLS	10/01-12/01
	Mississippi	Y	25230 FQ	40440 AW	57070 TQ	MSBLS	10/01-12/01
	Missouri	Y	22690 FQ	42960 AW	68780 TQ	MOBLS	10/01-12/01
	Montana	Y	12260 FQ	25880 AW	54830 TQ	MTBLS	10/01-12/01
	Nebraska	Y	23050 FQ	45390 AW	71930 TQ	NEBLS	10/01-12/01
	Nevada	Y	26100 FQ	49170 AW	73770 TQ	NVBLS	10/01-12/01
	New Hampshire	Y	26750 FQ	48040 AW	64100 TQ	NHBLS	10/01-12/01
	New Jersey	Y	27850 FQ	58590 AW	90300 TQ	NJBLS	10/01-12/01
	New Mexico	Y	25340 FQ	42380 AW	64230 TQ	NMBLS	10/01-12/01
	New York	Y	25170 FQ	53240 AW	88570 TQ	NYBLS	10/01-12/01
	North Carolina	Y	26090 FQ	44490 AW	66340 TQ	NCBLS	10/01-12/01
	North Dakota	Y	31400 FQ	50300 AW	70230 TQ	NDBLS	10/01-12/01
	Ohio	Y	25590 FQ	47330 AW	71030 TQ	OHBLS	10/01-12/01
	Oklahoma	Y	24670 FQ	40370 AW	59550 TQ	OKBLS	10/01-12/01
	Oregon	Y	30370 FQ	49230 AW	73370 TQ	ORBLS	10/01-12/01
	Pennsylvania	Y	24320 FQ	42340 AW	66800 TQ	PABLS	10/01-12/01
	Rhode Island	Y	17430 FQ	47040 AW	76900 TQ	RIBLS	10/01-12/01
	South Carolina	Y	21460 FQ	46840 AW	75890 TQ	SCBLS	10/01-12/01
	South Dakota	Y	29110 FQ	40980 AW	55540 TQ	SDBLS	10/01-12/01
	Tennessee	Y	22820 FQ	37510 AW	55730 TQ	TNBLS	10/01-12/01
	Texas	Y	33310 FQ	52340 AW	71460 TQ	TXBLS	10/01-12/01
	Utah	Y	20220 FQ	33630 AW	55360 TQ	UTBLS	10/01-12/01
	Vermont	Y	25120 FQ	41180 AW	55890 TQ	VTBLS	10/01-12/01
	Virginia	Y	24830 FQ	51110 AW	77110 TQ	VABLS	10/01-12/01
	Washington	Y	28340 FQ	46960 AW	69140 TQ	WABLS	10/01-12/01
	West Virginia	Y	21500 FQ	44590 AW	61560 TQ	WVBLS	10/01-12/01
	Wisconsin	Y	22710 FQ	46700 AW	73350 TQ	WIBLS	10/01-12/01
	Wyoming	Y	33430 FQ	47060 AW	65670 TQ	WYBLS	10/01-12/01
	Puerto Rico	Y	15590 FQ	22810 AW	30150 TQ	PRBLS	10/01-12/01
	Virgin Islands	Y	44500 FQ	57550 AW	73190 TQ	VIBLS	10/01-12/01
	Guam	Y	17330 FQ	36120 AW	55660 TQ	GUBLS	10/01-12/01
Insulation Worker	Alabama	H	7.36 FQ	12.98 AW	19.24 TQ	ALBLS	10/01-12/01
	Alaska	H	12.36 FQ	19.68 AW	26.77 TQ	AKBLS	10/01-12/01
	Arizona	H	7.25 FQ	12.50 AW	21.74 TQ	AZBLS	10/01-12/01
	Arkansas	H	7.51 FQ	10.33 AW	13.61 TQ	ARBLS	10/01-12/01
	California	H	8.78 FQ	18.25 AW	32.06 TQ	CABLS	10/01-12/01
	Colorado	H	7.96 FQ	13.30 AW	20.87 TQ	COBLS	10/01-12/01
	Connecticut	H	8.80 FQ	14.67 AW	23.60 TQ	CTBLS	10/01-12/01
	Delaware	H	8.17 FQ	14.50 AW	22.22 TQ	DEBLS	10/01-12/01
	Florida	H	6.94 FQ	13.54 AW	21.89 TQ	FLBLS	10/01-12/01
	Georgia	H	7.27 FQ	10.50 AW	15.69 TQ	GABLS	10/01-12/01
	Hawaii	H	14.44 FQ	21.84 AW	31.37 TQ	HIBLS	10/01-12/01
	Idaho	H	7.40 FQ	13.10 AW	25.74 TQ	IDBLS	10/01-12/01
	Illinois	H	8.55 FQ	19.45 AW	32.64 TQ	ILBLS	10/01-12/01
	Indiana	H	9.74 FQ	18.04 AW	30.54 TQ	INBLS	10/01-12/01
	Iowa	H	8.59 FQ	13.70 AW	23.06 TQ	IABLS	10/01-12/01
	Kansas	H	10.55 FQ	17.99 AW	26.25 TQ	KSBLS	10/01-12/01
	Kentucky	H	9.40 FQ	14.06 AW	24.69 TQ	KYBLS	10/01-12/01
	Louisiana	H	8.02 FQ	14.37 AW	19.45 TQ	LABLS	10/01-12/01
	Maine	H	8.45 FQ	14.01 AW	18.11 TQ	MEBLS	10/01-12/01
	Maryland	H	8.30 FQ	13.09 AW	19.84 TQ	MDBLS	10/01-12/01
	Massachusetts	H	10.55 FQ	19.63 AW	29.36 TQ	MABLS	10/01-12/01
	Michigan	H	9.15 FQ	14.66 AW	24.51 TQ	MIBLS	10/01-12/01
	Minnesota	H	11.24 FQ	19.93 AW	33.70 TQ	MNBLS	10/01-12/01
	Missouri	H	7.62 FQ	18.00 AW	33.77 TQ	MOBLS	10/01-12/01
	Montana	H	7.65 FQ	12.45 AW	24.80 TQ	MTBLS	10/01-12/01
	Nebraska	H	9.66 FQ	15.49 AW	26.45 TQ	NEBLS	10/01-12/01
	Nevada	H	10.68 FQ	22.06 AW	33.74 TQ	NVBLS	10/01-12/01
	New Hampshire	H	9.23 FQ	13.39 AW	19.63 TQ	NHBLS	10/01-12/01
	New Jersey	H	9.20 FQ	21.44 AW	34.81 TQ	NJBLS	10/01-12/01

AAW	Average annual wage	**AOH**	Average offered, high	**ASH**	Average starting, high	**H**	Hourly	**M**	Monthly	**S**	Special: hourly and annual
AE	Average entry wage	**AOL**	Average offered, low	**ASL**	Average starting, low	**HI**	Highest wage paid	**MTC**	Median total compensation	**TQ**	Third quartile wage
AEX	Average experienced wage	**APH**	Average pay, high range	**AW**	Average wage paid	**HR**	High end range	**MW**	Median wage paid	**W**	Weekly
AO	Average offered	**APL**	Average pay, low range	**FQ**	First quartile wage	**LR**	Low end range	**SQ**	Second quartile wage	**Y**	Yearly

Occupation/Type/Industry	Location	Per	Low	Mid	High	Source	Date
Insulation Worker	New Mexico	H	8.37 FQ	12.37 AW	16.65 TQ	NMBLS	10/01-12/01
	New York	H	10.95 FQ	32.11 AW	67.47 TQ	NYBLS	10/01-12/01
	North Carolina	H	7.80 FQ	12.43 AW	17.40 TQ	NCBLS	10/01-12/01
	North Dakota	H	8.12 FQ	13.75 AW	26.14 TQ	NDBLS	10/01-12/01
	Ohio	H	9.47 FQ	15.96 AW	26.11 TQ	OHBLS	10/01-12/01
	Oklahoma	H	8.47 FQ	14.60 AW	21.71 TQ	OKBLS	10/01-12/01
	Oregon	H	8.70 FQ	13.84 AW	19.98 TQ	ORBLS	10/01-12/01
	Pennsylvania	H	9.27 FQ	16.54 AW	26.91 TQ	PABLS	10/01-12/01
	Rhode Island	H	9.75 FQ	15.64 AW	22.07 TQ	RIBLS	10/01-12/01
	South Carolina	H	7.80 FQ	13.15 AW	17.63 TQ	SCBLS	10/01-12/01
	South Dakota	H	7.15 FQ	9.15 AW	11.06 TQ	SDBLS	10/01-12/01
	Tennessee	H	6.30 FQ	12.49 AW	19.38 TQ	TNBLS	10/01-12/01
	Texas	H	8.01 FQ	12.22 AW	17.04 TQ	TXBLS	10/01-12/01
	Utah	H	8.39 FQ	14.56 AW	22.63 TQ	UTBLS	10/01-12/01
	Vermont	H	10.38 FQ	12.76 AW	16.34 TQ	VTBLS	10/01-12/01
	Virginia	H	8.94 FQ	13.72 AW	18.32 TQ	VABLS	10/01-12/01
	Washington	H	10.99 FQ	18.24 AW	25.80 TQ	WABLS	10/01-12/01
	West Virginia	H	10.55 FQ	18.66 AW	27.66 TQ	WVBLS	10/01-12/01
	Wisconsin	H	10.00 FQ	16.01 AW	25.72 TQ	WIBLS	10/01-12/01
	Wyoming	H	9.41 FQ	12.97 AW	17.78 TQ	WYBLS	10/01-12/01
	Puerto Rico	H	5.80 FQ	7.53 AW	8.71 TQ	PRBLS	10/01-12/01
Insurance Appraiser							
Auto Damage	Alabama	Y	32150 FQ	46740 AW	71260 TQ	ALBLS	10/01-12/01
Auto Damage	Arizona	Y	34760 FQ	45080 AW	58580 TQ	AZBLS	10/01-12/01
Auto Damage	Arkansas	Y	26920 FQ	44040 AW	56310 TQ	ARBLS	10/01-12/01
Auto Damage	California	Y	33220 FQ	46890 AW	63310 TQ	CABLS	10/01-12/01
Auto Damage	Colorado	Y	27230 FQ	42450 AW	55350 TQ	COBLS	10/01-12/01
Auto Damage	Connecticut	Y	33590 FQ	45300 AW	58440 TQ	CTBLS	10/01-12/01
Auto Damage	Florida	Y	20300 FQ	40410 AW	58460 TQ	FLBLS	10/01-12/01
Auto Damage	Georgia	Y	31890 FQ	44510 AW	57670 TQ	GABLS	10/01-12/01
Auto Damage	Hawaii	Y	36320 FQ	47000 AW	57580 TQ	HIBLS	10/01-12/01
Auto Damage	Illinois	Y	31140 FQ	41720 AW	56770 TQ	ILBLS	10/01-12/01
Auto Damage	Indiana	Y	25700 FQ	42400 AW	57350 TQ	INBLS	10/01-12/01
Auto Damage	Iowa	Y	26700 FQ	40590 AW	62630 TQ	IABLS	10/01-12/01
Auto Damage	Kansas	Y	13750 FQ	29270 AW	53860 TQ	KSBLS	10/01-12/01
Auto Damage	Kentucky	Y	29640 FQ	45330 AW	67850 TQ	KYBLS	10/01-12/01
Auto Damage	Louisiana	Y	29930 FQ	38470 AW	49160 TQ	LABLS	10/01-12/01
Auto Damage	Maryland	Y	29700 FQ	42650 AW	59800 TQ	MDBLS	10/01-12/01
Auto Damage	Massachusetts	Y	41840 FQ	52370 AW	65350 TQ	MABLS	10/01-12/01
Auto Damage	Michigan	Y	20990 FQ	34480 AW	54070 TQ	MIBLS	10/01-12/01
Auto Damage	Minnesota	Y	28670 FQ	42520 AW	55710 TQ	MNBLS	10/01-12/01
Auto Damage	Mississippi	Y	27460 FQ	39550 AW	54520 TQ	MSBLS	10/01-12/01
Auto Damage	Missouri	Y	30940 FQ	44380 AW	57660 TQ	MOBLS	10/01-12/01
Auto Damage	New Hampshire	Y	32920 FQ	47960 AW	66590 TQ	NHBLS	10/01-12/01
Auto Damage	New Jersey	Y	26960 FQ	42930 AW	56390 TQ	NJBLS	10/01-12/01
Auto Damage	New Mexico	Y	31020 FQ	45450 AW	57560 TQ	NMBLS	10/01-12/01
Auto Damage	New York	Y	30710 FQ	46480 AW	62000 TQ	NYBLS	10/01-12/01
Auto Damage	North Carolina	Y	24210 FQ	36300 AW	52920 TQ	NCBLS	10/01-12/01
Auto Damage	North Dakota	Y	28360 FQ	39370 AW	52190 TQ	NDBLS	10/01-12/01
Auto Damage	Ohio	Y	30910 FQ	44090 AW	57900 TQ	OHBLS	10/01-12/01
Auto Damage	Oklahoma	Y	31600 FQ	45780 AW	69710 TQ	OKBLS	10/01-12/01
Auto Damage	Oregon	Y	40020 FQ	53640 AW	80550 TQ	ORBLS	10/01-12/01
Auto Damage	Pennsylvania	Y	32270 FQ	47010 AW	63830 TQ	PABLS	10/01-12/01
Auto Damage	Rhode Island	Y	36790 FQ	50350 AW	58780 TQ	RIBLS	10/01-12/01
Auto Damage	South Carolina	Y	24340 FQ	39070 AW	62770 TQ	SCBLS	10/01-12/01
Auto Damage	Tennessee	Y	23580 FQ	38770 AW	56400 TQ	TNBLS	10/01-12/01
Auto Damage	Texas	Y	31030 FQ	40520 AW	54290 TQ	TXBLS	10/01-12/01
Auto Damage	Utah	Y	25780 FQ	43930 AW	67490 TQ	UTBLS	10/01-12/01
Auto Damage	Virginia	Y	36370 FQ	46730 AW	61390 TQ	VABLS	10/01-12/01
Auto Damage	Washington	Y	30160 FQ	43120 AW	58550 TQ	WABLS	10/01-12/01
Auto Damage	West Virginia	Y	30980 FQ	45140 AW	75350 TQ	WVBLS	10/01-12/01
Auto Damage	Wisconsin	Y	28490 FQ	41100 AW	56140 TQ	WIBLS	10/01-12/01
Auto Damage	Puerto Rico	Y	14960 FQ	22890 AW	36620 TQ	PRBLS	10/01-12/01
Insurance Claim and Policy Processing Clerk	Alabama	H	8.44 FQ	13.83 AW	20.56 TQ	ALBLS	10/01-12/01
	Alaska	H	11.95 FQ	16.93 AW	22.60 TQ	AKBLS	10/01-12/01
	Arizona	H	9.80 FQ	14.76 AW	21.13 TQ	AZBLS	10/01-12/01
	Arkansas	H	7.85 FQ	11.82 AW	17.01 TQ	ARBLS	10/01-12/01
	California	H	10.66 FQ	17.08 AW	28.04 TQ	CABLS	10/01-12/01
	Colorado	H	9.46 FQ	14.96 AW	21.35 TQ	COBLS	10/01-12/01

AAW	Average annual wage	**AOH**	Average offered, high	**ASH**	Average starting, high	**H**	Hourly	**M**	Monthly	**S**	Special: hourly and annual
AE	Average entry wage	**AOL**	Average offered, low	**ASL**	Average starting, low	**HI**	Highest wage paid	**MTC**	Median total compensation	**TQ**	Third quartile wage
AEX	Average experienced wage	**APH**	Average pay, high range	**AW**	Average wage paid	**HR**	High end range	**MW**	Median wage paid	**W**	Weekly
AO	Average offered	**APL**	Average pay, low range	**FQ**	First quartile wage	**LR**	Low end range	**SQ**	Second quartile wage	**Y**	Yearly

Occupation/Type/Industry	Location	Per	Low	Mid	High	Source	Date
Insurance Claim and Policy Processing Clerk	Connecticut	H	11.70 FQ	16.34 AW	21.91 TQ	CTBLS	10/01-12/01
	Delaware	H	11.71 FQ	15.01 AW	19.86 TQ	DEBLS	10/01-12/01
	District of Columbia	H	9.61 FQ	13.87 AW	19.02 TQ	DCBLS	10/01-12/01
	Florida	H	9.30 FQ	14.25 AW	22.27 TQ	FLBLS	10/01-12/01
	Georgia	H	8.99 FQ	14.72 AW	21.90 TQ	GABLS	10/01-12/01
	Hawaii	H	9.60 FQ	14.61 AW	20.68 TQ	HIBLS	10/01-12/01
	Idaho	H	8.89 FQ	11.98 AW	16.33 TQ	IDBLS	10/01-12/01
	Illinois	H	9.26 FQ	15.24 AW	23.43 TQ	ILBLS	10/01-12/01
	Indiana	H	9.08 FQ	14.06 AW	20.19 TQ	INBLS	10/01-12/01
	Iowa	H	9.44 FQ	13.48 AW	18.29 TQ	IABLS	10/01-12/01
	Kansas	H	8.25 FQ	13.47 AW	20.06 TQ	KSBLS	10/01-12/01
	Kentucky	H	9.55 FQ	14.57 AW	21.81 TQ	KYBLS	10/01-12/01
	Louisiana	H	8.48 FQ	12.74 AW	19.45 TQ	LABLS	10/01-12/01
	Maine	H	9.45 FQ	12.63 AW	16.66 TQ	MEBLS	10/01-12/01
	Maryland	H	10.61 FQ	16.38 AW	22.45 TQ	MDBLS	10/01-12/01
	Massachusetts	H	10.01 FQ	14.52 AW	20.32 TQ	MABLS	10/01-12/01
	Michigan	H	9.32 FQ	14.29 AW	20.42 TQ	MIBLS	10/01-12/01
	Minnesota	H	9.83 FQ	14.41 AW	20.07 TQ	MNBLS	10/01-12/01
	Mississippi	H	8.17 FQ	11.95 AW	17.29 TQ	MSBLS	10/01-12/01
	Missouri	H	8.17 FQ	13.72 AW	20.30 TQ	MOBLS	10/01-12/01
	Montana	H	8.22 FQ	11.81 AW	15.23 TQ	MTBLS	10/01-12/01
	Nebraska	H	7.89 FQ	13.10 AW	19.66 TQ	NEBLS	10/01-12/01
	Nevada	H	8.11 FQ	13.20 AW	17.17 TQ	NVBLS	10/01-12/01
	New Hampshire	H	9.95 FQ	16.11 AW	25.20 TQ	NHBLS	10/01-12/01
	New Jersey	H	10.21 FQ	16.62 AW	24.80 TQ	NJBLS	10/01-12/01
	New Mexico	H	8.64 FQ	12.35 AW	18.35 TQ	NMBLS	10/01-12/01
	New York	H	10.66 FQ	16.75 AW	25.52 TQ	NYBLS	10/01-12/01
	North Carolina	H	9.77 FQ	14.70 AW	21.55 TQ	NCBLS	10/01-12/01
	North Dakota	H	8.14 FQ	14.77 AW	28.37 TQ	NDBLS	10/01-12/01
	Ohio	H	9.62 FQ	14.65 AW	21.30 TQ	OHBLS	10/01-12/01
	Oklahoma	H	7.91 FQ	13.98 AW	21.42 TQ	OKBLS	10/01-12/01
	Oregon	H	9.33 FQ	13.38 AW	17.78 TQ	ORBLS	10/01-12/01
	Pennsylvania	H	9.66 FQ	16.11 AW	26.52 TQ	PABLS	10/01-12/01
	Rhode Island	H	9.88 FQ	14.53 AW	20.01 TQ	RIBLS	10/01-12/01
	South Carolina	H	8.06 FQ	11.08 AW	14.22 TQ	SCBLS	10/01-12/01
	South Dakota	H	7.25 FQ	9.94 AW	13.44 TQ	SDBLS	10/01-12/01
	Tennessee	H	8.07 FQ	12.81 AW	18.12 TQ	TNBLS	10/01-12/01
	Texas	H	9.17 FQ	14.73 AW	21.26 TQ	TXBLS	10/01-12/01
	Utah	H	9.18 FQ	12.26 AW	16.55 TQ	UTBLS	10/01-12/01
	Vermont	H	9.42 FQ	12.83 AW	16.54 TQ	VTBLS	10/01-12/01
	Virginia	H	9.05 FQ	14.40 AW	21.62 TQ	VABLS	10/01-12/01
	Washington	H	9.92 FQ	13.79 AW	18.47 TQ	WABLS	10/01-12/01
	West Virginia	H	6.27 FQ	10.33 AW	15.39 TQ	WVBLS	10/01-12/01
	Wisconsin	H	9.20 FQ	12.64 AW	17.11 TQ	WIBLS	10/01-12/01
	Wyoming	H	6.64 FQ	10.50 AW	14.86 TQ	WYBLS	10/01-12/01
	Puerto Rico	H	6.10 FQ	8.87 AW	12.62 TQ	PRBLS	10/01-12/01
	Virgin Islands	H	7.23 FQ	9.38 AW	11.11 TQ	VIBLS	10/01-12/01
	Guam	H	6.76 FQ	11.09 AW	16.66 TQ	GUBLS	10/01-12/01
Insurance Sales Agent	Alabama	Y	21040 FQ	50700 AW	95060 TQ	ALBLS	10/01-12/01
	Birmingham MSA, AL	Y	24680 FQ	56020 AW	126730 TQ	ALBLS	10/01-12/01
	Huntsville MSA, AL	Y	22140 FQ	47400 AW	99380 TQ	ALBLS	10/01-12/01
	Mobile MSA, AL	Y	25420 FQ	63430 AW		ALBLS	10/01-12/01
	Montgomery MSA, AL	Y	24620 FQ	49080 AW	92940 TQ	ALBLS	10/01-12/01
	Alaska	Y	25240 FQ	36410 AW	44650 TQ	AKBLS	10/01-12/01
	Anchorage MSA, AK	Y	24870 FQ	39200 AW	45680 TQ	AKBLS	10/01-12/01
	Arizona	Y	22640 FQ	42780 AW	66460 TQ	AZBLS	10/01-12/01
	Phoenix-Mesa MSA, AZ	Y	28560 FQ	45140 AW	68430 TQ	AZBLS	10/01-12/01
	Tucson MSA, AZ	Y	19210 FQ	35130 AW	52130 TQ	AZBLS	10/01-12/01
	Arkansas	Y	19670 FQ	45900 AW	80600 TQ	ARBLS	10/01-12/01
	Fayetteville-Springdale-Rogers MSA, AR	Y	13170 FQ	31720 AW	64400 TQ	ARBLS	10/01-12/01
	Fort Smith MSA, AR-OK	Y	18070 FQ	36560 AW	65710 TQ	ARBLS	10/01-12/01
	Little Rock-North Little Rock MSA, AR	Y	28240 FQ	57160 AW	103370 TQ	ARBLS	10/01-12/01
	California	Y	23500 FQ	53580 AW	116400 TQ	CABLS	10/01-12/01
	Bakersfield MSA, CA	Y	23210 FQ	49940 AW	101400 TQ	CABLS	10/01-12/01
	Chico-Paradise MSA, CA	Y	14010 FQ	40350 AW	84310 TQ	CABLS	10/01-12/01
	Fresno MSA, CA	Y	23530 FQ	57030 AW	94830 TQ	CABLS	10/01-12/01
	Los Angeles-Long Beach PMSA, CA	Y	15280 FQ	45240 AW	86810 TQ	CABLS	10/01-12/01

AAW	Average annual wage	AOH	Average offered, high	ASH	Average starting, high	H	Hourly	M	Monthly	S	Special: hourly and annual
AE	Average entry wage	AOL	Average offered, low	ASL	Average starting, low	HI	Highest wage paid	MTC	Median total compensation	TQ	Third quartile wage
AEX	Average experienced wage	APH	Average pay, high range	AW	Average wage paid	HR	High end range	MW	Median wage paid	W	Weekly
AO	Average offered	APL	Average pay, low range	FQ	First quartile wage	LR	Low end range	SQ	Second quartile wage	Y	Yearly

Occupation/Type/Industry	Location	Per	Low	Mid	High	Source	Date
Insurance Sales Agent	Merced MSA, CA	Y	25820 FQ	51620 AW	90340 TQ	CABLS	10/01-12/01
	Modesto MSA, CA	Y	27130 FQ	66520 AW	141070 TQ	CABLS	10/01-12/01
	Oakland PMSA, CA	Y	29110 FQ	52720 AW	100090 TQ	CABLS	10/01-12/01
	Orange County PMSA, CA	Y	25230 FQ	70760 AW		CABLS	10/01-12/01
	Redding MSA, CA	Y	23500 FQ	46590 AW	76350 TQ	CABLS	10/01-12/01
	Riverside-San Bernardino PMSA, CA	Y	20690 FQ	54230 AW	117760 TQ	CABLS	10/01-12/01
	Sacramento PMSA, CA	Y	25810 FQ	46840 AW	72930 TQ	CABLS	10/01-12/01
	Salinas MSA, CA	Y	25270 FQ	67840 AW		CABLS	10/01-12/01
	San Diego MSA, CA	Y	23340 FQ	49500 AW	87330 TQ	CABLS	10/01-12/01
	San Francisco PMSA, CA	Y	32000 FQ	72930 AW		CABLS	10/01-12/01
	San Jose PMSA, CA	Y	32610 FQ	64260 AW	113690 TQ	CABLS	10/01-12/01
	San Luis Obispo-Atascadero-Paso Robles MSA, CA	Y	23690 FQ	47650 AW	73260 TQ	CABLS	10/01-12/01
	Santa Barbara-Santa Maria-Lompoc MSA, CA	Y	26060 FQ	61690 AW		CABLS	10/01-12/01
	Santa Cruz-Watsonville PMSA, CA	Y	24100 FQ	55040 AW	138380 TQ	CABLS	10/01-12/01
	Santa Rosa PMSA, CA	Y	25050 FQ	50850 AW	85690 TQ	CABLS	10/01-12/01
	Stockton-Lodi MSA, CA	Y	28680 FQ	73000 AW		CABLS	10/01-12/01
	Vallejo-Fairfield-Napa PMSA, CA	Y	27790 FQ	47330 AW	69430 TQ	CABLS	10/01-12/01
	Ventura PMSA, CA	Y	26340 FQ	67170 AW	138810 TQ	CABLS	10/01-12/01
	Visalia-Tulare-Porterville MSA, CA	Y	19810 FQ	40190 AW	75850 TQ	CABLS	10/01-12/01
	Colorado	Y	28210 FQ	56240 AW	88510 TQ	COBLS	10/01-12/01
	Boulder-Longmont PMSA, CO	Y	28670 FQ	75530 AW		COBLS	10/01-12/01
	Colorado Springs MSA, CO	Y	23790 FQ	42360 AW	77780 TQ	COBLS	10/01-12/01
	Denver PMSA, CO	Y	35250 FQ	59440 AW	87440 TQ	COBLS	10/01-12/01
	Fort Collins-Loveland MSA, CO	Y	31010 FQ	54230 AW	83380 TQ	COBLS	10/01-12/01
	Greeley PMSA, CO	Y	25720 FQ	52270 AW	115060 TQ	COBLS	10/01-12/01
	Connecticut	Y	30730 FQ	58920 AW	97900 TQ	CTBLS	10/01-12/01
	Bridgeport PMSA, CT	Y	30230 FQ	69940 AW		CTBLS	10/01-12/01
	Danbury PMSA, CT	Y	35930 FQ	53370 AW	77610 TQ	CTBLS	10/01-12/01
	Hartford MSA, CT	Y	31580 FQ	55750 AW	86840 TQ	CTBLS	10/01-12/01
	New Haven-Meriden PMSA, CT	Y	24750 FQ	50620 AW	82120 TQ	CTBLS	10/01-12/01
	New London-Norwich MSA, CT-RI	Y	30680 FQ	53210 AW	84030 TQ	CTBLS	10/01-12/01
	Stamford-Norwalk PMSA, CT	Y	39820 FQ	70820 AW	145530 TQ	CTBLS	10/01-12/01
	Waterbury PMSA, CT	Y	34150 FQ	88330 AW	139540 TQ	CTBLS	10/01-12/01
	Delaware	Y	23890 FQ	43910 AW	68750 TQ	DEBLS	10/01-12/01
	Wilmington-Newark PMSA, DE-MD	Y	25150 FQ	42910 AW	64850 TQ	DEBLS	10/01-12/01
	District of Columbia	Y	22640 FQ	53840 AW		DCBLS	10/01-12/01
	Washington PMSA, DC-MD-VA-WV	Y	23620 FQ	49450 AW	86470 TQ	DCBLS	10/01-12/01
	Florida	Y	19220 FQ	44950 AW	85530 TQ	FLBLS	10/01-12/01
	Daytona Beach MSA, FL	Y	19090 FQ	31960 AW	46390 TQ	FLBLS	10/01-12/01
	Fort Lauderdale PMSA, FL	Y	24230 FQ	45970 AW	81280 TQ	FLBLS	10/01-12/01
	Fort Myers-Cape Coral MSA, FL	Y	13620 FQ	40900 AW	84040 TQ	FLBLS	10/01-12/01
	Fort Pierce-Port St. Lucie MSA, FL	Y	12330 FQ	33380 AW	63130 TQ	FLBLS	10/01-12/01
	Fort Walton Beach MSA, FL	Y	20100 FQ	51430 AW	139590 TQ	FLBLS	10/01-12/01
	Gainesville MSA, FL	Y	15230 FQ	41880 AW	72590 TQ	FLBLS	10/01-12/01
	Jacksonville MSA, FL	Y	13510 FQ	36940 AW	71880 TQ	FLBLS	10/01-12/01
	Lakeland-Winter Haven MSA, FL	Y	22550 FQ	36730 AW	54510 TQ	FLBLS	10/01-12/01
	Melbourne-Titusville-Palm Bay MSA, FL	Y	19020 FQ	52700 AW		FLBLS	10/01-12/01
	Miami PMSA, FL	Y	18960 FQ	47990 AW	98470 TQ	FLBLS	10/01-12/01
	Naples MSA, FL	Y	25890 FQ	51840 AW	75680 TQ	FLBLS	10/01-12/01
	Ocala MSA, FL	Y	19190 FQ	60600 AW		FLBLS	10/01-12/01
	Orlando MSA, FL	Y	19480 FQ	46780 AW	84910 TQ	FLBLS	10/01-12/01
	Pensacola MSA, FL	Y	12200 FQ	38000 AW	80900 TQ	FLBLS	10/01-12/01
	Sarasota-Bradenton MSA, FL	Y	23420 FQ	54780 AW	106660 TQ	FLBLS	10/01-12/01
	Tallahassee MSA, FL	Y	13850 FQ	46030 AW	74050 TQ	FLBLS	10/01-12/01
	Tampa-St. Petersburg-Clearwater MSA, FL	Y	23820 FQ	44210 AW	76110 TQ	FLBLS	10/01-12/01

AAW	Average annual wage	AOH	Average offered, high	ASH	Average starting, high	H	Hourly	M	Monthly	S	Special: hourly and annual
AE	Average entry wage	AOL	Average offered, low	ASL	Average starting, low	HI	Highest wage paid	MTC	Median total compensation	TQ	Third quartile wage
AEX	Average experienced wage	APH	Average pay, high range	AW	Average wage paid	HR	High end range	MW	Median wage paid	W	Weekly
AO	Average offered	APL	Average pay, low range	FQ	First quartile wage	LR	Low end range	SQ	Second quartile wage	Y	Yearly

Occupation/Type/Industry	Location	Per	Low	Mid	High	Source	Date
Insurance Sales Agent	West Palm Beach-Boca Raton MSA, FL	Y	23900 FQ	52510 AW	132780 TQ	FLBLS	10/01-12/01
	Georgia	Y	24090 FQ	45270 AW	86560 TQ	GABLS	10/01-12/01
	Atlanta MSA, GA	Y	27560 FQ	50180 AW	111050 TQ	GABLS	10/01-12/01
	Augusta-Aiken MSA, GA-SC	Y	19890 FQ	35810 AW	58940 TQ	GABLS	10/01-12/01
	Columbus MSA, GA-AL	Y	30050 FQ	46330 AW	74160 TQ	GABLS	10/01-12/01
	Macon MSA, GA	Y	24420 FQ	39260 AW	71780 TQ	GABLS	10/01-12/01
	Savannah MSA, GA	Y	26840 FQ	48780 AW	87420 TQ	GABLS	10/01-12/01
	Hawaii	Y	19470 FQ	42910 AW	76780 TQ	HIBLS	10/01-12/01
	Honolulu MSA, HI	Y	21090 FQ	43490 AW	77790 TQ	HIBLS	10/01-12/01
	Idaho	Y	24330 FQ	48370 AW	89860 TQ	IDBLS	10/01-12/01
	Boise City MSA, ID	Y	24640 FQ	47770 AW	101100 TQ	IDBLS	10/01-12/01
	Illinois	Y	23630 FQ	48610 AW	96160 TQ	ILBLS	10/01-12/01
	Champaign-Urbana MSA, IL	Y	31430 FQ	54100 AW	115440 TQ	ILBLS	10/01-12/01
	Chicago PMSA, IL	Y	26620 FQ	51150 AW	101520 TQ	ILBLS	10/01-12/01
	Peoria-Pekin MSA, IL	Y	17380 FQ	51630 AW	95220 TQ	ILBLS	10/01-12/01
	Rockford MSA, IL	Y	24070 FQ	42350 AW	73240 TQ	ILBLS	10/01-12/01
	Springfield MSA, IL	Y	19260 FQ	37360 AW	69680 TQ	ILBLS	10/01-12/01
	Indiana	Y	14870 FQ	44300 AW	83680 TQ	INBLS	10/01-12/01
	Elkhart-Goshen MSA, IN	Y	25020 FQ	54950 AW		INBLS	10/01-12/01
	Evansville-Henderson MSA, IN-KY	Y	13590 FQ	46710 AW		INBLS	10/01-12/01
	Fort Wayne MSA, IN	Y	27390 FQ	56350 AW	99840 TQ	INBLS	10/01-12/01
	Gary PMSA, IN	Y	28740 FQ	51430 AW	85930 TQ	INBLS	10/01-12/01
	Indianapolis MSA, IN	Y	12510 FQ	39740 AW	67420 TQ	INBLS	10/01-12/01
	Lafayette MSA, IN	Y	16160 FQ	42370 AW	94880 TQ	INBLS	10/01-12/01
	South Bend MSA, IN	Y	16220 FQ	54950 AW	92330 TQ	INBLS	10/01-12/01
	Iowa	Y	20330 FQ	43140 AW	79140 TQ	IABLS	10/01-12/01
	Cedar Rapids MSA, IA	Y	22440 FQ	46800 AW	100700 TQ	IABLS	10/01-12/01
	Davenport-Moline-Rock Island MSA, IA-IL	Y	22910 FQ	50660 AW	117340 TQ	IABLS	10/01-12/01
	Des Moines MSA, IA	Y	28870 FQ	57460 AW	109850 TQ	IABLS	10/01-12/01
	Kansas	Y	16010 FQ	37840 AW	71740 TQ	KSBLS	10/01-12/01
	Topeka MSA, KS	Y	25050 FQ	61270 AW	115820 TQ	KSBLS	10/01-12/01
	Wichita MSA, KS	Y	17100 FQ	54000 AW	122940 TQ	KSBLS	10/01-12/01
	Kentucky	Y	16430 FQ	46170 AW	92120 TQ	KYBLS	10/01-12/01
	Lexington MSA, KY	Y	14820 FQ	44360 AW	90150 TQ	KYBLS	10/01-12/01
	Louisville MSA, KY-IN	Y	19040 FQ	59410 AW	102240 TQ	KYBLS	10/01-12/01
	Louisiana	Y	15670 FQ	42570 AW	81380 TQ	LABLS	10/01-12/01
	Baton Rouge MSA, LA	Y	21180 FQ	57750 AW	141070 TQ	LABLS	10/01-12/01
	Houma MSA, LA	Y	24090 FQ	60270 AW		LABLS	10/01-12/01
	Lafayette MSA, LA	Y	14140 FQ	65150 AW		LABLS	10/01-12/01
	Lake Charles MSA, LA	Y	17930 FQ	40290 AW	47530 TQ	LABLS	10/01-12/01
	New Orleans MSA, LA	Y	16950 FQ	37100 AW	66530 TQ	LABLS	10/01-12/01
	Shreveport-Bossier City MSA, LA	Y	21790 FQ	44590 AW	74780 TQ	LABLS	10/01-12/01
	Maine	Y	20470 FQ	41690 AW	74260 TQ	MEBLS	10/01-12/01
	Portland MSA, ME	Y	30640 FQ	50150 AW	85760 TQ	MEBLS	10/01-12/01
	Maryland	Y	22740 FQ	52350 AW	96050 TQ	MDBLS	10/01-12/01
	Baltimore PMSA, MD	Y	21220 FQ	54870 AW	110380 TQ	MDBLS	10/01-12/01
	Massachusetts	Y	27850 FQ	54190 AW	93180 TQ	MABLS	10/01-12/01
	Boston PMSA, MA-NH	Y	30480 FQ	60750 AW	108710 TQ	MABLS	10/01-12/01
	Brockton PMSA, MA	Y	30710 FQ	63070 AW		MABLS	10/01-12/01
	Lawrence PMSA, MA-NH	Y	21080 FQ	45550 AW	81190 TQ	MABLS	10/01-12/01
	Lowell PMSA, MA-NH	Y	34410 FQ	59560 AW	82030 TQ	MABLS	10/01-12/01
	New Bedford PMSA, MA	Y	20050 FQ	41160 AW	78610 TQ	MABLS	10/01-12/01
	Worcester PMSA, MA-CT	Y	25400 FQ	45650 AW	70110 TQ	MABLS	10/01-12/01
	Michigan	Y	21220 FQ	54260 AW	118770 TQ	MIBLS	10/01-12/01
	Ann Arbor PMSA, MI	Y	24050 FQ	43620 AW	75470 TQ	MIBLS	10/01-12/01
	Detroit PMSA, MI	Y	23960 FQ	62570 AW	130070 TQ	MIBLS	10/01-12/01
	Flint PMSA, MI	Y	24630 FQ	50740 AW	105890 TQ	MIBLS	10/01-12/01
	Grand Rapids-Muskegon-Holland MSA, MI	Y	20670 FQ	48380 AW	115670 TQ	MIBLS	10/01-12/01
	Kalamazoo-Battle Creek MSA, MI	Y	24490 FQ	49710 AW	85780 TQ	MIBLS	10/01-12/01
	Lansing-East Lansing MSA, MI	Y	18230 FQ	60850 AW		MIBLS	10/01-12/01
	Saginaw-Bay City-Midland MSA, MI	Y	12910 FQ	36760 AW	73800 TQ	MIBLS	10/01-12/01
	Minnesota	Y	26480 FQ	53850 AW	102340 TQ	MNBLS	10/01-12/01
	Duluth-Superior MSA, MN-WI	Y	14270 FQ	42920 AW	74140 TQ	MNBLS	10/01-12/01
	Minneapolis-St. Paul MSA, MN-WI	Y	30550 FQ	60420 AW	116940 TQ	MNBLS	10/01-12/01

AAW	Average annual wage	**AOH**	Average offered, high	**ASH**	Average starting, high	**H**	Hourly	**M**	Monthly	**S**	Special: hourly and annual
AE	Average entry wage	**AOL**	Average offered, low	**ASL**	Average starting, low	**HI**	Highest wage paid	**MTC**	Median total compensation	**TQ**	Third quartile wage
AEX	Average experienced wage	**APH**	Average pay, high range	**AW**	Average wage paid	**HR**	High end range	**MW**	Median wage paid	**W**	Weekly
AO	Average offered	**APL**	Average pay, low range	**FQ**	First quartile wage	**LR**	Low end range	**SQ**	Second quartile wage	**Y**	Yearly

Occupation/Type/Industry	Location	Per	Low	Mid	High	Source	Date
Insurance Sales Agent	St. Cloud MSA, MN	Y	25490 FQ	49350 AW	82350 TQ	MNBLS	10/01-12/01
	Mississippi	Y	22870 FQ	42010 AW	76070 TQ	MSBLS	10/01-12/01
	Biloxi-Gulfport-Pascagoula MSA, MS	Y	16440 FQ	40580 AW	87760 TQ	MSBLS	10/01-12/01
	Jackson MSA, MS	Y	24430 FQ	52880 AW	112280 TQ	MSBLS	10/01-12/01
	Missouri	Y	19220 FQ	43720 AW	81120 TQ	MOBLS	10/01-12/01
	Kansas City MSA, MO-KS	Y	15610 FQ	41150 AW	87660 TQ	MOBLS	10/01-12/01
	St. Louis MSA, MO-IL	Y	24560 FQ	46160 AW	80330 TQ	MOBLS	10/01-12/01
	Springfield MSA, MO	Y	33590 FQ	47680 AW	70360 TQ	MOBLS	10/01-12/01
	Montana	Y	13400 FQ	41760 AW	99080 TQ	MTBLS	10/01-12/01
	Billings MSA, MT	Y	16850 FQ	44700 AW	123950 TQ	MTBLS	10/01-12/01
	Nebraska	Y	19680 FQ	38990 AW	71730 TQ	NEBLS	10/01-12/01
	Lincoln MSA, NE	Y	19340 FQ	30910 AW	47370 TQ	NEBLS	10/01-12/01
	Omaha MSA, NE-IA	Y	22960 FQ	43210 AW	75750 TQ	NEBLS	10/01-12/01
	Nevada	Y	25450 FQ	49690 AW	82140 TQ	NVBLS	10/01-12/01
	Las Vegas MSA, NV-AZ	Y	24030 FQ	47580 AW	81300 TQ	NVBLS	10/01-12/01
	Reno MSA, NV	Y	25910 FQ	51110 AW	73050 TQ	NVBLS	10/01-12/01
	New Hampshire	Y	21770 FQ	41830 AW	66280 TQ	NHBLS	10/01-12/01
	Manchester PMSA, NH	Y	29160 FQ	42480 AW	70010 TQ	NHBLS	10/01-12/01
	Nashua PMSA, NH	Y	25320 FQ	46720 AW	95560 TQ	NHBLS	10/01-12/01
	Portsmouth-Rochester PMSA, NH-ME	Y	28210 FQ	42460 AW	71930 TQ	NHBLS	10/01-12/01
	New Jersey	Y	25270 FQ	56900 AW	118180 TQ	NJBLS	10/01-12/01
	Atlantic-Cape May PMSA, NJ	Y	46500 FQ	70990 AW	137960 TQ	NJBLS	10/01-12/01
	Bergen-Passaic PMSA, NJ	Y	29870 FQ	60250 AW	132520 TQ	NJBLS	10/01-12/01
	Jersey City PMSA, NJ	Y	26050 FQ	49420 AW	93250 TQ	NJBLS	10/01-12/01
	Middlesex-Somerset-Hunterdon PMSA, NJ	Y	29860 FQ	58600 AW	118400 TQ	NJBLS	10/01-12/01
	Monmouth-Ocean PMSA, NJ	Y	29610 FQ	56100 AW	101390 TQ	NJBLS	10/01-12/01
	Newark PMSA, NJ	Y	22960 FQ	54880 AW	118030 TQ	NJBLS	10/01-12/01
	Trenton PMSA, NJ	Y	26880 FQ	54650 AW	90960 TQ	NJBLS	10/01-12/01
	New Mexico	Y	20550 FQ	39150 AW	61340 TQ	NMBLS	10/01-12/01
	Albuquerque MSA, NM	Y	29360 FQ	43200 AW	69220 TQ	NMBLS	10/01-12/01
	Las Cruces MSA, NM	Y	11700 FQ	26020 AW	36180 TQ	NMBLS	10/01-12/01
	New York	Y	22610 FQ	55370 AW	107410 TQ	NYBLS	10/01-12/01
	Albany-Schenectady-Troy MSA, NY	Y	18390 FQ	41830 AW	71930 TQ	NYBLS	10/01-12/01
	Binghamton MSA, NY	Y	25630 FQ	53620 AW	91040 TQ	NYBLS	10/01-12/01
	Buffalo-Niagara Falls MSA, NY	Y	21860 FQ	39330 AW	63690 TQ	NYBLS	10/01-12/01
	Dutchess County PMSA, NY	Y	30380 FQ	63700 AW	114690 TQ	NYBLS	10/01-12/01
	Nassau-Suffolk PMSA, NY	Y	23000 FQ	47770 AW	86630 TQ	NYBLS	10/01-12/01
	New York PMSA, NY	Y	23720 FQ	66730 AW	121500 TQ	NYBLS	10/01-12/01
	Newburgh PMSA, NY-PA	Y	25340 FQ	58750 AW	93050 TQ	NYBLS	10/01-12/01
	Rochester MSA, NY	Y	22330 FQ	42820 AW	66130 TQ	NYBLS	10/01-12/01
	Syracuse MSA, NY	Y	21000 FQ	42070 AW	68060 TQ	NYBLS	10/01-12/01
	Utica-Rome MSA, NY	Y	36630 FQ	49060 AW	81570 TQ	NYBLS	10/01-12/01
	North Carolina	Y	19280 FQ	44040 AW	74010 TQ	NCBLS	10/01-12/01
	Asheville MSA, NC	Y	20560 FQ	45540 AW	69710 TQ	NCBLS	10/01-12/01
	Charlotte-Gastonia-Rock Hill MSA, NC-SC	Y	22810 FQ	52660 AW	93650 TQ	NCBLS	10/01-12/01
	Fayetteville MSA, NC	Y	12810 FQ	25670 AW	39510 TQ	NCBLS	10/01-12/01
	Greensboro-Winston-Salem-High Point MSA, NC	Y	21240 FQ	43980 AW	84350 TQ	NCBLS	10/01-12/01
	Hickory-Morganton-Lenoir MSA, NC	Y	18550 FQ	42760 AW	94590 TQ	NCBLS	10/01-12/01
	Raleigh-Durham-Chapel Hill MSA, NC	Y	23510 FQ	50590 AW	71340 TQ	NCBLS	10/01-12/01
	Wilmington MSA, NC	Y	19400 FQ	35050 AW	73200 TQ	NCBLS	10/01-12/01
	North Dakota	Y	15950 FQ	38630 AW	79180 TQ	NDBLS	10/01-12/01
	Fargo-Moorhead MSA, ND-MN	Y	14270 FQ	54170 AW	113500 TQ	NDBLS	10/01-12/01
	Ohio	Y	21140 FQ	53480 AW	112680 TQ	OHBLS	10/01-12/01
	Akron PMSA, OH	Y	23360 FQ	56980 AW		OHBLS	10/01-12/01
	Canton-Massillon MSA, OH	Y	23610 FQ	49520 AW	82120 TQ	OHBLS	10/01-12/01
	Cincinnati PMSA, OH-KY-IN	Y	20410 FQ	44840 AW	98690 TQ	OHBLS	10/01-12/01
	Cleveland-Lorain-Elyria PMSA, OH	Y	25510 FQ	61370 AW	121690 TQ	OHBLS	10/01-12/01
	Columbus MSA, OH	Y	20180 FQ	43280 AW	79120 TQ	OHBLS	10/01-12/01
	Dayton-Springfield MSA, OH	Y	22060 FQ	63400 AW	116210 TQ	OHBLS	10/01-12/01
	Hamilton-Middletown PMSA, OH	Y	29880 FQ	61280 AW	89920 TQ	OHBLS	10/01-12/01

AAW Average annual wage; AE Average entry wage; AEX Average experienced wage; AO Average offered; AOH Average offered, high; AOL Average offered, low; APH Average pay, high range; APL Average pay, low range; ASH Average starting, high; ASL Average starting, low; AW Average wage paid; FQ First quartile wage; H Hourly; HI Highest wage paid; HR High end range; LR Low end range; M Monthly; MTC Median total compensation; MW Median wage paid; SQ Second quartile wage; S Special: hourly and annual; TQ Third quartile wage; W Weekly; Y Yearly

Occupation/Type/Industry	Location	Per	Low	Mid	High	Source	Date
Insurance Sales Agent	Mansfield MSA, OH	Y	15840 FQ	34560 AW	62740 TQ	OHBLS	10/01-12/01
	Toledo MSA, OH	Y	25910 FQ	69590 AW	136380 TQ	OHBLS	10/01-12/01
	Youngstown-Warren MSA, OH	Y	27060 FQ	62380 AW	124240 TQ	OHBLS	10/01-12/01
	Oklahoma	Y	20200 FQ	44650 AW	81100 TQ	OKBLS	10/01-12/01
	Oklahoma City MSA, OK	Y	24270 FQ	53710 AW		OKBLS	10/01-12/01
	Tulsa MSA, OK	Y	22440 FQ	40150 AW	65770 TQ	OKBLS	10/01-12/01
	Oregon	Y	26670 FQ	49150 AW	86750 TQ	ORBLS	10/01-12/01
	Eugene-Springfield MSA, OR	Y	23060 FQ	47610 AW	103690 TQ	ORBLS	10/01-12/01
	Medford-Ashland MSA, OR	Y	25600 FQ	52500 AW	89620 TQ	ORBLS	10/01-12/01
	Portland-Vancouver PMSA, OR-WA	Y	27000 FQ	52650 AW	90920 TQ	ORBLS	10/01-12/01
	Salem PMSA, OR	Y	29330 FQ	33350 AW	35950 TQ	ORBLS	10/01-12/01
	Pennsylvania	Y	20020 FQ	48960 AW	98630 TQ	PABLS	10/01-12/01
	Allentown-Bethlehem-Easton MSA, PA	Y	26480 FQ	55090 AW	127810 TQ	PABLS	10/01-12/01
	Erie MSA, PA	Y	22650 FQ	47970 AW	101370 TQ	PABLS	10/01-12/01
	Harrisburg-Lebanon-Carlisle MSA, PA	Y	23690 FQ	44820 AW	63550 TQ	PABLS	10/01-12/01
	Johnstown MSA, PA	Y	12080 FQ	20430 AW	36390 TQ	PABLS	10/01-12/01
	Lancaster MSA, PA	Y	26870 FQ	54040 AW	89960 TQ	PABLS	10/01-12/01
	Philadelphia PMSA, PA-NJ	Y	24290 FQ	57380 AW	122570 TQ	PABLS	10/01-12/01
	Pittsburgh MSA, PA	Y	18070 FQ	45960 AW	108280 TQ	PABLS	10/01-12/01
	Reading MSA, PA	Y	23590 FQ	37730 AW	61600 TQ	PABLS	10/01-12/01
	Scranton-Wilkes-Barre-Hazleton MSA, PA	Y	22020 FQ	43490 AW	73170 TQ	PABLS	10/01-12/01
	York MSA, PA	Y	12790 FQ	48330 AW	98910 TQ	PABLS	10/01-12/01
	Rhode Island	Y	23360 FQ	51940 AW	108930 TQ	RIBLS	10/01-12/01
	Providence-Fall River-Warwick MSA, RI-MA	Y	24500 FQ	52880 AW	102110 TQ	RIBLS	10/01-12/01
	South Carolina	Y	19410 FQ	38830 AW	76630 TQ	SCBLS	10/01-12/01
	Charleston-North Charleston MSA, SC	Y	21880 FQ	36240 AW	53870 TQ	SCBLS	10/01-12/01
	Columbia MSA, SC	Y	22930 FQ	59990 AW	92440 TQ	SCBLS	10/01-12/01
	Greenville-Spartanburg-Anderson MSA, SC	Y	18540 FQ	32800 AW	52740 TQ	SCBLS	10/01-12/01
	Myrtle Beach MSA, SC	Y	12460 FQ	24080 AW	38300 TQ	SCBLS	10/01-12/01
	South Dakota	Y	21210 FQ	38100 AW	57050 TQ	SDBLS	10/01-12/01
	Sioux Falls MSA, SD	Y	20460 FQ	34580 AW	55220 TQ	SDBLS	10/01-12/01
	Tennessee	Y	17850 FQ	36540 AW	65960 TQ	TNBLS	10/01-12/01
	Chattanooga MSA, TN-GA	Y	16970 FQ	38450 AW	76440 TQ	TNBLS	10/01-12/01
	Johnson City-Kingsport-Bristol MSA, TN-VA	Y	20940 FQ	51770 AW	81700 TQ	TNBLS	10/01-12/01
	Knoxville MSA, TN	Y	20990 FQ	45520 AW	72650 TQ	TNBLS	10/01-12/01
	Memphis MSA, TN-AR-MS	Y	16760 FQ	39200 AW	76740 TQ	TNBLS	10/01-12/01
	Nashville MSA, TN	Y	18160 FQ	34820 AW	62700 TQ	TNBLS	10/01-12/01
	Texas	Y	18340 FQ	45990 AW	96550 TQ	TXBLS	10/01-12/01
	Austin-San Marcos MSA, TX	Y	23960 FQ	57700 AW		TXBLS	10/01-12/01
	Beaumont-Port Arthur MSA, TX	Y	13130 FQ	53220 AW	116670 TQ	TXBLS	10/01-12/01
	Brazoria PMSA, TX	Y	13250 FQ	28620 AW	46230 TQ	TXBLS	10/01-12/01
	Brownsville-Harlingen-San Benito MSA, TX	Y	20650 FQ	36480 AW	55670 TQ	TXBLS	10/01-12/01
	Corpus Christi MSA, TX	Y	12830 FQ	35200 AW	55930 TQ	TXBLS	10/01-12/01
	Dallas PMSA, TX	Y	19320 FQ	39530 AW	71800 TQ	TXBLS	10/01-12/01
	El Paso MSA, TX	Y	12450 FQ	27770 AW	55400 TQ	TXBLS	10/01-12/01
	Fort Worth-Arlington PMSA, TX	Y	23440 FQ	61030 AW	109870 TQ	TXBLS	10/01-12/01
	Galveston-Texas City PMSA, TX	Y	19850 FQ	42650 AW	80120 TQ	TXBLS	10/01-12/01
	Houston PMSA, TX	Y	23750 FQ	56260 AW	144180 TQ	TXBLS	10/01-12/01
	Killeen-Temple MSA, TX	Y	15260 FQ	24610 AW	36420 TQ	TXBLS	10/01-12/01
	Longview-Marshall MSA, TX	Y	14860 FQ	25600 AW	50740 TQ	TXBLS	10/01-12/01
	Lubbock MSA, TX	Y	20360 FQ	43360 AW	70810 TQ	TXBLS	10/01-12/01
	McAllen-Edinburg-Mission MSA, TX	Y	17450 FQ	37370 AW	68520 TQ	TXBLS	10/01-12/01
	Odessa-Midland MSA, TX	Y	12740 FQ	39970 AW	103020 TQ	TXBLS	10/01-12/01
	San Antonio MSA, TX	Y	21400 FQ	44270 AW	82380 TQ	TXBLS	10/01-12/01
	Tyler MSA, TX	Y	18900 FQ	41640 AW	87790 TQ	TXBLS	10/01-12/01
	Waco MSA, TX	Y	21850 FQ	58720 AW	133690 TQ	TXBLS	10/01-12/01
	Utah	Y	25350 FQ	49580 AW	87620 TQ	UTBLS	10/01-12/01
	Provo-Orem MSA, UT	Y	23550 FQ	49720 AW		UTBLS	10/01-12/01

AAW	Average annual wage	**AOH**	Average offered, high	**ASH**	Average starting, high	**H**	Hourly	**M**	Monthly	**S**	Special: hourly and annual
AE	Average entry wage	**AOL**	Average offered, low	**ASL**	Average starting, low	**HI**	Highest wage paid	**MTC**	Median total compensation	**TQ**	Third quartile wage
AEX	Average experienced wage	**APH**	Average pay, high range	**AW**	Average wage paid	**HR**	High end range	**MW**	Median wage paid	**W**	Weekly
AO	Average offered	**APL**	Average pay, low range	**FQ**	First quartile wage	**LR**	Low end range	**SQ**	Second quartile wage	**Y**	Yearly

Occupation/Type/Industry	Location	Per	Low	Mid	High	Source	Date
Insurance Sales Agent	Salt Lake City-Ogden MSA, UT	Y	30070 FQ	51810 AW	87370 TQ	UTBLS	10/01-12/01
	Vermont	Y	29380 FQ	46850 AW	68750 TQ	VTBLS	10/01-12/01
	Burlington MSA, VT	Y	29170 FQ	53020 AW	70920 TQ	VTBLS	10/01-12/01
	Virginia	Y	19450 FQ	44400 AW	84070 TQ	VABLS	10/01-12/01
	Lynchburg MSA, VA	Y	19630 FQ	37400 AW	55060 TQ	VABLS	10/01-12/01
	Norfolk-Virginia Beach-Newport News MSA, VA-NC	Y	19960 FQ	45130 AW	98910 TQ	VABLS	10/01-12/01
	Richmond-Petersburg MSA, VA	Y	23500 FQ	50430 AW	86860 TQ	VABLS	10/01-12/01
	Roanoke MSA, VA	Y	19850 FQ	39560 AW	55720 TQ	VABLS	10/01-12/01
	Washington	Y	28210 FQ	51290 AW	97580 TQ	WABLS	10/01-12/01
	Bremerton PMSA, WA	Y	29190 FQ	38170 AW	53570 TQ	WABLS	10/01-12/01
	Olympia PMSA, WA	Y	23970 FQ	43190 AW	70260 TQ	WABLS	10/01-12/01
	Richland-Kennewick-Pasco MSA, WA	Y	18280 FQ	38090 AW	72030 TQ	WABLS	10/01-12/01
	Seattle-Bellevue-Everett PMSA, WA	Y	30410 FQ	53220 AW	103280 TQ	WABLS	10/01-12/01
	Spokane MSA, WA	Y	27180 FQ	56440 AW	120600 TQ	WABLS	10/01-12/01
	Tacoma PMSA, WA	Y	20040 FQ	44460 AW	71810 TQ	WABLS	10/01-12/01
	Yakima MSA, WA	Y	29360 FQ	52870 AW	102990 TQ	WABLS	10/01-12/01
	West Virginia	Y	15300 FQ	34800 AW	77050 TQ	WVBLS	10/01-12/01
	Huntington-Ashland MSA, WV-KY-OH	Y	13550 FQ	30250 AW	52430 TQ	WVBLS	10/01-12/01
	Wisconsin	Y	15810 FQ	46640 AW	82780 TQ	WIBLS	10/01-12/01
	Appleton-Oshkosh-Neenah MSA, WI	Y	24330 FQ	44830 AW	71700 TQ	WIBLS	10/01-12/01
	Green Bay MSA, WI	Y	40800 FQ	70740 AW	110530 TQ	WIBLS	10/01-12/01
	Madison MSA, WI	Y	21480 FQ	49860 AW	81060 TQ	WIBLS	10/01-12/01
	Milwaukee-Waukesha PMSA, WI	Y	13040 FQ	50640 AW	84190 TQ	WIBLS	10/01-12/01
	Racine PMSA, WI	Y	26400 FQ	52410 AW	91310 TQ	WIBLS	10/01-12/01
	Wyoming	Y	19160 FQ	36340 AW	55900 TQ	WYBLS	10/01-12/01
	Cheyenne MSA, WY	Y	16410 FQ	23600 AW	46920 TQ	WYBLS	10/01-12/01
	Puerto Rico	Y	12750 FQ	29510 AW	55700 TQ	PRBLS	10/01-12/01
	Guam	Y	16620 FQ	40010 AW	74960 TQ	GUBLS	10/01-12/01
Insurance Underwriter	Alabama	Y	28440 FQ	44330 AW	68900 TQ	ALBLS	10/01-12/01
	Birmingham MSA, AL	Y	31570 FQ	49680 AW	74550 TQ	ALBLS	10/01-12/01
	Mobile MSA, AL	Y	21480 FQ	34500 AW	50880 TQ	ALBLS	10/01-12/01
	Alaska	Y	29390 FQ	49370 AW	69760 TQ	AKBLS	10/01-12/01
	Anchorage MSA, AK	Y	29150 FQ	49040 AW	69510 TQ	AKBLS	10/01-12/01
	Arizona	Y	28130 FQ	49230 AW	78860 TQ	AZBLS	10/01-12/01
	Phoenix-Mesa MSA, AZ	Y	28510 FQ	49350 AW	78960 TQ	AZBLS	10/01-12/01
	Tucson MSA, AZ	Y	24700 FQ	50250 AW	84960 TQ	AZBLS	10/01-12/01
	Arkansas	Y	29880 FQ	58530 AW	83680 TQ	ARBLS	10/01-12/01
	Little Rock-North Little Rock MSA, AR	Y	38960 FQ	60800 AW	84440 TQ	ARBLS	10/01-12/01
	California	Y	28670 FQ	52730 AW	84970 TQ	CABLS	10/01-12/01
	Fresno MSA, CA	Y	29940 FQ	40760 AW	56980 TQ	CABLS	10/01-12/01
	Los Angeles-Long Beach PMSA, CA	Y	31630 FQ	53640 AW	78770 TQ	CABLS	10/01-12/01
	Modesto MSA, CA	Y	24500 FQ	44050 AW	83000 TQ	CABLS	10/01-12/01
	Oakland PMSA, CA	Y	32550 FQ	53970 AW	74660 TQ	CABLS	10/01-12/01
	Orange County PMSA, CA	Y	29230 FQ	51670 AW	83290 TQ	CABLS	10/01-12/01
	Sacramento PMSA, CA	Y	26710 FQ	54820 AW	94920 TQ	CABLS	10/01-12/01
	Salinas MSA, CA	Y	24590 FQ	41850 AW	64510 TQ	CABLS	10/01-12/01
	San Diego MSA, CA	Y	26700 FQ	50460 AW	80720 TQ	CABLS	10/01-12/01
	San Francisco PMSA, CA	Y	32870 FQ	62190 AW	95030 TQ	CABLS	10/01-12/01
	San Jose PMSA, CA	Y	32560 FQ	76620 AW	138880 TQ	CABLS	10/01-12/01
	Santa Rosa PMSA, CA	Y	33650 FQ	51950 AW	72130 TQ	CABLS	10/01-12/01
	Stockton-Lodi MSA, CA	Y	25560 FQ	43830 AW	68000 TQ	CABLS	10/01-12/01
	Colorado	Y	32280 FQ	55130 AW	83730 TQ	COBLS	10/01-12/01
	Colorado Springs MSA, CO	Y	30300 FQ	50290 AW	72800 TQ	COBLS	10/01-12/01
	Denver PMSA, CO	Y	31890 FQ	56450 AW	85550 TQ	COBLS	10/01-12/01
	Connecticut	Y	35720 FQ	59120 AW	93080 TQ	CTBLS	10/01-12/01
	Bridgeport PMSA, CT	Y	28780 FQ	52030 AW	87990 TQ	CTBLS	10/01-12/01
	Hartford MSA, CT	Y	35960 FQ	57420 AW	85660 TQ	CTBLS	10/01-12/01
	New Haven-Meriden PMSA, CT	Y	34090 FQ	51450 AW	69760 TQ	CTBLS	10/01-12/01
	Stamford-Norwalk PMSA, CT	Y	39220 FQ	74630 AW		CTBLS	10/01-12/01
	Delaware	Y	24980 FQ	47220 AW	71230 TQ	DEBLS	10/01-12/01

AAW Average annual wage; **AE** Average entry wage; **AEX** Average experienced wage; **AO** Average offered; **AOH** Average offered, high; **AOL** Average offered, low; **APH** Average pay, high range; **APL** Average pay, low range; **ASH** Average starting, high; **ASL** Average starting, low; **AW** Average wage paid; **FQ** First quartile wage; **H** Hourly; **HI** Highest wage paid; **HR** High end range; **LR** Low end range; **M** Monthly; **MTC** Median total compensation; **MW** Median wage paid; **SQ** Second quartile wage; **S** Special: hourly and annual; **TQ** Third quartile wage; **W** Weekly; **Y** Yearly

Occupation/Type/Industry	Location	Per	Low	Mid	High	Source	Date
Insurance Underwriter	Wilmington-Newark PMSA, DE-MD	Y	25290 FQ	43850 AW	66210 TQ	DEBLS	10/01-12/01
	District of Columbia	Y	34730 FQ	52900 AW	74840 TQ	DCBLS	10/01-12/01
	Washington PMSA, DC-MD-VA-WV	Y	27550 FQ	47650 AW	76690 TQ	DCBLS	10/01-12/01
	Florida	Y	24330 FQ	45880 AW	73590 TQ	FLBLS	10/01-12/01
	Daytona Beach MSA, FL	Y	21000 FQ	41290 AW	78230 TQ	FLBLS	10/01-12/01
	Fort Lauderdale PMSA, FL	Y	24610 FQ	47250 AW	87950 TQ	FLBLS	10/01-12/01
	Fort Myers-Cape Coral MSA, FL	Y	23930 FQ	31950 AW	55000 TQ	FLBLS	10/01-12/01
	Gainesville MSA, FL	Y	27900 FQ	44680 AW	64960 TQ	FLBLS	10/01-12/01
	Jacksonville MSA, FL	Y	16890 FQ	43700 AW	71600 TQ	FLBLS	10/01-12/01
	Melbourne-Titusville-Palm Bay MSA, FL	Y	20630 FQ	34630 AW	53840 TQ	FLBLS	10/01-12/01
	Miami PMSA, FL	Y	21800 FQ	40530 AW	62980 TQ	FLBLS	10/01-12/01
	Orlando MSA, FL	Y	31870 FQ	51630 AW	80830 TQ	FLBLS	10/01-12/01
	Sarasota-Bradenton MSA, FL	Y	25360 FQ	46190 AW	59390 TQ	FLBLS	10/01-12/01
	Tallahassee MSA, FL	Y	36080 FQ	57950 AW	87750 TQ	FLBLS	10/01-12/01
	Tampa-St. Petersburg-Clearwater MSA, FL	Y	27040 FQ	45250 AW	66560 TQ	FLBLS	10/01-12/01
	West Palm Beach-Boca Raton MSA, FL	Y	29320 FQ	64470 AW	98240 TQ	FLBLS	10/01-12/01
	Georgia	Y	30870 FQ	49310 AW	76040 TQ	GABLS	10/01-12/01
	Atlanta MSA, GA	Y	30840 FQ	49520 AW	76970 TQ	GABLS	10/01-12/01
	Columbus MSA, GA-AL	Y	31360 FQ	50710 AW	79870 TQ	GABLS	10/01-12/01
	Macon MSA, GA	Y	27760 FQ	41000 AW	61430 TQ	GABLS	10/01-12/01
	Savannah MSA, GA	Y	30330 FQ	41780 AW	65570 TQ	GABLS	10/01-12/01
	Hawaii	Y	26580 FQ	42550 AW	64370 TQ	HIBLS	10/01-12/01
	Honolulu MSA, HI	Y	29840 FQ	44240 AW	65720 TQ	HIBLS	10/01-12/01
	Idaho	Y	27970 FQ	44920 AW	72920 TQ	IDBLS	10/01-12/01
	Boise City MSA, ID	Y	28600 FQ	48850 AW	80340 TQ	IDBLS	10/01-12/01
	Illinois	Y	30610 FQ	49380 AW	73090 TQ	ILBLS	10/01-12/01
	Chicago PMSA, IL	Y	32050 FQ	50680 AW	73570 TQ	ILBLS	10/01-12/01
	Peoria-Pekin MSA, IL	Y	23920 FQ	45910 AW	70570 TQ	ILBLS	10/01-12/01
	Rockford MSA, IL	Y	26160 FQ	41300 AW	67650 TQ	ILBLS	10/01-12/01
	Indiana	Y	29220 FQ	48830 AW	72290 TQ	INBLS	10/01-12/01
	Fort Wayne MSA, IN	Y	29080 FQ	55770 AW	89000 TQ	INBLS	10/01-12/01
	Indianapolis MSA, IN	Y	30590 FQ	47020 AW	68780 TQ	INBLS	10/01-12/01
	South Bend MSA, IN	Y	24250 FQ	40140 AW	60100 TQ	INBLS	10/01-12/01
	Iowa	Y	24170 FQ	40390 AW	58710 TQ	IABLS	10/01-12/01
	Cedar Rapids MSA, IA	Y	25890 FQ	43670 AW	61050 TQ	IABLS	10/01-12/01
	Davenport-Moline-Rock Island MSA, IA-IL	Y	24650 FQ	41670 AW	60550 TQ	IABLS	10/01-12/01
	Des Moines MSA, IA	Y	27670 FQ	40200 AW	56580 TQ	IABLS	10/01-12/01
	Kansas	Y	29510 FQ	55230 AW	94330 TQ	KSBLS	10/01-12/01
	Wichita MSA, KS	Y	23470 FQ	43600 AW	74950 TQ	KSBLS	10/01-12/01
	Kentucky	Y	24650 FQ	38140 AW	56460 TQ	KYBLS	10/01-12/01
	Louisville MSA, KY-IN	Y	25030 FQ	37910 AW	56380 TQ	KYBLS	10/01-12/01
	Louisiana	Y	18910 FQ	36140 AW	60490 TQ	LABLS	10/01-12/01
	Baton Rouge MSA, LA	Y	19870 FQ	40370 AW	63590 TQ	LABLS	10/01-12/01
	New Orleans MSA, LA	Y	18750 FQ	31190 AW	50540 TQ	LABLS	10/01-12/01
	Shreveport-Bossier City MSA, LA	Y	15350 FQ	28060 AW	50410 TQ	LABLS	10/01-12/01
	Maine	Y	25930 FQ	43760 AW	67660 TQ	MEBLS	10/01-12/01
	Portland MSA, ME	Y	28770 FQ	46030 AW	69670 TQ	MEBLS	10/01-12/01
	Maryland	Y	31290 FQ	54980 AW	94810 TQ	MDBLS	10/01-12/01
	Baltimore PMSA, MD	Y	34990 FQ	61530 AW	103730 TQ	MDBLS	10/01-12/01
	Massachusetts	Y	33130 FQ	55080 AW	84160 TQ	MABLS	10/01-12/01
	Boston PMSA, MA-NH	Y	33510 FQ	55830 AW	85420 TQ	MABLS	10/01-12/01
	Lawrence PMSA, MA-NH	Y	42350 FQ	60880 AW	75290 TQ	MABLS	10/01-12/01
	Worcester PMSA, MA-CT	Y	33730 FQ	52340 AW	75470 TQ	MABLS	10/01-12/01
	Michigan	Y	28250 FQ	45050 AW	67970 TQ	MIBLS	10/01-12/01
	Ann Arbor PMSA, MI	Y	29550 FQ	47740 AW	71290 TQ	MIBLS	10/01-12/01
	Detroit PMSA, MI	Y	28940 FQ	46090 AW	69770 TQ	MIBLS	10/01-12/01
	Grand Rapids-Muskegon-Holland MSA, MI	Y	30050 FQ	43400 AW	62390 TQ	MIBLS	10/01-12/01
	Lansing-East Lansing MSA, MI	Y	29290 FQ	43870 AW	63190 TQ	MIBLS	10/01-12/01
	Minnesota	Y	32080 FQ	48220 AW	69090 TQ	MNBLS	10/01-12/01
	Minneapolis-St. Paul MSA, MN-WI	Y	33500 FQ	49320 AW	69750 TQ	MNBLS	10/01-12/01
	Mississippi	Y	25190 FQ	39080 AW	57590 TQ	MSBLS	10/01-12/01
	Jackson MSA, MS	Y	25450 FQ	38040 AW	56350 TQ	MSBLS	10/01-12/01

AAW Average annual wage; **AE** Average entry wage; **AEX** Average experienced wage; **AO** Average offered; **AOH** Average offered, high; **AOL** Average offered, low; **APH** Average pay, high range; **APL** Average pay, low range; **ASH** Average starting, high; **ASL** Average starting, low; **AW** Average wage paid; **FQ** First quartile wage; **H** Hourly; **HI** Highest wage paid; **HR** High end range; **LR** Low end range; **M** Monthly; **MTC** Median total compensation; **MW** Median wage paid; **SQ** Second quartile wage; **S** Special: hourly and annual; **TQ** Third quartile wage; **W** Weekly; **Y** Yearly

Occupation/Type/Industry	Location	Per	Low	Mid	High	Source	Date
Insurance Underwriter	Missouri	Y	25010 FQ	45860 AW	71150 TQ	MOBLS	10/01-12/01
	Kansas City MSA, MO-KS	Y	29070 FQ	54670 AW	91280 TQ	MOBLS	10/01-12/01
	St. Louis MSA, MO-IL	Y	24300 FQ	46000 AW	70920 TQ	MOBLS	10/01-12/01
	Montana	Y	25020 FQ	46840 AW	75080 TQ	MTBLS	10/01-12/01
	Nebraska	Y	27490 FQ	44010 AW	67690 TQ	NEBLS	10/01-12/01
	Lincoln MSA, NE	Y	30970 FQ	46310 AW	72510 TQ	NEBLS	10/01-12/01
	Omaha MSA, NE-IA	Y	27380 FQ	43750 AW	64080 TQ	NEBLS	10/01-12/01
	Nevada	Y	22510 FQ	41520 AW	68990 TQ	NVBLS	10/01-12/01
	Las Vegas MSA, NV-AZ	Y	29290 FQ	46040 AW	68850 TQ	NVBLS	10/01-12/01
	Reno MSA, NV	Y	26600 FQ	50330 AW	86440 TQ	NVBLS	10/01-12/01
	New Hampshire	Y	28120 FQ	44120 AW	63280 TQ	NHBLS	10/01-12/01
	Manchester PMSA, NH	Y	31480 FQ	45750 AW	64380 TQ	NHBLS	10/01-12/01
	New Jersey	Y	29840 FQ	56990 AW	115720 TQ	NJBLS	10/01-12/01
	Atlantic-Cape May PMSA, NJ	Y	23260 FQ	43260 AW	98530 TQ	NJBLS	10/01-12/01
	Bergen-Passaic PMSA, NJ	Y	28300 FQ	48230 AW	80390 TQ	NJBLS	10/01-12/01
	Jersey City PMSA, NJ	Y	31580 FQ	72650 AW	143550 TQ	NJBLS	10/01-12/01
	Middlesex-Somerset-Hunterdon PMSA, NJ	Y	31450 FQ	72550 AW	142300 TQ	NJBLS	10/01-12/01
	Monmouth-Ocean PMSA, NJ	Y	28130 FQ	46740 AW	82330 TQ	NJBLS	10/01-12/01
	Newark PMSA, NJ	Y	30710 FQ	55120 AW	88170 TQ	NJBLS	10/01-12/01
	Trenton PMSA, NJ	Y	30780 FQ	46570 AW	68450 TQ	NJBLS	10/01-12/01
	New Mexico	Y	24620 FQ	42140 AW	70120 TQ	NMBLS	10/01-12/01
	Albuquerque MSA, NM	Y	24620 FQ	42590 AW	71050 TQ	NMBLS	10/01-12/01
	New York	Y	30710 FQ	56840 AW	103000 TQ	NYBLS	10/01-12/01
	Albany-Schenectady-Troy MSA, NY	Y	30350 FQ	49700 AW	80040 TQ	NYBLS	10/01-12/01
	Buffalo-Niagara Falls MSA, NY	Y	29640 FQ	46200 AW	72260 TQ	NYBLS	10/01-12/01
	Nassau-Suffolk PMSA, NY	Y	27630 FQ	56490 AW	92220 TQ	NYBLS	10/01-12/01
	New York PMSA, NY	Y	33130 FQ	61840 AW	112550 TQ	NYBLS	10/01-12/01
	Rochester MSA, NY	Y	27700 FQ	40830 AW	63810 TQ	NYBLS	10/01-12/01
	Syracuse MSA, NY	Y	30940 FQ	46560 AW	65050 TQ	NYBLS	10/01-12/01
	North Carolina	Y	26040 FQ	48380 AW	79110 TQ	NCBLS	10/01-12/01
	Charlotte-Gastonia-Rock Hill MSA, NC-SC	Y	33130 FQ	57040 AW	92530 TQ	NCBLS	10/01-12/01
	Fayetteville MSA, NC	Y	20520 FQ	32200 AW	52030 TQ	NCBLS	10/01-12/01
	Greensboro-Winston-Salem-High Point MSA, NC	Y	30940 FQ	48430 AW	73250 TQ	NCBLS	10/01-12/01
	Raleigh-Durham-Chapel Hill MSA, NC	Y	22340 FQ	40910 AW	65520 TQ	NCBLS	10/01-12/01
	North Dakota	Y	24340 FQ	31470 AW	41670 TQ	NDBLS	10/01-12/01
	Fargo-Moorhead MSA, ND-MN	Y	23270 FQ	31860 AW	49990 TQ	NDBLS	10/01-12/01
	Ohio	Y	30360 FQ	47030 AW	68480 TQ	OHBLS	10/01-12/01
	Akron PMSA, OH	Y	30780 FQ	47960 AW	74530 TQ	OHBLS	10/01-12/01
	Cincinnati PMSA, OH-KY-IN	Y	30960 FQ	51120 AW	78330 TQ	OHBLS	10/01-12/01
	Cleveland-Lorain-Elyria PMSA, OH	Y	28150 FQ	44820 AW	68950 TQ	OHBLS	10/01-12/01
	Columbus MSA, OH	Y	32380 FQ	47750 AW	67010 TQ	OHBLS	10/01-12/01
	Dayton-Springfield MSA, OH	Y	30930 FQ	42600 AW	58080 TQ	OHBLS	10/01-12/01
	Toledo MSA, OH	Y	32320 FQ	47320 AW	65530 TQ	OHBLS	10/01-12/01
	Youngstown-Warren MSA, OH	Y	42000 FQ	55110 AW	68520 TQ	OHBLS	10/01-12/01
	Oklahoma	Y	23780 FQ	39620 AW	59260 TQ	OKBLS	10/01-12/01
	Oklahoma City MSA, OK	Y	24800 FQ	39270 AW	54240 TQ	OKBLS	10/01-12/01
	Oregon	Y	31870 FQ	48280 AW	69150 TQ	ORBLS	10/01-12/01
	Portland-Vancouver PMSA, OR-WA	Y	32170 FQ	47220 AW	65800 TQ	ORBLS	10/01-12/01
	Pennsylvania	Y	30750 FQ	51830 AW	81580 TQ	PABLS	10/01-12/01
	Allentown-Bethlehem-Easton MSA, PA	Y	31560 FQ	51540 AW	81520 TQ	PABLS	10/01-12/01
	Harrisburg-Lebanon-Carlisle MSA, PA	Y	33330 FQ	48920 AW	69650 TQ	PABLS	10/01-12/01
	Lancaster MSA, PA	Y	28840 FQ	44990 AW	69090 TQ	PABLS	10/01-12/01
	Philadelphia PMSA, PA-NJ	Y	33010 FQ	55410 AW	87080 TQ	PABLS	10/01-12/01
	Pittsburgh MSA, PA	Y	25340 FQ	46090 AW	71470 TQ	PABLS	10/01-12/01
	Reading MSA, PA	Y	32500 FQ	52270 AW	84640 TQ	PABLS	10/01-12/01
	Scranton-Wilkes-Barre-Hazleton MSA, PA	Y	34620 FQ	46230 AW	58340 TQ	PABLS	10/01-12/01
	York MSA, PA	Y	27080 FQ	39790 AW	59580 TQ	PABLS	10/01-12/01
	Rhode Island	Y	31150 FQ	51590 AW	81440 TQ	RIBLS	10/01-12/01
	Providence-Fall River-Warwick MSA, RI-MA	Y	29920 FQ	49100 AW	76690 TQ	RIBLS	10/01-12/01

AAW	Average annual wage	**AOH**	Average offered, high	**ASH**	Average starting, high	**H**	Hourly	**M**	Monthly	**S**	Special: hourly and annual
AE	Average entry wage	**AOL**	Average offered, low	**ASL**	Average starting, low	**HI**	Highest wage paid	**MTC**	Median total compensation	**TQ**	Third quartile wage
AEX	Average experienced wage	**APH**	Average pay, high range	**AW**	Average wage paid	**HR**	High end range	**MW**	Median wage paid	**W**	Weekly
AO	Average offered	**APL**	Average pay, low range	**FQ**	First quartile wage	**LR**	Low end range	**SQ**	Second quartile wage	**Y**	Yearly

Occupation/Type/Industry	Location	Per	Low	Mid	High	Source	Date
Insurance Underwriter	Charleston-North Charleston MSA, SC	Y	18670 FQ	37500 AW	52800 TQ	SCBLS	10/01-12/01
	Greenville-Spartanburg-Anderson MSA, SC	Y	23940 FQ	37930 AW	56070 TQ	SCBLS	10/01-12/01
	South Dakota	Y	24290 FQ	42140 AW	65100 TQ	SDBLS	10/01-12/01
	Sioux Falls MSA, SD	Y	24210 FQ	40790 AW	58520 TQ	SDBLS	10/01-12/01
	Tennessee	Y	22050 FQ	40350 AW	62780 TQ	TNBLS	10/01-12/01
	Chattanooga MSA, TN-GA	Y	25630 FQ	33730 AW	43370 TQ	TNBLS	10/01-12/01
	Johnson City-Kingsport-Bristol MSA, TN-VA	Y	23670 FQ	39710 AW	64470 TQ	TNBLS	10/01-12/01
	Knoxville MSA, TN	Y	32800 FQ	59700 AW	92860 TQ	TNBLS	10/01-12/01
	Memphis MSA, TN-AR-MS	Y	30960 FQ	45180 AW	58180 TQ	TNBLS	10/01-12/01
	Nashville MSA, TN	Y	21500 FQ	39710 AW	61440 TQ	TNBLS	10/01-12/01
	Texas	Y	27360 FQ	45240 AW	69990 TQ	TXBLS	10/01-12/01
	Amarillo MSA, TX	Y	29540 FQ	46250 AW	77360 TQ	TXBLS	10/01-12/01
	Austin-San Marcos MSA, TX	Y	29180 FQ	45130 AW	67880 TQ	TXBLS	10/01-12/01
	Beaumont-Port Arthur MSA, TX	Y	17770 FQ	26810 AW	35210 TQ	TXBLS	10/01-12/01
	Corpus Christi MSA, TX	Y	15770 FQ	28520 AW	49650 TQ	TXBLS	10/01-12/01
	Dallas PMSA, TX	Y	30460 FQ	46850 AW	71500 TQ	TXBLS	10/01-12/01
	Fort Worth-Arlington PMSA, TX	Y	28360 FQ	47930 AW	75790 TQ	TXBLS	10/01-12/01
	Galveston-Texas City PMSA, TX	Y	23150 FQ	40600 AW	61990 TQ	TXBLS	10/01-12/01
	Houston PMSA, TX	Y	25820 FQ	43940 AW	64070 TQ	TXBLS	10/01-12/01
	Longview-Marshall MSA, TX	Y	17950 FQ	33970 AW	64320 TQ	TXBLS	10/01-12/01
	Lubbock MSA, TX	Y	19040 FQ	30750 AW	44890 TQ	TXBLS	10/01-12/01
	San Antonio MSA, TX	Y	28140 FQ	45640 AW	71220 TQ	TXBLS	10/01-12/01
	Tyler MSA, TX	Y	26370 FQ	48630 AW	77010 TQ	TXBLS	10/01-12/01
	Waco MSA, TX	Y	28850 FQ	40650 AW	54130 TQ	TXBLS	10/01-12/01
	Utah	Y	25000 FQ	39850 AW	58160 TQ	UTBLS	10/01-12/01
	Provo-Orem MSA, UT	Y	23090 FQ	32160 AW	54550 TQ	UTBLS	10/01-12/01
	Salt Lake City-Ogden MSA, UT	Y	29400 FQ	42630 AW	61140 TQ	UTBLS	10/01-12/01
	Vermont	Y	26110 FQ	42210 AW	68060 TQ	VTBLS	10/01-12/01
	Burlington MSA, VT	Y	27180 FQ	42810 AW	69890 TQ	VTBLS	10/01-12/01
	Virginia	Y	25210 FQ	44090 AW	71010 TQ	VABLS	10/01-12/01
	Norfolk-Virginia Beach-Newport News MSA, VA-NC	Y	20730 FQ	38810 AW	69120 TQ	VABLS	10/01-12/01
	Richmond-Petersburg MSA, VA	Y	29560 FQ	46620 AW	70660 TQ	VABLS	10/01-12/01
	Roanoke MSA, VA	Y	26670 FQ	44640 AW	68050 TQ	VABLS	10/01-12/01
	Washington	Y	33630 FQ	53990 AW	84310 TQ	WABLS	10/01-12/01
	Olympia PMSA, WA	Y	33240 FQ	41880 AW	53070 TQ	WABLS	10/01-12/01
	Seattle-Bellevue-Everett PMSA, WA	Y	34100 FQ	55750 AW	88020 TQ	WABLS	10/01-12/01
	Spokane MSA, WA	Y	30460 FQ	45830 AW	66490 TQ	WABLS	10/01-12/01
	West Virginia	Y	12700 FQ	32060 AW	53700 TQ	WVBLS	10/01-12/01
	Charleston MSA, WV	Y	12460 FQ	30680 AW	50560 TQ	WVBLS	10/01-12/01
	Wisconsin	Y	24760 FQ	40410 AW	61950 TQ	WIBLS	10/01-12/01
	Appleton-Oshkosh-Neenah MSA, WI	Y	25620 FQ	37730 AW	55980 TQ	WIBLS	10/01-12/01
	Green Bay MSA, WI	Y	25450 FQ	38810 AW	57310 TQ	WIBLS	10/01-12/01
	Madison MSA, WI	Y	30570 FQ	44560 AW	62980 TQ	WIBLS	10/01-12/01
	Milwaukee-Waukesha PMSA, WI	Y	25780 FQ	39850 AW	60810 TQ	WIBLS	10/01-12/01
	Wyoming	Y	20710 FQ	40840 AW	70420 TQ	WYBLS	10/01-12/01
	Puerto Rico	Y	17070 FQ	27780 AW	42010 TQ	PRBLS	10/01-12/01
	Virgin Islands	Y	20440 FQ	35820 AW	58560 TQ	VIBLS	10/01-12/01
	Guam	Y	15790 FQ	25940 AW	37010 TQ	GUBLS	10/01-12/01
Interior Designer	Alabama	Y	19620 FQ	36430 AW	60040 TQ	ALBLS	10/01-12/01
	Birmingham MSA, AL	Y	21760 FQ	32560 AW	44510 TQ	ALBLS	10/01-12/01
	Huntsville MSA, AL	Y	23890 FQ	46030 AW	68490 TQ	ALBLS	10/01-12/01
	Mobile MSA, AL	Y	23800 FQ	52560 AW	137310 TQ	ALBLS	10/01-12/01
	Montgomery MSA, AL	Y	21770 FQ	42110 AW	57210 TQ	ALBLS	10/01-12/01
	Arizona	Y	24640 FQ	44340 AW	74910 TQ	AZBLS	10/01-12/01
	Phoenix-Mesa MSA, AZ	Y	28040 FQ	47120 AW	76170 TQ	AZBLS	10/01-12/01
	Tucson MSA, AZ	Y	19420 FQ	35200 AW	60970 TQ	AZBLS	10/01-12/01
	Arkansas	Y	19730 FQ	28040 AW	45110 TQ	ARBLS	10/01-12/01
	California	Y	20440 FQ	47880 AW	78270 TQ	CABLS	10/01-12/01

AAW	Average annual wage	**AOH**	Average offered, high	**ASH**	Average starting, high	**H**	Hourly	**M**	Monthly	**S**	Special: hourly and annual
AE	Average entry wage	**AOL**	Average offered, low	**ASL**	Average starting, low	**HI**	Highest wage paid	**MTC**	Median total compensation	**TQ**	Third quartile wage
AEX	Average experienced wage	**APH**	Average pay, high range	**AW**	Average wage paid	**HR**	High end range	**MW**	Median wage paid	**W**	Weekly
AO	Average offered	**APL**	Average pay, low range	**FQ**	First quartile wage	**LR**	Low end range	**SQ**	Second quartile wage	**Y**	Yearly

Occupation/Type/Industry	Location	Per	Low	Mid	High	Source	Date
Interior Designer	Los Angeles-Long Beach PMSA, CA	Y	37290 FQ	57330 AW	82070 TQ	CABLS	10/01-12/01
	Oakland PMSA, CA	Y	26350 FQ	57730 AW	93280 TQ	CABLS	10/01-12/01
	Orange County PMSA, CA	Y	18400 FQ	28570 AW	52000 TQ	CABLS	10/01-12/01
	Riverside-San Bernardino PMSA, CA	Y	26880 FQ	44840 AW	60510 TQ	CABLS	10/01-12/01
	Sacramento PMSA, CA	Y	25410 FQ	42230 AW	59570 TQ	CABLS	10/01-12/01
	Salinas MSA, CA	Y	22480 FQ	37320 AW	53410 TQ	CABLS	10/01-12/01
	San Diego MSA, CA	Y	29290 FQ	50310 AW	75290 TQ	CABLS	10/01-12/01
	San Francisco PMSA, CA	Y	32550 FQ	52340 AW	77820 TQ	CABLS	10/01-12/01
	San Jose PMSA, CA	Y	27690 FQ	49220 AW	70570 TQ	CABLS	10/01-12/01
	Ventura PMSA, CA	Y	30280 FQ	87650 AW		CABLS	10/01-12/01
	Colorado	Y	31580 FQ	55070 AW	73100 TQ	COBLS	10/01-12/01
	Boulder-Longmont PMSA, CO	Y	28030 FQ	48780 AW	71420 TQ	COBLS	10/01-12/01
	Colorado Springs MSA, CO	Y	25670 FQ	54160 AW	91120 TQ	COBLS	10/01-12/01
	Denver PMSA, CO	Y	36050 FQ	59430 AW	72810 TQ	COBLS	10/01-12/01
	Fort Collins-Loveland MSA, CO	Y	30780 FQ	43690 AW	65830 TQ	COBLS	10/01-12/01
	Connecticut	Y	33390 FQ	59850 AW	90710 TQ	CTBLS	10/01-12/01
	Bridgeport PMSA, CT	Y	29850 FQ	48480 AW	69440 TQ	CTBLS	10/01-12/01
	Hartford MSA, CT	Y	28350 FQ	48540 AW	70200 TQ	CTBLS	10/01-12/01
	New Haven-Meriden PMSA, CT	Y	37200 FQ	42970 AW	50710 TQ	CTBLS	10/01-12/01
	Stamford-Norwalk PMSA, CT	Y	44590 FQ	78040 AW		CTBLS	10/01-12/01
	Delaware	Y	17120 FQ	26740 AW	36830 TQ	DEBLS	10/01-12/01
	District of Columbia	Y	31310 FQ	51520 AW	80110 TQ	DCBLS	10/01-12/01
	Washington PMSA, DC-MD-VA-WV	Y	26660 FQ	45230 AW	73440 TQ	DCBLS	10/01-12/01
	Florida	Y	27390 FQ	48380 AW	79980 TQ	FLBLS	10/01-12/01
	Fort Lauderdale PMSA, FL	Y	26790 FQ	57590 AW	108710 TQ	FLBLS	10/01-12/01
	Fort Myers-Cape Coral MSA, FL	Y	28460 FQ	42810 AW	62410 TQ	FLBLS	10/01-12/01
	Fort Pierce-Port St. Lucie MSA, FL	Y	29610 FQ	34940 AW	47680 TQ	FLBLS	10/01-12/01
	Fort Walton Beach MSA, FL	Y	27400 FQ	34940 AW	44130 TQ	FLBLS	10/01-12/01
	Jacksonville MSA, FL	Y	20560 FQ	35590 AW	54760 TQ	FLBLS	10/01-12/01
	Melbourne-Titusville-Palm Bay MSA, FL	Y	23870 FQ	32600 AW	42670 TQ	FLBLS	10/01-12/01
	Miami PMSA, FL	Y	35220 FQ	48290 AW	75490 TQ	FLBLS	10/01-12/01
	Naples MSA, FL	Y	28260 FQ	42770 AW	77740 TQ	FLBLS	10/01-12/01
	Orlando MSA, FL	Y	23710 FQ	37910 AW	57980 TQ	FLBLS	10/01-12/01
	Sarasota-Bradenton MSA, FL	Y	14260 FQ	30280 AW	43810 TQ	FLBLS	10/01-12/01
	Tampa-St. Petersburg-Clearwater MSA, FL	Y	23340 FQ	39100 AW	61970 TQ	FLBLS	10/01-12/01
	West Palm Beach-Boca Raton MSA, FL	Y	37030 FQ	70280 AW	113190 TQ	FLBLS	10/01-12/01
	Georgia	Y	26270 FQ	40660 AW	64550 TQ	GABLS	10/01-12/01
	Atlanta MSA, GA	Y	28190 FQ	41750 AW	65080 TQ	GABLS	10/01-12/01
	Hawaii	Y	24900 FQ	42580 AW	69270 TQ	HIBLS	10/01-12/01
	Honolulu MSA, HI	Y	24810 FQ	42290 AW	70300 TQ	HIBLS	10/01-12/01
	Idaho	Y	19380 FQ	34700 AW	55270 TQ	IDBLS	10/01-12/01
	Boise City MSA, ID	Y	18730 FQ	37020 AW	59010 TQ	IDBLS	10/01-12/01
	Illinois	Y	20020 FQ	45160 AW	74180 TQ	ILBLS	10/01-12/01
	Chicago PMSA, IL	Y	24270 FQ	49590 AW	80000 TQ	ILBLS	10/01-12/01
	Peoria-Pekin MSA, IL	Y	14850 FQ	21490 AW	35250 TQ	ILBLS	10/01-12/01
	Indiana	Y	18900 FQ	36110 AW	49570 TQ	INBLS	10/01-12/01
	Gary PMSA, IN	Y	19430 FQ	32270 AW	45400 TQ	INBLS	10/01-12/01
	Indianapolis MSA, IN	Y	23580 FQ	38200 AW	53740 TQ	INBLS	10/01-12/01
	South Bend MSA, IN	Y	18990 FQ	25070 AW	30840 TQ	INBLS	10/01-12/01
	Iowa	Y	19660 FQ	34630 AW	47360 TQ	IABLS	10/01-12/01
	Davenport-Moline-Rock Island MSA, IA-IL	Y	19970 FQ	28560 AW	42320 TQ	IABLS	10/01-12/01
	Des Moines MSA, IA	Y	22960 FQ	36160 AW	46130 TQ	IABLS	10/01-12/01
	Kansas	Y	21500 FQ	39540 AW	69320 TQ	KSBLS	10/01-12/01
	Topeka MSA, KS	Y	26530 FQ	55540 AW	72290 TQ	KSBLS	10/01-12/01
	Wichita MSA, KS	Y	27330 FQ	32030 AW	35240 TQ	KSBLS	10/01-12/01
	Kentucky	Y	16420 FQ	32480 AW	53720 TQ	KYBLS	10/01-12/01
	Lexington MSA, KY	Y	24060 FQ	37030 AW	53910 TQ	KYBLS	10/01-12/01
	Louisville MSA, KY-IN	Y	16690 FQ	35130 AW	53820 TQ	KYBLS	10/01-12/01
	Louisiana	Y	19060 FQ	33540 AW	54400 TQ	LABLS	10/01-12/01
	Baton Rouge MSA, LA	Y	30690 FQ	42630 AW	58370 TQ	LABLS	10/01-12/01
	Lafayette MSA, LA	Y	22950 FQ	34270 AW	47860 TQ	LABLS	10/01-12/01

AAW	Average annual wage	AOH	Average offered, high	ASH	Average starting, high	H	Hourly	M	Monthly	S	Special: hourly and annual
AE	Average entry wage	AOL	Average offered, low	ASL	Average starting, low	HI	Highest wage paid	MTC	Median total compensation	TQ	Third quartile wage
AEX	Average experienced wage	APH	Average pay, high range	AW	Average wage paid	HR	High end range	MW	Median wage paid	W	Weekly
AO	Average offered	APL	Average pay, low range	FQ	First quartile wage	LR	Low end range	SQ	Second quartile wage	Y	Yearly

Occupation/Type/Industry	Location	Per	Low	Mid	High	Source	Date
Interior Designer	New Orleans MSA, LA	Y	20430 FQ	33640 AW	48800 TQ	LABLS	10/01-12/01
	Maine	Y	20270 FQ	38140 AW	66820 TQ	MEBLS	10/01-12/01
	Portland MSA, ME	Y	22310 FQ	42060 AW	65590 TQ	MEBLS	10/01-12/01
	Maryland	Y	25550 FQ	42700 AW	68320 TQ	MDBLS	10/01-12/01
	Baltimore PMSA, MD	Y	21720 FQ	38780 AW	61950 TQ	MDBLS	10/01-12/01
	Massachusetts	Y	29130 FQ	49010 AW	76790 TQ	MABLS	10/01-12/01
	Boston PMSA, MA-NH	Y	29870 FQ	49370 AW	74270 TQ	MABLS	10/01-12/01
	Worcester PMSA, MA-CT	Y	29350 FQ	44470 AW	79330 TQ	MABLS	10/01-12/01
	Michigan	Y	25670 FQ	45690 AW	55830 TQ	MIBLS	10/01-12/01
	Ann Arbor PMSA, MI	Y	24640 FQ	42570 AW	65270 TQ	MIBLS	10/01-12/01
	Detroit PMSA, MI	Y	35430 FQ	49800 AW	55980 TQ	MIBLS	10/01-12/01
	Flint PMSA, MI	Y	13210 FQ	36110 AW	55670 TQ	MIBLS	10/01-12/01
	Grand Rapids-Muskegon-Holland MSA, MI	Y	23850 FQ	34840 AW	50060 TQ	MIBLS	10/01-12/01
	Kalamazoo-Battle Creek MSA, MI	Y	17780 FQ	37370 AW	50940 TQ	MIBLS	10/01-12/01
	Lansing-East Lansing MSA, MI	Y	18380 FQ	30030 AW	46210 TQ	MIBLS	10/01-12/01
	Saginaw-Bay City-Midland MSA, MI	Y	18100 FQ	29000 AW	44960 TQ	MIBLS	10/01-12/01
	Minnesota	Y	23410 FQ	37940 AW	55870 TQ	MNBLS	10/01-12/01
	Minneapolis-St. Paul MSA, MN-WI	Y	25910 FQ	40950 AW	58520 TQ	MNBLS	10/01-12/01
	Mississippi	Y	15850 FQ	33730 AW	56270 TQ	MSBLS	10/01-12/01
	Jackson MSA, MS	Y	21760 FQ	47400 AW	89610 TQ	MSBLS	10/01-12/01
	Missouri	Y	20270 FQ	37680 AW	56500 TQ	MOBLS	10/01-12/01
	Kansas City MSA, MO-KS	Y	19110 FQ	36490 AW	63770 TQ	MOBLS	10/01-12/01
	St. Louis MSA, MO-IL	Y	24590 FQ	41060 AW	60690 TQ	MOBLS	10/01-12/01
	Springfield MSA, MO	Y	18240 FQ	36680 AW	55170 TQ	MOBLS	10/01-12/01
	Montana	Y	22120 FQ	46910 AW	102550 TQ	MTBLS	10/01-12/01
	Nebraska	Y	16130 FQ	31510 AW	46330 TQ	NEBLS	10/01-12/01
	Lincoln MSA, NE	Y	15410 FQ	32870 AW	44320 TQ	NEBLS	10/01-12/01
	Omaha MSA, NE-IA	Y	16400 FQ	28530 AW	44660 TQ	NEBLS	10/01-12/01
	Nevada	Y	29540 FQ	54730 AW	85930 TQ	NVBLS	10/01-12/01
	Las Vegas MSA, NV-AZ	Y	24290 FQ	52760 AW	84670 TQ	NVBLS	10/01-12/01
	Reno MSA, NV	Y	31980 FQ	55730 AW	135600 TQ	NVBLS	10/01-12/01
	New Hampshire	Y	24030 FQ	36460 AW	53450 TQ	NHBLS	10/01-12/01
	New Jersey	Y	28840 FQ	50690 AW	86340 TQ	NJBLS	10/01-12/01
	Atlantic-Cape May PMSA, NJ	Y	34390 FQ	45270 AW	65570 TQ	NJBLS	10/01-12/01
	Bergen-Passaic PMSA, NJ	Y	30800 FQ	66660 AW	94600 TQ	NJBLS	10/01-12/01
	Jersey City PMSA, NJ	Y	23460 FQ	40290 AW	47810 TQ	NJBLS	10/01-12/01
	Middlesex-Somerset-Hunterdon PMSA, NJ	Y	31980 FQ	53980 AW	80330 TQ	NJBLS	10/01-12/01
	Monmouth-Ocean PMSA, NJ	Y	13410 FQ	36170 AW	59740 TQ	NJBLS	10/01-12/01
	Newark PMSA, NJ	Y	30620 FQ	47150 AW	68860 TQ	NJBLS	10/01-12/01
	New Mexico	Y	20510 FQ	37830 AW	57890 TQ	NMBLS	10/01-12/01
	Albuquerque MSA, NM	Y	22420 FQ	39690 AW	58450 TQ	NMBLS	10/01-12/01
	New York	Y	25540 FQ	49330 AW	78840 TQ	NYBLS	10/01-12/01
	Albany-Schenectady-Troy MSA, NY	Y	24210 FQ	45220 AW	60630 TQ	NYBLS	10/01-12/01
	Buffalo-Niagara Falls MSA, NY	Y	24100 FQ	34120 AW	41280 TQ	NYBLS	10/01-12/01
	Nassau-Suffolk PMSA, NY	Y	14470 FQ	40070 AW	68780 TQ	NYBLS	10/01-12/01
	New York PMSA, NY	Y	33000 FQ	56020 AW	91470 TQ	NYBLS	10/01-12/01
	Newburgh PMSA, NY-PA	Y	26370 FQ	40990 AW	60970 TQ	NYBLS	10/01-12/01
	Rochester MSA, NY	Y	24360 FQ	33560 AW	47550 TQ	NYBLS	10/01-12/01
	Syracuse MSA, NY	Y	14800 FQ	28940 AW	43380 TQ	NYBLS	10/01-12/01
	North Carolina	Y	17120 FQ	33850 AW	51650 TQ	NCBLS	10/01-12/01
	Charlotte-Gastonia-Rock Hill MSA, NC-SC	Y	15850 FQ	30840 AW	53740 TQ	NCBLS	10/01-12/01
	Greensboro-Winston-Salem-High Point MSA, NC	Y	16270 FQ	33230 AW	55760 TQ	NCBLS	10/01-12/01
	Hickory-Morganton-Lenoir MSA, NC	Y	21220 FQ	32240 AW	45070 TQ	NCBLS	10/01-12/01
	Raleigh-Durham-Chapel Hill MSA, NC	Y	22420 FQ	35800 AW	53170 TQ	NCBLS	10/01-12/01
	Wilmington MSA, NC	Y	28640 FQ	39890 AW	44090 TQ	NCBLS	10/01-12/01
	North Dakota	Y	17680 FQ	37220 AW	49320 TQ	NDBLS	10/01-12/01
	Fargo-Moorhead MSA, ND-MN	Y	19480 FQ	34710 AW	45930 TQ	NDBLS	10/01-12/01
	Ohio	Y	19930 FQ	37270 AW	55510 TQ	OHBLS	10/01-12/01
	Akron PMSA, OH	Y	22550 FQ	34140 AW	45970 TQ	OHBLS	10/01-12/01
	Cincinnati PMSA, OH-KY-IN	Y	23230 FQ	39520 AW	62480 TQ	OHBLS	10/01-12/01

AAW	Average annual wage	**AOH**	Average offered, high	**ASH**	Average starting, high	**H**	Hourly	**M**	Monthly	**S**	Special: hourly and annual
AE	Average entry wage	**AOL**	Average offered, low	**ASL**	Average starting, low	**HI**	Highest wage paid	**MTC**	Median total compensation	**TQ**	Third quartile wage
AEX	Average experienced wage	**APH**	Average pay, high range	**AW**	Average wage paid	**HR**	High end range	**MW**	Median wage paid	**W**	Weekly
AO	Average offered	**APL**	Average pay, low range	**FQ**	First quartile wage	**LR**	Low end range	**SQ**	Second quartile wage	**Y**	Yearly

Occupation/Type/Industry	Location	Per	Low	Mid	High	Source	Date
Interior Designer	Cleveland-Lorain-Elyria PMSA, OH	Y	12000 FQ	35340 AW	56330 TQ	OHBLS	10/01-12/01
	Columbus MSA, OH	Y	22020 FQ	39620 AW	56320 TQ	OHBLS	10/01-12/01
	Dayton-Springfield MSA, OH	Y	20690 FQ	32050 AW	50300 TQ	OHBLS	10/01-12/01
	Toledo MSA, OH	Y	16900 FQ	37740 AW	56970 TQ	OHBLS	10/01-12/01
	Oklahoma	Y	23730 FQ	34640 AW	51940 TQ	OKBLS	10/01-12/01
	Oklahoma City MSA, OK	Y	23930 FQ	32800 AW	47230 TQ	OKBLS	10/01-12/01
	Tulsa MSA, OK	Y	23930 FQ	38940 AW	58650 TQ	OKBLS	10/01-12/01
	Oregon	Y	28080 FQ	46010 AW	69160 TQ	ORBLS	10/01-12/01
	Portland-Vancouver PMSA, OR-WA	Y	27130 FQ	43070 AW	67260 TQ	ORBLS	10/01-12/01
	Salem PMSA, OR	Y	47450 FQ	56850 AW	71110 TQ	ORBLS	10/01-12/01
	Pennsylvania	Y	19400 FQ	36410 AW	55640 TQ	PABLS	10/01-12/01
	Allentown-Bethlehem-Easton MSA, PA	Y	23830 FQ	44790 AW	88800 TQ	PABLS	10/01-12/01
	Harrisburg-Lebanon-Carlisle MSA, PA	Y	20170 FQ	35510 AW	52730 TQ	PABLS	10/01-12/01
	Lancaster MSA, PA	Y	27000 FQ	39400 AW	46140 TQ	PABLS	10/01-12/01
	Philadelphia PMSA, PA-NJ	Y	23240 FQ	39800 AW	58080 TQ	PABLS	10/01-12/01
	Pittsburgh MSA, PA	Y	20310 FQ	34960 AW	56820 TQ	PABLS	10/01-12/01
	Rhode Island	Y	13820 FQ	42520 AW	80770 TQ	RIBLS	10/01-12/01
	Providence-Fall River-Warwick MSA, RI-MA	Y	26870 FQ	50710 AW	82580 TQ	RIBLS	10/01-12/01
	South Carolina	Y	24390 FQ	42530 AW	65130 TQ	SCBLS	10/01-12/01
	Charleston-North Charleston MSA, SC	Y	23590 FQ	46670 AW	94600 TQ	SCBLS	10/01-12/01
	Columbia MSA, SC	Y	30850 FQ	59180 AW		SCBLS	10/01-12/01
	Greenville-Spartanburg-Anderson MSA, SC	Y	26590 FQ	41850 AW	57030 TQ	SCBLS	10/01-12/01
	South Dakota	Y	13430 FQ	28920 AW	50090 TQ	SDBLS	10/01-12/01
	Tennessee	Y	15480 FQ	30460 AW	48130 TQ	TNBLS	10/01-12/01
	Johnson City-Kingsport-Bristol MSA, TN-VA	Y	14430 FQ	16700 AW	17550 TQ	TNBLS	10/01-12/01
	Knoxville MSA, TN	Y	19450 FQ	32260 AW	47620 TQ	TNBLS	10/01-12/01
	Memphis MSA, TN-AR-MS	Y	20270 FQ	36370 AW	58790 TQ	TNBLS	10/01-12/01
	Nashville MSA, TN	Y	16020 FQ	27870 AW	47030 TQ	TNBLS	10/01-12/01
	Texas	Y	12950 FQ	35250 AW	58280 TQ	TXBLS	10/01-12/01
	Austin-San Marcos MSA, TX	Y	23820 FQ	38750 AW	54980 TQ	TXBLS	10/01-12/01
	Dallas PMSA, TX	Y	25750 FQ	44250 AW	64580 TQ	TXBLS	10/01-12/01
	Fort Worth-Arlington PMSA, TX	Y	11540 FQ	19090 AW	42590 TQ	TXBLS	10/01-12/01
	Houston PMSA, TX	Y	19860 FQ	41290 AW	72420 TQ	TXBLS	10/01-12/01
	Lubbock MSA, TX	Y	28820 FQ	32490 AW	34880 TQ	TXBLS	10/01-12/01
	San Antonio MSA, TX	Y	15500 FQ	37970 AW	61420 TQ	TXBLS	10/01-12/01
	Utah	Y	15830 FQ	42810 AW	60200 TQ	UTBLS	10/01-12/01
	Provo-Orem MSA, UT	Y	12370 FQ	33420 AW	54430 TQ	UTBLS	10/01-12/01
	Salt Lake City-Ogden MSA, UT	Y	28670 FQ	37030 AW	44710 TQ	UTBLS	10/01-12/01
	Vermont	Y	28170 FQ	43620 AW	66850 TQ	VTBLS	10/01-12/01
	Virginia	Y	20290 FQ	40460 AW	68030 TQ	VABLS	10/01-12/01
	Norfolk-Virginia Beach-Newport News MSA, VA-NC	Y	17470 FQ	35580 AW	59150 TQ	VABLS	10/01-12/01
	Richmond-Petersburg MSA, VA	Y	26470 FQ	42140 AW	58240 TQ	VABLS	10/01-12/01
	Roanoke MSA, VA	Y	24590 FQ	36480 AW	55220 TQ	VABLS	10/01-12/01
	Washington	Y	27400 FQ	47670 AW	74590 TQ	WABLS	10/01-12/01
	Seattle-Bellevue-Everett PMSA, WA	Y	30380 FQ	50650 AW	79490 TQ	WABLS	10/01-12/01
	Spokane MSA, WA	Y	22480 FQ	44570 AW	72100 TQ	WABLS	10/01-12/01
	Tacoma PMSA, WA	Y	20180 FQ	36030 AW	49890 TQ	WABLS	10/01-12/01
	Yakima MSA, WA	Y	25400 FQ	50450 AW	88780 TQ	WABLS	10/01-12/01
	West Virginia	Y	17980 FQ	31080 AW	48500 TQ	WVBLS	10/01-12/01
	Wisconsin	Y	20150 FQ	34910 AW	56780 TQ	WIBLS	10/01-12/01
	Appleton-Oshkosh-Neenah MSA, WI	Y	18940 FQ	32470 AW	45720 TQ	WIBLS	10/01-12/01
	Green Bay MSA, WI	Y	19220 FQ	34470 AW	51880 TQ	WIBLS	10/01-12/01
	Madison MSA, WI	Y	23740 FQ	37530 AW	57330 TQ	WIBLS	10/01-12/01
	Milwaukee-Waukesha PMSA, WI	Y	20620 FQ	36030 AW	61200 TQ	WIBLS	10/01-12/01
	Puerto Rico	Y	19320 FQ	38200 AW	57400 TQ	PRBLS	10/01-12/01

AAW	Average annual wage	**AOH**	Average offered, high	**ASH**	Average starting, high	**H**	Hourly	**M**	Monthly	**S**	Special: hourly and annual
AE	Average entry wage	**AOL**	Average offered, low	**ASL**	Average starting, low	**HI**	Highest wage paid	**MTC**	Median total compensation	**TQ**	Third quartile wage
AEX	Average experienced wage	**APH**	Average pay, high range	**AW**	Average wage paid	**HR**	High end range	**MW**	Median wage paid	**W**	Weekly
AO	Average offered	**APL**	Average pay, low range	**FQ**	First quartile wage	**LR**	Low end range	**SQ**	Second quartile wage	**Y**	Yearly

Occupation/Type/Industry	Location	Per	Low	Mid	High	Source	Date
Intermediate Appellate Court Judge							
State Court	United States	Y		114280 MW		OOH7	1999-2000
Internet and Intranet Manager	United States	Y		58000-82500 AW		WW	1/00-1/01
Internet Manager	United States	Y		92833 AW		INFO6	1/99-1/00
Internet Manager and Director	United States	Y		78200 AW		INFO4	1/01-1/02
Internist	United States	Y		145000 AW		HHN	1/01-1/02
	Alabama	Y	91670 FQ	127950 AW		ALBLS	10/01-12/01
	Birmingham MSA, AL	Y	106360 FQ	135210 AW		ALBLS	10/01-12/01
	Huntsville MSA, AL	Y	80920 FQ	119720 AW		ALBLS	10/01-12/01
	Mobile MSA, AL	Y	95790 FQ	118670 AW		ALBLS	10/01-12/01
	Alaska	Y	99650 FQ	134270 AW		AKBLS	10/01-12/01
	Arizona	Y	106370 FQ	134570 AW		AZBLS	10/01-12/01
	Arkansas	Y	126360 FQ	140460 AW		ARBLS	10/01-12/01
	California	Y	110650 FQ	136190 AW		CABLS	10/01-12/01
	Fresno MSA, CA	Y	97340 FQ	121600 AW		CABLS	10/01-12/01
	Los Angeles-Long Beach PMSA, CA	Y	98750 FQ	122360 AW		CABLS	10/01-12/01
	Modesto MSA, CA	Y	78210 FQ	129010 AW		CABLS	10/01-12/01
	Oakland PMSA, CA	Y	58830 FQ	119330 AW		CABLS	10/01-12/01
	Orange County PMSA, CA	Y	46040 FQ	119160 AW		CABLS	10/01-12/01
	San Jose PMSA, CA	Y	102020 FQ	127620 AW		CABLS	10/01-12/01
	Santa Cruz-Watsonville PMSA, CA	Y	99760 FQ	129060 AW		CABLS	10/01-12/01
	Ventura PMSA, CA	Y	127410 FQ	139930 AW		CABLS	10/01-12/01
	Colorado	Y	24880 FQ	79310 AW		COBLS	10/01-12/01
	Boulder-Longmont PMSA, CO	Y	23860 FQ	29780 AW	29050 TQ	COBLS	10/01-12/01
	Colorado Springs MSA, CO	Y	88460 FQ	121780 AW		COBLS	10/01-12/01
	Connecticut	Y	38970 FQ	107450 AW		CTBLS	10/01-12/01
	New Haven-Meriden PMSA, CT	Y	94720 FQ	119370 AW		CTBLS	10/01-12/01
	New London-Norwich MSA, CT-RI	Y	98220 FQ	129160 AW		CTBLS	10/01-12/01
	Stamford-Norwalk PMSA, CT	Y	118260 FQ	135520 AW		CTBLS	10/01-12/01
	Waterbury PMSA, CT	Y	141250 FQ	142820 AW		CTBLS	10/01-12/01
	Washington PMSA, DC-MD-VA-WV	Y	75460 FQ	121750 AW		DCBLS	10/01-12/01
	Florida	Y	112880 FQ	135760 AW		FLBLS	10/01-12/01
	Fort Lauderdale PMSA, FL	Y	108450 FQ	133670 AW		FLBLS	10/01-12/01
	Fort Myers-Cape Coral MSA, FL	Y	49620 FQ	117710 AW		FLBLS	10/01-12/01
	Gainesville MSA, FL	Y	122990 FQ	137650 AW		FLBLS	10/01-12/01
	Jacksonville MSA, FL	Y	103600 FQ	130210 AW		FLBLS	10/01-12/01
	Lakeland-Winter Haven MSA, FL	Y	116260 FQ	137970 AW		FLBLS	10/01-12/01
	Melbourne-Titusville-Palm Bay MSA, FL	Y	100530 FQ	132050 AW		FLBLS	10/01-12/01
	Miami PMSA, FL	Y	89450 FQ	125020 AW		FLBLS	10/01-12/01
	Sarasota-Bradenton MSA, FL	Y	125050 FQ	138810 AW		FLBLS	10/01-12/01
	Tallahassee MSA, FL	Y		144010 AW		FLBLS	10/01-12/01
	West Palm Beach-Boca Raton MSA, FL	Y	123170 FQ	138530 AW		FLBLS	10/01-12/01
	Georgia	Y	64030 FQ	120250 AW		GABLS	10/01-12/01
	Atlanta MSA, GA	Y	61770 FQ	108020 AW		GABLS	10/01-12/01
	Augusta-Aiken MSA, GA-SC	Y	45880 FQ	90210 AW		GABLS	10/01-12/01
	Columbus MSA, GA-AL	Y	125730 FQ	138920 AW		GABLS	10/01-12/01
	Macon MSA, GA	Y	115980 FQ	138680 AW		GABLS	10/01-12/01
	Honolulu MSA, HI	Y	40480 FQ	87600 AW		HIBLS	10/01-12/01
	Illinois	Y	71320 FQ	124760 AW		ILBLS	10/01-12/01
	Chicago PMSA, IL	Y	102030 FQ	131570 AW		ILBLS	10/01-12/01
	Indiana	Y	98700 FQ	135170 AW		INBLS	10/01-12/01
	Fort Wayne MSA, IN	Y	80560 FQ	103310 AW		INBLS	10/01-12/01
	Iowa	Y	17590 FQ	110530 AW		IABLS	10/01-12/01
	Kansas	Y	80100 FQ	123160 AW		KSBLS	10/01-12/01
	Topeka MSA, KS	Y	98540 FQ	121300 AW		KSBLS	10/01-12/01
	Wichita MSA, KS	Y	77910 FQ	121890 AW		KSBLS	10/01-12/01
	Kentucky	Y	98920 FQ	131440 AW		KYBLS	10/01-12/01
	Louisville MSA, KY-IN	Y	73750 FQ	127110 AW		KYBLS	10/01-12/01

AAW Average annual wage **AOH** Average offered, high **ASH** Average starting, high **H** Hourly **M** Monthly **S** Special: hourly and annual
AE Average entry wage **AOL** Average offered, low **ASL** Average starting, low **HI** Highest wage paid **MTC** Median total compensation **TQ** Third quartile wage
AEX Average experienced wage **APH** Average pay, high range **AW** Average wage paid **HR** High end range **MW** Median wage paid **W** Weekly
AO Average offered **APL** Average pay, low range **FQ** First quartile wage **LR** Low end range **SQ** Second quartile wage **Y** Yearly

Occupation/Type/Industry	Location	Per	Low	Mid	High	Source	Date
Internist	Louisiana	Y		143310 AW		LABLS	10/01-12/01
	Maine	Y	87890 FQ	119800 AW		MEBLS	10/01-12/01
	Portland MSA, ME	Y	82710 FQ	110740 AW		MEBLS	10/01-12/01
	Maryland	Y	80840 FQ	119370 AW		MDBLS	10/01-12/01
	Baltimore PMSA, MD	Y	89950 FQ	120990 AW		MDBLS	10/01-12/01
	Massachusetts	Y	77010 FQ	121510 AW		MABLS	10/01-12/01
	Boston PMSA, MA-NH	Y	77190 FQ	119600 AW		MABLS	10/01-12/01
	Lawrence PMSA, MA-NH	Y	125570 FQ	139810 AW		MABLS	10/01-12/01
	Springfield MSA, MA	Y	117130 FQ	132730 AW		MABLS	10/01-12/01
	Worcester PMSA, MA-CT	Y	93170 FQ	109320 AW		MABLS	10/01-12/01
	Michigan	Y	107800 FQ	135850 AW		MIBLS	10/01-12/01
	Ann Arbor PMSA, MI	Y	94760 FQ	118590 AW		MIBLS	10/01-12/01
	Flint PMSA, MI	Y	108760 FQ	134680 AW		MIBLS	10/01-12/01
	Grand Rapids-Muskegon-Holland MSA, MI	Y	56090 FQ	112620 AW		MIBLS	10/01-12/01
	Lansing-East Lansing MSA, MI	Y	103930 FQ	130120 AW		MIBLS	10/01-12/01
	Minnesota	Y	104220 FQ	130580 AW		MNBLS	10/01-12/01
	Minneapolis-St. Paul MSA, MN-WI	Y	104430 FQ	130660 AW		MNBLS	10/01-12/01
	Mississippi	Y	51870 FQ	123920 AW		MSBLS	10/01-12/01
	Missouri	Y	102050 FQ	131170 AW		MOBLS	10/01-12/01
	Kansas City MSA, MO-KS	Y	82680 FQ	127780 AW		MOBLS	10/01-12/01
	St. Louis MSA, MO-IL	Y	103870 FQ	132090 AW		MOBLS	10/01-12/01
	Montana	Y	85980 FQ	118260 AW		MTBLS	10/01-12/01
	Nebraska	Y	104480 FQ	131250 AW		NEBLS	10/01-12/01
	Lincoln MSA, NE	Y	100410 FQ	128390 AW		NEBLS	10/01-12/01
	Omaha MSA, NE-IA	Y	118040 FQ	137870 AW		NEBLS	10/01-12/01
	Reno MSA, NV	Y	145480 FQ	143070 AW		NVBLS	10/01-12/01
	New Hampshire	Y	94230 FQ	127390 AW		NHBLS	10/01-12/01
	Portsmouth-Rochester PMSA, NH-ME	Y	82790 FQ	118110 AW		NHBLS	10/01-12/01
	New Jersey	Y	105480 FQ	130550 AW		NJBLS	10/01-12/01
	Bergen-Passaic PMSA, NJ	Y	117350 FQ	134710 AW		NJBLS	10/01-12/01
	Jersey City PMSA, NJ	Y	105800 FQ	125850 AW		NJBLS	10/01-12/01
	Middlesex-Somerset-Hunterdon PMSA, NJ	Y	53360 FQ	111470 AW		NJBLS	10/01-12/01
	Monmouth-Ocean PMSA, NJ	Y	125700 FQ	140520 AW		NJBLS	10/01-12/01
	Newark PMSA, NJ	Y	104870 FQ	135260 AW		NJBLS	10/01-12/01
	Trenton PMSA, NJ	Y	106560 FQ	131810 AW		NJBLS	10/01-12/01
	New Mexico	Y	86250 FQ	116030 AW		NMBLS	10/01-12/01
	New York	Y	54510 FQ	124350 AW		NYBLS	10/01-12/01
	Albany-Schenectady-Troy MSA, NY	Y	73460 FQ	118610 AW		NYBLS	10/01-12/01
	Buffalo-Niagara Falls MSA, NY	Y	59150 FQ	126870 AW		NYBLS	10/01-12/01
	New York PMSA, NY	Y	85110 FQ	130770 AW		NYBLS	10/01-12/01
	Newburgh PMSA, NY-PA	Y	45840 FQ	91520 AW		NYBLS	10/01-12/01
	Rochester MSA, NY	Y	54000 FQ	118140 AW		NYBLS	10/01-12/01
	Syracuse MSA, NY	Y	132930 FQ	141300 AW		NYBLS	10/01-12/01
	North Carolina	Y	63240 FQ	119910 AW		NCBLS	10/01-12/01
	Charlotte-Gastonia-Rock Hill MSA, NC-SC	Y	80570 FQ	126290 AW		NCBLS	10/01-12/01
	Greensboro-Winston-Salem-High Point MSA, NC	Y	34360 FQ	107560 AW		NCBLS	10/01-12/01
	Hickory-Morganton-Lenoir MSA, NC	Y	57350 FQ	109620 AW		NCBLS	10/01-12/01
	Raleigh-Durham-Chapel Hill MSA, NC	Y	81060 FQ	119110 AW		NCBLS	10/01-12/01
	Wilmington MSA, NC	Y		143870 AW		NCBLS	10/01-12/01
	North Dakota	Y	108700 FQ	134460 AW		NDBLS	10/01-12/01
	Ohio	Y	96270 FQ	129040 AW		OHBLS	10/01-12/01
	Akron PMSA, OH	Y	74570 FQ	119280 AW		OHBLS	10/01-12/01
	Canton-Massillon MSA, OH	Y	115500 FQ	128090 AW		OHBLS	10/01-12/01
	Cincinnati PMSA, OH-KY-IN	Y	96980 FQ	132080 AW		OHBLS	10/01-12/01
	Cleveland-Lorain-Elyria PMSA, OH	Y	83560 FQ	112570 AW		OHBLS	10/01-12/01
	Columbus MSA, OH	Y	128470 FQ	140790 AW		OHBLS	10/01-12/01
	Dayton-Springfield MSA, OH	Y	94920 FQ	129590 AW		OHBLS	10/01-12/01
	Hamilton-Middletown PMSA, OH	Y	79840 FQ	119720 AW		OHBLS	10/01-12/01
	Youngstown-Warren MSA, OH	Y	41990 FQ	121300 AW		OHBLS	10/01-12/01
	Oklahoma	Y	121130 FQ	134480 AW		OKBLS	10/01-12/01

AAW Average annual wage **AOH** Average offered, high **ASH** Average starting, high **H** Hourly **M** Monthly **S** Special: hourly and annual
AE Average entry wage **AOL** Average offered, low **ASL** Average starting, low **HI** Highest wage paid **MTC** Median total compensation **TQ** Third quartile wage
AEX Average experienced wage **APH** Average pay, high range **AW** Average wage paid **HR** High end range **MW** Median wage paid **W** Weekly
AO Average offered **APL** Average pay, low range **FQ** First quartile wage **LR** Low end range **SQ** Second quartile wage **Y** Yearly

Occupation/Type/Industry	Location	Per	Low	Mid	High	Source	Date
Internist	Oklahoma City MSA, OK	Y	101970 FQ	130580 AW		OKBLS	10/01-12/01
	Oregon	Y	79570 FQ	116750 AW		ORBLS	10/01-12/01
	Portland-Vancouver PMSA, OR-WA	Y	75980 FQ	113690 AW		ORBLS	10/01-12/01
	Pennsylvania	Y	61320 FQ	124130 AW		PABLS	10/01-12/01
	Allentown-Bethlehem-Easton MSA, PA	Y	105020 FQ	129390 AW		PABLS	10/01-12/01
	Erie MSA, PA	Y	125530 FQ	139110 AW		PABLS	10/01-12/01
	Philadelphia PMSA, PA-NJ	Y	60680 FQ	120260 AW		PABLS	10/01-12/01
	York MSA, PA	Y	98510 FQ	130060 AW		PABLS	10/01-12/01
	Rhode Island	Y	92660 FQ	107480 AW		RIBLS	10/01-12/01
	Providence-Fall River-Warwick MSA, RI-MA	Y	88690 FQ	104200 AW		RIBLS	10/01-12/01
	South Carolina	Y	83160 FQ	126230 AW		SCBLS	10/01-12/01
	Columbia MSA, SC	Y	78720 FQ	108480 AW		SCBLS	10/01-12/01
	Greenville-Spartanburg-Anderson MSA, SC	Y	105960 FQ	135330 AW		SCBLS	10/01-12/01
	South Dakota	Y	99800 FQ	129840 AW		SDBLS	10/01-12/01
	Sioux Falls MSA, SD	Y	105600 FQ	134750 AW		SDBLS	10/01-12/01
	Tennessee	Y	105640 FQ	133240 AW		TNBLS	10/01-12/01
	Chattanooga MSA, TN-GA	Y	118160 FQ	140660 AW		TNBLS	10/01-12/01
	Johnson City-Kingsport-Bristol MSA, TN-VA	Y	83580 FQ	124250 AW		TNBLS	10/01-12/01
	Knoxville MSA, TN	Y	97400 FQ	133660 AW		TNBLS	10/01-12/01
	Memphis MSA, TN-AR-MS	Y	110290 FQ	135560 AW		TNBLS	10/01-12/01
	Nashville MSA, TN	Y	101310 FQ	131990 AW		TNBLS	10/01-12/01
	Texas	Y	38370 FQ	117360 AW		TXBLS	10/01-12/01
	Fort Worth-Arlington PMSA, TX	Y	35940 FQ	106700 AW		TXBLS	10/01-12/01
	Galveston-Texas City PMSA, TX	Y	32020 FQ	70580 AW		TXBLS	10/01-12/01
	Houston PMSA, TX	Y	32250 FQ	73200 AW		TXBLS	10/01-12/01
	Utah	Y	104360 FQ	131350 AW		UTBLS	10/01-12/01
	Salt Lake City-Ogden MSA, UT	Y	99220 FQ	129310 AW		UTBLS	10/01-12/01
	Vermont	Y	39870 FQ	95010 AW		VTBLS	10/01-12/01
	Virginia	Y	81710 FQ	122150 AW		VABLS	10/01-12/01
	Norfolk-Virginia Beach-Newport News MSA, VA-NC	Y	122090 FQ	138170 AW		VABLS	10/01-12/01
	Roanoke MSA, VA	Y	37440 FQ	88040 AW		VABLS	10/01-12/01
	Washington	Y	91080 FQ	124620 AW		WABLS	10/01-12/01
	Seattle-Bellevue-Everett PMSA, WA	Y	93120 FQ	127780 AW		WABLS	10/01-12/01
	Spokane MSA, WA	Y	99370 FQ	124980 AW		WABLS	10/01-12/01
	Tacoma PMSA, WA	Y	98600 FQ	128020 AW		WABLS	10/01-12/01
	West Virginia	Y	84580 FQ	123410 AW		WVBLS	10/01-12/01
	Huntington-Ashland MSA, WV-KY-OH	Y	76540 FQ	115750 AW		WVBLS	10/01-12/01
	Wisconsin	Y	95620 FQ	130380 AW		WIBLS	10/01-12/01
	Green Bay MSA, WI	Y	126450 FQ	139300 AW		WIBLS	10/01-12/01
	Madison MSA, WI	Y	121410 FQ	135420 AW		WIBLS	10/01-12/01
	Milwaukee-Waukesha PMSA, WI	Y	89950 FQ	128810 AW		WIBLS	10/01-12/01
	Wyoming	Y	103990 FQ	126390 AW		WYBLS	10/01-12/01
	Puerto Rico	Y	40690 FQ	69120 AW	123610 TQ	PRBLS	10/01-12/01
Interpreter and Translator	Alabama	Y	16410 FQ	29760 AW	40420 TQ	ALBLS	10/01-12/01
	Alaska	Y	25850 FQ	35710 AW	46800 TQ	AKBLS	10/01-12/01
	Arkansas	Y	13450 FQ	23200 AW	33330 TQ	ARBLS	10/01-12/01
	California	Y	21490 FQ	34560 AW	51290 TQ	CABLS	10/01-12/01
	Colorado	Y	22040 FQ	34510 AW	51510 TQ	COBLS	10/01-12/01
	Connecticut	Y	29150 FQ	46150 AW	80060 TQ	CTBLS	10/01-12/01
	District of Columbia	Y	36920 FQ	62080 AW	101400 TQ	DCBLS	10/01-12/01
	Florida	Y	15290 FQ	43340 AW	122520 TQ	FLBLS	10/01-12/01
	Georgia	Y	16150 FQ	27760 AW	43090 TQ	GABLS	10/01-12/01
	Hawaii	Y	17870 FQ	33960 AW	46480 TQ	HIBLS	10/01-12/01
	Idaho	Y	16220 FQ	26780 AW	35900 TQ	IDBLS	10/01-12/01
	Illinois	Y	14430 FQ	30220 AW	46350 TQ	ILBLS	10/01-12/01
	Indiana	Y	13730 FQ	27060 AW	46760 TQ	INBLS	10/01-12/01
	Iowa	Y	16010 FQ	26150 AW	39190 TQ	IABLS	10/01-12/01
	Kansas	Y	16170 FQ	30500 AW	45170 TQ	KSBLS	10/01-12/01
	Kentucky	Y	19110 FQ	32400 AW	43630 TQ	KYBLS	10/01-12/01

AAW Average annual wage **AE** Average entry wage **AEX** Average experienced wage **AO** Average offered **AOH** Average offered, high **AOL** Average offered, low **APH** Average pay, high range **APL** Average pay, low range **ASH** Average starting, high **ASL** Average starting, low **AW** Average wage paid **FQ** First quartile wage **H** Hourly **HI** Highest wage paid **HR** High end range **LR** Low end range **M** Monthly **MTC** Median total compensation **MW** Median wage paid **SQ** Second quartile wage **S** Special: hourly and annual **TQ** Third quartile wage **W** Weekly **Y** Yearly

Occupation/Type/Industry	Location	Per	Low	Mid	High	Source	Date
Interpreter and Translator	Louisiana	Y	18300 FQ	37480 AW	55440 TQ	LABLS	10/01-12/01
	Maine	Y	28400 FQ	38870 AW	56280 TQ	MEBLS	10/01-12/01
	Maryland	Y	25620 FQ	43870 AW	66290 TQ	MDBLS	10/01-12/01
	Massachusetts	Y	24090 FQ	35880 AW	51600 TQ	MABLS	10/01-12/01
	Michigan	Y	20510 FQ	31780 AW	43540 TQ	MIBLS	10/01-12/01
	Minnesota	Y	21040 FQ	33640 AW	48030 TQ	MNBLS	10/01-12/01
	Mississippi	Y	12070 FQ	24730 AW	42280 TQ	MSBLS	10/01-12/01
	Missouri	Y	23940 FQ	36400 AW	52750 TQ	MOBLS	10/01-12/01
	Nebraska	Y	18380 FQ	29570 AW	40140 TQ	NEBLS	10/01-12/01
	Nevada	Y	18780 FQ	28840 AW	41740 TQ	NVBLS	10/01-12/01
	New Jersey	Y	16170 FQ	35740 AW	54520 TQ	NJBLS	10/01-12/01
	New Mexico	Y	21100 FQ	36100 AW	56780 TQ	NMBLS	10/01-12/01
	New York	Y	21230 FQ	38800 AW	55620 TQ	NYBLS	10/01-12/01
	North Carolina	Y	20160 FQ	29080 AW	39470 TQ	NCBLS	10/01-12/01
	North Dakota	Y	19730 FQ	31230 AW	43480 TQ	NDBLS	10/01-12/01
	Ohio	Y	17670 FQ	32750 AW	51260 TQ	OHBLS	10/01-12/01
	Oklahoma	Y	18140 FQ	29030 AW	34910 TQ	OKBLS	10/01-12/01
	Oregon	Y	20240 FQ	31720 AW	43950 TQ	ORBLS	10/01-12/01
	Pennsylvania	Y	19400 FQ	34330 AW	48580 TQ	PABLS	10/01-12/01
	Rhode Island	Y	22850 FQ	31850 AW	42260 TQ	RIBLS	10/01-12/01
	South Carolina	Y	15310 FQ	28310 AW	47310 TQ	SCBLS	10/01-12/01
	Tennessee	Y	13530 FQ	24010 AW	36010 TQ	TNBLS	10/01-12/01
	Texas	Y	16120 FQ	28770 AW	44250 TQ	TXBLS	10/01-12/01
	Utah	Y	16160 FQ	25960 AW	40330 TQ	UTBLS	10/01-12/01
	Virginia	Y	19440 FQ	37960 AW	66200 TQ	VABLS	10/01-12/01
	Washington	Y	25930 FQ	45830 AW	76210 TQ	WABLS	10/01-12/01
	West Virginia	Y	17750 FQ	25420 AW	40690 TQ	WVBLS	10/01-12/01
	Wisconsin	Y	20180 FQ	31720 AW	42630 TQ	WIBLS	10/01-12/01
	Puerto Rico	Y	16540 FQ	26880 AW	40550 TQ	PRBLS	10/01-12/01
	Guam	Y	16640 FQ	34150 AW	51740 TQ	GUBLS	10/01-12/01
Interviewer							
Except Eligibility and Loan	Alabama	H	7.24 FQ	10.38 AW	15.21 TQ	ALBLS	10/01-12/01
Except Eligibility and Loan	Alaska	H	11.88 FQ	14.48 AW	17.34 TQ	AKBLS	10/01-12/01
Except Eligibility and Loan	Arizona	H	6.20 FQ	10.32 AW	14.07 TQ	AZBLS	10/01-12/01
Except Eligibility and Loan	Arkansas	H	6.93 FQ	9.15 AW	12.01 TQ	ARBLS	10/01-12/01
Except Eligibility and Loan	California	H	7.64 FQ	13.62 AW	22.99 TQ	CABLS	10/01-12/01
Except Eligibility and Loan	Colorado	H	8.49 FQ	12.17 AW	16.69 TQ	COBLS	10/01-12/01
Except Eligibility and Loan	Connecticut	H	7.83 FQ	12.42 AW	17.60 TQ	CTBLS	10/01-12/01
Except Eligibility and Loan	Delaware	H	9.03 FQ	12.27 AW	17.52 TQ	DEBLS	10/01-12/01
Except Eligibility and Loan	District of Columbia	H	7.26 FQ	11.31 AW	17.08 TQ	DCBLS	10/01-12/01
Except Eligibility and Loan	Florida	H	6.93 FQ	9.52 AW	12.83 TQ	FLBLS	10/01-12/01
Except Eligibility and Loan	Georgia	H	7.55 FQ	10.74 AW	14.79 TQ	GABLS	10/01-12/01
Except Eligibility and Loan	Hawaii	H	6.73 FQ	11.19 AW	14.39 TQ	HIBLS	10/01-12/01
Except Eligibility and Loan	Idaho	H	6.50 FQ	8.63 AW	11.15 TQ	IDBLS	10/01-12/01
Except Eligibility and Loan	Illinois	H	7.39 FQ	10.71 AW	15.34 TQ	ILBLS	10/01-12/01
Except Eligibility and Loan	Indiana	H	7.74 FQ	10.62 AW	14.09 TQ	INBLS	10/01-12/01
Except Eligibility and Loan	Iowa	H	7.42 FQ	10.06 AW	13.39 TQ	IABLS	10/01-12/01
Except Eligibility and Loan	Kansas	H	7.56 FQ	11.28 AW	16.48 TQ	KSBLS	10/01-12/01
Except Eligibility and Loan	Kentucky	H	7.45 FQ	9.88 AW	13.12 TQ	KYBLS	10/01-12/01
Except Eligibility and Loan	Louisiana	H	6.33 FQ	8.95 AW	12.56 TQ	LABLS	10/01-12/01
Except Eligibility and Loan	Maine	H	7.35 FQ	9.32 AW	12.01 TQ	MEBLS	10/01-12/01
Except Eligibility and Loan	Maryland	H	7.82 FQ	11.53 AW	15.70 TQ	MDBLS	10/01-12/01
Except Eligibility and Loan	Massachusetts	H	9.78 FQ	13.48 AW	17.69 TQ	MABLS	10/01-12/01
Except Eligibility and Loan	Michigan	H	8.70 FQ	11.53 AW	14.87 TQ	MIBLS	10/01-12/01
Except Eligibility and Loan	Minnesota	H	8.46 FQ	11.17 AW	14.25 TQ	MNBLS	10/01-12/01
Except Eligibility and Loan	Mississippi	H	6.88 FQ	9.38 AW	12.76 TQ	MSBLS	10/01-12/01
Except Eligibility and Loan	Missouri	H	7.62 FQ	10.82 AW	14.07 TQ	MOBLS	10/01-12/01
Except Eligibility and Loan	Montana	H	6.42 FQ	8.86 AW	11.46 TQ	MTBLS	10/01-12/01
Except Eligibility and Loan	Nebraska	H	7.58 FQ	10.86 AW	15.47 TQ	NEBLS	10/01-12/01
Except Eligibility and Loan	Nevada	H	9.23 FQ	11.80 AW	15.48 TQ	NVBLS	10/01-12/01
Except Eligibility and Loan	New Hampshire	H	8.81 FQ	11.49 AW	14.02 TQ	NHBLS	10/01-12/01
Except Eligibility and Loan	New Jersey	H	7.67 FQ	11.32 AW	15.78 TQ	NJBLS	10/01-12/01
Except Eligibility and Loan	New Mexico	H	7.68 FQ	10.22 AW	13.07 TQ	NMBLS	10/01-12/01
Except Eligibility and Loan	New York	H	6.53 FQ	12.11 AW	18.24 TQ	NYBLS	10/01-12/01
Except Eligibility and Loan	North Carolina	H	7.51 FQ	10.45 AW	13.92 TQ	NCBLS	10/01-12/01
Except Eligibility and Loan	North Dakota	H	7.42 FQ	9.39 AW	11.86 TQ	NDBLS	10/01-12/01
Except Eligibility and Loan	Ohio	H	7.69 FQ	10.62 AW	14.09 TQ	OHBLS	10/01-12/01
Except Eligibility and Loan	Oklahoma	H	6.16 FQ	9.29 AW	12.95 TQ	OKBLS	10/01-12/01
Except Eligibility and Loan	Oregon	H	7.60 FQ	10.81 AW	14.59 TQ	ORBLS	10/01-12/01
Except Eligibility and Loan	Pennsylvania	H	6.45 FQ	10.42 AW	15.70 TQ	PABLS	10/01-12/01
Except Eligibility and Loan	Rhode Island	H	9.70 FQ	12.75 AW	16.41 TQ	RIBLS	10/01-12/01
Except Eligibility and Loan	South Carolina	H	8.04 FQ	12.09 AW	19.44 TQ	SCBLS	10/01-12/01

AAW	Average annual wage	**AOH**	Average offered, high	**ASH**	Average starting, high	**H**	Hourly	**M**	Monthly	**S**	Special: hourly and annual
AE	Average entry wage	**AOL**	Average offered, low	**ASL**	Average starting, low	**HI**	Highest wage paid	**MTC**	Median total compensation	**TQ**	Third quartile wage
AEX	Average experienced wage	**APH**	Average pay, high range	**AW**	Average wage paid	**HR**	High end range	**MW**	Median wage paid	**W**	Weekly
AO	Average offered	**APL**	Average pay, low range	**FQ**	First quartile wage	**LR**	Low end range	**SQ**	Second quartile wage	**Y**	Yearly

Occupation/Type/Industry	Location	Per	Low	Mid	High	Source	Date
Interviewer							
Except Eligibility and Loan	South Dakota	H	7.43 FQ	9.73 AW	12.89 TQ	SDBLS	10/01-12/01
Except Eligibility and Loan	Tennessee	H	7.34 FQ	10.36 AW	13.56 TQ	TNBLS	10/01-12/01
Except Eligibility and Loan	Texas	H	7.92 FQ	12.10 AW	16.60 TQ	TXBLS	10/01-12/01
Except Eligibility and Loan	Utah	H	5.76 FQ	7.89 AW	10.91 TQ	UTBLS	10/01-12/01
Except Eligibility and Loan	Vermont	H	7.55 FQ	10.70 AW	14.22 TQ	VTBLS	10/01-12/01
Except Eligibility and Loan	Virginia	H	6.94 FQ	10.43 AW	14.53 TQ	VABLS	10/01-12/01
Except Eligibility and Loan	Washington	H	7.71 FQ	11.35 AW	15.72 TQ	WABLS	10/01-12/01
Except Eligibility and Loan	West Virginia	H	7.23 FQ	10.14 AW	13.68 TQ	WVBLS	10/01-12/01
Except Eligibility and Loan	Wisconsin	H	7.77 FQ	11.63 AW	15.92 TQ	WIBLS	10/01-12/01
Except Eligibility and Loan	Wyoming	H	7.40 FQ	9.79 AW	13.22 TQ	WYBLS	10/01-12/01
Except Eligibility and Loan	Puerto Rico	H	5.67 FQ	7.18 AW	9.12 TQ	PRBLS	10/01-12/01
Except Eligibility and Loan	Guam	H	7.25 FQ	11.66 AW	35.76 TQ	GUBLS	10/01-12/01
Jail Officer	Indiana	H	11.00 AE	11.78 AEX		CORPRO	1/01-1/02
Janitor							
Nonunion	Los Angeles, CA	H		5.15-6.00 AW		WSJ1	1/00-1/01
Nonunion	Baltimore, MD	H		5.15-5.75 AW		WSJ1	1/00-1/01
Nonunion	Northern New Jersey, NJ	H		6.50 AW		WSJ1	1/00-1/01
Nonunion, Suburbs	Chicago, IL	H		5.15-9.00 AW		WSJ1	1/00-1/01
Nonunion, Suburbs	Philadelphia, PA	H		6.00-8.00 AW		WSJ1	1/00-1/01
Union	Los Angeles, CA	H		8.10 AW		WSJ1	1/00-1/01
Union	Washington, DC	H		7.40 AW		WSJ1	1/00-1/01
Union	New York, NY	H		17.00 AW		WSJ1	1/00-1/01
Union, Downtown area	Chicago, IL	H		12.10 AW		WSJ1	1/00-1/01
Union, Downtown area	Philadelphia, PA	H		12.45 AW		WSJ1	1/00-1/01
Janitor and Cleaner							
Except Maid and Housekeeping Cleaner	Alabama	H	5.68 FQ	7.71 AW	10.67 TQ	ALBLS	10/01-12/01
Except Maid and Housekeeping Cleaner	Birmingham MSA, AL	H	5.60 FQ	7.57 AW	10.72 TQ	ALBLS	10/01-12/01
Except Maid and Housekeeping Cleaner	Huntsville MSA, AL	H	5.93 FQ	8.55 AW	11.63 TQ	ALBLS	10/01-12/01
Except Maid and Housekeeping Cleaner	Mobile MSA, AL	H	5.71 FQ	7.76 AW	10.46 TQ	ALBLS	10/01-12/01
Except Maid and Housekeeping Cleaner	Montgomery MSA, AL	H	5.56 FQ	7.30 AW	10.34 TQ	ALBLS	10/01-12/01
Except Maid and Housekeeping Cleaner	Alaska	H	7.54 FQ	11.68 AW	17.48 TQ	AKBLS	10/01-12/01
Except Maid and Housekeeping Cleaner	Anchorage MSA, AK	H	7.47 FQ	11.44 AW	17.00 TQ	AKBLS	10/01-12/01
Except Maid and Housekeeping Cleaner	Arizona	H	5.88 FQ	8.61 AW	13.13 TQ	AZBLS	10/01-12/01
Except Maid and Housekeeping Cleaner	Phoenix-Mesa MSA, AZ	H	5.86 FQ	8.68 AW	13.69 TQ	AZBLS	10/01-12/01
Except Maid and Housekeeping Cleaner	Tucson MSA, AZ	H	5.96 FQ	8.86 AW	13.07 TQ	AZBLS	10/01-12/01
Except Maid and Housekeeping Cleaner	Arkansas	H	5.74 FQ	7.53 AW	10.15 TQ	ARBLS	10/01-12/01
Except Maid and Housekeeping Cleaner	Fayetteville-Springdale-Rogers MSA, AR	H	6.24 FQ	8.26 AW	10.69 TQ	ARBLS	10/01-12/01
Except Maid and Housekeeping Cleaner	Fort Smith MSA, AR-OK	H	6.00 FQ	8.11 AW	10.58 TQ	ARBLS	10/01-12/01
Except Maid and Housekeeping Cleaner	Little Rock-North Little Rock MSA, AR	H	5.68 FQ	7.32 AW	9.85 TQ	ARBLS	10/01-12/01
Except Maid and Housekeeping Cleaner	California	H	6.70 FQ	10.15 AW	15.77 TQ	CABLS	10/01-12/01
Except Maid and Housekeeping Cleaner	Bakersfield MSA, CA	H	6.52 FQ	10.09 AW	15.00 TQ	CABLS	10/01-12/01
Except Maid and Housekeeping Cleaner	Chico-Paradise MSA, CA	H	6.47 FQ	8.87 AW	13.03 TQ	CABLS	10/01-12/01
Except Maid and Housekeeping Cleaner	Fresno MSA, CA	H	6.54 FQ	8.87 AW	13.22 TQ	CABLS	10/01-12/01
Except Maid and Housekeeping Cleaner	Los Angeles-Long Beach PMSA, CA	H	6.73 FQ	10.25 AW	16.42 TQ	CABLS	10/01-12/01
Except Maid and Housekeeping Cleaner	Merced MSA, CA	H	6.46 FQ	9.03 AW	13.51 TQ	CABLS	10/01-12/01
Except Maid and Housekeeping Cleaner	Modesto MSA, CA	H	6.53 FQ	9.22 AW	14.26 TQ	CABLS	10/01-12/01
Except Maid and Housekeeping Cleaner	Oakland PMSA, CA	H	7.27 FQ	11.47 AW	16.75 TQ	CABLS	10/01-12/01
Except Maid and Housekeeping Cleaner	Orange County PMSA, CA	H	6.61 FQ	9.51 AW	15.48 TQ	CABLS	10/01-12/01
Except Maid and Housekeeping Cleaner	Redding MSA, CA	H	6.54 FQ	9.54 AW	14.45 TQ	CABLS	10/01-12/01
Except Maid and Housekeeping Cleaner	Riverside-San Bernardino PMSA, CA	H	6.52 FQ	9.92 AW	15.53 TQ	CABLS	10/01-12/01
Except Maid and Housekeeping Cleaner	Sacramento PMSA, CA	H	6.79 FQ	10.30 AW	14.18 TQ	CABLS	10/01-12/01
Except Maid and Housekeeping Cleaner	Salinas MSA, CA	H	6.59 FQ	10.11 AW	15.10 TQ	CABLS	10/01-12/01
Except Maid and Housekeeping Cleaner	San Diego MSA, CA	H	6.68 FQ	9.38 AW	13.96 TQ	CABLS	10/01-12/01
Except Maid and Housekeeping Cleaner	San Francisco PMSA, CA	H	7.25 FQ	11.53 AW	16.45 TQ	CABLS	10/01-12/01
Except Maid and Housekeeping Cleaner	San Jose PMSA, CA	H	7.24 FQ	10.40 AW	16.15 TQ	CABLS	10/01-12/01
Except Maid and Housekeeping Cleaner	San Luis Obispo-Atascadero-Paso Robles MSA, CA	H	7.18 FQ	10.42 AW	14.40 TQ	CABLS	10/01-12/01
Except Maid and Housekeeping Cleaner	Santa Barbara-Santa Maria-Lompoc MSA, CA	H	6.53 FQ	10.21 AW	16.62 TQ	CABLS	10/01-12/01
Except Maid and Housekeeping Cleaner	Santa Cruz-Watsonville PMSA, CA	H	6.71 FQ	10.08 AW	15.71 TQ	CABLS	10/01-12/01

AAW Average annual wage · **AE** Average entry wage · **AEX** Average experienced wage · **AO** Average offered · **AOH** Average offered, high · **AOL** Average offered, low · **APH** Average pay, high range · **APL** Average pay, low range · **ASH** Average starting, high · **ASL** Average starting, low · **AW** Average wage paid · **FQ** First quartile wage · **H** Hourly · **HI** Highest wage paid · **HR** High end range · **LR** Low end range · **M** Monthly · **MTC** Median total compensation · **MW** Median wage paid · **SQ** Second quartile wage · **S** Special: hourly and annual · **TQ** Third quartile wage · **W** Weekly · **Y** Yearly

Occupation/Type/Industry	Location	Per	Low	Mid	High	Source	Date
Janitor and Cleaner							
Except Maid and Housekeeping Cleaner	Santa Rosa PMSA, CA	H	6.71 FQ	10.01 AW	14.74 TQ	CABLS	10/01-12/01
Except Maid and Housekeeping Cleaner	Stockton-Lodi MSA, CA	H	6.56 FQ	9.51 AW	14.87 TQ	CABLS	10/01-12/01
Except Maid and Housekeeping Cleaner	Vallejo-Fairfield-Napa PMSA, CA	H	7.05 FQ	9.97 AW	14.07 TQ	CABLS	10/01-12/01
Except Maid and Housekeeping Cleaner	Ventura PMSA, CA	H	6.48 FQ	9.53 AW	15.52 TQ	CABLS	10/01-12/01
Except Maid and Housekeeping Cleaner	Visalia-Tulare-Porterville MSA, CA	H	6.60 FQ	10.07 AW	14.53 TQ	CABLS	10/01-12/01
Except Maid and Housekeeping Cleaner	Colorado	H	6.49 FQ	9.32 AW	13.27 TQ	COBLS	10/01-12/01
Except Maid and Housekeeping Cleaner	Boulder-Longmont PMSA, CO	H	6.63 FQ	9.66 AW	13.73 TQ	COBLS	10/01-12/01
Except Maid and Housekeeping Cleaner	Colorado Springs MSA, CO	H	6.17 FQ	8.65 AW	12.12 TQ	COBLS	10/01-12/01
Except Maid and Housekeeping Cleaner	Denver PMSA, CO	H	6.87 FQ	9.52 AW	13.59 TQ	COBLS	10/01-12/01
Except Maid and Housekeeping Cleaner	Fort Collins-Loveland MSA, CO	H	6.55 FQ	8.79 AW	11.18 TQ	COBLS	10/01-12/01
Except Maid and Housekeeping Cleaner	Greeley PMSA, CO	H	6.11 FQ	8.46 AW	11.30 TQ	COBLS	10/01-12/01
Except Maid and Housekeeping Cleaner	Connecticut	H	6.79 FQ	10.84 AW	16.90 TQ	CTBLS	10/01-12/01
Except Maid and Housekeeping Cleaner	Bridgeport PMSA, CT	H	6.85 FQ	10.36 AW	15.32 TQ	CTBLS	10/01-12/01
Except Maid and Housekeeping Cleaner	Danbury PMSA, CT	H	6.62 FQ	11.38 AW	16.95 TQ	CTBLS	10/01-12/01
Except Maid and Housekeeping Cleaner	Hartford MSA, CT	H	6.83 FQ	11.11 AW	16.99 TQ	CTBLS	10/01-12/01
Except Maid and Housekeeping Cleaner	New Haven-Meriden PMSA, CT	H	6.87 FQ	10.87 AW	17.01 TQ	CTBLS	10/01-12/01
Except Maid and Housekeeping Cleaner	New London-Norwich MSA, CT-RI	H	7.65 FQ	11.43 AW	16.28 TQ	CTBLS	10/01-12/01
Except Maid and Housekeeping Cleaner	Stamford-Norwalk PMSA, CT	H	6.66 FQ	10.65 AW	19.17 TQ	CTBLS	10/01-12/01
Except Maid and Housekeeping Cleaner	Waterbury PMSA, CT	H	7.17 FQ	11.31 AW	16.82 TQ	CTBLS	10/01-12/01
Except Maid and Housekeeping Cleaner	Delaware	H	6.57 FQ	9.58 AW	13.92 TQ	DEBLS	10/01-12/01
Except Maid and Housekeeping Cleaner	Wilmington-Newark PMSA, DE-MD	H	6.55 FQ	9.57 AW	14.38 TQ	DEBLS	10/01-12/01
Except Maid and Housekeeping Cleaner	District of Columbia	H	7.34 FQ	9.54 AW	12.85 TQ	DCBLS	10/01-12/01
Except Maid and Housekeeping Cleaner	Washington PMSA, DC-MD-VA-WV	H	6.10 FQ	8.88 AW	12.90 TQ	DCBLS	10/01-12/01
Except Maid and Housekeeping Cleaner	Florida	H	5.83 FQ	8.17 AW	11.21 TQ	FLBLS	10/01-12/01
Except Maid and Housekeeping Cleaner	Daytona Beach MSA, FL	H	5.92 FQ	7.87 AW	10.32 TQ	FLBLS	10/01-12/01
Except Maid and Housekeeping Cleaner	Fort Lauderdale PMSA, FL	H	5.84 FQ	8.11 AW	11.75 TQ	FLBLS	10/01-12/01
Except Maid and Housekeeping Cleaner	Fort Myers-Cape Coral MSA, FL	H	5.82 FQ	8.15 AW	12.01 TQ	FLBLS	10/01-12/01
Except Maid and Housekeeping Cleaner	Fort Pierce-Port St. Lucie MSA, FL	H	5.85 FQ	8.34 AW	10.96 TQ	FLBLS	10/01-12/01
Except Maid and Housekeeping Cleaner	Fort Walton Beach MSA, FL	H	6.05 FQ	8.83 AW	12.93 TQ	FLBLS	10/01-12/01
Except Maid and Housekeeping Cleaner	Gainesville MSA, FL	H	6.42 FQ	8.60 AW	11.19 TQ	FLBLS	10/01-12/01
Except Maid and Housekeeping Cleaner	Jacksonville MSA, FL	H	5.90 FQ	8.58 AW	12.26 TQ	FLBLS	10/01-12/01
Except Maid and Housekeeping Cleaner	Lakeland-Winter Haven MSA, FL	H	5.97 FQ	8.45 AW	11.41 TQ	FLBLS	10/01-12/01
Except Maid and Housekeeping Cleaner	Melbourne-Titusville-Palm Bay MSA, FL	H	6.18 FQ	9.10 AW	14.89 TQ	FLBLS	10/01-12/01
Except Maid and Housekeeping Cleaner	Miami PMSA, FL	H	5.77 FQ	8.05 AW	10.63 TQ	FLBLS	10/01-12/01
Except Maid and Housekeeping Cleaner	Naples MSA, FL	H	6.13 FQ	9.47 AW	13.26 TQ	FLBLS	10/01-12/01
Except Maid and Housekeeping Cleaner	Ocala MSA, FL	H	5.56 FQ	7.65 AW	10.61 TQ	FLBLS	10/01-12/01
Except Maid and Housekeeping Cleaner	Orlando MSA, FL	H	5.90 FQ	8.13 AW	11.08 TQ	FLBLS	10/01-12/01
Except Maid and Housekeeping Cleaner	Pensacola MSA, FL	H	5.56 FQ	7.22 AW	9.92 TQ	FLBLS	10/01-12/01
Except Maid and Housekeeping Cleaner	Sarasota-Bradenton MSA, FL	H	5.85 FQ	8.69 AW	12.83 TQ	FLBLS	10/01-12/01
Except Maid and Housekeeping Cleaner	Tallahassee MSA, FL	H	5.84 FQ	7.75 AW	10.49 TQ	FLBLS	10/01-12/01
Except Maid and Housekeeping Cleaner	Tampa-St. Petersburg-Clearwater MSA, FL	H	5.80 FQ	7.96 AW	10.78 TQ	FLBLS	10/01-12/01
Except Maid and Housekeeping Cleaner	West Palm Beach-Boca Raton MSA, FL	H	5.88 FQ	8.31 AW	11.29 TQ	FLBLS	10/01-12/01
Except Maid and Housekeeping Cleaner	Georgia	H	5.83 FQ	8.24 AW	11.41 TQ	GABLS	10/01-12/01
Except Maid and Housekeeping Cleaner	Atlanta MSA, GA	H	6.03 FQ	8.87 AW	12.54 TQ	GABLS	10/01-12/01
Except Maid and Housekeeping Cleaner	Augusta-Aiken MSA, GA-SC	H	5.68 FQ	7.72 AW	10.71 TQ	GABLS	10/01-12/01
Except Maid and Housekeeping Cleaner	Columbus MSA, GA-AL	H	5.78 FQ	7.87 AW	10.63 TQ	GABLS	10/01-12/01
Except Maid and Housekeeping Cleaner	Macon MSA, GA	H	5.66 FQ	7.38 AW	10.19 TQ	GABLS	10/01-12/01
Except Maid and Housekeeping Cleaner	Savannah MSA, GA	H	5.84 FQ	7.63 AW	9.88 TQ	GABLS	10/01-12/01
Except Maid and Housekeeping Cleaner	Hawaii	H	5.96 FQ	9.18 AW	12.82 TQ	HIBLS	10/01-12/01
Except Maid and Housekeeping Cleaner	Honolulu MSA, HI	H	5.89 FQ	8.98 AW	12.69 TQ	HIBLS	10/01-12/01
Except Maid and Housekeeping Cleaner	Idaho	H	5.94 FQ	8.73 AW	12.23 TQ	IDBLS	10/01-12/01
Except Maid and Housekeeping Cleaner	Boise City MSA, ID	H	5.73 FQ	8.39 AW	11.46 TQ	IDBLS	10/01-12/01
Except Maid and Housekeeping Cleaner	Illinois	H	6.25 FQ	10.55 AW	17.08 TQ	ILBLS	10/01-12/01
Except Maid and Housekeeping Cleaner	Champaign-Urbana MSA, IL	H	7.30 FQ	12.57 AW	17.58 TQ	ILBLS	10/01-12/01
Except Maid and Housekeeping Cleaner	Chicago PMSA, IL	H	6.41 FQ	10.87 AW	17.90 TQ	ILBLS	10/01-12/01
Except Maid and Housekeeping Cleaner	Peoria-Pekin MSA, IL	H	6.18 FQ	10.44 AW	16.74 TQ	ILBLS	10/01-12/01
Except Maid and Housekeeping Cleaner	Rockford MSA, IL	H	6.36 FQ	9.33 AW	13.38 TQ	ILBLS	10/01-12/01
Except Maid and Housekeeping Cleaner	Springfield MSA, IL	H	6.24 FQ	10.69 AW	16.68 TQ	ILBLS	10/01-12/01

AAW	Average annual wage	AOH	Average offered, high	ASH	Average starting, high	H	Hourly	M	Monthly	S	Special: hourly and annual
AE	Average entry wage	AOL	Average offered, low	ASL	Average starting, low	HI	Highest wage paid	MTC	Median total compensation	TQ	Third quartile wage
AEX	Average experienced wage	APH	Average pay, high range	AW	Average wage paid	HR	High end range	MW	Median wage paid	W	Weekly
AO	Average offered	APL	Average pay, low range	FQ	First quartile wage	LR	Low end range	SQ	Second quartile wage	Y	Yearly

Occupation/Type/Industry	Location	Per	Low	Mid	High	Source	Date
Janitor and Cleaner							
Except Maid and Housekeeping Cleaner	Indiana	H	6.13 FQ	9.47 AW	13.69 TQ	INBLS	10/01-12/01
Except Maid and Housekeeping Cleaner	Elkhart-Goshen MSA, IN	H	7.08 FQ	10.37 AW	15.00 TQ	INBLS	10/01-12/01
Except Maid and Housekeeping Cleaner	Evansville-Henderson MSA, IN-KY	H	6.10 FQ	9.30 AW	14.70 TQ	INBLS	10/01-12/01
Except Maid and Housekeeping Cleaner	Fort Wayne MSA, IN	H	6.86 FQ	9.50 AW	13.39 TQ	INBLS	10/01-12/01
Except Maid and Housekeeping Cleaner	Gary PMSA, IN	H	5.95 FQ	9.37 AW	14.47 TQ	INBLS	10/01-12/01
Except Maid and Housekeeping Cleaner	Indianapolis MSA, IN	H	5.99 FQ	9.15 AW	13.39 TQ	INBLS	10/01-12/01
Except Maid and Housekeeping Cleaner	Lafayette MSA, IN	H	6.92 FQ	9.59 AW	13.30 TQ	INBLS	10/01-12/01
Except Maid and Housekeeping Cleaner	South Bend MSA, IN	H	6.05 FQ	9.62 AW	13.62 TQ	INBLS	10/01-12/01
Except Maid and Housekeeping Cleaner	Iowa	H	6.19 FQ	9.24 AW	13.20 TQ	IABLS	10/01-12/01
Except Maid and Housekeeping Cleaner	Cedar Rapids MSA, IA	H	7.17 FQ	11.11 AW	16.53 TQ	IABLS	10/01-12/01
Except Maid and Housekeeping Cleaner	Davenport-Moline-Rock Island MSA, IA-IL	H	6.16 FQ	9.28 AW	14.10 TQ	IABLS	10/01-12/01
Except Maid and Housekeeping Cleaner	Des Moines MSA, IA	H	6.89 FQ	9.61 AW	13.26 TQ	IABLS	10/01-12/01
Except Maid and Housekeeping Cleaner	Kansas	H	5.93 FQ	8.74 AW	12.43 TQ	KSBLS	10/01-12/01
Except Maid and Housekeeping Cleaner	Topeka MSA, KS	H	5.87 FQ	8.44 AW	12.22 TQ	KSBLS	10/01-12/01
Except Maid and Housekeeping Cleaner	Wichita MSA, KS	H	5.64 FQ	8.21 AW	11.93 TQ	KSBLS	10/01-12/01
Except Maid and Housekeeping Cleaner	Kentucky	H	5.98 FQ	8.49 AW	11.48 TQ	KYBLS	10/01-12/01
Except Maid and Housekeeping Cleaner	Lexington MSA, KY	H	6.45 FQ	8.71 AW	11.16 TQ	KYBLS	10/01-12/01
Except Maid and Housekeeping Cleaner	Louisville MSA, KY-IN	H	6.20 FQ	9.13 AW	12.81 TQ	KYBLS	10/01-12/01
Except Maid and Housekeeping Cleaner	Louisiana	H	5.62 FQ	7.41 AW	10.38 TQ	LABLS	10/01-12/01
Except Maid and Housekeeping Cleaner	Baton Rouge MSA, LA	H	5.67 FQ	7.85 AW	11.88 TQ	LABLS	10/01-12/01
Except Maid and Housekeeping Cleaner	Houma MSA, LA	H	5.71 FQ	7.73 AW	10.39 TQ	LABLS	10/01-12/01
Except Maid and Housekeeping Cleaner	Lafayette MSA, LA	H	5.63 FQ	7.55 AW	10.87 TQ	LABLS	10/01-12/01
Except Maid and Housekeeping Cleaner	Lake Charles MSA, LA	H	5.62 FQ	7.38 AW	9.91 TQ	LABLS	10/01-12/01
Except Maid and Housekeeping Cleaner	New Orleans MSA, LA	H	5.62 FQ	7.39 AW	10.52 TQ	LABLS	10/01-12/01
Except Maid and Housekeeping Cleaner	Shreveport-Bossier City MSA, LA	H	5.52 FQ	6.98 AW	9.26 TQ	LABLS	10/01-12/01
Except Maid and Housekeeping Cleaner	Maine	H	6.81 FQ	9.87 AW	13.65 TQ	MEBLS	10/01-12/01
Except Maid and Housekeeping Cleaner	Portland MSA, ME	H	7.33 FQ	10.25 AW	14.21 TQ	MEBLS	10/01-12/01
Except Maid and Housekeeping Cleaner	Maryland	H	5.84 FQ	8.70 AW	13.23 TQ	MDBLS	10/01-12/01
Except Maid and Housekeeping Cleaner	Baltimore PMSA, MD	H	5.76 FQ	8.61 AW	13.12 TQ	MDBLS	10/01-12/01
Except Maid and Housekeeping Cleaner	Massachusetts	H	7.85 FQ	11.19 AW	16.16 TQ	MABLS	10/01-12/01
Except Maid and Housekeeping Cleaner	Boston PMSA, MA-NH	H	8.56 FQ	11.15 AW	16.03 TQ	MABLS	10/01-12/01
Except Maid and Housekeeping Cleaner	Brockton PMSA, MA	H	7.65 FQ	12.06 AW	17.12 TQ	MABLS	10/01-12/01
Except Maid and Housekeeping Cleaner	Lawrence PMSA, MA-NH	H	7.16 FQ	10.36 AW	15.28 TQ	MABLS	10/01-12/01
Except Maid and Housekeeping Cleaner	Lowell PMSA, MA-NH	H	7.41 FQ	11.43 AW	16.93 TQ	MABLS	10/01-12/01
Except Maid and Housekeeping Cleaner	New Bedford PMSA, MA	H	7.12 FQ	10.73 AW	14.84 TQ	MABLS	10/01-12/01
Except Maid and Housekeeping Cleaner	Springfield MSA, MA	H	6.98 FQ	10.73 AW	15.39 TQ	MABLS	10/01-12/01
Except Maid and Housekeeping Cleaner	Worcester PMSA, MA-CT	H	7.33 FQ	11.72 AW	16.56 TQ	MABLS	10/01-12/01
Except Maid and Housekeeping Cleaner	Michigan	H	6.70 FQ	11.15 AW	17.37 TQ	MIBLS	10/01-12/01
Except Maid and Housekeeping Cleaner	Ann Arbor PMSA, MI	H	7.14 FQ	11.92 AW	17.35 TQ	MIBLS	10/01-12/01
Except Maid and Housekeeping Cleaner	Detroit PMSA, MI	H	7.03 FQ	11.60 AW	19.27 TQ	MIBLS	10/01-12/01
Except Maid and Housekeeping Cleaner	Flint PMSA, MI	H	5.98 FQ	12.98 AW	24.92 TQ	MIBLS	10/01-12/01
Except Maid and Housekeeping Cleaner	Grand Rapids-Muskegon-Holland MSA, MI	H	6.89 FQ	10.47 AW	15.77 TQ	MIBLS	10/01-12/01
Except Maid and Housekeeping Cleaner	Kalamazoo-Battle Creek MSA, MI	H	6.95 FQ	10.66 AW	16.01 TQ	MIBLS	10/01-12/01
Except Maid and Housekeeping Cleaner	Lansing-East Lansing MSA, MI	H	7.12 FQ	11.71 AW	16.75 TQ	MIBLS	10/01-12/01
Except Maid and Housekeeping Cleaner	Saginaw-Bay City-Midland MSA, MI	H	5.97 FQ	9.94 AW	15.97 TQ	MIBLS	10/01-12/01
Except Maid and Housekeeping Cleaner	Minnesota	H	6.86 FQ	10.05 AW	14.31 TQ	MNBLS	10/01-12/01
Except Maid and Housekeeping Cleaner	Duluth-Superior MSA, MN-WI	H	5.80 FQ	8.72 AW	13.83 TQ	MNBLS	10/01-12/01
Except Maid and Housekeeping Cleaner	Minneapolis-St. Paul MSA, MN-WI	H	7.20 FQ	10.20 AW	14.25 TQ	MNBLS	10/01-12/01
Except Maid and Housekeeping Cleaner	St. Cloud MSA, MN	H	6.76 FQ	9.79 AW	14.50 TQ	MNBLS	10/01-12/01
Except Maid and Housekeeping Cleaner	Mississippi	H	5.67 FQ	7.49 AW	10.31 TQ	MSBLS	10/01-12/01
Except Maid and Housekeeping Cleaner	Biloxi-Gulfport-Pascagoula MSA, MS	H	5.84 FQ	8.06 AW	11.01 TQ	MSBLS	10/01-12/01
Except Maid and Housekeeping Cleaner	Jackson MSA, MS	H	5.62 FQ	7.34 AW	9.77 TQ	MSBLS	10/01-12/01
Except Maid and Housekeeping Cleaner	Missouri	H	6.03 FQ	8.89 AW	12.67 TQ	MOBLS	10/01-12/01
Except Maid and Housekeeping Cleaner	Kansas City MSA, MO-KS	H	6.12 FQ	9.44 AW	13.89 TQ	MOBLS	10/01-12/01
Except Maid and Housekeeping Cleaner	St. Louis MSA, MO-IL	H	6.14 FQ	9.18 AW	13.38 TQ	MOBLS	10/01-12/01
Except Maid and Housekeeping Cleaner	Springfield MSA, MO	H	5.83 FQ	8.61 AW	12.52 TQ	MOBLS	10/01-12/01
Except Maid and Housekeeping Cleaner	Montana	H	5.89 FQ	8.42 AW	11.66 TQ	MTBLS	10/01-12/01
Except Maid and Housekeeping Cleaner	Billings MSA, MT	H	5.81 FQ	7.95 AW	11.32 TQ	MTBLS	10/01-12/01
Except Maid and Housekeeping Cleaner	Nebraska	H	6.13 FQ	8.81 AW	12.47 TQ	NEBLS	10/01-12/01
Except Maid and Housekeeping Cleaner	Lincoln MSA, NE	H	6.01 FQ	8.42 AW	11.19 TQ	NEBLS	10/01-12/01
Except Maid and Housekeeping Cleaner	Omaha MSA, NE-IA	H	6.93 FQ	9.45 AW	13.48 TQ	NEBLS	10/01-12/01
Except Maid and Housekeeping Cleaner	Nevada	H	6.28 FQ	10.12 AW	13.73 TQ	NVBLS	10/01-12/01
Except Maid and Housekeeping Cleaner	Las Vegas MSA, NV-AZ	H	6.71 FQ	10.61 AW	13.79 TQ	NVBLS	10/01-12/01

AAW Average annual wage **AOH** Average offered, high **ASH** Average starting, high **H** Hourly **M** Monthly **S** Special: hourly and annual
AE Average entry wage **AOL** Average offered, low **ASL** Average starting, low **HI** Highest wage paid **MTC** Median total compensation **TQ** Third quartile wage
AEX Average experienced wage **APH** Average pay, high range **AW** Average wage paid **HR** High end range **MW** Median wage paid **W** Weekly
AO Average offered **APL** Average pay, low range **FQ** First quartile wage **LR** Low end range **SQ** Second quartile wage **Y** Yearly

Occupation/Type/Industry	Location	Per	Low	Mid	High	Source	Date
Janitor and Cleaner							
Except Maid and Housekeeping Cleaner	Reno MSA, NV	H	5.92 FQ	8.86 AW	13.20 TQ	NVBLS	10/01-12/01
Except Maid and Housekeeping Cleaner	New Hampshire	H	7.02 FQ	9.83 AW	13.36 TQ	NHBLS	10/01-12/01
Except Maid and Housekeeping Cleaner	Manchester PMSA, NH	H	6.64 FQ	9.83 AW	13.85 TQ	NHBLS	10/01-12/01
Except Maid and Housekeeping Cleaner	Nashua PMSA, NH	H	6.32 FQ	10.14 AW	13.73 TQ	NHBLS	10/01-12/01
Except Maid and Housekeeping Cleaner	Portsmouth-Rochester PMSA, NH-ME	H	7.50 FQ	9.87 AW	13.16 TQ	NHBLS	10/01-12/01
Except Maid and Housekeeping Cleaner	New Jersey	H	6.03 FQ	10.17 AW	16.36 TQ	NJBLS	10/01-12/01
Except Maid and Housekeeping Cleaner	Atlantic-Cape May PMSA, NJ	H	7.12 FQ	10.84 AW	14.10 TQ	NJBLS	10/01-12/01
Except Maid and Housekeeping Cleaner	Bergen-Passaic PMSA, NJ	H	5.81 FQ	10.10 AW	17.12 TQ	NJBLS	10/01-12/01
Except Maid and Housekeeping Cleaner	Jersey City PMSA, NJ	H	5.88 FQ	10.01 AW	16.21 TQ	NJBLS	10/01-12/01
Except Maid and Housekeeping Cleaner	Middlesex-Somerset-Hunterdon PMSA, NJ	H	6.05 FQ	10.47 AW	16.98 TQ	NJBLS	10/01-12/01
Except Maid and Housekeeping Cleaner	Monmouth-Ocean PMSA, NJ	H	6.35 FQ	10.85 AW	16.95 TQ	NJBLS	10/01-12/01
Except Maid and Housekeeping Cleaner	Newark PMSA, NJ	H	6.07 FQ	9.83 AW	16.18 TQ	NJBLS	10/01-12/01
Except Maid and Housekeeping Cleaner	Trenton PMSA, NJ	H	5.80 FQ	9.55 AW	14.60 TQ	NJBLS	10/01-12/01
Except Maid and Housekeeping Cleaner	New Mexico	H	5.79 FQ	8.03 AW	11.16 TQ	NMBLS	10/01-12/01
Except Maid and Housekeeping Cleaner	Albuquerque MSA, NM	H	5.79 FQ	8.11 AW	11.28 TQ	NMBLS	10/01-12/01
Except Maid and Housekeeping Cleaner	Las Cruces MSA, NM	H	5.65 FQ	7.24 AW	9.76 TQ	NMBLS	10/01-12/01
Except Maid and Housekeeping Cleaner	New York	H	6.33 FQ	11.56 AW	17.47 TQ	NYBLS	10/01-12/01
Except Maid and Housekeeping Cleaner	Albany-Schenectady-Troy MSA, NY	H	6.78 FQ	10.67 AW	16.18 TQ	NYBLS	10/01-12/01
Except Maid and Housekeeping Cleaner	Binghamton MSA, NY	H	6.18 FQ	9.30 AW	13.02 TQ	NYBLS	10/01-12/01
Except Maid and Housekeeping Cleaner	Buffalo-Niagara Falls MSA, NY	H	5.91 FQ	9.70 AW	15.20 TQ	NYBLS	10/01-12/01
Except Maid and Housekeeping Cleaner	Dutchess County PMSA, NY	H	6.44 FQ	10.62 AW	15.76 TQ	NYBLS	10/01-12/01
Except Maid and Housekeeping Cleaner	Nassau-Suffolk PMSA, NY	H	6.74 FQ	11.42 AW	18.76 TQ	NYBLS	10/01-12/01
Except Maid and Housekeeping Cleaner	New York PMSA, NY	H	6.47 FQ	12.60 AW	17.94 TQ	NYBLS	10/01-12/01
Except Maid and Housekeeping Cleaner	Newburgh PMSA, NY-PA	H	7.28 FQ	10.79 AW	15.33 TQ	NYBLS	10/01-12/01
Except Maid and Housekeeping Cleaner	Rochester MSA, NY	H	6.01 FQ	9.26 AW	14.03 TQ	NYBLS	10/01-12/01
Except Maid and Housekeeping Cleaner	Syracuse MSA, NY	H	6.09 FQ	9.49 AW	13.95 TQ	NYBLS	10/01-12/01
Except Maid and Housekeeping Cleaner	Utica Rome MSA, NY	H	5.98 FQ	9.16 AW	13.50 TQ	NYBLS	10/01-12/01
Except Maid and Housekeeping Cleaner	North Carolina	H	5.88 FQ	8.30 AW	11.00 TQ	NCBLS	10/01-12/01
Except Maid and Housekeeping Cleaner	Asheville MSA, NC	H	6.83 FQ	8.78 AW	11.21 TQ	NCBLS	10/01-12/01
Except Maid and Housekeeping Cleaner	Charlotte-Gastonia-Rock Hill MSA, NC-SC	H	6.18 FQ	8.91 AW	11.34 TQ	NCBLS	10/01-12/01
Except Maid and Housekeeping Cleaner	Fayetteville MSA, NC	H	5.86 FQ	8.16 AW	10.86 TQ	NCBLS	10/01-12/01
Except Maid and Housekeeping Cleaner	Greensboro-Winston-Salem-High Point MSA, NC	H	5.73 FQ	7.92 AW	10.75 TQ	NCBLS	10/01-12/01
Except Maid and Housekeeping Cleaner	Hickory-Morganton-Lenoir MSA, NC	H	6.13 FQ	8.68 AW	11.40 TQ	NCBLS	10/01-12/01
Except Maid and Housekeeping Cleaner	Raleigh-Durham-Chapel Hill MSA, NC	H	5.90 FQ	8.20 AW	10.97 TQ	NCBLS	10/01-12/01
Except Maid and Housekeeping Cleaner	Wilmington MSA, NC	H	5.94 FQ	7.91 AW	10.54 TQ	NCBLS	10/01-12/01
Except Maid and Housekeeping Cleaner	North Dakota	H	6.08 FQ	8.69 AW	12.00 TQ	NDBLS	10/01-12/01
Except Maid and Housekeeping Cleaner	Fargo-Moorhead MSA, ND-MN	H	6.52 FQ	9.27 AW	13.68 TQ	NDBLS	10/01-12/01
Except Maid and Housekeeping Cleaner	Ohio	H	6.09 FQ	9.86 AW	15.11 TQ	OHBLS	10/01-12/01
Except Maid and Housekeeping Cleaner	Akron PMSA, OH	H	6.02 FQ	10.03 AW	16.01 TQ	OHBLS	10/01-12/01
Except Maid and Housekeeping Cleaner	Canton-Massillon MSA, OH	H	6.05 FQ	9.77 AW	14.09 TQ	OHBLS	10/01-12/01
Except Maid and Housekeeping Cleaner	Cincinnati PMSA, OH-KY-IN	H	6.58 FQ	9.78 AW	13.62 TQ	OHBLS	10/01-12/01
Except Maid and Housekeeping Cleaner	Cleveland-Lorain-Elyria PMSA, OH	H	5.85 FQ	9.85 AW	16.08 TQ	OHBLS	10/01-12/01
Except Maid and Housekeeping Cleaner	Columbus MSA, OH	H	6.48 FQ	10.02 AW	15.10 TQ	OHBLS	10/01-12/01
Except Maid and Housekeeping Cleaner	Dayton-Springfield MSA, OH	H	6.65 FQ	10.18 AW	16.11 TQ	OHBLS	10/01-12/01
Except Maid and Housekeeping Cleaner	Hamilton-Middletown PMSA, OH	H	6.65 FQ	10.69 AW	15.94 TQ	OHBLS	10/01-12/01
Except Maid and Housekeeping Cleaner	Mansfield MSA, OH	H	5.73 FQ	8.95 AW	13.60 TQ	OHBLS	10/01-12/01
Except Maid and Housekeeping Cleaner	Toledo MSA, OH	H	6.60 FQ	10.81 AW	16.84 TQ	OHBLS	10/01-12/01
Except Maid and Housekeeping Cleaner	Youngstown-Warren MSA, OH	H	5.85 FQ	9.10 AW	13.63 TQ	OHBLS	10/01-12/01
Except Maid and Housekeeping Cleaner	Oklahoma	H	5.77 FQ	7.84 AW	10.60 TQ	OKBLS	10/01-12/01
Except Maid and Housekeeping Cleaner	Oklahoma City MSA, OK	H	5.76 FQ	7.77 AW	10.44 TQ	OKBLS	10/01-12/01
Except Maid and Housekeeping Cleaner	Tulsa MSA, OK	H	5.79 FQ	7.99 AW	10.85 TQ	OKBLS	10/01-12/01
Except Maid and Housekeeping Cleaner	Oregon	H	7.11 FQ	10.25 AW	14.61 TQ	ORBLS	10/01-12/01
Except Maid and Housekeeping Cleaner	Eugene-Springfield MSA, OR	H	6.75 FQ	9.69 AW	14.28 TQ	ORBLS	10/01-12/01
Except Maid and Housekeeping Cleaner	Medford-Ashland MSA, OR	H	7.08 FQ	9.37 AW	12.89 TQ	ORBLS	10/01-12/01
Except Maid and Housekeeping Cleaner	Portland-Vancouver PMSA, OR-WA	H	7.23 FQ	10.57 AW	15.33 TQ	ORBLS	10/01-12/01
Except Maid and Housekeeping Cleaner	Salem PMSA, OR	H	6.97 FQ	10.16 AW	14.32 TQ	ORBLS	10/01-12/01
Except Maid and Housekeeping Cleaner	Pennsylvania	H	6.16 FQ	9.72 AW	14.45 TQ	PABLS	10/01-12/01
Except Maid and Housekeeping Cleaner	Allentown-Bethlehem-Easton MSA, PA	H	6.43 FQ	9.18 AW	14.23 TQ	PABLS	10/01-12/01

AAW Average annual wage; **AE** Average entry wage; **AEX** Average experienced wage; **AO** Average offered; **AOH** Average offered, high; **AOL** Average offered, low; **APH** Average pay, high range; **APL** Average pay, low range; **ASH** Average starting, high; **ASL** Average starting, low; **AW** Average wage paid; **FQ** First quartile wage; **H** Hourly; **HI** Highest wage paid; **HR** High end range; **LR** Low end range; **M** Monthly; **MTC** Median total compensation; **MW** Median wage paid; **SQ** Second quartile wage; **S** Special: hourly and annual; **TQ** Third quartile wage; **W** Weekly; **Y** Yearly

Occupation/Type/Industry	Location	Per	Low	Mid	High	Source	Date
Janitor and Cleaner							
Except Maid and Housekeeping Cleaner	Erie MSA, PA	H	5.87 FQ	9.20 AW	15.46 TQ	PABLS	10/01-12/01
Except Maid and Housekeeping Cleaner	Harrisburg-Lebanon-Carlisle MSA, PA	H	6.33 FQ	9.22 AW	12.91 TQ	PABLS	10/01-12/01
Except Maid and Housekeeping Cleaner	Johnstown MSA, PA	H	5.74 FQ	8.06 AW	11.73 TQ	PABLS	10/01-12/01
Except Maid and Housekeeping Cleaner	Lancaster MSA, PA	H	6.35 FQ	10.04 AW	14.89 TQ	PABLS	10/01-12/01
Except Maid and Housekeeping Cleaner	Philadelphia PMSA, PA-NJ	H	6.90 FQ	10.65 AW	15.84 TQ	PABLS	10/01-12/01
Except Maid and Housekeeping Cleaner	Pittsburgh MSA, PA	H	5.94 FQ	9.68 AW	15.12 TQ	PABLS	10/01-12/01
Except Maid and Housekeeping Cleaner	Reading MSA, PA	H	6.05 FQ	9.18 AW	13.27 TQ	PABLS	10/01-12/01
Except Maid and Housekeeping Cleaner	Scranton-Wilkes-Barre-Hazleton MSA, PA	H	5.92 FQ	8.90 AW	13.02 TQ	PABLS	10/01-12/01
Except Maid and Housekeeping Cleaner	York MSA, PA	H	6.48 FQ	9.05 AW	12.70 TQ	PABLS	10/01-12/01
Except Maid and Housekeeping Cleaner	Rhode Island	H	6.91 FQ	10.66 AW	15.61 TQ	RIBLS	10/01-12/01
Except Maid and Housekeeping Cleaner	Providence-Fall River-Warwick MSA, RI-MA	H	6.97 FQ	10.67 AW	15.53 TQ	RIBLS	10/01-12/01
Except Maid and Housekeeping Cleaner	South Carolina	H	5.83 FQ	8.02 AW	10.76 TQ	SCBLS	10/01-12/01
Except Maid and Housekeeping Cleaner	Charleston-North Charleston MSA, SC	H	5.77 FQ	7.90 AW	10.66 TQ	SCBLS	10/01-12/01
Except Maid and Housekeeping Cleaner	Columbia MSA, SC	H	5.77 FQ	7.96 AW	10.88 TQ	SCBLS	10/01-12/01
Except Maid and Housekeeping Cleaner	Greenville-Spartanburg-Anderson MSA, SC	H	5.81 FQ	7.87 AW	10.58 TQ	SCBLS	10/01-12/01
Except Maid and Housekeeping Cleaner	Myrtle Beach MSA, SC	H	6.09 FQ	8.40 AW	10.99 TQ	SCBLS	10/01-12/01
Except Maid and Housekeeping Cleaner	South Dakota	H	6.08 FQ	8.38 AW	11.13 TQ	SDBLS	10/01-12/01
Except Maid and Housekeeping Cleaner	Sioux Falls MSA, SD	H	6.31 FQ	8.93 AW	12.15 TQ	SDBLS	10/01-12/01
Except Maid and Housekeeping Cleaner	Tennessee	H	5.89 FQ	8.61 AW	12.68 TQ	TNBLS	10/01-12/01
Except Maid and Housekeeping Cleaner	Chattanooga MSA, TN-GA	H	5.98 FQ	9.00 AW	13.13 TQ	TNBLS	10/01-12/01
Except Maid and Housekeeping Cleaner	Clarksville-Hopkinsville MSA, TN-KY	H	6.22 FQ	8.96 AW	12.31 TQ	TNBLS	10/01-12/01
Except Maid and Housekeeping Cleaner	Johnson City-Kingsport-Bristol MSA, TN-VA	H	5.79 FQ	8.08 AW	10.78 TQ	TNBLS	10/01-12/01
Except Maid and Housekeeping Cleaner	Knoxville MSA, TN	H	5.77 FQ	8.18 AW	10.97 TQ	TNBLS	10/01-12/01
Except Maid and Housekeeping Cleaner	Memphis MSA, TN-AR-MS	H	5.96 FQ	8.11 AW	10.56 TQ	TNBLS	10/01-12/01
Except Maid and Housekeeping Cleaner	Nashville MSA, TN	H	6.05 FQ	9.37 AW	14.69 TQ	TNBLS	10/01-12/01
Except Maid and Housekeeping Cleaner	Texas	H	5.71 FQ	7.80 AW	10.94 TQ	TXBLS	10/01-12/01
Except Maid and Housekeeping Cleaner	Amarillo MSA, TX	H	5.86 FQ	8.08 AW	10.97 TQ	TXBLS	10/01-12/01
Except Maid and Housekeeping Cleaner	Austin-San Marcos MSA, TX	H	5.87 FQ	8.10 AW	10.89 TQ	TXBLS	10/01-12/01
Except Maid and Housekeeping Cleaner	Beaumont-Port Arthur MSA, TX	H	5.62 FQ	7.47 AW	10.74 TQ	TXBLS	10/01-12/01
Except Maid and Housekeeping Cleaner	Brazoria PMSA, TX	H	5.77 FQ	7.73 AW	10.37 TQ	TXBLS	10/01-12/01
Except Maid and Housekeeping Cleaner	Brownsville-Harlingen-San Benito MSA, TX	H	5.69 FQ	7.37 AW	9.99 TQ	TXBLS	10/01-12/01
Except Maid and Housekeeping Cleaner	Corpus Christi MSA, TX	H	5.67 FQ	7.23 AW	8.90 TQ	TXBLS	10/01-12/01
Except Maid and Housekeeping Cleaner	Dallas PMSA, TX	H	5.83 FQ	8.42 AW	12.47 TQ	TXBLS	10/01-12/01
Except Maid and Housekeeping Cleaner	El Paso MSA, TX	H	5.68 FQ	7.35 AW	9.95 TQ	TXBLS	10/01-12/01
Except Maid and Housekeeping Cleaner	Fort Worth-Arlington PMSA, TX	H	6.10 FQ	9.31 AW	14.01 TQ	TXBLS	10/01-12/01
Except Maid and Housekeeping Cleaner	Galveston-Texas City PMSA, TX	H	5.79 FQ	7.95 AW	11.07 TQ	TXBLS	10/01-12/01
Except Maid and Housekeeping Cleaner	Houston PMSA, TX	H	5.63 FQ	7.28 AW	10.38 TQ	TXBLS	10/01-12/01
Except Maid and Housekeeping Cleaner	Killeen-Temple MSA, TX	H	5.62 FQ	7.29 AW	9.85 TQ	TXBLS	10/01-12/01
Except Maid and Housekeeping Cleaner	Laredo MSA, TX	H	5.75 FQ	7.47 AW	10.03 TQ	TXBLS	10/01-12/01
Except Maid and Housekeeping Cleaner	Longview-Marshall MSA, TX	H	5.76 FQ	7.79 AW	10.52 TQ	TXBLS	10/01-12/01
Except Maid and Housekeeping Cleaner	Lubbock MSA, TX	H	5.79 FQ	8.24 AW	11.15 TQ	TXBLS	10/01-12/01
Except Maid and Housekeeping Cleaner	McAllen-Edinburg-Mission MSA, TX	H	5.71 FQ	7.25 AW	8.93 TQ	TXBLS	10/01-12/01
Except Maid and Housekeeping Cleaner	Odessa-Midland MSA, TX	H	5.64 FQ	7.49 AW	10.31 TQ	TXBLS	10/01-12/01
Except Maid and Housekeeping Cleaner	San Antonio MSA, TX	H	5.78 FQ	8.01 AW	10.92 TQ	TXBLS	10/01-12/01
Except Maid and Housekeeping Cleaner	Tyler MSA, TX	H	5.69 FQ	7.83 AW	10.99 TQ	TXBLS	10/01-12/01
Except Maid and Housekeeping Cleaner	Waco MSA, TX	H	5.72 FQ	7.63 AW	10.20 TQ	TXBLS	10/01-12/01
Except Maid and Housekeeping Cleaner	Utah	H	5.96 FQ	8.67 AW	12.38 TQ	UTBLS	10/01-12/01
Except Maid and Housekeeping Cleaner	Provo-Orem MSA, UT	H	5.83 FQ	8.00 AW	11.38 TQ	UTBLS	10/01-12/01
Except Maid and Housekeeping Cleaner	Salt Lake City-Ogden MSA, UT	H	6.04 FQ	8.68 AW	11.69 TQ	UTBLS	10/01-12/01
Except Maid and Housekeeping Cleaner	Vermont	H	7.06 FQ	9.89 AW	13.23 TQ	VTBLS	10/01-12/01
Except Maid and Housekeeping Cleaner	Burlington MSA, VT	H	7.31 FQ	9.57 AW	12.89 TQ	VTBLS	10/01-12/01
Except Maid and Housekeeping Cleaner	Virginia	H	5.80 FQ	8.25 AW	11.36 TQ	VABLS	10/01-12/01
Except Maid and Housekeeping Cleaner	Lynchburg MSA, VA	H	5.70 FQ	7.70 AW	10.40 TQ	VABLS	10/01-12/01
Except Maid and Housekeeping Cleaner	Norfolk-Virginia Beach-Newport News MSA, VA-NC	H	5.73 FQ	8.06 AW	11.36 TQ	VABLS	10/01-12/01
Except Maid and Housekeeping Cleaner	Richmond-Petersburg MSA, VA	H	5.77 FQ	8.08 AW	11.20 TQ	VABLS	10/01-12/01

AAW Average annual wage **AE** Average entry wage **AEX** Average experienced wage **AO** Average offered **AOH** Average offered, high **AOL** Average offered, low **APH** Average pay, high range **APL** Average pay, low range **ASH** Average starting, high **ASL** Average starting, low **AW** Average wage paid **FQ** First quartile wage **H** Hourly **HI** Highest wage paid **HR** High end range **LR** Low end range **M** Monthly **MTC** Median total compensation **MW** Median wage paid **SQ** Second quartile wage **S** Special: hourly and annual **TQ** Third quartile wage **W** Weekly **Y** Yearly

Occupation/Type/Industry	Location	Per	Low	Mid	High	Source	Date
Janitor and Cleaner							
Except Maid and Housekeeping Cleaner	Roanoke MSA, VA	H	5.61 FQ	10.16 AW	11.14 TQ	VABLS	10/01-12/01
Except Maid and Housekeeping Cleaner	Washington	H	7.22 FQ	10.62 AW	14.88 TQ	WABLS	10/01-12/01
Except Maid and Housekeeping Cleaner	Bremerton PMSA, WA	H	7.21 FQ	11.12 AW	15.44 TQ	WABLS	10/01-12/01
Except Maid and Housekeeping Cleaner	Olympia PMSA, WA	H	7.06 FQ	10.09 AW	13.51 TQ	WABLS	10/01-12/01
Except Maid and Housekeeping Cleaner	Richland-Kennewick-Pasco MSA, WA	H	7.07 FQ	10.41 AW	14.51 TQ	WABLS	10/01-12/01
Except Maid and Housekeeping Cleaner	Seattle-Bellevue-Everett PMSA, WA	H	7.88 FQ	11.15 AW	15.54 TQ	WABLS	10/01-12/01
Except Maid and Housekeeping Cleaner	Spokane MSA, WA	H	7.00 FQ	9.77 AW	14.01 TQ	WABLS	10/01-12/01
Except Maid and Housekeeping Cleaner	Tacoma PMSA, WA	H	6.91 FQ	10.29 AW	15.15 TQ	WABLS	10/01-12/01
Except Maid and Housekeeping Cleaner	Yakima MSA, WA	H	7.13 FQ	10.08 AW	13.84 TQ	WABLS	10/01-12/01
Except Maid and Housekeeping Cleaner	West Virginia	H	5.74 FQ	8.36 AW	12.33 TQ	WVBLS	10/01-12/01
Except Maid and Housekeeping Cleaner	Charleston MSA, WV	H	5.74 FQ	7.81 AW	10.37 TQ	WVBLS	10/01-12/01
Except Maid and Housekeeping Cleaner	Huntington-Ashland MSA, WV-KY-OH	H	5.83 FQ	8.69 AW	12.60 TQ	WVBLS	10/01-12/01
Except Maid and Housekeeping Cleaner	Wisconsin	H	6.63 FQ	9.68 AW	13.92 TQ	WIBLS	10/01-12/01
Except Maid and Housekeeping Cleaner	Appleton-Oshkosh-Neenah MSA, WI	H	7.05 FQ	9.81 AW	14.05 TQ	WIBLS	10/01-12/01
Except Maid and Housekeeping Cleaner	Green Bay MSA, WI	H	6.91 FQ	9.85 AW	15.30 TQ	WIBLS	10/01-12/01
Except Maid and Housekeeping Cleaner	Madison MSA, WI	H	6.94 FQ	9.85 AW	14.40 TQ	WIBLS	10/01-12/01
Except Maid and Housekeeping Cleaner	Milwaukee-Waukesha PMSA, WI	H	6.87 FQ	9.73 AW	14.03 TQ	WIBLS	10/01-12/01
Except Maid and Housekeeping Cleaner	Racine PMSA, WI	H	6.12 FQ	8.97 AW	13.15 TQ	WIBLS	10/01-12/01
Except Maid and Housekeeping Cleaner	Wyoming	H	6.05 FQ	8.96 AW	12.80 TQ	WYBLS	10/01-12/01
Except Maid and Housekeeping Cleaner	Cheyenne MSA, WY	H	6.19 FQ	8.42 AW	11.05 TQ	WYBLS	10/01-12/01
Except Maid and Housekeeping Cleaner	Puerto Rico	H	5.45 FQ	6.32 AW	7.29 TQ	PRBLS	10/01-12/01
Except Maid and Housekeeping Cleaner	Virgin Islands	H	5.63 FQ	7.21 AW	9.12 TQ	VIBLS	10/01-12/01
Except Maid and Housekeeping Cleaner	Guam	H	5.61 FQ	7.73 AW	12.21 TQ	GUBLS	10/01-12/01
Jeweler and Precious Stone and Metal Worker							
	Alabama	H	8.18 FQ	15.00 AW	21.09 TQ	ALBLS	10/01-12/01
	Birmingham MSA, AL	H	7.29 FQ	13.35 AW	18.17 TQ	ALBLS	10/01-12/01
	Mobile MSA, AL	H	9.77 FQ	13.96 AW	19.27 TQ	ALBLS	10/01-12/01
	Alaska	H	9.74 FQ	16.95 AW	31.06 TQ	AKBLS	10/01-12/01
	Anchorage MSA, AK	H	9.96 FQ	17.25 AW	31.47 TQ	AKBLS	10/01-12/01
	Arizona	H	7.55 FQ	14.09 AW	23.26 TQ	AZBLS	10/01-12/01
	Phoenix-Mesa MSA, AZ	H	9.54 FQ	17.13 AW	25.17 TQ	AZBLS	10/01-12/01
	Tucson MSA, AZ	H	7.57 FQ	11.48 AW	20.96 TQ	AZBLS	10/01-12/01
	Arkansas	H	7.81 FQ	22.41 AW	60.20 TQ	ARBLS	10/01-12/01
	California	H	6.53 FQ	11.60 AW	20.54 TQ	CABLS	10/01-12/01
	Fresno MSA, CA	H	12.07 FQ	18.00 AW	22.23 TQ	CABLS	10/01-12/01
	Los Angeles-Long Beach PMSA, CA	H	6.48 FQ	10.31 AW	18.22 TQ	CABLS	10/01-12/01
	Oakland PMSA, CA	H	6.51 FQ	13.11 AW	21.46 TQ	CABLS	10/01-12/01
	Orange County PMSA, CA	H	6.48 FQ	10.46 AW	19.12 TQ	CABLS	10/01-12/01
	Riverside-San Bernardino PMSA, CA	H	6.69 FQ	17.94 AW	22.56 TQ	CABLS	10/01-12/01
	Sacramento PMSA, CA	H	8.40 FQ	14.62 AW	26.23 TQ	CABLS	10/01-12/01
	San Diego MSA, CA	H	6.54 FQ	12.18 AW	22.95 TQ	CABLS	10/01-12/01
	San Francisco PMSA, CA	H	7.95 FQ	14.43 AW	21.27 TQ	CABLS	10/01-12/01
	San Jose PMSA, CA	H	14.66 FQ	23.73 AW	34.91 TQ	CABLS	10/01-12/01
	Colorado	H	8.07 FQ	15.54 AW	21.43 TQ	COBLS	10/01-12/01
	Boulder-Longmont PMSA, CO	H	17.86 FQ	19.30 AW	21.85 TQ	COBLS	10/01-12/01
	Denver PMSA, CO	H	8.88 FQ	13.69 AW	17.17 TQ	COBLS	10/01-12/01
	Connecticut	H	9.75 FQ	18.10 AW	26.86 TQ	CTBLS	10/01-12/01
	Danbury PMSA, CT	H	14.48 FQ	17.27 AW	22.52 TQ	CTBLS	10/01-12/01
	Hartford MSA, CT	H	9.03 FQ	18.02 AW	27.64 TQ	CTBLS	10/01-12/01
	Stamford-Norwalk PMSA, CT	H	7.04 FQ	22.28 AW	44.29 TQ	CTBLS	10/01-12/01
	Washington PMSA, DC-MD-VA-WV	H	11.50 FQ	19.86 AW	28.50 TQ	DCBLS	10/01-12/01
	Florida	H	6.70 FQ	14.10 AW	21.79 TQ	FLBLS	10/01-12/01
	Daytona Beach MSA, FL	H	8.17 FQ	15.47 AW	32.79 TQ	FLBLS	10/01-12/01
	Fort Lauderdale PMSA, FL	H	6.33 FQ	12.83 AW	17.74 TQ	FLBLS	10/01-12/01
	Fort Myers-Cape Coral MSA, FL	H	10.63 FQ	16.32 AW	26.55 TQ	FLBLS	10/01-12/01
	Jacksonville MSA, FL	H	12.77 FQ	17.25 AW	24.98 TQ	FLBLS	10/01-12/01
	Miami PMSA, FL	H	6.47 FQ	13.19 AW	18.49 TQ	FLBLS	10/01-12/01
	Orlando MSA, FL	H	6.23 FQ	15.45 AW	28.73 TQ	FLBLS	10/01-12/01
	Pensacola MSA, FL	H	6.09 FQ	12.83 AW	18.75 TQ	FLBLS	10/01-12/01
	Tampa-St. Petersburg-Clearwater MSA, FL	H	11.19 FQ	14.15 AW	17.25 TQ	FLBLS	10/01-12/01

AAW	Average annual wage	AOH	Average offered, high	ASH	Average starting, high	H	Hourly	M	Monthly	S	Special: hourly and annual
AE	Average entry wage	AOL	Average offered, low	ASL	Average starting, low	HI	Highest wage paid	MTC	Median total compensation	TQ	Third quartile wage
AEX	Average experienced wage	APH	Average pay, high range	AW	Average wage paid	HR	High end range	MW	Median wage paid	W	Weekly
AO	Average offered	APL	Average pay, low range	FQ	First quartile wage	LR	Low end range	SQ	Second quartile wage	Y	Yearly

Occupation/Type/Industry	Location	Per	Low	Mid	High	Source	Date
Jeweler and Precious Stone and Metal Worker	West Palm Beach-Boca Raton MSA, FL	H	5.79 FQ	13.81 AW	29.16 TQ	FLBLS	10/01-12/01
	Georgia	H	6.96 FQ	16.05 AW	27.17 TQ	GABLS	10/01-12/01
	Atlanta MSA, GA	H	6.67 FQ	17.01 AW	28.37 TQ	GABLS	10/01-12/01
	Hawaii	H	6.87 FQ	10.22 AW	15.61 TQ	HIBLS	10/01-12/01
	Honolulu MSA, HI	H	6.85 FQ	10.05 AW	15.12 TQ	HIBLS	10/01-12/01
	Idaho	H	11.47 FQ	15.53 AW	21.49 TQ	IDBLS	10/01-12/01
	Boise City MSA, ID	H	12.16 FQ	17.84 AW	26.63 TQ	IDBLS	10/01-12/01
	Illinois	H	12.71 FQ	17.36 AW	21.61 TQ	ILBLS	10/01-12/01
	Chicago PMSA, IL	H	14.08 FQ	17.72 AW	21.61 TQ	ILBLS	10/01-12/01
	Indiana	H	6.51 FQ	11.87 AW	17.50 TQ	INBLS	10/01-12/01
	Evansville-Henderson MSA, IN-KY	H	6.96 FQ	11.97 AW	16.52 TQ	INBLS	10/01-12/01
	Gary PMSA, IN	H	9.20 FQ	12.44 AW	17.21 TQ	INBLS	10/01-12/01
	Indianapolis MSA, IN	H	7.15 FQ	11.67 AW	14.65 TQ	INBLS	10/01-12/01
	Iowa	H	7.65 FQ	14.04 AW	21.20 TQ	IABLS	10/01-12/01
	Kansas	H	8.46 FQ	14.16 AW	17.44 TQ	KSBLS	10/01-12/01
	Kentucky	H	8.56 FQ	13.89 AW	20.84 TQ	KYBLS	10/01-12/01
	Lexington MSA, KY	H	10.89 FQ	16.02 AW	22.12 TQ	KYBLS	10/01-12/01
	Louisville MSA, KY-IN	H	7.87 FQ	14.76 AW	24.88 TQ	KYBLS	10/01-12/01
	Louisiana	H	7.79 FQ	12.81 AW	19.31 TQ	LABLS	10/01-12/01
	New Orleans MSA, LA	H	8.85 FQ	13.31 AW	22.24 TQ	LABLS	10/01-12/01
	Maine	H	7.66 FQ	13.31 AW	16.89 TQ	MEBLS	10/01-12/01
	Maryland	H	8.33 FQ	15.28 AW	22.19 TQ	MDBLS	10/01-12/01
	Baltimore PMSA, MD	H	7.24 FQ	13.51 AW	17.52 TQ	MDBLS	10/01-12/01
	Massachusetts	H	9.43 FQ	14.77 AW	24.70 TQ	MABLS	10/01-12/01
	Boston PMSA, MA-NH	H	9.62 FQ	15.23 AW	25.53 TQ	MABLS	10/01-12/01
	Michigan	H	8.61 FQ	27.73 AW		MIBLS	10/01-12/01
	Ann Arbor PMSA, MI	H	7.06 FQ	10.60 AW	16.33 TQ	MIBLS	10/01-12/01
	Detroit PMSA, MI	H	16.90 FQ	35.17 AW		MIBLS	10/01-12/01
	Grand Rapids-Muskegon-Holland MSA, MI	H	9.30 FQ	13.41 AW	18.22 TQ	MIBLS	10/01-12/01
	Kalamazoo-Battle Creek MSA, MI	H	7.24 FQ	9.69 AW	13.35 TQ	MIBLS	10/01-12/01
	Minnesota	H	7.75 FQ	14.54 AW	21.10 TQ	MNBLS	10/01-12/01
	Minneapolis-St. Paul MSA, MN-WI	H	10.92 FQ	15.84 AW	21.49 TQ	MNBLS	10/01-12/01
	Mississippi	H	8.50 FQ	13.06 AW	18.17 TQ	MSBLS	10/01-12/01
	Missouri	H	8.59 FQ	19.31 AW	34.75 TQ	MOBLS	10/01-12/01
	Kansas City MSA, MO-KS	H	10.42 FQ	15.88 AW	22.78 TQ	MOBLS	10/01-12/01
	St. Louis MSA, MO-IL	H	11.68 FQ	18.74 AW	33.26 TQ	MOBLS	10/01-12/01
	Montana	H	8.79 FQ	11.46 AW	15.83 TQ	MTBLS	10/01-12/01
	Billings MSA, MT	H	8.96 FQ	10.58 AW	13.13 TQ	MTBLS	10/01-12/01
	Nebraska	H	7.30 FQ	12.70 AW	17.83 TQ	NEBLS	10/01-12/01
	Nevada	H	8.47 FQ	16.43 AW	24.01 TQ	NVBLS	10/01-12/01
	Las Vegas MSA, NV-AZ	H	9.32 FQ	18.63 AW	29.56 TQ	NVBLS	10/01-12/01
	Reno MSA, NV	H	7.53 FQ	11.10 AW	14.00 TQ	NVBLS	10/01-12/01
	New Hampshire	H	9.21 FQ	15.67 AW	22.08 TQ	NHBLS	10/01-12/01
	Portsmouth-Rochester PMSA, NH-ME	H	9.19 FQ	15.33 AW	19.83 TQ	NHBLS	10/01-12/01
	New Jersey	H	7.48 FQ	16.26 AW	25.70 TQ	NJBLS	10/01-12/01
	Bergen-Passaic PMSA, NJ	H	6.22 FQ	12.61 AW	22.94 TQ	NJBLS	10/01-12/01
	Middlesex-Somerset-Hunterdon PMSA, NJ	H	11.18 FQ	18.41 AW	22.72 TQ	NJBLS	10/01-12/01
	Newark PMSA, NJ	H	9.79 FQ	18.13 AW	27.50 TQ	NJBLS	10/01-12/01
	New Mexico	H	7.39 FQ	9.95 AW	12.51 TQ	NMBLS	10/01-12/01
	Albuquerque MSA, NM	H	7.65 FQ	10.07 AW	12.71 TQ	NMBLS	10/01-12/01
	New York	H	6.03 FQ	12.95 AW	21.81 TQ	NYBLS	10/01-12/01
	Buffalo-Niagara Falls MSA, NY	H	10.81 FQ	16.04 AW	21.54 TQ	NYBLS	10/01-12/01
	Nassau-Suffolk PMSA, NY	H	6.54 FQ	16.46 AW	26.76 TQ	NYBLS	10/01-12/01
	New York PMSA, NY	H	5.90 FQ	12.52 AW	21.83 TQ	NYBLS	10/01-12/01
	North Carolina	H	9.65 FQ	14.16 AW	18.70 TQ	NCBLS	10/01-12/01
	Charlotte-Gastonia-Rock Hill MSA, NC-SC	H	8.83 FQ	15.06 AW	20.99 TQ	NCBLS	10/01-12/01
	Greensboro-Winston-Salem-High Point MSA, NC	H	9.17 FQ	12.61 AW	16.98 TQ	NCBLS	10/01-12/01
	Raleigh-Durham-Chapel Hill MSA, NC	H	12.66 FQ	20.30 AW	29.33 TQ	NCBLS	10/01-12/01
	Ohio	H	7.86 FQ	14.95 AW	23.03 TQ	OHBLS	10/01-12/01
	Cincinnati PMSA, OH-KY-IN	H	8.41 FQ	14.98 AW	21.12 TQ	OHBLS	10/01-12/01

AAW	Average annual wage	AOH	Average offered, high	ASH	Average starting, high	H	Hourly	M	Monthly	S	Special: hourly and annual
AE	Average entry wage	AOL	Average offered, low	ASL	Average starting, low	HI	Highest wage paid	MTC	Median total compensation	TQ	Third quartile wage
AEX	Average experienced wage	APH	Average pay, high range	AW	Average wage paid	HR	High end range	MW	Median wage paid	W	Weekly
AO	Average offered	APL	Average pay, low range	FQ	First quartile wage	LR	Low end range	SQ	Second quartile wage	Y	Yearly

Occupation/Type/Industry	Location	Per	Low	Mid	High	Source	Date
Jeweler and Precious Stone and Metal Worker	Cleveland-Lorain-Elyria PMSA, OH	H	7.52 FQ	11.50 AW	19.96 TQ	OHBLS	10/01-12/01
	Columbus MSA, OH	H	12.03 FQ	18.65 AW	26.74 TQ	OHBLS	10/01-12/01
	Dayton-Springfield MSA, OH	H	12.84 FQ	18.04 AW	22.06 TQ	OHBLS	10/01-12/01
	Mansfield MSA, OH	H	9.39 FQ	15.10 AW	20.49 TQ	OHBLS	10/01-12/01
	Oklahoma	H	7.81 FQ	14.29 AW	20.84 TQ	OKBLS	10/01-12/01
	Oklahoma City MSA, OK	H	6.96 FQ	12.84 AW	24.21 TQ	OKBLS	10/01-12/01
	Tulsa MSA, OK	H	8.55 FQ	15.00 AW	19.71 TQ	OKBLS	10/01-12/01
	Oregon	H	9.34 FQ	17.02 AW	26.58 TQ	ORBLS	10/01-12/01
	Portland-Vancouver PMSA, OR-WA	H	9.91 FQ	18.78 AW	29.46 TQ	ORBLS	10/01-12/01
	Pennsylvania	H	8.79 FQ	14.03 AW	20.34 TQ	PABLS	10/01-12/01
	Allentown-Bethlehem-Easton MSA, PA	H	8.22 FQ	19.16 AW	29.54 TQ	PABLS	10/01-12/01
	Philadelphia PMSA, PA-NJ	H	8.28 FQ	13.71 AW	20.10 TQ	PABLS	10/01-12/01
	Pittsburgh MSA, PA	H	11.33 FQ	13.97 AW	19.78 TQ	PABLS	10/01-12/01
	Rhode Island	H	6.80 FQ	11.35 AW	17.41 TQ	RIBLS	10/01-12/01
	Providence-Fall River-Warwick MSA, RI-MA	H	6.90 FQ	11.80 AW	17.83 TQ	RIBLS	10/01-12/01
	South Carolina	H	6.68 FQ	14.65 AW	22.82 TQ	SCBLS	10/01-12/01
	Columbia MSA, SC	H	8.58 FQ	14.74 AW	23.19 TQ	SCBLS	10/01-12/01
	Greenville-Spartanburg-Anderson MSA, SC	H	11.66 FQ	16.18 AW	24.25 TQ	SCBLS	10/01-12/01
	South Dakota	H	6.58 FQ	9.91 AW	13.44 TQ	SDBLS	10/01-12/01
	Tennessee	H	7.59 FQ	13.19 AW	21.96 TQ	TNBLS	10/01-12/01
	Knoxville MSA, TN	H	11.93 FQ	14.34 AW	19.49 TQ	TNBLS	10/01-12/01
	Nashville MSA, TN	H	6.41 FQ	11.88 AW	17.39 TQ	TNBLS	10/01-12/01
	Texas	H	6.66 FQ	13.10 AW	19.59 TQ	TXBLS	10/01-12/01
	Austin-San Marcos MSA, TX	H	9.22 FQ	24.16 AW	53.60 TQ	TXBLS	10/01-12/01
	Dallas PMSA, TX	H	7.62 FQ	13.34 AW	18.63 TQ	TXBLS	10/01-12/01
	El Paso MSA, TX	H	5.91 FQ	10.85 AW	16.81 TQ	TXBLS	10/01-12/01
	Fort Worth-Arlington PMSA, TX	H	6.49 FQ	11.31 AW	17.02 TQ	TXBLS	10/01-12/01
	Houston PMSA, TX	H	6.08 FQ	12.02 AW	17.22 TQ	TXBLS	10/01-12/01
	San Antonio MSA, TX	H	9.12 FQ	16.85 AW	26.94 TQ	TXBLS	10/01-12/01
	Virginia	H	7.52 FQ	13.67 AW	21.25 TQ	VABLS	10/01-12/01
	Norfolk-Virginia Beach-Newport News MSA, VA-NC	H	6.13 FQ	9.85 AW	13.02 TQ	VABLS	10/01-12/01
	Richmond-Petersburg MSA, VA	H	9.23 FQ	13.58 AW	17.70 TQ	VABLS	10/01-12/01
	Washington	H	9.30 FQ	16.55 AW	21.78 TQ	WABLS	10/01-12/01
	Seattle-Bellevue-Everett PMSA, WA	H	9.64 FQ	17.50 AW	21.94 TQ	WABLS	10/01-12/01
	Spokane MSA, WA	H	9.05 FQ	13.89 AW	18.89 TQ	WABLS	10/01-12/01
	West Virginia	H	6.14 FQ	10.43 AW	16.40 TQ	WVBLS	10/01-12/01
	Huntington-Ashland MSA, WV-KY-OH	H	5.84 FQ	9.44 AW	16.81 TQ	WVBLS	10/01-12/01
	Wisconsin	H	10.19 FQ	16.38 AW	24.30 TQ	WIBLS	10/01-12/01
	Milwaukee-Waukesha PMSA, WI	H	13.53 FQ	18.82 AW	26.64 TQ	WIBLS	10/01-12/01
	Puerto Rico	H	7.10 FQ	8.25 AW	10.02 TQ	PRBLS	10/01-12/01
	Virgin Islands	H	9.79 FQ	15.18 AW	22.06 TQ	VIBLS	10/01-12/01
Job Printer	Alabama	H	7.62 FQ	12.54 AW	17.08 TQ	ALBLS	10/01-12/01
	Birmingham MSA, AL	H	9.36 FQ	14.27 AW	18.20 TQ	ALBLS	10/01-12/01
	Huntsville MSA, AL	H	8.93 FQ	13.47 AW	17.16 TQ	ALBLS	10/01-12/01
	Mobile MSA, AL	H	9.58 FQ	13.54 AW	17.10 TQ	ALBLS	10/01-12/01
	Arizona	H	8.12 FQ	12.56 AW	18.26 TQ	AZBLS	10/01-12/01
	Phoenix-Mesa MSA, AZ	H	8.38 FQ	13.11 AW	18.99 TQ	AZBLS	10/01-12/01
	Tucson MSA, AZ	H	7.99 FQ	11.44 AW	16.15 TQ	AZBLS	10/01-12/01
	Arkansas	H	5.95 FQ	10.79 AW	17.00 TQ	ARBLS	10/01-12/01
	Fayetteville-Springdale-Rogers MSA, AR	H	7.71 FQ	10.25 AW	15.27 TQ	ARBLS	10/01-12/01
	Little Rock-North Little Rock MSA, AR	H	5.59 FQ	9.37 AW	15.96 TQ	ARBLS	10/01-12/01
	California	H	10.26 FQ	16.97 AW	24.84 TQ	CABLS	10/01-12/01
	Fresno MSA, CA	H	8.40 FQ	12.24 AW	18.79 TQ	CABLS	10/01-12/01
	Los Angeles-Long Beach PMSA, CA	H	10.81 FQ	17.71 AW	29.16 TQ	CABLS	10/01-12/01
	Modesto MSA, CA	H	11.20 FQ	14.84 AW	20.39 TQ	CABLS	10/01-12/01

AAW Average annual wage; AE Average entry wage; AEX Average experienced wage; AO Average offered; AOH Average offered, high; AOL Average offered, low; APH Average pay, high range; APL Average pay, low range; ASH Average starting, high; ASL Average starting, low; AW Average wage paid; FQ First quartile wage; H Hourly; HI Highest wage paid; HR High end range; LR Low end range; M Monthly; MTC Median total compensation; MW Median wage paid; SQ Second quartile wage; S Special: hourly and annual; TQ Third quartile wage; W Weekly; Y Yearly

Occupation/Type/Industry	Location	Per	Low	Mid	High	Source	Date
Job Printer	Oakland PMSA, CA	H	13.16 FQ	18.12 AW	21.16 TQ	CABLS	10/01-12/01
	Orange County PMSA, CA	H	8.93 FQ	16.11 AW	24.55 TQ	CABLS	10/01-12/01
	Riverside-San Bernardino PMSA, CA	H	10.67 FQ	16.35 AW	22.16 TQ	CABLS	10/01-12/01
	Sacramento PMSA, CA	H	9.92 FQ	15.91 AW	24.99 TQ	CABLS	10/01-12/01
	Salinas MSA, CA	H	12.34 FQ	17.17 AW	23.37 TQ	CABLS	10/01-12/01
	San Diego MSA, CA	H	9.81 FQ	16.11 AW	20.86 TQ	CABLS	10/01-12/01
	San Francisco PMSA, CA	H	12.10 FQ	23.80 AW	34.44 TQ	CABLS	10/01-12/01
	San Jose PMSA, CA	H	9.39 FQ	17.37 AW	25.24 TQ	CABLS	10/01-12/01
	San Luis Obispo-Atascadero-Paso Robles MSA, CA	H	11.32 FQ	16.02 AW	21.07 TQ	CABLS	10/01-12/01
	Santa Rosa PMSA, CA	H	10.95 FQ	13.15 AW	16.87 TQ	CABLS	10/01-12/01
	Stockton-Lodi MSA, CA	H	9.45 FQ	11.98 AW	14.16 TQ	CABLS	10/01-12/01
	Vallejo-Fairfield-Napa PMSA, CA	H	12.02 FQ	18.34 AW	27.07 TQ	CABLS	10/01-12/01
	Ventura PMSA, CA	H	10.28 FQ	16.10 AW	22.10 TQ	CABLS	10/01-12/01
	Colorado	H	9.99 FQ	16.49 AW	21.19 TQ	COBLS	10/01-12/01
	Boulder-Longmont PMSA, CO	H	10.67 FQ	15.37 AW	19.90 TQ	COBLS	10/01-12/01
	Colorado Springs MSA, CO	H	9.55 FQ	13.75 AW	16.95 TQ	COBLS	10/01-12/01
	Denver PMSA, CO	H	15.66 FQ	18.92 AW	21.43 TQ	COBLS	10/01-12/01
	Connecticut	H	10.49 FQ	16.90 AW	22.58 TQ	CTBLS	10/01-12/01
	Bridgeport PMSA, CT	H	12.45 FQ	17.46 AW	21.57 TQ	CTBLS	10/01-12/01
	Hartford MSA, CT	H	11.72 FQ	17.00 AW	22.49 TQ	CTBLS	10/01-12/01
	New Haven-Meriden PMSA, CT	H	9.79 FQ	17.25 AW	23.17 TQ	CTBLS	10/01-12/01
	Stamford-Norwalk PMSA, CT	H	9.62 FQ	16.36 AW	21.81 TQ	CTBLS	10/01-12/01
	Waterbury PMSA, CT	H	9.02 FQ	16.69 AW	24.05 TQ	CTBLS	10/01-12/01
	District of Columbia	H	9.67 FQ	16.05 AW	23.75 TQ	DCBLS	10/01-12/01
	Washington PMSA, DC-MD-VA-WV	H	11.22 FQ	16.79 AW	24.49 TQ	DCBLS	10/01-12/01
	Florida	H	7.32 FQ	11.09 AW	18.03 TQ	FLBLS	10/01-12/01
	Daytona Beach MSA, FL	H	9.06 FQ	14.19 AW	22.85 TQ	FLBLS	10/01-12/01
	Fort Lauderdale PMSA, FL	H	10.67 FQ	16.51 AW	24.35 TQ	FLBLS	10/01-12/01
	Fort Myers-Cape Coral MSA, FL	H	9.70 FQ	15.01 AW	24.78 TQ	FLBLS	10/01-12/01
	Fort Pierce-Port St. Lucie MSA, FL	H	11.79 FQ	15.83 AW	20.35 TQ	FLBLS	10/01-12/01
	Jacksonville MSA, FL	H	6.56 FQ	11.30 AW	16.41 TQ	FLBLS	10/01-12/01
	Melbourne-Titusville-Palm Bay MSA, FL	H	11.40 FQ	14.52 AW	19.69 TQ	FLBLS	10/01-12/01
	Miami PMSA, FL	H	8.17 FQ	14.41 AW	21.71 TQ	FLBLS	10/01-12/01
	Naples MSA, FL	H	8.13 FQ	15.62 AW	24.57 TQ	FLBLS	10/01-12/01
	Ocala MSA, FL	H	7.46 FQ	11.97 AW	16.98 TQ	FLBLS	10/01-12/01
	Orlando MSA, FL	H	7.23 FQ	13.00 AW	18.39 TQ	FLBLS	10/01-12/01
	Pensacola MSA, FL	H	7.67 FQ	13.22 AW	20.28 TQ	FLBLS	10/01-12/01
	Sarasota-Bradenton MSA, FL	H	8.36 FQ	13.64 AW	19.47 TQ	FLBLS	10/01-12/01
	Tallahassee MSA, FL	H	11.76 FQ	14.56 AW	16.75 TQ	FLBLS	10/01-12/01
	Tampa-St. Petersburg-Clearwater MSA, FL	H	7.24 FQ	8.77 AW	10.68 TQ	FLBLS	10/01-12/01
	West Palm Beach-Boca Raton MSA, FL	H	10.27 FQ	16.49 AW	22.80 TQ	FLBLS	10/01-12/01
	Georgia	H	9.37 FQ	16.50 AW	24.96 TQ	GABLS	10/01-12/01
	Atlanta MSA, GA	H	11.78 FQ	19.32 AW	26.09 TQ	GABLS	10/01-12/01
	Columbus MSA, GA-AL	H	9.65 FQ	13.51 AW	17.87 TQ	GABLS	10/01-12/01
	Macon MSA, GA	H	11.02 FQ	15.69 AW	20.43 TQ	GABLS	10/01-12/01
	Savannah MSA, GA	H	7.86 FQ	15.78 AW	25.87 TQ	GABLS	10/01-12/01
	Hawaii	H	10.60 FQ	16.55 AW	22.25 TQ	HIBLS	10/01-12/01
	Honolulu MSA, HI	H	9.90 FQ	16.29 AW	24.90 TQ	HIBLS	10/01-12/01
	Idaho	H	8.88 FQ	14.24 AW	20.53 TQ	IDBLS	10/01-12/01
	Boise City MSA, ID	H	8.71 FQ	14.39 AW	22.47 TQ	IDBLS	10/01-12/01
	Illinois	H	9.17 FQ	16.17 AW	24.55 TQ	ILBLS	10/01-12/01
	Chicago PMSA, IL	H	9.88 FQ	17.01 AW	25.21 TQ	ILBLS	10/01-12/01
	Peoria-Pekin MSA, IL	H	10.95 FQ	19.20 AW	26.73 TQ	ILBLS	10/01-12/01
	Rockford MSA, IL	H	14.17 FQ	18.09 AW	24.54 TQ	ILBLS	10/01-12/01
	Indiana	H	9.15 FQ	13.80 AW	20.31 TQ	INBLS	10/01-12/01
	Elkhart-Goshen MSA, IN	H	9.42 FQ	13.34 AW	17.37 TQ	INBLS	10/01-12/01
	Evansville-Henderson MSA, IN-KY	H	8.62 FQ	12.86 AW	19.04 TQ	INBLS	10/01-12/01
	Fort Wayne MSA, IN	H	9.27 FQ	13.46 AW	20.51 TQ	INBLS	10/01-12/01
	Indianapolis MSA, IN	H	9.26 FQ	13.56 AW	19.73 TQ	INBLS	10/01-12/01
	Iowa	H	8.19 FQ	12.53 AW	18.99 TQ	IABLS	10/01-12/01
	Cedar Rapids MSA, IA	H	9.71 FQ	14.29 AW	19.83 TQ	IABLS	10/01-12/01

AAW Average annual wage **AE** Average entry wage **AEX** Average experienced wage **AO** Average offered **AOH** Average offered, high **AOL** Average offered, low **APH** Average pay, high range **APL** Average pay, low range **ASH** Average starting, high **ASL** Average starting, low **AW** Average wage paid **FQ** First quartile wage **H** Hourly **HI** Highest wage paid **HR** High end range **LR** Low end range **M** Monthly **MTC** Median total compensation **MW** Median wage paid **SQ** Second quartile wage **S** Special: hourly and annual **TQ** Third quartile wage **W** Weekly **Y** Yearly

Occupation/Type/Industry	Location	Per	Low	Mid	High	Source	Date
Job Printer	Des Moines MSA, IA	H	11.67 FQ	16.18 AW	21.82 TQ	IABLS	10/01-12/01
	Kansas	H	7.59 FQ	12.28 AW	17.60 TQ	KSBLS	10/01-12/01
	Wichita MSA, KS	H	8.20 FQ	11.53 AW	13.50 TQ	KSBLS	10/01-12/01
	Kentucky	H	7.47 FQ	13.11 AW	24.20 TQ	KYBLS	10/01-12/01
	Lexington MSA, KY	H	6.94 FQ	12.12 AW	21.11 TQ	KYBLS	10/01-12/01
	Louisville MSA, KY-IN	H	7.02 FQ	10.32 AW	15.17 TQ	KYBLS	10/01-12/01
	Louisiana	H	7.78 FQ	12.48 AW	19.02 TQ	LABLS	10/01-12/01
	Baton Rouge MSA, LA	H	8.93 FQ	13.54 AW	19.13 TQ	LABLS	10/01-12/01
	New Orleans MSA, LA	H	7.54 FQ	11.45 AW	16.68 TQ	LABLS	10/01-12/01
	Shreveport-Bossier City MSA, LA	H	9.63 FQ	14.70 AW	20.79 TQ	LABLS	10/01-12/01
	Maine	H	9.77 FQ	13.83 AW	17.72 TQ	MEBLS	10/01-12/01
	Portland MSA, ME	H	11.33 FQ	14.48 AW	17.33 TQ	MEBLS	10/01-12/01
	Maryland	H	9.79 FQ	16.84 AW	24.26 TQ	MDBLS	10/01-12/01
	Baltimore PMSA, MD	H	9.49 FQ	15.75 AW	22.21 TQ	MDBLS	10/01-12/01
	Massachusetts	H	9.31 FQ	14.45 AW	22.13 TQ	MABLS	10/01-12/01
	Boston PMSA, MA-NH	H	11.03 FQ	14.74 AW	22.34 TQ	MABLS	10/01-12/01
	Brockton PMSA, MA	H	6.95 FQ	10.17 AW	16.42 TQ	MABLS	10/01-12/01
	Springfield MSA, MA	H	7.49 FQ	13.73 AW	20.26 TQ	MABLS	10/01-12/01
	Worcester PMSA, MA-CT	H	7.16 FQ	13.20 AW	21.68 TQ	MABLS	10/01-12/01
	Michigan	H	9.47 FQ	16.02 AW	22.32 TQ	MIBLS	10/01-12/01
	Ann Arbor PMSA, MI	H	10.35 FQ	15.08 AW	20.61 TQ	MIBLS	10/01-12/01
	Detroit PMSA, MI	H	10.84 FQ	19.67 AW	26.73 TQ	MIBLS	10/01-12/01
	Grand Rapids-Muskegon-Holland MSA, MI	H	9.34 FQ	14.98 AW	21.92 TQ	MIBLS	10/01-12/01
	Kalamazoo-Battle Creek MSA, MI	H	10.41 FQ	13.90 AW	17.03 TQ	MIBLS	10/01-12/01
	Lansing-East Lansing MSA, MI	H	9.62 FQ	14.36 AW	20.72 TQ	MIBLS	10/01-12/01
	Saginaw-Bay City-Midland MSA, MI	H	9.94 FQ	13.65 AW	17.60 TQ	MIBLS	10/01-12/01
	Minnesota	H	10.51 FQ	17.40 AW	26.39 TQ	MNBLS	10/01-12/01
	Minneapolis-St. Paul MSA, MN-WI	H	11.77 FQ	18.75 AW	27.51 TQ	MNBLS	10/01-12/01
	Mississippi	H	7.23 FQ	13.35 AW	20.11 TQ	MSBLS	10/01-12/01
	Jackson MSA, MS	H	8.91 FQ	12.66 AW	17.96 TQ	MSBLS	10/01-12/01
	Missouri	H	7.80 FQ	12.65 AW	19.13 TQ	MOBLS	10/01-12/01
	Kansas City MSA, MO-KS	H	10.05 FQ	13.99 AW	19.16 TQ	MOBLS	10/01-12/01
	St. Louis MSA, MO-IL	H	7.43 FQ	12.56 AW	20.40 TQ	MOBLS	10/01-12/01
	Springfield MSA, MO	H	8.71 FQ	13.54 AW	21.49 TQ	MOBLS	10/01-12/01
	Montana	H	8.21 FQ	12.74 AW	19.29 TQ	MTBLS	10/01-12/01
	Nebraska	H	8.50 FQ	12.79 AW	18.22 TQ	NEBLS	10/01-12/01
	Lincoln MSA, NE	H	7.53 FQ	11.86 AW	18.16 TQ	NEBLS	10/01-12/01
	Omaha MSA, NE-IA	H	9.10 FQ	13.63 AW	19.34 TQ	NEBLS	10/01-12/01
	Nevada	H	8.86 FQ	14.84 AW	20.80 TQ	NVBLS	10/01-12/01
	Las Vegas MSA, NV-AZ	H	8.80 FQ	14.11 AW	20.41 TQ	NVBLS	10/01-12/01
	New Hampshire	H	10.84 FQ	16.29 AW	21.92 TQ	NHBLS	10/01-12/01
	Manchester PMSA, NH	H	10.53 FQ	14.59 AW	17.81 TQ	NHBLS	10/01-12/01
	Nashua PMSA, NH	H	15.86 FQ	20.91 AW	28.09 TQ	NHBLS	10/01-12/01
	Portsmouth-Rochester PMSA, NH-ME	H	11.20 FQ	15.17 AW	20.54 TQ	NHBLS	10/01-12/01
	New Jersey	H	9.35 FQ	20.42 AW	28.63 TQ	NJBLS	10/01-12/01
	Atlantic-Cape May PMSA, NJ	H	8.06 FQ	16.45 AW	27.34 TQ	NJBLS	10/01-12/01
	Bergen-Passaic PMSA, NJ	H	7.18 FQ	17.74 AW	27.76 TQ	NJBLS	10/01-12/01
	Jersey City PMSA, NJ	H	13.53 FQ	22.56 AW	31.88 TQ	NJBLS	10/01-12/01
	Middlesex-Somerset-Hunterdon PMSA, NJ	H	10.15 FQ	20.96 AW	30.86 TQ	NJBLS	10/01-12/01
	Monmouth-Ocean PMSA, NJ	H	9.02 FQ	16.92 AW	26.42 TQ	NJBLS	10/01-12/01
	Newark PMSA, NJ	H	12.53 FQ	21.97 AW	30.59 TQ	NJBLS	10/01-12/01
	New Mexico	H	6.24 FQ	11.31 AW	16.27 TQ	NMBLS	10/01-12/01
	Albuquerque MSA, NM	H	9.50 FQ	13.07 AW	17.35 TQ	NMBLS	10/01-12/01
	New York	H	10.80 FQ	16.29 AW	21.49 TQ	NYBLS	10/01-12/01
	Albany-Schenectady-Troy MSA, NY	H	9.11 FQ	14.44 AW	20.18 TQ	NYBLS	10/01-12/01
	Binghamton MSA, NY	H	8.06 FQ	12.04 AW	16.92 TQ	NYBLS	10/01-12/01
	Buffalo-Niagara Falls MSA, NY	H	6.43 FQ	11.73 AW	19.10 TQ	NYBLS	10/01-12/01
	Nassau-Suffolk PMSA, NY	H	12.32 FQ	18.89 AW	26.52 TQ	NYBLS	10/01-12/01
	New York PMSA, NY	H	11.10 FQ	16.65 AW	21.33 TQ	NYBLS	10/01-12/01
	Newburgh PMSA, NY-PA	H	13.25 FQ	17.15 AW	21.30 TQ	NYBLS	10/01-12/01
	Rochester MSA, NY	H	8.73 FQ	13.57 AW	18.14 TQ	NYBLS	10/01-12/01
	Syracuse MSA, NY	H	10.45 FQ	15.90 AW	24.43 TQ	NYBLS	10/01-12/01
	Utica-Rome MSA, NY	H	12.08 FQ	17.36 AW	24.17 TQ	NYBLS	10/01-12/01

AAW	Average annual wage	**AOH**	Average offered, high	**ASH**	Average starting, high	**H**	Hourly	**M**	Monthly	**S**	Special: hourly and annual
AE	Average entry wage	**AOL**	Average offered, low	**ASL**	Average starting, low	**HI**	Highest wage paid	**MTC**	Median total compensation	**TQ**	Third quartile wage
AEX	Average experienced wage	**APH**	Average pay, high range	**AW**	Average wage paid	**HR**	High end range	**MW**	Median wage paid	**W**	Weekly
AO	Average offered	**APL**	Average pay, low range	**FQ**	First quartile wage	**LR**	Low end range	**SQ**	Second quartile wage	**Y**	Yearly

Occupation/Type/Industry	Location	Per	Low	Mid	High	Source	Date
Job Printer	North Carolina	H	8.93 FQ	13.95 AW	19.80 TQ	NCBLS	10/01-12/01
	Charlotte-Gastonia-Rock Hill MSA, NC-SC	H	8.95 FQ	13.56 AW	19.16 TQ	NCBLS	10/01-12/01
	Greensboro-Winston-Salem-High Point MSA, NC	H	10.27 FQ	15.70 AW	22.04 TQ	NCBLS	10/01-12/01
	Raleigh-Durham-Chapel Hill MSA, NC	H	11.46 FQ	16.30 AW	21.54 TQ	NCBLS	10/01-12/01
	North Dakota	H	6.63 FQ	11.54 AW	16.70 TQ	NDBLS	10/01-12/01
	Ohio	H	9.59 FQ	16.18 AW	23.87 TQ	OHBLS	10/01-12/01
	Akron PMSA, OH	H	9.38 FQ	15.02 AW	23.83 TQ	OHBLS	10/01-12/01
	Canton-Massillon MSA, OH	H	10.19 FQ	13.96 AW	17.14 TQ	OHBLS	10/01-12/01
	Cincinnati PMSA, OH-KY-IN	H	10.46 FQ	17.29 AW	26.08 TQ	OHBLS	10/01-12/01
	Cleveland-Lorain-Elyria PMSA, OH	H	10.24 FQ	19.49 AW	27.34 TQ	OHBLS	10/01-12/01
	Columbus MSA, OH	H	9.46 FQ	16.00 AW	24.10 TQ	OHBLS	10/01-12/01
	Dayton-Springfield MSA, OH	H	8.38 FQ	17.12 AW	21.92 TQ	OHBLS	10/01-12/01
	Hamilton-Middletown PMSA, OH	H	11.98 FQ	15.55 AW	19.62 TQ	OHBLS	10/01-12/01
	Toledo MSA, OH	H	9.63 FQ	15.80 AW	21.91 TQ	OHBLS	10/01-12/01
	Youngstown-Warren MSA, OH	H	13.55 FQ	20.56 AW	28.20 TQ	OHBLS	10/01-12/01
	Oklahoma	H	7.87 FQ	12.48 AW	17.42 TQ	OKBLS	10/01-12/01
	Oklahoma City MSA, OK	H	7.72 FQ	13.08 AW	18.52 TQ	OKBLS	10/01-12/01
	Tulsa MSA, OK	H	8.78 FQ	12.76 AW	17.31 TQ	OKBLS	10/01-12/01
	Oregon	H	9.56 FQ	15.39 AW	21.41 TQ	ORBLS	10/01-12/01
	Portland-Vancouver PMSA, OR-WA	H	11.38 FQ	17.76 AW	22.67 TQ	ORBLS	10/01-12/01
	Salem PMSA, OR	H	12.22 FQ	14.71 AW	16.78 TQ	ORBLS	10/01-12/01
	Pennsylvania	H	8.30 FQ	15.19 AW	22.52 TQ	PABLS	10/01-12/01
	Allentown-Bethlehem-Easton MSA, PA	H	7.64 FQ	14.00 AW	20.99 TQ	PABLS	10/01-12/01
	Erie MSA, PA	H	9.82 FQ	15.40 AW	21.04 TQ	PABLS	10/01-12/01
	Harrisburg-Lebanon-Carlisle MSA, PA	H	7.61 FQ	14.60 AW	20.65 TQ	PABLS	10/01-12/01
	Lancaster MSA, PA	H	10.28 FQ	16.94 AW	25.95 TQ	PABLS	10/01-12/01
	Philadelphia PMSA, PA-NJ	H	9.00 FQ	19.09 AW	27.21 TQ	PABLS	10/01-12/01
	Pittsburgh MSA, PA	H	8.21 FQ	13.11 AW	19.55 TQ	PABLS	10/01-12/01
	Reading MSA, PA	H	8.03 FQ	14.33 AW	18.26 TQ	PABLS	10/01-12/01
	Scranton-Wilkes-Barre-Hazleton MSA, PA	H	13.10 FQ	17.37 AW	20.96 TQ	PABLS	10/01-12/01
	York MSA, PA	H	10.21 FQ	14.56 AW	19.92 TQ	PABLS	10/01-12/01
	Rhode Island	H	9.16 FQ	12.28 AW	17.38 TQ	RIBLS	10/01-12/01
	Providence-Fall River-Warwick MSA, RI-MA	H	9.19 FQ	12.54 AW	18.21 TQ	RIBLS	10/01-12/01
	South Carolina	H	7.55 FQ	11.71 AW	18.66 TQ	SCBLS	10/01-12/01
	Columbia MSA, SC	H	10.01 FQ	13.61 AW	17.54 TQ	SCBLS	10/01-12/01
	Greenville-Spartanburg-Anderson MSA, SC	H	8.57 FQ	11.10 AW	16.11 TQ	SCBLS	10/01-12/01
	Tennessee	H	9.17 FQ	14.31 AW	20.93 TQ	TNBLS	10/01-12/01
	Chattanooga MSA, TN-GA	H	9.54 FQ	12.76 AW	16.52 TQ	TNBLS	10/01-12/01
	Johnson City-Kingsport-Bristol MSA, TN-VA	H	8.14 FQ	11.97 AW	16.74 TQ	TNBLS	10/01-12/01
	Knoxville MSA, TN	H	9.44 FQ	13.85 AW	18.29 TQ	TNBLS	10/01-12/01
	Memphis MSA, TN-AR-MS	H	9.07 FQ	15.37 AW	21.89 TQ	TNBLS	10/01-12/01
	Nashville MSA, TN	H	10.11 FQ	15.01 AW	20.85 TQ	TNBLS	10/01-12/01
	Texas	H	7.88 FQ	13.32 AW	19.27 TQ	TXBLS	10/01-12/01
	Amarillo MSA, TX	H	8.97 FQ	12.14 AW	16.25 TQ	TXBLS	10/01-12/01
	Beaumont-Port Arthur MSA, TX	H	7.84 FQ	10.77 AW	14.76 TQ	TXBLS	10/01-12/01
	Brownsville-Harlingen-San Benito MSA, TX	H	6.15 FQ	9.41 AW	15.99 TQ	TXBLS	10/01-12/01
	Corpus Christi MSA, TX	H	9.00 FQ	12.10 AW	15.44 TQ	TXBLS	10/01-12/01
	Dallas PMSA, TX	H	7.60 FQ	13.45 AW	20.74 TQ	TXBLS	10/01-12/01
	El Paso MSA, TX	H	6.43 FQ	11.76 AW	16.00 TQ	TXBLS	10/01-12/01
	Fort Worth-Arlington PMSA, TX	H	9.15 FQ	14.75 AW	18.76 TQ	TXBLS	10/01-12/01
	Houston PMSA, TX	H	10.79 FQ	14.30 AW	19.72 TQ	TXBLS	10/01-12/01
	Lubbock MSA, TX	H	7.36 FQ	11.07 AW	13.83 TQ	TXBLS	10/01-12/01
	McAllen-Edinburg-Mission MSA, TX	H	5.74 FQ	8.77 AW	11.76 TQ	TXBLS	10/01-12/01
	Odessa-Midland MSA, TX	H	10.85 FQ	12.43 AW	15.13 TQ	TXBLS	10/01-12/01
	San Antonio MSA, TX	H	7.22 FQ	11.76 AW	16.63 TQ	TXBLS	10/01-12/01
	Tyler MSA, TX	H	9.35 FQ	15.52 AW	21.91 TQ	TXBLS	10/01-12/01

AAW	Average annual wage	**AOH**	Average offered, high	**ASH**	Average starting, high	**H**	Hourly	**M**	Monthly	**S**	Special: hourly and annual
AE	Average entry wage	**AOL**	Average offered, low	**ASL**	Average starting, low	**HI**	Highest wage paid	**MTC**	Median total compensation	**TQ**	Third quartile wage
AEX	Average experienced wage	**APH**	Average pay, high range	**AW**	Average wage paid	**HR**	High end range	**MW**	Median wage paid	**W**	Weekly
AO	Average offered	**APL**	Average pay, low range	**FQ**	First quartile wage	**LR**	Low end range	**SQ**	Second quartile wage	**Y**	Yearly

Occupation/Type/Industry	Location	Per	Low	Mid	High	Source	Date
Job Printer	Waco MSA, TX	H	6.87 FQ	14.66 AW	21.26 TQ	TXBLS	10/01-12/01
	Utah	H	8.65 FQ	14.60 AW	21.62 TQ	UTBLS	10/01-12/01
	Provo-Orem MSA, UT	H	6.19 FQ	10.59 AW	13.42 TQ	UTBLS	10/01-12/01
	Salt Lake City-Ogden MSA, UT	H	8.84 FQ	14.86 AW	22.07 TQ	UTBLS	10/01-12/01
	Vermont	H	10.62 FQ	15.31 AW	22.13 TQ	VTBLS	10/01-12/01
	Burlington MSA, VT	H	11.95 FQ	15.84 AW	23.00 TQ	VTBLS	10/01-12/01
	Virginia	H	8.96 FQ	13.74 AW	18.59 TQ	VABLS	10/01-12/01
	Lynchburg MSA, VA	H	8.65 FQ	15.11 AW	20.32 TQ	VABLS	10/01-12/01
	Norfolk-Virginia Beach-Newport News MSA, VA-NC	H	8.66 FQ	13.02 AW	17.97 TQ	VABLS	10/01-12/01
	Richmond-Petersburg MSA, VA	H	8.79 FQ	11.89 AW	16.92 TQ	VABLS	10/01-12/01
	Washington	H	9.30 FQ	15.04 AW	20.88 TQ	WABLS	10/01-12/01
	Seattle-Bellevue-Everett PMSA, WA	H	11.01 FQ	16.02 AW	21.32 TQ	WABLS	10/01-12/01
	Tacoma PMSA, WA	H	9.98 FQ	14.42 AW	17.53 TQ	WABLS	10/01-12/01
	West Virginia	H	7.75 FQ	12.35 AW	19.09 TQ	WVBLS	10/01-12/01
	Huntington-Ashland MSA, WV-KY-OH	H	7.79 FQ	12.35 AW	18.24 TQ	WVBLS	10/01-12/01
	Wisconsin	H	9.37 FQ	16.46 AW	27.84 TQ	WIBLS	10/01-12/01
	Appleton-Oshkosh-Neenah MSA, WI	H	10.94 FQ	16.02 AW	20.96 TQ	WIBLS	10/01-12/01
	Green Bay MSA, WI	H	6.22 FQ	11.11 AW	18.66 TQ	WIBLS	10/01-12/01
	Madison MSA, WI	H	11.39 FQ	15.54 AW	20.03 TQ	WIBLS	10/01-12/01
	Milwaukee-Waukesha PMSA, WI	H	10.62 FQ	20.05 AW	31.91 TQ	WIBLS	10/01-12/01
	Wyoming	H	6.35 FQ	11.21 AW	16.39 TQ	WYBLS	10/01-12/01
	Puerto Rico	H	5.80 FQ	9.35 AW	16.03 TQ	PRBLS	10/01-12/01
Judge							
Bankruptcy Court, United States	United States	Y		138000 AW		SCJS	1/1/02
Circuit Court, United States	United States	Y		159100 AW		SCJS	1/1/02
District Court, United States	United States	Y		150000 AW		SCJS	1/1/02
Magistrate Court, United States	United States	Y		138000 AW		SCJS	1/1/02
United States Court of Federal Claims	United States	Y		150000 AW		SCJS	1/1/02
United States Court of International Trade	United States	Y		150000 AW		SCJS	1/1/02
Judge and Magistrate	United States	Y		86760 MW		OOH7	1999-2000
	Alabama	Y	12810 FQ	30090 AW	56920 TQ	ALBLS	10/01-12/01
	Birmingham MSA, AL	Y	12210 FQ	23940 AW	42080 TQ	ALBLS	10/01-12/01
	Mobile MSA, AL	Y	14600 FQ	50650 AW	91900 TQ	ALBLS	10/01-12/01
	Montgomery MSA, AL	Y	12490 FQ	34040 AW	80070 TQ	ALBLS	10/01-12/01
	Alaska	Y	57830 FQ	82550 AW	109890 TQ	AKBLS	10/01-12/01
	Arizona	Y	30570 FQ	70310 AW	112340 TQ	AZBLS	10/01-12/01
	Phoenix-Mesa MSA, AZ	Y	58670 FQ	89740 AW	118610 TQ	AZBLS	10/01-12/01
	Arkansas	Y	12880 FQ	31860 AW	66960 TQ	ARBLS	10/01-12/01
	California	Y	42670 FQ	101060 AW	142670 TQ	CABLS	10/01-12/01
	Oakland PMSA, CA	Y	42110 FQ	95440 AW	140060 TQ	CABLS	10/01-12/01
	Sacramento PMSA, CA	Y	97450 FQ	122890 AW		CABLS	10/01-12/01
	San Francisco PMSA, CA	Y	105790 FQ	122960 AW	143720 TQ	CABLS	10/01-12/01
	Colorado	Y	66160 FQ	88060 AW	128310 TQ	COBLS	10/01-12/01
	Denver PMSA, CO	Y	69960 FQ	89740 AW	116110 TQ	COBLS	10/01-12/01
	Connecticut	Y	101050 FQ	119680 AW	141950 TQ	CTBLS	10/01-12/01
	Washington PMSA, DC-MD-VA-WV	Y	24980 FQ	61280 AW	105680 TQ	DCBLS	10/01-12/01
	Florida	Y		61280 AW		FLBLS	10/01-12/01
	Georgia	Y	29450 FQ	68950 AW	112020 TQ	GABLS	10/01-12/01
	Atlanta MSA, GA	Y	49120 FQ	79580 AW	119660 TQ	GABLS	10/01-12/01
	Augusta-Aiken MSA, GA-SC	Y	13030 FQ	56970 AW	106540 TQ	GABLS	10/01-12/01
	Macon MSA, GA	Y	13570 FQ	66210 AW	111680 TQ	GABLS	10/01-12/01
	Hawaii	Y	93540 FQ	101800 AW	113900 TQ	HIBLS	10/01-12/01
	Idaho	Y	36070 FQ	72260 AW		IDBLS	10/01-12/01
	Illinois	Y	12620 FQ	84590 AW	140940 TQ	ILBLS	10/01-12/01
	Indiana	Y	16430 FQ	57830 AW	112950 TQ	INBLS	10/01-12/01
	Indianapolis MSA, IN	Y	19300 FQ	61970 AW	112590 TQ	INBLS	10/01-12/01
	South Bend MSA, IN	Y	21780 FQ	62130 AW	112640 TQ	INBLS	10/01-12/01
	Iowa	Y	22620 FQ	65960 AW	111820 TQ	IABLS	10/01-12/01
	Kansas	Y	62500 FQ	96470 AW	134860 TQ	KSBLS	10/01-12/01
	Wichita MSA, KS	Y	46120 FQ	94920 AW	131480 TQ	KSBLS	10/01-12/01
	Kentucky	Y	51940 FQ	101060 AW	138140 TQ	KYBLS	10/01-12/01
	Louisville MSA, KY-IN	Y	35920 FQ	76520 AW	129710 TQ	KYBLS	10/01-12/01

AAW Average annual wage	**AOH** Average offered, high	**ASH** Average starting, high	**H** Hourly	**M** Monthly	**S** Special: hourly and annual
AE Average entry wage	**AOL** Average offered, low	**ASL** Average starting, low	**HI** Highest wage paid	**MTC** Median total compensation	**TQ** Third quartile wage
AEX Average experienced wage	**APH** Average pay, high range	**AW** Average wage paid	**HR** High end range	**MW** Median wage paid	**W** Weekly
AO Average offered	**APL** Average pay, low range	**FQ** First quartile wage	**LR** Low end range	**SQ** Second quartile wage	**Y** Yearly

Occupation/Type/Industry	Location	Per	Low	Mid	High	Source	Date
Judge and Magistrate	Louisiana	Y	12820 FQ	28820 AW	45560 TQ	LABLS	10/01-12/01
	Maine	Y	49100 FQ	88010 AW	112550 TQ	MEBLS	10/01-12/01
	Maryland	Y	30860 FQ	77320 AW	114190 TQ	MDBLS	10/01-12/01
	Michigan	Y	38860 FQ	81830 AW		MIBLS	10/01-12/01
	Detroit PMSA, MI	Y	49390 FQ	87720 AW		MIBLS	10/01-12/01
	Flint PMSA, MI	Y	55260 FQ	98080 AW	137410 TQ	MIBLS	10/01-12/01
	Grand Rapids-Muskegon-Holland MSA, MI	Y	49590 FQ	88060 AW	140690 TQ	MIBLS	10/01-12/01
	Kalamazoo-Battle Creek MSA, MI	Y	48760 FQ	71830 AW	140570 TQ	MIBLS	10/01-12/01
	Lansing-East Lansing MSA, MI	Y	53710 FQ	94530 AW	139270 TQ	MIBLS	10/01-12/01
	Minnesota	Y	80410 FQ	96530 AW	112920 TQ	MNBLS	10/01-12/01
	Minneapolis-St. Paul MSA, MN-WI	Y	78120 FQ	95110 AW	113090 TQ	MNBLS	10/01-12/01
	Mississippi	Y	12330 FQ	26990 AW	50520 TQ	MSBLS	10/01-12/01
	Kansas City MSA, MO-KS	Y	32860 FQ	68380 AW	102150 TQ	MOBLS	10/01-12/01
	St. Louis MSA, MO-IL	Y	21550 FQ	82780 AW	142350 TQ	MOBLS	10/01-12/01
	Montana	Y	13840 FQ	28110 AW	44200 TQ	MTBLS	10/01-12/01
	Nevada	Y	32770 FQ	91470 AW	134880 TQ	NVBLS	10/01-12/01
	Las Vegas MSA, NV-AZ	Y	38500 FQ	81170 AW	131910 TQ	NVBLS	10/01-12/01
	Atlantic-Cape May PMSA, NJ	Y	88150 FQ	117070 AW	144910 TQ	NJBLS	10/01-12/01
	Middlesex-Somerset-Hunterdon PMSA, NJ	Y	67410 FQ	118480 AW		NJBLS	10/01-12/01
	New Mexico	Y	15820 FQ	59540 AW	89380 TQ	NMBLS	10/01-12/01
	Albuquerque MSA, NM	Y	56780 FQ	75660 AW	89970 TQ	NMBLS	10/01-12/01
	New York	Y	35250 FQ	100310 AW	143010 TQ	NYBLS	10/01-12/01
	Albany-Schenectady-Troy MSA, NY	Y	75790 FQ	107900 AW	145050 TQ	NYBLS	10/01-12/01
	Binghamton MSA, NY	Y	15090 FQ	78970 AW	131870 TQ	NYBLS	10/01-12/01
	Buffalo-Niagara Falls MSA, NY	Y	57360 FQ	98810 AW	142210 TQ	NYBLS	10/01-12/01
	Dutchess County PMSA, NY	Y	12270 FQ	53510 AW	134060 TQ	NYBLS	10/01-12/01
	Nassau-Suffolk PMSA, NY	Y	27350 FQ	101570 AW		NYBLS	10/01-12/01
	New York PMSA, NY	Y	96690 FQ	119280 AW	142240 TQ	NYBLS	10/01-12/01
	Newburgh PMSA, NY-PA	Y	34680 FQ	94970 AW		NYBLS	10/01-12/01
	Rochester MSA, NY	Y	26890 FQ	85900 AW	138750 TQ	NYBLS	10/01-12/01
	Syracuse MSA, NY	Y	56470 FQ	92860 AW	130390 TQ	NYBLS	10/01-12/01
	Utica-Rome MSA, NY	Y	18940 FQ	72560 AW	129640 TQ	NYBLS	10/01-12/01
	North Carolina	Y	28110 FQ	56560 AW	108100 TQ	NCBLS	10/01-12/01
	Charlotte-Gastonia-Rock Hill MSA, NC-SC	Y	23760 FQ	54670 AW	107730 TQ	NCBLS	10/01-12/01
	North Dakota	Y	11980 FQ	23920 AW	44380 TQ	NDBLS	10/01-12/01
	Ohio	Y	15100 FQ	59750 AW	101250 TQ	OHBLS	10/01-12/01
	Canton-Massillon MSA, OH	Y	14020 FQ	61760 AW	106490 TQ	OHBLS	10/01-12/01
	Cincinnati PMSA, OH-KY-IN	Y	13830 FQ	61440 AW	106380 TQ	OHBLS	10/01-12/01
	Cleveland-Lorain-Elyria PMSA, OH	Y	36490 FQ	59400 AW	93950 TQ	OHBLS	10/01-12/01
	Dayton-Springfield MSA, OH	Y	13460 FQ	53470 AW	93880 TQ	OHBLS	10/01-12/01
	Mansfield MSA, OH	Y	13700 FQ	70580 AW	124840 TQ	OHBLS	10/01-12/01
	Toledo MSA, OH	Y	20270 FQ	64900 AW	98070 TQ	OHBLS	10/01-12/01
	Youngstown-Warren MSA, OH	Y	21310 FQ	59760 AW	99620 TQ	OHBLS	10/01-12/01
	Oklahoma	Y	31720 FQ	79750 AW	114810 TQ	OKBLS	10/01-12/01
	Oregon	Y	59610 FQ	83810 AW	111080 TQ	ORBLS	10/01-12/01
	Portland-Vancouver PMSA, OR-WA	Y	63370 FQ	84800 AW	110190 TQ	ORBLS	10/01-12/01
	Rhode Island	Y	30250 FQ	114130 AW		RIBLS	10/01-12/01
	Providence-Fall River-Warwick MSA, RI-MA	Y	32860 FQ	109380 AW		RIBLS	10/01-12/01
	South Carolina	Y	15340 FQ	52000 AW	105580 TQ	SCBLS	10/01-12/01
	Charleston-North Charleston MSA, SC	Y	14070 FQ	52110 AW	109880 TQ	SCBLS	10/01-12/01
	Columbia MSA, SC	Y	21050 FQ	58460 AW	106910 TQ	SCBLS	10/01-12/01
	Greenville-Spartanburg-Anderson MSA, SC	Y	21460 FQ	57540 AW	105770 TQ	SCBLS	10/01-12/01
	South Dakota	Y	60720 FQ	73590 AW	87930 TQ	SDBLS	10/01-12/01
	Tennessee	Y	12480 FQ	42640 AW	96780 TQ	TNBLS	10/01-12/01
	Chattanooga MSA, TN-GA	Y	28880 FQ	55870 AW	108410 TQ	TNBLS	10/01-12/01
	Memphis MSA, TN-AR-MS	Y	11830 FQ	32650 AW	87880 TQ	TNBLS	10/01-12/01
	Nashville MSA, TN	Y	19810 FQ	58720 AW		TNBLS	10/01-12/01
	Texas	Y	13220 FQ	59390 AW	111710 TQ	TXBLS	10/01-12/01
	Beaumont-Port Arthur MSA, TX	Y	14710 FQ	60710 AW	109690 TQ	TXBLS	10/01-12/01

AAW Average annual wage **AE** Average entry wage **AEX** Average experienced wage **AO** Average offered **AOH** Average offered, high **AOL** Average offered, low **APH** Average pay, high range **APL** Average pay, low range **ASH** Average starting, high **ASL** Average starting, low **AW** Average wage paid **FQ** First quartile wage **H** Hourly **HI** Highest wage paid **HR** High end range **LR** Low end range **M** Monthly **MTC** Median total compensation **MW** Median wage paid **SQ** Second quartile wage **S** Special: hourly and annual **TQ** Third quartile wage **W** Weekly **Y** Yearly

Occupation/Type/Industry	Location	Per	Low	Mid	High	Source	Date
Judge and Magistrate	Corpus Christi MSA, TX	Y	12420 FQ	70380 AW	114650 TQ	TXBLS	10/01-12/01
	Dallas PMSA, TX	Y	24460 FQ	78990 AW	113020 TQ	TXBLS	10/01-12/01
	Fort Worth-Arlington PMSA, TX	Y	21900 FQ	63120 AW	107120 TQ	TXBLS	10/01-12/01
	Houston PMSA, TX	Y	12650 FQ	74970 AW		TXBLS	10/01-12/01
	Longview-Marshall MSA, TX	Y	11880 FQ	37040 AW	99080 TQ	TXBLS	10/01-12/01
	Utah	Y	20780 FQ	74240 AW	111730 TQ	UTBLS	10/01-12/01
	Salt Lake City-Ogden MSA, UT	Y	68570 FQ	94820 AW	113640 TQ	UTBLS	10/01-12/01
	Washington	Y	59030 FQ	94580 AW	138710 TQ	WABLS	10/01-12/01
	Tacoma PMSA, WA	Y	59740 FQ	79080 AW	126660 TQ	WABLS	10/01-12/01
	Yakima MSA, WA	Y	61680 FQ	92910 AW	123020 TQ	WABLS	10/01-12/01
	West Virginia	Y	26150 FQ	46980 AW	83500 TQ	WVBLS	10/01-12/01
	Huntington-Ashland MSA, WV-KY-OH	Y	12950 FQ	60350 AW	113070 TQ	WVBLS	10/01-12/01
	Wisconsin	Y	12210 FQ	51510 AW	113450 TQ	WIBLS	10/01-12/01
	Milwaukee-Waukesha PMSA, WI	Y	13550 FQ	71870 AW	115610 TQ	WIBLS	10/01-12/01
	Puerto Rico	Y	62550 FQ	78510 AW	90690 TQ	PRBLS	10/01-12/01
Local Government	United States	Y		50150 MW		OOH7	1999-2000
State General Trial Court	United States	Y		104400 MW		OOH7	1999-2000
State Government	United States	Y		104560 MW		OOH7	1999-2000
Junior Architect							
Web Design	United States	Y		42072 AW		DFMAR	1/01-1/02
Kindergarten Teacher							
Except Special Education	Alabama	Y	22560 FQ	37120 AW	49170 TQ	ALBLS	10/01-12/01
Except Special Education	Birmingham MSA, AL	Y	13330 FQ	28500 AW	42900 TQ	ALBLS	10/01-12/01
Except Special Education	Huntsville MSA, AL	Y	31070 FQ	39180 AW	48510 TQ	ALBLS	10/01-12/01
Except Special Education	Montgomery MSA, AL	Y	12390 FQ	27140 AW	43590 TQ	ALBLS	10/01-12/01
Except Special Education	Alaska	Y	32280 FQ	49710 AW	69180 TQ	AKBLS	10/01-12/01
Except Special Education	Arizona	Y	20780 FQ	36510 AW	58610 TQ	AZBLS	10/01-12/01
Except Special Education	Phoenix-Mesa MSA, AZ	Y	18430 FQ	35590 AW	57950 TQ	AZBLS	10/01-12/01
Except Special Education	Tucson MSA, AZ	Y	25960 FQ	44620 AW	67160 TQ	AZBLS	10/01-12/01
Except Special Education	Arkansas	Y	24570 FQ	33360 AW	43910 TQ	ARBLS	10/01-12/01
Except Special Education	Fayetteville-Springdale-Rogers MSA, AR	Y	28180 FQ	34670 AW	43860 TQ	ARBLS	10/01-12/01
Except Special Education	Fort Smith MSA, AR-OK	Y	24320 FQ	32010 AW	42980 TQ	ARBLS	10/01-12/01
Except Special Education	Little Rock-North Little Rock MSA, AR	Y	25420 FQ	35600 AW	47090 TQ	ARBLS	10/01-12/01
Except Special Education	California	Y	23870 FQ	45900 AW	68100 TQ	CABLS	10/01-12/01
Except Special Education	Bakersfield MSA, CA	Y	37790 FQ	51640 AW	68630 TQ	CABLS	10/01-12/01
Except Special Education	Chico-Paradise MSA, CA	Y	32730 FQ	49160 AW	68640 TQ	CABLS	10/01-12/01
Except Special Education	Fresno MSA, CA	Y	15580 FQ	35390 AW	58880 TQ	CABLS	10/01-12/01
Except Special Education	Los Angeles-Long Beach PMSA, CA	Y	29650 FQ	48490 AW	70330 TQ	CABLS	10/01-12/01
Except Special Education	Merced MSA, CA	Y	34120 FQ	48710 AW	67730 TQ	CABLS	10/01-12/01
Except Special Education	Modesto MSA, CA	Y	30900 FQ	48300 AW	69730 TQ	CABLS	10/01-12/01
Except Special Education	Oakland PMSA, CA	Y	32660 FQ	49900 AW	69020 TQ	CABLS	10/01-12/01
Except Special Education	Orange County PMSA, CA	Y	19210 FQ	40710 AW	57840 TQ	CABLS	10/01-12/01
Except Special Education	Riverside-San Bernardino PMSA, CA	Y	31510 FQ	47100 AW	68350 TQ	CABLS	10/01-12/01
Except Special Education	Sacramento PMSA, CA	Y	33700 FQ	50150 AW	70370 TQ	CABLS	10/01-12/01
Except Special Education	Salinas MSA, CA	Y	20830 FQ	46560 AW	72670 TQ	CABLS	10/01-12/01
Except Special Education	San Diego MSA, CA	Y	28260 FQ	42440 AW	63970 TQ	CABLS	10/01-12/01
Except Special Education	San Francisco PMSA, CA	Y	35470 FQ	49320 AW	66800 TQ	CABLS	10/01-12/01
Except Special Education	San Jose PMSA, CA	Y	20360 FQ	39300 AW	69230 TQ	CABLS	10/01-12/01
Except Special Education	San Luis Obispo-Atascadero-Paso Robles MSA, CA	Y	21590 FQ	43980 AW	63730 TQ	CABLS	10/01-12/01
Except Special Education	Santa Barbara-Santa Maria-Lompoc MSA, CA	Y	31870 FQ	47130 AW	67570 TQ	CABLS	10/01-12/01
Except Special Education	Santa Cruz-Watsonville PMSA, CA	Y	27690 FQ	44480 AW	60260 TQ	CABLS	10/01-12/01
Except Special Education	Santa Rosa PMSA, CA	Y	33820 FQ	49150 AW	66820 TQ	CABLS	10/01-12/01
Except Special Education	Stockton-Lodi MSA, CA	Y	20950 FQ	44080 AW	67360 TQ	CABLS	10/01-12/01
Except Special Education	Vallejo-Fairfield-Napa PMSA, CA	Y	15960 FQ	32250 AW	55750 TQ	CABLS	10/01-12/01
Except Special Education	Ventura PMSA, CA	Y	34080 FQ	50940 AW	74900 TQ	CABLS	10/01-12/01
Except Special Education	Visalia-Tulare-Porterville MSA, CA	Y	31100 FQ	45420 AW	64110 TQ	CABLS	10/01-12/01
Except Special Education	Colorado	Y	17920 FQ	36640 AW	57170 TQ	COBLS	10/01-12/01
Except Special Education	Boulder-Longmont PMSA, CO	Y	12080 FQ	31390 AW	57450 TQ	COBLS	10/01-12/01

AAW	Average annual wage	**AOH**	Average offered, high	**ASH**	Average starting, high	**H**	Hourly	**M**	Monthly	**S**	Special: hourly and annual
AE	Average entry wage	**AOL**	Average offered, low	**ASL**	Average starting, low	**HI**	Highest wage paid	**MTC**	Median total compensation	**TQ**	Third quartile wage
AEX	Average experienced wage	**APH**	Average pay, high range	**AW**	Average wage paid	**HR**	High end range	**MW**	Median wage paid	**W**	Weekly
AO	Average offered	**APL**	Average pay, low range	**FQ**	First quartile wage	**LR**	Low end range	**SQ**	Second quartile wage	**Y**	Yearly

Occupation/Type/Industry	Location	Per	Low	Mid	High	Source	Date
Kindergarten Teacher							
Except Special Education	Colorado Springs MSA, CO	Y	24730 FQ	39060 AW	57800 TQ	COBLS	10/01-12/01
Except Special Education	Denver PMSA, CO	Y	17950 FQ	38520 AW	59370 TQ	COBLS	10/01-12/01
Except Special Education	Greeley PMSA, CO	Y	21050 FQ	31280 AW	50650 TQ	COBLS	10/01-12/01
Except Special Education	Connecticut	Y	31040 FQ	50980 AW	70950 TQ	CTBLS	10/01-12/01
Except Special Education	Bridgeport PMSA, CT	Y	32080 FQ	51940 AW	70680 TQ	CTBLS	10/01-12/01
Except Special Education	Danbury PMSA, CT	Y	24010 FQ	44380 AW	69510 TQ	CTBLS	10/01-12/01
Except Special Education	Hartford MSA, CT	Y	30330 FQ	49840 AW	70520 TQ	CTBLS	10/01-12/01
Except Special Education	New Haven-Meriden PMSA, CT	Y	32460 FQ	52860 AW	71390 TQ	CTBLS	10/01-12/01
Except Special Education	New London-Norwich MSA, CT-RI	Y	29270 FQ	48840 AW	69600 TQ	CTBLS	10/01-12/01
Except Special Education	Stamford-Norwalk PMSA, CT	Y	38320 FQ	54580 AW	75130 TQ	CTBLS	10/01-12/01
Except Special Education	Waterbury PMSA, CT	Y	35210 FQ	54570 AW	73250 TQ	CTBLS	10/01-12/01
Except Special Education	Delaware	Y	24790 FQ	45490 AW	73040 TQ	DEBLS	10/01-12/01
Except Special Education	Wilmington-Newark PMSA, DE-MD	Y	26250 FQ	48360 AW	74550 TQ	DEBLS	10/01-12/01
Except Special Education	District of Columbia	Y	19720 FQ	28880 AW	42680 TQ	DCBLS	10/01-12/01
Except Special Education	Washington PMSA, DC-MD-VA-WV	Y	22670 FQ	40530 AW	59180 TQ	DCBLS	10/01-12/01
Except Special Education	Florida	Y	25430 FQ	41130 AW	59850 TQ	FLBLS	10/01-12/01
Except Special Education	Fort Myers-Cape Coral MSA, FL	Y	29980 FQ	41460 AW	57210 TQ	FLBLS	10/01-12/01
Except Special Education	Jacksonville MSA, FL	Y	27490 FQ	45470 AW	69980 TQ	FLBLS	10/01-12/01
Except Special Education	Melbourne-Titusville-Palm Bay MSA, FL	Y	18560 FQ	26040 AW	38050 TQ	FLBLS	10/01-12/01
Except Special Education	Orlando MSA, FL	Y	24840 FQ	36620 AW	52910 TQ	FLBLS	10/01-12/01
Except Special Education	Pensacola MSA, FL	Y	26310 FQ	41960 AW	63540 TQ	FLBLS	10/01-12/01
Except Special Education	Sarasota-Bradenton MSA, FL	Y	23160 FQ	33810 AW	47400 TQ	FLBLS	10/01-12/01
Except Special Education	Tampa-St. Petersburg-Clearwater MSA, FL	Y	24130 FQ	40130 AW	57660 TQ	FLBLS	10/01-12/01
Except Special Education	Georgia	Y	25980 FQ	40790 AW	56990 TQ	GABLS	10/01-12/01
Except Special Education	Atlanta MSA, GA	Y	26260 FQ	41300 AW	57720 TQ	GABLS	10/01-12/01
Except Special Education	Augusta-Aiken MSA, GA-SC	Y	25320 FQ	40180 AW	57120 TQ	GABLS	10/01-12/01
Except Special Education	Columbus MSA, GA-AL	Y	30970 FQ	43800 AW	60180 TQ	GABLS	10/01-12/01
Except Special Education	Macon MSA, GA	Y	29340 FQ	39450 AW	54770 TQ	GABLS	10/01-12/01
Except Special Education	Savannah MSA, GA	Y	29800 FQ	39970 AW	52820 TQ	GABLS	10/01-12/01
Except Special Education	Hawaii	Y	25180 FQ	36410 AW	54450 TQ	HIBLS	10/01-12/01
Except Special Education	Honolulu MSA, HI	Y	25200 FQ	36900 AW	55510 TQ	HIBLS	10/01-12/01
Except Special Education	Idaho	Y	13500 FQ	18340 AW	23070 TQ	IDBLS	10/01-12/01
Except Special Education	Boise City MSA, ID	Y	13070 FQ	17170 AW	22320 TQ	IDBLS	10/01-12/01
Except Special Education	Illinois	Y	20750 FQ	37180 AW	58470 TQ	ILBLS	10/01-12/01
Except Special Education	Champaign-Urbana MSA, IL	Y	25380 FQ	39460 AW	58070 TQ	ILBLS	10/01-12/01
Except Special Education	Chicago PMSA, IL	Y	20220 FQ	37700 AW	63620 TQ	ILBLS	10/01-12/01
Except Special Education	Peoria-Pekin MSA, IL	Y	15980 FQ	33510 AW	57780 TQ	ILBLS	10/01-12/01
Except Special Education	Rockford MSA, IL	Y	18950 FQ	27920 AW	45730 TQ	ILBLS	10/01-12/01
Except Special Education	Springfield MSA, IL	Y	17650 FQ	36290 AW	57280 TQ	ILBLS	10/01-12/01
Except Special Education	Indiana	Y	21560 FQ	39670 AW	57530 TQ	INBLS	10/01-12/01
Except Special Education	Elkhart-Goshen MSA, IN	Y	23870 FQ	37050 AW	55150 TQ	INBLS	10/01-12/01
Except Special Education	Fort Wayne MSA, IN	Y	26940 FQ	42300 AW	57930 TQ	INBLS	10/01-12/01
Except Special Education	Gary PMSA, IN	Y	24740 FQ	40360 AW	57220 TQ	INBLS	10/01-12/01
Except Special Education	Indianapolis MSA, IN	Y	18020 FQ	37010 AW	57630 TQ	INBLS	10/01-12/01
Except Special Education	Lafayette MSA, IN	Y	29770 FQ	42920 AW	57830 TQ	INBLS	10/01-12/01
Except Special Education	South Bend MSA, IN	Y	22720 FQ	35830 AW	52080 TQ	INBLS	10/01-12/01
Except Special Education	Iowa	Y	23560 FQ	33510 AW	45950 TQ	IABLS	10/01-12/01
Except Special Education	Cedar Rapids MSA, IA	Y	24170 FQ	31130 AW	42910 TQ	IABLS	10/01-12/01
Except Special Education	Davenport-Moline-Rock Island MSA, IA-IL	Y	25780 FQ	36890 AW	48210 TQ	IABLS	10/01-12/01
Except Special Education	Des Moines MSA, IA	Y	21050 FQ	35120 AW	54150 TQ	IABLS	10/01-12/01
Except Special Education	Kansas	Y	23980 FQ	33980 AW	44600 TQ	KSBLS	10/01-12/01
Except Special Education	Wichita MSA, KS	Y	20680 FQ	34730 AW	45270 TQ	KSBLS	10/01-12/01
Except Special Education	Kentucky	Y	25370 FQ	38870 AW	54280 TQ	KYBLS	10/01-12/01
Except Special Education	Louisiana	Y	25250 FQ	34230 AW	44340 TQ	LABLS	10/01-12/01
Except Special Education	Lafayette MSA, LA	Y	26510 FQ	35290 AW	45260 TQ	LABLS	10/01-12/01
Except Special Education	New Orleans MSA, LA	Y	26290 FQ	36370 AW	45260 TQ	LABLS	10/01-12/01
Except Special Education	Maine	Y	26120 FQ	36190 AW	46640 TQ	MEBLS	10/01-12/01
Except Special Education	Portland MSA, ME	Y	28510 FQ	41310 AW	54290 TQ	MEBLS	10/01-12/01
Except Special Education	Maryland	Y	22800 FQ	40460 AW	60740 TQ	MDBLS	10/01-12/01
Except Special Education	Baltimore PMSA, MD	Y	16310 FQ	36960 AW	59560 TQ	MDBLS	10/01-12/01
Except Special Education	Massachusetts	Y	27800 FQ	44540 AW	60500 TQ	MABLS	10/01-12/01
Except Special Education	Boston PMSA, MA-NH	Y	29300 FQ	45030 AW	60980 TQ	MABLS	10/01-12/01
Except Special Education	Brockton PMSA, MA	Y	31070 FQ	47320 AW	64640 TQ	MABLS	10/01-12/01

AAW	Average annual wage	**AOH**	Average offered, high	**ASH**	Average starting, high	**H**	Hourly	**M**	Monthly	**S**	Special: hourly and annual
AE	Average entry wage	**AOL**	Average offered, low	**ASL**	Average starting, low	**HI**	Highest wage paid	**MTC**	Median total compensation	**TQ**	Third quartile wage
AEX	Average experienced wage	**APH**	Average pay, high range	**AW**	Average wage paid	**HR**	High end range	**MW**	Median wage paid	**W**	Weekly
AO	Average offered	**APL**	Average pay, low range	**FQ**	First quartile wage	**LR**	Low end range	**SQ**	Second quartile wage	**Y**	Yearly

Occupation/Type/Industry	Location	Per	Low	Mid	High	Source	Date
Kindergarten Teacher							
Except Special Education	Lawrence PMSA, MA-NH	Y	20230 FQ	39300 AW	64230 TQ	MABLS	10/01-12/01
Except Special Education	Lowell PMSA, MA-NH	Y	24330 FQ	41930 AW	59190 TQ	MABLS	10/01-12/01
Except Special Education	New Bedford PMSA, MA	Y	26520 FQ	43740 AW	60120 TQ	MABLS	10/01-12/01
Except Special Education	Springfield MSA, MA	Y	25200 FQ	44890 AW	66530 TQ	MABLS	10/01-12/01
Except Special Education	Worcester PMSA, MA-CT	Y	29930 FQ	44790 AW	58030 TQ	MABLS	10/01-12/01
Except Special Education	Michigan	Y	27320 FQ	44000 AW	63220 TQ	MIBLS	10/01-12/01
Except Special Education	Ann Arbor PMSA, MI	Y	29570 FQ	47550 AW	70110 TQ	MIBLS	10/01-12/01
Except Special Education	Detroit PMSA, MI	Y	25470 FQ	44410 AW	68140 TQ	MIBLS	10/01-12/01
Except Special Education	Flint PMSA, MI	Y	29210 FQ	34160 AW	45120 TQ	MIBLS	10/01-12/01
Except Special Education	Grand Rapids-Muskegon-Holland MSA, MI	Y	29800 FQ	41980 AW	59830 TQ	MIBLS	10/01-12/01
Except Special Education	Kalamazoo-Battle Creek MSA, MI	Y	26830 FQ	46290 AW	56520 TQ	MIBLS	10/01-12/01
Except Special Education	Lansing-East Lansing MSA, MI	Y	30850 FQ	44450 AW	57410 TQ	MIBLS	10/01-12/01
Except Special Education	Saginaw-Bay City-Midland MSA, MI	Y	35970 FQ	45740 AW	62930 TQ	MIBLS	10/01-12/01
Except Special Education	Minnesota	Y	27270 FQ	41120 AW	56190 TQ	MNBLS	10/01-12/01
Except Special Education	Duluth-Superior MSA, MN-WI	Y	23740 FQ	40650 AW	54460 TQ	MNBLS	10/01-12/01
Except Special Education	Minneapolis-St. Paul MSA, MN-WI	Y	30440 FQ	44090 AW	59870 TQ	MNBLS	10/01-12/01
Except Special Education	St. Cloud MSA, MN	Y	23470 FQ	36970 AW	51130 TQ	MNBLS	10/01-12/01
Except Special Education	Mississippi	Y	22090 FQ	30110 AW	38020 TQ	MSBLS	10/01-12/01
Except Special Education	Biloxi-Gulfport-Pascagoula MSA, MS	Y	26040 FQ	31470 AW	37570 TQ	MSBLS	10/01-12/01
Except Special Education	Jackson MSA, MS	Y	13730 FQ	26400 AW	37960 TQ	MSBLS	10/01-12/01
Except Special Education	Missouri	Y	20100 FQ	32900 AW	47840 TQ	MOBLS	10/01-12/01
Except Special Education	Kansas City MSA, MO-KS	Y	19200 FQ	33690 AW	50420 TQ	MOBLS	10/01-12/01
Except Special Education	St. Louis MSA, MO-IL	Y	20890 FQ	38400 AW	59790 TQ	MOBLS	10/01-12/01
Except Special Education	Springfield MSA, MO	Y	23850 FQ	31350 AW	42610 TQ	MOBLS	10/01-12/01
Except Special Education	Montana	Y	19670 FQ	32260 AW	44560 TQ	MTBLS	10/01-12/01
Except Special Education	Nebraska	Y	24250 FQ	36390 AW	52190 TQ	NEBLS	10/01-12/01
Except Special Education	Lincoln MSA, NE	Y	24040 FQ	35070 AW	49400 TQ	NEBLS	10/01-12/01
Except Special Education	Omaha MSA, NE-IA	Y	25220 FQ	39460 AW	57920 TQ	NEBLS	10/01-12/01
Except Special Education	New Hampshire	Y	15860 FQ	31800 AW	49290 TQ	NHBLS	10/01-12/01
Except Special Education	Nashua PMSA, NH	Y	18080 FQ	30260 AW	48670 TQ	NHBLS	10/01-12/01
Except Special Education	Portsmouth-Rochester PMSA, NH-ME	Y	12110 FQ	25950 AW	47560 TQ	NHBLS	10/01-12/01
Except Special Education	New Jersey	Y	28940 FQ	47260 AW	70790 TQ	NJBLS	10/01-12/01
Except Special Education	Atlantic-Cape May PMSA, NJ	Y	31070 FQ	46650 AW	68480 TQ	NJBLS	10/01-12/01
Except Special Education	Bergen-Passaic PMSA, NJ	Y	29530 FQ	49170 AW	76460 TQ	NJBLS	10/01-12/01
Except Special Education	Jersey City PMSA, NJ	Y	31610 FQ	48170 AW	77450 TQ	NJBLS	10/01-12/01
Except Special Education	Middlesex-Somerset-Hunterdon PMSA, NJ	Y	26180 FQ	45410 AW	68430 TQ	NJBLS	10/01-12/01
Except Special Education	Monmouth-Ocean PMSA, NJ	Y	26430 FQ	45140 AW	69200 TQ	NJBLS	10/01-12/01
Except Special Education	Newark PMSA, NJ	Y	29700 FQ	49140 AW	73090 TQ	NJBLS	10/01-12/01
Except Special Education	Trenton PMSA, NJ	Y	25710 FQ	44890 AW	67190 TQ	NJBLS	10/01-12/01
Except Special Education	New Mexico	Y	24610 FQ	35490 AW	49610 TQ	NMBLS	10/01-12/01
Except Special Education	Las Cruces MSA, NM	Y	25320 FQ	32520 AW	42330 TQ	NMBLS	10/01-12/01
Except Special Education	New York	Y	25670 FQ	58800 AW	103180 TQ	NYBLS	10/01-12/01
Except Special Education	Albany-Schenectady-Troy MSA, NY	Y	21790 FQ	40430 AW	68710 TQ	NYBLS	10/01-12/01
Except Special Education	Binghamton MSA, NY	Y	14220 FQ	31120 AW	44490 TQ	NYBLS	10/01-12/01
Except Special Education	Buffalo-Niagara Falls MSA, NY	Y	19520 FQ	43150 AW	67700 TQ	NYBLS	10/01-12/01
Except Special Education	Dutchess County PMSA, NY	Y	25120 FQ	53550 AW	90230 TQ	NYBLS	10/01-12/01
Except Special Education	Nassau-Suffolk PMSA, NY	Y	30200 FQ	56880 AW	93570 TQ	NYBLS	10/01-12/01
Except Special Education	Newburgh PMSA, NY-PA	Y	36660 FQ	52770 AW	71200 TQ	NYBLS	10/01-12/01
Except Special Education	Rochester MSA, NY	Y	32850 FQ	46280 AW	66950 TQ	NYBLS	10/01-12/01
Except Special Education	Syracuse MSA, NY	Y	24940 FQ	41010 AW	57990 TQ	NYBLS	10/01-12/01
Except Special Education	Utica-Rome MSA, NY	Y	28060 FQ	49440 AW	71510 TQ	NYBLS	10/01-12/01
Except Special Education	North Carolina	Y	21370 FQ	35880 AW	50380 TQ	NCBLS	10/01-12/01
Except Special Education	Asheville MSA, NC	Y	27900 FQ	40960 AW	57610 TQ	NCBLS	10/01-12/01
Except Special Education	Charlotte-Gastonia-Rock Hill MSA, NC-SC	Y	19250 FQ	36710 AW	53090 TQ	NCBLS	10/01-12/01
Except Special Education	Fayetteville MSA, NC	Y	26390 FQ	36570 AW	46990 TQ	NCBLS	10/01-12/01
Except Special Education	Greensboro-Winston-Salem-High Point MSA, NC	Y	13760 FQ	33730 AW	53820 TQ	NCBLS	10/01-12/01
Except Special Education	Hickory-Morganton-Lenoir MSA, NC	Y	31140 FQ	40140 AW	53910 TQ	NCBLS	10/01-12/01
Except Special Education	Raleigh-Durham-Chapel Hill MSA, NC	Y	24340 FQ	35860 AW	53750 TQ	NCBLS	10/01-12/01

AAW	Average annual wage	**AOH**	Average offered, high	**ASH**	Average starting, high	**H**	Hourly	**M**	Monthly	**S**	Special: hourly and annual
AE	Average entry wage	**AOL**	Average offered, low	**ASL**	Average starting, low	**HI**	Highest wage paid	**MTC**	Median total compensation	**TQ**	Third quartile wage
AEX	Average experienced wage	**APH**	Average pay, high range	**AW**	Average wage paid	**HR**	High end range	**MW**	Median wage paid	**W**	Weekly
AO	Average offered	**APL**	Average pay, low range	**FQ**	First quartile wage	**LR**	Low end range	**SQ**	Second quartile wage	**Y**	Yearly

Occupation/Type/Industry	Location	Per	Low	Mid	High	Source	Date
Kindergarten Teacher							
Except Special Education	Wilmington MSA, NC	Y	28890 FQ	37040 AW	47610 TQ	NCBLS	10/01-12/01
Except Special Education	North Dakota	Y	17620 FQ	27160 AW	37980 TQ	NDBLS	10/01-12/01
Except Special Education	Fargo-Moorhead MSA, ND-MN	Y	18060 FQ	30390 AW	46210 TQ	NDBLS	10/01-12/01
Except Special Education	Ohio	Y	24700 FQ	40800 AW	58400 TQ	OHBLS	10/01-12/01
Except Special Education	Akron PMSA, OH	Y	27820 FQ	42000 AW	58020 TQ	OHBLS	10/01-12/01
Except Special Education	Canton-Massillon MSA, OH	Y	29180 FQ	41280 AW	56690 TQ	OHBLS	10/01-12/01
Except Special Education	Cincinnati PMSA, OH-KY-IN	Y	26410 FQ	42730 AW	58950 TQ	OHBLS	10/01-12/01
Except Special Education	Cleveland-Lorain-Elyria PMSA, OH	Y	23260 FQ	42860 AW	67510 TQ	OHBLS	10/01-12/01
Except Special Education	Columbus MSA, OH	Y	27630 FQ	43530 AW	60530 TQ	OHBLS	10/01-12/01
Except Special Education	Dayton-Springfield MSA, OH	Y	20630 FQ	39560 AW	56510 TQ	OHBLS	10/01-12/01
Except Special Education	Hamilton-Middletown PMSA, OH	Y	27660 FQ	43160 AW	55820 TQ	OHBLS	10/01-12/01
Except Special Education	Mansfield MSA, OH	Y	26500 FQ	41830 AW	59310 TQ	OHBLS	10/01-12/01
Except Special Education	Toledo MSA, OH	Y	16580 FQ	36750 AW	57040 TQ	OHBLS	10/01-12/01
Except Special Education	Youngstown-Warren MSA, OH	Y	25020 FQ	39100 AW	54250 TQ	OHBLS	10/01-12/01
Except Special Education	Oklahoma	Y	13930 FQ	28480 AW	37080 TQ	OKBLS	10/01-12/01
Except Special Education	Oklahoma City MSA, OK	Y	20890 FQ	28770 AW	37200 TQ	OKBLS	10/01-12/01
Except Special Education	Tulsa MSA, OK	Y	23200 FQ	30690 AW	39280 TQ	OKBLS	10/01-12/01
Except Special Education	Oregon	Y	26620 FQ	38990 AW	55140 TQ	ORBLS	10/01-12/01
Except Special Education	Eugene-Springfield MSA, OR	Y	24780 FQ	38680 AW	54220 TQ	ORBLS	10/01-12/01
Except Special Education	Medford-Ashland MSA, OR	Y	30130 FQ	41290 AW	55200 TQ	ORBLS	10/01-12/01
Except Special Education	Portland-Vancouver PMSA, OR-WA	Y	25080 FQ	38460 AW	55860 TQ	ORBLS	10/01-12/01
Except Special Education	Salem PMSA, OR	Y	28170 FQ	39200 AW	55170 TQ	ORBLS	10/01-12/01
Except Special Education	Pennsylvania	Y	20480 FQ	42680 AW	68650 TQ	PABLS	10/01-12/01
Except Special Education	Allentown-Bethlehem-Easton MSA, PA	Y	19010 FQ	38400 AW	62520 TQ	PABLS	10/01-12/01
Except Special Education	Erie MSA, PA	Y	21030 FQ	43040 AW	58690 TQ	PABLS	10/01-12/01
Except Special Education	Harrisburg-Lebanon-Carlisle MSA, PA	Y	19890 FQ	36680 AW	57000 TQ	PABLS	10/01-12/01
Except Special Education	Johnstown MSA, PA	Y	21780 FQ	41790 AW	64710 TQ	PABLS	10/01-12/01
Except Special Education	Lancaster MSA, PA	Y	24210 FQ	41840 AW	56700 TQ	PABLS	10/01-12/01
Except Special Education	Philadelphia PMSA, PA-NJ	Y	20690 FQ	45070 AW	72920 TQ	PABLS	10/01-12/01
Except Special Education	Pittsburgh MSA, PA	Y	25240 FQ	41590 AW	61120 TQ	PABLS	10/01-12/01
Except Special Education	Reading MSA, PA	Y	24160 FQ	47870 AW	69530 TQ	PABLS	10/01-12/01
Except Special Education	Scranton-Wilkes-Barre-Hazleton MSA, PA	Y	24240 FQ	49240 AW	68880 TQ	PABLS	10/01-12/01
Except Special Education	York MSA, PA	Y	17670 FQ	36930 AW	59690 TQ	PABLS	10/01-12/01
Except Special Education	Rhode Island	Y	21060 FQ	42080 AW	64290 TQ	RIBLS	10/01-12/01
Except Special Education	South Carolina	Y	25010 FQ	37120 AW	52700 TQ	SCBLS	10/01-12/01
Except Special Education	Charleston-North Charleston MSA, SC	Y	23310 FQ	34600 AW	49320 TQ	SCBLS	10/01-12/01
Except Special Education	Columbia MSA, SC	Y	25170 FQ	36950 AW	54960 TQ	SCBLS	10/01-12/01
Except Special Education	Greenville-Spartanburg-Anderson MSA, SC	Y	30190 FQ	39570 AW	53610 TQ	SCBLS	10/01-12/01
Except Special Education	South Dakota	Y	22370 FQ	30590 AW	40920 TQ	SDBLS	10/01-12/01
Except Special Education	Tennessee	Y	18900 FQ	32450 AW	43730 TQ	TNBLS	10/01-12/01
Except Special Education	Chattanooga MSA, TN-GA	Y	28370 FQ	38110 AW	54030 TQ	TNBLS	10/01-12/01
Except Special Education	Johnson City-Kingsport-Bristol MSA, TN-VA	Y	25520 FQ	35230 AW	44980 TQ	TNBLS	10/01-12/01
Except Special Education	Knoxville MSA, TN	Y	28190 FQ	36600 AW	47700 TQ	TNBLS	10/01-12/01
Except Special Education	Memphis MSA, TN-AR-MS	Y	14930 FQ	24690 AW	39350 TQ	TNBLS	10/01-12/01
Except Special Education	Nashville MSA, TN	Y	26220 FQ	34340 AW	43790 TQ	TNBLS	10/01-12/01
Except Special Education	Texas	Y	27190 FQ	38060 AW	51940 TQ	TXBLS	10/01-12/01
Except Special Education	Austin-San Marcos MSA, TX	Y	29450 FQ	37570 AW	49980 TQ	TXBLS	10/01-12/01
Except Special Education	Beaumont-Port Arthur MSA, TX	Y	29020 FQ	38130 AW	52070 TQ	TXBLS	10/01-12/01
Except Special Education	Brazoria PMSA, TX	Y	29980 FQ	38650 AW	50680 TQ	TXBLS	10/01-12/01
Except Special Education	Corpus Christi MSA, TX	Y	31900 FQ	46900 AW	61030 TQ	TXBLS	10/01-12/01
Except Special Education	Dallas PMSA, TX	Y	22150 FQ	36270 AW	49100 TQ	TXBLS	10/01-12/01
Except Special Education	El Paso MSA, TX	Y	29910 FQ	37890 AW	50190 TQ	TXBLS	10/01-12/01
Except Special Education	Fort Worth-Arlington PMSA, TX	Y	30280 FQ	38900 AW	48950 TQ	TXBLS	10/01-12/01
Except Special Education	Houston PMSA, TX	Y	29970 FQ	40640 AW	55400 TQ	TXBLS	10/01-12/01
Except Special Education	Killeen-Temple MSA, TX	Y	25630 FQ	42720 AW	64500 TQ	TXBLS	10/01-12/01
Except Special Education	Laredo MSA, TX	Y	29600 FQ	38010 AW	51720 TQ	TXBLS	10/01-12/01
Except Special Education	Longview-Marshall MSA, TX	Y	25450 FQ	34020 AW	44110 TQ	TXBLS	10/01-12/01
Except Special Education	McAllen-Edinburg-Mission MSA, TX	Y	29440 FQ	38300 AW	52450 TQ	TXBLS	10/01-12/01

AAW	Average annual wage	AOH	Average offered, high	ASH	Average starting, high	H	Hourly	M	Monthly	S	Special: hourly and annual
AE	Average entry wage	AOL	Average offered, low	ASL	Average starting, low	HI	Highest wage paid	MTC	Median total compensation	TQ	Third quartile wage
AEX	Average experienced wage	APH	Average pay, high range	AW	Average wage paid	HR	High end range	MW	Median wage paid	W	Weekly
AO	Average offered	APL	Average pay, low range	FQ	First quartile wage	LR	Low end range	SQ	Second quartile wage	Y	Yearly

Occupation/Type/Industry	Location	Per	Low	Mid	High	Source	Date
Kindergarten Teacher							
Except Special Education	Odessa-Midland MSA, TX	Y	28600 FQ	34980 AW	44870 TQ	TXBLS	10/01-12/01
Except Special Education	San Antonio MSA, TX	Y	30230 FQ	40090 AW	55500 TQ	TXBLS	10/01-12/01
Except Special Education	Tyler MSA, TX	Y	23660 FQ	35060 AW	45440 TQ	TXBLS	10/01-12/01
Except Special Education	Waco MSA, TX	Y	25640 FQ	34780 AW	44410 TQ	TXBLS	10/01-12/01
Except Special Education	Utah	Y	19570 FQ	33450 AW	46420 TQ	UTBLS	10/01-12/01
Except Special Education	Provo-Orem MSA, UT	Y	23570 FQ	41320 AW	60430 TQ	UTBLS	10/01-12/01
Except Special Education	Salt Lake City-Ogden MSA, UT	Y	18700 FQ	30630 AW	43850 TQ	UTBLS	10/01-12/01
Except Special Education	Vermont	Y	25680 FQ	38340 AW	48370 TQ	VTBLS	10/01-12/01
Except Special Education	Burlington MSA, VT	Y	20800 FQ	35060 AW	52550 TQ	VTBLS	10/01-12/01
Except Special Education	Virginia	Y	25740 FQ	38390 AW	54620 TQ	VABLS	10/01-12/01
Except Special Education	Lynchburg MSA, VA	Y	28190 FQ	34670 AW	46980 TQ	VABLS	10/01-12/01
Except Special Education	Norfolk-Virginia Beach-Newport News MSA, VA-NC	Y	28590 FQ	35220 AW	46060 TQ	VABLS	10/01-12/01
Except Special Education	Washington	Y	25550 FQ	39110 AW	54370 TQ	WABLS	10/01-12/01
Except Special Education	Bremerton PMSA, WA	Y	23190 FQ	40330 AW	54760 TQ	WABLS	10/01-12/01
Except Special Education	Olympia PMSA, WA	Y	25440 FQ	40390 AW	55850 TQ	WABLS	10/01-12/01
Except Special Education	Richland-Kennewick-Pasco MSA, WA	Y	23800 FQ	40790 AW	56840 TQ	WABLS	10/01-12/01
Except Special Education	Seattle-Bellevue-Everett PMSA, WA	Y	27450 FQ	38370 AW	52350 TQ	WABLS	10/01-12/01
Except Special Education	Spokane MSA, WA	Y	21670 FQ	38430 AW	54040 TQ	WABLS	10/01-12/01
Except Special Education	Tacoma PMSA, WA	Y	26170 FQ	40370 AW	55710 TQ	WABLS	10/01-12/01
Except Special Education	Yakima MSA, WA	Y	15080 FQ	36720 AW	53910 TQ	WABLS	10/01-12/01
Except Special Education	West Virginia	Y	29120 FQ	36300 AW	44340 TQ	WVBLS	10/01-12/01
Except Special Education	Huntington-Ashland MSA, WV-KY-OH	Y	25290 FQ	35810 AW	46540 TQ	WVBLS	10/01-12/01
Except Special Education	Wisconsin	Y	22550 FQ	36640 AW	52710 TQ	WIBLS	10/01-12/01
Except Special Education	Appleton-Oshkosh-Neenah MSA, WI	Y	21130 FQ	34400 AW	48010 TQ	WIBLS	10/01-12/01
Except Special Education	Green Bay MSA, WI	Y	23330 FQ	34030 AW	51630 TQ	WIBLS	10/01-12/01
Except Special Education	Madison MSA, WI	Y	16780 FQ	32800 AW	50240 TQ	WIBLS	10/01-12/01
Except Special Education	Milwaukee-Waukesha PMSA, WI	Y	22770 FQ	35740 AW	49900 TQ	WIBLS	10/01-12/01
Except Special Education	Wyoming	Y	25360 FQ	34520 AW	44640 TQ	WYBLS	10/01-12/01
Except Special Education	Puerto Rico	Y	14950 FQ	19960 AW	23450 TQ	PRBLS	10/01-12/01
Except Special Education	Virgin Islands	Y	15070 FQ	17890 AW	23110 TQ	VIBLS	10/01-12/01
Except Special Education	Guam	Y	14570 FQ	30410 AW	42970 TQ	GUBLS	10/01-12/01
Laborer and Freight, Stock, and Material Mover							
Hand	Alabama	H	6.19 FQ	9.24 AW	13.31 TQ	ALBLS	10/01-12/01
Hand	Alaska	H	7.88 FQ	13.32 AW	20.44 TQ	AKBLS	10/01-12/01
Hand	Arizona	H	5.94 FQ	9.26 AW	13.83 TQ	AZBLS	10/01-12/01
Hand	Arkansas	H	6.08 FQ	8.91 AW	12.83 TQ	ARBLS	10/01-12/01
Hand	California	H	6.66 FQ	10.17 AW	15.69 TQ	CABLS	10/01-12/01
Hand	Colorado	H	7.07 FQ	10.55 AW	14.84 TQ	COBLS	10/01-12/01
Hand	Connecticut	H	7.38 FQ	11.65 AW	17.45 TQ	CTBLS	10/01-12/01
Hand	Delaware	H	7.25 FQ	12.11 AW	20.90 TQ	DEBLS	10/01-12/01
Hand	District of Columbia	H	7.27 FQ	10.20 AW	14.30 TQ	DCBLS	10/01-12/01
Hand	Florida	H	5.94 FQ	9.05 AW	13.09 TQ	FLBLS	10/01-12/01
Hand	Georgia	H	6.53 FQ	9.83 AW	14.36 TQ	GABLS	10/01-12/01
Hand	Hawaii	H	7.46 FQ	12.66 AW	22.18 TQ	HIBLS	10/01-12/01
Hand	Idaho	H	6.26 FQ	9.89 AW	14.57 TQ	IDBLS	10/01-12/01
Hand	Illinois	H	5.96 FQ	9.91 AW	15.58 TQ	ILBLS	10/01-12/01
Hand	Indiana	H	7.03 FQ	10.84 AW	16.61 TQ	INBLS	10/01-12/01
Hand	Iowa	H	6.93 FQ	10.20 AW	14.59 TQ	IABLS	10/01-12/01
Hand	Kansas	H	6.53 FQ	9.66 AW	14.02 TQ	KSBLS	10/01-12/01
Hand	Kentucky	H	6.28 FQ	10.24 AW	17.87 TQ	KYBLS	10/01-12/01
Hand	Louisiana	H	5.81 FQ	8.65 AW	13.11 TQ	LABLS	10/01-12/01
Hand	Maine	H	6.38 FQ	9.75 AW	14.43 TQ	MEBLS	10/01-12/01
Hand	Maryland	H	6.73 FQ	10.26 AW	14.97 TQ	MDBLS	10/01-12/01
Hand	Massachusetts	H	7.54 FQ	11.69 AW	16.86 TQ	MABLS	10/01-12/01
Hand	Michigan	H	7.11 FQ	11.99 AW	21.17 TQ	MIBLS	10/01-12/01
Hand	Minnesota	H	6.59 FQ	11.29 AW	17.28 TQ	MNBLS	10/01-12/01
Hand	Mississippi	H	5.89 FQ	8.78 AW	12.57 TQ	MSBLS	10/01-12/01
Hand	Missouri	H	6.51 FQ	10.61 AW	16.15 TQ	MOBLS	10/01-12/01
Hand	Montana	H	6.21 FQ	9.25 AW	13.45 TQ	MTBLS	10/01-12/01
Hand	Nebraska	H	6.52 FQ	9.88 AW	14.36 TQ	NEBLS	10/01-12/01
Hand	Nevada	H	6.74 FQ	10.98 AW	16.34 TQ	NVBLS	10/01-12/01

AAW	Average annual wage	AOH	Average offered, high	ASH	Average starting, high	H	Hourly	M	Monthly	S	Special: hourly and annual
AE	Average entry wage	AOL	Average offered, low	ASL	Average starting, low	HI	Highest wage paid	MTC	Median total compensation	TQ	Third quartile wage
AEX	Average experienced wage	APH	Average pay, high range	AW	Average wage paid	HR	High end range	MW	Median wage paid	W	Weekly
AO	Average offered	APL	Average pay, low range	FQ	First quartile wage	LR	Low end range	SQ	Second quartile wage	Y	Yearly

Occupation/Type/Industry	Location	Per	Low	Mid	High	Source	Date
Laborer and Freight, Stock, and Material Mover							
Hand	New Hampshire	H	7.50 FQ	10.35 AW	13.76 TQ	NHBLS	10/01-12/01
Hand	New Jersey	H	6.35 FQ	10.62 AW	16.67 TQ	NJBLS	10/01-12/01
Hand	New Mexico	H	5.79 FQ	8.80 AW	13.46 TQ	NMBLS	10/01-12/01
Hand	New York	H	6.63 FQ	11.07 AW	17.23 TQ	NYBLS	10/01-12/01
Hand	North Carolina	H	6.69 FQ	9.67 AW	13.54 TQ	NCBLS	10/01-12/01
Hand	North Dakota	H	6.29 FQ	9.60 AW	13.54 TQ	NDBLS	10/01-12/01
Hand	Ohio	H	6.88 FQ	11.03 AW	16.69 TQ	OHBLS	10/01-12/01
Hand	Oklahoma	H	6.09 FQ	9.02 AW	13.00 TQ	OKBLS	10/01-12/01
Hand	Oregon	H	7.32 FQ	10.53 AW	15.34 TQ	ORBLS	10/01-12/01
Hand	Pennsylvania	H	6.91 FQ	10.88 AW	16.40 TQ	PABLS	10/01-12/01
Hand	Rhode Island	H	6.89 FQ	10.48 AW	14.70 TQ	RIBLS	10/01-12/01
Hand	South Carolina	H	6.74 FQ	9.54 AW	13.15 TQ	SCBLS	10/01-12/01
Hand	South Dakota	H	6.28 FQ	8.76 AW	11.96 TQ	SDBLS	10/01-12/01
Hand	Tennessee	H	6.56 FQ	9.93 AW	14.56 TQ	TNBLS	10/01-12/01
Hand	Texas	H	6.10 FQ	9.23 AW	13.37 TQ	TXBLS	10/01-12/01
Hand	Utah	H	6.51 FQ	9.94 AW	14.29 TQ	UTBLS	10/01-12/01
Hand	Vermont	H	7.20 FQ	10.34 AW	14.72 TQ	VTBLS	10/01-12/01
Hand	Virginia	H	6.39 FQ	9.67 AW	13.67 TQ	VABLS	10/01-12/01
Hand	Washington	H	7.22 FQ	11.17 AW	16.96 TQ	WABLS	10/01-12/01
Hand	West Virginia	H	5.80 FQ	7.99 AW	12.15 TQ	WVBLS	10/01-12/01
Hand	Wisconsin	H	6.81 FQ	10.51 AW	15.47 TQ	WIBLS	10/01-12/01
Hand	Wyoming	H	6.00 FQ	9.16 AW	13.57 TQ	WYBLS	10/01-12/01
Hand	Puerto Rico	H	5.58 FQ	7.65 AW	12.12 TQ	PRBLS	10/01-12/01
Hand	Virgin Islands	H	6.07 FQ	7.90 AW	10.11 TQ	VIBLS	10/01-12/01
Hand	Guam	H	5.80 FQ	7.78 AW	10.51 TQ	GUBLS	10/01-12/01
Landscape Architect	Alabama	Y	20830 FQ	43940 AW	71470 TQ	ALBLS	10/01-12/01
	Alaska	Y	29350 FQ	49080 AW	75030 TQ	AKBLS	10/01-12/01
	Anchorage MSA, AK	Y	30530 FQ	46530 AW	71050 TQ	AKBLS	10/01-12/01
	Arizona	Y	27010 FQ	45550 AW	68260 TQ	AZBLS	10/01-12/01
	Phoenix-Mesa MSA, AZ	Y	27320 FQ	47870 AW	71900 TQ	AZBLS	10/01-12/01
	Tucson MSA, AZ	Y	27970 FQ	44590 AW	60810 TQ	AZBLS	10/01-12/01
	Arkansas	Y	19790 FQ	36700 AW	54560 TQ	ARBLS	10/01-12/01
	Fayetteville-Springdale-Rogers MSA, AR	Y	18690 FQ	33750 AW	53600 TQ	ARBLS	10/01-12/01
	California	Y	25980 FQ	59490 AW	104650 TQ	CABLS	10/01-12/01
	Fresno MSA, CA	Y	27390 FQ	51980 AW	79110 TQ	CABLS	10/01-12/01
	Los Angeles-Long Beach PMSA, CA	Y	23910 FQ	31020 AW	47360 TQ	CABLS	10/01-12/01
	Oakland PMSA, CA	Y	45610 FQ	61630 AW	86870 TQ	CABLS	10/01-12/01
	Orange County PMSA, CA	Y	29660 FQ	52790 AW	79380 TQ	CABLS	10/01-12/01
	Riverside-San Bernardino PMSA, CA	Y	38020 FQ	57550 AW	74680 TQ	CABLS	10/01-12/01
	Sacramento PMSA, CA	Y	39450 FQ	64530 AW	86480 TQ	CABLS	10/01-12/01
	San Diego MSA, CA	Y	36740 FQ	57450 AW	75420 TQ	CABLS	10/01-12/01
	San Francisco PMSA, CA	Y	34610 FQ	57280 AW	87160 TQ	CABLS	10/01-12/01
	San Luis Obispo-Atascadero-Paso Robles MSA, CA	Y	26060 FQ	47710 AW	70520 TQ	CABLS	10/01-12/01
	Santa Barbara-Santa Maria-Lompoc MSA, CA	Y	39080 FQ	66410 AW	105540 TQ	CABLS	10/01-12/01
	Vallejo-Fairfield-Napa PMSA, CA	Y	43520 FQ	79930 AW		CABLS	10/01-12/01
	Colorado	Y	26420 FQ	48530 AW	76140 TQ	COBLS	10/01-12/01
	Boulder-Longmont PMSA, CO	Y	26270 FQ	49490 AW	91350 TQ	COBLS	10/01-12/01
	Denver PMSA, CO	Y	25060 FQ	48540 AW	76020 TQ	COBLS	10/01-12/01
	Fort Collins-Loveland MSA, CO	Y	31430 FQ	52860 AW	86700 TQ	COBLS	10/01-12/01
	Connecticut	Y	30660 FQ	50930 AW	73010 TQ	CTBLS	10/01-12/01
	Hartford MSA, CT	Y	33530 FQ	51510 AW	74800 TQ	CTBLS	10/01-12/01
	New Haven-Meriden PMSA, CT	Y	30980 FQ	47540 AW	68760 TQ	CTBLS	10/01-12/01
	Delaware	Y	36180 FQ	57210 AW	86230 TQ	DEBLS	10/01-12/01
	Wilmington-Newark PMSA, DE-MD	Y	35270 FQ	55790 AW	85570 TQ	DEBLS	10/01-12/01
	District of Columbia	Y	37660 FQ	53380 AW	73630 TQ	DCBLS	10/01-12/01
	Washington PMSA, DC-MD-VA-WV	Y	25040 FQ	48310 AW	72750 TQ	DCBLS	10/01-12/01
	Florida	Y	31470 FQ	54410 AW	99300 TQ	FLBLS	10/01-12/01
	Fort Lauderdale PMSA, FL	Y	35160 FQ	55860 AW	86730 TQ	FLBLS	10/01-12/01

AAW	Average annual wage	**AOH**	Average offered, high	**ASH**	Average starting, high	**H**	Hourly	**M**	Monthly	**S**	Special: hourly and annual
AE	Average entry wage	**AOL**	Average offered, low	**ASL**	Average starting, low	**HI**	Highest wage paid	**MTC**	Median total compensation	**TQ**	Third quartile wage
AEX	Average experienced wage	**APH**	Average pay, high range	**AW**	Average wage paid	**HR**	High end range	**MW**	Median wage paid	**W**	Weekly
AO	Average offered	**APL**	Average pay, low range	**FQ**	First quartile wage	**LR**	Low end range	**SQ**	Second quartile wage	**Y**	Yearly

Occupation/Type/Industry	Location	Per	Low	Mid	High	Source	Date
Landscape Architect	Lakeland-Winter Haven MSA, FL	Y	62420 FQ	92830 AW	141480 TQ	FLBLS	10/01-12/01
	Miami PMSA, FL	Y	35160 FQ	54130 AW	77770 TQ	FLBLS	10/01-12/01
	Naples MSA, FL	Y	31430 FQ	58000 AW	95030 TQ	FLBLS	10/01-12/01
	Orlando MSA, FL	Y	31240 FQ	52490 AW	102500 TQ	FLBLS	10/01-12/01
	Sarasota-Bradenton MSA, FL	Y	33550 FQ	45880 AW	64520 TQ	FLBLS	10/01-12/01
	Tampa-St. Petersburg-Clearwater MSA, FL	Y	34330 FQ	56030 AW	100170 TQ	FLBLS	10/01-12/01
	West Palm Beach-Boca Raton MSA, FL	Y	27500 FQ	48920 AW	77710 TQ	FLBLS	10/01-12/01
	Georgia	Y	31750 FQ	45960 AW	66970 TQ	GABLS	10/01-12/01
	Atlanta MSA, GA	Y	31840 FQ	45660 AW	65810 TQ	GABLS	10/01-12/01
	Hawaii	Y	32820 FQ	54860 AW	80630 TQ	HIBLS	10/01-12/01
	Honolulu MSA, HI	Y	32610 FQ	55030 AW	81470 TQ	HIBLS	10/01-12/01
	Idaho	Y	25100 FQ	38240 AW	54560 TQ	IDBLS	10/01-12/01
	Boise City MSA, ID	Y	25110 FQ	37410 AW	52960 TQ	IDBLS	10/01-12/01
	Illinois	Y	30760 FQ	49240 AW	70610 TQ	ILBLS	10/01-12/01
	Chicago PMSA, IL	Y	31950 FQ	50230 AW	70520 TQ	ILBLS	10/01-12/01
	Peoria-Pekin MSA, IL	Y	29650 FQ	34040 AW	36490 TQ	ILBLS	10/01-12/01
	Indiana	Y	24180 FQ	40420 AW	57940 TQ	INBLS	10/01-12/01
	Fort Wayne MSA, IN	Y	25320 FQ	37240 AW	54270 TQ	INBLS	10/01-12/01
	Gary PMSA, IN	Y	18550 FQ	30020 AW	50440 TQ	INBLS	10/01-12/01
	Indianapolis MSA, IN	Y	29330 FQ	43890 AW	56610 TQ	INBLS	10/01-12/01
	Iowa	Y	24410 FQ	39240 AW	58460 TQ	IABLS	10/01-12/01
	Des Moines MSA, IA	Y	24350 FQ	35500 AW	52890 TQ	IABLS	10/01-12/01
	Kansas	Y	27890 FQ	61240 AW	108840 TQ	KSBLS	10/01-12/01
	Kentucky	Y	31660 FQ	49260 AW	69890 TQ	KYBLS	10/01-12/01
	Lexington MSA, KY	Y	33550 FQ	46530 AW	62290 TQ	KYBLS	10/01-12/01
	Louisville MSA, KY-IN	Y	30200 FQ	52670 AW	75870 TQ	KYBLS	10/01-12/01
	Louisiana	Y	26320 FQ	40860 AW	62280 TQ	LABLS	10/01-12/01
	Baton Rouge MSA, LA	Y	28160 FQ	41730 AW	59800 TQ	LABLS	10/01-12/01
	Maine	Y	29330 FQ	44440 AW	60720 TQ	MEBLS	10/01-12/01
	Maryland	Y	29270 FQ	46940 AW	71250 TQ	MDBLS	10/01-12/01
	Baltimore PMSA, MD	Y	33340 FQ	54430 AW	83200 TQ	MDBLS	10/01-12/01
	Massachusetts	Y	31380 FQ	51800 AW	81960 TQ	MABLS	10/01-12/01
	Boston PMSA, MA-NH	Y	31460 FQ	52200 AW	81920 TQ	MABLS	10/01-12/01
	Michigan	Y	28190 FQ	51020 AW	78300 TQ	MIBLS	10/01-12/01
	Ann Arbor PMSA, MI	Y	32270 FQ	50690 AW	70860 TQ	MIBLS	10/01-12/01
	Detroit PMSA, MI	Y	30640 FQ	47860 AW	69700 TQ	MIBLS	10/01-12/01
	Grand Rapids-Muskegon-Holland MSA, MI	Y	25720 FQ	44850 AW	82760 TQ	MIBLS	10/01-12/01
	Kalamazoo-Battle Creek MSA, MI	Y	31170 FQ	49950 AW	73790 TQ	MIBLS	10/01-12/01
	Minnesota	Y	38720 FQ	58640 AW	85060 TQ	MNBLS	10/01-12/01
	Minneapolis-St. Paul MSA, MN-WI	Y	38440 FQ	60100 AW	86440 TQ	MNBLS	10/01-12/01
	Mississippi	Y	32940 FQ	56760 AW	72780 TQ	MSBLS	10/01-12/01
	Jackson MSA, MS	Y	40340 FQ	61950 AW	73470 TQ	MSBLS	10/01-12/01
	Missouri	Y	25900 FQ	49190 AW	78110 TQ	MOBLS	10/01-12/01
	Kansas City MSA, MO-KS	Y	26020 FQ	62090 AW	109170 TQ	MOBLS	10/01-12/01
	St. Louis MSA, MO-IL	Y	27790 FQ	49960 AW	77450 TQ	MOBLS	10/01-12/01
	Nebraska	Y	25360 FQ	48950 AW	75730 TQ	NEBLS	10/01-12/01
	Omaha MSA, NE-IA	Y	27940 FQ	51370 AW	76470 TQ	NEBLS	10/01-12/01
	Nevada	Y	38620 FQ	58640 AW	84270 TQ	NVBLS	10/01-12/01
	Las Vegas MSA, NV-AZ	Y	29080 FQ	47220 AW	69860 TQ	NVBLS	10/01-12/01
	New Hampshire	Y	30340 FQ	40190 AW	49650 TQ	NHBLS	10/01-12/01
	New Jersey	Y	32910 FQ	57140 AW	96090 TQ	NJBLS	10/01-12/01
	Bergen-Passaic PMSA, NJ	Y	47050 FQ	67760 AW	100990 TQ	NJBLS	10/01-12/01
	Middlesex-Somerset-Hunterdon PMSA, NJ	Y	41850 FQ	68400 AW	104480 TQ	NJBLS	10/01-12/01
	Monmouth-Ocean PMSA, NJ	Y	30890 FQ	43060 AW	61620 TQ	NJBLS	10/01-12/01
	Newark PMSA, NJ	Y	32370 FQ	46430 AW	61080 TQ	NJBLS	10/01-12/01
	Trenton PMSA, NJ	Y	33000 FQ	58830 AW	101970 TQ	NJBLS	10/01-12/01
	New Mexico	Y	33120 FQ	51300 AW	69030 TQ	NMBLS	10/01-12/01
	New York	Y	30820 FQ	53420 AW	79580 TQ	NYBLS	10/01-12/01
	Albany-Schenectady-Troy MSA, NY	Y	32280 FQ	56210 AW	86080 TQ	NYBLS	10/01-12/01
	Nassau-Suffolk PMSA, NY	Y	31260 FQ	55380 AW	87260 TQ	NYBLS	10/01-12/01
	New York PMSA, NY	Y	40400 FQ	57530 AW	76780 TQ	NYBLS	10/01-12/01
	Syracuse MSA, NY	Y	26770 FQ	45400 AW	70810 TQ	NYBLS	10/01-12/01
	North Carolina	Y	31380 FQ	51280 AW	73810 TQ	NCBLS	10/01-12/01

AAW	Average annual wage	AOH	Average offered, high	ASH	Average starting, high	H	Hourly	M	Monthly	S	Special: hourly and annual
AE	Average entry wage	AOL	Average offered, low	ASL	Average starting, low	HI	Highest wage paid	MTC	Median total compensation	TQ	Third quartile wage
AEX	Average experienced wage	APH	Average pay, high range	AW	Average wage paid	HR	High end range	MW	Median wage paid	W	Weekly
AO	Average offered	APL	Average pay, low range	FQ	First quartile wage	LR	Low end range	SQ	Second quartile wage	Y	Yearly

Occupation/Type/Industry	Location	Per	Low	Mid	High	Source	Date
Landscape Architect	Charlotte-Gastonia-Rock Hill MSA, NC-SC	Y	30400 FQ	46740 AW	69190 TQ	NCBLS	10/01-12/01
	Raleigh-Durham-Chapel Hill MSA, NC	Y	30360 FQ	60980 AW	109250 TQ	NCBLS	10/01-12/01
	Ohio	Y	27500 FQ	49450 AW	69790 TQ	OHBLS	10/01-12/01
	Cincinnati PMSA, OH-KY-IN	Y	29040 FQ	42940 AW	66230 TQ	OHBLS	10/01-12/01
	Cleveland-Lorain-Elyria PMSA, OH	Y	28700 FQ	53190 AW	70360 TQ	OHBLS	10/01-12/01
	Columbus MSA, OH	Y	28900 FQ	47900 AW	68650 TQ	OHBLS	10/01-12/01
	Oklahoma	Y	17640 FQ	39250 AW	61000 TQ	OKBLS	10/01-12/01
	Oklahoma City MSA, OK	Y	17480 FQ	37720 AW	58150 TQ	OKBLS	10/01-12/01
	Oregon	Y	36320 FQ	51460 AW	71680 TQ	ORBLS	10/01-12/01
	Portland-Vancouver PMSA, OR-WA	Y	37370 FQ	52780 AW	74300 TQ	ORBLS	10/01-12/01
	Pennsylvania	Y	29380 FQ	49410 AW	70690 TQ	PABLS	10/01-12/01
	Allentown-Bethlehem-Easton MSA, PA	Y	26620 FQ	51920 AW	82610 TQ	PABLS	10/01-12/01
	Lancaster MSA, PA	Y	29530 FQ	52280 AW	69440 TQ	PABLS	10/01-12/01
	Philadelphia PMSA, PA-NJ	Y	32890 FQ	52060 AW	73000 TQ	PABLS	10/01-12/01
	Pittsburgh MSA, PA	Y	19000 FQ	39880 AW	57920 TQ	PABLS	10/01-12/01
	South Carolina	Y	24020 FQ	45840 AW	71150 TQ	SCBLS	10/01-12/01
	Tennessee	Y	27240 FQ	46750 AW	71140 TQ	TNBLS	10/01-12/01
	Memphis MSA, TN-AR-MS	Y	27010 FQ	44060 AW	69170 TQ	TNBLS	10/01-12/01
	Texas	Y	34090 FQ	58990 AW	81370 TQ	TXBLS	10/01-12/01
	Austin-San Marcos MSA, TX	Y	30570 FQ	49160 AW	79490 TQ	TXBLS	10/01-12/01
	Dallas PMSA, TX	Y	29900 FQ	53830 AW	89490 TQ	TXBLS	10/01-12/01
	Fort Worth-Arlington PMSA, TX	Y	45880 FQ	94140 AW		TXBLS	10/01-12/01
	Houston PMSA, TX	Y	35700 FQ	44980 AW	67530 TQ	TXBLS	10/01-12/01
	San Antonio MSA, TX	Y	59650 FQ	64370 AW	72880 TQ	TXBLS	10/01-12/01
	Utah	Y	31760 FQ	48850 AW	68870 TQ	UTBLS	10/01-12/01
	Salt Lake City-Ogden MSA, UT	Y	32940 FQ	47300 AW	67100 TQ	UTBLS	10/01-12/01
	Vermont	Y	25550 FQ	49410 AW	111900 TQ	VTBLS	10/01-12/01
	Virginia	Y	24140 FQ	42710 AW	66200 TQ	VABLS	10/01-12/01
	Norfolk-Virginia Beach-Newport News MSA, VA-NC	Y	28340 FQ	48010 AW	71790 TQ	VABLS	10/01-12/01
	Richmond-Petersburg MSA, VA	Y	28780 FQ	48040 AW	70670 TQ	VABLS	10/01-12/01
	Washington	Y	30910 FQ	48580 AW	73410 TQ	WABLS	10/01-12/01
	Bremerton PMSA, WA	Y	28820 FQ	31850 AW	34780 TQ	WABLS	10/01-12/01
	Seattle-Bellevue-Everett PMSA, WA	Y	33990 FQ	51160 AW	75960 TQ	WABLS	10/01-12/01
	Wisconsin	Y	23190 FQ	42390 AW	65560 TQ	WIBLS	10/01-12/01
	Madison MSA, WI	Y	22370 FQ	37740 AW	53800 TQ	WIBLS	10/01-12/01
	Milwaukee-Waukesha PMSA, WI	Y	27050 FQ	53720 AW	91690 TQ	WIBLS	10/01-12/01
Landscaping and Groundskeeping Worker	Alabama	H	6.24 FQ	9.03 AW	12.64 TQ	ALBLS	10/01-12/01
	Alaska	H	7.30 FQ	12.64 AW	19.71 TQ	AKBLS	10/01-12/01
	Arizona	H	6.07 FQ	8.62 AW	12.45 TQ	AZBLS	10/01-12/01
	Arkansas	H	5.85 FQ	8.06 AW	10.81 TQ	ARBLS	10/01-12/01
	California	H	6.79 FQ	10.61 AW	16.81 TQ	CABLS	10/01-12/01
	Colorado	H	7.25 FQ	10.30 AW	14.63 TQ	COBLS	10/01-12/01
	Connecticut	H	7.88 FQ	12.34 AW	17.47 TQ	CTBLS	10/01-12/01
	Delaware	H	7.20 FQ	9.93 AW	13.62 TQ	DEBLS	10/01-12/01
	District of Columbia	H	7.59 FQ	12.04 AW	19.15 TQ	DCBLS	10/01-12/01
	Florida	H	6.26 FQ	9.23 AW	13.09 TQ	FLBLS	10/01-12/01
	Georgia	H	6.84 FQ	9.19 AW	12.14 TQ	GABLS	10/01-12/01
	Hawaii	H	7.54 FQ	11.23 AW	14.90 TQ	HIBLS	10/01-12/01
	Idaho	H	6.35 FQ	9.21 AW	12.72 TQ	IDBLS	10/01-12/01
	Illinois	H	6.70 FQ	10.58 AW	16.26 TQ	ILBLS	10/01-12/01
	Indiana	H	6.42 FQ	9.30 AW	12.93 TQ	INBLS	10/01-12/01
	Iowa	H	6.13 FQ	9.32 AW	13.99 TQ	IABLS	10/01-12/01
	Kansas	H	6.47 FQ	10.07 AW	15.31 TQ	KSBLS	10/01-12/01
	Kentucky	H	6.66 FQ	9.34 AW	13.19 TQ	KYBLS	10/01-12/01
	Louisiana	H	5.91 FQ	8.42 AW	11.30 TQ	LABLS	10/01-12/01
	Maine	H	6.57 FQ	9.83 AW	13.49 TQ	MEBLS	10/01-12/01
	Maryland	H	6.88 FQ	9.96 AW	14.00 TQ	MDBLS	10/01-12/01
	Massachusetts	H	7.86 FQ	12.26 AW	17.88 TQ	MABLS	10/01-12/01

AAW	Average annual wage	AOH	Average offered, high	ASH	Average starting, high	H	Hourly	M	Monthly	S	Special: hourly and annual
AE	Average entry wage	AOL	Average offered, low	ASL	Average starting, low	HI	Highest wage paid	MTC	Median total compensation	TQ	Third quartile wage
AEX	Average experienced wage	APH	Average pay, high range	AW	Average wage paid	HR	High end range	MW	Median wage paid	W	Weekly
AO	Average offered	APL	Average pay, low range	FQ	First quartile wage	LR	Low end range	SQ	Second quartile wage	Y	Yearly

Occupation/Type/Industry	Location	Per	Low	Mid	High	Source	Date
Landscaping and Groundskeeping Worker							
	Michigan	H	6.97 FQ	10.50 AW	14.91 TQ	MIBLS	10/01-12/01
	Minnesota	H	7.04 FQ	11.18 AW	16.72 TQ	MNBLS	10/01-12/01
	Mississippi	H	5.91 FQ	8.56 AW	11.89 TQ	MSBLS	10/01-12/01
	Missouri	H	6.59 FQ	9.90 AW	13.78 TQ	MOBLS	10/01-12/01
	Montana	H	5.97 FQ	8.62 AW	12.49 TQ	MTBLS	10/01-12/01
	Nebraska	H	6.55 FQ	9.90 AW	13.40 TQ	NEBLS	10/01-12/01
	Nevada	H	6.54 FQ	9.93 AW	15.26 TQ	NVBLS	10/01-12/01
	New Hampshire	H	7.43 FQ	11.03 AW	15.67 TQ	NHBLS	10/01-12/01
	New Jersey	H	7.35 FQ	11.66 AW	17.88 TQ	NJBLS	10/01-12/01
	New Mexico	H	6.03 FQ	8.87 AW	12.56 TQ	NMBLS	10/01-12/01
	New York	H	6.89 FQ	11.32 AW	17.38 TQ	NYBLS	10/01-12/01
	North Carolina	H	7.00 FQ	9.55 AW	13.14 TQ	NCBLS	10/01-12/01
	North Dakota	H	6.14 FQ	9.08 AW	13.13 TQ	NDBLS	10/01-12/01
	Ohio	H	6.53 FQ	10.29 AW	15.75 TQ	OHBLS	10/01-12/01
	Oklahoma	H	5.94 FQ	8.56 AW	12.18 TQ	OKBLS	10/01-12/01
	Oregon	H	7.41 FQ	10.76 AW	15.15 TQ	ORBLS	10/01-12/01
	Pennsylvania	H	6.12 FQ	9.81 AW	14.47 TQ	PABLS	10/01-12/01
	Rhode Island	H	6.94 FQ	10.66 AW	15.08 TQ	RIBLS	10/01-12/01
	South Carolina	H	6.67 FQ	9.04 AW	11.83 TQ	SCBLS	10/01-12/01
	South Dakota	H	6.96 FQ	8.93 AW	11.51 TQ	SDBLS	10/01-12/01
	Tennessee	H	6.44 FQ	9.32 AW	13.22 TQ	TNBLS	10/01-12/01
	Texas	H	6.15 FQ	8.75 AW	12.20 TQ	TXBLS	10/01-12/01
	Utah	H	6.54 FQ	9.54 AW	13.56 TQ	UTBLS	10/01-12/01
	Vermont	H	7.41 FQ	10.30 AW	14.92 TQ	VTBLS	10/01-12/01
	Virginia	H	6.95 FQ	9.68 AW	13.33 TQ	VABLS	10/01-12/01
	Washington	H	7.43 FQ	11.62 AW	17.21 TQ	WABLS	10/01-12/01
	West Virginia	H	5.74 FQ	8.10 AW	11.39 TQ	WVBLS	10/01-12/01
	Wisconsin	H	6.38 FQ	10.36 AW	16.05 TQ	WIBLS	10/01-12/01
	Wyoming	H	6.54 FQ	9.63 AW	13.72 TQ	WYBLS	10/01-12/01
	Puerto Rico	H	5.52 FQ	6.64 AW	8.28 TQ	PRBLS	10/01-12/01
	Virgin Islands	H	6.10 FQ	8.24 AW	10.66 TQ	VIBLS	10/01-12/01
	Guam	H	5.73 FQ	7.75 AW	10.80 TQ	GUBLS	10/01-12/01
Lathe and Turning Machine Tool Setter, Operator, and Tender							
Metals and Plastics	Alabama	H	9.47 FQ	17.05 AW	26.82 TQ	ALBLS	10/01-12/01
Metals and Plastics	Birmingham MSA, AL	H	9.41 FQ	15.06 AW	21.21 TQ	ALBLS	10/01-12/01
Metals and Plastics	Arizona	H	9.74 FQ	15.21 AW	22.24 TQ	AZBLS	10/01-12/01
Metals and Plastics	Phoenix-Mesa MSA, AZ	H	9.85 FQ	15.04 AW	21.93 TQ	AZBLS	10/01-12/01
Metals and Plastics	Tucson MSA, AZ	H	9.88 FQ	15.39 AW	22.63 TQ	AZBLS	10/01-12/01
Metals and Plastics	Arkansas	H	9.39 FQ	12.83 AW	16.83 TQ	ARBLS	10/01-12/01
Metals and Plastics	Fayetteville-Springdale-Rogers MSA, AR	H	11.21 FQ	12.46 AW	13.84 TQ	ARBLS	10/01-12/01
Metals and Plastics	Fort Smith MSA, AR-OK	H	9.20 FQ	14.43 AW	17.50 TQ	ARBLS	10/01-12/01
Metals and Plastics	Little Rock-North Little Rock MSA, AR	H	9.10 FQ	12.14 AW	17.00 TQ	ARBLS	10/01-12/01
Metals and Plastics	California	H	8.09 FQ	14.23 AW	21.49 TQ	CABLS	10/01-12/01
Metals and Plastics	Fresno MSA, CA	H	8.97 FQ	14.25 AW	21.28 TQ	CABLS	10/01-12/01
Metals and Plastics	Los Angeles-Long Beach PMSA, CA	H	7.87 FQ	13.41 AW	20.15 TQ	CABLS	10/01-12/01
Metals and Plastics	Modesto MSA, CA	H	8.90 FQ	13.09 AW	17.99 TQ	CABLS	10/01-12/01
Metals and Plastics	Oakland PMSA, CA	H	9.83 FQ	19.63 AW	28.37 TQ	CABLS	10/01-12/01
Metals and Plastics	Orange County PMSA, CA	H	8.03 FQ	14.79 AW	22.81 TQ	CABLS	10/01-12/01
Metals and Plastics	Riverside-San Bernardino PMSA, CA	H	8.09 FQ	13.25 AW	19.40 TQ	CABLS	10/01-12/01
Metals and Plastics	Sacramento PMSA, CA	H	8.95 FQ	16.30 AW	25.41 TQ	CABLS	10/01-12/01
Metals and Plastics	San Diego MSA, CA	H	6.86 FQ	13.40 AW	19.92 TQ	CABLS	10/01-12/01
Metals and Plastics	San Francisco PMSA, CA	H	9.93 FQ	16.45 AW	24.81 TQ	CABLS	10/01-12/01
Metals and Plastics	San Jose PMSA, CA	H	11.50 FQ	18.37 AW	26.97 TQ	CABLS	10/01-12/01
Metals and Plastics	Santa Barbara-Santa Maria-Lompoc MSA, CA	H	8.51 FQ	12.06 AW	17.23 TQ	CABLS	10/01-12/01
Metals and Plastics	Ventura PMSA, CA	H	9.72 FQ	14.88 AW	21.97 TQ	CABLS	10/01-12/01
Metals and Plastics	Colorado	H	7.93 FQ	12.64 AW	18.70 TQ	COBLS	10/01-12/01
Metals and Plastics	Boulder-Longmont PMSA, CO	H	11.76 FQ	18.26 AW	30.42 TQ	COBLS	10/01-12/01
Metals and Plastics	Denver PMSA, CO	H	11.46 FQ	14.51 AW	20.99 TQ	COBLS	10/01-12/01
Metals and Plastics	Fort Collins-Loveland MSA, CO	H	8.98 FQ	13.77 AW	17.28 TQ	COBLS	10/01-12/01
Metals and Plastics	Connecticut	H	10.12 FQ	16.12 AW	22.21 TQ	CTBLS	10/01-12/01
Metals and Plastics	Bridgeport PMSA, CT	H	11.50 FQ	15.84 AW	21.04 TQ	CTBLS	10/01-12/01
Metals and Plastics	Danbury PMSA, CT	H	9.84 FQ	15.17 AW	20.72 TQ	CTBLS	10/01-12/01
Metals and Plastics	Hartford MSA, CT	H	10.10 FQ	16.14 AW	22.26 TQ	CTBLS	10/01-12/01

AAW	Average annual wage	AOH	Average offered, high	ASH	Average starting, high	H	Hourly	M	Monthly	S	Special: hourly and annual
AE	Average entry wage	AOL	Average offered, low	ASL	Average starting, low	HI	Highest wage paid	MTC	Median total compensation	TQ	Third quartile wage
AEX	Average experienced wage	APH	Average pay, high range	AW	Average wage paid	HR	High end range	MW	Median wage paid	W	Weekly
AO	Average offered	APL	Average pay, low range	FQ	First quartile wage	LR	Low end range	SQ	Second quartile wage	Y	Yearly

Occupation/Type/Industry	Location	Per	Low	Mid	High	Source	Date
Lathe and Turning Machine Tool Setter, Operator, and Tender							
Metals and Plastics	New Haven-Meriden PMSA, CT	H	10.55 FQ	15.90 AW	22.07 TQ	CTBLS	10/01-12/01
Metals and Plastics	Stamford-Norwalk PMSA, CT	H	13.12 FQ	18.00 AW	22.24 TQ	CTBLS	10/01-12/01
Metals and Plastics	Waterbury PMSA, CT	H	9.05 FQ	16.26 AW	24.94 TQ	CTBLS	10/01-12/01
Metals and Plastics	Delaware	H	11.57 FQ	15.83 AW	21.18 TQ	DEBLS	10/01-12/01
Metals and Plastics	Washington PMSA, DC-MD-VA-WV	H	8.84 FQ	14.99 AW	24.00 TQ	DCBLS	10/01-12/01
Metals and Plastics	Florida	H	9.24 FQ	13.56 AW	18.36 TQ	FLBLS	10/01-12/01
Metals and Plastics	Fort Lauderdale PMSA, FL	H	9.35 FQ	12.59 AW	17.04 TQ	FLBLS	10/01-12/01
Metals and Plastics	Gainesville MSA, FL	H	9.69 FQ	14.47 AW	19.99 TQ	FLBLS	10/01-12/01
Metals and Plastics	Jacksonville MSA, FL	H	11.55 FQ	13.55 AW	16.19 TQ	FLBLS	10/01-12/01
Metals and Plastics	Melbourne-Titusville-Palm Bay MSA, FL	H	10.64 FQ	13.71 AW	17.33 TQ	FLBLS	10/01-12/01
Metals and Plastics	Miami PMSA, FL	H	7.67 FQ	12.07 AW	18.83 TQ	FLBLS	10/01-12/01
Metals and Plastics	Orlando MSA, FL	H	10.48 FQ	13.55 AW	16.58 TQ	FLBLS	10/01-12/01
Metals and Plastics	Pensacola MSA, FL	H	9.06 FQ	14.00 AW	19.52 TQ	FLBLS	10/01-12/01
Metals and Plastics	Sarasota-Bradenton MSA, FL	H	9.73 FQ	13.31 AW	17.11 TQ	FLBLS	10/01-12/01
Metals and Plastics	Tampa-St. Petersburg-Clearwater MSA, FL	H	9.40 FQ	13.97 AW	20.25 TQ	FLBLS	10/01-12/01
Metals and Plastics	West Palm Beach-Boca Raton MSA, FL	H	10.60 FQ	15.83 AW	21.13 TQ	FLBLS	10/01-12/01
Metals and Plastics	Georgia	H	8.24 FQ	13.35 AW	18.08 TQ	GABLS	10/01-12/01
Metals and Plastics	Atlanta MSA, GA	H	8.02 FQ	13.02 AW	17.07 TQ	GABLS	10/01-12/01
Metals and Plastics	Augusta-Aiken MSA, GA-SC	H	11.26 FQ	15.07 AW	20.95 TQ	GABLS	10/01-12/01
Metals and Plastics	Idaho	H	8.20 FQ	12.47 AW	16.78 TQ	IDBLS	10/01-12/01
Metals and Plastics	Boise City MSA, ID	H	10.62 FQ	13.89 AW	16.96 TQ	IDBLS	10/01-12/01
Metals and Plastics	Illinois	H	9.01 FQ	13.46 AW	20.18 TQ	ILBLS	10/01-12/01
Metals and Plastics	Chicago PMSA, IL	H	8.95 FQ	14.00 AW	20.24 TQ	ILBLS	10/01-12/01
Metals and Plastics	Peoria-Pekin MSA, IL	H	13.00 FQ	21.99 AW	28.01 TQ	ILBLS	10/01-12/01
Metals and Plastics	Rockford MSA, IL	H	9.94 FQ	14.84 AW	20.42 TQ	ILBLS	10/01-12/01
Metals and Plastics	Indiana	H	9.76 FQ	15.00 AW	22.74 TQ	INBLS	10/01-12/01
Metals and Plastics	Elkhart-Goshen MSA, IN	H	8.84 FQ	12.31 AW	17.32 TQ	INBLS	10/01-12/01
Metals and Plastics	Evansville-Henderson MSA, IN-KY	H	10.11 FQ	14.81 AW	20.30 TQ	INBLS	10/01-12/01
Metals and Plastics	Fort Wayne MSA, IN	H	12.25 FQ	15.97 AW	20.33 TQ	INBLS	10/01-12/01
Metals and Plastics	Gary PMSA, IN	H	11.23 FQ	17.68 AW	24.21 TQ	INBLS	10/01-12/01
Metals and Plastics	Indianapolis MSA, IN	H	10.78 FQ	17.86 AW	26.01 TQ	INBLS	10/01-12/01
Metals and Plastics	South Bend MSA, IN	H	10.87 FQ	13.61 AW	17.45 TQ	INBLS	10/01-12/01
Metals and Plastics	Iowa	H	9.45 FQ	13.65 AW	17.25 TQ	IABLS	10/01-12/01
Metals and Plastics	Davenport-Moline-Rock Island MSA, IA-IL	H	9.94 FQ	13.99 AW	17.87 TQ	IABLS	10/01-12/01
Metals and Plastics	Kansas	H	7.46 FQ	13.74 AW	22.60 TQ	KSBLS	10/01-12/01
Metals and Plastics	Topeka MSA, KS	H	10.88 FQ	11.83 AW	13.21 TQ	KSBLS	10/01-12/01
Metals and Plastics	Wichita MSA, KS	H	11.77 FQ	18.48 AW	26.57 TQ	KSBLS	10/01-12/01
Metals and Plastics	Kentucky	H	9.67 FQ	13.34 AW	16.96 TQ	KYBLS	10/01-12/01
Metals and Plastics	Lexington MSA, KY	H	10.13 FQ	13.79 AW	18.87 TQ	KYBLS	10/01-12/01
Metals and Plastics	Louisville MSA, KY-IN	H	10.53 FQ	13.57 AW	17.01 TQ	KYBLS	10/01-12/01
Metals and Plastics	Louisiana	H	8.71 FQ	15.20 AW	24.51 TQ	LABLS	10/01-12/01
Metals and Plastics	Baton Rouge MSA, LA	H	10.56 FQ	18.70 AW	28.17 TQ	LABLS	10/01-12/01
Metals and Plastics	Houma MSA, LA	H	9.49 FQ	17.04 AW	38.88 TQ	LABLS	10/01-12/01
Metals and Plastics	Lafayette MSA, LA	H	8.78 FQ	12.59 AW	16.90 TQ	LABLS	10/01-12/01
Metals and Plastics	New Orleans MSA, LA	H	7.43 FQ	12.85 AW	20.31 TQ	LABLS	10/01-12/01
Metals and Plastics	Shreveport-Bossier City MSA, LA	H	10.72 FQ	12.08 AW	13.60 TQ	LABLS	10/01-12/01
Metals and Plastics	Maine	H	10.50 FQ	15.70 AW	21.11 TQ	MEBLS	10/01-12/01
Metals and Plastics	Maryland	H	10.83 FQ	17.18 AW	24.88 TQ	MDBLS	10/01-12/01
Metals and Plastics	Baltimore PMSA, MD	H	9.62 FQ	15.06 AW	20.60 TQ	MDBLS	10/01-12/01
Metals and Plastics	Massachusetts	H	11.71 FQ	16.93 AW	22.33 TQ	MABLS	10/01-12/01
Metals and Plastics	Boston PMSA, MA-NH	H	12.38 FQ	17.90 AW	24.23 TQ	MABLS	10/01-12/01
Metals and Plastics	Brockton PMSA, MA	H	12.25 FQ	17.47 AW	20.95 TQ	MABLS	10/01-12/01
Metals and Plastics	Lowell PMSA, MA-NH	H	9.90 FQ	15.84 AW	21.41 TQ	MABLS	10/01-12/01
Metals and Plastics	Springfield MSA, MA	H	11.58 FQ	16.04 AW	20.69 TQ	MABLS	10/01-12/01
Metals and Plastics	Worcester PMSA, MA-CT	H	11.95 FQ	17.38 AW	23.14 TQ	MABLS	10/01-12/01
Metals and Plastics	Michigan	H	10.18 FQ	17.23 AW	26.02 TQ	MIBLS	10/01-12/01
Metals and Plastics	Detroit PMSA, MI	H	9.50 FQ	17.51 AW	26.25 TQ	MIBLS	10/01-12/01
Metals and Plastics	Grand Rapids-Muskegon-Holland MSA, MI	H	10.38 FQ	19.30 AW	27.14 TQ	MIBLS	10/01-12/01
Metals and Plastics	Kalamazoo-Battle Creek MSA, MI	H	12.09 FQ	16.41 AW	23.03 TQ	MIBLS	10/01-12/01
Metals and Plastics	Lansing-East Lansing MSA, MI	H	11.06 FQ	14.75 AW	17.78 TQ	MIBLS	10/01-12/01

Occupation/Type/Industry	Location	Per	Low	Mid	High	Source	Date
Lathe and Turning Machine Tool Setter, Operator, and Tender							
Metals and Plastics	Saginaw-Bay City-Midland MSA, MI	H	10.21 FQ	18.12 AW	27.02 TQ	MIBLS	10/01-12/01
Metals and Plastics	Minnesota	H	11.64 FQ	16.65 AW	21.71 TQ	MNBLS	10/01-12/01
Metals and Plastics	Minneapolis-St. Paul MSA, MN-WI	H	12.66 FQ	17.15 AW	21.92 TQ	MNBLS	10/01-12/01
Metals and Plastics	Mississippi	H	8.96 FQ	13.48 AW	19.53 TQ	MSBLS	10/01-12/01
Metals and Plastics	Missouri	H	9.41 FQ	13.69 AW	17.86 TQ	MOBLS	10/01-12/01
Metals and Plastics	Kansas City MSA, MO-KS	H	9.61 FQ	14.33 AW	18.96 TQ	MOBLS	10/01-12/01
Metals and Plastics	St. Louis MSA, MO-IL	H	9.01 FQ	14.07 AW	20.55 TQ	MOBLS	10/01-12/01
Metals and Plastics	Springfield MSA, MO	H	9.43 FQ	12.37 AW	16.21 TQ	MOBLS	10/01-12/01
Metals and Plastics	Nebraska	H	9.30 FQ	13.05 AW	18.69 TQ	NEBLS	10/01-12/01
Metals and Plastics	Lincoln MSA, NE	H	9.61 FQ	13.07 AW	16.96 TQ	NEBLS	10/01-12/01
Metals and Plastics	Omaha MSA, NE-IA	H	9.35 FQ	13.34 AW	20.00 TQ	NEBLS	10/01-12/01
Metals and Plastics	Nevada	H	8.89 FQ	13.27 AW	18.94 TQ	NVBLS	10/01-12/01
Metals and Plastics	Reno MSA, NV	H	8.66 FQ	13.64 AW	20.56 TQ	NVBLS	10/01-12/01
Metals and Plastics	New Hampshire	H	9.82 FQ	14.51 AW	19.45 TQ	NHBLS	10/01-12/01
Metals and Plastics	Manchester PMSA, NH	H	9.59 FQ	12.09 AW	15.89 TQ	NHBLS	10/01-12/01
Metals and Plastics	Nashua PMSA, NH	H	9.66 FQ	15.46 AW	21.27 TQ	NHBLS	10/01-12/01
Metals and Plastics	New Jersey	H	7.14 FQ	14.03 AW	22.12 TQ	NJBLS	10/01-12/01
Metals and Plastics	Bergen-Passaic PMSA, NJ	H	8.63 FQ	14.10 AW	20.85 TQ	NJBLS	10/01-12/01
Metals and Plastics	Middlesex-Somerset-Hunterdon PMSA, NJ	H	6.16 FQ	13.94 AW	22.48 TQ	NJBLS	10/01-12/01
Metals and Plastics	Monmouth-Ocean PMSA, NJ	H	8.01 FQ	15.81 AW	22.02 TQ	NJBLS	10/01-12/01
Metals and Plastics	Newark PMSA, NJ	H	6.96 FQ	13.08 AW	23.27 TQ	NJBLS	10/01-12/01
Metals and Plastics	New Mexico	H	8.40 FQ	11.43 AW	15.12 TQ	NMBLS	10/01-12/01
Metals and Plastics	New York	H	9.54 FQ	15.03 AW	20.99 TQ	NYBLS	10/01-12/01
Metals and Plastics	Albany-Schenectady-Troy MSA, NY	H	11.72 FQ	15.08 AW	18.77 TQ	NYBLS	10/01-12/01
Metals and Plastics	Buffalo-Niagara Falls MSA, NY	H	8.84 FQ	14.67 AW	20.45 TQ	NYBLS	10/01-12/01
Metals and Plastics	Nassau-Suffolk PMSA, NY	H	8.07 FQ	13.53 AW	20.29 TQ	NYBLS	10/01-12/01
Metals and Plastics	New York PMSA, NY	H	8.57 FQ	13.41 AW	20.35 TQ	NYBLS	10/01-12/01
Metals and Plastics	Syracuse MSA, NY	H	9.70 FQ	13.31 AW	17.31 TQ	NYBLS	10/01-12/01
Metals and Plastics	Utica-Rome MSA, NY	H	7.75 FQ	12.23 AW	16.90 TQ	NYBLS	10/01-12/01
Metals and Plastics	North Carolina	H	10.43 FQ	14.78 AW	19.56 TQ	NCBLS	10/01-12/01
Metals and Plastics	Asheville MSA, NC	H	9.85 FQ	13.84 AW	17.41 TQ	NCBLS	10/01-12/01
Metals and Plastics	Charlotte-Gastonia-Rock Hill MSA, NC-SC	H	10.28 FQ	15.34 AW	20.96 TQ	NCBLS	10/01-12/01
Metals and Plastics	Greensboro-Winston-Salem-High Point MSA, NC	H	10.04 FQ	15.52 AW	21.23 TQ	NCBLS	10/01-12/01
Metals and Plastics	Raleigh-Durham-Chapel Hill MSA, NC	H	11.29 FQ	15.10 AW	19.20 TQ	NCBLS	10/01-12/01
Metals and Plastics	Ohio	H	9.92 FQ	15.16 AW	21.41 TQ	OHBLS	10/01-12/01
Metals and Plastics	Akron PMSA, OH	H	10.67 FQ	14.21 AW	17.23 TQ	OHBLS	10/01-12/01
Metals and Plastics	Canton-Massillon MSA, OH	H	11.18 FQ	16.50 AW	25.24 TQ	OHBLS	10/01-12/01
Metals and Plastics	Cincinnati PMSA, OH-KY-IN	H	10.50 FQ	14.49 AW	18.00 TQ	OHBLS	10/01-12/01
Metals and Plastics	Cleveland-Lorain-Elyria PMSA, OH	H	9.04 FQ	14.18 AW	19.70 TQ	OHBLS	10/01-12/01
Metals and Plastics	Columbus MSA, OH	H	9.18 FQ	11.88 AW	17.29 TQ	OHBLS	10/01-12/01
Metals and Plastics	Dayton-Springfield MSA, OH	H	11.64 FQ	18.39 AW	26.07 TQ	OHBLS	10/01-12/01
Metals and Plastics	Hamilton-Middletown PMSA, OH	H	8.04 FQ	12.00 AW	17.23 TQ	OHBLS	10/01-12/01
Metals and Plastics	Mansfield MSA, OH	H	11.25 FQ	14.48 AW	18.94 TQ	OHBLS	10/01-12/01
Metals and Plastics	Toledo MSA, OH	H	8.31 FQ	12.48 AW	17.07 TQ	OHBLS	10/01-12/01
Metals and Plastics	Youngstown-Warren MSA, OH	H	9.39 FQ	16.25 AW	26.32 TQ	OHBLS	10/01-12/01
Metals and Plastics	Oklahoma	H	7.37 FQ	11.91 AW	16.45 TQ	OKBLS	10/01-12/01
Metals and Plastics	Oklahoma City MSA, OK	H	7.07 FQ	10.21 AW	13.92 TQ	OKBLS	10/01-12/01
Metals and Plastics	Tulsa MSA, OK	H	9.90 FQ	14.30 AW	17.28 TQ	OKBLS	10/01-12/01
Metals and Plastics	Oregon	H	9.35 FQ	17.27 AW	26.65 TQ	ORBLS	10/01-12/01
Metals and Plastics	Portland-Vancouver PMSA, OR-WA	H	10.37 FQ	18.94 AW	27.42 TQ	ORBLS	10/01-12/01
Metals and Plastics	Pennsylvania	H	9.73 FQ	14.90 AW	20.85 TQ	PABLS	10/01-12/01
Metals and Plastics	Allentown-Bethlehem-Easton MSA, PA	H	12.13 FQ	15.44 AW	18.61 TQ	PABLS	10/01-12/01
Metals and Plastics	Erie MSA, PA	H	9.26 FQ	13.01 AW	17.86 TQ	PABLS	10/01-12/01
Metals and Plastics	Harrisburg-Lebanon-Carlisle MSA, PA	H	11.66 FQ	14.11 AW	17.32 TQ	PABLS	10/01-12/01
Metals and Plastics	Johnstown MSA, PA	H	8.39 FQ	12.26 AW	16.41 TQ	PABLS	10/01-12/01
Metals and Plastics	Lancaster MSA, PA	H	8.11 FQ	15.05 AW	21.12 TQ	PABLS	10/01-12/01
Metals and Plastics	Philadelphia PMSA, PA-NJ	H	11.76 FQ	17.55 AW	22.12 TQ	PABLS	10/01-12/01

AAW	Average annual wage	AOH	Average offered, high	ASH	Average starting, high	H	Hourly	M	Monthly	S	Special: hourly and annual
AE	Average entry wage	AOL	Average offered, low	ASL	Average starting, low	HI	Highest wage paid	MTC	Median total compensation	TQ	Third quartile wage
AEX	Average experienced wage	APH	Average pay, high range	AW	Average wage paid	HR	High end range	MW	Median wage paid	W	Weekly
AO	Average offered	APL	Average pay, low range	FQ	First quartile wage	LR	Low end range	SQ	Second quartile wage	Y	Yearly

Occupation/Type/Industry	Location	Per	Low	Mid	High	Source	Date
Lathe and Turning Machine Tool Setter, Operator, and Tender							
Metals and Plastics	Pittsburgh MSA, PA	H	9.61 FQ	13.86 AW	19.58 TQ	PABLS	10/01-12/01
Metals and Plastics	Reading MSA, PA	H	9.55 FQ	14.92 AW	24.63 TQ	PABLS	10/01-12/01
Metals and Plastics	Scranton-Wilkes-Barre-Hazleton MSA, PA	H	7.39 FQ	11.33 AW	15.99 TQ	PABLS	10/01-12/01
Metals and Plastics	York MSA, PA	H	12.34 FQ	17.08 AW	21.73 TQ	PABLS	10/01-12/01
Metals and Plastics	Rhode Island	H	8.49 FQ	13.39 AW	20.54 TQ	RIBLS	10/01-12/01
Metals and Plastics	Providence-Fall River-Warwick MSA, RI-MA	H	8.42 FQ	13.26 AW	20.34 TQ	RIBLS	10/01-12/01
Metals and Plastics	South Carolina	H	9.96 FQ	14.55 AW	19.36 TQ	SCBLS	10/01-12/01
Metals and Plastics	Charleston-North Charleston MSA, SC	H	8.98 FQ	14.87 AW	20.19 TQ	SCBLS	10/01-12/01
Metals and Plastics	Greenville-Spartanburg-Anderson MSA, SC	H	9.55 FQ	14.57 AW	20.28 TQ	SCBLS	10/01-12/01
Metals and Plastics	South Dakota	H	9.39 FQ	12.01 AW	14.93 TQ	SDBLS	10/01-12/01
Metals and Plastics	Tennessee	H	9.19 FQ	12.94 AW	17.48 TQ	TNBLS	10/01-12/01
Metals and Plastics	Chattanooga MSA, TN-GA	H	9.63 FQ	13.86 AW	18.46 TQ	TNBLS	10/01-12/01
Metals and Plastics	Johnson City-Kingsport-Bristol MSA, TN-VA	H	9.76 FQ	12.43 AW	16.10 TQ	TNBLS	10/01-12/01
Metals and Plastics	Knoxville MSA, TN	H	8.15 FQ	13.62 AW	17.29 TQ	TNBLS	10/01-12/01
Metals and Plastics	Memphis MSA, TN-AR-MS	H	10.72 FQ	13.45 AW	16.86 TQ	TNBLS	10/01-12/01
Metals and Plastics	Nashville MSA, TN	H	9.81 FQ	14.55 AW	19.69 TQ	TNBLS	10/01-12/01
Metals and Plastics	Texas	H	7.94 FQ	13.34 AW	20.17 TQ	TXBLS	10/01-12/01
Metals and Plastics	Austin-San Marcos MSA, TX	H	10.24 FQ	16.61 AW	22.16 TQ	TXBLS	10/01-12/01
Metals and Plastics	Beaumont-Port Arthur MSA, TX	H	9.08 FQ	14.04 AW	19.44 TQ	TXBLS	10/01-12/01
Metals and Plastics	Brazoria PMSA, TX	H	5.54 FQ	10.62 AW	18.85 TQ	TXBLS	10/01-12/01
Metals and Plastics	Dallas PMSA, TX	H	8.71 FQ	14.95 AW	21.04 TQ	TXBLS	10/01-12/01
Metals and Plastics	El Paso MSA, TX	H	7.28 FQ	10.13 AW	13.84 TQ	TXBLS	10/01-12/01
Metals and Plastics	Fort Worth-Arlington PMSA, TX	H	8.96 FQ	14.79 AW	25.57 TQ	TXBLS	10/01-12/01
Metals and Plastics	Houston PMSA, TX	H	8.08 FQ	13.06 AW	19.28 TQ	TXBLS	10/01-12/01
Metals and Plastics	Killeen-Temple MSA, TX	H	7.97 FQ	12.78 AW	19.65 TQ	TXBLS	10/01-12/01
Metals and Plastics	Lubbock MSA, TX	H	7.05 FQ	11.34 AW	15.96 TQ	TXBLS	10/01-12/01
Metals and Plastics	Odessa-Midland MSA, TX	H	9.15 FQ	12.30 AW	16.96 TQ	TXBLS	10/01-12/01
Metals and Plastics	San Antonio MSA, TX	H	9.32 FQ	12.48 AW	16.74 TQ	TXBLS	10/01-12/01
Metals and Plastics	Utah	H	8.53 FQ	13.49 AW	19.67 TQ	UTBLS	10/01-12/01
Metals and Plastics	Provo-Orem MSA, UT	H	8.94 FQ	14.11 AW	20.03 TQ	UTBLS	10/01-12/01
Metals and Plastics	Salt Lake City-Ogden MSA, UT	H	8.76 FQ	13.64 AW	19.78 TQ	UTBLS	10/01-12/01
Metals and Plastics	Vermont	H	9.48 FQ	13.16 AW	17.65 TQ	VTBLS	10/01-12/01
Metals and Plastics	Virginia	H	9.30 FQ	12.46 AW	16.26 TQ	VABLS	10/01-12/01
Metals and Plastics	Norfolk-Virginia Beach-Newport News MSA, VA-NC	H	6.48 FQ	13.47 AW	18.25 TQ	VABLS	10/01-12/01
Metals and Plastics	Washington	H	9.74 FQ	16.88 AW	25.06 TQ	WABLS	10/01-12/01
Metals and Plastics	Seattle-Bellevue-Everett PMSA, WA	H	12.13 FQ	18.84 AW	25.99 TQ	WABLS	10/01-12/01
Metals and Plastics	Spokane MSA, WA	H	8.41 FQ	11.37 AW	15.66 TQ	WABLS	10/01-12/01
Metals and Plastics	West Virginia	H	8.57 FQ	13.32 AW	18.56 TQ	WVBLS	10/01-12/01
Metals and Plastics	Charleston MSA, WV	H	9.44 FQ	14.89 AW	18.10 TQ	WVBLS	10/01-12/01
Metals and Plastics	Huntington-Ashland MSA, WV-KY-OH	H	10.23 FQ	13.88 AW	19.74 TQ	WVBLS	10/01-12/01
Metals and Plastics	Wisconsin	H	9.95 FQ	15.03 AW	20.70 TQ	WIBLS	10/01-12/01
Metals and Plastics	Appleton-Oshkosh-Neenah MSA, WI	H	10.57 FQ	16.51 AW	20.92 TQ	WIBLS	10/01-12/01
Metals and Plastics	Green Bay MSA, WI	H	13.81 FQ	16.88 AW	21.27 TQ	WIBLS	10/01-12/01
Metals and Plastics	Milwaukee-Waukesha PMSA, WI	H	9.72 FQ	15.64 AW	22.02 TQ	WIBLS	10/01-12/01
Metals and Plastics	Racine PMSA, WI	H	10.00 FQ	15.47 AW	21.30 TQ	WIBLS	10/01-12/01
Metals and Plastics	Puerto Rico	H	6.53 FQ	9.15 AW	12.71 TQ	PRBLS	10/01-12/01
Laundry and Dry-Cleaning Worker	Alabama	H	5.72 FQ	7.32 AW	9.08 TQ	ALBLS	10/01-12/01
	Alaska	H	7.36 FQ	10.24 AW	13.63 TQ	AKBLS	10/01-12/01
	Arizona	H	5.54 FQ	6.87 AW	8.80 TQ	AZBLS	10/01-12/01
	Arkansas	H	5.62 FQ	7.03 AW	9.04 TQ	ARBLS	10/01-12/01
	California	H	6.58 FQ	8.65 AW	11.65 TQ	CABLS	10/01-12/01
	Colorado	H	6.47 FQ	8.63 AW	11.13 TQ	COBLS	10/01-12/01
	Connecticut	H	7.00 FQ	9.71 AW	13.44 TQ	CTBLS	10/01-12/01
	Delaware	H	6.94 FQ	9.53 AW	12.47 TQ	DEBLS	10/01-12/01

AAW Average annual wage; AE Average entry wage; AEX Average experienced wage; AO Average offered; AOH Average offered, high; AOL Average offered, low; APH Average pay, high range; APL Average pay, low range; ASH Average starting, high; ASL Average starting, low; AW Average wage paid; FQ First quartile wage; H Hourly; HI Highest wage paid; HR High end range; LR Low end range; M Monthly; MTC Median total compensation; MW Median wage paid; SQ Second quartile wage; S Special: hourly and annual; TQ Third quartile wage; W Weekly; Y Yearly

Occupation/Type/Industry	Location	Per	Low	Mid	High	Source	Date
Laundry and Dry-Cleaning Worker	District of Columbia	H	6.65 FQ	10.48 AW	13.92 TQ	DCBLS	10/01-12/01
	Florida	H	5.74 FQ	7.54 AW	10.00 TQ	FLBLS	10/01-12/01
	Georgia	H	5.95 FQ	8.12 AW	10.69 TQ	GABLS	10/01-12/01
	Hawaii	H	6.39 FQ	10.47 AW	13.66 TQ	HIBLS	10/01-12/01
	Idaho	H	5.74 FQ	7.24 AW	8.79 TQ	IDBLS	10/01-12/01
	Illinois	H	5.85 FQ	8.16 AW	11.12 TQ	ILBLS	10/01-12/01
	Indiana	H	5.85 FQ	7.79 AW	10.35 TQ	INBLS	10/01-12/01
	Iowa	H	6.16 FQ	8.10 AW	10.53 TQ	IABLS	10/01-12/01
	Kansas	H	5.73 FQ	7.28 AW	9.20 TQ	KSBLS	10/01-12/01
	Kentucky	H	5.74 FQ	7.50 AW	9.82 TQ	KYBLS	10/01-12/01
	Louisiana	H	5.56 FQ	6.64 AW	8.37 TQ	LABLS	10/01-12/01
	Maine	H	5.97 FQ	7.95 AW	10.34 TQ	MEBLS	10/01-12/01
	Maryland	H	6.03 FQ	9.56 AW	15.65 TQ	MDBLS	10/01-12/01
	Massachusetts	H	6.93 FQ	9.22 AW	12.79 TQ	MABLS	10/01-12/01
	Michigan	H	6.29 FQ	8.85 AW	11.48 TQ	MIBLS	10/01-12/01
	Minnesota	H	7.21 FQ	9.65 AW	12.96 TQ	MNBLS	10/01-12/01
	Mississippi	H	5.60 FQ	7.08 AW	9.44 TQ	MSBLS	10/01-12/01
	Missouri	H	5.66 FQ	7.69 AW	10.46 TQ	MOBLS	10/01-12/01
	Montana	H	5.69 FQ	7.45 AW	9.74 TQ	MTBLS	10/01-12/01
	Nebraska	H	5.90 FQ	8.77 AW	10.66 TQ	NEBLS	10/01-12/01
	Nevada	H	6.25 FQ	8.54 AW	11.18 TQ	NVBLS	10/01-12/01
	New Hampshire	H	6.51 FQ	9.24 AW	12.51 TQ	NHBLS	10/01-12/01
	New Jersey	H	6.25 FQ	9.19 AW	13.18 TQ	NJBLS	10/01-12/01
	New Mexico	H	5.72 FQ	7.23 AW	9.05 TQ	NMBLS	10/01-12/01
	New York	H	6.00 FQ	9.70 AW	13.47 TQ	NYBLS	10/01-12/01
	North Carolina	H	5.93 FQ	7.90 AW	10.29 TQ	NCBLS	10/01-12/01
	North Dakota	H	5.90 FQ	7.95 AW	10.33 TQ	NDBLS	10/01-12/01
	Ohio	H	5.97 FQ	8.27 AW	11.03 TQ	OHBLS	10/01-12/01
	Oklahoma	H	5.66 FQ	7.17 AW	9.69 TQ	OKBLS	10/01-12/01
	Oregon	H	7.07 FQ	8.61 AW	10.70 TQ	ORBLS	10/01-12/01
	Pennsylvania	H	6.04 FQ	8.29 AW	10.91 TQ	PABLS	10/01-12/01
	Rhode Island	H	6.42 FQ	8.36 AW	12.21 TQ	RIBLS	10/01-12/01
	South Carolina	H	5.73 FQ	7.37 AW	9.64 TQ	SCBLS	10/01-12/01
	South Dakota	H	5.88 FQ	7.65 AW	9.68 TQ	SDBLS	10/01-12/01
	Tennessee	H	5.91 FQ	7.85 AW	10.43 TQ	TNBLS	10/01-12/01
	Texas	H	5.67 FQ	7.40 AW	10.15 TQ	TXBLS	10/01-12/01
	Utah	H	6.18 FQ	8.07 AW	10.30 TQ	UTBLS	10/01-12/01
	Vermont	H	6.59 FQ	8.53 AW	11.33 TQ	VTBLS	10/01-12/01
	Virginia	H	5.89 FQ	7.99 AW	10.44 TQ	VABLS	10/01-12/01
	Washington	H	7.04 FQ	9.51 AW	12.99 TQ	WABLS	10/01-12/01
	West Virginia	H	5.72 FQ	7.62 AW	10.26 TQ	WVBLS	10/01-12/01
	Wisconsin	H	5.86 FQ	8.07 AW	10.61 TQ	WIBLS	10/01-12/01
	Wyoming	H	5.81 FQ	7.57 AW	10.04 TQ	WYBLS	10/01-12/01
	Puerto Rico	H	5.53 FQ	6.55 AW	8.25 TQ	PRBLS	10/01-12/01
	Virgin Islands	H	5.69 FQ	7.20 AW	8.67 TQ	VIBLS	10/01-12/01
	Guam	H	5.54 FQ	6.58 AW	8.28 TQ	GUBLS	10/01-12/01
Law Clerk	Alabama	Y	13990 FQ	24170 AW	40000 TQ	ALBLS	10/01-12/01
	Birmingham MSA, AL	Y	13800 FQ	22820 AW	40200 TQ	ALBLS	10/01-12/01
	Alaska	Y	29400 FQ	36780 AW	43720 TQ	AKBLS	10/01-12/01
	Phoenix-Mesa MSA, AZ	Y	23940 FQ	34870 AW	49850 TQ	AZBLS	10/01-12/01
	Arkansas	Y	13590 FQ	25720 AW	40040 TQ	ARBLS	10/01-12/01
	Fayetteville-Springdale-Rogers MSA, AR	Y	18880 FQ	21860 AW	26920 TQ	ARBLS	10/01-12/01
	Little Rock-North Little Rock MSA, AR	Y	12720 FQ	25820 AW	41590 TQ	ARBLS	10/01-12/01
	California	Y	23040 FQ	33250 AW	48280 TQ	CABLS	10/01-12/01
	Fresno MSA, CA	Y	20170 FQ	33910 AW	62270 TQ	CABLS	10/01-12/01
	Los Angeles-Long Beach PMSA, CA	Y	24700 FQ	34660 AW	46970 TQ	CABLS	10/01-12/01
	Oakland PMSA, CA	Y	22950 FQ	27180 AW	30010 TQ	CABLS	10/01-12/01
	Orange County PMSA, CA	Y	24090 FQ	37670 AW	56130 TQ	CABLS	10/01-12/01
	Redding MSA, CA	Y	23240 FQ	28750 AW	37090 TQ	CABLS	10/01-12/01
	Riverside-San Bernardino PMSA, CA	Y	15560 FQ	28970 AW	43710 TQ	CABLS	10/01-12/01
	Sacramento PMSA, CA	Y	16730 FQ	30040 AW	43070 TQ	CABLS	10/01-12/01
	San Diego MSA, CA	Y	28250 FQ	42410 AW	50840 TQ	CABLS	10/01-12/01
	San Francisco PMSA, CA	Y	27480 FQ	45180 AW	77690 TQ	CABLS	10/01-12/01
	San Jose PMSA, CA	Y	22120 FQ	33500 AW	43590 TQ	CABLS	10/01-12/01
	San Luis Obispo-Atascadero-Paso Robles MSA, CA	Y	31010 FQ	34000 AW	37560 TQ	CABLS	10/01-12/01

AAW	Average annual wage	**AOH**	Average offered, high	**ASH**	Average starting, high	**H**	Hourly	**M**	Monthly	**S**	Special: hourly and annual
AE	Average entry wage	**AOL**	Average offered, low	**ASL**	Average starting, low	**HI**	Highest wage paid	**MTC**	Median total compensation	**TQ**	Third quartile wage
AEX	Average experienced wage	**APH**	Average pay, high range	**AW**	Average wage paid	**HR**	High end range	**MW**	Median wage paid	**W**	Weekly
AO	Average offered	**APL**	Average pay, low range	**FQ**	First quartile wage	**LR**	Low end range	**SQ**	Second quartile wage	**Y**	Yearly

Occupation/Type/Industry	Location	Per	Low	Mid	High	Source	Date
Law Clerk	Colorado	Y	25310 FQ	35630 AW	43950 TQ	COBLS	10/01-12/01
	Denver PMSA, CO	Y	26080 FQ	36550 AW	44150 TQ	COBLS	10/01-12/01
	Connecticut	Y	23680 FQ	38100 AW	62270 TQ	CTBLS	10/01-12/01
	Bridgeport PMSA, CT	Y	15780 FQ	28670 AW	42330 TQ	CTBLS	10/01-12/01
	Hartford MSA, CT	Y	23480 FQ	37140 AW	59930 TQ	CTBLS	10/01-12/01
	New Haven-Meriden PMSA, CT	Y	25240 FQ	35630 AW	44470 TQ	CTBLS	10/01-12/01
	Stamford-Norwalk PMSA, CT	Y	32130 FQ	53320 AW	84850 TQ	CTBLS	10/01-12/01
	Delaware	Y	21240 FQ	35020 AW	47400 TQ	DEBLS	10/01-12/01
	Wilmington-Newark PMSA, DE-MD	Y	24940 FQ	38630 AW	54660 TQ	DEBLS	10/01-12/01
	District of Columbia	Y	26040 FQ	38890 AW	52640 TQ	DCBLS	10/01-12/01
	Washington PMSA, DC-MD-VA-WV	Y	25110 FQ	37470 AW	50810 TQ	DCBLS	10/01-12/01
	Florida	Y	18920 FQ	33640 AW	58600 TQ	FLBLS	10/01-12/01
	Fort Lauderdale PMSA, FL	Y	23210 FQ	27950 AW	36260 TQ	FLBLS	10/01-12/01
	Jacksonville MSA, FL	Y	16270 FQ	25240 AW	38310 TQ	FLBLS	10/01-12/01
	Lakeland-Winter Haven MSA, FL	Y	21280 FQ	36710 AW	74250 TQ	FLBLS	10/01-12/01
	Melbourne-Titusville-Palm Bay MSA, FL	Y	18790 FQ	22350 AW	23000 TQ	FLBLS	10/01-12/01
	Miami PMSA, FL	Y	24950 FQ	42290 AW	73740 TQ	FLBLS	10/01-12/01
	Orlando MSA, FL	Y	16000 FQ	24850 AW	40230 TQ	FLBLS	10/01-12/01
	Pensacola MSA, FL	Y	15580 FQ	26130 AW	39340 TQ	FLBLS	10/01-12/01
	Sarasota-Bradenton MSA, FL	Y	20120 FQ	30250 AW	40470 TQ	FLBLS	10/01-12/01
	Tallahassee MSA, FL	Y	24750 FQ	57200 AW	102440 TQ	FLBLS	10/01-12/01
	Tampa-St. Petersburg-Clearwater MSA, FL	Y	23150 FQ	36790 AW	54190 TQ	FLBLS	10/01-12/01
	West Palm Beach-Boca Raton MSA, FL	Y	25210 FQ	48600 AW	92690 TQ	FLBLS	10/01-12/01
	Georgia	Y	15070 FQ	29940 AW	43430 TQ	GABLS	10/01-12/01
	Atlanta MSA, GA	Y	22970 FQ	34250 AW	48200 TQ	GABLS	10/01-12/01
	Augusta-Aiken MSA, GA-SC	Y	12490 FQ	20140 AW	28680 TQ	GABLS	10/01-12/01
	Macon MSA, GA	Y	14990 FQ	30260 AW	42650 TQ	GABLS	10/01-12/01
	Hawaii	Y	24220 FQ	33210 AW	42860 TQ	HIBLS	10/01-12/01
	Honolulu MSA, HI	Y	24180 FQ	33600 AW	43150 TQ	HIBLS	10/01-12/01
	Idaho	Y	23310 FQ	43850 AW	113390 TQ	IDBLS	10/01-12/01
	Boise City MSA, ID	Y	28350 FQ	53910 AW		IDBLS	10/01-12/01
	Illinois	Y	15130 FQ	29520 AW	43790 TQ	ILBLS	10/01-12/01
	Chicago PMSA, IL	Y	15510 FQ	29910 AW	43270 TQ	ILBLS	10/01-12/01
	Rockford MSA, IL	Y	14900 FQ	26030 AW	47150 TQ	ILBLS	10/01-12/01
	Springfield MSA, IL	Y	14710 FQ	29180 AW	47590 TQ	ILBLS	10/01-12/01
	Indiana	Y	16160 FQ	29370 AW	48350 TQ	INBLS	10/01-12/01
	Evansville-Henderson MSA, IN-KY	Y	13270 FQ	29300 AW	43040 TQ	INBLS	10/01-12/01
	Fort Wayne MSA, IN	Y	29120 FQ	35680 AW	44680 TQ	INBLS	10/01-12/01
	Gary PMSA, IN	Y	13270 FQ	25260 AW	37760 TQ	INBLS	10/01-12/01
	Indianapolis MSA, IN	Y	20520 FQ	35170 AW	55240 TQ	INBLS	10/01-12/01
	South Bend MSA, IN	Y	18540 FQ	22720 AW	29690 TQ	INBLS	10/01-12/01
	Iowa	Y	20010 FQ	30550 AW	45760 TQ	IABLS	10/01-12/01
	Des Moines MSA, IA	Y	23600 FQ	34110 AW	50190 TQ	IABLS	10/01-12/01
	Kansas	Y	15250 FQ	25850 AW	40730 TQ	KSBLS	10/01-12/01
	Topeka MSA, KS	Y	16000 FQ	22960 AW	31350 TQ	KSBLS	10/01-12/01
	Wichita MSA, KS	Y	14950 FQ	26610 AW	41040 TQ	KSBLS	10/01-12/01
	Kentucky	Y	15980 FQ	27760 AW	41670 TQ	KYBLS	10/01-12/01
	Lexington MSA, KY	Y	21520 FQ	29830 AW	42280 TQ	KYBLS	10/01-12/01
	Louisville MSA, KY-IN	Y	16560 FQ	28690 AW	42790 TQ	KYBLS	10/01-12/01
	Louisiana	Y	22410 FQ	29250 AW	42170 TQ	LABLS	10/01-12/01
	Baton Rouge MSA, LA	Y	22810 FQ	29060 AW	42950 TQ	LABLS	10/01-12/01
	New Orleans MSA, LA	Y	23930 FQ	32100 AW	44900 TQ	LABLS	10/01-12/01
	Shreveport-Bossier City MSA, LA	Y	20020 FQ	31110 AW	42540 TQ	LABLS	10/01-12/01
	Maine	Y	24950 FQ	36520 AW	44510 TQ	MEBLS	10/01-12/01
	Portland MSA, ME	Y	26850 FQ	36060 AW	43620 TQ	MEBLS	10/01-12/01
	Maryland	Y	25510 FQ	35150 AW	46690 TQ	MDBLS	10/01-12/01
	Baltimore PMSA, MD	Y	24530 FQ	33120 AW	42670 TQ	MDBLS	10/01-12/01
	Massachusetts	Y	24470 FQ	36320 AW	51030 TQ	MABLS	10/01-12/01
	Boston PMSA, MA-NH	Y	23920 FQ	36230 AW	50930 TQ	MABLS	10/01-12/01
	Michigan	Y	23210 FQ	30960 AW	42670 TQ	MIBLS	10/01-12/01
	Detroit PMSA, MI	Y	23260 FQ	30850 AW	42640 TQ	MIBLS	10/01-12/01
	Grand Rapids-Muskegon-Holland MSA, MI	Y	23910 FQ	32520 AW	42360 TQ	MIBLS	10/01-12/01

AAW	Average annual wage	**AOH**	Average offered, high	**ASH**	Average starting, high	**H**	Hourly	**M**	Monthly	**S**	Special: hourly and annual
AE	Average entry wage	**AOL**	Average offered, low	**ASL**	Average starting, low	**HI**	Highest wage paid	**MTC**	Median total compensation	**TQ**	Third quartile wage
AEX	Average experienced wage	**APH**	Average pay, high range	**AW**	Average wage paid	**HR**	High end range	**MW**	Median wage paid	**W**	Weekly
AO	Average offered	**APL**	Average pay, low range	**FQ**	First quartile wage	**LR**	Low end range	**SQ**	Second quartile wage	**Y**	Yearly

Occupation/Type/Industry	Location	Per	Low	Mid	High	Source	Date
Law Clerk	Kalamazoo-Battle Creek MSA, MI	Y	35510 FQ	39370 AW	44200 TQ	MIBLS	10/01-12/01
	Lansing-East Lansing MSA, MI	Y	17780 FQ	33550 AW	43950 TQ	MIBLS	10/01-12/01
	Minnesota	Y	27240 FQ	39750 AW	74660 TQ	MNBLS	10/01-12/01
	Minneapolis-St. Paul MSA, MN-WI	Y	26720 FQ	42000 AW	79080 TQ	MNBLS	10/01-12/01
	Mississippi	Y	24570 FQ	32000 AW	39530 TQ	MSBLS	10/01-12/01
	Jackson MSA, MS	Y	29670 FQ	33570 AW	38960 TQ	MSBLS	10/01-12/01
	Missouri	Y	14670 FQ	29030 AW	42000 TQ	MOBLS	10/01-12/01
	Kansas City MSA, MO-KS	Y	11740 FQ	26500 AW	41840 TQ	MOBLS	10/01-12/01
	St. Louis MSA, MO-IL	Y	23240 FQ	30510 AW	41810 TQ	MOBLS	10/01-12/01
	Montana	Y	15030 FQ	27220 AW	40750 TQ	MTBLS	10/01-12/01
	Billings MSA, MT	Y	24240 FQ	31080 AW	41270 TQ	MTBLS	10/01-12/01
	Nebraska	Y	16600 FQ	27970 AW	43320 TQ	NEBLS	10/01-12/01
	Lincoln MSA, NE	Y	17010 FQ	24500 AW	33160 TQ	NEBLS	10/01-12/01
	Omaha MSA, NE-IA	Y	16750 FQ	28900 AW	44160 TQ	NEBLS	10/01-12/01
	Nevada	Y	23180 FQ	41050 AW	55120 TQ	NVBLS	10/01-12/01
	Las Vegas MSA, NV-AZ	Y	21690 FQ	40100 AW	55230 TQ	NVBLS	10/01-12/01
	Reno MSA, NV	Y	37240 FQ	43510 AW	53510 TQ	NVBLS	10/01-12/01
	New Hampshire	Y	24900 FQ	35730 AW	44670 TQ	NHBLS	10/01-12/01
	Newark PMSA, NJ	Y	25370 FQ	33710 AW	43650 TQ	NJBLS	10/01-12/01
	New Mexico	Y	23270 FQ	33360 AW	43100 TQ	NMBLS	10/01-12/01
	Albuquerque MSA, NM	Y	23520 FQ	33430 AW	43110 TQ	NMBLS	10/01-12/01
	New York	Y	21260 FQ	39790 AW	66180 TQ	NYBLS	10/01-12/01
	Albany-Schenectady-Troy MSA, NY	Y	19850 FQ	28390 AW	39710 TQ	NYBLS	10/01-12/01
	Buffalo-Niagara Falls MSA, NY	Y	18990 FQ	27110 AW	39830 TQ	NYBLS	10/01-12/01
	Nassau-Suffolk PMSA, NY	Y	24400 FQ	34490 AW	44450 TQ	NYBLS	10/01-12/01
	New York PMSA, NY	Y	22510 FQ	45440 AW	101330 TQ	NYBLS	10/01-12/01
	Rochester MSA, NY	Y	24610 FQ	44700 AW	99920 TQ	NYBLS	10/01-12/01
	Syracuse MSA, NY	Y	19600 FQ	35170 AW	57310 TQ	NYBLS	10/01-12/01
	North Carolina	Y	22800 FQ	35680 AW	45850 TQ	NCBLS	10/01-12/01
	Charlotte-Gastonia-Rock Hill MSA, NC-SC	Y	18870 FQ	29590 AW	43160 TQ	NCBLS	10/01-12/01
	Greensboro-Winston-Salem-High Point MSA, NC	Y	26480 FQ	37910 AW	53150 TQ	NCBLS	10/01-12/01
	Raleigh-Durham-Chapel Hill MSA, NC	Y	28540 FQ	36590 AW	44000 TQ	NCBLS	10/01-12/01
	North Dakota	Y	14110 FQ	26490 AW	42270 TQ	NDBLS	10/01-12/01
	Ohio	Y	16420 FQ	27850 AW	42550 TQ	OHBLS	10/01-12/01
	Akron PMSA, OH	Y	14810 FQ	27620 AW	41300 TQ	OHBLS	10/01-12/01
	Canton-Massillon MSA, OH	Y	18700 FQ	26010 AW	40980 TQ	OHBLS	10/01-12/01
	Cincinnati PMSA, OH-KY-IN	Y	17860 FQ	24720 AW	36850 TQ	OHBLS	10/01-12/01
	Cleveland-Lorain-Elyria PMSA, OH	Y	19870 FQ	32130 AW	46390 TQ	OHBLS	10/01-12/01
	Columbus MSA, OH	Y	11460 FQ	22010 AW	39760 TQ	OHBLS	10/01-12/01
	Dayton-Springfield MSA, OH	Y	18910 FQ	30590 AW	43480 TQ	OHBLS	10/01-12/01
	Toledo MSA, OH	Y	17590 FQ	30960 AW	50580 TQ	OHBLS	10/01-12/01
	Youngstown-Warren MSA, OH	Y	19060 FQ	28830 AW	43910 TQ	OHBLS	10/01-12/01
	Oklahoma	Y	15910 FQ	27920 AW	44160 TQ	OKBLS	10/01-12/01
	Oklahoma City MSA, OK	Y	24280 FQ	34250 AW	50070 TQ	OKBLS	10/01-12/01
	Tulsa MSA, OK	Y	14150 FQ	23370 AW	38330 TQ	OKBLS	10/01-12/01
	Oregon	Y	23960 FQ	35190 AW	44100 TQ	ORBLS	10/01-12/01
	Eugene-Springfield MSA, OR	Y	25590 FQ	35950 AW	46720 TQ	ORBLS	10/01-12/01
	Portland-Vancouver PMSA, OR-WA	Y	28210 FQ	36070 AW	43500 TQ	ORBLS	10/01-12/01
	Pennsylvania	Y	22720 FQ	36450 AW	44870 TQ	PABLS	10/01-12/01
	Allentown-Bethlehem-Easton MSA, PA	Y	21420 FQ	30840 AW	42400 TQ	PABLS	10/01-12/01
	Philadelphia PMSA, PA-NJ	Y	23460 FQ	35720 AW	43850 TQ	PABLS	10/01-12/01
	Pittsburgh MSA, PA	Y	20230 FQ	31590 AW	42880 TQ	PABLS	10/01-12/01
	Scranton-Wilkes-Barre-Hazleton MSA, PA	Y	16300 FQ	31580 AW	42780 TQ	PABLS	10/01-12/01
	Rhode Island	Y	29130 FQ	40960 AW	55610 TQ	RIBLS	10/01-12/01
	Providence-Fall River-Warwick MSA, RI-MA	Y	29020 FQ	41110 AW	55910 TQ	RIBLS	10/01-12/01
	South Carolina	Y	18140 FQ	22590 AW	30320 TQ	SCBLS	10/01-12/01
	Charleston-North Charleston MSA, SC	Y	18680 FQ	23320 AW	27620 TQ	SCBLS	10/01-12/01
	Columbia MSA, SC	Y	18810 FQ	24170 AW	35860 TQ	SCBLS	10/01-12/01

AAW Average annual wage; AE Average entry wage; AEX Average experienced wage; AO Average offered; AOH Average offered, high; AOL Average offered, low; APH Average pay, high range; APL Average pay, low range; ASH Average starting, high; ASL Average starting, low; AW Average wage paid; FQ First quartile wage; H Hourly; HI Highest wage paid; HR High end range; LR Low end range; M Monthly; MTC Median total compensation; MW Median wage paid; SQ Second quartile wage; S Special: hourly and annual; TQ Third quartile wage; W Weekly; Y Yearly

Occupation/Type/Industry	Location	Per	Low	Mid	High	Source	Date
Law Clerk	Greenville-Spartanburg-Anderson MSA, SC	Y	17810 FQ	22260 AW	33850 TQ	SCBLS	10/01-12/01
	South Dakota	Y	28290 FQ	32690 AW	41130 TQ	SDBLS	10/01-12/01
	Tennessee	Y	15020 FQ	26390 AW	42380 TQ	TNBLS	10/01-12/01
	Chattanooga MSA, TN-GA	Y	13420 FQ	26980 AW	41300 TQ	TNBLS	10/01-12/01
	Knoxville MSA, TN	Y	12180 FQ	22970 AW	38860 TQ	TNBLS	10/01-12/01
	Memphis MSA, TN-AR-MS	Y	13540 FQ	28630 AW	44610 TQ	TNBLS	10/01-12/01
	Nashville MSA, TN	Y	17300 FQ	28620 AW	41820 TQ	TNBLS	10/01-12/01
	Texas	Y	17180 FQ	35020 AW	54260 TQ	TXBLS	10/01-12/01
	Austin-San Marcos MSA, TX	Y	23340 FQ	41960 AW	67050 TQ	TXBLS	10/01-12/01
	Beaumont-Port Arthur MSA, TX	Y	14030 FQ	41460 AW	70640 TQ	TXBLS	10/01-12/01
	Dallas PMSA, TX	Y	21440 FQ	33680 AW	44280 TQ	TXBLS	10/01-12/01
	Fort Worth-Arlington PMSA, TX	Y	18870 FQ	30320 AW	43800 TQ	TXBLS	10/01-12/01
	Houston PMSA, TX	Y	26050 FQ	43090 AW	55040 TQ	TXBLS	10/01-12/01
	Killeen-Temple MSA, TX	Y	15360 FQ	23840 AW	41520 TQ	TXBLS	10/01-12/01
	San Antonio MSA, TX	Y	24100 FQ	32390 AW	42750 TQ	TXBLS	10/01-12/01
	Utah	Y	18800 FQ	29150 AW	42300 TQ	UTBLS	10/01-12/01
	Provo-Orem MSA, UT	Y	18910 FQ	24010 AW	28310 TQ	UTBLS	10/01-12/01
	Salt Lake City-Ogden MSA, UT	Y	20160 FQ	32530 AW	44330 TQ	UTBLS	10/01-12/01
	Vermont	Y	22870 FQ	27480 AW	34720 TQ	VTBLS	10/01-12/01
	Burlington MSA, VT	Y	22830 FQ	27050 AW	33860 TQ	VTBLS	10/01-12/01
	Virginia	Y	24190 FQ	34690 AW	43980 TQ	VABLS	10/01-12/01
	Norfolk-Virginia Beach-Newport News MSA, VA-NC	Y	24990 FQ	33300 AW	42760 TQ	VABLS	10/01-12/01
	Richmond-Petersburg MSA, VA	Y	25530 FQ	34140 AW	43700 TQ	VABLS	10/01-12/01
	Washington	Y	20740 FQ	35630 AW	44620 TQ	WABLS	10/01-12/01
	Seattle-Bellevue-Everett PMSA, WA	Y	20730 FQ	40160 AW	98290 TQ	WABLS	10/01-12/01
	Spokane MSA, WA	Y	19440 FQ	28190 AW	39270 TQ	WABLS	10/01-12/01
	West Virginia	Y	17320 FQ	33810 AW	50590 TQ	WVBLS	10/01-12/01
	Charleston MSA, WV	Y	24960 FQ	38900 AW	65770 TQ	WVBLS	10/01-12/01
	Huntington-Ashland MSA, WV-KY-OH	Y	22790 FQ	31340 AW	43170 TQ	WVBLS	10/01-12/01
	Wisconsin	Y	22940 FQ	30070 AW	42050 TQ	WIBLS	10/01-12/01
	Madison MSA, WI	Y	23360 FQ	32470 AW	45040 TQ	WIBLS	10/01-12/01
	Milwaukee-Waukesha PMSA, WI	Y	22900 FQ	29000 AW	40600 TQ	WIBLS	10/01-12/01
	Wyoming	Y	20230 FQ	27580 AW	36340 TQ	WYBLS	10/01-12/01
	Puerto Rico	Y	20030 FQ	30660 AW	42190 TQ	PRBLS	10/01-12/01
	Virgin Islands	Y	28940 FQ	38790 AW	44900 TQ	VIBLS	10/01-12/01
Law Teacher							
Postsecondary	Alabama	Y	24430 FQ	63370 AW	128560 TQ	ALBLS	10/01-12/01
Postsecondary	California	Y	44960 FQ	82090 AW	137210 TQ	CABLS	10/01-12/01
Postsecondary	Los Angeles-Long Beach PMSA, CA	Y	44270 FQ	95770 AW		CABLS	10/01-12/01
Postsecondary	Orange County PMSA, CA	Y	37550 FQ	78700 AW	136110 TQ	CABLS	10/01-12/01
Postsecondary	District of Columbia	Y	49040 FQ	90360 AW		DCBLS	10/01-12/01
Postsecondary	Washington PMSA, DC-MD-VA-WV	Y	35890 FQ	87270 AW		DCBLS	10/01-12/01
Postsecondary	Florida	Y	36750 FQ	81970 AW	142930 TQ	FLBLS	10/01-12/01
Postsecondary	Gainesville MSA, FL	Y	47030 FQ	90870 AW		FLBLS	10/01-12/01
Postsecondary	Miami PMSA, FL	Y	41470 FQ	84260 AW	128060 TQ	FLBLS	10/01-12/01
Postsecondary	Tallahassee MSA, FL	Y	50220 FQ	97500 AW		FLBLS	10/01-12/01
Postsecondary	Georgia	Y	35950 FQ	91790 AW		GABLS	10/01-12/01
Postsecondary	Hawaii	Y	34830 FQ	80640 AW	136330 TQ	HIBLS	10/01-12/01
Postsecondary	Honolulu MSA, HI	Y	34830 FQ	80640 AW	136330 TQ	HIBLS	10/01-12/01
Postsecondary	Illinois	Y	30030 FQ	71370 AW	118700 TQ	ILBLS	10/01-12/01
Postsecondary	Chicago PMSA, IL	Y	38230 FQ	74690 AW	132180 TQ	ILBLS	10/01-12/01
Postsecondary	Indiana	Y	34610 FQ	81420 AW	135110 TQ	INBLS	10/01-12/01
Postsecondary	Kansas	Y	27560 FQ	80550 AW		KSBLS	10/01-12/01
Postsecondary	Louisiana	Y	30390 FQ	70280 AW	116750 TQ	LABLS	10/01-12/01
Postsecondary	Maine	Y	40100 FQ	73720 AW	110710 TQ	MEBLS	10/01-12/01
Postsecondary	Massachusetts	Y	34250 FQ	83630 AW		MABLS	10/01-12/01
Postsecondary	Boston PMSA, MA-NH	Y	35370 FQ	84930 AW		MABLS	10/01-12/01
Postsecondary	Springfield MSA, MA	Y	16790 FQ	74130 AW		MABLS	10/01-12/01
Postsecondary	Michigan	Y	45630 FQ	99480 AW	140850 TQ	MIBLS	10/01-12/01
Postsecondary	Detroit PMSA, MI	Y	35380 FQ	93900 AW	140240 TQ	MIBLS	10/01-12/01

AAW	Average annual wage	AOH	Average offered, high	ASH	Average starting, high	H	Hourly	M	Monthly	S	Special: hourly and annual
AE	Average entry wage	AOL	Average offered, low	ASL	Average starting, low	HI	Highest wage paid	MTC	Median total compensation	TQ	Third quartile wage
AEX	Average experienced wage	APH	Average pay, high range	AW	Average wage paid	HR	High end range	MW	Median wage paid	W	Weekly
AO	Average offered	APL	Average pay, low range	FQ	First quartile wage	LR	Low end range	SQ	Second quartile wage	Y	Yearly

Occupation/Type/Industry	Location	Per	Low	Mid	High	Source	Date
Law Teacher							
Postsecondary	Minnesota	Y	43060 FQ	95200 AW		MNBLS	10/01-12/01
Postsecondary	Minneapolis-St. Paul MSA, MN-WI	Y	47670 FQ	98980 AW		MNBLS	10/01-12/01
Postsecondary	Mississippi	Y	36750 FQ	69650 AW	111260 TQ	MSBLS	10/01-12/01
Postsecondary	Missouri	Y	34840 FQ	82300 AW	144590 TQ	MOBLS	10/01-12/01
Postsecondary	St. Louis MSA, MO-IL	Y	36440 FQ	84740 AW		MOBLS	10/01-12/01
Postsecondary	Nebraska	Y	42580 FQ	91110 AW		NEBLS	10/01-12/01
Postsecondary	Nevada	Y	22870 FQ	61640 AW	124210 TQ	NVBLS	10/01-12/01
Postsecondary	Las Vegas MSA, NV-AZ	Y	22120 FQ	67750 AW	132200 TQ	NVBLS	10/01-12/01
Postsecondary	New Hampshire	Y	20060 FQ	68550 AW	115790 TQ	NHBLS	10/01-12/01
Postsecondary	New Jersey	Y	34480 FQ	79080 AW		NJBLS	10/01-12/01
Postsecondary	Newark PMSA, NJ	Y	35890 FQ	71340 AW	134680 TQ	NJBLS	10/01-12/01
Postsecondary	New York	Y	49790 FQ	96700 AW		NYBLS	10/01-12/01
Postsecondary	New York PMSA, NY	Y	63050 FQ	100110 AW		NYBLS	10/01-12/01
Postsecondary	North Carolina	Y	33290 FQ	57000 AW	122460 TQ	NCBLS	10/01-12/01
Postsecondary	Charlotte-Gastonia-Rock Hill MSA, NC-SC	Y	36970 FQ	40190 AW	45560 TQ	NCBLS	10/01-12/01
Postsecondary	Greensboro-Winston-Salem-High Point MSA, NC	Y	37790 FQ	43020 AW	52210 TQ	NCBLS	10/01-12/01
Postsecondary	Raleigh-Durham-Chapel Hill MSA, NC	Y	25060 FQ	73570 AW	145230 TQ	NCBLS	10/01-12/01
Postsecondary	Ohio	Y	24450 FQ	70570 AW	118510 TQ	OHBLS	10/01-12/01
Postsecondary	Dayton-Springfield MSA, OH	Y	17190 FQ	31070 AW	53580 TQ	OHBLS	10/01-12/01
Postsecondary	Oklahoma	Y	40660 FQ	82990 AW	120520 TQ	OKBLS	10/01-12/01
Postsecondary	Pennsylvania	Y	24310 FQ	66930 AW		PABLS	10/01-12/01
Postsecondary	Philadelphia PMSA, PA-NJ	Y	24210 FQ	54650 AW	130160 TQ	PABLS	10/01-12/01
Postsecondary	South Carolina	Y	29240 FQ	35900 AW	49600 TQ	SCBLS	10/01-12/01
Postsecondary	Tennessee	Y	28360 FQ	81390 AW		TNBLS	10/01-12/01
Postsecondary	Knoxville MSA, TN	Y	39260 FQ	88550 AW	140490 TQ	TNBLS	10/01-12/01
Postsecondary	Texas	Y	38390 FQ	83320 AW	140200 TQ	TXBLS	10/01-12/01
Postsecondary	Fort Worth-Arlington PMSA, TX	Y	25480 FQ	47270 AW	71380 TQ	TXBLS	10/01-12/01
Postsecondary	Vermont	Y	30060 FQ	46730 AW	99310 TQ	VTBLS	10/01-12/01
Postsecondary	Virginia	Y	26190 FQ	83390 AW		VABLS	10/01-12/01
Postsecondary	Norfolk-Virginia Beach-Newport News MSA, VA-NC	Y	36370 FQ	82890 AW		VABLS	10/01-12/01
Postsecondary	Washington	Y	40780 FQ	84640 AW	137060 TQ	WABLS	10/01-12/01
Postsecondary	Puerto Rico	Y	24930 FQ	63290 AW	131740 TQ	PRBLS	10/01-12/01
Lawyer	Alabama	Y	48050 FQ	87280 AW		ALBLS	10/01-12/01
	Birmingham MSA, AL	Y	48920 FQ	87490 AW		ALBLS	10/01-12/01
	Huntsville MSA, AL	Y	61060 FQ	93140 AW		ALBLS	10/01-12/01
	Mobile MSA, AL	Y	49250 FQ	81820 AW	128620 TQ	ALBLS	10/01-12/01
	Montgomery MSA, AL	Y	50400 FQ	89080 AW		ALBLS	10/01-12/01
	Alaska	Y	44460 FQ	85370 AW	139480 TQ	AKBLS	10/01-12/01
	Anchorage MSA, AK	Y	46140 FQ	87840 AW	144050 TQ	AKBLS	10/01-12/01
	Arizona	Y	44500 FQ	89040 AW		AZBLS	10/01-12/01
	Phoenix-Mesa MSA, AZ	Y	57040 FQ	98710 AW		AZBLS	10/01-12/01
	Arkansas	Y	35580 FQ	70750 AW		ARBLS	10/01-12/01
	Fort Smith MSA, AR-OK	Y	38000 FQ	75150 AW		ARBLS	10/01-12/01
	Little Rock-North Little Rock MSA, AR	Y	37320 FQ	73180 AW		ARBLS	10/01-12/01
	California	Y	60960 FQ	104900 AW		CABLS	10/01-12/01
	Bakersfield MSA, CA	Y	61450 FQ	110000 AW		CABLS	10/01-12/01
	Chico-Paradise MSA, CA	Y	49230 FQ	76000 AW	125160 TQ	CABLS	10/01-12/01
	Fresno MSA, CA	Y	53910 FQ	89620 AW		CABLS	10/01-12/01
	Los Angeles-Long Beach PMSA, CA	Y	61110 FQ	105210 AW		CABLS	10/01-12/01
	Merced MSA, CA	Y	57810 FQ	96270 AW		CABLS	10/01-12/01
	Modesto MSA, CA	Y	50130 FQ	75000 AW	112730 TQ	CABLS	10/01-12/01
	Oakland PMSA, CA	Y	54170 FQ	98860 AW		CABLS	10/01-12/01
	Orange County PMSA, CA	Y	72080 FQ	112580 AW		CABLS	10/01-12/01
	Redding MSA, CA	Y	60800 FQ	92280 AW	118280 TQ	CABLS	10/01-12/01
	Riverside-San Bernardino PMSA, CA	Y	63010 FQ	96860 AW		CABLS	10/01-12/01
	Sacramento PMSA, CA	Y	59440 FQ	97650 AW		CABLS	10/01-12/01
	Salinas MSA, CA	Y	71750 FQ	103160 AW		CABLS	10/01-12/01
	San Diego MSA, CA	Y	56000 FQ	96900 AW		CABLS	10/01-12/01
	San Francisco PMSA, CA	Y	69880 FQ	112340 AW		CABLS	10/01-12/01
	San Jose PMSA, CA	Y	87010 FQ	123600 AW		CABLS	10/01-12/01

AAW	Average annual wage	**AOH**	Average offered, high	**ASH**	Average starting, high	**H**	Hourly	**M**	Monthly	**S**	Special: hourly and annual
AE	Average entry wage	**AOL**	Average offered, low	**ASL**	Average starting, low	**HI**	Highest wage paid	**MTC**	Median total compensation	**TQ**	Third quartile wage
AEX	Average experienced wage	**APH**	Average pay, high range	**AW**	Average wage paid	**HR**	High end range	**MW**	Median wage paid	**W**	Weekly
AO	Average offered	**APL**	Average pay, low range	**FQ**	First quartile wage	**LR**	Low end range	**SQ**	Second quartile wage	**Y**	Yearly

Occupation/Type/Industry	Location	Per	Low	Mid	High	Source	Date
Lawyer	San Luis Obispo-Atascadero-Paso Robles MSA, CA	Y	46540 FQ	89490 AW		CABLS	10/01-12/01
	Santa Barbara-Santa Maria-Lompoc MSA, CA	Y	48790 FQ	86290 AW		CABLS	10/01-12/01
	Santa Cruz-Watsonville PMSA, CA	Y	66650 FQ	92010 AW	142720 TQ	CABLS	10/01-12/01
	Santa Rosa PMSA, CA	Y	50810 FQ	94340 AW		CABLS	10/01-12/01
	Stockton-Lodi MSA, CA	Y	50650 FQ	78070 AW	98060 TQ	CABLS	10/01-12/01
	Vallejo-Fairfield-Napa PMSA, CA	Y	53400 FQ	86770 AW	141320 TQ	CABLS	10/01-12/01
	Ventura PMSA, CA	Y	67480 FQ	101100 AW		CABLS	10/01-12/01
	Visalia-Tulare-Porterville MSA, CA	Y	44800 FQ	75730 AW	114320 TQ	CABLS	10/01-12/01
	Colorado	Y	48750 FQ	86700 AW		COBLS	10/01-12/01
	Boulder-Longmont PMSA, CO	Y	43490 FQ	76960 AW	141860 TQ	COBLS	10/01-12/01
	Colorado Springs MSA, CO	Y	49800 FQ	87750 AW	119770 TQ	COBLS	10/01-12/01
	Denver PMSA, CO	Y	51530 FQ	90950 AW		COBLS	10/01-12/01
	Fort Collins-Loveland MSA, CO	Y	36800 FQ	79860 AW	135970 TQ	COBLS	10/01-12/01
	Greeley PMSA, CO	Y	33540 FQ	70150 AW	113340 TQ	COBLS	10/01-12/01
	Connecticut	Y	54610 FQ	99170 AW		CTBLS	10/01-12/01
	Bridgeport PMSA, CT	Y	63380 FQ	108630 AW		CTBLS	10/01-12/01
	Danbury PMSA, CT	Y	81300 FQ	118730 AW		CTBLS	10/01-12/01
	Hartford MSA, CT	Y	57800 FQ	95500 AW		CTBLS	10/01-12/01
	New Haven-Meriden PMSA, CT	Y	49780 FQ	91850 AW		CTBLS	10/01-12/01
	New London-Norwich MSA, CT-RI	Y	48410 FQ	97390 AW		CTBLS	10/01-12/01
	Stamford-Norwalk PMSA, CT	Y	50470 FQ	105780 AW		CTBLS	10/01-12/01
	Waterbury PMSA, CT	Y	61070 FQ	85460 AW	143420 TQ	CTBLS	10/01-12/01
	Delaware	Y	49140 FQ	92080 AW		DEBLS	10/01-12/01
	Wilmington-Newark PMSA, DE-MD	Y	50030 FQ	93770 AW		DEBLS	10/01-12/01
	District of Columbia	Y	64630 FQ	102780 AW		DCBLS	10/01-12/01
	Washington PMSA, DC-MD-VA-WV	Y	55490 FQ	98760 AW		DCBLS	10/01-12/01
	Florida	Y	39660 FQ	96970 AW		FLBLS	10/01-12/01
	Daytona Beach MSA, FL	Y	47220 FQ	98650 AW		FLBLS	10/01-12/01
	Fort Lauderdale PMSA, FL	Y	59970 FQ	107770 AW		FLBLS	10/01-12/01
	Fort Myers-Cape Coral MSA, FL	Y	37150 FQ	73190 AW	127550 TQ	FLBLS	10/01-12/01
	Fort Pierce-Port St. Lucie MSA, FL	Y	38790 FQ	82710 AW		FLBLS	10/01-12/01
	Fort Walton Beach MSA, FL	Y	60050 FQ	82050 AW	137930 TQ	FLBLS	10/01-12/01
	Gainesville MSA, FL	Y	41590 FQ	91800 AW		FLBLS	10/01-12/01
	Jacksonville MSA, FL	Y	61790 FQ	113190 AW		FLBLS	10/01-12/01
	Lakeland-Winter Haven MSA, FL	Y	56760 FQ	101470 AW		FLBLS	10/01-12/01
	Melbourne-Titusville-Palm Bay MSA, FL	Y	53920 FQ	96270 AW		FLBLS	10/01-12/01
	Miami PMSA, FL	Y	31290 FQ	93170 AW		FLBLS	10/01-12/01
	Naples MSA, FL	Y	53410 FQ	116560 AW		FLBLS	10/01-12/01
	Ocala MSA, FL	Y	73330 FQ	120140 AW		FLBLS	10/01-12/01
	Orlando MSA, FL	Y	56650 FQ	103110 AW		FLBLS	10/01-12/01
	Pensacola MSA, FL	Y	48800 FQ	94460 AW		FLBLS	10/01-12/01
	Tallahassee MSA, FL	Y	52050 FQ	87910 AW		FLBLS	10/01-12/01
	Tampa-St. Petersburg-Clearwater MSA, FL	Y	57130 FQ	101250 AW		FLBLS	10/01-12/01
	West Palm Beach-Boca Raton MSA, FL	Y	50480 FQ	94510 AW		FLBLS	10/01-12/01
	Georgia	Y	31500 FQ	82380 AW		GABLS	10/01-12/01
	Atlanta MSA, GA	Y	31240 FQ	82610 AW		GABLS	10/01-12/01
	Augusta-Aiken MSA, GA-SC	Y	42850 FQ	85560 AW	145260 TQ	GABLS	10/01-12/01
	Columbus MSA, GA-AL	Y	45970 FQ	84840 AW		GABLS	10/01-12/01
	Macon MSA, GA	Y	50340 FQ	76890 AW	102680 TQ	GABLS	10/01-12/01
	Savannah MSA, GA	Y	26020 FQ	61120 AW	111340 TQ	GABLS	10/01-12/01
	Hawaii	Y	46640 FQ	77040 AW	136850 TQ	HIBLS	10/01-12/01
	Honolulu MSA, HI	Y	46650 FQ	77920 AW	138620 TQ	HIBLS	10/01-12/01
	Idaho	Y	31470 FQ	67660 AW	123350 TQ	IDBLS	10/01-12/01
	Boise City MSA, ID	Y	46520 FQ	73400 AW	109300 TQ	IDBLS	10/01-12/01
	Illinois	Y	45620 FQ	97240 AW		ILBLS	10/01-12/01
	Champaign-Urbana MSA, IL	Y	48190 FQ	83940 AW	127400 TQ	ILBLS	10/01-12/01

AAW Average annual wage	**AOH** Average offered, high	**ASH** Average starting, high	**H** Hourly	**M** Monthly	**S** Special: hourly and annual
AE Average entry wage	**AOL** Average offered, low	**ASL** Average starting, low	**HI** Highest wage paid	**MTC** Median total compensation	**TQ** Third quartile wage
AEX Average experienced wage	**APH** Average pay, high range	**AW** Average wage paid	**HR** High end range	**MW** Median wage paid	**W** Weekly
AO Average offered	**APL** Average pay, low range	**FQ** First quartile wage	**LR** Low end range	**SQ** Second quartile wage	**Y** Yearly

Occupation/Type/Industry	Location	Per	Low	Mid	High	Source	Date
Lawyer	Chicago PMSA, IL	Y	46910 FQ	99410 AW		ILBLS	10/01-12/01
	Peoria-Pekin MSA, IL	Y	37580 FQ	70970 AW	129990 TQ	ILBLS	10/01-12/01
	Rockford MSA, IL	Y	49710 FQ	107550 AW		ILBLS	10/01-12/01
	Springfield MSA, IL	Y	34390 FQ	74220 AW	131610 TQ	ILBLS	10/01-12/01
	Indiana	Y	35210 FQ	74950 AW	144110 TQ	INBLS	10/01-12/01
	Elkhart-Goshen MSA, IN	Y	22060 FQ	46100 AW	80610 TQ	INBLS	10/01-12/01
	Evansville-Henderson MSA, IN-KY	Y	38300 FQ	71810 AW		INBLS	10/01-12/01
	Fort Wayne MSA, IN	Y	28610 FQ	76380 AW		INBLS	10/01-12/01
	Gary PMSA, IN	Y	41870 FQ	88580 AW		INBLS	10/01-12/01
	Indianapolis MSA, IN	Y	39040 FQ	77470 AW	140980 TQ	INBLS	10/01-12/01
	Lafayette MSA, IN	Y	37860 FQ	65790 AW	144910 TQ	INBLS	10/01-12/01
	South Bend MSA, IN	Y	32240 FQ	75610 AW	136630 TQ	INBLS	10/01-12/01
	Iowa	Y	39950 FQ	79130 AW		IABLS	10/01-12/01
	Cedar Rapids MSA, IA	Y	47420 FQ	72120 AW	112060 TQ	IABLS	10/01-12/01
	Davenport-Moline-Rock Island MSA, IA-IL	Y	41730 FQ	79260 AW	142140 TQ	IABLS	10/01-12/01
	Des Moines MSA, IA	Y	47350 FQ	89110 AW		IABLS	10/01-12/01
	Kansas	Y	37630 FQ	76470 AW		KSBLS	10/01-12/01
	Topeka MSA, KS	Y	42170 FQ	67860 AW	122210 TQ	KSBLS	10/01-12/01
	Wichita MSA, KS	Y	37360 FQ	73990 AW		KSBLS	10/01-12/01
	Kentucky	Y	32120 FQ	73360 AW	141110 TQ	KYBLS	10/01-12/01
	Lexington MSA, KY	Y	46200 FQ	90250 AW		KYBLS	10/01-12/01
	Louisville MSA, KY-IN	Y	30660 FQ	69010 AW		KYBLS	10/01-12/01
	Louisiana	Y	30640 FQ	79800 AW		LABLS	10/01-12/01
	Baton Rouge MSA, LA	Y	42500 FQ	72430 AW	118980 TQ	LABLS	10/01-12/01
	Houma MSA, LA	Y	13740 FQ	60760 AW		LABLS	10/01-12/01
	Lafayette MSA, LA	Y	16840 FQ	63550 AW		LABLS	10/01-12/01
	Lake Charles MSA, LA	Y	34490 FQ	101670 AW		LABLS	10/01-12/01
	New Orleans MSA, LA	Y	50940 FQ	97980 AW		LABLS	10/01-12/01
	Shreveport-Bossier City MSA, LA	Y	25850 FQ	63500 AW	136070 TQ	LABLS	10/01-12/01
	Maine	Y	33050 FQ	79160 AW		MEBLS	10/01-12/01
	Portland MSA, ME	Y	32740 FQ	86930 AW		MEBLS	10/01-12/01
	Maryland	Y	35460 FQ	76300 AW	142830 TQ	MDBLS	10/01-12/01
	Baltimore PMSA, MD	Y	37620 FQ	75090 AW	133680 TQ	MDBLS	10/01-12/01
	Massachusetts	Y	47450 FQ	93610 AW		MABLS	10/01-12/01
	Boston PMSA, MA-NH	Y	47770 FQ	94770 AW		MABLS	10/01-12/01
	Brockton PMSA, MA	Y	48420 FQ	71870 AW	133530 TQ	MABLS	10/01-12/01
	Lawrence PMSA, MA-NH	Y	47320 FQ	92740 AW		MABLS	10/01-12/01
	Lowell PMSA, MA-NH	Y	43180 FQ	85810 AW	120810 TQ	MABLS	10/01-12/01
	New Bedford PMSA, MA	Y	46230 FQ	90300 AW		MABLS	10/01-12/01
	Springfield MSA, MA	Y	46510 FQ	91020 AW	131910 TQ	MABLS	10/01-12/01
	Worcester PMSA, MA-CT	Y	46190 FQ	86060 AW		MABLS	10/01-12/01
	Michigan	Y	38620 FQ	79540 AW		MIBLS	10/01-12/01
	Ann Arbor PMSA, MI	Y	72940 FQ	90660 AW	114440 TQ	MIBLS	10/01-12/01
	Detroit PMSA, MI	Y	38110 FQ	76870 AW		MIBLS	10/01-12/01
	Flint PMSA, MI	Y	30590 FQ	64730 AW	109570 TQ	MIBLS	10/01-12/01
	Grand Rapids-Muskegon-Holland MSA, MI	Y	47320 FQ	93130 AW		MIBLS	10/01-12/01
	Kalamazoo-Battle Creek MSA, MI	Y	46900 FQ	75160 AW		MIBLS	10/01-12/01
	Lansing-East Lansing MSA, MI	Y	48790 FQ	85380 AW		MIBLS	10/01-12/01
	Saginaw-Bay City-Midland MSA, MI	Y	42320 FQ	84660 AW	142920 TQ	MIBLS	10/01-12/01
	Minnesota	Y	43770 FQ	83110 AW		MNBLS	10/01-12/01
	Duluth-Superior MSA, MN-WI	Y	38020 FQ	78130 AW		MNBLS	10/01-12/01
	Minneapolis-St. Paul MSA, MN-WI	Y	47130 FQ	86770 AW		MNBLS	10/01-12/01
	St. Cloud MSA, MN	Y	39790 FQ	74390 AW	129880 TQ	MNBLS	10/01-12/01
	Mississippi	Y	29620 FQ	60710 AW	109650 TQ	MSBLS	10/01-12/01
	Biloxi-Gulfport-Pascagoula MSA, MS	Y	35980 FQ	57330 AW	114160 TQ	MSBLS	10/01-12/01
	Jackson MSA, MS	Y	30840 FQ	62960 AW	110900 TQ	MSBLS	10/01-12/01
	Missouri	Y	43550 FQ	94090 AW		MOBLS	10/01-12/01
	Kansas City MSA, MO-KS	Y	55940 FQ	100730 AW		MOBLS	10/01-12/01
	St. Louis MSA, MO-IL	Y	46000 FQ	94640 AW		MOBLS	10/01-12/01
	Springfield MSA, MO	Y	37360 FQ	87560 AW		MOBLS	10/01-12/01
	Montana	Y	31480 FQ	65050 AW	123740 TQ	MTBLS	10/01-12/01
	Billings MSA, MT	Y	35880 FQ	74510 AW		MTBLS	10/01-12/01
	Nebraska	Y	38820 FQ	82690 AW		NEBLS	10/01-12/01
	Lincoln MSA, NE	Y	40480 FQ	78360 AW	137260 TQ	NEBLS	10/01-12/01

AAW	Average annual wage	**AOH**	Average offered, high	**ASH**	Average starting, high	**H**	Hourly	**M**	Monthly	**S**	Special: hourly and annual
AE	Average entry wage	**AOL**	Average offered, low	**ASL**	Average starting, low	**HI**	Highest wage paid	**MTC**	Median total compensation	**TQ**	Third quartile wage
AEX	Average experienced wage	**APH**	Average pay, high range	**AW**	Average wage paid	**HR**	High end range	**MW**	Median wage paid	**W**	Weekly
AO	Average offered	**APL**	Average pay, low range	**FQ**	First quartile wage	**LR**	Low end range	**SQ**	Second quartile wage	**Y**	Yearly

Occupation/Type/Industry	Location	Per	Low	Mid	High	Source	Date
Lawyer	Omaha MSA, NE-IA	Y	43570 FQ	87830 AW		NEBLS	10/01-12/01
	Nevada	Y	32960 FQ	80780 AW		NVBLS	10/01-12/01
	Las Vegas MSA, NV-AZ	Y	31790 FQ	77340 AW	142270 TQ	NVBLS	10/01-12/01
	Reno MSA, NV	Y	59790 FQ	99170 AW		NVBLS	10/01-12/01
	New Hampshire	Y	34430 FQ	73750 AW	142280 TQ	NHBLS	10/01-12/01
	Manchester PMSA, NH	Y	50820 FQ	95990 AW		NHBLS	10/01-12/01
	Nashua PMSA, NH	Y	47250 FQ	84820 AW		NHBLS	10/01-12/01
	Portsmouth-Rochester PMSA, NH-ME	Y	33430 FQ	69020 AW	110570 TQ	NHBLS	10/01-12/01
	New Jersey	Y	47030 FQ	94150 AW		NJBLS	10/01-12/01
	Atlantic-Cape May PMSA, NJ	Y	54060 FQ	96570 AW		NJBLS	10/01-12/01
	Bergen-Passaic PMSA, NJ	Y	64740 FQ	111050 AW		NJBLS	10/01-12/01
	Jersey City PMSA, NJ	Y	47260 FQ	86740 AW		NJBLS	10/01-12/01
	Middlesex-Somerset-Hunterdon PMSA, NJ	Y	65660 FQ	107880 AW		NJBLS	10/01-12/01
	Monmouth-Ocean PMSA, NJ	Y	47520 FQ	83530 AW		NJBLS	10/01-12/01
	Newark PMSA, NJ	Y	50480 FQ	99280 AW		NJBLS	10/01-12/01
	Trenton PMSA, NJ	Y	48440 FQ	84460 AW		NJBLS	10/01-12/01
	New Mexico	Y	37630 FQ	63360 AW	115140 TQ	NMBLS	10/01-12/01
	Albuquerque MSA, NM	Y	37290 FQ	58580 AW	95670 TQ	NMBLS	10/01-12/01
	Las Cruces MSA, NM	Y	39720 FQ	67560 AW	113440 TQ	NMBLS	10/01-12/01
	New York	Y	53650 FQ	101370 AW		NYBLS	10/01-12/01
	Albany-Schenectady-Troy MSA, NY	Y	50680 FQ	80870 AW	127280 TQ	NYBLS	10/01-12/01
	Binghamton MSA, NY	Y	37950 FQ	63540 AW	111970 TQ	NYBLS	10/01-12/01
	Buffalo-Niagara Falls MSA, NY	Y	38060 FQ	69660 AW	113420 TQ	NYBLS	10/01-12/01
	Dutchess County PMSA, NY	Y	46110 FQ	84090 AW		NYBLS	10/01-12/01
	Nassau-Suffolk PMSA, NY	Y	58470 FQ	89040 AW		NYBLS	10/01-12/01
	New York PMSA, NY	Y	57960 FQ	108600 AW		NYBLS	10/01-12/01
	Newburgh PMSA, NY-PA	Y	48030 FQ	72880 AW	112610 TQ	NYBLS	10/01-12/01
	Rochester MSA, NY	Y	52670 FQ	91550 AW		NYBLS	10/01-12/01
	Syracuse MSA, NY	Y	46510 FQ	77280 AW	134980 TQ	NYBLS	10/01-12/01
	Utica-Rome MSA, NY	Y	35460 FQ	66980 AW	106490 TQ	NYBLS	10/01-12/01
	North Carolina	Y	41370 FQ	84650 AW		NCBLS	10/01-12/01
	Asheville MSA, NC	Y	42190 FQ	87840 AW		NCBLS	10/01-12/01
	Charlotte-Gastonia-Rock Hill MSA, NC-SC	Y	49680 FQ	101460 AW		NCBLS	10/01-12/01
	Fayetteville MSA, NC	Y	49030 FQ	78200 AW	127920 TQ	NCBLS	10/01-12/01
	Greensboro-Winston-Salem-High Point MSA, NC	Y	46980 FQ	93000 AW		NCBLS	10/01-12/01
	Hickory-Morganton-Lenoir MSA, NC	Y	40640 FQ	67520 AW	120900 TQ	NCBLS	10/01-12/01
	Raleigh-Durham-Chapel Hill MSA, NC	Y	45920 FQ	80480 AW		NCBLS	10/01-12/01
	Wilmington MSA, NC	Y	37040 FQ	73580 AW		NCBLS	10/01-12/01
	North Dakota	Y	29950 FQ	58840 AW	121560 TQ	NDBLS	10/01-12/01
	Fargo-Moorhead MSA, ND-MN	Y	38620 FQ	81440 AW		NDBLS	10/01-12/01
	Ohio	Y	40610 FQ	86670 AW		OHBLS	10/01-12/01
	Akron PMSA, OH	Y	34750 FQ	84240 AW		OHBLS	10/01-12/01
	Canton-Massillon MSA, OH	Y	49070 FQ	98260 AW		OHBLS	10/01-12/01
	Cincinnati PMSA, OH-KY-IN	Y	35170 FQ	85970 AW		OHBLS	10/01-12/01
	Cleveland-Lorain-Elyria PMSA, OH	Y	49500 FQ	102020 AW		OHBLS	10/01-12/01
	Columbus MSA, OH	Y	40390 FQ	73090 AW	117700 TQ	OHBLS	10/01-12/01
	Dayton-Springfield MSA, OH	Y	41080 FQ	75340 AW	134970 TQ	OHBLS	10/01-12/01
	Hamilton-Middletown PMSA, OH	Y	46810 FQ	82090 AW		OHBLS	10/01-12/01
	Mansfield MSA, OH	Y	33050 FQ	77530 AW		OHBLS	10/01-12/01
	Toledo MSA, OH	Y	38890 FQ	77390 AW		OHBLS	10/01-12/01
	Youngstown-Warren MSA, OH	Y	31130 FQ	73850 AW		OHBLS	10/01-12/01
	Oklahoma	Y	37300 FQ	78770 AW		OKBLS	10/01-12/01
	Oklahoma City MSA, OK	Y	41790 FQ	86040 AW		OKBLS	10/01-12/01
	Tulsa MSA, OK	Y	43920 FQ	79940 AW		OKBLS	10/01-12/01
	Oregon	Y	36300 FQ	79100 AW	143770 TQ	ORBLS	10/01-12/01
	Eugene-Springfield MSA, OR	Y	48760 FQ	74670 AW		ORBLS	10/01-12/01
	Medford-Ashland MSA, OR	Y	37180 FQ	52400 AW	86010 TQ	ORBLS	10/01-12/01
	Salem PMSA, OR	Y	50530 FQ	98680 AW	141580 TQ	ORBLS	10/01-12/01
	Pennsylvania	Y	33130 FQ	84460 AW		PABLS	10/01-12/01
	Allentown-Bethlehem-Easton MSA, PA	Y	32710 FQ	96010 AW		PABLS	10/01-12/01

AAW Average annual wage **AOH** Average offered, high **ASH** Average starting, high **H** Hourly **M** Monthly **S** Special: hourly and annual
AE Average entry wage **AOL** Average offered, low **ASL** Average starting, low **HI** Highest wage paid **MTC** Median total compensation **TQ** Third quartile wage
AEX Average experienced wage **APH** Average pay, high range **AW** Average wage paid **HR** High end range **MW** Median wage paid **W** Weekly
AO Average offered **APL** Average pay, low range **FQ** First quartile wage **LR** Low end range **SQ** Second quartile wage **Y** Yearly

Occupation/Type/Industry	Location	Per	Low	Mid	High	Source	Date
Lawyer	Erie MSA, PA	Y	43020 FQ	91450 AW		PABLS	10/01-12/01
	Harrisburg-Lebanon-Carlisle MSA, PA	Y	44680 FQ	82730 AW	136180 TQ	PABLS	10/01-12/01
	Johnstown MSA, PA	Y	23740 FQ	54580 AW	107250 TQ	PABLS	10/01-12/01
	Lancaster MSA, PA	Y	37520 FQ	74680 AW	144010 TQ	PABLS	10/01-12/01
	Philadelphia PMSA, PA-NJ	Y	37680 FQ	86860 AW		PABLS	10/01-12/01
	Pittsburgh MSA, PA	Y	24750 FQ	73740 AW		PABLS	10/01-12/01
	Reading MSA, PA	Y	33880 FQ	79530 AW		PABLS	10/01-12/01
	Scranton-Wilkes-Barre-Hazleton MSA, PA	Y	29620 FQ	76340 AW		PABLS	10/01-12/01
	York MSA, PA	Y	37800 FQ	76830 AW		PABLS	10/01-12/01
	Rhode Island	Y	30620 FQ	71160 AW		RIBLS	10/01-12/01
	South Carolina	Y	46190 FQ	86670 AW		SCBLS	10/01-12/01
	Charleston-North Charleston MSA, SC	Y	52440 FQ	100920 AW		SCBLS	10/01-12/01
	Columbia MSA, SC	Y	48860 FQ	79940 AW	104600 TQ	SCBLS	10/01-12/01
	Greenville-Spartanburg-Anderson MSA, SC	Y	31960 FQ	76750 AW	137850 TQ	SCBLS	10/01-12/01
	Myrtle Beach MSA, SC	Y	52650 FQ	92460 AW	141900 TQ	SCBLS	10/01-12/01
	South Dakota	Y	38010 FQ	59240 AW	96650 TQ	SDBLS	10/01-12/01
	Sioux Falls MSA, SD	Y	43200 FQ	64870 AW	108020 TQ	SDBLS	10/01-12/01
	Tennessee	Y	38010 FQ	85410 AW		TNBLS	10/01-12/01
	Chattanooga MSA, TN-GA	Y	52370 FQ	87750 AW		TNBLS	10/01-12/01
	Clarksville-Hopkinsville MSA, TN-KY	Y	34020 FQ	73930 AW		TNBLS	10/01-12/01
	Johnson City-Kingsport-Bristol MSA, TN-VA	Y	57750 FQ	87400 AW	113830 TQ	TNBLS	10/01-12/01
	Knoxville MSA, TN	Y	38000 FQ	79810 AW	140900 TQ	TNBLS	10/01-12/01
	Memphis MSA, TN-AR-MS	Y	32680 FQ	76530 AW		TNBLS	10/01-12/01
	Nashville MSA, TN	Y	47250 FQ	100690 AW		TNBLS	10/01-12/01
	Texas	Y	49820 FQ	100220 AW		TXBLS	10/01-12/01
	Amarillo MSA, TX	Y	57340 FQ	101810 AW		TXBLS	10/01-12/01
	Austin-San Marcos MSA, TX	Y	42980 FQ	80970 AW		TXBLS	10/01-12/01
	Beaumont-Port Arthur MSA, TX	Y	47630 FQ	94210 AW		TXBLS	10/01-12/01
	Brownsville-Harlingen-San Benito MSA, TX	Y	49840 FQ	94450 AW		TXBLS	10/01-12/01
	Corpus Christi MSA, TX	Y	48080 FQ	98510 AW		TXBLS	10/01-12/01
	Dallas PMSA, TX	Y	60870 FQ	101880 AW		TXBLS	10/01-12/01
	El Paso MSA, TX	Y	59540 FQ	101640 AW		TXBLS	10/01-12/01
	Fort Worth-Arlington PMSA, TX	Y	50110 FQ	86040 AW		TXBLS	10/01-12/01
	Galveston-Texas City PMSA, TX	Y	52900 FQ	94510 AW		TXBLS	10/01-12/01
	Houston PMSA, TX	Y	62660 FQ	118490 AW		TXBLS	10/01-12/01
	Killeen-Temple MSA, TX	Y	47130 FQ	90900 AW		TXBLS	10/01-12/01
	Laredo MSA, TX	Y	60280 FQ	96210 AW		TXBLS	10/01-12/01
	Longview-Marshall MSA, TX	Y	43670 FQ	81080 AW		TXBLS	10/01-12/01
	Lubbock MSA, TX	Y	55490 FQ	65000 AW	71880 TQ	TXBLS	10/01-12/01
	McAllen-Edinburg-Mission MSA, TX	Y	60830 FQ	100150 AW		TXBLS	10/01-12/01
	Odessa-Midland MSA, TX	Y	67940 FQ	101420 AW		TXBLS	10/01-12/01
	San Antonio MSA, TX	Y	22200 FQ	83350 AW		TXBLS	10/01-12/01
	Tyler MSA, TX	Y	58630 FQ	107570 AW		TXBLS	10/01-12/01
	Waco MSA, TX	Y	49530 FQ	94820 AW		TXBLS	10/01-12/01
	Utah	Y	53110 FQ	102340 AW		UTBLS	10/01-12/01
	Provo-Orem MSA, UT	Y	48980 FQ	88340 AW	114920 TQ	UTBLS	10/01-12/01
	Salt Lake City-Ogden MSA, UT	Y	62830 FQ	107990 AW		UTBLS	10/01-12/01
	Vermont	Y	29320 FQ	64990 AW	140170 TQ	VTBLS	10/01-12/01
	Burlington MSA, VT	Y	33740 FQ	76690 AW		VTBLS	10/01-12/01
	Virginia	Y	39130 FQ	86520 AW		VABLS	10/01-12/01
	Lynchburg MSA, VA	Y	47710 FQ	70270 AW	117920 TQ	VABLS	10/01-12/01
	Norfolk-Virginia Beach-Newport News MSA, VA-NC	Y	45010 FQ	83970 AW		VABLS	10/01-12/01
	Richmond-Petersburg MSA, VA	Y	38760 FQ	77030 AW		VABLS	10/01-12/01
	Roanoke MSA, VA	Y	48910 FQ	84500 AW		VABLS	10/01-12/01
	Washington	Y	33960 FQ	79920 AW		WABLS	10/01-12/01
	Bremerton PMSA, WA	Y	41730 FQ	80390 AW		WABLS	10/01-12/01
	Olympia PMSA, WA	Y	42370 FQ	71610 AW	107330 TQ	WABLS	10/01-12/01

AAW	Average annual wage	**AOH**	Average offered, high	**ASH**	Average starting, high	**H**	Hourly	**M**	Monthly	**S**	Special: hourly and annual
AE	Average entry wage	**AOL**	Average offered, low	**ASL**	Average starting, low	**HI**	Highest wage paid	**MTC**	Median total compensation	**TQ**	Third quartile wage
AEX	Average experienced wage	**APH**	Average pay, high range	**AW**	Average wage paid	**HR**	High end range	**MW**	Median wage paid	**W**	Weekly
AO	Average offered	**APL**	Average pay, low range	**FQ**	First quartile wage	**LR**	Low end range	**SQ**	Second quartile wage	**Y**	Yearly

Occupation/Type/Industry	Location	Per	Low	Mid	High	Source	Date
Lawyer	Richland-Kennewick-Pasco MSA, WA	Y	47480 FQ	75640 AW	124320 TQ	WABLS	10/01-12/01
	Seattle-Bellevue-Everett PMSA, WA	Y	32960 FQ	83660 AW		WABLS	10/01-12/01
	Yakima MSA, WA	Y	42520 FQ	72250 AW	116820 TQ	WABLS	10/01-12/01
	West Virginia	Y	39150 FQ	68070 AW	137320 TQ	WVBLS	10/01-12/01
	Charleston MSA, WV	Y	45560 FQ	73470 AW		WVBLS	10/01-12/01
	Huntington-Ashland MSA, WV-KY-OH	Y	41850 FQ	72290 AW	136320 TQ	WVBLS	10/01-12/01
	Wisconsin	Y	45250 FQ	87880 AW		WIBLS	10/01-12/01
	Appleton-Oshkosh-Neenah MSA, WI	Y	47590 FQ	93210 AW		WIBLS	10/01-12/01
	Green Bay MSA, WI	Y	49550 FQ	92270 AW		WIBLS	10/01-12/01
	Madison MSA, WI	Y	49740 FQ	80040 AW	112590 TQ	WIBLS	10/01-12/01
	Milwaukee-Waukesha PMSA, WI	Y	47740 FQ	97720 AW		WIBLS	10/01-12/01
	Racine PMSA, WI	Y	36390 FQ	66490 AW	127760 TQ	WIBLS	10/01-12/01
	Wyoming	Y	35370 FQ	57710 AW	113600 TQ	WYBLS	10/01-12/01
	Cheyenne MSA, WY	Y	37870 FQ	50280 AW	71720 TQ	WYBLS	10/01-12/01
	Puerto Rico	Y	27200 FQ	50610 AW	83910 TQ	PRBLS	10/01-12/01
	Virgin Islands	Y	45510 FQ	78520 AW		VIBLS	10/01-12/01
	Guam	Y	51580 FQ	80990 AW	114180 TQ	GUBLS	10/01-12/01
Lay-Out Worker							
Metals and Plastics	Alabama	H	9.78 FQ	13.67 AW	18.98 TQ	ALBLS	10/01-12/01
Metals and Plastics	Arizona	H	7.20 FQ	12.58 AW	19.39 TQ	AZBLS	10/01-12/01
Metals and Plastics	Arkansas	H	9.17 FQ	13.30 AW	18.58 TQ	ARBLS	10/01-12/01
Metals and Plastics	California	H	8.14 FQ	14.25 AW	21.55 TQ	CABLS	10/01-12/01
Metals and Plastics	Colorado	H	7.81 FQ	13.40 AW	20.55 TQ	COBLS	10/01-12/01
Metals and Plastics	Connecticut	H	9.35 FQ	15.13 AW	20.95 TQ	CTBLS	10/01-12/01
Metals and Plastics	Florida	H	8.58 FQ	12.93 AW	16.96 TQ	FLBLS	10/01-12/01
Metals and Plastics	Georgia	H	10.23 FQ	15.13 AW	20.03 TQ	GABLS	10/01-12/01
Metals and Plastics	Idaho	H	11.45 FQ	14.56 AW	17.47 TQ	IDBLS	10/01-12/01
Metals and Plastics	Illinois	H	12.20 FQ	17.56 AW	25.44 TQ	ILBLS	10/01-12/01
Metals and Plastics	Indiana	H	11.28 FQ	17.85 AW	30.88 TQ	INBLS	10/01-12/01
Metals and Plastics	Iowa	H	10.18 FQ	15.99 AW	24.71 TQ	IABLS	10/01-12/01
Metals and Plastics	Kansas	H	7.98 FQ	12.04 AW	16.66 TQ	KSBLS	10/01-12/01
Metals and Plastics	Kentucky	H	9.57 FQ	13.49 AW	17.67 TQ	KYBLS	10/01-12/01
Metals and Plastics	Louisiana	H	9.18 FQ	13.52 AW	18.60 TQ	LABLS	10/01-12/01
Metals and Plastics	Maine	H	9.04 FQ	12.63 AW	16.92 TQ	MEBLS	10/01-12/01
Metals and Plastics	Maryland	H	11.48 FQ	14.61 AW	18.13 TQ	MDBLS	10/01-12/01
Metals and Plastics	Massachusetts	H	10.69 FQ	17.30 AW	25.17 TQ	MABLS	10/01-12/01
Metals and Plastics	Michigan	H	13.04 FQ	21.64 AW	33.18 TQ	MIBLS	10/01-12/01
Metals and Plastics	Minnesota	H	11.24 FQ	17.11 AW	22.02 TQ	MNBLS	10/01-12/01
Metals and Plastics	Mississippi	H	11.26 FQ	14.35 AW	17.47 TQ	MSBLS	10/01-12/01
Metals and Plastics	Missouri	H	9.59 FQ	13.00 AW	16.97 TQ	MOBLS	10/01-12/01
Metals and Plastics	Nevada	H	10.63 FQ	16.64 AW	26.74 TQ	NVBLS	10/01-12/01
Metals and Plastics	New Hampshire	H	11.38 FQ	14.62 AW	18.14 TQ	NHBLS	10/01-12/01
Metals and Plastics	New Jersey	H	12.15 FQ	18.71 AW	25.21 TQ	NJBLS	10/01-12/01
Metals and Plastics	New Mexico	H	9.62 FQ	14.74 AW	23.63 TQ	NMBLS	10/01-12/01
Metals and Plastics	New York	H	8.14 FQ	12.83 AW	18.00 TQ	NYBLS	10/01-12/01
Metals and Plastics	North Carolina	H	10.75 FQ	14.50 AW	19.53 TQ	NCBLS	10/01-12/01
Metals and Plastics	Ohio	H	11.52 FQ	18.47 AW	32.87 TQ	OHBLS	10/01-12/01
Metals and Plastics	Oklahoma	H	8.38 FQ	13.44 AW	21.28 TQ	OKBLS	10/01-12/01
Metals and Plastics	Oregon	H	9.65 FQ	16.74 AW	26.48 TQ	ORBLS	10/01-12/01
Metals and Plastics	Pennsylvania	H	11.66 FQ	19.42 AW	32.43 TQ	PABLS	10/01-12/01
Metals and Plastics	Rhode Island	H	9.54 FQ	16.47 AW	20.92 TQ	RIBLS	10/01-12/01
Metals and Plastics	Tennessee	H	9.60 FQ	13.46 AW	17.00 TQ	TNBLS	10/01-12/01
Metals and Plastics	Texas	H	8.31 FQ	12.73 AW	18.48 TQ	TXBLS	10/01-12/01
Metals and Plastics	Utah	H	9.59 FQ	13.42 AW	17.41 TQ	UTBLS	10/01-12/01
Metals and Plastics	Vermont	H	11.35 FQ	15.44 AW	19.88 TQ	VTBLS	10/01-12/01
Metals and Plastics	Virginia	H	8.74 FQ	12.37 AW	16.84 TQ	VABLS	10/01-12/01
Metals and Plastics	Washington	H	13.37 FQ	19.87 AW	31.05 TQ	WABLS	10/01-12/01
Metals and Plastics	West Virginia	H	9.89 FQ	13.45 AW	19.32 TQ	WVBLS	10/01-12/01
Metals and Plastics	Wisconsin	H	12.75 FQ	17.30 AW	21.91 TQ	WIBLS	10/01-12/01
Legal Secretary	Alabama	H	8.44 FQ	13.97 AW	21.55 TQ	ALBLS	10/01-12/01
	Birmingham MSA, AL	H	11.62 FQ	18.26 AW	24.61 TQ	ALBLS	10/01-12/01
	Huntsville MSA, AL	H	8.78 FQ	11.96 AW	16.87 TQ	ALBLS	10/01-12/01
	Mobile MSA, AL	H	9.70 FQ	14.89 AW	21.41 TQ	ALBLS	10/01-12/01
	Montgomery MSA, AL	H	9.47 FQ	14.05 AW	19.39 TQ	ALBLS	10/01-12/01
	Alaska	H	13.18 FQ	19.27 AW	25.68 TQ	AKBLS	10/01-12/01
	Anchorage MSA, AK	H	13.02 FQ	19.82 AW	26.09 TQ	AKBLS	10/01-12/01

AAW Average annual wage **AOH** Average offered, high **ASH** Average starting, high **H** Hourly **M** Monthly **S** Special: hourly and annual
AE Average entry wage **AOL** Average offered, low **ASL** Average starting, low **HI** Highest wage paid **MTC** Median total compensation **TQ** Third quartile wage
AEX Average experienced wage **APH** Average pay, high range **AW** Average wage paid **HR** High end range **MW** Median wage paid **W** Weekly
AO Average offered **APL** Average pay, low range **FQ** First quartile wage **LR** Low end range **SQ** Second quartile wage **Y** Yearly

Occupation/Type/Industry	Location	Per	Low	Mid	High	Source	Date
Legal Secretary	Arizona	H	10.43 FQ	17.19 AW	22.50 TQ	AZBLS	10/01-12/01
	Phoenix-Mesa MSA, AZ	H	13.51 FQ	19.25 AW	24.37 TQ	AZBLS	10/01-12/01
	Tucson MSA, AZ	H	9.50 FQ	14.39 AW	19.42 TQ	AZBLS	10/01-12/01
	Arkansas	H	8.86 FQ	11.96 AW	15.91 TQ	ARBLS	10/01-12/01
	Fayetteville-Springdale-Rogers MSA, AR	H	9.83 FQ	12.50 AW	15.61 TQ	ARBLS	10/01-12/01
	Fort Smith MSA, AR-OK	H	8.99 FQ	12.95 AW	23.61 TQ	ARBLS	10/01-12/01
	Little Rock-North Little Rock MSA, AR	H	9.36 FQ	12.83 AW	16.79 TQ	ARBLS	10/01-12/01
	California	H	12.00 FQ	19.42 AW	28.09 TQ	CABLS	10/01-12/01
	Bakersfield MSA, CA	H	10.84 FQ	15.76 AW	20.66 TQ	CABLS	10/01-12/01
	Chico-Paradise MSA, CA	H	9.07 FQ	12.46 AW	17.59 TQ	CABLS	10/01-12/01
	Fresno MSA, CA	H	10.69 FQ	16.08 AW	21.23 TQ	CABLS	10/01-12/01
	Los Angeles-Long Beach PMSA, CA	H	11.54 FQ	17.73 AW	25.18 TQ	CABLS	10/01-12/01
	Merced MSA, CA	H	10.94 FQ	14.09 AW	16.77 TQ	CABLS	10/01-12/01
	Oakland PMSA, CA	H	17.08 FQ	25.74 AW	33.96 TQ	CABLS	10/01-12/01
	Orange County PMSA, CA	H	15.70 FQ	23.44 AW	32.52 TQ	CABLS	10/01-12/01
	Redding MSA, CA	H	12.02 FQ	15.67 AW	20.46 TQ	CABLS	10/01-12/01
	Riverside-San Bernardino PMSA, CA	H	12.15 FQ	17.34 AW	21.98 TQ	CABLS	10/01-12/01
	Sacramento PMSA, CA	H	15.53 FQ	19.60 AW	23.99 TQ	CABLS	10/01-12/01
	Salinas MSA, CA	H	11.49 FQ	15.32 AW	20.70 TQ	CABLS	10/01-12/01
	San Diego MSA, CA	H	14.03 FQ	18.16 AW	24.97 TQ	CABLS	10/01-12/01
	San Francisco PMSA, CA	H	17.07 FQ	24.66 AW	33.11 TQ	CABLS	10/01-12/01
	San Jose PMSA, CA	H	14.83 FQ	24.98 AW	33.78 TQ	CABLS	10/01-12/01
	San Luis Obispo-Atascadero-Paso Robles MSA, CA	H	11.86 FQ	13.38 AW	14.66 TQ	CABLS	10/01-12/01
	Santa Barbara-Santa Maria-Lompoc MSA, CA	H	13.21 FQ	19.51 AW	25.49 TQ	CABLS	10/01-12/01
	Santa Cruz-Watsonville PMSA, CA	H	14.68 FQ	20.06 AW	25.76 TQ	CABLS	10/01-12/01
	Santa Rosa PMSA, CA	H	10.19 FQ	16.32 AW	22.85 TQ	CABLS	10/01-12/01
	Stockton-Lodi MSA, CA	H	15.22 FQ	18.19 AW	21.43 TQ	CABLS	10/01-12/01
	Vallejo-Fairfield-Napa PMSA, CA	H	13.09 FQ	16.39 AW	20.77 TQ	CABLS	10/01-12/01
	Ventura PMSA, CA	H	13.18 FQ	18.32 AW	22.81 TQ	CABLS	10/01-12/01
	Visalia-Tulare-Porterville MSA, CA	H	10.12 FQ	14.30 AW	20.76 TQ	CABLS	10/01-12/01
	Colorado	H	12.86 FQ	15.83 AW	20.53 TQ	COBLS	10/01-12/01
	Boulder-Longmont PMSA, CO	H	11.28 FQ	15.44 AW	22.12 TQ	COBLS	10/01-12/01
	Colorado Springs MSA, CO	H	10.16 FQ	14.34 AW	20.05 TQ	COBLS	10/01-12/01
	Denver PMSA, CO	H	13.97 FQ	16.40 AW	20.76 TQ	COBLS	10/01-12/01
	Fort Collins-Loveland MSA, CO	H	12.70 FQ	15.32 AW	17.46 TQ	COBLS	10/01-12/01
	Greeley PMSA, CO	H	9.43 FQ	11.38 AW	15.54 TQ	COBLS	10/01-12/01
	Connecticut	H	12.81 FQ	17.62 AW	22.72 TQ	CTBLS	10/01-12/01
	Bridgeport PMSA, CT	H	11.29 FQ	15.66 AW	21.63 TQ	CTBLS	10/01-12/01
	Danbury PMSA, CT	H	15.01 FQ	19.06 AW	25.45 TQ	CTBLS	10/01-12/01
	Hartford MSA, CT	H	14.22 FQ	18.41 AW	22.36 TQ	CTBLS	10/01-12/01
	New Haven-Meriden PMSA, CT	H	14.13 FQ	17.08 AW	21.68 TQ	CTBLS	10/01-12/01
	New London-Norwich MSA, CT-RI	H	11.87 FQ	15.88 AW	20.77 TQ	CTBLS	10/01-12/01
	Stamford-Norwalk PMSA, CT	H	14.62 FQ	19.49 AW	25.81 TQ	CTBLS	10/01-12/01
	Waterbury PMSA, CT	H	14.18 FQ	16.05 AW	18.83 TQ	CTBLS	10/01-12/01
	Delaware	H	10.42 FQ	17.07 AW	24.80 TQ	DEBLS	10/01-12/01
	Wilmington-Newark PMSA, DE-MD	H	10.54 FQ	17.22 AW	24.77 TQ	DEBLS	10/01-12/01
	District of Columbia	H	14.64 FQ	21.16 AW	28.40 TQ	DCBLS	10/01-12/01
	Washington PMSA, DC-MD-VA-WV	H	14.38 FQ	20.90 AW	28.27 TQ	DCBLS	10/01-12/01
	Florida	H	12.19 FQ	18.32 AW	26.19 TQ	FLBLS	10/01-12/01
	Daytona Beach MSA, FL	H	11.86 FQ	18.99 AW	32.43 TQ	FLBLS	10/01-12/01
	Fort Lauderdale PMSA, FL	H	16.85 FQ	20.84 AW	26.24 TQ	FLBLS	10/01-12/01
	Fort Myers-Cape Coral MSA, FL	H	10.89 FQ	15.26 AW	19.57 TQ	FLBLS	10/01-12/01
	Fort Pierce-Port St. Lucie MSA, FL	H	11.61 FQ	14.80 AW	19.10 TQ	FLBLS	10/01-12/01
	Fort Walton Beach MSA, FL	H	13.69 FQ	20.82 AW	27.78 TQ	FLBLS	10/01-12/01
	Gainesville MSA, FL	H	11.52 FQ	15.81 AW	26.87 TQ	FLBLS	10/01-12/01
	Jacksonville MSA, FL	H	12.27 FQ	19.03 AW	29.92 TQ	FLBLS	10/01-12/01

AAW	Average annual wage	**AOH**	Average offered, high	**ASH**	Average starting, high	**H**	Hourly	**M**	Monthly	**S**	Special: hourly and annual
AE	Average entry wage	**AOL**	Average offered, low	**ASL**	Average starting, low	**HI**	Highest wage paid	**MTC**	Median total compensation	**TQ**	Third quartile wage
AEX	Average experienced wage	**APH**	Average pay, high range	**AW**	Average wage paid	**HR**	High end range	**MW**	Median wage paid	**W**	Weekly
AO	Average offered	**APL**	Average pay, low range	**FQ**	First quartile wage	**LR**	Low end range	**SQ**	Second quartile wage	**Y**	Yearly

Occupation/Type/Industry	Location	Per	Low	Mid	High	Source	Date
Legal Secretary	Lakeland-Winter Haven MSA, FL	H	12.09 FQ	17.34 AW	26.71 TQ	FLBLS	10/01-12/01
	Melbourne-Titusville-Palm Bay MSA, FL	H	9.98 FQ	15.40 AW	22.15 TQ	FLBLS	10/01-12/01
	Miami PMSA, FL	H	14.40 FQ	20.03 AW	26.81 TQ	FLBLS	10/01-12/01
	Naples MSA, FL	H	13.67 FQ	16.76 AW	21.37 TQ	FLBLS	10/01-12/01
	Ocala MSA, FL	H	12.24 FQ	16.19 AW	22.74 TQ	FLBLS	10/01-12/01
	Orlando MSA, FL	H	11.88 FQ	16.63 AW	22.20 TQ	FLBLS	10/01-12/01
	Pensacola MSA, FL	H	9.93 FQ	16.20 AW	26.45 TQ	FLBLS	10/01-12/01
	Sarasota-Bradenton MSA, FL	H	11.83 FQ	17.69 AW	22.70 TQ	FLBLS	10/01-12/01
	Tallahassee MSA, FL	H	14.82 FQ	19.77 AW	26.07 TQ	FLBLS	10/01-12/01
	Tampa-St. Petersburg-Clearwater MSA, FL	H	10.45 FQ	16.59 AW	25.03 TQ	FLBLS	10/01-12/01
	West Palm Beach-Boca Raton MSA, FL	H	15.23 FQ	19.80 AW	23.44 TQ	FLBLS	10/01-12/01
	Georgia	H	10.99 FQ	18.89 AW	26.32 TQ	GABLS	10/01-12/01
	Atlanta MSA, GA	H	15.28 FQ	21.39 AW	26.77 TQ	GABLS	10/01-12/01
	Augusta-Aiken MSA, GA-SC	H	9.01 FQ	14.57 AW	21.46 TQ	GABLS	10/01-12/01
	Columbus MSA, GA-AL	H	9.38 FQ	13.21 AW	17.11 TQ	GABLS	10/01-12/01
	Macon MSA, GA	H	11.21 FQ	13.71 AW	17.30 TQ	GABLS	10/01-12/01
	Savannah MSA, GA	H	10.38 FQ	13.83 AW	16.92 TQ	GABLS	10/01-12/01
	Hawaii	H	11.38 FQ	16.79 AW	22.39 TQ	HIBLS	10/01-12/01
	Honolulu MSA, HI	H	11.76 FQ	17.25 AW	22.71 TQ	HIBLS	10/01-12/01
	Idaho	H	6.72 FQ	13.46 AW	19.64 TQ	IDBLS	10/01-12/01
	Boise City MSA, ID	H	6.00 FQ	14.48 AW	20.42 TQ	IDBLS	10/01-12/01
	Illinois	H	12.08 FQ	18.83 AW	25.95 TQ	ILBLS	10/01-12/01
	Champaign-Urbana MSA, IL	H	11.11 FQ	14.56 AW	17.70 TQ	ILBLS	10/01-12/01
	Chicago PMSA, IL	H	13.67 FQ	19.94 AW	26.41 TQ	ILBLS	10/01-12/01
	Peoria-Pekin MSA, IL	H	9.07 FQ	11.32 AW	14.24 TQ	ILBLS	10/01-12/01
	Rockford MSA, IL	H	10.11 FQ	12.90 AW	16.43 TQ	ILBLS	10/01-12/01
	Springfield MSA, IL	H	7.76 FQ	12.74 AW	16.71 TQ	ILBLS	10/01-12/01
	Indiana	H	9.26 FQ	12.94 AW	17.99 TQ	INBLS	10/01-12/01
	Evansville-Henderson MSA, IN-KY	H	9.18 FQ	11.64 AW	15.63 TQ	INBLS	10/01-12/01
	Fort Wayne MSA, IN	H	9.94 FQ	14.27 AW	19.33 TQ	INBLS	10/01-12/01
	Gary PMSA, IN	H	9.35 FQ	11.76 AW	14.05 TQ	INBLS	10/01-12/01
	Indianapolis MSA, IN	H	9.39 FQ	13.95 AW	19.75 TQ	INBLS	10/01-12/01
	Lafayette MSA, IN	H	9.60 FQ	12.95 AW	16.73 TQ	INBLS	10/01-12/01
	South Bend MSA, IN	H	11.20 FQ	14.71 AW	17.70 TQ	INBLS	10/01-12/01
	Iowa	H	9.97 FQ	14.25 AW	18.13 TQ	IABLS	10/01-12/01
	Cedar Rapids MSA, IA	H	12.06 FQ	15.13 AW	18.27 TQ	IABLS	10/01-12/01
	Davenport-Moline-Rock Island MSA, IA-IL	H	9.47 FQ	12.56 AW	17.29 TQ	IABLS	10/01-12/01
	Des Moines MSA, IA	H	12.16 FQ	16.05 AW	20.38 TQ	IABLS	10/01-12/01
	Kansas	H	9.64 FQ	12.81 AW	16.54 TQ	KSBLS	10/01-12/01
	Topeka MSA, KS	H	10.76 FQ	12.86 AW	16.12 TQ	KSBLS	10/01-12/01
	Wichita MSA, KS	H	11.03 FQ	13.95 AW	17.00 TQ	KSBLS	10/01-12/01
	Kentucky	H	9.13 FQ	14.45 AW	20.21 TQ	KYBLS	10/01-12/01
	Lexington MSA, KY	H	11.57 FQ	15.75 AW	20.90 TQ	KYBLS	10/01-12/01
	Louisville MSA, KY-IN	H	10.85 FQ	15.07 AW	19.74 TQ	KYBLS	10/01-12/01
	Louisiana	H	9.60 FQ	14.28 AW	20.52 TQ	LABLS	10/01-12/01
	Baton Rouge MSA, LA	H	10.76 FQ	13.02 AW	17.55 TQ	LABLS	10/01-12/01
	Houma MSA, LA	H	9.14 FQ	13.88 AW	20.96 TQ	LABLS	10/01-12/01
	Lafayette MSA, LA	H	9.49 FQ	13.33 AW	17.56 TQ	LABLS	10/01-12/01
	Lake Charles MSA, LA	H	8.81 FQ	11.04 AW	13.43 TQ	LABLS	10/01-12/01
	New Orleans MSA, LA	H	9.85 FQ	16.51 AW	21.53 TQ	LABLS	10/01-12/01
	Shreveport-Bossier City MSA, LA	H	10.63 FQ	12.65 AW	14.05 TQ	LABLS	10/01-12/01
	Maine	H	11.50 FQ	15.03 AW	19.39 TQ	MEBLS	10/01-12/01
	Portland MSA, ME	H	12.63 FQ	16.44 AW	20.91 TQ	MEBLS	10/01-12/01
	Maryland	H	12.44 FQ	17.59 AW	22.63 TQ	MDBLS	10/01-12/01
	Baltimore PMSA, MD	H	13.46 FQ	17.82 AW	22.33 TQ	MDBLS	10/01-12/01
	Massachusetts	H	12.37 FQ	18.96 AW	26.69 TQ	MABLS	10/01-12/01
	Boston PMSA, MA-NH	H	13.80 FQ	20.46 AW	27.27 TQ	MABLS	10/01-12/01
	Brockton PMSA, MA	H	14.37 FQ	16.31 AW	19.00 TQ	MABLS	10/01-12/01
	Lawrence PMSA, MA-NH	H	12.77 FQ	17.62 AW	23.07 TQ	MABLS	10/01-12/01
	Lowell PMSA, MA-NH	H	14.13 FQ	17.25 AW	18.03 TQ	MABLS	10/01-12/01
	New Bedford PMSA, MA	H	11.22 FQ	12.97 AW	16.17 TQ	MABLS	10/01-12/01
	Springfield MSA, MA	H	12.70 FQ	15.37 AW	18.27 TQ	MABLS	10/01-12/01
	Worcester PMSA, MA-CT	H	14.16 FQ	17.42 AW	21.42 TQ	MABLS	10/01-12/01
	Michigan	H	9.40 FQ	15.21 AW	22.24 TQ	MIBLS	10/01-12/01
	Ann Arbor PMSA, MI	H	11.84 FQ	15.34 AW	19.89 TQ	MIBLS	10/01-12/01

AAW Average annual wage; **AE** Average entry wage; **AEX** Average experienced wage; **AO** Average offered; **AOH** Average offered, high; **AOL** Average offered, low; **APH** Average pay, high range; **APL** Average pay, low range; **ASH** Average starting, high; **ASL** Average starting, low; **AW** Average wage paid; **FQ** First quartile wage; **H** Hourly; **HI** Highest wage paid; **HR** High end range; **LR** Low end range; **M** Monthly; **MTC** Median total compensation; **MW** Median wage paid; **SQ** Second quartile wage; **S** Special: hourly and annual; **TQ** Third quartile wage; **W** Weekly; **Y** Yearly

Occupation/Type/Industry	Location	Per	Low	Mid	High	Source	Date
Legal Secretary	Detroit PMSA, MI	H	9.37 FQ	16.34 AW	24.61 TQ	MIBLS	10/01-12/01
	Flint PMSA, MI	H	9.04 FQ	11.70 AW	15.09 TQ	MIBLS	10/01-12/01
	Grand Rapids-Muskegon-Holland MSA, MI	H	12.58 FQ	16.92 AW	21.14 TQ	MIBLS	10/01-12/01
	Kalamazoo-Battle Creek MSA, MI	H	10.87 FQ	14.36 AW	18.34 TQ	MIBLS	10/01-12/01
	Lansing-East Lansing MSA, MI	H	11.98 FQ	17.18 AW	21.38 TQ	MIBLS	10/01-12/01
	Saginaw-Bay City-Midland MSA, MI	H	9.50 FQ	12.19 AW	15.38 TQ	MIBLS	10/01-12/01
	Minnesota	H	11.09 FQ	17.82 AW	25.48 TQ	MNBLS	10/01-12/01
	Duluth-Superior MSA, MN-WI	H	10.22 FQ	13.89 AW	19.36 TQ	MNBLS	10/01-12/01
	Minneapolis-St. Paul MSA, MN-WI	H	12.53 FQ	19.24 AW	26.05 TQ	MNBLS	10/01-12/01
	St. Cloud MSA, MN	H	9.66 FQ	13.20 AW	17.04 TQ	MNBLS	10/01-12/01
	Mississippi	H	10.20 FQ	13.27 AW	16.95 TQ	MSBLS	10/01-12/01
	Biloxi-Gulfport-Pascagoula MSA, MS	H	10.96 FQ	12.35 AW	14.14 TQ	MSBLS	10/01-12/01
	Jackson MSA, MS	H	10.89 FQ	14.07 AW	17.87 TQ	MSBLS	10/01-12/01
	Missouri	H	11.00 FQ	15.93 AW	20.69 TQ	MOBLS	10/01-12/01
	Kansas City MSA, MO-KS	H	12.36 FQ	16.28 AW	20.82 TQ	MOBLS	10/01-12/01
	St. Louis MSA, MO-IL	H	13.09 FQ	16.67 AW	20.81 TQ	MOBLS	10/01-12/01
	Springfield MSA, MO	H	9.79 FQ	13.72 AW	19.54 TQ	MOBLS	10/01-12/01
	Montana	H	7.52 FQ	11.44 AW	16.50 TQ	MTBLS	10/01-12/01
	Billings MSA, MT	H	12.99 FQ	16.02 AW	20.16 TQ	MTBLS	10/01-12/01
	Nebraska	H	9.16 FQ	14.14 AW	19.27 TQ	NEBLS	10/01-12/01
	Lincoln MSA, NE	H	9.47 FQ	12.75 AW	16.44 TQ	NEBLS	10/01-12/01
	Omaha MSA, NE-IA	H	12.38 FQ	15.97 AW	20.34 TQ	NEBLS	10/01-12/01
	Nevada	H	13.05 FQ	17.88 AW	23.37 TQ	NVBLS	10/01-12/01
	Las Vegas MSA, NV-AZ	H	13.05 FQ	17.82 AW	23.75 TQ	NVBLS	10/01-12/01
	Reno MSA, NV	H	14.89 FQ	18.63 AW	22.97 TQ	NVBLS	10/01-12/01
	New Hampshire	H	9.12 FQ	13.30 AW	19.04 TQ	NHBLS	10/01-12/01
	Manchester PMSA, NH	H	8.74 FQ	12.06 AW	18.84 TQ	NHBLS	10/01-12/01
	Nashua PMSA, NH	H	11.57 FQ	13.88 AW	18.97 TQ	NHBLS	10/01-12/01
	Portsmouth-Rochester PMSA, NH-ME	H	11.75 FQ	15.89 AW	20.59 TQ	NHBLS	10/01-12/01
	New Jersey	H	13.24 FQ	17.46 AW	22.82 TQ	NJBLS	10/01-12/01
	Atlantic-Cape May PMSA, NJ	H	14.24 FQ	20.05 AW	30.51 TQ	NJBLS	10/01-12/01
	Bergen-Passaic PMSA, NJ	H	11.46 FQ	16.64 AW	22.13 TQ	NJBLS	10/01-12/01
	Jersey City PMSA, NJ	H	10.74 FQ	14.46 AW	20.78 TQ	NJBLS	10/01-12/01
	Middlesex-Somerset-Hunterdon PMSA, NJ	H	14.01 FQ	16.90 AW	21.65 TQ	NJBLS	10/01-12/01
	Monmouth-Ocean PMSA, NJ	H	13.88 FQ	17.60 AW	27.94 TQ	NJBLS	10/01-12/01
	Newark PMSA, NJ	H	14.30 FQ	18.28 AW	23.28 TQ	NJBLS	10/01-12/01
	Trenton PMSA, NJ	H	13.62 FQ	18.66 AW	25.69 TQ	NJBLS	10/01-12/01
	New Mexico	H	8.57 FQ	13.65 AW	18.48 TQ	NMBLS	10/01-12/01
	Albuquerque MSA, NM	H	11.74 FQ	15.83 AW	20.63 TQ	NMBLS	10/01-12/01
	Las Cruces MSA, NM	H	6.80 FQ	11.42 AW	15.89 TQ	NMBLS	10/01-12/01
	New York	H	12.61 FQ	21.32 AW	30.54 TQ	NYBLS	10/01-12/01
	Albany-Schenectady-Troy MSA, NY	H	11.12 FQ	15.09 AW	19.62 TQ	NYBLS	10/01-12/01
	Binghamton MSA, NY	H	9.58 FQ	13.77 AW	20.47 TQ	NYBLS	10/01-12/01
	Buffalo-Niagara Falls MSA, NY	H	11.26 FQ	14.50 AW	18.42 TQ	NYBLS	10/01-12/01
	Dutchess County PMSA, NY	H	9.50 FQ	15.19 AW	21.33 TQ	NYBLS	10/01-12/01
	Nassau-Suffolk PMSA, NY	H	9.96 FQ	16.98 AW	25.17 TQ	NYBLS	10/01-12/01
	New York PMSA, NY	H	17.43 FQ	23.65 AW	31.75 TQ	NYBLS	10/01-12/01
	Newburgh PMSA, NY-PA	H	10.99 FQ	15.41 AW	20.89 TQ	NYBLS	10/01-12/01
	Rochester MSA, NY	H	9.04 FQ	15.57 AW	26.24 TQ	NYBLS	10/01-12/01
	Syracuse MSA, NY	H	14.08 FQ	16.58 AW	20.66 TQ	NYBLS	10/01-12/01
	Utica-Rome MSA, NY	H	9.67 FQ	14.59 AW	18.03 TQ	NYBLS	10/01-12/01
	North Carolina	H	9.44 FQ	14.59 AW	20.84 TQ	NCBLS	10/01-12/01
	Asheville MSA, NC	H	9.83 FQ	14.88 AW	22.33 TQ	NCBLS	10/01-12/01
	Charlotte-Gastonia-Rock Hill MSA, NC-SC	H	9.85 FQ	15.18 AW	21.54 TQ	NCBLS	10/01-12/01
	Fayetteville MSA, NC	H	8.43 FQ	11.13 AW	14.11 TQ	NCBLS	10/01-12/01
	Greensboro-Winston-Salem-High Point MSA, NC	H	11.80 FQ	16.10 AW	21.08 TQ	NCBLS	10/01-12/01
	Hickory-Morganton-Lenoir MSA, NC	H	10.18 FQ	13.66 AW	16.62 TQ	NCBLS	10/01-12/01
	Raleigh-Durham-Chapel Hill MSA, NC	H	12.00 FQ	17.57 AW	22.08 TQ	NCBLS	10/01-12/01
	Wilmington MSA, NC	H	13.58 FQ	14.84 AW	16.70 TQ	NCBLS	10/01-12/01

AAW	Average annual wage	**AOH**	Average offered, high	**ASH**	Average starting, high	**H**	Hourly	**M**	Monthly	**S**	Special: hourly and annual
AE	Average entry wage	**AOL**	Average offered, low	**ASL**	Average starting, low	**HI**	Highest wage paid	**MTC**	Median total compensation	**TQ**	Third quartile wage
AEX	Average experienced wage	**APH**	Average pay, high range	**AW**	Average wage paid	**HR**	High end range	**MW**	Median wage paid	**W**	Weekly
AO	Average offered	**APL**	Average pay, low range	**FQ**	First quartile wage	**LR**	Low end range	**SQ**	Second quartile wage	**Y**	Yearly

Occupation/Type/Industry	Location	Per	Low	Mid	High	Source	Date
Legal Secretary	North Dakota	H	6.74 FQ	9.99 AW	13.30 TQ	NDBLS	10/01-12/01
	Fargo-Moorhead MSA, ND-MN	H	9.26 FQ	11.86 AW	15.26 TQ	NDBLS	10/01-12/01
	Ohio	H	10.62 FQ	15.27 AW	20.81 TQ	OHBLS	10/01-12/01
	Akron PMSA, OH	H	12.30 FQ	15.23 AW	18.59 TQ	OHBLS	10/01-12/01
	Canton-Massillon MSA, OH	H	11.87 FQ	14.21 AW	16.99 TQ	OHBLS	10/01-12/01
	Cincinnati PMSA, OH-KY-IN	H	9.57 FQ	14.61 AW	19.93 TQ	OHBLS	10/01-12/01
	Cleveland-Lorain-Elyria PMSA, OH	H	11.94 FQ	16.40 AW	21.32 TQ	OHBLS	10/01-12/01
	Columbus MSA, OH	H	12.01 FQ	17.07 AW	21.93 TQ	OHBLS	10/01-12/01
	Dayton-Springfield MSA, OH	H	9.91 FQ	13.66 AW	18.66 TQ	OHBLS	10/01-12/01
	Hamilton-Middletown PMSA, OH	H	9.51 FQ	12.39 AW	16.20 TQ	OHBLS	10/01-12/01
	Mansfield MSA, OH	H	7.86 FQ	11.68 AW	14.44 TQ	OHBLS	10/01-12/01
	Toledo MSA, OH	H	11.02 FQ	13.88 AW	16.98 TQ	OHBLS	10/01-12/01
	Youngstown-Warren MSA, OH	H	6.91 FQ	11.36 AW	17.05 TQ	OHBLS	10/01-12/01
	Oklahoma	H	9.02 FQ	12.67 AW	16.95 TQ	OKBLS	10/01-12/01
	Oklahoma City MSA, OK	H	11.29 FQ	14.87 AW	18.00 TQ	OKBLS	10/01-12/01
	Tulsa MSA, OK	H	9.59 FQ	12.58 AW	16.34 TQ	OKBLS	10/01-12/01
	Oregon	H	10.02 FQ	15.46 AW	21.49 TQ	ORBLS	10/01-12/01
	Eugene-Springfield MSA, OR	H	11.34 FQ	14.79 AW	19.49 TQ	ORBLS	10/01-12/01
	Medford-Ashland MSA, OR	H	9.27 FQ	11.52 AW	15.40 TQ	ORBLS	10/01-12/01
	Portland-Vancouver PMSA, OR-WA	H	12.80 FQ	17.40 AW	22.71 TQ	ORBLS	10/01-12/01
	Salem PMSA, OR	H	10.98 FQ	14.05 AW	16.90 TQ	ORBLS	10/01-12/01
	Pennsylvania	H	9.27 FQ	15.35 AW	22.60 TQ	PABLS	10/01-12/01
	Allentown-Bethlehem-Easton MSA, PA	H	10.07 FQ	14.02 AW	18.11 TQ	PABLS	10/01-12/01
	Erie MSA, PA	H	9.65 FQ	13.01 AW	17.27 TQ	PABLS	10/01-12/01
	Harrisburg-Lebanon-Carlisle MSA, PA	H	7.96 FQ	12.95 AW	18.05 TQ	PABLS	10/01-12/01
	Johnstown MSA, PA	H	6.79 FQ	10.24 AW	13.77 TQ	PABLS	10/01-12/01
	Lancaster MSA, PA	H	9.64 FQ	13.04 AW	16.80 TQ	PABLS	10/01-12/01
	Philadelphia PMSA, PA-NJ	H	10.13 FQ	17.04 AW	24.29 TQ	PABLS	10/01-12/01
	Pittsburgh MSA, PA	H	9.84 FQ	15.41 AW	20.91 TQ	PABLS	10/01-12/01
	Reading MSA, PA	H	9.47 FQ	14.55 AW	20.16 TQ	PABLS	10/01-12/01
	Scranton-Wilkes-Barre-Hazleton MSA, PA	H	8.88 FQ	12.29 AW	16.10 TQ	PABLS	10/01-12/01
	York MSA, PA	H	7.70 FQ	11.38 AW	15.94 TQ	PABLS	10/01-12/01
	Rhode Island	H	11.77 FQ	15.98 AW	21.37 TQ	RIBLS	10/01-12/01
	Providence-Fall River-Warwick MSA, RI-MA	H	10.51 FQ	14.93 AW	20.55 TQ	RIBLS	10/01-12/01
	South Carolina	H	9.49 FQ	14.30 AW	20.28 TQ	SCBLS	10/01-12/01
	Charleston-North Charleston MSA, SC	H	11.31 FQ	14.66 AW	19.07 TQ	SCBLS	10/01-12/01
	Columbia MSA, SC	H	11.49 FQ	15.36 AW	19.57 TQ	SCBLS	10/01-12/01
	Greenville-Spartanburg-Anderson MSA, SC	H	11.09 FQ	16.48 AW	24.33 TQ	SCBLS	10/01-12/01
	Myrtle Beach MSA, SC	H	7.66 FQ	12.32 AW	20.01 TQ	SCBLS	10/01-12/01
	South Dakota	H	7.54 FQ	11.08 AW	14.74 TQ	SDBLS	10/01-12/01
	Sioux Falls MSA, SD	H	9.92 FQ	13.29 AW	16.85 TQ	SDBLS	10/01-12/01
	Tennessee	H	9.02 FQ	13.27 AW	17.47 TQ	TNBLS	10/01-12/01
	Chattanooga MSA, TN-GA	H	10.26 FQ	14.17 AW	18.81 TQ	TNBLS	10/01-12/01
	Clarksville-Hopkinsville MSA, TN-KY	H	7.18 FQ	11.39 AW	14.67 TQ	TNBLS	10/01-12/01
	Johnson City-Kingsport-Bristol MSA, TN-VA	H	8.75 FQ	10.13 AW	12.18 TQ	TNBLS	10/01-12/01
	Knoxville MSA, TN	H	8.89 FQ	11.73 AW	16.43 TQ	TNBLS	10/01-12/01
	Memphis MSA, TN-AR-MS	H	11.32 FQ	15.52 AW	20.08 TQ	TNBLS	10/01-12/01
	Nashville MSA, TN	H	10.62 FQ	14.46 AW	17.39 TQ	TNBLS	10/01-12/01
	Texas	H	10.48 FQ	16.25 AW	24.44 TQ	TXBLS	10/01-12/01
	Amarillo MSA, TX	H	10.35 FQ	14.73 AW	19.26 TQ	TXBLS	10/01-12/01
	Austin-San Marcos MSA, TX	H	11.77 FQ	18.89 AW	26.18 TQ	TXBLS	10/01-12/01
	Beaumont-Port Arthur MSA, TX	H	12.04 FQ	15.98 AW	22.51 TQ	TXBLS	10/01-12/01
	Brazoria PMSA, TX	H	7.40 FQ	10.91 AW	16.25 TQ	TXBLS	10/01-12/01
	Brownsville-Harlingen-San Benito MSA, TX	H	5.93 FQ	12.20 AW	17.42 TQ	TXBLS	10/01-12/01
	Corpus Christi MSA, TX	H	10.81 FQ	15.59 AW	21.75 TQ	TXBLS	10/01-12/01
	Dallas PMSA, TX	H	13.11 FQ	19.40 AW	25.86 TQ	TXBLS	10/01-12/01
	El Paso MSA, TX	H	9.29 FQ	13.30 AW	19.77 TQ	TXBLS	10/01-12/01

AAW Average annual wage	**AOH** Average offered, high	**ASH** Average starting, high	**H** Hourly	**M** Monthly	**S** Special: hourly and annual
AE Average entry wage	**AOL** Average offered, low	**ASL** Average starting, low	**HI** Highest wage paid	**MTC** Median total compensation	**TQ** Third quartile wage
AEX Average experienced wage	**APH** Average pay, high range	**AW** Average wage paid	**HR** High end range	**MW** Median wage paid	**W** Weekly
AO Average offered	**APL** Average pay, low range	**FQ** First quartile wage	**LR** Low end range	**SQ** Second quartile wage	**Y** Yearly

Occupation/Type/Industry	Location	Per	Low	Mid	High	Source	Date
Legal Secretary	Fort Worth-Arlington PMSA, TX	H	12.07 FQ	17.01 AW	21.14 TQ	TXBLS	10/01-12/01
	Galveston-Texas City PMSA, TX	H	11.77 FQ	13.31 AW	15.65 TQ	TXBLS	10/01-12/01
	Houston PMSA, TX	H	11.17 FQ	15.67 AW	24.55 TQ	TXBLS	10/01-12/01
	Killeen-Temple MSA, TX	H	9.00 FQ	9.95 AW	11.08 TQ	TXBLS	10/01-12/01
	Laredo MSA, TX	H	9.40 FQ	11.80 AW	14.20 TQ	TXBLS	10/01-12/01
	Longview-Marshall MSA, TX	H	10.46 FQ	13.32 AW	16.78 TQ	TXBLS	10/01-12/01
	Lubbock MSA, TX	H	9.71 FQ	13.95 AW	17.26 TQ	TXBLS	10/01-12/01
	McAllen-Edinburg-Mission MSA, TX	H	9.64 FQ	13.72 AW	16.70 TQ	TXBLS	10/01-12/01
	Odessa-Midland MSA, TX	H	7.31 FQ	13.72 AW	20.13 TQ	TXBLS	10/01-12/01
	San Antonio MSA, TX	H	10.06 FQ	17.66 AW	25.27 TQ	TXBLS	10/01-12/01
	Tyler MSA, TX	H	9.15 FQ	11.15 AW	16.10 TQ	TXBLS	10/01-12/01
	Waco MSA, TX	H	11.98 FQ	14.64 AW	17.27 TQ	TXBLS	10/01-12/01
	Utah	H	11.19 FQ	14.71 AW	20.30 TQ	UTBLS	10/01-12/01
	Provo-Orem MSA, UT	H	8.97 FQ	11.62 AW	14.17 TQ	UTBLS	10/01-12/01
	Salt Lake City-Ogden MSA, UT	H	11.35 FQ	15.05 AW	20.59 TQ	UTBLS	10/01-12/01
	Vermont	H	11.16 FQ	13.94 AW	19.24 TQ	VTBLS	10/01-12/01
	Burlington MSA, VT	H	11.64 FQ	14.84 AW	20.00 TQ	VTBLS	10/01-12/01
	Virginia	H	9.42 FQ	16.11 AW	22.88 TQ	VABLS	10/01-12/01
	Lynchburg MSA, VA	H	9.26 FQ	11.74 AW	16.42 TQ	VABLS	10/01-12/01
	Norfolk-Virginia Beach-Newport News MSA, VA-NC	H	10.92 FQ	14.51 AW	17.69 TQ	VABLS	10/01-12/01
	Richmond-Petersburg MSA, VA	H	11.49 FQ	17.43 AW	23.45 TQ	VABLS	10/01-12/01
	Roanoke MSA, VA	H	8.88 FQ	12.10 AW	18.31 TQ	VABLS	10/01-12/01
	Washington	H	10.67 FQ	16.20 AW	24.08 TQ	WABLS	10/01-12/01
	Bremerton PMSA, WA	H	11.14 FQ	12.21 AW	13.50 TQ	WABLS	10/01-12/01
	Olympia PMSA, WA	H	11.78 FQ	15.37 AW	19.71 TQ	WABLS	10/01-12/01
	Richland-Kennewick-Pasco MSA, WA	H	9.32 FQ	12.34 AW	16.83 TQ	WABLS	10/01-12/01
	Seattle-Bellevue-Everett PMSA, WA	H	11.94 FQ	17.92 AW	25.40 TQ	WABLS	10/01-12/01
	Spokane MSA, WA	H	9.31 FQ	12.99 AW	17.82 TQ	WABLS	10/01-12/01
	Tacoma PMSA, WA	H	11.17 FQ	13.99 AW	19.58 TQ	WABLS	10/01-12/01
	Yakima MSA, WA	H	10.62 FQ	14.40 AW	17.77 TQ	WABLS	10/01-12/01
	West Virginia	H	9.93 FQ	12.78 AW	16.13 TQ	WVBLS	10/01-12/01
	Charleston MSA, WV	H	10.92 FQ	13.07 AW	16.57 TQ	WVBLS	10/01-12/01
	Huntington-Ashland MSA, WV-KY-OH	H	6.69 FQ	11.50 AW	15.87 TQ	WVBLS	10/01-12/01
	Wisconsin	H	9.93 FQ	15.26 AW	20.74 TQ	WIBLS	10/01-12/01
	Appleton-Oshkosh-Neenah MSA, WI	H	8.74 FQ	13.75 AW	17.52 TQ	WIBLS	10/01-12/01
	Green Bay MSA, WI	H	10.42 FQ	13.87 AW	17.51 TQ	WIBLS	10/01-12/01
	Madison MSA, WI	H	13.61 FQ	16.54 AW	20.51 TQ	WIBLS	10/01-12/01
	Milwaukee-Waukesha PMSA, WI	H	13.33 FQ	17.62 AW	21.82 TQ	WIBLS	10/01-12/01
	Racine PMSA, WI	H	11.96 FQ	13.31 AW	14.65 TQ	WIBLS	10/01-12/01
	Wyoming	H	8.92 FQ	11.35 AW	13.86 TQ	WYBLS	10/01-12/01
	Cheyenne MSA, WY	H	9.08 FQ	11.09 AW	15.47 TQ	WYBLS	10/01-12/01
	Puerto Rico	H	6.13 FQ	8.58 AW	11.11 TQ	PRBLS	10/01-12/01
	Virgin Islands	H	11.59 FQ	14.99 AW	17.73 TQ	VIBLS	10/01-12/01
	Guam	H	6.44 FQ	12.88 AW	20.82 TQ	GUBLS	10/01-12/01
Legislative Assistant	United States	Y		32000 AW		AM	1/01-1/02
Legislator	Alabama	Y	11510 FQ	15760 AW	20820 TQ	ALBLS	10/01-12/01
	Birmingham MSA, AL	Y	11320 FQ	16860 AW	30920 TQ	ALBLS	10/01-12/01
	Huntsville MSA, AL	Y	13030 FQ	15750 AW	18030 TQ	ALBLS	10/01-12/01
	Mobile MSA, AL	Y	11940 FQ	14860 AW	20960 TQ	ALBLS	10/01-12/01
	Montgomery MSA, AL	Y	12600 FQ	23950 AW	55580 TQ	ALBLS	10/01-12/01
	Alaska	Y	12460 FQ	20210 AW	27580 TQ	AKBLS	10/01-12/01
	Arizona	Y	11670 FQ	21290 AW	51120 TQ	AZBLS	10/01-12/01
	Arkansas	Y	11910 FQ	22760 AW	53820 TQ	ARBLS	10/01-12/01
	Fayetteville-Springdale-Rogers MSA, AR	Y	12340 FQ	40270 AW	84400 TQ	ARBLS	10/01-12/01
	Fort Smith MSA, AR-OK	Y	11620 FQ	29750 AW	70630 TQ	ARBLS	10/01-12/01
	Little Rock-North Little Rock MSA, AR	Y	11870 FQ	19040 AW	40770 TQ	ARBLS	10/01-12/01
	California	Y	31140 FQ	44580 AW	58020 TQ	CABLS	10/01-12/01

AAW Average annual wage; **AE** Average entry wage; **AEX** Average experienced wage; **AO** Average offered; **AOH** Average offered, high; **AOL** Average offered, low; **APH** Average pay, high range; **APL** Average pay, low range; **ASH** Average starting, high; **ASL** Average starting, low; **AW** Average wage paid; **FQ** First quartile wage; **H** Hourly; **HI** Highest wage paid; **HR** High end range; **LR** Low end range; **M** Monthly; **MTC** Median total compensation; **MW** Median wage paid; **SQ** Second quartile wage; **S** Special: hourly and annual; **TQ** Third quartile wage; **W** Weekly; **Y** Yearly

Occupation/Type/Industry	Location	Per	Low	Mid	High	Source	Date
Legislator	Bakersfield MSA, CA	Y	30160 FQ	34930 AW	42690 TQ	CABLS	10/01-12/01
	Chico-Paradise MSA, CA	Y	27350 FQ	50840 AW	105980 TQ	CABLS	10/01-12/01
	Los Angeles-Long Beach PMSA, CA	Y	33580 FQ	42500 AW	50150 TQ	CABLS	10/01-12/01
	Merced MSA, CA	Y	24980 FQ	44030 AW	66740 TQ	CABLS	10/01-12/01
	Modesto MSA, CA	Y	37470 FQ	43160 AW	46320 TQ	CABLS	10/01-12/01
	Oakland PMSA, CA	Y	31970 FQ	43770 AW	53090 TQ	CABLS	10/01-12/01
	Orange County PMSA, CA	Y	31130 FQ	46100 AW	82150 TQ	CABLS	10/01-12/01
	Riverside-San Bernardino PMSA, CA	Y	32940 FQ	43460 AW	56570 TQ	CABLS	10/01-12/01
	Sacramento PMSA, CA	Y	31710 FQ	54630 AW	106700 TQ	CABLS	10/01-12/01
	San Diego MSA, CA	Y	30940 FQ	49240 AW	82270 TQ	CABLS	10/01-12/01
	San Francisco PMSA, CA	Y	20400 FQ	38520 AW	46420 TQ	CABLS	10/01-12/01
	San Jose PMSA, CA	Y	33950 FQ	42880 AW	53320 TQ	CABLS	10/01-12/01
	San Luis Obispo-Atascadero-Paso Robles MSA, CA	Y	15020 FQ	38760 AW	45780 TQ	CABLS	10/01-12/01
	Santa Barbara-Santa Maria-Lompoc MSA, CA	Y	29420 FQ	39340 AW	54600 TQ	CABLS	10/01-12/01
	Santa Rosa PMSA, CA	Y	37980 FQ	42770 AW	45980 TQ	CABLS	10/01-12/01
	Stockton-Lodi MSA, CA	Y	33570 FQ	51770 AW	105850 TQ	CABLS	10/01-12/01
	Vallejo-Fairfield-Napa PMSA, CA	Y	25030 FQ	38540 AW	52330 TQ	CABLS	10/01-12/01
	Ventura PMSA, CA	Y	25790 FQ	40420 AW	51420 TQ	CABLS	10/01-12/01
	Visalia-Tulare-Porterville MSA, CA	Y	33380 FQ	45220 AW	57190 TQ	CABLS	10/01-12/01
	Colorado	Y	11610 FQ	25300 AW	50590 TQ	COBLS	10/01-12/01
	Denver PMSA, CO	Y	11510 FQ	26580 AW	56170 TQ	COBLS	10/01-12/01
	Greeley PMSA, CO	Y	11460 FQ	25870 AW	57020 TQ	COBLS	10/01-12/01
	Connecticut	Y	13940 FQ	42010 AW	75610 TQ	CTBLS	10/01-12/01
	Hartford MSA, CT	Y	23770 FQ	49080 AW	74260 TQ	CTBLS	10/01-12/01
	New Haven-Meriden PMSA, CT	Y	13570 FQ	29960 AW	66570 TQ	CTBLS	10/01-12/01
	New London-Norwich MSA, CT-RI	Y	14130 FQ	32280 AW	75280 TQ	CTBLS	10/01-12/01
	Delaware	Y	13380 FQ	39170 AW	94600 TQ	DEBLS	10/01-12/01
	Wilmington-Newark PMSA, DE-MD	Y	13220 FQ	36700 AW	126840 TQ	DEBLS	10/01-12/01
	Washington PMSA, DC-MD-VA-WV	Y	12510 FQ	48270 AW	111460 TQ	DCBLS	10/01-12/01
	Florida	Y	11990 FQ	25550 AW	52320 TQ	FLBLS	10/01-12/01
	Daytona Beach MSA, FL	Y	11630 FQ	17980 AW	41220 TQ	FLBLS	10/01-12/01
	Fort Lauderdale PMSA, FL	Y	12230 FQ	24760 AW	36470 TQ	FLBLS	10/01-12/01
	Fort Myers-Cape Coral MSA, FL	Y	11670 FQ	22070 AW	64210 TQ	FLBLS	10/01-12/01
	Jacksonville MSA, FL	Y	13740 FQ	29860 AW	46280 TQ	FLBLS	10/01-12/01
	Lakeland-Winter Haven MSA, FL	Y	11670 FQ	12700 AW	14580 TQ	FLBLS	10/01-12/01
	Melbourne-Titusville-Palm Bay MSA, FL	Y	11820 FQ	20840 AW	41770 TQ	FLBLS	10/01-12/01
	Miami PMSA, FL	Y	11950 FQ	26710 AW	50600 TQ	FLBLS	10/01-12/01
	Orlando MSA, FL	Y	12390 FQ	26810 AW	62260 TQ	FLBLS	10/01-12/01
	Sarasota-Bradenton MSA, FL	Y	12200 FQ	27370 AW	57020 TQ	FLBLS	10/01-12/01
	Tallahassee MSA, FL	Y	13280 FQ	35290 AW	72490 TQ	FLBLS	10/01-12/01
	Tampa-St. Petersburg-Clearwater MSA, FL	Y	11960 FQ	24630 AW	36800 TQ	FLBLS	10/01-12/01
	West Palm Beach-Boca Raton MSA, FL	Y	12060 FQ	30330 AW	86640 TQ	FLBLS	10/01-12/01
	Georgia	Y	12620 FQ	22590 AW	35610 TQ	GABLS	10/01-12/01
	Atlanta MSA, GA	Y	14630 FQ	31440 AW	61010 TQ	GABLS	10/01-12/01
	Augusta-Aiken MSA, GA-SC	Y	13220 FQ	29910 AW	55560 TQ	GABLS	10/01-12/01
	Macon MSA, GA	Y	14420 FQ	24050 AW	35160 TQ	GABLS	10/01-12/01
	Hawaii	Y	29140 FQ	36170 AW	46600 TQ	HIBLS	10/01-12/01
	Idaho	Y	11740 FQ	45850 AW	106870 TQ	IDBLS	10/01-12/01
	Boise City MSA, ID	Y	12340 FQ	74820 AW	111320 TQ	IDBLS	10/01-12/01
	Illinois	Y	11580 FQ	18590 AW	24810 TQ	ILBLS	10/01-12/01
	Chicago PMSA, IL	Y	11650 FQ	21170 AW	47890 TQ	ILBLS	10/01-12/01
	Peoria-Pekin MSA, IL	Y	11550 FQ	13890 AW	14410 TQ	ILBLS	10/01-12/01
	Rockford MSA, IL	Y	11690 FQ	24950 AW	66750 TQ	ILBLS	10/01-12/01
	Springfield MSA, IL	Y	12210 FQ	28830 AW	58610 TQ	ILBLS	10/01-12/01
	Indiana	Y	11870 FQ	23780 AW	36000 TQ	INBLS	10/01-12/01
	Elkhart-Goshen MSA, IN	Y	11130 FQ	15750 AW	33000 TQ	INBLS	10/01-12/01

AAW	Average annual wage	**AOH**	Average offered, high	**ASH**	Average starting, high	**H**	Hourly	**M**	Monthly	**S**	Special: hourly and annual
AE	Average entry wage	**AOL**	Average offered, low	**ASL**	Average starting, low	**HI**	Highest wage paid	**MTC**	Median total compensation	**TQ**	Third quartile wage
AEX	Average experienced wage	**APH**	Average pay, high range	**AW**	Average wage paid	**HR**	High end range	**MW**	Median wage paid	**W**	Weekly
AO	Average offered	**APL**	Average pay, low range	**FQ**	First quartile wage	**LR**	Low end range	**SQ**	Second quartile wage	**Y**	Yearly

Occupation/Type/Industry	Location	Per	Low	Mid	High	Source	Date
Legislator	Evansville-Henderson MSA, IN-KY	Y	16350 FQ	27550 AW	35270 TQ	INBLS	10/01-12/01
	Fort Wayne MSA, IN	Y	12060 FQ	40630 AW		INBLS	10/01-12/01
	Gary PMSA, IN	Y	12280 FQ	26930 AW	38450 TQ	INBLS	10/01-12/01
	Indianapolis MSA, IN	Y	11360 FQ	17230 AW	33000 TQ	INBLS	10/01-12/01
	Lafayette MSA, IN	Y	14300 FQ	25900 AW	32640 TQ	INBLS	10/01-12/01
	Iowa	Y	11420 FQ	20720 AW	42360 TQ	IABLS	10/01-12/01
	Cedar Rapids MSA, IA	Y	11050 FQ	12150 AW	13710 TQ	IABLS	10/01-12/01
	Davenport-Moline-Rock Island MSA, IA-IL	Y	11880 FQ	23220 AW	69220 TQ	IABLS	10/01-12/01
	Kansas	Y	12280 FQ	35370 AW	56480 TQ	KSBLS	10/01-12/01
	Topeka MSA, KS	Y	11430 FQ	25460 AW	48960 TQ	KSBLS	10/01-12/01
	Wichita MSA, KS	Y	23130 FQ	32730 AW	37660 TQ	KSBLS	10/01-12/01
	Kentucky	Y	13850 FQ	53490 AW	103050 TQ	KYBLS	10/01-12/01
	Louisville MSA, KY-IN	Y	15950 FQ	31690 AW	40510 TQ	KYBLS	10/01-12/01
	Louisiana	Y	11670 FQ	14070 AW	17270 TQ	LABLS	10/01-12/01
	Baton Rouge MSA, LA	Y	11800 FQ	14960 AW	18040 TQ	LABLS	10/01-12/01
	Houma MSA, LA	Y	11470 FQ	12580 AW	14240 TQ	LABLS	10/01-12/01
	Lafayette MSA, LA	Y	11230 FQ	13010 AW	14760 TQ	LABLS	10/01-12/01
	New Orleans MSA, LA	Y	11930 FQ	15700 AW	23040 TQ	LABLS	10/01-12/01
	Shreveport-Bossier City MSA, LA	Y	12430 FQ	17330 AW	31540 TQ	LABLS	10/01-12/01
	Maine	Y	11950 FQ	20120 AW	37620 TQ	MEBLS	10/01-12/01
	Portland MSA, ME	Y	12170 FQ	25260 AW	52900 TQ	MEBLS	10/01-12/01
	Maryland	Y	11890 FQ	34570 AW	73290 TQ	MDBLS	10/01-12/01
	Baltimore PMSA, MD	Y	12110 FQ	36080 AW	83950 TQ	MDBLS	10/01-12/01
	Massachusetts	Y	14110 FQ	19850 AW	37470 TQ	MABLS	10/01-12/01
	Boston PMSA, MA-NH	Y	14060 FQ	22070 AW	46900 TQ	MABLS	10/01-12/01
	Brockton PMSA, MA	Y	14140 FQ	16010 AW	16460 TQ	MABLS	10/01-12/01
	Lawrence PMSA, MA-NH	Y	11720 FQ	15490 AW	19800 TQ	MABLS	10/01-12/01
	Lowell PMSA, MA-NH	Y	13420 FQ	16600 AW	18160 TQ	MABLS	10/01-12/01
	Springfield MSA, MA	Y	14100 FQ	16930 AW	30930 TQ	MABLS	10/01-12/01
	Worcester PMSA, MA-CT	Y	14180 FQ	16430 AW	18310 TQ	MABLS	10/01-12/01
	Michigan	Y	12210 FQ	36570 AW	72950 TQ	MIBLS	10/01-12/01
	Detroit PMSA, MI	Y	12740 FQ	40870 AW	70610 TQ	MIBLS	10/01-12/01
	Flint PMSA, MI	Y	17460 FQ	32900 AW	44680 TQ	MIBLS	10/01-12/01
	Grand Rapids-Muskegon-Holland MSA, MI	Y	13800 FQ	39210 AW	58380 TQ	MIBLS	10/01-12/01
	Saginaw-Bay City-Midland MSA, MI	Y	12110 FQ	29930 AW	81830 TQ	MIBLS	10/01-12/01
	Minnesota	Y	11540 FQ	15960 AW	22390 TQ	MNBLS	10/01-12/01
	Duluth-Superior MSA, MN-WI	Y	11460 FQ	17260 AW	29030 TQ	MNBLS	10/01-12/01
	Minneapolis-St. Paul MSA, MN-WI	Y	11310 FQ	16550 AW	29020 TQ	MNBLS	10/01-12/01
	St. Cloud MSA, MN	Y	13380 FQ	20630 AW	22350 TQ	MNBLS	10/01-12/01
	Mississippi	Y	11810 FQ	19800 AW	38290 TQ	MSBLS	10/01-12/01
	Biloxi-Gulfport-Pascagoula MSA, MS	Y	11830 FQ	26780 AW	58460 TQ	MSBLS	10/01-12/01
	Jackson MSA, MS	Y	11740 FQ	25430 AW	56770 TQ	MSBLS	10/01-12/01
	Missouri	Y	11770 FQ	24170 AW	41510 TQ	MOBLS	10/01-12/01
	Kansas City MSA, MO-KS	Y	11400 FQ	17280 AW	38180 TQ	MOBLS	10/01-12/01
	St. Louis MSA, MO-IL	Y	11530 FQ	17990 AW	25800 TQ	MOBLS	10/01-12/01
	Montana	Y	11890 FQ	32360 AW	67530 TQ	MTBLS	10/01-12/01
	Billings MSA, MT	Y	11290 FQ	17850 AW	50620 TQ	MTBLS	10/01-12/01
	Nebraska	Y	11660 FQ	16800 AW	35680 TQ	NEBLS	10/01-12/01
	Omaha MSA, NE-IA	Y	11620 FQ	16440 AW	27880 TQ	NEBLS	10/01-12/01
	Nevada	Y	20350 FQ	39310 AW	69090 TQ	NVBLS	10/01-12/01
	Las Vegas MSA, NV-AZ	Y	13310 FQ	31320 AW	64200 TQ	NVBLS	10/01-12/01
	Reno MSA, NV	Y	26490 FQ	45980 AW	74950 TQ	NVBLS	10/01-12/01
	New Hampshire	Y	11440 FQ	12970 AW	14460 TQ	NHBLS	10/01-12/01
	Portsmouth-Rochester PMSA, NH-ME	Y	11120 FQ	12570 AW	13910 TQ	NHBLS	10/01-12/01
	New Jersey	Y	11760 FQ	28200 AW	62900 TQ	NJBLS	10/01-12/01
	Atlantic-Cape May PMSA, NJ	Y	11980 FQ	32180 AW	66670 TQ	NJBLS	10/01-12/01
	Bergen-Passaic PMSA, NJ	Y	11720 FQ	29930 AW	66890 TQ	NJBLS	10/01-12/01
	Middlesex-Somerset-Hunterdon PMSA, NJ	Y	11990 FQ	30390 AW	61590 TQ	NJBLS	10/01-12/01
	Monmouth-Ocean PMSA, NJ	Y	11830 FQ	23090 AW	44110 TQ	NJBLS	10/01-12/01
	Newark PMSA, NJ	Y	11630 FQ	27550 AW	70540 TQ	NJBLS	10/01-12/01
	Trenton PMSA, NJ	Y	11930 FQ	33680 AW	89030 TQ	NJBLS	10/01-12/01
	New Mexico	Y	11720 FQ	16910 AW	30750 TQ	NMBLS	10/01-12/01
	Albuquerque MSA, NM	Y	11590 FQ	23470 AW	66000 TQ	NMBLS	10/01-12/01

AAW Average annual wage **AE** Average entry wage **AEX** Average experienced wage **AO** Average offered **AOH** Average offered, high **AOL** Average offered, low **APH** Average pay, high range **APL** Average pay, low range **ASH** Average starting, high **ASL** Average starting, low **AW** Average wage paid **FQ** First quartile wage **H** Hourly **HI** Highest wage paid **HR** High end range **LR** Low end range **M** Monthly **MTC** Median total compensation **MW** Median wage paid **SQ** Second quartile wage **S** Special: hourly and annual **TQ** Third quartile wage **W** Weekly **Y** Yearly

Occupation/Type/Industry	Location	Per	Low	Mid	High	Source	Date
Legislator	New York	Y	13990 FQ	60240 AW	107670 TQ	NYBLS	10/01-12/01
	Albany-Schenectady-Troy MSA, NY	Y	13400 FQ	63430 AW	95130 TQ	NYBLS	10/01-12/01
	Binghamton MSA, NY	Y	15360 FQ	49140 AW	78090 TQ	NYBLS	10/01-12/01
	Buffalo-Niagara Falls MSA, NY	Y	12800 FQ	39310 AW	84410 TQ	NYBLS	10/01-12/01
	Dutchess County PMSA, NY	Y	11960 FQ	29010 AW	88860 TQ	NYBLS	10/01-12/01
	Nassau-Suffolk PMSA, NY	Y	28040 FQ	70000 AW	103690 TQ	NYBLS	10/01-12/01
	New York PMSA, NY	Y	30890 FQ	57330 AW	97370 TQ	NYBLS	10/01-12/01
	Newburgh PMSA, NY-PA	Y	18780 FQ	74030 AW		NYBLS	10/01-12/01
	Rochester MSA, NY	Y	24940 FQ	66940 AW	89930 TQ	NYBLS	10/01-12/01
	Syracuse MSA, NY	Y	13780 FQ	64860 AW	111100 TQ	NYBLS	10/01-12/01
	Utica-Rome MSA, NY	Y	12840 FQ	42740 AW	73110 TQ	NYBLS	10/01-12/01
	North Carolina	Y	11940 FQ	17830 AW	34960 TQ	NCBLS	10/01-12/01
	Charlotte-Gastonia-Rock Hill MSA, NC-SC	Y	11900 FQ	17640 AW	27670 TQ	NCBLS	10/01-12/01
	Raleigh-Durham-Chapel Hill MSA, NC	Y	11870 FQ	12850 AW	14730 TQ	NCBLS	10/01-12/01
	North Dakota	Y	11570 FQ	14700 AW	24400 TQ	NDBLS	10/01-12/01
	Fargo-Moorhead MSA, ND-MN	Y	11980 FQ	19380 AW	27930 TQ	NDBLS	10/01-12/01
	Ohio	Y	12030 FQ	25610 AW	54890 TQ	OHBLS	10/01-12/01
	Akron PMSA, OH	Y	12150 FQ	18840 AW	28390 TQ	OHBLS	10/01-12/01
	Cincinnati PMSA, OH-KY-IN	Y	12480 FQ	35100 AW	55060 TQ	OHBLS	10/01-12/01
	Columbus MSA, OH	Y	11810 FQ	25700 AW	45870 TQ	OHBLS	10/01-12/01
	Dayton-Springfield MSA, OH	Y	11880 FQ	16780 AW	28960 TQ	OHBLS	10/01-12/01
	Youngstown-Warren MSA, OH	Y	11880 FQ	13250 AW	14790 TQ	OHBLS	10/01-12/01
	Oklahoma	Y	11650 FQ	21180 AW	39930 TQ	OKBLS	10/01-12/01
	Oklahoma City MSA, OK	Y	11640 FQ	26500 AW	72480 TQ	OKBLS	10/01-12/01
	Tulsa MSA, OK	Y	11650 FQ	18680 AW	62120 TQ	OKBLS	10/01-12/01
	Oregon	Y	15010 FQ	29350 AW	55330 TQ	ORBLS	10/01-12/01
	Pennsylvania	Y	11540 FQ	21370 AW	51780 TQ	PABLS	10/01-12/01
	Allentown-Bethlehem-Easton MSA, PA	Y	11340 FQ	15260 AW	25480 TQ	PABLS	10/01-12/01
	Erie MSA, PA	Y	11530 FQ	20390 AW	61690 TQ	PABLS	10/01-12/01
	Harrisburg-Lebanon-Carlisle MSA, PA	Y	11260 FQ	36620 AW	105930 TQ	PABLS	10/01-12/01
	Johnstown MSA, PA	Y	11650 FQ	14940 AW	14720 TQ	PABLS	10/01-12/01
	Lancaster MSA, PA	Y	11780 FQ	22630 AW	54940 TQ	PABLS	10/01-12/01
	Philadelphia PMSA, PA-NJ	Y	11970 FQ	37890 AW	94820 TQ	PABLS	10/01-12/01
	Pittsburgh MSA, PA	Y	11710 FQ	16180 AW	14900 TQ	PABLS	10/01-12/01
	Reading MSA, PA	Y	11330 FQ	12460 AW	14200 TQ	PABLS	10/01-12/01
	Scranton-Wilkes-Barre-Hazleton MSA, PA	Y	11400 FQ	15300 AW	14470 TQ	PABLS	10/01-12/01
	York MSA, PA	Y	11620 FQ	12740 AW	14440 TQ	PABLS	10/01-12/01
	Rhode Island	Y	13460 FQ	24680 AW	76780 TQ	RIBLS	10/01-12/01
	Providence-Fall River-Warwick MSA, RI-MA	Y	13510 FQ	24480 AW	75950 TQ	RIBLS	10/01-12/01
	South Carolina	Y	11780 FQ	23520 AW	50420 TQ	SCBLS	10/01-12/01
	Charleston-North Charleston MSA, SC	Y	11740 FQ	22570 AW	54250 TQ	SCBLS	10/01-12/01
	Columbia MSA, SC	Y	12060 FQ	18860 AW	28040 TQ	SCBLS	10/01-12/01
	Greenville-Spartanburg-Anderson MSA, SC	Y	11890 FQ	21210 AW	43380 TQ	SCBLS	10/01-12/01
	Myrtle Beach MSA, SC	Y	12580 FQ	33730 AW	62740 TQ	SCBLS	10/01-12/01
	South Dakota	Y	23980 FQ	29470 AW	35040 TQ	SDBLS	10/01-12/01
	Sioux Falls MSA, SD	Y	24870 FQ	33980 AW	50840 TQ	SDBLS	10/01-12/01
	Tennessee	Y	11780 FQ	16810 AW	20610 TQ	TNBLS	10/01-12/01
	Knoxville MSA, TN	Y	12420 FQ	15940 AW	18970 TQ	TNBLS	10/01-12/01
	Memphis MSA, TN-AR-MS	Y	11580 FQ	14940 AW	20870 TQ	TNBLS	10/01-12/01
	Nashville MSA, TN	Y	11710 FQ	16450 AW	25800 TQ	TNBLS	10/01-12/01
	Texas	Y	11610 FQ	18020 AW	31120 TQ	TXBLS	10/01-12/01
	Austin-San Marcos MSA, TX	Y	11630 FQ	22730 AW	54380 TQ	TXBLS	10/01-12/01
	Beaumont-Port Arthur MSA, TX	Y	11730 FQ	33440 AW	73170 TQ	TXBLS	10/01-12/01
	Corpus Christi MSA, TX	Y	11530 FQ	22850 AW	45420 TQ	TXBLS	10/01-12/01
	Dallas PMSA, TX	Y	11800 FQ	15540 AW	14850 TQ	TXBLS	10/01-12/01
	Fort Worth-Arlington PMSA, TX	Y	11520 FQ	14110 AW	14480 TQ	TXBLS	10/01-12/01
	Houston PMSA, TX	Y	11130 FQ	17630 AW	22350 TQ	TXBLS	10/01-12/01
	Killeen-Temple MSA, TX	Y	11870 FQ	12850 AW	14730 TQ	TXBLS	10/01-12/01
	Longview-Marshall MSA, TX	Y	11220 FQ	18030 AW	41210 TQ	TXBLS	10/01-12/01

AAW Average annual wage **AOH** Average offered, high **ASH** Average starting, high **H** Hourly **M** Monthly **S** Special: hourly and annual
AE Average entry wage **AOL** Average offered, low **ASL** Average starting, low **HI** Highest wage paid **MTC** Median total compensation **TQ** Third quartile wage
AEX Average experienced wage **APH** Average pay, high range **AW** Average wage paid **HR** High end range **MW** Median wage paid **W** Weekly
AO Average offered **APL** Average pay, low range **FQ** First quartile wage **LR** Low end range **SQ** Second quartile wage **Y** Yearly

Occupation/Type/Industry	Location	Per	Low	Mid	High	Source	Date
Legislator	McAllen-Edinburg-Mission MSA, TX	Y	11490 FQ	13960 AW	14530 TQ	TXBLS	10/01-12/01
	San Antonio MSA, TX	Y	11300 FQ	12410 AW	14020 TQ	TXBLS	10/01-12/01
	Utah	Y	11860 FQ	20390 AW	32230 TQ	UTBLS	10/01-12/01
	Provo-Orem MSA, UT	Y	12030 FQ	14220 AW	18070 TQ	UTBLS	10/01-12/01
	Salt Lake City-Ogden MSA, UT	Y	12290 FQ	23900 AW	34290 TQ	UTBLS	10/01-12/01
	Virginia	Y	19530 FQ	74320 AW		VABLS	10/01-12/01
	Lynchburg MSA, VA	Y	26960 FQ	90590 AW		VABLS	10/01-12/01
	Norfolk-Virginia Beach-Newport News MSA, VA-NC	Y	14010 FQ	91490 AW		VABLS	10/01-12/01
	Richmond-Petersburg MSA, VA	Y	17290 FQ	76460 AW	120090 TQ	VABLS	10/01-12/01
	Roanoke MSA, VA	Y	13030 FQ	53520 AW	138420 TQ	VABLS	10/01-12/01
	Washington	Y	21240 FQ	55490 AW	104230 TQ	WABLS	10/01-12/01
	Bremerton PMSA, WA	Y	37750 FQ	61500 AW	133470 TQ	WABLS	10/01-12/01
	Olympia PMSA, WA	Y	29240 FQ	42590 AW	67870 TQ	WABLS	10/01-12/01
	Richland-Kennewick-Pasco MSA, WA	Y	47480 FQ	58720 AW	87670 TQ	WABLS	10/01-12/01
	Seattle-Bellevue-Everett PMSA, WA	Y	32990 FQ	65370 AW	110850 TQ	WABLS	10/01-12/01
	Spokane MSA, WA	Y	22440 FQ	52580 AW	86040 TQ	WABLS	10/01-12/01
	Tacoma PMSA, WA	Y	20010 FQ	39680 AW	65820 TQ	WABLS	10/01-12/01
	Yakima MSA, WA	Y	28740 FQ	56200 AW	94360 TQ	WABLS	10/01-12/01
	West Virginia	Y	11950 FQ	23730 AW	44860 TQ	WVBLS	10/01-12/01
	Wisconsin	Y	11540 FQ	19080 AW	27540 TQ	WIBLS	10/01-12/01
	Appleton-Oshkosh-Neenah MSA, WI	Y	11410 FQ	18950 AW	49470 TQ	WIBLS	10/01-12/01
	Green Bay MSA, WI	Y	11740 FQ	24050 AW	64780 TQ	WIBLS	10/01-12/01
	Madison MSA, WI	Y	12210 FQ	43180 AW	70070 TQ	WIBLS	10/01-12/01
	Milwaukee-Waukesha PMSA, WI	Y	11630 FQ	21900 AW	54910 TQ	WIBLS	10/01-12/01
	Racine PMSA, WI	Y	11540 FQ	14730 AW	19760 TQ	WIBLS	10/01-12/01
	Wyoming	Y	11530 FQ	15900 AW	25470 TQ	WYBLS	10/01-12/01
Librarian	Alabama	Y	22220 FQ	38060 AW	52610 TQ	ALBLS	10/01-12/01
	Birmingham MSA, AL	Y	24540 FQ	37460 AW	55680 TQ	ALBLS	10/01-12/01
	Huntsville MSA, AL	Y	25420 FQ	40480 AW	55410 TQ	ALBLS	10/01-12/01
	Mobile MSA, AL	Y	24450 FQ	37430 AW	50670 TQ	ALBLS	10/01-12/01
	Montgomery MSA, AL	Y	16740 FQ	33100 AW	48840 TQ	ALBLS	10/01-12/01
	Alaska	Y	24460 FQ	47740 AW	69180 TQ	AKBLS	10/01-12/01
	Anchorage MSA, AK	Y	32350 FQ	49830 AW	70340 TQ	AKBLS	10/01-12/01
	Arizona	Y	26170 FQ	41420 AW	59230 TQ	AZBLS	10/01-12/01
	Phoenix-Mesa MSA, AZ	Y	28690 FQ	43910 AW	64440 TQ	AZBLS	10/01-12/01
	Tucson MSA, AZ	Y	26510 FQ	41220 AW	56460 TQ	AZBLS	10/01-12/01
	Arkansas	Y	21620 FQ	36460 AW	50940 TQ	ARBLS	10/01-12/01
	Fayetteville-Springdale-Rogers MSA, AR	Y	17240 FQ	38030 AW	56240 TQ	ARBLS	10/01-12/01
	Fort Smith MSA, AR-OK	Y	31590 FQ	41690 AW	53140 TQ	ARBLS	10/01-12/01
	Little Rock-North Little Rock MSA, AR	Y	29640 FQ	39780 AW	52650 TQ	ARBLS	10/01-12/01
	California	Y	29180 FQ	50980 AW	73980 TQ	CABLS	10/01-12/01
	Bakersfield MSA, CA	Y	19700 FQ	39760 AW	68850 TQ	CABLS	10/01-12/01
	Chico-Paradise MSA, CA	Y	34220 FQ	55140 AW	84230 TQ	CABLS	10/01-12/01
	Fresno MSA, CA	Y	28580 FQ	48440 AW	73600 TQ	CABLS	10/01-12/01
	Los Angeles-Long Beach PMSA, CA	Y	38370 FQ	54750 AW	75120 TQ	CABLS	10/01-12/01
	Merced MSA, CA	Y	28600 FQ	52770 AW	73120 TQ	CABLS	10/01-12/01
	Modesto MSA, CA	Y	26230 FQ	47460 AW	73050 TQ	CABLS	10/01-12/01
	Oakland PMSA, CA	Y	28780 FQ	46250 AW	65390 TQ	CABLS	10/01-12/01
	Orange County PMSA, CA	Y	27880 FQ	51060 AW	69700 TQ	CABLS	10/01-12/01
	Redding MSA, CA	Y	36390 FQ	48850 AW	62550 TQ	CABLS	10/01-12/01
	Riverside-San Bernardino PMSA, CA	Y	30660 FQ	51420 AW	74760 TQ	CABLS	10/01-12/01
	Sacramento PMSA, CA	Y	27040 FQ	49780 AW	74610 TQ	CABLS	10/01-12/01
	Salinas MSA, CA	Y	35220 FQ	50280 AW	67990 TQ	CABLS	10/01-12/01
	San Diego MSA, CA	Y	33290 FQ	49250 AW	68980 TQ	CABLS	10/01-12/01
	San Francisco PMSA, CA	Y	32840 FQ	55890 AW	83650 TQ	CABLS	10/01-12/01
	San Jose PMSA, CA	Y	32920 FQ	55940 AW	78340 TQ	CABLS	10/01-12/01
	San Luis Obispo-Atascadero-Paso Robles MSA, CA	Y	20480 FQ	41910 AW	68760 TQ	CABLS	10/01-12/01

AAW	Average annual wage	**AOH**	Average offered, high	**ASH**	Average starting, high	**H**	Hourly	**M**	Monthly	**S**	Special: hourly and annual
AE	Average entry wage	**AOL**	Average offered, low	**ASL**	Average starting, low	**HI**	Highest wage paid	**MTC**	Median total compensation	**TQ**	Third quartile wage
AEX	Average experienced wage	**APH**	Average pay, high range	**AW**	Average wage paid	**HR**	High end range	**MW**	Median wage paid	**W**	Weekly
AO	Average offered	**APL**	Average pay, low range	**FQ**	First quartile wage	**LR**	Low end range	**SQ**	Second quartile wage	**Y**	Yearly

Occupation/Type/Industry	Location	Per	Low	Mid	High	Source	Date
Librarian	Santa Barbara-Santa Maria-Lompoc MSA, CA	Y	26430 FQ	42940 AW	59130 TQ	CABLS	10/01-12/01
	Santa Cruz-Watsonville PMSA, CA	Y	30160 FQ	50430 AW	72600 TQ	CABLS	10/01-12/01
	Santa Rosa PMSA, CA	Y	39860 FQ	53660 AW	72530 TQ	CABLS	10/01-12/01
	Stockton-Lodi MSA, CA	Y	24010 FQ	48100 AW	83060 TQ	CABLS	10/01-12/01
	Vallejo-Fairfield-Napa PMSA, CA	Y	29440 FQ	53270 AW	71660 TQ	CABLS	10/01-12/01
	Ventura PMSA, CA	Y	29900 FQ	56530 AW	84640 TQ	CABLS	10/01-12/01
	Visalia-Tulare-Porterville MSA, CA	Y	30970 FQ	47870 AW	69110 TQ	CABLS	10/01-12/01
	Colorado	Y	27450 FQ	41570 AW	57650 TQ	COBLS	10/01-12/01
	Boulder-Longmont PMSA, CO	Y	29270 FQ	43310 AW	58690 TQ	COBLS	10/01-12/01
	Colorado Springs MSA, CO	Y	29440 FQ	40690 AW	55070 TQ	COBLS	10/01-12/01
	Denver PMSA, CO	Y	30410 FQ	44160 AW	60220 TQ	COBLS	10/01-12/01
	Fort Collins-Loveland MSA, CO	Y	24590 FQ	39040 AW	56000 TQ	COBLS	10/01-12/01
	Greeley PMSA, CO	Y	30520 FQ	40080 AW	52380 TQ	COBLS	10/01-12/01
	Connecticut	Y	31990 FQ	49560 AW	70830 TQ	CTBLS	10/01-12/01
	Bridgeport PMSA, CT	Y	33710 FQ	48170 AW	68480 TQ	CTBLS	10/01-12/01
	Danbury PMSA, CT	Y	28380 FQ	51620 AW	80670 TQ	CTBLS	10/01-12/01
	Hartford MSA, CT	Y	34180 FQ	50950 AW	70940 TQ	CTBLS	10/01-12/01
	New Haven-Meriden PMSA, CT	Y	33120 FQ	47830 AW	67990 TQ	CTBLS	10/01-12/01
	New London-Norwich MSA, CT-RI	Y	28810 FQ	45380 AW	62100 TQ	CTBLS	10/01-12/01
	Stamford-Norwalk PMSA, CT	Y	39780 FQ	56760 AW	84190 TQ	CTBLS	10/01-12/01
	Waterbury PMSA, CT	Y	34600 FQ	51970 AW	72270 TQ	CTBLS	10/01-12/01
	Delaware	Y	29490 FQ	50960 AW	74630 TQ	DEBLS	10/01-12/01
	Wilmington-Newark PMSA, DE-MD	Y	30810 FQ	52090 AW	75150 TQ	DEBLS	10/01-12/01
	District of Columbia	Y	13700 FQ	47200 AW	73260 TQ	DCBLS	10/01-12/01
	Washington PMSA, DC-MD-VA-WV	Y	30940 FQ	50710 AW	73410 TQ	DCBLS	10/01-12/01
	Florida	Y	29220 FQ	43810 AW	63370 TQ	FLBLS	10/01-12/01
	Daytona Beach MSA, FL	Y	30960 FQ	47750 AW	70400 TQ	FLBLS	10/01-12/01
	Fort Myers-Cape Coral MSA, FL	Y	29920 FQ	45520 AW	78820 TQ	FLBLS	10/01-12/01
	Fort Pierce-Port St. Lucie MSA, FL	Y	29370 FQ	48620 AW	70100 TQ	FLBLS	10/01-12/01
	Gainesville MSA, FL	Y	32730 FQ	50490 AW	72920 TQ	FLBLS	10/01-12/01
	Jacksonville MSA, FL	Y	28290 FQ	41400 AW	58370 TQ	FLBLS	10/01-12/01
	Lakeland-Winter Haven MSA, FL	Y	25130 FQ	36320 AW	55820 TQ	FLBLS	10/01-12/01
	Melbourne-Titusville-Palm Bay MSA, FL	Y	25750 FQ	41450 AW	59850 TQ	FLBLS	10/01-12/01
	Naples MSA, FL	Y	21270 FQ	36690 AW	49510 TQ	FLBLS	10/01-12/01
	Ocala MSA, FL	Y	28970 FQ	42500 AW	62690 TQ	FLBLS	10/01-12/01
	Orlando MSA, FL	Y	28300 FQ	41260 AW	55940 TQ	FLBLS	10/01-12/01
	Pensacola MSA, FL	Y	28440 FQ	44700 AW	61900 TQ	FLBLS	10/01-12/01
	Sarasota-Bradenton MSA, FL	Y	30140 FQ	40940 AW	56670 TQ	FLBLS	10/01-12/01
	Tallahassee MSA, FL	Y	29050 FQ	48900 AW	76690 TQ	FLBLS	10/01-12/01
	Tampa-St. Petersburg-Clearwater MSA, FL	Y	29730 FQ	42750 AW	58180 TQ	FLBLS	10/01-12/01
	West Palm Beach-Boca Raton MSA, FL	Y	30280 FQ	43430 AW	64540 TQ	FLBLS	10/01-12/01
	Georgia	Y	34880 FQ	49130 AW	62900 TQ	GABLS	10/01-12/01
	Atlanta MSA, GA	Y	36320 FQ	50360 AW	64470 TQ	GABLS	10/01-12/01
	Augusta-Aiken MSA, GA-SC	Y	29130 FQ	46030 AW	63560 TQ	GABLS	10/01-12/01
	Columbus MSA, GA-AL	Y	36870 FQ	49200 AW	61200 TQ	GABLS	10/01-12/01
	Macon MSA, GA	Y	26350 FQ	49830 AW	71460 TQ	GABLS	10/01-12/01
	Savannah MSA, GA	Y	31230 FQ	43510 AW	58900 TQ	GABLS	10/01-12/01
	Hawaii	Y	28490 FQ	45150 AW	62720 TQ	HIBLS	10/01-12/01
	Honolulu MSA, HI	Y	28160 FQ	45350 AW	64220 TQ	HIBLS	10/01-12/01
	Idaho	Y	13580 FQ	35120 AW	54110 TQ	IDBLS	10/01-12/01
	Boise City MSA, ID	Y	30080 FQ	44310 AW	56990 TQ	IDBLS	10/01-12/01
	Illinois	Y	14230 FQ	40300 AW	69490 TQ	ILBLS	10/01-12/01
	Champaign-Urbana MSA, IL	Y	16540 FQ	43350 AW	68860 TQ	ILBLS	10/01-12/01
	Chicago PMSA, IL	Y	18700 FQ	42740 AW	74380 TQ	ILBLS	10/01-12/01
	Peoria-Pekin MSA, IL	Y	11810 FQ	23140 AW	45610 TQ	ILBLS	10/01-12/01
	Rockford MSA, IL	Y	15170 FQ	37040 AW	56210 TQ	ILBLS	10/01-12/01
	Springfield MSA, IL	Y	17180 FQ	41030 AW	61070 TQ	ILBLS	10/01-12/01

AAW	Average annual wage	AOH	Average offered, high	ASH	Average starting, high	H	Hourly	M	Monthly	S	Special: hourly and annual
AE	Average entry wage	AOL	Average offered, low	ASL	Average starting, low	HI	Highest wage paid	MTC	Median total compensation	TQ	Third quartile wage
AEX	Average experienced wage	APH	Average pay, high range	AW	Average wage paid	HR	High end range	MW	Median wage paid	W	Weekly
AO	Average offered	APL	Average pay, low range	FQ	First quartile wage	LR	Low end range	SQ	Second quartile wage	Y	Yearly

Occupation/Type/Industry	Location	Per	Low	Mid	High	Source	Date
Librarian	Indiana	Y	14890 FQ	36890 AW	56990 TQ	INBLS	10/01-12/01
	Elkhart-Goshen MSA, IN	Y	25480 FQ	42150 AW	58540 TQ	INBLS	10/01-12/01
	Evansville-Henderson MSA, IN-KY	Y	25650 FQ	40130 AW	55780 TQ	INBLS	10/01-12/01
	Fort Wayne MSA, IN	Y	23860 FQ	36620 AW	53680 TQ	INBLS	10/01-12/01
	Gary PMSA, IN	Y	12820 FQ	30120 AW	56860 TQ	INBLS	10/01-12/01
	Indianapolis MSA, IN	Y	12740 FQ	33410 AW	58100 TQ	INBLS	10/01-12/01
	Lafayette MSA, IN	Y	27730 FQ	44210 AW	60570 TQ	INBLS	10/01-12/01
	South Bend MSA, IN	Y	18570 FQ	38110 AW	53010 TQ	INBLS	10/01-12/01
	Iowa	Y	16280 FQ	35910 AW	55980 TQ	IABLS	10/01-12/01
	Cedar Rapids MSA, IA	Y	20230 FQ	36410 AW	55880 TQ	IABLS	10/01-12/01
	Davenport-Moline-Rock Island MSA, IA-IL	Y	21570 FQ	43000 AW	67730 TQ	IABLS	10/01-12/01
	Des Moines MSA, IA	Y	27790 FQ	44720 AW	60190 TQ	IABLS	10/01-12/01
	Kansas	Y	25400 FQ	38290 AW	51520 TQ	KSBLS	10/01-12/01
	Topeka MSA, KS	Y	31740 FQ	41080 AW	51420 TQ	KSBLS	10/01-12/01
	Wichita MSA, KS	Y	30870 FQ	41120 AW	53420 TQ	KSBLS	10/01-12/01
	Kentucky	Y	16100 FQ	37240 AW	55090 TQ	KYBLS	10/01-12/01
	Lexington MSA, KY	Y	29620 FQ	43790 AW	58190 TQ	KYBLS	10/01-12/01
	Louisville MSA, KY-IN	Y	29800 FQ	46560 AW	57900 TQ	KYBLS	10/01-12/01
	Louisiana	Y	22250 FQ	36120 AW	46680 TQ	LABLS	10/01-12/01
	Baton Rouge MSA, LA	Y	30060 FQ	40130 AW	47950 TQ	LABLS	10/01-12/01
	Houma MSA, LA	Y	21000 FQ	34270 AW	45070 TQ	LABLS	10/01-12/01
	Lafayette MSA, LA	Y	29150 FQ	36810 AW	44990 TQ	LABLS	10/01-12/01
	New Orleans MSA, LA	Y	19070 FQ	36040 AW	46270 TQ	LABLS	10/01-12/01
	Shreveport-Bossier City MSA, LA	Y	20570 FQ	38690 AW	53030 TQ	LABLS	10/01-12/01
	Maine	Y	23880 FQ	37780 AW	53300 TQ	MEBLS	10/01-12/01
	Portland MSA, ME	Y	25480 FQ	38020 AW	53820 TQ	MEBLS	10/01-12/01
	Maryland	Y	31100 FQ	49640 AW	72310 TQ	MDBLS	10/01-12/01
	Baltimore PMSA, MD	Y	30450 FQ	48730 AW	74400 TQ	MDBLS	10/01-12/01
	Massachusetts	Y	28750 FQ	44860 AW	63450 TQ	MABLS	10/01-12/01
	Boston PMSA, MA-NH	Y	29590 FQ	45450 AW	65030 TQ	MABLS	10/01-12/01
	Brockton PMSA, MA	Y	29060 FQ	43380 AW	61310 TQ	MABLS	10/01-12/01
	Lawrence PMSA, MA-NH	Y	27120 FQ	43660 AW	61360 TQ	MABLS	10/01-12/01
	Lowell PMSA, MA-NH	Y	29840 FQ	46630 AW	67170 TQ	MABLS	10/01-12/01
	New Bedford PMSA, MA	Y	27310 FQ	43420 AW	59160 TQ	MABLS	10/01-12/01
	Springfield MSA, MA	Y	25440 FQ	43680 AW	61120 TQ	MABLS	10/01-12/01
	Worcester PMSA, MA-CT	Y	31460 FQ	45070 AW	58960 TQ	MABLS	10/01-12/01
	Michigan	Y	29650 FQ	47560 AW	70300 TQ	MIBLS	10/01-12/01
	Ann Arbor PMSA, MI	Y	29600 FQ	45160 AW	66640 TQ	MIBLS	10/01-12/01
	Detroit PMSA, MI	Y	35810 FQ	53010 AW	81120 TQ	MIBLS	10/01-12/01
	Flint PMSA, MI	Y	30600 FQ	47220 AW	70490 TQ	MIBLS	10/01-12/01
	Grand Rapids-Muskegon-Holland MSA, MI	Y	28460 FQ	47030 AW	66700 TQ	MIBLS	10/01-12/01
	Kalamazoo-Battle Creek MSA, MI	Y	23580 FQ	41870 AW	60000 TQ	MIBLS	10/01-12/01
	Lansing-East Lansing MSA, MI	Y	30410 FQ	46450 AW	64080 TQ	MIBLS	10/01-12/01
	Saginaw-Bay City-Midland MSA, MI	Y	25010 FQ	45950 AW	71000 TQ	MIBLS	10/01-12/01
	Minnesota	Y	26890 FQ	42760 AW	58760 TQ	MNBLS	10/01-12/01
	Duluth-Superior MSA, MN-WI	Y	30790 FQ	43530 AW	56940 TQ	MNBLS	10/01-12/01
	Minneapolis-St. Paul MSA, MN-WI	Y	28460 FQ	44730 AW	61290 TQ	MNBLS	10/01-12/01
	St. Cloud MSA, MN	Y	29310 FQ	39100 AW	53410 TQ	MNBLS	10/01-12/01
	Mississippi	Y	13110 FQ	30850 AW	46610 TQ	MSBLS	10/01-12/01
	Biloxi-Gulfport-Pascagoula MSA, MS	Y	28390 FQ	38410 AW	50490 TQ	MSBLS	10/01-12/01
	Jackson MSA, MS	Y	21360 FQ	33210 AW	44860 TQ	MSBLS	10/01-12/01
	Missouri	Y	17610 FQ	37260 AW	57480 TQ	MOBLS	10/01-12/01
	Kansas City MSA, MO-KS	Y	25670 FQ	40100 AW	56160 TQ	MOBLS	10/01-12/01
	St. Louis MSA, MO-IL	Y	24400 FQ	43370 AW	65710 TQ	MOBLS	10/01-12/01
	Springfield MSA, MO	Y	21620 FQ	37880 AW	54140 TQ	MOBLS	10/01-12/01
	Montana	Y	19080 FQ	31400 AW	43820 TQ	MTBLS	10/01-12/01
	Billings MSA, MT	Y	23670 FQ	35650 AW	48050 TQ	MTBLS	10/01-12/01
	Nebraska	Y	14930 FQ	32160 AW	48040 TQ	NEBLS	10/01-12/01
	Lincoln MSA, NE	Y	27980 FQ	39600 AW	53560 TQ	NEBLS	10/01-12/01
	Omaha MSA, NE-IA	Y	20640 FQ	39930 AW	57420 TQ	NEBLS	10/01-12/01
	Nevada	Y	35920 FQ	51260 AW	69580 TQ	NVBLS	10/01-12/01
	Las Vegas MSA, NV-AZ	Y	34120 FQ	50810 AW	69570 TQ	NVBLS	10/01-12/01
	Reno MSA, NV	Y	33830 FQ	51010 AW	69280 TQ	NVBLS	10/01-12/01
	New Hampshire	Y	22750 FQ	38620 AW	54400 TQ	NHBLS	10/01-12/01

AAW Average annual wage **AE** Average entry wage **AEX** Average experienced wage **AO** Average offered **AOH** Average offered, high **AOL** Average offered, low **APH** Average pay, high range **APL** Average pay, low range **ASH** Average starting, high **ASL** Average starting, low **AW** Average wage paid **FQ** First quartile wage **H** Hourly **HI** Highest wage paid **HR** High end range **LR** Low end range **M** Monthly **MTC** Median total compensation **MW** Median wage paid **SQ** Second quartile wage **S** Special: hourly and annual **TQ** Third quartile wage **W** Weekly **Y** Yearly

Occupation/Type/Industry	Location	Per	Low	Mid	High	Source	Date
Librarian	Manchester PMSA, NH	Y	26520 FQ	40390 AW	57300 TQ	NHBLS	10/01-12/01
	Nashua PMSA, NH	Y	29830 FQ	41150 AW	55670 TQ	NHBLS	10/01-12/01
	Portsmouth-Rochester PMSA, NH-ME	Y	28680 FQ	40360 AW	55590 TQ	NHBLS	10/01-12/01
	New Jersey	Y	31700 FQ	52620 AW	78090 TQ	NJBLS	10/01-12/01
	Atlantic-Cape May PMSA, NJ	Y	31050 FQ	56330 AW	88680 TQ	NJBLS	10/01-12/01
	Bergen-Passaic PMSA, NJ	Y	31850 FQ	55400 AW	85140 TQ	NJBLS	10/01-12/01
	Jersey City PMSA, NJ	Y	31580 FQ	59660 AW	89950 TQ	NJBLS	10/01-12/01
	Middlesex-Somerset-Hunterdon PMSA, NJ	Y	33610 FQ	52910 AW	73440 TQ	NJBLS	10/01-12/01
	Monmouth-Ocean PMSA, NJ	Y	27440 FQ	49460 AW	77550 TQ	NJBLS	10/01-12/01
	Newark PMSA, NJ	Y	31220 FQ	52350 AW	77490 TQ	NJBLS	10/01-12/01
	Trenton PMSA, NJ	Y	34730 FQ	54400 AW	80150 TQ	NJBLS	10/01-12/01
	New Mexico	Y	20680 FQ	35240 AW	50550 TQ	NMBLS	10/01-12/01
	Albuquerque MSA, NM	Y	24270 FQ	35140 AW	48270 TQ	NMBLS	10/01-12/01
	Las Cruces MSA, NM	Y	30350 FQ	39170 AW	51400 TQ	NMBLS	10/01-12/01
	New York	Y	30240 FQ	47890 AW	71570 TQ	NYBLS	10/01-12/01
	Albany-Schenectady-Troy MSA, NY	Y	29800 FQ	48250 AW	69240 TQ	NYBLS	10/01-12/01
	Binghamton MSA, NY	Y	27460 FQ	51450 AW	70160 TQ	NYBLS	10/01-12/01
	Buffalo-Niagara Falls MSA, NY	Y	30970 FQ	45400 AW	64070 TQ	NYBLS	10/01-12/01
	Dutchess County PMSA, NY	Y	35800 FQ	48710 AW	70370 TQ	NYBLS	10/01-12/01
	Nassau-Suffolk PMSA, NY	Y	30730 FQ	51750 AW	83160 TQ	NYBLS	10/01-12/01
	New York PMSA, NY	Y	31440 FQ	47020 AW	70080 TQ	NYBLS	10/01-12/01
	Newburgh PMSA, NY-PA	Y	22870 FQ	44650 AW	68200 TQ	NYBLS	10/01-12/01
	Rochester MSA, NY	Y	31060 FQ	52780 AW	74630 TQ	NYBLS	10/01-12/01
	Syracuse MSA, NY	Y	25540 FQ	42060 AW	63090 TQ	NYBLS	10/01-12/01
	Utica-Rome MSA, NY	Y	18770 FQ	39980 AW	65760 TQ	NYBLS	10/01-12/01
	North Carolina	Y	26550 FQ	42130 AW	57710 TQ	NCBLS	10/01-12/01
	Asheville MSA, NC	Y	29410 FQ	38100 AW	54420 TQ	NCBLS	10/01-12/01
	Charlotte-Gastonia-Rock Hill MSA, NC-SC	Y	30940 FQ	44080 AW	58510 TQ	NCBLS	10/01-12/01
	Fayetteville MSA, NC	Y	30940 FQ	42060 AW	55660 TQ	NCBLS	10/01-12/01
	Greensboro-Winston-Salem-High Point MSA, NC	Y	28250 FQ	42480 AW	58100 TQ	NCBLS	10/01-12/01
	Hickory-Morganton-Lenoir MSA, NC	Y	29310 FQ	37410 AW	47990 TQ	NCBLS	10/01-12/01
	Raleigh-Durham-Chapel Hill MSA, NC	Y	32620 FQ	49530 AW	69210 TQ	NCBLS	10/01-12/01
	Wilmington MSA, NC	Y	29210 FQ	42640 AW	56570 TQ	NCBLS	10/01-12/01
	North Dakota	Y	14140 FQ	30760 AW	45760 TQ	NDBLS	10/01-12/01
	Fargo-Moorhead MSA, ND-MN	Y	24120 FQ	37680 AW	53020 TQ	NDBLS	10/01-12/01
	Ohio	Y	24260 FQ	43830 AW	66890 TQ	OHBLS	10/01-12/01
	Akron PMSA, OH	Y	28630 FQ	42980 AW	59060 TQ	OHBLS	10/01-12/01
	Canton-Massillon MSA, OH	Y	24210 FQ	43410 AW	65450 TQ	OHBLS	10/01-12/01
	Cincinnati PMSA, OH-KY-IN	Y	29250 FQ	46570 AW	65710 TQ	OHBLS	10/01-12/01
	Cleveland-Lorain-Elyria PMSA, OH	Y	21420 FQ	46850 AW	74630 TQ	OHBLS	10/01-12/01
	Columbus MSA, OH	Y	30620 FQ	46350 AW	67800 TQ	OHBLS	10/01-12/01
	Dayton-Springfield MSA, OH	Y	24390 FQ	41410 AW	59420 TQ	OHBLS	10/01-12/01
	Hamilton-Middletown PMSA, OH	Y	29600 FQ	49440 AW	67360 TQ	OHBLS	10/01-12/01
	Mansfield MSA, OH	Y	22790 FQ	40720 AW	61490 TQ	OHBLS	10/01-12/01
	Toledo MSA, OH	Y	13610 FQ	43000 AW	62420 TQ	OHBLS	10/01-12/01
	Youngstown-Warren MSA, OH	Y	29220 FQ	40040 AW	55180 TQ	OHBLS	10/01-12/01
	Oklahoma	Y	21400 FQ	34460 AW	46590 TQ	OKBLS	10/01-12/01
	Oklahoma City MSA, OK	Y	22770 FQ	36560 AW	52280 TQ	OKBLS	10/01-12/01
	Tulsa MSA, OK	Y	24580 FQ	35470 AW	47250 TQ	OKBLS	10/01-12/01
	Oregon	Y	29400 FQ	45690 AW	62500 TQ	ORBLS	10/01-12/01
	Eugene-Springfield MSA, OR	Y	29900 FQ	45950 AW	62480 TQ	ORBLS	10/01-12/01
	Medford-Ashland MSA, OR	Y	31670 FQ	43940 AW	56350 TQ	ORBLS	10/01-12/01
	Portland-Vancouver PMSA, OR-WA	Y	33350 FQ	48500 AW	67260 TQ	ORBLS	10/01-12/01
	Salem PMSA, OR	Y	31500 FQ	44940 AW	56910 TQ	ORBLS	10/01-12/01
	Pennsylvania	Y	22060 FQ	43930 AW	68370 TQ	PABLS	10/01-12/01
	Allentown-Bethlehem-Easton MSA, PA	Y	26310 FQ	48360 AW	78190 TQ	PABLS	10/01-12/01
	Erie MSA, PA	Y	28760 FQ	45590 AW	66630 TQ	PABLS	10/01-12/01
	Harrisburg-Lebanon-Carlisle MSA, PA	Y	23720 FQ	40910 AW	59120 TQ	PABLS	10/01-12/01

AAW	Average annual wage	AOH	Average offered, high	ASH	Average starting, high	H	Hourly	M	Monthly	S	Special: hourly and annual
AE	Average entry wage	AOL	Average offered, low	ASL	Average starting, low	HI	Highest wage paid	MTC	Median total compensation	TQ	Third quartile wage
AEX	Average experienced wage	APH	Average pay, high range	AW	Average wage paid	HR	High end range	MW	Median wage paid	W	Weekly
AO	Average offered	APL	Average pay, low range	FQ	First quartile wage	LR	Low end range	SQ	Second quartile wage	Y	Yearly

Occupation/Type/Industry	Location	Per	Low	Mid	High	Source	Date
Librarian	Johnstown MSA, PA	Y	12580 FQ	27840 AW	55470 TQ	PABLS	10/01-12/01
	Lancaster MSA, PA	Y	23630 FQ	47160 AW	68190 TQ	PABLS	10/01-12/01
	Philadelphia PMSA, PA-NJ	Y	26070 FQ	45410 AW	69820 TQ	PABLS	10/01-12/01
	Pittsburgh MSA, PA	Y	22660 FQ	46900 AW	70480 TQ	PABLS	10/01-12/01
	Reading MSA, PA	Y	22740 FQ	46170 AW	68260 TQ	PABLS	10/01-12/01
	Scranton-Wilkes-Barre-Hazleton MSA, PA	Y	22230 FQ	42440 AW	62820 TQ	PABLS	10/01-12/01
	York MSA, PA	Y	19630 FQ	41700 AW	60850 TQ	PABLS	10/01-12/01
	Rhode Island	Y	27860 FQ	46020 AW	66610 TQ	RIBLS	10/01-12/01
	Providence-Fall River-Warwick MSA, RI-MA	Y	29600 FQ	46290 AW	66070 TQ	RIBLS	10/01-12/01
	South Carolina	Y	28020 FQ	40070 AW	55230 TQ	SCBLS	10/01-12/01
	Charleston-North Charleston MSA, SC	Y	29210 FQ	37830 AW	52280 TQ	SCBLS	10/01-12/01
	Columbia MSA, SC	Y	28920 FQ	38990 AW	56640 TQ	SCBLS	10/01-12/01
	Greenville-Spartanburg-Anderson MSA, SC	Y	27630 FQ	41930 AW	57110 TQ	SCBLS	10/01-12/01
	Myrtle Beach MSA, SC	Y	27320 FQ	40730 AW	54670 TQ	SCBLS	10/01-12/01
	South Dakota	Y	17650 FQ	30140 AW	45340 TQ	SDBLS	10/01-12/01
	Sioux Falls MSA, SD	Y	25500 FQ	38500 AW	55790 TQ	SDBLS	10/01-12/01
	Tennessee	Y	26140 FQ	41560 AW	59080 TQ	TNBLS	10/01-12/01
	Chattanooga MSA, TN-GA	Y	21160 FQ	38490 AW	55190 TQ	TNBLS	10/01-12/01
	Clarksville-Hopkinsville MSA, TN-KY	Y	24450 FQ	37070 AW	50300 TQ	TNBLS	10/01-12/01
	Johnson City-Kingsport-Bristol MSA, TN-VA	Y	25960 FQ	36280 AW	46170 TQ	TNBLS	10/01-12/01
	Knoxville MSA, TN	Y	23330 FQ	39710 AW	56130 TQ	TNBLS	10/01-12/01
	Memphis MSA, TN-AR-MS	Y	26430 FQ	39900 AW	53760 TQ	TNBLS	10/01-12/01
	Nashville MSA, TN	Y	29700 FQ	43630 AW	59370 TQ	TNBLS	10/01-12/01
	Texas	Y	28910 FQ	42390 AW	56890 TQ	TXBLS	10/01-12/01
	Amarillo MSA, TX	Y	29610 FQ	39850 AW	47820 TQ	TXBLS	10/01-12/01
	Austin-San Marcos MSA, TX	Y	29370 FQ	41230 AW	55860 TQ	TXBLS	10/01-12/01
	Beaumont-Port Arthur MSA, TX	Y	30950 FQ	41800 AW	55170 TQ	TXBLS	10/01-12/01
	Brazoria PMSA, TX	Y	32950 FQ	42340 AW	54430 TQ	TXBLS	10/01-12/01
	Brownsville-Harlingen-San Benito MSA, TX	Y	25380 FQ	40360 AW	54850 TQ	TXBLS	10/01-12/01
	Corpus Christi MSA, TX	Y	31560 FQ	47470 AW	69270 TQ	TXBLS	10/01-12/01
	Dallas PMSA, TX	Y	29800 FQ	43240 AW	58610 TQ	TXBLS	10/01-12/01
	El Paso MSA, TX	Y	32440 FQ	43750 AW	55990 TQ	TXBLS	10/01-12/01
	Fort Worth-Arlington PMSA, TX	Y	32500 FQ	45650 AW	57720 TQ	TXBLS	10/01-12/01
	Galveston-Texas City PMSA, TX	Y	24300 FQ	39430 AW	55630 TQ	TXBLS	10/01-12/01
	Houston PMSA, TX	Y	33030 FQ	45450 AW	57570 TQ	TXBLS	10/01-12/01
	Killeen-Temple MSA, TX	Y	25940 FQ	44820 AW	68160 TQ	TXBLS	10/01-12/01
	Laredo MSA, TX	Y	35340 FQ	45720 AW	56390 TQ	TXBLS	10/01-12/01
	Longview-Marshall MSA, TX	Y	27270 FQ	41330 AW	54830 TQ	TXBLS	10/01-12/01
	Lubbock MSA, TX	Y	33310 FQ	41800 AW	52710 TQ	TXBLS	10/01-12/01
	McAllen-Edinburg-Mission MSA, TX	Y	29630 FQ	41770 AW	55160 TQ	TXBLS	10/01-12/01
	Odessa-Midland MSA, TX	Y	25770 FQ	40830 AW	54980 TQ	TXBLS	10/01-12/01
	San Antonio MSA, TX	Y	30850 FQ	44770 AW	59490 TQ	TXBLS	10/01-12/01
	Tyler MSA, TX	Y	22960 FQ	39060 AW	54530 TQ	TXBLS	10/01-12/01
	Waco MSA, TX	Y	21200 FQ	35640 AW	44970 TQ	TXBLS	10/01-12/01
	Utah	Y	22390 FQ	37990 AW	56920 TQ	UTBLS	10/01-12/01
	Provo-Orem MSA, UT	Y	19610 FQ	38330 AW	57220 TQ	UTBLS	10/01-12/01
	Salt Lake City-Ogden MSA, UT	Y	24350 FQ	40290 AW	59550 TQ	UTBLS	10/01-12/01
	Vermont	Y	22200 FQ	39690 AW	55080 TQ	VTBLS	10/01-12/01
	Burlington MSA, VT	Y	21770 FQ	41520 AW	57150 TQ	VTBLS	10/01-12/01
	Virginia	Y	30670 FQ	47600 AW	68530 TQ	VABLS	10/01-12/01
	Lynchburg MSA, VA	Y	26220 FQ	41210 AW	55980 TQ	VABLS	10/01-12/01
	Norfolk-Virginia Beach-Newport News MSA, VA-NC	Y	30610 FQ	44090 AW	60050 TQ	VABLS	10/01-12/01
	Richmond-Petersburg MSA, VA	Y	33520 FQ	48040 AW	65010 TQ	VABLS	10/01-12/01
	Roanoke MSA, VA	Y	29830 FQ	61680 AW		VABLS	10/01-12/01
	Washington	Y	31200 FQ	47470 AW	61200 TQ	WABLS	10/01-12/01
	Bremerton PMSA, WA	Y	38340 FQ	48620 AW	59850 TQ	WABLS	10/01-12/01
	Olympia PMSA, WA	Y	29340 FQ	46000 AW	58240 TQ	WABLS	10/01-12/01

AAW	Average annual wage	**AOH**	Average offered, high	**ASH**	Average starting, high	**H**	Hourly	**M**	Monthly	**S**	Special: hourly and annual
AE	Average entry wage	**AOL**	Average offered, low	**ASL**	Average starting, low	**HI**	Highest wage paid	**MTC**	Median total compensation	**TQ**	Third quartile wage
AEX	Average experienced wage	**APH**	Average pay, high range	**AW**	Average wage paid	**HR**	High end range	**MW**	Median wage paid	**W**	Weekly
AO	Average offered	**APL**	Average pay, low range	**FQ**	First quartile wage	**LR**	Low end range	**SQ**	Second quartile wage	**Y**	Yearly

Occupation/Type/Industry	Location	Per	Low	Mid	High	Source	Date
Librarian	Richland-Kennewick-Pasco MSA, WA	Y	36660 FQ	44670 AW	55540 TQ	WABLS	10/01-12/01
	Seattle-Bellevue-Everett PMSA, WA	Y	38600 FQ	51320 AW	67080 TQ	WABLS	10/01-12/01
	Spokane MSA, WA	Y	32150 FQ	44900 AW	57790 TQ	WABLS	10/01-12/01
	Tacoma PMSA, WA	Y	32490 FQ	45910 AW	58300 TQ	WABLS	10/01-12/01
	Yakima MSA, WA	Y	31210 FQ	45790 AW	57120 TQ	WABLS	10/01-12/01
	West Virginia	Y	24360 FQ	35750 AW	46250 TQ	WVBLS	10/01-12/01
	Charleston MSA, WV	Y	29340 FQ	36880 AW	50700 TQ	WVBLS	10/01-12/01
	Huntington-Ashland MSA, WV-KY-OH	Y	23720 FQ	38040 AW	53840 TQ	WVBLS	10/01-12/01
	Wisconsin	Y	28830 FQ	44300 AW	59500 TQ	WIBLS	10/01-12/01
	Appleton-Oshkosh-Neenah MSA, WI	Y	29200 FQ	42100 AW	57690 TQ	WIBLS	10/01-12/01
	Green Bay MSA, WI	Y	35450 FQ	48800 AW	60050 TQ	WIBLS	10/01-12/01
	Madison MSA, WI	Y	31060 FQ	46190 AW	61540 TQ	WIBLS	10/01-12/01
	Milwaukee-Waukesha PMSA, WI	Y	33100 FQ	46800 AW	64660 TQ	WIBLS	10/01-12/01
	Racine PMSA, WI	Y	31610 FQ	45770 AW	57470 TQ	WIBLS	10/01-12/01
	Wyoming	Y	24550 FQ	37020 AW	47730 TQ	WYBLS	10/01-12/01
	Puerto Rico	Y	19020 FQ	25540 AW	34670 TQ	PRBLS	10/01-12/01
	Virgin Islands	Y	26100 FQ	38040 AW	55330 TQ	VIBLS	10/01-12/01
	Guam	Y	13900 FQ	30170 AW	42960 TQ	GUBLS	10/01-12/01
Library Assistant	Alabama	H	5.85 FQ	9.02 AW	13.89 TQ	ALBLS	10/01-12/01
	Alaska	H	8.54 FQ	13.47 AW	18.17 TQ	AKBLS	10/01-12/01
	Arizona	H	6.62 FQ	9.82 AW	13.94 TQ	AZBLS	10/01-12/01
	Arkansas	H	5.69 FQ	7.40 AW	10.34 TQ	ARBLS	10/01-12/01
	California	H	7.26 FQ	12.04 AW	17.04 TQ	CABLS	10/01-12/01
	Colorado	H	6.73 FQ	9.61 AW	13.26 TQ	COBLS	10/01-12/01
	Connecticut	H	6.71 FQ	10.37 AW	15.87 TQ	CTBLS	10/01-12/01
	Delaware	H	6.69 FQ	11.45 AW	16.41 TQ	DEBLS	10/01-12/01
	District of Columbia	H	7.46 FQ	11.83 AW	17.61 TQ	DCBLS	10/01-12/01
	Florida	H	6.02 FQ	8.80 AW	12.62 TQ	FLBLS	10/01-12/01
	Georgia	H	6.00 FQ	9.16 AW	12.91 TQ	GABLS	10/01-12/01
	Hawaii	H	9.14 FQ	11.99 AW	15.75 TQ	HIBLS	10/01-12/01
	Idaho	H	6.00 FQ	9.15 AW	12.76 TQ	IDBLS	10/01-12/01
	Illinois	H	6.03 FQ	9.81 AW	15.06 TQ	ILBLS	10/01-12/01
	Indiana	H	5.86 FQ	8.35 AW	11.34 TQ	INBLS	10/01-12/01
	Iowa	H	5.74 FQ	8.63 AW	13.98 TQ	IABLS	10/01-12/01
	Kansas	H	5.91 FQ	8.32 AW	12.22 TQ	KSBLS	10/01-12/01
	Kentucky	H	5.80 FQ	7.82 AW	11.16 TQ	KYBLS	10/01-12/01
	Louisiana	H	5.90 FQ	8.97 AW	13.92 TQ	LABLS	10/01-12/01
	Maine	H	6.01 FQ	8.86 AW	12.62 TQ	MEBLS	10/01-12/01
	Maryland	H	6.29 FQ	11.54 AW	17.49 TQ	MDBLS	10/01-12/01
	Massachusetts	H	7.22 FQ	11.65 AW	16.78 TQ	MABLS	10/01-12/01
	Michigan	H	5.89 FQ	8.73 AW	12.76 TQ	MIBLS	10/01-12/01
	Minnesota	H	6.18 FQ	9.68 AW	13.78 TQ	MNBLS	10/01-12/01
	Mississippi	H	5.71 FQ	7.50 AW	10.60 TQ	MSBLS	10/01-12/01
	Missouri	H	6.02 FQ	9.16 AW	13.34 TQ	MOBLS	10/01-12/01
	Montana	H	5.75 FQ	7.86 AW	11.62 TQ	MTBLS	10/01-12/01
	Nebraska	H	5.85 FQ	8.09 AW	11.70 TQ	NEBLS	10/01-12/01
	Nevada	H	9.32 FQ	13.33 AW	17.71 TQ	NVBLS	10/01-12/01
	New Hampshire	H	6.32 FQ	9.30 AW	12.92 TQ	NHBLS	10/01-12/01
	New Jersey	H	6.24 FQ	10.41 AW	15.75 TQ	NJBLS	10/01-12/01
	New Mexico	H	6.09 FQ	9.34 AW	13.02 TQ	NMBLS	10/01-12/01
	New York	H	5.99 FQ	10.19 AW	16.34 TQ	NYBLS	10/01-12/01
	North Carolina	H	5.87 FQ	9.13 AW	13.24 TQ	NCBLS	10/01-12/01
	North Dakota	H	5.57 FQ	6.47 AW	7.91 TQ	NDBLS	10/01-12/01
	Ohio	H	5.99 FQ	8.72 AW	12.65 TQ	OHBLS	10/01-12/01
	Oklahoma	H	5.74 FQ	8.28 AW	11.32 TQ	OKBLS	10/01-12/01
	Oregon	H	7.86 FQ	11.17 AW	14.28 TQ	ORBLS	10/01-12/01
	Pennsylvania	H	5.89 FQ	8.91 AW	13.82 TQ	PABLS	10/01-12/01
	Rhode Island	H	6.84 FQ	10.94 AW	15.85 TQ	RIBLS	10/01-12/01
	South Carolina	H	6.13 FQ	8.76 AW	11.16 TQ	SCBLS	10/01-12/01
	South Dakota	H	5.76 FQ	7.42 AW	9.65 TQ	SDBLS	10/01-12/01
	Tennessee	H	5.76 FQ	8.05 AW	11.60 TQ	TNBLS	10/01-12/01
	Texas	H	5.89 FQ	8.57 AW	12.21 TQ	TXBLS	10/01-12/01
	Utah	H	5.87 FQ	7.56 AW	10.29 TQ	UTBLS	10/01-12/01
	Vermont	H	6.61 FQ	8.84 AW	12.42 TQ	VTBLS	10/01-12/01
	Virginia	H	6.13 FQ	10.71 AW	16.82 TQ	VABLS	10/01-12/01
	Washington	H	7.40 FQ	10.33 AW	14.74 TQ	WABLS	10/01-12/01
	West Virginia	H	5.69 FQ	7.54 AW	10.98 TQ	WVBLS	10/01-12/01

AAW Average annual wage	**AOH** Average offered, high	**ASH** Average starting, high	**H** Hourly	**M** Monthly	**S** Special: hourly and annual
AE Average entry wage	**AOL** Average offered, low	**ASL** Average starting, low	**HI** Highest wage paid	**MTC** Median total compensation	**TQ** Third quartile wage
AEX Average experienced wage	**APH** Average pay, high range	**AW** Average wage paid	**HR** High end range	**MW** Median wage paid	**W** Weekly
AO Average offered	**APL** Average pay, low range	**FQ** First quartile wage	**LR** Low end range	**SQ** Second quartile wage	**Y** Yearly

Occupation/Type/Industry	Location	Per	Low	Mid	High	Source	Date
Library Assistant	Wisconsin	H	6.53 FQ	9.27 AW	13.32 TQ	WIBLS	10/01-12/01
	Wyoming	H	6.78 FQ	9.85 AW	13.76 TQ	WYBLS	10/01-12/01
	Puerto Rico	H	5.86 FQ	8.01 AW	11.21 TQ	PRBLS	10/01-12/01
	Virgin Islands	H	6.35 FQ	8.73 AW	12.33 TQ	VIBLS	10/01-12/01
Library Science Teacher							
Postsecondary	Alabama	Y	28560 FQ	46010 AW	69240 TQ	ALBLS	10/01-12/01
Postsecondary	California	Y	36620 FQ	63360 AW	102120 TQ	CABLS	10/01-12/01
Postsecondary	Colorado	Y	31220 FQ	53500 AW	83070 TQ	COBLS	10/01-12/01
Postsecondary	Denver PMSA, CO	Y	35570 FQ	56700 AW	86790 TQ	COBLS	10/01-12/01
Postsecondary	Washington PMSA, DC-MD-VA-WV	Y	40220 FQ	63180 AW	97890 TQ	DCBLS	10/01-12/01
Postsecondary	Florida	Y	28810 FQ	56190 AW	92980 TQ	FLBLS	10/01-12/01
Postsecondary	Tallahassee MSA, FL	Y	44360 FQ	70390 AW	126550 TQ	FLBLS	10/01-12/01
Postsecondary	Tampa-St. Petersburg-Clearwater MSA, FL	Y	33620 FQ	54050 AW	83480 TQ	FLBLS	10/01-12/01
Postsecondary	Georgia	Y	30540 FQ	51430 AW	71300 TQ	GABLS	10/01-12/01
Postsecondary	Atlanta MSA, GA	Y	30280 FQ	48950 AW	68940 TQ	GABLS	10/01-12/01
Postsecondary	Hawaii	Y	40260 FQ	54270 AW	71670 TQ	HIBLS	10/01-12/01
Postsecondary	Honolulu MSA, HI	Y	40260 FQ	55180 AW	73850 TQ	HIBLS	10/01-12/01
Postsecondary	Illinois	Y	23180 FQ	55490 AW	91670 TQ	ILBLS	10/01-12/01
Postsecondary	Chicago PMSA, IL	Y	22390 FQ	63490 AW	95910 TQ	ILBLS	10/01-12/01
Postsecondary	Indiana	Y	31420 FQ	53080 AW	79030 TQ	INBLS	10/01-12/01
Postsecondary	Iowa	Y	32320 FQ	54500 AW	83660 TQ	IABLS	10/01-12/01
Postsecondary	Kansas	Y	32360 FQ	45040 AW	62200 TQ	KSBLS	10/01-12/01
Postsecondary	Louisiana	Y	28230 FQ	48520 AW	74490 TQ	LABLS	10/01-12/01
Postsecondary	New Orleans MSA, LA	Y	26460 FQ	51660 AW	83000 TQ	LABLS	10/01-12/01
Postsecondary	Michigan	Y	37660 FQ	53470 AW	70510 TQ	MIBLS	10/01-12/01
Postsecondary	Minnesota	Y	37380 FQ	55100 AW	78960 TQ	MNBLS	10/01-12/01
Postsecondary	Minneapolis-St. Paul MSA, MN-WI	Y	36590 FQ	59060 AW	88110 TQ	MNBLS	10/01-12/01
Postsecondary	Mississippi	Y	29440 FQ	40790 AW	56070 TQ	MSBLS	10/01-12/01
Postsecondary	Missouri	Y	30650 FQ	53580 AW	85840 TQ	MOBLS	10/01-12/01
Postsecondary	Kansas City MSA, MO-KS	Y	31170 FQ	50390 AW	80970 TQ	MOBLS	10/01-12/01
Postsecondary	St. Louis MSA, MO-IL	Y	29370 FQ	55800 AW	88230 TQ	MOBLS	10/01-12/01
Postsecondary	Nebraska	Y	33540 FQ	51080 AW	69620 TQ	NEBLS	10/01-12/01
Postsecondary	New Hampshire	Y	38670 FQ	50980 AW	67640 TQ	NHBLS	10/01-12/01
Postsecondary	New Jersey	Y	30200 FQ	54190 AW	84180 TQ	NJBLS	10/01-12/01
Postsecondary	New York	Y	40670 FQ	63310 AW	99630 TQ	NYBLS	10/01-12/01
Postsecondary	New York PMSA, NY	Y	40380 FQ	54730 AW	75390 TQ	NYBLS	10/01-12/01
Postsecondary	North Carolina	Y	35920 FQ	55960 AW	77980 TQ	NCBLS	10/01-12/01
Postsecondary	Ohio	Y	28340 FQ	45600 AW	67810 TQ	OHBLS	10/01-12/01
Postsecondary	Oklahoma	Y	30500 FQ	48140 AW	73560 TQ	OKBLS	10/01-12/01
Postsecondary	Oregon	Y	38120 FQ	52200 AW	69130 TQ	ORBLS	10/01-12/01
Postsecondary	Pennsylvania	Y	37280 FQ	55120 AW	79710 TQ	PABLS	10/01-12/01
Postsecondary	Philadelphia PMSA, PA-NJ	Y	33140 FQ	52930 AW	78570 TQ	PABLS	10/01-12/01
Postsecondary	Tennessee	Y	32620 FQ	48220 AW	73280 TQ	TNBLS	10/01-12/01
Postsecondary	Texas	Y	32010 FQ	52420 AW	79570 TQ	TXBLS	10/01-12/01
Postsecondary	Houston PMSA, TX	Y	30100 FQ	53960 AW	81380 TQ	TXBLS	10/01-12/01
Postsecondary	Vermont	Y	27730 FQ	47390 AW	67700 TQ	VTBLS	10/01-12/01
Postsecondary	Virginia	Y	32990 FQ	50370 AW	70120 TQ	VABLS	10/01-12/01
Postsecondary	Washington	Y	37820 FQ	67700 AW	109760 TQ	WABLS	10/01-12/01
Postsecondary	Seattle-Bellevue-Everett PMSA, WA	Y	42490 FQ	81390 AW	116150 TQ	WABLS	10/01-12/01
Postsecondary	Wisconsin	Y	38690 FQ	51230 AW	72400 TQ	WIBLS	10/01-12/01
Postsecondary	Puerto Rico	Y	32230 FQ	56300 AW	86750 TQ	PRBLS	10/01-12/01
Library Technician	Alabama	Y	12760 FQ	20530 AW	32010 TQ	ALBLS	10/01-12/01
	Birmingham MSA, AL	Y	12170 FQ	21090 AW	34030 TQ	ALBLS	10/01-12/01
	Huntsville MSA, AL	Y	12090 FQ	21160 AW	33180 TQ	ALBLS	10/01-12/01
	Mobile MSA, AL	Y	13170 FQ	20850 AW	29100 TQ	ALBLS	10/01-12/01
	Montgomery MSA, AL	Y	13310 FQ	22540 AW	33470 TQ	ALBLS	10/01-12/01
	Alaska	Y	21650 FQ	33760 AW	44570 TQ	AKBLS	10/01-12/01
	Arizona	Y	14290 FQ	24640 AW	38180 TQ	AZBLS	10/01-12/01
	Phoenix-Mesa MSA, AZ	Y	13850 FQ	24750 AW	38880 TQ	AZBLS	10/01-12/01
	Tucson MSA, AZ	Y	15590 FQ	31640 AW	58300 TQ	AZBLS	10/01-12/01
	Arkansas	Y	11830 FQ	16630 AW	23840 TQ	ARBLS	10/01-12/01
	Little Rock-North Little Rock MSA, AR	Y	12070 FQ	18480 AW	27140 TQ	ARBLS	10/01-12/01
	California	Y	20500 FQ	30990 AW	41740 TQ	CABLS	10/01-12/01
	Bakersfield MSA, CA	Y	18670 FQ	25640 AW	36150 TQ	CABLS	10/01-12/01
	Chico-Paradise MSA, CA	Y	23890 FQ	33000 AW	44620 TQ	CABLS	10/01-12/01
	Fresno MSA, CA	Y	19170 FQ	29380 AW	40920 TQ	CABLS	10/01-12/01

AAW	Average annual wage	**AOH**	Average offered, high	**ASH**	Average starting, high	**H**	Hourly	**M**	Monthly	**S**	Special: hourly and annual
AE	Average entry wage	**AOL**	Average offered, low	**ASL**	Average starting, low	**HI**	Highest wage paid	**MTC**	Median total compensation	**TQ**	Third quartile wage
AEX	Average experienced wage	**APH**	Average pay, high range	**AW**	Average wage paid	**HR**	High end range	**MW**	Median wage paid	**W**	Weekly
AO	Average offered	**APL**	Average pay, low range	**FQ**	First quartile wage	**LR**	Low end range	**SQ**	Second quartile wage	**Y**	Yearly

Occupation/Type/Industry	Location	Per	Low	Mid	High	Source	Date
Library Technician	Los Angeles-Long Beach PMSA, CA	Y	22420 FQ	33210 AW	43080 TQ	CABLS	10/01-12/01
	Merced MSA, CA	Y	16620 FQ	27880 AW	41730 TQ	CABLS	10/01-12/01
	Modesto MSA, CA	Y	23130 FQ	29760 AW	41130 TQ	CABLS	10/01-12/01
	Oakland PMSA, CA	Y	19010 FQ	26980 AW	37240 TQ	CABLS	10/01-12/01
	Orange County PMSA, CA	Y	20910 FQ	32000 AW	43370 TQ	CABLS	10/01-12/01
	Riverside-San Bernardino PMSA, CA	Y	20750 FQ	28330 AW	36290 TQ	CABLS	10/01-12/01
	Sacramento PMSA, CA	Y	20760 FQ	30960 AW	40360 TQ	CABLS	10/01-12/01
	Salinas MSA, CA	Y	18060 FQ	29780 AW	40360 TQ	CABLS	10/01-12/01
	San Diego MSA, CA	Y	19570 FQ	28090 AW	38800 TQ	CABLS	10/01-12/01
	San Francisco PMSA, CA	Y	22570 FQ	34950 AW	47260 TQ	CABLS	10/01-12/01
	San Jose PMSA, CA	Y	23870 FQ	34000 AW	43370 TQ	CABLS	10/01-12/01
	San Luis Obispo-Atascadero-Paso Robles MSA, CA	Y	22570 FQ	37330 AW	52650 TQ	CABLS	10/01-12/01
	Santa Barbara-Santa Maria-Lompoc MSA, CA	Y	20480 FQ	29240 AW	36680 TQ	CABLS	10/01-12/01
	Santa Cruz-Watsonville PMSA, CA	Y	23810 FQ	34040 AW	45570 TQ	CABLS	10/01-12/01
	Santa Rosa PMSA, CA	Y	21660 FQ	28420 AW	35810 TQ	CABLS	10/01-12/01
	Stockton-Lodi MSA, CA	Y	20030 FQ	28100 AW	37060 TQ	CABLS	10/01-12/01
	Vallejo-Fairfield-Napa PMSA, CA	Y	20800 FQ	31060 AW	42280 TQ	CABLS	10/01-12/01
	Ventura PMSA, CA	Y	21010 FQ	30000 AW	38010 TQ	CABLS	10/01-12/01
	Visalia-Tulare-Porterville MSA, CA	Y	20620 FQ	29200 AW	36790 TQ	CABLS	10/01-12/01
	Colorado	Y	16580 FQ	25400 AW	35670 TQ	COBLS	10/01-12/01
	Boulder-Longmont PMSA, CO	Y	16220 FQ	25290 AW	36080 TQ	COBLS	10/01-12/01
	Colorado Springs MSA, CO	Y	19210 FQ	25510 AW	34200 TQ	COBLS	10/01-12/01
	Denver PMSA, CO	Y	19500 FQ	27850 AW	37680 TQ	COBLS	10/01-12/01
	Fort Collins-Loveland MSA, CO	Y	14790 FQ	23740 AW	33790 TQ	COBLS	10/01-12/01
	Greeley PMSA, CO	Y	15830 FQ	24290 AW	34270 TQ	COBLS	10/01-12/01
	Connecticut	Y	16550 FQ	29240 AW	44830 TQ	CTBLS	10/01-12/01
	Bridgeport PMSA, CT	Y	19900 FQ	27350 AW	37450 TQ	CTBLS	10/01-12/01
	Danbury PMSA, CT	Y	13890 FQ	25420 AW	41890 TQ	CTBLS	10/01-12/01
	Hartford MSA, CT	Y	16870 FQ	30230 AW	47050 TQ	CTBLS	10/01-12/01
	New Haven-Meriden PMSA, CT	Y	16740 FQ	26880 AW	37300 TQ	CTBLS	10/01-12/01
	New London-Norwich MSA, CT-RI	Y	13840 FQ	31210 AW	49470 TQ	CTBLS	10/01-12/01
	Stamford-Norwalk PMSA, CT	Y	24480 FQ	31250 AW	38230 TQ	CTBLS	10/01-12/01
	Waterbury PMSA, CT	Y	16390 FQ	27460 AW	40150 TQ	CTBLS	10/01-12/01
	Delaware	Y	16120 FQ	25720 AW	36980 TQ	DEBLS	10/01-12/01
	Wilmington-Newark PMSA, DE-MD	Y	19230 FQ	27380 AW	38110 TQ	DEBLS	10/01-12/01
	District of Columbia	Y	20520 FQ	34780 AW	54000 TQ	DCBLS	10/01-12/01
	Washington PMSA, DC-MD-VA-WV	Y	21280 FQ	33870 AW	45870 TQ	DCBLS	10/01-12/01
	Florida	Y	16760 FQ	23640 AW	31640 TQ	FLBLS	10/01-12/01
	Daytona Beach MSA, FL	Y	17230 FQ	23570 AW	32640 TQ	FLBLS	10/01-12/01
	Fort Lauderdale PMSA, FL	Y	19900 FQ	27670 AW	39730 TQ	FLBLS	10/01-12/01
	Fort Walton Beach MSA, FL	Y	15250 FQ	21720 AW	31790 TQ	FLBLS	10/01-12/01
	Gainesville MSA, FL	Y	18770 FQ	22870 AW	28300 TQ	FLBLS	10/01-12/01
	Jacksonville MSA, FL	Y	15860 FQ	21560 AW	28830 TQ	FLBLS	10/01-12/01
	Lakeland-Winter Haven MSA, FL	Y	13580 FQ	19840 AW	27940 TQ	FLBLS	10/01-12/01
	Melbourne-Titusville-Palm Bay MSA, FL	Y	13730 FQ	22240 AW	29770 TQ	FLBLS	10/01-12/01
	Miami PMSA, FL	Y	18490 FQ	24600 AW	30680 TQ	FLBLS	10/01-12/01
	Naples MSA, FL	Y	18580 FQ	24540 AW	33980 TQ	FLBLS	10/01-12/01
	Ocala MSA, FL	Y	15530 FQ	22350 AW	29400 TQ	FLBLS	10/01-12/01
	Orlando MSA, FL	Y	16620 FQ	21510 AW	27420 TQ	FLBLS	10/01-12/01
	Pensacola MSA, FL	Y	17760 FQ	23200 AW	29330 TQ	FLBLS	10/01-12/01
	Tallahassee MSA, FL	Y	17180 FQ	25830 AW	33070 TQ	FLBLS	10/01-12/01
	Tampa-St. Petersburg-Clearwater MSA, FL	Y	16710 FQ	24250 AW	34230 TQ	FLBLS	10/01-12/01
	West Palm Beach-Boca Raton MSA, FL	Y	19030 FQ	24680 AW	33000 TQ	FLBLS	10/01-12/01
	Georgia	Y	13190 FQ	23000 AW	35340 TQ	GABLS	10/01-12/01
	Atlanta MSA, GA	Y	12910 FQ	25790 AW	36740 TQ	GABLS	10/01-12/01
	Augusta-Aiken MSA, GA-SC	Y	12660 FQ	23160 AW	33480 TQ	GABLS	10/01-12/01

AAW Average annual wage **AOH** Average offered, high **ASH** Average starting, high **H** Hourly **M** Monthly **S** Special: hourly and annual
AE Average entry wage **AOL** Average offered, low **ASL** Average starting, low **HI** Highest wage paid **MTC** Median total compensation **TQ** Third quartile wage
AEX Average experienced wage **APH** Average pay, high range **AW** Average wage paid **HR** High end range **MW** Median wage paid **W** Weekly
AO Average offered **APL** Average pay, low range **FQ** First quartile wage **LR** Low end range **SQ** Second quartile wage **Y** Yearly

Occupation/Type/Industry	Location	Per	Low	Mid	High	Source	Date
Library Technician	Columbus MSA, GA-AL	Y	19380 FQ	26420 AW	35290 TQ	GABLS	10/01-12/01
	Hawaii	Y	18750 FQ	29740 AW	40790 TQ	HIBLS	10/01-12/01
	Honolulu MSA, HI	Y	18260 FQ	29740 AW	41220 TQ	HIBLS	10/01-12/01
	Idaho	Y	16270 FQ	21780 AW	28290 TQ	IDBLS	10/01-12/01
	Illinois	Y	12760 FQ	24140 AW	39940 TQ	ILBLS	10/01-12/01
	Champaign-Urbana MSA, IL	Y	16190 FQ	34120 AW	46310 TQ	ILBLS	10/01-12/01
	Chicago PMSA, IL	Y	12890 FQ	24970 AW	42430 TQ	ILBLS	10/01-12/01
	Peoria-Pekin MSA, IL	Y	13280 FQ	20290 AW	30010 TQ	ILBLS	10/01-12/01
	Rockford MSA, IL	Y	14660 FQ	20120 AW	28370 TQ	ILBLS	10/01-12/01
	Springfield MSA, IL	Y	12890 FQ	22250 AW	37270 TQ	ILBLS	10/01-12/01
	Indiana	Y	14310 FQ	21060 AW	29010 TQ	INBLS	10/01-12/01
	Evansville-Henderson MSA, IN-KY	Y	15460 FQ	22060 AW	29900 TQ	INBLS	10/01-12/01
	Fort Wayne MSA, IN	Y	14520 FQ	17720 AW	24480 TQ	INBLS	10/01-12/01
	Gary PMSA, IN	Y	15120 FQ	20720 AW	28450 TQ	INBLS	10/01-12/01
	Indianapolis MSA, IN	Y	14340 FQ	25370 AW	47030 TQ	INBLS	10/01-12/01
	South Bend MSA, IN	Y	18910 FQ	23670 AW	28450 TQ	INBLS	10/01-12/01
	Iowa	Y	13330 FQ	20920 AW	30670 TQ	IABLS	10/01-12/01
	Cedar Rapids MSA, IA	Y	18090 FQ	24160 AW	36400 TQ	IABLS	10/01-12/01
	Davenport-Moline-Rock Island MSA, IA-IL	Y	13700 FQ	21540 AW	30490 TQ	IABLS	10/01-12/01
	Des Moines MSA, IA	Y	14000 FQ	21560 AW	31290 TQ	IABLS	10/01-12/01
	Kansas	Y	12890 FQ	19230 AW	29000 TQ	KSBLS	10/01-12/01
	Topeka MSA, KS	Y	17270 FQ	24580 AW	33150 TQ	KSBLS	10/01-12/01
	Wichita MSA, KS	Y	15220 FQ	24450 AW	34660 TQ	KSBLS	10/01-12/01
	Kentucky	Y	12080 FQ	20140 AW	28570 TQ	KYBLS	10/01-12/01
	Lexington MSA, KY	Y	19290 FQ	23610 AW	29290 TQ	KYBLS	10/01-12/01
	Louisville MSA, KY-IN	Y	17310 FQ	26030 AW	35840 TQ	KYBLS	10/01-12/01
	Louisiana	Y	12680 FQ	20220 AW	29310 TQ	LABLS	10/01-12/01
	Baton Rouge MSA, LA	Y	13200 FQ	22730 AW	34430 TQ	LABLS	10/01-12/01
	New Orleans MSA, LA	Y	14380 FQ	22410 AW	30060 TQ	LABLS	10/01-12/01
	Shreveport-Bossier City MSA, LA	Y	12750 FQ	18130 AW	25180 TQ	LABLS	10/01-12/01
	Maine	Y	15620 FQ	22700 AW	30680 TQ	MEBLS	10/01-12/01
	Portland MSA, ME	Y	16340 FQ	23090 AW	30090 TQ	MEBLS	10/01-12/01
	Maryland	Y	13260 FQ	28750 AW	43150 TQ	MDBLS	10/01-12/01
	Baltimore PMSA, MD	Y	12330 FQ	25410 AW	41160 TQ	MDBLS	10/01-12/01
	Massachusetts	Y	14960 FQ	25860 AW	37450 TQ	MABLS	10/01-12/01
	Boston PMSA, MA-NH	Y	15180 FQ	26700 AW	39150 TQ	MABLS	10/01-12/01
	Brockton PMSA, MA	Y	14700 FQ	25960 AW	36630 TQ	MABLS	10/01-12/01
	Lawrence PMSA, MA-NH	Y	15770 FQ	26020 AW	37260 TQ	MABLS	10/01-12/01
	Lowell PMSA, MA-NH	Y	14330 FQ	23290 AW	34270 TQ	MABLS	10/01-12/01
	New Bedford PMSA, MA	Y	14860 FQ	22550 AW	32740 TQ	MABLS	10/01-12/01
	Springfield MSA, MA	Y	15540 FQ	26550 AW	38910 TQ	MABLS	10/01-12/01
	Worcester PMSA, MA-CT	Y	14860 FQ	24920 AW	34850 TQ	MABLS	10/01-12/01
	Michigan	Y	16150 FQ	26370 AW	38500 TQ	MIBLS	10/01-12/01
	Ann Arbor PMSA, MI	Y	20880 FQ	29340 AW	44030 TQ	MIBLS	10/01-12/01
	Detroit PMSA, MI	Y	16670 FQ	28680 AW	42320 TQ	MIBLS	10/01-12/01
	Flint PMSA, MI	Y	14550 FQ	25550 AW	35980 TQ	MIBLS	10/01-12/01
	Grand Rapids-Muskegon-Holland MSA, MI	Y	17270 FQ	24860 AW	33850 TQ	MIBLS	10/01-12/01
	Kalamazoo-Battle Creek MSA, MI	Y	15040 FQ	23790 AW	35770 TQ	MIBLS	10/01-12/01
	Lansing-East Lansing MSA, MI	Y	16260 FQ	28400 AW	41630 TQ	MIBLS	10/01-12/01
	Saginaw-Bay City-Midland MSA, MI	Y	13930 FQ	23660 AW	34770 TQ	MIBLS	10/01-12/01
	Minnesota	Y	17610 FQ	28760 AW	41660 TQ	MNBLS	10/01-12/01
	Duluth-Superior MSA, MN-WI	Y	24130 FQ	31690 AW	40100 TQ	MNBLS	10/01-12/01
	Minneapolis-St. Paul MSA, MN-WI	Y	22410 FQ	30630 AW	42790 TQ	MNBLS	10/01-12/01
	St. Cloud MSA, MN	Y	21250 FQ	29400 AW	40660 TQ	MNBLS	10/01-12/01
	Mississippi	Y	12300 FQ	19040 AW	30080 TQ	MSBLS	10/01-12/01
	Biloxi-Gulfport-Pascagoula MSA, MS	Y	12850 FQ	18890 AW	26460 TQ	MSBLS	10/01-12/01
	Jackson MSA, MS	Y	12460 FQ	18910 AW	27460 TQ	MSBLS	10/01-12/01
	Missouri	Y	13360 FQ	22230 AW	33400 TQ	MOBLS	10/01-12/01
	Kansas City MSA, MO-KS	Y	14220 FQ	21260 AW	31710 TQ	MOBLS	10/01-12/01
	St. Louis MSA, MO-IL	Y	12890 FQ	23020 AW	34740 TQ	MOBLS	10/01-12/01
	Springfield MSA, MO	Y	15660 FQ	21550 AW	28460 TQ	MOBLS	10/01-12/01
	Montana	Y	12530 FQ	19010 AW	27010 TQ	MTBLS	10/01-12/01
	Nebraska	Y	13790 FQ	23110 AW	35180 TQ	NEBLS	10/01-12/01
	Lincoln MSA, NE	Y	18970 FQ	25710 AW	35410 TQ	NEBLS	10/01-12/01

AAW	Average annual wage	**AOH**	Average offered, high	**ASH**	Average starting, high	**H**	Hourly	**M**	Monthly	**S**	Special: hourly and annual
AE	Average entry wage	**AOL**	Average offered, low	**ASL**	Average starting, low	**HI**	Highest wage paid	**MTC**	Median total compensation	**TQ**	Third quartile wage
AEX	Average experienced wage	**APH**	Average pay, high range	**AW**	Average wage paid	**HR**	High end range	**MW**	Median wage paid	**W**	Weekly
AO	Average offered	**APL**	Average pay, low range	**FQ**	First quartile wage	**LR**	Low end range	**SQ**	Second quartile wage	**Y**	Yearly

Occupation/Type/Industry	Location	Per	Low	Mid	High	Source	Date
Library Technician	Omaha MSA, NE-IA	Y	12980 FQ	23960 AW	35580 TQ	NEBLS	10/01-12/01
	Nevada	Y	21390 FQ	31430 AW	42990 TQ	NVBLS	10/01-12/01
	Las Vegas MSA, NV-AZ	Y	16300 FQ	24310 AW	37600 TQ	NVBLS	10/01-12/01
	Reno MSA, NV	Y	24400 FQ	33390 AW	44280 TQ	NVBLS	10/01-12/01
	New Hampshire	Y	17580 FQ	24680 AW	33950 TQ	NHBLS	10/01-12/01
	Manchester PMSA, NH	Y	15880 FQ	23220 AW	32460 TQ	NHBLS	10/01-12/01
	Nashua PMSA, NH	Y	19030 FQ	27130 AW	40910 TQ	NHBLS	10/01-12/01
	Portsmouth-Rochester PMSA, NH-ME	Y	18360 FQ	24240 AW	32410 TQ	NHBLS	10/01-12/01
	New Jersey	Y	15840 FQ	27420 AW	40890 TQ	NJBLS	10/01-12/01
	Atlantic-Cape May PMSA, NJ	Y	20530 FQ	29270 AW	40890 TQ	NJBLS	10/01-12/01
	Bergen-Passaic PMSA, NJ	Y	14510 FQ	23850 AW	35450 TQ	NJBLS	10/01-12/01
	Jersey City PMSA, NJ	Y	12680 FQ	24650 AW	40480 TQ	NJBLS	10/01-12/01
	Middlesex-Somerset-Hunterdon PMSA, NJ	Y	15790 FQ	28280 AW	43850 TQ	NJBLS	10/01-12/01
	Monmouth-Ocean PMSA, NJ	Y	19110 FQ	26190 AW	35350 TQ	NJBLS	10/01-12/01
	Newark PMSA, NJ	Y	18700 FQ	29120 AW	42360 TQ	NJBLS	10/01-12/01
	Trenton PMSA, NJ	Y	21960 FQ	30030 AW	35860 TQ	NJBLS	10/01-12/01
	New Mexico	Y	12420 FQ	18850 AW	28750 TQ	NMBLS	10/01-12/01
	Albuquerque MSA, NM	Y	12660 FQ	20170 AW	28090 TQ	NMBLS	10/01-12/01
	Las Cruces MSA, NM	Y	12170 FQ	18090 AW	26240 TQ	NMBLS	10/01-12/01
	New York	Y	12620 FQ	23390 AW	38610 TQ	NYBLS	10/01-12/01
	Albany-Schenectady-Troy MSA, NY	Y	13620 FQ	25170 AW	41270 TQ	NYBLS	10/01-12/01
	Binghamton MSA, NY	Y	11910 FQ	22040 AW	40520 TQ	NYBLS	10/01-12/01
	Buffalo-Niagara Falls MSA, NY	Y	11870 FQ	20470 AW	36260 TQ	NYBLS	10/01-12/01
	Dutchess County PMSA, NY	Y	19410 FQ	26910 AW	36280 TQ	NYBLS	10/01-12/01
	Nassau-Suffolk PMSA, NY	Y	12680 FQ	20220 AW	33170 TQ	NYBLS	10/01-12/01
	New York PMSA, NY	Y	13240 FQ	25160 AW	40990 TQ	NYBLS	10/01-12/01
	Newburgh PMSA, NY-PA	Y	13620 FQ	25720 AW	37920 TQ	NYBLS	10/01-12/01
	Rochester MSA, NY	Y	11980 FQ	25350 AW	44750 TQ	NYBLS	10/01-12/01
	Syracuse MSA, NY	Y	14110 FQ	22060 AW	30190 TQ	NYBLS	10/01-12/01
	Utica-Rome MSA, NY	Y	13370 FQ	21310 AW	35320 TQ	NYBLS	10/01-12/01
	North Carolina	Y	15570 FQ	23600 AW	33370 TQ	NCBLS	10/01-12/01
	Asheville MSA, NC	Y	20200 FQ	26460 AW	32270 TQ	NCBLS	10/01-12/01
	Charlotte-Gastonia-Rock Hill MSA, NC-SC	Y	17990 FQ	24190 AW	33260 TQ	NCBLS	10/01-12/01
	Greensboro-Winston-Salem-High Point MSA, NC	Y	15970 FQ	24680 AW	34850 TQ	NCBLS	10/01-12/01
	Hickory-Morganton-Lenoir MSA, NC	Y	15450 FQ	20840 AW	29610 TQ	NCBLS	10/01-12/01
	Raleigh-Durham-Chapel Hill MSA, NC	Y	17690 FQ	26900 AW	37160 TQ	NCBLS	10/01-12/01
	Wilmington MSA, NC	Y	12690 FQ	22260 AW	33700 TQ	NCBLS	10/01-12/01
	North Dakota	Y	13290 FQ	20760 AW	31130 TQ	NDBLS	10/01-12/01
	Fargo-Moorhead MSA, ND-MN	Y	14630 FQ	21580 AW	31450 TQ	NDBLS	10/01-12/01
	Ohio	Y	17760 FQ	26700 AW	37700 TQ	OHBLS	10/01-12/01
	Akron PMSA, OH	Y	18480 FQ	25300 AW	33330 TQ	OHBLS	10/01-12/01
	Cincinnati PMSA, OH-KY-IN	Y	20270 FQ	30310 AW	45490 TQ	OHBLS	10/01-12/01
	Cleveland-Lorain-Elyria PMSA, OH	Y	17930 FQ	31300 AW	49570 TQ	OHBLS	10/01-12/01
	Columbus MSA, OH	Y	19900 FQ	26530 AW	34400 TQ	OHBLS	10/01-12/01
	Dayton-Springfield MSA, OH	Y	17870 FQ	24600 AW	32990 TQ	OHBLS	10/01-12/01
	Hamilton-Middletown PMSA, OH	Y	19630 FQ	25240 AW	33720 TQ	OHBLS	10/01-12/01
	Toledo MSA, OH	Y	20080 FQ	28980 AW	40220 TQ	OHBLS	10/01-12/01
	Youngstown-Warren MSA, OH	Y	21500 FQ	35930 AW	53350 TQ	OHBLS	10/01-12/01
	Oklahoma	Y	12040 FQ	17360 AW	24800 TQ	OKBLS	10/01-12/01
	Oklahoma City MSA, OK	Y	11950 FQ	18360 AW	26720 TQ	OKBLS	10/01-12/01
	Tulsa MSA, OK	Y	12360 FQ	17300 AW	23120 TQ	OKBLS	10/01-12/01
	Oregon	Y	20200 FQ	27780 AW	35520 TQ	ORBLS	10/01-12/01
	Eugene-Springfield MSA, OR	Y	19580 FQ	28010 AW	35860 TQ	ORBLS	10/01-12/01
	Medford-Ashland MSA, OR	Y	19480 FQ	28850 AW	40650 TQ	ORBLS	10/01-12/01
	Portland-Vancouver PMSA, OR-WA	Y	23020 FQ	29360 AW	35880 TQ	ORBLS	10/01-12/01
	Salem PMSA, OR	Y	19710 FQ	25810 AW	33970 TQ	ORBLS	10/01-12/01
	Pennsylvania	Y	13030 FQ	22420 AW	33750 TQ	PABLS	10/01-12/01
	Allentown-Bethlehem-Easton MSA, PA	Y	16650 FQ	27390 AW	37820 TQ	PABLS	10/01-12/01
	Erie MSA, PA	Y	15500 FQ	26990 AW	42070 TQ	PABLS	10/01-12/01

AAW Average annual wage; **AE** Average entry wage; **AEX** Average experienced wage; **AO** Average offered; **AOH** Average offered, high; **AOL** Average offered, low; **APH** Average pay, high range; **APL** Average pay, low range; **ASH** Average starting, high; **ASL** Average starting, low; **AW** Average wage paid; **FQ** First quartile wage; **H** Hourly; **HI** Highest wage paid; **HR** High end range; **LR** Low end range; **M** Monthly; **MTC** Median total compensation; **MW** Median wage paid; **SQ** Second quartile wage; **S** Special: hourly and annual; **TQ** Third quartile wage; **W** Weekly; **Y** Yearly

Occupation/Type/Industry	Location	Per	Low	Mid	High	Source	Date
Library Technician	Harrisburg-Lebanon-Carlisle MSA, PA	Y	14130 FQ	23370 AW	36170 TQ	PABLS	10/01-12/01
	Johnstown MSA, PA	Y	12820 FQ	21260 AW	32330 TQ	PABLS	10/01-12/01
	Lancaster MSA, PA	Y	16230 FQ	23790 AW	33770 TQ	PABLS	10/01-12/01
	Philadelphia PMSA, PA-NJ	Y	12860 FQ	22930 AW	34710 TQ	PABLS	10/01-12/01
	Pittsburgh MSA, PA	Y	13750 FQ	21720 AW	29780 TQ	PABLS	10/01-12/01
	Reading MSA, PA	Y	12900 FQ	23070 AW	33870 TQ	PABLS	10/01-12/01
	Scranton-Wilkes-Barre-Hazleton MSA, PA	Y	12870 FQ	23840 AW	40050 TQ	PABLS	10/01-12/01
	York MSA, PA	Y	12120 FQ	17840 AW	25860 TQ	PABLS	10/01-12/01
	Rhode Island	Y	14720 FQ	23730 AW	33780 TQ	RIBLS	10/01-12/01
	Providence-Fall River-Warwick MSA, RI-MA	Y	14770 FQ	24110 AW	33870 TQ	RIBLS	10/01-12/01
	South Carolina	Y	12940 FQ	23670 AW	40530 TQ	SCBLS	10/01-12/01
	Charleston-North Charleston MSA, SC	Y	15660 FQ	25310 AW	41270 TQ	SCBLS	10/01-12/01
	Columbia MSA, SC	Y	18800 FQ	31050 AW	46320 TQ	SCBLS	10/01-12/01
	Greenville-Spartanburg-Anderson MSA, SC	Y	12450 FQ	21540 AW	33740 TQ	SCBLS	10/01-12/01
	South Dakota	Y	15990 FQ	21720 AW	28970 TQ	SDBLS	10/01-12/01
	Sioux Falls MSA, SD	Y	18390 FQ	26040 AW	40220 TQ	SDBLS	10/01-12/01
	Tennessee	Y	12780 FQ	20670 AW	31800 TQ	TNBLS	10/01-12/01
	Chattanooga MSA, TN-GA	Y	15280 FQ	25230 AW	35050 TQ	TNBLS	10/01-12/01
	Clarksville-Hopkinsville MSA, TN-KY	Y	17270 FQ	24930 AW	36860 TQ	TNBLS	10/01-12/01
	Johnson City-Kingsport-Bristol MSA, TN-VA	Y	14140 FQ	20050 AW	28050 TQ	TNBLS	10/01-12/01
	Memphis MSA, TN-AR-MS	Y	12540 FQ	20350 AW	32300 TQ	TNBLS	10/01-12/01
	Nashville MSA, TN	Y	13320 FQ	21870 AW	32900 TQ	TNBLS	10/01-12/01
	Texas	Y	12800 FQ	21320 AW	32620 TQ	TXBLS	10/01-12/01
	Austin-San Marcos MSA, TX	Y	15020 FQ	23110 AW	30700 TQ	TXBLS	10/01-12/01
	Beaumont-Port Arthur MSA, TX	Y	12470 FQ	21060 AW	33180 TQ	TXBLS	10/01-12/01
	Brownsville-Harlingen-San Benito MSA, TX	Y	13170 FQ	20510 AW	30500 TQ	TXBLS	10/01-12/01
	Corpus Christi MSA, TX	Y	12580 FQ	19530 AW	27990 TQ	TXBLS	10/01-12/01
	Dallas PMSA, TX	Y	13480 FQ	23190 AW	34540 TQ	TXBLS	10/01-12/01
	El Paso MSA, TX	Y	19390 FQ	24160 AW	29990 TQ	TXBLS	10/01-12/01
	Fort Worth-Arlington PMSA, TX	Y	12770 FQ	20440 AW	29010 TQ	TXBLS	10/01-12/01
	Galveston-Texas City PMSA, TX	Y	14330 FQ	24710 AW	49220 TQ	TXBLS	10/01-12/01
	Houston PMSA, TX	Y	13880 FQ	25440 AW	43170 TQ	TXBLS	10/01-12/01
	Killeen-Temple MSA, TX	Y	12690 FQ	18470 AW	25990 TQ	TXBLS	10/01-12/01
	Longview-Marshall MSA, TX	Y	11770 FQ	15800 AW	22030 TQ	TXBLS	10/01-12/01
	Lubbock MSA, TX	Y	14900 FQ	24340 AW	34930 TQ	TXBLS	10/01-12/01
	McAllen-Edinburg-Mission MSA, TX	Y	12340 FQ	18630 AW	28790 TQ	TXBLS	10/01-12/01
	Odessa-Midland MSA, TX	Y	14150 FQ	20770 AW	29830 TQ	TXBLS	10/01-12/01
	San Antonio MSA, TX	Y	15470 FQ	23450 AW	32610 TQ	TXBLS	10/01-12/01
	Waco MSA, TX	Y	13090 FQ	17370 AW	21840 TQ	TXBLS	10/01-12/01
	Utah	Y	13840 FQ	20160 AW	28370 TQ	UTBLS	10/01-12/01
	Provo-Orem MSA, UT	Y	13760 FQ	18200 AW	24930 TQ	UTBLS	10/01-12/01
	Salt Lake City-Ogden MSA, UT	Y	13610 FQ	20420 AW	28710 TQ	UTBLS	10/01-12/01
	Vermont	Y	14340 FQ	21490 AW	29180 TQ	VTBLS	10/01-12/01
	Burlington MSA, VT	Y	17730 FQ	22400 AW	28870 TQ	VTBLS	10/01-12/01
	Virginia	Y	14250 FQ	27260 AW	41380 TQ	VABLS	10/01-12/01
	Lynchburg MSA, VA	Y	13900 FQ	19320 AW	27060 TQ	VABLS	10/01-12/01
	Norfolk-Virginia Beach-Newport News MSA, VA-NC	Y	13870 FQ	26350 AW	39220 TQ	VABLS	10/01-12/01
	Richmond-Petersburg MSA, VA	Y	18880 FQ	30440 AW	43010 TQ	VABLS	10/01-12/01
	Roanoke MSA, VA	Y	12730 FQ	20150 AW	29270 TQ	VABLS	10/01-12/01
	Washington	Y	21400 FQ	29650 AW	38590 TQ	WABLS	10/01-12/01
	Olympia PMSA, WA	Y	22170 FQ	29570 AW	36530 TQ	WABLS	10/01-12/01
	Richland-Kennewick-Pasco MSA, WA	Y	24460 FQ	29110 AW	36130 TQ	WABLS	10/01-12/01
	Seattle-Bellevue-Everett PMSA, WA	Y	24060 FQ	32070 AW	42180 TQ	WABLS	10/01-12/01
	Spokane MSA, WA	Y	19340 FQ	26000 AW	34880 TQ	WABLS	10/01-12/01

AAW Average annual wage **AE** Average entry wage **AEX** Average experienced wage **AO** Average offered **AOH** Average offered, high **AOL** Average offered, low **APH** Average pay, high range **APL** Average pay, low range **ASH** Average starting, high **ASL** Average starting, low **AW** Average wage paid **FQ** First quartile wage **H** Hourly **HI** Highest wage paid **HR** High end range **LR** Low end range **M** Monthly **MTC** Median total compensation **MW** Median wage paid **SQ** Second quartile wage **S** Special: hourly and annual **TQ** Third quartile wage **W** Weekly **Y** Yearly

Occupation/Type/Industry	Location	Per	Low	Mid	High	Source	Date
Library Technician	Tacoma PMSA, WA	Y	22740 FQ	28100 AW	34940 TQ	WABLS	10/01-12/01
	Yakima MSA, WA	Y	16410 FQ	25370 AW	41150 TQ	WABLS	10/01-12/01
	West Virginia	Y	13090 FQ	20950 AW	30240 TQ	WVBLS	10/01-12/01
	Huntington-Ashland MSA, WV-KY-OH	Y	12930 FQ	18760 AW	26790 TQ	WVBLS	10/01-12/01
	Wisconsin	Y	14130 FQ	23200 AW	33900 TQ	WIBLS	10/01-12/01
	Appleton-Oshkosh-Neenah MSA, WI	Y	12940 FQ	21930 AW	32780 TQ	WIBLS	10/01-12/01
	Green Bay MSA, WI	Y	15020 FQ	24420 AW	34210 TQ	WIBLS	10/01-12/01
	Milwaukee-Waukesha PMSA, WI	Y	14320 FQ	24280 AW	34930 TQ	WIBLS	10/01-12/01
	Racine PMSA, WI	Y	17330 FQ	27830 AW	37510 TQ	WIBLS	10/01-12/01
	Wyoming	Y	13460 FQ	19970 AW	27280 TQ	WYBLS	10/01-12/01
	Puerto Rico	Y	11620 FQ	15740 AW	21920 TQ	PRBLS	10/01-12/01
	Virgin Islands	Y	15130 FQ	19190 AW	24180 TQ	VIBLS	10/01-12/01
	Guam	Y	22740 FQ	27600 AW	34200 TQ	GUBLS	10/01-12/01
Licensed Practical and Licensed Vocational Nurse	Alabama	Y	18840 FQ	25330 AW	33300 TQ	ALBLS	10/01-12/01
	Birmingham MSA, AL	Y	20150 FQ	27230 AW	34990 TQ	ALBLS	10/01-12/01
	Huntsville MSA, AL	Y	16820 FQ	24350 AW	32440 TQ	ALBLS	10/01-12/01
	Mobile MSA, AL	Y	19580 FQ	25180 AW	32330 TQ	ALBLS	10/01-12/01
	Montgomery MSA, AL	Y	19600 FQ	26850 AW	36550 TQ	ALBLS	10/01-12/01
	Alaska	Y	29350 FQ	37170 AW	45730 TQ	AKBLS	10/01-12/01
	Anchorage MSA, AK	Y	28620 FQ	36100 AW	44890 TQ	AKBLS	10/01-12/01
	Arizona	Y	23530 FQ	31820 AW	41510 TQ	AZBLS	10/01-12/01
	Phoenix-Mesa MSA, AZ	Y	23340 FQ	31940 AW	42180 TQ	AZBLS	10/01-12/01
	Tucson MSA, AZ	Y	25640 FQ	32500 AW	39250 TQ	AZBLS	10/01-12/01
	Arkansas	Y	19430 FQ	25360 AW	32960 TQ	ARBLS	10/01-12/01
	Fayetteville-Springdale-Rogers MSA, AR	Y	21120 FQ	26960 AW	33910 TQ	ARBLS	10/01-12/01
	Fort Smith MSA, AR-OK	Y	19500 FQ	23980 AW	29070 TQ	ARBLS	10/01-12/01
	Little Rock-North Little Rock MSA, AR	Y	24030 FQ	29290 AW	35210 TQ	ARBLS	10/01-12/01
	California	Y	27570 FQ	36970 AW	48000 TQ	CABLS	10/01-12/01
	Bakersfield MSA, CA	Y	25790 FQ	34270 AW	43890 TQ	CABLS	10/01-12/01
	Chico-Paradise MSA, CA	Y	24500 FQ	32730 AW	41660 TQ	CABLS	10/01-12/01
	Fresno MSA, CA	Y	25060 FQ	32990 AW	43130 TQ	CABLS	10/01-12/01
	Los Angeles-Long Beach PMSA, CA	Y	28290 FQ	36690 AW	46090 TQ	CABLS	10/01-12/01
	Merced MSA, CA	Y	25930 FQ	33120 AW	42330 TQ	CABLS	10/01-12/01
	Modesto MSA, CA	Y	31780 FQ	38930 AW	45290 TQ	CABLS	10/01-12/01
	Oakland PMSA, CA	Y	35690 FQ	43930 AW	54230 TQ	CABLS	10/01-12/01
	Orange County PMSA, CA	Y	28740 FQ	38470 AW	50990 TQ	CABLS	10/01-12/01
	Redding MSA, CA	Y	24210 FQ	32790 AW	42070 TQ	CABLS	10/01-12/01
	Riverside-San Bernardino PMSA, CA	Y	24850 FQ	32500 AW	39440 TQ	CABLS	10/01-12/01
	Sacramento PMSA, CA	Y	29640 FQ	38200 AW	49610 TQ	CABLS	10/01-12/01
	Salinas MSA, CA	Y	29500 FQ	37720 AW	45480 TQ	CABLS	10/01-12/01
	San Diego MSA, CA	Y	25550 FQ	33740 AW	41850 TQ	CABLS	10/01-12/01
	San Francisco PMSA, CA	Y	32890 FQ	43130 AW	54540 TQ	CABLS	10/01-12/01
	San Jose PMSA, CA	Y	32580 FQ	42450 AW	53790 TQ	CABLS	10/01-12/01
	San Luis Obispo-Atascadero-Paso Robles MSA, CA	Y	29440 FQ	34850 AW	41980 TQ	CABLS	10/01-12/01
	Santa Barbara-Santa Maria-Lompoc MSA, CA	Y	29530 FQ	36490 AW	44170 TQ	CABLS	10/01-12/01
	Santa Cruz-Watsonville PMSA, CA	Y	31210 FQ	40070 AW	52590 TQ	CABLS	10/01-12/01
	Santa Rosa PMSA, CA	Y	32600 FQ	41630 AW	52400 TQ	CABLS	10/01-12/01
	Stockton-Lodi MSA, CA	Y	29040 FQ	35720 AW	44740 TQ	CABLS	10/01-12/01
	Vallejo-Fairfield-Napa PMSA, CA	Y	27660 FQ	37210 AW	48070 TQ	CABLS	10/01-12/01
	Ventura PMSA, CA	Y	26800 FQ	34990 AW	44490 TQ	CABLS	10/01-12/01
	Visalia-Tulare-Porterville MSA, CA	Y	28010 FQ	34310 AW	44560 TQ	CABLS	10/01-12/01
	Colorado	Y	24300 FQ	32130 AW	40490 TQ	COBLS	10/01-12/01
	Boulder-Longmont PMSA, CO	Y	28480 FQ	32660 AW	37370 TQ	COBLS	10/01-12/01
	Colorado Springs MSA, CO	Y	24470 FQ	31740 AW	38180 TQ	COBLS	10/01-12/01
	Denver PMSA, CO	Y	28540 FQ	35040 AW	43550 TQ	COBLS	10/01-12/01
	Fort Collins-Loveland MSA, CO	Y	23160 FQ	31240 AW	40790 TQ	COBLS	10/01-12/01
	Greeley PMSA, CO	Y	25930 FQ	32160 AW	37540 TQ	COBLS	10/01-12/01

AAW Average annual wage **AE** Average entry wage **AEX** Average experienced wage **AO** Average offered **AOH** Average offered, high **AOL** Average offered, low **APH** Average pay, high range **APL** Average pay, low range **ASH** Average starting, high **ASL** Average starting, low **AW** Average wage paid **FQ** First quartile wage **H** Hourly **HI** Highest wage paid **HR** High end range **LR** Low end range **M** Monthly **MTC** Median total compensation **MW** Median wage paid **SQ** Second quartile wage **S** Special: hourly and annual **TQ** Third quartile wage **W** Weekly **Y** Yearly

Occupation/Type/Industry	Location	Per	Low	Mid	High	Source	Date
Licensed Practical and Licensed Vocational Nurse	Connecticut	Y	33930 FQ	42690 AW	53160 TQ	CTBLS	10/01-12/01
	Bridgeport PMSA, CT	Y	38350 FQ	44380 AW	53660 TQ	CTBLS	10/01-12/01
	Danbury PMSA, CT	Y	35750 FQ	42660 AW	52570 TQ	CTBLS	10/01-12/01
	Hartford MSA, CT	Y	35040 FQ	43100 AW	53260 TQ	CTBLS	10/01-12/01
	New Haven-Meriden PMSA, CT	Y	33870 FQ	42530 AW	52690 TQ	CTBLS	10/01-12/01
	New London-Norwich MSA, CT-RI	Y	32180 FQ	41500 AW	53270 TQ	CTBLS	10/01-12/01
	Stamford-Norwalk PMSA, CT	Y	33240 FQ	42860 AW	54510 TQ	CTBLS	10/01-12/01
	Waterbury PMSA, CT	Y	32840 FQ	42060 AW	52300 TQ	CTBLS	10/01-12/01
	Delaware	Y	27330 FQ	38160 AW	52630 TQ	DEBLS	10/01-12/01
	Wilmington-Newark PMSA, DE-MD	Y	28520 FQ	39750 AW	53640 TQ	DEBLS	10/01-12/01
	District of Columbia	Y	23880 FQ	38450 AW	55220 TQ	DCBLS	10/01-12/01
	Washington PMSA, DC-MD-VA-WV	Y	26790 FQ	36590 AW	45960 TQ	DCBLS	10/01-12/01
	Florida	Y	23910 FQ	31520 AW	41460 TQ	FLBLS	10/01-12/01
	Daytona Beach MSA, FL	Y	22660 FQ	29600 AW	37250 TQ	FLBLS	10/01-12/01
	Fort Lauderdale PMSA, FL	Y	25740 FQ	36060 AW	46020 TQ	FLBLS	10/01-12/01
	Fort Myers-Cape Coral MSA, FL	Y	21030 FQ	28680 AW	36150 TQ	FLBLS	10/01-12/01
	Fort Pierce-Port St. Lucie MSA, FL	Y	29500 FQ	33970 AW	39560 TQ	FLBLS	10/01-12/01
	Fort Walton Beach MSA, FL	Y	18360 FQ	24550 AW	31300 TQ	FLBLS	10/01-12/01
	Gainesville MSA, FL	Y	23900 FQ	29320 AW	35530 TQ	FLBLS	10/01-12/01
	Jacksonville MSA, FL	Y	24190 FQ	32390 AW	43200 TQ	FLBLS	10/01-12/01
	Lakeland-Winter Haven MSA, FL	Y	21410 FQ	29910 AW	37070 TQ	FLBLS	10/01-12/01
	Melbourne-Titusville-Palm Bay MSA, FL	Y	23900 FQ	32610 AW	42560 TQ	FLBLS	10/01-12/01
	Miami PMSA, FL	Y	24170 FQ	31290 AW	38220 TQ	FLBLS	10/01-12/01
	Naples MSA, FL	Y	24790 FQ	31860 AW	42020 TQ	FLBLS	10/01-12/01
	Ocala MSA, FL	Y	19610 FQ	28450 AW	36150 TQ	FLBLS	10/01-12/01
	Orlando MSA, FL	Y	24510 FQ	30360 AW	37060 TQ	FLBLS	10/01-12/01
	Pensacola MSA, FL	Y	20380 FQ	28260 AW	36450 TQ	FLBLS	10/01-12/01
	Sarasota-Bradenton MSA, FL	Y	23330 FQ	30840 AW	38740 TQ	FLBLS	10/01-12/01
	Tallahassee MSA, FL	Y	24990 FQ	31010 AW	36900 TQ	FLBLS	10/01-12/01
	Tampa-St. Petersburg-Clearwater MSA, FL	Y	24320 FQ	31200 AW	37770 TQ	FLBLS	10/01-12/01
	West Palm Beach-Boca Raton MSA, FL	Y	25480 FQ	33640 AW	43970 TQ	FLBLS	10/01-12/01
	Georgia	Y	20470 FQ	27170 AW	34910 TQ	GABLS	10/01-12/01
	Atlanta MSA, GA	Y	23860 FQ	30200 AW	37030 TQ	GABLS	10/01-12/01
	Augusta-Aiken MSA, GA-SC	Y	21630 FQ	27550 AW	34300 TQ	GABLS	10/01-12/01
	Columbus MSA, GA-AL	Y	19840 FQ	26280 AW	33660 TQ	GABLS	10/01-12/01
	Macon MSA, GA	Y	18650 FQ	25790 AW	33740 TQ	GABLS	10/01-12/01
	Savannah MSA, GA	Y	20810 FQ	25830 AW	30560 TQ	GABLS	10/01-12/01
	Hawaii	Y	25600 FQ	31900 AW	37810 TQ	HIBLS	10/01-12/01
	Honolulu MSA, HI	Y	26290 FQ	32360 AW	38400 TQ	HIBLS	10/01-12/01
	Idaho	Y	23390 FQ	29090 AW	36260 TQ	IDBLS	10/01-12/01
	Boise City MSA, ID	Y	24490 FQ	31360 AW	38120 TQ	IDBLS	10/01-12/01
	Illinois	Y	22720 FQ	31840 AW	42670 TQ	ILBLS	10/01-12/01
	Champaign-Urbana MSA, IL	Y	20640 FQ	32910 AW	55240 TQ	ILBLS	10/01-12/01
	Chicago PMSA, IL	Y	24710 FQ	34410 AW	45280 TQ	ILBLS	10/01-12/01
	Peoria-Pekin MSA, IL	Y	22570 FQ	33900 AW	54070 TQ	ILBLS	10/01-12/01
	Rockford MSA, IL	Y	25930 FQ	33480 AW	39660 TQ	ILBLS	10/01-12/01
	Springfield MSA, IL	Y	22180 FQ	30350 AW	39250 TQ	ILBLS	10/01-12/01
	Indiana	Y	23960 FQ	31620 AW	41150 TQ	INBLS	10/01-12/01
	Elkhart-Goshen MSA, IN	Y	20670 FQ	30760 AW	40700 TQ	INBLS	10/01-12/01
	Evansville-Henderson MSA, IN-KY	Y	23980 FQ	29970 AW	36350 TQ	INBLS	10/01-12/01
	Fort Wayne MSA, IN	Y	24810 FQ	31190 AW	37190 TQ	INBLS	10/01-12/01
	Gary PMSA, IN	Y	23870 FQ	29950 AW	37470 TQ	INBLS	10/01-12/01
	Indianapolis MSA, IN	Y	25330 FQ	35930 AW	49620 TQ	INBLS	10/01-12/01
	Lafayette MSA, IN	Y	25640 FQ	33290 AW	43850 TQ	INBLS	10/01-12/01
	South Bend MSA, IN	Y	24560 FQ	30910 AW	37530 TQ	INBLS	10/01-12/01
	Iowa	Y	21820 FQ	27720 AW	35300 TQ	IABLS	10/01-12/01
	Cedar Rapids MSA, IA	Y	22210 FQ	28800 AW	35860 TQ	IABLS	10/01-12/01
	Davenport-Moline-Rock Island MSA, IA-IL	Y	20200 FQ	27940 AW	36780 TQ	IABLS	10/01-12/01
	Des Moines MSA, IA	Y	24670 FQ	31660 AW	39110 TQ	IABLS	10/01-12/01

AAW	Average annual wage	**AOH**	Average offered, high	**ASH**	Average starting, high	**H**	Hourly	**M**	Monthly	**S**	Special: hourly and annual
AE	Average entry wage	**AOL**	Average offered, low	**ASL**	Average starting, low	**HI**	Highest wage paid	**MTC**	Median total compensation	**TQ**	Third quartile wage
AEX	Average experienced wage	**APH**	Average pay, high range	**AW**	Average wage paid	**HR**	High end range	**MW**	Median wage paid	**W**	Weekly
AO	Average offered	**APL**	Average pay, low range	**FQ**	First quartile wage	**LR**	Low end range	**SQ**	Second quartile wage	**Y**	Yearly

Occupation/Type/Industry	Location	Per	Low	Mid	High	Source	Date
Licensed Practical and Licensed Vocational Nurse	Kansas	Y	22410 FQ	29350 AW	37620 TQ	KSBLS	10/01-12/01
	Topeka MSA, KS	Y	22990 FQ	28760 AW	35100 TQ	KSBLS	10/01-12/01
	Wichita MSA, KS	Y	24630 FQ	30450 AW	36900 TQ	KSBLS	10/01-12/01
	Kentucky	Y	20120 FQ	27870 AW	36540 TQ	KYBLS	10/01-12/01
	Lexington MSA, KY	Y	24350 FQ	30510 AW	36910 TQ	KYBLS	10/01-12/01
	Louisville MSA, KY-IN	Y	24280 FQ	31330 AW	40160 TQ	KYBLS	10/01-12/01
	Louisiana	Y	19750 FQ	26290 AW	33990 TQ	LABLS	10/01-12/01
	Baton Rouge MSA, LA	Y	20270 FQ	26820 AW	34480 TQ	LABLS	10/01-12/01
	Houma MSA, LA	Y	19220 FQ	24270 AW	30680 TQ	LABLS	10/01-12/01
	Lafayette MSA, LA	Y	19800 FQ	26050 AW	33140 TQ	LABLS	10/01-12/01
	Lake Charles MSA, LA	Y	19860 FQ	28840 AW	33990 TQ	LABLS	10/01-12/01
	New Orleans MSA, LA	Y	22670 FQ	28860 AW	35980 TQ	LABLS	10/01-12/01
	Shreveport-Bossier City MSA, LA	Y	19370 FQ	25080 AW	31520 TQ	LABLS	10/01-12/01
	Maine	Y	20240 FQ	29200 AW	36810 TQ	MEBLS	10/01-12/01
	Portland MSA, ME	Y	26570 FQ	33090 AW	37810 TQ	MEBLS	10/01-12/01
	Maryland	Y	29120 FQ	37500 AW	47320 TQ	MDBLS	10/01-12/01
	Baltimore PMSA, MD	Y	29830 FQ	37820 AW	48250 TQ	MDBLS	10/01-12/01
	Massachusetts	Y	30120 FQ	38420 AW	47940 TQ	MABLS	10/01-12/01
	Boston PMSA, MA-NH	Y	30580 FQ	38920 AW	47970 TQ	MABLS	10/01-12/01
	Brockton PMSA, MA	Y	27730 FQ	37630 AW	47230 TQ	MABLS	10/01-12/01
	Lawrence PMSA, MA-NH	Y	32640 FQ	41290 AW	50710 TQ	MABLS	10/01-12/01
	Lowell PMSA, MA-NH	Y	30600 FQ	37530 AW	44890 TQ	MABLS	10/01-12/01
	New Bedford PMSA, MA	Y	30860 FQ	38390 AW	46160 TQ	MABLS	10/01-12/01
	Springfield MSA, MA	Y	29840 FQ	37690 AW	46900 TQ	MABLS	10/01-12/01
	Worcester PMSA, MA-CT	Y	30440 FQ	39190 AW	52910 TQ	MABLS	10/01-12/01
	Michigan	Y	25030 FQ	33170 AW	42680 TQ	MIBLS	10/01-12/01
	Ann Arbor PMSA, MI	Y	28110 FQ	35140 AW	43800 TQ	MIBLS	10/01-12/01
	Detroit PMSA, MI	Y	29570 FQ	35590 AW	43730 TQ	MIBLS	10/01-12/01
	Flint PMSA, MI	Y	28330 FQ	34030 AW	41450 TQ	MIBLS	10/01-12/01
	Grand Rapids-Muskegon-Holland MSA, MI	Y	25370 FQ	32340 AW	40610 TQ	MIBLS	10/01-12/01
	Kalamazoo-Battle Creek MSA, MI	Y	26540 FQ	33240 AW	41610 TQ	MIBLS	10/01-12/01
	Lansing-East Lansing MSA, MI	Y	26460 FQ	32730 AW	41140 TQ	MIBLS	10/01-12/01
	Saginaw-Bay City-Midland MSA, MI	Y	24860 FQ	31480 AW	37520 TQ	MIBLS	10/01-12/01
	Minnesota	Y	23950 FQ	31160 AW	40070 TQ	MNBLS	10/01-12/01
	Duluth-Superior MSA, MN-WI	Y	24220 FQ	30500 AW	36420 TQ	MNBLS	10/01-12/01
	Minneapolis-St. Paul MSA, MN-WI	Y	25650 FQ	33500 AW	43100 TQ	MNBLS	10/01-12/01
	St. Cloud MSA, MN	Y	23870 FQ	29780 AW	35340 TQ	MNBLS	10/01-12/01
	Mississippi	Y	19270 FQ	24510 AW	30580 TQ	MSBLS	10/01-12/01
	Biloxi-Gulfport-Pascagoula MSA, MS	Y	19130 FQ	24910 AW	31900 TQ	MSBLS	10/01-12/01
	Jackson MSA, MS	Y	19150 FQ	25270 AW	33310 TQ	MSBLS	10/01-12/01
	Missouri	Y	20490 FQ	28220 AW	37390 TQ	MOBLS	10/01-12/01
	Kansas City MSA, MO-KS	Y	24050 FQ	31540 AW	39800 TQ	MOBLS	10/01-12/01
	St. Louis MSA, MO-IL	Y	24320 FQ	32050 AW	42290 TQ	MOBLS	10/01-12/01
	Springfield MSA, MO	Y	19560 FQ	25310 AW	31860 TQ	MOBLS	10/01-12/01
	Montana	Y	19800 FQ	25450 AW	32140 TQ	MTBLS	10/01-12/01
	Billings MSA, MT	Y	21060 FQ	26270 AW	33020 TQ	MTBLS	10/01-12/01
	Nebraska	Y	20680 FQ	28210 AW	36050 TQ	NEBLS	10/01-12/01
	Lincoln MSA, NE	Y	24020 FQ	30500 AW	36410 TQ	NEBLS	10/01-12/01
	Omaha MSA, NE-IA	Y	22270 FQ	31350 AW	40590 TQ	NEBLS	10/01-12/01
	Nevada	Y	28990 FQ	35710 AW	44280 TQ	NVBLS	10/01-12/01
	Las Vegas MSA, NV-AZ	Y	26180 FQ	34300 AW	43530 TQ	NVBLS	10/01-12/01
	Reno MSA, NV	Y	30270 FQ	36740 AW	44460 TQ	NVBLS	10/01-12/01
	New Hampshire	Y	26130 FQ	32620 AW	39760 TQ	NHBLS	10/01-12/01
	Manchester PMSA, NH	Y	29070 FQ	33450 AW	40130 TQ	NHBLS	10/01-12/01
	Nashua PMSA, NH	Y	26150 FQ	33700 AW	42980 TQ	NHBLS	10/01-12/01
	Portsmouth-Rochester PMSA, NH-ME	Y	26680 FQ	33540 AW	42250 TQ	NHBLS	10/01-12/01
	New Jersey	Y	29960 FQ	38440 AW	47880 TQ	NJBLS	10/01-12/01
	Atlantic-Cape May PMSA, NJ	Y	28150 FQ	35110 AW	43420 TQ	NJBLS	10/01-12/01
	Bergen-Passaic PMSA, NJ	Y	25070 FQ	38240 AW	50990 TQ	NJBLS	10/01-12/01
	Jersey City PMSA, NJ	Y	32250 FQ	38850 AW	44490 TQ	NJBLS	10/01-12/01
	Middlesex-Somerset-Hunterdon PMSA, NJ	Y	30120 FQ	37150 AW	45360 TQ	NJBLS	10/01-12/01
	Monmouth-Ocean PMSA, NJ	Y	28070 FQ	36400 AW	45370 TQ	NJBLS	10/01-12/01
	Newark PMSA, NJ	Y	30790 FQ	39200 AW	48280 TQ	NJBLS	10/01-12/01

AAW	Average annual wage	**AOH**	Average offered, high	**ASH**	Average starting, high	**H**	Hourly	**M**	Monthly	**S**	Special: hourly and annual
AE	Average entry wage	**AOL**	Average offered, low	**ASL**	Average starting, low	**HI**	Highest wage paid	**MTC**	Median total compensation	**TQ**	Third quartile wage
AEX	Average experienced wage	**APH**	Average pay, high range	**AW**	Average wage paid	**HR**	High end range	**MW**	Median wage paid	**W**	Weekly
AO	Average offered	**APL**	Average pay, low range	**FQ**	First quartile wage	**LR**	Low end range	**SQ**	Second quartile wage	**Y**	Yearly

Occupation/Type/Industry	Location	Per	Low	Mid	High	Source	Date
Licensed Practical and Licensed Vocational Nurse	Trenton PMSA, NJ	Y	29010 FQ	36270 AW	44220 TQ	NJBLS	10/01-12/01
	New Mexico	Y	24000 FQ	31460 AW	40500 TQ	NMBLS	10/01-12/01
	Albuquerque MSA, NM	Y	24750 FQ	31480 AW	39070 TQ	NMBLS	10/01-12/01
	Las Cruces MSA, NM	Y	24560 FQ	31190 AW	41330 TQ	NMBLS	10/01-12/01
	New York	Y	23510 FQ	32120 AW	43520 TQ	NYBLS	10/01-12/01
	Albany-Schenectady-Troy MSA, NY	Y	23800 FQ	29470 AW	36560 TQ	NYBLS	10/01-12/01
	Binghamton MSA, NY	Y	23200 FQ	28240 AW	34980 TQ	NYBLS	10/01-12/01
	Buffalo-Niagara Falls MSA, NY	Y	21170 FQ	27560 AW	34480 TQ	NYBLS	10/01-12/01
	Dutchess County PMSA, NY	Y	23920 FQ	30800 AW	41050 TQ	NYBLS	10/01-12/01
	Nassau-Suffolk PMSA, NY	Y	30530 FQ	38570 AW	46690 TQ	NYBLS	10/01-12/01
	New York PMSA, NY	Y	25660 FQ	35000 AW	45080 TQ	NYBLS	10/01-12/01
	Newburgh PMSA, NY-PA	Y	25050 FQ	31740 AW	37940 TQ	NYBLS	10/01-12/01
	Rochester MSA, NY	Y	23300 FQ	29910 AW	37300 TQ	NYBLS	10/01-12/01
	Syracuse MSA, NY	Y	21450 FQ	27670 AW	34710 TQ	NYBLS	10/01-12/01
	Utica-Rome MSA, NY	Y	20330 FQ	26270 AW	33740 TQ	NYBLS	10/01-12/01
	North Carolina	Y	23180 FQ	30680 AW	39050 TQ	NCBLS	10/01-12/01
	Asheville MSA, NC	Y	20730 FQ	28800 AW	36760 TQ	NCBLS	10/01-12/01
	Charlotte-Gastonia-Rock Hill MSA, NC-SC	Y	25320 FQ	33500 AW	43210 TQ	NCBLS	10/01-12/01
	Fayetteville MSA, NC	Y	22400 FQ	28630 AW	35030 TQ	NCBLS	10/01-12/01
	Greensboro-Winston-Salem-High Point MSA, NC	Y	25340 FQ	31730 AW	37370 TQ	NCBLS	10/01-12/01
	Hickory-Morganton-Lenoir MSA, NC	Y	18390 FQ	29830 AW	38230 TQ	NCBLS	10/01-12/01
	Raleigh-Durham-Chapel Hill MSA, NC	Y	27420 FQ	34910 AW	44670 TQ	NCBLS	10/01-12/01
	Wilmington MSA, NC	Y	24090 FQ	30610 AW	38810 TQ	NCBLS	10/01-12/01
	North Dakota	Y	21150 FQ	26540 AW	33160 TQ	NDBLS	10/01-12/01
	Fargo-Moorhead MSA, ND-MN	Y	21040 FQ	27630 AW	35110 TQ	NDBLS	10/01-12/01
	Ohio	Y	24520 FQ	32610 AW	42590 TQ	OHBLS	10/01-12/01
	Akron PMSA, OH	Y	25730 FQ	32520 AW	40770 TQ	OHBLS	10/01-12/01
	Canton-Massillon MSA, OH	Y	24330 FQ	30810 AW	38180 TQ	OHBLS	10/01-12/01
	Cincinnati PMSA, OH-KY-IN	Y	30120 FQ	38160 AW	51450 TQ	OHBLS	10/01-12/01
	Cleveland-Lorain-Elyria PMSA, OH	Y	25810 FQ	33310 AW	41940 TQ	OHBLS	10/01-12/01
	Columbus MSA, OH	Y	25350 FQ	33990 AW	43910 TQ	OHBLS	10/01-12/01
	Dayton-Springfield MSA, OH	Y	25810 FQ	34120 AW	44210 TQ	OHBLS	10/01-12/01
	Hamilton-Middletown PMSA, OH	Y	23850 FQ	31480 AW	38820 TQ	OHBLS	10/01-12/01
	Mansfield MSA, OH	Y	24890 FQ	30750 AW	37060 TQ	OHBLS	10/01-12/01
	Toledo MSA, OH	Y	24770 FQ	30030 AW	35990 TQ	OHBLS	10/01-12/01
	Youngstown-Warren MSA, OH	Y	23300 FQ	29700 AW	36180 TQ	OHBLS	10/01-12/01
	Oklahoma	Y	19500 FQ	26130 AW	33970 TQ	OKBLS	10/01-12/01
	Oklahoma City MSA, OK	Y	20550 FQ	26670 AW	34160 TQ	OKBLS	10/01-12/01
	Tulsa MSA, OK	Y	20260 FQ	29040 AW	43940 TQ	OKBLS	10/01-12/01
	Oregon	Y	25970 FQ	33990 AW	43320 TQ	ORBLS	10/01-12/01
	Eugene-Springfield MSA, OR	Y	26540 FQ	33640 AW	43020 TQ	ORBLS	10/01-12/01
	Medford-Ashland MSA, OR	Y	24070 FQ	31100 AW	41330 TQ	ORBLS	10/01-12/01
	Portland-Vancouver PMSA, OR-WA	Y	29140 FQ	35880 AW	44290 TQ	ORBLS	10/01-12/01
	Salem PMSA, OR	Y	25810 FQ	32410 AW	37740 TQ	ORBLS	10/01-12/01
	Pennsylvania	Y	22590 FQ	32200 AW	44350 TQ	PABLS	10/01-12/01
	Allentown-Bethlehem-Easton MSA, PA	Y	25110 FQ	34640 AW	44450 TQ	PABLS	10/01-12/01
	Erie MSA, PA	Y	24070 FQ	30470 AW	39800 TQ	PABLS	10/01-12/01
	Harrisburg-Lebanon-Carlisle MSA, PA	Y	24640 FQ	31840 AW	39690 TQ	PABLS	10/01-12/01
	Johnstown MSA, PA	Y	19830 FQ	24950 AW	30900 TQ	PABLS	10/01-12/01
	Lancaster MSA, PA	Y	21250 FQ	29450 AW	37860 TQ	PABLS	10/01-12/01
	Philadelphia PMSA, PA-NJ	Y	30020 FQ	39630 AW	52270 TQ	PABLS	10/01-12/01
	Pittsburgh MSA, PA	Y	22210 FQ	30590 AW	39870 TQ	PABLS	10/01-12/01
	Reading MSA, PA	Y	25900 FQ	35760 AW	46250 TQ	PABLS	10/01-12/01
	Scranton-Wilkes-Barre-Hazleton MSA, PA	Y	23000 FQ	29650 AW	39420 TQ	PABLS	10/01-12/01
	York MSA, PA	Y	22080 FQ	30770 AW	42390 TQ	PABLS	10/01-12/01
	Rhode Island	Y	31360 FQ	39820 AW	47840 TQ	RIBLS	10/01-12/01
	Providence-Fall River-Warwick MSA, RI-MA	Y	29940 FQ	38680 AW	47520 TQ	RIBLS	10/01-12/01

AAW Average annual wage **AOH** Average offered, high **ASH** Average starting, high **H** Hourly **M** Monthly **S** Special: hourly and annual
AE Average entry wage **AOL** Average offered, low **ASL** Average starting, low **HI** Highest wage paid **MTC** Median total compensation **TQ** Third quartile wage
AEX Average experienced wage **APH** Average pay, high range **AW** Average wage paid **HR** High end range **MW** Median wage paid **W** Weekly
AO Average offered **APL** Average pay, low range **FQ** First quartile wage **LR** Low end range **SQ** Second quartile wage **Y** Yearly

Occupation/Type/Industry	Location	Per	Low	Mid	High	Source	Date
Licensed Practical and Licensed Vocational Nurse	South Carolina	Y	21850 FQ	29020 AW	36470 TQ	SCBLS	10/01-12/01
	Charleston-North Charleston MSA, SC	Y	21260 FQ	28390 AW	35970 TQ	SCBLS	10/01-12/01
	Columbia MSA, SC	Y	24210 FQ	29520 AW	35680 TQ	SCBLS	10/01-12/01
	Greenville-Spartanburg-Anderson MSA, SC	Y	20650 FQ	28850 AW	37180 TQ	SCBLS	10/01-12/01
	Myrtle Beach MSA, SC	Y	19860 FQ	25170 AW	32430 TQ	SCBLS	10/01-12/01
	South Dakota	Y	20390 FQ	25890 AW	32530 TQ	SDBLS	10/01-12/01
	Sioux Falls MSA, SD	Y	21860 FQ	27070 AW	34050 TQ	SDBLS	10/01-12/01
	Tennessee	Y	20570 FQ	28530 AW	39290 TQ	TNBLS	10/01-12/01
	Chattanooga MSA, TN-GA	Y	22810 FQ	28400 AW	35500 TQ	TNBLS	10/01-12/01
	Clarksville-Hopkinsville MSA, TN-KY	Y	19020 FQ	26210 AW	34630 TQ	TNBLS	10/01-12/01
	Johnson City-Kingsport-Bristol MSA, TN-VA	Y	17170 FQ	27180 AW	47570 TQ	TNBLS	10/01-12/01
	Knoxville MSA, TN	Y	20570 FQ	25960 AW	31900 TQ	TNBLS	10/01-12/01
	Memphis MSA, TN-AR-MS	Y	20960 FQ	28070 AW	35930 TQ	TNBLS	10/01-12/01
	Nashville MSA, TN	Y	24870 FQ	33230 AW	43670 TQ	TNBLS	10/01-12/01
	Texas	Y	22750 FQ	31330 AW	43350 TQ	TXBLS	10/01-12/01
	Amarillo MSA, TX	Y	23590 FQ	28900 AW	36450 TQ	TXBLS	10/01-12/01
	Austin-San Marcos MSA, TX	Y	23520 FQ	31850 AW	43990 TQ	TXBLS	10/01-12/01
	Beaumont-Port Arthur MSA, TX	Y	22150 FQ	27280 AW	34400 TQ	TXBLS	10/01-12/01
	Brazoria PMSA, TX	Y	22460 FQ	28900 AW	37020 TQ	TXBLS	10/01-12/01
	Brownsville-Harlingen-San Benito MSA, TX	Y	22000 FQ	29230 AW	38800 TQ	TXBLS	10/01-12/01
	Corpus Christi MSA, TX	Y	22400 FQ	29430 AW	38070 TQ	TXBLS	10/01-12/01
	Dallas PMSA, TX	Y	25570 FQ	37890 AW	54430 TQ	TXBLS	10/01-12/01
	El Paso MSA, TX	Y	24440 FQ	32860 AW	43320 TQ	TXBLS	10/01-12/01
	Fort Worth-Arlington PMSA, TX	Y	25650 FQ	32230 AW	38010 TQ	TXBLS	10/01-12/01
	Houston PMSA, TX	Y	25430 FQ	34450 AW	44510 TQ	TXBLS	10/01-12/01
	Killeen-Temple MSA, TX	Y	20970 FQ	27150 AW	34740 TQ	TXBLS	10/01-12/01
	Laredo MSA, TX	Y	23490 FQ	29570 AW	37940 TQ	TXBLS	10/01-12/01
	Longview-Marshall MSA, TX	Y	19650 FQ	26510 AW	34560 TQ	TXBLS	10/01-12/01
	Lubbock MSA, TX	Y	23160 FQ	28890 AW	36020 TQ	TXBLS	10/01-12/01
	McAllen-Edinburg-Mission MSA, TX	Y	23450 FQ	30300 AW	37780 TQ	TXBLS	10/01-12/01
	Odessa-Midland MSA, TX	Y	20060 FQ	27830 AW	35340 TQ	TXBLS	10/01-12/01
	San Antonio MSA, TX	Y	21540 FQ	28920 AW	37680 TQ	TXBLS	10/01-12/01
	Tyler MSA, TX	Y	22230 FQ	29990 AW	37620 TQ	TXBLS	10/01-12/01
	Waco MSA, TX	Y	24190 FQ	29330 AW	35900 TQ	TXBLS	10/01-12/01
	Utah	Y	21170 FQ	29360 AW	37740 TQ	UTBLS	10/01-12/01
	Provo-Orem MSA, UT	Y	19800 FQ	31330 AW	51950 TQ	UTBLS	10/01-12/01
	Salt Lake City-Ogden MSA, UT	Y	23820 FQ	30110 AW	37430 TQ	UTBLS	10/01-12/01
	Vermont	Y	23360 FQ	29690 AW	36470 TQ	VTBLS	10/01-12/01
	Burlington MSA, VT	Y	25300 FQ	32220 AW	39600 TQ	VTBLS	10/01-12/01
	Virginia	Y	22390 FQ	30170 AW	40280 TQ	VABLS	10/01-12/01
	Lynchburg MSA, VA	Y	22240 FQ	28970 AW	35630 TQ	VABLS	10/01-12/01
	Norfolk-Virginia Beach-Newport News MSA, VA-NC	Y	22380 FQ	27070 AW	33760 TQ	VABLS	10/01-12/01
	Richmond-Petersburg MSA, VA	Y	24590 FQ	32850 AW	46400 TQ	VABLS	10/01-12/01
	Roanoke MSA, VA	Y	23250 FQ	28640 AW	35530 TQ	VABLS	10/01-12/01
	Washington	Y	26250 FQ	33510 AW	42390 TQ	WABLS	10/01-12/01
	Bremerton PMSA, WA	Y	29340 FQ	33610 AW	40470 TQ	WABLS	10/01-12/01
	Olympia PMSA, WA	Y	24650 FQ	30680 AW	37510 TQ	WABLS	10/01-12/01
	Richland-Kennewick-Pasco MSA, WA	Y	24630 FQ	30440 AW	37530 TQ	WABLS	10/01-12/01
	Seattle-Bellevue-Everett PMSA, WA	Y	28160 FQ	35100 AW	43950 TQ	WABLS	10/01-12/01
	Spokane MSA, WA	Y	26300 FQ	34060 AW	43310 TQ	WABLS	10/01-12/01
	Tacoma PMSA, WA	Y	27420 FQ	34150 AW	42680 TQ	WABLS	10/01-12/01
	Yakima MSA, WA	Y	24710 FQ	32140 AW	40900 TQ	WABLS	10/01-12/01
	West Virginia	Y	17830 FQ	24500 AW	33010 TQ	WVBLS	10/01-12/01
	Charleston MSA, WV	Y	19780 FQ	25460 AW	32760 TQ	WVBLS	10/01-12/01
	Huntington-Ashland MSA, WV-KY-OH	Y	19240 FQ	25490 AW	33520 TQ	WVBLS	10/01-12/01
	Wisconsin	Y	24600 FQ	32420 AW	42520 TQ	WIBLS	10/01-12/01

AAW Average annual wage **AOH** Average offered, high **ASH** Average starting, high **H** Hourly **M** Monthly **S** Special: hourly and annual
AE Average entry wage **AOL** Average offered, low **ASL** Average starting, low **HI** Highest wage paid **MTC** Median total compensation **TQ** Third quartile wage
AEX Average experienced wage **APH** Average pay, high range **AW** Average wage paid **HR** High end range **MW** Median wage paid **W** Weekly
AO Average offered **APL** Average pay, low range **FQ** First quartile wage **LR** Low end range **SQ** Second quartile wage **Y** Yearly

Occupation/Type/Industry	Location	Per	Low	Mid	High	Source	Date
Licensed Practical and Licensed Vocational Nurse	Appleton-Oshkosh-Neenah MSA, WI	Y	23810 FQ	30700 AW	38920 TQ	WIBLS	10/01-12/01
	Green Bay MSA, WI	Y	25210 FQ	30680 AW	36340 TQ	WIBLS	10/01-12/01
	Madison MSA, WI	Y	25300 FQ	33320 AW	43110 TQ	WIBLS	10/01-12/01
	Milwaukee-Waukesha PMSA, WI	Y	28350 FQ	36450 AW	45740 TQ	WIBLS	10/01-12/01
	Racine PMSA, WI	Y	25180 FQ	31950 AW	40870 TQ	WIBLS	10/01-12/01
	Wyoming	Y	19820 FQ	27550 AW	35890 TQ	WYBLS	10/01-12/01
	Cheyenne MSA, WY	Y	19410 FQ	27110 AW	36920 TQ	WYBLS	10/01-12/01
	Puerto Rico	Y	11830 FQ	15290 AW	20430 TQ	PRBLS	10/01-12/01
	Virgin Islands	Y	19190 FQ	24320 AW	32480 TQ	VIBLS	10/01-12/01
	Guam	Y	23980 FQ	29430 AW	35900 TQ	GUBLS	10/01-12/01
Loading Machine Operator							
Underground Mining	Alabama	H	9.83 FQ	11.96 AW	13.51 TQ	ALBLS	10/01-12/01
Underground Mining	Arizona	H	7.23 FQ	11.50 AW	19.49 TQ	AZBLS	10/01-12/01
Underground Mining	Colorado	H	14.63 FQ	17.96 AW	23.64 TQ	COBLS	10/01-12/01
Underground Mining	Georgia	H	9.80 FQ	12.43 AW	15.68 TQ	GABLS	10/01-12/01
Underground Mining	Illinois	H	9.03 FQ	12.51 AW	19.72 TQ	ILBLS	10/01-12/01
Underground Mining	Indiana	H	10.30 FQ	14.60 AW	19.14 TQ	INBLS	10/01-12/01
Underground Mining	Kentucky	H	12.95 FQ	15.07 AW	17.16 TQ	KYBLS	10/01-12/01
Underground Mining	Michigan	H	12.97 FQ	17.66 AW	21.01 TQ	MIBLS	10/01-12/01
Underground Mining	Minnesota	H	12.24 FQ	17.27 AW	21.39 TQ	MNBLS	10/01-12/01
Underground Mining	New York	H	14.14 FQ	15.56 AW	17.40 TQ	NYBLS	10/01-12/01
Underground Mining	Ohio	H	11.33 FQ	14.03 AW	16.93 TQ	OHBLS	10/01-12/01
Underground Mining	Oklahoma	H	6.37 FQ	9.99 AW	13.80 TQ	OKBLS	10/01-12/01
Underground Mining	Pennsylvania	H	8.95 FQ	13.57 AW	21.61 TQ	PABLS	10/01-12/01
Underground Mining	South Carolina	H	11.73 FQ	13.49 AW	16.58 TQ	SCBLS	10/01-12/01
Underground Mining	Tennessee	H	10.39 FQ	12.67 AW	15.36 TQ	TNBLS	10/01-12/01
Underground Mining	Texas	H	8.45 FQ	12.02 AW	17.40 TQ	TXBLS	10/01-12/01
Underground Mining	Virginia	H	11.65 FQ	14.66 AW	17.19 TQ	VABLS	10/01-12/01
Underground Mining	Washington	H	12.98 FQ	19.95 AW	27.39 TQ	WABLS	10/01-12/01
Underground Mining	West Virginia	H	11.94 FQ	17.55 AW	21.22 TQ	WVBLS	10/01-12/01
Underground Mining	Puerto Rico	H	5.91 FQ	8.36 AW	11.25 TQ	PRBLS	10/01-12/01
Loan Counselor	Alabama	Y	20900 FQ	31350 AW	46350 TQ	ALBLS	10/01-12/01
	Alaska	Y	23650 FQ	43830 AW	88060 TQ	AKBLS	10/01-12/01
	Arizona	Y	23960 FQ	51290 AW	78330 TQ	AZBLS	10/01-12/01
	Arkansas	Y	23820 FQ	34260 AW	49410 TQ	ARBLS	10/01-12/01
	California	Y	24920 FQ	43930 AW	75220 TQ	CABLS	10/01-12/01
	Connecticut	Y	26030 FQ	47170 AW	75000 TQ	CTBLS	10/01-12/01
	Delaware	Y	22820 FQ	40980 AW	74950 TQ	DEBLS	10/01-12/01
	District of Columbia	Y	23040 FQ	35720 AW	61940 TQ	DCBLS	10/01-12/01
	Florida	Y	24170 FQ	37930 AW	66510 TQ	FLBLS	10/01-12/01
	Georgia	Y	23600 FQ	45240 AW	68420 TQ	GABLS	10/01-12/01
	Idaho	Y	20970 FQ	38990 AW	71480 TQ	IDBLS	10/01-12/01
	Illinois	Y	22040 FQ	34190 AW	45590 TQ	ILBLS	10/01-12/01
	Indiana	Y	23720 FQ	32430 AW	44110 TQ	INBLS	10/01-12/01
	Iowa	Y	19850 FQ	31100 AW	51600 TQ	IABLS	10/01-12/01
	Kansas	Y	21500 FQ	29470 AW	38980 TQ	KSBLS	10/01-12/01
	Kentucky	Y	18430 FQ	28150 AW	41340 TQ	KYBLS	10/01-12/01
	Louisiana	Y	18960 FQ	26210 AW	34700 TQ	LABLS	10/01-12/01
	Maine	Y	26040 FQ	33950 AW	43910 TQ	MEBLS	10/01-12/01
	Maryland	Y	22930 FQ	31010 AW	42520 TQ	MDBLS	10/01-12/01
	Massachusetts	Y	19690 FQ	36470 AW	62280 TQ	MABLS	10/01-12/01
	Michigan	Y	24640 FQ	36950 AW	52600 TQ	MIBLS	10/01-12/01
	Minnesota	Y	23390 FQ	31650 AW	42140 TQ	MNBLS	10/01-12/01
	Mississippi	Y	20470 FQ	29460 AW	42270 TQ	MSBLS	10/01-12/01
	Missouri	Y	24030 FQ	35070 AW	47000 TQ	MOBLS	10/01-12/01
	Montana	Y	27640 FQ	42550 AW	60140 TQ	MTBLS	10/01-12/01
	Nebraska	Y	18370 FQ	30200 AW	54790 TQ	NEBLS	10/01-12/01
	Nevada	Y	22570 FQ	33320 AW	45880 TQ	NVBLS	10/01-12/01
	New Hampshire	Y	26170 FQ	36700 AW	45920 TQ	NHBLS	10/01-12/01
	New Jersey	Y	16700 FQ	37210 AW	68320 TQ	NJBLS	10/01-12/01
	New Mexico	Y	24120 FQ	30350 AW	36690 TQ	NMBLS	10/01-12/01
	New York	Y	24330 FQ	40600 AW	68230 TQ	NYBLS	10/01-12/01
	North Carolina	Y	19780 FQ	28280 AW	38380 TQ	NCBLS	10/01-12/01
	North Dakota	Y	24870 FQ	32210 AW	37180 TQ	NDBLS	10/01-12/01
	Ohio	Y	20560 FQ	32590 AW	50020 TQ	OHBLS	10/01-12/01
	Oklahoma	Y	19460 FQ	28550 AW	40150 TQ	OKBLS	10/01-12/01
	Pennsylvania	Y	22930 FQ	39120 AW	68900 TQ	PABLS	10/01-12/01

AAW Average annual wage; **AE** Average entry wage; **AEX** Average experienced wage; **AO** Average offered; **AOH** Average offered, high; **AOL** Average offered, low; **APH** Average pay, high range; **APL** Average pay, low range; **ASH** Average starting, high; **ASL** Average starting, low; **AW** Average wage paid; **FQ** First quartile wage; **H** Hourly; **HI** Highest wage paid; **HR** High end range; **LR** Low end range; **M** Monthly; **MTC** Median total compensation; **MW** Median wage paid; **SQ** Second quartile wage; **S** Special: hourly and annual; **TQ** Third quartile wage; **W** Weekly; **Y** Yearly

Occupation/Type/Industry	Location	Per	Low	Mid	High	Source	Date
Loan Counselor	Rhode Island	Y	15070 FQ	38590 AW	53840 TQ	RIBLS	10/01-12/01
	South Carolina	Y	22900 FQ	35110 AW	57940 TQ	SCBLS	10/01-12/01
	South Dakota	Y	25560 FQ	36270 AW	46080 TQ	SDBLS	10/01-12/01
	Tennessee	Y	23910 FQ	36880 AW	49540 TQ	TNBLS	10/01-12/01
	Texas	Y	22540 FQ	31540 AW	46200 TQ	TXBLS	10/01-12/01
	Utah	Y	18540 FQ	25930 AW	36010 TQ	UTBLS	10/01-12/01
	Vermont	Y	25580 FQ	40140 AW	60370 TQ	VTBLS	10/01-12/01
	Virginia	Y	24000 FQ	36440 AW	45820 TQ	VABLS	10/01-12/01
	Washington	Y	24430 FQ	34870 AW	49340 TQ	WABLS	10/01-12/01
	West Virginia	Y	21420 FQ	36880 AW	54990 TQ	WVBLS	10/01-12/01
	Wisconsin	Y	25830 FQ	41850 AW	64180 TQ	WIBLS	10/01-12/01
	Puerto Rico	Y	21140 FQ	28650 AW	38830 TQ	PRBLS	10/01-12/01
Loan Interviewer and Clerk	Alabama	H	7.31 FQ	10.64 AW	14.51 TQ	ALBLS	10/01-12/01
	Alaska	H	11.31 FQ	16.16 AW	21.85 TQ	AKBLS	10/01-12/01
	Arizona	H	8.81 FQ	14.04 AW	20.56 TQ	AZBLS	10/01-12/01
	Arkansas	H	7.78 FQ	10.87 AW	14.19 TQ	ARBLS	10/01-12/01
	California	H	10.54 FQ	15.40 AW	21.25 TQ	CABLS	10/01-12/01
	Colorado	H	10.55 FQ	15.53 AW	21.18 TQ	COBLS	10/01-12/01
	Connecticut	H	10.45 FQ	14.63 AW	20.33 TQ	CTBLS	10/01-12/01
	Delaware	H	8.95 FQ	12.60 AW	17.58 TQ	DEBLS	10/01-12/01
	District of Columbia	H	10.88 FQ	15.33 AW	20.74 TQ	DCBLS	10/01-12/01
	Florida	H	9.35 FQ	13.57 AW	19.05 TQ	FLBLS	10/01-12/01
	Georgia	H	8.70 FQ	12.77 AW	17.55 TQ	GABLS	10/01-12/01
	Hawaii	H	9.41 FQ	13.73 AW	19.61 TQ	HIBLS	10/01-12/01
	Idaho	H	9.25 FQ	12.19 AW	16.47 TQ	IDBLS	10/01-12/01
	Illinois	H	9.52 FQ	15.61 AW	22.82 TQ	ILBLS	10/01-12/01
	Indiana	H	8.82 FQ	12.52 AW	17.34 TQ	INBLS	10/01-12/01
	Iowa	H	8.88 FQ	11.71 AW	15.86 TQ	IABLS	10/01-12/01
	Kansas	H	8.63 FQ	11.77 AW	16.27 TQ	KSBLS	10/01-12/01
	Kentucky	H	7.35 FQ	11.02 AW	15.95 TQ	KYBLS	10/01-12/01
	Louisiana	H	7.72 FQ	11.52 AW	15.90 TQ	LABLS	10/01-12/01
	Maine	H	8.60 FQ	11.43 AW	14.44 TQ	MEBLS	10/01-12/01
	Maryland	H	10.07 FQ	14.72 AW	20.22 TQ	MDBLS	10/01-12/01
	Massachusetts	H	10.64 FQ	15.30 AW	21.18 TQ	MABLS	10/01-12/01
	Michigan	H	8.93 FQ	13.63 AW	19.84 TQ	MIBLS	10/01-12/01
	Minnesota	H	9.57 FQ	13.40 AW	17.66 TQ	MNBLS	10/01-12/01
	Mississippi	H	7.72 FQ	11.45 AW	16.18 TQ	MSBLS	10/01-12/01
	Missouri	H	8.99 FQ	12.99 AW	17.84 TQ	MOBLS	10/01-12/01
	Montana	H	7.73 FQ	10.40 AW	13.25 TQ	MTBLS	10/01-12/01
	Nebraska	H	8.34 FQ	11.98 AW	16.58 TQ	NEBLS	10/01-12/01
	Nevada	H	10.20 FQ	14.71 AW	21.01 TQ	NVBLS	10/01-12/01
	New Hampshire	H	9.43 FQ	12.57 AW	16.27 TQ	NHBLS	10/01-12/01
	New Jersey	H	11.15 FQ	15.07 AW	20.38 TQ	NJBLS	10/01-12/01
	New Mexico	H	7.48 FQ	11.05 AW	15.57 TQ	NMBLS	10/01-12/01
	New York	H	8.99 FQ	14.42 AW	21.63 TQ	NYBLS	10/01-12/01
	North Carolina	H	9.64 FQ	14.29 AW	20.10 TQ	NCBLS	10/01-12/01
	North Dakota	H	7.49 FQ	10.22 AW	13.45 TQ	NDBLS	10/01-12/01
	Ohio	H	9.07 FQ	13.84 AW	21.31 TQ	OHBLS	10/01-12/01
	Oklahoma	H	8.06 FQ	12.22 AW	18.25 TQ	OKBLS	10/01-12/01
	Oregon	H	8.93 FQ	12.69 AW	18.31 TQ	ORBLS	10/01-12/01
	Pennsylvania	H	8.84 FQ	13.20 AW	18.71 TQ	PABLS	10/01-12/01
	Rhode Island	H	10.77 FQ	13.01 AW	16.64 TQ	RIBLS	10/01-12/01
	South Carolina	H	9.11 FQ	12.28 AW	16.16 TQ	SCBLS	10/01-12/01
	South Dakota	H	8.60 FQ	10.59 AW	13.12 TQ	SDBLS	10/01-12/01
	Tennessee	H	7.83 FQ	12.39 AW	17.00 TQ	TNBLS	10/01-12/01
	Texas	H	8.37 FQ	13.19 AW	19.28 TQ	TXBLS	10/01-12/01
	Utah	H	9.45 FQ	13.11 AW	16.98 TQ	UTBLS	10/01-12/01
	Vermont	H	8.39 FQ	13.00 AW	19.85 TQ	VTBLS	10/01-12/01
	Virginia	H	9.75 FQ	14.10 AW	20.15 TQ	VABLS	10/01-12/01
	Washington	H	10.30 FQ	14.93 AW	20.63 TQ	WABLS	10/01-12/01
	West Virginia	H	7.15 FQ	10.27 AW	13.88 TQ	WVBLS	10/01-12/01
	Wisconsin	H	8.79 FQ	12.83 AW	17.48 TQ	WIBLS	10/01-12/01
	Wyoming	H	8.17 FQ	11.17 AW	14.89 TQ	WYBLS	10/01-12/01
	Puerto Rico	H	5.75 FQ	8.15 AW	11.22 TQ	PRBLS	10/01-12/01
	Virgin Islands	H	9.30 FQ	12.43 AW	15.82 TQ	VIBLS	10/01-12/01
	Guam	H	8.56 FQ	10.61 AW	13.99 TQ	GUBLS	10/01-12/01
Loan Officer	Alabama	Y	23800 FQ	41150 AW	67240 TQ	ALBLS	10/01-12/01
	Birmingham MSA, AL	Y	23470 FQ	41920 AW	72390 TQ	ALBLS	10/01-12/01
	Huntsville MSA, AL	Y	23820 FQ	39870 AW	68220 TQ	ALBLS	10/01-12/01
	Mobile MSA, AL	Y	27160 FQ	40180 AW	57240 TQ	ALBLS	10/01-12/01
	Montgomery MSA, AL	Y	22980 FQ	42620 AW	70770 TQ	ALBLS	10/01-12/01

AAW	Average annual wage	**AOH**	Average offered, high	**ASH**	Average starting, high	**H**	Hourly	**M**	Monthly	**S**	Special: hourly and annual
AE	Average entry wage	**AOL**	Average offered, low	**ASL**	Average starting, low	**HI**	Highest wage paid	**MTC**	Median total compensation	**TQ**	Third quartile wage
AEX	Average experienced wage	**APH**	Average pay, high range	**AW**	Average wage paid	**HR**	High end range	**MW**	Median wage paid	**W**	Weekly
AO	Average offered	**APL**	Average pay, low range	**FQ**	First quartile wage	**LR**	Low end range	**SQ**	Second quartile wage	**Y**	Yearly

Occupation/Type/Industry	Location	Per	Low	Mid	High	Source	Date
Loan Officer	Alaska	Y	24090 FQ	53220 AW	90080 TQ	AKBLS	10/01-12/01
	Anchorage MSA, AK	Y	23410 FQ	52600 AW	92880 TQ	AKBLS	10/01-12/01
	Arizona	Y	26090 FQ	59970 AW	128000 TQ	AZBLS	10/01-12/01
	Phoenix-Mesa MSA, AZ	Y	28020 FQ	64440 AW	143270 TQ	AZBLS	10/01-12/01
	Tucson MSA, AZ	Y	25390 FQ	47780 AW	72630 TQ	AZBLS	10/01-12/01
	Arkansas	Y	26630 FQ	44690 AW	68750 TQ	ARBLS	10/01-12/01
	Fayetteville-Springdale-Rogers MSA, AR	Y	27370 FQ	46640 AW	70870 TQ	ARBLS	10/01-12/01
	Fort Smith MSA, AR-OK	Y	26410 FQ	39190 AW	58090 TQ	ARBLS	10/01-12/01
	Little Rock-North Little Rock MSA, AR	Y	26600 FQ	46100 AW	71330 TQ	ARBLS	10/01-12/01
	California	Y	31290 FQ	57890 AW	102220 TQ	CABLS	10/01-12/01
	Bakersfield MSA, CA	Y	27750 FQ	50010 AW	103890 TQ	CABLS	10/01-12/01
	Chico-Paradise MSA, CA	Y	23430 FQ	47760 AW	73480 TQ	CABLS	10/01-12/01
	Fresno MSA, CA	Y	23240 FQ	43580 AW	71540 TQ	CABLS	10/01-12/01
	Los Angeles-Long Beach PMSA, CA	Y	31430 FQ	62040 AW	109580 TQ	CABLS	10/01-12/01
	Merced MSA, CA	Y	24560 FQ	45610 AW	74220 TQ	CABLS	10/01-12/01
	Modesto MSA, CA	Y	30980 FQ	53320 AW	79100 TQ	CABLS	10/01-12/01
	Oakland PMSA, CA	Y	32090 FQ	65740 AW		CABLS	10/01-12/01
	Orange County PMSA, CA	Y	32500 FQ	57520 AW	91750 TQ	CABLS	10/01-12/01
	Redding MSA, CA	Y	24720 FQ	47150 AW	71150 TQ	CABLS	10/01-12/01
	Riverside-San Bernardino PMSA, CA	Y	28200 FQ	47380 AW	80860 TQ	CABLS	10/01-12/01
	Sacramento PMSA, CA	Y	31000 FQ	50620 AW	70260 TQ	CABLS	10/01-12/01
	Salinas MSA, CA	Y	31020 FQ	46240 AW	74980 TQ	CABLS	10/01-12/01
	San Diego MSA, CA	Y	31130 FQ	49280 AW	73460 TQ	CABLS	10/01-12/01
	San Francisco PMSA, CA	Y	38450 FQ	74430 AW	139230 TQ	CABLS	10/01-12/01
	San Jose PMSA, CA	Y	31540 FQ	56550 AW	108420 TQ	CABLS	10/01-12/01
	San Luis Obispo-Atascadero-Paso Robles MSA, CA	Y	29390 FQ	67880 AW	137990 TQ	CABLS	10/01-12/01
	Santa Barbara-Santa Maria-Lompoc MSA, CA	Y	31550 FQ	55740 AW	101650 TQ	CABLS	10/01-12/01
	Santa Cruz-Watsonville PMSA, CA	Y	21490 FQ	59190 AW	118830 TQ	CABLS	10/01-12/01
	Santa Rosa PMSA, CA	Y	32490 FQ	53770 AW	74250 TQ	CABLS	10/01-12/01
	Stockton-Lodi MSA, CA	Y	30070 FQ	54680 AW	89950 TQ	CABLS	10/01-12/01
	Vallejo-Fairfield-Napa PMSA, CA	Y	28210 FQ	43260 AW	66400 TQ	CABLS	10/01-12/01
	Ventura PMSA, CA	Y	38630 FQ	50510 AW	78420 TQ	CABLS	10/01-12/01
	Visalia-Tulare-Porterville MSA, CA	Y	26020 FQ	51290 AW	78730 TQ	CABLS	10/01-12/01
	Colorado	Y	27290 FQ	58330 AW	115050 TQ	COBLS	10/01-12/01
	Boulder-Longmont PMSA, CO	Y	30060 FQ	57860 AW	107330 TQ	COBLS	10/01-12/01
	Colorado Springs MSA, CO	Y	26840 FQ	40760 AW	57130 TQ	COBLS	10/01-12/01
	Denver PMSA, CO	Y	27840 FQ	64260 AW	143240 TQ	COBLS	10/01-12/01
	Fort Collins-Loveland MSA, CO	Y	28370 FQ	55390 AW	87600 TQ	COBLS	10/01-12/01
	Greeley PMSA, CO	Y	29310 FQ	52000 AW	71300 TQ	COBLS	10/01-12/01
	Connecticut	Y	31070 FQ	64030 AW	109500 TQ	CTBLS	10/01-12/01
	Bridgeport PMSA, CT	Y	27720 FQ	62410 AW	112630 TQ	CTBLS	10/01-12/01
	Danbury PMSA, CT	Y	34500 FQ	61610 AW	96120 TQ	CTBLS	10/01-12/01
	Hartford MSA, CT	Y	30600 FQ	60030 AW	92310 TQ	CTBLS	10/01-12/01
	New Haven-Meriden PMSA, CT	Y	31570 FQ	61810 AW	92820 TQ	CTBLS	10/01-12/01
	New London-Norwich MSA, CT-RI	Y	29900 FQ	55830 AW	106590 TQ	CTBLS	10/01-12/01
	Stamford-Norwalk PMSA, CT	Y	31780 FQ	80980 AW	139740 TQ	CTBLS	10/01-12/01
	Waterbury PMSA, CT	Y	31230 FQ	60950 AW	97420 TQ	CTBLS	10/01-12/01
	Delaware	Y	25510 FQ	39180 AW	59790 TQ	DEBLS	10/01-12/01
	Wilmington-Newark PMSA, DE-MD	Y	26130 FQ	40520 AW	65050 TQ	DEBLS	10/01-12/01
	District of Columbia	Y	36310 FQ	61290 AW	90060 TQ	DCBLS	10/01-12/01
	Washington PMSA, DC-MD-VA-WV	Y	24550 FQ	54430 AW	101780 TQ	DCBLS	10/01-12/01
	Florida	Y	24330 FQ	49270 AW	87800 TQ	FLBLS	10/01-12/01
	Daytona Beach MSA, FL	Y	23900 FQ	41310 AW	73980 TQ	FLBLS	10/01-12/01
	Fort Lauderdale PMSA, FL	Y	21010 FQ	39720 AW	62570 TQ	FLBLS	10/01-12/01
	Fort Myers-Cape Coral MSA, FL	Y	22590 FQ	52760 AW	134960 TQ	FLBLS	10/01-12/01
	Fort Pierce-Port St. Lucie MSA, FL	Y	23000 FQ	45030 AW	71670 TQ	FLBLS	10/01-12/01

AAW	Average annual wage	**AOH**	Average offered, high	**ASH**	Average starting, high	**H**	Hourly	**M**	Monthly	**S**	Special: hourly and annual
AE	Average entry wage	**AOL**	Average offered, low	**ASL**	Average starting, low	**HI**	Highest wage paid	**MTC**	Median total compensation	**TQ**	Third quartile wage
AEX	Average experienced wage	**APH**	Average pay, high range	**AW**	Average wage paid	**HR**	High end range	**MW**	Median wage paid	**W**	Weekly
AO	Average offered	**APL**	Average pay, low range	**FQ**	First quartile wage	**LR**	Low end range	**SQ**	Second quartile wage	**Y**	Yearly

Occupation/Type/Industry	Location	Per	Low	Mid	High	Source	Date
Loan Officer	Fort Walton Beach MSA, FL	Y	25670 FQ	49550 AW	80590 TQ	FLBLS	10/01-12/01
	Gainesville MSA, FL	Y	24410 FQ	37460 AW	64730 TQ	FLBLS	10/01-12/01
	Jacksonville MSA, FL	Y	28430 FQ	56870 AW	105780 TQ	FLBLS	10/01-12/01
	Lakeland-Winter Haven MSA, FL	Y	27100 FQ	49850 AW	73420 TQ	FLBLS	10/01-12/01
	Melbourne-Titusville-Palm Bay MSA, FL	Y	12770 FQ	36720 AW	61630 TQ	FLBLS	10/01-12/01
	Miami PMSA, FL	Y	24150 FQ	51700 AW	103360 TQ	FLBLS	10/01-12/01
	Naples MSA, FL	Y	35030 FQ	53050 AW	80310 TQ	FLBLS	10/01-12/01
	Ocala MSA, FL	Y	24670 FQ	47010 AW	72270 TQ	FLBLS	10/01-12/01
	Orlando MSA, FL	Y	25230 FQ	51880 AW	89920 TQ	FLBLS	10/01-12/01
	Pensacola MSA, FL	Y	23080 FQ	39680 AW	66820 TQ	FLBLS	10/01-12/01
	Sarasota-Bradenton MSA, FL	Y	28150 FQ	55460 AW	88780 TQ	FLBLS	10/01-12/01
	Tallahassee MSA, FL	Y	22840 FQ	41450 AW	69930 TQ	FLBLS	10/01-12/01
	Tampa-St. Petersburg-Clearwater MSA, FL	Y	32510 FQ	52450 AW	84400 TQ	FLBLS	10/01-12/01
	West Palm Beach-Boca Raton MSA, FL	Y	14030 FQ	43880 AW	86760 TQ	FLBLS	10/01-12/01
	Georgia	Y	24280 FQ	48640 AW	85060 TQ	GABLS	10/01-12/01
	Atlanta MSA, GA	Y	23700 FQ	50690 AW	90330 TQ	GABLS	10/01-12/01
	Augusta-Aiken MSA, GA-SC	Y	21350 FQ	38050 AW	61650 TQ	GABLS	10/01-12/01
	Columbus MSA, GA-AL	Y	26210 FQ	41170 AW	65680 TQ	GABLS	10/01-12/01
	Macon MSA, GA	Y	26590 FQ	41180 AW	71590 TQ	GABLS	10/01-12/01
	Savannah MSA, GA	Y	22690 FQ	48350 AW	72740 TQ	GABLS	10/01-12/01
	Hawaii	Y	21090 FQ	44520 AW	79780 TQ	HIBLS	10/01-12/01
	Honolulu MSA, HI	Y	17460 FQ	42270 AW	72520 TQ	HIBLS	10/01-12/01
	Idaho	Y	22910 FQ	40100 AW	60750 TQ	IDBLS	10/01-12/01
	Boise City MSA, ID	Y	23740 FQ	41180 AW	59770 TQ	IDBLS	10/01-12/01
	Illinois	Y	23810 FQ	50590 AW	95550 TQ	ILBLS	10/01-12/01
	Champaign-Urbana MSA, IL	Y	19830 FQ	42620 AW	71630 TQ	ILBLS	10/01-12/01
	Chicago PMSA, IL	Y	24230 FQ	54710 AW	111930 TQ	ILBLS	10/01-12/01
	Peoria-Pekin MSA, IL	Y	27340 FQ	43950 AW	65160 TQ	ILBLS	10/01-12/01
	Rockford MSA, IL	Y	14050 FQ	43610 AW	84310 TQ	ILBLS	10/01-12/01
	Springfield MSA, IL	Y	16210 FQ	36270 AW	65700 TQ	ILBLS	10/01-12/01
	Indiana	Y	24440 FQ	44660 AW	70470 TQ	INBLS	10/01-12/01
	Elkhart-Goshen MSA, IN	Y	24700 FQ	45110 AW	64210 TQ	INBLS	10/01-12/01
	Evansville-Henderson MSA, IN-KY	Y	25070 FQ	39590 AW	55540 TQ	INBLS	10/01-12/01
	Fort Wayne MSA, IN	Y	22030 FQ	46470 AW	73600 TQ	INBLS	10/01-12/01
	Gary PMSA, IN	Y	23870 FQ	40430 AW	61440 TQ	INBLS	10/01-12/01
	Indianapolis MSA, IN	Y	24310 FQ	43290 AW	70840 TQ	INBLS	10/01-12/01
	Lafayette MSA, IN	Y	27800 FQ	44090 AW	63740 TQ	INBLS	10/01-12/01
	South Bend MSA, IN	Y	24250 FQ	42410 AW	62430 TQ	INBLS	10/01-12/01
	Iowa	Y	26020 FQ	42510 AW	63020 TQ	IABLS	10/01-12/01
	Cedar Rapids MSA, IA	Y	26480 FQ	43890 AW	68670 TQ	IABLS	10/01-12/01
	Davenport-Moline-Rock Island MSA, IA-IL	Y	20450 FQ	38970 AW	58390 TQ	IABLS	10/01-12/01
	Des Moines MSA, IA	Y	26310 FQ	43900 AW	70030 TQ	IABLS	10/01-12/01
	Kansas	Y	24090 FQ	44840 AW	68610 TQ	KSBLS	10/01-12/01
	Topeka MSA, KS	Y	23290 FQ	38990 AW	58980 TQ	KSBLS	10/01-12/01
	Wichita MSA, KS	Y	28360 FQ	46230 AW	70630 TQ	KSBLS	10/01-12/01
	Kentucky	Y	23540 FQ	42250 AW	67790 TQ	KYBLS	10/01-12/01
	Lexington MSA, KY	Y	28470 FQ	43840 AW	71160 TQ	KYBLS	10/01-12/01
	Louisville MSA, KY-IN	Y	26450 FQ	52000 AW	83330 TQ	KYBLS	10/01-12/01
	Louisiana	Y	24540 FQ	38430 AW	55960 TQ	LABLS	10/01-12/01
	Baton Rouge MSA, LA	Y	24000 FQ	39550 AW	54400 TQ	LABLS	10/01-12/01
	Houma MSA, LA	Y	29930 FQ	47270 AW	76360 TQ	LABLS	10/01-12/01
	Lafayette MSA, LA	Y	24580 FQ	39730 AW	60660 TQ	LABLS	10/01-12/01
	Lake Charles MSA, LA	Y	25060 FQ	38170 AW	56990 TQ	LABLS	10/01-12/01
	New Orleans MSA, LA	Y	25480 FQ	35730 AW	45610 TQ	LABLS	10/01-12/01
	Shreveport-Bossier City MSA, LA	Y	23610 FQ	35770 AW	53610 TQ	LABLS	10/01-12/01
	Maine	Y	25600 FQ	44440 AW	68200 TQ	MEBLS	10/01-12/01
	Portland MSA, ME	Y	26640 FQ	50930 AW	74360 TQ	MEBLS	10/01-12/01
	Maryland	Y	21630 FQ	47900 AW	84900 TQ	MDBLS	10/01-12/01
	Baltimore PMSA, MD	Y	23880 FQ	57060 AW	90290 TQ	MDBLS	10/01-12/01
	Massachusetts	Y	30510 FQ	58370 AW	97290 TQ	MABLS	10/01-12/01
	Boston PMSA, MA-NH	Y	35250 FQ	60830 AW	97940 TQ	MABLS	10/01-12/01
	Brockton PMSA, MA	Y	34330 FQ	69870 AW	125550 TQ	MABLS	10/01-12/01
	Lawrence PMSA, MA-NH	Y	29040 FQ	54280 AW	90720 TQ	MABLS	10/01-12/01
	Lowell PMSA, MA-NH	Y	14630 FQ	48850 AW	76380 TQ	MABLS	10/01-12/01
	New Bedford PMSA, MA	Y	27520 FQ	52400 AW	85520 TQ	MABLS	10/01-12/01

AAW Average annual wage; **AE** Average entry wage; **AEX** Average experienced wage; **AO** Average offered; **AOH** Average offered, high; **AOL** Average offered, low; **APH** Average pay, high range; **APL** Average pay, low range; **ASH** Average starting, high; **ASL** Average starting, low; **AW** Average wage paid; **FQ** First quartile wage; **H** Hourly; **HI** Highest wage paid; **HR** High end range; **LR** Low end range; **M** Monthly; **MTC** Median total compensation; **MW** Median wage paid; **SQ** Second quartile wage; **S** Special: hourly and annual; **TQ** Third quartile wage; **W** Weekly; **Y** Yearly

Occupation/Type/Industry	Location	Per	Low	Mid	High	Source	Date
Loan Officer	Springfield MSA, MA	Y	24840 FQ	44700 AW	76000 TQ	MABLS	10/01-12/01
	Worcester PMSA, MA-CT	Y	27280 FQ	60760 AW	103940 TQ	MABLS	10/01-12/01
	Michigan	Y	24030 FQ	45940 AW	82130 TQ	MIBLS	10/01-12/01
	Ann Arbor PMSA, MI	Y	25610 FQ	45130 AW	71030 TQ	MIBLS	10/01-12/01
	Detroit PMSA, MI	Y	24020 FQ	51450 AW	93030 TQ	MIBLS	10/01-12/01
	Flint PMSA, MI	Y	24140 FQ	52240 AW	88940 TQ	MIBLS	10/01-12/01
	Grand Rapids-Muskegon-Holland MSA, MI	Y	23920 FQ	40930 AW	66090 TQ	MIBLS	10/01-12/01
	Kalamazoo-Battle Creek MSA, MI	Y	23710 FQ	37490 AW	54770 TQ	MIBLS	10/01-12/01
	Lansing-East Lansing MSA, MI	Y	26130 FQ	44110 AW	71260 TQ	MIBLS	10/01-12/01
	Saginaw-Bay City-Midland MSA, MI	Y	23760 FQ	35220 AW	43960 TQ	MIBLS	10/01-12/01
	Minnesota	Y	28080 FQ	49530 AW	82090 TQ	MNBLS	10/01-12/01
	Duluth-Superior MSA, MN-WI	Y	22250 FQ	34660 AW	53500 TQ	MNBLS	10/01-12/01
	Minneapolis-St. Paul MSA, MN-WI	Y	30050 FQ	54170 AW	88510 TQ	MNBLS	10/01-12/01
	St. Cloud MSA, MN	Y	28240 FQ	46550 AW	71130 TQ	MNBLS	10/01-12/01
	Mississippi	Y	23190 FQ	40130 AW	61790 TQ	MSBLS	10/01-12/01
	Biloxi-Gulfport-Pascagoula MSA, MS	Y	21640 FQ	37620 AW	55260 TQ	MSBLS	10/01-12/01
	Jackson MSA, MS	Y	20330 FQ	39010 AW	64460 TQ	MSBLS	10/01-12/01
	Missouri	Y	23550 FQ	47080 AW	79630 TQ	MOBLS	10/01-12/01
	Kansas City MSA, MO-KS	Y	26030 FQ	48280 AW	78520 TQ	MOBLS	10/01-12/01
	St. Louis MSA, MO-IL	Y	23650 FQ	48260 AW	82190 TQ	MOBLS	10/01-12/01
	Springfield MSA, MO	Y	18700 FQ	44420 AW	88090 TQ	MOBLS	10/01-12/01
	Montana	Y	22810 FQ	39330 AW	64860 TQ	MTBLS	10/01-12/01
	Billings MSA, MT	Y	21890 FQ	40700 AW	68470 TQ	MTBLS	10/01-12/01
	Nebraska	Y	24860 FQ	43600 AW	69040 TQ	NEBLS	10/01-12/01
	Lincoln MSA, NE	Y	29650 FQ	43930 AW	60960 TQ	NEBLS	10/01-12/01
	Omaha MSA, NE-IA	Y	25130 FQ	47890 AW	81070 TQ	NEBLS	10/01-12/01
	Nevada	Y	26760 FQ	51440 AW	88980 TQ	NVBLS	10/01-12/01
	Las Vegas MSA, NV-AZ	Y	25860 FQ	50300 AW	95050 TQ	NVBLS	10/01-12/01
	Reno MSA, NV	Y	33790 FQ	57600 AW	71040 TQ	NVBLS	10/01-12/01
	New Hampshire	Y	26590 FQ	48560 AW	80070 TQ	NHBLS	10/01-12/01
	Manchester PMSA, NH	Y	27190 FQ	49680 AW	88390 TQ	NHBLS	10/01-12/01
	Nashua PMSA, NH	Y	26960 FQ	50560 AW	71620 TQ	NHBLS	10/01-12/01
	Portsmouth-Rochester PMSA, NH-ME	Y	13640 FQ	46830 AW	82930 TQ	NHBLS	10/01-12/01
	New Jersey	Y	27960 FQ	49350 AW	84020 TQ	NJBLS	10/01-12/01
	Atlantic-Cape May PMSA, NJ	Y	28720 FQ	36010 AW	44850 TQ	NJBLS	10/01-12/01
	Bergen-Passaic PMSA, NJ	Y	24780 FQ	46230 AW	75520 TQ	NJBLS	10/01-12/01
	Jersey City PMSA, NJ	Y	27460 FQ	55550 AW	130840 TQ	NJBLS	10/01-12/01
	Middlesex-Somerset-Hunterdon PMSA, NJ	Y	32250 FQ	56580 AW	89220 TQ	NJBLS	10/01-12/01
	Monmouth-Ocean PMSA, NJ	Y	26410 FQ	51290 AW	87570 TQ	NJBLS	10/01-12/01
	Newark PMSA, NJ	Y	30090 FQ	55510 AW	96710 TQ	NJBLS	10/01-12/01
	Trenton PMSA, NJ	Y	26360 FQ	46660 AW	90340 TQ	NJBLS	10/01-12/01
	New Mexico	Y	22760 FQ	40910 AW	68000 TQ	NMBLS	10/01-12/01
	Albuquerque MSA, NM	Y	23700 FQ	41380 AW	71700 TQ	NMBLS	10/01-12/01
	Las Cruces MSA, NM	Y	17200 FQ	40220 AW	65460 TQ	NMBLS	10/01-12/01
	New York	Y	31530 FQ	63840 AW	120020 TQ	NYBLS	10/01-12/01
	Albany-Schenectady-Troy MSA, NY	Y	29290 FQ	49840 AW	82810 TQ	NYBLS	10/01-12/01
	Binghamton MSA, NY	Y	27700 FQ	45650 AW	78870 TQ	NYBLS	10/01-12/01
	Buffalo-Niagara Falls MSA, NY	Y	28250 FQ	43970 AW	67760 TQ	NYBLS	10/01-12/01
	Dutchess County PMSA, NY	Y	31370 FQ	48440 AW	77070 TQ	NYBLS	10/01-12/01
	Nassau-Suffolk PMSA, NY	Y	29420 FQ	59560 AW	102290 TQ	NYBLS	10/01-12/01
	New York PMSA, NY	Y	43370 FQ	79180 AW	138780 TQ	NYBLS	10/01-12/01
	Newburgh PMSA, NY-PA	Y	32550 FQ	53470 AW	83200 TQ	NYBLS	10/01-12/01
	Rochester MSA, NY	Y	36110 FQ	54440 AW	80820 TQ	NYBLS	10/01-12/01
	Syracuse MSA, NY	Y	29140 FQ	43760 AW	66890 TQ	NYBLS	10/01-12/01
	Utica-Rome MSA, NY	Y	32660 FQ	48710 AW	75730 TQ	NYBLS	10/01-12/01
	North Carolina	Y	25360 FQ	50160 AW	90550 TQ	NCBLS	10/01-12/01
	Asheville MSA, NC	Y	20800 FQ	32090 AW	51410 TQ	NCBLS	10/01-12/01
	Charlotte-Gastonia-Rock Hill MSA, NC-SC	Y	29900 FQ	58970 AW	142340 TQ	NCBLS	10/01-12/01
	Fayetteville MSA, NC	Y	18400 FQ	33190 AW	46400 TQ	NCBLS	10/01-12/01
	Greensboro-Winston-Salem-High Point MSA, NC	Y	27910 FQ	49700 AW	89020 TQ	NCBLS	10/01-12/01

AAW	Average annual wage	**AOH**	Average offered, high	**ASH**	Average starting, high	**H**	Hourly	**M**	Monthly	**S**	Special: hourly and annual
AE	Average entry wage	**AOL**	Average offered, low	**ASL**	Average starting, low	**HI**	Highest wage paid	**MTC**	Median total compensation	**TQ**	Third quartile wage
AEX	Average experienced wage	**APH**	Average pay, high range	**AW**	Average wage paid	**HR**	High end range	**MW**	Median wage paid	**W**	Weekly
AO	Average offered	**APL**	Average pay, low range	**FQ**	First quartile wage	**LR**	Low end range	**SQ**	Second quartile wage	**Y**	Yearly

Occupation/Type/Industry	Location	Per	Low	Mid	High	Source	Date
Loan Officer	Hickory-Morganton-Lenoir MSA, NC	Y	25110 FQ	45030 AW	77920 TQ	NCBLS	10/01-12/01
	Raleigh-Durham-Chapel Hill MSA, NC	Y	21470 FQ	42830 AW	74220 TQ	NCBLS	10/01-12/01
	Wilmington MSA, NC	Y	27330 FQ	53660 AW	91070 TQ	NCBLS	10/01-12/01
	North Dakota	Y	26250 FQ	42770 AW	60040 TQ	NDBLS	10/01-12/01
	Fargo-Moorhead MSA, ND-MN	Y	28950 FQ	44680 AW	64080 TQ	NDBLS	10/01-12/01
	Ohio	Y	24020 FQ	46500 AW	79930 TQ	OHBLS	10/01-12/01
	Akron PMSA, OH	Y	24040 FQ	40620 AW	63230 TQ	OHBLS	10/01-12/01
	Canton-Massillon MSA, OH	Y	24140 FQ	46060 AW	88700 TQ	OHBLS	10/01-12/01
	Cincinnati PMSA, OH-KY-IN	Y	25570 FQ	53520 AW	92560 TQ	OHBLS	10/01-12/01
	Cleveland-Lorain-Elyria PMSA, OH	Y	21430 FQ	48990 AW	94410 TQ	OHBLS	10/01-12/01
	Columbus MSA, OH	Y	25470 FQ	44890 AW	73760 TQ	OHBLS	10/01-12/01
	Dayton-Springfield MSA, OH	Y	27820 FQ	51310 AW	70740 TQ	OHBLS	10/01-12/01
	Hamilton-Middletown PMSA, OH	Y	25710 FQ	44200 AW	73600 TQ	OHBLS	10/01-12/01
	Mansfield MSA, OH	Y	23890 FQ	39570 AW	55370 TQ	OHBLS	10/01-12/01
	Toledo MSA, OH	Y	22200 FQ	46340 AW	80100 TQ	OHBLS	10/01-12/01
	Youngstown-Warren MSA, OH	Y	17200 FQ	36980 AW	60370 TQ	OHBLS	10/01-12/01
	Oklahoma	Y	20920 FQ	43270 AW	69630 TQ	OKBLS	10/01-12/01
	Oklahoma City MSA, OK	Y	20760 FQ	46520 AW	82960 TQ	OKBLS	10/01-12/01
	Tulsa MSA, OK	Y	22200 FQ	46520 AW	72530 TQ	OKBLS	10/01-12/01
	Oregon	Y	26700 FQ	48360 AW	72080 TQ	ORBLS	10/01-12/01
	Eugene-Springfield MSA, OR	Y	27870 FQ	46700 AW	72730 TQ	ORBLS	10/01-12/01
	Medford-Ashland MSA, OR	Y	26030 FQ	48080 AW	74320 TQ	ORBLS	10/01-12/01
	Portland-Vancouver PMSA, OR-WA	Y	26770 FQ	49540 AW	73700 TQ	ORBLS	10/01-12/01
	Salem PMSA, OR	Y	30040 FQ	46760 AW	68730 TQ	ORBLS	10/01-12/01
	Pennsylvania	Y	25030 FQ	41870 AW	71210 TQ	PABLS	10/01-12/01
	Allentown-Bethlehem-Easton MSA, PA	Y	23740 FQ	51130 AW	86000 TQ	PABLS	10/01-12/01
	Erie MSA, PA	Y	22930 FQ	31390 AW	42910 TQ	PABLS	10/01-12/01
	Harrisburg-Lebanon-Carlisle MSA, PA	Y	25670 FQ	41890 AW	73410 TQ	PABLS	10/01-12/01
	Johnstown MSA, PA	Y	21190 FQ	36830 AW	59630 TQ	PABLS	10/01-12/01
	Lancaster MSA, PA	Y	25950 FQ	51200 AW	86930 TQ	PABLS	10/01-12/01
	Philadelphia PMSA, PA-NJ	Y	25550 FQ	45360 AW	81110 TQ	PABLS	10/01-12/01
	Pittsburgh MSA, PA	Y	24240 FQ	37530 AW	56500 TQ	PABLS	10/01-12/01
	Reading MSA, PA	Y	22740 FQ	39750 AW	71940 TQ	PABLS	10/01-12/01
	Scranton-Wilkes-Barre-Hazleton MSA, PA	Y	28370 FQ	33150 AW	38110 TQ	PABLS	10/01-12/01
	York MSA, PA	Y	26870 FQ	35010 AW	52580 TQ	PABLS	10/01-12/01
	Rhode Island	Y	31050 FQ	76580 AW	142180 TQ	RIBLS	10/01-12/01
	Providence-Fall River-Warwick MSA, RI-MA	Y	30220 FQ	74080 AW	140940 TQ	RIBLS	10/01-12/01
	South Carolina	Y	24930 FQ	41870 AW	66650 TQ	SCBLS	10/01-12/01
	Charleston-North Charleston MSA, SC	Y	25330 FQ	39980 AW	57560 TQ	SCBLS	10/01-12/01
	Columbia MSA, SC	Y	25120 FQ	37810 AW	61140 TQ	SCBLS	10/01-12/01
	Greenville-Spartanburg-Anderson MSA, SC	Y	22990 FQ	42770 AW	56380 TQ	SCBLS	10/01-12/01
	Myrtle Beach MSA, SC	Y	30680 FQ	45230 AW	59410 TQ	SCBLS	10/01-12/01
	South Dakota	Y	27180 FQ	38900 AW	54190 TQ	SDBLS	10/01-12/01
	Sioux Falls MSA, SD	Y	29030 FQ	39680 AW	55490 TQ	SDBLS	10/01-12/01
	Tennessee	Y	19630 FQ	42760 AW	74410 TQ	TNBLS	10/01-12/01
	Chattanooga MSA, TN-GA	Y	20340 FQ	40800 AW	69480 TQ	TNBLS	10/01-12/01
	Clarksville-Hopkinsville MSA, TN-KY	Y	20980 FQ	40560 AW	69500 TQ	TNBLS	10/01-12/01
	Johnson City-Kingsport-Bristol MSA, TN-VA	Y	24970 FQ	44470 AW	71410 TQ	TNBLS	10/01-12/01
	Knoxville MSA, TN	Y	21590 FQ	45730 AW	75110 TQ	TNBLS	10/01-12/01
	Memphis MSA, TN-AR-MS	Y	24600 FQ	51020 AW	106730 TQ	TNBLS	10/01-12/01
	Nashville MSA, TN	Y	13100 FQ	41420 AW	93550 TQ	TNBLS	10/01-12/01
	Texas	Y	24140 FQ	53180 AW	98800 TQ	TXBLS	10/01-12/01
	Amarillo MSA, TX	Y	24590 FQ	41350 AW	71730 TQ	TXBLS	10/01-12/01
	Austin-San Marcos MSA, TX	Y	28350 FQ	46720 AW	70000 TQ	TXBLS	10/01-12/01
	Beaumont-Port Arthur MSA, TX	Y	21650 FQ	37990 AW	64830 TQ	TXBLS	10/01-12/01
	Brazoria PMSA, TX	Y	20370 FQ	36700 AW	66740 TQ	TXBLS	10/01-12/01

AAW Average annual wage **AOH** Average offered, high **ASH** Average starting, high **H** Hourly **M** Monthly **S** Special: hourly and annual
AE Average entry wage **AOL** Average offered, low **ASL** Average starting, low **HI** Highest wage paid **MTC** Median total compensation **TQ** Third quartile wage
AEX Average experienced wage **APH** Average pay, high range **AW** Average wage paid **HR** High end range **MW** Median wage paid **W** Weekly
AO Average offered **APL** Average pay, low range **FQ** First quartile wage **LR** Low end range **SQ** Second quartile wage **Y** Yearly

Occupation/Type/Industry	Location	Per	Low	Mid	High	Source	Date
Loan Officer	Brownsville-Harlingen-San Benito MSA, TX	Y	23510 FQ	41550 AW	70180 TQ	TXBLS	10/01-12/01
	Corpus Christi MSA, TX	Y	25750 FQ	44670 AW	69150 TQ	TXBLS	10/01-12/01
	Dallas PMSA, TX	Y	29490 FQ	67790 AW	129860 TQ	TXBLS	10/01-12/01
	El Paso MSA, TX	Y	15770 FQ	32010 AW	47640 TQ	TXBLS	10/01-12/01
	Fort Worth-Arlington PMSA, TX	Y	22940 FQ	43180 AW	70530 TQ	TXBLS	10/01-12/01
	Galveston-Texas City PMSA, TX	Y	24260 FQ	43280 AW	71400 TQ	TXBLS	10/01-12/01
	Houston PMSA, TX	Y	25860 FQ	52160 AW	88520 TQ	TXBLS	10/01-12/01
	Killeen-Temple MSA, TX	Y	24260 FQ	50580 AW	87220 TQ	TXBLS	10/01-12/01
	Laredo MSA, TX	Y	23460 FQ	40840 AW	68000 TQ	TXBLS	10/01-12/01
	Longview-Marshall MSA, TX	Y	23410 FQ	52360 AW	98400 TQ	TXBLS	10/01-12/01
	Lubbock MSA, TX	Y	30900 FQ	62570 AW	94540 TQ	TXBLS	10/01-12/01
	McAllen-Edinburg-Mission MSA, TX	Y	20240 FQ	35710 AW	58260 TQ	TXBLS	10/01-12/01
	Odessa-Midland MSA, TX	Y	22280 FQ	45040 AW	77340 TQ	TXBLS	10/01-12/01
	San Antonio MSA, TX	Y	18220 FQ	41530 AW	70070 TQ	TXBLS	10/01-12/01
	Tyler MSA, TX	Y	19700 FQ	39580 AW	70990 TQ	TXBLS	10/01-12/01
	Waco MSA, TX	Y	25580 FQ	42210 AW	65840 TQ	TXBLS	10/01-12/01
	Utah	Y	22720 FQ	42140 AW	63880 TQ	UTBLS	10/01-12/01
	Provo-Orem MSA, UT	Y	20970 FQ	43030 AW	67810 TQ	UTBLS	10/01-12/01
	Salt Lake City-Ogden MSA, UT	Y	22800 FQ	41020 AW	61820 TQ	UTBLS	10/01-12/01
	Vermont	Y	26220 FQ	53280 AW	85770 TQ	VTBLS	10/01-12/01
	Burlington MSA, VT	Y	31580 FQ	60220 AW	87130 TQ	VTBLS	10/01-12/01
	Virginia	Y	25110 FQ	53010 AW	96350 TQ	VABLS	10/01-12/01
	Lynchburg MSA, VA	Y	22000 FQ	43360 AW	67860 TQ	VABLS	10/01-12/01
	Norfolk-Virginia Beach-Newport News MSA, VA-NC	Y	24600 FQ	47690 AW	83400 TQ	VABLS	10/01-12/01
	Richmond-Petersburg MSA, VA	Y	24700 FQ	46940 AW	74280 TQ	VABLS	10/01-12/01
	Roanoke MSA, VA	Y	30500 FQ	58910 AW	106360 TQ	VABLS	10/01-12/01
	Washington	Y	25630 FQ	52200 AW	89670 TQ	WABLS	10/01-12/01
	Bremerton PMSA, WA	Y	23550 FQ	71160 AW		WABLS	10/01-12/01
	Olympia PMSA, WA	Y	25120 FQ	49630 AW	86720 TQ	WABLS	10/01-12/01
	Richland-Kennewick-Pasco MSA, WA	Y	30450 FQ	53680 AW	80930 TQ	WABLS	10/01-12/01
	Seattle-Bellevue-Everett PMSA, WA	Y	26930 FQ	54670 AW	92800 TQ	WABLS	10/01-12/01
	Spokane MSA, WA	Y	20270 FQ	48140 AW	87460 TQ	WABLS	10/01-12/01
	Tacoma PMSA, WA	Y	25800 FQ	51130 AW	104420 TQ	WABLS	10/01-12/01
	Yakima MSA, WA	Y	30290 FQ	56550 AW	91100 TQ	WABLS	10/01-12/01
	West Virginia	Y	20830 FQ	35470 AW	56870 TQ	WVBLS	10/01-12/01
	Charleston MSA, WV	Y	15610 FQ	32640 AW	48840 TQ	WVBLS	10/01-12/01
	Huntington-Ashland MSA, WV-KY-OH	Y	22540 FQ	36140 AW	56970 TQ	WVBLS	10/01-12/01
	Wisconsin	Y	25440 FQ	47740 AW	78600 TQ	WIBLS	10/01-12/01
	Appleton-Oshkosh-Neenah MSA, WI	Y	28530 FQ	52440 AW	86690 TQ	WIBLS	10/01-12/01
	Green Bay MSA, WI	Y	26010 FQ	45400 AW	69630 TQ	WIBLS	10/01-12/01
	Madison MSA, WI	Y	20680 FQ	41030 AW	71570 TQ	WIBLS	10/01-12/01
	Milwaukee-Waukesha PMSA, WI	Y	30920 FQ	56430 AW	91400 TQ	WIBLS	10/01-12/01
	Racine PMSA, WI	Y	24620 FQ	37870 AW	63680 TQ	WIBLS	10/01-12/01
	Wyoming	Y	24260 FQ	42680 AW	68040 TQ	WYBLS	10/01-12/01
	Cheyenne MSA, WY	Y	21030 FQ	33080 AW	44640 TQ	WYBLS	10/01-12/01
	Puerto Rico	Y	17450 FQ	40660 AW	78180 TQ	PRBLS	10/01-12/01
	Virgin Islands	Y	20850 FQ	35000 AW	55300 TQ	VIBLS	10/01-12/01
	Guam	Y	23910 FQ	39540 AW	59620 TQ	GUBLS	10/01-12/01
Locker Room, Coatroom, and Dressing Room Attendant	Arizona	H	5.88 FQ	8.34 AW	11.06 TQ	AZBLS	10/01-12/01
	California	H	6.65 FQ	8.99 AW	13.32 TQ	CABLS	10/01-12/01
	Colorado	H	5.87 FQ	8.26 AW	11.41 TQ	COBLS	10/01-12/01
	Connecticut	H	6.71 FQ	9.64 AW	13.35 TQ	CTBLS	10/01-12/01
	Delaware	H	7.04 FQ	8.72 AW	11.38 TQ	DEBLS	10/01-12/01
	District of Columbia	H	6.81 FQ	8.71 AW	10.71 TQ	DCBLS	10/01-12/01
	Florida	H	5.95 FQ	7.93 AW	10.51 TQ	FLBLS	10/01-12/01
	Georgia	H	6.40 FQ	8.81 AW	11.38 TQ	GABLS	10/01-12/01
	Hawaii	H	6.83 FQ	9.35 AW	12.11 TQ	HIBLS	10/01-12/01

AAW	Average annual wage	AOH	Average offered, high	ASH	Average starting, high	H	Hourly	M	Monthly	S	Special: hourly and annual
AE	Average entry wage	AOL	Average offered, low	ASL	Average starting, low	HI	Highest wage paid	MTC	Median total compensation	TQ	Third quartile wage
AEX	Average experienced wage	APH	Average pay, high range	AW	Average wage paid	HR	High end range	MW	Median wage paid	W	Weekly
AO	Average offered	APL	Average pay, low range	FQ	First quartile wage	LR	Low end range	SQ	Second quartile wage	Y	Yearly

Occupation/Type/Industry	Location	Per	Low	Mid	High	Source	Date
Locker Room, Coatroom, and Dressing Room Attendant	Idaho	H	5.91 FQ	7.48 AW	8.81 TQ	IDBLS	10/01-12/01
	Illinois	H	5.97 FQ	8.46 AW	11.26 TQ	ILBLS	10/01-12/01
	Indiana	H	5.81 FQ	7.58 AW	9.95 TQ	INBLS	10/01-12/01
	Iowa	H	6.02 FQ	7.81 AW	10.09 TQ	IABLS	10/01-12/01
	Kansas	H	5.87 FQ	7.73 AW	10.38 TQ	KSBLS	10/01-12/01
	Kentucky	H	5.84 FQ	7.78 AW	10.28 TQ	KYBLS	10/01-12/01
	Louisiana	H	5.90 FQ	8.10 AW	10.23 TQ	LABLS	10/01-12/01
	Maine	H	5.98 FQ	7.68 AW	9.76 TQ	MEBLS	10/01-12/01
	Maryland	H	6.08 FQ	7.86 AW	9.90 TQ	MDBLS	10/01-12/01
	Massachusetts	H	6.90 FQ	9.35 AW	12.91 TQ	MABLS	10/01-12/01
	Michigan	H	6.01 FQ	8.28 AW	10.89 TQ	MIBLS	10/01-12/01
	Minnesota	H	6.11 FQ	8.08 AW	10.48 TQ	MNBLS	10/01-12/01
	Mississippi	H	5.71 FQ	7.42 AW	9.53 TQ	MSBLS	10/01-12/01
	Missouri	H	6.03 FQ	8.31 AW	10.71 TQ	MOBLS	10/01-12/01
	Montana	H	5.84 FQ	7.09 AW	8.65 TQ	MTBLS	10/01-12/01
	Nebraska	H	6.19 FQ	8.19 AW	10.86 TQ	NEBLS	10/01-12/01
	Nevada	H	6.60 FQ	9.74 AW	12.99 TQ	NVBLS	10/01-12/01
	New Hampshire	H	6.23 FQ	8.37 AW	10.85 TQ	NHBLS	10/01-12/01
	New Jersey	H	6.11 FQ	8.54 AW	11.02 TQ	NJBLS	10/01-12/01
	New Mexico	H	5.83 FQ	7.36 AW	9.59 TQ	NMBLS	10/01-12/01
	New York	H	6.03 FQ	9.40 AW	15.67 TQ	NYBLS	10/01-12/01
	North Carolina	H	6.11 FQ	8.21 AW	10.74 TQ	NCBLS	10/01-12/01
	Ohio	H	5.64 FQ	7.52 AW	9.98 TQ	OHBLS	10/01-12/01
	Oklahoma	H	5.88 FQ	7.80 AW	10.49 TQ	OKBLS	10/01-12/01
	Oregon	H	6.95 FQ	8.39 AW	10.61 TQ	ORBLS	10/01-12/01
	Pennsylvania	H	5.83 FQ	7.76 AW	10.74 TQ	PABLS	10/01-12/01
	Rhode Island	H	6.63 FQ	8.26 AW	10.84 TQ	RIBLS	10/01-12/01
	South Carolina	H	6.05 FQ	8.14 AW	10.50 TQ	SCBLS	10/01-12/01
	South Dakota	H	6.91 FQ	7.68 AW	8.44 TQ	SDBLS	10/01-12/01
	Tennessee	H	6.22 FQ	8.28 AW	10.62 TQ	TNBLS	10/01-12/01
	Texas	H	6.07 FQ	8.05 AW	10.51 TQ	TXBLS	10/01-12/01
	Utah	H	5.78 FQ	8.30 AW	11.92 TQ	UTBLS	10/01-12/01
	Virginia	H	6.07 FQ	8.16 AW	10.61 TQ	VABLS	10/01-12/01
	Washington	H	7.08 FQ	8.96 AW	11.64 TQ	WABLS	10/01-12/01
	West Virginia	H	5.66 FQ	7.22 AW	8.69 TQ	WVBLS	10/01-12/01
	Wisconsin	H	5.87 FQ	7.84 AW	10.51 TQ	WIBLS	10/01-12/01
	Wyoming	H	5.65 FQ	6.97 AW	9.06 TQ	WYBLS	10/01-12/01
	Puerto Rico	H	5.95 FQ	7.98 AW	10.48 TQ	PRBLS	10/01-12/01
Locksmith and Safe Repairer	Alabama	H	9.65 FQ	12.76 AW	16.50 TQ	ALBLS	10/01-12/01
	Birmingham MSA, AL	H	10.31 FQ	13.13 AW	16.54 TQ	ALBLS	10/01-12/01
	Arizona	H	8.45 FQ	15.10 AW	21.50 TQ	AZBLS	10/01-12/01
	Phoenix-Mesa MSA, AZ	H	8.41 FQ	15.51 AW	22.03 TQ	AZBLS	10/01-12/01
	Tucson MSA, AZ	H	9.43 FQ	14.50 AW	16.94 TQ	AZBLS	10/01-12/01
	Arkansas	H	8.41 FQ	12.01 AW	19.67 TQ	ARBLS	10/01-12/01
	Little Rock-North Little Rock MSA, AR	H	8.62 FQ	13.95 AW	21.06 TQ	ARBLS	10/01-12/01
	California	H	9.23 FQ	15.91 AW	22.08 TQ	CABLS	10/01-12/01
	Los Angeles-Long Beach PMSA, CA	H	9.26 FQ	16.06 AW	21.12 TQ	CABLS	10/01-12/01
	Oakland PMSA, CA	H	6.80 FQ	20.40 AW	43.79 TQ	CABLS	10/01-12/01
	Orange County PMSA, CA	H	9.93 FQ	14.79 AW	21.87 TQ	CABLS	10/01-12/01
	Riverside-San Bernardino PMSA, CA	H	9.61 FQ	15.28 AW	22.43 TQ	CABLS	10/01-12/01
	Sacramento PMSA, CA	H	11.96 FQ	15.07 AW	18.70 TQ	CABLS	10/01-12/01
	San Diego MSA, CA	H	9.03 FQ	16.16 AW	21.98 TQ	CABLS	10/01-12/01
	San Francisco PMSA, CA	H	8.69 FQ	16.88 AW	25.33 TQ	CABLS	10/01-12/01
	Santa Barbara-Santa Maria-Lompoc MSA, CA	H	7.77 FQ	14.50 AW	21.20 TQ	CABLS	10/01-12/01
	Santa Rosa PMSA, CA	H	9.07 FQ	16.05 AW	21.69 TQ	CABLS	10/01-12/01
	Vallejo-Fairfield-Napa PMSA, CA	H	9.56 FQ	15.72 AW	21.53 TQ	CABLS	10/01-12/01
	Ventura PMSA, CA	H	9.34 FQ	13.79 AW	18.95 TQ	CABLS	10/01-12/01
	Colorado	H	9.29 FQ	14.93 AW	22.21 TQ	COBLS	10/01-12/01
	Denver PMSA, CO	H	10.26 FQ	16.27 AW	23.52 TQ	COBLS	10/01-12/01
	Connecticut	H	11.75 FQ	16.93 AW	21.94 TQ	CTBLS	10/01-12/01
	New Haven-Meriden PMSA, CT	H	11.13 FQ	15.08 AW	21.03 TQ	CTBLS	10/01-12/01
	Delaware	H	10.14 FQ	17.23 AW	23.17 TQ	DEBLS	10/01-12/01
	Wilmington-Newark PMSA, DE-MD	H	10.14 FQ	17.33 AW	23.17 TQ	DEBLS	10/01-12/01

Occupation/Type/Industry	Location	Per	Low	Mid	High	Source	Date
Locksmith and Safe Repairer	District of Columbia	H	14.16 FQ	18.95 AW	23.38 TQ	DCBLS	10/01-12/01
	Washington PMSA, DC-MD-VA-WV	H	10.29 FQ	17.06 AW	25.01 TQ	DCBLS	10/01-12/01
	Florida	H	7.45 FQ	12.68 AW	18.73 TQ	FLBLS	10/01-12/01
	Daytona Beach MSA, FL	H	7.89 FQ	11.44 AW	15.93 TQ	FLBLS	10/01-12/01
	Fort Lauderdale PMSA, FL	H	13.05 FQ	15.31 AW	17.35 TQ	FLBLS	10/01-12/01
	Jacksonville MSA, FL	H	9.45 FQ	10.86 AW	12.36 TQ	FLBLS	10/01-12/01
	Miami PMSA, FL	H	6.33 FQ	11.27 AW	15.86 TQ	FLBLS	10/01-12/01
	Orlando MSA, FL	H	7.26 FQ	11.47 AW	21.42 TQ	FLBLS	10/01-12/01
	Sarasota-Bradenton MSA, FL	H	11.16 FQ	13.06 AW	15.45 TQ	FLBLS	10/01-12/01
	Tampa-St. Petersburg-Clearwater MSA, FL	H	5.59 FQ	8.93 AW	13.59 TQ	FLBLS	10/01-12/01
	West Palm Beach-Boca Raton MSA, FL	H	10.40 FQ	15.37 AW	20.69 TQ	FLBLS	10/01-12/01
	Georgia	H	8.60 FQ	14.07 AW	18.02 TQ	GABLS	10/01-12/01
	Atlanta MSA, GA	H	12.15 FQ	15.15 AW	17.48 TQ	GABLS	10/01-12/01
	Hawaii	H	11.33 FQ	14.50 AW	18.32 TQ	HIBLS	10/01-12/01
	Honolulu MSA, HI	H	11.83 FQ	14.89 AW	18.30 TQ	HIBLS	10/01-12/01
	Illinois	H	8.41 FQ	15.10 AW	22.23 TQ	ILBLS	10/01-12/01
	Chicago PMSA, IL	H	8.92 FQ	15.67 AW	22.04 TQ	ILBLS	10/01-12/01
	Indiana	H	8.20 FQ	12.44 AW	18.27 TQ	INBLS	10/01-12/01
	Iowa	H	6.92 FQ	12.90 AW	17.74 TQ	IABLS	10/01-12/01
	Des Moines MSA, IA	H	6.70 FQ	13.93 AW	21.12 TQ	IABLS	10/01-12/01
	Kansas	H	9.38 FQ	14.83 AW	20.68 TQ	KSBLS	10/01-12/01
	Kentucky	H	7.46 FQ	13.07 AW	18.64 TQ	KYBLS	10/01-12/01
	Lexington MSA, KY	H	10.75 FQ	13.71 AW	18.66 TQ	KYBLS	10/01-12/01
	Louisville MSA, KY-IN	H	5.52 FQ	9.93 AW	15.99 TQ	KYBLS	10/01-12/01
	Louisiana	H	6.82 FQ	11.68 AW	16.54 TQ	LABLS	10/01-12/01
	New Orleans MSA, LA	H	11.05 FQ	13.00 AW	16.12 TQ	LABLS	10/01-12/01
	Maine	H	6.20 FQ	13.59 AW	17.91 TQ	MEBLS	10/01-12/01
	Maryland	H	9.80 FQ	17.06 AW	27.26 TQ	MDBLS	10/01-12/01
	Baltimore PMSA, MD	H	11.15 FQ	15.85 AW	23.26 TQ	MDBLS	10/01-12/01
	Massachusetts	H	9.23 FQ	15.25 AW	23.42 TQ	MABLS	10/01-12/01
	Boston PMSA, MA-NH	H	9.05 FQ	15.59 AW	24.25 TQ	MABLS	10/01-12/01
	Springfield MSA, MA	H	9.81 FQ	16.87 AW	24.28 TQ	MABLS	10/01-12/01
	Michigan	H	7.11 FQ	12.91 AW	24.22 TQ	MIBLS	10/01-12/01
	Detroit PMSA, MI	H	7.08 FQ	12.76 AW	24.67 TQ	MIBLS	10/01-12/01
	Minnesota	H	10.53 FQ	17.47 AW	29.41 TQ	MNBLS	10/01-12/01
	Minneapolis-St. Paul MSA, MN-WI	H	10.67 FQ	17.73 AW	30.11 TQ	MNBLS	10/01-12/01
	Mississippi	H	9.68 FQ	12.39 AW	15.30 TQ	MSBLS	10/01-12/01
	Jackson MSA, MS	H	11.34 FQ	12.60 AW	13.93 TQ	MSBLS	10/01-12/01
	Missouri	H	9.09 FQ	13.26 AW	17.92 TQ	MOBLS	10/01-12/01
	Kansas City MSA, MO-KS	H	9.20 FQ	15.27 AW	20.89 TQ	MOBLS	10/01-12/01
	St. Louis MSA, MO-IL	H	10.08 FQ	12.45 AW	15.59 TQ	MOBLS	10/01-12/01
	Springfield MSA, MO	H	9.06 FQ	12.85 AW	13.98 TQ	MOBLS	10/01-12/01
	Nebraska	H	11.67 FQ	16.94 AW	23.47 TQ	NEBLS	10/01-12/01
	Omaha MSA, NE-IA	H	11.80 FQ	17.29 AW	23.30 TQ	NEBLS	10/01-12/01
	Nevada	H	12.63 FQ	17.81 AW	25.19 TQ	NVBLS	10/01-12/01
	Las Vegas MSA, NV-AZ	H	11.79 FQ	19.06 AW	26.13 TQ	NVBLS	10/01-12/01
	Reno MSA, NV	H	13.64 FQ	15.27 AW	16.90 TQ	NVBLS	10/01-12/01
	New Jersey	H	11.76 FQ	17.92 AW	24.77 TQ	NJBLS	10/01-12/01
	Bergen-Passaic PMSA, NJ	H	12.83 FQ	19.80 AW	31.34 TQ	NJBLS	10/01-12/01
	Middlesex-Somerset-Hunterdon PMSA, NJ	H	9.65 FQ	16.22 AW	21.73 TQ	NJBLS	10/01-12/01
	Monmouth-Ocean PMSA, NJ	H	11.29 FQ	16.30 AW	22.46 TQ	NJBLS	10/01-12/01
	Newark PMSA, NJ	H	17.19 FQ	18.79 AW	21.09 TQ	NJBLS	10/01-12/01
	Trenton PMSA, NJ	H	11.63 FQ	15.45 AW	20.33 TQ	NJBLS	10/01-12/01
	New Mexico	H	8.55 FQ	13.04 AW	17.50 TQ	NMBLS	10/01-12/01
	New York	H	7.72 FQ	15.10 AW	22.86 TQ	NYBLS	10/01-12/01
	Albany-Schenectady-Troy MSA, NY	H	7.98 FQ	12.84 AW	18.96 TQ	NYBLS	10/01-12/01
	Nassau-Suffolk PMSA, NY	H	10.39 FQ	15.19 AW	21.15 TQ	NYBLS	10/01-12/01
	New York PMSA, NY	H	7.12 FQ	15.10 AW	23.96 TQ	NYBLS	10/01-12/01
	Syracuse MSA, NY	H	8.97 FQ	14.40 AW	19.86 TQ	NYBLS	10/01-12/01
	North Carolina	H	8.65 FQ	12.95 AW	18.24 TQ	NCBLS	10/01-12/01
	Charlotte-Gastonia-Rock Hill MSA, NC-SC	H	9.59 FQ	14.41 AW	21.07 TQ	NCBLS	10/01-12/01
	Raleigh-Durham-Chapel Hill MSA, NC	H	11.23 FQ	15.22 AW	18.16 TQ	NCBLS	10/01-12/01
	Ohio	H	9.41 FQ	13.21 AW	18.53 TQ	OHBLS	10/01-12/01
	Akron PMSA, OH	H	9.90 FQ	12.75 AW	17.04 TQ	OHBLS	10/01-12/01

AAW	Average annual wage	**AOH**	Average offered, high	**ASH**	Average starting, high	**H**	Hourly	**M**	Monthly	**S**	Special: hourly and annual
AE	Average entry wage	**AOL**	Average offered, low	**ASL**	Average starting, low	**HI**	Highest wage paid	**MTC**	Median total compensation	**TQ**	Third quartile wage
AEX	Average experienced wage	**APH**	Average pay, high range	**AW**	Average wage paid	**HR**	High end range	**MW**	Median wage paid	**W**	Weekly
AO	Average offered	**APL**	Average pay, low range	**FQ**	First quartile wage	**LR**	Low end range	**SQ**	Second quartile wage	**Y**	Yearly

Occupation/Type/Industry	Location	Per	Low	Mid	High	Source	Date
Locksmith and Safe Repairer	Cincinnati PMSA, OH-KY-IN	H	9.57 FQ	13.55 AW	19.65 TQ	OHBLS	10/01-12/01
	Columbus MSA, OH	H	9.00 FQ	13.15 AW	19.50 TQ	OHBLS	10/01-12/01
	Oklahoma	H	12.14 FQ	14.54 AW	16.74 TQ	OKBLS	10/01-12/01
	Oklahoma City MSA, OK	H	13.81 FQ	15.07 AW	16.67 TQ	OKBLS	10/01-12/01
	Oregon	H	9.48 FQ	14.27 AW	20.45 TQ	ORBLS	10/01-12/01
	Portland-Vancouver PMSA, OR-WA	H	9.97 FQ	14.19 AW	19.88 TQ	ORBLS	10/01-12/01
	Pennsylvania	H	7.94 FQ	14.75 AW	23.93 TQ	PABLS	10/01-12/01
	Harrisburg-Lebanon-Carlisle MSA, PA	H	8.16 FQ	13.69 AW	18.63 TQ	PABLS	10/01-12/01
	Philadelphia PMSA, PA-NJ	H	10.83 FQ	17.25 AW	25.20 TQ	PABLS	10/01-12/01
	York MSA, PA	H	7.10 FQ	10.47 AW	16.62 TQ	PABLS	10/01-12/01
	Rhode Island	H	10.18 FQ	14.29 AW	17.40 TQ	RIBLS	10/01-12/01
	Providence-Fall River-Warwick MSA, RI-MA	H	9.42 FQ	13.63 AW	17.36 TQ	RIBLS	10/01-12/01
	South Carolina	H	8.95 FQ	13.31 AW	20.69 TQ	SCBLS	10/01-12/01
	Columbia MSA, SC	H	6.25 FQ	12.99 AW	25.10 TQ	SCBLS	10/01-12/01
	Tennessee	H	8.96 FQ	12.28 AW	16.86 TQ	TNBLS	10/01-12/01
	Knoxville MSA, TN	H	8.41 FQ	11.18 AW	13.54 TQ	TNBLS	10/01-12/01
	Memphis MSA, TN-AR-MS	H	10.35 FQ	12.17 AW	13.74 TQ	TNBLS	10/01-12/01
	Texas	H	9.72 FQ	14.17 AW	18.39 TQ	TXBLS	10/01-12/01
	Dallas PMSA, TX	H	11.91 FQ	16.15 AW	21.21 TQ	TXBLS	10/01-12/01
	Fort Worth-Arlington PMSA, TX	H	9.35 FQ	13.30 AW	17.73 TQ	TXBLS	10/01-12/01
	Houston PMSA, TX	H	13.56 FQ	14.99 AW	16.82 TQ	TXBLS	10/01-12/01
	Lubbock MSA, TX	H	7.60 FQ	13.32 AW	19.63 TQ	TXBLS	10/01-12/01
	McAllen-Edinburg-Mission MSA, TX	H	9.16 FQ	10.99 AW	14.13 TQ	TXBLS	10/01-12/01
	San Antonio MSA, TX	H	9.30 FQ	13.01 AW	16.44 TQ	TXBLS	10/01-12/01
	Utah	H	8.22 FQ	14.02 AW	21.11 TQ	UTBLS	10/01-12/01
	Virginia	H	9.50 FQ	15.53 AW	22.34 TQ	VABLS	10/01-12/01
	Lynchburg MSA, VA	H	9.63 FQ	13.90 AW	18.52 TQ	VABLS	10/01-12/01
	Norfolk-Virginia Beach-Newport News MSA, VA-NC	H	8.74 FQ	18.17 AW	27.29 TQ	VABLS	10/01-12/01
	Washington	H	7.16 FQ	14.49 AW	23.17 TQ	WABLS	10/01-12/01
	Bremerton PMSA, WA	H	6.85 FQ	9.29 AW	11.57 TQ	WABLS	10/01-12/01
	Seattle-Bellevue-Everett PMSA, WA	H	12.34 FQ	18.40 AW	26.13 TQ	WABLS	10/01-12/01
	West Virginia	H	9.94 FQ	13.82 AW	16.97 TQ	WVBLS	10/01-12/01
	Wisconsin	H	7.85 FQ	13.05 AW	18.54 TQ	WIBLS	10/01-12/01
	Milwaukee-Waukesha PMSA, WI	H	7.52 FQ	13.91 AW	23.32 TQ	WIBLS	10/01-12/01
	Puerto Rico	H	5.53 FQ	8.20 AW	14.43 TQ	PRBLS	10/01-12/01
Locomotive Engineer	Alabama	H	10.44 FQ	21.72 AW	36.47 TQ	ALBLS	10/01-12/01
	Arkansas	H	12.00 FQ	21.98 AW	33.03 TQ	ARBLS	10/01-12/01
	California	H	15.57 FQ	25.39 AW	36.61 TQ	CABLS	10/01-12/01
	Colorado	H	14.12 FQ	22.71 AW	34.34 TQ	COBLS	10/01-12/01
	Florida	H	12.11 FQ	17.21 AW	26.03 TQ	FLBLS	10/01-12/01
	Georgia	H	12.25 FQ	17.37 AW	22.82 TQ	GABLS	10/01-12/01
	Idaho	H	15.85 FQ	22.07 AW	28.43 TQ	IDBLS	10/01-12/01
	Illinois	H	14.37 FQ	23.56 AW	36.29 TQ	ILBLS	10/01-12/01
	Indiana	H	13.88 FQ	18.66 AW	23.11 TQ	INBLS	10/01-12/01
	Iowa	H	15.28 FQ	24.39 AW	37.16 TQ	IABLS	10/01-12/01
	Kansas	H	13.57 FQ	21.60 AW	33.57 TQ	KSBLS	10/01-12/01
	Kentucky	H	14.33 FQ	25.10 AW	38.97 TQ	KYBLS	10/01-12/01
	Louisiana	H	15.56 FQ	27.42 AW	40.81 TQ	LABLS	10/01-12/01
	Michigan	H	14.07 FQ	23.46 AW	34.03 TQ	MIBLS	10/01-12/01
	Minnesota	H	19.01 FQ	29.32 AW	41.40 TQ	MNBLS	10/01-12/01
	Mississippi	H	14.74 FQ	27.62 AW	41.42 TQ	MSBLS	10/01-12/01
	Missouri	H	13.46 FQ	23.09 AW	38.39 TQ	MOBLS	10/01-12/01
	Montana	H	13.31 FQ	22.47 AW	37.61 TQ	MTBLS	10/01-12/01
	Nebraska	H	11.78 FQ	18.62 AW	25.35 TQ	NEBLS	10/01-12/01
	Nevada	H	13.28 FQ	22.79 AW	38.34 TQ	NVBLS	10/01-12/01
	New Jersey	H	15.32 FQ	22.87 AW	28.41 TQ	NJBLS	10/01-12/01
	New York	H	15.63 FQ	25.42 AW	33.15 TQ	NYBLS	10/01-12/01
	North Carolina	H	12.71 FQ	22.14 AW	27.56 TQ	NCBLS	10/01-12/01
	North Dakota	H	16.65 FQ	22.32 AW	28.48 TQ	NDBLS	10/01-12/01
	Ohio	H	13.67 FQ	18.63 AW	26.74 TQ	OHBLS	10/01-12/01
	Oklahoma	H	16.49 FQ	22.53 AW	28.78 TQ	OKBLS	10/01-12/01
	Oregon	H	15.28 FQ	26.11 AW	37.70 TQ	ORBLS	10/01-12/01
	Pennsylvania	H	13.59 FQ	18.90 AW	22.98 TQ	PABLS	10/01-12/01

AAW	Average annual wage	**AOH**	Average offered, high	**ASH**	Average starting, high	**H**	Hourly	**M**	Monthly	**S**	Special: hourly and annual
AE	Average entry wage	**AOL**	Average offered, low	**ASL**	Average starting, low	**HI**	Highest wage paid	**MTC**	Median total compensation	**TQ**	Third quartile wage
AEX	Average experienced wage	**APH**	Average pay, high range	**AW**	Average wage paid	**HR**	High end range	**MW**	Median wage paid	**W**	Weekly
AO	Average offered	**APL**	Average pay, low range	**FQ**	First quartile wage	**LR**	Low end range	**SQ**	Second quartile wage	**Y**	Yearly

Occupation/Type/Industry	Location	Per	Low	Mid	High	Source	Date
Locomotive Engineer	South Carolina	H	16.36 FQ	23.07 AW	29.90 TQ	SCBLS	10/01-12/01
	South Dakota	H	13.75 FQ	19.07 AW	23.99 TQ	SDBLS	10/01-12/01
	Tennessee	H	11.76 FQ	18.67 AW	38.78 TQ	TNBLS	10/01-12/01
	Texas	H	13.30 FQ	19.33 AW	27.01 TQ	TXBLS	10/01-12/01
	Utah	H	17.89 FQ	22.81 AW	28.89 TQ	UTBLS	10/01-12/01
	Virginia	H	14.92 FQ	25.81 AW	38.70 TQ	VABLS	10/01-12/01
	Washington	H	13.75 FQ	22.68 AW	36.76 TQ	WABLS	10/01-12/01
	West Virginia	H	14.13 FQ	24.44 AW	38.83 TQ	WVBLS	10/01-12/01
	Wisconsin	H	14.89 FQ	26.05 AW	34.44 TQ	WIBLS	10/01-12/01
	Wyoming	H	14.50 FQ	26.80 AW	40.70 TQ	WYBLS	10/01-12/01
Locomotive Firer	Illinois	H	12.61 FQ	19.67 AW	27.54 TQ	ILBLS	10/01-12/01
	Pennsylvania	H	17.90 FQ	20.95 AW	26.33 TQ	PABLS	10/01-12/01
Lodging Manager	Alabama	Y	19730 FQ	31440 AW	45610 TQ	ALBLS	10/01-12/01
	Birmingham MSA, AL	Y	21080 FQ	33960 AW	49650 TQ	ALBLS	10/01-12/01
	Mobile MSA, AL	Y	24300 FQ	32860 AW	44990 TQ	ALBLS	10/01-12/01
	Montgomery MSA, AL	Y	23690 FQ	32990 AW	51760 TQ	ALBLS	10/01-12/01
	Alaska	Y	21790 FQ	35750 AW	51670 TQ	AKBLS	10/01-12/01
	Anchorage MSA, AK	Y	23380 FQ	31710 AW	43390 TQ	AKBLS	10/01-12/01
	Arizona	Y	18160 FQ	36360 AW	57640 TQ	AZBLS	10/01-12/01
	Phoenix-Mesa MSA, AZ	Y	19970 FQ	40230 AW	80470 TQ	AZBLS	10/01-12/01
	Tucson MSA, AZ	Y	21690 FQ	35900 AW	51820 TQ	AZBLS	10/01-12/01
	Arkansas	Y	12580 FQ	27060 AW	42560 TQ	ARBLS	10/01-12/01
	Fayetteville-Springdale-Rogers MSA, AR	Y	12360 FQ	29490 AW	43270 TQ	ARBLS	10/01-12/01
	Little Rock-North Little Rock MSA, AR	Y	20000 FQ	37340 AW	56510 TQ	ARBLS	10/01-12/01
	California	Y	25080 FQ	42250 AW	68610 TQ	CABLS	10/01-12/01
	Fresno MSA, CA	Y	23030 FQ	33540 AW	49350 TQ	CABLS	10/01-12/01
	Los Angeles-Long Beach PMSA, CA	Y	26970 FQ	43560 AW	60070 TQ	CABLS	10/01-12/01
	Oakland PMSA, CA	Y	30870 FQ	42590 AW	56630 TQ	CABLS	10/01-12/01
	Orange County PMSA, CA	Y	33380 FQ	45230 AW	63330 TQ	CABLS	10/01-12/01
	Riverside-San Bernardino PMSA, CA	Y	28170 FQ	44190 AW	75690 TQ	CABLS	10/01-12/01
	Sacramento PMSA, CA	Y	24720 FQ	36570 AW	52480 TQ	CABLS	10/01-12/01
	Salinas MSA, CA	Y	24410 FQ	37430 AW	49160 TQ	CABLS	10/01-12/01
	San Diego MSA, CA	Y	29780 FQ	55340 AW	85900 TQ	CABLS	10/01-12/01
	San Francisco PMSA, CA	Y	34640 FQ	50790 AW	82440 TQ	CABLS	10/01-12/01
	San Jose PMSA, CA	Y	24450 FQ	37490 AW	65430 TQ	CABLS	10/01-12/01
	San Luis Obispo-Atascadero-Paso Robles MSA, CA	Y	18230 FQ	28220 AW	36010 TQ	CABLS	10/01-12/01
	Santa Barbara-Santa Maria-Lompoc MSA, CA	Y	25350 FQ	39330 AW	56770 TQ	CABLS	10/01-12/01
	Santa Rosa PMSA, CA	Y	25140 FQ	43670 AW	85390 TQ	CABLS	10/01-12/01
	Vallejo-Fairfield-Napa PMSA, CA	Y	29540 FQ	44290 AW	57930 TQ	CABLS	10/01-12/01
	Ventura PMSA, CA	Y	23910 FQ	33950 AW	51430 TQ	CABLS	10/01-12/01
	Colorado	Y	21570 FQ	37080 AW	56400 TQ	COBLS	10/01-12/01
	Boulder-Longmont PMSA, CO	Y	24510 FQ	39140 AW	55570 TQ	COBLS	10/01-12/01
	Colorado Springs MSA, CO	Y	25180 FQ	37990 AW	53750 TQ	COBLS	10/01-12/01
	Denver PMSA, CO	Y	22250 FQ	35820 AW	52450 TQ	COBLS	10/01-12/01
	Connecticut	Y	25620 FQ	49600 AW	76650 TQ	CTBLS	10/01-12/01
	Hartford MSA, CT	Y	25370 FQ	48620 AW	99610 TQ	CTBLS	10/01-12/01
	New Haven-Meriden PMSA, CT	Y	20890 FQ	34440 AW	44280 TQ	CTBLS	10/01-12/01
	New London-Norwich MSA, CT-RI	Y	25250 FQ	42580 AW	71420 TQ	CTBLS	10/01-12/01
	Stamford-Norwalk PMSA, CT	Y	46610 FQ	65100 AW	76100 TQ	CTBLS	10/01-12/01
	Delaware	Y	14080 FQ	33440 AW	44520 TQ	DEBLS	10/01-12/01
	Wilmington-Newark PMSA, DE-MD	Y	13950 FQ	28740 AW	44500 TQ	DEBLS	10/01-12/01
	District of Columbia	Y	23750 FQ	43230 AW	67080 TQ	DCBLS	10/01-12/01
	Washington PMSA, DC-MD-VA-WV	Y	24410 FQ	39650 AW	62970 TQ	DCBLS	10/01-12/01
	Florida	Y	24660 FQ	43530 AW	77070 TQ	FLBLS	10/01-12/01
	Daytona Beach MSA, FL	Y	29800 FQ	50870 AW	88150 TQ	FLBLS	10/01-12/01
	Fort Lauderdale PMSA, FL	Y	25610 FQ	46230 AW	95780 TQ	FLBLS	10/01-12/01
	Fort Myers-Cape Coral MSA, FL	Y	22630 FQ	45600 AW	117470 TQ	FLBLS	10/01-12/01
	Fort Pierce-Port St. Lucie MSA, FL	Y	25460 FQ	35520 AW	54130 TQ	FLBLS	10/01-12/01

AAW Average annual wage · AE Average entry wage · AEX Average experienced wage · AO Average offered · AOH Average offered, high · AOL Average offered, low · APH Average pay, high range · APL Average pay, low range · ASH Average starting, high · ASL Average starting, low · AW Average wage paid · FQ First quartile wage · H Hourly · HI Highest wage paid · HR High end range · LR Low end range · M Monthly · MTC Median total compensation · MW Median wage paid · SQ Second quartile wage · S Special: hourly and annual · TQ Third quartile wage · W Weekly · Y Yearly

Occupation/Type/Industry	Location	Per	Low	Mid	High	Source	Date
Lodging Manager	Gainesville MSA, FL	Y	20980 FQ	42970 AW	55970 TQ	FLBLS	10/01-12/01
	Jacksonville MSA, FL	Y	31410 FQ	44770 AW	57800 TQ	FLBLS	10/01-12/01
	Miami PMSA, FL	Y	28310 FQ	37610 AW	57700 TQ	FLBLS	10/01-12/01
	Naples MSA, FL	Y	25040 FQ	37740 AW	60450 TQ	FLBLS	10/01-12/01
	Orlando MSA, FL	Y	30350 FQ	56170 AW	95150 TQ	FLBLS	10/01-12/01
	Pensacola MSA, FL	Y	24170 FQ	36140 AW	64910 TQ	FLBLS	10/01-12/01
	Sarasota-Bradenton MSA, FL	Y	32980 FQ	53450 AW	86040 TQ	FLBLS	10/01-12/01
	Tallahassee MSA, FL	Y	31360 FQ	46300 AW	60160 TQ	FLBLS	10/01-12/01
	Tampa-St. Petersburg-Clearwater MSA, FL	Y	25440 FQ	40920 AW	63760 TQ	FLBLS	10/01-12/01
	West Palm Beach-Boca Raton MSA, FL	Y	23890 FQ	39800 AW	58890 TQ	FLBLS	10/01-12/01
	Georgia	Y	23480 FQ	33530 AW	48270 TQ	GABLS	10/01-12/01
	Atlanta MSA, GA	Y	24720 FQ	35460 AW	51920 TQ	GABLS	10/01-12/01
	Augusta-Aiken MSA, GA-SC	Y	22660 FQ	32840 AW	47200 TQ	GABLS	10/01-12/01
	Macon MSA, GA	Y	20640 FQ	30220 AW	37050 TQ	GABLS	10/01-12/01
	Savannah MSA, GA	Y	23740 FQ	33700 AW	47410 TQ	GABLS	10/01-12/01
	Hawaii	Y	26780 FQ	48760 AW	72740 TQ	HIBLS	10/01-12/01
	Honolulu MSA, HI	Y	25400 FQ	45430 AW	71400 TQ	HIBLS	10/01-12/01
	Idaho	Y	12180 FQ	27370 AW	45370 TQ	IDBLS	10/01-12/01
	Boise City MSA, ID	Y	11340 FQ	20130 AW	34250 TQ	IDBLS	10/01-12/01
	Illinois	Y	16670 FQ	31810 AW	59600 TQ	ILBLS	10/01-12/01
	Chicago PMSA, IL	Y	16420 FQ	31580 AW	60600 TQ	ILBLS	10/01-12/01
	Rockford MSA, IL	Y	22780 FQ	38890 AW	62420 TQ	ILBLS	10/01-12/01
	Springfield MSA, IL	Y	17330 FQ	44010 AW	68130 TQ	ILBLS	10/01-12/01
	Indiana	Y	20050 FQ	32610 AW	50220 TQ	INBLS	10/01-12/01
	Evansville-Henderson MSA, IN-KY	Y	19680 FQ	31210 AW	44600 TQ	INBLS	10/01-12/01
	Fort Wayne MSA, IN	Y	20650 FQ	30770 AW	36300 TQ	INBLS	10/01-12/01
	Gary PMSA, IN	Y	28260 FQ	37790 AW	52320 TQ	INBLS	10/01-12/01
	Indianapolis MSA, IN	Y	19530 FQ	35180 AW	58680 TQ	INBLS	10/01-12/01
	Iowa	Y	19240 FQ	38120 AW	55310 TQ	IABLS	10/01-12/01
	Des Moines MSA, IA	Y	18330 FQ	35260 AW	53990 TQ	IABLS	10/01-12/01
	Kansas	Y	19110 FQ	27680 AW	41580 TQ	KSBLS	10/01-12/01
	Wichita MSA, KS	Y	19400 FQ	33580 AW	59190 TQ	KSBLS	10/01-12/01
	Kentucky	Y	20450 FQ	34390 AW	55070 TQ	KYBLS	10/01-12/01
	Lexington MSA, KY	Y	19850 FQ	31640 AW	48700 TQ	KYBLS	10/01-12/01
	Louisville MSA, KY-IN	Y	24200 FQ	38510 AW	61520 TQ	KYBLS	10/01-12/01
	Louisiana	Y	20780 FQ	35040 AW	55430 TQ	LABLS	10/01-12/01
	New Orleans MSA, LA	Y	28270 FQ	34640 AW	45760 TQ	LABLS	10/01-12/01
	Shreveport-Bossier City MSA, LA	Y	14620 FQ	38210 AW	67540 TQ	LABLS	10/01-12/01
	Maine	Y	19870 FQ	35350 AW	58610 TQ	MEBLS	10/01-12/01
	Portland MSA, ME	Y	25660 FQ	34310 AW	45320 TQ	MEBLS	10/01-12/01
	Maryland	Y	18880 FQ	31790 AW	45440 TQ	MDBLS	10/01-12/01
	Baltimore PMSA, MD	Y	19950 FQ	29540 AW	41610 TQ	MDBLS	10/01-12/01
	Massachusetts	Y	25150 FQ	40930 AW	59070 TQ	MABLS	10/01-12/01
	Boston PMSA, MA-NH	Y	26990 FQ	43290 AW	62540 TQ	MABLS	10/01-12/01
	Lawrence PMSA, MA-NH	Y	20910 FQ	34000 AW	52460 TQ	MABLS	10/01-12/01
	Springfield MSA, MA	Y	25550 FQ	35100 AW	43050 TQ	MABLS	10/01-12/01
	Worcester PMSA, MA-CT	Y	26620 FQ	39420 AW	64240 TQ	MABLS	10/01-12/01
	Michigan	Y	19620 FQ	34700 AW	54940 TQ	MIBLS	10/01-12/01
	Detroit PMSA, MI	Y	21070 FQ	33130 AW	45380 TQ	MIBLS	10/01-12/01
	Grand Rapids-Muskegon-Holland MSA, MI	Y	27310 FQ	39080 AW	59420 TQ	MIBLS	10/01-12/01
	Saginaw-Bay City-Midland MSA, MI	Y	24100 FQ	30860 AW	40720 TQ	MIBLS	10/01-12/01
	Minnesota	Y	17970 FQ	35320 AW	52100 TQ	MNBLS	10/01-12/01
	Minneapolis-St. Paul MSA, MN-WI	Y	24820 FQ	41350 AW	60790 TQ	MNBLS	10/01-12/01
	Mississippi	Y	19030 FQ	31150 AW	53100 TQ	MSBLS	10/01-12/01
	Biloxi-Gulfport-Pascagoula MSA, MS	Y	20130 FQ	31980 AW	62540 TQ	MSBLS	10/01-12/01
	Jackson MSA, MS	Y	23860 FQ	31800 AW	40360 TQ	MSBLS	10/01-12/01
	Missouri	Y	16170 FQ	34070 AW	52750 TQ	MOBLS	10/01-12/01
	Kansas City MSA, MO-KS	Y	19770 FQ	31440 AW	49810 TQ	MOBLS	10/01-12/01
	St. Louis MSA, MO-IL	Y	23420 FQ	36630 AW	53510 TQ	MOBLS	10/01-12/01
	Springfield MSA, MO	Y	17340 FQ	31230 AW	43660 TQ	MOBLS	10/01-12/01
	Montana	Y	12520 FQ	23100 AW	36280 TQ	MTBLS	10/01-12/01
	Nebraska	Y	16860 FQ	32310 AW	53400 TQ	NEBLS	10/01-12/01
	Lincoln MSA, NE	Y	14270 FQ	27880 AW	37590 TQ	NEBLS	10/01-12/01
	Omaha MSA, NE-IA	Y	18010 FQ	36190 AW	57120 TQ	NEBLS	10/01-12/01

AAW Average annual wage **AE** Average entry wage **AEX** Average experienced wage **AO** Average offered **AOH** Average offered, high **AOL** Average offered, low **APH** Average pay, high range **APL** Average pay, low range **ASH** Average starting, high **ASL** Average starting, low **AW** Average wage paid **FQ** First quartile wage **H** Hourly **HI** Highest wage paid **HR** High end range **LR** Low end range **M** Monthly **MTC** Median total compensation **MW** Median wage paid **SQ** Second quartile wage **S** Special: hourly and annual **TQ** Third quartile wage **W** Weekly **Y** Yearly

Occupation/Type/Industry	Location	Per	Low	Mid	High	Source	Date
Lodging Manager	Nevada	Y	25830 FQ	45850 AW	68270 TQ	NVBLS	10/01-12/01
	Las Vegas MSA, NV-AZ	Y	25300 FQ	46380 AW	69680 TQ	NVBLS	10/01-12/01
	Reno MSA, NV	Y	26580 FQ	44040 AW	66370 TQ	NVBLS	10/01-12/01
	New Hampshire	Y	16990 FQ	31530 AW	52830 TQ	NHBLS	10/01-12/01
	Portsmouth-Rochester PMSA, NH-ME	Y	21800 FQ	36080 AW	52550 TQ	NHBLS	10/01-12/01
	New Jersey	Y	29200 FQ	53110 AW	92140 TQ	NJBLS	10/01-12/01
	Atlantic-Cape May PMSA, NJ	Y	26680 FQ	54150 AW	102510 TQ	NJBLS	10/01-12/01
	Bergen-Passaic PMSA, NJ	Y	39120 FQ	66430 AW	108310 TQ	NJBLS	10/01-12/01
	Middlesex-Somerset-Hunterdon PMSA, NJ	Y	31230 FQ	55490 AW	99640 TQ	NJBLS	10/01-12/01
	Monmouth-Ocean PMSA, NJ	Y	28490 FQ	51820 AW	93450 TQ	NJBLS	10/01-12/01
	Newark PMSA, NJ	Y	25650 FQ	49540 AW	74270 TQ	NJBLS	10/01-12/01
	New Mexico	Y	19060 FQ	33170 AW	57910 TQ	NMBLS	10/01-12/01
	Albuquerque MSA, NM	Y	20950 FQ	34970 AW	63000 TQ	NMBLS	10/01-12/01
	New York	Y	24370 FQ	47500 AW	82760 TQ	NYBLS	10/01-12/01
	Albany-Schenectady-Troy MSA, NY	Y	23820 FQ	38100 AW	65780 TQ	NYBLS	10/01-12/01
	Buffalo-Niagara Falls MSA, NY	Y	22780 FQ	38020 AW	55280 TQ	NYBLS	10/01-12/01
	Nassau-Suffolk PMSA, NY	Y	31330 FQ	59250 AW		NYBLS	10/01-12/01
	New York PMSA, NY	Y	28090 FQ	57160 AW	137770 TQ	NYBLS	10/01-12/01
	Newburgh PMSA, NY-PA	Y	23440 FQ	47030 AW	72900 TQ	NYBLS	10/01-12/01
	Rochester MSA, NY	Y	24900 FQ	39320 AW	65340 TQ	NYBLS	10/01-12/01
	Syracuse MSA, NY	Y	21020 FQ	37390 AW	68140 TQ	NYBLS	10/01-12/01
	North Carolina	Y	21490 FQ	37750 AW	54600 TQ	NCBLS	10/01-12/01
	Asheville MSA, NC	Y	22220 FQ	31090 AW	43750 TQ	NCBLS	10/01-12/01
	Charlotte-Gastonia-Rock Hill MSA, NC-SC	Y	26520 FQ	43380 AW	55040 TQ	NCBLS	10/01-12/01
	Greensboro-Winston-Salem-High Point MSA, NC	Y	15810 FQ	32680 AW	53100 TQ	NCBLS	10/01-12/01
	Hickory-Morganton-Lenoir MSA, NC	Y	20660 FQ	33430 AW	50020 TQ	NCBLS	10/01-12/01
	Raleigh-Durham-Chapel Hill MSA, NC	Y	23360 FQ	47200 AW	94250 TQ	NCBLS	10/01-12/01
	Wilmington MSA, NC	Y	19410 FQ	26170 AW	40530 TQ	NCBLS	10/01-12/01
	North Dakota	Y	16630 FQ	27440 AW	39250 TQ	NDBLS	10/01-12/01
	Ohio	Y	20550 FQ	35870 AW	57490 TQ	OHBLS	10/01-12/01
	Akron PMSA, OH	Y	30200 FQ	41940 AW	54480 TQ	OHBLS	10/01-12/01
	Cincinnati PMSA, OH-KY-IN	Y	24070 FQ	36450 AW	56620 TQ	OHBLS	10/01-12/01
	Cleveland-Lorain-Elyria PMSA, OH	Y	23450 FQ	34980 AW	56200 TQ	OHBLS	10/01-12/01
	Columbus MSA, OH	Y	18160 FQ	40920 AW	68620 TQ	OHBLS	10/01-12/01
	Dayton-Springfield MSA, OH	Y	23860 FQ	33910 AW	45270 TQ	OHBLS	10/01-12/01
	Toledo MSA, OH	Y	19930 FQ	34300 AW	52960 TQ	OHBLS	10/01-12/01
	Oklahoma	Y	17500 FQ	28870 AW	51320 TQ	OKBLS	10/01-12/01
	Oklahoma City MSA, OK	Y	23570 FQ	34440 AW	55460 TQ	OKBLS	10/01-12/01
	Tulsa MSA, OK	Y	15590 FQ	25940 AW	51500 TQ	OKBLS	10/01-12/01
	Oregon	Y	22900 FQ	37460 AW	56090 TQ	ORBLS	10/01-12/01
	Eugene-Springfield MSA, OR	Y	24590 FQ	37650 AW	60980 TQ	ORBLS	10/01-12/01
	Medford-Ashland MSA, OR	Y	25240 FQ	36400 AW	62110 TQ	ORBLS	10/01-12/01
	Portland-Vancouver PMSA, OR-WA	Y	21410 FQ	35490 AW	50460 TQ	ORBLS	10/01-12/01
	Salem PMSA, OR	Y	24450 FQ	40930 AW	60600 TQ	ORBLS	10/01-12/01
	Pennsylvania	Y	17850 FQ	38020 AW	62860 TQ	PABLS	10/01-12/01
	Allentown-Bethlehem-Easton MSA, PA	Y	22540 FQ	34350 AW	51010 TQ	PABLS	10/01-12/01
	Harrisburg-Lebanon-Carlisle MSA, PA	Y	24260 FQ	38780 AW	53340 TQ	PABLS	10/01-12/01
	Lancaster MSA, PA	Y	26480 FQ	40880 AW	56310 TQ	PABLS	10/01-12/01
	Philadelphia PMSA, PA-NJ	Y	27320 FQ	45600 AW	72290 TQ	PABLS	10/01-12/01
	Pittsburgh MSA, PA	Y	13280 FQ	31870 AW	56760 TQ	PABLS	10/01-12/01
	Scranton-Wilkes-Barre-Hazleton MSA, PA	Y	23400 FQ	51880 AW		PABLS	10/01-12/01
	Rhode Island	Y	27360 FQ	45200 AW	73550 TQ	RIBLS	10/01-12/01
	Providence-Fall River-Warwick MSA, RI-MA	Y	23080 FQ	45600 AW	82880 TQ	RIBLS	10/01-12/01
	South Carolina	Y	21260 FQ	31670 AW	43650 TQ	SCBLS	10/01-12/01
	Charleston-North Charleston MSA, SC	Y	19860 FQ	30710 AW	42530 TQ	SCBLS	10/01-12/01
	Columbia MSA, SC	Y	22140 FQ	29460 AW	34740 TQ	SCBLS	10/01-12/01

AAW	Average annual wage	AOH	Average offered, high	ASH	Average starting, high	H	Hourly	M	Monthly	S	Special: hourly and annual
AE	Average entry wage	AOL	Average offered, low	ASL	Average starting, low	HI	Highest wage paid	MTC	Median total compensation	TQ	Third quartile wage
AEX	Average experienced wage	APH	Average pay, high range	AW	Average wage paid	HR	High end range	MW	Median wage paid	W	Weekly
AO	Average offered	APL	Average pay, low range	FQ	First quartile wage	LR	Low end range	SQ	Second quartile wage	Y	Yearly

Occupation/Type/Industry	Location	Per	Low	Mid	High	Source	Date
Lodging Manager	Greenville-Spartanburg-Anderson MSA, SC	Y	20930 FQ	30300 AW	42710 TQ	SCBLS	10/01-12/01
	Myrtle Beach MSA, SC	Y	22130 FQ	32280 AW	44040 TQ	SCBLS	10/01-12/01
	South Dakota	Y	31310 FQ	39470 AW	46940 TQ	SDBLS	10/01-12/01
	Sioux Falls MSA, SD	Y	31350 FQ	40530 AW	51710 TQ	SDBLS	10/01-12/01
	Tennessee	Y	17660 FQ	32840 AW	49290 TQ	TNBLS	10/01-12/01
	Chattanooga MSA, TN-GA	Y	20080 FQ	32260 AW	45660 TQ	TNBLS	10/01-12/01
	Johnson City-Kingsport-Bristol MSA, TN-VA	Y	16390 FQ	26070 AW	44390 TQ	TNBLS	10/01-12/01
	Knoxville MSA, TN	Y	16100 FQ	28450 AW	42290 TQ	TNBLS	10/01-12/01
	Memphis MSA, TN-AR-MS	Y	14650 FQ	30290 AW	46740 TQ	TNBLS	10/01-12/01
	Nashville MSA, TN	Y	22840 FQ	36810 AW	58790 TQ	TNBLS	10/01-12/01
	Texas	Y	18480 FQ	31640 AW	48280 TQ	TXBLS	10/01-12/01
	Austin-San Marcos MSA, TX	Y	14160 FQ	33510 AW	44910 TQ	TXBLS	10/01-12/01
	Brownsville-Harlingen-San Benito MSA, TX	Y	13870 FQ	25820 AW	40330 TQ	TXBLS	10/01-12/01
	Corpus Christi MSA, TX	Y	20340 FQ	32910 AW	51320 TQ	TXBLS	10/01-12/01
	Dallas PMSA, TX	Y	18660 FQ	29740 AW	38660 TQ	TXBLS	10/01-12/01
	El Paso MSA, TX	Y	16330 FQ	26790 AW	36730 TQ	TXBLS	10/01-12/01
	Fort Worth-Arlington PMSA, TX	Y	18950 FQ	34870 AW	55270 TQ	TXBLS	10/01-12/01
	Galveston-Texas City PMSA, TX	Y	20240 FQ	33160 AW	52140 TQ	TXBLS	10/01-12/01
	Houston PMSA, TX	Y	22350 FQ	34330 AW	54000 TQ	TXBLS	10/01-12/01
	Lubbock MSA, TX	Y	24930 FQ	33600 AW	51240 TQ	TXBLS	10/01-12/01
	McAllen-Edinburg-Mission MSA, TX	Y	16650 FQ	28620 AW	42350 TQ	TXBLS	10/01-12/01
	San Antonio MSA, TX	Y	21870 FQ	30490 AW	39840 TQ	TXBLS	10/01-12/01
	Utah	Y	22450 FQ	34050 AW	53320 TQ	UTBLS	10/01-12/01
	Provo-Orem MSA, UT	Y	19980 FQ	31500 AW	49580 TQ	UTBLS	10/01-12/01
	Salt Lake City-Ogden MSA, UT	Y	25210 FQ	37240 AW	55820 TQ	UTBLS	10/01-12/01
	Vermont	Y	28360 FQ	55890 AW		VTBLS	10/01-12/01
	Virginia	Y	20540 FQ	35100 AW	54690 TQ	VABLS	10/01-12/01
	Norfolk-Virginia Beach-Newport News MSA, VA-NC	Y	17970 FQ	32850 AW	46060 TQ	VABLS	10/01-12/01
	Richmond-Petersburg MSA, VA	Y	24040 FQ	35130 AW	55120 TQ	VABLS	10/01-12/01
	Roanoke MSA, VA	Y	20050 FQ	28790 AW	37660 TQ	VABLS	10/01-12/01
	Washington	Y	26500 FQ	57960 AW	93970 TQ	WABLS	10/01-12/01
	Seattle-Bellevue-Everett PMSA, WA	Y	28910 FQ	65430 AW	92940 TQ	WABLS	10/01-12/01
	Tacoma PMSA, WA	Y	26430 FQ	46420 AW	69050 TQ	WABLS	10/01-12/01
	West Virginia	Y	16400 FQ	28080 AW	42060 TQ	WVBLS	10/01-12/01
	Charleston MSA, WV	Y	18590 FQ	25320 AW	40890 TQ	WVBLS	10/01-12/01
	Huntington-Ashland MSA, WV-KY-OH	Y	20340 FQ	30890 AW	49190 TQ	WVBLS	10/01-12/01
	Wisconsin	Y	20030 FQ	33170 AW	55030 TQ	WIBLS	10/01-12/01
	Appleton-Oshkosh-Neenah MSA, WI	Y	24020 FQ	36310 AW	53490 TQ	WIBLS	10/01-12/01
	Green Bay MSA, WI	Y	24800 FQ	33470 AW	45380 TQ	WIBLS	10/01-12/01
	Madison MSA, WI	Y	22350 FQ	42810 AW	66070 TQ	WIBLS	10/01-12/01
	Milwaukee-Waukesha PMSA, WI	Y	23240 FQ	41170 AW	73470 TQ	WIBLS	10/01-12/01
	Wyoming	Y	15940 FQ	29630 AW	43470 TQ	WYBLS	10/01-12/01
	Puerto Rico	Y	20610 FQ	41060 AW	95540 TQ	PRBLS	10/01-12/01
	Virgin Islands	Y	30410 FQ	47610 AW	74190 TQ	VIBLS	10/01-12/01
Log Grader and Scaler	Alabama	H	7.11 FQ	10.44 AW	15.92 TQ	ALBLS	10/01-12/01
	Arkansas	H	8.12 FQ	12.25 AW	16.78 TQ	ARBLS	10/01-12/01
	California	H	13.13 FQ	17.15 AW	21.56 TQ	CABLS	10/01-12/01
	Florida	H	7.54 FQ	11.45 AW	17.76 TQ	FLBLS	10/01-12/01
	Georgia	H	9.12 FQ	12.16 AW	18.79 TQ	GABLS	10/01-12/01
	Idaho	H	12.55 FQ	15.67 AW	18.34 TQ	IDBLS	10/01-12/01
	Indiana	H	9.09 FQ	16.48 AW	29.91 TQ	INBLS	10/01-12/01
	Kentucky	H	7.82 FQ	13.93 AW	20.21 TQ	KYBLS	10/01-12/01
	Louisiana	H	9.10 FQ	12.28 AW	15.97 TQ	LABLS	10/01-12/01
	Maine	H	10.37 FQ	13.97 AW	19.53 TQ	MEBLS	10/01-12/01
	Michigan	H	9.40 FQ	14.35 AW	19.08 TQ	MIBLS	10/01-12/01
	Minnesota	H	9.68 FQ	15.23 AW	21.78 TQ	MNBLS	10/01-12/01
	Mississippi	H	9.34 FQ	13.78 AW	23.19 TQ	MSBLS	10/01-12/01
	Missouri	H	8.98 FQ	12.41 AW	19.28 TQ	MOBLS	10/01-12/01

AAW Average annual wage	**AOH** Average offered, high	**ASH** Average starting, high	**H** Hourly	**M** Monthly	**S** Special: hourly and annual
AE Average entry wage	**AOL** Average offered, low	**ASL** Average starting, low	**HI** Highest wage paid	**MTC** Median total compensation	**TQ** Third quartile wage
AEX Average experienced wage	**APH** Average pay, high range	**AW** Average wage paid	**HR** High end range	**MW** Median wage paid	**W** Weekly
AO Average offered	**APL** Average pay, low range	**FQ** First quartile wage	**LR** Low end range	**SQ** Second quartile wage	**Y** Yearly

Occupation/Type/Industry	Location	Per	Low	Mid	High	Source	Date
Log Grader and Scaler	Montana	H	10.16 FQ	14.25 AW	19.52 TQ	MTBLS	10/01-12/01
	New Hampshire	H	10.95 FQ	13.87 AW	17.27 TQ	NHBLS	10/01-12/01
	New York	H	8.80 FQ	15.42 AW	25.26 TQ	NYBLS	10/01-12/01
	North Carolina	H	8.52 FQ	13.99 AW	20.67 TQ	NCBLS	10/01-12/01
	Ohio	H	6.63 FQ	14.72 AW	22.98 TQ	OHBLS	10/01-12/01
	Oregon	H	11.65 FQ	17.74 AW	24.70 TQ	ORBLS	10/01-12/01
	Pennsylvania	H	6.75 FQ	12.21 AW	17.40 TQ	PABLS	10/01-12/01
	South Carolina	H	7.77 FQ	11.50 AW	15.29 TQ	SCBLS	10/01-12/01
	Tennessee	H	8.29 FQ	14.90 AW	24.77 TQ	TNBLS	10/01-12/01
	Texas	H	8.42 FQ	12.88 AW	17.39 TQ	TXBLS	10/01-12/01
	Vermont	H	11.37 FQ	13.53 AW	17.32 TQ	VTBLS	10/01-12/01
	Virginia	H	9.19 FQ	14.50 AW	19.35 TQ	VABLS	10/01-12/01
	Washington	H	12.14 FQ	16.64 AW	22.40 TQ	WABLS	10/01-12/01
	West Virginia	H	7.55 FQ	11.84 AW	16.64 TQ	WVBLS	10/01-12/01
	Wisconsin	H	7.32 FQ	12.82 AW	20.81 TQ	WIBLS	10/01-12/01
Logging Equipment Operator	Alabama	H	7.73 FQ	12.08 AW	16.66 TQ	ALBLS	10/01-12/01
	Alaska	H	15.24 FQ	19.69 AW	23.04 TQ	AKBLS	10/01-12/01
	Arizona	H	7.71 FQ	12.38 AW	20.97 TQ	AZBLS	10/01-12/01
	Arkansas	H	5.80 FQ	9.94 AW	15.60 TQ	ARBLS	10/01-12/01
	California	H	11.03 FQ	15.52 AW	20.12 TQ	CABLS	10/01-12/01
	Colorado	H	9.39 FQ	16.84 AW	21.29 TQ	COBLS	10/01-12/01
	Florida	H	7.74 FQ	12.08 AW	17.43 TQ	FLBLS	10/01-12/01
	Georgia	H	7.36 FQ	11.52 AW	16.79 TQ	GABLS	10/01-12/01
	Idaho	H	12.47 FQ	18.49 AW	27.97 TQ	IDBLS	10/01-12/01
	Illinois	H	9.20 FQ	12.20 AW	15.95 TQ	ILBLS	10/01-12/01
	Indiana	H	7.79 FQ	10.98 AW	13.87 TQ	INBLS	10/01-12/01
	Kentucky	H	7.19 FQ	9.73 AW	13.05 TQ	KYBLS	10/01-12/01
	Louisiana	H	9.73 FQ	13.89 AW	17.55 TQ	LABLS	10/01-12/01
	Maine	H	9.32 FQ	12.05 AW	16.30 TQ	MEBLS	10/01-12/01
	Maryland	H	10.07 FQ	14.07 AW	20.61 TQ	MDBLS	10/01-12/01
	Michigan	H	8.95 FQ	11.23 AW	15.63 TQ	MIBLS	10/01-12/01
	Minnesota	H	7.49 FQ	12.09 AW	16.79 TQ	MNBLS	10/01-12/01
	Mississippi	H	9.00 FQ	11.95 AW	16.24 TQ	MSBLS	10/01-12/01
	Missouri	H	7.28 FQ	9.49 AW	12.52 TQ	MOBLS	10/01-12/01
	Montana	H	12.54 FQ	15.50 AW	18.14 TQ	MTBLS	10/01-12/01
	New Hampshire	H	8.34 FQ	14.06 AW	17.25 TQ	NHBLS	10/01-12/01
	New Mexico	H	5.79 FQ	10.03 AW	13.66 TQ	NMBLS	10/01-12/01
	New York	H	9.55 FQ	14.15 AW	17.57 TQ	NYBLS	10/01-12/01
	North Carolina	H	8.81 FQ	12.70 AW	17.84 TQ	NCBLS	10/01-12/01
	Ohio	H	9.29 FQ	11.35 AW	13.52 TQ	OHBLS	10/01-12/01
	Oklahoma	H	6.35 FQ	14.17 AW	22.44 TQ	OKBLS	10/01-12/01
	Oregon	H	12.67 FQ	16.66 AW	21.59 TQ	ORBLS	10/01-12/01
	Pennsylvania	H	8.68 FQ	13.00 AW	21.49 TQ	PABLS	10/01-12/01
	South Carolina	H	8.73 FQ	12.71 AW	18.86 TQ	SCBLS	10/01-12/01
	South Dakota	H	8.85 FQ	14.02 AW	17.85 TQ	SDBLS	10/01-12/01
	Tennessee	H	8.25 FQ	12.22 AW	16.60 TQ	TNBLS	10/01-12/01
	Texas	H	8.34 FQ	12.89 AW	17.02 TQ	TXBLS	10/01-12/01
	Utah	H	7.76 FQ	11.88 AW	17.64 TQ	UTBLS	10/01-12/01
	Vermont	H	9.38 FQ	12.51 AW	16.69 TQ	VTBLS	10/01-12/01
	Virginia	H	6.34 FQ	10.32 AW	13.81 TQ	VABLS	10/01-12/01
	Washington	H	13.10 FQ	17.51 AW	21.72 TQ	WABLS	10/01-12/01
	West Virginia	H	7.79 FQ	10.85 AW	13.71 TQ	WVBLS	10/01-12/01
	Wisconsin	H	7.60 FQ	12.01 AW	17.26 TQ	WIBLS	10/01-12/01
	Wyoming	H	11.18 FQ	15.13 AW	17.72 TQ	WYBLS	10/01-12/01
Longshoreman							
Experienced	West	Y		167000 Y		VIRPIL	10/1/02
Full time	West	Y		80000 Y		VIRPIL	10/1/02
Machine Feeder and Offbearer	Alabama	H	6.54 FQ	11.80 AW	20.41 TQ	ALBLS	10/01-12/01
	Huntsville MSA, AL	H	6.50 FQ	12.88 AW	21.43 TQ	ALBLS	10/01-12/01
	Mobile MSA, AL	H	6.86 FQ	10.07 AW	13.08 TQ	ALBLS	10/01-12/01
	Montgomery MSA, AL	H	6.27 FQ	10.97 AW	18.73 TQ	ALBLS	10/01-12/01
	Arizona	H	5.97 FQ	8.77 AW	13.59 TQ	AZBLS	10/01-12/01
	Phoenix-Mesa MSA, AZ	H	6.27 FQ	9.69 AW	14.45 TQ	AZBLS	10/01-12/01
	Arkansas	H	7.51 FQ	12.00 AW	16.34 TQ	ARBLS	10/01-12/01
	Fayetteville-Springdale-Rogers MSA, AR	H	7.33 FQ	9.67 AW	13.35 TQ	ARBLS	10/01-12/01
	Little Rock-North Little Rock MSA, AR	H	8.17 FQ	12.02 AW	17.14 TQ	ARBLS	10/01-12/01
	California	H	7.03 FQ	10.21 AW	14.85 TQ	CABLS	10/01-12/01
	Bakersfield MSA, CA	H	7.09 FQ	9.22 AW	15.01 TQ	CABLS	10/01-12/01

AAW	Average annual wage	**AOH**	Average offered, high	**ASH**	Average starting, high	**H**	Hourly	**M**	Monthly	**S**	Special: hourly and annual
AE	Average entry wage	**AOL**	Average offered, low	**ASL**	Average starting, low	**HI**	Highest wage paid	**MTC**	Median total compensation	**TQ**	Third quartile wage
AEX	Average experienced wage	**APH**	Average pay, high range	**AW**	Average wage paid	**HR**	High end range	**MW**	Median wage paid	**W**	Weekly
AO	Average offered	**APL**	Average pay, low range	**FQ**	First quartile wage	**LR**	Low end range	**SQ**	Second quartile wage	**Y**	Yearly

Occupation/Type/Industry	Location	Per	Low	Mid	High	Source	Date
Machine Feeder and Offbearer	Chico-Paradise MSA, CA	H	6.56 FQ	9.48 AW	15.65 TQ	CABLS	10/01-12/01
	Fresno MSA, CA	H	6.73 FQ	9.42 AW	13.35 TQ	CABLS	10/01-12/01
	Los Angeles-Long Beach PMSA, CA	H	7.11 FQ	9.91 AW	13.57 TQ	CABLS	10/01-12/01
	Merced MSA, CA	H	7.44 FQ	11.23 AW	14.30 TQ	CABLS	10/01-12/01
	Modesto MSA, CA	H	7.71 FQ	14.48 AW	20.47 TQ	CABLS	10/01-12/01
	Oakland PMSA, CA	H	6.55 FQ	9.72 AW	16.08 TQ	CABLS	10/01-12/01
	Orange County PMSA, CA	H	6.84 FQ	10.31 AW	17.66 TQ	CABLS	10/01-12/01
	Redding MSA, CA	H	7.57 FQ	14.06 AW	20.51 TQ	CABLS	10/01-12/01
	Riverside-San Bernardino PMSA, CA	H	6.95 FQ	10.34 AW	15.28 TQ	CABLS	10/01-12/01
	Sacramento PMSA, CA	H	7.02 FQ	9.91 AW	15.39 TQ	CABLS	10/01-12/01
	Salinas MSA, CA	H	8.21 FQ	11.53 AW	14.04 TQ	CABLS	10/01-12/01
	San Diego MSA, CA	H	6.88 FQ	8.23 AW	10.13 TQ	CABLS	10/01-12/01
	San Francisco PMSA, CA	H	6.74 FQ	11.60 AW	17.66 TQ	CABLS	10/01-12/01
	San Jose PMSA, CA	H	8.60 FQ	13.14 AW	16.85 TQ	CABLS	10/01-12/01
	Stockton-Lodi MSA, CA	H	7.89 FQ	13.05 AW	17.67 TQ	CABLS	10/01-12/01
	Vallejo-Fairfield-Napa PMSA, CA	H	7.21 FQ	11.70 AW	16.59 TQ	CABLS	10/01-12/01
	Visalia-Tulare-Porterville MSA, CA	H	6.62 FQ	9.77 AW	15.18 TQ	CABLS	10/01-12/01
	Colorado	H	7.65 FQ	10.81 AW	15.07 TQ	COBLS	10/01-12/01
	Boulder-Longmont PMSA, CO	H	7.62 FQ	10.97 AW	16.54 TQ	COBLS	10/01-12/01
	Colorado Springs MSA, CO	H	7.37 FQ	9.12 AW	11.19 TQ	COBLS	10/01-12/01
	Denver PMSA, CO	H	8.68 FQ	11.29 AW	14.64 TQ	COBLS	10/01-12/01
	Connecticut	H	7.53 FQ	10.43 AW	14.14 TQ	CTBLS	10/01-12/01
	Bridgeport PMSA, CT	H	7.56 FQ	9.15 AW	12.66 TQ	CTBLS	10/01-12/01
	Danbury PMSA, CT	H	10.82 FQ	13.80 AW	18.57 TQ	CTBLS	10/01-12/01
	Hartford MSA, CT	H	7.83 FQ	11.82 AW	14.62 TQ	CTBLS	10/01-12/01
	New Haven-Meriden PMSA, CT	H	7.42 FQ	9.73 AW	12.48 TQ	CTBLS	10/01-12/01
	Waterbury PMSA, CT	H	7.26 FQ	9.29 AW	11.46 TQ	CTBLS	10/01-12/01
	Delaware	H	9.01 FQ	12.62 AW	17.30 TQ	DEBLS	10/01-12/01
	Wilmington-Newark PMSA, DE-MD	H	9.14 FQ	13.02 AW	17.63 TQ	DEBLS	10/01-12/01
	Washington PMSA, DC-MD-VA-WV	H	7.78 FQ	11.82 AW	18.12 TQ	DCBLS	10/01-12/01
	Florida	H	6.43 FQ	9.02 AW	12.80 TQ	FLBLS	10/01-12/01
	Daytona Beach MSA, FL	H	5.97 FQ	9.54 AW	15.67 TQ	FLBLS	10/01-12/01
	Fort Lauderdale PMSA, FL	H	6.22 FQ	8.66 AW	13.33 TQ	FLBLS	10/01-12/01
	Fort Pierce-Port St. Lucie MSA, FL	H	10.08 FQ	12.99 AW	16.21 TQ	FLBLS	10/01-12/01
	Jacksonville MSA, FL	H	7.13 FQ	9.29 AW	12.74 TQ	FLBLS	10/01-12/01
	Lakeland-Winter Haven MSA, FL	H	7.67 FQ	12.13 AW	15.67 TQ	FLBLS	10/01-12/01
	Miami PMSA, FL	H	5.72 FQ	6.93 AW	9.45 TQ	FLBLS	10/01-12/01
	Ocala MSA, FL	H	7.12 FQ	8.37 AW	10.47 TQ	FLBLS	10/01-12/01
	Orlando MSA, FL	H	7.64 FQ	10.26 AW	13.46 TQ	FLBLS	10/01-12/01
	Sarasota-Bradenton MSA, FL	H	6.76 FQ	8.92 AW	12.42 TQ	FLBLS	10/01-12/01
	Tallahassee MSA, FL	H	6.49 FQ	8.68 AW	10.84 TQ	FLBLS	10/01-12/01
	Tampa-St. Petersburg-Clearwater MSA, FL	H	6.90 FQ	9.19 AW	12.82 TQ	FLBLS	10/01-12/01
	Georgia	H	6.97 FQ	10.05 AW	13.65 TQ	GABLS	10/01-12/01
	Atlanta MSA, GA	H	7.22 FQ	10.64 AW	15.30 TQ	GABLS	10/01-12/01
	Augusta-Aiken MSA, GA-SC	H	8.08 FQ	10.04 AW	13.19 TQ	GABLS	10/01-12/01
	Columbus MSA, GA-AL	H	7.49 FQ	10.42 AW	14.12 TQ	GABLS	10/01-12/01
	Macon MSA, GA	H	5.93 FQ	14.22 AW	21.52 TQ	GABLS	10/01-12/01
	Savannah MSA, GA	H	7.60 FQ	11.89 AW	16.43 TQ	GABLS	10/01-12/01
	Hawaii	H	7.71 FQ	12.50 AW	20.57 TQ	HIBLS	10/01-12/01
	Honolulu MSA, HI	H	7.54 FQ	12.51 AW	20.15 TQ	HIBLS	10/01-12/01
	Idaho	H	7.20 FQ	11.44 AW	16.10 TQ	IDBLS	10/01-12/01
	Boise City MSA, ID	H	6.94 FQ	9.58 AW	12.37 TQ	IDBLS	10/01-12/01
	Illinois	H	7.33 FQ	11.31 AW	17.29 TQ	ILBLS	10/01-12/01
	Chicago PMSA, IL	H	7.46 FQ	11.47 AW	17.03 TQ	ILBLS	10/01-12/01
	Rockford MSA, IL	H	7.46 FQ	11.13 AW	16.92 TQ	ILBLS	10/01-12/01
	Indiana	H	7.65 FQ	11.69 AW	18.28 TQ	INBLS	10/01-12/01
	Elkhart-Goshen MSA, IN	H	7.78 FQ	10.73 AW	13.76 TQ	INBLS	10/01-12/01
	Evansville-Henderson MSA, IN-KY	H	8.54 FQ	11.01 AW	13.36 TQ	INBLS	10/01-12/01
	Fort Wayne MSA, IN	H	8.85 FQ	11.03 AW	13.42 TQ	INBLS	10/01-12/01
	Gary PMSA, IN	H	7.37 FQ	16.79 AW	22.85 TQ	INBLS	10/01-12/01
	Indianapolis MSA, IN	H	7.47 FQ	10.79 AW	14.20 TQ	INBLS	10/01-12/01

AAW Average annual wage **AOH** Average offered, high **ASH** Average starting, high **H** Hourly **M** Monthly **S** Special: hourly and annual
AE Average entry wage **AOL** Average offered, low **ASL** Average starting, low **HI** Highest wage paid **MTC** Median total compensation **TQ** Third quartile wage
AEX Average experienced wage **APH** Average pay, high range **AW** Average wage paid **HR** High end range **MW** Median wage paid **W** Weekly
AO Average offered **APL** Average pay, low range **FQ** First quartile wage **LR** Low end range **SQ** Second quartile wage **Y** Yearly

Occupation/Type/Industry	Location	Per	Low	Mid	High	Source	Date
Machine Feeder and Offbearer	Lafayette MSA, IN	H	6.59 FQ	10.13 AW	13.36 TQ	INBLS	10/01-12/01
	South Bend MSA, IN	H	6.48 FQ	9.32 AW	11.47 TQ	INBLS	10/01-12/01
	Iowa	H	7.18 FQ	9.59 AW	13.41 TQ	IABLS	10/01-12/01
	Davenport-Moline-Rock Island MSA, IA-IL	H	6.66 FQ	10.91 AW	14.60 TQ	IABLS	10/01-12/01
	Des Moines MSA, IA	H	8.97 FQ	11.17 AW	14.49 TQ	IABLS	10/01-12/01
	Kansas	H	7.56 FQ	11.65 AW	18.00 TQ	KSBLS	10/01-12/01
	Topeka MSA, KS	H	9.03 FQ	13.58 AW	17.69 TQ	KSBLS	10/01-12/01
	Wichita MSA, KS	H	7.63 FQ	10.64 AW	14.56 TQ	KSBLS	10/01-12/01
	Kentucky	H	7.20 FQ	10.29 AW	14.46 TQ	KYBLS	10/01-12/01
	Lexington MSA, KY	H	7.67 FQ	10.65 AW	14.95 TQ	KYBLS	10/01-12/01
	Louisville MSA, KY-IN	H	6.79 FQ	11.46 AW	16.50 TQ	KYBLS	10/01-12/01
	Louisiana	H	5.90 FQ	9.78 AW	14.00 TQ	LABLS	10/01-12/01
	Baton Rouge MSA, LA	H	6.86 FQ	7.70 AW	8.74 TQ	LABLS	10/01-12/01
	Houma MSA, LA	H	5.84 FQ	8.10 AW	10.46 TQ	LABLS	10/01-12/01
	Lafayette MSA, LA	H	6.00 FQ	10.04 AW	13.63 TQ	LABLS	10/01-12/01
	New Orleans MSA, LA	H	5.77 FQ	7.98 AW	11.33 TQ	LABLS	10/01-12/01
	Shreveport-Bossier City MSA, LA	H	5.99 FQ	12.55 AW	20.78 TQ	LABLS	10/01-12/01
	Maine	H	7.46 FQ	10.05 AW	13.14 TQ	MEBLS	10/01-12/01
	Maryland	H	7.17 FQ	10.17 AW	13.67 TQ	MDBLS	10/01-12/01
	Baltimore PMSA, MD	H	7.36 FQ	10.62 AW	14.12 TQ	MDBLS	10/01-12/01
	Massachusetts	H	7.83 FQ	11.55 AW	16.11 TQ	MABLS	10/01-12/01
	Boston PMSA, MA-NH	H	9.08 FQ	12.90 AW	17.83 TQ	MABLS	10/01-12/01
	Brockton PMSA, MA	H	7.57 FQ	11.15 AW	15.68 TQ	MABLS	10/01-12/01
	Lawrence PMSA, MA-NH	H	7.06 FQ	10.39 AW	15.25 TQ	MABLS	10/01-12/01
	Lowell PMSA, MA-NH	H	8.44 FQ	11.67 AW	15.31 TQ	MABLS	10/01-12/01
	New Bedford PMSA, MA	H	6.88 FQ	8.70 AW	12.09 TQ	MABLS	10/01-12/01
	Springfield MSA, MA	H	7.44 FQ	10.31 AW	13.23 TQ	MABLS	10/01-12/01
	Worcester PMSA, MA-CT	H	8.60 FQ	11.81 AW	16.13 TQ	MABLS	10/01-12/01
	Michigan	H	7.28 FQ	14.15 AW	26.58 TQ	MIBLS	10/01-12/01
	Ann Arbor PMSA, MI	H	7.59 FQ	10.67 AW	13.77 TQ	MIBLS	10/01-12/01
	Detroit PMSA, MI	H	7.54 FQ	11.45 AW	16.76 TQ	MIBLS	10/01-12/01
	Flint PMSA, MI	H	5.81 FQ	18.02 AW	28.22 TQ	MIBLS	10/01-12/01
	Grand Rapids-Muskegon-Holland MSA, MI	H	8.79 FQ	19.33 AW	28.42 TQ	MIBLS	10/01-12/01
	Kalamazoo-Battle Creek MSA, MI	H	9.39 FQ	12.00 AW	14.00 TQ	MIBLS	10/01-12/01
	Lansing-East Lansing MSA, MI	H	7.42 FQ	9.85 AW	15.45 TQ	MIBLS	10/01-12/01
	Saginaw-Bay City-Midland MSA, MI	H	6.78 FQ	10.21 AW	13.48 TQ	MIBLS	10/01-12/01
	Minnesota	H	8.99 FQ	12.65 AW	18.48 TQ	MNBLS	10/01-12/01
	Minneapolis-St. Paul MSA, MN-WI	H	9.47 FQ	13.43 AW	19.16 TQ	MNBLS	10/01-12/01
	St. Cloud MSA, MN	H	6.73 FQ	9.02 AW	11.41 TQ	MNBLS	10/01-12/01
	Mississippi	H	5.91 FQ	9.13 AW	13.01 TQ	MSBLS	10/01-12/01
	Jackson MSA, MS	H	6.74 FQ	9.57 AW	13.22 TQ	MSBLS	10/01-12/01
	Missouri	H	7.47 FQ	10.96 AW	13.99 TQ	MOBLS	10/01-12/01
	Kansas City MSA, MO-KS	H	7.53 FQ	12.01 AW	18.33 TQ	MOBLS	10/01-12/01
	St. Louis MSA, MO-IL	H	7.95 FQ	12.05 AW	17.51 TQ	MOBLS	10/01-12/01
	Springfield MSA, MO	H	7.60 FQ	12.00 AW	16.54 TQ	MOBLS	10/01-12/01
	Montana	H	6.48 FQ	10.45 AW	15.40 TQ	MTBLS	10/01-12/01
	Nebraska	H	7.23 FQ	9.73 AW	13.50 TQ	NEBLS	10/01-12/01
	Omaha MSA, NE-IA	H	7.23 FQ	9.34 AW	12.61 TQ	NEBLS	10/01-12/01
	Reno MSA, NV	H	7.63 FQ	9.57 AW	11.22 TQ	NVBLS	10/01-12/01
	New Hampshire	H	7.61 FQ	10.38 AW	13.51 TQ	NHBLS	10/01-12/01
	Manchester PMSA, NH	H	7.47 FQ	9.53 AW	12.39 TQ	NHBLS	10/01-12/01
	Nashua PMSA, NH	H	9.46 FQ	12.29 AW	15.56 TQ	NHBLS	10/01-12/01
	Portsmouth-Rochester PMSA, NH-ME	H	7.81 FQ	10.37 AW	13.22 TQ	NHBLS	10/01-12/01
	New Jersey	H	6.08 FQ	9.83 AW	14.99 TQ	NJBLS	10/01-12/01
	Atlantic-Cape May PMSA, NJ	H	8.61 FQ	11.80 AW	17.07 TQ	NJBLS	10/01-12/01
	Bergen-Passaic PMSA, NJ	H	5.97 FQ	8.95 AW	12.79 TQ	NJBLS	10/01-12/01
	Jersey City PMSA, NJ	H	7.34 FQ	9.59 AW	12.98 TQ	NJBLS	10/01-12/01
	Middlesex-Somerset-Hunterdon PMSA, NJ	H	6.27 FQ	10.29 AW	16.82 TQ	NJBLS	10/01-12/01
	Monmouth-Ocean PMSA, NJ	H	5.54 FQ	7.57 AW	10.20 TQ	NJBLS	10/01-12/01
	Newark PMSA, NJ	H	5.87 FQ	9.71 AW	15.54 TQ	NJBLS	10/01-12/01
	Trenton PMSA, NJ	H	6.85 FQ	9.92 AW	14.96 TQ	NJBLS	10/01-12/01
	Albuquerque MSA, NM	H	7.23 FQ	8.91 AW	10.92 TQ	NMBLS	10/01-12/01
	New York	H	7.22 FQ	10.67 AW	15.83 TQ	NYBLS	10/01-12/01

AAW	Average annual wage	**AOH**	Average offered, high	**ASH**	Average starting, high	**H**	Hourly	**M**	Monthly	**S**	Special: hourly and annual
AE	Average entry wage	**AOL**	Average offered, low	**ASL**	Average starting, low	**HI**	Highest wage paid	**MTC**	Median total compensation	**TQ**	Third quartile wage
AEX	Average experienced wage	**APH**	Average pay, high range	**AW**	Average wage paid	**HR**	High end range	**MW**	Median wage paid	**W**	Weekly
AO	Average offered	**APL**	Average pay, low range	**FQ**	First quartile wage	**LR**	Low end range	**SQ**	Second quartile wage	**Y**	Yearly

Occupation/Type/Industry	Location	Per	Low	Mid	High	Source	Date
Machine Feeder and Offbearer	Albany-Schenectady-Troy MSA, NY	H	7.51 FQ	10.04 AW	13.07 TQ	NYBLS	10/01-12/01
	Binghamton MSA, NY	H	7.39 FQ	10.74 AW	15.78 TQ	NYBLS	10/01-12/01
	Buffalo-Niagara Falls MSA, NY	H	9.30 FQ	12.66 AW	18.67 TQ	NYBLS	10/01-12/01
	Nassau-Suffolk PMSA, NY	H	6.30 FQ	9.71 AW	15.29 TQ	NYBLS	10/01-12/01
	New York PMSA, NY	H	7.09 FQ	10.00 AW	16.28 TQ	NYBLS	10/01-12/01
	Rochester MSA, NY	H	8.06 FQ	10.86 AW	13.82 TQ	NYBLS	10/01-12/01
	Syracuse MSA, NY	H	9.72 FQ	13.72 AW	18.02 TQ	NYBLS	10/01-12/01
	Utica-Rome MSA, NY	H	8.46 FQ	10.16 AW	12.79 TQ	NYBLS	10/01-12/01
	North Carolina	H	7.33 FQ	10.30 AW	13.52 TQ	NCBLS	10/01-12/01
	Asheville MSA, NC	H	7.25 FQ	8.61 AW	10.59 TQ	NCBLS	10/01-12/01
	Charlotte-Gastonia-Rock Hill MSA, NC-SC	H	7.80 FQ	11.39 AW	14.39 TQ	NCBLS	10/01-12/01
	Fayetteville MSA, NC	H	6.63 FQ	9.82 AW	14.92 TQ	NCBLS	10/01-12/01
	Greensboro-Winston-Salem-High Point MSA, NC	H	7.38 FQ	10.34 AW	15.08 TQ	NCBLS	10/01-12/01
	Hickory-Morganton-Lenoir MSA, NC	H	7.86 FQ	9.80 AW	11.63 TQ	NCBLS	10/01-12/01
	Raleigh-Durham-Chapel Hill MSA, NC	H	7.26 FQ	9.54 AW	12.77 TQ	NCBLS	10/01-12/01
	Wilmington MSA, NC	H	5.94 FQ	9.33 AW	15.98 TQ	NCBLS	10/01-12/01
	North Dakota	H	6.18 FQ	9.28 AW	13.54 TQ	NDBLS	10/01-12/01
	Fargo-Moorhead MSA, ND-MN	H	6.41 FQ	9.74 AW	13.70 TQ	NDBLS	10/01-12/01
	Ohio	H	7.82 FQ	13.44 AW	23.47 TQ	OHBLS	10/01-12/01
	Akron PMSA, OH	H	7.47 FQ	10.25 AW	16.08 TQ	OHBLS	10/01-12/01
	Canton-Massillon MSA, OH	H	7.57 FQ	10.17 AW	12.48 TQ	OHBLS	10/01-12/01
	Cincinnati PMSA, OH-KY-IN	H	8.54 FQ	11.48 AW	16.40 TQ	OHBLS	10/01-12/01
	Cleveland-Lorain-Elyria PMSA, OH	H	7.71 FQ	18.21 AW	27.04 TQ	OHBLS	10/01-12/01
	Columbus MSA, OH	H	7.12 FQ	14.03 AW	25.82 TQ	OHBLS	10/01-12/01
	Dayton-Springfield MSA, OH	H	8.58 FQ	11.83 AW	15.51 TQ	OHBLS	10/01-12/01
	Hamilton-Middletown PMSA, OH	H	9.01 FQ	12.12 AW	16.04 TQ	OHBLS	10/01-12/01
	Mansfield MSA, OH	H	7.60 FQ	10.94 AW	15.90 TQ	OHBLS	10/01-12/01
	Toledo MSA, OH	H	11.19 FQ	14.74 AW	17.25 TQ	OHBLS	10/01-12/01
	Oklahoma	H	6.98 FQ	10.34 AW	15.81 TQ	OKBLS	10/01-12/01
	Oklahoma City MSA, OK	H	6.78 FQ	10.31 AW	16.17 TQ	OKBLS	10/01-12/01
	Tulsa MSA, OK	H	8.67 FQ	11.04 AW	15.94 TQ	OKBLS	10/01-12/01
	Oregon	H	7.64 FQ	11.73 AW	16.63 TQ	ORBLS	10/01-12/01
	Eugene-Springfield MSA, OR	H	7.75 FQ	12.28 AW	16.90 TQ	ORBLS	10/01-12/01
	Medford-Ashland MSA, OR	H	8.77 FQ	13.03 AW	17.06 TQ	ORBLS	10/01-12/01
	Portland-Vancouver PMSA, OR-WA	H	7.48 FQ	10.81 AW	14.35 TQ	ORBLS	10/01-12/01
	Salem PMSA, OR	H	7.14 FQ	10.14 AW	15.94 TQ	ORBLS	10/01-12/01
	Pennsylvania	H	7.73 FQ	12.04 AW	17.47 TQ	PABLS	10/01-12/01
	Allentown-Bethlehem-Easton MSA, PA	H	9.01 FQ	11.72 AW	16.56 TQ	PABLS	10/01-12/01
	Erie MSA, PA	H	7.76 FQ	11.34 AW	15.65 TQ	PABLS	10/01-12/01
	Harrisburg-Lebanon-Carlisle MSA, PA	H	7.30 FQ	11.49 AW	16.70 TQ	PABLS	10/01-12/01
	Johnstown MSA, PA	H	7.26 FQ	9.88 AW	15.49 TQ	PABLS	10/01-12/01
	Lancaster MSA, PA	H	8.55 FQ	11.84 AW	16.03 TQ	PABLS	10/01-12/01
	Philadelphia PMSA, PA-NJ	H	7.92 FQ	12.14 AW	16.89 TQ	PABLS	10/01-12/01
	Pittsburgh MSA, PA	H	7.76 FQ	15.35 AW	21.98 TQ	PABLS	10/01-12/01
	Reading MSA, PA	H	9.41 FQ	13.53 AW	16.58 TQ	PABLS	10/01-12/01
	Scranton-Wilkes-Barre-Hazleton MSA, PA	H	7.72 FQ	10.08 AW	13.30 TQ	PABLS	10/01-12/01
	York MSA, PA	H	8.42 FQ	11.61 AW	14.57 TQ	PABLS	10/01-12/01
	Rhode Island	H	7.55 FQ	11.44 AW	16.81 TQ	RIBLS	10/01-12/01
	Providence-Fall River-Warwick MSA, RI-MA	H	7.64 FQ	11.32 AW	16.52 TQ	RIBLS	10/01-12/01
	South Carolina	H	7.35 FQ	10.23 AW	13.67 TQ	SCBLS	10/01-12/01
	Charleston-North Charleston MSA, SC	H	7.58 FQ	11.89 AW	20.21 TQ	SCBLS	10/01-12/01
	Columbia MSA, SC	H	6.38 FQ	10.94 AW	15.78 TQ	SCBLS	10/01-12/01
	Greenville-Spartanburg-Anderson MSA, SC	H	8.28 FQ	10.58 AW	13.76 TQ	SCBLS	10/01-12/01
	Myrtle Beach MSA, SC	H	6.28 FQ	9.39 AW	12.16 TQ	SCBLS	10/01-12/01
	South Dakota	H	6.71 FQ	9.77 AW	13.47 TQ	SDBLS	10/01-12/01
	Sioux Falls MSA, SD	H	6.91 FQ	10.65 AW	13.44 TQ	SDBLS	10/01-12/01

AAW	Average annual wage	**AOH**	Average offered, high	**ASH**	Average starting, high	**H**	Hourly	**M**	Monthly	**S**	Special: hourly and annual
AE	Average entry wage	**AOL**	Average offered, low	**ASL**	Average starting, low	**HI**	Highest wage paid	**MTC**	Median total compensation	**TQ**	Third quartile wage
AEX	Average experienced wage	**APH**	Average pay, high range	**AW**	Average wage paid	**HR**	High end range	**MW**	Median wage paid	**W**	Weekly
AO	Average offered	**APL**	Average pay, low range	**FQ**	First quartile wage	**LR**	Low end range	**SQ**	Second quartile wage	**Y**	Yearly

Occupation/Type/Industry	Location	Per	Low	Mid	High	Source	Date
Machine Feeder and Offbearer	Tennessee	H	7.38 FQ	10.30 AW	13.68 TQ	TNBLS	10/01-12/01
	Chattanooga MSA, TN-GA	H	7.58 FQ	10.26 AW	12.99 TQ	TNBLS	10/01-12/01
	Clarksville-Hopkinsville MSA, TN-KY	H	6.41 FQ	9.39 AW	11.65 TQ	TNBLS	10/01-12/01
	Johnson City-Kingsport-Bristol MSA, TN-VA	H	7.65 FQ	11.41 AW	14.86 TQ	TNBLS	10/01-12/01
	Knoxville MSA, TN	H	7.31 FQ	10.06 AW	15.49 TQ	TNBLS	10/01-12/01
	Memphis MSA, TN-AR-MS	H	7.34 FQ	9.56 AW	12.95 TQ	TNBLS	10/01-12/01
	Nashville MSA, TN	H	8.89 FQ	11.69 AW	14.49 TQ	TNBLS	10/01-12/01
	Texas	H	6.12 FQ	9.49 AW	13.20 TQ	TXBLS	10/01-12/01
	Austin-San Marcos MSA, TX	H	7.67 FQ	10.13 AW	12.42 TQ	TXBLS	10/01-12/01
	Beaumont-Port Arthur MSA, TX	H	6.04 FQ	9.34 AW	12.76 TQ	TXBLS	10/01-12/01
	Brazoria PMSA, TX	H	5.69 FQ	7.36 AW	9.76 TQ	TXBLS	10/01-12/01
	Dallas PMSA, TX	H	6.17 FQ	9.69 AW	13.01 TQ	TXBLS	10/01-12/01
	El Paso MSA, TX	H	5.85 FQ	8.34 AW	12.26 TQ	TXBLS	10/01-12/01
	Fort Worth-Arlington PMSA, TX	H	6.11 FQ	9.81 AW	13.44 TQ	TXBLS	10/01-12/01
	Houston PMSA, TX	H	5.87 FQ	9.19 AW	13.32 TQ	TXBLS	10/01-12/01
	Killeen-Temple MSA, TX	H	6.97 FQ	9.17 AW	12.26 TQ	TXBLS	10/01-12/01
	Longview-Marshall MSA, TX	H	5.86 FQ	8.15 AW	11.28 TQ	TXBLS	10/01-12/01
	Lubbock MSA, TX	H	6.72 FQ	9.15 AW	10.89 TQ	TXBLS	10/01-12/01
	McAllen-Edinburg-Mission MSA, TX	H	5.83 FQ	8.66 AW	13.10 TQ	TXBLS	10/01-12/01
	San Antonio MSA, TX	H	5.99 FQ	8.74 AW	12.60 TQ	TXBLS	10/01-12/01
	Tyler MSA, TX	H	5.68 FQ	8.47 AW	13.42 TQ	TXBLS	10/01-12/01
	Waco MSA, TX	H	5.59 FQ	7.50 AW	10.33 TQ	TXBLS	10/01-12/01
	Utah	H	6.19 FQ	10.05 AW	14.59 TQ	UTBLS	10/01-12/01
	Provo-Orem MSA, UT	H	6.91 FQ	10.40 AW	14.45 TQ	UTBLS	10/01-12/01
	Salt Lake City-Ogden MSA, UT	H	6.22 FQ	9.58 AW	13.18 TQ	UTBLS	10/01-12/01
	Vermont	H	7.53 FQ	9.81 AW	12.80 TQ	VTBLS	10/01-12/01
	Burlington MSA, VT	H	7.23 FQ	8.92 AW	10.83 TQ	VTBLS	10/01-12/01
	Virginia	H	7.31 FQ	11.42 AW	16.82 TQ	VABLS	10/01-12/01
	Lynchburg MSA, VA	H	7.91 FQ	10.91 AW	13.34 TQ	VABLS	10/01-12/01
	Norfolk-Virginia Beach-Newport News MSA, VA-NC	H	7.74 FQ	11.62 AW	18.70 TQ	VABLS	10/01-12/01
	Richmond-Petersburg MSA, VA	H	8.01 FQ	12.23 AW	19.75 TQ	VABLS	10/01-12/01
	Roanoke MSA, VA	H	7.97 FQ	10.22 AW	12.78 TQ	VABLS	10/01-12/01
	Washington	H	7.78 FQ	12.53 AW	17.70 TQ	WABLS	10/01-12/01
	Seattle-Bellevue-Everett PMSA, WA	H	7.39 FQ	11.84 AW	17.62 TQ	WABLS	10/01-12/01
	Spokane MSA, WA	H	7.36 FQ	10.16 AW	14.37 TQ	WABLS	10/01-12/01
	Tacoma PMSA, WA	H	8.41 FQ	12.28 AW	16.80 TQ	WABLS	10/01-12/01
	Yakima MSA, WA	H	7.48 FQ	10.96 AW	16.76 TQ	WABLS	10/01-12/01
	West Virginia	H	5.72 FQ	9.17 AW	16.10 TQ	WVBLS	10/01-12/01
	Huntington-Ashland MSA, WV-KY-OH	H	7.39 FQ	12.17 AW	16.37 TQ	WVBLS	10/01-12/01
	Wisconsin	H	7.78 FQ	11.14 AW	15.18 TQ	WIBLS	10/01-12/01
	Appleton-Oshkosh-Neenah MSA, WI	H	7.84 FQ	11.59 AW	16.43 TQ	WIBLS	10/01-12/01
	Green Bay MSA, WI	H	7.34 FQ	10.76 AW	15.59 TQ	WIBLS	10/01-12/01
	Madison MSA, WI	H	9.24 FQ	11.41 AW	13.76 TQ	WIBLS	10/01-12/01
	Milwaukee-Waukesha PMSA, WI	H	8.50 FQ	12.46 AW	16.47 TQ	WIBLS	10/01-12/01
	Racine PMSA, WI	H	7.25 FQ	10.07 AW	13.22 TQ	WIBLS	10/01-12/01
	Puerto Rico	H	5.67 FQ	7.11 AW	9.82 TQ	PRBLS	10/01-12/01
Machine Tool Setter, Operator, and Tender							
Metals and Plastics	Alabama	H	8.50 FQ	13.21 AW	19.12 TQ	ALBLS	10/01-12/01
Metals and Plastics	Arizona	H	8.02 FQ	12.98 AW	18.80 TQ	AZBLS	10/01-12/01
Metals and Plastics	Arkansas	H	8.21 FQ	12.34 AW	16.54 TQ	ARBLS	10/01-12/01
Metals and Plastics	California	H	7.54 FQ	12.65 AW	21.00 TQ	CABLS	10/01-12/01
Metals and Plastics	Colorado	H	8.80 FQ	13.60 AW	20.11 TQ	COBLS	10/01-12/01
Metals and Plastics	Connecticut	H	11.56 FQ	16.12 AW	21.66 TQ	CTBLS	10/01-12/01
Metals and Plastics	Delaware	H	9.90 FQ	14.59 AW	18.98 TQ	DEBLS	10/01-12/01
Metals and Plastics	Florida	H	7.44 FQ	11.61 AW	19.22 TQ	FLBLS	10/01-12/01
Metals and Plastics	Georgia	H	9.25 FQ	12.78 AW	16.94 TQ	GABLS	10/01-12/01
Metals and Plastics	Idaho	H	7.66 FQ	11.61 AW	17.07 TQ	IDBLS	10/01-12/01

AAW	Average annual wage	AOH	Average offered, high	ASH	Average starting, high	H	Hourly	M	Monthly	S	Special: hourly and annual
AE	Average entry wage	AOL	Average offered, low	ASL	Average starting, low	HI	Highest wage paid	MTC	Median total compensation	TQ	Third quartile wage
AEX	Average experienced wage	APH	Average pay, high range	AW	Average wage paid	HR	High end range	MW	Median wage paid	W	Weekly
AO	Average offered	APL	Average pay, low range	FQ	First quartile wage	LR	Low end range	SQ	Second quartile wage	Y	Yearly

Occupation/Type/Industry	Location	Per	Low	Mid	High	Source	Date
Machine Tool Setter, Operator, and Tender							
Metals and Plastics	Illinois	H	8.34 FQ	13.23 AW	19.62 TQ	ILBLS	10/01-12/01
Metals and Plastics	Indiana	H	9.54 FQ	16.34 AW	26.22 TQ	INBLS	10/01-12/01
Metals and Plastics	Iowa	H	9.19 FQ	12.51 AW	16.66 TQ	IABLS	10/01-12/01
Metals and Plastics	Kansas	H	8.74 FQ	12.47 AW	16.78 TQ	KSBLS	10/01-12/01
Metals and Plastics	Kentucky	H	9.00 FQ	15.80 AW	22.19 TQ	KYBLS	10/01-12/01
Metals and Plastics	Louisiana	H	6.91 FQ	12.69 AW	19.85 TQ	LABLS	10/01-12/01
Metals and Plastics	Maine	H	8.84 FQ	12.80 AW	18.60 TQ	MEBLS	10/01-12/01
Metals and Plastics	Maryland	H	9.07 FQ	14.93 AW	21.79 TQ	MDBLS	10/01-12/01
Metals and Plastics	Massachusetts	H	9.21 FQ	13.57 AW	19.70 TQ	MABLS	10/01-12/01
Metals and Plastics	Michigan	H	11.66 FQ	20.93 AW	27.39 TQ	MIBLS	10/01-12/01
Metals and Plastics	Minnesota	H	11.03 FQ	16.54 AW	21.40 TQ	MNBLS	10/01-12/01
Metals and Plastics	Mississippi	H	9.28 FQ	13.06 AW	16.91 TQ	MSBLS	10/01-12/01
Metals and Plastics	Missouri	H	8.12 FQ	11.73 AW	16.92 TQ	MOBLS	10/01-12/01
Metals and Plastics	Montana	H	7.17 FQ	12.36 AW	20.63 TQ	MTBLS	10/01-12/01
Metals and Plastics	Nebraska	H	9.84 FQ	12.42 AW	15.37 TQ	NEBLS	10/01-12/01
Metals and Plastics	Nevada	H	7.65 FQ	12.35 AW	19.16 TQ	NVBLS	10/01-12/01
Metals and Plastics	New Hampshire	H	8.18 FQ	12.08 AW	16.91 TQ	NHBLS	10/01-12/01
Metals and Plastics	New Jersey	H	8.78 FQ	14.43 AW	21.13 TQ	NJBLS	10/01-12/01
Metals and Plastics	New York	H	7.77 FQ	12.56 AW	19.04 TQ	NYBLS	10/01-12/01
Metals and Plastics	North Carolina	H	9.22 FQ	13.31 AW	19.81 TQ	NCBLS	10/01-12/01
Metals and Plastics	North Dakota	H	9.11 FQ	12.86 AW	16.88 TQ	NDBLS	10/01-12/01
Metals and Plastics	Ohio	H	10.40 FQ	17.85 AW	26.38 TQ	OHBLS	10/01-12/01
Metals and Plastics	Oklahoma	H	8.05 FQ	12.35 AW	17.26 TQ	OKBLS	10/01-12/01
Metals and Plastics	Oregon	H	8.83 FQ	13.25 AW	18.91 TQ	ORBLS	10/01-12/01
Metals and Plastics	Pennsylvania	H	8.67 FQ	13.10 AW	17.85 TQ	PABLS	10/01-12/01
Metals and Plastics	Rhode Island	H	8.29 FQ	14.21 AW	20.17 TQ	RIBLS	10/01-12/01
Metals and Plastics	South Carolina	H	9.84 FQ	13.96 AW	17.85 TQ	SCBLS	10/01-12/01
Metals and Plastics	South Dakota	H	7.64 FQ	10.76 AW	14.85 TQ	SDBLS	10/01-12/01
Metals and Plastics	Tennessee	H	7.70 FQ	11.68 AW	16.36 TQ	TNBLS	10/01-12/01
Metals and Plastics	Texas	H	7.48 FQ	10.95 AW	15.91 TQ	TXBLS	10/01-12/01
Metals and Plastics	Utah	H	9.13 FQ	13.73 AW	20.47 TQ	UTBLS	10/01-12/01
Metals and Plastics	Vermont	H	7.55 FQ	11.29 AW	16.37 TQ	VTBLS	10/01-12/01
Metals and Plastics	Virginia	H	9.34 FQ	13.59 AW	18.73 TQ	VABLS	10/01-12/01
Metals and Plastics	Washington	H	8.71 FQ	12.63 AW	16.89 TQ	WABLS	10/01-12/01
Metals and Plastics	West Virginia	H	7.54 FQ	13.92 AW	19.99 TQ	WVBLS	10/01-12/01
Metals and Plastics	Wisconsin	H	10.71 FQ	14.60 AW	18.08 TQ	WIBLS	10/01-12/01
Metals and Plastics	Puerto Rico	H	5.92 FQ	8.37 AW	11.60 TQ	PRBLS	10/01-12/01
Machinist	Alabama	H	9.02 FQ	14.71 AW	21.64 TQ	ALBLS	10/01-12/01
	Birmingham MSA, AL	H	9.06 FQ	15.17 AW	24.34 TQ	ALBLS	10/01-12/01
	Huntsville MSA, AL	H	10.98 FQ	15.56 AW	21.44 TQ	ALBLS	10/01-12/01
	Mobile MSA, AL	H	11.06 FQ	15.54 AW	20.97 TQ	ALBLS	10/01-12/01
	Montgomery MSA, AL	H	8.40 FQ	15.42 AW	23.84 TQ	ALBLS	10/01-12/01
	Alaska	H	13.74 FQ	21.28 AW	28.56 TQ	AKBLS	10/01-12/01
	Anchorage MSA, AK	H	15.41 FQ	22.41 AW	29.17 TQ	AKBLS	10/01-12/01
	Arizona	H	8.38 FQ	15.34 AW	22.03 TQ	AZBLS	10/01-12/01
	Phoenix-Mesa MSA, AZ	H	10.31 FQ	16.27 AW	22.40 TQ	AZBLS	10/01-12/01
	Tucson MSA, AZ	H	6.07 FQ	12.43 AW	20.26 TQ	AZBLS	10/01-12/01
	Arkansas	H	9.18 FQ	14.27 AW	19.99 TQ	ARBLS	10/01-12/01
	Fayetteville-Springdale-Rogers MSA, AR	H	9.26 FQ	13.16 AW	17.04 TQ	ARBLS	10/01-12/01
	Fort Smith MSA, AR-OK	H	10.29 FQ	14.15 AW	18.21 TQ	ARBLS	10/01-12/01
	Little Rock-North Little Rock MSA, AR	H	10.32 FQ	14.51 AW	19.90 TQ	ARBLS	10/01-12/01
	California	H	8.39 FQ	16.23 AW	25.81 TQ	CABLS	10/01-12/01
	Bakersfield MSA, CA	H	8.39 FQ	15.99 AW	23.62 TQ	CABLS	10/01-12/01
	Chico-Paradise MSA, CA	H	7.93 FQ	13.91 AW	18.67 TQ	CABLS	10/01-12/01
	Fresno MSA, CA	H	7.43 FQ	10.59 AW	16.19 TQ	CABLS	10/01-12/01
	Los Angeles-Long Beach PMSA, CA	H	8.47 FQ	15.38 AW	23.23 TQ	CABLS	10/01-12/01
	Merced MSA, CA	H	8.80 FQ	15.15 AW	24.17 TQ	CABLS	10/01-12/01
	Modesto MSA, CA	H	9.95 FQ	16.65 AW	24.89 TQ	CABLS	10/01-12/01
	Oakland PMSA, CA	H	10.92 FQ	20.21 AW	28.53 TQ	CABLS	10/01-12/01
	Orange County PMSA, CA	H	8.33 FQ	16.54 AW	26.14 TQ	CABLS	10/01-12/01
	Redding MSA, CA	H	8.45 FQ	15.44 AW	27.32 TQ	CABLS	10/01-12/01
	Riverside-San Bernardino PMSA, CA	H	8.45 FQ	14.09 AW	21.52 TQ	CABLS	10/01-12/01
	Sacramento PMSA, CA	H	12.29 FQ	17.82 AW	22.85 TQ	CABLS	10/01-12/01
	Salinas MSA, CA	H	8.06 FQ	13.78 AW	21.40 TQ	CABLS	10/01-12/01
	San Diego MSA, CA	H	9.01 FQ	15.66 AW	24.41 TQ	CABLS	10/01-12/01

AAW	Average annual wage	AOH	Average offered, high	ASH	Average starting, high	H	Hourly	M	Monthly
AE	Average entry wage	AOL	Average offered, low	ASL	Average starting, low	HI	Highest wage paid	MTC	Median total compensation
AEX	Average experienced wage	APH	Average pay, high range	AW	Average wage paid	HR	High end range	MW	Median wage paid
AO	Average offered	APL	Average pay, low range	FQ	First quartile wage	LR	Low end range	SQ	Second quartile wage

S	Special: hourly and annual
TQ	Third quartile wage
W	Weekly
Y	Yearly

Occupation/Type/Industry	Location	Per	Low	Mid	High	Source	Date
Machinist	San Francisco PMSA, CA	H	8.16 FQ	18.58 AW	27.75 TQ	CABLS	10/01-12/01
	San Jose PMSA, CA	H	12.02 FQ	21.27 AW	31.54 TQ	CABLS	10/01-12/01
	San Luis Obispo-Atascadero-Paso Robles MSA, CA	H	7.43 FQ	16.94 AW	32.90 TQ	CABLS	10/01-12/01
	Santa Barbara-Santa Maria-Lompoc MSA, CA	H	11.50 FQ	18.77 AW	27.62 TQ	CABLS	10/01-12/01
	Santa Cruz-Watsonville PMSA, CA	H	8.39 FQ	16.61 AW	26.14 TQ	CABLS	10/01-12/01
	Santa Rosa PMSA, CA	H	10.02 FQ	17.53 AW	26.11 TQ	CABLS	10/01-12/01
	Stockton-Lodi MSA, CA	H	7.45 FQ	14.89 AW	23.27 TQ	CABLS	10/01-12/01
	Vallejo-Fairfield-Napa PMSA, CA	H	14.97 FQ	23.15 AW	33.54 TQ	CABLS	10/01-12/01
	Ventura PMSA, CA	H	8.15 FQ	13.69 AW	20.39 TQ	CABLS	10/01-12/01
	Colorado	H	9.43 FQ	16.01 AW	22.70 TQ	COBLS	10/01-12/01
	Boulder-Longmont PMSA, CO	H	8.23 FQ	16.84 AW	25.44 TQ	COBLS	10/01-12/01
	Colorado Springs MSA, CO	H	8.84 FQ	13.11 AW	19.02 TQ	COBLS	10/01-12/01
	Denver PMSA, CO	H	10.79 FQ	16.60 AW	23.39 TQ	COBLS	10/01-12/01
	Fort Collins-Loveland MSA, CO	H	11.62 FQ	17.28 AW	22.17 TQ	COBLS	10/01-12/01
	Greeley PMSA, CO	H	10.36 FQ	16.48 AW	22.77 TQ	COBLS	10/01-12/01
	Connecticut	H	10.01 FQ	16.75 AW	22.95 TQ	CTBLS	10/01-12/01
	Bridgeport PMSA, CT	H	10.27 FQ	18.05 AW	24.90 TQ	CTBLS	10/01-12/01
	Danbury PMSA, CT	H	9.99 FQ	16.60 AW	23.03 TQ	CTBLS	10/01-12/01
	Hartford MSA, CT	H	10.28 FQ	16.81 AW	22.46 TQ	CTBLS	10/01-12/01
	New Haven-Meriden PMSA, CT	H	9.77 FQ	15.57 AW	22.28 TQ	CTBLS	10/01-12/01
	New London-Norwich MSA, CT-RI	H	13.73 FQ	17.34 AW	21.14 TQ	CTBLS	10/01-12/01
	Stamford-Norwalk PMSA, CT	H	10.25 FQ	17.27 AW	25.33 TQ	CTBLS	10/01-12/01
	Waterbury PMSA, CT	H	8.94 FQ	17.02 AW	28.67 TQ	CTBLS	10/01-12/01
	Delaware	H	10.34 FQ	17.41 AW	24.04 TQ	DEBLS	10/01-12/01
	Wilmington-Newark PMSA, DE-MD	H	12.33 FQ	18.82 AW	26.06 TQ	DEBLS	10/01-12/01
	District of Columbia	H	11.62 FQ	19.95 AW	31.12 TQ	DCBLS	10/01-12/01
	Washington PMSA, DC-MD-VA-WV	H	9.86 FQ	17.42 AW	25.90 TQ	DCBLS	10/01-12/01
	Florida	H	8.52 FQ	14.38 AW	21.12 TQ	FLBLS	10/01-12/01
	Daytona Beach MSA, FL	H	9.67 FQ	14.80 AW	20.56 TQ	FLBLS	10/01-12/01
	Fort Lauderdale PMSA, FL	H	9.69 FQ	15.67 AW	21.41 TQ	FLBLS	10/01-12/01
	Fort Myers-Cape Coral MSA, FL	H	7.44 FQ	13.25 AW	18.12 TQ	FLBLS	10/01-12/01
	Fort Pierce-Port St. Lucie MSA, FL	H	9.26 FQ	15.04 AW	20.61 TQ	FLBLS	10/01-12/01
	Fort Walton Beach MSA, FL	H	7.56 FQ	13.64 AW	35.00 TQ	FLBLS	10/01-12/01
	Gainesville MSA, FL	H	9.58 FQ	15.01 AW	24.90 TQ	FLBLS	10/01-12/01
	Jacksonville MSA, FL	H	9.63 FQ	14.55 AW	20.61 TQ	FLBLS	10/01-12/01
	Lakeland-Winter Haven MSA, FL	H	9.27 FQ	14.49 AW	21.22 TQ	FLBLS	10/01-12/01
	Melbourne-Titusville-Palm Bay MSA, FL	H	8.95 FQ	14.81 AW	21.61 TQ	FLBLS	10/01-12/01
	Miami PMSA, FL	H	8.19 FQ	13.27 AW	18.65 TQ	FLBLS	10/01-12/01
	Naples MSA, FL	H	11.62 FQ	16.76 AW	21.62 TQ	FLBLS	10/01-12/01
	Ocala MSA, FL	H	9.18 FQ	12.30 AW	16.34 TQ	FLBLS	10/01-12/01
	Orlando MSA, FL	H	9.92 FQ	15.42 AW	22.14 TQ	FLBLS	10/01-12/01
	Pensacola MSA, FL	H	5.95 FQ	12.59 AW	22.64 TQ	FLBLS	10/01-12/01
	Sarasota-Bradenton MSA, FL	H	8.86 FQ	13.89 AW	18.18 TQ	FLBLS	10/01-12/01
	Tallahassee MSA, FL	H	10.15 FQ	14.69 AW	19.66 TQ	FLBLS	10/01-12/01
	Tampa-St. Petersburg-Clearwater MSA, FL	H	8.00 FQ	13.47 AW	20.45 TQ	FLBLS	10/01-12/01
	West Palm Beach-Boca Raton MSA, FL	H	11.17 FQ	17.10 AW	22.82 TQ	FLBLS	10/01-12/01
	Georgia	H	10.37 FQ	15.48 AW	21.97 TQ	GABLS	10/01-12/01
	Atlanta MSA, GA	H	11.47 FQ	16.60 AW	25.13 TQ	GABLS	10/01-12/01
	Augusta-Aiken MSA, GA-SC	H	11.23 FQ	15.22 AW	20.37 TQ	GABLS	10/01-12/01
	Columbus MSA, GA-AL	H	9.96 FQ	13.97 AW	18.68 TQ	GABLS	10/01-12/01
	Macon MSA, GA	H	11.18 FQ	15.21 AW	20.14 TQ	GABLS	10/01-12/01
	Savannah MSA, GA	H	11.62 FQ	18.62 AW	26.53 TQ	GABLS	10/01-12/01
	Hawaii	H	13.20 FQ	21.67 AW	30.70 TQ	HIBLS	10/01-12/01
	Honolulu MSA, HI	H	13.43 FQ	22.07 AW	31.02 TQ	HIBLS	10/01-12/01
	Idaho	H	8.08 FQ	14.92 AW	21.91 TQ	IDBLS	10/01-12/01
	Boise City MSA, ID	H	8.46 FQ	14.73 AW	21.24 TQ	IDBLS	10/01-12/01
	Illinois	H	9.86 FQ	16.22 AW	23.22 TQ	ILBLS	10/01-12/01

AAW Average annual wage; **AE** Average entry wage; **AEX** Average experienced wage; **AO** Average offered; **AOH** Average offered, high; **AOL** Average offered, low; **APH** Average pay, high range; **APL** Average pay, low range; **ASH** Average starting, high; **ASL** Average starting, low; **AW** Average wage paid; **FQ** First quartile wage; **H** Hourly; **HI** Highest wage paid; **HR** High end range; **LR** Low end range; **M** Monthly; **MTC** Median total compensation; **MW** Median wage paid; **SQ** Second quartile wage; **S** Special: hourly and annual; **TQ** Third quartile wage; **W** Weekly; **Y** Yearly

Occupation/Type/Industry	Location	Per	Low	Mid	High	Source	Date
Machinist	Champaign-Urbana MSA, IL	H	9.63 FQ	13.65 AW	17.92 TQ	ILBLS	10/01-12/01
	Chicago PMSA, IL	H	9.83 FQ	16.40 AW	23.62 TQ	ILBLS	10/01-12/01
	Peoria-Pekin MSA, IL	H	10.73 FQ	16.67 AW	26.21 TQ	ILBLS	10/01-12/01
	Rockford MSA, IL	H	11.00 FQ	15.85 AW	20.91 TQ	ILBLS	10/01-12/01
	Indiana	H	10.13 FQ	15.64 AW	21.25 TQ	INBLS	10/01-12/01
	Elkhart-Goshen MSA, IN	H	9.36 FQ	12.98 AW	17.14 TQ	INBLS	10/01-12/01
	Evansville-Henderson MSA, IN-KY	H	8.69 FQ	14.32 AW	20.20 TQ	INBLS	10/01-12/01
	Fort Wayne MSA, IN	H	9.56 FQ	14.95 AW	20.78 TQ	INBLS	10/01-12/01
	Gary PMSA, IN	H	11.43 FQ	19.04 AW	26.73 TQ	INBLS	10/01-12/01
	Indianapolis MSA, IN	H	10.82 FQ	15.37 AW	20.97 TQ	INBLS	10/01-12/01
	Lafayette MSA, IN	H	13.22 FQ	18.00 AW	21.37 TQ	INBLS	10/01-12/01
	South Bend MSA, IN	H	10.25 FQ	15.20 AW	20.90 TQ	INBLS	10/01-12/01
	Iowa	H	9.33 FQ	13.75 AW	18.95 TQ	IABLS	10/01-12/01
	Cedar Rapids MSA, IA	H	10.08 FQ	16.26 AW	22.36 TQ	IABLS	10/01-12/01
	Davenport-Moline-Rock Island MSA, IA-IL	H	9.28 FQ	16.62 AW	25.70 TQ	IABLS	10/01-12/01
	Des Moines MSA, IA	H	6.32 FQ	12.28 AW	18.46 TQ	IABLS	10/01-12/01
	Kansas	H	10.01 FQ	15.18 AW	22.02 TQ	KSBLS	10/01-12/01
	Topeka MSA, KS	H	10.38 FQ	13.96 AW	19.89 TQ	KSBLS	10/01-12/01
	Wichita MSA, KS	H	10.43 FQ	16.39 AW	26.11 TQ	KSBLS	10/01-12/01
	Kentucky	H	8.70 FQ	14.98 AW	21.17 TQ	KYBLS	10/01-12/01
	Lexington MSA, KY	H	9.51 FQ	14.84 AW	20.37 TQ	KYBLS	10/01-12/01
	Louisville MSA, KY-IN	H	10.03 FQ	16.51 AW	22.84 TQ	KYBLS	10/01-12/01
	Louisiana	H	9.86 FQ	15.90 AW	22.53 TQ	LABLS	10/01-12/01
	Baton Rouge MSA, LA	H	12.12 FQ	17.56 AW	24.63 TQ	LABLS	10/01-12/01
	Houma MSA, LA	H	10.04 FQ	15.19 AW	20.06 TQ	LABLS	10/01-12/01
	Lafayette MSA, LA	H	8.98 FQ	13.67 AW	19.53 TQ	LABLS	10/01-12/01
	Lake Charles MSA, LA	H	10.99 FQ	18.45 AW	26.04 TQ	LABLS	10/01-12/01
	New Orleans MSA, LA	H	9.98 FQ	15.88 AW	22.33 TQ	LABLS	10/01-12/01
	Shreveport-Bossier City MSA, LA	H	9.13 FQ	16.35 AW	23.55 TQ	LABLS	10/01-12/01
	Maine	H	9.53 FQ	14.96 AW	20.26 TQ	MEBLS	10/01-12/01
	Portland MSA, ME	H	9.68 FQ	13.91 AW	18.64 TQ	MEBLS	10/01-12/01
	Maryland	H	9.72 FQ	16.30 AW	23.97 TQ	MDBLS	10/01-12/01
	Baltimore PMSA, MD	H	10.51 FQ	16.10 AW	21.71 TQ	MDBLS	10/01-12/01
	Massachusetts	H	11.89 FQ	17.88 AW	24.81 TQ	MABLS	10/01-12/01
	Boston PMSA, MA-NH	H	12.43 FQ	18.85 AW	26.17 TQ	MABLS	10/01-12/01
	Brockton PMSA, MA	H	10.52 FQ	15.92 AW	21.35 TQ	MABLS	10/01-12/01
	Lawrence PMSA, MA-NH	H	11.30 FQ	18.65 AW	25.41 TQ	MABLS	10/01-12/01
	Lowell PMSA, MA-NH	H	9.45 FQ	16.78 AW	23.74 TQ	MABLS	10/01-12/01
	New Bedford PMSA, MA	H	12.35 FQ	18.56 AW	24.98 TQ	MABLS	10/01-12/01
	Springfield MSA, MA	H	12.21 FQ	16.57 AW	21.29 TQ	MABLS	10/01-12/01
	Worcester PMSA, MA-CT	H	11.61 FQ	16.93 AW	22.22 TQ	MABLS	10/01-12/01
	Michigan	H	9.70 FQ	16.16 AW	24.06 TQ	MIBLS	10/01-12/01
	Ann Arbor PMSA, MI	H	10.92 FQ	19.08 AW	29.95 TQ	MIBLS	10/01-12/01
	Detroit PMSA, MI	H	9.75 FQ	16.26 AW	24.30 TQ	MIBLS	10/01-12/01
	Flint PMSA, MI	H	9.77 FQ	19.23 AW	32.35 TQ	MIBLS	10/01-12/01
	Grand Rapids-Muskegon-Holland MSA, MI	H	9.58 FQ	15.53 AW	21.47 TQ	MIBLS	10/01-12/01
	Kalamazoo-Battle Creek MSA, MI	H	9.61 FQ	13.79 AW	19.35 TQ	MIBLS	10/01-12/01
	Lansing-East Lansing MSA, MI	H	11.05 FQ	20.48 AW	32.22 TQ	MIBLS	10/01-12/01
	Saginaw-Bay City-Midland MSA, MI	H	7.87 FQ	15.05 AW	23.53 TQ	MIBLS	10/01-12/01
	Minnesota	H	11.36 FQ	17.24 AW	23.99 TQ	MNBLS	10/01-12/01
	Duluth-Superior MSA, MN-WI	H	9.62 FQ	15.82 AW	21.52 TQ	MNBLS	10/01-12/01
	Minneapolis-St. Paul MSA, MN-WI	H	12.72 FQ	18.22 AW	24.87 TQ	MNBLS	10/01-12/01
	St. Cloud MSA, MN	H	10.70 FQ	16.57 AW	24.04 TQ	MNBLS	10/01-12/01
	Mississippi	H	8.95 FQ	13.60 AW	17.65 TQ	MSBLS	10/01-12/01
	Jackson MSA, MS	H	9.69 FQ	13.83 AW	17.69 TQ	MSBLS	10/01-12/01
	Missouri	H	9.20 FQ	15.26 AW	22.86 TQ	MOBLS	10/01-12/01
	Kansas City MSA, MO-KS	H	9.18 FQ	15.30 AW	21.17 TQ	MOBLS	10/01-12/01
	St. Louis MSA, MO-IL	H	10.52 FQ	17.49 AW	25.67 TQ	MOBLS	10/01-12/01
	Springfield MSA, MO	H	9.24 FQ	13.11 AW	17.25 TQ	MOBLS	10/01-12/01
	Montana	H	9.30 FQ	14.77 AW	20.96 TQ	MTBLS	10/01-12/01
	Billings MSA, MT	H	8.85 FQ	15.33 AW	23.15 TQ	MTBLS	10/01-12/01
	Nebraska	H	9.66 FQ	14.71 AW	20.42 TQ	NEBLS	10/01-12/01
	Lincoln MSA, NE	H	10.27 FQ	15.18 AW	18.90 TQ	NEBLS	10/01-12/01
	Omaha MSA, NE-IA	H	9.21 FQ	14.17 AW	20.04 TQ	NEBLS	10/01-12/01
	Nevada	H	10.15 FQ	17.52 AW	25.06 TQ	NVBLS	10/01-12/01

AAW	Average annual wage	**AOH**	Average offered, high	**ASH**	Average starting, high	**H**	Hourly	**M**	Monthly	**S**	Special: hourly and annual
AE	Average entry wage	**AOL**	Average offered, low	**ASL**	Average starting, low	**HI**	Highest wage paid	**MTC**	Median total compensation	**TQ**	Third quartile wage
AEX	Average experienced wage	**APH**	Average pay, high range	**AW**	Average wage paid	**HR**	High end range	**MW**	Median wage paid	**W**	Weekly
AO	Average offered	**APL**	Average pay, low range	**FQ**	First quartile wage	**LR**	Low end range	**SQ**	Second quartile wage	**Y**	Yearly

Occupation/Type/Industry	Location	Per	Low	Mid	High	Source	Date
Machinist	Las Vegas MSA, NV-AZ	H	9.15 FQ	15.42 AW	23.05 TQ	NVBLS	10/01-12/01
	Reno MSA, NV	H	11.78 FQ	21.06 AW	38.96 TQ	NVBLS	10/01-12/01
	New Hampshire	H	10.72 FQ	16.42 AW	22.11 TQ	NHBLS	10/01-12/01
	Manchester PMSA, NH	H	11.42 FQ	17.47 AW	23.75 TQ	NHBLS	10/01-12/01
	Nashua PMSA, NH	H	11.88 FQ	17.36 AW	22.96 TQ	NHBLS	10/01-12/01
	Portsmouth-Rochester PMSA, NH-ME	H	12.91 FQ	17.79 AW	22.87 TQ	NHBLS	10/01-12/01
	New Jersey	H	10.86 FQ	17.59 AW	25.03 TQ	NJBLS	10/01-12/01
	Atlantic-Cape May PMSA, NJ	H	12.09 FQ	18.17 AW	26.62 TQ	NJBLS	10/01-12/01
	Bergen-Passaic PMSA, NJ	H	9.93 FQ	17.30 AW	24.74 TQ	NJBLS	10/01-12/01
	Jersey City PMSA, NJ	H	12.28 FQ	18.68 AW	26.88 TQ	NJBLS	10/01-12/01
	Middlesex-Somerset-Hunterdon PMSA, NJ	H	11.72 FQ	18.55 AW	27.09 TQ	NJBLS	10/01-12/01
	Monmouth-Ocean PMSA, NJ	H	11.14 FQ	17.25 AW	24.46 TQ	NJBLS	10/01-12/01
	Newark PMSA, NJ	H	10.40 FQ	17.26 AW	24.20 TQ	NJBLS	10/01-12/01
	Trenton PMSA, NJ	H	12.24 FQ	18.34 AW	25.44 TQ	NJBLS	10/01-12/01
	New Mexico	H	9.89 FQ	17.91 AW	25.94 TQ	NMBLS	10/01-12/01
	Albuquerque MSA, NM	H	10.08 FQ	19.22 AW	26.34 TQ	NMBLS	10/01-12/01
	New York	H	8.85 FQ	15.54 AW	22.90 TQ	NYBLS	10/01-12/01
	Albany-Schenectady-Troy MSA, NY	H	11.93 FQ	18.14 AW	24.76 TQ	NYBLS	10/01-12/01
	Binghamton MSA, NY	H	9.10 FQ	13.50 AW	19.30 TQ	NYBLS	10/01-12/01
	Buffalo-Niagara Falls MSA, NY	H	10.38 FQ	17.00 AW	24.85 TQ	NYBLS	10/01-12/01
	Dutchess County PMSA, NY	H	10.20 FQ	13.99 AW	18.47 TQ	NYBLS	10/01-12/01
	Nassau-Suffolk PMSA, NY	H	9.29 FQ	16.12 AW	23.79 TQ	NYBLS	10/01-12/01
	New York PMSA, NY	H	7.16 FQ	14.22 AW	22.69 TQ	NYBLS	10/01-12/01
	Newburgh PMSA, NY-PA	H	8.03 FQ	15.72 AW	23.90 TQ	NYBLS	10/01-12/01
	Rochester MSA, NY	H	8.61 FQ	15.06 AW	21.38 TQ	NYBLS	10/01-12/01
	Syracuse MSA, NY	H	9.48 FQ	15.07 AW	21.02 TQ	NYBLS	10/01-12/01
	Utica-Rome MSA, NY	H	5.79 FQ	10.17 AW	16.47 TQ	NYBLS	10/01-12/01
	North Carolina	H	9.68 FQ	15.14 AW	21.49 TQ	NCBLS	10/01-12/01
	Asheville MSA, NC	H	9.86 FQ	13.88 AW	17.92 TQ	NCBLS	10/01-12/01
	Charlotte-Gastonia-Rock Hill MSA, NC-SC	H	9.97 FQ	16.38 AW	24.35 TQ	NCBLS	10/01-12/01
	Fayetteville MSA, NC	H	9.38 FQ	13.94 AW	19.45 TQ	NCBLS	10/01-12/01
	Greensboro-Winston-Salem-High Point MSA, NC	H	9.90 FQ	15.31 AW	21.53 TQ	NCBLS	10/01-12/01
	Hickory-Morganton-Lenoir MSA, NC	H	10.18 FQ	15.39 AW	24.05 TQ	NCBLS	10/01-12/01
	Raleigh-Durham-Chapel Hill MSA, NC	H	9.83 FQ	14.29 AW	18.27 TQ	NCBLS	10/01-12/01
	Wilmington MSA, NC	H	9.32 FQ	14.19 AW	21.73 TQ	NCBLS	10/01-12/01
	North Dakota	H	9.85 FQ	15.61 AW	21.90 TQ	NDBLS	10/01-12/01
	Fargo-Moorhead MSA, ND-MN	H	10.72 FQ	14.36 AW	17.69 TQ	NDBLS	10/01-12/01
	Ohio	H	9.97 FQ	15.80 AW	21.96 TQ	OHBLS	10/01-12/01
	Akron PMSA, OH	H	10.85 FQ	15.90 AW	21.41 TQ	OHBLS	10/01-12/01
	Canton-Massillon MSA, OH	H	9.44 FQ	13.75 AW	18.77 TQ	OHBLS	10/01-12/01
	Cincinnati PMSA, OH-KY-IN	H	9.73 FQ	14.65 AW	20.36 TQ	OHBLS	10/01-12/01
	Cleveland-Lorain-Elyria PMSA, OH	H	9.86 FQ	15.77 AW	21.45 TQ	OHBLS	10/01-12/01
	Columbus MSA, OH	H	10.31 FQ	15.68 AW	21.38 TQ	OHBLS	10/01-12/01
	Dayton-Springfield MSA, OH	H	10.39 FQ	17.21 AW	22.11 TQ	OHBLS	10/01-12/01
	Hamilton-Middletown PMSA, OH	H	10.98 FQ	16.65 AW	25.59 TQ	OHBLS	10/01-12/01
	Mansfield MSA, OH	H	9.48 FQ	16.71 AW	30.60 TQ	OHBLS	10/01-12/01
	Toledo MSA, OH	H	11.18 FQ	15.57 AW	21.25 TQ	OHBLS	10/01-12/01
	Youngstown-Warren MSA, OH	H	8.07 FQ	14.72 AW	21.23 TQ	OHBLS	10/01-12/01
	Oklahoma	H	8.47 FQ	14.17 AW	20.70 TQ	OKBLS	10/01-12/01
	Oklahoma City MSA, OK	H	8.30 FQ	14.27 AW	20.99 TQ	OKBLS	10/01-12/01
	Tulsa MSA, OK	H	10.06 FQ	15.22 AW	20.68 TQ	OKBLS	10/01-12/01
	Oregon	H	11.50 FQ	17.47 AW	23.96 TQ	ORBLS	10/01-12/01
	Eugene-Springfield MSA, OR	H	10.33 FQ	15.10 AW	20.67 TQ	ORBLS	10/01-12/01
	Medford-Ashland MSA, OR	H	10.31 FQ	15.96 AW	21.29 TQ	ORBLS	10/01-12/01
	Portland-Vancouver PMSA, OR-WA	H	11.39 FQ	17.93 AW	25.09 TQ	ORBLS	10/01-12/01
	Salem PMSA, OR	H	11.40 FQ	15.84 AW	21.13 TQ	ORBLS	10/01-12/01
	Pennsylvania	H	9.96 FQ	15.45 AW	21.75 TQ	PABLS	10/01-12/01
	Allentown-Bethlehem-Easton MSA, PA	H	10.38 FQ	14.66 AW	20.00 TQ	PABLS	10/01-12/01
	Erie MSA, PA	H	9.94 FQ	15.78 AW	23.80 TQ	PABLS	10/01-12/01

AAW	Average annual wage	**AOH**	Average offered, high	**ASH**	Average starting, high	**H**	Hourly	**M**	Monthly	**S**	Special: hourly and annual
AE	Average entry wage	**AOL**	Average offered, low	**ASL**	Average starting, low	**HI**	Highest wage paid	**MTC**	Median total compensation	**TQ**	Third quartile wage
AEX	Average experienced wage	**APH**	Average pay, high range	**AW**	Average wage paid	**HR**	High end range	**MW**	Median wage paid	**W**	Weekly
AO	Average offered	**APL**	Average pay, low range	**FQ**	First quartile wage	**LR**	Low end range	**SQ**	Second quartile wage	**Y**	Yearly

Occupation/Type/Industry	Location	Per	Low	Mid	High	Source	Date
Machinist	Harrisburg-Lebanon-Carlisle MSA, PA	H	8.16 FQ	14.37 AW	20.51 TQ	PABLS	10/01-12/01
	Johnstown MSA, PA	H	8.96 FQ	12.18 AW	16.77 TQ	PABLS	10/01-12/01
	Lancaster MSA, PA	H	9.52 FQ	14.09 AW	19.83 TQ	PABLS	10/01-12/01
	Philadelphia PMSA, PA-NJ	H	10.58 FQ	16.37 AW	22.51 TQ	PABLS	10/01-12/01
	Pittsburgh MSA, PA	H	10.25 FQ	15.17 AW	20.48 TQ	PABLS	10/01-12/01
	Reading MSA, PA	H	9.39 FQ	15.55 AW	21.64 TQ	PABLS	10/01-12/01
	Scranton-Wilkes-Barre-Hazleton MSA, PA	H	10.51 FQ	15.91 AW	20.90 TQ	PABLS	10/01-12/01
	York MSA, PA	H	11.67 FQ	17.43 AW	26.17 TQ	PABLS	10/01-12/01
	Rhode Island	H	7.89 FQ	14.45 AW	21.20 TQ	RIBLS	10/01-12/01
	Providence-Fall River-Warwick MSA, RI-MA	H	7.92 FQ	14.60 AW	21.29 TQ	RIBLS	10/01-12/01
	South Carolina	H	9.92 FQ	15.92 AW	21.72 TQ	SCBLS	10/01-12/01
	Charleston-North Charleston MSA, SC	H	9.24 FQ	13.71 AW	18.01 TQ	SCBLS	10/01-12/01
	Columbia MSA, SC	H	7.67 FQ	12.77 AW	19.93 TQ	SCBLS	10/01-12/01
	Greenville-Spartanburg-Anderson MSA, SC	H	11.61 FQ	17.00 AW	22.05 TQ	SCBLS	10/01-12/01
	Myrtle Beach MSA, SC	H	8.54 FQ	13.65 AW	17.41 TQ	SCBLS	10/01-12/01
	South Dakota	H	9.24 FQ	12.34 AW	16.45 TQ	SDBLS	10/01-12/01
	Sioux Falls MSA, SD	H	9.42 FQ	12.57 AW	16.88 TQ	SDBLS	10/01-12/01
	Tennessee	H	9.64 FQ	15.47 AW	22.09 TQ	TNBLS	10/01-12/01
	Chattanooga MSA, TN-GA	H	10.25 FQ	14.96 AW	20.72 TQ	TNBLS	10/01-12/01
	Clarksville-Hopkinsville MSA, TN-KY	H	9.29 FQ	14.68 AW	19.64 TQ	TNBLS	10/01-12/01
	Johnson City-Kingsport-Bristol MSA, TN-VA	H	8.99 FQ	13.56 AW	17.87 TQ	TNBLS	10/01-12/01
	Knoxville MSA, TN	H	10.25 FQ	15.92 AW	21.22 TQ	TNBLS	10/01-12/01
	Memphis MSA, TN-AR-MS	H	10.51 FQ	16.41 AW	22.05 TQ	TNBLS	10/01-12/01
	Nashville MSA, TN	H	10.69 FQ	16.64 AW	21.57 TQ	TNBLS	10/01-12/01
	Texas	H	8.80 FQ	14.55 AW	21.19 TQ	TXBLS	10/01-12/01
	Amarillo MSA, TX	H	9.10 FQ	13.44 AW	20.29 TQ	TXBLS	10/01-12/01
	Austin-San Marcos MSA, TX	H	9.37 FQ	15.33 AW	21.66 TQ	TXBLS	10/01-12/01
	Beaumont-Port Arthur MSA, TX	H	9.86 FQ	14.98 AW	21.30 TQ	TXBLS	10/01-12/01
	Brazoria PMSA, TX	H	9.88 FQ	17.07 AW	24.70 TQ	TXBLS	10/01-12/01
	Brownsville-Harlingen-San Benito MSA, TX	H	6.18 FQ	9.45 AW	13.58 TQ	TXBLS	10/01-12/01
	Corpus Christi MSA, TX	H	10.80 FQ	16.46 AW	22.42 TQ	TXBLS	10/01-12/01
	Dallas PMSA, TX	H	9.50 FQ	14.81 AW	21.05 TQ	TXBLS	10/01-12/01
	El Paso MSA, TX	H	6.08 FQ	10.86 AW	18.73 TQ	TXBLS	10/01-12/01
	Fort Worth-Arlington PMSA, TX	H	8.66 FQ	14.06 AW	20.15 TQ	TXBLS	10/01-12/01
	Galveston-Texas City PMSA, TX	H	11.75 FQ	16.93 AW	23.81 TQ	TXBLS	10/01-12/01
	Houston PMSA, TX	H	9.23 FQ	15.10 AW	21.68 TQ	TXBLS	10/01-12/01
	Killeen-Temple MSA, TX	H	9.13 FQ	14.66 AW	21.16 TQ	TXBLS	10/01-12/01
	Longview-Marshall MSA, TX	H	9.90 FQ	14.70 AW	20.03 TQ	TXBLS	10/01-12/01
	Lubbock MSA, TX	H	8.02 FQ	11.76 AW	16.31 TQ	TXBLS	10/01-12/01
	McAllen-Edinburg-Mission MSA, TX	H	7.82 FQ	11.13 AW	14.39 TQ	TXBLS	10/01-12/01
	Odessa-Midland MSA, TX	H	8.06 FQ	13.51 AW	19.44 TQ	TXBLS	10/01-12/01
	San Antonio MSA, TX	H	8.00 FQ	12.24 AW	16.69 TQ	TXBLS	10/01-12/01
	Tyler MSA, TX	H	7.94 FQ	13.49 AW	19.59 TQ	TXBLS	10/01-12/01
	Waco MSA, TX	H	9.24 FQ	13.69 AW	19.40 TQ	TXBLS	10/01-12/01
	Utah	H	10.76 FQ	16.02 AW	21.30 TQ	UTBLS	10/01-12/01
	Provo-Orem MSA, UT	H	11.11 FQ	16.42 AW	21.33 TQ	UTBLS	10/01-12/01
	Salt Lake City-Ogden MSA, UT	H	10.17 FQ	15.79 AW	21.10 TQ	UTBLS	10/01-12/01
	Vermont	H	10.13 FQ	14.89 AW	19.78 TQ	VTBLS	10/01-12/01
	Burlington MSA, VT	H	9.52 FQ	15.26 AW	20.78 TQ	VTBLS	10/01-12/01
	Virginia	H	10.20 FQ	16.19 AW	21.91 TQ	VABLS	10/01-12/01
	Lynchburg MSA, VA	H	13.87 FQ	19.22 AW	22.64 TQ	VABLS	10/01-12/01
	Norfolk-Virginia Beach-Newport News MSA, VA-NC	H	11.34 FQ	15.98 AW	20.52 TQ	VABLS	10/01-12/01
	Richmond-Petersburg MSA, VA	H	12.63 FQ	18.70 AW	25.39 TQ	VABLS	10/01-12/01
	Roanoke MSA, VA	H	10.06 FQ	14.23 AW	19.10 TQ	VABLS	10/01-12/01
	Washington	H	11.12 FQ	18.76 AW	26.88 TQ	WABLS	10/01-12/01
	Bremerton PMSA, WA	H	18.24 FQ	23.09 AW	26.91 TQ	WABLS	10/01-12/01

AAW	Average annual wage	**AOH**	Average offered, high	**ASH**	Average starting, high	**H**	Hourly	**M**	Monthly	**S**	Special: hourly and annual
AE	Average entry wage	**AOL**	Average offered, low	**ASL**	Average starting, low	**HI**	Highest wage paid	**MTC**	Median total compensation	**TQ**	Third quartile wage
AEX	Average experienced wage	**APH**	Average pay, high range	**AW**	Average wage paid	**HR**	High end range	**MW**	Median wage paid	**W**	Weekly
AO	Average offered	**APL**	Average pay, low range	**FQ**	First quartile wage	**LR**	Low end range	**SQ**	Second quartile wage	**Y**	Yearly

Occupation/Type/Industry	Location	Per	Low	Mid	High	Source	Date
Machinist	Olympia PMSA, WA	H	8.10 FQ	13.93 AW	21.20 TQ	WABLS	10/01-12/01
	Richland-Kennewick-Pasco MSA, WA	H	11.59 FQ	19.14 AW	26.31 TQ	WABLS	10/01-12/01
	Seattle-Bellevue-Everett PMSA, WA	H	11.91 FQ	19.75 AW	27.82 TQ	WABLS	10/01-12/01
	Spokane MSA, WA	H	9.19 FQ	14.47 AW	20.95 TQ	WABLS	10/01-12/01
	Tacoma PMSA, WA	H	12.82 FQ	19.43 AW	26.77 TQ	WABLS	10/01-12/01
	Yakima MSA, WA	H	10.48 FQ	15.18 AW	20.68 TQ	WABLS	10/01-12/01
	West Virginia	H	8.17 FQ	14.37 AW	21.85 TQ	WVBLS	10/01-12/01
	Charleston MSA, WV	H	8.40 FQ	14.33 AW	23.93 TQ	WVBLS	10/01-12/01
	Huntington-Ashland MSA, WV-KY-OH	H	9.67 FQ	16.03 AW	23.13 TQ	WVBLS	10/01-12/01
	Wisconsin	H	10.96 FQ	16.70 AW	23.16 TQ	WIBLS	10/01-12/01
	Appleton-Oshkosh-Neenah MSA, WI	H	11.88 FQ	16.57 AW	21.21 TQ	WIBLS	10/01-12/01
	Green Bay MSA, WI	H	13.34 FQ	20.00 AW	27.42 TQ	WIBLS	10/01-12/01
	Madison MSA, WI	H	10.29 FQ	15.70 AW	21.23 TQ	WIBLS	10/01-12/01
	Milwaukee-Waukesha PMSA, WI	H	10.31 FQ	17.64 AW	25.75 TQ	WIBLS	10/01-12/01
	Racine PMSA, WI	H	10.31 FQ	15.02 AW	19.25 TQ	WIBLS	10/01-12/01
	Wyoming	H	8.65 FQ	15.53 AW	23.12 TQ	WYBLS	10/01-12/01
	Puerto Rico	H	6.06 FQ	9.70 AW	15.46 TQ	PRBLS	10/01-12/01
Maid and Housekeeping Cleaner	Alabama	H	5.60 FQ	6.79 AW	8.62 TQ	ALBLS	10/01-12/01
	Birmingham MSA, AL	H	5.61 FQ	6.83 AW	8.65 TQ	ALBLS	10/01-12/01
	Huntsville MSA, AL	H	5.64 FQ	6.67 AW	8.45 TQ	ALBLS	10/01-12/01
	Mobile MSA, AL	H	5.63 FQ	7.02 AW	8.77 TQ	ALBLS	10/01-12/01
	Montgomery MSA, AL	H	5.62 FQ	6.65 AW	8.62 TQ	ALBLS	10/01-12/01
	Alaska	H	7.15 FQ	9.91 AW	13.44 TQ	AKBLS	10/01-12/01
	Anchorage MSA, AK	H	7.95 FQ	10.25 AW	13.40 TQ	AKBLS	10/01-12/01
	Arizona	H	5.69 FQ	7.17 AW	9.06 TQ	AZBLS	10/01-12/01
	Phoenix-Mesa MSA, AZ	H	5.70 FQ	7.37 AW	9.39 TQ	AZBLS	10/01-12/01
	Tucson MSA, AZ	H	5.75 FQ	7.14 AW	8.88 TQ	AZBLS	10/01-12/01
	Arkansas	H	5.64 FQ	6.67 AW	8.34 TQ	ARBLS	10/01-12/01
	Fayetteville-Springdale-Rogers MSA, AR	H	5.76 FQ	7.00 AW	8.59 TQ	ARBLS	10/01-12/01
	Fort Smith MSA, AR-OK	H	5.65 FQ	6.90 AW	8.93 TQ	ARBLS	10/01-12/01
	Little Rock-North Little Rock MSA, AR	H	5.74 FQ	6.88 AW	8.42 TQ	ARBLS	10/01-12/01
	California	H	6.58 FQ	8.52 AW	11.46 TQ	CABLS	10/01-12/01
	Bakersfield MSA, CA	H	6.37 FQ	7.31 AW	9.00 TQ	CABLS	10/01-12/01
	Chico-Paradise MSA, CA	H	6.45 FQ	7.68 AW	9.24 TQ	CABLS	10/01-12/01
	Fresno MSA, CA	H	6.39 FQ	7.31 AW	8.70 TQ	CABLS	10/01-12/01
	Los Angeles-Long Beach PMSA, CA	H	6.73 FQ	8.49 AW	10.95 TQ	CABLS	10/01-12/01
	Merced MSA, CA	H	6.39 FQ	7.35 AW	8.82 TQ	CABLS	10/01-12/01
	Modesto MSA, CA	H	6.44 FQ	7.69 AW	9.04 TQ	CABLS	10/01-12/01
	Oakland PMSA, CA	H	6.73 FQ	9.35 AW	13.23 TQ	CABLS	10/01-12/01
	Orange County PMSA, CA	H	6.61 FQ	7.85 AW	9.44 TQ	CABLS	10/01-12/01
	Redding MSA, CA	H	6.38 FQ	7.29 AW	8.63 TQ	CABLS	10/01-12/01
	Riverside-San Bernardino PMSA, CA	H	6.46 FQ	7.67 AW	9.40 TQ	CABLS	10/01-12/01
	Sacramento PMSA, CA	H	6.51 FQ	8.19 AW	10.72 TQ	CABLS	10/01-12/01
	Salinas MSA, CA	H	6.81 FQ	8.59 AW	10.83 TQ	CABLS	10/01-12/01
	San Diego MSA, CA	H	6.68 FQ	8.35 AW	10.43 TQ	CABLS	10/01-12/01
	San Francisco PMSA, CA	H	7.53 FQ	11.04 AW	14.37 TQ	CABLS	10/01-12/01
	San Jose PMSA, CA	H	6.65 FQ	8.77 AW	11.02 TQ	CABLS	10/01-12/01
	San Luis Obispo-Atascadero-Paso Robles MSA, CA	H	6.59 FQ	7.70 AW	8.68 TQ	CABLS	10/01-12/01
	Santa Barbara-Santa Maria-Lompoc MSA, CA	H	6.41 FQ	7.71 AW	10.03 TQ	CABLS	10/01-12/01
	Santa Cruz-Watsonville PMSA, CA	H	6.55 FQ	8.48 AW	11.20 TQ	CABLS	10/01-12/01
	Santa Rosa PMSA, CA	H	6.44 FQ	8.07 AW	10.66 TQ	CABLS	10/01-12/01
	Stockton-Lodi MSA, CA	H	6.50 FQ	9.11 AW	13.22 TQ	CABLS	10/01-12/01
	Vallejo-Fairfield-Napa PMSA, CA	H	6.67 FQ	9.25 AW	13.34 TQ	CABLS	10/01-12/01
	Ventura PMSA, CA	H	6.46 FQ	7.84 AW	10.05 TQ	CABLS	10/01-12/01
	Visalia-Tulare-Porterville MSA, CA	H	6.42 FQ	7.51 AW	9.37 TQ	CABLS	10/01-12/01
	Colorado	H	6.06 FQ	8.44 AW	11.11 TQ	COBLS	10/01-12/01
	Boulder-Longmont PMSA, CO	H	6.51 FQ	8.76 AW	11.36 TQ	COBLS	10/01-12/01
	Colorado Springs MSA, CO	H	6.18 FQ	7.67 AW	9.09 TQ	COBLS	10/01-12/01

AAW Average annual wage **AOH** Average offered, high **ASH** Average starting, high **H** Hourly **M** Monthly **S** Special: hourly and annual
AE Average entry wage **AOL** Average offered, low **ASL** Average starting, low **HI** Highest wage paid **MTC** Median total compensation **TQ** Third quartile wage
AEX Average experienced wage **APH** Average pay, high range **AW** Average wage paid **HR** High end range **MW** Median wage paid **W** Weekly
AO Average offered **APL** Average pay, low range **FQ** First quartile wage **LR** Low end range **SQ** Second quartile wage **Y** Yearly

Occupation/Type/Industry	Location	Per	Low	Mid	High	Source	Date
Maid and Housekeeping Cleaner	Denver PMSA, CO	H	6.18 FQ	8.48 AW	11.05 TQ	COBLS	10/01-12/01
	Fort Collins-Loveland MSA, CO	H	6.29 FQ	8.00 AW	10.16 TQ	COBLS	10/01-12/01
	Greeley PMSA, CO	H	5.59 FQ	7.00 AW	9.45 TQ	COBLS	10/01-12/01
	Connecticut	H	6.76 FQ	9.34 AW	12.94 TQ	CTBLS	10/01-12/01
	Bridgeport PMSA, CT	H	6.92 FQ	9.83 AW	13.28 TQ	CTBLS	10/01-12/01
	Danbury PMSA, CT	H	7.34 FQ	9.62 AW	12.72 TQ	CTBLS	10/01-12/01
	Hartford MSA, CT	H	6.62 FQ	9.06 AW	13.10 TQ	CTBLS	10/01-12/01
	New Haven-Meriden PMSA, CT	H	6.82 FQ	9.47 AW	12.71 TQ	CTBLS	10/01-12/01
	New London-Norwich MSA, CT-RI	H	7.15 FQ	9.14 AW	11.56 TQ	CTBLS	10/01-12/01
	Stamford-Norwalk PMSA, CT	H	6.96 FQ	10.02 AW	13.55 TQ	CTBLS	10/01-12/01
	Waterbury PMSA, CT	H	7.22 FQ	9.79 AW	13.80 TQ	CTBLS	10/01-12/01
	Delaware	H	6.71 FQ	8.17 AW	10.24 TQ	DEBLS	10/01-12/01
	Wilmington-Newark PMSA, DE-MD	H	6.60 FQ	8.12 AW	10.49 TQ	DEBLS	10/01-12/01
	District of Columbia	H	7.68 FQ	11.19 AW	14.47 TQ	DCBLS	10/01-12/01
	Washington PMSA, DC-MD-VA-WV	H	6.23 FQ	9.13 AW	13.03 TQ	DCBLS	10/01-12/01
	Florida	H	5.77 FQ	7.48 AW	9.62 TQ	FLBLS	10/01-12/01
	Daytona Beach MSA, FL	H	5.59 FQ	6.88 AW	8.60 TQ	FLBLS	10/01-12/01
	Fort Lauderdale PMSA, FL	H	5.76 FQ	7.66 AW	10.01 TQ	FLBLS	10/01-12/01
	Fort Myers-Cape Coral MSA, FL	H	5.93 FQ	7.79 AW	9.74 TQ	FLBLS	10/01-12/01
	Fort Pierce-Port St. Lucie MSA, FL	H	5.62 FQ	7.12 AW	8.89 TQ	FLBLS	10/01-12/01
	Fort Walton Beach MSA, FL	H	5.81 FQ	7.32 AW	8.87 TQ	FLBLS	10/01-12/01
	Gainesville MSA, FL	H	6.05 FQ	7.76 AW	9.69 TQ	FLBLS	10/01-12/01
	Jacksonville MSA, FL	H	5.96 FQ	7.52 AW	8.90 TQ	FLBLS	10/01-12/01
	Lakeland-Winter Haven MSA, FL	H	5.63 FQ	6.88 AW	8.81 TQ	FLBLS	10/01-12/01
	Melbourne-Titusville-Palm Bay MSA, FL	H	5.59 FQ	7.01 AW	8.74 TQ	FLBLS	10/01-12/01
	Miami PMSA, FL	H	5.69 FQ	7.20 AW	9.05 TQ	FLBLS	10/01-12/01
	Naples MSA, FL	H	5.97 FQ	8.09 AW	10.73 TQ	FLBLS	10/01-12/01
	Ocala MSA, FL	H	5.67 FQ	6.88 AW	8.68 TQ	FLBLS	10/01-12/01
	Orlando MSA, FL	H	5.80 FQ	7.51 AW	9.79 TQ	FLBLS	10/01-12/01
	Pensacola MSA, FL	H	5.58 FQ	6.56 AW	8.16 TQ	FLBLS	10/01-12/01
	Sarasota-Bradenton MSA, FL	H	6.19 FQ	8.02 AW	10.16 TQ	FLBLS	10/01-12/01
	Tallahassee MSA, FL	H	5.64 FQ	7.14 AW	9.07 TQ	FLBLS	10/01-12/01
	Tampa-St. Petersburg-Clearwater MSA, FL	H	5.81 FQ	7.60 AW	9.96 TQ	FLBLS	10/01-12/01
	West Palm Beach-Boca Raton MSA, FL	H	6.31 FQ	8.02 AW	9.96 TQ	FLBLS	10/01-12/01
	Georgia	H	5.82 FQ	7.45 AW	9.24 TQ	GABLS	10/01-12/01
	Atlanta MSA, GA	H	6.80 FQ	8.03 AW	9.79 TQ	GABLS	10/01-12/01
	Augusta-Aiken MSA, GA-SC	H	5.67 FQ	7.10 AW	9.10 TQ	GABLS	10/01-12/01
	Columbus MSA, GA-AL	H	5.45 FQ	6.52 AW	8.35 TQ	GABLS	10/01-12/01
	Macon MSA, GA	H	5.67 FQ	6.70 AW	8.44 TQ	GABLS	10/01-12/01
	Savannah MSA, GA	H	5.69 FQ	6.73 AW	8.37 TQ	GABLS	10/01-12/01
	Hawaii	H	7.09 FQ	11.16 AW	13.82 TQ	HIBLS	10/01-12/01
	Honolulu MSA, HI	H	6.39 FQ	10.57 AW	13.60 TQ	HIBLS	10/01-12/01
	Idaho	H	5.72 FQ	7.32 AW	9.57 TQ	IDBLS	10/01-12/01
	Boise City MSA, ID	H	5.83 FQ	7.45 AW	9.64 TQ	IDBLS	10/01-12/01
	Illinois	H	5.88 FQ	8.15 AW	11.49 TQ	ILBLS	10/01-12/01
	Champaign-Urbana MSA, IL	H	5.71 FQ	7.41 AW	9.77 TQ	ILBLS	10/01-12/01
	Chicago PMSA, IL	H	6.13 FQ	8.67 AW	12.10 TQ	ILBLS	10/01-12/01
	Peoria-Pekin MSA, IL	H	5.62 FQ	6.72 AW	8.42 TQ	ILBLS	10/01-12/01
	Rockford MSA, IL	H	5.77 FQ	7.36 AW	9.12 TQ	ILBLS	10/01-12/01
	Springfield MSA, IL	H	5.84 FQ	7.70 AW	9.22 TQ	ILBLS	10/01-12/01
	Indiana	H	5.79 FQ	7.51 AW	9.87 TQ	INBLS	10/01-12/01
	Elkhart-Goshen MSA, IN	H	5.88 FQ	7.79 AW	10.40 TQ	INBLS	10/01-12/01
	Evansville-Henderson MSA, IN-KY	H	5.73 FQ	7.44 AW	10.10 TQ	INBLS	10/01-12/01
	Fort Wayne MSA, IN	H	5.86 FQ	7.52 AW	9.13 TQ	INBLS	10/01-12/01
	Gary PMSA, IN	H	5.74 FQ	7.14 AW	8.60 TQ	INBLS	10/01-12/01
	Indianapolis MSA, IN	H	5.88 FQ	7.66 AW	10.05 TQ	INBLS	10/01-12/01
	Lafayette MSA, IN	H	6.06 FQ	8.00 AW	10.41 TQ	INBLS	10/01-12/01
	South Bend MSA, IN	H	5.87 FQ	7.87 AW	10.54 TQ	INBLS	10/01-12/01
	Iowa	H	5.93 FQ	7.74 AW	9.83 TQ	IABLS	10/01-12/01
	Cedar Rapids MSA, IA	H	6.19 FQ	8.05 AW	10.37 TQ	IABLS	10/01-12/01

AAW Average annual wage **AE** Average entry wage **AEX** Average experienced wage **AO** Average offered **AOH** Average offered, high **AOL** Average offered, low **APH** Average pay, high range **APL** Average pay, low range **ASH** Average starting, high **ASL** Average starting, low **AW** Average wage paid **FQ** First quartile wage **H** Hourly **HI** Highest wage paid **HR** High end range **LR** Low end range **M** Monthly **MTC** Median total compensation **MW** Median wage paid **SQ** Second quartile wage **S** Special: hourly and annual **TQ** Third quartile wage **W** Weekly **Y** Yearly

Occupation/Type/Industry	Location	Per	Low	Mid	High	Source	Date
Maid and Housekeeping Cleaner	Davenport-Moline-Rock Island MSA, IA-IL	H	5.74 FQ	7.32 AW	9.60 TQ	IABLS	10/01-12/01
	Des Moines MSA, IA	H	7.07 FQ	8.21 AW	10.01 TQ	IABLS	10/01-12/01
	Kansas	H	5.78 FQ	7.28 AW	9.09 TQ	KSBLS	10/01-12/01
	Topeka MSA, KS	H	5.81 FQ	7.13 AW	8.90 TQ	KSBLS	10/01-12/01
	Wichita MSA, KS	H	5.78 FQ	7.38 AW	9.44 TQ	KSBLS	10/01-12/01
	Kentucky	H	5.77 FQ	7.64 AW	10.32 TQ	KYBLS	10/01-12/01
	Lexington MSA, KY	H	6.04 FQ	7.75 AW	9.69 TQ	KYBLS	10/01-12/01
	Louisville MSA, KY-IN	H	5.97 FQ	8.21 AW	11.12 TQ	KYBLS	10/01-12/01
	Louisiana	H	5.61 FQ	6.58 AW	8.22 TQ	LABLS	10/01-12/01
	Baton Rouge MSA, LA	H	5.60 FQ	6.66 AW	8.45 TQ	LABLS	10/01-12/01
	Houma MSA, LA	H	5.59 FQ	6.47 AW	7.62 TQ	LABLS	10/01-12/01
	Lafayette MSA, LA	H	5.52 FQ	6.24 AW	7.13 TQ	LABLS	10/01-12/01
	Lake Charles MSA, LA	H	5.60 FQ	6.28 AW	7.18 TQ	LABLS	10/01-12/01
	New Orleans MSA, LA	H	5.66 FQ	6.78 AW	8.45 TQ	LABLS	10/01-12/01
	Shreveport-Bossier City MSA, LA	H	5.59 FQ	6.51 AW	8.03 TQ	LABLS	10/01-12/01
	Maine	H	6.02 FQ	8.30 AW	11.48 TQ	MEBLS	10/01-12/01
	Portland MSA, ME	H	7.02 FQ	8.63 AW	11.16 TQ	MEBLS	10/01-12/01
	Maryland	H	6.15 FQ	8.88 AW	12.85 TQ	MDBLS	10/01-12/01
	Baltimore PMSA, MD	H	6.59 FQ	9.18 AW	13.03 TQ	MDBLS	10/01-12/01
	Massachusetts	H	7.22 FQ	9.52 AW	12.67 TQ	MABLS	10/01-12/01
	Boston PMSA, MA-NH	H	7.41 FQ	9.94 AW	13.04 TQ	MABLS	10/01-12/01
	Brockton PMSA, MA	H	7.41 FQ	9.56 AW	12.94 TQ	MABLS	10/01-12/01
	Lawrence PMSA, MA-NH	H	7.19 FQ	8.90 AW	11.08 TQ	MABLS	10/01-12/01
	Lowell PMSA, MA-NH	H	7.35 FQ	9.36 AW	11.63 TQ	MABLS	10/01-12/01
	New Bedford PMSA, MA	H	7.02 FQ	8.51 AW	11.12 TQ	MABLS	10/01-12/01
	Springfield MSA, MA	H	6.99 FQ	8.82 AW	11.17 TQ	MABLS	10/01-12/01
	Worcester PMSA, MA-CT	H	7.06 FQ	8.79 AW	11.07 TQ	MABLS	10/01-12/01
	Michigan	H	6.06 FQ	8.35 AW	10.91 TQ	MIBLS	10/01-12/01
	Ann Arbor PMSA, MI	H	7.00 FQ	8.93 AW	11.15 TQ	MIBLS	10/01-12/01
	Detroit PMSA, MI	H	7.27 FQ	9.15 AW	11.59 TQ	MIBLS	10/01-12/01
	Flint PMSA, MI	H	5.69 FQ	7.75 AW	10.75 TQ	MIBLS	10/01-12/01
	Grand Rapids-Muskegon-Holland MSA, MI	H	6.10 FQ	8.28 AW	10.61 TQ	MIBLS	10/01-12/01
	Kalamazoo-Battle Creek MSA, MI	H	6.10 FQ	8.39 AW	11.25 TQ	MIBLS	10/01-12/01
	Lansing-East Lansing MSA, MI	H	5.92 FQ	8.12 AW	10.56 TQ	MIBLS	10/01-12/01
	Saginaw-Bay City-Midland MSA, MI	H	5.59 FQ	7.32 AW	9.66 TQ	MIBLS	10/01-12/01
	Minnesota	H	6.16 FQ	8.64 AW	11.75 TQ	MNBLS	10/01-12/01
	Duluth-Superior MSA, MN-WI	H	5.70 FQ	7.44 AW	10.60 TQ	MNBLS	10/01-12/01
	Minneapolis-St. Paul MSA, MN-WI	H	7.01 FQ	9.42 AW	12.78 TQ	MNBLS	10/01-12/01
	St. Cloud MSA, MN	H	5.86 FQ	7.87 AW	10.46 TQ	MNBLS	10/01-12/01
	Mississippi	H	5.59 FQ	6.75 AW	8.42 TQ	MSBLS	10/01-12/01
	Biloxi-Gulfport-Pascagoula MSA, MS	H	5.63 FQ	6.96 AW	8.54 TQ	MSBLS	10/01-12/01
	Jackson MSA, MS	H	5.71 FQ	6.85 AW	8.40 TQ	MSBLS	10/01-12/01
	Missouri	H	5.80 FQ	7.45 AW	9.68 TQ	MOBLS	10/01-12/01
	Kansas City MSA, MO-KS	H	5.93 FQ	7.73 AW	10.02 TQ	MOBLS	10/01-12/01
	St. Louis MSA, MO-IL	H	5.89 FQ	7.66 AW	9.94 TQ	MOBLS	10/01-12/01
	Springfield MSA, MO	H	5.72 FQ	6.95 AW	8.53 TQ	MOBLS	10/01-12/01
	Montana	H	5.64 FQ	6.96 AW	8.88 TQ	MTBLS	10/01-12/01
	Billings MSA, MT	H	5.64 FQ	6.91 AW	8.64 TQ	MTBLS	10/01-12/01
	Nebraska	H	5.88 FQ	7.54 AW	9.82 TQ	NEBLS	10/01-12/01
	Lincoln MSA, NE	H	5.91 FQ	7.55 AW	9.84 TQ	NEBLS	10/01-12/01
	Omaha MSA, NE-IA	H	6.80 FQ	8.00 AW	9.85 TQ	NEBLS	10/01-12/01
	Nevada	H	6.62 FQ	9.45 AW	12.28 TQ	NVBLS	10/01-12/01
	Las Vegas MSA, NV-AZ	H	6.92 FQ	9.77 AW	12.51 TQ	NVBLS	10/01-12/01
	Reno MSA, NV	H	5.99 FQ	8.06 AW	10.49 TQ	NVBLS	10/01-12/01
	New Hampshire	H	7.21 FQ	8.86 AW	10.83 TQ	NHBLS	10/01-12/01
	Manchester PMSA, NH	H	7.33 FQ	9.09 AW	11.45 TQ	NHBLS	10/01-12/01
	Nashua PMSA, NH	H	7.35 FQ	9.06 AW	11.44 TQ	NHBLS	10/01-12/01
	Portsmouth-Rochester PMSA, NH-ME	H	7.14 FQ	8.65 AW	10.78 TQ	NHBLS	10/01-12/01
	New Jersey	H	6.65 FQ	9.04 AW	12.29 TQ	NJBLS	10/01-12/01
	Atlantic-Cape May PMSA, NJ	H	7.12 FQ	9.65 AW	12.95 TQ	NJBLS	10/01-12/01
	Bergen-Passaic PMSA, NJ	H	6.54 FQ	8.95 AW	12.09 TQ	NJBLS	10/01-12/01
	Jersey City PMSA, NJ	H	5.84 FQ	8.12 AW	11.30 TQ	NJBLS	10/01-12/01
	Middlesex-Somerset-Hunterdon PMSA, NJ	H	6.98 FQ	8.87 AW	11.50 TQ	NJBLS	10/01-12/01

AAW	Average annual wage	**AOH**	Average offered, high	**ASH**	Average starting, high	**H**	Hourly	**M**	Monthly	**S**	Special: hourly and annual
AE	Average entry wage	**AOL**	Average offered, low	**ASL**	Average starting, low	**HI**	Highest wage paid	**MTC**	Median total compensation	**TQ**	Third quartile wage
AEX	Average experienced wage	**APH**	Average pay, high range	**AW**	Average wage paid	**HR**	High end range	**MW**	Median wage paid	**W**	Weekly
AO	Average offered	**APL**	Average pay, low range	**FQ**	First quartile wage	**LR**	Low end range	**SQ**	Second quartile wage	**Y**	Yearly

Occupation/Type/Industry	Location	Per	Low	Mid	High	Source	Date
Maid and Housekeeping Cleaner	Monmouth-Ocean PMSA, NJ	H	6.02 FQ	8.26 AW	10.59 TQ	NJBLS	10/01-12/01
	Newark PMSA, NJ	H	6.53 FQ	9.30 AW	12.76 TQ	NJBLS	10/01-12/01
	Trenton PMSA, NJ	H	7.03 FQ	9.80 AW	12.82 TQ	NJBLS	10/01-12/01
	New Mexico	H	5.62 FQ	6.85 AW	8.60 TQ	NMBLS	10/01-12/01
	Albuquerque MSA, NM	H	5.62 FQ	6.87 AW	8.52 TQ	NMBLS	10/01-12/01
	Las Cruces MSA, NM	H	5.67 FQ	6.63 AW	8.28 TQ	NMBLS	10/01-12/01
	New York	H	6.11 FQ	10.92 AW	17.64 TQ	NYBLS	10/01-12/01
	Albany-Schenectady-Troy MSA, NY	H	5.96 FQ	7.77 AW	10.07 TQ	NYBLS	10/01-12/01
	Binghamton MSA, NY	H	5.70 FQ	6.99 AW	8.72 TQ	NYBLS	10/01-12/01
	Buffalo-Niagara Falls MSA, NY	H	5.65 FQ	7.53 AW	11.43 TQ	NYBLS	10/01-12/01
	Dutchess County PMSA, NY	H	5.83 FQ	7.76 AW	10.46 TQ	NYBLS	10/01-12/01
	Nassau-Suffolk PMSA, NY	H	6.55 FQ	9.88 AW	14.14 TQ	NYBLS	10/01-12/01
	New York PMSA, NY	H	7.59 FQ	13.66 AW	19.40 TQ	NYBLS	10/01-12/01
	Newburgh PMSA, NY-PA	H	5.92 FQ	7.97 AW	10.63 TQ	NYBLS	10/01-12/01
	Rochester MSA, NY	H	5.87 FQ	7.48 AW	9.22 TQ	NYBLS	10/01-12/01
	Syracuse MSA, NY	H	5.73 FQ	7.11 AW	8.86 TQ	NYBLS	10/01-12/01
	Utica-Rome MSA, NY	H	5.77 FQ	7.67 AW	10.26 TQ	NYBLS	10/01-12/01
	North Carolina	H	5.80 FQ	7.71 AW	10.13 TQ	NCBLS	10/01-12/01
	Asheville MSA, NC	H	5.77 FQ	7.50 AW	9.64 TQ	NCBLS	10/01-12/01
	Charlotte-Gastonia-Rock Hill MSA, NC-SC	H	6.02 FQ	7.83 AW	10.07 TQ	NCBLS	10/01-12/01
	Fayetteville MSA, NC	H	5.55 FQ	6.75 AW	8.47 TQ	NCBLS	10/01-12/01
	Greensboro-Winston-Salem-High Point MSA, NC	H	5.80 FQ	7.49 AW	9.55 TQ	NCBLS	10/01-12/01
	Hickory-Morganton-Lenoir MSA, NC	H	5.93 FQ	7.71 AW	9.88 TQ	NCBLS	10/01-12/01
	Raleigh-Durham-Chapel Hill MSA, NC	H	6.33 FQ	8.28 AW	10.37 TQ	NCBLS	10/01-12/01
	Wilmington MSA, NC	H	5.82 FQ	7.81 AW	10.20 TQ	NCBLS	10/01-12/01
	North Dakota	H	5.64 FQ	7.02 AW	8.85 TQ	NDBLS	10/01-12/01
	Fargo-Moorhead MSA, ND-MN	H	5.77 FQ	7.45 AW	9.66 TQ	NDBLS	10/01-12/01
	Ohio	H	5.99 FQ	8.01 AW	10.54 TQ	OHBLS	10/01-12/01
	Akron PMSA, OH	H	6.12 FQ	8.03 AW	10.34 TQ	OHBLS	10/01-12/01
	Canton-Massillon MSA, OH	H	5.86 FQ	7.91 AW	10.58 TQ	OHBLS	10/01-12/01
	Cincinnati PMSA, OH-KY-IN	H	6.88 FQ	8.57 AW	10.94 TQ	OHBLS	10/01-12/01
	Cleveland-Lorain-Elyria PMSA, OH	H	6.17 FQ	8.17 AW	10.64 TQ	OHBLS	10/01-12/01
	Columbus MSA, OH	H	6.26 FQ	8.44 AW	11.05 TQ	OHBLS	10/01-12/01
	Dayton-Springfield MSA, OH	H	6.01 FQ	8.00 AW	10.54 TQ	OHBLS	10/01-12/01
	Hamilton-Middletown PMSA, OH	H	6.10 FQ	8.36 AW	10.61 TQ	OHBLS	10/01-12/01
	Mansfield MSA, OH	H	5.78 FQ	7.43 AW	9.37 TQ	OHBLS	10/01-12/01
	Toledo MSA, OH	H	5.76 FQ	7.68 AW	10.29 TQ	OHBLS	10/01-12/01
	Youngstown-Warren MSA, OH	H	5.79 FQ	7.56 AW	9.84 TQ	OHBLS	10/01-12/01
	Oklahoma	H	5.65 FQ	6.92 AW	8.66 TQ	OKBLS	10/01-12/01
	Oklahoma City MSA, OK	H	5.73 FQ	7.04 AW	8.79 TQ	OKBLS	10/01-12/01
	Tulsa MSA, OK	H	5.66 FQ	7.01 AW	8.68 TQ	OKBLS	10/01-12/01
	Oregon	H	6.88 FQ	8.30 AW	10.57 TQ	ORBLS	10/01-12/01
	Eugene-Springfield MSA, OR	H	6.84 FQ	7.96 AW	10.09 TQ	ORBLS	10/01-12/01
	Medford-Ashland MSA, OR	H	7.04 FQ	8.34 AW	10.45 TQ	ORBLS	10/01-12/01
	Portland-Vancouver PMSA, OR-WA	H	6.85 FQ	8.58 AW	11.37 TQ	ORBLS	10/01-12/01
	Salem PMSA, OR	H	6.96 FQ	9.02 AW	12.74 TQ	ORBLS	10/01-12/01
	Pennsylvania	H	5.96 FQ	8.23 AW	10.88 TQ	PABLS	10/01-12/01
	Allentown-Bethlehem-Easton MSA, PA	H	6.52 FQ	9.58 AW	15.03 TQ	PABLS	10/01-12/01
	Erie MSA, PA	H	5.91 FQ	7.53 AW	9.50 TQ	PABLS	10/01-12/01
	Harrisburg-Lebanon-Carlisle MSA, PA	H	5.99 FQ	8.16 AW	10.75 TQ	PABLS	10/01-12/01
	Johnstown MSA, PA	H	5.62 FQ	7.19 AW	9.82 TQ	PABLS	10/01-12/01
	Lancaster MSA, PA	H	6.95 FQ	8.43 AW	10.74 TQ	PABLS	10/01-12/01
	Philadelphia PMSA, PA-NJ	H	6.71 FQ	8.95 AW	11.59 TQ	PABLS	10/01-12/01
	Pittsburgh MSA, PA	H	5.86 FQ	7.91 AW	10.46 TQ	PABLS	10/01-12/01
	Reading MSA, PA	H	5.86 FQ	8.06 AW	10.60 TQ	PABLS	10/01-12/01
	Scranton-Wilkes-Barre-Hazleton MSA, PA	H	5.95 FQ	7.69 AW	9.56 TQ	PABLS	10/01-12/01
	York MSA, PA	H	5.84 FQ	7.60 AW	9.37 TQ	PABLS	10/01-12/01
	Rhode Island	H	6.86 FQ	9.14 AW	12.77 TQ	RIBLS	10/01-12/01

AAW Average annual wage **AOH** Average offered, high **ASH** Average starting, high **H** Hourly **M** Monthly **S** Special: hourly and annual
AE Average entry wage **AOL** Average offered, low **ASL** Average starting, low **HI** Highest wage paid **MTC** Median total compensation **TQ** Third quartile wage
AEX Average experienced wage **APH** Average pay, high range **AW** Average wage paid **HR** High end range **MW** Median wage paid **W** Weekly
AO Average offered **APL** Average pay, low range **FQ** First quartile wage **LR** Low end range **SQ** Second quartile wage **Y** Yearly

Occupation/Type/Industry	Location	Per	Low	Mid	High	Source	Date
Maid and Housekeeping Cleaner	Providence-Fall River-Warwick MSA, RI-MA	H	6.85 FQ	9.03 AW	12.70 TQ	RIBLS	10/01-12/01
	South Carolina	H	5.75 FQ	7.33 AW	9.56 TQ	SCBLS	10/01-12/01
	Charleston-North Charleston MSA, SC	H	5.75 FQ	7.24 AW	9.47 TQ	SCBLS	10/01-12/01
	Columbia MSA, SC	H	5.74 FQ	7.37 AW	9.86 TQ	SCBLS	10/01-12/01
	Greenville-Spartanburg-Anderson MSA, SC	H	5.79 FQ	7.28 AW	9.14 TQ	SCBLS	10/01-12/01
	Myrtle Beach MSA, SC	H	5.96 FQ	7.68 AW	9.81 TQ	SCBLS	10/01-12/01
	South Dakota	H	5.76 FQ	7.29 AW	9.17 TQ	SDBLS	10/01-12/01
	Sioux Falls MSA, SD	H	6.19 FQ	8.01 AW	10.30 TQ	SDBLS	10/01-12/01
	Tennessee	H	5.80 FQ	7.33 AW	9.07 TQ	TNBLS	10/01-12/01
	Chattanooga MSA, TN-GA	H	5.73 FQ	7.44 AW	9.70 TQ	TNBLS	10/01-12/01
	Clarksville-Hopkinsville MSA, TN-KY	H	5.67 FQ	7.90 AW	10.98 TQ	TNBLS	10/01-12/01
	Johnson City-Kingsport-Bristol MSA, TN-VA	H	5.65 FQ	6.71 AW	8.46 TQ	TNBLS	10/01-12/01
	Knoxville MSA, TN	H	6.01 FQ	7.50 AW	8.76 TQ	TNBLS	10/01-12/01
	Memphis MSA, TN-AR-MS	H	5.81 FQ	7.29 AW	9.11 TQ	TNBLS	10/01-12/01
	Nashville MSA, TN	H	5.87 FQ	7.58 AW	9.81 TQ	TNBLS	10/01-12/01
	Texas	H	5.62 FQ	7.02 AW	8.90 TQ	TXBLS	10/01-12/01
	Amarillo MSA, TX	H	5.66 FQ	6.73 AW	8.49 TQ	TXBLS	10/01-12/01
	Austin-San Marcos MSA, TX	H	6.02 FQ	7.68 AW	9.63 TQ	TXBLS	10/01-12/01
	Beaumont-Port Arthur MSA, TX	H	5.59 FQ	6.37 AW	7.62 TQ	TXBLS	10/01-12/01
	Brazoria PMSA, TX	H	5.65 FQ	6.86 AW	8.82 TQ	TXBLS	10/01-12/01
	Brownsville-Harlingen-San Benito MSA, TX	H	5.52 FQ	6.38 AW	7.76 TQ	TXBLS	10/01-12/01
	Corpus Christi MSA, TX	H	5.64 FQ	6.66 AW	8.26 TQ	TXBLS	10/01-12/01
	Dallas PMSA, TX	H	5.65 FQ	7.35 AW	11.42 TQ	TXBLS	10/01-12/01
	El Paso MSA, TX	H	5.57 FQ	6.44 AW	7.92 TQ	TXBLS	10/01-12/01
	Fort Worth-Arlington PMSA, TX	H	5.71 FQ	7.31 AW	8.87 TQ	TXBLS	10/01-12/01
	Galveston-Texas City PMSA, TX	H	5.61 FQ	7.16 AW	11.45 TQ	TXBLS	10/01-12/01
	Houston PMSA, TX	H	5.60 FQ	6.97 AW	8.75 TQ	TXBLS	10/01-12/01
	Killeen-Temple MSA, TX	H	5.57 FQ	6.52 AW	8.17 TQ	TXBLS	10/01-12/01
	Laredo MSA, TX	H	5.58 FQ	6.28 AW	7.20 TQ	TXBLS	10/01-12/01
	Longview-Marshall MSA, TX	H	5.56 FQ	6.40 AW	7.78 TQ	TXBLS	10/01-12/01
	Lubbock MSA, TX	H	5.61 FQ	6.69 AW	8.31 TQ	TXBLS	10/01-12/01
	McAllen-Edinburg-Mission MSA, TX	H	5.53 FQ	6.15 AW	7.05 TQ	TXBLS	10/01-12/01
	Odessa-Midland MSA, TX	H	5.47 FQ	6.40 AW	7.98 TQ	TXBLS	10/01-12/01
	San Antonio MSA, TX	H	5.61 FQ	7.14 AW	9.55 TQ	TXBLS	10/01-12/01
	Tyler MSA, TX	H	5.70 FQ	6.88 AW	8.65 TQ	TXBLS	10/01-12/01
	Waco MSA, TX	H	5.56 FQ	6.63 AW	8.35 TQ	TXBLS	10/01-12/01
	Utah	H	5.78 FQ	7.52 AW	9.96 TQ	UTBLS	10/01-12/01
	Provo-Orem MSA, UT	H	5.95 FQ	7.97 AW	10.54 TQ	UTBLS	10/01-12/01
	Salt Lake City-Ogden MSA, UT	H	5.86 FQ	7.55 AW	9.62 TQ	UTBLS	10/01-12/01
	Vermont	H	6.58 FQ	8.21 AW	10.37 TQ	VTBLS	10/01-12/01
	Burlington MSA, VT	H	6.94 FQ	8.81 AW	10.85 TQ	VTBLS	10/01-12/01
	Virginia	H	5.78 FQ	7.49 AW	9.90 TQ	VABLS	10/01-12/01
	Lynchburg MSA, VA	H	5.52 FQ	6.86 AW	9.74 TQ	VABLS	10/01-12/01
	Norfolk-Virginia Beach-Newport News MSA, VA-NC	H	5.75 FQ	7.41 AW	9.55 TQ	VABLS	10/01-12/01
	Richmond-Petersburg MSA, VA	H	5.82 FQ	7.24 AW	8.97 TQ	VABLS	10/01-12/01
	Roanoke MSA, VA	H	5.86 FQ	7.52 AW	9.42 TQ	VABLS	10/01-12/01
	Washington	H	6.92 FQ	8.64 AW	10.91 TQ	WABLS	10/01-12/01
	Bremerton PMSA, WA	H	6.83 FQ	8.62 AW	11.77 TQ	WABLS	10/01-12/01
	Olympia PMSA, WA	H	7.09 FQ	9.19 AW	11.76 TQ	WABLS	10/01-12/01
	Richland-Kennewick-Pasco MSA, WA	H	6.83 FQ	7.85 AW	10.01 TQ	WABLS	10/01-12/01
	Seattle-Bellevue-Everett PMSA, WA	H	7.31 FQ	9.14 AW	11.14 TQ	WABLS	10/01-12/01
	Spokane MSA, WA	H	6.81 FQ	8.02 AW	10.18 TQ	WABLS	10/01-12/01
	Tacoma PMSA, WA	H	6.92 FQ	8.75 AW	12.24 TQ	WABLS	10/01-12/01
	Yakima MSA, WA	H	6.74 FQ	7.86 AW	9.62 TQ	WABLS	10/01-12/01
	West Virginia	H	5.57 FQ	6.74 AW	8.51 TQ	WVBLS	10/01-12/01
	Charleston MSA, WV	H	5.57 FQ	6.56 AW	8.34 TQ	WVBLS	10/01-12/01

AAW Average annual wage; **AE** Average entry wage; **AEX** Average experienced wage; **AO** Average offered; **AOH** Average offered, high; **AOL** Average offered, low; **APH** Average pay, high range; **APL** Average pay, low range; **ASH** Average starting, high; **ASL** Average starting, low; **AW** Average wage paid; **FQ** First quartile wage; **H** Hourly; **HI** Highest wage paid; **HR** High end range; **LR** Low end range; **M** Monthly; **MTC** Median total compensation; **MW** Median wage paid; **SQ** Second quartile wage; **S** Special: hourly and annual; **TQ** Third quartile wage; **W** Weekly; **Y** Yearly

Occupation/Type/Industry	Location	Per	Low	Mid	High	Source	Date
Maid and Housekeeping Cleaner	Huntington-Ashland MSA, WV-KY-OH	H	5.57 FQ	6.77 AW	9.03 TQ	WVBLS	10/01-12/01
	Wisconsin	H	6.16 FQ	8.15 AW	10.60 TQ	WIBLS	10/01-12/01
	Appleton-Oshkosh-Neenah MSA, WI	H	6.34 FQ	8.38 AW	11.07 TQ	WIBLS	10/01-12/01
	Green Bay MSA, WI	H	6.30 FQ	8.01 AW	10.19 TQ	WIBLS	10/01-12/01
	Madison MSA, WI	H	6.72 FQ	8.34 AW	10.63 TQ	WIBLS	10/01-12/01
	Milwaukee-Waukesha PMSA, WI	H	6.55 FQ	8.23 AW	10.46 TQ	WIBLS	10/01-12/01
	Racine PMSA, WI	H	6.08 FQ	8.03 AW	10.31 TQ	WIBLS	10/01-12/01
	Wyoming	H	5.68 FQ	7.36 AW	9.82 TQ	WYBLS	10/01-12/01
	Cheyenne MSA, WY	H	5.74 FQ	7.16 AW	9.02 TQ	WYBLS	10/01-12/01
	Puerto Rico	H	5.60 FQ	6.91 AW	9.51 TQ	PRBLS	10/01-12/01
	Virgin Islands	H	5.73 FQ	7.18 AW	8.73 TQ	VIBLS	10/01-12/01
	Guam	H	5.52 FQ	6.42 AW	7.92 TQ	GUBLS	10/01-12/01
Mail Clerk and Mail Machine Operator							
Except Postal Service	Alabama	H	6.27 FQ	8.95 AW	12.49 TQ	ALBLS	10/01-12/01
Except Postal Service	Alaska	H	6.64 FQ	10.14 AW	15.30 TQ	AKBLS	10/01-12/01
Except Postal Service	Arizona	H	6.22 FQ	9.77 AW	14.65 TQ	AZBLS	10/01-12/01
Except Postal Service	Arkansas	H	5.95 FQ	8.28 AW	11.41 TQ	ARBLS	10/01-12/01
Except Postal Service	California	H	7.08 FQ	10.87 AW	15.67 TQ	CABLS	10/01-12/01
Except Postal Service	Colorado	H	7.73 FQ	11.00 AW	14.62 TQ	COBLS	10/01-12/01
Except Postal Service	Connecticut	H	7.63 FQ	11.23 AW	15.63 TQ	CTBLS	10/01-12/01
Except Postal Service	Delaware	H	7.45 FQ	9.82 AW	13.09 TQ	DEBLS	10/01-12/01
Except Postal Service	District of Columbia	H	7.32 FQ	11.80 AW	16.63 TQ	DCBLS	10/01-12/01
Except Postal Service	Florida	H	6.97 FQ	9.60 AW	13.28 TQ	FLBLS	10/01-12/01
Except Postal Service	Georgia	H	6.89 FQ	10.22 AW	14.73 TQ	GABLS	10/01-12/01
Except Postal Service	Hawaii	H	7.30 FQ	11.00 AW	15.89 TQ	HIBLS	10/01-12/01
Except Postal Service	Idaho	H	7.50 FQ	9.65 AW	12.00 TQ	IDBLS	10/01-12/01
Except Postal Service	Illinois	H	6.66 FQ	9.52 AW	12.77 TQ	ILBLS	10/01-12/01
Except Postal Service	Indiana	H	6.99 FQ	11.06 AW	15.86 TQ	INBLS	10/01-12/01
Except Postal Service	Iowa	H	7.13 FQ	10.51 AW	16.11 TQ	IABLS	10/01-12/01
Except Postal Service	Kansas	H	7.07 FQ	9.26 AW	12.18 TQ	KSBLS	10/01-12/01
Except Postal Service	Kentucky	H	7.09 FQ	9.91 AW	13.68 TQ	KYBLS	10/01-12/01
Except Postal Service	Louisiana	H	5.79 FQ	8.41 AW	12.67 TQ	LABLS	10/01-12/01
Except Postal Service	Maine	H	7.06 FQ	10.88 AW	17.85 TQ	MEBLS	10/01-12/01
Except Postal Service	Maryland	H	7.03 FQ	10.37 AW	14.54 TQ	MDBLS	10/01-12/01
Except Postal Service	Massachusetts	H	8.33 FQ	12.00 AW	16.57 TQ	MABLS	10/01-12/01
Except Postal Service	Michigan	H	7.01 FQ	10.32 AW	14.09 TQ	MIBLS	10/01-12/01
Except Postal Service	Minnesota	H	8.51 FQ	11.20 AW	14.36 TQ	MNBLS	10/01-12/01
Except Postal Service	Mississippi	H	6.21 FQ	9.37 AW	13.07 TQ	MSBLS	10/01-12/01
Except Postal Service	Missouri	H	7.12 FQ	9.92 AW	13.10 TQ	MOBLS	10/01-12/01
Except Postal Service	Montana	H	6.05 FQ	8.39 AW	10.83 TQ	MTBLS	10/01-12/01
Except Postal Service	Nebraska	H	6.83 FQ	9.30 AW	12.39 TQ	NEBLS	10/01-12/01
Except Postal Service	Nevada	H	7.48 FQ	10.34 AW	13.62 TQ	NVBLS	10/01-12/01
Except Postal Service	New Hampshire	H	7.59 FQ	10.20 AW	13.55 TQ	NHBLS	10/01-12/01
Except Postal Service	New Jersey	H	7.67 FQ	11.40 AW	16.20 TQ	NJBLS	10/01-12/01
Except Postal Service	New Mexico	H	6.25 FQ	10.22 AW	15.84 TQ	NMBLS	10/01-12/01
Except Postal Service	New York	H	6.99 FQ	10.82 AW	15.41 TQ	NYBLS	10/01-12/01
Except Postal Service	North Carolina	H	6.93 FQ	10.09 AW	13.85 TQ	NCBLS	10/01-12/01
Except Postal Service	North Dakota	H	7.34 FQ	9.77 AW	13.15 TQ	NDBLS	10/01-12/01
Except Postal Service	Ohio	H	6.93 FQ	10.11 AW	13.67 TQ	OHBLS	10/01-12/01
Except Postal Service	Oklahoma	H	6.52 FQ	9.14 AW	12.63 TQ	OKBLS	10/01-12/01
Except Postal Service	Oregon	H	7.81 FQ	11.05 AW	15.12 TQ	ORBLS	10/01-12/01
Except Postal Service	Pennsylvania	H	7.09 FQ	10.10 AW	13.98 TQ	PABLS	10/01-12/01
Except Postal Service	Rhode Island	H	7.77 FQ	11.08 AW	15.34 TQ	RIBLS	10/01-12/01
Except Postal Service	South Carolina	H	6.26 FQ	9.18 AW	12.42 TQ	SCBLS	10/01-12/01
Except Postal Service	South Dakota	H	7.39 FQ	9.92 AW	13.79 TQ	SDBLS	10/01-12/01
Except Postal Service	Tennessee	H	7.14 FQ	9.83 AW	13.16 TQ	TNBLS	10/01-12/01
Except Postal Service	Texas	H	6.36 FQ	9.85 AW	14.09 TQ	TXBLS	10/01-12/01
Except Postal Service	Utah	H	7.40 FQ	9.67 AW	12.24 TQ	UTBLS	10/01-12/01
Except Postal Service	Vermont	H	8.16 FQ	10.51 AW	13.37 TQ	VTBLS	10/01-12/01
Except Postal Service	Virginia	H	6.79 FQ	11.24 AW	18.87 TQ	VABLS	10/01-12/01
Except Postal Service	Washington	H	7.53 FQ	11.30 AW	16.70 TQ	WABLS	10/01-12/01
Except Postal Service	West Virginia	H	6.18 FQ	9.18 AW	13.02 TQ	WVBLS	10/01-12/01
Except Postal Service	Wisconsin	H	7.60 FQ	10.41 AW	13.69 TQ	WIBLS	10/01-12/01
Except Postal Service	Wyoming	H	5.62 FQ	8.55 AW	12.64 TQ	WYBLS	10/01-12/01
Except Postal Service	Puerto Rico	H	6.00 FQ	8.87 AW	12.91 TQ	PRBLS	10/01-12/01
Except Postal Service	Virgin Islands	H	7.41 FQ	9.38 AW	11.31 TQ	VIBLS	10/01-12/01

AAW Average annual wage; AE Average entry wage; AEX Average experienced wage; AO Average offered; AOH Average offered, high; AOL Average offered, low; APH Average pay, high range; APL Average pay, low range; ASH Average starting, high; ASL Average starting, low; AW Average wage paid; FQ First quartile wage; H Hourly; HI Highest wage paid; HR High end range; LR Low end range; M Monthly; MTC Median total compensation; MW Median wage paid; SQ Second quartile wage; S Special: hourly and annual; TQ Third quartile wage; W Weekly; Y Yearly

Occupation/Type/Industry	Location	Per	Low	Mid	High	Source	Date
Maintenance and Repair Worker							
General	Alabama	H	7.90 FQ	13.62 AW	20.68 TQ	ALBLS	10/01-12/01
General	Alaska	H	10.26 FQ	19.62 AW	29.27 TQ	AKBLS	10/01-12/01
General	Arizona	H	7.61 FQ	12.72 AW	19.26 TQ	AZBLS	10/01-12/01
General	Arkansas	H	7.36 FQ	12.68 AW	18.99 TQ	ARBLS	10/01-12/01
General	California	H	7.79 FQ	15.36 AW	24.57 TQ	CABLS	10/01-12/01
General	Colorado	H	8.59 FQ	14.29 AW	21.07 TQ	COBLS	10/01-12/01
General	Connecticut	H	10.62 FQ	16.80 AW	23.03 TQ	CTBLS	10/01-12/01
General	Delaware	H	9.53 FQ	16.19 AW	24.63 TQ	DEBLS	10/01-12/01
General	District of Columbia	H	9.63 FQ	17.38 AW	25.55 TQ	DCBLS	10/01-12/01
General	Florida	H	7.56 FQ	12.36 AW	18.62 TQ	FLBLS	10/01-12/01
General	Georgia	H	8.74 FQ	13.82 AW	20.25 TQ	GABLS	10/01-12/01
General	Hawaii	H	9.83 FQ	15.46 AW	22.30 TQ	HIBLS	10/01-12/01
General	Idaho	H	8.37 FQ	13.47 AW	19.95 TQ	IDBLS	10/01-12/01
General	Illinois	H	8.79 FQ	16.51 AW	24.48 TQ	ILBLS	10/01-12/01
General	Indiana	H	9.18 FQ	15.35 AW	22.79 TQ	INBLS	10/01-12/01
General	Iowa	H	8.27 FQ	13.72 AW	20.34 TQ	IABLS	10/01-12/01
General	Kansas	H	7.80 FQ	13.71 AW	21.01 TQ	KSBLS	10/01-12/01
General	Kentucky	H	7.51 FQ	14.09 AW	22.56 TQ	KYBLS	10/01-12/01
General	Louisiana	H	7.33 FQ	13.68 AW	22.39 TQ	LABLS	10/01-12/01
General	Maine	H	8.34 FQ	14.47 AW	24.24 TQ	MEBLS	10/01-12/01
General	Maryland	H	8.24 FQ	14.03 AW	21.05 TQ	MDBLS	10/01-12/01
General	Massachusetts	H	9.35 FQ	15.79 AW	22.61 TQ	MABLS	10/01-12/01
General	Michigan	H	8.91 FQ	16.37 AW	25.52 TQ	MIBLS	10/01-12/01
General	Minnesota	H	9.95 FQ	15.90 AW	21.89 TQ	MNBLS	10/01-12/01
General	Mississippi	H	7.25 FQ	12.25 AW	18.65 TQ	MSBLS	10/01-12/01
General	Missouri	H	8.31 FQ	14.35 AW	22.32 TQ	MOBLS	10/01-12/01
General	Montana	H	6.79 FQ	12.99 AW	20.41 TQ	MTBLS	10/01-12/01
General	Nebraska	H	7.73 FQ	12.47 AW	18.00 TQ	NEBLS	10/01-12/01
General	Nevada	H	8.58 FQ	16.01 AW	25.09 TQ	NVBLS	10/01-12/01
General	New Hampshire	H	8.93 FQ	14.17 AW	21.00 TQ	NHBLS	10/01-12/01
General	New Jersey	H	9.85 FQ	17.05 AW	24.85 TQ	NJBLS	10/01-12/01
General	New Mexico	H	7.33 FQ	11.84 AW	18.41 TQ	NMBLS	10/01-12/01
General	New York	H	8.20 FQ	15.82 AW	23.21 TQ	NYBLS	10/01-12/01
General	North Carolina	H	8.96 FQ	14.20 AW	20.71 TQ	NCBLS	10/01-12/01
General	North Dakota	H	8.03 FQ	13.73 AW	21.78 TQ	NDBLS	10/01-12/01
General	Ohio	H	8.52 FQ	15.01 AW	22.21 TQ	OHBLS	10/01-12/01
General	Oklahoma	H	7.38 FQ	12.26 AW	18.61 TQ	OKBLS	10/01-12/01
General	Oregon	H	8.78 FQ	14.82 AW	21.88 TQ	ORBLS	10/01-12/01
General	Pennsylvania	H	7.99 FQ	14.34 AW	21.27 TQ	PABLS	10/01-12/01
General	Rhode Island	H	8.98 FQ	15.29 AW	21.47 TQ	RIBLS	10/01-12/01
General	South Carolina	H	8.23 FQ	14.30 AW	21.46 TQ	SCBLS	10/01-12/01
General	South Dakota	H	7.65 FQ	10.77 AW	14.47 TQ	SDBLS	10/01-12/01
General	Tennessee	H	8.29 FQ	14.24 AW	21.38 TQ	TNBLS	10/01-12/01
General	Texas	H	7.15 FQ	12.57 AW	19.92 TQ	TXBLS	10/01-12/01
General	Utah	H	7.84 FQ	13.67 AW	20.38 TQ	UTBLS	10/01-12/01
General	Vermont	H	8.48 FQ	13.10 AW	18.71 TQ	VTBLS	10/01-12/01
General	Virginia	H	8.00 FQ	13.78 AW	20.83 TQ	VABLS	10/01-12/01
General	Washington	H	9.63 FQ	16.40 AW	24.16 TQ	WABLS	10/01-12/01
General	West Virginia	H	6.55 FQ	12.37 AW	20.29 TQ	WVBLS	10/01-12/01
General	Wisconsin	H	8.92 FQ	15.08 AW	21.31 TQ	WIBLS	10/01-12/01
General	Wyoming	H	6.67 FQ	13.88 AW	24.21 TQ	WYBLS	10/01-12/01
General	Puerto Rico	H	5.75 FQ	9.39 AW	14.83 TQ	PRBLS	10/01-12/01
General	Virgin Islands	H	6.22 FQ	9.37 AW	12.92 TQ	VIBLS	10/01-12/01
General	Guam	H	6.36 FQ	10.19 AW	14.75 TQ	GUBLS	10/01-12/01
Maintenance Worker							
Machinery	Alabama	H	7.47 FQ	12.75 AW	18.47 TQ	ALBLS	10/01-12/01
Machinery	Alaska	H	9.85 FQ	18.02 AW	25.70 TQ	AKBLS	10/01-12/01
Machinery	Arizona	H	10.00 FQ	18.29 AW	28.02 TQ	AZBLS	10/01-12/01
Machinery	Arkansas	H	8.92 FQ	12.53 AW	17.15 TQ	ARBLS	10/01-12/01
Machinery	California	H	9.19 FQ	16.93 AW	25.79 TQ	CABLS	10/01-12/01
Machinery	Colorado	H	7.24 FQ	15.16 AW	23.09 TQ	COBLS	10/01-12/01
Machinery	Connecticut	H	11.62 FQ	18.18 AW	25.61 TQ	CTBLS	10/01-12/01
Machinery	Delaware	H	12.43 FQ	18.85 AW	25.41 TQ	DEBLS	10/01-12/01
Machinery	District of Columbia	H	8.99 FQ	13.60 AW	20.99 TQ	DCBLS	10/01-12/01
Machinery	Florida	H	9.34 FQ	15.04 AW	21.39 TQ	FLBLS	10/01-12/01
Machinery	Georgia	H	9.46 FQ	14.66 AW	21.87 TQ	GABLS	10/01-12/01
Machinery	Hawaii	H	7.84 FQ	16.78 AW	28.51 TQ	HIBLS	10/01-12/01
Machinery	Idaho	H	8.27 FQ	13.14 AW	17.60 TQ	IDBLS	10/01-12/01
Machinery	Illinois	H	9.76 FQ	16.60 AW	22.82 TQ	ILBLS	10/01-12/01
Machinery	Indiana	H	10.02 FQ	16.78 AW	25.91 TQ	INBLS	10/01-12/01
Machinery	Iowa	H	8.18 FQ	14.59 AW	21.00 TQ	IABLS	10/01-12/01

AAW	Average annual wage	AOH	Average offered, high	ASH	Average starting, high	H	Hourly	M	Monthly	S	Special: hourly and annual
AE	Average entry wage	AOL	Average offered, low	ASL	Average starting, low	HI	Highest wage paid	MTC	Median total compensation	TQ	Third quartile wage
AEX	Average experienced wage	APH	Average pay, high range	AW	Average wage paid	HR	High end range	MW	Median wage paid	W	Weekly
AO	Average offered	APL	Average pay, low range	FQ	First quartile wage	LR	Low end range	SQ	Second quartile wage	Y	Yearly

Occupation/Type/Industry	Location	Per	Low	Mid	High	Source	Date
Maintenance Worker							
Machinery	Kansas	H	8.78 FQ	14.27 AW	20.68 TQ	KSBLS	10/01-12/01
Machinery	Kentucky	H	9.40 FQ	14.64 AW	21.17 TQ	KYBLS	10/01-12/01
Machinery	Louisiana	H	8.09 FQ	12.54 AW	20.54 TQ	LABLS	10/01-12/01
Machinery	Maine	H	9.61 FQ	15.65 AW	23.80 TQ	MEBLS	10/01-12/01
Machinery	Maryland	H	10.54 FQ	15.61 AW	21.72 TQ	MDBLS	10/01-12/01
Machinery	Massachusetts	H	10.78 FQ	17.28 AW	22.04 TQ	MABLS	10/01-12/01
Machinery	Michigan	H	11.19 FQ	18.76 AW	28.20 TQ	MIBLS	10/01-12/01
Machinery	Minnesota	H	10.09 FQ	16.02 AW	21.59 TQ	MNBLS	10/01-12/01
Machinery	Mississippi	H	8.60 FQ	13.56 AW	20.63 TQ	MSBLS	10/01-12/01
Machinery	Missouri	H	7.99 FQ	15.37 AW	24.57 TQ	MOBLS	10/01-12/01
Machinery	Montana	H	7.95 FQ	12.30 AW	17.78 TQ	MTBLS	10/01-12/01
Machinery	Nebraska	H	9.62 FQ	13.76 AW	19.49 TQ	NEBLS	10/01-12/01
Machinery	Nevada	H	9.62 FQ	16.59 AW	22.87 TQ	NVBLS	10/01-12/01
Machinery	New Hampshire	H	9.78 FQ	14.65 AW	19.29 TQ	NHBLS	10/01-12/01
Machinery	New Jersey	H	10.32 FQ	18.79 AW	26.89 TQ	NJBLS	10/01-12/01
Machinery	New Mexico	H	6.53 FQ	13.54 AW	23.69 TQ	NMBLS	10/01-12/01
Machinery	New York	H	10.16 FQ	17.13 AW	25.41 TQ	NYBLS	10/01-12/01
Machinery	North Carolina	H	9.36 FQ	14.14 AW	20.37 TQ	NCBLS	10/01-12/01
Machinery	North Dakota	H	7.81 FQ	13.00 AW	23.82 TQ	NDBLS	10/01-12/01
Machinery	Ohio	H	11.35 FQ	18.26 AW	27.16 TQ	OHBLS	10/01-12/01
Machinery	Oklahoma	H	7.90 FQ	14.98 AW	22.98 TQ	OKBLS	10/01-12/01
Machinery	Oregon	H	8.94 FQ	15.32 AW	21.26 TQ	ORBLS	10/01-12/01
Machinery	Pennsylvania	H	10.77 FQ	16.28 AW	22.06 TQ	PABLS	10/01-12/01
Machinery	Rhode Island	H	11.21 FQ	15.59 AW	20.79 TQ	RIBLS	10/01-12/01
Machinery	South Carolina	H	10.00 FQ	14.82 AW	20.91 TQ	SCBLS	10/01-12/01
Machinery	South Dakota	H	7.52 FQ	9.78 AW	12.79 TQ	SDBLS	10/01-12/01
Machinery	Tennessee	H	9.89 FQ	14.65 AW	20.47 TQ	TNBLS	10/01-12/01
Machinery	Texas	H	8.13 FQ	14.45 AW	23.61 TQ	TXBLS	10/01-12/01
Machinery	Utah	H	10.54 FQ	15.91 AW	21.75 TQ	UTBLS	10/01-12/01
Machinery	Vermont	H	9.30 FQ	13.02 AW	17.33 TQ	VTBLS	10/01-12/01
Machinery	Virginia	H	9.46 FQ	15.08 AW	21.23 TQ	VABLS	10/01-12/01
Machinery	Washington	H	9.65 FQ	15.66 AW	24.17 TQ	WABLS	10/01-12/01
Machinery	West Virginia	H	9.71 FQ	15.40 AW	21.06 TQ	WVBLS	10/01-12/01
Machinery	Wisconsin	H	10.87 FQ	15.91 AW	22.81 TQ	WIBLS	10/01-12/01
Machinery	Wyoming	H	11.29 FQ	19.51 AW	26.39 TQ	WYBLS	10/01-12/01
Machinery	Puerto Rico	H	6.83 FQ	12.53 AW	17.07 TQ	PRBLS	10/01-12/01
Machinery	Virgin Islands	H	6.97 FQ	10.48 AW	16.18 TQ	VIBLS	10/01-12/01
Machinery	Guam	H	9.33 FQ	14.86 AW	21.06 TQ	GUBLS	10/01-12/01
Maitre d'							
Golf Course	St. Louis, MO	Y		34700 AW		SLBJ	1/00-1/01
Makeup Artist							
Theatrical and Performance	California	H	9.70 FQ	20.53 AW	33.13 TQ	CABLS	10/01-12/01
Theatrical and Performance	Georgia	H	8.89 FQ	16.02 AW	30.28 TQ	GABLS	10/01-12/01
Theatrical and Performance	Illinois	H	9.03 FQ	17.25 AW	33.69 TQ	ILBLS	10/01-12/01
Theatrical and Performance	Massachusetts	H	8.80 FQ	10.16 AW	12.44 TQ	MABLS	10/01-12/01
Theatrical and Performance	New York	H	13.52 FQ	15.55 AW	16.98 TQ	NYBLS	10/01-12/01
Theatrical and Performance	Pennsylvania	H	9.06 FQ	11.14 AW	14.50 TQ	PABLS	10/01-12/01
Theatrical and Performance	Washington	H	7.58 FQ	15.61 AW	27.31 TQ	WABLS	10/01-12/01
Management Analyst	Alabama	Y	32970 FQ	59070 AW	87560 TQ	ALBLS	10/01-12/01
	Birmingham MSA, AL	Y	34280 FQ	59540 AW	92110 TQ	ALBLS	10/01-12/01
	Huntsville MSA, AL	Y	37220 FQ	60400 AW	86380 TQ	ALBLS	10/01-12/01
	Mobile MSA, AL	Y	31860 FQ	60020 AW	93200 TQ	ALBLS	10/01-12/01
	Montgomery MSA, AL	Y	25580 FQ	50720 AW	84560 TQ	ALBLS	10/01-12/01
	Alaska	Y	30510 FQ	55560 AW	89680 TQ	AKBLS	10/01-12/01
	Anchorage MSA, AK	Y	29400 FQ	52130 AW	81420 TQ	AKBLS	10/01-12/01
	Arizona	Y	31090 FQ	54980 AW	84660 TQ	AZBLS	10/01-12/01
	Phoenix-Mesa MSA, AZ	Y	31450 FQ	55840 AW	85560 TQ	AZBLS	10/01-12/01
	Tucson MSA, AZ	Y	31010 FQ	52330 AW	80340 TQ	AZBLS	10/01-12/01
	Arkansas	Y	20730 FQ	40320 AW	63640 TQ	ARBLS	10/01-12/01
	Fort Smith MSA, AR-OK	Y	32420 FQ	57150 AW	82400 TQ	ARBLS	10/01-12/01
	Little Rock-North Little Rock MSA, AR	Y	25720 FQ	40990 AW	57140 TQ	ARBLS	10/01-12/01
	California	Y	37660 FQ	69930 AW	121740 TQ	CABLS	10/01-12/01
	Bakersfield MSA, CA	Y	42860 FQ	73290 AW	115080 TQ	CABLS	10/01-12/01
	Chico-Paradise MSA, CA	Y	32040 FQ	71560 AW	130390 TQ	CABLS	10/01-12/01
	Fresno MSA, CA	Y	38850 FQ	54090 AW	71800 TQ	CABLS	10/01-12/01
	Los Angeles-Long Beach PMSA, CA	Y	38410 FQ	71300 AW	117770 TQ	CABLS	10/01-12/01
	Modesto MSA, CA	Y	40100 FQ	62270 AW	93190 TQ	CABLS	10/01-12/01

AAW	Average annual wage	**AOH**	Average offered, high	**ASH**	Average starting, high	**H**	Hourly	**M**	Monthly	**S**	Special: hourly and annual
AE	Average entry wage	**AOL**	Average offered, low	**ASL**	Average starting, low	**HI**	Highest wage paid	**MTC**	Median total compensation	**TQ**	Third quartile wage
AEX	Average experienced wage	**APH**	Average pay, high range	**AW**	Average wage paid	**HR**	High end range	**MW**	Median wage paid	**W**	Weekly
AO	Average offered	**APL**	Average pay, low range	**FQ**	First quartile wage	**LR**	Low end range	**SQ**	Second quartile wage	**Y**	Yearly

Occupation/Type/Industry	Location	Per	Low	Mid	High	Source	Date
Management Analyst	Oakland PMSA, CA	Y	42440 FQ	84300 AW		CABLS	10/01-12/01
	Orange County PMSA, CA	Y	39460 FQ	66740 AW	102720 TQ	CABLS	10/01-12/01
	Redding MSA, CA	Y	38350 FQ	52080 AW	69580 TQ	CABLS	10/01-12/01
	Riverside-San Bernardino PMSA, CA	Y	36420 FQ	52780 AW	73610 TQ	CABLS	10/01-12/01
	Sacramento PMSA, CA	Y	13950 FQ	56150 AW	90320 TQ	CABLS	10/01-12/01
	Salinas MSA, CA	Y	34410 FQ	53410 AW	74480 TQ	CABLS	10/01-12/01
	San Diego MSA, CA	Y	26690 FQ	52760 AW	81290 TQ	CABLS	10/01-12/01
	San Francisco PMSA, CA	Y	43720 FQ	78620 AW		CABLS	10/01-12/01
	San Jose PMSA, CA	Y	45030 FQ	78630 AW		CABLS	10/01-12/01
	San Luis Obispo-Atascadero-Paso Robles MSA, CA	Y	31630 FQ	56180 AW	92700 TQ	CABLS	10/01-12/01
	Santa Barbara-Santa Maria-Lompoc MSA, CA	Y	41370 FQ	59440 AW	74170 TQ	CABLS	10/01-12/01
	Santa Cruz-Watsonville PMSA, CA	Y	39590 FQ	74040 AW	120710 TQ	CABLS	10/01-12/01
	Santa Rosa PMSA, CA	Y	42280 FQ	86470 AW		CABLS	10/01-12/01
	Stockton-Lodi MSA, CA	Y	30810 FQ	55150 AW	82410 TQ	CABLS	10/01-12/01
	Vallejo-Fairfield-Napa PMSA, CA	Y	41720 FQ	75350 AW		CABLS	10/01-12/01
	Ventura PMSA, CA	Y	43610 FQ	72050 AW	110780 TQ	CABLS	10/01-12/01
	Colorado	Y	35110 FQ	62030 AW	94420 TQ	COBLS	10/01-12/01
	Boulder-Longmont PMSA, CO	Y	28480 FQ	60360 AW	88070 TQ	COBLS	10/01-12/01
	Colorado Springs MSA, CO	Y	30210 FQ	49440 AW	73240 TQ	COBLS	10/01-12/01
	Denver PMSA, CO	Y	39810 FQ	66520 AW	103820 TQ	COBLS	10/01-12/01
	Fort Collins-Loveland MSA, CO	Y	31650 FQ	56200 AW	84980 TQ	COBLS	10/01-12/01
	Greeley PMSA, CO	Y	37040 FQ	56070 AW	80390 TQ	COBLS	10/01-12/01
	Connecticut	Y	39720 FQ	71930 AW	138320 TQ	CTBLS	10/01-12/01
	Bridgeport PMSA, CT	Y	35640 FQ	72520 AW		CTBLS	10/01-12/01
	Danbury PMSA, CT	Y	38500 FQ	67440 AW	110140 TQ	CTBLS	10/01-12/01
	Hartford MSA, CT	Y	39360 FQ	67780 AW	117740 TQ	CTBLS	10/01-12/01
	New Haven-Meriden PMSA, CT	Y	38060 FQ	61590 AW	91080 TQ	CTBLS	10/01-12/01
	Stamford-Norwalk PMSA, CT	Y	46520 FQ	85410 AW		CTBLS	10/01-12/01
	Waterbury PMSA, CT	Y	48320 FQ	67280 AW	101240 TQ	CTBLS	10/01-12/01
	Delaware	Y	35910 FQ	66090 AW	110880 TQ	DEBLS	10/01-12/01
	Wilmington-Newark PMSA, DE-MD	Y	36220 FQ	67020 AW	111140 TQ	DEBLS	10/01-12/01
	District of Columbia	Y	36880 FQ	62890 AW	91670 TQ	DCBLS	10/01-12/01
	Washington PMSA, DC-MD-VA-WV	Y	38440 FQ	68830 AW	108250 TQ	DCBLS	10/01-12/01
	Florida	Y	30820 FQ	62570 AW	114630 TQ	FLBLS	10/01-12/01
	Daytona Beach MSA, FL	Y	36750 FQ	56750 AW	85620 TQ	FLBLS	10/01-12/01
	Fort Lauderdale PMSA, FL	Y	31630 FQ	52950 AW	89620 TQ	FLBLS	10/01-12/01
	Fort Myers-Cape Coral MSA, FL	Y	34110 FQ	66970 AW	131370 TQ	FLBLS	10/01-12/01
	Fort Pierce-Port St. Lucie MSA, FL	Y	33060 FQ	60290 AW	108250 TQ	FLBLS	10/01-12/01
	Fort Walton Beach MSA, FL	Y	37950 FQ	61700 AW	86700 TQ	FLBLS	10/01-12/01
	Gainesville MSA, FL	Y	31620 FQ	50300 AW	79550 TQ	FLBLS	10/01-12/01
	Jacksonville MSA, FL	Y	34180 FQ	66490 AW		FLBLS	10/01-12/01
	Lakeland-Winter Haven MSA, FL	Y	31220 FQ	58070 AW		FLBLS	10/01-12/01
	Melbourne-Titusville-Palm Bay MSA, FL	Y	36700 FQ	56460 AW	82410 TQ	FLBLS	10/01-12/01
	Miami PMSA, FL	Y	15650 FQ	42950 AW	89200 TQ	FLBLS	10/01-12/01
	Naples MSA, FL	Y	28490 FQ	61830 AW		FLBLS	10/01-12/01
	Ocala MSA, FL	Y	28390 FQ	49240 AW	71620 TQ	FLBLS	10/01-12/01
	Orlando MSA, FL	Y	32500 FQ	67840 AW	113540 TQ	FLBLS	10/01-12/01
	Pensacola MSA, FL	Y	32160 FQ	51310 AW	75120 TQ	FLBLS	10/01-12/01
	Sarasota-Bradenton MSA, FL	Y	38160 FQ	75710 AW	132880 TQ	FLBLS	10/01-12/01
	Tallahassee MSA, FL	Y	35460 FQ	66830 AW	113270 TQ	FLBLS	10/01-12/01
	Tampa-St. Petersburg-Clearwater MSA, FL	Y	32320 FQ	66560 AW	120950 TQ	FLBLS	10/01-12/01
	West Palm Beach-Boca Raton MSA, FL	Y	36080 FQ	80210 AW		FLBLS	10/01-12/01
	Georgia	Y	32740 FQ	58000 AW	91600 TQ	GABLS	10/01-12/01
	Atlanta MSA, GA	Y	32740 FQ	57600 AW	91590 TQ	GABLS	10/01-12/01
	Augusta-Aiken MSA, GA-SC	Y	35540 FQ	52150 AW	71610 TQ	GABLS	10/01-12/01
	Columbus MSA, GA-AL	Y	28730 FQ	45110 AW	67530 TQ	GABLS	10/01-12/01
	Macon MSA, GA	Y	36490 FQ	52510 AW	71260 TQ	GABLS	10/01-12/01

AAW Average annual wage **AOH** Average offered, high **ASH** Average starting, high **H** Hourly **M** Monthly **S** Special: hourly and annual
AE Average entry wage **AOL** Average offered, low **ASL** Average starting, low **HI** Highest wage paid **MTC** Median total compensation **TQ** Third quartile wage
AEX Average experienced wage **APH** Average pay, high range **AW** Average wage paid **HR** High end range **MW** Median wage paid **W** Weekly
AO Average offered **APL** Average pay, low range **FQ** First quartile wage **LR** Low end range **SQ** Second quartile wage **Y** Yearly

Occupation/Type/Industry	Location	Per	Low	Mid	High	Source	Date
Management Analyst	Savannah MSA, GA	Y	28860 FQ	46930 AW	69560 TQ	GABLS	10/01-12/01
	Hawaii	Y	38210 FQ	59730 AW	86000 TQ	HIBLS	10/01-12/01
	Honolulu MSA, HI	Y	38630 FQ	59940 AW	85600 TQ	HIBLS	10/01-12/01
	Idaho	Y	35360 FQ	71300 AW		IDBLS	10/01-12/01
	Boise City MSA, ID	Y	36620 FQ	79790 AW		IDBLS	10/01-12/01
	Illinois	Y	34570 FQ	74910 AW		ILBLS	10/01-12/01
	Champaign-Urbana MSA, IL	Y	21590 FQ	56820 AW	101490 TQ	ILBLS	10/01-12/01
	Chicago PMSA, IL	Y	34460 FQ	78330 AW		ILBLS	10/01-12/01
	Peoria-Pekin MSA, IL	Y	31330 FQ	54310 AW	89380 TQ	ILBLS	10/01-12/01
	Rockford MSA, IL	Y	34390 FQ	57300 AW	99270 TQ	ILBLS	10/01-12/01
	Springfield MSA, IL	Y	32260 FQ	51220 AW	72890 TQ	ILBLS	10/01-12/01
	Indiana	Y	30970 FQ	55710 AW	89590 TQ	INBLS	10/01-12/01
	Elkhart-Goshen MSA, IN	Y	18050 FQ	41400 AW	61830 TQ	INBLS	10/01-12/01
	Evansville-Henderson MSA, IN-KY	Y	29060 FQ	54160 AW	136700 TQ	INBLS	10/01-12/01
	Fort Wayne MSA, IN	Y	31750 FQ	47350 AW	77580 TQ	INBLS	10/01-12/01
	Gary PMSA, IN	Y	27770 FQ	58660 AW	90870 TQ	INBLS	10/01-12/01
	Indianapolis MSA, IN	Y	33280 FQ	54980 AW	78970 TQ	INBLS	10/01-12/01
	Lafayette MSA, IN	Y	24490 FQ	45850 AW	86600 TQ	INBLS	10/01-12/01
	South Bend MSA, IN	Y	32550 FQ	53780 AW	77520 TQ	INBLS	10/01-12/01
	Iowa	Y	30610 FQ	51570 AW	77240 TQ	IABLS	10/01-12/01
	Cedar Rapids MSA, IA	Y	24640 FQ	43630 AW	68290 TQ	IABLS	10/01-12/01
	Davenport-Moline-Rock Island MSA, IA-IL	Y	37770 FQ	57800 AW	77550 TQ	IABLS	10/01-12/01
	Des Moines MSA, IA	Y	31580 FQ	53090 AW	77300 TQ	IABLS	10/01-12/01
	Kansas	Y	34240 FQ	54990 AW	82620 TQ	KSBLS	10/01-12/01
	Topeka MSA, KS	Y	32440 FQ	44910 AW	55340 TQ	KSBLS	10/01-12/01
	Kentucky	Y	21590 FQ	46830 AW	77500 TQ	KYBLS	10/01-12/01
	Lexington MSA, KY	Y	21610 FQ	46060 AW	78540 TQ	KYBLS	10/01-12/01
	Louisville MSA, KY-IN	Y	20230 FQ	40710 AW	70900 TQ	KYBLS	10/01-12/01
	Louisiana	Y	30290 FQ	54550 AW	88460 TQ	LABLS	10/01-12/01
	Baton Rouge MSA, LA	Y	31760 FQ	54120 AW	99480 TQ	LABLS	10/01-12/01
	Lafayette MSA, LA	Y	26860 FQ	48120 AW	72490 TQ	LABLS	10/01-12/01
	Lake Charles MSA, LA	Y	40820 FQ	62980 AW	92230 TQ	LABLS	10/01-12/01
	New Orleans MSA, LA	Y	29490 FQ	51660 AW	86120 TQ	LABLS	10/01-12/01
	Shreveport-Bossier City MSA, LA	Y	31890 FQ	60730 AW	127910 TQ	LABLS	10/01-12/01
	Maine	Y	34310 FQ	52800 AW	75610 TQ	MEBLS	10/01-12/01
	Portland MSA, ME	Y	31800 FQ	49080 AW	70390 TQ	MEBLS	10/01-12/01
	Maryland	Y	36830 FQ	63090 AW	97750 TQ	MDBLS	10/01-12/01
	Baltimore PMSA, MD	Y	37340 FQ	61310 AW	95350 TQ	MDBLS	10/01-12/01
	Massachusetts	Y	40330 FQ	73510 AW	118510 TQ	MABLS	10/01-12/01
	Boston PMSA, MA-NH	Y	41560 FQ	74470 AW	119370 TQ	MABLS	10/01-12/01
	Brockton PMSA, MA	Y	41930 FQ	69120 AW	110060 TQ	MABLS	10/01-12/01
	Lawrence PMSA, MA-NH	Y	34930 FQ	65370 AW	111380 TQ	MABLS	10/01-12/01
	Lowell PMSA, MA-NH	Y	36940 FQ	64880 AW	95010 TQ	MABLS	10/01-12/01
	Springfield MSA, MA	Y	32540 FQ	62850 AW	98150 TQ	MABLS	10/01-12/01
	Worcester PMSA, MA-CT	Y	42780 FQ	73280 AW	132940 TQ	MABLS	10/01-12/01
	Michigan	Y	34620 FQ	65860 AW	111060 TQ	MIBLS	10/01-12/01
	Ann Arbor PMSA, MI	Y	26280 FQ	59470 AW	128160 TQ	MIBLS	10/01-12/01
	Detroit PMSA, MI	Y	37000 FQ	67620 AW	108980 TQ	MIBLS	10/01-12/01
	Flint PMSA, MI	Y	38130 FQ	56990 AW	83350 TQ	MIBLS	10/01-12/01
	Grand Rapids-Muskegon-Holland MSA, MI	Y	48710 FQ	85810 AW		MIBLS	10/01-12/01
	Kalamazoo-Battle Creek MSA, MI	Y	39260 FQ	63330 AW	92500 TQ	MIBLS	10/01-12/01
	Lansing-East Lansing MSA, MI	Y	36030 FQ	56170 AW	76370 TQ	MIBLS	10/01-12/01
	Saginaw-Bay City-Midland MSA, MI	Y	43070 FQ	74010 AW	114100 TQ	MIBLS	10/01-12/01
	Minnesota	Y	39290 FQ	68260 AW	110370 TQ	MNBLS	10/01-12/01
	Duluth-Superior MSA, MN-WI	Y	33300 FQ	60900 AW	119290 TQ	MNBLS	10/01-12/01
	Minneapolis-St. Paul MSA, MN-WI	Y	39850 FQ	68950 AW	110720 TQ	MNBLS	10/01-12/01
	St. Cloud MSA, MN	Y	38480 FQ	57700 AW	86140 TQ	MNBLS	10/01-12/01
	Mississippi	Y	29890 FQ	50050 AW	74110 TQ	MSBLS	10/01-12/01
	Biloxi-Gulfport-Pascagoula MSA, MS	Y	37360 FQ	55490 AW	79690 TQ	MSBLS	10/01-12/01
	Jackson MSA, MS	Y	28740 FQ	46320 AW	71650 TQ	MSBLS	10/01-12/01
	Missouri	Y	32990 FQ	56150 AW	85870 TQ	MOBLS	10/01-12/01
	Kansas City MSA, MO-KS	Y	35220 FQ	58700 AW	91070 TQ	MOBLS	10/01-12/01
	St. Louis MSA, MO-IL	Y	33360 FQ	56990 AW	86460 TQ	MOBLS	10/01-12/01
	Springfield MSA, MO	Y	29590 FQ	50680 AW	71580 TQ	MOBLS	10/01-12/01

AAW Average annual wage	**AOH** Average offered, high	**ASH** Average starting, high	**H** Hourly	**M** Monthly	**S** Special: hourly and annual
AE Average entry wage	**AOL** Average offered, low	**ASL** Average starting, low	**HI** Highest wage paid	**MTC** Median total compensation	**TQ** Third quartile wage
AEX Average experienced wage	**APH** Average pay, high range	**AW** Average wage paid	**HR** High end range	**MW** Median wage paid	**W** Weekly
AO Average offered	**APL** Average pay, low range	**FQ** First quartile wage	**LR** Low end range	**SQ** Second quartile wage	**Y** Yearly

Occupation/Type/Industry	Location	Per	Low	Mid	High	Source	Date
Management Analyst	Montana	Y	30730 FQ	59180 AW	97530 TQ	MTBLS	10/01-12/01
	Nebraska	Y	22120 FQ	53310 AW	87700 TQ	NEBLS	10/01-12/01
	Lincoln MSA, NE	Y	15950 FQ	46110 AW	88870 TQ	NEBLS	10/01-12/01
	Omaha MSA, NE-IA	Y	31310 FQ	56630 AW	87450 TQ	NEBLS	10/01-12/01
	Nevada	Y	35370 FQ	57400 AW	91520 TQ	NVBLS	10/01-12/01
	Las Vegas MSA, NV-AZ	Y	39800 FQ	63290 AW	99950 TQ	NVBLS	10/01-12/01
	Reno MSA, NV	Y	30590 FQ	47630 AW	68850 TQ	NVBLS	10/01-12/01
	New Hampshire	Y	35700 FQ	73530 AW		NHBLS	10/01-12/01
	Manchester PMSA, NH	Y	51250 FQ	103560 AW		NHBLS	10/01-12/01
	Nashua PMSA, NH	Y	39910 FQ	65220 AW	94580 TQ	NHBLS	10/01-12/01
	Portsmouth-Rochester PMSA, NH-ME	Y	31070 FQ	54290 AW	86070 TQ	NHBLS	10/01-12/01
	New Jersey	Y	41320 FQ	72150 AW		NJBLS	10/01-12/01
	Atlantic-Cape May PMSA, NJ	Y	33400 FQ	65240 AW	109540 TQ	NJBLS	10/01-12/01
	Bergen-Passaic PMSA, NJ	Y	42160 FQ	69160 AW	101960 TQ	NJBLS	10/01-12/01
	Jersey City PMSA, NJ	Y	40490 FQ	64980 AW	97250 TQ	NJBLS	10/01-12/01
	Middlesex-Somerset-Hunterdon PMSA, NJ	Y	40350 FQ	77130 AW	139310 TQ	NJBLS	10/01-12/01
	Monmouth-Ocean PMSA, NJ	Y	41310 FQ	58870 AW	88710 TQ	NJBLS	10/01-12/01
	Newark PMSA, NJ	Y	41130 FQ	81740 AW		NJBLS	10/01-12/01
	New Mexico	Y	30060 FQ	51860 AW	82820 TQ	NMBLS	10/01-12/01
	Albuquerque MSA, NM	Y	31390 FQ	54230 AW	83750 TQ	NMBLS	10/01-12/01
	Las Cruces MSA, NM	Y	38650 FQ	57430 AW	76270 TQ	NMBLS	10/01-12/01
	New York	Y	38180 FQ	64220 AW	103000 TQ	NYBLS	10/01-12/01
	Albany-Schenectady-Troy MSA, NY	Y	35520 FQ	53940 AW	77980 TQ	NYBLS	10/01-12/01
	Binghamton MSA, NY	Y	34890 FQ	64040 AW	107730 TQ	NYBLS	10/01-12/01
	Buffalo-Niagara Falls MSA, NY	Y	32490 FQ	51340 AW	77180 TQ	NYBLS	10/01-12/01
	Dutchess County PMSA, NY	Y	42680 FQ	58810 AW	77630 TQ	NYBLS	10/01-12/01
	Nassau-Suffolk PMSA, NY	Y	35890 FQ	58960 AW	89220 TQ	NYBLS	10/01-12/01
	New York PMSA, NY	Y	40800 FQ	68130 AW	110550 TQ	NYBLS	10/01-12/01
	Newburgh PMSA, NY-PA	Y	36560 FQ	55260 AW	80160 TQ	NYBLS	10/01-12/01
	Rochester MSA, NY	Y	37720 FQ	58780 AW	82600 TQ	NYBLS	10/01-12/01
	Syracuse MSA, NY	Y	33090 FQ	53470 AW	73650 TQ	NYBLS	10/01-12/01
	Utica-Rome MSA, NY	Y	28110 FQ	43900 AW	70750 TQ	NYBLS	10/01-12/01
	North Carolina	Y	31460 FQ	64480 AW	109250 TQ	NCBLS	10/01-12/01
	Charlotte-Gastonia-Rock Hill MSA, NC-SC	Y	23310 FQ	63230 AW	111510 TQ	NCBLS	10/01-12/01
	Fayetteville MSA, NC	Y	36390 FQ	54360 AW	78930 TQ	NCBLS	10/01-12/01
	Greensboro-Winston-Salem-High Point MSA, NC	Y	36250 FQ	60690 AW	97300 TQ	NCBLS	10/01-12/01
	Raleigh-Durham-Chapel Hill MSA, NC	Y	37240 FQ	70850 AW	116830 TQ	NCBLS	10/01-12/01
	Wilmington MSA, NC	Y	28400 FQ	63060 AW	118720 TQ	NCBLS	10/01-12/01
	North Dakota	Y	27700 FQ	52060 AW	83870 TQ	NDBLS	10/01-12/01
	Fargo-Moorhead MSA, ND-MN	Y	26340 FQ	47790 AW	71350 TQ	NDBLS	10/01-12/01
	Ohio	Y	32410 FQ	56860 AW	86450 TQ	OHBLS	10/01-12/01
	Akron PMSA, OH	Y	36190 FQ	67800 AW		OHBLS	10/01-12/01
	Canton-Massillon MSA, OH	Y	37290 FQ	61230 AW	90470 TQ	OHBLS	10/01-12/01
	Cincinnati PMSA, OH-KY-IN	Y	32200 FQ	58250 AW	95210 TQ	OHBLS	10/01-12/01
	Cleveland-Lorain-Elyria PMSA, OH	Y	32430 FQ	54490 AW	80220 TQ	OHBLS	10/01-12/01
	Columbus MSA, OH	Y	27280 FQ	53460 AW	79460 TQ	OHBLS	10/01-12/01
	Dayton-Springfield MSA, OH	Y	36890 FQ	58280 AW	83040 TQ	OHBLS	10/01-12/01
	Hamilton-Middletown PMSA, OH	Y	37200 FQ	67040 AW	116650 TQ	OHBLS	10/01-12/01
	Toledo MSA, OH	Y	38270 FQ	65370 AW	106960 TQ	OHBLS	10/01-12/01
	Youngstown-Warren MSA, OH	Y	36800 FQ	56870 AW	79810 TQ	OHBLS	10/01-12/01
	Oklahoma	Y	27150 FQ	51400 AW	76530 TQ	OKBLS	10/01-12/01
	Oklahoma City MSA, OK	Y	25490 FQ	45760 AW	69130 TQ	OKBLS	10/01-12/01
	Tulsa MSA, OK	Y	34320 FQ	63390 AW	94040 TQ	OKBLS	10/01-12/01
	Oregon	Y	35540 FQ	61620 AW	102200 TQ	ORBLS	10/01-12/01
	Eugene-Springfield MSA, OR	Y	35760 FQ	55270 AW	80940 TQ	ORBLS	10/01-12/01
	Medford-Ashland MSA, OR	Y	39940 FQ	63610 AW	90590 TQ	ORBLS	10/01-12/01
	Portland-Vancouver PMSA, OR-WA	Y	37530 FQ	62580 AW	109560 TQ	ORBLS	10/01-12/01
	Salem PMSA, OR	Y	21960 FQ	48430 AW	69580 TQ	ORBLS	10/01-12/01
	Pennsylvania	Y	34040 FQ	61020 AW	94060 TQ	PABLS	10/01-12/01
	Allentown-Bethlehem-Easton MSA, PA	Y	29740 FQ	57130 AW	92000 TQ	PABLS	10/01-12/01

AAW Average annual wage **AE** Average entry wage **AEX** Average experienced wage **AO** Average offered **AOH** Average offered, high **AOL** Average offered, low **APH** Average pay, high range **APL** Average pay, low range **ASH** Average starting, high **ASL** Average starting, low **AW** Average wage paid **FQ** First quartile wage **H** Hourly **HI** Highest wage paid **HR** High end range **LR** Low end range **M** Monthly **MTC** Median total compensation **MW** Median wage paid **SQ** Second quartile wage **S** Special: hourly and annual **TQ** Third quartile wage **W** Weekly **Y** Yearly

Occupation/Type/Industry	Location	Per	Low	Mid	High	Source	Date
Management Analyst	Erie MSA, PA	Y	38340 FQ	59560 AW	87300 TQ	PABLS	10/01-12/01
	Harrisburg-Lebanon-Carlisle MSA, PA	Y	35790 FQ	53750 AW	74780 TQ	PABLS	10/01-12/01
	Johnstown MSA, PA	Y	34340 FQ	57970 AW	90040 TQ	PABLS	10/01-12/01
	Lancaster MSA, PA	Y	31990 FQ	54280 AW	85200 TQ	PABLS	10/01-12/01
	Philadelphia PMSA, PA-NJ	Y	35620 FQ	64680 AW	99770 TQ	PABLS	10/01-12/01
	Pittsburgh MSA, PA	Y	33120 FQ	57870 AW	90130 TQ	PABLS	10/01-12/01
	Reading MSA, PA	Y	34400 FQ	82160 AW		PABLS	10/01-12/01
	Scranton-Wilkes-Barre-Hazleton MSA, PA	Y	37110 FQ	53800 AW	83660 TQ	PABLS	10/01-12/01
	York MSA, PA	Y	30080 FQ	46440 AW	69540 TQ	PABLS	10/01-12/01
	Rhode Island	Y	38970 FQ	83640 AW	143480 TQ	RIBLS	10/01-12/01
	Providence-Fall River-Warwick MSA, RI-MA	Y	38350 FQ	87380 AW	142720 TQ	RIBLS	10/01-12/01
	South Carolina	Y	30960 FQ	58490 AW	89510 TQ	SCBLS	10/01-12/01
	Charleston-North Charleston MSA, SC	Y	22850 FQ	51920 AW	80380 TQ	SCBLS	10/01-12/01
	Greenville-Spartanburg-Anderson MSA, SC	Y	16480 FQ	47770 AW	79100 TQ	SCBLS	10/01-12/01
	Myrtle Beach MSA, SC	Y	31570 FQ	60790 AW	105350 TQ	SCBLS	10/01-12/01
	South Dakota	Y	32340 FQ	50960 AW	71830 TQ	SDBLS	10/01-12/01
	Sioux Falls MSA, SD	Y	32250 FQ	50390 AW	67810 TQ	SDBLS	10/01-12/01
	Tennessee	Y	28330 FQ	57880 AW	91760 TQ	TNBLS	10/01-12/01
	Chattanooga MSA, TN-GA	Y	29570 FQ	46850 AW	82860 TQ	TNBLS	10/01-12/01
	Clarksville-Hopkinsville MSA, TN-KY	Y	36210 FQ	49530 AW	68080 TQ	TNBLS	10/01-12/01
	Johnson City-Kingsport-Bristol MSA, TN-VA	Y	22640 FQ	43150 AW	67840 TQ	TNBLS	10/01-12/01
	Knoxville MSA, TN	Y	19750 FQ	43710 AW	75570 TQ	TNBLS	10/01-12/01
	Memphis MSA, TN-AR-MS	Y	38190 FQ	58920 AW	82360 TQ	TNBLS	10/01-12/01
	Nashville MSA, TN	Y	32960 FQ	64440 AW	135110 TQ	TNBLS	10/01-12/01
	Texas	Y	36230 FQ	59320 AW	95540 TQ	TXBLS	10/01-12/01
	Amarillo MSA, TX	Y	30750 FQ	52070 AW	72140 TQ	TXBLS	10/01-12/01
	Beaumont-Port Arthur MSA, TX	Y	41510 FQ	67490 AW	96590 TQ	TXBLS	10/01-12/01
	Brazoria PMSA, TX	Y	30110 FQ	64390 AW	106800 TQ	TXBLS	10/01-12/01
	Brownsville-Harlingen-San Benito MSA, TX	Y	35360 FQ	51610 AW	81890 TQ	TXBLS	10/01-12/01
	Corpus Christi MSA, TX	Y	39030 FQ	62900 AW	92310 TQ	TXBLS	10/01-12/01
	Dallas PMSA, TX	Y	38720 FQ	64070 AW	96600 TQ	TXBLS	10/01-12/01
	El Paso MSA, TX	Y	37400 FQ	69370 AW		TXBLS	10/01-12/01
	Fort Worth-Arlington PMSA, TX	Y	36480 FQ	56770 AW	86750 TQ	TXBLS	10/01-12/01
	Galveston-Texas City PMSA, TX	Y	28800 FQ	49740 AW	74060 TQ	TXBLS	10/01-12/01
	Houston PMSA, TX	Y	37570 FQ	62500 AW	107020 TQ	TXBLS	10/01-12/01
	Killeen-Temple MSA, TX	Y	37590 FQ	48580 AW	58170 TQ	TXBLS	10/01-12/01
	Laredo MSA, TX	Y	33090 FQ	54580 AW	85440 TQ	TXBLS	10/01-12/01
	Longview-Marshall MSA, TX	Y	37560 FQ	64860 AW	95840 TQ	TXBLS	10/01-12/01
	Lubbock MSA, TX	Y	39770 FQ	85950 AW	130450 TQ	TXBLS	10/01-12/01
	McAllen-Edinburg-Mission MSA, TX	Y	33300 FQ	54090 AW	85050 TQ	TXBLS	10/01-12/01
	Odessa-Midland MSA, TX	Y	12390 FQ	49930 AW	87920 TQ	TXBLS	10/01-12/01
	San Antonio MSA, TX	Y	36030 FQ	56420 AW	82850 TQ	TXBLS	10/01-12/01
	Waco MSA, TX	Y	32730 FQ	59190 AW	96460 TQ	TXBLS	10/01-12/01
	Utah	Y	35150 FQ	65090 AW	126670 TQ	UTBLS	10/01-12/01
	Provo-Orem MSA, UT	Y	40600 FQ	80190 AW		UTBLS	10/01-12/01
	Salt Lake City-Ogden MSA, UT	Y	34700 FQ	64050 AW	123920 TQ	UTBLS	10/01-12/01
	Vermont	Y	36210 FQ	61190 AW	107380 TQ	VTBLS	10/01-12/01
	Burlington MSA, VT	Y	38200 FQ	73920 AW	129530 TQ	VTBLS	10/01-12/01
	Virginia	Y	38060 FQ	71310 AW	128810 TQ	VABLS	10/01-12/01
	Lynchburg MSA, VA	Y	31130 FQ	68390 AW		VABLS	10/01-12/01
	Norfolk-Virginia Beach-Newport News MSA, VA-NC	Y	36080 FQ	70330 AW	145410 TQ	VABLS	10/01-12/01
	Richmond-Petersburg MSA, VA	Y	35080 FQ	54150 AW	79510 TQ	VABLS	10/01-12/01
	Washington	Y	41550 FQ	65190 AW	98330 TQ	WABLS	10/01-12/01
	Bremerton PMSA, WA	Y	40600 FQ	56370 AW	71910 TQ	WABLS	10/01-12/01
	Olympia PMSA, WA	Y	35610 FQ	49410 AW	67510 TQ	WABLS	10/01-12/01

AAW Average annual wage · **AE** Average entry wage · **AEX** Average experienced wage · **AO** Average offered · **AOH** Average offered, high · **AOL** Average offered, low · **APH** Average pay, high range · **APL** Average pay, low range · **ASH** Average starting, high · **ASL** Average starting, low · **AW** Average wage paid · **FQ** First quartile wage · **H** Hourly · **HI** Highest wage paid · **HR** High end range · **LR** Low end range · **M** Monthly · **MTC** Median total compensation · **MW** Median wage paid · **SQ** Second quartile wage · **S** Special: hourly and annual · **TQ** Third quartile wage · **W** Weekly · **Y** Yearly

Occupation/Type/Industry	Location	Per	Low	Mid	High	Source	Date
Management Analyst	Richland-Kennewick-Pasco MSA, WA	Y	37180 FQ	74300 AW	113920 TQ	WABLS	10/01-12/01
	Seattle-Bellevue-Everett PMSA, WA	Y	44280 FQ	66420 AW	99760 TQ	WABLS	10/01-12/01
	Spokane MSA, WA	Y	40830 FQ	79360 AW		WABLS	10/01-12/01
	Tacoma PMSA, WA	Y	32070 FQ	51160 AW	79030 TQ	WABLS	10/01-12/01
	Yakima MSA, WA	Y	32070 FQ	49090 AW	70100 TQ	WABLS	10/01-12/01
	West Virginia	Y	36220 FQ	57580 AW	87200 TQ	WVBLS	10/01-12/01
	Charleston MSA, WV	Y	30950 FQ	54910 AW	94300 TQ	WVBLS	10/01-12/01
	Huntington-Ashland MSA, WV-KY-OH	Y	37750 FQ	51100 AW	71330 TQ	WVBLS	10/01-12/01
	Wisconsin	Y	33360 FQ	57600 AW	87510 TQ	WIBLS	10/01-12/01
	Appleton-Oshkosh-Neenah MSA, WI	Y	30860 FQ	47350 AW	70830 TQ	WIBLS	10/01-12/01
	Green Bay MSA, WI	Y	33020 FQ	51220 AW	73600 TQ	WIBLS	10/01-12/01
	Milwaukee-Waukesha PMSA, WI	Y	35140 FQ	58800 AW	77080 TQ	WIBLS	10/01-12/01
	Racine PMSA, WI	Y	32840 FQ	52810 AW	72850 TQ	WIBLS	10/01-12/01
	Wyoming	Y	28730 FQ	66070 AW		WYBLS	10/01-12/01
	Puerto Rico	Y	23690 FQ	44880 AW	70570 TQ	PRBLS	10/01-12/01
	Guam	Y	32790 FQ	49990 AW	71310 TQ	GUBLS	10/01-12/01
Manager							
Business	United States	Y		130700 AW		EBN	1/01-1/02
Operations	United States	Y		87700 AW		EBN	1/01-1/02
Procurement	United States	Y		73900 AW		EBN	1/01-1/02
Manager of Applications Development							
Information Technology	United States	Y	76750 AOL			IOMA5	1/01-1/02
Manager of Data Mining and Warehousing							
Information Technology	United States	Y	69500 AOL			IOMA5	1/01-1/02
Manager of Help Desk and Information Technology Support							
Information Technology	United States	Y	48000 AOL			IOMA5	1/01-1/02
Manager of Web Content Development							
Information Technology	United States	Y	51750 AOL			IOMA5	1/01-1/02
Manager of Web Design and Development							
Information Technology	United States	Y	63750 AOL			IOMA5	1/01-1/02
Manicurist and Pedicurist	Alabama	H	6.20 FQ	12.70 AW	19.87 TQ	ALBLS	10/01-12/01
	Arizona	H	5.55 FQ	7.09 AW	8.85 TQ	AZBLS	10/01-12/01
	Phoenix-Mesa MSA, AZ	H	5.54 FQ	7.19 AW	8.97 TQ	AZBLS	10/01-12/01
	Tucson MSA, AZ	H	5.56 FQ	6.86 AW	8.46 TQ	AZBLS	10/01-12/01
	Arkansas	H	6.15 FQ	10.10 AW	15.11 TQ	ARBLS	10/01-12/01
	California	H	6.43 FQ	7.92 AW	10.18 TQ	CABLS	10/01-12/01
	Los Angeles-Long Beach PMSA, CA	H	6.46 FQ	10.85 AW	18.11 TQ	CABLS	10/01-12/01
	Modesto MSA, CA	H	6.95 FQ	8.21 AW	9.78 TQ	CABLS	10/01-12/01
	Oakland PMSA, CA	H	6.50 FQ	7.76 AW	9.58 TQ	CABLS	10/01-12/01
	Orange County PMSA, CA	H	6.36 FQ	7.13 AW	8.47 TQ	CABLS	10/01-12/01
	Riverside-San Bernardino PMSA, CA	H	8.37 FQ	9.35 AW	10.56 TQ	CABLS	10/01-12/01
	Salinas MSA, CA	H	6.35 FQ	6.72 AW	7.17 TQ	CABLS	10/01-12/01
	San Diego MSA, CA	H	7.04 FQ	7.88 AW	8.80 TQ	CABLS	10/01-12/01
	San Francisco PMSA, CA	H	6.50 FQ	7.73 AW	8.71 TQ	CABLS	10/01-12/01
	San Jose PMSA, CA	H	6.39 FQ	7.61 AW	9.67 TQ	CABLS	10/01-12/01
	Santa Rosa PMSA, CA	H	6.43 FQ	8.50 AW	11.38 TQ	CABLS	10/01-12/01
	Vallejo-Fairfield-Napa PMSA, CA	H	6.38 FQ	7.08 AW	8.43 TQ	CABLS	10/01-12/01
	Colorado	H	6.15 FQ	9.27 AW	15.01 TQ	COBLS	10/01-12/01
	Colorado Springs MSA, CO	H	6.78 FQ	9.56 AW	15.34 TQ	COBLS	10/01-12/01
	Denver PMSA, CO	H	6.17 FQ	8.77 AW	14.44 TQ	COBLS	10/01-12/01

AAW Average annual wage; **AE** Average entry wage; **AEX** Average experienced wage; **AO** Average offered; **AOH** Average offered, high; **AOL** Average offered, low; **APH** Average pay, high range; **APL** Average pay, low range; **ASH** Average starting, high; **ASL** Average starting, low; **AW** Average wage paid; **FQ** First quartile wage; **H** Hourly; **HI** Highest wage paid; **HR** High end range; **LR** Low end range; **M** Monthly; **MTC** Median total compensation; **MW** Median wage paid; **SQ** Second quartile wage; **S** Special: hourly and annual; **TQ** Third quartile wage; **W** Weekly; **Y** Yearly

Occupation/Type/Industry	Location	Per	Low	Mid	High	Source	Date
Manicurist and Pedicurist	Connecticut	H	6.99 FQ	10.26 AW	12.95 TQ	CTBLS	10/01-12/01
	Hartford MSA, CT	H	7.95 FQ	10.31 AW	12.86 TQ	CTBLS	10/01-12/01
	New Haven-Meriden PMSA, CT	H	7.89 FQ	9.87 AW	11.64 TQ	CTBLS	10/01-12/01
	Stamford-Norwalk PMSA, CT	H	7.07 FQ	11.58 AW	16.84 TQ	CTBLS	10/01-12/01
	Waterbury PMSA, CT	H	6.53 FQ	8.79 AW	13.08 TQ	CTBLS	10/01-12/01
	Delaware	H	6.32 FQ	8.09 AW	10.23 TQ	DEBLS	10/01-12/01
	Wilmington-Newark PMSA, DE-MD	H	6.31 FQ	7.94 AW	10.11 TQ	DEBLS	10/01-12/01
	District of Columbia	H	7.37 FQ	10.23 AW	13.39 TQ	DCBLS	10/01-12/01
	Washington PMSA, DC-MD-VA-WV	H	6.02 FQ	9.72 AW	17.67 TQ	DCBLS	10/01-12/01
	Florida	H	5.78 FQ	7.94 AW	11.16 TQ	FLBLS	10/01-12/01
	Daytona Beach MSA, FL	H	5.75 FQ	6.62 AW	8.24 TQ	FLBLS	10/01-12/01
	Fort Lauderdale PMSA, FL	H	5.56 FQ	6.85 AW	8.59 TQ	FLBLS	10/01-12/01
	Fort Myers-Cape Coral MSA, FL	H	6.08 FQ	9.11 AW	12.24 TQ	FLBLS	10/01-12/01
	Fort Pierce-Port St. Lucie MSA, FL	H	5.60 FQ	7.48 AW	11.81 TQ	FLBLS	10/01-12/01
	Gainesville MSA, FL	H	5.46 FQ	7.07 AW	10.06 TQ	FLBLS	10/01-12/01
	Jacksonville MSA, FL	H	5.69 FQ	7.09 AW	8.66 TQ	FLBLS	10/01-12/01
	Miami PMSA, FL	H	6.04 FQ	8.74 AW	13.03 TQ	FLBLS	10/01-12/01
	Naples MSA, FL	H	5.96 FQ	8.60 AW	12.52 TQ	FLBLS	10/01-12/01
	Orlando MSA, FL	H	6.77 FQ	8.27 AW	10.49 TQ	FLBLS	10/01-12/01
	Sarasota-Bradenton MSA, FL	H	5.97 FQ	10.67 AW	16.51 TQ	FLBLS	10/01-12/01
	Tallahassee MSA, FL	H	5.70 FQ	7.09 AW	8.58 TQ	FLBLS	10/01-12/01
	Tampa-St. Petersburg-Clearwater MSA, FL	H	5.79 FQ	7.59 AW	10.44 TQ	FLBLS	10/01-12/01
	West Palm Beach-Boca Raton MSA, FL	H	6.57 FQ	9.55 AW	14.08 TQ	FLBLS	10/01-12/01
	Georgia	H	5.54 FQ	6.35 AW	6.97 TQ	GABLS	10/01-12/01
	Atlanta MSA, GA	H	5.53 FQ	6.18 AW	6.89 TQ	GABLS	10/01-12/01
	Hawaii	H	6.96 FQ	9.27 AW	13.62 TQ	HIBLS	10/01-12/01
	Honolulu MSA, HI	H	6.96 FQ	8.28 AW	11.11 TQ	HIBLS	10/01-12/01
	Illinois	H	7.29 FQ	9.40 AW	12.85 TQ	ILBLS	10/01-12/01
	Chicago PMSA, IL	H	7.29 FQ	9.40 AW	12.86 TQ	ILBLS	10/01-12/01
	Indiana	H	5.67 FQ	7.81 AW	11.48 TQ	INBLS	10/01-12/01
	Fort Wayne MSA, IN	H	5.54 FQ	6.89 AW	8.74 TQ	INBLS	10/01-12/01
	Indianapolis MSA, IN	H	6.11 FQ	9.00 AW	11.15 TQ	INBLS	10/01-12/01
	South Bend MSA, IN	H	6.10 FQ	7.96 AW	10.30 TQ	INBLS	10/01-12/01
	Iowa	H	7.37 FQ	9.54 AW	12.20 TQ	IABLS	10/01-12/01
	Davenport-Moline-Rock Island MSA, IA-IL	H	7.44 FQ	8.29 AW	9.22 TQ	IABLS	10/01-12/01
	Des Moines MSA, IA	H	6.80 FQ	10.02 AW	13.39 TQ	IABLS	10/01-12/01
	Kansas	H	6.79 FQ	11.51 AW	20.64 TQ	KSBLS	10/01-12/01
	Kentucky	H	7.08 FQ	11.16 AW	14.93 TQ	KYBLS	10/01-12/01
	Louisville MSA, KY-IN	H	8.05 FQ	11.93 AW	14.12 TQ	KYBLS	10/01-12/01
	Louisiana	H	5.91 FQ	8.27 AW	11.16 TQ	LABLS	10/01-12/01
	Baton Rouge MSA, LA	H	6.02 FQ	9.19 AW	12.22 TQ	LABLS	10/01-12/01
	Lafayette MSA, LA	H	5.56 FQ	6.90 AW	8.55 TQ	LABLS	10/01-12/01
	New Orleans MSA, LA	H	6.31 FQ	8.62 AW	11.10 TQ	LABLS	10/01-12/01
	Maryland	H	5.91 FQ	8.57 AW	11.48 TQ	MDBLS	10/01-12/01
	Baltimore PMSA, MD	H	5.74 FQ	7.37 AW	10.25 TQ	MDBLS	10/01-12/01
	Massachusetts	H	7.10 FQ	9.26 AW	10.64 TQ	MABLS	10/01-12/01
	Boston PMSA, MA-NH	H	7.37 FQ	9.37 AW	10.63 TQ	MABLS	10/01-12/01
	Lawrence PMSA, MA-NH	H	5.63 FQ	6.91 AW	8.53 TQ	MABLS	10/01-12/01
	Springfield MSA, MA	H	6.88 FQ	8.53 AW	10.59 TQ	MABLS	10/01-12/01
	Worcester PMSA, MA-CT	H	6.81 FQ	8.23 AW	12.96 TQ	MABLS	10/01-12/01
	Michigan	H	6.04 FQ	8.86 AW	11.55 TQ	MIBLS	10/01-12/01
	Ann Arbor PMSA, MI	H	6.09 FQ	10.15 AW	13.45 TQ	MIBLS	10/01-12/01
	Detroit PMSA, MI	H	6.16 FQ	9.32 AW	11.51 TQ	MIBLS	10/01-12/01
	Grand Rapids-Muskegon-Holland MSA, MI	H	5.71 FQ	7.77 AW	10.63 TQ	MIBLS	10/01-12/01
	Saginaw-Bay City-Midland MSA, MI	H	5.82 FQ	8.04 AW	10.51 TQ	MIBLS	10/01-12/01
	Minnesota	H	7.16 FQ	8.82 AW	10.61 TQ	MNBLS	10/01-12/01
	Minneapolis-St. Paul MSA, MN-WI	H	7.28 FQ	8.91 AW	10.60 TQ	MNBLS	10/01-12/01
	Mississippi	H	6.35 FQ	9.28 AW	13.45 TQ	MSBLS	10/01-12/01
	Missouri	H	5.66 FQ	8.41 AW	14.33 TQ	MOBLS	10/01-12/01
	Kansas City MSA, MO-KS	H	5.72 FQ	9.52 AW	13.69 TQ	MOBLS	10/01-12/01
	St. Louis MSA, MO-IL	H	5.93 FQ	9.95 AW	15.37 TQ	MOBLS	10/01-12/01

AAW Average annual wage; AE Average entry wage; AEX Average experienced wage; AO Average offered; AOH Average offered, high; AOL Average offered, low; APH Average pay, high range; APL Average pay, low range; ASH Average starting, high; ASL Average starting, low; AW Average wage paid; FQ First quartile wage; H Hourly; HI Highest wage paid; HR High end range; LR Low end range; M Monthly; MTC Median total compensation; MW Median wage paid; SQ Second quartile wage; S Special: hourly and annual; TQ Third quartile wage; W Weekly; Y Yearly

Occupation/Type/Industry	Location	Per	Low	Mid	High	Source	Date
Manicurist and Pedicurist	Nebraska	H	6.07 FQ	8.51 AW	14.22 TQ	NEBLS	10/01-12/01
	Omaha MSA, NE-IA	H	5.89 FQ	8.55 AW	14.26 TQ	NEBLS	10/01-12/01
	Nevada	H	6.00 FQ	10.66 AW	18.80 TQ	NVBLS	10/01-12/01
	Las Vegas MSA, NV-AZ	H	5.90 FQ	10.18 AW	18.03 TQ	NVBLS	10/01-12/01
	New Hampshire	H	6.13 FQ	8.31 AW	11.11 TQ	NHBLS	10/01-12/01
	Nashua PMSA, NH	H	7.46 FQ	8.11 AW	8.99 TQ	NHBLS	10/01-12/01
	Portsmouth-Rochester PMSA, NH-ME	H	6.19 FQ	10.84 AW	15.82 TQ	NHBLS	10/01-12/01
	New Jersey	H	6.21 FQ	9.90 AW	15.53 TQ	NJBLS	10/01-12/01
	Atlantic-Cape May PMSA, NJ	H	5.78 FQ	8.88 AW	12.02 TQ	NJBLS	10/01-12/01
	Bergen-Passaic PMSA, NJ	H	6.61 FQ	8.31 AW	11.21 TQ	NJBLS	10/01-12/01
	Middlesex-Somerset-Hunterdon PMSA, NJ	H	5.87 FQ	11.22 AW	20.74 TQ	NJBLS	10/01-12/01
	Monmouth-Ocean PMSA, NJ	H	6.59 FQ	8.75 AW	10.76 TQ	NJBLS	10/01-12/01
	Newark PMSA, NJ	H	7.58 FQ	12.31 AW	16.61 TQ	NJBLS	10/01-12/01
	New York	H	5.52 FQ	7.02 AW	10.15 TQ	NYBLS	10/01-12/01
	Albany-Schenectady-Troy MSA, NY	H	5.86 FQ	7.98 AW	10.54 TQ	NYBLS	10/01-12/01
	Dutchess County PMSA, NY	H	5.34 FQ	5.96 AW	6.69 TQ	NYBLS	10/01-12/01
	Nassau-Suffolk PMSA, NY	H	5.55 FQ	6.75 AW	9.66 TQ	NYBLS	10/01-12/01
	New York PMSA, NY	H	5.44 FQ	7.33 AW	11.00 TQ	NYBLS	10/01-12/01
	Rochester MSA, NY	H	5.75 FQ	7.18 AW	10.14 TQ	NYBLS	10/01-12/01
	Syracuse MSA, NY	H	5.71 FQ	7.73 AW	10.34 TQ	NYBLS	10/01-12/01
	North Carolina	H	6.43 FQ	10.16 AW	13.48 TQ	NCBLS	10/01-12/01
	Charlotte-Gastonia-Rock Hill MSA, NC-SC	H	7.40 FQ	10.66 AW	14.16 TQ	NCBLS	10/01-12/01
	Fayetteville MSA, NC	H	6.90 FQ	9.81 AW	13.43 TQ	NCBLS	10/01-12/01
	Greensboro-Winston-Salem-High Point MSA, NC	H	7.63 FQ	11.10 AW	13.60 TQ	NCBLS	10/01-12/01
	Raleigh-Durham-Chapel Hill MSA, NC	H	5.86 FQ	8.60 AW	12.64 TQ	NCBLS	10/01-12/01
	Ohio	H	5.81 FQ	8.68 AW	13.38 TQ	OHBLS	10/01-12/01
	Akron PMSA, OH	H	6.23 FQ	7.54 AW	8.62 TQ	OHBLS	10/01-12/01
	Canton-Massillon MSA, OH	H	5.66 FQ	7.46 AW	10.88 TQ	OHBLS	10/01-12/01
	Cincinnati PMSA, OH-KY-IN	H	5.79 FQ	10.30 AW	17.45 TQ	OHBLS	10/01-12/01
	Cleveland-Lorain-Elyria PMSA, OH	H	6.16 FQ	10.42 AW	13.92 TQ	OHBLS	10/01-12/01
	Columbus MSA, OH	H	7.49 FQ	11.39 AW	15.92 TQ	OHBLS	10/01-12/01
	Dayton-Springfield MSA, OH	H	5.54 FQ	6.39 AW	7.42 TQ	OHBLS	10/01-12/01
	Hamilton-Middletown PMSA, OH	H	5.80 FQ	8.20 AW	12.95 TQ	OHBLS	10/01-12/01
	Toledo MSA, OH	H	6.79 FQ	9.25 AW	12.85 TQ	OHBLS	10/01-12/01
	Youngstown-Warren MSA, OH	H	7.06 FQ	7.93 AW	8.82 TQ	OHBLS	10/01-12/01
	Oklahoma	H	5.87 FQ	8.02 AW	11.51 TQ	OKBLS	10/01-12/01
	Oregon	H	7.17 FQ	10.36 AW	15.60 TQ	ORBLS	10/01-12/01
	Portland-Vancouver PMSA, OR-WA	H	7.15 FQ	10.00 AW	15.49 TQ	ORBLS	10/01-12/01
	Pennsylvania	H	5.75 FQ	7.79 AW	10.71 TQ	PABLS	10/01-12/01
	Erie MSA, PA	H	5.71 FQ	6.59 AW	7.25 TQ	PABLS	10/01-12/01
	Philadelphia PMSA, PA-NJ	H	5.74 FQ	8.41 AW	13.63 TQ	PABLS	10/01-12/01
	Pittsburgh MSA, PA	H	5.61 FQ	7.59 AW	10.93 TQ	PABLS	10/01-12/01
	York MSA, PA	H	6.62 FQ	7.67 AW	8.68 TQ	PABLS	10/01-12/01
	Rhode Island	H	6.82 FQ	9.81 AW	12.93 TQ	RIBLS	10/01-12/01
	Providence-Fall River-Warwick MSA, RI-MA	H	6.84 FQ	9.84 AW	12.92 TQ	RIBLS	10/01-12/01
	South Carolina	H	7.37 FQ	8.32 AW	9.68 TQ	SCBLS	10/01-12/01
	Charleston-North Charleston MSA, SC	H	7.49 FQ	8.37 AW	9.63 TQ	SCBLS	10/01-12/01
	Tennessee	H	5.90 FQ	10.20 AW	16.18 TQ	TNBLS	10/01-12/01
	Knoxville MSA, TN	H	6.88 FQ	12.96 AW	17.22 TQ	TNBLS	10/01-12/01
	Memphis MSA, TN-AR-MS	H	5.71 FQ	10.26 AW	16.86 TQ	TNBLS	10/01-12/01
	Nashville MSA, TN	H	5.79 FQ	8.29 AW	12.75 TQ	TNBLS	10/01-12/01
	Texas	H	5.97 FQ	9.61 AW	13.80 TQ	TXBLS	10/01-12/01
	Austin-San Marcos MSA, TX	H	7.22 FQ	9.91 AW	16.86 TQ	TXBLS	10/01-12/01
	El Paso MSA, TX	H	6.34 FQ	10.34 AW	13.44 TQ	TXBLS	10/01-12/01
	Fort Worth-Arlington PMSA, TX	H	6.22 FQ	11.02 AW	16.60 TQ	TXBLS	10/01-12/01
	Houston PMSA, TX	H	8.97 FQ	11.35 AW	16.02 TQ	TXBLS	10/01-12/01
	San Antonio MSA, TX	H	5.65 FQ	7.84 AW	12.66 TQ	TXBLS	10/01-12/01
	Utah	H	8.66 FQ	12.90 AW	16.93 TQ	UTBLS	10/01-12/01
	Salt Lake City-Ogden MSA, UT	H	9.10 FQ	13.53 AW	17.11 TQ	UTBLS	10/01-12/01

AAW	Average annual wage	**AOH**	Average offered, high	**ASH**	Average starting, high	**H**	Hourly	**M**	Monthly	**S**	Special: hourly and annual
AE	Average entry wage	**AOL**	Average offered, low	**ASL**	Average starting, low	**HI**	Highest wage paid	**MTC**	Median total compensation	**TQ**	Third quartile wage
AEX	Average experienced wage	**APH**	Average pay, high range	**AW**	Average wage paid	**HR**	High end range	**MW**	Median wage paid	**W**	Weekly
AO	Average offered	**APL**	Average pay, low range	**FQ**	First quartile wage	**LR**	Low end range	**SQ**	Second quartile wage	**Y**	Yearly

Occupation/Type/Industry	Location	Per	Low	Mid	High	Source	Date
Manicurist and Pedicurist	Virginia	H	5.96 FQ	8.67 AW	13.53 TQ	VABLS	10/01-12/01
	Norfolk-Virginia Beach-Newport News MSA, VA-NC	H	6.17 FQ	8.48 AW	12.43 TQ	VABLS	10/01-12/01
	Richmond-Petersburg MSA, VA	H	7.26 FQ	8.40 AW	10.14 TQ	VABLS	10/01-12/01
	Roanoke MSA, VA	H	5.73 FQ	6.73 AW	7.23 TQ	VABLS	10/01-12/01
	Washington	H	7.49 FQ	13.37 AW	19.86 TQ	WABLS	10/01-12/01
	Seattle-Bellevue-Everett PMSA, WA	H	10.18 FQ	15.72 AW	21.31 TQ	WABLS	10/01-12/01
	West Virginia	H	5.65 FQ	7.95 AW	10.32 TQ	WVBLS	10/01-12/01
	Wisconsin	H	6.25 FQ	9.61 AW	15.41 TQ	WIBLS	10/01-12/01
	Milwaukee-Waukesha PMSA, WI	H	7.35 FQ	9.42 AW	14.65 TQ	WIBLS	10/01-12/01
	Wyoming	H	9.28 FQ	10.13 AW	11.34 TQ	WYBLS	10/01-12/01
	Puerto Rico	H	5.50 FQ	6.39 AW	7.08 TQ	PRBLS	10/01-12/01
Manufactured Building and Mobile Home Installer	Alabama	H	7.18 FQ	11.93 AW	16.59 TQ	ALBLS	10/01-12/01
	Mobile MSA, AL	H	7.28 FQ	11.47 AW	17.22 TQ	ALBLS	10/01-12/01
	Arizona	H	7.43 FQ	13.03 AW	19.14 TQ	AZBLS	10/01-12/01
	Phoenix-Mesa MSA, AZ	H	9.49 FQ	14.35 AW	20.44 TQ	AZBLS	10/01-12/01
	Arkansas	H	6.81 FQ	11.92 AW	17.44 TQ	ARBLS	10/01-12/01
	Little Rock-North Little Rock MSA, AR	H	7.34 FQ	15.44 AW	24.08 TQ	ARBLS	10/01-12/01
	California	H	7.98 FQ	11.11 AW	15.27 TQ	CABLS	10/01-12/01
	Riverside-San Bernardino PMSA, CA	H	8.58 FQ	12.36 AW	15.84 TQ	CABLS	10/01-12/01
	San Diego MSA, CA	H	7.76 FQ	9.49 AW	10.90 TQ	CABLS	10/01-12/01
	Delaware	H	6.63 FQ	10.07 AW	13.89 TQ	DEBLS	10/01-12/01
	Washington PMSA, DC-MD-VA-WV	H	6.92 FQ	10.19 AW	15.58 TQ	DCBLS	10/01-12/01
	Florida	H	8.04 FQ	11.68 AW	16.16 TQ	FLBLS	10/01-12/01
	Tampa-St. Petersburg-Clearwater MSA, FL	H	8.02 FQ	11.55 AW	15.79 TQ	FLBLS	10/01-12/01
	Georgia	H	7.21 FQ	11.06 AW	13.94 TQ	GABLS	10/01-12/01
	Atlanta MSA, GA	H	6.29 FQ	8.10 AW	10.15 TQ	GABLS	10/01-12/01
	Macon MSA, GA	H	6.82 FQ	10.24 AW	18.23 TQ	GABLS	10/01-12/01
	Idaho	H	7.15 FQ	10.60 AW	14.95 TQ	IDBLS	10/01-12/01
	Illinois	H	8.94 FQ	12.20 AW	14.29 TQ	ILBLS	10/01-12/01
	Indiana	H	8.91 FQ	13.55 AW	19.96 TQ	INBLS	10/01-12/01
	Elkhart-Goshen MSA, IN	H	9.45 FQ	15.80 AW	26.64 TQ	INBLS	10/01-12/01
	Indianapolis MSA, IN	H	10.92 FQ	15.43 AW	18.46 TQ	INBLS	10/01-12/01
	Iowa	H	8.50 FQ	12.18 AW	16.13 TQ	IABLS	10/01-12/01
	Kansas	H	7.17 FQ	10.64 AW	16.58 TQ	KSBLS	10/01-12/01
	Kentucky	H	7.56 FQ	10.82 AW	15.74 TQ	KYBLS	10/01-12/01
	Louisville MSA, KY-IN	H	8.70 FQ	12.81 AW	17.24 TQ	KYBLS	10/01-12/01
	Louisiana	H	6.26 FQ	11.61 AW	19.99 TQ	LABLS	10/01-12/01
	Baton Rouge MSA, LA	H	9.77 FQ	14.89 AW	22.85 TQ	LABLS	10/01-12/01
	Maine	H	7.91 FQ	11.39 AW	15.98 TQ	MEBLS	10/01-12/01
	Maryland	H	7.20 FQ	10.32 AW	15.48 TQ	MDBLS	10/01-12/01
	Baltimore PMSA, MD	H	7.35 FQ	10.61 AW	16.20 TQ	MDBLS	10/01-12/01
	Michigan	H	8.17 FQ	12.38 AW	16.23 TQ	MIBLS	10/01-12/01
	Detroit PMSA, MI	H	10.97 FQ	13.25 AW	16.29 TQ	MIBLS	10/01-12/01
	Flint PMSA, MI	H	5.74 FQ	8.29 AW	11.06 TQ	MIBLS	10/01-12/01
	Lansing-East Lansing MSA, MI	H	7.10 FQ	11.19 AW	16.54 TQ	MIBLS	10/01-12/01
	Minnesota	H	8.92 FQ	12.19 AW	17.25 TQ	MNBLS	10/01-12/01
	Mississippi	H	7.77 FQ	10.59 AW	14.20 TQ	MSBLS	10/01-12/01
	Missouri	H	7.90 FQ	11.76 AW	17.65 TQ	MOBLS	10/01-12/01
	St. Louis MSA, MO-IL	H	9.30 FQ	13.58 AW	17.44 TQ	MOBLS	10/01-12/01
	Montana	H	6.89 FQ	10.99 AW	13.96 TQ	MTBLS	10/01-12/01
	Omaha MSA, NE-IA	H	9.59 FQ	11.38 AW	13.86 TQ	NEBLS	10/01-12/01
	Nevada	H	8.73 FQ	11.91 AW	16.33 TQ	NVBLS	10/01-12/01
	Las Vegas MSA, NV-AZ	H	8.69 FQ	11.89 AW	16.22 TQ	NVBLS	10/01-12/01
	New Mexico	H	7.28 FQ	10.92 AW	17.18 TQ	NMBLS	10/01-12/01
	Albuquerque MSA, NM	H	6.36 FQ	10.31 AW	16.27 TQ	NMBLS	10/01-12/01
	Las Cruces MSA, NM	H	7.41 FQ	8.23 AW	9.14 TQ	NMBLS	10/01-12/01
	New York	H	7.41 FQ	11.67 AW	16.76 TQ	NYBLS	10/01-12/01
	Nassau-Suffolk PMSA, NY	H	10.99 FQ	16.01 AW	20.55 TQ	NYBLS	10/01-12/01
	North Carolina	H	5.60 FQ	9.17 AW	13.43 TQ	NCBLS	10/01-12/01
	Charlotte-Gastonia-Rock Hill MSA, NC-SC	H	8.89 FQ	14.71 AW	21.33 TQ	NCBLS	10/01-12/01

AAW Average annual wage; AE Average entry wage; AEX Average experienced wage; AO Average offered; AOH Average offered, high; AOL Average offered, low; APH Average pay, high range; APL Average pay, low range; ASH Average starting, high; ASL Average starting, low; AW Average wage paid; FQ First quartile wage; H Hourly; HI Highest wage paid; HR High end range; LR Low end range; M Monthly; MTC Median total compensation; MW Median wage paid; SQ Second quartile wage; S Special: hourly and annual; TQ Third quartile wage; W Weekly; Y Yearly

Occupation/Type/Industry	Location	Per	Low	Mid	High	Source	Date
Manufactured Building and Mobile Home Installer	Greensboro-Winston-Salem-High Point MSA, NC	H	5.38 FQ	7.24 AW	10.33 TQ	NCBLS	10/01-12/01
	Raleigh-Durham-Chapel Hill MSA, NC	H	7.83 FQ	12.75 AW	20.94 TQ	NCBLS	10/01-12/01
	North Dakota	H	6.95 FQ	10.41 AW	14.42 TQ	NDBLS	10/01-12/01
	Ohio	H	8.54 FQ	11.60 AW	15.93 TQ	OHBLS	10/01-12/01
	Oklahoma	H	9.25 FQ	12.99 AW	20.77 TQ	OKBLS	10/01-12/01
	Oregon	H	9.72 FQ	12.83 AW	17.28 TQ	ORBLS	10/01-12/01
	Portland-Vancouver PMSA, OR-WA	H	7.81 FQ	11.36 AW	16.33 TQ	ORBLS	10/01-12/01
	Pennsylvania	H	7.82 FQ	11.87 AW	16.82 TQ	PABLS	10/01-12/01
	Harrisburg-Lebanon-Carlisle MSA, PA	H	7.83 FQ	12.45 AW	17.18 TQ	PABLS	10/01-12/01
	Pittsburgh MSA, PA	H	6.91 FQ	10.59 AW	16.40 TQ	PABLS	10/01-12/01
	York MSA, PA	H	10.16 FQ	13.01 AW	16.38 TQ	PABLS	10/01-12/01
	South Carolina	H	8.11 FQ	12.62 AW	19.90 TQ	SCBLS	10/01-12/01
	Greenville-Spartanburg-Anderson MSA, SC	H	9.24 FQ	15.68 AW	20.88 TQ	SCBLS	10/01-12/01
	South Dakota	H	7.60 FQ	10.20 AW	13.25 TQ	SDBLS	10/01-12/01
	Tennessee	H	7.53 FQ	10.17 AW	13.00 TQ	TNBLS	10/01-12/01
	Clarksville-Hopkinsville MSA, TN-KY	H	9.51 FQ	12.55 AW	16.98 TQ	TNBLS	10/01-12/01
	Johnson City-Kingsport-Bristol MSA, TN-VA	H	7.10 FQ	9.32 AW	11.27 TQ	TNBLS	10/01-12/01
	Memphis MSA, TN-AR-MS	H	7.57 FQ	11.45 AW	16.76 TQ	TNBLS	10/01-12/01
	Texas	H	7.39 FQ	11.02 AW	15.93 TQ	TXBLS	10/01-12/01
	Austin-San Marcos MSA, TX	H	9.87 FQ	12.80 AW	14.47 TQ	TXBLS	10/01-12/01
	Dallas PMSA, TX	H	7.16 FQ	9.13 AW	12.36 TQ	TXBLS	10/01-12/01
	Fort Worth-Arlington PMSA, TX	H	7.57 FQ	9.73 AW	12.43 TQ	TXBLS	10/01-12/01
	Houston PMSA, TX	H	7.47 FQ	9.82 AW	12.45 TQ	TXBLS	10/01-12/01
	San Antonio MSA, TX	H	6.98 FQ	13.17 AW	19.32 TQ	TXBLS	10/01-12/01
	Virginia	H	8.05 FQ	10.79 AW	14.16 TQ	VABLS	10/01-12/01
	Washington	H	7.67 FQ	11.70 AW	16.88 TQ	WABLS	10/01-12/01
	West Virginia	H	6.11 FQ	9.74 AW	15.16 TQ	WVBLS	10/01-12/01
	Charleston MSA, WV	H	7.85 FQ	12.78 AW	16.66 TQ	WVBLS	10/01-12/01
	Huntington-Ashland MSA, WV-KY-OH	H	7.25 FQ	9.96 AW	14.04 TQ	WVBLS	10/01-12/01
	Wisconsin	H	7.53 FQ	13.17 AW	19.56 TQ	WIBLS	10/01-12/01
	Wyoming	H	7.75 FQ	10.85 AW	14.99 TQ	WYBLS	10/01-12/01
Marine Engineer and Naval Architect	Alabama	Y	46220 FQ	66820 AW	94320 TQ	ALBLS	10/01-12/01
	California	Y	40680 FQ	65200 AW	95040 TQ	CABLS	10/01-12/01
	Florida	Y	33100 FQ	55400 AW	83990 TQ	FLBLS	10/01-12/01
	Hawaii	Y	13380 FQ	59130 AW	97910 TQ	HIBLS	10/01-12/01
	Louisiana	Y	33490 FQ	58900 AW	85950 TQ	LABLS	10/01-12/01
	Maine	Y	41640 FQ	60480 AW	83550 TQ	MEBLS	10/01-12/01
	Maryland	Y	48420 FQ	76420 AW	104980 TQ	MDBLS	10/01-12/01
	Massachusetts	Y	52630 FQ	67700 AW	86980 TQ	MABLS	10/01-12/01
	Mississippi	Y	33350 FQ	51170 AW	72250 TQ	MSBLS	10/01-12/01
	New Jersey	Y	52550 FQ	75060 AW	100630 TQ	NJBLS	10/01-12/01
	New York	Y	51170 FQ	79160 AW	112900 TQ	NYBLS	10/01-12/01
	Pennsylvania	Y	47080 FQ	74180 AW	107790 TQ	PABLS	10/01-12/01
	South Carolina	Y	39480 FQ	60120 AW	84530 TQ	SCBLS	10/01-12/01
	Texas	Y	46150 FQ	72870 AW	103550 TQ	TXBLS	10/01-12/01
	Virginia	Y	38900 FQ	65970 AW	99840 TQ	VABLS	10/01-12/01
	Washington	Y	47100 FQ	63960 AW	86820 TQ	WABLS	10/01-12/01
Market Research Analyst	Alabama	Y	31760 FQ	60210 AW	94010 TQ	ALBLS	10/01-12/01
	Alaska	Y	30330 FQ	50670 AW	85090 TQ	AKBLS	10/01-12/01
	Arizona	Y	20940 FQ	50670 AW	95290 TQ	AZBLS	10/01-12/01
	Arkansas	Y	15080 FQ	45500 AW	82210 TQ	ARBLS	10/01-12/01
	California	Y	31600 FQ	65270 AW	113060 TQ	CABLS	10/01-12/01
	Colorado	Y	32250 FQ	60350 AW	99990 TQ	COBLS	10/01-12/01
	Connecticut	Y	34400 FQ	63750 AW	102690 TQ	CTBLS	10/01-12/01
	Delaware	Y	21100 FQ	50110 AW	96430 TQ	DEBLS	10/01-12/01
	District of Columbia	Y	38830 FQ	63160 AW	87130 TQ	DCBLS	10/01-12/01
	Florida	Y	28910 FQ	52290 AW	87270 TQ	FLBLS	10/01-12/01
	Georgia	Y	30080 FQ	50480 AW	80640 TQ	GABLS	10/01-12/01
	Hawaii	Y	35390 FQ	52630 AW	72100 TQ	HIBLS	10/01-12/01

AAW	Average annual wage	AOH	Average offered, high	ASH	Average starting, high	H	Hourly	M	Monthly	S	Special: hourly and annual
AE	Average entry wage	AOL	Average offered, low	ASL	Average starting, low	HI	Highest wage paid	MTC	Median total compensation	TQ	Third quartile wage
AEX	Average experienced wage	APH	Average pay, high range	AW	Average wage paid	HR	High end range	MW	Median wage paid	W	Weekly
AO	Average offered	APL	Average pay, low range	FQ	First quartile wage	LR	Low end range	SQ	Second quartile wage	Y	Yearly

Occupation/Type/Industry	Location	Per	Low	Mid	High	Source	Date
Market Research Analyst	Idaho	Y	18500 FQ	44500 AW	81930 TQ	IDBLS	10/01-12/01
	Illinois	Y	19850 FQ	45800 AW	79990 TQ	ILBLS	10/01-12/01
	Indiana	Y	29480 FQ	50320 AW	78940 TQ	INBLS	10/01-12/01
	Iowa	Y	24990 FQ	46550 AW	70480 TQ	IABLS	10/01-12/01
	Kansas	Y	25890 FQ	49510 AW	82700 TQ	KSBLS	10/01-12/01
	Kentucky	Y	23280 FQ	49130 AW	84450 TQ	KYBLS	10/01-12/01
	Louisiana	Y	23770 FQ	47770 AW	84880 TQ	LABLS	10/01-12/01
	Maine	Y	22050 FQ	41960 AW	64340 TQ	MEBLS	10/01-12/01
	Maryland	Y	25590 FQ	52530 AW	89610 TQ	MDBLS	10/01-12/01
	Massachusetts	Y	32590 FQ	62290 AW	110770 TQ	MABLS	10/01-12/01
	Michigan	Y	31750 FQ	61230 AW	101500 TQ	MIBLS	10/01-12/01
	Minnesota	Y	35330 FQ	65160 AW	104970 TQ	MNBLS	10/01-12/01
	Mississippi	Y	25670 FQ	54130 AW	86900 TQ	MSBLS	10/01-12/01
	Missouri	Y	13520 FQ	45550 AW	78970 TQ	MOBLS	10/01-12/01
	Montana	Y	26310 FQ	50190 AW	76410 TQ	MTBLS	10/01-12/01
	Nebraska	Y	24000 FQ	45430 AW	83440 TQ	NEBLS	10/01-12/01
	Nevada	Y	28540 FQ	50600 AW	81880 TQ	NVBLS	10/01-12/01
	New Hampshire	Y	27910 FQ	58110 AW	104390 TQ	NHBLS	10/01-12/01
	New Jersey	Y	28930 FQ	58890 AW	95410 TQ	NJBLS	10/01-12/01
	New Mexico	Y	30630 FQ	51750 AW	87250 TQ	NMBLS	10/01-12/01
	New York	Y	27700 FQ	60750 AW	100350 TQ	NYBLS	10/01-12/01
	North Carolina	Y	28530 FQ	60780 AW	105510 TQ	NCBLS	10/01-12/01
	North Dakota	Y	28520 FQ	53990 AW	82920 TQ	NDBLS	10/01-12/01
	Ohio	Y	30300 FQ	57590 AW	93810 TQ	OHBLS	10/01-12/01
	Oklahoma	Y	21170 FQ	43130 AW	70790 TQ	OKBLS	10/01-12/01
	Oregon	Y	32190 FQ	68030 AW	122940 TQ	ORBLS	10/01-12/01
	Pennsylvania	Y	25010 FQ	46620 AW	79710 TQ	PABLS	10/01-12/01
	Rhode Island	Y	34630 FQ	58580 AW	86530 TQ	RIBLS	10/01-12/01
	South Carolina	Y	23480 FQ	50900 AW	87230 TQ	SCBLS	10/01-12/01
	South Dakota	Y	24450 FQ	38290 AW	60260 TQ	SDBLS	10/01-12/01
	Tennessee	Y	32970 FQ	60070 AW	88600 TQ	TNBLS	10/01-12/01
	Texas	Y	31480 FQ	61240 AW	104040 TQ	TXBLS	10/01-12/01
	Utah	Y	24610 FQ	48660 AW	84380 TQ	UTBLS	10/01-12/01
	Vermont	Y	33090 FQ	54890 AW	91540 TQ	VTBLS	10/01-12/01
	Virginia	Y	31450 FQ	57180 AW	89710 TQ	VABLS	10/01-12/01
	Washington	Y	39020 FQ	75540 AW	114330 TQ	WABLS	10/01-12/01
	West Virginia	Y	21050 FQ	49510 AW	87280 TQ	WVBLS	10/01-12/01
	Wisconsin	Y	28830 FQ	49420 AW	80820 TQ	WIBLS	10/01-12/01
	Wyoming	Y	21550 FQ	40800 AW	68400 TQ	WYBLS	10/01-12/01
	Puerto Rico	Y	18960 FQ	37070 AW	64340 TQ	PRBLS	10/01-12/01
Marketing Director							
Web Design	United States	Y		57358 AW		DFMAR	1/01-1/02
Marketing Manager	Alabama	Y	31820 FQ	64740 AW	107130 TQ	ALBLS	10/01-12/01
	Birmingham MSA, AL	Y	35140 FQ	66380 AW	103640 TQ	ALBLS	10/01-12/01
	Huntsville MSA, AL	Y	30060 FQ	70590 AW	130720 TQ	ALBLS	10/01-12/01
	Mobile MSA, AL	Y	27490 FQ	48500 AW	79760 TQ	ALBLS	10/01-12/01
	Montgomery MSA, AL	Y	33770 FQ	61620 AW	103030 TQ	ALBLS	10/01-12/01
	Alaska	Y	41210 FQ	69380 AW	118090 TQ	AKBLS	10/01-12/01
	Anchorage MSA, AK	Y	40700 FQ	69270 AW	120520 TQ	AKBLS	10/01-12/01
	Arizona	Y	33150 FQ	67590 AW	116320 TQ	AZBLS	10/01-12/01
	Phoenix-Mesa MSA, AZ	Y	34370 FQ	68880 AW	117760 TQ	AZBLS	10/01-12/01
	Tucson MSA, AZ	Y	28750 FQ	58260 AW	105760 TQ	AZBLS	10/01-12/01
	Arkansas	Y	31200 FQ	62970 AW	106060 TQ	ARBLS	10/01-12/01
	Fayetteville-Springdale-Rogers MSA, AR	Y	28580 FQ	55600 AW	96500 TQ	ARBLS	10/01-12/01
	Fort Smith MSA, AR-OK	Y	31580 FQ	58330 AW	95390 TQ	ARBLS	10/01-12/01
	Little Rock-North Little Rock MSA, AR	Y	32670 FQ	69030 AW	114680 TQ	ARBLS	10/01-12/01
	California	Y	44820 FQ	88340 AW		CABLS	10/01-12/01
	Bakersfield MSA, CA	Y	35510 FQ	74550 AW	118150 TQ	CABLS	10/01-12/01
	Chico-Paradise MSA, CA	Y	26130 FQ	54590 AW	95310 TQ	CABLS	10/01-12/01
	Fresno MSA, CA	Y	35330 FQ	66680 AW	108100 TQ	CABLS	10/01-12/01
	Los Angeles-Long Beach PMSA, CA	Y	44750 FQ	84320 AW		CABLS	10/01-12/01
	Modesto MSA, CA	Y	41990 FQ	82710 AW	140810 TQ	CABLS	10/01-12/01
	Oakland PMSA, CA	Y	54680 FQ	93600 AW		CABLS	10/01-12/01
	Orange County PMSA, CA	Y	43210 FQ	86150 AW		CABLS	10/01-12/01
	Redding MSA, CA	Y	31730 FQ	50770 AW	104100 TQ	CABLS	10/01-12/01
	Riverside-San Bernardino PMSA, CA	Y	34100 FQ	70730 AW	114710 TQ	CABLS	10/01-12/01
	Sacramento PMSA, CA	Y	40820 FQ	77270 AW	121440 TQ	CABLS	10/01-12/01

AAW	Average annual wage	**AOH**	Average offered, high	**ASH**	Average starting, high	**H**	Hourly	**M**	Monthly	**S**	Special: hourly and annual
AE	Average entry wage	**AOL**	Average offered, low	**ASL**	Average starting, low	**HI**	Highest wage paid	**MTC**	Median total compensation	**TQ**	Third quartile wage
AEX	Average experienced wage	**APH**	Average pay, high range	**AW**	Average wage paid	**HR**	High end range	**MW**	Median wage paid	**W**	Weekly
AO	Average offered	**APL**	Average pay, low range	**FQ**	First quartile wage	**LR**	Low end range	**SQ**	Second quartile wage	**Y**	Yearly

Occupation/Type/Industry	Location	Per	Low	Mid	High	Source	Date
Marketing Manager	Salinas MSA, CA	Y	51990 FQ	93680 AW		CABLS	10/01-12/01
	San Diego MSA, CA	Y	41470 FQ	83590 AW		CABLS	10/01-12/01
	San Francisco PMSA, CA	Y	47160 FQ	90750 AW		CABLS	10/01-12/01
	San Jose PMSA, CA	Y	66540 FQ	109950 AW		CABLS	10/01-12/01
	San Luis Obispo-Atascadero-Paso Robles MSA, CA	Y	44080 FQ	75130 AW	117990 TQ	CABLS	10/01-12/01
	Santa Barbara-Santa Maria-Lompoc MSA, CA	Y	43960 FQ	82980 AW	144170 TQ	CABLS	10/01-12/01
	Santa Cruz-Watsonville PMSA, CA	Y	48890 FQ	83710 AW	133260 TQ	CABLS	10/01-12/01
	Santa Rosa PMSA, CA	Y	41450 FQ	89670 AW		CABLS	10/01-12/01
	Stockton-Lodi MSA, CA	Y	35610 FQ	66580 AW	111760 TQ	CABLS	10/01-12/01
	Vallejo-Fairfield-Napa PMSA, CA	Y	44810 FQ	81970 AW	141220 TQ	CABLS	10/01-12/01
	Ventura PMSA, CA	Y	47160 FQ	83990 AW	119380 TQ	CABLS	10/01-12/01
	Visalia-Tulare-Porterville MSA, CA	Y	31220 FQ	63130 AW	105290 TQ	CABLS	10/01-12/01
	Colorado	Y	41050 FQ	77710 AW	123090 TQ	COBLS	10/01-12/01
	Boulder-Longmont PMSA, CO	Y	46450 FQ	86660 AW	141080 TQ	COBLS	10/01-12/01
	Colorado Springs MSA, CO	Y	36410 FQ	74130 AW	125580 TQ	COBLS	10/01-12/01
	Denver PMSA, CO	Y	44570 FQ	78910 AW	122130 TQ	COBLS	10/01-12/01
	Fort Collins-Loveland MSA, CO	Y	43980 FQ	78080 AW	115410 TQ	COBLS	10/01-12/01
	Greeley PMSA, CO	Y	32950 FQ	63320 AW	105920 TQ	COBLS	10/01-12/01
	Connecticut	Y	50800 FQ	92880 AW		CTBLS	10/01-12/01
	Bridgeport PMSA, CT	Y	49040 FQ	83650 AW	134810 TQ	CTBLS	10/01-12/01
	Danbury PMSA, CT	Y	47600 FQ	99290 AW		CTBLS	10/01-12/01
	Hartford MSA, CT	Y	49270 FQ	87800 AW	143090 TQ	CTBLS	10/01-12/01
	New Haven-Meriden PMSA, CT	Y	40350 FQ	82310 AW	125620 TQ	CTBLS	10/01-12/01
	New London-Norwich MSA, CT-RI	Y	51450 FQ	97340 AW		CTBLS	10/01-12/01
	Stamford-Norwalk PMSA, CT	Y	59960 FQ	103590 AW		CTBLS	10/01-12/01
	Waterbury PMSA, CT	Y	36430 FQ	89160 AW	136470 TQ	CTBLS	10/01-12/01
	Delaware	Y	40190 FQ	79870 AW	140370 TQ	DEBLS	10/01-12/01
	Wilmington-Newark PMSA, DE-MD	Y	41310 FQ	81170 AW	141470 TQ	DEBLS	10/01-12/01
	District of Columbia	Y	34920 FQ	69230 AW	111430 TQ	DCBLS	10/01-12/01
	Washington PMSA, DC-MD-VA-WV	Y	38170 FQ	79900 AW	133200 TQ	DCBLS	10/01-12/01
	Florida	Y	31690 FQ	69280 AW	129390 TQ	FLBLS	10/01-12/01
	Daytona Beach MSA, FL	Y	30900 FQ	63770 AW	113220 TQ	FLBLS	10/01-12/01
	Fort Lauderdale PMSA, FL	Y	34070 FQ	68980 AW	122910 TQ	FLBLS	10/01-12/01
	Fort Myers-Cape Coral MSA, FL	Y	35990 FQ	60630 AW	95850 TQ	FLBLS	10/01-12/01
	Fort Pierce-Port St. Lucie MSA, FL	Y	33480 FQ	65640 AW	127510 TQ	FLBLS	10/01-12/01
	Fort Walton Beach MSA, FL	Y	44930 FQ	71100 AW	108830 TQ	FLBLS	10/01-12/01
	Gainesville MSA, FL	Y	33420 FQ	70700 AW	109850 TQ	FLBLS	10/01-12/01
	Jacksonville MSA, FL	Y	38820 FQ	73140 AW	135940 TQ	FLBLS	10/01-12/01
	Lakeland-Winter Haven MSA, FL	Y	23210 FQ	38550 AW	70960 TQ	FLBLS	10/01-12/01
	Melbourne-Titusville-Palm Bay MSA, FL	Y	36310 FQ	77180 AW	122060 TQ	FLBLS	10/01-12/01
	Miami PMSA, FL	Y	35890 FQ	76410 AW	138400 TQ	FLBLS	10/01-12/01
	Naples MSA, FL	Y	25320 FQ	53630 AW	98430 TQ	FLBLS	10/01-12/01
	Ocala MSA, FL	Y	30580 FQ	57700 AW	96520 TQ	FLBLS	10/01-12/01
	Orlando MSA, FL	Y	39420 FQ	78210 AW	139070 TQ	FLBLS	10/01-12/01
	Pensacola MSA, FL	Y	30770 FQ	53560 AW	76170 TQ	FLBLS	10/01-12/01
	Sarasota-Bradenton MSA, FL	Y	27540 FQ	63180 AW	112090 TQ	FLBLS	10/01-12/01
	Tallahassee MSA, FL	Y	34180 FQ	73180 AW		FLBLS	10/01-12/01
	Tampa-St. Petersburg-Clearwater MSA, FL	Y	35790 FQ	69970 AW	138150 TQ	FLBLS	10/01-12/01
	West Palm Beach-Boca Raton MSA, FL	Y	36930 FQ	72310 AW	142670 TQ	FLBLS	10/01-12/01
	Georgia	Y	41390 FQ	79810 AW	133040 TQ	GABLS	10/01-12/01
	Atlanta MSA, GA	Y	43020 FQ	82130 AW	134660 TQ	GABLS	10/01-12/01
	Augusta-Aiken MSA, GA-SC	Y	35630 FQ	67160 AW	126580 TQ	GABLS	10/01-12/01
	Columbus MSA, GA-AL	Y	37590 FQ	72450 AW	113490 TQ	GABLS	10/01-12/01
	Macon MSA, GA	Y	35690 FQ	62030 AW	94860 TQ	GABLS	10/01-12/01
	Savannah MSA, GA	Y	37960 FQ	67910 AW	109740 TQ	GABLS	10/01-12/01
	Hawaii	Y	34520 FQ	71510 AW	115780 TQ	HIBLS	10/01-12/01

AAW	Average annual wage	AOH	Average offered, high	ASH	Average starting, high	H	Hourly	M	Monthly	S	Special: hourly and annual
AE	Average entry wage	AOL	Average offered, low	ASL	Average starting, low	HI	Highest wage paid	MTC	Median total compensation	TQ	Third quartile wage
AEX	Average experienced wage	APH	Average pay, high range	AW	Average wage paid	HR	High end range	MW	Median wage paid	W	Weekly
AO	Average offered	APL	Average pay, low range	FQ	First quartile wage	LR	Low end range	SQ	Second quartile wage	Y	Yearly

Occupation/Type/Industry	Location	Per	Low	Mid	High	Source	Date
Marketing Manager	Honolulu MSA, HI	Y	33760 FQ	70790 AW	116530 TQ	HIBLS	10/01-12/01
	Idaho	Y	36410 FQ	64180 AW	113550 TQ	IDBLS	10/01-12/01
	Boise City MSA, ID	Y	39580 FQ	66170 AW	113600 TQ	IDBLS	10/01-12/01
	Illinois	Y	33270 FQ	73140 AW	129380 TQ	ILBLS	10/01-12/01
	Champaign-Urbana MSA, IL	Y	23800 FQ	56270 AW	100210 TQ	ILBLS	10/01-12/01
	Chicago PMSA, IL	Y	34750 FQ	75230 AW	132480 TQ	ILBLS	10/01-12/01
	Peoria-Pekin MSA, IL	Y	30410 FQ	63440 AW	113160 TQ	ILBLS	10/01-12/01
	Rockford MSA, IL	Y	28670 FQ	60160 AW	93310 TQ	ILBLS	10/01-12/01
	Springfield MSA, IL	Y	17010 FQ	51290 AW	88290 TQ	ILBLS	10/01-12/01
	Indiana	Y	33160 FQ	66580 AW	114630 TQ	INBLS	10/01-12/01
	Elkhart-Goshen MSA, IN	Y	36810 FQ	69970 AW	113710 TQ	INBLS	10/01-12/01
	Evansville-Henderson MSA, IN-KY	Y	30970 FQ	59570 AW	91590 TQ	INBLS	10/01-12/01
	Fort Wayne MSA, IN	Y	32890 FQ	62440 AW	101350 TQ	INBLS	10/01-12/01
	Gary PMSA, IN	Y	32880 FQ	63130 AW	112840 TQ	INBLS	10/01-12/01
	Indianapolis MSA, IN	Y	36900 FQ	69440 AW	119610 TQ	INBLS	10/01-12/01
	Lafayette MSA, IN	Y	49830 FQ	83180 AW	140580 TQ	INBLS	10/01-12/01
	South Bend MSA, IN	Y	31570 FQ	67810 AW	111030 TQ	INBLS	10/01-12/01
	Iowa	Y	32200 FQ	63060 AW	105930 TQ	IABLS	10/01-12/01
	Cedar Rapids MSA, IA	Y	34180 FQ	70160 AW	113770 TQ	IABLS	10/01-12/01
	Davenport-Moline-Rock Island MSA, IA-IL	Y	28380 FQ	54320 AW	93100 TQ	IABLS	10/01-12/01
	Des Moines MSA, IA	Y	35550 FQ	66970 AW	112160 TQ	IABLS	10/01-12/01
	Kansas	Y	33450 FQ	69530 AW	115620 TQ	KSBLS	10/01-12/01
	Topeka MSA, KS	Y	31620 FQ	63570 AW	111310 TQ	KSBLS	10/01-12/01
	Wichita MSA, KS	Y	39280 FQ	68240 AW	109380 TQ	KSBLS	10/01-12/01
	Kentucky	Y	34450 FQ	66000 AW	108700 TQ	KYBLS	10/01-12/01
	Lexington MSA, KY	Y	37930 FQ	68800 AW	110470 TQ	KYBLS	10/01-12/01
	Louisville MSA, KY-IN	Y	37050 FQ	69750 AW	120090 TQ	KYBLS	10/01-12/01
	Louisiana	Y	28770 FQ	60110 AW	97780 TQ	LABLS	10/01-12/01
	Baton Rouge MSA, LA	Y	29160 FQ	60640 AW	104460 TQ	LABLS	10/01-12/01
	Houma MSA, LA	Y	14490 FQ	55920 AW	106540 TQ	LABLS	10/01-12/01
	Lafayette MSA, LA	Y	25400 FQ	56670 AW	101930 TQ	LABLS	10/01-12/01
	Lake Charles MSA, LA	Y	28690 FQ	58240 AW	106210 TQ	LABLS	10/01-12/01
	New Orleans MSA, LA	Y	29470 FQ	60870 AW	91440 TQ	LABLS	10/01-12/01
	Shreveport-Bossier City MSA, LA	Y	28630 FQ	52860 AW	88880 TQ	LABLS	10/01-12/01
	Maine	Y	32810 FQ	64570 AW	107550 TQ	MEBLS	10/01-12/01
	Portland MSA, ME	Y	35440 FQ	72610 AW	132630 TQ	MEBLS	10/01-12/01
	Maryland	Y	36590 FQ	71280 AW	118150 TQ	MDBLS	10/01-12/01
	Baltimore PMSA, MD	Y	37600 FQ	70810 AW	116020 TQ	MDBLS	10/01-12/01
	Massachusetts	Y	45060 FQ	87510 AW	143710 TQ	MABLS	10/01-12/01
	Boston PMSA, MA-NH	Y	47540 FQ	90540 AW		MABLS	10/01-12/01
	Brockton PMSA, MA	Y	49130 FQ	90380 AW	143800 TQ	MABLS	10/01-12/01
	Lawrence PMSA, MA-NH	Y	41350 FQ	82330 AW	135270 TQ	MABLS	10/01-12/01
	Lowell PMSA, MA-NH	Y	51800 FQ	83060 AW	125400 TQ	MABLS	10/01-12/01
	New Bedford PMSA, MA	Y	37120 FQ	69950 AW	112210 TQ	MABLS	10/01-12/01
	Springfield MSA, MA	Y	26410 FQ	62050 AW	110540 TQ	MABLS	10/01-12/01
	Worcester PMSA, MA-CT	Y	41960 FQ	78150 AW	129140 TQ	MABLS	10/01-12/01
	Michigan	Y	41120 FQ	83770 AW		MIBLS	10/01-12/01
	Ann Arbor PMSA, MI	Y	40760 FQ	80120 AW	130510 TQ	MIBLS	10/01-12/01
	Detroit PMSA, MI	Y	43980 FQ	90790 AW		MIBLS	10/01-12/01
	Flint PMSA, MI	Y	46380 FQ	76110 AW	103580 TQ	MIBLS	10/01-12/01
	Grand Rapids-Muskegon-Holland MSA, MI	Y	43650 FQ	78060 AW	120930 TQ	MIBLS	10/01-12/01
	Kalamazoo-Battle Creek MSA, MI	Y	44220 FQ	87160 AW		MIBLS	10/01-12/01
	Lansing-East Lansing MSA, MI	Y	32990 FQ	64280 AW	119330 TQ	MIBLS	10/01-12/01
	Saginaw-Bay City-Midland MSA, MI	Y	48290 FQ	79140 AW		MIBLS	10/01-12/01
	Minnesota	Y	54090 FQ	90240 AW	142510 TQ	MNBLS	10/01-12/01
	Duluth-Superior MSA, MN-WI	Y	27310 FQ	71170 AW	127070 TQ	MNBLS	10/01-12/01
	Minneapolis-St. Paul MSA, MN-WI	Y	58320 FQ	91990 AW	144130 TQ	MNBLS	10/01-12/01
	St. Cloud MSA, MN	Y	50590 FQ	83990 AW		MNBLS	10/01-12/01
	Mississippi	Y	30990 FQ	57860 AW	91820 TQ	MSBLS	10/01-12/01
	Biloxi-Gulfport-Pascagoula MSA, MS	Y	35580 FQ	63120 AW	94330 TQ	MSBLS	10/01-12/01
	Jackson MSA, MS	Y	29500 FQ	57220 AW	89760 TQ	MSBLS	10/01-12/01
	Missouri	Y	34760 FQ	70710 AW	121520 TQ	MOBLS	10/01-12/01
	Kansas City MSA, MO-KS	Y	34370 FQ	69560 AW	116770 TQ	MOBLS	10/01-12/01
	St. Louis MSA, MO-IL	Y	34450 FQ	73710 AW	129420 TQ	MOBLS	10/01-12/01

AAW Average annual wage **AOH** Average offered, high **ASH** Average starting, high **H** Hourly **M** Monthly **S** Special: hourly and annual
AE Average entry wage **AOL** Average offered, low **ASL** Average starting, low **HI** Highest wage paid **MTC** Median total compensation **TQ** Third quartile wage
AEX Average experienced wage **APH** Average pay, high range **AW** Average wage paid **HR** High end range **MW** Median wage paid **W** Weekly
AO Average offered **APL** Average pay, low range **FQ** First quartile wage **LR** Low end range **SQ** Second quartile wage **Y** Yearly

Occupation/Type/Industry	Location	Per	Low	Mid	High	Source	Date
Marketing Manager	Springfield MSA, MO	Y	26380 FQ	58860 AW	104850 TQ	MOBLS	10/01-12/01
	Montana	Y	26010 FQ	52900 AW	85590 TQ	MTBLS	10/01-12/01
	Billings MSA, MT	Y	25550 FQ	53560 AW	85280 TQ	MTBLS	10/01-12/01
	Nebraska	Y	32110 FQ	68940 AW	115950 TQ	NEBLS	10/01-12/01
	Lincoln MSA, NE	Y	29940 FQ	61790 AW	107080 TQ	NEBLS	10/01-12/01
	Omaha MSA, NE-IA	Y	35460 FQ	72600 AW	122230 TQ	NEBLS	10/01-12/01
	Nevada	Y	36920 FQ	72160 AW	141370 TQ	NVBLS	10/01-12/01
	Las Vegas MSA, NV-AZ	Y	37320 FQ	73910 AW		NVBLS	10/01-12/01
	Reno MSA, NV	Y	34560 FQ	68150 AW	112380 TQ	NVBLS	10/01-12/01
	New Hampshire	Y	39660 FQ	73250 AW	117510 TQ	NHBLS	10/01-12/01
	Manchester PMSA, NH	Y	36110 FQ	70130 AW	114970 TQ	NHBLS	10/01-12/01
	Nashua PMSA, NH	Y	48750 FQ	80100 AW	126440 TQ	NHBLS	10/01-12/01
	Portsmouth-Rochester PMSA, NH-ME	Y	43960 FQ	73640 AW	112070 TQ	NHBLS	10/01-12/01
	New Jersey	Y	54830 FQ	95530 AW		NJBLS	10/01-12/01
	Atlantic-Cape May PMSA, NJ	Y	35970 FQ	72420 AW	126410 TQ	NJBLS	10/01-12/01
	Bergen-Passaic PMSA, NJ	Y	45690 FQ	91090 AW		NJBLS	10/01-12/01
	Jersey City PMSA, NJ	Y	53900 FQ	98260 AW		NJBLS	10/01-12/01
	Middlesex-Somerset-Hunterdon PMSA, NJ	Y	61080 FQ	98060 AW		NJBLS	10/01-12/01
	Monmouth-Ocean PMSA, NJ	Y	52200 FQ	92640 AW		NJBLS	10/01-12/01
	Newark PMSA, NJ	Y	59530 FQ	99070 AW		NJBLS	10/01-12/01
	Trenton PMSA, NJ	Y	53550 FQ	90140 AW		NJBLS	10/01-12/01
	New Mexico	Y	29430 FQ	60340 AW	105380 TQ	NMBLS	10/01-12/01
	Albuquerque MSA, NM	Y	26810 FQ	61200 AW	101850 TQ	NMBLS	10/01-12/01
	Las Cruces MSA, NM	Y	33180 FQ	57400 AW	105680 TQ	NMBLS	10/01-12/01
	New York	Y	49770 FQ	96410 AW		NYBLS	10/01-12/01
	Albany-Schenectady-Troy MSA, NY	Y	40610 FQ	84410 AW		NYBLS	10/01-12/01
	Binghamton MSA, NY	Y	39530 FQ	73510 AW	136810 TQ	NYBLS	10/01-12/01
	Buffalo-Niagara Falls MSA, NY	Y	47870 FQ	76150 AW	127140 TQ	NYBLS	10/01-12/01
	Dutchess County PMSA, NY	Y	40440 FQ	80820 AW	140180 TQ	NYBLS	10/01-12/01
	Nassau-Suffolk PMSA, NY	Y	54070 FQ	95100 AW		NYBLS	10/01-12/01
	New York PMSA, NY	Y	54720 FQ	101520 AW		NYBLS	10/01-12/01
	Newburgh PMSA, NY-PA	Y	34820 FQ	72080 AW	132730 TQ	NYBLS	10/01-12/01
	Rochester MSA, NY	Y	47970 FQ	89850 AW	142340 TQ	NYBLS	10/01-12/01
	Syracuse MSA, NY	Y	47830 FQ	89510 AW	144970 TQ	NYBLS	10/01-12/01
	Utica-Rome MSA, NY	Y	36160 FQ	66470 AW	110270 TQ	NYBLS	10/01-12/01
	North Carolina	Y	40280 FQ	81780 AW	139580 TQ	NCBLS	10/01-12/01
	Asheville MSA, NC	Y	35290 FQ	63650 AW	103020 TQ	NCBLS	10/01-12/01
	Charlotte-Gastonia-Rock Hill MSA, NC-SC	Y	40100 FQ	81180 AW		NCBLS	10/01-12/01
	Fayetteville MSA, NC	Y	30420 FQ	54300 AW	83250 TQ	NCBLS	10/01-12/01
	Greensboro-Winston-Salem-High Point MSA, NC	Y	42270 FQ	80390 AW	139720 TQ	NCBLS	10/01-12/01
	Hickory-Morganton-Lenoir MSA, NC	Y	36320 FQ	77900 AW		NCBLS	10/01-12/01
	Raleigh-Durham-Chapel Hill MSA, NC	Y	48330 FQ	91230 AW	142520 TQ	NCBLS	10/01-12/01
	Wilmington MSA, NC	Y	40710 FQ	73810 AW	115450 TQ	NCBLS	10/01-12/01
	North Dakota	Y	31090 FQ	57060 AW	85900 TQ	NDBLS	10/01-12/01
	Fargo-Moorhead MSA, ND-MN	Y	35300 FQ	60200 AW	86750 TQ	NDBLS	10/01-12/01
	Ohio	Y	34570 FQ	72570 AW	121400 TQ	OHBLS	10/01-12/01
	Akron PMSA, OH	Y	38300 FQ	76570 AW	118400 TQ	OHBLS	10/01-12/01
	Canton-Massillon MSA, OH	Y	32380 FQ	66920 AW	125820 TQ	OHBLS	10/01-12/01
	Cincinnati PMSA, OH-KY-IN	Y	34640 FQ	70700 AW	131170 TQ	OHBLS	10/01-12/01
	Cleveland-Lorain-Elyria PMSA, OH	Y	37020 FQ	74500 AW	123330 TQ	OHBLS	10/01-12/01
	Columbus MSA, OH	Y	40190 FQ	78490 AW	132830 TQ	OHBLS	10/01-12/01
	Dayton-Springfield MSA, OH	Y	30990 FQ	69220 AW	113670 TQ	OHBLS	10/01-12/01
	Hamilton-Middletown PMSA, OH	Y	37030 FQ	75340 AW	122550 TQ	OHBLS	10/01-12/01
	Mansfield MSA, OH	Y	30490 FQ	61340 AW	96160 TQ	OHBLS	10/01-12/01
	Toledo MSA, OH	Y	30320 FQ	67350 AW	110820 TQ	OHBLS	10/01-12/01
	Youngstown-Warren MSA, OH	Y	28510 FQ	64960 AW	118940 TQ	OHBLS	10/01-12/01
	Oklahoma	Y	28400 FQ	61020 AW	106570 TQ	OKBLS	10/01-12/01
	Oklahoma City MSA, OK	Y	26550 FQ	55840 AW	91640 TQ	OKBLS	10/01-12/01
	Tulsa MSA, OK	Y	33190 FQ	69700 AW	114880 TQ	OKBLS	10/01-12/01
	Oregon	Y	40910 FQ	79090 AW	130790 TQ	ORBLS	10/01-12/01
	Eugene-Springfield MSA, OR	Y	33340 FQ	59880 AW	89260 TQ	ORBLS	10/01-12/01

AAW	Average annual wage	**AOH**	Average offered, high	**ASH**	Average starting, high	**H**	Hourly	**M**	Monthly	**S**	Special: hourly and annual
AE	Average entry wage	**AOL**	Average offered, low	**ASL**	Average starting, low	**HI**	Highest wage paid	**MTC**	Median total compensation	**TQ**	Third quartile wage
AEX	Average experienced wage	**APH**	Average pay, high range	**AW**	Average wage paid	**HR**	High end range	**MW**	Median wage paid	**W**	Weekly
AO	Average offered	**APL**	Average pay, low range	**FQ**	First quartile wage	**LR**	Low end range	**SQ**	Second quartile wage	**Y**	Yearly

Occupation/Type/Industry	Location	Per	Low	Mid	High	Source	Date
Marketing Manager	Medford-Ashland MSA, OR	Y	36220 FQ	60280 AW	89510 TQ	ORBLS	10/01-12/01
	Portland-Vancouver PMSA, OR-WA	Y	42840 FQ	82310 AW	135240 TQ	ORBLS	10/01-12/01
	Salem PMSA, OR	Y	31580 FQ	69760 AW	115590 TQ	ORBLS	10/01-12/01
	Pennsylvania	Y	37090 FQ	70640 AW	113010 TQ	PABLS	10/01-12/01
	Allentown-Bethlehem-Easton MSA, PA	Y	37320 FQ	66380 AW	106760 TQ	PABLS	10/01-12/01
	Erie MSA, PA	Y	27540 FQ	56710 AW	90750 TQ	PABLS	10/01-12/01
	Harrisburg-Lebanon-Carlisle MSA, PA	Y	32660 FQ	60820 AW	91450 TQ	PABLS	10/01-12/01
	Johnstown MSA, PA	Y	24910 FQ	61870 AW	131740 TQ	PABLS	10/01-12/01
	Lancaster MSA, PA	Y	32970 FQ	71090 AW	114250 TQ	PABLS	10/01-12/01
	Philadelphia PMSA, PA-NJ	Y	41370 FQ	78160 AW	132800 TQ	PABLS	10/01-12/01
	Pittsburgh MSA, PA	Y	36290 FQ	68150 AW	102420 TQ	PABLS	10/01-12/01
	Reading MSA, PA	Y	35020 FQ	65890 AW	109910 TQ	PABLS	10/01-12/01
	Scranton-Wilkes-Barre-Hazleton MSA, PA	Y	32420 FQ	60370 AW	93030 TQ	PABLS	10/01-12/01
	York MSA, PA	Y	36300 FQ	68580 AW	116460 TQ	PABLS	10/01-12/01
	Rhode Island	Y	39320 FQ	72940 AW	123880 TQ	RIBLS	10/01-12/01
	Providence-Fall River-Warwick MSA, RI-MA	Y	39620 FQ	71410 AW	117360 TQ	RIBLS	10/01-12/01
	South Carolina	Y	29220 FQ	62960 AW	107090 TQ	SCBLS	10/01-12/01
	Charleston-North Charleston MSA, SC	Y	26900 FQ	53170 AW	82780 TQ	SCBLS	10/01-12/01
	Columbia MSA, SC	Y	34630 FQ	67860 AW	114410 TQ	SCBLS	10/01-12/01
	Greenville-Spartanburg-Anderson MSA, SC	Y	30910 FQ	66540 AW	114080 TQ	SCBLS	10/01-12/01
	Myrtle Beach MSA, SC	Y	13840 FQ	44990 AW	73920 TQ	SCBLS	10/01-12/01
	South Dakota	Y	45230 FQ	73830 AW	112220 TQ	SDBLS	10/01-12/01
	Sioux Falls MSA, SD	Y	44140 FQ	74200 AW	109630 TQ	SDBLS	10/01-12/01
	Tennessee	Y	33390 FQ	65600 AW	114290 TQ	TNBLS	10/01-12/01
	Chattanooga MSA, TN-GA	Y	31000 FQ	57980 AW	98520 TQ	TNBLS	10/01-12/01
	Clarksville-Hopkinsville MSA, TN-KY	Y	28720 FQ	64330 AW	99870 TQ	TNBLS	10/01-12/01
	Johnson City-Kingsport-Bristol MSA, TN-VA	Y	25850 FQ	63790 AW	115620 TQ	TNBLS	10/01-12/01
	Knoxville MSA, TN	Y	32150 FQ	62970 AW	109150 TQ	TNBLS	10/01-12/01
	Memphis MSA, TN-AR-MS	Y	36180 FQ	72850 AW	135860 TQ	TNBLS	10/01-12/01
	Nashville MSA, TN	Y	36350 FQ	62510 AW	105090 TQ	TNBLS	10/01-12/01
	Texas	Y	35900 FQ	73580 AW	121900 TQ	TXBLS	10/01-12/01
	Amarillo MSA, TX	Y	30730 FQ	57040 AW	101780 TQ	TXBLS	10/01-12/01
	Austin-San Marcos MSA, TX	Y	30900 FQ	71060 AW	130230 TQ	TXBLS	10/01-12/01
	Beaumont-Port Arthur MSA, TX	Y	33340 FQ	67930 AW	114310 TQ	TXBLS	10/01-12/01
	Brazoria PMSA, TX	Y	28450 FQ	66770 AW	117170 TQ	TXBLS	10/01-12/01
	Brownsville-Harlingen-San Benito MSA, TX	Y	32310 FQ	67440 AW	105870 TQ	TXBLS	10/01-12/01
	Corpus Christi MSA, TX	Y	32710 FQ	56690 AW	94690 TQ	TXBLS	10/01-12/01
	Dallas PMSA, TX	Y	44970 FQ	82750 AW	134870 TQ	TXBLS	10/01-12/01
	El Paso MSA, TX	Y	24170 FQ	64870 AW	118650 TQ	TXBLS	10/01-12/01
	Fort Worth-Arlington PMSA, TX	Y	35230 FQ	73660 AW	130020 TQ	TXBLS	10/01-12/01
	Galveston-Texas City PMSA, TX	Y	25220 FQ	68850 AW	118160 TQ	TXBLS	10/01-12/01
	Houston PMSA, TX	Y	37230 FQ	72090 AW	117920 TQ	TXBLS	10/01-12/01
	Laredo MSA, TX	Y	29780 FQ	51960 AW	91270 TQ	TXBLS	10/01-12/01
	Longview-Marshall MSA, TX	Y	24250 FQ	67450 AW	130070 TQ	TXBLS	10/01-12/01
	Lubbock MSA, TX	Y	31320 FQ	49290 AW	83000 TQ	TXBLS	10/01-12/01
	McAllen-Edinburg-Mission MSA, TX	Y	28010 FQ	56970 AW	100670 TQ	TXBLS	10/01-12/01
	Odessa-Midland MSA, TX	Y	28410 FQ	62220 AW	105970 TQ	TXBLS	10/01-12/01
	San Antonio MSA, TX	Y	33760 FQ	68400 AW	109290 TQ	TXBLS	10/01-12/01
	Tyler MSA, TX	Y	32430 FQ	63350 AW	104660 TQ	TXBLS	10/01-12/01
	Waco MSA, TX	Y	36990 FQ	67170 AW	108430 TQ	TXBLS	10/01-12/01
	Utah	Y	34990 FQ	71680 AW	122350 TQ	UTBLS	10/01-12/01
	Provo-Orem MSA, UT	Y	33660 FQ	81560 AW	137380 TQ	UTBLS	10/01-12/01
	Salt Lake City-Ogden MSA, UT	Y	36000 FQ	69700 AW	112540 TQ	UTBLS	10/01-12/01
	Vermont	Y	44830 FQ	76900 AW	139310 TQ	VTBLS	10/01-12/01
	Burlington MSA, VT	Y	45060 FQ	77660 AW	140340 TQ	VTBLS	10/01-12/01
	Virginia	Y	41150 FQ	84770 AW	139990 TQ	VABLS	10/01-12/01
	Lynchburg MSA, VA	Y	50240 FQ	93190 AW		VABLS	10/01-12/01

AAW	Average annual wage	**AOH**	Average offered, high	**ASH**	Average starting, high	**H**	Hourly	**M**	Monthly	**S**	Special: hourly and annual
AE	Average entry wage	**AOL**	Average offered, low	**ASL**	Average starting, low	**HI**	Highest wage paid	**MTC**	Median total compensation	**TQ**	Third quartile wage
AEX	Average experienced wage	**APH**	Average pay, high range	**AW**	Average wage paid	**HR**	High end range	**MW**	Median wage paid	**W**	Weekly
AO	Average offered	**APL**	Average pay, low range	**FQ**	First quartile wage	**LR**	Low end range	**SQ**	Second quartile wage	**Y**	Yearly

Occupation/Type/Industry	Location	Per	Low	Mid	High	Source	Date
Marketing Manager	Norfolk-Virginia Beach-Newport News MSA, VA-NC	Y	34230 FQ	69880 AW	110200 TQ	VABLS	10/01-12/01
	Richmond-Petersburg MSA, VA	Y	37040 FQ	75140 AW	129090 TQ	VABLS	10/01-12/01
	Roanoke MSA, VA	Y	35810 FQ	71150 AW	116740 TQ	VABLS	10/01-12/01
	Washington	Y	49470 FQ	85900 AW	138050 TQ	WABLS	10/01-12/01
	Richland-Kennewick-Pasco MSA, WA	Y	51960 FQ	84350 AW	134430 TQ	WABLS	10/01-12/01
	Seattle-Bellevue-Everett PMSA, WA	Y	52860 FQ	89560 AW	140200 TQ	WABLS	10/01-12/01
	Spokane MSA, WA	Y	40690 FQ	71990 AW	126670 TQ	WABLS	10/01-12/01
	Tacoma PMSA, WA	Y	39060 FQ	66200 AW	94500 TQ	WABLS	10/01-12/01
	Yakima MSA, WA	Y	48930 FQ	74570 AW	111410 TQ	WABLS	10/01-12/01
	West Virginia	Y	26210 FQ	65160 AW	137510 TQ	WVBLS	10/01-12/01
	Charleston MSA, WV	Y	28860 FQ	63260 AW	131910 TQ	WVBLS	10/01-12/01
	Huntington-Ashland MSA, WV-KY-OH	Y	28640 FQ	63090 AW	117730 TQ	WVBLS	10/01-12/01
	Wisconsin	Y	38550 FQ	72040 AW	124190 TQ	WIBLS	10/01-12/01
	Appleton-Oshkosh-Neenah MSA, WI	Y	40350 FQ	83020 AW		WIBLS	10/01-12/01
	Green Bay MSA, WI	Y	40080 FQ	70160 AW	113660 TQ	WIBLS	10/01-12/01
	Madison MSA, WI	Y	39990 FQ	69840 AW	110350 TQ	WIBLS	10/01-12/01
	Milwaukee-Waukesha PMSA, WI	Y	43330 FQ	74380 AW	126230 TQ	WIBLS	10/01-12/01
	Racine PMSA, WI	Y	44170 FQ	78030 AW	120830 TQ	WIBLS	10/01-12/01
	Wyoming	Y	30350 FQ	54950 AW	95730 TQ	WYBLS	10/01-12/01
	Puerto Rico	Y	27070 FQ	59900 AW	95950 TQ	PRBLS	10/01-12/01
	Guam	Y	15880 FQ	47120 AW	82310 TQ	GUBLS	10/01-12/01
Marriage and Family Therapist	Alabama	Y	26090 FQ	36740 AW	49340 TQ	ALBLS	10/01-12/01
	Alaska	Y	30920 FQ	40700 AW	55290 TQ	AKBLS	10/01-12/01
	Arizona	Y	25370 FQ	33040 AW	41960 TQ	AZBLS	10/01-12/01
	Arkansas	Y	28090 FQ	32230 AW	36180 TQ	ARBLS	10/01-12/01
	California	Y	18410 FQ	30860 AW	52580 TQ	CABLS	10/01-12/01
	Colorado	Y	25840 FQ	32890 AW	41960 TQ	COBLS	10/01-12/01
	Connecticut	Y	30640 FQ	41650 AW	55480 TQ	CTBLS	10/01-12/01
	Florida	Y	24290 FQ	45440 AW	86430 TQ	FLBLS	10/01-12/01
	Georgia	Y	23540 FQ	32630 AW	47520 TQ	GABLS	10/01-12/01
	Hawaii	Y	24050 FQ	33320 AW	54680 TQ	HIBLS	10/01-12/01
	Idaho	Y	35370 FQ	40300 AW	48920 TQ	IDBLS	10/01-12/01
	Illinois	Y	18810 FQ	32430 AW	54820 TQ	ILBLS	10/01-12/01
	Indiana	Y	25880 FQ	38910 AW	52590 TQ	INBLS	10/01-12/01
	Iowa	Y	23220 FQ	31510 AW	43920 TQ	IABLS	10/01-12/01
	Kansas	Y	29190 FQ	45990 AW	85350 TQ	KSBLS	10/01-12/01
	Kentucky	Y	12770 FQ	31520 AW	50510 TQ	KYBLS	10/01-12/01
	Louisiana	Y	22460 FQ	34330 AW	53890 TQ	LABLS	10/01-12/01
	Maine	Y	25280 FQ	31860 AW	39750 TQ	MEBLS	10/01-12/01
	Massachusetts	Y	26580 FQ	40350 AW	63440 TQ	MABLS	10/01-12/01
	Michigan	Y	25800 FQ	47920 AW	96790 TQ	MIBLS	10/01-12/01
	Minnesota	Y	28530 FQ	39210 AW	51690 TQ	MNBLS	10/01-12/01
	Missouri	Y	22510 FQ	37020 AW	65170 TQ	MOBLS	10/01-12/01
	Nebraska	Y	25770 FQ	35980 AW	49530 TQ	NEBLS	10/01-12/01
	Nevada	Y	29900 FQ	45590 AW	66250 TQ	NVBLS	10/01-12/01
	New Hampshire	Y	22380 FQ	32330 AW	43260 TQ	NHBLS	10/01-12/01
	New Jersey	Y	26360 FQ	42760 AW	62960 TQ	NJBLS	10/01-12/01
	New York	Y	22500 FQ	43010 AW	76440 TQ	NYBLS	10/01-12/01
	North Carolina	Y	26930 FQ	40020 AW	57970 TQ	NCBLS	10/01-12/01
	North Dakota	Y	21670 FQ	35780 AW	46040 TQ	NDBLS	10/01-12/01
	Ohio	Y	24490 FQ	37690 AW	54950 TQ	OHBLS	10/01-12/01
	Oklahoma	Y	26040 FQ	37730 AW	48340 TQ	OKBLS	10/01-12/01
	Oregon	Y	26060 FQ	36970 AW	58070 TQ	ORBLS	10/01-12/01
	Pennsylvania	Y	20700 FQ	35800 AW	54590 TQ	PABLS	10/01-12/01
	South Carolina	Y	15360 FQ	30540 AW	51120 TQ	SCBLS	10/01-12/01
	South Dakota	Y	21640 FQ	29690 AW	43280 TQ	SDBLS	10/01-12/01
	Tennessee	Y	23380 FQ	30980 AW	41110 TQ	TNBLS	10/01-12/01
	Texas	Y	26040 FQ	45030 AW	71590 TQ	TXBLS	10/01-12/01
	Utah	Y	28890 FQ	39460 AW	56400 TQ	UTBLS	10/01-12/01
	Vermont	Y	29640 FQ	39180 AW	50860 TQ	VTBLS	10/01-12/01
	Virginia	Y	18800 FQ	31250 AW	50220 TQ	VABLS	10/01-12/01
	Washington	Y	26380 FQ	38610 AW	52520 TQ	WABLS	10/01-12/01
	Wisconsin	Y	17250 FQ	33970 AW	55490 TQ	WIBLS	10/01-12/01

AAW	Average annual wage	**AOH**	Average offered, high	**ASH**	Average starting, high	**H**	Hourly	**M**	Monthly	**S**	Special: hourly and annual
AE	Average entry wage	**AOL**	Average offered, low	**ASL**	Average starting, low	**HI**	Highest wage paid	**MTC**	Median total compensation	**TQ**	Third quartile wage
AEX	Average experienced wage	**APH**	Average pay, high range	**AW**	Average wage paid	**HR**	High end range	**MW**	Median wage paid	**W**	Weekly
AO	Average offered	**APL**	Average pay, low range	**FQ**	First quartile wage	**LR**	Low end range	**SQ**	Second quartile wage	**Y**	Yearly

Occupation/Type/Industry	Location	Per	Low	Mid	High	Source	Date
Massage Therapist	Alabama	H	6.12 FQ	10.61 AW	19.51 TQ	ALBLS	10/01-12/01
	Alaska	H	6.20 FQ	16.57 AW	29.12 TQ	AKBLS	10/01-12/01
	Arizona	H	7.46 FQ	17.30 AW	28.94 TQ	AZBLS	10/01-12/01
	Arkansas	H	5.66 FQ	8.81 AW	16.31 TQ	ARBLS	10/01-12/01
	California	H	6.81 FQ	15.93 AW	28.02 TQ	CABLS	10/01-12/01
	Colorado	H	10.04 FQ	16.97 AW	36.78 TQ	COBLS	10/01-12/01
	Connecticut	H	10.70 FQ	21.82 AW	40.90 TQ	CTBLS	10/01-12/01
	Delaware	H	6.67 FQ	14.47 AW	30.35 TQ	DEBLS	10/01-12/01
	District of Columbia	H	7.70 FQ	16.31 AW	28.90 TQ	DCBLS	10/01-12/01
	Florida	H	6.02 FQ	11.54 AW	20.83 TQ	FLBLS	10/01-12/01
	Georgia	H	9.60 FQ	19.45 AW	38.17 TQ	GABLS	10/01-12/01
	Hawaii	H	6.01 FQ	12.73 AW	25.84 TQ	HIBLS	10/01-12/01
	Idaho	H	8.12 FQ	13.03 AW	17.70 TQ	IDBLS	10/01-12/01
	Illinois	H	7.03 FQ	16.68 AW	28.24 TQ	ILBLS	10/01-12/01
	Indiana	H	6.43 FQ	16.47 AW	39.13 TQ	INBLS	10/01-12/01
	Iowa	H	9.05 FQ	11.70 AW	14.92 TQ	IABLS	10/01-12/01
	Kansas	H	9.54 FQ	13.62 AW	17.49 TQ	KSBLS	10/01-12/01
	Kentucky	H	5.90 FQ	12.32 AW	19.71 TQ	KYBLS	10/01-12/01
	Louisiana	H	7.02 FQ	11.94 AW	16.78 TQ	LABLS	10/01-12/01
	Maine	H	6.05 FQ	14.97 AW	20.72 TQ	MEBLS	10/01-12/01
	Maryland	H	5.64 FQ	7.90 AW	10.97 TQ	MDBLS	10/01-12/01
	Massachusetts	H	8.41 FQ	20.06 AW	38.43 TQ	MABLS	10/01-12/01
	Michigan	H	5.92 FQ	11.89 AW	23.95 TQ	MIBLS	10/01-12/01
	Minnesota	H	12.09 FQ	20.60 AW	27.93 TQ	MNBLS	10/01-12/01
	Mississippi	H	7.19 FQ	12.36 AW	17.81 TQ	MSBLS	10/01-12/01
	Missouri	H	7.46 FQ	15.84 AW	25.16 TQ	MOBLS	10/01-12/01
	Montana	H	6.11 FQ	10.86 AW	19.92 TQ	MTBLS	10/01-12/01
	Nebraska	H	6.81 FQ	15.51 AW	25.32 TQ	NEBLS	10/01-12/01
	Nevada	H	5.97 FQ	17.86 AW	33.80 TQ	NVBLS	10/01-12/01
	New Hampshire	H	6.77 FQ	14.70 AW	21.89 TQ	NHBLS	10/01-12/01
	New Jersey	H	9.93 FQ	21.84 AW	33.44 TQ	NJBLS	10/01-12/01
	New Mexico	H	12.33 FQ	17.56 AW	28.61 TQ	NMBLS	10/01-12/01
	New York	H	8.20 FQ	24.46 AW	34.86 TQ	NYBLS	10/01-12/01
	North Carolina	H	7.11 FQ	17.81 AW	28.59 TQ	NCBLS	10/01-12/01
	Ohio	H	6.19 FQ	14.78 AW	25.64 TQ	OHBLS	10/01-12/01
	Oklahoma	H	6.07 FQ	14.81 AW	20.90 TQ	OKBLS	10/01-12/01
	Oregon	H	7.53 FQ	15.06 AW	26.32 TQ	ORBLS	10/01-12/01
	Pennsylvania	H	5.71 FQ	11.34 AW	21.73 TQ	PABLS	10/01-12/01
	Rhode Island	H	8.51 FQ	17.89 AW	26.93 TQ	RIBLS	10/01-12/01
	South Carolina	H	7.49 FQ	13.33 AW	21.74 TQ	SCBLS	10/01-12/01
	South Dakota	H	8.49 FQ	10.64 AW	13.14 TQ	SDBLS	10/01-12/01
	Tennessee	H	6.86 FQ	13.83 AW	21.33 TQ	TNBLS	10/01-12/01
	Texas	H	7.74 FQ	15.26 AW	24.74 TQ	TXBLS	10/01-12/01
	Utah	H	6.65 FQ	17.85 AW	27.12 TQ	UTBLS	10/01-12/01
	Virginia	H	6.67 FQ	15.46 AW	30.96 TQ	VABLS	10/01-12/01
	Washington	H	8.90 FQ	16.86 AW	30.46 TQ	WABLS	10/01-12/01
	West Virginia	H	5.71 FQ	12.06 AW	21.25 TQ	WVBLS	10/01-12/01
	Wisconsin	H	6.68 FQ	17.30 AW	26.73 TQ	WIBLS	10/01-12/01
	Wyoming	H	9.30 FQ	21.53 AW	28.89 TQ	WYBLS	10/01-12/01
Materials Engineer	Alabama	Y	41570 FQ	66200 AW	90140 TQ	ALBLS	10/01-12/01
	Alaska	Y	51490 FQ	71990 AW	97600 TQ	AKBLS	10/01-12/01
	Arizona	Y	38220 FQ	65880 AW	92110 TQ	AZBLS	10/01-12/01
	Arkansas	Y	39320 FQ	56410 AW	77340 TQ	ARBLS	10/01-12/01
	California	Y	40130 FQ	66310 AW	96630 TQ	CABLS	10/01-12/01
	Colorado	Y	43800 FQ	70650 AW	101500 TQ	COBLS	10/01-12/01
	Connecticut	Y	42260 FQ	67060 AW	91760 TQ	CTBLS	10/01-12/01
	Delaware	Y	43030 FQ	72060 AW	94730 TQ	DEBLS	10/01-12/01
	Florida	Y	39630 FQ	61470 AW	89030 TQ	FLBLS	10/01-12/01
	Georgia	Y	35740 FQ	56040 AW	80110 TQ	GABLS	10/01-12/01
	Illinois	Y	38650 FQ	60100 AW	83300 TQ	ILBLS	10/01-12/01
	Indiana	Y	38610 FQ	55090 AW	74650 TQ	INBLS	10/01-12/01
	Iowa	Y	39620 FQ	58940 AW	81860 TQ	IABLS	10/01-12/01
	Kansas	Y	30760 FQ	53650 AW	85410 TQ	KSBLS	10/01-12/01
	Kentucky	Y	44210 FQ	60520 AW	81680 TQ	KYBLS	10/01-12/01
	Louisiana	Y	30400 FQ	60690 AW	90630 TQ	LABLS	10/01-12/01
	Maine	Y	35280 FQ	63800 AW	93530 TQ	MEBLS	10/01-12/01
	Maryland	Y	49490 FQ	72740 AW	102820 TQ	MDBLS	10/01-12/01
	Massachusetts	Y	42950 FQ	69660 AW	103440 TQ	MABLS	10/01-12/01
	Michigan	Y	39350 FQ	58830 AW	83490 TQ	MIBLS	10/01-12/01
	Minnesota	Y	40640 FQ	61130 AW	87100 TQ	MNBLS	10/01-12/01
	Mississippi	Y	32700 FQ	52500 AW	77860 TQ	MSBLS	10/01-12/01
	Missouri	Y	28170 FQ	58510 AW	88130 TQ	MOBLS	10/01-12/01

AAW Average annual wage **AE** Average entry wage **AEX** Average experienced wage **AO** Average offered **AOH** Average offered, high **AOL** Average offered, low **APH** Average pay, high range **APL** Average pay, low range **ASH** Average starting, high **ASL** Average starting, low **AW** Average wage paid **FQ** First quartile wage **H** Hourly **HI** Highest wage paid **HR** High end range **LR** Low end range **M** Monthly **MTC** Median total compensation **MW** Median wage paid **SQ** Second quartile wage **S** Special: hourly and annual **TQ** Third quartile wage **W** Weekly **Y** Yearly

Occupation/Type/Industry	Location	Per	Low	Mid	High	Source	Date
Materials Engineer	Nebraska	Y	43190 FQ	58250 AW	80500 TQ	NEBLS	10/01-12/01
	Nevada	Y	47920 FQ	73210 AW		NVBLS	10/01-12/01
	New Hampshire	Y	39150 FQ	59740 AW	86140 TQ	NHBLS	10/01-12/01
	New Jersey	Y	45820 FQ	64550 AW	90410 TQ	NJBLS	10/01-12/01
	New Mexico	Y	46130 FQ	76500 AW	118010 TQ	NMBLS	10/01-12/01
	New York	Y	38260 FQ	63380 AW	93360 TQ	NYBLS	10/01-12/01
	North Carolina	Y	33990 FQ	58290 AW	87880 TQ	NCBLS	10/01-12/01
	Ohio	Y	40030 FQ	62850 AW	92330 TQ	OHBLS	10/01-12/01
	Oklahoma	Y	23070 FQ	57210 AW	86920 TQ	OKBLS	10/01-12/01
	Oregon	Y	34820 FQ	60930 AW	87200 TQ	ORBLS	10/01-12/01
	Pennsylvania	Y	37980 FQ	58590 AW	82180 TQ	PABLS	10/01-12/01
	Rhode Island	Y	42640 FQ	60900 AW	77700 TQ	RIBLS	10/01-12/01
	South Carolina	Y	39490 FQ	66910 AW	94860 TQ	SCBLS	10/01-12/01
	Tennessee	Y	44900 FQ	67690 AW	94190 TQ	TNBLS	10/01-12/01
	Texas	Y	39980 FQ	63670 AW	90370 TQ	TXBLS	10/01-12/01
	Utah	Y	35510 FQ	60420 AW	89580 TQ	UTBLS	10/01-12/01
	Vermont	Y	41230 FQ	58180 AW	86090 TQ	VTBLS	10/01-12/01
	Virginia	Y	38860 FQ	59280 AW	87700 TQ	VABLS	10/01-12/01
	Washington	Y	33020 FQ	58620 AW	87370 TQ	WABLS	10/01-12/01
	West Virginia	Y	41890 FQ	59940 AW	82700 TQ	WVBLS	10/01-12/01
	Wisconsin	Y	40250 FQ	57450 AW	80610 TQ	WIBLS	10/01-12/01
	Puerto Rico	Y	40210 FQ	50310 AW	61580 TQ	PRBLS	10/01-12/01
Materials Scientist	Alabama	Y	31150 FQ	47780 AW	78830 TQ	ALBLS	10/01-12/01
	Arizona	Y	30760 FQ	57200 AW	100300 TQ	AZBLS	10/01-12/01
	Phoenix-Mesa MSA, AZ	Y	30070 FQ	53120 AW	99020 TQ	AZBLS	10/01-12/01
	California	Y	37990 FQ	63760 AW	98940 TQ	CABLS	10/01-12/01
	Los Angeles-Long Beach PMSA, CA	Y	40410 FQ	67530 AW	100760 TQ	CABLS	10/01-12/01
	Oakland PMSA, CA	Y	28250 FQ	63780 AW	109380 TQ	CABLS	10/01-12/01
	Orange County PMSA, CA	Y	36920 FQ	61870 AW	91160 TQ	CABLS	10/01-12/01
	Riverside-San Bernardino PMSA, CA	Y	34240 FQ	56570 AW	84720 TQ	CABLS	10/01-12/01
	San Diego MSA, CA	Y	38770 FQ	58660 AW	90290 TQ	CABLS	10/01-12/01
	San Francisco PMSA, CA	Y	59910 FQ	79750 AW	106760 TQ	CABLS	10/01-12/01
	Santa Barbara-Santa Maria-Lompoc MSA, CA	Y	39150 FQ	65960 AW	113780 TQ	CABLS	10/01-12/01
	Colorado	Y	51050 FQ	81910 AW	117360 TQ	COBLS	10/01-12/01
	Denver PMSA, CO	Y	53050 FQ	83530 AW	117180 TQ	COBLS	10/01-12/01
	Connecticut	Y	41310 FQ	70140 AW	109340 TQ	CTBLS	10/01-12/01
	District of Columbia	Y	42770 FQ	74970 AW	110000 TQ	DCBLS	10/01-12/01
	Washington PMSA, DC-MD-VA-WV	Y	46100 FQ	82140 AW	118750 TQ	DCBLS	10/01-12/01
	Florida	Y	50140 FQ	74110 AW	108080 TQ	FLBLS	10/01-12/01
	Miami PMSA, FL	Y	43850 FQ	74430 AW	116850 TQ	FLBLS	10/01-12/01
	Georgia	Y	22810 FQ	37860 AW	58380 TQ	GABLS	10/01-12/01
	Atlanta MSA, GA	Y	21970 FQ	34810 AW	52590 TQ	GABLS	10/01-12/01
	Illinois	Y	38400 FQ	69670 AW	102760 TQ	ILBLS	10/01-12/01
	Chicago PMSA, IL	Y	40060 FQ	71140 AW	105360 TQ	ILBLS	10/01-12/01
	Indiana	Y	23920 FQ	46520 AW	86760 TQ	INBLS	10/01-12/01
	Indianapolis MSA, IN	Y	23560 FQ	38420 AW	70500 TQ	INBLS	10/01-12/01
	Louisiana	Y	35850 FQ	50440 AW	85580 TQ	LABLS	10/01-12/01
	Maryland	Y	46890 FQ	88760 AW	128600 TQ	MDBLS	10/01-12/01
	Massachusetts	Y	49660 FQ	78750 AW	115650 TQ	MABLS	10/01-12/01
	Boston PMSA, MA-NH	Y	48800 FQ	78520 AW	118380 TQ	MABLS	10/01-12/01
	Lowell PMSA, MA-NH	Y	57620 FQ	80600 AW	115470 TQ	MABLS	10/01-12/01
	Michigan	Y	31410 FQ	53260 AW	86860 TQ	MIBLS	10/01-12/01
	Detroit PMSA, MI	Y	29050 FQ	54300 AW	96290 TQ	MIBLS	10/01-12/01
	Grand Rapids-Muskegon-Holland MSA, MI	Y	36670 FQ	52800 AW	77520 TQ	MIBLS	10/01-12/01
	Minnesota	Y	35860 FQ	74420 AW	131610 TQ	MNBLS	10/01-12/01
	Minneapolis-St. Paul MSA, MN-WI	Y	36260 FQ	75230 AW	132880 TQ	MNBLS	10/01-12/01
	Mississippi	Y	33590 FQ	43530 AW	46330 TQ	MSBLS	10/01-12/01
	New Jersey	Y	38170 FQ	83980 AW	128390 TQ	NJBLS	10/01-12/01
	Bergen-Passaic PMSA, NJ	Y	32400 FQ	84470 AW		NJBLS	10/01-12/01
	Middlesex-Somerset-Hunterdon PMSA, NJ	Y	35090 FQ	77480 AW	116000 TQ	NJBLS	10/01-12/01
	Newark PMSA, NJ	Y	62130 FQ	93490 AW	124460 TQ	NJBLS	10/01-12/01
	New York	Y	49790 FQ	79750 AW	112370 TQ	NYBLS	10/01-12/01
	Buffalo-Niagara Falls MSA, NY	Y	31260 FQ	57290 AW	76770 TQ	NYBLS	10/01-12/01
	New York PMSA, NY	Y	60040 FQ	81600 AW	108040 TQ	NYBLS	10/01-12/01

AAW	Average annual wage	**AOH**	Average offered, high	**ASH**	Average starting, high	**H**	Hourly	**M**	Monthly	**S**	Special: hourly and annual
AE	Average entry wage	**AOL**	Average offered, low	**ASL**	Average starting, low	**HI**	Highest wage paid	**MTC**	Median total compensation	**TQ**	Third quartile wage
AEX	Average experienced wage	**APH**	Average pay, high range	**AW**	Average wage paid	**HR**	High end range	**MW**	Median wage paid	**W**	Weekly
AO	Average offered	**APL**	Average pay, low range	**FQ**	First quartile wage	**LR**	Low end range	**SQ**	Second quartile wage	**Y**	Yearly

Occupation/Type/Industry	Location	Per	Low	Mid	High	Source	Date
Materials Scientist	Rochester MSA, NY	Y	60030 FQ	92230 AW	128630 TQ	NYBLS	10/01-12/01
	North Carolina	Y	35440 FQ	65850 AW	93290 TQ	NCBLS	10/01-12/01
	Raleigh-Durham-Chapel Hill MSA, NC	Y	36200 FQ	72440 AW	98420 TQ	NCBLS	10/01-12/01
	Ohio	Y	25960 FQ	53670 AW	94610 TQ	OHBLS	10/01-12/01
	Akron PMSA, OH	Y	25480 FQ	43830 AW	84830 TQ	OHBLS	10/01-12/01
	Cleveland-Lorain-Elyria PMSA, OH	Y	25290 FQ	56070 AW	92140 TQ	OHBLS	10/01-12/01
	Oklahoma	Y	42470 FQ	72070 AW	109450 TQ	OKBLS	10/01-12/01
	Oklahoma City MSA, OK	Y	48370 FQ	73690 AW	109210 TQ	OKBLS	10/01-12/01
	Tulsa MSA, OK	Y	37620 FQ	71370 AW	111440 TQ	OKBLS	10/01-12/01
	Pennsylvania	Y	32900 FQ	59940 AW	92460 TQ	PABLS	10/01-12/01
	Philadelphia PMSA, PA-NJ	Y	42040 FQ	61930 AW	88750 TQ	PABLS	10/01-12/01
	Pittsburgh MSA, PA	Y	32250 FQ	60750 AW	113060 TQ	PABLS	10/01-12/01
	Rhode Island	Y	37280 FQ	53530 AW	79720 TQ	RIBLS	10/01-12/01
	Tennessee	Y	39250 FQ	67040 AW	105480 TQ	TNBLS	10/01-12/01
	Texas	Y	28160 FQ	67380 AW	104130 TQ	TXBLS	10/01-12/01
	Brazoria PMSA, TX	Y	42690 FQ	64680 AW	87450 TQ	TXBLS	10/01-12/01
	Dallas PMSA, TX	Y	33230 FQ	70180 AW	105690 TQ	TXBLS	10/01-12/01
	Houston PMSA, TX	Y	37950 FQ	64870 AW	90220 TQ	TXBLS	10/01-12/01
	Utah	Y	23410 FQ	38780 AW	58250 TQ	UTBLS	10/01-12/01
	Virginia	Y	40020 FQ	63330 AW	101680 TQ	VABLS	10/01-12/01
	Norfolk-Virginia Beach-Newport News MSA, VA-NC	Y	51140 FQ	75470 AW	108830 TQ	VABLS	10/01-12/01
	Washington	Y	37320 FQ	59080 AW	92020 TQ	WABLS	10/01-12/01
	Seattle-Bellevue-Everett PMSA, WA	Y	28660 FQ	58410 AW	96260 TQ	WABLS	10/01-12/01
	Wisconsin	Y	32530 FQ	54670 AW	72950 TQ	WIBLS	10/01-12/01
	Milwaukee-Waukesha PMSA, WI	Y	33200 FQ	53670 AW	81580 TQ	WIBLS	10/01-12/01
Mathematical Science Teacher							
Postsecondary	Alabama	Y	18470 FQ	44790 AW	71500 TQ	ALBLS	10/01-12/01
Postsecondary	Birmingham MSA, AL	Y	33190 FQ	57000 AW	87320 TQ	ALBLS	10/01-12/01
Postsecondary	Huntsville MSA, AL	Y	18820 FQ	43240 AW	61300 TQ	ALBLS	10/01-12/01
Postsecondary	Mobile MSA, AL	Y	12140 FQ	32790 AW	52660 TQ	ALBLS	10/01-12/01
Postsecondary	Montgomery MSA, AL	Y	31740 FQ	43270 AW	66540 TQ	ALBLS	10/01-12/01
Postsecondary	Arkansas	Y	21230 FQ	46390 AW	87000 TQ	ARBLS	10/01-12/01
Postsecondary	California	Y	36590 FQ	68150 AW	107480 TQ	CABLS	10/01-12/01
Postsecondary	Fresno MSA, CA	Y	26050 FQ	55010 AW	91510 TQ	CABLS	10/01-12/01
Postsecondary	Los Angeles-Long Beach PMSA, CA	Y	40200 FQ	69470 AW	103810 TQ	CABLS	10/01-12/01
Postsecondary	Orange County PMSA, CA	Y	33100 FQ	64600 AW	97780 TQ	CABLS	10/01-12/01
Postsecondary	Riverside-San Bernardino PMSA, CA	Y	33070 FQ	62380 AW	98070 TQ	CABLS	10/01-12/01
Postsecondary	San Diego MSA, CA	Y	32280 FQ	64430 AW	99180 TQ	CABLS	10/01-12/01
Postsecondary	San Francisco PMSA, CA	Y	57950 FQ	86920 AW	118900 TQ	CABLS	10/01-12/01
Postsecondary	San Jose PMSA, CA	Y	38920 FQ	62980 AW	86400 TQ	CABLS	10/01-12/01
Postsecondary	Santa Cruz-Watsonville PMSA, CA	Y	32560 FQ	57360 AW	90220 TQ	CABLS	10/01-12/01
Postsecondary	Colorado	Y	29170 FQ	48520 AW	78500 TQ	COBLS	10/01-12/01
Postsecondary	Colorado Springs MSA, CO	Y	32730 FQ	53640 AW	83740 TQ	COBLS	10/01-12/01
Postsecondary	Denver PMSA, CO	Y	27820 FQ	46930 AW	78780 TQ	COBLS	10/01-12/01
Postsecondary	Fort Collins-Loveland MSA, CO	Y	33130 FQ	49680 AW	76970 TQ	COBLS	10/01-12/01
Postsecondary	Connecticut	Y	40360 FQ	59910 AW	81590 TQ	CTBLS	10/01-12/01
Postsecondary	Bridgeport PMSA, CT	Y	43770 FQ	65820 AW	86880 TQ	CTBLS	10/01-12/01
Postsecondary	New Haven-Meriden PMSA, CT	Y	50930 FQ	61390 AW	74440 TQ	CTBLS	10/01-12/01
Postsecondary	Delaware	Y	38760 FQ	59920 AW	87400 TQ	DEBLS	10/01-12/01
Postsecondary	Wilmington-Newark PMSA, DE-MD	Y	38100 FQ	61330 AW	91170 TQ	DEBLS	10/01-12/01
Postsecondary	District of Columbia	Y	36750 FQ	62590 AW	94310 TQ	DCBLS	10/01-12/01
Postsecondary	Washington PMSA, DC-MD-VA-WV	Y	26350 FQ	61010 AW	108400 TQ	DCBLS	10/01-12/01
Postsecondary	Florida	Y	27020 FQ	56610 AW	95150 TQ	FLBLS	10/01-12/01
Postsecondary	Fort Lauderdale PMSA, FL	Y	32020 FQ	55070 AW	86220 TQ	FLBLS	10/01-12/01
Postsecondary	Gainesville MSA, FL	Y	37550 FQ	73270 AW	119480 TQ	FLBLS	10/01-12/01
Postsecondary	Jacksonville MSA, FL	Y	34780 FQ	55530 AW	85540 TQ	FLBLS	10/01-12/01
Postsecondary	Miami PMSA, FL	Y	39530 FQ	65590 AW	110880 TQ	FLBLS	10/01-12/01
Postsecondary	Orlando MSA, FL	Y	23880 FQ	47860 AW	83280 TQ	FLBLS	10/01-12/01
Postsecondary	Pensacola MSA, FL	Y	33760 FQ	55580 AW	83880 TQ	FLBLS	10/01-12/01

Occupation/Type/Industry	Location	Per	Low	Mid	High	Source	Date
Mathematical Science Teacher							
Postsecondary	Tallahassee MSA, FL	Y	38050 FQ	67090 AW	106350 TQ	FLBLS	10/01-12/01
Postsecondary	Tampa-St. Petersburg-Clearwater MSA, FL	Y	30260 FQ	52200 AW	82820 TQ	FLBLS	10/01-12/01
Postsecondary	West Palm Beach-Boca Raton MSA, FL	Y	36830 FQ	58770 AW	89020 TQ	FLBLS	10/01-12/01
Postsecondary	Georgia	Y	33410 FQ	52680 AW	80170 TQ	GABLS	10/01-12/01
Postsecondary	Atlanta MSA, GA	Y	36100 FQ	55700 AW	83340 TQ	GABLS	10/01-12/01
Postsecondary	Savannah MSA, GA	Y	22820 FQ	43510 AW	59610 TQ	GABLS	10/01-12/01
Postsecondary	Hawaii	Y	35330 FQ	55940 AW	83340 TQ	HIBLS	10/01-12/01
Postsecondary	Honolulu MSA, HI	Y	33460 FQ	56890 AW	85160 TQ	HIBLS	10/01-12/01
Postsecondary	Idaho	Y	22000 FQ	42210 AW	57970 TQ	IDBLS	10/01-12/01
Postsecondary	Illinois	Y	21790 FQ	54840 AW	92860 TQ	ILBLS	10/01-12/01
Postsecondary	Champaign-Urbana MSA, IL	Y	23120 FQ	56250 AW	92800 TQ	ILBLS	10/01-12/01
Postsecondary	Chicago PMSA, IL	Y	22420 FQ	60660 AW	95090 TQ	ILBLS	10/01-12/01
Postsecondary	Indiana	Y	21080 FQ	46130 AW	71830 TQ	INBLS	10/01-12/01
Postsecondary	Evansville-Henderson MSA, IN-KY	Y	22910 FQ	47000 AW	67660 TQ	INBLS	10/01-12/01
Postsecondary	South Bend MSA, IN	Y	22780 FQ	40720 AW	66520 TQ	INBLS	10/01-12/01
Postsecondary	Iowa	Y	30750 FQ	54170 AW	81460 TQ	IABLS	10/01-12/01
Postsecondary	Davenport-Moline-Rock Island MSA, IA-IL	Y	30800 FQ	49160 AW	68990 TQ	IABLS	10/01-12/01
Postsecondary	Des Moines MSA, IA	Y	30730 FQ	45280 AW	65370 TQ	IABLS	10/01-12/01
Postsecondary	Kansas	Y	16480 FQ	39910 AW	67390 TQ	KSBLS	10/01-12/01
Postsecondary	Kentucky	Y	23140 FQ	47130 AW	76870 TQ	KYBLS	10/01-12/01
Postsecondary	Lexington MSA, KY	Y	34690 FQ	57790 AW	87460 TQ	KYBLS	10/01-12/01
Postsecondary	Louisville MSA, KY-IN	Y	29990 FQ	54050 AW	89240 TQ	KYBLS	10/01-12/01
Postsecondary	Louisiana	Y	23410 FQ	42220 AW	67090 TQ	LABLS	10/01-12/01
Postsecondary	New Orleans MSA, LA	Y	13900 FQ	41060 AW	62850 TQ	LABLS	10/01-12/01
Postsecondary	Maine	Y	33390 FQ	48320 AW	68720 TQ	MEBLS	10/01-12/01
Postsecondary	Maryland	Y	36030 FQ	60840 AW	103500 TQ	MDBLS	10/01-12/01
Postsecondary	Baltimore PMSA, MD	Y	37790 FQ	58760 AW	88420 TQ	MDBLS	10/01-12/01
Postsecondary	Massachusetts	Y	33540 FQ	54690 AW	84660 TQ	MABLS	10/01-12/01
Postsecondary	Boston PMSA, MA-NH	Y	32980 FQ	55540 AW	85750 TQ	MABLS	10/01-12/01
Postsecondary	Brockton PMSA, MA	Y	36480 FQ	48860 AW	69360 TQ	MABLS	10/01-12/01
Postsecondary	Springfield MSA, MA	Y	36800 FQ	56960 AW	92000 TQ	MABLS	10/01-12/01
Postsecondary	Michigan	Y	31280 FQ	60120 AW	94990 TQ	MIBLS	10/01-12/01
Postsecondary	Ann Arbor PMSA, MI	Y	29400 FQ	54690 AW	89490 TQ	MIBLS	10/01-12/01
Postsecondary	Detroit PMSA, MI	Y	27870 FQ	57870 AW	93560 TQ	MIBLS	10/01-12/01
Postsecondary	Grand Rapids-Muskegon-Holland MSA, MI	Y	34310 FQ	53870 AW	83080 TQ	MIBLS	10/01-12/01
Postsecondary	Minnesota	Y	34440 FQ	57840 AW	88620 TQ	MNBLS	10/01-12/01
Postsecondary	Duluth-Superior MSA, MN-WI	Y	33780 FQ	52680 AW	76970 TQ	MNBLS	10/01-12/01
Postsecondary	Minneapolis-St. Paul MSA, MN-WI	Y	35660 FQ	62730 AW	104030 TQ	MNBLS	10/01-12/01
Postsecondary	Mississippi	Y	23840 FQ	42250 AW	61740 TQ	MSBLS	10/01-12/01
Postsecondary	Jackson MSA, MS	Y	13100 FQ	32700 AW	49900 TQ	MSBLS	10/01-12/01
Postsecondary	Missouri	Y	25750 FQ	44940 AW	66360 TQ	MOBLS	10/01-12/01
Postsecondary	Kansas City MSA, MO-KS	Y	17670 FQ	39630 AW	58590 TQ	MOBLS	10/01-12/01
Postsecondary	St. Louis MSA, MO-IL	Y	25420 FQ	46280 AW	70340 TQ	MOBLS	10/01-12/01
Postsecondary	Springfield MSA, MO	Y	36980 FQ	53850 AW	73890 TQ	MOBLS	10/01-12/01
Postsecondary	Montana	Y	25100 FQ	49660 AW	83190 TQ	MTBLS	10/01-12/01
Postsecondary	Nebraska	Y	27860 FQ	47670 AW	73700 TQ	NEBLS	10/01-12/01
Postsecondary	Lincoln MSA, NE	Y	38350 FQ	62410 AW	93850 TQ	NEBLS	10/01-12/01
Postsecondary	Omaha MSA, NE-IA	Y	31640 FQ	46160 AW	67040 TQ	NEBLS	10/01-12/01
Postsecondary	Nevada	Y	25900 FQ	45040 AW	70830 TQ	NVBLS	10/01-12/01
Postsecondary	Las Vegas MSA, NV-AZ	Y	25890 FQ	42800 AW	66060 TQ	NVBLS	10/01-12/01
Postsecondary	New Hampshire	Y	34600 FQ	59230 AW	93540 TQ	NHBLS	10/01-12/01
Postsecondary	New Jersey	Y	31830 FQ	65990 AW	111490 TQ	NJBLS	10/01-12/01
Postsecondary	Bergen-Passaic PMSA, NJ	Y	31890 FQ	59790 AW	102070 TQ	NJBLS	10/01-12/01
Postsecondary	Jersey City PMSA, NJ	Y	34860 FQ	73880 AW	127360 TQ	NJBLS	10/01-12/01
Postsecondary	Monmouth-Ocean PMSA, NJ	Y	35630 FQ	57820 AW	87240 TQ	NJBLS	10/01-12/01
Postsecondary	Newark PMSA, NJ	Y	21820 FQ	60110 AW	103900 TQ	NJBLS	10/01-12/01
Postsecondary	New Mexico	Y	26930 FQ	44970 AW	61620 TQ	NMBLS	10/01-12/01
Postsecondary	New York	Y	34870 FQ	62910 AW	108290 TQ	NYBLS	10/01-12/01
Postsecondary	Albany-Schenectady-Troy MSA, NY	Y	36930 FQ	51260 AW	79770 TQ	NYBLS	10/01-12/01
Postsecondary	Buffalo-Niagara Falls MSA, NY	Y	31550 FQ	48610 AW	71290 TQ	NYBLS	10/01-12/01
Postsecondary	Nassau-Suffolk PMSA, NY	Y	40750 FQ	65350 AW	103210 TQ	NYBLS	10/01-12/01
Postsecondary	New York PMSA, NY	Y	39760 FQ	70090 AW	120340 TQ	NYBLS	10/01-12/01
Postsecondary	North Carolina	Y	32480 FQ	48760 AW	71530 TQ	NCBLS	10/01-12/01

AAW	Average annual wage	**AOH**	Average offered, high	**ASH**	Average starting, high	**H**	Hourly	**M**	Monthly	**S**	Special: hourly and annual
AE	Average entry wage	**AOL**	Average offered, low	**ASL**	Average starting, low	**HI**	Highest wage paid	**MTC**	Median total compensation	**TQ**	Third quartile wage
AEX	Average experienced wage	**APH**	Average pay, high range	**AW**	Average wage paid	**HR**	High end range	**MW**	Median wage paid	**W**	Weekly
AO	Average offered	**APL**	Average pay, low range	**FQ**	First quartile wage	**LR**	Low end range	**SQ**	Second quartile wage	**Y**	Yearly

Occupation/Type/Industry	Location	Per	Low	Mid	High	Source	Date
Mathematical Science Teacher							
Postsecondary	Asheville MSA, NC	Y	39510 FQ	50470 AW	60200 TQ	NCBLS	10/01-12/01
Postsecondary	Charlotte-Gastonia-Rock Hill MSA, NC-SC	Y	32910 FQ	52060 AW	80340 TQ	NCBLS	10/01-12/01
Postsecondary	Fayetteville MSA, NC	Y	29840 FQ	46960 AW	67580 TQ	NCBLS	10/01-12/01
Postsecondary	Greensboro-Winston-Salem-High Point MSA, NC	Y	36020 FQ	49140 AW	65920 TQ	NCBLS	10/01-12/01
Postsecondary	Hickory-Morganton-Lenoir MSA, NC	Y	31750 FQ	38130 AW	45050 TQ	NCBLS	10/01-12/01
Postsecondary	Raleigh-Durham-Chapel Hill MSA, NC	Y	32440 FQ	53100 AW	83920 TQ	NCBLS	10/01-12/01
Postsecondary	Wilmington MSA, NC	Y	37000 FQ	53660 AW	81470 TQ	NCBLS	10/01-12/01
Postsecondary	North Dakota	Y	22640 FQ	38610 AW	56550 TQ	NDBLS	10/01-12/01
Postsecondary	Fargo-Moorhead MSA, ND-MN	Y	26470 FQ	48870 AW	72020 TQ	NDBLS	10/01-12/01
Postsecondary	Ohio	Y	24150 FQ	50130 AW	80490 TQ	OHBLS	10/01-12/01
Postsecondary	Canton-Massillon MSA, OH	Y	30420 FQ	52820 AW	69570 TQ	OHBLS	10/01-12/01
Postsecondary	Cincinnati PMSA, OH-KY-IN	Y	28200 FQ	53680 AW	84440 TQ	OHBLS	10/01-12/01
Postsecondary	Cleveland-Lorain-Elyria PMSA, OH	Y	30160 FQ	54270 AW	84970 TQ	OHBLS	10/01-12/01
Postsecondary	Columbus MSA, OH	Y	32090 FQ	57620 AW	95570 TQ	OHBLS	10/01-12/01
Postsecondary	Dayton-Springfield MSA, OH	Y	19160 FQ	41660 AW	69960 TQ	OHBLS	10/01-12/01
Postsecondary	Toledo MSA, OH	Y	23120 FQ	50820 AW	81830 TQ	OHBLS	10/01-12/01
Postsecondary	Youngstown-Warren MSA, OH	Y	25810 FQ	51160 AW	92210 TQ	OHBLS	10/01-12/01
Postsecondary	Oklahoma	Y	25030 FQ	38800 AW	56850 TQ	OKBLS	10/01-12/01
Postsecondary	Oklahoma City MSA, OK	Y	25080 FQ	37950 AW	56070 TQ	OKBLS	10/01-12/01
Postsecondary	Tulsa MSA, OK	Y	22520 FQ	40190 AW	61150 TQ	OKBLS	10/01-12/01
Postsecondary	Oregon	Y	27800 FQ	57550 AW	89990 TQ	ORBLS	10/01-12/01
Postsecondary	Portland-Vancouver PMSA, OR-WA	Y	29730 FQ	56950 AW	88200 TQ	ORBLS	10/01-12/01
Postsecondary	Salem PMSA, OR	Y	25820 FQ	56300 AW	90080 TQ	ORBLS	10/01-12/01
Postsecondary	Pennsylvania	Y	27280 FQ	59370 AW	96660 TQ	PABLS	10/01-12/01
Postsecondary	Allentown-Bethlehem-Easton MSA, PA	Y	25570 FQ	47900 AW	77090 TQ	PABLS	10/01-12/01
Postsecondary	Harrisburg-Lebanon-Carlisle MSA, PA	Y	26110 FQ	54450 AW	90310 TQ	PABLS	10/01-12/01
Postsecondary	Lancaster MSA, PA	Y	47370 FQ	65960 AW	91060 TQ	PABLS	10/01-12/01
Postsecondary	Philadelphia PMSA, PA-NJ	Y	28750 FQ	61410 AW	97790 TQ	PABLS	10/01-12/01
Postsecondary	Pittsburgh MSA, PA	Y	25090 FQ	54420 AW	98130 TQ	PABLS	10/01-12/01
Postsecondary	Reading MSA, PA	Y	35610 FQ	65040 AW	130140 TQ	PABLS	10/01-12/01
Postsecondary	Scranton-Wilkes-Barre-Hazleton MSA, PA	Y	33270 FQ	54190 AW	81170 TQ	PABLS	10/01-12/01
Postsecondary	Rhode Island	Y	35480 FQ	62750 AW	90690 TQ	RIBLS	10/01-12/01
Postsecondary	Providence-Fall River-Warwick MSA, RI-MA	Y	35500 FQ	62010 AW	90110 TQ	RIBLS	10/01-12/01
Postsecondary	South Carolina	Y	29160 FQ	46750 AW	74810 TQ	SCBLS	10/01-12/01
Postsecondary	Columbia MSA, SC	Y	30080 FQ	47600 AW	74080 TQ	SCBLS	10/01-12/01
Postsecondary	Greenville-Spartanburg-Anderson MSA, SC	Y	31580 FQ	52130 AW	83950 TQ	SCBLS	10/01-12/01
Postsecondary	South Dakota	Y	29840 FQ	44370 AW	63820 TQ	SDBLS	10/01-12/01
Postsecondary	Tennessee	Y	24860 FQ	47120 AW	71040 TQ	TNBLS	10/01-12/01
Postsecondary	Chattanooga MSA, TN-GA	Y	22500 FQ	43900 AW	58670 TQ	TNBLS	10/01-12/01
Postsecondary	Clarksville-Hopkinsville MSA, TN-KY	Y	21880 FQ	43350 AW	71340 TQ	TNBLS	10/01-12/01
Postsecondary	Johnson City-Kingsport-Bristol MSA, TN-VA	Y	20760 FQ	38100 AW	59980 TQ	TNBLS	10/01-12/01
Postsecondary	Knoxville MSA, TN	Y	30600 FQ	48930 AW	72710 TQ	TNBLS	10/01-12/01
Postsecondary	Memphis MSA, TN-AR-MS	Y	27230 FQ	49320 AW	74000 TQ	TNBLS	10/01-12/01
Postsecondary	Nashville MSA, TN	Y	32420 FQ	54200 AW	80440 TQ	TNBLS	10/01-12/01
Postsecondary	Texas	Y	21200 FQ	51930 AW	86740 TQ	TXBLS	10/01-12/01
Postsecondary	Austin-San Marcos MSA, TX	Y	38850 FQ	57500 AW	74390 TQ	TXBLS	10/01-12/01
Postsecondary	Beaumont-Port Arthur MSA, TX	Y	30520 FQ	39510 AW	52390 TQ	TXBLS	10/01-12/01
Postsecondary	Dallas PMSA, TX	Y	21180 FQ	63040 AW	141280 TQ	TXBLS	10/01-12/01
Postsecondary	Fort Worth-Arlington PMSA, TX	Y	17100 FQ	50760 AW	85530 TQ	TXBLS	10/01-12/01
Postsecondary	Houston PMSA, TX	Y	32740 FQ	57580 AW	92770 TQ	TXBLS	10/01-12/01
Postsecondary	Longview-Marshall MSA, TX	Y	24330 FQ	50250 AW	88440 TQ	TXBLS	10/01-12/01
Postsecondary	San Antonio MSA, TX	Y	19920 FQ	52490 AW	91150 TQ	TXBLS	10/01-12/01
Postsecondary	Tyler MSA, TX	Y	26430 FQ	42670 AW	64750 TQ	TXBLS	10/01-12/01
Postsecondary	Utah	Y	37720 FQ	70430 AW	126440 TQ	UTBLS	10/01-12/01

AAW Average annual wage **AOH** Average offered, high **ASH** Average starting, high **H** Hourly **M** Monthly **S** Special: hourly and annual
AE Average entry wage **AOL** Average offered, low **ASL** Average starting, low **HI** Highest wage paid **MTC** Median total compensation **TQ** Third quartile wage
AEX Average experienced wage **APH** Average pay, high range **AW** Average wage paid **HR** High end range **MW** Median wage paid **W** Weekly
AO Average offered **APL** Average pay, low range **FQ** First quartile wage **LR** Low end range **SQ** Second quartile wage **Y** Yearly

Occupation/Type/Industry	Location	Per	Low	Mid	High	Source	Date
Mathematical Science Teacher							
Postsecondary	Salt Lake City-Ogden MSA, UT	Y	38450 FQ	74770 AW	134680 TQ	UTBLS	10/01-12/01
Postsecondary	Vermont	Y	35900 FQ	51710 AW	76660 TQ	VTBLS	10/01-12/01
Postsecondary	Burlington MSA, VT	Y	36520 FQ	54110 AW	87330 TQ	VTBLS	10/01-12/01
Postsecondary	Virginia	Y	24450 FQ	51320 AW	87270 TQ	VABLS	10/01-12/01
Postsecondary	Norfolk-Virginia Beach-Newport News MSA, VA-NC	Y	31610 FQ	56750 AW	90970 TQ	VABLS	10/01-12/01
Postsecondary	Richmond-Petersburg MSA, VA	Y	19390 FQ	41150 AW	67150 TQ	VABLS	10/01-12/01
Postsecondary	Roanoke MSA, VA	Y	32620 FQ	50010 AW	73300 TQ	VABLS	10/01-12/01
Postsecondary	Washington	Y	29430 FQ	56330 AW	95820 TQ	WABLS	10/01-12/01
Postsecondary	Seattle-Bellevue-Everett PMSA, WA	Y	31380 FQ	63600 AW	117140 TQ	WABLS	10/01-12/01
Postsecondary	Tacoma PMSA, WA	Y	30600 FQ	55320 AW	90040 TQ	WABLS	10/01-12/01
Postsecondary	West Virginia	Y	27870 FQ	48710 AW	71570 TQ	WVBLS	10/01-12/01
Postsecondary	Wisconsin	Y	27890 FQ	48250 AW	74110 TQ	WIBLS	10/01-12/01
Postsecondary	Appleton-Oshkosh-Neenah MSA, WI	Y	29400 FQ	44380 AW	63350 TQ	WIBLS	10/01-12/01
Postsecondary	Milwaukee-Waukesha PMSA, WI	Y	24700 FQ	41840 AW	65510 TQ	WIBLS	10/01-12/01
Postsecondary	Wyoming	Y	30030 FQ	47240 AW	74010 TQ	WYBLS	10/01-12/01
Postsecondary	Puerto Rico	Y	24020 FQ	36100 AW	48330 TQ	PRBLS	10/01-12/01
Mathematical Technician	California	Y	20730 FQ	54040 AW	87000 TQ	CABLS	10/01-12/01
	San Francisco PMSA, CA	Y	72610 FQ	81550 AW	97060 TQ	CABLS	10/01-12/01
	Washington PMSA, DC-MD-VA-WV	Y	28920 FQ	47900 AW	72420 TQ	DCBLS	10/01-12/01
	Florida	Y	24320 FQ	41250 AW	87600 TQ	FLBLS	10/01-12/01
	Orlando MSA, FL	Y	24470 FQ	50290 AW	104150 TQ	FLBLS	10/01-12/01
	Georgia	Y	22630 FQ	30710 AW	41610 TQ	GABLS	10/01-12/01
	Atlanta MSA, GA	Y	22980 FQ	32000 AW	42660 TQ	GABLS	10/01-12/01
	Illinois	Y	15890 FQ	33800 AW	61950 TQ	ILBLS	10/01-12/01
	Maryland	Y	28610 FQ	43550 AW	57680 TQ	MDBLS	10/01-12/01
	Massachusetts	Y	25800 FQ	44330 AW	72290 TQ	MABLS	10/01-12/01
	Michigan	Y	29920 FQ	57470 AW	112570 TQ	MIBLS	10/01-12/01
	Minnesota	Y	31170 FQ	40410 AW	54890 TQ	MNBLS	10/01-12/01
	Minneapolis-St. Paul MSA, MN-WI	Y	31470 FQ	40840 AW	55170 TQ	MNBLS	10/01-12/01
	New York	Y	19240 FQ	58680 AW	110820 TQ	NYBLS	10/01-12/01
	New York PMSA, NY	Y	37760 FQ	86260 AW	120090 TQ	NYBLS	10/01-12/01
	Ohio	Y	27210 FQ	38860 AW	50330 TQ	OHBLS	10/01-12/01
	Pennsylvania	Y	23990 FQ	47020 AW	84730 TQ	PABLS	10/01-12/01
	Tennessee	Y	23280 FQ	34370 AW	45720 TQ	TNBLS	10/01-12/01
	Texas	Y	27010 FQ	59740 AW	109010 TQ	TXBLS	10/01-12/01
	Houston PMSA, TX	Y	32350 FQ	71190 AW	113640 TQ	TXBLS	10/01-12/01
	Virginia	Y	20610 FQ	47690 AW	71360 TQ	VABLS	10/01-12/01
	Washington	Y	28220 FQ	43400 AW	58530 TQ	WABLS	10/01-12/01
Mathematician	Arizona	Y	65490 FQ	81690 AW	100680 TQ	AZBLS	10/01-12/01
	California	Y	58440 FQ	77220 AW	100840 TQ	CABLS	10/01-12/01
	Los Angeles-Long Beach PMSA, CA	Y	58980 FQ	73130 AW	93710 TQ	CABLS	10/01-12/01
	San Diego MSA, CA	Y	61210 FQ	80170 AW	105200 TQ	CABLS	10/01-12/01
	Colorado	Y	57040 FQ	80700 AW	107290 TQ	COBLS	10/01-12/01
	Colorado Springs MSA, CO	Y	47240 FQ	80860 AW	107620 TQ	COBLS	10/01-12/01
	Connecticut	Y	40500 FQ	72300 AW	115510 TQ	CTBLS	10/01-12/01
	Washington PMSA, DC-MD-VA-WV	Y	50650 FQ	77520 AW	109500 TQ	DCBLS	10/01-12/01
	Florida	Y	36990 FQ	63610 AW	88840 TQ	FLBLS	10/01-12/01
	Illinois	Y	26250 FQ	62980 AW	108670 TQ	ILBLS	10/01-12/01
	Maryland	Y	59000 FQ	87560 AW	125730 TQ	MDBLS	10/01-12/01
	Baltimore PMSA, MD	Y	59670 FQ	90950 AW	139860 TQ	MDBLS	10/01-12/01
	Massachusetts	Y	22820 FQ	75340 AW	108650 TQ	MABLS	10/01-12/01
	Boston PMSA, MA-NH	Y	21450 FQ	74040 AW	107930 TQ	MABLS	10/01-12/01
	Michigan	Y	44390 FQ	64720 AW	99750 TQ	MIBLS	10/01-12/01
	Mississippi	Y	46810 FQ	62210 AW	83730 TQ	MSBLS	10/01-12/01
	Newark PMSA, NJ	Y	61910 FQ	94340 AW	138940 TQ	NJBLS	10/01-12/01
	New Mexico	Y	50290 FQ	81880 AW	114770 TQ	NMBLS	10/01-12/01
	Albuquerque MSA, NM	Y	44150 FQ	76710 AW	109930 TQ	NMBLS	10/01-12/01
	New York	Y	25920 FQ	62050 AW		NYBLS	10/01-12/01
	New York PMSA, NY	Y	28430 FQ	64810 AW		NYBLS	10/01-12/01

AAW	Average annual wage	**AOH**	Average offered, high	**ASH**	Average starting, high	**H**	Hourly	**M**	Monthly	**S**	Special: hourly and annual
AE	Average entry wage	**AOL**	Average offered, low	**ASL**	Average starting, low	**HI**	Highest wage paid	**MTC**	Median total compensation	**TQ**	Third quartile wage
AEX	Average experienced wage	**APH**	Average pay, high range	**AW**	Average wage paid	**HR**	High end range	**MW**	Median wage paid	**W**	Weekly
AO	Average offered	**APL**	Average pay, low range	**FQ**	First quartile wage	**LR**	Low end range	**SQ**	Second quartile wage	**Y**	Yearly

Occupation/Type/Industry	Location	Per	Low	Mid	High	Source	Date
Mathematician	Ohio	Y	38050 FQ	70260 AW	104990 TQ	OHBLS	10/01-12/01
	Philadelphia PMSA, PA-NJ	Y	33590 FQ	67110 AW	109170 TQ	PABLS	10/01-12/01
	Rhode Island	Y	25260 FQ	65320 AW	110810 TQ	RIBLS	10/01-12/01
	Virginia	Y	47060 FQ	73270 AW	106700 TQ	VABLS	10/01-12/01
	Washington	Y	53340 FQ	81750 AW	106350 TQ	WABLS	10/01-12/01
	Seattle-Bellevue-Everett PMSA, WA	Y	61030 FQ	83850 AW	101640 TQ	WABLS	10/01-12/01
	Wisconsin	Y	26600 FQ	53130 AW	94350 TQ	WIBLS	10/01-12/01
Meat, Poultry, and Fish Cutter and Trimmer	Alabama	H	6.93 FQ	7.99 AW	9.50 TQ	ALBLS	10/01-12/01
	Mobile MSA, AL	H	5.62 FQ	8.13 AW	12.53 TQ	ALBLS	10/01-12/01
	Alaska	H	6.34 FQ	8.69 AW	12.11 TQ	AKBLS	10/01-12/01
	Arizona	H	7.37 FQ	12.85 AW	16.84 TQ	AZBLS	10/01-12/01
	Phoenix-Mesa MSA, AZ	H	7.21 FQ	12.91 AW	16.92 TQ	AZBLS	10/01-12/01
	Tucson MSA, AZ	H	8.99 FQ	12.21 AW	16.03 TQ	AZBLS	10/01-12/01
	Arkansas	H	7.01 FQ	7.94 AW	9.04 TQ	ARBLS	10/01-12/01
	Fayetteville-Springdale-Rogers MSA, AR	H	7.24 FQ	8.05 AW	8.97 TQ	ARBLS	10/01-12/01
	Little Rock-North Little Rock MSA, AR	H	7.47 FQ	9.37 AW	12.42 TQ	ARBLS	10/01-12/01
	California	H	6.57 FQ	9.33 AW	13.81 TQ	CABLS	10/01-12/01
	Bakersfield MSA, CA	H	7.48 FQ	10.52 AW	15.84 TQ	CABLS	10/01-12/01
	Los Angeles-Long Beach PMSA, CA	H	6.51 FQ	8.73 AW	12.81 TQ	CABLS	10/01-12/01
	Merced MSA, CA	H	6.52 FQ	8.68 AW	12.45 TQ	CABLS	10/01-12/01
	Modesto MSA, CA	H	6.61 FQ	8.71 AW	12.33 TQ	CABLS	10/01-12/01
	Oakland PMSA, CA	H	7.68 FQ	12.84 AW	17.16 TQ	CABLS	10/01-12/01
	Orange County PMSA, CA	H	6.55 FQ	9.93 AW	13.58 TQ	CABLS	10/01-12/01
	Riverside-San Bernardino PMSA, CA	H	6.66 FQ	10.03 AW	13.79 TQ	CABLS	10/01-12/01
	Sacramento PMSA, CA	H	11.39 FQ	13.16 AW	16.48 TQ	CABLS	10/01-12/01
	Salinas MSA, CA	H	6.85 FQ	9.20 AW	12.44 TQ	CABLS	10/01-12/01
	San Diego MSA, CA	H	6.76 FQ	9.84 AW	13.48 TQ	CABLS	10/01-12/01
	San Francisco PMSA, CA	H	7.88 FQ	12.68 AW	17.33 TQ	CABLS	10/01-12/01
	San Jose PMSA, CA	H	7.40 FQ	13.22 AW	17.77 TQ	CABLS	10/01-12/01
	Santa Rosa PMSA, CA	H	7.83 FQ	12.28 AW	17.29 TQ	CABLS	10/01-12/01
	Stockton-Lodi MSA, CA	H	8.24 FQ	13.33 AW	19.26 TQ	CABLS	10/01-12/01
	Vallejo-Fairfield-Napa PMSA, CA	H	7.12 FQ	10.29 AW	16.05 TQ	CABLS	10/01-12/01
	Ventura PMSA, CA	H	6.39 FQ	8.06 AW	12.26 TQ	CABLS	10/01-12/01
	Visalia-Tulare-Porterville MSA, CA	H	6.39 FQ	9.84 AW	18.39 TQ	CABLS	10/01-12/01
	Denver PMSA, CO	H	8.31 FQ	11.58 AW	17.97 TQ	COBLS	10/01-12/01
	Greeley PMSA, CO	H	8.93 FQ	10.18 AW	11.76 TQ	COBLS	10/01-12/01
	Connecticut	H	7.06 FQ	10.31 AW	13.72 TQ	CTBLS	10/01-12/01
	Hartford MSA, CT	H	6.97 FQ	9.79 AW	15.93 TQ	CTBLS	10/01-12/01
	New Haven-Meriden PMSA, CT	H	6.66 FQ	8.38 AW	12.26 TQ	CTBLS	10/01-12/01
	New London-Norwich MSA, CT-RI	H	7.31 FQ	10.89 AW	21.23 TQ	CTBLS	10/01-12/01
	Delaware	H	6.91 FQ	8.14 AW	10.11 TQ	DEBLS	10/01-12/01
	Wilmington-Newark PMSA, DE-MD	H	7.39 FQ	10.09 AW	13.49 TQ	DEBLS	10/01-12/01
	District of Columbia	H	12.06 FQ	15.79 AW	20.15 TQ	DCBLS	10/01-12/01
	Washington PMSA, DC-MD-VA-WV	H	6.20 FQ	10.92 AW	16.56 TQ	DCBLS	10/01-12/01
	Florida	H	5.90 FQ	8.12 AW	10.74 TQ	FLBLS	10/01-12/01
	Daytona Beach MSA, FL	H	6.08 FQ	8.95 AW	11.51 TQ	FLBLS	10/01-12/01
	Fort Lauderdale PMSA, FL	H	6.03 FQ	8.40 AW	10.85 TQ	FLBLS	10/01-12/01
	Fort Myers-Cape Coral MSA, FL	H	6.59 FQ	8.84 AW	11.00 TQ	FLBLS	10/01-12/01
	Fort Pierce-Port St. Lucie MSA, FL	H	6.16 FQ	9.59 AW	13.54 TQ	FLBLS	10/01-12/01
	Jacksonville MSA, FL	H	6.58 FQ	8.23 AW	10.40 TQ	FLBLS	10/01-12/01
	Lakeland-Winter Haven MSA, FL	H	6.69 FQ	8.95 AW	11.03 TQ	FLBLS	10/01-12/01
	Melbourne-Titusville-Palm Bay MSA, FL	H	6.07 FQ	8.90 AW	12.06 TQ	FLBLS	10/01-12/01
	Miami PMSA, FL	H	5.68 FQ	7.82 AW	10.96 TQ	FLBLS	10/01-12/01
	Naples MSA, FL	H	6.12 FQ	8.59 AW	10.77 TQ	FLBLS	10/01-12/01
	Orlando MSA, FL	H	5.94 FQ	8.66 AW	11.00 TQ	FLBLS	10/01-12/01

AAW	Average annual wage	**AOH**	Average offered, high	**ASH**	Average starting, high	**H**	Hourly	**M**	Monthly	**S**	Special: hourly and annual
AE	Average entry wage	**AOL**	Average offered, low	**ASL**	Average starting, low	**HI**	Highest wage paid	**MTC**	Median total compensation	**TQ**	Third quartile wage
AEX	Average experienced wage	**APH**	Average pay, high range	**AW**	Average wage paid	**HR**	High end range	**MW**	Median wage paid	**W**	Weekly
AO	Average offered	**APL**	Average pay, low range	**FQ**	First quartile wage	**LR**	Low end range	**SQ**	Second quartile wage	**Y**	Yearly

Occupation/Type/Industry	Location	Per	Low	Mid	High	Source	Date
Meat, Poultry, and Fish Cutter and Trimmer	Pensacola MSA, FL	H	5.95 FQ	7.88 AW	10.05 TQ	FLBLS	10/01-12/01
	Sarasota-Bradenton MSA, FL	H	5.67 FQ	8.57 AW	11.45 TQ	FLBLS	10/01-12/01
	Tampa-St. Petersburg-Clearwater MSA, FL	H	5.61 FQ	7.36 AW	10.49 TQ	FLBLS	10/01-12/01
	West Palm Beach-Boca Raton MSA, FL	H	6.21 FQ	8.66 AW	10.97 TQ	FLBLS	10/01-12/01
	Georgia	H	6.23 FQ	8.17 AW	10.60 TQ	GABLS	10/01-12/01
	Atlanta MSA, GA	H	6.95 FQ	8.82 AW	11.00 TQ	GABLS	10/01-12/01
	Macon MSA, GA	H	7.27 FQ	7.99 AW	8.95 TQ	GABLS	10/01-12/01
	Hawaii	H	6.86 FQ	12.21 AW	16.72 TQ	HIBLS	10/01-12/01
	Honolulu MSA, HI	H	6.55 FQ	12.07 AW	16.69 TQ	HIBLS	10/01-12/01
	Idaho	H	5.85 FQ	8.36 AW	10.97 TQ	IDBLS	10/01-12/01
	Illinois	H	7.08 FQ	8.95 AW	12.13 TQ	ILBLS	10/01-12/01
	Chicago PMSA, IL	H	7.16 FQ	8.98 AW	12.18 TQ	ILBLS	10/01-12/01
	Peoria-Pekin MSA, IL	H	5.86 FQ	8.46 AW	11.18 TQ	ILBLS	10/01-12/01
	Indiana	H	7.03 FQ	8.54 AW	10.91 TQ	INBLS	10/01-12/01
	Gary PMSA, IN	H	6.09 FQ	8.68 AW	12.52 TQ	INBLS	10/01-12/01
	Indianapolis MSA, IN	H	6.12 FQ	9.10 AW	12.56 TQ	INBLS	10/01-12/01
	Iowa	H	7.23 FQ	10.92 AW	15.71 TQ	IABLS	10/01-12/01
	Davenport-Moline-Rock Island MSA, IA-IL	H	7.09 FQ	8.86 AW	11.90 TQ	IABLS	10/01-12/01
	Kansas	H	8.54 FQ	10.55 AW	13.57 TQ	KSBLS	10/01-12/01
	Wichita MSA, KS	H	7.30 FQ	9.28 AW	11.78 TQ	KSBLS	10/01-12/01
	Kentucky	H	7.34 FQ	8.81 AW	10.93 TQ	KYBLS	10/01-12/01
	Louisiana	H	5.87 FQ	8.01 AW	10.76 TQ	LABLS	10/01-12/01
	Baton Rouge MSA, LA	H	5.50 FQ	7.66 AW	11.83 TQ	LABLS	10/01-12/01
	Houma MSA, LA	H	5.54 FQ	6.78 AW	9.18 TQ	LABLS	10/01-12/01
	Lafayette MSA, LA	H	5.72 FQ	7.17 AW	9.83 TQ	LABLS	10/01-12/01
	Lake Charles MSA, LA	H	5.54 FQ	7.86 AW	11.11 TQ	LABLS	10/01-12/01
	New Orleans MSA, LA	H	5.81 FQ	8.99 AW	12.72 TQ	LABLS	10/01-12/01
	Shreveport-Bossier City MSA, LA	H	6.31 FQ	8.44 AW	10.96 TQ	LABLS	10/01-12/01
	Maine	H	6.87 FQ	9.14 AW	12.18 TQ	MEBLS	10/01-12/01
	Portland MSA, ME	H	7.93 FQ	9.87 AW	12.21 TQ	MEBLS	10/01-12/01
	Maryland	H	6.07 FQ	8.30 AW	11.28 TQ	MDBLS	10/01-12/01
	Baltimore PMSA, MD	H	6.00 FQ	9.31 AW	13.95 TQ	MDBLS	10/01-12/01
	Massachusetts	H	7.33 FQ	11.39 AW	17.77 TQ	MABLS	10/01-12/01
	Boston PMSA, MA-NH	H	7.44 FQ	11.07 AW	17.35 TQ	MABLS	10/01-12/01
	New Bedford PMSA, MA	H	7.36 FQ	12.05 AW	19.10 TQ	MABLS	10/01-12/01
	Springfield MSA, MA	H	6.92 FQ	10.51 AW	15.90 TQ	MABLS	10/01-12/01
	Michigan	H	6.35 FQ	9.24 AW	11.32 TQ	MIBLS	10/01-12/01
	Detroit PMSA, MI	H	6.32 FQ	9.20 AW	11.25 TQ	MIBLS	10/01-12/01
	Minnesota	H	7.29 FQ	9.81 AW	13.02 TQ	MNBLS	10/01-12/01
	Minneapolis-St. Paul MSA, MN-WI	H	7.37 FQ	10.02 AW	12.82 TQ	MNBLS	10/01-12/01
	Mississippi	H	6.22 FQ	7.83 AW	9.72 TQ	MSBLS	10/01-12/01
	Biloxi-Gulfport-Pascagoula MSA, MS	H	5.91 FQ	7.40 AW	9.05 TQ	MSBLS	10/01-12/01
	Jackson MSA, MS	H	6.99 FQ	7.80 AW	8.79 TQ	MSBLS	10/01-12/01
	Missouri	H	7.11 FQ	9.12 AW	11.65 TQ	MOBLS	10/01-12/01
	Kansas City MSA, MO-KS	H	5.98 FQ	8.58 AW	12.67 TQ	MOBLS	10/01-12/01
	St. Louis MSA, MO-IL	H	7.19 FQ	9.56 AW	13.51 TQ	MOBLS	10/01-12/01
	Montana	H	7.87 FQ	10.78 AW	13.60 TQ	MTBLS	10/01-12/01
	Billings MSA, MT	H	7.57 FQ	10.93 AW	14.00 TQ	MTBLS	10/01-12/01
	Nebraska	H	6.41 FQ	10.23 AW	13.19 TQ	NEBLS	10/01-12/01
	Omaha MSA, NE-IA	H	6.14 FQ	10.16 AW	13.45 TQ	NEBLS	10/01-12/01
	Nevada	H	7.51 FQ	10.69 AW	13.91 TQ	NVBLS	10/01-12/01
	Las Vegas MSA, NV-AZ	H	7.92 FQ	11.04 AW	14.06 TQ	NVBLS	10/01-12/01
	New Hampshire	H	7.25 FQ	9.28 AW	12.72 TQ	NHBLS	10/01-12/01
	Manchester PMSA, NH	H	7.11 FQ	8.65 AW	11.12 TQ	NHBLS	10/01-12/01
	New Jersey	H	6.78 FQ	10.52 AW	16.31 TQ	NJBLS	10/01-12/01
	Atlantic-Cape May PMSA, NJ	H	6.17 FQ	10.22 AW	13.94 TQ	NJBLS	10/01-12/01
	Bergen-Passaic PMSA, NJ	H	6.69 FQ	14.60 AW	21.07 TQ	NJBLS	10/01-12/01
	Jersey City PMSA, NJ	H	6.10 FQ	9.82 AW	16.40 TQ	NJBLS	10/01-12/01
	Middlesex-Somerset-Hunterdon PMSA, NJ	H	6.64 FQ	9.28 AW	12.87 TQ	NJBLS	10/01-12/01
	Monmouth-Ocean PMSA, NJ	H	7.01 FQ	9.56 AW	13.03 TQ	NJBLS	10/01-12/01
	Newark PMSA, NJ	H	7.76 FQ	11.99 AW	15.91 TQ	NJBLS	10/01-12/01
	Trenton PMSA, NJ	H	9.36 FQ	12.38 AW	16.97 TQ	NJBLS	10/01-12/01
	New Mexico	H	5.78 FQ	7.58 AW	10.92 TQ	NMBLS	10/01-12/01
	New York	H	5.77 FQ	9.15 AW	13.80 TQ	NYBLS	10/01-12/01

AAW	Average annual wage	**AOH**	Average offered, high	**ASH**	Average starting, high	**H**	Hourly	**M**	Monthly	**S**	Special: hourly and annual
AE	Average entry wage	**AOL**	Average offered, low	**ASL**	Average starting, low	**HI**	Highest wage paid	**MTC**	Median total compensation	**TQ**	Third quartile wage
AEX	Average experienced wage	**APH**	Average pay, high range	**AW**	Average wage paid	**HR**	High end range	**MW**	Median wage paid	**W**	Weekly
AO	Average offered	**APL**	Average pay, low range	**FQ**	First quartile wage	**LR**	Low end range	**SQ**	Second quartile wage	**Y**	Yearly

Occupation/Type/Industry	Location	Per	Low	Mid	High	Source	Date
Meat, Poultry, and Fish Cutter and Trimmer	Albany-Schenectady-Troy MSA, NY	H	5.80 FQ	8.08 AW	11.55 TQ	NYBLS	10/01-12/01
	Binghamton MSA, NY	H	6.11 FQ	9.04 AW	14.49 TQ	NYBLS	10/01-12/01
	Buffalo-Niagara Falls MSA, NY	H	5.52 FQ	6.99 AW	9.55 TQ	NYBLS	10/01-12/01
	Nassau-Suffolk PMSA, NY	H	7.51 FQ	11.28 AW	18.92 TQ	NYBLS	10/01-12/01
	New York PMSA, NY	H	6.07 FQ	10.31 AW	15.31 TQ	NYBLS	10/01-12/01
	Newburgh PMSA, NY-PA	H	6.37 FQ	10.21 AW	13.68 TQ	NYBLS	10/01-12/01
	Rochester MSA, NY	H	5.59 FQ	7.47 AW	10.55 TQ	NYBLS	10/01-12/01
	Syracuse MSA, NY	H	5.56 FQ	7.49 AW	11.04 TQ	NYBLS	10/01-12/01
	North Carolina	H	6.52 FQ	8.46 AW	10.66 TQ	NCBLS	10/01-12/01
	Charlotte-Gastonia-Rock Hill MSA, NC-SC	H	7.11 FQ	8.81 AW	10.88 TQ	NCBLS	10/01-12/01
	Greensboro-Winston-Salem-High Point MSA, NC	H	7.09 FQ	8.05 AW	9.39 TQ	NCBLS	10/01-12/01
	Wilmington MSA, NC	H	6.66 FQ	9.67 AW	12.41 TQ	NCBLS	10/01-12/01
	Ohio	H	7.23 FQ	9.68 AW	12.77 TQ	OHBLS	10/01-12/01
	Canton-Massillon MSA, OH	H	7.14 FQ	8.51 AW	10.61 TQ	OHBLS	10/01-12/01
	Cincinnati PMSA, OH-KY-IN	H	7.53 FQ	9.77 AW	13.18 TQ	OHBLS	10/01-12/01
	Cleveland-Lorain-Elyria PMSA, OH	H	7.90 FQ	10.87 AW	13.75 TQ	OHBLS	10/01-12/01
	Columbus MSA, OH	H	7.18 FQ	9.53 AW	13.29 TQ	OHBLS	10/01-12/01
	Dayton-Springfield MSA, OH	H	8.97 FQ	11.14 AW	13.51 TQ	OHBLS	10/01-12/01
	Toledo MSA, OH	H	6.91 FQ	9.18 AW	13.28 TQ	OHBLS	10/01-12/01
	Oklahoma	H	7.28 FQ	9.12 AW	11.61 TQ	OKBLS	10/01-12/01
	Oregon	H	7.31 FQ	11.24 AW	16.84 TQ	ORBLS	10/01-12/01
	Portland-Vancouver PMSA, OR-WA	H	7.68 FQ	12.89 AW	17.26 TQ	ORBLS	10/01-12/01
	Salem PMSA, OR	H	7.61 FQ	13.27 AW	17.48 TQ	ORBLS	10/01-12/01
	Pennsylvania	H	7.70 FQ	10.22 AW	13.02 TQ	PABLS	10/01-12/01
	Allentown-Bethlehem-Easton MSA, PA	H	7.31 FQ	10.09 AW	13.46 TQ	PABLS	10/01-12/01
	Erie MSA, PA	H	8.12 FQ	10.68 AW	13.50 TQ	PABLS	10/01-12/01
	Lancaster MSA, PA	H	7.89 FQ	10.12 AW	12.54 TQ	PABLS	10/01-12/01
	Philadelphia PMSA, PA-NJ	H	7.07 FQ	10.01 AW	13.65 TQ	PABLS	10/01-12/01
	Pittsburgh MSA, PA	H	7.44 FQ	9.79 AW	13.00 TQ	PABLS	10/01-12/01
	Reading MSA, PA	H	7.13 FQ	9.24 AW	11.02 TQ	PABLS	10/01-12/01
	Scranton-Wilkes-Barre-Hazleton MSA, PA	H	7.32 FQ	9.53 AW	12.12 TQ	PABLS	10/01-12/01
	York MSA, PA	H	7.50 FQ	9.79 AW	12.94 TQ	PABLS	10/01-12/01
	Rhode Island	H	8.90 FQ	12.12 AW	17.33 TQ	RIBLS	10/01-12/01
	Providence-Fall River-Warwick MSA, RI-MA	H	7.27 FQ	11.25 AW	16.72 TQ	RIBLS	10/01-12/01
	Greenville-Spartanburg-Anderson MSA, SC	H	6.83 FQ	8.33 AW	10.43 TQ	SCBLS	10/01-12/01
	Myrtle Beach MSA, SC	H	5.71 FQ	7.37 AW	8.73 TQ	SCBLS	10/01-12/01
	Tennessee	H	6.89 FQ	8.61 AW	10.70 TQ	TNBLS	10/01-12/01
	Memphis MSA, TN-AR-MS	H	6.72 FQ	8.77 AW	11.00 TQ	TNBLS	10/01-12/01
	Texas	H	5.96 FQ	8.15 AW	10.95 TQ	TXBLS	10/01-12/01
	Dallas PMSA, TX	H	5.84 FQ	8.27 AW	12.52 TQ	TXBLS	10/01-12/01
	El Paso MSA, TX	H	5.68 FQ	7.52 AW	10.34 TQ	TXBLS	10/01-12/01
	Fort Worth-Arlington PMSA, TX	H	6.82 FQ	11.91 AW	17.02 TQ	TXBLS	10/01-12/01
	Galveston-Texas City PMSA, TX	H	5.75 FQ	7.78 AW	10.05 TQ	TXBLS	10/01-12/01
	Houston PMSA, TX	H	5.92 FQ	8.88 AW	15.59 TQ	TXBLS	10/01-12/01
	Longview-Marshall MSA, TX	H	6.57 FQ	8.30 AW	10.47 TQ	TXBLS	10/01-12/01
	Provo-Orem MSA, UT	H	6.10 FQ	9.52 AW	13.35 TQ	UTBLS	10/01-12/01
	Salt Lake City-Ogden MSA, UT	H	7.61 FQ	10.86 AW	13.70 TQ	UTBLS	10/01-12/01
	Vermont	H	6.61 FQ	8.94 AW	12.77 TQ	VTBLS	10/01-12/01
	Burlington MSA, VT	H	6.55 FQ	9.12 AW	13.83 TQ	VTBLS	10/01-12/01
	Virginia	H	6.66 FQ	8.76 AW	10.62 TQ	VABLS	10/01-12/01
	Norfolk-Virginia Beach-Newport News MSA, VA-NC	H	5.62 FQ	7.03 AW	9.90 TQ	VABLS	10/01-12/01
	Richmond-Petersburg MSA, VA	H	7.44 FQ	9.33 AW	10.67 TQ	VABLS	10/01-12/01
	Washington	H	7.18 FQ	9.53 AW	13.95 TQ	WABLS	10/01-12/01
	Bremerton PMSA, WA	H	8.83 FQ	12.97 AW	16.73 TQ	WABLS	10/01-12/01

AAW Average annual wage **AE** Average entry wage **AEX** Average experienced wage **AO** Average offered **AOH** Average offered, high **AOL** Average offered, low **APH** Average pay, high range **APL** Average pay, low range **ASH** Average starting, high **ASL** Average starting, low **AW** Average wage paid **FQ** First quartile wage **H** Hourly **HI** Highest wage paid **HR** High end range **LR** Low end range **M** Monthly **MTC** Median total compensation **MW** Median wage paid **SQ** Second quartile wage **S** Special: hourly and annual **TQ** Third quartile wage **W** Weekly **Y** Yearly

Occupation/Type/Industry	Location	Per	Low	Mid	High	Source	Date
Meat, Poultry, and Fish Cutter and Trimmer	Seattle-Bellevue-Everett PMSA, WA	H	7.26 FQ	9.58 AW	14.20 TQ	WABLS	10/01-12/01
	Spokane MSA, WA	H	7.46 FQ	11.01 AW	14.01 TQ	WABLS	10/01-12/01
	Tacoma PMSA, WA	H	7.38 FQ	12.97 AW	17.78 TQ	WABLS	10/01-12/01
	West Virginia	H	6.80 FQ	8.42 AW	10.57 TQ	WVBLS	10/01-12/01
	Wisconsin	H	8.14 FQ	11.73 AW	15.94 TQ	WIBLS	10/01-12/01
	Appleton-Oshkosh-Neenah MSA, WI	H	9.10 FQ	13.15 AW	16.39 TQ	WIBLS	10/01-12/01
	Green Bay MSA, WI	H	9.60 FQ	13.30 AW	16.39 TQ	WIBLS	10/01-12/01
	Madison MSA, WI	H	8.73 FQ	11.04 AW	13.49 TQ	WIBLS	10/01-12/01
	Milwaukee-Waukesha PMSA, WI	H	10.24 FQ	13.81 AW	16.93 TQ	WIBLS	10/01-12/01
	Wyoming	H	5.85 FQ	8.07 AW	12.31 TQ	WYBLS	10/01-12/01
Mechanic							
Automotive Body Shop, Collision Repair	United States	Y		40059 AW		BSB	1/01-1/02
Outdoor Power and Small Engine	Alabama	H	7.39 FQ	10.78 AW	15.33 TQ	ALBLS	10/01-12/01
Outdoor Power and Small Engine	Birmingham MSA, AL	H	7.62 FQ	11.63 AW	17.16 TQ	ALBLS	10/01-12/01
Outdoor Power and Small Engine	Huntsville MSA, AL	H	9.19 FQ	12.43 AW	16.93 TQ	ALBLS	10/01-12/01
Outdoor Power and Small Engine	Mobile MSA, AL	H	9.25 FQ	12.89 AW	17.50 TQ	ALBLS	10/01-12/01
Outdoor Power and Small Engine	Montgomery MSA, AL	H	9.15 FQ	11.36 AW	16.19 TQ	ALBLS	10/01-12/01
Outdoor Power and Small Engine	Alaska	H	9.73 FQ	15.85 AW	24.14 TQ	AKBLS	10/01-12/01
Outdoor Power and Small Engine	Anchorage MSA, AK	H	13.46 FQ	19.97 AW	27.77 TQ	AKBLS	10/01-12/01
Outdoor Power and Small Engine	Arizona	H	8.09 FQ	12.51 AW	17.17 TQ	AZBLS	10/01-12/01
Outdoor Power and Small Engine	Phoenix-Mesa MSA, AZ	H	9.95 FQ	13.43 AW	18.06 TQ	AZBLS	10/01-12/01
Outdoor Power and Small Engine	Tucson MSA, AZ	H	6.58 FQ	9.73 AW	12.98 TQ	AZBLS	10/01-12/01
Outdoor Power and Small Engine	Arkansas	H	6.20 FQ	10.54 AW	16.03 TQ	ARBLS	10/01-12/01
Outdoor Power and Small Engine	Fort Smith MSA, AR-OK	H	5.66 FQ	7.27 AW	8.34 TQ	ARBLS	10/01-12/01
Outdoor Power and Small Engine	Little Rock-North Little Rock MSA, AR	H	5.99 FQ	10.29 AW	15.74 TQ	ARBLS	10/01-12/01
Outdoor Power and Small Engine	California	H	8.97 FQ	12.95 AW	17.84 TQ	CABLS	10/01-12/01
Outdoor Power and Small Engine	Bakersfield MSA, CA	H	9.33 FQ	12.67 AW	16.72 TQ	CABLS	10/01-12/01
Outdoor Power and Small Engine	Fresno MSA, CA	H	9.00 FQ	12.16 AW	18.14 TQ	CABLS	10/01-12/01
Outdoor Power and Small Engine	Los Angeles-Long Beach PMSA, CA	H	10.92 FQ	15.57 AW	18.86 TQ	CABLS	10/01-12/01
Outdoor Power and Small Engine	Modesto MSA, CA	H	10.22 FQ	14.24 AW	17.83 TQ	CABLS	10/01-12/01
Outdoor Power and Small Engine	Oakland PMSA, CA	H	6.91 FQ	13.74 AW	22.30 TQ	CABLS	10/01-12/01
Outdoor Power and Small Engine	Orange County PMSA, CA	H	8.80 FQ	11.10 AW	13.27 TQ	CABLS	10/01-12/01
Outdoor Power and Small Engine	Riverside-San Bernardino PMSA, CA	H	7.34 FQ	13.01 AW	19.74 TQ	CABLS	10/01-12/01
Outdoor Power and Small Engine	Sacramento PMSA, CA	H	9.60 FQ	13.85 AW	19.59 TQ	CABLS	10/01-12/01
Outdoor Power and Small Engine	San Diego MSA, CA	H	10.84 FQ	13.50 AW	16.81 TQ	CABLS	10/01-12/01
Outdoor Power and Small Engine	San Francisco PMSA, CA	H	10.57 FQ	14.92 AW	17.02 TQ	CABLS	10/01-12/01
Outdoor Power and Small Engine	San Jose PMSA, CA	H	9.96 FQ	13.06 AW	16.54 TQ	CABLS	10/01-12/01
Outdoor Power and Small Engine	Santa Rosa PMSA, CA	H	11.91 FQ	14.96 AW	17.52 TQ	CABLS	10/01-12/01
Outdoor Power and Small Engine	Stockton-Lodi MSA, CA	H	9.60 FQ	13.74 AW	20.53 TQ	CABLS	10/01-12/01
Outdoor Power and Small Engine	Colorado	H	7.55 FQ	12.08 AW	17.76 TQ	COBLS	10/01-12/01
Outdoor Power and Small Engine	Boulder-Longmont PMSA, CO	H	6.96 FQ	12.01 AW	18.08 TQ	COBLS	10/01-12/01
Outdoor Power and Small Engine	Colorado Springs MSA, CO	H	7.09 FQ	10.53 AW	16.77 TQ	COBLS	10/01-12/01
Outdoor Power and Small Engine	Denver PMSA, CO	H	7.75 FQ	11.85 AW	17.34 TQ	COBLS	10/01-12/01
Outdoor Power and Small Engine	Connecticut	H	8.86 FQ	14.44 AW	19.38 TQ	CTBLS	10/01-12/01
Outdoor Power and Small Engine	Bridgeport PMSA, CT	H	7.66 FQ	13.51 AW	17.31 TQ	CTBLS	10/01-12/01
Outdoor Power and Small Engine	Danbury PMSA, CT	H	11.78 FQ	17.02 AW	21.45 TQ	CTBLS	10/01-12/01
Outdoor Power and Small Engine	Hartford MSA, CT	H	9.39 FQ	13.82 AW	17.13 TQ	CTBLS	10/01-12/01
Outdoor Power and Small Engine	New Haven-Meriden PMSA, CT	H	11.12 FQ	14.42 AW	18.44 TQ	CTBLS	10/01-12/01
Outdoor Power and Small Engine	Delaware	H	8.88 FQ	13.64 AW	19.88 TQ	DEBLS	10/01-12/01
Outdoor Power and Small Engine	Wilmington-Newark PMSA, DE-MD	H	9.36 FQ	13.94 AW	20.46 TQ	DEBLS	10/01-12/01
Outdoor Power and Small Engine	Washington PMSA, DC-MD-VA-WV	H	7.73 FQ	12.56 AW	18.09 TQ	DCBLS	10/01-12/01
Outdoor Power and Small Engine	Florida	H	8.71 FQ	13.51 AW	18.92 TQ	FLBLS	10/01-12/01
Outdoor Power and Small Engine	Fort Lauderdale PMSA, FL	H	8.16 FQ	17.55 AW	31.21 TQ	FLBLS	10/01-12/01
Outdoor Power and Small Engine	Fort Myers-Cape Coral MSA, FL	H	9.91 FQ	12.87 AW	16.65 TQ	FLBLS	10/01-12/01
Outdoor Power and Small Engine	Fort Pierce-Port St. Lucie MSA, FL	H	6.61 FQ	13.51 AW	20.25 TQ	FLBLS	10/01-12/01
Outdoor Power and Small Engine	Jacksonville MSA, FL	H	7.59 FQ	11.63 AW	17.28 TQ	FLBLS	10/01-12/01
Outdoor Power and Small Engine	Lakeland-Winter Haven MSA, FL	H	9.29 FQ	12.51 AW	17.85 TQ	FLBLS	10/01-12/01
Outdoor Power and Small Engine	Miami PMSA, FL	H	10.73 FQ	14.22 AW	17.38 TQ	FLBLS	10/01-12/01

AAW	Average annual wage	**AOH**	Average offered, high	**ASH**	Average starting, high	**H**	Hourly	**M**	Monthly	**S**	Special: hourly and annual
AE	Average entry wage	**AOL**	Average offered, low	**ASL**	Average starting, low	**HI**	Highest wage paid	**MTC**	Median total compensation	**TQ**	Third quartile wage
AEX	Average experienced wage	**APH**	Average pay, high range	**AW**	Average wage paid	**HR**	High end range	**MW**	Median wage paid	**W**	Weekly
AO	Average offered	**APL**	Average pay, low range	**FQ**	First quartile wage	**LR**	Low end range	**SQ**	Second quartile wage	**Y**	Yearly

Occupation/Type/Industry	Location	Per	Low	Mid	High	Source	Date
Mechanic							
Outdoor Power and Small Engine	Naples MSA, FL	H	11.25 FQ	14.52 AW	19.97 TQ	FLBLS	10/01-12/01
Outdoor Power and Small Engine	Ocala MSA, FL	H	9.13 FQ	12.16 AW	16.70 TQ	FLBLS	10/01-12/01
Outdoor Power and Small Engine	Orlando MSA, FL	H	7.97 FQ	14.76 AW	27.04 TQ	FLBLS	10/01-12/01
Outdoor Power and Small Engine	Pensacola MSA, FL	H	8.91 FQ	12.27 AW	17.53 TQ	FLBLS	10/01-12/01
Outdoor Power and Small Engine	Sarasota-Bradenton MSA, FL	H	9.68 FQ	13.17 AW	17.29 TQ	FLBLS	10/01-12/01
Outdoor Power and Small Engine	Tampa-St. Petersburg-Clearwater MSA, FL	H	9.01 FQ	12.01 AW	16.66 TQ	FLBLS	10/01-12/01
Outdoor Power and Small Engine	West Palm Beach-Boca Raton MSA, FL	H	7.95 FQ	12.82 AW	17.56 TQ	FLBLS	10/01-12/01
Outdoor Power and Small Engine	Georgia	H	7.92 FQ	12.56 AW	18.50 TQ	GABLS	10/01-12/01
Outdoor Power and Small Engine	Atlanta MSA, GA	H	8.88 FQ	13.93 AW	20.47 TQ	GABLS	10/01-12/01
Outdoor Power and Small Engine	Macon MSA, GA	H	7.47 FQ	12.04 AW	18.89 TQ	GABLS	10/01-12/01
Outdoor Power and Small Engine	Hawaii	H	9.98 FQ	15.44 AW	20.94 TQ	HIBLS	10/01-12/01
Outdoor Power and Small Engine	Honolulu MSA, HI	H	10.89 FQ	16.15 AW	21.68 TQ	HIBLS	10/01-12/01
Outdoor Power and Small Engine	Idaho	H	5.91 FQ	10.77 AW	16.19 TQ	IDBLS	10/01-12/01
Outdoor Power and Small Engine	Boise City MSA, ID	H	5.77 FQ	10.41 AW	16.32 TQ	IDBLS	10/01-12/01
Outdoor Power and Small Engine	Illinois	H	7.27 FQ	13.08 AW	20.83 TQ	ILBLS	10/01-12/01
Outdoor Power and Small Engine	Chicago PMSA, IL	H	10.19 FQ	14.15 AW	20.98 TQ	ILBLS	10/01-12/01
Outdoor Power and Small Engine	Peoria-Pekin MSA, IL	H	7.89 FQ	12.00 AW	19.22 TQ	ILBLS	10/01-12/01
Outdoor Power and Small Engine	Rockford MSA, IL	H	7.66 FQ	12.57 AW	20.24 TQ	ILBLS	10/01-12/01
Outdoor Power and Small Engine	Indiana	H	8.22 FQ	12.35 AW	18.28 TQ	INBLS	10/01-12/01
Outdoor Power and Small Engine	Fort Wayne MSA, IN	H	6.79 FQ	13.39 AW	20.19 TQ	INBLS	10/01-12/01
Outdoor Power and Small Engine	Gary PMSA, IN	H	9.58 FQ	15.31 AW	20.57 TQ	INBLS	10/01-12/01
Outdoor Power and Small Engine	Indianapolis MSA, IN	H	9.18 FQ	13.24 AW	18.95 TQ	INBLS	10/01-12/01
Outdoor Power and Small Engine	Iowa	H	6.61 FQ	9.97 AW	14.16 TQ	IABLS	10/01-12/01
Outdoor Power and Small Engine	Davenport-Moline-Rock Island MSA, IA-IL	H	7.73 FQ	16.95 AW	27.58 TQ	IABLS	10/01-12/01
Outdoor Power and Small Engine	Des Moines MSA, IA	H	6.09 FQ	11.47 AW	16.50 TQ	IABLS	10/01-12/01
Outdoor Power and Small Engine	Kansas	H	6.39 FQ	10.91 AW	16.78 TQ	KSBLS	10/01-12/01
Outdoor Power and Small Engine	Wichita MSA, KS	H	8.60 FQ	9.63 AW	10.69 TQ	KSBLS	10/01-12/01
Outdoor Power and Small Engine	Kentucky	H	6.35 FQ	10.01 AW	15.20 TQ	KYBLS	10/01-12/01
Outdoor Power and Small Engine	Lexington MSA, KY	H	7.23 FQ	11.79 AW	18.55 TQ	KYBLS	10/01-12/01
Outdoor Power and Small Engine	Louisville MSA, KY-IN	H	8.79 FQ	12.57 AW	17.50 TQ	KYBLS	10/01-12/01
Outdoor Power and Small Engine	Louisiana	H	6.50 FQ	9.97 AW	14.65 TQ	LABLS	10/01-12/01
Outdoor Power and Small Engine	Baton Rouge MSA, LA	H	7.34 FQ	10.94 AW	16.52 TQ	LABLS	10/01-12/01
Outdoor Power and Small Engine	Houma MSA, LA	H	7.51 FQ	10.41 AW	16.37 TQ	LABLS	10/01-12/01
Outdoor Power and Small Engine	Lafayette MSA, LA	H	5.75 FQ	9.69 AW	14.53 TQ	LABLS	10/01-12/01
Outdoor Power and Small Engine	New Orleans MSA, LA	H	7.04 FQ	9.30 AW	12.98 TQ	LABLS	10/01-12/01
Outdoor Power and Small Engine	Maine	H	7.93 FQ	11.41 AW	14.87 TQ	MEBLS	10/01-12/01
Outdoor Power and Small Engine	Portland MSA, ME	H	9.59 FQ	12.51 AW	16.62 TQ	MEBLS	10/01-12/01
Outdoor Power and Small Engine	Maryland	H	8.12 FQ	13.40 AW	19.23 TQ	MDBLS	10/01-12/01
Outdoor Power and Small Engine	Baltimore PMSA, MD	H	9.33 FQ	14.48 AW	20.78 TQ	MDBLS	10/01-12/01
Outdoor Power and Small Engine	Massachusetts	H	9.28 FQ	13.62 AW	18.50 TQ	MABLS	10/01-12/01
Outdoor Power and Small Engine	Boston PMSA, MA-NH	H	10.33 FQ	15.41 AW	20.26 TQ	MABLS	10/01-12/01
Outdoor Power and Small Engine	Lawrence PMSA, MA-NH	H	9.63 FQ	14.69 AW	21.86 TQ	MABLS	10/01-12/01
Outdoor Power and Small Engine	Springfield MSA, MA	H	9.33 FQ	13.03 AW	17.35 TQ	MABLS	10/01-12/01
Outdoor Power and Small Engine	Worcester PMSA, MA-CT	H	9.54 FQ	13.56 AW	19.06 TQ	MABLS	10/01-12/01
Outdoor Power and Small Engine	Michigan	H	7.03 FQ	13.11 AW	19.46 TQ	MIBLS	10/01-12/01
Outdoor Power and Small Engine	Ann Arbor PMSA, MI	H	7.87 FQ	12.77 AW	17.52 TQ	MIBLS	10/01-12/01
Outdoor Power and Small Engine	Detroit PMSA, MI	H	10.24 FQ	16.28 AW	23.85 TQ	MIBLS	10/01-12/01
Outdoor Power and Small Engine	Flint PMSA, MI	H	7.94 FQ	12.03 AW	18.07 TQ	MIBLS	10/01-12/01
Outdoor Power and Small Engine	Grand Rapids-Muskegon-Holland MSA, MI	H	9.12 FQ	14.53 AW	21.97 TQ	MIBLS	10/01-12/01
Outdoor Power and Small Engine	Kalamazoo-Battle Creek MSA, MI	H	7.82 FQ	12.03 AW	16.60 TQ	MIBLS	10/01-12/01
Outdoor Power and Small Engine	Lansing-East Lansing MSA, MI	H	8.43 FQ	14.71 AW	19.55 TQ	MIBLS	10/01-12/01
Outdoor Power and Small Engine	Minnesota	H	8.29 FQ	13.10 AW	18.19 TQ	MNBLS	10/01-12/01
Outdoor Power and Small Engine	Minneapolis-St. Paul MSA, MN-WI	H	9.73 FQ	14.38 AW	19.47 TQ	MNBLS	10/01-12/01
Outdoor Power and Small Engine	St. Cloud MSA, MN	H	9.61 FQ	13.15 AW	19.04 TQ	MNBLS	10/01-12/01
Outdoor Power and Small Engine	Mississippi	H	6.31 FQ	10.30 AW	13.65 TQ	MSBLS	10/01-12/01
Outdoor Power and Small Engine	Biloxi-Gulfport-Pascagoula MSA, MS	H	8.17 FQ	11.50 AW	14.22 TQ	MSBLS	10/01-12/01
Outdoor Power and Small Engine	Missouri	H	7.06 FQ	11.71 AW	16.28 TQ	MOBLS	10/01-12/01
Outdoor Power and Small Engine	Kansas City MSA, MO-KS	H	6.49 FQ	11.89 AW	18.13 TQ	MOBLS	10/01-12/01
Outdoor Power and Small Engine	St. Louis MSA, MO-IL	H	7.18 FQ	12.00 AW	17.28 TQ	MOBLS	10/01-12/01
Outdoor Power and Small Engine	Montana	H	6.89 FQ	10.28 AW	14.76 TQ	MTBLS	10/01-12/01
Outdoor Power and Small Engine	Nebraska	H	7.25 FQ	11.31 AW	15.67 TQ	NEBLS	10/01-12/01
Outdoor Power and Small Engine	Lincoln MSA, NE	H	9.52 FQ	12.95 AW	16.65 TQ	NEBLS	10/01-12/01
Outdoor Power and Small Engine	Omaha MSA, NE-IA	H	7.44 FQ	10.81 AW	14.84 TQ	NEBLS	10/01-12/01
Outdoor Power and Small Engine	Nevada	H	9.13 FQ	12.84 AW	18.19 TQ	NVBLS	10/01-12/01

AAW Average annual wage **AE** Average entry wage **AEX** Average experienced wage **AO** Average offered **AOH** Average offered, high **AOL** Average offered, low **APH** Average pay, high range **APL** Average pay, low range **ASH** Average starting, high **ASL** Average starting, low **AW** Average wage paid **FQ** First quartile wage **H** Hourly **HI** Highest wage paid **HR** High end range **LR** Low end range **M** Monthly **MTC** Median total compensation **MW** Median wage paid **SQ** Second quartile wage **S** Special: hourly and annual **TQ** Third quartile wage **W** Weekly **Y** Yearly

Occupation/Type/Industry	Location	Per	Low	Mid	High	Source	Date
Mechanic							
Outdoor Power and Small Engine	Las Vegas MSA, NV-AZ	H	9.19 FQ	12.38 AW	17.43 TQ	NVBLS	10/01-12/01
Outdoor Power and Small Engine	Reno MSA, NV	H	8.32 FQ	13.86 AW	19.95 TQ	NVBLS	10/01-12/01
Outdoor Power and Small Engine	New Hampshire	H	9.74 FQ	13.73 AW	18.95 TQ	NHBLS	10/01-12/01
Outdoor Power and Small Engine	Manchester PMSA, NH	H	11.66 FQ	14.44 AW	17.20 TQ	NHBLS	10/01-12/01
Outdoor Power and Small Engine	Nashua PMSA, NH	H	9.99 FQ	13.46 AW	17.66 TQ	NHBLS	10/01-12/01
Outdoor Power and Small Engine	Portsmouth-Rochester PMSA, NH-ME	H	10.66 FQ	14.59 AW	20.17 TQ	NHBLS	10/01-12/01
Outdoor Power and Small Engine	New Jersey	H	11.11 FQ	16.10 AW	22.85 TQ	NJBLS	10/01-12/01
Outdoor Power and Small Engine	Bergen-Passaic PMSA, NJ	H	11.24 FQ	13.75 AW	20.11 TQ	NJBLS	10/01-12/01
Outdoor Power and Small Engine	Middlesex-Somerset-Hunterdon PMSA, NJ	H	11.62 FQ	17.22 AW	23.98 TQ	NJBLS	10/01-12/01
Outdoor Power and Small Engine	Monmouth-Ocean PMSA, NJ	H	11.35 FQ	15.87 AW	20.72 TQ	NJBLS	10/01-12/01
Outdoor Power and Small Engine	Newark PMSA, NJ	H	11.69 FQ	17.15 AW	24.61 TQ	NJBLS	10/01-12/01
Outdoor Power and Small Engine	New Mexico	H	7.85 FQ	11.84 AW	16.65 TQ	NMBLS	10/01-12/01
Outdoor Power and Small Engine	Albuquerque MSA, NM	H	9.40 FQ	12.06 AW	16.23 TQ	NMBLS	10/01-12/01
Outdoor Power and Small Engine	New York	H	7.38 FQ	12.32 AW	18.48 TQ	NYBLS	10/01-12/01
Outdoor Power and Small Engine	Albany-Schenectady-Troy MSA, NY	H	7.61 FQ	11.90 AW	16.73 TQ	NYBLS	10/01-12/01
Outdoor Power and Small Engine	Binghamton MSA, NY	H	6.05 FQ	8.84 AW	14.24 TQ	NYBLS	10/01-12/01
Outdoor Power and Small Engine	Buffalo-Niagara Falls MSA, NY	H	8.45 FQ	11.88 AW	15.70 TQ	NYBLS	10/01-12/01
Outdoor Power and Small Engine	Dutchess County PMSA, NY	H	7.90 FQ	13.39 AW	20.78 TQ	NYBLS	10/01-12/01
Outdoor Power and Small Engine	Nassau-Suffolk PMSA, NY	H	6.20 FQ	11.55 AW	18.10 TQ	NYBLS	10/01-12/01
Outdoor Power and Small Engine	New York PMSA, NY	H	9.12 FQ	13.87 AW	21.04 TQ	NYBLS	10/01-12/01
Outdoor Power and Small Engine	Rochester MSA, NY	H	6.15 FQ	12.09 AW	17.17 TQ	NYBLS	10/01-12/01
Outdoor Power and Small Engine	North Carolina	H	6.32 FQ	11.08 AW	17.22 TQ	NCBLS	10/01-12/01
Outdoor Power and Small Engine	Charlotte-Gastonia-Rock Hill MSA, NC-SC	H	8.73 FQ	12.23 AW	18.13 TQ	NCBLS	10/01-12/01
Outdoor Power and Small Engine	Fayetteville MSA, NC	H	5.74 FQ	6.51 AW	7.22 TQ	NCBLS	10/01-12/01
Outdoor Power and Small Engine	Greensboro-Winston-Salem-High Point MSA, NC	H	9.83 FQ	14.11 AW	21.06 TQ	NCBLS	10/01-12/01
Outdoor Power and Small Engine	Raleigh-Durham-Chapel Hill MSA, NC	H	9.29 FQ	12.95 AW	16.83 TQ	NCBLS	10/01-12/01
Outdoor Power and Small Engine	North Dakota	H	6.75 FQ	10.98 AW	15.14 TQ	NDBLS	10/01-12/01
Outdoor Power and Small Engine	Ohio	H	8.05 FQ	12.46 AW	17.16 TQ	OHBLS	10/01-12/01
Outdoor Power and Small Engine	Akron PMSA, OH	H	9.30 FQ	13.55 AW	21.55 TQ	OHBLS	10/01-12/01
Outdoor Power and Small Engine	Canton-Massillon MSA, OH	H	8.00 FQ	12.86 AW	19.16 TQ	OHBLS	10/01-12/01
Outdoor Power and Small Engine	Cincinnati PMSA, OH-KY-IN	H	8.03 FQ	11.98 AW	16.22 TQ	OHBLS	10/01-12/01
Outdoor Power and Small Engine	Cleveland-Lorain-Elyria PMSA, OH	H	10.05 FQ	13.65 AW	17.24 TQ	OHBLS	10/01-12/01
Outdoor Power and Small Engine	Columbus MSA, OH	H	7.93 FQ	13.84 AW	21.21 TQ	OHBLS	10/01-12/01
Outdoor Power and Small Engine	Dayton-Springfield MSA, OH	H	8.94 FQ	12.09 AW	16.98 TQ	OHBLS	10/01-12/01
Outdoor Power and Small Engine	Toledo MSA, OH	H	8.17 FQ	11.29 AW	13.92 TQ	OHBLS	10/01-12/01
Outdoor Power and Small Engine	Youngstown-Warren MSA, OH	H	7.74 FQ	12.78 AW	19.77 TQ	OHBLS	10/01-12/01
Outdoor Power and Small Engine	Oklahoma	H	5.38 FQ	7.84 AW	13.22 TQ	OKBLS	10/01-12/01
Outdoor Power and Small Engine	Oklahoma City MSA, OK	H	5.34 FQ	6.78 AW	9.76 TQ	OKBLS	10/01-12/01
Outdoor Power and Small Engine	Tulsa MSA, OK	H	9.56 FQ	14.53 AW	20.10 TQ	OKBLS	10/01-12/01
Outdoor Power and Small Engine	Oregon	H	9.05 FQ	13.15 AW	17.60 TQ	ORBLS	10/01-12/01
Outdoor Power and Small Engine	Portland-Vancouver PMSA, OR-WA	H	8.98 FQ	13.23 AW	19.46 TQ	ORBLS	10/01-12/01
Outdoor Power and Small Engine	Salem PMSA, OR	H	10.78 FQ	12.92 AW	16.70 TQ	ORBLS	10/01-12/01
Outdoor Power and Small Engine	Pennsylvania	H	6.33 FQ	11.91 AW	21.12 TQ	PABLS	10/01-12/01
Outdoor Power and Small Engine	Harrisburg-Lebanon-Carlisle MSA, PA	H	9.22 FQ	14.12 AW	18.25 TQ	PABLS	10/01-12/01
Outdoor Power and Small Engine	Johnstown MSA, PA	H	6.74 FQ	10.27 AW	15.62 TQ	PABLS	10/01-12/01
Outdoor Power and Small Engine	Lancaster MSA, PA	H	9.03 FQ	11.72 AW	14.39 TQ	PABLS	10/01-12/01
Outdoor Power and Small Engine	Philadelphia PMSA, PA-NJ	H	6.30 FQ	15.39 AW	24.95 TQ	PABLS	10/01-12/01
Outdoor Power and Small Engine	Pittsburgh MSA, PA	H	7.76 FQ	13.28 AW	20.65 TQ	PABLS	10/01-12/01
Outdoor Power and Small Engine	Reading MSA, PA	H	6.80 FQ	9.40 AW	13.07 TQ	PABLS	10/01-12/01
Outdoor Power and Small Engine	Scranton-Wilkes-Barre-Hazleton MSA, PA	H	7.77 FQ	11.61 AW	20.16 TQ	PABLS	10/01-12/01
Outdoor Power and Small Engine	York MSA, PA	H	7.42 FQ	11.44 AW	14.02 TQ	PABLS	10/01-12/01
Outdoor Power and Small Engine	Rhode Island	H	7.53 FQ	13.27 AW	20.06 TQ	RIBLS	10/01-12/01
Outdoor Power and Small Engine	Providence-Fall River-Warwick MSA, RI-MA	H	7.55 FQ	13.18 AW	20.09 TQ	RIBLS	10/01-12/01
Outdoor Power and Small Engine	South Carolina	H	6.23 FQ	10.25 AW	14.83 TQ	SCBLS	10/01-12/01
Outdoor Power and Small Engine	Charleston-North Charleston MSA, SC	H	7.85 FQ	13.18 AW	17.57 TQ	SCBLS	10/01-12/01
Outdoor Power and Small Engine	Columbia MSA, SC	H	8.63 FQ	12.14 AW	17.09 TQ	SCBLS	10/01-12/01
Outdoor Power and Small Engine	Greenville-Spartanburg-Anderson MSA, SC	H	5.65 FQ	8.27 AW	12.88 TQ	SCBLS	10/01-12/01

AAW	Average annual wage	AOH	Average offered, high	ASH	Average starting, high	H	Hourly	M	Monthly	S	Special: hourly and annual
AE	Average entry wage	AOL	Average offered, low	ASL	Average starting, low	HI	Highest wage paid	MTC	Median total compensation	TQ	Third quartile wage
AEX	Average experienced wage	APH	Average pay, high range	AW	Average wage paid	HR	High end range	MW	Median wage paid	W	Weekly
AO	Average offered	APL	Average pay, low range	FQ	First quartile wage	LR	Low end range	SQ	Second quartile wage	Y	Yearly

Occupation/Type/Industry	Location	Per	Low	Mid	High	Source	Date
Mechanic							
Outdoor Power and Small Engine	Myrtle Beach MSA, SC	H	8.61 FQ	10.81 AW	13.48 TQ	SCBLS	10/01-12/01
Outdoor Power and Small Engine	South Dakota	H	7.10 FQ	9.49 AW	13.66 TQ	SDBLS	10/01-12/01
Outdoor Power and Small Engine	Tennessee	H	7.71 FQ	11.41 AW	15.44 TQ	TNBLS	10/01-12/01
Outdoor Power and Small Engine	Chattanooga MSA, TN-GA	H	8.31 FQ	11.30 AW	14.65 TQ	TNBLS	10/01-12/01
Outdoor Power and Small Engine	Johnson City-Kingsport-Bristol MSA, TN-VA	H	6.38 FQ	10.39 AW	15.58 TQ	TNBLS	10/01-12/01
Outdoor Power and Small Engine	Knoxville MSA, TN	H	7.08 FQ	8.10 AW	9.56 TQ	TNBLS	10/01-12/01
Outdoor Power and Small Engine	Memphis MSA, TN-AR-MS	H	9.43 FQ	11.84 AW	15.38 TQ	TNBLS	10/01-12/01
Outdoor Power and Small Engine	Nashville MSA, TN	H	11.38 FQ	13.50 AW	17.41 TQ	TNBLS	10/01-12/01
Outdoor Power and Small Engine	Texas	H	7.49 FQ	11.73 AW	16.88 TQ	TXBLS	10/01-12/01
Outdoor Power and Small Engine	Austin-San Marcos MSA, TX	H	7.75 FQ	11.44 AW	16.95 TQ	TXBLS	10/01-12/01
Outdoor Power and Small Engine	Dallas PMSA, TX	H	7.53 FQ	11.67 AW	16.84 TQ	TXBLS	10/01-12/01
Outdoor Power and Small Engine	El Paso MSA, TX	H	6.19 FQ	11.59 AW	19.80 TQ	TXBLS	10/01-12/01
Outdoor Power and Small Engine	Fort Worth-Arlington PMSA, TX	H	9.54 FQ	13.32 AW	17.16 TQ	TXBLS	10/01-12/01
Outdoor Power and Small Engine	Houston PMSA, TX	H	7.54 FQ	10.23 AW	13.10 TQ	TXBLS	10/01-12/01
Outdoor Power and Small Engine	McAllen-Edinburg-Mission MSA, TX	H	6.42 FQ	12.11 AW	17.31 TQ	TXBLS	10/01-12/01
Outdoor Power and Small Engine	San Antonio MSA, TX	H	9.49 FQ	15.77 AW	31.13 TQ	TXBLS	10/01-12/01
Outdoor Power and Small Engine	Utah	H	7.16 FQ	10.82 AW	16.06 TQ	UTBLS	10/01-12/01
Outdoor Power and Small Engine	Salt Lake City-Ogden MSA, UT	H	7.47 FQ	11.03 AW	16.31 TQ	UTBLS	10/01-12/01
Outdoor Power and Small Engine	Vermont	H	9.01 FQ	11.83 AW	15.63 TQ	VTBLS	10/01-12/01
Outdoor Power and Small Engine	Burlington MSA, VT	H	9.51 FQ	12.80 AW	16.49 TQ	VTBLS	10/01-12/01
Outdoor Power and Small Engine	Virginia	H	8.00 FQ	11.73 AW	16.16 TQ	VABLS	10/01-12/01
Outdoor Power and Small Engine	Lynchburg MSA, VA	H	7.63 FQ	11.20 AW	15.42 TQ	VABLS	10/01-12/01
Outdoor Power and Small Engine	Norfolk-Virginia Beach-Newport News MSA, VA-NC	H	8.53 FQ	11.32 AW	14.81 TQ	VABLS	10/01-12/01
Outdoor Power and Small Engine	Richmond-Petersburg MSA, VA	H	8.64 FQ	12.16 AW	16.86 TQ	VABLS	10/01-12/01
Outdoor Power and Small Engine	Washington	H	9.24 FQ	12.97 AW	17.32 TQ	WABLS	10/01-12/01
Outdoor Power and Small Engine	Olympia PMSA, WA	H	9.35 FQ	12.83 AW	17.34 TQ	WABLS	10/01-12/01
Outdoor Power and Small Engine	Seattle-Bellevue-Everett PMSA, WA	H	10.91 FQ	12.98 AW	16.73 TQ	WABLS	10/01-12/01
Outdoor Power and Small Engine	Spokane MSA, WA	H	9.18 FQ	13.95 AW	19.44 TQ	WABLS	10/01-12/01
Outdoor Power and Small Engine	Tacoma PMSA, WA	H	7.79 FQ	11.96 AW	17.48 TQ	WABLS	10/01-12/01
Outdoor Power and Small Engine	Yakima MSA, WA	H	9.51 FQ	12.52 AW	16.14 TQ	WABLS	10/01-12/01
Outdoor Power and Small Engine	West Virginia	H	6.52 FQ	10.09 AW	14.91 TQ	WVBLS	10/01-12/01
Outdoor Power and Small Engine	Huntington-Ashland MSA, WV-KY-OH	H	5.84 FQ	9.29 AW	13.95 TQ	WVBLS	10/01-12/01
Outdoor Power and Small Engine	Wisconsin	H	7.98 FQ	12.66 AW	17.10 TQ	WIBLS	10/01-12/01
Outdoor Power and Small Engine	Green Bay MSA, WI	H	8.46 FQ	12.60 AW	17.48 TQ	WIBLS	10/01-12/01
Outdoor Power and Small Engine	Milwaukee-Waukesha PMSA, WI	H	7.76 FQ	13.19 AW	17.73 TQ	WIBLS	10/01-12/01
Outdoor Power and Small Engine	Wyoming	H	7.52 FQ	11.06 AW	18.92 TQ	WYBLS	10/01-12/01
Outdoor Power and Small Engine	Puerto Rico	H	6.43 FQ	10.95 AW	16.62 TQ	PRBLS	10/01-12/01
Mechanical Door Repairer	Arkansas	H	6.55 FQ	10.34 AW	15.26 TQ	ARBLS	10/01-12/01
	California	H	11.11 FQ	17.73 AW	22.37 TQ	CABLS	10/01-12/01
	Colorado	H	11.31 FQ	16.69 AW	21.90 TQ	COBLS	10/01-12/01
	Connecticut	H	11.20 FQ	14.71 AW	17.95 TQ	CTBLS	10/01-12/01
	Florida	H	8.88 FQ	12.06 AW	17.54 TQ	FLBLS	10/01-12/01
	Georgia	H	9.40 FQ	13.13 AW	20.39 TQ	GABLS	10/01-12/01
	Idaho	H	9.57 FQ	11.04 AW	13.05 TQ	IDBLS	10/01-12/01
	Illinois	H	10.19 FQ	24.04 AW	33.17 TQ	ILBLS	10/01-12/01
	Indiana	H	8.99 FQ	21.28 AW	33.04 TQ	INBLS	10/01-12/01
	Kansas	H	10.20 FQ	15.95 AW	21.67 TQ	KSBLS	10/01-12/01
	Kentucky	H	8.81 FQ	13.61 AW	17.78 TQ	KYBLS	10/01-12/01
	Massachusetts	H	10.76 FQ	17.32 AW	26.93 TQ	MABLS	10/01-12/01
	Michigan	H	7.66 FQ	13.28 AW	20.18 TQ	MIBLS	10/01-12/01
	Minnesota	H	5.50 FQ	12.60 AW	22.29 TQ	MNBLS	10/01-12/01
	Mississippi	H	9.28 FQ	12.06 AW	14.41 TQ	MSBLS	10/01-12/01
	Missouri	H	9.96 FQ	17.49 AW	28.06 TQ	MOBLS	10/01-12/01
	Montana	H	9.64 FQ	12.57 AW	16.19 TQ	MTBLS	10/01-12/01
	Nebraska	H	8.92 FQ	14.37 AW	22.09 TQ	NEBLS	10/01-12/01
	Nevada	H	13.14 FQ	19.79 AW	27.64 TQ	NVBLS	10/01-12/01
	New Hampshire	H	12.92 FQ	15.32 AW	17.54 TQ	NHBLS	10/01-12/01
	New Jersey	H	16.59 FQ	24.08 AW	32.28 TQ	NJBLS	10/01-12/01
	New York	H	7.81 FQ	12.69 AW	16.99 TQ	NYBLS	10/01-12/01
	North Carolina	H	9.79 FQ	14.59 AW	19.79 TQ	NCBLS	10/01-12/01
	Ohio	H	7.06 FQ	13.63 AW	19.31 TQ	OHBLS	10/01-12/01

AAW Average annual wage; **AE** Average entry wage; **AEX** Average experienced wage; **AO** Average offered; **AOH** Average offered, high; **AOL** Average offered, low; **APH** Average pay, high range; **APL** Average pay, low range; **ASH** Average starting, high; **ASL** Average starting, low; **AW** Average wage paid; **FQ** First quartile wage; **H** Hourly; **HI** Highest wage paid; **HR** High end range; **LR** Low end range; **M** Monthly; **MTC** Median total compensation; **MW** Median wage paid; **SQ** Second quartile wage; **S** Special: hourly and annual; **TQ** Third quartile wage; **W** Weekly; **Y** Yearly

Occupation/Type/Industry	Location	Per	Low	Mid	High	Source	Date
Mechanical Door Repairer	Oklahoma	H	7.77 FQ	12.12 AW	15.27 TQ	OKBLS	10/01-12/01
	Oregon	H	6.58 FQ	12.10 AW	20.82 TQ	ORBLS	10/01-12/01
	Pennsylvania	H	9.52 FQ	15.13 AW	21.76 TQ	PABLS	10/01-12/01
	Tennessee	H	8.71 FQ	16.02 AW	29.07 TQ	TNBLS	10/01-12/01
	Texas	H	8.33 FQ	15.57 AW	24.37 TQ	TXBLS	10/01-12/01
	Utah	H	12.61 FQ	17.42 AW	22.00 TQ	UTBLS	10/01-12/01
	Virginia	H	9.70 FQ	15.32 AW	21.55 TQ	VABLS	10/01-12/01
	Washington	H	10.59 FQ	19.36 AW	32.86 TQ	WABLS	10/01-12/01
	West Virginia	H	7.61 FQ	15.87 AW	23.88 TQ	WVBLS	10/01-12/01
	Wisconsin	H	9.02 FQ	13.08 AW	17.40 TQ	WIBLS	10/01-12/01
Mechanical Drafter	Alabama	Y	22490 FQ	39570 AW	60720 TQ	ALBLS	10/01-12/01
	Birmingham MSA, AL	Y	25010 FQ	39820 AW	56850 TQ	ALBLS	10/01-12/01
	Huntsville MSA, AL	Y	29810 FQ	48710 AW	72070 TQ	ALBLS	10/01-12/01
	Mobile MSA, AL	Y	20490 FQ	37440 AW	64660 TQ	ALBLS	10/01-12/01
	Montgomery MSA, AL	Y	20350 FQ	31980 AW	46400 TQ	ALBLS	10/01-12/01
	Alaska	Y	31610 FQ	46900 AW	64270 TQ	AKBLS	10/01-12/01
	Anchorage MSA, AK	Y	32410 FQ	46770 AW	59870 TQ	AKBLS	10/01-12/01
	Arizona	Y	26470 FQ	43460 AW	58900 TQ	AZBLS	10/01-12/01
	Phoenix-Mesa MSA, AZ	Y	27110 FQ	44630 AW	59990 TQ	AZBLS	10/01-12/01
	Tucson MSA, AZ	Y	25880 FQ	39460 AW	55130 TQ	AZBLS	10/01-12/01
	Arkansas	Y	23290 FQ	34250 AW	50110 TQ	ARBLS	10/01-12/01
	Fayetteville-Springdale-Rogers MSA, AR	Y	23980 FQ	37620 AW	53800 TQ	ARBLS	10/01-12/01
	Fort Smith MSA, AR-OK	Y	23030 FQ	30770 AW	43340 TQ	ARBLS	10/01-12/01
	Little Rock-North Little Rock MSA, AR	Y	22930 FQ	33240 AW	49880 TQ	ARBLS	10/01-12/01
	California	Y	27360 FQ	44600 AW	67070 TQ	CABLS	10/01-12/01
	Bakersfield MSA, CA	Y	31080 FQ	42560 AW	60530 TQ	CABLS	10/01-12/01
	Fresno MSA, CA	Y	23500 FQ	38020 AW	53580 TQ	CABLS	10/01-12/01
	Los Angeles-Long Beach PMSA, CA	Y	26130 FQ	42970 AW	66740 TQ	CABLS	10/01-12/01
	Modesto MSA, CA	Y	22430 FQ	33480 AW	47500 TQ	CABLS	10/01-12/01
	Oakland PMSA, CA	Y	34180 FQ	53530 AW	74960 TQ	CABLS	10/01-12/01
	Orange County PMSA, CA	Y	30520 FQ	44050 AW	60930 TQ	CABLS	10/01-12/01
	Riverside-San Bernardino PMSA, CA	Y	24980 FQ	37710 AW	51790 TQ	CABLS	10/01-12/01
	Sacramento PMSA, CA	Y	25890 FQ	42180 AW	63380 TQ	CABLS	10/01-12/01
	San Diego MSA, CA	Y	27860 FQ	44560 AW	71000 TQ	CABLS	10/01-12/01
	San Francisco PMSA, CA	Y	35710 FQ	50550 AW	70290 TQ	CABLS	10/01-12/01
	San Jose PMSA, CA	Y	34350 FQ	52760 AW	73730 TQ	CABLS	10/01-12/01
	San Luis Obispo-Atascadero-Paso Robles MSA, CA	Y	25480 FQ	35590 AW	46200 TQ	CABLS	10/01-12/01
	Santa Barbara-Santa Maria-Lompoc MSA, CA	Y	33560 FQ	50160 AW	68080 TQ	CABLS	10/01-12/01
	Santa Rosa PMSA, CA	Y	33690 FQ	45970 AW	56100 TQ	CABLS	10/01-12/01
	Stockton-Lodi MSA, CA	Y	19270 FQ	31720 AW	49110 TQ	CABLS	10/01-12/01
	Ventura PMSA, CA	Y	26340 FQ	42500 AW	65660 TQ	CABLS	10/01-12/01
	Colorado	Y	28130 FQ	40730 AW	56680 TQ	COBLS	10/01-12/01
	Boulder-Longmont PMSA, CO	Y	30690 FQ	46560 AW	62900 TQ	COBLS	10/01-12/01
	Colorado Springs MSA, CO	Y	29660 FQ	40490 AW	54180 TQ	COBLS	10/01-12/01
	Denver PMSA, CO	Y	29640 FQ	41080 AW	57550 TQ	COBLS	10/01-12/01
	Fort Collins-Loveland MSA, CO	Y	24980 FQ	38300 AW	51620 TQ	COBLS	10/01-12/01
	Connecticut	Y	30400 FQ	43470 AW	56470 TQ	CTBLS	10/01-12/01
	Bridgeport PMSA, CT	Y	31070 FQ	44260 AW	60780 TQ	CTBLS	10/01-12/01
	Danbury PMSA, CT	Y	35610 FQ	46840 AW	63880 TQ	CTBLS	10/01-12/01
	Hartford MSA, CT	Y	29310 FQ	43610 AW	60770 TQ	CTBLS	10/01-12/01
	New Haven-Meriden PMSA, CT	Y	33070 FQ	46010 AW	59460 TQ	CTBLS	10/01-12/01
	Stamford-Norwalk PMSA, CT	Y	31350 FQ	44700 AW	57140 TQ	CTBLS	10/01-12/01
	Waterbury PMSA, CT	Y	24280 FQ	41740 AW	64650 TQ	CTBLS	10/01-12/01
	Delaware	Y	20390 FQ	41320 AW	60160 TQ	DEBLS	10/01-12/01
	Wilmington-Newark PMSA, DE-MD	Y	18890 FQ	42570 AW	60990 TQ	DEBLS	10/01-12/01
	Washington PMSA, DC-MD-VA-WV	Y	24640 FQ	40490 AW	65540 TQ	DCBLS	10/01-12/01
	Florida	Y	22440 FQ	38660 AW	55860 TQ	FLBLS	10/01-12/01
	Daytona Beach MSA, FL	Y	28710 FQ	56660 AW		FLBLS	10/01-12/01
	Fort Lauderdale PMSA, FL	Y	28210 FQ	41050 AW	54310 TQ	FLBLS	10/01-12/01
	Fort Myers-Cape Coral MSA, FL	Y	23520 FQ	40020 AW	55380 TQ	FLBLS	10/01-12/01
	Fort Walton Beach MSA, FL	Y	19590 FQ	38520 AW	58210 TQ	FLBLS	10/01-12/01

AAW Average annual wage; AE Average entry wage; AEX Average experienced wage; AO Average offered; AOH Average offered, high; AOL Average offered, low; APH Average pay, high range; APL Average pay, low range; ASH Average starting, high; ASL Average starting, low; AW Average wage paid; FQ First quartile wage; H Hourly; HI Highest wage paid; HR High end range; LR Low end range; M Monthly; MTC Median total compensation; MW Median wage paid; SQ Second quartile wage; S Special: hourly and annual; TQ Third quartile wage; W Weekly; Y Yearly

Occupation/Type/Industry	Location	Per	Low	Mid	High	Source	Date
Mechanical Drafter	Jacksonville MSA, FL	Y	24370 FQ	37500 AW	52210 TQ	FLBLS	10/01-12/01
	Lakeland-Winter Haven MSA, FL	Y	30710 FQ	49210 AW	82440 TQ	FLBLS	10/01-12/01
	Melbourne-Titusville-Palm Bay MSA, FL	Y	25680 FQ	37520 AW	47220 TQ	FLBLS	10/01-12/01
	Miami PMSA, FL	Y	23040 FQ	38250 AW	57580 TQ	FLBLS	10/01-12/01
	Ocala MSA, FL	Y	19840 FQ	26650 AW	32440 TQ	FLBLS	10/01-12/01
	Orlando MSA, FL	Y	19090 FQ	33080 AW	49310 TQ	FLBLS	10/01-12/01
	Pensacola MSA, FL	Y	21000 FQ	35020 AW	61930 TQ	FLBLS	10/01-12/01
	Sarasota-Bradenton MSA, FL	Y	27160 FQ	38160 AW	52910 TQ	FLBLS	10/01-12/01
	Tampa-St. Petersburg-Clearwater MSA, FL	Y	26170 FQ	41380 AW	59870 TQ	FLBLS	10/01-12/01
	West Palm Beach-Boca Raton MSA, FL	Y	25320 FQ	40430 AW	58250 TQ	FLBLS	10/01-12/01
	Georgia	Y	24810 FQ	42130 AW	65980 TQ	GABLS	10/01-12/01
	Atlanta MSA, GA	Y	26540 FQ	45330 AW	70370 TQ	GABLS	10/01-12/01
	Augusta-Aiken MSA, GA-SC	Y	21220 FQ	42200 AW	73890 TQ	GABLS	10/01-12/01
	Macon MSA, GA	Y	27350 FQ	45260 AW	67620 TQ	GABLS	10/01-12/01
	Hawaii	Y	23860 FQ	27470 AW	29060 TQ	HIBLS	10/01-12/01
	Honolulu MSA, HI	Y	23820 FQ	26540 AW	28710 TQ	HIBLS	10/01-12/01
	Idaho	Y	21300 FQ	33480 AW	50310 TQ	IDBLS	10/01-12/01
	Boise City MSA, ID	Y	24270 FQ	33220 AW	46510 TQ	IDBLS	10/01-12/01
	Illinois	Y	27480 FQ	41110 AW	57540 TQ	ILBLS	10/01-12/01
	Chicago PMSA, IL	Y	28930 FQ	42360 AW	58380 TQ	ILBLS	10/01-12/01
	Peoria-Pekin MSA, IL	Y	29200 FQ	40030 AW	56070 TQ	ILBLS	10/01-12/01
	Rockford MSA, IL	Y	28610 FQ	39150 AW	53850 TQ	ILBLS	10/01-12/01
	Springfield MSA, IL	Y	28640 FQ	37610 AW	44580 TQ	ILBLS	10/01-12/01
	Indiana	Y	25230 FQ	39050 AW	56480 TQ	INBLS	10/01-12/01
	Elkhart-Goshen MSA, IN	Y	15730 FQ	31030 AW	42830 TQ	INBLS	10/01-12/01
	Evansville-Henderson MSA, IN-KY	Y	23300 FQ	33950 AW	44100 TQ	INBLS	10/01-12/01
	Fort Wayne MSA, IN	Y	28490 FQ	44190 AW	66770 TQ	INBLS	10/01-12/01
	Gary PMSA, IN	Y	30430 FQ	42760 AW	57200 TQ	INBLS	10/01-12/01
	Indianapolis MSA, IN	Y	24770 FQ	39490 AW	60070 TQ	INBLS	10/01-12/01
	Lafayette MSA, IN	Y	29750 FQ	38980 AW	51190 TQ	INBLS	10/01-12/01
	South Bend MSA, IN	Y	26140 FQ	36770 AW	53310 TQ	INBLS	10/01-12/01
	Iowa	Y	24730 FQ	35460 AW	48330 TQ	IABLS	10/01-12/01
	Cedar Rapids MSA, IA	Y	29450 FQ	40510 AW	51730 TQ	IABLS	10/01-12/01
	Davenport-Moline-Rock Island MSA, IA-IL	Y	22760 FQ	34050 AW	47860 TQ	IABLS	10/01-12/01
	Des Moines MSA, IA	Y	25150 FQ	40270 AW	64380 TQ	IABLS	10/01-12/01
	Kansas	Y	22480 FQ	35290 AW	52420 TQ	KSBLS	10/01-12/01
	Wichita MSA, KS	Y	24480 FQ	38890 AW	63510 TQ	KSBLS	10/01-12/01
	Kentucky	Y	25010 FQ	36110 AW	50650 TQ	KYBLS	10/01-12/01
	Lexington MSA, KY	Y	27700 FQ	34420 AW	43090 TQ	KYBLS	10/01-12/01
	Louisville MSA, KY-IN	Y	26050 FQ	41530 AW	58910 TQ	KYBLS	10/01-12/01
	Louisiana	Y	24390 FQ	44470 AW	73700 TQ	LABLS	10/01-12/01
	Baton Rouge MSA, LA	Y	30850 FQ	56880 AW	87290 TQ	LABLS	10/01-12/01
	Lafayette MSA, LA	Y	21230 FQ	33180 AW	47710 TQ	LABLS	10/01-12/01
	Lake Charles MSA, LA	Y	30640 FQ	51670 AW	79230 TQ	LABLS	10/01-12/01
	New Orleans MSA, LA	Y	24100 FQ	40460 AW	67820 TQ	LABLS	10/01-12/01
	Shreveport-Bossier City MSA, LA	Y	21230 FQ	36720 AW	54850 TQ	LABLS	10/01-12/01
	Maine	Y	24060 FQ	37700 AW	52310 TQ	MEBLS	10/01-12/01
	Portland MSA, ME	Y	27720 FQ	40430 AW	55780 TQ	MEBLS	10/01-12/01
	Maryland	Y	24090 FQ	39060 AW	61750 TQ	MDBLS	10/01-12/01
	Baltimore PMSA, MD	Y	23660 FQ	39930 AW	58680 TQ	MDBLS	10/01-12/01
	Massachusetts	Y	29740 FQ	47530 AW	70980 TQ	MABLS	10/01-12/01
	Boston PMSA, MA-NH	Y	30400 FQ	49970 AW	73360 TQ	MABLS	10/01-12/01
	Lawrence PMSA, MA-NH	Y	28370 FQ	41530 AW	56110 TQ	MABLS	10/01-12/01
	Lowell PMSA, MA-NH	Y	36110 FQ	46670 AW	59110 TQ	MABLS	10/01-12/01
	Springfield MSA, MA	Y	25050 FQ	37000 AW	51840 TQ	MABLS	10/01-12/01
	Worcester PMSA, MA-CT	Y	32910 FQ	53520 AW	80520 TQ	MABLS	10/01-12/01
	Michigan	Y	28070 FQ	50180 AW	81480 TQ	MIBLS	10/01-12/01
	Ann Arbor PMSA, MI	Y	32310 FQ	53620 AW	86470 TQ	MIBLS	10/01-12/01
	Detroit PMSA, MI	Y	32190 FQ	56390 AW	91140 TQ	MIBLS	10/01-12/01
	Flint PMSA, MI	Y	37460 FQ	54460 AW	76980 TQ	MIBLS	10/01-12/01
	Grand Rapids-Muskegon-Holland MSA, MI	Y	24950 FQ	41640 AW	58220 TQ	MIBLS	10/01-12/01
	Kalamazoo-Battle Creek MSA, MI	Y	29530 FQ	43160 AW	62660 TQ	MIBLS	10/01-12/01
	Lansing-East Lansing MSA, MI	Y	23250 FQ	39350 AW	60250 TQ	MIBLS	10/01-12/01

AAW Average annual wage **AE** Average entry wage **AEX** Average experienced wage **AO** Average offered **AOH** Average offered, high **AOL** Average offered, low **APH** Average pay, high range **APL** Average pay, low range **ASH** Average starting, high **ASL** Average starting, low **AW** Average wage paid **FQ** First quartile wage **H** Hourly **HI** Highest wage paid **HR** High end range **LR** Low end range **M** Monthly **MTC** Median total compensation **MW** Median wage paid **SQ** Second quartile wage **S** Special: hourly and annual **TQ** Third quartile wage **W** Weekly **Y** Yearly

Occupation/Type/Industry	Location	Per	Low	Mid	High	Source	Date
Mechanical Drafter	Saginaw-Bay City-Midland MSA, MI	Y	17810 FQ	33670 AW	53810 TQ	MIBLS	10/01-12/01
	Minnesota	Y	27350 FQ	40150 AW	55590 TQ	MNBLS	10/01-12/01
	Duluth-Superior MSA, MN-WI	Y	24420 FQ	33430 AW	44940 TQ	MNBLS	10/01-12/01
	Minneapolis-St. Paul MSA, MN-WI	Y	30340 FQ	42820 AW	57980 TQ	MNBLS	10/01-12/01
	Mississippi	Y	23520 FQ	33780 AW	47200 TQ	MSBLS	10/01-12/01
	Biloxi-Gulfport-Pascagoula MSA, MS	Y	23790 FQ	33500 AW	45060 TQ	MSBLS	10/01-12/01
	Jackson MSA, MS	Y	18630 FQ	32300 AW	44780 TQ	MSBLS	10/01-12/01
	Missouri	Y	25360 FQ	38780 AW	55450 TQ	MOBLS	10/01-12/01
	Kansas City MSA, MO-KS	Y	29220 FQ	41020 AW	56140 TQ	MOBLS	10/01-12/01
	St. Louis MSA, MO-IL	Y	25110 FQ	40540 AW	58340 TQ	MOBLS	10/01-12/01
	Springfield MSA, MO	Y	24840 FQ	33610 AW	43520 TQ	MOBLS	10/01-12/01
	Montana	Y	20690 FQ	28760 AW	42830 TQ	MTBLS	10/01-12/01
	Billings MSA, MT	Y	22630 FQ	28200 AW	39140 TQ	MTBLS	10/01-12/01
	Nebraska	Y	20790 FQ	30130 AW	42680 TQ	NEBLS	10/01-12/01
	Lincoln MSA, NE	Y	21480 FQ	30950 AW	41250 TQ	NEBLS	10/01-12/01
	Omaha MSA, NE-IA	Y	21230 FQ	31510 AW	44720 TQ	NEBLS	10/01-12/01
	Nevada	Y	27410 FQ	43480 AW	65020 TQ	NVBLS	10/01-12/01
	Las Vegas MSA, NV-AZ	Y	25320 FQ	37090 AW	51350 TQ	NVBLS	10/01-12/01
	Reno MSA, NV	Y	25940 FQ	39850 AW	57540 TQ	NVBLS	10/01-12/01
	New Hampshire	Y	30140 FQ	41330 AW	56700 TQ	NHBLS	10/01-12/01
	Nashua PMSA, NH	Y	30640 FQ	44580 AW	60290 TQ	NHBLS	10/01-12/01
	Portsmouth-Rochester PMSA, NH-ME	Y	27600 FQ	38170 AW	51540 TQ	NHBLS	10/01-12/01
	New Jersey	Y	27740 FQ	45730 AW	68460 TQ	NJBLS	10/01-12/01
	Bergen-Passaic PMSA, NJ	Y	25310 FQ	39640 AW	55470 TQ	NJBLS	10/01-12/01
	Middlesex-Somerset-Hunterdon PMSA, NJ	Y	30030 FQ	53370 AW	79210 TQ	NJBLS	10/01-12/01
	Monmouth-Ocean PMSA, NJ	Y	27330 FQ	41960 AW	58370 TQ	NJBLS	10/01-12/01
	Newark PMSA, NJ	Y	27640 FQ	44030 AW	62080 TQ	NJBLS	10/01-12/01
	Trenton PMSA, NJ	Y	30850 FQ	43920 AW	58360 TQ	NJBLS	10/01-12/01
	New Mexico	Y	24220 FQ	38180 AW	60470 TQ	NMBLS	10/01-12/01
	Albuquerque MSA, NM	Y	24420 FQ	34810 AW	52100 TQ	NMBLS	10/01-12/01
	New York	Y	25450 FQ	41830 AW	59120 TQ	NYBLS	10/01-12/01
	Albany-Schenectady-Troy MSA, NY	Y	25010 FQ	37600 AW	52640 TQ	NYBLS	10/01-12/01
	Binghamton MSA, NY	Y	29060 FQ	42700 AW	56140 TQ	NYBLS	10/01-12/01
	Buffalo-Niagara Falls MSA, NY	Y	27700 FQ	40900 AW	55950 TQ	NYBLS	10/01-12/01
	Nassau-Suffolk PMSA, NY	Y	27220 FQ	48220 AW	71770 TQ	NYBLS	10/01-12/01
	New York PMSA, NY	Y	25590 FQ	43400 AW	60360 TQ	NYBLS	10/01-12/01
	Newburgh PMSA, NY-PA	Y	25280 FQ	39710 AW	56920 TQ	NYBLS	10/01-12/01
	Rochester MSA, NY	Y	30300 FQ	45430 AW	62490 TQ	NYBLS	10/01-12/01
	Syracuse MSA, NY	Y	25060 FQ	37960 AW	54250 TQ	NYBLS	10/01-12/01
	Utica-Rome MSA, NY	Y	24280 FQ	36340 AW	53680 TQ	NYBLS	10/01-12/01
	North Carolina	Y	27580 FQ	41890 AW	59810 TQ	NCBLS	10/01-12/01
	Asheville MSA, NC	Y	30370 FQ	38990 AW	46760 TQ	NCBLS	10/01-12/01
	Charlotte-Gastonia-Rock Hill MSA, NC-SC	Y	28810 FQ	46290 AW	67980 TQ	NCBLS	10/01-12/01
	Greensboro-Winston-Salem-High Point MSA, NC	Y	27340 FQ	39940 AW	54980 TQ	NCBLS	10/01-12/01
	Hickory-Morganton-Lenoir MSA, NC	Y	30080 FQ	39170 AW	54210 TQ	NCBLS	10/01-12/01
	Raleigh-Durham-Chapel Hill MSA, NC	Y	31350 FQ	46650 AW	67050 TQ	NCBLS	10/01-12/01
	North Dakota	Y	18740 FQ	27580 AW	37280 TQ	NDBLS	10/01-12/01
	Fargo-Moorhead MSA, ND-MN	Y	20480 FQ	26600 AW	33700 TQ	NDBLS	10/01-12/01
	Ohio	Y	25730 FQ	41000 AW	60340 TQ	OHBLS	10/01-12/01
	Akron PMSA, OH	Y	26280 FQ	39920 AW	55160 TQ	OHBLS	10/01-12/01
	Canton-Massillon MSA, OH	Y	25560 FQ	39880 AW	57950 TQ	OHBLS	10/01-12/01
	Cincinnati PMSA, OH-KY-IN	Y	26120 FQ	42400 AW	64760 TQ	OHBLS	10/01-12/01
	Cleveland-Lorain-Elyria PMSA, OH	Y	28160 FQ	42740 AW	62140 TQ	OHBLS	10/01-12/01
	Columbus MSA, OH	Y	26280 FQ	40180 AW	54920 TQ	OHBLS	10/01-12/01
	Dayton-Springfield MSA, OH	Y	23620 FQ	43000 AW	65180 TQ	OHBLS	10/01-12/01
	Hamilton-Middletown PMSA, OH	Y	32860 FQ	50460 AW	69760 TQ	OHBLS	10/01-12/01
	Mansfield MSA, OH	Y	24270 FQ	32450 AW	44750 TQ	OHBLS	10/01-12/01
	Toledo MSA, OH	Y	25300 FQ	40360 AW	61070 TQ	OHBLS	10/01-12/01

AAW	Average annual wage	AOH	Average offered, high	ASH	Average starting, high	H	Hourly	M	Monthly	S	Special: hourly and annual
AE	Average entry wage	AOL	Average offered, low	ASL	Average starting, low	HI	Highest wage paid	MTC	Median total compensation	TQ	Third quartile wage
AEX	Average experienced wage	APH	Average pay, high range	AW	Average wage paid	HR	High end range	MW	Median wage paid	W	Weekly
AO	Average offered	APL	Average pay, low range	FQ	First quartile wage	LR	Low end range	SQ	Second quartile wage	Y	Yearly

Occupation/Type/Industry	Location	Per	Low	Mid	High	Source	Date
Mechanical Drafter	Youngstown-Warren MSA, OH	Y	20370 FQ	39190 AW	72700 TQ	OHBLS	10/01-12/01
	Oklahoma	Y	24430 FQ	37580 AW	54710 TQ	OKBLS	10/01-12/01
	Oklahoma City MSA, OK	Y	23760 FQ	33240 AW	45310 TQ	OKBLS	10/01-12/01
	Tulsa MSA, OK	Y	28110 FQ	40800 AW	55800 TQ	OKBLS	10/01-12/01
	Oregon	Y	24080 FQ	38480 AW	55110 TQ	ORBLS	10/01-12/01
	Eugene-Springfield MSA, OR	Y	23350 FQ	35780 AW	47620 TQ	ORBLS	10/01-12/01
	Portland-Vancouver PMSA, OR-WA	Y	25860 FQ	40480 AW	58810 TQ	ORBLS	10/01-12/01
	Salem PMSA, OR	Y	27930 FQ	39510 AW	52310 TQ	ORBLS	10/01-12/01
	Pennsylvania	Y	22230 FQ	39940 AW	61460 TQ	PABLS	10/01-12/01
	Allentown-Bethlehem-Easton MSA, PA	Y	25580 FQ	41610 AW	58360 TQ	PABLS	10/01-12/01
	Erie MSA, PA	Y	29660 FQ	48470 AW	66280 TQ	PABLS	10/01-12/01
	Harrisburg-Lebanon-Carlisle MSA, PA	Y	29870 FQ	38200 AW	51730 TQ	PABLS	10/01-12/01
	Johnstown MSA, PA	Y	19500 FQ	29810 AW	45120 TQ	PABLS	10/01-12/01
	Lancaster MSA, PA	Y	24300 FQ	34870 AW	48350 TQ	PABLS	10/01-12/01
	Philadelphia PMSA, PA-NJ	Y	28580 FQ	43130 AW	60000 TQ	PABLS	10/01-12/01
	Pittsburgh MSA, PA	Y	20130 FQ	39870 AW	64960 TQ	PABLS	10/01-12/01
	Reading MSA, PA	Y	28760 FQ	41430 AW	56410 TQ	PABLS	10/01-12/01
	Scranton-Wilkes-Barre-Hazleton MSA, PA	Y	23040 FQ	33290 AW	44440 TQ	PABLS	10/01-12/01
	York MSA, PA	Y	23230 FQ	35070 AW	48830 TQ	PABLS	10/01-12/01
	Rhode Island	Y	28530 FQ	45570 AW	70180 TQ	RIBLS	10/01-12/01
	Providence-Fall River-Warwick MSA, RI-MA	Y	26600 FQ	44250 AW	68690 TQ	RIBLS	10/01-12/01
	South Carolina	Y	28630 FQ	44510 AW	70210 TQ	SCBLS	10/01-12/01
	Charleston-North Charleston MSA, SC	Y	28450 FQ	38470 AW	53710 TQ	SCBLS	10/01-12/01
	Columbia MSA, SC	Y	28380 FQ	38190 AW	53520 TQ	SCBLS	10/01-12/01
	Greenville-Spartanburg-Anderson MSA, SC	Y	31040 FQ	49040 AW	74680 TQ	SCBLS	10/01-12/01
	Myrtle Beach MSA, SC	Y	36960 FQ	40580 AW	45610 TQ	SCBLS	10/01-12/01
	South Dakota	Y	23050 FQ	29860 AW	37860 TQ	SDBLS	10/01-12/01
	Tennessee	Y	24510 FQ	39550 AW	57770 TQ	TNBLS	10/01-12/01
	Chattanooga MSA, TN-GA	Y	24990 FQ	34750 AW	50610 TQ	TNBLS	10/01-12/01
	Clarksville-Hopkinsville MSA, TN-KY	Y	27380 FQ	40340 AW	53460 TQ	TNBLS	10/01-12/01
	Johnson City-Kingsport-Bristol MSA, TN-VA	Y	21720 FQ	33500 AW	45130 TQ	TNBLS	10/01-12/01
	Knoxville MSA, TN	Y	25970 FQ	42070 AW	60470 TQ	TNBLS	10/01-12/01
	Memphis MSA, TN-AR-MS	Y	28730 FQ	40860 AW	56680 TQ	TNBLS	10/01-12/01
	Nashville MSA, TN	Y	23400 FQ	38240 AW	56950 TQ	TNBLS	10/01-12/01
	Texas	Y	24750 FQ	42540 AW	64820 TQ	TXBLS	10/01-12/01
	Austin-San Marcos MSA, TX	Y	24460 FQ	37730 AW	50780 TQ	TXBLS	10/01-12/01
	Beaumont-Port Arthur MSA, TX	Y	23700 FQ	43580 AW	71610 TQ	TXBLS	10/01-12/01
	Brazoria PMSA, TX	Y	23710 FQ	35900 AW	55210 TQ	TXBLS	10/01-12/01
	Brownsville-Harlingen-San Benito MSA, TX	Y	18610 FQ	28830 AW	47660 TQ	TXBLS	10/01-12/01
	Corpus Christi MSA, TX	Y	29890 FQ	38140 AW	51130 TQ	TXBLS	10/01-12/01
	Dallas PMSA, TX	Y	24040 FQ	40160 AW	59740 TQ	TXBLS	10/01-12/01
	El Paso MSA, TX	Y	19350 FQ	31550 AW	47120 TQ	TXBLS	10/01-12/01
	Fort Worth-Arlington PMSA, TX	Y	23520 FQ	38320 AW	56140 TQ	TXBLS	10/01-12/01
	Galveston-Texas City PMSA, TX	Y	24640 FQ	52700 AW	88290 TQ	TXBLS	10/01-12/01
	Houston PMSA, TX	Y	30990 FQ	48770 AW	69730 TQ	TXBLS	10/01-12/01
	Killeen-Temple MSA, TX	Y	22140 FQ	34760 AW	47340 TQ	TXBLS	10/01-12/01
	Longview-Marshall MSA, TX	Y	20940 FQ	33640 AW	46180 TQ	TXBLS	10/01-12/01
	Odessa-Midland MSA, TX	Y	28650 FQ	51060 AW	67900 TQ	TXBLS	10/01-12/01
	San Antonio MSA, TX	Y	24770 FQ	39210 AW	62840 TQ	TXBLS	10/01-12/01
	Tyler MSA, TX	Y	23850 FQ	34890 AW	46830 TQ	TXBLS	10/01-12/01
	Waco MSA, TX	Y	24290 FQ	30140 AW	37440 TQ	TXBLS	10/01-12/01
	Utah	Y	25790 FQ	39910 AW	56850 TQ	UTBLS	10/01-12/01
	Provo-Orem MSA, UT	Y	25430 FQ	34560 AW	45540 TQ	UTBLS	10/01-12/01
	Salt Lake City-Ogden MSA, UT	Y	25390 FQ	39840 AW	57080 TQ	UTBLS	10/01-12/01
	Vermont	Y	28030 FQ	37080 AW	48710 TQ	VTBLS	10/01-12/01
	Burlington MSA, VT	Y	27650 FQ	36700 AW	50300 TQ	VTBLS	10/01-12/01
	Virginia	Y	25270 FQ	40180 AW	56420 TQ	VABLS	10/01-12/01
	Lynchburg MSA, VA	Y	19280 FQ	31310 AW	46670 TQ	VABLS	10/01-12/01

AAW Average annual wage; **AE** Average entry wage; **AEX** Average experienced wage; **AO** Average offered; **AOH** Average offered, high; **AOL** Average offered, low; **APH** Average pay, high range; **APL** Average pay, low range; **ASH** Average starting, high; **ASL** Average starting, low; **AW** Average wage paid; **FQ** First quartile wage; **H** Hourly; **HI** Highest wage paid; **HR** High end range; **LR** Low end range; **M** Monthly; **MTC** Median total compensation; **MW** Median wage paid; **SQ** Second quartile wage; **S** Special: hourly and annual; **TQ** Third quartile wage; **W** Weekly; **Y** Yearly

Occupation/Type/Industry	Location	Per	Low	Mid	High	Source	Date
Mechanical Drafter	Richmond-Petersburg MSA, VA	Y	23440 FQ	37070 AW	61840 TQ	VABLS	10/01-12/01
	Washington	Y	25670 FQ	42910 AW	66460 TQ	WABLS	10/01-12/01
	Bremerton PMSA, WA	Y	28500 FQ	50660 AW	71580 TQ	WABLS	10/01-12/01
	Richland-Kennewick-Pasco MSA, WA	Y	26980 FQ	49920 AW	69650 TQ	WABLS	10/01-12/01
	Seattle-Bellevue-Everett PMSA, WA	Y	28010 FQ	45110 AW	69140 TQ	WABLS	10/01-12/01
	Spokane MSA, WA	Y	23290 FQ	32530 AW	43070 TQ	WABLS	10/01-12/01
	Tacoma PMSA, WA	Y	21120 FQ	36750 AW	51120 TQ	WABLS	10/01-12/01
	Yakima MSA, WA	Y	16690 FQ	30230 AW	44630 TQ	WABLS	10/01-12/01
	West Virginia	Y	24710 FQ	39870 AW	60800 TQ	WVBLS	10/01-12/01
	Charleston MSA, WV	Y	24810 FQ	35660 AW	48130 TQ	WVBLS	10/01-12/01
	Huntington-Ashland MSA, WV-KY-OH	Y	24930 FQ	34970 AW	46220 TQ	WVBLS	10/01-12/01
	Wisconsin	Y	25470 FQ	37970 AW	52720 TQ	WIBLS	10/01-12/01
	Appleton-Oshkosh-Neenah MSA, WI	Y	29500 FQ	38750 AW	50820 TQ	WIBLS	10/01-12/01
	Green Bay MSA, WI	Y	23250 FQ	37050 AW	51050 TQ	WIBLS	10/01-12/01
	Madison MSA, WI	Y	26670 FQ	38050 AW	53490 TQ	WIBLS	10/01-12/01
	Milwaukee-Waukesha PMSA, WI	Y	28740 FQ	41070 AW	55200 TQ	WIBLS	10/01-12/01
	Racine PMSA, WI	Y	20680 FQ	39440 AW	54370 TQ	WIBLS	10/01-12/01
	Wyoming	Y	29310 FQ	42670 AW	61230 TQ	WYBLS	10/01-12/01
	Puerto Rico	Y	11900 FQ	26210 AW	44510 TQ	PRBLS	10/01-12/01
Mechanical Engineer	Alabama	Y	37570 FQ	61080 AW	89170 TQ	ALBLS	10/01-12/01
	Birmingham MSA, AL	Y	29350 FQ	55970 AW	86700 TQ	ALBLS	10/01-12/01
	Huntsville MSA, AL	Y	39420 FQ	64740 AW	90760 TQ	ALBLS	10/01-12/01
	Mobile MSA, AL	Y	34990 FQ	60080 AW	85750 TQ	ALBLS	10/01-12/01
	Montgomery MSA, AL	Y	35940 FQ	52270 AW	82030 TQ	ALBLS	10/01-12/01
	Alaska	Y	46350 FQ	71910 AW	97370 TQ	AKBLS	10/01-12/01
	Anchorage MSA, AK	Y	48210 FQ	72210 AW	95390 TQ	AKBLS	10/01-12/01
	Arizona	Y	40850 FQ	67480 AW	106560 TQ	AZBLS	10/01-12/01
	Phoenix-Mesa MSA, AZ	Y	42070 FQ	69250 AW	108790 TQ	AZBLS	10/01-12/01
	Tucson MSA, AZ	Y	38010 FQ	55120 AW	75820 TQ	AZBLS	10/01-12/01
	Arkansas	Y	39660 FQ	55480 AW	74120 TQ	ARBLS	10/01-12/01
	Fayetteville-Springdale-Rogers MSA, AR	Y	38880 FQ	52190 AW	69150 TQ	ARBLS	10/01-12/01
	Fort Smith MSA, AR-OK	Y	42810 FQ	54240 AW	68930 TQ	ARBLS	10/01-12/01
	Little Rock-North Little Rock MSA, AR	Y	38970 FQ	56400 AW	78030 TQ	ARBLS	10/01-12/01
	California	Y	45350 FQ	70180 AW	102370 TQ	CABLS	10/01-12/01
	Bakersfield MSA, CA	Y	50280 FQ	74320 AW	97780 TQ	CABLS	10/01-12/01
	Fresno MSA, CA	Y	32190 FQ	50900 AW	69450 TQ	CABLS	10/01-12/01
	Los Angeles-Long Beach PMSA, CA	Y	44270 FQ	69190 AW	101440 TQ	CABLS	10/01-12/01
	Modesto MSA, CA	Y	38430 FQ	65180 AW	97600 TQ	CABLS	10/01-12/01
	Oakland PMSA, CA	Y	51740 FQ	77270 AW	110430 TQ	CABLS	10/01-12/01
	Orange County PMSA, CA	Y	44410 FQ	68390 AW	102340 TQ	CABLS	10/01-12/01
	Redding MSA, CA	Y	27890 FQ	55730 AW	105170 TQ	CABLS	10/01-12/01
	Riverside-San Bernardino PMSA, CA	Y	41760 FQ	63420 AW	88420 TQ	CABLS	10/01-12/01
	Sacramento PMSA, CA	Y	49130 FQ	67370 AW	91430 TQ	CABLS	10/01-12/01
	Salinas MSA, CA	Y	34880 FQ	62550 AW	87330 TQ	CABLS	10/01-12/01
	San Diego MSA, CA	Y	45320 FQ	67280 AW	90800 TQ	CABLS	10/01-12/01
	San Francisco PMSA, CA	Y	48720 FQ	69390 AW	97770 TQ	CABLS	10/01-12/01
	San Jose PMSA, CA	Y	50190 FQ	77310 AW	112200 TQ	CABLS	10/01-12/01
	San Luis Obispo-Atascadero-Paso Robles MSA, CA	Y	39080 FQ	53990 AW	75440 TQ	CABLS	10/01-12/01
	Santa Barbara-Santa Maria-Lompoc MSA, CA	Y	51180 FQ	72740 AW	96780 TQ	CABLS	10/01-12/01
	Santa Cruz-Watsonville PMSA, CA	Y	27850 FQ	65820 AW	113410 TQ	CABLS	10/01-12/01
	Santa Rosa PMSA, CA	Y	50980 FQ	73250 AW	102740 TQ	CABLS	10/01-12/01
	Stockton-Lodi MSA, CA	Y	40250 FQ	59470 AW	82420 TQ	CABLS	10/01-12/01
	Vallejo-Fairfield-Napa PMSA, CA	Y	43530 FQ	56790 AW	73720 TQ	CABLS	10/01-12/01
	Ventura PMSA, CA	Y	40860 FQ	65430 AW	91450 TQ	CABLS	10/01-12/01
	Visalia-Tulare-Porterville MSA, CA	Y	35460 FQ	55430 AW	77510 TQ	CABLS	10/01-12/01
	Colorado	Y	44450 FQ	68750 AW	103600 TQ	COBLS	10/01-12/01
	Boulder-Longmont PMSA, CO	Y	52150 FQ	78350 AW	113160 TQ	COBLS	10/01-12/01

AAW Average annual wage; **AE** Average entry wage; **AEX** Average experienced wage; **AO** Average offered; **AOH** Average offered, high; **AOL** Average offered, low; **APH** Average pay, high range; **APL** Average pay, low range; **ASH** Average starting, high; **ASL** Average starting, low; **AW** Average wage paid; **FQ** First quartile wage; **H** Hourly; **HI** Highest wage paid; **HR** High end range; **LR** Low end range; **M** Monthly; **MTC** Median total compensation; **MW** Median wage paid; **SQ** Second quartile wage; **S** Special: hourly and annual; **TQ** Third quartile wage; **W** Weekly; **Y** Yearly

Occupation/Type/Industry	Location	Per	Low	Mid	High	Source	Date
Mechanical Engineer	Colorado Springs MSA, CO	Y	46350 FQ	65120 AW	100140 TQ	COBLS	10/01-12/01
	Denver PMSA, CO	Y	43750 FQ	68610 AW	104840 TQ	COBLS	10/01-12/01
	Fort Collins-Loveland MSA, CO	Y	40040 FQ	59200 AW	81780 TQ	COBLS	10/01-12/01
	Greeley PMSA, CO	Y	28480 FQ	55050 AW	78970 TQ	COBLS	10/01-12/01
	Connecticut	Y	45950 FQ	63090 AW	85580 TQ	CTBLS	10/01-12/01
	Bridgeport PMSA, CT	Y	49830 FQ	70410 AW	97610 TQ	CTBLS	10/01-12/01
	Danbury PMSA, CT	Y	47030 FQ	67140 AW	95590 TQ	CTBLS	10/01-12/01
	Hartford MSA, CT	Y	39940 FQ	60760 AW	85310 TQ	CTBLS	10/01-12/01
	New Haven-Meriden PMSA, CT	Y	41530 FQ	61600 AW	86510 TQ	CTBLS	10/01-12/01
	Stamford-Norwalk PMSA, CT	Y	42970 FQ	60810 AW	82160 TQ	CTBLS	10/01-12/01
	Waterbury PMSA, CT	Y	35680 FQ	58500 AW	75940 TQ	CTBLS	10/01-12/01
	Delaware	Y	46270 FQ	71020 AW	107100 TQ	DEBLS	10/01-12/01
	Wilmington-Newark PMSA, DE-MD	Y	47680 FQ	72250 AW	108200 TQ	DEBLS	10/01-12/01
	District of Columbia	Y	48850 FQ	72220 AW	99760 TQ	DCBLS	10/01-12/01
	Washington PMSA, DC-MD-VA-WV	Y	43320 FQ	67310 AW	94490 TQ	DCBLS	10/01-12/01
	Florida	Y	38120 FQ	62620 AW	89340 TQ	FLBLS	10/01-12/01
	Daytona Beach MSA, FL	Y	41330 FQ	60510 AW	86620 TQ	FLBLS	10/01-12/01
	Fort Lauderdale PMSA, FL	Y	37410 FQ	53970 AW	71400 TQ	FLBLS	10/01-12/01
	Fort Myers-Cape Coral MSA, FL	Y	45970 FQ	65020 AW	91010 TQ	FLBLS	10/01-12/01
	Fort Pierce-Port St. Lucie MSA, FL	Y	38700 FQ	64570 AW	90280 TQ	FLBLS	10/01-12/01
	Fort Walton Beach MSA, FL	Y	48070 FQ	65640 AW	86750 TQ	FLBLS	10/01-12/01
	Gainesville MSA, FL	Y	39740 FQ	52590 AW	72360 TQ	FLBLS	10/01-12/01
	Jacksonville MSA, FL	Y	38240 FQ	61240 AW	90130 TQ	FLBLS	10/01-12/01
	Lakeland-Winter Haven MSA, FL	Y	36940 FQ	58550 AW	85870 TQ	FLBLS	10/01-12/01
	Melbourne-Titusville-Palm Bay MSA, FL	Y	35020 FQ	54760 AW	79820 TQ	FLBLS	10/01-12/01
	Miami PMSA, FL	Y	34390 FQ	59190 AW	85770 TQ	FLBLS	10/01-12/01
	Ocala MSA, FL	Y	29800 FQ	50860 AW	69880 TQ	FLBLS	10/01-12/01
	Orlando MSA, FL	Y	40820 FQ	64250 AW	89090 TQ	FLBLS	10/01-12/01
	Pensacola MSA, FL	Y	40380 FQ	62150 AW	89700 TQ	FLBLS	10/01-12/01
	Sarasota-Bradenton MSA, FL	Y	35180 FQ	54110 AW	74320 TQ	FLBLS	10/01-12/01
	Tampa-St. Petersburg-Clearwater MSA, FL	Y	34290 FQ	63360 AW	94170 TQ	FLBLS	10/01-12/01
	West Palm Beach-Boca Raton MSA, FL	Y	48820 FQ	68290 AW	91620 TQ	FLBLS	10/01-12/01
	Georgia	Y	38620 FQ	58700 AW	84530 TQ	GABLS	10/01-12/01
	Atlanta MSA, GA	Y	37770 FQ	58620 AW	84930 TQ	GABLS	10/01-12/01
	Augusta-Aiken MSA, GA-SC	Y	50830 FQ	73950 AW	106270 TQ	GABLS	10/01-12/01
	Columbus MSA, GA-AL	Y	45190 FQ	60210 AW	80500 TQ	GABLS	10/01-12/01
	Macon MSA, GA	Y	41460 FQ	60990 AW	85150 TQ	GABLS	10/01-12/01
	Savannah MSA, GA	Y	41370 FQ	54750 AW	70890 TQ	GABLS	10/01-12/01
	Hawaii	Y	27220 FQ	57910 AW	88010 TQ	HIBLS	10/01-12/01
	Honolulu MSA, HI	Y	27150 FQ	57700 AW	87930 TQ	HIBLS	10/01-12/01
	Idaho	Y	39640 FQ	59110 AW	84850 TQ	IDBLS	10/01-12/01
	Boise City MSA, ID	Y	37990 FQ	50890 AW	69510 TQ	IDBLS	10/01-12/01
	Illinois	Y	39480 FQ	60830 AW	88270 TQ	ILBLS	10/01-12/01
	Champaign-Urbana MSA, IL	Y	35150 FQ	54670 AW	80580 TQ	ILBLS	10/01-12/01
	Chicago PMSA, IL	Y	39800 FQ	61790 AW	90920 TQ	ILBLS	10/01-12/01
	Peoria-Pekin MSA, IL	Y	50830 FQ	67670 AW	90480 TQ	ILBLS	10/01-12/01
	Rockford MSA, IL	Y	38140 FQ	50710 AW	67380 TQ	ILBLS	10/01-12/01
	Springfield MSA, IL	Y	41560 FQ	67670 AW	102120 TQ	ILBLS	10/01-12/01
	Indiana	Y	39250 FQ	57280 AW	81080 TQ	INBLS	10/01-12/01
	Elkhart-Goshen MSA, IN	Y	34540 FQ	49440 AW	69240 TQ	INBLS	10/01-12/01
	Evansville-Henderson MSA, IN-KY	Y	37340 FQ	51690 AW	72610 TQ	INBLS	10/01-12/01
	Fort Wayne MSA, IN	Y	39560 FQ	58590 AW	84830 TQ	INBLS	10/01-12/01
	Gary PMSA, IN	Y	47310 FQ	65600 AW	88350 TQ	INBLS	10/01-12/01
	Indianapolis MSA, IN	Y	39750 FQ	59760 AW	84880 TQ	INBLS	10/01-12/01
	Lafayette MSA, IN	Y	44520 FQ	61870 AW	86220 TQ	INBLS	10/01-12/01
	South Bend MSA, IN	Y	39400 FQ	60100 AW	86760 TQ	INBLS	10/01-12/01
	Iowa	Y	37350 FQ	55830 AW	77950 TQ	IABLS	10/01-12/01
	Cedar Rapids MSA, IA	Y	47500 FQ	62890 AW	82860 TQ	IABLS	10/01-12/01
	Davenport-Moline-Rock Island MSA, IA-IL	Y	27880 FQ	53000 AW	73340 TQ	IABLS	10/01-12/01
	Des Moines MSA, IA	Y	36180 FQ	55130 AW	79920 TQ	IABLS	10/01-12/01

AAW	Average annual wage	**AOH**	Average offered, high	**ASH**	Average starting, high	**H**	Hourly	**M**	Monthly	**S**	Special: hourly and annual
AE	Average entry wage	**AOL**	Average offered, low	**ASL**	Average starting, low	**HI**	Highest wage paid	**MTC**	Median total compensation	**TQ**	Third quartile wage
AEX	Average experienced wage	**APH**	Average pay, high range	**AW**	Average wage paid	**HR**	High end range	**MW**	Median wage paid	**W**	Weekly
AO	Average offered	**APL**	Average pay, low range	**FQ**	First quartile wage	**LR**	Low end range	**SQ**	Second quartile wage	**Y**	Yearly

Occupation/Type/Industry	Location	Per	Low	Mid	High	Source	Date
Mechanical Engineer	Kansas	Y	37620 FQ	53440 AW	72670 TQ	KSBLS	10/01-12/01
	Topeka MSA, KS	Y	43050 FQ	68320 AW	109030 TQ	KSBLS	10/01-12/01
	Wichita MSA, KS	Y	38730 FQ	58500 AW	82460 TQ	KSBLS	10/01-12/01
	Kentucky	Y	40370 FQ	58300 AW	80810 TQ	KYBLS	10/01-12/01
	Lexington MSA, KY	Y	38940 FQ	54440 AW	73430 TQ	KYBLS	10/01-12/01
	Louisville MSA, KY-IN	Y	44230 FQ	63290 AW	86990 TQ	KYBLS	10/01-12/01
	Louisiana	Y	45270 FQ	69320 AW	100920 TQ	LABLS	10/01-12/01
	Baton Rouge MSA, LA	Y	47810 FQ	69890 AW	96740 TQ	LABLS	10/01-12/01
	Houma MSA, LA	Y	47070 FQ	69960 AW	114050 TQ	LABLS	10/01-12/01
	Lafayette MSA, LA	Y	37670 FQ	53250 AW	77570 TQ	LABLS	10/01-12/01
	Lake Charles MSA, LA	Y	55020 FQ	74770 AW	100440 TQ	LABLS	10/01-12/01
	New Orleans MSA, LA	Y	49770 FQ	74200 AW	107200 TQ	LABLS	10/01-12/01
	Shreveport-Bossier City MSA, LA	Y	39140 FQ	62530 AW	90030 TQ	LABLS	10/01-12/01
	Maine	Y	40690 FQ	63270 AW	92730 TQ	MEBLS	10/01-12/01
	Portland MSA, ME	Y	39020 FQ	58740 AW	87350 TQ	MEBLS	10/01-12/01
	Maryland	Y	40860 FQ	65570 AW	93300 TQ	MDBLS	10/01-12/01
	Baltimore PMSA, MD	Y	39680 FQ	64430 AW	91960 TQ	MDBLS	10/01-12/01
	Massachusetts	Y	47140 FQ	69060 AW	97850 TQ	MABLS	10/01-12/01
	Boston PMSA, MA-NH	Y	48760 FQ	71820 AW	102250 TQ	MABLS	10/01-12/01
	Brockton PMSA, MA	Y	40290 FQ	59370 AW	83350 TQ	MABLS	10/01-12/01
	Lawrence PMSA, MA-NH	Y	45070 FQ	64000 AW	90120 TQ	MABLS	10/01-12/01
	Lowell PMSA, MA-NH	Y	50540 FQ	71820 AW	97050 TQ	MABLS	10/01-12/01
	New Bedford PMSA, MA	Y	45890 FQ	61660 AW	90160 TQ	MABLS	10/01-12/01
	Springfield MSA, MA	Y	42560 FQ	62830 AW	91910 TQ	MABLS	10/01-12/01
	Worcester PMSA, MA-CT	Y	43630 FQ	60220 AW	84900 TQ	MABLS	10/01-12/01
	Michigan	Y	40200 FQ	62780 AW	89430 TQ	MIBLS	10/01-12/01
	Ann Arbor PMSA, MI	Y	42520 FQ	66510 AW	90970 TQ	MIBLS	10/01-12/01
	Detroit PMSA, MI	Y	43220 FQ	66260 AW	91860 TQ	MIBLS	10/01-12/01
	Flint PMSA, MI	Y	34050 FQ	62120 AW	89710 TQ	MIBLS	10/01-12/01
	Grand Rapids-Muskegon-Holland MSA, MI	Y	36660 FQ	56610 AW	81450 TQ	MIBLS	10/01-12/01
	Kalamazoo-Battle Creek MSA, MI	Y	42590 FQ	61350 AW	84220 TQ	MIBLS	10/01-12/01
	Lansing-East Lansing MSA, MI	Y	37090 FQ	57640 AW	81890 TQ	MIBLS	10/01-12/01
	Saginaw-Bay City-Midland MSA, MI	Y	35380 FQ	57340 AW	83230 TQ	MIBLS	10/01-12/01
	Minnesota	Y	41190 FQ	59990 AW	83770 TQ	MNBLS	10/01-12/01
	Duluth-Superior MSA, MN-WI	Y	38090 FQ	51460 AW	68840 TQ	MNBLS	10/01-12/01
	Minneapolis-St. Paul MSA, MN-WI	Y	44630 FQ	62230 AW	86140 TQ	MNBLS	10/01-12/01
	St. Cloud MSA, MN	Y	40300 FQ	55890 AW	74610 TQ	MNBLS	10/01-12/01
	Mississippi	Y	33390 FQ	52430 AW	73000 TQ	MSBLS	10/01-12/01
	Biloxi-Gulfport-Pascagoula MSA, MS	Y	27950 FQ	49700 AW	70700 TQ	MSBLS	10/01-12/01
	Jackson MSA, MS	Y	41430 FQ	54410 AW	74790 TQ	MSBLS	10/01-12/01
	Missouri	Y	39230 FQ	59410 AW	85810 TQ	MOBLS	10/01-12/01
	Kansas City MSA, MO-KS	Y	37930 FQ	52820 AW	72860 TQ	MOBLS	10/01-12/01
	St. Louis MSA, MO-IL	Y	38590 FQ	60610 AW	88960 TQ	MOBLS	10/01-12/01
	Springfield MSA, MO	Y	39540 FQ	52890 AW	70450 TQ	MOBLS	10/01-12/01
	Montana	Y	31030 FQ	51450 AW	76110 TQ	MTBLS	10/01-12/01
	Billings MSA, MT	Y	43360 FQ	59810 AW	85700 TQ	MTBLS	10/01-12/01
	Nebraska	Y	38720 FQ	59500 AW	87980 TQ	NEBLS	10/01-12/01
	Lincoln MSA, NE	Y	41550 FQ	58320 AW	80120 TQ	NEBLS	10/01-12/01
	Omaha MSA, NE-IA	Y	40190 FQ	63440 AW	96360 TQ	NEBLS	10/01-12/01
	Nevada	Y	45280 FQ	65000 AW	89950 TQ	NVBLS	10/01-12/01
	Las Vegas MSA, NV-AZ	Y	46310 FQ	68970 AW	101010 TQ	NVBLS	10/01-12/01
	Reno MSA, NV	Y	35250 FQ	59710 AW	90340 TQ	NVBLS	10/01-12/01
	New Hampshire	Y	40960 FQ	58600 AW	84050 TQ	NHBLS	10/01-12/01
	Manchester PMSA, NH	Y	45940 FQ	57860 AW	77280 TQ	NHBLS	10/01-12/01
	Nashua PMSA, NH	Y	46010 FQ	66770 AW	93000 TQ	NHBLS	10/01-12/01
	Portsmouth-Rochester PMSA, NH-ME	Y	40060 FQ	55220 AW	71020 TQ	NHBLS	10/01-12/01
	New Jersey	Y	44300 FQ	68490 AW	99430 TQ	NJBLS	10/01-12/01
	Atlantic-Cape May PMSA, NJ	Y	38110 FQ	72530 AW	108970 TQ	NJBLS	10/01-12/01
	Bergen-Passaic PMSA, NJ	Y	43160 FQ	65070 AW	95770 TQ	NJBLS	10/01-12/01
	Jersey City PMSA, NJ	Y	41160 FQ	63530 AW	90320 TQ	NJBLS	10/01-12/01
	Middlesex-Somerset-Hunterdon PMSA, NJ	Y	45400 FQ	72010 AW	104790 TQ	NJBLS	10/01-12/01
	Monmouth-Ocean PMSA, NJ	Y	45810 FQ	68060 AW	94120 TQ	NJBLS	10/01-12/01
	Newark PMSA, NJ	Y	42240 FQ	68310 AW	99560 TQ	NJBLS	10/01-12/01
	Trenton PMSA, NJ	Y	43080 FQ	66470 AW	96920 TQ	NJBLS	10/01-12/01

AAW	Average annual wage	**AOH**	Average offered, high	**ASH**	Average starting, high	**H**	Hourly	**M**	Monthly	**S**	Special: hourly and annual
AE	Average entry wage	**AOL**	Average offered, low	**ASL**	Average starting, low	**HI**	Highest wage paid	**MTC**	Median total compensation	**TQ**	Third quartile wage
AEX	Average experienced wage	**APH**	Average pay, high range	**AW**	Average wage paid	**HR**	High end range	**MW**	Median wage paid	**W**	Weekly
AO	Average offered	**APL**	Average pay, low range	**FQ**	First quartile wage	**LR**	Low end range	**SQ**	Second quartile wage	**Y**	Yearly

Occupation/Type/Industry	Location	Per	Low	Mid	High	Source	Date
Mechanical Engineer	New Mexico	Y	46220 FQ	76400 AW	112510 TQ	NMBLS	10/01-12/01
	Albuquerque MSA, NM	Y	45830 FQ	70950 AW	103790 TQ	NMBLS	10/01-12/01
	New York	Y	38780 FQ	61910 AW	91790 TQ	NYBLS	10/01-12/01
	Albany-Schenectady-Troy MSA, NY	Y	39960 FQ	61840 AW	86480 TQ	NYBLS	10/01-12/01
	Binghamton MSA, NY	Y	32720 FQ	52450 AW	84830 TQ	NYBLS	10/01-12/01
	Buffalo-Niagara Falls MSA, NY	Y	38730 FQ	59110 AW	82300 TQ	NYBLS	10/01-12/01
	Dutchess County PMSA, NY	Y	37740 FQ	62690 AW	92840 TQ	NYBLS	10/01-12/01
	Nassau-Suffolk PMSA, NY	Y	39620 FQ	67080 AW	105580 TQ	NYBLS	10/01-12/01
	New York PMSA, NY	Y	39040 FQ	63290 AW	97720 TQ	NYBLS	10/01-12/01
	Newburgh PMSA, NY-PA	Y	37320 FQ	55860 AW	75680 TQ	NYBLS	10/01-12/01
	Rochester MSA, NY	Y	40810 FQ	64470 AW	94550 TQ	NYBLS	10/01-12/01
	Syracuse MSA, NY	Y	40420 FQ	62900 AW	90390 TQ	NYBLS	10/01-12/01
	Utica-Rome MSA, NY	Y	26830 FQ	48240 AW	73230 TQ	NYBLS	10/01-12/01
	North Carolina	Y	40320 FQ	62630 AW	89380 TQ	NCBLS	10/01-12/01
	Asheville MSA, NC	Y	31960 FQ	57110 AW	78090 TQ	NCBLS	10/01-12/01
	Charlotte-Gastonia-Rock Hill MSA, NC-SC	Y	41960 FQ	63060 AW	89590 TQ	NCBLS	10/01-12/01
	Fayetteville MSA, NC	Y	45750 FQ	68570 AW	100470 TQ	NCBLS	10/01-12/01
	Greensboro-Winston-Salem-High Point MSA, NC	Y	39450 FQ	61680 AW	90740 TQ	NCBLS	10/01-12/01
	Hickory-Morganton-Lenoir MSA, NC	Y	32390 FQ	53720 AW	76110 TQ	NCBLS	10/01-12/01
	Raleigh-Durham-Chapel Hill MSA, NC	Y	42830 FQ	69340 AW	110660 TQ	NCBLS	10/01-12/01
	North Dakota	Y	28290 FQ	53200 AW	75380 TQ	NDBLS	10/01-12/01
	Fargo-Moorhead MSA, ND-MN	Y	35640 FQ	52220 AW	73490 TQ	NDBLS	10/01-12/01
	Ohio	Y	37870 FQ	56690 AW	80280 TQ	OHBLS	10/01-12/01
	Akron PMSA, OH	Y	38390 FQ	55280 AW	75190 TQ	OHBLS	10/01-12/01
	Canton-Massillon MSA, OH	Y	38680 FQ	54840 AW	74090 TQ	OHBLS	10/01-12/01
	Cincinnati PMSA, OH-KY-IN	Y	39590 FQ	60150 AW	88070 TQ	OHBLS	10/01-12/01
	Cleveland-Lorain-Elyria PMSA, OH	Y	38020 FQ	55680 AW	76120 TQ	OHBLS	10/01-12/01
	Columbus MSA, OH	Y	39200 FQ	60350 AW	85960 TQ	OHBLS	10/01-12/01
	Dayton-Springfield MSA, OH	Y	38630 FQ	60780 AW	87170 TQ	OHBLS	10/01-12/01
	Hamilton-Middletown PMSA, OH	Y	36710 FQ	54790 AW	77150 TQ	OHBLS	10/01-12/01
	Mansfield MSA, OH	Y	31490 FQ	50360 AW	69230 TQ	OHBLS	10/01-12/01
	Toledo MSA, OH	Y	34000 FQ	51970 AW	72100 TQ	OHBLS	10/01-12/01
	Youngstown-Warren MSA, OH	Y	33390 FQ	53560 AW	82600 TQ	OHBLS	10/01-12/01
	Oklahoma	Y	37410 FQ	58300 AW	83620 TQ	OKBLS	10/01-12/01
	Oklahoma City MSA, OK	Y	37680 FQ	56160 AW	75940 TQ	OKBLS	10/01-12/01
	Tulsa MSA, OK	Y	43000 FQ	63340 AW	87760 TQ	OKBLS	10/01-12/01
	Oregon	Y	38240 FQ	62650 AW	100930 TQ	ORBLS	10/01-12/01
	Eugene-Springfield MSA, OR	Y	35990 FQ	56190 AW	82320 TQ	ORBLS	10/01-12/01
	Portland-Vancouver PMSA, OR-WA	Y	38810 FQ	64260 AW	102510 TQ	ORBLS	10/01-12/01
	Salem PMSA, OR	Y	32490 FQ	48620 AW	71150 TQ	ORBLS	10/01-12/01
	Pennsylvania	Y	39160 FQ	59960 AW	86710 TQ	PABLS	10/01-12/01
	Allentown-Bethlehem-Easton MSA, PA	Y	42550 FQ	60710 AW	82380 TQ	PABLS	10/01-12/01
	Erie MSA, PA	Y	39790 FQ	52930 AW	67640 TQ	PABLS	10/01-12/01
	Harrisburg-Lebanon-Carlisle MSA, PA	Y	37620 FQ	55250 AW	77870 TQ	PABLS	10/01-12/01
	Johnstown MSA, PA	Y	36930 FQ	54400 AW	76190 TQ	PABLS	10/01-12/01
	Lancaster MSA, PA	Y	37730 FQ	53920 AW	77250 TQ	PABLS	10/01-12/01
	Philadelphia PMSA, PA-NJ	Y	42460 FQ	64770 AW	91000 TQ	PABLS	10/01-12/01
	Pittsburgh MSA, PA	Y	39720 FQ	62950 AW	89210 TQ	PABLS	10/01-12/01
	Reading MSA, PA	Y	37730 FQ	59910 AW	100260 TQ	PABLS	10/01-12/01
	Scranton-Wilkes-Barre-Hazleton MSA, PA	Y	39000 FQ	55240 AW	72670 TQ	PABLS	10/01-12/01
	York MSA, PA	Y	38630 FQ	53140 AW	71060 TQ	PABLS	10/01-12/01
	Rhode Island	Y	41140 FQ	63950 AW	88640 TQ	RIBLS	10/01-12/01
	Providence-Fall River-Warwick MSA, RI-MA	Y	39990 FQ	58010 AW	81240 TQ	RIBLS	10/01-12/01
	South Carolina	Y	39160 FQ	61380 AW	90730 TQ	SCBLS	10/01-12/01
	Charleston-North Charleston MSA, SC	Y	26200 FQ	47230 AW	70970 TQ	SCBLS	10/01-12/01
	Columbia MSA, SC	Y	39550 FQ	60910 AW	88280 TQ	SCBLS	10/01-12/01

AAW	Average annual wage	**AOH**	Average offered, high	**ASH**	Average starting, high	**H**	Hourly	**M**	Monthly	**S**	Special: hourly and annual
AE	Average entry wage	**AOL**	Average offered, low	**ASL**	Average starting, low	**HI**	Highest wage paid	**MTC**	Median total compensation	**TQ**	Third quartile wage
AEX	Average experienced wage	**APH**	Average pay, high range	**AW**	Average wage paid	**HR**	High end range	**MW**	Median wage paid	**W**	Weekly
AO	Average offered	**APL**	Average pay, low range	**FQ**	First quartile wage	**LR**	Low end range	**SQ**	Second quartile wage	**Y**	Yearly

Occupation/Type/Industry	Location	Per	Low	Mid	High	Source	Date
Mechanical Engineer	Greenville-Spartanburg-Anderson MSA, SC	Y	41650 FQ	61370 AW	87950 TQ	SCBLS	10/01-12/01
	South Dakota	Y	40210 FQ	57020 AW	81020 TQ	SDBLS	10/01-12/01
	Sioux Falls MSA, SD	Y	39770 FQ	52340 AW	70440 TQ	SDBLS	10/01-12/01
	Tennessee	Y	40410 FQ	60400 AW	85450 TQ	TNBLS	10/01-12/01
	Chattanooga MSA, TN-GA	Y	45290 FQ	64910 AW	85370 TQ	TNBLS	10/01-12/01
	Clarksville-Hopkinsville MSA, TN-KY	Y	44320 FQ	68620 AW	101900 TQ	TNBLS	10/01-12/01
	Johnson City-Kingsport-Bristol MSA, TN-VA	Y	37720 FQ	52570 AW	70410 TQ	TNBLS	10/01-12/01
	Knoxville MSA, TN	Y	41540 FQ	63330 AW	89430 TQ	TNBLS	10/01-12/01
	Memphis MSA, TN-AR-MS	Y	42580 FQ	61730 AW	87620 TQ	TNBLS	10/01-12/01
	Nashville MSA, TN	Y	39420 FQ	56920 AW	76810 TQ	TNBLS	10/01-12/01
	Texas	Y	46430 FQ	73150 AW	100130 TQ	TXBLS	10/01-12/01
	Amarillo MSA, TX	Y	40630 FQ	65870 AW	95330 TQ	TXBLS	10/01-12/01
	Austin-San Marcos MSA, TX	Y	42390 FQ	66140 AW	92030 TQ	TXBLS	10/01-12/01
	Beaumont-Port Arthur MSA, TX	Y	43790 FQ	69540 AW	94440 TQ	TXBLS	10/01-12/01
	Brazoria PMSA, TX	Y	46160 FQ	77800 AW	126240 TQ	TXBLS	10/01-12/01
	Brownsville-Harlingen-San Benito MSA, TX	Y	35520 FQ	61770 AW	100790 TQ	TXBLS	10/01-12/01
	Corpus Christi MSA, TX	Y	39500 FQ	61420 AW	88710 TQ	TXBLS	10/01-12/01
	Dallas PMSA, TX	Y	46430 FQ	69520 AW	102500 TQ	TXBLS	10/01-12/01
	El Paso MSA, TX	Y	39110 FQ	56960 AW	80090 TQ	TXBLS	10/01-12/01
	Fort Worth-Arlington PMSA, TX	Y	45420 FQ	66350 AW	103520 TQ	TXBLS	10/01-12/01
	Galveston-Texas City PMSA, TX	Y	36210 FQ	66850 AW	97090 TQ	TXBLS	10/01-12/01
	Houston PMSA, TX	Y	49230 FQ	78800 AW	102430 TQ	TXBLS	10/01-12/01
	Killeen-Temple MSA, TX	Y	38790 FQ	57510 AW	80730 TQ	TXBLS	10/01-12/01
	Longview-Marshall MSA, TX	Y	41150 FQ	61410 AW	87550 TQ	TXBLS	10/01-12/01
	Lubbock MSA, TX	Y	36620 FQ	51860 AW	71720 TQ	TXBLS	10/01-12/01
	Odessa-Midland MSA, TX	Y	44770 FQ	64650 AW	87140 TQ	TXBLS	10/01-12/01
	San Antonio MSA, TX	Y	39670 FQ	60300 AW	88940 TQ	TXBLS	10/01-12/01
	Tyler MSA, TX	Y	44830 FQ	62230 AW	88910 TQ	TXBLS	10/01-12/01
	Waco MSA, TX	Y	38730 FQ	59890 AW	87790 TQ	TXBLS	10/01-12/01
	Utah	Y	41860 FQ	60520 AW	83560 TQ	UTBLS	10/01-12/01
	Provo-Orem MSA, UT	Y	37020 FQ	63170 AW	90740 TQ	UTBLS	10/01-12/01
	Salt Lake City-Ogden MSA, UT	Y	40890 FQ	59570 AW	83500 TQ	UTBLS	10/01-12/01
	Vermont	Y	38680 FQ	57880 AW	84140 TQ	VTBLS	10/01-12/01
	Burlington MSA, VT	Y	37850 FQ	58170 AW	85730 TQ	VTBLS	10/01-12/01
	Virginia	Y	43220 FQ	61730 AW	84690 TQ	VABLS	10/01-12/01
	Norfolk-Virginia Beach-Newport News MSA, VA-NC	Y	45020 FQ	58370 AW	73210 TQ	VABLS	10/01-12/01
	Richmond-Petersburg MSA, VA	Y	46420 FQ	65450 AW	88750 TQ	VABLS	10/01-12/01
	Roanoke MSA, VA	Y	37180 FQ	56100 AW	92630 TQ	VABLS	10/01-12/01
	Washington	Y	44690 FQ	64200 AW	90210 TQ	WABLS	10/01-12/01
	Bremerton PMSA, WA	Y	46420 FQ	61400 AW	75870 TQ	WABLS	10/01-12/01
	Richland-Kennewick-Pasco MSA, WA	Y	57290 FQ	79800 AW	109280 TQ	WABLS	10/01-12/01
	Seattle-Bellevue-Everett PMSA, WA	Y	45970 FQ	64090 AW	88680 TQ	WABLS	10/01-12/01
	Spokane MSA, WA	Y	37410 FQ	55050 AW	74860 TQ	WABLS	10/01-12/01
	Tacoma PMSA, WA	Y	40120 FQ	58980 AW	82440 TQ	WABLS	10/01-12/01
	Yakima MSA, WA	Y	31020 FQ	49730 AW	78710 TQ	WABLS	10/01-12/01
	West Virginia	Y	38060 FQ	61570 AW	100130 TQ	WVBLS	10/01-12/01
	Huntington-Ashland MSA, WV-KY-OH	Y	35190 FQ	52640 AW	71470 TQ	WVBLS	10/01-12/01
	Wisconsin	Y	39180 FQ	57030 AW	77590 TQ	WIBLS	10/01-12/01
	Appleton-Oshkosh-Neenah MSA, WI	Y	40120 FQ	56270 AW	73170 TQ	WIBLS	10/01-12/01
	Green Bay MSA, WI	Y	39650 FQ	59970 AW	87490 TQ	WIBLS	10/01-12/01
	Madison MSA, WI	Y	29810 FQ	51690 AW	74540 TQ	WIBLS	10/01-12/01
	Milwaukee-Waukesha PMSA, WI	Y	42150 FQ	58750 AW	80040 TQ	WIBLS	10/01-12/01
	Racine PMSA, WI	Y	39620 FQ	56860 AW	74320 TQ	WIBLS	10/01-12/01
	Wyoming	Y	33100 FQ	51470 AW	72820 TQ	WYBLS	10/01-12/01
	Puerto Rico	Y	29670 FQ	47010 AW	68670 TQ	PRBLS	10/01-12/01

AAW	Average annual wage	**AOH**	Average offered, high	**ASH**	Average starting, high	**H**	Hourly	**M**	Monthly	**S**	Special: hourly and annual
AE	Average entry wage	**AOL**	Average offered, low	**ASL**	Average starting, low	**HI**	Highest wage paid	**MTC**	Median total compensation	**TQ**	Third quartile wage
AEX	Average experienced wage	**APH**	Average pay, high range	**AW**	Average wage paid	**HR**	High end range	**MW**	Median wage paid	**W**	Weekly
AO	Average offered	**APL**	Average pay, low range	**FQ**	First quartile wage	**LR**	Low end range	**SQ**	Second quartile wage	**Y**	Yearly

Occupation/Type/Industry	Location	Per	Low	Mid	High	Source	Date
Mechanical Engineering Technician	Alabama	Y	22390 FQ	37970 AW	57550 TQ	ALBLS	10/01-12/01
	Birmingham MSA, AL	Y	20350 FQ	40210 AW	70410 TQ	ALBLS	10/01-12/01
	Huntsville MSA, AL	Y	21860 FQ	36960 AW	55850 TQ	ALBLS	10/01-12/01
	Mobile MSA, AL	Y	27420 FQ	49110 AW	70910 TQ	ALBLS	10/01-12/01
	Arizona	Y	25300 FQ	38760 AW	53890 TQ	AZBLS	10/01-12/01
	Phoenix-Mesa MSA, AZ	Y	25370 FQ	38460 AW	53240 TQ	AZBLS	10/01-12/01
	Tucson MSA, AZ	Y	24700 FQ	40840 AW	56620 TQ	AZBLS	10/01-12/01
	Arkansas	Y	25960 FQ	43430 AW	72550 TQ	ARBLS	10/01-12/01
	Little Rock-North Little Rock MSA, AR	Y	25940 FQ	37450 AW	60900 TQ	ARBLS	10/01-12/01
	California	Y	27850 FQ	47530 AW	72440 TQ	CABLS	10/01-12/01
	Los Angeles-Long Beach PMSA, CA	Y	23720 FQ	38610 AW	57510 TQ	CABLS	10/01-12/01
	Modesto MSA, CA	Y	27900 FQ	40120 AW	55010 TQ	CABLS	10/01-12/01
	Oakland PMSA, CA	Y	28570 FQ	43700 AW	67970 TQ	CABLS	10/01-12/01
	Orange County PMSA, CA	Y	27050 FQ	45140 AW	66210 TQ	CABLS	10/01-12/01
	Riverside-San Bernardino PMSA, CA	Y	25520 FQ	38980 AW	56640 TQ	CABLS	10/01-12/01
	Sacramento PMSA, CA	Y	40220 FQ	66690 AW	121510 TQ	CABLS	10/01-12/01
	San Diego MSA, CA	Y	28400 FQ	43700 AW	62070 TQ	CABLS	10/01-12/01
	San Francisco PMSA, CA	Y	28540 FQ	42170 AW	60560 TQ	CABLS	10/01-12/01
	San Jose PMSA, CA	Y	34530 FQ	56410 AW	83570 TQ	CABLS	10/01-12/01
	Santa Barbara-Santa Maria-Lompoc MSA, CA	Y	28100 FQ	39680 AW	55210 TQ	CABLS	10/01-12/01
	Santa Rosa PMSA, CA	Y	31320 FQ	44360 AW	57970 TQ	CABLS	10/01-12/01
	Ventura PMSA, CA	Y	30240 FQ	46060 AW	61560 TQ	CABLS	10/01-12/01
	Colorado	Y	26170 FQ	41200 AW	57280 TQ	COBLS	10/01-12/01
	Boulder-Longmont PMSA, CO	Y	28760 FQ	43180 AW	57980 TQ	COBLS	10/01-12/01
	Colorado Springs MSA, CO	Y	23790 FQ	35430 AW	43890 TQ	COBLS	10/01-12/01
	Denver PMSA, CO	Y	29470 FQ	43550 AW	65560 TQ	COBLS	10/01-12/01
	Fort Collins-Loveland MSA, CO	Y	34750 FQ	48240 AW	60470 TQ	COBLS	10/01-12/01
	Connecticut	Y	29280 FQ	42670 AW	55920 TQ	CTBLS	10/01-12/01
	Bridgeport PMSA, CT	Y	36040 FQ	50460 AW	68860 TQ	CTBLS	10/01-12/01
	Danbury PMSA, CT	Y	33490 FQ	48560 AW	65960 TQ	CTBLS	10/01-12/01
	Hartford MSA, CT	Y	24340 FQ	36930 AW	49510 TQ	CTBLS	10/01-12/01
	New Haven-Meriden PMSA, CT	Y	32400 FQ	46720 AW	68530 TQ	CTBLS	10/01-12/01
	Stamford-Norwalk PMSA, CT	Y	26680 FQ	44450 AW	65180 TQ	CTBLS	10/01-12/01
	Delaware	Y	29840 FQ	43820 AW	60380 TQ	DEBLS	10/01-12/01
	Wilmington-Newark PMSA, DE-MD	Y	30680 FQ	45730 AW	63520 TQ	DEBLS	10/01-12/01
	District of Columbia	Y	29080 FQ	43690 AW	60420 TQ	DCBLS	10/01-12/01
	Washington PMSA, DC-MD-VA-WV	Y	23080 FQ	40380 AW	57190 TQ	DCBLS	10/01-12/01
	Florida	Y	25590 FQ	38700 AW	53360 TQ	FLBLS	10/01-12/01
	Daytona Beach MSA, FL	Y	31680 FQ	38840 AW	46070 TQ	FLBLS	10/01-12/01
	Fort Lauderdale PMSA, FL	Y	23670 FQ	35390 AW	50040 TQ	FLBLS	10/01-12/01
	Fort Walton Beach MSA, FL	Y	26910 FQ	42470 AW	56220 TQ	FLBLS	10/01-12/01
	Jacksonville MSA, FL	Y	29130 FQ	45510 AW	68900 TQ	FLBLS	10/01-12/01
	Melbourne-Titusville-Palm Bay MSA, FL	Y	25000 FQ	38780 AW	53490 TQ	FLBLS	10/01-12/01
	Miami PMSA, FL	Y	23590 FQ	36440 AW	46520 TQ	FLBLS	10/01-12/01
	Orlando MSA, FL	Y	28800 FQ	39690 AW	50770 TQ	FLBLS	10/01-12/01
	Sarasota-Bradenton MSA, FL	Y	26230 FQ	37010 AW	45250 TQ	FLBLS	10/01-12/01
	Tampa-St. Petersburg-Clearwater MSA, FL	Y	26470 FQ	39000 AW	55370 TQ	FLBLS	10/01-12/01
	West Palm Beach-Boca Raton MSA, FL	Y	26900 FQ	39390 AW	55840 TQ	FLBLS	10/01-12/01
	Georgia	Y	26820 FQ	42870 AW	67630 TQ	GABLS	10/01-12/01
	Atlanta MSA, GA	Y	27990 FQ	45840 AW	76080 TQ	GABLS	10/01-12/01
	Augusta-Aiken MSA, GA-SC	Y	24870 FQ	48720 AW	83910 TQ	GABLS	10/01-12/01
	Macon MSA, GA	Y	23170 FQ	35480 AW	48680 TQ	GABLS	10/01-12/01
	Hawaii	Y	22990 FQ	41640 AW	55380 TQ	HIBLS	10/01-12/01
	Honolulu MSA, HI	Y	24530 FQ	40790 AW	55320 TQ	HIBLS	10/01-12/01
	Idaho	Y	21280 FQ	33180 AW	47740 TQ	IDBLS	10/01-12/01
	Boise City MSA, ID	Y	23110 FQ	31260 AW	42220 TQ	IDBLS	10/01-12/01
	Illinois	Y	25900 FQ	41380 AW	59280 TQ	ILBLS	10/01-12/01
	Champaign-Urbana MSA, IL	Y	32010 FQ	49890 AW	71300 TQ	ILBLS	10/01-12/01
	Chicago PMSA, IL	Y	25670 FQ	41190 AW	59620 TQ	ILBLS	10/01-12/01
	Rockford MSA, IL	Y	26160 FQ	39590 AW	48250 TQ	ILBLS	10/01-12/01

Occupation/Type/Industry	Location	Per	Low	Mid	High	Source	Date
Mechanical Engineering Technician	Indiana	Y	27260 FQ	40260 AW	54750 TQ	INBLS	10/01-12/01
	Elkhart-Goshen MSA, IN	Y	25440 FQ	34000 AW	45520 TQ	INBLS	10/01-12/01
	Evansville-Henderson MSA, IN-KY	Y	25770 FQ	40080 AW	59860 TQ	INBLS	10/01-12/01
	Fort Wayne MSA, IN	Y	27060 FQ	42320 AW	58340 TQ	INBLS	10/01-12/01
	Gary PMSA, IN	Y	24200 FQ	43390 AW	55870 TQ	INBLS	10/01-12/01
	Indianapolis MSA, IN	Y	30450 FQ	41500 AW	54840 TQ	INBLS	10/01-12/01
	Lafayette MSA, IN	Y	29550 FQ	39150 AW	49920 TQ	INBLS	10/01-12/01
	South Bend MSA, IN	Y	29080 FQ	40290 AW	53020 TQ	INBLS	10/01-12/01
	Iowa	Y	26050 FQ	39900 AW	56770 TQ	IABLS	10/01-12/01
	Davenport-Moline-Rock Island MSA, IA-IL	Y	26830 FQ	44010 AW	66700 TQ	IABLS	10/01-12/01
	Des Moines MSA, IA	Y	27000 FQ	44670 AW	57320 TQ	IABLS	10/01-12/01
	Kansas	Y	27220 FQ	40180 AW	56120 TQ	KSBLS	10/01-12/01
	Topeka MSA, KS	Y	34310 FQ	40580 AW	50120 TQ	KSBLS	10/01-12/01
	Wichita MSA, KS	Y	28460 FQ	42320 AW	62500 TQ	KSBLS	10/01-12/01
	Kentucky	Y	24890 FQ	36640 AW	54070 TQ	KYBLS	10/01-12/01
	Lexington MSA, KY	Y	24530 FQ	35510 AW	54290 TQ	KYBLS	10/01-12/01
	Louisville MSA, KY-IN	Y	25140 FQ	36120 AW	52600 TQ	KYBLS	10/01-12/01
	Louisiana	Y	30490 FQ	46670 AW	68790 TQ	LABLS	10/01-12/01
	Baton Rouge MSA, LA	Y	31070 FQ	49120 AW	70710 TQ	LABLS	10/01-12/01
	Lafayette MSA, LA	Y	27170 FQ	41800 AW	57670 TQ	LABLS	10/01-12/01
	New Orleans MSA, LA	Y	33530 FQ	47690 AW	68930 TQ	LABLS	10/01-12/01
	Maine	Y	26420 FQ	39750 AW	57430 TQ	MEBLS	10/01-12/01
	Portland MSA, ME	Y	28350 FQ	38970 AW	54430 TQ	MEBLS	10/01-12/01
	Maryland	Y	27270 FQ	42130 AW	57890 TQ	MDBLS	10/01-12/01
	Baltimore PMSA, MD	Y	30220 FQ	44020 AW	58480 TQ	MDBLS	10/01-12/01
	Massachusetts	Y	31270 FQ	45120 AW	60700 TQ	MABLS	10/01-12/01
	Boston PMSA, MA-NH	Y	32380 FQ	46240 AW	62360 TQ	MABLS	10/01-12/01
	Lawrence PMSA, MA-NH	Y	35390 FQ	45290 AW	57800 TQ	MABLS	10/01-12/01
	Lowell PMSA, MA-NH	Y	26300 FQ	41020 AW	59080 TQ	MABLS	10/01-12/01
	New Bedford PMSA, MA	Y	30880 FQ	41480 AW	54460 TQ	MABLS	10/01-12/01
	Springfield MSA, MA	Y	27240 FQ	44720 AW	64190 TQ	MABLS	10/01-12/01
	Worcester PMSA, MA-CT	Y	30770 FQ	44280 AW	59790 TQ	MABLS	10/01-12/01
	Michigan	Y	29640 FQ	45240 AW	62240 TQ	MIBLS	10/01-12/01
	Ann Arbor PMSA, MI	Y	36220 FQ	51290 AW	69080 TQ	MIBLS	10/01-12/01
	Detroit PMSA, MI	Y	29690 FQ	46800 AW	66520 TQ	MIBLS	10/01-12/01
	Flint PMSA, MI	Y	27150 FQ	42920 AW	59340 TQ	MIBLS	10/01-12/01
	Grand Rapids-Muskegon-Holland MSA, MI	Y	28990 FQ	41770 AW	57550 TQ	MIBLS	10/01-12/01
	Kalamazoo-Battle Creek MSA, MI	Y	33910 FQ	47840 AW	59180 TQ	MIBLS	10/01-12/01
	Lansing-East Lansing MSA, MI	Y	25990 FQ	41280 AW	66560 TQ	MIBLS	10/01-12/01
	Saginaw-Bay City-Midland MSA, MI	Y	29120 FQ	44540 AW	62170 TQ	MIBLS	10/01-12/01
	Minnesota	Y	31360 FQ	44200 AW	59840 TQ	MNBLS	10/01-12/01
	Minneapolis-St. Paul MSA, MN-WI	Y	32940 FQ	45950 AW	61940 TQ	MNBLS	10/01-12/01
	Mississippi	Y	24400 FQ	36620 AW	50990 TQ	MSBLS	10/01-12/01
	Biloxi-Gulfport-Pascagoula MSA, MS	Y	30560 FQ	39440 AW	48530 TQ	MSBLS	10/01-12/01
	Jackson MSA, MS	Y	21720 FQ	35420 AW	51070 TQ	MSBLS	10/01-12/01
	Missouri	Y	28640 FQ	46180 AW	72530 TQ	MOBLS	10/01-12/01
	Kansas City MSA, MO-KS	Y	25480 FQ	41090 AW	59950 TQ	MOBLS	10/01-12/01
	St. Louis MSA, MO-IL	Y	28400 FQ	48230 AW	80850 TQ	MOBLS	10/01-12/01
	Springfield MSA, MO	Y	25150 FQ	37940 AW	52620 TQ	MOBLS	10/01-12/01
	Montana	Y	20370 FQ	37550 AW	56450 TQ	MTBLS	10/01-12/01
	Nebraska	Y	25790 FQ	39610 AW	57800 TQ	NEBLS	10/01-12/01
	Lincoln MSA, NE	Y	29740 FQ	44200 AW	56810 TQ	NEBLS	10/01-12/01
	Omaha MSA, NE-IA	Y	25690 FQ	37070 AW	52500 TQ	NEBLS	10/01-12/01
	Nevada	Y	31680 FQ	46590 AW	64320 TQ	NVBLS	10/01-12/01
	Las Vegas MSA, NV-AZ	Y	37850 FQ	48270 AW	64930 TQ	NVBLS	10/01-12/01
	Reno MSA, NV	Y	28710 FQ	39750 AW	54050 TQ	NVBLS	10/01-12/01
	New Hampshire	Y	28220 FQ	39220 AW	52140 TQ	NHBLS	10/01-12/01
	Manchester PMSA, NH	Y	30170 FQ	38630 AW	47230 TQ	NHBLS	10/01-12/01
	Nashua PMSA, NH	Y	30020 FQ	39180 AW	49010 TQ	NHBLS	10/01-12/01
	Portsmouth-Rochester PMSA, NH-ME	Y	24160 FQ	37780 AW	51690 TQ	NHBLS	10/01-12/01
	New Jersey	Y	34270 FQ	50750 AW	73560 TQ	NJBLS	10/01-12/01
	Bergen-Passaic PMSA, NJ	Y	31430 FQ	51640 AW	72950 TQ	NJBLS	10/01-12/01

AAW	Average annual wage	**AOH**	Average offered, high	**ASH**	Average starting, high	**H**	Hourly	**M**	Monthly	**S**	Special: hourly and annual
AE	Average entry wage	**AOL**	Average offered, low	**ASL**	Average starting, low	**HI**	Highest wage paid	**MTC**	Median total compensation	**TQ**	Third quartile wage
AEX	Average experienced wage	**APH**	Average pay, high range	**AW**	Average wage paid	**HR**	High end range	**MW**	Median wage paid	**W**	Weekly
AO	Average offered	**APL**	Average pay, low range	**FQ**	First quartile wage	**LR**	Low end range	**SQ**	Second quartile wage	**Y**	Yearly

Occupation/Type/Industry	Location	Per	Low	Mid	High	Source	Date
Mechanical Engineering Technician	Middlesex-Somerset-Hunterdon PMSA, NJ	Y	37200 FQ	52110 AW	75590 TQ	NJBLS	10/01-12/01
	Monmouth-Ocean PMSA, NJ	Y	39910 FQ	65120 AW	87530 TQ	NJBLS	10/01-12/01
	Newark PMSA, NJ	Y	32580 FQ	46760 AW	59890 TQ	NJBLS	10/01-12/01
	Albuquerque MSA, NM	Y	34550 FQ	47070 AW	59850 TQ	NMBLS	10/01-12/01
	New York	Y	25980 FQ	40350 AW	56490 TQ	NYBLS	10/01-12/01
	Albany-Schenectady-Troy MSA, NY	Y	26080 FQ	38830 AW	55650 TQ	NYBLS	10/01-12/01
	Buffalo-Niagara Falls MSA, NY	Y	27550 FQ	42640 AW	56900 TQ	NYBLS	10/01-12/01
	Nassau-Suffolk PMSA, NY	Y	31590 FQ	43010 AW	57260 TQ	NYBLS	10/01-12/01
	New York PMSA, NY	Y	22890 FQ	40180 AW	57690 TQ	NYBLS	10/01-12/01
	Rochester MSA, NY	Y	30390 FQ	42780 AW	57200 TQ	NYBLS	10/01-12/01
	Syracuse MSA, NY	Y	26120 FQ	41420 AW	56020 TQ	NYBLS	10/01-12/01
	North Carolina	Y	27010 FQ	42470 AW	62640 TQ	NCBLS	10/01-12/01
	Charlotte-Gastonia-Rock Hill MSA, NC-SC	Y	26410 FQ	41820 AW	59600 TQ	NCBLS	10/01-12/01
	Fayetteville MSA, NC	Y	29660 FQ	40850 AW	53240 TQ	NCBLS	10/01-12/01
	Greensboro-Winston-Salem-High Point MSA, NC	Y	27740 FQ	41730 AW	56130 TQ	NCBLS	10/01-12/01
	Raleigh-Durham-Chapel Hill MSA, NC	Y	29110 FQ	45370 AW	77130 TQ	NCBLS	10/01-12/01
	Wilmington MSA, NC	Y	30880 FQ	49510 AW	81110 TQ	NCBLS	10/01-12/01
	North Dakota	Y	22210 FQ	34310 AW	51940 TQ	NDBLS	10/01-12/01
	Fargo-Moorhead MSA, ND-MN	Y	20840 FQ	30770 AW	44710 TQ	NDBLS	10/01-12/01
	Ohio	Y	25690 FQ	38540 AW	53740 TQ	OHBLS	10/01-12/01
	Akron PMSA, OH	Y	28970 FQ	39660 AW	58250 TQ	OHBLS	10/01-12/01
	Canton-Massillon MSA, OH	Y	30430 FQ	40450 AW	53190 TQ	OHBLS	10/01-12/01
	Cincinnati PMSA, OH-KY-IN	Y	24570 FQ	39290 AW	56120 TQ	OHBLS	10/01-12/01
	Cleveland-Lorain-Elyria PMSA, OH	Y	30710 FQ	42410 AW	55970 TQ	OHBLS	10/01-12/01
	Columbus MSA, OH	Y	28220 FQ	41140 AW	54330 TQ	OHBLS	10/01-12/01
	Dayton-Springfield MSA, OH	Y	24750 FQ	36200 AW	50460 TQ	OHBLS	10/01-12/01
	Hamilton-Middletown PMSA, OH	Y	32980 FQ	58350 AW	90830 TQ	OHBLS	10/01-12/01
	Toledo MSA, OH	Y	29450 FQ	43200 AW	57090 TQ	OHBLS	10/01-12/01
	Youngstown-Warren MSA, OH	Y	20190 FQ	31830 AW	51170 TQ	OHBLS	10/01-12/01
	Tulsa MSA, OK	Y	21290 FQ	39070 AW	63230 TQ	OKBLS	10/01-12/01
	Oregon	Y	35040 FQ	43160 AW	57150 TQ	ORBLS	10/01-12/01
	Eugene-Springfield MSA, OR	Y	29640 FQ	38910 AW	48730 TQ	ORBLS	10/01-12/01
	Portland-Vancouver PMSA, OR-WA	Y	35820 FQ	44190 AW	59650 TQ	ORBLS	10/01-12/01
	Pennsylvania	Y	25220 FQ	41880 AW	60940 TQ	PABLS	10/01-12/01
	Allentown-Bethlehem-Easton MSA, PA	Y	30660 FQ	44070 AW	58340 TQ	PABLS	10/01-12/01
	Johnstown MSA, PA	Y	22690 FQ	33310 AW	45790 TQ	PABLS	10/01-12/01
	Lancaster MSA, PA	Y	26430 FQ	45770 AW	71420 TQ	PABLS	10/01-12/01
	Philadelphia PMSA, PA-NJ	Y	25560 FQ	43900 AW	65080 TQ	PABLS	10/01-12/01
	Pittsburgh MSA, PA	Y	25920 FQ	44940 AW	66990 TQ	PABLS	10/01-12/01
	Reading MSA, PA	Y	22290 FQ	38200 AW	54320 TQ	PABLS	10/01-12/01
	York MSA, PA	Y	31810 FQ	44290 AW	56530 TQ	PABLS	10/01-12/01
	Rhode Island	Y	28700 FQ	42440 AW	56390 TQ	RIBLS	10/01-12/01
	Providence-Fall River-Warwick MSA, RI-MA	Y	25910 FQ	40040 AW	56240 TQ	RIBLS	10/01-12/01
	South Carolina	Y	25630 FQ	42500 AW	63250 TQ	SCBLS	10/01-12/01
	Charleston-North Charleston MSA, SC	Y	26770 FQ	42800 AW	63820 TQ	SCBLS	10/01-12/01
	Columbia MSA, SC	Y	31510 FQ	43380 AW	55360 TQ	SCBLS	10/01-12/01
	Greenville-Spartanburg-Anderson MSA, SC	Y	30150 FQ	46150 AW	66460 TQ	SCBLS	10/01-12/01
	South Dakota	Y	24390 FQ	33540 AW	43280 TQ	SDBLS	10/01-12/01
	Sioux Falls MSA, SD	Y	24170 FQ	32970 AW	43630 TQ	SDBLS	10/01-12/01
	Tennessee	Y	27400 FQ	41120 AW	57790 TQ	TNBLS	10/01-12/01
	Knoxville MSA, TN	Y	28700 FQ	41860 AW	55120 TQ	TNBLS	10/01-12/01
	Memphis MSA, TN-AR-MS	Y	27140 FQ	40860 AW	60540 TQ	TNBLS	10/01-12/01
	Nashville MSA, TN	Y	28630 FQ	40220 AW	56280 TQ	TNBLS	10/01-12/01
	Texas	Y	26580 FQ	41640 AW	57420 TQ	TXBLS	10/01-12/01
	Austin-San Marcos MSA, TX	Y	29940 FQ	43150 AW	60780 TQ	TXBLS	10/01-12/01
	Dallas PMSA, TX	Y	25060 FQ	41870 AW	56490 TQ	TXBLS	10/01-12/01
	El Paso MSA, TX	Y	22770 FQ	37370 AW	54230 TQ	TXBLS	10/01-12/01

AAW Average annual wage; AE Average entry wage; AEX Average experienced wage; AO Average offered; AOH Average offered, high; AOL Average offered, low; APH Average pay, high range; APL Average pay, low range; ASH Average starting, high; ASL Average starting, low; AW Average wage paid; FQ First quartile wage; H Hourly; HI Highest wage paid; HR High end range; LR Low end range; M Monthly; MTC Median total compensation; MW Median wage paid; SQ Second quartile wage; S Special: hourly and annual; TQ Third quartile wage; W Weekly; Y Yearly

Occupation/Type/Industry	Location	Per	Low	Mid	High	Source	Date
Mechanical Engineering Technician	Fort Worth-Arlington PMSA, TX	Y	28950 FQ	39350 AW	52850 TQ	TXBLS	10/01-12/01
	Houston PMSA, TX	Y	28310 FQ	41940 AW	58320 TQ	TXBLS	10/01-12/01
	Longview-Marshall MSA, TX	Y	26120 FQ	45550 AW	61050 TQ	TXBLS	10/01-12/01
	San Antonio MSA, TX	Y	21280 FQ	35160 AW	55410 TQ	TXBLS	10/01-12/01
	Tyler MSA, TX	Y	25340 FQ	37630 AW	48810 TQ	TXBLS	10/01-12/01
	Waco MSA, TX	Y	27630 FQ	44300 AW	63350 TQ	TXBLS	10/01-12/01
	Utah	Y	29870 FQ	41520 AW	54940 TQ	UTBLS	10/01-12/01
	Salt Lake City-Ogden MSA, UT	Y	25850 FQ	39050 AW	52390 TQ	UTBLS	10/01-12/01
	Vermont	Y	30550 FQ	42870 AW	56330 TQ	VTBLS	10/01-12/01
	Burlington MSA, VT	Y	34690 FQ	46630 AW	62240 TQ	VTBLS	10/01-12/01
	Virginia	Y	26290 FQ	39330 AW	54240 TQ	VABLS	10/01-12/01
	Lynchburg MSA, VA	Y	27090 FQ	38960 AW	50610 TQ	VABLS	10/01-12/01
	Norfolk-Virginia Beach-Newport News MSA, VA-NC	Y	27360 FQ	38770 AW	49250 TQ	VABLS	10/01-12/01
	Richmond-Petersburg MSA, VA	Y	24630 FQ	37580 AW	52030 TQ	VABLS	10/01-12/01
	Roanoke MSA, VA	Y	20330 FQ	37600 AW	58620 TQ	VABLS	10/01-12/01
	Washington	Y	30790 FQ	44730 AW	61950 TQ	WABLS	10/01-12/01
	Bremerton PMSA, WA	Y	24240 FQ	32360 AW	43480 TQ	WABLS	10/01-12/01
	Richland-Kennewick-Pasco MSA, WA	Y	36540 FQ	52820 AW	79240 TQ	WABLS	10/01-12/01
	Seattle-Bellevue-Everett PMSA, WA	Y	30890 FQ	43620 AW	57430 TQ	WABLS	10/01-12/01
	Spokane MSA, WA	Y	31790 FQ	44280 AW	63690 TQ	WABLS	10/01-12/01
	Tacoma PMSA, WA	Y	30130 FQ	43250 AW	56260 TQ	WABLS	10/01-12/01
	West Virginia	Y	24180 FQ	40780 AW	62230 TQ	WVBLS	10/01-12/01
	Charleston MSA, WV	Y	26470 FQ	47830 AW	72670 TQ	WVBLS	10/01-12/01
	Huntington-Ashland MSA, WV-KY-OH	Y	25490 FQ	37440 AW	55000 TQ	WVBLS	10/01-12/01
	Wisconsin	Y	27260 FQ	42680 AW	61690 TQ	WIBLS	10/01-12/01
	Green Bay MSA, WI	Y	24210 FQ	42520 AW	60840 TQ	WIBLS	10/01-12/01
	Madison MSA, WI	Y	28620 FQ	43010 AW	59500 TQ	WIBLS	10/01-12/01
	Milwaukee-Waukesha PMSA, WI	Y	27700 FQ	41720 AW	61000 TQ	WIBLS	10/01-12/01
	Puerto Rico	Y	13660 FQ	26480 AW	42280 TQ	PRBLS	10/01-12/01
Media Director							
Advertising	East	Y		74000 AW		ADAGE	1/00-1/01
Advertising	Midwest	Y		68000 AW		ADAGE	1/00-1/01
Advertising	South	Y		65000 AW		ADAGE	1/00-1/01
Advertising	West	Y		83000 AW		ADAGE	1/00-1/01
Medical and Clinical Laboratory Technician	Alabama	Y	16330 FQ	27040 AW	40380 TQ	ALBLS	10/01-12/01
	Birmingham MSA, AL	Y	17990 FQ	28910 AW	43830 TQ	ALBLS	10/01-12/01
	Huntsville MSA, AL	Y	17020 FQ	27480 AW	40990 TQ	ALBLS	10/01-12/01
	Mobile MSA, AL	Y	15040 FQ	26830 AW	40920 TQ	ALBLS	10/01-12/01
	Montgomery MSA, AL	Y	15210 FQ	23560 AW	33610 TQ	ALBLS	10/01-12/01
	Alaska	Y	24820 FQ	35680 AW	45860 TQ	AKBLS	10/01-12/01
	Anchorage MSA, AK	Y	27640 FQ	34910 AW	43750 TQ	AKBLS	10/01-12/01
	Arizona	Y	17770 FQ	26310 AW	35870 TQ	AZBLS	10/01-12/01
	Phoenix-Mesa MSA, AZ	Y	17870 FQ	26370 AW	35730 TQ	AZBLS	10/01-12/01
	Tucson MSA, AZ	Y	16930 FQ	25250 AW	34800 TQ	AZBLS	10/01-12/01
	Arkansas	Y	17650 FQ	26760 AW	37220 TQ	ARBLS	10/01-12/01
	Fayetteville-Springdale-Rogers MSA, AR	Y	16960 FQ	24150 AW	34520 TQ	ARBLS	10/01-12/01
	Fort Smith MSA, AR-OK	Y	19810 FQ	29300 AW	37970 TQ	ARBLS	10/01-12/01
	Little Rock-North Little Rock MSA, AR	Y	17000 FQ	28120 AW	41810 TQ	ARBLS	10/01-12/01
	California	Y	21390 FQ	34560 AW	52940 TQ	CABLS	10/01-12/01
	Bakersfield MSA, CA	Y	19620 FQ	34870 AW	55180 TQ	CABLS	10/01-12/01
	Chico-Paradise MSA, CA	Y	24300 FQ	37630 AW	58090 TQ	CABLS	10/01-12/01
	Fresno MSA, CA	Y	21280 FQ	31740 AW	51670 TQ	CABLS	10/01-12/01
	Los Angeles-Long Beach PMSA, CA	Y	21240 FQ	32930 AW	48620 TQ	CABLS	10/01-12/01
	Modesto MSA, CA	Y	17820 FQ	34240 AW	53300 TQ	CABLS	10/01-12/01
	Oakland PMSA, CA	Y	28390 FQ	39110 AW	60040 TQ	CABLS	10/01-12/01
	Orange County PMSA, CA	Y	21980 FQ	33870 AW	53930 TQ	CABLS	10/01-12/01

AAW Average annual wage; AE Average entry wage; AEX Average experienced wage; AO Average offered; AOH Average offered, high; AOL Average offered, low; APH Average pay, high range; APL Average pay, low range; ASH Average starting, high; ASL Average starting, low; AW Average wage paid; FQ First quartile wage; H Hourly; HI Highest wage paid; HR High end range; LR Low end range; M Monthly; MTC Median total compensation; MW Median wage paid; SQ Second quartile wage; S Special: hourly and annual; TQ Third quartile wage; W Weekly; Y Yearly

Occupation/Type/Industry	Location	Per	Low	Mid	High	Source	Date
Medical and Clinical Laboratory Technician	Riverside-San Bernardino PMSA, CA	Y	21910 FQ	37830 AW	55890 TQ	CABLS	10/01-12/01
	Sacramento PMSA, CA	Y	26510 FQ	36610 AW	52950 TQ	CABLS	10/01-12/01
	Salinas MSA, CA	Y	23360 FQ	47040 AW	67590 TQ	CABLS	10/01-12/01
	San Diego MSA, CA	Y	18880 FQ	31430 AW	45420 TQ	CABLS	10/01-12/01
	San Francisco PMSA, CA	Y	23860 FQ	35380 AW	52980 TQ	CABLS	10/01-12/01
	San Jose PMSA, CA	Y	28920 FQ	38490 AW	53430 TQ	CABLS	10/01-12/01
	San Luis Obispo-Atascadero-Paso Robles MSA, CA	Y	20300 FQ	43310 AW	56060 TQ	CABLS	10/01-12/01
	Santa Barbara-Santa Maria-Lompoc MSA, CA	Y	19960 FQ	26440 AW	33020 TQ	CABLS	10/01-12/01
	Santa Cruz-Watsonville PMSA, CA	Y	21960 FQ	33680 AW	57840 TQ	CABLS	10/01-12/01
	Santa Rosa PMSA, CA	Y	25190 FQ	37990 AW	56840 TQ	CABLS	10/01-12/01
	Stockton-Lodi MSA, CA	Y	20270 FQ	33540 AW	53230 TQ	CABLS	10/01-12/01
	Vallejo-Fairfield-Napa PMSA, CA	Y	20660 FQ	36800 AW	57700 TQ	CABLS	10/01-12/01
	Ventura PMSA, CA	Y	19710 FQ	28520 AW	44040 TQ	CABLS	10/01-12/01
	Colorado	Y	20770 FQ	31720 AW	44390 TQ	COBLS	10/01-12/01
	Boulder-Longmont PMSA, CO	Y	23620 FQ	33400 AW	44050 TQ	COBLS	10/01-12/01
	Denver PMSA, CO	Y	21060 FQ	31720 AW	44070 TQ	COBLS	10/01-12/01
	Fort Collins-Loveland MSA, CO	Y	21150 FQ	29140 AW	40160 TQ	COBLS	10/01-12/01
	Connecticut	Y	24970 FQ	38880 AW	57210 TQ	CTBLS	10/01-12/01
	Bridgeport PMSA, CT	Y	22600 FQ	38920 AW	59690 TQ	CTBLS	10/01-12/01
	Hartford MSA, CT	Y	25670 FQ	36730 AW	46640 TQ	CTBLS	10/01-12/01
	New London-Norwich MSA, CT-RI	Y	23030 FQ	36120 AW	46630 TQ	CTBLS	10/01-12/01
	Stamford-Norwalk PMSA, CT	Y	35980 FQ	39730 AW	44130 TQ	CTBLS	10/01-12/01
	Delaware	Y	18300 FQ	30340 AW	43490 TQ	DEBLS	10/01-12/01
	Wilmington-Newark PMSA, DE-MD	Y	19420 FQ	31220 AW	44310 TQ	DEBLS	10/01-12/01
	District of Columbia	Y	20800 FQ	33580 AW	47500 TQ	DCBLS	10/01-12/01
	Washington PMSA, DC-MD-VA-WV	Y	21920 FQ	35260 AW	50430 TQ	DCBLS	10/01-12/01
	Florida	Y	17820 FQ	28310 AW	42630 TQ	FLBLS	10/01-12/01
	Daytona Beach MSA, FL	Y	22260 FQ	32200 AW	44450 TQ	FLBLS	10/01-12/01
	Fort Lauderdale PMSA, FL	Y	17300 FQ	34100 AW	55730 TQ	FLBLS	10/01-12/01
	Fort Myers-Cape Coral MSA, FL	Y	15710 FQ	26220 AW	43480 TQ	FLBLS	10/01-12/01
	Fort Pierce-Port St. Lucie MSA, FL	Y	18160 FQ	28710 AW	44750 TQ	FLBLS	10/01-12/01
	Gainesville MSA, FL	Y	19660 FQ	28030 AW	37200 TQ	FLBLS	10/01-12/01
	Jacksonville MSA, FL	Y	18290 FQ	26720 AW	39150 TQ	FLBLS	10/01-12/01
	Lakeland-Winter Haven MSA, FL	Y	18390 FQ	30130 AW	42160 TQ	FLBLS	10/01-12/01
	Melbourne-Titusville-Palm Bay MSA, FL	Y	18900 FQ	30460 AW	43800 TQ	FLBLS	10/01-12/01
	Miami PMSA, FL	Y	19210 FQ	32320 AW	45980 TQ	FLBLS	10/01-12/01
	Ocala MSA, FL	Y	18150 FQ	28940 AW	43770 TQ	FLBLS	10/01-12/01
	Orlando MSA, FL	Y	16630 FQ	22010 AW	29980 TQ	FLBLS	10/01-12/01
	Pensacola MSA, FL	Y	15180 FQ	29450 AW	43950 TQ	FLBLS	10/01-12/01
	Sarasota-Bradenton MSA, FL	Y	19440 FQ	28430 AW	41840 TQ	FLBLS	10/01-12/01
	Tallahassee MSA, FL	Y	16780 FQ	25820 AW	38650 TQ	FLBLS	10/01-12/01
	Tampa-St. Petersburg-Clearwater MSA, FL	Y	19320 FQ	28120 AW	39680 TQ	FLBLS	10/01-12/01
	West Palm Beach-Boca Raton MSA, FL	Y	17370 FQ	26720 AW	35810 TQ	FLBLS	10/01-12/01
	Georgia	Y	16290 FQ	25400 AW	34970 TQ	GABLS	10/01-12/01
	Atlanta MSA, GA	Y	16540 FQ	26010 AW	35290 TQ	GABLS	10/01-12/01
	Augusta-Aiken MSA, GA-SC	Y	17370 FQ	25150 AW	35270 TQ	GABLS	10/01-12/01
	Columbus MSA, GA-AL	Y	15610 FQ	24540 AW	38130 TQ	GABLS	10/01-12/01
	Macon MSA, GA	Y	15880 FQ	22390 AW	30810 TQ	GABLS	10/01-12/01
	Savannah MSA, GA	Y	18040 FQ	24620 AW	34120 TQ	GABLS	10/01-12/01
	Hawaii	Y	25350 FQ	33370 AW	42930 TQ	HIBLS	10/01-12/01
	Honolulu MSA, HI	Y	25320 FQ	33580 AW	43190 TQ	HIBLS	10/01-12/01
	Idaho	Y	20560 FQ	31300 AW	43180 TQ	IDBLS	10/01-12/01
	Boise City MSA, ID	Y	21340 FQ	30110 AW	36570 TQ	IDBLS	10/01-12/01
	Illinois	Y	20190 FQ	30960 AW	44170 TQ	ILBLS	10/01-12/01
	Champaign-Urbana MSA, IL	Y	16660 FQ	24350 AW	34050 TQ	ILBLS	10/01-12/01
	Chicago PMSA, IL	Y	21200 FQ	32040 AW	45990 TQ	ILBLS	10/01-12/01

AAW	Average annual wage	**AOH**	Average offered, high	**ASH**	Average starting, high	**H**	Hourly	**M**	Monthly	**S**	Special: hourly and annual
AE	Average entry wage	**AOL**	Average offered, low	**ASL**	Average starting, low	**HI**	Highest wage paid	**MTC**	Median total compensation	**TQ**	Third quartile wage
AEX	Average experienced wage	**APH**	Average pay, high range	**AW**	Average wage paid	**HR**	High end range	**MW**	Median wage paid	**W**	Weekly
AO	Average offered	**APL**	Average pay, low range	**FQ**	First quartile wage	**LR**	Low end range	**SQ**	Second quartile wage	**Y**	Yearly

Occupation/Type/Industry	Location	Per	Low	Mid	High	Source	Date
Medical and Clinical Laboratory Technician	Peoria-Pekin MSA, IL	Y	17370 FQ	26760 AW	35860 TQ	ILBLS	10/01-12/01
	Rockford MSA, IL	Y	19130 FQ	27200 AW	34250 TQ	ILBLS	10/01-12/01
	Springfield MSA, IL	Y	19350 FQ	31760 AW	45840 TQ	ILBLS	10/01-12/01
	Indiana	Y	18120 FQ	27760 AW	39360 TQ	INBLS	10/01-12/01
	Elkhart-Goshen MSA, IN	Y	20020 FQ	29920 AW	39460 TQ	INBLS	10/01-12/01
	Evansville-Henderson MSA, IN-KY	Y	19320 FQ	30490 AW	40590 TQ	INBLS	10/01-12/01
	Fort Wayne MSA, IN	Y	18190 FQ	28270 AW	43010 TQ	INBLS	10/01-12/01
	Gary PMSA, IN	Y	21360 FQ	32210 AW	42850 TQ	INBLS	10/01-12/01
	Indianapolis MSA, IN	Y	17910 FQ	26290 AW	36640 TQ	INBLS	10/01-12/01
	Lafayette MSA, IN	Y	19510 FQ	26380 AW	35070 TQ	INBLS	10/01-12/01
	South Bend MSA, IN	Y	20350 FQ	28910 AW	36500 TQ	INBLS	10/01-12/01
	Iowa	Y	18200 FQ	27600 AW	37740 TQ	IABLS	10/01-12/01
	Davenport-Moline-Rock Island MSA, IA-IL	Y	17340 FQ	27740 AW	37620 TQ	IABLS	10/01-12/01
	Des Moines MSA, IA	Y	18090 FQ	28470 AW	41470 TQ	IABLS	10/01-12/01
	Kansas	Y	18170 FQ	27250 AW	37360 TQ	KSBLS	10/01-12/01
	Topeka MSA, KS	Y	19500 FQ	25960 AW	35170 TQ	KSBLS	10/01-12/01
	Wichita MSA, KS	Y	18910 FQ	27710 AW	36680 TQ	KSBLS	10/01-12/01
	Kentucky	Y	20080 FQ	28070 AW	36900 TQ	KYBLS	10/01-12/01
	Lexington MSA, KY	Y	19050 FQ	27400 AW	36540 TQ	KYBLS	10/01-12/01
	Louisville MSA, KY-IN	Y	18600 FQ	27070 AW	36630 TQ	KYBLS	10/01-12/01
	Louisiana	Y	15920 FQ	26410 AW	40040 TQ	LABLS	10/01-12/01
	Baton Rouge MSA, LA	Y	18340 FQ	28390 AW	42250 TQ	LABLS	10/01-12/01
	Houma MSA, LA	Y	17280 FQ	29750 AW	41760 TQ	LABLS	10/01-12/01
	Lafayette MSA, LA	Y	14850 FQ	25910 AW	37690 TQ	LABLS	10/01-12/01
	Lake Charles MSA, LA	Y	14870 FQ	27470 AW	43330 TQ	LABLS	10/01-12/01
	New Orleans MSA, LA	Y	17120 FQ	27770 AW	42620 TQ	LABLS	10/01-12/01
	Shreveport-Bossier City MSA, LA	Y	15780 FQ	23680 AW	35250 TQ	LABLS	10/01-12/01
	Maine	Y	19340 FQ	28800 AW	41990 TQ	MEBLS	10/01-12/01
	Portland MSA, ME	Y	19400 FQ	26430 AW	38030 TQ	MEBLS	10/01-12/01
	Maryland	Y	22530 FQ	34990 AW	49440 TQ	MDBLS	10/01-12/01
	Baltimore PMSA, MD	Y	23030 FQ	32680 AW	44710 TQ	MDBLS	10/01-12/01
	Massachusetts	Y	21550 FQ	33640 AW	50390 TQ	MABLS	10/01-12/01
	Boston PMSA, MA-NH	Y	21550 FQ	33730 AW	50850 TQ	MABLS	10/01-12/01
	Brockton PMSA, MA	Y	23160 FQ	36920 AW	51410 TQ	MABLS	10/01-12/01
	Lawrence PMSA, MA-NH	Y	19880 FQ	31470 AW	50530 TQ	MABLS	10/01-12/01
	Lowell PMSA, MA-NH	Y	19820 FQ	34090 AW	50750 TQ	MABLS	10/01-12/01
	New Bedford PMSA, MA	Y	20890 FQ	33000 AW	50540 TQ	MABLS	10/01-12/01
	Springfield MSA, MA	Y	22290 FQ	31990 AW	47120 TQ	MABLS	10/01-12/01
	Worcester PMSA, MA-CT	Y	21090 FQ	36330 AW	51800 TQ	MABLS	10/01-12/01
	Michigan	Y	20400 FQ	30820 AW	42740 TQ	MIBLS	10/01-12/01
	Ann Arbor PMSA, MI	Y	20340 FQ	29090 AW	41290 TQ	MIBLS	10/01-12/01
	Detroit PMSA, MI	Y	22130 FQ	32800 AW	45620 TQ	MIBLS	10/01-12/01
	Flint PMSA, MI	Y	20030 FQ	29990 AW	41490 TQ	MIBLS	10/01-12/01
	Grand Rapids-Muskegon-Holland MSA, MI	Y	21110 FQ	28370 AW	35060 TQ	MIBLS	10/01-12/01
	Kalamazoo-Battle Creek MSA, MI	Y	19690 FQ	30440 AW	42400 TQ	MIBLS	10/01-12/01
	Lansing-East Lansing MSA, MI	Y	16520 FQ	23780 AW	31990 TQ	MIBLS	10/01-12/01
	Saginaw-Bay City-Midland MSA, MI	Y	19850 FQ	29540 AW	38910 TQ	MIBLS	10/01-12/01
	Minnesota	Y	24020 FQ	32880 AW	43850 TQ	MNBLS	10/01-12/01
	Duluth-Superior MSA, MN-WI	Y	22440 FQ	30400 AW	39380 TQ	MNBLS	10/01-12/01
	Minneapolis-St. Paul MSA, MN-WI	Y	24760 FQ	32990 AW	44220 TQ	MNBLS	10/01-12/01
	St. Cloud MSA, MN	Y	21670 FQ	30600 AW	40950 TQ	MNBLS	10/01-12/01
	Mississippi	Y	17780 FQ	26250 AW	37220 TQ	MSBLS	10/01-12/01
	Biloxi-Gulfport-Pascagoula MSA, MS	Y	17970 FQ	28030 AW	43240 TQ	MSBLS	10/01-12/01
	Jackson MSA, MS	Y	17680 FQ	25440 AW	34740 TQ	MSBLS	10/01-12/01
	Missouri	Y	17900 FQ	25690 AW	35150 TQ	MOBLS	10/01-12/01
	Kansas City MSA, MO-KS	Y	18790 FQ	27500 AW	37660 TQ	MOBLS	10/01-12/01
	St. Louis MSA, MO-IL	Y	18740 FQ	26750 AW	35730 TQ	MOBLS	10/01-12/01
	Springfield MSA, MO	Y	16320 FQ	22670 AW	30090 TQ	MOBLS	10/01-12/01
	Montana	Y	19270 FQ	29330 AW	40540 TQ	MTBLS	10/01-12/01
	Billings MSA, MT	Y	17480 FQ	26800 AW	36470 TQ	MTBLS	10/01-12/01
	Nebraska	Y	17500 FQ	26180 AW	36560 TQ	NEBLS	10/01-12/01
	Lincoln MSA, NE	Y	17690 FQ	28190 AW	40410 TQ	NEBLS	10/01-12/01
	Omaha MSA, NE-IA	Y	17060 FQ	24570 AW	35160 TQ	NEBLS	10/01-12/01

AAW Average annual wage **AOH** Average offered, high **ASH** Average starting, high **H** Hourly **M** Monthly **S** Special: hourly and annual
AE Average entry wage **AOL** Average offered, low **ASL** Average starting, low **HI** Highest wage paid **MTC** Median total compensation **TQ** Third quartile wage
AEX Average experienced wage **APH** Average pay, high range **AW** Average wage paid **HR** High end range **MW** Median wage paid **W** Weekly
AO Average offered **APL** Average pay, low range **FQ** First quartile wage **LR** Low end range **SQ** Second quartile wage **Y** Yearly

Occupation/Type/Industry	Location	Per	Low	Mid	High	Source	Date
Medical and Clinical Laboratory Technician	Nevada	Y	22400 FQ	32830 AW	52740 TQ	NVBLS	10/01-12/01
	Las Vegas MSA, NV-AZ	Y	20990 FQ	31340 AW	48120 TQ	NVBLS	10/01-12/01
	Reno MSA, NV	Y	22510 FQ	33850 AW	54810 TQ	NVBLS	10/01-12/01
	New Hampshire	Y	24140 FQ	35310 AW	44670 TQ	NHBLS	10/01-12/01
	Manchester PMSA, NH	Y	18180 FQ	34250 AW	45550 TQ	NHBLS	10/01-12/01
	Nashua PMSA, NH	Y	36870 FQ	40930 AW	45770 TQ	NHBLS	10/01-12/01
	Portsmouth-Rochester PMSA, NH-ME	Y	26040 FQ	33660 AW	42160 TQ	NHBLS	10/01-12/01
	New Jersey	Y	23730 FQ	36030 AW	47790 TQ	NJBLS	10/01-12/01
	Atlantic-Cape May PMSA, NJ	Y	29320 FQ	39990 AW	48170 TQ	NJBLS	10/01-12/01
	Bergen-Passaic PMSA, NJ	Y	23450 FQ	36930 AW	51560 TQ	NJBLS	10/01-12/01
	Jersey City PMSA, NJ	Y	23700 FQ	36520 AW	48020 TQ	NJBLS	10/01-12/01
	Middlesex-Somerset-Hunterdon PMSA, NJ	Y	22490 FQ	35210 AW	47320 TQ	NJBLS	10/01-12/01
	Monmouth-Ocean PMSA, NJ	Y	25240 FQ	37070 AW	49500 TQ	NJBLS	10/01-12/01
	Newark PMSA, NJ	Y	24300 FQ	36010 AW	47510 TQ	NJBLS	10/01-12/01
	Trenton PMSA, NJ	Y	27140 FQ	38060 AW	51230 TQ	NJBLS	10/01-12/01
	New Mexico	Y	20300 FQ	34980 AW	49750 TQ	NMBLS	10/01-12/01
	Albuquerque MSA, NM	Y	24750 FQ	38310 AW	52120 TQ	NMBLS	10/01-12/01
	New York	Y	22630 FQ	34700 AW	50240 TQ	NYBLS	10/01-12/01
	Albany-Schenectady-Troy MSA, NY	Y	20380 FQ	28010 AW	36540 TQ	NYBLS	10/01-12/01
	Binghamton MSA, NY	Y	19790 FQ	27380 AW	37770 TQ	NYBLS	10/01-12/01
	Buffalo-Niagara Falls MSA, NY	Y	20250 FQ	29270 AW	39060 TQ	NYBLS	10/01-12/01
	Dutchess County PMSA, NY	Y	20230 FQ	33390 AW	49790 TQ	NYBLS	10/01-12/01
	Nassau-Suffolk PMSA, NY	Y	23720 FQ	36650 AW	53760 TQ	NYBLS	10/01-12/01
	New York PMSA, NY	Y	24380 FQ	36590 AW	52450 TQ	NYBLS	10/01-12/01
	Newburgh PMSA, NY-PA	Y	25880 FQ	39120 AW	53720 TQ	NYBLS	10/01-12/01
	Rochester MSA, NY	Y	20930 FQ	32630 AW	46510 TQ	NYBLS	10/01-12/01
	Syracuse MSA, NY	Y	22680 FQ	34230 AW	46280 TQ	NYBLS	10/01-12/01
	Utica-Rome MSA, NY	Y	18350 FQ	26290 AW	35870 TQ	NYBLS	10/01-12/01
	North Carolina	Y	19510 FQ	28170 AW	38350 TQ	NCBLS	10/01-12/01
	Asheville MSA, NC	Y	20140 FQ	27100 AW	36350 TQ	NCBLS	10/01-12/01
	Charlotte-Gastonia-Rock Hill MSA, NC-SC	Y	19390 FQ	29910 AW	43840 TQ	NCBLS	10/01-12/01
	Fayetteville MSA, NC	Y	19290 FQ	26430 AW	34280 TQ	NCBLS	10/01-12/01
	Greensboro-Winston-Salem-High Point MSA, NC	Y	20000 FQ	28630 AW	38310 TQ	NCBLS	10/01-12/01
	Hickory-Morganton-Lenoir MSA, NC	Y	20900 FQ	28220 AW	37370 TQ	NCBLS	10/01-12/01
	Raleigh-Durham-Chapel Hill MSA, NC	Y	19170 FQ	28100 AW	36540 TQ	NCBLS	10/01-12/01
	North Dakota	Y	20080 FQ	28290 AW	39540 TQ	NDBLS	10/01-12/01
	Fargo-Moorhead MSA, ND-MN	Y	19760 FQ	27530 AW	39710 TQ	NDBLS	10/01-12/01
	Ohio	Y	19650 FQ	28680 AW	39310 TQ	OHBLS	10/01-12/01
	Akron PMSA, OH	Y	19410 FQ	27470 AW	35390 TQ	OHBLS	10/01-12/01
	Canton-Massillon MSA, OH	Y	19940 FQ	27860 AW	36240 TQ	OHBLS	10/01-12/01
	Cincinnati PMSA, OH-KY-IN	Y	20070 FQ	29320 AW	40130 TQ	OHBLS	10/01-12/01
	Cleveland-Lorain-Elyria PMSA, OH	Y	19840 FQ	29770 AW	42640 TQ	OHBLS	10/01-12/01
	Columbus MSA, OH	Y	19980 FQ	28600 AW	36660 TQ	OHBLS	10/01-12/01
	Dayton-Springfield MSA, OH	Y	18100 FQ	27670 AW	39720 TQ	OHBLS	10/01-12/01
	Hamilton-Middletown PMSA, OH	Y	20500 FQ	29010 AW	39570 TQ	OHBLS	10/01-12/01
	Toledo MSA, OH	Y	19260 FQ	27080 AW	36210 TQ	OHBLS	10/01-12/01
	Youngstown-Warren MSA, OH	Y	19240 FQ	26240 AW	33800 TQ	OHBLS	10/01-12/01
	Oklahoma	Y	16560 FQ	26920 AW	38160 TQ	OKBLS	10/01-12/01
	Oklahoma City MSA, OK	Y	17670 FQ	25850 AW	35330 TQ	OKBLS	10/01-12/01
	Tulsa MSA, OK	Y	17570 FQ	30040 AW	47150 TQ	OKBLS	10/01-12/01
	Oregon	Y	21080 FQ	31430 AW	45890 TQ	ORBLS	10/01-12/01
	Portland-Vancouver PMSA, OR-WA	Y	21900 FQ	31450 AW	46130 TQ	ORBLS	10/01-12/01
	Salem PMSA, OR	Y	21260 FQ	34590 AW	43070 TQ	ORBLS	10/01-12/01
	Pennsylvania	Y	21300 FQ	31260 AW	41440 TQ	PABLS	10/01-12/01
	Allentown-Bethlehem-Easton MSA, PA	Y	21800 FQ	30330 AW	42140 TQ	PABLS	10/01-12/01
	Erie MSA, PA	Y	24260 FQ	32190 AW	41710 TQ	PABLS	10/01-12/01
	Harrisburg-Lebanon-Carlisle MSA, PA	Y	22960 FQ	34830 AW	44110 TQ	PABLS	10/01-12/01

AAW Average annual wage; **AE** Average entry wage; **AEX** Average experienced wage; **AO** Average offered; **AOH** Average offered, high; **AOL** Average offered, low; **APH** Average pay, high range; **APL** Average pay, low range; **ASH** Average starting, high; **ASL** Average starting, low; **AW** Average wage paid; **FQ** First quartile wage; **H** Hourly; **HI** Highest wage paid; **HR** High end range; **LR** Low end range; **M** Monthly; **MTC** Median total compensation; **MW** Median wage paid; **SQ** Second quartile wage; **S** Special: hourly and annual; **TQ** Third quartile wage; **W** Weekly; **Y** Yearly

Occupation/Type/Industry	Location	Per	Low	Mid	High	Source	Date
Medical and Clinical Laboratory Technician	Johnstown MSA, PA	Y	17390 FQ	28840 AW	41170 TQ	PABLS	10/01-12/01
	Lancaster MSA, PA	Y	20420 FQ	32110 AW	43580 TQ	PABLS	10/01-12/01
	Philadelphia PMSA, PA-NJ	Y	21550 FQ	32040 AW	42470 TQ	PABLS	10/01-12/01
	Pittsburgh MSA, PA	Y	24990 FQ	31580 AW	37540 TQ	PABLS	10/01-12/01
	Reading MSA, PA	Y	18860 FQ	26830 AW	36810 TQ	PABLS	10/01-12/01
	Scranton-Wilkes-Barre-Hazleton MSA, PA	Y	19430 FQ	29140 AW	43360 TQ	PABLS	10/01-12/01
	York MSA, PA	Y	22600 FQ	35220 AW	53440 TQ	PABLS	10/01-12/01
	Rhode Island	Y	27020 FQ	40900 AW	61730 TQ	RIBLS	10/01-12/01
	Providence-Fall River-Warwick MSA, RI-MA	Y	24940 FQ	39610 AW	60310 TQ	RIBLS	10/01-12/01
	South Carolina	Y	19410 FQ	30120 AW	43620 TQ	SCBLS	10/01-12/01
	Charleston-North Charleston MSA, SC	Y	19210 FQ	29750 AW	45540 TQ	SCBLS	10/01-12/01
	Columbia MSA, SC	Y	22290 FQ	32290 AW	45920 TQ	SCBLS	10/01-12/01
	Greenville-Spartanburg-Anderson MSA, SC	Y	19910 FQ	29910 AW	41740 TQ	SCBLS	10/01-12/01
	Myrtle Beach MSA, SC	Y	17070 FQ	25590 AW	30780 TQ	SCBLS	10/01-12/01
	South Dakota	Y	19590 FQ	26110 AW	34380 TQ	SDBLS	10/01-12/01
	Sioux Falls MSA, SD	Y	19700 FQ	25190 AW	32330 TQ	SDBLS	10/01-12/01
	Tennessee	Y	16970 FQ	25950 AW	35170 TQ	TNBLS	10/01-12/01
	Chattanooga MSA, TN-GA	Y	15790 FQ	24210 AW	34820 TQ	TNBLS	10/01-12/01
	Clarksville-Hopkinsville MSA, TN-KY	Y	21240 FQ	29190 AW	39160 TQ	TNBLS	10/01-12/01
	Johnson City-Kingsport-Bristol MSA, TN-VA	Y	15180 FQ	22320 AW	32220 TQ	TNBLS	10/01-12/01
	Knoxville MSA, TN	Y	18420 FQ	25490 AW	33690 TQ	TNBLS	10/01-12/01
	Memphis MSA, TN-AR-MS	Y	16980 FQ	25480 AW	35900 TQ	TNBLS	10/01-12/01
	Nashville MSA, TN	Y	18420 FQ	28120 AW	36610 TQ	TNBLS	10/01-12/01
	Texas	Y	18610 FQ	27370 AW	38800 TQ	TXBLS	10/01-12/01
	Amarillo MSA, TX	Y	14740 FQ	18860 AW	25030 TQ	TXBLS	10/01-12/01
	Austin-San Marcos MSA, TX	Y	19260 FQ	28860 AW	40530 TQ	TXBLS	10/01-12/01
	Beaumont-Port Arthur MSA, TX	Y	19340 FQ	28260 AW	40090 TQ	TXBLS	10/01-12/01
	Brownsville-Harlingen-San Benito MSA, TX	Y	15610 FQ	22470 AW	30470 TQ	TXBLS	10/01-12/01
	Corpus Christi MSA, TX	Y	15980 FQ	23330 AW	36220 TQ	TXBLS	10/01-12/01
	Dallas PMSA, TX	Y	18900 FQ	28150 AW	40310 TQ	TXBLS	10/01-12/01
	El Paso MSA, TX	Y	18130 FQ	24980 AW	34870 TQ	TXBLS	10/01-12/01
	Fort Worth-Arlington PMSA, TX	Y	18960 FQ	27420 AW	39750 TQ	TXBLS	10/01-12/01
	Galveston-Texas City PMSA, TX	Y	18810 FQ	29010 AW	42580 TQ	TXBLS	10/01-12/01
	Houston PMSA, TX	Y	20660 FQ	28300 AW	40270 TQ	TXBLS	10/01-12/01
	Killeen-Temple MSA, TX	Y	23190 FQ	28250 AW	34990 TQ	TXBLS	10/01-12/01
	Longview-Marshall MSA, TX	Y	20290 FQ	25950 AW	33640 TQ	TXBLS	10/01-12/01
	Lubbock MSA, TX	Y	19320 FQ	27180 AW	36470 TQ	TXBLS	10/01-12/01
	McAllen-Edinburg-Mission MSA, TX	Y	15710 FQ	26400 AW	37560 TQ	TXBLS	10/01-12/01
	Odessa-Midland MSA, TX	Y	21190 FQ	28820 AW	38250 TQ	TXBLS	10/01-12/01
	San Antonio MSA, TX	Y	17240 FQ	24540 AW	32740 TQ	TXBLS	10/01-12/01
	Tyler MSA, TX	Y	16190 FQ	23360 AW	34270 TQ	TXBLS	10/01-12/01
	Waco MSA, TX	Y	19190 FQ	24920 AW	32130 TQ	TXBLS	10/01-12/01
	Utah	Y	15270 FQ	22590 AW	34280 TQ	UTBLS	10/01-12/01
	Provo-Orem MSA, UT	Y	16380 FQ	21970 AW	28580 TQ	UTBLS	10/01-12/01
	Vermont	Y	21620 FQ	30300 AW	41460 TQ	VTBLS	10/01-12/01
	Burlington MSA, VT	Y	21010 FQ	28640 AW	38920 TQ	VTBLS	10/01-12/01
	Virginia	Y	19250 FQ	27840 AW	38040 TQ	VABLS	10/01-12/01
	Lynchburg MSA, VA	Y	24400 FQ	31560 AW	43070 TQ	VABLS	10/01-12/01
	Norfolk-Virginia Beach-Newport News MSA, VA-NC	Y	17190 FQ	25250 AW	35070 TQ	VABLS	10/01-12/01
	Richmond-Petersburg MSA, VA	Y	20370 FQ	29530 AW	41700 TQ	VABLS	10/01-12/01
	Roanoke MSA, VA	Y	23280 FQ	30520 AW	36390 TQ	VABLS	10/01-12/01
	Washington	Y	22400 FQ	30900 AW	42290 TQ	WABLS	10/01-12/01
	Bremerton PMSA, WA	Y	23750 FQ	32980 AW	45170 TQ	WABLS	10/01-12/01
	Richland-Kennewick-Pasco MSA, WA	Y	20480 FQ	26940 AW	35040 TQ	WABLS	10/01-12/01
	Seattle-Bellevue-Everett PMSA, WA	Y	23890 FQ	32320 AW	44420 TQ	WABLS	10/01-12/01

AAW Average annual wage; AE Average entry wage; AEX Average experienced wage; AO Average offered; AOH Average offered, high; AOL Average offered, low; APH Average pay, high range; APL Average pay, low range; ASH Average starting, high; ASL Average starting, low; AW Average wage paid; FQ First quartile wage; H Hourly; HI Highest wage paid; HR High end range; LR Low end range; M Monthly; MTC Median total compensation; MW Median wage paid; SQ Second quartile wage; S Special: hourly and annual; TQ Third quartile wage; W Weekly; Y Yearly

Occupation/Type/Industry	Location	Per	Low	Mid	High	Source	Date
Medical and Clinical Laboratory Technician	Spokane MSA, WA	Y	22580 FQ	30590 AW	40440 TQ	WABLS	10/01-12/01
	Tacoma PMSA, WA	Y	23510 FQ	32120 AW	42640 TQ	WABLS	10/01-12/01
	Yakima MSA, WA	Y	23370 FQ	30860 AW	40330 TQ	WABLS	10/01-12/01
	West Virginia	Y	18130 FQ	26740 AW	36720 TQ	WVBLS	10/01-12/01
	Charleston MSA, WV	Y	17540 FQ	26700 AW	37170 TQ	WVBLS	10/01-12/01
	Huntington-Ashland MSA, WV-KY-OH	Y	20010 FQ	28810 AW	41980 TQ	WVBLS	10/01-12/01
	Wisconsin	Y	21820 FQ	30680 AW	40850 TQ	WIBLS	10/01-12/01
	Appleton-Oshkosh-Neenah MSA, WI	Y	22970 FQ	29880 AW	35740 TQ	WIBLS	10/01-12/01
	Green Bay MSA, WI	Y	24450 FQ	31640 AW	40450 TQ	WIBLS	10/01-12/01
	Madison MSA, WI	Y	23280 FQ	30430 AW	39040 TQ	WIBLS	10/01-12/01
	Milwaukee-Waukesha PMSA, WI	Y	23280 FQ	32660 AW	43990 TQ	WIBLS	10/01-12/01
	Racine PMSA, WI	Y	23470 FQ	30970 AW	42070 TQ	WIBLS	10/01-12/01
	Wyoming	Y	17100 FQ	27070 AW	40040 TQ	WYBLS	10/01-12/01
	Cheyenne MSA, WY	Y	16280 FQ	22220 AW	30980 TQ	WYBLS	10/01-12/01
	Puerto Rico	Y	11970 FQ	16580 AW	24280 TQ	PRBLS	10/01-12/01
	Virgin Islands	Y	18460 FQ	24220 AW	31130 TQ	VIBLS	10/01-12/01
Medical and Clinical Laboratory Technologist	Alabama	Y	28380 FQ	40050 AW	55000 TQ	ALBLS	10/01-12/01
	Alaska	Y	42880 FQ	52410 AW	64660 TQ	AKBLS	10/01-12/01
	Arizona	Y	31790 FQ	43190 AW	56190 TQ	AZBLS	10/01-12/01
	Arkansas	Y	28190 FQ	38140 AW	49690 TQ	ARBLS	10/01-12/01
	California	Y	38780 FQ	54890 AW	72690 TQ	CABLS	10/01-12/01
	Colorado	Y	29930 FQ	41610 AW	54920 TQ	COBLS	10/01-12/01
	Connecticut	Y	38380 FQ	49810 AW	60910 TQ	CTBLS	10/01-12/01
	Delaware	Y	34660 FQ	53380 AW	71010 TQ	DEBLS	10/01-12/01
	District of Columbia	Y	30050 FQ	44450 AW	57210 TQ	DCBLS	10/01-12/01
	Florida	Y	30990 FQ	41450 AW	54100 TQ	FLBLS	10/01-12/01
	Georgia	Y	30320 FQ	40540 AW	52130 TQ	GABLS	10/01-12/01
	Hawaii	Y	39300 FQ	49590 AW	61290 TQ	HIBLS	10/01-12/01
	Idaho	Y	30880 FQ	41780 AW	53360 TQ	IDBLS	10/01-12/01
	Illinois	Y	29500 FQ	43040 AW	62720 TQ	ILBLS	10/01-12/01
	Indiana	Y	29860 FQ	39200 AW	51280 TQ	INBLS	10/01-12/01
	Iowa	Y	24210 FQ	35430 AW	47410 TQ	IABLS	10/01-12/01
	Kansas	Y	29750 FQ	38500 AW	51360 TQ	KSBLS	10/01-12/01
	Kentucky	Y	29300 FQ	39110 AW	49690 TQ	KYBLS	10/01-12/01
	Louisiana	Y	27870 FQ	38750 AW	51610 TQ	LABLS	10/01-12/01
	Maine	Y	30260 FQ	40050 AW	51820 TQ	MEBLS	10/01-12/01
	Maryland	Y	36740 FQ	48600 AW	60480 TQ	MDBLS	10/01-12/01
	Massachusetts	Y	33080 FQ	45660 AW	58490 TQ	MABLS	10/01-12/01
	Michigan	Y	34340 FQ	43240 AW	54550 TQ	MIBLS	10/01-12/01
	Minnesota	Y	30150 FQ	41460 AW	55120 TQ	MNBLS	10/01-12/01
	Mississippi	Y	25130 FQ	36620 AW	50440 TQ	MSBLS	10/01-12/01
	Missouri	Y	30800 FQ	40520 AW	51490 TQ	MOBLS	10/01-12/01
	Montana	Y	27730 FQ	38230 AW	50140 TQ	MTBLS	10/01-12/01
	Nebraska	Y	22960 FQ	37490 AW	49260 TQ	NEBLS	10/01-12/01
	Nevada	Y	37620 FQ	48360 AW	58040 TQ	NVBLS	10/01-12/01
	New Hampshire	Y	32710 FQ	40520 AW	48020 TQ	NHBLS	10/01-12/01
	New Jersey	Y	34630 FQ	48060 AW	63960 TQ	NJBLS	10/01-12/01
	New Mexico	Y	23710 FQ	35490 AW	46690 TQ	NMBLS	10/01-12/01
	New York	Y	31600 FQ	45040 AW	59210 TQ	NYBLS	10/01-12/01
	North Carolina	Y	29180 FQ	39150 AW	51260 TQ	NCBLS	10/01-12/01
	North Dakota	Y	24280 FQ	35240 AW	45910 TQ	NDBLS	10/01-12/01
	Ohio	Y	31610 FQ	41090 AW	51750 TQ	OHBLS	10/01-12/01
	Oklahoma	Y	23060 FQ	37800 AW	50720 TQ	OKBLS	10/01-12/01
	Oregon	Y	35120 FQ	45780 AW	56550 TQ	ORBLS	10/01-12/01
	Pennsylvania	Y	29350 FQ	40050 AW	52130 TQ	PABLS	10/01-12/01
	Rhode Island	Y	37790 FQ	47740 AW	58620 TQ	RIBLS	10/01-12/01
	South Carolina	Y	24330 FQ	37770 AW	52580 TQ	SCBLS	10/01-12/01
	South Dakota	Y	25400 FQ	36530 AW	48960 TQ	SDBLS	10/01-12/01
	Tennessee	Y	27500 FQ	40620 AW	55730 TQ	TNBLS	10/01-12/01
	Texas	Y	28790 FQ	40040 AW	53870 TQ	TXBLS	10/01-12/01
	Utah	Y	24980 FQ	39760 AW	55570 TQ	UTBLS	10/01-12/01
	Vermont	Y	25580 FQ	41230 AW	56010 TQ	VTBLS	10/01-12/01
	Virginia	Y	29830 FQ	40640 AW	54000 TQ	VABLS	10/01-12/01
	Washington	Y	35690 FQ	47400 AW	58680 TQ	WABLS	10/01-12/01
	West Virginia	Y	26420 FQ	38500 AW	53450 TQ	WVBLS	10/01-12/01
	Wisconsin	Y	32970 FQ	42700 AW	54210 TQ	WIBLS	10/01-12/01

AAW Average annual wage **AE** Average entry wage **AEX** Average experienced wage **AO** Average offered **AOH** Average offered, high **AOL** Average offered, low **APH** Average pay, high range **APL** Average pay, low range **ASH** Average starting, high **ASL** Average starting, low **AW** Average wage paid **FQ** First quartile wage **H** Hourly **HI** Highest wage paid **HR** High end range **LR** Low end range **M** Monthly **MTC** Median total compensation **MW** Median wage paid **SQ** Second quartile wage **S** Special: hourly and annual **TQ** Third quartile wage **W** Weekly **Y** Yearly

Occupation/Type/Industry	Location	Per	Low	Mid	High	Source	Date
Medical and Clinical Laboratory Technologist	Wyoming	Y	28490 FQ	38420 AW	49650 TQ	WYBLS	10/01-12/01
	Puerto Rico	Y	15660 FQ	23730 AW	33680 TQ	PRBLS	10/01-12/01
Medical and Health Services Manager	Alabama	Y	33930 FQ	60550 AW	92660 TQ	ALBLS	10/01-12/01
	Birmingham MSA, AL	Y	38600 FQ	65060 AW	99030 TQ	ALBLS	10/01-12/01
	Huntsville MSA, AL	Y	33220 FQ	61040 AW	92060 TQ	ALBLS	10/01-12/01
	Mobile MSA, AL	Y	37930 FQ	59350 AW	84680 TQ	ALBLS	10/01-12/01
	Montgomery MSA, AL	Y	35530 FQ	60330 AW	92370 TQ	ALBLS	10/01-12/01
	Alaska	Y	42580 FQ	64830 AW	90350 TQ	AKBLS	10/01-12/01
	Anchorage MSA, AK	Y	42040 FQ	69070 AW	109120 TQ	AKBLS	10/01-12/01
	Arizona	Y	32420 FQ	60810 AW	93650 TQ	AZBLS	10/01-12/01
	Phoenix-Mesa MSA, AZ	Y	33490 FQ	62710 AW	95940 TQ	AZBLS	10/01-12/01
	Tucson MSA, AZ	Y	29510 FQ	55470 AW	88740 TQ	AZBLS	10/01-12/01
	Arkansas	Y	31500 FQ	55660 AW	86000 TQ	ARBLS	10/01-12/01
	Fayetteville-Springdale-Rogers MSA, AR	Y	31260 FQ	51840 AW	76200 TQ	ARBLS	10/01-12/01
	Fort Smith MSA, AR-OK	Y	39140 FQ	63130 AW	88290 TQ	ARBLS	10/01-12/01
	Little Rock-North Little Rock MSA, AR	Y	39220 FQ	64990 AW	97910 TQ	ARBLS	10/01-12/01
	California	Y	42740 FQ	74150 AW	116720 TQ	CABLS	10/01-12/01
	Bakersfield MSA, CA	Y	30010 FQ	64730 AW	105220 TQ	CABLS	10/01-12/01
	Chico-Paradise MSA, CA	Y	39540 FQ	63870 AW	96580 TQ	CABLS	10/01-12/01
	Fresno MSA, CA	Y	47340 FQ	82720 AW	120100 TQ	CABLS	10/01-12/01
	Los Angeles-Long Beach PMSA, CA	Y	42010 FQ	74420 AW	119680 TQ	CABLS	10/01-12/01
	Merced MSA, CA	Y	41080 FQ	63610 AW	82690 TQ	CABLS	10/01-12/01
	Modesto MSA, CA	Y	34950 FQ	59080 AW	87950 TQ	CABLS	10/01-12/01
	Oakland PMSA, CA	Y	50540 FQ	85900 AW	140110 TQ	CABLS	10/01-12/01
	Orange County PMSA, CA	Y	44690 FQ	71000 AW	105210 TQ	CABLS	10/01-12/01
	Redding MSA, CA	Y	37570 FQ	53980 AW	73290 TQ	CABLS	10/01-12/01
	Riverside-San Bernardino PMSA, CA	Y	46600 FQ	68450 AW	96910 TQ	CABLS	10/01-12/01
	Sacramento PMSA, CA	Y	42390 FQ	80850 AW	126010 TQ	CABLS	10/01-12/01
	Salinas MSA, CA	Y	42810 FQ	76480 AW	112510 TQ	CABLS	10/01-12/01
	San Diego MSA, CA	Y	43340 FQ	72810 AW	116820 TQ	CABLS	10/01-12/01
	San Francisco PMSA, CA	Y	47870 FQ	79880 AW	117710 TQ	CABLS	10/01-12/01
	San Jose PMSA, CA	Y	48900 FQ	81750 AW	118120 TQ	CABLS	10/01-12/01
	San Luis Obispo-Atascadero-Paso Robles MSA, CA	Y	43100 FQ	62730 AW	82980 TQ	CABLS	10/01-12/01
	Santa Barbara-Santa Maria-Lompoc MSA, CA	Y	43910 FQ	67440 AW	106130 TQ	CABLS	10/01-12/01
	Santa Cruz-Watsonville PMSA, CA	Y	34070 FQ	62530 AW	91510 TQ	CABLS	10/01-12/01
	Santa Rosa PMSA, CA	Y	41170 FQ	65380 AW	95220 TQ	CABLS	10/01-12/01
	Stockton-Lodi MSA, CA	Y	39090 FQ	69440 AW	93350 TQ	CABLS	10/01-12/01
	Vallejo-Fairfield-Napa PMSA, CA	Y	49090 FQ	71500 AW	97760 TQ	CABLS	10/01-12/01
	Ventura PMSA, CA	Y	43590 FQ	66860 AW	94740 TQ	CABLS	10/01-12/01
	Visalia-Tulare-Porterville MSA, CA	Y	46240 FQ	64760 AW	81490 TQ	CABLS	10/01-12/01
	Colorado	Y	38110 FQ	64080 AW	97310 TQ	COBLS	10/01-12/01
	Boulder-Longmont PMSA, CO	Y	48590 FQ	71610 AW	95370 TQ	COBLS	10/01-12/01
	Colorado Springs MSA, CO	Y	36920 FQ	57190 AW	88910 TQ	COBLS	10/01-12/01
	Denver PMSA, CO	Y	39690 FQ	68150 AW	105160 TQ	COBLS	10/01-12/01
	Fort Collins-Loveland MSA, CO	Y	43470 FQ	71900 AW	118670 TQ	COBLS	10/01-12/01
	Greeley PMSA, CO	Y	32380 FQ	51420 AW	70570 TQ	COBLS	10/01-12/01
	Connecticut	Y	48470 FQ	76580 AW	129890 TQ	CTBLS	10/01-12/01
	Bridgeport PMSA, CT	Y	44100 FQ	73670 AW		CTBLS	10/01-12/01
	Danbury PMSA, CT	Y	52080 FQ	72090 AW	97440 TQ	CTBLS	10/01-12/01
	Hartford MSA, CT	Y	50320 FQ	80440 AW		CTBLS	10/01-12/01
	New Haven-Meriden PMSA, CT	Y	49210 FQ	74600 AW	105710 TQ	CTBLS	10/01-12/01
	New London-Norwich MSA, CT-RI	Y	41370 FQ	71660 AW	112310 TQ	CTBLS	10/01-12/01
	Stamford-Norwalk PMSA, CT	Y	49750 FQ	75710 AW	111630 TQ	CTBLS	10/01-12/01
	Waterbury PMSA, CT	Y	47020 FQ	82810 AW		CTBLS	10/01-12/01
	Delaware	Y	37690 FQ	69340 AW	123290 TQ	DEBLS	10/01-12/01
	Wilmington-Newark PMSA, DE-MD	Y	36790 FQ	71720 AW	135630 TQ	DEBLS	10/01-12/01

AAW Average annual wage **AE** Average entry wage **AEX** Average experienced wage **AO** Average offered
AOH Average offered, high **AOL** Average offered, low **APH** Average pay, high range **APL** Average pay, low range
ASH Average starting, high **ASL** Average starting, low **AW** Average wage paid **FQ** First quartile wage
H Hourly **HI** Highest wage paid **HR** High end range **LR** Low end range
M Monthly **MTC** Median total compensation **MW** Median wage paid **SQ** Second quartile wage
S Special: hourly and annual **TQ** Third quartile wage **W** Weekly **Y** Yearly

Occupation/Type/Industry	Location	Per	Low	Mid	High	Source	Date
Medical and Health Services Manager	District of Columbia	Y	42150 FQ	71540 AW	108080 TQ	DCBLS	10/01-12/01
	Washington PMSA, DC-MD-VA-WV	Y	37680 FQ	70590 AW	108210 TQ	DCBLS	10/01-12/01
	Florida	Y	38370 FQ	66280 AW	111070 TQ	FLBLS	10/01-12/01
	Daytona Beach MSA, FL	Y	39010 FQ	69480 AW	134430 TQ	FLBLS	10/01-12/01
	Fort Lauderdale PMSA, FL	Y	41540 FQ	69470 AW	119300 TQ	FLBLS	10/01-12/01
	Fort Myers-Cape Coral MSA, FL	Y	37980 FQ	62860 AW	127520 TQ	FLBLS	10/01-12/01
	Fort Pierce-Port St. Lucie MSA, FL	Y	41410 FQ	62120 AW	89270 TQ	FLBLS	10/01-12/01
	Fort Walton Beach MSA, FL	Y	44710 FQ	64250 AW	89520 TQ	FLBLS	10/01-12/01
	Gainesville MSA, FL	Y	39540 FQ	67770 AW	103630 TQ	FLBLS	10/01-12/01
	Jacksonville MSA, FL	Y	40860 FQ	66100 AW	96150 TQ	FLBLS	10/01-12/01
	Lakeland-Winter Haven MSA, FL	Y	36330 FQ	73740 AW		FLBLS	10/01-12/01
	Melbourne-Titusville-Palm Bay MSA, FL	Y	38990 FQ	69450 AW	134120 TQ	FLBLS	10/01-12/01
	Miami PMSA, FL	Y	46260 FQ	78230 AW	122420 TQ	FLBLS	10/01-12/01
	Naples MSA, FL	Y	39050 FQ	64180 AW	94370 TQ	FLBLS	10/01-12/01
	Ocala MSA, FL	Y	44420 FQ	78410 AW	135200 TQ	FLBLS	10/01-12/01
	Orlando MSA, FL	Y	42170 FQ	64860 AW	121290 TQ	FLBLS	10/01-12/01
	Pensacola MSA, FL	Y	40540 FQ	57490 AW	81340 TQ	FLBLS	10/01-12/01
	Sarasota-Bradenton MSA, FL	Y	38930 FQ	59900 AW	90340 TQ	FLBLS	10/01-12/01
	Tallahassee MSA, FL	Y	41570 FQ	79910 AW		FLBLS	10/01-12/01
	Tampa-St. Petersburg-Clearwater MSA, FL	Y	32100 FQ	63070 AW	108180 TQ	FLBLS	10/01-12/01
	West Palm Beach-Boca Raton MSA, FL	Y	37800 FQ	58490 AW	90470 TQ	FLBLS	10/01-12/01
	Georgia	Y	37350 FQ	62680 AW	94090 TQ	GABLS	10/01-12/01
	Atlanta MSA, GA	Y	41070 FQ	64100 AW	92660 TQ	GABLS	10/01-12/01
	Augusta-Aiken MSA, GA-SC	Y	38730 FQ	71180 AW	130120 TQ	GABLS	10/01-12/01
	Columbus MSA, GA-AL	Y	33540 FQ	61250 AW	97650 TQ	GABLS	10/01-12/01
	Macon MSA, GA	Y	35610 FQ	68420 AW		GABLS	10/01-12/01
	Savannah MSA, GA	Y	32100 FQ	49080 AW	73410 TQ	GABLS	10/01-12/01
	Hawaii	Y	45470 FQ	70470 AW	97770 TQ	HIBLS	10/01-12/01
	Honolulu MSA, HI	Y	50170 FQ	73170 AW	100290 TQ	HIBLS	10/01-12/01
	Idaho	Y	31650 FQ	57220 AW	87430 TQ	IDBLS	10/01-12/01
	Boise City MSA, ID	Y	31930 FQ	57210 AW	86220 TQ	IDBLS	10/01-12/01
	Illinois	Y	36340 FQ	67690 AW	115350 TQ	ILBLS	10/01-12/01
	Champaign-Urbana MSA, IL	Y	36360 FQ	63120 AW	96120 TQ	ILBLS	10/01-12/01
	Chicago PMSA, IL	Y	40380 FQ	73500 AW	131650 TQ	ILBLS	10/01-12/01
	Peoria-Pekin MSA, IL	Y	38690 FQ	63840 AW	91830 TQ	ILBLS	10/01-12/01
	Rockford MSA, IL	Y	31620 FQ	54600 AW	83080 TQ	ILBLS	10/01-12/01
	Springfield MSA, IL	Y	31700 FQ	54560 AW	76870 TQ	ILBLS	10/01-12/01
	Indiana	Y	31740 FQ	53860 AW	80830 TQ	INBLS	10/01-12/01
	Elkhart-Goshen MSA, IN	Y	39710 FQ	59100 AW	89790 TQ	INBLS	10/01-12/01
	Evansville-Henderson MSA, IN-KY	Y	26820 FQ	50400 AW	83290 TQ	INBLS	10/01-12/01
	Fort Wayne MSA, IN	Y	30330 FQ	51380 AW	74280 TQ	INBLS	10/01-12/01
	Gary PMSA, IN	Y	26070 FQ	49760 AW	80520 TQ	INBLS	10/01-12/01
	Indianapolis MSA, IN	Y	35470 FQ	57790 AW	84890 TQ	INBLS	10/01-12/01
	Lafayette MSA, IN	Y	30800 FQ	52680 AW	82540 TQ	INBLS	10/01-12/01
	South Bend MSA, IN	Y	32180 FQ	47240 AW	66140 TQ	INBLS	10/01-12/01
	Iowa	Y	31620 FQ	51070 AW	73700 TQ	IABLS	10/01-12/01
	Cedar Rapids MSA, IA	Y	36990 FQ	55070 AW	82480 TQ	IABLS	10/01-12/01
	Davenport-Moline-Rock Island MSA, IA-IL	Y	33230 FQ	55160 AW	80270 TQ	IABLS	10/01-12/01
	Des Moines MSA, IA	Y	34540 FQ	51360 AW	71500 TQ	IABLS	10/01-12/01
	Kansas	Y	35590 FQ	57120 AW	89530 TQ	KSBLS	10/01-12/01
	Topeka MSA, KS	Y	33350 FQ	53330 AW	83670 TQ	KSBLS	10/01-12/01
	Wichita MSA, KS	Y	37420 FQ	65650 AW		KSBLS	10/01-12/01
	Kentucky	Y	35960 FQ	57430 AW	85750 TQ	KYBLS	10/01-12/01
	Lexington MSA, KY	Y	39220 FQ	62550 AW	93630 TQ	KYBLS	10/01-12/01
	Louisville MSA, KY-IN	Y	37540 FQ	61130 AW	91740 TQ	KYBLS	10/01-12/01
	Louisiana	Y	33580 FQ	54760 AW	78410 TQ	LABLS	10/01-12/01
	Baton Rouge MSA, LA	Y	38750 FQ	64430 AW	117470 TQ	LABLS	10/01-12/01
	Houma MSA, LA	Y	28420 FQ	53670 AW	73300 TQ	LABLS	10/01-12/01
	Lafayette MSA, LA	Y	26420 FQ	51200 AW	72870 TQ	LABLS	10/01-12/01
	Lake Charles MSA, LA	Y	34560 FQ	47550 AW	59480 TQ	LABLS	10/01-12/01
	New Orleans MSA, LA	Y	31820 FQ	52590 AW	73450 TQ	LABLS	10/01-12/01

AAW Average annual wage **AOH** Average offered, high **ASH** Average starting, high **H** Hourly **M** Monthly **S** Special: hourly and annual
AE Average entry wage **AOL** Average offered, low **ASL** Average starting, low **HI** Highest wage paid **MTC** Median total compensation **TQ** Third quartile wage
AEX Average experienced wage **APH** Average pay, high range **AW** Average wage paid **HR** High end range **MW** Median wage paid **W** Weekly
AO Average offered **APL** Average pay, low range **FQ** First quartile wage **LR** Low end range **SQ** Second quartile wage **Y** Yearly

Occupation/Type/Industry	Location	Per	Low	Mid	High	Source	Date
Medical and Health Services Manager	Shreveport-Bossier City MSA, LA	Y	33660 FQ	54480 AW	91610 TQ	LABLS	10/01-12/01
	Maine	Y	37010 FQ	59020 AW	90510 TQ	MEBLS	10/01-12/01
	Portland MSA, ME	Y	34330 FQ	60090 AW	99360 TQ	MEBLS	10/01-12/01
	Maryland	Y	35100 FQ	66420 AW	104000 TQ	MDBLS	10/01-12/01
	Baltimore PMSA, MD	Y	38430 FQ	67250 AW	103180 TQ	MDBLS	10/01-12/01
	Massachusetts	Y	37620 FQ	63900 AW	96400 TQ	MABLS	10/01-12/01
	Boston PMSA, MA-NH	Y	38080 FQ	66500 AW	104650 TQ	MABLS	10/01-12/01
	Brockton PMSA, MA	Y	33740 FQ	56460 AW	87310 TQ	MABLS	10/01-12/01
	Lawrence PMSA, MA-NH	Y	41940 FQ	60950 AW	79340 TQ	MABLS	10/01-12/01
	Lowell PMSA, MA-NH	Y	35140 FQ	54710 AW	77690 TQ	MABLS	10/01-12/01
	New Bedford PMSA, MA	Y	35320 FQ	71220 AW	115990 TQ	MABLS	10/01-12/01
	Springfield MSA, MA	Y	42500 FQ	60530 AW	77060 TQ	MABLS	10/01-12/01
	Worcester PMSA, MA-CT	Y	30750 FQ	55110 AW	75710 TQ	MABLS	10/01-12/01
	Michigan	Y	38920 FQ	67860 AW	116370 TQ	MIBLS	10/01-12/01
	Ann Arbor PMSA, MI	Y	32810 FQ	61530 AW	108250 TQ	MIBLS	10/01-12/01
	Detroit PMSA, MI	Y	48700 FQ	80330 AW		MIBLS	10/01-12/01
	Flint PMSA, MI	Y	30580 FQ	63390 AW	91650 TQ	MIBLS	10/01-12/01
	Grand Rapids-Muskegon-Holland MSA, MI	Y	37520 FQ	58080 AW	82870 TQ	MIBLS	10/01-12/01
	Kalamazoo-Battle Creek MSA, MI	Y	38370 FQ	55700 AW	77120 TQ	MIBLS	10/01-12/01
	Lansing-East Lansing MSA, MI	Y	42160 FQ	64750 AW	88710 TQ	MIBLS	10/01-12/01
	Saginaw-Bay City-Midland MSA, MI	Y	44770 FQ	72050 AW	129290 TQ	MIBLS	10/01-12/01
	Minnesota	Y	39470 FQ	64770 AW	99110 TQ	MNBLS	10/01-12/01
	Duluth-Superior MSA, MN-WI	Y	39070 FQ	56520 AW	78040 TQ	MNBLS	10/01-12/01
	Minneapolis-St. Paul MSA, MN-WI	Y	40690 FQ	68920 AW	110870 TQ	MNBLS	10/01-12/01
	St. Cloud MSA, MN	Y	43500 FQ	65700 AW	104020 TQ	MNBLS	10/01-12/01
	Mississippi	Y	35610 FQ	60340 AW	96490 TQ	MSBLS	10/01-12/01
	Biloxi-Gulfport-Pascagoula MSA, MS	Y	37370 FQ	64500 AW	103750 TQ	MSBLS	10/01-12/01
	Jackson MSA, MS	Y	36490 FQ	63840 AW	111150 TQ	MSBLS	10/01-12/01
	Missouri	Y	34370 FQ	59280 AW	93800 TQ	MOBLS	10/01-12/01
	Kansas City MSA, MO-KS	Y	37170 FQ	58550 AW	91000 TQ	MOBLS	10/01-12/01
	St. Louis MSA, MO-IL	Y	36700 FQ	61700 AW	102760 TQ	MOBLS	10/01-12/01
	Springfield MSA, MO	Y	30340 FQ	49190 AW	70490 TQ	MOBLS	10/01-12/01
	Montana	Y	24720 FQ	51280 AW	80590 TQ	MTBLS	10/01-12/01
	Nebraska	Y	29510 FQ	54610 AW	84200 TQ	NEBLS	10/01-12/01
	Lincoln MSA, NE	Y	30470 FQ	57400 AW	85960 TQ	NEBLS	10/01-12/01
	Omaha MSA, NE-IA	Y	35990 FQ	59800 AW	90400 TQ	NEBLS	10/01-12/01
	Nevada	Y	32310 FQ	63320 AW	95630 TQ	NVBLS	10/01-12/01
	Las Vegas MSA, NV-AZ	Y	32520 FQ	62200 AW	94610 TQ	NVBLS	10/01-12/01
	Reno MSA, NV	Y	31590 FQ	64940 AW	96900 TQ	NVBLS	10/01-12/01
	New Hampshire	Y	37720 FQ	62560 AW	92320 TQ	NHBLS	10/01-12/01
	Manchester PMSA, NH	Y	44830 FQ	75870 AW	115540 TQ	NHBLS	10/01-12/01
	Nashua PMSA, NH	Y	40860 FQ	63440 AW	87530 TQ	NHBLS	10/01-12/01
	Portsmouth-Rochester PMSA, NH-ME	Y	39360 FQ	61020 AW	88980 TQ	NHBLS	10/01-12/01
	New Jersey	Y	49490 FQ	79320 AW	120530 TQ	NJBLS	10/01-12/01
	Atlantic-Cape May PMSA, NJ	Y	43310 FQ	81100 AW		NJBLS	10/01-12/01
	Bergen-Passaic PMSA, NJ	Y	58600 FQ	87850 AW	129110 TQ	NJBLS	10/01-12/01
	Jersey City PMSA, NJ	Y	49510 FQ	75930 AW	108450 TQ	NJBLS	10/01-12/01
	Middlesex-Somerset-Hunterdon PMSA, NJ	Y	49520 FQ	83980 AW	140990 TQ	NJBLS	10/01-12/01
	Monmouth-Ocean PMSA, NJ	Y	49200 FQ	79200 AW	117800 TQ	NJBLS	10/01-12/01
	Newark PMSA, NJ	Y	48760 FQ	79020 AW	120090 TQ	NJBLS	10/01-12/01
	Trenton PMSA, NJ	Y	53900 FQ	78820 AW	112440 TQ	NJBLS	10/01-12/01
	New Mexico	Y	35970 FQ	60850 AW	99660 TQ	NMBLS	10/01-12/01
	Albuquerque MSA, NM	Y	38830 FQ	63820 AW	102860 TQ	NMBLS	10/01-12/01
	Las Cruces MSA, NM	Y	27220 FQ	43510 AW	56460 TQ	NMBLS	10/01-12/01
	New York	Y	44090 FQ	77880 AW	135640 TQ	NYBLS	10/01-12/01
	Albany-Schenectady-Troy MSA, NY	Y	44170 FQ	72660 AW	120190 TQ	NYBLS	10/01-12/01
	Binghamton MSA, NY	Y	33680 FQ	57490 AW	102950 TQ	NYBLS	10/01-12/01
	Buffalo-Niagara Falls MSA, NY	Y	37520 FQ	68810 AW	118690 TQ	NYBLS	10/01-12/01
	Dutchess County PMSA, NY	Y	46560 FQ	70630 AW	120690 TQ	NYBLS	10/01-12/01
	Nassau-Suffolk PMSA, NY	Y	50590 FQ	81130 AW	133500 TQ	NYBLS	10/01-12/01
	New York PMSA, NY	Y	49290 FQ	84660 AW	144500 TQ	NYBLS	10/01-12/01

AAW Average annual wage; **AE** Average entry wage; **AEX** Average experienced wage; **AO** Average offered; **AOH** Average offered, high; **AOL** Average offered, low; **APH** Average pay, high range; **APL** Average pay, low range; **ASH** Average starting, high; **ASL** Average starting, low; **AW** Average wage paid; **FQ** First quartile wage; **H** Hourly; **HI** Highest wage paid; **HR** High end range; **LR** Low end range; **M** Monthly; **MTC** Median total compensation; **MW** Median wage paid; **SQ** Second quartile wage; **S** Special: hourly and annual; **TQ** Third quartile wage; **W** Weekly; **Y** Yearly

Occupation/Type/Industry	Location	Per	Low	Mid	High	Source	Date
Medical and Health Services Manager	Newburgh PMSA, NY-PA	Y	47460 FQ	67140 AW	102790 TQ	NYBLS	10/01-12/01
	Rochester MSA, NY	Y	39840 FQ	66030 AW	117280 TQ	NYBLS	10/01-12/01
	Syracuse MSA, NY	Y	32370 FQ	58100 AW	93550 TQ	NYBLS	10/01-12/01
	Utica-Rome MSA, NY	Y	41620 FQ	64860 AW	97230 TQ	NYBLS	10/01-12/01
	North Carolina	Y	38700 FQ	63430 AW	96840 TQ	NCBLS	10/01-12/01
	Asheville MSA, NC	Y	36490 FQ	64970 AW	114410 TQ	NCBLS	10/01-12/01
	Charlotte-Gastonia-Rock Hill MSA, NC-SC	Y	42110 FQ	71020 AW	110890 TQ	NCBLS	10/01-12/01
	Fayetteville MSA, NC	Y	45060 FQ	65730 AW	98830 TQ	NCBLS	10/01-12/01
	Greensboro-Winston-Salem-High Point MSA, NC	Y	41660 FQ	63330 AW	94120 TQ	NCBLS	10/01-12/01
	Hickory-Morganton-Lenoir MSA, NC	Y	43050 FQ	61880 AW	84030 TQ	NCBLS	10/01-12/01
	Raleigh-Durham-Chapel Hill MSA, NC	Y	39570 FQ	68170 AW	110030 TQ	NCBLS	10/01-12/01
	North Dakota	Y	14790 FQ	48730 AW	74890 TQ	NDBLS	10/01-12/01
	Fargo-Moorhead MSA, ND-MN	Y	38890 FQ	59150 AW	84960 TQ	NDBLS	10/01-12/01
	Ohio	Y	38100 FQ	60740 AW	89890 TQ	OHBLS	10/01-12/01
	Akron PMSA, OH	Y	38740 FQ	62240 AW	93770 TQ	OHBLS	10/01-12/01
	Canton-Massillon MSA, OH	Y	32470 FQ	55580 AW	77880 TQ	OHBLS	10/01-12/01
	Cincinnati PMSA, OH-KY-IN	Y	39050 FQ	59670 AW	88380 TQ	OHBLS	10/01-12/01
	Cleveland-Lorain-Elyria PMSA, OH	Y	40860 FQ	63260 AW	91000 TQ	OHBLS	10/01-12/01
	Columbus MSA, OH	Y	39410 FQ	66300 AW	96150 TQ	OHBLS	10/01-12/01
	Dayton-Springfield MSA, OH	Y	36540 FQ	57650 AW	86060 TQ	OHBLS	10/01-12/01
	Hamilton-Middletown PMSA, OH	Y	31100 FQ	66880 AW		OHBLS	10/01-12/01
	Mansfield MSA, OH	Y	31300 FQ	51000 AW	71900 TQ	OHBLS	10/01-12/01
	Toledo MSA, OH	Y	41230 FQ	65060 AW	95090 TQ	OHBLS	10/01-12/01
	Youngstown-Warren MSA, OH	Y	31980 FQ	59490 AW	120170 TQ	OHBLS	10/01-12/01
	Oklahoma	Y	33660 FQ	57950 AW	89900 TQ	OKBLS	10/01-12/01
	Oklahoma City MSA, OK	Y	35860 FQ	60680 AW	94830 TQ	OKBLS	10/01-12/01
	Tulsa MSA, OK	Y	38450 FQ	64630 AW	110560 TQ	OKBLS	10/01-12/01
	Oregon	Y	39600 FQ	67320 AW	107790 TQ	ORBLS	10/01-12/01
	Eugene-Springfield MSA, OR	Y	37370 FQ	63450 AW	107460 TQ	ORBLS	10/01-12/01
	Medford-Ashland MSA, OR	Y	37790 FQ	59530 AW	84270 TQ	ORBLS	10/01-12/01
	Portland-Vancouver PMSA, OR-WA	Y	42920 FQ	72420 AW	115180 TQ	ORBLS	10/01-12/01
	Salem PMSA, OR	Y	37010 FQ	61890 AW	106390 TQ	ORBLS	10/01-12/01
	Pennsylvania	Y	35150 FQ	62080 AW	95300 TQ	PABLS	10/01-12/01
	Allentown-Bethlehem-Easton MSA, PA	Y	46780 FQ	69200 AW	113320 TQ	PABLS	10/01-12/01
	Erie MSA, PA	Y	31660 FQ	49790 AW	71380 TQ	PABLS	10/01-12/01
	Harrisburg-Lebanon-Carlisle MSA, PA	Y	39480 FQ	61910 AW	90860 TQ	PABLS	10/01-12/01
	Johnstown MSA, PA	Y	26360 FQ	58210 AW	102530 TQ	PABLS	10/01-12/01
	Lancaster MSA, PA	Y	35840 FQ	53830 AW	75500 TQ	PABLS	10/01-12/01
	Philadelphia PMSA, PA-NJ	Y	38850 FQ	66680 AW	102740 TQ	PABLS	10/01-12/01
	Pittsburgh MSA, PA	Y	32970 FQ	60680 AW	93920 TQ	PABLS	10/01-12/01
	Reading MSA, PA	Y	37760 FQ	60460 AW	86820 TQ	PABLS	10/01-12/01
	Scranton-Wilkes-Barre-Hazleton MSA, PA	Y	36830 FQ	61340 AW	94760 TQ	PABLS	10/01-12/01
	York MSA, PA	Y	27130 FQ	48940 AW	86920 TQ	PABLS	10/01-12/01
	Rhode Island	Y	42320 FQ	73070 AW	123480 TQ	RIBLS	10/01-12/01
	Providence-Fall River-Warwick MSA, RI-MA	Y	41620 FQ	70760 AW	118220 TQ	RIBLS	10/01-12/01
	South Carolina	Y	27480 FQ	56140 AW	92610 TQ	SCBLS	10/01-12/01
	Charleston-North Charleston MSA, SC	Y	30880 FQ	57260 AW	92610 TQ	SCBLS	10/01-12/01
	Columbia MSA, SC	Y	26580 FQ	58660 AW	101190 TQ	SCBLS	10/01-12/01
	Greenville-Spartanburg-Anderson MSA, SC	Y	25440 FQ	64000 AW	114290 TQ	SCBLS	10/01-12/01
	Myrtle Beach MSA, SC	Y	28170 FQ	50660 AW	83400 TQ	SCBLS	10/01-12/01
	South Dakota	Y	42710 FQ	62550 AW	92690 TQ	SDBLS	10/01-12/01
	Sioux Falls MSA, SD	Y	48950 FQ	70800 AW	99770 TQ	SDBLS	10/01-12/01
	Tennessee	Y	30780 FQ	62490 AW	122330 TQ	TNBLS	10/01-12/01
	Chattanooga MSA, TN-GA	Y	33520 FQ	59300 AW	97460 TQ	TNBLS	10/01-12/01
	Clarksville-Hopkinsville MSA, TN-KY	Y	31460 FQ	54320 AW	84280 TQ	TNBLS	10/01-12/01

AAW Average annual wage	**AOH** Average offered, high	**ASH** Average starting, high	**H** Hourly	**M** Monthly	**S** Special: hourly and annual
AE Average entry wage	**AOL** Average offered, low	**ASL** Average starting, low	**HI** Highest wage paid	**MTC** Median total compensation	**TQ** Third quartile wage
AEX Average experienced wage	**APH** Average pay, high range	**AW** Average wage paid	**HR** High end range	**MW** Median wage paid	**W** Weekly
AO Average offered	**APL** Average pay, low range	**FQ** First quartile wage	**LR** Low end range	**SQ** Second quartile wage	**Y** Yearly

Occupation/Type/Industry	Location	Per	Low	Mid	High	Source	Date
Medical and Health Services Manager	Johnson City-Kingsport-Bristol MSA, TN-VA	Y	24940 FQ	54090 AW	99070 TQ	TNBLS	10/01-12/01
	Knoxville MSA, TN	Y	29530 FQ	55290 AW	102140 TQ	TNBLS	10/01-12/01
	Memphis MSA, TN-AR-MS	Y	36330 FQ	76910 AW		TNBLS	10/01-12/01
	Nashville MSA, TN	Y	33790 FQ	66360 AW	125330 TQ	TNBLS	10/01-12/01
	Texas	Y	33550 FQ	57160 AW	85090 TQ	TXBLS	10/01-12/01
	Amarillo MSA, TX	Y	39220 FQ	62270 AW	92390 TQ	TXBLS	10/01-12/01
	Austin-San Marcos MSA, TX	Y	29180 FQ	56370 AW	101040 TQ	TXBLS	10/01-12/01
	Beaumont-Port Arthur MSA, TX	Y	24740 FQ	40690 AW	68430 TQ	TXBLS	10/01-12/01
	Brazoria PMSA, TX	Y	31260 FQ	56000 AW	73210 TQ	TXBLS	10/01-12/01
	Brownsville-Harlingen-San Benito MSA, TX	Y	19020 FQ	49280 AW	77300 TQ	TXBLS	10/01-12/01
	Corpus Christi MSA, TX	Y	33400 FQ	61690 AW	128250 TQ	TXBLS	10/01-12/01
	Dallas PMSA, TX	Y	39250 FQ	58780 AW	76350 TQ	TXBLS	10/01-12/01
	El Paso MSA, TX	Y	35620 FQ	58880 AW	84250 TQ	TXBLS	10/01-12/01
	Fort Worth-Arlington PMSA, TX	Y	35620 FQ	61250 AW	98540 TQ	TXBLS	10/01-12/01
	Galveston-Texas City PMSA, TX	Y	28100 FQ	57920 AW	89620 TQ	TXBLS	10/01-12/01
	Houston PMSA, TX	Y	37480 FQ	60650 AW	88930 TQ	TXBLS	10/01-12/01
	Killeen-Temple MSA, TX	Y	34690 FQ	53030 AW	72580 TQ	TXBLS	10/01-12/01
	Laredo MSA, TX	Y	21050 FQ	50090 AW	80850 TQ	TXBLS	10/01-12/01
	Longview-Marshall MSA, TX	Y	18170 FQ	42940 AW	73050 TQ	TXBLS	10/01-12/01
	Lubbock MSA, TX	Y	37950 FQ	55750 AW	75630 TQ	TXBLS	10/01-12/01
	McAllen-Edinburg-Mission MSA, TX	Y	22960 FQ	55080 AW	81760 TQ	TXBLS	10/01-12/01
	Odessa-Midland MSA, TX	Y	24070 FQ	45160 AW	76740 TQ	TXBLS	10/01-12/01
	San Antonio MSA, TX	Y	34280 FQ	56340 AW	83400 TQ	TXBLS	10/01-12/01
	Tyler MSA, TX	Y	33300 FQ	62370 AW	109780 TQ	TXBLS	10/01-12/01
	Waco MSA, TX	Y	31980 FQ	47840 AW	61820 TQ	TXBLS	10/01-12/01
	Utah	Y	31610 FQ	61680 AW	93420 TQ	UTBLS	10/01-12/01
	Provo-Orem MSA, UT	Y	37160 FQ	65570 AW	105760 TQ	UTBLS	10/01-12/01
	Salt Lake City-Ogden MSA, UT	Y	30160 FQ	61740 AW	93630 TQ	UTBLS	10/01-12/01
	Vermont	Y	46180 FQ	70970 AW	108850 TQ	VTBLS	10/01-12/01
	Burlington MSA, VT	Y	49860 FQ	79930 AW	127750 TQ	VTBLS	10/01-12/01
	Virginia	Y	35120 FQ	62450 AW	99900 TQ	VABLS	10/01-12/01
	Lynchburg MSA, VA	Y	43210 FQ	67560 AW	97250 TQ	VABLS	10/01-12/01
	Norfolk-Virginia Beach-Newport News MSA, VA-NC	Y	37830 FQ	62130 AW	97300 TQ	VABLS	10/01-12/01
	Richmond-Petersburg MSA, VA	Y	31710 FQ	57610 AW	90820 TQ	VABLS	10/01-12/01
	Roanoke MSA, VA	Y	28740 FQ	65260 AW	110300 TQ	VABLS	10/01-12/01
	Washington	Y	47320 FQ	79280 AW		WABLS	10/01-12/01
	Bremerton PMSA, WA	Y	44350 FQ	64230 AW	88940 TQ	WABLS	10/01-12/01
	Olympia PMSA, WA	Y	48130 FQ	77440 AW	140020 TQ	WABLS	10/01-12/01
	Richland-Kennewick-Pasco MSA, WA	Y	45320 FQ	71550 AW	127480 TQ	WABLS	10/01-12/01
	Seattle-Bellevue-Everett PMSA, WA	Y	49910 FQ	87570 AW		WABLS	10/01-12/01
	Spokane MSA, WA	Y	44960 FQ	81030 AW	137490 TQ	WABLS	10/01-12/01
	Tacoma PMSA, WA	Y	49140 FQ	74960 AW	113830 TQ	WABLS	10/01-12/01
	Yakima MSA, WA	Y	42760 FQ	70200 AW	112240 TQ	WABLS	10/01-12/01
	West Virginia	Y	26120 FQ	48940 AW	73070 TQ	WVBLS	10/01-12/01
	Charleston MSA, WV	Y	36540 FQ	54040 AW	82460 TQ	WVBLS	10/01-12/01
	Huntington-Ashland MSA, WV-KY-OH	Y	32850 FQ	52730 AW	86120 TQ	WVBLS	10/01-12/01
	Wisconsin	Y	36890 FQ	60590 AW	91860 TQ	WIBLS	10/01-12/01
	Appleton-Oshkosh-Neenah MSA, WI	Y	20850 FQ	52000 AW	84910 TQ	WIBLS	10/01-12/01
	Green Bay MSA, WI	Y	39160 FQ	59820 AW	86790 TQ	WIBLS	10/01-12/01
	Madison MSA, WI	Y	34650 FQ	64080 AW	104820 TQ	WIBLS	10/01-12/01
	Milwaukee-Waukesha PMSA, WI	Y	39510 FQ	64030 AW	99340 TQ	WIBLS	10/01-12/01
	Racine PMSA, WI	Y	36870 FQ	56910 AW	76900 TQ	WIBLS	10/01-12/01
	Wyoming	Y	29180 FQ	51160 AW	73900 TQ	WYBLS	10/01-12/01
	Cheyenne MSA, WY	Y	30910 FQ	54510 AW	92290 TQ	WYBLS	10/01-12/01
	Puerto Rico	Y	28720 FQ	55850 AW	105900 TQ	PRBLS	10/01-12/01
	Guam	Y	31840 FQ	55070 AW	88520 TQ	GUBLS	10/01-12/01

AAW Average annual wage; **AE** Average entry wage; **AEX** Average experienced wage; **AO** Average offered; **AOH** Average offered, high; **AOL** Average offered, low; **APH** Average pay, high range; **APL** Average pay, low range; **ASH** Average starting, high; **ASL** Average starting, low; **AW** Average wage paid; **FQ** First quartile wage; **H** Hourly; **HI** Highest wage paid; **HR** High end range; **LR** Low end range; **M** Monthly; **MTC** Median total compensation; **MW** Median wage paid; **SQ** Second quartile wage; **S** Special: hourly and annual; **TQ** Third quartile wage; **W** Weekly; **Y** Yearly

Occupation/Type/Industry	Location	Per	Low	Mid	High	Source	Date
Medical and Public Health Social Worker	Alabama	Y	23140 FQ	31360 AW	43030 TQ	ALBLS	10/01-12/01
	Alaska	Y	26190 FQ	38490 AW	57670 TQ	AKBLS	10/01-12/01
	Arizona	Y	22750 FQ	37020 AW	56270 TQ	AZBLS	10/01-12/01
	Arkansas	Y	21890 FQ	35640 AW	51020 TQ	ARBLS	10/01-12/01
	California	Y	28630 FQ	44710 AW	63370 TQ	CABLS	10/01-12/01
	Colorado	Y	26220 FQ	37810 AW	52680 TQ	COBLS	10/01-12/01
	Connecticut	Y	28690 FQ	43680 AW	61240 TQ	CTBLS	10/01-12/01
	Delaware	Y	25350 FQ	37020 AW	52460 TQ	DEBLS	10/01-12/01
	Florida	Y	24100 FQ	36550 AW	53700 TQ	FLBLS	10/01-12/01
	Georgia	Y	23020 FQ	34480 AW	50010 TQ	GABLS	10/01-12/01
	Hawaii	Y	30340 FQ	42260 AW	56140 TQ	HIBLS	10/01-12/01
	Idaho	Y	25170 FQ	35030 AW	47140 TQ	IDBLS	10/01-12/01
	Illinois	Y	20470 FQ	31830 AW	46030 TQ	ILBLS	10/01-12/01
	Indiana	Y	23290 FQ	34370 AW	47960 TQ	INBLS	10/01-12/01
	Iowa	Y	19710 FQ	32100 AW	46720 TQ	IABLS	10/01-12/01
	Kansas	Y	22970 FQ	34800 AW	47920 TQ	KSBLS	10/01-12/01
	Kentucky	Y	21610 FQ	32600 AW	45090 TQ	KYBLS	10/01-12/01
	Louisiana	Y	13550 FQ	31950 AW	48430 TQ	LABLS	10/01-12/01
	Maine	Y	26180 FQ	35930 AW	46090 TQ	MEBLS	10/01-12/01
	Maryland	Y	22550 FQ	40280 AW	55240 TQ	MDBLS	10/01-12/01
	Massachusetts	Y	24470 FQ	40150 AW	57640 TQ	MABLS	10/01-12/01
	Michigan	Y	27600 FQ	40290 AW	54180 TQ	MIBLS	10/01-12/01
	Minnesota	Y	26220 FQ	37550 AW	53550 TQ	MNBLS	10/01-12/01
	Mississippi	Y	19370 FQ	33070 AW	47740 TQ	MSBLS	10/01-12/01
	Missouri	Y	21910 FQ	37340 AW	52840 TQ	MOBLS	10/01-12/01
	Montana	Y	20600 FQ	32900 AW	44570 TQ	MTBLS	10/01-12/01
	Nebraska	Y	16540 FQ	28740 AW	44230 TQ	NEBLS	10/01-12/01
	Nevada	Y	32280 FQ	46700 AW	57150 TQ	NVBLS	10/01-12/01
	New Hampshire	Y	20640 FQ	34560 AW	48270 TQ	NHBLS	10/01-12/01
	New Jersey	Y	25570 FQ	43470 AW	61110 TQ	NJBLS	10/01-12/01
	New Mexico	Y	22050 FQ	35080 AW	48330 TQ	NMBLS	10/01-12/01
	New York	Y	27580 FQ	43810 AW	62790 TQ	NYBLS	10/01-12/01
	North Carolina	Y	25360 FQ	37330 AW	52940 TQ	NCBLS	10/01-12/01
	North Dakota	Y	22370 FQ	31350 AW	42470 TQ	NDBLS	10/01-12/01
	Ohio	Y	24600 FQ	36180 AW	48240 TQ	OHBLS	10/01-12/01
	Oklahoma	Y	15730 FQ	31840 AW	49920 TQ	OKBLS	10/01-12/01
	Oregon	Y	29100 FQ	43420 AW	56250 TQ	ORBLS	10/01-12/01
	Pennsylvania	Y	24610 FQ	37910 AW	53370 TQ	PABLS	10/01-12/01
	Rhode Island	Y	26440 FQ	41530 AW	59020 TQ	RIBLS	10/01-12/01
	South Carolina	Y	19380 FQ	32960 AW	53390 TQ	SCBLS	10/01-12/01
	South Dakota	Y	20040 FQ	31980 AW	46530 TQ	SDBLS	10/01-12/01
	Tennessee	Y	20410 FQ	34520 AW	50930 TQ	TNBLS	10/01-12/01
	Texas	Y	23260 FQ	35220 AW	50380 TQ	TXBLS	10/01-12/01
	Utah	Y	20720 FQ	39340 AW	58880 TQ	UTBLS	10/01-12/01
	Vermont	Y	29290 FQ	39860 AW	53170 TQ	VTBLS	10/01-12/01
	Virginia	Y	25480 FQ	37740 AW	52690 TQ	VABLS	10/01-12/01
	Washington	Y	29730 FQ	41150 AW	54670 TQ	WABLS	10/01-12/01
	West Virginia	Y	18560 FQ	27970 AW	39670 TQ	WVBLS	10/01-12/01
	Wisconsin	Y	26790 FQ	37950 AW	51360 TQ	WIBLS	10/01-12/01
	Wyoming	Y	19210 FQ	31450 AW	45180 TQ	WYBLS	10/01-12/01
	Puerto Rico	Y	12490 FQ	20010 AW	29530 TQ	PRBLS	10/01-12/01
Medical Appliance Technician	Alabama	H	7.44 FQ	14.81 AW	26.94 TQ	ALBLS	10/01-12/01
	Arkansas	H	8.94 FQ	12.50 AW	17.54 TQ	ARBLS	10/01-12/01
	California	H	8.50 FQ	15.24 AW	23.98 TQ	CABLS	10/01-12/01
	Colorado	H	10.47 FQ	13.93 AW	17.72 TQ	COBLS	10/01-12/01
	Connecticut	H	7.05 FQ	14.02 AW	24.90 TQ	CTBLS	10/01-12/01
	Florida	H	9.13 FQ	12.50 AW	16.19 TQ	FLBLS	10/01-12/01
	Georgia	H	8.06 FQ	14.27 AW	22.26 TQ	GABLS	10/01-12/01
	Indiana	H	8.41 FQ	12.18 AW	16.84 TQ	INBLS	10/01-12/01
	Iowa	H	7.76 FQ	15.83 AW	28.76 TQ	IABLS	10/01-12/01
	Kansas	H	5.68 FQ	8.21 AW	13.41 TQ	KSBLS	10/01-12/01
	Louisiana	H	11.58 FQ	16.76 AW	24.44 TQ	LABLS	10/01-12/01
	Maine	H	8.34 FQ	13.58 AW	20.11 TQ	MEBLS	10/01-12/01
	Maryland	H	9.34 FQ	15.11 AW	22.20 TQ	MDBLS	10/01-12/01
	Massachusetts	H	11.10 FQ	16.47 AW	23.00 TQ	MABLS	10/01-12/01
	Michigan	H	9.94 FQ	17.70 AW	25.64 TQ	MIBLS	10/01-12/01
	Minnesota	H	10.24 FQ	18.08 AW	32.32 TQ	MNBLS	10/01-12/01
	Mississippi	H	8.76 FQ	14.59 AW	22.51 TQ	MSBLS	10/01-12/01
	Missouri	H	9.24 FQ	13.90 AW	21.65 TQ	MOBLS	10/01-12/01
	Montana	H	5.88 FQ	9.57 AW	18.70 TQ	MTBLS	10/01-12/01

AAW Average annual wage; **AE** Average entry wage; **AEX** Average experienced wage; **AO** Average offered; **AOH** Average offered, high; **AOL** Average offered, low; **APH** Average pay, high range; **APL** Average pay, low range; **ASH** Average starting, high; **ASL** Average starting, low; **AW** Average wage paid; **FQ** First quartile wage; **H** Hourly; **HI** Highest wage paid; **HR** High end range; **LR** Low end range; **M** Monthly; **MTC** Median total compensation; **MW** Median wage paid; **SQ** Second quartile wage; **S** Special: hourly and annual; **TQ** Third quartile wage; **W** Weekly; **Y** Yearly

Occupation/Type/Industry	Location	Per	Low	Mid	High	Source	Date
Medical Appliance Technician	Nevada	H	13.55 FQ	15.37 AW	18.48 TQ	NVBLS	10/01-12/01
	New Hampshire	H	11.46 FQ	14.83 AW	17.41 TQ	NHBLS	10/01-12/01
	New Jersey	H	9.21 FQ	18.20 AW	31.35 TQ	NJBLS	10/01-12/01
	New Mexico	H	9.88 FQ	12.71 AW	16.27 TQ	NMBLS	10/01-12/01
	New York	H	6.83 FQ	16.14 AW	25.07 TQ	NYBLS	10/01-12/01
	North Carolina	H	9.41 FQ	13.77 AW	17.55 TQ	NCBLS	10/01-12/01
	Ohio	H	9.33 FQ	18.07 AW	37.41 TQ	OHBLS	10/01-12/01
	Oklahoma	H	8.63 FQ	14.47 AW	20.93 TQ	OKBLS	10/01-12/01
	Oregon	H	7.68 FQ	13.06 AW	19.64 TQ	ORBLS	10/01-12/01
	Pennsylvania	H	7.92 FQ	12.90 AW	18.77 TQ	PABLS	10/01-12/01
	South Carolina	H	11.03 FQ	17.81 AW	28.00 TQ	SCBLS	10/01-12/01
	Tennessee	H	9.28 FQ	14.89 AW	21.02 TQ	TNBLS	10/01-12/01
	Texas	H	9.81 FQ	17.25 AW	32.01 TQ	TXBLS	10/01-12/01
	Utah	H	8.11 FQ	11.67 AW	14.55 TQ	UTBLS	10/01-12/01
	Virginia	H	10.19 FQ	15.53 AW	22.18 TQ	VABLS	10/01-12/01
	Washington	H	8.65 FQ	13.84 AW	20.58 TQ	WABLS	10/01-12/01
	Wisconsin	H	9.29 FQ	15.86 AW	23.61 TQ	WIBLS	10/01-12/01
Medical Assistant	United States	Y		18500-25760 AW		FREEP1	1/00-1/00
	Alabama	H	7.19 FQ	9.92 AW	13.45 TQ	ALBLS	10/01-12/01
	Alaska	H	11.59 FQ	14.93 AW	20.17 TQ	AKBLS	10/01-12/01
	Arizona	H	7.65 FQ	10.95 AW	15.02 TQ	AZBLS	10/01-12/01
	Arkansas	H	7.18 FQ	10.20 AW	13.84 TQ	ARBLS	10/01-12/01
	California	H	8.71 FQ	12.76 AW	17.25 TQ	CABLS	10/01-12/01
	Colorado	H	9.26 FQ	12.85 AW	16.88 TQ	COBLS	10/01-12/01
	Connecticut	H	9.87 FQ	13.89 AW	17.74 TQ	CTBLS	10/01-12/01
	Delaware	H	7.53 FQ	11.23 AW	16.33 TQ	DEBLS	10/01-12/01
	District of Columbia	H	11.31 FQ	15.26 AW	19.96 TQ	DCBLS	10/01-12/01
	Florida	H	8.29 FQ	11.23 AW	14.91 TQ	FLBLS	10/01-12/01
	Georgia	H	8.93 FQ	11.61 AW	13.82 TQ	GABLS	10/01-12/01
	Hawaii	H	9.21 FQ	12.36 AW	16.99 TQ	HIBLS	10/01-12/01
	Idaho	H	8.98 FQ	10.86 AW	13.46 TQ	IDBLS	10/01-12/01
	Illinois	H	8.93 FQ	12.80 AW	17.63 TQ	ILBLS	10/01-12/01
	Indiana	H	8.69 FQ	11.53 AW	15.75 TQ	INBLS	10/01-12/01
	Iowa	H	8.32 FQ	10.89 AW	13.87 TQ	IABLS	10/01-12/01
	Kansas	H	7.41 FQ	10.13 AW	13.89 TQ	KSBLS	10/01-12/01
	Kentucky	H	7.83 FQ	10.96 AW	15.95 TQ	KYBLS	10/01-12/01
	Louisiana	H	7.18 FQ	9.63 AW	12.72 TQ	LABLS	10/01-12/01
	Maine	H	8.93 FQ	11.90 AW	16.07 TQ	MEBLS	10/01-12/01
	Maryland	H	8.84 FQ	12.24 AW	16.52 TQ	MDBLS	10/01-12/01
	Massachusetts	H	9.55 FQ	13.29 AW	16.90 TQ	MABLS	10/01-12/01
	Michigan	H	9.09 FQ	11.73 AW	14.56 TQ	MIBLS	10/01-12/01
	Minnesota	H	9.49 FQ	12.62 AW	16.19 TQ	MNBLS	10/01-12/01
	Mississippi	H	6.92 FQ	9.48 AW	12.69 TQ	MSBLS	10/01-12/01
	Missouri	H	7.97 FQ	10.78 AW	13.83 TQ	MOBLS	10/01-12/01
	Montana	H	7.90 FQ	10.54 AW	13.81 TQ	MTBLS	10/01-12/01
	Nebraska	H	7.95 FQ	10.39 AW	13.25 TQ	NEBLS	10/01-12/01
	Nevada	H	8.10 FQ	12.41 AW	16.12 TQ	NVBLS	10/01-12/01
	New Hampshire	H	9.63 FQ	12.14 AW	14.78 TQ	NHBLS	10/01-12/01
	New Jersey	H	7.60 FQ	11.82 AW	16.51 TQ	NJBLS	10/01-12/01
	New Mexico	H	7.66 FQ	10.76 AW	14.03 TQ	NMBLS	10/01-12/01
	New York	H	9.13 FQ	12.79 AW	16.95 TQ	NYBLS	10/01-12/01
	North Carolina	H	8.35 FQ	11.67 AW	16.06 TQ	NCBLS	10/01-12/01
	North Dakota	H	7.44 FQ	10.71 AW	13.85 TQ	NDBLS	10/01-12/01
	Ohio	H	8.21 FQ	10.86 AW	13.96 TQ	OHBLS	10/01-12/01
	Oklahoma	H	7.35 FQ	9.80 AW	12.82 TQ	OKBLS	10/01-12/01
	Oregon	H	9.65 FQ	12.96 AW	17.07 TQ	ORBLS	10/01-12/01
	Pennsylvania	H	8.27 FQ	11.33 AW	15.18 TQ	PABLS	10/01-12/01
	Rhode Island	H	8.83 FQ	11.10 AW	13.96 TQ	RIBLS	10/01-12/01
	South Carolina	H	6.87 FQ	10.42 AW	13.81 TQ	SCBLS	10/01-12/01
	South Dakota	H	7.56 FQ	9.81 AW	12.66 TQ	SDBLS	10/01-12/01
	Tennessee	H	7.87 FQ	11.11 AW	15.35 TQ	TNBLS	10/01-12/01
	Texas	H	7.34 FQ	10.65 AW	14.40 TQ	TXBLS	10/01-12/01
	Utah	H	7.75 FQ	10.05 AW	12.91 TQ	UTBLS	10/01-12/01
	Vermont	H	9.53 FQ	13.14 AW	18.24 TQ	VTBLS	10/01-12/01
	Virginia	H	8.39 FQ	11.37 AW	16.12 TQ	VABLS	10/01-12/01
	Washington	H	9.60 FQ	12.77 AW	16.49 TQ	WABLS	10/01-12/01
	West Virginia	H	6.41 FQ	9.10 AW	11.82 TQ	WVBLS	10/01-12/01
	Wisconsin	H	9.22 FQ	12.04 AW	15.80 TQ	WIBLS	10/01-12/01
	Wyoming	H	7.59 FQ	9.92 AW	11.43 TQ	WYBLS	10/01-12/01
	Puerto Rico	H	5.98 FQ	11.35 AW	18.92 TQ	PRBLS	10/01-12/01
	Guam	H	7.46 FQ	10.68 AW	13.60 TQ	GUBLS	10/01-12/01

AAW	Average annual wage	**AOH**	Average offered, high	**ASH**	Average starting, high	**H**	Hourly	**M**	Monthly	**S**	Special: hourly and annual
AE	Average entry wage	**AOL**	Average offered, low	**ASL**	Average starting, low	**HI**	Highest wage paid	**MTC**	Median total compensation	**TQ**	Third quartile wage
AEX	Average experienced wage	**APH**	Average pay, high range	**AW**	Average wage paid	**HR**	High end range	**MW**	Median wage paid	**W**	Weekly
AO	Average offered	**APL**	Average pay, low range	**FQ**	First quartile wage	**LR**	Low end range	**SQ**	Second quartile wage	**Y**	Yearly

Occupation/Type/Industry	Location	Per	Low	Mid	High	Source	Date
Medical Equipment Preparer	Alabama	H	6.64 FQ	8.87 AW	12.06 TQ	ALBLS	10/01-12/01
	Alaska	H	7.91 FQ	13.52 AW	17.48 TQ	AKBLS	10/01-12/01
	Arizona	H	8.26 FQ	11.62 AW	15.59 TQ	AZBLS	10/01-12/01
	Arkansas	H	7.46 FQ	10.38 AW	13.99 TQ	ARBLS	10/01-12/01
	California	H	8.85 FQ	13.59 AW	17.46 TQ	CABLS	10/01-12/01
	Colorado	H	8.82 FQ	11.72 AW	15.11 TQ	COBLS	10/01-12/01
	Connecticut	H	11.07 FQ	13.80 AW	17.19 TQ	CTBLS	10/01-12/01
	Delaware	H	9.38 FQ	13.76 AW	19.72 TQ	DEBLS	10/01-12/01
	District of Columbia	H	9.30 FQ	13.35 AW	16.85 TQ	DCBLS	10/01-12/01
	Florida	H	7.47 FQ	9.70 AW	12.59 TQ	FLBLS	10/01-12/01
	Georgia	H	7.70 FQ	10.43 AW	13.53 TQ	GABLS	10/01-12/01
	Hawaii	H	9.03 FQ	11.18 AW	13.86 TQ	HIBLS	10/01-12/01
	Idaho	H	7.60 FQ	10.15 AW	13.43 TQ	IDBLS	10/01-12/01
	Illinois	H	7.87 FQ	11.43 AW	15.34 TQ	ILBLS	10/01-12/01
	Indiana	H	7.70 FQ	10.32 AW	13.17 TQ	INBLS	10/01-12/01
	Iowa	H	7.19 FQ	10.50 AW	15.03 TQ	IABLS	10/01-12/01
	Kansas	H	7.14 FQ	9.76 AW	12.71 TQ	KSBLS	10/01-12/01
	Kentucky	H	8.38 FQ	10.86 AW	13.43 TQ	KYBLS	10/01-12/01
	Louisiana	H	6.81 FQ	9.49 AW	13.15 TQ	LABLS	10/01-12/01
	Maine	H	8.72 FQ	10.74 AW	13.44 TQ	MEBLS	10/01-12/01
	Maryland	H	7.79 FQ	12.01 AW	16.90 TQ	MDBLS	10/01-12/01
	Massachusetts	H	8.85 FQ	12.24 AW	16.37 TQ	MABLS	10/01-12/01
	Michigan	H	9.18 FQ	11.75 AW	14.93 TQ	MIBLS	10/01-12/01
	Minnesota	H	9.09 FQ	11.56 AW	15.68 TQ	MNBLS	10/01-12/01
	Mississippi	H	6.83 FQ	8.58 AW	10.78 TQ	MSBLS	10/01-12/01
	Missouri	H	6.62 FQ	10.04 AW	13.16 TQ	MOBLS	10/01-12/01
	Montana	H	7.60 FQ	10.06 AW	13.05 TQ	MTBLS	10/01-12/01
	Nebraska	H	8.36 FQ	10.65 AW	13.39 TQ	NEBLS	10/01-12/01
	Nevada	H	9.61 FQ	12.56 AW	15.80 TQ	NVBLS	10/01-12/01
	New Hampshire	H	9.16 FQ	11.79 AW	14.61 TQ	NHBLS	10/01-12/01
	New Jersey	H	9.19 FQ	11.98 AW	15.63 TQ	NJBLS	10/01-12/01
	New Mexico	H	7.31 FQ	9.51 AW	13.15 TQ	NMBLS	10/01-12/01
	New York	H	9.01 FQ	13.29 AW	17.94 TQ	NYBLS	10/01-12/01
	North Carolina	H	8.26 FQ	10.90 AW	14.07 TQ	NCBLS	10/01-12/01
	Ohio	H	8.71 FQ	11.15 AW	14.03 TQ	OHBLS	10/01-12/01
	Oklahoma	H	6.58 FQ	9.47 AW	12.61 TQ	OKBLS	10/01-12/01
	Oregon	H	9.03 FQ	11.78 AW	15.15 TQ	ORBLS	10/01-12/01
	Pennsylvania	H	8.13 FQ	11.89 AW	16.31 TQ	PABLS	10/01-12/01
	Rhode Island	H	9.36 FQ	12.18 AW	15.77 TQ	RIBLS	10/01-12/01
	South Carolina	H	7.70 FQ	11.49 AW	16.61 TQ	SCBLS	10/01-12/01
	Tennessee	H	7.61 FQ	10.21 AW	13.49 TQ	TNBLS	10/01-12/01
	Texas	H	6.83 FQ	9.34 AW	12.89 TQ	TXBLS	10/01-12/01
	Utah	H	6.46 FQ	9.15 AW	12.03 TQ	UTBLS	10/01-12/01
	Virginia	H	7.49 FQ	10.26 AW	14.44 TQ	VABLS	10/01-12/01
	Washington	H	7.40 FQ	11.88 AW	16.17 TQ	WABLS	10/01-12/01
	West Virginia	H	7.47 FQ	10.73 AW	14.53 TQ	WVBLS	10/01-12/01
	Wisconsin	H	7.79 FQ	10.62 AW	13.94 TQ	WIBLS	10/01-12/01
	Wyoming	H	8.12 FQ	10.45 AW	14.26 TQ	WYBLS	10/01-12/01
	Puerto Rico	H	5.52 FQ	7.54 AW	11.63 TQ	PRBLS	10/01-12/01
Medical Equipment Repairer	Alabama	H	9.07 FQ	14.37 AW	21.28 TQ	ALBLS	10/01-12/01
	Alaska	H	16.67 FQ	24.04 AW	32.02 TQ	AKBLS	10/01-12/01
	Arizona	H	12.80 FQ	29.04 AW	52.38 TQ	AZBLS	10/01-12/01
	Arkansas	H	11.76 FQ	18.16 AW	28.20 TQ	ARBLS	10/01-12/01
	California	H	11.04 FQ	16.67 AW	28.21 TQ	CABLS	10/01-12/01
	Colorado	H	14.85 FQ	22.42 AW	28.27 TQ	COBLS	10/01-12/01
	Connecticut	H	11.73 FQ	18.42 AW	26.22 TQ	CTBLS	10/01-12/01
	Delaware	H	14.66 FQ	21.32 AW	29.00 TQ	DEBLS	10/01-12/01
	District of Columbia	H	13.99 FQ	18.79 AW	25.67 TQ	DCBLS	10/01-12/01
	Florida	H	10.09 FQ	16.76 AW	24.81 TQ	FLBLS	10/01-12/01
	Georgia	H	8.96 FQ	17.86 AW	26.19 TQ	GABLS	10/01-12/01
	Hawaii	H	14.08 FQ	21.07 AW	26.97 TQ	HIBLS	10/01-12/01
	Idaho	H	11.53 FQ	17.79 AW	25.73 TQ	IDBLS	10/01-12/01
	Illinois	H	10.57 FQ	18.61 AW	27.07 TQ	ILBLS	10/01-12/01
	Indiana	H	11.63 FQ	18.02 AW	25.66 TQ	INBLS	10/01-12/01
	Iowa	H	7.99 FQ	15.09 AW	21.56 TQ	IABLS	10/01-12/01
	Kansas	H	11.17 FQ	17.10 AW	24.97 TQ	KSBLS	10/01-12/01
	Kentucky	H	9.75 FQ	16.54 AW	24.63 TQ	KYBLS	10/01-12/01
	Louisiana	H	9.65 FQ	15.87 AW	25.04 TQ	LABLS	10/01-12/01
	Maine	H	11.26 FQ	18.60 AW	26.67 TQ	MEBLS	10/01-12/01
	Maryland	H	10.08 FQ	16.66 AW	24.38 TQ	MDBLS	10/01-12/01
	Massachusetts	H	11.63 FQ	19.31 AW	28.27 TQ	MABLS	10/01-12/01
	Michigan	H	12.18 FQ	20.47 AW	31.99 TQ	MIBLS	10/01-12/01

AAW Average annual wage	**AOH** Average offered, high	**ASH** Average starting, high	**H** Hourly	**M** Monthly	**S** Special: hourly and annual
AE Average entry wage	**AOL** Average offered, low	**ASL** Average starting, low	**HI** Highest wage paid	**MTC** Median total compensation	**TQ** Third quartile wage
AEX Average experienced wage	**APH** Average pay, high range	**AW** Average wage paid	**HR** High end range	**MW** Median wage paid	**W** Weekly
AO Average offered	**APL** Average pay, low range	**FQ** First quartile wage	**LR** Low end range	**SQ** Second quartile wage	**Y** Yearly

Occupation/Type/Industry	Location	Per	Low	Mid	High	Source	Date
Medical Equipment Repairer	Minnesota	H	12.53 FQ	19.12 AW	26.06 TQ	MNBLS	10/01-12/01
	Mississippi	H	11.08 FQ	15.44 AW	23.38 TQ	MSBLS	10/01-12/01
	Missouri	H	10.69 FQ	22.26 AW	37.15 TQ	MOBLS	10/01-12/01
	Montana	H	9.06 FQ	16.80 AW	26.64 TQ	MTBLS	10/01-12/01
	Nebraska	H	9.46 FQ	17.28 AW	26.29 TQ	NEBLS	10/01-12/01
	Nevada	H	9.07 FQ	14.55 AW	22.49 TQ	NVBLS	10/01-12/01
	New Hampshire	H	8.74 FQ	18.14 AW	27.55 TQ	NHBLS	10/01-12/01
	New Jersey	H	12.05 FQ	23.66 AW	40.39 TQ	NJBLS	10/01-12/01
	New Mexico	H	8.93 FQ	16.24 AW	26.76 TQ	NMBLS	10/01-12/01
	New York	H	10.05 FQ	18.76 AW	30.22 TQ	NYBLS	10/01-12/01
	North Carolina	H	10.03 FQ	16.97 AW	25.12 TQ	NCBLS	10/01-12/01
	Ohio	H	12.70 FQ	19.44 AW	26.78 TQ	OHBLS	10/01-12/01
	Oklahoma	H	9.75 FQ	17.51 AW	26.40 TQ	OKBLS	10/01-12/01
	Oregon	H	12.50 FQ	19.97 AW	27.77 TQ	ORBLS	10/01-12/01
	Pennsylvania	H	10.38 FQ	17.57 AW	26.32 TQ	PABLS	10/01-12/01
	Rhode Island	H	10.85 FQ	17.42 AW	26.10 TQ	RIBLS	10/01-12/01
	South Carolina	H	10.81 FQ	16.11 AW	21.40 TQ	SCBLS	10/01-12/01
	South Dakota	H	10.93 FQ	17.93 AW	22.18 TQ	SDBLS	10/01-12/01
	Tennessee	H	10.52 FQ	17.14 AW	25.26 TQ	TNBLS	10/01-12/01
	Texas	H	6.21 FQ	14.47 AW	25.63 TQ	TXBLS	10/01-12/01
	Utah	H	11.84 FQ	14.13 AW	18.83 TQ	UTBLS	10/01-12/01
	Virginia	H	9.75 FQ	17.44 AW	25.32 TQ	VABLS	10/01-12/01
	Washington	H	10.61 FQ	19.39 AW	27.29 TQ	WABLS	10/01-12/01
	West Virginia	H	7.62 FQ	14.69 AW	23.61 TQ	WVBLS	10/01-12/01
	Wisconsin	H	12.96 FQ	18.80 AW	25.34 TQ	WIBLS	10/01-12/01
	Wyoming	H	9.13 FQ	15.75 AW	22.26 TQ	WYBLS	10/01-12/01
	Puerto Rico	H	6.01 FQ	10.46 AW	17.49 TQ	PRBLS	10/01-12/01
Medical Marketing and Media Professional	United States	Y	20000 AOL	111000 AW	425000 HI	MM&M	1/01-1/02
Medical Record and Health Information Technician	United States	Y		18500-25760 AW		FREEP1	1/00-1/00
	Alabama	Y	14220 FQ	20650 AW	30040 TQ	ALBLS	10/01-12/01
	Alaska	Y	23710 FQ	30950 AW	41910 TQ	AKBLS	10/01-12/01
	Arizona	Y	15840 FQ	25040 AW	37090 TQ	AZBLS	10/01-12/01
	Arkansas	Y	15440 FQ	23170 AW	32880 TQ	ARBLS	10/01-12/01
	California	Y	17420 FQ	28570 AW	43100 TQ	CABLS	10/01-12/01
	Colorado	Y	19260 FQ	28300 AW	41200 TQ	COBLS	10/01-12/01
	Connecticut	Y	20650 FQ	32040 AW	48320 TQ	CTBLS	10/01-12/01
	Delaware	Y	18620 FQ	25830 AW	33820 TQ	DEBLS	10/01-12/01
	District of Columbia	Y	19990 FQ	30670 AW	42650 TQ	DCBLS	10/01-12/01
	Florida	Y	16090 FQ	24330 AW	35460 TQ	FLBLS	10/01-12/01
	Georgia	Y	16090 FQ	25340 AW	36610 TQ	GABLS	10/01-12/01
	Hawaii	Y	22460 FQ	29370 AW	42470 TQ	HIBLS	10/01-12/01
	Idaho	Y	15130 FQ	22910 AW	33060 TQ	IDBLS	10/01-12/01
	Illinois	Y	15530 FQ	23920 AW	35420 TQ	ILBLS	10/01-12/01
	Indiana	Y	16330 FQ	23620 AW	33730 TQ	INBLS	10/01-12/01
	Iowa	Y	15530 FQ	23290 AW	34300 TQ	IABLS	10/01-12/01
	Kansas	Y	15550 FQ	22810 AW	33940 TQ	KSBLS	10/01-12/01
	Kentucky	Y	16130 FQ	24190 AW	34740 TQ	KYBLS	10/01-12/01
	Louisiana	Y	13620 FQ	22540 AW	35900 TQ	LABLS	10/01-12/01
	Maine	Y	16520 FQ	23310 AW	32980 TQ	MEBLS	10/01-12/01
	Maryland	Y	18730 FQ	27590 AW	39330 TQ	MDBLS	10/01-12/01
	Massachusetts	Y	18760 FQ	27060 AW	36270 TQ	MABLS	10/01-12/01
	Michigan	Y	18010 FQ	26010 AW	38220 TQ	MIBLS	10/01-12/01
	Minnesota	Y	17860 FQ	25800 AW	36250 TQ	MNBLS	10/01-12/01
	Mississippi	Y	14190 FQ	20210 AW	29450 TQ	MSBLS	10/01-12/01
	Missouri	Y	15860 FQ	24680 AW	39170 TQ	MOBLS	10/01-12/01
	Montana	Y	14690 FQ	21250 AW	31400 TQ	MTBLS	10/01-12/01
	Nebraska	Y	15740 FQ	24370 AW	36300 TQ	NEBLS	10/01-12/01
	Nevada	Y	18320 FQ	26610 AW	41300 TQ	NVBLS	10/01-12/01
	New Hampshire	Y	18310 FQ	25770 AW	35770 TQ	NHBLS	10/01-12/01
	New Jersey	Y	20180 FQ	30960 AW	44560 TQ	NJBLS	10/01-12/01
	New Mexico	Y	15860 FQ	23320 AW	32930 TQ	NMBLS	10/01-12/01
	New York	Y	18130 FQ	29960 AW	42840 TQ	NYBLS	10/01-12/01
	North Carolina	Y	16710 FQ	24530 AW	35420 TQ	NCBLS	10/01-12/01
	North Dakota	Y	14120 FQ	20730 AW	29400 TQ	NDBLS	10/01-12/01
	Ohio	Y	16470 FQ	24860 AW	35650 TQ	OHBLS	10/01-12/01
	Oklahoma	Y	14590 FQ	22500 AW	32500 TQ	OKBLS	10/01-12/01
	Oregon	Y	17640 FQ	26110 AW	36690 TQ	ORBLS	10/01-12/01

AAW Average annual wage **AE** Average entry wage **AEX** Average experienced wage **AO** Average offered **AOH** Average offered, high **AOL** Average offered, low **APH** Average pay, high range **APL** Average pay, low range **ASH** Average starting, high **ASL** Average starting, low **AW** Average wage paid **FQ** First quartile wage **H** Hourly **HI** Highest wage paid **HR** High end range **LR** Low end range **M** Monthly **MTC** Median total compensation **MW** Median wage paid **SQ** Second quartile wage **S** Special: hourly and annual **TQ** Third quartile wage **W** Weekly **Y** Yearly

Occupation/Type/Industry	Location	Per	Low	Mid	High	Source	Date
Medical Record and Health Information Technician							
	Pennsylvania	Y	16520 FQ	25970 AW	38430 TQ	PABLS	10/01-12/01
	Rhode Island	Y	19150 FQ	29560 AW	42630 TQ	RIBLS	10/01-12/01
	South Carolina	Y	15990 FQ	23220 AW	33310 TQ	SCBLS	10/01-12/01
	South Dakota	Y	16560 FQ	24160 AW	34220 TQ	SDBLS	10/01-12/01
	Tennessee	Y	15830 FQ	22970 AW	32160 TQ	TNBLS	10/01-12/01
	Texas	Y	15370 FQ	23480 AW	34270 TQ	TXBLS	10/01-12/01
	Utah	Y	15770 FQ	23220 AW	32850 TQ	UTBLS	10/01-12/01
	Vermont	Y	19270 FQ	31900 AW	46150 TQ	VTBLS	10/01-12/01
	Virginia	Y	16280 FQ	24870 AW	35750 TQ	VABLS	10/01-12/01
	Washington	Y	18680 FQ	27500 AW	38750 TQ	WABLS	10/01-12/01
	West Virginia	Y	13600 FQ	19820 AW	28910 TQ	WVBLS	10/01-12/01
	Wisconsin	Y	16700 FQ	24060 AW	34730 TQ	WIBLS	10/01-12/01
	Wyoming	Y	16260 FQ	22710 AW	31050 TQ	WYBLS	10/01-12/01
	Puerto Rico	Y	11730 FQ	15610 AW	20990 TQ	PRBLS	10/01-12/01
	Guam	Y	15550 FQ	25510 AW	35280 TQ	GUBLS	10/01-12/01
Medical Scientist							
Except Epidemiologist	Alabama	Y	25500 FQ	53150 AW	97720 TQ	ALBLS	10/01-12/01
Except Epidemiologist	Arizona	Y	25750 FQ	53370 AW	86700 TQ	AZBLS	10/01-12/01
Except Epidemiologist	Phoenix-Mesa MSA, AZ	Y	25600 FQ	50330 AW	74010 TQ	AZBLS	10/01-12/01
Except Epidemiologist	Arkansas	Y	30070 FQ	60480 AW	107070 TQ	ARBLS	10/01-12/01
Except Epidemiologist	Little Rock-North Little Rock MSA, AR	Y	28410 FQ	48360 AW	70530 TQ	ARBLS	10/01-12/01
Except Epidemiologist	California	Y	33560 FQ	63790 AW	104600 TQ	CABLS	10/01-12/01
Except Epidemiologist	Los Angeles-Long Beach PMSA, CA	Y	28230 FQ	54650 AW	87000 TQ	CABLS	10/01-12/01
Except Epidemiologist	Oakland PMSA, CA	Y	47990 FQ	76750 AW	118140 TQ	CABLS	10/01-12/01
Except Epidemiologist	Orange County PMSA, CA	Y	36320 FQ	60200 AW	88800 TQ	CABLS	10/01-12/01
Except Epidemiologist	Riverside-San Bernardino PMSA, CA	Y	36480 FQ	50200 AW	65400 TQ	CABLS	10/01-12/01
Except Epidemiologist	San Diego MSA, CA	Y	36830 FQ	70600 AW	121850 TQ	CABLS	10/01-12/01
Except Epidemiologist	San Francisco PMSA, CA	Y	40020 FQ	67550 AW	103170 TQ	CABLS	10/01-12/01
Except Epidemiologist	San Jose PMSA, CA	Y	45280 FQ	71440 AW	109310 TQ	CABLS	10/01-12/01
Except Epidemiologist	Santa Barbara-Santa Maria-Lompoc MSA, CA	Y	31900 FQ	51420 AW	82950 TQ	CABLS	10/01-12/01
Except Epidemiologist	Colorado	Y	32700 FQ	62250 AW	108560 TQ	COBLS	10/01-12/01
Except Epidemiologist	Denver PMSA, CO	Y	41770 FQ	66240 AW	109640 TQ	COBLS	10/01-12/01
Except Epidemiologist	Fort Collins-Loveland MSA, CO	Y	23080 FQ	52230 AW	104730 TQ	COBLS	10/01-12/01
Except Epidemiologist	Connecticut	Y	47590 FQ	82650 AW	115200 TQ	CTBLS	10/01-12/01
Except Epidemiologist	New Haven-Meriden PMSA, CT	Y	42660 FQ	86630 AW	127440 TQ	CTBLS	10/01-12/01
Except Epidemiologist	Stamford-Norwalk PMSA, CT	Y	51300 FQ	79410 AW	109830 TQ	CTBLS	10/01-12/01
Except Epidemiologist	District of Columbia	Y	31000 FQ	60320 AW	102870 TQ	DCBLS	10/01-12/01
Except Epidemiologist	Washington PMSA, DC-MD-VA-WV	Y	35300 FQ	66050 AW	104750 TQ	DCBLS	10/01-12/01
Except Epidemiologist	Florida	Y	41280 FQ	73150 AW	145050 TQ	FLBLS	10/01-12/01
Except Epidemiologist	Fort Lauderdale PMSA, FL	Y	42940 FQ	73820 AW		FLBLS	10/01-12/01
Except Epidemiologist	Gainesville MSA, FL	Y	58710 FQ	74960 AW	99900 TQ	FLBLS	10/01-12/01
Except Epidemiologist	Jacksonville MSA, FL	Y	41500 FQ	65900 AW	97880 TQ	FLBLS	10/01-12/01
Except Epidemiologist	Miami PMSA, FL	Y	39170 FQ	60350 AW	90620 TQ	FLBLS	10/01-12/01
Except Epidemiologist	Orlando MSA, FL	Y	40300 FQ	69150 AW	137610 TQ	FLBLS	10/01-12/01
Except Epidemiologist	Tampa-St. Petersburg-Clearwater MSA, FL	Y	44000 FQ	89920 AW		FLBLS	10/01-12/01
Except Epidemiologist	Georgia	Y	32730 FQ	56590 AW	94420 TQ	GABLS	10/01-12/01
Except Epidemiologist	Atlanta MSA, GA	Y	34030 FQ	57610 AW	94320 TQ	GABLS	10/01-12/01
Except Epidemiologist	Augusta-Aiken MSA, GA-SC	Y	24230 FQ	43770 AW	66290 TQ	GABLS	10/01-12/01
Except Epidemiologist	Illinois	Y	31900 FQ	59850 AW	90280 TQ	ILBLS	10/01-12/01
Except Epidemiologist	Chicago PMSA, IL	Y	32950 FQ	61910 AW	90920 TQ	ILBLS	10/01-12/01
Except Epidemiologist	Rockford MSA, IL	Y	25070 FQ	40130 AW	62860 TQ	ILBLS	10/01-12/01
Except Epidemiologist	Indiana	Y	29730 FQ	65220 AW	134120 TQ	INBLS	10/01-12/01
Except Epidemiologist	Kansas	Y	25800 FQ	60420 AW	120860 TQ	KSBLS	10/01-12/01
Except Epidemiologist	Louisiana	Y	27300 FQ	44380 AW	66470 TQ	LABLS	10/01-12/01
Except Epidemiologist	New Orleans MSA, LA	Y	28420 FQ	43080 AW	56210 TQ	LABLS	10/01-12/01
Except Epidemiologist	Maryland	Y	42720 FQ	71040 AW	104490 TQ	MDBLS	10/01-12/01
Except Epidemiologist	Baltimore PMSA, MD	Y	36240 FQ	65750 AW	110780 TQ	MDBLS	10/01-12/01
Except Epidemiologist	Massachusetts	Y	33060 FQ	64450 AW	110780 TQ	MABLS	10/01-12/01
Except Epidemiologist	Boston PMSA, MA-NH	Y	33010 FQ	64830 AW	111070 TQ	MABLS	10/01-12/01
Except Epidemiologist	Lawrence PMSA, MA-NH	Y	32470 FQ	58550 AW	95120 TQ	MABLS	10/01-12/01
Except Epidemiologist	Worcester PMSA, MA-CT	Y	34850 FQ	62480 AW	108500 TQ	MABLS	10/01-12/01
Except Epidemiologist	Michigan	Y	30370 FQ	51270 AW	82440 TQ	MIBLS	10/01-12/01

AAW Average annual wage	**AOH** Average offered, high	**ASH** Average starting, high	**H** Hourly	**M** Monthly	**S** Special: hourly and annual
AE Average entry wage	**AOL** Average offered, low	**ASL** Average starting, low	**HI** Highest wage paid	**MTC** Median total compensation	**TQ** Third quartile wage
AEX Average experienced wage	**APH** Average pay, high range	**AW** Average wage paid	**HR** High end range	**MW** Median wage paid	**W** Weekly
AO Average offered	**APL** Average pay, low range	**FQ** First quartile wage	**LR** Low end range	**SQ** Second quartile wage	**Y** Yearly

Occupation/Type/Industry	Location	Per	Low	Mid	High	Source	Date
Medical Scientist							
Except Epidemiologist	Ann Arbor PMSA, MI	Y	39600 FQ	47840 AW	58540 TQ	MIBLS	10/01-12/01
Except Epidemiologist	Detroit PMSA, MI	Y	31450 FQ	52900 AW	80560 TQ	MIBLS	10/01-12/01
Except Epidemiologist	Minnesota	Y	36240 FQ	61980 AW	96160 TQ	MNBLS	10/01-12/01
Except Epidemiologist	Minneapolis-St. Paul MSA, MN-WI	Y	36060 FQ	61350 AW	95600 TQ	MNBLS	10/01-12/01
Except Epidemiologist	Mississippi	Y	25830 FQ	45400 AW	71800 TQ	MSBLS	10/01-12/01
Except Epidemiologist	Kansas City MSA, MO-KS	Y	46680 FQ	81270 AW		MOBLS	10/01-12/01
Except Epidemiologist	Montana	Y	29760 FQ	53920 AW	82980 TQ	MTBLS	10/01-12/01
Except Epidemiologist	Nebraska	Y	24380 FQ	43650 AW	82920 TQ	NEBLS	10/01-12/01
Except Epidemiologist	Omaha MSA, NE-IA	Y	24020 FQ	38580 AW	60150 TQ	NEBLS	10/01-12/01
Except Epidemiologist	New Jersey	Y	47590 FQ	80490 AW	126360 TQ	NJBLS	10/01-12/01
Except Epidemiologist	Middlesex-Somerset-Hunterdon PMSA, NJ	Y	49080 FQ	76190 AW	109640 TQ	NJBLS	10/01-12/01
Except Epidemiologist	Newark PMSA, NJ	Y	48530 FQ	78040 AW	110780 TQ	NJBLS	10/01-12/01
Except Epidemiologist	New Mexico	Y	34940 FQ	71460 AW	116250 TQ	NMBLS	10/01-12/01
Except Epidemiologist	Albuquerque MSA, NM	Y	35930 FQ	72000 AW	118960 TQ	NMBLS	10/01-12/01
Except Epidemiologist	New York	Y	35650 FQ	73610 AW	136010 TQ	NYBLS	10/01-12/01
Except Epidemiologist	Buffalo-Niagara Falls MSA, NY	Y	33760 FQ	67110 AW	115630 TQ	NYBLS	10/01-12/01
Except Epidemiologist	New York PMSA, NY	Y	37930 FQ	78030 AW	139570 TQ	NYBLS	10/01-12/01
Except Epidemiologist	North Carolina	Y	39000 FQ	73770 AW	134110 TQ	NCBLS	10/01-12/01
Except Epidemiologist	Charlotte-Gastonia-Rock Hill MSA, NC-SC	Y	46870 FQ	61380 AW	86840 TQ	NCBLS	10/01-12/01
Except Epidemiologist	Greensboro-Winston-Salem-High Point MSA, NC	Y	32820 FQ	58340 AW	80260 TQ	NCBLS	10/01-12/01
Except Epidemiologist	Raleigh-Durham-Chapel Hill MSA, NC	Y	35380 FQ	61920 AW	95820 TQ	NCBLS	10/01-12/01
Except Epidemiologist	North Dakota	Y	30520 FQ	57680 AW	94680 TQ	NDBLS	10/01-12/01
Except Epidemiologist	Ohio	Y	26880 FQ	48070 AW	72260 TQ	OHBLS	10/01-12/01
Except Epidemiologist	Cleveland-Lorain-Elyria PMSA, OH	Y	30350 FQ	45710 AW	57210 TQ	OHBLS	10/01-12/01
Except Epidemiologist	Columbus MSA, OH	Y	25630 FQ	44630 AW	69220 TQ	OHBLS	10/01-12/01
Except Epidemiologist	Toledo MSA, OH	Y	23960 FQ	43040 AW	64320 TQ	OHBLS	10/01-12/01
Except Epidemiologist	Oklahoma	Y	27750 FQ	49110 AW	83960 TQ	OKBLS	10/01-12/01
Except Epidemiologist	Oklahoma City MSA, OK	Y	26470 FQ	48900 AW	90200 TQ	OKBLS	10/01-12/01
Except Epidemiologist	Tulsa MSA, OK	Y	32940 FQ	51170 AW	77290 TQ	OKBLS	10/01-12/01
Except Epidemiologist	Pennsylvania	Y	20820 FQ	38250 AW	66860 TQ	PABLS	10/01-12/01
Except Epidemiologist	Philadelphia PMSA, PA-NJ	Y	23760 FQ	48370 AW	82500 TQ	PABLS	10/01-12/01
Except Epidemiologist	Rhode Island	Y	24080 FQ	37790 AW	56460 TQ	RIBLS	10/01-12/01
Except Epidemiologist	Providence-Fall River-Warwick MSA, RI-MA	Y	24080 FQ	37800 AW	56470 TQ	RIBLS	10/01-12/01
Except Epidemiologist	South Carolina	Y	37260 FQ	51280 AW	70170 TQ	SCBLS	10/01-12/01
Except Epidemiologist	Tennessee	Y	30420 FQ	50840 AW	73490 TQ	TNBLS	10/01-12/01
Except Epidemiologist	Nashville MSA, TN	Y	35060 FQ	52940 AW	75140 TQ	TNBLS	10/01-12/01
Except Epidemiologist	Texas	Y	26770 FQ	52390 AW	88140 TQ	TXBLS	10/01-12/01
Except Epidemiologist	Austin-San Marcos MSA, TX	Y	38460 FQ	53060 AW	73410 TQ	TXBLS	10/01-12/01
Except Epidemiologist	Dallas PMSA, TX	Y	25840 FQ	47430 AW	84660 TQ	TXBLS	10/01-12/01
Except Epidemiologist	El Paso MSA, TX	Y	35860 FQ	85370 AW	115970 TQ	TXBLS	10/01-12/01
Except Epidemiologist	Houston PMSA, TX	Y	24990 FQ	46130 AW	75150 TQ	TXBLS	10/01-12/01
Except Epidemiologist	San Antonio MSA, TX	Y	33050 FQ	60370 AW	101680 TQ	TXBLS	10/01-12/01
Except Epidemiologist	Utah	Y	27110 FQ	41040 AW	51340 TQ	UTBLS	10/01-12/01
Except Epidemiologist	Salt Lake City-Ogden MSA, UT	Y	27210 FQ	40550 AW	50390 TQ	UTBLS	10/01-12/01
Except Epidemiologist	Vermont	Y	23430 FQ	50500 AW	104330 TQ	VTBLS	10/01-12/01
Except Epidemiologist	Burlington MSA, VT	Y	23200 FQ	49820 AW	105970 TQ	VTBLS	10/01-12/01
Except Epidemiologist	Virginia	Y	37920 FQ	79980 AW	118350 TQ	VABLS	10/01-12/01
Except Epidemiologist	Richmond-Petersburg MSA, VA	Y	41090 FQ	73980 AW	118700 TQ	VABLS	10/01-12/01
Except Epidemiologist	Washington	Y	34070 FQ	67740 AW	130200 TQ	WABLS	10/01-12/01
Except Epidemiologist	West Virginia	Y	45110 FQ	74780 AW	109770 TQ	WVBLS	10/01-12/01
Medical Secretary	Alabama	H	6.80 FQ	9.52 AW	12.72 TQ	ALBLS	10/01-12/01
	Birmingham MSA, AL	H	7.90 FQ	10.50 AW	13.21 TQ	ALBLS	10/01-12/01
	Huntsville MSA, AL	H	6.39 FQ	9.67 AW	12.99 TQ	ALBLS	10/01-12/01
	Mobile MSA, AL	H	6.61 FQ	9.17 AW	11.75 TQ	ALBLS	10/01-12/01
	Montgomery MSA, AL	H	7.30 FQ	9.16 AW	11.63 TQ	ALBLS	10/01-12/01
	Alaska	H	11.53 FQ	14.31 AW	17.21 TQ	AKBLS	10/01-12/01
	Anchorage MSA, AK	H	11.47 FQ	13.88 AW	16.76 TQ	AKBLS	10/01-12/01
	Arizona	H	8.81 FQ	11.88 AW	15.94 TQ	AZBLS	10/01-12/01
	Phoenix-Mesa MSA, AZ	H	9.33 FQ	12.19 AW	15.89 TQ	AZBLS	10/01-12/01
	Tucson MSA, AZ	H	7.98 FQ	12.14 AW	19.38 TQ	AZBLS	10/01-12/01
	Arkansas	H	7.91 FQ	10.27 AW	13.28 TQ	ARBLS	10/01-12/01

AAW	Average annual wage	AOH	Average offered, high	ASH	Average starting, high	H	Hourly	M	Monthly	S	Special: hourly and annual
AE	Average entry wage	AOL	Average offered, low	ASL	Average starting, low	HI	Highest wage paid	MTC	Median total compensation	TQ	Third quartile wage
AEX	Average experienced wage	APH	Average pay, high range	AW	Average wage paid	HR	High end range	MW	Median wage paid	W	Weekly
AO	Average offered	APL	Average pay, low range	FQ	First quartile wage	LR	Low end range	SQ	Second quartile wage	Y	Yearly

Occupation/Type/Industry	Location	Per	Low	Mid	High	Source	Date
Medical Secretary	Fayetteville-Springdale-Rogers MSA, AR	H	8.68 FQ	10.00 AW	11.92 TQ	ARBLS	10/01-12/01
	Fort Smith MSA, AR-OK	H	7.37 FQ	10.41 AW	13.31 TQ	ARBLS	10/01-12/01
	Little Rock-North Little Rock MSA, AR	H	9.07 FQ	10.90 AW	13.73 TQ	ARBLS	10/01-12/01
	California	H	9.49 FQ	14.10 AW	17.87 TQ	CABLS	10/01-12/01
	Bakersfield MSA, CA	H	8.02 FQ	11.13 AW	16.17 TQ	CABLS	10/01-12/01
	Chico-Paradise MSA, CA	H	8.21 FQ	11.87 AW	16.54 TQ	CABLS	10/01-12/01
	Fresno MSA, CA	H	7.25 FQ	10.54 AW	15.69 TQ	CABLS	10/01-12/01
	Los Angeles-Long Beach PMSA, CA	H	11.03 FQ	14.76 AW	17.60 TQ	CABLS	10/01-12/01
	Merced MSA, CA	H	7.22 FQ	9.68 AW	12.30 TQ	CABLS	10/01-12/01
	Modesto MSA, CA	H	9.47 FQ	13.31 AW	16.60 TQ	CABLS	10/01-12/01
	Oakland PMSA, CA	H	13.83 FQ	15.62 AW	18.17 TQ	CABLS	10/01-12/01
	Orange County PMSA, CA	H	6.46 FQ	11.28 AW	16.34 TQ	CABLS	10/01-12/01
	Redding MSA, CA	H	8.66 FQ	10.47 AW	12.86 TQ	CABLS	10/01-12/01
	Riverside-San Bernardino PMSA, CA	H	9.63 FQ	12.97 AW	16.40 TQ	CABLS	10/01-12/01
	Sacramento PMSA, CA	H	8.89 FQ	11.30 AW	15.34 TQ	CABLS	10/01-12/01
	Salinas MSA, CA	H	8.95 FQ	14.08 AW	20.19 TQ	CABLS	10/01-12/01
	San Diego MSA, CA	H	9.16 FQ	13.46 AW	19.36 TQ	CABLS	10/01-12/01
	San Francisco PMSA, CA	H	11.57 FQ	16.15 AW	22.20 TQ	CABLS	10/01-12/01
	San Jose PMSA, CA	H	9.75 FQ	16.71 AW	26.63 TQ	CABLS	10/01-12/01
	San Luis Obispo-Atascadero-Paso Robles MSA, CA	H	8.04 FQ	12.15 AW	17.68 TQ	CABLS	10/01-12/01
	Santa Barbara-Santa Maria-Lompoc MSA, CA	H	10.20 FQ	12.54 AW	15.55 TQ	CABLS	10/01-12/01
	Santa Cruz-Watsonville PMSA, CA	H	9.46 FQ	13.45 AW	17.98 TQ	CABLS	10/01-12/01
	Santa Rosa PMSA, CA	H	11.28 FQ	14.24 AW	17.67 TQ	CABLS	10/01-12/01
	Stockton-Lodi MSA, CA	H	7.54 FQ	10.74 AW	13.33 TQ	CABLS	10/01-12/01
	Vallejo-Fairfield-Napa PMSA, CA	H	9.20 FQ	13.16 AW	17.88 TQ	CABLS	10/01-12/01
	Ventura PMSA, CA	H	9.45 FQ	13.12 AW	16.85 TQ	CABLS	10/01-12/01
	Visalia-Tulare-Porterville MSA, CA	H	8.71 FQ	12.67 AW	16.32 TQ	CABLS	10/01-12/01
	Colorado	H	9.60 FQ	15.17 AW	24.44 TQ	COBLS	10/01-12/01
	Boulder-Longmont PMSA, CO	H	10.01 FQ	13.36 AW	16.82 TQ	COBLS	10/01-12/01
	Colorado Springs MSA, CO	H	10.19 FQ	16.51 AW	24.69 TQ	COBLS	10/01-12/01
	Denver PMSA, CO	H	10.66 FQ	16.43 AW	25.30 TQ	COBLS	10/01-12/01
	Fort Collins-Loveland MSA, CO	H	8.30 FQ	12.42 AW	16.26 TQ	COBLS	10/01-12/01
	Greeley PMSA, CO	H	9.02 FQ	11.98 AW	16.18 TQ	COBLS	10/01-12/01
	Connecticut	H	11.01 FQ	14.82 AW	19.61 TQ	CTBLS	10/01-12/01
	Bridgeport PMSA, CT	H	11.70 FQ	15.12 AW	19.81 TQ	CTBLS	10/01-12/01
	Danbury PMSA, CT	H	11.22 FQ	14.00 AW	17.78 TQ	CTBLS	10/01-12/01
	Hartford MSA, CT	H	11.59 FQ	15.61 AW	20.23 TQ	CTBLS	10/01-12/01
	New Haven-Meriden PMSA, CT	H	10.35 FQ	15.11 AW	20.20 TQ	CTBLS	10/01-12/01
	New London-Norwich MSA, CT-RI	H	9.61 FQ	13.00 AW	16.76 TQ	CTBLS	10/01-12/01
	Stamford-Norwalk PMSA, CT	H	12.46 FQ	16.34 AW	21.60 TQ	CTBLS	10/01-12/01
	Waterbury PMSA, CT	H	11.30 FQ	13.98 AW	17.49 TQ	CTBLS	10/01-12/01
	Delaware	H	8.72 FQ	12.19 AW	16.18 TQ	DEBLS	10/01-12/01
	Wilmington-Newark PMSA, DE-MD	H	9.40 FQ	12.70 AW	16.62 TQ	DEBLS	10/01-12/01
	District of Columbia	H	10.36 FQ	13.76 AW	17.68 TQ	DCBLS	10/01-12/01
	Washington PMSA, DC-MD-VA-WV	H	9.67 FQ	13.92 AW	19.77 TQ	DCBLS	10/01-12/01
	Florida	H	8.19 FQ	11.40 AW	16.31 TQ	FLBLS	10/01-12/01
	Daytona Beach MSA, FL	H	8.35 FQ	12.68 AW	23.71 TQ	FLBLS	10/01-12/01
	Fort Lauderdale PMSA, FL	H	9.02 FQ	13.34 AW	19.67 TQ	FLBLS	10/01-12/01
	Fort Myers-Cape Coral MSA, FL	H	8.57 FQ	10.80 AW	13.31 TQ	FLBLS	10/01-12/01
	Fort Pierce-Port St. Lucie MSA, FL	H	9.81 FQ	12.45 AW	15.03 TQ	FLBLS	10/01-12/01
	Fort Walton Beach MSA, FL	H	7.82 FQ	11.52 AW	14.27 TQ	FLBLS	10/01-12/01
	Gainesville MSA, FL	H	7.51 FQ	9.79 AW	11.64 TQ	FLBLS	10/01-12/01
	Jacksonville MSA, FL	H	6.55 FQ	10.91 AW	15.60 TQ	FLBLS	10/01-12/01
	Lakeland-Winter Haven MSA, FL	H	6.58 FQ	10.13 AW	13.78 TQ	FLBLS	10/01-12/01

AAW Average annual wage, **AE** Average entry wage, **AEX** Average experienced wage, **AO** Average offered, **AOH** Average offered, high, **AOL** Average offered, low, **APH** Average pay, high range, **APL** Average pay, low range, **ASH** Average starting, high, **ASL** Average starting, low, **AW** Average wage paid, **FQ** First quartile wage, **H** Hourly, **HI** Highest wage paid, **HR** High end range, **LR** Low end range, **M** Monthly, **MTC** Median total compensation, **MW** Median wage paid, **SQ** Second quartile wage, **S** Special: hourly and annual, **TQ** Third quartile wage, **W** Weekly, **Y** Yearly

Occupation/Type/Industry	Location	Per	Low	Mid	High	Source	Date
Medical Secretary	Melbourne-Titusville-Palm Bay MSA, FL	H	7.48 FQ	9.77 AW	12.52 TQ	FLBLS	10/01-12/01
	Miami PMSA, FL	H	8.66 FQ	11.37 AW	15.59 TQ	FLBLS	10/01-12/01
	Naples MSA, FL	H	9.26 FQ	11.56 AW	13.82 TQ	FLBLS	10/01-12/01
	Ocala MSA, FL	H	7.95 FQ	10.63 AW	14.55 TQ	FLBLS	10/01-12/01
	Orlando MSA, FL	H	8.71 FQ	10.39 AW	13.19 TQ	FLBLS	10/01-12/01
	Pensacola MSA, FL	H	7.39 FQ	11.00 AW	15.75 TQ	FLBLS	10/01-12/01
	Sarasota-Bradenton MSA, FL	H	8.82 FQ	11.66 AW	17.01 TQ	FLBLS	10/01-12/01
	Tallahassee MSA, FL	H	8.71 FQ	10.82 AW	13.45 TQ	FLBLS	10/01-12/01
	Tampa-St. Petersburg-Clearwater MSA, FL	H	7.75 FQ	11.87 AW	19.02 TQ	FLBLS	10/01-12/01
	West Palm Beach-Boca Raton MSA, FL	H	9.38 FQ	11.83 AW	13.61 TQ	FLBLS	10/01-12/01
	Georgia	H	7.29 FQ	11.65 AW	17.85 TQ	GABLS	10/01-12/01
	Atlanta MSA, GA	H	9.19 FQ	12.85 AW	17.50 TQ	GABLS	10/01-12/01
	Augusta-Aiken MSA, GA-SC	H	7.35 FQ	9.94 AW	13.82 TQ	GABLS	10/01-12/01
	Columbus MSA, GA-AL	H	7.84 FQ	10.44 AW	14.19 TQ	GABLS	10/01-12/01
	Macon MSA, GA	H	6.01 FQ	10.50 AW	15.42 TQ	GABLS	10/01-12/01
	Savannah MSA, GA	H	7.95 FQ	10.35 AW	13.14 TQ	GABLS	10/01-12/01
	Hawaii	H	10.34 FQ	17.74 AW	26.39 TQ	HIBLS	10/01-12/01
	Honolulu MSA, HI	H	11.83 FQ	19.54 AW	26.88 TQ	HIBLS	10/01-12/01
	Idaho	H	8.93 FQ	10.94 AW	13.85 TQ	IDBLS	10/01-12/01
	Boise City MSA, ID	H	9.24 FQ	11.27 AW	14.49 TQ	IDBLS	10/01-12/01
	Illinois	H	8.11 FQ	15.51 AW	25.33 TQ	ILBLS	10/01-12/01
	Champaign-Urbana MSA, IL	H	7.75 FQ	11.19 AW	15.14 TQ	ILBLS	10/01-12/01
	Chicago PMSA, IL	H	8.96 FQ	17.45 AW	25.88 TQ	ILBLS	10/01-12/01
	Peoria-Pekin MSA, IL	H	7.89 FQ	9.95 AW	11.59 TQ	ILBLS	10/01-12/01
	Rockford MSA, IL	H	8.12 FQ	10.94 AW	14.02 TQ	ILBLS	10/01-12/01
	Springfield MSA, IL	H	7.64 FQ	12.09 AW	16.34 TQ	ILBLS	10/01-12/01
	Indiana	H	7.52 FQ	10.62 AW	14.31 TQ	INBLS	10/01-12/01
	Evansville-Henderson MSA, IN-KY	H	8.38 FQ	10.42 AW	13.06 TQ	INBLS	10/01-12/01
	Fort Wayne MSA, IN	H	8.75 FQ	12.33 AW	18.30 TQ	INBLS	10/01-12/01
	Gary PMSA, IN	H	7.22 FQ	9.80 AW	14.86 TQ	INBLS	10/01-12/01
	Indianapolis MSA, IN	H	6.48 FQ	10.23 AW	13.36 TQ	INBLS	10/01-12/01
	Lafayette MSA, IN	H	8.57 FQ	11.98 AW	14.01 TQ	INBLS	10/01-12/01
	South Bend MSA, IN	H	8.96 FQ	12.14 AW	15.87 TQ	INBLS	10/01-12/01
	Iowa	H	7.91 FQ	10.66 AW	13.59 TQ	IABLS	10/01-12/01
	Cedar Rapids MSA, IA	H	8.39 FQ	10.34 AW	12.43 TQ	IABLS	10/01-12/01
	Davenport-Moline-Rock Island MSA, IA-IL	H	7.27 FQ	9.67 AW	12.58 TQ	IABLS	10/01-12/01
	Des Moines MSA, IA	H	9.73 FQ	12.34 AW	15.58 TQ	IABLS	10/01-12/01
	Kansas	H	7.62 FQ	10.82 AW	14.82 TQ	KSBLS	10/01-12/01
	Topeka MSA, KS	H	9.23 FQ	13.21 AW	16.88 TQ	KSBLS	10/01-12/01
	Wichita MSA, KS	H	7.99 FQ	10.70 AW	14.27 TQ	KSBLS	10/01-12/01
	Kentucky	H	7.97 FQ	10.68 AW	13.70 TQ	KYBLS	10/01-12/01
	Lexington MSA, KY	H	8.37 FQ	10.61 AW	13.18 TQ	KYBLS	10/01-12/01
	Louisville MSA, KY-IN	H	9.05 FQ	11.79 AW	14.36 TQ	KYBLS	10/01-12/01
	Louisiana	H	7.34 FQ	9.71 AW	12.73 TQ	LABLS	10/01-12/01
	Baton Rouge MSA, LA	H	7.23 FQ	9.33 AW	13.02 TQ	LABLS	10/01-12/01
	Houma MSA, LA	H	5.80 FQ	8.46 AW	12.17 TQ	LABLS	10/01-12/01
	Lafayette MSA, LA	H	6.49 FQ	10.57 AW	15.21 TQ	LABLS	10/01-12/01
	Lake Charles MSA, LA	H	7.24 FQ	9.12 AW	11.61 TQ	LABLS	10/01-12/01
	New Orleans MSA, LA	H	7.84 FQ	10.00 AW	12.74 TQ	LABLS	10/01-12/01
	Shreveport-Bossier City MSA, LA	H	8.25 FQ	9.98 AW	11.50 TQ	LABLS	10/01-12/01
	Maine	H	9.22 FQ	12.08 AW	16.09 TQ	MEBLS	10/01-12/01
	Portland MSA, ME	H	10.66 FQ	13.92 AW	18.96 TQ	MEBLS	10/01-12/01
	Maryland	H	7.11 FQ	12.48 AW	17.49 TQ	MDBLS	10/01-12/01
	Baltimore PMSA, MD	H	6.16 FQ	11.30 AW	16.21 TQ	MDBLS	10/01-12/01
	Massachusetts	H	10.85 FQ	14.97 AW	19.97 TQ	MABLS	10/01-12/01
	Boston PMSA, MA-NH	H	11.72 FQ	15.54 AW	20.00 TQ	MABLS	10/01-12/01
	Brockton PMSA, MA	H	11.59 FQ	14.89 AW	20.04 TQ	MABLS	10/01-12/01
	Lawrence PMSA, MA-NH	H	9.17 FQ	13.26 AW	17.16 TQ	MABLS	10/01-12/01
	Lowell PMSA, MA-NH	H	10.05 FQ	13.55 AW	17.03 TQ	MABLS	10/01-12/01
	New Bedford PMSA, MA	H	8.46 FQ	13.08 AW	19.54 TQ	MABLS	10/01-12/01
	Springfield MSA, MA	H	10.97 FQ	15.07 AW	19.95 TQ	MABLS	10/01-12/01
	Worcester PMSA, MA-CT	H	9.39 FQ	15.10 AW	22.28 TQ	MABLS	10/01-12/01
	Michigan	H	8.66 FQ	11.63 AW	16.32 TQ	MIBLS	10/01-12/01
	Ann Arbor PMSA, MI	H	9.20 FQ	13.90 AW	18.02 TQ	MIBLS	10/01-12/01
	Detroit PMSA, MI	H	8.76 FQ	11.18 AW	15.90 TQ	MIBLS	10/01-12/01
	Flint PMSA, MI	H	10.31 FQ	14.21 AW	17.44 TQ	MIBLS	10/01-12/01

AAW Average annual wage; AE Average entry wage; AEX Average experienced wage; AO Average offered; AOH Average offered, high; AOL Average offered, low; APH Average pay, high range; APL Average pay, low range; ASH Average starting, high; ASL Average starting, low; AW Average wage paid; FQ First quartile wage; H Hourly; HI Highest wage paid; HR High end range; LR Low end range; M Monthly; MTC Median total compensation; MW Median wage paid; SQ Second quartile wage; S Special: hourly and annual; TQ Third quartile wage; W Weekly; Y Yearly

Occupation/Type/Industry	Location	Per	Low	Mid	High	Source	Date
Medical Secretary	Grand Rapids-Muskegon-Holland MSA, MI	H	9.28 FQ	12.53 AW	15.98 TQ	MIBLS	10/01-12/01
	Kalamazoo-Battle Creek MSA, MI	H	9.03 FQ	11.26 AW	13.93 TQ	MIBLS	10/01-12/01
	Lansing-East Lansing MSA, MI	H	7.91 FQ	13.05 AW	19.60 TQ	MIBLS	10/01-12/01
	Saginaw-Bay City-Midland MSA, MI	H	7.41 FQ	10.75 AW	15.95 TQ	MIBLS	10/01-12/01
	Minnesota	H	9.89 FQ	12.91 AW	16.59 TQ	MNBLS	10/01-12/01
	Duluth-Superior MSA, MN-WI	H	9.38 FQ	12.05 AW	15.33 TQ	MNBLS	10/01-12/01
	Minneapolis-St. Paul MSA, MN-WI	H	10.95 FQ	13.45 AW	16.93 TQ	MNBLS	10/01-12/01
	St. Cloud MSA, MN	H	9.44 FQ	12.05 AW	15.89 TQ	MNBLS	10/01-12/01
	Mississippi	H	7.22 FQ	13.89 AW	15.46 TQ	MSBLS	10/01-12/01
	Biloxi-Gulfport-Pascagoula MSA, MS	H	7.26 FQ	9.45 AW	11.65 TQ	MSBLS	10/01-12/01
	Jackson MSA, MS	H	7.50 FQ	11.52 AW	15.98 TQ	MSBLS	10/01-12/01
	Missouri	H	7.78 FQ	10.79 AW	14.25 TQ	MOBLS	10/01-12/01
	Kansas City MSA, MO-KS	H	8.63 FQ	11.35 AW	14.74 TQ	MOBLS	10/01-12/01
	St. Louis MSA, MO-IL	H	8.71 FQ	11.36 AW	15.26 TQ	MOBLS	10/01-12/01
	Springfield MSA, MO	H	7.53 FQ	10.02 AW	13.47 TQ	MOBLS	10/01-12/01
	Montana	H	7.97 FQ	10.11 AW	12.96 TQ	MTBLS	10/01-12/01
	Billings MSA, MT	H	8.79 FQ	11.19 AW	15.03 TQ	MTBLS	10/01-12/01
	Nebraska	H	8.09 FQ	10.72 AW	14.04 TQ	NEBLS	10/01-12/01
	Lincoln MSA, NE	H	8.91 FQ	11.24 AW	13.99 TQ	NEBLS	10/01-12/01
	Omaha MSA, NE-IA	H	9.08 FQ	11.31 AW	14.69 TQ	NEBLS	10/01-12/01
	Nevada	H	9.32 FQ	13.16 AW	17.32 TQ	NVBLS	10/01-12/01
	Las Vegas MSA, NV-AZ	H	9.38 FQ	13.81 AW	18.03 TQ	NVBLS	10/01-12/01
	Reno MSA, NV	H	9.34 FQ	12.24 AW	14.65 TQ	NVBLS	10/01-12/01
	New Hampshire	H	9.44 FQ	12.94 AW	16.85 TQ	NHBLS	10/01-12/01
	Manchester PMSA, NH	H	10.88 FQ	13.62 AW	16.66 TQ	NHBLS	10/01-12/01
	Nashua PMSA, NH	H	10.04 FQ	15.14 AW	21.06 TQ	NHBLS	10/01-12/01
	Portsmouth-Rochester PMSA, NH-ME	H	9.88 FQ	14.11 AW	19.02 TQ	NHBLS	10/01-12/01
	New Jersey	H	8.91 FQ	12.93 AW	19.28 TQ	NJBLS	10/01-12/01
	Atlantic-Cape May PMSA, NJ	H	8.97 FQ	11.44 AW	14.35 TQ	NJBLS	10/01-12/01
	Bergen-Passaic PMSA, NJ	H	9.22 FQ	14.74 AW	23.72 TQ	NJBLS	10/01-12/01
	Jersey City PMSA, NJ	H	8.82 FQ	11.87 AW	16.26 TQ	NJBLS	10/01-12/01
	Middlesex-Somerset-Hunterdon PMSA, NJ	H	9.90 FQ	12.51 AW	16.02 TQ	NJBLS	10/01-12/01
	Monmouth-Ocean PMSA, NJ	H	9.09 FQ	12.24 AW	16.49 TQ	NJBLS	10/01-12/01
	Newark PMSA, NJ	H	8.21 FQ	12.53 AW	20.99 TQ	NJBLS	10/01-12/01
	Trenton PMSA, NJ	H	10.74 FQ	13.74 AW	17.87 TQ	NJBLS	10/01-12/01
	New Mexico	H	8.50 FQ	12.26 AW	18.30 TQ	NMBLS	10/01-12/01
	Albuquerque MSA, NM	H	9.53 FQ	13.90 AW	19.79 TQ	NMBLS	10/01-12/01
	Las Cruces MSA, NM	H	7.22 FQ	9.11 AW	11.12 TQ	NMBLS	10/01-12/01
	New York	H	9.31 FQ	13.37 AW	19.31 TQ	NYBLS	10/01-12/01
	Albany-Schenectady-Troy MSA, NY	H	9.39 FQ	11.92 AW	14.43 TQ	NYBLS	10/01-12/01
	Binghamton MSA, NY	H	7.63 FQ	9.66 AW	12.90 TQ	NYBLS	10/01-12/01
	Buffalo-Niagara Falls MSA, NY	H	8.26 FQ	11.20 AW	14.09 TQ	NYBLS	10/01-12/01
	Dutchess County PMSA, NY	H	9.71 FQ	12.05 AW	14.73 TQ	NYBLS	10/01-12/01
	Nassau-Suffolk PMSA, NY	H	10.86 FQ	14.76 AW	19.90 TQ	NYBLS	10/01-12/01
	New York PMSA, NY	H	11.31 FQ	15.23 AW	21.37 TQ	NYBLS	10/01-12/01
	Newburgh PMSA, NY-PA	H	7.53 FQ	10.58 AW	13.67 TQ	NYBLS	10/01-12/01
	Rochester MSA, NY	H	8.78 FQ	11.46 AW	14.75 TQ	NYBLS	10/01-12/01
	Syracuse MSA, NY	H	9.11 FQ	11.05 AW	13.42 TQ	NYBLS	10/01-12/01
	Utica-Rome MSA, NY	H	8.38 FQ	10.33 AW	12.72 TQ	NYBLS	10/01-12/01
	North Carolina	H	8.27 FQ	11.12 AW	14.68 TQ	NCBLS	10/01-12/01
	Asheville MSA, NC	H	7.92 FQ	11.05 AW	14.68 TQ	NCBLS	10/01-12/01
	Charlotte-Gastonia-Rock Hill MSA, NC-SC	H	9.10 FQ	12.51 AW	17.05 TQ	NCBLS	10/01-12/01
	Fayetteville MSA, NC	H	7.09 FQ	9.14 AW	12.31 TQ	NCBLS	10/01-12/01
	Greensboro-Winston-Salem-High Point MSA, NC	H	9.07 FQ	11.50 AW	13.92 TQ	NCBLS	10/01-12/01
	Hickory-Morganton-Lenoir MSA, NC	H	8.77 FQ	11.54 AW	15.84 TQ	NCBLS	10/01-12/01
	Raleigh-Durham-Chapel Hill MSA, NC	H	8.85 FQ	11.16 AW	14.53 TQ	NCBLS	10/01-12/01
	Wilmington MSA, NC	H	8.95 FQ	11.03 AW	13.26 TQ	NCBLS	10/01-12/01
	North Dakota	H	7.43 FQ	9.35 AW	11.20 TQ	NDBLS	10/01-12/01

AAW Average annual wage; AE Average entry wage; AEX Average experienced wage; AO Average offered; AOH Average offered, high; AOL Average offered, low; APH Average pay, high range; APL Average pay, low range; ASH Average starting, high; ASL Average starting, low; AW Average wage paid; FQ First quartile wage; H Hourly; HI Highest wage paid; HR High end range; LR Low end range; M Monthly; MTC Median total compensation; MW Median wage paid; SQ Second quartile wage; S Special: hourly and annual; TQ Third quartile wage; W Weekly; Y Yearly

Occupation/Type/Industry	Location	Per	Low	Mid	High	Source	Date
Medical Secretary	Fargo-Moorhead MSA, ND-MN	H	7.75 FQ	9.85 AW	12.60 TQ	NDBLS	10/01-12/01
	Ohio	H	8.00 FQ	11.42 AW	15.60 TQ	OHBLS	10/01-12/01
	Akron PMSA, OH	H	8.35 FQ	11.02 AW	13.96 TQ	OHBLS	10/01-12/01
	Canton-Massillon MSA, OH	H	7.96 FQ	10.74 AW	13.36 TQ	OHBLS	10/01-12/01
	Cincinnati PMSA, OH-KY-IN	H	8.80 FQ	11.23 AW	14.53 TQ	OHBLS	10/01-12/01
	Cleveland-Lorain-Elyria PMSA, OH	H	9.78 FQ	13.20 AW	16.64 TQ	OHBLS	10/01-12/01
	Columbus MSA, OH	H	7.38 FQ	11.26 AW	15.98 TQ	OHBLS	10/01-12/01
	Dayton-Springfield MSA, OH	H	8.42 FQ	11.19 AW	14.25 TQ	OHBLS	10/01-12/01
	Hamilton-Middletown PMSA, OH	H	8.72 FQ	11.44 AW	15.14 TQ	OHBLS	10/01-12/01
	Toledo MSA, OH	H	8.39 FQ	11.27 AW	14.55 TQ	OHBLS	10/01-12/01
	Youngstown-Warren MSA, OH	H	7.72 FQ	9.87 AW	11.91 TQ	OHBLS	10/01-12/01
	Oklahoma	H	7.61 FQ	10.02 AW	12.97 TQ	OKBLS	10/01-12/01
	Oklahoma City MSA, OK	H	7.41 FQ	9.73 AW	13.17 TQ	OKBLS	10/01-12/01
	Tulsa MSA, OK	H	8.59 FQ	10.40 AW	13.12 TQ	OKBLS	10/01-12/01
	Oregon	H	9.03 FQ	13.41 AW	19.12 TQ	ORBLS	10/01-12/01
	Eugene-Springfield MSA, OR	H	9.57 FQ	12.71 AW	16.51 TQ	ORBLS	10/01-12/01
	Medford-Ashland MSA, OR	H	9.09 FQ	11.67 AW	14.59 TQ	ORBLS	10/01-12/01
	Portland-Vancouver PMSA, OR-WA	H	9.89 FQ	14.63 AW	20.24 TQ	ORBLS	10/01-12/01
	Salem PMSA, OR	H	9.48 FQ	12.46 AW	16.22 TQ	ORBLS	10/01-12/01
	Pennsylvania	H	8.58 FQ	11.88 AW	16.27 TQ	PABLS	10/01-12/01
	Allentown-Bethlehem-Easton MSA, PA	H	9.35 FQ	12.15 AW	15.72 TQ	PABLS	10/01-12/01
	Erie MSA, PA	H	7.61 FQ	9.55 AW	11.88 TQ	PABLS	10/01-12/01
	Harrisburg-Lebanon-Carlisle MSA, PA	H	8.93 FQ	12.07 AW	15.88 TQ	PABLS	10/01-12/01
	Johnstown MSA, PA	H	7.05 FQ	9.25 AW	11.79 TQ	PABLS	10/01-12/01
	Lancaster MSA, PA	H	8.55 FQ	11.27 AW	14.76 TQ	PABLS	10/01-12/01
	Philadelphia PMSA, PA-NJ	H	9.08 FQ	12.98 AW	18.80 TQ	PABLS	10/01-12/01
	Pittsburgh MSA, PA	H	8.76 FQ	11.72 AW	14.64 TQ	PABLS	10/01-12/01
	Reading MSA, PA	H	8.92 FQ	11.45 AW	15.07 TQ	PABLS	10/01-12/01
	Scranton-Wilkes-Barre-Hazleton MSA, PA	H	6.46 FQ	10.17 AW	13.75 TQ	PABLS	10/01-12/01
	York MSA, PA	H	8.93 FQ	10.82 AW	13.14 TQ	PABLS	10/01-12/01
	Rhode Island	H	9.30 FQ	12.80 AW	16.63 TQ	RIBLS	10/01-12/01
	Providence-Fall River-Warwick MSA, RI-MA	H	9.40 FQ	12.64 AW	16.36 TQ	RIBLS	10/01-12/01
	South Carolina	H	8.16 FQ	11.15 AW	14.67 TQ	SCBLS	10/01-12/01
	Charleston-North Charleston MSA, SC	H	7.45 FQ	10.32 AW	13.44 TQ	SCBLS	10/01-12/01
	Columbia MSA, SC	H	8.95 FQ	11.33 AW	14.96 TQ	SCBLS	10/01-12/01
	Greenville-Spartanburg-Anderson MSA, SC	H	8.25 FQ	11.53 AW	15.40 TQ	SCBLS	10/01-12/01
	Myrtle Beach MSA, SC	H	7.62 FQ	9.93 AW	13.24 TQ	SCBLS	10/01-12/01
	South Dakota	H	8.25 FQ	10.88 AW	13.59 TQ	SDBLS	10/01-12/01
	Sioux Falls MSA, SD	H	7.97 FQ	11.20 AW	13.89 TQ	SDBLS	10/01-12/01
	Tennessee	H	8.01 FQ	11.98 AW	16.93 TQ	TNBLS	10/01-12/01
	Chattanooga MSA, TN-GA	H	9.33 FQ	13.54 AW	17.64 TQ	TNBLS	10/01-12/01
	Clarksville-Hopkinsville MSA, TN-KY	H	7.14 FQ	8.72 AW	11.39 TQ	TNBLS	10/01-12/01
	Johnson City-Kingsport-Bristol MSA, TN-VA	H	7.54 FQ	10.12 AW	14.24 TQ	TNBLS	10/01-12/01
	Knoxville MSA, TN	H	7.94 FQ	10.28 AW	13.19 TQ	TNBLS	10/01-12/01
	Memphis MSA, TN-AR-MS	H	9.59 FQ	13.99 AW	22.84 TQ	TNBLS	10/01-12/01
	Nashville MSA, TN	H	9.31 FQ	12.73 AW	19.15 TQ	TNBLS	10/01-12/01
	Texas	H	7.32 FQ	10.91 AW	15.62 TQ	TXBLS	10/01-12/01
	Amarillo MSA, TX	H	5.89 FQ	8.79 AW	12.35 TQ	TXBLS	10/01-12/01
	Austin-San Marcos MSA, TX	H	8.38 FQ	10.98 AW	13.91 TQ	TXBLS	10/01-12/01
	Beaumont-Port Arthur MSA, TX	H	7.32 FQ	10.43 AW	15.01 TQ	TXBLS	10/01-12/01
	Brazoria PMSA, TX	H	8.63 FQ	12.05 AW	15.93 TQ	TXBLS	10/01-12/01
	Brownsville-Harlingen-San Benito MSA, TX	H	7.08 FQ	10.25 AW	15.16 TQ	TXBLS	10/01-12/01
	Corpus Christi MSA, TX	H	6.45 FQ	8.87 AW	11.40 TQ	TXBLS	10/01-12/01
	Dallas PMSA, TX	H	8.64 FQ	12.58 AW	16.56 TQ	TXBLS	10/01-12/01
	El Paso MSA, TX	H	6.40 FQ	9.49 AW	13.65 TQ	TXBLS	10/01-12/01
	Fort Worth-Arlington PMSA, TX	H	9.31 FQ	12.38 AW	16.01 TQ	TXBLS	10/01-12/01

AAW	Average annual wage	**AOH**	Average offered, high	**ASH**	Average starting, high	**H**	Hourly	**M**	Monthly	**S**	Special: hourly and annual
AE	Average entry wage	**AOL**	Average offered, low	**ASL**	Average starting, low	**HI**	Highest wage paid	**MTC**	Median total compensation	**TQ**	Third quartile wage
AEX	Average experienced wage	**APH**	Average pay, high range	**AW**	Average wage paid	**HR**	High end range	**MW**	Median wage paid	**W**	Weekly
AO	Average offered	**APL**	Average pay, low range	**FQ**	First quartile wage	**LR**	Low end range	**SQ**	Second quartile wage	**Y**	Yearly

Occupation/Type/Industry	Location	Per	Low	Mid	High	Source	Date
Medical Secretary	Galveston-Texas City PMSA, TX	H	8.40 FQ	15.00 AW	20.65 TQ	TXBLS	10/01-12/01
	Houston PMSA, TX	H	7.81 FQ	11.73 AW	16.31 TQ	TXBLS	10/01-12/01
	Killeen-Temple MSA, TX	H	8.15 FQ	11.12 AW	17.59 TQ	TXBLS	10/01-12/01
	Laredo MSA, TX	H	6.80 FQ	8.81 AW	10.58 TQ	TXBLS	10/01-12/01
	Longview-Marshall MSA, TX	H	7.34 FQ	9.38 AW	11.42 TQ	TXBLS	10/01-12/01
	Lubbock MSA, TX	H	8.63 FQ	9.94 AW	10.88 TQ	TXBLS	10/01-12/01
	McAllen-Edinburg-Mission MSA, TX	H	6.02 FQ	9.82 AW	14.59 TQ	TXBLS	10/01-12/01
	Odessa-Midland MSA, TX	H	6.87 FQ	8.00 AW	9.92 TQ	TXBLS	10/01-12/01
	San Antonio MSA, TX	H	7.76 FQ	11.51 AW	17.77 TQ	TXBLS	10/01-12/01
	Tyler MSA, TX	H	7.57 FQ	10.67 AW	15.96 TQ	TXBLS	10/01-12/01
	Waco MSA, TX	H	7.70 FQ	10.30 AW	13.86 TQ	TXBLS	10/01-12/01
	Utah	H	8.55 FQ	11.52 AW	15.93 TQ	UTBLS	10/01-12/01
	Provo-Orem MSA, UT	H	8.30 FQ	10.62 AW	13.25 TQ	UTBLS	10/01-12/01
	Salt Lake City-Ogden MSA, UT	H	8.87 FQ	11.86 AW	16.87 TQ	UTBLS	10/01-12/01
	Vermont	H	9.01 FQ	12.63 AW	19.13 TQ	VTBLS	10/01-12/01
	Burlington MSA, VT	H	8.67 FQ	10.82 AW	13.86 TQ	VTBLS	10/01-12/01
	Virginia	H	8.64 FQ	12.24 AW	17.91 TQ	VABLS	10/01-12/01
	Lynchburg MSA, VA	H	6.07 FQ	10.22 AW	13.65 TQ	VABLS	10/01-12/01
	Norfolk-Virginia Beach-Newport News MSA, VA-NC	H	8.13 FQ	11.44 AW	18.87 TQ	VABLS	10/01-12/01
	Richmond-Petersburg MSA, VA	H	8.41 FQ	11.46 AW	14.67 TQ	VABLS	10/01-12/01
	Roanoke MSA, VA	H	8.85 FQ	11.81 AW	15.21 TQ	VABLS	10/01-12/01
	Washington	H	9.79 FQ	13.95 AW	19.68 TQ	WABLS	10/01-12/01
	Bremerton PMSA, WA	H	9.69 FQ	13.41 AW	17.21 TQ	WABLS	10/01-12/01
	Olympia PMSA, WA	H	9.44 FQ	12.49 AW	16.55 TQ	WABLS	10/01-12/01
	Richland-Kennewick-Pasco MSA, WA	H	8.78 FQ	12.37 AW	18.19 TQ	WABLS	10/01-12/01
	Seattle-Bellevue-Everett PMSA, WA	H	10.18 FQ	14.44 AW	20.49 TQ	WABLS	10/01-12/01
	Spokane MSA, WA	H	9.31 FQ	12.57 AW	16.80 TQ	WABLS	10/01-12/01
	Tacoma PMSA, WA	H	10.25 FQ	15.00 AW	20.55 TQ	WABLS	10/01-12/01
	Yakima MSA, WA	H	10.10 FQ	13.11 AW	16.57 TQ	WABLS	10/01-12/01
	West Virginia	H	6.97 FQ	9.54 AW	13.02 TQ	WVBLS	10/01-12/01
	Charleston MSA, WV	H	7.09 FQ	10.03 AW	14.39 TQ	WVBLS	10/01-12/01
	Huntington-Ashland MSA, WV-KY-OH	H	6.61 FQ	9.13 AW	11.91 TQ	WVBLS	10/01-12/01
	Wisconsin	H	8.89 FQ	11.57 AW	14.67 TQ	WIBLS	10/01-12/01
	Appleton-Oshkosh-Neenah MSA, WI	H	8.93 FQ	11.32 AW	14.07 TQ	WIBLS	10/01-12/01
	Green Bay MSA, WI	H	9.43 FQ	10.69 AW	11.77 TQ	WIBLS	10/01-12/01
	Madison MSA, WI	H	9.59 FQ	13.40 AW	17.17 TQ	WIBLS	10/01-12/01
	Milwaukee-Waukesha PMSA, WI	H	9.02 FQ	12.09 AW	16.11 TQ	WIBLS	10/01-12/01
	Racine PMSA, WI	H	9.09 FQ	11.44 AW	13.94 TQ	WIBLS	10/01-12/01
	Wyoming	H	7.63 FQ	10.21 AW	13.36 TQ	WYBLS	10/01-12/01
	Cheyenne MSA, WY	H	7.42 FQ	9.59 AW	12.28 TQ	WYBLS	10/01-12/01
	Puerto Rico	H	5.73 FQ	7.22 AW	9.24 TQ	PRBLS	10/01-12/01
	Virgin Islands	H	9.00 FQ	10.40 AW	12.36 TQ	VIBLS	10/01-12/01
	Guam	H	7.23 FQ	11.41 AW	19.46 TQ	GUBLS	10/01-12/01
Medical Transcriptionist	Alabama	H	8.58 FQ	11.57 AW	14.80 TQ	ALBLS	10/01-12/01
	Alaska	H	13.43 FQ	17.13 AW	21.59 TQ	AKBLS	10/01-12/01
	Arizona	H	9.70 FQ	13.63 AW	18.12 TQ	AZBLS	10/01-12/01
	Arkansas	H	7.79 FQ	10.52 AW	13.71 TQ	ARBLS	10/01-12/01
	California	H	10.59 FQ	15.46 AW	20.69 TQ	CABLS	10/01-12/01
	Colorado	H	9.53 FQ	13.91 AW	18.18 TQ	COBLS	10/01-12/01
	Connecticut	H	11.66 FQ	15.70 AW	21.78 TQ	CTBLS	10/01-12/01
	Delaware	H	10.12 FQ	13.34 AW	16.71 TQ	DEBLS	10/01-12/01
	District of Columbia	H	10.20 FQ	14.25 AW	18.91 TQ	DCBLS	10/01-12/01
	Florida	H	8.75 FQ	12.53 AW	16.79 TQ	FLBLS	10/01-12/01
	Georgia	H	8.73 FQ	12.24 AW	16.60 TQ	GABLS	10/01-12/01
	Hawaii	H	11.61 FQ	15.90 AW	20.72 TQ	HIBLS	10/01-12/01
	Idaho	H	8.83 FQ	12.15 AW	15.85 TQ	IDBLS	10/01-12/01
	Illinois	H	8.18 FQ	12.54 AW	17.11 TQ	ILBLS	10/01-12/01
	Indiana	H	9.52 FQ	12.40 AW	15.93 TQ	INBLS	10/01-12/01
	Iowa	H	8.66 FQ	11.23 AW	14.14 TQ	IABLS	10/01-12/01
	Kansas	H	7.69 FQ	10.75 AW	14.02 TQ	KSBLS	10/01-12/01
	Kentucky	H	9.09 FQ	11.92 AW	14.98 TQ	KYBLS	10/01-12/01

AAW Average annual wage **AE** Average entry wage **AEX** Average experienced wage **AO** Average offered **AOH** Average offered, high **AOL** Average offered, low **APH** Average pay, high range **APL** Average pay, low range **ASH** Average starting, high **ASL** Average starting, low **AW** Average wage paid **FQ** First quartile wage **H** Hourly **HI** Highest wage paid **HR** High end range **LR** Low end range **M** Monthly **MTC** Median total compensation **MW** Median wage paid **SQ** Second quartile wage **S** Special: hourly and annual **TQ** Third quartile wage **W** Weekly **Y** Yearly

Occupation/Type/Industry	Location	Per	Low	Mid	High	Source	Date
Medical Transcriptionist	Louisiana	H	7.56 FQ	10.60 AW	14.01 TQ	LABLS	10/01-12/01
	Maine	H	9.20 FQ	12.28 AW	16.55 TQ	MEBLS	10/01-12/01
	Maryland	H	11.49 FQ	16.49 AW	21.40 TQ	MDBLS	10/01-12/01
	Massachusetts	H	9.20 FQ	14.01 AW	17.85 TQ	MABLS	10/01-12/01
	Michigan	H	9.25 FQ	12.73 AW	16.74 TQ	MIBLS	10/01-12/01
	Minnesota	H	10.09 FQ	13.52 AW	17.22 TQ	MNBLS	10/01-12/01
	Mississippi	H	7.96 FQ	10.71 AW	13.53 TQ	MSBLS	10/01-12/01
	Missouri	H	9.09 FQ	12.34 AW	16.38 TQ	MOBLS	10/01-12/01
	Montana	H	8.21 FQ	11.51 AW	14.48 TQ	MTBLS	10/01-12/01
	Nebraska	H	8.29 FQ	10.93 AW	13.89 TQ	NEBLS	10/01-12/01
	Nevada	H	10.79 FQ	15.64 AW	21.40 TQ	NVBLS	10/01-12/01
	New Hampshire	H	10.33 FQ	13.21 AW	16.92 TQ	NHBLS	10/01-12/01
	New Jersey	H	10.74 FQ	15.10 AW	19.82 TQ	NJBLS	10/01-12/01
	New Mexico	H	9.29 FQ	11.91 AW	15.42 TQ	NMBLS	10/01-12/01
	New York	H	9.44 FQ	13.73 AW	18.68 TQ	NYBLS	10/01-12/01
	North Carolina	H	9.75 FQ	13.09 AW	16.92 TQ	NCBLS	10/01-12/01
	North Dakota	H	7.82 FQ	10.64 AW	14.05 TQ	NDBLS	10/01-12/01
	Ohio	H	9.25 FQ	12.42 AW	16.20 TQ	OHBLS	10/01-12/01
	Oklahoma	H	7.63 FQ	11.68 AW	16.31 TQ	OKBLS	10/01-12/01
	Oregon	H	9.21 FQ	13.32 AW	17.40 TQ	ORBLS	10/01-12/01
	Pennsylvania	H	9.02 FQ	12.24 AW	16.24 TQ	PABLS	10/01-12/01
	Rhode Island	H	11.37 FQ	13.86 AW	16.89 TQ	RIBLS	10/01-12/01
	South Carolina	H	9.44 FQ	12.80 AW	17.02 TQ	SCBLS	10/01-12/01
	South Dakota	H	8.92 FQ	11.24 AW	13.92 TQ	SDBLS	10/01-12/01
	Tennessee	H	8.07 FQ	11.54 AW	15.32 TQ	TNBLS	10/01-12/01
	Texas	H	8.14 FQ	13.05 AW	19.31 TQ	TXBLS	10/01-12/01
	Utah	H	8.14 FQ	12.03 AW	17.28 TQ	UTBLS	10/01-12/01
	Vermont	H	9.88 FQ	13.08 AW	16.50 TQ	VTBLS	10/01-12/01
	Virginia	H	8.97 FQ	13.07 AW	19.43 TQ	VABLS	10/01-12/01
	Washington	H	10.89 FQ	14.77 AW	18.48 TQ	WABLS	10/01-12/01
	West Virginia	H	7.09 FQ	10.52 AW	14.58 TQ	WVBLS	10/01-12/01
	Wisconsin	H	9.78 FQ	13.12 AW	16.75 TQ	WIBLS	10/01-12/01
	Wyoming	H	8.52 FQ	11.19 AW	14.90 TQ	WYBLS	10/01-12/01
	Puerto Rico	H	6.03 FQ	8.57 AW	11.38 TQ	PRBLS	10/01-12/01
Meeting and Convention Planner	Alabama	Y	19990 FQ	33220 AW	51940 TQ	ALBLS	10/01-12/01
	Birmingham MSA, AL	Y	20840 FQ	32770 AW	48550 TQ	ALBLS	10/01-12/01
	Huntsville MSA, AL	Y	20480 FQ	33900 AW	52240 TQ	ALBLS	10/01-12/01
	Alaska	Y	30790 FQ	39770 AW	56400 TQ	AKBLS	10/01-12/01
	Arizona	Y	21730 FQ	37770 AW	55220 TQ	AZBLS	10/01-12/01
	Phoenix-Mesa MSA, AZ	Y	26710 FQ	40600 AW	56940 TQ	AZBLS	10/01-12/01
	Tucson MSA, AZ	Y	23540 FQ	34550 AW	49790 TQ	AZBLS	10/01-12/01
	Arkansas	Y	20710 FQ	32140 AW	49880 TQ	ARBLS	10/01-12/01
	Little Rock-North Little Rock MSA, AR	Y	23240 FQ	34960 AW	52750 TQ	ARBLS	10/01-12/01
	California	Y	25160 FQ	44190 AW	68330 TQ	CABLS	10/01-12/01
	Los Angeles-Long Beach PMSA, CA	Y	22300 FQ	39500 AW	57840 TQ	CABLS	10/01-12/01
	Oakland PMSA, CA	Y	31360 FQ	48280 AW	67760 TQ	CABLS	10/01-12/01
	Orange County PMSA, CA	Y	25800 FQ	43240 AW	71880 TQ	CABLS	10/01-12/01
	Riverside-San Bernardino PMSA, CA	Y	24710 FQ	38950 AW	57920 TQ	CABLS	10/01-12/01
	Sacramento PMSA, CA	Y	20600 FQ	38130 AW	60580 TQ	CABLS	10/01-12/01
	Salinas MSA, CA	Y	24150 FQ	44100 AW	66480 TQ	CABLS	10/01-12/01
	San Diego MSA, CA	Y	25560 FQ	40710 AW	60240 TQ	CABLS	10/01-12/01
	San Francisco PMSA, CA	Y	32680 FQ	55850 AW	83380 TQ	CABLS	10/01-12/01
	San Jose PMSA, CA	Y	32310 FQ	49950 AW	77370 TQ	CABLS	10/01-12/01
	San Luis Obispo-Atascadero-Paso Robles MSA, CA	Y	25490 FQ	36580 AW	46910 TQ	CABLS	10/01-12/01
	Santa Barbara-Santa Maria-Lompoc MSA, CA	Y	24220 FQ	38810 AW	58370 TQ	CABLS	10/01-12/01
	Santa Cruz-Watsonville PMSA, CA	Y	32240 FQ	53540 AW	89010 TQ	CABLS	10/01-12/01
	Santa Rosa PMSA, CA	Y	28110 FQ	45950 AW	66300 TQ	CABLS	10/01-12/01
	Vallejo-Fairfield-Napa PMSA, CA	Y	30460 FQ	48070 AW	62240 TQ	CABLS	10/01-12/01
	Colorado	Y	24560 FQ	38360 AW	55300 TQ	COBLS	10/01-12/01
	Boulder-Longmont PMSA, CO	Y	29090 FQ	40880 AW	55090 TQ	COBLS	10/01-12/01
	Colorado Springs MSA, CO	Y	21060 FQ	36670 AW	57610 TQ	COBLS	10/01-12/01
	Denver PMSA, CO	Y	27390 FQ	40690 AW	56030 TQ	COBLS	10/01-12/01
	Connecticut	Y	29790 FQ	45420 AW	68890 TQ	CTBLS	10/01-12/01
	Hartford MSA, CT	Y	30050 FQ	43500 AW	58540 TQ	CTBLS	10/01-12/01
	Stamford-Norwalk PMSA, CT	Y	31590 FQ	48980 AW	79070 TQ	CTBLS	10/01-12/01

AAW	Average annual wage	AOH	Average offered, high	ASH	Average starting, high	H	Hourly	M	Monthly	S	Special: hourly and annual
AE	Average entry wage	AOL	Average offered, low	ASL	Average starting, low	HI	Highest wage paid	MTC	Median total compensation	TQ	Third quartile wage
AEX	Average experienced wage	APH	Average pay, high range	AW	Average wage paid	HR	High end range	MW	Median wage paid	W	Weekly
AO	Average offered	APL	Average pay, low range	FQ	First quartile wage	LR	Low end range	SQ	Second quartile wage	Y	Yearly

Occupation/Type/Industry	Location	Per	Low	Mid	High	Source	Date
Meeting and Convention Planner	Delaware	Y	30440 FQ	44950 AW	58810 TQ	DEBLS	10/01-12/01
	Wilmington-Newark PMSA, DE-MD	Y	31780 FQ	45730 AW	59210 TQ	DEBLS	10/01-12/01
	District of Columbia	Y	31560 FQ	48540 AW	71660 TQ	DCBLS	10/01-12/01
	Washington PMSA, DC-MD-VA-WV	Y	30760 FQ	47840 AW	71300 TQ	DCBLS	10/01-12/01
	Florida	Y	17910 FQ	33000 AW	50570 TQ	FLBLS	10/01-12/01
	Fort Lauderdale PMSA, FL	Y	23970 FQ	37260 AW	64730 TQ	FLBLS	10/01-12/01
	Jacksonville MSA, FL	Y	23400 FQ	30660 AW	41860 TQ	FLBLS	10/01-12/01
	Melbourne-Titusville-Palm Bay MSA, FL	Y	14380 FQ	36090 AW	67310 TQ	FLBLS	10/01-12/01
	Miami PMSA, FL	Y	25650 FQ	35700 AW	49910 TQ	FLBLS	10/01-12/01
	Orlando MSA, FL	Y	12970 FQ	29180 AW	49980 TQ	FLBLS	10/01-12/01
	Pensacola MSA, FL	Y	17600 FQ	24110 AW	27890 TQ	FLBLS	10/01-12/01
	Sarasota-Bradenton MSA, FL	Y	14780 FQ	35270 AW	54240 TQ	FLBLS	10/01-12/01
	Tallahassee MSA, FL	Y	18890 FQ	32290 AW	42860 TQ	FLBLS	10/01-12/01
	Tampa-St. Petersburg-Clearwater MSA, FL	Y	23390 FQ	35520 AW	49910 TQ	FLBLS	10/01-12/01
	West Palm Beach-Boca Raton MSA, FL	Y	26480 FQ	36150 AW	48010 TQ	FLBLS	10/01-12/01
	Georgia	Y	23840 FQ	36500 AW	54880 TQ	GABLS	10/01-12/01
	Atlanta MSA, GA	Y	24430 FQ	37400 AW	56050 TQ	GABLS	10/01-12/01
	Columbus MSA, GA-AL	Y	21490 FQ	31310 AW	43320 TQ	GABLS	10/01-12/01
	Hawaii	Y	28340 FQ	43800 AW	74450 TQ	HIBLS	10/01-12/01
	Honolulu MSA, HI	Y	25600 FQ	37910 AW	55310 TQ	HIBLS	10/01-12/01
	Idaho	Y	24410 FQ	33760 AW	46680 TQ	IDBLS	10/01-12/01
	Boise City MSA, ID	Y	25680 FQ	34990 AW	47620 TQ	IDBLS	10/01-12/01
	Illinois	Y	25440 FQ	44270 AW	67820 TQ	ILBLS	10/01-12/01
	Chicago PMSA, IL	Y	28860 FQ	46220 AW	68960 TQ	ILBLS	10/01-12/01
	Springfield MSA, IL	Y	24990 FQ	39690 AW	55370 TQ	ILBLS	10/01-12/01
	Indiana	Y	22090 FQ	35840 AW	60560 TQ	INBLS	10/01-12/01
	Gary PMSA, IN	Y	19170 FQ	26920 AW	36490 TQ	INBLS	10/01-12/01
	Indianapolis MSA, IN	Y	24810 FQ	39940 AW	67640 TQ	INBLS	10/01-12/01
	Iowa	Y	22860 FQ	31930 AW	45160 TQ	IABLS	10/01-12/01
	Des Moines MSA, IA	Y	25010 FQ	34180 AW	44390 TQ	IABLS	10/01-12/01
	Kansas	Y	21650 FQ	36750 AW	54240 TQ	KSBLS	10/01-12/01
	Topeka MSA, KS	Y	15910 FQ	34750 AW	46950 TQ	KSBLS	10/01-12/01
	Wichita MSA, KS	Y	24870 FQ	34770 AW	49800 TQ	KSBLS	10/01-12/01
	Kentucky	Y	23060 FQ	33940 AW	51620 TQ	KYBLS	10/01-12/01
	Lexington MSA, KY	Y	25250 FQ	34310 AW	44490 TQ	KYBLS	10/01-12/01
	Louisville MSA, KY-IN	Y	21380 FQ	34820 AW	53360 TQ	KYBLS	10/01-12/01
	Louisiana	Y	22320 FQ	36810 AW	60640 TQ	LABLS	10/01-12/01
	Baton Rouge MSA, LA	Y	23380 FQ	32980 AW	60630 TQ	LABLS	10/01-12/01
	New Orleans MSA, LA	Y	24500 FQ	41700 AW	65210 TQ	LABLS	10/01-12/01
	Maine	Y	22150 FQ	31600 AW	44000 TQ	MEBLS	10/01-12/01
	Maryland	Y	25430 FQ	41100 AW	64360 TQ	MDBLS	10/01-12/01
	Baltimore PMSA, MD	Y	23480 FQ	39970 AW	66160 TQ	MDBLS	10/01-12/01
	Massachusetts	Y	28210 FQ	42300 AW	59840 TQ	MABLS	10/01-12/01
	Boston PMSA, MA-NH	Y	28260 FQ	42510 AW	60090 TQ	MABLS	10/01-12/01
	Lowell PMSA, MA-NH	Y	28300 FQ	42970 AW	58730 TQ	MABLS	10/01-12/01
	Springfield MSA, MA	Y	29290 FQ	44680 AW	64510 TQ	MABLS	10/01-12/01
	Worcester PMSA, MA-CT	Y	30320 FQ	42690 AW	65860 TQ	MABLS	10/01-12/01
	Michigan	Y	22360 FQ	35760 AW	53890 TQ	MIBLS	10/01-12/01
	Ann Arbor PMSA, MI	Y	24380 FQ	36380 AW	51610 TQ	MIBLS	10/01-12/01
	Detroit PMSA, MI	Y	26260 FQ	39230 AW	58560 TQ	MIBLS	10/01-12/01
	Lansing-East Lansing MSA, MI	Y	29420 FQ	39750 AW	55210 TQ	MIBLS	10/01-12/01
	Saginaw-Bay City-Midland MSA, MI	Y	19870 FQ	30050 AW	45580 TQ	MIBLS	10/01-12/01
	Minnesota	Y	25010 FQ	38900 AW	56690 TQ	MNBLS	10/01-12/01
	Minneapolis-St. Paul MSA, MN-WI	Y	25700 FQ	40080 AW	58740 TQ	MNBLS	10/01-12/01
	St. Cloud MSA, MN	Y	23540 FQ	31380 AW	43030 TQ	MNBLS	10/01-12/01
	Mississippi	Y	20140 FQ	32600 AW	53090 TQ	MSBLS	10/01-12/01
	Missouri	Y	19350 FQ	30780 AW	47080 TQ	MOBLS	10/01-12/01
	Kansas City MSA, MO-KS	Y	19330 FQ	30290 AW	49800 TQ	MOBLS	10/01-12/01
	St. Louis MSA, MO-IL	Y	22530 FQ	35100 AW	54160 TQ	MOBLS	10/01-12/01
	Montana	Y	17890 FQ	26040 AW	36640 TQ	MTBLS	10/01-12/01
	Nebraska	Y	19820 FQ	32950 AW	50790 TQ	NEBLS	10/01-12/01
	Omaha MSA, NE-IA	Y	23250 FQ	33960 AW	50150 TQ	NEBLS	10/01-12/01
	Nevada	Y	15380 FQ	36230 AW	58660 TQ	NVBLS	10/01-12/01
	Las Vegas MSA, NV-AZ	Y	25800 FQ	41670 AW	61980 TQ	NVBLS	10/01-12/01
	Reno MSA, NV	Y	12700 FQ	28390 AW	52050 TQ	NVBLS	10/01-12/01

AAW Average annual wage **AOH** Average offered, high **ASH** Average starting, high **H** Hourly **M** Monthly **S** Special: hourly and annual
AE Average entry wage **AOL** Average offered, low **ASL** Average starting, low **HI** Highest wage paid **MTC** Median total compensation **TQ** Third quartile wage
AEX Average experienced wage **APH** Average pay, high range **AW** Average wage paid **HR** High end range **MW** Median wage paid **W** Weekly
AO Average offered **APL** Average pay, low range **FQ** First quartile wage **LR** Low end range **SQ** Second quartile wage **Y** Yearly

Occupation/Type/Industry	Location	Per	Low	Mid	High	Source	Date
Meeting and Convention Planner	New Hampshire	Y	23220 FQ	35530 AW	47180 TQ	NHBLS	10/01-12/01
	Portsmouth-Rochester PMSA, NH-ME	Y	20030 FQ	35250 AW	52620 TQ	NHBLS	10/01-12/01
	New Jersey	Y	27740 FQ	49440 AW	71350 TQ	NJBLS	10/01-12/01
	Atlantic-Cape May PMSA, NJ	Y	29920 FQ	44910 AW	68290 TQ	NJBLS	10/01-12/01
	Bergen-Passaic PMSA, NJ	Y	29820 FQ	54590 AW	103390 TQ	NJBLS	10/01-12/01
	Jersey City PMSA, NJ	Y	30820 FQ	46230 AW	66000 TQ	NJBLS	10/01-12/01
	Middlesex-Somerset-Hunterdon PMSA, NJ	Y	29820 FQ	45650 AW	67860 TQ	NJBLS	10/01-12/01
	Monmouth-Ocean PMSA, NJ	Y	32370 FQ	50730 AW	69200 TQ	NJBLS	10/01-12/01
	Newark PMSA, NJ	Y	33690 FQ	59510 AW		NJBLS	10/01-12/01
	Trenton PMSA, NJ	Y	28450 FQ	49800 AW	71470 TQ	NJBLS	10/01-12/01
	New Mexico	Y	23390 FQ	33740 AW	45740 TQ	NMBLS	10/01-12/01
	Albuquerque MSA, NM	Y	24760 FQ	34120 AW	45810 TQ	NMBLS	10/01-12/01
	New York	Y	26190 FQ	47490 AW	76250 TQ	NYBLS	10/01-12/01
	Albany-Schenectady-Troy MSA, NY	Y	26390 FQ	47850 AW	70450 TQ	NYBLS	10/01-12/01
	Binghamton MSA, NY	Y	30170 FQ	48410 AW	67860 TQ	NYBLS	10/01-12/01
	Buffalo-Niagara Falls MSA, NY	Y	24400 FQ	38210 AW	57450 TQ	NYBLS	10/01-12/01
	Nassau-Suffolk PMSA, NY	Y	24570 FQ	44880 AW	69090 TQ	NYBLS	10/01-12/01
	New York PMSA, NY	Y	30880 FQ	51990 AW	84680 TQ	NYBLS	10/01-12/01
	Rochester MSA, NY	Y	18940 FQ	29410 AW	45040 TQ	NYBLS	10/01-12/01
	North Carolina	Y	22330 FQ	34500 AW	49910 TQ	NCBLS	10/01-12/01
	Charlotte-Gastonia-Rock Hill MSA, NC-SC	Y	26620 FQ	37800 AW	53180 TQ	NCBLS	10/01-12/01
	Greensboro-Winston-Salem-High Point MSA, NC	Y	24060 FQ	32390 AW	44700 TQ	NCBLS	10/01-12/01
	Raleigh-Durham-Chapel Hill MSA, NC	Y	20720 FQ	33740 AW	51010 TQ	NCBLS	10/01-12/01
	North Dakota	Y	22060 FQ	31410 AW	43800 TQ	NDBLS	10/01-12/01
	Ohio	Y	23180 FQ	36150 AW	54100 TQ	OHBLS	10/01-12/01
	Cincinnati PMSA, OH-KY-IN	Y	23400 FQ	34880 AW	50410 TQ	OHBLS	10/01-12/01
	Cleveland-Lorain-Elyria PMSA, OH	Y	23910 FQ	35150 AW	51720 TQ	OHBLS	10/01-12/01
	Columbus MSA, OH	Y	25650 FQ	38540 AW	55850 TQ	OHBLS	10/01-12/01
	Dayton-Springfield MSA, OH	Y	24410 FQ	39960 AW	56660 TQ	OHBLS	10/01-12/01
	Toledo MSA, OH	Y	24980 FQ	39850 AW	64110 TQ	OHBLS	10/01-12/01
	Oklahoma	Y	18490 FQ	34520 AW	55550 TQ	OKBLS	10/01-12/01
	Oklahoma City MSA, OK	Y	17530 FQ	36260 AW	58080 TQ	OKBLS	10/01-12/01
	Tulsa MSA, OK	Y	16580 FQ	34130 AW	55900 TQ	OKBLS	10/01-12/01
	Oregon	Y	22260 FQ	36980 AW	53800 TQ	ORBLS	10/01-12/01
	Portland-Vancouver PMSA, OR-WA	Y	24430 FQ	37500 AW	52840 TQ	ORBLS	10/01-12/01
	Pennsylvania	Y	18420 FQ	36850 AW	57730 TQ	PABLS	10/01-12/01
	Harrisburg-Lebanon-Carlisle MSA, PA	Y	16120 FQ	34810 AW	65450 TQ	PABLS	10/01-12/01
	Philadelphia PMSA, PA-NJ	Y	22000 FQ	38970 AW	57950 TQ	PABLS	10/01-12/01
	Pittsburgh MSA, PA	Y	13130 FQ	35150 AW	60920 TQ	PABLS	10/01-12/01
	Rhode Island	Y	30950 FQ	46610 AW	66780 TQ	RIBLS	10/01-12/01
	Providence-Fall River-Warwick MSA, RI-MA	Y	30790 FQ	45340 AW	64640 TQ	RIBLS	10/01-12/01
	South Carolina	Y	21960 FQ	35660 AW	53760 TQ	SCBLS	10/01-12/01
	Greenville-Spartanburg-Anderson MSA, SC	Y	18640 FQ	28730 AW	40100 TQ	SCBLS	10/01-12/01
	Myrtle Beach MSA, SC	Y	17710 FQ	34030 AW	57560 TQ	SCBLS	10/01-12/01
	South Dakota	Y	21620 FQ	29550 AW	39750 TQ	SDBLS	10/01-12/01
	Tennessee	Y	24510 FQ	38920 AW	56040 TQ	TNBLS	10/01-12/01
	Knoxville MSA, TN	Y	21670 FQ	29690 AW	40920 TQ	TNBLS	10/01-12/01
	Memphis MSA, TN-AR-MS	Y	27940 FQ	41380 AW	55660 TQ	TNBLS	10/01-12/01
	Nashville MSA, TN	Y	27570 FQ	42080 AW	57260 TQ	TNBLS	10/01-12/01
	Texas	Y	21670 FQ	38140 AW	57120 TQ	TXBLS	10/01-12/01
	Austin-San Marcos MSA, TX	Y	22470 FQ	36810 AW	55310 TQ	TXBLS	10/01-12/01
	Dallas PMSA, TX	Y	23900 FQ	38880 AW	56730 TQ	TXBLS	10/01-12/01
	Fort Worth-Arlington PMSA, TX	Y	21530 FQ	37720 AW	57420 TQ	TXBLS	10/01-12/01
	Houston PMSA, TX	Y	23620 FQ	43850 AW	82490 TQ	TXBLS	10/01-12/01
	McAllen-Edinburg-Mission MSA, TX	Y	17410 FQ	29530 AW	49660 TQ	TXBLS	10/01-12/01
	San Antonio MSA, TX	Y	25680 FQ	36700 AW	46070 TQ	TXBLS	10/01-12/01
	Utah	Y	20090 FQ	31140 AW	44120 TQ	UTBLS	10/01-12/01
	Provo-Orem MSA, UT	Y	20220 FQ	29940 AW	44120 TQ	UTBLS	10/01-12/01

AAW	Average annual wage	**AOH**	Average offered, high	**ASH**	Average starting, high	**H**	Hourly	**M**	Monthly	**S**	Special: hourly and annual
AE	Average entry wage	**AOL**	Average offered, low	**ASL**	Average starting, low	**HI**	Highest wage paid	**MTC**	Median total compensation	**TQ**	Third quartile wage
AEX	Average experienced wage	**APH**	Average pay, high range	**AW**	Average wage paid	**HR**	High end range	**MW**	Median wage paid	**W**	Weekly
AO	Average offered	**APL**	Average pay, low range	**FQ**	First quartile wage	**LR**	Low end range	**SQ**	Second quartile wage	**Y**	Yearly

Occupation/Type/Industry	Location	Per	Low	Mid	High	Source	Date
Meeting and Convention Planner	Salt Lake City-Ogden MSA, UT	Y	20310 FQ	31070 AW	43720 TQ	UTBLS	10/01-12/01
	Vermont	Y	25850 FQ	42220 AW	67660 TQ	VTBLS	10/01-12/01
	Burlington MSA, VT	Y	29210 FQ	45730 AW	68440 TQ	VTBLS	10/01-12/01
	Virginia	Y	26380 FQ	45330 AW	70470 TQ	VABLS	10/01-12/01
	Norfolk-Virginia Beach-Newport News MSA, VA-NC	Y	20670 FQ	34240 AW	53940 TQ	VABLS	10/01-12/01
	Richmond-Petersburg MSA, VA	Y	21880 FQ	36200 AW	52980 TQ	VABLS	10/01-12/01
	Washington	Y	25550 FQ	39550 AW	57330 TQ	WABLS	10/01-12/01
	Seattle-Bellevue-Everett PMSA, WA	Y	26590 FQ	42530 AW	60890 TQ	WABLS	10/01-12/01
	West Virginia	Y	17660 FQ	27860 AW	37250 TQ	WVBLS	10/01-12/01
	Charleston MSA, WV	Y	17610 FQ	28700 AW	37950 TQ	WVBLS	10/01-12/01
	Wisconsin	Y	19560 FQ	35150 AW	53110 TQ	WIBLS	10/01-12/01
	Madison MSA, WI	Y	26260 FQ	38870 AW	47960 TQ	WIBLS	10/01-12/01
	Milwaukee-Waukesha PMSA, WI	Y	14050 FQ	34930 AW	54420 TQ	WIBLS	10/01-12/01
	Puerto Rico	Y	15610 FQ	29690 AW	45420 TQ	PRBLS	10/01-12/01
Meeting Professional							
Corporations	United States	Y		60714 AW		CMI	2002
Mental Health and Substance Abuse Social Worker	United States	Y		25760-39660 AW		FREEP1	1/00-1/00
	Alabama	Y	15990 FQ	26330 AW	45280 TQ	ALBLS	10/01-12/01
	Birmingham MSA, AL	Y	17400 FQ	32400 AW	50110 TQ	ALBLS	10/01-12/01
	Mobile MSA, AL	Y	24700 FQ	39090 AW	53540 TQ	ALBLS	10/01-12/01
	Montgomery MSA, AL	Y	16070 FQ	29710 AW	51950 TQ	ALBLS	10/01-12/01
	Alaska	Y	22290 FQ	33250 AW	46990 TQ	AKBLS	10/01-12/01
	Anchorage MSA, AK	Y	20110 FQ	33790 AW	51070 TQ	AKBLS	10/01-12/01
	Arizona	Y	16770 FQ	25700 AW	39290 TQ	AZBLS	10/01-12/01
	Phoenix-Mesa MSA, AZ	Y	17530 FQ	25890 AW	39740 TQ	AZBLS	10/01-12/01
	Tucson MSA, AZ	Y	16290 FQ	26960 AW	42190 TQ	AZBLS	10/01-12/01
	Arkansas	Y	16650 FQ	29500 AW	44540 TQ	ARBLS	10/01-12/01
	Little Rock-North Little Rock MSA, AR	Y	15400 FQ	25880 AW	41920 TQ	ARBLS	10/01-12/01
	California	Y	22130 FQ	36000 AW	54620 TQ	CABLS	10/01-12/01
	Bakersfield MSA, CA	Y	22300 FQ	37200 AW	47660 TQ	CABLS	10/01-12/01
	Los Angeles-Long Beach PMSA, CA	Y	22310 FQ	34650 AW	51710 TQ	CABLS	10/01-12/01
	Oakland PMSA, CA	Y	30660 FQ	48970 AW	64090 TQ	CABLS	10/01-12/01
	Orange County PMSA, CA	Y	23660 FQ	32000 AW	43290 TQ	CABLS	10/01-12/01
	Riverside-San Bernardino PMSA, CA	Y	20630 FQ	43750 AW	81760 TQ	CABLS	10/01-12/01
	Sacramento PMSA, CA	Y	26960 FQ	38560 AW	53590 TQ	CABLS	10/01-12/01
	Salinas MSA, CA	Y	20040 FQ	25020 AW	31360 TQ	CABLS	10/01-12/01
	San Diego MSA, CA	Y	19580 FQ	28610 AW	40600 TQ	CABLS	10/01-12/01
	San Francisco PMSA, CA	Y	25980 FQ	41490 AW	59500 TQ	CABLS	10/01-12/01
	San Jose PMSA, CA	Y	27780 FQ	35650 AW	47010 TQ	CABLS	10/01-12/01
	Santa Barbara-Santa Maria-Lompoc MSA, CA	Y	22640 FQ	28180 AW	35270 TQ	CABLS	10/01-12/01
	Santa Cruz-Watsonville PMSA, CA	Y	23540 FQ	40680 AW	56330 TQ	CABLS	10/01-12/01
	Santa Rosa PMSA, CA	Y	22600 FQ	32140 AW	52550 TQ	CABLS	10/01-12/01
	Visalia-Tulare-Porterville MSA, CA	Y	22530 FQ	27380 AW	34720 TQ	CABLS	10/01-12/01
	Colorado	Y	23570 FQ	35690 AW	52190 TQ	COBLS	10/01-12/01
	Denver PMSA, CO	Y	23280 FQ	34550 AW	49530 TQ	COBLS	10/01-12/01
	Fort Collins-Loveland MSA, CO	Y	22120 FQ	29910 AW	39690 TQ	COBLS	10/01-12/01
	Connecticut	Y	29740 FQ	46020 AW	65800 TQ	CTBLS	10/01-12/01
	Bridgeport PMSA, CT	Y	28980 FQ	38360 AW	53030 TQ	CTBLS	10/01-12/01
	Danbury PMSA, CT	Y	31820 FQ	45960 AW	68280 TQ	CTBLS	10/01-12/01
	Hartford MSA, CT	Y	36530 FQ	50230 AW	67940 TQ	CTBLS	10/01-12/01
	New Haven-Meriden PMSA, CT	Y	26780 FQ	38840 AW	55210 TQ	CTBLS	10/01-12/01
	New London-Norwich MSA, CT-RI	Y	27130 FQ	46390 AW	66890 TQ	CTBLS	10/01-12/01
	Stamford-Norwalk PMSA, CT	Y	38300 FQ	52350 AW	67510 TQ	CTBLS	10/01-12/01

Occupation/Type/Industry	Location	Per	Low	Mid	High	Source	Date
Mental Health and Substance Abuse Social Worker	Delaware	Y	27740 FQ	34960 AW	44800 TQ	DEBLS	10/01-12/01
	Wilmington-Newark PMSA, DE-MD	Y	26490 FQ	34590 AW	45560 TQ	DEBLS	10/01-12/01
	District of Columbia	Y	30220 FQ	44360 AW	65600 TQ	DCBLS	10/01-12/01
	Washington PMSA, DC-MD-VA-WV	Y	30990 FQ	47560 AW	69490 TQ	DCBLS	10/01-12/01
	Florida	Y	20890 FQ	31200 AW	44000 TQ	FLBLS	10/01-12/01
	Daytona Beach MSA, FL	Y	22080 FQ	34290 AW	44490 TQ	FLBLS	10/01-12/01
	Fort Lauderdale PMSA, FL	Y	24330 FQ	33870 AW	44580 TQ	FLBLS	10/01-12/01
	Fort Myers-Cape Coral MSA, FL	Y	23670 FQ	33270 AW	44480 TQ	FLBLS	10/01-12/01
	Fort Pierce-Port St. Lucie MSA, FL	Y	25070 FQ	32970 AW	49320 TQ	FLBLS	10/01-12/01
	Gainesville MSA, FL	Y	23890 FQ	28000 AW	34030 TQ	FLBLS	10/01-12/01
	Jacksonville MSA, FL	Y	20080 FQ	31350 AW	46400 TQ	FLBLS	10/01-12/01
	Melbourne-Titusville-Palm Bay MSA, FL	Y	20980 FQ	31640 AW	44670 TQ	FLBLS	10/01-12/01
	Miami PMSA, FL	Y	23710 FQ	36520 AW	78030 TQ	FLBLS	10/01-12/01
	Naples MSA, FL	Y	18330 FQ	28560 AW	40790 TQ	FLBLS	10/01-12/01
	Ocala MSA, FL	Y	24500 FQ	31930 AW	42870 TQ	FLBLS	10/01-12/01
	Orlando MSA, FL	Y	21620 FQ	28080 AW	37670 TQ	FLBLS	10/01-12/01
	Sarasota-Bradenton MSA, FL	Y	19700 FQ	27150 AW	40870 TQ	FLBLS	10/01-12/01
	Tallahassee MSA, FL	Y	24840 FQ	31340 AW	37450 TQ	FLBLS	10/01-12/01
	Tampa-St. Petersburg-Clearwater MSA, FL	Y	19020 FQ	27970 AW	40980 TQ	FLBLS	10/01-12/01
	West Palm Beach-Boca Raton MSA, FL	Y	20520 FQ	30650 AW	43260 TQ	FLBLS	10/01-12/01
	Georgia	Y	15990 FQ	36780 AW	55790 TQ	GABLS	10/01-12/01
	Atlanta MSA, GA	Y	25080 FQ	36640 AW	53640 TQ	GABLS	10/01-12/01
	Columbus MSA, GA-AL	Y	30250 FQ	49910 AW	91940 TQ	GABLS	10/01-12/01
	Macon MSA, GA	Y	13420 FQ	28670 AW	51060 TQ	GABLS	10/01-12/01
	Savannah MSA, GA	Y	25530 FQ	36120 AW	44570 TQ	GABLS	10/01-12/01
	Hawaii	Y	27640 FQ	39470 AW	47020 TQ	HIBLS	10/01-12/01
	Idaho	Y	16450 FQ	36120 AW	58060 TQ	IDBLS	10/01-12/01
	Boise City MSA, ID	Y	19240 FQ	36840 AW	55110 TQ	IDBLS	10/01-12/01
	Illinois	Y	19900 FQ	31090 AW	45480 TQ	ILBLS	10/01-12/01
	Champaign-Urbana MSA, IL	Y	16820 FQ	24760 AW	37470 TQ	ILBLS	10/01-12/01
	Chicago PMSA, IL	Y	20460 FQ	31840 AW	46390 TQ	ILBLS	10/01-12/01
	Peoria-Pekin MSA, IL	Y	30590 FQ	48650 AW	67850 TQ	ILBLS	10/01-12/01
	Springfield MSA, IL	Y	16970 FQ	28730 AW	37500 TQ	ILBLS	10/01-12/01
	Indiana	Y	20860 FQ	29770 AW	40540 TQ	INBLS	10/01-12/01
	Fort Wayne MSA, IN	Y	22490 FQ	28350 AW	37260 TQ	INBLS	10/01-12/01
	Indianapolis MSA, IN	Y	24390 FQ	32840 AW	43450 TQ	INBLS	10/01-12/01
	South Bend MSA, IN	Y	24480 FQ	32710 AW	44080 TQ	INBLS	10/01-12/01
	Iowa	Y	16880 FQ	28930 AW	43400 TQ	IABLS	10/01-12/01
	Des Moines MSA, IA	Y	20410 FQ	29040 AW	42250 TQ	IABLS	10/01-12/01
	Kansas	Y	19760 FQ	31650 AW	44860 TQ	KSBLS	10/01-12/01
	Topeka MSA, KS	Y	19910 FQ	30970 AW	41860 TQ	KSBLS	10/01-12/01
	Wichita MSA, KS	Y	19060 FQ	28750 AW	39380 TQ	KSBLS	10/01-12/01
	Kentucky	Y	20230 FQ	32290 AW	46270 TQ	KYBLS	10/01-12/01
	Lexington MSA, KY	Y	22800 FQ	29080 AW	38310 TQ	KYBLS	10/01-12/01
	Louisville MSA, KY-IN	Y	20810 FQ	31230 AW	43360 TQ	KYBLS	10/01-12/01
	Louisiana	Y	15340 FQ	27910 AW	42270 TQ	LABLS	10/01-12/01
	Baton Rouge MSA, LA	Y	22910 FQ	32850 AW	42630 TQ	LABLS	10/01-12/01
	Lafayette MSA, LA	Y	15070 FQ	25340 AW	40590 TQ	LABLS	10/01-12/01
	New Orleans MSA, LA	Y	21240 FQ	35060 AW	46270 TQ	LABLS	10/01-12/01
	Shreveport-Bossier City MSA, LA	Y	14630 FQ	21780 AW	35100 TQ	LABLS	10/01-12/01
	Maine	Y	22060 FQ	33650 AW	44500 TQ	MEBLS	10/01-12/01
	Portland MSA, ME	Y	20460 FQ	31050 AW	43020 TQ	MEBLS	10/01-12/01
	Maryland	Y	20910 FQ	41370 AW	66810 TQ	MDBLS	10/01-12/01
	Baltimore PMSA, MD	Y	20170 FQ	39720 AW	64080 TQ	MDBLS	10/01-12/01
	Massachusetts	Y	22110 FQ	37210 AW	59210 TQ	MABLS	10/01-12/01
	Boston PMSA, MA-NH	Y	22630 FQ	38610 AW	60660 TQ	MABLS	10/01-12/01
	Brockton PMSA, MA	Y	26140 FQ	37630 AW	44260 TQ	MABLS	10/01-12/01
	Lawrence PMSA, MA-NH	Y	25180 FQ	39850 AW	64830 TQ	MABLS	10/01-12/01
	Lowell PMSA, MA-NH	Y	25540 FQ	46530 AW	59140 TQ	MABLS	10/01-12/01
	New Bedford PMSA, MA	Y	19300 FQ	32000 AW	56890 TQ	MABLS	10/01-12/01
	Springfield MSA, MA	Y	20480 FQ	33560 AW	61360 TQ	MABLS	10/01-12/01
	Worcester PMSA, MA-CT	Y	24260 FQ	31810 AW	42930 TQ	MABLS	10/01-12/01
	Michigan	Y	26080 FQ	38230 AW	49790 TQ	MIBLS	10/01-12/01

AAW Average annual wage; **AE** Average entry wage; **AEX** Average experienced wage; **AO** Average offered; **AOH** Average offered, high; **AOL** Average offered, low; **APH** Average pay, high range; **APL** Average pay, low range; **ASH** Average starting, high; **ASL** Average starting, low; **AW** Average wage paid; **FQ** First quartile wage; **H** Hourly; **HI** Highest wage paid; **HR** High end range; **LR** Low end range; **M** Monthly; **MTC** Median total compensation; **MW** Median wage paid; **SQ** Second quartile wage; **S** Special: hourly and annual; **TQ** Third quartile wage; **W** Weekly; **Y** Yearly

Occupation/Type/Industry	Location	Per	Low	Mid	High	Source	Date
Mental Health and Substance Abuse Social Worker	Ann Arbor PMSA, MI	Y	24280 FQ	35150 AW	46760 TQ	MIBLS	10/01-12/01
	Detroit PMSA, MI	Y	29340 FQ	41820 AW	53020 TQ	MIBLS	10/01-12/01
	Grand Rapids-Muskegon-Holland MSA, MI	Y	22630 FQ	33960 AW	46540 TQ	MIBLS	10/01-12/01
	Kalamazoo-Battle Creek MSA, MI	Y	31400 FQ	39950 AW	53020 TQ	MIBLS	10/01-12/01
	Lansing-East Lansing MSA, MI	Y	25810 FQ	34360 AW	44920 TQ	MIBLS	10/01-12/01
	Minnesota	Y	26070 FQ	38100 AW	53330 TQ	MNBLS	10/01-12/01
	Duluth-Superior MSA, MN-WI	Y	26450 FQ	38250 AW	56250 TQ	MNBLS	10/01-12/01
	Minneapolis-St. Paul MSA, MN-WI	Y	24510 FQ	36380 AW	53590 TQ	MNBLS	10/01-12/01
	Mississippi	Y	13770 FQ	26310 AW	40400 TQ	MSBLS	10/01-12/01
	Jackson MSA, MS	Y	13530 FQ	26570 AW	40820 TQ	MSBLS	10/01-12/01
	Missouri	Y	22770 FQ	33430 AW	45800 TQ	MOBLS	10/01-12/01
	Kansas City MSA, MO-KS	Y	20510 FQ	32670 AW	46620 TQ	MOBLS	10/01-12/01
	St. Louis MSA, MO-IL	Y	21270 FQ	32860 AW	47780 TQ	MOBLS	10/01-12/01
	Springfield MSA, MO	Y	24620 FQ	35580 AW	45930 TQ	MOBLS	10/01-12/01
	Montana	Y	21300 FQ	27480 AW	34950 TQ	MTBLS	10/01-12/01
	Nebraska	Y	19290 FQ	29130 AW	41390 TQ	NEBLS	10/01-12/01
	Lincoln MSA, NE	Y	19890 FQ	28940 AW	41760 TQ	NEBLS	10/01-12/01
	Omaha MSA, NE-IA	Y	16530 FQ	26800 AW	36130 TQ	NEBLS	10/01-12/01
	Nevada	Y	32800 FQ	42850 AW	53820 TQ	NVBLS	10/01-12/01
	Las Vegas MSA, NV-AZ	Y	16820 FQ	35580 AW	51170 TQ	NVBLS	10/01-12/01
	New Hampshire	Y	23690 FQ	34450 AW	44260 TQ	NHBLS	10/01-12/01
	Manchester PMSA, NH	Y	26000 FQ	35440 AW	43450 TQ	NHBLS	10/01-12/01
	New Jersey	Y	27730 FQ	41120 AW	56770 TQ	NJBLS	10/01-12/01
	Atlantic-Cape May PMSA, NJ	Y	22450 FQ	33210 AW	45620 TQ	NJBLS	10/01-12/01
	Bergen-Passaic PMSA, NJ	Y	27460 FQ	39300 AW	54450 TQ	NJBLS	10/01-12/01
	Jersey City PMSA, NJ	Y	32120 FQ	43740 AW	56590 TQ	NJBLS	10/01-12/01
	Middlesex-Somerset-Hunterdon PMSA, NJ	Y	29190 FQ	39460 AW	54160 TQ	NJBLS	10/01-12/01
	Monmouth-Ocean PMSA, NJ	Y	28480 FQ	42450 AW	58660 TQ	NJBLS	10/01-12/01
	Newark PMSA, NJ	Y	24320 FQ	38880 AW	54210 TQ	NJBLS	10/01-12/01
	Trenton PMSA, NJ	Y	34030 FQ	47340 AW	64030 TQ	NJBLS	10/01-12/01
	New Mexico	Y	22550 FQ	34470 AW	51180 TQ	NMBLS	10/01-12/01
	Albuquerque MSA, NM	Y	20520 FQ	38920 AW	55100 TQ	NMBLS	10/01-12/01
	Las Cruces MSA, NM	Y	24730 FQ	32540 AW	50830 TQ	NMBLS	10/01-12/01
	New York	Y	22780 FQ	37410 AW	56400 TQ	NYBLS	10/01-12/01
	Albany-Schenectady-Troy MSA, NY	Y	17590 FQ	31090 AW	49470 TQ	NYBLS	10/01-12/01
	Binghamton MSA, NY	Y	23660 FQ	31920 AW	41270 TQ	NYBLS	10/01-12/01
	Buffalo-Niagara Falls MSA, NY	Y	24460 FQ	31820 AW	43070 TQ	NYBLS	10/01-12/01
	Dutchess County PMSA, NY	Y	25390 FQ	43660 AW	62090 TQ	NYBLS	10/01-12/01
	Nassau-Suffolk PMSA, NY	Y	20070 FQ	36840 AW	58180 TQ	NYBLS	10/01-12/01
	New York PMSA, NY	Y	24070 FQ	38720 AW	57560 TQ	NYBLS	10/01-12/01
	Rochester MSA, NY	Y	20510 FQ	34100 AW	46630 TQ	NYBLS	10/01-12/01
	Syracuse MSA, NY	Y	21450 FQ	42700 AW	60500 TQ	NYBLS	10/01-12/01
	Utica-Rome MSA, NY	Y	23520 FQ	34430 AW	56780 TQ	NYBLS	10/01-12/01
	North Carolina	Y	23880 FQ	34060 AW	44910 TQ	NCBLS	10/01-12/01
	Charlotte-Gastonia-Rock Hill MSA, NC-SC	Y	24860 FQ	35660 AW	54080 TQ	NCBLS	10/01-12/01
	Fayetteville MSA, NC	Y	30660 FQ	40180 AW	51440 TQ	NCBLS	10/01-12/01
	Greensboro-Winston-Salem-High Point MSA, NC	Y	28450 FQ	36690 AW	46290 TQ	NCBLS	10/01-12/01
	Hickory-Morganton-Lenoir MSA, NC	Y	23800 FQ	32770 AW	45370 TQ	NCBLS	10/01-12/01
	North Dakota	Y	15490 FQ	24700 AW	36720 TQ	NDBLS	10/01-12/01
	Fargo-Moorhead MSA, ND-MN	Y	23810 FQ	32380 AW	43440 TQ	NDBLS	10/01-12/01
	Ohio	Y	21200 FQ	30830 AW	43440 TQ	OHBLS	10/01-12/01
	Canton-Massillon MSA, OH	Y	23610 FQ	32230 AW	42820 TQ	OHBLS	10/01-12/01
	Cincinnati PMSA, OH-KY-IN	Y	23520 FQ	31270 AW	41720 TQ	OHBLS	10/01-12/01
	Cleveland-Lorain-Elyria PMSA, OH	Y	19780 FQ	30750 AW	46920 TQ	OHBLS	10/01-12/01
	Columbus MSA, OH	Y	23900 FQ	30280 AW	39010 TQ	OHBLS	10/01-12/01
	Dayton-Springfield MSA, OH	Y	24280 FQ	32270 AW	43680 TQ	OHBLS	10/01-12/01
	Hamilton-Middletown PMSA, OH	Y	20850 FQ	28200 AW	35210 TQ	OHBLS	10/01-12/01
	Toledo MSA, OH	Y	20250 FQ	29190 AW	37570 TQ	OHBLS	10/01-12/01
	Youngstown-Warren MSA, OH	Y	23220 FQ	34880 AW	50640 TQ	OHBLS	10/01-12/01

AAW Average annual wage; **AE** Average entry wage; **AEX** Average experienced wage; **AO** Average offered; **AOH** Average offered, high; **AOL** Average offered, low; **APH** Average pay, high range; **APL** Average pay, low range; **ASH** Average starting, high; **ASL** Average starting, low; **AW** Average wage paid; **FQ** First quartile wage; **H** Hourly; **HI** Highest wage paid; **HR** High end range; **LR** Low end range; **M** Monthly; **MTC** Median total compensation; **MW** Median wage paid; **SQ** Second quartile wage; **S** Special: hourly and annual; **TQ** Third quartile wage; **W** Weekly; **Y** Yearly

Occupation/Type/Industry	Location	Per	Low	Mid	High	Source	Date
Mental Health and Substance Abuse Social Worker	Oklahoma	Y	16490 FQ	28110 AW	42730 TQ	OKBLS	10/01-12/01
	Tulsa MSA, OK	Y	23080 FQ	30400 AW	37330 TQ	OKBLS	10/01-12/01
	Oregon	Y	19840 FQ	32670 AW	46430 TQ	ORBLS	10/01-12/01
	Eugene-Springfield MSA, OR	Y	19330 FQ	29320 AW	47410 TQ	ORBLS	10/01-12/01
	Portland-Vancouver PMSA, OR-WA	Y	19890 FQ	33890 AW	48340 TQ	ORBLS	10/01-12/01
	Pennsylvania	Y	21610 FQ	30470 AW	43430 TQ	PABLS	10/01-12/01
	Allentown-Bethlehem-Easton MSA, PA	Y	20620 FQ	30280 AW	46010 TQ	PABLS	10/01-12/01
	Harrisburg-Lebanon-Carlisle MSA, PA	Y	20320 FQ	31030 AW	45180 TQ	PABLS	10/01-12/01
	Philadelphia PMSA, PA-NJ	Y	20680 FQ	33240 AW	51680 TQ	PABLS	10/01-12/01
	Pittsburgh MSA, PA	Y	20760 FQ	33460 AW	47930 TQ	PABLS	10/01-12/01
	Scranton-Wilkes-Barre-Hazleton MSA, PA	Y	22230 FQ	31950 AW	51780 TQ	PABLS	10/01-12/01
	Rhode Island	Y	22830 FQ	37870 AW	57420 TQ	RIBLS	10/01-12/01
	Providence-Fall River-Warwick MSA, RI-MA	Y	22990 FQ	36870 AW	56310 TQ	RIBLS	10/01-12/01
	South Carolina	Y	15250 FQ	26870 AW	51710 TQ	SCBLS	10/01-12/01
	Charleston-North Charleston MSA, SC	Y	20490 FQ	36310 AW	56890 TQ	SCBLS	10/01-12/01
	Myrtle Beach MSA, SC	Y	24660 FQ	36490 AW	53420 TQ	SCBLS	10/01-12/01
	South Dakota	Y	22520 FQ	30960 AW	38480 TQ	SDBLS	10/01-12/01
	Sioux Falls MSA, SD	Y	20220 FQ	27380 AW	37060 TQ	SDBLS	10/01-12/01
	Tennessee	Y	18620 FQ	26110 AW	35630 TQ	TNBLS	10/01-12/01
	Chattanooga MSA, TN-GA	Y	18670 FQ	24350 AW	31690 TQ	TNBLS	10/01-12/01
	Johnson City-Kingsport-Bristol MSA, TN-VA	Y	17410 FQ	22090 AW	28110 TQ	TNBLS	10/01-12/01
	Knoxville MSA, TN	Y	18740 FQ	26630 AW	35180 TQ	TNBLS	10/01-12/01
	Memphis MSA, TN-AR-MS	Y	18650 FQ	26140 AW	36250 TQ	TNBLS	10/01-12/01
	Nashville MSA, TN	Y	19360 FQ	28450 AW	39070 TQ	TNBLS	10/01-12/01
	Texas	Y	20060 FQ	29710 AW	42160 TQ	TXBLS	10/01-12/01
	Amarillo MSA, TX	Y	20960 FQ	29670 AW	35630 TQ	TXBLS	10/01-12/01
	Austin-San Marcos MSA, TX	Y	23900 FQ	30390 AW	40920 TQ	TXBLS	10/01-12/01
	Beaumont-Port Arthur MSA, TX	Y	19140 FQ	27850 AW	41200 TQ	TXBLS	10/01-12/01
	Brownsville-Harlingen-San Benito MSA, TX	Y	28010 FQ	35010 AW	37990 TQ	TXBLS	10/01-12/01
	Corpus Christi MSA, TX	Y	13980 FQ	25060 AW	37760 TQ	TXBLS	10/01-12/01
	Dallas PMSA, TX	Y	22680 FQ	30050 AW	40930 TQ	TXBLS	10/01-12/01
	El Paso MSA, TX	Y	16210 FQ	27040 AW	42530 TQ	TXBLS	10/01-12/01
	Fort Worth-Arlington PMSA, TX	Y	17110 FQ	27750 AW	39590 TQ	TXBLS	10/01-12/01
	Galveston-Texas City PMSA, TX	Y	20780 FQ	28950 AW	41690 TQ	TXBLS	10/01-12/01
	Houston PMSA, TX	Y	22100 FQ	34940 AW	50200 TQ	TXBLS	10/01-12/01
	Killeen-Temple MSA, TX	Y	20370 FQ	25170 AW	28990 TQ	TXBLS	10/01-12/01
	Longview-Marshall MSA, TX	Y	19780 FQ	26950 AW	38390 TQ	TXBLS	10/01-12/01
	San Antonio MSA, TX	Y	18350 FQ	30390 AW	41860 TQ	TXBLS	10/01-12/01
	Waco MSA, TX	Y	18680 FQ	31710 AW	43270 TQ	TXBLS	10/01-12/01
	Utah	Y	23540 FQ	36510 AW	50240 TQ	UTBLS	10/01-12/01
	Provo-Orem MSA, UT	Y	29760 FQ	38670 AW	50570 TQ	UTBLS	10/01-12/01
	Salt Lake City-Ogden MSA, UT	Y	23330 FQ	35130 AW	50060 TQ	UTBLS	10/01-12/01
	Vermont	Y	26380 FQ	39760 AW	54920 TQ	VTBLS	10/01-12/01
	Burlington MSA, VT	Y	28160 FQ	45880 AW	60390 TQ	VTBLS	10/01-12/01
	Virginia	Y	27430 FQ	43190 AW	64710 TQ	VABLS	10/01-12/01
	Norfolk-Virginia Beach-Newport News MSA, VA-NC	Y	29210 FQ	41400 AW	56480 TQ	VABLS	10/01-12/01
	Richmond-Petersburg MSA, VA	Y	25580 FQ	41450 AW	67180 TQ	VABLS	10/01-12/01
	Roanoke MSA, VA	Y	23600 FQ	32980 AW	51280 TQ	VABLS	10/01-12/01
	Washington	Y	25650 FQ	39240 AW	53190 TQ	WABLS	10/01-12/01
	Bremerton PMSA, WA	Y	26520 FQ	39230 AW	52630 TQ	WABLS	10/01-12/01
	Olympia PMSA, WA	Y	28050 FQ	40980 AW	53740 TQ	WABLS	10/01-12/01
	Richland-Kennewick-Pasco MSA, WA	Y	19410 FQ	34630 AW	51580 TQ	WABLS	10/01-12/01
	Seattle-Bellevue-Everett PMSA, WA	Y	25920 FQ	39290 AW	53430 TQ	WABLS	10/01-12/01
	Spokane MSA, WA	Y	24120 FQ	38920 AW	53160 TQ	WABLS	10/01-12/01

AAW	Average annual wage	AOH	Average offered, high	ASH	Average starting, high	H	Hourly	M	Monthly	S	Special: hourly and annual
AE	Average entry wage	AOL	Average offered, low	ASL	Average starting, low	HI	Highest wage paid	MTC	Median total compensation	TQ	Third quartile wage
AEX	Average experienced wage	APH	Average pay, high range	AW	Average wage paid	HR	High end range	MW	Median wage paid	W	Weekly
AO	Average offered	APL	Average pay, low range	FQ	First quartile wage	LR	Low end range	SQ	Second quartile wage	Y	Yearly

Occupation/Type/Industry	Location	Per	Low	Mid	High	Source	Date
Mental Health and Substance Abuse Social Worker	Tacoma PMSA, WA	Y	29410 FQ	41530 AW	54320 TQ	WABLS	10/01-12/01
	Yakima MSA, WA	Y	20830 FQ	34290 AW	51000 TQ	WABLS	10/01-12/01
	West Virginia	Y	13600 FQ	21230 AW	28910 TQ	WVBLS	10/01-12/01
	Charleston MSA, WV	Y	15100 FQ	22790 AW	34970 TQ	WVBLS	10/01-12/01
	Huntington-Ashland MSA, WV-KY-OH	Y	14800 FQ	23540 AW	34530 TQ	WVBLS	10/01-12/01
	Wisconsin	Y	21920 FQ	38480 AW	53230 TQ	WIBLS	10/01-12/01
	Milwaukee-Waukesha PMSA, WI	Y	18700 FQ	34030 AW	51390 TQ	WIBLS	10/01-12/01
	Wyoming	Y	22580 FQ	33630 AW	48410 TQ	WYBLS	10/01-12/01
	Puerto Rico	Y	18410 FQ	25040 AW	33100 TQ	PRBLS	10/01-12/01
	Virgin Islands	Y	19890 FQ	27500 AW	45610 TQ	VIBLS	10/01-12/01
Mental Health Counselor	Alabama	Y	16610 FQ	26820 AW	41440 TQ	ALBLS	10/01-12/01
	Birmingham MSA, AL	Y	17160 FQ	23470 AW	32390 TQ	ALBLS	10/01-12/01
	Huntsville MSA, AL	Y	16120 FQ	23390 AW	30270 TQ	ALBLS	10/01-12/01
	Alaska	Y	25250 FQ	38040 AW	48230 TQ	AKBLS	10/01-12/01
	Anchorage MSA, AK	Y	30670 FQ	38100 AW	46320 TQ	AKBLS	10/01-12/01
	Arizona	Y	20360 FQ	31880 AW	47060 TQ	AZBLS	10/01-12/01
	Phoenix-Mesa MSA, AZ	Y	20900 FQ	32990 AW	48360 TQ	AZBLS	10/01-12/01
	Tucson MSA, AZ	Y	19970 FQ	30140 AW	44340 TQ	AZBLS	10/01-12/01
	Arkansas	Y	27180 FQ	37560 AW	55530 TQ	ARBLS	10/01-12/01
	Little Rock-North Little Rock MSA, AR	Y	27300 FQ	37110 AW	52650 TQ	ARBLS	10/01-12/01
	California	Y	19200 FQ	32400 AW	51020 TQ	CABLS	10/01-12/01
	Bakersfield MSA, CA	Y	24520 FQ	36000 AW	51870 TQ	CABLS	10/01-12/01
	Chico-Paradise MSA, CA	Y	15160 FQ	36310 AW	53580 TQ	CABLS	10/01-12/01
	Fresno MSA, CA	Y	24800 FQ	42600 AW	54990 TQ	CABLS	10/01-12/01
	Los Angeles-Long Beach PMSA, CA	Y	21150 FQ	32550 AW	52210 TQ	CABLS	10/01-12/01
	Oakland PMSA, CA	Y	19980 FQ	31730 AW	47430 TQ	CABLS	10/01-12/01
	Orange County PMSA, CA	Y	20500 FQ	33550 AW	53790 TQ	CABLS	10/01-12/01
	Riverside-San Bernardino PMSA, CA	Y	15170 FQ	21790 AW	28340 TQ	CABLS	10/01-12/01
	Sacramento PMSA, CA	Y	20380 FQ	41490 AW	62220 TQ	CABLS	10/01-12/01
	San Diego MSA, CA	Y	19370 FQ	31190 AW	48330 TQ	CABLS	10/01-12/01
	San Francisco PMSA, CA	Y	19260 FQ	28830 AW	38890 TQ	CABLS	10/01-12/01
	San Jose PMSA, CA	Y	33170 FQ	39280 AW	44330 TQ	CABLS	10/01-12/01
	Santa Barbara-Santa Maria-Lompoc MSA, CA	Y	19640 FQ	26580 AW	34810 TQ	CABLS	10/01-12/01
	Santa Cruz-Watsonville PMSA, CA	Y	19940 FQ	35230 AW	55270 TQ	CABLS	10/01-12/01
	Santa Rosa PMSA, CA	Y	20540 FQ	36720 AW	55100 TQ	CABLS	10/01-12/01
	Stockton-Lodi MSA, CA	Y	24830 FQ	32620 AW	43470 TQ	CABLS	10/01-12/01
	Vallejo-Fairfield-Napa PMSA, CA	Y	21780 FQ	50950 AW	70140 TQ	CABLS	10/01-12/01
	Colorado	Y	20230 FQ	32020 AW	50940 TQ	COBLS	10/01-12/01
	Boulder-Longmont PMSA, CO	Y	20950 FQ	37250 AW	60650 TQ	COBLS	10/01-12/01
	Colorado Springs MSA, CO	Y	25100 FQ	43970 AW	56980 TQ	COBLS	10/01-12/01
	Denver PMSA, CO	Y	20080 FQ	27650 AW	36560 TQ	COBLS	10/01-12/01
	Fort Collins-Loveland MSA, CO	Y	18850 FQ	28910 AW	44760 TQ	COBLS	10/01-12/01
	Greeley PMSA, CO	Y	24800 FQ	32580 AW	42720 TQ	COBLS	10/01-12/01
	Connecticut	Y	21050 FQ	33250 AW	51820 TQ	CTBLS	10/01-12/01
	Bridgeport PMSA, CT	Y	21860 FQ	32090 AW	46490 TQ	CTBLS	10/01-12/01
	Danbury PMSA, CT	Y	13900 FQ	27160 AW	35640 TQ	CTBLS	10/01-12/01
	Hartford MSA, CT	Y	20100 FQ	35370 AW	62090 TQ	CTBLS	10/01-12/01
	New Haven-Meriden PMSA, CT	Y	20350 FQ	34690 AW	55230 TQ	CTBLS	10/01-12/01
	New London-Norwich MSA, CT-RI	Y	20930 FQ	35360 AW	52620 TQ	CTBLS	10/01-12/01
	Stamford-Norwalk PMSA, CT	Y	23800 FQ	32120 AW	42550 TQ	CTBLS	10/01-12/01
	Waterbury PMSA, CT	Y	24990 FQ	34620 AW	44680 TQ	CTBLS	10/01-12/01
	Delaware	Y	19230 FQ	29660 AW	42890 TQ	DEBLS	10/01-12/01
	Wilmington-Newark PMSA, DE-MD	Y	18870 FQ	28540 AW	40970 TQ	DEBLS	10/01-12/01
	District of Columbia	Y	15490 FQ	34290 AW	70020 TQ	DCBLS	10/01-12/01
	Washington PMSA, DC-MD-VA-WV	Y	16400 FQ	33010 AW	57630 TQ	DCBLS	10/01-12/01
	Florida	Y	19990 FQ	31550 AW	50210 TQ	FLBLS	10/01-12/01
	Daytona Beach MSA, FL	Y	28310 FQ	32740 AW	39300 TQ	FLBLS	10/01-12/01

AAW	Average annual wage	**AOH**	Average offered, high	**ASH**	Average starting, high	**H**	Hourly	**M**	Monthly	**S**	Special: hourly and annual
AE	Average entry wage	**AOL**	Average offered, low	**ASL**	Average starting, low	**HI**	Highest wage paid	**MTC**	Median total compensation	**TQ**	Third quartile wage
AEX	Average experienced wage	**APH**	Average pay, high range	**AW**	Average wage paid	**HR**	High end range	**MW**	Median wage paid	**W**	Weekly
AO	Average offered	**APL**	Average pay, low range	**FQ**	First quartile wage	**LR**	Low end range	**SQ**	Second quartile wage	**Y**	Yearly

Occupation/Type/Industry	Location	Per	Low	Mid	High	Source	Date
Mental Health Counselor	Fort Lauderdale PMSA, FL	Y	21070 FQ	33370 AW	51890 TQ	FLBLS	10/01-12/01
	Fort Myers-Cape Coral MSA, FL	Y	24610 FQ	37840 AW	53660 TQ	FLBLS	10/01-12/01
	Fort Pierce-Port St. Lucie MSA, FL	Y	20940 FQ	29620 AW	49510 TQ	FLBLS	10/01-12/01
	Gainesville MSA, FL	Y	19130 FQ	35140 AW	55380 TQ	FLBLS	10/01-12/01
	Jacksonville MSA, FL	Y	20690 FQ	29420 AW	40440 TQ	FLBLS	10/01-12/01
	Lakeland-Winter Haven MSA, FL	Y	25610 FQ	41380 AW	55410 TQ	FLBLS	10/01-12/01
	Melbourne-Titusville-Palm Bay MSA, FL	Y	23980 FQ	36700 AW	58600 TQ	FLBLS	10/01-12/01
	Miami PMSA, FL	Y	23840 FQ	34470 AW	52590 TQ	FLBLS	10/01-12/01
	Naples MSA, FL	Y	22620 FQ	33490 AW	46000 TQ	FLBLS	10/01-12/01
	Orlando MSA, FL	Y	19480 FQ	29990 AW	47070 TQ	FLBLS	10/01-12/01
	Sarasota-Bradenton MSA, FL	Y	19790 FQ	29860 AW	43590 TQ	FLBLS	10/01-12/01
	Tallahassee MSA, FL	Y	23320 FQ	32700 AW	61460 TQ	FLBLS	10/01-12/01
	Tampa-St. Petersburg-Clearwater MSA, FL	Y	19860 FQ	28470 AW	45260 TQ	FLBLS	10/01-12/01
	West Palm Beach-Boca Raton MSA, FL	Y	11580 FQ	27340 AW	46640 TQ	FLBLS	10/01-12/01
	Georgia	Y	20730 FQ	36370 AW	58760 TQ	GABLS	10/01-12/01
	Atlanta MSA, GA	Y	20770 FQ	38240 AW	63730 TQ	GABLS	10/01-12/01
	Augusta-Aiken MSA, GA-SC	Y	16030 FQ	29730 AW	55520 TQ	GABLS	10/01-12/01
	Hawaii	Y	17380 FQ	30710 AW	45060 TQ	HIBLS	10/01-12/01
	Honolulu MSA, HI	Y	17040 FQ	30520 AW	44320 TQ	HIBLS	10/01-12/01
	Idaho	Y	23430 FQ	38080 AW	53240 TQ	IDBLS	10/01-12/01
	Boise City MSA, ID	Y	26300 FQ	37550 AW	50610 TQ	IDBLS	10/01-12/01
	Illinois	Y	20010 FQ	29670 AW	41620 TQ	ILBLS	10/01-12/01
	Champaign-Urbana MSA, IL	Y	23810 FQ	30100 AW	42140 TQ	ILBLS	10/01-12/01
	Chicago PMSA, IL	Y	20100 FQ	29200 AW	40590 TQ	ILBLS	10/01-12/01
	Peoria-Pekin MSA, IL	Y	21840 FQ	32500 AW	44060 TQ	ILBLS	10/01-12/01
	Rockford MSA, IL	Y	20710 FQ	30320 AW	43380 TQ	ILBLS	10/01-12/01
	Springfield MSA, IL	Y	22600 FQ	27640 AW	35630 TQ	ILBLS	10/01-12/01
	Indiana	Y	17320 FQ	26600 AW	37180 TQ	INBLS	10/01-12/01
	Evansville-Henderson MSA, IN-KY	Y	16050 FQ	22430 AW	34030 TQ	INBLS	10/01-12/01
	Fort Wayne MSA, IN	Y	17500 FQ	28330 AW	37380 TQ	INBLS	10/01-12/01
	Gary PMSA, IN	Y	19090 FQ	24910 AW	35910 TQ	INBLS	10/01-12/01
	Indianapolis MSA, IN	Y	20890 FQ	29000 AW	40460 TQ	INBLS	10/01-12/01
	South Bend MSA, IN	Y	15260 FQ	22960 AW	34330 TQ	INBLS	10/01-12/01
	Iowa	Y	15240 FQ	30210 AW	49280 TQ	IABLS	10/01-12/01
	Davenport-Moline-Rock Island MSA, IA-IL	Y	15840 FQ	19800 AW	27570 TQ	IABLS	10/01-12/01
	Des Moines MSA, IA	Y	16180 FQ	24840 AW	40440 TQ	IABLS	10/01-12/01
	Kansas	Y	19950 FQ	30360 AW	44280 TQ	KSBLS	10/01-12/01
	Topeka MSA, KS	Y	19280 FQ	26260 AW	34930 TQ	KSBLS	10/01-12/01
	Kentucky	Y	16740 FQ	27870 AW	40640 TQ	KYBLS	10/01-12/01
	Lexington MSA, KY	Y	14970 FQ	24590 AW	38120 TQ	KYBLS	10/01-12/01
	Louisville MSA, KY-IN	Y	19390 FQ	28510 AW	41950 TQ	KYBLS	10/01-12/01
	Louisiana	Y	16850 FQ	32370 AW	51590 TQ	LABLS	10/01-12/01
	Baton Rouge MSA, LA	Y	19640 FQ	34150 AW	49950 TQ	LABLS	10/01-12/01
	Houma MSA, LA	Y	24580 FQ	36050 AW	45960 TQ	LABLS	10/01-12/01
	Lafayette MSA, LA	Y	23160 FQ	48390 AW	68510 TQ	LABLS	10/01-12/01
	Lake Charles MSA, LA	Y	25930 FQ	35390 AW	48920 TQ	LABLS	10/01-12/01
	New Orleans MSA, LA	Y	16950 FQ	30330 AW	50020 TQ	LABLS	10/01-12/01
	Shreveport-Bossier City MSA, LA	Y	23240 FQ	34470 AW	47010 TQ	LABLS	10/01-12/01
	Maine	Y	19800 FQ	32830 AW	45230 TQ	MEBLS	10/01-12/01
	Maryland	Y	20640 FQ	31570 AW	47390 TQ	MDBLS	10/01-12/01
	Baltimore PMSA, MD	Y	24840 FQ	33510 AW	47710 TQ	MDBLS	10/01-12/01
	Massachusetts	Y	20540 FQ	36390 AW	61570 TQ	MABLS	10/01-12/01
	Boston PMSA, MA-NH	Y	20860 FQ	36380 AW	62520 TQ	MABLS	10/01-12/01
	Brockton PMSA, MA	Y	20860 FQ	41850 AW	55650 TQ	MABLS	10/01-12/01
	Lawrence PMSA, MA-NH	Y	20320 FQ	34180 AW	56280 TQ	MABLS	10/01-12/01
	Lowell PMSA, MA-NH	Y	24190 FQ	39450 AW	55830 TQ	MABLS	10/01-12/01
	Springfield MSA, MA	Y	20690 FQ	37770 AW	65740 TQ	MABLS	10/01-12/01
	Worcester PMSA, MA-CT	Y	19240 FQ	24590 AW	32250 TQ	MABLS	10/01-12/01
	Michigan	Y	24890 FQ	36840 AW	51580 TQ	MIBLS	10/01-12/01
	Ann Arbor PMSA, MI	Y	22560 FQ	41960 AW	65760 TQ	MIBLS	10/01-12/01
	Detroit PMSA, MI	Y	25170 FQ	34390 AW	46590 TQ	MIBLS	10/01-12/01
	Flint PMSA, MI	Y	27190 FQ	38930 AW	45480 TQ	MIBLS	10/01-12/01

AAW Average annual wage; **AE** Average entry wage; **AEX** Average experienced wage; **AO** Average offered; **AOH** Average offered, high; **AOL** Average offered, low; **APH** Average pay, high range; **APL** Average pay, low range; **ASH** Average starting, high; **ASL** Average starting, low; **AW** Average wage paid; **FQ** First quartile wage; **H** Hourly; **HI** Highest wage paid; **HR** High end range; **LR** Low end range; **M** Monthly; **MTC** Median total compensation; **MW** Median wage paid; **SQ** Second quartile wage; **S** Special: hourly and annual; **TQ** Third quartile wage; **W** Weekly; **Y** Yearly

Occupation/Type/Industry	Location	Per	Low	Mid	High	Source	Date
Mental Health Counselor	Grand Rapids-Muskegon-Holland MSA, MI	Y	26630 FQ	35350 AW	51320 TQ	MIBLS	10/01-12/01
	Kalamazoo-Battle Creek MSA, MI	Y	24890 FQ	35390 AW	50910 TQ	MIBLS	10/01-12/01
	Lansing-East Lansing MSA, MI	Y	23450 FQ	36840 AW	55440 TQ	MIBLS	10/01-12/01
	Saginaw-Bay City-Midland MSA, MI	Y	25230 FQ	42250 AW	57550 TQ	MIBLS	10/01-12/01
	Minnesota	Y	21260 FQ	35220 AW	55290 TQ	MNBLS	10/01-12/01
	Minneapolis-St. Paul MSA, MN-WI	Y	25030 FQ	40490 AW	66510 TQ	MNBLS	10/01-12/01
	Mississippi	Y	13130 FQ	25640 AW	35770 TQ	MSBLS	10/01-12/01
	Jackson MSA, MS	Y	11870 FQ	19460 AW	29170 TQ	MSBLS	10/01-12/01
	Missouri	Y	23750 FQ	36450 AW	52820 TQ	MOBLS	10/01-12/01
	Kansas City MSA, MO-KS	Y	23340 FQ	32800 AW	45650 TQ	MOBLS	10/01-12/01
	St. Louis MSA, MO-IL	Y	24030 FQ	35200 AW	44960 TQ	MOBLS	10/01-12/01
	Montana	Y	18720 FQ	29950 AW	43200 TQ	MTBLS	10/01-12/01
	Billings MSA, MT	Y	16660 FQ	22400 AW	28140 TQ	MTBLS	10/01-12/01
	Nebraska	Y	23950 FQ	37430 AW	60140 TQ	NEBLS	10/01-12/01
	Omaha MSA, NE-IA	Y	24750 FQ	40070 AW	61830 TQ	NEBLS	10/01-12/01
	Nevada	Y	23920 FQ	38720 AW	54540 TQ	NVBLS	10/01-12/01
	Las Vegas MSA, NV-AZ	Y	23460 FQ	37660 AW	53230 TQ	NVBLS	10/01-12/01
	New Hampshire	Y	21140 FQ	34200 AW	46600 TQ	NHBLS	10/01-12/01
	Portsmouth-Rochester PMSA, NH-ME	Y	18380 FQ	25410 AW	37130 TQ	NHBLS	10/01-12/01
	New Jersey	Y	22840 FQ	33830 AW	48400 TQ	NJBLS	10/01-12/01
	Atlantic-Cape May PMSA, NJ	Y	25840 FQ	38990 AW	55920 TQ	NJBLS	10/01-12/01
	Bergen-Passaic PMSA, NJ	Y	22200 FQ	32670 AW	46680 TQ	NJBLS	10/01-12/01
	Middlesex-Somerset-Hunterdon PMSA, NJ	Y	23540 FQ	36480 AW	56920 TQ	NJBLS	10/01-12/01
	Monmouth-Ocean PMSA, NJ	Y	23050 FQ	32630 AW	47220 TQ	NJBLS	10/01-12/01
	Newark PMSA, NJ	Y	23050 FQ	35670 AW	51380 TQ	NJBLS	10/01-12/01
	Trenton PMSA, NJ	Y	23500 FQ	30610 AW	42440 TQ	NJBLS	10/01-12/01
	New Mexico	Y	24420 FQ	34770 AW	46640 TQ	NMBLS	10/01-12/01
	Albuquerque MSA, NM	Y	31480 FQ	42330 AW	55220 TQ	NMBLS	10/01-12/01
	New York	Y	19560 FQ	32680 AW	54730 TQ	NYBLS	10/01-12/01
	Albany-Schenectady-Troy MSA, NY	Y	17310 FQ	28890 AW	54590 TQ	NYBLS	10/01-12/01
	Buffalo-Niagara Falls MSA, NY	Y	20320 FQ	34970 AW	53820 TQ	NYBLS	10/01-12/01
	Dutchess County PMSA, NY	Y	21490 FQ	33990 AW	54340 TQ	NYBLS	10/01-12/01
	Nassau-Suffolk PMSA, NY	Y	19530 FQ	32740 AW	52970 TQ	NYBLS	10/01-12/01
	New York PMSA, NY	Y	19800 FQ	32360 AW	53970 TQ	NYBLS	10/01-12/01
	Rochester MSA, NY	Y	21860 FQ	34870 AW	48340 TQ	NYBLS	10/01-12/01
	Syracuse MSA, NY	Y	23490 FQ	38230 AW	65760 TQ	NYBLS	10/01-12/01
	North Carolina	Y	24490 FQ	34070 AW	45380 TQ	NCBLS	10/01-12/01
	Charlotte-Gastonia-Rock Hill MSA, NC-SC	Y	25900 FQ	31940 AW	39020 TQ	NCBLS	10/01-12/01
	Greensboro-Winston-Salem-High Point MSA, NC	Y	24760 FQ	33950 AW	44760 TQ	NCBLS	10/01-12/01
	Hickory-Morganton-Lenoir MSA, NC	Y	28160 FQ	35500 AW	45280 TQ	NCBLS	10/01-12/01
	Raleigh-Durham-Chapel Hill MSA, NC	Y	31020 FQ	41150 AW	52010 TQ	NCBLS	10/01-12/01
	Wilmington MSA, NC	Y	14510 FQ	18620 AW	30910 TQ	NCBLS	10/01-12/01
	North Dakota	Y	25120 FQ	35480 AW	47700 TQ	NDBLS	10/01-12/01
	Ohio	Y	23340 FQ	34920 AW	46250 TQ	OHBLS	10/01-12/01
	Akron PMSA, OH	Y	23410 FQ	35100 AW	45580 TQ	OHBLS	10/01-12/01
	Canton-Massillon MSA, OH	Y	20670 FQ	34560 AW	52190 TQ	OHBLS	10/01-12/01
	Cincinnati PMSA, OH-KY-IN	Y	23580 FQ	30640 AW	41320 TQ	OHBLS	10/01-12/01
	Cleveland-Lorain-Elyria PMSA, OH	Y	19470 FQ	33030 AW	45590 TQ	OHBLS	10/01-12/01
	Columbus MSA, OH	Y	29280 FQ	35680 AW	44270 TQ	OHBLS	10/01-12/01
	Mansfield MSA, OH	Y	25610 FQ	32930 AW	43060 TQ	OHBLS	10/01-12/01
	Toledo MSA, OH	Y	29800 FQ	38490 AW	45700 TQ	OHBLS	10/01-12/01
	Youngstown-Warren MSA, OH	Y	25700 FQ	37280 AW	55510 TQ	OHBLS	10/01-12/01
	Oklahoma	Y	19260 FQ	29480 AW	43010 TQ	OKBLS	10/01-12/01
	Oklahoma City MSA, OK	Y	18590 FQ	29500 AW	44930 TQ	OKBLS	10/01-12/01
	Tulsa MSA, OK	Y	17610 FQ	29480 AW	41720 TQ	OKBLS	10/01-12/01
	Oregon	Y	19720 FQ	33400 AW	50430 TQ	ORBLS	10/01-12/01
	Eugene-Springfield MSA, OR	Y	16520 FQ	22680 AW	32030 TQ	ORBLS	10/01-12/01
	Medford-Ashland MSA, OR	Y	17750 FQ	26490 AW	38520 TQ	ORBLS	10/01-12/01

AAW	Average annual wage	**AOH**	Average offered, high	**ASH**	Average starting, high	**H**	Hourly	**M**	Monthly	**S**	Special: hourly and annual
AE	Average entry wage	**AOL**	Average offered, low	**ASL**	Average starting, low	**HI**	Highest wage paid	**MTC**	Median total compensation	**TQ**	Third quartile wage
AEX	Average experienced wage	**APH**	Average pay, high range	**AW**	Average wage paid	**HR**	High end range	**MW**	Median wage paid	**W**	Weekly
AO	Average offered	**APL**	Average pay, low range	**FQ**	First quartile wage	**LR**	Low end range	**SQ**	Second quartile wage	**Y**	Yearly

Occupation/Type/Industry	Location	Per	Low	Mid	High	Source	Date
Mental Health Counselor	Portland-Vancouver PMSA, OR-WA	Y	24390 FQ	36210 AW	52510 TQ	ORBLS	10/01-12/01
	Salem PMSA, OR	Y	28340 FQ	39010 AW	50680 TQ	ORBLS	10/01-12/01
	Pennsylvania	Y	18330 FQ	26280 AW	39360 TQ	PABLS	10/01-12/01
	Harrisburg-Lebanon-Carlisle MSA, PA	Y	19330 FQ	24350 AW	32990 TQ	PABLS	10/01-12/01
	Philadelphia PMSA, PA-NJ	Y	19160 FQ	29230 AW	44310 TQ	PABLS	10/01-12/01
	Pittsburgh MSA, PA	Y	21230 FQ	31390 AW	44910 TQ	PABLS	10/01-12/01
	Reading MSA, PA	Y	15550 FQ	22650 AW	30350 TQ	PABLS	10/01-12/01
	Rhode Island	Y	21460 FQ	29400 AW	40780 TQ	RIBLS	10/01-12/01
	Providence-Fall River-Warwick MSA, RI-MA	Y	21170 FQ	30140 AW	44870 TQ	RIBLS	10/01-12/01
	South Carolina	Y	19850 FQ	26500 AW	34620 TQ	SCBLS	10/01-12/01
	South Dakota	Y	25150 FQ	33460 AW	44240 TQ	SDBLS	10/01-12/01
	Tennessee	Y	16350 FQ	25330 AW	35350 TQ	TNBLS	10/01-12/01
	Chattanooga MSA, TN-GA	Y	24060 FQ	32100 AW	40670 TQ	TNBLS	10/01-12/01
	Johnson City-Kingsport-Bristol MSA, TN-VA	Y	13100 FQ	22730 AW	34340 TQ	TNBLS	10/01-12/01
	Knoxville MSA, TN	Y	17870 FQ	22830 AW	28700 TQ	TNBLS	10/01-12/01
	Memphis MSA, TN-AR-MS	Y	17980 FQ	28630 AW	42000 TQ	TNBLS	10/01-12/01
	Nashville MSA, TN	Y	17060 FQ	24980 AW	34270 TQ	TNBLS	10/01-12/01
	Texas	Y	17930 FQ	33240 AW	50310 TQ	TXBLS	10/01-12/01
	Austin-San Marcos MSA, TX	Y	26010 FQ	39080 AW	54900 TQ	TXBLS	10/01-12/01
	Brazoria PMSA, TX	Y	15290 FQ	21230 AW	30780 TQ	TXBLS	10/01-12/01
	Corpus Christi MSA, TX	Y	25670 FQ	43920 AW	66500 TQ	TXBLS	10/01-12/01
	Dallas PMSA, TX	Y	19900 FQ	30360 AW	45650 TQ	TXBLS	10/01-12/01
	Fort Worth-Arlington PMSA, TX	Y	20030 FQ	33420 AW	43870 TQ	TXBLS	10/01-12/01
	Houston PMSA, TX	Y	29310 FQ	37810 AW	46480 TQ	TXBLS	10/01-12/01
	Killeen-Temple MSA, TX	Y	31490 FQ	36640 AW	44380 TQ	TXBLS	10/01-12/01
	McAllen-Edinburg-Mission MSA, TX	Y	24650 FQ	43260 AW	67460 TQ	TXBLS	10/01-12/01
	San Antonio MSA, TX	Y	16030 FQ	26450 AW	42460 TQ	TXBLS	10/01-12/01
	Utah	Y	17740 FQ	30090 AW	54050 TQ	UTBLS	10/01-12/01
	Salt Lake City-Ogden MSA, UT	Y	18360 FQ	31240 AW	55390 TQ	UTBLS	10/01-12/01
	Vermont	Y	24450 FQ	36760 AW	55790 TQ	VTBLS	10/01-12/01
	Virginia	Y	16080 FQ	29830 AW	48180 TQ	VABLS	10/01-12/01
	Lynchburg MSA, VA	Y	17910 FQ	26170 AW	37280 TQ	VABLS	10/01-12/01
	Richmond-Petersburg MSA, VA	Y	30810 FQ	42910 AW	58790 TQ	VABLS	10/01-12/01
	Washington	Y	25500 FQ	36400 AW	47910 TQ	WABLS	10/01-12/01
	Olympia PMSA, WA	Y	28210 FQ	35630 AW	43520 TQ	WABLS	10/01-12/01
	Richland-Kennewick-Pasco MSA, WA	Y	26270 FQ	36520 AW	47560 TQ	WABLS	10/01-12/01
	Seattle-Bellevue-Everett PMSA, WA	Y	26000 FQ	38080 AW	51900 TQ	WABLS	10/01-12/01
	Spokane MSA, WA	Y	29250 FQ	37650 AW	46080 TQ	WABLS	10/01-12/01
	Tacoma PMSA, WA	Y	24240 FQ	33010 AW	43440 TQ	WABLS	10/01-12/01
	West Virginia	Y	13110 FQ	25880 AW	42260 TQ	WVBLS	10/01-12/01
	Charleston MSA, WV	Y	24520 FQ	31740 AW	37310 TQ	WVBLS	10/01-12/01
	Huntington-Ashland MSA, WV-KY-OH	Y	14980 FQ	26300 AW	36220 TQ	WVBLS	10/01-12/01
	Wisconsin	Y	25440 FQ	49220 AW	90000 TQ	WIBLS	10/01-12/01
	Appleton-Oshkosh-Neenah MSA, WI	Y	27630 FQ	46270 AW	66700 TQ	WIBLS	10/01-12/01
	Madison MSA, WI	Y	24110 FQ	31800 AW	51750 TQ	WIBLS	10/01-12/01
	Milwaukee-Waukesha PMSA, WI	Y	27400 FQ	62030 AW	94950 TQ	WIBLS	10/01-12/01
	Wyoming	Y	25540 FQ	36720 AW	52090 TQ	WYBLS	10/01-12/01
	Puerto Rico	Y	12610 FQ	17430 AW	22120 TQ	PRBLS	10/01-12/01
Merchandise Displayer and Window Trimmer	Alabama	Y	14090 FQ	25240 AW	40070 TQ	ALBLS	10/01-12/01
	Alaska	Y	14700 FQ	24780 AW	36780 TQ	AKBLS	10/01-12/01
	Arizona	Y	12630 FQ	21230 AW	34690 TQ	AZBLS	10/01-12/01
	Arkansas	Y	13250 FQ	24700 AW	40810 TQ	ARBLS	10/01-12/01
	California	Y	14310 FQ	24240 AW	37480 TQ	CABLS	10/01-12/01
	Colorado	Y	15510 FQ	25010 AW	36220 TQ	COBLS	10/01-12/01
	Connecticut	Y	18340 FQ	27930 AW	37420 TQ	CTBLS	10/01-12/01
	Delaware	Y	17330 FQ	25160 AW	36730 TQ	DEBLS	10/01-12/01
	Florida	Y	15340 FQ	22700 AW	32620 TQ	FLBLS	10/01-12/01

AAW	Average annual wage	AOH	Average offered, high	ASH	Average starting, high	H	Hourly	M	Monthly	S	Special: hourly and annual
AE	Average entry wage	AOL	Average offered, low	ASL	Average starting, low	HI	Highest wage paid	MTC	Median total compensation	TQ	Third quartile wage
AEX	Average experienced wage	APH	Average pay, high range	AW	Average wage paid	HR	High end range	MW	Median wage paid	W	Weekly
AO	Average offered	APL	Average pay, low range	FQ	First quartile wage	LR	Low end range	SQ	Second quartile wage	Y	Yearly

Occupation/Type/Industry	Location	Per	Low	Mid	High	Source	Date
Merchandise Displayer and Window Trimmer							
	Georgia	Y	13550 FQ	23660 AW	35530 TQ	GABLS	10/01-12/01
	Hawaii	Y	15100 FQ	26950 AW	48720 TQ	HIBLS	10/01-12/01
	Idaho	Y	15540 FQ	22270 AW	37320 TQ	IDBLS	10/01-12/01
	Illinois	Y	17570 FQ	25340 AW	38050 TQ	ILBLS	10/01-12/01
	Indiana	Y	16220 FQ	23120 AW	30230 TQ	INBLS	10/01-12/01
	Kansas	Y	13680 FQ	21560 AW	28430 TQ	KSBLS	10/01-12/01
	Kentucky	Y	14000 FQ	21790 AW	29930 TQ	KYBLS	10/01-12/01
	Louisiana	Y	15280 FQ	22560 AW	31060 TQ	LABLS	10/01-12/01
	Maine	Y	13120 FQ	19030 AW	28410 TQ	MEBLS	10/01-12/01
	Maryland	Y	15680 FQ	25870 AW	35690 TQ	MDBLS	10/01-12/01
	Massachusetts	Y	15570 FQ	26120 AW	42440 TQ	MABLS	10/01-12/01
	Michigan	Y	15820 FQ	24510 AW	36010 TQ	MIBLS	10/01-12/01
	Minnesota	Y	15350 FQ	23370 AW	35780 TQ	MNBLS	10/01-12/01
	Mississippi	Y	12510 FQ	19280 AW	27370 TQ	MSBLS	10/01-12/01
	Missouri	Y	13430 FQ	21930 AW	34330 TQ	MOBLS	10/01-12/01
	Montana	Y	12860 FQ	19780 AW	26610 TQ	MTBLS	10/01-12/01
	Nebraska	Y	14860 FQ	21900 AW	32140 TQ	NEBLS	10/01-12/01
	Nevada	Y	15680 FQ	22360 AW	29100 TQ	NVBLS	10/01-12/01
	New Hampshire	Y	17420 FQ	28740 AW	45730 TQ	NHBLS	10/01-12/01
	New Jersey	Y	17870 FQ	28180 AW	47740 TQ	NJBLS	10/01-12/01
	New Mexico	Y	12780 FQ	19550 AW	29580 TQ	NMBLS	10/01-12/01
	New York	Y	17730 FQ	36790 AW	69950 TQ	NYBLS	10/01-12/01
	North Carolina	Y	15130 FQ	23670 AW	36510 TQ	NCBLS	10/01-12/01
	North Dakota	Y	13470 FQ	18090 AW	24140 TQ	NDBLS	10/01-12/01
	Ohio	Y	16250 FQ	25350 AW	36100 TQ	OHBLS	10/01-12/01
	Oklahoma	Y	14840 FQ	24890 AW	40380 TQ	OKBLS	10/01-12/01
	Oregon	Y	15720 FQ	25140 AW	38270 TQ	ORBLS	10/01-12/01
	Pennsylvania	Y	14370 FQ	25100 AW	38200 TQ	PABLS	10/01-12/01
	Rhode Island	Y	17350 FQ	29170 AW	49330 TQ	RIBLS	10/01-12/01
	South Carolina	Y	15290 FQ	22830 AW	34290 TQ	SCBLS	10/01-12/01
	South Dakota	Y	15320 FQ	18880 AW	23250 TQ	SDBLS	10/01-12/01
	Tennessee	Y	12050 FQ	18810 AW	28660 TQ	TNBLS	10/01-12/01
	Texas	Y	13190 FQ	24580 AW	41400 TQ	TXBLS	10/01-12/01
	Utah	Y	14660 FQ	22110 AW	35920 TQ	UTBLS	10/01-12/01
	Vermont	Y	13320 FQ	19380 AW	28070 TQ	VTBLS	10/01-12/01
	Virginia	Y	16020 FQ	24220 AW	33450 TQ	VABLS	10/01-12/01
	Washington	Y	16670 FQ	25800 AW	36350 TQ	WABLS	10/01-12/01
	West Virginia	Y	12150 FQ	17980 AW	26980 TQ	WVBLS	10/01-12/01
	Wisconsin	Y	15460 FQ	22810 AW	32000 TQ	WIBLS	10/01-12/01
	Puerto Rico	Y	11790 FQ	16220 AW	21810 TQ	PRBLS	10/01-12/01
	Virgin Islands	Y	14330 FQ	17460 AW	21900 TQ	VIBLS	10/01-12/01
Metal-Refining Furnace Operator and Tender							
	Alabama	H	10.28 FQ	14.80 AW	20.00 TQ	ALBLS	10/01-12/01
	Arizona	H	9.85 FQ	14.82 AW	20.64 TQ	AZBLS	10/01-12/01
	Arkansas	H	10.00 FQ	15.03 AW	22.46 TQ	ARBLS	10/01-12/01
	California	H	8.42 FQ	12.66 AW	18.60 TQ	CABLS	10/01-12/01
	Connecticut	H	9.91 FQ	15.21 AW	20.69 TQ	CTBLS	10/01-12/01
	Florida	H	8.64 FQ	11.38 AW	14.66 TQ	FLBLS	10/01-12/01
	Georgia	H	9.36 FQ	12.35 AW	15.23 TQ	GABLS	10/01-12/01
	Illinois	H	9.11 FQ	13.15 AW	16.93 TQ	ILBLS	10/01-12/01
	Indiana	H	11.11 FQ	16.86 AW	23.64 TQ	INBLS	10/01-12/01
	Iowa	H	9.55 FQ	12.80 AW	16.99 TQ	IABLS	10/01-12/01
	Kentucky	H	10.58 FQ	14.13 AW	19.07 TQ	KYBLS	10/01-12/01
	Maine	H	9.66 FQ	14.23 AW	20.67 TQ	MEBLS	10/01-12/01
	Maryland	H	12.08 FQ	16.91 AW	21.12 TQ	MDBLS	10/01-12/01
	Massachusetts	H	11.82 FQ	16.37 AW	21.27 TQ	MABLS	10/01-12/01
	Michigan	H	10.60 FQ	15.30 AW	21.46 TQ	MIBLS	10/01-12/01
	Minnesota	H	11.77 FQ	16.54 AW	21.34 TQ	MNBLS	10/01-12/01
	Mississippi	H	10.25 FQ	13.06 AW	16.24 TQ	MSBLS	10/01-12/01
	Missouri	H	10.21 FQ	14.21 AW	17.51 TQ	MOBLS	10/01-12/01
	Montana	H	8.31 FQ	12.64 AW	16.96 TQ	MTBLS	10/01-12/01
	Nebraska	H	9.66 FQ	12.28 AW	14.28 TQ	NEBLS	10/01-12/01
	New Jersey	H	11.43 FQ	16.46 AW	21.70 TQ	NJBLS	10/01-12/01
	New York	H	8.97 FQ	16.53 AW	24.81 TQ	NYBLS	10/01-12/01
	North Carolina	H	11.75 FQ	15.90 AW	20.84 TQ	NCBLS	10/01-12/01
	Ohio	H	10.76 FQ	16.02 AW	24.18 TQ	OHBLS	10/01-12/01
	Oklahoma	H	8.70 FQ	12.11 AW	17.09 TQ	OKBLS	10/01-12/01
	Oregon	H	9.38 FQ	15.50 AW	21.62 TQ	ORBLS	10/01-12/01
	Pennsylvania	H	11.22 FQ	15.49 AW	20.65 TQ	PABLS	10/01-12/01
	Rhode Island	H	9.49 FQ	14.95 AW	23.64 TQ	RIBLS	10/01-12/01

AAW Average annual wage, **AE** Average entry wage, **AEX** Average experienced wage, **AO** Average offered, **AOH** Average offered, high, **AOL** Average offered, low, **APH** Average pay, high range, **APL** Average pay, low range, **ASH** Average starting, high, **ASL** Average starting, low, **AW** Average wage paid, **FQ** First quartile wage, **H** Hourly, **HI** Highest wage paid, **HR** High end range, **LR** Low end range, **M** Monthly, **MTC** Median total compensation, **MW** Median wage paid, **SQ** Second quartile wage, **S** Special: hourly and annual, **TQ** Third quartile wage, **W** Weekly, **Y** Yearly

Occupation/Type/Industry	Location	Per	Low	Mid	High	Source	Date
Metal-Refining Furnace Operator and Tender	South Carolina	H	9.13 FQ	13.00 AW	18.64 TQ	SCBLS	10/01-12/01
	Tennessee	H	9.68 FQ	12.54 AW	15.85 TQ	TNBLS	10/01-12/01
	Texas	H	7.31 FQ	11.83 AW	16.50 TQ	TXBLS	10/01-12/01
	Utah	H	10.01 FQ	15.35 AW	22.04 TQ	UTBLS	10/01-12/01
	Virginia	H	9.03 FQ	13.10 AW	17.27 TQ	VABLS	10/01-12/01
	Washington	H	13.19 FQ	17.66 AW	21.15 TQ	WABLS	10/01-12/01
	West Virginia	H	12.20 FQ	17.01 AW	21.14 TQ	WVBLS	10/01-12/01
	Wisconsin	H	11.58 FQ	15.83 AW	20.81 TQ	WIBLS	10/01-12/01
Metal Technician							
Automotive Body Shop	United States	Y		42059 AW		BSB	1/01-1/02
Automotive Body Shop	East North Central	Y		44508 AW		BSB	1/01-1/02
Automotive Body Shop	East South Central	Y		39750 AW		BSB	1/01-1/02
Automotive Body Shop	Middle Atlantic	Y		37561 AW		BSB	1/01-1/02
Automotive Body Shop	Mountain	Y		37200 AW		BSB	1/01-1/02
Automotive Body Shop	New England	Y		43350 AW		BSB	1/01-1/02
Automotive Body Shop	Pacific	Y		46571 AW		BSB	1/01-1/02
Automotive Body Shop	South Atlantic	Y		41463 AW		BSB	1/01-1/02
Automotive Body Shop	West North Central	Y		37682 AW		BSB	1/01-1/02
Automotive Body Shop	West South Central	Y		46847 AW		BSB	1/01-1/02
Meteorologist	United States	Y	17000 ASL		47000 ASH	AEAC	1/99-1/99
Meter Reader							
Utilities	Alabama	H	8.51 FQ	13.99 AW	21.11 TQ	ALBLS	10/01-12/01
Utilities	Birmingham MSA, AL	H	11.52 FQ	16.95 AW	21.74 TQ	ALBLS	10/01-12/01
Utilities	Mobile MSA, AL	H	7.79 FQ	12.53 AW	19.24 TQ	ALBLS	10/01-12/01
Utilities	Montgomery MSA, AL	H	8.58 FQ	12.12 AW	19.07 TQ	ALBLS	10/01-12/01
Utilities	Alaska	H	10.82 FQ	22.63 AW	34.65 TQ	AKBLS	10/01-12/01
Utilities	Arizona	H	11.36 FQ	16.11 AW	21.82 TQ	AZBLS	10/01-12/01
Utilities	Phoenix-Mesa MSA, AZ	H	12.51 FQ	17.16 AW	22.20 TQ	AZBLS	10/01-12/01
Utilities	Tucson MSA, AZ	H	7.96 FQ	12.76 AW	17.40 TQ	AZBLS	10/01-12/01
Utilities	Arkansas	H	6.07 FQ	10.40 AW	15.89 TQ	ARBLS	10/01-12/01
Utilities	Fayetteville-Springdale-Rogers MSA, AR	H	7.69 FQ	11.36 AW	19.68 TQ	ARBLS	10/01-12/01
Utilities	Fort Smith MSA, AR-OK	H	8.34 FQ	12.22 AW	16.64 TQ	ARBLS	10/01-12/01
Utilities	Little Rock-North Little Rock MSA, AR	H	6.90 FQ	11.39 AW	16.11 TQ	ARBLS	10/01-12/01
Utilities	California	H	11.81 FQ	18.56 AW	25.49 TQ	CABLS	10/01-12/01
Utilities	Bakersfield MSA, CA	H	13.85 FQ	19.44 AW	24.90 TQ	CABLS	10/01-12/01
Utilities	Chico-Paradise MSA, CA	H	14.17 FQ	19.09 AW	23.14 TQ	CABLS	10/01-12/01
Utilities	Fresno MSA, CA	H	15.53 FQ	20.18 AW	24.64 TQ	CABLS	10/01-12/01
Utilities	Merced MSA, CA	H	15.09 FQ	18.86 AW	22.73 TQ	CABLS	10/01-12/01
Utilities	Modesto MSA, CA	H	16.23 FQ	20.27 AW	23.66 TQ	CABLS	10/01-12/01
Utilities	Orange County PMSA, CA	H	13.26 FQ	17.48 AW	22.20 TQ	CABLS	10/01-12/01
Utilities	Riverside-San Bernardino PMSA, CA	H	13.79 FQ	18.66 AW	24.92 TQ	CABLS	10/01-12/01
Utilities	Sacramento PMSA, CA	H	11.54 FQ	16.72 AW	24.85 TQ	CABLS	10/01-12/01
Utilities	Salinas MSA, CA	H	9.82 FQ	20.68 AW	26.54 TQ	CABLS	10/01-12/01
Utilities	San Jose PMSA, CA	H	14.61 FQ	21.64 AW	27.30 TQ	CABLS	10/01-12/01
Utilities	Santa Barbara-Santa Maria-Lompoc MSA, CA	H	6.46 FQ	17.09 AW	23.20 TQ	CABLS	10/01-12/01
Utilities	Santa Cruz-Watsonville PMSA, CA	H	17.64 FQ	22.52 AW	26.65 TQ	CABLS	10/01-12/01
Utilities	Vallejo-Fairfield-Napa PMSA, CA	H	14.82 FQ	22.04 AW	26.84 TQ	CABLS	10/01-12/01
Utilities	Colorado	H	11.38 FQ	16.38 AW	23.14 TQ	COBLS	10/01-12/01
Utilities	Boulder-Longmont PMSA, CO	H	11.25 FQ	16.55 AW	22.93 TQ	COBLS	10/01-12/01
Utilities	Denver PMSA, CO	H	11.91 FQ	17.92 AW	25.78 TQ	COBLS	10/01-12/01
Utilities	Fort Collins-Loveland MSA, CO	H	9.71 FQ	14.98 AW	22.94 TQ	COBLS	10/01-12/01
Utilities	Connecticut	H	11.45 FQ	17.66 AW	24.82 TQ	CTBLS	10/01-12/01
Utilities	Bridgeport PMSA, CT	H	11.48 FQ	17.64 AW	25.25 TQ	CTBLS	10/01-12/01
Utilities	Hartford MSA, CT	H	10.86 FQ	16.75 AW	23.40 TQ	CTBLS	10/01-12/01
Utilities	New Haven-Meriden PMSA, CT	H	12.81 FQ	18.83 AW	26.22 TQ	CTBLS	10/01-12/01
Utilities	New London-Norwich MSA, CT-RI	H	15.06 FQ	19.20 AW	23.43 TQ	CTBLS	10/01-12/01
Utilities	Stamford-Norwalk PMSA, CT	H	11.10 FQ	17.72 AW	25.60 TQ	CTBLS	10/01-12/01
Utilities	Washington PMSA, DC-MD-VA-WV	H	11.79 FQ	17.18 AW	22.02 TQ	DCBLS	10/01-12/01

AAW	Average annual wage	**AOH**	Average offered, high	**ASH**	Average starting, high	**H**	Hourly	**M**	Monthly	**S**	Special: hourly and annual
AE	Average entry wage	**AOL**	Average offered, low	**ASL**	Average starting, low	**HI**	Highest wage paid	**MTC**	Median total compensation	**TQ**	Third quartile wage
AEX	Average experienced wage	**APH**	Average pay, high range	**AW**	Average wage paid	**HR**	High end range	**MW**	Median wage paid	**W**	Weekly
AO	Average offered	**APL**	Average pay, low range	**FQ**	First quartile wage	**LR**	Low end range	**SQ**	Second quartile wage	**Y**	Yearly

Occupation/Type/Industry	Location	Per	Low	Mid	High	Source	Date
Meter Reader							
Utilities	Florida	H	8.78 FQ	13.01 AW	18.96 TQ	FLBLS	10/01-12/01
Utilities	Daytona Beach MSA, FL	H	7.59 FQ	11.36 AW	16.68 TQ	FLBLS	10/01-12/01
Utilities	Fort Lauderdale PMSA, FL	H	10.03 FQ	13.47 AW	17.03 TQ	FLBLS	10/01-12/01
Utilities	Fort Walton Beach MSA, FL	H	8.08 FQ	12.50 AW	19.04 TQ	FLBLS	10/01-12/01
Utilities	Jacksonville MSA, FL	H	8.96 FQ	12.48 AW	18.83 TQ	FLBLS	10/01-12/01
Utilities	Lakeland-Winter Haven MSA, FL	H	8.03 FQ	11.36 AW	14.61 TQ	FLBLS	10/01-12/01
Utilities	Melbourne-Titusville-Palm Bay MSA, FL	H	9.67 FQ	11.88 AW	15.63 TQ	FLBLS	10/01-12/01
Utilities	Orlando MSA, FL	H	9.58 FQ	14.15 AW	21.21 TQ	FLBLS	10/01-12/01
Utilities	Pensacola MSA, FL	H	8.81 FQ	12.25 AW	18.94 TQ	FLBLS	10/01-12/01
Utilities	Sarasota-Bradenton MSA, FL	H	8.33 FQ	11.45 AW	16.78 TQ	FLBLS	10/01-12/01
Utilities	Tampa-St. Petersburg-Clearwater MSA, FL	H	9.27 FQ	14.87 AW	20.85 TQ	FLBLS	10/01-12/01
Utilities	West Palm Beach-Boca Raton MSA, FL	H	9.12 FQ	13.94 AW	19.51 TQ	FLBLS	10/01-12/01
Utilities	Georgia	H	8.60 FQ	12.62 AW	18.04 TQ	GABLS	10/01-12/01
Utilities	Atlanta MSA, GA	H	10.00 FQ	13.51 AW	19.23 TQ	GABLS	10/01-12/01
Utilities	Augusta-Aiken MSA, GA-SC	H	9.03 FQ	13.32 AW	20.25 TQ	GABLS	10/01-12/01
Utilities	Columbus MSA, GA-AL	H	7.40 FQ	13.32 AW	22.68 TQ	GABLS	10/01-12/01
Utilities	Macon MSA, GA	H	7.91 FQ	10.95 AW	14.38 TQ	GABLS	10/01-12/01
Utilities	Savannah MSA, GA	H	8.18 FQ	12.77 AW	18.31 TQ	GABLS	10/01-12/01
Utilities	Hawaii	H	10.44 FQ	15.88 AW	21.62 TQ	HIBLS	10/01-12/01
Utilities	Honolulu MSA, HI	H	10.72 FQ	17.34 AW	22.01 TQ	HIBLS	10/01-12/01
Utilities	Idaho	H	11.63 FQ	15.84 AW	20.74 TQ	IDBLS	10/01-12/01
Utilities	Boise City MSA, ID	H	11.81 FQ	16.17 AW	20.51 TQ	IDBLS	10/01-12/01
Utilities	Illinois	H	7.97 FQ	14.07 AW	20.18 TQ	ILBLS	10/01-12/01
Utilities	Chicago PMSA, IL	H	6.50 FQ	14.59 AW	21.26 TQ	ILBLS	10/01-12/01
Utilities	Peoria-Pekin MSA, IL	H	14.22 FQ	15.71 AW	17.64 TQ	ILBLS	10/01-12/01
Utilities	Rockford MSA, IL	H	6.19 FQ	11.82 AW	16.61 TQ	ILBLS	10/01-12/01
Utilities	Springfield MSA, IL	H	5.75 FQ	12.43 AW	21.09 TQ	ILBLS	10/01-12/01
Utilities	Indiana	H	6.22 FQ	12.39 AW	19.10 TQ	INBLS	10/01-12/01
Utilities	Elkhart-Goshen MSA, IN	H	7.59 FQ	12.95 AW	17.08 TQ	INBLS	10/01-12/01
Utilities	Evansville-Henderson MSA, IN-KY	H	6.05 FQ	11.57 AW	18.71 TQ	INBLS	10/01-12/01
Utilities	Gary PMSA, IN	H	6.43 FQ	10.29 AW	16.29 TQ	INBLS	10/01-12/01
Utilities	Indianapolis MSA, IN	H	10.28 FQ	16.14 AW	21.08 TQ	INBLS	10/01-12/01
Utilities	Iowa	H	6.17 FQ	11.80 AW	17.78 TQ	IABLS	10/01-12/01
Utilities	Davenport-Moline-Rock Island MSA, IA-IL	H	8.99 FQ	12.34 AW	17.07 TQ	IABLS	10/01-12/01
Utilities	Des Moines MSA, IA	H	5.71 FQ	11.04 AW	18.53 TQ	IABLS	10/01-12/01
Utilities	Kansas	H	6.14 FQ	12.38 AW	18.70 TQ	KSBLS	10/01-12/01
Utilities	Wichita MSA, KS	H	5.86 FQ	10.46 AW	15.06 TQ	KSBLS	10/01-12/01
Utilities	Kentucky	H	8.51 FQ	12.62 AW	18.27 TQ	KYBLS	10/01-12/01
Utilities	Lexington MSA, KY	H	9.03 FQ	13.04 AW	18.65 TQ	KYBLS	10/01-12/01
Utilities	Louisville MSA, KY-IN	H	8.64 FQ	14.29 AW	21.34 TQ	KYBLS	10/01-12/01
Utilities	Louisiana	H	6.89 FQ	10.61 AW	14.71 TQ	LABLS	10/01-12/01
Utilities	Baton Rouge MSA, LA	H	7.33 FQ	11.27 AW	15.82 TQ	LABLS	10/01-12/01
Utilities	Houma MSA, LA	H	7.32 FQ	10.77 AW	15.19 TQ	LABLS	10/01-12/01
Utilities	Lafayette MSA, LA	H	7.97 FQ	11.07 AW	15.40 TQ	LABLS	10/01-12/01
Utilities	Lake Charles MSA, LA	H	6.45 FQ	9.69 AW	13.54 TQ	LABLS	10/01-12/01
Utilities	New Orleans MSA, LA	H	7.11 FQ	10.77 AW	13.33 TQ	LABLS	10/01-12/01
Utilities	Shreveport-Bossier City MSA, LA	H	7.71 FQ	11.10 AW	13.36 TQ	LABLS	10/01-12/01
Utilities	Maine	H	9.40 FQ	13.38 AW	17.60 TQ	MEBLS	10/01-12/01
Utilities	Maryland	H	11.54 FQ	16.56 AW	22.02 TQ	MDBLS	10/01-12/01
Utilities	Baltimore PMSA, MD	H	11.91 FQ	16.58 AW	22.21 TQ	MDBLS	10/01-12/01
Utilities	Massachusetts	H	11.72 FQ	17.99 AW	25.59 TQ	MABLS	10/01-12/01
Utilities	Boston PMSA, MA-NH	H	11.73 FQ	18.41 AW	26.48 TQ	MABLS	10/01-12/01
Utilities	Lawrence PMSA, MA-NH	H	12.09 FQ	16.19 AW	20.65 TQ	MABLS	10/01-12/01
Utilities	Springfield MSA, MA	H	10.16 FQ	17.31 AW	24.85 TQ	MABLS	10/01-12/01
Utilities	Worcester PMSA, MA-CT	H	10.19 FQ	17.21 AW	23.43 TQ	MABLS	10/01-12/01
Utilities	Michigan	H	10.81 FQ	14.61 AW	20.33 TQ	MIBLS	10/01-12/01
Utilities	Ann Arbor PMSA, MI	H	10.12 FQ	13.60 AW	19.88 TQ	MIBLS	10/01-12/01
Utilities	Detroit PMSA, MI	H	11.24 FQ	14.79 AW	20.30 TQ	MIBLS	10/01-12/01
Utilities	Flint PMSA, MI	H	11.13 FQ	14.87 AW	19.99 TQ	MIBLS	10/01-12/01
Utilities	Grand Rapids-Muskegon-Holland MSA, MI	H	10.50 FQ	14.51 AW	19.81 TQ	MIBLS	10/01-12/01
Utilities	Kalamazoo-Battle Creek MSA, MI	H	11.42 FQ	15.11 AW	19.97 TQ	MIBLS	10/01-12/01
Utilities	Lansing-East Lansing MSA, MI	H	11.57 FQ	15.53 AW	20.76 TQ	MIBLS	10/01-12/01

AAW	Average annual wage	**AOH**	Average offered, high	**ASH**	Average starting, high	**H**	Hourly	**M**	Monthly	**S**	Special: hourly and annual
AE	Average entry wage	**AOL**	Average offered, low	**ASL**	Average starting, low	**HI**	Highest wage paid	**MTC**	Median total compensation	**TQ**	Third quartile wage
AEX	Average experienced wage	**APH**	Average pay, high range	**AW**	Average wage paid	**HR**	High end range	**MW**	Median wage paid	**W**	Weekly
AO	Average offered	**APL**	Average pay, low range	**FQ**	First quartile wage	**LR**	Low end range	**SQ**	Second quartile wage	**Y**	Yearly

Occupation/Type/Industry	Location	Per	Low	Mid	High	Source	Date
Meter Reader							
Utilities	Saginaw-Bay City-Midland MSA, MI	H	6.66 FQ	13.55 AW	20.02 TQ	MIBLS	10/01-12/01
Utilities	Minnesota	H	11.97 FQ	18.03 AW	25.97 TQ	MNBLS	10/01-12/01
Utilities	Duluth-Superior MSA, MN-WI	H	11.34 FQ	16.86 AW	21.54 TQ	MNBLS	10/01-12/01
Utilities	Minneapolis-St. Paul MSA, MN-WI	H	11.08 FQ	18.05 AW	26.59 TQ	MNBLS	10/01-12/01
Utilities	Mississippi	H	7.05 FQ	10.90 AW	16.60 TQ	MSBLS	10/01-12/01
Utilities	Biloxi-Gulfport-Pascagoula MSA, MS	H	7.96 FQ	13.96 AW	18.22 TQ	MSBLS	10/01-12/01
Utilities	Jackson MSA, MS	H	7.88 FQ	12.67 AW	17.56 TQ	MSBLS	10/01-12/01
Utilities	Missouri	H	9.76 FQ	14.55 AW	18.41 TQ	MOBLS	10/01-12/01
Utilities	Kansas City MSA, MO-KS	H	10.95 FQ	15.51 AW	20.37 TQ	MOBLS	10/01-12/01
Utilities	St. Louis MSA, MO-IL	H	10.96 FQ	14.76 AW	18.97 TQ	MOBLS	10/01-12/01
Utilities	Springfield MSA, MO	H	11.74 FQ	15.93 AW	18.33 TQ	MOBLS	10/01-12/01
Utilities	Montana	H	8.06 FQ	13.33 AW	18.55 TQ	MTBLS	10/01-12/01
Utilities	Billings MSA, MT	H	6.40 FQ	11.45 AW	17.50 TQ	MTBLS	10/01-12/01
Utilities	Nebraska	H	9.79 FQ	14.64 AW	20.53 TQ	NEBLS	10/01-12/01
Utilities	Lincoln MSA, NE	H	12.33 FQ	15.93 AW	20.58 TQ	NEBLS	10/01-12/01
Utilities	Omaha MSA, NE-IA	H	10.26 FQ	16.01 AW	21.71 TQ	NEBLS	10/01-12/01
Utilities	Nevada	H	11.73 FQ	17.30 AW	23.86 TQ	NVBLS	10/01-12/01
Utilities	Las Vegas MSA, NV-AZ	H	9.78 FQ	15.12 AW	21.19 TQ	NVBLS	10/01-12/01
Utilities	Reno MSA, NV	H	11.11 FQ	17.47 AW	24.96 TQ	NVBLS	10/01-12/01
Utilities	New Hampshire	H	9.67 FQ	15.87 AW	20.99 TQ	NHBLS	10/01-12/01
Utilities	Manchester PMSA, NH	H	14.16 FQ	16.67 AW	20.80 TQ	NHBLS	10/01-12/01
Utilities	Portsmouth-Rochester PMSA, NH-ME	H	9.35 FQ	15.26 AW	20.93 TQ	NHBLS	10/01-12/01
Utilities	New Jersey	H	14.69 FQ	21.68 AW	28.92 TQ	NJBLS	10/01-12/01
Utilities	Atlantic-Cape May PMSA, NJ	H	17.43 FQ	21.99 AW	27.61 TQ	NJBLS	10/01-12/01
Utilities	Bergen-Passaic PMSA, NJ	H	7.63 FQ	18.35 AW	27.76 TQ	NJBLS	10/01-12/01
Utilities	Middlesex-Somerset-Hunterdon PMSA, NJ	H	17.68 FQ	22.71 AW	28.23 TQ	NJBLS	10/01-12/01
Utilities	Monmouth-Ocean PMSA, NJ	H	14.79 FQ	21.85 AW	31.11 TQ	NJBLS	10/01-12/01
Utilities	Newark PMSA, NJ	H	15.22 FQ	22.34 AW	31.71 TQ	NJBLS	10/01-12/01
Utilities	Trenton PMSA, NJ	H	15.37 FQ	21.65 AW	28.70 TQ	NJBLS	10/01-12/01
Utilities	New Mexico	H	7.37 FQ	12.24 AW	19.85 TQ	NMBLS	10/01-12/01
Utilities	Albuquerque MSA, NM	H	8.76 FQ	15.74 AW	22.30 TQ	NMBLS	10/01-12/01
Utilities	Las Cruces MSA, NM	H	9.02 FQ	10.76 AW	13.87 TQ	NMBLS	10/01-12/01
Utilities	New York	H	9.94 FQ	16.97 AW	25.31 TQ	NYBLS	10/01-12/01
Utilities	Buffalo-Niagara Falls MSA, NY	H	8.55 FQ	15.63 AW	22.98 TQ	NYBLS	10/01-12/01
Utilities	Nassau-Suffolk PMSA, NY	H	17.03 FQ	22.13 AW	27.66 TQ	NYBLS	10/01-12/01
Utilities	New York PMSA, NY	H	9.21 FQ	14.78 AW	23.38 TQ	NYBLS	10/01-12/01
Utilities	Rochester MSA, NY	H	10.28 FQ	15.68 AW	21.34 TQ	NYBLS	10/01-12/01
Utilities	Syracuse MSA, NY	H	11.44 FQ	16.66 AW	24.38 TQ	NYBLS	10/01-12/01
Utilities	North Carolina	H	9.02 FQ	11.70 AW	16.46 TQ	NCBLS	10/01-12/01
Utilities	Charlotte-Gastonia-Rock Hill MSA, NC-SC	H	9.46 FQ	12.74 AW	17.40 TQ	NCBLS	10/01-12/01
Utilities	Fayetteville MSA, NC	H	9.33 FQ	12.45 AW	16.63 TQ	NCBLS	10/01-12/01
Utilities	Hickory-Morganton-Lenoir MSA, NC	H	8.87 FQ	11.59 AW	16.70 TQ	NCBLS	10/01-12/01
Utilities	Raleigh-Durham-Chapel Hill MSA, NC	H	9.11 FQ	11.72 AW	17.31 TQ	NCBLS	10/01-12/01
Utilities	Wilmington MSA, NC	H	7.74 FQ	12.02 AW	20.42 TQ	NCBLS	10/01-12/01
Utilities	North Dakota	H	9.30 FQ	14.67 AW	23.45 TQ	NDBLS	10/01-12/01
Utilities	Fargo-Moorhead MSA, ND-MN	H	11.98 FQ	19.02 AW	26.49 TQ	NDBLS	10/01-12/01
Utilities	Ohio	H	9.34 FQ	14.92 AW	21.14 TQ	OHBLS	10/01-12/01
Utilities	Akron PMSA, OH	H	11.07 FQ	15.50 AW	22.26 TQ	OHBLS	10/01-12/01
Utilities	Canton-Massillon MSA, OH	H	10.73 FQ	14.57 AW	19.89 TQ	OHBLS	10/01-12/01
Utilities	Cincinnati PMSA, OH-KY-IN	H	9.45 FQ	14.74 AW	20.91 TQ	OHBLS	10/01-12/01
Utilities	Cleveland-Lorain-Elyria PMSA, OH	H	10.22 FQ	15.60 AW	20.88 TQ	OHBLS	10/01-12/01
Utilities	Columbus MSA, OH	H	10.27 FQ	14.81 AW	18.32 TQ	OHBLS	10/01-12/01
Utilities	Hamilton-Middletown PMSA, OH	H	11.35 FQ	15.12 AW	21.59 TQ	OHBLS	10/01-12/01
Utilities	Mansfield MSA, OH	H	10.23 FQ	14.20 AW	17.70 TQ	OHBLS	10/01-12/01
Utilities	Oklahoma	H	6.71 FQ	10.43 AW	15.00 TQ	OKBLS	10/01-12/01
Utilities	Oklahoma City MSA, OK	H	7.03 FQ	11.18 AW	15.74 TQ	OKBLS	10/01-12/01
Utilities	Tulsa MSA, OK	H	9.33 FQ	12.20 AW	17.98 TQ	OKBLS	10/01-12/01
Utilities	Oregon	H	11.63 FQ	15.74 AW	20.33 TQ	ORBLS	10/01-12/01
Utilities	Eugene-Springfield MSA, OR	H	12.43 FQ	15.47 AW	18.18 TQ	ORBLS	10/01-12/01

AAW Average annual wage; **AE** Average entry wage; **AEX** Average experienced wage; **AO** Average offered; **AOH** Average offered, high; **AOL** Average offered, low; **APH** Average pay, high range; **APL** Average pay, low range; **ASH** Average starting, high; **ASL** Average starting, low; **AW** Average wage paid; **FQ** First quartile wage; **H** Hourly; **HI** Highest wage paid; **HR** High end range; **LR** Low end range; **M** Monthly; **MTC** Median total compensation; **MW** Median wage paid; **SQ** Second quartile wage; **S** Special: hourly and annual; **TQ** Third quartile wage; **W** Weekly; **Y** Yearly

Occupation/Type/Industry	Location	Per	Low	Mid	High	Source	Date
Meter Reader							
Utilities	Medford-Ashland MSA, OR	H	9.61 FQ	14.54 AW	18.50 TQ	ORBLS	10/01-12/01
Utilities	Portland-Vancouver PMSA, OR-WA	H	11.82 FQ	15.55 AW	19.67 TQ	ORBLS	10/01-12/01
Utilities	Salem PMSA, OR	H	11.51 FQ	15.38 AW	20.91 TQ	ORBLS	10/01-12/01
Utilities	Pennsylvania	H	12.57 FQ	18.58 AW	25.33 TQ	PABLS	10/01-12/01
Utilities	Allentown-Bethlehem-Easton MSA, PA	H	15.67 FQ	20.81 AW	26.83 TQ	PABLS	10/01-12/01
Utilities	Erie MSA, PA	H	9.07 FQ	16.85 AW	25.44 TQ	PABLS	10/01-12/01
Utilities	Harrisburg-Lebanon-Carlisle MSA, PA	H	13.10 FQ	19.70 AW	26.37 TQ	PABLS	10/01-12/01
Utilities	Johnstown MSA, PA	H	6.80 FQ	19.36 AW	26.36 TQ	PABLS	10/01-12/01
Utilities	Philadelphia PMSA, PA-NJ	H	14.34 FQ	18.86 AW	24.08 TQ	PABLS	10/01-12/01
Utilities	Pittsburgh MSA, PA	H	9.74 FQ	15.95 AW	22.70 TQ	PABLS	10/01-12/01
Utilities	Reading MSA, PA	H	17.89 FQ	20.90 AW	25.80 TQ	PABLS	10/01-12/01
Utilities	Scranton-Wilkes-Barre-Hazleton MSA, PA	H	16.80 FQ	20.53 AW	24.63 TQ	PABLS	10/01-12/01
Utilities	York MSA, PA	H	11.86 FQ	17.53 AW	21.57 TQ	PABLS	10/01-12/01
Utilities	Rhode Island	H	8.67 FQ	15.28 AW	23.06 TQ	RIBLS	10/01-12/01
Utilities	Providence-Fall River-Warwick MSA, RI-MA	H	9.17 FQ	15.69 AW	22.32 TQ	RIBLS	10/01-12/01
Utilities	South Carolina	H	9.30 FQ	13.06 AW	17.46 TQ	SCBLS	10/01-12/01
Utilities	Charleston-North Charleston MSA, SC	H	9.73 FQ	14.25 AW	16.88 TQ	SCBLS	10/01-12/01
Utilities	Greenville-Spartanburg-Anderson MSA, SC	H	10.48 FQ	14.24 AW	19.61 TQ	SCBLS	10/01-12/01
Utilities	Myrtle Beach MSA, SC	H	9.48 FQ	11.71 AW	15.38 TQ	SCBLS	10/01-12/01
Utilities	South Dakota	H	7.90 FQ	12.40 AW	17.63 TQ	SDBLS	10/01-12/01
Utilities	Tennessee	H	7.81 FQ	13.86 AW	21.06 TQ	TNBLS	10/01-12/01
Utilities	Chattanooga MSA, TN-GA	H	6.46 FQ	13.33 AW	19.71 TQ	TNBLS	10/01-12/01
Utilities	Johnson City-Kingsport-Bristol MSA, TN-VA	H	8.19 FQ	11.84 AW	16.68 TQ	TNBLS	10/01-12/01
Utilities	Knoxville MSA, TN	H	9.17 FQ	15.21 AW	22.03 TQ	TNBLS	10/01-12/01
Utilities	Memphis MSA, TN-AR-MS	H	6.55 FQ	10.36 AW	13.99 TQ	TNBLS	10/01-12/01
Utilities	Nashville MSA, TN	H	10.10 FQ	17.05 AW	24.41 TQ	TNBLS	10/01-12/01
Utilities	Texas	H	8.04 FQ	11.18 AW	15.56 TQ	TXBLS	10/01-12/01
Utilities	Austin-San Marcos MSA, TX	H	8.16 FQ	11.53 AW	16.73 TQ	TXBLS	10/01-12/01
Utilities	Beaumont-Port Arthur MSA, TX	H	7.93 FQ	12.14 AW	17.04 TQ	TXBLS	10/01-12/01
Utilities	Brazoria PMSA, TX	H	8.43 FQ	11.39 AW	15.96 TQ	TXBLS	10/01-12/01
Utilities	Brownsville-Harlingen-San Benito MSA, TX	H	7.99 FQ	11.38 AW	15.72 TQ	TXBLS	10/01-12/01
Utilities	Corpus Christi MSA, TX	H	7.68 FQ	9.65 AW	12.12 TQ	TXBLS	10/01-12/01
Utilities	Dallas PMSA, TX	H	8.72 FQ	11.51 AW	14.59 TQ	TXBLS	10/01-12/01
Utilities	El Paso MSA, TX	H	9.04 FQ	10.59 AW	12.92 TQ	TXBLS	10/01-12/01
Utilities	Fort Worth-Arlington PMSA, TX	H	8.03 FQ	11.40 AW	15.85 TQ	TXBLS	10/01-12/01
Utilities	Galveston-Texas City PMSA, TX	H	8.39 FQ	12.01 AW	14.87 TQ	TXBLS	10/01-12/01
Utilities	Houston PMSA, TX	H	8.11 FQ	11.33 AW	15.95 TQ	TXBLS	10/01-12/01
Utilities	Killeen-Temple MSA, TX	H	7.62 FQ	9.23 AW	11.01 TQ	TXBLS	10/01-12/01
Utilities	Laredo MSA, TX	H	7.78 FQ	10.87 AW	15.77 TQ	TXBLS	10/01-12/01
Utilities	Longview-Marshall MSA, TX	H	7.83 FQ	11.18 AW	14.85 TQ	TXBLS	10/01-12/01
Utilities	Lubbock MSA, TX	H	7.85 FQ	11.41 AW	15.36 TQ	TXBLS	10/01-12/01
Utilities	McAllen-Edinburg-Mission MSA, TX	H	6.90 FQ	9.99 AW	14.90 TQ	TXBLS	10/01-12/01
Utilities	San Antonio MSA, TX	H	9.16 FQ	13.37 AW	17.88 TQ	TXBLS	10/01-12/01
Utilities	Tyler MSA, TX	H	8.11 FQ	12.33 AW	17.47 TQ	TXBLS	10/01-12/01
Utilities	Waco MSA, TX	H	6.49 FQ	9.57 AW	14.88 TQ	TXBLS	10/01-12/01
Utilities	Utah	H	8.98 FQ	12.74 AW	17.28 TQ	UTBLS	10/01-12/01
Utilities	Provo-Orem MSA, UT	H	7.17 FQ	11.37 AW	18.05 TQ	UTBLS	10/01-12/01
Utilities	Salt Lake City-Ogden MSA, UT	H	9.66 FQ	12.81 AW	17.00 TQ	UTBLS	10/01-12/01
Utilities	Vermont	H	12.37 FQ	16.78 AW	21.40 TQ	VTBLS	10/01-12/01
Utilities	Virginia	H	9.33 FQ	14.85 AW	21.54 TQ	VABLS	10/01-12/01
Utilities	Norfolk-Virginia Beach-Newport News MSA, VA-NC	H	10.22 FQ	15.89 AW	22.27 TQ	VABLS	10/01-12/01
Utilities	Richmond-Petersburg MSA, VA	H	9.30 FQ	13.24 AW	20.73 TQ	VABLS	10/01-12/01
Utilities	Roanoke MSA, VA	H	8.86 FQ	13.02 AW	17.75 TQ	VABLS	10/01-12/01
Utilities	Washington	H	11.84 FQ	16.14 AW	20.92 TQ	WABLS	10/01-12/01

AAW	Average annual wage	**AOH**	Average offered, high	**ASH**	Average starting, high	**H**	Hourly	**M**	Monthly	**S**	Special: hourly and annual
AE	Average entry wage	**AOL**	Average offered, low	**ASL**	Average starting, low	**HI**	Highest wage paid	**MTC**	Median total compensation	**TQ**	Third quartile wage
AEX	Average experienced wage	**APH**	Average pay, high range	**AW**	Average wage paid	**HR**	High end range	**MW**	Median wage paid	**W**	Weekly
AO	Average offered	**APL**	Average pay, low range	**FQ**	First quartile wage	**LR**	Low end range	**SQ**	Second quartile wage	**Y**	Yearly

Occupation/Type/Industry	Location	Per	Low	Mid	High	Source	Date
Meter Reader							
Utilities	Richland-Kennewick-Pasco MSA, WA	H	13.27 FQ	17.24 AW	21.35 TQ	WABLS	10/01-12/01
Utilities	Seattle-Bellevue-Everett PMSA, WA	H	9.77 FQ	14.82 AW	18.41 TQ	WABLS	10/01-12/01
Utilities	Tacoma PMSA, WA	H	12.61 FQ	17.12 AW	21.67 TQ	WABLS	10/01-12/01
Utilities	Yakima MSA, WA	H	14.18 FQ	16.45 AW	20.22 TQ	WABLS	10/01-12/01
Utilities	West Virginia	H	6.31 FQ	12.53 AW	20.24 TQ	WVBLS	10/01-12/01
Utilities	Charleston MSA, WV	H	10.33 FQ	15.13 AW	20.96 TQ	WVBLS	10/01-12/01
Utilities	Huntington-Ashland MSA, WV-KY-OH	H	7.64 FQ	11.99 AW	16.90 TQ	WVBLS	10/01-12/01
Utilities	Wisconsin	H	6.07 FQ	13.92 AW	22.45 TQ	WIBLS	10/01-12/01
Utilities	Appleton-Oshkosh-Neenah MSA, WI	H	11.22 FQ	13.75 AW	19.72 TQ	WIBLS	10/01-12/01
Utilities	Green Bay MSA, WI	H	10.36 FQ	17.50 AW	26.82 TQ	WIBLS	10/01-12/01
Utilities	Madison MSA, WI	H	14.12 FQ	19.05 AW	25.19 TQ	WIBLS	10/01-12/01
Utilities	Milwaukee-Waukesha PMSA, WI	H	12.49 FQ	18.07 AW	25.61 TQ	WIBLS	10/01-12/01
Utilities	Racine PMSA, WI	H	13.57 FQ	20.76 AW	28.83 TQ	WIBLS	10/01-12/01
Utilities	Wyoming	H	10.29 FQ	14.76 AW	20.03 TQ	WYBLS	10/01-12/01
Microbiologist	Alabama	Y	28240 FQ	49840 AW	81620 TQ	ALBLS	10/01-12/01
	Birmingham MSA, AL	Y	26140 FQ	41270 AW	56270 TQ	ALBLS	10/01-12/01
	Arizona	Y	25060 FQ	42440 AW	63530 TQ	AZBLS	10/01-12/01
	Phoenix-Mesa MSA, AZ	Y	24800 FQ	42840 AW	65330 TQ	AZBLS	10/01-12/01
	Arkansas	Y	32730 FQ	49580 AW	70920 TQ	ARBLS	10/01-12/01
	California	Y	32010 FQ	57390 AW	89060 TQ	CABLS	10/01-12/01
	Los Angeles-Long Beach PMSA, CA	Y	31760 FQ	53390 AW	80660 TQ	CABLS	10/01-12/01
	Oakland PMSA, CA	Y	44410 FQ	66220 AW	90160 TQ	CABLS	10/01-12/01
	Orange County PMSA, CA	Y	36540 FQ	55800 AW	82450 TQ	CABLS	10/01-12/01
	Riverside-San Bernardino PMSA, CA	Y	26480 FQ	53940 AW	86510 TQ	CABLS	10/01-12/01
	San Diego MSA, CA	Y	30550 FQ	50160 AW	77490 TQ	CABLS	10/01-12/01
	San Francisco PMSA, CA	Y	44130 FQ	68010 AW	99530 TQ	CABLS	10/01-12/01
	San Jose PMSA, CA	Y	42600 FQ	76660 AW	124170 TQ	CABLS	10/01-12/01
	Ventura PMSA, CA	Y	33330 FQ	59610 AW	101230 TQ	CABLS	10/01-12/01
	Colorado	Y	30390 FQ	51350 AW	72320 TQ	COBLS	10/01-12/01
	Denver PMSA, CO	Y	36810 FQ	53680 AW	72080 TQ	COBLS	10/01-12/01
	Fort Collins-Loveland MSA, CO	Y	23330 FQ	47280 AW	79120 TQ	COBLS	10/01-12/01
	New Haven-Meriden PMSA, CT	Y	47880 FQ	67020 AW	92200 TQ	CTBLS	10/01-12/01
	Stamford-Norwalk PMSA, CT	Y	32960 FQ	58240 AW	89310 TQ	CTBLS	10/01-12/01
	District of Columbia	Y	36240 FQ	56450 AW	88390 TQ	DCBLS	10/01-12/01
	Washington PMSA, DC-MD-VA-WV	Y	35760 FQ	65240 AW	101810 TQ	DCBLS	10/01-12/01
	Florida	Y	21270 FQ	44320 AW	74160 TQ	FLBLS	10/01-12/01
	Gainesville MSA, FL	Y	18570 FQ	27390 AW	48770 TQ	FLBLS	10/01-12/01
	Miami PMSA, FL	Y	25170 FQ	55530 AW	104350 TQ	FLBLS	10/01-12/01
	Tampa-St. Petersburg-Clearwater MSA, FL	Y	26450 FQ	37650 AW	52150 TQ	FLBLS	10/01-12/01
	Georgia	Y	33450 FQ	55840 AW	84330 TQ	GABLS	10/01-12/01
	Atlanta MSA, GA	Y	36840 FQ	59250 AW	86520 TQ	GABLS	10/01-12/01
	Augusta-Aiken MSA, GA-SC	Y	25770 FQ	36890 AW	44530 TQ	GABLS	10/01-12/01
	Hawaii	Y	29790 FQ	43390 AW	61130 TQ	HIBLS	10/01-12/01
	Honolulu MSA, HI	Y	28780 FQ	42790 AW	60760 TQ	HIBLS	10/01-12/01
	Idaho	Y	26910 FQ	48010 AW	79140 TQ	IDBLS	10/01-12/01
	Boise City MSA, ID	Y	26490 FQ	36080 AW	45580 TQ	IDBLS	10/01-12/01
	Illinois	Y	30350 FQ	45700 AW	68550 TQ	ILBLS	10/01-12/01
	Chicago PMSA, IL	Y	30270 FQ	45620 AW	68630 TQ	ILBLS	10/01-12/01
	Indiana	Y	29090 FQ	47470 AW	63640 TQ	INBLS	10/01-12/01
	Evansville-Henderson MSA, IN-KY	Y	24790 FQ	56930 AW		INBLS	10/01-12/01
	Indianapolis MSA, IN	Y	31410 FQ	47320 AW	60170 TQ	INBLS	10/01-12/01
	Iowa	Y	36920 FQ	59220 AW	89700 TQ	IABLS	10/01-12/01
	Kansas	Y	28620 FQ	40680 AW	55880 TQ	KSBLS	10/01-12/01
	Kentucky	Y	24720 FQ	40890 AW	66140 TQ	KYBLS	10/01-12/01
	Louisiana	Y	30740 FQ	52300 AW	75310 TQ	LABLS	10/01-12/01
	New Orleans MSA, LA	Y	30930 FQ	51940 AW	76510 TQ	LABLS	10/01-12/01
	Maine	Y	25880 FQ	44640 AW	80720 TQ	MEBLS	10/01-12/01
	Maryland	Y	40970 FQ	68640 AW	103690 TQ	MDBLS	10/01-12/01
	Baltimore PMSA, MD	Y	36130 FQ	56790 AW	79920 TQ	MDBLS	10/01-12/01

AAW	Average annual wage	AOH	Average offered, high	ASH	Average starting, high	H	Hourly	M	Monthly	S	Special: hourly and annual
AE	Average entry wage	AOL	Average offered, low	ASL	Average starting, low	HI	Highest wage paid	MTC	Median total compensation	TQ	Third quartile wage
AEX	Average experienced wage	APH	Average pay, high range	AW	Average wage paid	HR	High end range	MW	Median wage paid	W	Weekly
AO	Average offered	APL	Average pay, low range	FQ	First quartile wage	LR	Low end range	SQ	Second quartile wage	Y	Yearly

Occupation/Type/Industry	Location	Per	Low	Mid	High	Source	Date
Microbiologist	Massachusetts	Y	36010 FQ	61860 AW	106990 TQ	MABLS	10/01-12/01
	Boston PMSA, MA-NH	Y	37540 FQ	63850 AW	111540 TQ	MABLS	10/01-12/01
	Springfield MSA, MA	Y	30230 FQ	38480 AW	50950 TQ	MABLS	10/01-12/01
	Michigan	Y	32520 FQ	48800 AW	67340 TQ	MIBLS	10/01-12/01
	Detroit PMSA, MI	Y	37790 FQ	47290 AW	58490 TQ	MIBLS	10/01-12/01
	Minnesota	Y	23940 FQ	47030 AW	72520 TQ	MNBLS	10/01-12/01
	Minneapolis-St. Paul MSA, MN-WI	Y	23240 FQ	47500 AW	73200 TQ	MNBLS	10/01-12/01
	Mississippi	Y	24280 FQ	42750 AW	67580 TQ	MSBLS	10/01-12/01
	Missouri	Y	29460 FQ	47370 AW	72280 TQ	MOBLS	10/01-12/01
	Kansas City MSA, MO-KS	Y	27630 FQ	48380 AW	76570 TQ	MOBLS	10/01-12/01
	St. Louis MSA, MO-IL	Y	28440 FQ	45300 AW	61720 TQ	MOBLS	10/01-12/01
	Montana	Y	24430 FQ	43520 AW	64730 TQ	MTBLS	10/01-12/01
	Nebraska	Y	28460 FQ	53160 AW		NEBLS	10/01-12/01
	Lincoln MSA, NE	Y	31850 FQ	54630 AW		NEBLS	10/01-12/01
	Omaha MSA, NE-IA	Y	26080 FQ	51160 AW		NEBLS	10/01-12/01
	Nevada	Y	33940 FQ	53750 AW	70900 TQ	NVBLS	10/01-12/01
	New Hampshire	Y	39270 FQ	48100 AW	59290 TQ	NHBLS	10/01-12/01
	New Jersey	Y	37260 FQ	63020 AW	97800 TQ	NJBLS	10/01-12/01
	Bergen-Passaic PMSA, NJ	Y	33280 FQ	55680 AW	78020 TQ	NJBLS	10/01-12/01
	Middlesex-Somerset-Hunterdon PMSA, NJ	Y	38360 FQ	56320 AW	89390 TQ	NJBLS	10/01-12/01
	Newark PMSA, NJ	Y	38020 FQ	60510 AW	88550 TQ	NJBLS	10/01-12/01
	New Mexico	Y	27520 FQ	51280 AW	99460 TQ	NMBLS	10/01-12/01
	Albuquerque MSA, NM	Y	25780 FQ	38760 AW	54540 TQ	NMBLS	10/01-12/01
	New York	Y	30390 FQ	50540 AW	81340 TQ	NYBLS	10/01-12/01
	Albany-Schenectady-Troy MSA, NY	Y	37080 FQ	52120 AW	79530 TQ	NYBLS	10/01-12/01
	Buffalo-Niagara Falls MSA, NY	Y	28710 FQ	55300 AW	96740 TQ	NYBLS	10/01-12/01
	Nassau-Suffolk PMSA, NY	Y	24610 FQ	47890 AW	82850 TQ	NYBLS	10/01-12/01
	New York PMSA, NY	Y	33230 FQ	51480 AW	78510 TQ	NYBLS	10/01-12/01
	North Carolina	Y	32130 FQ	55410 AW	88920 TQ	NCBLS	10/01-12/01
	Raleigh-Durham-Chapel Hill MSA, NC	Y	33050 FQ	58130 AW	91610 TQ	NCBLS	10/01-12/01
	North Dakota	Y	28820 FQ	37380 AW	55580 TQ	NDBLS	10/01-12/01
	Ohio	Y	26400 FQ	44960 AW	68280 TQ	OHBLS	10/01-12/01
	Cincinnati PMSA, OH-KY-IN	Y	28390 FQ	51520 AW	79320 TQ	OHBLS	10/01-12/01
	Cleveland-Lorain-Elyria PMSA, OH	Y	30890 FQ	43660 AW	58260 TQ	OHBLS	10/01-12/01
	Columbus MSA, OH	Y	24370 FQ	40630 AW	60780 TQ	OHBLS	10/01-12/01
	Oklahoma	Y	35370 FQ	45720 AW	65480 TQ	OKBLS	10/01-12/01
	Oregon	Y	31360 FQ	47770 AW	73470 TQ	ORBLS	10/01-12/01
	Portland-Vancouver PMSA, OR-WA	Y	30240 FQ	44590 AW	71610 TQ	ORBLS	10/01-12/01
	Pennsylvania	Y	32100 FQ	49290 AW	74130 TQ	PABLS	10/01-12/01
	Philadelphia PMSA, PA-NJ	Y	33310 FQ	54230 AW	82840 TQ	PABLS	10/01-12/01
	Pittsburgh MSA, PA	Y	27650 FQ	44090 AW	57450 TQ	PABLS	10/01-12/01
	Rhode Island	Y	35820 FQ	47050 AW	58150 TQ	RIBLS	10/01-12/01
	Providence-Fall River-Warwick MSA, RI-MA	Y	32610 FQ	46720 AW	58620 TQ	RIBLS	10/01-12/01
	South Carolina	Y	27680 FQ	39740 AW	57160 TQ	SCBLS	10/01-12/01
	Tennessee	Y	29730 FQ	46990 AW	66770 TQ	TNBLS	10/01-12/01
	Knoxville MSA, TN	Y	28490 FQ	41720 AW	56400 TQ	TNBLS	10/01-12/01
	Nashville MSA, TN	Y	27870 FQ	42700 AW	58830 TQ	TNBLS	10/01-12/01
	Texas	Y	29560 FQ	53050 AW	89420 TQ	TXBLS	10/01-12/01
	Dallas PMSA, TX	Y	30900 FQ	45330 AW	61780 TQ	TXBLS	10/01-12/01
	Houston PMSA, TX	Y	37350 FQ	50970 AW	67330 TQ	TXBLS	10/01-12/01
	Utah	Y	27660 FQ	45340 AW	74290 TQ	UTBLS	10/01-12/01
	Salt Lake City-Ogden MSA, UT	Y	26640 FQ	42400 AW	69560 TQ	UTBLS	10/01-12/01
	Vermont	Y	26990 FQ	46320 AW	74790 TQ	VTBLS	10/01-12/01
	Virginia	Y	27060 FQ	52200 AW	88360 TQ	VABLS	10/01-12/01
	Norfolk-Virginia Beach-Newport News MSA, VA-NC	Y	29980 FQ	54390 AW	95690 TQ	VABLS	10/01-12/01
	Washington	Y	28780 FQ	49570 AW	73840 TQ	WABLS	10/01-12/01
	Seattle-Bellevue-Everett PMSA, WA	Y	28160 FQ	50510 AW	77910 TQ	WABLS	10/01-12/01
	West Virginia	Y	28210 FQ	45110 AW	70470 TQ	WVBLS	10/01-12/01
	Milwaukee-Waukesha PMSA, WI	Y	24990 FQ	49880 AW	80510 TQ	WIBLS	10/01-12/01

AAW Average annual wage **AOH** Average offered, high **ASH** Average starting, high **H** Hourly **M** Monthly **S** Special: hourly and annual
AE Average entry wage **AOL** Average offered, low **ASL** Average starting, low **HI** Highest wage paid **MTC** Median total compensation **TQ** Third quartile wage
AEX Average experienced wage **APH** Average pay, high range **AW** Average wage paid **HR** High end range **MW** Median wage paid **W** Weekly
AO Average offered **APL** Average pay, low range **FQ** First quartile wage **LR** Low end range **SQ** Second quartile wage **Y** Yearly

Occupation/Type/Industry	Location	Per	Low	Mid	High	Source	Date
Microbiologist	Puerto Rico	Y	22450 FQ	39580 AW	61670 TQ	PRBLS	10/01-12/01
Middle School Teacher							
Except Special and Vocational Education	Alabama	Y	30810 FQ	39320 AW	50110 TQ	ALBLS	10/01-12/01
Except Special and Vocational Education	Alaska	Y	34040 FQ	49050 AW	67600 TQ	AKBLS	10/01-12/01
Except Special and Vocational Education	Arizona	Y	26220 FQ	39110 AW	58060 TQ	AZBLS	10/01-12/01
Except Special and Vocational Education	Arkansas	Y	25320 FQ	35400 AW	46910 TQ	ARBLS	10/01-12/01
Except Special and Vocational Education	California	Y	33110 FQ	49590 AW	69270 TQ	CABLS	10/01-12/01
Except Special and Vocational Education	Colorado	Y	26940 FQ	39590 AW	56440 TQ	COBLS	10/01-12/01
Except Special and Vocational Education	Connecticut	Y	34160 FQ	53460 AW	72200 TQ	CTBLS	10/01-12/01
Except Special and Vocational Education	Delaware	Y	31090 FQ	47530 AW	68510 TQ	DEBLS	10/01-12/01
Except Special and Vocational Education	Florida	Y	28510 FQ	41980 AW	60210 TQ	FLBLS	10/01-12/01
Except Special and Vocational Education	Georgia	Y	29690 FQ	42480 AW	57420 TQ	GABLS	10/01-12/01
Except Special and Vocational Education	Hawaii	Y	25320 FQ	39110 AW	56120 TQ	HIBLS	10/01-12/01
Except Special and Vocational Education	Illinois	Y	26130 FQ	42650 AW	65030 TQ	ILBLS	10/01-12/01
Except Special and Vocational Education	Indiana	Y	27070 FQ	41770 AW	57010 TQ	INBLS	10/01-12/01
Except Special and Vocational Education	Iowa	Y	24770 FQ	35000 AW	46570 TQ	IABLS	10/01-12/01
Except Special and Vocational Education	Kansas	Y	25570 FQ	36280 AW	46200 TQ	KSBLS	10/01-12/01
Except Special and Vocational Education	Kentucky	Y	26860 FQ	39190 AW	52970 TQ	KYBLS	10/01-12/01
Except Special and Vocational Education	Louisiana	Y	17880 FQ	23410 AW	31310 TQ	LABLS	10/01-12/01
Except Special and Vocational Education	Maine	Y	25570 FQ	38130 AW	51670 TQ	MEBLS	10/01-12/01
Except Special and Vocational Education	Maryland	Y	28770 FQ	44360 AW	63340 TQ	MDBLS	10/01-12/01
Except Special and Vocational Education	Massachusetts	Y	27970 FQ	45430 AW	63050 TQ	MABLS	10/01-12/01
Except Special and Vocational Education	Michigan	Y	28880 FQ	45180 AW	64530 TQ	MIBLS	10/01-12/01
Except Special and Vocational Education	Minnesota	Y	28330 FQ	41700 AW	58840 TQ	MNBLS	10/01-12/01
Except Special and Vocational Education	Mississippi	Y	22660 FQ	31610 AW	43160 TQ	MSBLS	10/01-12/01
Except Special and Vocational Education	Missouri	Y	21840 FQ	36750 AW	56330 TQ	MOBLS	10/01-12/01
Except Special and Vocational Education	Montana	Y	16190 FQ	31030 AW	44420 TQ	MTBLS	10/01-12/01
Except Special and Vocational Education	Nebraska	Y	25090 FQ	38540 AW	54010 TQ	NEBLS	10/01-12/01
Except Special and Vocational Education	New Hampshire	Y	26150 FQ	38390 AW	53180 TQ	NHBLS	10/01-12/01
Except Special and Vocational Education	New Jersey	Y	30980 FQ	51460 AW	77250 TQ	NJBLS	10/01-12/01
Except Special and Vocational Education	New Mexico	Y	27520 FQ	37590 AW	52160 TQ	NMBLS	10/01-12/01
Except Special and Vocational Education	New York	Y	29630 FQ	59420 AW	97840 TQ	NYBLS	10/01-12/01
Except Special and Vocational Education	North Carolina	Y	24800 FQ	35760 AW	50210 TQ	NCBLS	10/01-12/01
Except Special and Vocational Education	Ohio	Y	28510 FQ	43470 AW	60340 TQ	OHBLS	10/01-12/01
Except Special and Vocational Education	Oklahoma	Y	24540 FQ	33770 AW	44050 TQ	OKBLS	10/01-12/01
Except Special and Vocational Education	Oregon	Y	30130 FQ	42340 AW	57650 TQ	ORBLS	10/01-12/01
Except Special and Vocational Education	Pennsylvania	Y	29500 FQ	49070 AW	72060 TQ	PABLS	10/01-12/01
Except Special and Vocational Education	Rhode Island	Y	31710 FQ	46210 AW	63070 TQ	RIBLS	10/01-12/01
Except Special and Vocational Education	South Carolina	Y	27390 FQ	39030 AW	53440 TQ	SCBLS	10/01-12/01
Except Special and Vocational Education	South Dakota	Y	23730 FQ	33210 AW	45170 TQ	SDBLS	10/01-12/01
Except Special and Vocational Education	Tennessee	Y	26180 FQ	35530 AW	45680 TQ	TNBLS	10/01-12/01
Except Special and Vocational Education	Texas	Y	29940 FQ	39870 AW	53760 TQ	TXBLS	10/01-12/01
Except Special and Vocational Education	Utah	Y	25770 FQ	38930 AW	53300 TQ	UTBLS	10/01-12/01
Except Special and Vocational Education	Vermont	Y	29930 FQ	41220 AW	54580 TQ	VTBLS	10/01-12/01
Except Special and Vocational Education	Virginia	Y	28010 FQ	43150 AW	61400 TQ	VABLS	10/01-12/01
Except Special and Vocational Education	Washington	Y	29110 FQ	43000 AW	56930 TQ	WABLS	10/01-12/01
Except Special and Vocational Education	West Virginia	Y	29220 FQ	36720 AW	44660 TQ	WVBLS	10/01-12/01
Except Special and Vocational Education	Wisconsin	Y	26880 FQ	43670 AW	62370 TQ	WIBLS	10/01-12/01
Except Special and Vocational Education	Wyoming	Y	25660 FQ	36360 AW	46810 TQ	WYBLS	10/01-12/01
Except Special and Vocational Education	Puerto Rico	Y	18030 FQ	21730 AW	26620 TQ	PRBLS	10/01-12/01
Except Special and Vocational Education	Virgin Islands	Y	20650 FQ	34920 AW	54830 TQ	VIBLS	10/01-12/01
Except Special and Vocational Education	Guam	Y	20540 FQ	29680 AW	41590 TQ	GUBLS	10/01-12/01
Milling and Planing Machine Setter, Operator, and Tender							
Metals and Plastics	Alabama	H	7.68 FQ	15.59 AW	25.82 TQ	ALBLS	10/01-12/01
Metals and Plastics	Arizona	H	9.92 FQ	14.09 AW	19.35 TQ	AZBLS	10/01-12/01
Metals and Plastics	Phoenix-Mesa MSA, AZ	H	9.91 FQ	13.92 AW	18.57 TQ	AZBLS	10/01-12/01
Metals and Plastics	Arkansas	H	7.97 FQ	13.21 AW	18.97 TQ	ARBLS	10/01-12/01
Metals and Plastics	Fayetteville-Springdale-Rogers MSA, AR	H	7.26 FQ	11.00 AW	14.24 TQ	ARBLS	10/01-12/01
Metals and Plastics	California	H	7.83 FQ	13.23 AW	19.87 TQ	CABLS	10/01-12/01
Metals and Plastics	Fresno MSA, CA	H	9.75 FQ	13.63 AW	16.56 TQ	CABLS	10/01-12/01
Metals and Plastics	Los Angeles-Long Beach PMSA, CA	H	7.27 FQ	12.68 AW	18.40 TQ	CABLS	10/01-12/01
Metals and Plastics	Oakland PMSA, CA	H	7.81 FQ	11.65 AW	17.71 TQ	CABLS	10/01-12/01
Metals and Plastics	Orange County PMSA, CA	H	8.96 FQ	13.95 AW	20.28 TQ	CABLS	10/01-12/01
Metals and Plastics	Riverside-San Bernardino PMSA, CA	H	8.22 FQ	14.81 AW	21.46 TQ	CABLS	10/01-12/01
Metals and Plastics	Sacramento PMSA, CA	H	9.41 FQ	13.96 AW	21.33 TQ	CABLS	10/01-12/01
Metals and Plastics	San Diego MSA, CA	H	7.67 FQ	11.74 AW	16.81 TQ	CABLS	10/01-12/01

AAW	Average annual wage	AOH	Average offered, high	ASH	Average starting, high	H	Hourly	M	Monthly	S	Special: hourly and annual
AE	Average entry wage	AOL	Average offered, low	ASL	Average starting, low	HI	Highest wage paid	MTC	Median total compensation	TQ	Third quartile wage
AEX	Average experienced wage	APH	Average pay, high range	AW	Average wage paid	HR	High end range	MW	Median wage paid	W	Weekly
AO	Average offered	APL	Average pay, low range	FQ	First quartile wage	LR	Low end range	SQ	Second quartile wage	Y	Yearly

Occupation/Type/Industry	Location	Per	Low	Mid	High	Source	Date
Milling and Planing Machine Setter, Operator, and Tender							
Metals and Plastics	San Francisco PMSA, CA	H	7.87 FQ	13.94 AW	19.88 TQ	CABLS	10/01-12/01
Metals and Plastics	San Jose PMSA, CA	H	9.87 FQ	15.90 AW	24.92 TQ	CABLS	10/01-12/01
Metals and Plastics	Santa Barbara-Santa Maria-Lompoc MSA, CA	H	7.78 FQ	13.20 AW	20.84 TQ	CABLS	10/01-12/01
Metals and Plastics	Ventura PMSA, CA	H	7.52 FQ	11.83 AW	16.32 TQ	CABLS	10/01-12/01
Metals and Plastics	Colorado	H	9.15 FQ	14.82 AW	21.54 TQ	COBLS	10/01-12/01
Metals and Plastics	Colorado Springs MSA, CO	H	10.71 FQ	15.14 AW	20.58 TQ	COBLS	10/01-12/01
Metals and Plastics	Denver PMSA, CO	H	8.31 FQ	15.25 AW	24.24 TQ	COBLS	10/01-12/01
Metals and Plastics	Greeley PMSA, CO	H	8.92 FQ	11.84 AW	16.57 TQ	COBLS	10/01-12/01
Metals and Plastics	Connecticut	H	9.76 FQ	15.58 AW	21.24 TQ	CTBLS	10/01-12/01
Metals and Plastics	Bridgeport PMSA, CT	H	12.71 FQ	17.50 AW	22.22 TQ	CTBLS	10/01-12/01
Metals and Plastics	Hartford MSA, CT	H	9.44 FQ	15.15 AW	20.86 TQ	CTBLS	10/01-12/01
Metals and Plastics	New Haven-Meriden PMSA, CT	H	10.36 FQ	15.69 AW	22.31 TQ	CTBLS	10/01-12/01
Metals and Plastics	Waterbury PMSA, CT	H	8.87 FQ	12.33 AW	19.86 TQ	CTBLS	10/01-12/01
Metals and Plastics	Delaware	H	9.08 FQ	12.66 AW	17.76 TQ	DEBLS	10/01-12/01
Metals and Plastics	Washington PMSA, DC-MD-VA-WV	H	7.28 FQ	11.95 AW	17.04 TQ	DCBLS	10/01-12/01
Metals and Plastics	Florida	H	9.20 FQ	13.80 AW	20.13 TQ	FLBLS	10/01-12/01
Metals and Plastics	Fort Lauderdale PMSA, FL	H	9.93 FQ	14.69 AW	21.24 TQ	FLBLS	10/01-12/01
Metals and Plastics	Melbourne-Titusville-Palm Bay MSA, FL	H	10.90 FQ	12.87 AW	15.90 TQ	FLBLS	10/01-12/01
Metals and Plastics	Miami PMSA, FL	H	6.98 FQ	13.23 AW	20.04 TQ	FLBLS	10/01-12/01
Metals and Plastics	Orlando MSA, FL	H	9.87 FQ	14.09 AW	19.56 TQ	FLBLS	10/01-12/01
Metals and Plastics	Sarasota-Bradenton MSA, FL	H	9.23 FQ	12.11 AW	16.56 TQ	FLBLS	10/01-12/01
Metals and Plastics	Tampa-St. Petersburg-Clearwater MSA, FL	H	8.85 FQ	10.70 AW	14.07 TQ	FLBLS	10/01-12/01
Metals and Plastics	West Palm Beach-Boca Raton MSA, FL	H	14.43 FQ	17.95 AW	21.85 TQ	FLBLS	10/01-12/01
Metals and Plastics	Georgia	H	8.94 FQ	12.52 AW	16.86 TQ	GABLS	10/01-12/01
Metals and Plastics	Atlanta MSA, GA	H	8.85 FQ	11.76 AW	16.61 TQ	GABLS	10/01-12/01
Metals and Plastics	Augusta-Aiken MSA, GA-SC	H	8.76 FQ	12.45 AW	17.31 TQ	GABLS	10/01-12/01
Metals and Plastics	Idaho	H	7.75 FQ	12.46 AW	16.63 TQ	IDBLS	10/01-12/01
Metals and Plastics	Boise City MSA, ID	H	9.69 FQ	13.22 AW	16.80 TQ	IDBLS	10/01-12/01
Metals and Plastics	Illinois	H	8.71 FQ	14.27 AW	20.29 TQ	ILBLS	10/01-12/01
Metals and Plastics	Chicago PMSA, IL	H	8.60 FQ	14.03 AW	19.84 TQ	ILBLS	10/01-12/01
Metals and Plastics	Indiana	H	10.19 FQ	17.29 AW	25.88 TQ	INBLS	10/01-12/01
Metals and Plastics	Elkhart-Goshen MSA, IN	H	12.48 FQ	21.20 AW	26.55 TQ	INBLS	10/01-12/01
Metals and Plastics	Fort Wayne MSA, IN	H	9.54 FQ	15.25 AW	21.97 TQ	INBLS	10/01-12/01
Metals and Plastics	Gary PMSA, IN	H	12.47 FQ	18.97 AW	26.38 TQ	INBLS	10/01-12/01
Metals and Plastics	Indianapolis MSA, IN	H	13.67 FQ	19.88 AW	26.53 TQ	INBLS	10/01-12/01
Metals and Plastics	Iowa	H	11.01 FQ	15.49 AW	22.19 TQ	IABLS	10/01-12/01
Metals and Plastics	Des Moines MSA, IA	H	10.45 FQ	15.03 AW	21.06 TQ	IABLS	10/01-12/01
Metals and Plastics	Kansas	H	9.56 FQ	17.35 AW	26.11 TQ	KSBLS	10/01-12/01
Metals and Plastics	Wichita MSA, KS	H	11.58 FQ	19.90 AW	26.91 TQ	KSBLS	10/01-12/01
Metals and Plastics	Kentucky	H	8.82 FQ	13.88 AW	19.89 TQ	KYBLS	10/01-12/01
Metals and Plastics	Louisville MSA, KY-IN	H	8.97 FQ	12.09 AW	16.14 TQ	KYBLS	10/01-12/01
Metals and Plastics	Louisiana	H	9.02 FQ	15.95 AW	21.03 TQ	LABLS	10/01-12/01
Metals and Plastics	Baton Rouge MSA, LA	H	12.20 FQ	17.09 AW	21.43 TQ	LABLS	10/01-12/01
Metals and Plastics	Maine	H	6.23 FQ	11.78 AW	17.99 TQ	MEBLS	10/01-12/01
Metals and Plastics	Maryland	H	8.92 FQ	18.27 AW	25.96 TQ	MDBLS	10/01-12/01
Metals and Plastics	Baltimore PMSA, MD	H	8.03 FQ	14.92 AW	21.62 TQ	MDBLS	10/01-12/01
Metals and Plastics	Massachusetts	H	10.44 FQ	16.88 AW	22.90 TQ	MABLS	10/01-12/01
Metals and Plastics	Boston PMSA, MA-NH	H	14.57 FQ	19.43 AW	27.92 TQ	MABLS	10/01-12/01
Metals and Plastics	Lawrence PMSA, MA-NH	H	11.29 FQ	15.38 AW	19.82 TQ	MABLS	10/01-12/01
Metals and Plastics	Lowell PMSA, MA-NH	H	11.65 FQ	15.15 AW	17.43 TQ	MABLS	10/01-12/01
Metals and Plastics	Springfield MSA, MA	H	12.30 FQ	16.89 AW	21.37 TQ	MABLS	10/01-12/01
Metals and Plastics	Worcester PMSA, MA-CT	H	7.72 FQ	13.23 AW	19.69 TQ	MABLS	10/01-12/01
Metals and Plastics	Michigan	H	8.55 FQ	16.87 AW	28.72 TQ	MIBLS	10/01-12/01
Metals and Plastics	Ann Arbor PMSA, MI	H	11.78 FQ	16.27 AW	22.59 TQ	MIBLS	10/01-12/01
Metals and Plastics	Detroit PMSA, MI	H	10.94 FQ	18.87 AW	28.21 TQ	MIBLS	10/01-12/01
Metals and Plastics	Grand Rapids-Muskegon-Holland MSA, MI	H	9.88 FQ	18.38 AW	32.35 TQ	MIBLS	10/01-12/01
Metals and Plastics	Kalamazoo-Battle Creek MSA, MI	H	8.50 FQ	22.35 AW	34.99 TQ	MIBLS	10/01-12/01
Metals and Plastics	Minnesota	H	11.11 FQ	16.09 AW	21.39 TQ	MNBLS	10/01-12/01
Metals and Plastics	Minneapolis-St. Paul MSA, MN-WI	H	11.67 FQ	16.56 AW	21.64 TQ	MNBLS	10/01-12/01
Metals and Plastics	Mississippi	H	8.19 FQ	11.72 AW	15.03 TQ	MSBLS	10/01-12/01
Metals and Plastics	Missouri	H	7.34 FQ	11.85 AW	18.98 TQ	MOBLS	10/01-12/01

AAW Average annual wage	**AOH** Average offered, high	**ASH** Average starting, high	**H** Hourly	**M** Monthly	**S** Special: hourly and annual
AE Average entry wage	**AOL** Average offered, low	**ASL** Average starting, low	**HI** Highest wage paid	**MTC** Median total compensation	**TQ** Third quartile wage
AEX Average experienced wage	**APH** Average pay, high range	**AW** Average wage paid	**HR** High end range	**MW** Median wage paid	**W** Weekly
AO Average offered	**APL** Average pay, low range	**FQ** First quartile wage	**LR** Low end range	**SQ** Second quartile wage	**Y** Yearly

Occupation/Type/Industry	Location	Per	Low	Mid	High	Source	Date
Milling and Planing Machine Setter, Operator, and Tender							
Metals and Plastics	Kansas City MSA, MO-KS	H	7.84 FQ	13.55 AW	20.72 TQ	MOBLS	10/01-12/01
Metals and Plastics	St. Louis MSA, MO-IL	H	8.12 FQ	14.42 AW	20.51 TQ	MOBLS	10/01-12/01
Metals and Plastics	Springfield MSA, MO	H	7.26 FQ	10.19 AW	13.45 TQ	MOBLS	10/01-12/01
Metals and Plastics	Montana	H	8.96 FQ	13.53 AW	17.49 TQ	MTBLS	10/01-12/01
Metals and Plastics	Nebraska	H	9.43 FQ	14.38 AW	23.07 TQ	NEBLS	10/01-12/01
Metals and Plastics	Lincoln MSA, NE	H	10.17 FQ	16.75 AW	25.99 TQ	NEBLS	10/01-12/01
Metals and Plastics	Nevada	H	10.81 FQ	17.84 AW	24.27 TQ	NVBLS	10/01-12/01
Metals and Plastics	Las Vegas MSA, NV-AZ	H	10.64 FQ	15.51 AW	21.52 TQ	NVBLS	10/01-12/01
Metals and Plastics	Reno MSA, NV	H	9.61 FQ	15.08 AW	22.33 TQ	NVBLS	10/01-12/01
Metals and Plastics	New Hampshire	H	9.48 FQ	14.34 AW	19.30 TQ	NHBLS	10/01-12/01
Metals and Plastics	Nashua PMSA, NH	H	9.20 FQ	14.91 AW	20.61 TQ	NHBLS	10/01-12/01
Metals and Plastics	New Jersey	H	8.32 FQ	13.54 AW	18.93 TQ	NJBLS	10/01-12/01
Metals and Plastics	Bergen-Passaic PMSA, NJ	H	7.20 FQ	12.22 AW	18.28 TQ	NJBLS	10/01-12/01
Metals and Plastics	Newark PMSA, NJ	H	8.57 FQ	14.30 AW	19.00 TQ	NJBLS	10/01-12/01
Metals and Plastics	New York	H	7.39 FQ	12.16 AW	17.24 TQ	NYBLS	10/01-12/01
Metals and Plastics	Albany-Schenectady-Troy MSA, NY	H	7.64 FQ	12.31 AW	17.63 TQ	NYBLS	10/01-12/01
Metals and Plastics	Buffalo-Niagara Falls MSA, NY	H	9.27 FQ	12.61 AW	16.88 TQ	NYBLS	10/01-12/01
Metals and Plastics	Nassau-Suffolk PMSA, NY	H	6.45 FQ	11.09 AW	18.24 TQ	NYBLS	10/01-12/01
Metals and Plastics	New York PMSA, NY	H	9.40 FQ	17.90 AW	25.59 TQ	NYBLS	10/01-12/01
Metals and Plastics	Rochester MSA, NY	H	7.04 FQ	10.42 AW	14.95 TQ	NYBLS	10/01-12/01
Metals and Plastics	Syracuse MSA, NY	H	9.54 FQ	13.98 AW	19.66 TQ	NYBLS	10/01-12/01
Metals and Plastics	North Carolina	H	8.64 FQ	12.80 AW	18.57 TQ	NCBLS	10/01-12/01
Metals and Plastics	Charlotte-Gastonia-Rock Hill MSA, NC-SC	H	7.95 FQ	13.16 AW	19.33 TQ	NCBLS	10/01-12/01
Metals and Plastics	Greensboro-Winston-Salem-High Point MSA, NC	H	8.70 FQ	12.59 AW	20.01 TQ	NCBLS	10/01-12/01
Metals and Plastics	Hickory-Morganton-Lenoir MSA, NC	H	9.37 FQ	11.90 AW	13.72 TQ	NCBLS	10/01-12/01
Metals and Plastics	Raleigh-Durham-Chapel Hill MSA, NC	H	9.34 FQ	12.30 AW	17.07 TQ	NCBLS	10/01-12/01
Metals and Plastics	Ohio	H	9.76 FQ	14.61 AW	20.24 TQ	OHBLS	10/01-12/01
Metals and Plastics	Akron PMSA, OH	H	9.86 FQ	14.08 AW	19.02 TQ	OHBLS	10/01-12/01
Metals and Plastics	Canton-Massillon MSA, OH	H	10.47 FQ	15.33 AW	21.75 TQ	OHBLS	10/01-12/01
Metals and Plastics	Cincinnati PMSA, OH-KY-IN	H	10.03 FQ	15.16 AW	20.60 TQ	OHBLS	10/01-12/01
Metals and Plastics	Cleveland-Lorain-Elyria PMSA, OH	H	9.99 FQ	15.11 AW	20.48 TQ	OHBLS	10/01-12/01
Metals and Plastics	Columbus MSA, OH	H	10.58 FQ	13.90 AW	16.86 TQ	OHBLS	10/01-12/01
Metals and Plastics	Dayton-Springfield MSA, OH	H	9.95 FQ	15.75 AW	20.79 TQ	OHBLS	10/01-12/01
Metals and Plastics	Hamilton-Middletown PMSA, OH	H	11.16 FQ	13.19 AW	16.22 TQ	OHBLS	10/01-12/01
Metals and Plastics	Mansfield MSA, OH	H	8.94 FQ	13.60 AW	17.19 TQ	OHBLS	10/01-12/01
Metals and Plastics	Toledo MSA, OH	H	10.98 FQ	16.11 AW	24.48 TQ	OHBLS	10/01-12/01
Metals and Plastics	Youngstown-Warren MSA, OH	H	9.22 FQ	15.64 AW	20.00 TQ	OHBLS	10/01-12/01
Metals and Plastics	Oklahoma	H	10.11 FQ	12.97 AW	16.43 TQ	OKBLS	10/01-12/01
Metals and Plastics	Tulsa MSA, OK	H	10.37 FQ	13.74 AW	17.37 TQ	OKBLS	10/01-12/01
Metals and Plastics	Oregon	H	9.55 FQ	16.84 AW	26.81 TQ	ORBLS	10/01-12/01
Metals and Plastics	Portland-Vancouver PMSA, OR-WA	H	11.68 FQ	18.63 AW	27.24 TQ	ORBLS	10/01-12/01
Metals and Plastics	Pennsylvania	H	8.82 FQ	13.91 AW	19.97 TQ	PABLS	10/01-12/01
Metals and Plastics	Allentown-Bethlehem-Easton MSA, PA	H	8.90 FQ	13.58 AW	17.18 TQ	PABLS	10/01-12/01
Metals and Plastics	Erie MSA, PA	H	6.19 FQ	13.58 AW	20.86 TQ	PABLS	10/01-12/01
Metals and Plastics	Harrisburg-Lebanon-Carlisle MSA, PA	H	7.65 FQ	11.80 AW	14.65 TQ	PABLS	10/01-12/01
Metals and Plastics	Philadelphia PMSA, PA-NJ	H	10.51 FQ	16.37 AW	25.04 TQ	PABLS	10/01-12/01
Metals and Plastics	Pittsburgh MSA, PA	H	9.62 FQ	14.48 AW	20.08 TQ	PABLS	10/01-12/01
Metals and Plastics	York MSA, PA	H	11.66 FQ	14.37 AW	17.87 TQ	PABLS	10/01-12/01
Metals and Plastics	Rhode Island	H	8.73 FQ	14.01 AW	19.81 TQ	RIBLS	10/01-12/01
Metals and Plastics	Providence-Fall River-Warwick MSA, RI-MA	H	8.86 FQ	13.81 AW	19.60 TQ	RIBLS	10/01-12/01
Metals and Plastics	South Carolina	H	9.11 FQ	12.51 AW	16.96 TQ	SCBLS	10/01-12/01
Metals and Plastics	Greenville-Spartanburg-Anderson MSA, SC	H	9.59 FQ	13.62 AW	17.54 TQ	SCBLS	10/01-12/01
Metals and Plastics	South Dakota	H	9.21 FQ	12.25 AW	15.85 TQ	SDBLS	10/01-12/01
Metals and Plastics	Tennessee	H	9.62 FQ	13.24 AW	16.75 TQ	TNBLS	10/01-12/01
Metals and Plastics	Chattanooga MSA, TN-GA	H	7.76 FQ	11.96 AW	16.85 TQ	TNBLS	10/01-12/01
Metals and Plastics	Knoxville MSA, TN	H	9.48 FQ	12.66 AW	16.15 TQ	TNBLS	10/01-12/01
Metals and Plastics	Nashville MSA, TN	H	9.52 FQ	13.19 AW	19.71 TQ	TNBLS	10/01-12/01

AAW	Average annual wage	**AOH**	Average offered, high	**ASH**	Average starting, high	**H**	Hourly	**M**	Monthly	**S**	Special: hourly and annual		
AE	Average entry wage	**AOL**	Average offered, low	**ASL**	Average starting, low	**HI**	Highest wage paid	**MTC**	Median total compensation	**TQ**	Third quartile wage		
AEX	Average experienced wage	**APH**	Average pay, high range	**AW**	Average wage paid	**HR**	High end range	**MW**	Median wage paid	**W**	Weekly		
AO	Average offered	**APL**	Average pay, low range	**FQ**	First quartile wage	**LR**	Low end range	**SQ**	Second quartile wage	**Y**	Yearly		

Occupation/Type/Industry	Location	Per	Low	Mid	High	Source	Date
Milling and Planing Machine Setter, Operator, and Tender							
Metals and Plastics	Texas	H	7.26 FQ	14.12 AW	24.94 TQ	TXBLS	10/01-12/01
Metals and Plastics	Dallas PMSA, TX	H	7.62 FQ	14.26 AW	22.72 TQ	TXBLS	10/01-12/01
Metals and Plastics	Fort Worth-Arlington PMSA, TX	H	8.89 FQ	18.29 AW	27.09 TQ	TXBLS	10/01-12/01
Metals and Plastics	Houston PMSA, TX	H	6.90 FQ	14.57 AW	25.82 TQ	TXBLS	10/01-12/01
Metals and Plastics	San Antonio MSA, TX	H	5.95 FQ	9.21 AW	11.36 TQ	TXBLS	10/01-12/01
Metals and Plastics	Utah	H	8.58 FQ	11.38 AW	15.66 TQ	UTBLS	10/01-12/01
Metals and Plastics	Salt Lake City-Ogden MSA, UT	H	8.84 FQ	11.26 AW	14.24 TQ	UTBLS	10/01-12/01
Metals and Plastics	Vermont	H	9.17 FQ	13.48 AW	17.42 TQ	VTBLS	10/01-12/01
Metals and Plastics	Virginia	H	8.04 FQ	11.83 AW	16.25 TQ	VABLS	10/01-12/01
Metals and Plastics	Lynchburg MSA, VA	H	9.73 FQ	12.75 AW	16.20 TQ	VABLS	10/01-12/01
Metals and Plastics	Washington	H	10.32 FQ	15.07 AW	21.63 TQ	WABLS	10/01-12/01
Metals and Plastics	Seattle-Bellevue-Everett PMSA, WA	H	10.63 FQ	15.22 AW	21.49 TQ	WABLS	10/01-12/01
Metals and Plastics	West Virginia	H	9.72 FQ	14.82 AW	21.99 TQ	WVBLS	10/01-12/01
Metals and Plastics	Wisconsin	H	9.37 FQ	13.55 AW	18.19 TQ	WIBLS	10/01-12/01
Metals and Plastics	Appleton-Oshkosh-Neenah MSA, WI	H	11.60 FQ	14.97 AW	19.27 TQ	WIBLS	10/01-12/01
Metals and Plastics	Green Bay MSA, WI	H	11.91 FQ	16.25 AW	20.64 TQ	WIBLS	10/01-12/01
Metals and Plastics	Madison MSA, WI	H	12.70 FQ	15.90 AW	18.11 TQ	WIBLS	10/01-12/01
Metals and Plastics	Milwaukee-Waukesha PMSA, WI	H	10.53 FQ	15.17 AW	20.79 TQ	WIBLS	10/01-12/01
Millwright	Alabama	H	10.41 FQ	15.88 AW	21.38 TQ	ALBLS	10/01-12/01
	Birmingham MSA, AL	H	10.04 FQ	14.69 AW	20.83 TQ	ALBLS	10/01-12/01
	Mobile MSA, AL	H	11.65 FQ	16.39 AW	21.07 TQ	ALBLS	10/01-12/01
	Arizona	H	15.17 FQ	19.55 AW	25.73 TQ	AZBLS	10/01-12/01
	Phoenix-Mesa MSA, AZ	H	15.26 FQ	19.60 AW	25.75 TQ	AZBLS	10/01-12/01
	Arkansas	H	10.83 FQ	15.95 AW	23.38 TQ	ARBLS	10/01-12/01
	Fayetteville-Springdale-Rogers MSA, AR	H	12.22 FQ	15.22 AW	18.10 TQ	ARBLS	10/01-12/01
	Little Rock-North Little Rock MSA, AR	H	11.71 FQ	15.66 AW	20.07 TQ	ARBLS	10/01-12/01
	California	H	10.21 FQ	20.18 AW	30.92 TQ	CABLS	10/01-12/01
	Bakersfield MSA, CA	H	9.22 FQ	14.30 AW	20.83 TQ	CABLS	10/01-12/01
	Fresno MSA, CA	H	9.77 FQ	18.22 AW	27.93 TQ	CABLS	10/01-12/01
	Los Angeles-Long Beach PMSA, CA	H	6.90 FQ	18.05 AW	28.26 TQ	CABLS	10/01-12/01
	Modesto MSA, CA	H	15.05 FQ	24.42 AW	33.28 TQ	CABLS	10/01-12/01
	Oakland PMSA, CA	H	18.72 FQ	24.31 AW	31.68 TQ	CABLS	10/01-12/01
	Orange County PMSA, CA	H	11.62 FQ	19.62 AW	30.86 TQ	CABLS	10/01-12/01
	Riverside-San Bernardino PMSA, CA	H	11.18 FQ	23.65 AW	34.08 TQ	CABLS	10/01-12/01
	Sacramento PMSA, CA	H	10.94 FQ	22.59 AW	33.17 TQ	CABLS	10/01-12/01
	San Diego MSA, CA	H	13.07 FQ	23.50 AW	41.20 TQ	CABLS	10/01-12/01
	San Jose PMSA, CA	H	11.83 FQ	23.45 AW	33.93 TQ	CABLS	10/01-12/01
	Stockton-Lodi MSA, CA	H	10.01 FQ	17.93 AW	25.63 TQ	CABLS	10/01-12/01
	Vallejo-Fairfield-Napa PMSA, CA	H	12.09 FQ	21.68 AW	37.63 TQ	CABLS	10/01-12/01
	Colorado	H	9.61 FQ	13.83 AW	20.81 TQ	COBLS	10/01-12/01
	Denver PMSA, CO	H	17.14 FQ	19.23 AW	21.82 TQ	COBLS	10/01-12/01
	Greeley PMSA, CO	H	9.48 FQ	11.47 AW	16.07 TQ	COBLS	10/01-12/01
	Connecticut	H	14.91 FQ	20.65 AW	27.10 TQ	CTBLS	10/01-12/01
	Bridgeport PMSA, CT	H	14.46 FQ	19.01 AW	24.89 TQ	CTBLS	10/01-12/01
	Hartford MSA, CT	H	18.23 FQ	22.49 AW	27.42 TQ	CTBLS	10/01-12/01
	New Haven-Meriden PMSA, CT	H	14.27 FQ	19.78 AW	27.18 TQ	CTBLS	10/01-12/01
	Delaware	H	14.40 FQ	20.48 AW	27.67 TQ	DEBLS	10/01-12/01
	Wilmington-Newark PMSA, DE-MD	H	17.01 FQ	23.34 AW	28.92 TQ	DEBLS	10/01-12/01
	Washington PMSA, DC-MD-VA-WV	H	13.73 FQ	19.70 AW	28.92 TQ	DCBLS	10/01-12/01
	Florida	H	9.40 FQ	16.74 AW	24.43 TQ	FLBLS	10/01-12/01
	Fort Lauderdale PMSA, FL	H	10.88 FQ	20.69 AW	30.93 TQ	FLBLS	10/01-12/01
	Jacksonville MSA, FL	H	7.90 FQ	14.39 AW	20.75 TQ	FLBLS	10/01-12/01
	Lakeland-Winter Haven MSA, FL	H	14.50 FQ	16.58 AW	19.13 TQ	FLBLS	10/01-12/01
	Melbourne-Titusville-Palm Bay MSA, FL	H	14.04 FQ	18.37 AW	22.63 TQ	FLBLS	10/01-12/01

AAW	Average annual wage	AOH	Average offered, high	ASH	Average starting, high	H	Hourly	M	Monthly	S	Special: hourly and annual
AE	Average entry wage	AOL	Average offered, low	ASL	Average starting, low	HI	Highest wage paid	MTC	Median total compensation	TQ	Third quartile wage
AEX	Average experienced wage	APH	Average pay, high range	AW	Average wage paid	HR	High end range	MW	Median wage paid	W	Weekly
AO	Average offered	APL	Average pay, low range	FQ	First quartile wage	LR	Low end range	SQ	Second quartile wage	Y	Yearly

Occupation/Type/Industry	Location	Per	Low	Mid	High	Source	Date
Millwright	Miami PMSA, FL	H	16.03 FQ	19.47 AW	22.16 TQ	FLBLS	10/01-12/01
	Orlando MSA, FL	H	12.22 FQ	17.16 AW	22.70 TQ	FLBLS	10/01-12/01
	Sarasota-Bradenton MSA, FL	H	12.43 FQ	16.48 AW	21.12 TQ	FLBLS	10/01-12/01
	Tampa-St. Petersburg-Clearwater MSA, FL	H	11.35 FQ	16.86 AW	22.45 TQ	FLBLS	10/01-12/01
	Georgia	H	12.74 FQ	19.85 AW	28.16 TQ	GABLS	10/01-12/01
	Atlanta MSA, GA	H	12.99 FQ	19.62 AW	30.85 TQ	GABLS	10/01-12/01
	Columbus MSA, GA-AL	H	12.68 FQ	20.84 AW	29.56 TQ	GABLS	10/01-12/01
	Macon MSA, GA	H	11.66 FQ	19.03 AW	27.66 TQ	GABLS	10/01-12/01
	Savannah MSA, GA	H	15.01 FQ	19.23 AW	22.50 TQ	GABLS	10/01-12/01
	Honolulu MSA, HI	H	18.94 FQ	21.74 AW	25.41 TQ	HIBLS	10/01-12/01
	Idaho	H	12.84 FQ	18.99 AW	26.08 TQ	IDBLS	10/01-12/01
	Boise City MSA, ID	H	10.10 FQ	14.77 AW	20.73 TQ	IDBLS	10/01-12/01
	Illinois	H	13.69 FQ	20.60 AW	27.16 TQ	ILBLS	10/01-12/01
	Chicago PMSA, IL	H	14.15 FQ	20.34 AW	26.72 TQ	ILBLS	10/01-12/01
	Indiana	H	14.65 FQ	21.95 AW	31.70 TQ	INBLS	10/01-12/01
	Elkhart-Goshen MSA, IN	H	14.57 FQ	20.68 AW	31.70 TQ	INBLS	10/01-12/01
	Evansville-Henderson MSA, IN-KY	H	15.29 FQ	22.41 AW	32.99 TQ	INBLS	10/01-12/01
	Fort Wayne MSA, IN	H	15.09 FQ	19.96 AW	26.77 TQ	INBLS	10/01-12/01
	Gary PMSA, IN	H	14.73 FQ	19.76 AW	25.81 TQ	INBLS	10/01-12/01
	Indianapolis MSA, IN	H	17.41 FQ	25.76 AW	34.26 TQ	INBLS	10/01-12/01
	South Bend MSA, IN	H	16.84 FQ	21.54 AW	27.96 TQ	INBLS	10/01-12/01
	Iowa	H	10.88 FQ	17.24 AW	25.17 TQ	IABLS	10/01-12/01
	Davenport-Moline-Rock Island MSA, IA-IL	H	13.10 FQ	20.03 AW	26.88 TQ	IABLS	10/01-12/01
	Des Moines MSA, IA	H	9.70 FQ	16.23 AW	25.95 TQ	IABLS	10/01-12/01
	Kansas	H	13.05 FQ	18.90 AW	26.12 TQ	KSBLS	10/01-12/01
	Wichita MSA, KS	H	14.02 FQ	18.47 AW	25.30 TQ	KSBLS	10/01-12/01
	Kentucky	H	12.59 FQ	21.16 AW	31.65 TQ	KYBLS	10/01-12/01
	Lexington MSA, KY	H	9.81 FQ	27.50 AW	36.12 TQ	KYBLS	10/01-12/01
	Louisville MSA, KY-IN	H	15.59 FQ	21.64 AW	29.53 TQ	KYBLS	10/01-12/01
	Louisiana	H	11.64 FQ	16.92 AW	22.34 TQ	LABLS	10/01-12/01
	Baton Rouge MSA, LA	H	13.73 FQ	17.16 AW	22.13 TQ	LABLS	10/01-12/01
	Houma MSA, LA	H	7.89 FQ	14.26 AW	21.96 TQ	LABLS	10/01-12/01
	Lafayette MSA, LA	H	11.84 FQ	18.95 AW	28.39 TQ	LABLS	10/01-12/01
	Lake Charles MSA, LA	H	9.20 FQ	15.63 AW	22.62 TQ	LABLS	10/01-12/01
	New Orleans MSA, LA	H	12.87 FQ	18.40 AW	23.00 TQ	LABLS	10/01-12/01
	Maine	H	13.53 FQ	17.85 AW	22.47 TQ	MEBLS	10/01-12/01
	Portland MSA, ME	H	18.58 FQ	22.20 AW	27.64 TQ	MEBLS	10/01-12/01
	Maryland	H	14.21 FQ	19.19 AW	26.65 TQ	MDBLS	10/01-12/01
	Baltimore PMSA, MD	H	14.42 FQ	19.33 AW	26.53 TQ	MDBLS	10/01-12/01
	Massachusetts	H	14.41 FQ	21.44 AW	27.43 TQ	MABLS	10/01-12/01
	Boston PMSA, MA-NH	H	15.90 FQ	22.24 AW	27.51 TQ	MABLS	10/01-12/01
	Lawrence PMSA, MA-NH	H	21.27 FQ	25.23 AW	33.26 TQ	MABLS	10/01-12/01
	Lowell PMSA, MA-NH	H	10.73 FQ	14.52 AW	19.77 TQ	MABLS	10/01-12/01
	New Bedford PMSA, MA	H	17.38 FQ	21.46 AW	26.09 TQ	MABLS	10/01-12/01
	Springfield MSA, MA	H	13.46 FQ	19.44 AW	26.78 TQ	MABLS	10/01-12/01
	Michigan	H	19.72 FQ	26.00 AW	32.94 TQ	MIBLS	10/01-12/01
	Detroit PMSA, MI	H	22.59 FQ	26.69 AW	32.78 TQ	MIBLS	10/01-12/01
	Grand Rapids-Muskegon-Holland MSA, MI	H	15.65 FQ	23.36 AW	29.65 TQ	MIBLS	10/01-12/01
	Kalamazoo-Battle Creek MSA, MI	H	15.40 FQ	21.52 AW	27.65 TQ	MIBLS	10/01-12/01
	Saginaw-Bay City-Midland MSA, MI	H	20.92 FQ	27.43 AW	34.35 TQ	MIBLS	10/01-12/01
	Minnesota	H	16.12 FQ	21.73 AW	27.79 TQ	MNBLS	10/01-12/01
	Minneapolis-St. Paul MSA, MN-WI	H	17.55 FQ	23.24 AW	28.40 TQ	MNBLS	10/01-12/01
	St. Cloud MSA, MN	H	19.63 FQ	24.35 AW	28.42 TQ	MNBLS	10/01-12/01
	Mississippi	H	11.94 FQ	17.30 AW	22.58 TQ	MSBLS	10/01-12/01
	Biloxi-Gulfport-Pascagoula MSA, MS	H	14.77 FQ	18.02 AW	21.09 TQ	MSBLS	10/01-12/01
	Jackson MSA, MS	H	11.34 FQ	13.17 AW	16.21 TQ	MSBLS	10/01-12/01
	Missouri	H	15.34 FQ	22.59 AW	28.93 TQ	MOBLS	10/01-12/01
	Kansas City MSA, MO-KS	H	16.79 FQ	22.68 AW	28.26 TQ	MOBLS	10/01-12/01
	St. Louis MSA, MO-IL	H	14.96 FQ	21.87 AW	29.01 TQ	MOBLS	10/01-12/01
	Montana	H	11.69 FQ	16.34 AW	21.13 TQ	MTBLS	10/01-12/01
	Nebraska	H	9.25 FQ	14.06 AW	20.30 TQ	NEBLS	10/01-12/01
	Nevada	H	8.51 FQ	17.70 AW	26.17 TQ	NVBLS	10/01-12/01
	Las Vegas MSA, NV-AZ	H	8.32 FQ	18.26 AW	26.47 TQ	NVBLS	10/01-12/01
	New Hampshire	H	13.97 FQ	17.72 AW	21.86 TQ	NHBLS	10/01-12/01

AAW	Average annual wage	AOH	Average offered, high	ASH	Average starting, high	H	Hourly	M	Monthly	S	Special: hourly and annual
AE	Average entry wage	AOL	Average offered, low	ASL	Average starting, low	HI	Highest wage paid	MTC	Median total compensation	TQ	Third quartile wage
AEX	Average experienced wage	APH	Average pay, high range	AW	Average wage paid	HR	High end range	MW	Median wage paid	W	Weekly
AO	Average offered	APL	Average pay, low range	FQ	First quartile wage	LR	Low end range	SQ	Second quartile wage	Y	Yearly

Occupation/Type/Industry	Location	Per	Low	Mid	High	Source	Date
Millwright	Nashua PMSA, NH	H	13.64 FQ	17.45 AW	23.53 TQ	NHBLS	10/01-12/01
	Portsmouth-Rochester PMSA, NH-ME	H	13.86 FQ	16.99 AW	20.71 TQ	NHBLS	10/01-12/01
	New Jersey	H	17.50 FQ	26.08 AW	33.76 TQ	NJBLS	10/01-12/01
	Bergen-Passaic PMSA, NJ	H	17.01 FQ	25.18 AW	34.16 TQ	NJBLS	10/01-12/01
	Middlesex-Somerset-Hunterdon PMSA, NJ	H	19.84 FQ	27.97 AW	34.15 TQ	NJBLS	10/01-12/01
	Monmouth-Ocean PMSA, NJ	H	23.56 FQ	29.21 AW	34.19 TQ	NJBLS	10/01-12/01
	Newark PMSA, NJ	H	16.55 FQ	22.05 AW	26.92 TQ	NJBLS	10/01-12/01
	New Mexico	H	9.61 FQ	14.07 AW	20.59 TQ	NMBLS	10/01-12/01
	New York	H	15.29 FQ	20.44 AW	26.32 TQ	NYBLS	10/01-12/01
	Albany-Schenectady-Troy MSA, NY	H	15.85 FQ	19.43 AW	22.67 TQ	NYBLS	10/01-12/01
	Buffalo-Niagara Falls MSA, NY	H	16.10 FQ	21.04 AW	26.89 TQ	NYBLS	10/01-12/01
	Nassau-Suffolk PMSA, NY	H	18.53 FQ	21.14 AW	23.11 TQ	NYBLS	10/01-12/01
	New York PMSA, NY	H	15.71 FQ	21.21 AW	26.77 TQ	NYBLS	10/01-12/01
	Syracuse MSA, NY	H	16.17 FQ	19.29 AW	22.09 TQ	NYBLS	10/01-12/01
	Utica-Rome MSA, NY	H	10.61 FQ	18.02 AW	22.95 TQ	NYBLS	10/01-12/01
	North Carolina	H	11.48 FQ	15.25 AW	20.67 TQ	NCBLS	10/01-12/01
	Charlotte-Gastonia-Rock Hill MSA, NC-SC	H	13.52 FQ	19.26 AW	26.40 TQ	NCBLS	10/01-12/01
	Fayetteville MSA, NC	H	10.47 FQ	14.59 AW	18.00 TQ	NCBLS	10/01-12/01
	Greensboro-Winston-Salem-High Point MSA, NC	H	12.92 FQ	16.64 AW	21.10 TQ	NCBLS	10/01-12/01
	Hickory-Morganton-Lenoir MSA, NC	H	6.82 FQ	11.41 AW	16.45 TQ	NCBLS	10/01-12/01
	Raleigh-Durham-Chapel Hill MSA, NC	H	11.58 FQ	15.44 AW	19.13 TQ	NCBLS	10/01-12/01
	Wilmington MSA, NC	H	11.47 FQ	15.37 AW	20.49 TQ	NCBLS	10/01-12/01
	North Dakota	H	6.68 FQ	18.34 AW	26.71 TQ	NDBLS	10/01-12/01
	Ohio	H	15.67 FQ	22.87 AW	30.30 TQ	OHBLS	10/01-12/01
	Akron PMSA, OH	H	14.22 FQ	22.18 AW	27.58 TQ	OHBLS	10/01-12/01
	Canton-Massillon MSA, OH	H	15.52 FQ	22.34 AW	30.03 TQ	OHBLS	10/01-12/01
	Cincinnati PMSA, OH-KY-IN	H	13.27 FQ	21.57 AW	28.42 TQ	OHBLS	10/01-12/01
	Cleveland-Lorain-Elyria PMSA, OH	H	18.75 FQ	23.70 AW	27.87 TQ	OHBLS	10/01-12/01
	Columbus MSA, OH	H	12.78 FQ	19.85 AW	26.75 TQ	OHBLS	10/01-12/01
	Dayton-Springfield MSA, OH	H	20.04 FQ	28.28 AW	34.64 TQ	OHBLS	10/01-12/01
	Toledo MSA, OH	H	19.39 FQ	24.17 AW	28.12 TQ	OHBLS	10/01-12/01
	Oklahoma	H	7.85 FQ	15.02 AW	25.47 TQ	OKBLS	10/01-12/01
	Oklahoma City MSA, OK	H	7.45 FQ	11.96 AW	20.35 TQ	OKBLS	10/01-12/01
	Oregon	H	14.50 FQ	20.25 AW	26.72 TQ	ORBLS	10/01-12/01
	Eugene-Springfield MSA, OR	H	16.78 FQ	20.60 AW	25.96 TQ	ORBLS	10/01-12/01
	Portland-Vancouver PMSA, OR-WA	H	15.59 FQ	22.51 AW	28.23 TQ	ORBLS	10/01-12/01
	Salem PMSA, OR	H	9.92 FQ	19.96 AW	27.66 TQ	ORBLS	10/01-12/01
	Pennsylvania	H	12.84 FQ	18.74 AW	25.95 TQ	PABLS	10/01-12/01
	Allentown-Bethlehem-Easton MSA, PA	H	14.91 FQ	18.41 AW	23.47 TQ	PABLS	10/01-12/01
	Erie MSA, PA	H	11.89 FQ	16.43 AW	23.25 TQ	PABLS	10/01-12/01
	Harrisburg-Lebanon-Carlisle MSA, PA	H	12.81 FQ	19.12 AW	26.93 TQ	PABLS	10/01-12/01
	Johnstown MSA, PA	H	14.27 FQ	16.65 AW	20.74 TQ	PABLS	10/01-12/01
	Lancaster MSA, PA	H	13.68 FQ	17.66 AW	22.74 TQ	PABLS	10/01-12/01
	Philadelphia PMSA, PA-NJ	H	14.81 FQ	21.37 AW	27.82 TQ	PABLS	10/01-12/01
	Pittsburgh MSA, PA	H	11.16 FQ	18.76 AW	25.31 TQ	PABLS	10/01-12/01
	Reading MSA, PA	H	14.36 FQ	18.93 AW	24.48 TQ	PABLS	10/01-12/01
	Scranton-Wilkes-Barre-Hazleton MSA, PA	H	12.32 FQ	18.80 AW	27.92 TQ	PABLS	10/01-12/01
	York MSA, PA	H	14.54 FQ	20.41 AW	27.02 TQ	PABLS	10/01-12/01
	Rhode Island	H	12.16 FQ	16.51 AW	24.78 TQ	RIBLS	10/01-12/01
	Providence-Fall River-Warwick MSA, RI-MA	H	12.05 FQ	15.93 AW	23.56 TQ	RIBLS	10/01-12/01
	South Carolina	H	11.78 FQ	18.27 AW	28.06 TQ	SCBLS	10/01-12/01
	Charleston-North Charleston MSA, SC	H	11.63 FQ	14.69 AW	18.58 TQ	SCBLS	10/01-12/01
	Greenville-Spartanburg-Anderson MSA, SC	H	14.21 FQ	17.81 AW	24.02 TQ	SCBLS	10/01-12/01
	South Dakota	H	12.29 FQ	14.82 AW	17.49 TQ	SDBLS	10/01-12/01
	Tennessee	H	10.39 FQ	16.61 AW	24.27 TQ	TNBLS	10/01-12/01
	Chattanooga MSA, TN-GA	H	11.60 FQ	17.14 AW	21.58 TQ	TNBLS	10/01-12/01

AAW	Average annual wage	**AOH**	Average offered, high	**ASH**	Average starting, high	**H**	Hourly	**M**	Monthly	**S**	Special: hourly and annual
AE	Average entry wage	**AOL**	Average offered, low	**ASL**	Average starting, low	**HI**	Highest wage paid	**MTC**	Median total compensation	**TQ**	Third quartile wage
AEX	Average experienced wage	**APH**	Average pay, high range	**AW**	Average wage paid	**HR**	High end range	**MW**	Median wage paid	**W**	Weekly
AO	Average offered	**APL**	Average pay, low range	**FQ**	First quartile wage	**LR**	Low end range	**SQ**	Second quartile wage	**Y**	Yearly

Occupation/Type/Industry	Location	Per	Low	Mid	High	Source	Date
Millwright	Johnson City-Kingsport-Bristol MSA, TN-VA	H	10.16 FQ	14.33 AW	20.15 TQ	TNBLS	10/01-12/01
	Memphis MSA, TN-AR-MS	H	12.27 FQ	16.87 AW	21.60 TQ	TNBLS	10/01-12/01
	Nashville MSA, TN	H	17.47 FQ	22.09 AW	30.11 TQ	TNBLS	10/01-12/01
	Texas	H	10.57 FQ	17.73 AW	25.81 TQ	TXBLS	10/01-12/01
	Austin-San Marcos MSA, TX	H	10.30 FQ	17.00 AW	21.65 TQ	TXBLS	10/01-12/01
	Beaumont-Port Arthur MSA, TX	H	12.32 FQ	19.31 AW	26.96 TQ	TXBLS	10/01-12/01
	Dallas PMSA, TX	H	11.61 FQ	18.95 AW	26.51 TQ	TXBLS	10/01-12/01
	El Paso MSA, TX	H	9.79 FQ	16.11 AW	21.90 TQ	TXBLS	10/01-12/01
	Galveston-Texas City PMSA, TX	H	10.94 FQ	16.10 AW	21.64 TQ	TXBLS	10/01-12/01
	Houston PMSA, TX	H	12.48 FQ	19.02 AW	25.63 TQ	TXBLS	10/01-12/01
	San Antonio MSA, TX	H	11.75 FQ	18.71 AW	26.65 TQ	TXBLS	10/01-12/01
	Waco MSA, TX	H	9.47 FQ	14.19 AW	18.16 TQ	TXBLS	10/01-12/01
	Utah	H	10.35 FQ	17.96 AW	26.06 TQ	UTBLS	10/01-12/01
	Salt Lake City-Ogden MSA, UT	H	9.33 FQ	15.77 AW	21.49 TQ	UTBLS	10/01-12/01
	Vermont	H	14.72 FQ	21.65 AW	28.95 TQ	VTBLS	10/01-12/01
	Virginia	H	12.14 FQ	18.21 AW	26.40 TQ	VABLS	10/01-12/01
	Lynchburg MSA, VA	H	11.30 FQ	16.02 AW	21.64 TQ	VABLS	10/01-12/01
	Norfolk-Virginia Beach-Newport News MSA, VA-NC	H	13.12 FQ	19.87 AW	27.89 TQ	VABLS	10/01-12/01
	Richmond-Petersburg MSA, VA	H	14.55 FQ	20.97 AW	27.24 TQ	VABLS	10/01-12/01
	Roanoke MSA, VA	H	11.35 FQ	17.04 AW	25.78 TQ	VABLS	10/01-12/01
	Washington	H	15.59 FQ	22.25 AW	28.29 TQ	WABLS	10/01-12/01
	Seattle-Bellevue-Everett PMSA, WA	H	18.86 FQ	24.46 AW	30.30 TQ	WABLS	10/01-12/01
	Spokane MSA, WA	H	11.46 FQ	15.90 AW	21.78 TQ	WABLS	10/01-12/01
	Tacoma PMSA, WA	H	14.79 FQ	21.74 AW	28.69 TQ	WABLS	10/01-12/01
	West Virginia	H	13.67 FQ	19.03 AW	26.20 TQ	WVBLS	10/01-12/01
	Wisconsin	H	15.67 FQ	22.80 AW	29.85 TQ	WIBLS	10/01-12/01
	Appleton-Oshkosh-Neenah MSA, WI	H	18.51 FQ	24.44 AW	33.41 TQ	WIBLS	10/01-12/01
	Milwaukee-Waukesha PMSA, WI	H	17.65 FQ	22.70 AW	27.72 TQ	WIBLS	10/01-12/01
	Wyoming	H	11.25 FQ	15.71 AW	21.58 TQ	WYBLS	10/01-12/01
	Puerto Rico	H	10.56 FQ	18.95 AW	28.90 TQ	PRBLS	10/01-12/01
Mine Cutting and Channeling Machine Operator	Alabama	H	10.47 FQ	14.42 AW	20.61 TQ	ALBLS	10/01-12/01
	Arizona	H	16.59 FQ	20.78 AW	25.90 TQ	AZBLS	10/01-12/01
	California	H	12.54 FQ	16.13 AW	19.74 TQ	CABLS	10/01-12/01
	Illinois	H	12.00 FQ	18.90 AW	27.46 TQ	ILBLS	10/01-12/01
	Indiana	H	13.11 FQ	16.08 AW	20.00 TQ	INBLS	10/01-12/01
	Iowa	H	11.04 FQ	13.99 AW	16.55 TQ	IABLS	10/01-12/01
	Kentucky	H	11.04 FQ	14.70 AW	20.53 TQ	KYBLS	10/01-12/01
	Missouri	H	9.82 FQ	13.30 AW	17.37 TQ	MOBLS	10/01-12/01
	Nevada	H	18.11 FQ	21.38 AW	27.04 TQ	NVBLS	10/01-12/01
	New York	H	11.56 FQ	15.93 AW	20.33 TQ	NYBLS	10/01-12/01
	North Carolina	H	10.27 FQ	13.29 AW	16.73 TQ	NCBLS	10/01-12/01
	Ohio	H	11.48 FQ	15.72 AW	21.30 TQ	OHBLS	10/01-12/01
	Pennsylvania	H	12.83 FQ	18.96 AW	22.76 TQ	PABLS	10/01-12/01
	Texas	H	8.22 FQ	10.35 AW	12.91 TQ	TXBLS	10/01-12/01
	Virginia	H	11.77 FQ	15.61 AW	20.18 TQ	VABLS	10/01-12/01
	West Virginia	H	12.39 FQ	15.87 AW	20.10 TQ	WVBLS	10/01-12/01
	Wisconsin	H	10.45 FQ	15.65 AW	20.75 TQ	WIBLS	10/01-12/01
Mining and Geological Engineer							
Including Mining Safety Engineer	Alabama	Y	35030 FQ	58790 AW	85760 TQ	ALBLS	10/01-12/01
Including Mining Safety Engineer	Arizona	Y	30190 FQ	49640 AW	80140 TQ	AZBLS	10/01-12/01
Including Mining Safety Engineer	California	Y	43180 FQ	77700 AW		CABLS	10/01-12/01
Including Mining Safety Engineer	Colorado	Y	39140 FQ	69230 AW	100250 TQ	COBLS	10/01-12/01
Including Mining Safety Engineer	Florida	Y	35780 FQ	56670 AW	76590 TQ	FLBLS	10/01-12/01
Including Mining Safety Engineer	Georgia	Y	39640 FQ	63360 AW	99220 TQ	GABLS	10/01-12/01
Including Mining Safety Engineer	Idaho	Y	44770 FQ	67020 AW	102840 TQ	IDBLS	10/01-12/01
Including Mining Safety Engineer	Illinois	Y	38510 FQ	55010 AW	76500 TQ	ILBLS	10/01-12/01
Including Mining Safety Engineer	Indiana	Y	39680 FQ	58160 AW	82660 TQ	INBLS	10/01-12/01
Including Mining Safety Engineer	Kentucky	Y	30150 FQ	58810 AW	90970 TQ	KYBLS	10/01-12/01
Including Mining Safety Engineer	Louisiana	Y	48480 FQ	73390 AW	107830 TQ	LABLS	10/01-12/01

AAW Average annual wage; **AE** Average entry wage; **AEX** Average experienced wage; **AO** Average offered; **AOH** Average offered, high; **AOL** Average offered, low; **APH** Average pay, high range; **APL** Average pay, low range; **ASH** Average starting, high; **ASL** Average starting, low; **AW** Average wage paid; **FQ** First quartile wage; **H** Hourly; **HI** Highest wage paid; **HR** High end range; **LR** Low end range; **M** Monthly; **MTC** Median total compensation; **MW** Median wage paid; **SQ** Second quartile wage; **S** Special: hourly and annual; **TQ** Third quartile wage; **W** Weekly; **Y** Yearly

Occupation/Type/Industry	Location	Per	Low	Mid	High	Source	Date
Mining and Geological Engineer							
Including Mining Safety Engineer	Massachusetts	Y	39080 FQ	57650 AW	88190 TQ	MABLS	10/01-12/01
Including Mining Safety Engineer	Michigan	Y	42350 FQ	62740 AW	90290 TQ	MIBLS	10/01-12/01
Including Mining Safety Engineer	Minnesota	Y	38920 FQ	61790 AW	94290 TQ	MNBLS	10/01-12/01
Including Mining Safety Engineer	Mississippi	Y	34030 FQ	54140 AW	84690 TQ	MSBLS	10/01-12/01
Including Mining Safety Engineer	Missouri	Y	36380 FQ	59960 AW	90050 TQ	MOBLS	10/01-12/01
Including Mining Safety Engineer	Montana	Y	44830 FQ	51930 AW	58820 TQ	MTBLS	10/01-12/01
Including Mining Safety Engineer	Nevada	Y	46710 FQ	64610 AW	88400 TQ	NVBLS	10/01-12/01
Including Mining Safety Engineer	New Mexico	Y	40810 FQ	63550 AW	88980 TQ	NMBLS	10/01-12/01
Including Mining Safety Engineer	New York	Y	38300 FQ	58180 AW	86410 TQ	NYBLS	10/01-12/01
Including Mining Safety Engineer	North Carolina	Y	32300 FQ	51980 AW	80420 TQ	NCBLS	10/01-12/01
Including Mining Safety Engineer	North Dakota	Y	36900 FQ	51270 AW	79340 TQ	NDBLS	10/01-12/01
Including Mining Safety Engineer	Ohio	Y	37760 FQ	59050 AW	85190 TQ	OHBLS	10/01-12/01
Including Mining Safety Engineer	Oklahoma	Y	39080 FQ	72780 AW	138510 TQ	OKBLS	10/01-12/01
Including Mining Safety Engineer	Pennsylvania	Y	36200 FQ	57940 AW	77060 TQ	PABLS	10/01-12/01
Including Mining Safety Engineer	South Carolina	Y	35580 FQ	49710 AW	63580 TQ	SCBLS	10/01-12/01
Including Mining Safety Engineer	Texas	Y	38060 FQ	75600 AW	125160 TQ	TXBLS	10/01-12/01
Including Mining Safety Engineer	Utah	Y	42800 FQ	74180 AW	115300 TQ	UTBLS	10/01-12/01
Including Mining Safety Engineer	Virginia	Y	38830 FQ	62710 AW	88810 TQ	VABLS	10/01-12/01
Including Mining Safety Engineer	Washington	Y	44020 FQ	69470 AW	95520 TQ	WABLS	10/01-12/01
Including Mining Safety Engineer	West Virginia	Y	21730 FQ	52470 AW	77810 TQ	WVBLS	10/01-12/01
Including Mining Safety Engineer	Wyoming	Y	46380 FQ	62120 AW	82770 TQ	WYBLS	10/01-12/01
Mixing and Blending Machine Setter, Operator, and Tender	Alabama	H	7.56 FQ	13.24 AW	20.36 TQ	ALBLS	10/01-12/01
	Birmingham MSA, AL	H	8.45 FQ	13.09 AW	20.11 TQ	ALBLS	10/01-12/01
	Mobile MSA, AL	H	6.48 FQ	10.72 AW	17.28 TQ	ALBLS	10/01-12/01
	Montgomery MSA, AL	H	8.91 FQ	12.35 AW	16.59 TQ	ALBLS	10/01-12/01
	Alaska	H	9.74 FQ	13.11 AW	16.64 TQ	AKBLS	10/01-12/01
	Arizona	H	6.96 FQ	12.32 AW	17.67 TQ	AZBLS	10/01-12/01
	Phoenix-Mesa MSA, AZ	H	7.08 FQ	12.49 AW	17.86 TQ	AZBLS	10/01-12/01
	Tucson MSA, AZ	H	6.55 FQ	11.07 AW	16.51 TQ	AZBLS	10/01-12/01
	Arkansas	H	8.11 FQ	11.38 AW	15.87 TQ	ARBLS	10/01-12/01
	Fayetteville-Springdale-Rogers MSA, AR	H	8.14 FQ	10.43 AW	13.49 TQ	ARBLS	10/01-12/01
	Fort Smith MSA, AR-OK	H	7.66 FQ	10.50 AW	15.63 TQ	ARBLS	10/01-12/01
	Little Rock-North Little Rock MSA, AR	H	7.60 FQ	10.97 AW	14.86 TQ	ARBLS	10/01-12/01
	California	H	7.66 FQ	13.34 AW	19.73 TQ	CABLS	10/01-12/01
	Bakersfield MSA, CA	H	6.69 FQ	11.14 AW	17.39 TQ	CABLS	10/01-12/01
	Fresno MSA, CA	H	7.52 FQ	12.16 AW	18.98 TQ	CABLS	10/01-12/01
	Los Angeles-Long Beach PMSA, CA	H	7.19 FQ	12.53 AW	18.66 TQ	CABLS	10/01-12/01
	Merced MSA, CA	H	7.60 FQ	12.85 AW	17.54 TQ	CABLS	10/01-12/01
	Modesto MSA, CA	H	8.77 FQ	14.17 AW	18.19 TQ	CABLS	10/01-12/01
	Oakland PMSA, CA	H	7.68 FQ	14.76 AW	20.57 TQ	CABLS	10/01-12/01
	Orange County PMSA, CA	H	7.85 FQ	12.97 AW	19.17 TQ	CABLS	10/01-12/01
	Riverside-San Bernardino PMSA, CA	H	7.59 FQ	11.91 AW	16.73 TQ	CABLS	10/01-12/01
	Sacramento PMSA, CA	H	9.92 FQ	16.47 AW	27.93 TQ	CABLS	10/01-12/01
	Salinas MSA, CA	H	7.71 FQ	13.23 AW	19.70 TQ	CABLS	10/01-12/01
	San Diego MSA, CA	H	9.18 FQ	13.38 AW	19.37 TQ	CABLS	10/01-12/01
	San Francisco PMSA, CA	H	6.63 FQ	14.08 AW	21.88 TQ	CABLS	10/01-12/01
	Santa Rosa PMSA, CA	H	9.86 FQ	14.74 AW	19.59 TQ	CABLS	10/01-12/01
	Stockton-Lodi MSA, CA	H	8.65 FQ	12.48 AW	17.96 TQ	CABLS	10/01-12/01
	Vallejo-Fairfield-Napa PMSA, CA	H	9.39 FQ	13.54 AW	17.84 TQ	CABLS	10/01-12/01
	Ventura PMSA, CA	H	10.72 FQ	15.70 AW	21.96 TQ	CABLS	10/01-12/01
	Visalia-Tulare-Porterville MSA, CA	H	7.32 FQ	13.40 AW	20.29 TQ	CABLS	10/01-12/01
	Colorado	H	8.97 FQ	13.10 AW	17.32 TQ	COBLS	10/01-12/01
	Colorado Springs MSA, CO	H	8.30 FQ	11.66 AW	14.68 TQ	COBLS	10/01-12/01
	Denver PMSA, CO	H	9.62 FQ	13.85 AW	17.97 TQ	COBLS	10/01-12/01
	Fort Collins-Loveland MSA, CO	H	8.97 FQ	13.89 AW	19.82 TQ	COBLS	10/01-12/01
	Greeley PMSA, CO	H	9.14 FQ	12.14 AW	15.71 TQ	COBLS	10/01-12/01
	Connecticut	H	9.98 FQ	15.88 AW	22.15 TQ	CTBLS	10/01-12/01
	Bridgeport PMSA, CT	H	9.97 FQ	13.44 AW	17.51 TQ	CTBLS	10/01-12/01
	Danbury PMSA, CT	H	9.56 FQ	17.71 AW	29.48 TQ	CTBLS	10/01-12/01
	Hartford MSA, CT	H	11.09 FQ	16.79 AW	21.76 TQ	CTBLS	10/01-12/01
	New Haven-Meriden PMSA, CT	H	9.51 FQ	14.84 AW	21.24 TQ	CTBLS	10/01-12/01

AAW	Average annual wage	AOH	Average offered, high	ASH	Average starting, high	H	Hourly	M	Monthly	S	Special: hourly and annual
AE	Average entry wage	AOL	Average offered, low	ASL	Average starting, low	HI	Highest wage paid	MTC	Median total compensation	TQ	Third quartile wage
AEX	Average experienced wage	APH	Average pay, high range	AW	Average wage paid	HR	High end range	MW	Median wage paid	W	Weekly
AO	Average offered	APL	Average pay, low range	FQ	First quartile wage	LR	Low end range	SQ	Second quartile wage	Y	Yearly

Occupation/Type/Industry	Location	Per	Low	Mid	High	Source	Date
Mixing and Blending Machine Setter, Operator, and Tender	New London-Norwich MSA, CT-RI	H	10.68 FQ	14.35 AW	17.90 TQ	CTBLS	10/01-12/01
	Waterbury PMSA, CT	H	9.21 FQ	12.36 AW	18.69 TQ	CTBLS	10/01-12/01
	Delaware	H	9.82 FQ	15.21 AW	20.65 TQ	DEBLS	10/01-12/01
	Wilmington-Newark PMSA, DE-MD	H	10.95 FQ	16.64 AW	21.17 TQ	DEBLS	10/01-12/01
	Washington PMSA, DC-MD-VA-WV	H	8.19 FQ	12.76 AW	16.88 TQ	DCBLS	10/01-12/01
	Florida	H	6.15 FQ	10.74 AW	16.31 TQ	FLBLS	10/01-12/01
	Daytona Beach MSA, FL	H	7.35 FQ	10.35 AW	13.73 TQ	FLBLS	10/01-12/01
	Fort Lauderdale PMSA, FL	H	6.71 FQ	11.45 AW	17.36 TQ	FLBLS	10/01-12/01
	Fort Myers-Cape Coral MSA, FL	H	7.07 FQ	9.36 AW	12.56 TQ	FLBLS	10/01-12/01
	Fort Pierce-Port St. Lucie MSA, FL	H	7.79 FQ	10.41 AW	13.48 TQ	FLBLS	10/01-12/01
	Fort Walton Beach MSA, FL	H	7.22 FQ	10.40 AW	14.94 TQ	FLBLS	10/01-12/01
	Gainesville MSA, FL	H	7.02 FQ	9.02 AW	12.35 TQ	FLBLS	10/01-12/01
	Jacksonville MSA, FL	H	5.42 FQ	9.19 AW	16.83 TQ	FLBLS	10/01-12/01
	Lakeland-Winter Haven MSA, FL	H	8.83 FQ	12.67 AW	16.77 TQ	FLBLS	10/01-12/01
	Melbourne-Titusville-Palm Bay MSA, FL	H	7.52 FQ	10.42 AW	13.86 TQ	FLBLS	10/01-12/01
	Miami PMSA, FL	H	7.27 FQ	11.38 AW	16.39 TQ	FLBLS	10/01-12/01
	Naples MSA, FL	H	7.58 FQ	11.08 AW	14.40 TQ	FLBLS	10/01-12/01
	Ocala MSA, FL	H	8.65 FQ	10.77 AW	13.40 TQ	FLBLS	10/01-12/01
	Orlando MSA, FL	H	7.22 FQ	10.28 AW	13.67 TQ	FLBLS	10/01-12/01
	Pensacola MSA, FL	H	7.26 FQ	10.67 AW	15.91 TQ	FLBLS	10/01-12/01
	Sarasota-Bradenton MSA, FL	H	7.54 FQ	9.96 AW	12.93 TQ	FLBLS	10/01-12/01
	Tampa-St. Petersburg-Clearwater MSA, FL	H	7.30 FQ	11.61 AW	17.26 TQ	FLBLS	10/01-12/01
	West Palm Beach-Boca Raton MSA, FL	H	6.60 FQ	11.09 AW	14.97 TQ	FLBLS	10/01-12/01
	Georgia	H	6.62 FQ	11.85 AW	17.88 TQ	GABLS	10/01-12/01
	Atlanta MSA, GA	H	6.19 FQ	12.10 AW	19.21 TQ	GABLS	10/01-12/01
	Augusta-Aiken MSA, GA-SC	H	8.35 FQ	13.88 AW	19.65 TQ	GABLS	10/01-12/01
	Columbus MSA, GA-AL	H	7.02 FQ	10.54 AW	15.12 TQ	GABLS	10/01-12/01
	Macon MSA, GA	H	7.66 FQ	12.61 AW	16.42 TQ	GABLS	10/01-12/01
	Savannah MSA, GA	H	6.24 FQ	12.04 AW	17.15 TQ	GABLS	10/01-12/01
	Hawaii	H	7.39 FQ	12.06 AW	17.11 TQ	HIBLS	10/01-12/01
	Honolulu MSA, HI	H	7.12 FQ	11.84 AW	17.03 TQ	HIBLS	10/01-12/01
	Idaho	H	8.04 FQ	13.62 AW	20.84 TQ	IDBLS	10/01-12/01
	Boise City MSA, ID	H	7.68 FQ	10.90 AW	14.20 TQ	IDBLS	10/01-12/01
	Illinois	H	8.05 FQ	13.66 AW	20.22 TQ	ILBLS	10/01-12/01
	Champaign-Urbana MSA, IL	H	11.63 FQ	16.35 AW	21.58 TQ	ILBLS	10/01-12/01
	Chicago PMSA, IL	H	8.99 FQ	14.52 AW	20.74 TQ	ILBLS	10/01-12/01
	Peoria-Pekin MSA, IL	H	11.60 FQ	19.99 AW	26.12 TQ	ILBLS	10/01-12/01
	Rockford MSA, IL	H	8.91 FQ	13.54 AW	20.19 TQ	ILBLS	10/01-12/01
	Springfield MSA, IL	H	11.27 FQ	15.77 AW	23.13 TQ	ILBLS	10/01-12/01
	Indiana	H	9.46 FQ	14.24 AW	19.90 TQ	INBLS	10/01-12/01
	Elkhart-Goshen MSA, IN	H	9.22 FQ	12.97 AW	16.89 TQ	INBLS	10/01-12/01
	Evansville-Henderson MSA, IN-KY	H	9.39 FQ	13.60 AW	18.87 TQ	INBLS	10/01-12/01
	Fort Wayne MSA, IN	H	11.19 FQ	15.81 AW	21.21 TQ	INBLS	10/01-12/01
	Gary PMSA, IN	H	10.14 FQ	16.94 AW	22.16 TQ	INBLS	10/01-12/01
	Indianapolis MSA, IN	H	9.63 FQ	13.90 AW	18.53 TQ	INBLS	10/01-12/01
	Lafayette MSA, IN	H	10.23 FQ	15.24 AW	20.90 TQ	INBLS	10/01-12/01
	South Bend MSA, IN	H	8.13 FQ	12.45 AW	19.73 TQ	INBLS	10/01-12/01
	Iowa	H	7.38 FQ	11.71 AW	16.85 TQ	IABLS	10/01-12/01
	Cedar Rapids MSA, IA	H	7.36 FQ	11.58 AW	19.02 TQ	IABLS	10/01-12/01
	Davenport-Moline-Rock Island MSA, IA-IL	H	6.00 FQ	11.33 AW	16.25 TQ	IABLS	10/01-12/01
	Des Moines MSA, IA	H	6.63 FQ	11.47 AW	16.15 TQ	IABLS	10/01-12/01
	Kansas	H	8.49 FQ	12.06 AW	16.24 TQ	KSBLS	10/01-12/01
	Topeka MSA, KS	H	10.13 FQ	13.35 AW	18.35 TQ	KSBLS	10/01-12/01
	Wichita MSA, KS	H	8.65 FQ	13.34 AW	21.28 TQ	KSBLS	10/01-12/01
	Kentucky	H	8.89 FQ	13.20 AW	17.93 TQ	KYBLS	10/01-12/01
	Lexington MSA, KY	H	8.84 FQ	13.74 AW	18.30 TQ	KYBLS	10/01-12/01
	Louisville MSA, KY-IN	H	9.26 FQ	14.16 AW	20.13 TQ	KYBLS	10/01-12/01
	Louisiana	H	7.29 FQ	12.89 AW	20.54 TQ	LABLS	10/01-12/01
	Baton Rouge MSA, LA	H	9.14 FQ	16.24 AW	23.69 TQ	LABLS	10/01-12/01
	Lafayette MSA, LA	H	6.67 FQ	9.23 AW	11.31 TQ	LABLS	10/01-12/01

AAW Average annual wage · **AE** Average entry wage · **AEX** Average experienced wage · **AO** Average offered · **AOH** Average offered, high · **AOL** Average offered, low · **APH** Average pay, high range · **APL** Average pay, low range · **ASH** Average starting, high · **ASL** Average starting, low · **AW** Average wage paid · **FQ** First quartile wage · **H** Hourly · **HI** Highest wage paid · **HR** High end range · **LR** Low end range · **M** Monthly · **MTC** Median total compensation · **MW** Median wage paid · **SQ** Second quartile wage · **S** Special: hourly and annual · **TQ** Third quartile wage · **W** Weekly · **Y** Yearly

Occupation/Type/Industry	Location	Per	Low	Mid	High	Source	Date
Mixing and Blending Machine Setter, Operator, and Tender	Lake Charles MSA, LA	H	7.23 FQ	14.58 AW	24.08 TQ	LABLS	10/01-12/01
	New Orleans MSA, LA	H	7.48 FQ	12.83 AW	20.71 TQ	LABLS	10/01-12/01
	Shreveport-Bossier City MSA, LA	H	7.91 FQ	12.01 AW	16.95 TQ	LABLS	10/01-12/01
	Maine	H	10.77 FQ	16.04 AW	22.56 TQ	MEBLS	10/01-12/01
	Portland MSA, ME	H	9.68 FQ	16.20 AW	22.70 TQ	MEBLS	10/01-12/01
	Maryland	H	9.31 FQ	13.69 AW	19.17 TQ	MDBLS	10/01-12/01
	Baltimore PMSA, MD	H	9.35 FQ	13.69 AW	19.31 TQ	MDBLS	10/01-12/01
	Massachusetts	H	9.92 FQ	14.10 AW	18.20 TQ	MABLS	10/01-12/01
	Boston PMSA, MA-NH	H	9.73 FQ	13.68 AW	17.78 TQ	MABLS	10/01-12/01
	Brockton PMSA, MA	H	10.67 FQ	15.46 AW	21.15 TQ	MABLS	10/01-12/01
	Lawrence PMSA, MA-NH	H	11.11 FQ	14.47 AW	17.67 TQ	MABLS	10/01-12/01
	Lowell PMSA, MA-NH	H	10.71 FQ	14.43 AW	19.20 TQ	MABLS	10/01-12/01
	Springfield MSA, MA	H	11.58 FQ	16.51 AW	23.20 TQ	MABLS	10/01-12/01
	Worcester PMSA, MA-CT	H	10.00 FQ	13.72 AW	18.32 TQ	MABLS	10/01-12/01
	Michigan	H	9.11 FQ	13.84 AW	20.08 TQ	MIBLS	10/01-12/01
	Ann Arbor PMSA, MI	H	8.56 FQ	13.99 AW	20.28 TQ	MIBLS	10/01-12/01
	Detroit PMSA, MI	H	9.96 FQ	15.23 AW	21.10 TQ	MIBLS	10/01-12/01
	Flint PMSA, MI	H	6.25 FQ	14.60 AW	26.44 TQ	MIBLS	10/01-12/01
	Grand Rapids-Muskegon-Holland MSA, MI	H	9.20 FQ	12.05 AW	16.21 TQ	MIBLS	10/01-12/01
	Kalamazoo-Battle Creek MSA, MI	H	9.83 FQ	14.80 AW	20.17 TQ	MIBLS	10/01-12/01
	Lansing-East Lansing MSA, MI	H	6.43 FQ	10.76 AW	16.57 TQ	MIBLS	10/01-12/01
	Saginaw-Bay City-Midland MSA, MI	H	7.96 FQ	15.08 AW	23.18 TQ	MIBLS	10/01-12/01
	Minnesota	H	10.24 FQ	15.44 AW	20.71 TQ	MNBLS	10/01-12/01
	Duluth-Superior MSA, MN-WI	H	8.00 FQ	13.57 AW	19.55 TQ	MNBLS	10/01-12/01
	Minneapolis-St. Paul MSA, MN-WI	H	11.06 FQ	15.84 AW	20.74 TQ	MNBLS	10/01-12/01
	Mississippi	H	8.13 FQ	11.78 AW	16.65 TQ	MSBLS	10/01-12/01
	Jackson MSA, MS	H	8.26 FQ	11.27 AW	15.45 TQ	MSBLS	10/01-12/01
	Missouri	H	9.13 FQ	14.53 AW	20.22 TQ	MOBLS	10/01-12/01
	Kansas City MSA, MO-KS	H	9.76 FQ	14.78 AW	20.48 TQ	MOBLS	10/01-12/01
	St. Louis MSA, MO-IL	H	10.18 FQ	15.43 AW	20.62 TQ	MOBLS	10/01-12/01
	Springfield MSA, MO	H	7.67 FQ	11.36 AW	16.15 TQ	MOBLS	10/01-12/01
	Montana	H	8.12 FQ	13.44 AW	20.21 TQ	MTBLS	10/01-12/01
	Nebraska	H	7.63 FQ	11.35 AW	16.51 TQ	NEBLS	10/01-12/01
	Lincoln MSA, NE	H	7.36 FQ	11.22 AW	17.37 TQ	NEBLS	10/01-12/01
	Omaha MSA, NE-IA	H	7.73 FQ	11.04 AW	16.14 TQ	NEBLS	10/01-12/01
	Nevada	H	8.67 FQ	15.74 AW	29.35 TQ	NVBLS	10/01-12/01
	Las Vegas MSA, NV-AZ	H	8.70 FQ	16.73 AW	31.51 TQ	NVBLS	10/01-12/01
	Reno MSA, NV	H	9.72 FQ	14.36 AW	20.60 TQ	NVBLS	10/01-12/01
	New Hampshire	H	9.34 FQ	13.73 AW	19.06 TQ	NHBLS	10/01-12/01
	Nashua PMSA, NH	H	8.74 FQ	13.91 AW	20.86 TQ	NHBLS	10/01-12/01
	Portsmouth-Rochester PMSA, NH-ME	H	8.93 FQ	13.04 AW	18.90 TQ	NHBLS	10/01-12/01
	New Jersey	H	8.84 FQ	14.99 AW	22.08 TQ	NJBLS	10/01-12/01
	Atlantic-Cape May PMSA, NJ	H	5.85 FQ	12.25 AW	16.89 TQ	NJBLS	10/01-12/01
	Bergen-Passaic PMSA, NJ	H	8.25 FQ	13.97 AW	21.36 TQ	NJBLS	10/01-12/01
	Jersey City PMSA, NJ	H	7.07 FQ	13.76 AW	23.44 TQ	NJBLS	10/01-12/01
	Middlesex-Somerset-Hunterdon PMSA, NJ	H	10.27 FQ	17.35 AW	24.85 TQ	NJBLS	10/01-12/01
	Monmouth-Ocean PMSA, NJ	H	9.00 FQ	12.64 AW	17.55 TQ	NJBLS	10/01-12/01
	Newark PMSA, NJ	H	8.69 FQ	14.65 AW	20.90 TQ	NJBLS	10/01-12/01
	Trenton PMSA, NJ	H	7.72 FQ	13.73 AW	20.39 TQ	NJBLS	10/01-12/01
	New Mexico	H	7.01 FQ	12.03 AW	17.62 TQ	NMBLS	10/01-12/01
	Albuquerque MSA, NM	H	8.35 FQ	13.33 AW	17.69 TQ	NMBLS	10/01-12/01
	New York	H	7.50 FQ	13.56 AW	21.36 TQ	NYBLS	10/01-12/01
	Albany-Schenectady-Troy MSA, NY	H	9.61 FQ	16.83 AW	25.31 TQ	NYBLS	10/01-12/01
	Binghamton MSA, NY	H	7.96 FQ	12.16 AW	16.69 TQ	NYBLS	10/01-12/01
	Buffalo-Niagara Falls MSA, NY	H	8.77 FQ	13.71 AW	17.91 TQ	NYBLS	10/01-12/01
	Dutchess County PMSA, NY	H	6.40 FQ	9.24 AW	14.09 TQ	NYBLS	10/01-12/01
	Nassau-Suffolk PMSA, NY	H	7.27 FQ	12.11 AW	19.74 TQ	NYBLS	10/01-12/01
	New York PMSA, NY	H	6.30 FQ	13.26 AW	23.43 TQ	NYBLS	10/01-12/01
	Newburgh PMSA, NY-PA	H	8.35 FQ	12.32 AW	16.80 TQ	NYBLS	10/01-12/01
	Rochester MSA, NY	H	11.46 FQ	17.02 AW	22.12 TQ	NYBLS	10/01-12/01
	Syracuse MSA, NY	H	8.18 FQ	13.47 AW	18.28 TQ	NYBLS	10/01-12/01
	Utica-Rome MSA, NY	H	7.16 FQ	11.02 AW	14.79 TQ	NYBLS	10/01-12/01

AAW	Average annual wage	**AOH**	Average offered, high	**ASH**	Average starting, high	**H**	Hourly	**M**	Monthly	**S**	Special: hourly and annual
AE	Average entry wage	**AOL**	Average offered, low	**ASL**	Average starting, low	**HI**	Highest wage paid	**MTC**	Median total compensation	**TQ**	Third quartile wage
AEX	Average experienced wage	**APH**	Average pay, high range	**AW**	Average wage paid	**HR**	High end range	**MW**	Median wage paid	**W**	Weekly
AO	Average offered	**APL**	Average pay, low range	**FQ**	First quartile wage	**LR**	Low end range	**SQ**	Second quartile wage	**Y**	Yearly

Occupation/Type/Industry	Location	Per	Low	Mid	High	Source	Date
Mixing and Blending Machine Setter, Operator, and Tender	North Carolina	H	8.57 FQ	13.60 AW	19.58 TQ	NCBLS	10/01-12/01
	Asheville MSA, NC	H	9.32 FQ	12.32 AW	15.07 TQ	NCBLS	10/01-12/01
	Charlotte-Gastonia-Rock Hill MSA, NC-SC	H	9.62 FQ	13.61 AW	18.47 TQ	NCBLS	10/01-12/01
	Greensboro-Winston-Salem-High Point MSA, NC	H	9.91 FQ	15.46 AW	21.57 TQ	NCBLS	10/01-12/01
	Hickory-Morganton-Lenoir MSA, NC	H	9.27 FQ	12.51 AW	16.65 TQ	NCBLS	10/01-12/01
	Raleigh-Durham-Chapel Hill MSA, NC	H	9.07 FQ	13.48 AW	17.30 TQ	NCBLS	10/01-12/01
	North Dakota	H	7.65 FQ	11.50 AW	15.55 TQ	NDBLS	10/01-12/01
	Fargo-Moorhead MSA, ND-MN	H	9.43 FQ	11.67 AW	13.54 TQ	NDBLS	10/01-12/01
	Ohio	H	9.08 FQ	13.63 AW	18.58 TQ	OHBLS	10/01-12/01
	Akron PMSA, OH	H	9.69 FQ	13.55 AW	17.59 TQ	OHBLS	10/01-12/01
	Canton-Massillon MSA, OH	H	9.07 FQ	11.83 AW	13.99 TQ	OHBLS	10/01-12/01
	Cincinnati PMSA, OH-KY-IN	H	10.06 FQ	14.88 AW	20.29 TQ	OHBLS	10/01-12/01
	Cleveland-Lorain-Elyria PMSA, OH	H	6.42 FQ	12.75 AW	18.23 TQ	OHBLS	10/01-12/01
	Columbus MSA, OH	H	9.96 FQ	13.92 AW	17.63 TQ	OHBLS	10/01-12/01
	Dayton-Springfield MSA, OH	H	9.60 FQ	13.31 AW	17.53 TQ	OHBLS	10/01-12/01
	Hamilton-Middletown PMSA, OH	H	8.18 FQ	15.34 AW	20.58 TQ	OHBLS	10/01-12/01
	Mansfield MSA, OH	H	9.66 FQ	12.31 AW	15.19 TQ	OHBLS	10/01-12/01
	Toledo MSA, OH	H	8.80 FQ	13.71 AW	17.54 TQ	OHBLS	10/01-12/01
	Youngstown-Warren MSA, OH	H	6.79 FQ	10.95 AW	16.03 TQ	OHBLS	10/01-12/01
	Oklahoma	H	8.71 FQ	14.68 AW	21.61 TQ	OKBLS	10/01-12/01
	Oklahoma City MSA, OK	H	8.64 FQ	13.12 AW	17.02 TQ	OKBLS	10/01-12/01
	Tulsa MSA, OK	H	9.01 FQ	16.42 AW	28.05 TQ	OKBLS	10/01-12/01
	Oregon	H	8.92 FQ	14.56 AW	20.52 TQ	ORBLS	10/01-12/01
	Eugene-Springfield MSA, OR	H	9.00 FQ	12.86 AW	18.99 TQ	ORBLS	10/01-12/01
	Portland-Vancouver PMSA, OR-WA	H	9.06 FQ	14.40 AW	20.35 TQ	ORBLS	10/01-12/01
	Salem PMSA, OR	H	9.06 FQ	14.71 AW	21.50 TQ	ORBLS	10/01-12/01
	Pennsylvania	H	8.77 FQ	13.55 AW	19.22 TQ	PABLS	10/01-12/01
	Allentown-Bethlehem-Easton MSA, PA	H	7.61 FQ	12.98 AW	19.82 TQ	PABLS	10/01-12/01
	Erie MSA, PA	H	7.78 FQ	10.33 AW	13.89 TQ	PABLS	10/01-12/01
	Harrisburg-Lebanon-Carlisle MSA, PA	H	10.10 FQ	13.22 AW	16.70 TQ	PABLS	10/01-12/01
	Johnstown MSA, PA	H	7.73 FQ	10.54 AW	15.74 TQ	PABLS	10/01-12/01
	Lancaster MSA, PA	H	9.58 FQ	13.77 AW	18.58 TQ	PABLS	10/01-12/01
	Philadelphia PMSA, PA-NJ	H	9.80 FQ	15.40 AW	21.28 TQ	PABLS	10/01-12/01
	Pittsburgh MSA, PA	H	8.14 FQ	12.92 AW	18.08 TQ	PABLS	10/01-12/01
	Reading MSA, PA	H	9.50 FQ	13.47 AW	16.98 TQ	PABLS	10/01-12/01
	Scranton-Wilkes-Barre-Hazleton MSA, PA	H	8.72 FQ	12.16 AW	16.13 TQ	PABLS	10/01-12/01
	York MSA, PA	H	9.86 FQ	12.94 AW	16.61 TQ	PABLS	10/01-12/01
	Rhode Island	H	9.84 FQ	15.64 AW	21.75 TQ	RIBLS	10/01-12/01
	Providence-Fall River-Warwick MSA, RI-MA	H	9.64 FQ	15.62 AW	21.75 TQ	RIBLS	10/01-12/01
	South Carolina	H	9.12 FQ	13.41 AW	19.79 TQ	SCBLS	10/01-12/01
	Columbia MSA, SC	H	9.43 FQ	13.65 AW	19.82 TQ	SCBLS	10/01-12/01
	Greenville-Spartanburg-Anderson MSA, SC	H	10.95 FQ	14.82 AW	20.63 TQ	SCBLS	10/01-12/01
	South Dakota	H	8.85 FQ	12.38 AW	16.23 TQ	SDBLS	10/01-12/01
	Tennessee	H	8.67 FQ	13.16 AW	17.47 TQ	TNBLS	10/01-12/01
	Chattanooga MSA, TN-GA	H	10.40 FQ	13.39 AW	16.40 TQ	TNBLS	10/01-12/01
	Clarksville-Hopkinsville MSA, TN-KY	H	7.64 FQ	11.33 AW	14.18 TQ	TNBLS	10/01-12/01
	Johnson City-Kingsport-Bristol MSA, TN-VA	H	8.69 FQ	12.50 AW	17.53 TQ	TNBLS	10/01-12/01
	Knoxville MSA, TN	H	9.49 FQ	13.80 AW	18.67 TQ	TNBLS	10/01-12/01
	Memphis MSA, TN-AR-MS	H	8.54 FQ	13.38 AW	19.91 TQ	TNBLS	10/01-12/01
	Nashville MSA, TN	H	9.57 FQ	13.71 AW	17.91 TQ	TNBLS	10/01-12/01
	Texas	H	7.58 FQ	12.25 AW	18.53 TQ	TXBLS	10/01-12/01
	Amarillo MSA, TX	H	7.15 FQ	11.38 AW	16.91 TQ	TXBLS	10/01-12/01
	Austin-San Marcos MSA, TX	H	7.28 FQ	11.06 AW	15.26 TQ	TXBLS	10/01-12/01
	Beaumont-Port Arthur MSA, TX	H	7.56 FQ	16.20 AW	25.07 TQ	TXBLS	10/01-12/01
	Brazoria PMSA, TX	H	7.40 FQ	12.90 AW	21.17 TQ	TXBLS	10/01-12/01

AAW	Average annual wage	**AOH**	Average offered, high	**ASH**	Average starting, high	**H**	Hourly	**M**	Monthly	**S**	Special: hourly and annual
AE	Average entry wage	**AOL**	Average offered, low	**ASL**	Average starting, low	**HI**	Highest wage paid	**MTC**	Median total compensation	**TQ**	Third quartile wage
AEX	Average experienced wage	**APH**	Average pay, high range	**AW**	Average wage paid	**HR**	High end range	**MW**	Median wage paid	**W**	Weekly
AO	Average offered	**APL**	Average pay, low range	**FQ**	First quartile wage	**LR**	Low end range	**SQ**	Second quartile wage	**Y**	Yearly

Occupation/Type/Industry	Location	Per	Low	Mid	High	Source	Date
Mixing and Blending Machine Setter, Operator, and Tender	Brownsville-Harlingen-San Benito MSA, TX	H	6.21 FQ	12.62 AW	24.09 TQ	TXBLS	10/01-12/01
	Dallas PMSA, TX	H	8.71 FQ	12.18 AW	17.48 TQ	TXBLS	10/01-12/01
	El Paso MSA, TX	H	6.19 FQ	9.77 AW	15.15 TQ	TXBLS	10/01-12/01
	Fort Worth-Arlington PMSA, TX	H	7.95 FQ	12.75 AW	17.35 TQ	TXBLS	10/01-12/01
	Galveston-Texas City PMSA, TX	H	9.06 FQ	15.81 AW	26.26 TQ	TXBLS	10/01-12/01
	Houston PMSA, TX	H	7.87 FQ	13.18 AW	21.54 TQ	TXBLS	10/01-12/01
	Longview-Marshall MSA, TX	H	6.47 FQ	10.45 AW	16.14 TQ	TXBLS	10/01-12/01
	Lubbock MSA, TX	H	7.31 FQ	10.40 AW	14.88 TQ	TXBLS	10/01-12/01
	McAllen-Edinburg-Mission MSA, TX	H	5.68 FQ	8.86 AW	13.36 TQ	TXBLS	10/01-12/01
	San Antonio MSA, TX	H	7.33 FQ	9.96 AW	13.24 TQ	TXBLS	10/01-12/01
	Tyler MSA, TX	H	8.87 FQ	12.29 AW	16.40 TQ	TXBLS	10/01-12/01
	Waco MSA, TX	H	9.52 FQ	12.21 AW	15.55 TQ	TXBLS	10/01-12/01
	Utah	H	7.69 FQ	11.28 AW	16.15 TQ	UTBLS	10/01-12/01
	Salt Lake City-Ogden MSA, UT	H	7.80 FQ	11.98 AW	17.30 TQ	UTBLS	10/01-12/01
	Vermont	H	9.17 FQ	12.95 AW	17.21 TQ	VTBLS	10/01-12/01
	Burlington MSA, VT	H	9.21 FQ	12.93 AW	17.25 TQ	VTBLS	10/01-12/01
	Virginia	H	8.80 FQ	14.25 AW	20.58 TQ	VABLS	10/01-12/01
	Lynchburg MSA, VA	H	8.63 FQ	14.04 AW	19.43 TQ	VABLS	10/01-12/01
	Norfolk-Virginia Beach-Newport News MSA, VA-NC	H	7.85 FQ	12.71 AW	19.09 TQ	VABLS	10/01-12/01
	Richmond-Petersburg MSA, VA	H	8.95 FQ	16.00 AW	23.49 TQ	VABLS	10/01-12/01
	Roanoke MSA, VA	H	9.98 FQ	14.83 AW	21.02 TQ	VABLS	10/01-12/01
	Washington	H	9.52 FQ	14.62 AW	20.67 TQ	WABLS	10/01-12/01
	Seattle-Bellevue-Everett PMSA, WA	H	9.31 FQ	14.28 AW	20.42 TQ	WABLS	10/01-12/01
	Spokane MSA, WA	H	9.75 FQ	14.25 AW	17.72 TQ	WABLS	10/01-12/01
	Tacoma PMSA, WA	H	12.01 FQ	16.26 AW	20.60 TQ	WABLS	10/01-12/01
	Yakima MSA, WA	H	8.26 FQ	13.32 AW	18.75 TQ	WABLS	10/01-12/01
	West Virginia	H	7.83 FQ	12.21 AW	17.07 TQ	WVBLS	10/01-12/01
	Charleston MSA, WV	H	7.37 FQ	10.56 AW	15.01 TQ	WVBLS	10/01-12/01
	Huntington-Ashland MSA, WV-KY-OH	H	7.44 FQ	10.87 AW	14.41 TQ	WVBLS	10/01-12/01
	Wisconsin	H	9.55 FQ	14.02 AW	19.86 TQ	WIBLS	10/01-12/01
	Appleton-Oshkosh-Neenah MSA, WI	H	11.47 FQ	16.30 AW	21.37 TQ	WIBLS	10/01-12/01
	Green Bay MSA, WI	H	8.94 FQ	12.59 AW	17.67 TQ	WIBLS	10/01-12/01
	Madison MSA, WI	H	9.77 FQ	14.52 AW	24.89 TQ	WIBLS	10/01-12/01
	Milwaukee-Waukesha PMSA, WI	H	9.75 FQ	13.94 AW	19.38 TQ	WIBLS	10/01-12/01
	Racine PMSA, WI	H	8.92 FQ	11.23 AW	15.29 TQ	WIBLS	10/01-12/01
	Wyoming	H	7.96 FQ	13.69 AW	18.11 TQ	WYBLS	10/01-12/01
	Puerto Rico	H	6.07 FQ	10.81 AW	15.88 TQ	PRBLS	10/01-12/01
Mobile Heavy Equipment Mechanic							
Except Engine	Alabama	H	10.83 FQ	16.24 AW	21.51 TQ	ALBLS	10/01-12/01
Except Engine	Alaska	H	15.47 FQ	24.01 AW	32.78 TQ	AKBLS	10/01-12/01
Except Engine	Arizona	H	12.35 FQ	17.22 AW	22.03 TQ	AZBLS	10/01-12/01
Except Engine	Arkansas	H	9.42 FQ	13.88 AW	18.08 TQ	ARBLS	10/01-12/01
Except Engine	California	H	13.60 FQ	20.75 AW	29.19 TQ	CABLS	10/01-12/01
Except Engine	Colorado	H	13.00 FQ	17.69 AW	22.33 TQ	COBLS	10/01-12/01
Except Engine	Connecticut	H	14.20 FQ	19.86 AW	27.01 TQ	CTBLS	10/01-12/01
Except Engine	Delaware	H	12.90 FQ	16.79 AW	21.50 TQ	DEBLS	10/01-12/01
Except Engine	Florida	H	9.93 FQ	14.93 AW	20.63 TQ	FLBLS	10/01-12/01
Except Engine	Georgia	H	11.24 FQ	15.94 AW	21.26 TQ	GABLS	10/01-12/01
Except Engine	Hawaii	H	13.93 FQ	21.50 AW	28.98 TQ	HIBLS	10/01-12/01
Except Engine	Idaho	H	9.17 FQ	14.99 AW	20.96 TQ	IDBLS	10/01-12/01
Except Engine	Illinois	H	12.13 FQ	19.28 AW	27.24 TQ	ILBLS	10/01-12/01
Except Engine	Indiana	H	11.71 FQ	17.09 AW	22.35 TQ	INBLS	10/01-12/01
Except Engine	Iowa	H	11.73 FQ	16.53 AW	21.79 TQ	IABLS	10/01-12/01
Except Engine	Kansas	H	10.82 FQ	15.65 AW	21.16 TQ	KSBLS	10/01-12/01
Except Engine	Kentucky	H	11.91 FQ	17.09 AW	22.09 TQ	KYBLS	10/01-12/01
Except Engine	Louisiana	H	10.22 FQ	15.82 AW	22.04 TQ	LABLS	10/01-12/01
Except Engine	Maine	H	11.01 FQ	15.23 AW	20.56 TQ	MEBLS	10/01-12/01

AAW	Average annual wage	**AOH**	Average offered, high	**ASH**	Average starting, high	**H**	Hourly	**M**	Monthly	**S**	Special: hourly and annual
AE	Average entry wage	**AOL**	Average offered, low	**ASL**	Average starting, low	**HI**	Highest wage paid	**MTC**	Median total compensation	**TQ**	Third quartile wage
AEX	Average experienced wage	**APH**	Average pay, high range	**AW**	Average wage paid	**HR**	High end range	**MW**	Median wage paid	**W**	Weekly
AO	Average offered	**APL**	Average pay, low range	**FQ**	First quartile wage	**LR**	Low end range	**SQ**	Second quartile wage	**Y**	Yearly

Occupation/Type/Industry	Location	Per	Low	Mid	High	Source	Date
Mobile Heavy Equipment Mechanic							
Except Engine	Maryland	H	11.64 FQ	17.56 AW	23.50 TQ	MDBLS	10/01-12/01
Except Engine	Massachusetts	H	15.02 FQ	20.51 AW	28.69 TQ	MABLS	10/01-12/01
Except Engine	Michigan	H	12.65 FQ	19.08 AW	25.96 TQ	MIBLS	10/01-12/01
Except Engine	Minnesota	H	13.65 FQ	18.55 AW	23.17 TQ	MNBLS	10/01-12/01
Except Engine	Mississippi	H	9.39 FQ	13.61 AW	18.91 TQ	MSBLS	10/01-12/01
Except Engine	Missouri	H	12.04 FQ	17.08 AW	22.24 TQ	MOBLS	10/01-12/01
Except Engine	Montana	H	12.17 FQ	17.92 AW	24.91 TQ	MTBLS	10/01-12/01
Except Engine	Nebraska	H	10.84 FQ	15.89 AW	20.83 TQ	NEBLS	10/01-12/01
Except Engine	Nevada	H	15.07 FQ	20.81 AW	27.13 TQ	NVBLS	10/01-12/01
Except Engine	New Hampshire	H	11.95 FQ	16.64 AW	21.98 TQ	NHBLS	10/01-12/01
Except Engine	New Jersey	H	11.87 FQ	19.07 AW	26.51 TQ	NJBLS	10/01-12/01
Except Engine	New Mexico	H	11.55 FQ	17.78 AW	25.83 TQ	NMBLS	10/01-12/01
Except Engine	New York	H	12.08 FQ	18.11 AW	25.60 TQ	NYBLS	10/01-12/01
Except Engine	North Carolina	H	10.92 FQ	15.66 AW	21.15 TQ	NCBLS	10/01-12/01
Except Engine	North Dakota	H	12.65 FQ	17.79 AW	25.37 TQ	NDBLS	10/01-12/01
Except Engine	Ohio	H	11.82 FQ	17.46 AW	22.87 TQ	OHBLS	10/01-12/01
Except Engine	Oklahoma	H	10.64 FQ	14.74 AW	20.44 TQ	OKBLS	10/01-12/01
Except Engine	Oregon	H	11.42 FQ	17.71 AW	24.59 TQ	ORBLS	10/01-12/01
Except Engine	Pennsylvania	H	11.20 FQ	17.11 AW	24.05 TQ	PABLS	10/01-12/01
Except Engine	Rhode Island	H	12.03 FQ	17.53 AW	25.00 TQ	RIBLS	10/01-12/01
Except Engine	South Carolina	H	10.29 FQ	16.19 AW	24.22 TQ	SCBLS	10/01-12/01
Except Engine	South Dakota	H	10.09 FQ	15.23 AW	20.33 TQ	SDBLS	10/01-12/01
Except Engine	Tennessee	H	10.71 FQ	15.23 AW	20.62 TQ	TNBLS	10/01-12/01
Except Engine	Texas	H	9.43 FQ	14.91 AW	21.37 TQ	TXBLS	10/01-12/01
Except Engine	Utah	H	11.65 FQ	17.11 AW	22.35 TQ	UTBLS	10/01-12/01
Except Engine	Vermont	H	11.61 FQ	15.99 AW	21.01 TQ	VTBLS	10/01-12/01
Except Engine	Virginia	H	10.62 FQ	16.25 AW	22.05 TQ	VABLS	10/01-12/01
Except Engine	Washington	H	15.00 FQ	20.62 AW	26.97 TQ	WABLS	10/01-12/01
Except Engine	West Virginia	H	10.90 FQ	17.22 AW	22.87 TQ	WVBLS	10/01-12/01
Except Engine	Wisconsin	H	12.75 FQ	18.03 AW	24.63 TQ	WIBLS	10/01-12/01
Except Engine	Wyoming	H	12.31 FQ	19.69 AW	26.61 TQ	WYBLS	10/01-12/01
Except Engine	Puerto Rico	H	6.82 FQ	10.18 AW	13.77 TQ	PRBLS	10/01-12/01
Except Engine	Virgin Islands	H	7.95 FQ	12.76 AW	19.70 TQ	VIBLS	10/01-12/01
Except Engine	Guam	H	10.20 FQ	14.19 AW	18.81 TQ	GUBLS	10/01-12/01
Model	Arizona	Y	13060 FQ	21860 AW	32420 TQ	AZBLS	10/01-12/01
	Phoenix-Mesa MSA, AZ	Y	12070 FQ	22280 AW	32240 TQ	AZBLS	10/01-12/01
	California	Y	13880 FQ	23580 AW	35310 TQ	CABLS	10/01-12/01
	Orange County PMSA, CA	Y	13820 FQ	19560 AW	26940 TQ	CABLS	10/01-12/01
	Florida	Y	11840 FQ	22640 AW	51630 TQ	FLBLS	10/01-12/01
	Illinois	Y	12650 FQ	22530 AW	50460 TQ	ILBLS	10/01-12/01
	Chicago PMSA, IL	Y	12890 FQ	23270 AW	51210 TQ	ILBLS	10/01-12/01
	Indiana	Y	15500 FQ	21200 AW	30910 TQ	INBLS	10/01-12/01
	Iowa	Y	11770 FQ	13080 AW	14760 TQ	IABLS	10/01-12/01
	Maryland	Y	14360 FQ	17500 AW	21030 TQ	MDBLS	10/01-12/01
	Michigan	Y	16990 FQ	20970 AW	27320 TQ	MIBLS	10/01-12/01
	Minnesota	Y	11870 FQ	14020 AW	17430 TQ	MNBLS	10/01-12/01
	New York	Y	15220 FQ	28820 AW	60380 TQ	NYBLS	10/01-12/01
	New York PMSA, NY	Y	14870 FQ	26410 AW	60550 TQ	NYBLS	10/01-12/01
	Ohio	Y	18290 FQ	23020 AW	33430 TQ	OHBLS	10/01-12/01
	Oregon	Y	14800 FQ	20740 AW	27580 TQ	ORBLS	10/01-12/01
	Texas	Y	20490 FQ	33680 AW	37190 TQ	TXBLS	10/01-12/01
	Dallas PMSA, TX	Y	20080 FQ	41200 AW	103110 TQ	TXBLS	10/01-12/01
	Virginia	Y	12800 FQ	24810 AW	51660 TQ	VABLS	10/01-12/01
	Washington	Y	14610 FQ	20730 AW	25840 TQ	WABLS	10/01-12/01
	Seattle-Bellevue-Everett PMSA, WA	Y	18990 FQ	21560 AW	24800 TQ	WABLS	10/01-12/01
Model Bartender	United States	H		30.00 AW		MC	1/01-1/01
Model Maker							
Metals and Plastics	Alabama	H	7.90 FQ	12.95 AW	20.06 TQ	ALBLS	10/01-12/01
Metals and Plastics	Arkansas	H	12.14 FQ	18.71 AW	31.07 TQ	ARBLS	10/01-12/01
Metals and Plastics	California	H	9.39 FQ	18.95 AW	27.67 TQ	CABLS	10/01-12/01
Metals and Plastics	Colorado	H	11.48 FQ	20.78 AW	29.12 TQ	COBLS	10/01-12/01
Metals and Plastics	Connecticut	H	14.65 FQ	22.48 AW	27.98 TQ	CTBLS	10/01-12/01
Metals and Plastics	Florida	H	11.05 FQ	17.13 AW	22.12 TQ	FLBLS	10/01-12/01
Metals and Plastics	Georgia	H	7.75 FQ	11.51 AW	20.08 TQ	GABLS	10/01-12/01
Metals and Plastics	Illinois	H	6.71 FQ	14.31 AW	24.72 TQ	ILBLS	10/01-12/01
Metals and Plastics	Indiana	H	11.77 FQ	22.16 AW	33.73 TQ	INBLS	10/01-12/01

AAW	Average annual wage	**AOH**	Average offered, high	**ASH**	Average starting, high	**H**	Hourly	**M**	Monthly	**S**	Special: hourly and annual
AE	Average entry wage	**AOL**	Average offered, low	**ASL**	Average starting, low	**HI**	Highest wage paid	**MTC**	Median total compensation	**TQ**	Third quartile wage
AEX	Average experienced wage	**APH**	Average pay, high range	**AW**	Average wage paid	**HR**	High end range	**MW**	Median wage paid	**W**	Weekly
AO	Average offered	**APL**	Average pay, low range	**FQ**	First quartile wage	**LR**	Low end range	**SQ**	Second quartile wage	**Y**	Yearly

Occupation/Type/Industry	Location	Per	Low	Mid	High	Source	Date
Model Maker							
Metals and Plastics	Iowa	H	6.55 FQ	12.32 AW	20.42 TQ	IABLS	10/01-12/01
Metals and Plastics	Kansas	H	10.20 FQ	18.28 AW	26.38 TQ	KSBLS	10/01-12/01
Metals and Plastics	Kentucky	H	14.07 FQ	19.70 AW	27.39 TQ	KYBLS	10/01-12/01
Metals and Plastics	Maryland	H	11.85 FQ	20.13 AW	32.91 TQ	MDBLS	10/01-12/01
Metals and Plastics	Massachusetts	H	10.63 FQ	18.92 AW	25.85 TQ	MABLS	10/01-12/01
Metals and Plastics	Michigan	H	18.55 FQ	27.41 AW	35.78 TQ	MIBLS	10/01-12/01
Metals and Plastics	Minnesota	H	11.97 FQ	18.70 AW	26.15 TQ	MNBLS	10/01-12/01
Metals and Plastics	Missouri	H	10.24 FQ	18.78 AW	26.56 TQ	MOBLS	10/01-12/01
Metals and Plastics	Nebraska	H	9.72 FQ	12.40 AW	16.05 TQ	NEBLS	10/01-12/01
Metals and Plastics	New Hampshire	H	13.69 FQ	17.40 AW	24.90 TQ	NHBLS	10/01-12/01
Metals and Plastics	New Jersey	H	14.23 FQ	20.54 AW	30.67 TQ	NJBLS	10/01-12/01
Metals and Plastics	New York	H	6.51 FQ	17.30 AW	27.01 TQ	NYBLS	10/01-12/01
Metals and Plastics	North Carolina	H	6.46 FQ	11.57 AW	17.24 TQ	NCBLS	10/01-12/01
Metals and Plastics	Ohio	H	11.40 FQ	20.05 AW	31.64 TQ	OHBLS	10/01-12/01
Metals and Plastics	Pennsylvania	H	7.53 FQ	14.58 AW	22.79 TQ	PABLS	10/01-12/01
Metals and Plastics	Rhode Island	H	8.95 FQ	17.94 AW	26.49 TQ	RIBLS	10/01-12/01
Metals and Plastics	South Carolina	H	8.88 FQ	13.11 AW	21.38 TQ	SCBLS	10/01-12/01
Metals and Plastics	Tennessee	H	8.91 FQ	15.16 AW	21.10 TQ	TNBLS	10/01-12/01
Metals and Plastics	Texas	H	7.06 FQ	14.25 AW	22.01 TQ	TXBLS	10/01-12/01
Metals and Plastics	Virginia	H	10.42 FQ	14.97 AW	20.11 TQ	VABLS	10/01-12/01
Metals and Plastics	Washington	H	16.11 FQ	24.73 AW	29.92 TQ	WABLS	10/01-12/01
Metals and Plastics	Wisconsin	H	14.94 FQ	19.91 AW	25.88 TQ	WIBLS	10/01-12/01
Wood	California	H	7.06 FQ	12.04 AW	21.21 TQ	CABLS	10/01-12/01
Wood	Connecticut	H	10.49 FQ	14.63 AW	17.69 TQ	CTBLS	10/01-12/01
Wood	Florida	H	7.35 FQ	13.26 AW	22.24 TQ	FLBLS	10/01-12/01
Wood	Georgia	H	7.39 FQ	10.20 AW	16.32 TQ	GABLS	10/01-12/01
Wood	Illinois	H	7.44 FQ	12.26 AW	19.70 TQ	ILBLS	10/01-12/01
Wood	Indiana	H	8.27 FQ	14.55 AW	21.64 TQ	INBLS	10/01-12/01
Wood	Iowa	H	7.23 FQ	14.64 AW	24.19 TQ	IABLS	10/01-12/01
Wood	Michigan	H	15.50 FQ	25.00 AW	34.13 TQ	MIBLS	10/01-12/01
Wood	Mississippi	H	7.88 FQ	12.35 AW	22.24 TQ	MSBLS	10/01-12/01
Wood	Missouri	H	10.61 FQ	15.23 AW	21.84 TQ	MOBLS	10/01-12/01
Wood	New Jersey	H	11.65 FQ	18.29 AW	23.86 TQ	NJBLS	10/01-12/01
Wood	New York	H	8.60 FQ	15.78 AW	22.90 TQ	NYBLS	10/01-12/01
Wood	North Carolina	H	7.92 FQ	11.51 AW	14.86 TQ	NCBLS	10/01-12/01
Wood	Ohio	H	8.50 FQ	13.72 AW	21.45 TQ	OHBLS	10/01-12/01
Wood	Pennsylvania	H	9.25 FQ	12.62 AW	15.75 TQ	PABLS	10/01-12/01
Wood	South Carolina	H	8.20 FQ	11.23 AW	13.58 TQ	SCBLS	10/01-12/01
Wood	Tennessee	H	6.91 FQ	14.70 AW	24.97 TQ	TNBLS	10/01-12/01
Wood	Texas	H	8.02 FQ	11.59 AW	15.89 TQ	TXBLS	10/01-12/01
Wood	Utah	H	7.89 FQ	10.93 AW	17.16 TQ	UTBLS	10/01-12/01
Wood	Virginia	H	8.30 FQ	11.85 AW	17.59 TQ	VABLS	10/01-12/01
Wood	Wisconsin	H	8.13 FQ	13.74 AW	19.56 TQ	WIBLS	10/01-12/01
Molder, Shaper, and Caster							
Except Metals and Plastics	Alabama	H	7.70 FQ	11.38 AW	18.84 TQ	ALBLS	10/01-12/01
Except Metals and Plastics	Birmingham MSA, AL	H	7.23 FQ	12.91 AW	20.00 TQ	ALBLS	10/01-12/01
Except Metals and Plastics	Arizona	H	6.41 FQ	10.88 AW	16.46 TQ	AZBLS	10/01-12/01
Except Metals and Plastics	Phoenix-Mesa MSA, AZ	H	7.47 FQ	11.79 AW	16.66 TQ	AZBLS	10/01-12/01
Except Metals and Plastics	Tucson MSA, AZ	H	5.74 FQ	9.02 AW	12.41 TQ	AZBLS	10/01-12/01
Except Metals and Plastics	Arkansas	H	6.25 FQ	9.17 AW	11.52 TQ	ARBLS	10/01-12/01
Except Metals and Plastics	Fayetteville-Springdale-Rogers MSA, AR	H	7.83 FQ	10.36 AW	13.73 TQ	ARBLS	10/01-12/01
Except Metals and Plastics	Little Rock-North Little Rock MSA, AR	H	5.85 FQ	8.09 AW	10.68 TQ	ARBLS	10/01-12/01
Except Metals and Plastics	California	H	7.26 FQ	12.39 AW	19.99 TQ	CABLS	10/01-12/01
Except Metals and Plastics	Los Angeles-Long Beach PMSA, CA	H	6.93 FQ	9.73 AW	13.44 TQ	CABLS	10/01-12/01
Except Metals and Plastics	Oakland PMSA, CA	H	7.76 FQ	12.61 AW	16.84 TQ	CABLS	10/01-12/01
Except Metals and Plastics	Orange County PMSA, CA	H	7.99 FQ	17.78 AW	32.31 TQ	CABLS	10/01-12/01
Except Metals and Plastics	Riverside-San Bernardino PMSA, CA	H	7.19 FQ	10.09 AW	13.42 TQ	CABLS	10/01-12/01
Except Metals and Plastics	Sacramento PMSA, CA	H	8.32 FQ	12.34 AW	18.81 TQ	CABLS	10/01-12/01
Except Metals and Plastics	San Diego MSA, CA	H	6.74 FQ	10.80 AW	18.68 TQ	CABLS	10/01-12/01
Except Metals and Plastics	San Francisco PMSA, CA	H	9.56 FQ	14.06 AW	19.84 TQ	CABLS	10/01-12/01
Except Metals and Plastics	San Jose PMSA, CA	H	8.77 FQ	18.70 AW	33.89 TQ	CABLS	10/01-12/01
Except Metals and Plastics	Santa Rosa PMSA, CA	H	8.97 FQ	11.14 AW	15.17 TQ	CABLS	10/01-12/01
Except Metals and Plastics	Vallejo-Fairfield-Napa PMSA, CA	H	7.90 FQ	13.69 AW	20.62 TQ	CABLS	10/01-12/01
Except Metals and Plastics	Colorado	H	7.38 FQ	14.42 AW	20.69 TQ	COBLS	10/01-12/01
Except Metals and Plastics	Boulder-Longmont PMSA, CO	H	9.83 FQ	15.49 AW	21.97 TQ	COBLS	10/01-12/01
Except Metals and Plastics	Colorado Springs MSA, CO	H	8.64 FQ	12.43 AW	20.14 TQ	COBLS	10/01-12/01

AAW Average annual wage; AE Average entry wage; AEX Average experienced wage; AO Average offered; AOH Average offered, high; AOL Average offered, low; APH Average pay, high range; APL Average pay, low range; ASH Average starting, high; ASL Average starting, low; AW Average wage paid; FQ First quartile wage; H Hourly; HI Highest wage paid; HR High end range; LR Low end range; M Monthly; MTC Median total compensation; MW Median wage paid; SQ Second quartile wage; S Special: hourly and annual; TQ Third quartile wage; W Weekly; Y Yearly

Occupation/Type/Industry	Location	Per	Low	Mid	High	Source	Date
Molder, Shaper, and Caster							
Except Metals and Plastics	Denver PMSA, CO	H	7.46 FQ	13.30 AW	16.97 TQ	COBLS	10/01-12/01
Except Metals and Plastics	Fort Collins-Loveland MSA, CO	H	5.95 FQ	21.39 AW	53.32 TQ	COBLS	10/01-12/01
Except Metals and Plastics	Connecticut	H	9.04 FQ	11.86 AW	16.45 TQ	CTBLS	10/01-12/01
Except Metals and Plastics	Hartford MSA, CT	H	9.04 FQ	12.62 AW	16.62 TQ	CTBLS	10/01-12/01
Except Metals and Plastics	Washington PMSA, DC-MD-VA-WV	H	7.01 FQ	13.09 AW	24.85 TQ	DCBLS	10/01-12/01
Except Metals and Plastics	Florida	H	6.95 FQ	10.11 AW	13.48 TQ	FLBLS	10/01-12/01
Except Metals and Plastics	Fort Lauderdale PMSA, FL	H	5.90 FQ	8.90 AW	12.15 TQ	FLBLS	10/01-12/01
Except Metals and Plastics	Fort Pierce-Port St. Lucie MSA, FL	H	7.09 FQ	9.13 AW	11.52 TQ	FLBLS	10/01-12/01
Except Metals and Plastics	Jacksonville MSA, FL	H	8.57 FQ	14.18 AW	24.69 TQ	FLBLS	10/01-12/01
Except Metals and Plastics	Miami PMSA, FL	H	6.91 FQ	9.28 AW	12.75 TQ	FLBLS	10/01-12/01
Except Metals and Plastics	Orlando MSA, FL	H	9.17 FQ	10.36 AW	11.83 TQ	FLBLS	10/01-12/01
Except Metals and Plastics	Pensacola MSA, FL	H	7.24 FQ	8.25 AW	9.74 TQ	FLBLS	10/01-12/01
Except Metals and Plastics	Sarasota-Bradenton MSA, FL	H	7.39 FQ	10.38 AW	14.22 TQ	FLBLS	10/01-12/01
Except Metals and Plastics	Tampa-St. Petersburg-Clearwater MSA, FL	H	6.17 FQ	10.34 AW	13.73 TQ	FLBLS	10/01-12/01
Except Metals and Plastics	West Palm Beach-Boca Raton MSA, FL	H	7.84 FQ	12.25 AW	19.81 TQ	FLBLS	10/01-12/01
Except Metals and Plastics	Georgia	H	7.94 FQ	11.58 AW	15.90 TQ	GABLS	10/01-12/01
Except Metals and Plastics	Atlanta MSA, GA	H	8.69 FQ	11.95 AW	16.14 TQ	GABLS	10/01-12/01
Except Metals and Plastics	Hawaii	H	7.54 FQ	13.22 AW	21.72 TQ	HIBLS	10/01-12/01
Except Metals and Plastics	Honolulu MSA, HI	H	7.21 FQ	13.93 AW	22.82 TQ	HIBLS	10/01-12/01
Except Metals and Plastics	Idaho	H	7.57 FQ	10.79 AW	16.14 TQ	IDBLS	10/01-12/01
Except Metals and Plastics	Illinois	H	9.10 FQ	13.46 AW	19.58 TQ	ILBLS	10/01-12/01
Except Metals and Plastics	Chicago PMSA, IL	H	9.09 FQ	12.39 AW	16.68 TQ	ILBLS	10/01-12/01
Except Metals and Plastics	Indiana	H	8.77 FQ	12.41 AW	15.10 TQ	INBLS	10/01-12/01
Except Metals and Plastics	Elkhart-Goshen MSA, IN	H	12.13 FQ	15.28 AW	18.27 TQ	INBLS	10/01-12/01
Except Metals and Plastics	Fort Wayne MSA, IN	H	10.90 FQ	12.58 AW	14.32 TQ	INBLS	10/01-12/01
Except Metals and Plastics	Gary PMSA, IN	H	7.58 FQ	10.81 AW	15.94 TQ	INBLS	10/01-12/01
Except Metals and Plastics	Indianapolis MSA, IN	H	7.71 FQ	11.71 AW	15.76 TQ	INBLS	10/01-12/01
Except Metals and Plastics	Iowa	H	7.35 FQ	10.29 AW	14.58 TQ	IABLS	10/01-12/01
Except Metals and Plastics	Des Moines MSA, IA	H	8.32 FQ	12.43 AW	16.17 TQ	IABLS	10/01-12/01
Except Metals and Plastics	Kansas	H	7.12 FQ	9.93 AW	12.65 TQ	KSBLS	10/01-12/01
Except Metals and Plastics	Kentucky	H	7.00 FQ	9.71 AW	13.62 TQ	KYBLS	10/01-12/01
Except Metals and Plastics	Lexington MSA, KY	H	7.27 FQ	10.34 AW	14.85 TQ	KYBLS	10/01-12/01
Except Metals and Plastics	Louisville MSA, KY-IN	H	8.74 FQ	12.20 AW	14.95 TQ	KYBLS	10/01-12/01
Except Metals and Plastics	Louisiana	H	5.89 FQ	8.47 AW	12.68 TQ	LABLS	10/01-12/01
Except Metals and Plastics	New Orleans MSA, LA	H	5.87 FQ	7.37 AW	9.78 TQ	LABLS	10/01-12/01
Except Metals and Plastics	Maine	H	6.47 FQ	10.64 AW	19.24 TQ	MEBLS	10/01-12/01
Except Metals and Plastics	Maryland	H	7.41 FQ	12.14 AW	20.88 TQ	MDBLS	10/01-12/01
Except Metals and Plastics	Baltimore PMSA, MD	H	7.70 FQ	10.72 AW	13.95 TQ	MDBLS	10/01-12/01
Except Metals and Plastics	Massachusetts	H	9.01 FQ	12.52 AW	17.77 TQ	MABLS	10/01-12/01
Except Metals and Plastics	Boston PMSA, MA-NH	H	9.36 FQ	13.65 AW	19.34 TQ	MABLS	10/01-12/01
Except Metals and Plastics	New Bedford PMSA, MA	H	8.20 FQ	11.43 AW	16.12 TQ	MABLS	10/01-12/01
Except Metals and Plastics	Springfield MSA, MA	H	8.04 FQ	12.80 AW	19.53 TQ	MABLS	10/01-12/01
Except Metals and Plastics	Michigan	H	7.67 FQ	13.50 AW	18.78 TQ	MIBLS	10/01-12/01
Except Metals and Plastics	Ann Arbor PMSA, MI	H	8.52 FQ	12.61 AW	17.37 TQ	MIBLS	10/01-12/01
Except Metals and Plastics	Detroit PMSA, MI	H	8.15 FQ	13.96 AW	17.78 TQ	MIBLS	10/01-12/01
Except Metals and Plastics	Grand Rapids-Muskegon-Holland MSA, MI	H	11.24 FQ	16.66 AW	27.44 TQ	MIBLS	10/01-12/01
Except Metals and Plastics	Kalamazoo-Battle Creek MSA, MI	H	9.24 FQ	12.69 AW	16.10 TQ	MIBLS	10/01-12/01
Except Metals and Plastics	Minnesota	H	9.40 FQ	14.05 AW	17.70 TQ	MNBLS	10/01-12/01
Except Metals and Plastics	Minneapolis-St. Paul MSA, MN-WI	H	9.56 FQ	14.30 AW	17.74 TQ	MNBLS	10/01-12/01
Except Metals and Plastics	St. Cloud MSA, MN	H	8.53 FQ	13.10 AW	17.07 TQ	MNBLS	10/01-12/01
Except Metals and Plastics	Mississippi	H	9.10 FQ	13.09 AW	17.70 TQ	MSBLS	10/01-12/01
Except Metals and Plastics	Missouri	H	8.45 FQ	12.73 AW	17.02 TQ	MOBLS	10/01-12/01
Except Metals and Plastics	Kansas City MSA, MO-KS	H	7.49 FQ	11.38 AW	16.60 TQ	MOBLS	10/01-12/01
Except Metals and Plastics	St. Louis MSA, MO-IL	H	12.08 FQ	15.31 AW	17.91 TQ	MOBLS	10/01-12/01
Except Metals and Plastics	Springfield MSA, MO	H	7.21 FQ	8.50 AW	11.73 TQ	MOBLS	10/01-12/01
Except Metals and Plastics	Montana	H	7.27 FQ	10.34 AW	15.28 TQ	MTBLS	10/01-12/01
Except Metals and Plastics	Nebraska	H	7.90 FQ	12.41 AW	16.27 TQ	NEBLS	10/01-12/01
Except Metals and Plastics	Nevada	H	8.95 FQ	15.19 AW	25.03 TQ	NVBLS	10/01-12/01
Except Metals and Plastics	Las Vegas MSA, NV-AZ	H	10.20 FQ	16.43 AW	25.48 TQ	NVBLS	10/01-12/01
Except Metals and Plastics	New Hampshire	H	7.54 FQ	11.35 AW	15.63 TQ	NHBLS	10/01-12/01
Except Metals and Plastics	Portsmouth-Rochester PMSA, NH-ME	H	7.70 FQ	12.41 AW	19.56 TQ	NHBLS	10/01-12/01
Except Metals and Plastics	New Jersey	H	8.26 FQ	13.40 AW	18.21 TQ	NJBLS	10/01-12/01

AAW	Average annual wage	**AOH**	Average offered, high	**ASH**	Average starting, high	**H**	Hourly	**M**	Monthly	**S**	Special: hourly and annual
AE	Average entry wage	**AOL**	Average offered, low	**ASL**	Average starting, low	**HI**	Highest wage paid	**MTC**	Median total compensation	**TQ**	Third quartile wage
AEX	Average experienced wage	**APH**	Average pay, high range	**AW**	Average wage paid	**HR**	High end range	**MW**	Median wage paid	**W**	Weekly
AO	Average offered	**APL**	Average pay, low range	**FQ**	First quartile wage	**LR**	Low end range	**SQ**	Second quartile wage	**Y**	Yearly

Occupation/Type/Industry	Location	Per	Low	Mid	High	Source	Date
Molder, Shaper, and Caster							
Except Metals and Plastics	Bergen-Passaic PMSA, NJ	H	9.37 FQ	13.89 AW	17.39 TQ	NJBLS	10/01-12/01
Except Metals and Plastics	Jersey City PMSA, NJ	H	6.42 FQ	10.03 AW	14.54 TQ	NJBLS	10/01-12/01
Except Metals and Plastics	Middlesex-Somerset-Hunterdon PMSA, NJ	H	7.44 FQ	11.78 AW	16.75 TQ	NJBLS	10/01-12/01
Except Metals and Plastics	Monmouth-Ocean PMSA, NJ	H	9.30 FQ	12.45 AW	14.82 TQ	NJBLS	10/01-12/01
Except Metals and Plastics	Newark PMSA, NJ	H	9.38 FQ	14.68 AW	19.77 TQ	NJBLS	10/01-12/01
Except Metals and Plastics	Trenton PMSA, NJ	H	8.46 FQ	13.70 AW	17.96 TQ	NJBLS	10/01-12/01
Except Metals and Plastics	New Mexico	H	6.03 FQ	10.11 AW	16.90 TQ	NMBLS	10/01-12/01
Except Metals and Plastics	New York	H	6.65 FQ	11.84 AW	17.21 TQ	NYBLS	10/01-12/01
Except Metals and Plastics	Albany-Schenectady-Troy MSA, NY	H	6.99 FQ	12.93 AW	21.88 TQ	NYBLS	10/01-12/01
Except Metals and Plastics	Buffalo-Niagara Falls MSA, NY	H	8.95 FQ	13.03 AW	21.03 TQ	NYBLS	10/01-12/01
Except Metals and Plastics	Nassau-Suffolk PMSA, NY	H	7.32 FQ	11.09 AW	18.33 TQ	NYBLS	10/01-12/01
Except Metals and Plastics	New York PMSA, NY	H	6.23 FQ	11.45 AW	16.83 TQ	NYBLS	10/01-12/01
Except Metals and Plastics	Rochester MSA, NY	H	7.29 FQ	12.47 AW	20.33 TQ	NYBLS	10/01-12/01
Except Metals and Plastics	Syracuse MSA, NY	H	9.34 FQ	10.81 AW	12.53 TQ	NYBLS	10/01-12/01
Except Metals and Plastics	North Carolina	H	7.49 FQ	10.77 AW	14.36 TQ	NCBLS	10/01-12/01
Except Metals and Plastics	Charlotte-Gastonia-Rock Hill MSA, NC-SC	H	7.40 FQ	10.64 AW	13.83 TQ	NCBLS	10/01-12/01
Except Metals and Plastics	Fayetteville MSA, NC	H	7.58 FQ	10.55 AW	13.50 TQ	NCBLS	10/01-12/01
Except Metals and Plastics	Greensboro-Winston-Salem-High Point MSA, NC	H	7.37 FQ	9.48 AW	12.86 TQ	NCBLS	10/01-12/01
Except Metals and Plastics	Raleigh-Durham-Chapel Hill MSA, NC	H	7.96 FQ	13.79 AW	22.25 TQ	NCBLS	10/01-12/01
Except Metals and Plastics	North Dakota	H	8.36 FQ	12.21 AW	15.76 TQ	NDBLS	10/01-12/01
Except Metals and Plastics	Ohio	H	9.01 FQ	13.03 AW	19.59 TQ	OHBLS	10/01-12/01
Except Metals and Plastics	Akron PMSA, OH	H	9.40 FQ	11.03 AW	14.96 TQ	OHBLS	10/01-12/01
Except Metals and Plastics	Canton-Massillon MSA, OH	H	9.32 FQ	11.89 AW	16.04 TQ	OHBLS	10/01-12/01
Except Metals and Plastics	Cincinnati PMSA, OH-KY-IN	H	8.87 FQ	11.43 AW	15.85 TQ	OHBLS	10/01-12/01
Except Metals and Plastics	Cleveland-Lorain-Elyria PMSA, OH	H	7.80 FQ	11.76 AW	16.80 TQ	OHBLS	10/01-12/01
Except Metals and Plastics	Dayton-Springfield MSA, OH	H	11.83 FQ	14.52 AW	18.08 TQ	OHBLS	10/01-12/01
Except Metals and Plastics	Youngstown-Warren MSA, OH	H	9.06 FQ	11.81 AW	14.82 TQ	OHBLS	10/01-12/01
Except Metals and Plastics	Oklahoma	H	7.09 FQ	10.45 AW	15.49 TQ	OKBLS	10/01-12/01
Except Metals and Plastics	Oregon	H	8.03 FQ	12.19 AW	17.93 TQ	ORBLS	10/01-12/01
Except Metals and Plastics	Eugene-Springfield MSA, OR	H	8.98 FQ	12.90 AW	19.48 TQ	ORBLS	10/01-12/01
Except Metals and Plastics	Portland-Vancouver PMSA, OR-WA	H	8.90 FQ	12.76 AW	17.97 TQ	ORBLS	10/01-12/01
Except Metals and Plastics	Pennsylvania	H	7.93 FQ	12.87 AW	18.18 TQ	PABLS	10/01-12/01
Except Metals and Plastics	Allentown-Bethlehem-Easton MSA, PA	H	6.45 FQ	12.40 AW	17.83 TQ	PABLS	10/01-12/01
Except Metals and Plastics	Lancaster MSA, PA	H	10.68 FQ	12.31 AW	15.06 TQ	PABLS	10/01-12/01
Except Metals and Plastics	Philadelphia PMSA, PA-NJ	H	7.24 FQ	11.56 AW	19.49 TQ	PABLS	10/01-12/01
Except Metals and Plastics	Pittsburgh MSA, PA	H	8.67 FQ	12.46 AW	16.49 TQ	PABLS	10/01-12/01
Except Metals and Plastics	Reading MSA, PA	H	6.21 FQ	12.94 AW	21.18 TQ	PABLS	10/01-12/01
Except Metals and Plastics	York MSA, PA	H	7.55 FQ	10.55 AW	15.19 TQ	PABLS	10/01-12/01
Except Metals and Plastics	Rhode Island	H	7.90 FQ	10.91 AW	15.32 TQ	RIBLS	10/01-12/01
Except Metals and Plastics	Providence-Fall River-Warwick MSA, RI-MA	H	7.93 FQ	11.23 AW	16.17 TQ	RIBLS	10/01-12/01
Except Metals and Plastics	South Carolina	H	11.13 FQ	16.65 AW	21.01 TQ	SCBLS	10/01-12/01
Except Metals and Plastics	Charleston-North Charleston MSA, SC	H	5.67 FQ	8.26 AW	12.40 TQ	SCBLS	10/01-12/01
Except Metals and Plastics	Greenville-Spartanburg-Anderson MSA, SC	H	11.31 FQ	16.69 AW	21.05 TQ	SCBLS	10/01-12/01
Except Metals and Plastics	Tennessee	H	7.97 FQ	11.19 AW	13.68 TQ	TNBLS	10/01-12/01
Except Metals and Plastics	Knoxville MSA, TN	H	7.16 FQ	8.36 AW	10.38 TQ	TNBLS	10/01-12/01
Except Metals and Plastics	Memphis MSA, TN-AR-MS	H	9.74 FQ	13.45 AW	17.51 TQ	TNBLS	10/01-12/01
Except Metals and Plastics	Nashville MSA, TN	H	9.80 FQ	12.13 AW	14.28 TQ	TNBLS	10/01-12/01
Except Metals and Plastics	Texas	H	5.89 FQ	9.59 AW	15.38 TQ	TXBLS	10/01-12/01
Except Metals and Plastics	Austin-San Marcos MSA, TX	H	6.18 FQ	8.77 AW	12.39 TQ	TXBLS	10/01-12/01
Except Metals and Plastics	Dallas PMSA, TX	H	7.71 FQ	11.18 AW	15.27 TQ	TXBLS	10/01-12/01
Except Metals and Plastics	Fort Worth-Arlington PMSA, TX	H	7.22 FQ	10.08 AW	13.29 TQ	TXBLS	10/01-12/01
Except Metals and Plastics	Houston PMSA, TX	H	5.97 FQ	11.08 AW	23.39 TQ	TXBLS	10/01-12/01
Except Metals and Plastics	Longview-Marshall MSA, TX	H	5.88 FQ	9.69 AW	19.84 TQ	TXBLS	10/01-12/01
Except Metals and Plastics	Odessa-Midland MSA, TX	H	6.35 FQ	9.36 AW	11.17 TQ	TXBLS	10/01-12/01
Except Metals and Plastics	San Antonio MSA, TX	H	5.90 FQ	7.86 AW	10.36 TQ	TXBLS	10/01-12/01
Except Metals and Plastics	Utah	H	7.47 FQ	11.17 AW	16.25 TQ	UTBLS	10/01-12/01
Except Metals and Plastics	Provo-Orem MSA, UT	H	7.78 FQ	12.61 AW	17.06 TQ	UTBLS	10/01-12/01

AAW Average annual wage	**AOH** Average offered, high	**ASH** Average starting, high	**H** Hourly	**M** Monthly	**S** Special: hourly and annual
AE Average entry wage	**AOL** Average offered, low	**ASL** Average starting, low	**HI** Highest wage paid	**MTC** Median total compensation	**TQ** Third quartile wage
AEX Average experienced wage	**APH** Average pay, high range	**AW** Average wage paid	**HR** High end range	**MW** Median wage paid	**W** Weekly
AO Average offered	**APL** Average pay, low range	**FQ** First quartile wage	**LR** Low end range	**SQ** Second quartile wage	**Y** Yearly

Occupation/Type/Industry	Location	Per	Low	Mid	High	Source	Date
Molder, Shaper, and Caster							
Except Metals and Plastics	Salt Lake City-Ogden MSA, UT	H	7.45 FQ	10.71 AW	15.06 TQ	UTBLS	10/01-12/01
Except Metals and Plastics	Vermont	H	7.88 FQ	11.52 AW	15.05 TQ	VTBLS	10/01-12/01
Except Metals and Plastics	Virginia	H	6.15 FQ	9.70 AW	13.43 TQ	VABLS	10/01-12/01
Except Metals and Plastics	Norfolk-Virginia Beach-Newport News MSA, VA-NC	H	6.33 FQ	12.28 AW	20.50 TQ	VABLS	10/01-12/01
Except Metals and Plastics	Richmond-Petersburg MSA, VA	H	7.10 FQ	10.54 AW	13.70 TQ	VABLS	10/01-12/01
Except Metals and Plastics	Washington	H	7.72 FQ	12.78 AW	20.24 TQ	WABLS	10/01-12/01
Except Metals and Plastics	Seattle-Bellevue-Everett PMSA, WA	H	9.21 FQ	14.20 AW	22.23 TQ	WABLS	10/01-12/01
Except Metals and Plastics	Spokane MSA, WA	H	7.42 FQ	10.05 AW	13.35 TQ	WABLS	10/01-12/01
Except Metals and Plastics	Tacoma PMSA, WA	H	8.09 FQ	14.01 AW	21.00 TQ	WABLS	10/01-12/01
Except Metals and Plastics	West Virginia	H	5.52 FQ	9.17 AW	15.53 TQ	WVBLS	10/01-12/01
Except Metals and Plastics	Huntington-Ashland MSA, WV-KY-OH	H	7.58 FQ	11.07 AW	14.93 TQ	WVBLS	10/01-12/01
Except Metals and Plastics	Wisconsin	H	9.34 FQ	12.79 AW	16.39 TQ	WIBLS	10/01-12/01
Except Metals and Plastics	Green Bay MSA, WI	H	9.78 FQ	13.74 AW	16.65 TQ	WIBLS	10/01-12/01
Except Metals and Plastics	Milwaukee-Waukesha PMSA, WI	H	10.35 FQ	13.65 AW	17.06 TQ	WIBLS	10/01-12/01
Except Metals and Plastics	Wyoming	H	8.07 FQ	10.56 AW	13.50 TQ	WYBLS	10/01-12/01
Molding, Coremaking, and Casting Machine Setter, Operator, and Tender							
Metals and Plastics	Alabama	H	7.48 FQ	11.44 AW	17.36 TQ	ALBLS	10/01-12/01
Metals and Plastics	Birmingham MSA, AL	H	7.73 FQ	14.06 AW	23.77 TQ	ALBLS	10/01-12/01
Metals and Plastics	Huntsville MSA, AL	H	7.43 FQ	9.94 AW	14.30 TQ	ALBLS	10/01-12/01
Metals and Plastics	Mobile MSA, AL	H	8.27 FQ	11.62 AW	16.39 TQ	ALBLS	10/01-12/01
Metals and Plastics	Montgomery MSA, AL	H	11.13 FQ	12.86 AW	15.73 TQ	ALBLS	10/01-12/01
Metals and Plastics	Arizona	H	7.38 FQ	11.14 AW	16.68 TQ	AZBLS	10/01-12/01
Metals and Plastics	Phoenix-Mesa MSA, AZ	H	7.27 FQ	11.16 AW	17.15 TQ	AZBLS	10/01-12/01
Metals and Plastics	Tucson MSA, AZ	H	6.64 FQ	11.09 AW	16.79 TQ	AZBLS	10/01-12/01
Metals and Plastics	Arkansas	H	7.46 FQ	11.68 AW	16.45 TQ	ARBLS	10/01-12/01
Metals and Plastics	Little Rock-North Little Rock MSA, AR	H	8.92 FQ	12.77 AW	16.71 TQ	ARBLS	10/01-12/01
Metals and Plastics	California	H	6.54 FQ	9.95 AW	15.09 TQ	CABLS	10/01-12/01
Metals and Plastics	Bakersfield MSA, CA	H	6.94 FQ	9.81 AW	12.31 TQ	CABLS	10/01-12/01
Metals and Plastics	Fresno MSA, CA	H	6.64 FQ	10.07 AW	15.44 TQ	CABLS	10/01-12/01
Metals and Plastics	Los Angeles-Long Beach PMSA, CA	H	6.47 FQ	9.23 AW	13.43 TQ	CABLS	10/01-12/01
Metals and Plastics	Modesto MSA, CA	H	9.60 FQ	12.60 AW	16.14 TQ	CABLS	10/01-12/01
Metals and Plastics	Oakland PMSA, CA	H	7.24 FQ	11.10 AW	16.76 TQ	CABLS	10/01-12/01
Metals and Plastics	Orange County PMSA, CA	H	6.45 FQ	8.74 AW	13.06 TQ	CABLS	10/01-12/01
Metals and Plastics	Riverside-San Bernardino PMSA, CA	H	6.77 FQ	10.06 AW	15.93 TQ	CABLS	10/01-12/01
Metals and Plastics	Sacramento PMSA, CA	H	6.98 FQ	10.07 AW	14.31 TQ	CABLS	10/01-12/01
Metals and Plastics	San Diego MSA, CA	H	6.73 FQ	11.14 AW	16.87 TQ	CABLS	10/01-12/01
Metals and Plastics	San Francisco PMSA, CA	H	7.07 FQ	15.57 AW	30.38 TQ	CABLS	10/01-12/01
Metals and Plastics	San Jose PMSA, CA	H	6.64 FQ	10.34 AW	14.39 TQ	CABLS	10/01-12/01
Metals and Plastics	Santa Cruz-Watsonville PMSA, CA	H	7.48 FQ	12.39 AW	21.06 TQ	CABLS	10/01-12/01
Metals and Plastics	Santa Rosa PMSA, CA	H	8.64 FQ	12.93 AW	17.90 TQ	CABLS	10/01-12/01
Metals and Plastics	Stockton-Lodi MSA, CA	H	7.42 FQ	10.89 AW	14.30 TQ	CABLS	10/01-12/01
Metals and Plastics	Vallejo-Fairfield-Napa PMSA, CA	H	9.25 FQ	12.17 AW	16.86 TQ	CABLS	10/01-12/01
Metals and Plastics	Ventura PMSA, CA	H	6.36 FQ	7.65 AW	10.09 TQ	CABLS	10/01-12/01
Metals and Plastics	Colorado	H	7.45 FQ	11.67 AW	17.36 TQ	COBLS	10/01-12/01
Metals and Plastics	Boulder-Longmont PMSA, CO	H	7.33 FQ	11.77 AW	17.35 TQ	COBLS	10/01-12/01
Metals and Plastics	Colorado Springs MSA, CO	H	8.34 FQ	13.37 AW	20.87 TQ	COBLS	10/01-12/01
Metals and Plastics	Denver PMSA, CO	H	7.67 FQ	11.52 AW	16.54 TQ	COBLS	10/01-12/01
Metals and Plastics	Fort Collins-Loveland MSA, CO	H	7.67 FQ	11.98 AW	19.45 TQ	COBLS	10/01-12/01
Metals and Plastics	Connecticut	H	8.08 FQ	13.60 AW	21.05 TQ	CTBLS	10/01-12/01
Metals and Plastics	Bridgeport PMSA, CT	H	8.05 FQ	13.81 AW	21.60 TQ	CTBLS	10/01-12/01
Metals and Plastics	Danbury PMSA, CT	H	10.56 FQ	17.52 AW	24.56 TQ	CTBLS	10/01-12/01
Metals and Plastics	Hartford MSA, CT	H	8.05 FQ	13.28 AW	20.06 TQ	CTBLS	10/01-12/01
Metals and Plastics	New Haven-Meriden PMSA, CT	H	7.77 FQ	12.59 AW	21.87 TQ	CTBLS	10/01-12/01

Occupation/Type/Industry	Location	Per	Low	Mid	High	Source	Date
Molding, Coremaking, and Casting Machine Setter, Operator, and Tender							
Metals and Plastics	New London-Norwich MSA, CT-RI	H	8.55 FQ	12.18 AW	16.17 TQ	CTBLS	10/01-12/01
Metals and Plastics	Stamford-Norwalk PMSA, CT	H	6.90 FQ	10.27 AW	15.60 TQ	CTBLS	10/01-12/01
Metals and Plastics	Waterbury PMSA, CT	H	8.94 FQ	13.36 AW	21.38 TQ	CTBLS	10/01-12/01
Metals and Plastics	Washington PMSA, DC-MD-VA-WV	H	7.53 FQ	11.84 AW	16.50 TQ	DCBLS	10/01-12/01
Metals and Plastics	Florida	H	6.57 FQ	9.98 AW	15.47 TQ	FLBLS	10/01-12/01
Metals and Plastics	Fort Lauderdale PMSA, FL	H	7.22 FQ	11.40 AW	19.05 TQ	FLBLS	10/01-12/01
Metals and Plastics	Lakeland-Winter Haven MSA, FL	H	7.31 FQ	10.14 AW	13.05 TQ	FLBLS	10/01-12/01
Metals and Plastics	Miami PMSA, FL	H	6.22 FQ	8.67 AW	11.96 TQ	FLBLS	10/01-12/01
Metals and Plastics	Orlando MSA, FL	H	7.47 FQ	10.62 AW	16.09 TQ	FLBLS	10/01-12/01
Metals and Plastics	Sarasota-Bradenton MSA, FL	H	6.18 FQ	8.83 AW	11.40 TQ	FLBLS	10/01-12/01
Metals and Plastics	Tampa-St. Petersburg-Clearwater MSA, FL	H	6.33 FQ	9.24 AW	13.49 TQ	FLBLS	10/01-12/01
Metals and Plastics	West Palm Beach-Boca Raton MSA, FL	H	5.85 FQ	8.48 AW	10.76 TQ	FLBLS	10/01-12/01
Metals and Plastics	Georgia	H	7.15 FQ	10.70 AW	16.19 TQ	GABLS	10/01-12/01
Metals and Plastics	Atlanta MSA, GA	H	7.04 FQ	11.28 AW	17.63 TQ	GABLS	10/01-12/01
Metals and Plastics	Augusta-Aiken MSA, GA-SC	H	6.31 FQ	8.92 AW	12.50 TQ	GABLS	10/01-12/01
Metals and Plastics	Idaho	H	6.03 FQ	8.48 AW	12.32 TQ	IDBLS	10/01-12/01
Metals and Plastics	Boise City MSA, ID	H	6.33 FQ	8.62 AW	12.11 TQ	IDBLS	10/01-12/01
Metals and Plastics	Illinois	H	7.50 FQ	12.46 AW	18.10 TQ	ILBLS	10/01-12/01
Metals and Plastics	Chicago PMSA, IL	H	7.67 FQ	12.44 AW	16.89 TQ	ILBLS	10/01-12/01
Metals and Plastics	Rockford MSA, IL	H	6.78 FQ	11.96 AW	18.98 TQ	ILBLS	10/01-12/01
Metals and Plastics	Indiana	H	8.13 FQ	12.34 AW	18.56 TQ	INBLS	10/01-12/01
Metals and Plastics	Elkhart-Goshen MSA, IN	H	7.90 FQ	10.66 AW	14.26 TQ	INBLS	10/01-12/01
Metals and Plastics	Evansville-Henderson MSA, IN-KY	H	7.54 FQ	11.09 AW	16.28 TQ	INBLS	10/01-12/01
Metals and Plastics	Fort Wayne MSA, IN	H	9.14 FQ	12.41 AW	16.86 TQ	INBLS	10/01-12/01
Metals and Plastics	Gary PMSA, IN	H	7.65 FQ	15.78 AW	26.68 TQ	INBLS	10/01-12/01
Metals and Plastics	Indianapolis MSA, IN	H	9.00 FQ	12.09 AW	16.22 TQ	INBLS	10/01-12/01
Metals and Plastics	South Bend MSA, IN	H	7.72 FQ	11.57 AW	17.81 TQ	INBLS	10/01-12/01
Metals and Plastics	Iowa	H	8.16 FQ	11.42 AW	15.47 TQ	IABLS	10/01-12/01
Metals and Plastics	Davenport-Moline-Rock Island MSA, IA-IL	H	7.77 FQ	12.48 AW	16.76 TQ	IABLS	10/01-12/01
Metals and Plastics	Des Moines MSA, IA	H	8.97 FQ	13.26 AW	17.19 TQ	IABLS	10/01-12/01
Metals and Plastics	Kansas	H	6.42 FQ	10.25 AW	15.21 TQ	KSBLS	10/01-12/01
Metals and Plastics	Kentucky	H	7.60 FQ	11.42 AW	16.32 TQ	KYBLS	10/01-12/01
Metals and Plastics	Lexington MSA, KY	H	8.56 FQ	12.95 AW	16.49 TQ	KYBLS	10/01-12/01
Metals and Plastics	Louisville MSA, KY-IN	H	7.97 FQ	10.85 AW	15.01 TQ	KYBLS	10/01-12/01
Metals and Plastics	Louisiana	H	6.37 FQ	13.37 AW	21.80 TQ	LABLS	10/01-12/01
Metals and Plastics	Baton Rouge MSA, LA	H	9.95 FQ	17.97 AW	26.77 TQ	LABLS	10/01-12/01
Metals and Plastics	New Orleans MSA, LA	H	7.04 FQ	13.78 AW	18.48 TQ	LABLS	10/01-12/01
Metals and Plastics	Shreveport-Bossier City MSA, LA	H	6.46 FQ	11.86 AW	20.36 TQ	LABLS	10/01-12/01
Metals and Plastics	Maine	H	7.75 FQ	10.96 AW	14.29 TQ	MEBLS	10/01-12/01
Metals and Plastics	Maryland	H	8.79 FQ	11.82 AW	14.24 TQ	MDBLS	10/01-12/01
Metals and Plastics	Baltimore PMSA, MD	H	9.24 FQ	12.34 AW	15.52 TQ	MDBLS	10/01-12/01
Metals and Plastics	Massachusetts	H	8.13 FQ	12.00 AW	16.95 TQ	MABLS	10/01-12/01
Metals and Plastics	Boston PMSA, MA-NH	H	9.07 FQ	12.19 AW	16.68 TQ	MABLS	10/01-12/01
Metals and Plastics	Brockton PMSA, MA	H	7.74 FQ	12.65 AW	17.30 TQ	MABLS	10/01-12/01
Metals and Plastics	Lawrence PMSA, MA-NH	H	8.13 FQ	12.25 AW	18.95 TQ	MABLS	10/01-12/01
Metals and Plastics	New Bedford PMSA, MA	H	10.96 FQ	14.61 AW	18.94 TQ	MABLS	10/01-12/01
Metals and Plastics	Springfield MSA, MA	H	7.71 FQ	12.89 AW	17.86 TQ	MABLS	10/01-12/01
Metals and Plastics	Worcester PMSA, MA-CT	H	7.54 FQ	11.36 AW	16.07 TQ	MABLS	10/01-12/01
Metals and Plastics	Michigan	H	8.40 FQ	12.79 AW	23.88 TQ	MIBLS	10/01-12/01
Metals and Plastics	Ann Arbor PMSA, MI	H	10.49 FQ	16.28 AW	26.13 TQ	MIBLS	10/01-12/01
Metals and Plastics	Detroit PMSA, MI	H	8.61 FQ	12.46 AW	24.55 TQ	MIBLS	10/01-12/01
Metals and Plastics	Grand Rapids-Muskegon-Holland MSA, MI	H	8.28 FQ	11.60 AW	16.36 TQ	MIBLS	10/01-12/01
Metals and Plastics	Kalamazoo-Battle Creek MSA, MI	H	8.30 FQ	11.88 AW	17.72 TQ	MIBLS	10/01-12/01
Metals and Plastics	Lansing-East Lansing MSA, MI	H	7.06 FQ	10.47 AW	15.11 TQ	MIBLS	10/01-12/01
Metals and Plastics	Minnesota	H	9.20 FQ	13.12 AW	18.13 TQ	MNBLS	10/01-12/01
Metals and Plastics	Duluth-Superior MSA, MN-WI	H	9.48 FQ	13.17 AW	16.98 TQ	MNBLS	10/01-12/01
Metals and Plastics	Minneapolis-St. Paul MSA, MN-WI	H	9.31 FQ	13.40 AW	19.07 TQ	MNBLS	10/01-12/01
Metals and Plastics	St. Cloud MSA, MN	H	9.60 FQ	14.61 AW	20.52 TQ	MNBLS	10/01-12/01

AAW	Average annual wage	**AOH**	Average offered, high	**ASH**	Average starting, high	**H**	Hourly	**M**	Monthly	**S**	Special: hourly and annual
AE	Average entry wage	**AOL**	Average offered, low	**ASL**	Average starting, low	**HI**	Highest wage paid	**MTC**	Median total compensation	**TQ**	Third quartile wage
AEX	Average experienced wage	**APH**	Average pay, high range	**AW**	Average wage paid	**HR**	High end range	**MW**	Median wage paid	**W**	Weekly
AO	Average offered	**APL**	Average pay, low range	**FQ**	First quartile wage	**LR**	Low end range	**SQ**	Second quartile wage	**Y**	Yearly

Occupation/Type/Industry	Location	Per	Low	Mid	High	Source	Date
Molding, Coremaking, and Casting Machine Setter, Operator, and Tender							
Metals and Plastics	Mississippi	H	6.37 FQ	9.64 AW	13.20 TQ	MSBLS	10/01-12/01
Metals and Plastics	Jackson MSA, MS	H	6.06 FQ	9.89 AW	16.03 TQ	MSBLS	10/01-12/01
Metals and Plastics	Missouri	H	7.32 FQ	10.33 AW	14.60 TQ	MOBLS	10/01-12/01
Metals and Plastics	Kansas City MSA, MO-KS	H	7.40 FQ	10.86 AW	15.03 TQ	MOBLS	10/01-12/01
Metals and Plastics	St. Louis MSA, MO-IL	H	7.23 FQ	9.90 AW	15.10 TQ	MOBLS	10/01-12/01
Metals and Plastics	Springfield MSA, MO	H	8.26 FQ	12.30 AW	16.18 TQ	MOBLS	10/01-12/01
Metals and Plastics	Lincoln MSA, NE	H	7.51 FQ	12.02 AW	16.93 TQ	NEBLS	10/01-12/01
Metals and Plastics	Nevada	H	5.67 FQ	7.76 AW	11.30 TQ	NVBLS	10/01-12/01
Metals and Plastics	New Hampshire	H	8.83 FQ	11.76 AW	15.71 TQ	NHBLS	10/01-12/01
Metals and Plastics	Manchester PMSA, NH	H	9.05 FQ	12.30 AW	17.87 TQ	NHBLS	10/01-12/01
Metals and Plastics	Nashua PMSA, NH	H	9.20 FQ	11.77 AW	15.42 TQ	NHBLS	10/01-12/01
Metals and Plastics	New Jersey	H	6.16 FQ	10.12 AW	16.14 TQ	NJBLS	10/01-12/01
Metals and Plastics	Bergen-Passaic PMSA, NJ	H	5.89 FQ	10.05 AW	16.08 TQ	NJBLS	10/01-12/01
Metals and Plastics	Middlesex-Somerset-Hunterdon PMSA, NJ	H	6.28 FQ	11.00 AW	17.20 TQ	NJBLS	10/01-12/01
Metals and Plastics	Monmouth-Ocean PMSA, NJ	H	6.39 FQ	10.83 AW	17.52 TQ	NJBLS	10/01-12/01
Metals and Plastics	Newark PMSA, NJ	H	6.25 FQ	9.14 AW	13.56 TQ	NJBLS	10/01-12/01
Metals and Plastics	Trenton PMSA, NJ	H	6.35 FQ	10.02 AW	14.66 TQ	NJBLS	10/01-12/01
Metals and Plastics	New Mexico	H	6.91 FQ	9.56 AW	14.25 TQ	NMBLS	10/01-12/01
Metals and Plastics	New York	H	6.47 FQ	10.99 AW	16.71 TQ	NYBLS	10/01-12/01
Metals and Plastics	Albany-Schenectady-Troy MSA, NY	H	8.06 FQ	10.32 AW	12.77 TQ	NYBLS	10/01-12/01
Metals and Plastics	Binghamton MSA, NY	H	6.36 FQ	9.70 AW	13.20 TQ	NYBLS	10/01-12/01
Metals and Plastics	Buffalo-Niagara Falls MSA, NY	H	8.00 FQ	10.89 AW	14.64 TQ	NYBLS	10/01-12/01
Metals and Plastics	Nassau-Suffolk PMSA, NY	H	5.83 FQ	8.93 AW	13.91 TQ	NYBLS	10/01-12/01
Metals and Plastics	New York PMSA, NY	H	5.85 FQ	9.66 AW	13.82 TQ	NYBLS	10/01-12/01
Metals and Plastics	Rochester MSA, NY	H	7.96 FQ	13.14 AW	22.00 TQ	NYBLS	10/01-12/01
Metals and Plastics	Syracuse MSA, NY	H	7.25 FQ	12.35 AW	19.30 TQ	NYBLS	10/01-12/01
Metals and Plastics	Utica-Rome MSA, NY	H	5.74 FQ	7.41 AW	9.89 TQ	NYBLS	10/01-12/01
Metals and Plastics	North Carolina	H	7.52 FQ	11.25 AW	16.41 TQ	NCBLS	10/01-12/01
Metals and Plastics	Asheville MSA, NC	H	7.28 FQ	8.89 AW	10.74 TQ	NCBLS	10/01-12/01
Metals and Plastics	Charlotte-Gastonia-Rock Hill MSA, NC-SC	H	8.74 FQ	13.03 AW	17.99 TQ	NCBLS	10/01-12/01
Metals and Plastics	Greensboro-Winston-Salem-High Point MSA, NC	H	8.38 FQ	11.31 AW	16.07 TQ	NCBLS	10/01-12/01
Metals and Plastics	Raleigh-Durham-Chapel Hill MSA, NC	H	7.73 FQ	11.27 AW	16.60 TQ	NCBLS	10/01-12/01
Metals and Plastics	Wilmington MSA, NC	H	7.00 FQ	8.13 AW	9.98 TQ	NCBLS	10/01-12/01
Metals and Plastics	North Dakota	H	7.19 FQ	9.41 AW	12.62 TQ	NDBLS	10/01-12/01
Metals and Plastics	Ohio	H	7.79 FQ	13.45 AW	24.84 TQ	OHBLS	10/01-12/01
Metals and Plastics	Akron PMSA, OH	H	7.68 FQ	11.80 AW	16.09 TQ	OHBLS	10/01-12/01
Metals and Plastics	Canton-Massillon MSA, OH	H	6.90 FQ	12.31 AW	23.29 TQ	OHBLS	10/01-12/01
Metals and Plastics	Cincinnati PMSA, OH-KY-IN	H	7.80 FQ	11.12 AW	15.69 TQ	OHBLS	10/01-12/01
Metals and Plastics	Cleveland-Lorain-Elyria PMSA, OH	H	8.22 FQ	16.98 AW	27.15 TQ	OHBLS	10/01-12/01
Metals and Plastics	Columbus MSA, OH	H	7.98 FQ	12.22 AW	16.79 TQ	OHBLS	10/01-12/01
Metals and Plastics	Dayton-Springfield MSA, OH	H	7.50 FQ	11.77 AW	19.06 TQ	OHBLS	10/01-12/01
Metals and Plastics	Hamilton-Middletown PMSA, OH	H	7.45 FQ	10.25 AW	13.64 TQ	OHBLS	10/01-12/01
Metals and Plastics	Mansfield MSA, OH	H	6.80 FQ	10.43 AW	13.75 TQ	OHBLS	10/01-12/01
Metals and Plastics	Toledo MSA, OH	H	8.83 FQ	14.64 AW	26.22 TQ	OHBLS	10/01-12/01
Metals and Plastics	Youngstown-Warren MSA, OH	H	6.63 FQ	13.02 AW	24.38 TQ	OHBLS	10/01-12/01
Metals and Plastics	Oklahoma	H	6.56 FQ	10.15 AW	14.12 TQ	OKBLS	10/01-12/01
Metals and Plastics	Oklahoma City MSA, OK	H	7.04 FQ	10.10 AW	14.01 TQ	OKBLS	10/01-12/01
Metals and Plastics	Tulsa MSA, OK	H	6.27 FQ	10.68 AW	16.35 TQ	OKBLS	10/01-12/01
Metals and Plastics	Oregon	H	8.29 FQ	13.32 AW	18.83 TQ	ORBLS	10/01-12/01
Metals and Plastics	Eugene-Springfield MSA, OR	H	7.43 FQ	9.80 AW	14.21 TQ	ORBLS	10/01-12/01
Metals and Plastics	Medford-Ashland MSA, OR	H	8.22 FQ	10.76 AW	14.37 TQ	ORBLS	10/01-12/01
Metals and Plastics	Portland-Vancouver PMSA, OR-WA	H	8.86 FQ	13.55 AW	18.07 TQ	ORBLS	10/01-12/01
Metals and Plastics	Pennsylvania	H	8.17 FQ	12.94 AW	17.88 TQ	PABLS	10/01-12/01
Metals and Plastics	Allentown-Bethlehem-Easton MSA, PA	H	7.64 FQ	10.40 AW	13.72 TQ	PABLS	10/01-12/01
Metals and Plastics	Erie MSA, PA	H	7.09 FQ	11.87 AW	16.35 TQ	PABLS	10/01-12/01
Metals and Plastics	Harrisburg-Lebanon-Carlisle MSA, PA	H	8.24 FQ	13.04 AW	20.52 TQ	PABLS	10/01-12/01
Metals and Plastics	Philadelphia PMSA, PA-NJ	H	8.91 FQ	13.84 AW	19.17 TQ	PABLS	10/01-12/01
Metals and Plastics	Pittsburgh MSA, PA	H	8.95 FQ	15.69 AW	26.00 TQ	PABLS	10/01-12/01

AAW Average annual wage; AE Average entry wage; AEX Average experienced wage; AO Average offered; AOH Average offered, high; AOL Average offered, low; APH Average pay, high range; APL Average pay, low range; ASH Average starting, high; ASL Average starting, low; AW Average wage paid; FQ First quartile wage; H Hourly; HI Highest wage paid; HR High end range; LR Low end range; M Monthly; MTC Median total compensation; MW Median wage paid; SQ Second quartile wage; S Special: hourly and annual; TQ Third quartile wage; W Weekly; Y Yearly

Occupation/Type/Industry	Location	Per	Low	Mid	High	Source	Date
Molding, Coremaking, and Casting Machine Setter, Operator, and Tender							
Metals and Plastics	Reading MSA, PA	H	8.81 FQ	13.78 AW	19.90 TQ	PABLS	10/01-12/01
Metals and Plastics	Scranton-Wilkes-Barre-Hazleton MSA, PA	H	8.77 FQ	12.31 AW	15.50 TQ	PABLS	10/01-12/01
Metals and Plastics	York MSA, PA	H	8.84 FQ	11.55 AW	13.95 TQ	PABLS	10/01-12/01
Metals and Plastics	Rhode Island	H	8.06 FQ	11.31 AW	15.75 TQ	RIBLS	10/01-12/01
Metals and Plastics	Providence-Fall River-Warwick MSA, RI-MA	H	8.20 FQ	11.47 AW	15.87 TQ	RIBLS	10/01-12/01
Metals and Plastics	South Carolina	H	7.82 FQ	11.33 AW	15.88 TQ	SCBLS	10/01-12/01
Metals and Plastics	Charleston-North Charleston MSA, SC	H	8.36 FQ	11.46 AW	14.34 TQ	SCBLS	10/01-12/01
Metals and Plastics	Columbia MSA, SC	H	11.22 FQ	12.43 AW	13.79 TQ	SCBLS	10/01-12/01
Metals and Plastics	Greenville-Spartanburg-Anderson MSA, SC	H	7.67 FQ	10.52 AW	15.15 TQ	SCBLS	10/01-12/01
Metals and Plastics	South Dakota	H	8.15 FQ	10.90 AW	14.54 TQ	SDBLS	10/01-12/01
Metals and Plastics	Sioux Falls MSA, SD	H	9.10 FQ	12.19 AW	18.82 TQ	SDBLS	10/01-12/01
Metals and Plastics	Tennessee	H	7.72 FQ	10.47 AW	14.10 TQ	TNBLS	10/01-12/01
Metals and Plastics	Clarksville-Hopkinsville MSA, TN-KY	H	8.37 FQ	12.73 AW	17.26 TQ	TNBLS	10/01-12/01
Metals and Plastics	Johnson City-Kingsport-Bristol MSA, TN-VA	H	7.16 FQ	9.72 AW	13.33 TQ	TNBLS	10/01-12/01
Metals and Plastics	Knoxville MSA, TN	H	7.67 FQ	9.48 AW	11.39 TQ	TNBLS	10/01-12/01
Metals and Plastics	Memphis MSA, TN-AR-MS	H	7.20 FQ	11.63 AW	18.35 TQ	TNBLS	10/01-12/01
Metals and Plastics	Nashville MSA, TN	H	9.08 FQ	11.20 AW	16.05 TQ	TNBLS	10/01-12/01
Metals and Plastics	Texas	H	6.15 FQ	9.49 AW	14.61 TQ	TXBLS	10/01-12/01
Metals and Plastics	Austin-San Marcos MSA, TX	H	7.24 FQ	9.82 AW	14.95 TQ	TXBLS	10/01-12/01
Metals and Plastics	Brownsville-Harlingen-San Benito MSA, TX	H	7.30 FQ	11.33 AW	15.27 TQ	TXBLS	10/01-12/01
Metals and Plastics	Dallas PMSA, TX	H	6.30 FQ	9.33 AW	15.00 TQ	TXBLS	10/01-12/01
Metals and Plastics	El Paso MSA, TX	H	6.70 FQ	9.38 AW	12.86 TQ	TXBLS	10/01-12/01
Metals and Plastics	Fort Worth-Arlington PMSA, TX	H	5.66 FQ	8.99 AW	14.40 TQ	TXBLS	10/01-12/01
Metals and Plastics	Houston PMSA, TX	H	7.47 FQ	10.42 AW	14.57 TQ	TXBLS	10/01-12/01
Metals and Plastics	Killeen-Temple MSA, TX	H	5.67 FQ	8.90 AW	14.02 TQ	TXBLS	10/01-12/01
Metals and Plastics	Longview-Marshall MSA, TX	H	5.73 FQ	7.65 AW	11.13 TQ	TXBLS	10/01-12/01
Metals and Plastics	McAllen-Edinburg-Mission MSA, TX	H	5.83 FQ	7.64 AW	9.91 TQ	TXBLS	10/01-12/01
Metals and Plastics	San Antonio MSA, TX	H	7.30 FQ	9.27 AW	12.29 TQ	TXBLS	10/01-12/01
Metals and Plastics	Utah	H	7.82 FQ	10.79 AW	14.44 TQ	UTBLS	10/01-12/01
Metals and Plastics	Provo-Orem MSA, UT	H	7.22 FQ	10.98 AW	16.16 TQ	UTBLS	10/01-12/01
Metals and Plastics	Salt Lake City-Ogden MSA, UT	H	8.51 FQ	11.11 AW	14.95 TQ	UTBLS	10/01-12/01
Metals and Plastics	Vermont	H	8.12 FQ	11.88 AW	17.02 TQ	VTBLS	10/01-12/01
Metals and Plastics	Virginia	H	7.92 FQ	11.44 AW	15.22 TQ	VABLS	10/01-12/01
Metals and Plastics	Lynchburg MSA, VA	H	7.65 FQ	10.26 AW	13.00 TQ	VABLS	10/01-12/01
Metals and Plastics	Norfolk-Virginia Beach-Newport News MSA, VA-NC	H	7.29 FQ	10.96 AW	15.02 TQ	VABLS	10/01-12/01
Metals and Plastics	Richmond-Petersburg MSA, VA	H	7.38 FQ	10.89 AW	15.86 TQ	VABLS	10/01-12/01
Metals and Plastics	Roanoke MSA, VA	H	8.37 FQ	11.36 AW	15.85 TQ	VABLS	10/01-12/01
Metals and Plastics	Washington	H	8.34 FQ	12.28 AW	17.11 TQ	WABLS	10/01-12/01
Metals and Plastics	Seattle-Bellevue-Everett PMSA, WA	H	8.27 FQ	13.59 AW	18.78 TQ	WABLS	10/01-12/01
Metals and Plastics	Spokane MSA, WA	H	8.73 FQ	11.39 AW	15.12 TQ	WABLS	10/01-12/01
Metals and Plastics	Tacoma PMSA, WA	H	7.64 FQ	10.29 AW	13.53 TQ	WABLS	10/01-12/01
Metals and Plastics	Yakima MSA, WA	H	8.68 FQ	9.61 AW	10.59 TQ	WABLS	10/01-12/01
Metals and Plastics	West Virginia	H	6.84 FQ	12.81 AW	20.64 TQ	WVBLS	10/01-12/01
Metals and Plastics	Wisconsin	H	8.48 FQ	13.01 AW	19.24 TQ	WIBLS	10/01-12/01
Metals and Plastics	Appleton-Oshkosh-Neenah MSA, WI	H	8.08 FQ	11.74 AW	15.91 TQ	WIBLS	10/01-12/01
Metals and Plastics	Madison MSA, WI	H	10.55 FQ	13.80 AW	17.51 TQ	WIBLS	10/01-12/01
Metals and Plastics	Milwaukee-Waukesha PMSA, WI	H	7.85 FQ	13.29 AW	20.34 TQ	WIBLS	10/01-12/01
Metals and Plastics	Racine PMSA, WI	H	8.93 FQ	11.36 AW	13.35 TQ	WIBLS	10/01-12/01
Metals and Plastics	Puerto Rico	H	5.62 FQ	7.49 AW	10.28 TQ	PRBLS	10/01-12/01
Motion Picture Projectionist	Alabama	H	5.51 FQ	6.73 AW	8.44 TQ	ALBLS	10/01-12/01
	Arizona	H	5.57 FQ	7.68 AW	10.27 TQ	AZBLS	10/01-12/01
	Arkansas	H	5.73 FQ	7.81 AW	11.02 TQ	ARBLS	10/01-12/01

AAW	Average annual wage	AOH	Average offered, high	ASH	Average starting, high	H	Hourly	M	Monthly	S	Special: hourly and annual
AE	Average entry wage	AOL	Average offered, low	ASL	Average starting, low	HI	Highest wage paid	MTC	Median total compensation	TQ	Third quartile wage
AEX	Average experienced wage	APH	Average pay, high range	AW	Average wage paid	HR	High end range	MW	Median wage paid	W	Weekly
AO	Average offered	APL	Average pay, low range	FQ	First quartile wage	LR	Low end range	SQ	Second quartile wage	Y	Yearly

Occupation/Type/Industry	Location	Per	Low	Mid	High	Source	Date
Motion Picture Projectionist	California	H	6.79 FQ	11.43 AW	13.44 TQ	CABLS	10/01-12/01
	Colorado	H	6.41 FQ	9.50 AW	12.98 TQ	COBLS	10/01-12/01
	Connecticut	H	6.73 FQ	9.79 AW	13.44 TQ	CTBLS	10/01-12/01
	Florida	H	5.66 FQ	7.37 AW	9.46 TQ	FLBLS	10/01-12/01
	Georgia	H	5.64 FQ	6.75 AW	8.47 TQ	GABLS	10/01-12/01
	Hawaii	H	6.36 FQ	12.18 AW	20.11 TQ	HIBLS	10/01-12/01
	Idaho	H	5.57 FQ	8.09 AW	11.93 TQ	IDBLS	10/01-12/01
	Illinois	H	6.98 FQ	14.72 AW	24.42 TQ	ILBLS	10/01-12/01
	Indiana	H	5.84 FQ	8.83 AW	15.37 TQ	INBLS	10/01-12/01
	Iowa	H	5.62 FQ	6.68 AW	8.71 TQ	IABLS	10/01-12/01
	Kansas	H	5.79 FQ	7.43 AW	9.06 TQ	KSBLS	10/01-12/01
	Kentucky	H	5.62 FQ	7.98 AW	12.40 TQ	KYBLS	10/01-12/01
	Louisiana	H	5.54 FQ	6.72 AW	8.94 TQ	LABLS	10/01-12/01
	Maine	H	6.17 FQ	7.79 AW	9.89 TQ	MEBLS	10/01-12/01
	Maryland	H	6.12 FQ	8.10 AW	10.30 TQ	MDBLS	10/01-12/01
	Massachusetts	H	6.95 FQ	9.60 AW	12.98 TQ	MABLS	10/01-12/01
	Michigan	H	5.69 FQ	8.58 AW	13.66 TQ	MIBLS	10/01-12/01
	Minnesota	H	5.58 FQ	7.03 AW	9.88 TQ	MNBLS	10/01-12/01
	Mississippi	H	5.61 FQ	7.28 AW	10.21 TQ	MSBLS	10/01-12/01
	Missouri	H	5.47 FQ	6.65 AW	7.37 TQ	MOBLS	10/01-12/01
	Montana	H	5.67 FQ	7.03 AW	8.41 TQ	MTBLS	10/01-12/01
	Nebraska	H	5.40 FQ	6.80 AW	9.84 TQ	NEBLS	10/01-12/01
	Nevada	H	5.51 FQ	7.40 AW	10.10 TQ	NVBLS	10/01-12/01
	New Hampshire	H	7.19 FQ	8.56 AW	11.40 TQ	NHBLS	10/01-12/01
	New Jersey	H	5.94 FQ	10.05 AW	16.97 TQ	NJBLS	10/01-12/01
	New Mexico	H	5.51 FQ	6.25 AW	7.00 TQ	NMBLS	10/01-12/01
	New York	H	6.03 FQ	15.04 AW	31.00 TQ	NYBLS	10/01-12/01
	North Carolina	H	5.75 FQ	7.68 AW	10.92 TQ	NCBLS	10/01-12/01
	North Dakota	H	5.49 FQ	6.30 AW	7.07 TQ	NDBLS	10/01-12/01
	Ohio	H	5.68 FQ	7.48 AW	9.48 TQ	OHBLS	10/01-12/01
	Oklahoma	H	5.41 FQ	6.78 AW	8.95 TQ	OKBLS	10/01-12/01
	Oregon	H	6.71 FQ	8.38 AW	10.34 TQ	ORBLS	10/01-12/01
	Pennsylvania	H	5.56 FQ	7.27 AW	9.39 TQ	PABLS	10/01-12/01
	Rhode Island	H	8.04 FQ	12.63 AW	18.94 TQ	RIBLS	10/01-12/01
	South Carolina	H	5.52 FQ	6.71 AW	8.86 TQ	SCBLS	10/01-12/01
	Tennessee	H	5.52 FQ	6.93 AW	8.53 TQ	TNBLS	10/01-12/01
	Texas	H	5.70 FQ	8.06 AW	13.64 TQ	TXBLS	10/01-12/01
	Utah	H	5.72 FQ	7.59 AW	9.87 TQ	UTBLS	10/01-12/01
	Vermont	H	6.92 FQ	8.79 AW	12.56 TQ	VTBLS	10/01-12/01
	Virginia	H	5.62 FQ	7.18 AW	9.00 TQ	VABLS	10/01-12/01
	Washington	H	7.00 FQ	9.66 AW	14.26 TQ	WABLS	10/01-12/01
	Wisconsin	H	5.81 FQ	8.99 AW	17.31 TQ	WIBLS	10/01-12/01
	Puerto Rico	H	5.64 FQ	6.58 AW	8.30 TQ	PRBLS	10/01-12/01
Motorboat Mechanic	Alabama	H	8.15 FQ	13.31 AW	16.93 TQ	ALBLS	10/01-12/01
	Alaska	H	11.94 FQ	16.69 AW	21.66 TQ	AKBLS	10/01-12/01
	Arizona	H	7.89 FQ	12.54 AW	16.92 TQ	AZBLS	10/01-12/01
	Arkansas	H	6.78 FQ	10.89 AW	16.53 TQ	ARBLS	10/01-12/01
	California	H	9.08 FQ	15.36 AW	22.77 TQ	CABLS	10/01-12/01
	Colorado	H	9.82 FQ	14.51 AW	20.31 TQ	COBLS	10/01-12/01
	Connecticut	H	11.86 FQ	16.91 AW	22.75 TQ	CTBLS	10/01-12/01
	Delaware	H	6.88 FQ	10.55 AW	14.23 TQ	DEBLS	10/01-12/01
	Florida	H	9.39 FQ	15.17 AW	21.64 TQ	FLBLS	10/01-12/01
	Georgia	H	9.09 FQ	14.33 AW	20.73 TQ	GABLS	10/01-12/01
	Hawaii	H	7.15 FQ	15.28 AW	25.33 TQ	HIBLS	10/01-12/01
	Idaho	H	8.72 FQ	13.28 AW	21.64 TQ	IDBLS	10/01-12/01
	Illinois	H	9.10 FQ	13.60 AW	20.18 TQ	ILBLS	10/01-12/01
	Indiana	H	8.66 FQ	13.27 AW	18.11 TQ	INBLS	10/01-12/01
	Iowa	H	8.56 FQ	12.84 AW	17.77 TQ	IABLS	10/01-12/01
	Kansas	H	7.94 FQ	12.22 AW	17.41 TQ	KSBLS	10/01-12/01
	Kentucky	H	7.63 FQ	12.13 AW	19.58 TQ	KYBLS	10/01-12/01
	Louisiana	H	7.74 FQ	14.29 AW	22.29 TQ	LABLS	10/01-12/01
	Maine	H	10.00 FQ	14.71 AW	19.66 TQ	MEBLS	10/01-12/01
	Maryland	H	9.03 FQ	16.21 AW	24.69 TQ	MDBLS	10/01-12/01
	Massachusetts	H	10.39 FQ	16.57 AW	21.62 TQ	MABLS	10/01-12/01
	Michigan	H	9.68 FQ	14.13 AW	18.76 TQ	MIBLS	10/01-12/01
	Minnesota	H	10.26 FQ	15.11 AW	20.76 TQ	MNBLS	10/01-12/01
	Mississippi	H	9.31 FQ	13.87 AW	20.61 TQ	MSBLS	10/01-12/01
	Missouri	H	6.87 FQ	12.71 AW	18.60 TQ	MOBLS	10/01-12/01
	Montana	H	8.08 FQ	13.37 AW	17.73 TQ	MTBLS	10/01-12/01
	Nebraska	H	9.10 FQ	12.95 AW	19.38 TQ	NEBLS	10/01-12/01
	Nevada	H	8.16 FQ	14.02 AW	21.43 TQ	NVBLS	10/01-12/01
	New Hampshire	H	10.68 FQ	14.04 AW	18.56 TQ	NHBLS	10/01-12/01

AAW Average annual wage; **AE** Average entry wage; **AEX** Average experienced wage; **AO** Average offered; **AOH** Average offered, high; **AOL** Average offered, low; **APH** Average pay, high range; **APL** Average pay, low range; **ASH** Average starting, high; **ASL** Average starting, low; **AW** Average wage paid; **FQ** First quartile wage; **H** Hourly; **HI** Highest wage paid; **HR** High end range; **LR** Low end range; **M** Monthly; **MTC** Median total compensation; **MW** Median wage paid; **SQ** Second quartile wage; **S** Special: hourly and annual; **TQ** Third quartile wage; **W** Weekly; **Y** Yearly

Occupation/Type/Industry	Location	Per	Low	Mid	High	Source	Date
Motorboat Mechanic	New Jersey	H	9.75 FQ	14.51 AW	20.53 TQ	NJBLS	10/01-12/01
	New York	H	8.72 FQ	15.12 AW	23.15 TQ	NYBLS	10/01-12/01
	North Carolina	H	8.98 FQ	13.54 AW	18.27 TQ	NCBLS	10/01-12/01
	North Dakota	H	9.12 FQ	11.91 AW	16.32 TQ	NDBLS	10/01-12/01
	Ohio	H	8.48 FQ	13.19 AW	18.24 TQ	OHBLS	10/01-12/01
	Oklahoma	H	6.77 FQ	11.63 AW	17.39 TQ	OKBLS	10/01-12/01
	Oregon	H	7.39 FQ	12.47 AW	17.23 TQ	ORBLS	10/01-12/01
	Pennsylvania	H	7.02 FQ	11.46 AW	18.72 TQ	PABLS	10/01-12/01
	Rhode Island	H	12.51 FQ	17.23 AW	21.86 TQ	RIBLS	10/01-12/01
	South Carolina	H	8.82 FQ	12.63 AW	17.06 TQ	SCBLS	10/01-12/01
	South Dakota	H	7.90 FQ	11.15 AW	14.82 TQ	SDBLS	10/01-12/01
	Tennessee	H	7.33 FQ	12.01 AW	17.11 TQ	TNBLS	10/01-12/01
	Texas	H	7.76 FQ	12.78 AW	19.80 TQ	TXBLS	10/01-12/01
	Utah	H	9.62 FQ	13.87 AW	19.91 TQ	UTBLS	10/01-12/01
	Vermont	H	9.62 FQ	14.65 AW	19.48 TQ	VTBLS	10/01-12/01
	Virginia	H	8.00 FQ	12.56 AW	19.28 TQ	VABLS	10/01-12/01
	Washington	H	9.83 FQ	14.82 AW	19.86 TQ	WABLS	10/01-12/01
	West Virginia	H	6.73 FQ	9.80 AW	14.41 TQ	WVBLS	10/01-12/01
	Wisconsin	H	8.75 FQ	12.81 AW	17.42 TQ	WIBLS	10/01-12/01
	Puerto Rico	H	6.04 FQ	9.48 AW	15.06 TQ	PRBLS	10/01-12/01
	Virgin Islands	H	11.51 FQ	14.79 AW	19.99 TQ	VIBLS	10/01-12/01
Motorboat Operator	Alabama	H	9.04 FQ	16.87 AW	23.03 TQ	ALBLS	10/01-12/01
	California	H	11.95 FQ	21.06 AW	27.21 TQ	CABLS	10/01-12/01
	Florida	H	6.14 FQ	13.44 AW	24.28 TQ	FLBLS	10/01-12/01
	Illinois	H	14.40 FQ	17.31 AW	21.20 TQ	ILBLS	10/01-12/01
	Louisiana	H	9.65 FQ	15.38 AW	21.70 TQ	LABLS	10/01-12/01
	Maryland	H	6.76 FQ	16.91 AW	23.00 TQ	MDBLS	10/01-12/01
	Michigan	H	8.18 FQ	15.64 AW	30.64 TQ	MIBLS	10/01-12/01
	New York	H	7.18 FQ	9.05 AW	12.98 TQ	NYBLS	10/01-12/01
	North Carolina	H	6.15 FQ	16.50 AW	25.89 TQ	NCBLS	10/01-12/01
	Pennsylvania	H	6.97 FQ	17.32 AW	25.66 TQ	PABLS	10/01-12/01
	Tennessee	H	10.77 FQ	13.65 AW	20.41 TQ	TNBLS	10/01-12/01
	Texas	H	9.91 FQ	17.07 AW	23.74 TQ	TXBLS	10/01-12/01
	Virginia	H	10.60 FQ	17.41 AW	21.73 TQ	VABLS	10/01-12/01
	Washington	H	14.66 FQ	20.95 AW	28.55 TQ	WABLS	10/01-12/01
Motorcycle Mechanic	Alabama	H	8.70 FQ	12.85 AW	18.88 TQ	ALBLS	10/01-12/01
	Birmingham MSA, AL	H	10.87 FQ	12.97 AW	18.43 TQ	ALBLS	10/01-12/01
	Alaska	H	7.86 FQ	14.61 AW	20.85 TQ	AKBLS	10/01-12/01
	Arizona	H	7.97 FQ	14.49 AW	21.64 TQ	AZBLS	10/01-12/01
	Phoenix-Mesa MSA, AZ	H	9.09 FQ	15.47 AW	22.56 TQ	AZBLS	10/01-12/01
	Arkansas	H	8.18 FQ	11.79 AW	16.99 TQ	ARBLS	10/01-12/01
	Little Rock-North Little Rock MSA, AR	H	9.02 FQ	13.06 AW	17.51 TQ	ARBLS	10/01-12/01
	California	H	9.47 FQ	15.60 AW	22.44 TQ	CABLS	10/01-12/01
	Los Angeles-Long Beach PMSA, CA	H	8.33 FQ	14.95 AW	22.93 TQ	CABLS	10/01-12/01
	Modesto MSA, CA	H	9.10 FQ	13.71 AW	20.38 TQ	CABLS	10/01-12/01
	Oakland PMSA, CA	H	13.00 FQ	20.35 AW	26.78 TQ	CABLS	10/01-12/01
	Orange County PMSA, CA	H	12.26 FQ	16.53 AW	21.65 TQ	CABLS	10/01-12/01
	Riverside-San Bernardino PMSA, CA	H	8.86 FQ	15.41 AW	24.61 TQ	CABLS	10/01-12/01
	Sacramento PMSA, CA	H	11.75 FQ	16.64 AW	21.29 TQ	CABLS	10/01-12/01
	San Diego MSA, CA	H	9.41 FQ	15.01 AW	21.93 TQ	CABLS	10/01-12/01
	San Francisco PMSA, CA	H	13.68 FQ	17.41 AW	23.64 TQ	CABLS	10/01-12/01
	San Jose PMSA, CA	H	9.54 FQ	17.52 AW	28.33 TQ	CABLS	10/01-12/01
	Santa Rosa PMSA, CA	H	8.02 FQ	13.65 AW	20.08 TQ	CABLS	10/01-12/01
	Vallejo-Fairfield-Napa PMSA, CA	H	9.72 FQ	14.27 AW	17.79 TQ	CABLS	10/01-12/01
	Colorado	H	9.10 FQ	15.03 AW	22.87 TQ	COBLS	10/01-12/01
	Boulder-Longmont PMSA, CO	H	9.75 FQ	15.02 AW	23.83 TQ	COBLS	10/01-12/01
	Denver PMSA, CO	H	10.45 FQ	16.33 AW	28.51 TQ	COBLS	10/01-12/01
	Connecticut	H	9.45 FQ	14.84 AW	21.27 TQ	CTBLS	10/01-12/01
	Hartford MSA, CT	H	9.45 FQ	12.69 AW	17.40 TQ	CTBLS	10/01-12/01
	Delaware	H	8.41 FQ	14.06 AW	20.29 TQ	DEBLS	10/01-12/01
	Washington PMSA, DC-MD-VA-WV	H	8.39 FQ	14.51 AW	20.99 TQ	DCBLS	10/01-12/01
	Florida	H	7.68 FQ	13.03 AW	19.52 TQ	FLBLS	10/01-12/01
	Fort Lauderdale PMSA, FL	H	10.66 FQ	15.64 AW	23.62 TQ	FLBLS	10/01-12/01
	Fort Myers-Cape Coral MSA, FL	H	9.10 FQ	14.40 AW	20.71 TQ	FLBLS	10/01-12/01
	Jacksonville MSA, FL	H	7.93 FQ	11.89 AW	18.73 TQ	FLBLS	10/01-12/01

AAW Average annual wage; **AE** Average entry wage; **AEX** Average experienced wage; **AO** Average offered; **AOH** Average offered, high; **AOL** Average offered, low; **APH** Average pay, high range; **APL** Average pay, low range; **ASH** Average starting, high; **ASL** Average starting, low; **AW** Average wage paid; **FQ** First quartile wage; **H** Hourly; **HI** Highest wage paid; **HR** High end range; **LR** Low end range; **M** Monthly; **MTC** Median total compensation; **MW** Median wage paid; **SQ** Second quartile wage; **S** Special: hourly and annual; **TQ** Third quartile wage; **W** Weekly; **Y** Yearly

Occupation/Type/Industry	Location	Per	Low	Mid	High	Source	Date
Motorcycle Mechanic	Orlando MSA, FL	H	9.77 FQ	13.79 AW	18.38 TQ	FLBLS	10/01-12/01
	Tampa-St. Petersburg-Clearwater MSA, FL	H	8.43 FQ	13.53 AW	16.86 TQ	FLBLS	10/01-12/01
	West Palm Beach-Boca Raton MSA, FL	H	5.72 FQ	10.85 AW	19.66 TQ	FLBLS	10/01-12/01
	Georgia	H	9.38 FQ	12.78 AW	17.42 TQ	GABLS	10/01-12/01
	Atlanta MSA, GA	H	11.01 FQ	14.29 AW	20.47 TQ	GABLS	10/01-12/01
	Augusta-Aiken MSA, GA-SC	H	9.59 FQ	12.66 AW	17.26 TQ	GABLS	10/01-12/01
	Hawaii	H	8.67 FQ	15.15 AW	20.55 TQ	HIBLS	10/01-12/01
	Idaho	H	8.59 FQ	14.56 AW	20.87 TQ	IDBLS	10/01-12/01
	Boise City MSA, ID	H	8.12 FQ	14.81 AW	21.27 TQ	IDBLS	10/01-12/01
	Illinois	H	7.48 FQ	12.52 AW	19.61 TQ	ILBLS	10/01-12/01
	Chicago PMSA, IL	H	9.93 FQ	16.18 AW	21.98 TQ	ILBLS	10/01-12/01
	Indiana	H	8.57 FQ	13.12 AW	19.69 TQ	INBLS	10/01-12/01
	Gary PMSA, IN	H	7.40 FQ	10.58 AW	13.90 TQ	INBLS	10/01-12/01
	Indianapolis MSA, IN	H	10.66 FQ	16.20 AW	24.58 TQ	INBLS	10/01-12/01
	Iowa	H	6.05 FQ	11.31 AW	16.41 TQ	IABLS	10/01-12/01
	Des Moines MSA, IA	H	6.49 FQ	11.33 AW	16.23 TQ	IABLS	10/01-12/01
	Kansas	H	8.70 FQ	13.01 AW	18.05 TQ	KSBLS	10/01-12/01
	Kentucky	H	6.84 FQ	10.16 AW	15.27 TQ	KYBLS	10/01-12/01
	Lexington MSA, KY	H	7.70 FQ	11.59 AW	16.96 TQ	KYBLS	10/01-12/01
	Louisville MSA, KY-IN	H	7.61 FQ	10.12 AW	13.96 TQ	KYBLS	10/01-12/01
	Louisiana	H	7.51 FQ	12.30 AW	18.58 TQ	LABLS	10/01-12/01
	Baton Rouge MSA, LA	H	8.94 FQ	16.06 AW	21.44 TQ	LABLS	10/01-12/01
	New Orleans MSA, LA	H	9.07 FQ	14.09 AW	21.49 TQ	LABLS	10/01-12/01
	Maine	H	7.14 FQ	10.55 AW	14.19 TQ	MEBLS	10/01-12/01
	Maryland	H	7.28 FQ	13.54 AW	20.83 TQ	MDBLS	10/01-12/01
	Baltimore PMSA, MD	H	6.02 FQ	13.07 AW	20.43 TQ	MDBLS	10/01-12/01
	Massachusetts	H	8.29 FQ	15.96 AW	27.98 TQ	MABLS	10/01-12/01
	Boston PMSA, MA-NH	H	7.32 FQ	12.65 AW	18.20 TQ	MABLS	10/01-12/01
	Springfield MSA, MA	H	9.29 FQ	12.19 AW	16.23 TQ	MABLS	10/01-12/01
	Michigan	H	9.32 FQ	14.11 AW	21.48 TQ	MIBLS	10/01-12/01
	Ann Arbor PMSA, MI	H	10.78 FQ	13.69 AW	22.86 TQ	MIBLS	10/01-12/01
	Detroit PMSA, MI	H	9.55 FQ	14.77 AW	24.62 TQ	MIBLS	10/01-12/01
	Grand Rapids-Muskegon-Holland MSA, MI	H	9.77 FQ	16.27 AW	20.92 TQ	MIBLS	10/01-12/01
	Minnesota	H	8.81 FQ	13.15 AW	17.54 TQ	MNBLS	10/01-12/01
	Minneapolis-St. Paul MSA, MN-WI	H	8.88 FQ	13.68 AW	18.32 TQ	MNBLS	10/01-12/01
	Mississippi	H	7.42 FQ	11.35 AW	16.52 TQ	MSBLS	10/01-12/01
	Jackson MSA, MS	H	7.26 FQ	11.96 AW	20.50 TQ	MSBLS	10/01-12/01
	Missouri	H	7.58 FQ	11.11 AW	16.14 TQ	MOBLS	10/01-12/01
	Kansas City MSA, MO-KS	H	8.44 FQ	12.56 AW	19.52 TQ	MOBLS	10/01-12/01
	St. Louis MSA, MO-IL	H	8.07 FQ	13.13 AW	21.52 TQ	MOBLS	10/01-12/01
	Montana	H	7.42 FQ	10.57 AW	14.00 TQ	MTBLS	10/01-12/01
	Nebraska	H	6.87 FQ	11.48 AW	17.42 TQ	NEBLS	10/01-12/01
	Omaha MSA, NE-IA	H	9.15 FQ	11.61 AW	16.09 TQ	NEBLS	10/01-12/01
	Nevada	H	8.90 FQ	14.61 AW	20.95 TQ	NVBLS	10/01-12/01
	Las Vegas MSA, NV-AZ	H	11.10 FQ	15.65 AW	21.79 TQ	NVBLS	10/01-12/01
	Reno MSA, NV	H	7.76 FQ	12.61 AW	18.54 TQ	NVBLS	10/01-12/01
	New Hampshire	H	9.11 FQ	13.78 AW	17.52 TQ	NHBLS	10/01-12/01
	Manchester PMSA, NH	H	9.01 FQ	13.39 AW	17.50 TQ	NHBLS	10/01-12/01
	New Jersey	H	9.94 FQ	15.46 AW	24.26 TQ	NJBLS	10/01-12/01
	Middlesex-Somerset-Hunterdon PMSA, NJ	H	9.31 FQ	14.49 AW	20.34 TQ	NJBLS	10/01-12/01
	Monmouth-Ocean PMSA, NJ	H	10.48 FQ	16.34 AW	25.03 TQ	NJBLS	10/01-12/01
	Newark PMSA, NJ	H	11.34 FQ	16.38 AW	26.40 TQ	NJBLS	10/01-12/01
	New Mexico	H	7.25 FQ	12.09 AW	20.01 TQ	NMBLS	10/01-12/01
	Albuquerque MSA, NM	H	7.64 FQ	13.35 AW	21.81 TQ	NMBLS	10/01-12/01
	New York	H	6.94 FQ	11.84 AW	17.74 TQ	NYBLS	10/01-12/01
	Albany-Schenectady-Troy MSA, NY	H	5.50 FQ	10.28 AW	16.82 TQ	NYBLS	10/01-12/01
	Buffalo-Niagara Falls MSA, NY	H	7.76 FQ	10.93 AW	14.74 TQ	NYBLS	10/01-12/01
	Nassau-Suffolk PMSA, NY	H	7.44 FQ	15.17 AW	24.41 TQ	NYBLS	10/01-12/01
	New York PMSA, NY	H	9.04 FQ	14.51 AW	20.39 TQ	NYBLS	10/01-12/01
	Rochester MSA, NY	H	7.49 FQ	10.14 AW	13.97 TQ	NYBLS	10/01-12/01
	Syracuse MSA, NY	H	5.95 FQ	10.42 AW	16.04 TQ	NYBLS	10/01-12/01
	Utica-Rome MSA, NY	H	7.52 FQ	10.01 AW	13.07 TQ	NYBLS	10/01-12/01
	North Carolina	H	8.07 FQ	13.41 AW	19.86 TQ	NCBLS	10/01-12/01
	Charlotte-Gastonia-Rock Hill MSA, NC-SC	H	7.94 FQ	14.34 AW	21.09 TQ	NCBLS	10/01-12/01

AAW	Average annual wage	**AOH**	Average offered, high	**ASH**	Average starting, high	**H**	Hourly	**M**	Monthly	**S**	Special: hourly and annual
AE	Average entry wage	**AOL**	Average offered, low	**ASL**	Average starting, low	**HI**	Highest wage paid	**MTC**	Median total compensation	**TQ**	Third quartile wage
AEX	Average experienced wage	**APH**	Average pay, high range	**AW**	Average wage paid	**HR**	High end range	**MW**	Median wage paid	**W**	Weekly
AO	Average offered	**APL**	Average pay, low range	**FQ**	First quartile wage	**LR**	Low end range	**SQ**	Second quartile wage	**Y**	Yearly

Occupation/Type/Industry	Location	Per	Low	Mid	High	Source	Date
Motorcycle Mechanic	Greensboro-Winston-Salem-High Point MSA, NC	H	8.16 FQ	14.49 AW	21.21 TQ	NCBLS	10/01-12/01
	Raleigh-Durham-Chapel Hill MSA, NC	H	10.01 FQ	14.86 AW	20.41 TQ	NCBLS	10/01-12/01
	North Dakota	H	7.76 FQ	11.80 AW	16.75 TQ	NDBLS	10/01-12/01
	Ohio	H	6.96 FQ	12.65 AW	18.93 TQ	OHBLS	10/01-12/01
	Cincinnati PMSA, OH-KY-IN	H	8.07 FQ	12.49 AW	17.41 TQ	OHBLS	10/01-12/01
	Cleveland-Lorain-Elyria PMSA, OH	H	7.86 FQ	12.71 AW	17.56 TQ	OHBLS	10/01-12/01
	Columbus MSA, OH	H	8.99 FQ	14.23 AW	20.59 TQ	OHBLS	10/01-12/01
	Oklahoma	H	6.95 FQ	12.76 AW	21.26 TQ	OKBLS	10/01-12/01
	Oklahoma City MSA, OK	H	8.80 FQ	18.29 AW	27.48 TQ	OKBLS	10/01-12/01
	Tulsa MSA, OK	H	8.49 FQ	13.13 AW	18.16 TQ	OKBLS	10/01-12/01
	Oregon	H	9.42 FQ	13.90 AW	20.28 TQ	ORBLS	10/01-12/01
	Portland-Vancouver PMSA, OR-WA	H	9.35 FQ	14.42 AW	21.35 TQ	ORBLS	10/01-12/01
	Salem PMSA, OR	H	7.90 FQ	13.77 AW	20.72 TQ	ORBLS	10/01-12/01
	Pennsylvania	H	8.00 FQ	12.49 AW	16.91 TQ	PABLS	10/01-12/01
	Allentown-Bethlehem-Easton MSA, PA	H	10.28 FQ	13.30 AW	16.70 TQ	PABLS	10/01-12/01
	Harrisburg-Lebanon-Carlisle MSA, PA	H	9.05 FQ	12.65 AW	17.15 TQ	PABLS	10/01-12/01
	Johnstown MSA, PA	H	9.09 FQ	11.94 AW	14.94 TQ	PABLS	10/01-12/01
	Lancaster MSA, PA	H	9.20 FQ	13.64 AW	19.43 TQ	PABLS	10/01-12/01
	Philadelphia PMSA, PA-NJ	H	9.08 FQ	15.72 AW	28.56 TQ	PABLS	10/01-12/01
	Pittsburgh MSA, PA	H	7.51 FQ	10.34 AW	13.84 TQ	PABLS	10/01-12/01
	Rhode Island	H	8.40 FQ	12.84 AW	18.07 TQ	RIBLS	10/01-12/01
	Providence-Fall River-Warwick MSA, RI-MA	H	8.54 FQ	12.67 AW	17.76 TQ	RIBLS	10/01-12/01
	South Carolina	H	9.05 FQ	13.60 AW	19.19 TQ	SCBLS	10/01-12/01
	Greenville-Spartanburg-Anderson MSA, SC	H	11.97 FQ	14.42 AW	16.95 TQ	SCBLS	10/01-12/01
	South Dakota	H	9.16 FQ	12.01 AW	16.45 TQ	SDBLS	10/01-12/01
	Tennessee	H	7.75 FQ	12.41 AW	18.34 TQ	TNBLS	10/01-12/01
	Johnson City-Kingsport-Bristol MSA, TN-VA	H	7.34 FQ	10.70 AW	17.22 TQ	TNBLS	10/01-12/01
	Knoxville MSA, TN	H	6.64 FQ	10.73 AW	14.40 TQ	TNBLS	10/01-12/01
	Memphis MSA, TN-AR-MS	H	9.79 FQ	13.02 AW	17.41 TQ	TNBLS	10/01-12/01
	Nashville MSA, TN	H	7.90 FQ	14.17 AW	21.61 TQ	TNBLS	10/01-12/01
	Texas	H	7.92 FQ	14.36 AW	22.97 TQ	TXBLS	10/01-12/01
	Austin-San Marcos MSA, TX	H	11.23 FQ	16.33 AW	23.42 TQ	TXBLS	10/01-12/01
	Beaumont-Port Arthur MSA, TX	H	8.94 FQ	14.40 AW	23.39 TQ	TXBLS	10/01-12/01
	Dallas PMSA, TX	H	9.88 FQ	19.00 AW	33.50 TQ	TXBLS	10/01-12/01
	El Paso MSA, TX	H	6.81 FQ	10.32 AW	13.77 TQ	TXBLS	10/01-12/01
	Fort Worth-Arlington PMSA, TX	H	9.33 FQ	13.35 AW	19.65 TQ	TXBLS	10/01-12/01
	Houston PMSA, TX	H	7.85 FQ	14.40 AW	24.24 TQ	TXBLS	10/01-12/01
	Longview-Marshall MSA, TX	H	11.90 FQ	15.83 AW	22.25 TQ	TXBLS	10/01-12/01
	San Antonio MSA, TX	H	8.89 FQ	15.99 AW	25.36 TQ	TXBLS	10/01-12/01
	Utah	H	8.57 FQ	14.11 AW	20.65 TQ	UTBLS	10/01-12/01
	Salt Lake City-Ogden MSA, UT	H	8.78 FQ	14.70 AW	21.60 TQ	UTBLS	10/01-12/01
	Vermont	H	9.02 FQ	12.45 AW	16.40 TQ	VTBLS	10/01-12/01
	Virginia	H	7.69 FQ	13.65 AW	22.17 TQ	VABLS	10/01-12/01
	Norfolk-Virginia Beach-Newport News MSA, VA-NC	H	7.62 FQ	14.26 AW	25.48 TQ	VABLS	10/01-12/01
	Richmond-Petersburg MSA, VA	H	6.96 FQ	13.25 AW	20.55 TQ	VABLS	10/01-12/01
	Washington	H	9.26 FQ	13.75 AW	18.52 TQ	WABLS	10/01-12/01
	Seattle-Bellevue-Everett PMSA, WA	H	9.74 FQ	13.79 AW	18.60 TQ	WABLS	10/01-12/01
	West Virginia	H	6.49 FQ	9.96 AW	15.88 TQ	WVBLS	10/01-12/01
	Wisconsin	H	9.83 FQ	16.65 AW	25.37 TQ	WIBLS	10/01-12/01
	Appleton-Oshkosh-Neenah MSA, WI	H	9.47 FQ	13.26 AW	17.35 TQ	WIBLS	10/01-12/01
	Milwaukee-Waukesha PMSA, WI	H	11.95 FQ	20.35 AW	26.30 TQ	WIBLS	10/01-12/01
	Wyoming	H	7.64 FQ	15.05 AW	22.09 TQ	WYBLS	10/01-12/01
Multi-Media Artist and Animator	Alabama	Y	19960 FQ	36680 AW	57660 TQ	ALBLS	10/01-12/01
	Alaska	Y	23790 FQ	29810 AW	41340 TQ	AKBLS	10/01-12/01

AAW Average annual wage **AE** Average entry wage **AEX** Average experienced wage **AO** Average offered **AOH** Average offered, high **AOL** Average offered, low **APH** Average pay, high range **APL** Average pay, low range **ASH** Average starting, high **ASL** Average starting, low **AW** Average wage paid **FQ** First quartile wage **H** Hourly **HI** Highest wage paid **HR** High end range **LR** Low end range **M** Monthly **MTC** Median total compensation **MW** Median wage paid **SQ** Second quartile wage **S** Special: hourly and annual **TQ** Third quartile wage **W** Weekly **Y** Yearly

Occupation/Type/Industry	Location	Per	Low	Mid	High	Source	Date
Multi-Media Artist and Animator	Arkansas	Y	14850 FQ	28610 AW	49780 TQ	ARBLS	10/01-12/01
	California	Y	31950 FQ	60680 AW	96860 TQ	CABLS	10/01-12/01
	Colorado	Y	21390 FQ	45410 AW	73550 TQ	COBLS	10/01-12/01
	Connecticut	Y	30660 FQ	56210 AW	101820 TQ	CTBLS	10/01-12/01
	District of Columbia	Y	26830 FQ	46120 AW	75020 TQ	DCBLS	10/01-12/01
	Florida	Y	24730 FQ	44520 AW	66270 TQ	FLBLS	10/01-12/01
	Georgia	Y	29680 FQ	48140 AW	80550 TQ	GABLS	10/01-12/01
	Hawaii	Y	27120 FQ	45440 AW	79530 TQ	HIBLS	10/01-12/01
	Idaho	Y	21080 FQ	35760 AW	52770 TQ	IDBLS	10/01-12/01
	Illinois	Y	24450 FQ	40690 AW	60530 TQ	ILBLS	10/01-12/01
	Indiana	Y	20490 FQ	37070 AW	57450 TQ	INBLS	10/01-12/01
	Iowa	Y	19660 FQ	31280 AW	51850 TQ	IABLS	10/01-12/01
	Kansas	Y	24980 FQ	38080 AW	58840 TQ	KSBLS	10/01-12/01
	Kentucky	Y	23430 FQ	42550 AW	66260 TQ	KYBLS	10/01-12/01
	Louisiana	Y	25320 FQ	33280 AW	42690 TQ	LABLS	10/01-12/01
	Maine	Y	29370 FQ	38440 AW	54080 TQ	MEBLS	10/01-12/01
	Maryland	Y	28260 FQ	47960 AW	75960 TQ	MDBLS	10/01-12/01
	Massachusetts	Y	28480 FQ	43990 AW	72030 TQ	MABLS	10/01-12/01
	Michigan	Y	27050 FQ	46570 AW	74290 TQ	MIBLS	10/01-12/01
	Minnesota	Y	25380 FQ	45440 AW	71520 TQ	MNBLS	10/01-12/01
	Missouri	Y	12770 FQ	36340 AW	61250 TQ	MOBLS	10/01-12/01
	Nebraska	Y	23090 FQ	32420 AW	44100 TQ	NEBLS	10/01-12/01
	Nevada	Y	24810 FQ	44380 AW	68770 TQ	NVBLS	10/01-12/01
	New Hampshire	Y	28680 FQ	38730 AW	56890 TQ	NHBLS	10/01-12/01
	New Jersey	Y	24640 FQ	42500 AW	69970 TQ	NJBLS	10/01-12/01
	New Mexico	Y	20270 FQ	42430 AW	63060 TQ	NMBLS	10/01-12/01
	New York	Y	24920 FQ	47740 AW	79420 TQ	NYBLS	10/01-12/01
	North Carolina	Y	16300 FQ	38440 AW	61500 TQ	NCBLS	10/01-12/01
	Ohio	Y	23410 FQ	38730 AW	58350 TQ	OHBLS	10/01-12/01
	Oklahoma	Y	19670 FQ	31650 AW	46320 TQ	OKBLS	10/01-12/01
	Oregon	Y	28530 FQ	44120 AW	67340 TQ	ORBLS	10/01-12/01
	Pennsylvania	Y	28010 FQ	47650 AW	81090 TQ	PABLS	10/01-12/01
	Rhode Island	Y	24870 FQ	43360 AW	66370 TQ	RIBLS	10/01-12/01
	South Carolina	Y	22450 FQ	37380 AW	60360 TQ	SCBLS	10/01-12/01
	South Dakota	Y	18320 FQ	28910 AW	42220 TQ	SDBLS	10/01-12/01
	Tennessee	Y	23370 FQ	33740 AW	49360 TQ	TNBLS	10/01-12/01
	Texas	Y	27050 FQ	46300 AW	77130 TQ	TXBLS	10/01-12/01
	Utah	Y	17820 FQ	38820 AW	58900 TQ	UTBLS	10/01-12/01
	Vermont	Y	29940 FQ	49830 AW	82750 TQ	VTBLS	10/01-12/01
	Virginia	Y	28450 FQ	44660 AW	62940 TQ	VABLS	10/01-12/01
	Washington	Y	25720 FQ	51610 AW	81630 TQ	WABLS	10/01-12/01
	West Virginia	Y	19600 FQ	30350 AW	43010 TQ	WVBLS	10/01-12/01
	Wisconsin	Y	22780 FQ	39830 AW	56360 TQ	WIBLS	10/01-12/01
	Puerto Rico	Y	18150 FQ	31600 AW	49130 TQ	PRBLS	10/01-12/01
Music Director and Composer	Arizona	Y	15070 FQ	33560 AW	98010 TQ	AZBLS	10/01-12/01
	Phoenix-Mesa MSA, AZ	Y	14970 FQ	21100 AW	38180 TQ	AZBLS	10/01-12/01
	California	Y	14530 FQ	35730 AW	60680 TQ	CABLS	10/01-12/01
	Los Angeles-Long Beach PMSA, CA	Y	14330 FQ	38970 AW	64680 TQ	CABLS	10/01-12/01
	Orange County PMSA, CA	Y	23140 FQ	37120 AW	45170 TQ	CABLS	10/01-12/01
	Riverside-San Bernardino PMSA, CA	Y	14270 FQ	28630 AW	43430 TQ	CABLS	10/01-12/01
	San Diego MSA, CA	Y	15960 FQ	28820 AW	43020 TQ	CABLS	10/01-12/01
	San Francisco PMSA, CA	Y	13730 FQ	38240 AW	63580 TQ	CABLS	10/01-12/01
	San Jose PMSA, CA	Y	21940 FQ	38550 AW	55850 TQ	CABLS	10/01-12/01
	Colorado	Y	12680 FQ	40500 AW	80550 TQ	COBLS	10/01-12/01
	Connecticut	Y	19780 FQ	45580 AW	72020 TQ	CTBLS	10/01-12/01
	Hartford MSA, CT	Y	25100 FQ	42240 AW	55100 TQ	CTBLS	10/01-12/01
	Washington PMSA, DC-MD-VA-WV	Y	21070 FQ	51950 AW	96040 TQ	DCBLS	10/01-12/01
	Florida	Y	12970 FQ	29590 AW	47590 TQ	FLBLS	10/01-12/01
	Fort Lauderdale PMSA, FL	Y	15240 FQ	27490 AW	36780 TQ	FLBLS	10/01-12/01
	Miami PMSA, FL	Y	13460 FQ	30670 AW	48190 TQ	FLBLS	10/01-12/01
	Orlando MSA, FL	Y	12440 FQ	25140 AW	40880 TQ	FLBLS	10/01-12/01
	Pensacola MSA, FL	Y	11830 FQ	14030 AW	15120 TQ	FLBLS	10/01-12/01
	Sarasota-Bradenton MSA, FL	Y	26670 FQ	47330 AW	86580 TQ	FLBLS	10/01-12/01
	Tampa-St. Petersburg-Clearwater MSA, FL	Y	15030 FQ	32710 AW	52100 TQ	FLBLS	10/01-12/01
	Georgia	Y	19580 FQ	44180 AW	67270 TQ	GABLS	10/01-12/01
	Atlanta MSA, GA	Y	24730 FQ	45100 AW	58270 TQ	GABLS	10/01-12/01
	Hawaii	Y	13670 FQ	31530 AW	56480 TQ	HIBLS	10/01-12/01
	Honolulu MSA, HI	Y	13500 FQ	30880 AW	38040 TQ	HIBLS	10/01-12/01

AAW	Average annual wage	**AOH**	Average offered, high	**ASH**	Average starting, high	**H**	Hourly	**M**	Monthly	**S**	Special: hourly and annual
AE	Average entry wage	**AOL**	Average offered, low	**ASL**	Average starting, low	**HI**	Highest wage paid	**MTC**	Median total compensation	**TQ**	Third quartile wage
AEX	Average experienced wage	**APH**	Average pay, high range	**AW**	Average wage paid	**HR**	High end range	**MW**	Median wage paid	**W**	Weekly
AO	Average offered	**APL**	Average pay, low range	**FQ**	First quartile wage	**LR**	Low end range	**SQ**	Second quartile wage	**Y**	Yearly

Occupation/Type/Industry	Location	Per	Low	Mid	High	Source	Date
Music Director and Composer	Illinois	Y	13220 FQ	38490 AW	71670 TQ	ILBLS	10/01-12/01
	Chicago PMSA, IL	Y	14040 FQ	43790 AW	76730 TQ	ILBLS	10/01-12/01
	Indiana	Y	12950 FQ	32250 AW	60460 TQ	INBLS	10/01-12/01
	Iowa	Y	28440 FQ	37920 AW	54650 TQ	IABLS	10/01-12/01
	Louisiana	Y	22660 FQ	40960 AW	60280 TQ	LABLS	10/01-12/01
	Maryland	Y	12870 FQ	39010 AW	86940 TQ	MDBLS	10/01-12/01
	Baltimore PMSA, MD	Y	12500 FQ	33010 AW	49390 TQ	MDBLS	10/01-12/01
	Massachusetts	Y	31030 FQ	45630 AW	60350 TQ	MABLS	10/01-12/01
	Boston PMSA, MA-NH	Y	34540 FQ	48420 AW	60500 TQ	MABLS	10/01-12/01
	Michigan	Y	13230 FQ	34500 AW	64030 TQ	MIBLS	10/01-12/01
	Ann Arbor PMSA, MI	Y	12090 FQ	48320 AW	71610 TQ	MIBLS	10/01-12/01
	Detroit PMSA, MI	Y	12820 FQ	32830 AW	63670 TQ	MIBLS	10/01-12/01
	Grand Rapids-Muskegon-Holland MSA, MI	Y	23920 FQ	30340 AW	35100 TQ	MIBLS	10/01-12/01
	Saginaw-Bay City-Midland MSA, MI	Y	13870 FQ	41740 AW	65700 TQ	MIBLS	10/01-12/01
	Minnesota	Y	23690 FQ	42040 AW	57090 TQ	MNBLS	10/01-12/01
	Minneapolis-St. Paul MSA, MN-WI	Y	23340 FQ	41150 AW	56240 TQ	MNBLS	10/01-12/01
	Missouri	Y	12700 FQ	38370 AW	65090 TQ	MOBLS	10/01-12/01
	Montana	Y	13170 FQ	21210 AW	27590 TQ	MTBLS	10/01-12/01
	Billings MSA, MT	Y	14300 FQ	19140 AW	17500 TQ	MTBLS	10/01-12/01
	New Jersey	Y	12490 FQ	38900 AW	70640 TQ	NJBLS	10/01-12/01
	Middlesex-Somerset-Hunterdon PMSA, NJ	Y	19530 FQ	49060 AW	71760 TQ	NJBLS	10/01-12/01
	Monmouth-Ocean PMSA, NJ	Y	11760 FQ	20360 AW	34420 TQ	NJBLS	10/01-12/01
	New York	Y	12620 FQ	47030 AW	134340 TQ	NYBLS	10/01-12/01
	Binghamton MSA, NY	Y	24460 FQ	36760 AW	45140 TQ	NYBLS	10/01-12/01
	Buffalo-Niagara Falls MSA, NY	Y	11280 FQ	16190 AW	29110 TQ	NYBLS	10/01-12/01
	Nassau-Suffolk PMSA, NY	Y	11470 FQ	19490 AW	32910 TQ	NYBLS	10/01-12/01
	New York PMSA, NY	Y	22730 FQ	82030 AW		NYBLS	10/01-12/01
	Rochester MSA, NY	Y	12430 FQ	25420 AW	38970 TQ	NYBLS	10/01-12/01
	Syracuse MSA, NY	Y	29380 FQ	40140 AW	55160 TQ	NYBLS	10/01-12/01
	North Carolina	Y	29250 FQ	44960 AW	64660 TQ	NCBLS	10/01-12/01
	Charlotte-Gastonia-Rock Hill MSA, NC-SC	Y	13330 FQ	29180 AW	40320 TQ	NCBLS	10/01-12/01
	Greensboro-Winston-Salem-High Point MSA, NC	Y	38240 FQ	50660 AW	69510 TQ	NCBLS	10/01-12/01
	Ohio	Y	12210 FQ	33340 AW	56270 TQ	OHBLS	10/01-12/01
	Cincinnati PMSA, OH-KY-IN	Y	13320 FQ	41890 AW	77970 TQ	OHBLS	10/01-12/01
	Cleveland-Lorain-Elyria PMSA, OH	Y	11440 FQ	31510 AW	92070 TQ	OHBLS	10/01-12/01
	Columbus MSA, OH	Y	24200 FQ	42330 AW	58300 TQ	OHBLS	10/01-12/01
	Dayton-Springfield MSA, OH	Y	14520 FQ	25330 AW	35800 TQ	OHBLS	10/01-12/01
	Oklahoma	Y	21160 FQ	30670 AW	44390 TQ	OKBLS	10/01-12/01
	Oregon	Y	23610 FQ	44320 AW	56510 TQ	ORBLS	10/01-12/01
	Eugene-Springfield MSA, OR	Y	45480 FQ	49710 AW	55800 TQ	ORBLS	10/01-12/01
	Portland-Vancouver PMSA, OR-WA	Y	24490 FQ	42850 AW	55270 TQ	ORBLS	10/01-12/01
	Pennsylvania	Y	12970 FQ	44480 AW	94810 TQ	PABLS	10/01-12/01
	Philadelphia PMSA, PA-NJ	Y	14120 FQ	56380 AW	126180 TQ	PABLS	10/01-12/01
	Rhode Island	Y	15310 FQ	27910 AW	42430 TQ	RIBLS	10/01-12/01
	Providence-Fall River-Warwick MSA, RI-MA	Y	15480 FQ	27910 AW	43260 TQ	RIBLS	10/01-12/01
	South Carolina	Y	13360 FQ	36520 AW	58570 TQ	SCBLS	10/01-12/01
	Greenville-Spartanburg-Anderson MSA, SC	Y	13590 FQ	34510 AW	57080 TQ	SCBLS	10/01-12/01
	Tennessee	Y	23580 FQ	36540 AW	72200 TQ	TNBLS	10/01-12/01
	Nashville MSA, TN	Y	23820 FQ	27660 AW	28730 TQ	TNBLS	10/01-12/01
	Texas	Y	12880 FQ	43470 AW	102180 TQ	TXBLS	10/01-12/01
	Dallas PMSA, TX	Y	14450 FQ	51650 AW	137740 TQ	TXBLS	10/01-12/01
	Virginia	Y	14240 FQ	39980 AW	61200 TQ	VABLS	10/01-12/01
	Washington	Y	14410 FQ	48020 AW	73730 TQ	WABLS	10/01-12/01
	Seattle-Bellevue-Everett PMSA, WA	Y	26630 FQ	47280 AW	68950 TQ	WABLS	10/01-12/01
	Wisconsin	Y	12530 FQ	32480 AW	61380 TQ	WIBLS	10/01-12/01
Musical Instrument Repairer and Tuner	Alabama	H	6.38 FQ	14.15 AW	21.90 TQ	ALBLS	10/01-12/01
	Arizona	H	28.33 FQ	30.00 AW	35.02 TQ	AZBLS	10/01-12/01
	California	H	11.23 FQ	14.97 AW	18.92 TQ	CABLS	10/01-12/01

AAW Average annual wage; **AE** Average entry wage; **AEX** Average experienced wage; **AO** Average offered; **AOH** Average offered, high; **AOL** Average offered, low; **APH** Average pay, high range; **APL** Average pay, low range; **ASH** Average starting, high; **ASL** Average starting, low; **AW** Average wage paid; **FQ** First quartile wage; **H** Hourly; **HI** Highest wage paid; **HR** High end range; **LR** Low end range; **M** Monthly; **MTC** Median total compensation; **MW** Median wage paid; **SQ** Second quartile wage; **S** Special: hourly and annual; **TQ** Third quartile wage; **W** Weekly; **Y** Yearly

Occupation/Type/Industry	Location	Per	Low	Mid	High	Source	Date
Musical Instrument Repairer and Tuner	Colorado	H	5.81 FQ	9.33 AW	15.20 TQ	COBLS	10/01-12/01
	Florida	H	5.93 FQ	11.63 AW	19.29 TQ	FLBLS	10/01-12/01
	Georgia	H	7.19 FQ	11.09 AW	17.13 TQ	GABLS	10/01-12/01
	Illinois	H	8.72 FQ	15.80 AW	21.35 TQ	ILBLS	10/01-12/01
	Indiana	H	7.80 FQ	16.52 AW	26.38 TQ	INBLS	10/01-12/01
	Iowa	H	7.68 FQ	15.13 AW	22.49 TQ	IABLS	10/01-12/01
	Kansas	H	6.37 FQ	12.44 AW	22.85 TQ	KSBLS	10/01-12/01
	Kentucky	H	6.03 FQ	10.50 AW	15.95 TQ	KYBLS	10/01-12/01
	Maryland	H	10.56 FQ	16.53 AW	22.97 TQ	MDBLS	10/01-12/01
	Massachusetts	H	9.14 FQ	17.86 AW	27.35 TQ	MABLS	10/01-12/01
	Michigan	H	8.07 FQ	16.72 AW	27.35 TQ	MIBLS	10/01-12/01
	Minnesota	H	8.43 FQ	14.23 AW	21.24 TQ	MNBLS	10/01-12/01
	Missouri	H	8.48 FQ	13.72 AW	19.65 TQ	MOBLS	10/01-12/01
	New Jersey	H	9.51 FQ	15.07 AW	21.09 TQ	NJBLS	10/01-12/01
	New Mexico	H	14.23 FQ	15.57 AW	17.31 TQ	NMBLS	10/01-12/01
	New York	H	9.43 FQ	15.83 AW	22.39 TQ	NYBLS	10/01-12/01
	Ohio	H	9.09 FQ	17.06 AW	22.35 TQ	OHBLS	10/01-12/01
	Oklahoma	H	7.38 FQ	12.86 AW	25.43 TQ	OKBLS	10/01-12/01
	Oregon	H	8.14 FQ	13.77 AW	29.94 TQ	ORBLS	10/01-12/01
	Pennsylvania	H	7.68 FQ	12.28 AW	18.64 TQ	PABLS	10/01-12/01
	Rhode Island	H	7.77 FQ	9.78 AW	11.43 TQ	RIBLS	10/01-12/01
	South Dakota	H	9.36 FQ	11.80 AW	17.41 TQ	SDBLS	10/01-12/01
	Tennessee	H	6.67 FQ	9.79 AW	14.57 TQ	TNBLS	10/01-12/01
	Texas	H	6.63 FQ	15.23 AW	29.21 TQ	TXBLS	10/01-12/01
	Utah	H	9.77 FQ	18.73 AW	28.75 TQ	UTBLS	10/01-12/01
	Virginia	H	6.15 FQ	12.12 AW	19.39 TQ	VABLS	10/01-12/01
	Washington	H	8.26 FQ	15.49 AW	25.81 TQ	WABLS	10/01-12/01
	West Virginia	H	5.97 FQ	10.13 AW	18.10 TQ	WVBLS	10/01-12/01
	Wisconsin	H	8.85 FQ	14.45 AW	22.09 TQ	WIBLS	10/01-12/01
Musician							
Boston Symphony	Boston, MA	Y	91520 ASL			FREEP	2001
Chicago Symphony Orchestra	Chicago, IL	Y	92040 ASL			FREEP	2001
Cincinnati Symphony	Cincinnati, OH	Y	78910 ASL			FREEP	2001
Cleveland Orchestra	Cleveland, OH	Y	88920 ASL			FREEP	2001
Detroit Symphony Orchestra	Detroit, MI	Y	83100 ASL			FREEP	2001
Los Angeles Philharmonic	Los Angeles, CA	Y	91260 ASL			FREEP	2001
Metropolitan Opera	New York, NY	Y	81016 ASL			FREEP	2001
Minnesota Orchestra	Minneapolis, MN	Y	79430 ASL			FREEP	2001
National Symphony Orchestra	Washington, DC	Y	82810 ASL			FREEP	2001
New York Philharmonic Orchestra	New York, NY	Y	92300 ASL			FREEP	2001
Philadelphia Orchestra	Philadelphia, PA	Y	91520 ASL			FREEP	2001
Pittsburgh Symphony	Pittsburgh, PA	Y	85280 ASL			FREEP	2001
San Francisco Symphony	San Francisco, CA	Y	90220 ASL			FREEP	2001
Musician and Singer	Alabama	Y	21010 FQ	43150 AW	59070 TQ	ALBLS	10/01-12/01
	Arizona	Y	12780 FQ	52640 AW	91740 TQ	AZBLS	10/01-12/01
	Phoenix-Mesa MSA, AZ	Y	12360 FQ	48420 AW	92570 TQ	AZBLS	10/01-12/01
	Arkansas	Y	11600 FQ	18510 AW	37260 TQ	ARBLS	10/01-12/01
	California	Y	13780 FQ	49060 AW	128860 TQ	CABLS	10/01-12/01
	Fresno MSA, CA	Y	14060 FQ	36730 AW	45230 TQ	CABLS	10/01-12/01
	Los Angeles-Long Beach PMSA, CA	Y	13470 FQ	34400 AW	71420 TQ	CABLS	10/01-12/01
	Oakland PMSA, CA	Y	15560 FQ	82530 AW		CABLS	10/01-12/01
	Orange County PMSA, CA	Y	23010 FQ	45280 AW	58720 TQ	CABLS	10/01-12/01
	Riverside-San Bernardino PMSA, CA	Y	13170 FQ	17880 AW	28990 TQ	CABLS	10/01-12/01
	Sacramento PMSA, CA	Y	46000 FQ	86860 AW	143840 TQ	CABLS	10/01-12/01
	San Diego MSA, CA	Y	15880 FQ	46260 AW	100630 TQ	CABLS	10/01-12/01
	San Francisco PMSA, CA	Y	37310 FQ	85590 AW		CABLS	10/01-12/01
	San Jose PMSA, CA	Y	14010 FQ	27390 AW	42810 TQ	CABLS	10/01-12/01
	San Luis Obispo-Atascadero-Paso Robles MSA, CA	Y	17420 FQ	27110 AW	34420 TQ	CABLS	10/01-12/01
	Santa Cruz-Watsonville PMSA, CA	Y	13230 FQ	25540 AW	36490 TQ	CABLS	10/01-12/01
	Vallejo-Fairfield-Napa PMSA, CA	Y	17520 FQ	63700 AW	132700 TQ	CABLS	10/01-12/01
	Colorado	Y	13280 FQ	75770 AW		COBLS	10/01-12/01
	Denver PMSA, CO	Y	14720 FQ	89150 AW		COBLS	10/01-12/01
	Connecticut	Y	30550 FQ	64840 AW		CTBLS	10/01-12/01

AAW	Average annual wage	AOH	Average offered, high	ASH	Average starting, high	H	Hourly	M	Monthly	S	Special: hourly and annual
AE	Average entry wage	AOL	Average offered, low	ASL	Average starting, low	HI	Highest wage paid	MTC	Median total compensation	TQ	Third quartile wage
AEX	Average experienced wage	APH	Average pay, high range	AW	Average wage paid	HR	High end range	MW	Median wage paid	W	Weekly
AO	Average offered	APL	Average pay, low range	FQ	First quartile wage	LR	Low end range	SQ	Second quartile wage	Y	Yearly

Occupation/Type/Industry	Location	Per	Low	Mid	High	Source	Date
Musician and Singer	New Haven-Meriden PMSA, CT	Y	37830 FQ	80630 AW	115590 TQ	CTBLS	10/01-12/01
	District of Columbia	Y	30890 FQ	40320 AW	59060 TQ	DCBLS	10/01-12/01
	Washington PMSA, DC-MD-VA-WV	Y	11330 FQ	38740 AW	110710 TQ	DCBLS	10/01-12/01
	Florida	Y	12330 FQ	30420 AW	46210 TQ	FLBLS	10/01-12/01
	Jacksonville MSA, FL	Y	12270 FQ	29140 AW	44390 TQ	FLBLS	10/01-12/01
	Tampa-St. Petersburg-Clearwater MSA, FL	Y	11860 FQ	26170 AW	39950 TQ	FLBLS	10/01-12/01
	West Palm Beach-Boca Raton MSA, FL	Y	11750 FQ	26680 AW	44120 TQ	FLBLS	10/01-12/01
	Georgia	Y	12920 FQ	43660 AW	92670 TQ	GABLS	10/01-12/01
	Atlanta MSA, GA	Y	14260 FQ	50020 AW	99750 TQ	GABLS	10/01-12/01
	Hawaii	Y	18450 FQ	40640 AW	57520 TQ	HIBLS	10/01-12/01
	Honolulu MSA, HI	Y	22280 FQ	41680 AW	57230 TQ	HIBLS	10/01-12/01
	Idaho	Y	13670 FQ	44710 AW	92600 TQ	IDBLS	10/01-12/01
	Boise City MSA, ID	Y	13670 FQ	44710 AW	92600 TQ	IDBLS	10/01-12/01
	Illinois	Y	12890 FQ	40110 AW	88500 TQ	ILBLS	10/01-12/01
	Chicago PMSA, IL	Y	12760 FQ	40310 AW	89920 TQ	ILBLS	10/01-12/01
	Indiana	Y	12050 FQ	35520 AW	66730 TQ	INBLS	10/01-12/01
	Indianapolis MSA, IN	Y	46510 FQ	60630 AW	70300 TQ	INBLS	10/01-12/01
	Iowa	Y	15380 FQ	45010 AW	92520 TQ	IABLS	10/01-12/01
	Kansas	Y	14070 FQ	26670 AW	44890 TQ	KSBLS	10/01-12/01
	Kentucky	Y	11840 FQ	24950 AW	42860 TQ	KYBLS	10/01-12/01
	Louisiana	Y	12520 FQ	27710 AW	42900 TQ	LABLS	10/01-12/01
	New Orleans MSA, LA	Y	12500 FQ	28470 AW	43060 TQ	LABLS	10/01-12/01
	Maryland	Y	13010 FQ	64850 AW	112990 TQ	MDBLS	10/01-12/01
	Baltimore PMSA, MD	Y	25590 FQ	67530 AW	111040 TQ	MDBLS	10/01-12/01
	Massachusetts	Y	18420 FQ	39190 AW	55560 TQ	MABLS	10/01-12/01
	Boston PMSA, MA-NH	Y	24860 FQ	46020 AW	56000 TQ	MABLS	10/01-12/01
	Springfield MSA, MA	Y	17720 FQ	20440 AW	22230 TQ	MABLS	10/01-12/01
	Michigan	Y	15670 FQ	51030 AW	88690 TQ	MIBLS	10/01-12/01
	Detroit PMSA, MI	Y	15610 FQ	54920 AW	90480 TQ	MIBLS	10/01-12/01
	Flint PMSA, MI	Y	12950 FQ	65570 AW	118720 TQ	MIBLS	10/01-12/01
	Grand Rapids-Muskegon-Holland MSA, MI	Y	17930 FQ	27100 AW	38510 TQ	MIBLS	10/01-12/01
	Kalamazoo-Battle Creek MSA, MI	Y	47150 FQ	59700 AW	70680 TQ	MIBLS	10/01-12/01
	Minnesota	Y	20790 FQ	56350 AW		MNBLS	10/01-12/01
	Minneapolis-St. Paul MSA, MN-WI	Y	20470 FQ	58370 AW		MNBLS	10/01-12/01
	Missouri	Y	21040 FQ	48220 AW	73670 TQ	MOBLS	10/01-12/01
	Kansas City MSA, MO-KS	Y	12580 FQ	31510 AW	45040 TQ	MOBLS	10/01-12/01
	Springfield MSA, MO	Y	25440 FQ	40840 AW	58880 TQ	MOBLS	10/01-12/01
	Montana	Y	11260 FQ	18070 AW	40160 TQ	MTBLS	10/01-12/01
	Nebraska	Y	18230 FQ	23540 AW	40860 TQ	NEBLS	10/01-12/01
	Lincoln MSA, NE	Y	18320 FQ	23830 AW	42240 TQ	NEBLS	10/01-12/01
	Nevada	Y	35490 FQ	78560 AW	121870 TQ	NVBLS	10/01-12/01
	Las Vegas MSA, NV-AZ	Y	34380 FQ	83160 AW	127470 TQ	NVBLS	10/01-12/01
	New Jersey	Y	12060 FQ	53180 AW	90540 TQ	NJBLS	10/01-12/01
	Monmouth-Ocean PMSA, NJ	Y	20700 FQ	54430 AW	137450 TQ	NJBLS	10/01-12/01
	Newark PMSA, NJ	Y	11760 FQ	48730 AW	88210 TQ	NJBLS	10/01-12/01
	New York	Y	13350 FQ	49890 AW	94040 TQ	NYBLS	10/01-12/01
	Binghamton MSA, NY	Y	12240 FQ	19910 AW	40940 TQ	NYBLS	10/01-12/01
	Buffalo-Niagara Falls MSA, NY	Y	11330 FQ	13960 AW	14570 TQ	NYBLS	10/01-12/01
	Nassau-Suffolk PMSA, NY	Y	12020 FQ	82930 AW	138130 TQ	NYBLS	10/01-12/01
	New York PMSA, NY	Y	24370 FQ	51330 AW	73440 TQ	NYBLS	10/01-12/01
	Newburgh PMSA, NY-PA	Y	20530 FQ	29530 AW	29880 TQ	NYBLS	10/01-12/01
	Syracuse MSA, NY	Y	11620 FQ	20710 AW	33730 TQ	NYBLS	10/01-12/01
	North Carolina	Y	12300 FQ	32360 AW	78550 TQ	NCBLS	10/01-12/01
	Greensboro-Winston-Salem-High Point MSA, NC	Y	11920 FQ	15600 AW	18330 TQ	NCBLS	10/01-12/01
	Ohio	Y	11820 FQ	45860 AW	110270 TQ	OHBLS	10/01-12/01
	Cincinnati PMSA, OH-KY-IN	Y	44290 FQ	85190 AW		OHBLS	10/01-12/01
	Cleveland-Lorain-Elyria PMSA, OH	Y	11250 FQ	22300 AW	34030 TQ	OHBLS	10/01-12/01
	Toledo MSA, OH	Y	12580 FQ	27230 AW	46550 TQ	OHBLS	10/01-12/01
	Oklahoma	Y	14120 FQ	45630 AW	83670 TQ	OKBLS	10/01-12/01
	Oklahoma City MSA, OK	Y	14110 FQ	47230 AW	91500 TQ	OKBLS	10/01-12/01
	Tulsa MSA, OK	Y	14070 FQ	40590 AW	68000 TQ	OKBLS	10/01-12/01
	Oregon	Y	14550 FQ	45240 AW	75470 TQ	ORBLS	10/01-12/01

AAW Average annual wage **AE** Average entry wage **AEX** Average experienced wage **AO** Average offered **AOH** Average offered, high **AOL** Average offered, low **APH** Average pay, high range **APL** Average pay, low range **ASH** Average starting, high **ASL** Average starting, low **AW** Average wage paid **FQ** First quartile wage **H** Hourly **HI** Highest wage paid **HR** High end range **LR** Low end range **M** Monthly **MTC** Median total compensation **MW** Median wage paid **SQ** Second quartile wage **S** Special: hourly and annual **TQ** Third quartile wage **W** Weekly **Y** Yearly

Occupation/Type/Industry	Location	Per	Low	Mid	High	Source	Date
Musician and Singer	Portland-Vancouver PMSA, OR-WA	Y	14440 FQ	36810 AW	66400 TQ	ORBLS	10/01-12/01
	Pennsylvania	Y	12570 FQ	44000 AW	77000 TQ	PABLS	10/01-12/01
	Allentown-Bethlehem-Easton MSA, PA	Y	62770 FQ	68070 AW	75990 TQ	PABLS	10/01-12/01
	Harrisburg-Lebanon-Carlisle MSA, PA	Y	14260 FQ	50350 AW	70820 TQ	PABLS	10/01-12/01
	Philadelphia PMSA, PA-NJ	Y	12410 FQ	39130 AW	86000 TQ	PABLS	10/01-12/01
	Pittsburgh MSA, PA	Y	15230 FQ	49730 AW	113530 TQ	PABLS	10/01-12/01
	Scranton-Wilkes-Barre-Hazleton MSA, PA	Y	11060 FQ	12170 AW	13730 TQ	PABLS	10/01-12/01
	Rhode Island	Y	13970 FQ	24690 AW	29110 TQ	RIBLS	10/01-12/01
	Providence-Fall River-Warwick MSA, RI-MA	Y	18900 FQ	23890 AW	28960 TQ	RIBLS	10/01-12/01
	South Carolina	Y	18970 FQ	38780 AW	57520 TQ	SCBLS	10/01-12/01
	Charleston-North Charleston MSA, SC	Y	13520 FQ	25020 AW	31500 TQ	SCBLS	10/01-12/01
	Tennessee	Y	17410 FQ	39380 AW	73430 TQ	TNBLS	10/01-12/01
	Nashville MSA, TN	Y	19500 FQ	36220 AW	64170 TQ	TNBLS	10/01-12/01
	Texas	Y	12730 FQ	38280 AW	64250 TQ	TXBLS	10/01-12/01
	Austin-San Marcos MSA, TX	Y	11630 FQ	24590 AW	47000 TQ	TXBLS	10/01-12/01
	Beaumont-Port Arthur MSA, TX	Y	13170 FQ	38850 AW	54040 TQ	TXBLS	10/01-12/01
	Dallas PMSA, TX	Y	36500 FQ	55800 AW	92740 TQ	TXBLS	10/01-12/01
	Fort Worth-Arlington PMSA, TX	Y	12800 FQ	35250 AW	55570 TQ	TXBLS	10/01-12/01
	Houston PMSA, TX	Y	12100 FQ	25920 AW	44640 TQ	TXBLS	10/01-12/01
	San Antonio MSA, TX	Y	29760 FQ	40380 AW	47510 TQ	TXBLS	10/01-12/01
	Utah	Y	11800 FQ	37950 AW	55130 TQ	UTBLS	10/01-12/01
	Salt Lake City-Ogden MSA, UT	Y	11720 FQ	36780 AW	55000 TQ	UTBLS	10/01-12/01
	Vermont	Y	13790 FQ	44370 AW	91090 TQ	VTBLS	10/01-12/01
	Virginia	Y	11490 FQ	27550 AW	66280 TQ	VABLS	10/01-12/01
	Lynchburg MSA, VA	Y	12270 FQ	19230 AW	27020 TQ	VABLS	10/01-12/01
	Norfolk-Virginia Beach-Newport News MSA, VA-NC	Y	11710 FQ	29030 AW	66880 TQ	VABLS	10/01-12/01
	Richmond-Petersburg MSA, VA	Y	12320 FQ	34140 AW	67030 TQ	VABLS	10/01-12/01
	Washington	Y	21350 FQ	60350 AW	115210 TQ	WABLS	10/01-12/01
	Seattle-Bellevue-Everett PMSA, WA	Y	39690 FQ	70260 AW	122320 TQ	WABLS	10/01-12/01
	Wisconsin	Y	25550 FQ	59360 AW	131840 TQ	WIBLS	10/01-12/01
	Milwaukee-Waukesha PMSA, WI	Y	24540 FQ	71880 AW		WIBLS	10/01-12/01
	Wyoming	Y	13090 FQ	43560 AW	94200 TQ	WYBLS	10/01-12/01
	Puerto Rico	Y	13100 FQ	26760 AW	63160 TQ	PRBLS	10/01-12/01
National Guard Commander	Alabama	Y		95000 AW		USATOD2	1/99-1/99
	Alaska	Y		84000 AW		USATOD2	1/99-1/99
	Arizona	Y		110000 AW		USATOD2	1/99-1/99
	Arkansas	Y		117500 AW		USATOD2	1/99-1/99
	California	Y		149300 AW		USATOD2	1/99-1/99
	Colorado	Y		114500 AW		USATOD2	1/99-1/99
	Connecticut	Y		166300 AW		USATOD2	1/99-1/99
	Delaware	Y		107600 AW		USATOD2	1/99-1/99
	Florida	Y		140600 AW		USATOD2	1/99-1/99
	Georgia	Y		141200 AW		USATOD2	1/99-1/99
	Hawaii	Y		136800 AW		USATOD2	1/99-1/99
	Idaho	Y		117100 AW		USATOD2	1/99-1/99
	Illinois	Y		108760 AW		USATOD2	1/99-1/99
	Indiana	Y		98050 AW		USATOD2	1/99-1/99
	Iowa	Y		112860 AW		USATOD2	1/99-1/99
	Kansas	Y		127300 AW		USATOD2	1/99-1/99
	Kentucky	Y		109800 AW		USATOD2	1/99-1/99
	Louisiana	Y		102400 AW		USATOD2	1/99-1/99
	Maine	Y		112670 AW		USATOD2	1/99-1/99
	Maryland	Y		103600 AW		USATOD2	1/99-1/99
	Massachusetts	Y		126200 AW		USATOD2	1/99-1/99
	Michigan	Y		127580 AW		USATOD2	1/99-1/99
	Minnesota	Y		141500 AW		USATOD2	1/99-1/99
	Mississippi	Y		113780 AW		USATOD2	1/99-1/99
	Missouri	Y		116340 AW		USATOD2	1/99-1/99

AAW	Average annual wage	**AOH**	Average offered, high	**ASH**	Average starting, high	**H**	Hourly	**M**	Monthly	**S**	Special: hourly and annual
AE	Average entry wage	**AOL**	Average offered, low	**ASL**	Average starting, low	**HI**	Highest wage paid	**MTC**	Median total compensation	**TQ**	Third quartile wage
AEX	Average experienced wage	**APH**	Average pay, high range	**AW**	Average wage paid	**HR**	High end range	**MW**	Median wage paid	**W**	Weekly
AO	Average offered	**APL**	Average pay, low range	**FQ**	First quartile wage	**LR**	Low end range	**SQ**	Second quartile wage	**Y**	Yearly

Occupation/Type/Industry	Location	Per	Low	Mid	High	Source	Date
National Guard Commander	Montana	Y		111000 AW		USATOD2	1/99-1/99
	Nebraska	Y		98400 AW		USATOD2	1/99-1/99
	Nevada	Y		112600 AW		USATOD2	1/99-1/99
	New Hampshire	Y		105305 AW		USATOD2	1/99-1/99
	New Jersey	Y		134000 AW		USATOD2	1/99-1/99
	New Mexico	Y		103500 AW		USATOD2	1/99-1/99
	New York	Y		158500 AW		USATOD2	1/99-1/99
	North Carolina	Y		121900 AW		USATOD2	1/99-1/99
	North Dakota	Y		114500 AW		USATOD2	1/99-1/99
	Ohio	Y		139000 AW		USATOD2	1/99-1/99
	Oklahoma	Y		154200 AW		USATOD2	1/99-1/99
	Oregon	Y		126400 AW		USATOD2	1/99-1/99
	Pennsylvania	Y		115000 AW		USATOD2	1/99-1/99
	Rhode Island	Y		107200 AW		USATOD2	1/99-1/99
	South Carolina	Y		138700 AW		USATOD2	1/99-1/99
	South Dakota	Y		110000 AW		USATOD2	1/99-1/99
	Tennessee	Y		117590 AW		USATOD2	1/99-1/99
	Texas	Y		134660 AW		USATOD2	1/99-1/99
	Utah	Y		104140 AW		USATOD2	1/99-1/99
	Vermont	Y		99670 AW		USATOD2	1/99-1/99
	Virginia	Y		115570 AW		USATOD2	1/99-1/99
	Washington	Y		138800 AW		USATOD2	1/99-1/99
	West Virginia	Y		108560 AW		USATOD2	1/99-1/99
	Wisconsin	Y		109200 AW		USATOD2	1/99-1/99
	Wyoming	Y		121800 AW		USATOD2	1/99-1/99
Natural Sciences Manager	Alabama	Y	48040 FQ	81450 AW	117550 TQ	ALBLS	10/01-12/01
	Alaska	Y	52360 FQ	77620 AW	112050 TQ	AKBLS	10/01-12/01
	Arizona	Y	33730 FQ	62730 AW	95820 TQ	AZBLS	10/01-12/01
	Arkansas	Y	43850 FQ	71570 AW	109120 TQ	ARBLS	10/01-12/01
	California	Y	41600 FQ	81760 AW	140800 TQ	CABLS	10/01-12/01
	Colorado	Y	46980 FQ	78860 AW	112150 TQ	COBLS	10/01-12/01
	Connecticut	Y	69310 FQ	114180 AW		CTBLS	10/01-12/01
	Delaware	Y	59730 FQ	97250 AW		DEBLS	10/01-12/01
	District of Columbia	Y	52540 FQ	88470 AW	122490 TQ	DCBLS	10/01-12/01
	Florida	Y	45840 FQ	78300 AW	127640 TQ	FLBLS	10/01-12/01
	Georgia	Y	48850 FQ	75310 AW	109970 TQ	GABLS	10/01-12/01
	Hawaii	Y	49920 FQ	75230 AW	109060 TQ	HIBLS	10/01-12/01
	Idaho	Y	33870 FQ	58100 AW	89010 TQ	IDBLS	10/01-12/01
	Illinois	Y	36000 FQ	82930 AW	141500 TQ	ILBLS	10/01-12/01
	Iowa	Y	40030 FQ	73640 AW	114090 TQ	IABLS	10/01-12/01
	Kansas	Y	42780 FQ	70470 AW	107020 TQ	KSBLS	10/01-12/01
	Kentucky	Y	40930 FQ	74300 AW	118550 TQ	KYBLS	10/01-12/01
	Louisiana	Y	39120 FQ	69360 AW	110160 TQ	LABLS	10/01-12/01
	Maine	Y	38420 FQ	60100 AW	85030 TQ	MEBLS	10/01-12/01
	Maryland	Y	56950 FQ	86180 AW	112220 TQ	MDBLS	10/01-12/01
	Massachusetts	Y	53670 FQ	103440 AW		MABLS	10/01-12/01
	Michigan	Y	46400 FQ	78060 AW	129250 TQ	MIBLS	10/01-12/01
	Minnesota	Y	50850 FQ	83670 AW	141690 TQ	MNBLS	10/01-12/01
	Mississippi	Y	40820 FQ	71570 AW	103090 TQ	MSBLS	10/01-12/01
	Missouri	Y	46260 FQ	73110 AW	113380 TQ	MOBLS	10/01-12/01
	Montana	Y	32210 FQ	57150 AW	88730 TQ	MTBLS	10/01-12/01
	Nebraska	Y	45670 FQ	76610 AW	114820 TQ	NEBLS	10/01-12/01
	Nevada	Y	35050 FQ	67700 AW	103690 TQ	NVBLS	10/01-12/01
	New Hampshire	Y	52050 FQ	83570 AW	126670 TQ	NHBLS	10/01-12/01
	New Jersey	Y	72750 FQ	110790 AW		NJBLS	10/01-12/01
	New Mexico	Y	36190 FQ	84480 AW		NMBLS	10/01-12/01
	New York	Y	56480 FQ	97610 AW		NYBLS	10/01-12/01
	North Carolina	Y	59270 FQ	93690 AW		NCBLS	10/01-12/01
	North Dakota	Y	46720 FQ	70880 AW	100770 TQ	NDBLS	10/01-12/01
	Ohio	Y	40490 FQ	72430 AW	111900 TQ	OHBLS	10/01-12/01
	Oklahoma	Y	30860 FQ	56730 AW	93080 TQ	OKBLS	10/01-12/01
	Oregon	Y	37110 FQ	63040 AW	100380 TQ	ORBLS	10/01-12/01
	Pennsylvania	Y	54250 FQ	89200 AW	138080 TQ	PABLS	10/01-12/01
	Rhode Island	Y	34680 FQ	69670 AW	103730 TQ	RIBLS	10/01-12/01
	South Carolina	Y	33830 FQ	77820 AW	113730 TQ	SCBLS	10/01-12/01
	South Dakota	Y	44380 FQ	68610 AW	100350 TQ	SDBLS	10/01-12/01
	Tennessee	Y	40940 FQ	72930 AW	108750 TQ	TNBLS	10/01-12/01
	Texas	Y	34300 FQ	72680 AW	124190 TQ	TXBLS	10/01-12/01
	Utah	Y	38410 FQ	66770 AW	106030 TQ	UTBLS	10/01-12/01
	Vermont	Y	36900 FQ	62230 AW	86800 TQ	VTBLS	10/01-12/01
	Virginia	Y	51480 FQ	86500 AW	115110 TQ	VABLS	10/01-12/01
	Washington	Y	48430 FQ	80780 AW	134820 TQ	WABLS	10/01-12/01

AAW	Average annual wage	**AOH**	Average offered, high	**ASH**	Average starting, high	**H**	Hourly	**M**	Monthly	**S**	Special: hourly and annual
AE	Average entry wage	**AOL**	Average offered, low	**ASL**	Average starting, low	**HI**	Highest wage paid	**MTC**	Median total compensation	**TQ**	Third quartile wage
AEX	Average experienced wage	**APH**	Average pay, high range	**AW**	Average wage paid	**HR**	High end range	**MW**	Median wage paid	**W**	Weekly
AO	Average offered	**APL**	Average pay, low range	**FQ**	First quartile wage	**LR**	Low end range	**SQ**	Second quartile wage	**Y**	Yearly

Occupation/Type/Industry	Location	Per	Low	Mid	High	Source	Date
Natural Sciences Manager	West Virginia	Y	40720 FQ	73580 AW	122470 TQ	WVBLS	10/01-12/01
	Wisconsin	Y	46490 FQ	72100 AW	108060 TQ	WIBLS	10/01-12/01
	Wyoming	Y	30910 FQ	63380 AW	101120 TQ	WYBLS	10/01-12/01
	Puerto Rico	Y	45430 FQ	70860 AW	106740 TQ	PRBLS	10/01-12/01
Network Administrator	United States	Y		59300 AW		INFO4	1/01-1/02
	United States	Y		48000-69250 AW		IW	1/00-1/01
Network and Computer Systems Administrator	United States	Y		39700 AW		FREEP1	1/00-1/00
	Alabama	Y	31040 FQ	49120 AW	70710 TQ	ALBLS	10/01-12/01
	Birmingham MSA, AL	Y	31780 FQ	50800 AW	75310 TQ	ALBLS	10/01-12/01
	Huntsville MSA, AL	Y	28460 FQ	49130 AW	65710 TQ	ALBLS	10/01-12/01
	Mobile MSA, AL	Y	31020 FQ	43350 AW	58210 TQ	ALBLS	10/01-12/01
	Montgomery MSA, AL	Y	33660 FQ	54450 AW	78350 TQ	ALBLS	10/01-12/01
	Alaska	Y	36000 FQ	52630 AW	72670 TQ	AKBLS	10/01-12/01
	Anchorage MSA, AK	Y	35100 FQ	52170 AW	72250 TQ	AKBLS	10/01-12/01
	Arizona	Y	35030 FQ	55570 AW	82270 TQ	AZBLS	10/01-12/01
	Phoenix-Mesa MSA, AZ	Y	36680 FQ	57140 AW	85800 TQ	AZBLS	10/01-12/01
	Tucson MSA, AZ	Y	31220 FQ	47260 AW	69910 TQ	AZBLS	10/01-12/01
	Arkansas	Y	20420 FQ	42290 AW	66450 TQ	ARBLS	10/01-12/01
	Fayetteville-Springdale-Rogers MSA, AR	Y	15200 FQ	36230 AW	57880 TQ	ARBLS	10/01-12/01
	Fort Smith MSA, AR-OK	Y	23590 FQ	38970 AW	66400 TQ	ARBLS	10/01-12/01
	Little Rock-North Little Rock MSA, AR	Y	28720 FQ	48030 AW	78190 TQ	ARBLS	10/01-12/01
	California	Y	37510 FQ	61600 AW	91340 TQ	CABLS	10/01-12/01
	Bakersfield MSA, CA	Y	32020 FQ	51110 AW	72200 TQ	CABLS	10/01-12/01
	Chico-Paradise MSA, CA	Y	23020 FQ	47320 AW	73060 TQ	CABLS	10/01-12/01
	Fresno MSA, CA	Y	30090 FQ	44710 AW	65790 TQ	CABLS	10/01-12/01
	Los Angeles-Long Beach PMSA, CA	Y	37380 FQ	59390 AW	90280 TQ	CABLS	10/01-12/01
	Merced MSA, CA	Y	33450 FQ	47990 AW	65380 TQ	CABLS	10/01-12/01
	Modesto MSA, CA	Y	24960 FQ	48730 AW	76810 TQ	CABLS	10/01-12/01
	Oakland PMSA, CA	Y	39920 FQ	63520 AW	90190 TQ	CABLS	10/01-12/01
	Orange County PMSA, CA	Y	35370 FQ	58070 AW	86460 TQ	CABLS	10/01-12/01
	Redding MSA, CA	Y	14420 FQ	37220 AW	59270 TQ	CABLS	10/01-12/01
	Riverside-San Bernardino PMSA, CA	Y	33550 FQ	52380 AW	74060 TQ	CABLS	10/01-12/01
	Sacramento PMSA, CA	Y	36900 FQ	54910 AW	76590 TQ	CABLS	10/01-12/01
	Salinas MSA, CA	Y	29880 FQ	52690 AW	83070 TQ	CABLS	10/01-12/01
	San Diego MSA, CA	Y	36970 FQ	58210 AW	83940 TQ	CABLS	10/01-12/01
	San Francisco PMSA, CA	Y	42250 FQ	69070 AW	102620 TQ	CABLS	10/01-12/01
	San Jose PMSA, CA	Y	48090 FQ	72170 AW	103300 TQ	CABLS	10/01-12/01
	San Luis Obispo-Atascadero-Paso Robles MSA, CA	Y	31510 FQ	54290 AW	80730 TQ	CABLS	10/01-12/01
	Santa Barbara-Santa Maria-Lompoc MSA, CA	Y	36880 FQ	54580 AW	82280 TQ	CABLS	10/01-12/01
	Santa Cruz-Watsonville PMSA, CA	Y	32770 FQ	59910 AW	93060 TQ	CABLS	10/01-12/01
	Santa Rosa PMSA, CA	Y	37990 FQ	56230 AW	81650 TQ	CABLS	10/01-12/01
	Stockton-Lodi MSA, CA	Y	29140 FQ	45670 AW	64940 TQ	CABLS	10/01-12/01
	Vallejo-Fairfield-Napa PMSA, CA	Y	34240 FQ	57430 AW	86390 TQ	CABLS	10/01-12/01
	Ventura PMSA, CA	Y	39970 FQ	59060 AW	82830 TQ	CABLS	10/01-12/01
	Visalia-Tulare-Porterville MSA, CA	Y	30760 FQ	51820 AW	78160 TQ	CABLS	10/01-12/01
	Colorado	Y	38850 FQ	63380 AW	92630 TQ	COBLS	10/01-12/01
	Boulder-Longmont PMSA, CO	Y	37050 FQ	59060 AW	86520 TQ	COBLS	10/01-12/01
	Colorado Springs MSA, CO	Y	37290 FQ	64080 AW	90760 TQ	COBLS	10/01-12/01
	Denver PMSA, CO	Y	40800 FQ	65420 AW	96260 TQ	COBLS	10/01-12/01
	Fort Collins-Loveland MSA, CO	Y	34620 FQ	54410 AW	78550 TQ	COBLS	10/01-12/01
	Greeley PMSA, CO	Y	33860 FQ	53240 AW	71460 TQ	COBLS	10/01-12/01
	Connecticut	Y	40570 FQ	63080 AW	90290 TQ	CTBLS	10/01-12/01
	Bridgeport PMSA, CT	Y	44820 FQ	67260 AW	93400 TQ	CTBLS	10/01-12/01
	Danbury PMSA, CT	Y	40820 FQ	65230 AW	91310 TQ	CTBLS	10/01-12/01
	Hartford MSA, CT	Y	39240 FQ	57770 AW	83050 TQ	CTBLS	10/01-12/01
	New Haven-Meriden PMSA, CT	Y	41080 FQ	61360 AW	85250 TQ	CTBLS	10/01-12/01

AAW	Average annual wage	**AOH**	Average offered, high	**ASH**	Average starting, high	**H**	Hourly	**M**	Monthly	**S**	Special: hourly and annual
AE	Average entry wage	**AOL**	Average offered, low	**ASL**	Average starting, low	**HI**	Highest wage paid	**MTC**	Median total compensation	**TQ**	Third quartile wage
AEX	Average experienced wage	**APH**	Average pay, high range	**AW**	Average wage paid	**HR**	High end range	**MW**	Median wage paid	**W**	Weekly
AO	Average offered	**APL**	Average pay, low range	**FQ**	First quartile wage	**LR**	Low end range	**SQ**	Second quartile wage	**Y**	Yearly

Occupation/Type/Industry	Location	Per	Low	Mid	High	Source	Date
Network and Computer Systems Administrator	New London-Norwich MSA, CT-RI	Y	38120 FQ	57320 AW	80440 TQ	CTBLS	10/01-12/01
	Stamford-Norwalk PMSA, CT	Y	44580 FQ	70080 AW	105450 TQ	CTBLS	10/01-12/01
	Waterbury PMSA, CT	Y	38550 FQ	57320 AW	76580 TQ	CTBLS	10/01-12/01
	Delaware	Y	37560 FQ	61560 AW	87510 TQ	DEBLS	10/01-12/01
	Wilmington-Newark PMSA, DE-MD	Y	38150 FQ	62330 AW	87850 TQ	DEBLS	10/01-12/01
	District of Columbia	Y	38620 FQ	58020 AW	82440 TQ	DCBLS	10/01-12/01
	Washington PMSA, DC-MD-VA-WV	Y	38860 FQ	59260 AW	85670 TQ	DCBLS	10/01-12/01
	Florida	Y	33710 FQ	54120 AW	78980 TQ	FLBLS	10/01-12/01
	Daytona Beach MSA, FL	Y	30800 FQ	47850 AW	67650 TQ	FLBLS	10/01-12/01
	Fort Lauderdale PMSA, FL	Y	32250 FQ	52800 AW	74140 TQ	FLBLS	10/01-12/01
	Fort Myers-Cape Coral MSA, FL	Y	33380 FQ	49520 AW	67560 TQ	FLBLS	10/01-12/01
	Fort Pierce-Port St. Lucie MSA, FL	Y	35490 FQ	46950 AW	65990 TQ	FLBLS	10/01-12/01
	Fort Walton Beach MSA, FL	Y	34830 FQ	51750 AW	74830 TQ	FLBLS	10/01-12/01
	Gainesville MSA, FL	Y	30850 FQ	47440 AW	64780 TQ	FLBLS	10/01-12/01
	Jacksonville MSA, FL	Y	36890 FQ	54460 AW	76490 TQ	FLBLS	10/01-12/01
	Lakeland-Winter Haven MSA, FL	Y	28700 FQ	47880 AW	71700 TQ	FLBLS	10/01-12/01
	Melbourne-Titusville-Palm Bay MSA, FL	Y	33810 FQ	47950 AW	66540 TQ	FLBLS	10/01-12/01
	Miami PMSA, FL	Y	34930 FQ	54640 AW	77280 TQ	FLBLS	10/01-12/01
	Naples MSA, FL	Y	31670 FQ	48550 AW	68840 TQ	FLBLS	10/01-12/01
	Ocala MSA, FL	Y	32230 FQ	50450 AW	67530 TQ	FLBLS	10/01-12/01
	Orlando MSA, FL	Y	33970 FQ	52530 AW	73890 TQ	FLBLS	10/01-12/01
	Pensacola MSA, FL	Y	30620 FQ	42760 AW	56690 TQ	FLBLS	10/01-12/01
	Sarasota-Bradenton MSA, FL	Y	32930 FQ	54240 AW	74550 TQ	FLBLS	10/01-12/01
	Tallahassee MSA, FL	Y	37730 FQ	72450 AW	123320 TQ	FLBLS	10/01-12/01
	Tampa-St. Petersburg-Clearwater MSA, FL	Y	33130 FQ	52170 AW	77720 TQ	FLBLS	10/01-12/01
	West Palm Beach-Boca Raton MSA, FL	Y	35790 FQ	54170 AW	76070 TQ	FLBLS	10/01-12/01
	Georgia	Y	34380 FQ	56440 AW	84940 TQ	GABLS	10/01-12/01
	Atlanta MSA, GA	Y	35760 FQ	58190 AW	87580 TQ	GABLS	10/01-12/01
	Augusta-Aiken MSA, GA-SC	Y	36230 FQ	52310 AW	72670 TQ	GABLS	10/01-12/01
	Columbus MSA, GA-AL	Y	27450 FQ	46450 AW	68820 TQ	GABLS	10/01-12/01
	Macon MSA, GA	Y	31970 FQ	54120 AW	78390 TQ	GABLS	10/01-12/01
	Savannah MSA, GA	Y	31660 FQ	47510 AW	68170 TQ	GABLS	10/01-12/01
	Hawaii	Y	32570 FQ	54690 AW	96830 TQ	HIBLS	10/01-12/01
	Honolulu MSA, HI	Y	32680 FQ	55470 AW	99920 TQ	HIBLS	10/01-12/01
	Idaho	Y	28220 FQ	45760 AW	68120 TQ	IDBLS	10/01-12/01
	Boise City MSA, ID	Y	28730 FQ	44410 AW	65290 TQ	IDBLS	10/01-12/01
	Illinois	Y	36750 FQ	58200 AW	87250 TQ	ILBLS	10/01-12/01
	Champaign-Urbana MSA, IL	Y	34930 FQ	50760 AW	69810 TQ	ILBLS	10/01-12/01
	Chicago PMSA, IL	Y	39420 FQ	60590 AW	89050 TQ	ILBLS	10/01-12/01
	Peoria-Pekin MSA, IL	Y	21550 FQ	42900 AW	63430 TQ	ILBLS	10/01-12/01
	Rockford MSA, IL	Y	31070 FQ	51880 AW	72120 TQ	ILBLS	10/01-12/01
	Springfield MSA, IL	Y	29820 FQ	48970 AW	69160 TQ	ILBLS	10/01-12/01
	Indiana	Y	31320 FQ	48600 AW	69070 TQ	INBLS	10/01-12/01
	Elkhart-Goshen MSA, IN	Y	32320 FQ	53140 AW	75720 TQ	INBLS	10/01-12/01
	Evansville-Henderson MSA, IN-KY	Y	32020 FQ	46390 AW	56380 TQ	INBLS	10/01-12/01
	Fort Wayne MSA, IN	Y	30600 FQ	45510 AW	64930 TQ	INBLS	10/01-12/01
	Gary PMSA, IN	Y	31930 FQ	47590 AW	67950 TQ	INBLS	10/01-12/01
	Indianapolis MSA, IN	Y	33840 FQ	52110 AW	72360 TQ	INBLS	10/01-12/01
	Lafayette MSA, IN	Y	27770 FQ	43610 AW	59950 TQ	INBLS	10/01-12/01
	South Bend MSA, IN	Y	34390 FQ	50450 AW	69500 TQ	INBLS	10/01-12/01
	Iowa	Y	28800 FQ	47300 AW	71400 TQ	IABLS	10/01-12/01
	Cedar Rapids MSA, IA	Y	28610 FQ	48020 AW	72910 TQ	IABLS	10/01-12/01
	Davenport-Moline-Rock Island MSA, IA-IL	Y	29890 FQ	47540 AW	68770 TQ	IABLS	10/01-12/01
	Des Moines MSA, IA	Y	33420 FQ	53870 AW	79140 TQ	IABLS	10/01-12/01
	Kansas	Y	31800 FQ	48550 AW	69810 TQ	KSBLS	10/01-12/01
	Topeka MSA, KS	Y	30740 FQ	48840 AW	74600 TQ	KSBLS	10/01-12/01
	Wichita MSA, KS	Y	32240 FQ	50600 AW	76890 TQ	KSBLS	10/01-12/01
	Kentucky	Y	29610 FQ	46640 AW	68110 TQ	KYBLS	10/01-12/01
	Lexington MSA, KY	Y	29080 FQ	47620 AW	70020 TQ	KYBLS	10/01-12/01
	Louisville MSA, KY-IN	Y	31230 FQ	50120 AW	71800 TQ	KYBLS	10/01-12/01

AAW Average annual wage **AE** Average entry wage **AEX** Average experienced wage **AO** Average offered **AOH** Average offered, high **AOL** Average offered, low **APH** Average pay, high range **APL** Average pay, low range **ASH** Average starting, high **ASL** Average starting, low **AW** Average wage paid **FQ** First quartile wage **H** Hourly **HI** Highest wage paid **HR** High end range **LR** Low end range **M** Monthly **MTC** Median total compensation **MW** Median wage paid **SQ** Second quartile wage **S** Special: hourly and annual **TQ** Third quartile wage **W** Weekly **Y** Yearly

Occupation/Type/Industry	Location	Per	Low	Mid	High	Source	Date
Network and Computer Systems Administrator	Louisiana	Y	27250 FQ	55500 AW	94500 TQ	LABLS	10/01-12/01
	Baton Rouge MSA, LA	Y	31210 FQ	47600 AW	70540 TQ	LABLS	10/01-12/01
	Lafayette MSA, LA	Y	29940 FQ	49600 AW	69080 TQ	LABLS	10/01-12/01
	Lake Charles MSA, LA	Y	30560 FQ	50340 AW	75460 TQ	LABLS	10/01-12/01
	New Orleans MSA, LA	Y	29330 FQ	72740 AW		LABLS	10/01-12/01
	Shreveport-Bossier City MSA, LA	Y	19530 FQ	36430 AW	63200 TQ	LABLS	10/01-12/01
	Maine	Y	31300 FQ	46980 AW	65750 TQ	MEBLS	10/01-12/01
	Portland MSA, ME	Y	31930 FQ	50300 AW	71840 TQ	MEBLS	10/01-12/01
	Maryland	Y	36640 FQ	58300 AW	84930 TQ	MDBLS	10/01-12/01
	Baltimore PMSA, MD	Y	37370 FQ	56990 AW	80860 TQ	MDBLS	10/01-12/01
	Massachusetts	Y	38990 FQ	60980 AW	88120 TQ	MABLS	10/01-12/01
	Boston PMSA, MA-NH	Y	39880 FQ	62150 AW	89660 TQ	MABLS	10/01-12/01
	Brockton PMSA, MA	Y	37680 FQ	53990 AW	76400 TQ	MABLS	10/01-12/01
	Lawrence PMSA, MA-NH	Y	39140 FQ	60550 AW	86080 TQ	MABLS	10/01-12/01
	Lowell PMSA, MA-NH	Y	40050 FQ	61080 AW	83050 TQ	MABLS	10/01-12/01
	New Bedford PMSA, MA	Y	36640 FQ	54100 AW	73790 TQ	MABLS	10/01-12/01
	Springfield MSA, MA	Y	35280 FQ	52510 AW	72170 TQ	MABLS	10/01-12/01
	Worcester PMSA, MA-CT	Y	35830 FQ	59000 AW	86850 TQ	MABLS	10/01-12/01
	Michigan	Y	35080 FQ	52570 AW	72050 TQ	MIBLS	10/01-12/01
	Ann Arbor PMSA, MI	Y	29060 FQ	50880 AW	70620 TQ	MIBLS	10/01-12/01
	Detroit PMSA, MI	Y	37530 FQ	56310 AW	76840 TQ	MIBLS	10/01-12/01
	Flint PMSA, MI	Y	37610 FQ	50510 AW	67070 TQ	MIBLS	10/01-12/01
	Grand Rapids-Muskegon-Holland MSA, MI	Y	35670 FQ	51920 AW	70270 TQ	MIBLS	10/01-12/01
	Kalamazoo-Battle Creek MSA, MI	Y	27780 FQ	46290 AW	65210 TQ	MIBLS	10/01-12/01
	Lansing-East Lansing MSA, MI	Y	33990 FQ	48440 AW	67870 TQ	MIBLS	10/01-12/01
	Saginaw-Bay City-Midland MSA, MI	Y	29990 FQ	45760 AW	61160 TQ	MIBLS	10/01-12/01
	Minnesota	Y	34680 FQ	53910 AW	75990 TQ	MNBLS	10/01-12/01
	Duluth-Superior MSA, MN-WI	Y	29470 FQ	44750 AW	66850 TQ	MNBLS	10/01-12/01
	Minneapolis-St. Paul MSA, MN-WI	Y	35880 FQ	55020 AW	76860 TQ	MNBLS	10/01-12/01
	St. Cloud MSA, MN	Y	37040 FQ	55140 AW	77990 TQ	MNBLS	10/01-12/01
	Mississippi	Y	21930 FQ	39920 AW	58910 TQ	MSBLS	10/01-12/01
	Biloxi-Gulfport-Pascagoula MSA, MS	Y	24540 FQ	45680 AW	63270 TQ	MSBLS	10/01-12/01
	Jackson MSA, MS	Y	21620 FQ	37930 AW	55330 TQ	MSBLS	10/01-12/01
	Missouri	Y	30750 FQ	51300 AW	75020 TQ	MOBLS	10/01-12/01
	Kansas City MSA, MO-KS	Y	31950 FQ	49100 AW	70430 TQ	MOBLS	10/01-12/01
	St. Louis MSA, MO-IL	Y	32610 FQ	54410 AW	77990 TQ	MOBLS	10/01-12/01
	Springfield MSA, MO	Y	31690 FQ	48170 AW	68070 TQ	MOBLS	10/01-12/01
	Montana	Y	27840 FQ	42060 AW	57470 TQ	MTBLS	10/01-12/01
	Billings MSA, MT	Y	29090 FQ	41450 AW	58380 TQ	MTBLS	10/01-12/01
	Nebraska	Y	32120 FQ	51730 AW	74300 TQ	NEBLS	10/01-12/01
	Lincoln MSA, NE	Y	32670 FQ	48380 AW	68660 TQ	NEBLS	10/01-12/01
	Omaha MSA, NE-IA	Y	35630 FQ	54900 AW	78640 TQ	NEBLS	10/01-12/01
	Nevada	Y	32390 FQ	50510 AW	70230 TQ	NVBLS	10/01-12/01
	Las Vegas MSA, NV-AZ	Y	33460 FQ	50480 AW	69560 TQ	NVBLS	10/01-12/01
	Reno MSA, NV	Y	32970 FQ	51410 AW	71400 TQ	NVBLS	10/01-12/01
	New Hampshire	Y	31850 FQ	49740 AW	69960 TQ	NHBLS	10/01-12/01
	Manchester PMSA, NH	Y	30150 FQ	47450 AW	69430 TQ	NHBLS	10/01-12/01
	Nashua PMSA, NH	Y	36980 FQ	52460 AW	74880 TQ	NHBLS	10/01-12/01
	Portsmouth-Rochester PMSA, NH-ME	Y	35270 FQ	51080 AW	73770 TQ	NHBLS	10/01-12/01
	New Jersey	Y	40020 FQ	66120 AW	99410 TQ	NJBLS	10/01-12/01
	Atlantic-Cape May PMSA, NJ	Y	32580 FQ	57490 AW	86550 TQ	NJBLS	10/01-12/01
	Bergen-Passaic PMSA, NJ	Y	41610 FQ	69250 AW	103030 TQ	NJBLS	10/01-12/01
	Jersey City PMSA, NJ	Y	39030 FQ	67910 AW	104820 TQ	NJBLS	10/01-12/01
	Middlesex-Somerset-Hunterdon PMSA, NJ	Y	41340 FQ	70230 AW	105240 TQ	NJBLS	10/01-12/01
	Monmouth-Ocean PMSA, NJ	Y	38710 FQ	61670 AW	89580 TQ	NJBLS	10/01-12/01
	Newark PMSA, NJ	Y	41130 FQ	66920 AW	104120 TQ	NJBLS	10/01-12/01
	Trenton PMSA, NJ	Y	40300 FQ	60150 AW	83500 TQ	NJBLS	10/01-12/01
	New Mexico	Y	30710 FQ	46940 AW	68390 TQ	NMBLS	10/01-12/01
	Albuquerque MSA, NM	Y	32880 FQ	49950 AW	70930 TQ	NMBLS	10/01-12/01
	Las Cruces MSA, NM	Y	27590 FQ	39060 AW	55700 TQ	NMBLS	10/01-12/01
	New York	Y	36830 FQ	62480 AW	94360 TQ	NYBLS	10/01-12/01
	Albany-Schenectady-Troy MSA, NY	Y	28660 FQ	52360 AW	82410 TQ	NYBLS	10/01-12/01

AAW	Average annual wage	**AOH**	Average offered, high	**ASH**	Average starting, high	**H**	Hourly	**M**	Monthly	**S**	Special: hourly and annual
AE	Average entry wage	**AOL**	Average offered, low	**ASL**	Average starting, low	**HI**	Highest wage paid	**MTC**	Median total compensation	**TQ**	Third quartile wage
AEX	Average experienced wage	**APH**	Average pay, high range	**AW**	Average wage paid	**HR**	High end range	**MW**	Median wage paid	**W**	Weekly
AO	Average offered	**APL**	Average pay, low range	**FQ**	First quartile wage	**LR**	Low end range	**SQ**	Second quartile wage	**Y**	Yearly

Occupation/Type/Industry	Location	Per	Low	Mid	High	Source	Date
Network and Computer Systems Administrator	Binghamton MSA, NY	Y	28080 FQ	46490 AW	60010 TQ	NYBLS	10/01-12/01
	Buffalo-Niagara Falls MSA, NY	Y	29380 FQ	48770 AW	72450 TQ	NYBLS	10/01-12/01
	Dutchess County PMSA, NY	Y	29610 FQ	58200 AW	90680 TQ	NYBLS	10/01-12/01
	Nassau-Suffolk PMSA, NY	Y	38470 FQ	59590 AW	87120 TQ	NYBLS	10/01-12/01
	New York PMSA, NY	Y	42720 FQ	70150 AW	104490 TQ	NYBLS	10/01-12/01
	Newburgh PMSA, NY-PA	Y	32840 FQ	53410 AW	81010 TQ	NYBLS	10/01-12/01
	Rochester MSA, NY	Y	38530 FQ	60510 AW	89870 TQ	NYBLS	10/01-12/01
	Syracuse MSA, NY	Y	33580 FQ	50520 AW	71270 TQ	NYBLS	10/01-12/01
	Utica-Rome MSA, NY	Y	29190 FQ	48200 AW	74950 TQ	NYBLS	10/01-12/01
	North Carolina	Y	35400 FQ	61470 AW	103210 TQ	NCBLS	10/01-12/01
	Asheville MSA, NC	Y	32670 FQ	47020 AW	68250 TQ	NCBLS	10/01-12/01
	Charlotte-Gastonia-Rock Hill MSA, NC-SC	Y	35650 FQ	55050 AW	80170 TQ	NCBLS	10/01-12/01
	Fayetteville MSA, NC	Y	30620 FQ	49820 AW	71570 TQ	NCBLS	10/01-12/01
	Greensboro-Winston-Salem-High Point MSA, NC	Y	34770 FQ	53460 AW	79000 TQ	NCBLS	10/01-12/01
	Hickory-Morganton-Lenoir MSA, NC	Y	29940 FQ	48160 AW	67270 TQ	NCBLS	10/01-12/01
	Raleigh-Durham-Chapel Hill MSA, NC	Y	40210 FQ	71750 AW	109380 TQ	NCBLS	10/01-12/01
	Wilmington MSA, NC	Y	30340 FQ	47230 AW	68580 TQ	NCBLS	10/01-12/01
	North Dakota	Y	26700 FQ	37860 AW	54640 TQ	NDBLS	10/01-12/01
	Fargo-Moorhead MSA, ND-MN	Y	24700 FQ	40860 AW	57800 TQ	NDBLS	10/01-12/01
	Ohio	Y	33360 FQ	52770 AW	77930 TQ	OHBLS	10/01-12/01
	Akron PMSA, OH	Y	33100 FQ	55480 AW	83650 TQ	OHBLS	10/01-12/01
	Canton-Massillon MSA, OH	Y	30950 FQ	47620 AW	67210 TQ	OHBLS	10/01-12/01
	Cincinnati PMSA, OH-KY-IN	Y	33730 FQ	57280 AW	87640 TQ	OHBLS	10/01-12/01
	Cleveland-Lorain-Elyria PMSA, OH	Y	34940 FQ	53610 AW	80090 TQ	OHBLS	10/01-12/01
	Columbus MSA, OH	Y	37480 FQ	54820 AW	73990 TQ	OHBLS	10/01-12/01
	Dayton-Springfield MSA, OH	Y	32980 FQ	48470 AW	69320 TQ	OHBLS	10/01-12/01
	Hamilton-Middletown PMSA, OH	Y	37130 FQ	56990 AW	84670 TQ	OHBLS	10/01-12/01
	Mansfield MSA, OH	Y	36950 FQ	52580 AW	71600 TQ	OHBLS	10/01-12/01
	Toledo MSA, OH	Y	30200 FQ	45620 AW	64000 TQ	OHBLS	10/01-12/01
	Youngstown-Warren MSA, OH	Y	29830 FQ	44630 AW	66380 TQ	OHBLS	10/01-12/01
	Oklahoma	Y	29620 FQ	46900 AW	67970 TQ	OKBLS	10/01-12/01
	Oklahoma City MSA, OK	Y	30270 FQ	48540 AW	68590 TQ	OKBLS	10/01-12/01
	Tulsa MSA, OK	Y	31070 FQ	46870 AW	67810 TQ	OKBLS	10/01-12/01
	Oregon	Y	28430 FQ	49270 AW	72340 TQ	ORBLS	10/01-12/01
	Eugene-Springfield MSA, OR	Y	23900 FQ	43160 AW	67570 TQ	ORBLS	10/01-12/01
	Medford-Ashland MSA, OR	Y	31880 FQ	51300 AW	72260 TQ	ORBLS	10/01-12/01
	Portland-Vancouver PMSA, OR-WA	Y	28780 FQ	51050 AW	74640 TQ	ORBLS	10/01-12/01
	Salem PMSA, OR	Y	32840 FQ	46530 AW	65750 TQ	ORBLS	10/01-12/01
	Pennsylvania	Y	30870 FQ	51870 AW	76310 TQ	PABLS	10/01-12/01
	Allentown-Bethlehem-Easton MSA, PA	Y	32430 FQ	48520 AW	72590 TQ	PABLS	10/01-12/01
	Erie MSA, PA	Y	27730 FQ	45620 AW	58360 TQ	PABLS	10/01-12/01
	Harrisburg-Lebanon-Carlisle MSA, PA	Y	32330 FQ	51630 AW	78050 TQ	PABLS	10/01-12/01
	Johnstown MSA, PA	Y	25930 FQ	45700 AW	69800 TQ	PABLS	10/01-12/01
	Lancaster MSA, PA	Y	31260 FQ	48630 AW	70460 TQ	PABLS	10/01-12/01
	Philadelphia PMSA, PA-NJ	Y	37150 FQ	58480 AW	84670 TQ	PABLS	10/01-12/01
	Pittsburgh MSA, PA	Y	26300 FQ	45220 AW	68500 TQ	PABLS	10/01-12/01
	Reading MSA, PA	Y	29940 FQ	47670 AW	63690 TQ	PABLS	10/01-12/01
	Scranton-Wilkes-Barre-Hazleton MSA, PA	Y	26880 FQ	44440 AW	66010 TQ	PABLS	10/01-12/01
	York MSA, PA	Y	30270 FQ	47450 AW	71810 TQ	PABLS	10/01-12/01
	Rhode Island	Y	38620 FQ	56490 AW	80140 TQ	RIBLS	10/01-12/01
	Providence-Fall River-Warwick MSA, RI-MA	Y	38110 FQ	55950 AW	79390 TQ	RIBLS	10/01-12/01
	South Carolina	Y	25800 FQ	47980 AW	71490 TQ	SCBLS	10/01-12/01
	Charleston-North Charleston MSA, SC	Y	23140 FQ	44090 AW	62300 TQ	SCBLS	10/01-12/01
	Columbia MSA, SC	Y	28770 FQ	48580 AW	70290 TQ	SCBLS	10/01-12/01
	Greenville-Spartanburg-Anderson MSA, SC	Y	30080 FQ	50410 AW	72230 TQ	SCBLS	10/01-12/01
	Myrtle Beach MSA, SC	Y	28810 FQ	44730 AW	68910 TQ	SCBLS	10/01-12/01

Occupation/Type/Industry	Location	Per	Low	Mid	High	Source	Date
Network and Computer Systems Administrator	South Dakota	Y	32610 FQ	46650 AW	63910 TQ	SDBLS	10/01-12/01
	Sioux Falls MSA, SD	Y	33980 FQ	47960 AW	65460 TQ	SDBLS	10/01-12/01
	Tennessee	Y	30910 FQ	52590 AW	78260 TQ	TNBLS	10/01-12/01
	Chattanooga MSA, TN-GA	Y	27880 FQ	45780 AW	64140 TQ	TNBLS	10/01-12/01
	Clarksville-Hopkinsville MSA, TN-KY	Y	31040 FQ	41360 AW	50480 TQ	TNBLS	10/01-12/01
	Johnson City-Kingsport-Bristol MSA, TN-VA	Y	25460 FQ	42470 AW	60140 TQ	TNBLS	10/01-12/01
	Knoxville MSA, TN	Y	32280 FQ	56350 AW	87570 TQ	TNBLS	10/01-12/01
	Memphis MSA, TN-AR-MS	Y	32220 FQ	54430 AW	82170 TQ	TNBLS	10/01-12/01
	Nashville MSA, TN	Y	33600 FQ	56290 AW	84130 TQ	TNBLS	10/01-12/01
	Texas	Y	32370 FQ	55890 AW	88270 TQ	TXBLS	10/01-12/01
	Amarillo MSA, TX	Y	31240 FQ	49840 AW	70440 TQ	TXBLS	10/01-12/01
	Austin-San Marcos MSA, TX	Y	36960 FQ	77120 AW	131350 TQ	TXBLS	10/01-12/01
	Beaumont-Port Arthur MSA, TX	Y	33110 FQ	50340 AW	78000 TQ	TXBLS	10/01-12/01
	Brazoria PMSA, TX	Y	30670 FQ	53070 AW	73800 TQ	TXBLS	10/01-12/01
	Brownsville-Harlingen-San Benito MSA, TX	Y	28330 FQ	44050 AW	65870 TQ	TXBLS	10/01-12/01
	Corpus Christi MSA, TX	Y	29780 FQ	39260 AW	54060 TQ	TXBLS	10/01-12/01
	Dallas PMSA, TX	Y	36750 FQ	58430 AW	86970 TQ	TXBLS	10/01-12/01
	El Paso MSA, TX	Y	30520 FQ	46090 AW	68950 TQ	TXBLS	10/01-12/01
	Fort Worth-Arlington PMSA, TX	Y	32500 FQ	50960 AW	77940 TQ	TXBLS	10/01-12/01
	Galveston-Texas City PMSA, TX	Y	36250 FQ	49740 AW	69770 TQ	TXBLS	10/01-12/01
	Houston PMSA, TX	Y	31780 FQ	51540 AW	73870 TQ	TXBLS	10/01-12/01
	Killeen-Temple MSA, TX	Y	27050 FQ	49850 AW	101180 TQ	TXBLS	10/01-12/01
	Laredo MSA, TX	Y	30410 FQ	51020 AW	73550 TQ	TXBLS	10/01-12/01
	Longview-Marshall MSA, TX	Y	29550 FQ	42560 AW	57480 TQ	TXBLS	10/01-12/01
	Lubbock MSA, TX	Y	26390 FQ	41650 AW	61480 TQ	TXBLS	10/01-12/01
	McAllen-Edinburg-Mission MSA, TX	Y	25720 FQ	42960 AW	56710 TQ	TXBLS	10/01-12/01
	Odessa-Midland MSA, TX	Y	16680 FQ	42090 AW	65140 TQ	TXBLS	10/01-12/01
	San Antonio MSA, TX	Y	30030 FQ	48000 AW	71030 TQ	TXBLS	10/01-12/01
	Tyler MSA, TX	Y	22520 FQ	41190 AW	58370 TQ	TXBLS	10/01-12/01
	Waco MSA, TX	Y	25200 FQ	44670 AW	67420 TQ	TXBLS	10/01-12/01
	Utah	Y	31810 FQ	50460 AW	71510 TQ	UTBLS	10/01-12/01
	Provo-Orem MSA, UT	Y	28310 FQ	45660 AW	65800 TQ	UTBLS	10/01-12/01
	Salt Lake City-Ogden MSA, UT	Y	34160 FQ	52090 AW	73240 TQ	UTBLS	10/01-12/01
	Vermont	Y	32200 FQ	46940 AW	65970 TQ	VTBLS	10/01-12/01
	Burlington MSA, VT	Y	33070 FQ	47900 AW	67860 TQ	VTBLS	10/01-12/01
	Virginia	Y	37400 FQ	57530 AW	84310 TQ	VABLS	10/01-12/01
	Lynchburg MSA, VA	Y	34050 FQ	48970 AW	68780 TQ	VABLS	10/01-12/01
	Norfolk-Virginia Beach-Newport News MSA, VA-NC	Y	36670 FQ	53610 AW	70310 TQ	VABLS	10/01-12/01
	Richmond-Petersburg MSA, VA	Y	35420 FQ	58520 AW	88530 TQ	VABLS	10/01-12/01
	Roanoke MSA, VA	Y	32510 FQ	50000 AW	70630 TQ	VABLS	10/01-12/01
	Washington	Y	36220 FQ	56000 AW	81870 TQ	WABLS	10/01-12/01
	Bremerton PMSA, WA	Y	33100 FQ	49810 AW	69020 TQ	WABLS	10/01-12/01
	Olympia PMSA, WA	Y	38290 FQ	54490 AW	77200 TQ	WABLS	10/01-12/01
	Richland-Kennewick-Pasco MSA, WA	Y	33320 FQ	48450 AW	68580 TQ	WABLS	10/01-12/01
	Seattle-Bellevue-Everett PMSA, WA	Y	38600 FQ	58480 AW	85330 TQ	WABLS	10/01-12/01
	Spokane MSA, WA	Y	27800 FQ	48840 AW	70560 TQ	WABLS	10/01-12/01
	Tacoma PMSA, WA	Y	32460 FQ	52040 AW	75780 TQ	WABLS	10/01-12/01
	Yakima MSA, WA	Y	32460 FQ	47580 AW	69150 TQ	WABLS	10/01-12/01
	West Virginia	Y	22770 FQ	41500 AW	62250 TQ	WVBLS	10/01-12/01
	Charleston MSA, WV	Y	26770 FQ	43700 AW	60200 TQ	WVBLS	10/01-12/01
	Huntington-Ashland MSA, WV-KY-OH	Y	19460 FQ	34720 AW	57280 TQ	WVBLS	10/01-12/01
	Wisconsin	Y	28530 FQ	48940 AW	72690 TQ	WIBLS	10/01-12/01
	Appleton-Oshkosh-Neenah MSA, WI	Y	35170 FQ	53060 AW	74320 TQ	WIBLS	10/01-12/01
	Green Bay MSA, WI	Y	30730 FQ	46770 AW	66190 TQ	WIBLS	10/01-12/01
	Madison MSA, WI	Y	36360 FQ	53690 AW	75180 TQ	WIBLS	10/01-12/01

AAW Average annual wage **AOH** Average offered, high **ASH** Average starting, high **H** Hourly **M** Monthly **S** Special: hourly and annual
AE Average entry wage **AOL** Average offered, low **ASL** Average starting, low **HI** Highest wage paid **MTC** Median total compensation **TQ** Third quartile wage
AEX Average experienced wage **APH** Average pay, high range **AW** Average wage paid **HR** High end range **MW** Median wage paid **W** Weekly
AO Average offered **APL** Average pay, low range **FQ** First quartile wage **LR** Low end range **SQ** Second quartile wage **Y** Yearly

Occupation/Type/Industry	Location	Per	Low	Mid	High	Source	Date
Network and Computer Systems Administrator	Milwaukee-Waukesha PMSA, WI	Y	33070 FQ	52860 AW	81400 TQ	WIBLS	10/01-12/01
	Racine PMSA, WI	Y	31980 FQ	47930 AW	64510 TQ	WIBLS	10/01-12/01
	Wyoming	Y	24680 FQ	42910 AW	68240 TQ	WYBLS	10/01-12/01
	Cheyenne MSA, WY	Y	27900 FQ	39900 AW	58620 TQ	WYBLS	10/01-12/01
	Puerto Rico	Y	25040 FQ	40070 AW	58650 TQ	PRBLS	10/01-12/01
	Virgin Islands	Y	32520 FQ	49370 AW	71490 TQ	VIBLS	10/01-12/01
Network Architect	United States	Y		72250-102000 AW		WW	1/00-1/01
Network Engineer	United States	Y		62500-85250 AW		IW	1/00-1/01
Network Services Professional	Baltimore, MD	Y		86150 AW		INFO5	1/00-1/01
Network System and Data Communications Analyst	Alabama	Y	30140 FQ	52910 AW	78800 TQ	ALBLS	10/01-12/01
	Alaska	Y	30610 FQ	53770 AW	79660 TQ	AKBLS	10/01-12/01
	Arizona	Y	40910 FQ	63340 AW	87760 TQ	AZBLS	10/01-12/01
	Arkansas	Y	23170 FQ	42440 AW	64530 TQ	ARBLS	10/01-12/01
	California	Y	38600 FQ	68750 AW	113220 TQ	CABLS	10/01-12/01
	Colorado	Y	38580 FQ	61240 AW	90050 TQ	COBLS	10/01-12/01
	Connecticut	Y	39380 FQ	62370 AW	93860 TQ	CTBLS	10/01-12/01
	Delaware	Y	40830 FQ	68090 AW	92240 TQ	DEBLS	10/01-12/01
	District of Columbia	Y	40470 FQ	63400 AW	89550 TQ	DCBLS	10/01-12/01
	Florida	Y	34330 FQ	59790 AW	88770 TQ	FLBLS	10/01-12/01
	Georgia	Y	32510 FQ	57190 AW	94100 TQ	GABLS	10/01-12/01
	Hawaii	Y	36690 FQ	48600 AW	59710 TQ	HIBLS	10/01-12/01
	Idaho	Y	32480 FQ	49720 AW	73390 TQ	IDBLS	10/01-12/01
	Illinois	Y	36580 FQ	60070 AW	89760 TQ	ILBLS	10/01-12/01
	Indiana	Y	27530 FQ	47960 AW	71510 TQ	INBLS	10/01-12/01
	Iowa	Y	28950 FQ	52980 AW	84740 TQ	IABLS	10/01-12/01
	Kansas	Y	37910 FQ	60100 AW	90720 TQ	KSBLS	10/01-12/01
	Kentucky	Y	30430 FQ	49840 AW	71480 TQ	KYBLS	10/01-12/01
	Louisiana	Y	32060 FQ	48490 AW	77370 TQ	LABLS	10/01-12/01
	Maine	Y	27200 FQ	47700 AW	72920 TQ	MEBLS	10/01-12/01
	Maryland	Y	35440 FQ	65290 AW	102650 TQ	MDBLS	10/01-12/01
	Massachusetts	Y	41590 FQ	69940 AW	106630 TQ	MABLS	10/01-12/01
	Michigan	Y	35470 FQ	55890 AW	83170 TQ	MIBLS	10/01-12/01
	Minnesota	Y	37370 FQ	56020 AW	81690 TQ	MNBLS	10/01-12/01
	Mississippi	Y	27830 FQ	43760 AW	69330 TQ	MSBLS	10/01-12/01
	Missouri	Y	35880 FQ	61570 AW	97340 TQ	MOBLS	10/01-12/01
	Montana	Y	20600 FQ	36690 AW	53360 TQ	MTBLS	10/01-12/01
	Nebraska	Y	25370 FQ	47110 AW	72690 TQ	NEBLS	10/01-12/01
	Nevada	Y	33380 FQ	47570 AW	66530 TQ	NVBLS	10/01-12/01
	New Hampshire	Y	30110 FQ	45660 AW	64340 TQ	NHBLS	10/01-12/01
	New Jersey	Y	40190 FQ	66720 AW	96420 TQ	NJBLS	10/01-12/01
	New Mexico	Y	31200 FQ	50000 AW	71320 TQ	NMBLS	10/01-12/01
	New York	Y	37110 FQ	62950 AW	94480 TQ	NYBLS	10/01-12/01
	North Carolina	Y	37490 FQ	61490 AW	89040 TQ	NCBLS	10/01-12/01
	North Dakota	Y	27000 FQ	41690 AW	60830 TQ	NDBLS	10/01-12/01
	Ohio	Y	37000 FQ	58980 AW	86710 TQ	OHBLS	10/01-12/01
	Oklahoma	Y	23990 FQ	42410 AW	68980 TQ	OKBLS	10/01-12/01
	Oregon	Y	36110 FQ	59280 AW	87410 TQ	ORBLS	10/01-12/01
	Pennsylvania	Y	32760 FQ	59090 AW	89920 TQ	PABLS	10/01-12/01
	Rhode Island	Y	35920 FQ	54580 AW	79860 TQ	RIBLS	10/01-12/01
	South Carolina	Y	30850 FQ	66760 AW	107890 TQ	SCBLS	10/01-12/01
	South Dakota	Y	29310 FQ	42730 AW	63650 TQ	SDBLS	10/01-12/01
	Tennessee	Y	27730 FQ	48160 AW	71510 TQ	TNBLS	10/01-12/01
	Texas	Y	33450 FQ	56070 AW	84680 TQ	TXBLS	10/01-12/01
	Utah	Y	28360 FQ	50850 AW	72600 TQ	UTBLS	10/01-12/01
	Vermont	Y	33700 FQ	55760 AW	84730 TQ	VTBLS	10/01-12/01
	Virginia	Y	37410 FQ	62310 AW	95500 TQ	VABLS	10/01-12/01
	Washington	Y	34840 FQ	60780 AW	89220 TQ	WABLS	10/01-12/01
	West Virginia	Y	20810 FQ	39720 AW	67450 TQ	WVBLS	10/01-12/01
	Wisconsin	Y	29080 FQ	47950 AW	71390 TQ	WIBLS	10/01-12/01
	Wyoming	Y	23570 FQ	40570 AW	67830 TQ	WYBLS	10/01-12/01
	Puerto Rico	Y	21440 FQ	40090 AW	67410 TQ	PRBLS	10/01-12/01

AAW	Average annual wage	**AOH**	Average offered, high	**ASH**	Average starting, high	**H**	Hourly	**M**	Monthly	**S**	Special: hourly and annual
AE	Average entry wage	**AOL**	Average offered, low	**ASL**	Average starting, low	**HI**	Highest wage paid	**MTC**	Median total compensation	**TQ**	Third quartile wage
AEX	Average experienced wage	**APH**	Average pay, high range	**AW**	Average wage paid	**HR**	High end range	**MW**	Median wage paid	**W**	Weekly
AO	Average offered	**APL**	Average pay, low range	**FQ**	First quartile wage	**LR**	Low end range	**SQ**	Second quartile wage	**Y**	Yearly

Occupation/Type/Industry	Location	Per	Low	Mid	High	Source	Date
Network Systems and Data Communications Analyst	United States	Y		39700 AW		FREEP1	1/00-1/00
Neurologist	United States	Y		174000 AW		HHN	1/01-1/02
New Accounts Clerk	Alabama	H	7.66 FQ	9.70 AW	12.05 TQ	ALBLS	10/01-12/01
	Alaska	H	9.54 FQ	12.97 AW	17.52 TQ	AKBLS	10/01-12/01
	Arizona	H	9.27 FQ	13.54 AW	19.27 TQ	AZBLS	10/01-12/01
	Arkansas	H	7.82 FQ	11.67 AW	15.67 TQ	ARBLS	10/01-12/01
	California	H	9.32 FQ	13.57 AW	18.53 TQ	CABLS	10/01-12/01
	Colorado	H	9.21 FQ	11.88 AW	14.87 TQ	COBLS	10/01-12/01
	Connecticut	H	11.21 FQ	14.25 AW	17.76 TQ	CTBLS	10/01-12/01
	Delaware	H	9.28 FQ	11.52 AW	14.58 TQ	DEBLS	10/01-12/01
	District of Columbia	H	9.36 FQ	13.04 AW	16.58 TQ	DCBLS	10/01-12/01
	Florida	H	9.09 FQ	12.56 AW	16.90 TQ	FLBLS	10/01-12/01
	Georgia	H	8.71 FQ	11.85 AW	15.45 TQ	GABLS	10/01-12/01
	Hawaii	H	9.18 FQ	13.01 AW	16.93 TQ	HIBLS	10/01-12/01
	Idaho	H	8.79 FQ	12.02 AW	16.74 TQ	IDBLS	10/01-12/01
	Illinois	H	9.09 FQ	13.19 AW	19.26 TQ	ILBLS	10/01-12/01
	Indiana	H	8.53 FQ	11.23 AW	14.56 TQ	INBLS	10/01-12/01
	Iowa	H	8.74 FQ	11.65 AW	16.34 TQ	IABLS	10/01-12/01
	Kansas	H	9.15 FQ	12.38 AW	16.74 TQ	KSBLS	10/01-12/01
	Kentucky	H	8.78 FQ	11.15 AW	14.65 TQ	KYBLS	10/01-12/01
	Louisiana	H	7.18 FQ	9.74 AW	14.50 TQ	LABLS	10/01-12/01
	Maine	H	9.12 FQ	11.60 AW	15.06 TQ	MEBLS	10/01-12/01
	Maryland	H	8.99 FQ	12.51 AW	16.51 TQ	MDBLS	10/01-12/01
	Massachusetts	H	9.89 FQ	12.56 AW	15.91 TQ	MABLS	10/01-12/01
	Michigan	H	8.82 FQ	12.61 AW	16.49 TQ	MIBLS	10/01-12/01
	Minnesota	H	9.54 FQ	12.49 AW	16.25 TQ	MNBLS	10/01-12/01
	Mississippi	H	9.06 FQ	11.33 AW	13.63 TQ	MSBLS	10/01-12/01
	Missouri	H	8.37 FQ	11.65 AW	15.93 TQ	MOBLS	10/01-12/01
	Montana	H	7.45 FQ	10.18 AW	13.26 TQ	MTBLS	10/01-12/01
	Nebraska	H	8.81 FQ	12.06 AW	15.29 TQ	NEBLS	10/01-12/01
	Nevada	H	9.24 FQ	13.13 AW	16.97 TQ	NVBLS	10/01-12/01
	New Hampshire	H	9.02 FQ	11.55 AW	14.67 TQ	NHBLS	10/01-12/01
	New Jersey	H	9.44 FQ	13.45 AW	17.76 TQ	NJBLS	10/01-12/01
	New Mexico	H	7.55 FQ	10.37 AW	13.59 TQ	NMBLS	10/01-12/01
	New York	H	8.80 FQ	12.51 AW	17.67 TQ	NYBLS	10/01-12/01
	North Carolina	H	8.94 FQ	18.24 AW	47.15 TQ	NCBLS	10/01-12/01
	North Dakota	H	8.40 FQ	11.61 AW	15.80 TQ	NDBLS	10/01-12/01
	Ohio	H	9.02 FQ	11.08 AW	14.65 TQ	OHBLS	10/01-12/01
	Oklahoma	H	7.64 FQ	10.78 AW	13.99 TQ	OKBLS	10/01-12/01
	Oregon	H	9.45 FQ	12.38 AW	16.01 TQ	ORBLS	10/01-12/01
	Pennsylvania	H	8.98 FQ	11.60 AW	14.83 TQ	PABLS	10/01-12/01
	Rhode Island	H	9.12 FQ	13.68 AW	17.76 TQ	RIBLS	10/01-12/01
	South Carolina	H	7.79 FQ	10.99 AW	14.29 TQ	SCBLS	10/01-12/01
	South Dakota	H	8.00 FQ	11.51 AW	16.84 TQ	SDBLS	10/01-12/01
	Tennessee	H	7.72 FQ	10.72 AW	14.50 TQ	TNBLS	10/01-12/01
	Texas	H	8.69 FQ	11.92 AW	15.86 TQ	TXBLS	10/01-12/01
	Utah	H	8.95 FQ	10.57 AW	12.94 TQ	UTBLS	10/01-12/01
	Vermont	H	9.18 FQ	11.12 AW	13.67 TQ	VTBLS	10/01-12/01
	Virginia	H	8.63 FQ	13.03 AW	19.08 TQ	VABLS	10/01-12/01
	Washington	H	9.28 FQ	13.15 AW	18.30 TQ	WABLS	10/01-12/01
	West Virginia	H	7.34 FQ	10.45 AW	13.86 TQ	WVBLS	10/01-12/01
	Wisconsin	H	9.10 FQ	11.77 AW	15.39 TQ	WIBLS	10/01-12/01
	Wyoming	H	7.61 FQ	10.57 AW	13.96 TQ	WYBLS	10/01-12/01
	Puerto Rico	H	6.45 FQ	9.32 AW	12.65 TQ	PRBLS	10/01-12/01
	Guam	H	9.37 FQ	11.20 AW	13.60 TQ	GUBLS	10/01-12/01
News Analyst, Reporter and Correspondent	Alabama	Y	14970 FQ	28690 AW	42590 TQ	ALBLS	10/01-12/01
	Birmingham MSA, AL	Y	16580 FQ	37480 AW	75040 TQ	ALBLS	10/01-12/01
	Huntsville MSA, AL	Y	16430 FQ	30070 AW	36590 TQ	ALBLS	10/01-12/01
	Mobile MSA, AL	Y	14850 FQ	26060 AW	36260 TQ	ALBLS	10/01-12/01
	Montgomery MSA, AL	Y	16710 FQ	29420 AW	42520 TQ	ALBLS	10/01-12/01
	Alaska	Y	23130 FQ	33780 AW	47630 TQ	AKBLS	10/01-12/01
	Anchorage MSA, AK	Y	23680 FQ	36350 AW	57160 TQ	AKBLS	10/01-12/01
	Arizona	Y	19720 FQ	43300 AW	67410 TQ	AZBLS	10/01-12/01
	Phoenix-Mesa MSA, AZ	Y	23420 FQ	49390 AW	70940 TQ	AZBLS	10/01-12/01
	Tucson MSA, AZ	Y	19860 FQ	39920 AW	59130 TQ	AZBLS	10/01-12/01
	Arkansas	Y	17140 FQ	27440 AW	43040 TQ	ARBLS	10/01-12/01

AAW	Average annual wage	**AOH**	Average offered, high	**ASH**	Average starting, high	**H**	Hourly	**M**	Monthly	**S**	Special: hourly and annual
AE	Average entry wage	**AOL**	Average offered, low	**ASL**	Average starting, low	**HI**	Highest wage paid	**MTC**	Median total compensation	**TQ**	Third quartile wage
AEX	Average experienced wage	**APH**	Average pay, high range	**AW**	Average wage paid	**HR**	High end range	**MW**	Median wage paid	**W**	Weekly
AO	Average offered	**APL**	Average pay, low range	**FQ**	First quartile wage	**LR**	Low end range	**SQ**	Second quartile wage	**Y**	Yearly

Occupation/Type/Industry	Location	Per	Low	Mid	High	Source	Date
News Analyst, Reporter and Correspondent	Fayetteville-Springdale-Rogers MSA, AR	Y	19250 FQ	29310 AW	46900 TQ	ARBLS	10/01-12/01
	Fort Smith MSA, AR-OK	Y	18740 FQ	25670 AW	32300 TQ	ARBLS	10/01-12/01
	Little Rock-North Little Rock MSA, AR	Y	16900 FQ	33440 AW	56750 TQ	ARBLS	10/01-12/01
	California	Y	20320 FQ	45980 AW	89310 TQ	CABLS	10/01-12/01
	Bakersfield MSA, CA	Y	16290 FQ	35560 AW	70390 TQ	CABLS	10/01-12/01
	Chico-Paradise MSA, CA	Y	16190 FQ	29110 AW	46860 TQ	CABLS	10/01-12/01
	Fresno MSA, CA	Y	19510 FQ	41620 AW	71880 TQ	CABLS	10/01-12/01
	Los Angeles-Long Beach PMSA, CA	Y	22400 FQ	51940 AW	110450 TQ	CABLS	10/01-12/01
	Modesto MSA, CA	Y	19120 FQ	32010 AW	60840 TQ	CABLS	10/01-12/01
	Oakland PMSA, CA	Y	18530 FQ	38280 AW	67550 TQ	CABLS	10/01-12/01
	Orange County PMSA, CA	Y	20770 FQ	41250 AW	75700 TQ	CABLS	10/01-12/01
	Riverside-San Bernardino PMSA, CA	Y	18410 FQ	33130 AW	55320 TQ	CABLS	10/01-12/01
	Sacramento PMSA, CA	Y	21140 FQ	43240 AW	73070 TQ	CABLS	10/01-12/01
	San Diego MSA, CA	Y	18220 FQ	54030 AW	85190 TQ	CABLS	10/01-12/01
	San Francisco PMSA, CA	Y	21700 FQ	54350 AW	110350 TQ	CABLS	10/01-12/01
	San Jose PMSA, CA	Y	22460 FQ	44600 AW	85280 TQ	CABLS	10/01-12/01
	San Luis Obispo-Atascadero-Paso Robles MSA, CA	Y	18990 FQ	33480 AW	51520 TQ	CABLS	10/01-12/01
	Santa Barbara-Santa Maria-Lompoc MSA, CA	Y	19280 FQ	47450 AW	102910 TQ	CABLS	10/01-12/01
	Santa Cruz-Watsonville PMSA, CA	Y	17820 FQ	34990 AW	52610 TQ	CABLS	10/01-12/01
	Vallejo-Fairfield-Napa PMSA, CA	Y	19930 FQ	27390 AW	37310 TQ	CABLS	10/01-12/01
	Visalia-Tulare-Porterville MSA, CA	Y	18330 FQ	26260 AW	38130 TQ	CABLS	10/01-12/01
	Colorado	Y	17500 FQ	43220 AW	79350 TQ	COBLS	10/01-12/01
	Boulder-Longmont PMSA, CO	Y	23720 FQ	37610 AW	56780 TQ	COBLS	10/01-12/01
	Colorado Springs MSA, CO	Y	20940 FQ	42260 AW	87160 TQ	COBLS	10/01-12/01
	Denver PMSA, CO	Y	21680 FQ	57760 AW	103170 TQ	COBLS	10/01-12/01
	Fort Collins-Loveland MSA, CO	Y	23440 FQ	31440 AW	40880 TQ	COBLS	10/01-12/01
	Connecticut	Y	20730 FQ	36910 AW	59300 TQ	CTBLS	10/01-12/01
	Danbury PMSA, CT	Y	23000 FQ	37620 AW	56120 TQ	CTBLS	10/01-12/01
	Hartford MSA, CT	Y	20410 FQ	38120 AW	66830 TQ	CTBLS	10/01-12/01
	New Haven-Meriden PMSA, CT	Y	20530 FQ	35040 AW	53270 TQ	CTBLS	10/01-12/01
	Stamford-Norwalk PMSA, CT	Y	25140 FQ	39200 AW	59670 TQ	CTBLS	10/01-12/01
	Waterbury PMSA, CT	Y	17100 FQ	28390 AW	42590 TQ	CTBLS	10/01-12/01
	Delaware	Y	18320 FQ	28950 AW	40480 TQ	DEBLS	10/01-12/01
	Wilmington-Newark PMSA, DE-MD	Y	18460 FQ	29080 AW	40710 TQ	DEBLS	10/01-12/01
	District of Columbia	Y	24020 FQ	51260 AW	86380 TQ	DCBLS	10/01-12/01
	Washington PMSA, DC-MD-VA-WV	Y	22860 FQ	48370 AW	87870 TQ	DCBLS	10/01-12/01
	Florida	Y	19090 FQ	46590 AW	85640 TQ	FLBLS	10/01-12/01
	Daytona Beach MSA, FL	Y	13930 FQ	35990 AW	54910 TQ	FLBLS	10/01-12/01
	Fort Lauderdale PMSA, FL	Y	15400 FQ	43130 AW	83920 TQ	FLBLS	10/01-12/01
	Jacksonville MSA, FL	Y	16300 FQ	44210 AW	89200 TQ	FLBLS	10/01-12/01
	Miami PMSA, FL	Y	20420 FQ	60720 AW	107420 TQ	FLBLS	10/01-12/01
	Orlando MSA, FL	Y	31340 FQ	58830 AW	98420 TQ	FLBLS	10/01-12/01
	Pensacola MSA, FL	Y	22980 FQ	45730 AW	85820 TQ	FLBLS	10/01-12/01
	Sarasota-Bradenton MSA, FL	Y	19520 FQ	36980 AW	58370 TQ	FLBLS	10/01-12/01
	Tallahassee MSA, FL	Y	23360 FQ	49980 AW	121140 TQ	FLBLS	10/01-12/01
	Tampa-St. Petersburg-Clearwater MSA, FL	Y	19710 FQ	42090 AW	70100 TQ	FLBLS	10/01-12/01
	West Palm Beach-Boca Raton MSA, FL	Y	18170 FQ	40950 AW	65040 TQ	FLBLS	10/01-12/01
	Georgia	Y	13030 FQ	26610 AW	36310 TQ	GABLS	10/01-12/01
	Atlanta MSA, GA	Y	12840 FQ	27450 AW	36880 TQ	GABLS	10/01-12/01
	Augusta-Aiken MSA, GA-SC	Y	16990 FQ	25030 AW	36370 TQ	GABLS	10/01-12/01
	Columbus MSA, GA-AL	Y	21560 FQ	31190 AW	42690 TQ	GABLS	10/01-12/01
	Savannah MSA, GA	Y	18560 FQ	24600 AW	33420 TQ	GABLS	10/01-12/01
	Hawaii	Y	23620 FQ	54720 AW	79790 TQ	HIBLS	10/01-12/01
	Honolulu MSA, HI	Y	24240 FQ	58310 AW	85140 TQ	HIBLS	10/01-12/01
	Idaho	Y	15950 FQ	30590 AW	53520 TQ	IDBLS	10/01-12/01
	Boise City MSA, ID	Y	18610 FQ	39860 AW	82310 TQ	IDBLS	10/01-12/01

AAW Average annual wage; AE Average entry wage; AEX Average experienced wage; AO Average offered; AOH Average offered, high; AOL Average offered, low; APH Average pay, high range; APL Average pay, low range; ASH Average starting, high; ASL Average starting, low; AW Average wage paid; FQ First quartile wage; H Hourly; HI Highest wage paid; HR High end range; LR Low end range; M Monthly; MTC Median total compensation; MW Median wage paid; SQ Second quartile wage; S Special: hourly and annual; TQ Third quartile wage; W Weekly; Y Yearly

Occupation/Type/Industry	Location	Per	Low	Mid	High	Source	Date
News Analyst, Reporter and Correspondent	Illinois	Y	13390 FQ	29610 AW	52510 TQ	ILBLS	10/01-12/01
	Chicago PMSA, IL	Y	14370 FQ	32450 AW	56210 TQ	ILBLS	10/01-12/01
	Peoria-Pekin MSA, IL	Y	18960 FQ	37870 AW	55300 TQ	ILBLS	10/01-12/01
	Rockford MSA, IL	Y	17420 FQ	33370 AW	51710 TQ	ILBLS	10/01-12/01
	Indiana	Y	14760 FQ	26600 AW	41230 TQ	INBLS	10/01-12/01
	Elkhart-Goshen MSA, IN	Y	15860 FQ	29050 AW	47600 TQ	INBLS	10/01-12/01
	Evansville-Henderson MSA, IN-KY	Y	18300 FQ	33640 AW	56390 TQ	INBLS	10/01-12/01
	Fort Wayne MSA, IN	Y	18340 FQ	32180 AW	55120 TQ	INBLS	10/01-12/01
	Gary PMSA, IN	Y	15290 FQ	28110 AW	40070 TQ	INBLS	10/01-12/01
	Indianapolis MSA, IN	Y	16600 FQ	31810 AW	53990 TQ	INBLS	10/01-12/01
	Lafayette MSA, IN	Y	14310 FQ	27610 AW	43810 TQ	INBLS	10/01-12/01
	Iowa	Y	15300 FQ	26920 AW	46390 TQ	IABLS	10/01-12/01
	Cedar Rapids MSA, IA	Y	16090 FQ	31710 AW	53430 TQ	IABLS	10/01-12/01
	Davenport-Moline-Rock Island MSA, IA-IL	Y	17320 FQ	29520 AW	44480 TQ	IABLS	10/01-12/01
	Des Moines MSA, IA	Y	19250 FQ	40390 AW	69070 TQ	IABLS	10/01-12/01
	Kansas	Y	15040 FQ	29690 AW	51260 TQ	KSBLS	10/01-12/01
	Topeka MSA, KS	Y	16870 FQ	36400 AW	66670 TQ	KSBLS	10/01-12/01
	Kentucky	Y	16880 FQ	34280 AW	60890 TQ	KYBLS	10/01-12/01
	Lexington MSA, KY	Y	17470 FQ	35800 AW	61190 TQ	KYBLS	10/01-12/01
	Louisville MSA, KY-IN	Y	18930 FQ	43500 AW	76750 TQ	KYBLS	10/01-12/01
	Louisiana	Y	14320 FQ	32030 AW	54650 TQ	LABLS	10/01-12/01
	Baton Rouge MSA, LA	Y	18300 FQ	34390 AW	47390 TQ	LABLS	10/01-12/01
	Lafayette MSA, LA	Y	17680 FQ	35240 AW	60200 TQ	LABLS	10/01-12/01
	Lake Charles MSA, LA	Y	15090 FQ	28110 AW	44560 TQ	LABLS	10/01-12/01
	New Orleans MSA, LA	Y	13260 FQ	30700 AW	62740 TQ	LABLS	10/01-12/01
	Shreveport-Bossier City MSA, LA	Y	18930 FQ	41290 AW	83120 TQ	LABLS	10/01-12/01
	Maine	Y	16750 FQ	29830 AW	46760 TQ	MEBLS	10/01-12/01
	Portland MSA, ME	Y	18690 FQ	37540 AW	56220 TQ	MEBLS	10/01-12/01
	Maryland	Y	21500 FQ	39610 AW	56030 TQ	MDBLS	10/01-12/01
	Baltimore PMSA, MD	Y	22170 FQ	40900 AW	56160 TQ	MDBLS	10/01-12/01
	Massachusetts	Y	21150 FQ	37810 AW	58830 TQ	MABLS	10/01-12/01
	Boston PMSA, MA-NH	Y	21880 FQ	41890 AW	72240 TQ	MABLS	10/01-12/01
	Springfield MSA, MA	Y	20730 FQ	32760 AW	43550 TQ	MABLS	10/01-12/01
	Michigan	Y	16390 FQ	39200 AW	73050 TQ	MIBLS	10/01-12/01
	Ann Arbor PMSA, MI	Y	18800 FQ	41710 AW	76510 TQ	MIBLS	10/01-12/01
	Detroit PMSA, MI	Y	16980 FQ	46000 AW	94520 TQ	MIBLS	10/01-12/01
	Flint PMSA, MI	Y	16270 FQ	27860 AW	43900 TQ	MIBLS	10/01-12/01
	Grand Rapids-Muskegon-Holland MSA, MI	Y	14790 FQ	38400 AW	71890 TQ	MIBLS	10/01-12/01
	Kalamazoo-Battle Creek MSA, MI	Y	19600 FQ	42820 AW	72970 TQ	MIBLS	10/01-12/01
	Lansing-East Lansing MSA, MI	Y	20800 FQ	43190 AW	70510 TQ	MIBLS	10/01-12/01
	Saginaw-Bay City-Midland MSA, MI	Y	15050 FQ	30040 AW	50400 TQ	MIBLS	10/01-12/01
	Minnesota	Y	15510 FQ	34600 AW	68180 TQ	MNBLS	10/01-12/01
	Duluth-Superior MSA, MN-WI	Y	18360 FQ	31500 AW	44750 TQ	MNBLS	10/01-12/01
	Minneapolis-St. Paul MSA, MN-WI	Y	18830 FQ	45640 AW	73940 TQ	MNBLS	10/01-12/01
	Mississippi	Y	17820 FQ	28950 AW	41600 TQ	MSBLS	10/01-12/01
	Missouri	Y	17740 FQ	35530 AW	63650 TQ	MOBLS	10/01-12/01
	Kansas City MSA, MO-KS	Y	19320 FQ	42940 AW	70120 TQ	MOBLS	10/01-12/01
	St. Louis MSA, MO-IL	Y	18200 FQ	35630 AW	62640 TQ	MOBLS	10/01-12/01
	Springfield MSA, MO	Y	18280 FQ	36420 AW	71950 TQ	MOBLS	10/01-12/01
	Montana	Y	19210 FQ	31080 AW	51480 TQ	MTBLS	10/01-12/01
	Billings MSA, MT	Y	17270 FQ	29550 AW	42840 TQ	MTBLS	10/01-12/01
	Nebraska	Y	12740 FQ	22720 AW	35600 TQ	NEBLS	10/01-12/01
	Omaha MSA, NE-IA	Y	12910 FQ	25720 AW	43410 TQ	NEBLS	10/01-12/01
	Nevada	Y	19910 FQ	37370 AW	57800 TQ	NVBLS	10/01-12/01
	Las Vegas MSA, NV-AZ	Y	20470 FQ	39660 AW	63140 TQ	NVBLS	10/01-12/01
	Reno MSA, NV	Y	17830 FQ	34590 AW	54560 TQ	NVBLS	10/01-12/01
	New Hampshire	Y	18760 FQ	33950 AW	61100 TQ	NHBLS	10/01-12/01
	Portsmouth-Rochester PMSA, NH-ME	Y	20190 FQ	30760 AW	58310 TQ	NHBLS	10/01-12/01
	New Jersey	Y	19890 FQ	37260 AW	60210 TQ	NJBLS	10/01-12/01
	Atlantic-Cape May PMSA, NJ	Y	20650 FQ	32400 AW	51530 TQ	NJBLS	10/01-12/01
	Bergen-Passaic PMSA, NJ	Y	20700 FQ	42710 AW	83060 TQ	NJBLS	10/01-12/01
	Jersey City PMSA, NJ	Y	19930 FQ	39900 AW	63760 TQ	NJBLS	10/01-12/01

AAW Average annual wage **AE** Average entry wage **AEX** Average experienced wage **AO** Average offered **AOH** Average offered, high **AOL** Average offered, low **APH** Average pay, high range **APL** Average pay, low range **ASH** Average starting, high **ASL** Average starting, low **AW** Average wage paid **FQ** First quartile wage **H** Hourly **HI** Highest wage paid **HR** High end range **LR** Low end range **M** Monthly **MTC** Median total compensation **MW** Median wage paid **SQ** Second quartile wage **S** Special: hourly and annual **TQ** Third quartile wage **W** Weekly **Y** Yearly

Occupation/Type/Industry	Location	Per	Low	Mid	High	Source	Date
News Analyst, Reporter and Correspondent	Middlesex-Somerset-Hunterdon PMSA, NJ	Y	20080 FQ	31850 AW	49740 TQ	NJBLS	10/01-12/01
	Newark PMSA, NJ	Y	19810 FQ	35900 AW	56580 TQ	NJBLS	10/01-12/01
	Trenton PMSA, NJ	Y	20470 FQ	31680 AW	43080 TQ	NJBLS	10/01-12/01
	New Mexico	Y	17140 FQ	34410 AW	59390 TQ	NMBLS	10/01-12/01
	Albuquerque MSA, NM	Y	22140 FQ	49040 AW	106520 TQ	NMBLS	10/01-12/01
	New York	Y	20660 FQ	47900 AW	98990 TQ	NYBLS	10/01-12/01
	Albany-Schenectady-Troy MSA, NY	Y	21630 FQ	49880 AW	105950 TQ	NYBLS	10/01-12/01
	Binghamton MSA, NY	Y	16180 FQ	36860 AW	66400 TQ	NYBLS	10/01-12/01
	Nassau-Suffolk PMSA, NY	Y	23670 FQ	57800 AW	109800 TQ	NYBLS	10/01-12/01
	New York PMSA, NY	Y	21920 FQ	48960 AW	101440 TQ	NYBLS	10/01-12/01
	Rochester MSA, NY	Y	19110 FQ	41450 AW	70490 TQ	NYBLS	10/01-12/01
	Syracuse MSA, NY	Y	18960 FQ	38080 AW	68890 TQ	NYBLS	10/01-12/01
	Utica-Rome MSA, NY	Y	17540 FQ	43350 AW	85920 TQ	NYBLS	10/01-12/01
	North Carolina	Y	18970 FQ	36690 AW	62330 TQ	NCBLS	10/01-12/01
	Charlotte-Gastonia-Rock Hill MSA, NC-SC	Y	24200 FQ	45980 AW	71520 TQ	NCBLS	10/01-12/01
	Greensboro-Winston-Salem-High Point MSA, NC	Y	20020 FQ	34460 AW	51390 TQ	NCBLS	10/01-12/01
	Hickory-Morganton-Lenoir MSA, NC	Y	17330 FQ	23510 AW	30220 TQ	NCBLS	10/01-12/01
	Raleigh-Durham-Chapel Hill MSA, NC	Y	19120 FQ	42870 AW	74200 TQ	NCBLS	10/01-12/01
	Wilmington MSA, NC	Y	19260 FQ	37840 AW	80290 TQ	NCBLS	10/01-12/01
	North Dakota	Y	14020 FQ	25820 AW	44250 TQ	NDBLS	10/01-12/01
	Fargo-Moorhead MSA, ND-MN	Y	13210 FQ	26760 AW	45270 TQ	NDBLS	10/01-12/01
	Ohio	Y	17630 FQ	35250 AW	63740 TQ	OHBLS	10/01-12/01
	Canton-Massillon MSA, OH	Y	13780 FQ	27090 AW	43340 TQ	OHBLS	10/01-12/01
	Cincinnati PMSA, OH-KY-IN	Y	18890 FQ	36540 AW	62450 TQ	OHBLS	10/01-12/01
	Cleveland-Lorain-Elyria PMSA, OH	Y	17630 FQ	34830 AW	65580 TQ	OHBLS	10/01-12/01
	Columbus MSA, OH	Y	21370 FQ	41630 AW	70800 TQ	OHBLS	10/01-12/01
	Dayton-Springfield MSA, OH	Y	16320 FQ	39820 AW	68120 TQ	OHBLS	10/01-12/01
	Hamilton-Middletown PMSA, OH	Y	19710 FQ	30150 AW	40860 TQ	OHBLS	10/01-12/01
	Mansfield MSA, OH	Y	17930 FQ	28290 AW	42340 TQ	OHBLS	10/01-12/01
	Toledo MSA, OH	Y	16700 FQ	43050 AW	69450 TQ	OHBLS	10/01-12/01
	Youngstown-Warren MSA, OH	Y	22300 FQ	34380 AW	44050 TQ	OHBLS	10/01-12/01
	Oklahoma	Y	14730 FQ	32340 AW	65060 TQ	OKBLS	10/01-12/01
	Oklahoma City MSA, OK	Y	18320 FQ	36670 AW	70430 TQ	OKBLS	10/01-12/01
	Tulsa MSA, OK	Y	14220 FQ	31990 AW	75500 TQ	OKBLS	10/01-12/01
	Oregon	Y	15160 FQ	35820 AW	61600 TQ	ORBLS	10/01-12/01
	Eugene-Springfield MSA, OR	Y	14720 FQ	26290 AW	55320 TQ	ORBLS	10/01-12/01
	Medford-Ashland MSA, OR	Y	18380 FQ	41040 AW	90740 TQ	ORBLS	10/01-12/01
	Portland-Vancouver PMSA, OR-WA	Y	23860 FQ	45100 AW	78690 TQ	ORBLS	10/01-12/01
	Salem PMSA, OR	Y	17870 FQ	30410 AW	46770 TQ	ORBLS	10/01-12/01
	Pennsylvania	Y	17680 FQ	33880 AW	53390 TQ	PABLS	10/01-12/01
	Allentown-Bethlehem-Easton MSA, PA	Y	19900 FQ	38850 AW	56710 TQ	PABLS	10/01-12/01
	Erie MSA, PA	Y	18770 FQ	32170 AW	50600 TQ	PABLS	10/01-12/01
	Johnstown MSA, PA	Y	15670 FQ	30330 AW	48230 TQ	PABLS	10/01-12/01
	Lancaster MSA, PA	Y	16310 FQ	33100 AW	48810 TQ	PABLS	10/01-12/01
	Philadelphia PMSA, PA-NJ	Y	18190 FQ	39080 AW	61710 TQ	PABLS	10/01-12/01
	Pittsburgh MSA, PA	Y	18480 FQ	27530 AW	45260 TQ	PABLS	10/01-12/01
	Scranton-Wilkes-Barre-Hazleton MSA, PA	Y	20890 FQ	36630 AW	47910 TQ	PABLS	10/01-12/01
	South Carolina	Y	20540 FQ	38500 AW	55950 TQ	SCBLS	10/01-12/01
	Columbia MSA, SC	Y	26010 FQ	44890 AW	56610 TQ	SCBLS	10/01-12/01
	Greenville-Spartanburg-Anderson MSA, SC	Y	19000 FQ	35480 AW	56160 TQ	SCBLS	10/01-12/01
	South Dakota	Y	16910 FQ	27940 AW	47290 TQ	SDBLS	10/01-12/01
	Sioux Falls MSA, SD	Y	19690 FQ	34490 AW	57240 TQ	SDBLS	10/01-12/01
	Tennessee	Y	16990 FQ	38640 AW	60220 TQ	TNBLS	10/01-12/01
	Chattanooga MSA, TN-GA	Y	21580 FQ	37550 AW	57180 TQ	TNBLS	10/01-12/01
	Johnson City-Kingsport-Bristol MSA, TN-VA	Y	14680 FQ	34000 AW	56400 TQ	TNBLS	10/01-12/01
	Knoxville MSA, TN	Y	20270 FQ	35510 AW	46780 TQ	TNBLS	10/01-12/01
	Memphis MSA, TN-AR-MS	Y	20670 FQ	42560 AW	59790 TQ	TNBLS	10/01-12/01

AAW	Average annual wage	**AOH**	Average offered, high	**ASH**	Average starting, high	**H**	Hourly	**M**	Monthly	**S**	Special: hourly and annual
AE	Average entry wage	**AOL**	Average offered, low	**ASL**	Average starting, low	**HI**	Highest wage paid	**MTC**	Median total compensation	**TQ**	Third quartile wage
AEX	Average experienced wage	**APH**	Average pay, high range	**AW**	Average wage paid	**HR**	High end range	**MW**	Median wage paid	**W**	Weekly
AO	Average offered	**APL**	Average pay, low range	**FQ**	First quartile wage	**LR**	Low end range	**SQ**	Second quartile wage	**Y**	Yearly

Occupation/Type/Industry	Location	Per	Low	Mid	High	Source	Date
News Analyst, Reporter and Correspondent	Nashville MSA, TN	Y	19450 FQ	46530 AW	113410 TQ	TNBLS	10/01-12/01
	Texas	Y	16730 FQ	33410 AW	60400 TQ	TXBLS	10/01-12/01
	Amarillo MSA, TX	Y	19810 FQ	33810 AW	54550 TQ	TXBLS	10/01-12/01
	Austin-San Marcos MSA, TX	Y	18110 FQ	38530 AW	67040 TQ	TXBLS	10/01-12/01
	Beaumont-Port Arthur MSA, TX	Y	16890 FQ	30080 AW	54200 TQ	TXBLS	10/01-12/01
	Brownsville-Harlingen-San Benito MSA, TX	Y	15970 FQ	22920 AW	29670 TQ	TXBLS	10/01-12/01
	Corpus Christi MSA, TX	Y	17610 FQ	36720 AW	68400 TQ	TXBLS	10/01-12/01
	Dallas PMSA, TX	Y	16840 FQ	33500 AW	62350 TQ	TXBLS	10/01-12/01
	Houston PMSA, TX	Y	18370 FQ	40670 AW	78160 TQ	TXBLS	10/01-12/01
	Lubbock MSA, TX	Y	20600 FQ	36160 AW	62720 TQ	TXBLS	10/01-12/01
	McAllen-Edinburg-Mission MSA, TX	Y	18400 FQ	32350 AW	60230 TQ	TXBLS	10/01-12/01
	San Antonio MSA, TX	Y	24810 FQ	49530 AW	86290 TQ	TXBLS	10/01-12/01
	Utah	Y	20710 FQ	39990 AW	61410 TQ	UTBLS	10/01-12/01
	Provo-Orem MSA, UT	Y	21990 FQ	32920 AW	55280 TQ	UTBLS	10/01-12/01
	Salt Lake City-Ogden MSA, UT	Y	21230 FQ	41670 AW	64670 TQ	UTBLS	10/01-12/01
	Vermont	Y	19300 FQ	31780 AW	52460 TQ	VTBLS	10/01-12/01
	Burlington MSA, VT	Y	20620 FQ	34740 AW	52460 TQ	VTBLS	10/01-12/01
	Virginia	Y	17780 FQ	40040 AW	81860 TQ	VABLS	10/01-12/01
	Norfolk-Virginia Beach-Newport News MSA, VA-NC	Y	17820 FQ	40830 AW	77150 TQ	VABLS	10/01-12/01
	Richmond-Petersburg MSA, VA	Y	18830 FQ	43970 AW	90000 TQ	VABLS	10/01-12/01
	Roanoke MSA, VA	Y	18360 FQ	35390 AW	64870 TQ	VABLS	10/01-12/01
	Washington	Y	20500 FQ	47420 AW	83650 TQ	WABLS	10/01-12/01
	Richland-Kennewick-Pasco MSA, WA	Y	17780 FQ	35960 AW	68030 TQ	WABLS	10/01-12/01
	Seattle-Bellevue-Everett PMSA, WA	Y	22550 FQ	56910 AW	106730 TQ	WABLS	10/01-12/01
	Spokane MSA, WA	Y	21360 FQ	47630 AW	100550 TQ	WABLS	10/01-12/01
	Yakima MSA, WA	Y	15810 FQ	25470 AW	40770 TQ	WABLS	10/01-12/01
	West Virginia	Y	13560 FQ	28730 AW	57000 TQ	WVBLS	10/01-12/01
	Huntington-Ashland MSA, WV-KY-OH	Y	17990 FQ	37040 AW	66660 TQ	WVBLS	10/01-12/01
	Wisconsin	Y	16110 FQ	30890 AW	47080 TQ	WIBLS	10/01-12/01
	Green Bay MSA, WI	Y	18420 FQ	33220 AW	65090 TQ	WIBLS	10/01-12/01
	Madison MSA, WI	Y	18730 FQ	33480 AW	45660 TQ	WIBLS	10/01-12/01
	Milwaukee-Waukesha PMSA, WI	Y	17860 FQ	39100 AW	84240 TQ	WIBLS	10/01-12/01
	Wyoming	Y	15110 FQ	23570 AW	33010 TQ	WYBLS	10/01-12/01
	Puerto Rico	Y	17890 FQ	32040 AW	47340 TQ	PRBLS	10/01-12/01
	Virgin Islands	Y	24660 FQ	36280 AW	51950 TQ	VIBLS	10/01-12/01
Nonfarm Animal Caretaker	Alabama	H	5.76 FQ	8.13 AW	11.62 TQ	ALBLS	10/01-12/01
	Alaska	H	7.02 FQ	9.26 AW	12.13 TQ	AKBLS	10/01-12/01
	Arizona	H	5.82 FQ	7.87 AW	10.32 TQ	AZBLS	10/01-12/01
	Arkansas	H	5.65 FQ	7.38 AW	10.57 TQ	ARBLS	10/01-12/01
	California	H	6.60 FQ	9.68 AW	15.41 TQ	CABLS	10/01-12/01
	Colorado	H	6.19 FQ	9.41 AW	13.49 TQ	COBLS	10/01-12/01
	Connecticut	H	6.69 FQ	9.92 AW	16.07 TQ	CTBLS	10/01-12/01
	Delaware	H	6.42 FQ	8.92 AW	13.05 TQ	DEBLS	10/01-12/01
	District of Columbia	H	7.01 FQ	9.43 AW	13.32 TQ	DCBLS	10/01-12/01
	Florida	H	5.85 FQ	8.34 AW	12.22 TQ	FLBLS	10/01-12/01
	Georgia	H	6.02 FQ	8.98 AW	13.40 TQ	GABLS	10/01-12/01
	Hawaii	H	7.15 FQ	11.46 AW	16.02 TQ	HIBLS	10/01-12/01
	Idaho	H	5.59 FQ	7.86 AW	12.32 TQ	IDBLS	10/01-12/01
	Illinois	H	6.15 FQ	10.60 AW	18.18 TQ	ILBLS	10/01-12/01
	Indiana	H	5.76 FQ	7.94 AW	11.74 TQ	INBLS	10/01-12/01
	Iowa	H	5.71 FQ	7.88 AW	12.27 TQ	IABLS	10/01-12/01
	Kansas	H	5.71 FQ	7.67 AW	10.83 TQ	KSBLS	10/01-12/01
	Kentucky	H	5.70 FQ	8.07 AW	11.19 TQ	KYBLS	10/01-12/01
	Louisiana	H	5.69 FQ	7.70 AW	10.64 TQ	LABLS	10/01-12/01
	Maine	H	5.92 FQ	8.17 AW	10.82 TQ	MEBLS	10/01-12/01
	Maryland	H	5.97 FQ	9.43 AW	14.12 TQ	MDBLS	10/01-12/01
	Massachusetts	H	7.02 FQ	9.89 AW	15.00 TQ	MABLS	10/01-12/01
	Michigan	H	5.80 FQ	8.69 AW	13.40 TQ	MIBLS	10/01-12/01
	Minnesota	H	5.85 FQ	8.52 AW	11.96 TQ	MNBLS	10/01-12/01

AAW	Average annual wage	AOH	Average offered, high	ASH	Average starting, high	H	Hourly	M	Monthly	S	Special: hourly and annual
AE	Average entry wage	AOL	Average offered, low	ASL	Average starting, low	HI	Highest wage paid	MTC	Median total compensation	TQ	Third quartile wage
AEX	Average experienced wage	APH	Average pay, high range	AW	Average wage paid	HR	High end range	MW	Median wage paid	W	Weekly
AO	Average offered	APL	Average pay, low range	FQ	First quartile wage	LR	Low end range	SQ	Second quartile wage	Y	Yearly

Occupation/Type/Industry	Location	Per	Low	Mid	High	Source	Date
Nonfarm Animal Caretaker	Mississippi	H	5.77 FQ	7.76 AW	10.38 TQ	MSBLS	10/01-12/01
	Missouri	H	6.00 FQ	8.35 AW	12.01 TQ	MOBLS	10/01-12/01
	Montana	H	5.63 FQ	7.62 AW	11.40 TQ	MTBLS	10/01-12/01
	Nebraska	H	5.78 FQ	8.32 AW	11.57 TQ	NEBLS	10/01-12/01
	Nevada	H	6.06 FQ	9.25 AW	13.57 TQ	NVBLS	10/01-12/01
	New Hampshire	H	6.01 FQ	8.72 AW	12.65 TQ	NHBLS	10/01-12/01
	New Jersey	H	5.96 FQ	8.68 AW	12.24 TQ	NJBLS	10/01-12/01
	New Mexico	H	6.10 FQ	9.69 AW	14.25 TQ	NMBLS	10/01-12/01
	New York	H	5.90 FQ	8.96 AW	13.67 TQ	NYBLS	10/01-12/01
	North Carolina	H	6.09 FQ	9.04 AW	12.73 TQ	NCBLS	10/01-12/01
	North Dakota	H	5.71 FQ	7.66 AW	10.97 TQ	NDBLS	10/01-12/01
	Ohio	H	5.90 FQ	8.41 AW	12.34 TQ	OHBLS	10/01-12/01
	Oklahoma	H	5.89 FQ	8.69 AW	12.84 TQ	OKBLS	10/01-12/01
	Oregon	H	6.94 FQ	9.56 AW	14.97 TQ	ORBLS	10/01-12/01
	Pennsylvania	H	5.77 FQ	8.00 AW	10.86 TQ	PABLS	10/01-12/01
	Rhode Island	H	6.67 FQ	9.21 AW	14.84 TQ	RIBLS	10/01-12/01
	South Carolina	H	5.82 FQ	7.81 AW	10.33 TQ	SCBLS	10/01-12/01
	South Dakota	H	5.65 FQ	7.86 AW	11.10 TQ	SDBLS	10/01-12/01
	Tennessee	H	5.86 FQ	8.48 AW	12.97 TQ	TNBLS	10/01-12/01
	Texas	H	5.79 FQ	8.18 AW	12.25 TQ	TXBLS	10/01-12/01
	Utah	H	6.07 FQ	9.07 AW	12.77 TQ	UTBLS	10/01-12/01
	Vermont	H	6.47 FQ	8.69 AW	12.00 TQ	VTBLS	10/01-12/01
	Virginia	H	5.97 FQ	8.53 AW	11.67 TQ	VABLS	10/01-12/01
	Washington	H	6.94 FQ	10.35 AW	17.57 TQ	WABLS	10/01-12/01
	West Virginia	H	5.61 FQ	7.06 AW	9.16 TQ	WVBLS	10/01-12/01
	Wisconsin	H	5.96 FQ	9.01 AW	14.22 TQ	WIBLS	10/01-12/01
	Wyoming	H	6.10 FQ	8.82 AW	11.06 TQ	WYBLS	10/01-12/01
	Puerto Rico	H	5.59 FQ	6.46 AW	7.86 TQ	PRBLS	10/01-12/01
Nuclear Engineer	Alabama	Y	54340 FQ	79020 AW	104770 TQ	ALBLS	10/01-12/01
	California	Y	66640 FQ	86350 AW	112620 TQ	CABLS	10/01-12/01
	Connecticut	Y	61140 FQ	81900 AW	108380 TQ	CTBLS	10/01-12/01
	Florida	Y	57610 FQ	76280 AW	95000 TQ	FLBLS	10/01-12/01
	Georgia	Y	60040 FQ	82910 AW	111840 TQ	GABLS	10/01-12/01
	Illinois	Y	57490 FQ	79870 AW	116270 TQ	ILBLS	10/01-12/01
	Kansas	Y	60290 FQ	83480 AW	114120 TQ	KSBLS	10/01-12/01
	Louisiana	Y	56980 FQ	79460 AW	103120 TQ	LABLS	10/01-12/01
	Maine	Y	43600 FQ	63740 AW	84620 TQ	MEBLS	10/01-12/01
	Maryland	Y	62280 FQ	91870 AW	121630 TQ	MDBLS	10/01-12/01
	Massachusetts	Y	56360 FQ	74310 AW	93150 TQ	MABLS	10/01-12/01
	Michigan	Y	65870 FQ	107130 AW		MIBLS	10/01-12/01
	Mississippi	Y	43150 FQ	64360 AW	87210 TQ	MSBLS	10/01-12/01
	Missouri	Y	57130 FQ	73110 AW	94750 TQ	MOBLS	10/01-12/01
	New Jersey	Y	58030 FQ	74320 AW	98820 TQ	NJBLS	10/01-12/01
	New Mexico	Y	61770 FQ	92670 AW	136270 TQ	NMBLS	10/01-12/01
	North Carolina	Y	62420 FQ	81430 AW	107440 TQ	NCBLS	10/01-12/01
	Ohio	Y	62490 FQ	80470 AW	97210 TQ	OHBLS	10/01-12/01
	Pennsylvania	Y	61690 FQ	79080 AW	96000 TQ	PABLS	10/01-12/01
	South Carolina	Y	61610 FQ	78290 AW	97450 TQ	SCBLS	10/01-12/01
	Texas	Y	60430 FQ	83510 AW	113410 TQ	TXBLS	10/01-12/01
	Virginia	Y	49380 FQ	69080 AW	92470 TQ	VABLS	10/01-12/01
	Washington	Y	48710 FQ	74540 AW	118680 TQ	WABLS	10/01-12/01
	Wisconsin	Y	57190 FQ	77710 AW	111780 TQ	WIBLS	10/01-12/01
Nuclear Medicine Technologist	Alabama	Y	31530 FQ	42420 AW	56010 TQ	ALBLS	10/01-12/01
	Arizona	Y	36370 FQ	46970 AW	56450 TQ	AZBLS	10/01-12/01
	Arkansas	Y	32420 FQ	46690 AW	61040 TQ	ARBLS	10/01-12/01
	California	Y	45870 FQ	56380 AW	70880 TQ	CABLS	10/01-12/01
	Colorado	Y	37830 FQ	46730 AW	56810 TQ	COBLS	10/01-12/01
	Connecticut	Y	44360 FQ	56940 AW	73430 TQ	CTBLS	10/01-12/01
	Delaware	Y	38770 FQ	50520 AW	66600 TQ	DEBLS	10/01-12/01
	District of Columbia	Y	37070 FQ	48990 AW	64410 TQ	DCBLS	10/01-12/01
	Florida	Y	35740 FQ	48050 AW	60650 TQ	FLBLS	10/01-12/01
	Georgia	Y	32820 FQ	46280 AW	62920 TQ	GABLS	10/01-12/01
	Hawaii	Y	41100 FQ	50730 AW	58630 TQ	HIBLS	10/01-12/01
	Illinois	Y	39120 FQ	50780 AW	64350 TQ	ILBLS	10/01-12/01
	Indiana	Y	33790 FQ	43470 AW	54890 TQ	INBLS	10/01-12/01
	Iowa	Y	27100 FQ	40470 AW	55340 TQ	IABLS	10/01-12/01
	Kansas	Y	35620 FQ	45930 AW	58820 TQ	KSBLS	10/01-12/01
	Kentucky	Y	31190 FQ	39700 AW	48060 TQ	KYBLS	10/01-12/01
	Louisiana	Y	36390 FQ	45840 AW	57310 TQ	LABLS	10/01-12/01
	Maine	Y	35730 FQ	44220 AW	55330 TQ	MEBLS	10/01-12/01
	Maryland	Y	43280 FQ	56620 AW	72460 TQ	MDBLS	10/01-12/01

AAW Average annual wage **AE** Average entry wage **AEX** Average experienced wage **AO** Average offered **AOH** Average offered, high **AOL** Average offered, low **APH** Average pay, high range **APL** Average pay, low range **ASH** Average starting, high **ASL** Average starting, low **AW** Average wage paid **FQ** First quartile wage **H** Hourly **HI** Highest wage paid **HR** High end range **LR** Low end range **M** Monthly **MTC** Median total compensation **MW** Median wage paid **SQ** Second quartile wage **S** Special: hourly and annual **TQ** Third quartile wage **W** Weekly **Y** Yearly

Occupation/Type/Industry	Location	Per	Low	Mid	High	Source	Date
Nuclear Medicine Technologist	Massachusetts	Y	37750 FQ	48970 AW	60480 TQ	MABLS	10/01-12/01
	Michigan	Y	37570 FQ	46690 AW	57510 TQ	MIBLS	10/01-12/01
	Minnesota	Y	37210 FQ	47280 AW	58210 TQ	MNBLS	10/01-12/01
	Mississippi	Y	33580 FQ	44200 AW	55720 TQ	MSBLS	10/01-12/01
	Missouri	Y	38000 FQ	47490 AW	56970 TQ	MOBLS	10/01-12/01
	Montana	Y	32350 FQ	42270 AW	53870 TQ	MTBLS	10/01-12/01
	Nebraska	Y	37680 FQ	48270 AW	61100 TQ	NEBLS	10/01-12/01
	Nevada	Y	25050 FQ	43490 AW	61010 TQ	NVBLS	10/01-12/01
	New Hampshire	Y	39500 FQ	48870 AW	58280 TQ	NHBLS	10/01-12/01
	New Jersey	Y	43930 FQ	56950 AW	73260 TQ	NJBLS	10/01-12/01
	New Mexico	Y	38350 FQ	47610 AW	58820 TQ	NMBLS	10/01-12/01
	New York	Y	38630 FQ	49640 AW	64810 TQ	NYBLS	10/01-12/01
	North Carolina	Y	15890 FQ	39430 AW	54370 TQ	NCBLS	10/01-12/01
	North Dakota	Y	31910 FQ	42590 AW	55420 TQ	NDBLS	10/01-12/01
	Ohio	Y	25710 FQ	39720 AW	52590 TQ	OHBLS	10/01-12/01
	Oklahoma	Y	34340 FQ	48220 AW	63850 TQ	OKBLS	10/01-12/01
	Oregon	Y	40380 FQ	51350 AW	63140 TQ	ORBLS	10/01-12/01
	Pennsylvania	Y	32160 FQ	42800 AW	55590 TQ	PABLS	10/01-12/01
	Rhode Island	Y	41100 FQ	53160 AW	67970 TQ	RIBLS	10/01-12/01
	South Dakota	Y	32250 FQ	41160 AW	52400 TQ	SDBLS	10/01-12/01
	Tennessee	Y	29430 FQ	40580 AW	54130 TQ	TNBLS	10/01-12/01
	Texas	Y	33630 FQ	48120 AW	68080 TQ	TXBLS	10/01-12/01
	Utah	Y	37210 FQ	45310 AW	55650 TQ	UTBLS	10/01-12/01
	Virginia	Y	37510 FQ	44860 AW	55090 TQ	VABLS	10/01-12/01
	Washington	Y	37100 FQ	51760 AW	67850 TQ	WABLS	10/01-12/01
	West Virginia	Y	30180 FQ	41380 AW	55470 TQ	WVBLS	10/01-12/01
	Wisconsin	Y	37040 FQ	48650 AW	64610 TQ	WIBLS	10/01-12/01
	Puerto Rico	Y	20000 FQ	24600 AW	28710 TQ	PRBLS	10/01-12/01
Nuclear Power Reactor Operator	Florida	H	24.50 FQ	30.07 AW	35.98 TQ	FLBLS	10/01-12/01
	Louisiana	H	23.53 FQ	28.16 AW	34.16 TQ	LABLS	10/01-12/01
	Michigan	H	23.91 FQ	29.19 AW	35.55 TQ	MIBLS	10/01-12/01
	North Carolina	H	24.58 FQ	32.17 AW	41.38 TQ	NCBLS	10/01-12/01
	Pennsylvania	H	25.22 FQ	33.04 AW	42.77 TQ	PABLS	10/01-12/01
Nuclear Technician	California	Y	32480 FQ	73400 AW	111690 TQ	CABLS	10/01-12/01
	Connecticut	Y	48050 FQ	66240 AW	88210 TQ	CTBLS	10/01-12/01
	Florida	Y	46470 FQ	57440 AW	70480 TQ	FLBLS	10/01-12/01
	Illinois	Y	50910 FQ	72480 AW	106240 TQ	ILBLS	10/01-12/01
	Louisiana	Y	49000 FQ	62870 AW	79710 TQ	LABLS	10/01-12/01
	Missouri	Y	33250 FQ	51170 AW	70110 TQ	MOBLS	10/01-12/01
	Nebraska	Y	26510 FQ	41550 AW	54830 TQ	NEBLS	10/01-12/01
	New Jersey	Y	43570 FQ	67000 AW	100590 TQ	NJBLS	10/01-12/01
	Oregon	Y	42380 FQ	58090 AW	74840 TQ	ORBLS	10/01-12/01
	Pennsylvania	Y	35680 FQ	52980 AW	79890 TQ	PABLS	10/01-12/01
	Texas	Y	59090 FQ	68350 AW	87030 TQ	TXBLS	10/01-12/01
	Washington	Y	39860 FQ	53790 AW	68440 TQ	WABLS	10/01-12/01
	Wisconsin	Y	44290 FQ	58530 AW	74010 TQ	WIBLS	10/01-12/01
Numerical Tool and Process Control Programmer	Alabama	H	10.70 FQ	15.88 AW	21.88 TQ	ALBLS	10/01-12/01
	Arizona	H	8.89 FQ	16.72 AW	27.16 TQ	AZBLS	10/01-12/01
	Arkansas	H	11.73 FQ	14.99 AW	17.80 TQ	ARBLS	10/01-12/01
	Fayetteville-Springdale-Rogers MSA, AR	H	12.45 FQ	15.00 AW	16.94 TQ	ARBLS	10/01-12/01
	California	H	13.21 FQ	21.93 AW	33.36 TQ	CABLS	10/01-12/01
	Los Angeles-Long Beach PMSA, CA	H	12.56 FQ	20.75 AW	30.21 TQ	CABLS	10/01-12/01
	Oakland PMSA, CA	H	18.53 FQ	27.98 AW	40.09 TQ	CABLS	10/01-12/01
	Orange County PMSA, CA	H	13.80 FQ	22.57 AW	36.72 TQ	CABLS	10/01-12/01
	Riverside-San Bernardino PMSA, CA	H	11.42 FQ	17.22 AW	22.56 TQ	CABLS	10/01-12/01
	Sacramento PMSA, CA	H	12.47 FQ	24.97 AW		CABLS	10/01-12/01
	San Diego MSA, CA	H	10.30 FQ	20.90 AW	31.49 TQ	CABLS	10/01-12/01
	San Francisco PMSA, CA	H	13.88 FQ	20.38 AW	29.51 TQ	CABLS	10/01-12/01
	San Jose PMSA, CA	H	15.80 FQ	24.39 AW	32.24 TQ	CABLS	10/01-12/01
	Ventura PMSA, CA	H	15.79 FQ	20.80 AW	26.16 TQ	CABLS	10/01-12/01
	Colorado	H	14.50 FQ	22.28 AW	32.92 TQ	COBLS	10/01-12/01
	Boulder-Longmont PMSA, CO	H	15.26 FQ	19.64 AW	23.71 TQ	COBLS	10/01-12/01
	Denver PMSA, CO	H	10.37 FQ	24.70 AW	34.34 TQ	COBLS	10/01-12/01
	Connecticut	H	15.30 FQ	22.63 AW	30.64 TQ	CTBLS	10/01-12/01
	Bridgeport PMSA, CT	H	14.94 FQ	22.24 AW	31.30 TQ	CTBLS	10/01-12/01

AAW	Average annual wage	**AOH**	Average offered, high	**ASH**	Average starting, high	**H**	Hourly	**M**	Monthly	**S**	Special: hourly and annual
AE	Average entry wage	**AOL**	Average offered, low	**ASL**	Average starting, low	**HI**	Highest wage paid	**MTC**	Median total compensation	**TQ**	Third quartile wage
AEX	Average experienced wage	**APH**	Average pay, high range	**AW**	Average wage paid	**HR**	High end range	**MW**	Median wage paid	**W**	Weekly
AO	Average offered	**APL**	Average pay, low range	**FQ**	First quartile wage	**LR**	Low end range	**SQ**	Second quartile wage	**Y**	Yearly

Occupation/Type/Industry	Location	Per	Low	Mid	High	Source	Date
Numerical Tool and Process Control Programmer	Hartford MSA, CT	H	15.05 FQ	22.53 AW	31.11 TQ	CTBLS	10/01-12/01
	Stamford-Norwalk PMSA, CT	H	16.64 FQ	23.55 AW	28.16 TQ	CTBLS	10/01-12/01
	Florida	H	10.84 FQ	17.48 AW	25.96 TQ	FLBLS	10/01-12/01
	Sarasota-Bradenton MSA, FL	H	11.77 FQ	14.84 AW	19.43 TQ	FLBLS	10/01-12/01
	Tampa-St. Petersburg-Clearwater MSA, FL	H	11.46 FQ	18.90 AW	26.31 TQ	FLBLS	10/01-12/01
	Georgia	H	6.50 FQ	17.05 AW	30.40 TQ	GABLS	10/01-12/01
	Atlanta MSA, GA	H	6.25 FQ	17.47 AW	32.09 TQ	GABLS	10/01-12/01
	Illinois	H	10.48 FQ	18.81 AW	27.00 TQ	ILBLS	10/01-12/01
	Chicago PMSA, IL	H	9.97 FQ	19.01 AW	27.14 TQ	ILBLS	10/01-12/01
	Peoria-Pekin MSA, IL	H	9.77 FQ	14.78 AW	20.96 TQ	ILBLS	10/01-12/01
	Rockford MSA, IL	H	15.33 FQ	20.48 AW	27.91 TQ	ILBLS	10/01-12/01
	Indiana	H	11.69 FQ	16.91 AW	22.54 TQ	INBLS	10/01-12/01
	Elkhart-Goshen MSA, IN	H	11.41 FQ	17.01 AW	25.64 TQ	INBLS	10/01-12/01
	Evansville-Henderson MSA, IN-KY	H	10.34 FQ	15.13 AW	21.16 TQ	INBLS	10/01-12/01
	Fort Wayne MSA, IN	H	12.05 FQ	16.28 AW	20.63 TQ	INBLS	10/01-12/01
	Indianapolis MSA, IN	H	11.98 FQ	19.98 AW	32.54 TQ	INBLS	10/01-12/01
	Davenport-Moline-Rock Island MSA, IA-IL	H	10.93 FQ	19.48 AW	27.18 TQ	IABLS	10/01-12/01
	Kansas	H	11.27 FQ	18.42 AW	27.08 TQ	KSBLS	10/01-12/01
	Wichita MSA, KS	H	13.65 FQ	21.92 AW	29.38 TQ	KSBLS	10/01-12/01
	Kentucky	H	11.69 FQ	16.03 AW	20.40 TQ	KYBLS	10/01-12/01
	Lexington MSA, KY	H	11.69 FQ	15.88 AW	20.56 TQ	KYBLS	10/01-12/01
	Louisville MSA, KY-IN	H	10.58 FQ	16.25 AW	21.15 TQ	KYBLS	10/01-12/01
	Louisiana	H	15.21 FQ	18.92 AW	21.60 TQ	LABLS	10/01-12/01
	Maryland	H	7.26 FQ	18.80 AW	24.65 TQ	MDBLS	10/01-12/01
	Baltimore PMSA, MD	H	17.45 FQ	20.36 AW	25.67 TQ	MDBLS	10/01-12/01
	Massachusetts	H	15.05 FQ	20.99 AW	27.36 TQ	MABLS	10/01-12/01
	Boston PMSA, MA-NH	H	15.89 FQ	22.13 AW	28.01 TQ	MABLS	10/01-12/01
	Lawrence PMSA, MA-NH	H	16.47 FQ	19.44 AW	22.11 TQ	MABLS	10/01-12/01
	Worcester PMSA, MA-CT	H	16.63 FQ	23.86 AW	32.69 TQ	MABLS	10/01-12/01
	Michigan	H	13.75 FQ	21.57 AW	28.94 TQ	MIBLS	10/01-12/01
	Ann Arbor PMSA, MI	H	10.58 FQ	20.26 AW	28.94 TQ	MIBLS	10/01-12/01
	Detroit PMSA, MI	H	18.28 FQ	24.06 AW	31.01 TQ	MIBLS	10/01-12/01
	Grand Rapids-Muskegon-Holland MSA, MI	H	14.38 FQ	19.54 AW	26.50 TQ	MIBLS	10/01-12/01
	Kalamazoo-Battle Creek MSA, MI	H	10.07 FQ	19.10 AW	27.18 TQ	MIBLS	10/01-12/01
	Lansing-East Lansing MSA, MI	H	14.56 FQ	20.39 AW	27.93 TQ	MIBLS	10/01-12/01
	Minnesota	H	14.74 FQ	20.80 AW	27.16 TQ	MNBLS	10/01-12/01
	Minneapolis-St. Paul MSA, MN-WI	H	15.78 FQ	21.69 AW	27.79 TQ	MNBLS	10/01-12/01
	Mississippi	H	11.67 FQ	15.06 AW	19.53 TQ	MSBLS	10/01-12/01
	Biloxi-Gulfport-Pascagoula MSA, MS	H	11.44 FQ	14.70 AW	18.20 TQ	MSBLS	10/01-12/01
	Missouri	H	11.64 FQ	17.97 AW	26.70 TQ	MOBLS	10/01-12/01
	Kansas City MSA, MO-KS	H	12.98 FQ	18.86 AW	25.21 TQ	MOBLS	10/01-12/01
	St. Louis MSA, MO-IL	H	11.49 FQ	21.26 AW	33.56 TQ	MOBLS	10/01-12/01
	New Hampshire	H	11.15 FQ	16.79 AW	22.22 TQ	NHBLS	10/01-12/01
	Nashua PMSA, NH	H	6.16 FQ	17.04 AW	26.55 TQ	NHBLS	10/01-12/01
	Portsmouth-Rochester PMSA, NH-ME	H	12.78 FQ	17.24 AW	23.43 TQ	NHBLS	10/01-12/01
	New Jersey	H	14.81 FQ	23.12 AW	33.16 TQ	NJBLS	10/01-12/01
	Bergen-Passaic PMSA, NJ	H	18.97 FQ	25.96 AW	40.78 TQ	NJBLS	10/01-12/01
	Newark PMSA, NJ	H	13.18 FQ	21.70 AW	32.05 TQ	NJBLS	10/01-12/01
	New York	H	9.69 FQ	17.15 AW	27.08 TQ	NYBLS	10/01-12/01
	Buffalo-Niagara Falls MSA, NY	H	6.10 FQ	13.61 AW	21.20 TQ	NYBLS	10/01-12/01
	Nassau-Suffolk PMSA, NY	H	10.21 FQ	20.22 AW	34.60 TQ	NYBLS	10/01-12/01
	New York PMSA, NY	H	13.36 FQ	22.54 AW	31.51 TQ	NYBLS	10/01-12/01
	Rochester MSA, NY	H	14.58 FQ	20.00 AW	26.30 TQ	NYBLS	10/01-12/01
	Syracuse MSA, NY	H	9.23 FQ	13.96 AW	20.22 TQ	NYBLS	10/01-12/01
	Utica-Rome MSA, NY	H	12.35 FQ	23.43 AW	32.84 TQ	NYBLS	10/01-12/01
	North Carolina	H	6.43 FQ	13.63 AW	21.01 TQ	NCBLS	10/01-12/01
	Asheville MSA, NC	H	14.21 FQ	16.04 AW	17.72 TQ	NCBLS	10/01-12/01
	Charlotte-Gastonia-Rock Hill MSA, NC-SC	H	8.40 FQ	15.91 AW	22.60 TQ	NCBLS	10/01-12/01
	Greensboro-Winston-Salem-High Point MSA, NC	H	11.32 FQ	17.37 AW	24.80 TQ	NCBLS	10/01-12/01

AAW	Average annual wage	**AOH**	Average offered, high	**ASH**	Average starting, high	**H**	Hourly	**M**	Monthly	**S**	Special: hourly and annual
AE	Average entry wage	**AOL**	Average offered, low	**ASL**	Average starting, low	**HI**	Highest wage paid	**MTC**	Median total compensation	**TQ**	Third quartile wage
AEX	Average experienced wage	**APH**	Average pay, high range	**AW**	Average wage paid	**HR**	High end range	**MW**	Median wage paid	**W**	Weekly
AO	Average offered	**APL**	Average pay, low range	**FQ**	First quartile wage	**LR**	Low end range	**SQ**	Second quartile wage	**Y**	Yearly

Occupation/Type/Industry	Location	Per	Low	Mid	High	Source	Date
Numerical Tool and Process Control Programmer	Raleigh-Durham-Chapel Hill MSA, NC	H	15.93 FQ	19.84 AW	24.19 TQ	NCBLS	10/01-12/01
	Ohio	H	10.99 FQ	17.51 AW	24.40 TQ	OHBLS	10/01-12/01
	Akron PMSA, OH	H	14.44 FQ	18.96 AW	25.70 TQ	OHBLS	10/01-12/01
	Canton-Massillon MSA, OH	H	13.24 FQ	17.90 AW	21.96 TQ	OHBLS	10/01-12/01
	Cincinnati PMSA, OH-KY-IN	H	13.54 FQ	17.29 AW	22.91 TQ	OHBLS	10/01-12/01
	Cleveland-Lorain-Elyria PMSA, OH	H	13.79 FQ	18.76 AW	25.87 TQ	OHBLS	10/01-12/01
	Columbus MSA, OH	H	11.13 FQ	16.54 AW	21.19 TQ	OHBLS	10/01-12/01
	Dayton-Springfield MSA, OH	H	9.20 FQ	17.91 AW	25.84 TQ	OHBLS	10/01-12/01
	Youngstown-Warren MSA, OH	H	12.50 FQ	15.72 AW	20.34 TQ	OHBLS	10/01-12/01
	Oklahoma	H	7.81 FQ	15.66 AW	22.46 TQ	OKBLS	10/01-12/01
	Tulsa MSA, OK	H	14.55 FQ	17.85 AW	22.26 TQ	OKBLS	10/01-12/01
	Oregon	H	15.70 FQ	22.91 AW	33.57 TQ	ORBLS	10/01-12/01
	Portland-Vancouver PMSA, OR-WA	H	15.99 FQ	24.10 AW	34.43 TQ	ORBLS	10/01-12/01
	Pennsylvania	H	9.06 FQ	17.04 AW	25.88 TQ	PABLS	10/01-12/01
	Allentown-Bethlehem-Easton MSA, PA	H	12.39 FQ	19.08 AW	26.73 TQ	PABLS	10/01-12/01
	Erie MSA, PA	H	11.52 FQ	15.59 AW	21.52 TQ	PABLS	10/01-12/01
	Philadelphia PMSA, PA-NJ	H	7.66 FQ	18.45 AW	30.00 TQ	PABLS	10/01-12/01
	Pittsburgh MSA, PA	H	11.18 FQ	17.89 AW	25.82 TQ	PABLS	10/01-12/01
	Scranton-Wilkes-Barre-Hazleton MSA, PA	H	11.59 FQ	17.43 AW	25.96 TQ	PABLS	10/01-12/01
	York MSA, PA	H	14.59 FQ	19.92 AW	26.71 TQ	PABLS	10/01-12/01
	Rhode Island	H	13.65 FQ	18.08 AW	22.23 TQ	RIBLS	10/01-12/01
	Providence-Fall River-Warwick MSA, RI-MA	H	13.07 FQ	18.19 AW	24.20 TQ	RIBLS	10/01-12/01
	South Carolina	H	11.95 FQ	16.90 AW	22.47 TQ	SCBLS	10/01-12/01
	Greenville-Spartanburg-Anderson MSA, SC	H	13.15 FQ	17.52 AW	22.55 TQ	SCBLS	10/01-12/01
	South Dakota	H	8.40 FQ	13.56 AW	18.20 TQ	SDBLS	10/01-12/01
	Tennessee	H	11.01 FQ	17.60 AW	22.96 TQ	TNBLS	10/01-12/01
	Johnson City-Kingsport-Bristol MSA, TN-VA	H	11.11 FQ	15.26 AW	21.31 TQ	TNBLS	10/01-12/01
	Nashville MSA, TN	H	14.52 FQ	19.43 AW	24.86 TQ	TNBLS	10/01-12/01
	Texas	H	11.67 FQ	18.54 AW	26.23 TQ	TXBLS	10/01-12/01
	Austin-San Marcos MSA, TX	H	9.47 FQ	16.44 AW	26.64 TQ	TXBLS	10/01-12/01
	Dallas PMSA, TX	H	10.44 FQ	17.32 AW	22.31 TQ	TXBLS	10/01-12/01
	El Paso MSA, TX	H	8.80 FQ	15.77 AW	20.58 TQ	TXBLS	10/01-12/01
	Fort Worth-Arlington PMSA, TX	H	14.63 FQ	18.20 AW	25.09 TQ	TXBLS	10/01-12/01
	Houston PMSA, TX	H	13.40 FQ	21.12 AW	27.62 TQ	TXBLS	10/01-12/01
	Utah	H	12.70 FQ	16.98 AW	22.71 TQ	UTBLS	10/01-12/01
	Salt Lake City-Ogden MSA, UT	H	12.54 FQ	16.38 AW	21.48 TQ	UTBLS	10/01-12/01
	Vermont	H	11.26 FQ	15.86 AW	21.29 TQ	VTBLS	10/01-12/01
	Virginia	H	11.44 FQ	16.82 AW	22.64 TQ	VABLS	10/01-12/01
	Norfolk-Virginia Beach-Newport News MSA, VA-NC	H	16.30 FQ	20.17 AW	25.38 TQ	VABLS	10/01-12/01
	Washington	H	14.72 FQ	21.54 AW	32.24 TQ	WABLS	10/01-12/01
	Seattle-Bellevue-Everett PMSA, WA	H	14.98 FQ	21.32 AW	31.24 TQ	WABLS	10/01-12/01
	West Virginia	H	12.01 FQ	17.44 AW	25.18 TQ	WVBLS	10/01-12/01
	Wisconsin	H	13.12 FQ	19.93 AW	28.21 TQ	WIBLS	10/01-12/01
	Appleton-Oshkosh-Neenah MSA, WI	H	14.95 FQ	18.42 AW	21.24 TQ	WIBLS	10/01-12/01
	Madison MSA, WI	H	11.38 FQ	15.23 AW	21.06 TQ	WIBLS	10/01-12/01
	Milwaukee-Waukesha PMSA, WI	H	12.74 FQ	21.43 AW	30.01 TQ	WIBLS	10/01-12/01
	Racine PMSA, WI	H	15.01 FQ	20.59 AW	28.40 TQ	WIBLS	10/01-12/01
Nurse	United States	Y	34682 AE			TIME	1/00-1/01
	East North Central	Y		43702 AW		NURSE	1/99-1/00
	East South Central	Y		38456 AW		NURSE	1/99-1/00
	Middle Atlantic	Y		44329 AW		NURSE	1/99-1/00
	Mountain	Y		42351 AW		NURSE	1/99-1/00
	New England	Y		43102 AW		NURSE	1/99-1/00
	Pacific	Y		49088 AW		NURSE	1/99-1/00
	South Atlantic	Y		42847 AW		NURSE	1/99-1/00

AAW	Average annual wage	**AOH**	Average offered, high	**ASH**	Average starting, high	**H**	Hourly	**M**	Monthly	**S**	Special: hourly and annual
AE	Average entry wage	**AOL**	Average offered, low	**ASL**	Average starting, low	**HI**	Highest wage paid	**MTC**	Median total compensation	**TQ**	Third quartile wage
AEX	Average experienced wage	**APH**	Average pay, high range	**AW**	Average wage paid	**HR**	High end range	**MW**	Median wage paid	**W**	Weekly
AO	Average offered	**APL**	Average pay, low range	**FQ**	First quartile wage	**LR**	Low end range	**SQ**	Second quartile wage	**Y**	Yearly

Occupation/Type/Industry	Location	Per	Low	Mid	High	Source	Date
Nurse	West North Central	Y		39656 AW		NURSE	1/99-1/00
	West South Central	Y		41024 AW		NURSE	1/99-1/00
	Long Island, NY	Y	45000-60000 AE			LIBN	1/01-1/02
	Seattle, WA	Y		49016 AW		KRTNS	1/01-1/02
Nurse Anesthetist	United States	Y	90000 ASL	118000 AW	180000 ASH	USATOD3	1/01-1/02
	Machias, ME	Y		110000 AW		USATOD3	1/01-1/02
	Minneapolis-St. Paul, MN	Y		110000-130000 AW		USATOD3	1/01-1/02
Nurse Practitioner	United States	Y	53000 ASL	65000 AW	80000 ASH	USATOD3	1/01-1/02
Family Planning	United States	Y		55710 AW	55313 MW	CTU	1/01-1/02
Nursing Aide, Orderly, and Attendant	Alabama	H	5.97 FQ	7.90 AW	10.21 TQ	ALBLS	10/01-12/01
	Birmingham MSA, AL	H	7.10 FQ	8.64 AW	10.71 TQ	ALBLS	10/01-12/01
	Huntsville MSA, AL	H	5.82 FQ	7.66 AW	9.96 TQ	ALBLS	10/01-12/01
	Mobile MSA, AL	H	5.88 FQ	7.71 AW	9.85 TQ	ALBLS	10/01-12/01
	Montgomery MSA, AL	H	6.49 FQ	8.52 AW	11.00 TQ	ALBLS	10/01-12/01
	Alaska	H	10.77 FQ	13.06 AW	16.30 TQ	AKBLS	10/01-12/01
	Anchorage MSA, AK	H	10.22 FQ	12.37 AW	14.50 TQ	AKBLS	10/01-12/01
	Arizona	H	7.00 FQ	9.33 AW	12.12 TQ	AZBLS	10/01-12/01
	Phoenix-Mesa MSA, AZ	H	7.22 FQ	9.55 AW	12.45 TQ	AZBLS	10/01-12/01
	Tucson MSA, AZ	H	6.88 FQ	9.27 AW	11.52 TQ	AZBLS	10/01-12/01
	Arkansas	H	5.86 FQ	7.60 AW	9.93 TQ	ARBLS	10/01-12/01
	Fayetteville-Springdale-Rogers MSA, AR	H	6.53 FQ	8.51 AW	10.70 TQ	ARBLS	10/01-12/01
	Fort Smith MSA, AR-OK	H	5.64 FQ	7.12 AW	9.34 TQ	ARBLS	10/01-12/01
	Little Rock-North Little Rock MSA, AR	H	6.37 FQ	8.45 AW	10.93 TQ	ARBLS	10/01-12/01
	California	H	7.44 FQ	10.15 AW	13.77 TQ	CABLS	10/01-12/01
	Bakersfield MSA, CA	H	7.09 FQ	8.88 AW	10.84 TQ	CABLS	10/01-12/01
	Chico-Paradise MSA, CA	H	7.36 FQ	9.86 AW	12.44 TQ	CABLS	10/01-12/01
	Fresno MSA, CA	H	7.02 FQ	9.06 AW	12.21 TQ	CABLS	10/01-12/01
	Los Angeles-Long Beach PMSA, CA	H	7.31 FQ	9.61 AW	13.04 TQ	CABLS	10/01-12/01
	Merced MSA, CA	H	7.31 FQ	8.42 AW	10.18 TQ	CABLS	10/01-12/01
	Modesto MSA, CA	H	7.46 FQ	9.36 AW	11.52 TQ	CABLS	10/01-12/01
	Oakland PMSA, CA	H	9.02 FQ	12.53 AW	16.18 TQ	CABLS	10/01-12/01
	Orange County PMSA, CA	H	7.83 FQ	10.03 AW	12.88 TQ	CABLS	10/01-12/01
	Redding MSA, CA	H	7.55 FQ	9.49 AW	11.94 TQ	CABLS	10/01-12/01
	Riverside-San Bernardino PMSA, CA	H	7.14 FQ	9.49 AW	12.61 TQ	CABLS	10/01-12/01
	Sacramento PMSA, CA	H	7.59 FQ	10.33 AW	13.32 TQ	CABLS	10/01-12/01
	Salinas MSA, CA	H	7.88 FQ	10.11 AW	13.28 TQ	CABLS	10/01-12/01
	San Diego MSA, CA	H	7.48 FQ	10.01 AW	13.22 TQ	CABLS	10/01-12/01
	San Francisco PMSA, CA	H	8.88 FQ	12.30 AW	16.35 TQ	CABLS	10/01-12/01
	San Jose PMSA, CA	H	8.65 FQ	11.75 AW	15.90 TQ	CABLS	10/01-12/01
	Santa Barbara-Santa Maria-Lompoc MSA, CA	H	7.55 FQ	10.00 AW	13.01 TQ	CABLS	10/01-12/01
	Santa Cruz-Watsonville PMSA, CA	H	8.54 FQ	11.50 AW	18.89 TQ	CABLS	10/01-12/01
	Santa Rosa PMSA, CA	H	8.92 FQ	11.17 AW	13.68 TQ	CABLS	10/01-12/01
	Stockton-Lodi MSA, CA	H	7.40 FQ	9.54 AW	11.77 TQ	CABLS	10/01-12/01
	Vallejo-Fairfield-Napa PMSA, CA	H	7.89 FQ	11.02 AW	14.55 TQ	CABLS	10/01-12/01
	Ventura PMSA, CA	H	7.58 FQ	9.93 AW	12.79 TQ	CABLS	10/01-12/01
	Visalia-Tulare-Porterville MSA, CA	H	6.93 FQ	8.45 AW	10.45 TQ	CABLS	10/01-12/01
	Colorado	H	7.60 FQ	10.14 AW	13.20 TQ	COBLS	10/01-12/01
	Boulder-Longmont PMSA, CO	H	8.22 FQ	10.65 AW	13.51 TQ	COBLS	10/01-12/01
	Colorado Springs MSA, CO	H	7.76 FQ	9.83 AW	12.34 TQ	COBLS	10/01-12/01
	Denver PMSA, CO	H	8.82 FQ	10.88 AW	13.56 TQ	COBLS	10/01-12/01
	Fort Collins-Loveland MSA, CO	H	7.61 FQ	9.91 AW	13.30 TQ	COBLS	10/01-12/01
	Greeley PMSA, CO	H	7.61 FQ	9.50 AW	11.57 TQ	COBLS	10/01-12/01
	Connecticut	H	9.77 FQ	12.37 AW	15.21 TQ	CTBLS	10/01-12/01
	Bridgeport PMSA, CT	H	9.82 FQ	12.30 AW	14.51 TQ	CTBLS	10/01-12/01
	Danbury PMSA, CT	H	9.22 FQ	12.14 AW	15.25 TQ	CTBLS	10/01-12/01
	Hartford MSA, CT	H	9.95 FQ	12.59 AW	15.69 TQ	CTBLS	10/01-12/01

AAW Average annual wage; **AE** Average entry wage; **AEX** Average experienced wage; **AO** Average offered; **AOH** Average offered, high; **AOL** Average offered, low; **APH** Average pay, high range; **APL** Average pay, low range; **ASH** Average starting, high; **ASL** Average starting, low; **AW** Average wage paid; **FQ** First quartile wage; **H** Hourly; **HI** Highest wage paid; **HR** High end range; **LR** Low end range; **M** Monthly; **MTC** Median total compensation; **MW** Median wage paid; **SQ** Second quartile wage; **S** Special: hourly and annual; **TQ** Third quartile wage; **W** Weekly; **Y** Yearly

Occupation/Type/Industry	Location	Per	Low	Mid	High	Source	Date
Nursing Aide, Orderly, and Attendant	New Haven-Meriden PMSA, CT	H	9.95 FQ	12.42 AW	14.90 TQ	CTBLS	10/01-12/01
	New London-Norwich MSA, CT-RI	H	9.28 FQ	11.46 AW	13.98 TQ	CTBLS	10/01-12/01
	Stamford-Norwalk PMSA, CT	H	9.77 FQ	12.37 AW	15.31 TQ	CTBLS	10/01-12/01
	Waterbury PMSA, CT	H	10.02 FQ	12.64 AW	15.65 TQ	CTBLS	10/01-12/01
	Delaware	H	7.91 FQ	10.81 AW	13.82 TQ	DEBLS	10/01-12/01
	Wilmington-Newark PMSA, DE-MD	H	8.14 FQ	10.98 AW	14.44 TQ	DEBLS	10/01-12/01
	District of Columbia	H	7.65 FQ	10.53 AW	13.89 TQ	DCBLS	10/01-12/01
	Washington PMSA, DC-MD-VA-WV	H	7.84 FQ	10.72 AW	14.48 TQ	DCBLS	10/01-12/01
	Florida	H	7.15 FQ	9.05 AW	11.28 TQ	FLBLS	10/01-12/01
	Daytona Beach MSA, FL	H	7.29 FQ	9.13 AW	11.16 TQ	FLBLS	10/01-12/01
	Fort Lauderdale PMSA, FL	H	7.08 FQ	8.96 AW	11.13 TQ	FLBLS	10/01-12/01
	Fort Myers-Cape Coral MSA, FL	H	6.92 FQ	8.82 AW	11.79 TQ	FLBLS	10/01-12/01
	Fort Pierce-Port St. Lucie MSA, FL	H	7.49 FQ	9.06 AW	11.17 TQ	FLBLS	10/01-12/01
	Fort Walton Beach MSA, FL	H	6.37 FQ	8.18 AW	10.50 TQ	FLBLS	10/01-12/01
	Gainesville MSA, FL	H	6.99 FQ	8.69 AW	10.92 TQ	FLBLS	10/01-12/01
	Jacksonville MSA, FL	H	7.43 FQ	9.31 AW	11.45 TQ	FLBLS	10/01-12/01
	Lakeland-Winter Haven MSA, FL	H	7.21 FQ	9.50 AW	11.97 TQ	FLBLS	10/01-12/01
	Melbourne-Titusville-Palm Bay MSA, FL	H	7.15 FQ	8.77 AW	10.76 TQ	FLBLS	10/01-12/01
	Miami PMSA, FL	H	6.66 FQ	8.74 AW	11.15 TQ	FLBLS	10/01-12/01
	Naples MSA, FL	H	7.53 FQ	9.17 AW	11.66 TQ	FLBLS	10/01-12/01
	Ocala MSA, FL	H	7.36 FQ	9.37 AW	11.80 TQ	FLBLS	10/01-12/01
	Orlando MSA, FL	H	7.37 FQ	9.06 AW	11.27 TQ	FLBLS	10/01-12/01
	Pensacola MSA, FL	H	6.81 FQ	8.46 AW	10.84 TQ	FLBLS	10/01-12/01
	Sarasota-Bradenton MSA, FL	H	7.54 FQ	9.33 AW	11.22 TQ	FLBLS	10/01-12/01
	Tallahassee MSA, FL	H	6.93 FQ	8.71 AW	10.97 TQ	FLBLS	10/01-12/01
	Tampa-St. Petersburg-Clearwater MSA, FL	H	7.41 FQ	9.52 AW	11.57 TQ	FLBLS	10/01-12/01
	West Palm Beach-Boca Raton MSA, FL	H	7.18 FQ	8.88 AW	11.16 TQ	FLBLS	10/01-12/01
	Georgia	H	6.01 FQ	8.37 AW	11.12 TQ	GABLS	10/01-12/01
	Atlanta MSA, GA	H	7.34 FQ	9.54 AW	12.87 TQ	GABLS	10/01-12/01
	Augusta-Aiken MSA, GA-SC	H	5.85 FQ	7.98 AW	10.63 TQ	GABLS	10/01-12/01
	Columbus MSA, GA-AL	H	5.98 FQ	7.88 AW	10.29 TQ	GABLS	10/01-12/01
	Macon MSA, GA	H	5.93 FQ	7.91 AW	10.46 TQ	GABLS	10/01-12/01
	Savannah MSA, GA	H	6.04 FQ	7.27 AW	8.42 TQ	GABLS	10/01-12/01
	Hawaii	H	9.03 FQ	11.04 AW	13.64 TQ	HIBLS	10/01-12/01
	Honolulu MSA, HI	H	9.05 FQ	10.99 AW	13.54 TQ	HIBLS	10/01-12/01
	Idaho	H	6.26 FQ	8.38 AW	10.68 TQ	IDBLS	10/01-12/01
	Boise City MSA, ID	H	7.05 FQ	8.91 AW	10.79 TQ	IDBLS	10/01-12/01
	Illinois	H	6.59 FQ	9.20 AW	12.46 TQ	ILBLS	10/01-12/01
	Champaign-Urbana MSA, IL	H	7.75 FQ	10.06 AW	12.61 TQ	ILBLS	10/01-12/01
	Chicago PMSA, IL	H	6.52 FQ	9.45 AW	12.94 TQ	ILBLS	10/01-12/01
	Peoria-Pekin MSA, IL	H	7.18 FQ	9.45 AW	12.75 TQ	ILBLS	10/01-12/01
	Rockford MSA, IL	H	7.32 FQ	9.59 AW	12.36 TQ	ILBLS	10/01-12/01
	Springfield MSA, IL	H	6.14 FQ	8.32 AW	11.37 TQ	ILBLS	10/01-12/01
	Indiana	H	7.15 FQ	9.51 AW	12.53 TQ	INBLS	10/01-12/01
	Elkhart-Goshen MSA, IN	H	7.59 FQ	9.90 AW	12.62 TQ	INBLS	10/01-12/01
	Evansville-Henderson MSA, IN-KY	H	7.25 FQ	8.99 AW	11.03 TQ	INBLS	10/01-12/01
	Fort Wayne MSA, IN	H	7.62 FQ	9.59 AW	11.29 TQ	INBLS	10/01-12/01
	Gary PMSA, IN	H	6.95 FQ	8.86 AW	11.22 TQ	INBLS	10/01-12/01
	Indianapolis MSA, IN	H	7.71 FQ	10.25 AW	13.17 TQ	INBLS	10/01-12/01
	Lafayette MSA, IN	H	7.67 FQ	11.27 AW	16.23 TQ	INBLS	10/01-12/01
	South Bend MSA, IN	H	6.23 FQ	9.14 AW	11.36 TQ	INBLS	10/01-12/01
	Iowa	H	7.48 FQ	9.42 AW	11.61 TQ	IABLS	10/01-12/01
	Cedar Rapids MSA, IA	H	8.21 FQ	10.11 AW	12.06 TQ	IABLS	10/01-12/01
	Davenport-Moline-Rock Island MSA, IA-IL	H	7.50 FQ	9.84 AW	13.12 TQ	IABLS	10/01-12/01
	Des Moines MSA, IA	H	8.23 FQ	10.64 AW	13.84 TQ	IABLS	10/01-12/01
	Kansas	H	7.02 FQ	8.86 AW	11.11 TQ	KSBLS	10/01-12/01
	Topeka MSA, KS	H	7.26 FQ	9.03 AW	11.53 TQ	KSBLS	10/01-12/01
	Wichita MSA, KS	H	7.51 FQ	9.30 AW	11.15 TQ	KSBLS	10/01-12/01
	Kentucky	H	6.19 FQ	8.60 AW	11.21 TQ	KYBLS	10/01-12/01

AAW	Average annual wage	**AOH**	Average offered, high	**ASH**	Average starting, high	**H**	Hourly	**M**	Monthly	**S**	Special: hourly and annual
AE	Average entry wage	**AOL**	Average offered, low	**ASL**	Average starting, low	**HI**	Highest wage paid	**MTC**	Median total compensation	**TQ**	Third quartile wage
AEX	Average experienced wage	**APH**	Average pay, high range	**AW**	Average wage paid	**HR**	High end range	**MW**	Median wage paid	**W**	Weekly
AO	Average offered	**APL**	Average pay, low range	**FQ**	First quartile wage	**LR**	Low end range	**SQ**	Second quartile wage	**Y**	Yearly

Occupation/Type/Industry	Location	Per	Low	Mid	High	Source	Date
Nursing Aide, Orderly, and Attendant	Lexington MSA, KY	H	7.60 FQ	9.70 AW	12.19 TQ	KYBLS	10/01-12/01
	Louisville MSA, KY-IN	H	7.43 FQ	9.63 AW	12.04 TQ	KYBLS	10/01-12/01
	Louisiana	H	5.69 FQ	6.89 AW	8.92 TQ	LABLS	10/01-12/01
	Baton Rouge MSA, LA	H	5.66 FQ	6.92 AW	9.07 TQ	LABLS	10/01-12/01
	Houma MSA, LA	H	5.59 FQ	6.49 AW	8.10 TQ	LABLS	10/01-12/01
	Lafayette MSA, LA	H	5.62 FQ	6.36 AW	7.25 TQ	LABLS	10/01-12/01
	Lake Charles MSA, LA	H	5.68 FQ	6.68 AW	8.27 TQ	LABLS	10/01-12/01
	New Orleans MSA, LA	H	5.79 FQ	7.25 AW	9.56 TQ	LABLS	10/01-12/01
	Shreveport-Bossier City MSA, LA	H	5.66 FQ	6.80 AW	8.82 TQ	LABLS	10/01-12/01
	Maine	H	7.33 FQ	9.37 AW	11.57 TQ	MEBLS	10/01-12/01
	Portland MSA, ME	H	8.27 FQ	10.15 AW	12.46 TQ	MEBLS	10/01-12/01
	Maryland	H	7.70 FQ	10.95 AW	15.48 TQ	MDBLS	10/01-12/01
	Baltimore PMSA, MD	H	7.70 FQ	11.12 AW	15.82 TQ	MDBLS	10/01-12/01
	Massachusetts	H	8.92 FQ	11.36 AW	14.40 TQ	MABLS	10/01-12/01
	Boston PMSA, MA-NH	H	9.12 FQ	11.55 AW	14.50 TQ	MABLS	10/01-12/01
	Brockton PMSA, MA	H	9.37 FQ	11.82 AW	15.50 TQ	MABLS	10/01-12/01
	Lawrence PMSA, MA-NH	H	9.34 FQ	11.86 AW	14.50 TQ	MABLS	10/01-12/01
	Lowell PMSA, MA-NH	H	9.24 FQ	11.27 AW	14.49 TQ	MABLS	10/01-12/01
	New Bedford PMSA, MA	H	7.63 FQ	10.15 AW	13.27 TQ	MABLS	10/01-12/01
	Springfield MSA, MA	H	8.58 FQ	11.12 AW	14.57 TQ	MABLS	10/01-12/01
	Worcester PMSA, MA-CT	H	8.86 FQ	11.33 AW	14.27 TQ	MABLS	10/01-12/01
	Michigan	H	7.95 FQ	10.17 AW	12.85 TQ	MIBLS	10/01-12/01
	Ann Arbor PMSA, MI	H	9.25 FQ	10.86 AW	13.33 TQ	MIBLS	10/01-12/01
	Detroit PMSA, MI	H	8.54 FQ	10.51 AW	13.07 TQ	MIBLS	10/01-12/01
	Flint PMSA, MI	H	7.52 FQ	9.84 AW	12.84 TQ	MIBLS	10/01-12/01
	Grand Rapids-Muskegon-Holland MSA, MI	H	8.59 FQ	10.43 AW	13.00 TQ	MIBLS	10/01-12/01
	Kalamazoo-Battle Creek MSA, MI	H	7.66 FQ	9.90 AW	12.66 TQ	MIBLS	10/01-12/01
	Lansing-East Lansing MSA, MI	H	8.15 FQ	9.98 AW	12.21 TQ	MIBLS	10/01-12/01
	Saginaw-Bay City-Midland MSA, MI	H	7.83 FQ	10.21 AW	13.40 TQ	MIBLS	10/01-12/01
	Minnesota	H	8.22 FQ	10.88 AW	13.84 TQ	MNBLS	10/01-12/01
	Duluth-Superior MSA, MN-WI	H	7.85 FQ	10.45 AW	13.43 TQ	MNBLS	10/01-12/01
	Minneapolis-St. Paul MSA, MN-WI	H	9.46 FQ	11.89 AW	14.37 TQ	MNBLS	10/01-12/01
	St. Cloud MSA, MN	H	7.59 FQ	9.76 AW	12.14 TQ	MNBLS	10/01-12/01
	Mississippi	H	5.76 FQ	7.42 AW	9.73 TQ	MSBLS	10/01-12/01
	Biloxi-Gulfport-Pascagoula MSA, MS	H	6.05 FQ	8.60 AW	12.16 TQ	MSBLS	10/01-12/01
	Jackson MSA, MS	H	5.98 FQ	7.92 AW	10.22 TQ	MSBLS	10/01-12/01
	Missouri	H	6.21 FQ	8.45 AW	11.02 TQ	MOBLS	10/01-12/01
	Kansas City MSA, MO-KS	H	7.66 FQ	9.81 AW	12.56 TQ	MOBLS	10/01-12/01
	St. Louis MSA, MO-IL	H	7.17 FQ	9.07 AW	11.42 TQ	MOBLS	10/01-12/01
	Springfield MSA, MO	H	6.07 FQ	8.28 AW	10.80 TQ	MOBLS	10/01-12/01
	Montana	H	6.27 FQ	8.20 AW	10.55 TQ	MTBLS	10/01-12/01
	Billings MSA, MT	H	7.08 FQ	8.93 AW	11.53 TQ	MTBLS	10/01-12/01
	Nebraska	H	7.22 FQ	9.36 AW	12.08 TQ	NEBLS	10/01-12/01
	Lincoln MSA, NE	H	8.02 FQ	9.97 AW	12.31 TQ	NEBLS	10/01-12/01
	Omaha MSA, NE-IA	H	8.64 FQ	10.49 AW	13.01 TQ	NEBLS	10/01-12/01
	Nevada	H	8.12 FQ	10.75 AW	13.55 TQ	NVBLS	10/01-12/01
	Las Vegas MSA, NV-AZ	H	7.64 FQ	10.46 AW	13.40 TQ	NVBLS	10/01-12/01
	Reno MSA, NV	H	8.87 FQ	11.05 AW	13.78 TQ	NVBLS	10/01-12/01
	New Hampshire	H	8.65 FQ	10.82 AW	13.64 TQ	NHBLS	10/01-12/01
	Manchester PMSA, NH	H	9.03 FQ	11.22 AW	14.14 TQ	NHBLS	10/01-12/01
	Nashua PMSA, NH	H	9.23 FQ	11.36 AW	13.79 TQ	NHBLS	10/01-12/01
	Portsmouth-Rochester PMSA, NH-ME	H	8.55 FQ	10.48 AW	13.19 TQ	NHBLS	10/01-12/01
	New Jersey	H	8.41 FQ	10.84 AW	13.91 TQ	NJBLS	10/01-12/01
	Atlantic-Cape May PMSA, NJ	H	7.05 FQ	9.66 AW	12.40 TQ	NJBLS	10/01-12/01
	Bergen-Passaic PMSA, NJ	H	8.64 FQ	11.13 AW	14.28 TQ	NJBLS	10/01-12/01
	Jersey City PMSA, NJ	H	8.69 FQ	10.92 AW	13.68 TQ	NJBLS	10/01-12/01
	Middlesex-Somerset-Hunterdon PMSA, NJ	H	8.54 FQ	10.91 AW	13.90 TQ	NJBLS	10/01-12/01
	Monmouth-Ocean PMSA, NJ	H	8.44 FQ	10.41 AW	13.07 TQ	NJBLS	10/01-12/01
	Newark PMSA, NJ	H	8.87 FQ	11.32 AW	14.50 TQ	NJBLS	10/01-12/01
	Trenton PMSA, NJ	H	8.98 FQ	11.61 AW	15.34 TQ	NJBLS	10/01-12/01
	New Mexico	H	6.12 FQ	8.77 AW	12.28 TQ	NMBLS	10/01-12/01
	Albuquerque MSA, NM	H	7.52 FQ	10.08 AW	13.25 TQ	NMBLS	10/01-12/01
	Las Cruces MSA, NM	H	5.93 FQ	7.87 AW	10.80 TQ	NMBLS	10/01-12/01

AAW	Average annual wage	**AOH**	Average offered, high	**ASH**	Average starting, high	**H**	Hourly	**M**	Monthly	**S**	Special: hourly and annual
AE	Average entry wage	**AOL**	Average offered, low	**ASL**	Average starting, low	**HI**	Highest wage paid	**MTC**	Median total compensation	**TQ**	Third quartile wage
AEX	Average experienced wage	**APH**	Average pay, high range	**AW**	Average wage paid	**HR**	High end range	**MW**	Median wage paid	**W**	Weekly
AO	Average offered	**APL**	Average pay, low range	**FQ**	First quartile wage	**LR**	Low end range	**SQ**	Second quartile wage	**Y**	Yearly

Occupation/Type/Industry	Location	Per	Low	Mid	High	Source	Date
Nursing Aide, Orderly, and Attendant	New York	H	8.13 FQ	11.95 AW	15.99 TQ	NYBLS	10/01-12/01
	Albany-Schenectady-Troy MSA, NY	H	7.57 FQ	9.84 AW	12.67 TQ	NYBLS	10/01-12/01
	Binghamton MSA, NY	H	7.14 FQ	8.80 AW	10.93 TQ	NYBLS	10/01-12/01
	Buffalo-Niagara Falls MSA, NY	H	7.57 FQ	10.52 AW	14.32 TQ	NYBLS	10/01-12/01
	Dutchess County PMSA, NY	H	8.22 FQ	11.16 AW	14.84 TQ	NYBLS	10/01-12/01
	Nassau-Suffolk PMSA, NY	H	10.95 FQ	13.96 AW	17.16 TQ	NYBLS	10/01-12/01
	New York PMSA, NY	H	10.45 FQ	13.05 AW	16.26 TQ	NYBLS	10/01-12/01
	Newburgh PMSA, NY-PA	H	7.78 FQ	10.08 AW	12.96 TQ	NYBLS	10/01-12/01
	Rochester MSA, NY	H	7.38 FQ	9.73 AW	12.46 TQ	NYBLS	10/01-12/01
	Syracuse MSA, NY	H	7.50 FQ	9.99 AW	13.38 TQ	NYBLS	10/01-12/01
	Utica-Rome MSA, NY	H	6.98 FQ	8.21 AW	10.07 TQ	NYBLS	10/01-12/01
	North Carolina	H	6.82 FQ	8.84 AW	11.31 TQ	NCBLS	10/01-12/01
	Asheville MSA, NC	H	7.06 FQ	9.35 AW	11.50 TQ	NCBLS	10/01-12/01
	Charlotte-Gastonia-Rock Hill MSA, NC-SC	H	7.26 FQ	9.57 AW	12.64 TQ	NCBLS	10/01-12/01
	Fayetteville MSA, NC	H	6.85 FQ	8.55 AW	11.10 TQ	NCBLS	10/01-12/01
	Greensboro-Winston-Salem-High Point MSA, NC	H	7.16 FQ	9.06 AW	11.36 TQ	NCBLS	10/01-12/01
	Hickory-Morganton-Lenoir MSA, NC	H	6.73 FQ	9.10 AW	12.07 TQ	NCBLS	10/01-12/01
	Raleigh-Durham-Chapel Hill MSA, NC	H	7.44 FQ	9.36 AW	11.94 TQ	NCBLS	10/01-12/01
	Wilmington MSA, NC	H	6.95 FQ	8.47 AW	10.62 TQ	NCBLS	10/01-12/01
	North Dakota	H	6.75 FQ	8.44 AW	10.60 TQ	NDBLS	10/01-12/01
	Fargo-Moorhead MSA, ND-MN	H	7.50 FQ	9.20 AW	11.32 TQ	NDBLS	10/01-12/01
	Ohio	H	7.20 FQ	9.60 AW	12.86 TQ	OHBLS	10/01-12/01
	Akron PMSA, OH	H	7.33 FQ	9.32 AW	11.54 TQ	OHBLS	10/01-12/01
	Canton-Massillon MSA, OH	H	7.48 FQ	10.01 AW	13.04 TQ	OHBLS	10/01-12/01
	Cincinnati PMSA, OH-KY-IN	H	7.76 FQ	10.15 AW	13.09 TQ	OHBLS	10/01-12/01
	Cleveland-Lorain-Elyria PMSA, OH	H	7.36 FQ	9.47 AW	12.38 TQ	OHBLS	10/01-12/01
	Columbus MSA, OH	H	7.88 FQ	10.41 AW	13.65 TQ	OHBLS	10/01-12/01
	Dayton-Springfield MSA, OH	H	7.16 FQ	10.10 AW	13.60 TQ	OHBLS	10/01-12/01
	Hamilton-Middletown PMSA, OH	H	7.59 FQ	9.62 AW	11.44 TQ	OHBLS	10/01-12/01
	Mansfield MSA, OH	H	6.82 FQ	8.76 AW	11.03 TQ	OHBLS	10/01-12/01
	Toledo MSA, OH	H	7.59 FQ	9.96 AW	13.22 TQ	OHBLS	10/01-12/01
	Youngstown-Warren MSA, OH	H	7.06 FQ	9.01 AW	11.19 TQ	OHBLS	10/01-12/01
	Oklahoma	H	6.01 FQ	7.80 AW	10.03 TQ	OKBLS	10/01-12/01
	Oklahoma City MSA, OK	H	6.05 FQ	8.01 AW	10.48 TQ	OKBLS	10/01-12/01
	Tulsa MSA, OK	H	6.41 FQ	8.32 AW	10.46 TQ	OKBLS	10/01-12/01
	Oregon	H	7.56 FQ	10.20 AW	13.36 TQ	ORBLS	10/01-12/01
	Eugene-Springfield MSA, OR	H	8.31 FQ	10.97 AW	15.13 TQ	ORBLS	10/01-12/01
	Medford-Ashland MSA, OR	H	7.75 FQ	9.90 AW	12.44 TQ	ORBLS	10/01-12/01
	Portland-Vancouver PMSA, OR-WA	H	7.73 FQ	10.42 AW	13.40 TQ	ORBLS	10/01-12/01
	Salem PMSA, OR	H	8.07 FQ	11.04 AW	13.95 TQ	ORBLS	10/01-12/01
	Pennsylvania	H	7.46 FQ	9.90 AW	12.95 TQ	PABLS	10/01-12/01
	Allentown-Bethlehem-Easton MSA, PA	H	7.86 FQ	10.14 AW	12.97 TQ	PABLS	10/01-12/01
	Erie MSA, PA	H	7.55 FQ	10.02 AW	13.85 TQ	PABLS	10/01-12/01
	Harrisburg-Lebanon-Carlisle MSA, PA	H	8.45 FQ	10.65 AW	13.61 TQ	PABLS	10/01-12/01
	Johnstown MSA, PA	H	6.23 FQ	8.45 AW	10.86 TQ	PABLS	10/01-12/01
	Lancaster MSA, PA	H	8.05 FQ	10.36 AW	13.39 TQ	PABLS	10/01-12/01
	Philadelphia PMSA, PA-NJ	H	8.18 FQ	10.48 AW	13.46 TQ	PABLS	10/01-12/01
	Pittsburgh MSA, PA	H	7.32 FQ	9.57 AW	12.61 TQ	PABLS	10/01-12/01
	Reading MSA, PA	H	7.74 FQ	10.17 AW	12.92 TQ	PABLS	10/01-12/01
	Scranton-Wilkes-Barre-Hazleton MSA, PA	H	7.01 FQ	9.36 AW	11.60 TQ	PABLS	10/01-12/01
	York MSA, PA	H	7.84 FQ	10.23 AW	13.16 TQ	PABLS	10/01-12/01
	Rhode Island	H	7.96 FQ	10.64 AW	13.76 TQ	RIBLS	10/01-12/01
	Providence-Fall River-Warwick MSA, RI-MA	H	8.00 FQ	10.62 AW	13.62 TQ	RIBLS	10/01-12/01
	South Carolina	H	6.39 FQ	8.55 AW	11.16 TQ	SCBLS	10/01-12/01
	Charleston-North Charleston MSA, SC	H	6.86 FQ	8.47 AW	10.68 TQ	SCBLS	10/01-12/01
	Columbia MSA, SC	H	7.42 FQ	9.60 AW	12.70 TQ	SCBLS	10/01-12/01

AAW Average annual wage **AOH** Average offered, high **ASH** Average starting, high **H** Hourly **M** Monthly **S** Special: hourly and annual
AE Average entry wage **AOL** Average offered, low **ASL** Average starting, low **HI** Highest wage paid **MTC** Median total compensation **TQ** Third quartile wage
AEX Average experienced wage **APH** Average pay, high range **AW** Average wage paid **HR** High end range **MW** Median wage paid **W** Weekly
AO Average offered **APL** Average pay, low range **FQ** First quartile wage **LR** Low end range **SQ** Second quartile wage **Y** Yearly

Occupation/Type/Industry	Location	Per	Low	Mid	High	Source	Date
Nursing Aide, Orderly, and Attendant	Greenville-Spartanburg-Anderson MSA, SC	H	6.98 FQ	8.78 AW	11.10 TQ	SCBLS	10/01-12/01
	Myrtle Beach MSA, SC	H	6.00 FQ	7.50 AW	9.20 TQ	SCBLS	10/01-12/01
	South Dakota	H	6.94 FQ	8.60 AW	10.83 TQ	SDBLS	10/01-12/01
	Sioux Falls MSA, SD	H	7.39 FQ	9.34 AW	11.43 TQ	SDBLS	10/01-12/01
	Tennessee	H	6.51 FQ	8.50 AW	10.83 TQ	TNBLS	10/01-12/01
	Chattanooga MSA, TN-GA	H	7.27 FQ	8.87 AW	11.04 TQ	TNBLS	10/01-12/01
	Clarksville-Hopkinsville MSA, TN-KY	H	6.54 FQ	8.69 AW	11.26 TQ	TNBLS	10/01-12/01
	Johnson City-Kingsport-Bristol MSA, TN-VA	H	6.17 FQ	7.93 AW	10.06 TQ	TNBLS	10/01-12/01
	Knoxville MSA, TN	H	7.01 FQ	8.37 AW	10.42 TQ	TNBLS	10/01-12/01
	Memphis MSA, TN-AR-MS	H	6.57 FQ	9.10 AW	12.12 TQ	TNBLS	10/01-12/01
	Nashville MSA, TN	H	7.19 FQ	9.00 AW	11.07 TQ	TNBLS	10/01-12/01
	Texas	H	5.84 FQ	7.75 AW	10.38 TQ	TXBLS	10/01-12/01
	Amarillo MSA, TX	H	6.67 FQ	8.78 AW	10.79 TQ	TXBLS	10/01-12/01
	Austin-San Marcos MSA, TX	H	6.39 FQ	9.02 AW	12.05 TQ	TXBLS	10/01-12/01
	Beaumont-Port Arthur MSA, TX	H	5.74 FQ	7.28 AW	9.84 TQ	TXBLS	10/01-12/01
	Brazoria PMSA, TX	H	5.92 FQ	7.43 AW	8.97 TQ	TXBLS	10/01-12/01
	Brownsville-Harlingen-San Benito MSA, TX	H	5.70 FQ	6.75 AW	8.56 TQ	TXBLS	10/01-12/01
	Corpus Christi MSA, TX	H	5.75 FQ	6.71 AW	8.44 TQ	TXBLS	10/01-12/01
	Dallas PMSA, TX	H	5.92 FQ	8.14 AW	10.83 TQ	TXBLS	10/01-12/01
	El Paso MSA, TX	H	5.76 FQ	7.35 AW	9.64 TQ	TXBLS	10/01-12/01
	Fort Worth-Arlington PMSA, TX	H	6.82 FQ	8.74 AW	10.93 TQ	TXBLS	10/01-12/01
	Galveston-Texas City PMSA, TX	H	6.54 FQ	8.07 AW	9.67 TQ	TXBLS	10/01-12/01
	Houston PMSA, TX	H	5.82 FQ	7.98 AW	10.89 TQ	TXBLS	10/01-12/01
	Killeen-Temple MSA, TX	H	5.98 FQ	8.22 AW	11.33 TQ	TXBLS	10/01-12/01
	Laredo MSA, TX	H	5.62 FQ	7.28 AW	9.83 TQ	TXBLS	10/01-12/01
	Longview-Marshall MSA, TX	H	5.86 FQ	7.27 AW	8.96 TQ	TXBLS	10/01-12/01
	Lubbock MSA, TX	H	5.88 FQ	7.53 AW	9.28 TQ	TXBLS	10/01-12/01
	McAllen-Edinburg-Mission MSA, TX	H	5.55 FQ	6.48 AW	8.11 TQ	TXBLS	10/01-12/01
	Odessa-Midland MSA, TX	H	5.98 FQ	7.63 AW	9.66 TQ	TXBLS	10/01-12/01
	San Antonio MSA, TX	H	6.00 FQ	7.81 AW	10.38 TQ	TXBLS	10/01-12/01
	Tyler MSA, TX	H	5.72 FQ	7.44 AW	9.08 TQ	TXBLS	10/01-12/01
	Waco MSA, TX	H	6.77 FQ	8.74 AW	12.90 TQ	TXBLS	10/01-12/01
	Utah	H	7.19 FQ	8.69 AW	10.73 TQ	UTBLS	10/01-12/01
	Provo-Orem MSA, UT	H	7.28 FQ	8.77 AW	10.68 TQ	UTBLS	10/01-12/01
	Salt Lake City-Ogden MSA, UT	H	7.29 FQ	8.82 AW	10.89 TQ	UTBLS	10/01-12/01
	Vermont	H	7.48 FQ	9.75 AW	12.68 TQ	VTBLS	10/01-12/01
	Burlington MSA, VT	H	7.99 FQ	10.29 AW	13.08 TQ	VTBLS	10/01-12/01
	Virginia	H	6.85 FQ	9.04 AW	11.75 TQ	VABLS	10/01-12/01
	Lynchburg MSA, VA	H	7.03 FQ	8.78 AW	11.57 TQ	VABLS	10/01-12/01
	Norfolk-Virginia Beach-Newport News MSA, VA-NC	H	6.56 FQ	8.49 AW	10.71 TQ	VABLS	10/01-12/01
	Richmond-Petersburg MSA, VA	H	7.46 FQ	9.71 AW	12.64 TQ	VABLS	10/01-12/01
	Roanoke MSA, VA	H	6.45 FQ	8.86 AW	11.28 TQ	VABLS	10/01-12/01
	Washington	H	7.71 FQ	10.32 AW	13.41 TQ	WABLS	10/01-12/01
	Bremerton PMSA, WA	H	7.70 FQ	10.26 AW	13.49 TQ	WABLS	10/01-12/01
	Olympia PMSA, WA	H	7.42 FQ	9.90 AW	13.09 TQ	WABLS	10/01-12/01
	Richland-Kennewick-Pasco MSA, WA	H	8.05 FQ	9.89 AW	12.53 TQ	WABLS	10/01-12/01
	Seattle-Bellevue-Everett PMSA, WA	H	9.36 FQ	11.47 AW	14.02 TQ	WABLS	10/01-12/01
	Spokane MSA, WA	H	7.73 FQ	9.58 AW	11.64 TQ	WABLS	10/01-12/01
	Tacoma PMSA, WA	H	7.71 FQ	10.44 AW	13.42 TQ	WABLS	10/01-12/01
	Yakima MSA, WA	H	7.41 FQ	9.02 AW	11.44 TQ	WABLS	10/01-12/01
	West Virginia	H	5.85 FQ	7.65 AW	10.11 TQ	WVBLS	10/01-12/01
	Charleston MSA, WV	H	5.95 FQ	7.64 AW	9.76 TQ	WVBLS	10/01-12/01
	Huntington-Ashland MSA, WV-KY-OH	H	6.08 FQ	7.95 AW	10.61 TQ	WVBLS	10/01-12/01
	Wisconsin	H	7.61 FQ	9.97 AW	12.98 TQ	WIBLS	10/01-12/01
	Appleton-Oshkosh-Neenah MSA, WI	H	7.51 FQ	9.48 AW	11.64 TQ	WIBLS	10/01-12/01

AAW Average annual wage; **AE** Average entry wage; **AEX** Average experienced wage; **AO** Average offered; **AOH** Average offered, high; **AOL** Average offered, low; **APH** Average pay, high range; **APL** Average pay, low range; **ASH** Average starting, high; **ASL** Average starting, low; **AW** Average wage paid; **FQ** First quartile wage; **H** Hourly; **HI** Highest wage paid; **HR** High end range; **LR** Low end range; **M** Monthly; **MTC** Median total compensation; **MW** Median wage paid; **SQ** Second quartile wage; **S** Special: hourly and annual; **TQ** Third quartile wage; **W** Weekly; **Y** Yearly

Occupation/Type/Industry	Location	Per	Low	Mid	High	Source	Date
Nursing Aide, Orderly, and Attendant	Green Bay MSA, WI	H	8.81 FQ	10.28 AW	12.36 TQ	WIBLS	10/01-12/01
	Madison MSA, WI	H	8.98 FQ	11.57 AW	15.14 TQ	WIBLS	10/01-12/01
	Milwaukee-Waukesha PMSA, WI	H	7.63 FQ	9.98 AW	13.01 TQ	WIBLS	10/01-12/01
	Racine PMSA, WI	H	8.69 FQ	11.06 AW	14.95 TQ	WIBLS	10/01-12/01
	Wyoming	H	6.81 FQ	8.63 AW	10.75 TQ	WYBLS	10/01-12/01
	Cheyenne MSA, WY	H	7.45 FQ	9.23 AW	11.06 TQ	WYBLS	10/01-12/01
	Puerto Rico	H	5.64 FQ	7.29 AW	10.64 TQ	PRBLS	10/01-12/01
	Virgin Islands	H	7.56 FQ	9.31 AW	10.86 TQ	VIBLS	10/01-12/01
	Guam	H	7.26 FQ	10.65 AW	14.14 TQ	GUBLS	10/01-12/01
Nursing Home Administrator	United States	Y		65773 AW		CLTC	1/00-1/02
Nursing Instructor and Teacher							
Postsecondary	Alabama	Y	29600 FQ	47380 AW	72340 TQ	ALBLS	10/01-12/01
Postsecondary	Birmingham MSA, AL	Y	40980 FQ	62790 AW	88140 TQ	ALBLS	10/01-12/01
Postsecondary	Huntsville MSA, AL	Y	32170 FQ	42030 AW	53720 TQ	ALBLS	10/01-12/01
Postsecondary	Mobile MSA, AL	Y	30890 FQ	41080 AW	55080 TQ	ALBLS	10/01-12/01
Postsecondary	Arizona	Y	25020 FQ	51900 AW	76670 TQ	AZBLS	10/01-12/01
Postsecondary	Arkansas	Y	25720 FQ	41390 AW	55580 TQ	ARBLS	10/01-12/01
Postsecondary	Fayetteville-Springdale-Rogers MSA, AR	Y	27650 FQ	43390 AW	58370 TQ	ARBLS	10/01-12/01
Postsecondary	California	Y	39420 FQ	59590 AW	81060 TQ	CABLS	10/01-12/01
Postsecondary	Fresno MSA, CA	Y	35570 FQ	55380 AW	74990 TQ	CABLS	10/01-12/01
Postsecondary	Los Angeles-Long Beach PMSA, CA	Y	46110 FQ	62740 AW	80880 TQ	CABLS	10/01-12/01
Postsecondary	Oakland PMSA, CA	Y	42810 FQ	61240 AW	85420 TQ	CABLS	10/01-12/01
Postsecondary	Orange County PMSA, CA	Y	35440 FQ	54460 AW	72000 TQ	CABLS	10/01-12/01
Postsecondary	Riverside-San Bernardino PMSA, CA	Y	39420 FQ	58090 AW	76380 TQ	CABLS	10/01-12/01
Postsecondary	Sacramento PMSA, CA	Y	41900 FQ	62150 AW	88320 TQ	CABLS	10/01-12/01
Postsecondary	San Diego MSA, CA	Y	29910 FQ	56520 AW	77470 TQ	CABLS	10/01-12/01
Postsecondary	San Francisco PMSA, CA	Y	31590 FQ	56220 AW	80850 TQ	CABLS	10/01-12/01
Postsecondary	San Jose PMSA, CA	Y	39470 FQ	60130 AW	87210 TQ	CABLS	10/01-12/01
Postsecondary	Colorado	Y	31670 FQ	46310 AW	60650 TQ	COBLS	10/01-12/01
Postsecondary	Boulder-Longmont PMSA, CO	Y	31090 FQ	40730 AW	55600 TQ	COBLS	10/01-12/01
Postsecondary	Colorado Springs MSA, CO	Y	34730 FQ	49470 AW	67650 TQ	COBLS	10/01-12/01
Postsecondary	Denver PMSA, CO	Y	32730 FQ	50890 AW	63080 TQ	COBLS	10/01-12/01
Postsecondary	Fort Collins-Loveland MSA, CO	Y	31740 FQ	45600 AW	62830 TQ	COBLS	10/01-12/01
Postsecondary	Connecticut	Y	40220 FQ	61220 AW	77450 TQ	CTBLS	10/01-12/01
Postsecondary	Bridgeport PMSA, CT	Y	25660 FQ	51810 AW	78440 TQ	CTBLS	10/01-12/01
Postsecondary	Hartford MSA, CT	Y	45090 FQ	63190 AW	83550 TQ	CTBLS	10/01-12/01
Postsecondary	New Haven-Meriden PMSA, CT	Y	48390 FQ	63300 AW	76500 TQ	CTBLS	10/01-12/01
Postsecondary	Delaware	Y	35690 FQ	54300 AW	82480 TQ	DEBLS	10/01-12/01
Postsecondary	Wilmington-Newark PMSA, DE-MD	Y	36950 FQ	58630 AW	90650 TQ	DEBLS	10/01-12/01
Postsecondary	District of Columbia	Y	41360 FQ	57010 AW	71380 TQ	DCBLS	10/01-12/01
Postsecondary	Washington PMSA, DC-MD-VA-WV	Y	39120 FQ	58920 AW	77140 TQ	DCBLS	10/01-12/01
Postsecondary	Florida	Y	34490 FQ	57650 AW	85080 TQ	FLBLS	10/01-12/01
Postsecondary	Daytona Beach MSA, FL	Y	31830 FQ	50040 AW	90460 TQ	FLBLS	10/01-12/01
Postsecondary	Fort Lauderdale PMSA, FL	Y	39460 FQ	54530 AW	72880 TQ	FLBLS	10/01-12/01
Postsecondary	Gainesville MSA, FL	Y	45180 FQ	67400 AW	92480 TQ	FLBLS	10/01-12/01
Postsecondary	Jacksonville MSA, FL	Y	35960 FQ	54580 AW	71600 TQ	FLBLS	10/01-12/01
Postsecondary	Miami PMSA, FL	Y	37550 FQ	57400 AW	76990 TQ	FLBLS	10/01-12/01
Postsecondary	Orlando MSA, FL	Y	33140 FQ	57220 AW	79970 TQ	FLBLS	10/01-12/01
Postsecondary	Tallahassee MSA, FL	Y	41500 FQ	63530 AW	95530 TQ	FLBLS	10/01-12/01
Postsecondary	Tampa-St. Petersburg-Clearwater MSA, FL	Y	34250 FQ	61870 AW	94320 TQ	FLBLS	10/01-12/01
Postsecondary	West Palm Beach-Boca Raton MSA, FL	Y	32420 FQ	57380 AW	94170 TQ	FLBLS	10/01-12/01
Postsecondary	Georgia	Y	36810 FQ	53110 AW	77140 TQ	GABLS	10/01-12/01
Postsecondary	Atlanta MSA, GA	Y	38270 FQ	53490 AW	75640 TQ	GABLS	10/01-12/01
Postsecondary	Augusta-Aiken MSA, GA-SC	Y	26790 FQ	45630 AW	78220 TQ	GABLS	10/01-12/01
Postsecondary	Columbus MSA, GA-AL	Y	39290 FQ	71770 AW	91740 TQ	GABLS	10/01-12/01
Postsecondary	Hawaii	Y	16230 FQ	47690 AW	75990 TQ	HIBLS	10/01-12/01
Postsecondary	Honolulu MSA, HI	Y	16100 FQ	47330 AW	76230 TQ	HIBLS	10/01-12/01
Postsecondary	Idaho	Y	37470 FQ	49680 AW	62130 TQ	IDBLS	10/01-12/01
Postsecondary	Illinois	Y	23690 FQ	47010 AW	71540 TQ	ILBLS	10/01-12/01

AAW	Average annual wage	**AOH**	Average offered, high	**ASH**	Average starting, high	**H**	Hourly	**M**	Monthly	**S**	Special: hourly and annual
AE	Average entry wage	**AOL**	Average offered, low	**ASL**	Average starting, low	**HI**	Highest wage paid	**MTC**	Median total compensation	**TQ**	Third quartile wage
AEX	Average experienced wage	**APH**	Average pay, high range	**AW**	Average wage paid	**HR**	High end range	**MW**	Median wage paid	**W**	Weekly
AO	Average offered	**APL**	Average pay, low range	**FQ**	First quartile wage	**LR**	Low end range	**SQ**	Second quartile wage	**Y**	Yearly

Occupation/Type/Industry	Location	Per	Low	Mid	High	Source	Date
Nursing Instructor and Teacher							
Postsecondary	Chicago PMSA, IL	Y	29840 FQ	50580 AW	74660 TQ	ILBLS	10/01-12/01
Postsecondary	Indiana	Y	29420 FQ	44330 AW	61190 TQ	INBLS	10/01-12/01
Postsecondary	Evansville-Henderson MSA, IN-KY	Y	35630 FQ	47520 AW	66330 TQ	INBLS	10/01-12/01
Postsecondary	Fort Wayne MSA, IN	Y	34220 FQ	47280 AW	60280 TQ	INBLS	10/01-12/01
Postsecondary	Gary PMSA, IN	Y	33250 FQ	49520 AW	71280 TQ	INBLS	10/01-12/01
Postsecondary	Indianapolis MSA, IN	Y	36150 FQ	46860 AW	61000 TQ	INBLS	10/01-12/01
Postsecondary	South Bend MSA, IN	Y	29540 FQ	41690 AW	57840 TQ	INBLS	10/01-12/01
Postsecondary	Iowa	Y	32080 FQ	47530 AW	67120 TQ	IABLS	10/01-12/01
Postsecondary	Davenport-Moline-Rock Island MSA, IA-IL	Y	33520 FQ	50430 AW	70480 TQ	IABLS	10/01-12/01
Postsecondary	Des Moines MSA, IA	Y	31110 FQ	45830 AW	65580 TQ	IABLS	10/01-12/01
Postsecondary	Kansas	Y	24710 FQ	38700 AW	56910 TQ	KSBLS	10/01-12/01
Postsecondary	Kentucky	Y	31250 FQ	49180 AW	69330 TQ	KYBLS	10/01-12/01
Postsecondary	Lexington MSA, KY	Y	45950 FQ	54740 AW	71090 TQ	KYBLS	10/01-12/01
Postsecondary	Louisville MSA, KY-IN	Y	30020 FQ	48140 AW	70590 TQ	KYBLS	10/01-12/01
Postsecondary	Louisiana	Y	32250 FQ	45500 AW	62650 TQ	LABLS	10/01-12/01
Postsecondary	New Orleans MSA, LA	Y	32070 FQ	47080 AW	70170 TQ	LABLS	10/01-12/01
Postsecondary	Shreveport-Bossier City MSA, LA	Y	31650 FQ	44400 AW	61560 TQ	LABLS	10/01-12/01
Postsecondary	Maine	Y	35830 FQ	50300 AW	66670 TQ	MEBLS	10/01-12/01
Postsecondary	Maryland	Y	43550 FQ	60920 AW	77840 TQ	MDBLS	10/01-12/01
Postsecondary	Baltimore PMSA, MD	Y	43610 FQ	61190 AW	80140 TQ	MDBLS	10/01-12/01
Postsecondary	Massachusetts	Y	31030 FQ	53720 AW	87190 TQ	MABLS	10/01-12/01
Postsecondary	Boston PMSA, MA-NH	Y	31870 FQ	53950 AW	86830 TQ	MABLS	10/01-12/01
Postsecondary	Springfield MSA, MA	Y	38850 FQ	64670 AW	100620 TQ	MABLS	10/01-12/01
Postsecondary	Worcester PMSA, MA-CT	Y	50280 FQ	74380 AW	103240 TQ	MABLS	10/01-12/01
Postsecondary	Michigan	Y	39330 FQ	55900 AW	79170 TQ	MIBLS	10/01-12/01
Postsecondary	Detroit PMSA, MI	Y	39990 FQ	56960 AW	83370 TQ	MIBLS	10/01-12/01
Postsecondary	Grand Rapids-Muskegon-Holland MSA, MI	Y	40430 FQ	52330 AW	67830 TQ	MIBLS	10/01-12/01
Postsecondary	Kalamazoo-Battle Creek MSA, MI	Y	41200 FQ	55140 AW	74560 TQ	MIBLS	10/01-12/01
Postsecondary	Minnesota	Y	34790 FQ	49640 AW	68490 TQ	MNBLS	10/01-12/01
Postsecondary	Duluth-Superior MSA, MN-WI	Y	34890 FQ	48550 AW	64870 TQ	MNBLS	10/01-12/01
Postsecondary	Minneapolis-St. Paul MSA, MN-WI	Y	36360 FQ	49850 AW	67780 TQ	MNBLS	10/01-12/01
Postsecondary	St. Cloud MSA, MN	Y	37280 FQ	49140 AW	66390 TQ	MNBLS	10/01-12/01
Postsecondary	Mississippi	Y	31720 FQ	48530 AW	61940 TQ	MSBLS	10/01-12/01
Postsecondary	Missouri	Y	30950 FQ	45910 AW	59820 TQ	MOBLS	10/01-12/01
Postsecondary	Kansas City MSA, MO-KS	Y	33890 FQ	45710 AW	57800 TQ	MOBLS	10/01-12/01
Postsecondary	St. Louis MSA, MO-IL	Y	21580 FQ	44190 AW	60330 TQ	MOBLS	10/01-12/01
Postsecondary	Springfield MSA, MO	Y	31500 FQ	46540 AW	62760 TQ	MOBLS	10/01-12/01
Postsecondary	Montana	Y	30390 FQ	45310 AW	63840 TQ	MTBLS	10/01-12/01
Postsecondary	Nebraska	Y	36380 FQ	52260 AW	75580 TQ	NEBLS	10/01-12/01
Postsecondary	Lincoln MSA, NE	Y	37240 FQ	48330 AW	65550 TQ	NEBLS	10/01-12/01
Postsecondary	Omaha MSA, NE-IA	Y	36070 FQ	57020 AW	86320 TQ	NEBLS	10/01-12/01
Postsecondary	Nevada	Y	25930 FQ	48170 AW	75420 TQ	NVBLS	10/01-12/01
Postsecondary	Las Vegas MSA, NV-AZ	Y	25840 FQ	47580 AW	79170 TQ	NVBLS	10/01-12/01
Postsecondary	New Hampshire	Y	38370 FQ	50650 AW	68210 TQ	NHBLS	10/01-12/01
Postsecondary	New Jersey	Y	37260 FQ	57190 AW	75260 TQ	NJBLS	10/01-12/01
Postsecondary	Atlantic-Cape May PMSA, NJ	Y	55120 FQ	64700 AW	74280 TQ	NJBLS	10/01-12/01
Postsecondary	Bergen-Passaic PMSA, NJ	Y	36800 FQ	59090 AW	78230 TQ	NJBLS	10/01-12/01
Postsecondary	Jersey City PMSA, NJ	Y	34040 FQ	52880 AW	72260 TQ	NJBLS	10/01-12/01
Postsecondary	Monmouth-Ocean PMSA, NJ	Y	39490 FQ	54010 AW	69510 TQ	NJBLS	10/01-12/01
Postsecondary	Newark PMSA, NJ	Y	28130 FQ	53310 AW	72700 TQ	NJBLS	10/01-12/01
Postsecondary	Trenton PMSA, NJ	Y	45290 FQ	58160 AW	71660 TQ	NJBLS	10/01-12/01
Postsecondary	New Mexico	Y	30680 FQ	44530 AW	56380 TQ	NMBLS	10/01-12/01
Postsecondary	New York	Y	39190 FQ	66170 AW	106920 TQ	NYBLS	10/01-12/01
Postsecondary	Albany-Schenectady-Troy MSA, NY	Y	42450 FQ	64370 AW	102860 TQ	NYBLS	10/01-12/01
Postsecondary	Binghamton MSA, NY	Y	28000 FQ	41440 AW	53610 TQ	NYBLS	10/01-12/01
Postsecondary	Buffalo-Niagara Falls MSA, NY	Y	39270 FQ	53240 AW	73630 TQ	NYBLS	10/01-12/01
Postsecondary	Nassau-Suffolk PMSA, NY	Y	46180 FQ	73090 AW	109660 TQ	NYBLS	10/01-12/01
Postsecondary	New York PMSA, NY	Y	41510 FQ	70590 AW	111980 TQ	NYBLS	10/01-12/01
Postsecondary	Rochester MSA, NY	Y	38950 FQ	64390 AW	114740 TQ	NYBLS	10/01-12/01
Postsecondary	Syracuse MSA, NY	Y	39430 FQ	64680 AW	101850 TQ	NYBLS	10/01-12/01
Postsecondary	Utica-Rome MSA, NY	Y	36300 FQ	49430 AW	63490 TQ	NYBLS	10/01-12/01
Postsecondary	North Carolina	Y	29030 FQ	46040 AW	63200 TQ	NCBLS	10/01-12/01

AAW	Average annual wage	**AOH**	Average offered, high	**ASH**	Average starting, high	**H**	Hourly	**M**	Monthly	**S**	Special: hourly and annual
AE	Average entry wage	**AOL**	Average offered, low	**ASL**	Average starting, low	**HI**	Highest wage paid	**MTC**	Median total compensation	**TQ**	Third quartile wage
AEX	Average experienced wage	**APH**	Average pay, high range	**AW**	Average wage paid	**HR**	High end range	**MW**	Median wage paid	**W**	Weekly
AO	Average offered	**APL**	Average pay, low range	**FQ**	First quartile wage	**LR**	Low end range	**SQ**	Second quartile wage	**Y**	Yearly

Occupation/Type/Industry	Location	Per	Low	Mid	High	Source	Date
Nursing Instructor and Teacher							
Postsecondary	Charlotte-Gastonia-Rock Hill MSA, NC-SC	Y	34800 FQ	48700 AW	60740 TQ	NCBLS	10/01-12/01
Postsecondary	Greensboro-Winston-Salem-High Point MSA, NC	Y	35920 FQ	49390 AW	65610 TQ	NCBLS	10/01-12/01
Postsecondary	Hickory-Morganton-Lenoir MSA, NC	Y	31860 FQ	40520 AW	54120 TQ	NCBLS	10/01-12/01
Postsecondary	Raleigh-Durham-Chapel Hill MSA, NC	Y	39120 FQ	51440 AW	66780 TQ	NCBLS	10/01-12/01
Postsecondary	Wilmington MSA, NC	Y	34700 FQ	54560 AW	83190 TQ	NCBLS	10/01-12/01
Postsecondary	North Dakota	Y	28830 FQ	42390 AW	56490 TQ	NDBLS	10/01-12/01
Postsecondary	Fargo-Moorhead MSA, ND-MN	Y	35100 FQ	45390 AW	60940 TQ	NDBLS	10/01-12/01
Postsecondary	Ohio	Y	31670 FQ	49300 AW	65740 TQ	OHBLS	10/01-12/01
Postsecondary	Canton-Massillon MSA, OH	Y	38150 FQ	55140 AW	69550 TQ	OHBLS	10/01-12/01
Postsecondary	Cincinnati PMSA, OH-KY-IN	Y	34220 FQ	54230 AW	73690 TQ	OHBLS	10/01-12/01
Postsecondary	Cleveland-Lorain-Elyria PMSA, OH	Y	36760 FQ	50320 AW	64110 TQ	OHBLS	10/01-12/01
Postsecondary	Columbus MSA, OH	Y	30230 FQ	51850 AW	71280 TQ	OHBLS	10/01-12/01
Postsecondary	Dayton-Springfield MSA, OH	Y	30100 FQ	45600 AW	62140 TQ	OHBLS	10/01-12/01
Postsecondary	Toledo MSA, OH	Y	29710 FQ	47480 AW	61670 TQ	OHBLS	10/01-12/01
Postsecondary	Youngstown-Warren MSA, OH	Y	30910 FQ	47920 AW	63970 TQ	OHBLS	10/01-12/01
Postsecondary	Oklahoma	Y	28960 FQ	41350 AW	56580 TQ	OKBLS	10/01-12/01
Postsecondary	Oklahoma City MSA, OK	Y	30620 FQ	42240 AW	56610 TQ	OKBLS	10/01-12/01
Postsecondary	Tulsa MSA, OK	Y	24420 FQ	43590 AW	65320 TQ	OKBLS	10/01-12/01
Postsecondary	Oregon	Y	29860 FQ	51550 AW	82140 TQ	ORBLS	10/01-12/01
Postsecondary	Portland-Vancouver PMSA, OR-WA	Y	38310 FQ	55060 AW	82760 TQ	ORBLS	10/01-12/01
Postsecondary	Pennsylvania	Y	27270 FQ	49730 AW	72080 TQ	PABLS	10/01-12/01
Postsecondary	Allentown-Bethlehem-Easton MSA, PA	Y	32950 FQ	48380 AW	65700 TQ	PABLS	10/01-12/01
Postsecondary	Philadelphia PMSA, PA NJ	Y	26360 FQ	51380 AW	80450 TQ	PABLS	10/01-12/01
Postsecondary	Pittsburgh MSA, PA	Y	25790 FQ	47360 AW	68460 TQ	PABLS	10/01-12/01
Postsecondary	Reading MSA, PA	Y	28720 FQ	35050 AW	49350 TQ	PABLS	10/01-12/01
Postsecondary	Scranton-Wilkes-Barre-Hazleton MSA, PA	Y	34080 FQ	52410 AW	72440 TQ	PABLS	10/01-12/01
Postsecondary	York MSA, PA	Y	32340 FQ	48450 AW	69510 TQ	PABLS	10/01-12/01
Postsecondary	Rhode Island	Y	36780 FQ	52300 AW	71570 TQ	RIBLS	10/01-12/01
Postsecondary	Providence-Fall River-Warwick MSA, RI-MA	Y	35560 FQ	51500 AW	71300 TQ	RIBLS	10/01-12/01
Postsecondary	South Carolina	Y	26190 FQ	45180 AW	64660 TQ	SCBLS	10/01-12/01
Postsecondary	Charleston-North Charleston MSA, SC	Y	21480 FQ	36590 AW	53910 TQ	SCBLS	10/01-12/01
Postsecondary	Columbia MSA, SC	Y	26050 FQ	42980 AW	56090 TQ	SCBLS	10/01-12/01
Postsecondary	Greenville-Spartanburg-Anderson MSA, SC	Y	25380 FQ	46600 AW	74610 TQ	SCBLS	10/01-12/01
Postsecondary	South Dakota	Y	30260 FQ	39950 AW	52720 TQ	SDBLS	10/01-12/01
Postsecondary	Tennessee	Y	22450 FQ	45560 AW	70860 TQ	TNBLS	10/01-12/01
Postsecondary	Chattanooga MSA, TN-GA	Y	31210 FQ	40990 AW	54850 TQ	TNBLS	10/01-12/01
Postsecondary	Johnson City-Kingsport-Bristol MSA, TN-VA	Y	12790 FQ	39290 AW	65340 TQ	TNBLS	10/01-12/01
Postsecondary	Knoxville MSA, TN	Y	19250 FQ	34360 AW	53710 TQ	TNBLS	10/01-12/01
Postsecondary	Memphis MSA, TN-AR-MS	Y	21870 FQ	43570 AW	64390 TQ	TNBLS	10/01-12/01
Postsecondary	Nashville MSA, TN	Y	32930 FQ	55310 AW	82130 TQ	TNBLS	10/01-12/01
Postsecondary	Texas	Y	30560 FQ	46280 AW	66490 TQ	TXBLS	10/01-12/01
Postsecondary	Beaumont-Port Arthur MSA, TX	Y	31620 FQ	41180 AW	54400 TQ	TXBLS	10/01-12/01
Postsecondary	Dallas PMSA, TX	Y	21620 FQ	44860 AW	62160 TQ	TXBLS	10/01-12/01
Postsecondary	El Paso MSA, TX	Y	29160 FQ	45040 AW	64330 TQ	TXBLS	10/01-12/01
Postsecondary	Fort Worth-Arlington PMSA, TX	Y	37950 FQ	54000 AW	73970 TQ	TXBLS	10/01-12/01
Postsecondary	Houston PMSA, TX	Y	36280 FQ	50160 AW	67920 TQ	TXBLS	10/01-12/01
Postsecondary	Killeen-Temple MSA, TX	Y	36600 FQ	47420 AW	63240 TQ	TXBLS	10/01-12/01
Postsecondary	Laredo MSA, TX	Y	33540 FQ	52290 AW	75190 TQ	TXBLS	10/01-12/01
Postsecondary	San Antonio MSA, TX	Y	30590 FQ	46020 AW	67320 TQ	TXBLS	10/01-12/01
Postsecondary	Tyler MSA, TX	Y	14370 FQ	39790 AW	55680 TQ	TXBLS	10/01-12/01
Postsecondary	Utah	Y	37180 FQ	54750 AW	72480 TQ	UTBLS	10/01-12/01
Postsecondary	Provo-Orem MSA, UT	Y	40650 FQ	54520 AW	70020 TQ	UTBLS	10/01-12/01
Postsecondary	Salt Lake City-Ogden MSA, UT	Y	40960 FQ	60060 AW	84110 TQ	UTBLS	10/01-12/01
Postsecondary	Vermont	Y	31220 FQ	48270 AW	74120 TQ	VTBLS	10/01-12/01
Postsecondary	Burlington MSA, VT	Y	31310 FQ	49080 AW	74370 TQ	VTBLS	10/01-12/01

AAW	Average annual wage	AOH	Average offered, high	ASH	Average starting, high	H	Hourly	M	Monthly	S	Special: hourly and annual
AE	Average entry wage	AOL	Average offered, low	ASL	Average starting, low	HI	Highest wage paid	MTC	Median total compensation	TQ	Third quartile wage
AEX	Average experienced wage	APH	Average pay, high range	AW	Average wage paid	HR	High end range	MW	Median wage paid	W	Weekly
AO	Average offered	APL	Average pay, low range	FQ	First quartile wage	LR	Low end range	SQ	Second quartile wage	Y	Yearly

Occupation/Type/Industry	Location	Per	Low	Mid	High	Source	Date
Nursing Instructor and Teacher							
Postsecondary	Virginia	Y	24510 FQ	52360 AW	85450 TQ	VABLS	10/01-12/01
Postsecondary	Norfolk-Virginia Beach-Newport News MSA, VA-NC	Y	26690 FQ	45520 AW	63060 TQ	VABLS	10/01-12/01
Postsecondary	Richmond-Petersburg MSA, VA	Y	17200 FQ	51220 AW	91950 TQ	VABLS	10/01-12/01
Postsecondary	Roanoke MSA, VA	Y	22600 FQ	57380 AW	91020 TQ	VABLS	10/01-12/01
Postsecondary	Washington	Y	32260 FQ	53030 AW	77130 TQ	WABLS	10/01-12/01
Postsecondary	Seattle-Bellevue-Everett PMSA, WA	Y	33420 FQ	58530 AW	86420 TQ	WABLS	10/01-12/01
Postsecondary	Spokane MSA, WA	Y	32320 FQ	52510 AW	81100 TQ	WABLS	10/01-12/01
Postsecondary	Tacoma PMSA, WA	Y	38330 FQ	55100 AW	72090 TQ	WABLS	10/01-12/01
Postsecondary	West Virginia	Y	31720 FQ	53220 AW	83780 TQ	WVBLS	10/01-12/01
Postsecondary	Wisconsin	Y	33220 FQ	49990 AW	71050 TQ	WIBLS	10/01-12/01
Postsecondary	Milwaukee-Waukesha PMSA, WI	Y	32250 FQ	50070 AW	71960 TQ	WIBLS	10/01-12/01
Postsecondary	Wyoming	Y	31020 FQ	43130 AW	56210 TQ	WYBLS	10/01-12/01
Postsecondary	Puerto Rico	Y	19660 FQ	29330 AW	39620 TQ	PRBLS	10/01-12/01
Obstetrician and Gynecologist	United States	Y		227000 AW		HHN	1/01-1/02
	Alabama	Y	81460 FQ	132090 AW		ALBLS	10/01-12/01
	Birmingham MSA, AL	Y		143810 AW		ALBLS	10/01-12/01
	Montgomery MSA, AL	Y	138970 FQ	143750 AW		ALBLS	10/01-12/01
	Arizona	Y		145280 AW		AZBLS	10/01-12/01
	Phoenix-Mesa MSA, AZ	Y		144630 AW		AZBLS	10/01-12/01
	California	Y	93430 FQ	133470 AW		CABLS	10/01-12/01
	Los Angeles-Long Beach PMSA, CA	Y	77330 FQ	119520 AW		CABLS	10/01-12/01
	San Jose PMSA, CA	Y	108430 FQ	136310 AW		CABLS	10/01-12/01
	Ventura PMSA, CA	Y	94270 FQ	112020 AW		CABLS	10/01-12/01
	Colorado	Y	130680 FQ	140090 AW		COBLS	10/01-12/01
	Denver PMSA, CO	Y	136430 FQ	141060 AW		COBLS	10/01-12/01
	Connecticut	Y	44590 FQ	130110 AW		CTBLS	10/01-12/01
	Bridgeport PMSA, CT	Y	99480 FQ	126150 AW		CTBLS	10/01-12/01
	Hartford MSA, CT	Y	42050 FQ	125970 AW		CTBLS	10/01-12/01
	Delaware	Y	99140 FQ	122240 AW		DEBLS	10/01-12/01
	District of Columbia	Y	57680 FQ	78380 AW	108490 TQ	DCBLS	10/01-12/01
	Washington PMSA, DC-MD-VA-WV	Y	59980 FQ	95710 AW		DCBLS	10/01-12/01
	Florida	Y	89920 FQ	136980 AW		FLBLS	10/01-12/01
	Orlando MSA, FL	Y	78410 FQ	113370 AW		FLBLS	10/01-12/01
	Georgia	Y	116390 FQ	139220 AW		GABLS	10/01-12/01
	Hawaii	Y	116490 FQ	123390 AW	144650 TQ	HIBLS	10/01-12/01
	Honolulu MSA, HI	Y	116230 FQ	122630 AW	144620 TQ	HIBLS	10/01-12/01
	Idaho	Y	107970 FQ	136640 AW		IDBLS	10/01-12/01
	Illinois	Y	70230 FQ	128240 AW		ILBLS	10/01-12/01
	Chicago PMSA, IL	Y	54120 FQ	122240 AW		ILBLS	10/01-12/01
	Indiana	Y	117270 FQ	139280 AW		INBLS	10/01-12/01
	Fort Wayne MSA, IN	Y	123170 FQ	138090 AW		INBLS	10/01-12/01
	Indianapolis MSA, IN	Y	102370 FQ	129790 AW		INBLS	10/01-12/01
	Kansas	Y	95160 FQ	132020 AW		KSBLS	10/01-12/01
	Kentucky	Y	138930 FQ	137830 AW		KYBLS	10/01-12/01
	Louisiana	Y		143190 AW		LABLS	10/01-12/01
	Maine	Y		141080 AW		MEBLS	10/01-12/01
	Portland MSA, ME	Y		138050 AW		MEBLS	10/01-12/01
	Maryland	Y	101700 FQ	121300 AW		MDBLS	10/01-12/01
	Baltimore PMSA, MD	Y	101510 FQ	119800 AW		MDBLS	10/01-12/01
	Massachusetts	Y	94260 FQ	132190 AW		MABLS	10/01-12/01
	Boston PMSA, MA-NH	Y	55960 FQ	128210 AW		MABLS	10/01-12/01
	Michigan	Y		142530 AW		MIBLS	10/01-12/01
	Detroit PMSA, MI	Y		145180 AW		MIBLS	10/01-12/01
	Grand Rapids-Muskegon-Holland MSA, MI	Y	126100 FQ	141020 AW		MIBLS	10/01-12/01
	Minnesota	Y	133240 FQ	141840 AW		MNBLS	10/01-12/01
	Minneapolis-St. Paul MSA, MN-WI	Y	129290 FQ	140840 AW		MNBLS	10/01-12/01
	Mississippi	Y	131340 FQ	138970 AW		MSBLS	10/01-12/01
	Missouri	Y	116190 FQ	139680 AW		MOBLS	10/01-12/01
	Kansas City MSA, MO-KS	Y	101460 FQ	134080 AW		MOBLS	10/01-12/01
	St. Louis MSA, MO-IL	Y	113920 FQ	139130 AW		MOBLS	10/01-12/01
	Montana	Y	107010 FQ	137810 AW		MTBLS	10/01-12/01
	Nebraska	Y	61160 FQ	130320 AW		NEBLS	10/01-12/01

AAW	Average annual wage	**AOH**	Average offered, high	**ASH**	Average starting, high	**H**	Hourly	**M**	Monthly	**S**	Special: hourly and annual		
AE	Average entry wage	**AOL**	Average offered, low	**ASL**	Average starting, low	**HI**	Highest wage paid	**MTC**	Median total compensation	**TQ**	Third quartile wage		
AEX	Average experienced wage	**APH**	Average pay, high range	**AW**	Average wage paid	**HR**	High end range	**MW**	Median wage paid	**W**	Weekly		
AO	Average offered	**APL**	Average pay, low range	**FQ**	First quartile wage	**LR**	Low end range	**SQ**	Second quartile wage	**Y**	Yearly		

Occupation/Type/Industry	Location	Per	Low	Mid	High	Source	Date
Obstetrician and Gynecologist	Omaha MSA, NE-IA	Y	63460 FQ	128120 AW		NEBLS	10/01-12/01
	Nevada	Y	100470 FQ	133350 AW		NVBLS	10/01-12/01
	New Jersey	Y	89730 FQ	134370 AW		NJBLS	10/01-12/01
	Jersey City PMSA, NJ	Y	74360 FQ	96330 AW		NJBLS	10/01-12/01
	Newark PMSA, NJ	Y	120350 FQ	139570 AW		NJBLS	10/01-12/01
	New Mexico	Y	83770 FQ	118650 AW		NMBLS	10/01-12/01
	New York	Y	79640 FQ	130130 AW		NYBLS	10/01-12/01
	Nassau-Suffolk PMSA, NY	Y	66660 FQ	117020 AW		NYBLS	10/01-12/01
	New York PMSA, NY	Y	56530 FQ	122810 AW		NYBLS	10/01-12/01
	Newburgh PMSA, NY-PA	Y	117420 FQ	128040 AW		NYBLS	10/01-12/01
	North Carolina	Y	80310 FQ	130790 AW		NCBLS	10/01-12/01
	Charlotte-Gastonia-Rock Hill MSA, NC-SC	Y	109980 FQ	138850 AW		NCBLS	10/01-12/01
	North Dakota	Y	132240 FQ	141420 AW		NDBLS	10/01-12/01
	Ohio	Y	122670 FQ	139500 AW		OHBLS	10/01-12/01
	Akron PMSA, OH	Y	84790 FQ	125110 AW		OHBLS	10/01-12/01
	Cincinnati PMSA, OH-KY-IN	Y	142330 FQ	143190 AW		OHBLS	10/01-12/01
	Cleveland-Lorain-Elyria PMSA, OH	Y	118950 FQ	136820 AW		OHBLS	10/01-12/01
	Columbus MSA, OH	Y		145290 AW		OHBLS	10/01-12/01
	Oklahoma	Y	112210 FQ	136420 AW		OKBLS	10/01-12/01
	Oregon	Y	111790 FQ	137280 AW		ORBLS	10/01-12/01
	Portland-Vancouver PMSA, OR-WA	Y	104460 FQ	132590 AW		ORBLS	10/01-12/01
	Pennsylvania	Y	120070 FQ	138080 AW		PABLS	10/01-12/01
	Allentown-Bethlehem-Easton MSA, PA	Y	103550 FQ	135230 AW		PABLS	10/01-12/01
	Harrisburg-Lebanon-Carlisle MSA, PA	Y	60550 FQ	91700 AW		PABLS	10/01-12/01
	Philadelphia PMSA, PA-NJ	Y	103030 FQ	133480 AW		PABLS	10/01-12/01
	Rhode Island	Y	99360 FQ	135100 AW		RIBLS	10/01-12/01
	Providence-Fall River-Warwick MSA, RI-MA	Y	58520 FQ	133320 AW		RIBLS	10/01-12/01
	South Carolina	Y	115310 FQ	138520 AW		SCBLS	10/01-12/01
	Greenville-Spartanburg-Anderson MSA, SC	Y	98210 FQ	127810 AW		SCBLS	10/01-12/01
	South Dakota	Y	86610 FQ	126020 AW		SDBLS	10/01-12/01
	Tennessee	Y	34950 FQ	120490 AW		TNBLS	10/01-12/01
	Texas	Y	115800 FQ	134180 AW		TXBLS	10/01-12/01
	Dallas PMSA, TX	Y	32250 FQ	114720 AW		TXBLS	10/01-12/01
	Houston PMSA, TX	Y	107390 FQ	123430 AW		TXBLS	10/01-12/01
	San Antonio MSA, TX	Y	99210 FQ	120830 AW		TXBLS	10/01-12/01
	Utah	Y	133320 FQ	138410 AW		UTBLS	10/01-12/01
	Salt Lake City-Ogden MSA, UT	Y	134420 FQ	141980 AW		UTBLS	10/01-12/01
	Vermont	Y	42290 FQ	116010 AW		VTBLS	10/01-12/01
	Virginia	Y	135000 FQ	141500 AW		VABLS	10/01-12/01
	Washington	Y	81430 FQ	128660 AW		WABLS	10/01-12/01
	Seattle-Bellevue-Everett PMSA, WA	Y	44720 FQ	121830 AW		WABLS	10/01-12/01
	West Virginia	Y	113800 FQ	138060 AW		WVBLS	10/01-12/01
	Wisconsin	Y	143580 FQ	142900 AW		WIBLS	10/01-12/01
	Milwaukee-Waukesha PMSA, WI	Y	123630 FQ	138320 AW		WIBLS	10/01-12/01
	Wyoming	Y	97260 FQ	108700 AW	119740 TQ	WYBLS	10/01-12/01
	Puerto Rico	Y	41240 FQ	64360 AW	96340 TQ	PRBLS	10/01-12/01
Occupational Health and Safety Specialist and Technician	Alabama	Y	27870 FQ	48980 AW	77990 TQ	ALBLS	10/01-12/01
	Alaska	Y	45450 FQ	72850 AW	112050 TQ	AKBLS	10/01-12/01
	Arizona	Y	24890 FQ	42150 AW	64210 TQ	AZBLS	10/01-12/01
	Arkansas	Y	16170 FQ	34200 AW	53690 TQ	ARBLS	10/01-12/01
	California	Y	30680 FQ	54000 AW	76600 TQ	CABLS	10/01-12/01
	Colorado	Y	31110 FQ	53130 AW	78070 TQ	COBLS	10/01-12/01
	Connecticut	Y	32620 FQ	50900 AW	70400 TQ	CTBLS	10/01-12/01
	Delaware	Y	28010 FQ	52730 AW	73460 TQ	DEBLS	10/01-12/01
	District of Columbia	Y	26510 FQ	61820 AW	89600 TQ	DCBLS	10/01-12/01
	Florida	Y	28830 FQ	47320 AW	66770 TQ	FLBLS	10/01-12/01
	Georgia	Y	23440 FQ	47370 AW	74870 TQ	GABLS	10/01-12/01
	Hawaii	Y	31440 FQ	47030 AW	71820 TQ	HIBLS	10/01-12/01
	Idaho	Y	29020 FQ	46730 AW	68660 TQ	IDBLS	10/01-12/01
	Illinois	Y	28680 FQ	46270 AW	67270 TQ	ILBLS	10/01-12/01

AAW	Average annual wage	**AOH**	Average offered, high	**ASH**	Average starting, high	**H**	Hourly	**M**	Monthly	**S**	Special: hourly and annual
AE	Average entry wage	**AOL**	Average offered, low	**ASL**	Average starting, low	**HI**	Highest wage paid	**MTC**	Median total compensation	**TQ**	Third quartile wage
AEX	Average experienced wage	**APH**	Average pay, high range	**AW**	Average wage paid	**HR**	High end range	**MW**	Median wage paid	**W**	Weekly
AO	Average offered	**APL**	Average pay, low range	**FQ**	First quartile wage	**LR**	Low end range	**SQ**	Second quartile wage	**Y**	Yearly

Occupation/Type/Industry	Location	Per	Low	Mid	High	Source	Date
Occupational Health and Safety Specialist and Technician	Indiana	Y	22100 FQ	41680 AW	64900 TQ	INBLS	10/01-12/01
	Iowa	Y	26620 FQ	42310 AW	60320 TQ	IABLS	10/01-12/01
	Kansas	Y	20350 FQ	42010 AW	65090 TQ	KSBLS	10/01-12/01
	Kentucky	Y	28070 FQ	46560 AW	67430 TQ	KYBLS	10/01-12/01
	Louisiana	Y	24370 FQ	42950 AW	65640 TQ	LABLS	10/01-12/01
	Maine	Y	25800 FQ	42870 AW	58760 TQ	MEBLS	10/01-12/01
	Maryland	Y	24800 FQ	50170 AW	72050 TQ	MDBLS	10/01-12/01
	Massachusetts	Y	27870 FQ	48740 AW	70810 TQ	MABLS	10/01-12/01
	Michigan	Y	23510 FQ	44760 AW	67760 TQ	MIBLS	10/01-12/01
	Minnesota	Y	29410 FQ	49310 AW	69420 TQ	MNBLS	10/01-12/01
	Mississippi	Y	18670 FQ	38560 AW	62890 TQ	MSBLS	10/01-12/01
	Missouri	Y	24300 FQ	45720 AW	69830 TQ	MOBLS	10/01-12/01
	Montana	Y	26100 FQ	42400 AW	64780 TQ	MTBLS	10/01-12/01
	Nebraska	Y	15760 FQ	32020 AW	56290 TQ	NEBLS	10/01-12/01
	Nevada	Y	32220 FQ	47110 AW	65000 TQ	NVBLS	10/01-12/01
	New Hampshire	Y	31020 FQ	47550 AW	67140 TQ	NHBLS	10/01-12/01
	New Jersey	Y	24360 FQ	45960 AW	69210 TQ	NJBLS	10/01-12/01
	New Mexico	Y	25330 FQ	41680 AW	65080 TQ	NMBLS	10/01-12/01
	New York	Y	31730 FQ	49620 AW	69560 TQ	NYBLS	10/01-12/01
	North Carolina	Y	28170 FQ	45160 AW	69670 TQ	NCBLS	10/01-12/01
	North Dakota	Y	25000 FQ	47060 AW	73610 TQ	NDBLS	10/01-12/01
	Ohio	Y	25720 FQ	45580 AW	68860 TQ	OHBLS	10/01-12/01
	Oklahoma	Y	23410 FQ	46540 AW	71100 TQ	OKBLS	10/01-12/01
	Oregon	Y	23330 FQ	43510 AW	61710 TQ	ORBLS	10/01-12/01
	Pennsylvania	Y	25720 FQ	49060 AW	79060 TQ	PABLS	10/01-12/01
	Rhode Island	Y	27460 FQ	45470 AW	67830 TQ	RIBLS	10/01-12/01
	South Carolina	Y	19860 FQ	35130 AW	54820 TQ	SCBLS	10/01-12/01
	South Dakota	Y	29960 FQ	42730 AW	58630 TQ	SDBLS	10/01-12/01
	Tennessee	Y	22400 FQ	43110 AW	67030 TQ	TNBLS	10/01-12/01
	Texas	Y	25150 FQ	42260 AW	66630 TQ	TXBLS	10/01-12/01
	Utah	Y	29620 FQ	55720 AW	85260 TQ	UTBLS	10/01-12/01
	Vermont	Y	27880 FQ	43500 AW	64870 TQ	VTBLS	10/01-12/01
	Virginia	Y	29770 FQ	48770 AW	70080 TQ	VABLS	10/01-12/01
	Washington	Y	33330 FQ	50720 AW	71370 TQ	WABLS	10/01-12/01
	West Virginia	Y	32780 FQ	55320 AW	71820 TQ	WVBLS	10/01-12/01
	Wisconsin	Y	20590 FQ	40920 AW	65540 TQ	WIBLS	10/01-12/01
	Wyoming	Y	28270 FQ	47680 AW	67230 TQ	WYBLS	10/01-12/01
	Puerto Rico	Y	19500 FQ	31790 AW	52510 TQ	PRBLS	10/01-12/01
Occupational Therapist	Alabama	Y	38940 FQ	56210 AW	78020 TQ	ALBLS	10/01-12/01
	Alaska	Y	35270 FQ	56410 AW	72360 TQ	AKBLS	10/01-12/01
	Arizona	Y	29870 FQ	52560 AW	74110 TQ	AZBLS	10/01-12/01
	Arkansas	Y	38310 FQ	51350 AW	67700 TQ	ARBLS	10/01-12/01
	California	Y	37790 FQ	59240 AW	82230 TQ	CABLS	10/01-12/01
	Colorado	Y	35640 FQ	48580 AW	59610 TQ	COBLS	10/01-12/01
	Connecticut	Y	39370 FQ	58330 AW	82280 TQ	CTBLS	10/01-12/01
	Delaware	Y	22900 FQ	36710 AW	65980 TQ	DEBLS	10/01-12/01
	District of Columbia	Y	35180 FQ	50140 AW	70130 TQ	DCBLS	10/01-12/01
	Florida	Y	28070 FQ	50660 AW	71280 TQ	FLBLS	10/01-12/01
	Georgia	Y	38790 FQ	59300 AW	86970 TQ	GABLS	10/01-12/01
	Hawaii	Y	38390 FQ	53900 AW	70990 TQ	HIBLS	10/01-12/01
	Idaho	Y	16260 FQ	35600 AW	60440 TQ	IDBLS	10/01-12/01
	Illinois	Y	15510 FQ	45850 AW	64860 TQ	ILBLS	10/01-12/01
	Indiana	Y	32140 FQ	51720 AW	74100 TQ	INBLS	10/01-12/01
	Iowa	Y	30010 FQ	44410 AW	58230 TQ	IABLS	10/01-12/01
	Kansas	Y	33630 FQ	51800 AW	78540 TQ	KSBLS	10/01-12/01
	Kentucky	Y	38570 FQ	51910 AW	69160 TQ	KYBLS	10/01-12/01
	Louisiana	Y	36660 FQ	53920 AW	76210 TQ	LABLS	10/01-12/01
	Maine	Y	36350 FQ	48860 AW	64320 TQ	MEBLS	10/01-12/01
	Maryland	Y	39860 FQ	57900 AW	83010 TQ	MDBLS	10/01-12/01
	Massachusetts	Y	35600 FQ	53940 AW	76510 TQ	MABLS	10/01-12/01
	Michigan	Y	35620 FQ	48270 AW	66750 TQ	MIBLS	10/01-12/01
	Minnesota	Y	35170 FQ	46190 AW	57290 TQ	MNBLS	10/01-12/01
	Mississippi	Y	33170 FQ	52640 AW	71860 TQ	MSBLS	10/01-12/01
	Missouri	Y	36410 FQ	50480 AW	68720 TQ	MOBLS	10/01-12/01
	Montana	Y	29340 FQ	45990 AW	61160 TQ	MTBLS	10/01-12/01
	Nebraska	Y	22500 FQ	41530 AW	57790 TQ	NEBLS	10/01-12/01
	Nevada	Y	41270 FQ	63890 AW	90160 TQ	NVBLS	10/01-12/01
	New Hampshire	Y	29750 FQ	49500 AW	68690 TQ	NHBLS	10/01-12/01
	New Jersey	Y	38900 FQ	59310 AW	89050 TQ	NJBLS	10/01-12/01
	New Mexico	Y	26860 FQ	46710 AW	67960 TQ	NMBLS	10/01-12/01

AAW	Average annual wage	**AOH**	Average offered, high	**ASH**	Average starting, high	**H**	Hourly	**M**	Monthly	**S**	Special: hourly and annual
AE	Average entry wage	**AOL**	Average offered, low	**ASL**	Average starting, low	**HI**	Highest wage paid	**MTC**	Median total compensation	**TQ**	Third quartile wage
AEX	Average experienced wage	**APH**	Average pay, high range	**AW**	Average wage paid	**HR**	High end range	**MW**	Median wage paid	**W**	Weekly
AO	Average offered	**APL**	Average pay, low range	**FQ**	First quartile wage	**LR**	Low end range	**SQ**	Second quartile wage	**Y**	Yearly

Occupation/Type/Industry	Location	Per	Low	Mid	High	Source	Date
Occupational Therapist	New York	Y	36390 FQ	52910 AW	71800 TQ	NYBLS	10/01-12/01
	North Carolina	Y	36580 FQ	54800 AW	75110 TQ	NCBLS	10/01-12/01
	North Dakota	Y	24530 FQ	41490 AW	59460 TQ	NDBLS	10/01-12/01
	Ohio	Y	37180 FQ	53600 AW	73400 TQ	OHBLS	10/01-12/01
	Oklahoma	Y	19630 FQ	49730 AW	78980 TQ	OKBLS	10/01-12/01
	Oregon	Y	38790 FQ	51380 AW	66420 TQ	ORBLS	10/01-12/01
	Pennsylvania	Y	36800 FQ	53610 AW	74560 TQ	PABLS	10/01-12/01
	Rhode Island	Y	36370 FQ	50150 AW	68430 TQ	RIBLS	10/01-12/01
	South Carolina	Y	35590 FQ	56200 AW	82110 TQ	SCBLS	10/01-12/01
	South Dakota	Y	34820 FQ	46160 AW	59500 TQ	SDBLS	10/01-12/01
	Tennessee	Y	27390 FQ	48360 AW	67940 TQ	TNBLS	10/01-12/01
	Texas	Y	33580 FQ	52380 AW	77300 TQ	TXBLS	10/01-12/01
	Utah	Y	24450 FQ	44890 AW	69920 TQ	UTBLS	10/01-12/01
	Vermont	Y	31900 FQ	46930 AW	60540 TQ	VTBLS	10/01-12/01
	Virginia	Y	36450 FQ	53150 AW	72390 TQ	VABLS	10/01-12/01
	Washington	Y	37530 FQ	50970 AW	65870 TQ	WABLS	10/01-12/01
	West Virginia	Y	21790 FQ	46370 AW	65620 TQ	WVBLS	10/01-12/01
	Wisconsin	Y	31950 FQ	47350 AW	63480 TQ	WIBLS	10/01-12/01
	Wyoming	Y	30980 FQ	47360 AW	64890 TQ	WYBLS	10/01-12/01
	Puerto Rico	Y	15990 FQ	24510 AW	40130 TQ	PRBLS	10/01-12/01
Occupational Therapist Aide	United States	Y		25760-39660 AW		FREEP1	1/00-1/00
	United States	Y		18500-25760 AW		FREEP1	1/00-1/00
	Alabama	H	6.86 FQ	14.37 AW	22.25 TQ	ALBLS	10/01-12/01
	Alabama	H	12.10 FQ	17.84 AW	21.85 TQ	ALBLS	10/01-12/01
	Arizona	H	9.02 FQ	13.31 AW	20.59 TQ	AZBLS	10/01-12/01
	Arizona	H	11.61 FQ	16.11 AW	20.81 TQ	AZBLS	10/01-12/01
	Arkansas	H	8.63 FQ	15.67 AW	21.96 TQ	ARBLS	10/01-12/01
	Arkansas	H	6.78 FQ	10.91 AW	17.24 TQ	ARBLS	10/01-12/01
	California	H	14.35 FQ	19.81 AW	26.63 TQ	CABLS	10/01-12/01
	California	H	7.45 FQ	13.32 AW	25.43 TQ	CABLS	10/01-12/01
	Colorado	H	7.44 FQ	10.51 AW	15.41 TQ	COBLS	10/01-12/01
	Colorado	H	12.03 FQ	15.58 AW	20.16 TQ	COBLS	10/01-12/01
	Connecticut	H	15.51 FQ	19.41 AW	24.01 TQ	CTBLS	10/01-12/01
	Connecticut	H	8.73 FQ	13.64 AW	19.84 TQ	CTBLS	10/01-12/01
	Delaware	H	13.83 FQ	17.97 AW	24.00 TQ	DEBLS	10/01-12/01
	District of Columbia	H	9.18 FQ	15.09 AW	21.99 TQ	DCBLS	10/01-12/01
	Florida	H	14.77 FQ	19.25 AW	25.12 TQ	FLBLS	10/01-12/01
	Florida	H	7.55 FQ	11.68 AW	19.91 TQ	FLBLS	10/01-12/01
	Georgia	H	12.94 FQ	18.11 AW	22.97 TQ	GABLS	10/01-12/01
	Georgia	H	5.97 FQ	8.93 AW	12.70 TQ	GABLS	10/01-12/01
	Hawaii	H	12.43 FQ	16.19 AW	20.50 TQ	HIBLS	10/01-12/01
	Idaho	H	13.31 FQ	16.74 AW	21.71 TQ	IDBLS	10/01-12/01
	Illinois	H	13.70 FQ	18.00 AW	22.66 TQ	ILBLS	10/01-12/01
	Illinois	H	6.67 FQ	10.25 AW	14.03 TQ	ILBLS	10/01-12/01
	Indiana	H	6.29 FQ	10.42 AW	18.90 TQ	INBLS	10/01-12/01
	Indiana	H	12.72 FQ	17.40 AW	23.57 TQ	INBLS	10/01-12/01
	Iowa	H	10.89 FQ	15.52 AW	21.06 TQ	IABLS	10/01-12/01
	Kansas	H	12.74 FQ	16.89 AW	21.00 TQ	KSBLS	10/01-12/01
	Kansas	H	6.18 FQ	11.39 AW	17.81 TQ	KSBLS	10/01-12/01
	Kentucky	H	6.85 FQ	13.22 AW	21.12 TQ	KYBLS	10/01-12/01
	Kentucky	H	12.77 FQ	17.10 AW	21.57 TQ	KYBLS	10/01-12/01
	Louisiana	H	14.67 FQ	19.37 AW	25.15 TQ	LABLS	10/01-12/01
	Louisiana	H	5.54 FQ	7.56 AW	11.37 TQ	LABLS	10/01-12/01
	Maine	H	8.48 FQ	10.96 AW	15.85 TQ	MEBLS	10/01-12/01
	Maine	H	11.82 FQ	15.05 AW	18.46 TQ	MEBLS	10/01-12/01
	Maryland	H	11.78 FQ	16.33 AW	21.19 TQ	MDBLS	10/01-12/01
	Maryland	H	9.35 FQ	12.39 AW	18.48 TQ	MDBLS	10/01-12/01
	Massachusetts	H	14.07 FQ	17.82 AW	21.88 TQ	MABLS	10/01-12/01
	Massachusetts	H	9.55 FQ	14.91 AW	21.54 TQ	MABLS	10/01-12/01
	Michigan	H	7.78 FQ	11.50 AW	16.97 TQ	MIBLS	10/01-12/01
	Michigan	H	11.28 FQ	15.25 AW	20.37 TQ	MIBLS	10/01-12/01
	Minnesota	H	9.23 FQ	13.00 AW	17.64 TQ	MNBLS	10/01-12/01
	Minnesota	H	11.29 FQ	15.52 AW	20.81 TQ	MNBLS	10/01-12/01
	Mississippi	H	11.59 FQ	16.27 AW	21.50 TQ	MSBLS	10/01-12/01
	Mississippi	H	5.78 FQ	9.14 AW	12.44 TQ	MSBLS	10/01-12/01
	Missouri	H	13.26 FQ	17.79 AW	23.41 TQ	MOBLS	10/01-12/01
	Missouri	H	7.83 FQ	11.85 AW	20.15 TQ	MOBLS	10/01-12/01
	Montana	H	11.19 FQ	14.71 AW	18.51 TQ	MTBLS	10/01-12/01
	Nebraska	H	6.51 FQ	12.44 AW	18.31 TQ	NEBLS	10/01-12/01
	Nevada	H	11.22 FQ	19.76 AW	27.01 TQ	NVBLS	10/01-12/01

AAW Average annual wage **AOH** Average offered, high **ASH** Average starting, high **H** Hourly **M** Monthly **S** Special: hourly and annual
AE Average entry wage **AOL** Average offered, low **ASL** Average starting, low **HI** Highest wage paid **MTC** Median total compensation **TQ** Third quartile wage
AEX Average experienced wage **APH** Average pay, high range **AW** Average wage paid **HR** High end range **MW** Median wage paid **W** Weekly
AO Average offered **APL** Average pay, low range **FQ** First quartile wage **LR** Low end range **SQ** Second quartile wage **Y** Yearly

Occupation/Type/Industry	Location	Per	Low	Mid	High	Source	Date
Occupational Therapist Aide	New Hampshire	H	12.05 FQ	15.87 AW	20.84 TQ	NHBLS	10/01-12/01
	New Jersey	H	7.60 FQ	12.95 AW	21.94 TQ	NJBLS	10/01-12/01
	New Mexico	H	8.21 FQ	14.24 AW	24.68 TQ	NMBLS	10/01-12/01
	New Mexico	H	7.58 FQ	12.01 AW	20.03 TQ	NMBLS	10/01-12/01
	New York	H	8.37 FQ	13.23 AW	17.51 TQ	NYBLS	10/01-12/01
	New York	H	11.66 FQ	16.80 AW	22.25 TQ	NYBLS	10/01-12/01
	North Carolina	H	9.01 FQ	16.56 AW	22.15 TQ	NCBLS	10/01-12/01
	North Carolina	H	8.98 FQ	13.48 AW	20.47 TQ	NCBLS	10/01-12/01
	North Dakota	H	10.76 FQ	13.66 AW	17.16 TQ	NDBLS	10/01-12/01
	Ohio	H	7.93 FQ	14.18 AW	22.01 TQ	OHBLS	10/01-12/01
	Ohio	H	14.11 FQ	18.09 AW	22.26 TQ	OHBLS	10/01-12/01
	Oklahoma	H	8.04 FQ	15.04 AW	21.01 TQ	OKBLS	10/01-12/01
	Oklahoma	H	6.93 FQ	8.01 AW	8.70 TQ	OKBLS	10/01-12/01
	Oregon	H	8.44 FQ	12.98 AW	19.35 TQ	ORBLS	10/01-12/01
	Oregon	H	13.19 FQ	17.25 AW	21.24 TQ	ORBLS	10/01-12/01
	Pennsylvania	H	6.76 FQ	11.38 AW	16.84 TQ	PABLS	10/01-12/01
	Pennsylvania	H	12.05 FQ	16.40 AW	21.11 TQ	PABLS	10/01-12/01
	Rhode Island	H	11.79 FQ	16.26 AW	21.13 TQ	RIBLS	10/01-12/01
	South Carolina	H	5.99 FQ	10.59 AW	17.23 TQ	SCBLS	10/01-12/01
	South Carolina	H	12.94 FQ	17.41 AW	22.03 TQ	SCBLS	10/01-12/01
	Tennessee	H	9.04 FQ	20.75 AW	33.46 TQ	TNBLS	10/01-12/01
	Tennessee	H	7.47 FQ	11.15 AW	17.15 TQ	TNBLS	10/01-12/01
	Texas	H	12.96 FQ	17.60 AW	23.03 TQ	TXBLS	10/01-12/01
	Texas	H	7.14 FQ	10.01 AW	14.44 TQ	TXBLS	10/01-12/01
	Utah	H	10.29 FQ	14.88 AW	20.13 TQ	UTBLS	10/01-12/01
	Utah	H	7.88 FQ	9.90 AW	11.31 TQ	UTBLS	10/01-12/01
	Virginia	H	7.83 FQ	14.11 AW	22.14 TQ	VABLS	10/01-12/01
	Virginia	H	12.20 FQ	17.59 AW	24.08 TQ	VABLS	10/01-12/01
	Washington	H	8.27 FQ	12.42 AW	16.80 TQ	WABLS	10/01-12/01
	Washington	H	12.16 FQ	16.06 AW	20.52 TQ	WABLS	10/01-12/01
	West Virginia	H	7.79 FQ	10.63 AW	14.82 TQ	WVBLS	10/01-12/01
	West Virginia	H	12.87 FQ	16.82 AW	23.09 TQ	WVBLS	10/01-12/01
	Wisconsin	H	8.21 FQ	11.46 AW	15.57 TQ	WIBLS	10/01-12/01
	Wisconsin	H	11.73 FQ	15.76 AW	20.50 TQ	WIBLS	10/01-12/01
	Wyoming	H	11.65 FQ	15.80 AW	20.97 TQ	WYBLS	10/01-12/01
	Puerto Rico	H	6.13 FQ	8.57 AW	11.32 TQ	PRBLS	10/01-12/01
Office Building Cleaner	Indianapolis, IN	H		6.00-8.00 AW		IBJ	1/00-1/01
Office Clerk							
General	Alabama	H	6.16 FQ	9.63 AW	13.79 TQ	ALBLS	10/01-12/01
General	Birmingham MSA, AL	H	6.11 FQ	10.01 AW	15.25 TQ	ALBLS	10/01-12/01
General	Huntsville MSA, AL	H	6.25 FQ	9.96 AW	14.68 TQ	ALBLS	10/01-12/01
General	Mobile MSA, AL	H	6.35 FQ	9.11 AW	12.80 TQ	ALBLS	10/01-12/01
General	Montgomery MSA, AL	H	6.44 FQ	9.98 AW	13.75 TQ	ALBLS	10/01-12/01
General	Alaska	H	8.58 FQ	13.02 AW	18.55 TQ	AKBLS	10/01-12/01
General	Anchorage MSA, AK	H	8.92 FQ	13.48 AW	19.38 TQ	AKBLS	10/01-12/01
General	Arizona	H	6.59 FQ	10.21 AW	15.29 TQ	AZBLS	10/01-12/01
General	Phoenix-Mesa MSA, AZ	H	6.76 FQ	10.35 AW	15.65 TQ	AZBLS	10/01-12/01
General	Tucson MSA, AZ	H	6.55 FQ	10.28 AW	14.72 TQ	AZBLS	10/01-12/01
General	Arkansas	H	6.02 FQ	8.88 AW	12.68 TQ	ARBLS	10/01-12/01
General	Fayetteville-Springdale-Rogers MSA, AR	H	6.09 FQ	8.87 AW	12.89 TQ	ARBLS	10/01-12/01
General	Fort Smith MSA, AR-OK	H	6.06 FQ	9.86 AW	15.25 TQ	ARBLS	10/01-12/01
General	Little Rock-North Little Rock MSA, AR	H	6.27 FQ	9.32 AW	13.06 TQ	ARBLS	10/01-12/01
General	California	H	7.35 FQ	12.09 AW	17.40 TQ	CABLS	10/01-12/01
General	Bakersfield MSA, CA	H	7.13 FQ	10.74 AW	15.53 TQ	CABLS	10/01-12/01
General	Chico-Paradise MSA, CA	H	6.91 FQ	10.34 AW	14.67 TQ	CABLS	10/01-12/01
General	Fresno MSA, CA	H	7.13 FQ	11.38 AW	16.06 TQ	CABLS	10/01-12/01
General	Los Angeles-Long Beach PMSA, CA	H	7.49 FQ	12.05 AW	17.38 TQ	CABLS	10/01-12/01
General	Merced MSA, CA	H	6.63 FQ	10.15 AW	14.15 TQ	CABLS	10/01-12/01
General	Modesto MSA, CA	H	7.20 FQ	10.92 AW	15.45 TQ	CABLS	10/01-12/01
General	Oakland PMSA, CA	H	7.47 FQ	13.14 AW	19.36 TQ	CABLS	10/01-12/01
General	Orange County PMSA, CA	H	7.72 FQ	12.28 AW	17.32 TQ	CABLS	10/01-12/01
General	Redding MSA, CA	H	6.88 FQ	10.96 AW	15.79 TQ	CABLS	10/01-12/01
General	Riverside-San Bernardino PMSA, CA	H	7.21 FQ	11.38 AW	16.40 TQ	CABLS	10/01-12/01
General	Sacramento PMSA, CA	H	7.30 FQ	12.16 AW	16.62 TQ	CABLS	10/01-12/01
General	Salinas MSA, CA	H	7.30 FQ	12.18 AW	16.97 TQ	CABLS	10/01-12/01
General	San Diego MSA, CA	H	7.57 FQ	11.81 AW	16.67 TQ	CABLS	10/01-12/01

AAW Average annual wage **AOH** Average offered, high **ASH** Average starting, high **H** Hourly **M** Monthly **S** Special: hourly and annual
AE Average entry wage **AOL** Average offered, low **ASL** Average starting, low **HI** Highest wage paid **MTC** Median total compensation **TQ** Third quartile wage
AEX Average experienced wage **APH** Average pay, high range **AW** Average wage paid **HR** High end range **MW** Median wage paid **W** Weekly
AO Average offered **APL** Average pay, low range **FQ** First quartile wage **LR** Low end range **SQ** Second quartile wage **Y** Yearly

Occupation/Type/Industry	Location	Per	Low	Mid	High	Source	Date
Office Clerk							
General	San Francisco PMSA, CA	H	7.09 FQ	13.18 AW	19.84 TQ	CABLS	10/01-12/01
General	San Jose PMSA, CA	H	7.43 FQ	13.06 AW	19.85 TQ	CABLS	10/01-12/01
General	San Luis Obispo-Atascadero-Paso Robles MSA, CA	H	7.43 FQ	11.73 AW	16.51 TQ	CABLS	10/01-12/01
General	Santa Barbara-Santa Maria-Lompoc MSA, CA	H	7.26 FQ	11.17 AW	15.89 TQ	CABLS	10/01-12/01
General	Santa Cruz-Watsonville PMSA, CA	H	7.67 FQ	11.86 AW	16.54 TQ	CABLS	10/01-12/01
General	Santa Rosa PMSA, CA	H	6.93 FQ	12.05 AW	17.37 TQ	CABLS	10/01-12/01
General	Stockton-Lodi MSA, CA	H	6.75 FQ	10.82 AW	14.78 TQ	CABLS	10/01-12/01
General	Vallejo-Fairfield-Napa PMSA, CA	H	7.44 FQ	12.01 AW	16.76 TQ	CABLS	10/01-12/01
General	Ventura PMSA, CA	H	6.79 FQ	11.83 AW	17.94 TQ	CABLS	10/01-12/01
General	Visalia-Tulare-Porterville MSA, CA	H	7.28 FQ	10.73 AW	15.26 TQ	CABLS	10/01-12/01
General	Colorado	H	7.35 FQ	12.08 AW	17.08 TQ	COBLS	10/01-12/01
General	Boulder-Longmont PMSA, CO	H	8.69 FQ	13.02 AW	18.92 TQ	COBLS	10/01-12/01
General	Colorado Springs MSA, CO	H	7.57 FQ	11.73 AW	16.66 TQ	COBLS	10/01-12/01
General	Denver PMSA, CO	H	8.15 FQ	12.60 AW	17.37 TQ	COBLS	10/01-12/01
General	Fort Collins-Loveland MSA, CO	H	7.19 FQ	11.07 AW	15.90 TQ	COBLS	10/01-12/01
General	Greeley PMSA, CO	H	7.05 FQ	12.67 AW	16.46 TQ	COBLS	10/01-12/01
General	Connecticut	H	7.71 FQ	12.47 AW	17.54 TQ	CTBLS	10/01-12/01
General	Bridgeport PMSA, CT	H	7.79 FQ	12.91 AW	17.75 TQ	CTBLS	10/01-12/01
General	Danbury PMSA, CT	H	7.96 FQ	13.20 AW	18.91 TQ	CTBLS	10/01-12/01
General	Hartford MSA, CT	H	8.01 FQ	12.38 AW	17.29 TQ	CTBLS	10/01-12/01
General	New Haven-Meriden PMSA, CT	H	8.16 FQ	12.22 AW	17.03 TQ	CTBLS	10/01-12/01
General	New London-Norwich MSA, CT-RI	H	6.99 FQ	11.74 AW	16.82 TQ	CTBLS	10/01-12/01
General	Stamford-Norwalk PMSA, CT	H	7.29 FQ	13.20 AW	18.49 TQ	CTBLS	10/01 12/01
General	Waterbury PMSA, CT	H	7.14 FQ	11.35 AW	16.75 TQ	CTBLS	10/01-12/01
General	Delaware	H	6.62 FQ	11.16 AW	16.85 TQ	DEBLS	10/01-12/01
General	Wilmington-Newark PMSA, DE-MD	H	6.59 FQ	11.32 AW	17.00 TQ	DEBLS	10/01-12/01
General	District of Columbia	H	8.78 FQ	13.24 AW	18.99 TQ	DCBLS	10/01-12/01
General	Washington PMSA, DC-MD-VA-WV	H	7.67 FQ	12.66 AW	18.84 TQ	DCBLS	10/01-12/01
General	Florida	H	6.33 FQ	10.22 AW	14.71 TQ	FLBLS	10/01-12/01
General	Daytona Beach MSA, FL	H	6.33 FQ	9.47 AW	13.33 TQ	FLBLS	10/01-12/01
General	Fort Lauderdale PMSA, FL	H	7.05 FQ	10.87 AW	15.40 TQ	FLBLS	10/01-12/01
General	Fort Myers-Cape Coral MSA, FL	H	6.58 FQ	10.00 AW	13.57 TQ	FLBLS	10/01-12/01
General	Fort Pierce-Port St. Lucie MSA, FL	H	6.09 FQ	9.61 AW	13.69 TQ	FLBLS	10/01-12/01
General	Fort Walton Beach MSA, FL	H	5.93 FQ	9.17 AW	13.28 TQ	FLBLS	10/01-12/01
General	Gainesville MSA, FL	H	7.22 FQ	11.23 AW	16.02 TQ	FLBLS	10/01-12/01
General	Jacksonville MSA, FL	H	6.27 FQ	9.89 AW	14.46 TQ	FLBLS	10/01-12/01
General	Lakeland-Winter Haven MSA, FL	H	6.12 FQ	9.75 AW	14.01 TQ	FLBLS	10/01-12/01
General	Melbourne-Titusville-Palm Bay MSA, FL	H	6.36 FQ	9.76 AW	13.46 TQ	FLBLS	10/01-12/01
General	Miami PMSA, FL	H	6.55 FQ	10.55 AW	15.31 TQ	FLBLS	10/01-12/01
General	Naples MSA, FL	H	6.26 FQ	10.53 AW	15.02 TQ	FLBLS	10/01-12/01
General	Ocala MSA, FL	H	6.27 FQ	9.40 AW	13.29 TQ	FLBLS	10/01-12/01
General	Orlando MSA, FL	H	6.49 FQ	10.26 AW	14.55 TQ	FLBLS	10/01-12/01
General	Pensacola MSA, FL	H	6.39 FQ	9.72 AW	13.50 TQ	FLBLS	10/01-12/01
General	Sarasota-Bradenton MSA, FL	H	5.82 FQ	8.92 AW	12.63 TQ	FLBLS	10/01-12/01
General	Tallahassee MSA, FL	H	7.23 FQ	13.18 AW	23.83 TQ	FLBLS	10/01-12/01
General	Tampa-St. Petersburg-Clearwater MSA, FL	H	6.35 FQ	10.07 AW	14.57 TQ	FLBLS	10/01-12/01
General	West Palm Beach-Boca Raton MSA, FL	H	6.00 FQ	10.20 AW	15.36 TQ	FLBLS	10/01-12/01
General	Georgia	H	6.52 FQ	11.14 AW	16.19 TQ	GABLS	10/01-12/01
General	Atlanta MSA, GA	H	7.18 FQ	12.16 AW	16.98 TQ	GABLS	10/01-12/01
General	Augusta-Aiken MSA, GA-SC	H	6.26 FQ	10.16 AW	14.35 TQ	GABLS	10/01-12/01
General	Columbus MSA, GA-AL	H	6.19 FQ	9.30 AW	12.96 TQ	GABLS	10/01-12/01
General	Macon MSA, GA	H	6.28 FQ	9.43 AW	13.42 TQ	GABLS	10/01-12/01
General	Savannah MSA, GA	H	6.61 FQ	9.93 AW	13.99 TQ	GABLS	10/01-12/01
General	Hawaii	H	6.68 FQ	11.27 AW	16.35 TQ	HIBLS	10/01-12/01
General	Honolulu MSA, HI	H	6.60 FQ	11.27 AW	16.33 TQ	HIBLS	10/01-12/01

AAW Average annual wage **AOH** Average offered, high **ASH** Average starting, high **H** Hourly **M** Monthly **S** Special: hourly and annual
AE Average entry wage **AOL** Average offered, low **ASL** Average starting, low **HI** Highest wage paid **MTC** Median total compensation **TQ** Third quartile wage
AEX Average experienced wage **APH** Average pay, high range **AW** Average wage paid **HR** High end range **MW** Median wage paid **W** Weekly
AO Average offered **APL** Average pay, low range **FQ** First quartile wage **LR** Low end range **SQ** Second quartile wage **Y** Yearly

Occupation/Type/Industry	Location	Per	Low	Mid	High	Source	Date
Office Clerk							
General	Idaho	H	6.67 FQ	10.63 AW	15.37 TQ	IDBLS	10/01-12/01
General	Boise City MSA, ID	H	7.26 FQ	10.92 AW	14.95 TQ	IDBLS	10/01-12/01
General	Illinois	H	6.72 FQ	11.11 AW	16.17 TQ	ILBLS	10/01-12/01
General	Champaign-Urbana MSA, IL	H	6.78 FQ	10.25 AW	14.35 TQ	ILBLS	10/01-12/01
General	Chicago PMSA, IL	H	7.09 FQ	11.49 AW	16.45 TQ	ILBLS	10/01-12/01
General	Peoria-Pekin MSA, IL	H	6.73 FQ	10.09 AW	14.17 TQ	ILBLS	10/01-12/01
General	Rockford MSA, IL	H	7.27 FQ	10.75 AW	14.55 TQ	ILBLS	10/01-12/01
General	Springfield MSA, IL	H	6.35 FQ	11.52 AW	16.26 TQ	ILBLS	10/01-12/01
General	Indiana	H	6.35 FQ	9.71 AW	13.39 TQ	INBLS	10/01-12/01
General	Elkhart-Goshen MSA, IN	H	6.51 FQ	10.03 AW	13.32 TQ	INBLS	10/01-12/01
General	Evansville-Henderson MSA, IN-KY	H	6.29 FQ	9.16 AW	12.23 TQ	INBLS	10/01-12/01
General	Fort Wayne MSA, IN	H	6.57 FQ	10.04 AW	13.49 TQ	INBLS	10/01-12/01
General	Gary PMSA, IN	H	6.57 FQ	10.27 AW	14.94 TQ	INBLS	10/01-12/01
General	Indianapolis MSA, IN	H	6.68 FQ	10.08 AW	13.65 TQ	INBLS	10/01-12/01
General	Lafayette MSA, IN	H	6.08 FQ	9.24 AW	12.88 TQ	INBLS	10/01-12/01
General	South Bend MSA, IN	H	6.26 FQ	9.47 AW	13.14 TQ	INBLS	10/01-12/01
General	Iowa	H	6.52 FQ	10.23 AW	14.72 TQ	IABLS	10/01-12/01
General	Cedar Rapids MSA, IA	H	6.74 FQ	10.28 AW	13.99 TQ	IABLS	10/01-12/01
General	Davenport-Moline-Rock Island MSA, IA-IL	H	6.51 FQ	10.08 AW	14.04 TQ	IABLS	10/01-12/01
General	Des Moines MSA, IA	H	7.53 FQ	11.11 AW	15.54 TQ	IABLS	10/01-12/01
General	Kansas	H	6.52 FQ	10.03 AW	14.15 TQ	KSBLS	10/01-12/01
General	Topeka MSA, KS	H	7.38 FQ	10.47 AW	14.34 TQ	KSBLS	10/01-12/01
General	Wichita MSA, KS	H	6.88 FQ	9.87 AW	13.91 TQ	KSBLS	10/01-12/01
General	Kentucky	H	6.41 FQ	10.20 AW	14.59 TQ	KYBLS	10/01-12/01
General	Lexington MSA, KY	H	6.78 FQ	10.16 AW	14.90 TQ	KYBLS	10/01-12/01
General	Louisville MSA, KY-IN	H	7.35 FQ	11.18 AW	16.14 TQ	KYBLS	10/01-12/01
General	Louisiana	H	5.93 FQ	9.24 AW	13.57 TQ	LABLS	10/01-12/01
General	Baton Rouge MSA, LA	H	6.16 FQ	8.81 AW	12.89 TQ	LABLS	10/01-12/01
General	Houma MSA, LA	H	5.85 FQ	8.76 AW	12.54 TQ	LABLS	10/01-12/01
General	Lafayette MSA, LA	H	5.90 FQ	8.84 AW	13.29 TQ	LABLS	10/01-12/01
General	Lake Charles MSA, LA	H	5.77 FQ	8.83 AW	13.93 TQ	LABLS	10/01-12/01
General	New Orleans MSA, LA	H	6.16 FQ	10.05 AW	14.67 TQ	LABLS	10/01-12/01
General	Shreveport-Bossier City MSA, LA	H	5.96 FQ	9.59 AW	13.96 TQ	LABLS	10/01-12/01
General	Maine	H	6.83 FQ	10.43 AW	15.02 TQ	MEBLS	10/01-12/01
General	Portland MSA, ME	H	7.66 FQ	11.44 AW	15.92 TQ	MEBLS	10/01-12/01
General	Maryland	H	7.41 FQ	11.79 AW	16.96 TQ	MDBLS	10/01-12/01
General	Baltimore PMSA, MD	H	7.49 FQ	11.76 AW	16.69 TQ	MDBLS	10/01-12/01
General	Massachusetts	H	8.03 FQ	12.62 AW	17.51 TQ	MABLS	10/01-12/01
General	Boston PMSA, MA-NH	H	8.45 FQ	13.03 AW	17.83 TQ	MABLS	10/01-12/01
General	Brockton PMSA, MA	H	7.26 FQ	11.41 AW	16.49 TQ	MABLS	10/01-12/01
General	Lawrence PMSA, MA-NH	H	8.41 FQ	12.15 AW	16.61 TQ	MABLS	10/01-12/01
General	Lowell PMSA, MA-NH	H	8.57 FQ	12.47 AW	17.63 TQ	MABLS	10/01-12/01
General	New Bedford PMSA, MA	H	7.10 FQ	10.67 AW	15.48 TQ	MABLS	10/01-12/01
General	Springfield MSA, MA	H	7.71 FQ	12.07 AW	16.96 TQ	MABLS	10/01-12/01
General	Worcester PMSA, MA-CT	H	7.96 FQ	12.02 AW	16.35 TQ	MABLS	10/01-12/01
General	Michigan	H	7.44 FQ	11.86 AW	16.88 TQ	MIBLS	10/01-12/01
General	Ann Arbor PMSA, MI	H	7.09 FQ	11.13 AW	16.12 TQ	MIBLS	10/01-12/01
General	Detroit PMSA, MI	H	8.30 FQ	12.82 AW	17.90 TQ	MIBLS	10/01-12/01
General	Flint PMSA, MI	H	6.84 FQ	10.71 AW	15.49 TQ	MIBLS	10/01-12/01
General	Grand Rapids-Muskegon-Holland MSA, MI	H	7.81 FQ	11.33 AW	16.01 TQ	MIBLS	10/01-12/01
General	Kalamazoo-Battle Creek MSA, MI	H	6.97 FQ	11.00 AW	16.09 TQ	MIBLS	10/01-12/01
General	Lansing-East Lansing MSA, MI	H	7.05 FQ	12.21 AW	18.55 TQ	MIBLS	10/01-12/01
General	Saginaw-Bay City-Midland MSA, MI	H	6.51 FQ	10.31 AW	15.20 TQ	MIBLS	10/01-12/01
General	Minnesota	H	7.34 FQ	11.65 AW	16.76 TQ	MNBLS	10/01-12/01
General	Duluth-Superior MSA, MN-WI	H	6.41 FQ	10.87 AW	15.78 TQ	MNBLS	10/01-12/01
General	Minneapolis-St. Paul MSA, MN-WI	H	8.09 FQ	12.41 AW	17.47 TQ	MNBLS	10/01-12/01
General	St. Cloud MSA, MN	H	7.41 FQ	10.54 AW	14.48 TQ	MNBLS	10/01-12/01
General	Mississippi	H	6.19 FQ	9.36 AW	13.16 TQ	MSBLS	10/01-12/01
General	Biloxi-Gulfport-Pascagoula MSA, MS	H	6.00 FQ	9.61 AW	14.58 TQ	MSBLS	10/01-12/01
General	Jackson MSA, MS	H	6.35 FQ	10.04 AW	14.62 TQ	MSBLS	10/01-12/01
General	Missouri	H	6.94 FQ	10.68 AW	15.61 TQ	MOBLS	10/01-12/01
General	Kansas City MSA, MO-KS	H	7.59 FQ	11.51 AW	16.40 TQ	MOBLS	10/01-12/01
General	St. Louis MSA, MO-IL	H	7.19 FQ	11.21 AW	16.20 TQ	MOBLS	10/01-12/01

AAW	Average annual wage	**AOH**	Average offered, high	**ASH**	Average starting, high	**H**	Hourly	**M**	Monthly	**S**	Special: hourly and annual
AE	Average entry wage	**AOL**	Average offered, low	**ASL**	Average starting, low	**HI**	Highest wage paid	**MTC**	Median total compensation	**TQ**	Third quartile wage
AEX	Average experienced wage	**APH**	Average pay, high range	**AW**	Average wage paid	**HR**	High end range	**MW**	Median wage paid	**W**	Weekly
AO	Average offered	**APL**	Average pay, low range	**FQ**	First quartile wage	**LR**	Low end range	**SQ**	Second quartile wage	**Y**	Yearly

Occupation/Type/Industry	Location	Per	Low	Mid	High	Source	Date
Office Clerk							
General	Springfield MSA, MO	H	6.52 FQ	9.52 AW	13.35 TQ	MOBLS	10/01-12/01
General	Montana	H	6.15 FQ	9.43 AW	13.44 TQ	MTBLS	10/01-12/01
General	Billings MSA, MT	H	6.79 FQ	10.16 AW	13.52 TQ	MTBLS	10/01-12/01
General	Nebraska	H	6.57 FQ	10.16 AW	14.22 TQ	NEBLS	10/01-12/01
General	Lincoln MSA, NE	H	7.27 FQ	10.53 AW	14.36 TQ	NEBLS	10/01-12/01
General	Omaha MSA, NE-IA	H	7.16 FQ	10.77 AW	14.71 TQ	NEBLS	10/01-12/01
General	Nevada	H	6.73 FQ	10.57 AW	15.53 TQ	NVBLS	10/01-12/01
General	Las Vegas MSA, NV-AZ	H	6.80 FQ	10.63 AW	15.66 TQ	NVBLS	10/01-12/01
General	Reno MSA, NV	H	6.99 FQ	10.69 AW	15.31 TQ	NVBLS	10/01-12/01
General	New Hampshire	H	7.13 FQ	11.22 AW	16.08 TQ	NHBLS	10/01-12/01
General	Manchester PMSA, NH	H	7.63 FQ	11.78 AW	16.67 TQ	NHBLS	10/01-12/01
General	Nashua PMSA, NH	H	7.85 FQ	12.66 AW	18.55 TQ	NHBLS	10/01-12/01
General	Portsmouth-Rochester PMSA, NH-ME	H	6.37 FQ	10.79 AW	15.82 TQ	NHBLS	10/01-12/01
General	New Jersey	H	6.66 FQ	11.71 AW	17.43 TQ	NJBLS	10/01-12/01
General	Atlantic-Cape May PMSA, NJ	H	6.43 FQ	10.71 AW	15.57 TQ	NJBLS	10/01-12/01
General	Bergen-Passaic PMSA, NJ	H	6.75 FQ	12.38 AW	18.08 TQ	NJBLS	10/01-12/01
General	Jersey City PMSA, NJ	H	7.51 FQ	12.04 AW	17.68 TQ	NJBLS	10/01-12/01
General	Middlesex-Somerset-Hunterdon PMSA, NJ	H	6.21 FQ	11.53 AW	17.86 TQ	NJBLS	10/01-12/01
General	Monmouth-Ocean PMSA, NJ	H	6.32 FQ	10.42 AW	16.11 TQ	NJBLS	10/01-12/01
General	Newark PMSA, NJ	H	7.15 FQ	12.16 AW	17.60 TQ	NJBLS	10/01-12/01
General	Trenton PMSA, NJ	H	7.28 FQ	12.54 AW	18.84 TQ	NJBLS	10/01-12/01
General	New Mexico	H	6.23 FQ	9.33 AW	13.30 TQ	NMBLS	10/01-12/01
General	Albuquerque MSA, NM	H	6.62 FQ	9.66 AW	13.83 TQ	NMBLS	10/01-12/01
General	Las Cruces MSA, NM	H	5.78 FQ	7.96 AW	10.91 TQ	NMBLS	10/01-12/01
General	New York	H	6.50 FQ	11.79 AW	17.61 TQ	NYBLS	10/01-12/01
General	Albany-Schenectady-Troy MSA, NY	H	6.99 FQ	11.22 AW	16.01 TQ	NYBLS	10/01-12/01
General	Binghamton MSA, NY	H	6.40 FQ	10.00 AW	15.10 TQ	NYBLS	10/01-12/01
General	Buffalo-Niagara Falls MSA, NY	H	6.32 FQ	10.34 AW	15.06 TQ	NYBLS	10/01-12/01
General	Dutchess County PMSA, NY	H	6.28 FQ	11.79 AW	18.43 TQ	NYBLS	10/01-12/01
General	Nassau-Suffolk PMSA, NY	H	6.56 FQ	12.23 AW	18.80 TQ	NYBLS	10/01-12/01
General	New York PMSA, NY	H	6.54 FQ	12.32 AW	18.14 TQ	NYBLS	10/01-12/01
General	Newburgh PMSA, NY-PA	H	6.69 FQ	10.86 AW	16.31 TQ	NYBLS	10/01-12/01
General	Rochester MSA, NY	H	6.52 FQ	10.88 AW	15.94 TQ	NYBLS	10/01-12/01
General	Syracuse MSA, NY	H	6.51 FQ	11.15 AW	17.07 TQ	NYBLS	10/01-12/01
General	Utica-Rome MSA, NY	H	6.47 FQ	9.66 AW	13.50 TQ	NYBLS	10/01-12/01
General	North Carolina	H	6.90 FQ	10.96 AW	15.64 TQ	NCBLS	10/01-12/01
General	Asheville MSA, NC	H	6.19 FQ	10.38 AW	14.61 TQ	NCBLS	10/01-12/01
General	Charlotte-Gastonia-Rock Hill MSA, NC-SC	H	7.55 FQ	11.58 AW	16.50 TQ	NCBLS	10/01-12/01
General	Fayetteville MSA, NC	H	7.22 FQ	10.29 AW	13.50 TQ	NCBLS	10/01-12/01
General	Greensboro-Winston-Salem-High Point MSA, NC	H	6.83 FQ	10.76 AW	15.02 TQ	NCBLS	10/01-12/01
General	Hickory-Morganton-Lenoir MSA, NC	H	7.14 FQ	10.72 AW	15.45 TQ	NCBLS	10/01-12/01
General	Raleigh-Durham-Chapel Hill MSA, NC	H	7.97 FQ	11.78 AW	16.39 TQ	NCBLS	10/01-12/01
General	Wilmington MSA, NC	H	7.24 FQ	10.88 AW	15.36 TQ	NCBLS	10/01-12/01
General	North Dakota	H	6.36 FQ	9.40 AW	13.20 TQ	NDBLS	10/01-12/01
General	Fargo-Moorhead MSA, ND-MN	H	7.23 FQ	10.33 AW	13.77 TQ	NDBLS	10/01-12/01
General	Ohio	H	6.59 FQ	10.75 AW	15.62 TQ	OHBLS	10/01-12/01
General	Akron PMSA, OH	H	7.03 FQ	10.69 AW	15.33 TQ	OHBLS	10/01-12/01
General	Canton-Massillon MSA, OH	H	7.06 FQ	10.40 AW	14.23 TQ	OHBLS	10/01-12/01
General	Cincinnati PMSA, OH-KY-IN	H	6.70 FQ	11.07 AW	15.88 TQ	OHBLS	10/01-12/01
General	Cleveland-Lorain-Elyria PMSA, OH	H	6.38 FQ	11.36 AW	16.53 TQ	OHBLS	10/01-12/01
General	Columbus MSA, OH	H	7.47 FQ	11.21 AW	15.76 TQ	OHBLS	10/01-12/01
General	Dayton-Springfield MSA, OH	H	6.64 FQ	10.91 AW	16.04 TQ	OHBLS	10/01-12/01
General	Hamilton-Middletown PMSA, OH	H	7.51 FQ	10.44 AW	14.72 TQ	OHBLS	10/01-12/01
General	Mansfield MSA, OH	H	6.01 FQ	10.10 AW	14.97 TQ	OHBLS	10/01-12/01
General	Toledo MSA, OH	H	6.95 FQ	10.85 AW	15.92 TQ	OHBLS	10/01-12/01
General	Youngstown-Warren MSA, OH	H	6.28 FQ	9.67 AW	13.64 TQ	OHBLS	10/01-12/01
General	Oklahoma	H	6.18 FQ	9.42 AW	13.45 TQ	OKBLS	10/01-12/01
General	Oklahoma City MSA, OK	H	6.22 FQ	9.35 AW	13.40 TQ	OKBLS	10/01-12/01
General	Tulsa MSA, OK	H	6.88 FQ	10.31 AW	14.57 TQ	OKBLS	10/01-12/01
General	Oregon	H	7.86 FQ	11.96 AW	16.68 TQ	ORBLS	10/01-12/01

AAW	Average annual wage	**AOH**	Average offered, high	**ASH**	Average starting, high	**H**	Hourly	**M**	Monthly	**S**	Special: hourly and annual
AE	Average entry wage	**AOL**	Average offered, low	**ASL**	Average starting, low	**HI**	Highest wage paid	**MTC**	Median total compensation	**TQ**	Third quartile wage
AEX	Average experienced wage	**APH**	Average pay, high range	**AW**	Average wage paid	**HR**	High end range	**MW**	Median wage paid	**W**	Weekly
AO	Average offered	**APL**	Average pay, low range	**FQ**	First quartile wage	**LR**	Low end range	**SQ**	Second quartile wage	**Y**	Yearly

Occupation/Type/Industry	Location	Per	Low	Mid	High	Source	Date
Office Clerk							
General	Eugene-Springfield MSA, OR	H	7.41 FQ	11.40 AW	16.28 TQ	ORBLS	10/01-12/01
General	Medford-Ashland MSA, OR	H	7.14 FQ	10.60 AW	14.93 TQ	ORBLS	10/01-12/01
General	Portland-Vancouver PMSA, OR-WA	H	8.43 FQ	12.52 AW	17.17 TQ	ORBLS	10/01-12/01
General	Salem PMSA, OR	H	8.26 FQ	11.77 AW	16.15 TQ	ORBLS	10/01-12/01
General	Pennsylvania	H	6.42 FQ	10.55 AW	15.86 TQ	PABLS	10/01-12/01
General	Allentown-Bethlehem-Easton MSA, PA	H	6.95 FQ	10.47 AW	14.25 TQ	PABLS	10/01-12/01
General	Erie MSA, PA	H	6.11 FQ	9.57 AW	14.00 TQ	PABLS	10/01-12/01
General	Harrisburg-Lebanon-Carlisle MSA, PA	H	7.17 FQ	11.80 AW	17.99 TQ	PABLS	10/01-12/01
General	Johnstown MSA, PA	H	6.05 FQ	9.10 AW	13.29 TQ	PABLS	10/01-12/01
General	Lancaster MSA, PA	H	6.99 FQ	10.76 AW	14.88 TQ	PABLS	10/01-12/01
General	Philadelphia PMSA, PA-NJ	H	6.49 FQ	11.08 AW	16.43 TQ	PABLS	10/01-12/01
General	Pittsburgh MSA, PA	H	6.36 FQ	9.83 AW	14.53 TQ	PABLS	10/01-12/01
General	Reading MSA, PA	H	7.31 FQ	10.54 AW	14.37 TQ	PABLS	10/01-12/01
General	Scranton-Wilkes-Barre-Hazleton MSA, PA	H	6.29 FQ	9.95 AW	14.51 TQ	PABLS	10/01-12/01
General	York MSA, PA	H	5.93 FQ	9.85 AW	13.87 TQ	PABLS	10/01-12/01
General	Rhode Island	H	6.70 FQ	10.85 AW	15.96 TQ	RIBLS	10/01-12/01
General	Providence-Fall River-Warwick MSA, RI-MA	H	6.78 FQ	10.94 AW	15.88 TQ	RIBLS	10/01-12/01
General	South Carolina	H	6.50 FQ	10.30 AW	14.73 TQ	SCBLS	10/01-12/01
General	Charleston-North Charleston MSA, SC	H	6.60 FQ	10.26 AW	14.55 TQ	SCBLS	10/01-12/01
General	Columbia MSA, SC	H	7.36 FQ	10.57 AW	14.59 TQ	SCBLS	10/01-12/01
General	Greenville-Spartanburg-Anderson MSA, SC	H	6.31 FQ	10.56 AW	15.76 TQ	SCBLS	10/01-12/01
General	Myrtle Beach MSA, SC	H	6.34 FQ	9.79 AW	14.94 TQ	SCBLS	10/01-12/01
General	South Dakota	H	6.06 FQ	8.31 AW	10.95 TQ	SDBLS	10/01-12/01
General	Sioux Falls MSA, SD	H	6.55 FQ	8.95 AW	11.51 TQ	SDBLS	10/01-12/01
General	Tennessee	H	6.62 FQ	10.37 AW	15.06 TQ	TNBLS	10/01-12/01
General	Chattanooga MSA, TN-GA	H	6.48 FQ	10.06 AW	14.50 TQ	TNBLS	10/01-12/01
General	Clarksville-Hopkinsville MSA, TN-KY	H	6.34 FQ	9.20 AW	13.01 TQ	TNBLS	10/01-12/01
General	Johnson City-Kingsport-Bristol MSA, TN-VA	H	6.28 FQ	9.63 AW	13.87 TQ	TNBLS	10/01-12/01
General	Knoxville MSA, TN	H	6.82 FQ	10.27 AW	14.75 TQ	TNBLS	10/01-12/01
General	Memphis MSA, TN-AR-MS	H	7.35 FQ	10.90 AW	15.57 TQ	TNBLS	10/01-12/01
General	Nashville MSA, TN	H	6.75 FQ	10.92 AW	15.92 TQ	TNBLS	10/01-12/01
General	Texas	H	6.31 FQ	10.29 AW	15.36 TQ	TXBLS	10/01-12/01
General	Amarillo MSA, TX	H	6.05 FQ	8.77 AW	12.60 TQ	TXBLS	10/01-12/01
General	Austin-San Marcos MSA, TX	H	7.26 FQ	11.26 AW	16.14 TQ	TXBLS	10/01-12/01
General	Beaumont-Port Arthur MSA, TX	H	5.96 FQ	9.32 AW	13.75 TQ	TXBLS	10/01-12/01
General	Brazoria PMSA, TX	H	6.31 FQ	9.86 AW	14.31 TQ	TXBLS	10/01-12/01
General	Brownsville-Harlingen-San Benito MSA, TX	H	5.83 FQ	8.45 AW	11.31 TQ	TXBLS	10/01-12/01
General	Corpus Christi MSA, TX	H	5.82 FQ	8.81 AW	13.11 TQ	TXBLS	10/01-12/01
General	Dallas PMSA, TX	H	6.95 FQ	11.43 AW	16.64 TQ	TXBLS	10/01-12/01
General	El Paso MSA, TX	H	6.00 FQ	8.70 AW	12.22 TQ	TXBLS	10/01-12/01
General	Fort Worth-Arlington PMSA, TX	H	7.07 FQ	10.88 AW	15.80 TQ	TXBLS	10/01-12/01
General	Galveston-Texas City PMSA, TX	H	6.89 FQ	10.18 AW	13.63 TQ	TXBLS	10/01-12/01
General	Houston PMSA, TX	H	6.64 FQ	11.01 AW	16.30 TQ	TXBLS	10/01-12/01
General	Killeen-Temple MSA, TX	H	6.23 FQ	8.94 AW	12.32 TQ	TXBLS	10/01-12/01
General	Laredo MSA, TX	H	5.93 FQ	8.38 AW	11.55 TQ	TXBLS	10/01-12/01
General	Longview-Marshall MSA, TX	H	6.11 FQ	8.90 AW	12.23 TQ	TXBLS	10/01-12/01
General	Lubbock MSA, TX	H	6.12 FQ	8.80 AW	12.54 TQ	TXBLS	10/01-12/01
General	McAllen-Edinburg-Mission MSA, TX	H	5.88 FQ	8.22 AW	11.17 TQ	TXBLS	10/01-12/01
General	Odessa-Midland MSA, TX	H	6.11 FQ	9.79 AW	14.54 TQ	TXBLS	10/01-12/01
General	San Antonio MSA, TX	H	6.71 FQ	9.70 AW	13.63 TQ	TXBLS	10/01-12/01
General	Tyler MSA, TX	H	6.36 FQ	9.66 AW	13.96 TQ	TXBLS	10/01-12/01
General	Waco MSA, TX	H	6.49 FQ	9.51 AW	13.52 TQ	TXBLS	10/01-12/01
General	Utah	H	6.80 FQ	10.37 AW	14.63 TQ	UTBLS	10/01-12/01
General	Provo-Orem MSA, UT	H	6.49 FQ	9.85 AW	13.52 TQ	UTBLS	10/01-12/01
General	Salt Lake City-Ogden MSA, UT	H	7.24 FQ	10.82 AW	15.42 TQ	UTBLS	10/01-12/01
General	Vermont	H	7.00 FQ	10.21 AW	13.80 TQ	VTBLS	10/01-12/01

AAW Average annual wage **AOH** Average offered, high **ASH** Average starting, high **H** Hourly **M** Monthly **S** Special: hourly and annual
AE Average entry wage **AOL** Average offered, low **ASL** Average starting, low **HI** Highest wage paid **MTC** Median total compensation **TQ** Third quartile wage
AEX Average experienced wage **APH** Average pay, high range **AW** Average wage paid **HR** High end range **MW** Median wage paid **W** Weekly
AO Average offered **APL** Average pay, low range **FQ** First quartile wage **LR** Low end range **SQ** Second quartile wage **Y** Yearly

Occupation/Type/Industry	Location	Per	Low	Mid	High	Source	Date
Office Clerk							
General	Burlington MSA, VT	H	7.16 FQ	10.75 AW	14.97 TQ	VTBLS	10/01-12/01
General	Virginia	H	6.64 FQ	10.97 AW	16.44 TQ	VABLS	10/01-12/01
General	Lynchburg MSA, VA	H	6.61 FQ	9.98 AW	13.59 TQ	VABLS	10/01-12/01
General	Norfolk-Virginia Beach-Newport News MSA, VA-NC	H	6.31 FQ	9.77 AW	14.16 TQ	VABLS	10/01-12/01
General	Richmond-Petersburg MSA, VA	H	6.93 FQ	11.07 AW	16.22 TQ	VABLS	10/01-12/01
General	Roanoke MSA, VA	H	6.60 FQ	9.97 AW	13.96 TQ	VABLS	10/01-12/01
General	Washington	H	7.89 FQ	12.19 AW	17.18 TQ	WABLS	10/01-12/01
General	Bremerton PMSA, WA	H	7.39 FQ	11.31 AW	16.04 TQ	WABLS	10/01-12/01
General	Olympia PMSA, WA	H	8.60 FQ	11.82 AW	15.79 TQ	WABLS	10/01-12/01
General	Richland-Kennewick-Pasco MSA, WA	H	7.25 FQ	11.44 AW	16.25 TQ	WABLS	10/01-12/01
General	Seattle-Bellevue-Everett PMSA, WA	H	8.88 FQ	12.99 AW	18.37 TQ	WABLS	10/01-12/01
General	Spokane MSA, WA	H	7.27 FQ	10.87 AW	15.34 TQ	WABLS	10/01-12/01
General	Tacoma PMSA, WA	H	7.88 FQ	12.07 AW	16.58 TQ	WABLS	10/01-12/01
General	Yakima MSA, WA	H	7.23 FQ	10.94 AW	14.66 TQ	WABLS	10/01-12/01
General	West Virginia	H	5.99 FQ	9.19 AW	13.31 TQ	WVBLS	10/01-12/01
General	Charleston MSA, WV	H	5.98 FQ	9.67 AW	13.92 TQ	WVBLS	10/01-12/01
General	Huntington-Ashland MSA, WV-KY-OH	H	5.94 FQ	8.68 AW	12.22 TQ	WVBLS	10/01-12/01
General	Wisconsin	H	6.95 FQ	10.85 AW	15.67 TQ	WIBLS	10/01-12/01
General	Appleton-Oshkosh-Neenah MSA, WI	H	6.68 FQ	10.92 AW	15.93 TQ	WIBLS	10/01-12/01
General	Green Bay MSA, WI	H	7.46 FQ	11.11 AW	15.97 TQ	WIBLS	10/01-12/01
General	Madison MSA, WI	H	8.02 FQ	12.30 AW	17.29 TQ	WIBLS	10/01-12/01
General	Milwaukee-Waukesha PMSA, WI	H	6.99 FQ	11.25 AW	16.61 TQ	WIBLS	10/01-12/01
General	Racine PMSA, WI	H	7.21 FQ	10.77 AW	15.08 TQ	WIBLS	10/01-12/01
General	Wyoming	H	5.99 FQ	8.95 AW	12.82 TQ	WYBLS	10/01-12/01
General	Cheyenne MSA, WY	H	6.18 FQ	9.06 AW	12.63 TQ	WYBLS	10/01-12/01
General	Puerto Rico	H	5.55 FQ	7.22 AW	10.39 TQ	PRBLS	10/01-12/01
General	Virgin Islands	H	6.42 FQ	8.32 AW	10.54 TQ	VIBLS	10/01-12/01
General	Guam	H	5.83 FQ	8.70 AW	12.96 TQ	GUBLS	10/01-12/01
Office Machine Operator							
Except Computer	Alabama	H	7.29 FQ	9.69 AW	13.26 TQ	ALBLS	10/01-12/01
Except Computer	Alaska	H	8.97 FQ	11.58 AW	16.15 TQ	AKBLS	10/01-12/01
Except Computer	Arizona	H	6.28 FQ	9.67 AW	15.35 TQ	AZBLS	10/01-12/01
Except Computer	Arkansas	H	6.84 FQ	9.34 AW	12.80 TQ	ARBLS	10/01-12/01
Except Computer	California	H	7.66 FQ	12.22 AW	17.90 TQ	CABLS	10/01-12/01
Except Computer	Colorado	H	7.69 FQ	11.13 AW	15.38 TQ	COBLS	10/01-12/01
Except Computer	Connecticut	H	7.71 FQ	12.24 AW	17.63 TQ	CTBLS	10/01-12/01
Except Computer	Delaware	H	7.53 FQ	11.18 AW	15.27 TQ	DEBLS	10/01-12/01
Except Computer	District of Columbia	H	9.17 FQ	13.36 AW	17.64 TQ	DCBLS	10/01-12/01
Except Computer	Florida	H	7.16 FQ	9.91 AW	13.52 TQ	FLBLS	10/01-12/01
Except Computer	Georgia	H	7.57 FQ	11.07 AW	15.65 TQ	GABLS	10/01-12/01
Except Computer	Hawaii	H	6.88 FQ	9.39 AW	13.32 TQ	HIBLS	10/01-12/01
Except Computer	Idaho	H	7.75 FQ	12.69 AW	17.75 TQ	IDBLS	10/01-12/01
Except Computer	Illinois	H	7.92 FQ	13.43 AW	22.02 TQ	ILBLS	10/01-12/01
Except Computer	Indiana	H	7.38 FQ	10.77 AW	15.71 TQ	INBLS	10/01-12/01
Except Computer	Iowa	H	7.83 FQ	11.02 AW	14.91 TQ	IABLS	10/01-12/01
Except Computer	Kansas	H	6.28 FQ	9.31 AW	13.55 TQ	KSBLS	10/01-12/01
Except Computer	Kentucky	H	7.47 FQ	10.04 AW	13.68 TQ	KYBLS	10/01-12/01
Except Computer	Louisiana	H	6.26 FQ	11.26 AW	18.67 TQ	LABLS	10/01-12/01
Except Computer	Maine	H	6.12 FQ	9.84 AW	13.40 TQ	MEBLS	10/01-12/01
Except Computer	Maryland	H	7.69 FQ	11.86 AW	19.01 TQ	MDBLS	10/01-12/01
Except Computer	Massachusetts	H	7.96 FQ	11.66 AW	16.36 TQ	MABLS	10/01-12/01
Except Computer	Michigan	H	7.20 FQ	13.39 AW	23.37 TQ	MIBLS	10/01-12/01
Except Computer	Minnesota	H	8.04 FQ	11.46 AW	15.89 TQ	MNBLS	10/01-12/01
Except Computer	Mississippi	H	6.41 FQ	9.60 AW	14.40 TQ	MSBLS	10/01-12/01
Except Computer	Missouri	H	7.03 FQ	11.83 AW	24.62 TQ	MOBLS	10/01-12/01
Except Computer	Montana	H	6.36 FQ	9.61 AW	14.35 TQ	MTBLS	10/01-12/01
Except Computer	Nevada	H	7.95 FQ	10.56 AW	13.57 TQ	NVBLS	10/01-12/01
Except Computer	New Hampshire	H	7.52 FQ	12.35 AW	16.76 TQ	NHBLS	10/01-12/01
Except Computer	New Jersey	H	7.16 FQ	11.02 AW	15.77 TQ	NJBLS	10/01-12/01
Except Computer	New Mexico	H	8.91 FQ	11.66 AW	15.59 TQ	NMBLS	10/01-12/01
Except Computer	New York	H	7.54 FQ	12.08 AW	18.33 TQ	NYBLS	10/01-12/01
Except Computer	North Carolina	H	7.18 FQ	10.30 AW	14.14 TQ	NCBLS	10/01-12/01
Except Computer	North Dakota	H	7.29 FQ	10.04 AW	13.71 TQ	NDBLS	10/01-12/01

AAW Average annual wage; **AE** Average entry wage; **AEX** Average experienced wage; **AO** Average offered; **AOH** Average offered, high; **AOL** Average offered, low; **APH** Average pay, high range; **APL** Average pay, low range; **ASH** Average starting, high; **ASL** Average starting, low; **AW** Average wage paid; **FQ** First quartile wage; **H** Hourly; **HI** Highest wage paid; **HR** High end range; **LR** Low end range; **M** Monthly; **MTC** Median total compensation; **MW** Median wage paid; **SQ** Second quartile wage; **S** Special: hourly and annual; **TQ** Third quartile wage; **W** Weekly; **Y** Yearly

Occupation/Type/Industry	Location	Per	Low	Mid	High	Source	Date
Office Machine Operator							
Except Computer	Ohio	H	7.82 FQ	11.59 AW	16.82 TQ	OHBLS	10/01-12/01
Except Computer	Oklahoma	H	6.65 FQ	10.36 AW	16.23 TQ	OKBLS	10/01-12/01
Except Computer	Oregon	H	7.31 FQ	11.46 AW	17.12 TQ	ORBLS	10/01-12/01
Except Computer	Pennsylvania	H	7.08 FQ	10.33 AW	15.59 TQ	PABLS	10/01-12/01
Except Computer	Rhode Island	H	7.49 FQ	10.46 AW	13.66 TQ	RIBLS	10/01-12/01
Except Computer	South Carolina	H	6.89 FQ	10.29 AW	13.69 TQ	SCBLS	10/01-12/01
Except Computer	South Dakota	H	7.32 FQ	10.01 AW	13.42 TQ	SDBLS	10/01-12/01
Except Computer	Tennessee	H	7.46 FQ	10.14 AW	13.65 TQ	TNBLS	10/01-12/01
Except Computer	Texas	H	7.19 FQ	10.48 AW	14.43 TQ	TXBLS	10/01-12/01
Except Computer	Utah	H	7.49 FQ	12.34 AW	19.80 TQ	UTBLS	10/01-12/01
Except Computer	Vermont	H	7.65 FQ	10.51 AW	13.49 TQ	VTBLS	10/01-12/01
Except Computer	Virginia	H	7.16 FQ	10.87 AW	16.21 TQ	VABLS	10/01-12/01
Except Computer	Washington	H	7.78 FQ	11.93 AW	18.55 TQ	WABLS	10/01-12/01
Except Computer	West Virginia	H	5.72 FQ	8.14 AW	12.55 TQ	WVBLS	10/01-12/01
Except Computer	Wisconsin	H	6.87 FQ	10.62 AW	15.31 TQ	WIBLS	10/01-12/01
Except Computer	Wyoming	H	7.14 FQ	9.96 AW	15.37 TQ	WYBLS	10/01-12/01
Except Computer	Puerto Rico	H	5.84 FQ	7.99 AW	11.11 TQ	PRBLS	10/01-12/01
Office Manager							
Golf Course	St. Louis, MO	Y		30200 AW		SLBJ	1/00-1/01
Operating Engineer and Other Construction Equipment Operator	Alabama	H	9.09 FQ	13.14 AW	18.19 TQ	ALBLS	10/01-12/01
	Alaska	H	17.70 FQ	25.23 AW	34.32 TQ	AKBLS	10/01-12/01
	Arizona	H	11.67 FQ	16.48 AW	21.54 TQ	AZBLS	10/01-12/01
	Arkansas	H	8.68 FQ	12.31 AW	16.50 TQ	ARBLS	10/01-12/01
	California	H	15.03 FQ	25.13 AW	35.31 TQ	CABLS	10/01-12/01
	Colorado	H	12.34 FQ	17.60 AW	22.79 TQ	COBLS	10/01-12/01
	Connecticut	H	14.89 FQ	21.75 AW	29.10 TQ	CTBLS	10/01-12/01
	Delaware	H	10.45 FQ	17.26 AW	25.63 TQ	DEBLS	10/01-12/01
	District of Columbia	H	14.54 FQ	18.33 AW	22.21 TQ	DCBLS	10/01-12/01
	Florida	H	9.19 FQ	13.30 AW	19.08 TQ	FLBLS	10/01-12/01
	Georgia	H	9.09 FQ	12.99 AW	18.06 TQ	GABLS	10/01-12/01
	Hawaii	H	14.27 FQ	25.43 AW	34.80 TQ	HIBLS	10/01-12/01
	Idaho	H	11.33 FQ	15.90 AW	21.16 TQ	IDBLS	10/01-12/01
	Illinois	H	12.59 FQ	24.12 AW	33.83 TQ	ILBLS	10/01-12/01
	Indiana	H	12.20 FQ	19.56 AW	27.56 TQ	INBLS	10/01-12/01
	Iowa	H	10.54 FQ	15.22 AW	20.75 TQ	IABLS	10/01-12/01
	Kansas	H	9.43 FQ	14.26 AW	22.19 TQ	KSBLS	10/01-12/01
	Kentucky	H	10.94 FQ	16.29 AW	22.77 TQ	KYBLS	10/01-12/01
	Louisiana	H	8.30 FQ	12.92 AW	18.40 TQ	LABLS	10/01-12/01
	Maine	H	9.76 FQ	13.33 AW	18.34 TQ	MEBLS	10/01-12/01
	Maryland	H	11.82 FQ	16.99 AW	23.25 TQ	MDBLS	10/01-12/01
	Massachusetts	H	15.27 FQ	25.80 AW	36.27 TQ	MABLS	10/01-12/01
	Michigan	H	12.97 FQ	20.14 AW	28.12 TQ	MIBLS	10/01-12/01
	Minnesota	H	12.84 FQ	20.04 AW	26.90 TQ	MNBLS	10/01-12/01
	Mississippi	H	8.89 FQ	12.49 AW	16.91 TQ	MSBLS	10/01-12/01
	Missouri	H	10.34 FQ	18.46 AW	26.94 TQ	MOBLS	10/01-12/01
	Montana	H	10.02 FQ	16.07 AW	23.49 TQ	MTBLS	10/01-12/01
	Nebraska	H	10.40 FQ	14.99 AW	20.65 TQ	NEBLS	10/01-12/01
	Nevada	H	14.34 FQ	22.22 AW	32.89 TQ	NVBLS	10/01-12/01
	New Hampshire	H	12.02 FQ	16.56 AW	21.48 TQ	NHBLS	10/01-12/01
	New Jersey	H	13.89 FQ	23.37 AW	34.29 TQ	NJBLS	10/01-12/01
	New Mexico	H	9.86 FQ	15.14 AW	21.36 TQ	NMBLS	10/01-12/01
	New York	H	11.80 FQ	22.10 AW	34.92 TQ	NYBLS	10/01-12/01
	North Carolina	H	9.76 FQ	13.45 AW	17.57 TQ	NCBLS	10/01-12/01
	North Dakota	H	11.46 FQ	16.36 AW	24.08 TQ	NDBLS	10/01-12/01
	Ohio	H	12.37 FQ	19.47 AW	27.20 TQ	OHBLS	10/01-12/01
	Oklahoma	H	9.40 FQ	13.25 AW	18.55 TQ	OKBLS	10/01-12/01
	Oregon	H	12.58 FQ	19.39 AW	26.99 TQ	ORBLS	10/01-12/01
	Pennsylvania	H	11.40 FQ	17.65 AW	25.93 TQ	PABLS	10/01-12/01
	Rhode Island	H	15.86 FQ	21.16 AW	27.13 TQ	RIBLS	10/01-12/01
	South Carolina	H	9.30 FQ	12.78 AW	17.55 TQ	SCBLS	10/01-12/01
	South Dakota	H	9.24 FQ	13.28 AW	17.92 TQ	SDBLS	10/01-12/01
	Tennessee	H	8.85 FQ	13.00 AW	18.09 TQ	TNBLS	10/01-12/01
	Texas	H	9.14 FQ	13.56 AW	19.82 TQ	TXBLS	10/01-12/01
	Utah	H	11.51 FQ	16.09 AW	21.54 TQ	UTBLS	10/01-12/01
	Vermont	H	10.34 FQ	13.76 AW	17.41 TQ	VTBLS	10/01-12/01
	Virginia	H	9.81 FQ	14.33 AW	19.90 TQ	VABLS	10/01-12/01
	Washington	H	15.72 FQ	22.64 AW	29.62 TQ	WABLS	10/01-12/01

AAW Average annual wage **AE** Average entry wage **AEX** Average experienced wage **AO** Average offered **AOH** Average offered, high **AOL** Average offered, low **APH** Average pay, high range **APL** Average pay, low range **ASH** Average starting, high **ASL** Average starting, low **AW** Average wage paid **FQ** First quartile wage **H** Hourly **HI** Highest wage paid **HR** High end range **LR** Low end range **M** Monthly **MTC** Median total compensation **MW** Median wage paid **SQ** Second quartile wage **S** Special: hourly and annual **TQ** Third quartile wage **W** Weekly **Y** Yearly

Occupation/Type/Industry	Location	Per	Low	Mid	High	Source	Date
Operating Engineer and Other Construction Equipment Operator	West Virginia	H	9.39 FQ	14.76 AW	23.46 TQ	WVBLS	10/01-12/01
	Wisconsin	H	13.22 FQ	20.92 AW	28.29 TQ	WIBLS	10/01-12/01
	Wyoming	H	11.33 FQ	15.32 AW	20.81 TQ	WYBLS	10/01-12/01
	Puerto Rico	H	5.89 FQ	9.25 AW	14.97 TQ	PRBLS	10/01-12/01
	Virgin Islands	H	10.83 FQ	15.16 AW	20.12 TQ	VIBLS	10/01-12/01
	Guam	H	8.17 FQ	12.39 AW	16.93 TQ	GUBLS	10/01-12/01
Operations Research Analyst	Alabama	Y	31740 FQ	59810 AW	87760 TQ	ALBLS	10/01-12/01
	Arizona	Y	26600 FQ	49580 AW	77830 TQ	AZBLS	10/01-12/01
	Arkansas	Y	23820 FQ	48420 AW	86470 TQ	ARBLS	10/01-12/01
	California	Y	39120 FQ	66350 AW	104440 TQ	CABLS	10/01-12/01
	Colorado	Y	37880 FQ	57370 AW	82110 TQ	COBLS	10/01-12/01
	Connecticut	Y	36530 FQ	63050 AW	103700 TQ	CTBLS	10/01-12/01
	Delaware	Y	26180 FQ	61630 AW	122080 TQ	DEBLS	10/01-12/01
	District of Columbia	Y	45490 FQ	72580 AW	103680 TQ	DCBLS	10/01-12/01
	Florida	Y	32530 FQ	56720 AW	88840 TQ	FLBLS	10/01-12/01
	Georgia	Y	30490 FQ	50430 AW	80920 TQ	GABLS	10/01-12/01
	Hawaii	Y	32950 FQ	51010 AW	73520 TQ	HIBLS	10/01-12/01
	Idaho	Y	33820 FQ	50170 AW	71750 TQ	IDBLS	10/01-12/01
	Illinois	Y	28940 FQ	60810 AW	100770 TQ	ILBLS	10/01-12/01
	Indiana	Y	29530 FQ	51380 AW	79970 TQ	INBLS	10/01-12/01
	Iowa	Y	29670 FQ	44070 AW	63540 TQ	IABLS	10/01-12/01
	Kansas	Y	38320 FQ	53280 AW	71970 TQ	KSBLS	10/01-12/01
	Kentucky	Y	32260 FQ	51520 AW	75230 TQ	KYBLS	10/01-12/01
	Louisiana	Y	26900 FQ	46240 AW	74140 TQ	LABLS	10/01-12/01
	Maine	Y	29390 FQ	46360 AW	62350 TQ	MEBLS	10/01-12/01
	Maryland	Y	32630 FQ	59760 AW	90500 TQ	MDBLS	10/01-12/01
	Massachusetts	Y	33920 FQ	57100 AW	92450 TQ	MABLS	10/01-12/01
	Michigan	Y	40010 FQ	62830 AW	90590 TQ	MIBLS	10/01-12/01
	Minnesota	Y	33270 FQ	50530 AW	74510 TQ	MNBLS	10/01-12/01
	Missouri	Y	27380 FQ	48370 AW	73740 TQ	MOBLS	10/01-12/01
	Montana	Y	25370 FQ	52130 AW	93600 TQ	MTBLS	10/01-12/01
	Nebraska	Y	26660 FQ	50220 AW	80220 TQ	NEBLS	10/01-12/01
	Nevada	Y	33480 FQ	49380 AW	68530 TQ	NVBLS	10/01-12/01
	New Hampshire	Y	37930 FQ	65070 AW	104650 TQ	NHBLS	10/01-12/01
	New Jersey	Y	39210 FQ	69220 AW	110020 TQ	NJBLS	10/01-12/01
	New Mexico	Y	33520 FQ	62330 AW	89880 TQ	NMBLS	10/01-12/01
	New York	Y	35700 FQ	64110 AW	104240 TQ	NYBLS	10/01-12/01
	North Carolina	Y	32640 FQ	53270 AW	82340 TQ	NCBLS	10/01-12/01
	North Dakota	Y	30770 FQ	49200 AW	78100 TQ	NDBLS	10/01-12/01
	Ohio	Y	33090 FQ	53740 AW	80770 TQ	OHBLS	10/01-12/01
	Oklahoma	Y	29530 FQ	46630 AW	69090 TQ	OKBLS	10/01-12/01
	Oregon	Y	34270 FQ	57450 AW	90000 TQ	ORBLS	10/01-12/01
	Pennsylvania	Y	31320 FQ	50180 AW	75760 TQ	PABLS	10/01-12/01
	Rhode Island	Y	37850 FQ	59240 AW	89090 TQ	RIBLS	10/01-12/01
	South Carolina	Y	30310 FQ	50050 AW	79750 TQ	SCBLS	10/01-12/01
	South Dakota	Y	28270 FQ	44340 AW	73540 TQ	SDBLS	10/01-12/01
	Tennessee	Y	32380 FQ	51360 AW	79770 TQ	TNBLS	10/01-12/01
	Texas	Y	33600 FQ	66360 AW	108380 TQ	TXBLS	10/01-12/01
	Utah	Y	30910 FQ	56210 AW	89360 TQ	UTBLS	10/01-12/01
	Vermont	Y	25060 FQ	40850 AW	64210 TQ	VTBLS	10/01-12/01
	Virginia	Y	41210 FQ	66610 AW	93270 TQ	VABLS	10/01-12/01
	Washington	Y	39080 FQ	61450 AW	91150 TQ	WABLS	10/01-12/01
	West Virginia	Y	31960 FQ	51100 AW	72020 TQ	WVBLS	10/01-12/01
	Wisconsin	Y	35980 FQ	59520 AW	90970 TQ	WIBLS	10/01-12/01
Ophthalmic Laboratory Technician	Alabama	H	7.20 FQ	9.87 AW	13.37 TQ	ALBLS	10/01-12/01
	Birmingham MSA, AL	H	7.32 FQ	9.06 AW	11.68 TQ	ALBLS	10/01-12/01
	Montgomery MSA, AL	H	8.38 FQ	13.36 AW	20.32 TQ	ALBLS	10/01-12/01
	Arizona	H	7.95 FQ	11.42 AW	15.92 TQ	AZBLS	10/01-12/01
	Phoenix-Mesa MSA, AZ	H	8.00 FQ	11.64 AW	16.27 TQ	AZBLS	10/01-12/01
	Tucson MSA, AZ	H	8.22 FQ	10.91 AW	13.72 TQ	AZBLS	10/01-12/01
	Arkansas	H	6.23 FQ	8.95 AW	12.86 TQ	ARBLS	10/01-12/01
	Little Rock-North Little Rock MSA, AR	H	7.29 FQ	8.68 AW	10.52 TQ	ARBLS	10/01-12/01
	California	H	7.58 FQ	12.64 AW	21.14 TQ	CABLS	10/01-12/01
	Los Angeles-Long Beach PMSA, CA	H	7.39 FQ	12.67 AW	24.72 TQ	CABLS	10/01-12/01
	Oakland PMSA, CA	H	7.89 FQ	11.98 AW	16.66 TQ	CABLS	10/01-12/01

AAW Average annual wage; AE Average entry wage; AEX Average experienced wage; AO Average offered; AOH Average offered, high; AOL Average offered, low; APH Average pay, high range; APL Average pay, low range; ASH Average starting, high; ASL Average starting, low; AW Average wage paid; FQ First quartile wage; H Hourly; HI Highest wage paid; HR High end range; LR Low end range; M Monthly; MTC Median total compensation; MW Median wage paid; SQ Second quartile wage; S Special: hourly and annual; TQ Third quartile wage; W Weekly; Y Yearly

Occupation/Type/Industry	Location	Per	Low	Mid	High	Source	Date
Ophthalmic Laboratory Technician	Orange County PMSA, CA	H	8.32 FQ	14.64 AW	23.96 TQ	CABLS	10/01-12/01
	Riverside-San Bernardino PMSA, CA	H	7.35 FQ	9.82 AW	13.69 TQ	CABLS	10/01-12/01
	Sacramento PMSA, CA	H	7.07 FQ	9.37 AW	13.40 TQ	CABLS	10/01-12/01
	San Diego MSA, CA	H	7.31 FQ	10.10 AW	13.95 TQ	CABLS	10/01-12/01
	San Francisco PMSA, CA	H	12.88 FQ	16.23 AW	19.56 TQ	CABLS	10/01-12/01
	Santa Rosa PMSA, CA	H	7.24 FQ	9.89 AW	15.18 TQ	CABLS	10/01-12/01
	Colorado	H	8.03 FQ	11.86 AW	16.70 TQ	COBLS	10/01-12/01
	Denver PMSA, CO	H	8.14 FQ	11.97 AW	16.82 TQ	COBLS	10/01-12/01
	Connecticut	H	9.33 FQ	14.03 AW	19.90 TQ	CTBLS	10/01-12/01
	Hartford MSA, CT	H	9.34 FQ	14.33 AW	19.86 TQ	CTBLS	10/01-12/01
	Washington PMSA, DC-MD-VA-WV	H	7.52 FQ	12.42 AW	21.28 TQ	DCBLS	10/01-12/01
	Florida	H	7.55 FQ	10.79 AW	13.83 TQ	FLBLS	10/01-12/01
	Fort Lauderdale PMSA, FL	H	7.51 FQ	12.14 AW	19.39 TQ	FLBLS	10/01-12/01
	Jacksonville MSA, FL	H	7.56 FQ	10.07 AW	13.18 TQ	FLBLS	10/01-12/01
	Miami PMSA, FL	H	7.24 FQ	9.96 AW	13.42 TQ	FLBLS	10/01-12/01
	Orlando MSA, FL	H	7.50 FQ	10.76 AW	13.97 TQ	FLBLS	10/01-12/01
	Sarasota-Bradenton MSA, FL	H	7.21 FQ	9.05 AW	12.00 TQ	FLBLS	10/01-12/01
	Tampa-St. Petersburg-Clearwater MSA, FL	H	8.40 FQ	11.71 AW	13.78 TQ	FLBLS	10/01-12/01
	West Palm Beach-Boca Raton MSA, FL	H	7.62 FQ	10.19 AW	13.15 TQ	FLBLS	10/01-12/01
	Augusta-Aiken MSA, GA-SC	H	8.26 FQ	9.69 AW	10.99 TQ	GABLS	10/01-12/01
	Columbus MSA, GA-AL	H	5.78 FQ	7.78 AW	10.51 TQ	GABLS	10/01-12/01
	Macon MSA, GA	H	6.35 FQ	8.52 AW	10.99 TQ	GABLS	10/01-12/01
	Hawaii	H	6.46 FQ	11.08 AW	16.60 TQ	HIBLS	10/01-12/01
	Honolulu MSA, HI	H	6.34 FQ	11.18 AW	16.91 TQ	HIBLS	10/01-12/01
	Idaho	H	7.61 FQ	13.06 AW	17.53 TQ	IDBLS	10/01-12/01
	Boise City MSA, ID	H	7.58 FQ	13.01 AW	17.51 TQ	IDBLS	10/01-12/01
	Illinois	H	7.73 FQ	10.18 AW	13.31 TQ	ILBLS	10/01-12/01
	Chicago PMSA, IL	H	7.76 FQ	10.14 AW	13.13 TQ	ILBLS	10/01-12/01
	Indiana	H	6.85 FQ	10.43 AW	13.95 TQ	INBLS	10/01-12/01
	Evansville-Henderson MSA, IN-KY	H	7.51 FQ	10.30 AW	13.94 TQ	INBLS	10/01-12/01
	Indianapolis MSA, IN	H	7.84 FQ	10.50 AW	13.71 TQ	INBLS	10/01-12/01
	South Bend MSA, IN	H	8.05 FQ	11.84 AW	16.48 TQ	INBLS	10/01-12/01
	Iowa	H	6.83 FQ	10.97 AW	15.97 TQ	IABLS	10/01-12/01
	Des Moines MSA, IA	H	7.75 FQ	13.84 AW	30.40 TQ	IABLS	10/01-12/01
	Kansas	H	7.74 FQ	10.92 AW	14.24 TQ	KSBLS	10/01-12/01
	Wichita MSA, KS	H	8.62 FQ	11.34 AW	15.84 TQ	KSBLS	10/01-12/01
	Kentucky	H	7.87 FQ	10.55 AW	13.56 TQ	KYBLS	10/01-12/01
	Lexington MSA, KY	H	6.86 FQ	10.63 AW	13.81 TQ	KYBLS	10/01-12/01
	Louisville MSA, KY-IN	H	7.80 FQ	10.39 AW	13.47 TQ	KYBLS	10/01-12/01
	Louisiana	H	6.66 FQ	9.46 AW	13.11 TQ	LABLS	10/01-12/01
	Baton Rouge MSA, LA	H	6.40 FQ	9.16 AW	11.60 TQ	LABLS	10/01-12/01
	New Orleans MSA, LA	H	7.39 FQ	10.37 AW	13.56 TQ	LABLS	10/01-12/01
	Maine	H	6.06 FQ	9.70 AW	15.88 TQ	MEBLS	10/01-12/01
	Maryland	H	7.54 FQ	12.36 AW	21.25 TQ	MDBLS	10/01-12/01
	Baltimore PMSA, MD	H	7.37 FQ	10.43 AW	16.11 TQ	MDBLS	10/01-12/01
	Massachusetts	H	7.63 FQ	11.06 AW	15.95 TQ	MABLS	10/01-12/01
	Boston PMSA, MA-NH	H	7.38 FQ	9.55 AW	12.03 TQ	MABLS	10/01-12/01
	Springfield MSA, MA	H	8.10 FQ	11.03 AW	18.58 TQ	MABLS	10/01-12/01
	Michigan	H	7.58 FQ	11.32 AW	16.62 TQ	MIBLS	10/01-12/01
	Ann Arbor PMSA, MI	H	8.94 FQ	10.91 AW	13.55 TQ	MIBLS	10/01-12/01
	Detroit PMSA, MI	H	7.49 FQ	11.26 AW	16.61 TQ	MIBLS	10/01-12/01
	Flint PMSA, MI	H	7.73 FQ	12.46 AW	17.41 TQ	MIBLS	10/01-12/01
	Lansing-East Lansing MSA, MI	H	7.57 FQ	10.98 AW	15.56 TQ	MIBLS	10/01-12/01
	Minnesota	H	8.39 FQ	10.74 AW	13.89 TQ	MNBLS	10/01-12/01
	Minneapolis-St. Paul MSA, MN-WI	H	8.73 FQ	11.96 AW	16.07 TQ	MNBLS	10/01-12/01
	St. Cloud MSA, MN	H	8.18 FQ	10.05 AW	12.74 TQ	MNBLS	10/01-12/01
	Mississippi	H	8.86 FQ	11.19 AW	14.22 TQ	MSBLS	10/01-12/01
	Biloxi-Gulfport-Pascagoula MSA, MS	H	9.36 FQ	11.14 AW	13.87 TQ	MSBLS	10/01-12/01
	Missouri	H	8.35 FQ	11.54 AW	15.60 TQ	MOBLS	10/01-12/01
	Kansas City MSA, MO-KS	H	8.00 FQ	10.98 AW	14.21 TQ	MOBLS	10/01-12/01
	St. Louis MSA, MO-IL	H	7.79 FQ	10.54 AW	15.18 TQ	MOBLS	10/01-12/01
	Springfield MSA, MO	H	9.05 FQ	12.49 AW	16.19 TQ	MOBLS	10/01-12/01
	Montana	H	8.90 FQ	12.15 AW	14.25 TQ	MTBLS	10/01-12/01
	Nebraska	H	6.93 FQ	9.87 AW	13.32 TQ	NEBLS	10/01-12/01

AAW Average annual wage **AOH** Average offered, high **ASH** Average starting, high **H** Hourly **M** Monthly **S** Special: hourly and annual
AE Average entry wage **AOL** Average offered, low **ASL** Average starting, low **HI** Highest wage paid **MTC** Median total compensation **TQ** Third quartile wage
AEX Average experienced wage **APH** Average pay, high range **AW** Average wage paid **HR** High end range **MW** Median wage paid **W** Weekly
AO Average offered **APL** Average pay, low range **FQ** First quartile wage **LR** Low end range **SQ** Second quartile wage **Y** Yearly

Occupation/Type/Industry	Location	Per	Low	Mid	High	Source	Date
Ophthalmic Laboratory Technician	Omaha MSA, NE-IA	H	6.88 FQ	9.62 AW	13.07 TQ	NEBLS	10/01-12/01
	Nevada	H	7.72 FQ	11.11 AW	16.48 TQ	NVBLS	10/01-12/01
	Las Vegas MSA, NV-AZ	H	7.89 FQ	11.58 AW	16.85 TQ	NVBLS	10/01-12/01
	New Hampshire	H	8.48 FQ	10.73 AW	13.49 TQ	NHBLS	10/01-12/01
	Manchester PMSA, NH	H	8.19 FQ	10.60 AW	14.24 TQ	NHBLS	10/01-12/01
	New Jersey	H	8.05 FQ	12.54 AW	19.85 TQ	NJBLS	10/01-12/01
	Bergen-Passaic PMSA, NJ	H	8.05 FQ	12.59 AW	21.13 TQ	NJBLS	10/01-12/01
	Middlesex-Somerset-Hunterdon PMSA, NJ	H	7.68 FQ	12.12 AW	19.76 TQ	NJBLS	10/01-12/01
	Monmouth-Ocean PMSA, NJ	H	8.30 FQ	12.32 AW	20.31 TQ	NJBLS	10/01-12/01
	Newark PMSA, NJ	H	9.49 FQ	13.47 AW	20.26 TQ	NJBLS	10/01-12/01
	Trenton PMSA, NJ	H	11.00 FQ	14.53 AW	17.34 TQ	NJBLS	10/01-12/01
	New Mexico	H	8.95 FQ	11.77 AW	16.91 TQ	NMBLS	10/01-12/01
	Albuquerque MSA, NM	H	9.38 FQ	12.26 AW	17.25 TQ	NMBLS	10/01-12/01
	New York	H	8.29 FQ	11.75 AW	15.66 TQ	NYBLS	10/01-12/01
	Buffalo-Niagara Falls MSA, NY	H	7.94 FQ	11.07 AW	14.90 TQ	NYBLS	10/01-12/01
	Nassau-Suffolk PMSA, NY	H	7.76 FQ	10.78 AW	14.38 TQ	NYBLS	10/01-12/01
	New York PMSA, NY	H	9.67 FQ	12.02 AW	14.86 TQ	NYBLS	10/01-12/01
	Rochester MSA, NY	H	8.40 FQ	13.49 AW	20.63 TQ	NYBLS	10/01-12/01
	Syracuse MSA, NY	H	7.49 FQ	10.80 AW	15.47 TQ	NYBLS	10/01-12/01
	North Carolina	H	7.38 FQ	10.46 AW	14.09 TQ	NCBLS	10/01-12/01
	Charlotte-Gastonia-Rock Hill MSA, NC-SC	H	6.69 FQ	9.24 AW	11.21 TQ	NCBLS	10/01-12/01
	Greensboro-Winston-Salem-High Point MSA, NC	H	8.21 FQ	11.46 AW	15.45 TQ	NCBLS	10/01-12/01
	Wilmington MSA, NC	H	7.61 FQ	12.14 AW	18.16 TQ	NCBLS	10/01-12/01
	North Dakota	H	8.63 FQ	10.62 AW	13.33 TQ	NDBLS	10/01-12/01
	Ohio	H	7.15 FQ	10.39 AW	15.26 TQ	OHBLS	10/01-12/01
	Cincinnati PMSA, OH-KY-IN	H	7.40 FQ	10.39 AW	13.91 TQ	OHBLS	10/01-12/01
	Cleveland-Lorain-Elyria PMSA, OH	H	7.09 FQ	10.71 AW	16.18 TQ	OHBLS	10/01-12/01
	Columbus MSA, OH	H	8.07 FQ	10.21 AW	12.55 TQ	OHBLS	10/01-12/01
	Dayton-Springfield MSA, OH	H	7.78 FQ	11.95 AW	17.20 TQ	OHBLS	10/01-12/01
	Youngstown-Warren MSA, OH	H	6.24 FQ	8.28 AW	10.83 TQ	OHBLS	10/01-12/01
	Oklahoma	H	7.35 FQ	9.73 AW	11.12 TQ	OKBLS	10/01-12/01
	Oklahoma City MSA, OK	H	5.79 FQ	8.70 AW	12.77 TQ	OKBLS	10/01-12/01
	Tulsa MSA, OK	H	8.93 FQ	9.92 AW	11.03 TQ	OKBLS	10/01-12/01
	Oregon	H	8.49 FQ	11.04 AW	15.20 TQ	ORBLS	10/01-12/01
	Eugene-Springfield MSA, OR	H	8.22 FQ	10.77 AW	15.11 TQ	ORBLS	10/01-12/01
	Portland-Vancouver PMSA, OR-WA	H	8.62 FQ	11.10 AW	15.27 TQ	ORBLS	10/01-12/01
	Pennsylvania	H	8.40 FQ	12.18 AW	16.97 TQ	PABLS	10/01-12/01
	Erie MSA, PA	H	7.35 FQ	10.92 AW	15.09 TQ	PABLS	10/01-12/01
	Lancaster MSA, PA	H	10.06 FQ	14.29 AW	20.49 TQ	PABLS	10/01-12/01
	Philadelphia PMSA, PA-NJ	H	7.09 FQ	10.74 AW	16.02 TQ	PABLS	10/01-12/01
	Pittsburgh MSA, PA	H	8.41 FQ	12.89 AW	17.30 TQ	PABLS	10/01-12/01
	York MSA, PA	H	10.15 FQ	13.11 AW	16.88 TQ	PABLS	10/01-12/01
	Rhode Island	H	7.42 FQ	9.75 AW	13.27 TQ	RIBLS	10/01-12/01
	Providence-Fall River-Warwick MSA, RI-MA	H	7.85 FQ	12.53 AW	16.36 TQ	RIBLS	10/01-12/01
	South Carolina	H	7.64 FQ	10.09 AW	13.01 TQ	SCBLS	10/01-12/01
	Columbia MSA, SC	H	7.77 FQ	10.70 AW	13.79 TQ	SCBLS	10/01-12/01
	Greenville-Spartanburg-Anderson MSA, SC	H	7.38 FQ	9.71 AW	12.85 TQ	SCBLS	10/01-12/01
	South Dakota	H	7.59 FQ	10.08 AW	13.43 TQ	SDBLS	10/01-12/01
	Tennessee	H	6.33 FQ	9.12 AW	12.65 TQ	TNBLS	10/01-12/01
	Chattanooga MSA, TN-GA	H	7.88 FQ	10.25 AW	14.98 TQ	TNBLS	10/01-12/01
	Memphis MSA, TN-AR-MS	H	6.99 FQ	10.19 AW	14.27 TQ	TNBLS	10/01-12/01
	Nashville MSA, TN	H	6.02 FQ	8.28 AW	11.41 TQ	TNBLS	10/01-12/01
	Texas	H	7.19 FQ	9.55 AW	13.25 TQ	TXBLS	10/01-12/01
	Austin-San Marcos MSA, TX	H	7.47 FQ	10.28 AW	13.43 TQ	TXBLS	10/01-12/01
	Brownsville-Harlingen-San Benito MSA, TX	H	6.01 FQ	7.58 AW	9.08 TQ	TXBLS	10/01-12/01
	Corpus Christi MSA, TX	H	7.29 FQ	9.55 AW	13.16 TQ	TXBLS	10/01-12/01
	Dallas PMSA, TX	H	7.28 FQ	9.62 AW	13.33 TQ	TXBLS	10/01-12/01
	El Paso MSA, TX	H	6.13 FQ	8.04 AW	10.53 TQ	TXBLS	10/01-12/01
	Fort Worth-Arlington PMSA, TX	H	7.01 FQ	8.79 AW	11.75 TQ	TXBLS	10/01-12/01
	Houston PMSA, TX	H	6.52 FQ	12.08 AW	17.30 TQ	TXBLS	10/01-12/01
	Odessa-Midland MSA, TX	H	7.30 FQ	9.12 AW	11.03 TQ	TXBLS	10/01-12/01

AAW Average annual wage **AOH** Average offered, high **ASH** Average starting, high **H** Hourly **M** Monthly **S** Special: hourly and annual
AE Average entry wage **AOL** Average offered, low **ASL** Average starting, low **HI** Highest wage paid **MTC** Median total compensation **TQ** Third quartile wage
AEX Average experienced wage **APH** Average pay, high range **AW** Average wage paid **HR** High end range **MW** Median wage paid **W** Weekly
AO Average offered **APL** Average pay, low range **FQ** First quartile wage **LR** Low end range **SQ** Second quartile wage **Y** Yearly

Occupation/Type/Industry	Location	Per	Low	Mid	High	Source	Date
Ophthalmic Laboratory Technician	San Antonio MSA, TX	H	7.87 FQ	10.55 AW	13.70 TQ	TXBLS	10/01-12/01
	Utah	H	7.51 FQ	10.55 AW	13.84 TQ	UTBLS	10/01-12/01
	Vermont	H	7.74 FQ	11.65 AW	16.67 TQ	VTBLS	10/01-12/01
	Virginia	H	7.31 FQ	10.03 AW	14.02 TQ	VABLS	10/01-12/01
	Norfolk-Virginia Beach-Newport News MSA, VA-NC	H	7.04 FQ	9.73 AW	14.20 TQ	VABLS	10/01-12/01
	Richmond-Petersburg MSA, VA	H	7.96 FQ	10.20 AW	12.92 TQ	VABLS	10/01-12/01
	Washington	H	8.22 FQ	11.30 AW	14.55 TQ	WABLS	10/01-12/01
	Richland-Kennewick-Pasco MSA, WA	H	7.97 FQ	10.01 AW	11.52 TQ	WABLS	10/01-12/01
	Seattle-Bellevue-Everett PMSA, WA	H	8.23 FQ	11.21 AW	13.91 TQ	WABLS	10/01-12/01
	Wisconsin	H	8.15 FQ	11.75 AW	17.01 TQ	WIBLS	10/01-12/01
	Madison MSA, WI	H	9.24 FQ	12.91 AW	19.13 TQ	WIBLS	10/01-12/01
	Milwaukee-Waukesha PMSA, WI	H	8.09 FQ	11.07 AW	15.16 TQ	WIBLS	10/01-12/01
Optician, Dispensing	Alabama	Y	15240 FQ	22160 AW	32120 TQ	ALBLS	10/01-12/01
	Alaska	Y	20230 FQ	36360 AW	45990 TQ	AKBLS	10/01-12/01
	Arizona	Y	16950 FQ	24540 AW	34420 TQ	AZBLS	10/01-12/01
	Arkansas	Y	16310 FQ	25240 AW	35790 TQ	ARBLS	10/01-12/01
	California	Y	19610 FQ	30900 AW	43500 TQ	CABLS	10/01-12/01
	Colorado	Y	18870 FQ	28940 AW	39030 TQ	COBLS	10/01-12/01
	Connecticut	Y	26240 FQ	42020 AW	55780 TQ	CTBLS	10/01-12/01
	Delaware	Y	15410 FQ	22530 AW	35170 TQ	DEBLS	10/01-12/01
	District of Columbia	Y	16570 FQ	25460 AW	33080 TQ	DCBLS	10/01-12/01
	Florida	Y	21550 FQ	33200 AW	43750 TQ	FLBLS	10/01-12/01
	Georgia	Y	15510 FQ	25580 AW	41190 TQ	GABLS	10/01-12/01
	Hawaii	Y	17050 FQ	27100 AW	39120 TQ	HIBLS	10/01-12/01
	Idaho	Y	13040 FQ	20080 AW	28350 TQ	IDBLS	10/01-12/01
	Illinois	Y	16770 FQ	25740 AW	34840 TQ	ILBLS	10/01-12/01
	Indiana	Y	16620 FQ	24100 AW	32510 TQ	INBLS	10/01-12/01
	Iowa	Y	15660 FQ	20920 AW	28340 TQ	IABLS	10/01-12/01
	Kansas	Y	15330 FQ	19950 AW	27000 TQ	KSBLS	10/01-12/01
	Kentucky	Y	15670 FQ	27070 AW	41670 TQ	KYBLS	10/01-12/01
	Louisiana	Y	13210 FQ	19660 AW	27570 TQ	LABLS	10/01-12/01
	Maine	Y	18680 FQ	26720 AW	36710 TQ	MEBLS	10/01-12/01
	Maryland	Y	17080 FQ	28250 AW	48710 TQ	MDBLS	10/01-12/01
	Massachusetts	Y	19180 FQ	34870 AW	77420 TQ	MABLS	10/01-12/01
	Michigan	Y	18510 FQ	26730 AW	36090 TQ	MIBLS	10/01-12/01
	Minnesota	Y	17540 FQ	26540 AW	40720 TQ	MNBLS	10/01-12/01
	Mississippi	Y	15410 FQ	24680 AW	34290 TQ	MSBLS	10/01-12/01
	Missouri	Y	15510 FQ	21580 AW	29490 TQ	MOBLS	10/01-12/01
	Montana	Y	16200 FQ	24310 AW	30100 TQ	MTBLS	10/01-12/01
	Nebraska	Y	15450 FQ	22220 AW	32060 TQ	NEBLS	10/01-12/01
	Nevada	Y	20270 FQ	33120 AW	43720 TQ	NVBLS	10/01-12/01
	New Hampshire	Y	17280 FQ	34130 AW	66950 TQ	NHBLS	10/01-12/01
	New Jersey	Y	24570 FQ	42550 AW	56240 TQ	NJBLS	10/01-12/01
	New Mexico	Y	15860 FQ	26370 AW	39360 TQ	NMBLS	10/01-12/01
	New York	Y	28280 FQ	41260 AW	54610 TQ	NYBLS	10/01-12/01
	North Carolina	Y	18760 FQ	30040 AW	44240 TQ	NCBLS	10/01-12/01
	North Dakota	Y	16700 FQ	23100 AW	34270 TQ	NDBLS	10/01-12/01
	Ohio	Y	17060 FQ	27900 AW	37920 TQ	OHBLS	10/01-12/01
	Oklahoma	Y	14240 FQ	24130 AW	48230 TQ	OKBLS	10/01-12/01
	Oregon	Y	18500 FQ	26090 AW	37010 TQ	ORBLS	10/01-12/01
	Pennsylvania	Y	16160 FQ	25950 AW	41860 TQ	PABLS	10/01-12/01
	Rhode Island	Y	18920 FQ	31010 AW	52650 TQ	RIBLS	10/01-12/01
	South Carolina	Y	17030 FQ	28060 AW	39570 TQ	SCBLS	10/01-12/01
	South Dakota	Y	16330 FQ	21720 AW	28420 TQ	SDBLS	10/01-12/01
	Tennessee	Y	16080 FQ	26910 AW	44220 TQ	TNBLS	10/01-12/01
	Texas	Y	14490 FQ	21860 AW	31330 TQ	TXBLS	10/01-12/01
	Utah	Y	15810 FQ	21980 AW	29050 TQ	UTBLS	10/01-12/01
	Vermont	Y	20870 FQ	32820 AW	50700 TQ	VTBLS	10/01-12/01
	Virginia	Y	16410 FQ	30040 AW	44330 TQ	VABLS	10/01-12/01
	Washington	Y	20310 FQ	31920 AW	44220 TQ	WABLS	10/01-12/01
	West Virginia	Y	13260 FQ	20800 AW	31930 TQ	WVBLS	10/01-12/01
	Wisconsin	Y	16960 FQ	26710 AW	41240 TQ	WIBLS	10/01-12/01
	Wyoming	Y	15620 FQ	21690 AW	29350 TQ	WYBLS	10/01-12/01
	Puerto Rico	Y	11780 FQ	18460 AW	28710 TQ	PRBLS	10/01-12/01

Occupation/Type/Industry	Location	Per	Low	Mid	High	Source	Date
Optician, Dispensing	Virgin Islands	Y	14460 FQ	20250 AW	26600 TQ	VIBLS	10/01-12/01
Optometrist	Alabama	Y	27080 FQ	67150 AW	123790 TQ	ALBLS	10/01-12/01
	Birmingham MSA, AL	Y	49230 FQ	64410 AW	90790 TQ	ALBLS	10/01-12/01
	Alaska	Y	84340 FQ	106350 AW	135720 TQ	AKBLS	10/01-12/01
	Arizona	Y	26410 FQ	87340 AW		AZBLS	10/01-12/01
	Phoenix-Mesa MSA, AZ	Y	66000 FQ	101360 AW		AZBLS	10/01-12/01
	Arkansas	Y	30850 FQ	104290 AW		ARBLS	10/01-12/01
	California	Y	62810 FQ	90310 AW		CABLS	10/01-12/01
	Bakersfield MSA, CA	Y	65460 FQ	93590 AW	117010 TQ	CABLS	10/01-12/01
	Fresno MSA, CA	Y	48010 FQ	68530 AW	105860 TQ	CABLS	10/01-12/01
	Los Angeles-Long Beach PMSA, CA	Y	62860 FQ	91020 AW		CABLS	10/01-12/01
	Modesto MSA, CA	Y	75570 FQ	100390 AW		CABLS	10/01-12/01
	Oakland PMSA, CA	Y	78700 FQ	89390 AW	107780 TQ	CABLS	10/01-12/01
	Orange County PMSA, CA	Y	42940 FQ	81610 AW	116930 TQ	CABLS	10/01-12/01
	Riverside-San Bernardino PMSA, CA	Y	78570 FQ	107050 AW		CABLS	10/01-12/01
	Sacramento PMSA, CA	Y	62080 FQ	83570 AW	110320 TQ	CABLS	10/01-12/01
	San Diego MSA, CA	Y	62070 FQ	75370 AW	90380 TQ	CABLS	10/01-12/01
	San Francisco PMSA, CA	Y	63720 FQ	91030 AW	143610 TQ	CABLS	10/01-12/01
	San Jose PMSA, CA	Y	77790 FQ	108460 AW		CABLS	10/01-12/01
	Santa Rosa PMSA, CA	Y	62560 FQ	78750 AW	107930 TQ	CABLS	10/01-12/01
	Vallejo-Fairfield-Napa PMSA, CA	Y	72500 FQ	80490 AW	90800 TQ	CABLS	10/01-12/01
	Colorado	Y	55600 FQ	81980 AW	126590 TQ	COBLS	10/01-12/01
	Boulder-Longmont PMSA, CO	Y	61520 FQ	72660 AW	89580 TQ	COBLS	10/01-12/01
	Colorado Springs MSA, CO	Y	74240 FQ	106690 AW		COBLS	10/01-12/01
	Denver PMSA, CO	Y	53980 FQ	79730 AW	124760 TQ	COBLS	10/01-12/01
	Fort Collins-Loveland MSA, CO	Y	62710 FQ	93800 AW	116350 TQ	COBLS	10/01-12/01
	Connecticut	Y	43240 FQ	93300 AW	140330 TQ	CTBLS	10/01-12/01
	Hartford MSA, CT	Y	78090 FQ	112090 AW	141230 TQ	CTBLS	10/01-12/01
	Stamford-Norwalk PMSA, CT	Y	37370 FQ	52750 AW	70080 TQ	CTBLS	10/01-12/01
	Delaware	Y	26930 FQ	57550 AW		DEBLS	10/01-12/01
	Wilmington-Newark PMSA, DE-MD	Y	26750 FQ	57990 AW		DEBLS	10/01-12/01
	District of Columbia	Y	55960 FQ	70100 AW	88160 TQ	DCBLS	10/01-12/01
	Washington PMSA, DC-MD-VA-WV	Y	41630 FQ	68000 AW	107250 TQ	DCBLS	10/01-12/01
	Florida	Y	69490 FQ	114370 AW		FLBLS	10/01-12/01
	Fort Lauderdale PMSA, FL	Y	94920 FQ	102650 AW	116970 TQ	FLBLS	10/01-12/01
	Fort Myers-Cape Coral MSA, FL	Y	94930 FQ	101890 AW	117600 TQ	FLBLS	10/01-12/01
	Jacksonville MSA, FL	Y	73610 FQ	87910 AW	130630 TQ	FLBLS	10/01-12/01
	Miami PMSA, FL	Y	87320 FQ	120400 AW		FLBLS	10/01-12/01
	Tampa-St. Petersburg-Clearwater MSA, FL	Y	120210 FQ	128300 AW		FLBLS	10/01-12/01
	West Palm Beach-Boca Raton MSA, FL	Y	55030 FQ	92830 AW		FLBLS	10/01-12/01
	Georgia	Y	45870 FQ	75110 AW	143470 TQ	GABLS	10/01-12/01
	Atlanta MSA, GA	Y	47020 FQ	81930 AW		GABLS	10/01-12/01
	Augusta-Aiken MSA, GA-SC	Y	56270 FQ	117760 AW		GABLS	10/01-12/01
	Savannah MSA, GA	Y	45260 FQ	52740 AW	65500 TQ	GABLS	10/01-12/01
	Hawaii	Y	63150 FQ	94720 AW	142900 TQ	HIBLS	10/01-12/01
	Honolulu MSA, HI	Y	64110 FQ	94200 AW	124110 TQ	HIBLS	10/01-12/01
	Idaho	Y	42760 FQ	68860 AW	115060 TQ	IDBLS	10/01-12/01
	Boise City MSA, ID	Y	40050 FQ	70890 AW		IDBLS	10/01-12/01
	Illinois	Y	47620 FQ	85920 AW	145230 TQ	ILBLS	10/01-12/01
	Champaign-Urbana MSA, IL	Y	47950 FQ	61360 AW	88810 TQ	ILBLS	10/01-12/01
	Chicago PMSA, IL	Y	49380 FQ	83910 AW	136080 TQ	ILBLS	10/01-12/01
	Peoria-Pekin MSA, IL	Y	23840 FQ	73910 AW	135870 TQ	ILBLS	10/01-12/01
	Springfield MSA, IL	Y	72500 FQ	103470 AW	144680 TQ	ILBLS	10/01-12/01
	Indiana	Y	40490 FQ	94380 AW		INBLS	10/01-12/01
	Indianapolis MSA, IN	Y	52390 FQ	97240 AW		INBLS	10/01-12/01
	Iowa	Y	33280 FQ	90670 AW		IABLS	10/01-12/01
	Kansas	Y	54490 FQ	100950 AW		KSBLS	10/01-12/01
	Wichita MSA, KS	Y	49670 FQ	79210 AW	140630 TQ	KSBLS	10/01-12/01
	Kentucky	Y	22620 FQ	65930 AW	116250 TQ	KYBLS	10/01-12/01
	Louisville MSA, KY-IN	Y	32640 FQ	68110 AW	109560 TQ	KYBLS	10/01-12/01
	Louisiana	Y	40490 FQ	96020 AW		LABLS	10/01-12/01
	New Orleans MSA, LA	Y	81300 FQ	107430 AW	141650 TQ	LABLS	10/01-12/01
	Maine	Y	27540 FQ	83180 AW		MEBLS	10/01-12/01

AAW	Average annual wage	**AOH**	Average offered, high	**ASH**	Average starting, high	**H**	Hourly	**M**	Monthly	**S**	Special: hourly and annual
AE	Average entry wage	**AOL**	Average offered, low	**ASL**	Average starting, low	**HI**	Highest wage paid	**MTC**	Median total compensation	**TQ**	Third quartile wage
AEX	Average experienced wage	**APH**	Average pay, high range	**AW**	Average wage paid	**HR**	High end range	**MW**	Median wage paid	**W**	Weekly
AO	Average offered	**APL**	Average pay, low range	**FQ**	First quartile wage	**LR**	Low end range	**SQ**	Second quartile wage	**Y**	Yearly

Occupation/Type/Industry	Location	Per	Low	Mid	High	Source	Date
Optometrist	Portland MSA, ME	Y	74680 FQ	85090 AW	93900 TQ	MEBLS	10/01-12/01
	Maryland	Y	50460 FQ	96120 AW		MDBLS	10/01-12/01
	Baltimore PMSA, MD	Y	73230 FQ	99130 AW		MDBLS	10/01-12/01
	Massachusetts	Y	44300 FQ	91360 AW		MABLS	10/01-12/01
	Boston PMSA, MA-NH	Y	64500 FQ	98510 AW		MABLS	10/01-12/01
	Springfield MSA, MA	Y	19040 FQ	34910 AW	78870 TQ	MABLS	10/01-12/01
	Worcester PMSA, MA-CT	Y	69080 FQ	82360 AW	95470 TQ	MABLS	10/01-12/01
	Michigan	Y	42460 FQ	84660 AW		MIBLS	10/01-12/01
	Detroit PMSA, MI	Y	64290 FQ	102110 AW		MIBLS	10/01-12/01
	Grand Rapids-Muskegon-Holland MSA, MI	Y	58630 FQ	75660 AW	106130 TQ	MIBLS	10/01-12/01
	Kalamazoo-Battle Creek MSA, MI	Y	60940 FQ	92730 AW	117880 TQ	MIBLS	10/01-12/01
	Lansing-East Lansing MSA, MI	Y	25520 FQ	59230 AW	97120 TQ	MIBLS	10/01-12/01
	Saginaw-Bay City-Midland MSA, MI	Y	37940 FQ	60340 AW	130800 TQ	MIBLS	10/01-12/01
	Minnesota	Y	23030 FQ	83380 AW		MNBLS	10/01-12/01
	Minneapolis-St. Paul MSA, MN-WI	Y	61330 FQ	90710 AW		MNBLS	10/01-12/01
	Mississippi	Y	48290 FQ	82530 AW		MSBLS	10/01-12/01
	Missouri	Y	53100 FQ	97570 AW		MOBLS	10/01-12/01
	Kansas City MSA, MO-KS	Y	76320 FQ	100370 AW	144120 TQ	MOBLS	10/01-12/01
	St. Louis MSA, MO-IL	Y	53480 FQ	93860 AW		MOBLS	10/01-12/01
	Montana	Y	11480 FQ	50660 AW	113370 TQ	MTBLS	10/01-12/01
	Nebraska	Y	52850 FQ	92060 AW		NEBLS	10/01-12/01
	Lincoln MSA, NE	Y	33010 FQ	70950 AW	121840 TQ	NEBLS	10/01-12/01
	Omaha MSA, NE-IA	Y	50080 FQ	80040 AW		NEBLS	10/01-12/01
	Nevada	Y	64160 FQ	92950 AW		NVBLS	10/01-12/01
	Las Vegas MSA, NV-AZ	Y	67920 FQ	104090 AW		NVBLS	10/01-12/01
	Reno MSA, NV	Y	59170 FQ	81210 AW	106230 TQ	NVBLS	10/01-12/01
	New Hampshire	Y	27890 FQ	67200 AW	112130 TQ	NHBLS	10/01-12/01
	Nashua PMSA, NH	Y	26260 FQ	51520 AW	61080 TQ	NHBLS	10/01-12/01
	New Jersey	Y	52810 FQ	83860 AW	116050 TQ	NJBLS	10/01-12/01
	Bergen-Passaic PMSA, NJ	Y	70370 FQ	82720 AW	95530 TQ	NJBLS	10/01-12/01
	Middlesex-Somerset-Hunterdon PMSA, NJ	Y	50240 FQ	92310 AW	142950 TQ	NJBLS	10/01-12/01
	Monmouth-Ocean PMSA, NJ	Y	41780 FQ	74690 AW	110310 TQ	NJBLS	10/01-12/01
	Newark PMSA, NJ	Y	74720 FQ	81460 AW	93100 TQ	NJBLS	10/01-12/01
	Trenton PMSA, NJ	Y	57290 FQ	79380 AW	92560 TQ	NJBLS	10/01-12/01
	New Mexico	Y	53340 FQ	87180 AW	121420 TQ	NMBLS	10/01-12/01
	Albuquerque MSA, NM	Y	52680 FQ	84350 AW	115340 TQ	NMBLS	10/01-12/01
	New York	Y	46610 FQ	72050 AW	111450 TQ	NYBLS	10/01-12/01
	Buffalo-Niagara Falls MSA, NY	Y	61530 FQ	86340 AW	117940 TQ	NYBLS	10/01-12/01
	Nassau-Suffolk PMSA, NY	Y	48510 FQ	77700 AW	110060 TQ	NYBLS	10/01-12/01
	New York PMSA, NY	Y	45750 FQ	66360 AW	111090 TQ	NYBLS	10/01-12/01
	Newburgh PMSA, NY-PA	Y	52260 FQ	66070 AW	85360 TQ	NYBLS	10/01-12/01
	Rochester MSA, NY	Y	69270 FQ	80610 AW	92650 TQ	NYBLS	10/01-12/01
	Syracuse MSA, NY	Y	60810 FQ	69200 AW	83090 TQ	NYBLS	10/01-12/01
	North Carolina	Y	44410 FQ	100450 AW		NCBLS	10/01-12/01
	Charlotte-Gastonia-Rock Hill MSA, NC-SC	Y	69810 FQ	110450 AW		NCBLS	10/01-12/01
	Greensboro-Winston-Salem-High Point MSA, NC	Y	44630 FQ	108770 AW	143240 TQ	NCBLS	10/01-12/01
	Raleigh-Durham-Chapel Hill MSA, NC	Y	43690 FQ	86300 AW	120610 TQ	NCBLS	10/01-12/01
	North Dakota	Y	42410 FQ	78410 AW	137190 TQ	NDBLS	10/01-12/01
	Fargo-Moorhead MSA, ND-MN	Y	18970 FQ	57900 AW	112420 TQ	NDBLS	10/01-12/01
	Ohio	Y	59740 FQ	94500 AW		OHBLS	10/01-12/01
	Akron PMSA, OH	Y	55150 FQ	90330 AW	115660 TQ	OHBLS	10/01-12/01
	Cincinnati PMSA, OH-KY-IN	Y	43290 FQ	104970 AW		OHBLS	10/01-12/01
	Cleveland-Lorain-Elyria PMSA, OH	Y	34450 FQ	89260 AW		OHBLS	10/01-12/01
	Columbus MSA, OH	Y	80710 FQ	95910 AW	113260 TQ	OHBLS	10/01-12/01
	Dayton-Springfield MSA, OH	Y	60460 FQ	78590 AW	125100 TQ	OHBLS	10/01-12/01
	Toledo MSA, OH	Y	118040 FQ	126900 AW	142540 TQ	OHBLS	10/01-12/01
	Youngstown-Warren MSA, OH	Y	71840 FQ	77930 AW	89050 TQ	OHBLS	10/01-12/01
	Oklahoma	Y	45520 FQ	85720 AW		OKBLS	10/01-12/01
	Oklahoma City MSA, OK	Y	76010 FQ	100560 AW		OKBLS	10/01-12/01
	Tulsa MSA, OK	Y	67920 FQ	90610 AW	113820 TQ	OKBLS	10/01-12/01
	Oregon	Y	31840 FQ	61890 AW	105740 TQ	ORBLS	10/01-12/01

AAW Average annual wage **AE** Average entry wage **AEX** Average experienced wage **AO** Average offered **AOH** Average offered, high **AOL** Average offered, low **APH** Average pay, high range **APL** Average pay, low range **ASH** Average starting, high **ASL** Average starting, low **AW** Average wage paid **FQ** First quartile wage **H** Hourly **HI** Highest wage paid **HR** High end range **LR** Low end range **M** Monthly **MTC** Median total compensation **MW** Median wage paid **SQ** Second quartile wage **S** Special: hourly and annual **TQ** Third quartile wage **W** Weekly **Y** Yearly

Occupation/Type/Industry	Location	Per	Low	Mid	High	Source	Date
Optometrist	Portland-Vancouver PMSA, OR-WA	Y	31590 FQ	57190 AW	99460 TQ	ORBLS	10/01-12/01
	Pennsylvania	Y	31870 FQ	93630 AW		PABLS	10/01-12/01
	Allentown-Bethlehem-Easton MSA, PA	Y	29050 FQ	79600 AW	105410 TQ	PABLS	10/01-12/01
	Harrisburg-Lebanon-Carlisle MSA, PA	Y	36880 FQ	97860 AW	139930 TQ	PABLS	10/01-12/01
	Lancaster MSA, PA	Y	61240 FQ	82190 AW		PABLS	10/01-12/01
	Pittsburgh MSA, PA	Y	27320 FQ	58010 AW	109870 TQ	PABLS	10/01-12/01
	Reading MSA, PA	Y	59150 FQ	75820 AW		PABLS	10/01-12/01
	York MSA, PA	Y	60520 FQ	81110 AW	139410 TQ	PABLS	10/01-12/01
	Rhode Island	Y	66310 FQ	97000 AW	116950 TQ	RIBLS	10/01-12/01
	Providence-Fall River-Warwick MSA, RI-MA	Y	65290 FQ	95860 AW	115010 TQ	RIBLS	10/01-12/01
	South Carolina	Y	42450 FQ	97700 AW		SCBLS	10/01-12/01
	Greenville-Spartanburg-Anderson MSA, SC	Y	46580 FQ	95530 AW		SCBLS	10/01-12/01
	South Dakota	Y	54720 FQ	101880 AW		SDBLS	10/01-12/01
	Tennessee	Y	69980 FQ	100480 AW	141540 TQ	TNBLS	10/01-12/01
	Knoxville MSA, TN	Y	75530 FQ	99440 AW		TNBLS	10/01-12/01
	Memphis MSA, TN-AR-MS	Y	62450 FQ	95020 AW		TNBLS	10/01-12/01
	Nashville MSA, TN	Y	96800 FQ	108370 AW	129190 TQ	TNBLS	10/01-12/01
	Texas	Y	37100 FQ	107890 AW		TXBLS	10/01-12/01
	El Paso MSA, TX	Y	93110 FQ	101470 AW	113820 TQ	TXBLS	10/01-12/01
	Houston PMSA, TX	Y	60640 FQ	82400 AW	109790 TQ	TXBLS	10/01-12/01
	Utah	Y	37720 FQ	69750 AW	137160 TQ	UTBLS	10/01-12/01
	Provo-Orem MSA, UT	Y	60680 FQ	72540 AW	93740 TQ	UTBLS	10/01-12/01
	Salt Lake City-Ogden MSA, UT	Y	37110 FQ	59360 AW	89370 TQ	UTBLS	10/01-12/01
	Vermont	Y	76060 FQ	97710 AW	118300 TQ	VTBLS	10/01-12/01
	Virginia	Y	40450 FQ	80080 AW	136490 TQ	VABLS	10/01-12/01
	Norfolk-Virginia Beach-Newport News MSA, VA-NC	Y	59040 FQ	91370 AW	139940 TQ	VABLS	10/01-12/01
	Richmond-Petersburg MSA, VA	Y	75190 FQ	105150 AW	141670 TQ	VABLS	10/01-12/01
	Roanoke MSA, VA	Y	19680 FQ	32060 AW	36170 TQ	VABLS	10/01-12/01
	Washington	Y	64730 FQ	93710 AW		WABLS	10/01-12/01
	Bremerton PMSA, WA	Y	60860 FQ	74630 AW	92010 TQ	WABLS	10/01-12/01
	Seattle-Bellevue-Everett PMSA, WA	Y	74100 FQ	93830 AW	112250 TQ	WABLS	10/01-12/01
	Spokane MSA, WA	Y	63400 FQ	79160 AW	95060 TQ	WABLS	10/01-12/01
	West Virginia	Y	23260 FQ	70960 AW	140090 TQ	WVBLS	10/01-12/01
	Wisconsin	Y	39920 FQ	84420 AW	139720 TQ	WIBLS	10/01-12/01
	Appleton-Oshkosh-Neenah MSA, WI	Y	49690 FQ	88850 AW		WIBLS	10/01-12/01
	Green Bay MSA, WI	Y	30180 FQ	50700 AW	112730 TQ	WIBLS	10/01-12/01
	Madison MSA, WI	Y	60100 FQ	80930 AW	114520 TQ	WIBLS	10/01-12/01
	Milwaukee-Waukesha PMSA, WI	Y	80140 FQ	116960 AW		WIBLS	10/01-12/01
	Wyoming	Y	18830 FQ	43150 AW	107570 TQ	WYBLS	10/01-12/01
	Puerto Rico	Y	42530 FQ	51140 AW	59810 TQ	PRBLS	10/01-12/01
Order Clerk	Alabama	H	6.37 FQ	10.23 AW	15.82 TQ	ALBLS	10/01-12/01
	Birmingham MSA, AL	H	6.46 FQ	10.65 AW	16.65 TQ	ALBLS	10/01-12/01
	Huntsville MSA, AL	H	7.37 FQ	10.68 AW	15.34 TQ	ALBLS	10/01-12/01
	Mobile MSA, AL	H	7.08 FQ	10.69 AW	16.01 TQ	ALBLS	10/01-12/01
	Montgomery MSA, AL	H	6.06 FQ	10.49 AW	17.12 TQ	ALBLS	10/01-12/01
	Alaska	H	9.89 FQ	15.22 AW	21.32 TQ	AKBLS	10/01-12/01
	Anchorage MSA, AK	H	9.97 FQ	15.43 AW	21.33 TQ	AKBLS	10/01-12/01
	Arizona	H	7.51 FQ	11.13 AW	16.14 TQ	AZBLS	10/01-12/01
	Phoenix-Mesa MSA, AZ	H	7.59 FQ	11.28 AW	16.20 TQ	AZBLS	10/01-12/01
	Tucson MSA, AZ	H	7.47 FQ	10.65 AW	16.19 TQ	AZBLS	10/01-12/01
	Arkansas	H	6.65 FQ	10.11 AW	14.51 TQ	ARBLS	10/01-12/01
	Fayetteville-Springdale-Rogers MSA, AR	H	6.39 FQ	9.40 AW	13.06 TQ	ARBLS	10/01-12/01
	Fort Smith MSA, AR-OK	H	7.02 FQ	10.80 AW	14.37 TQ	ARBLS	10/01-12/01
	Little Rock-North Little Rock MSA, AR	H	7.54 FQ	11.10 AW	17.12 TQ	ARBLS	10/01-12/01
	California	H	7.33 FQ	13.06 AW	19.98 TQ	CABLS	10/01-12/01
	Bakersfield MSA, CA	H	6.78 FQ	12.99 AW	25.88 TQ	CABLS	10/01-12/01
	Chico-Paradise MSA, CA	H	6.61 FQ	10.82 AW	17.51 TQ	CABLS	10/01-12/01
	Fresno MSA, CA	H	7.26 FQ	11.85 AW	18.26 TQ	CABLS	10/01-12/01

AAW	Average annual wage	**AOH**	Average offered, high	**ASH**	Average starting, high	**H**	Hourly	**M**	Monthly	**S**	Special: hourly and annual
AE	Average entry wage	**AOL**	Average offered, low	**ASL**	Average starting, low	**HI**	Highest wage paid	**MTC**	Median total compensation	**TQ**	Third quartile wage
AEX	Average experienced wage	**APH**	Average pay, high range	**AW**	Average wage paid	**HR**	High end range	**MW**	Median wage paid	**W**	Weekly
AO	Average offered	**APL**	Average pay, low range	**FQ**	First quartile wage	**LR**	Low end range	**SQ**	Second quartile wage	**Y**	Yearly

Occupation/Type/Industry	Location	Per	Low	Mid	High	Source	Date
Order Clerk	Los Angeles-Long Beach PMSA, CA	H	7.31 FQ	12.86 AW	19.47 TQ	CABLS	10/01-12/01
	Merced MSA, CA	H	6.75 FQ	11.92 AW	20.78 TQ	CABLS	10/01-12/01
	Modesto MSA, CA	H	7.70 FQ	12.56 AW	18.08 TQ	CABLS	10/01-12/01
	Oakland PMSA, CA	H	8.13 FQ	14.41 AW	21.18 TQ	CABLS	10/01-12/01
	Orange County PMSA, CA	H	6.58 FQ	12.19 AW	19.52 TQ	CABLS	10/01-12/01
	Redding MSA, CA	H	7.35 FQ	11.98 AW	17.55 TQ	CABLS	10/01-12/01
	Riverside-San Bernardino PMSA, CA	H	7.92 FQ	12.23 AW	18.39 TQ	CABLS	10/01-12/01
	Sacramento PMSA, CA	H	7.59 FQ	12.77 AW	18.00 TQ	CABLS	10/01-12/01
	Salinas MSA, CA	H	9.25 FQ	13.79 AW	18.44 TQ	CABLS	10/01-12/01
	San Diego MSA, CA	H	8.15 FQ	13.10 AW	19.28 TQ	CABLS	10/01-12/01
	San Francisco PMSA, CA	H	9.41 FQ	14.72 AW	21.22 TQ	CABLS	10/01-12/01
	San Jose PMSA, CA	H	11.18 FQ	16.52 AW	23.72 TQ	CABLS	10/01-12/01
	San Luis Obispo-Atascadero-Paso Robles MSA, CA	H	8.56 FQ	12.06 AW	16.58 TQ	CABLS	10/01-12/01
	Santa Barbara-Santa Maria-Lompoc MSA, CA	H	7.11 FQ	12.02 AW	17.41 TQ	CABLS	10/01-12/01
	Santa Cruz-Watsonville PMSA, CA	H	7.51 FQ	11.62 AW	16.94 TQ	CABLS	10/01-12/01
	Santa Rosa PMSA, CA	H	8.14 FQ	13.45 AW	19.44 TQ	CABLS	10/01-12/01
	Stockton-Lodi MSA, CA	H	6.89 FQ	11.53 AW	16.79 TQ	CABLS	10/01-12/01
	Vallejo-Fairfield-Napa PMSA, CA	H	7.67 FQ	12.95 AW	18.48 TQ	CABLS	10/01-12/01
	Ventura PMSA, CA	H	7.85 FQ	13.31 AW	20.30 TQ	CABLS	10/01-12/01
	Visalia-Tulare-Porterville MSA, CA	H	7.18 FQ	10.46 AW	14.58 TQ	CABLS	10/01-12/01
	Colorado	H	8.17 FQ	12.57 AW	17.57 TQ	COBLS	10/01-12/01
	Boulder-Longmont PMSA, CO	H	9.23 FQ	13.57 AW	18.27 TQ	COBLS	10/01-12/01
	Colorado Springs MSA, CO	H	6.69 FQ	11.13 AW	16.58 TQ	COBLS	10/01-12/01
	Denver PMSA, CO	H	9.15 FQ	13.21 AW	17.97 TQ	COBLS	10/01-12/01
	Fort Collins-Loveland MSA, CO	H	7.52 FQ	12.44 AW	20.16 TQ	COBLS	10/01-12/01
	Greeley PMSA, CO	H	8.72 FQ	12.38 AW	16.73 TQ	COBLS	10/01-12/01
	Connecticut	H	8.37 FQ	14.16 AW	21.11 TQ	CTBLS	10/01-12/01
	Bridgeport PMSA, CT	H	9.36 FQ	14.27 AW	20.46 TQ	CTBLS	10/01-12/01
	Danbury PMSA, CT	H	10.13 FQ	15.75 AW	20.65 TQ	CTBLS	10/01-12/01
	Hartford MSA, CT	H	8.94 FQ	13.68 AW	20.23 TQ	CTBLS	10/01-12/01
	New Haven-Meriden PMSA, CT	H	7.81 FQ	13.21 AW	19.56 TQ	CTBLS	10/01-12/01
	New London-Norwich MSA, CT-RI	H	7.59 FQ	11.17 AW	17.33 TQ	CTBLS	10/01-12/01
	Stamford-Norwalk PMSA, CT	H	8.52 FQ	16.75 AW	24.87 TQ	CTBLS	10/01-12/01
	Waterbury PMSA, CT	H	7.78 FQ	12.40 AW	17.97 TQ	CTBLS	10/01-12/01
	Delaware	H	8.55 FQ	13.71 AW	19.23 TQ	DEBLS	10/01-12/01
	Wilmington-Newark PMSA, DE-MD	H	9.44 FQ	14.56 AW	19.96 TQ	DEBLS	10/01-12/01
	District of Columbia	H	8.09 FQ	13.35 AW	20.54 TQ	DCBLS	10/01-12/01
	Washington PMSA, DC-MD-VA-WV	H	8.15 FQ	13.34 AW	19.95 TQ	DCBLS	10/01-12/01
	Florida	H	7.49 FQ	11.80 AW	16.96 TQ	FLBLS	10/01-12/01
	Daytona Beach MSA, FL	H	6.99 FQ	10.17 AW	13.69 TQ	FLBLS	10/01-12/01
	Fort Lauderdale PMSA, FL	H	7.59 FQ	11.34 AW	16.48 TQ	FLBLS	10/01-12/01
	Fort Myers-Cape Coral MSA, FL	H	8.25 FQ	13.11 AW	17.63 TQ	FLBLS	10/01-12/01
	Fort Pierce-Port St. Lucie MSA, FL	H	7.02 FQ	11.19 AW	15.97 TQ	FLBLS	10/01-12/01
	Fort Walton Beach MSA, FL	H	7.04 FQ	10.60 AW	16.63 TQ	FLBLS	10/01-12/01
	Gainesville MSA, FL	H	6.65 FQ	9.76 AW	14.09 TQ	FLBLS	10/01-12/01
	Jacksonville MSA, FL	H	7.61 FQ	11.46 AW	15.81 TQ	FLBLS	10/01-12/01
	Lakeland-Winter Haven MSA, FL	H	7.71 FQ	12.57 AW	18.49 TQ	FLBLS	10/01-12/01
	Melbourne-Titusville-Palm Bay MSA, FL	H	5.99 FQ	8.78 AW	12.37 TQ	FLBLS	10/01-12/01
	Miami PMSA, FL	H	7.41 FQ	11.95 AW	17.29 TQ	FLBLS	10/01-12/01
	Naples MSA, FL	H	9.15 FQ	13.15 AW	20.10 TQ	FLBLS	10/01-12/01
	Ocala MSA, FL	H	7.36 FQ	9.88 AW	13.89 TQ	FLBLS	10/01-12/01
	Orlando MSA, FL	H	7.97 FQ	12.42 AW	18.69 TQ	FLBLS	10/01-12/01
	Pensacola MSA, FL	H	6.71 FQ	10.19 AW	15.25 TQ	FLBLS	10/01-12/01
	Sarasota-Bradenton MSA, FL	H	7.71 FQ	12.28 AW	17.58 TQ	FLBLS	10/01-12/01
	Tallahassee MSA, FL	H	7.22 FQ	10.52 AW	15.06 TQ	FLBLS	10/01-12/01

AAW Average annual wage **AOH** Average offered, high **ASH** Average starting, high **H** Hourly **M** Monthly **S** Special: hourly and annual
AE Average entry wage **AOL** Average offered, low **ASL** Average starting, low **HI** Highest wage paid **MTC** Median total compensation **TQ** Third quartile wage
AEX Average experienced wage **APH** Average pay, high range **AW** Average wage paid **HR** High end range **MW** Median wage paid **W** Weekly
AO Average offered **APL** Average pay, low range **FQ** First quartile wage **LR** Low end range **SQ** Second quartile wage **Y** Yearly

Occupation/Type/Industry	Location	Per	Low	Mid	High	Source	Date
Order Clerk	Tampa-St. Petersburg-Clearwater MSA, FL	H	7.54 FQ	12.38 AW	17.82 TQ	FLBLS	10/01-12/01
	West Palm Beach-Boca Raton MSA, FL	H	8.46 FQ	12.22 AW	16.43 TQ	FLBLS	10/01-12/01
	Georgia	H	8.11 FQ	12.30 AW	17.24 TQ	GABLS	10/01-12/01
	Atlanta MSA, GA	H	8.85 FQ	13.03 AW	17.84 TQ	GABLS	10/01-12/01
	Augusta-Aiken MSA, GA-SC	H	6.89 FQ	10.57 AW	14.51 TQ	GABLS	10/01-12/01
	Columbus MSA, GA-AL	H	6.57 FQ	10.39 AW	15.78 TQ	GABLS	10/01-12/01
	Macon MSA, GA	H	7.53 FQ	11.55 AW	15.31 TQ	GABLS	10/01-12/01
	Savannah MSA, GA	H	6.63 FQ	10.59 AW	14.35 TQ	GABLS	10/01-12/01
	Hawaii	H	7.92 FQ	12.31 AW	16.81 TQ	HIBLS	10/01-12/01
	Honolulu MSA, HI	H	8.13 FQ	12.61 AW	16.87 TQ	HIBLS	10/01-12/01
	Idaho	H	7.34 FQ	9.96 AW	14.32 TQ	IDBLS	10/01-12/01
	Boise City MSA, ID	H	8.70 FQ	11.74 AW	16.04 TQ	IDBLS	10/01-12/01
	Illinois	H	7.74 FQ	12.63 AW	18.36 TQ	ILBLS	10/01-12/01
	Champaign-Urbana MSA, IL	H	6.72 FQ	13.64 AW	22.82 TQ	ILBLS	10/01-12/01
	Chicago PMSA, IL	H	8.00 FQ	13.00 AW	18.90 TQ	ILBLS	10/01-12/01
	Peoria-Pekin MSA, IL	H	7.79 FQ	11.49 AW	16.69 TQ	ILBLS	10/01-12/01
	Rockford MSA, IL	H	8.92 FQ	13.65 AW	19.77 TQ	ILBLS	10/01-12/01
	Springfield MSA, IL	H	7.84 FQ	13.76 AW	20.15 TQ	ILBLS	10/01-12/01
	Indiana	H	7.40 FQ	11.81 AW	17.41 TQ	INBLS	10/01-12/01
	Elkhart-Goshen MSA, IN	H	9.14 FQ	12.50 AW	16.66 TQ	INBLS	10/01-12/01
	Evansville-Henderson MSA, IN-KY	H	7.04 FQ	12.29 AW	19.82 TQ	INBLS	10/01-12/01
	Fort Wayne MSA, IN	H	8.10 FQ	12.28 AW	16.72 TQ	INBLS	10/01-12/01
	Gary PMSA, IN	H	6.74 FQ	11.21 AW	16.62 TQ	INBLS	10/01-12/01
	Indianapolis MSA, IN	H	7.66 FQ	12.46 AW	19.04 TQ	INBLS	10/01-12/01
	Lafayette MSA, IN	H	7.42 FQ	11.56 AW	16.84 TQ	INBLS	10/01-12/01
	South Bend MSA, IN	H	6.05 FQ	11.22 AW	16.72 TQ	INBLS	10/01-12/01
	Iowa	H	6.66 FQ	11.02 AW	16.20 TQ	IABLS	10/01-12/01
	Cedar Rapids MSA, IA	H	8.05 FQ	12.67 AW	18.34 TQ	IABLS	10/01-12/01
	Davenport-Moline-Rock Island MSA, IA-IL	H	7.63 FQ	11.11 AW	16.05 TQ	IABLS	10/01-12/01
	Des Moines MSA, IA	H	8.95 FQ	13.21 AW	18.28 TQ	IABLS	10/01-12/01
	Kansas	H	7.38 FQ	11.23 AW	16.74 TQ	KSBLS	10/01-12/01
	Topeka MSA, KS	H	6.26 FQ	10.71 AW	15.03 TQ	KSBLS	10/01-12/01
	Wichita MSA, KS	H	7.27 FQ	11.14 AW	18.98 TQ	KSBLS	10/01-12/01
	Kentucky	H	6.90 FQ	11.05 AW	15.97 TQ	KYBLS	10/01-12/01
	Lexington MSA, KY	H	6.63 FQ	10.26 AW	15.13 TQ	KYBLS	10/01-12/01
	Louisville MSA, KY-IN	H	8.46 FQ	12.44 AW	17.03 TQ	KYBLS	10/01-12/01
	Louisiana	H	6.39 FQ	11.70 AW	18.49 TQ	LABLS	10/01-12/01
	Baton Rouge MSA, LA	H	6.34 FQ	11.64 AW	17.98 TQ	LABLS	10/01-12/01
	Houma MSA, LA	H	6.44 FQ	12.10 AW	18.16 TQ	LABLS	10/01-12/01
	Lafayette MSA, LA	H	6.05 FQ	9.83 AW	14.53 TQ	LABLS	10/01-12/01
	Lake Charles MSA, LA	H	6.38 FQ	9.05 AW	12.37 TQ	LABLS	10/01-12/01
	New Orleans MSA, LA	H	6.87 FQ	13.70 AW	23.55 TQ	LABLS	10/01-12/01
	Shreveport-Bossier City MSA, LA	H	7.13 FQ	12.07 AW	20.06 TQ	LABLS	10/01-12/01
	Maine	H	7.52 FQ	11.04 AW	16.08 TQ	MEBLS	10/01-12/01
	Portland MSA, ME	H	9.41 FQ	13.32 AW	17.65 TQ	MEBLS	10/01-12/01
	Maryland	H	7.99 FQ	13.13 AW	19.56 TQ	MDBLS	10/01-12/01
	Baltimore PMSA, MD	H	7.96 FQ	13.05 AW	19.29 TQ	MDBLS	10/01-12/01
	Massachusetts	H	8.30 FQ	14.21 AW	20.52 TQ	MABLS	10/01-12/01
	Boston PMSA, MA-NH	H	8.80 FQ	14.89 AW	20.94 TQ	MABLS	10/01-12/01
	Lawrence PMSA, MA-NH	H	9.38 FQ	14.87 AW	22.83 TQ	MABLS	10/01-12/01
	Lowell PMSA, MA-NH	H	8.53 FQ	14.75 AW	21.84 TQ	MABLS	10/01-12/01
	New Bedford PMSA, MA	H	7.39 FQ	10.46 AW	14.74 TQ	MABLS	10/01-12/01
	Springfield MSA, MA	H	8.18 FQ	12.87 AW	18.41 TQ	MABLS	10/01-12/01
	Worcester PMSA, MA-CT	H	8.30 FQ	13.80 AW	18.62 TQ	MABLS	10/01-12/01
	Michigan	H	7.98 FQ	13.04 AW	18.77 TQ	MIBLS	10/01-12/01
	Ann Arbor PMSA, MI	H	8.72 FQ	12.62 AW	17.19 TQ	MIBLS	10/01-12/01
	Detroit PMSA, MI	H	8.24 FQ	13.77 AW	19.89 TQ	MIBLS	10/01-12/01
	Flint PMSA, MI	H	7.89 FQ	12.98 AW	16.83 TQ	MIBLS	10/01-12/01
	Grand Rapids-Muskegon-Holland MSA, MI	H	7.89 FQ	12.72 AW	18.12 TQ	MIBLS	10/01-12/01
	Kalamazoo-Battle Creek MSA, MI	H	8.54 FQ	13.09 AW	18.76 TQ	MIBLS	10/01-12/01
	Lansing-East Lansing MSA, MI	H	7.78 FQ	11.72 AW	16.80 TQ	MIBLS	10/01-12/01
	Saginaw-Bay City-Midland MSA, MI	H	8.00 FQ	13.26 AW	20.71 TQ	MIBLS	10/01-12/01
	Minnesota	H	8.68 FQ	13.04 AW	18.34 TQ	MNBLS	10/01-12/01
	Duluth-Superior MSA, MN-WI	H	7.58 FQ	11.37 AW	16.41 TQ	MNBLS	10/01-12/01

AAW	Average annual wage	AOH	Average offered, high	ASH	Average starting, high	H	Hourly	M	Monthly	S	Special: hourly and annual
AE	Average entry wage	AOL	Average offered, low	ASL	Average starting, low	HI	Highest wage paid	MTC	Median total compensation	TQ	Third quartile wage
AEX	Average experienced wage	APH	Average pay, high range	AW	Average wage paid	HR	High end range	MW	Median wage paid	W	Weekly
AO	Average offered	APL	Average pay, low range	FQ	First quartile wage	LR	Low end range	SQ	Second quartile wage	Y	Yearly

Occupation/Type/Industry	Location	Per	Low	Mid	High	Source	Date
Order Clerk	Minneapolis-St. Paul MSA, MN-WI	H	9.91 FQ	14.19 AW	19.63 TQ	MNBLS	10/01-12/01
	St. Cloud MSA, MN	H	7.43 FQ	10.09 AW	13.19 TQ	MNBLS	10/01-12/01
	Mississippi	H	6.55 FQ	11.06 AW	16.91 TQ	MSBLS	10/01-12/01
	Biloxi-Gulfport-Pascagoula MSA, MS	H	6.72 FQ	13.32 AW	22.86 TQ	MSBLS	10/01-12/01
	Jackson MSA, MS	H	7.37 FQ	11.46 AW	16.64 TQ	MSBLS	10/01-12/01
	Missouri	H	7.14 FQ	11.50 AW	16.87 TQ	MOBLS	10/01-12/01
	Kansas City MSA, MO-KS	H	7.98 FQ	12.40 AW	17.71 TQ	MOBLS	10/01-12/01
	St. Louis MSA, MO-IL	H	8.06 FQ	12.33 AW	16.99 TQ	MOBLS	10/01-12/01
	Springfield MSA, MO	H	6.61 FQ	9.25 AW	12.84 TQ	MOBLS	10/01-12/01
	Montana	H	6.54 FQ	10.35 AW	15.53 TQ	MTBLS	10/01-12/01
	Billings MSA, MT	H	7.46 FQ	10.72 AW	16.44 TQ	MTBLS	10/01-12/01
	Nebraska	H	7.38 FQ	10.33 AW	15.08 TQ	NEBLS	10/01-12/01
	Lincoln MSA, NE	H	7.25 FQ	10.92 AW	16.41 TQ	NEBLS	10/01-12/01
	Omaha MSA, NE-IA	H	7.75 FQ	11.73 AW	17.10 TQ	NEBLS	10/01-12/01
	Nevada	H	7.86 FQ	11.70 AW	16.68 TQ	NVBLS	10/01-12/01
	Las Vegas MSA, NV-AZ	H	7.85 FQ	11.74 AW	16.71 TQ	NVBLS	10/01-12/01
	Reno MSA, NV	H	7.90 FQ	11.56 AW	17.03 TQ	NVBLS	10/01-12/01
	New Hampshire	H	8.03 FQ	11.88 AW	16.71 TQ	NHBLS	10/01-12/01
	Manchester PMSA, NH	H	9.52 FQ	13.41 AW	17.33 TQ	NHBLS	10/01-12/01
	Nashua PMSA, NH	H	7.43 FQ	11.65 AW	16.73 TQ	NHBLS	10/01-12/01
	Portsmouth-Rochester PMSA, NH-ME	H	8.82 FQ	12.30 AW	17.10 TQ	NHBLS	10/01-12/01
	New Jersey	H	9.30 FQ	14.38 AW	20.60 TQ	NJBLS	10/01-12/01
	Atlantic-Cape May PMSA, NJ	H	6.78 FQ	12.56 AW	18.31 TQ	NJBLS	10/01-12/01
	Bergen-Passaic PMSA, NJ	H	9.39 FQ	14.69 AW	21.02 TQ	NJBLS	10/01-12/01
	Jersey City PMSA, NJ	H	7.99 FQ	13.57 AW	19.25 TQ	NJBLS	10/01-12/01
	Middlesex-Somerset-Hunterdon PMSA, NJ	H	9.72 FQ	14.87 AW	20.99 TQ	NJBLS	10/01-12/01
	Monmouth-Ocean PMSA, NJ	H	8.94 FQ	12.77 AW	17.35 TQ	NJBLS	10/01-12/01
	Newark PMSA, NJ	H	9.73 FQ	14.45 AW	20.15 TQ	NJBLS	10/01-12/01
	Trenton PMSA, NJ	H	9.38 FQ	14.25 AW	19.03 TQ	NJBLS	10/01-12/01
	New Mexico	H	6.86 FQ	10.54 AW	15.13 TQ	NMBLS	10/01-12/01
	Albuquerque MSA, NM	H	7.03 FQ	10.39 AW	13.79 TQ	NMBLS	10/01-12/01
	Las Cruces MSA, NM	H	6.56 FQ	10.41 AW	15.54 TQ	NMBLS	10/01-12/01
	New York	H	8.03 FQ	13.66 AW	20.57 TQ	NYBLS	10/01-12/01
	Albany-Schenectady-Troy MSA, NY	H	7.92 FQ	12.16 AW	17.28 TQ	NYBLS	10/01-12/01
	Binghamton MSA, NY	H	8.16 FQ	12.18 AW	17.35 TQ	NYBLS	10/01-12/01
	Buffalo-Niagara Falls MSA, NY	H	7.25 FQ	11.32 AW	16.42 TQ	NYBLS	10/01-12/01
	Dutchess County PMSA, NY	H	8.61 FQ	12.30 AW	16.82 TQ	NYBLS	10/01-12/01
	Nassau-Suffolk PMSA, NY	H	8.75 FQ	14.10 AW	21.34 TQ	NYBLS	10/01-12/01
	New York PMSA, NY	H	8.67 FQ	14.92 AW	22.62 TQ	NYBLS	10/01-12/01
	Newburgh PMSA, NY-PA	H	7.70 FQ	12.19 AW	17.25 TQ	NYBLS	10/01-12/01
	Rochester MSA, NY	H	7.89 FQ	12.24 AW	17.80 TQ	NYBLS	10/01-12/01
	Syracuse MSA, NY	H	7.38 FQ	12.55 AW	18.90 TQ	NYBLS	10/01-12/01
	Utica-Rome MSA, NY	H	6.79 FQ	10.83 AW	15.84 TQ	NYBLS	10/01-12/01
	North Carolina	H	8.03 FQ	12.54 AW	17.50 TQ	NCBLS	10/01-12/01
	Asheville MSA, NC	H	7.13 FQ	11.26 AW	15.71 TQ	NCBLS	10/01-12/01
	Charlotte-Gastonia-Rock Hill MSA, NC-SC	H	8.80 FQ	13.41 AW	19.21 TQ	NCBLS	10/01-12/01
	Fayetteville MSA, NC	H	7.89 FQ	12.35 AW	16.42 TQ	NCBLS	10/01-12/01
	Greensboro-Winston-Salem-High Point MSA, NC	H	9.16 FQ	13.09 AW	17.48 TQ	NCBLS	10/01-12/01
	Hickory-Morganton-Lenoir MSA, NC	H	8.76 FQ	11.63 AW	15.63 TQ	NCBLS	10/01-12/01
	Raleigh-Durham-Chapel Hill MSA, NC	H	8.47 FQ	13.18 AW	19.51 TQ	NCBLS	10/01-12/01
	Wilmington MSA, NC	H	7.50 FQ	10.38 AW	14.64 TQ	NCBLS	10/01-12/01
	North Dakota	H	7.80 FQ	11.09 AW	15.64 TQ	NDBLS	10/01-12/01
	Fargo-Moorhead MSA, ND-MN	H	8.03 FQ	11.34 AW	16.25 TQ	NDBLS	10/01-12/01
	Ohio	H	7.73 FQ	12.32 AW	18.06 TQ	OHBLS	10/01-12/01
	Akron PMSA, OH	H	8.79 FQ	12.53 AW	17.20 TQ	OHBLS	10/01-12/01
	Canton-Massillon MSA, OH	H	6.60 FQ	11.66 AW	19.11 TQ	OHBLS	10/01-12/01
	Cincinnati PMSA, OH-KY-IN	H	8.63 FQ	12.38 AW	17.14 TQ	OHBLS	10/01-12/01
	Cleveland-Lorain-Elyria PMSA, OH	H	8.11 FQ	13.04 AW	19.62 TQ	OHBLS	10/01-12/01
	Columbus MSA, OH	H	7.85 FQ	12.92 AW	20.53 TQ	OHBLS	10/01-12/01
	Dayton-Springfield MSA, OH	H	8.01 FQ	12.95 AW	19.47 TQ	OHBLS	10/01-12/01

AAW	Average annual wage	**AOH**	Average offered, high	**ASH**	Average starting, high	**H**	Hourly	**M**	Monthly	**S**	Special: hourly and annual
AE	Average entry wage	**AOL**	Average offered, low	**ASL**	Average starting, low	**HI**	Highest wage paid	**MTC**	Median total compensation	**TQ**	Third quartile wage
AEX	Average experienced wage	**APH**	Average pay, high range	**AW**	Average wage paid	**HR**	High end range	**MW**	Median wage paid	**W**	Weekly
AO	Average offered	**APL**	Average pay, low range	**FQ**	First quartile wage	**LR**	Low end range	**SQ**	Second quartile wage	**Y**	Yearly

Occupation/Type/Industry	Location	Per	Low	Mid	High	Source	Date
Order Clerk	Hamilton-Middletown PMSA, OH	H	7.44 FQ	11.05 AW	16.80 TQ	OHBLS	10/01-12/01
	Mansfield MSA, OH	H	8.02 FQ	13.00 AW	18.28 TQ	OHBLS	10/01-12/01
	Toledo MSA, OH	H	8.33 FQ	12.33 AW	17.12 TQ	OHBLS	10/01-12/01
	Youngstown-Warren MSA, OH	H	7.29 FQ	11.89 AW	16.99 TQ	OHBLS	10/01-12/01
	Oklahoma	H	6.69 FQ	11.07 AW	17.04 TQ	OKBLS	10/01-12/01
	Oklahoma City MSA, OK	H	6.66 FQ	10.43 AW	15.66 TQ	OKBLS	10/01-12/01
	Tulsa MSA, OK	H	6.63 FQ	11.38 AW	17.42 TQ	OKBLS	10/01-12/01
	Oregon	H	7.97 FQ	12.53 AW	17.99 TQ	ORBLS	10/01-12/01
	Eugene-Springfield MSA, OR	H	8.42 FQ	11.91 AW	16.94 TQ	ORBLS	10/01-12/01
	Medford-Ashland MSA, OR	H	8.51 FQ	11.31 AW	16.14 TQ	ORBLS	10/01-12/01
	Portland-Vancouver PMSA, OR-WA	H	9.37 FQ	13.74 AW	19.38 TQ	ORBLS	10/01-12/01
	Salem PMSA, OR	H	9.07 FQ	13.54 AW	19.84 TQ	ORBLS	10/01-12/01
	Pennsylvania	H	7.62 FQ	12.29 AW	17.67 TQ	PABLS	10/01-12/01
	Allentown-Bethlehem-Easton MSA, PA	H	8.01 FQ	12.40 AW	17.42 TQ	PABLS	10/01-12/01
	Erie MSA, PA	H	7.20 FQ	9.39 AW	13.84 TQ	PABLS	10/01-12/01
	Harrisburg-Lebanon-Carlisle MSA, PA	H	7.24 FQ	12.10 AW	17.66 TQ	PABLS	10/01-12/01
	Johnstown MSA, PA	H	7.25 FQ	10.54 AW	14.41 TQ	PABLS	10/01-12/01
	Lancaster MSA, PA	H	8.39 FQ	12.23 AW	16.71 TQ	PABLS	10/01-12/01
	Philadelphia PMSA, PA-NJ	H	8.58 FQ	13.67 AW	20.04 TQ	PABLS	10/01-12/01
	Pittsburgh MSA, PA	H	7.54 FQ	11.79 AW	16.75 TQ	PABLS	10/01-12/01
	Reading MSA, PA	H	9.19 FQ	13.96 AW	20.27 TQ	PABLS	10/01-12/01
	Scranton-Wilkes-Barre-Hazleton MSA, PA	H	6.79 FQ	11.22 AW	16.28 TQ	PABLS	10/01-12/01
	York MSA, PA	H	8.38 FQ	12.19 AW	16.53 TQ	PABLS	10/01-12/01
	Rhode Island	H	7.98 FQ	11.64 AW	16.90 TQ	RIBLS	10/01-12/01
	Providence-Fall River-Warwick MSA, RI-MA	H	7.56 FQ	11.71 AW	16.61 TQ	RIBLS	10/01-12/01
	South Carolina	H	7.49 FQ	12.22 AW	17.75 TQ	SCBLS	10/01-12/01
	Charleston-North Charleston MSA, SC	H	7.62 FQ	11.28 AW	15.40 TQ	SCBLS	10/01-12/01
	Columbia MSA, SC	H	7.57 FQ	11.84 AW	17.67 TQ	SCBLS	10/01-12/01
	Greenville-Spartanburg-Anderson MSA, SC	H	7.92 FQ	13.51 AW	19.62 TQ	SCBLS	10/01-12/01
	Myrtle Beach MSA, SC	H	7.16 FQ	11.71 AW	19.54 TQ	SCBLS	10/01-12/01
	South Dakota	H	7.17 FQ	9.20 AW	12.21 TQ	SDBLS	10/01-12/01
	Sioux Falls MSA, SD	H	6.93 FQ	9.35 AW	12.82 TQ	SDBLS	10/01-12/01
	Tennessee	H	7.45 FQ	11.85 AW	17.06 TQ	TNBLS	10/01-12/01
	Chattanooga MSA, TN-GA	H	6.92 FQ	11.31 AW	16.42 TQ	TNBLS	10/01-12/01
	Clarksville-Hopkinsville MSA, TN-KY	H	7.16 FQ	11.03 AW	16.90 TQ	TNBLS	10/01-12/01
	Johnson City-Kingsport-Bristol MSA, TN-VA	H	7.17 FQ	10.26 AW	13.67 TQ	TNBLS	10/01-12/01
	Knoxville MSA, TN	H	7.40 FQ	11.11 AW	15.82 TQ	TNBLS	10/01-12/01
	Memphis MSA, TN-AR-MS	H	7.74 FQ	12.26 AW	16.81 TQ	TNBLS	10/01-12/01
	Nashville MSA, TN	H	8.03 FQ	12.29 AW	18.81 TQ	TNBLS	10/01-12/01
	Texas	H	7.17 FQ	12.23 AW	18.19 TQ	TXBLS	10/01-12/01
	Amarillo MSA, TX	H	5.86 FQ	8.79 AW	11.57 TQ	TXBLS	10/01-12/01
	Austin-San Marcos MSA, TX	H	7.48 FQ	12.38 AW	17.65 TQ	TXBLS	10/01-12/01
	Beaumont-Port Arthur MSA, TX	H	5.73 FQ	8.76 AW	14.88 TQ	TXBLS	10/01-12/01
	Brazoria PMSA, TX	H	6.49 FQ	11.13 AW	17.29 TQ	TXBLS	10/01-12/01
	Brownsville-Harlingen-San Benito MSA, TX	H	6.08 FQ	9.07 AW	12.93 TQ	TXBLS	10/01-12/01
	Corpus Christi MSA, TX	H	7.23 FQ	11.64 AW	16.44 TQ	TXBLS	10/01-12/01
	Dallas PMSA, TX	H	8.16 FQ	13.60 AW	20.20 TQ	TXBLS	10/01-12/01
	El Paso MSA, TX	H	6.14 FQ	9.96 AW	15.60 TQ	TXBLS	10/01-12/01
	Fort Worth-Arlington PMSA, TX	H	7.22 FQ	12.23 AW	18.44 TQ	TXBLS	10/01-12/01
	Galveston-Texas City PMSA, TX	H	6.60 FQ	10.98 AW	18.35 TQ	TXBLS	10/01-12/01
	Houston PMSA, TX	H	7.54 FQ	12.95 AW	17.90 TQ	TXBLS	10/01-12/01
	Killeen-Temple MSA, TX	H	6.22 FQ	10.69 AW	17.07 TQ	TXBLS	10/01-12/01
	Laredo MSA, TX	H	6.04 FQ	10.02 AW	18.64 TQ	TXBLS	10/01-12/01
	Longview-Marshall MSA, TX	H	6.28 FQ	10.14 AW	15.93 TQ	TXBLS	10/01-12/01
	Lubbock MSA, TX	H	6.77 FQ	10.25 AW	13.42 TQ	TXBLS	10/01-12/01
	McAllen-Edinburg-Mission MSA, TX	H	6.47 FQ	10.38 AW	16.34 TQ	TXBLS	10/01-12/01
	Odessa-Midland MSA, TX	H	6.88 FQ	11.13 AW	15.50 TQ	TXBLS	10/01-12/01

AAW Average annual wage; **AE** Average entry wage; **AEX** Average experienced wage; **AO** Average offered; **AOH** Average offered, high; **AOL** Average offered, low; **APH** Average pay, high range; **APL** Average pay, low range; **ASH** Average starting, high; **ASL** Average starting, low; **AW** Average wage paid; **FQ** First quartile wage; **H** Hourly; **HI** Highest wage paid; **HR** High end range; **LR** Low end range; **M** Monthly; **MTC** Median total compensation; **MW** Median wage paid; **SQ** Second quartile wage; **S** Special: hourly and annual; **TQ** Third quartile wage; **W** Weekly; **Y** Yearly

Occupation/Type/Industry	Location	Per	Low	Mid	High	Source	Date
Order Clerk	San Antonio MSA, TX	H	7.26 FQ	10.76 AW	14.15 TQ	TXBLS	10/01-12/01
	Tyler MSA, TX	H	6.06 FQ	9.08 AW	13.55 TQ	TXBLS	10/01-12/01
	Waco MSA, TX	H	6.90 FQ	10.56 AW	15.61 TQ	TXBLS	10/01-12/01
	Utah	H	7.99 FQ	11.60 AW	16.25 TQ	UTBLS	10/01-12/01
	Provo-Orem MSA, UT	H	7.67 FQ	11.05 AW	16.39 TQ	UTBLS	10/01-12/01
	Salt Lake City-Ogden MSA, UT	H	8.60 FQ	12.01 AW	16.50 TQ	UTBLS	10/01-12/01
	Vermont	H	7.63 FQ	11.27 AW	15.58 TQ	VTBLS	10/01-12/01
	Burlington MSA, VT	H	8.55 FQ	11.56 AW	15.63 TQ	VTBLS	10/01-12/01
	Virginia	H	6.05 FQ	10.68 AW	17.11 TQ	VABLS	10/01-12/01
	Norfolk-Virginia Beach-Newport News MSA, VA-NC	H	6.05 FQ	9.53 AW	15.64 TQ	VABLS	10/01-12/01
	Richmond-Petersburg MSA, VA	H	5.51 FQ	9.51 AW	16.55 TQ	VABLS	10/01-12/01
	Roanoke MSA, VA	H	7.38 FQ	11.59 AW	17.88 TQ	VABLS	10/01-12/01
	Washington	H	9.03 FQ	13.69 AW	19.55 TQ	WABLS	10/01-12/01
	Bremerton PMSA, WA	H	7.42 FQ	11.57 AW	16.68 TQ	WABLS	10/01-12/01
	Olympia PMSA, WA	H	8.02 FQ	11.25 AW	16.05 TQ	WABLS	10/01-12/01
	Richland-Kennewick-Pasco MSA, WA	H	8.55 FQ	12.04 AW	16.37 TQ	WABLS	10/01-12/01
	Seattle-Bellevue-Everett PMSA, WA	H	9.74 FQ	14.48 AW	20.70 TQ	WABLS	10/01-12/01
	Spokane MSA, WA	H	7.53 FQ	11.30 AW	15.95 TQ	WABLS	10/01-12/01
	Tacoma PMSA, WA	H	9.37 FQ	12.95 AW	17.18 TQ	WABLS	10/01-12/01
	Yakima MSA, WA	H	8.28 FQ	12.31 AW	18.80 TQ	WABLS	10/01-12/01
	West Virginia	H	6.31 FQ	10.14 AW	15.88 TQ	WVBLS	10/01-12/01
	Charleston MSA, WV	H	7.54 FQ	10.96 AW	17.70 TQ	WVBLS	10/01-12/01
	Huntington-Ashland MSA, WV-KY-OH	H	6.45 FQ	10.18 AW	14.08 TQ	WVBLS	10/01-12/01
	Wisconsin	H	7.30 FQ	11.41 AW	16.40 TQ	WIBLS	10/01-12/01
	Appleton-Oshkosh-Neenah MSA, WI	H	7.10 FQ	10.17 AW	14.04 TQ	WIBLS	10/01-12/01
	Madison MSA, WI	H	9.09 FQ	11.90 AW	15.98 TQ	WIBLS	10/01-12/01
	Milwaukee-Waukesha PMSA, WI	H	9.58 FQ	14.24 AW	20.27 TQ	WIBLS	10/01-12/01
	Racine PMSA, WI	H	8.76 FQ	11.63 AW	15.94 TQ	WIBLS	10/01-12/01
	Wyoming	H	6.36 FQ	10.33 AW	16.82 TQ	WYBLS	10/01-12/01
	Cheyenne MSA, WY	H	6.89 FQ	11.23 AW	17.20 TQ	WYBLS	10/01-12/01
	Puerto Rico	H	5.86 FQ	9.02 AW	14.04 TQ	PRBLS	10/01-12/01
	Guam	H	5.82 FQ	8.77 AW	13.63 TQ	GUBLS	10/01-12/01
Orthopedic Surgeon	United States	Y		287000 AW		HHN	1/01-1/02
Orthotist and Prosthetist	Alaska	Y	50950 FQ	81470 AW		AKBLS	10/01-12/01
	California	Y	33790 FQ	60760 AW	74060 TQ	CABLS	10/01-12/01
	Colorado	Y	30240 FQ	39490 AW	56000 TQ	COBLS	10/01-12/01
	Florida	Y	24130 FQ	53590 AW	89340 TQ	FLBLS	10/01-12/01
	Illinois	Y	14650 FQ	31040 AW	60780 TQ	ILBLS	10/01-12/01
	Indiana	Y	15310 FQ	33190 AW	75160 TQ	INBLS	10/01-12/01
	Iowa	Y	28360 FQ	59840 AW	123250 TQ	IABLS	10/01-12/01
	Kansas	Y	23270 FQ	36980 AW	73900 TQ	KSBLS	10/01-12/01
	Louisiana	Y	18520 FQ	42000 AW	65930 TQ	LABLS	10/01-12/01
	Maine	Y	24820 FQ	39930 AW	68580 TQ	MEBLS	10/01-12/01
	Maryland	Y	28470 FQ	41040 AW	67370 TQ	MDBLS	10/01-12/01
	Massachusetts	Y	29600 FQ	61010 AW	92750 TQ	MABLS	10/01-12/01
	Michigan	Y	30550 FQ	47170 AW	70620 TQ	MIBLS	10/01-12/01
	Minnesota	Y	31530 FQ	54470 AW	72340 TQ	MNBLS	10/01-12/01
	Mississippi	Y	20940 FQ	34480 AW	48400 TQ	MSBLS	10/01-12/01
	Missouri	Y	26070 FQ	44350 AW	71990 TQ	MOBLS	10/01-12/01
	Nevada	Y	40470 FQ	73020 AW	92150 TQ	NVBLS	10/01-12/01
	New Hampshire	Y	29300 FQ	49700 AW	67380 TQ	NHBLS	10/01-12/01
	New Jersey	Y	32490 FQ	53420 AW	71130 TQ	NJBLS	10/01-12/01
	New York	Y	35690 FQ	67980 AW	132470 TQ	NYBLS	10/01-12/01
	North Carolina	Y	24080 FQ	35740 AW	55410 TQ	NCBLS	10/01-12/01
	Ohio	Y	24510 FQ	51080 AW	89270 TQ	OHBLS	10/01-12/01
	Oregon	Y	30520 FQ	53270 AW	112440 TQ	ORBLS	10/01-12/01
	Pennsylvania	Y	22790 FQ	44570 AW	59120 TQ	PABLS	10/01-12/01
	South Carolina	Y	22380 FQ	58400 AW		SCBLS	10/01-12/01
	Tennessee	Y	29990 FQ	46900 AW	62720 TQ	TNBLS	10/01-12/01
	Texas	Y	20920 FQ	55420 AW	88610 TQ	TXBLS	10/01-12/01
	Virginia	Y	29680 FQ	63460 AW	116640 TQ	VABLS	10/01-12/01
	Washington	Y	31660 FQ	56520 AW	96180 TQ	WABLS	10/01-12/01

AAW Average annual wage **AOH** Average offered, high **ASH** Average starting, high **H** Hourly **M** Monthly **S** Special: hourly and annual
AE Average entry wage **AOL** Average offered, low **ASL** Average starting, low **HI** Highest wage paid **MTC** Median total compensation **TQ** Third quartile wage
AEX Average experienced wage **APH** Average pay, high range **AW** Average wage paid **HR** High end range **MW** Median wage paid **W** Weekly
AO Average offered **APL** Average pay, low range **FQ** First quartile wage **LR** Low end range **SQ** Second quartile wage **Y** Yearly

Occupation/Type/Industry	Location	Per	Low	Mid	High	Source	Date
Orthotist and Prosthetist	Wisconsin	Y	24000 FQ	42970 AW	72260 TQ	WIBLS	10/01-12/01
Packaging and Filling Machine Operator and Tender	Alabama	H	6.69 FQ	9.54 AW	13.22 TQ	ALBLS	10/01-12/01
	Birmingham MSA, AL	H	7.08 FQ	9.80 AW	13.37 TQ	ALBLS	10/01-12/01
	Huntsville MSA, AL	H	6.97 FQ	10.32 AW	16.12 TQ	ALBLS	10/01-12/01
	Mobile MSA, AL	H	6.40 FQ	10.19 AW	13.95 TQ	ALBLS	10/01-12/01
	Montgomery MSA, AL	H	6.48 FQ	9.40 AW	11.90 TQ	ALBLS	10/01-12/01
	Alaska	H	6.98 FQ	10.93 AW	16.28 TQ	AKBLS	10/01-12/01
	Anchorage MSA, AK	H	7.30 FQ	10.36 AW	15.94 TQ	AKBLS	10/01-12/01
	Arizona	H	6.34 FQ	9.85 AW	13.83 TQ	AZBLS	10/01-12/01
	Phoenix-Mesa MSA, AZ	H	6.45 FQ	10.00 AW	13.84 TQ	AZBLS	10/01-12/01
	Tucson MSA, AZ	H	5.84 FQ	7.64 AW	9.50 TQ	AZBLS	10/01-12/01
	Arkansas	H	7.28 FQ	9.06 AW	12.23 TQ	ARBLS	10/01-12/01
	Fayetteville-Springdale-Rogers MSA, AR	H	7.46 FQ	8.88 AW	10.81 TQ	ARBLS	10/01-12/01
	Fort Smith MSA, AR-OK	H	7.33 FQ	9.95 AW	15.64 TQ	ARBLS	10/01-12/01
	Little Rock-North Little Rock MSA, AR	H	6.42 FQ	9.39 AW	12.96 TQ	ARBLS	10/01-12/01
	California	H	6.62 FQ	10.61 AW	17.42 TQ	CABLS	10/01-12/01
	Bakersfield MSA, CA	H	6.48 FQ	10.85 AW	18.29 TQ	CABLS	10/01-12/01
	Chico-Paradise MSA, CA	H	6.45 FQ	9.28 AW	14.05 TQ	CABLS	10/01-12/01
	Fresno MSA, CA	H	6.79 FQ	11.88 AW	19.76 TQ	CABLS	10/01-12/01
	Los Angeles-Long Beach PMSA, CA	H	6.66 FQ	10.25 AW	17.55 TQ	CABLS	10/01-12/01
	Merced MSA, CA	H	7.37 FQ	12.68 AW	17.16 TQ	CABLS	10/01-12/01
	Modesto MSA, CA	H	7.20 FQ	12.45 AW	17.60 TQ	CABLS	10/01-12/01
	Oakland PMSA, CA	H	6.60 FQ	11.45 AW	19.67 TQ	CABLS	10/01-12/01
	Orange County PMSA, CA	H	6.43 FQ	9.76 AW	16.09 TQ	CABLS	10/01-12/01
	Redding MSA, CA	H	7.35 FQ	10.45 AW	16.98 TQ	CABLS	10/01-12/01
	Riverside-San Bernardino PMSA, CA	H	6.53 FQ	9.30 AW	14.58 TQ	CABLS	10/01-12/01
	Sacramento PMSA, CA	H	7.29 FQ	12.57 AW	17.02 TQ	CABLS	10/01-12/01
	Salinas MSA, CA	H	6.58 FQ	10.47 AW	16.54 TQ	CABLS	10/01-12/01
	San Diego MSA, CA	H	6.85 FQ	10.29 AW	15.90 TQ	CABLS	10/01-12/01
	San Francisco PMSA, CA	H	7.40 FQ	11.21 AW	18.14 TQ	CABLS	10/01-12/01
	San Jose PMSA, CA	H	6.83 FQ	12.15 AW	18.81 TQ	CABLS	10/01-12/01
	San Luis Obispo-Atascadero-Paso Robles MSA, CA	H	6.47 FQ	9.21 AW	12.25 TQ	CABLS	10/01-12/01
	Santa Barbara-Santa Maria-Lompoc MSA, CA	H	6.48 FQ	8.35 AW	11.10 TQ	CABLS	10/01-12/01
	Santa Cruz-Watsonville PMSA, CA	H	7.36 FQ	9.16 AW	11.91 TQ	CABLS	10/01-12/01
	Santa Rosa PMSA, CA	H	7.48 FQ	11.75 AW	17.89 TQ	CABLS	10/01-12/01
	Stockton-Lodi MSA, CA	H	7.10 FQ	12.61 AW	21.61 TQ	CABLS	10/01-12/01
	Vallejo-Fairfield-Napa PMSA, CA	H	7.60 FQ	12.01 AW	19.27 TQ	CABLS	10/01-12/01
	Ventura PMSA, CA	H	6.72 FQ	9.39 AW	14.08 TQ	CABLS	10/01-12/01
	Visalia-Tulare-Porterville MSA, CA	H	6.55 FQ	10.75 AW	16.18 TQ	CABLS	10/01-12/01
	Colorado	H	6.95 FQ	10.85 AW	16.10 TQ	COBLS	10/01-12/01
	Boulder-Longmont PMSA, CO	H	6.71 FQ	10.18 AW	13.91 TQ	COBLS	10/01-12/01
	Colorado Springs MSA, CO	H	6.38 FQ	10.76 AW	15.71 TQ	COBLS	10/01-12/01
	Denver PMSA, CO	H	8.40 FQ	12.32 AW	17.09 TQ	COBLS	10/01-12/01
	Fort Collins-Loveland MSA, CO	H	6.01 FQ	9.60 AW	12.87 TQ	COBLS	10/01-12/01
	Greeley PMSA, CO	H	6.63 FQ	9.26 AW	12.77 TQ	COBLS	10/01-12/01
	Connecticut	H	7.25 FQ	11.07 AW	16.17 TQ	CTBLS	10/01-12/01
	Bridgeport PMSA, CT	H	7.05 FQ	9.93 AW	14.44 TQ	CTBLS	10/01-12/01
	Danbury PMSA, CT	H	7.81 FQ	11.88 AW	16.50 TQ	CTBLS	10/01-12/01
	Hartford MSA, CT	H	7.15 FQ	10.11 AW	14.69 TQ	CTBLS	10/01-12/01
	New Haven-Meriden PMSA, CT	H	7.22 FQ	11.45 AW	16.35 TQ	CTBLS	10/01-12/01
	New London-Norwich MSA, CT-RI	H	7.36 FQ	8.94 AW	11.19 TQ	CTBLS	10/01-12/01
	Stamford-Norwalk PMSA, CT	H	8.38 FQ	12.27 AW	16.74 TQ	CTBLS	10/01-12/01
	Waterbury PMSA, CT	H	6.54 FQ	9.18 AW	12.91 TQ	CTBLS	10/01-12/01
	Delaware	H	7.43 FQ	12.51 AW	18.60 TQ	DEBLS	10/01-12/01
	District of Columbia	H	7.81 FQ	12.24 AW	16.36 TQ	DCBLS	10/01-12/01
	Washington PMSA, DC-MD-VA-WV	H	6.05 FQ	11.09 AW	17.75 TQ	DCBLS	10/01-12/01
	Florida	H	5.57 FQ	8.16 AW	12.40 TQ	FLBLS	10/01-12/01

AAW	Average annual wage	AOH	Average offered, high	ASH	Average starting, high	H	Hourly	M	Monthly	S	Special: hourly and annual
AE	Average entry wage	AOL	Average offered, low	ASL	Average starting, low	HI	Highest wage paid	MTC	Median total compensation	TQ	Third quartile wage
AEX	Average experienced wage	APH	Average pay, high range	AW	Average wage paid	HR	High end range	MW	Median wage paid	W	Weekly
AO	Average offered	APL	Average pay, low range	FQ	First quartile wage	LR	Low end range	SQ	Second quartile wage	Y	Yearly

Occupation/Type/Industry	Location	Per	Low	Mid	High	Source	Date
Packaging and Filling Machine Operator and Tender	Daytona Beach MSA, FL	H	6.88 FQ	9.33 AW	12.89 TQ	FLBLS	10/01-12/01
	Fort Lauderdale PMSA, FL	H	5.84 FQ	9.26 AW	13.28 TQ	FLBLS	10/01-12/01
	Fort Myers-Cape Coral MSA, FL	H	8.66 FQ	11.17 AW	13.65 TQ	FLBLS	10/01-12/01
	Fort Pierce-Port St. Lucie MSA, FL	H	8.66 FQ	12.53 AW	16.33 TQ	FLBLS	10/01-12/01
	Fort Walton Beach MSA, FL	H	5.85 FQ	7.35 AW	9.20 TQ	FLBLS	10/01-12/01
	Gainesville MSA, FL	H	5.44 FQ	7.43 AW	10.57 TQ	FLBLS	10/01-12/01
	Jacksonville MSA, FL	H	5.41 FQ	7.55 AW	11.69 TQ	FLBLS	10/01-12/01
	Lakeland-Winter Haven MSA, FL	H	5.86 FQ	9.15 AW	13.36 TQ	FLBLS	10/01-12/01
	Melbourne-Titusville-Palm Bay MSA, FL	H	6.25 FQ	9.02 AW	12.96 TQ	FLBLS	10/01-12/01
	Miami PMSA, FL	H	6.15 FQ	8.72 AW	12.65 TQ	FLBLS	10/01-12/01
	Orlando MSA, FL	H	7.02 FQ	10.49 AW	16.76 TQ	FLBLS	10/01-12/01
	Sarasota-Bradenton MSA, FL	H	5.53 FQ	7.33 AW	10.96 TQ	FLBLS	10/01-12/01
	Tampa-St. Petersburg-Clearwater MSA, FL	H	5.42 FQ	7.47 AW	11.15 TQ	FLBLS	10/01-12/01
	West Palm Beach-Boca Raton MSA, FL	H	5.49 FQ	8.34 AW	13.03 TQ	FLBLS	10/01-12/01
	Georgia	H	6.40 FQ	10.61 AW	16.66 TQ	GABLS	10/01-12/01
	Atlanta MSA, GA	H	7.06 FQ	11.25 AW	17.08 TQ	GABLS	10/01-12/01
	Augusta-Aiken MSA, GA-SC	H	6.11 FQ	11.83 AW	18.12 TQ	GABLS	10/01-12/01
	Columbus MSA, GA-AL	H	6.15 FQ	8.63 AW	12.11 TQ	GABLS	10/01-12/01
	Macon MSA, GA	H	6.98 FQ	10.94 AW	19.84 TQ	GABLS	10/01-12/01
	Savannah MSA, GA	H	5.95 FQ	10.53 AW	16.47 TQ	GABLS	10/01-12/01
	Hawaii	H	6.93 FQ	10.53 AW	15.39 TQ	HIBLS	10/01-12/01
	Honolulu MSA, HI	H	6.87 FQ	10.63 AW	16.21 TQ	HIBLS	10/01-12/01
	Idaho	H	6.72 FQ	9.79 AW	12.84 TQ	IDBLS	10/01-12/01
	Boise City MSA, ID	H	6.99 FQ	10.03 AW	13.08 TQ	IDBLS	10/01-12/01
	Illinois	H	6.14 FQ	11.20 AW	18.28 TQ	ILBLS	10/01-12/01
	Champaign-Urbana MSA, IL	H	9.13 FQ	14.76 AW	20.55 TQ	ILBLS	10/01-12/01
	Chicago PMSA, IL	H	6.30 FQ	11.51 AW	18.53 TQ	ILBLS	10/01-12/01
	Peoria-Pekin MSA, IL	H	6.89 FQ	10.99 AW	17.25 TQ	ILBLS	10/01-12/01
	Indiana	H	7.22 FQ	11.55 AW	17.52 TQ	INBLS	10/01-12/01
	Elkhart-Goshen MSA, IN	H	8.80 FQ	13.76 AW	24.12 TQ	INBLS	10/01-12/01
	Evansville-Henderson MSA, IN-KY	H	8.42 FQ	13.89 AW	24.15 TQ	INBLS	10/01-12/01
	Fort Wayne MSA, IN	H	7.79 FQ	11.93 AW	16.18 TQ	INBLS	10/01-12/01
	Gary PMSA, IN	H	6.11 FQ	12.00 AW	23.02 TQ	INBLS	10/01-12/01
	Indianapolis MSA, IN	H	7.29 FQ	11.63 AW	17.15 TQ	INBLS	10/01-12/01
	South Bend MSA, IN	H	6.71 FQ	10.25 AW	16.39 TQ	INBLS	10/01-12/01
	Iowa	H	8.08 FQ	12.33 AW	17.00 TQ	IABLS	10/01-12/01
	Davenport-Moline-Rock Island MSA, IA-IL	H	7.73 FQ	12.84 AW	20.10 TQ	IABLS	10/01-12/01
	Des Moines MSA, IA	H	7.76 FQ	10.87 AW	14.94 TQ	IABLS	10/01-12/01
	Kansas	H	7.20 FQ	11.91 AW	17.16 TQ	KSBLS	10/01-12/01
	Topeka MSA, KS	H	9.37 FQ	15.46 AW	20.47 TQ	KSBLS	10/01-12/01
	Wichita MSA, KS	H	8.64 FQ	12.80 AW	16.71 TQ	KSBLS	10/01-12/01
	Kentucky	H	7.03 FQ	11.49 AW	16.91 TQ	KYBLS	10/01-12/01
	Lexington MSA, KY	H	9.27 FQ	13.68 AW	18.63 TQ	KYBLS	10/01-12/01
	Louisville MSA, KY-IN	H	7.57 FQ	12.03 AW	18.46 TQ	KYBLS	10/01-12/01
	Louisiana	H	5.86 FQ	9.53 AW	14.58 TQ	LABLS	10/01-12/01
	Baton Rouge MSA, LA	H	5.97 FQ	10.27 AW	14.93 TQ	LABLS	10/01-12/01
	Houma MSA, LA	H	7.26 FQ	9.52 AW	12.69 TQ	LABLS	10/01-12/01
	Lafayette MSA, LA	H	5.84 FQ	9.45 AW	12.69 TQ	LABLS	10/01-12/01
	New Orleans MSA, LA	H	6.06 FQ	10.22 AW	16.40 TQ	LABLS	10/01-12/01
	Maine	H	7.17 FQ	10.89 AW	16.26 TQ	MEBLS	10/01-12/01
	Portland MSA, ME	H	7.45 FQ	10.62 AW	13.64 TQ	MEBLS	10/01-12/01
	Maryland	H	7.03 FQ	12.12 AW	19.05 TQ	MDBLS	10/01-12/01
	Baltimore PMSA, MD	H	7.42 FQ	11.99 AW	18.08 TQ	MDBLS	10/01-12/01
	Massachusetts	H	7.21 FQ	10.59 AW	14.95 TQ	MABLS	10/01-12/01
	Boston PMSA, MA-NH	H	7.11 FQ	10.60 AW	15.48 TQ	MABLS	10/01-12/01
	Brockton PMSA, MA	H	7.77 FQ	11.77 AW	16.36 TQ	MABLS	10/01-12/01
	Lawrence PMSA, MA-NH	H	7.15 FQ	9.71 AW	12.93 TQ	MABLS	10/01-12/01
	Lowell PMSA, MA-NH	H	7.81 FQ	11.76 AW	16.08 TQ	MABLS	10/01-12/01
	New Bedford PMSA, MA	H	7.84 FQ	11.11 AW	16.13 TQ	MABLS	10/01-12/01
	Springfield MSA, MA	H	7.20 FQ	10.64 AW	14.43 TQ	MABLS	10/01-12/01
	Worcester PMSA, MA-CT	H	8.50 FQ	11.64 AW	15.10 TQ	MABLS	10/01-12/01
	Michigan	H	7.48 FQ	11.47 AW	17.27 TQ	MIBLS	10/01-12/01
	Ann Arbor PMSA, MI	H	7.81 FQ	12.39 AW	19.85 TQ	MIBLS	10/01-12/01

AAW Average annual wage	**AOH** Average offered, high	**ASH** Average starting, high	**H** Hourly	**M** Monthly	**S** Special: hourly and annual
AE Average entry wage	**AOL** Average offered, low	**ASL** Average starting, low	**HI** Highest wage paid	**MTC** Median total compensation	**TQ** Third quartile wage
AEX Average experienced wage	**APH** Average pay, high range	**AW** Average wage paid	**HR** High end range	**MW** Median wage paid	**W** Weekly
AO Average offered	**APL** Average pay, low range	**FQ** First quartile wage	**LR** Low end range	**SQ** Second quartile wage	**Y** Yearly

Occupation/Type/Industry	Location	Per	Low	Mid	High	Source	Date
Packaging and Filling Machine Operator and Tender	Detroit PMSA, MI	H	7.29 FQ	11.18 AW	16.78 TQ	MIBLS	10/01-12/01
	Flint PMSA, MI	H	7.22 FQ	11.60 AW	19.90 TQ	MIBLS	10/01-12/01
	Grand Rapids-Muskegon-Holland MSA, MI	H	8.65 FQ	11.16 AW	15.87 TQ	MIBLS	10/01-12/01
	Kalamazoo-Battle Creek MSA, MI	H	7.72 FQ	14.35 AW	26.37 TQ	MIBLS	10/01-12/01
	Lansing-East Lansing MSA, MI	H	7.65 FQ	11.57 AW	16.52 TQ	MIBLS	10/01-12/01
	Saginaw-Bay City-Midland MSA, MI	H	7.20 FQ	10.15 AW	15.91 TQ	MIBLS	10/01-12/01
	Minnesota	H	8.12 FQ	12.21 AW	17.19 TQ	MNBLS	10/01-12/01
	Duluth-Superior MSA, MN-WI	H	7.23 FQ	10.71 AW	14.16 TQ	MNBLS	10/01-12/01
	Minneapolis-St. Paul MSA, MN-WI	H	8.23 FQ	12.44 AW	17.49 TQ	MNBLS	10/01-12/01
	St. Cloud MSA, MN	H	8.31 FQ	11.37 AW	15.97 TQ	MNBLS	10/01-12/01
	Mississippi	H	6.27 FQ	9.08 AW	12.31 TQ	MSBLS	10/01-12/01
	Jackson MSA, MS	H	6.07 FQ	9.07 AW	12.51 TQ	MSBLS	10/01-12/01
	Missouri	H	6.70 FQ	11.48 AW	18.94 TQ	MOBLS	10/01-12/01
	Kansas City MSA, MO-KS	H	6.88 FQ	12.50 AW	19.91 TQ	MOBLS	10/01-12/01
	St. Louis MSA, MO-IL	H	7.17 FQ	12.31 AW	19.48 TQ	MOBLS	10/01-12/01
	Springfield MSA, MO	H	6.31 FQ	9.33 AW	13.51 TQ	MOBLS	10/01-12/01
	Montana	H	6.74 FQ	9.43 AW	13.34 TQ	MTBLS	10/01-12/01
	Billings MSA, MT	H	7.32 FQ	9.61 AW	13.27 TQ	MTBLS	10/01-12/01
	Nebraska	H	7.28 FQ	10.13 AW	13.84 TQ	NEBLS	10/01-12/01
	Lincoln MSA, NE	H	7.18 FQ	9.06 AW	10.93 TQ	NEBLS	10/01-12/01
	Omaha MSA, NE-IA	H	7.24 FQ	10.25 AW	22.24 TQ	NEBLS	10/01-12/01
	Nevada	H	7.39 FQ	10.88 AW	16.47 TQ	NVBLS	10/01-12/01
	Las Vegas MSA, NV-AZ	H	7.50 FQ	12.08 AW	17.11 TQ	NVBLS	10/01-12/01
	Reno MSA, NV	H	7.37 FQ	9.90 AW	14.82 TQ	NVBLS	10/01-12/01
	New Hampshire	H	7.78 FQ	13.81 AW	24.29 TQ	NHBLS	10/01-12/01
	Portsmouth-Rochester PMSA, NH-ME	H	7.24 FQ	10.65 AW	15.85 TQ	NHBLS	10/01-12/01
	New Jersey	H	6.66 FQ	12.12 AW	18.16 TQ	NJBLS	10/01-12/01
	Atlantic-Cape May PMSA, NJ	H	6.59 FQ	10.24 AW	14.38 TQ	NJBLS	10/01-12/01
	Bergen-Passaic PMSA, NJ	H	5.95 FQ	10.49 AW	16.32 TQ	NJBLS	10/01-12/01
	Jersey City PMSA, NJ	H	6.14 FQ	12.20 AW	19.96 TQ	NJBLS	10/01-12/01
	Middlesex-Somerset-Hunterdon PMSA, NJ	H	7.53 FQ	13.41 AW	20.66 TQ	NJBLS	10/01-12/01
	Monmouth-Ocean PMSA, NJ	H	7.09 FQ	9.86 AW	13.31 TQ	NJBLS	10/01-12/01
	Newark PMSA, NJ	H	6.64 FQ	12.44 AW	19.20 TQ	NJBLS	10/01-12/01
	Trenton PMSA, NJ	H	6.30 FQ	12.55 AW	17.51 TQ	NJBLS	10/01-12/01
	New Mexico	H	6.15 FQ	9.00 AW	13.20 TQ	NMBLS	10/01-12/01
	Albuquerque MSA, NM	H	6.17 FQ	9.75 AW	13.76 TQ	NMBLS	10/01-12/01
	Las Cruces MSA, NM	H	7.01 FQ	8.87 AW	10.80 TQ	NMBLS	10/01-12/01
	New York	H	6.21 FQ	11.33 AW	17.77 TQ	NYBLS	10/01-12/01
	Albany-Schenectady-Troy MSA, NY	H	6.78 FQ	13.37 AW	19.50 TQ	NYBLS	10/01-12/01
	Binghamton MSA, NY	H	9.24 FQ	12.28 AW	16.51 TQ	NYBLS	10/01-12/01
	Buffalo-Niagara Falls MSA, NY	H	6.21 FQ	11.21 AW	16.64 TQ	NYBLS	10/01-12/01
	Nassau-Suffolk PMSA, NY	H	6.41 FQ	10.63 AW	15.79 TQ	NYBLS	10/01-12/01
	New York PMSA, NY	H	5.97 FQ	12.11 AW	21.87 TQ	NYBLS	10/01-12/01
	Rochester MSA, NY	H	7.85 FQ	12.23 AW	17.37 TQ	NYBLS	10/01-12/01
	Syracuse MSA, NY	H	7.56 FQ	11.08 AW	16.74 TQ	NYBLS	10/01-12/01
	Utica-Rome MSA, NY	H	5.81 FQ	8.08 AW	12.63 TQ	NYBLS	10/01-12/01
	North Carolina	H	6.87 FQ	11.72 AW	17.81 TQ	NCBLS	10/01-12/01
	Charlotte-Gastonia-Rock Hill MSA, NC-SC	H	7.51 FQ	10.45 AW	14.51 TQ	NCBLS	10/01-12/01
	Fayetteville MSA, NC	H	5.80 FQ	8.58 AW	14.57 TQ	NCBLS	10/01-12/01
	Greensboro-Winston-Salem-High Point MSA, NC	H	6.71 FQ	13.37 AW	24.37 TQ	NCBLS	10/01-12/01
	Hickory-Morganton-Lenoir MSA, NC	H	7.86 FQ	10.79 AW	13.82 TQ	NCBLS	10/01-12/01
	Raleigh-Durham-Chapel Hill MSA, NC	H	7.11 FQ	12.05 AW	16.74 TQ	NCBLS	10/01-12/01
	Wilmington MSA, NC	H	5.76 FQ	10.15 AW	17.95 TQ	NCBLS	10/01-12/01
	North Dakota	H	6.97 FQ	9.94 AW	13.09 TQ	NDBLS	10/01-12/01
	Fargo-Moorhead MSA, ND-MN	H	7.29 FQ	10.35 AW	13.37 TQ	NDBLS	10/01-12/01
	Ohio	H	7.30 FQ	11.35 AW	16.70 TQ	OHBLS	10/01-12/01
	Akron PMSA, OH	H	7.45 FQ	11.33 AW	16.20 TQ	OHBLS	10/01-12/01
	Canton-Massillon MSA, OH	H	6.31 FQ	9.73 AW	13.46 TQ	OHBLS	10/01-12/01

AAW	Average annual wage	**AOH**	Average offered, high	**ASH**	Average starting, high	**H**	Hourly	**M**	Monthly	**S**	Special: hourly and annual
AE	Average entry wage	**AOL**	Average offered, low	**ASL**	Average starting, low	**HI**	Highest wage paid	**MTC**	Median total compensation	**TQ**	Third quartile wage
AEX	Average experienced wage	**APH**	Average pay, high range	**AW**	Average wage paid	**HR**	High end range	**MW**	Median wage paid	**W**	Weekly
AO	Average offered	**APL**	Average pay, low range	**FQ**	First quartile wage	**LR**	Low end range	**SQ**	Second quartile wage	**Y**	Yearly

Occupation/Type/Industry	Location	Per	Low	Mid	High	Source	Date
Packaging and Filling Machine Operator and Tender	Cincinnati PMSA, OH-KY-IN	H	8.17 FQ	12.33 AW	17.26 TQ	OHBLS	10/01-12/01
	Cleveland-Lorain-Elyria PMSA, OH	H	7.31 FQ	10.87 AW	15.35 TQ	OHBLS	10/01-12/01
	Columbus MSA, OH	H	7.27 FQ	9.92 AW	14.13 TQ	OHBLS	10/01-12/01
	Dayton-Springfield MSA, OH	H	5.88 FQ	9.49 AW	14.97 TQ	OHBLS	10/01-12/01
	Hamilton-Middletown PMSA, OH	H	9.47 FQ	13.00 AW	17.21 TQ	OHBLS	10/01-12/01
	Toledo MSA, OH	H	8.90 FQ	14.41 AW	19.63 TQ	OHBLS	10/01-12/01
	Youngstown-Warren MSA, OH	H	6.89 FQ	10.05 AW	15.45 TQ	OHBLS	10/01-12/01
	Oklahoma	H	6.37 FQ	9.26 AW	13.06 TQ	OKBLS	10/01-12/01
	Oklahoma City MSA, OK	H	6.68 FQ	10.06 AW	13.69 TQ	OKBLS	10/01-12/01
	Tulsa MSA, OK	H	6.92 FQ	8.74 AW	11.69 TQ	OKBLS	10/01-12/01
	Oregon	H	6.89 FQ	10.78 AW	16.73 TQ	ORBLS	10/01-12/01
	Eugene-Springfield MSA, OR	H	8.58 FQ	13.64 AW	18.14 TQ	ORBLS	10/01-12/01
	Medford-Ashland MSA, OR	H	8.71 FQ	11.76 AW	15.83 TQ	ORBLS	10/01-12/01
	Portland-Vancouver PMSA, OR-WA	H	7.18 FQ	11.96 AW	18.35 TQ	ORBLS	10/01-12/01
	Pennsylvania	H	7.16 FQ	11.85 AW	17.42 TQ	PABLS	10/01-12/01
	Allentown-Bethlehem-Easton MSA, PA	H	7.90 FQ	14.21 AW	20.28 TQ	PABLS	10/01-12/01
	Erie MSA, PA	H	5.86 FQ	8.85 AW	12.33 TQ	PABLS	10/01-12/01
	Harrisburg-Lebanon-Carlisle MSA, PA	H	8.26 FQ	14.45 AW	21.54 TQ	PABLS	10/01-12/01
	Johnstown MSA, PA	H	7.24 FQ	10.65 AW	15.47 TQ	PABLS	10/01-12/01
	Lancaster MSA, PA	H	6.41 FQ	11.49 AW	16.04 TQ	PABLS	10/01-12/01
	Philadelphia PMSA, PA-NJ	H	7.62 FQ	11.90 AW	17.29 TQ	PABLS	10/01-12/01
	Pittsburgh MSA, PA	H	6.16 FQ	11.08 AW	18.87 TQ	PABLS	10/01-12/01
	Reading MSA, PA	H	7.76 FQ	12.48 AW	16.76 TQ	PABLS	10/01-12/01
	Scranton-Wilkes-Barre-Hazleton MSA, PA	H	7.49 FQ	10.75 AW	14.42 TQ	PABLS	10/01-12/01
	York MSA, PA	H	8.98 FQ	12.87 AW	18.59 TQ	PABLS	10/01-12/01
	Rhode Island	H	6.78 FQ	10.10 AW	13.91 TQ	RIBLS	10/01-12/01
	Providence-Fall River-Warwick MSA, RI-MA	H	6.97 FQ	10.16 AW	13.76 TQ	RIBLS	10/01-12/01
	South Carolina	H	7.41 FQ	11.28 AW	16.26 TQ	SCBLS	10/01-12/01
	Charleston-North Charleston MSA, SC	H	7.03 FQ	11.47 AW	16.25 TQ	SCBLS	10/01-12/01
	Columbia MSA, SC	H	8.54 FQ	11.02 AW	13.47 TQ	SCBLS	10/01-12/01
	Greenville-Spartanburg-Anderson MSA, SC	H	7.88 FQ	12.26 AW	17.76 TQ	SCBLS	10/01-12/01
	South Dakota	H	7.70 FQ	10.60 AW	13.35 TQ	SDBLS	10/01-12/01
	Sioux Falls MSA, SD	H	9.52 FQ	11.66 AW	13.63 TQ	SDBLS	10/01-12/01
	Tennessee	H	6.40 FQ	10.72 AW	15.71 TQ	TNBLS	10/01-12/01
	Chattanooga MSA, TN-GA	H	6.79 FQ	11.15 AW	16.13 TQ	TNBLS	10/01-12/01
	Clarksville-Hopkinsville MSA, TN-KY	H	5.88 FQ	8.42 AW	11.70 TQ	TNBLS	10/01-12/01
	Johnson City-Kingsport-Bristol MSA, TN-VA	H	6.41 FQ	10.30 AW	13.93 TQ	TNBLS	10/01-12/01
	Knoxville MSA, TN	H	7.18 FQ	8.97 AW	11.06 TQ	TNBLS	10/01-12/01
	Memphis MSA, TN-AR-MS	H	6.38 FQ	11.72 AW	16.78 TQ	TNBLS	10/01-12/01
	Nashville MSA, TN	H	6.01 FQ	10.09 AW	14.06 TQ	TNBLS	10/01-12/01
	Texas	H	6.03 FQ	10.25 AW	16.47 TQ	TXBLS	10/01-12/01
	Amarillo MSA, TX	H	5.95 FQ	8.32 AW	12.36 TQ	TXBLS	10/01-12/01
	Austin-San Marcos MSA, TX	H	7.37 FQ	9.25 AW	11.05 TQ	TXBLS	10/01-12/01
	Beaumont-Port Arthur MSA, TX	H	5.77 FQ	9.84 AW	13.89 TQ	TXBLS	10/01-12/01
	Brazoria PMSA, TX	H	6.46 FQ	9.32 AW	13.52 TQ	TXBLS	10/01-12/01
	Corpus Christi MSA, TX	H	5.71 FQ	8.88 AW	14.94 TQ	TXBLS	10/01-12/01
	Dallas PMSA, TX	H	7.05 FQ	11.34 AW	16.31 TQ	TXBLS	10/01-12/01
	El Paso MSA, TX	H	6.06 FQ	9.32 AW	13.17 TQ	TXBLS	10/01-12/01
	Fort Worth-Arlington PMSA, TX	H	6.66 FQ	13.61 AW	24.90 TQ	TXBLS	10/01-12/01
	Galveston-Texas City PMSA, TX	H	5.47 FQ	7.87 AW	13.99 TQ	TXBLS	10/01-12/01
	Houston PMSA, TX	H	5.84 FQ	9.70 AW	16.84 TQ	TXBLS	10/01-12/01
	Killeen-Temple MSA, TX	H	7.59 FQ	11.97 AW	16.33 TQ	TXBLS	10/01-12/01
	Laredo MSA, TX	H	5.92 FQ	10.27 AW	16.92 TQ	TXBLS	10/01-12/01
	Longview-Marshall MSA, TX	H	6.22 FQ	9.28 AW	13.45 TQ	TXBLS	10/01-12/01
	Lubbock MSA, TX	H	6.02 FQ	8.04 AW	11.15 TQ	TXBLS	10/01-12/01
	McAllen-Edinburg-Mission MSA, TX	H	5.59 FQ	7.77 AW	11.67 TQ	TXBLS	10/01-12/01

AAW	Average annual wage	AOH	Average offered, high	ASH	Average starting, high	H	Hourly	M	Monthly	S	Special: hourly and annual
AE	Average entry wage	AOL	Average offered, low	ASL	Average starting, low	HI	Highest wage paid	MTC	Median total compensation	TQ	Third quartile wage
AEX	Average experienced wage	APH	Average pay, high range	AW	Average wage paid	HR	High end range	MW	Median wage paid	W	Weekly
AO	Average offered	APL	Average pay, low range	FQ	First quartile wage	LR	Low end range	SQ	Second quartile wage	Y	Yearly

Occupation/Type/Industry	Location	Per	Low	Mid	High	Source	Date
Packaging and Filling Machine Operator and Tender	Odessa-Midland MSA, TX	H	5.62 FQ	8.12 AW	14.25 TQ	TXBLS	10/01-12/01
	San Antonio MSA, TX	H	5.99 FQ	9.02 AW	12.94 TQ	TXBLS	10/01-12/01
	Waco MSA, TX	H	7.36 FQ	11.00 AW	15.55 TQ	TXBLS	10/01-12/01
	Utah	H	7.04 FQ	10.28 AW	13.20 TQ	UTBLS	10/01-12/01
	Provo-Orem MSA, UT	H	8.32 FQ	11.12 AW	13.14 TQ	UTBLS	10/01-12/01
	Salt Lake City-Ogden MSA, UT	H	6.32 FQ	9.58 AW	13.33 TQ	UTBLS	10/01-12/01
	Vermont	H	7.62 FQ	10.55 AW	14.78 TQ	VTBLS	10/01-12/01
	Burlington MSA, VT	H	7.55 FQ	10.86 AW	14.87 TQ	VTBLS	10/01-12/01
	Virginia	H	7.52 FQ	13.65 AW	22.26 TQ	VABLS	10/01-12/01
	Lynchburg MSA, VA	H	9.10 FQ	13.88 AW	16.89 TQ	VABLS	10/01-12/01
	Norfolk-Virginia Beach-Newport News MSA, VA-NC	H	7.53 FQ	16.09 AW	26.38 TQ	VABLS	10/01-12/01
	Richmond-Petersburg MSA, VA	H	7.55 FQ	14.32 AW	21.20 TQ	VABLS	10/01-12/01
	Roanoke MSA, VA	H	6.97 FQ	10.95 AW	16.49 TQ	VABLS	10/01-12/01
	Washington	H	7.11 FQ	11.14 AW	16.75 TQ	WABLS	10/01-12/01
	Olympia PMSA, WA	H	7.10 FQ	9.68 AW	15.88 TQ	WABLS	10/01-12/01
	Richland-Kennewick-Pasco MSA, WA	H	6.98 FQ	10.35 AW	15.04 TQ	WABLS	10/01-12/01
	Seattle-Bellevue-Everett PMSA, WA	H	7.64 FQ	12.94 AW	17.89 TQ	WABLS	10/01-12/01
	Spokane MSA, WA	H	7.37 FQ	10.85 AW	16.21 TQ	WABLS	10/01-12/01
	Tacoma PMSA, WA	H	7.80 FQ	12.40 AW	17.46 TQ	WABLS	10/01-12/01
	Yakima MSA, WA	H	7.33 FQ	9.86 AW	13.51 TQ	WABLS	10/01-12/01
	West Virginia	H	6.42 FQ	11.12 AW	16.46 TQ	WVBLS	10/01-12/01
	Charleston MSA, WV	H	7.29 FQ	10.42 AW	13.50 TQ	WVBLS	10/01-12/01
	Huntington-Ashland MSA, WV-KY-OH	H	7.73 FQ	12.65 AW	18.69 TQ	WVBLS	10/01-12/01
	Wisconsin	H	7.02 FQ	11.57 AW	16.91 TQ	WIBLS	10/01-12/01
	Appleton-Oshkosh-Neenah MSA, WI	H	6.56 FQ	11.68 AW	16.92 TQ	WIBLS	10/01-12/01
	Green Bay MSA, WI	H	6.78 FQ	13.82 AW	20.25 TQ	WIBLS	10/01-12/01
	Madison MSA, WI	H	7.57 FQ	11.52 AW	16.53 TQ	WIBLS	10/01-12/01
	Milwaukee-Waukesha PMSA, WI	H	6.30 FQ	10.28 AW	15.42 TQ	WIBLS	10/01-12/01
	Racine PMSA, WI	H	7.42 FQ	11.18 AW	16.55 TQ	WIBLS	10/01-12/01
	Wyoming	H	6.67 FQ	11.90 AW	17.29 TQ	WYBLS	10/01-12/01
	Puerto Rico	H	5.77 FQ	8.77 AW	13.36 TQ	PRBLS	10/01-12/01
	Virgin Islands	H	5.64 FQ	7.85 AW	10.69 TQ	VIBLS	10/01-12/01
Packer and Packager							
Hand	Alabama	H	5.67 FQ	7.66 AW	11.00 TQ	ALBLS	10/01-12/01
Hand	Alaska	H	6.28 FQ	8.65 AW	13.22 TQ	AKBLS	10/01-12/01
Hand	Arizona	H	5.63 FQ	7.54 AW	11.53 TQ	AZBLS	10/01-12/01
Hand	Arkansas	H	5.92 FQ	8.41 AW	11.93 TQ	ARBLS	10/01-12/01
Hand	California	H	6.47 FQ	8.49 AW	12.28 TQ	CABLS	10/01-12/01
Hand	Colorado	H	5.89 FQ	8.25 AW	11.57 TQ	COBLS	10/01-12/01
Hand	Connecticut	H	6.67 FQ	8.96 AW	12.78 TQ	CTBLS	10/01-12/01
Hand	Delaware	H	6.66 FQ	10.21 AW	15.57 TQ	DEBLS	10/01-12/01
Hand	District of Columbia	H	6.49 FQ	7.99 AW	10.42 TQ	DCBLS	10/01-12/01
Hand	Florida	H	5.67 FQ	7.17 AW	9.64 TQ	FLBLS	10/01-12/01
Hand	Georgia	H	5.96 FQ	8.41 AW	11.37 TQ	GABLS	10/01-12/01
Hand	Hawaii	H	6.06 FQ	8.68 AW	12.59 TQ	HIBLS	10/01-12/01
Hand	Idaho	H	5.80 FQ	7.49 AW	11.10 TQ	IDBLS	10/01-12/01
Hand	Illinois	H	5.96 FQ	8.85 AW	12.76 TQ	ILBLS	10/01-12/01
Hand	Indiana	H	6.08 FQ	9.09 AW	12.53 TQ	INBLS	10/01-12/01
Hand	Iowa	H	5.85 FQ	8.59 AW	12.56 TQ	IABLS	10/01-12/01
Hand	Kansas	H	5.87 FQ	8.40 AW	12.75 TQ	KSBLS	10/01-12/01
Hand	Kentucky	H	5.86 FQ	8.58 AW	12.16 TQ	KYBLS	10/01-12/01
Hand	Louisiana	H	5.70 FQ	7.69 AW	10.68 TQ	LABLS	10/01-12/01
Hand	Maine	H	5.84 FQ	8.05 AW	11.21 TQ	MEBLS	10/01-12/01
Hand	Maryland	H	6.14 FQ	9.16 AW	13.03 TQ	MDBLS	10/01-12/01
Hand	Massachusetts	H	6.94 FQ	9.18 AW	13.00 TQ	MABLS	10/01-12/01
Hand	Michigan	H	5.77 FQ	8.49 AW	12.94 TQ	MIBLS	10/01-12/01
Hand	Minnesota	H	6.12 FQ	9.09 AW	12.94 TQ	MNBLS	10/01-12/01
Hand	Mississippi	H	5.82 FQ	8.37 AW	11.93 TQ	MSBLS	10/01-12/01
Hand	Missouri	H	5.93 FQ	8.37 AW	11.82 TQ	MOBLS	10/01-12/01
Hand	Montana	H	5.76 FQ	8.27 AW	13.08 TQ	MTBLS	10/01-12/01
Hand	Nebraska	H	5.79 FQ	8.95 AW	13.63 TQ	NEBLS	10/01-12/01

AAW	Average annual wage	AOH	Average offered, high	ASH	Average starting, high	H	Hourly	M	Monthly	S	Special: hourly and annual
AE	Average entry wage	AOL	Average offered, low	ASL	Average starting, low	HI	Highest wage paid	MTC	Median total compensation	TQ	Third quartile wage
AEX	Average experienced wage	APH	Average pay, high range	AW	Average wage paid	HR	High end range	MW	Median wage paid	W	Weekly
AO	Average offered	APL	Average pay, low range	FQ	First quartile wage	LR	Low end range	SQ	Second quartile wage	Y	Yearly

Occupation/Type/Industry	Location	Per	Low	Mid	High	Source	Date
Packer and Packager							
Hand	Nevada	H	5.71 FQ	7.67 AW	10.98 TQ	NVBLS	10/01-12/01
Hand	New Hampshire	H	5.87 FQ	8.11 AW	11.31 TQ	NHBLS	10/01-12/01
Hand	New Jersey	H	5.79 FQ	8.49 AW	13.09 TQ	NJBLS	10/01-12/01
Hand	New Mexico	H	5.67 FQ	6.97 AW	9.16 TQ	NMBLS	10/01-12/01
Hand	New York	H	5.86 FQ	9.08 AW	13.48 TQ	NYBLS	10/01-12/01
Hand	North Carolina	H	5.98 FQ	8.46 AW	11.21 TQ	NCBLS	10/01-12/01
Hand	North Dakota	H	5.71 FQ	7.41 AW	9.85 TQ	NDBLS	10/01-12/01
Hand	Ohio	H	5.91 FQ	8.93 AW	13.26 TQ	OHBLS	10/01-12/01
Hand	Oklahoma	H	5.70 FQ	7.69 AW	10.64 TQ	OKBLS	10/01-12/01
Hand	Oregon	H	7.01 FQ	9.51 AW	15.43 TQ	ORBLS	10/01-12/01
Hand	Pennsylvania	H	6.18 FQ	9.33 AW	13.93 TQ	PABLS	10/01-12/01
Hand	Rhode Island	H	6.58 FQ	8.15 AW	10.95 TQ	RIBLS	10/01-12/01
Hand	South Carolina	H	5.94 FQ	8.29 AW	11.12 TQ	SCBLS	10/01-12/01
Hand	South Dakota	H	5.81 FQ	8.33 AW	12.08 TQ	SDBLS	10/01-12/01
Hand	Tennessee	H	5.98 FQ	8.50 AW	11.49 TQ	TNBLS	10/01-12/01
Hand	Texas	H	5.80 FQ	8.10 AW	12.08 TQ	TXBLS	10/01-12/01
Hand	Utah	H	5.73 FQ	8.04 AW	12.17 TQ	UTBLS	10/01-12/01
Hand	Vermont	H	6.78 FQ	8.98 AW	12.04 TQ	VTBLS	10/01-12/01
Hand	Virginia	H	5.88 FQ	8.09 AW	11.05 TQ	VABLS	10/01-12/01
Hand	Washington	H	6.87 FQ	8.97 AW	13.03 TQ	WABLS	10/01-12/01
Hand	West Virginia	H	5.84 FQ	8.83 AW	12.78 TQ	WVBLS	10/01-12/01
Hand	Wisconsin	H	6.15 FQ	9.48 AW	13.62 TQ	WIBLS	10/01-12/01
Hand	Wyoming	H	5.66 FQ	7.18 AW	10.39 TQ	WYBLS	10/01-12/01
Hand	Puerto Rico	H	5.54 FQ	6.23 AW	7.15 TQ	PRBLS	10/01-12/01
Hand	Virgin Islands	H	5.59 FQ	6.37 AW	7.72 TQ	VIBLS	10/01-12/01
Hand	Guam	H	5.64 FQ	6.18 AW	7.08 TQ	GUBLS	10/01-12/01
Painter							
Automotive Body Shop	United States	Y		42524 AW		BSB	1/01-1/02
Construction and Maintenance	Alabama	H	8.03 FQ	12.67 AW	17.44 TQ	ALBLS	10/01-12/01
Construction and Maintenance	Birmingham MSA, AL	H	8.03 FQ	12.49 AW	17.22 TQ	ALBLS	10/01-12/01
Construction and Maintenance	Huntsville MSA, AL	H	9.26 FQ	12.63 AW	17.09 TQ	ALBLS	10/01-12/01
Construction and Maintenance	Mobile MSA, AL	H	8.05 FQ	13.13 AW	19.15 TQ	ALBLS	10/01-12/01
Construction and Maintenance	Montgomery MSA, AL	H	8.44 FQ	12.39 AW	16.28 TQ	ALBLS	10/01-12/01
Construction and Maintenance	Alaska	H	13.27 FQ	19.50 AW	26.93 TQ	AKBLS	10/01-12/01
Construction and Maintenance	Anchorage MSA, AK	H	13.34 FQ	18.35 AW	25.12 TQ	AKBLS	10/01-12/01
Construction and Maintenance	Arizona	H	8.32 FQ	12.39 AW	17.15 TQ	AZBLS	10/01-12/01
Construction and Maintenance	Phoenix-Mesa MSA, AZ	H	8.44 FQ	12.78 AW	17.42 TQ	AZBLS	10/01-12/01
Construction and Maintenance	Tucson MSA, AZ	H	8.36 FQ	11.09 AW	15.84 TQ	AZBLS	10/01-12/01
Construction and Maintenance	Arkansas	H	8.22 FQ	11.82 AW	16.26 TQ	ARBLS	10/01-12/01
Construction and Maintenance	Fayetteville-Springdale-Rogers MSA, AR	H	7.17 FQ	10.70 AW	16.09 TQ	ARBLS	10/01-12/01
Construction and Maintenance	Fort Smith MSA, AR-OK	H	7.69 FQ	10.29 AW	14.18 TQ	ARBLS	10/01-12/01
Construction and Maintenance	Little Rock-North Little Rock MSA, AR	H	9.51 FQ	12.65 AW	16.68 TQ	ARBLS	10/01-12/01
Construction and Maintenance	California	H	8.98 FQ	15.63 AW	24.64 TQ	CABLS	10/01-12/01
Construction and Maintenance	Bakersfield MSA, CA	H	9.02 FQ	14.29 AW	23.87 TQ	CABLS	10/01-12/01
Construction and Maintenance	Chico-Paradise MSA, CA	H	9.33 FQ	13.42 AW	17.32 TQ	CABLS	10/01-12/01
Construction and Maintenance	Fresno MSA, CA	H	7.28 FQ	13.14 AW	21.47 TQ	CABLS	10/01-12/01
Construction and Maintenance	Los Angeles-Long Beach PMSA, CA	H	7.61 FQ	14.92 AW	25.22 TQ	CABLS	10/01-12/01
Construction and Maintenance	Merced MSA, CA	H	7.59 FQ	13.87 AW	21.61 TQ	CABLS	10/01-12/01
Construction and Maintenance	Modesto MSA, CA	H	10.34 FQ	16.06 AW	21.83 TQ	CABLS	10/01-12/01
Construction and Maintenance	Oakland PMSA, CA	H	11.52 FQ	18.13 AW	26.57 TQ	CABLS	10/01-12/01
Construction and Maintenance	Orange County PMSA, CA	H	9.20 FQ	13.91 AW	20.06 TQ	CABLS	10/01-12/01
Construction and Maintenance	Redding MSA, CA	H	9.23 FQ	13.00 AW	20.52 TQ	CABLS	10/01-12/01
Construction and Maintenance	Riverside-San Bernardino PMSA, CA	H	8.80 FQ	13.81 AW	21.01 TQ	CABLS	10/01-12/01
Construction and Maintenance	Sacramento PMSA, CA	H	7.85 FQ	14.23 AW	21.05 TQ	CABLS	10/01-12/01
Construction and Maintenance	Salinas MSA, CA	H	11.52 FQ	18.56 AW	26.00 TQ	CABLS	10/01-12/01
Construction and Maintenance	San Diego MSA, CA	H	9.21 FQ	15.04 AW	21.87 TQ	CABLS	10/01-12/01
Construction and Maintenance	San Francisco PMSA, CA	H	12.16 FQ	19.84 AW	30.36 TQ	CABLS	10/01-12/01
Construction and Maintenance	San Jose PMSA, CA	H	10.56 FQ	17.39 AW	25.51 TQ	CABLS	10/01-12/01
Construction and Maintenance	San Luis Obispo-Atascadero-Paso Robles MSA, CA	H	9.06 FQ	14.88 AW	21.81 TQ	CABLS	10/01-12/01
Construction and Maintenance	Santa Barbara-Santa Maria-Lompoc MSA, CA	H	7.90 FQ	14.33 AW	21.54 TQ	CABLS	10/01-12/01
Construction and Maintenance	Santa Cruz-Watsonville PMSA, CA	H	11.06 FQ	16.37 AW	23.75 TQ	CABLS	10/01-12/01
Construction and Maintenance	Santa Rosa PMSA, CA	H	10.64 FQ	16.75 AW	23.80 TQ	CABLS	10/01-12/01
Construction and Maintenance	Stockton-Lodi MSA, CA	H	8.51 FQ	12.89 AW	19.37 TQ	CABLS	10/01-12/01

AAW Average annual wage **AOH** Average offered, high **ASH** Average starting, high **H** Hourly **M** Monthly **S** Special: hourly and annual
AE Average entry wage **AOL** Average offered, low **ASL** Average starting, low **HI** Highest wage paid **MTC** Median total compensation **TQ** Third quartile wage
AEX Average experienced wage **APH** Average pay, high range **AW** Average wage paid **HR** High end range **MW** Median wage paid **W** Weekly
AO Average offered **APL** Average pay, low range **FQ** First quartile wage **LR** Low end range **SQ** Second quartile wage **Y** Yearly

Occupation/Type/Industry	Location	Per	Low	Mid	High	Source	Date
Painter							
Construction and Maintenance	Vallejo-Fairfield-Napa PMSA, CA	H	9.90 FQ	17.95 AW	26.12 TQ	CABLS	10/01-12/01
Construction and Maintenance	Ventura PMSA, CA	H	9.43 FQ	14.05 AW	18.75 TQ	CABLS	10/01-12/01
Construction and Maintenance	Visalia-Tulare-Porterville MSA, CA	H	7.34 FQ	12.67 AW	21.04 TQ	CABLS	10/01-12/01
Construction and Maintenance	Colorado	H	9.67 FQ	14.47 AW	20.49 TQ	COBLS	10/01-12/01
Construction and Maintenance	Boulder-Longmont PMSA, CO	H	8.02 FQ	12.80 AW	18.56 TQ	COBLS	10/01-12/01
Construction and Maintenance	Colorado Springs MSA, CO	H	11.28 FQ	14.44 AW	18.04 TQ	COBLS	10/01-12/01
Construction and Maintenance	Denver PMSA, CO	H	10.25 FQ	14.77 AW	20.83 TQ	COBLS	10/01-12/01
Construction and Maintenance	Fort Collins-Loveland MSA, CO	H	8.76 FQ	12.26 AW	16.67 TQ	COBLS	10/01-12/01
Construction and Maintenance	Greeley PMSA, CO	H	9.13 FQ	14.56 AW	21.02 TQ	COBLS	10/01-12/01
Construction and Maintenance	Connecticut	H	9.32 FQ	16.12 AW	22.27 TQ	CTBLS	10/01-12/01
Construction and Maintenance	Bridgeport PMSA, CT	H	8.07 FQ	15.77 AW	22.54 TQ	CTBLS	10/01-12/01
Construction and Maintenance	Danbury PMSA, CT	H	7.47 FQ	13.61 AW	19.07 TQ	CTBLS	10/01-12/01
Construction and Maintenance	Hartford MSA, CT	H	10.21 FQ	16.16 AW	21.79 TQ	CTBLS	10/01-12/01
Construction and Maintenance	New Haven-Meriden PMSA, CT	H	9.41 FQ	16.79 AW	25.97 TQ	CTBLS	10/01-12/01
Construction and Maintenance	New London-Norwich MSA, CT-RI	H	10.39 FQ	15.50 AW	20.67 TQ	CTBLS	10/01-12/01
Construction and Maintenance	Stamford-Norwalk PMSA, CT	H	11.30 FQ	17.19 AW	24.32 TQ	CTBLS	10/01-12/01
Construction and Maintenance	Waterbury PMSA, CT	H	9.31 FQ	14.35 AW	20.68 TQ	CTBLS	10/01-12/01
Construction and Maintenance	Delaware	H	9.80 FQ	16.33 AW	25.25 TQ	DEBLS	10/01-12/01
Construction and Maintenance	Wilmington-Newark PMSA, DE-MD	H	11.63 FQ	17.40 AW	25.67 TQ	DEBLS	10/01-12/01
Construction and Maintenance	District of Columbia	H	8.99 FQ	16.78 AW	21.22 TQ	DCBLS	10/01-12/01
Construction and Maintenance	Washington PMSA, DC-MD-VA-WV	H	9.37 FQ	14.24 AW	19.63 TQ	DCBLS	10/01-12/01
Construction and Maintenance	Florida	H	8.56 FQ	12.51 AW	17.21 TQ	FLBLS	10/01-12/01
Construction and Maintenance	Daytona Beach MSA, FL	H	6.38 FQ	9.93 AW	13.43 TQ	FLBLS	10/01-12/01
Construction and Maintenance	Fort Lauderdale PMSA, FL	H	9.02 FQ	12.99 AW	17.32 TQ	FLBLS	10/01-12/01
Construction and Maintenance	Fort Myers-Cape Coral MSA, FL	H	8.28 FQ	12.41 AW	16.67 TQ	FLBLS	10/01-12/01
Construction and Maintenance	Fort Pierce-Port St. Lucie MSA, FL	H	9.39 FQ	12.91 AW	16.90 TQ	FLBLS	10/01-12/01
Construction and Maintenance	Fort Walton Beach MSA, FL	H	9.25 FQ	11.53 AW	15.55 TQ	FLBLS	10/01-12/01
Construction and Maintenance	Gainesville MSA, FL	H	7.59 FQ	11.09 AW	13.96 TQ	FLBLS	10/01-12/01
Construction and Maintenance	Jacksonville MSA, FL	H	7.83 FQ	12.12 AW	16.75 TQ	FLBLS	10/01-12/01
Construction and Maintenance	Lakeland-Winter Haven MSA, FL	H	9.83 FQ	13.90 AW	17.45 TQ	FLBLS	10/01-12/01
Construction and Maintenance	Melbourne-Titusville-Palm Bay MSA, FL	H	8.14 FQ	14.99 AW	22.03 TQ	FLBLS	10/01-12/01
Construction and Maintenance	Miami PMSA, FL	H	8.39 FQ	12.61 AW	17.53 TQ	FLBLS	10/01-12/01
Construction and Maintenance	Naples MSA, FL	H	9.23 FQ	13.17 AW	16.87 TQ	FLBLS	10/01-12/01
Construction and Maintenance	Ocala MSA, FL	H	8.04 FQ	11.19 AW	14.41 TQ	FLBLS	10/01-12/01
Construction and Maintenance	Orlando MSA, FL	H	9.29 FQ	13.37 AW	17.31 TQ	FLBLS	10/01-12/01
Construction and Maintenance	Pensacola MSA, FL	H	7.45 FQ	11.44 AW	16.52 TQ	FLBLS	10/01-12/01
Construction and Maintenance	Sarasota-Bradenton MSA, FL	H	7.62 FQ	11.87 AW	17.57 TQ	FLBLS	10/01-12/01
Construction and Maintenance	Tallahassee MSA, FL	H	8.44 FQ	11.51 AW	15.58 TQ	FLBLS	10/01-12/01
Construction and Maintenance	Tampa-St. Petersburg-Clearwater MSA, FL	H	8.62 FQ	11.79 AW	15.91 TQ	FLBLS	10/01-12/01
Construction and Maintenance	West Palm Beach-Boca Raton MSA, FL	H	8.08 FQ	13.33 AW	19.48 TQ	FLBLS	10/01-12/01
Construction and Maintenance	Georgia	H	8.61 FQ	14.05 AW	19.97 TQ	GABLS	10/01-12/01
Construction and Maintenance	Atlanta MSA, GA	H	10.02 FQ	15.12 AW	21.16 TQ	GABLS	10/01-12/01
Construction and Maintenance	Augusta-Aiken MSA, GA-SC	H	8.52 FQ	13.49 AW	21.27 TQ	GABLS	10/01-12/01
Construction and Maintenance	Columbus MSA, GA-AL	H	7.64 FQ	11.13 AW	15.76 TQ	GABLS	10/01-12/01
Construction and Maintenance	Macon MSA, GA	H	7.69 FQ	13.54 AW	19.54 TQ	GABLS	10/01-12/01
Construction and Maintenance	Savannah MSA, GA	H	7.38 FQ	13.51 AW	23.53 TQ	GABLS	10/01-12/01
Construction and Maintenance	Hawaii	H	11.23 FQ	20.12 AW	29.21 TQ	HIBLS	10/01-12/01
Construction and Maintenance	Honolulu MSA, HI	H	10.76 FQ	20.49 AW	30.31 TQ	HIBLS	10/01-12/01
Construction and Maintenance	Idaho	H	9.48 FQ	14.34 AW	20.47 TQ	IDBLS	10/01-12/01
Construction and Maintenance	Boise City MSA, ID	H	9.53 FQ	14.04 AW	18.98 TQ	IDBLS	10/01-12/01
Construction and Maintenance	Illinois	H	7.45 FQ	17.23 AW	30.36 TQ	ILBLS	10/01-12/01
Construction and Maintenance	Champaign-Urbana MSA, IL	H	12.31 FQ	24.74 AW	35.13 TQ	ILBLS	10/01-12/01
Construction and Maintenance	Chicago PMSA, IL	H	7.34 FQ	17.28 AW	30.91 TQ	ILBLS	10/01-12/01
Construction and Maintenance	Peoria-Pekin MSA, IL	H	9.01 FQ	20.04 AW	26.60 TQ	ILBLS	10/01-12/01
Construction and Maintenance	Rockford MSA, IL	H	7.89 FQ	13.15 AW	23.67 TQ	ILBLS	10/01-12/01
Construction and Maintenance	Springfield MSA, IL	H	11.81 FQ	22.30 AW	32.96 TQ	ILBLS	10/01-12/01
Construction and Maintenance	Indiana	H	9.12 FQ	15.28 AW	22.74 TQ	INBLS	10/01-12/01
Construction and Maintenance	Elkhart-Goshen MSA, IN	H	9.69 FQ	15.92 AW	30.92 TQ	INBLS	10/01-12/01

AAW	Average annual wage	**AOH**	Average offered, high	**ASH**	Average starting, high	**H**	Hourly	**M**	Monthly	**S**	Special: hourly and annual
AE	Average entry wage	**AOL**	Average offered, low	**ASL**	Average starting, low	**HI**	Highest wage paid	**MTC**	Median total compensation	**TQ**	Third quartile wage
AEX	Average experienced wage	**APH**	Average pay, high range	**AW**	Average wage paid	**HR**	High end range	**MW**	Median wage paid	**W**	Weekly
AO	Average offered	**APL**	Average pay, low range	**FQ**	First quartile wage	**LR**	Low end range	**SQ**	Second quartile wage	**Y**	Yearly

Occupation/Type/Industry	Location	Per	Low	Mid	High	Source	Date
Painter							
Construction and Maintenance	Evansville-Henderson MSA, IN-KY	H	9.41 FQ	15.86 AW	25.50 TQ	INBLS	10/01-12/01
Construction and Maintenance	Fort Wayne MSA, IN	H	9.10 FQ	14.18 AW	20.58 TQ	INBLS	10/01-12/01
Construction and Maintenance	Gary PMSA, IN	H	8.39 FQ	17.09 AW	26.44 TQ	INBLS	10/01-12/01
Construction and Maintenance	Indianapolis MSA, IN	H	9.62 FQ	15.99 AW	21.86 TQ	INBLS	10/01-12/01
Construction and Maintenance	Lafayette MSA, IN	H	9.00 FQ	14.00 AW	21.37 TQ	INBLS	10/01-12/01
Construction and Maintenance	South Bend MSA, IN	H	9.39 FQ	15.17 AW	22.14 TQ	INBLS	10/01-12/01
Construction and Maintenance	Iowa	H	8.17 FQ	13.61 AW	20.10 TQ	IABLS	10/01-12/01
Construction and Maintenance	Cedar Rapids MSA, IA	H	9.03 FQ	15.97 AW	22.14 TQ	IABLS	10/01-12/01
Construction and Maintenance	Davenport-Moline-Rock Island MSA, IA-IL	H	7.69 FQ	13.91 AW	22.54 TQ	IABLS	10/01-12/01
Construction and Maintenance	Des Moines MSA, IA	H	8.82 FQ	15.10 AW	21.38 TQ	IABLS	10/01-12/01
Construction and Maintenance	Kansas	H	8.94 FQ	13.71 AW	20.73 TQ	KSBLS	10/01-12/01
Construction and Maintenance	Topeka MSA, KS	H	7.39 FQ	13.86 AW	21.13 TQ	KSBLS	10/01-12/01
Construction and Maintenance	Wichita MSA, KS	H	8.36 FQ	13.01 AW	17.65 TQ	KSBLS	10/01-12/01
Construction and Maintenance	Kentucky	H	8.65 FQ	12.35 AW	17.00 TQ	KYBLS	10/01-12/01
Construction and Maintenance	Lexington MSA, KY	H	7.01 FQ	11.08 AW	14.60 TQ	KYBLS	10/01-12/01
Construction and Maintenance	Louisville MSA, KY-IN	H	9.26 FQ	13.00 AW	17.44 TQ	KYBLS	10/01-12/01
Construction and Maintenance	Louisiana	H	9.04 FQ	13.41 AW	18.56 TQ	LABLS	10/01-12/01
Construction and Maintenance	Baton Rouge MSA, LA	H	9.71 FQ	13.33 AW	16.85 TQ	LABLS	10/01-12/01
Construction and Maintenance	Houma MSA, LA	H	9.53 FQ	14.10 AW	18.50 TQ	LABLS	10/01-12/01
Construction and Maintenance	Lafayette MSA, LA	H	8.06 FQ	11.87 AW	16.20 TQ	LABLS	10/01-12/01
Construction and Maintenance	Lake Charles MSA, LA	H	10.63 FQ	14.95 AW	21.45 TQ	LABLS	10/01-12/01
Construction and Maintenance	New Orleans MSA, LA	H	9.41 FQ	13.40 AW	18.12 TQ	LABLS	10/01-12/01
Construction and Maintenance	Shreveport-Bossier City MSA, LA	H	9.08 FQ	13.08 AW	18.47 TQ	LABLS	10/01-12/01
Construction and Maintenance	Maine	H	9.10 FQ	14.39 AW	18.26 TQ	MEBLS	10/01-12/01
Construction and Maintenance	Portland MSA, ME	H	8.25 FQ	12.78 AW	18.78 TQ	MEBLS	10/01-12/01
Construction and Maintenance	Maryland	H	9.37 FQ	13.94 AW	18.48 TQ	MDBLS	10/01-12/01
Construction and Maintenance	Baltimore PMSA, MD	H	10.74 FQ	14.58 AW	18.39 TQ	MDBLS	10/01-12/01
Construction and Maintenance	Massachusetts	H	9.44 FQ	16.20 AW	27.27 TQ	MABLS	10/01-12/01
Construction and Maintenance	Boston PMSA, MA-NH	H	9.44 FQ	16.62 AW	28.43 TQ	MABLS	10/01-12/01
Construction and Maintenance	Brockton PMSA, MA	H	7.96 FQ	15.49 AW	25.66 TQ	MABLS	10/01-12/01
Construction and Maintenance	Lawrence PMSA, MA-NH	H	10.79 FQ	15.80 AW	22.45 TQ	MABLS	10/01-12/01
Construction and Maintenance	Lowell PMSA, MA-NH	H	11.49 FQ	18.06 AW	28.31 TQ	MABLS	10/01-12/01
Construction and Maintenance	New Bedford PMSA, MA	H	9.02 FQ	13.98 AW	22.02 TQ	MABLS	10/01-12/01
Construction and Maintenance	Springfield MSA, MA	H	8.95 FQ	14.05 AW	21.35 TQ	MABLS	10/01-12/01
Construction and Maintenance	Worcester PMSA, MA-CT	H	9.77 FQ	14.75 AW	20.42 TQ	MABLS	10/01-12/01
Construction and Maintenance	Michigan	H	9.97 FQ	16.69 AW	25.68 TQ	MIBLS	10/01-12/01
Construction and Maintenance	Ann Arbor PMSA, MI	H	10.14 FQ	19.68 AW	28.21 TQ	MIBLS	10/01-12/01
Construction and Maintenance	Detroit PMSA, MI	H	10.92 FQ	18.29 AW	26.62 TQ	MIBLS	10/01-12/01
Construction and Maintenance	Flint PMSA, MI	H	11.68 FQ	19.54 AW	28.90 TQ	MIBLS	10/01-12/01
Construction and Maintenance	Grand Rapids-Muskegon-Holland MSA, MI	H	9.48 FQ	14.00 AW	20.35 TQ	MIBLS	10/01-12/01
Construction and Maintenance	Kalamazoo-Battle Creek MSA, MI	H	9.40 FQ	14.11 AW	19.88 TQ	MIBLS	10/01-12/01
Construction and Maintenance	Lansing-East Lansing MSA, MI	H	8.35 FQ	16.32 AW	23.17 TQ	MIBLS	10/01-12/01
Construction and Maintenance	Saginaw-Bay City-Midland MSA, MI	H	9.31 FQ	15.74 AW	21.87 TQ	MIBLS	10/01-12/01
Construction and Maintenance	Minnesota	H	11.34 FQ	18.30 AW	26.57 TQ	MNBLS	10/01-12/01
Construction and Maintenance	Duluth-Superior MSA, MN-WI	H	11.58 FQ	20.34 AW	27.22 TQ	MNBLS	10/01-12/01
Construction and Maintenance	Minneapolis-St. Paul MSA, MN-WI	H	11.74 FQ	18.63 AW	26.52 TQ	MNBLS	10/01-12/01
Construction and Maintenance	St. Cloud MSA, MN	H	10.06 FQ	14.64 AW	20.49 TQ	MNBLS	10/01-12/01
Construction and Maintenance	Mississippi	H	8.01 FQ	12.22 AW	17.10 TQ	MSBLS	10/01-12/01
Construction and Maintenance	Biloxi-Gulfport-Pascagoula MSA, MS	H	11.02 FQ	13.62 AW	17.24 TQ	MSBLS	10/01-12/01
Construction and Maintenance	Jackson MSA, MS	H	8.91 FQ	11.79 AW	14.26 TQ	MSBLS	10/01-12/01
Construction and Maintenance	Missouri	H	9.73 FQ	17.69 AW	26.61 TQ	MOBLS	10/01-12/01
Construction and Maintenance	Kansas City MSA, MO-KS	H	9.77 FQ	16.35 AW	25.49 TQ	MOBLS	10/01-12/01
Construction and Maintenance	St. Louis MSA, MO-IL	H	10.83 FQ	19.11 AW	27.06 TQ	MOBLS	10/01-12/01
Construction and Maintenance	Springfield MSA, MO	H	8.10 FQ	13.73 AW	20.16 TQ	MOBLS	10/01-12/01
Construction and Maintenance	Montana	H	8.32 FQ	13.55 AW	18.77 TQ	MTBLS	10/01-12/01
Construction and Maintenance	Billings MSA, MT	H	8.76 FQ	15.24 AW	21.90 TQ	MTBLS	10/01-12/01
Construction and Maintenance	Nebraska	H	8.64 FQ	12.82 AW	17.75 TQ	NEBLS	10/01-12/01
Construction and Maintenance	Lincoln MSA, NE	H	6.56 FQ	12.35 AW	17.45 TQ	NEBLS	10/01-12/01
Construction and Maintenance	Omaha MSA, NE-IA	H	9.68 FQ	13.78 AW	19.08 TQ	NEBLS	10/01-12/01
Construction and Maintenance	Nevada	H	9.95 FQ	16.38 AW	25.09 TQ	NVBLS	10/01-12/01
Construction and Maintenance	Las Vegas MSA, NV-AZ	H	10.03 FQ	16.66 AW	25.66 TQ	NVBLS	10/01-12/01
Construction and Maintenance	Reno MSA, NV	H	9.36 FQ	15.19 AW	21.80 TQ	NVBLS	10/01-12/01
Construction and Maintenance	New Hampshire	H	9.49 FQ	13.25 AW	17.15 TQ	NHBLS	10/01-12/01

AAW Average annual wage **AOH** Average offered, high **ASH** Average starting, high **H** Hourly **M** Monthly **S** Special: hourly and annual
AE Average entry wage **AOL** Average offered, low **ASL** Average starting, low **HI** Highest wage paid **MTC** Median total compensation **TQ** Third quartile wage
AEX Average experienced wage **APH** Average pay, high range **AW** Average wage paid **HR** High end range **MW** Median wage paid **W** Weekly
AO Average offered **APL** Average pay, low range **FQ** First quartile wage **LR** Low end range **SQ** Second quartile wage **Y** Yearly

Occupation/Type/Industry	Location	Per	Low	Mid	High	Source	Date
Painter							
Construction and Maintenance	Manchester PMSA, NH	H	11.18 FQ	14.65 AW	19.78 TQ	NHBLS	10/01-12/01
Construction and Maintenance	Nashua PMSA, NH	H	6.69 FQ	12.77 AW	17.18 TQ	NHBLS	10/01-12/01
Construction and Maintenance	Portsmouth-Rochester PMSA, NH-ME	H	10.78 FQ	14.82 AW	20.14 TQ	NHBLS	10/01-12/01
Construction and Maintenance	New Jersey	H	10.01 FQ	18.26 AW	31.54 TQ	NJBLS	10/01-12/01
Construction and Maintenance	Atlantic-Cape May PMSA, NJ	H	11.11 FQ	17.40 AW	28.36 TQ	NJBLS	10/01-12/01
Construction and Maintenance	Bergen-Passaic PMSA, NJ	H	10.16 FQ	16.73 AW	26.61 TQ	NJBLS	10/01-12/01
Construction and Maintenance	Jersey City PMSA, NJ	H	10.97 FQ	16.46 AW	24.96 TQ	NJBLS	10/01-12/01
Construction and Maintenance	Middlesex-Somerset-Hunterdon PMSA, NJ	H	10.54 FQ	18.87 AW	32.15 TQ	NJBLS	10/01-12/01
Construction and Maintenance	Monmouth-Ocean PMSA, NJ	H	7.54 FQ	14.66 AW	22.66 TQ	NJBLS	10/01-12/01
Construction and Maintenance	Newark PMSA, NJ	H	11.13 FQ	21.53 AW	34.36 TQ	NJBLS	10/01-12/01
Construction and Maintenance	Trenton PMSA, NJ	H	9.18 FQ	16.22 AW	23.19 TQ	NJBLS	10/01-12/01
Construction and Maintenance	New Mexico	H	8.34 FQ	12.12 AW	16.43 TQ	NMBLS	10/01-12/01
Construction and Maintenance	Albuquerque MSA, NM	H	9.39 FQ	12.47 AW	16.38 TQ	NMBLS	10/01-12/01
Construction and Maintenance	Las Cruces MSA, NM	H	6.34 FQ	9.33 AW	13.67 TQ	NMBLS	10/01-12/01
Construction and Maintenance	New York	H	9.29 FQ	17.94 AW	31.48 TQ	NYBLS	10/01-12/01
Construction and Maintenance	Albany-Schenectady-Troy MSA, NY	H	9.39 FQ	15.03 AW	21.12 TQ	NYBLS	10/01-12/01
Construction and Maintenance	Binghamton MSA, NY	H	8.70 FQ	13.64 AW	18.23 TQ	NYBLS	10/01-12/01
Construction and Maintenance	Buffalo-Niagara Falls MSA, NY	H	10.20 FQ	19.10 AW	32.31 TQ	NYBLS	10/01-12/01
Construction and Maintenance	Dutchess County PMSA, NY	H	10.04 FQ	15.34 AW	21.06 TQ	NYBLS	10/01-12/01
Construction and Maintenance	Nassau-Suffolk PMSA, NY	H	7.83 FQ	17.36 AW	31.91 TQ	NYBLS	10/01-12/01
Construction and Maintenance	New York PMSA, NY	H	11.15 FQ	20.12 AW	33.18 TQ	NYBLS	10/01-12/01
Construction and Maintenance	Newburgh PMSA, NY-PA	H	8.06 FQ	14.22 AW	20.87 TQ	NYBLS	10/01-12/01
Construction and Maintenance	Rochester MSA, NY	H	9.21 FQ	14.37 AW	20.93 TQ	NYBLS	10/01-12/01
Construction and Maintenance	Syracuse MSA, NY	H	8.56 FQ	14.73 AW	21.01 TQ	NYBLS	10/01-12/01
Construction and Maintenance	Utica-Rome MSA, NY	H	8.07 FQ	13.97 AW	24.65 TQ	NYBLS	10/01-12/01
Construction and Maintenance	North Carolina	H	8.16 FQ	11.86 AW	16.38 TQ	NCBLS	10/01-12/01
Construction and Maintenance	Asheville MSA, NC	H	9.40 FQ	11.89 AW	13.85 TQ	NCBLS	10/01-12/01
Construction and Maintenance	Charlotte-Gastonia-Rock Hill MSA, NC-SC	H	8.79 FQ	12.44 AW	16.51 TQ	NCBLS	10/01-12/01
Construction and Maintenance	Fayetteville MSA, NC	H	8.84 FQ	11.29 AW	14.00 TQ	NCBLS	10/01-12/01
Construction and Maintenance	Greensboro-Winston-Salem-High Point MSA, NC	H	7.75 FQ	11.35 AW	15.93 TQ	NCBLS	10/01-12/01
Construction and Maintenance	Hickory-Morganton-Lenoir MSA, NC	H	9.55 FQ	12.04 AW	14.80 TQ	NCBLS	10/01-12/01
Construction and Maintenance	Raleigh-Durham-Chapel Hill MSA, NC	H	8.09 FQ	11.68 AW	16.37 TQ	NCBLS	10/01-12/01
Construction and Maintenance	Wilmington MSA, NC	H	7.83 FQ	11.01 AW	14.01 TQ	NCBLS	10/01-12/01
Construction and Maintenance	North Dakota	H	8.88 FQ	13.89 AW	20.79 TQ	NDBLS	10/01-12/01
Construction and Maintenance	Fargo-Moorhead MSA, ND-MN	H	9.63 FQ	14.41 AW	21.10 TQ	NDBLS	10/01-12/01
Construction and Maintenance	Ohio	H	9.41 FQ	15.43 AW	23.05 TQ	OHBLS	10/01-12/01
Construction and Maintenance	Akron PMSA, OH	H	7.95 FQ	14.30 AW	21.49 TQ	OHBLS	10/01-12/01
Construction and Maintenance	Canton-Massillon MSA, OH	H	9.28 FQ	13.18 AW	19.78 TQ	OHBLS	10/01-12/01
Construction and Maintenance	Cincinnati PMSA, OH-KY-IN	H	9.91 FQ	15.23 AW	21.04 TQ	OHBLS	10/01-12/01
Construction and Maintenance	Cleveland-Lorain-Elyria PMSA, OH	H	9.43 FQ	16.44 AW	25.31 TQ	OHBLS	10/01-12/01
Construction and Maintenance	Columbus MSA, OH	H	10.33 FQ	15.43 AW	20.29 TQ	OHBLS	10/01-12/01
Construction and Maintenance	Dayton-Springfield MSA, OH	H	9.20 FQ	13.26 AW	19.27 TQ	OHBLS	10/01-12/01
Construction and Maintenance	Hamilton-Middletown PMSA, OH	H	9.74 FQ	14.39 AW	19.75 TQ	OHBLS	10/01-12/01
Construction and Maintenance	Mansfield MSA, OH	H	10.36 FQ	16.43 AW	21.79 TQ	OHBLS	10/01-12/01
Construction and Maintenance	Toledo MSA, OH	H	9.76 FQ	17.22 AW	25.64 TQ	OHBLS	10/01-12/01
Construction and Maintenance	Youngstown-Warren MSA, OH	H	10.43 FQ	18.17 AW	26.94 TQ	OHBLS	10/01-12/01
Construction and Maintenance	Oklahoma	H	7.58 FQ	12.13 AW	17.45 TQ	OKBLS	10/01-12/01
Construction and Maintenance	Oklahoma City MSA, OK	H	7.17 FQ	12.70 AW	18.95 TQ	OKBLS	10/01-12/01
Construction and Maintenance	Tulsa MSA, OK	H	8.17 FQ	11.98 AW	16.43 TQ	OKBLS	10/01-12/01
Construction and Maintenance	Oregon	H	8.98 FQ	14.91 AW	20.90 TQ	ORBLS	10/01-12/01
Construction and Maintenance	Eugene-Springfield MSA, OR	H	9.13 FQ	13.00 AW	17.42 TQ	ORBLS	10/01-12/01
Construction and Maintenance	Medford-Ashland MSA, OR	H	10.90 FQ	15.15 AW	20.18 TQ	ORBLS	10/01-12/01
Construction and Maintenance	Portland-Vancouver PMSA, OR-WA	H	8.96 FQ	15.51 AW	21.37 TQ	ORBLS	10/01-12/01
Construction and Maintenance	Salem PMSA, OR	H	9.36 FQ	13.32 AW	18.11 TQ	ORBLS	10/01-12/01
Construction and Maintenance	Pennsylvania	H	9.39 FQ	16.47 AW	25.83 TQ	PABLS	10/01-12/01
Construction and Maintenance	Allentown-Bethlehem-Easton MSA, PA	H	10.22 FQ	14.67 AW	20.47 TQ	PABLS	10/01-12/01
Construction and Maintenance	Erie MSA, PA	H	8.95 FQ	13.25 AW	19.59 TQ	PABLS	10/01-12/01

AAW	Average annual wage	**AOH**	Average offered, high	**ASH**	Average starting, high	**H**	Hourly	**M**	Monthly	**S**	Special: hourly and annual
AE	Average entry wage	**AOL**	Average offered, low	**ASL**	Average starting, low	**HI**	Highest wage paid	**MTC**	Median total compensation	**TQ**	Third quartile wage
AEX	Average experienced wage	**APH**	Average pay, high range	**AW**	Average wage paid	**HR**	High end range	**MW**	Median wage paid	**W**	Weekly
AO	Average offered	**APL**	Average pay, low range	**FQ**	First quartile wage	**LR**	Low end range	**SQ**	Second quartile wage	**Y**	Yearly

Occupation/Type/Industry	Location	Per	Low	Mid	High	Source	Date
Painter							
Construction and Maintenance	Harrisburg-Lebanon-Carlisle MSA, PA	H	9.27 FQ	14.43 AW	21.53 TQ	PABLS	10/01-12/01
Construction and Maintenance	Johnstown MSA, PA	H	5.95 FQ	12.14 AW	23.94 TQ	PABLS	10/01-12/01
Construction and Maintenance	Lancaster MSA, PA	H	9.26 FQ	13.24 AW	17.90 TQ	PABLS	10/01-12/01
Construction and Maintenance	Philadelphia PMSA, PA-NJ	H	11.20 FQ	18.53 AW	28.19 TQ	PABLS	10/01-12/01
Construction and Maintenance	Pittsburgh MSA, PA	H	10.84 FQ	18.40 AW	26.03 TQ	PABLS	10/01-12/01
Construction and Maintenance	Reading MSA, PA	H	8.90 FQ	14.23 AW	20.88 TQ	PABLS	10/01-12/01
Construction and Maintenance	Scranton-Wilkes-Barre-Hazleton MSA, PA	H	8.56 FQ	15.69 AW	22.61 TQ	PABLS	10/01-12/01
Construction and Maintenance	York MSA, PA	H	9.55 FQ	12.94 AW	16.84 TQ	PABLS	10/01-12/01
Construction and Maintenance	Rhode Island	H	9.96 FQ	15.30 AW	23.92 TQ	RIBLS	10/01-12/01
Construction and Maintenance	Providence-Fall River-Warwick MSA, RI-MA	H	10.42 FQ	15.64 AW	24.66 TQ	RIBLS	10/01-12/01
Construction and Maintenance	South Carolina	H	8.59 FQ	12.03 AW	16.54 TQ	SCBLS	10/01-12/01
Construction and Maintenance	Charleston-North Charleston MSA, SC	H	8.28 FQ	12.20 AW	16.99 TQ	SCBLS	10/01-12/01
Construction and Maintenance	Columbia MSA, SC	H	9.26 FQ	11.73 AW	13.98 TQ	SCBLS	10/01-12/01
Construction and Maintenance	Greenville-Spartanburg-Anderson MSA, SC	H	9.26 FQ	12.29 AW	16.00 TQ	SCBLS	10/01-12/01
Construction and Maintenance	Myrtle Beach MSA, SC	H	8.63 FQ	10.81 AW	13.32 TQ	SCBLS	10/01-12/01
Construction and Maintenance	South Dakota	H	8.63 FQ	11.30 AW	14.77 TQ	SDBLS	10/01-12/01
Construction and Maintenance	Sioux Falls MSA, SD	H	9.25 FQ	11.24 AW	14.66 TQ	SDBLS	10/01-12/01
Construction and Maintenance	Tennessee	H	8.99 FQ	13.44 AW	18.09 TQ	TNBLS	10/01-12/01
Construction and Maintenance	Chattanooga MSA, TN-GA	H	9.26 FQ	13.12 AW	16.96 TQ	TNBLS	10/01-12/01
Construction and Maintenance	Clarksville-Hopkinsville MSA, TN-KY	H	7.89 FQ	13.06 AW	17.06 TQ	TNBLS	10/01-12/01
Construction and Maintenance	Johnson City-Kingsport-Bristol MSA, TN-VA	H	6.12 FQ	10.00 AW	13.72 TQ	TNBLS	10/01-12/01
Construction and Maintenance	Knoxville MSA, TN	H	9.19 FQ	13.03 AW	18.28 TQ	TNBLS	10/01-12/01
Construction and Maintenance	Memphis MSA, TN-AR-MS	H	9.55 FQ	14.60 AW	21.38 TQ	TNBLS	10/01-12/01
Construction and Maintenance	Nashville MSA, TN	H	9.68 FQ	13.61 AW	17.55 TQ	TNBLS	10/01-12/01
Construction and Maintenance	Texas	H	8.34 FQ	12.15 AW	16.55 TQ	TXBLS	10/01-12/01
Construction and Maintenance	Amarillo MSA, TX	H	8.28 FQ	12.25 AW	16.41 TQ	TXBLS	10/01-12/01
Construction and Maintenance	Austin-San Marcos MSA, TX	H	9.14 FQ	12.30 AW	15.96 TQ	TXBLS	10/01-12/01
Construction and Maintenance	Beaumont-Port Arthur MSA, TX	H	8.83 FQ	12.87 AW	16.87 TQ	TXBLS	10/01-12/01
Construction and Maintenance	Brazoria PMSA, TX	H	7.68 FQ	11.92 AW	16.18 TQ	TXBLS	10/01-12/01
Construction and Maintenance	Brownsville-Harlingen-San Benito MSA, TX	H	6.86 FQ	8.57 AW	11.23 TQ	TXBLS	10/01-12/01
Construction and Maintenance	Corpus Christi MSA, TX	H	8.65 FQ	12.11 AW	17.50 TQ	TXBLS	10/01-12/01
Construction and Maintenance	Dallas PMSA, TX	H	9.10 FQ	12.81 AW	17.06 TQ	TXBLS	10/01-12/01
Construction and Maintenance	El Paso MSA, TX	H	6.36 FQ	9.11 AW	12.70 TQ	TXBLS	10/01-12/01
Construction and Maintenance	Fort Worth-Arlington PMSA, TX	H	9.13 FQ	12.70 AW	16.73 TQ	TXBLS	10/01-12/01
Construction and Maintenance	Galveston-Texas City PMSA, TX	H	8.61 FQ	13.34 AW	17.58 TQ	TXBLS	10/01-12/01
Construction and Maintenance	Houston PMSA, TX	H	8.51 FQ	12.44 AW	16.65 TQ	TXBLS	10/01-12/01
Construction and Maintenance	Killeen-Temple MSA, TX	H	8.31 FQ	13.84 AW	21.02 TQ	TXBLS	10/01-12/01
Construction and Maintenance	Laredo MSA, TX	H	6.38 FQ	10.33 AW	14.59 TQ	TXBLS	10/01-12/01
Construction and Maintenance	Longview-Marshall MSA, TX	H	8.50 FQ	11.42 AW	15.23 TQ	TXBLS	10/01-12/01
Construction and Maintenance	Lubbock MSA, TX	H	7.10 FQ	10.35 AW	13.44 TQ	TXBLS	10/01-12/01
Construction and Maintenance	McAllen-Edinburg-Mission MSA, TX	H	6.54 FQ	9.94 AW	13.28 TQ	TXBLS	10/01-12/01
Construction and Maintenance	San Antonio MSA, TX	H	8.24 FQ	11.08 AW	15.32 TQ	TXBLS	10/01-12/01
Construction and Maintenance	Tyler MSA, TX	H	8.78 FQ	11.61 AW	14.85 TQ	TXBLS	10/01-12/01
Construction and Maintenance	Waco MSA, TX	H	8.69 FQ	11.66 AW	15.50 TQ	TXBLS	10/01-12/01
Construction and Maintenance	Utah	H	9.06 FQ	13.29 AW	18.26 TQ	UTBLS	10/01-12/01
Construction and Maintenance	Provo-Orem MSA, UT	H	8.86 FQ	13.29 AW	18.93 TQ	UTBLS	10/01-12/01
Construction and Maintenance	Salt Lake City-Ogden MSA, UT	H	9.16 FQ	13.18 AW	18.00 TQ	UTBLS	10/01-12/01
Construction and Maintenance	Vermont	H	9.28 FQ	12.00 AW	15.93 TQ	VTBLS	10/01-12/01
Construction and Maintenance	Burlington MSA, VT	H	9.71 FQ	13.22 AW	17.43 TQ	VTBLS	10/01-12/01
Construction and Maintenance	Virginia	H	8.83 FQ	13.01 AW	17.62 TQ	VABLS	10/01-12/01
Construction and Maintenance	Lynchburg MSA, VA	H	7.13 FQ	11.55 AW	16.20 TQ	VABLS	10/01-12/01
Construction and Maintenance	Norfolk-Virginia Beach-Newport News MSA, VA-NC	H	9.29 FQ	13.15 AW	17.50 TQ	VABLS	10/01-12/01
Construction and Maintenance	Richmond-Petersburg MSA, VA	H	7.30 FQ	11.50 AW	16.31 TQ	VABLS	10/01-12/01
Construction and Maintenance	Roanoke MSA, VA	H	8.78 FQ	11.43 AW	16.27 TQ	VABLS	10/01-12/01
Construction and Maintenance	Washington	H	10.07 FQ	16.53 AW	24.32 TQ	WABLS	10/01-12/01

AAW Average annual wage; **AE** Average entry wage; **AEX** Average experienced wage; **AO** Average offered; **AOH** Average offered, high; **AOL** Average offered, low; **APH** Average pay, high range; **APL** Average pay, low range; **ASH** Average starting, high; **ASL** Average starting, low; **AW** Average wage paid; **FQ** First quartile wage; **H** Hourly; **HI** Highest wage paid; **HR** High end range; **LR** Low end range; **M** Monthly; **MTC** Median total compensation; **MW** Median wage paid; **SQ** Second quartile wage; **S** Special: hourly and annual; **TQ** Third quartile wage; **W** Weekly; **Y** Yearly

Occupation/Type/Industry	Location	Per	Low	Mid	High	Source	Date
Painter							
Construction and Maintenance	Bremerton PMSA, WA	H	11.24 FQ	17.25 AW	24.96 TQ	WABLS	10/01-12/01
Construction and Maintenance	Olympia PMSA, WA	H	9.70 FQ	15.85 AW	23.12 TQ	WABLS	10/01-12/01
Construction and Maintenance	Richland-Kennewick-Pasco MSA, WA	H	9.70 FQ	16.31 AW	24.63 TQ	WABLS	10/01-12/01
Construction and Maintenance	Seattle-Bellevue-Everett PMSA, WA	H	10.39 FQ	17.26 AW	24.84 TQ	WABLS	10/01-12/01
Construction and Maintenance	Spokane MSA, WA	H	9.50 FQ	14.66 AW	20.53 TQ	WABLS	10/01-12/01
Construction and Maintenance	Tacoma PMSA, WA	H	9.04 FQ	15.65 AW	23.10 TQ	WABLS	10/01-12/01
Construction and Maintenance	Yakima MSA, WA	H	9.87 FQ	14.47 AW	18.39 TQ	WABLS	10/01-12/01
Construction and Maintenance	West Virginia	H	8.87 FQ	13.38 AW	19.65 TQ	WVBLS	10/01-12/01
Construction and Maintenance	Charleston MSA, WV	H	9.02 FQ	12.87 AW	20.06 TQ	WVBLS	10/01-12/01
Construction and Maintenance	Huntington-Ashland MSA, WV-KY-OH	H	7.90 FQ	14.67 AW	22.57 TQ	WVBLS	10/01-12/01
Construction and Maintenance	Wisconsin	H	9.70 FQ	16.26 AW	25.12 TQ	WIBLS	10/01-12/01
Construction and Maintenance	Appleton-Oshkosh-Neenah MSA, WI	H	9.50 FQ	14.41 AW	19.67 TQ	WIBLS	10/01-12/01
Construction and Maintenance	Green Bay MSA, WI	H	9.83 FQ	16.29 AW	22.97 TQ	WIBLS	10/01-12/01
Construction and Maintenance	Madison MSA, WI	H	9.67 FQ	16.42 AW	22.63 TQ	WIBLS	10/01-12/01
Construction and Maintenance	Milwaukee-Waukesha PMSA, WI	H	10.42 FQ	17.99 AW	26.86 TQ	WIBLS	10/01-12/01
Construction and Maintenance	Racine PMSA, WI	H	8.34 FQ	17.54 AW	31.43 TQ	WIBLS	10/01-12/01
Construction and Maintenance	Wyoming	H	8.54 FQ	13.45 AW	20.62 TQ	WYBLS	10/01-12/01
Construction and Maintenance	Cheyenne MSA, WY	H	8.21 FQ	11.73 AW	18.08 TQ	WYBLS	10/01-12/01
Construction and Maintenance	Puerto Rico	H	5.56 FQ	6.99 AW	9.80 TQ	PRBLS	10/01-12/01
Construction and Maintenance	Virgin Islands	H	8.51 FQ	11.33 AW	14.93 TQ	VIBLS	10/01-12/01
Construction and Maintenance	Guam	H	8.65 FQ	12.82 AW	17.56 TQ	GUBLS	10/01-12/01
Transportation Equipment	Alabama	H	9.01 FQ	13.44 AW	17.37 TQ	ALBLS	10/01-12/01
Transportation Equipment	Alaska	H	10.94 FQ	18.39 AW	26.26 TQ	AKBLS	10/01-12/01
Transportation Equipment	Arizona	H	9.14 FQ	17.81 AW	35.84 TQ	AZBLS	10/01-12/01
Transportation Equipment	Arkansas	H	6.99 FQ	14.71 AW	23.60 TQ	ARBLS	10/01-12/01
Transportation Equipment	California	H	9.47 FQ	18.34 AW	26.64 TQ	CABLS	10/01-12/01
Transportation Equipment	Colorado	H	8.20 FQ	15.98 AW	25.00 TQ	COBLS	10/01-12/01
Transportation Equipment	Connecticut	H	12.63 FQ	19.02 AW	25.15 TQ	CTBLS	10/01-12/01
Transportation Equipment	Delaware	H	13.02 FQ	17.14 AW	22.06 TQ	DEBLS	10/01-12/01
Transportation Equipment	Florida	H	8.92 FQ	14.11 AW	20.06 TQ	FLBLS	10/01-12/01
Transportation Equipment	Georgia	H	9.23 FQ	14.22 AW	20.93 TQ	GABLS	10/01-12/01
Transportation Equipment	Hawaii	H	11.80 FQ	19.43 AW	26.33 TQ	HIBLS	10/01-12/01
Transportation Equipment	Idaho	H	9.81 FQ	15.35 AW	21.20 TQ	IDBLS	10/01-12/01
Transportation Equipment	Illinois	H	10.56 FQ	17.00 AW	24.67 TQ	ILBLS	10/01-12/01
Transportation Equipment	Indiana	H	9.23 FQ	16.71 AW	25.45 TQ	INBLS	10/01-12/01
Transportation Equipment	Iowa	H	8.33 FQ	13.25 AW	19.94 TQ	IABLS	10/01-12/01
Transportation Equipment	Kansas	H	11.41 FQ	17.75 AW	24.71 TQ	KSBLS	10/01-12/01
Transportation Equipment	Kentucky	H	12.27 FQ	19.25 AW	25.84 TQ	KYBLS	10/01-12/01
Transportation Equipment	Louisiana	H	7.54 FQ	12.22 AW	17.66 TQ	LABLS	10/01-12/01
Transportation Equipment	Maine	H	6.14 FQ	11.10 AW	16.75 TQ	MEBLS	10/01-12/01
Transportation Equipment	Maryland	H	11.03 FQ	19.40 AW	30.92 TQ	MDBLS	10/01-12/01
Transportation Equipment	Massachusetts	H	11.22 FQ	16.59 AW	26.92 TQ	MABLS	10/01-12/01
Transportation Equipment	Michigan	H	12.08 FQ	22.96 AW	33.99 TQ	MIBLS	10/01-12/01
Transportation Equipment	Minnesota	H	10.41 FQ	17.25 AW	28.70 TQ	MNBLS	10/01-12/01
Transportation Equipment	Missouri	H	9.88 FQ	17.58 AW	26.73 TQ	MOBLS	10/01-12/01
Transportation Equipment	Montana	H	9.29 FQ	14.65 AW	21.74 TQ	MTBLS	10/01-12/01
Transportation Equipment	Nebraska	H	9.75 FQ	16.23 AW	24.40 TQ	NEBLS	10/01-12/01
Transportation Equipment	Nevada	H	10.73 FQ	16.05 AW	24.17 TQ	NVBLS	10/01-12/01
Transportation Equipment	New Hampshire	H	10.21 FQ	15.60 AW	20.30 TQ	NHBLS	10/01-12/01
Transportation Equipment	New Jersey	H	11.54 FQ	18.88 AW	26.52 TQ	NJBLS	10/01-12/01
Transportation Equipment	New Mexico	H	7.48 FQ	12.38 AW	17.02 TQ	NMBLS	10/01-12/01
Transportation Equipment	New York	H	8.90 FQ	16.25 AW	23.65 TQ	NYBLS	10/01-12/01
Transportation Equipment	North Carolina	H	10.26 FQ	16.83 AW	25.00 TQ	NCBLS	10/01-12/01
Transportation Equipment	North Dakota	H	7.49 FQ	14.70 AW	25.35 TQ	NDBLS	10/01-12/01
Transportation Equipment	Ohio	H	10.87 FQ	19.33 AW	26.80 TQ	OHBLS	10/01-12/01
Transportation Equipment	Oklahoma	H	9.09 FQ	13.19 AW	18.13 TQ	OKBLS	10/01-12/01
Transportation Equipment	Oregon	H	9.13 FQ	15.99 AW	26.30 TQ	ORBLS	10/01-12/01
Transportation Equipment	Pennsylvania	H	9.38 FQ	15.30 AW	22.58 TQ	PABLS	10/01-12/01
Transportation Equipment	Rhode Island	H	11.25 FQ	16.39 AW	20.89 TQ	RIBLS	10/01-12/01
Transportation Equipment	South Carolina	H	7.41 FQ	12.44 AW	19.76 TQ	SCBLS	10/01-12/01
Transportation Equipment	South Dakota	H	9.22 FQ	12.42 AW	16.47 TQ	SDBLS	10/01-12/01
Transportation Equipment	Tennessee	H	8.86 FQ	17.42 AW	25.92 TQ	TNBLS	10/01-12/01
Transportation Equipment	Texas	H	9.29 FQ	15.67 AW	28.30 TQ	TXBLS	10/01-12/01
Transportation Equipment	Utah	H	10.12 FQ	15.76 AW	26.17 TQ	UTBLS	10/01-12/01
Transportation Equipment	Virginia	H	9.41 FQ	17.27 AW	26.13 TQ	VABLS	10/01-12/01
Transportation Equipment	Washington	H	12.56 FQ	18.31 AW	26.22 TQ	WABLS	10/01-12/01

AAW	Average annual wage	**AOH**	Average offered, high	**ASH**	Average starting, high	**H**	Hourly	**M**	Monthly	**S**	Special: hourly and annual
AE	Average entry wage	**AOL**	Average offered, low	**ASL**	Average starting, low	**HI**	Highest wage paid	**MTC**	Median total compensation	**TQ**	Third quartile wage
AEX	Average experienced wage	**APH**	Average pay, high range	**AW**	Average wage paid	**HR**	High end range	**MW**	Median wage paid	**W**	Weekly
AO	Average offered	**APL**	Average pay, low range	**FQ**	First quartile wage	**LR**	Low end range	**SQ**	Second quartile wage	**Y**	Yearly

Occupation/Type/Industry	Location	Per	Low	Mid	High	Source	Date
Painter							
Transportation Equipment	West Virginia	H	7.43 FQ	13.07 AW	19.55 TQ	WVBLS	10/01-12/01
Transportation Equipment	Wisconsin	H	10.04 FQ	15.35 AW	20.97 TQ	WIBLS	10/01-12/01
Transportation Equipment	Wyoming	H	10.23 FQ	15.73 AW	24.14 TQ	WYBLS	10/01-12/01
Transportation Equipment	Puerto Rico	H	7.37 FQ	12.14 AW	17.38 TQ	PRBLS	10/01-12/01
Painting, Coating, and Decorating Worker	Alabama	H	6.24 FQ	9.82 AW	16.07 TQ	ALBLS	10/01-12/01
	Mobile MSA, AL	H	6.14 FQ	9.95 AW	16.45 TQ	ALBLS	10/01-12/01
	Arizona	H	6.89 FQ	9.79 AW	14.35 TQ	AZBLS	10/01-12/01
	Phoenix-Mesa MSA, AZ	H	6.86 FQ	10.05 AW	15.45 TQ	AZBLS	10/01-12/01
	Tucson MSA, AZ	H	7.00 FQ	8.80 AW	11.05 TQ	AZBLS	10/01-12/01
	Arkansas	H	5.86 FQ	8.55 AW	12.02 TQ	ARBLS	10/01-12/01
	Little Rock-North Little Rock MSA, AR	H	6.33 FQ	9.82 AW	13.15 TQ	ARBLS	10/01-12/01
	California	H	6.63 FQ	10.48 AW	16.53 TQ	CABLS	10/01-12/01
	Los Angeles-Long Beach PMSA, CA	H	6.50 FQ	9.61 AW	14.52 TQ	CABLS	10/01-12/01
	Modesto MSA, CA	H	7.20 FQ	9.59 AW	13.96 TQ	CABLS	10/01-12/01
	Oakland PMSA, CA	H	8.07 FQ	14.32 AW	21.34 TQ	CABLS	10/01-12/01
	Orange County PMSA, CA	H	6.83 FQ	10.48 AW	16.36 TQ	CABLS	10/01-12/01
	Riverside-San Bernardino PMSA, CA	H	6.78 FQ	10.21 AW	16.00 TQ	CABLS	10/01-12/01
	Sacramento PMSA, CA	H	7.39 FQ	10.46 AW	15.92 TQ	CABLS	10/01-12/01
	San Diego MSA, CA	H	6.71 FQ	10.28 AW	15.30 TQ	CABLS	10/01-12/01
	San Francisco PMSA, CA	H	8.26 FQ	16.42 AW	24.92 TQ	CABLS	10/01-12/01
	San Jose PMSA, CA	H	7.54 FQ	11.17 AW	16.54 TQ	CABLS	10/01-12/01
	Vallejo-Fairfield-Napa PMSA, CA	H	7.00 FQ	10.60 AW	15.09 TQ	CABLS	10/01-12/01
	Ventura PMSA, CA	H	6.58 FQ	10.33 AW	16.96 TQ	CABLS	10/01-12/01
	Colorado	H	7.97 FQ	11.97 AW	16.79 TQ	COBLS	10/01-12/01
	Boulder-Longmont PMSA, CO	H	6.06 FQ	9.52 AW	15.33 TQ	COBLS	10/01-12/01
	Colorado Springs MSA, CO	H	8.37 FQ	11.48 AW	16.17 TQ	COBLS	10/01-12/01
	Denver PMSA, CO	H	8.39 FQ	12.32 AW	16.78 TQ	COBLS	10/01-12/01
	Fort Collins-Loveland MSA, CO	H	8.79 FQ	12.13 AW	15.90 TQ	COBLS	10/01-12/01
	Connecticut	H	8.19 FQ	12.31 AW	17.59 TQ	CTBLS	10/01-12/01
	Bridgeport PMSA, CT	H	8.22 FQ	12.30 AW	16.64 TQ	CTBLS	10/01-12/01
	Hartford MSA, CT	H	8.41 FQ	12.57 AW	18.60 TQ	CTBLS	10/01-12/01
	New Haven-Meriden PMSA, CT	H	8.91 FQ	12.91 AW	22.98 TQ	CTBLS	10/01-12/01
	Washington PMSA, DC-MD-VA-WV	H	9.15 FQ	12.45 AW	17.17 TQ	DCBLS	10/01-12/01
	Florida	H	6.76 FQ	10.75 AW	14.36 TQ	FLBLS	10/01-12/01
	Fort Lauderdale PMSA, FL	H	7.53 FQ	10.24 AW	14.77 TQ	FLBLS	10/01-12/01
	Miami PMSA, FL	H	6.28 FQ	9.54 AW	13.66 TQ	FLBLS	10/01-12/01
	Orlando MSA, FL	H	9.76 FQ	14.66 AW	21.02 TQ	FLBLS	10/01-12/01
	Pensacola MSA, FL	H	5.56 FQ	7.98 AW	15.31 TQ	FLBLS	10/01-12/01
	Georgia	H	6.02 FQ	9.67 AW	14.22 TQ	GABLS	10/01-12/01
	Atlanta MSA, GA	H	6.59 FQ	12.38 AW	23.31 TQ	GABLS	10/01-12/01
	Columbus MSA, GA-AL	H	5.90 FQ	9.32 AW	13.29 TQ	GABLS	10/01-12/01
	Hawaii	H	6.54 FQ	9.78 AW	14.93 TQ	HIBLS	10/01-12/01
	Honolulu MSA, HI	H	6.51 FQ	9.63 AW	13.47 TQ	HIBLS	10/01-12/01
	Idaho	H	7.14 FQ	11.09 AW	17.10 TQ	IDBLS	10/01-12/01
	Illinois	H	6.82 FQ	11.45 AW	19.29 TQ	ILBLS	10/01-12/01
	Chicago PMSA, IL	H	6.67 FQ	11.37 AW	19.38 TQ	ILBLS	10/01-12/01
	Peoria-Pekin MSA, IL	H	8.10 FQ	11.39 AW	19.66 TQ	ILBLS	10/01-12/01
	Indiana	H	7.39 FQ	10.47 AW	14.38 TQ	INBLS	10/01-12/01
	Elkhart-Goshen MSA, IN	H	7.85 FQ	11.78 AW	16.90 TQ	INBLS	10/01-12/01
	Fort Wayne MSA, IN	H	7.68 FQ	10.64 AW	14.15 TQ	INBLS	10/01-12/01
	Gary PMSA, IN	H	7.12 FQ	11.17 AW	22.34 TQ	INBLS	10/01-12/01
	Indianapolis MSA, IN	H	7.10 FQ	9.02 AW	11.65 TQ	INBLS	10/01-12/01
	Iowa	H	6.08 FQ	9.78 AW	13.88 TQ	IABLS	10/01-12/01
	Davenport-Moline-Rock Island MSA, IA-IL	H	6.13 FQ	10.97 AW	19.76 TQ	IABLS	10/01-12/01
	Des Moines MSA, IA	H	5.68 FQ	9.05 AW	14.98 TQ	IABLS	10/01-12/01
	Kansas	H	6.63 FQ	10.21 AW	13.49 TQ	KSBLS	10/01-12/01
	Kentucky	H	7.30 FQ	12.95 AW	24.75 TQ	KYBLS	10/01-12/01
	Lexington MSA, KY	H	7.10 FQ	13.08 AW	25.80 TQ	KYBLS	10/01-12/01
	Louisville MSA, KY-IN	H	8.49 FQ	13.15 AW	22.67 TQ	KYBLS	10/01-12/01
	Louisiana	H	6.78 FQ	10.69 AW	14.68 TQ	LABLS	10/01-12/01
	Baton Rouge MSA, LA	H	7.43 FQ	9.94 AW	13.09 TQ	LABLS	10/01-12/01

AAW Average annual wage **AE** Average entry wage **AEX** Average experienced wage **AO** Average offered **AOH** Average offered, high **AOL** Average offered, low **APH** Average pay, high range **APL** Average pay, low range **ASH** Average starting, high **ASL** Average starting, low **AW** Average wage paid **FQ** First quartile wage **H** Hourly **HI** Highest wage paid **HR** High end range **LR** Low end range **M** Monthly **MTC** Median total compensation **MW** Median wage paid **SQ** Second quartile wage **S** Special: hourly and annual **TQ** Third quartile wage **W** Weekly **Y** Yearly

Occupation/Type/Industry	Location	Per	Low	Mid	High	Source	Date
Painting, Coating, and Decorating Worker	New Orleans MSA, LA	H	6.04 FQ	9.87 AW	16.12 TQ	LABLS	10/01-12/01
	Shreveport-Bossier City MSA, LA	H	8.74 FQ	17.40 AW	34.16 TQ	LABLS	10/01-12/01
	Maine	H	6.86 FQ	9.98 AW	13.62 TQ	MEBLS	10/01-12/01
	Portland MSA, ME	H	7.61 FQ	11.05 AW	14.54 TQ	MEBLS	10/01-12/01
	Maryland	H	8.85 FQ	11.58 AW	16.66 TQ	MDBLS	10/01-12/01
	Baltimore PMSA, MD	H	7.75 FQ	10.83 AW	15.58 TQ	MDBLS	10/01-12/01
	Massachusetts	H	7.93 FQ	11.88 AW	18.22 TQ	MABLS	10/01-12/01
	Boston PMSA, MA-NH	H	7.66 FQ	11.33 AW	17.46 TQ	MABLS	10/01-12/01
	Springfield MSA, MA	H	8.17 FQ	10.92 AW	16.05 TQ	MABLS	10/01-12/01
	Michigan	H	7.74 FQ	12.59 AW	24.38 TQ	MIBLS	10/01-12/01
	Ann Arbor PMSA, MI	H	8.09 FQ	10.76 AW	14.40 TQ	MIBLS	10/01-12/01
	Detroit PMSA, MI	H	7.63 FQ	13.98 AW	26.86 TQ	MIBLS	10/01-12/01
	Grand Rapids-Muskegon-Holland MSA, MI	H	8.31 FQ	11.29 AW	14.30 TQ	MIBLS	10/01-12/01
	Kalamazoo-Battle Creek MSA, MI	H	7.55 FQ	10.10 AW	13.91 TQ	MIBLS	10/01-12/01
	Saginaw-Bay City-Midland MSA, MI	H	6.06 FQ	10.23 AW	15.18 TQ	MIBLS	10/01-12/01
	Minnesota	H	7.43 FQ	11.26 AW	17.09 TQ	MNBLS	10/01-12/01
	Minneapolis-St. Paul MSA, MN-WI	H	7.46 FQ	11.46 AW	17.33 TQ	MNBLS	10/01-12/01
	Mississippi	H	6.37 FQ	9.82 AW	13.15 TQ	MSBLS	10/01-12/01
	Missouri	H	6.84 FQ	10.62 AW	16.23 TQ	MOBLS	10/01-12/01
	St. Louis MSA, MO-IL	H	7.12 FQ	12.65 AW	23.52 TQ	MOBLS	10/01-12/01
	Montana	H	7.52 FQ	11.56 AW	17.25 TQ	MTBLS	10/01-12/01
	Nebraska	H	7.53 FQ	10.64 AW	13.99 TQ	NEBLS	10/01-12/01
	Omaha MSA, NE-IA	H	8.51 FQ	12.41 AW	16.85 TQ	NEBLS	10/01-12/01
	Nevada	H	7.75 FQ	12.37 AW	17.84 TQ	NVBLS	10/01-12/01
	Las Vegas MSA, NV-AZ	H	7.78 FQ	12.72 AW	19.59 TQ	NVBLS	10/01-12/01
	Reno MSA, NV	H	7.44 FQ	10.38 AW	15.68 TQ	NVBLS	10/01-12/01
	New Hampshire	H	9.13 FQ	12.42 AW	16.31 TQ	NHBLS	10/01-12/01
	Manchester PMSA, NH	H	9.48 FQ	11.31 AW	13.37 TQ	NHBLS	10/01-12/01
	Nashua PMSA, NH	H	9.16 FQ	12.95 AW	16.27 TQ	NHBLS	10/01-12/01
	Portsmouth-Rochester PMSA, NH-ME	H	8.17 FQ	12.38 AW	16.29 TQ	NHBLS	10/01-12/01
	New Jersey	H	7.03 FQ	12.52 AW	20.72 TQ	NJBLS	10/01-12/01
	Bergen-Passaic PMSA, NJ	H	6.23 FQ	11.60 AW	20.29 TQ	NJBLS	10/01-12/01
	Jersey City PMSA, NJ	H	7.49 FQ	10.72 AW	15.85 TQ	NJBLS	10/01-12/01
	Middlesex-Somerset-Hunterdon PMSA, NJ	H	6.99 FQ	10.89 AW	16.56 TQ	NJBLS	10/01-12/01
	Monmouth-Ocean PMSA, NJ	H	6.33 FQ	10.30 AW	15.90 TQ	NJBLS	10/01-12/01
	Newark PMSA, NJ	H	6.74 FQ	11.31 AW	19.70 TQ	NJBLS	10/01-12/01
	Albuquerque MSA, NM	H	7.25 FQ	9.90 AW	14.09 TQ	NMBLS	10/01-12/01
	New York	H	6.40 FQ	11.04 AW	17.61 TQ	NYBLS	10/01-12/01
	Nassau-Suffolk PMSA, NY	H	8.43 FQ	13.94 AW	20.51 TQ	NYBLS	10/01-12/01
	New York PMSA, NY	H	6.02 FQ	10.73 AW	18.80 TQ	NYBLS	10/01-12/01
	Rochester MSA, NY	H	7.26 FQ	10.35 AW	16.15 TQ	NYBLS	10/01-12/01
	Syracuse MSA, NY	H	7.45 FQ	9.76 AW	13.00 TQ	NYBLS	10/01-12/01
	Utica-Rome MSA, NY	H	5.89 FQ	9.30 AW	13.09 TQ	NYBLS	10/01-12/01
	North Carolina	H	7.41 FQ	10.13 AW	13.81 TQ	NCBLS	10/01-12/01
	Charlotte-Gastonia-Rock Hill MSA, NC-SC	H	6.22 FQ	11.21 AW	17.42 TQ	NCBLS	10/01-12/01
	Greensboro-Winston-Salem-High Point MSA, NC	H	7.44 FQ	9.07 AW	11.94 TQ	NCBLS	10/01-12/01
	Hickory-Morganton-Lenoir MSA, NC	H	7.76 FQ	10.20 AW	13.13 TQ	NCBLS	10/01-12/01
	North Dakota	H	6.33 FQ	8.22 AW	10.48 TQ	NDBLS	10/01-12/01
	Ohio	H	6.18 FQ	10.01 AW	15.10 TQ	OHBLS	10/01-12/01
	Akron PMSA, OH	H	5.78 FQ	7.82 AW	11.10 TQ	OHBLS	10/01-12/01
	Cincinnati PMSA, OH-KY-IN	H	5.74 FQ	8.63 AW	11.72 TQ	OHBLS	10/01-12/01
	Columbus MSA, OH	H	7.60 FQ	11.64 AW	15.61 TQ	OHBLS	10/01-12/01
	Toledo MSA, OH	H	6.72 FQ	10.09 AW	13.43 TQ	OHBLS	10/01-12/01
	Youngstown-Warren MSA, OH	H	5.78 FQ	8.35 AW	12.37 TQ	OHBLS	10/01-12/01
	Oklahoma	H	6.68 FQ	11.31 AW	19.32 TQ	OKBLS	10/01-12/01
	Oklahoma City MSA, OK	H	7.47 FQ	9.98 AW	12.79 TQ	OKBLS	10/01-12/01
	Tulsa MSA, OK	H	6.43 FQ	11.00 AW	16.69 TQ	OKBLS	10/01-12/01
	Oregon	H	7.84 FQ	11.88 AW	16.19 TQ	ORBLS	10/01-12/01
	Eugene-Springfield MSA, OR	H	7.57 FQ	11.40 AW	16.21 TQ	ORBLS	10/01-12/01
	Portland-Vancouver PMSA, OR-WA	H	7.51 FQ	12.44 AW	17.01 TQ	ORBLS	10/01-12/01

AAW	Average annual wage	**AOH**	Average offered, high	**ASH**	Average starting, high	**H**	Hourly	**M**	Monthly	**S**	Special: hourly and annual
AE	Average entry wage	**AOL**	Average offered, low	**ASL**	Average starting, low	**HI**	Highest wage paid	**MTC**	Median total compensation	**TQ**	Third quartile wage
AEX	Average experienced wage	**APH**	Average pay, high range	**AW**	Average wage paid	**HR**	High end range	**MW**	Median wage paid	**W**	Weekly
AO	Average offered	**APL**	Average pay, low range	**FQ**	First quartile wage	**LR**	Low end range	**SQ**	Second quartile wage	**Y**	Yearly

Occupation/Type/Industry	Location	Per	Low	Mid	High	Source	Date
Painting, Coating, and Decorating Worker	Pennsylvania	H	7.25 FQ	11.87 AW	17.36 TQ	PABLS	10/01-12/01
	Allentown-Bethlehem-Easton MSA, PA	H	8.91 FQ	12.18 AW	16.20 TQ	PABLS	10/01-12/01
	Harrisburg-Lebanon-Carlisle MSA, PA	H	7.56 FQ	11.91 AW	16.57 TQ	PABLS	10/01-12/01
	Lancaster MSA, PA	H	9.21 FQ	13.22 AW	18.69 TQ	PABLS	10/01-12/01
	Philadelphia PMSA, PA-NJ	H	7.91 FQ	14.39 AW	24.56 TQ	PABLS	10/01-12/01
	Pittsburgh MSA, PA	H	7.37 FQ	14.30 AW	23.81 TQ	PABLS	10/01-12/01
	York MSA, PA	H	7.41 FQ	10.33 AW	17.14 TQ	PABLS	10/01-12/01
	Rhode Island	H	6.87 FQ	8.76 AW	11.47 TQ	RIBLS	10/01-12/01
	Providence-Fall River-Warwick MSA, RI-MA	H	7.06 FQ	10.30 AW	16.70 TQ	RIBLS	10/01-12/01
	South Carolina	H	7.52 FQ	11.66 AW	18.43 TQ	SCBLS	10/01-12/01
	Charleston-North Charleston MSA, SC	H	7.35 FQ	10.20 AW	13.50 TQ	SCBLS	10/01-12/01
	Greenville-Spartanburg-Anderson MSA, SC	H	7.91 FQ	13.08 AW	19.12 TQ	SCBLS	10/01-12/01
	South Dakota	H	6.76 FQ	8.85 AW	11.28 TQ	SDBLS	10/01-12/01
	Tennessee	H	7.37 FQ	10.22 AW	13.73 TQ	TNBLS	10/01-12/01
	Johnson City-Kingsport-Bristol MSA, TN-VA	H	8.59 FQ	11.09 AW	14.36 TQ	TNBLS	10/01-12/01
	Knoxville MSA, TN	H	7.51 FQ	10.11 AW	13.61 TQ	TNBLS	10/01-12/01
	Memphis MSA, TN-AR-MS	H	7.31 FQ	10.52 AW	16.32 TQ	TNBLS	10/01-12/01
	Nashville MSA, TN	H	7.73 FQ	11.63 AW	17.36 TQ	TNBLS	10/01-12/01
	Texas	H	6.13 FQ	8.95 AW	12.81 TQ	TXBLS	10/01-12/01
	Austin-San Marcos MSA, TX	H	5.57 FQ	8.51 AW	11.91 TQ	TXBLS	10/01-12/01
	Corpus Christi MSA, TX	H	5.89 FQ	9.26 AW	13.32 TQ	TXBLS	10/01-12/01
	Dallas PMSA, TX	H	6.65 FQ	9.77 AW	13.60 TQ	TXBLS	10/01-12/01
	Fort Worth-Arlington PMSA, TX	H	7.10 FQ	9.96 AW	14.22 TQ	TXBLS	10/01-12/01
	Houston PMSA, TX	H	6.79 FQ	9.63 AW	12.90 TQ	TXBLS	10/01-12/01
	Lubbock MSA, TX	H	7.12 FQ	8.89 AW	10.80 TQ	TXBLS	10/01-12/01
	San Antonio MSA, TX	H	5.78 FQ	7.88 AW	11.28 TQ	TXBLS	10/01-12/01
	Waco MSA, TX	H	5.44 FQ	7.07 AW	8.93 TQ	TXBLS	10/01-12/01
	Utah	H	7.18 FQ	10.27 AW	13.96 TQ	UTBLS	10/01-12/01
	Salt Lake City-Ogden MSA, UT	H	7.15 FQ	9.79 AW	13.74 TQ	UTBLS	10/01-12/01
	Virginia	H	7.01 FQ	10.65 AW	14.89 TQ	VABLS	10/01-12/01
	Norfolk-Virginia Beach-Newport News MSA, VA-NC	H	5.74 FQ	7.96 AW	10.35 TQ	VABLS	10/01-12/01
	Washington	H	7.93 FQ	12.63 AW	17.71 TQ	WABLS	10/01-12/01
	Seattle-Bellevue-Everett PMSA, WA	H	8.71 FQ	12.98 AW	18.01 TQ	WABLS	10/01-12/01
	Spokane MSA, WA	H	7.93 FQ	12.58 AW	17.43 TQ	WABLS	10/01-12/01
	Tacoma PMSA, WA	H	8.52 FQ	14.08 AW	22.61 TQ	WABLS	10/01-12/01
	West Virginia	H	5.91 FQ	8.86 AW	12.77 TQ	WVBLS	10/01-12/01
	Wisconsin	H	7.26 FQ	10.68 AW	15.54 TQ	WIBLS	10/01-12/01
	Appleton-Oshkosh-Neenah MSA, WI	H	7.28 FQ	10.97 AW	15.73 TQ	WIBLS	10/01-12/01
	Madison MSA, WI	H	8.39 FQ	10.94 AW	13.83 TQ	WIBLS	10/01-12/01
	Milwaukee-Waukesha PMSA, WI	H	7.05 FQ	10.21 AW	15.88 TQ	WIBLS	10/01-12/01
	Wyoming	H	5.97 FQ	10.44 AW	18.87 TQ	WYBLS	10/01-12/01
	Puerto Rico	H	5.53 FQ	6.85 AW	8.69 TQ	PRBLS	10/01-12/01
Paper Goods Machine Setter, Operator, and Tender	Alabama	H	8.02 FQ	12.93 AW	19.40 TQ	ALBLS	10/01-12/01
	Arizona	H	7.85 FQ	11.47 AW	16.18 TQ	AZBLS	10/01-12/01
	Arkansas	H	9.77 FQ	15.04 AW	22.03 TQ	ARBLS	10/01-12/01
	California	H	7.45 FQ	14.01 AW	20.98 TQ	CABLS	10/01-12/01
	Colorado	H	8.39 FQ	13.82 AW	18.98 TQ	COBLS	10/01-12/01
	Connecticut	H	6.87 FQ	12.38 AW	16.95 TQ	CTBLS	10/01-12/01
	Florida	H	7.63 FQ	11.33 AW	15.97 TQ	FLBLS	10/01-12/01
	Georgia	H	8.34 FQ	13.81 AW	20.46 TQ	GABLS	10/01-12/01
	Hawaii	H	6.58 FQ	18.05 AW	26.30 TQ	HIBLS	10/01-12/01
	Illinois	H	7.44 FQ	12.22 AW	17.68 TQ	ILBLS	10/01-12/01
	Indiana	H	9.19 FQ	13.06 AW	17.30 TQ	INBLS	10/01-12/01
	Iowa	H	7.79 FQ	12.30 AW	16.46 TQ	IABLS	10/01-12/01
	Kansas	H	9.08 FQ	14.49 AW	23.27 TQ	KSBLS	10/01-12/01
	Kentucky	H	8.81 FQ	13.68 AW	19.55 TQ	KYBLS	10/01-12/01

AAW	Average annual wage	**AOH**	Average offered, high	**ASH**	Average starting, high	**H**	Hourly	**M**	Monthly	**S**	Special: hourly and annual
AE	Average entry wage	**AOL**	Average offered, low	**ASL**	Average starting, low	**HI**	Highest wage paid	**MTC**	Median total compensation	**TQ**	Third quartile wage
AEX	Average experienced wage	**APH**	Average pay, high range	**AW**	Average wage paid	**HR**	High end range	**MW**	Median wage paid	**W**	Weekly
AO	Average offered	**APL**	Average pay, low range	**FQ**	First quartile wage	**LR**	Low end range	**SQ**	Second quartile wage	**Y**	Yearly

Occupation/Type/Industry	Location	Per	Low	Mid	High	Source	Date
Paper Goods Machine Setter, Operator, and Tender	Louisiana	H	9.46 FQ	17.45 AW	26.89 TQ	LABLS	10/01-12/01
	Maine	H	11.83 FQ	14.95 AW	18.44 TQ	MEBLS	10/01-12/01
	Maryland	H	8.90 FQ	13.14 AW	19.99 TQ	MDBLS	10/01-12/01
	Massachusetts	H	9.58 FQ	14.17 AW	17.91 TQ	MABLS	10/01-12/01
	Michigan	H	8.12 FQ	12.73 AW	17.25 TQ	MIBLS	10/01-12/01
	Minnesota	H	9.36 FQ	14.91 AW	21.50 TQ	MNBLS	10/01-12/01
	Mississippi	H	9.53 FQ	15.32 AW	21.94 TQ	MSBLS	10/01-12/01
	Missouri	H	8.60 FQ	12.79 AW	16.46 TQ	MOBLS	10/01-12/01
	Nebraska	H	9.26 FQ	12.60 AW	16.08 TQ	NEBLS	10/01-12/01
	Nevada	H	8.18 FQ	14.44 AW	21.06 TQ	NVBLS	10/01-12/01
	New Hampshire	H	7.79 FQ	12.66 AW	18.15 TQ	NHBLS	10/01-12/01
	New Jersey	H	7.61 FQ	12.64 AW	17.72 TQ	NJBLS	10/01-12/01
	New Mexico	H	7.32 FQ	9.45 AW	12.54 TQ	NMBLS	10/01-12/01
	New York	H	7.29 FQ	13.15 AW	19.80 TQ	NYBLS	10/01-12/01
	North Carolina	H	8.25 FQ	13.21 AW	19.39 TQ	NCBLS	10/01-12/01
	Ohio	H	9.24 FQ	13.26 AW	17.42 TQ	OHBLS	10/01-12/01
	Oklahoma	H	7.81 FQ	13.42 AW	20.57 TQ	OKBLS	10/01-12/01
	Oregon	H	10.02 FQ	16.38 AW	22.04 TQ	ORBLS	10/01-12/01
	Pennsylvania	H	8.09 FQ	14.62 AW	20.83 TQ	PABLS	10/01-12/01
	Rhode Island	H	6.97 FQ	11.14 AW	16.70 TQ	RIBLS	10/01-12/01
	South Carolina	H	9.16 FQ	13.43 AW	17.60 TQ	SCBLS	10/01-12/01
	Tennessee	H	9.05 FQ	15.49 AW	27.55 TQ	TNBLS	10/01-12/01
	Texas	H	7.63 FQ	12.32 AW	17.33 TQ	TXBLS	10/01-12/01
	Utah	H	8.51 FQ	12.12 AW	16.20 TQ	UTBLS	10/01-12/01
	Vermont	H	11.18 FQ	13.90 AW	17.29 TQ	VTBLS	10/01-12/01
	Virginia	H	9.03 FQ	13.20 AW	18.72 TQ	VABLS	10/01-12/01
	Washington	H	11.87 FQ	18.15 AW	24.45 TQ	WABLS	10/01-12/01
	West Virginia	H	8.80 FQ	12.95 AW	17.24 TQ	WVBLS	10/01-12/01
	Wisconsin	H	11.21 FQ	15.67 AW	21.22 TQ	WIBLS	10/01-12/01
	Puerto Rico	H	5.66 FQ	7.50 AW	11.19 TQ	PRBLS	10/01-12/01
Paperhanger	Alabama	H	7.80 FQ	12.37 AW	18.16 TQ	ALBLS	10/01-12/01
	Arizona	H	9.20 FQ	16.03 AW	21.55 TQ	AZBLS	10/01-12/01
	Phoenix-Mesa MSA, AZ	H	9.20 FQ	16.07 AW	21.56 TQ	AZBLS	10/01-12/01
	Arkansas	H	7.89 FQ	10.28 AW	13.05 TQ	ARBLS	10/01-12/01
	California	H	15.33 FQ	21.50 AW	27.37 TQ	CABLS	10/01-12/01
	Los Angeles-Long Beach PMSA, CA	H	14.59 FQ	20.13 AW	25.91 TQ	CABLS	10/01-12/01
	Riverside-San Bernardino PMSA, CA	H	21.50 FQ	23.52 AW	26.83 TQ	CABLS	10/01-12/01
	San Francisco PMSA, CA	H	16.86 FQ	25.10 AW	32.81 TQ	CABLS	10/01-12/01
	Santa Rosa PMSA, CA	H	15.06 FQ	17.20 AW	20.49 TQ	CABLS	10/01-12/01
	Colorado	H	14.15 FQ	16.87 AW	21.25 TQ	COBLS	10/01-12/01
	Denver PMSA, CO	H	14.36 FQ	17.15 AW	21.42 TQ	COBLS	10/01-12/01
	Delaware	H	11.21 FQ	15.86 AW	20.85 TQ	DEBLS	10/01-12/01
	Wilmington-Newark PMSA, DE-MD	H	11.81 FQ	16.12 AW	20.87 TQ	DEBLS	10/01-12/01
	Washington PMSA, DC-MD-VA-WV	H	10.01 FQ	15.70 AW	21.21 TQ	DCBLS	10/01-12/01
	Florida	H	8.56 FQ	13.05 AW	18.95 TQ	FLBLS	10/01-12/01
	Jacksonville MSA, FL	H	7.63 FQ	13.38 AW	17.74 TQ	FLBLS	10/01-12/01
	Miami PMSA, FL	H	7.82 FQ	11.49 AW	14.14 TQ	FLBLS	10/01-12/01
	Orlando MSA, FL	H	8.12 FQ	12.78 AW	20.41 TQ	FLBLS	10/01-12/01
	West Palm Beach-Boca Raton MSA, FL	H	9.56 FQ	15.91 AW	25.85 TQ	FLBLS	10/01-12/01
	Georgia	H	6.04 FQ	10.95 AW	16.09 TQ	GABLS	10/01-12/01
	Atlanta MSA, GA	H	5.80 FQ	11.69 AW	16.62 TQ	GABLS	10/01-12/01
	Illinois	H	5.64 FQ	12.72 AW	27.40 TQ	ILBLS	10/01-12/01
	Chicago PMSA, IL	H	5.59 FQ	11.17 AW	26.26 TQ	ILBLS	10/01-12/01
	Indiana	H	9.41 FQ	16.62 AW	22.13 TQ	INBLS	10/01-12/01
	Indianapolis MSA, IN	H	13.24 FQ	18.25 AW	22.30 TQ	INBLS	10/01-12/01
	Iowa	H	10.38 FQ	16.92 AW	22.66 TQ	IABLS	10/01-12/01
	Kansas	H	9.99 FQ	17.25 AW	21.80 TQ	KSBLS	10/01-12/01
	Kentucky	H	9.68 FQ	14.46 AW	20.02 TQ	KYBLS	10/01-12/01
	Louisville MSA, KY-IN	H	9.76 FQ	13.86 AW	19.91 TQ	KYBLS	10/01-12/01
	Louisiana	H	7.17 FQ	12.18 AW	16.74 TQ	LABLS	10/01-12/01
	Maine	H	9.59 FQ	12.64 AW	17.50 TQ	MEBLS	10/01-12/01
	Portland MSA, ME	H	10.40 FQ	12.61 AW	16.20 TQ	MEBLS	10/01-12/01
	Maryland	H	10.21 FQ	16.37 AW	21.89 TQ	MDBLS	10/01-12/01
	Baltimore PMSA, MD	H	10.36 FQ	17.95 AW	22.57 TQ	MDBLS	10/01-12/01
	Massachusetts	H	11.47 FQ	20.34 AW	31.00 TQ	MABLS	10/01-12/01

AAW	Average annual wage	AOH	Average offered, high	ASH	Average starting, high	H	Hourly	M	Monthly	S	Special: hourly and annual
AE	Average entry wage	AOL	Average offered, low	ASL	Average starting, low	HI	Highest wage paid	MTC	Median total compensation	TQ	Third quartile wage
AEX	Average experienced wage	APH	Average pay, high range	AW	Average wage paid	HR	High end range	MW	Median wage paid	W	Weekly
AO	Average offered	APL	Average pay, low range	FQ	First quartile wage	LR	Low end range	SQ	Second quartile wage	Y	Yearly

Occupation/Type/Industry	Location	Per	Low	Mid	High	Source	Date
Paperhanger	Boston PMSA, MA-NH	H	13.73 FQ	23.65 AW	32.67 TQ	MABLS	10/01-12/01
	Michigan	H	10.97 FQ	16.27 AW	21.40 TQ	MIBLS	10/01-12/01
	Detroit PMSA, MI	H	11.25 FQ	16.63 AW	21.59 TQ	MIBLS	10/01-12/01
	Grand Rapids-Muskegon-Holland MSA, MI	H	11.16 FQ	16.31 AW	21.15 TQ	MIBLS	10/01-12/01
	Kalamazoo-Battle Creek MSA, MI	H	7.97 FQ	14.25 AW	19.75 TQ	MIBLS	10/01-12/01
	Minnesota	H	14.00 FQ	22.67 AW	30.90 TQ	MNBLS	10/01-12/01
	Minneapolis-St. Paul MSA, MN-WI	H	13.32 FQ	21.94 AW	26.73 TQ	MNBLS	10/01-12/01
	Mississippi	H	9.46 FQ	15.66 AW	20.45 TQ	MSBLS	10/01-12/01
	Missouri	H	10.78 FQ	20.59 AW	27.44 TQ	MOBLS	10/01-12/01
	Kansas City MSA, MO-KS	H	22.93 FQ	25.04 AW	27.82 TQ	MOBLS	10/01-12/01
	St. Louis MSA, MO-IL	H	17.32 FQ	22.61 AW	27.54 TQ	MOBLS	10/01-12/01
	Nebraska	H	9.20 FQ	12.17 AW	17.20 TQ	NEBLS	10/01-12/01
	Nevada	H	9.40 FQ	18.32 AW	27.66 TQ	NVBLS	10/01-12/01
	Las Vegas MSA, NV-AZ	H	8.89 FQ	16.18 AW	27.61 TQ	NVBLS	10/01-12/01
	Reno MSA, NV	H	12.55 FQ	21.13 AW	27.65 TQ	NVBLS	10/01-12/01
	New Jersey	H	10.71 FQ	19.46 AW	31.22 TQ	NJBLS	10/01-12/01
	Newark PMSA, NJ	H	11.32 FQ	22.61 AW	34.70 TQ	NJBLS	10/01-12/01
	New York	H	9.22 FQ	16.25 AW	26.67 TQ	NYBLS	10/01-12/01
	Albany-Schenectady-Troy MSA, NY	H	12.42 FQ	17.22 AW	22.17 TQ	NYBLS	10/01-12/01
	Buffalo-Niagara Falls MSA, NY	H	9.86 FQ	14.56 AW	18.00 TQ	NYBLS	10/01-12/01
	Nassau-Suffolk PMSA, NY	H	8.76 FQ	13.28 AW	21.96 TQ	NYBLS	10/01-12/01
	New York PMSA, NY	H	8.93 FQ	16.94 AW	30.79 TQ	NYBLS	10/01-12/01
	Rochester MSA, NY	H	11.21 FQ	14.15 AW	19.83 TQ	NYBLS	10/01-12/01
	North Carolina	H	6.23 FQ	11.05 AW	16.11 TQ	NCBLS	10/01-12/01
	Charlotte-Gastonia-Rock Hill MSA, NC-SC	H	10.84 FQ	13.63 AW	22.47 TQ	NCBLS	10/01-12/01
	Ohio	H	12.16 FQ	19.37 AW	26.36 TQ	OHBLS	10/01-12/01
	Cincinnati PMSA, OH-KY-IN	H	14.44 FQ	18.49 AW	24.21 TQ	OHBLS	10/01-12/01
	Cleveland-Lorain-Elyria PMSA, OH	H	12.88 FQ	20.64 AW	26.73 TQ	OHBLS	10/01-12/01
	Oklahoma	H	7.45 FQ	12.07 AW	16.84 TQ	OKBLS	10/01-12/01
	Oregon	H	10.96 FQ	15.94 AW	21.87 TQ	ORBLS	10/01-12/01
	Eugene-Springfield MSA, OR	H	8.21 FQ	13.43 AW	18.47 TQ	ORBLS	10/01-12/01
	Pennsylvania	H	11.29 FQ	17.84 AW	25.52 TQ	PABLS	10/01-12/01
	Lancaster MSA, PA	H	11.39 FQ	14.36 AW	17.63 TQ	PABLS	10/01-12/01
	Philadelphia PMSA, PA-NJ	H	14.41 FQ	19.34 AW	24.94 TQ	PABLS	10/01-12/01
	Pittsburgh MSA, PA	H	15.16 FQ	21.24 AW	26.61 TQ	PABLS	10/01-12/01
	Scranton-Wilkes-Barre-Hazleton MSA, PA	H	9.31 FQ	14.52 AW	20.41 TQ	PABLS	10/01-12/01
	South Carolina	H	8.97 FQ	14.62 AW	21.47 TQ	SCBLS	10/01-12/01
	Tennessee	H	11.25 FQ	16.71 AW	25.09 TQ	TNBLS	10/01-12/01
	Chattanooga MSA, TN-GA	H	11.14 FQ	14.19 AW	17.12 TQ	TNBLS	10/01-12/01
	Memphis MSA, TN-AR-MS	H	14.07 FQ	20.65 AW	26.31 TQ	TNBLS	10/01-12/01
	Texas	H	7.72 FQ	11.98 AW	16.19 TQ	TXBLS	10/01-12/01
	Dallas PMSA, TX	H	9.93 FQ	12.80 AW	16.39 TQ	TXBLS	10/01-12/01
	Houston PMSA, TX	H	11.38 FQ	13.71 AW	16.81 TQ	TXBLS	10/01-12/01
	San Antonio MSA, TX	H	9.87 FQ	12.29 AW	15.57 TQ	TXBLS	10/01-12/01
	Virginia	H	9.12 FQ	15.77 AW	22.15 TQ	VABLS	10/01-12/01
	Washington	H	9.53 FQ	15.59 AW	22.02 TQ	WABLS	10/01-12/01
	Seattle-Bellevue-Everett PMSA, WA	H	9.53 FQ	15.86 AW	23.90 TQ	WABLS	10/01-12/01
	Wisconsin	H	9.12 FQ	16.07 AW	26.26 TQ	WIBLS	10/01-12/01
	Madison MSA, WI	H	9.79 FQ	20.12 AW	32.78 TQ	WIBLS	10/01-12/01
	Milwaukee-Waukesha PMSA, WI	H	8.75 FQ	10.63 AW	10.74 TQ	WIBLS	10/01-12/01
	Puerto Rico	H	5.44 FQ	6.72 AW	8.19 TQ	PRBLS	10/01-12/01
Paralegal and Legal Assistant	Alabama	Y	14920 FQ	34360 AW	54360 TQ	ALBLS	10/01-12/01
	Birmingham MSA, AL	Y	11920 FQ	33370 AW	55590 TQ	ALBLS	10/01-12/01
	Huntsville MSA, AL	Y	21570 FQ	33500 AW	51960 TQ	ALBLS	10/01-12/01
	Mobile MSA, AL	Y	15150 FQ	22760 AW	38450 TQ	ALBLS	10/01-12/01
	Montgomery MSA, AL	Y	31640 FQ	46720 AW	55470 TQ	ALBLS	10/01-12/01
	Alaska	Y	30220 FQ	44870 AW	62800 TQ	AKBLS	10/01-12/01
	Anchorage MSA, AK	Y	30180 FQ	43620 AW	63480 TQ	AKBLS	10/01-12/01
	Arizona	Y	22460 FQ	41450 AW	78010 TQ	AZBLS	10/01-12/01
	Phoenix-Mesa MSA, AZ	Y	20510 FQ	44590 AW	81450 TQ	AZBLS	10/01-12/01
	Tucson MSA, AZ	Y	28320 FQ	34040 AW	43170 TQ	AZBLS	10/01-12/01
	Arkansas	Y	18120 FQ	27230 AW	36430 TQ	ARBLS	10/01-12/01

AAW Average annual wage **AOH** Average offered, high **ASH** Average starting, high **H** Hourly **M** Monthly **S** Special: hourly and annual
AE Average entry wage **AOL** Average offered, low **ASL** Average starting, low **HI** Highest wage paid **MTC** Median total compensation **TQ** Third quartile wage
AEX Average experienced wage **APH** Average pay, high range **AW** Average wage paid **HR** High end range **MW** Median wage paid **W** Weekly
AO Average offered **APL** Average pay, low range **FQ** First quartile wage **LR** Low end range **SQ** Second quartile wage **Y** Yearly

Occupation/Type/Industry	Location	Per	Low	Mid	High	Source	Date
Paralegal and Legal Assistant	Fort Smith MSA, AR-OK	Y	20000 FQ	27860 AW	43560 TQ	ARBLS	10/01-12/01
	Little Rock-North Little Rock MSA, AR	Y	22530 FQ	29120 AW	38150 TQ	ARBLS	10/01-12/01
	California	Y	28430 FQ	48990 AW	70850 TQ	CABLS	10/01-12/01
	Bakersfield MSA, CA	Y	29410 FQ	40360 AW	51880 TQ	CABLS	10/01-12/01
	Chico-Paradise MSA, CA	Y	24320 FQ	31810 AW	42860 TQ	CABLS	10/01-12/01
	Fresno MSA, CA	Y	33050 FQ	43520 AW	56630 TQ	CABLS	10/01-12/01
	Los Angeles-Long Beach PMSA, CA	Y	39250 FQ	54330 AW	77490 TQ	CABLS	10/01-12/01
	Merced MSA, CA	Y	28910 FQ	39550 AW	53750 TQ	CABLS	10/01-12/01
	Modesto MSA, CA	Y	25670 FQ	37630 AW	48250 TQ	CABLS	10/01-12/01
	Oakland PMSA, CA	Y	32680 FQ	50100 AW	65660 TQ	CABLS	10/01-12/01
	Orange County PMSA, CA	Y	21130 FQ	45000 AW	73780 TQ	CABLS	10/01-12/01
	Redding MSA, CA	Y	25020 FQ	33830 AW	44760 TQ	CABLS	10/01-12/01
	Riverside-San Bernardino PMSA, CA	Y	28760 FQ	46310 AW	60070 TQ	CABLS	10/01-12/01
	Sacramento PMSA, CA	Y	20680 FQ	39540 AW	56420 TQ	CABLS	10/01-12/01
	Salinas MSA, CA	Y	29230 FQ	41330 AW	55110 TQ	CABLS	10/01-12/01
	San Diego MSA, CA	Y	26050 FQ	46170 AW	68080 TQ	CABLS	10/01-12/01
	San Francisco PMSA, CA	Y	34930 FQ	52880 AW	72730 TQ	CABLS	10/01-12/01
	San Jose PMSA, CA	Y	32890 FQ	52280 AW	70440 TQ	CABLS	10/01-12/01
	San Luis Obispo-Atascadero-Paso Robles MSA, CA	Y	30590 FQ	45810 AW	57840 TQ	CABLS	10/01-12/01
	Santa Barbara-Santa Maria-Lompoc MSA, CA	Y	30120 FQ	45170 AW	59530 TQ	CABLS	10/01-12/01
	Santa Cruz-Watsonville PMSA, CA	Y	30120 FQ	37640 AW	56080 TQ	CABLS	10/01-12/01
	Santa Rosa PMSA, CA	Y	18380 FQ	26920 AW	45630 TQ	CABLS	10/01-12/01
	Stockton-Lodi MSA, CA	Y	25650 FQ	41090 AW	55370 TQ	CABLS	10/01-12/01
	Vallejo-Fairfield-Napa PMSA, CA	Y	24770 FQ	37090 AW	48190 TQ	CABLS	10/01-12/01
	Ventura PMSA, CA	Y	40360 FQ	48910 AW	56390 TQ	CABLS	10/01-12/01
	Visalia-Tulare-Porterville MSA, CA	Y	25010 FQ	35660 AW	47320 TQ	CABLS	10/01-12/01
	Colorado	Y	26990 FQ	40600 AW	55250 TQ	COBLS	10/01-12/01
	Boulder-Longmont PMSA, CO	Y	24670 FQ	39670 AW	54180 TQ	COBLS	10/01-12/01
	Colorado Springs MSA, CO	Y	26090 FQ	36300 AW	46700 TQ	COBLS	10/01-12/01
	Denver PMSA, CO	Y	30960 FQ	43420 AW	57640 TQ	COBLS	10/01-12/01
	Fort Collins-Loveland MSA, CO	Y	22380 FQ	28660 AW	37870 TQ	COBLS	10/01-12/01
	Greeley PMSA, CO	Y	23930 FQ	30880 AW	43720 TQ	COBLS	10/01-12/01
	Connecticut	Y	31870 FQ	43310 AW	55750 TQ	CTBLS	10/01-12/01
	Bridgeport PMSA, CT	Y	32840 FQ	45100 AW	55910 TQ	CTBLS	10/01-12/01
	Danbury PMSA, CT	Y	39020 FQ	47520 AW	56450 TQ	CTBLS	10/01-12/01
	Hartford MSA, CT	Y	29690 FQ	42340 AW	56330 TQ	CTBLS	10/01-12/01
	New Haven-Meriden PMSA, CT	Y	36000 FQ	42910 AW	54980 TQ	CTBLS	10/01-12/01
	New London-Norwich MSA, CT-RI	Y	26430 FQ	39010 AW	52810 TQ	CTBLS	10/01-12/01
	Stamford-Norwalk PMSA, CT	Y	36650 FQ	45140 AW	55500 TQ	CTBLS	10/01-12/01
	Waterbury PMSA, CT	Y	28010 FQ	41150 AW	54620 TQ	CTBLS	10/01-12/01
	Delaware	Y	21400 FQ	34500 AW	48520 TQ	DEBLS	10/01-12/01
	Wilmington-Newark PMSA, DE-MD	Y	20920 FQ	34640 AW	49570 TQ	DEBLS	10/01-12/01
	District of Columbia	Y	23470 FQ	37990 AW	56180 TQ	DCBLS	10/01-12/01
	Washington PMSA, DC-MD-VA-WV	Y	23750 FQ	39040 AW	58760 TQ	DCBLS	10/01-12/01
	Florida	Y	25270 FQ	38920 AW	56290 TQ	FLBLS	10/01-12/01
	Daytona Beach MSA, FL	Y	28680 FQ	47570 AW	75810 TQ	FLBLS	10/01-12/01
	Fort Lauderdale PMSA, FL	Y	23810 FQ	31710 AW	44480 TQ	FLBLS	10/01-12/01
	Fort Myers-Cape Coral MSA, FL	Y	25580 FQ	38430 AW	59710 TQ	FLBLS	10/01-12/01
	Fort Pierce-Port St. Lucie MSA, FL	Y	27880 FQ	46740 AW	60890 TQ	FLBLS	10/01-12/01
	Gainesville MSA, FL	Y	23490 FQ	33260 AW	64880 TQ	FLBLS	10/01-12/01
	Jacksonville MSA, FL	Y	35130 FQ	50310 AW	66000 TQ	FLBLS	10/01-12/01
	Lakeland-Winter Haven MSA, FL	Y	23470 FQ	40470 AW	73430 TQ	FLBLS	10/01-12/01
	Melbourne-Titusville-Palm Bay MSA, FL	Y	25370 FQ	42200 AW	69810 TQ	FLBLS	10/01-12/01
	Miami PMSA, FL	Y	35310 FQ	50180 AW	68230 TQ	FLBLS	10/01-12/01
	Naples MSA, FL	Y	37640 FQ	47570 AW	55770 TQ	FLBLS	10/01-12/01

AAW Average annual wage; AE Average entry wage; AEX Average experienced wage; AO Average offered; AOH Average offered, high; AOL Average offered, low; APH Average pay, high range; APL Average pay, low range; ASH Average starting, high; ASL Average starting, low; AW Average wage paid; FQ First quartile wage; H Hourly; HI Highest wage paid; HR High end range; LR Low end range; M Monthly; MTC Median total compensation; MW Median wage paid; SQ Second quartile wage; S Special: hourly and annual; TQ Third quartile wage; W Weekly; Y Yearly

Occupation/Type/Industry	Location	Per	Low	Mid	High	Source	Date
Paralegal and Legal Assistant	Ocala MSA, FL	Y	24690 FQ	39430 AW	69030 TQ	FLBLS	10/01-12/01
	Orlando MSA, FL	Y	27040 FQ	38470 AW	44670 TQ	FLBLS	10/01-12/01
	Pensacola MSA, FL	Y	24480 FQ	35550 AW	44520 TQ	FLBLS	10/01-12/01
	Sarasota-Bradenton MSA, FL	Y	25260 FQ	36320 AW	59870 TQ	FLBLS	10/01-12/01
	Tallahassee MSA, FL	Y	25390 FQ	44330 AW	77370 TQ	FLBLS	10/01-12/01
	Tampa-St. Petersburg-Clearwater MSA, FL	Y	24920 FQ	34840 AW	44810 TQ	FLBLS	10/01-12/01
	West Palm Beach-Boca Raton MSA, FL	Y	31860 FQ	44230 AW	55710 TQ	FLBLS	10/01-12/01
	Georgia	Y	24320 FQ	37650 AW	56320 TQ	GABLS	10/01-12/01
	Atlanta MSA, GA	Y	28510 FQ	38290 AW	56380 TQ	GABLS	10/01-12/01
	Augusta-Aiken MSA, GA-SC	Y	29960 FQ	40650 AW	51190 TQ	GABLS	10/01-12/01
	Columbus MSA, GA-AL	Y	24310 FQ	39710 AW	59390 TQ	GABLS	10/01-12/01
	Macon MSA, GA	Y	23290 FQ	40570 AW	58780 TQ	GABLS	10/01-12/01
	Savannah MSA, GA	Y	21020 FQ	34310 AW	57590 TQ	GABLS	10/01-12/01
	Hawaii	Y	26830 FQ	39050 AW	53690 TQ	HIBLS	10/01-12/01
	Honolulu MSA, HI	Y	26790 FQ	39520 AW	53890 TQ	HIBLS	10/01-12/01
	Idaho	Y	23580 FQ	36770 AW	51060 TQ	IDBLS	10/01-12/01
	Boise City MSA, ID	Y	31970 FQ	42010 AW	53750 TQ	IDBLS	10/01-12/01
	Illinois	Y	25460 FQ	40740 AW	58090 TQ	ILBLS	10/01-12/01
	Champaign-Urbana MSA, IL	Y	30970 FQ	34400 AW	37780 TQ	ILBLS	10/01-12/01
	Chicago PMSA, IL	Y	26390 FQ	41810 AW	58750 TQ	ILBLS	10/01-12/01
	Peoria-Pekin MSA, IL	Y	23830 FQ	35240 AW	53230 TQ	ILBLS	10/01-12/01
	Springfield MSA, IL	Y	25960 FQ	41610 AW	58270 TQ	ILBLS	10/01-12/01
	Indiana	Y	21470 FQ	33080 AW	45080 TQ	INBLS	10/01-12/01
	Elkhart-Goshen MSA, IN	Y	23650 FQ	28050 AW	34890 TQ	INBLS	10/01-12/01
	Evansville-Henderson MSA, IN-KY	Y	18620 FQ	30510 AW	46030 TQ	INBLS	10/01-12/01
	Fort Wayne MSA, IN	Y	25030 FQ	33600 AW	44230 TQ	INBLS	10/01-12/01
	Gary PMSA, IN	Y	19590 FQ	28980 AW	41630 TQ	INBLS	10/01-12/01
	Indianapolis MSA, IN	Y	22220 FQ	36780 AW	50490 TQ	INBLS	10/01-12/01
	Lafayette MSA, IN	Y	23760 FQ	28570 AW	38200 TQ	INBLS	10/01-12/01
	South Bend MSA, IN	Y	20010 FQ	33050 AW	49250 TQ	INBLS	10/01-12/01
	Iowa	Y	24180 FQ	35410 AW	45740 TQ	IABLS	10/01-12/01
	Cedar Rapids MSA, IA	Y	24990 FQ	34920 AW	45080 TQ	IABLS	10/01-12/01
	Davenport-Moline-Rock Island MSA, IA-IL	Y	24800 FQ	34280 AW	47980 TQ	IABLS	10/01-12/01
	Des Moines MSA, IA	Y	29340 FQ	39150 AW	47160 TQ	IABLS	10/01-12/01
	Kansas	Y	21950 FQ	32020 AW	45820 TQ	KSBLS	10/01-12/01
	Topeka MSA, KS	Y	23390 FQ	30660 AW	41700 TQ	KSBLS	10/01-12/01
	Wichita MSA, KS	Y	20510 FQ	30950 AW	44030 TQ	KSBLS	10/01-12/01
	Kentucky	Y	19660 FQ	32250 AW	48720 TQ	KYBLS	10/01-12/01
	Lexington MSA, KY	Y	22640 FQ	35730 AW	51290 TQ	KYBLS	10/01-12/01
	Louisville MSA, KY-IN	Y	24140 FQ	35930 AW	47910 TQ	KYBLS	10/01-12/01
	Louisiana	Y	19430 FQ	31050 AW	47670 TQ	LABLS	10/01-12/01
	Baton Rouge MSA, LA	Y	19720 FQ	29510 AW	42760 TQ	LABLS	10/01-12/01
	Lafayette MSA, LA	Y	19190 FQ	32800 AW	47960 TQ	LABLS	10/01-12/01
	Lake Charles MSA, LA	Y	23240 FQ	36890 AW	55790 TQ	LABLS	10/01-12/01
	New Orleans MSA, LA	Y	24350 FQ	38250 AW	53490 TQ	LABLS	10/01-12/01
	Shreveport-Bossier City MSA, LA	Y	20840 FQ	27250 AW	34040 TQ	LABLS	10/01-12/01
	Maine	Y	24020 FQ	32550 AW	43390 TQ	MEBLS	10/01-12/01
	Portland MSA, ME	Y	23790 FQ	32420 AW	45780 TQ	MEBLS	10/01-12/01
	Maryland	Y	24080 FQ	36710 AW	55540 TQ	MDBLS	10/01-12/01
	Baltimore PMSA, MD	Y	24120 FQ	36620 AW	56230 TQ	MDBLS	10/01-12/01
	Massachusetts	Y	24100 FQ	37330 AW	54740 TQ	MABLS	10/01-12/01
	Boston PMSA, MA-NH	Y	23760 FQ	37620 AW	57720 TQ	MABLS	10/01-12/01
	Lawrence PMSA, MA-NH	Y	24790 FQ	32720 AW	41100 TQ	MABLS	10/01-12/01
	Lowell PMSA, MA-NH	Y	29530 FQ	38510 AW	46730 TQ	MABLS	10/01-12/01
	Springfield MSA, MA	Y	30120 FQ	37900 AW	44500 TQ	MABLS	10/01-12/01
	Worcester PMSA, MA-CT	Y	25840 FQ	38110 AW	44560 TQ	MABLS	10/01-12/01
	Michigan	Y	24000 FQ	36820 AW	55550 TQ	MIBLS	10/01-12/01
	Ann Arbor PMSA, MI	Y	25600 FQ	37660 AW	54680 TQ	MIBLS	10/01-12/01
	Detroit PMSA, MI	Y	24440 FQ	39890 AW	61790 TQ	MIBLS	10/01-12/01
	Flint PMSA, MI	Y	28040 FQ	37530 AW	49010 TQ	MIBLS	10/01-12/01
	Grand Rapids-Muskegon-Holland MSA, MI	Y	25860 FQ	34290 AW	43770 TQ	MIBLS	10/01-12/01
	Kalamazoo-Battle Creek MSA, MI	Y	23160 FQ	29170 AW	40190 TQ	MIBLS	10/01-12/01
	Lansing-East Lansing MSA, MI	Y	29510 FQ	42440 AW	58600 TQ	MIBLS	10/01-12/01
	Saginaw-Bay City-Midland MSA, MI	Y	20360 FQ	33380 AW	49660 TQ	MIBLS	10/01-12/01

Occupation/Type/Industry	Location	Per	Low	Mid	High	Source	Date
Paralegal and Legal Assistant	Minnesota	Y	29700 FQ	40800 AW	55480 TQ	MNBLS	10/01-12/01
	Duluth-Superior MSA, MN-WI	Y	21790 FQ	32490 AW	44880 TQ	MNBLS	10/01-12/01
	Minneapolis-St. Paul MSA, MN-WI	Y	31360 FQ	42150 AW	56510 TQ	MNBLS	10/01-12/01
	St. Cloud MSA, MN	Y	23820 FQ	32200 AW	41880 TQ	MNBLS	10/01-12/01
	Mississippi	Y	19540 FQ	27950 AW	36360 TQ	MSBLS	10/01-12/01
	Biloxi-Gulfport-Pascagoula MSA, MS	Y	24590 FQ	30700 AW	36480 TQ	MSBLS	10/01-12/01
	Jackson MSA, MS	Y	18770 FQ	26830 AW	37010 TQ	MSBLS	10/01-12/01
	Missouri	Y	22240 FQ	34280 AW	48440 TQ	MOBLS	10/01-12/01
	Kansas City MSA, MO-KS	Y	27480 FQ	36420 AW	51020 TQ	MOBLS	10/01-12/01
	St. Louis MSA, MO-IL	Y	28450 FQ	36240 AW	49690 TQ	MOBLS	10/01-12/01
	Springfield MSA, MO	Y	19200 FQ	26760 AW	41830 TQ	MOBLS	10/01-12/01
	Montana	Y	20020 FQ	31240 AW	48910 TQ	MTBLS	10/01-12/01
	Billings MSA, MT	Y	20490 FQ	31180 AW	47830 TQ	MTBLS	10/01-12/01
	Nebraska	Y	21110 FQ	34310 AW	45930 TQ	NEBLS	10/01-12/01
	Lincoln MSA, NE	Y	24280 FQ	36300 AW	45260 TQ	NEBLS	10/01-12/01
	Omaha MSA, NE-IA	Y	27620 FQ	37550 AW	51320 TQ	NEBLS	10/01-12/01
	Nevada	Y	23860 FQ	36510 AW	53350 TQ	NVBLS	10/01-12/01
	Las Vegas MSA, NV-AZ	Y	23710 FQ	35650 AW	53000 TQ	NVBLS	10/01-12/01
	Reno MSA, NV	Y	25950 FQ	39810 AW	53610 TQ	NVBLS	10/01-12/01
	New Hampshire	Y	26750 FQ	35210 AW	45720 TQ	NHBLS	10/01-12/01
	Manchester PMSA, NH	Y	30260 FQ	41170 AW	56530 TQ	NHBLS	10/01-12/01
	Nashua PMSA, NH	Y	30070 FQ	38300 AW	46160 TQ	NHBLS	10/01-12/01
	Portsmouth-Rochester PMSA, NH-ME	Y	28620 FQ	33420 AW	41490 TQ	NHBLS	10/01-12/01
	New Jersey	Y	29460 FQ	43380 AW	59520 TQ	NJBLS	10/01-12/01
	Atlantic-Cape May PMSA, NJ	Y	29480 FQ	40560 AW	53400 TQ	NJBLS	10/01-12/01
	Bergen-Passaic PMSA, NJ	Y	31680 FQ	46410 AW	56490 TQ	NJBLS	10/01-12/01
	Jersey City PMSA, NJ	Y	29190 FQ	43220 AW	63180 TQ	NJBLS	10/01-12/01
	Middlesex-Somerset-Hunterdon PMSA, NJ	Y	29750 FQ	43190 AW	56660 TQ	NJBLS	10/01-12/01
	Monmouth-Ocean PMSA, NJ	Y	36360 FQ	53850 AW	69290 TQ	NJBLS	10/01-12/01
	Newark PMSA, NJ	Y	31360 FQ	42870 AW	55630 TQ	NJBLS	10/01-12/01
	Trenton PMSA, NJ	Y	27700 FQ	36420 AW	47450 TQ	NJBLS	10/01-12/01
	New Mexico	Y	22010 FQ	31430 AW	42470 TQ	NMBLS	10/01-12/01
	Albuquerque MSA, NM	Y	21400 FQ	31240 AW	42480 TQ	NMBLS	10/01-12/01
	Las Cruces MSA, NM	Y	19950 FQ	30070 AW	50150 TQ	NMBLS	10/01-12/01
	New York	Y	28440 FQ	47090 AW	69390 TQ	NYBLS	10/01-12/01
	Albany-Schenectady-Troy MSA, NY	Y	29750 FQ	39190 AW	51440 TQ	NYBLS	10/01-12/01
	Binghamton MSA, NY	Y	19940 FQ	29030 AW	40090 TQ	NYBLS	10/01-12/01
	Buffalo-Niagara Falls MSA, NY	Y	25880 FQ	36380 AW	45990 TQ	NYBLS	10/01-12/01
	Dutchess County PMSA, NY	Y	28870 FQ	41960 AW	52820 TQ	NYBLS	10/01-12/01
	Nassau-Suffolk PMSA, NY	Y	25730 FQ	41100 AW	70310 TQ	NYBLS	10/01-12/01
	New York PMSA, NY	Y	30700 FQ	50450 AW	72870 TQ	NYBLS	10/01-12/01
	Newburgh PMSA, NY-PA	Y	22960 FQ	33970 AW	45340 TQ	NYBLS	10/01-12/01
	Rochester MSA, NY	Y	27540 FQ	40350 AW	58950 TQ	NYBLS	10/01-12/01
	Syracuse MSA, NY	Y	27290 FQ	38860 AW	53860 TQ	NYBLS	10/01-12/01
	Utica-Rome MSA, NY	Y	22950 FQ	36900 AW	53250 TQ	NYBLS	10/01-12/01
	North Carolina	Y	19810 FQ	32400 AW	46120 TQ	NCBLS	10/01-12/01
	Asheville MSA, NC	Y	18230 FQ	21920 AW	29830 TQ	NCBLS	10/01-12/01
	Charlotte-Gastonia-Rock Hill MSA, NC-SC	Y	19320 FQ	33810 AW	53700 TQ	NCBLS	10/01-12/01
	Fayetteville MSA, NC	Y	20110 FQ	27220 AW	35980 TQ	NCBLS	10/01-12/01
	Greensboro-Winston-Salem-High Point MSA, NC	Y	23800 FQ	34470 AW	44310 TQ	NCBLS	10/01-12/01
	Hickory-Morganton-Lenoir MSA, NC	Y	23720 FQ	29380 AW	35240 TQ	NCBLS	10/01-12/01
	Raleigh-Durham-Chapel Hill MSA, NC	Y	27240 FQ	37760 AW	51510 TQ	NCBLS	10/01-12/01
	Wilmington MSA, NC	Y	22810 FQ	37890 AW	64890 TQ	NCBLS	10/01-12/01
	North Dakota	Y	19350 FQ	30410 AW	44430 TQ	NDBLS	10/01-12/01
	Fargo-Moorhead MSA, ND-MN	Y	27870 FQ	34430 AW	47830 TQ	NDBLS	10/01-12/01
	Ohio	Y	24260 FQ	36580 AW	52460 TQ	OHBLS	10/01-12/01
	Akron PMSA, OH	Y	30670 FQ	37660 AW	44370 TQ	OHBLS	10/01-12/01
	Canton-Massillon MSA, OH	Y	26650 FQ	36870 AW	50700 TQ	OHBLS	10/01-12/01
	Cincinnati PMSA, OH-KY-IN	Y	22900 FQ	35480 AW	52520 TQ	OHBLS	10/01-12/01
	Cleveland-Lorain-Elyria PMSA, OH	Y	25660 FQ	37850 AW	52530 TQ	OHBLS	10/01-12/01

AAW	Average annual wage	AOH	Average offered, high	ASH	Average starting, high	H	Hourly	M	Monthly	S	Special: hourly and annual
AE	Average entry wage	AOL	Average offered, low	ASL	Average starting, low	HI	Highest wage paid	MTC	Median total compensation	TQ	Third quartile wage
AEX	Average experienced wage	APH	Average pay, high range	AW	Average wage paid	HR	High end range	MW	Median wage paid	W	Weekly
AO	Average offered	APL	Average pay, low range	FQ	First quartile wage	LR	Low end range	SQ	Second quartile wage	Y	Yearly

Occupation/Type/Industry	Location	Per	Low	Mid	High	Source	Date
Paralegal and Legal Assistant	Columbus MSA, OH	Y	28450 FQ	39690 AW	57110 TQ	OHBLS	10/01-12/01
	Dayton-Springfield MSA, OH	Y	24070 FQ	34530 AW	46990 TQ	OHBLS	10/01-12/01
	Hamilton-Middletown PMSA, OH	Y	23830 FQ	28180 AW	35040 TQ	OHBLS	10/01-12/01
	Toledo MSA, OH	Y	24630 FQ	36880 AW	54230 TQ	OHBLS	10/01-12/01
	Youngstown-Warren MSA, OH	Y	24750 FQ	34840 AW	46690 TQ	OHBLS	10/01-12/01
	Oklahoma	Y	22430 FQ	36200 AW	56060 TQ	OKBLS	10/01-12/01
	Oklahoma City MSA, OK	Y	24930 FQ	40770 AW	66800 TQ	OKBLS	10/01-12/01
	Tulsa MSA, OK	Y	23820 FQ	34410 AW	47340 TQ	OKBLS	10/01-12/01
	Oregon	Y	29200 FQ	40800 AW	53940 TQ	ORBLS	10/01-12/01
	Eugene-Springfield MSA, OR	Y	25690 FQ	38870 AW	51710 TQ	ORBLS	10/01-12/01
	Medford-Ashland MSA, OR	Y	19290 FQ	31250 AW	53520 TQ	ORBLS	10/01-12/01
	Portland-Vancouver PMSA, OR-WA	Y	31180 FQ	42020 AW	54470 TQ	ORBLS	10/01-12/01
	Salem PMSA, OR	Y	30050 FQ	37410 AW	44150 TQ	ORBLS	10/01-12/01
	Pennsylvania	Y	21080 FQ	36480 AW	54300 TQ	PABLS	10/01-12/01
	Allentown-Bethlehem-Easton MSA, PA	Y	24020 FQ	33380 AW	44450 TQ	PABLS	10/01-12/01
	Erie MSA, PA	Y	24260 FQ	30960 AW	38250 TQ	PABLS	10/01-12/01
	Harrisburg-Lebanon-Carlisle MSA, PA	Y	30690 FQ	39260 AW	47300 TQ	PABLS	10/01-12/01
	Lancaster MSA, PA	Y	24050 FQ	35660 AW	51130 TQ	PABLS	10/01-12/01
	Philadelphia PMSA, PA-NJ	Y	29160 FQ	43760 AW	57530 TQ	PABLS	10/01-12/01
	Pittsburgh MSA, PA	Y	19160 FQ	29720 AW	45290 TQ	PABLS	10/01-12/01
	Reading MSA, PA	Y	25270 FQ	39110 AW	53560 TQ	PABLS	10/01-12/01
	Scranton-Wilkes-Barre-Hazleton MSA, PA	Y	19470 FQ	28110 AW	41770 TQ	PABLS	10/01-12/01
	York MSA, PA	Y	23320 FQ	33700 AW	52560 TQ	PABLS	10/01-12/01
	Rhode Island	Y	24990 FQ	35930 AW	48780 TQ	RIBLS	10/01-12/01
	Providence-Fall River-Warwick MSA, RI-MA	Y	24890 FQ	35920 AW	48940 TQ	RIBLS	10/01-12/01
	South Carolina	Y	22780 FQ	31330 AW	42540 TQ	SCBLS	10/01-12/01
	Charleston-North Charleston MSA, SC	Y	23140 FQ	30670 AW	39180 TQ	SCBLS	10/01-12/01
	Columbia MSA, SC	Y	28130 FQ	33740 AW	42000 TQ	SCBLS	10/01-12/01
	Greenville-Spartanburg-Anderson MSA, SC	Y	22810 FQ	28750 AW	41120 TQ	SCBLS	10/01-12/01
	Myrtle Beach MSA, SC	Y	25150 FQ	40560 AW	67810 TQ	SCBLS	10/01-12/01
	South Dakota	Y	18240 FQ	28720 AW	40510 TQ	SDBLS	10/01-12/01
	Sioux Falls MSA, SD	Y	18530 FQ	30400 AW	41710 TQ	SDBLS	10/01-12/01
	Tennessee	Y	22370 FQ	33990 AW	46390 TQ	TNBLS	10/01-12/01
	Chattanooga MSA, TN-GA	Y	22170 FQ	34050 AW	48460 TQ	TNBLS	10/01-12/01
	Clarksville-Hopkinsville MSA, TN-KY	Y	21310 FQ	35370 AW	53380 TQ	TNBLS	10/01-12/01
	Johnson City-Kingsport-Bristol MSA, TN-VA	Y	20400 FQ	29690 AW	45040 TQ	TNBLS	10/01-12/01
	Knoxville MSA, TN	Y	21580 FQ	31180 AW	46620 TQ	TNBLS	10/01-12/01
	Memphis MSA, TN-AR-MS	Y	22640 FQ	34290 AW	50340 TQ	TNBLS	10/01-12/01
	Nashville MSA, TN	Y	30830 FQ	37940 AW	44890 TQ	TNBLS	10/01-12/01
	Texas	Y	23200 FQ	38490 AW	55290 TQ	TXBLS	10/01-12/01
	Amarillo MSA, TX	Y	29380 FQ	37610 AW	54520 TQ	TXBLS	10/01-12/01
	Austin-San Marcos MSA, TX	Y	24300 FQ	36870 AW	53150 TQ	TXBLS	10/01-12/01
	Beaumont-Port Arthur MSA, TX	Y	20460 FQ	35620 AW	52350 TQ	TXBLS	10/01-12/01
	Brazoria PMSA, TX	Y	17280 FQ	32450 AW	51010 TQ	TXBLS	10/01-12/01
	Corpus Christi MSA, TX	Y	28880 FQ	35970 AW	47690 TQ	TXBLS	10/01-12/01
	Dallas PMSA, TX	Y	28410 FQ	44370 AW	59320 TQ	TXBLS	10/01-12/01
	El Paso MSA, TX	Y	23200 FQ	30570 AW	44900 TQ	TXBLS	10/01-12/01
	Fort Worth-Arlington PMSA, TX	Y	29280 FQ	44170 AW	61700 TQ	TXBLS	10/01-12/01
	Galveston-Texas City PMSA, TX	Y	23880 FQ	39870 AW	57840 TQ	TXBLS	10/01-12/01
	Houston PMSA, TX	Y	28810 FQ	42950 AW	56940 TQ	TXBLS	10/01-12/01
	Killeen-Temple MSA, TX	Y	24170 FQ	31590 AW	36620 TQ	TXBLS	10/01-12/01
	Longview-Marshall MSA, TX	Y	15620 FQ	26560 AW	40130 TQ	TXBLS	10/01-12/01
	McAllen-Edinburg-Mission MSA, TX	Y	22510 FQ	29240 AW	38270 TQ	TXBLS	10/01-12/01
	Odessa-Midland MSA, TX	Y	15150 FQ	28270 AW	39010 TQ	TXBLS	10/01-12/01
	San Antonio MSA, TX	Y	18970 FQ	31810 AW	50920 TQ	TXBLS	10/01-12/01
	Tyler MSA, TX	Y	25680 FQ	36570 AW	50110 TQ	TXBLS	10/01-12/01
	Waco MSA, TX	Y	19280 FQ	28350 AW	35370 TQ	TXBLS	10/01-12/01
	Utah	Y	25650 FQ	38360 AW	51980 TQ	UTBLS	10/01-12/01

AAW	Average annual wage	**AOH**	Average offered, high	**ASH**	Average starting, high	**H**	Hourly	**M**	Monthly	**S**	Special: hourly and annual
AE	Average entry wage	**AOL**	Average offered, low	**ASL**	Average starting, low	**HI**	Highest wage paid	**MTC**	Median total compensation	**TQ**	Third quartile wage
AEX	Average experienced wage	**APH**	Average pay, high range	**AW**	Average wage paid	**HR**	High end range	**MW**	Median wage paid	**W**	Weekly
AO	Average offered	**APL**	Average pay, low range	**FQ**	First quartile wage	**LR**	Low end range	**SQ**	Second quartile wage	**Y**	Yearly

Occupation/Type/Industry	Location	Per	Low	Mid	High	Source	Date
Paralegal and Legal Assistant	Provo-Orem MSA, UT	Y	28710 FQ	37710 AW	45770 TQ	UTBLS	10/01-12/01
	Salt Lake City-Ogden MSA, UT	Y	27340 FQ	40660 AW	53750 TQ	UTBLS	10/01-12/01
	Vermont	Y	23270 FQ	34090 AW	47750 TQ	VTBLS	10/01-12/01
	Burlington MSA, VT	Y	26750 FQ	38520 AW	52960 TQ	VTBLS	10/01-12/01
	Virginia	Y	22940 FQ	34860 AW	54140 TQ	VABLS	10/01-12/01
	Lynchburg MSA, VA	Y	23720 FQ	28100 AW	35090 TQ	VABLS	10/01-12/01
	Norfolk-Virginia Beach-Newport News MSA, VA-NC	Y	23040 FQ	31430 AW	42390 TQ	VABLS	10/01-12/01
	Richmond-Petersburg MSA, VA	Y	23350 FQ	31550 AW	44740 TQ	VABLS	10/01-12/01
	Roanoke MSA, VA	Y	21400 FQ	30430 AW	42730 TQ	VABLS	10/01-12/01
	Washington	Y	25310 FQ	41110 AW	62170 TQ	WABLS	10/01-12/01
	Bremerton PMSA, WA	Y	25010 FQ	35220 AW	49290 TQ	WABLS	10/01-12/01
	Olympia PMSA, WA	Y	30070 FQ	38270 AW	45750 TQ	WABLS	10/01-12/01
	Richland-Kennewick-Pasco MSA, WA	Y	30170 FQ	48770 AW	68430 TQ	WABLS	10/01-12/01
	Seattle-Bellevue-Everett PMSA, WA	Y	30470 FQ	46970 AW	67860 TQ	WABLS	10/01-12/01
	Spokane MSA, WA	Y	23100 FQ	28650 AW	41720 TQ	WABLS	10/01-12/01
	Tacoma PMSA, WA	Y	26810 FQ	36780 AW	45610 TQ	WABLS	10/01-12/01
	Yakima MSA, WA	Y	28160 FQ	41680 AW	56430 TQ	WABLS	10/01-12/01
	West Virginia	Y	18180 FQ	26250 AW	35780 TQ	WVBLS	10/01-12/01
	Charleston MSA, WV	Y	19780 FQ	28170 AW	37260 TQ	WVBLS	10/01-12/01
	Huntington-Ashland MSA, WV-KY-OH	Y	17130 FQ	25260 AW	36390 TQ	WVBLS	10/01-12/01
	Wisconsin	Y	23320 FQ	35050 AW	48760 TQ	WIBLS	10/01-12/01
	Appleton-Oshkosh-Neenah MSA, WI	Y	27150 FQ	38800 AW	56210 TQ	WIBLS	10/01-12/01
	Green Bay MSA, WI	Y	24230 FQ	31930 AW	41530 TQ	WIBLS	10/01-12/01
	Madison MSA, WI	Y	21660 FQ	37420 AW	51570 TQ	WIBLS	10/01-12/01
	Milwaukee-Waukesha PMSA, WI	Y	25970 FQ	39680 AW	56190 TQ	WIBLS	10/01-12/01
	Wyoming	Y	20410 FQ	30600 AW	45660 TQ	WYBLS	10/01-12/01
	Puerto Rico	Y	15880 FQ	27260 AW	42010 TQ	PRBLS	10/01-12/01
	Virgin Islands	Y	28480 FQ	38640 AW	54480 TQ	VIBLS	10/01-12/01
Parking Enforcement Worker	Alabama	Y	18710 FQ	24220 AW	30670 TQ	ALBLS	10/01-12/01
	Arizona	Y	23420 FQ	34310 AW	45700 TQ	AZBLS	10/01-12/01
	California	Y	21680 FQ	33260 AW	43360 TQ	CABLS	10/01-12/01
	Colorado	Y	18450 FQ	25300 AW	34900 TQ	COBLS	10/01-12/01
	Connecticut	Y	14700 FQ	25490 AW	41840 TQ	CTBLS	10/01-12/01
	Delaware	Y	17390 FQ	27610 AW	39120 TQ	DEBLS	10/01-12/01
	Florida	Y	15660 FQ	25020 AW	35570 TQ	FLBLS	10/01-12/01
	Georgia	Y	19340 FQ	27190 AW	39050 TQ	GABLS	10/01-12/01
	Illinois	Y	13200 FQ	27830 AW	42660 TQ	ILBLS	10/01-12/01
	Indiana	Y	13280 FQ	20850 AW	29770 TQ	INBLS	10/01-12/01
	Iowa	Y	18960 FQ	27470 AW	34630 TQ	IABLS	10/01-12/01
	Kentucky	Y	14500 FQ	19430 AW	24650 TQ	KYBLS	10/01-12/01
	Louisiana	Y	17020 FQ	26420 AW	38590 TQ	LABLS	10/01-12/01
	Maine	Y	17730 FQ	25750 AW	30250 TQ	MEBLS	10/01-12/01
	Maryland	Y	17540 FQ	22880 AW	27680 TQ	MDBLS	10/01-12/01
	Massachusetts	Y	20170 FQ	30670 AW	42610 TQ	MABLS	10/01-12/01
	Michigan	Y	18480 FQ	25780 AW	34510 TQ	MIBLS	10/01-12/01
	Minnesota	Y	18380 FQ	26230 AW	34700 TQ	MNBLS	10/01-12/01
	Mississippi	Y	12610 FQ	19180 AW	27980 TQ	MSBLS	10/01-12/01
	Missouri	Y	16880 FQ	26750 AW	37470 TQ	MOBLS	10/01-12/01
	New Hampshire	Y	18570 FQ	23530 AW	29680 TQ	NHBLS	10/01-12/01
	New Jersey	Y	19400 FQ	26810 AW	37200 TQ	NJBLS	10/01-12/01
	New Mexico	Y	15660 FQ	17930 AW	22010 TQ	NMBLS	10/01-12/01
	New York	Y	19640 FQ	27970 AW	37850 TQ	NYBLS	10/01-12/01
	North Carolina	Y	16020 FQ	21020 AW	27000 TQ	NCBLS	10/01-12/01
	Ohio	Y	15020 FQ	24390 AW	35440 TQ	OHBLS	10/01-12/01
	Oklahoma	Y	14220 FQ	26010 AW	35500 TQ	OKBLS	10/01-12/01
	Oregon	Y	17120 FQ	28880 AW	40900 TQ	ORBLS	10/01-12/01
	Pennsylvania	Y	15870 FQ	25130 AW	36030 TQ	PABLS	10/01-12/01
	South Carolina	Y	13060 FQ	19820 AW	23880 TQ	SCBLS	10/01-12/01
	Tennessee	Y	15710 FQ	25920 AW	35990 TQ	TNBLS	10/01-12/01
	Texas	Y	14780 FQ	21530 AW	28280 TQ	TXBLS	10/01-12/01
	Virginia	Y	16900 FQ	26610 AW	36590 TQ	VABLS	10/01-12/01
	Washington	Y	19790 FQ	33270 AW	45470 TQ	WABLS	10/01-12/01
	West Virginia	Y	12260 FQ	16440 AW	22420 TQ	WVBLS	10/01-12/01

AAW	Average annual wage	**AOH**	Average offered, high	**ASH**	Average starting, high	**H**	Hourly	**M**	Monthly	**S**	Special: hourly and annual
AE	Average entry wage	**AOL**	Average offered, low	**ASL**	Average starting, low	**HI**	Highest wage paid	**MTC**	Median total compensation	**TQ**	Third quartile wage
AEX	Average experienced wage	**APH**	Average pay, high range	**AW**	Average wage paid	**HR**	High end range	**MW**	Median wage paid	**W**	Weekly
AO	Average offered	**APL**	Average pay, low range	**FQ**	First quartile wage	**LR**	Low end range	**SQ**	Second quartile wage	**Y**	Yearly

Occupation/Type/Industry	Location	Per	Low	Mid	High	Source	Date
Parking Enforcement Worker	Wisconsin	Y	15910 FQ	27700 AW	37120 TQ	WIBLS	10/01-12/01
Parking Lot Attendant	Alabama	H	5.64 FQ	7.18 AW	9.88 TQ	ALBLS	10/01-12/01
	Mobile MSA, AL	H	5.61 FQ	6.33 AW	7.47 TQ	ALBLS	10/01-12/01
	Alaska	H	7.01 FQ	9.00 AW	11.43 TQ	AKBLS	10/01-12/01
	Anchorage MSA, AK	H	7.26 FQ	8.95 AW	11.32 TQ	AKBLS	10/01-12/01
	Arizona	H	6.04 FQ	8.82 AW	13.15 TQ	AZBLS	10/01-12/01
	Phoenix-Mesa MSA, AZ	H	6.32 FQ	9.12 AW	13.33 TQ	AZBLS	10/01-12/01
	Tucson MSA, AZ	H	5.64 FQ	7.36 AW	10.75 TQ	AZBLS	10/01-12/01
	Arkansas	H	5.59 FQ	6.68 AW	8.81 TQ	ARBLS	10/01-12/01
	Little Rock-North Little Rock MSA, AR	H	5.65 FQ	6.59 AW	8.36 TQ	ARBLS	10/01-12/01
	California	H	6.47 FQ	8.00 AW	10.30 TQ	CABLS	10/01-12/01
	Fresno MSA, CA	H	6.46 FQ	7.39 AW	8.50 TQ	CABLS	10/01-12/01
	Los Angeles-Long Beach PMSA, CA	H	6.45 FQ	7.51 AW	8.80 TQ	CABLS	10/01-12/01
	Oakland PMSA, CA	H	6.42 FQ	8.10 AW	10.46 TQ	CABLS	10/01-12/01
	Orange County PMSA, CA	H	6.63 FQ	8.10 AW	9.64 TQ	CABLS	10/01-12/01
	Riverside-San Bernardino PMSA, CA	H	6.45 FQ	7.73 AW	9.13 TQ	CABLS	10/01-12/01
	Sacramento PMSA, CA	H	6.47 FQ	7.85 AW	9.86 TQ	CABLS	10/01-12/01
	Salinas MSA, CA	H	6.72 FQ	8.31 AW	10.41 TQ	CABLS	10/01-12/01
	San Diego MSA, CA	H	6.45 FQ	8.08 AW	10.30 TQ	CABLS	10/01-12/01
	San Francisco PMSA, CA	H	6.57 FQ	9.69 AW	14.14 TQ	CABLS	10/01-12/01
	San Jose PMSA, CA	H	6.72 FQ	8.15 AW	10.30 TQ	CABLS	10/01-12/01
	Santa Barbara-Santa Maria-Lompoc MSA, CA	H	6.55 FQ	7.58 AW	8.72 TQ	CABLS	10/01-12/01
	Santa Cruz-Watsonville PMSA, CA	H	6.36 FQ	7.02 AW	8.17 TQ	CABLS	10/01-12/01
	Santa Rosa PMSA, CA	H	6.84 FQ	9.77 AW	13.80 TQ	CABLS	10/01-12/01
	Vallejo-Fairfield-Napa PMSA, CA	H	6.46 FQ	7.82 AW	9.41 TQ	CABLS	10/01-12/01
	Ventura PMSA, CA	H	6.36 FQ	7.32 AW	8.47 TQ	CABLS	10/01-12/01
	Colorado	H	5.67 FQ	7.81 AW	10.89 TQ	COBLS	10/01-12/01
	Boulder-Longmont PMSA, CO	H	7.84 FQ	9.78 AW	12.34 TQ	COBLS	10/01-12/01
	Colorado Springs MSA, CO	H	6.11 FQ	7.63 AW	9.02 TQ	COBLS	10/01-12/01
	Denver PMSA, CO	H	5.61 FQ	7.62 AW	10.77 TQ	COBLS	10/01-12/01
	Connecticut	H	6.60 FQ	8.40 AW	10.71 TQ	CTBLS	10/01-12/01
	Bridgeport PMSA, CT	H	6.83 FQ	9.69 AW	13.46 TQ	CTBLS	10/01-12/01
	Hartford MSA, CT	H	6.90 FQ	8.36 AW	10.54 TQ	CTBLS	10/01-12/01
	New Haven-Meriden PMSA, CT	H	6.60 FQ	8.93 AW	11.77 TQ	CTBLS	10/01-12/01
	Stamford-Norwalk PMSA, CT	H	6.55 FQ	8.66 AW	10.89 TQ	CTBLS	10/01-12/01
	Delaware	H	6.62 FQ	8.23 AW	9.93 TQ	DEBLS	10/01-12/01
	Wilmington-Newark PMSA, DE-MD	H	6.60 FQ	8.31 AW	10.49 TQ	DEBLS	10/01-12/01
	District of Columbia	H	6.75 FQ	8.16 AW	10.45 TQ	DCBLS	10/01-12/01
	Washington PMSA, DC-MD-VA-WV	H	6.38 FQ	8.02 AW	10.42 TQ	DCBLS	10/01-12/01
	Florida	H	5.67 FQ	7.09 AW	9.30 TQ	FLBLS	10/01-12/01
	Daytona Beach MSA, FL	H	5.61 FQ	7.01 AW	9.08 TQ	FLBLS	10/01-12/01
	Fort Lauderdale PMSA, FL	H	5.70 FQ	6.76 AW	8.49 TQ	FLBLS	10/01-12/01
	Fort Myers-Cape Coral MSA, FL	H	5.42 FQ	7.76 AW	11.26 TQ	FLBLS	10/01-12/01
	Gainesville MSA, FL	H	5.51 FQ	6.93 AW	8.63 TQ	FLBLS	10/01-12/01
	Jacksonville MSA, FL	H	5.56 FQ	7.26 AW	10.23 TQ	FLBLS	10/01-12/01
	Lakeland-Winter Haven MSA, FL	H	5.68 FQ	7.02 AW	8.56 TQ	FLBLS	10/01-12/01
	Melbourne-Titusville-Palm Bay MSA, FL	H	5.95 FQ	7.17 AW	8.27 TQ	FLBLS	10/01-12/01
	Miami PMSA, FL	H	5.61 FQ	7.25 AW	10.13 TQ	FLBLS	10/01-12/01
	Naples MSA, FL	H	5.82 FQ	7.38 AW	8.86 TQ	FLBLS	10/01-12/01
	Orlando MSA, FL	H	5.70 FQ	7.17 AW	9.84 TQ	FLBLS	10/01-12/01
	Pensacola MSA, FL	H	5.68 FQ	6.73 AW	8.25 TQ	FLBLS	10/01-12/01
	Sarasota-Bradenton MSA, FL	H	6.95 FQ	7.87 AW	8.97 TQ	FLBLS	10/01-12/01
	Tallahassee MSA, FL	H	5.56 FQ	6.69 AW	8.14 TQ	FLBLS	10/01-12/01
	Tampa-St. Petersburg-Clearwater MSA, FL	H	5.64 FQ	7.19 AW	9.65 TQ	FLBLS	10/01-12/01
	West Palm Beach-Boca Raton MSA, FL	H	5.72 FQ	7.19 AW	9.86 TQ	FLBLS	10/01-12/01
	Georgia	H	5.71 FQ	7.39 AW	10.35 TQ	GABLS	10/01-12/01
	Atlanta MSA, GA	H	5.73 FQ	7.42 AW	10.42 TQ	GABLS	10/01-12/01
	Augusta-Aiken MSA, GA-SC	H	5.74 FQ	6.71 AW	8.40 TQ	GABLS	10/01-12/01

AAW	Average annual wage	**AOH**	Average offered, high	**ASH**	Average starting, high	**H**	Hourly	**M**	Monthly	**S**	Special: hourly and annual
AE	Average entry wage	**AOL**	Average offered, low	**ASL**	Average starting, low	**HI**	Highest wage paid	**MTC**	Median total compensation	**TQ**	Third quartile wage
AEX	Average experienced wage	**APH**	Average pay, high range	**AW**	Average wage paid	**HR**	High end range	**MW**	Median wage paid	**W**	Weekly
AO	Average offered	**APL**	Average pay, low range	**FQ**	First quartile wage	**LR**	Low end range	**SQ**	Second quartile wage	**Y**	Yearly

Occupation/Type/Industry	Location	Per	Low	Mid	High	Source	Date
Parking Lot Attendant	Savannah MSA, GA	H	5.85 FQ	8.37 AW	11.77 TQ	GABLS	10/01-12/01
	Hawaii	H	5.85 FQ	7.53 AW	9.88 TQ	HIBLS	10/01-12/01
	Honolulu MSA, HI	H	5.87 FQ	7.47 AW	9.71 TQ	HIBLS	10/01-12/01
	Idaho	H	5.78 FQ	7.30 AW	9.62 TQ	IDBLS	10/01-12/01
	Boise City MSA, ID	H	5.90 FQ	7.73 AW	10.22 TQ	IDBLS	10/01-12/01
	Illinois	H	5.83 FQ	8.41 AW	12.64 TQ	ILBLS	10/01-12/01
	Chicago PMSA, IL	H	5.90 FQ	8.56 AW	12.88 TQ	ILBLS	10/01-12/01
	Rockford MSA, IL	H	6.81 FQ	8.36 AW	12.09 TQ	ILBLS	10/01-12/01
	Indiana	H	5.99 FQ	8.43 AW	11.61 TQ	INBLS	10/01-12/01
	Fort Wayne MSA, IN	H	6.05 FQ	8.75 AW	11.71 TQ	INBLS	10/01-12/01
	Gary PMSA, IN	H	5.82 FQ	8.22 AW	12.23 TQ	INBLS	10/01-12/01
	Indianapolis MSA, IN	H	6.38 FQ	8.58 AW	11.39 TQ	INBLS	10/01-12/01
	South Bend MSA, IN	H	5.89 FQ	8.41 AW	12.82 TQ	INBLS	10/01-12/01
	Iowa	H	5.59 FQ	7.16 AW	8.98 TQ	IABLS	10/01-12/01
	Cedar Rapids MSA, IA	H	6.92 FQ	8.18 AW	9.54 TQ	IABLS	10/01-12/01
	Davenport-Moline-Rock Island MSA, IA-IL	H	5.58 FQ	6.96 AW	8.57 TQ	IABLS	10/01-12/01
	Des Moines MSA, IA	H	5.56 FQ	7.10 AW	8.69 TQ	IABLS	10/01-12/01
	Kansas	H	5.87 FQ	8.08 AW	12.17 TQ	KSBLS	10/01-12/01
	Wichita MSA, KS	H	5.89 FQ	8.23 AW	12.63 TQ	KSBLS	10/01-12/01
	Kentucky	H	5.74 FQ	8.12 AW	11.47 TQ	KYBLS	10/01-12/01
	Lexington MSA, KY	H	5.74 FQ	6.63 AW	7.85 TQ	KYBLS	10/01-12/01
	Louisiana	H	5.68 FQ	7.22 AW	9.95 TQ	LABLS	10/01-12/01
	Baton Rouge MSA, LA	H	5.73 FQ	7.69 AW	11.54 TQ	LABLS	10/01-12/01
	New Orleans MSA, LA	H	5.72 FQ	7.29 AW	9.86 TQ	LABLS	10/01-12/01
	Shreveport-Bossier City MSA, LA	H	5.63 FQ	7.08 AW	10.28 TQ	LABLS	10/01-12/01
	Maine	H	5.54 FQ	7.47 AW	10.64 TQ	MEBLS	10/01-12/01
	Portland MSA, ME	H	5.72 FQ	8.05 AW	11.43 TQ	MEBLS	10/01-12/01
	Maryland	H	5.81 FQ	7.71 AW	10.13 TQ	MDBLS	10/01-12/01
	Baltimore PMSA, MD	H	5.73 FQ	7.51 AW	9.39 TQ	MDBLS	10/01-12/01
	Massachusetts	H	6.92 FQ	8.82 AW	11.35 TQ	MABLS	10/01-12/01
	Boston PMSA, MA-NH	H	6.92 FQ	8.86 AW	11.32 TQ	MABLS	10/01-12/01
	Springfield MSA, MA	H	6.79 FQ	7.23 AW	8.22 TQ	MABLS	10/01-12/01
	Worcester PMSA, MA-CT	H	7.33 FQ	9.57 AW	12.78 TQ	MABLS	10/01-12/01
	Michigan	H	5.89 FQ	7.55 AW	9.68 TQ	MIBLS	10/01-12/01
	Detroit PMSA, MI	H	5.87 FQ	7.45 AW	9.40 TQ	MIBLS	10/01-12/01
	Grand Rapids-Muskegon-Holland MSA, MI	H	6.10 FQ	8.14 AW	11.38 TQ	MIBLS	10/01-12/01
	Kalamazoo-Battle Creek MSA, MI	H	6.84 FQ	7.78 AW	9.31 TQ	MIBLS	10/01-12/01
	Saginaw-Bay City-Midland MSA, MI	H	5.86 FQ	7.91 AW	11.04 TQ	MIBLS	10/01-12/01
	Minnesota	H	6.51 FQ	8.75 AW	11.15 TQ	MNBLS	10/01-12/01
	Minneapolis-St. Paul MSA, MN-WI	H	6.46 FQ	8.67 AW	10.95 TQ	MNBLS	10/01-12/01
	Mississippi	H	5.65 FQ	6.96 AW	8.46 TQ	MSBLS	10/01-12/01
	Biloxi-Gulfport-Pascagoula MSA, MS	H	5.67 FQ	6.77 AW	8.31 TQ	MSBLS	10/01-12/01
	Missouri	H	5.78 FQ	7.63 AW	9.43 TQ	MOBLS	10/01-12/01
	Kansas City MSA, MO-KS	H	5.65 FQ	7.03 AW	8.90 TQ	MOBLS	10/01-12/01
	St. Louis MSA, MO-IL	H	5.87 FQ	7.99 AW	10.35 TQ	MOBLS	10/01-12/01
	Montana	H	5.64 FQ	7.29 AW	9.48 TQ	MTBLS	10/01-12/01
	Billings MSA, MT	H	5.52 FQ	6.98 AW	9.78 TQ	MTBLS	10/01-12/01
	Nebraska	H	5.62 FQ	7.67 AW	10.84 TQ	NEBLS	10/01-12/01
	Lincoln MSA, NE	H	5.54 FQ	6.64 AW	8.68 TQ	NEBLS	10/01-12/01
	Omaha MSA, NE-IA	H	5.65 FQ	7.50 AW	10.44 TQ	NEBLS	10/01-12/01
	Nevada	H	5.76 FQ	7.76 AW	10.43 TQ	NVBLS	10/01-12/01
	Las Vegas MSA, NV-AZ	H	5.92 FQ	8.04 AW	10.66 TQ	NVBLS	10/01-12/01
	Reno MSA, NV	H	5.57 FQ	6.95 AW	8.89 TQ	NVBLS	10/01-12/01
	New Hampshire	H	5.80 FQ	8.10 AW	11.29 TQ	NHBLS	10/01-12/01
	Portsmouth-Rochester PMSA, NH-ME	H	5.66 FQ	7.23 AW	8.72 TQ	NHBLS	10/01-12/01
	New Jersey	H	5.72 FQ	7.50 AW	10.18 TQ	NJBLS	10/01-12/01
	Atlantic-Cape May PMSA, NJ	H	5.62 FQ	7.04 AW	9.38 TQ	NJBLS	10/01-12/01
	Bergen-Passaic PMSA, NJ	H	5.86 FQ	9.19 AW	15.63 TQ	NJBLS	10/01-12/01
	Jersey City PMSA, NJ	H	5.95 FQ	8.76 AW	12.61 TQ	NJBLS	10/01-12/01
	Middlesex-Somerset-Hunterdon PMSA, NJ	H	6.51 FQ	8.35 AW	11.18 TQ	NJBLS	10/01-12/01
	Monmouth-Ocean PMSA, NJ	H	6.16 FQ	8.45 AW	11.08 TQ	NJBLS	10/01-12/01
	Newark PMSA, NJ	H	5.72 FQ	7.14 AW	9.41 TQ	NJBLS	10/01-12/01
	Trenton PMSA, NJ	H	6.56 FQ	8.26 AW	10.80 TQ	NJBLS	10/01-12/01

AAW	Average annual wage	AOH	Average offered, high	ASH	Average starting, high	H	Hourly	M	Monthly	S	Special: hourly and annual
AE	Average entry wage	AOL	Average offered, low	ASL	Average starting, low	HI	Highest wage paid	MTC	Median total compensation	TQ	Third quartile wage
AEX	Average experienced wage	APH	Average pay, high range	AW	Average wage paid	HR	High end range	MW	Median wage paid	W	Weekly
AO	Average offered	APL	Average pay, low range	FQ	First quartile wage	LR	Low end range	SQ	Second quartile wage	Y	Yearly

Occupation/Type/Industry	Location	Per	Low	Mid	High	Source	Date
Parking Lot Attendant	New Mexico	H	5.83 FQ	7.62 AW	10.04 TQ	NMBLS	10/01-12/01
	Albuquerque MSA, NM	H	6.10 FQ	7.82 AW	9.08 TQ	NMBLS	10/01-12/01
	New York	H	6.34 FQ	8.95 AW	12.29 TQ	NYBLS	10/01-12/01
	Albany-Schenectady-Troy MSA, NY	H	6.36 FQ	10.00 AW	12.91 TQ	NYBLS	10/01-12/01
	Binghamton MSA, NY	H	5.82 FQ	8.41 AW	12.94 TQ	NYBLS	10/01-12/01
	Buffalo-Niagara Falls MSA, NY	H	5.55 FQ	7.21 AW	11.25 TQ	NYBLS	10/01-12/01
	Nassau-Suffolk PMSA, NY	H	6.79 FQ	8.79 AW	12.36 TQ	NYBLS	10/01-12/01
	New York PMSA, NY	H	6.58 FQ	9.04 AW	12.24 TQ	NYBLS	10/01-12/01
	Newburgh PMSA, NY-PA	H	5.61 FQ	8.84 AW	13.53 TQ	NYBLS	10/01-12/01
	Rochester MSA, NY	H	5.78 FQ	8.89 AW	14.28 TQ	NYBLS	10/01-12/01
	Utica-Rome MSA, NY	H	5.75 FQ	8.05 AW	10.68 TQ	NYBLS	10/01-12/01
	North Carolina	H	6.15 FQ	8.36 AW	10.81 TQ	NCBLS	10/01-12/01
	Charlotte-Gastonia-Rock Hill MSA, NC-SC	H	5.81 FQ	7.87 AW	10.52 TQ	NCBLS	10/01-12/01
	Greensboro-Winston-Salem-High Point MSA, NC	H	6.22 FQ	9.12 AW	13.72 TQ	NCBLS	10/01-12/01
	Raleigh-Durham-Chapel Hill MSA, NC	H	7.13 FQ	8.82 AW	10.78 TQ	NCBLS	10/01-12/01
	North Dakota	H	5.87 FQ	7.13 AW	8.41 TQ	NDBLS	10/01-12/01
	Fargo-Moorhead MSA, ND-MN	H	5.85 FQ	7.08 AW	8.51 TQ	NDBLS	10/01-12/01
	Ohio	H	5.75 FQ	7.66 AW	10.18 TQ	OHBLS	10/01-12/01
	Akron PMSA, OH	H	5.48 FQ	7.21 AW	10.24 TQ	OHBLS	10/01-12/01
	Canton-Massillon MSA, OH	H	5.58 FQ	6.63 AW	8.19 TQ	OHBLS	10/01-12/01
	Cincinnati PMSA, OH-KY-IN	H	5.82 FQ	8.10 AW	10.64 TQ	OHBLS	10/01-12/01
	Cleveland-Lorain-Elyria PMSA, OH	H	5.74 FQ	7.49 AW	9.30 TQ	OHBLS	10/01-12/01
	Dayton-Springfield MSA, OH	H	5.58 FQ	7.27 AW	9.40 TQ	OHBLS	10/01-12/01
	Toledo MSA, OH	H	5.71 FQ	7.27 AW	8.79 TQ	OHBLS	10/01-12/01
	Oklahoma	H	5.50 FQ	6.72 AW	8.62 TQ	OKBLS	10/01-12/01
	Oklahoma City MSA, OK	H	5.57 FQ	6.79 AW	8.65 TQ	OKBLS	10/01-12/01
	Tulsa MSA, OK	H	5.42 FQ	6.52 AW	8.46 TQ	OKBLS	10/01-12/01
	Oregon	H	7.09 FQ	9.12 AW	10.98 TQ	ORBLS	10/01-12/01
	Portland-Vancouver PMSA, OR-WA	H	7.14 FQ	9.18 AW	10.97 TQ	ORBLS	10/01-12/01
	Pennsylvania	H	5.77 FQ	7.73 AW	11.50 TQ	PABLS	10/01-12/01
	Allentown-Bethlehem-Easton MSA, PA	H	5.52 FQ	7.26 AW	11.01 TQ	PABLS	10/01-12/01
	Erie MSA, PA	H	5.75 FQ	7.58 AW	12.84 TQ	PABLS	10/01-12/01
	Harrisburg-Lebanon-Carlisle MSA, PA	H	5.83 FQ	7.98 AW	10.90 TQ	PABLS	10/01-12/01
	Lancaster MSA, PA	H	5.69 FQ	7.15 AW	8.64 TQ	PABLS	10/01-12/01
	Philadelphia PMSA, PA-NJ	H	5.77 FQ	7.35 AW	9.70 TQ	PABLS	10/01-12/01
	Pittsburgh MSA, PA	H	5.87 FQ	9.00 AW	13.35 TQ	PABLS	10/01-12/01
	Reading MSA, PA	H	5.74 FQ	8.13 AW	10.44 TQ	PABLS	10/01-12/01
	York MSA, PA	H	5.70 FQ	6.20 AW	7.11 TQ	PABLS	10/01-12/01
	Rhode Island	H	6.67 FQ	8.93 AW	12.57 TQ	RIBLS	10/01-12/01
	Providence-Fall River-Warwick MSA, RI-MA	H	6.75 FQ	9.10 AW	12.74 TQ	RIBLS	10/01-12/01
	South Carolina	H	5.67 FQ	8.34 AW	14.05 TQ	SCBLS	10/01-12/01
	Charleston-North Charleston MSA, SC	H	5.51 FQ	7.19 AW	9.66 TQ	SCBLS	10/01-12/01
	Greenville-Spartanburg-Anderson MSA, SC	H	5.91 FQ	7.96 AW	9.92 TQ	SCBLS	10/01-12/01
	South Dakota	H	7.06 FQ	8.41 AW	10.62 TQ	SDBLS	10/01-12/01
	Sioux Falls MSA, SD	H	6.82 FQ	8.83 AW	11.50 TQ	SDBLS	10/01-12/01
	Tennessee	H	5.63 FQ	7.08 AW	8.73 TQ	TNBLS	10/01-12/01
	Knoxville MSA, TN	H	5.61 FQ	6.81 AW	8.52 TQ	TNBLS	10/01-12/01
	Memphis MSA, TN-AR-MS	H	5.54 FQ	6.75 AW	8.55 TQ	TNBLS	10/01-12/01
	Nashville MSA, TN	H	6.49 FQ	8.15 AW	10.20 TQ	TNBLS	10/01-12/01
	Texas	H	5.78 FQ	7.52 AW	10.05 TQ	TXBLS	10/01-12/01
	Amarillo MSA, TX	H	5.70 FQ	7.21 AW	8.76 TQ	TXBLS	10/01-12/01
	Austin-San Marcos MSA, TX	H	5.74 FQ	6.97 AW	9.51 TQ	TXBLS	10/01-12/01
	Dallas PMSA, TX	H	5.82 FQ	7.83 AW	10.36 TQ	TXBLS	10/01-12/01
	El Paso MSA, TX	H	5.48 FQ	6.58 AW	8.38 TQ	TXBLS	10/01-12/01
	Fort Worth-Arlington PMSA, TX	H	5.70 FQ	6.93 AW	8.36 TQ	TXBLS	10/01-12/01
	Houston PMSA, TX	H	5.76 FQ	7.38 AW	9.64 TQ	TXBLS	10/01-12/01
	McAllen-Edinburg-Mission MSA, TX	H	5.81 FQ	7.41 AW	8.66 TQ	TXBLS	10/01-12/01

AAW	Average annual wage	AOH	Average offered, high	ASH	Average starting, high	H	Hourly	M	Monthly	S	Special: hourly and annual
AE	Average entry wage	AOL	Average offered, low	ASL	Average starting, low	HI	Highest wage paid	MTC	Median total compensation	TQ	Third quartile wage
AEX	Average experienced wage	APH	Average pay, high range	AW	Average wage paid	HR	High end range	MW	Median wage paid	W	Weekly
AO	Average offered	APL	Average pay, low range	FQ	First quartile wage	LR	Low end range	SQ	Second quartile wage	Y	Yearly

Occupation/Type/Industry	Location	Per	Low	Mid	High	Source	Date
Parking Lot Attendant	San Antonio MSA, TX	H	5.98 FQ	7.48 AW	8.71 TQ	TXBLS	10/01-12/01
	Utah	H	5.67 FQ	7.14 AW	8.86 TQ	UTBLS	10/01-12/01
	Salt Lake City-Ogden MSA, UT	H	5.70 FQ	7.18 AW	8.96 TQ	UTBLS	10/01-12/01
	Vermont	H	6.90 FQ	8.91 AW	11.08 TQ	VTBLS	10/01-12/01
	Virginia	H	5.79 FQ	7.39 AW	9.38 TQ	VABLS	10/01-12/01
	Norfolk-Virginia Beach-Newport News MSA, VA-NC	H	5.83 FQ	7.40 AW	8.89 TQ	VABLS	10/01-12/01
	Richmond-Petersburg MSA, VA	H	5.73 FQ	6.79 AW	8.40 TQ	VABLS	10/01-12/01
	Roanoke MSA, VA	H	6.30 FQ	7.49 AW	8.48 TQ	VABLS	10/01-12/01
	Washington	H	6.97 FQ	9.60 AW	12.95 TQ	WABLS	10/01-12/01
	Seattle-Bellevue-Everett PMSA, WA	H	7.12 FQ	9.90 AW	13.16 TQ	WABLS	10/01-12/01
	Spokane MSA, WA	H	6.95 FQ	7.80 AW	8.84 TQ	WABLS	10/01-12/01
	Tacoma PMSA, WA	H	6.81 FQ	8.04 AW	10.21 TQ	WABLS	10/01-12/01
	West Virginia	H	5.70 FQ	7.60 AW	10.19 TQ	WVBLS	10/01-12/01
	Charleston MSA, WV	H	5.79 FQ	7.17 AW	8.38 TQ	WVBLS	10/01-12/01
	Wisconsin	H	6.88 FQ	8.92 AW	12.19 TQ	WIBLS	10/01-12/01
	Milwaukee-Waukesha PMSA, WI	H	6.83 FQ	9.47 AW	15.01 TQ	WIBLS	10/01-12/01
	Wyoming	H	5.73 FQ	7.10 AW	8.66 TQ	WYBLS	10/01-12/01
	Puerto Rico	H	5.49 FQ	6.22 AW	6.98 TQ	PRBLS	10/01-12/01
	Guam	H	5.52 FQ	6.35 AW	7.62 TQ	GUBLS	10/01-12/01
Parts Salesperson	Alabama	Y	13650 FQ	25720 AW	41810 TQ	ALBLS	10/01-12/01
	Alaska	Y	19880 FQ	30070 AW	43390 TQ	AKBLS	10/01-12/01
	Arizona	Y	15750 FQ	28440 AW	44930 TQ	AZBLS	10/01-12/01
	Arkansas	Y	14080 FQ	22020 AW	33350 TQ	ARBLS	10/01-12/01
	California	Y	14980 FQ	29610 AW	46500 TQ	CABLS	10/01-12/01
	Colorado	Y	16840 FQ	30560 AW	52000 TQ	COBLS	10/01-12/01
	Connecticut	Y	16370 FQ	28330 AW	42910 TQ	CTBLS	10/01-12/01
	Delaware	Y	17260 FQ	28250 AW	42990 TQ	DEBLS	10/01-12/01
	District of Columbia	Y	14870 FQ	20530 AW	30560 TQ	DCBLS	10/01-12/01
	Florida	Y	14170 FQ	27020 AW	43000 TQ	FLBLS	10/01-12/01
	Georgia	Y	15020 FQ	26970 AW	42790 TQ	GABLS	10/01-12/01
	Hawaii	Y	15610 FQ	27030 AW	42180 TQ	HIBLS	10/01-12/01
	Idaho	Y	13840 FQ	23560 AW	35280 TQ	IDBLS	10/01-12/01
	Illinois	Y	14540 FQ	24940 AW	37970 TQ	ILBLS	10/01-12/01
	Indiana	Y	13700 FQ	24470 AW	36160 TQ	INBLS	10/01-12/01
	Iowa	Y	15150 FQ	26100 AW	37800 TQ	IABLS	10/01-12/01
	Kansas	Y	14370 FQ	22910 AW	33820 TQ	KSBLS	10/01-12/01
	Kentucky	Y	13670 FQ	22530 AW	34200 TQ	KYBLS	10/01-12/01
	Louisiana	Y	12790 FQ	22320 AW	35170 TQ	LABLS	10/01-12/01
	Maine	Y	14960 FQ	23080 AW	33800 TQ	MEBLS	10/01-12/01
	Maryland	Y	16000 FQ	28910 AW	47040 TQ	MDBLS	10/01-12/01
	Massachusetts	Y	17690 FQ	30860 AW	52810 TQ	MABLS	10/01-12/01
	Michigan	Y	15550 FQ	27160 AW	42930 TQ	MIBLS	10/01-12/01
	Minnesota	Y	16210 FQ	27390 AW	40610 TQ	MNBLS	10/01-12/01
	Mississippi	Y	14350 FQ	23840 AW	36600 TQ	MSBLS	10/01-12/01
	Missouri	Y	14460 FQ	25580 AW	40440 TQ	MOBLS	10/01-12/01
	Montana	Y	15410 FQ	24420 AW	35900 TQ	MTBLS	10/01-12/01
	Nebraska	Y	14640 FQ	24240 AW	36580 TQ	NEBLS	10/01-12/01
	Nevada	Y	16860 FQ	28210 AW	42710 TQ	NVBLS	10/01-12/01
	New Hampshire	Y	16460 FQ	27210 AW	42510 TQ	NHBLS	10/01-12/01
	New Jersey	Y	15410 FQ	30280 AW	46690 TQ	NJBLS	10/01-12/01
	New Mexico	Y	13370 FQ	22980 AW	35670 TQ	NMBLS	10/01-12/01
	New York	Y	13750 FQ	25900 AW	43170 TQ	NYBLS	10/01-12/01
	North Carolina	Y	14690 FQ	24400 AW	37380 TQ	NCBLS	10/01-12/01
	North Dakota	Y	15850 FQ	24310 AW	35290 TQ	NDBLS	10/01-12/01
	Ohio	Y	14630 FQ	24660 AW	37440 TQ	OHBLS	10/01-12/01
	Oklahoma	Y	12730 FQ	21740 AW	34180 TQ	OKBLS	10/01-12/01
	Oregon	Y	16950 FQ	28400 AW	42520 TQ	ORBLS	10/01-12/01
	Pennsylvania	Y	15040 FQ	24410 AW	36540 TQ	PABLS	10/01-12/01
	Rhode Island	Y	17010 FQ	28830 AW	42230 TQ	RIBLS	10/01-12/01
	South Carolina	Y	13550 FQ	23390 AW	34690 TQ	SCBLS	10/01-12/01
	South Dakota	Y	15860 FQ	22630 AW	31030 TQ	SDBLS	10/01-12/01
	Tennessee	Y	14500 FQ	23560 AW	36250 TQ	TNBLS	10/01-12/01
	Texas	Y	13470 FQ	23920 AW	41650 TQ	TXBLS	10/01-12/01
	Utah	Y	16860 FQ	26800 AW	39940 TQ	UTBLS	10/01-12/01
	Vermont	Y	15320 FQ	23500 AW	33550 TQ	VTBLS	10/01-12/01
	Virginia	Y	13750 FQ	24290 AW	38560 TQ	VABLS	10/01-12/01

AAW	Average annual wage	**AOH**	Average offered, high	**ASH**	Average starting, high	**H**	Hourly	**M**	Monthly	**S**	Special: hourly and annual
AE	Average entry wage	**AOL**	Average offered, low	**ASL**	Average starting, low	**HI**	Highest wage paid	**MTC**	Median total compensation	**TQ**	Third quartile wage
AEX	Average experienced wage	**APH**	Average pay, high range	**AW**	Average wage paid	**HR**	High end range	**MW**	Median wage paid	**W**	Weekly
AO	Average offered	**APL**	Average pay, low range	**FQ**	First quartile wage	**LR**	Low end range	**SQ**	Second quartile wage	**Y**	Yearly

Occupation/Type/Industry	Location	Per	Low	Mid	High	Source	Date
Parts Salesperson	Washington	Y	17850 FQ	29520 AW	43550 TQ	WABLS	10/01-12/01
	West Virginia	Y	11960 FQ	18550 AW	27830 TQ	WVBLS	10/01-12/01
	Wisconsin	Y	15780 FQ	27390 AW	40210 TQ	WIBLS	10/01-12/01
	Wyoming	Y	14600 FQ	21330 AW	31300 TQ	WYBLS	10/01-12/01
	Puerto Rico	Y	11560 FQ	15230 AW	21840 TQ	PRBLS	10/01-12/01
	Virgin Islands	Y	13180 FQ	17390 AW	22140 TQ	VIBLS	10/01-12/01
	Guam	Y	12070 FQ	18430 AW	27360 TQ	GUBLS	10/01-12/01
Patternmaker							
Metals and Plastics	Alabama	H	9.69 FQ	15.44 AW	20.61 TQ	ALBLS	10/01-12/01
Metals and Plastics	Arizona	H	12.23 FQ	15.38 AW	17.97 TQ	AZBLS	10/01-12/01
Metals and Plastics	Arkansas	H	7.97 FQ	14.02 AW	17.91 TQ	ARBLS	10/01-12/01
Metals and Plastics	California	H	7.33 FQ	14.69 AW	22.67 TQ	CABLS	10/01-12/01
Metals and Plastics	Connecticut	H	14.76 FQ	17.80 AW	25.22 TQ	CTBLS	10/01-12/01
Metals and Plastics	Florida	H	7.33 FQ	10.54 AW	16.92 TQ	FLBLS	10/01-12/01
Metals and Plastics	Georgia	H	10.35 FQ	15.19 AW	17.63 TQ	GABLS	10/01-12/01
Metals and Plastics	Illinois	H	9.91 FQ	17.42 AW	27.43 TQ	ILBLS	10/01-12/01
Metals and Plastics	Indiana	H	7.92 FQ	15.87 AW	23.91 TQ	INBLS	10/01-12/01
Metals and Plastics	Iowa	H	10.75 FQ	18.60 AW	26.04 TQ	IABLS	10/01-12/01
Metals and Plastics	Kansas	H	14.67 FQ	20.08 AW	25.37 TQ	KSBLS	10/01-12/01
Metals and Plastics	Kentucky	H	7.67 FQ	13.55 AW	21.10 TQ	KYBLS	10/01-12/01
Metals and Plastics	Louisiana	H	6.62 FQ	14.63 AW	21.64 TQ	LABLS	10/01-12/01
Metals and Plastics	Maryland	H	11.78 FQ	16.67 AW	21.26 TQ	MDBLS	10/01-12/01
Metals and Plastics	Massachusetts	H	13.52 FQ	19.31 AW	25.74 TQ	MABLS	10/01-12/01
Metals and Plastics	Michigan	H	11.36 FQ	22.49 AW	32.45 TQ	MIBLS	10/01-12/01
Metals and Plastics	Minnesota	H	13.53 FQ	17.33 AW	22.30 TQ	MNBLS	10/01-12/01
Metals and Plastics	Missouri	H	6.83 FQ	13.95 AW	21.30 TQ	MOBLS	10/01-12/01
Metals and Plastics	Nebraska	H	11.38 FQ	14.15 AW	17.65 TQ	NEBLS	10/01-12/01
Metals and Plastics	New Hampshire	H	8.30 FQ	13.55 AW	20.48 TQ	NHBLS	10/01-12/01
Metals and Plastics	New Jersey	H	9.46 FQ	15.34 AW	21.35 TQ	NJBLS	10/01-12/01
Metals and Plastics	New York	H	9.58 FQ	16.17 AW	22.13 TQ	NYBLS	10/01-12/01
Metals and Plastics	North Carolina	H	5.88 FQ	12.84 AW	23.03 TQ	NCBLS	10/01-12/01
Metals and Plastics	Ohio	H	9.62 FQ	20.76 AW	33.12 TQ	OHBLS	10/01-12/01
Metals and Plastics	Oklahoma	H	7.75 FQ	11.92 AW	16.58 TQ	OKBLS	10/01-12/01
Metals and Plastics	Pennsylvania	H	9.99 FQ	14.33 AW	19.97 TQ	PABLS	10/01-12/01
Metals and Plastics	Tennessee	H	6.75 FQ	14.94 AW	21.42 TQ	TNBLS	10/01-12/01
Metals and Plastics	Texas	H	7.77 FQ	12.33 AW	17.62 TQ	TXBLS	10/01-12/01
Metals and Plastics	Utah	H	7.24 FQ	12.41 AW	20.80 TQ	UTBLS	10/01-12/01
Metals and Plastics	Virginia	H	9.64 FQ	15.48 AW	22.85 TQ	VABLS	10/01-12/01
Metals and Plastics	Washington	H	10.93 FQ	16.60 AW	23.83 TQ	WABLS	10/01-12/01
Metals and Plastics	Wisconsin	H	11.69 FQ	16.26 AW	23.98 TQ	WIBLS	10/01-12/01
Wood	Alabama	H	8.62 FQ	12.25 AW	18.53 TQ	ALBLS	10/01-12/01
Wood	Arizona	H	9.44 FQ	14.37 AW	25.33 TQ	AZBLS	10/01-12/01
Wood	California	H	6.99 FQ	13.31 AW	25.03 TQ	CABLS	10/01-12/01
Wood	Florida	H	7.92 FQ	13.19 AW	18.66 TQ	FLBLS	10/01-12/01
Wood	Georgia	H	8.71 FQ	14.67 AW	20.56 TQ	GABLS	10/01-12/01
Wood	Illinois	H	7.96 FQ	14.55 AW	20.39 TQ	ILBLS	10/01-12/01
Wood	Indiana	H	11.16 FQ	19.30 AW	32.69 TQ	INBLS	10/01-12/01
Wood	Iowa	H	7.47 FQ	13.02 AW	22.26 TQ	IABLS	10/01-12/01
Wood	Kansas	H	11.17 FQ	14.40 AW	16.93 TQ	KSBLS	10/01-12/01
Wood	Louisiana	H	7.84 FQ	10.79 AW	13.61 TQ	LABLS	10/01-12/01
Wood	Massachusetts	H	10.97 FQ	19.96 AW	28.22 TQ	MABLS	10/01-12/01
Wood	Michigan	H	11.59 FQ	21.75 AW	31.45 TQ	MIBLS	10/01-12/01
Wood	Minnesota	H	9.36 FQ	13.01 AW	19.25 TQ	MNBLS	10/01-12/01
Wood	Mississippi	H	5.88 FQ	8.22 AW	11.17 TQ	MSBLS	10/01-12/01
Wood	Missouri	H	8.62 FQ	13.64 AW	21.25 TQ	MOBLS	10/01-12/01
Wood	New Jersey	H	11.97 FQ	16.13 AW	21.67 TQ	NJBLS	10/01-12/01
Wood	New York	H	8.12 FQ	11.87 AW	17.24 TQ	NYBLS	10/01-12/01
Wood	North Carolina	H	9.26 FQ	13.45 AW	17.72 TQ	NCBLS	10/01-12/01
Wood	Ohio	H	12.63 FQ	20.73 AW	30.61 TQ	OHBLS	10/01-12/01
Wood	Oregon	H	9.38 FQ	21.62 AW	29.20 TQ	ORBLS	10/01-12/01
Wood	Pennsylvania	H	10.19 FQ	15.49 AW	21.19 TQ	PABLS	10/01-12/01
Wood	South Carolina	H	7.76 FQ	11.11 AW	15.49 TQ	SCBLS	10/01-12/01
Wood	Tennessee	H	6.70 FQ	10.64 AW	16.35 TQ	TNBLS	10/01-12/01
Wood	Texas	H	6.24 FQ	11.20 AW	18.02 TQ	TXBLS	10/01-12/01
Wood	Utah	H	8.18 FQ	12.55 AW	17.67 TQ	UTBLS	10/01-12/01
Wood	Virginia	H	9.75 FQ	14.04 AW	20.21 TQ	VABLS	10/01-12/01
Wood	Washington	H	14.16 FQ	17.11 AW	24.70 TQ	WABLS	10/01-12/01
Wood	Wisconsin	H	9.84 FQ	15.69 AW	21.57 TQ	WIBLS	10/01-12/01
Paving, Surfacing, and Tamping Equipment Operator	Alabama	H	7.87 FQ	10.85 AW	14.03 TQ	ALBLS	10/01-12/01

AAW Average annual wage; AE Average entry wage; AEX Average experienced wage; AO Average offered; AOH Average offered, high; AOL Average offered, low; APH Average pay, high range; APL Average pay, low range; ASH Average starting, high; ASL Average starting, low; AW Average wage paid; FQ First quartile wage; H Hourly; HI Highest wage paid; HR High end range; LR Low end range; M Monthly; MTC Median total compensation; MW Median wage paid; SQ Second quartile wage; S Special: hourly and annual; TQ Third quartile wage; W Weekly; Y Yearly

Occupation/Type/Industry	Location	Per	Low	Mid	High	Source	Date
Paving, Surfacing, and Tamping Equipment Operator	Alaska	H	11.08 FQ	21.45 AW	29.94 TQ	AKBLS	10/01-12/01
	Arizona	H	7.49 FQ	13.73 AW	20.66 TQ	AZBLS	10/01-12/01
	Arkansas	H	8.40 FQ	11.42 AW	14.79 TQ	ARBLS	10/01-12/01
	California	H	11.49 FQ	20.70 AW	32.93 TQ	CABLS	10/01-12/01
	Colorado	H	11.06 FQ	15.38 AW	20.20 TQ	COBLS	10/01-12/01
	Connecticut	H	12.85 FQ	17.98 AW	24.81 TQ	CTBLS	10/01-12/01
	Delaware	H	12.21 FQ	17.08 AW	21.95 TQ	DEBLS	10/01-12/01
	Florida	H	7.39 FQ	11.06 AW	16.20 TQ	FLBLS	10/01-12/01
	Georgia	H	8.27 FQ	11.24 AW	14.31 TQ	GABLS	10/01-12/01
	Hawaii	H	12.26 FQ	21.61 AW	33.30 TQ	HIBLS	10/01-12/01
	Idaho	H	9.59 FQ	13.34 AW	17.54 TQ	IDBLS	10/01-12/01
	Illinois	H	9.87 FQ	22.86 AW	32.80 TQ	ILBLS	10/01-12/01
	Indiana	H	9.73 FQ	17.06 AW	26.52 TQ	INBLS	10/01-12/01
	Iowa	H	9.26 FQ	13.39 AW	17.78 TQ	IABLS	10/01-12/01
	Kansas	H	9.04 FQ	12.86 AW	22.15 TQ	KSBLS	10/01-12/01
	Kentucky	H	9.45 FQ	14.00 AW	19.95 TQ	KYBLS	10/01-12/01
	Louisiana	H	7.22 FQ	11.32 AW	16.40 TQ	LABLS	10/01-12/01
	Maine	H	8.96 FQ	11.98 AW	15.84 TQ	MEBLS	10/01-12/01
	Maryland	H	10.88 FQ	15.16 AW	20.20 TQ	MDBLS	10/01-12/01
	Massachusetts	H	9.49 FQ	17.43 AW	30.28 TQ	MABLS	10/01-12/01
	Michigan	H	10.50 FQ	17.12 AW	23.14 TQ	MIBLS	10/01-12/01
	Minnesota	H	11.72 FQ	18.74 AW	26.25 TQ	MNBLS	10/01-12/01
	Mississippi	H	7.33 FQ	9.98 AW	13.31 TQ	MSBLS	10/01-12/01
	Missouri	H	8.97 FQ	14.30 AW	22.42 TQ	MOBLS	10/01-12/01
	Montana	H	9.34 FQ	14.22 AW	19.90 TQ	MTBLS	10/01-12/01
	Nebraska	H	9.73 FQ	14.32 AW	20.43 TQ	NEBLS	10/01-12/01
	Nevada	H	13.91 FQ	23.72 AW	34.26 TQ	NVBLS	10/01-12/01
	New Hampshire	H	10.72 FQ	13.63 AW	17.19 TQ	NHBLS	10/01-12/01
	New Jersey	H	13.08 FQ	22.04 AW	32.05 TQ	NJBLS	10/01-12/01
	New Mexico	H	9.43 FQ	12.46 AW	16.25 TQ	NMBLS	10/01-12/01
	New York	H	11.13 FQ	21.60 AW	32.18 TQ	NYBLS	10/01-12/01
	North Carolina	H	8.43 FQ	12.10 AW	16.72 TQ	NCBLS	10/01-12/01
	North Dakota	H	9.93 FQ	15.54 AW	21.93 TQ	NDBLS	10/01-12/01
	Ohio	H	10.24 FQ	17.29 AW	26.38 TQ	OHBLS	10/01-12/01
	Oklahoma	H	8.61 FQ	11.59 AW	15.66 TQ	OKBLS	10/01-12/01
	Oregon	H	11.04 FQ	18.12 AW	26.73 TQ	ORBLS	10/01-12/01
	Pennsylvania	H	9.55 FQ	15.63 AW	21.98 TQ	PABLS	10/01-12/01
	Rhode Island	H	14.18 FQ	21.32 AW	27.38 TQ	RIBLS	10/01-12/01
	South Carolina	H	8.24 FQ	11.41 AW	15.74 TQ	SCBLS	10/01-12/01
	South Dakota	H	9.56 FQ	12.53 AW	16.45 TQ	SDBLS	10/01-12/01
	Tennessee	H	9.21 FQ	11.71 AW	14.43 TQ	TNBLS	10/01-12/01
	Texas	H	7.72 FQ	11.47 AW	16.11 TQ	TXBLS	10/01-12/01
	Utah	H	11.77 FQ	15.64 AW	20.39 TQ	UTBLS	10/01-12/01
	Vermont	H	9.65 FQ	12.84 AW	16.09 TQ	VTBLS	10/01-12/01
	Virginia	H	8.72 FQ	12.98 AW	18.40 TQ	VABLS	10/01-12/01
	Washington	H	11.90 FQ	18.97 AW	26.58 TQ	WABLS	10/01-12/01
	West Virginia	H	9.30 FQ	16.45 AW	22.41 TQ	WVBLS	10/01-12/01
	Wisconsin	H	10.37 FQ	16.70 AW	25.23 TQ	WIBLS	10/01-12/01
	Wyoming	H	11.68 FQ	15.29 AW	19.48 TQ	WYBLS	10/01-12/01
	Puerto Rico	H	5.70 FQ	7.31 AW	9.37 TQ	PRBLS	10/01-12/01
	Virgin Islands	H	8.63 FQ	10.52 AW	13.41 TQ	VIBLS	10/01-12/01
Payroll and Timekeeping Clerk	Alabama	H	8.11 FQ	12.50 AW	17.68 TQ	ALBLS	10/01-12/01
	Birmingham MSA, AL	H	9.11 FQ	13.52 AW	19.26 TQ	ALBLS	10/01-12/01
	Huntsville MSA, AL	H	7.36 FQ	11.92 AW	17.55 TQ	ALBLS	10/01-12/01
	Mobile MSA, AL	H	8.52 FQ	12.23 AW	17.79 TQ	ALBLS	10/01-12/01
	Montgomery MSA, AL	H	7.96 FQ	12.44 AW	17.16 TQ	ALBLS	10/01-12/01
	Alaska	H	11.82 FQ	17.40 AW	25.39 TQ	AKBLS	10/01-12/01
	Anchorage MSA, AK	H	11.68 FQ	16.47 AW	22.22 TQ	AKBLS	10/01-12/01
	Arizona	H	7.86 FQ	12.27 AW	17.16 TQ	AZBLS	10/01-12/01
	Phoenix-Mesa MSA, AZ	H	7.66 FQ	12.20 AW	17.20 TQ	AZBLS	10/01-12/01
	Tucson MSA, AZ	H	8.87 FQ	12.52 AW	17.07 TQ	AZBLS	10/01-12/01
	Arkansas	H	7.92 FQ	11.64 AW	16.28 TQ	ARBLS	10/01-12/01
	Fayetteville-Springdale-Rogers MSA, AR	H	8.14 FQ	11.24 AW	15.30 TQ	ARBLS	10/01-12/01
	Fort Smith MSA, AR-OK	H	8.14 FQ	11.81 AW	15.01 TQ	ARBLS	10/01-12/01
	Little Rock-North Little Rock MSA, AR	H	9.16 FQ	12.89 AW	17.19 TQ	ARBLS	10/01-12/01
	California	H	10.12 FQ	15.71 AW	21.91 TQ	CABLS	10/01-12/01
	Bakersfield MSA, CA	H	8.71 FQ	13.55 AW	18.94 TQ	CABLS	10/01-12/01
	Chico-Paradise MSA, CA	H	9.28 FQ	12.75 AW	17.28 TQ	CABLS	10/01-12/01

AAW	Average annual wage	AOH	Average offered, high	ASH	Average starting, high	H	Hourly	M	Monthly	S	Special: hourly and annual
AE	Average entry wage	AOL	Average offered, low	ASL	Average starting, low	HI	Highest wage paid	MTC	Median total compensation	TQ	Third quartile wage
AEX	Average experienced wage	APH	Average pay, high range	AW	Average wage paid	HR	High end range	MW	Median wage paid	W	Weekly
AO	Average offered	APL	Average pay, low range	FQ	First quartile wage	LR	Low end range	SQ	Second quartile wage	Y	Yearly

Occupation/Type/Industry	Location	Per	Low	Mid	High	Source	Date
Payroll and Timekeeping Clerk	Fresno MSA, CA	H	9.00 FQ	13.33 AW	19.01 TQ	CABLS	10/01-12/01
	Los Angeles-Long Beach PMSA, CA	H	11.08 FQ	16.04 AW	21.88 TQ	CABLS	10/01-12/01
	Merced MSA, CA	H	8.17 FQ	12.81 AW	17.94 TQ	CABLS	10/01-12/01
	Modesto MSA, CA	H	9.95 FQ	13.86 AW	18.36 TQ	CABLS	10/01-12/01
	Oakland PMSA, CA	H	11.64 FQ	17.51 AW	23.35 TQ	CABLS	10/01-12/01
	Orange County PMSA, CA	H	9.68 FQ	14.31 AW	20.77 TQ	CABLS	10/01-12/01
	Redding MSA, CA	H	8.49 FQ	13.46 AW	17.71 TQ	CABLS	10/01-12/01
	Riverside-San Bernardino PMSA, CA	H	8.41 FQ	14.05 AW	20.09 TQ	CABLS	10/01-12/01
	Sacramento PMSA, CA	H	10.98 FQ	16.01 AW	21.25 TQ	CABLS	10/01-12/01
	Salinas MSA, CA	H	9.64 FQ	14.35 AW	19.53 TQ	CABLS	10/01-12/01
	San Diego MSA, CA	H	10.84 FQ	15.31 AW	20.33 TQ	CABLS	10/01-12/01
	San Francisco PMSA, CA	H	11.65 FQ	19.53 AW	27.25 TQ	CABLS	10/01-12/01
	San Jose PMSA, CA	H	13.59 FQ	20.21 AW	27.10 TQ	CABLS	10/01-12/01
	San Luis Obispo-Atascadero-Paso Robles MSA, CA	H	9.78 FQ	14.67 AW	18.18 TQ	CABLS	10/01-12/01
	Santa Barbara-Santa Maria-Lompoc MSA, CA	H	10.40 FQ	15.82 AW	21.77 TQ	CABLS	10/01-12/01
	Santa Cruz-Watsonville PMSA, CA	H	10.27 FQ	16.27 AW	22.71 TQ	CABLS	10/01-12/01
	Santa Rosa PMSA, CA	H	11.43 FQ	16.64 AW	22.42 TQ	CABLS	10/01-12/01
	Stockton-Lodi MSA, CA	H	10.01 FQ	14.85 AW	20.16 TQ	CABLS	10/01-12/01
	Vallejo-Fairfield-Napa PMSA, CA	H	10.63 FQ	15.74 AW	21.00 TQ	CABLS	10/01-12/01
	Ventura PMSA, CA	H	11.07 FQ	16.02 AW	22.30 TQ	CABLS	10/01-12/01
	Visalia-Tulare-Porterville MSA, CA	H	6.58 FQ	11.68 AW	16.78 TQ	CABLS	10/01-12/01
	Colorado	H	10.96 FQ	16.40 AW	20.75 TQ	COBLS	10/01-12/01
	Boulder-Longmont PMSA, CO	H	10.71 FQ	15.67 AW	21.64 TQ	COBLS	10/01-12/01
	Colorado Springs MSA, CO	H	10.87 FQ	13.90 AW	17.67 TQ	COBLS	10/01-12/01
	Denver PMSA, CO	H	11.86 FQ	17.91 AW	21.40 TQ	COBLS	10/01-12/01
	Fort Collins-Loveland MSA, CO	H	9.58 FQ	13.47 AW	17.69 TQ	COBLS	10/01-12/01
	Greeley PMSA, CO	H	10.01 FQ	13.83 AW	17.23 TQ	COBLS	10/01-12/01
	Connecticut	H	11.54 FQ	16.74 AW	22.03 TQ	CTBLS	10/01-12/01
	Bridgeport PMSA, CT	H	12.15 FQ	16.45 AW	21.61 TQ	CTBLS	10/01-12/01
	Danbury PMSA, CT	H	12.37 FQ	17.03 AW	22.30 TQ	CTBLS	10/01-12/01
	Hartford MSA, CT	H	11.88 FQ	17.02 AW	22.13 TQ	CTBLS	10/01-12/01
	New Haven-Meriden PMSA, CT	H	11.06 FQ	16.37 AW	21.84 TQ	CTBLS	10/01-12/01
	New London-Norwich MSA, CT-RI	H	10.16 FQ	14.93 AW	20.78 TQ	CTBLS	10/01-12/01
	Stamford-Norwalk PMSA, CT	H	13.60 FQ	19.04 AW	24.36 TQ	CTBLS	10/01-12/01
	Waterbury PMSA, CT	H	9.99 FQ	15.10 AW	20.08 TQ	CTBLS	10/01-12/01
	Delaware	H	10.53 FQ	14.57 AW	19.79 TQ	DEBLS	10/01-12/01
	Wilmington-Newark PMSA, DE-MD	H	11.21 FQ	15.06 AW	20.18 TQ	DEBLS	10/01-12/01
	District of Columbia	H	11.20 FQ	16.56 AW	21.72 TQ	DCBLS	10/01-12/01
	Washington PMSA, DC-MD-VA-WV	H	10.83 FQ	15.99 AW	21.52 TQ	DCBLS	10/01-12/01
	Florida	H	9.01 FQ	12.90 AW	17.26 TQ	FLBLS	10/01-12/01
	Daytona Beach MSA, FL	H	8.88 FQ	12.40 AW	16.79 TQ	FLBLS	10/01-12/01
	Fort Lauderdale PMSA, FL	H	11.14 FQ	14.26 AW	18.61 TQ	FLBLS	10/01-12/01
	Fort Myers-Cape Coral MSA, FL	H	9.65 FQ	12.48 AW	16.17 TQ	FLBLS	10/01-12/01
	Fort Pierce-Port St. Lucie MSA, FL	H	9.26 FQ	12.44 AW	16.29 TQ	FLBLS	10/01-12/01
	Fort Walton Beach MSA, FL	H	8.19 FQ	12.23 AW	16.62 TQ	FLBLS	10/01-12/01
	Gainesville MSA, FL	H	8.78 FQ	13.10 AW	18.07 TQ	FLBLS	10/01-12/01
	Jacksonville MSA, FL	H	9.26 FQ	13.18 AW	18.75 TQ	FLBLS	10/01-12/01
	Lakeland-Winter Haven MSA, FL	H	9.00 FQ	12.24 AW	17.00 TQ	FLBLS	10/01-12/01
	Melbourne-Titusville-Palm Bay MSA, FL	H	9.06 FQ	12.69 AW	16.92 TQ	FLBLS	10/01-12/01
	Miami PMSA, FL	H	9.49 FQ	13.73 AW	18.79 TQ	FLBLS	10/01-12/01
	Naples MSA, FL	H	8.16 FQ	12.79 AW	16.70 TQ	FLBLS	10/01-12/01
	Ocala MSA, FL	H	8.63 FQ	11.52 AW	14.71 TQ	FLBLS	10/01-12/01
	Orlando MSA, FL	H	8.56 FQ	12.28 AW	16.72 TQ	FLBLS	10/01-12/01
	Pensacola MSA, FL	H	8.58 FQ	13.29 AW	18.58 TQ	FLBLS	10/01-12/01
	Sarasota-Bradenton MSA, FL	H	8.46 FQ	11.42 AW	15.55 TQ	FLBLS	10/01-12/01
	Tallahassee MSA, FL	H	8.96 FQ	13.45 AW	17.90 TQ	FLBLS	10/01-12/01

AAW Average annual wage **AOH** Average offered, high **ASH** Average starting, high **H** Hourly **M** Monthly **S** Special: hourly and annual
AE Average entry wage **AOL** Average offered, low **ASL** Average starting, low **HI** Highest wage paid **MTC** Median total compensation **TQ** Third quartile wage
AEX Average experienced wage **APH** Average pay, high range **AW** Average wage paid **HR** High end range **MW** Median wage paid **W** Weekly
AO Average offered **APL** Average pay, low range **FQ** First quartile wage **LR** Low end range **SQ** Second quartile wage **Y** Yearly

Occupation/Type/Industry	Location	Per	Low	Mid	High	Source	Date
Payroll and Timekeeping Clerk	Tampa-St. Petersburg-Clearwater MSA, FL	H	8.79 FQ	12.61 AW	16.69 TQ	FLBLS	10/01-12/01
	West Palm Beach-Boca Raton MSA, FL	H	10.17 FQ	14.07 AW	18.02 TQ	FLBLS	10/01-12/01
	Georgia	H	8.67 FQ	13.55 AW	19.75 TQ	GABLS	10/01-12/01
	Atlanta MSA, GA	H	10.11 FQ	15.38 AW	22.64 TQ	GABLS	10/01-12/01
	Augusta-Aiken MSA, GA-SC	H	8.94 FQ	12.48 AW	16.87 TQ	GABLS	10/01-12/01
	Columbus MSA, GA-AL	H	7.49 FQ	12.24 AW	16.62 TQ	GABLS	10/01-12/01
	Macon MSA, GA	H	5.95 FQ	10.34 AW	14.52 TQ	GABLS	10/01-12/01
	Savannah MSA, GA	H	6.46 FQ	11.28 AW	16.12 TQ	GABLS	10/01-12/01
	Hawaii	H	10.63 FQ	14.20 AW	19.57 TQ	HIBLS	10/01-12/01
	Honolulu MSA, HI	H	10.83 FQ	14.17 AW	19.61 TQ	HIBLS	10/01-12/01
	Idaho	H	8.22 FQ	12.40 AW	16.70 TQ	IDBLS	10/01-12/01
	Boise City MSA, ID	H	8.64 FQ	12.74 AW	16.87 TQ	IDBLS	10/01-12/01
	Illinois	H	8.56 FQ	13.98 AW	20.16 TQ	ILBLS	10/01-12/01
	Champaign-Urbana MSA, IL	H	9.74 FQ	13.54 AW	16.92 TQ	ILBLS	10/01-12/01
	Chicago PMSA, IL	H	9.94 FQ	14.90 AW	20.76 TQ	ILBLS	10/01-12/01
	Peoria-Pekin MSA, IL	H	8.51 FQ	12.24 AW	16.88 TQ	ILBLS	10/01-12/01
	Rockford MSA, IL	H	8.54 FQ	13.78 AW	18.54 TQ	ILBLS	10/01-12/01
	Springfield MSA, IL	H	9.57 FQ	14.27 AW	20.21 TQ	ILBLS	10/01-12/01
	Indiana	H	9.20 FQ	13.51 AW	18.94 TQ	INBLS	10/01-12/01
	Elkhart-Goshen MSA, IN	H	9.79 FQ	13.38 AW	17.28 TQ	INBLS	10/01-12/01
	Evansville-Henderson MSA, IN-KY	H	8.92 FQ	12.40 AW	17.13 TQ	INBLS	10/01-12/01
	Fort Wayne MSA, IN	H	9.19 FQ	12.79 AW	16.80 TQ	INBLS	10/01-12/01
	Gary PMSA, IN	H	8.27 FQ	13.10 AW	18.28 TQ	INBLS	10/01-12/01
	Indianapolis MSA, IN	H	10.81 FQ	15.02 AW	20.67 TQ	INBLS	10/01-12/01
	Lafayette MSA, IN	H	7.63 FQ	11.96 AW	16.62 TQ	INBLS	10/01-12/01
	South Bend MSA, IN	H	9.35 FQ	13.24 AW	18.29 TQ	INBLS	10/01-12/01
	Iowa	H	7.95 FQ	12.25 AW	17.20 TQ	IABLS	10/01-12/01
	Cedar Rapids MSA, IA	H	9.46 FQ	13.30 AW	18.85 TQ	IABLS	10/01-12/01
	Davenport-Molinc-Rock Island MSA, IA-IL	H	8.97 FQ	13.09 AW	17.83 TQ	IABLS	10/01-12/01
	Des Moines MSA, IA	H	9.95 FQ	14.27 AW	18.95 TQ	IABLS	10/01-12/01
	Kansas	H	9.01 FQ	13.17 AW	17.62 TQ	KSBLS	10/01-12/01
	Topeka MSA, KS	H	10.02 FQ	13.62 AW	17.51 TQ	KSBLS	10/01-12/01
	Wichita MSA, KS	H	9.21 FQ	13.62 AW	20.41 TQ	KSBLS	10/01-12/01
	Kentucky	H	7.97 FQ	12.65 AW	18.06 TQ	KYBLS	10/01-12/01
	Lexington MSA, KY	H	9.86 FQ	14.31 AW	20.56 TQ	KYBLS	10/01-12/01
	Louisville MSA, KY-IN	H	9.54 FQ	13.48 AW	17.93 TQ	KYBLS	10/01-12/01
	Louisiana	H	8.25 FQ	12.44 AW	17.27 TQ	LABLS	10/01-12/01
	Baton Rouge MSA, LA	H	8.65 FQ	12.50 AW	16.82 TQ	LABLS	10/01-12/01
	Houma MSA, LA	H	8.80 FQ	11.87 AW	16.59 TQ	LABLS	10/01-12/01
	Lafayette MSA, LA	H	7.26 FQ	11.14 AW	14.62 TQ	LABLS	10/01-12/01
	Lake Charles MSA, LA	H	8.89 FQ	12.94 AW	18.61 TQ	LABLS	10/01-12/01
	New Orleans MSA, LA	H	9.25 FQ	13.46 AW	17.76 TQ	LABLS	10/01-12/01
	Shreveport-Bossier City MSA, LA	H	7.75 FQ	12.23 AW	18.92 TQ	LABLS	10/01-12/01
	Maine	H	9.13 FQ	12.76 AW	16.85 TQ	MEBLS	10/01-12/01
	Portland MSA, ME	H	10.63 FQ	13.84 AW	16.97 TQ	MEBLS	10/01-12/01
	Maryland	H	9.05 FQ	14.29 AW	20.27 TQ	MDBLS	10/01-12/01
	Baltimore PMSA, MD	H	6.98 FQ	13.69 AW	19.52 TQ	MDBLS	10/01-12/01
	Massachusetts	H	11.05 FQ	15.86 AW	21.48 TQ	MABLS	10/01-12/01
	Boston PMSA, MA-NH	H	11.68 FQ	16.48 AW	22.00 TQ	MABLS	10/01-12/01
	Brockton PMSA, MA	H	11.27 FQ	15.09 AW	19.87 TQ	MABLS	10/01-12/01
	Lawrence PMSA, MA-NH	H	10.40 FQ	15.21 AW	20.31 TQ	MABLS	10/01-12/01
	Lowell PMSA, MA-NH	H	11.47 FQ	16.49 AW	21.84 TQ	MABLS	10/01-12/01
	New Bedford PMSA, MA	H	9.31 FQ	13.30 AW	17.54 TQ	MABLS	10/01-12/01
	Springfield MSA, MA	H	11.01 FQ	14.37 AW	18.50 TQ	MABLS	10/01-12/01
	Worcester PMSA, MA-CT	H	10.06 FQ	15.59 AW	22.64 TQ	MABLS	10/01-12/01
	Michigan	H	9.22 FQ	14.00 AW	19.23 TQ	MIBLS	10/01-12/01
	Ann Arbor PMSA, MI	H	6.02 FQ	12.02 AW	18.29 TQ	MIBLS	10/01-12/01
	Detroit PMSA, MI	H	10.79 FQ	14.87 AW	19.71 TQ	MIBLS	10/01-12/01
	Flint PMSA, MI	H	6.92 FQ	14.60 AW	20.41 TQ	MIBLS	10/01-12/01
	Grand Rapids-Muskegon-Holland MSA, MI	H	9.77 FQ	13.99 AW	19.58 TQ	MIBLS	10/01-12/01
	Kalamazoo-Battle Creek MSA, MI	H	9.94 FQ	16.11 AW	27.03 TQ	MIBLS	10/01-12/01
	Lansing-East Lansing MSA, MI	H	10.34 FQ	14.51 AW	19.08 TQ	MIBLS	10/01-12/01
	Saginaw-Bay City-Midland MSA, MI	H	8.60 FQ	13.08 AW	17.37 TQ	MIBLS	10/01-12/01
	Minnesota	H	10.52 FQ	14.78 AW	19.91 TQ	MNBLS	10/01-12/01

AAW Average annual wage; AE Average entry wage; AEX Average experienced wage; AO Average offered; AOH Average offered, high; AOL Average offered, low; APH Average pay, high range; APL Average pay, low range; ASH Average starting, high; ASL Average starting, low; AW Average wage paid; FQ First quartile wage; H Hourly; HI Highest wage paid; HR High end range; LR Low end range; M Monthly; MTC Median total compensation; MW Median wage paid; SQ Second quartile wage; S Special: hourly and annual; TQ Third quartile wage; W Weekly; Y Yearly

Occupation/Type/Industry	Location	Per	Low	Mid	High	Source	Date
Payroll and Timekeeping Clerk	Duluth-Superior MSA, MN-WI	H	9.17 FQ	13.33 AW	18.51 TQ	MNBLS	10/01-12/01
	Minneapolis-St. Paul MSA, MN-WI	H	11.72 FQ	15.69 AW	20.60 TQ	MNBLS	10/01-12/01
	St. Cloud MSA, MN	H	9.68 FQ	12.96 AW	16.86 TQ	MNBLS	10/01-12/01
	Mississippi	H	8.36 FQ	12.06 AW	16.48 TQ	MSBLS	10/01-12/01
	Biloxi-Gulfport-Pascagoula MSA, MS	H	8.81 FQ	12.24 AW	16.55 TQ	MSBLS	10/01-12/01
	Jackson MSA, MS	H	9.48 FQ	12.44 AW	16.61 TQ	MSBLS	10/01-12/01
	Missouri	H	8.65 FQ	12.97 AW	17.85 TQ	MOBLS	10/01-12/01
	Kansas City MSA, MO-KS	H	10.45 FQ	14.27 AW	18.78 TQ	MOBLS	10/01-12/01
	St. Louis MSA, MO-IL	H	7.52 FQ	12.77 AW	17.95 TQ	MOBLS	10/01-12/01
	Springfield MSA, MO	H	8.73 FQ	12.50 AW	19.15 TQ	MOBLS	10/01-12/01
	Montana	H	6.89 FQ	11.10 AW	16.51 TQ	MTBLS	10/01-12/01
	Billings MSA, MT	H	7.46 FQ	11.40 AW	16.46 TQ	MTBLS	10/01-12/01
	Nebraska	H	9.44 FQ	12.99 AW	17.09 TQ	NEBLS	10/01-12/01
	Lincoln MSA, NE	H	10.09 FQ	13.54 AW	17.62 TQ	NEBLS	10/01-12/01
	Omaha MSA, NE-IA	H	9.76 FQ	13.66 AW	17.51 TQ	NEBLS	10/01-12/01
	Nevada	H	9.16 FQ	13.42 AW	18.32 TQ	NVBLS	10/01-12/01
	Las Vegas MSA, NV-AZ	H	9.04 FQ	13.19 AW	18.19 TQ	NVBLS	10/01-12/01
	Reno MSA, NV	H	9.60 FQ	14.09 AW	18.61 TQ	NVBLS	10/01-12/01
	New Hampshire	H	9.16 FQ	13.31 AW	17.64 TQ	NHBLS	10/01-12/01
	Manchester PMSA, NH	H	8.60 FQ	13.03 AW	17.60 TQ	NHBLS	10/01-12/01
	Nashua PMSA, NH	H	9.87 FQ	14.84 AW	20.46 TQ	NHBLS	10/01-12/01
	Portsmouth-Rochester PMSA, NH-ME	H	7.92 FQ	13.65 AW	18.14 TQ	NHBLS	10/01-12/01
	New Jersey	H	10.53 FQ	15.83 AW	21.78 TQ	NJBLS	10/01-12/01
	Atlantic-Cape May PMSA, NJ	H	8.95 FQ	13.37 AW	20.45 TQ	NJBLS	10/01-12/01
	Bergen-Passaic PMSA, NJ	H	10.52 FQ	15.76 AW	21.52 TQ	NJBLS	10/01-12/01
	Jersey City PMSA, NJ	H	10.03 FQ	15.47 AW	21.60 TQ	NJBLS	10/01-12/01
	Middlesex-Somerset-Hunterdon PMSA, NJ	H	11.91 FQ	17.44 AW	23.25 TQ	NJBLS	10/01-12/01
	Monmouth-Ocean PMSA, NJ	H	9.79 FQ	14.66 AW	21.00 TQ	NJBLS	10/01-12/01
	Newark PMSA, NJ	H	11.43 FQ	16.47 AW	22.11 TQ	NJBLS	10/01-12/01
	Trenton PMSA, NJ	H	11.56 FQ	15.86 AW	20.69 TQ	NJBLS	10/01-12/01
	New Mexico	H	7.70 FQ	11.81 AW	16.54 TQ	NMBLS	10/01-12/01
	Albuquerque MSA, NM	H	9.04 FQ	12.73 AW	16.97 TQ	NMBLS	10/01-12/01
	Las Cruces MSA, NM	H	6.88 FQ	10.33 AW	14.15 TQ	NMBLS	10/01-12/01
	New York	H	10.01 FQ	16.25 AW	23.63 TQ	NYBLS	10/01-12/01
	Albany-Schenectady-Troy MSA, NY	H	9.91 FQ	14.34 AW	18.60 TQ	NYBLS	10/01-12/01
	Binghamton MSA, NY	H	8.16 FQ	13.43 AW	21.16 TQ	NYBLS	10/01-12/01
	Buffalo-Niagara Falls MSA, NY	H	9.58 FQ	13.64 AW	18.19 TQ	NYBLS	10/01-12/01
	Dutchess County PMSA, NY	H	9.96 FQ	15.16 AW	20.86 TQ	NYBLS	10/01-12/01
	Nassau-Suffolk PMSA, NY	H	11.28 FQ	17.08 AW	23.60 TQ	NYBLS	10/01-12/01
	New York PMSA, NY	H	11.32 FQ	18.32 AW	26.59 TQ	NYBLS	10/01-12/01
	Newburgh PMSA, NY-PA	H	9.23 FQ	14.03 AW	18.72 TQ	NYBLS	10/01-12/01
	Rochester MSA, NY	H	9.32 FQ	13.63 AW	19.24 TQ	NYBLS	10/01-12/01
	Syracuse MSA, NY	H	9.21 FQ	13.30 AW	18.12 TQ	NYBLS	10/01-12/01
	Utica-Rome MSA, NY	H	9.19 FQ	13.36 AW	19.43 TQ	NYBLS	10/01-12/01
	North Carolina	H	9.03 FQ	13.13 AW	17.71 TQ	NCBLS	10/01-12/01
	Asheville MSA, NC	H	9.24 FQ	12.23 AW	16.56 TQ	NCBLS	10/01-12/01
	Charlotte-Gastonia-Rock Hill MSA, NC-SC	H	9.68 FQ	13.67 AW	18.24 TQ	NCBLS	10/01-12/01
	Fayetteville MSA, NC	H	8.46 FQ	12.28 AW	16.97 TQ	NCBLS	10/01-12/01
	Greensboro-Winston-Salem-High Point MSA, NC	H	9.38 FQ	13.68 AW	19.08 TQ	NCBLS	10/01-12/01
	Hickory-Morganton-Lenoir MSA, NC	H	9.55 FQ	12.87 AW	17.31 TQ	NCBLS	10/01-12/01
	Raleigh-Durham-Chapel Hill MSA, NC	H	10.29 FQ	14.42 AW	19.08 TQ	NCBLS	10/01-12/01
	Wilmington MSA, NC	H	6.86 FQ	13.52 AW	20.61 TQ	NCBLS	10/01-12/01
	North Dakota	H	8.66 FQ	11.98 AW	16.56 TQ	NDBLS	10/01-12/01
	Fargo-Moorhead MSA, ND-MN	H	9.34 FQ	13.01 AW	17.20 TQ	NDBLS	10/01-12/01
	Ohio	H	9.38 FQ	14.36 AW	20.67 TQ	OHBLS	10/01-12/01
	Akron PMSA, OH	H	9.52 FQ	13.61 AW	17.94 TQ	OHBLS	10/01-12/01
	Canton-Massillon MSA, OH	H	9.36 FQ	12.61 AW	16.59 TQ	OHBLS	10/01-12/01
	Cincinnati PMSA, OH-KY-IN	H	10.31 FQ	15.70 AW	21.70 TQ	OHBLS	10/01-12/01
	Cleveland-Lorain-Elyria PMSA, OH	H	10.16 FQ	15.27 AW	21.29 TQ	OHBLS	10/01-12/01
	Columbus MSA, OH	H	9.64 FQ	14.99 AW	21.14 TQ	OHBLS	10/01-12/01

AAW Average annual wage; AE Average entry wage; AEX Average experienced wage; AO Average offered; AOH Average offered, high; AOL Average offered, low; APH Average pay, high range; APL Average pay, low range; ASH Average starting, high; ASL Average starting, low; AW Average wage paid; FQ First quartile wage; H Hourly; HI Highest wage paid; HR High end range; LR Low end range; M Monthly; MTC Median total compensation; MW Median wage paid; SQ Second quartile wage; S Special: hourly and annual; TQ Third quartile wage; W Weekly; Y Yearly

Occupation/Type/Industry	Location	Per	Low	Mid	High	Source	Date
Payroll and Timekeeping Clerk	Dayton-Springfield MSA, OH	H	9.34 FQ	13.36 AW	17.98 TQ	OHBLS	10/01-12/01
	Hamilton-Middletown PMSA, OH	H	9.85 FQ	13.80 AW	18.50 TQ	OHBLS	10/01-12/01
	Mansfield MSA, OH	H	7.81 FQ	12.26 AW	16.75 TQ	OHBLS	10/01-12/01
	Toledo MSA, OH	H	9.92 FQ	13.65 AW	18.23 TQ	OHBLS	10/01-12/01
	Youngstown-Warren MSA, OH	H	7.56 FQ	12.23 AW	16.98 TQ	OHBLS	10/01-12/01
	Oklahoma	H	7.49 FQ	11.98 AW	17.30 TQ	OKBLS	10/01-12/01
	Oklahoma City MSA, OK	H	7.68 FQ	12.15 AW	17.53 TQ	OKBLS	10/01-12/01
	Tulsa MSA, OK	H	8.66 FQ	12.92 AW	18.46 TQ	OKBLS	10/01-12/01
	Oregon	H	10.34 FQ	14.77 AW	19.64 TQ	ORBLS	10/01-12/01
	Eugene-Springfield MSA, OR	H	9.73 FQ	13.66 AW	18.34 TQ	ORBLS	10/01-12/01
	Medford-Ashland MSA, OR	H	9.18 FQ	13.26 AW	17.45 TQ	ORBLS	10/01-12/01
	Portland-Vancouver PMSA, OR-WA	H	11.25 FQ	15.04 AW	19.93 TQ	ORBLS	10/01-12/01
	Salem PMSA, OR	H	9.36 FQ	14.08 AW	20.05 TQ	ORBLS	10/01-12/01
	Pennsylvania	H	8.95 FQ	13.55 AW	19.41 TQ	PABLS	10/01-12/01
	Allentown-Bethlehem-Easton MSA, PA	H	9.12 FQ	13.77 AW	18.29 TQ	PABLS	10/01-12/01
	Erie MSA, PA	H	8.70 FQ	11.50 AW	14.81 TQ	PABLS	10/01-12/01
	Harrisburg-Lebanon-Carlisle MSA, PA	H	9.27 FQ	13.40 AW	18.72 TQ	PABLS	10/01-12/01
	Johnstown MSA, PA	H	7.77 FQ	11.67 AW	16.30 TQ	PABLS	10/01-12/01
	Lancaster MSA, PA	H	9.69 FQ	13.31 AW	17.53 TQ	PABLS	10/01-12/01
	Philadelphia PMSA, PA-NJ	H	9.97 FQ	15.05 AW	20.67 TQ	PABLS	10/01-12/01
	Pittsburgh MSA, PA	H	8.88 FQ	13.25 AW	18.74 TQ	PABLS	10/01-12/01
	Reading MSA, PA	H	8.41 FQ	12.94 AW	17.71 TQ	PABLS	10/01-12/01
	Scranton-Wilkes-Barre-Hazleton MSA, PA	H	8.38 FQ	12.46 AW	17.20 TQ	PABLS	10/01-12/01
	York MSA, PA	H	9.37 FQ	12.99 AW	16.98 TQ	PABLS	10/01-12/01
	Rhode Island	H	9.76 FQ	14.26 AW	19.38 TQ	RIBLS	10/01-12/01
	Providence-Fall River-Warwick MSA, RI-MA	H	9.41 FQ	14.05 AW	19.28 TQ	RIBLS	10/01-12/01
	South Carolina	H	8.91 FQ	12.70 AW	17.34 TQ	SCBLS	10/01-12/01
	Charleston-North Charleston MSA, SC	H	9.80 FQ	13.70 AW	18.75 TQ	SCBLS	10/01-12/01
	Columbia MSA, SC	H	9.47 FQ	12.97 AW	16.88 TQ	SCBLS	10/01-12/01
	Greenville-Spartanburg-Anderson MSA, SC	H	8.96 FQ	12.83 AW	17.57 TQ	SCBLS	10/01-12/01
	Myrtle Beach MSA, SC	H	7.52 FQ	11.11 AW	15.36 TQ	SCBLS	10/01-12/01
	South Dakota	H	8.38 FQ	10.99 AW	13.84 TQ	SDBLS	10/01-12/01
	Sioux Falls MSA, SD	H	9.34 FQ	11.59 AW	14.26 TQ	SDBLS	10/01-12/01
	Tennessee	H	8.77 FQ	13.15 AW	18.10 TQ	TNBLS	10/01-12/01
	Chattanooga MSA, TN-GA	H	8.99 FQ	12.58 AW	17.31 TQ	TNBLS	10/01-12/01
	Clarksville-Hopkinsville MSA, TN-KY	H	8.79 FQ	12.12 AW	16.60 TQ	TNBLS	10/01-12/01
	Johnson City-Kingsport-Bristol MSA, TN-VA	H	7.89 FQ	11.81 AW	16.88 TQ	TNBLS	10/01-12/01
	Knoxville MSA, TN	H	8.45 FQ	12.79 AW	17.42 TQ	TNBLS	10/01-12/01
	Memphis MSA, TN-AR-MS	H	9.76 FQ	14.71 AW	21.04 TQ	TNBLS	10/01-12/01
	Nashville MSA, TN	H	9.32 FQ	13.76 AW	18.52 TQ	TNBLS	10/01-12/01
	Texas	H	8.61 FQ	13.24 AW	18.27 TQ	TXBLS	10/01-12/01
	Amarillo MSA, TX	H	7.56 FQ	12.22 AW	18.24 TQ	TXBLS	10/01-12/01
	Austin-San Marcos MSA, TX	H	10.03 FQ	14.10 AW	18.80 TQ	TXBLS	10/01-12/01
	Beaumont-Port Arthur MSA, TX	H	8.74 FQ	14.75 AW	24.58 TQ	TXBLS	10/01-12/01
	Brazoria PMSA, TX	H	8.97 FQ	12.67 AW	16.73 TQ	TXBLS	10/01-12/01
	Brownsville-Harlingen-San Benito MSA, TX	H	7.00 FQ	9.97 AW	13.34 TQ	TXBLS	10/01-12/01
	Corpus Christi MSA, TX	H	7.75 FQ	11.96 AW	16.98 TQ	TXBLS	10/01-12/01
	Dallas PMSA, TX	H	9.94 FQ	14.69 AW	20.19 TQ	TXBLS	10/01-12/01
	El Paso MSA, TX	H	6.54 FQ	10.70 AW	15.39 TQ	TXBLS	10/01-12/01
	Fort Worth-Arlington PMSA, TX	H	9.30 FQ	13.33 AW	17.56 TQ	TXBLS	10/01-12/01
	Galveston-Texas City PMSA, TX	H	9.16 FQ	13.35 AW	19.69 TQ	TXBLS	10/01-12/01
	Houston PMSA, TX	H	10.34 FQ	14.78 AW	20.17 TQ	TXBLS	10/01-12/01
	Killeen-Temple MSA, TX	H	7.98 FQ	12.40 AW	17.05 TQ	TXBLS	10/01-12/01
	Laredo MSA, TX	H	6.63 FQ	10.04 AW	14.07 TQ	TXBLS	10/01-12/01
	Longview-Marshall MSA, TX	H	8.13 FQ	11.63 AW	15.62 TQ	TXBLS	10/01-12/01
	Lubbock MSA, TX	H	7.63 FQ	12.64 AW	17.14 TQ	TXBLS	10/01-12/01
	McAllen-Edinburg-Mission MSA, TX	H	7.15 FQ	10.59 AW	14.80 TQ	TXBLS	10/01-12/01

AAW	Average annual wage	**AOH**	Average offered, high	**ASH**	Average starting, high	**H**	Hourly	**M**	Monthly	**S**	Special: hourly and annual
AE	Average entry wage	**AOL**	Average offered, low	**ASL**	Average starting, low	**HI**	Highest wage paid	**MTC**	Median total compensation	**TQ**	Third quartile wage
AEX	Average experienced wage	**APH**	Average pay, high range	**AW**	Average wage paid	**HR**	High end range	**MW**	Median wage paid	**W**	Weekly
AO	Average offered	**APL**	Average pay, low range	**FQ**	First quartile wage	**LR**	Low end range	**SQ**	Second quartile wage	**Y**	Yearly

Occupation/Type/Industry	Location	Per	Low	Mid	High	Source	Date
Payroll and Timekeeping Clerk	Odessa-Midland MSA, TX	H	7.98 FQ	11.77 AW	17.72 TQ	TXBLS	10/01-12/01
	San Antonio MSA, TX	H	8.08 FQ	11.92 AW	16.20 TQ	TXBLS	10/01-12/01
	Tyler MSA, TX	H	7.33 FQ	11.42 AW	16.86 TQ	TXBLS	10/01-12/01
	Waco MSA, TX	H	8.93 FQ	12.86 AW	17.29 TQ	TXBLS	10/01-12/01
	Utah	H	9.22 FQ	13.38 AW	17.44 TQ	UTBLS	10/01-12/01
	Provo-Orem MSA, UT	H	9.51 FQ	13.86 AW	17.33 TQ	UTBLS	10/01-12/01
	Salt Lake City-Ogden MSA, UT	H	9.40 FQ	13.45 AW	17.51 TQ	UTBLS	10/01-12/01
	Vermont	H	8.61 FQ	13.06 AW	17.56 TQ	VTBLS	10/01-12/01
	Burlington MSA, VT	H	9.91 FQ	14.39 AW	18.84 TQ	VTBLS	10/01-12/01
	Virginia	H	8.96 FQ	13.87 AW	19.96 TQ	VABLS	10/01-12/01
	Lynchburg MSA, VA	H	9.47 FQ	13.16 AW	18.34 TQ	VABLS	10/01-12/01
	Norfolk-Virginia Beach-Newport News MSA, VA-NC	H	7.04 FQ	12.58 AW	17.69 TQ	VABLS	10/01-12/01
	Richmond-Petersburg MSA, VA	H	9.46 FQ	14.55 AW	20.32 TQ	VABLS	10/01-12/01
	Roanoke MSA, VA	H	9.38 FQ	13.39 AW	19.81 TQ	VABLS	10/01-12/01
	Washington	H	10.57 FQ	15.20 AW	20.23 TQ	WABLS	10/01-12/01
	Bremerton PMSA, WA	H	9.87 FQ	13.76 AW	17.65 TQ	WABLS	10/01-12/01
	Olympia PMSA, WA	H	8.91 FQ	14.84 AW	19.31 TQ	WABLS	10/01-12/01
	Richland-Kennewick-Pasco MSA, WA	H	7.90 FQ	13.11 AW	19.34 TQ	WABLS	10/01-12/01
	Seattle-Bellevue-Everett PMSA, WA	H	11.99 FQ	16.23 AW	21.10 TQ	WABLS	10/01-12/01
	Spokane MSA, WA	H	9.93 FQ	14.37 AW	19.05 TQ	WABLS	10/01-12/01
	Tacoma PMSA, WA	H	11.55 FQ	15.18 AW	19.05 TQ	WABLS	10/01-12/01
	Yakima MSA, WA	H	8.74 FQ	13.73 AW	17.82 TQ	WABLS	10/01-12/01
	West Virginia	H	7.46 FQ	12.00 AW	17.37 TQ	WVBLS	10/01-12/01
	Charleston MSA, WV	H	8.46 FQ	12.28 AW	16.88 TQ	WVBLS	10/01-12/01
	Huntington-Ashland MSA, WV-KY-OH	H	7.71 FQ	11.86 AW	16.95 TQ	WVBLS	10/01-12/01
	Wisconsin	H	9.42 FQ	13.48 AW	17.93 TQ	WIBLS	10/01-12/01
	Appleton-Oshkosh-Neenah MSA, WI	H	8.95 FQ	13.36 AW	18.51 TQ	WIBLS	10/01-12/01
	Green Bay MSA, WI	H	9.96 FQ	14.17 AW	18.32 TQ	WIBLS	10/01-12/01
	Madison MSA, WI	H	10.63 FQ	14.56 AW	19.52 TQ	WIBLS	10/01-12/01
	Milwaukee-Waukesha PMSA, WI	H	10.21 FQ	14.32 AW	19.09 TQ	WIBLS	10/01-12/01
	Racine PMSA, WI	H	10.18 FQ	13.75 AW	17.48 TQ	WIBLS	10/01-12/01
	Wyoming	H	8.70 FQ	12.89 AW	19.08 TQ	WYBLS	10/01-12/01
	Cheyenne MSA, WY	H	9.19 FQ	13.35 AW	19.19 TQ	WYBLS	10/01-12/01
	Puerto Rico	H	5.92 FQ	9.27 AW	13.61 TQ	PRBLS	10/01-12/01
	Virgin Islands	H	7.56 FQ	10.28 AW	13.76 TQ	VIBLS	10/01-12/01
	Guam	H	8.13 FQ	12.25 AW	16.69 TQ	GUBLS	10/01-12/01
Payroll Clerk							
Association	United States	Y		35000 AW		AM	1/01-1/02
Pediatrician	United States	Y		131000 AW		HHN	1/01-1/02
General	Alabama	Y	80220 FQ	116040 AW		ALBLS	10/01-12/01
General	Birmingham MSA, AL	Y	76730 FQ	110960 AW		ALBLS	10/01-12/01
General	Mobile MSA, AL	Y	81120 FQ	118500 AW		ALBLS	10/01-12/01
General	Arizona	Y	86420 FQ	114010 AW		AZBLS	10/01-12/01
General	Phoenix-Mesa MSA, AZ	Y	95310 FQ	122660 AW		AZBLS	10/01-12/01
General	Tucson MSA, AZ	Y	81480 FQ	105440 AW		AZBLS	10/01-12/01
General	Arkansas	Y	97640 FQ	112850 AW	140240 TQ	ARBLS	10/01-12/01
General	California	Y	36320 FQ	104820 AW		CABLS	10/01-12/01
General	Bakersfield MSA, CA	Y	102590 FQ	129180 AW		CABLS	10/01-12/01
General	Fresno MSA, CA	Y	34420 FQ	91590 AW		CABLS	10/01-12/01
General	Los Angeles-Long Beach PMSA, CA	Y	32480 FQ	81780 AW		CABLS	10/01-12/01
General	Orange County PMSA, CA	Y	33380 FQ	100030 AW		CABLS	10/01-12/01
General	Riverside-San Bernardino PMSA, CA	Y	111010 FQ	130940 AW		CABLS	10/01-12/01
General	Sacramento PMSA, CA	Y	80340 FQ	113270 AW		CABLS	10/01-12/01
General	San Diego MSA, CA	Y	86820 FQ	105220 AW	143810 TQ	CABLS	10/01-12/01
General	Stockton-Lodi MSA, CA	Y	91570 FQ	100040 AW	115730 TQ	CABLS	10/01-12/01
General	Ventura PMSA, CA	Y	100720 FQ	129330 AW		CABLS	10/01-12/01
General	Colorado	Y	67260 FQ	120620 AW		COBLS	10/01-12/01
General	Fort Collins-Loveland MSA, CO	Y	68730 FQ	113210 AW		COBLS	10/01-12/01
General	Connecticut	Y	40150 FQ	102780 AW		CTBLS	10/01-12/01

AAW	Average annual wage	AOH	Average offered, high	ASH	Average starting, high	H	Hourly	M	Monthly	S	Special: hourly and annual
AE	Average entry wage	AOL	Average offered, low	ASL	Average starting, low	HI	Highest wage paid	MTC	Median total compensation	TQ	Third quartile wage
AEX	Average experienced wage	APH	Average pay, high range	AW	Average wage paid	HR	High end range	MW	Median wage paid	W	Weekly
AO	Average offered	APL	Average pay, low range	FQ	First quartile wage	LR	Low end range	SQ	Second quartile wage	Y	Yearly

Occupation/Type/Industry	Location	Per	Low	Mid	High	Source	Date
Pediatrician							
General	Hartford MSA, CT	Y	38820 FQ	102390 AW		CTBLS	10/01-12/01
General	New Haven-Meriden PMSA, CT	Y	91100 FQ	103190 AW	140650 TQ	CTBLS	10/01-12/01
General	New London-Norwich MSA, CT-RI	Y	94070 FQ	117010 AW		CTBLS	10/01-12/01
General	Delaware	Y	76860 FQ	98880 AW	138560 TQ	DEBLS	10/01-12/01
General	Wilmington-Newark PMSA, DE-MD	Y	79090 FQ	104890 AW		DEBLS	10/01-12/01
General	District of Columbia	Y	53480 FQ	70140 AW	89600 TQ	DCBLS	10/01-12/01
General	Washington PMSA, DC-MD-VA-WV	Y	52880 FQ	81140 AW		DCBLS	10/01-12/01
General	Florida	Y	98750 FQ	126880 AW		FLBLS	10/01-12/01
General	Daytona Beach MSA, FL	Y	124610 FQ	137990 AW		FLBLS	10/01-12/01
General	Fort Lauderdale PMSA, FL	Y	96690 FQ	125910 AW		FLBLS	10/01-12/01
General	Melbourne-Titusville-Palm Bay MSA, FL	Y	122520 FQ	136550 AW		FLBLS	10/01-12/01
General	Miami PMSA, FL	Y	101030 FQ	126230 AW		FLBLS	10/01-12/01
General	Naples MSA, FL	Y	111630 FQ	137640 AW		FLBLS	10/01-12/01
General	Orlando MSA, FL	Y	97730 FQ	126990 AW		FLBLS	10/01-12/01
General	Tampa-St. Petersburg-Clearwater MSA, FL	Y	107500 FQ	129360 AW		FLBLS	10/01-12/01
General	West Palm Beach-Boca Raton MSA, FL	Y	95880 FQ	115670 AW		FLBLS	10/01-12/01
General	Georgia	Y	100200 FQ	126110 AW		GABLS	10/01-12/01
General	Atlanta MSA, GA	Y	94790 FQ	124400 AW		GABLS	10/01-12/01
General	Macon MSA, GA	Y	124380 FQ	138170 AW		GABLS	10/01-12/01
General	Hawaii	Y	40770 FQ	87780 AW		HIBLS	10/01-12/01
General	Honolulu MSA, HI	Y	40130 FQ	79760 AW		HIBLS	10/01-12/01
General	Idaho	Y	58400 FQ	110120 AW		IDBLS	10/01-12/01
General	Illinois	Y	20930 FQ	98570 AW		ILBLS	10/01-12/01
General	Chicago PMSA, IL	Y	20530 FQ	95610 AW		ILBLS	10/01-12/01
General	Indiana	Y	95080 FQ	121120 AW		INBLS	10/01-12/01
General	Indianapolis MSA, IN	Y	97200 FQ	122060 AW		INBLS	10/01-12/01
General	Iowa	Y	101480 FQ	132160 AW		IABLS	10/01-12/01
General	Kansas	Y	92820 FQ	113090 AW		KSBLS	10/01-12/01
General	Wichita MSA, KS	Y	97150 FQ	107200 AW	119100 TQ	KSBLS	10/01-12/01
General	Kentucky	Y	70210 FQ	112020 AW		KYBLS	10/01-12/01
General	Louisville MSA, KY-IN	Y	97070 FQ	128000 AW		KYBLS	10/01-12/01
General	Louisiana	Y	53590 FQ	111200 AW		LABLS	10/01-12/01
General	Maine	Y	74270 FQ	114160 AW		MEBLS	10/01-12/01
General	Maryland	Y	56530 FQ	109390 AW		MDBLS	10/01-12/01
General	Baltimore PMSA, MD	Y	85760 FQ	110530 AW	143630 TQ	MDBLS	10/01-12/01
General	Massachusetts	Y	99470 FQ	130730 AW		MABLS	10/01-12/01
General	Boston PMSA, MA-NH	Y	120670 FQ	136610 AW		MABLS	10/01-12/01
General	Lawrence PMSA, MA-NH	Y	51550 FQ	103320 AW		MABLS	10/01-12/01
General	Springfield MSA, MA	Y	49900 FQ	93880 AW	144640 TQ	MABLS	10/01-12/01
General	Michigan	Y	85370 FQ	120270 AW		MIBLS	10/01-12/01
General	Detroit PMSA, MI	Y	90270 FQ	123880 AW		MIBLS	10/01-12/01
General	Lansing-East Lansing MSA, MI	Y	86030 FQ	120270 AW		MIBLS	10/01-12/01
General	Minnesota	Y	95470 FQ	126300 AW		MNBLS	10/01-12/01
General	Minneapolis-St. Paul MSA, MN-WI	Y	95420 FQ	125720 AW		MNBLS	10/01-12/01
General	Mississippi	Y	113720 FQ	131000 AW		MSBLS	10/01-12/01
General	Jackson MSA, MS	Y	120710 FQ	128490 AW		MSBLS	10/01-12/01
General	Missouri	Y	96200 FQ	124470 AW		MOBLS	10/01-12/01
General	St. Louis MSA, MO-IL	Y	65840 FQ	111430 AW		MOBLS	10/01-12/01
General	Nebraska	Y	27100 FQ	90650 AW		NEBLS	10/01-12/01
General	Nevada	Y	115580 FQ	136720 AW		NVBLS	10/01-12/01
General	New Hampshire	Y	91850 FQ	130540 AW		NHBLS	10/01-12/01
General	New Jersey	Y	92920 FQ	107370 AW		NJBLS	10/01-12/01
General	Bergen-Passaic PMSA, NJ	Y	85290 FQ	124380 AW		NJBLS	10/01-12/01
General	Monmouth-Ocean PMSA, NJ	Y	90530 FQ	120830 AW		NJBLS	10/01-12/01
General	Newark PMSA, NJ	Y	92950 FQ	101530 AW	114120 TQ	NJBLS	10/01-12/01
General	Trenton PMSA, NJ	Y	95910 FQ	123260 AW		NJBLS	10/01-12/01
General	New Mexico	Y	48100 FQ	100970 AW		NMBLS	10/01-12/01
General	Albuquerque MSA, NM	Y	47110 FQ	82700 AW		NMBLS	10/01-12/01
General	New York	Y	96860 FQ	124220 AW		NYBLS	10/01-12/01
General	Buffalo-Niagara Falls MSA, NY	Y	89780 FQ	123710 AW		NYBLS	10/01-12/01
General	Nassau-Suffolk PMSA, NY	Y	98970 FQ	121250 AW		NYBLS	10/01-12/01
General	New York PMSA, NY	Y	95800 FQ	123920 AW		NYBLS	10/01-12/01

AAW Average annual wage · **AE** Average entry wage · **AEX** Average experienced wage · **AO** Average offered · **AOH** Average offered, high · **AOL** Average offered, low · **APH** Average pay, high range · **APL** Average pay, low range · **ASH** Average starting, high · **ASL** Average starting, low · **AW** Average wage paid · **FQ** First quartile wage · **H** Hourly · **HI** Highest wage paid · **HR** High end range · **LR** Low end range · **M** Monthly · **MTC** Median total compensation · **MW** Median wage paid · **SQ** Second quartile wage · **S** Special: hourly and annual · **TQ** Third quartile wage · **W** Weekly · **Y** Yearly

Occupation/Type/Industry	Location	Per	Low	Mid	High	Source	Date
Pediatrician							
General	Newburgh PMSA, NY-PA	Y	100550 FQ	129590 AW		NYBLS	10/01-12/01
General	North Carolina	Y	55750 FQ	118780 AW		NCBLS	10/01-12/01
General	Asheville MSA, NC	Y	61660 FQ	109250 AW		NCBLS	10/01-12/01
General	Raleigh-Durham-Chapel Hill MSA, NC	Y	107980 FQ	129630 AW		NCBLS	10/01-12/01
General	Wilmington MSA, NC	Y	126660 FQ	135560 AW		NCBLS	10/01-12/01
General	Ohio	Y	83680 FQ	118500 AW		OHBLS	10/01-12/01
General	Canton-Massillon MSA, OH	Y	95470 FQ	119550 AW		OHBLS	10/01-12/01
General	Cincinnati PMSA, OH-KY-IN	Y	85280 FQ	120260 AW		OHBLS	10/01-12/01
General	Cleveland-Lorain-Elyria PMSA, OH	Y	73960 FQ	108400 AW		OHBLS	10/01-12/01
General	Dayton-Springfield MSA, OH	Y	104140 FQ	131210 AW		OHBLS	10/01-12/01
General	Toledo MSA, OH	Y	87280 FQ	98570 AW	113020 TQ	OHBLS	10/01-12/01
General	Oklahoma	Y	116810 FQ	129940 AW		OKBLS	10/01-12/01
General	Oklahoma City MSA, OK	Y	85560 FQ	128010 AW		OKBLS	10/01-12/01
General	Oregon	Y	64840 FQ	111980 AW		ORBLS	10/01-12/01
General	Portland-Vancouver PMSA, OR-WA	Y	64630 FQ	111910 AW		ORBLS	10/01-12/01
General	Pennsylvania	Y	65540 FQ	118480 AW		PABLS	10/01-12/01
General	Harrisburg-Lebanon-Carlisle MSA, PA	Y	87320 FQ	121540 AW		PABLS	10/01-12/01
General	Philadelphia PMSA, PA-NJ	Y	61960 FQ	111080 AW		PABLS	10/01-12/01
General	Rhode Island	Y	93150 FQ	124710 AW		RIBLS	10/01-12/01
General	Providence-Fall River-Warwick MSA, RI-MA	Y	93440 FQ	124160 AW		RIBLS	10/01-12/01
General	South Carolina	Y	87260 FQ	120780 AW		SCBLS	10/01-12/01
General	Columbia MSA, SC	Y	79430 FQ	105480 AW	141890 TQ	SCBLS	10/01-12/01
General	Greenville-Spartanburg-Anderson MSA, SC	Y	98900 FQ	126460 AW		SCBLS	10/01-12/01
General	Tennessee	Y	79900 FQ	113200 AW		TNBLS	10/01-12/01
General	Knoxville MSA, TN	Y	42970 FQ	102580 AW		TNBLS	10/01-12/01
General	Memphis MSA, TN-AR-MS	Y	83730 FQ	121410 AW		TNBLS	10/01-12/01
General	Nashville MSA, TN	Y	76490 FQ	115360 AW		TNBLS	10/01-12/01
General	Texas	Y	35340 FQ	121410 AW		TXBLS	10/01-12/01
General	Brownsville-Harlingen-San Benito MSA, TX	Y	70230 FQ	121280 AW		TXBLS	10/01-12/01
General	El Paso MSA, TX	Y	98390 FQ	119380 AW		TXBLS	10/01-12/01
General	Fort Worth-Arlington PMSA, TX	Y	31330 FQ	99000 AW		TXBLS	10/01-12/01
General	Utah	Y	84120 FQ	124070 AW		UTBLS	10/01-12/01
General	Salt Lake City-Ogden MSA, UT	Y	85260 FQ	124260 AW		UTBLS	10/01-12/01
General	Vermont	Y	43380 FQ	100370 AW		VTBLS	10/01-12/01
General	Burlington MSA, VT	Y	39860 FQ	86940 AW		VTBLS	10/01-12/01
General	Virginia	Y	99580 FQ	124510 AW		VABLS	10/01-12/01
General	Roanoke MSA, VA	Y	36510 FQ	125170 AW		VABLS	10/01-12/01
General	Washington	Y	41640 FQ	103640 AW		WABLS	10/01-12/01
General	Seattle-Bellevue-Everett PMSA, WA	Y	35430 FQ	95920 AW		WABLS	10/01-12/01
General	West Virginia	Y	73450 FQ	104210 AW		WVBLS	10/01-12/01
General	Charleston MSA, WV	Y	73420 FQ	100220 AW		WVBLS	10/01-12/01
General	Huntington-Ashland MSA, WV-KY-OH	Y	73390 FQ	98910 AW		WVBLS	10/01-12/01
General	Wisconsin	Y	100200 FQ	127940 AW		WIBLS	10/01-12/01
General	Green Bay MSA, WI	Y	109400 FQ	131550 AW		WIBLS	10/01-12/01
General	Milwaukee-Waukesha PMSA, WI	Y	92710 FQ	125990 AW		WIBLS	10/01-12/01
General	Wyoming	Y	74660 FQ	101640 AW	133050 TQ	WYBLS	10/01-12/01
General	Puerto Rico	Y	41850 FQ	58530 AW	76510 TQ	PRBLS	10/01-12/01
Personal and Home Care Aide	United States	Y			18490 HI	FREEP1	1/00-1/00
	United States	H		7.50 MW		OOH10	1999-2000
	Alabama	H	5.68 FQ	7.18 AW	9.72 TQ	ALBLS	10/01-12/01
	Alaska	H	8.55 FQ	11.74 AW	16.42 TQ	AKBLS	10/01-12/01
	Arizona	H	7.17 FQ	10.34 AW	19.18 TQ	AZBLS	10/01-12/01
	Arkansas	H	5.73 FQ	6.89 AW	8.44 TQ	ARBLS	10/01-12/01
	California	H	6.67 FQ	9.02 AW	11.50 TQ	CABLS	10/01-12/01
	Colorado	H	6.14 FQ	8.09 AW	10.40 TQ	COBLS	10/01-12/01
	Connecticut	H	7.18 FQ	10.21 AW	14.79 TQ	CTBLS	10/01-12/01
	Delaware	H	6.48 FQ	7.27 AW	8.69 TQ	DEBLS	10/01-12/01
	District of Columbia	H	7.43 FQ	9.08 AW	12.33 TQ	DCBLS	10/01-12/01
	Florida	H	6.15 FQ	8.23 AW	10.60 TQ	FLBLS	10/01-12/01

AAW	Average annual wage	**AOH**	Average offered, high	**ASH**	Average starting, high	**H**	Hourly	**M**	Monthly	**S**	Special: hourly and annual
AE	Average entry wage	**AOL**	Average offered, low	**ASL**	Average starting, low	**HI**	Highest wage paid	**MTC**	Median total compensation	**TQ**	Third quartile wage
AEX	Average experienced wage	**APH**	Average pay, high range	**AW**	Average wage paid	**HR**	High end range	**MW**	Median wage paid	**W**	Weekly
AO	Average offered	**APL**	Average pay, low range	**FQ**	First quartile wage	**LR**	Low end range	**SQ**	Second quartile wage	**Y**	Yearly

Occupation/Type/Industry	Location	Per	Low	Mid	High	Source	Date
Personal and Home Care Aide	Georgia	H	5.73 FQ	7.94 AW	10.95 TQ	GABLS	10/01-12/01
	Hawaii	H	5.85 FQ	8.86 AW	12.47 TQ	HIBLS	10/01-12/01
	Idaho	H	5.79 FQ	7.35 AW	8.71 TQ	IDBLS	10/01-12/01
	Illinois	H	5.73 FQ	7.70 AW	10.46 TQ	ILBLS	10/01-12/01
	Indiana	H	6.75 FQ	8.92 AW	11.17 TQ	INBLS	10/01-12/01
	Iowa	H	6.83 FQ	8.14 AW	10.22 TQ	IABLS	10/01-12/01
	Kansas	H	6.86 FQ	8.13 AW	10.13 TQ	KSBLS	10/01-12/01
	Kentucky	H	5.79 FQ	7.55 AW	9.72 TQ	KYBLS	10/01-12/01
	Louisiana	H	5.50 FQ	6.36 AW	7.76 TQ	LABLS	10/01-12/01
	Maine	H	6.42 FQ	8.40 AW	10.74 TQ	MEBLS	10/01-12/01
	Maryland	H	6.86 FQ	8.83 AW	11.55 TQ	MDBLS	10/01-12/01
	Massachusetts	H	7.79 FQ	9.74 AW	11.93 TQ	MABLS	10/01-12/01
	Michigan	H	6.41 FQ	8.27 AW	10.50 TQ	MIBLS	10/01-12/01
	Minnesota	H	7.40 FQ	9.37 AW	11.51 TQ	MNBLS	10/01-12/01
	Mississippi	H	5.61 FQ	7.05 AW	9.71 TQ	MSBLS	10/01-12/01
	Missouri	H	5.97 FQ	7.53 AW	8.94 TQ	MOBLS	10/01-12/01
	Montana	H	5.81 FQ	7.29 AW	8.70 TQ	MTBLS	10/01-12/01
	Nebraska	H	6.16 FQ	8.54 AW	10.85 TQ	NEBLS	10/01-12/01
	Nevada	H	7.13 FQ	8.59 AW	10.45 TQ	NVBLS	10/01-12/01
	New Hampshire	H	6.32 FQ	8.39 AW	10.73 TQ	NHBLS	10/01-12/01
	New Jersey	H	7.56 FQ	9.73 AW	12.09 TQ	NJBLS	10/01-12/01
	New Mexico	H	5.87 FQ	7.68 AW	10.34 TQ	NMBLS	10/01-12/01
	New York	H	6.11 FQ	8.11 AW	10.18 TQ	NYBLS	10/01-12/01
	North Carolina	H	6.11 FQ	7.92 AW	10.16 TQ	NCBLS	10/01-12/01
	North Dakota	H	6.55 FQ	8.00 AW	9.69 TQ	NDBLS	10/01-12/01
	Ohio	H	6.65 FQ	8.41 AW	10.57 TQ	OHBLS	10/01-12/01
	Oklahoma	H	5.62 FQ	7.01 AW	8.44 TQ	OKBLS	10/01-12/01
	Oregon	H	7.30 FQ	9.36 AW	12.37 TQ	ORBLS	10/01-12/01
	Pennsylvania	H	6.08 FQ	8.48 AW	10.44 TQ	PABLS	10/01-12/01
	Rhode Island	H	7.17 FQ	10.47 AW	13.22 TQ	RIBLS	10/01-12/01
	South Carolina	H	6.20 FQ	7.97 AW	10.13 TQ	SCBLS	10/01-12/01
	South Dakota	H	6.03 FQ	8.00 AW	10.50 TQ	SDBLS	10/01-12/01
	Tennessee	H	6.04 FQ	7.94 AW	10.39 TQ	TNBLS	10/01-12/01
	Texas	H	5.50 FQ	6.32 AW	7.54 TQ	TXBLS	10/01-12/01
	Utah	H	6.42 FQ	7.83 AW	9.12 TQ	UTBLS	10/01-12/01
	Vermont	H	6.92 FQ	8.12 AW	10.09 TQ	VTBLS	10/01-12/01
	Virginia	H	5.66 FQ	7.40 AW	10.36 TQ	VABLS	10/01-12/01
	Washington	H	7.18 FQ	8.58 AW	10.62 TQ	WABLS	10/01-12/01
	West Virginia	H	5.57 FQ	6.59 AW	8.29 TQ	WVBLS	10/01-12/01
	Wisconsin	H	7.17 FQ	8.68 AW	10.60 TQ	WIBLS	10/01-12/01
	Puerto Rico	H	5.56 FQ	6.26 AW	7.00 TQ	PRBLS	10/01-12/01
Home Health Care Services	United States	H		6.49 MW		OOH10	1999-2000
Individual and Family Services	United States	H		7.75 MW		OOH10	1999-2000
Job Training and Related Services	United States	H		7.85 MW		OOH10	1999-2000
Nursing and Personal Care Facilities	United States	H		7.82 MW		OOH10	1999-2000
Residential Care	United States	H		7.97 MW		OOH10	1999-2000
Personal Financial Advisor	Alabama	Y	23500 FQ	56030 AW	116560 TQ	ALBLS	10/01-12/01
	Birmingham MSA, AL	Y	21750 FQ	47300 AW	97690 TQ	ALBLS	10/01-12/01
	Huntsville MSA, AL	Y	44280 FQ	93560 AW		ALBLS	10/01-12/01
	Mobile MSA, AL	Y	31900 FQ	59770 AW	102210 TQ	ALBLS	10/01-12/01
	Montgomery MSA, AL	Y	24990 FQ	50640 AW	83270 TQ	ALBLS	10/01-12/01
	Alaska	Y	27340 FQ	49170 AW	85080 TQ	AKBLS	10/01-12/01
	Anchorage MSA, AK	Y	28890 FQ	52540 AW	88070 TQ	AKBLS	10/01-12/01
	Tucson MSA, AZ	Y	31420 FQ	68430 AW		AZBLS	10/01-12/01
	Arkansas	Y	24580 FQ	55010 AW	143830 TQ	ARBLS	10/01-12/01
	Fayetteville-Springdale-Rogers MSA, AR	Y	14780 FQ	68150 AW		ARBLS	10/01-12/01
	Little Rock-North Little Rock MSA, AR	Y	24900 FQ	50680 AW	103050 TQ	ARBLS	10/01-12/01
	California	Y	31750 FQ	74500 AW		CABLS	10/01-12/01
	Chico-Paradise MSA, CA	Y	26020 FQ	73200 AW		CABLS	10/01-12/01
	Los Angeles-Long Beach PMSA, CA	Y	36020 FQ	77230 AW		CABLS	10/01-12/01
	Oakland PMSA, CA	Y	34610 FQ	66700 AW		CABLS	10/01-12/01
	Orange County PMSA, CA	Y	36980 FQ	80170 AW		CABLS	10/01-12/01
	Riverside-San Bernardino PMSA, CA	Y	40590 FQ	74570 AW	133020 TQ	CABLS	10/01-12/01
	Sacramento PMSA, CA	Y	24430 FQ	42770 AW	79050 TQ	CABLS	10/01-12/01
	San Diego MSA, CA	Y	38730 FQ	80220 AW		CABLS	10/01-12/01
	San Francisco PMSA, CA	Y	42960 FQ	80590 AW		CABLS	10/01-12/01
	San Jose PMSA, CA	Y	41850 FQ	91390 AW	142890 TQ	CABLS	10/01-12/01

AAW	Average annual wage	**AOH**	Average offered, high	**ASH**	Average starting, high	**H**	Hourly	**M**	Monthly	**S**	Special: hourly and annual
AE	Average entry wage	**AOL**	Average offered, low	**ASL**	Average starting, low	**HI**	Highest wage paid	**MTC**	Median total compensation	**TQ**	Third quartile wage
AEX	Average experienced wage	**APH**	Average pay, high range	**AW**	Average wage paid	**HR**	High end range	**MW**	Median wage paid	**W**	Weekly
AO	Average offered	**APL**	Average pay, low range	**FQ**	First quartile wage	**LR**	Low end range	**SQ**	Second quartile wage	**Y**	Yearly

Occupation/Type/Industry	Location	Per	Low	Mid	High	Source	Date
Personal Financial Advisor	Santa Barbara-Santa Maria-Lompoc MSA, CA	Y	44130 FQ	82810 AW		CABLS	10/01-12/01
	Santa Rosa PMSA, CA	Y	38700 FQ	84280 AW		CABLS	10/01-12/01
	Stockton-Lodi MSA, CA	Y	46470 FQ	71300 AW	139210 TQ	CABLS	10/01-12/01
	Ventura PMSA, CA	Y	41420 FQ	72940 AW	132080 TQ	CABLS	10/01-12/01
	Visalia-Tulare-Porterville MSA, CA	Y	23260 FQ	64870 AW		CABLS	10/01-12/01
	Colorado	Y	26830 FQ	62240 AW	142640 TQ	COBLS	10/01-12/01
	Boulder-Longmont PMSA, CO	Y	24730 FQ	57190 AW	122100 TQ	COBLS	10/01-12/01
	Denver PMSA, CO	Y	28240 FQ	63930 AW	135540 TQ	COBLS	10/01-12/01
	Connecticut	Y	35980 FQ	82410 AW		CTBLS	10/01-12/01
	Bridgeport PMSA, CT	Y	44470 FQ	97320 AW		CTBLS	10/01-12/01
	Danbury PMSA, CT	Y	35390 FQ	76300 AW		CTBLS	10/01-12/01
	Hartford MSA, CT	Y	32080 FQ	87840 AW		CTBLS	10/01-12/01
	New Haven-Meriden PMSA, CT	Y	53620 FQ	82500 AW		CTBLS	10/01-12/01
	New London-Norwich MSA, CT-RI	Y	35490 FQ	59180 AW	117070 TQ	CTBLS	10/01-12/01
	Stamford-Norwalk PMSA, CT	Y	37230 FQ	78990 AW		CTBLS	10/01-12/01
	Delaware	Y	30330 FQ	57170 AW	99610 TQ	DEBLS	10/01-12/01
	Wilmington-Newark PMSA, DE-MD	Y	30340 FQ	57870 AW	100610 TQ	DEBLS	10/01-12/01
	District of Columbia	Y	31950 FQ	83250 AW		DCBLS	10/01-12/01
	Washington PMSA, DC-MD-VA-WV	Y	25840 FQ	66760 AW		DCBLS	10/01-12/01
	Florida	Y	23230 FQ	57150 AW	143840 TQ	FLBLS	10/01-12/01
	Daytona Beach MSA, FL	Y	20570 FQ	40220 AW	67610 TQ	FLBLS	10/01-12/01
	Fort Lauderdale PMSA, FL	Y	28600 FQ	59020 AW	109380 TQ	FLBLS	10/01-12/01
	Fort Myers-Cape Coral MSA, FL	Y	19730 FQ	54930 AW		FLBLS	10/01-12/01
	Fort Pierce-Port St. Lucie MSA, FL	Y	14330 FQ	61140 AW	115950 TQ	FLBLS	10/01-12/01
	Jacksonville MSA, FL	Y	14290 FQ	69740 AW		FLBLS	10/01-12/01
	Lakeland-Winter Haven MSA, FL	Y	20550 FQ	39560 AW	80680 TQ	FLBLS	10/01-12/01
	Miami PMSA, FL	Y	22910 FQ	47680 AW	100460 TQ	FLBLS	10/01-12/01
	Naples MSA, FL	Y	34450 FQ	96020 AW		FLBLS	10/01-12/01
	Orlando MSA, FL	Y	23500 FQ	36190 AW	58910 TQ	FLBLS	10/01-12/01
	Pensacola MSA, FL	Y	19490 FQ	36040 AW	62290 TQ	FLBLS	10/01-12/01
	Sarasota-Bradenton MSA, FL	Y	26890 FQ	73610 AW		FLBLS	10/01-12/01
	Tallahassee MSA, FL	Y	31200 FQ	68540 AW		FLBLS	10/01-12/01
	Tampa-St. Petersburg-Clearwater MSA, FL	Y	23210 FQ	58500 AW		FLBLS	10/01-12/01
	West Palm Beach-Boca Raton MSA, FL	Y	24780 FQ	76000 AW		FLBLS	10/01-12/01
	Georgia	Y	34830 FQ	69350 AW		GABLS	10/01-12/01
	Atlanta MSA, GA	Y	37520 FQ	70120 AW		GABLS	10/01-12/01
	Augusta-Aiken MSA, GA-SC	Y	26170 FQ	74500 AW		GABLS	10/01-12/01
	Columbus MSA, GA-AL	Y	28430 FQ	41250 AW	60360 TQ	GABLS	10/01-12/01
	Macon MSA, GA	Y	29810 FQ	64130 AW	132680 TQ	GABLS	10/01-12/01
	Savannah MSA, GA	Y	44190 FQ	78550 AW		GABLS	10/01-12/01
	Hawaii	Y	27340 FQ	55250 AW	91160 TQ	HIBLS	10/01-12/01
	Honolulu MSA, HI	Y	30110 FQ	57000 AW	92050 TQ	HIBLS	10/01-12/01
	Idaho	Y	25820 FQ	60190 AW		IDBLS	10/01-12/01
	Boise City MSA, ID	Y	31310 FQ	69760 AW		IDBLS	10/01-12/01
	Illinois	Y	30120 FQ	66550 AW		ILBLS	10/01-12/01
	Champaign-Urbana MSA, IL	Y	25850 FQ	49250 AW	62380 TQ	ILBLS	10/01-12/01
	Chicago PMSA, IL	Y	30870 FQ	69080 AW		ILBLS	10/01-12/01
	Peoria-Pekin MSA, IL	Y	28620 FQ	51420 AW	88240 TQ	ILBLS	10/01-12/01
	Rockford MSA, IL	Y	13550 FQ	57520 AW	128940 TQ	ILBLS	10/01-12/01
	Indiana	Y	20510 FQ	54980 AW	119490 TQ	INBLS	10/01-12/01
	Evansville-Henderson MSA, IN-KY	Y	19710 FQ	42350 AW	73700 TQ	INBLS	10/01-12/01
	Fort Wayne MSA, IN	Y	18470 FQ	32320 AW	68590 TQ	INBLS	10/01-12/01
	Gary PMSA, IN	Y	22680 FQ	43540 AW	79350 TQ	INBLS	10/01-12/01
	Indianapolis MSA, IN	Y	29380 FQ	73010 AW		INBLS	10/01-12/01
	Lafayette MSA, IN	Y	30710 FQ	76480 AW	117910 TQ	INBLS	10/01-12/01
	South Bend MSA, IN	Y	21980 FQ	48330 AW	102010 TQ	INBLS	10/01-12/01
	Iowa	Y	21320 FQ	65690 AW	136080 TQ	IABLS	10/01-12/01
	Cedar Rapids MSA, IA	Y	19360 FQ	49920 AW	92930 TQ	IABLS	10/01-12/01
	Davenport-Moline-Rock Island MSA, IA-IL	Y	31040 FQ	70470 AW		IABLS	10/01-12/01

AAW	Average annual wage	**AOH**	Average offered, high	**ASH**	Average starting, high	**H**	Hourly	**M**	Monthly	**S**	Special: hourly and annual
AE	Average entry wage	**AOL**	Average offered, low	**ASL**	Average starting, low	**HI**	Highest wage paid	**MTC**	Median total compensation	**TQ**	Third quartile wage
AEX	Average experienced wage	**APH**	Average pay, high range	**AW**	Average wage paid	**HR**	High end range	**MW**	Median wage paid	**W**	Weekly
AO	Average offered	**APL**	Average pay, low range	**FQ**	First quartile wage	**LR**	Low end range	**SQ**	Second quartile wage	**Y**	Yearly

Occupation/Type/Industry	Location	Per	Low	Mid	High	Source	Date
Personal Financial Advisor	Des Moines MSA, IA	Y	31090 FQ	83980 AW		IABLS	10/01-12/01
	Kansas	Y	22060 FQ	62790 AW	131240 TQ	KSBLS	10/01-12/01
	Topeka MSA, KS	Y	29920 FQ	52530 AW	85400 TQ	KSBLS	10/01-12/01
	Wichita MSA, KS	Y	22520 FQ	69530 AW		KSBLS	10/01-12/01
	Kentucky	Y	27730 FQ	71880 AW		KYBLS	10/01-12/01
	Lexington MSA, KY	Y	27640 FQ	63600 AW	92120 TQ	KYBLS	10/01-12/01
	Louisville MSA, KY-IN	Y	28260 FQ	81080 AW		KYBLS	10/01-12/01
	Louisiana	Y	22580 FQ	57210 AW		LABLS	10/01-12/01
	Baton Rouge MSA, LA	Y	24180 FQ	43880 AW	93850 TQ	LABLS	10/01-12/01
	New Orleans MSA, LA	Y	26220 FQ	78030 AW		LABLS	10/01-12/01
	Shreveport-Bossier City MSA, LA	Y	24620 FQ	41180 AW	69730 TQ	LABLS	10/01-12/01
	Maine	Y	29340 FQ	51590 AW	107410 TQ	MEBLS	10/01-12/01
	Portland MSA, ME	Y	29320 FQ	50410 AW	107500 TQ	MEBLS	10/01-12/01
	Maryland	Y	25440 FQ	59670 AW		MDBLS	10/01-12/01
	Baltimore PMSA, MD	Y	26920 FQ	65640 AW		MDBLS	10/01-12/01
	Massachusetts	Y	36370 FQ	77480 AW	138940 TQ	MABLS	10/01-12/01
	Boston PMSA, MA-NH	Y	38360 FQ	79230 AW	138240 TQ	MABLS	10/01-12/01
	Springfield MSA, MA	Y	26230 FQ	45650 AW	77850 TQ	MABLS	10/01-12/01
	Worcester PMSA, MA-CT	Y	41440 FQ	83650 AW		MABLS	10/01-12/01
	Michigan	Y	26460 FQ	74450 AW		MIBLS	10/01-12/01
	Ann Arbor PMSA, MI	Y	24800 FQ	68150 AW		MIBLS	10/01-12/01
	Detroit PMSA, MI	Y	27730 FQ	70110 AW		MIBLS	10/01-12/01
	Grand Rapids-Muskegon-Holland MSA, MI	Y	30170 FQ	100670 AW		MIBLS	10/01-12/01
	Kalamazoo-Battle Creek MSA, MI	Y	31710 FQ	92440 AW		MIBLS	10/01-12/01
	Lansing-East Lansing MSA, MI	Y	22990 FQ	57370 AW	97500 TQ	MIBLS	10/01-12/01
	Saginaw-Bay City-Midland MSA, MI	Y	31910 FQ	86560 AW		MIBLS	10/01-12/01
	Minnesota	Y	30560 FQ	63620 AW	118940 TQ	MNBLS	10/01-12/01
	Minneapolis-St. Paul MSA, MN-WI	Y	38070 FQ	69090 AW	136660 TQ	MNBLS	10/01-12/01
	Mississippi	Y	22900 FQ	48070 AW	86520 TQ	MSBLS	10/01-12/01
	Jackson MSA, MS	Y	24800 FQ	55190 AW	104490 TQ	MSBLS	10/01-12/01
	Missouri	Y	19990 FQ	45890 AW	109780 TQ	MOBLS	10/01-12/01
	St. Louis MSA, MO-IL	Y	29230 FQ	68660 AW		MOBLS	10/01-12/01
	Springfield MSA, MO	Y	24240 FQ	63250 AW		MOBLS	10/01-12/01
	Montana	Y	21390 FQ	72210 AW	145310 TQ	MTBLS	10/01-12/01
	Billings MSA, MT	Y	22670 FQ	70530 AW	132330 TQ	MTBLS	10/01-12/01
	Nebraska	Y	20000 FQ	42730 AW	95320 TQ	NEBLS	10/01-12/01
	Lincoln MSA, NE	Y	21630 FQ	45920 AW	117000 TQ	NEBLS	10/01-12/01
	Omaha MSA, NE-IA	Y	25580 FQ	51600 AW	104680 TQ	NEBLS	10/01-12/01
	Nevada	Y	27460 FQ	71550 AW		NVBLS	10/01-12/01
	Las Vegas MSA, NV-AZ	Y	26320 FQ	67250 AW		NVBLS	10/01-12/01
	Reno MSA, NV	Y	31190 FQ	87470 AW		NVBLS	10/01-12/01
	New Hampshire	Y	26810 FQ	77080 AW		NHBLS	10/01-12/01
	Manchester PMSA, NH	Y	29070 FQ	63820 AW	142200 TQ	NHBLS	10/01-12/01
	New Jersey	Y	27950 FQ	74430 AW	137070 TQ	NJBLS	10/01-12/01
	Bergen-Passaic PMSA, NJ	Y	29920 FQ	66270 AW	114290 TQ	NJBLS	10/01-12/01
	Jersey City PMSA, NJ	Y	30920 FQ	70260 AW	118270 TQ	NJBLS	10/01-12/01
	Middlesex-Somerset-Hunterdon PMSA, NJ	Y	58120 FQ	101630 AW		NJBLS	10/01-12/01
	Monmouth-Ocean PMSA, NJ	Y	30050 FQ	69500 AW		NJBLS	10/01-12/01
	Newark PMSA, NJ	Y	25110 FQ	49450 AW	95650 TQ	NJBLS	10/01-12/01
	Trenton PMSA, NJ	Y	27310 FQ	74480 AW	134570 TQ	NJBLS	10/01-12/01
	New Mexico	Y	20070 FQ	53990 AW	83000 TQ	NMBLS	10/01-12/01
	Albuquerque MSA, NM	Y	19040 FQ	50590 AW	73050 TQ	NMBLS	10/01-12/01
	New York	Y	33590 FQ	81500 AW		NYBLS	10/01-12/01
	Albany-Schenectady-Troy MSA, NY	Y	40600 FQ	91840 AW		NYBLS	10/01-12/01
	Binghamton MSA, NY	Y	25220 FQ	48760 AW	104690 TQ	NYBLS	10/01-12/01
	Buffalo-Niagara Falls MSA, NY	Y	29440 FQ	69470 AW	119710 TQ	NYBLS	10/01-12/01
	Dutchess County PMSA, NY	Y	29100 FQ	78000 AW		NYBLS	10/01-12/01
	Nassau-Suffolk PMSA, NY	Y	37040 FQ	75620 AW		NYBLS	10/01-12/01
	New York PMSA, NY	Y	35610 FQ	83660 AW		NYBLS	10/01-12/01
	Newburgh PMSA, NY-PA	Y	25570 FQ	75220 AW		NYBLS	10/01-12/01
	Rochester MSA, NY	Y	23020 FQ	46720 AW	88510 TQ	NYBLS	10/01-12/01
	Utica-Rome MSA, NY	Y	39330 FQ	89070 AW		NYBLS	10/01-12/01
	North Carolina	Y	20700 FQ	56520 AW	117460 TQ	NCBLS	10/01-12/01
	Asheville MSA, NC	Y	28990 FQ	79120 AW		NCBLS	10/01-12/01

AAW	Average annual wage	**AOH**	Average offered, high	**ASH**	Average starting, high	**H**	Hourly	**M**	Monthly	**S**	Special: hourly and annual
AE	Average entry wage	**AOL**	Average offered, low	**ASL**	Average starting, low	**HI**	Highest wage paid	**MTC**	Median total compensation	**TQ**	Third quartile wage
AEX	Average experienced wage	**APH**	Average pay, high range	**AW**	Average wage paid	**HR**	High end range	**MW**	Median wage paid	**W**	Weekly
AO	Average offered	**APL**	Average pay, low range	**FQ**	First quartile wage	**LR**	Low end range	**SQ**	Second quartile wage	**Y**	Yearly

Occupation/Type/Industry	Location	Per	Low	Mid	High	Source	Date
Personal Financial Advisor	Charlotte-Gastonia-Rock Hill MSA, NC-SC	Y	15470 FQ	55090 AW	113460 TQ	NCBLS	10/01-12/01
	Fayetteville MSA, NC	Y	28140 FQ	49610 AW	89150 TQ	NCBLS	10/01-12/01
	Greensboro-Winston-Salem-High Point MSA, NC	Y	23590 FQ	54610 AW	102680 TQ	NCBLS	10/01-12/01
	Raleigh-Durham-Chapel Hill MSA, NC	Y	29790 FQ	72500 AW		NCBLS	10/01-12/01
	Wilmington MSA, NC	Y	20680 FQ	77980 AW		NCBLS	10/01-12/01
	North Dakota	Y	20840 FQ	42160 AW	80280 TQ	NDBLS	10/01-12/01
	Fargo-Moorhead MSA, ND-MN	Y	19580 FQ	40270 AW	59850 TQ	NDBLS	10/01-12/01
	Ohio	Y	29950 FQ	71790 AW		OHBLS	10/01-12/01
	Akron PMSA, OH	Y	32310 FQ	67360 AW		OHBLS	10/01-12/01
	Canton-Massillon MSA, OH	Y	31690 FQ	54200 AW	73670 TQ	OHBLS	10/01-12/01
	Cincinnati PMSA, OH-KY-IN	Y	25040 FQ	48410 AW	82480 TQ	OHBLS	10/01-12/01
	Cleveland-Lorain-Elyria PMSA, OH	Y	32550 FQ	96770 AW		OHBLS	10/01-12/01
	Columbus MSA, OH	Y	33550 FQ	59230 AW	92450 TQ	OHBLS	10/01-12/01
	Youngstown-Warren MSA, OH	Y	29590 FQ	77010 AW		OHBLS	10/01-12/01
	Oklahoma	Y	22360 FQ	55790 AW		OKBLS	10/01-12/01
	Tulsa MSA, OK	Y	21560 FQ	72720 AW		OKBLS	10/01-12/01
	Oregon	Y	32280 FQ	84960 AW		ORBLS	10/01-12/01
	Eugene-Springfield MSA, OR	Y	28770 FQ	69810 AW		ORBLS	10/01-12/01
	Portland-Vancouver PMSA, OR-WA	Y	43870 FQ	89610 AW		ORBLS	10/01-12/01
	Salem PMSA, OR	Y	25600 FQ	63030 AW		ORBLS	10/01-12/01
	Pennsylvania	Y	24800 FQ	63340 AW		PABLS	10/01-12/01
	Allentown-Bethlehem-Easton MSA, PA	Y	24900 FQ	61190 AW	97770 TQ	PABLS	10/01-12/01
	Erie MSA, PA	Y	27550 FQ	71570 AW		PABLS	10/01-12/01
	Harrisburg-Lebanon-Carlisle MSA, PA	Y	30920 FQ	64460 AW		PABLS	10/01-12/01
	Lancaster MSA, PA	Y	30420 FQ	69170 AW		PABLS	10/01-12/01
	Philadelphia PMSA, PA-NJ	Y	25780 FQ	67090 AW		PABLS	10/01-12/01
	Pittsburgh MSA, PA	Y	21300 FQ	55150 AW	137190 TQ	PABLS	10/01-12/01
	Reading MSA, PA	Y	31730 FQ	56910 AW	89720 TQ	PABLS	10/01-12/01
	Scranton-Wilkes-Barre-Hazleton MSA, PA	Y	25510 FQ	43460 AW	61680 TQ	PABLS	10/01-12/01
	York MSA, PA	Y	25310 FQ	56980 AW	135600 TQ	PABLS	10/01-12/01
	Rhode Island	Y	29770 FQ	57220 AW	106450 TQ	RIBLS	10/01-12/01
	Providence-Fall River-Warwick MSA, RI-MA	Y	29800 FQ	55810 AW	99810 TQ	RIBLS	10/01-12/01
	Columbia MSA, SC	Y	23320 FQ	34030 AW	46140 TQ	SCBLS	10/01-12/01
	Greenville-Spartanburg-Anderson MSA, SC	Y	28380 FQ	58230 AW	130980 TQ	SCBLS	10/01-12/01
	Myrtle Beach MSA, SC	Y	30710 FQ	83740 AW		SCBLS	10/01-12/01
	South Dakota	Y	37570 FQ	58600 AW	80570 TQ	SDBLS	10/01-12/01
	Sioux Falls MSA, SD	Y	36370 FQ	59970 AW	80280 TQ	SDBLS	10/01-12/01
	Tennessee	Y	27650 FQ	88020 AW		TNBLS	10/01-12/01
	Chattanooga MSA, TN-GA	Y	18570 FQ	59610 AW	116010 TQ	TNBLS	10/01-12/01
	Johnson City-Kingsport-Bristol MSA, TN-VA	Y	29110 FQ	94140 AW		TNBLS	10/01-12/01
	Memphis MSA, TN-AR-MS	Y	26570 FQ	77700 AW		TNBLS	10/01-12/01
	Texas	Y	24290 FQ	59940 AW	140660 TQ	TXBLS	10/01-12/01
	Austin-San Marcos MSA, TX	Y	24540 FQ	66130 AW		TXBLS	10/01-12/01
	Beaumont-Port Arthur MSA, TX	Y	32130 FQ	58700 AW	91480 TQ	TXBLS	10/01-12/01
	Corpus Christi MSA, TX	Y	23980 FQ	59970 AW		TXBLS	10/01-12/01
	Dallas PMSA, TX	Y	28370 FQ	56340 AW	113310 TQ	TXBLS	10/01-12/01
	El Paso MSA, TX	Y	19540 FQ	57580 AW		TXBLS	10/01-12/01
	Fort Worth-Arlington PMSA, TX	Y	20380 FQ	61960 AW		TXBLS	10/01-12/01
	Houston PMSA, TX	Y	22010 FQ	62610 AW		TXBLS	10/01-12/01
	Laredo MSA, TX	Y	24780 FQ	48270 AW	101100 TQ	TXBLS	10/01-12/01
	Lubbock MSA, TX	Y	20530 FQ	34110 AW	61440 TQ	TXBLS	10/01-12/01
	Odessa-Midland MSA, TX	Y	22260 FQ	54370 AW	91820 TQ	TXBLS	10/01-12/01
	San Antonio MSA, TX	Y	26540 FQ	62840 AW	144870 TQ	TXBLS	10/01-12/01
	Waco MSA, TX	Y	30350 FQ	61840 AW	129800 TQ	TXBLS	10/01-12/01
	Utah	Y	30360 FQ	52020 AW	126430 TQ	UTBLS	10/01-12/01
	Salt Lake City-Ogden MSA, UT	Y	30410 FQ	47150 AW	77350 TQ	UTBLS	10/01-12/01
	Vermont	Y	29000 FQ	63440 AW		VTBLS	10/01-12/01

AAW Average annual wage **AOH** Average offered, high **ASH** Average starting, high **H** Hourly **M** Monthly **S** Special: hourly and annual
AE Average entry wage **AOL** Average offered, low **ASL** Average starting, low **HI** Highest wage paid **MTC** Median total compensation **TQ** Third quartile wage
AEX Average experienced wage **APH** Average pay, high range **AW** Average wage paid **HR** High end range **MW** Median wage paid **W** Weekly
AO Average offered **APL** Average pay, low range **FQ** First quartile wage **LR** Low end range **SQ** Second quartile wage **Y** Yearly

Occupation/Type/Industry	Location	Per	Low	Mid	High	Source	Date
Personal Financial Advisor	Burlington MSA, VT	Y	30330 FQ	67190 AW		VTBLS	10/01-12/01
	Virginia	Y	31390 FQ	77710 AW		VABLS	10/01-12/01
	Lynchburg MSA, VA	Y	53530 FQ	101200 AW		VABLS	10/01-12/01
	Norfolk-Virginia Beach-Newport News MSA, VA-NC	Y	32840 FQ	84930 AW	140460 TQ	VABLS	10/01-12/01
	Richmond-Petersburg MSA, VA	Y	38040 FQ	85880 AW	114180 TQ	VABLS	10/01-12/01
	Roanoke MSA, VA	Y	30430 FQ	60220 AW	102720 TQ	VABLS	10/01-12/01
	Washington	Y	25210 FQ	61700 AW	142380 TQ	WABLS	10/01-12/01
	Bremerton PMSA, WA	Y	26240 FQ	56640 AW	117220 TQ	WABLS	10/01-12/01
	Seattle-Bellevue-Everett PMSA, WA	Y	24590 FQ	63380 AW		WABLS	10/01-12/01
	Spokane MSA, WA	Y	28400 FQ	49750 AW	91480 TQ	WABLS	10/01-12/01
	West Virginia	Y	19740 FQ	43050 AW	80820 TQ	WVBLS	10/01-12/01
	Charleston MSA, WV	Y	19070 FQ	33820 AW	58040 TQ	WVBLS	10/01-12/01
	Huntington-Ashland MSA, WV-KY-OH	Y	20570 FQ	50380 AW	115820 TQ	WVBLS	10/01-12/01
	Wisconsin	Y	27100 FQ	58900 AW	109640 TQ	WIBLS	10/01-12/01
	Appleton-Oshkosh-Neenah MSA, WI	Y	30420 FQ	55800 AW	84990 TQ	WIBLS	10/01-12/01
	Green Bay MSA, WI	Y	28730 FQ	76860 AW		WIBLS	10/01-12/01
	Madison MSA, WI	Y	30010 FQ	59070 AW	94570 TQ	WIBLS	10/01-12/01
	Milwaukee-Waukesha PMSA, WI	Y	28500 FQ	61510 AW	111690 TQ	WIBLS	10/01-12/01
Pest Control Worker	Alabama	H	6.46 FQ	10.76 AW	15.54 TQ	ALBLS	10/01-12/01
	Arizona	H	7.71 FQ	12.64 AW	22.02 TQ	AZBLS	10/01-12/01
	Arkansas	H	6.96 FQ	10.28 AW	15.36 TQ	ARBLS	10/01-12/01
	California	H	7.61 FQ	12.56 AW	19.86 TQ	CABLS	10/01-12/01
	Colorado	H	6.59 FQ	11.84 AW	18.12 TQ	COBLS	10/01-12/01
	Connecticut	H	8.28 FQ	12.73 AW	18.09 TQ	CTBLS	10/01-12/01
	Delaware	H	10.65 FQ	12.39 AW	13.81 TQ	DEBLS	10/01-12/01
	Florida	H	7.36 FQ	10.79 AW	15.22 TQ	FLBLS	10/01-12/01
	Georgia	H	8.79 FQ	12.53 AW	17.30 TQ	GABLS	10/01-12/01
	Hawaii	H	8.99 FQ	13.64 AW	24.17 TQ	HIBLS	10/01-12/01
	Idaho	H	10.82 FQ	13.68 AW	20.10 TQ	IDBLS	10/01-12/01
	Illinois	H	7.96 FQ	14.13 AW	21.74 TQ	ILBLS	10/01-12/01
	Indiana	H	7.53 FQ	12.60 AW	16.59 TQ	INBLS	10/01-12/01
	Iowa	H	10.58 FQ	12.85 AW	16.54 TQ	IABLS	10/01-12/01
	Kansas	H	9.07 FQ	13.08 AW	16.89 TQ	KSBLS	10/01-12/01
	Kentucky	H	6.53 FQ	10.80 AW	17.19 TQ	KYBLS	10/01-12/01
	Louisiana	H	5.97 FQ	10.80 AW	16.27 TQ	LABLS	10/01-12/01
	Maine	H	7.13 FQ	11.76 AW	17.40 TQ	MEBLS	10/01-12/01
	Maryland	H	7.73 FQ	13.98 AW	20.32 TQ	MDBLS	10/01-12/01
	Massachusetts	H	11.38 FQ	14.61 AW	18.15 TQ	MABLS	10/01-12/01
	Michigan	H	9.77 FQ	14.15 AW	19.79 TQ	MIBLS	10/01-12/01
	Minnesota	H	7.36 FQ	11.17 AW	17.35 TQ	MNBLS	10/01-12/01
	Mississippi	H	7.76 FQ	10.23 AW	13.34 TQ	MSBLS	10/01-12/01
	Missouri	H	7.55 FQ	12.22 AW	16.93 TQ	MOBLS	10/01-12/01
	Montana	H	5.88 FQ	11.76 AW	22.38 TQ	MTBLS	10/01-12/01
	Nebraska	H	6.50 FQ	11.21 AW	18.63 TQ	NEBLS	10/01-12/01
	Nevada	H	7.51 FQ	11.62 AW	19.26 TQ	NVBLS	10/01-12/01
	New Hampshire	H	12.15 FQ	14.82 AW	16.88 TQ	NHBLS	10/01-12/01
	New Jersey	H	9.69 FQ	14.37 AW	19.69 TQ	NJBLS	10/01-12/01
	New Mexico	H	8.85 FQ	11.22 AW	13.27 TQ	NMBLS	10/01-12/01
	New York	H	10.25 FQ	15.37 AW	20.41 TQ	NYBLS	10/01-12/01
	North Carolina	H	7.19 FQ	12.43 AW	16.94 TQ	NCBLS	10/01-12/01
	Ohio	H	9.62 FQ	17.18 AW	38.40 TQ	OHBLS	10/01-12/01
	Oklahoma	H	6.05 FQ	9.20 AW	13.33 TQ	OKBLS	10/01-12/01
	Oregon	H	9.00 FQ	12.15 AW	16.57 TQ	ORBLS	10/01-12/01
	Pennsylvania	H	8.55 FQ	13.12 AW	18.51 TQ	PABLS	10/01-12/01
	Rhode Island	H	7.96 FQ	13.88 AW	18.05 TQ	RIBLS	10/01-12/01
	South Carolina	H	7.04 FQ	11.06 AW	15.90 TQ	SCBLS	10/01-12/01
	Tennessee	H	8.06 FQ	11.49 AW	16.86 TQ	TNBLS	10/01-12/01
	Texas	H	6.00 FQ	10.82 AW	14.37 TQ	TXBLS	10/01-12/01
	Utah	H	8.74 FQ	9.80 AW	10.63 TQ	UTBLS	10/01-12/01
	Virginia	H	7.08 FQ	11.15 AW	16.16 TQ	VABLS	10/01-12/01
	Washington	H	10.95 FQ	14.99 AW	20.34 TQ	WABLS	10/01-12/01
	West Virginia	H	9.09 FQ	10.86 AW	14.08 TQ	WVBLS	10/01-12/01
	Wisconsin	H	7.27 FQ	13.10 AW	20.45 TQ	WIBLS	10/01-12/01
	Puerto Rico	H	5.46 FQ	6.73 AW	8.61 TQ	PRBLS	10/01-12/01

AAW	Average annual wage	**AOH**	Average offered, high	**ASH**	Average starting, high	**H**	Hourly	**M**	Monthly	**S**	Special: hourly and annual
AE	Average entry wage	**AOL**	Average offered, low	**ASL**	Average starting, low	**HI**	Highest wage paid	**MTC**	Median total compensation	**TQ**	Third quartile wage
AEX	Average experienced wage	**APH**	Average pay, high range	**AW**	Average wage paid	**HR**	High end range	**MW**	Median wage paid	**W**	Weekly
AO	Average offered	**APL**	Average pay, low range	**FQ**	First quartile wage	**LR**	Low end range	**SQ**	Second quartile wage	**Y**	Yearly

Occupation/Type/Industry	Location	Per	Low	Mid	High	Source	Date
Pesticide Handler, Sprayer, and Applicator	Alabama	H	7.90 FQ	10.83 AW	15.10 TQ	ALBLS	10/01-12/01
	Arizona	H	7.45 FQ	9.61 AW	13.24 TQ	AZBLS	10/01-12/01
	Arkansas	H	6.65 FQ	10.07 AW	15.29 TQ	ARBLS	10/01-12/01
	California	H	7.69 FQ	12.34 AW	18.31 TQ	CABLS	10/01-12/01
	Colorado	H	8.03 FQ	12.80 AW	18.91 TQ	COBLS	10/01-12/01
	Connecticut	H	10.30 FQ	13.47 AW	17.37 TQ	CTBLS	10/01-12/01
	Delaware	H	11.15 FQ	14.85 AW	21.67 TQ	DEBLS	10/01-12/01
	Florida	H	7.73 FQ	11.70 AW	16.23 TQ	FLBLS	10/01-12/01
	Georgia	H	6.60 FQ	12.78 AW	19.86 TQ	GABLS	10/01-12/01
	Hawaii	H	6.19 FQ	10.78 AW	14.43 TQ	HIBLS	10/01-12/01
	Idaho	H	9.35 FQ	11.68 AW	13.84 TQ	IDBLS	10/01-12/01
	Illinois	H	9.00 FQ	13.59 AW	20.94 TQ	ILBLS	10/01-12/01
	Indiana	H	8.71 FQ	13.16 AW	18.00 TQ	INBLS	10/01-12/01
	Iowa	H	8.06 FQ	11.52 AW	15.45 TQ	IABLS	10/01-12/01
	Kansas	H	7.90 FQ	11.29 AW	16.14 TQ	KSBLS	10/01-12/01
	Kentucky	H	8.23 FQ	11.31 AW	15.47 TQ	KYBLS	10/01-12/01
	Louisiana	H	7.36 FQ	10.18 AW	14.64 TQ	LABLS	10/01-12/01
	Maine	H	7.14 FQ	10.78 AW	16.03 TQ	MEBLS	10/01-12/01
	Maryland	H	9.24 FQ	12.29 AW	16.81 TQ	MDBLS	10/01-12/01
	Massachusetts	H	9.61 FQ	14.39 AW	18.39 TQ	MABLS	10/01-12/01
	Michigan	H	9.33 FQ	12.68 AW	16.66 TQ	MIBLS	10/01-12/01
	Minnesota	H	8.77 FQ	12.17 AW	16.65 TQ	MNBLS	10/01-12/01
	Mississippi	H	7.70 FQ	10.68 AW	13.90 TQ	MSBLS	10/01-12/01
	Missouri	H	9.11 FQ	11.78 AW	15.81 TQ	MOBLS	10/01-12/01
	Montana	H	6.68 FQ	9.61 AW	12.14 TQ	MTBLS	10/01-12/01
	Nebraska	H	8.11 FQ	11.65 AW	17.03 TQ	NEBLS	10/01-12/01
	New Hampshire	H	9.09 FQ	12.81 AW	16.94 TQ	NHBLS	10/01-12/01
	New Jersey	H	10.91 FQ	14.48 AW	18.13 TQ	NJBLS	10/01-12/01
	New York	H	9.52 FQ	18.73 AW	33.99 TQ	NYBLS	10/01-12/01
	North Carolina	H	9.31 FQ	12.52 AW	15.95 TQ	NCBLS	10/01-12/01
	North Dakota	H	7.59 FQ	10.30 AW	14.46 TQ	NDBLS	10/01-12/01
	Ohio	H	8.00 FQ	11.85 AW	15.91 TQ	OHBLS	10/01-12/01
	Oklahoma	H	6.16 FQ	9.68 AW	15.12 TQ	OKBLS	10/01-12/01
	Oregon	H	7.56 FQ	12.18 AW	16.80 TQ	ORBLS	10/01-12/01
	Pennsylvania	H	8.27 FQ	13.12 AW	18.38 TQ	PABLS	10/01-12/01
	South Carolina	H	7.39 FQ	11.23 AW	16.27 TQ	SCBLS	10/01-12/01
	South Dakota	H	7.65 FQ	10.74 AW	13.79 TQ	SDBLS	10/01-12/01
	Tennessee	H	8.63 FQ	11.69 AW	13.97 TQ	TNBLS	10/01-12/01
	Texas	H	5.74 FQ	10.13 AW	15.98 TQ	TXBLS	10/01-12/01
	Utah	H	9.31 FQ	11.45 AW	14.48 TQ	UTBLS	10/01-12/01
	Vermont	H	9.53 FQ	11.63 AW	14.18 TQ	VTBLS	10/01-12/01
	Virginia	H	7.93 FQ	12.08 AW	16.45 TQ	VABLS	10/01-12/01
	Washington	H	9.89 FQ	13.83 AW	17.91 TQ	WABLS	10/01-12/01
	West Virginia	H	7.09 FQ	10.93 AW	16.12 TQ	WVBLS	10/01-12/01
	Wisconsin	H	8.06 FQ	11.05 AW	14.63 TQ	WIBLS	10/01-12/01
	Wyoming	H	7.88 FQ	10.25 AW	12.85 TQ	WYBLS	10/01-12/01
Pet Sitter	United States	H		20.00-32.00 AW		EXAM	1/02-1/03
Petroleum Engineer	Alabama	Y	24550 FQ	63290 AW	108090 TQ	ALBLS	10/01-12/01
	Alaska	Y	68800 FQ	107620 AW		AKBLS	10/01-12/01
	California	Y	58150 FQ	82890 AW	115440 TQ	CABLS	10/01-12/01
	Colorado	Y	50090 FQ	84440 AW	128020 TQ	COBLS	10/01-12/01
	Florida	Y	61220 FQ	93140 AW		FLBLS	10/01-12/01
	Illinois	Y	55250 FQ	71980 AW	104330 TQ	ILBLS	10/01-12/01
	Kansas	Y	46420 FQ	68020 AW	106020 TQ	KSBLS	10/01-12/01
	Kentucky	Y	26840 FQ	72730 AW	113390 TQ	KYBLS	10/01-12/01
	Louisiana	Y	55640 FQ	84850 AW	116770 TQ	LABLS	10/01-12/01
	Michigan	Y	51520 FQ	69800 AW	94230 TQ	MIBLS	10/01-12/01
	Mississippi	Y	45860 FQ	69800 AW	105820 TQ	MSBLS	10/01-12/01
	Missouri	Y	36160 FQ	50330 AW	75650 TQ	MOBLS	10/01-12/01
	Montana	Y	51030 FQ	80890 AW	137350 TQ	MTBLS	10/01-12/01
	New Mexico	Y	50150 FQ	73460 AW	108240 TQ	NMBLS	10/01-12/01
	New York	Y	35980 FQ	53480 AW	76950 TQ	NYBLS	10/01-12/01
	North Dakota	Y	37180 FQ	58140 AW	91380 TQ	NDBLS	10/01-12/01
	Ohio	Y	31790 FQ	63010 AW	96370 TQ	OHBLS	10/01-12/01
	Oklahoma	Y	52730 FQ	89280 AW	135860 TQ	OKBLS	10/01-12/01
	Pennsylvania	Y	43620 FQ	57600 AW	81550 TQ	PABLS	10/01-12/01
	Texas	Y	49970 FQ	84160 AW	122270 TQ	TXBLS	10/01-12/01
	Utah	Y	30720 FQ	60620 AW	101440 TQ	UTBLS	10/01-12/01

AAW Average annual wage **AOH** Average offered, high **ASH** Average starting, high **H** Hourly **M** Monthly **S** Special: hourly and annual
AE Average entry wage **AOL** Average offered, low **ASL** Average starting, low **HI** Highest wage paid **MTC** Median total compensation **TQ** Third quartile wage
AEX Average experienced wage **APH** Average pay, high range **AW** Average wage paid **HR** High end range **MW** Median wage paid **W** Weekly
AO Average offered **APL** Average pay, low range **FQ** First quartile wage **LR** Low end range **SQ** Second quartile wage **Y** Yearly

Occupation/Type/Industry	Location	Per	Low	Mid	High	Source	Date
Petroleum Engineer	Virginia	Y	48250 FQ	74870 AW	107860 TQ	VABLS	10/01-12/01
	West Virginia	Y	29810 FQ	56660 AW	87160 TQ	WVBLS	10/01-12/01
	Wyoming	Y	49100 FQ	69630 AW	104830 TQ	WYBLS	10/01-12/01
Petroleum Pump System Operator, Refinery Operator, and Gauger	Alabama	H	12.04 FQ	19.23 AW	26.67 TQ	ALBLS	10/01-12/01
	Alaska	H	27.02 FQ	34.84 AW	42.44 TQ	AKBLS	10/01-12/01
	Arizona	H	9.30 FQ	16.76 AW	22.61 TQ	AZBLS	10/01-12/01
	Arkansas	H	15.78 FQ	21.96 AW	28.75 TQ	ARBLS	10/01-12/01
	California	H	18.59 FQ	24.18 AW	29.09 TQ	CABLS	10/01-12/01
	Colorado	H	13.17 FQ	21.05 AW	27.99 TQ	COBLS	10/01-12/01
	Delaware	H	11.27 FQ	21.26 AW	28.37 TQ	DEBLS	10/01-12/01
	Florida	H	9.86 FQ	15.03 AW	21.46 TQ	FLBLS	10/01-12/01
	Georgia	H	16.18 FQ	23.41 AW	33.34 TQ	GABLS	10/01-12/01
	Hawaii	H	16.34 FQ	22.59 AW	28.25 TQ	HIBLS	10/01-12/01
	Idaho	H	10.01 FQ	16.17 AW	23.70 TQ	IDBLS	10/01-12/01
	Illinois	H	18.06 FQ	24.06 AW	32.00 TQ	ILBLS	10/01-12/01
	Iowa	H	12.33 FQ	20.64 AW	28.20 TQ	IABLS	10/01-12/01
	Kansas	H	17.47 FQ	22.19 AW	27.14 TQ	KSBLS	10/01-12/01
	Louisiana	H	13.17 FQ	21.02 AW	26.97 TQ	LABLS	10/01-12/01
	Massachusetts	H	15.10 FQ	20.10 AW	26.17 TQ	MABLS	10/01-12/01
	Michigan	H	15.33 FQ	21.71 AW	27.42 TQ	MIBLS	10/01-12/01
	Missouri	H	15.38 FQ	22.75 AW	29.16 TQ	MOBLS	10/01-12/01
	Montana	H	18.13 FQ	25.54 AW	34.48 TQ	MTBLS	10/01-12/01
	Nebraska	H	8.38 FQ	18.21 AW	27.29 TQ	NEBLS	10/01-12/01
	Nevada	H	11.86 FQ	15.13 AW	19.10 TQ	NVBLS	10/01-12/01
	New Jersey	H	17.99 FQ	24.79 AW	32.26 TQ	NJBLS	10/01-12/01
	New Mexico	H	9.62 FQ	19.92 AW	27.39 TQ	NMBLS	10/01-12/01
	New York	H	14.46 FQ	18.07 AW	21.78 TQ	NYBLS	10/01-12/01
	North Carolina	H	14.26 FQ	19.36 AW	25.99 TQ	NCBLS	10/01-12/01
	Ohio	H	13.96 FQ	22.08 AW	27.26 TQ	OHBLS	10/01-12/01
	Oklahoma	H	10.25 FQ	19.87 AW	28.27 TQ	OKBLS	10/01-12/01
	Oregon	H	17.10 FQ	21.40 AW	26.52 TQ	ORBLS	10/01-12/01
	Pennsylvania	H	15.56 FQ	23.10 AW	30.71 TQ	PABLS	10/01-12/01
	South Carolina	H	8.77 FQ	16.03 AW	23.61 TQ	SCBLS	10/01-12/01
	Tennessee	H	10.29 FQ	17.45 AW	25.71 TQ	TNBLS	10/01-12/01
	Texas	H	13.15 FQ	21.79 AW	27.98 TQ	TXBLS	10/01-12/01
	Utah	H	15.08 FQ	21.65 AW	26.80 TQ	UTBLS	10/01-12/01
	Virginia	H	16.22 FQ	22.83 AW	29.71 TQ	VABLS	10/01-12/01
	Washington	H	17.59 FQ	21.90 AW	26.36 TQ	WABLS	10/01-12/01
	West Virginia	H	10.30 FQ	18.24 AW	23.53 TQ	WVBLS	10/01-12/01
	Wisconsin	H	16.72 FQ	23.03 AW	28.85 TQ	WIBLS	10/01-12/01
	Wyoming	H	18.66 FQ	22.50 AW	27.23 TQ	WYBLS	10/01-12/01
	Puerto Rico	H	12.03 FQ	18.29 AW	26.69 TQ	PRBLS	10/01-12/01
Pharmaceuticals Professional	San Diego, CA	Y		70259 AW		SDBJ1	1/99-1/00
Pharmacist	United States	Y	62000 ASL	74300 AW	96000 ASH	USATOD3	1/01-1/02
	United States	Y			96000 HI	DTHSE	1/00-1/01
	Northeast	Y		69871 AW		WW	1/00-1/01
	West	Y		84803 AW		WW	1/00-1/01
	Alabama	Y	54620 FQ	72210 AW	91190 TQ	ALBLS	10/01-12/01
	Birmingham MSA, AL	Y	55790 FQ	71210 AW	90500 TQ	ALBLS	10/01-12/01
	Huntsville MSA, AL	Y	62260 FQ	75820 AW	92300 TQ	ALBLS	10/01-12/01
	Mobile MSA, AL	Y	62070 FQ	75440 AW	91880 TQ	ALBLS	10/01-12/01
	Montgomery MSA, AL	Y	48260 FQ	72790 AW	91760 TQ	ALBLS	10/01-12/01
	Alaska	Y	63340 FQ	77180 AW	92870 TQ	AKBLS	10/01-12/01
	Anchorage MSA, AK	Y	63350 FQ	74910 AW	90560 TQ	AKBLS	10/01-12/01
	Arizona	Y	59130 FQ	73990 AW	90520 TQ	AZBLS	10/01-12/01
	Phoenix-Mesa MSA, AZ	Y	57950 FQ	73260 AW	90060 TQ	AZBLS	10/01-12/01
	Tucson MSA, AZ	Y	61510 FQ	75240 AW	90470 TQ	AZBLS	10/01-12/01
	Arkansas	Y	49090 FQ	65640 AW	88240 TQ	ARBLS	10/01-12/01
	Fayetteville-Springdale-Rogers MSA, AR	Y	55540 FQ	70180 AW	87760 TQ	ARBLS	10/01-12/01
	Fort Smith MSA, AR-OK	Y	28180 FQ	66930 AW	89450 TQ	ARBLS	10/01-12/01
	Little Rock-North Little Rock MSA, AR	Y	49990 FQ	66030 AW	88650 TQ	ARBLS	10/01-12/01
	California	Y	64880 FQ	83370 AW	105730 TQ	CABLS	10/01-12/01
	Bakersfield MSA, CA	Y	69500 FQ	85130 AW	107850 TQ	CABLS	10/01-12/01
	Chico-Paradise MSA, CA	Y	73170 FQ	86960 AW	109080 TQ	CABLS	10/01-12/01
	Fresno MSA, CA	Y	66460 FQ	86880 AW	113260 TQ	CABLS	10/01-12/01

AAW	Average annual wage	**AOH**	Average offered, high	**ASH**	Average starting, high	**H**	Hourly	**M**	Monthly	**S**	Special: hourly and annual
AE	Average entry wage	**AOL**	Average offered, low	**ASL**	Average starting, low	**HI**	Highest wage paid	**MTC**	Median total compensation	**TQ**	Third quartile wage
AEX	Average experienced wage	**APH**	Average pay, high range	**AW**	Average wage paid	**HR**	High end range	**MW**	Median wage paid	**W**	Weekly
AO	Average offered	**APL**	Average pay, low range	**FQ**	First quartile wage	**LR**	Low end range	**SQ**	Second quartile wage	**Y**	Yearly

Occupation/Type/Industry	Location	Per	Low	Mid	High	Source	Date
Pharmacist	Los Angeles-Long Beach PMSA, CA	Y	67990 FQ	85920 AW	112540 TQ	CABLS	10/01-12/01
	Merced MSA, CA	Y	63500 FQ	83320 AW	109800 TQ	CABLS	10/01-12/01
	Modesto MSA, CA	Y	75270 FQ	84820 AW	104630 TQ	CABLS	10/01-12/01
	Oakland PMSA, CA	Y	73400 FQ	84100 AW	102810 TQ	CABLS	10/01-12/01
	Orange County PMSA, CA	Y	64510 FQ	82690 AW	104470 TQ	CABLS	10/01-12/01
	Redding MSA, CA	Y	77840 FQ	93550 AW	123860 TQ	CABLS	10/01-12/01
	Riverside-San Bernardino PMSA, CA	Y	72240 FQ	83640 AW	100740 TQ	CABLS	10/01-12/01
	Sacramento PMSA, CA	Y	37750 FQ	81190 AW	101590 TQ	CABLS	10/01-12/01
	Salinas MSA, CA	Y	41990 FQ	79550 AW	104520 TQ	CABLS	10/01-12/01
	San Diego MSA, CA	Y	41220 FQ	76390 AW	100090 TQ	CABLS	10/01-12/01
	San Francisco PMSA, CA	Y	59440 FQ	80460 AW	98840 TQ	CABLS	10/01-12/01
	San Jose PMSA, CA	Y	70640 FQ	82650 AW	98250 TQ	CABLS	10/01-12/01
	San Luis Obispo-Atascadero-Paso Robles MSA, CA	Y	59600 FQ	79940 AW	107150 TQ	CABLS	10/01-12/01
	Santa Barbara-Santa Maria-Lompoc MSA, CA	Y	76360 FQ	87610 AW	107800 TQ	CABLS	10/01-12/01
	Santa Cruz-Watsonville PMSA, CA	Y	73430 FQ	85100 AW	108310 TQ	CABLS	10/01-12/01
	Santa Rosa PMSA, CA	Y	69390 FQ	83390 AW	103890 TQ	CABLS	10/01-12/01
	Stockton-Lodi MSA, CA	Y	34270 FQ	77200 AW	105850 TQ	CABLS	10/01-12/01
	Vallejo-Fairfield-Napa PMSA, CA	Y	61350 FQ	78470 AW	94860 TQ	CABLS	10/01-12/01
	Ventura PMSA, CA	Y	63100 FQ	83220 AW	105910 TQ	CABLS	10/01-12/01
	Visalia-Tulare-Porterville MSA, CA	Y	74890 FQ	92910 AW	113780 TQ	CABLS	10/01-12/01
	Colorado	Y	57940 FQ	70390 AW	88790 TQ	COBLS	10/01-12/01
	Boulder-Longmont PMSA, CO	Y	54340 FQ	68950 AW	88640 TQ	COBLS	10/01-12/01
	Colorado Springs MSA, CO	Y	61590 FQ	72630 AW	89260 TQ	COBLS	10/01-12/01
	Denver PMSA, CO	Y	57620 FQ	70320 AW	88960 TQ	COBLS	10/01-12/01
	Fort Collins-Loveland MSA, CO	Y	62290 FQ	70310 AW	82840 TQ	COBLS	10/01-12/01
	Greeley PMSA, CO	Y	60830 FQ	70250 AW	87670 TQ	COBLS	10/01-12/01
	Connecticut	Y	60660 FQ	76440 AW	93510 TQ	CTBLS	10/01-12/01
	Bridgeport PMSA, CT	Y	57960 FQ	77270 AW	94290 TQ	CTBLS	10/01-12/01
	Danbury PMSA, CT	Y	59440 FQ	77740 AW	93420 TQ	CTBLS	10/01-12/01
	Hartford MSA, CT	Y	61620 FQ	75280 AW	92090 TQ	CTBLS	10/01-12/01
	New Haven-Meriden PMSA, CT	Y	58190 FQ	76770 AW	97680 TQ	CTBLS	10/01-12/01
	New London-Norwich MSA, CT-RI	Y	63880 FQ	77440 AW	92750 TQ	CTBLS	10/01-12/01
	Stamford-Norwalk PMSA, CT	Y	60410 FQ	76230 AW	94420 TQ	CTBLS	10/01-12/01
	Waterbury PMSA, CT	Y	63480 FQ	78040 AW	93620 TQ	CTBLS	10/01-12/01
	Delaware	Y	60070 FQ	78720 AW	101020 TQ	DEBLS	10/01-12/01
	Wilmington-Newark PMSA, DE-MD	Y	59760 FQ	77810 AW	96830 TQ	DEBLS	10/01-12/01
	District of Columbia	Y	40410 FQ	67320 AW	89240 TQ	DCBLS	10/01-12/01
	Washington PMSA, DC-MD-VA-WV	Y	59780 FQ	73300 AW	93540 TQ	DCBLS	10/01-12/01
	Florida	Y	62440 FQ	77670 AW	93840 TQ	FLBLS	10/01-12/01
	Daytona Beach MSA, FL	Y	62720 FQ	77010 AW	93930 TQ	FLBLS	10/01-12/01
	Fort Lauderdale PMSA, FL	Y	49220 FQ	72210 AW	93020 TQ	FLBLS	10/01-12/01
	Fort Myers-Cape Coral MSA, FL	Y	65160 FQ	79860 AW	96500 TQ	FLBLS	10/01-12/01
	Fort Pierce-Port St. Lucie MSA, FL	Y	67830 FQ	79680 AW	93610 TQ	FLBLS	10/01-12/01
	Fort Walton Beach MSA, FL	Y	63650 FQ	76750 AW	90620 TQ	FLBLS	10/01-12/01
	Gainesville MSA, FL	Y	50290 FQ	74730 AW	91980 TQ	FLBLS	10/01-12/01
	Jacksonville MSA, FL	Y	64310 FQ	79460 AW	94360 TQ	FLBLS	10/01-12/01
	Lakeland-Winter Haven MSA, FL	Y	65970 FQ	78490 AW	93410 TQ	FLBLS	10/01-12/01
	Melbourne-Titusville-Palm Bay MSA, FL	Y	63740 FQ	78190 AW	93660 TQ	FLBLS	10/01-12/01
	Miami PMSA, FL	Y	63510 FQ	84690 AW	113660 TQ	FLBLS	10/01-12/01
	Naples MSA, FL	Y	71840 FQ	81620 AW	94290 TQ	FLBLS	10/01-12/01
	Ocala MSA, FL	Y	66500 FQ	79950 AW	96750 TQ	FLBLS	10/01-12/01
	Orlando MSA, FL	Y	65070 FQ	78160 AW	92470 TQ	FLBLS	10/01-12/01
	Pensacola MSA, FL	Y	60420 FQ	75140 AW	90760 TQ	FLBLS	10/01-12/01
	Sarasota-Bradenton MSA, FL	Y	63430 FQ	77030 AW	92800 TQ	FLBLS	10/01-12/01
	Tallahassee MSA, FL	Y	59420 FQ	75680 AW	91960 TQ	FLBLS	10/01-12/01

Occupation/Type/Industry	Location	Per	Low	Mid	High	Source	Date
Pharmacist	Tampa-St. Petersburg-Clearwater MSA, FL	Y	62260 FQ	76550 AW	92240 TQ	FLBLS	10/01-12/01
	West Palm Beach-Boca Raton MSA, FL	Y	63360 FQ	76440 AW	92230 TQ	FLBLS	10/01-12/01
	Georgia	Y	52860 FQ	71480 AW	90410 TQ	GABLS	10/01-12/01
	Atlanta MSA, GA	Y	53590 FQ	72690 AW	90640 TQ	GABLS	10/01-12/01
	Augusta-Aiken MSA, GA-SC	Y	54760 FQ	74300 AW	91400 TQ	GABLS	10/01-12/01
	Columbus MSA, GA-AL	Y	48620 FQ	69690 AW	90360 TQ	GABLS	10/01-12/01
	Macon MSA, GA	Y	54890 FQ	71160 AW	91110 TQ	GABLS	10/01-12/01
	Savannah MSA, GA	Y	57690 FQ	73710 AW	91020 TQ	GABLS	10/01-12/01
	Hawaii	Y	59920 FQ	74610 AW	92320 TQ	HIBLS	10/01-12/01
	Honolulu MSA, HI	Y	61230 FQ	74920 AW	92280 TQ	HIBLS	10/01-12/01
	Idaho	Y	56670 FQ	68670 AW	87070 TQ	IDBLS	10/01-12/01
	Boise City MSA, ID	Y	54670 FQ	70720 AW	89020 TQ	IDBLS	10/01-12/01
	Illinois	Y	51420 FQ	72780 AW	92010 TQ	ILBLS	10/01-12/01
	Champaign-Urbana MSA, IL	Y	52050 FQ	72510 AW	90790 TQ	ILBLS	10/01-12/01
	Chicago PMSA, IL	Y	50250 FQ	72200 AW	91750 TQ	ILBLS	10/01-12/01
	Peoria-Pekin MSA, IL	Y	48700 FQ	72550 AW	91560 TQ	ILBLS	10/01-12/01
	Rockford MSA, IL	Y	51840 FQ	73500 AW	93320 TQ	ILBLS	10/01-12/01
	Springfield MSA, IL	Y	48940 FQ	69600 AW	91300 TQ	ILBLS	10/01-12/01
	Indiana	Y	61540 FQ	73730 AW	90560 TQ	INBLS	10/01-12/01
	Elkhart-Goshen MSA, IN	Y	57690 FQ	77240 AW	93350 TQ	INBLS	10/01-12/01
	Evansville-Henderson MSA, IN-KY	Y	62690 FQ	76150 AW	92220 TQ	INBLS	10/01-12/01
	Fort Wayne MSA, IN	Y	62890 FQ	74120 AW	90130 TQ	INBLS	10/01-12/01
	Gary PMSA, IN	Y	60140 FQ	75830 AW	93520 TQ	INBLS	10/01-12/01
	Indianapolis MSA, IN	Y	60590 FQ	72140 AW	88990 TQ	INBLS	10/01-12/01
	Lafayette MSA, IN	Y	60810 FQ	73010 AW	89750 TQ	INBLS	10/01-12/01
	South Bend MSA, IN	Y	64280 FQ	76710 AW	91990 TQ	INBLS	10/01-12/01
	Iowa	Y	49880 FQ	68310 AW	88690 TQ	IABLS	10/01-12/01
	Cedar Rapids MSA, IA	Y	58180 FQ	71040 AW	92220 TQ	IABLS	10/01-12/01
	Davenport-Moline-Rock Island MSA, IA-IL	Y	59100 FQ	70820 AW	89550 TQ	IABLS	10/01-12/01
	Des Moines MSA, IA	Y	45570 FQ	64560 AW	83860 TQ	IABLS	10/01-12/01
	Kansas	Y	50140 FQ	69230 AW	90060 TQ	KSBLS	10/01-12/01
	Topeka MSA, KS	Y	49720 FQ	64980 AW	84460 TQ	KSBLS	10/01-12/01
	Wichita MSA, KS	Y	52930 FQ	69810 AW	88930 TQ	KSBLS	10/01-12/01
	Kentucky	Y	61440 FQ	75770 AW	92850 TQ	KYBLS	10/01-12/01
	Lexington MSA, KY	Y	57370 FQ	70610 AW	90150 TQ	KYBLS	10/01-12/01
	Louisville MSA, KY-IN	Y	64290 FQ	77480 AW	92340 TQ	KYBLS	10/01-12/01
	Louisiana	Y	44320 FQ	66150 AW	87440 TQ	LABLS	10/01-12/01
	Baton Rouge MSA, LA	Y	46370 FQ	68110 AW	88620 TQ	LABLS	10/01-12/01
	Houma MSA, LA	Y	38510 FQ	61280 AW	85920 TQ	LABLS	10/01-12/01
	Lafayette MSA, LA	Y	55940 FQ	66960 AW	84450 TQ	LABLS	10/01-12/01
	Lake Charles MSA, LA	Y	51630 FQ	66750 AW	84880 TQ	LABLS	10/01-12/01
	New Orleans MSA, LA	Y	49490 FQ	66860 AW	88040 TQ	LABLS	10/01-12/01
	Shreveport-Bossier City MSA, LA	Y	42790 FQ	67710 AW	88690 TQ	LABLS	10/01-12/01
	Maine	Y	59180 FQ	73050 AW	90530 TQ	MEBLS	10/01-12/01
	Portland MSA, ME	Y	58880 FQ	69290 AW	87380 TQ	MEBLS	10/01-12/01
	Maryland	Y	61180 FQ	72010 AW	90440 TQ	MDBLS	10/01-12/01
	Baltimore PMSA, MD	Y	61100 FQ	70060 AW	86300 TQ	MDBLS	10/01-12/01
	Massachusetts	Y	55850 FQ	69760 AW	88750 TQ	MABLS	10/01-12/01
	Boston PMSA, MA-NH	Y	54000 FQ	68550 AW	88180 TQ	MABLS	10/01-12/01
	Brockton PMSA, MA	Y	56250 FQ	70000 AW	88720 TQ	MABLS	10/01-12/01
	Lawrence PMSA, MA-NH	Y	60560 FQ	70900 AW	88220 TQ	MABLS	10/01-12/01
	Lowell PMSA, MA-NH	Y	58630 FQ	70870 AW	89020 TQ	MABLS	10/01-12/01
	New Bedford PMSA, MA	Y	40560 FQ	69120 AW	89010 TQ	MABLS	10/01-12/01
	Springfield MSA, MA	Y	58050 FQ	74750 AW	91680 TQ	MABLS	10/01-12/01
	Worcester PMSA, MA-CT	Y	61900 FQ	70980 AW	86840 TQ	MABLS	10/01-12/01
	Michigan	Y	57390 FQ	71800 AW	90260 TQ	MIBLS	10/01-12/01
	Ann Arbor PMSA, MI	Y	49760 FQ	68600 AW	89040 TQ	MIBLS	10/01-12/01
	Detroit PMSA, MI	Y	61650 FQ	72430 AW	90040 TQ	MIBLS	10/01-12/01
	Flint PMSA, MI	Y	57210 FQ	72720 AW	90220 TQ	MIBLS	10/01-12/01
	Grand Rapids-Muskegon-Holland MSA, MI	Y	54690 FQ	71310 AW	90170 TQ	MIBLS	10/01-12/01
	Kalamazoo-Battle Creek MSA, MI	Y	41060 FQ	66900 AW	88820 TQ	MIBLS	10/01-12/01
	Lansing-East Lansing MSA, MI	Y	48340 FQ	71190 AW	90620 TQ	MIBLS	10/01-12/01
	Saginaw-Bay City-Midland MSA, MI	Y	60070 FQ	74650 AW	91930 TQ	MIBLS	10/01-12/01
	Minnesota	Y	59960 FQ	73660 AW	91450 TQ	MNBLS	10/01-12/01

AAW Average annual wage **AOH** Average offered, high **ASH** Average starting, high **H** Hourly **M** Monthly **S** Special: hourly and annual
AE Average entry wage **AOL** Average offered, low **ASL** Average starting, low **HI** Highest wage paid **MTC** Median total compensation **TQ** Third quartile wage
AEX Average experienced wage **APH** Average pay, high range **AW** Average wage paid **HR** High end range **MW** Median wage paid **W** Weekly
AO Average offered **APL** Average pay, low range **FQ** First quartile wage **LR** Low end range **SQ** Second quartile wage **Y** Yearly

Occupation/Type/Industry	Location	Per	Low	Mid	High	Source	Date
Pharmacist	Duluth-Superior MSA, MN-WI	Y	44670 FQ	71730 AW	91210 TQ	MNBLS	10/01-12/01
	Minneapolis-St. Paul MSA, MN-WI	Y	61010 FQ	74030 AW	92160 TQ	MNBLS	10/01-12/01
	St. Cloud MSA, MN	Y	61960 FQ	76660 AW	91510 TQ	MNBLS	10/01-12/01
	Mississippi	Y	34830 FQ	62300 AW	85850 TQ	MSBLS	10/01-12/01
	Biloxi-Gulfport-Pascagoula MSA, MS	Y	48700 FQ	65860 AW	87740 TQ	MSBLS	10/01-12/01
	Jackson MSA, MS	Y	42550 FQ	63410 AW	84290 TQ	MSBLS	10/01-12/01
	Missouri	Y	53890 FQ	70780 AW	90940 TQ	MOBLS	10/01-12/01
	Kansas City MSA, MO-KS	Y	57930 FQ	69120 AW	87180 TQ	MOBLS	10/01-12/01
	St. Louis MSA, MO-IL	Y	48890 FQ	67590 AW	88990 TQ	MOBLS	10/01-12/01
	Springfield MSA, MO	Y	58250 FQ	75200 AW	93810 TQ	MOBLS	10/01-12/01
	Montana	Y	42830 FQ	62600 AW	78570 TQ	MTBLS	10/01-12/01
	Billings MSA, MT	Y	57330 FQ	67620 AW	84440 TQ	MTBLS	10/01-12/01
	Nebraska	Y	23100 FQ	62400 AW	84530 TQ	NEBLS	10/01-12/01
	Lincoln MSA, NE	Y	56180 FQ	64630 AW	76180 TQ	NEBLS	10/01-12/01
	Omaha MSA, NE-IA	Y	49600 FQ	65400 AW	84310 TQ	NEBLS	10/01-12/01
	Nevada	Y	60820 FQ	77740 AW	93560 TQ	NVBLS	10/01-12/01
	Las Vegas MSA, NV-AZ	Y	64320 FQ	78650 AW	93530 TQ	NVBLS	10/01-12/01
	Reno MSA, NV	Y	55100 FQ	78140 AW	93460 TQ	NVBLS	10/01-12/01
	New Hampshire	Y	56200 FQ	71260 AW	89390 TQ	NHBLS	10/01-12/01
	Manchester PMSA, NH	Y	59280 FQ	71400 AW	89170 TQ	NHBLS	10/01-12/01
	Nashua PMSA, NH	Y	59200 FQ	70170 AW	88260 TQ	NHBLS	10/01-12/01
	Portsmouth-Rochester PMSA, NH-ME	Y	56110 FQ	73750 AW	90170 TQ	NHBLS	10/01-12/01
	New Jersey	Y	53380 FQ	73510 AW	91300 TQ	NJBLS	10/01-12/01
	Atlantic-Cape May PMSA, NJ	Y	56640 FQ	73110 AW	92960 TQ	NJBLS	10/01-12/01
	Bergen-Passaic PMSA, NJ	Y	59630 FQ	73270 AW	90660 TQ	NJBLS	10/01-12/01
	Jersey City PMSA, NJ	Y	51430 FQ	81320 AW		NJBLS	10/01-12/01
	Middlesex-Somerset-Hunterdon PMSA, NJ	Y	51740 FQ	69710 AW	89810 TQ	NJBLS	10/01-12/01
	Monmouth-Ocean PMSA, NJ	Y	50470 FQ	74270 AW	92790 TQ	NJBLS	10/01-12/01
	Newark PMSA, NJ	Y	52920 FQ	72090 AW	89890 TQ	NJBLS	10/01-12/01
	Trenton PMSA, NJ	Y	55410 FQ	76990 AW	101590 TQ	NJBLS	10/01-12/01
	New Mexico	Y	58660 FQ	71300 AW	90470 TQ	NMBLS	10/01-12/01
	Albuquerque MSA, NM	Y	57530 FQ	69090 AW	88320 TQ	NMBLS	10/01-12/01
	Las Cruces MSA, NM	Y	62040 FQ	70650 AW	86270 TQ	NMBLS	10/01-12/01
	New York	Y	26900 FQ	66620 AW	89780 TQ	NYBLS	10/01-12/01
	Albany-Schenectady-Troy MSA, NY	Y	50800 FQ	65350 AW	84050 TQ	NYBLS	10/01-12/01
	Binghamton MSA, NY	Y	53660 FQ	69260 AW	87680 TQ	NYBLS	10/01-12/01
	Buffalo-Niagara Falls MSA, NY	Y	58910 FQ	71880 AW	88540 TQ	NYBLS	10/01-12/01
	Dutchess County PMSA, NY	Y	46840 FQ	71690 AW	95270 TQ	NYBLS	10/01-12/01
	Nassau-Suffolk PMSA, NY	Y	48830 FQ	68920 AW	90420 TQ	NYBLS	10/01-12/01
	New York PMSA, NY	Y	24100 FQ	62870 AW	89570 TQ	NYBLS	10/01-12/01
	Newburgh PMSA, NY-PA	Y	54430 FQ	75570 AW	101790 TQ	NYBLS	10/01-12/01
	Rochester MSA, NY	Y	54580 FQ	70790 AW	88890 TQ	NYBLS	10/01-12/01
	Syracuse MSA, NY	Y	56740 FQ	73570 AW	93270 TQ	NYBLS	10/01-12/01
	Utica-Rome MSA, NY	Y	40210 FQ	66170 AW	91430 TQ	NYBLS	10/01-12/01
	North Carolina	Y	58110 FQ	73930 AW	91640 TQ	NCBLS	10/01-12/01
	Asheville MSA, NC	Y	56080 FQ	75170 AW	93320 TQ	NCBLS	10/01-12/01
	Charlotte-Gastonia-Rock Hill MSA, NC-SC	Y	55770 FQ	74800 AW	90670 TQ	NCBLS	10/01-12/01
	Fayetteville MSA, NC	Y	55980 FQ	72480 AW	95410 TQ	NCBLS	10/01-12/01
	Greensboro-Winston-Salem-High Point MSA, NC	Y	59760 FQ	73290 AW	91550 TQ	NCBLS	10/01-12/01
	Hickory-Morganton-Lenoir MSA, NC	Y	60160 FQ	73060 AW	98840 TQ	NCBLS	10/01-12/01
	Raleigh-Durham-Chapel Hill MSA, NC	Y	59230 FQ	75180 AW	92850 TQ	NCBLS	10/01-12/01
	Wilmington MSA, NC	Y	59900 FQ	69520 AW	85790 TQ	NCBLS	10/01-12/01
	North Dakota	Y	45060 FQ	61230 AW	80510 TQ	NDBLS	10/01-12/01
	Fargo-Moorhead MSA, ND-MN	Y	49910 FQ	64900 AW	89470 TQ	NDBLS	10/01-12/01
	Ohio	Y	46770 FQ	69590 AW	90820 TQ	OHBLS	10/01-12/01
	Akron PMSA, OH	Y	58400 FQ	71890 AW	90400 TQ	OHBLS	10/01-12/01
	Canton-Massillon MSA, OH	Y	38110 FQ	69900 AW	89660 TQ	OHBLS	10/01-12/01
	Cincinnati PMSA, OH-KY-IN	Y	59060 FQ	72520 AW	90620 TQ	OHBLS	10/01-12/01
	Cleveland-Lorain-Elyria PMSA, OH	Y	62470 FQ	75470 AW	92830 TQ	OHBLS	10/01-12/01
	Columbus MSA, OH	Y	21970 FQ	62230 AW	88160 TQ	OHBLS	10/01-12/01

AAW Average annual wage **AE** Average entry wage **AEX** Average experienced wage **AO** Average offered **AOH** Average offered, high **AOL** Average offered, low **APH** Average pay, high range **APL** Average pay, low range **ASH** Average starting, high **ASL** Average starting, low **AW** Average wage paid **FQ** First quartile wage **H** Hourly **HI** Highest wage paid **HR** High end range **LR** Low end range **M** Monthly **MTC** Median total compensation **MW** Median wage paid **SQ** Second quartile wage **S** Special: hourly and annual **TQ** Third quartile wage **W** Weekly **Y** Yearly

Occupation/Type/Industry	Location	Per	Low	Mid	High	Source	Date
Pharmacist	Dayton-Springfield MSA, OH	Y	63200 FQ	77880 AW	93820 TQ	OHBLS	10/01-12/01
	Hamilton-Middletown PMSA, OH	Y	38900 FQ	69360 AW	90460 TQ	OHBLS	10/01-12/01
	Mansfield MSA, OH	Y	56730 FQ	71860 AW	91480 TQ	OHBLS	10/01-12/01
	Toledo MSA, OH	Y	23840 FQ	63810 AW	87170 TQ	OHBLS	10/01-12/01
	Youngstown-Warren MSA, OH	Y	29040 FQ	68580 AW	89770 TQ	OHBLS	10/01-12/01
	Oklahoma	Y	47080 FQ	67310 AW	88360 TQ	OKBLS	10/01-12/01
	Oklahoma City MSA, OK	Y	52550 FQ	67120 AW	86140 TQ	OKBLS	10/01-12/01
	Tulsa MSA, OK	Y	61360 FQ	75590 AW	90910 TQ	OKBLS	10/01-12/01
	Oregon	Y	60560 FQ	74930 AW	91190 TQ	ORBLS	10/01-12/01
	Eugene-Springfield MSA, OR	Y	62090 FQ	76880 AW	91870 TQ	ORBLS	10/01-12/01
	Medford-Ashland MSA, OR	Y	65090 FQ	77870 AW	91250 TQ	ORBLS	10/01-12/01
	Portland-Vancouver PMSA, OR-WA	Y	61460 FQ	74630 AW	90730 TQ	ORBLS	10/01-12/01
	Salem PMSA, OR	Y	61920 FQ	74060 AW	90920 TQ	ORBLS	10/01-12/01
	Pennsylvania	Y	51330 FQ	67930 AW	88730 TQ	PABLS	10/01-12/01
	Allentown-Bethlehem-Easton MSA, PA	Y	59710 FQ	70050 AW	87630 TQ	PABLS	10/01-12/01
	Erie MSA, PA	Y	51110 FQ	65680 AW	83300 TQ	PABLS	10/01-12/01
	Harrisburg-Lebanon-Carlisle MSA, PA	Y	56820 FQ	69440 AW	89150 TQ	PABLS	10/01-12/01
	Johnstown MSA, PA	Y	50080 FQ	68470 AW	92910 TQ	PABLS	10/01-12/01
	Lancaster MSA, PA	Y	47730 FQ	64340 AW	89180 TQ	PABLS	10/01-12/01
	Philadelphia PMSA, PA-NJ	Y	49390 FQ	68250 AW	89750 TQ	PABLS	10/01-12/01
	Pittsburgh MSA, PA	Y	54100 FQ	65150 AW	80080 TQ	PABLS	10/01-12/01
	Reading MSA, PA	Y	43890 FQ	67820 AW	88850 TQ	PABLS	10/01-12/01
	Scranton-Wilkes-Barre-Hazleton MSA, PA	Y	52160 FQ	65090 AW	76570 TQ	PABLS	10/01-12/01
	York MSA, PA	Y	54560 FQ	70280 AW	89430 TQ	PABLS	10/01-12/01
	Rhode Island	Y	54390 FQ	69270 AW	87070 TQ	RIBLS	10/01-12/01
	Providence-Fall River-Warwick MSA, RI-MA	Y	54760 FQ	69490 AW	87380 TQ	RIBLS	10/01-12/01
	South Carolina	Y	44980 FQ	71720 AW	95020 TQ	SCBLS	10/01-12/01
	Charleston-North Charleston MSA, SC	Y	47860 FQ	71970 AW	97220 TQ	SCBLS	10/01-12/01
	Columbia MSA, SC	Y	40590 FQ	68320 AW	90090 TQ	SCBLS	10/01-12/01
	Greenville-Spartanburg-Anderson MSA, SC	Y	45060 FQ	71500 AW	90990 TQ	SCBLS	10/01-12/01
	Myrtle Beach MSA, SC	Y	47730 FQ	65810 AW	87630 TQ	SCBLS	10/01-12/01
	South Dakota	Y	46550 FQ	65100 AW	87040 TQ	SDBLS	10/01-12/01
	Sioux Falls MSA, SD	Y	50630 FQ	65460 AW	84000 TQ	SDBLS	10/01-12/01
	Tennessee	Y	57520 FQ	75010 AW	92920 TQ	TNBLS	10/01-12/01
	Chattanooga MSA, TN-GA	Y	62070 FQ	76280 AW	94070 TQ	TNBLS	10/01-12/01
	Clarksville-Hopkinsville MSA, TN-KY	Y	50970 FQ	72270 AW	92960 TQ	TNBLS	10/01-12/01
	Johnson City-Kingsport-Bristol MSA, TN-VA	Y	61300 FQ	79020 AW	99370 TQ	TNBLS	10/01-12/01
	Knoxville MSA, TN	Y	60460 FQ	76500 AW	92650 TQ	TNBLS	10/01-12/01
	Memphis MSA, TN-AR-MS	Y	59840 FQ	73710 AW	90220 TQ	TNBLS	10/01-12/01
	Nashville MSA, TN	Y	62540 FQ	77870 AW	92510 TQ	TNBLS	10/01-12/01
	Texas	Y	59040 FQ	73280 AW	91430 TQ	TXBLS	10/01-12/01
	Amarillo MSA, TX	Y	57880 FQ	72290 AW	90500 TQ	TXBLS	10/01-12/01
	Austin-San Marcos MSA, TX	Y	55550 FQ	69860 AW	89450 TQ	TXBLS	10/01-12/01
	Beaumont-Port Arthur MSA, TX	Y	57500 FQ	70390 AW	90050 TQ	TXBLS	10/01-12/01
	Brazoria PMSA, TX	Y	62030 FQ	72180 AW	89860 TQ	TXBLS	10/01-12/01
	Brownsville-Harlingen-San Benito MSA, TX	Y	58910 FQ	71980 AW	89040 TQ	TXBLS	10/01-12/01
	Corpus Christi MSA, TX	Y	59310 FQ	75500 AW	93840 TQ	TXBLS	10/01-12/01
	Dallas PMSA, TX	Y	60090 FQ	75840 AW	93900 TQ	TXBLS	10/01-12/01
	El Paso MSA, TX	Y	62200 FQ	76470 AW	92730 TQ	TXBLS	10/01-12/01
	Fort Worth-Arlington PMSA, TX	Y	63190 FQ	76320 AW	92750 TQ	TXBLS	10/01-12/01
	Galveston-Texas City PMSA, TX	Y	39880 FQ	65150 AW	90540 TQ	TXBLS	10/01-12/01
	Houston PMSA, TX	Y	59550 FQ	73160 AW	90110 TQ	TXBLS	10/01-12/01
	Killeen-Temple MSA, TX	Y	60290 FQ	77740 AW	94950 TQ	TXBLS	10/01-12/01
	Laredo MSA, TX	Y	61220 FQ	73470 AW	89830 TQ	TXBLS	10/01-12/01
	Longview-Marshall MSA, TX	Y	59640 FQ	76530 AW	95350 TQ	TXBLS	10/01-12/01
	Lubbock MSA, TX	Y	56620 FQ	71490 AW	91260 TQ	TXBLS	10/01-12/01
	McAllen-Edinburg-Mission MSA, TX	Y	62880 FQ	77580 AW	94800 TQ	TXBLS	10/01-12/01

AAW	Average annual wage	**AOH**	Average offered, high	**ASH**	Average starting, high	**H**	Hourly	**M**	Monthly	**S**	Special: hourly and annual
AE	Average entry wage	**AOL**	Average offered, low	**ASL**	Average starting, low	**HI**	Highest wage paid	**MTC**	Median total compensation	**TQ**	Third quartile wage
AEX	Average experienced wage	**APH**	Average pay, high range	**AW**	Average wage paid	**HR**	High end range	**MW**	Median wage paid	**W**	Weekly
AO	Average offered	**APL**	Average pay, low range	**FQ**	First quartile wage	**LR**	Low end range	**SQ**	Second quartile wage	**Y**	Yearly

Occupation/Type/Industry	Location	Per	Low	Mid	High	Source	Date
Pharmacist	Odessa-Midland MSA, TX	Y	61180 FQ	75050 AW	90840 TQ	TXBLS	10/01-12/01
	San Antonio MSA, TX	Y	57300 FQ	68750 AW	86380 TQ	TXBLS	10/01-12/01
	Tyler MSA, TX	Y	53070 FQ	69690 AW	89920 TQ	TXBLS	10/01-12/01
	Waco MSA, TX	Y	50040 FQ	68150 AW	88730 TQ	TXBLS	10/01-12/01
	Utah	Y	60110 FQ	74420 AW	90820 TQ	UTBLS	10/01-12/01
	Provo-Orem MSA, UT	Y	61920 FQ	75650 AW	91960 TQ	UTBLS	10/01-12/01
	Salt Lake City-Ogden MSA, UT	Y	59520 FQ	73620 AW	90340 TQ	UTBLS	10/01-12/01
	Vermont	Y	53330 FQ	70460 AW	89560 TQ	VTBLS	10/01-12/01
	Burlington MSA, VT	Y	59740 FQ	73590 AW	90360 TQ	VTBLS	10/01-12/01
	Virginia	Y	59690 FQ	73570 AW	90830 TQ	VABLS	10/01-12/01
	Lynchburg MSA, VA	Y	51290 FQ	69590 AW	92340 TQ	VABLS	10/01-12/01
	Norfolk-Virginia Beach-Newport News MSA, VA-NC	Y	63100 FQ	76880 AW	92100 TQ	VABLS	10/01-12/01
	Richmond-Petersburg MSA, VA	Y	59480 FQ	73380 AW	91120 TQ	VABLS	10/01-12/01
	Roanoke MSA, VA	Y	51400 FQ	67290 AW	86480 TQ	VABLS	10/01-12/01
	Washington	Y	53480 FQ	71640 AW	90190 TQ	WABLS	10/01-12/01
	Bremerton PMSA, WA	Y	62820 FQ	76650 AW	95800 TQ	WABLS	10/01-12/01
	Olympia PMSA, WA	Y	56730 FQ	70930 AW	88310 TQ	WABLS	10/01-12/01
	Richland-Kennewick-Pasco MSA, WA	Y	51330 FQ	69650 AW	88160 TQ	WABLS	10/01-12/01
	Seattle-Bellevue-Everett PMSA, WA	Y	48730 FQ	69820 AW	90440 TQ	WABLS	10/01-12/01
	Spokane MSA, WA	Y	59620 FQ	73500 AW	89040 TQ	WABLS	10/01-12/01
	Tacoma PMSA, WA	Y	61920 FQ	75420 AW	91910 TQ	WABLS	10/01-12/01
	Yakima MSA, WA	Y	63590 FQ	76190 AW	91420 TQ	WABLS	10/01-12/01
	West Virginia	Y	56280 FQ	74390 AW	99080 TQ	WVBLS	10/01-12/01
	Charleston MSA, WV	Y	59030 FQ	76740 AW	103840 TQ	WVBLS	10/01-12/01
	Huntington-Ashland MSA, WV-KY-OH	Y	61330 FQ	78560 AW	101260 TQ	WVBLS	10/01-12/01
	Wisconsin	Y	62680 FQ	78510 AW	94240 TQ	WIBLS	10/01-12/01
	Appleton-Oshkosh-Neenah MSA, WI	Y	62850 FQ	76950 AW	93070 TQ	WIBLS	10/01-12/01
	Green Bay MSA, WI	Y	63300 FQ	77600 AW	94040 TQ	WIBLS	10/01-12/01
	Madison MSA, WI	Y	63960 FQ	77120 AW	90770 TQ	WIBLS	10/01-12/01
	Milwaukee-Waukesha PMSA, WI	Y	63810 FQ	79770 AW	95800 TQ	WIBLS	10/01-12/01
	Racine PMSA, WI	Y	74340 FQ	81680 AW	93680 TQ	WIBLS	10/01-12/01
	Wyoming	Y	46740 FQ	65670 AW	87550 TQ	WYBLS	10/01-12/01
	Cheyenne MSA, WY	Y	48070 FQ	62370 AW	76630 TQ	WYBLS	10/01-12/01
	Puerto Rico	Y	19550 FQ	38940 AW	54990 TQ	PRBLS	10/01-12/01
	Virgin Islands	Y	35830 FQ	55910 AW	70310 TQ	VIBLS	10/01-12/01
	Guam	Y	35310 FQ	64680 AW	93710 TQ	GUBLS	10/01-12/01
Hospital	East	Y	64000 AE			LIBN	1/01-1/02
Pharmacy Aide	Alabama	H	5.68 FQ	7.38 AW	9.78 TQ	ALBLS	10/01-12/01
	Alaska	H	7.46 FQ	11.79 AW	15.85 TQ	AKBLS	10/01-12/01
	Arizona	H	7.10 FQ	9.96 AW	12.95 TQ	AZBLS	10/01-12/01
	Arkansas	H	5.78 FQ	7.66 AW	10.19 TQ	ARBLS	10/01-12/01
	California	H	7.50 FQ	11.44 AW	15.98 TQ	CABLS	10/01-12/01
	Colorado	H	8.25 FQ	10.50 AW	13.35 TQ	COBLS	10/01-12/01
	Connecticut	H	7.07 FQ	9.46 AW	13.33 TQ	CTBLS	10/01-12/01
	Delaware	H	6.50 FQ	9.22 AW	13.13 TQ	DEBLS	10/01-12/01
	District of Columbia	H	9.83 FQ	13.75 AW	18.37 TQ	DCBLS	10/01-12/01
	Florida	H	5.61 FQ	8.04 AW	11.43 TQ	FLBLS	10/01-12/01
	Georgia	H	5.85 FQ	7.77 AW	10.31 TQ	GABLS	10/01-12/01
	Hawaii	H	6.23 FQ	9.84 AW	14.98 TQ	HIBLS	10/01-12/01
	Idaho	H	7.11 FQ	8.98 AW	12.31 TQ	IDBLS	10/01-12/01
	Illinois	H	6.36 FQ	9.30 AW	12.21 TQ	ILBLS	10/01-12/01
	Indiana	H	6.27 FQ	8.37 AW	10.75 TQ	INBLS	10/01-12/01
	Iowa	H	5.82 FQ	8.47 AW	11.03 TQ	IABLS	10/01-12/01
	Kansas	H	6.29 FQ	8.52 AW	10.74 TQ	KSBLS	10/01-12/01
	Kentucky	H	6.22 FQ	8.50 AW	11.45 TQ	KYBLS	10/01-12/01
	Louisiana	H	5.88 FQ	7.93 AW	10.51 TQ	LABLS	10/01-12/01
	Maine	H	5.95 FQ	8.09 AW	10.70 TQ	MEBLS	10/01-12/01
	Maryland	H	6.43 FQ	8.79 AW	11.94 TQ	MDBLS	10/01-12/01
	Massachusetts	H	7.01 FQ	9.42 AW	13.10 TQ	MABLS	10/01-12/01
	Michigan	H	6.46 FQ	8.97 AW	12.32 TQ	MIBLS	10/01-12/01
	Minnesota	H	7.26 FQ	9.68 AW	12.94 TQ	MNBLS	10/01-12/01
	Mississippi	H	6.12 FQ	9.00 AW	12.50 TQ	MSBLS	10/01-12/01
	Missouri	H	7.07 FQ	9.19 AW	11.87 TQ	MOBLS	10/01-12/01

AAW	Average annual wage	**AOH**	Average offered, high	**ASH**	Average starting, high	**H**	Hourly	**M**	Monthly	**S**	Special: hourly and annual
AE	Average entry wage	**AOL**	Average offered, low	**ASL**	Average starting, low	**HI**	Highest wage paid	**MTC**	Median total compensation	**TQ**	Third quartile wage
AEX	Average experienced wage	**APH**	Average pay, high range	**AW**	Average wage paid	**HR**	High end range	**MW**	Median wage paid	**W**	Weekly
AO	Average offered	**APL**	Average pay, low range	**FQ**	First quartile wage	**LR**	Low end range	**SQ**	Second quartile wage	**Y**	Yearly

Occupation/Type/Industry	Location	Per	Low	Mid	High	Source	Date
Pharmacy Aide	Montana	H	7.38 FQ	9.34 AW	12.12 TQ	MTBLS	10/01-12/01
	Nebraska	H	6.00 FQ	9.00 AW	11.16 TQ	NEBLS	10/01-12/01
	Nevada	H	8.47 FQ	11.22 AW	14.36 TQ	NVBLS	10/01-12/01
	New Hampshire	H	6.41 FQ	7.95 AW	9.61 TQ	NHBLS	10/01-12/01
	New Jersey	H	5.87 FQ	8.45 AW	11.72 TQ	NJBLS	10/01-12/01
	New Mexico	H	7.39 FQ	9.55 AW	12.23 TQ	NMBLS	10/01-12/01
	New York	H	5.95 FQ	9.78 AW	15.99 TQ	NYBLS	10/01-12/01
	North Carolina	H	6.73 FQ	9.25 AW	13.09 TQ	NCBLS	10/01-12/01
	North Dakota	H	5.79 FQ	8.20 AW	12.69 TQ	NDBLS	10/01-12/01
	Ohio	H	6.04 FQ	8.55 AW	11.45 TQ	OHBLS	10/01-12/01
	Oklahoma	H	6.05 FQ	7.98 AW	10.45 TQ	OKBLS	10/01-12/01
	Oregon	H	8.40 FQ	11.58 AW	15.04 TQ	ORBLS	10/01-12/01
	Pennsylvania	H	5.71 FQ	7.85 AW	11.03 TQ	PABLS	10/01-12/01
	Rhode Island	H	6.71 FQ	8.95 AW	13.18 TQ	RIBLS	10/01-12/01
	South Carolina	H	5.79 FQ	8.36 AW	10.96 TQ	SCBLS	10/01-12/01
	South Dakota	H	6.98 FQ	8.07 AW	9.91 TQ	SDBLS	10/01-12/01
	Tennessee	H	6.28 FQ	8.96 AW	12.55 TQ	TNBLS	10/01-12/01
	Texas	H	5.93 FQ	8.10 AW	10.72 TQ	TXBLS	10/01-12/01
	Utah	H	7.03 FQ	9.89 AW	12.76 TQ	UTBLS	10/01-12/01
	Vermont	H	6.64 FQ	7.95 AW	9.42 TQ	VTBLS	10/01-12/01
	Virginia	H	6.03 FQ	9.27 AW	13.38 TQ	VABLS	10/01-12/01
	Washington	H	7.30 FQ	10.44 AW	15.20 TQ	WABLS	10/01-12/01
	West Virginia	H	5.67 FQ	7.62 AW	11.30 TQ	WVBLS	10/01-12/01
	Wisconsin	H	7.45 FQ	9.96 AW	13.28 TQ	WIBLS	10/01-12/01
	Wyoming	H	7.20 FQ	8.83 AW	10.89 TQ	WYBLS	10/01-12/01
	Puerto Rico	H	5.55 FQ	6.54 AW	8.15 TQ	PRBLS	10/01-12/01
Pharmacy Technician	United States	Y		18500-25760 AW		FREEP1	1/00-1/00
	Alabama	Y	12610 FQ	17930 AW	24060 TQ	ALBLS	10/01-12/01
	Alaska	Y	21520 FQ	29000 AW	36630 TQ	AKBLS	10/01-12/01
	Arizona	Y	15860 FQ	21700 AW	28860 TQ	AZBLS	10/01-12/01
	Arkansas	Y	14220 FQ	18630 AW	23750 TQ	ARBLS	10/01-12/01
	California	Y	22520 FQ	30810 AW	37730 TQ	CABLS	10/01-12/01
	Colorado	Y	18770 FQ	26430 AW	34180 TQ	COBLS	10/01-12/01
	Connecticut	Y	15380 FQ	23020 AW	33170 TQ	CTBLS	10/01-12/01
	Delaware	Y	14780 FQ	20040 AW	26790 TQ	DEBLS	10/01-12/01
	District of Columbia	Y	15860 FQ	24380 AW	34080 TQ	DCBLS	10/01-12/01
	Florida	Y	14480 FQ	20450 AW	28460 TQ	FLBLS	10/01-12/01
	Georgia	Y	14800 FQ	20470 AW	27020 TQ	GABLS	10/01-12/01
	Hawaii	Y	16250 FQ	25720 AW	34870 TQ	HIBLS	10/01-12/01
	Idaho	Y	16710 FQ	23140 AW	29740 TQ	IDBLS	10/01-12/01
	Illinois	Y	15660 FQ	21700 AW	28780 TQ	ILBLS	10/01-12/01
	Indiana	Y	15320 FQ	20810 AW	27270 TQ	INBLS	10/01-12/01
	Iowa	Y	15400 FQ	20940 AW	27820 TQ	IABLS	10/01-12/01
	Kansas	Y	14440 FQ	20570 AW	28000 TQ	KSBLS	10/01-12/01
	Kentucky	Y	14640 FQ	20100 AW	27570 TQ	KYBLS	10/01-12/01
	Louisiana	Y	13690 FQ	19340 AW	26000 TQ	LABLS	10/01-12/01
	Maine	Y	15010 FQ	20110 AW	27000 TQ	MEBLS	10/01-12/01
	Maryland	Y	14110 FQ	22640 AW	32100 TQ	MDBLS	10/01-12/01
	Massachusetts	Y	15570 FQ	22970 AW	31870 TQ	MABLS	10/01-12/01
	Michigan	Y	15880 FQ	22380 AW	29270 TQ	MIBLS	10/01-12/01
	Minnesota	Y	17900 FQ	26060 AW	33970 TQ	MNBLS	10/01-12/01
	Mississippi	Y	14840 FQ	19550 AW	25350 TQ	MSBLS	10/01-12/01
	Missouri	Y	14630 FQ	19930 AW	26700 TQ	MOBLS	10/01-12/01
	Montana	Y	15920 FQ	22030 AW	28550 TQ	MTBLS	10/01-12/01
	Nebraska	Y	15740 FQ	21100 AW	27590 TQ	NEBLS	10/01-12/01
	Nevada	Y	19270 FQ	25870 AW	33160 TQ	NVBLS	10/01-12/01
	New Hampshire	Y	14760 FQ	20830 AW	28370 TQ	NHBLS	10/01-12/01
	New Jersey	Y	15150 FQ	23440 AW	34800 TQ	NJBLS	10/01-12/01
	New Mexico	Y	15170 FQ	21890 AW	28540 TQ	NMBLS	10/01-12/01
	New York	Y	14670 FQ	23300 AW	33890 TQ	NYBLS	10/01-12/01
	North Carolina	Y	13260 FQ	20080 AW	27790 TQ	NCBLS	10/01-12/01
	North Dakota	Y	16360 FQ	21240 AW	27590 TQ	NDBLS	10/01-12/01
	Ohio	Y	14590 FQ	20330 AW	27840 TQ	OHBLS	10/01-12/01
	Oklahoma	Y	14580 FQ	20100 AW	26790 TQ	OKBLS	10/01-12/01
	Oregon	Y	20130 FQ	27050 AW	34150 TQ	ORBLS	10/01-12/01
	Pennsylvania	Y	13860 FQ	20180 AW	27600 TQ	PABLS	10/01-12/01
	Rhode Island	Y	14340 FQ	20550 AW	28650 TQ	RIBLS	10/01-12/01
	South Carolina	Y	13670 FQ	20980 AW	28940 TQ	SCBLS	10/01-12/01
	South Dakota	Y	17500 FQ	22150 AW	28760 TQ	SDBLS	10/01-12/01
	Tennessee	Y	15220 FQ	21390 AW	27870 TQ	TNBLS	10/01-12/01
	Texas	Y	15630 FQ	21950 AW	28220 TQ	TXBLS	10/01-12/01

AAW	Average annual wage	**AOH**	Average offered, high	**ASH**	Average starting, high	**H**	Hourly	**M**	Monthly	**S**	Special: hourly and annual
AE	Average entry wage	**AOL**	Average offered, low	**ASL**	Average starting, low	**HI**	Highest wage paid	**MTC**	Median total compensation	**TQ**	Third quartile wage
AEX	Average experienced wage	**APH**	Average pay, high range	**AW**	Average wage paid	**HR**	High end range	**MW**	Median wage paid	**W**	Weekly
AO	Average offered	**APL**	Average pay, low range	**FQ**	First quartile wage	**LR**	Low end range	**SQ**	Second quartile wage	**Y**	Yearly

Occupation/Type/Industry	Location	Per	Low	Mid	High	Source	Date
Pharmacy Technician	Utah	Y	18780 FQ	24650 AW	30270 TQ	UTBLS	10/01-12/01
	Vermont	Y	15060 FQ	21950 AW	31130 TQ	VTBLS	10/01-12/01
	Virginia	Y	14110 FQ	21160 AW	29430 TQ	VABLS	10/01-12/01
	Washington	Y	20910 FQ	28160 AW	35320 TQ	WABLS	10/01-12/01
	West Virginia	Y	13170 FQ	19210 AW	26850 TQ	WVBLS	10/01-12/01
	Wisconsin	Y	16100 FQ	21860 AW	28960 TQ	WIBLS	10/01-12/01
	Wyoming	Y	16210 FQ	22900 AW	29060 TQ	WYBLS	10/01-12/01
	Puerto Rico	Y	12230 FQ	18300 AW	30430 TQ	PRBLS	10/01-12/01
	Guam	Y	19290 FQ	23930 AW	29780 TQ	GUBLS	10/01-12/01
Philosophy and Religion Teacher							
Postsecondary	Alabama	Y	21120 FQ	53740 AW	103430 TQ	ALBLS	10/01-12/01
Postsecondary	Birmingham MSA, AL	Y	24500 FQ	46010 AW	73020 TQ	ALBLS	10/01-12/01
Postsecondary	Arkansas	Y	22410 FQ	42350 AW	70260 TQ	ARBLS	10/01-12/01
Postsecondary	California	Y	28930 FQ	58380 AW	90270 TQ	CABLS	10/01-12/01
Postsecondary	Los Angeles-Long Beach PMSA, CA	Y	34850 FQ	61040 AW	89680 TQ	CABLS	10/01-12/01
Postsecondary	Riverside-San Bernardino PMSA, CA	Y	35070 FQ	55530 AW	76860 TQ	CABLS	10/01-12/01
Postsecondary	San Diego MSA, CA	Y	14240 FQ	56630 AW	90620 TQ	CABLS	10/01-12/01
Postsecondary	San Francisco PMSA, CA	Y	49470 FQ	72880 AW	104160 TQ	CABLS	10/01-12/01
Postsecondary	Colorado	Y	30620 FQ	52310 AW	82880 TQ	COBLS	10/01-12/01
Postsecondary	Denver PMSA, CO	Y	30930 FQ	52790 AW	81290 TQ	COBLS	10/01-12/01
Postsecondary	Connecticut	Y	32820 FQ	58080 AW	90020 TQ	CTBLS	10/01-12/01
Postsecondary	Hartford MSA, CT	Y	31980 FQ	62490 AW	98540 TQ	CTBLS	10/01-12/01
Postsecondary	District of Columbia	Y	26090 FQ	46270 AW	72520 TQ	DCBLS	10/01-12/01
Postsecondary	Washington PMSA, DC-MD-VA-WV	Y	25080 FQ	46860 AW	76260 TQ	DCBLS	10/01-12/01
Postsecondary	Florida	Y	32580 FQ	56240 AW	88310 TQ	FLBLS	10/01-12/01
Postsecondary	Gainesville MSA, FL	Y	27960 FQ	54170 AW	82340 TQ	FLBLS	10/01-12/01
Postsecondary	Miami PMSA, FL	Y	38990 FQ	59480 AW	89500 TQ	FLBLS	10/01-12/01
Postsecondary	Orlando MSA, FL	Y	31020 FQ	49480 AW	80880 TQ	FLBLS	10/01-12/01
Postsecondary	Tallahassee MSA, FL	Y	36030 FQ	60830 AW	95290 TQ	FLBLS	10/01-12/01
Postsecondary	Tampa-St. Petersburg-Clearwater MSA, FL	Y	36210 FQ	64610 AW	103540 TQ	FLBLS	10/01-12/01
Postsecondary	West Palm Beach-Boca Raton MSA, FL	Y	37980 FQ	53630 AW	85300 TQ	FLBLS	10/01-12/01
Postsecondary	Georgia	Y	32170 FQ	53290 AW	80030 TQ	GABLS	10/01-12/01
Postsecondary	Hawaii	Y	26560 FQ	53670 AW	83640 TQ	HIBLS	10/01-12/01
Postsecondary	Honolulu MSA, HI	Y	25990 FQ	53800 AW	86180 TQ	HIBLS	10/01-12/01
Postsecondary	Idaho	Y	42410 FQ	52180 AW	59990 TQ	IDBLS	10/01-12/01
Postsecondary	Illinois	Y	25550 FQ	51360 AW	83450 TQ	ILBLS	10/01-12/01
Postsecondary	Champaign-Urbana MSA, IL	Y	29020 FQ	50650 AW	82620 TQ	ILBLS	10/01-12/01
Postsecondary	Chicago PMSA, IL	Y	25290 FQ	52130 AW	84770 TQ	ILBLS	10/01-12/01
Postsecondary	Indiana	Y	29860 FQ	52120 AW	81750 TQ	INBLS	10/01-12/01
Postsecondary	South Bend MSA, IN	Y	34400 FQ	50700 AW	69450 TQ	INBLS	10/01-12/01
Postsecondary	Iowa	Y	31040 FQ	58460 AW	125130 TQ	IABLS	10/01-12/01
Postsecondary	Kansas	Y	18040 FQ	31180 AW	49710 TQ	KSBLS	10/01-12/01
Postsecondary	Kentucky	Y	31720 FQ	51390 AW	77430 TQ	KYBLS	10/01-12/01
Postsecondary	Louisiana	Y	23590 FQ	42540 AW	66950 TQ	LABLS	10/01-12/01
Postsecondary	Maine	Y	31160 FQ	42400 AW	62780 TQ	MEBLS	10/01-12/01
Postsecondary	Portland MSA, ME	Y	31270 FQ	42130 AW	62330 TQ	MEBLS	10/01-12/01
Postsecondary	Maryland	Y	24970 FQ	50160 AW	84980 TQ	MDBLS	10/01-12/01
Postsecondary	Baltimore PMSA, MD	Y	29030 FQ	53440 AW	85270 TQ	MDBLS	10/01-12/01
Postsecondary	Massachusetts	Y	31030 FQ	53020 AW	82680 TQ	MABLS	10/01-12/01
Postsecondary	Boston PMSA, MA-NH	Y	30630 FQ	52720 AW	82600 TQ	MABLS	10/01-12/01
Postsecondary	Springfield MSA, MA	Y	38240 FQ	68280 AW	102900 TQ	MABLS	10/01-12/01
Postsecondary	Worcester PMSA, MA-CT	Y	32950 FQ	52210 AW	76260 TQ	MABLS	10/01-12/01
Postsecondary	Michigan	Y	30540 FQ	53920 AW	85930 TQ	MIBLS	10/01-12/01
Postsecondary	Ann Arbor PMSA, MI	Y	29650 FQ	51810 AW	85900 TQ	MIBLS	10/01-12/01
Postsecondary	Detroit PMSA, MI	Y	27130 FQ	48860 AW	73160 TQ	MIBLS	10/01-12/01
Postsecondary	Grand Rapids-Muskegon-Holland MSA, MI	Y	31750 FQ	50090 AW	76670 TQ	MIBLS	10/01-12/01
Postsecondary	Minnesota	Y	31270 FQ	48540 AW	70490 TQ	MNBLS	10/01-12/01
Postsecondary	Minneapolis-St. Paul MSA, MN-WI	Y	30550 FQ	47520 AW	67730 TQ	MNBLS	10/01-12/01
Postsecondary	St. Cloud MSA, MN	Y	31910 FQ	48250 AW	69790 TQ	MNBLS	10/01-12/01
Postsecondary	Mississippi	Y	22450 FQ	39180 AW	55680 TQ	MSBLS	10/01-12/01
Postsecondary	Missouri	Y	22690 FQ	46400 AW	72300 TQ	MOBLS	10/01-12/01
Postsecondary	Kansas City MSA, MO-KS	Y	31690 FQ	48000 AW	69850 TQ	MOBLS	10/01-12/01
Postsecondary	St. Louis MSA, MO-IL	Y	21170 FQ	43560 AW	73000 TQ	MOBLS	10/01-12/01
Postsecondary	Springfield MSA, MO	Y	38920 FQ	54380 AW	80850 TQ	MOBLS	10/01-12/01
Postsecondary	Nebraska	Y	25640 FQ	45660 AW	71340 TQ	NEBLS	10/01-12/01

AAW	Average annual wage	**AOH**	Average offered, high	**ASH**	Average starting, high	**H**	Hourly	**M**	Monthly	**S**	Special: hourly and annual
AE	Average entry wage	**AOL**	Average offered, low	**ASL**	Average starting, low	**HI**	Highest wage paid	**MTC**	Median total compensation	**TQ**	Third quartile wage
AEX	Average experienced wage	**APH**	Average pay, high range	**AW**	Average wage paid	**HR**	High end range	**MW**	Median wage paid	**W**	Weekly
AO	Average offered	**APL**	Average pay, low range	**FQ**	First quartile wage	**LR**	Low end range	**SQ**	Second quartile wage	**Y**	Yearly

Occupation/Type/Industry	Location	Per	Low	Mid	High	Source	Date
Philosophy and Religion Teacher							
Postsecondary	Nevada	Y	24580 FQ	45860 AW	74790 TQ	NVBLS	10/01-12/01
Postsecondary	Las Vegas MSA, NV-AZ	Y	24100 FQ	41320 AW	56670 TQ	NVBLS	10/01-12/01
Postsecondary	New Hampshire	Y	36200 FQ	57330 AW	85290 TQ	NHBLS	10/01-12/01
Postsecondary	Manchester PMSA, NH	Y	40000 FQ	51380 AW	65440 TQ	NHBLS	10/01-12/01
Postsecondary	New Jersey	Y	35460 FQ	65260 AW	108770 TQ	NJBLS	10/01-12/01
Postsecondary	Jersey City PMSA, NJ	Y	36400 FQ	64750 AW	111850 TQ	NJBLS	10/01-12/01
Postsecondary	Monmouth-Ocean PMSA, NJ	Y	33140 FQ	52490 AW	83470 TQ	NJBLS	10/01-12/01
Postsecondary	Newark PMSA, NJ	Y	33750 FQ	60790 AW	94550 TQ	NJBLS	10/01-12/01
Postsecondary	New Mexico	Y	33870 FQ	49910 AW	68510 TQ	NMBLS	10/01-12/01
Postsecondary	New York	Y	32450 FQ	61860 AW	103740 TQ	NYBLS	10/01-12/01
Postsecondary	Nassau-Suffolk PMSA, NY	Y	21830 FQ	41080 AW	65040 TQ	NYBLS	10/01-12/01
Postsecondary	New York PMSA, NY	Y	34810 FQ	61510 AW	101400 TQ	NYBLS	10/01-12/01
Postsecondary	North Carolina	Y	28250 FQ	47460 AW	75810 TQ	NCBLS	10/01-12/01
Postsecondary	Charlotte-Gastonia-Rock Hill MSA, NC-SC	Y	26980 FQ	52270 AW	92780 TQ	NCBLS	10/01-12/01
Postsecondary	Greensboro-Winston-Salem-High Point MSA, NC	Y	28910 FQ	47500 AW	76110 TQ	NCBLS	10/01-12/01
Postsecondary	Raleigh-Durham-Chapel Hill MSA, NC	Y	29190 FQ	48940 AW	80550 TQ	NCBLS	10/01-12/01
Postsecondary	Ohio	Y	26640 FQ	50120 AW	76310 TQ	OHBLS	10/01-12/01
Postsecondary	Cincinnati PMSA, OH-KY-IN	Y	30220 FQ	52850 AW	81280 TQ	OHBLS	10/01-12/01
Postsecondary	Cleveland-Lorain-Elyria PMSA, OH	Y	22110 FQ	49020 AW	73770 TQ	OHBLS	10/01-12/01
Postsecondary	Columbus MSA, OH	Y	26260 FQ	45680 AW	73250 TQ	OHBLS	10/01-12/01
Postsecondary	Dayton-Springfield MSA, OH	Y	21840 FQ	45160 AW	66540 TQ	OHBLS	10/01-12/01
Postsecondary	Toledo MSA, OH	Y	36070 FQ	67890 AW	110720 TQ	OHBLS	10/01-12/01
Postsecondary	Oklahoma	Y	24700 FQ	39390 AW	59900 TQ	OKBLS	10/01-12/01
Postsecondary	Oklahoma City MSA, OK	Y	23910 FQ	37620 AW	61230 TQ	OKBLS	10/01-12/01
Postsecondary	Oregon	Y	38680 FQ	63360 AW	91270 TQ	ORBLS	10/01-12/01
Postsecondary	Portland-Vancouver PMSA, OR-WA	Y	39150 FQ	64010 AW	90670 TQ	ORBLS	10/01-12/01
Postsecondary	Pennsylvania	Y	28300 FQ	52880 AW	86750 TQ	PABLS	10/01-12/01
Postsecondary	Allentown-Bethlehem-Easton MSA, PA	Y	28110 FQ	47080 AW	72350 TQ	PABLS	10/01-12/01
Postsecondary	Philadelphia PMSA, PA-NJ	Y	28330 FQ	56650 AW	94160 TQ	PABLS	10/01-12/01
Postsecondary	Pittsburgh MSA, PA	Y	25790 FQ	57450 AW	106440 TQ	PABLS	10/01-12/01
Postsecondary	Scranton-Wilkes-Barre-Hazleton MSA, PA	Y	31080 FQ	43380 AW	63660 TQ	PABLS	10/01-12/01
Postsecondary	Rhode Island	Y	33000 FQ	54390 AW	86050 TQ	RIBLS	10/01-12/01
Postsecondary	South Carolina	Y	28280 FQ	48730 AW	73770 TQ	SCBLS	10/01-12/01
Postsecondary	Greenville-Spartanburg-Anderson MSA, SC	Y	28890 FQ	49070 AW	82470 TQ	SCBLS	10/01-12/01
Postsecondary	South Dakota	Y	29220 FQ	41830 AW	57500 TQ	SDBLS	10/01-12/01
Postsecondary	Tennessee	Y	25080 FQ	45310 AW	68840 TQ	TNBLS	10/01-12/01
Postsecondary	Johnson City-Kingsport-Bristol MSA, TN-VA	Y	23800 FQ	41470 AW	56150 TQ	TNBLS	10/01-12/01
Postsecondary	Knoxville MSA, TN	Y	28550 FQ	49130 AW	79970 TQ	TNBLS	10/01-12/01
Postsecondary	Memphis MSA, TN-AR-MS	Y	34410 FQ	51050 AW	75760 TQ	TNBLS	10/01-12/01
Postsecondary	Nashville MSA, TN	Y	30840 FQ	49190 AW	70590 TQ	TNBLS	10/01-12/01
Postsecondary	Texas	Y	24210 FQ	50100 AW	76110 TQ	TXBLS	10/01-12/01
Postsecondary	Dallas PMSA, TX	Y	19720 FQ	52600 AW	90830 TQ	TXBLS	10/01-12/01
Postsecondary	Fort Worth-Arlington PMSA, TX	Y	22460 FQ	48730 AW	80040 TQ	TXBLS	10/01-12/01
Postsecondary	Houston PMSA, TX	Y	38110 FQ	55910 AW	73640 TQ	TXBLS	10/01-12/01
Postsecondary	San Antonio MSA, TX	Y	25360 FQ	43760 AW	60900 TQ	TXBLS	10/01-12/01
Postsecondary	Utah	Y	41260 FQ	59750 AW	85430 TQ	UTBLS	10/01-12/01
Postsecondary	Vermont	Y	33710 FQ	52480 AW	80100 TQ	VTBLS	10/01-12/01
Postsecondary	Burlington MSA, VT	Y	39040 FQ	56430 AW	89060 TQ	VTBLS	10/01-12/01
Postsecondary	Virginia	Y	31080 FQ	52570 AW	86400 TQ	VABLS	10/01-12/01
Postsecondary	Norfolk-Virginia Beach-Newport News MSA, VA-NC	Y	36760 FQ	57330 AW	91300 TQ	VABLS	10/01-12/01
Postsecondary	Richmond-Petersburg MSA, VA	Y	25330 FQ	47590 AW	75820 TQ	VABLS	10/01-12/01
Postsecondary	Washington	Y	28060 FQ	46150 AW	70430 TQ	WABLS	10/01-12/01
Postsecondary	Seattle-Bellevue-Everett PMSA, WA	Y	28990 FQ	46340 AW	70460 TQ	WABLS	10/01-12/01
Postsecondary	Tacoma PMSA, WA	Y	31160 FQ	50890 AW	72560 TQ	WABLS	10/01-12/01
Postsecondary	Wisconsin	Y	28320 FQ	50640 AW	76220 TQ	WIBLS	10/01-12/01
Postsecondary	Milwaukee-Waukesha PMSA, WI	Y	25790 FQ	51130 AW	78640 TQ	WIBLS	10/01-12/01

AAW Average annual wage; AE Average entry wage; AEX Average experienced wage; AO Average offered; AOH Average offered, high; AOL Average offered, low; APH Average pay, high range; APL Average pay, low range; ASH Average starting, high; ASL Average starting, low; AW Average wage paid; FQ First quartile wage; H Hourly; HI Highest wage paid; HR High end range; LR Low end range; M Monthly; MTC Median total compensation; MW Median wage paid; SQ Second quartile wage; S Special: hourly and annual; TQ Third quartile wage; W Weekly; Y Yearly

Occupation/Type/Industry	Location	Per	Low	Mid	High	Source	Date
Philosophy and Religion Teacher							
Postsecondary	Puerto Rico	Y	24760 FQ	44950 AW	75540 TQ	PRBLS	10/01-12/01
Photographer	Alabama	Y	14660 FQ	22340 AW	34720 TQ	ALBLS	10/01-12/01
	Birmingham MSA, AL	Y	15680 FQ	29370 AW	45110 TQ	ALBLS	10/01-12/01
	Huntsville MSA, AL	Y	15550 FQ	22300 AW	29020 TQ	ALBLS	10/01-12/01
	Mobile MSA, AL	Y	15450 FQ	19930 AW	28690 TQ	ALBLS	10/01-12/01
	Montgomery MSA, AL	Y	14670 FQ	24290 AW	42070 TQ	ALBLS	10/01-12/01
	Alaska	Y	19590 FQ	28840 AW	40630 TQ	AKBLS	10/01-12/01
	Anchorage MSA, AK	Y	19840 FQ	28150 AW	37340 TQ	AKBLS	10/01-12/01
	Arizona	Y	16980 FQ	27640 AW	44480 TQ	AZBLS	10/01-12/01
	Phoenix-Mesa MSA, AZ	Y	17460 FQ	27460 AW	43870 TQ	AZBLS	10/01-12/01
	Tucson MSA, AZ	Y	17040 FQ	29420 AW	46710 TQ	AZBLS	10/01-12/01
	Arkansas	Y	12610 FQ	21500 AW	37360 TQ	ARBLS	10/01-12/01
	Fayetteville-Springdale-Rogers MSA, AR	Y	15940 FQ	22830 AW	33900 TQ	ARBLS	10/01-12/01
	Fort Smith MSA, AR-OK	Y	13410 FQ	18540 AW	25410 TQ	ARBLS	10/01-12/01
	Little Rock-North Little Rock MSA, AR	Y	12520 FQ	23010 AW	41780 TQ	ARBLS	10/01-12/01
	California	Y	14940 FQ	25680 AW	47620 TQ	CABLS	10/01-12/01
	Bakersfield MSA, CA	Y	14570 FQ	26190 AW	41280 TQ	CABLS	10/01-12/01
	Chico-Paradise MSA, CA	Y	15270 FQ	20560 AW	24060 TQ	CABLS	10/01-12/01
	Fresno MSA, CA	Y	15680 FQ	25000 AW	50500 TQ	CABLS	10/01-12/01
	Los Angeles-Long Beach PMSA, CA	Y	14510 FQ	26750 AW	52120 TQ	CABLS	10/01-12/01
	Modesto MSA, CA	Y	14550 FQ	22450 AW	31320 TQ	CABLS	10/01-12/01
	Oakland PMSA, CA	Y	15440 FQ	23770 AW	37970 TQ	CABLS	10/01-12/01
	Orange County PMSA, CA	Y	14560 FQ	22660 AW	38350 TQ	CABLS	10/01-12/01
	Riverside-San Bernardino PMSA, CA	Y	15720 FQ	23580 AW	35450 TQ	CABLS	10/01-12/01
	Sacramento PMSA, CA	Y	15660 FQ	23570 AW	37610 TQ	CABLS	10/01-12/01
	Salinas MSA, CA	Y	16040 FQ	27010 AW	48590 TQ	CABLS	10/01-12/01
	San Diego MSA, CA	Y	15680 FQ	23800 AW	37350 TQ	CABLS	10/01-12/01
	San Francisco PMSA, CA	Y	14230 FQ	36170 AW	67180 TQ	CABLS	10/01-12/01
	San Jose PMSA, CA	Y	15890 FQ	27000 AW	50010 TQ	CABLS	10/01-12/01
	San Luis Obispo-Atascadero-Paso Robles MSA, CA	Y	14600 FQ	21800 AW	36090 TQ	CABLS	10/01-12/01
	Santa Barbara-Santa Maria-Lompoc MSA, CA	Y	15950 FQ	30300 AW	47390 TQ	CABLS	10/01-12/01
	Santa Cruz-Watsonville PMSA, CA	Y	16460 FQ	38280 AW	96610 TQ	CABLS	10/01-12/01
	Santa Rosa PMSA, CA	Y	15320 FQ	25860 AW	50420 TQ	CABLS	10/01-12/01
	Stockton-Lodi MSA, CA	Y	13820 FQ	23060 AW	41500 TQ	CABLS	10/01-12/01
	Vallejo-Fairfield-Napa PMSA, CA	Y	14620 FQ	19590 AW	28380 TQ	CABLS	10/01-12/01
	Ventura PMSA, CA	Y	15940 FQ	24520 AW	32900 TQ	CABLS	10/01-12/01
	Visalia-Tulare-Porterville MSA, CA	Y	13950 FQ	19250 AW	26640 TQ	CABLS	10/01-12/01
	Colorado	Y	13900 FQ	25980 AW	43210 TQ	COBLS	10/01-12/01
	Boulder-Longmont PMSA, CO	Y	18730 FQ	33970 AW	63360 TQ	COBLS	10/01-12/01
	Colorado Springs MSA, CO	Y	14740 FQ	23770 AW	36390 TQ	COBLS	10/01-12/01
	Denver PMSA, CO	Y	15060 FQ	25850 AW	44520 TQ	COBLS	10/01-12/01
	Fort Collins-Loveland MSA, CO	Y	12800 FQ	25630 AW	39620 TQ	COBLS	10/01-12/01
	Greeley PMSA, CO	Y	13640 FQ	24560 AW	37810 TQ	COBLS	10/01-12/01
	Connecticut	Y	16230 FQ	30690 AW	54250 TQ	CTBLS	10/01-12/01
	Bridgeport PMSA, CT	Y	16490 FQ	25700 AW	38760 TQ	CTBLS	10/01-12/01
	Danbury PMSA, CT	Y	15640 FQ	36580 AW	56990 TQ	CTBLS	10/01-12/01
	Hartford MSA, CT	Y	16770 FQ	32060 AW	62160 TQ	CTBLS	10/01-12/01
	New Haven-Meriden PMSA, CT	Y	15590 FQ	32620 AW	52950 TQ	CTBLS	10/01-12/01
	New London-Norwich MSA, CT-RI	Y	15850 FQ	28780 AW	54710 TQ	CTBLS	10/01-12/01
	Stamford-Norwalk PMSA, CT	Y	28720 FQ	41700 AW	63130 TQ	CTBLS	10/01-12/01
	Waterbury PMSA, CT	Y	15730 FQ	23660 AW	40770 TQ	CTBLS	10/01-12/01
	Delaware	Y	15250 FQ	27760 AW	52380 TQ	DEBLS	10/01-12/01
	Wilmington-Newark PMSA, DE-MD	Y	16050 FQ	32660 AW	57450 TQ	DEBLS	10/01-12/01
	District of Columbia	Y	19360 FQ	36790 AW	61130 TQ	DCBLS	10/01-12/01
	Washington PMSA, DC-MD-VA-WV	Y	14610 FQ	26190 AW	43440 TQ	DCBLS	10/01-12/01
	Florida	Y	13410 FQ	26400 AW	47410 TQ	FLBLS	10/01-12/01
	Daytona Beach MSA, FL	Y	12460 FQ	22160 AW	36080 TQ	FLBLS	10/01-12/01

AAW Average annual wage	**AOH** Average offered, high	**ASH** Average starting, high	**H** Hourly	**M** Monthly	**S** Special: hourly and annual
AE Average entry wage	**AOL** Average offered, low	**ASL** Average starting, low	**HI** Highest wage paid	**MTC** Median total compensation	**TQ** Third quartile wage
AEX Average experienced wage	**APH** Average pay, high range	**AW** Average wage paid	**HR** High end range	**MW** Median wage paid	**W** Weekly
AO Average offered	**APL** Average pay, low range	**FQ** First quartile wage	**LR** Low end range	**SQ** Second quartile wage	**Y** Yearly

Occupation/Type/Industry	Location	Per	Low	Mid	High	Source	Date
Photographer	Fort Lauderdale PMSA, FL	Y	14690 FQ	23190 AW	34920 TQ	FLBLS	10/01-12/01
	Fort Myers-Cape Coral MSA, FL	Y	14710 FQ	20740 AW	34400 TQ	FLBLS	10/01-12/01
	Fort Walton Beach MSA, FL	Y	12430 FQ	21710 AW	35500 TQ	FLBLS	10/01-12/01
	Gainesville MSA, FL	Y	12170 FQ	20270 AW	31500 TQ	FLBLS	10/01-12/01
	Jacksonville MSA, FL	Y	12940 FQ	25150 AW	42460 TQ	FLBLS	10/01-12/01
	Melbourne-Titusville-Palm Bay MSA, FL	Y	12720 FQ	21850 AW	39540 TQ	FLBLS	10/01-12/01
	Miami PMSA, FL	Y	11980 FQ	26290 AW	50320 TQ	FLBLS	10/01-12/01
	Orlando MSA, FL	Y	14900 FQ	24700 AW	36580 TQ	FLBLS	10/01-12/01
	Pensacola MSA, FL	Y	13090 FQ	23950 AW	41970 TQ	FLBLS	10/01-12/01
	Sarasota-Bradenton MSA, FL	Y	12620 FQ	22700 AW	39340 TQ	FLBLS	10/01-12/01
	Tallahassee MSA, FL	Y	18890 FQ	29180 AW	52520 TQ	FLBLS	10/01-12/01
	Tampa-St. Petersburg-Clearwater MSA, FL	Y	17330 FQ	33560 AW	53760 TQ	FLBLS	10/01-12/01
	West Palm Beach-Boca Raton MSA, FL	Y	13590 FQ	31410 AW	55300 TQ	FLBLS	10/01-12/01
	Georgia	Y	17550 FQ	28430 AW	42780 TQ	GABLS	10/01-12/01
	Atlanta MSA, GA	Y	19150 FQ	30030 AW	44360 TQ	GABLS	10/01-12/01
	Augusta-Aiken MSA, GA-SC	Y	15890 FQ	33030 AW	56360 TQ	GABLS	10/01-12/01
	Columbus MSA, GA-AL	Y	16140 FQ	24330 AW	39340 TQ	GABLS	10/01-12/01
	Macon MSA, GA	Y	16000 FQ	22990 AW	34540 TQ	GABLS	10/01-12/01
	Savannah MSA, GA	Y	12550 FQ	26600 AW	41300 TQ	GABLS	10/01-12/01
	Hawaii	Y	14000 FQ	26220 AW	41870 TQ	HIBLS	10/01-12/01
	Honolulu MSA, HI	Y	13570 FQ	24050 AW	38540 TQ	HIBLS	10/01-12/01
	Idaho	Y	15010 FQ	23930 AW	40790 TQ	IDBLS	10/01-12/01
	Boise City MSA, ID	Y	15510 FQ	27380 AW	52650 TQ	IDBLS	10/01-12/01
	Illinois	Y	19770 FQ	35340 AW	52870 TQ	ILBLS	10/01-12/01
	Chicago PMSA, IL	Y	21660 FQ	36950 AW	54110 TQ	ILBLS	10/01-12/01
	Peoria-Pekin MSA, IL	Y	13240 FQ	27580 AW	52210 TQ	ILBLS	10/01-12/01
	Rockford MSA, IL	Y	12800 FQ	24860 AW	38520 TQ	ILBLS	10/01-12/01
	Springfield MSA, IL	Y	25010 FQ	36060 AW	44240 TQ	ILBLS	10/01-12/01
	Indiana	Y	13590 FQ	25020 AW	35990 TQ	INBLS	10/01-12/01
	Elkhart-Goshen MSA, IN	Y	13660 FQ	21970 AW	31040 TQ	INBLS	10/01-12/01
	Evansville-Henderson MSA, IN-KY	Y	12840 FQ	26430 AW	45280 TQ	INBLS	10/01-12/01
	Fort Wayne MSA, IN	Y	19480 FQ	24180 AW	32930 TQ	INBLS	10/01-12/01
	Gary PMSA, IN	Y	12490 FQ	21430 AW	37830 TQ	INBLS	10/01-12/01
	Indianapolis MSA, IN	Y	16830 FQ	24040 AW	34290 TQ	INBLS	10/01-12/01
	Lafayette MSA, IN	Y	13160 FQ	23670 AW	41170 TQ	INBLS	10/01-12/01
	South Bend MSA, IN	Y	14670 FQ	34130 AW	56980 TQ	INBLS	10/01-12/01
	Iowa	Y	12550 FQ	24890 AW	43160 TQ	IABLS	10/01-12/01
	Cedar Rapids MSA, IA	Y	14090 FQ	30040 AW	50530 TQ	IABLS	10/01-12/01
	Davenport-Moline-Rock Island MSA, IA-IL	Y	13030 FQ	24080 AW	34250 TQ	IABLS	10/01-12/01
	Des Moines MSA, IA	Y	15850 FQ	30160 AW	56920 TQ	IABLS	10/01-12/01
	Kansas	Y	12680 FQ	25510 AW	47550 TQ	KSBLS	10/01-12/01
	Topeka MSA, KS	Y	12260 FQ	23270 AW	49290 TQ	KSBLS	10/01-12/01
	Wichita MSA, KS	Y	13950 FQ	26090 AW	42950 TQ	KSBLS	10/01-12/01
	Kentucky	Y	12890 FQ	24080 AW	38650 TQ	KYBLS	10/01-12/01
	Lexington MSA, KY	Y	18990 FQ	28720 AW	42900 TQ	KYBLS	10/01-12/01
	Louisville MSA, KY-IN	Y	14490 FQ	28110 AW	46930 TQ	KYBLS	10/01-12/01
	Louisiana	Y	12280 FQ	21270 AW	36150 TQ	LABLS	10/01-12/01
	Baton Rouge MSA, LA	Y	16810 FQ	30920 AW	44090 TQ	LABLS	10/01-12/01
	Lafayette MSA, LA	Y	11810 FQ	17560 AW	26450 TQ	LABLS	10/01-12/01
	New Orleans MSA, LA	Y	11880 FQ	20960 AW	37140 TQ	LABLS	10/01-12/01
	Shreveport-Bossier City MSA, LA	Y	12860 FQ	20280 AW	27390 TQ	LABLS	10/01-12/01
	Maine	Y	11850 FQ	23110 AW	40780 TQ	MEBLS	10/01-12/01
	Portland MSA, ME	Y	11490 FQ	28830 AW	57750 TQ	MEBLS	10/01-12/01
	Maryland	Y	12360 FQ	21470 AW	39280 TQ	MDBLS	10/01-12/01
	Baltimore PMSA, MD	Y	12050 FQ	21570 AW	43300 TQ	MDBLS	10/01-12/01
	Massachusetts	Y	14790 FQ	32680 AW	50570 TQ	MABLS	10/01-12/01
	Boston PMSA, MA-NH	Y	15930 FQ	29870 AW	46540 TQ	MABLS	10/01-12/01
	Lawrence PMSA, MA-NH	Y	18170 FQ	36550 AW	66660 TQ	MABLS	10/01-12/01
	Springfield MSA, MA	Y	14270 FQ	24140 AW	40260 TQ	MABLS	10/01-12/01
	Worcester PMSA, MA-CT	Y	29790 FQ	84370 AW		MABLS	10/01-12/01
	Michigan	Y	15570 FQ	33400 AW	62240 TQ	MIBLS	10/01-12/01
	Ann Arbor PMSA, MI	Y	19810 FQ	36340 AW	58790 TQ	MIBLS	10/01-12/01
	Detroit PMSA, MI	Y	17420 FQ	42740 AW	73280 TQ	MIBLS	10/01-12/01
	Flint PMSA, MI	Y	12230 FQ	18790 AW	28630 TQ	MIBLS	10/01-12/01

AAW	Average annual wage	AOH	Average offered, high	ASH	Average starting, high	H	Hourly	M	Monthly	S	Special: hourly and annual
AE	Average entry wage	AOL	Average offered, low	ASL	Average starting, low	HI	Highest wage paid	MTC	Median total compensation	TQ	Third quartile wage
AEX	Average experienced wage	APH	Average pay, high range	AW	Average wage paid	HR	High end range	MW	Median wage paid	W	Weekly
AO	Average offered	APL	Average pay, low range	FQ	First quartile wage	LR	Low end range	SQ	Second quartile wage	Y	Yearly

Occupation/Type/Industry	Location	Per	Low	Mid	High	Source	Date
Photographer	Grand Rapids-Muskegon-Holland MSA, MI	Y	16290 FQ	27380 AW	45490 TQ	MIBLS	10/01-12/01
	Kalamazoo-Battle Creek MSA, MI	Y	13310 FQ	44860 AW	82760 TQ	MIBLS	10/01-12/01
	Lansing-East Lansing MSA, MI	Y	17680 FQ	30280 AW	50710 TQ	MIBLS	10/01-12/01
	Saginaw-Bay City-Midland MSA, MI	Y	17320 FQ	38690 AW	67860 TQ	MIBLS	10/01-12/01
	Minnesota	Y	17050 FQ	37900 AW	65690 TQ	MNBLS	10/01-12/01
	Minneapolis-St. Paul MSA, MN-WI	Y	17610 FQ	41250 AW	67950 TQ	MNBLS	10/01-12/01
	St. Cloud MSA, MN	Y	16760 FQ	29230 AW	43780 TQ	MNBLS	10/01-12/01
	Mississippi	Y	12210 FQ	19670 AW	29090 TQ	MSBLS	10/01-12/01
	Biloxi-Gulfport-Pascagoula MSA, MS	Y	12010 FQ	21520 AW	33990 TQ	MSBLS	10/01-12/01
	Jackson MSA, MS	Y	16850 FQ	25650 AW	36370 TQ	MSBLS	10/01-12/01
	Missouri	Y	13090 FQ	25300 AW	48050 TQ	MOBLS	10/01-12/01
	Kansas City MSA, MO-KS	Y	13410 FQ	25550 AW	47160 TQ	MOBLS	10/01-12/01
	St. Louis MSA, MO-IL	Y	13270 FQ	29440 AW	53560 TQ	MOBLS	10/01-12/01
	Springfield MSA, MO	Y	12780 FQ	19330 AW	27680 TQ	MOBLS	10/01-12/01
	Montana	Y	14610 FQ	23740 AW	36300 TQ	MTBLS	10/01-12/01
	Billings MSA, MT	Y	13140 FQ	21340 AW	31190 TQ	MTBLS	10/01-12/01
	Nebraska	Y	13410 FQ	27190 AW	46800 TQ	NEBLS	10/01-12/01
	Lincoln MSA, NE	Y	12230 FQ	26160 AW	51120 TQ	NEBLS	10/01-12/01
	Omaha MSA, NE-IA	Y	13390 FQ	25590 AW	47290 TQ	NEBLS	10/01-12/01
	Nevada	Y	18280 FQ	27580 AW	38790 TQ	NVBLS	10/01-12/01
	Las Vegas MSA, NV-AZ	Y	18450 FQ	27780 AW	38920 TQ	NVBLS	10/01-12/01
	Reno MSA, NV	Y	19280 FQ	29880 AW	43270 TQ	NVBLS	10/01-12/01
	New Hampshire	Y	14610 FQ	28090 AW	52010 TQ	NHBLS	10/01-12/01
	Manchester PMSA, NH	Y	16990 FQ	24250 AW	38970 TQ	NHBLS	10/01-12/01
	Portsmouth-Rochester PMSA, NH-ME	Y	12380 FQ	22030 AW	36100 TQ	NHBLS	10/01-12/01
	New Jersey	Y	13920 FQ	29240 AW	54510 TQ	NJBLS	10/01-12/01
	Atlantic-Cape May PMSA, NJ	Y	14780 FQ	25860 AW	51150 TQ	NJBLS	10/01-12/01
	Bergen-Passaic PMSA, NJ	Y	15080 FQ	30790 AW	56910 TQ	NJBLS	10/01-12/01
	Jersey City PMSA, NJ	Y	15660 FQ	30540 AW	56650 TQ	NJBLS	10/01-12/01
	Middlesex-Somerset-Hunterdon PMSA, NJ	Y	13520 FQ	26780 AW	55730 TQ	NJBLS	10/01-12/01
	Monmouth-Ocean PMSA, NJ	Y	12970 FQ	22120 AW	36150 TQ	NJBLS	10/01-12/01
	Newark PMSA, NJ	Y	18880 FQ	35600 AW	55900 TQ	NJBLS	10/01-12/01
	Trenton PMSA, NJ	Y	16110 FQ	37390 AW	77420 TQ	NJBLS	10/01-12/01
	New Mexico	Y	14830 FQ	26100 AW	37080 TQ	NMBLS	10/01-12/01
	Albuquerque MSA, NM	Y	18100 FQ	26970 AW	39400 TQ	NMBLS	10/01-12/01
	New York	Y	15580 FQ	38860 AW	72410 TQ	NYBLS	10/01-12/01
	Albany-Schenectady-Troy MSA, NY	Y	16130 FQ	32870 AW	55070 TQ	NYBLS	10/01-12/01
	Binghamton MSA, NY	Y	18440 FQ	43700 AW	83550 TQ	NYBLS	10/01-12/01
	Buffalo-Niagara Falls MSA, NY	Y	12150 FQ	22380 AW	38870 TQ	NYBLS	10/01-12/01
	Dutchess County PMSA, NY	Y	12940 FQ	24810 AW	41060 TQ	NYBLS	10/01-12/01
	Nassau-Suffolk PMSA, NY	Y	16860 FQ	33690 AW	59850 TQ	NYBLS	10/01-12/01
	New York PMSA, NY	Y	22610 FQ	49720 AW	126180 TQ	NYBLS	10/01-12/01
	Newburgh PMSA, NY-PA	Y	13640 FQ	27980 AW	37040 TQ	NYBLS	10/01-12/01
	Rochester MSA, NY	Y	13070 FQ	27930 AW	44660 TQ	NYBLS	10/01-12/01
	Syracuse MSA, NY	Y	12270 FQ	22310 AW	34340 TQ	NYBLS	10/01-12/01
	Utica-Rome MSA, NY	Y	15860 FQ	26220 AW	60590 TQ	NYBLS	10/01-12/01
	North Carolina	Y	14190 FQ	33030 AW	56370 TQ	NCBLS	10/01-12/01
	Asheville MSA, NC	Y	12170 FQ	29250 AW	78370 TQ	NCBLS	10/01-12/01
	Charlotte-Gastonia-Rock Hill MSA, NC-SC	Y	23090 FQ	40990 AW	81890 TQ	NCBLS	10/01-12/01
	Fayetteville MSA, NC	Y	14390 FQ	28390 AW	49010 TQ	NCBLS	10/01-12/01
	Greensboro-Winston-Salem-High Point MSA, NC	Y	13780 FQ	26910 AW	42690 TQ	NCBLS	10/01-12/01
	Hickory-Morganton-Lenoir MSA, NC	Y	12580 FQ	23290 AW	38590 TQ	NCBLS	10/01-12/01
	Raleigh-Durham-Chapel Hill MSA, NC	Y	11970 FQ	26900 AW	44740 TQ	NCBLS	10/01-12/01
	Wilmington MSA, NC	Y	19880 FQ	33350 AW	51760 TQ	NCBLS	10/01-12/01
	North Dakota	Y	14330 FQ	25480 AW	41920 TQ	NDBLS	10/01-12/01
	Fargo-Moorhead MSA, ND-MN	Y	15380 FQ	25420 AW	44830 TQ	NDBLS	10/01-12/01
	Ohio	Y	13700 FQ	26480 AW	45750 TQ	OHBLS	10/01-12/01
	Akron PMSA, OH	Y	15610 FQ	35850 AW	55050 TQ	OHBLS	10/01-12/01

AAW Average annual wage **AOH** Average offered, high **ASH** Average starting, high **H** Hourly **M** Monthly **S** Special: hourly and annual
AE Average entry wage **AOL** Average offered, low **ASL** Average starting, low **HI** Highest wage paid **MTC** Median total compensation **TQ** Third quartile wage
AEX Average experienced wage **APH** Average pay, high range **AW** Average wage paid **HR** High end range **MW** Median wage paid **W** Weekly
AO Average offered **APL** Average pay, low range **FQ** First quartile wage **LR** Low end range **SQ** Second quartile wage **Y** Yearly

Occupation/Type/Industry	Location	Per	Low	Mid	High	Source	Date
Photographer	Canton-Massillon MSA, OH	Y	13430 FQ	27210 AW	43030 TQ	OHBLS	10/01-12/01
	Cincinnati PMSA, OH-KY-IN	Y	13830 FQ	23550 AW	35200 TQ	OHBLS	10/01-12/01
	Cleveland-Lorain-Elyria PMSA, OH	Y	13080 FQ	29470 AW	50370 TQ	OHBLS	10/01-12/01
	Columbus MSA, OH	Y	15990 FQ	31560 AW	56280 TQ	OHBLS	10/01-12/01
	Dayton-Springfield MSA, OH	Y	15620 FQ	24640 AW	35460 TQ	OHBLS	10/01-12/01
	Hamilton-Middletown PMSA, OH	Y	12450 FQ	22300 AW	35930 TQ	OHBLS	10/01-12/01
	Mansfield MSA, OH	Y	12650 FQ	21680 AW	33070 TQ	OHBLS	10/01-12/01
	Toledo MSA, OH	Y	12610 FQ	24420 AW	36840 TQ	OHBLS	10/01-12/01
	Youngstown-Warren MSA, OH	Y	12590 FQ	21830 AW	35330 TQ	OHBLS	10/01-12/01
	Oklahoma	Y	13550 FQ	21580 AW	32450 TQ	OKBLS	10/01-12/01
	Oklahoma City MSA, OK	Y	14710 FQ	21970 AW	32610 TQ	OKBLS	10/01-12/01
	Tulsa MSA, OK	Y	14990 FQ	24080 AW	36520 TQ	OKBLS	10/01-12/01
	Oregon	Y	14790 FQ	24320 AW	46530 TQ	ORBLS	10/01-12/01
	Eugene-Springfield MSA, OR	Y	14780 FQ	20040 AW	28410 TQ	ORBLS	10/01-12/01
	Medford-Ashland MSA, OR	Y	14820 FQ	18130 AW	23210 TQ	ORBLS	10/01-12/01
	Portland-Vancouver PMSA, OR-WA	Y	14820 FQ	32390 AW	68110 TQ	ORBLS	10/01-12/01
	Salem PMSA, OR	Y	15450 FQ	19160 AW	26710 TQ	ORBLS	10/01-12/01
	Pennsylvania	Y	14180 FQ	27810 AW	44530 TQ	PABLS	10/01-12/01
	Allentown-Bethlehem-Easton MSA, PA	Y	12760 FQ	29540 AW	51820 TQ	PABLS	10/01-12/01
	Erie MSA, PA	Y	13540 FQ	24830 AW	43650 TQ	PABLS	10/01-12/01
	Harrisburg-Lebanon-Carlisle MSA, PA	Y	18920 FQ	38920 AW	56960 TQ	PABLS	10/01-12/01
	Johnstown MSA, PA	Y	14410 FQ	23580 AW	43900 TQ	PABLS	10/01-12/01
	Lancaster MSA, PA	Y	15510 FQ	27590 AW	48440 TQ	PABLS	10/01-12/01
	Philadelphia PMSA, PA-NJ	Y	13310 FQ	29380 AW	46830 TQ	PABLS	10/01-12/01
	Pittsburgh MSA, PA	Y	15340 FQ	21160 AW	31780 TQ	PABLS	10/01-12/01
	Scranton-Wilkes-Barre-Hazleton MSA, PA	Y	12730 FQ	23530 AW	37210 TQ	PABLS	10/01-12/01
	York MSA, PA	Y	13080 FQ	24580 AW	42600 TQ	PABLS	10/01-12/01
	Rhode Island	Y	13770 FQ	26670 AW	47240 TQ	RIBLS	10/01-12/01
	Providence-Fall River-Warwick MSA, RI-MA	Y	13890 FQ	25310 AW	45450 TQ	RIBLS	10/01-12/01
	South Carolina	Y	12960 FQ	29140 AW	56510 TQ	SCBLS	10/01-12/01
	Charleston-North Charleston MSA, SC	Y	13270 FQ	21460 AW	32560 TQ	SCBLS	10/01-12/01
	Columbia MSA, SC	Y	19300 FQ	32230 AW	51500 TQ	SCBLS	10/01-12/01
	Greenville-Spartanburg-Anderson MSA, SC	Y	14300 FQ	36880 AW	84340 TQ	SCBLS	10/01-12/01
	Myrtle Beach MSA, SC	Y	11680 FQ	18850 AW	34440 TQ	SCBLS	10/01-12/01
	South Dakota	Y	15530 FQ	24540 AW	37050 TQ	SDBLS	10/01-12/01
	Sioux Falls MSA, SD	Y	15440 FQ	25670 AW	37160 TQ	SDBLS	10/01-12/01
	Tennessee	Y	13540 FQ	23330 AW	39210 TQ	TNBLS	10/01-12/01
	Chattanooga MSA, TN-GA	Y	14420 FQ	22030 AW	34910 TQ	TNBLS	10/01-12/01
	Johnson City-Kingsport-Bristol MSA, TN-VA	Y	17740 FQ	23330 AW	34140 TQ	TNBLS	10/01-12/01
	Knoxville MSA, TN	Y	15410 FQ	23410 AW	38000 TQ	TNBLS	10/01-12/01
	Memphis MSA, TN-AR-MS	Y	15530 FQ	27840 AW	51240 TQ	TNBLS	10/01-12/01
	Nashville MSA, TN	Y	14840 FQ	24440 AW	45200 TQ	TNBLS	10/01-12/01
	Texas	Y	12950 FQ	22890 AW	38760 TQ	TXBLS	10/01-12/01
	Amarillo MSA, TX	Y	14360 FQ	19620 AW	26740 TQ	TXBLS	10/01-12/01
	Austin-San Marcos MSA, TX	Y	14590 FQ	24460 AW	37960 TQ	TXBLS	10/01-12/01
	Beaumont-Port Arthur MSA, TX	Y	12560 FQ	20630 AW	29820 TQ	TXBLS	10/01-12/01
	Corpus Christi MSA, TX	Y	15220 FQ	22750 AW	29400 TQ	TXBLS	10/01-12/01
	Dallas PMSA, TX	Y	15650 FQ	29330 AW	45920 TQ	TXBLS	10/01-12/01
	El Paso MSA, TX	Y	13280 FQ	20110 AW	28890 TQ	TXBLS	10/01-12/01
	Fort Worth-Arlington PMSA, TX	Y	12670 FQ	22500 AW	34720 TQ	TXBLS	10/01-12/01
	Galveston-Texas City PMSA, TX	Y	14520 FQ	18090 AW	23670 TQ	TXBLS	10/01-12/01
	Houston PMSA, TX	Y	12280 FQ	21490 AW	34780 TQ	TXBLS	10/01-12/01
	Laredo MSA, TX	Y	11450 FQ	17050 AW	31750 TQ	TXBLS	10/01-12/01
	Lubbock MSA, TX	Y	15400 FQ	20250 AW	27360 TQ	TXBLS	10/01-12/01
	McAllen-Edinburg-Mission MSA, TX	Y	12090 FQ	19380 AW	27490 TQ	TXBLS	10/01-12/01
	Odessa-Midland MSA, TX	Y	13180 FQ	19540 AW	25730 TQ	TXBLS	10/01-12/01
	San Antonio MSA, TX	Y	12530 FQ	20850 AW	36450 TQ	TXBLS	10/01-12/01
	Tyler MSA, TX	Y	11570 FQ	18700 AW	29360 TQ	TXBLS	10/01-12/01

AAW	Average annual wage	**AOH**	Average offered, high	**ASH**	Average starting, high	**H**	Hourly	**M**	Monthly	**S**	Special: hourly and annual
AE	Average entry wage	**AOL**	Average offered, low	**ASL**	Average starting, low	**HI**	Highest wage paid	**MTC**	Median total compensation	**TQ**	Third quartile wage
AEX	Average experienced wage	**APH**	Average pay, high range	**AW**	Average wage paid	**HR**	High end range	**MW**	Median wage paid	**W**	Weekly
AO	Average offered	**APL**	Average pay, low range	**FQ**	First quartile wage	**LR**	Low end range	**SQ**	Second quartile wage	**Y**	Yearly

Occupation/Type/Industry	Location	Per	Low	Mid	High	Source	Date
Photographer	Waco MSA, TX	Y	13250 FQ	20760 AW	31370 TQ	TXBLS	10/01-12/01
	Utah	Y	16150 FQ	33100 AW	52840 TQ	UTBLS	10/01-12/01
	Salt Lake City-Ogden MSA, UT	Y	17740 FQ	35850 AW	54940 TQ	UTBLS	10/01-12/01
	Vermont	Y	14500 FQ	30940 AW	54040 TQ	VTBLS	10/01-12/01
	Burlington MSA, VT	Y	15980 FQ	35140 AW	62940 TQ	VTBLS	10/01-12/01
	Virginia	Y	14970 FQ	24250 AW	35350 TQ	VABLS	10/01-12/01
	Lynchburg MSA, VA	Y	12460 FQ	21250 AW	36720 TQ	VABLS	10/01-12/01
	Norfolk-Virginia Beach-Newport News MSA, VA-NC	Y	15320 FQ	22130 AW	32800 TQ	VABLS	10/01-12/01
	Richmond-Petersburg MSA, VA	Y	15790 FQ	25090 AW	34930 TQ	VABLS	10/01-12/01
	Roanoke MSA, VA	Y	15390 FQ	21710 AW	34120 TQ	VABLS	10/01-12/01
	Washington	Y	20190 FQ	40190 AW	63200 TQ	WABLS	10/01-12/01
	Richland-Kennewick-Pasco MSA, WA	Y	16640 FQ	35100 AW	53870 TQ	WABLS	10/01-12/01
	Seattle-Bellevue-Everett PMSA, WA	Y	24180 FQ	42660 AW	60450 TQ	WABLS	10/01-12/01
	Spokane MSA, WA	Y	15020 FQ	25620 AW	42340 TQ	WABLS	10/01-12/01
	Tacoma PMSA, WA	Y	18720 FQ	39800 AW	69490 TQ	WABLS	10/01-12/01
	West Virginia	Y	15190 FQ	24960 AW	36990 TQ	WVBLS	10/01-12/01
	Charleston MSA, WV	Y	15240 FQ	23510 AW	32920 TQ	WVBLS	10/01-12/01
	Huntington-Ashland MSA, WV-KY-OH	Y	12730 FQ	23730 AW	38290 TQ	WVBLS	10/01-12/01
	Wisconsin	Y	16440 FQ	27530 AW	44110 TQ	WIBLS	10/01-12/01
	Appleton-Oshkosh-Neenah MSA, WI	Y	16900 FQ	31090 AW	57770 TQ	WIBLS	10/01-12/01
	Green Bay MSA, WI	Y	18000 FQ	26460 AW	41910 TQ	WIBLS	10/01-12/01
	Madison MSA, WI	Y	19360 FQ	24410 AW	37160 TQ	WIBLS	10/01-12/01
	Milwaukee-Waukesha PMSA, WI	Y	20250 FQ	31130 AW	45570 TQ	WIBLS	10/01-12/01
	Racine PMSA, WI	Y	12660 FQ	24480 AW	49500 TQ	WIBLS	10/01-12/01
	Wyoming	Y	15270 FQ	25600 AW	43400 TQ	WYBLS	10/01-12/01
	Puerto Rico	Y	13300 FQ	23530 AW	38080 TQ	PRBLS	10/01-12/01
Photographic Process Worker	Alabama	H	5.98 FQ	8.76 AW	12.78 TQ	ALBLS	10/01-12/01
	Birmingham MSA, AL	H	6.34 FQ	9.48 AW	13.29 TQ	ALBLS	10/01-12/01
	Alaska	H	8.20 FQ	11.58 AW	15.72 TQ	AKBLS	10/01-12/01
	Arizona	H	8.32 FQ	11.77 AW	14.51 TQ	AZBLS	10/01-12/01
	Phoenix-Mesa MSA, AZ	H	9.48 FQ	11.96 AW	14.50 TQ	AZBLS	10/01-12/01
	Tucson MSA, AZ	H	9.47 FQ	11.76 AW	13.53 TQ	AZBLS	10/01-12/01
	Arkansas	H	5.90 FQ	8.23 AW	11.57 TQ	ARBLS	10/01-12/01
	Fayetteville-Springdale-Rogers MSA, AR	H	6.80 FQ	8.56 AW	11.45 TQ	ARBLS	10/01-12/01
	California	H	7.29 FQ	13.02 AW	22.63 TQ	CABLS	10/01-12/01
	Los Angeles-Long Beach PMSA, CA	H	7.45 FQ	15.74 AW	26.28 TQ	CABLS	10/01-12/01
	Oakland PMSA, CA	H	8.38 FQ	11.54 AW	16.23 TQ	CABLS	10/01-12/01
	Orange County PMSA, CA	H	8.27 FQ	12.50 AW	21.60 TQ	CABLS	10/01-12/01
	Riverside-San Bernardino PMSA, CA	H	6.99 FQ	10.18 AW	15.88 TQ	CABLS	10/01-12/01
	Sacramento PMSA, CA	H	7.88 FQ	12.96 AW	17.36 TQ	CABLS	10/01-12/01
	San Diego MSA, CA	H	7.31 FQ	11.47 AW	17.71 TQ	CABLS	10/01-12/01
	San Francisco PMSA, CA	H	8.52 FQ	18.64 AW	29.18 TQ	CABLS	10/01-12/01
	San Jose PMSA, CA	H	8.55 FQ	15.40 AW	22.89 TQ	CABLS	10/01-12/01
	San Luis Obispo-Atascadero-Paso Robles MSA, CA	H	7.45 FQ	11.23 AW	16.89 TQ	CABLS	10/01-12/01
	Santa Rosa PMSA, CA	H	7.11 FQ	9.87 AW	15.16 TQ	CABLS	10/01-12/01
	Ventura PMSA, CA	H	7.75 FQ	16.84 AW	26.17 TQ	CABLS	10/01-12/01
	Visalia-Tulare-Porterville MSA, CA	H	6.95 FQ	9.03 AW	11.16 TQ	CABLS	10/01-12/01
	Colorado	H	7.39 FQ	11.01 AW	16.41 TQ	COBLS	10/01-12/01
	Colorado Springs MSA, CO	H	9.31 FQ	12.82 AW	18.84 TQ	COBLS	10/01-12/01
	Denver PMSA, CO	H	7.39 FQ	10.62 AW	16.72 TQ	COBLS	10/01-12/01
	Connecticut	H	7.07 FQ	10.55 AW	15.05 TQ	CTBLS	10/01-12/01
	Hartford MSA, CT	H	7.10 FQ	10.73 AW	15.29 TQ	CTBLS	10/01-12/01
	New Haven-Meriden PMSA, CT	H	6.68 FQ	9.72 AW	15.05 TQ	CTBLS	10/01-12/01
	New London-Norwich MSA, CT-RI	H	7.32 FQ	9.71 AW	13.50 TQ	CTBLS	10/01-12/01
	Delaware	H	7.25 FQ	9.95 AW	13.32 TQ	DEBLS	10/01-12/01

AAW	Average annual wage	**AOH**	Average offered, high	**ASH**	Average starting, high	**H**	Hourly	**M**	Monthly	**S**	Special: hourly and annual
AE	Average entry wage	**AOL**	Average offered, low	**ASL**	Average starting, low	**HI**	Highest wage paid	**MTC**	Median total compensation	**TQ**	Third quartile wage
AEX	Average experienced wage	**APH**	Average pay, high range	**AW**	Average wage paid	**HR**	High end range	**MW**	Median wage paid	**W**	Weekly
AO	Average offered	**APL**	Average pay, low range	**FQ**	First quartile wage	**LR**	Low end range	**SQ**	Second quartile wage	**Y**	Yearly

Occupation/Type/Industry	Location	Per	Low	Mid	High	Source	Date
Photographic Process Worker	Wilmington-Newark PMSA, DE-MD	H	7.47 FQ	10.36 AW	13.26 TQ	DEBLS	10/01-12/01
	District of Columbia	H	11.38 FQ	16.76 AW	21.90 TQ	DCBLS	10/01-12/01
	Washington PMSA, DC-MD-VA-WV	H	7.40 FQ	12.55 AW	21.18 TQ	DCBLS	10/01-12/01
	Florida	H	6.33 FQ	9.29 AW	14.27 TQ	FLBLS	10/01-12/01
	Daytona Beach MSA, FL	H	6.65 FQ	10.62 AW	16.62 TQ	FLBLS	10/01-12/01
	Fort Lauderdale PMSA, FL	H	7.16 FQ	11.31 AW	19.01 TQ	FLBLS	10/01-12/01
	Jacksonville MSA, FL	H	6.38 FQ	8.78 AW	12.19 TQ	FLBLS	10/01-12/01
	Lakeland-Winter Haven MSA, FL	H	5.99 FQ	8.17 AW	10.69 TQ	FLBLS	10/01-12/01
	Miami PMSA, FL	H	6.10 FQ	10.26 AW	17.36 TQ	FLBLS	10/01-12/01
	Orlando MSA, FL	H	7.00 FQ	9.55 AW	15.18 TQ	FLBLS	10/01-12/01
	Pensacola MSA, FL	H	6.64 FQ	8.87 AW	11.00 TQ	FLBLS	10/01-12/01
	Tampa-St. Petersburg-Clearwater MSA, FL	H	6.08 FQ	8.56 AW	11.52 TQ	FLBLS	10/01-12/01
	Georgia	H	6.75 FQ	10.58 AW	16.61 TQ	GABLS	10/01-12/01
	Atlanta MSA, GA	H	6.95 FQ	9.95 AW	15.16 TQ	GABLS	10/01-12/01
	Macon MSA, GA	H	6.77 FQ	11.98 AW	18.55 TQ	GABLS	10/01-12/01
	Hawaii	H	5.87 FQ	10.20 AW	18.87 TQ	HIBLS	10/01-12/01
	Honolulu MSA, HI	H	5.78 FQ	10.08 AW	18.66 TQ	HIBLS	10/01-12/01
	Idaho	H	6.61 FQ	8.31 AW	10.95 TQ	IDBLS	10/01-12/01
	Illinois	H	7.04 FQ	11.35 AW	17.66 TQ	ILBLS	10/01-12/01
	Chicago PMSA, IL	H	7.43 FQ	12.17 AW	21.98 TQ	ILBLS	10/01-12/01
	Indiana	H	5.95 FQ	9.64 AW	14.84 TQ	INBLS	10/01-12/01
	Indianapolis MSA, IN	H	7.31 FQ	11.30 AW	16.81 TQ	INBLS	10/01-12/01
	South Bend MSA, IN	H	7.48 FQ	9.10 AW	10.92 TQ	INBLS	10/01-12/01
	Iowa	H	5.72 FQ	8.94 AW	13.57 TQ	IABLS	10/01-12/01
	Davenport-Moline-Rock Island MSA, IA-IL	H	6.28 FQ	8.98 AW	12.05 TQ	IABLS	10/01-12/01
	Kansas	H	6.78 FQ	8.11 AW	10.16 TQ	KSBLS	10/01-12/01
	Kentucky	H	5.97 FQ	9.05 AW	13.90 TQ	KYBLS	10/01-12/01
	Lexington MSA, KY	H	6.09 FQ	8.31 AW	11.50 TQ	KYBLS	10/01-12/01
	Louisville MSA, KY-IN	H	7.41 FQ	10.82 AW	15.65 TQ	KYBLS	10/01-12/01
	Louisiana	H	6.11 FQ	8.90 AW	12.48 TQ	LABLS	10/01-12/01
	New Orleans MSA, LA	H	6.31 FQ	9.22 AW	13.01 TQ	LABLS	10/01-12/01
	Maine	H	7.19 FQ	11.23 AW	16.14 TQ	MEBLS	10/01-12/01
	Maryland	H	7.14 FQ	10.58 AW	17.93 TQ	MDBLS	10/01-12/01
	Baltimore PMSA, MD	H	7.25 FQ	11.43 AW	19.50 TQ	MDBLS	10/01-12/01
	Massachusetts	H	7.90 FQ	13.47 AW	21.44 TQ	MABLS	10/01-12/01
	Boston PMSA, MA-NH	H	8.09 FQ	13.79 AW	21.26 TQ	MABLS	10/01-12/01
	Springfield MSA, MA	H	7.93 FQ	16.11 AW	26.59 TQ	MABLS	10/01-12/01
	Worcester PMSA, MA-CT	H	7.28 FQ	11.40 AW	16.41 TQ	MABLS	10/01-12/01
	Michigan	H	5.91 FQ	10.25 AW	15.41 TQ	MIBLS	10/01-12/01
	Ann Arbor PMSA, MI	H	7.18 FQ	10.45 AW	13.79 TQ	MIBLS	10/01-12/01
	Detroit PMSA, MI	H	5.75 FQ	9.34 AW	14.28 TQ	MIBLS	10/01-12/01
	Grand Rapids-Muskegon-Holland MSA, MI	H	7.21 FQ	13.77 AW	29.86 TQ	MIBLS	10/01-12/01
	Kalamazoo-Battle Creek MSA, MI	H	7.26 FQ	10.33 AW	14.05 TQ	MIBLS	10/01-12/01
	Minnesota	H	6.97 FQ	10.87 AW	17.23 TQ	MNBLS	10/01-12/01
	Minneapolis-St. Paul MSA, MN-WI	H	7.42 FQ	13.05 AW	19.62 TQ	MNBLS	10/01-12/01
	St. Cloud MSA, MN	H	5.92 FQ	7.57 AW	9.60 TQ	MNBLS	10/01-12/01
	Mississippi	H	5.61 FQ	7.43 AW	11.61 TQ	MSBLS	10/01-12/01
	Jackson MSA, MS	H	5.45 FQ	8.04 AW	13.18 TQ	MSBLS	10/01-12/01
	Missouri	H	6.77 FQ	9.99 AW	15.80 TQ	MOBLS	10/01-12/01
	Kansas City MSA, MO-KS	H	7.36 FQ	11.39 AW	17.84 TQ	MOBLS	10/01-12/01
	St. Louis MSA, MO-IL	H	7.19 FQ	9.98 AW	15.07 TQ	MOBLS	10/01-12/01
	Springfield MSA, MO	H	7.28 FQ	10.65 AW	16.87 TQ	MOBLS	10/01-12/01
	Montana	H	6.99 FQ	9.39 AW	12.49 TQ	MTBLS	10/01-12/01
	Nebraska	H	6.21 FQ	11.24 AW	17.88 TQ	NEBLS	10/01-12/01
	Omaha MSA, NE-IA	H	6.23 FQ	12.57 AW	19.09 TQ	NEBLS	10/01-12/01
	Nevada	H	7.23 FQ	11.45 AW	16.73 TQ	NVBLS	10/01-12/01
	Las Vegas MSA, NV-AZ	H	7.62 FQ	12.26 AW	17.36 TQ	NVBLS	10/01-12/01
	Reno MSA, NV	H	6.94 FQ	7.69 AW	8.45 TQ	NVBLS	10/01-12/01
	New Hampshire	H	7.12 FQ	9.13 AW	12.07 TQ	NHBLS	10/01-12/01
	New Jersey	H	7.95 FQ	13.34 AW	20.67 TQ	NJBLS	10/01-12/01
	Bergen-Passaic PMSA, NJ	H	8.61 FQ	13.84 AW	23.40 TQ	NJBLS	10/01-12/01
	Middlesex-Somerset-Hunterdon PMSA, NJ	H	7.38 FQ	10.99 AW	13.89 TQ	NJBLS	10/01-12/01
	Newark PMSA, NJ	H	7.99 FQ	13.93 AW	21.23 TQ	NJBLS	10/01-12/01

AAW	Average annual wage	**AOH**	Average offered, high	**ASH**	Average starting, high	**H**	Hourly	**M**	Monthly	**S**	Special: hourly and annual
AE	Average entry wage	**AOL**	Average offered, low	**ASL**	Average starting, low	**HI**	Highest wage paid	**MTC**	Median total compensation	**TQ**	Third quartile wage
AEX	Average experienced wage	**APH**	Average pay, high range	**AW**	Average wage paid	**HR**	High end range	**MW**	Median wage paid	**W**	Weekly
AO	Average offered	**APL**	Average pay, low range	**FQ**	First quartile wage	**LR**	Low end range	**SQ**	Second quartile wage	**Y**	Yearly

Occupation/Type/Industry	Location	Per	Low	Mid	High	Source	Date
Photographic Process Worker	Trenton PMSA, NJ	H	8.94 FQ	14.32 AW	20.57 TQ	NJBLS	10/01-12/01
	New Mexico	H	6.61 FQ	9.91 AW	13.99 TQ	NMBLS	10/01-12/01
	Albuquerque MSA, NM	H	7.33 FQ	10.69 AW	15.02 TQ	NMBLS	10/01-12/01
	New York	H	6.86 FQ	14.26 AW	24.48 TQ	NYBLS	10/01-12/01
	Albany-Schenectady-Troy MSA, NY	H	6.12 FQ	10.97 AW	16.51 TQ	NYBLS	10/01-12/01
	Buffalo-Niagara Falls MSA, NY	H	6.85 FQ	11.17 AW	16.33 TQ	NYBLS	10/01-12/01
	Nassau-Suffolk PMSA, NY	H	7.07 FQ	12.82 AW	22.55 TQ	NYBLS	10/01-12/01
	New York PMSA, NY	H	7.75 FQ	16.33 AW	28.09 TQ	NYBLS	10/01-12/01
	Rochester MSA, NY	H	6.77 FQ	11.10 AW	17.76 TQ	NYBLS	10/01-12/01
	Syracuse MSA, NY	H	7.06 FQ	11.20 AW	16.02 TQ	NYBLS	10/01-12/01
	North Carolina	H	7.24 FQ	10.59 AW	14.01 TQ	NCBLS	10/01-12/01
	Charlotte-Gastonia-Rock Hill MSA, NC-SC	H	8.32 FQ	11.81 AW	14.42 TQ	NCBLS	10/01-12/01
	Greensboro-Winston-Salem-High Point MSA, NC	H	7.78 FQ	11.06 AW	14.54 TQ	NCBLS	10/01-12/01
	Ohio	H	6.24 FQ	10.21 AW	15.50 TQ	OHBLS	10/01-12/01
	Canton-Massillon MSA, OH	H	5.92 FQ	10.32 AW	17.26 TQ	OHBLS	10/01-12/01
	Cincinnati PMSA, OH-KY-IN	H	6.44 FQ	10.79 AW	16.49 TQ	OHBLS	10/01-12/01
	Cleveland-Lorain-Elyria PMSA, OH	H	6.44 FQ	9.83 AW	15.35 TQ	OHBLS	10/01-12/01
	Columbus MSA, OH	H	7.01 FQ	10.96 AW	18.00 TQ	OHBLS	10/01-12/01
	Dayton-Springfield MSA, OH	H	6.90 FQ	9.63 AW	12.96 TQ	OHBLS	10/01-12/01
	Mansfield MSA, OH	H	5.68 FQ	7.40 AW	10.11 TQ	OHBLS	10/01-12/01
	Youngstown-Warren MSA, OH	H	7.55 FQ	13.67 AW	17.85 TQ	OHBLS	10/01-12/01
	Oklahoma	H	5.72 FQ	8.52 AW	11.52 TQ	OKBLS	10/01-12/01
	Oklahoma City MSA, OK	H	5.66 FQ	8.35 AW	10.97 TQ	OKBLS	10/01-12/01
	Tulsa MSA, OK	H	6.53 FQ	9.31 AW	13.20 TQ	OKBLS	10/01-12/01
	Oregon	H	6.63 FQ	9.13 AW	13.17 TQ	ORBLS	10/01-12/01
	Portland-Vancouver PMSA, OR-WA	H	7.12 FQ	10.79 AW	14.94 TQ	ORBLS	10/01-12/01
	Salem PMSA, OR	H	6.56 FQ	7.64 AW	8.89 TQ	ORBLS	10/01-12/01
	Pennsylvania	H	6.28 FQ	11.11 AW	16.49 TQ	PABLS	10/01-12/01
	Philadelphia PMSA, PA-NJ	H	6.63 FQ	12.22 AW	20.09 TQ	PABLS	10/01-12/01
	Pittsburgh MSA, PA	H	7.02 FQ	11.48 AW	16.21 TQ	PABLS	10/01-12/01
	Scranton-Wilkes-Barre-Hazleton MSA, PA	H	6.21 FQ	13.48 AW	23.58 TQ	PABLS	10/01-12/01
	Rhode Island	H	7.31 FQ	11.12 AW	17.24 TQ	RIBLS	10/01-12/01
	Providence-Fall River-Warwick MSA, RI-MA	H	7.27 FQ	11.28 AW	17.61 TQ	RIBLS	10/01-12/01
	South Carolina	H	6.35 FQ	9.20 AW	13.04 TQ	SCBLS	10/01-12/01
	Columbia MSA, SC	H	6.00 FQ	8.08 AW	10.69 TQ	SCBLS	10/01-12/01
	Greenville-Spartanburg-Anderson MSA, SC	H	7.15 FQ	8.94 AW	12.25 TQ	SCBLS	10/01-12/01
	South Dakota	H	7.16 FQ	9.26 AW	12.27 TQ	SDBLS	10/01-12/01
	Tennessee	H	6.76 FQ	10.27 AW	16.15 TQ	TNBLS	10/01-12/01
	Memphis MSA, TN-AR-MS	H	7.03 FQ	9.86 AW	14.47 TQ	TNBLS	10/01-12/01
	Nashville MSA, TN	H	6.37 FQ	12.47 AW	20.85 TQ	TNBLS	10/01-12/01
	Texas	H	5.92 FQ	8.94 AW	14.79 TQ	TXBLS	10/01-12/01
	Austin-San Marcos MSA, TX	H	5.72 FQ	7.81 AW	11.84 TQ	TXBLS	10/01-12/01
	Dallas PMSA, TX	H	6.61 FQ	10.88 AW	16.67 TQ	TXBLS	10/01-12/01
	Fort Worth-Arlington PMSA, TX	H	5.97 FQ	8.13 AW	10.53 TQ	TXBLS	10/01-12/01
	Houston PMSA, TX	H	6.00 FQ	9.17 AW	15.56 TQ	TXBLS	10/01-12/01
	Longview-Marshall MSA, TX	H	6.28 FQ	8.38 AW	11.01 TQ	TXBLS	10/01-12/01
	Lubbock MSA, TX	H	6.03 FQ	9.08 AW	13.48 TQ	TXBLS	10/01-12/01
	McAllen-Edinburg-Mission MSA, TX	H	5.80 FQ	8.42 AW	12.16 TQ	TXBLS	10/01-12/01
	San Antonio MSA, TX	H	6.18 FQ	8.52 AW	11.16 TQ	TXBLS	10/01-12/01
	Waco MSA, TX	H	5.56 FQ	9.15 AW	20.23 TQ	TXBLS	10/01-12/01
	Utah	H	7.46 FQ	10.08 AW	13.58 TQ	UTBLS	10/01-12/01
	Salt Lake City-Ogden MSA, UT	H	7.61 FQ	10.37 AW	13.76 TQ	UTBLS	10/01-12/01
	Virginia	H	7.37 FQ	11.53 AW	16.74 TQ	VABLS	10/01-12/01
	Norfolk-Virginia Beach-Newport News MSA, VA-NC	H	6.57 FQ	9.51 AW	15.29 TQ	VABLS	10/01-12/01
	Richmond-Petersburg MSA, VA	H	7.30 FQ	11.23 AW	15.98 TQ	VABLS	10/01-12/01
	Roanoke MSA, VA	H	7.67 FQ	10.11 AW	13.48 TQ	VABLS	10/01-12/01
	Washington	H	7.55 FQ	11.84 AW	19.51 TQ	WABLS	10/01-12/01

AAW Average annual wage **AE** Average entry wage **AEX** Average experienced wage **AO** Average offered **AOH** Average offered, high **AOL** Average offered, low **APH** Average pay, high range **APL** Average pay, low range **ASH** Average starting, high **ASL** Average starting, low **AW** Average wage paid **FQ** First quartile wage **H** Hourly **HI** Highest wage paid **HR** High end range **LR** Low end range **M** Monthly **MTC** Median total compensation **MW** Median wage paid **SQ** Second quartile wage **S** Special: hourly and annual **TQ** Third quartile wage **W** Weekly **Y** Yearly

Occupation/Type/Industry	Location	Per	Low	Mid	High	Source	Date
Photographic Process Worker	Seattle-Bellevue-Everett PMSA, WA	H	8.19 FQ	14.10 AW	20.98 TQ	WABLS	10/01-12/01
	Spokane MSA, WA	H	7.33 FQ	9.25 AW	12.60 TQ	WABLS	10/01-12/01
	West Virginia	H	5.84 FQ	9.15 AW	13.03 TQ	WVBLS	10/01-12/01
	Huntington-Ashland MSA, WV-KY-OH	H	5.61 FQ	8.86 AW	19.04 TQ	WVBLS	10/01-12/01
	Wisconsin	H	6.91 FQ	11.06 AW	19.57 TQ	WIBLS	10/01-12/01
	Green Bay MSA, WI	H	6.85 FQ	9.90 AW	15.43 TQ	WIBLS	10/01-12/01
	Madison MSA, WI	H	8.15 FQ	12.88 AW	21.58 TQ	WIBLS	10/01-12/01
	Milwaukee-Waukesha PMSA, WI	H	7.37 FQ	12.08 AW	20.21 TQ	WIBLS	10/01-12/01
	Wyoming	H	6.00 FQ	9.28 AW	13.49 TQ	WYBLS	10/01-12/01
	Puerto Rico	H	5.70 FQ	7.55 AW	10.50 TQ	PRBLS	10/01-12/01
Photographic Processing Machine Operator	Alaska	H	8.98 FQ	11.41 AW	15.70 TQ	AKBLS	10/01-12/01
	Arizona	H	7.23 FQ	9.91 AW	14.45 TQ	AZBLS	10/01-12/01
	California	H	7.63 FQ	13.17 AW	21.09 TQ	CABLS	10/01-12/01
	Colorado	H	7.35 FQ	9.92 AW	13.09 TQ	COBLS	10/01-12/01
	Connecticut	H	6.70 FQ	9.81 AW	14.88 TQ	CTBLS	10/01-12/01
	Delaware	H	6.29 FQ	7.80 AW	10.17 TQ	DEBLS	10/01-12/01
	District of Columbia	H	7.34 FQ	11.26 AW	14.25 TQ	DCBLS	10/01-12/01
	Florida	H	5.66 FQ	8.28 AW	12.11 TQ	FLBLS	10/01-12/01
	Georgia	H	6.03 FQ	9.60 AW	13.94 TQ	GABLS	10/01-12/01
	Hawaii	H	8.03 FQ	12.32 AW	16.74 TQ	HIBLS	10/01-12/01
	Idaho	H	6.15 FQ	9.40 AW	13.62 TQ	IDBLS	10/01-12/01
	Illinois	H	7.45 FQ	11.36 AW	17.45 TQ	ILBLS	10/01-12/01
	Indiana	H	7.13 FQ	9.10 AW	12.10 TQ	INBLS	10/01-12/01
	Iowa	H	6.40 FQ	9.29 AW	14.56 TQ	IABLS	10/01-12/01
	Kansas	H	6.47 FQ	9.85 AW	15.30 TQ	KSBLS	10/01-12/01
	Kentucky	H	6.23 FQ	8.46 AW	11.53 TQ	KYBLS	10/01-12/01
	Louisiana	H	5.78 FQ	7.80 AW	10.50 TQ	LABLS	10/01-12/01
	Maine	H	6.56 FQ	9.28 AW	12.64 TQ	MEBLS	10/01-12/01
	Maryland	H	6.39 FQ	9.54 AW	14.41 TQ	MDBLS	10/01-12/01
	Massachusetts	H	6.96 FQ	9.40 AW	13.18 TQ	MABLS	10/01-12/01
	Michigan	H	7.25 FQ	11.84 AW	17.67 TQ	MIBLS	10/01-12/01
	Minnesota	H	8.02 FQ	12.27 AW	18.40 TQ	MNBLS	10/01-12/01
	Mississippi	H	6.20 FQ	8.48 AW	10.83 TQ	MSBLS	10/01-12/01
	Missouri	H	6.91 FQ	9.64 AW	14.84 TQ	MOBLS	10/01-12/01
	Montana	H	6.07 FQ	8.73 AW	12.17 TQ	MTBLS	10/01-12/01
	Nebraska	H	5.84 FQ	7.84 AW	10.26 TQ	NEBLS	10/01-12/01
	Nevada	H	6.85 FQ	9.60 AW	13.43 TQ	NVBLS	10/01-12/01
	New Hampshire	H	6.36 FQ	10.85 AW	23.78 TQ	NHBLS	10/01-12/01
	New Jersey	H	6.08 FQ	9.32 AW	14.15 TQ	NJBLS	10/01-12/01
	New Mexico	H	5.90 FQ	9.17 AW	15.73 TQ	NMBLS	10/01-12/01
	New York	H	5.73 FQ	9.13 AW	16.44 TQ	NYBLS	10/01-12/01
	North Carolina	H	6.35 FQ	9.38 AW	13.88 TQ	NCBLS	10/01-12/01
	North Dakota	H	6.38 FQ	8.37 AW	11.41 TQ	NDBLS	10/01-12/01
	Ohio	H	5.97 FQ	8.81 AW	12.04 TQ	OHBLS	10/01-12/01
	Oklahoma	H	5.73 FQ	7.41 AW	9.88 TQ	OKBLS	10/01-12/01
	Oregon	H	7.36 FQ	10.10 AW	13.66 TQ	ORBLS	10/01-12/01
	Pennsylvania	H	5.90 FQ	8.74 AW	12.15 TQ	PABLS	10/01-12/01
	Rhode Island	H	6.56 FQ	8.55 AW	10.89 TQ	RIBLS	10/01-12/01
	South Carolina	H	6.07 FQ	8.83 AW	12.88 TQ	SCBLS	10/01-12/01
	South Dakota	H	5.75 FQ	8.53 AW	12.87 TQ	SDBLS	10/01-12/01
	Tennessee	H	5.94 FQ	8.90 AW	12.87 TQ	TNBLS	10/01-12/01
	Texas	H	6.14 FQ	9.08 AW	13.22 TQ	TXBLS	10/01-12/01
	Utah	H	7.24 FQ	9.17 AW	11.34 TQ	UTBLS	10/01-12/01
	Vermont	H	6.56 FQ	9.36 AW	14.72 TQ	VTBLS	10/01-12/01
	Virginia	H	6.85 FQ	10.03 AW	13.09 TQ	VABLS	10/01-12/01
	Washington	H	7.69 FQ	11.51 AW	16.63 TQ	WABLS	10/01-12/01
	West Virginia	H	5.69 FQ	7.74 AW	11.03 TQ	WVBLS	10/01-12/01
	Wisconsin	H	7.36 FQ	9.83 AW	13.32 TQ	WIBLS	10/01-12/01
	Wyoming	H	5.68 FQ	7.55 AW	10.32 TQ	WYBLS	10/01-12/01
	Puerto Rico	H	5.67 FQ	7.38 AW	10.11 TQ	PRBLS	10/01-12/01
	Guam	H	6.93 FQ	8.94 AW	12.58 TQ	GUBLS	10/01-12/01
Physical Therapist	Alabama	Y	33450 FQ	58870 AW	86750 TQ	ALBLS	10/01-12/01
	Alaska	Y	43930 FQ	56620 AW	71340 TQ	AKBLS	10/01-12/01
	Arizona	Y	39740 FQ	58750 AW	81870 TQ	AZBLS	10/01-12/01
	Arkansas	Y	33810 FQ	53290 AW	77290 TQ	ARBLS	10/01-12/01
	California	Y	43620 FQ	64960 AW	88340 TQ	CABLS	10/01-12/01

AAW	Average annual wage	**AOH**	Average offered, high	**ASH**	Average starting, high	**H**	Hourly	**M**	Monthly	**S**	Special: hourly and annual
AE	Average entry wage	**AOL**	Average offered, low	**ASL**	Average starting, low	**HI**	Highest wage paid	**MTC**	Median total compensation	**TQ**	Third quartile wage
AEX	Average experienced wage	**APH**	Average pay, high range	**AW**	Average wage paid	**HR**	High end range	**MW**	Median wage paid	**W**	Weekly
AO	Average offered	**APL**	Average pay, low range	**FQ**	First quartile wage	**LR**	Low end range	**SQ**	Second quartile wage	**Y**	Yearly

Occupation/Type/Industry	Location	Per	Low	Mid	High	Source	Date
Physical Therapist	Colorado	Y	37560 FQ	51160 AW	66450 TQ	COBLS	10/01-12/01
	Connecticut	Y	42260 FQ	63170 AW	98100 TQ	CTBLS	10/01-12/01
	Delaware	Y	34690 FQ	59130 AW	85800 TQ	DEBLS	10/01-12/01
	District of Columbia	Y	37200 FQ	55140 AW	75120 TQ	DCBLS	10/01-12/01
	Florida	Y	40000 FQ	58940 AW	84320 TQ	FLBLS	10/01-12/01
	Georgia	Y	38900 FQ	57460 AW	80290 TQ	GABLS	10/01-12/01
	Hawaii	Y	43520 FQ	57720 AW	74420 TQ	HIBLS	10/01-12/01
	Idaho	Y	38480 FQ	52340 AW	71410 TQ	IDBLS	10/01-12/01
	Illinois	Y	43080 FQ	59900 AW	87390 TQ	ILBLS	10/01-12/01
	Indiana	Y	29680 FQ	56790 AW	86410 TQ	INBLS	10/01-12/01
	Iowa	Y	33930 FQ	53160 AW	72230 TQ	IABLS	10/01-12/01
	Kansas	Y	38140 FQ	54170 AW	75510 TQ	KSBLS	10/01-12/01
	Kentucky	Y	39320 FQ	54430 AW	72500 TQ	KYBLS	10/01-12/01
	Louisiana	Y	35070 FQ	64970 AW	107400 TQ	LABLS	10/01-12/01
	Maine	Y	34000 FQ	49080 AW	65630 TQ	MEBLS	10/01-12/01
	Maryland	Y	42800 FQ	61060 AW	82790 TQ	MDBLS	10/01-12/01
	Massachusetts	Y	38840 FQ	57410 AW	84140 TQ	MABLS	10/01-12/01
	Michigan	Y	42210 FQ	60490 AW	88490 TQ	MIBLS	10/01-12/01
	Minnesota	Y	42160 FQ	54200 AW	70200 TQ	MNBLS	10/01-12/01
	Mississippi	Y	34980 FQ	58270 AW	86120 TQ	MSBLS	10/01-12/01
	Missouri	Y	37970 FQ	52760 AW	71240 TQ	MOBLS	10/01-12/01
	Montana	Y	40480 FQ	52960 AW	68370 TQ	MTBLS	10/01-12/01
	Nebraska	Y	35920 FQ	51940 AW	70500 TQ	NEBLS	10/01-12/01
	Nevada	Y	46900 FQ	67240 AW	89540 TQ	NVBLS	10/01-12/01
	New Hampshire	Y	38090 FQ	52560 AW	70900 TQ	NHBLS	10/01-12/01
	New Jersey	Y	43850 FQ	65060 AW	95440 TQ	NJBLS	10/01-12/01
	New Mexico	Y	39220 FQ	57240 AW	74670 TQ	NMBLS	10/01-12/01
	New York	Y	39530 FQ	60640 AW	89430 TQ	NYBLS	10/01-12/01
	North Carolina	Y	41570 FQ	60870 AW	88490 TQ	NCBLS	10/01-12/01
	North Dakota	Y	28890 FQ	53350 AW	78370 TQ	NDBLS	10/01-12/01
	Ohio	Y	43090 FQ	60370 AW	85060 TQ	OHBLS	10/01-12/01
	Oklahoma	Y	39130 FQ	56950 AW	81180 TQ	OKBLS	10/01-12/01
	Oregon	Y	41830 FQ	54320 AW	69430 TQ	ORBLS	10/01-12/01
	Pennsylvania	Y	41090 FQ	59250 AW	81760 TQ	PABLS	10/01-12/01
	Rhode Island	Y	39640 FQ	58820 AW	83520 TQ	RIBLS	10/01-12/01
	South Carolina	Y	33660 FQ	59240 AW	86500 TQ	SCBLS	10/01-12/01
	South Dakota	Y	38430 FQ	51650 AW	68130 TQ	SDBLS	10/01-12/01
	Tennessee	Y	38710 FQ	55540 AW	74550 TQ	TNBLS	10/01-12/01
	Texas	Y	40460 FQ	60800 AW	89120 TQ	TXBLS	10/01-12/01
	Utah	Y	37080 FQ	52730 AW	71190 TQ	UTBLS	10/01-12/01
	Vermont	Y	38660 FQ	50820 AW	66890 TQ	VTBLS	10/01-12/01
	Virginia	Y	38060 FQ	58390 AW	83940 TQ	VABLS	10/01-12/01
	Washington	Y	43020 FQ	55390 AW	70730 TQ	WABLS	10/01-12/01
	West Virginia	Y	43680 FQ	67510 AW	112990 TQ	WVBLS	10/01-12/01
	Wisconsin	Y	40900 FQ	56800 AW	74720 TQ	WIBLS	10/01-12/01
	Wyoming	Y	38650 FQ	52900 AW	71560 TQ	WYBLS	10/01-12/01
	Puerto Rico	Y	13610 FQ	25830 AW	42660 TQ	PRBLS	10/01-12/01
	Virgin Islands	Y	26400 FQ	56500 AW	112620 TQ	VIBLS	10/01-12/01
Physical Therapist Aide	United States	Y		18500-25760 AW		FREEP1	1/00-1/00
	United States	Y		25760-39660 AW		FREEP1	1/00-1/00
	Alabama	H	6.19 FQ	8.64 AW	11.39 TQ	ALBLS	10/01-12/01
	Alabama	H	10.87 FQ	17.88 AW	23.62 TQ	ALBLS	10/01-12/01
	Alaska	H	11.07 FQ	15.94 AW	22.55 TQ	AKBLS	10/01-12/01
	Alaska	H	10.26 FQ	12.96 AW	16.24 TQ	AKBLS	10/01-12/01
	Arizona	H	6.34 FQ	9.08 AW	12.26 TQ	AZBLS	10/01-12/01
	Arizona	H	9.11 FQ	13.88 AW	18.92 TQ	AZBLS	10/01-12/01
	Arkansas	H	5.98 FQ	8.18 AW	10.78 TQ	ARBLS	10/01-12/01
	Arkansas	H	10.74 FQ	16.20 AW	20.97 TQ	ARBLS	10/01-12/01
	California	H	9.91 FQ	19.61 AW	27.57 TQ	CABLS	10/01-12/01
	California	H	7.64 FQ	11.02 AW	15.03 TQ	CABLS	10/01-12/01
	Colorado	H	10.17 FQ	14.96 AW	19.61 TQ	COBLS	10/01-12/01
	Colorado	H	7.26 FQ	9.98 AW	13.36 TQ	COBLS	10/01-12/01
	Connecticut	H	8.75 FQ	11.69 AW	15.43 TQ	CTBLS	10/01-12/01
	Connecticut	H	10.41 FQ	16.21 AW	21.63 TQ	CTBLS	10/01-12/01
	Delaware	H	7.90 FQ	10.34 AW	13.25 TQ	DEBLS	10/01-12/01
	Delaware	H	10.75 FQ	16.29 AW	22.01 TQ	DEBLS	10/01-12/01
	District of Columbia	H	7.85 FQ	12.98 AW	19.48 TQ	DCBLS	10/01-12/01
	District of Columbia	H	11.43 FQ	16.42 AW	21.79 TQ	DCBLS	10/01-12/01
	Florida	H	7.47 FQ	10.35 AW	14.37 TQ	FLBLS	10/01-12/01
	Florida	H	13.97 FQ	18.40 AW	23.19 TQ	FLBLS	10/01-12/01

AAW	Average annual wage	**AOH**	Average offered, high	**ASH**	Average starting, high	**H**	Hourly	**M**	Monthly	**S**	Special: hourly and annual
AE	Average entry wage	**AOL**	Average offered, low	**ASL**	Average starting, low	**HI**	Highest wage paid	**MTC**	Median total compensation	**TQ**	Third quartile wage
AEX	Average experienced wage	**APH**	Average pay, high range	**AW**	Average wage paid	**HR**	High end range	**MW**	Median wage paid	**W**	Weekly
AO	Average offered	**APL**	Average pay, low range	**FQ**	First quartile wage	**LR**	Low end range	**SQ**	Second quartile wage	**Y**	Yearly

Occupation/Type/Industry	Location	Per	Low	Mid	High	Source	Date
Physical Therapist Aide	Georgia	H	10.60 FQ	17.63 AW	24.09 TQ	GABLS	10/01-12/01
	Georgia	H	6.11 FQ	8.84 AW	12.17 TQ	GABLS	10/01-12/01
	Hawaii	H	9.06 FQ	13.16 AW	17.60 TQ	HIBLS	10/01-12/01
	Hawaii	H	13.06 FQ	17.19 AW	21.40 TQ	HIBLS	10/01-12/01
	Idaho	H	6.39 FQ	8.73 AW	12.08 TQ	IDBLS	10/01-12/01
	Idaho	H	7.35 FQ	12.66 AW	19.07 TQ	IDBLS	10/01-12/01
	Illinois	H	7.54 FQ	10.63 AW	14.10 TQ	ILBLS	10/01-12/01
	Illinois	H	10.41 FQ	16.04 AW	21.66 TQ	ILBLS	10/01-12/01
	Indiana	H	7.25 FQ	11.53 AW	20.16 TQ	INBLS	10/01-12/01
	Indiana	H	11.12 FQ	17.10 AW	23.08 TQ	INBLS	10/01-12/01
	Iowa	H	9.20 FQ	13.48 AW	18.24 TQ	IABLS	10/01-12/01
	Iowa	H	7.51 FQ	10.02 AW	14.04 TQ	IABLS	10/01-12/01
	Kansas	H	7.32 FQ	9.60 AW	11.70 TQ	KSBLS	10/01-12/01
	Kansas	H	11.28 FQ	16.65 AW	23.16 TQ	KSBLS	10/01-12/01
	Kentucky	H	10.08 FQ	15.86 AW	21.43 TQ	KYBLS	10/01-12/01
	Kentucky	H	6.82 FQ	9.47 AW	12.20 TQ	KYBLS	10/01-12/01
	Louisiana	H	5.93 FQ	8.02 AW	10.48 TQ	LABLS	10/01-12/01
	Louisiana	H	6.31 FQ	14.54 AW	23.47 TQ	LABLS	10/01-12/01
	Maine	H	13.26 FQ	16.78 AW	20.72 TQ	MEBLS	10/01-12/01
	Maine	H	7.47 FQ	9.87 AW	13.06 TQ	MEBLS	10/01-12/01
	Maryland	H	7.67 FQ	15.33 AW	21.68 TQ	MDBLS	10/01-12/01
	Maryland	H	7.45 FQ	10.83 AW	17.59 TQ	MDBLS	10/01-12/01
	Massachusetts	H	13.43 FQ	17.70 AW	22.14 TQ	MABLS	10/01-12/01
	Massachusetts	H	8.80 FQ	12.89 AW	20.45 TQ	MABLS	10/01-12/01
	Michigan	H	8.71 FQ	11.35 AW	15.06 TQ	MIBLS	10/01-12/01
	Michigan	H	11.54 FQ	15.90 AW	20.75 TQ	MIBLS	10/01-12/01
	Minnesota	H	12.01 FQ	16.01 AW	20.79 TQ	MNBLS	10/01-12/01
	Minnesota	H	8.59 FQ	10.88 AW	13.50 TQ	MNBLS	10/01-12/01
	Mississippi	H	6.18 FQ	9.51 AW	18.96 TQ	MSBLS	10/01-12/01
	Mississippi	H	8.28 FQ	14.85 AW	21.08 TQ	MSBLS	10/01-12/01
	Missouri	H	7.27 FQ	10.37 AW	14.51 TQ	MOBLS	10/01-12/01
	Missouri	H	11.04 FQ	17.09 AW	23.04 TQ	MOBLS	10/01-12/01
	Montana	H	7.98 FQ	13.58 AW	20.52 TQ	MTBLS	10/01-12/01
	Montana	H	6.20 FQ	8.78 AW	11.46 TQ	MTBLS	10/01-12/01
	Nebraska	H	6.07 FQ	8.45 AW	11.55 TQ	NEBLS	10/01-12/01
	Nebraska	H	7.53 FQ	13.22 AW	17.79 TQ	NEBLS	10/01-12/01
	Nevada	H	12.32 FQ	18.52 AW	23.83 TQ	NVBLS	10/01-12/01
	Nevada	H	7.72 FQ	10.56 AW	13.57 TQ	NVBLS	10/01-12/01
	New Hampshire	H	13.20 FQ	17.76 AW	21.87 TQ	NHBLS	10/01-12/01
	New Hampshire	H	8.69 FQ	11.43 AW	15.19 TQ	NHBLS	10/01-12/01
	New Jersey	H	7.52 FQ	10.30 AW	13.28 TQ	NJBLS	10/01-12/01
	New Jersey	H	11.99 FQ	18.04 AW	22.98 TQ	NJBLS	10/01-12/01
	New Mexico	H	7.35 FQ	10.34 AW	13.33 TQ	NMBLS	10/01-12/01
	New Mexico	H	10.94 FQ	15.10 AW	20.98 TQ	NMBLS	10/01-12/01
	New York	H	12.16 FQ	17.90 AW	24.98 TQ	NYBLS	10/01-12/01
	New York	H	7.84 FQ	11.34 AW	16.27 TQ	NYBLS	10/01-12/01
	North Carolina	H	7.77 FQ	10.82 AW	13.62 TQ	NCBLS	10/01-12/01
	North Carolina	H	13.62 FQ	17.98 AW	22.39 TQ	NCBLS	10/01-12/01
	North Dakota	H	8.50 FQ	11.99 AW	15.51 TQ	NDBLS	10/01-12/01
	North Dakota	H	7.42 FQ	9.42 AW	11.85 TQ	NDBLS	10/01-12/01
	Ohio	H	14.11 FQ	18.23 AW	22.81 TQ	OHBLS	10/01-12/01
	Ohio	H	7.71 FQ	11.31 AW	16.64 TQ	OHBLS	10/01-12/01
	Oklahoma	H	6.75 FQ	9.08 AW	12.28 TQ	OKBLS	10/01-12/01
	Oklahoma	H	11.06 FQ	16.08 AW	21.34 TQ	OKBLS	10/01-12/01
	Oregon	H	7.32 FQ	9.94 AW	12.57 TQ	ORBLS	10/01-12/01
	Oregon	H	12.74 FQ	17.43 AW	21.53 TQ	ORBLS	10/01-12/01
	Pennsylvania	H	7.25 FQ	10.13 AW	14.16 TQ	PABLS	10/01-12/01
	Pennsylvania	H	11.47 FQ	15.59 AW	20.76 TQ	PABLS	10/01-12/01
	Rhode Island	H	11.41 FQ	15.52 AW	21.30 TQ	RIBLS	10/01-12/01
	Rhode Island	H	14.23 FQ	17.39 AW	21.35 TQ	RIBLS	10/01-12/01
	South Carolina	H	13.63 FQ	18.70 AW	26.26 TQ	SCBLS	10/01-12/01
	South Carolina	H	7.05 FQ	11.91 AW	17.39 TQ	SCBLS	10/01-12/01
	South Dakota	H	8.53 FQ	11.48 AW	15.59 TQ	SDBLS	10/01-12/01
	South Dakota	H	7.48 FQ	9.07 AW	10.93 TQ	SDBLS	10/01-12/01
	Tennessee	H	7.00 FQ	9.48 AW	12.32 TQ	TNBLS	10/01-12/01
	Tennessee	H	12.22 FQ	17.19 AW	21.86 TQ	TNBLS	10/01-12/01
	Texas	H	14.44 FQ	19.51 AW	27.04 TQ	TXBLS	10/01-12/01
	Texas	H	6.44 FQ	11.54 AW	25.89 TQ	TXBLS	10/01-12/01
	Utah	H	6.84 FQ	8.58 AW	10.46 TQ	UTBLS	10/01-12/01
	Utah	H	10.57 FQ	14.95 AW	19.13 TQ	UTBLS	10/01-12/01
	Vermont	H	7.76 FQ	10.16 AW	13.62 TQ	VTBLS	10/01-12/01
	Vermont	H	11.42 FQ	14.60 AW	17.57 TQ	VTBLS	10/01-12/01

AAW Average annual wage **AOH** Average offered, high **ASH** Average starting, high **H** Hourly **M** Monthly **S** Special: hourly and annual
AE Average entry wage **AOL** Average offered, low **ASL** Average starting, low **HI** Highest wage paid **MTC** Median total compensation **TQ** Third quartile wage
AEX Average experienced wage **APH** Average pay, high range **AW** Average wage paid **HR** High end range **MW** Median wage paid **W** Weekly
AO Average offered **APL** Average pay, low range **FQ** First quartile wage **LR** Low end range **SQ** Second quartile wage **Y** Yearly

Occupation/Type/Industry	Location	Per	Low	Mid	High	Source	Date
Physical Therapist Aide	Virginia	H	6.77 FQ	8.99 AW	11.64 TQ	VABLS	10/01-12/01
	Virginia	H	13.38 FQ	18.30 AW	23.76 TQ	VABLS	10/01-12/01
	Washington	H	12.94 FQ	16.37 AW	20.55 TQ	WABLS	10/01-12/01
	Washington	H	8.35 FQ	10.62 AW	13.31 TQ	WABLS	10/01-12/01
	West Virginia	H	6.43 FQ	8.99 AW	10.79 TQ	WVBLS	10/01-12/01
	West Virginia	H	9.64 FQ	14.31 AW	18.02 TQ	WVBLS	10/01-12/01
	Wisconsin	H	7.81 FQ	10.30 AW	13.28 TQ	WIBLS	10/01-12/01
	Wisconsin	H	11.32 FQ	15.91 AW	20.88 TQ	WIBLS	10/01-12/01
	Wyoming	H	11.84 FQ	14.63 AW	17.46 TQ	WYBLS	10/01-12/01
	Wyoming	H	7.22 FQ	8.65 AW	10.70 TQ	WYBLS	10/01-12/01
	Puerto Rico	H	5.67 FQ	7.88 AW	10.80 TQ	PRBLS	10/01-12/01
	Puerto Rico	H	5.75 FQ	7.96 AW	10.97 TQ	PRBLS	10/01-12/01
Physician							
Family Practice	United States	Y	110000 ASL	136000 AW	195000 ASH	USATOD3	1/01-1/02
Family Practice	Midwest	Y		153649 AW		WW	1/00-1/01
Family Practice	West	Y		138018 AW		WW	1/00-1/01
Physician Assistant	United States	Y		39700 AW		FREEP1	1/00-1/00
	Alabama	Y	20900 FQ	56630 AW	92580 TQ	ALBLS	10/01-12/01
	Birmingham MSA, AL	Y	20100 FQ	60740 AW	127530 TQ	ALBLS	10/01-12/01
	Huntsville MSA, AL	Y	33670 FQ	51550 AW	66510 TQ	ALBLS	10/01-12/01
	Mobile MSA, AL	Y	45230 FQ	51360 AW	56580 TQ	ALBLS	10/01-12/01
	Alaska	Y	53070 FQ	78540 AW	109280 TQ	AKBLS	10/01-12/01
	Arizona	Y	36760 FQ	58010 AW	86560 TQ	AZBLS	10/01-12/01
	Phoenix-Mesa MSA, AZ	Y	36030 FQ	56500 AW	86250 TQ	AZBLS	10/01-12/01
	Tucson MSA, AZ	Y	47280 FQ	62180 AW	84280 TQ	AZBLS	10/01-12/01
	Arkansas	Y	46960 FQ	79870 AW	110310 TQ	ARBLS	10/01-12/01
	Little Rock-North Little Rock MSA, AR	Y	23180 FQ	80560 AW	111270 TQ	ARBLS	10/01-12/01
	California	Y	37530 FQ	68270 AW	92640 TQ	CABLS	10/01-12/01
	Bakersfield MSA, CA	Y	59440 FQ	72440 AW	90520 TQ	CABLS	10/01-12/01
	Fresno MSA, CA	Y	54000 FQ	70880 AW	88780 TQ	CABLS	10/01-12/01
	Los Angeles-Long Beach PMSA, CA	Y	39720 FQ	71000 AW	96040 TQ	CABLS	10/01-12/01
	Modesto MSA, CA	Y	51270 FQ	78250 AW		CABLS	10/01-12/01
	Oakland PMSA, CA	Y	38350 FQ	68080 AW	93130 TQ	CABLS	10/01-12/01
	Orange County PMSA, CA	Y	28870 FQ	67160 AW	90010 TQ	CABLS	10/01-12/01
	Redding MSA, CA	Y	64820 FQ	79010 AW	98640 TQ	CABLS	10/01-12/01
	Riverside-San Bernardino PMSA, CA	Y	45780 FQ	69930 AW	93240 TQ	CABLS	10/01-12/01
	Sacramento PMSA, CA	Y	41830 FQ	65940 AW	83020 TQ	CABLS	10/01-12/01
	Salinas MSA, CA	Y	59010 FQ	75780 AW	99910 TQ	CABLS	10/01-12/01
	San Diego MSA, CA	Y	50660 FQ	74020 AW	99740 TQ	CABLS	10/01-12/01
	San Francisco PMSA, CA	Y	26240 FQ	63100 AW	86960 TQ	CABLS	10/01-12/01
	San Jose PMSA, CA	Y	44720 FQ	70280 AW	90320 TQ	CABLS	10/01-12/01
	Santa Barbara-Santa Maria-Lompoc MSA, CA	Y	50270 FQ	61220 AW	75170 TQ	CABLS	10/01-12/01
	Santa Rosa PMSA, CA	Y	47160 FQ	56940 AW	69400 TQ	CABLS	10/01-12/01
	Vallejo-Fairfield-Napa PMSA, CA	Y	25770 FQ	46560 AW	79840 TQ	CABLS	10/01-12/01
	Ventura PMSA, CA	Y	57520 FQ	65710 AW	79690 TQ	CABLS	10/01-12/01
	Colorado	Y	32640 FQ	55300 AW	77060 TQ	COBLS	10/01-12/01
	Boulder-Longmont PMSA, CO	Y	54480 FQ	63770 AW	73740 TQ	COBLS	10/01-12/01
	Colorado Springs MSA, CO	Y	46430 FQ	58370 AW	76670 TQ	COBLS	10/01-12/01
	Denver PMSA, CO	Y	30250 FQ	55030 AW	80370 TQ	COBLS	10/01-12/01
	Fort Collins-Loveland MSA, CO	Y	30600 FQ	48060 AW	66030 TQ	COBLS	10/01-12/01
	Connecticut	Y	42350 FQ	67510 AW	91460 TQ	CTBLS	10/01-12/01
	Bridgeport PMSA, CT	Y	50580 FQ	74900 AW	101840 TQ	CTBLS	10/01-12/01
	Danbury PMSA, CT	Y	45620 FQ	73460 AW	97680 TQ	CTBLS	10/01-12/01
	Hartford MSA, CT	Y	42980 FQ	65670 AW	88560 TQ	CTBLS	10/01-12/01
	New Haven-Meriden PMSA, CT	Y	58080 FQ	69480 AW	89220 TQ	CTBLS	10/01-12/01
	New London-Norwich MSA, CT-RI	Y	49820 FQ	69690 AW	91290 TQ	CTBLS	10/01-12/01
	Stamford-Norwalk PMSA, CT	Y	30090 FQ	61870 AW	92230 TQ	CTBLS	10/01-12/01
	Delaware	Y	53640 FQ	84110 AW	112820 TQ	DEBLS	10/01-12/01
	Wilmington-Newark PMSA, DE-MD	Y	55620 FQ	84700 AW	112610 TQ	DEBLS	10/01-12/01
	District of Columbia	Y	38760 FQ	56160 AW	75910 TQ	DCBLS	10/01-12/01
	Washington PMSA, DC-MD-VA-WV	Y	39540 FQ	68460 AW	105220 TQ	DCBLS	10/01-12/01

AAW Average annual wage; **AE** Average entry wage; **AEX** Average experienced wage; **AO** Average offered; **AOH** Average offered, high; **AOL** Average offered, low; **APH** Average pay, high range; **APL** Average pay, low range; **ASH** Average starting, high; **ASL** Average starting, low; **AW** Average wage paid; **FQ** First quartile wage; **H** Hourly; **HI** Highest wage paid; **HR** High end range; **LR** Low end range; **M** Monthly; **MTC** Median total compensation; **MW** Median wage paid; **SQ** Second quartile wage; **S** Special: hourly and annual; **TQ** Third quartile wage; **W** Weekly; **Y** Yearly

Occupation/Type/Industry	Location	Per	Low	Mid	High	Source	Date
Physician Assistant	Florida	Y	27200 FQ	60920 AW	95490 TQ	FLBLS	10/01-12/01
	Fort Lauderdale PMSA, FL	Y	59450 FQ	83800 AW	139480 TQ	FLBLS	10/01-12/01
	Fort Myers-Cape Coral MSA, FL	Y	46270 FQ	63550 AW	73630 TQ	FLBLS	10/01-12/01
	Fort Pierce-Port St. Lucie MSA, FL	Y	29500 FQ	58940 AW	81890 TQ	FLBLS	10/01-12/01
	Gainesville MSA, FL	Y	28280 FQ	53140 AW	73910 TQ	FLBLS	10/01-12/01
	Jacksonville MSA, FL	Y	17100 FQ	41430 AW	74150 TQ	FLBLS	10/01-12/01
	Lakeland-Winter Haven MSA, FL	Y	24860 FQ	56110 AW	84780 TQ	FLBLS	10/01-12/01
	Melbourne-Titusville-Palm Bay MSA, FL	Y	26720 FQ	60720 AW	85580 TQ	FLBLS	10/01-12/01
	Miami PMSA, FL	Y	43860 FQ	61670 AW	76120 TQ	FLBLS	10/01-12/01
	Ocala MSA, FL	Y	72220 FQ	81720 AW	95810 TQ	FLBLS	10/01-12/01
	Orlando MSA, FL	Y	52500 FQ	67240 AW	88310 TQ	FLBLS	10/01-12/01
	Pensacola MSA, FL	Y	28370 FQ	58960 AW	86300 TQ	FLBLS	10/01-12/01
	Sarasota-Bradenton MSA, FL	Y	27580 FQ	42870 AW	64830 TQ	FLBLS	10/01-12/01
	Tallahassee MSA, FL	Y	47380 FQ	62660 AW	82180 TQ	FLBLS	10/01-12/01
	Tampa-St. Petersburg-Clearwater MSA, FL	Y	37430 FQ	67600 AW	112170 TQ	FLBLS	10/01-12/01
	West Palm Beach-Boca Raton MSA, FL	Y	25600 FQ	54550 AW	90350 TQ	FLBLS	10/01-12/01
	Georgia	Y	30980 FQ	71050 AW	113810 TQ	GABLS	10/01-12/01
	Atlanta MSA, GA	Y	31480 FQ	77440 AW		GABLS	10/01-12/01
	Augusta-Aiken MSA, GA-SC	Y	25460 FQ	58260 AW	83260 TQ	GABLS	10/01-12/01
	Columbus MSA, GA-AL	Y	32360 FQ	56200 AW	74380 TQ	GABLS	10/01-12/01
	Macon MSA, GA	Y	39710 FQ	82470 AW	142020 TQ	GABLS	10/01-12/01
	Savannah MSA, GA	Y	19820 FQ	55410 AW	88610 TQ	GABLS	10/01-12/01
	Idaho	Y	25630 FQ	51650 AW	72060 TQ	IDBLS	10/01-12/01
	Boise City MSA, ID	Y	46580 FQ	57990 AW	73200 TQ	IDBLS	10/01-12/01
	Illinois	Y	25600 FQ	47900 AW	74380 TQ	ILBLS	10/01-12/01
	Champaign-Urbana MSA, IL	Y	29060 FQ	65120 AW	88650 TQ	ILBLS	10/01-12/01
	Chicago PMSA, IL	Y	33980 FQ	49110 AW	69970 TQ	ILBLS	10/01-12/01
	Peoria-Pekin MSA, IL	Y	31680 FQ	44090 AW	57910 TQ	ILBLS	10/01-12/01
	Rockford MSA, IL	Y	22440 FQ	38850 AW	78860 TQ	ILBLS	10/01-12/01
	Springfield MSA, IL	Y	24330 FQ	49790 AW	97900 TQ	ILBLS	10/01-12/01
	Indiana	Y	30710 FQ	61320 AW	85680 TQ	INBLS	10/01-12/01
	Evansville-Henderson MSA, IN-KY	Y	60640 FQ	73170 AW	90370 TQ	INBLS	10/01-12/01
	Fort Wayne MSA, IN	Y	43220 FQ	66060 AW	76820 TQ	INBLS	10/01-12/01
	Gary PMSA, IN	Y	20360 FQ	53110 AW	73030 TQ	INBLS	10/01-12/01
	Indianapolis MSA, IN	Y	38130 FQ	58600 AW	85490 TQ	INBLS	10/01-12/01
	South Bend MSA, IN	Y	44790 FQ	66660 AW	87850 TQ	INBLS	10/01-12/01
	Iowa	Y	40880 FQ	60200 AW	83240 TQ	IABLS	10/01-12/01
	Davenport-Moline-Rock Island MSA, IA-IL	Y	36380 FQ	56520 AW	74150 TQ	IABLS	10/01-12/01
	Des Moines MSA, IA	Y	49670 FQ	65520 AW	86930 TQ	IABLS	10/01-12/01
	Kansas	Y	48180 FQ	70640 AW	93570 TQ	KSBLS	10/01-12/01
	Topeka MSA, KS	Y	47660 FQ	60780 AW	76750 TQ	KSBLS	10/01-12/01
	Wichita MSA, KS	Y	40800 FQ	59170 AW	77620 TQ	KSBLS	10/01-12/01
	Kentucky	Y	47780 FQ	61520 AW	80530 TQ	KYBLS	10/01-12/01
	Lexington MSA, KY	Y	46700 FQ	56200 AW	71900 TQ	KYBLS	10/01-12/01
	Louisville MSA, KY-IN	Y	42390 FQ	64770 AW	88040 TQ	KYBLS	10/01-12/01
	Louisiana	Y	15790 FQ	46630 AW	86210 TQ	LABLS	10/01-12/01
	Baton Rouge MSA, LA	Y	15060 FQ	23700 AW	59890 TQ	LABLS	10/01-12/01
	New Orleans MSA, LA	Y	25560 FQ	59010 AW	87530 TQ	LABLS	10/01-12/01
	Maine	Y	54000 FQ	74220 AW	94670 TQ	MEBLS	10/01-12/01
	Portland MSA, ME	Y	53230 FQ	79780 AW	128130 TQ	MEBLS	10/01-12/01
	Maryland	Y	21990 FQ	53920 AW	92040 TQ	MDBLS	10/01-12/01
	Baltimore PMSA, MD	Y	20940 FQ	46760 AW	80710 TQ	MDBLS	10/01-12/01
	Massachusetts	Y	29900 FQ	58890 AW	86490 TQ	MABLS	10/01-12/01
	Boston PMSA, MA-NH	Y	28550 FQ	55800 AW	83240 TQ	MABLS	10/01-12/01
	Lawrence PMSA, MA-NH	Y	39550 FQ	75440 AW	131840 TQ	MABLS	10/01-12/01
	Lowell PMSA, MA-NH	Y	26650 FQ	50500 AW	69610 TQ	MABLS	10/01-12/01
	Springfield MSA, MA	Y	46160 FQ	65350 AW	87600 TQ	MABLS	10/01-12/01
	Worcester PMSA, MA-CT	Y	37000 FQ	54510 AW	88410 TQ	MABLS	10/01-12/01
	Michigan	Y	41490 FQ	64840 AW	86550 TQ	MIBLS	10/01-12/01
	Ann Arbor PMSA, MI	Y	50960 FQ	68070 AW	90200 TQ	MIBLS	10/01-12/01
	Detroit PMSA, MI	Y	44730 FQ	68570 AW	89110 TQ	MIBLS	10/01-12/01
	Flint PMSA, MI	Y	55480 FQ	70800 AW	89470 TQ	MIBLS	10/01-12/01
	Grand Rapids-Muskegon-Holland MSA, MI	Y	29150 FQ	59510 AW	75320 TQ	MIBLS	10/01-12/01

AAW	Average annual wage	AOH	Average offered, high	ASH	Average starting, high	H	Hourly	M	Monthly	S	Special: hourly and annual
AE	Average entry wage	AOL	Average offered, low	ASL	Average starting, low	HI	Highest wage paid	MTC	Median total compensation	TQ	Third quartile wage
AEX	Average experienced wage	APH	Average pay, high range	AW	Average wage paid	HR	High end range	MW	Median wage paid	W	Weekly
AO	Average offered	APL	Average pay, low range	FQ	First quartile wage	LR	Low end range	SQ	Second quartile wage	Y	Yearly

Occupation/Type/Industry	Location	Per	Low	Mid	High	Source	Date
Physician Assistant	Kalamazoo-Battle Creek MSA, MI	Y	46200 FQ	59010 AW	74060 TQ	MIBLS	10/01-12/01
	Lansing-East Lansing MSA, MI	Y	57390 FQ	65250 AW	73940 TQ	MIBLS	10/01-12/01
	Saginaw-Bay City-Midland MSA, MI	Y	56870 FQ	71470 AW	91740 TQ	MIBLS	10/01-12/01
	Minnesota	Y	50620 FQ	68010 AW	90830 TQ	MNBLS	10/01-12/01
	Minneapolis-St. Paul MSA, MN-WI	Y	51090 FQ	69320 AW	92250 TQ	MNBLS	10/01-12/01
	St. Cloud MSA, MN	Y	57530 FQ	63860 AW	71530 TQ	MNBLS	10/01-12/01
	Mississippi	Y	16620 FQ	34150 AW	82430 TQ	MSBLS	10/01-12/01
	Missouri	Y	23870 FQ	53370 AW	76720 TQ	MOBLS	10/01-12/01
	Kansas City MSA, MO-KS	Y	45600 FQ	72280 AW	94270 TQ	MOBLS	10/01-12/01
	St. Louis MSA, MO-IL	Y	24310 FQ	50260 AW	73090 TQ	MOBLS	10/01-12/01
	Springfield MSA, MO	Y	53910 FQ	66800 AW	82040 TQ	MOBLS	10/01-12/01
	Montana	Y	38600 FQ	64120 AW	91200 TQ	MTBLS	10/01-12/01
	Nebraska	Y	27640 FQ	66270 AW	113130 TQ	NEBLS	10/01-12/01
	Lincoln MSA, NE	Y	25430 FQ	46210 AW	78360 TQ	NEBLS	10/01-12/01
	Omaha MSA, NE-IA	Y	32220 FQ	70640 AW	137640 TQ	NEBLS	10/01-12/01
	Nevada	Y	26080 FQ	57540 AW	92670 TQ	NVBLS	10/01-12/01
	Las Vegas MSA, NV-AZ	Y	25870 FQ	57380 AW	93350 TQ	NVBLS	10/01-12/01
	Reno MSA, NV	Y	57540 FQ	65760 AW	86770 TQ	NVBLS	10/01-12/01
	New Hampshire	Y	41020 FQ	64930 AW	88430 TQ	NHBLS	10/01-12/01
	Manchester PMSA, NH	Y	59050 FQ	66700 AW	77120 TQ	NHBLS	10/01-12/01
	Portsmouth-Rochester PMSA, NH-ME	Y	56930 FQ	76860 AW	91890 TQ	NHBLS	10/01-12/01
	New Jersey	Y	28860 FQ	58520 AW	82220 TQ	NJBLS	10/01-12/01
	Bergen-Passaic PMSA, NJ	Y	26040 FQ	53040 AW	83230 TQ	NJBLS	10/01-12/01
	Middlesex-Somerset-Hunterdon PMSA, NJ	Y	25750 FQ	45530 AW	76790 TQ	NJBLS	10/01-12/01
	Newark PMSA, NJ	Y	51480 FQ	68790 AW	89880 TQ	NJBLS	10/01-12/01
	Trenton PMSA, NJ	Y	41560 FQ	48640 AW	55650 TQ	NJBLS	10/01-12/01
	New Mexico	Y	43410 FQ	58440 AW	77440 TQ	NMBLS	10/01-12/01
	Albuquerque MSA, NM	Y	43390 FQ	58020 AW	76220 TQ	NMBLS	10/01-12/01
	New York	Y	50740 FQ	68370 AW	89700 TQ	NYBLS	10/01-12/01
	Albany-Schenectady-Troy MSA, NY	Y	45950 FQ	60750 AW	83380 TQ	NYBLS	10/01-12/01
	Binghamton MSA, NY	Y	52270 FQ	70610 AW	94090 TQ	NYBLS	10/01-12/01
	Buffalo-Niagara Falls MSA, NY	Y	52490 FQ	70370 AW	90320 TQ	NYBLS	10/01-12/01
	Dutchess County PMSA, NY	Y	46260 FQ	58320 AW	71380 TQ	NYBLS	10/01-12/01
	Nassau-Suffolk PMSA, NY	Y	49250 FQ	69160 AW	91340 TQ	NYBLS	10/01-12/01
	New York PMSA, NY	Y	54000 FQ	70710 AW	90790 TQ	NYBLS	10/01-12/01
	Newburgh PMSA, NY-PA	Y	56760 FQ	71960 AW	90450 TQ	NYBLS	10/01-12/01
	Rochester MSA, NY	Y	50310 FQ	65490 AW	85680 TQ	NYBLS	10/01-12/01
	Syracuse MSA, NY	Y	50340 FQ	65400 AW	84810 TQ	NYBLS	10/01-12/01
	Utica-Rome MSA, NY	Y	49890 FQ	64790 AW	85970 TQ	NYBLS	10/01-12/01
	North Carolina	Y	51650 FQ	70310 AW	97750 TQ	NCBLS	10/01-12/01
	Asheville MSA, NC	Y	50220 FQ	73920 AW	111550 TQ	NCBLS	10/01-12/01
	Charlotte-Gastonia-Rock Hill MSA, NC-SC	Y	35100 FQ	63880 AW	88550 TQ	NCBLS	10/01-12/01
	Fayetteville MSA, NC	Y	56680 FQ	79240 AW	117170 TQ	NCBLS	10/01-12/01
	Greensboro-Winston-Salem-High Point MSA, NC	Y	50650 FQ	62620 AW	74430 TQ	NCBLS	10/01-12/01
	Hickory-Morganton-Lenoir MSA, NC	Y	50870 FQ	70370 AW	101010 TQ	NCBLS	10/01-12/01
	Raleigh-Durham-Chapel Hill MSA, NC	Y	51580 FQ	73080 AW	109610 TQ	NCBLS	10/01-12/01
	Wilmington MSA, NC	Y	52190 FQ	72050 AW	95700 TQ	NCBLS	10/01-12/01
	North Dakota	Y	48710 FQ	60590 AW	73860 TQ	NDBLS	10/01-12/01
	Fargo-Moorhead MSA, ND-MN	Y	48970 FQ	59400 AW	71370 TQ	NDBLS	10/01-12/01
	Ohio	Y	48990 FQ	72520 AW	99490 TQ	OHBLS	10/01-12/01
	Akron PMSA, OH	Y	56370 FQ	76980 AW	91920 TQ	OHBLS	10/01-12/01
	Canton-Massillon MSA, OH	Y	76350 FQ	90240 AW	113160 TQ	OHBLS	10/01-12/01
	Cincinnati PMSA, OH-KY-IN	Y	47180 FQ	66920 AW	90350 TQ	OHBLS	10/01-12/01
	Cleveland-Lorain-Elyria PMSA, OH	Y	50160 FQ	71400 AW	102570 TQ	OHBLS	10/01-12/01
	Columbus MSA, OH	Y	46300 FQ	67320 AW	87840 TQ	OHBLS	10/01-12/01
	Dayton-Springfield MSA, OH	Y	41130 FQ	64210 AW	89290 TQ	OHBLS	10/01-12/01
	Oklahoma	Y	20770 FQ	44870 AW	82600 TQ	OKBLS	10/01-12/01
	Oklahoma City MSA, OK	Y	20100 FQ	35130 AW	68150 TQ	OKBLS	10/01-12/01
	Tulsa MSA, OK	Y	48590 FQ	63450 AW	83620 TQ	OKBLS	10/01-12/01

AAW	Average annual wage	**AOH**	Average offered, high	**ASH**	Average starting, high	**H**	Hourly	**M**	Monthly	**S**	Special: hourly and annual
AE	Average entry wage	**AOL**	Average offered, low	**ASL**	Average starting, low	**HI**	Highest wage paid	**MTC**	Median total compensation	**TQ**	Third quartile wage
AEX	Average experienced wage	**APH**	Average pay, high range	**AW**	Average wage paid	**HR**	High end range	**MW**	Median wage paid	**W**	Weekly
AO	Average offered	**APL**	Average pay, low range	**FQ**	First quartile wage	**LR**	Low end range	**SQ**	Second quartile wage	**Y**	Yearly

Occupation/Type/Industry	Location	Per	Low	Mid	High	Source	Date
Physician Assistant	Oregon	Y	51290 FQ	67480 AW	86530 TQ	ORBLS	10/01-12/01
	Medford-Ashland MSA, OR	Y	50400 FQ	67190 AW	85950 TQ	ORBLS	10/01-12/01
	Portland-Vancouver PMSA, OR-WA	Y	54000 FQ	68110 AW	85200 TQ	ORBLS	10/01-12/01
	Salem PMSA, OR	Y	53300 FQ	69540 AW	86830 TQ	ORBLS	10/01-12/01
	Pennsylvania	Y	28560 FQ	58180 AW	79920 TQ	PABLS	10/01-12/01
	Allentown-Bethlehem-Easton MSA, PA	Y	32220 FQ	58300 AW	79600 TQ	PABLS	10/01-12/01
	Harrisburg-Lebanon-Carlisle MSA, PA	Y	28690 FQ	58060 AW	75020 TQ	PABLS	10/01-12/01
	Johnstown MSA, PA	Y	27490 FQ	56140 AW	73690 TQ	PABLS	10/01-12/01
	Lancaster MSA, PA	Y	19550 FQ	60650 AW	102370 TQ	PABLS	10/01-12/01
	Philadelphia PMSA, PA-NJ	Y	47090 FQ	62170 AW	79370 TQ	PABLS	10/01-12/01
	Pittsburgh MSA, PA	Y	22230 FQ	50170 AW	74570 TQ	PABLS	10/01-12/01
	Reading MSA, PA	Y	46820 FQ	59910 AW	73660 TQ	PABLS	10/01-12/01
	Scranton-Wilkes-Barre-Hazleton MSA, PA	Y	48240 FQ	60590 AW	77890 TQ	PABLS	10/01-12/01
	York MSA, PA	Y	49370 FQ	68010 AW	87080 TQ	PABLS	10/01-12/01
	Rhode Island	Y	25350 FQ	63300 AW	92360 TQ	RIBLS	10/01-12/01
	Providence-Fall River-Warwick MSA, RI-MA	Y	26650 FQ	63970 AW	89000 TQ	RIBLS	10/01-12/01
	South Carolina	Y	29760 FQ	44610 AW	65230 TQ	SCBLS	10/01-12/01
	Charleston-North Charleston MSA, SC	Y	29760 FQ	55180 AW	84610 TQ	SCBLS	10/01-12/01
	Columbia MSA, SC	Y	33650 FQ	47550 AW	60410 TQ	SCBLS	10/01-12/01
	South Dakota	Y	50500 FQ	64300 AW	82570 TQ	SDBLS	10/01-12/01
	Sioux Falls MSA, SD	Y	51870 FQ	65800 AW	85150 TQ	SDBLS	10/01-12/01
	Tennessee	Y	23890 FQ	58030 AW	84910 TQ	TNBLS	10/01-12/01
	Chattanooga MSA, TN-GA	Y	16100 FQ	58670 AW	100090 TQ	TNBLS	10/01-12/01
	Johnson City-Kingsport-Bristol MSA, TN-VA	Y	28260 FQ	60420 AW	82130 TQ	TNBLS	10/01-12/01
	Knoxville MSA, TN	Y	22220 FQ	53000 AW	78740 TQ	TNBLS	10/01-12/01
	Memphis MSA, TN-AR-MS	Y	20480 FQ	49610 AW	85320 TQ	TNBLS	10/01-12/01
	Nashville MSA, TN	Y	21830 FQ	50750 AW	80560 TQ	TNBLS	10/01-12/01
	Texas	Y	41550 FQ	67030 AW	89200 TQ	TXBLS	10/01-12/01
	Amarillo MSA, TX	Y	26470 FQ	56780 AW	85590 TQ	TXBLS	10/01-12/01
	Austin-San Marcos MSA, TX	Y	38460 FQ	57880 AW	73710 TQ	TXBLS	10/01-12/01
	Beaumont-Port Arthur MSA, TX	Y	53630 FQ	64790 AW	75320 TQ	TXBLS	10/01-12/01
	Brazoria PMSA, TX	Y	55330 FQ	66420 AW	71710 TQ	TXBLS	10/01-12/01
	Brownsville-Harlingen-San Benito MSA, TX	Y	60580 FQ	69290 AW	85590 TQ	TXBLS	10/01-12/01
	Corpus Christi MSA, TX	Y	35070 FQ	62610 AW	76650 TQ	TXBLS	10/01-12/01
	Dallas PMSA, TX	Y	29830 FQ	63760 AW	86660 TQ	TXBLS	10/01-12/01
	El Paso MSA, TX	Y	25800 FQ	62270 AW	87520 TQ	TXBLS	10/01-12/01
	Fort Worth-Arlington PMSA, TX	Y	50000 FQ	64950 AW	84050 TQ	TXBLS	10/01-12/01
	Galveston-Texas City PMSA, TX	Y	18870 FQ	31920 AW	53230 TQ	TXBLS	10/01-12/01
	Houston PMSA, TX	Y	58210 FQ	70860 AW	89550 TQ	TXBLS	10/01-12/01
	Killeen-Temple MSA, TX	Y	61230 FQ	72500 AW	87710 TQ	TXBLS	10/01-12/01
	Laredo MSA, TX	Y	20040 FQ	34570 AW	57300 TQ	TXBLS	10/01-12/01
	Longview-Marshall MSA, TX	Y	49200 FQ	67560 AW	87310 TQ	TXBLS	10/01-12/01
	Lubbock MSA, TX	Y	54180 FQ	77800 AW	92860 TQ	TXBLS	10/01-12/01
	McAllen-Edinburg-Mission MSA, TX	Y	61830 FQ	73440 AW	92020 TQ	TXBLS	10/01-12/01
	San Antonio MSA, TX	Y	59440 FQ	69400 AW	88330 TQ	TXBLS	10/01-12/01
	Tyler MSA, TX	Y	62390 FQ	74420 AW	90840 TQ	TXBLS	10/01-12/01
	Waco MSA, TX	Y	60580 FQ	77330 AW	98630 TQ	TXBLS	10/01-12/01
	Utah	Y	35190 FQ	66150 AW	92540 TQ	UTBLS	10/01-12/01
	Salt Lake City-Ogden MSA, UT	Y	35980 FQ	68990 AW	94170 TQ	UTBLS	10/01-12/01
	Vermont	Y	47950 FQ	62770 AW	73880 TQ	VTBLS	10/01-12/01
	Burlington MSA, VT	Y	40610 FQ	63430 AW	87000 TQ	VTBLS	10/01-12/01
	Virginia	Y	41190 FQ	62170 AW	88420 TQ	VABLS	10/01-12/01
	Lynchburg MSA, VA	Y	26420 FQ	51870 AW	71070 TQ	VABLS	10/01-12/01
	Norfolk-Virginia Beach-Newport News MSA, VA-NC	Y	46990 FQ	62260 AW	73100 TQ	VABLS	10/01-12/01
	Richmond-Petersburg MSA, VA	Y	40230 FQ	58530 AW	84850 TQ	VABLS	10/01-12/01
	Washington	Y	56680 FQ	69280 AW	87760 TQ	WABLS	10/01-12/01

AAW	Average annual wage	AOH	Average offered, high	ASH	Average starting, high	H	Hourly	M	Monthly	S	Special: hourly and annual
AE	Average entry wage	AOL	Average offered, low	ASL	Average starting, low	HI	Highest wage paid	MTC	Median total compensation	TQ	Third quartile wage
AEX	Average experienced wage	APH	Average pay, high range	AW	Average wage paid	HR	High end range	MW	Median wage paid	W	Weekly
AO	Average offered	APL	Average pay, low range	FQ	First quartile wage	LR	Low end range	SQ	Second quartile wage	Y	Yearly

Occupation/Type/Industry	Location	Per	Low	Mid	High	Source	Date
Physician Assistant	Richland-Kennewick-Pasco MSA, WA	Y	57300 FQ	65470 AW	74890 TQ	WABLS	10/01-12/01
	Seattle-Bellevue-Everett PMSA, WA	Y	58790 FQ	70550 AW	87580 TQ	WABLS	10/01-12/01
	Spokane MSA, WA	Y	49930 FQ	62440 AW	75880 TQ	WABLS	10/01-12/01
	Tacoma PMSA, WA	Y	45980 FQ	60480 AW	74240 TQ	WABLS	10/01-12/01
	Yakima MSA, WA	Y	50680 FQ	64680 AW	80320 TQ	WABLS	10/01-12/01
	West Virginia	Y	45540 FQ	62150 AW	86000 TQ	WVBLS	10/01-12/01
	Charleston MSA, WV	Y	36850 FQ	58480 AW	86810 TQ	WVBLS	10/01-12/01
	Huntington-Ashland MSA, WV-KY-OH	Y	46670 FQ	60670 AW	83280 TQ	WVBLS	10/01-12/01
	Wisconsin	Y	47640 FQ	70950 AW	107550 TQ	WIBLS	10/01-12/01
	Appleton-Oshkosh-Neenah MSA, WI	Y	63030 FQ	98720 AW	121350 TQ	WIBLS	10/01-12/01
	Green Bay MSA, WI	Y	48490 FQ	81800 AW	124890 TQ	WIBLS	10/01-12/01
	Madison MSA, WI	Y	54780 FQ	73790 AW	96640 TQ	WIBLS	10/01-12/01
	Milwaukee-Waukesha PMSA, WI	Y	57680 FQ	73640 AW	97580 TQ	WIBLS	10/01-12/01
	Wyoming	Y	45830 FQ	64780 AW	86310 TQ	WYBLS	10/01-12/01
	Puerto Rico	Y	14870 FQ	32310 AW	63870 TQ	PRBLS	10/01-12/01
Family Planning	United States	Y			69567 MW	CTU	1/01-1/02
Family Practice	United States	Y		136000 AW		HHN	1/01-1/02
Physicist	Alabama	Y	56090 FQ	77090 AW	105190 TQ	ALBLS	10/01-12/01
	Huntsville MSA, AL	Y	61370 FQ	82540 AW	107760 TQ	ALBLS	10/01-12/01
	Arizona	Y	32280 FQ	65030 AW	103350 TQ	AZBLS	10/01-12/01
	California	Y	47390 FQ	78300 AW	113290 TQ	CABLS	10/01-12/01
	Los Angeles-Long Beach PMSA, CA	Y	46500 FQ	79730 AW	117520 TQ	CABLS	10/01-12/01
	Sacramento PMSA, CA	Y	49720 FQ	70150 AW	109210 TQ	CABLS	10/01-12/01
	San Diego MSA, CA	Y	48400 FQ	73050 AW	102480 TQ	CABLS	10/01-12/01
	San Francisco PMSA, CA	Y	44620 FQ	82470 AW	122600 TQ	CABLS	10/01-12/01
	San Jose PMSA, CA	Y	68880 FQ	95330 AW	122350 TQ	CABLS	10/01-12/01
	Colorado	Y	59830 FQ	88140 AW	127560 TQ	COBLS	10/01-12/01
	Boulder-Longmont PMSA, CO	Y	55390 FQ	91880 AW	133080 TQ	COBLS	10/01-12/01
	Denver PMSA, CO	Y	63160 FQ	82460 AW	108010 TQ	COBLS	10/01-12/01
	District of Columbia	Y	59060 FQ	85160 AW	112660 TQ	DCBLS	10/01-12/01
	Washington PMSA, DC-MD-VA-WV	Y	58250 FQ	89970 AW	129290 TQ	DCBLS	10/01-12/01
	Florida	Y	56940 FQ	82560 AW	112750 TQ	FLBLS	10/01-12/01
	Miami PMSA, FL	Y	67510 FQ	86400 AW	107250 TQ	FLBLS	10/01-12/01
	Tampa-St. Petersburg-Clearwater MSA, FL	Y	48610 FQ	79710 AW	113890 TQ	FLBLS	10/01-12/01
	Georgia	Y	60070 FQ	83180 AW	113610 TQ	GABLS	10/01-12/01
	Atlanta MSA, GA	Y	59400 FQ	83850 AW	111570 TQ	GABLS	10/01-12/01
	Hawaii	Y	60530 FQ	76710 AW	90220 TQ	HIBLS	10/01-12/01
	Honolulu MSA, HI	Y	61890 FQ	76650 AW	89730 TQ	HIBLS	10/01-12/01
	Indiana	Y	53800 FQ	83190 AW	117630 TQ	INBLS	10/01-12/01
	Kansas	Y	41790 FQ	74330 AW	128680 TQ	KSBLS	10/01-12/01
	Louisiana	Y	41790 FQ	69530 AW	106000 TQ	LABLS	10/01-12/01
	Maine	Y	51780 FQ	67740 AW	95010 TQ	MEBLS	10/01-12/01
	Maryland	Y	57480 FQ	86890 AW	114490 TQ	MDBLS	10/01-12/01
	Baltimore PMSA, MD	Y	49880 FQ	79190 AW	111010 TQ	MDBLS	10/01-12/01
	Massachusetts	Y	48260 FQ	88700 AW	134760 TQ	MABLS	10/01-12/01
	Boston PMSA, MA-NH	Y	48010 FQ	89130 AW	134220 TQ	MABLS	10/01-12/01
	Worcester PMSA, MA-CT	Y	44640 FQ	81780 AW	121920 TQ	MABLS	10/01-12/01
	Michigan	Y	52160 FQ	80920 AW	118590 TQ	MIBLS	10/01-12/01
	Ann Arbor PMSA, MI	Y	57330 FQ	92160 AW	143860 TQ	MIBLS	10/01-12/01
	Detroit PMSA, MI	Y	51960 FQ	81260 AW	115990 TQ	MIBLS	10/01-12/01
	Minnesota	Y	57890 FQ	80660 AW	113520 TQ	MNBLS	10/01-12/01
	Minneapolis-St. Paul MSA, MN-WI	Y	57550 FQ	80270 AW	113720 TQ	MNBLS	10/01-12/01
	Mississippi	Y	37700 FQ	68840 AW	107670 TQ	MSBLS	10/01-12/01
	Biloxi-Gulfport-Pascagoula MSA, MS	Y	50500 FQ	75370 AW	107150 TQ	MSBLS	10/01-12/01
	Missouri	Y	53950 FQ	79630 AW	110630 TQ	MOBLS	10/01-12/01
	Kansas City MSA, MO-KS	Y	58920 FQ	85780 AW	124030 TQ	MOBLS	10/01-12/01
	Nebraska	Y	49470 FQ	75860 AW	115840 TQ	NEBLS	10/01-12/01
	New Jersey	Y	50530 FQ	83070 AW	142880 TQ	NJBLS	10/01-12/01
	Newark PMSA, NJ	Y	62530 FQ	101100 AW		NJBLS	10/01-12/01
	Albuquerque MSA, NM	Y	63840 FQ	88610 AW	117920 TQ	NMBLS	10/01-12/01
	Las Cruces MSA, NM	Y	49920 FQ	76650 AW	107200 TQ	NMBLS	10/01-12/01
	New York	Y	49410 FQ	84690 AW	138770 TQ	NYBLS	10/01-12/01

AAW	Average annual wage	**AOH**	Average offered, high	**ASH**	Average starting, high	**H**	Hourly	**M**	Monthly	**S**	Special: hourly and annual
AE	Average entry wage	**AOL**	Average offered, low	**ASL**	Average starting, low	**HI**	Highest wage paid	**MTC**	Median total compensation	**TQ**	Third quartile wage
AEX	Average experienced wage	**APH**	Average pay, high range	**AW**	Average wage paid	**HR**	High end range	**MW**	Median wage paid	**W**	Weekly
AO	Average offered	**APL**	Average pay, low range	**FQ**	First quartile wage	**LR**	Low end range	**SQ**	Second quartile wage	**Y**	Yearly

Occupation/Type/Industry	Location	Per	Low	Mid	High	Source	Date
Physicist	Albany-Schenectady-Troy MSA, NY	Y	51560 FQ	74100 AW	99150 TQ	NYBLS	10/01-12/01
	Buffalo-Niagara Falls MSA, NY	Y	44310 FQ	74610 AW	113740 TQ	NYBLS	10/01-12/01
	New York PMSA, NY	Y	44590 FQ	80860 AW	125950 TQ	NYBLS	10/01-12/01
	Syracuse MSA, NY	Y	55820 FQ	96380 AW		NYBLS	10/01-12/01
	North Carolina	Y	39860 FQ	70820 AW	111130 TQ	NCBLS	10/01-12/01
	Raleigh-Durham-Chapel Hill MSA, NC	Y	39610 FQ	72910 AW	112670 TQ	NCBLS	10/01-12/01
	Ohio	Y	52150 FQ	79960 AW	113210 TQ	OHBLS	10/01-12/01
	Cincinnati PMSA, OH-KY-IN	Y	48960 FQ	77160 AW	114900 TQ	OHBLS	10/01-12/01
	Cleveland-Lorain-Elyria PMSA, OH	Y	62410 FQ	81340 AW	110440 TQ	OHBLS	10/01-12/01
	Dayton-Springfield MSA, OH	Y	49700 FQ	79010 AW	112570 TQ	OHBLS	10/01-12/01
	Pennsylvania	Y	51130 FQ	85000 AW	118400 TQ	PABLS	10/01-12/01
	Philadelphia PMSA, PA-NJ	Y	59730 FQ	88510 AW	120040 TQ	PABLS	10/01-12/01
	Pittsburgh MSA, PA	Y	47760 FQ	77400 AW	111860 TQ	PABLS	10/01-12/01
	Rhode Island	Y	61330 FQ	88970 AW	133310 TQ	RIBLS	10/01-12/01
	Tennessee	Y	49810 FQ	79430 AW	115290 TQ	TNBLS	10/01-12/01
	Chattanooga MSA, TN-GA	Y	31180 FQ	58710 AW	80210 TQ	TNBLS	10/01-12/01
	Nashville MSA, TN	Y	36830 FQ	84390 AW	134300 TQ	TNBLS	10/01-12/01
	Texas	Y	51580 FQ	88140 AW	130610 TQ	TXBLS	10/01-12/01
	Fort Worth-Arlington PMSA, TX	Y	55370 FQ	83780 AW	113750 TQ	TXBLS	10/01-12/01
	Houston PMSA, TX	Y	47470 FQ	84480 AW	124960 TQ	TXBLS	10/01-12/01
	Virginia	Y	47740 FQ	87640 AW	143290 TQ	VABLS	10/01-12/01
	Norfolk-Virginia Beach-Newport News MSA, VA-NC	Y	51480 FQ	72740 AW	108010 TQ	VABLS	10/01-12/01
	Washington	Y	50930 FQ	68590 AW	90040 TQ	WABLS	10/01-12/01
Physics Teacher							
Postsecondary	Alabama	Y	33590 FQ	53390 AW	73590 TQ	ALBLS	10/01-12/01
Postsecondary	Arkansas	Y	38180 FQ	69870 AW	112420 TQ	ARBLS	10/01-12/01
Postsecondary	California	Y	25590 FQ	64490 AW	99710 TQ	CABLS	10/01-12/01
Postsecondary	Los Angeles-Long Beach PMSA, CA	Y	39860 FQ	70130 AW	103710 TQ	CABLS	10/01-12/01
Postsecondary	Oakland PMSA, CA	Y	19670 FQ	50980 AW	94190 TQ	CABLS	10/01-12/01
Postsecondary	Orange County PMSA, CA	Y	26450 FQ	64680 AW	100220 TQ	CABLS	10/01-12/01
Postsecondary	San Francisco PMSA, CA	Y	43130 FQ	63710 AW	86580 TQ	CABLS	10/01-12/01
Postsecondary	Santa Cruz-Watsonville PMSA, CA	Y	33120 FQ	70020 AW	116280 TQ	CABLS	10/01-12/01
Postsecondary	Colorado	Y	36240 FQ	59040 AW	91850 TQ	COBLS	10/01-12/01
Postsecondary	Denver PMSA, CO	Y	37900 FQ	62650 AW	97530 TQ	COBLS	10/01-12/01
Postsecondary	Connecticut	Y	34770 FQ	68650 AW	108350 TQ	CTBLS	10/01-12/01
Postsecondary	District of Columbia	Y	46410 FQ	74610 AW	108300 TQ	DCBLS	10/01-12/01
Postsecondary	Washington PMSA, DC-MD-VA-WV	Y	39770 FQ	76600 AW	123010 TQ	DCBLS	10/01-12/01
Postsecondary	Florida	Y	43360 FQ	69600 AW	107260 TQ	FLBLS	10/01-12/01
Postsecondary	Gainesville MSA, FL	Y	44220 FQ	74760 AW	113160 TQ	FLBLS	10/01-12/01
Postsecondary	Miami PMSA, FL	Y	48220 FQ	68220 AW	95640 TQ	FLBLS	10/01-12/01
Postsecondary	Orlando MSA, FL	Y	40320 FQ	63550 AW	92060 TQ	FLBLS	10/01-12/01
Postsecondary	Tallahassee MSA, FL	Y	45880 FQ	70870 AW	110890 TQ	FLBLS	10/01-12/01
Postsecondary	Tampa-St. Petersburg-Clearwater MSA, FL	Y	42460 FQ	65610 AW	98500 TQ	FLBLS	10/01-12/01
Postsecondary	West Palm Beach-Boca Raton MSA, FL	Y	45570 FQ	70520 AW	107220 TQ	FLBLS	10/01-12/01
Postsecondary	Georgia	Y	38980 FQ	60500 AW	86170 TQ	GABLS	10/01-12/01
Postsecondary	Hawaii	Y	42760 FQ	74780 AW	115090 TQ	HIBLS	10/01-12/01
Postsecondary	Honolulu MSA, HI	Y	47120 FQ	79540 AW	117750 TQ	HIBLS	10/01-12/01
Postsecondary	Illinois	Y	19430 FQ	59480 AW	97050 TQ	ILBLS	10/01-12/01
Postsecondary	Champaign-Urbana MSA, IL	Y	17470 FQ	56010 AW	94200 TQ	ILBLS	10/01-12/01
Postsecondary	Chicago PMSA, IL	Y	19200 FQ	61560 AW	99520 TQ	ILBLS	10/01-12/01
Postsecondary	Indiana	Y	33730 FQ	61660 AW	97720 TQ	INBLS	10/01-12/01
Postsecondary	South Bend MSA, IN	Y	31370 FQ	59160 AW	100370 TQ	INBLS	10/01-12/01
Postsecondary	Iowa	Y	33330 FQ	65820 AW	132310 TQ	IABLS	10/01-12/01
Postsecondary	Kansas	Y	27930 FQ	64130 AW	101390 TQ	KSBLS	10/01-12/01
Postsecondary	Kentucky	Y	37470 FQ	59990 AW	87540 TQ	KYBLS	10/01-12/01
Postsecondary	Louisiana	Y	30650 FQ	53260 AW	85470 TQ	LABLS	10/01-12/01
Postsecondary	Maine	Y	36030 FQ	53380 AW	74740 TQ	MEBLS	10/01-12/01
Postsecondary	Maryland	Y	40190 FQ	76230 AW	131230 TQ	MDBLS	10/01-12/01
Postsecondary	Baltimore PMSA, MD	Y	37950 FQ	67580 AW	112850 TQ	MDBLS	10/01-12/01
Postsecondary	Massachusetts	Y	38150 FQ	70100 AW	113310 TQ	MABLS	10/01-12/01

AAW Average annual wage **AOH** Average offered, high **ASH** Average starting, high **H** Hourly **M** Monthly **S** Special: hourly and annual
AE Average entry wage **AOL** Average offered, low **ASL** Average starting, low **HI** Highest wage paid **MTC** Median total compensation **TQ** Third quartile wage
AEX Average experienced wage **APH** Average pay, high range **AW** Average wage paid **HR** High end range **MW** Median wage paid **W** Weekly
AO Average offered **APL** Average pay, low range **FQ** First quartile wage **LR** Low end range **SQ** Second quartile wage **Y** Yearly

Occupation/Type/Industry	Location	Per	Low	Mid	High	Source	Date
Physics Teacher							
Postsecondary	Boston PMSA, MA-NH	Y	38530 FQ	71110 AW	114530 TQ	MABLS	10/01-12/01
Postsecondary	Springfield MSA, MA	Y	37290 FQ	66040 AW	105670 TQ	MABLS	10/01-12/01
Postsecondary	Michigan	Y	39920 FQ	72310 AW	114400 TQ	MIBLS	10/01-12/01
Postsecondary	Minnesota	Y	39490 FQ	63430 AW	93780 TQ	MNBLS	10/01-12/01
Postsecondary	Minneapolis-St. Paul MSA, MN-WI	Y	46560 FQ	73010 AW	113630 TQ	MNBLS	10/01-12/01
Postsecondary	Mississippi	Y	36660 FQ	50090 AW	70430 TQ	MSBLS	10/01-12/01
Postsecondary	Missouri	Y	31880 FQ	54590 AW	75710 TQ	MOBLS	10/01-12/01
Postsecondary	Kansas City MSA, MO-KS	Y	33510 FQ	56160 AW	77170 TQ	MOBLS	10/01-12/01
Postsecondary	St. Louis MSA, MO-IL	Y	30910 FQ	54780 AW	76190 TQ	MOBLS	10/01-12/01
Postsecondary	Springfield MSA, MO	Y	36800 FQ	56740 AW	77000 TQ	MOBLS	10/01-12/01
Postsecondary	Nebraska	Y	39230 FQ	62260 AW	93520 TQ	NEBLS	10/01-12/01
Postsecondary	Lincoln MSA, NE	Y	40860 FQ	71780 AW	111570 TQ	NEBLS	10/01-12/01
Postsecondary	Nevada	Y	30760 FQ	57190 AW	87520 TQ	NVBLS	10/01-12/01
Postsecondary	New Hampshire	Y	33310 FQ	62570 AW	103040 TQ	NHBLS	10/01-12/01
Postsecondary	New Jersey	Y	41660 FQ	74400 AW	119660 TQ	NJBLS	10/01-12/01
Postsecondary	Jersey City PMSA, NJ	Y	32610 FQ	66420 AW	111090 TQ	NJBLS	10/01-12/01
Postsecondary	Newark PMSA, NJ	Y	49520 FQ	69080 AW	93570 TQ	NJBLS	10/01-12/01
Postsecondary	Trenton PMSA, NJ	Y	44050 FQ	72690 AW	118220 TQ	NJBLS	10/01-12/01
Postsecondary	New Mexico	Y	31360 FQ	55140 AW	78610 TQ	NMBLS	10/01-12/01
Postsecondary	New York	Y	41420 FQ	79580 AW	121120 TQ	NYBLS	10/01-12/01
Postsecondary	Albany-Schenectady-Troy MSA, NY	Y	44720 FQ	78680 AW	121220 TQ	NYBLS	10/01-12/01
Postsecondary	Nassau-Suffolk PMSA, NY	Y	42380 FQ	69350 AW	108760 TQ	NYBLS	10/01-12/01
Postsecondary	New York PMSA, NY	Y	42730 FQ	87320 AW	145420 TQ	NYBLS	10/01-12/01
Postsecondary	North Carolina	Y	39590 FQ	60890 AW	89930 TQ	NCBLS	10/01-12/01
Postsecondary	Charlotte-Gastonia-Rock Hill MSA, NC-SC	Y	33940 FQ	55810 AW	84330 TQ	NCBLS	10/01-12/01
Postsecondary	Greensboro-Winston-Salem-High Point MSA, NC	Y	40870 FQ	58550 AW	81180 TQ	NCBLS	10/01-12/01
Postsecondary	Raleigh-Durham-Chapel Hill MSA, NC	Y	39330 FQ	65510 AW	96480 TQ	NCBLS	10/01-12/01
Postsecondary	Ohio	Y	36390 FQ	60150 AW	91860 TQ	OHBLS	10/01-12/01
Postsecondary	Cincinnati PMSA, OH-KY-IN	Y	39580 FQ	63720 AW	88580 TQ	OHBLS	10/01-12/01
Postsecondary	Cleveland-Lorain-Elyria PMSA, OH	Y	41820 FQ	64370 AW	94370 TQ	OHBLS	10/01-12/01
Postsecondary	Columbus MSA, OH	Y	34670 FQ	63410 AW	109900 TQ	OHBLS	10/01-12/01
Postsecondary	Dayton-Springfield MSA, OH	Y	38000 FQ	53400 AW	85130 TQ	OHBLS	10/01-12/01
Postsecondary	Oklahoma	Y	33090 FQ	50070 AW	70250 TQ	OKBLS	10/01-12/01
Postsecondary	Oregon	Y	37160 FQ	73510 AW	111540 TQ	ORBLS	10/01-12/01
Postsecondary	Portland-Vancouver PMSA, OR-WA	Y	29840 FQ	64900 AW	107410 TQ	ORBLS	10/01-12/01
Postsecondary	Pennsylvania	Y	31970 FQ	67060 AW	104200 TQ	PABLS	10/01-12/01
Postsecondary	Allentown-Bethlehem-Easton MSA, PA	Y	29170 FQ	62310 AW	95650 TQ	PABLS	10/01-12/01
Postsecondary	Philadelphia PMSA, PA-NJ	Y	36960 FQ	70680 AW	109180 TQ	PABLS	10/01-12/01
Postsecondary	Pittsburgh MSA, PA	Y	26280 FQ	62240 AW	96570 TQ	PABLS	10/01-12/01
Postsecondary	Scranton-Wilkes-Barre-Hazleton MSA, PA	Y	33580 FQ	58550 AW	92610 TQ	PABLS	10/01-12/01
Postsecondary	Rhode Island	Y	35920 FQ	67750 AW	101420 TQ	RIBLS	10/01-12/01
Postsecondary	Providence-Fall River-Warwick MSA, RI-MA	Y	35570 FQ	68390 AW	103590 TQ	RIBLS	10/01-12/01
Postsecondary	South Carolina	Y	33590 FQ	48910 AW	71310 TQ	SCBLS	10/01-12/01
Postsecondary	Charleston-North Charleston MSA, SC	Y	34810 FQ	49250 AW	74170 TQ	SCBLS	10/01-12/01
Postsecondary	Tennessee	Y	37480 FQ	59330 AW	90400 TQ	TNBLS	10/01-12/01
Postsecondary	Memphis MSA, TN-AR-MS	Y	38500 FQ	51840 AW	69640 TQ	TNBLS	10/01-12/01
Postsecondary	Nashville MSA, TN	Y	38090 FQ	62900 AW	99540 TQ	TNBLS	10/01-12/01
Postsecondary	Texas	Y	35500 FQ	63230 AW	95340 TQ	TXBLS	10/01-12/01
Postsecondary	Dallas PMSA, TX	Y	32120 FQ	58370 AW	86680 TQ	TXBLS	10/01-12/01
Postsecondary	Fort Worth-Arlington PMSA, TX	Y	33420 FQ	57140 AW	80350 TQ	TXBLS	10/01-12/01
Postsecondary	Houston PMSA, TX	Y	49680 FQ	76710 AW	116820 TQ	TXBLS	10/01-12/01
Postsecondary	San Antonio MSA, TX	Y	35490 FQ	65920 AW	103740 TQ	TXBLS	10/01-12/01
Postsecondary	Utah	Y	41420 FQ	81870 AW	124030 TQ	UTBLS	10/01-12/01
Postsecondary	Virginia	Y	40400 FQ	79270 AW	139700 TQ	VABLS	10/01-12/01
Postsecondary	Norfolk-Virginia Beach-Newport News MSA, VA-NC	Y	49320 FQ	91420 AW		VABLS	10/01-12/01
Postsecondary	Washington	Y	32070 FQ	67450 AW	119610 TQ	WABLS	10/01-12/01

AAW	Average annual wage	**AOH**	Average offered, high	**ASH**	Average starting, high	**H**	Hourly	**M**	Monthly	**S**	Special: hourly and annual
AE	Average entry wage	**AOL**	Average offered, low	**ASL**	Average starting, low	**HI**	Highest wage paid	**MTC**	Median total compensation	**TQ**	Third quartile wage
AEX	Average experienced wage	**APH**	Average pay, high range	**AW**	Average wage paid	**HR**	High end range	**MW**	Median wage paid	**W**	Weekly
AO	Average offered	**APL**	Average pay, low range	**FQ**	First quartile wage	**LR**	Low end range	**SQ**	Second quartile wage	**Y**	Yearly

Occupation/Type/Industry	Location	Per	Low	Mid	High	Source	Date
Physics Teacher							
Postsecondary	Seattle-Bellevue-Everett PMSA, WA	Y	33990 FQ	75070 AW	133210 TQ	WABLS	10/01-12/01
Postsecondary	West Virginia	Y	39810 FQ	64190 AW	97290 TQ	WVBLS	10/01-12/01
Postsecondary	Wisconsin	Y	34680 FQ	59670 AW	92090 TQ	WIBLS	10/01-12/01
Postsecondary	Milwaukee-Waukesha PMSA, WI	Y	32610 FQ	56160 AW	85780 TQ	WIBLS	10/01-12/01
Postsecondary	Wyoming	Y	30240 FQ	41590 AW	57840 TQ	WYBLS	10/01-12/01
Postsecondary	Puerto Rico	Y	30620 FQ	48230 AW	76920 TQ	PRBLS	10/01-12/01
Pile-Driver Operator	Alabama	H	10.22 FQ	13.08 AW	16.65 TQ	ALBLS	10/01-12/01
	California	H	20.59 FQ	29.01 AW	35.47 TQ	CABLS	10/01-12/01
	Colorado	H	12.43 FQ	17.15 AW	21.64 TQ	COBLS	10/01-12/01
	Connecticut	H	17.15 FQ	22.65 AW	32.01 TQ	CTBLS	10/01-12/01
	Florida	H	11.53 FQ	17.72 AW	24.23 TQ	FLBLS	10/01-12/01
	Georgia	H	8.14 FQ	11.54 AW	16.69 TQ	GABLS	10/01-12/01
	Illinois	H	16.16 FQ	25.00 AW	32.79 TQ	ILBLS	10/01-12/01
	Indiana	H	12.50 FQ	19.81 AW	29.23 TQ	INBLS	10/01-12/01
	Kentucky	H	11.87 FQ	13.81 AW	18.27 TQ	KYBLS	10/01-12/01
	Louisiana	H	10.65 FQ	17.37 AW	27.77 TQ	LABLS	10/01-12/01
	Maryland	H	12.90 FQ	21.08 AW	29.25 TQ	MDBLS	10/01-12/01
	Massachusetts	H	23.12 FQ	26.09 AW	31.05 TQ	MABLS	10/01-12/01
	Michigan	H	11.52 FQ	18.72 AW	30.67 TQ	MIBLS	10/01-12/01
	Minnesota	H	16.99 FQ	22.39 AW	27.76 TQ	MNBLS	10/01-12/01
	Mississippi	H	8.96 FQ	11.88 AW	15.37 TQ	MSBLS	10/01-12/01
	Missouri	H	8.14 FQ	21.97 AW	32.89 TQ	MOBLS	10/01-12/01
	New Jersey	H	18.51 FQ	29.22 AW	39.42 TQ	NJBLS	10/01-12/01
	New York	H	15.46 FQ	29.03 AW	42.13 TQ	NYBLS	10/01-12/01
	North Carolina	H	9.87 FQ	12.34 AW	14.50 TQ	NCBLS	10/01-12/01
	Ohio	H	16.22 FQ	22.53 AW	27.24 TQ	OHBLS	10/01-12/01
	Oklahoma	H	8.89 FQ	17.24 AW	28.17 TQ	OKBLS	10/01-12/01
	Oregon	H	15.47 FQ	23.99 AW	37.46 TQ	ORBLS	10/01-12/01
	Pennsylvania	H	23.66 FQ	26.33 AW	29.23 TQ	PABLS	10/01-12/01
	South Carolina	H	8.41 FQ	12.50 AW	16.88 TQ	SCBLS	10/01-12/01
	Tennessee	H	11.81 FQ	18.56 AW	28.64 TQ	TNBLS	10/01-12/01
	Texas	H	10.42 FQ	16.96 AW	27.02 TQ	TXBLS	10/01-12/01
	Utah	H	10.54 FQ	17.76 AW	28.72 TQ	UTBLS	10/01-12/01
	Virginia	H	10.08 FQ	13.21 AW	18.99 TQ	VABLS	10/01-12/01
	Washington	H	20.00 FQ	27.02 AW	33.77 TQ	WABLS	10/01-12/01
	West Virginia	H	10.40 FQ	17.33 AW	25.98 TQ	WVBLS	10/01-12/01
	Wisconsin	H	12.78 FQ	24.00 AW	32.45 TQ	WIBLS	10/01-12/01
	Puerto Rico	H	5.37 FQ	7.55 AW	14.11 TQ	PRBLS	10/01-12/01
Pilot							
American Airlines	United States	H		186.51 AW		NYT	6/01
American Eagle Airlines	United States	H		80.27 AW		NYT	6/01
Chief, Corporations	United States	Y		70920 AW		AWST	2001-2001
Comair (Delta)	United States	H		69.69 AW		NYT	6/01
Continental Airlines	United States	H		156.70 AW		NYT	6/01
Continental Express Airlines	United States	H		76.70 AW		NYT	6/01
Delta Airlines	United States	H		201.65 AW		NYT	6/01
Southwest Airlines	United States	H		137.67 AW		NYT	6/01
United Airlines	United States	H		198.55 AW		NYT	6/01
Pipelayer	Alabama	H	7.97 FQ	11.43 AW	15.89 TQ	ALBLS	10/01-12/01
	Alaska	H	16.69 FQ	23.59 AW	28.21 TQ	AKBLS	10/01-12/01
	Arizona	H	9.23 FQ	13.26 AW	17.93 TQ	AZBLS	10/01-12/01
	Arkansas	H	7.69 FQ	10.74 AW	14.06 TQ	ARBLS	10/01-12/01
	California	H	12.11 FQ	20.18 AW	29.49 TQ	CABLS	10/01-12/01
	Colorado	H	9.67 FQ	13.92 AW	19.55 TQ	COBLS	10/01-12/01
	Connecticut	H	12.75 FQ	19.11 AW	25.35 TQ	CTBLS	10/01-12/01
	Delaware	H	9.91 FQ	14.02 AW	17.55 TQ	DEBLS	10/01-12/01
	Florida	H	8.61 FQ	12.37 AW	17.33 TQ	FLBLS	10/01-12/01
	Georgia	H	8.05 FQ	13.81 AW	19.72 TQ	GABLS	10/01-12/01
	Hawaii	H	10.38 FQ	15.41 AW	21.57 TQ	HIBLS	10/01-12/01
	Idaho	H	10.34 FQ	15.58 AW	23.74 TQ	IDBLS	10/01-12/01
	Illinois	H	12.55 FQ	22.97 AW	31.03 TQ	ILBLS	10/01-12/01
	Indiana	H	10.52 FQ	15.49 AW	21.27 TQ	INBLS	10/01-12/01
	Iowa	H	10.30 FQ	14.34 AW	18.19 TQ	IABLS	10/01-12/01
	Kansas	H	7.99 FQ	16.70 AW	25.12 TQ	KSBLS	10/01-12/01
	Kentucky	H	9.22 FQ	13.85 AW	20.06 TQ	KYBLS	10/01-12/01
	Louisiana	H	7.94 FQ	11.32 AW	16.21 TQ	LABLS	10/01-12/01
	Maine	H	9.64 FQ	13.49 AW	19.10 TQ	MEBLS	10/01-12/01

AAW	Average annual wage	**AOH**	Average offered, high	**ASH**	Average starting, high	**H**	Hourly	**M**	Monthly	**S**	Special: hourly and annual
AE	Average entry wage	**AOL**	Average offered, low	**ASL**	Average starting, low	**HI**	Highest wage paid	**MTC**	Median total compensation	**TQ**	Third quartile wage
AEX	Average experienced wage	**APH**	Average pay, high range	**AW**	Average wage paid	**HR**	High end range	**MW**	Median wage paid	**W**	Weekly
AO	Average offered	**APL**	Average pay, low range	**FQ**	First quartile wage	**LR**	Low end range	**SQ**	Second quartile wage	**Y**	Yearly

Occupation/Type/Industry	Location	Per	Low	Mid	High	Source	Date
Pipelayer	Maryland	H	8.71 FQ	12.87 AW	17.02 TQ	MDBLS	10/01-12/01
	Massachusetts	H	11.43 FQ	18.35 AW	27.97 TQ	MABLS	10/01-12/01
	Michigan	H	11.32 FQ	15.96 AW	21.21 TQ	MIBLS	10/01-12/01
	Minnesota	H	14.06 FQ	20.42 AW	26.56 TQ	MNBLS	10/01-12/01
	Mississippi	H	8.22 FQ	11.90 AW	17.42 TQ	MSBLS	10/01-12/01
	Missouri	H	10.75 FQ	15.46 AW	22.78 TQ	MOBLS	10/01-12/01
	Montana	H	12.31 FQ	16.56 AW	21.47 TQ	MTBLS	10/01-12/01
	Nebraska	H	9.42 FQ	12.87 AW	17.37 TQ	NEBLS	10/01-12/01
	Nevada	H	10.01 FQ	16.42 AW	22.55 TQ	NVBLS	10/01-12/01
	New Hampshire	H	11.50 FQ	15.26 AW	21.04 TQ	NHBLS	10/01-12/01
	New Jersey	H	13.73 FQ	23.02 AW	32.14 TQ	NJBLS	10/01-12/01
	New Mexico	H	7.77 FQ	11.77 AW	16.76 TQ	NMBLS	10/01-12/01
	New York	H	8.68 FQ	19.33 AW	32.62 TQ	NYBLS	10/01-12/01
	North Carolina	H	8.23 FQ	11.58 AW	15.87 TQ	NCBLS	10/01-12/01
	North Dakota	H	9.90 FQ	14.49 AW	23.27 TQ	NDBLS	10/01-12/01
	Ohio	H	9.87 FQ	16.17 AW	24.12 TQ	OHBLS	10/01-12/01
	Oklahoma	H	7.77 FQ	11.46 AW	16.43 TQ	OKBLS	10/01-12/01
	Oregon	H	12.78 FQ	18.41 AW	25.05 TQ	ORBLS	10/01-12/01
	Pennsylvania	H	10.64 FQ	17.74 AW	23.00 TQ	PABLS	10/01-12/01
	Rhode Island	H	16.68 FQ	20.90 AW	25.88 TQ	RIBLS	10/01-12/01
	South Carolina	H	7.73 FQ	11.97 AW	16.89 TQ	SCBLS	10/01-12/01
	South Dakota	H	9.36 FQ	12.71 AW	19.75 TQ	SDBLS	10/01-12/01
	Tennessee	H	9.04 FQ	12.35 AW	16.74 TQ	TNBLS	10/01-12/01
	Texas	H	8.02 FQ	11.51 AW	16.95 TQ	TXBLS	10/01-12/01
	Utah	H	9.26 FQ	12.72 AW	16.96 TQ	UTBLS	10/01-12/01
	Vermont	H	9.76 FQ	13.63 AW	19.46 TQ	VTBLS	10/01-12/01
	Virginia	H	8.31 FQ	12.44 AW	17.73 TQ	VABLS	10/01-12/01
	Washington	H	13.42 FQ	21.24 AW	27.45 TQ	WABLS	10/01-12/01
	West Virginia	H	6.82 FQ	13.39 AW	19.99 TQ	WVBLS	10/01-12/01
	Wisconsin	H	13.70 FQ	21.05 AW	27.76 TQ	WIBLS	10/01-12/01
	Wyoming	H	9.78 FQ	14.05 AW	19.77 TQ	WYBLS	10/01-12/01
	Puerto Rico	H	6.18 FQ	9.47 AW	14.25 TQ	PRBLS	10/01-12/01
	Guam	H	9.41 FQ	14.88 AW	20.22 TQ	GUBLS	10/01-12/01
Plasterer and Stucco Mason	Alabama	H	9.32 FQ	12.46 AW	16.74 TQ	ALBLS	10/01-12/01
	Birmingham MSA, AL	H	9.36 FQ	13.11 AW	17.61 TQ	ALBLS	10/01-12/01
	Mobile MSA, AL	H	9.09 FQ	10.32 AW	11.16 TQ	ALBLS	10/01-12/01
	Alaska	H	15.74 FQ	25.91 AW	35.19 TQ	AKBLS	10/01-12/01
	Arizona	H	9.12 FQ	14.65 AW	21.31 TQ	AZBLS	10/01-12/01
	Phoenix-Mesa MSA, AZ	H	9.08 FQ	14.60 AW	20.90 TQ	AZBLS	10/01-12/01
	Tucson MSA, AZ	H	8.41 FQ	13.22 AW	18.16 TQ	AZBLS	10/01-12/01
	Arkansas	H	10.80 FQ	14.08 AW	17.03 TQ	ARBLS	10/01-12/01
	Fayetteville-Springdale-Rogers MSA, AR	H	10.22 FQ	13.69 AW	17.15 TQ	ARBLS	10/01-12/01
	Little Rock-North Little Rock MSA, AR	H	11.53 FQ	14.39 AW	17.17 TQ	ARBLS	10/01-12/01
	California	H	9.44 FQ	16.58 AW	26.79 TQ	CABLS	10/01-12/01
	Bakersfield MSA, CA	H	9.25 FQ	16.43 AW	22.95 TQ	CABLS	10/01-12/01
	Fresno MSA, CA	H	6.64 FQ	15.11 AW	21.77 TQ	CABLS	10/01-12/01
	Los Angeles-Long Beach PMSA, CA	H	8.77 FQ	13.66 AW	20.35 TQ	CABLS	10/01-12/01
	Modesto MSA, CA	H	10.68 FQ	16.91 AW	26.87 TQ	CABLS	10/01-12/01
	Oakland PMSA, CA	H	11.27 FQ	22.67 AW	33.48 TQ	CABLS	10/01-12/01
	Orange County PMSA, CA	H	8.22 FQ	15.76 AW	27.44 TQ	CABLS	10/01-12/01
	Riverside-San Bernardino PMSA, CA	H	10.01 FQ	17.37 AW	26.40 TQ	CABLS	10/01-12/01
	Sacramento PMSA, CA	H	8.22 FQ	15.03 AW	22.85 TQ	CABLS	10/01-12/01
	Salinas MSA, CA	H	10.13 FQ	18.22 AW	26.84 TQ	CABLS	10/01-12/01
	San Diego MSA, CA	H	11.46 FQ	19.31 AW	29.19 TQ	CABLS	10/01-12/01
	San Francisco PMSA, CA	H	12.31 FQ	22.02 AW	29.79 TQ	CABLS	10/01-12/01
	San Jose PMSA, CA	H	13.43 FQ	18.59 AW	25.80 TQ	CABLS	10/01-12/01
	San Luis Obispo-Atascadero-Paso Robles MSA, CA	H	10.63 FQ	16.48 AW	21.73 TQ	CABLS	10/01-12/01
	Santa Barbara-Santa Maria-Lompoc MSA, CA	H	11.36 FQ	16.46 AW	23.30 TQ	CABLS	10/01-12/01
	Santa Rosa PMSA, CA	H	15.35 FQ	21.45 AW	28.17 TQ	CABLS	10/01-12/01
	Stockton-Lodi MSA, CA	H	11.21 FQ	14.78 AW	20.31 TQ	CABLS	10/01-12/01
	Vallejo-Fairfield-Napa PMSA, CA	H	11.99 FQ	20.37 AW	30.53 TQ	CABLS	10/01-12/01
	Ventura PMSA, CA	H	11.24 FQ	16.57 AW	21.47 TQ	CABLS	10/01-12/01
	Colorado	H	8.20 FQ	13.39 AW	17.62 TQ	COBLS	10/01-12/01
	Colorado Springs MSA, CO	H	9.96 FQ	14.65 AW	20.09 TQ	COBLS	10/01-12/01
	Denver PMSA, CO	H	11.26 FQ	13.91 AW	17.26 TQ	COBLS	10/01-12/01

AAW Average annual wage **AOH** Average offered, high **ASH** Average starting, high **H** Hourly **M** Monthly **S** Special: hourly and annual
AE Average entry wage **AOL** Average offered, low **ASL** Average starting, low **HI** Highest wage paid **MTC** Median total compensation **TQ** Third quartile wage
AEX Average experienced wage **APH** Average pay, high range **AW** Average wage paid **HR** High end range **MW** Median wage paid **W** Weekly
AO Average offered **APL** Average pay, low range **FQ** First quartile wage **LR** Low end range **SQ** Second quartile wage **Y** Yearly

Occupation/Type/Industry	Location	Per	Low	Mid	High	Source	Date
Plasterer and Stucco Mason	Greeley PMSA, CO	H	11.93 FQ	14.97 AW	18.32 TQ	COBLS	10/01-12/01
	Delaware	H	10.85 FQ	18.82 AW	23.00 TQ	DEBLS	10/01-12/01
	Wilmington-Newark PMSA, DE-MD	H	10.64 FQ	18.15 AW	22.43 TQ	DEBLS	10/01-12/01
	District of Columbia	H	11.49 FQ	18.21 AW	21.75 TQ	DCBLS	10/01-12/01
	Washington PMSA, DC-MD-VA-WV	H	13.96 FQ	18.65 AW	26.03 TQ	DCBLS	10/01-12/01
	Florida	H	11.15 FQ	16.04 AW	21.10 TQ	FLBLS	10/01-12/01
	Daytona Beach MSA, FL	H	13.62 FQ	14.97 AW	16.84 TQ	FLBLS	10/01-12/01
	Fort Lauderdale PMSA, FL	H	10.79 FQ	15.77 AW	20.64 TQ	FLBLS	10/01-12/01
	Fort Myers-Cape Coral MSA, FL	H	14.06 FQ	17.02 AW	21.15 TQ	FLBLS	10/01-12/01
	Gainesville MSA, FL	H	7.97 FQ	12.65 AW	17.52 TQ	FLBLS	10/01-12/01
	Jacksonville MSA, FL	H	10.90 FQ	14.26 AW	17.17 TQ	FLBLS	10/01-12/01
	Lakeland-Winter Haven MSA, FL	H	10.80 FQ	11.83 AW	13.27 TQ	FLBLS	10/01-12/01
	Melbourne-Titusville-Palm Bay MSA, FL	H	13.54 FQ	16.21 AW	20.53 TQ	FLBLS	10/01-12/01
	Miami PMSA, FL	H	12.92 FQ	22.59 AW	32.88 TQ	FLBLS	10/01-12/01
	Naples MSA, FL	H	13.85 FQ	18.02 AW	23.95 TQ	FLBLS	10/01-12/01
	Ocala MSA, FL	H	9.31 FQ	13.58 AW	16.57 TQ	FLBLS	10/01-12/01
	Orlando MSA, FL	H	11.94 FQ	17.26 AW	21.57 TQ	FLBLS	10/01-12/01
	Pensacola MSA, FL	H	8.40 FQ	13.21 AW	17.57 TQ	FLBLS	10/01-12/01
	Sarasota-Bradenton MSA, FL	H	11.18 FQ	14.05 AW	17.55 TQ	FLBLS	10/01-12/01
	Tallahassee MSA, FL	H	11.87 FQ	14.38 AW	16.61 TQ	FLBLS	10/01-12/01
	Tampa-St. Petersburg-Clearwater MSA, FL	H	11.03 FQ	13.90 AW	18.86 TQ	FLBLS	10/01-12/01
	West Palm Beach-Boca Raton MSA, FL	H	14.95 FQ	17.93 AW	21.23 TQ	FLBLS	10/01-12/01
	Georgia	H	9.95 FQ	14.09 AW	18.96 TQ	GABLS	10/01-12/01
	Atlanta MSA, GA	H	10.74 FQ	15.02 AW	20.95 TQ	GABLS	10/01-12/01
	Hawaii	H	15.44 FQ	23.27 AW	31.86 TQ	HIBLS	10/01-12/01
	Honolulu MSA, HI	H	13.22 FQ	25.53 AW	34.41 TQ	HIBLS	10/01-12/01
	Idaho	H	11.39 FQ	14.58 AW	18.28 TQ	IDBLS	10/01-12/01
	Boise City MSA, ID	H	11.63 FQ	15.08 AW	19.79 TQ	IDBLS	10/01-12/01
	Illinois	H	16.02 FQ	25.83 AW	35.61 TQ	ILBLS	10/01-12/01
	Chicago PMSA, IL	H	21.10 FQ	27.12 AW	35.00 TQ	ILBLS	10/01-12/01
	Peoria-Pekin MSA, IL	H	8.97 FQ	15.43 AW	26.13 TQ	ILBLS	10/01-12/01
	Indiana	H	14.30 FQ	19.20 AW	25.50 TQ	INBLS	10/01-12/01
	Evansville-Henderson MSA, IN-KY	H	17.48 FQ	19.09 AW	21.19 TQ	INBLS	10/01-12/01
	Indianapolis MSA, IN	H	15.32 FQ	20.97 AW	27.07 TQ	INBLS	10/01-12/01
	Iowa	H	10.58 FQ	16.33 AW	21.72 TQ	IABLS	10/01-12/01
	Davenport-Moline-Rock Island MSA, IA-IL	H	13.96 FQ	18.48 AW	25.89 TQ	IABLS	10/01-12/01
	Kansas	H	12.09 FQ	16.40 AW	21.48 TQ	KSBLS	10/01-12/01
	Wichita MSA, KS	H	12.37 FQ	15.34 AW	17.71 TQ	KSBLS	10/01-12/01
	Kentucky	H	9.10 FQ	11.10 AW	16.46 TQ	KYBLS	10/01-12/01
	Louisiana	H	9.93 FQ	15.23 AW	20.87 TQ	LABLS	10/01-12/01
	Baton Rouge MSA, LA	H	9.63 FQ	14.70 AW	20.34 TQ	LABLS	10/01-12/01
	Lafayette MSA, LA	H	11.88 FQ	16.96 AW	24.75 TQ	LABLS	10/01-12/01
	New Orleans MSA, LA	H	9.11 FQ	13.28 AW	17.47 TQ	LABLS	10/01-12/01
	Maine	H	5.91 FQ	10.66 AW	20.51 TQ	MEBLS	10/01-12/01
	Maryland	H	13.47 FQ	20.25 AW	26.81 TQ	MDBLS	10/01-12/01
	Baltimore PMSA, MD	H	13.05 FQ	18.12 AW	22.47 TQ	MDBLS	10/01-12/01
	Boston PMSA, MA-NH	H	21.39 FQ	31.88 AW	53.18 TQ	MABLS	10/01-12/01
	Brockton PMSA, MA	H	13.72 FQ	19.76 AW	28.34 TQ	MABLS	10/01-12/01
	Michigan	H	15.42 FQ	22.63 AW	28.17 TQ	MIBLS	10/01-12/01
	Detroit PMSA, MI	H	19.37 FQ	24.19 AW	28.46 TQ	MIBLS	10/01-12/01
	Grand Rapids-Muskegon-Holland MSA, MI	H	16.77 FQ	22.79 AW	28.28 TQ	MIBLS	10/01-12/01
	Minnesota	H	12.38 FQ	21.26 AW	28.04 TQ	MNBLS	10/01-12/01
	Minneapolis-St. Paul MSA, MN-WI	H	19.00 FQ	24.14 AW	28.56 TQ	MNBLS	10/01-12/01
	Missouri	H	12.75 FQ	18.49 AW	27.72 TQ	MOBLS	10/01-12/01
	Kansas City MSA, MO-KS	H	11.81 FQ	17.25 AW	22.62 TQ	MOBLS	10/01-12/01
	St. Louis MSA, MO-IL	H	11.69 FQ	19.68 AW	30.22 TQ	MOBLS	10/01-12/01
	Springfield MSA, MO	H	14.24 FQ	16.44 AW	19.79 TQ	MOBLS	10/01-12/01
	Nebraska	H	8.60 FQ	14.52 AW	21.30 TQ	NEBLS	10/01-12/01
	Lincoln MSA, NE	H	8.39 FQ	13.51 AW	20.69 TQ	NEBLS	10/01-12/01
	Omaha MSA, NE-IA	H	14.92 FQ	19.00 AW	24.95 TQ	NEBLS	10/01-12/01
	Nevada	H	12.50 FQ	17.00 AW	22.55 TQ	NVBLS	10/01-12/01

AAW	Average annual wage	**AOH**	Average offered, high	**ASH**	Average starting, high	**H**	Hourly	**M**	Monthly	**S**	Special: hourly and annual
AE	Average entry wage	**AOL**	Average offered, low	**ASL**	Average starting, low	**HI**	Highest wage paid	**MTC**	Median total compensation	**TQ**	Third quartile wage
AEX	Average experienced wage	**APH**	Average pay, high range	**AW**	Average wage paid	**HR**	High end range	**MW**	Median wage paid	**W**	Weekly
AO	Average offered	**APL**	Average pay, low range	**FQ**	First quartile wage	**LR**	Low end range	**SQ**	Second quartile wage	**Y**	Yearly

Occupation/Type/Industry	Location	Per	Low	Mid	High	Source	Date
Plasterer and Stucco Mason	Las Vegas MSA, NV-AZ	H	12.25 FQ	17.02 AW	24.10 TQ	NVBLS	10/01-12/01
	Reno MSA, NV	H	12.09 FQ	18.18 AW	22.35 TQ	NVBLS	10/01-12/01
	New Jersey	H	11.32 FQ	18.48 AW	26.52 TQ	NJBLS	10/01-12/01
	Bergen-Passaic PMSA, NJ	H	15.23 FQ	18.95 AW	23.71 TQ	NJBLS	10/01-12/01
	Newark PMSA, NJ	H	9.76 FQ	14.85 AW	18.24 TQ	NJBLS	10/01-12/01
	Trenton PMSA, NJ	H	15.67 FQ	25.49 AW	33.90 TQ	NJBLS	10/01-12/01
	New Mexico	H	8.97 FQ	13.71 AW	20.36 TQ	NMBLS	10/01-12/01
	Albuquerque MSA, NM	H	8.84 FQ	14.01 AW	21.23 TQ	NMBLS	10/01-12/01
	Las Cruces MSA, NM	H	7.43 FQ	11.98 AW	20.14 TQ	NMBLS	10/01-12/01
	New York	H	14.96 FQ	25.68 AW	39.39 TQ	NYBLS	10/01-12/01
	Albany-Schenectady-Troy MSA, NY	H	15.46 FQ	25.16 AW	40.58 TQ	NYBLS	10/01-12/01
	Buffalo-Niagara Falls MSA, NY	H	13.26 FQ	15.94 AW	21.05 TQ	NYBLS	10/01-12/01
	Nassau-Suffolk PMSA, NY	H	19.84 FQ	31.23 AW	41.03 TQ	NYBLS	10/01-12/01
	New York PMSA, NY	H	16.10 FQ	24.04 AW	28.92 TQ	NYBLS	10/01-12/01
	Rochester MSA, NY	H	11.74 FQ	27.76 AW	42.07 TQ	NYBLS	10/01-12/01
	North Carolina	H	8.31 FQ	12.69 AW	18.08 TQ	NCBLS	10/01-12/01
	Charlotte-Gastonia-Rock Hill MSA, NC-SC	H	11.55 FQ	16.12 AW	21.55 TQ	NCBLS	10/01-12/01
	Greensboro-Winston-Salem-High Point MSA, NC	H	7.96 FQ	11.60 AW	17.02 TQ	NCBLS	10/01-12/01
	Raleigh-Durham-Chapel Hill MSA, NC	H	11.08 FQ	13.68 AW	16.89 TQ	NCBLS	10/01-12/01
	Ohio	H	10.71 FQ	15.59 AW	24.21 TQ	OHBLS	10/01-12/01
	Cincinnati PMSA, OH-KY-IN	H	13.09 FQ	18.57 AW	22.29 TQ	OHBLS	10/01-12/01
	Cleveland-Lorain-Elyria PMSA, OH	H	8.77 FQ	15.34 AW	22.11 TQ	OHBLS	10/01-12/01
	Columbus MSA, OH	H	11.94 FQ	16.34 AW	22.36 TQ	OHBLS	10/01-12/01
	Dayton-Springfield MSA, OH	H	11.02 FQ	12.50 AW	13.42 TQ	OHBLS	10/01-12/01
	Hamilton-Middletown PMSA, OH	H	8.87 FQ	13.49 AW	21.36 TQ	OHBLS	10/01-12/01
	Toledo MSA, OH	H	18.42 FQ	24.05 AW	28.56 TQ	OHBLS	10/01-12/01
	Youngstown-Warren MSA, OH	H	12.97 FQ	19.49 AW	26.21 TQ	OHBLS	10/01-12/01
	Oklahoma	H	10.99 FQ	15.73 AW	21.14 TQ	OKBLS	10/01-12/01
	Tulsa MSA, OK	H	12.59 FQ	16.34 AW	21.78 TQ	OKBLS	10/01-12/01
	Oregon	H	10.43 FQ	18.70 AW	26.70 TQ	ORBLS	10/01-12/01
	Portland-Vancouver PMSA, OR-WA	H	10.89 FQ	19.01 AW	27.04 TQ	ORBLS	10/01-12/01
	Salem PMSA, OR	H	9.36 FQ	14.50 AW	21.28 TQ	ORBLS	10/01-12/01
	Pennsylvania	H	10.79 FQ	17.78 AW	28.08 TQ	PABLS	10/01-12/01
	Allentown-Bethlehem-Easton MSA, PA	H	9.35 FQ	17.84 AW	27.98 TQ	PABLS	10/01-12/01
	Philadelphia PMSA, PA-NJ	H	13.60 FQ	20.82 AW	32.84 TQ	PABLS	10/01-12/01
	Pittsburgh MSA, PA	H	11.49 FQ	17.48 AW	21.58 TQ	PABLS	10/01-12/01
	York MSA, PA	H	8.95 FQ	13.05 AW	18.81 TQ	PABLS	10/01-12/01
	Rhode Island	H	10.64 FQ	18.25 AW	27.21 TQ	RIBLS	10/01-12/01
	Providence-Fall River-Warwick MSA, RI-MA	H	10.45 FQ	18.77 AW	27.81 TQ	RIBLS	10/01-12/01
	South Carolina	H	9.02 FQ	11.82 AW	16.01 TQ	SCBLS	10/01-12/01
	Tennessee	H	11.85 FQ	15.15 AW	17.86 TQ	TNBLS	10/01-12/01
	Chattanooga MSA, TN-GA	H	11.60 FQ	14.72 AW	17.71 TQ	TNBLS	10/01-12/01
	Knoxville MSA, TN	H	12.18 FQ	15.01 AW	17.84 TQ	TNBLS	10/01-12/01
	Memphis MSA, TN-AR-MS	H	8.93 FQ	14.11 AW	18.05 TQ	TNBLS	10/01-12/01
	Nashville MSA, TN	H	14.62 FQ	15.82 AW	17.90 TQ	TNBLS	10/01-12/01
	Texas	H	9.10 FQ	13.87 AW	18.43 TQ	TXBLS	10/01-12/01
	Austin-San Marcos MSA, TX	H	10.80 FQ	14.36 AW	17.63 TQ	TXBLS	10/01-12/01
	Dallas PMSA, TX	H	8.93 FQ	14.00 AW	20.52 TQ	TXBLS	10/01-12/01
	El Paso MSA, TX	H	9.28 FQ	12.10 AW	17.00 TQ	TXBLS	10/01-12/01
	Houston PMSA, TX	H	9.82 FQ	15.23 AW	21.02 TQ	TXBLS	10/01-12/01
	San Antonio MSA, TX	H	8.71 FQ	12.91 AW	17.27 TQ	TXBLS	10/01-12/01
	Utah	H	9.81 FQ	15.05 AW	22.47 TQ	UTBLS	10/01-12/01
	Provo-Orem MSA, UT	H	10.63 FQ	15.99 AW	20.91 TQ	UTBLS	10/01-12/01
	Salt Lake City-Ogden MSA, UT	H	9.80 FQ	15.14 AW	23.21 TQ	UTBLS	10/01-12/01
	Virginia	H	11.90 FQ	15.19 AW	18.59 TQ	VABLS	10/01-12/01
	Norfolk-Virginia Beach-Newport News MSA, VA-NC	H	12.62 FQ	15.98 AW	20.19 TQ	VABLS	10/01-12/01
	Richmond-Petersburg MSA, VA	H	12.14 FQ	15.40 AW	19.58 TQ	VABLS	10/01-12/01
	Washington	H	14.39 FQ	21.19 AW	28.12 TQ	WABLS	10/01-12/01

AAW Average annual wage **AOH** Average offered, high **ASH** Average starting, high **H** Hourly **M** Monthly **S** Special: hourly and annual
AE Average entry wage **AOL** Average offered, low **ASL** Average starting, low **HI** Highest wage paid **MTC** Median total compensation **TQ** Third quartile wage
AEX Average experienced wage **APH** Average pay, high range **AW** Average wage paid **HR** High end range **MW** Median wage paid **W** Weekly
AO Average offered **APL** Average pay, low range **FQ** First quartile wage **LR** Low end range **SQ** Second quartile wage **Y** Yearly

Occupation/Type/Industry	Location	Per	Low	Mid	High	Source	Date
Plasterer and Stucco Mason	Seattle-Bellevue-Everett PMSA, WA	H	15.53 FQ	22.92 AW	28.38 TQ	WABLS	10/01-12/01
	Spokane MSA, WA	H	15.71 FQ	19.28 AW	22.12 TQ	WABLS	10/01-12/01
	West Virginia	H	9.78 FQ	16.59 AW	23.91 TQ	WVBLS	10/01-12/01
	Huntington-Ashland MSA, WV-KY-OH	H	10.25 FQ	16.83 AW	24.65 TQ	WVBLS	10/01-12/01
	Wisconsin	H	11.71 FQ	18.63 AW	27.08 TQ	WIBLS	10/01-12/01
	Appleton-Oshkosh-Neenah MSA, WI	H	10.77 FQ	18.30 AW	25.66 TQ	WIBLS	10/01-12/01
	Green Bay MSA, WI	H	11.83 FQ	14.83 AW	20.79 TQ	WIBLS	10/01-12/01
	Madison MSA, WI	H	10.65 FQ	18.42 AW	26.12 TQ	WIBLS	10/01-12/01
	Milwaukee-Waukesha PMSA, WI	H	16.52 FQ	23.77 AW	28.33 TQ	WIBLS	10/01-12/01
	Wyoming	H	7.48 FQ	11.79 AW	18.06 TQ	WYBLS	10/01-12/01
	Puerto Rico	H	5.98 FQ	10.82 AW	21.34 TQ	PRBLS	10/01-12/01
	Guam	H	9.24 FQ	10.81 AW	13.14 TQ	GUBLS	10/01-12/01
Plating and Coating Machine Setter, Operator, and Tender							
Metals and Plastics	Alabama	H	7.47 FQ	11.96 AW	17.93 TQ	ALBLS	10/01-12/01
Metals and Plastics	Birmingham MSA, AL	H	7.23 FQ	13.07 AW	19.89 TQ	ALBLS	10/01-12/01
Metals and Plastics	Huntsville MSA, AL	H	7.69 FQ	11.46 AW	18.04 TQ	ALBLS	10/01-12/01
Metals and Plastics	Montgomery MSA, AL	H	7.30 FQ	11.31 AW	15.00 TQ	ALBLS	10/01-12/01
Metals and Plastics	Arizona	H	6.94 FQ	10.67 AW	17.57 TQ	AZBLS	10/01-12/01
Metals and Plastics	Phoenix-Mesa MSA, AZ	H	6.84 FQ	10.62 AW	18.02 TQ	AZBLS	10/01-12/01
Metals and Plastics	Tucson MSA, AZ	H	7.21 FQ	11.21 AW	16.40 TQ	AZBLS	10/01-12/01
Metals and Plastics	Arkansas	H	8.79 FQ	11.82 AW	16.09 TQ	ARBLS	10/01-12/01
Metals and Plastics	Fayetteville-Springdale-Rogers MSA, AR	H	8.99 FQ	11.59 AW	15.68 TQ	ARBLS	10/01-12/01
Metals and Plastics	Fort Smith MSA, AR-OK	H	10.45 FQ	14.81 AW	20.67 TQ	ARBLS	10/01-12/01
Metals and Plastics	California	H	7.26 FQ	11.64 AW	17.54 TQ	CABLS	10/01-12/01
Metals and Plastics	Fresno MSA, CA	H	7.10 FQ	9.87 AW	12.41 TQ	CABLS	10/01 12/01
Metals and Plastics	Los Angeles-Long Beach PMSA, CA	H	7.04 FQ	10.47 AW	14.58 TQ	CABLS	10/01-12/01
Metals and Plastics	Oakland PMSA, CA	H	8.47 FQ	14.30 AW	20.57 TQ	CABLS	10/01-12/01
Metals and Plastics	Orange County PMSA, CA	H	6.95 FQ	10.86 AW	16.75 TQ	CABLS	10/01-12/01
Metals and Plastics	Riverside-San Bernardino PMSA, CA	H	8.85 FQ	16.98 AW	41.74 TQ	CABLS	10/01-12/01
Metals and Plastics	Sacramento PMSA, CA	H	6.68 FQ	13.24 AW	19.05 TQ	CABLS	10/01-12/01
Metals and Plastics	San Diego MSA, CA	H	8.03 FQ	11.30 AW	17.65 TQ	CABLS	10/01-12/01
Metals and Plastics	San Francisco PMSA, CA	H	9.92 FQ	15.79 AW	22.84 TQ	CABLS	10/01-12/01
Metals and Plastics	San Jose PMSA, CA	H	7.16 FQ	11.11 AW	16.11 TQ	CABLS	10/01-12/01
Metals and Plastics	Vallejo-Fairfield-Napa PMSA, CA	H	11.45 FQ	14.87 AW	19.63 TQ	CABLS	10/01-12/01
Metals and Plastics	Ventura PMSA, CA	H	7.31 FQ	9.75 AW	16.02 TQ	CABLS	10/01-12/01
Metals and Plastics	Colorado	H	7.96 FQ	11.88 AW	16.29 TQ	COBLS	10/01-12/01
Metals and Plastics	Boulder-Longmont PMSA, CO	H	9.23 FQ	13.97 AW	24.02 TQ	COBLS	10/01-12/01
Metals and Plastics	Colorado Springs MSA, CO	H	7.66 FQ	11.06 AW	14.88 TQ	COBLS	10/01-12/01
Metals and Plastics	Denver PMSA, CO	H	8.45 FQ	11.96 AW	16.46 TQ	COBLS	10/01-12/01
Metals and Plastics	Connecticut	H	8.63 FQ	13.25 AW	17.74 TQ	CTBLS	10/01-12/01
Metals and Plastics	Bridgeport PMSA, CT	H	9.66 FQ	14.57 AW	20.29 TQ	CTBLS	10/01-12/01
Metals and Plastics	Hartford MSA, CT	H	8.13 FQ	12.81 AW	17.30 TQ	CTBLS	10/01-12/01
Metals and Plastics	New Haven-Meriden PMSA, CT	H	9.09 FQ	12.90 AW	17.00 TQ	CTBLS	10/01-12/01
Metals and Plastics	Waterbury PMSA, CT	H	9.27 FQ	13.05 AW	16.99 TQ	CTBLS	10/01-12/01
Metals and Plastics	Washington PMSA, DC-MD-VA-WV	H	8.06 FQ	12.50 AW	18.58 TQ	DCBLS	10/01-12/01
Metals and Plastics	Florida	H	7.38 FQ	11.14 AW	17.35 TQ	FLBLS	10/01-12/01
Metals and Plastics	Fort Lauderdale PMSA, FL	H	8.09 FQ	10.59 AW	13.60 TQ	FLBLS	10/01-12/01
Metals and Plastics	Jacksonville MSA, FL	H	9.04 FQ	16.57 AW	23.11 TQ	FLBLS	10/01-12/01
Metals and Plastics	Miami PMSA, FL	H	6.94 FQ	10.13 AW	14.35 TQ	FLBLS	10/01-12/01
Metals and Plastics	Orlando MSA, FL	H	7.10 FQ	9.54 AW	13.83 TQ	FLBLS	10/01-12/01
Metals and Plastics	Tampa-St. Petersburg-Clearwater MSA, FL	H	7.31 FQ	9.77 AW	13.07 TQ	FLBLS	10/01-12/01
Metals and Plastics	West Palm Beach-Boca Raton MSA, FL	H	9.12 FQ	14.49 AW	20.23 TQ	FLBLS	10/01-12/01
Metals and Plastics	Georgia	H	7.85 FQ	11.22 AW	15.65 TQ	GABLS	10/01-12/01
Metals and Plastics	Atlanta MSA, GA	H	7.61 FQ	10.70 AW	14.71 TQ	GABLS	10/01-12/01
Metals and Plastics	Idaho	H	6.22 FQ	9.88 AW	15.60 TQ	IDBLS	10/01-12/01
Metals and Plastics	Illinois	H	7.10 FQ	11.82 AW	17.30 TQ	ILBLS	10/01-12/01
Metals and Plastics	Chicago PMSA, IL	H	6.75 FQ	11.93 AW	17.29 TQ	ILBLS	10/01-12/01
Metals and Plastics	Rockford MSA, IL	H	7.60 FQ	11.05 AW	14.62 TQ	ILBLS	10/01-12/01

AAW	Average annual wage	AOH	Average offered, high	ASH	Average starting, high	H	Hourly	M	Monthly	S	Special: hourly and annual
AE	Average entry wage	AOL	Average offered, low	ASL	Average starting, low	HI	Highest wage paid	MTC	Median total compensation	TQ	Third quartile wage
AEX	Average experienced wage	APH	Average pay, high range	AW	Average wage paid	HR	High end range	MW	Median wage paid	W	Weekly
AO	Average offered	APL	Average pay, low range	FQ	First quartile wage	LR	Low end range	SQ	Second quartile wage	Y	Yearly

Occupation/Type/Industry	Location	Per	Low	Mid	High	Source	Date
Plating and Coating Machine Setter, Operator, and Tender							
Metals and Plastics	Indiana	H	8.64 FQ	12.53 AW	16.64 TQ	INBLS	10/01-12/01
Metals and Plastics	Elkhart-Goshen MSA, IN	H	9.30 FQ	14.61 AW	18.05 TQ	INBLS	10/01-12/01
Metals and Plastics	Evansville-Henderson MSA, IN-KY	H	11.66 FQ	15.28 AW	25.61 TQ	INBLS	10/01-12/01
Metals and Plastics	Fort Wayne MSA, IN	H	8.07 FQ	11.01 AW	14.11 TQ	INBLS	10/01-12/01
Metals and Plastics	Gary PMSA, IN	H	8.63 FQ	15.58 AW	24.81 TQ	INBLS	10/01-12/01
Metals and Plastics	Indianapolis MSA, IN	H	9.46 FQ	12.82 AW	16.73 TQ	INBLS	10/01-12/01
Metals and Plastics	South Bend MSA, IN	H	8.06 FQ	10.50 AW	13.35 TQ	INBLS	10/01-12/01
Metals and Plastics	Iowa	H	8.05 FQ	12.11 AW	16.71 TQ	IABLS	10/01-12/01
Metals and Plastics	Cedar Rapids MSA, IA	H	10.74 FQ	15.50 AW	21.01 TQ	IABLS	10/01-12/01
Metals and Plastics	Kansas	H	8.46 FQ	11.91 AW	16.16 TQ	KSBLS	10/01-12/01
Metals and Plastics	Wichita MSA, KS	H	9.14 FQ	11.49 AW	14.71 TQ	KSBLS	10/01-12/01
Metals and Plastics	Kentucky	H	7.96 FQ	11.76 AW	16.64 TQ	KYBLS	10/01-12/01
Metals and Plastics	Lexington MSA, KY	H	9.17 FQ	12.44 AW	18.70 TQ	KYBLS	10/01-12/01
Metals and Plastics	Louisville MSA, KY-IN	H	8.03 FQ	11.76 AW	16.60 TQ	KYBLS	10/01-12/01
Metals and Plastics	Louisiana	H	6.39 FQ	10.31 AW	14.99 TQ	LABLS	10/01-12/01
Metals and Plastics	Maine	H	8.55 FQ	13.02 AW	19.77 TQ	MEBLS	10/01-12/01
Metals and Plastics	Maryland	H	9.47 FQ	13.14 AW	18.98 TQ	MDBLS	10/01-12/01
Metals and Plastics	Baltimore PMSA, MD	H	9.92 FQ	13.63 AW	19.52 TQ	MDBLS	10/01-12/01
Metals and Plastics	Massachusetts	H	8.86 FQ	13.34 AW	19.32 TQ	MABLS	10/01-12/01
Metals and Plastics	Boston PMSA, MA-NH	H	8.88 FQ	13.84 AW	19.79 TQ	MABLS	10/01-12/01
Metals and Plastics	Brockton PMSA, MA	H	9.36 FQ	13.55 AW	19.33 TQ	MABLS	10/01-12/01
Metals and Plastics	Lawrence PMSA, MA-NH	H	8.29 FQ	12.17 AW	17.04 TQ	MABLS	10/01-12/01
Metals and Plastics	Lowell PMSA, MA-NH	H	9.25 FQ	13.57 AW	20.01 TQ	MABLS	10/01-12/01
Metals and Plastics	New Bedford PMSA, MA	H	10.29 FQ	13.11 AW	17.81 TQ	MABLS	10/01-12/01
Metals and Plastics	Springfield MSA, MA	H	8.87 FQ	13.06 AW	19.33 TQ	MABLS	10/01-12/01
Metals and Plastics	Worcester PMSA, MA-CT	H	9.21 FQ	12.96 AW	19.97 TQ	MABLS	10/01-12/01
Metals and Plastics	Michigan	H	8.00 FQ	12.90 AW	18.90 TQ	MIBLS	10/01-12/01
Metals and Plastics	Detroit PMSA, MI	H	8.69 FQ	12.61 AW	18.09 TQ	MIBLS	10/01-12/01
Metals and Plastics	Grand Rapids-Muskegon-Holland MSA, MI	H	7.75 FQ	13.80 AW	19.64 TQ	MIBLS	10/01-12/01
Metals and Plastics	Kalamazoo-Battle Creek MSA, MI	H	8.56 FQ	11.78 AW	14.10 TQ	MIBLS	10/01-12/01
Metals and Plastics	Minnesota	H	9.09 FQ	13.47 AW	17.45 TQ	MNBLS	10/01-12/01
Metals and Plastics	Minneapolis-St. Paul MSA, MN-WI	H	10.18 FQ	14.45 AW	17.78 TQ	MNBLS	10/01-12/01
Metals and Plastics	Mississippi	H	8.67 FQ	12.20 AW	14.02 TQ	MSBLS	10/01-12/01
Metals and Plastics	Jackson MSA, MS	H	9.27 FQ	11.33 AW	13.26 TQ	MSBLS	10/01-12/01
Metals and Plastics	Missouri	H	7.96 FQ	12.15 AW	17.99 TQ	MOBLS	10/01-12/01
Metals and Plastics	Kansas City MSA, MO-KS	H	8.52 FQ	13.73 AW	20.48 TQ	MOBLS	10/01-12/01
Metals and Plastics	St. Louis MSA, MO-IL	H	7.77 FQ	11.45 AW	16.10 TQ	MOBLS	10/01-12/01
Metals and Plastics	Springfield MSA, MO	H	7.31 FQ	9.21 AW	12.94 TQ	MOBLS	10/01-12/01
Metals and Plastics	Nebraska	H	9.03 FQ	12.19 AW	16.41 TQ	NEBLS	10/01-12/01
Metals and Plastics	Lincoln MSA, NE	H	9.69 FQ	12.75 AW	16.89 TQ	NEBLS	10/01-12/01
Metals and Plastics	Nevada	H	7.27 FQ	10.91 AW	14.29 TQ	NVBLS	10/01-12/01
Metals and Plastics	Las Vegas MSA, NV-AZ	H	6.73 FQ	10.69 AW	14.19 TQ	NVBLS	10/01-12/01
Metals and Plastics	New Hampshire	H	9.11 FQ	12.84 AW	16.95 TQ	NHBLS	10/01-12/01
Metals and Plastics	Manchester PMSA, NH	H	9.61 FQ	12.61 AW	16.33 TQ	NHBLS	10/01-12/01
Metals and Plastics	Nashua PMSA, NH	H	10.33 FQ	13.76 AW	17.10 TQ	NHBLS	10/01-12/01
Metals and Plastics	Portsmouth-Rochester PMSA, NH-ME	H	7.40 FQ	11.45 AW	17.50 TQ	NHBLS	10/01-12/01
Metals and Plastics	New Jersey	H	9.18 FQ	13.52 AW	18.87 TQ	NJBLS	10/01-12/01
Metals and Plastics	Bergen-Passaic PMSA, NJ	H	7.85 FQ	13.09 AW	20.28 TQ	NJBLS	10/01-12/01
Metals and Plastics	Middlesex-Somerset-Hunterdon PMSA, NJ	H	11.01 FQ	13.79 AW	17.58 TQ	NJBLS	10/01-12/01
Metals and Plastics	Monmouth-Ocean PMSA, NJ	H	7.24 FQ	11.75 AW	16.49 TQ	NJBLS	10/01-12/01
Metals and Plastics	Newark PMSA, NJ	H	8.96 FQ	13.20 AW	18.94 TQ	NJBLS	10/01-12/01
Metals and Plastics	New Mexico	H	9.51 FQ	12.32 AW	15.07 TQ	NMBLS	10/01-12/01
Metals and Plastics	Albuquerque MSA, NM	H	7.52 FQ	10.12 AW	13.42 TQ	NMBLS	10/01-12/01
Metals and Plastics	New York	H	7.96 FQ	13.34 AW	20.00 TQ	NYBLS	10/01-12/01
Metals and Plastics	Albany-Schenectady-Troy MSA, NY	H	8.29 FQ	13.29 AW	20.18 TQ	NYBLS	10/01-12/01
Metals and Plastics	Buffalo-Niagara Falls MSA, NY	H	8.34 FQ	14.67 AW	21.74 TQ	NYBLS	10/01-12/01
Metals and Plastics	Nassau-Suffolk PMSA, NY	H	8.17 FQ	11.79 AW	16.22 TQ	NYBLS	10/01-12/01
Metals and Plastics	New York PMSA, NY	H	7.91 FQ	14.16 AW	20.51 TQ	NYBLS	10/01-12/01
Metals and Plastics	Rochester MSA, NY	H	7.55 FQ	13.14 AW	20.66 TQ	NYBLS	10/01-12/01
Metals and Plastics	Syracuse MSA, NY	H	7.93 FQ	12.75 AW	19.47 TQ	NYBLS	10/01-12/01
Metals and Plastics	Utica-Rome MSA, NY	H	6.95 FQ	11.80 AW	18.81 TQ	NYBLS	10/01-12/01
Metals and Plastics	North Carolina	H	8.13 FQ	12.40 AW	16.97 TQ	NCBLS	10/01-12/01

AAW Average annual wage **AE** Average entry wage **AEX** Average experienced wage **AO** Average offered **AOH** Average offered, high **AOL** Average offered, low **APH** Average pay, high range **APL** Average pay, low range **ASH** Average starting, high **ASL** Average starting, low **AW** Average wage paid **FQ** First quartile wage **H** Hourly **HI** Highest wage paid **HR** High end range **LR** Low end range **M** Monthly **MTC** Median total compensation **MW** Median wage paid **SQ** Second quartile wage **S** Special: hourly and annual **TQ** Third quartile wage **W** Weekly **Y** Yearly

Occupation/Type/Industry	Location	Per	Low	Mid	High	Source	Date
Plating and Coating Machine Setter, Operator, and Tender							
Metals and Plastics	Charlotte-Gastonia-Rock Hill MSA, NC-SC	H	8.57 FQ	13.29 AW	18.69 TQ	NCBLS	10/01-12/01
Metals and Plastics	Greensboro-Winston-Salem-High Point MSA, NC	H	7.50 FQ	10.69 AW	15.22 TQ	NCBLS	10/01-12/01
Metals and Plastics	North Dakota	H	8.05 FQ	11.40 AW	15.44 TQ	NDBLS	10/01-12/01
Metals and Plastics	Ohio	H	9.20 FQ	13.99 AW	19.99 TQ	OHBLS	10/01-12/01
Metals and Plastics	Canton-Massillon MSA, OH	H	7.52 FQ	10.20 AW	13.85 TQ	OHBLS	10/01-12/01
Metals and Plastics	Cincinnati PMSA, OH-KY-IN	H	9.53 FQ	12.91 AW	16.89 TQ	OHBLS	10/01-12/01
Metals and Plastics	Cleveland-Lorain-Elyria PMSA, OH	H	8.25 FQ	12.39 AW	19.08 TQ	OHBLS	10/01-12/01
Metals and Plastics	Columbus MSA, OH	H	10.32 FQ	16.47 AW	22.35 TQ	OHBLS	10/01-12/01
Metals and Plastics	Dayton-Springfield MSA, OH	H	8.85 FQ	12.80 AW	19.33 TQ	OHBLS	10/01-12/01
Metals and Plastics	Toledo MSA, OH	H	9.50 FQ	13.89 AW	20.75 TQ	OHBLS	10/01-12/01
Metals and Plastics	Youngstown-Warren MSA, OH	H	11.10 FQ	15.71 AW	21.02 TQ	OHBLS	10/01-12/01
Metals and Plastics	Oklahoma	H	7.89 FQ	12.29 AW	18.63 TQ	OKBLS	10/01-12/01
Metals and Plastics	Oklahoma City MSA, OK	H	7.84 FQ	13.15 AW	19.68 TQ	OKBLS	10/01-12/01
Metals and Plastics	Tulsa MSA, OK	H	7.73 FQ	10.91 AW	15.20 TQ	OKBLS	10/01-12/01
Metals and Plastics	Oregon	H	7.15 FQ	12.36 AW	18.03 TQ	ORBLS	10/01-12/01
Metals and Plastics	Eugene-Springfield MSA, OR	H	8.24 FQ	11.69 AW	15.04 TQ	ORBLS	10/01-12/01
Metals and Plastics	Portland-Vancouver PMSA, OR-WA	H	7.11 FQ	12.70 AW	18.82 TQ	ORBLS	10/01-12/01
Metals and Plastics	Pennsylvania	H	8.06 FQ	12.85 AW	17.65 TQ	PABLS	10/01-12/01
Metals and Plastics	Allentown-Bethlehem-Easton MSA, PA	H	12.08 FQ	15.54 AW	19.52 TQ	PABLS	10/01-12/01
Metals and Plastics	Erie MSA, PA	H	7.45 FQ	10.96 AW	15.48 TQ	PABLS	10/01-12/01
Metals and Plastics	Johnstown MSA, PA	H	8.96 FQ	14.55 AW	21.12 TQ	PABLS	10/01-12/01
Metals and Plastics	Lancaster MSA, PA	H	9.68 FQ	13.62 AW	17.66 TQ	PABLS	10/01-12/01
Metals and Plastics	Philadelphia PMSA, PA-NJ	H	8.28 FQ	13.22 AW	17.97 TQ	PABLS	10/01-12/01
Metals and Plastics	Pittsburgh MSA, PA	H	8.30 FQ	13.39 AW	21.63 TQ	PABLS	10/01-12/01
Metals and Plastics	Scranton-Wilkes-Barre-Hazleton MSA, PA	H	7.99 FQ	11.97 AW	16.67 TQ	PABLS	10/01-12/01
Metals and Plastics	York MSA, PA	H	8.20 FQ	12.69 AW	16.38 TQ	PABLS	10/01-12/01
Metals and Plastics	Rhode Island	H	7.19 FQ	10.92 AW	15.73 TQ	RIBLS	10/01-12/01
Metals and Plastics	Providence-Fall River-Warwick MSA, RI-MA	H	7.26 FQ	11.45 AW	16.44 TQ	RIBLS	10/01-12/01
Metals and Plastics	South Carolina	H	9.23 FQ	12.21 AW	16.27 TQ	SCBLS	10/01-12/01
Metals and Plastics	Columbia MSA, SC	H	8.98 FQ	11.76 AW	16.05 TQ	SCBLS	10/01-12/01
Metals and Plastics	Greenville-Spartanburg-Anderson MSA, SC	H	9.26 FQ	12.66 AW	16.67 TQ	SCBLS	10/01-12/01
Metals and Plastics	South Dakota	H	7.98 FQ	10.92 AW	14.64 TQ	SDBLS	10/01-12/01
Metals and Plastics	Tennessee	H	7.85 FQ	12.30 AW	16.78 TQ	TNBLS	10/01-12/01
Metals and Plastics	Johnson City-Kingsport-Bristol MSA, TN-VA	H	7.01 FQ	11.40 AW	16.28 TQ	TNBLS	10/01-12/01
Metals and Plastics	Knoxville MSA, TN	H	9.02 FQ	12.26 AW	17.96 TQ	TNBLS	10/01-12/01
Metals and Plastics	Nashville MSA, TN	H	9.51 FQ	13.45 AW	19.54 TQ	TNBLS	10/01-12/01
Metals and Plastics	Texas	H	7.72 FQ	11.81 AW	17.31 TQ	TXBLS	10/01-12/01
Metals and Plastics	Austin-San Marcos MSA, TX	H	6.85 FQ	9.65 AW	12.99 TQ	TXBLS	10/01-12/01
Metals and Plastics	Corpus Christi MSA, TX	H	9.88 FQ	17.16 AW	21.20 TQ	TXBLS	10/01-12/01
Metals and Plastics	Dallas PMSA, TX	H	8.57 FQ	12.69 AW	19.26 TQ	TXBLS	10/01-12/01
Metals and Plastics	El Paso MSA, TX	H	7.87 FQ	11.60 AW	17.16 TQ	TXBLS	10/01-12/01
Metals and Plastics	Fort Worth-Arlington PMSA, TX	H	7.43 FQ	12.11 AW	20.44 TQ	TXBLS	10/01-12/01
Metals and Plastics	Houston PMSA, TX	H	8.73 FQ	11.65 AW	16.01 TQ	TXBLS	10/01-12/01
Metals and Plastics	Odessa-Midland MSA, TX	H	6.28 FQ	9.32 AW	13.15 TQ	TXBLS	10/01-12/01
Metals and Plastics	San Antonio MSA, TX	H	6.42 FQ	11.20 AW	16.23 TQ	TXBLS	10/01-12/01
Metals and Plastics	Utah	H	9.45 FQ	13.66 AW	18.81 TQ	UTBLS	10/01-12/01
Metals and Plastics	Salt Lake City-Ogden MSA, UT	H	9.53 FQ	13.79 AW	18.94 TQ	UTBLS	10/01-12/01
Metals and Plastics	Vermont	H	9.39 FQ	12.55 AW	16.94 TQ	VTBLS	10/01-12/01
Metals and Plastics	Virginia	H	8.12 FQ	11.82 AW	16.23 TQ	VABLS	10/01-12/01
Metals and Plastics	Norfolk-Virginia Beach-Newport News MSA, VA-NC	H	8.49 FQ	12.07 AW	17.13 TQ	VABLS	10/01-12/01
Metals and Plastics	Washington	H	9.47 FQ	14.92 AW	21.11 TQ	WABLS	10/01-12/01
Metals and Plastics	Seattle-Bellevue-Everett PMSA, WA	H	9.95 FQ	15.12 AW	21.03 TQ	WABLS	10/01-12/01
Metals and Plastics	Spokane MSA, WA	H	7.35 FQ	11.60 AW	15.87 TQ	WABLS	10/01-12/01
Metals and Plastics	Tacoma PMSA, WA	H	7.88 FQ	12.52 AW	16.59 TQ	WABLS	10/01-12/01
Metals and Plastics	West Virginia	H	11.59 FQ	16.49 AW	21.59 TQ	WVBLS	10/01-12/01
Metals and Plastics	Wisconsin	H	8.04 FQ	12.32 AW	16.93 TQ	WIBLS	10/01-12/01

AAW Average annual wage; **AE** Average entry wage; **AEX** Average experienced wage; **AO** Average offered; **AOH** Average offered, high; **AOL** Average offered, low; **APH** Average pay, high range; **APL** Average pay, low range; **ASH** Average starting, high; **ASL** Average starting, low; **AW** Average wage paid; **FQ** First quartile wage; **H** Hourly; **HI** Highest wage paid; **HR** High end range; **LR** Low end range; **M** Monthly; **MTC** Median total compensation; **MW** Median wage paid; **SQ** Second quartile wage; **S** Special: hourly and annual; **TQ** Third quartile wage; **W** Weekly; **Y** Yearly

Occupation/Type/Industry	Location	Per	Low	Mid	High	Source	Date
Plating and Coating Machine Setter, Operator, and Tender							
Metals and Plastics	Appleton-Oshkosh-Neenah MSA, WI	H	6.85 FQ	9.75 AW	15.64 TQ	WIBLS	10/01-12/01
Metals and Plastics	Green Bay MSA, WI	H	9.96 FQ	14.10 AW	18.04 TQ	WIBLS	10/01-12/01
Metals and Plastics	Milwaukee-Waukesha PMSA, WI	H	9.25 FQ	12.38 AW	16.83 TQ	WIBLS	10/01-12/01
Metals and Plastics	Racine PMSA, WI	H	7.05 FQ	12.23 AW	19.78 TQ	WIBLS	10/01-12/01
Metals and Plastics	Puerto Rico	H	6.18 FQ	9.21 AW	12.62 TQ	PRBLS	10/01-12/01
Plumber, Pipefitter, and Steamfitter	Alabama	H	9.37 FQ	16.44 AW	22.97 TQ	ALBLS	10/01-12/01
	Birmingham MSA, AL	H	8.91 FQ	16.06 AW	22.43 TQ	ALBLS	10/01-12/01
	Huntsville MSA, AL	H	11.58 FQ	15.90 AW	22.30 TQ	ALBLS	10/01-12/01
	Mobile MSA, AL	H	11.34 FQ	17.19 AW	22.73 TQ	ALBLS	10/01-12/01
	Montgomery MSA, AL	H	11.30 FQ	17.80 AW	26.23 TQ	ALBLS	10/01-12/01
	Alaska	H	15.41 FQ	25.98 AW	36.14 TQ	AKBLS	10/01-12/01
	Anchorage MSA, AK	H	15.64 FQ	26.19 AW	35.37 TQ	AKBLS	10/01-12/01
	Arizona	H	11.10 FQ	17.40 AW	25.47 TQ	AZBLS	10/01-12/01
	Phoenix-Mesa MSA, AZ	H	11.83 FQ	18.36 AW	25.99 TQ	AZBLS	10/01-12/01
	Tucson MSA, AZ	H	10.79 FQ	16.15 AW	24.58 TQ	AZBLS	10/01-12/01
	Arkansas	H	10.27 FQ	15.89 AW	20.87 TQ	ARBLS	10/01-12/01
	Fayetteville-Springdale-Rogers MSA, AR	H	11.47 FQ	21.52 AW	50.76 TQ	ARBLS	10/01-12/01
	Fort Smith MSA, AR-OK	H	10.33 FQ	15.81 AW	21.32 TQ	ARBLS	10/01-12/01
	Little Rock-North Little Rock MSA, AR	H	9.92 FQ	15.65 AW	21.19 TQ	ARBLS	10/01-12/01
	California	H	10.08 FQ	20.36 AW	32.66 TQ	CABLS	10/01-12/01
	Bakersfield MSA, CA	H	9.72 FQ	17.32 AW	24.08 TQ	CABLS	10/01-12/01
	Chico-Paradise MSA, CA	H	13.52 FQ	15.89 AW	21.46 TQ	CABLS	10/01-12/01
	Fresno MSA, CA	H	10.29 FQ	19.51 AW	32.57 TQ	CABLS	10/01-12/01
	Los Angeles-Long Beach PMSA, CA	H	9.38 FQ	19.25 AW	32.08 TQ	CABLS	10/01-12/01
	Merced MSA, CA	H	11.57 FQ	17.34 AW	25.90 TQ	CABLS	10/01-12/01
	Modesto MSA, CA	H	9.32 FQ	18.11 AW	27.91 TQ	CABLS	10/01-12/01
	Oakland PMSA, CA	H	12.56 FQ	25.13 AW	40.82 TQ	CABLS	10/01-12/01
	Orange County PMSA, CA	H	11.04 FQ	18.86 AW	26.54 TQ	CABLS	10/01-12/01
	Redding MSA, CA	H	11.26 FQ	15.64 AW	21.26 TQ	CABLS	10/01-12/01
	Riverside-San Bernardino PMSA, CA	H	8.59 FQ	15.49 AW	24.60 TQ	CABLS	10/01-12/01
	Sacramento PMSA, CA	H	11.14 FQ	18.69 AW	26.49 TQ	CABLS	10/01-12/01
	Salinas MSA, CA	H	11.53 FQ	19.00 AW	26.44 TQ	CABLS	10/01-12/01
	San Diego MSA, CA	H	12.51 FQ	19.55 AW	28.32 TQ	CABLS	10/01-12/01
	San Francisco PMSA, CA	H	13.48 FQ	28.30 AW	43.44 TQ	CABLS	10/01-12/01
	San Jose PMSA, CA	H	16.17 FQ	28.20 AW	41.86 TQ	CABLS	10/01-12/01
	San Luis Obispo-Atascadero-Paso Robles MSA, CA	H	12.89 FQ	20.53 AW	27.31 TQ	CABLS	10/01-12/01
	Santa Barbara-Santa Maria-Lompoc MSA, CA	H	14.33 FQ	23.68 AW	33.95 TQ	CABLS	10/01-12/01
	Santa Cruz-Watsonville PMSA, CA	H	9.38 FQ	20.24 AW	35.11 TQ	CABLS	10/01-12/01
	Santa Rosa PMSA, CA	H	15.39 FQ	25.00 AW	43.54 TQ	CABLS	10/01-12/01
	Stockton-Lodi MSA, CA	H	10.79 FQ	20.53 AW	32.57 TQ	CABLS	10/01-12/01
	Vallejo-Fairfield-Napa PMSA, CA	H	9.63 FQ	19.23 AW	32.75 TQ	CABLS	10/01-12/01
	Ventura PMSA, CA	H	9.37 FQ	17.45 AW	25.14 TQ	CABLS	10/01-12/01
	Visalia-Tulare-Porterville MSA, CA	H	10.67 FQ	18.27 AW	27.60 TQ	CABLS	10/01-12/01
	Colorado	H	11.00 FQ	19.05 AW	27.33 TQ	COBLS	10/01-12/01
	Boulder-Longmont PMSA, CO	H	12.59 FQ	20.37 AW	27.67 TQ	COBLS	10/01-12/01
	Colorado Springs MSA, CO	H	11.84 FQ	17.41 AW	22.64 TQ	COBLS	10/01-12/01
	Denver PMSA, CO	H	10.51 FQ	19.42 AW	27.63 TQ	COBLS	10/01-12/01
	Fort Collins-Loveland MSA, CO	H	11.37 FQ	17.36 AW	23.96 TQ	COBLS	10/01-12/01
	Greeley PMSA, CO	H	11.19 FQ	19.00 AW	26.94 TQ	COBLS	10/01-12/01
	Connecticut	H	13.83 FQ	21.61 AW	29.55 TQ	CTBLS	10/01-12/01
	Bridgeport PMSA, CT	H	17.27 FQ	23.75 AW	32.52 TQ	CTBLS	10/01-12/01
	Danbury PMSA, CT	H	12.23 FQ	20.35 AW	28.47 TQ	CTBLS	10/01-12/01
	Hartford MSA, CT	H	11.07 FQ	20.00 AW	28.16 TQ	CTBLS	10/01-12/01
	New Haven-Meriden PMSA, CT	H	14.98 FQ	22.19 AW	29.33 TQ	CTBLS	10/01-12/01

AAW Average annual wage; AE Average entry wage; AEX Average experienced wage; AO Average offered; AOH Average offered, high; AOL Average offered, low; APH Average pay, high range; APL Average pay, low range; ASH Average starting, high; ASL Average starting, low; AW Average wage paid; FQ First quartile wage; H Hourly; HI Highest wage paid; HR High end range; LR Low end range; M Monthly; MTC Median total compensation; MW Median wage paid; SQ Second quartile wage; S Special: hourly and annual; TQ Third quartile wage; W Weekly; Y Yearly

Occupation/Type/Industry	Location	Per	Low	Mid	High	Source	Date
Plumber, Pipefitter, and Steamfitter	New London-Norwich MSA, CT-RI	H	14.39 FQ	21.27 AW	28.89 TQ	CTBLS	10/01-12/01
	Stamford-Norwalk PMSA, CT	H	18.67 FQ	24.02 AW	28.59 TQ	CTBLS	10/01-12/01
	Waterbury PMSA, CT	H	17.21 FQ	23.41 AW	32.74 TQ	CTBLS	10/01-12/01
	Delaware	H	12.59 FQ	21.20 AW	28.67 TQ	DEBLS	10/01-12/01
	Wilmington-Newark PMSA, DE-MD	H	14.13 FQ	22.04 AW	28.76 TQ	DEBLS	10/01-12/01
	District of Columbia	H	15.65 FQ	23.34 AW	31.63 TQ	DCBLS	10/01-12/01
	Washington PMSA, DC-MD-VA-WV	H	12.77 FQ	21.29 AW	29.70 TQ	DCBLS	10/01-12/01
	Florida	H	9.79 FQ	15.35 AW	21.47 TQ	FLBLS	10/01-12/01
	Daytona Beach MSA, FL	H	9.32 FQ	13.04 AW	17.60 TQ	FLBLS	10/01-12/01
	Fort Lauderdale PMSA, FL	H	10.22 FQ	16.22 AW	23.65 TQ	FLBLS	10/01-12/01
	Fort Myers-Cape Coral MSA, FL	H	11.55 FQ	16.23 AW	21.54 TQ	FLBLS	10/01-12/01
	Fort Pierce-Port St. Lucie MSA, FL	H	10.06 FQ	14.40 AW	19.27 TQ	FLBLS	10/01-12/01
	Fort Walton Beach MSA, FL	H	9.59 FQ	14.07 AW	20.13 TQ	FLBLS	10/01-12/01
	Gainesville MSA, FL	H	9.35 FQ	13.62 AW	17.47 TQ	FLBLS	10/01-12/01
	Jacksonville MSA, FL	H	10.17 FQ	16.09 AW	21.98 TQ	FLBLS	10/01-12/01
	Lakeland-Winter Haven MSA, FL	H	10.25 FQ	18.98 AW	29.54 TQ	FLBLS	10/01-12/01
	Melbourne-Titusville-Palm Bay MSA, FL	H	7.72 FQ	14.93 AW	21.93 TQ	FLBLS	10/01-12/01
	Miami PMSA, FL	H	10.87 FQ	15.51 AW	21.04 TQ	FLBLS	10/01-12/01
	Naples MSA, FL	H	9.91 FQ	14.58 AW	19.55 TQ	FLBLS	10/01-12/01
	Ocala MSA, FL	H	8.36 FQ	13.10 AW	16.90 TQ	FLBLS	10/01-12/01
	Orlando MSA, FL	H	10.40 FQ	15.49 AW	21.17 TQ	FLBLS	10/01-12/01
	Pensacola MSA, FL	H	9.39 FQ	14.40 AW	21.57 TQ	FLBLS	10/01-12/01
	Sarasota-Bradenton MSA, FL	H	9.87 FQ	14.38 AW	18.69 TQ	FLBLS	10/01-12/01
	Tallahassee MSA, FL	H	10.18 FQ	14.05 AW	19.07 TQ	FLBLS	10/01-12/01
	Tampa-St. Petersburg-Clearwater MSA, FL	H	9.45 FQ	14.93 AW	22.03 TQ	FLBLS	10/01-12/01
	West Palm Beach-Boca Raton MSA, FL	H	9.61 FQ	15.12 AW	20.71 TQ	FLBLS	10/01-12/01
	Georgia	H	11.84 FQ	18.47 AW	26.26 TQ	GABLS	10/01-12/01
	Atlanta MSA, GA	H	13.91 FQ	20.26 AW	27.07 TQ	GABLS	10/01-12/01
	Augusta-Aiken MSA, GA-SC	H	12.42 FQ	17.79 AW	25.76 TQ	GABLS	10/01-12/01
	Columbus MSA, GA-AL	H	9.10 FQ	13.66 AW	19.64 TQ	GABLS	10/01-12/01
	Macon MSA, GA	H	11.85 FQ	16.39 AW	21.20 TQ	GABLS	10/01-12/01
	Savannah MSA, GA	H	11.70 FQ	19.40 AW	28.59 TQ	GABLS	10/01-12/01
	Hawaii	H	14.00 FQ	22.30 AW	32.54 TQ	HIBLS	10/01-12/01
	Honolulu MSA, HI	H	13.83 FQ	22.53 AW	32.82 TQ	HIBLS	10/01-12/01
	Idaho	H	11.34 FQ	19.58 AW	27.58 TQ	IDBLS	10/01-12/01
	Boise City MSA, ID	H	11.75 FQ	20.57 AW	27.84 TQ	IDBLS	10/01-12/01
	Illinois	H	14.14 FQ	26.67 AW	36.43 TQ	ILBLS	10/01-12/01
	Champaign-Urbana MSA, IL	H	17.41 FQ	28.50 AW	42.87 TQ	ILBLS	10/01-12/01
	Chicago PMSA, IL	H	15.97 FQ	28.85 AW	39.30 TQ	ILBLS	10/01-12/01
	Peoria-Pekin MSA, IL	H	18.14 FQ	24.74 AW	32.11 TQ	ILBLS	10/01-12/01
	Rockford MSA, IL	H	14.76 FQ	25.83 AW	35.19 TQ	ILBLS	10/01-12/01
	Springfield MSA, IL	H	14.28 FQ	25.72 AW	34.22 TQ	ILBLS	10/01-12/01
	Indiana	H	11.94 FQ	21.55 AW	31.62 TQ	INBLS	10/01-12/01
	Elkhart-Goshen MSA, IN	H	10.98 FQ	18.69 AW	28.54 TQ	INBLS	10/01-12/01
	Evansville-Henderson MSA, IN-KY	H	11.57 FQ	21.46 AW	28.30 TQ	INBLS	10/01-12/01
	Fort Wayne MSA, IN	H	13.54 FQ	22.23 AW	28.81 TQ	INBLS	10/01-12/01
	Gary PMSA, IN	H	14.85 FQ	24.90 AW	34.13 TQ	INBLS	10/01-12/01
	Indianapolis MSA, IN	H	10.98 FQ	20.11 AW	31.54 TQ	INBLS	10/01-12/01
	Lafayette MSA, IN	H	11.42 FQ	18.44 AW	27.35 TQ	INBLS	10/01-12/01
	South Bend MSA, IN	H	15.16 FQ	23.43 AW	32.22 TQ	INBLS	10/01-12/01
	Iowa	H	10.36 FQ	17.77 AW	26.88 TQ	IABLS	10/01-12/01
	Cedar Rapids MSA, IA	H	11.53 FQ	20.36 AW	30.31 TQ	IABLS	10/01-12/01
	Davenport-Moline-Rock Island MSA, IA-IL	H	12.72 FQ	21.18 AW	30.08 TQ	IABLS	10/01-12/01
	Des Moines MSA, IA	H	11.71 FQ	21.00 AW	29.00 TQ	IABLS	10/01-12/01
	Kansas	H	11.39 FQ	18.88 AW	29.18 TQ	KSBLS	10/01-12/01
	Topeka MSA, KS	H	9.33 FQ	15.01 AW	26.26 TQ	KSBLS	10/01-12/01
	Wichita MSA, KS	H	12.96 FQ	19.03 AW	26.77 TQ	KSBLS	10/01-12/01
	Kentucky	H	11.34 FQ	19.07 AW	27.75 TQ	KYBLS	10/01-12/01
	Lexington MSA, KY	H	11.90 FQ	17.81 AW	28.48 TQ	KYBLS	10/01-12/01
	Louisville MSA, KY-IN	H	12.59 FQ	20.41 AW	27.96 TQ	KYBLS	10/01-12/01

AAW Average annual wage; AE Average entry wage; AEX Average experienced wage; AO Average offered; AOH Average offered, high; AOL Average offered, low; APH Average pay, high range; APL Average pay, low range; ASH Average starting, high; ASL Average starting, low; AW Average wage paid; FQ First quartile wage; H Hourly; HI Highest wage paid; HR High end range; LR Low end range; M Monthly; MTC Median total compensation; MW Median wage paid; SQ Second quartile wage; S Special: hourly and annual; TQ Third quartile wage; W Weekly; Y Yearly

Occupation/Type/Industry	Location	Per	Low	Mid	High	Source	Date
Plumber, Pipefitter, and Steamfitter	Louisiana	H	10.68 FQ	16.81 AW	22.23 TQ	LABLS	10/01-12/01
	Baton Rouge MSA, LA	H	11.29 FQ	17.12 AW	21.55 TQ	LABLS	10/01-12/01
	Houma MSA, LA	H	10.40 FQ	16.13 AW	22.81 TQ	LABLS	10/01-12/01
	Lafayette MSA, LA	H	7.55 FQ	13.61 AW	20.92 TQ	LABLS	10/01-12/01
	Lake Charles MSA, LA	H	14.57 FQ	19.06 AW	25.73 TQ	LABLS	10/01-12/01
	New Orleans MSA, LA	H	11.75 FQ	16.58 AW	21.71 TQ	LABLS	10/01-12/01
	Shreveport-Bossier City MSA, LA	H	9.69 FQ	18.13 AW	28.50 TQ	LABLS	10/01-12/01
	Maine	H	11.92 FQ	16.71 AW	21.51 TQ	MEBLS	10/01-12/01
	Portland MSA, ME	H	10.72 FQ	16.44 AW	23.59 TQ	MEBLS	10/01-12/01
	Maryland	H	12.44 FQ	20.54 AW	29.04 TQ	MDBLS	10/01-12/01
	Baltimore PMSA, MD	H	12.58 FQ	20.60 AW	32.08 TQ	MDBLS	10/01-12/01
	Massachusetts	H	13.51 FQ	21.46 AW	32.73 TQ	MABLS	10/01-12/01
	Boston PMSA, MA-NH	H	13.70 FQ	21.90 AW	34.35 TQ	MABLS	10/01-12/01
	Brockton PMSA, MA	H	12.83 FQ	20.04 AW	30.41 TQ	MABLS	10/01-12/01
	Lawrence PMSA, MA-NH	H	15.61 FQ	21.92 AW	28.44 TQ	MABLS	10/01-12/01
	Lowell PMSA, MA-NH	H	15.34 FQ	22.00 AW	30.49 TQ	MABLS	10/01-12/01
	New Bedford PMSA, MA	H	13.00 FQ	23.05 AW	33.05 TQ	MABLS	10/01-12/01
	Springfield MSA, MA	H	13.58 FQ	21.27 AW	28.20 TQ	MABLS	10/01-12/01
	Worcester PMSA, MA-CT	H	10.13 FQ	19.43 AW	29.47 TQ	MABLS	10/01-12/01
	Michigan	H	14.15 FQ	24.35 AW	34.36 TQ	MIBLS	10/01-12/01
	Ann Arbor PMSA, MI	H	14.20 FQ	23.41 AW	33.68 TQ	MIBLS	10/01-12/01
	Detroit PMSA, MI	H	15.64 FQ	25.90 AW	35.39 TQ	MIBLS	10/01-12/01
	Flint PMSA, MI	H	14.81 FQ	26.14 AW	34.25 TQ	MIBLS	10/01-12/01
	Grand Rapids-Muskegon-Holland MSA, MI	H	14.39 FQ	23.40 AW	33.68 TQ	MIBLS	10/01-12/01
	Kalamazoo-Battle Creek MSA, MI	H	9.40 FQ	22.48 AW	33.78 TQ	MIBLS	10/01-12/01
	Lansing-East Lansing MSA, MI	H	14.35 FQ	23.52 AW	33.49 TQ	MIBLS	10/01-12/01
	Saginaw-Bay City-Midland MSA, MI	H	14.70 FQ	25.03 AW	33.50 TQ	MIBLS	10/01-12/01
	Minnesota	H	12.73 FQ	23.65 AW	33.31 TQ	MNBLS	10/01-12/01
	Duluth-Superior MSA, MN-WI	H	13.36 FQ	21.37 AW	29.22 TQ	MNBLS	10/01-12/01
	Minneapolis-St. Paul MSA, MN-WI	H	17.02 FQ	25.32 AW	33.31 TQ	MNBLS	10/01-12/01
	St. Cloud MSA, MN	H	13.83 FQ	24.20 AW	41.66 TQ	MNBLS	10/01-12/01
	Mississippi	H	9.15 FQ	15.02 AW	21.58 TQ	MSBLS	10/01-12/01
	Biloxi-Gulfport-Pascagoula MSA, MS	H	10.09 FQ	17.13 AW	22.48 TQ	MSBLS	10/01-12/01
	Jackson MSA, MS	H	11.04 FQ	15.33 AW	19.76 TQ	MSBLS	10/01-12/01
	Missouri	H	11.35 FQ	21.73 AW	32.45 TQ	MOBLS	10/01-12/01
	Kansas City MSA, MO-KS	H	12.00 FQ	22.10 AW	33.05 TQ	MOBLS	10/01-12/01
	St. Louis MSA, MO-IL	H	14.68 FQ	24.55 AW	33.10 TQ	MOBLS	10/01-12/01
	Springfield MSA, MO	H	11.24 FQ	18.58 AW	28.23 TQ	MOBLS	10/01-12/01
	Montana	H	11.91 FQ	20.16 AW	27.47 TQ	MTBLS	10/01-12/01
	Billings MSA, MT	H	14.22 FQ	24.09 AW	31.92 TQ	MTBLS	10/01-12/01
	Nebraska	H	9.94 FQ	17.89 AW	26.99 TQ	NEBLS	10/01-12/01
	Lincoln MSA, NE	H	9.79 FQ	15.32 AW	21.49 TQ	NEBLS	10/01-12/01
	Omaha MSA, NE-IA	H	13.82 FQ	22.30 AW	29.33 TQ	NEBLS	10/01-12/01
	Nevada	H	12.90 FQ	20.17 AW	31.75 TQ	NVBLS	10/01-12/01
	Las Vegas MSA, NV-AZ	H	11.12 FQ	19.22 AW	32.06 TQ	NVBLS	10/01-12/01
	Reno MSA, NV	H	14.06 FQ	20.32 AW	28.95 TQ	NVBLS	10/01-12/01
	New Hampshire	H	11.90 FQ	17.85 AW	25.75 TQ	NHBLS	10/01-12/01
	Manchester PMSA, NH	H	11.31 FQ	17.33 AW	25.82 TQ	NHBLS	10/01-12/01
	Portsmouth-Rochester PMSA, NH-ME	H	12.12 FQ	17.20 AW	21.89 TQ	NHBLS	10/01-12/01
	New Jersey	H	12.62 FQ	23.72 AW	34.96 TQ	NJBLS	10/01-12/01
	Atlantic-Cape May PMSA, NJ	H	11.96 FQ	20.55 AW	32.25 TQ	NJBLS	10/01-12/01
	Bergen-Passaic PMSA, NJ	H	15.81 FQ	26.66 AW	37.16 TQ	NJBLS	10/01-12/01
	Jersey City PMSA, NJ	H	11.30 FQ	20.45 AW	39.17 TQ	NJBLS	10/01-12/01
	Middlesex-Somerset-Hunterdon PMSA, NJ	H	12.22 FQ	22.88 AW	34.50 TQ	NJBLS	10/01-12/01
	Monmouth-Ocean PMSA, NJ	H	12.42 FQ	22.32 AW	34.11 TQ	NJBLS	10/01-12/01
	Newark PMSA, NJ	H	13.74 FQ	25.00 AW	35.44 TQ	NJBLS	10/01-12/01
	Trenton PMSA, NJ	H	15.48 FQ	23.04 AW	33.18 TQ	NJBLS	10/01-12/01
	New Mexico	H	9.20 FQ	17.11 AW	25.96 TQ	NMBLS	10/01-12/01
	Albuquerque MSA, NM	H	12.11 FQ	18.61 AW	26.57 TQ	NMBLS	10/01-12/01
	Las Cruces MSA, NM	H	8.04 FQ	13.53 AW	21.29 TQ	NMBLS	10/01-12/01
	New York	H	12.43 FQ	22.11 AW	36.80 TQ	NYBLS	10/01-12/01
	Albany-Schenectady-Troy MSA, NY	H	14.25 FQ	20.96 AW	27.13 TQ	NYBLS	10/01-12/01

AAW	Average annual wage	**AOH**	Average offered, high	**ASH**	Average starting, high	**H**	Hourly	**M**	Monthly	**S**	Special: hourly and annual
AE	Average entry wage	**AOL**	Average offered, low	**ASL**	Average starting, low	**HI**	Highest wage paid	**MTC**	Median total compensation	**TQ**	Third quartile wage
AEX	Average experienced wage	**APH**	Average pay, high range	**AW**	Average wage paid	**HR**	High end range	**MW**	Median wage paid	**W**	Weekly
AO	Average offered	**APL**	Average pay, low range	**FQ**	First quartile wage	**LR**	Low end range	**SQ**	Second quartile wage	**Y**	Yearly

Occupation/Type/Industry	Location	Per	Low	Mid	High	Source	Date
Plumber, Pipefitter, and Steamfitter	Binghamton MSA, NY	H	12.11 FQ	20.88 AW	29.09 TQ	NYBLS	10/01-12/01
	Buffalo-Niagara Falls MSA, NY	H	12.64 FQ	22.28 AW	31.76 TQ	NYBLS	10/01-12/01
	Dutchess County PMSA, NY	H	13.13 FQ	21.67 AW	32.22 TQ	NYBLS	10/01-12/01
	Nassau-Suffolk PMSA, NY	H	13.91 FQ	21.33 AW	36.01 TQ	NYBLS	10/01-12/01
	New York PMSA, NY	H	10.98 FQ	23.25 AW	40.91 TQ	NYBLS	10/01-12/01
	Newburgh PMSA, NY-PA	H	12.38 FQ	18.84 AW	28.52 TQ	NYBLS	10/01-12/01
	Rochester MSA, NY	H	13.21 FQ	21.71 AW	28.70 TQ	NYBLS	10/01-12/01
	Syracuse MSA, NY	H	13.73 FQ	20.77 AW	28.65 TQ	NYBLS	10/01-12/01
	Utica-Rome MSA, NY	H	13.52 FQ	22.29 AW	33.07 TQ	NYBLS	10/01-12/01
	North Carolina	H	9.82 FQ	15.01 AW	20.74 TQ	NCBLS	10/01-12/01
	Asheville MSA, NC	H	9.58 FQ	12.96 AW	17.03 TQ	NCBLS	10/01-12/01
	Charlotte-Gastonia-Rock Hill MSA, NC-SC	H	9.94 FQ	15.48 AW	21.45 TQ	NCBLS	10/01-12/01
	Fayetteville MSA, NC	H	11.17 FQ	14.75 AW	18.12 TQ	NCBLS	10/01-12/01
	Greensboro-Winston-Salem-High Point MSA, NC	H	12.14 FQ	16.33 AW	21.47 TQ	NCBLS	10/01-12/01
	Hickory-Morganton-Lenoir MSA, NC	H	9.73 FQ	13.67 AW	17.76 TQ	NCBLS	10/01-12/01
	Raleigh-Durham-Chapel Hill MSA, NC	H	10.46 FQ	16.23 AW	24.06 TQ	NCBLS	10/01-12/01
	Wilmington MSA, NC	H	10.16 FQ	14.09 AW	17.49 TQ	NCBLS	10/01-12/01
	North Dakota	H	10.38 FQ	17.55 AW	25.75 TQ	NDBLS	10/01-12/01
	Fargo-Moorhead MSA, ND-MN	H	12.47 FQ	20.88 AW	32.19 TQ	NDBLS	10/01-12/01
	Ohio	H	11.87 FQ	20.64 AW	30.55 TQ	OHBLS	10/01-12/01
	Akron PMSA, OH	H	12.31 FQ	19.98 AW	27.46 TQ	OHBLS	10/01-12/01
	Canton-Massillon MSA, OH	H	12.88 FQ	20.51 AW	28.97 TQ	OHBLS	10/01-12/01
	Cincinnati PMSA, OH-KY-IN	H	11.50 FQ	19.13 AW	27.74 TQ	OHBLS	10/01-12/01
	Cleveland-Lorain-Elyria PMSA, OH	H	13.13 FQ	21.86 AW	32.08 TQ	OHBLS	10/01-12/01
	Columbus MSA, OH	H	13.59 FQ	21.67 AW	32.26 TQ	OHBLS	10/01-12/01
	Dayton-Springfield MSA, OH	H	10.35 FQ	18.85 AW	28.67 TQ	OHBLS	10/01-12/01
	Hamilton-Middletown PMSA, OH	H	10.89 FQ	17.72 AW	26.08 TQ	OHBLS	10/01-12/01
	Mansfield MSA, OH	H	10.73 FQ	19.07 AW	28.75 TQ	OHBLS	10/01-12/01
	Toledo MSA, OH	H	14.87 FQ	24.17 AW	33.42 TQ	OHBLS	10/01-12/01
	Youngstown-Warren MSA, OH	H	16.86 FQ	24.84 AW	32.54 TQ	OHBLS	10/01-12/01
	Oklahoma	H	9.25 FQ	16.34 AW	25.19 TQ	OKBLS	10/01-12/01
	Oklahoma City MSA, OK	H	9.53 FQ	17.52 AW	27.02 TQ	OKBLS	10/01-12/01
	Tulsa MSA, OK	H	10.17 FQ	16.73 AW	25.59 TQ	OKBLS	10/01-12/01
	Oregon	H	14.76 FQ	24.40 AW	35.16 TQ	ORBLS	10/01-12/01
	Eugene-Springfield MSA, OR	H	14.99 FQ	23.12 AW	33.65 TQ	ORBLS	10/01-12/01
	Medford-Ashland MSA, OR	H	14.24 FQ	20.49 AW	34.01 TQ	ORBLS	10/01-12/01
	Portland-Vancouver PMSA, OR-WA	H	15.68 FQ	25.45 AW	35.35 TQ	ORBLS	10/01-12/01
	Salem PMSA, OR	H	11.77 FQ	21.52 AW	38.35 TQ	ORBLS	10/01-12/01
	Pennsylvania	H	11.98 FQ	20.64 AW	32.26 TQ	PABLS	10/01-12/01
	Allentown-Bethlehem-Easton MSA, PA	H	14.04 FQ	20.90 AW	29.88 TQ	PABLS	10/01-12/01
	Erie MSA, PA	H	14.71 FQ	22.07 AW	27.91 TQ	PABLS	10/01-12/01
	Harrisburg-Lebanon-Carlisle MSA, PA	H	12.77 FQ	20.89 AW	27.21 TQ	PABLS	10/01-12/01
	Johnstown MSA, PA	H	9.29 FQ	16.38 AW	23.58 TQ	PABLS	10/01-12/01
	Lancaster MSA, PA	H	11.18 FQ	15.37 AW	20.80 TQ	PABLS	10/01-12/01
	Philadelphia PMSA, PA-NJ	H	14.51 FQ	22.33 AW	34.06 TQ	PABLS	10/01-12/01
	Pittsburgh MSA, PA	H	11.36 FQ	21.84 AW	33.71 TQ	PABLS	10/01-12/01
	Reading MSA, PA	H	10.99 FQ	17.72 AW	26.45 TQ	PABLS	10/01-12/01
	Scranton-Wilkes-Barre-Hazleton MSA, PA	H	9.93 FQ	17.33 AW	26.42 TQ	PABLS	10/01-12/01
	York MSA, PA	H	13.26 FQ	18.86 AW	25.69 TQ	PABLS	10/01-12/01
	Rhode Island	H	11.76 FQ	17.46 AW	26.66 TQ	RIBLS	10/01-12/01
	Providence-Fall River-Warwick MSA, RI-MA	H	11.79 FQ	17.57 AW	26.67 TQ	RIBLS	10/01-12/01
	South Carolina	H	9.54 FQ	15.54 AW	21.56 TQ	SCBLS	10/01-12/01
	Charleston-North Charleston MSA, SC	H	7.92 FQ	13.35 AW	18.24 TQ	SCBLS	10/01-12/01
	Columbia MSA, SC	H	11.26 FQ	14.59 AW	19.44 TQ	SCBLS	10/01-12/01
	Greenville-Spartanburg-Anderson MSA, SC	H	10.97 FQ	15.31 AW	19.44 TQ	SCBLS	10/01-12/01
	Myrtle Beach MSA, SC	H	9.12 FQ	13.22 AW	17.67 TQ	SCBLS	10/01-12/01

AAW	Average annual wage	**AOH**	Average offered, high	**ASH**	Average starting, high	**H**	Hourly	**M**	Monthly	**S**	Special: hourly and annual
AE	Average entry wage	**AOL**	Average offered, low	**ASL**	Average starting, low	**HI**	Highest wage paid	**MTC**	Median total compensation	**TQ**	Third quartile wage
AEX	Average experienced wage	**APH**	Average pay, high range	**AW**	Average wage paid	**HR**	High end range	**MW**	Median wage paid	**W**	Weekly
AO	Average offered	**APL**	Average pay, low range	**FQ**	First quartile wage	**LR**	Low end range	**SQ**	Second quartile wage	**Y**	Yearly

Occupation/Type/Industry	Location	Per	Low	Mid	High	Source	Date
Plumber, Pipefitter, and Steamfitter	South Dakota	H	10.96 FQ	15.10 AW	20.85 TQ	SDBLS	10/01-12/01
	Sioux Falls MSA, SD	H	11.57 FQ	16.91 AW	23.16 TQ	SDBLS	10/01-12/01
	Tennessee	H	11.82 FQ	17.53 AW	24.47 TQ	TNBLS	10/01-12/01
	Chattanooga MSA, TN-GA	H	12.07 FQ	16.61 AW	20.93 TQ	TNBLS	10/01-12/01
	Clarksville-Hopkinsville MSA, TN-KY	H	8.88 FQ	14.63 AW	21.21 TQ	TNBLS	10/01-12/01
	Johnson City-Kingsport-Bristol MSA, TN-VA	H	9.49 FQ	14.06 AW	19.52 TQ	TNBLS	10/01-12/01
	Knoxville MSA, TN	H	10.58 FQ	15.43 AW	21.14 TQ	TNBLS	10/01-12/01
	Memphis MSA, TN-AR-MS	H	12.56 FQ	18.38 AW	25.38 TQ	TNBLS	10/01-12/01
	Nashville MSA, TN	H	13.38 FQ	18.02 AW	23.17 TQ	TNBLS	10/01-12/01
	Texas	H	9.52 FQ	16.64 AW	24.77 TQ	TXBLS	10/01-12/01
	Amarillo MSA, TX	H	11.28 FQ	18.43 AW	24.84 TQ	TXBLS	10/01-12/01
	Austin-San Marcos MSA, TX	H	10.70 FQ	17.22 AW	22.98 TQ	TXBLS	10/01-12/01
	Beaumont-Port Arthur MSA, TX	H	11.72 FQ	19.87 AW	27.08 TQ	TXBLS	10/01-12/01
	Brazoria PMSA, TX	H	11.81 FQ	17.00 AW	22.40 TQ	TXBLS	10/01-12/01
	Brownsville-Harlingen-San Benito MSA, TX	H	7.70 FQ	10.69 AW	13.95 TQ	TXBLS	10/01-12/01
	Corpus Christi MSA, TX	H	9.86 FQ	17.88 AW	26.53 TQ	TXBLS	10/01-12/01
	Dallas PMSA, TX	H	9.31 FQ	15.79 AW	22.03 TQ	TXBLS	10/01-12/01
	El Paso MSA, TX	H	9.53 FQ	14.16 AW	21.46 TQ	TXBLS	10/01-12/01
	Fort Worth-Arlington PMSA, TX	H	11.59 FQ	17.91 AW	24.50 TQ	TXBLS	10/01-12/01
	Galveston-Texas City PMSA, TX	H	10.98 FQ	18.32 AW	26.21 TQ	TXBLS	10/01-12/01
	Houston PMSA, TX	H	11.07 FQ	18.51 AW	27.07 TQ	TXBLS	10/01-12/01
	Killeen-Temple MSA, TX	H	7.21 FQ	12.36 AW	19.19 TQ	TXBLS	10/01-12/01
	Laredo MSA, TX	H	6.54 FQ	10.30 AW	15.99 TQ	TXBLS	10/01-12/01
	Longview-Marshall MSA, TX	H	7.94 FQ	11.48 AW	17.51 TQ	TXBLS	10/01-12/01
	Lubbock MSA, TX	H	8.60 FQ	13.83 AW	18.85 TQ	TXBLS	10/01-12/01
	McAllen-Edinburg-Mission MSA, TX	H	7.17 FQ	11.06 AW	17.98 TQ	TXBLS	10/01-12/01
	Odessa-Midland MSA, TX	H	8.97 FQ	14.10 AW	19.67 TQ	TXBLS	10/01-12/01
	San Antonio MSA, TX	H	10.03 FQ	15.25 AW	21.99 TQ	TXBLS	10/01-12/01
	Tyler MSA, TX	H	7.86 FQ	13.14 AW	18.05 TQ	TXBLS	10/01-12/01
	Waco MSA, TX	H	9.34 FQ	15.57 AW	21.44 TQ	TXBLS	10/01-12/01
	Utah	H	11.92 FQ	19.06 AW	26.02 TQ	UTBLS	10/01-12/01
	Provo-Orem MSA, UT	H	10.80 FQ	17.39 AW	23.31 TQ	UTBLS	10/01-12/01
	Salt Lake City-Ogden MSA, UT	H	11.87 FQ	19.66 AW	26.28 TQ	UTBLS	10/01-12/01
	Vermont	H	10.02 FQ	15.81 AW	23.27 TQ	VTBLS	10/01-12/01
	Burlington MSA, VT	H	11.27 FQ	18.07 AW	25.88 TQ	VTBLS	10/01-12/01
	Virginia	H	10.89 FQ	16.51 AW	23.82 TQ	VABLS	10/01-12/01
	Lynchburg MSA, VA	H	10.58 FQ	17.54 AW	22.83 TQ	VABLS	10/01-12/01
	Norfolk-Virginia Beach-Newport News MSA, VA-NC	H	12.31 FQ	16.58 AW	20.88 TQ	VABLS	10/01-12/01
	Richmond-Petersburg MSA, VA	H	11.19 FQ	14.88 AW	20.84 TQ	VABLS	10/01-12/01
	Roanoke MSA, VA	H	5.81 FQ	10.89 AW	17.33 TQ	VABLS	10/01-12/01
	Washington	H	13.00 FQ	23.58 AW	33.95 TQ	WABLS	10/01-12/01
	Bremerton PMSA, WA	H	14.05 FQ	25.14 AW	38.77 TQ	WABLS	10/01-12/01
	Olympia PMSA, WA	H	16.00 FQ	21.84 AW	26.84 TQ	WABLS	10/01-12/01
	Richland-Kennewick-Pasco MSA, WA	H	17.74 FQ	25.17 AW	33.98 TQ	WABLS	10/01-12/01
	Seattle-Bellevue-Everett PMSA, WA	H	13.95 FQ	25.02 AW	34.87 TQ	WABLS	10/01-12/01
	Spokane MSA, WA	H	16.17 FQ	23.24 AW	29.37 TQ	WABLS	10/01-12/01
	Tacoma PMSA, WA	H	11.69 FQ	21.88 AW	33.38 TQ	WABLS	10/01-12/01
	Yakima MSA, WA	H	17.30 FQ	22.28 AW	27.65 TQ	WABLS	10/01-12/01
	West Virginia	H	8.43 FQ	17.44 AW	27.08 TQ	WVBLS	10/01-12/01
	Charleston MSA, WV	H	10.95 FQ	19.08 AW	29.95 TQ	WVBLS	10/01-12/01
	Huntington-Ashland MSA, WV-KY-OH	H	9.55 FQ	18.90 AW	27.25 TQ	WVBLS	10/01-12/01
	Wisconsin	H	10.54 FQ	21.50 AW	33.14 TQ	WIBLS	10/01-12/01
	Appleton-Oshkosh-Neenah MSA, WI	H	12.34 FQ	20.36 AW	28.83 TQ	WIBLS	10/01-12/01
	Green Bay MSA, WI	H	17.47 FQ	25.41 AW	34.47 TQ	WIBLS	10/01-12/01
	Madison MSA, WI	H	13.38 FQ	23.47 AW	33.57 TQ	WIBLS	10/01-12/01

AAW Average annual wage **AOH** Average offered, high **ASH** Average starting, high **H** Hourly **M** Monthly **S** Special: hourly and annual
AE Average entry wage **AOL** Average offered, low **ASL** Average starting, low **HI** Highest wage paid **MTC** Median total compensation **TQ** Third quartile wage
AEX Average experienced wage **APH** Average pay, high range **AW** Average wage paid **HR** High end range **MW** Median wage paid **W** Weekly
AO Average offered **APL** Average pay, low range **FQ** First quartile wage **LR** Low end range **SQ** Second quartile wage **Y** Yearly

Occupation/Type/Industry	Location	Per	Low	Mid	High	Source	Date
Plumber, Pipefitter, and Steamfitter	Milwaukee-Waukesha PMSA, WI	H	16.41 FQ	27.25 AW	37.84 TQ	WIBLS	10/01-12/01
	Racine PMSA, WI	H	13.56 FQ	27.52 AW	36.32 TQ	WIBLS	10/01-12/01
	Wyoming	H	8.97 FQ	15.68 AW	24.66 TQ	WYBLS	10/01-12/01
	Cheyenne MSA, WY	H	10.52 FQ	18.53 AW	25.96 TQ	WYBLS	10/01-12/01
	Puerto Rico	H	5.82 FQ	7.74 AW	10.32 TQ	PRBLS	10/01-12/01
	Virgin Islands	H	13.33 FQ	16.43 AW	20.68 TQ	VIBLS	10/01-12/01
	Guam	H	10.14 FQ	13.83 AW	19.17 TQ	GUBLS	10/01-12/01
Podiatrist	Arizona	Y	64330 FQ	105860 AW	140650 TQ	AZBLS	10/01-12/01
	Phoenix-Mesa MSA, AZ	Y	91110 FQ	110530 AW	141650 TQ	AZBLS	10/01-12/01
	California	Y	53950 FQ	77600 AW	117640 TQ	CABLS	10/01-12/01
	Fresno MSA, CA	Y	78680 FQ	95240 AW	116280 TQ	CABLS	10/01-12/01
	San Diego MSA, CA	Y	81150 FQ	109220 AW	143590 TQ	CABLS	10/01-12/01
	Colorado	Y	27500 FQ	86290 AW		COBLS	10/01-12/01
	Connecticut	Y	33080 FQ	96510 AW		CTBLS	10/01-12/01
	Washington PMSA, DC-MD-VA-WV	Y	65120 FQ	109490 AW		DCBLS	10/01-12/01
	Florida	Y	32240 FQ	88280 AW		FLBLS	10/01-12/01
	Fort Lauderdale PMSA, FL	Y	91300 FQ	98290 AW	115320 TQ	FLBLS	10/01-12/01
	Fort Myers-Cape Coral MSA, FL	Y	127160 FQ	138440 AW		FLBLS	10/01-12/01
	Miami PMSA, FL	Y	27460 FQ	71850 AW	114610 TQ	FLBLS	10/01-12/01
	West Palm Beach-Boca Raton MSA, FL	Y	37310 FQ	60810 AW	93240 TQ	FLBLS	10/01-12/01
	Georgia	Y	22890 FQ	82580 AW		GABLS	10/01-12/01
	Illinois	Y	25570 FQ	80450 AW		ILBLS	10/01-12/01
	Chicago PMSA, IL	Y	24110 FQ	75600 AW		ILBLS	10/01-12/01
	Indiana	Y	112610 FQ	127110 AW		INBLS	10/01-12/01
	Gary PMSA, IN	Y	122290 FQ	133170 AW		INBLS	10/01-12/01
	Iowa	Y	58800 FQ	103990 AW		IABLS	10/01-12/01
	Maryland	Y	27010 FQ	92110 AW		MDBLS	10/01-12/01
	Baltimore PMSA, MD	Y	24470 FQ	83080 AW		MDBLS	10/01-12/01
	Massachusetts	Y	43990 FQ	116940 AW		MABLS	10/01-12/01
	Boston PMSA, MA-NH	Y	47390 FQ	124140 AW		MABLS	10/01-12/01
	Minnesota	Y	54080 FQ	101050 AW		MNBLS	10/01-12/01
	Minneapolis-St. Paul MSA, MN-WI	Y	41760 FQ	97420 AW		MNBLS	10/01-12/01
	Kansas City MSA, MO-KS	Y	36290 FQ	58400 AW	98120 TQ	MOBLS	10/01-12/01
	Las Vegas MSA, NV-AZ	Y	117210 FQ	133330 AW		NVBLS	10/01-12/01
	New Jersey	Y	41850 FQ	80450 AW	136910 TQ	NJBLS	10/01-12/01
	Monmouth-Ocean PMSA, NJ	Y	62090 FQ	74350 AW	90350 TQ	NJBLS	10/01-12/01
	New York	Y	37790 FQ	72540 AW	143430 TQ	NYBLS	10/01-12/01
	Nassau-Suffolk PMSA, NY	Y	58220 FQ	71260 AW	108190 TQ	NYBLS	10/01-12/01
	New York PMSA, NY	Y	36280 FQ	63160 AW	140610 TQ	NYBLS	10/01-12/01
	Rochester MSA, NY	Y	81710 FQ	115150 AW	144540 TQ	NYBLS	10/01-12/01
	Ohio	Y	43060 FQ	88900 AW		OHBLS	10/01-12/01
	Canton-Massillon MSA, OH	Y	76570 FQ	84750 AW	93750 TQ	OHBLS	10/01-12/01
	Cincinnati PMSA, OH-KY-IN	Y	77010 FQ	96990 AW		OHBLS	10/01-12/01
	Cleveland-Lorain-Elyria PMSA, OH	Y	26250 FQ	65910 AW	104470 TQ	OHBLS	10/01-12/01
	Oregon	Y	53450 FQ	102930 AW		ORBLS	10/01-12/01
	Pennsylvania	Y	49990 FQ	86730 AW	133460 TQ	PABLS	10/01-12/01
	Erie MSA, PA	Y	77640 FQ	83410 AW	95990 TQ	PABLS	10/01-12/01
	Philadelphia PMSA, PA-NJ	Y	28760 FQ	80670 AW	136740 TQ	PABLS	10/01-12/01
	Pittsburgh MSA, PA	Y	50070 FQ	72520 AW	91670 TQ	PABLS	10/01-12/01
	Scranton-Wilkes-Barre-Hazleton MSA, PA	Y	89480 FQ	110920 AW	144340 TQ	PABLS	10/01-12/01
	York MSA, PA	Y	92540 FQ	104310 AW	135590 TQ	PABLS	10/01-12/01
	Rhode Island	Y	76200 FQ	109360 AW		RIBLS	10/01-12/01
	Providence-Fall River-Warwick MSA, RI-MA	Y	74280 FQ	108200 AW		RIBLS	10/01-12/01
	South Carolina	Y	76610 FQ	87150 AW	94010 TQ	SCBLS	10/01-12/01
	Tennessee	Y	17340 FQ	97450 AW		TNBLS	10/01-12/01
	Texas	Y	83050 FQ	120500 AW		TXBLS	10/01-12/01
	Virginia	Y	68410 FQ	109920 AW		VABLS	10/01-12/01
	Richmond-Petersburg MSA, VA	Y	78480 FQ	94360 AW	116290 TQ	VABLS	10/01-12/01
	Washington	Y	99050 FQ	119320 AW		WABLS	10/01-12/01
	Seattle-Bellevue-Everett PMSA, WA	Y	99260 FQ	119510 AW		WABLS	10/01-12/01

AAW	Average annual wage	**AOH**	Average offered, high	**ASH**	Average starting, high	**H**	Hourly	**M**	Monthly	**S**	Special: hourly and annual
AE	Average entry wage	**AOL**	Average offered, low	**ASL**	Average starting, low	**HI**	Highest wage paid	**MTC**	Median total compensation	**TQ**	Third quartile wage
AEX	Average experienced wage	**APH**	Average pay, high range	**AW**	Average wage paid	**HR**	High end range	**MW**	Median wage paid	**W**	Weekly
AO	Average offered	**APL**	Average pay, low range	**FQ**	First quartile wage	**LR**	Low end range	**SQ**	Second quartile wage	**Y**	Yearly

Occupation/Type/Industry	Location	Per	Low	Mid	High	Source	Date
Podiatrist	Wisconsin	Y	56640 FQ	109140 AW		WIBLS	10/01-12/01
Police and Detective Supervisor	United States	Y		57210 MW		OOH2	1/99-1/00
Federal government	United States	Y		74070 MW		OOH2	1/99-1/00
Local government	United States	Y		57030 MW		OOH2	1/99-1/00
State government	United States	Y		53960 MW		OOH2	1/99-1/00
Police and Sheriff's Patrol Officer	Alabama	Y	20970 FQ	30690 AW	41710 TQ	ALBLS	10/01-12/01
	Birmingham MSA, AL	Y	27340 FQ	35500 AW	47600 TQ	ALBLS	10/01-12/01
	Huntsville MSA, AL	Y	25150 FQ	34850 AW	45800 TQ	ALBLS	10/01-12/01
	Mobile MSA, AL	Y	23530 FQ	28700 AW	36410 TQ	ALBLS	10/01-12/01
	Alaska	Y	26720 FQ	49590 AW	69460 TQ	AKBLS	10/01-12/01
	Arizona	Y	29730 FQ	42080 AW	56200 TQ	AZBLS	10/01-12/01
	Phoenix-Mesa MSA, AZ	Y	33200 FQ	45860 AW	58150 TQ	AZBLS	10/01-12/01
	Tucson MSA, AZ	Y	29680 FQ	38840 AW	51800 TQ	AZBLS	10/01-12/01
	Arkansas	Y	18530 FQ	28210 AW	40730 TQ	ARBLS	10/01-12/01
	Fayetteville-Springdale-Rogers MSA, AR	Y	18980 FQ	26010 AW	34270 TQ	ARBLS	10/01-12/01
	Fort Smith MSA, AR-OK	Y	18140 FQ	28910 AW	42850 TQ	ARBLS	10/01-12/01
	Little Rock-North Little Rock MSA, AR	Y	22280 FQ	31830 AW	43100 TQ	ARBLS	10/01-12/01
	California	Y	38180 FQ	54500 AW	73810 TQ	CABLS	10/01-12/01
	Bakersfield MSA, CA	Y	40270 FQ	54020 AW	70050 TQ	CABLS	10/01-12/01
	Chico-Paradise MSA, CA	Y	38380 FQ	48690 AW	64650 TQ	CABLS	10/01-12/01
	Fresno MSA, CA	Y	32840 FQ	59570 AW	74420 TQ	CABLS	10/01-12/01
	Los Angeles-Long Beach PMSA, CA	Y	38790 FQ	51190 AW	71420 TQ	CABLS	10/01-12/01
	Merced MSA, CA	Y	35010 FQ	47740 AW	60300 TQ	CABLS	10/01-12/01
	Modesto MSA, CA	Y	38000 FQ	47750 AW	58960 TQ	CABLS	10/01-12/01
	Oakland PMSA, CA	Y	49420 FQ	65860 AW	87130 TQ	CABLS	10/01-12/01
	Orange County PMSA, CA	Y	40860 FQ	60730 AW	75990 TQ	CABLS	10/01-12/01
	Redding MSA, CA	Y	39700 FQ	55690 AW	71650 TQ	CABLS	10/01-12/01
	Riverside-San Bernardino PMSA, CA	Y	38980 FQ	53920 AW	69490 TQ	CABLS	10/01-12/01
	Sacramento PMSA, CA	Y	39820 FQ	55430 AW	72710 TQ	CABLS	10/01-12/01
	Salinas MSA, CA	Y	30720 FQ	49940 AW	70990 TQ	CABLS	10/01-12/01
	San Diego MSA, CA	Y	38970 FQ	56660 AW	73470 TQ	CABLS	10/01-12/01
	San Francisco PMSA, CA	Y	49060 FQ	66270 AW	89370 TQ	CABLS	10/01-12/01
	San Jose PMSA, CA	Y	39170 FQ	54700 AW	74570 TQ	CABLS	10/01-12/01
	San Luis Obispo-Atascadero-Paso Robles MSA, CA	Y	39360 FQ	50600 AW	66850 TQ	CABLS	10/01-12/01
	Santa Barbara-Santa Maria-Lompoc MSA, CA	Y	38930 FQ	52530 AW	71780 TQ	CABLS	10/01-12/01
	Santa Cruz-Watsonville PMSA, CA	Y	39160 FQ	52710 AW	72560 TQ	CABLS	10/01-12/01
	Santa Rosa PMSA, CA	Y	45580 FQ	57540 AW	73910 TQ	CABLS	10/01-12/01
	Stockton-Lodi MSA, CA	Y	38840 FQ	52090 AW	64400 TQ	CABLS	10/01-12/01
	Vallejo-Fairfield-Napa PMSA, CA	Y	50330 FQ	60100 AW	70830 TQ	CABLS	10/01-12/01
	Ventura PMSA, CA	Y	39290 FQ	53960 AW	71710 TQ	CABLS	10/01-12/01
	Visalia-Tulare-Porterville MSA, CA	Y	38190 FQ	50920 AW	67760 TQ	CABLS	10/01-12/01
	Colorado	Y	30880 FQ	45490 AW	61720 TQ	COBLS	10/01-12/01
	Boulder-Longmont PMSA, CO	Y	35640 FQ	50200 AW	68510 TQ	COBLS	10/01-12/01
	Denver PMSA, CO	Y	34490 FQ	48280 AW	65230 TQ	COBLS	10/01-12/01
	Fort Collins-Loveland MSA, CO	Y	28720 FQ	46980 AW	65350 TQ	COBLS	10/01-12/01
	Greeley PMSA, CO	Y	30370 FQ	37270 AW	50360 TQ	COBLS	10/01-12/01
	Connecticut	Y	37930 FQ	47680 AW	58110 TQ	CTBLS	10/01-12/01
	Bridgeport PMSA, CT	Y	38370 FQ	47150 AW	58230 TQ	CTBLS	10/01-12/01
	Danbury PMSA, CT	Y	36030 FQ	47040 AW	58150 TQ	CTBLS	10/01-12/01
	Hartford MSA, CT	Y	37650 FQ	47390 AW	57990 TQ	CTBLS	10/01-12/01
	New Haven-Meriden PMSA, CT	Y	38530 FQ	48710 AW	58220 TQ	CTBLS	10/01-12/01
	New London-Norwich MSA, CT-RI	Y	36320 FQ	45150 AW	56460 TQ	CTBLS	10/01-12/01
	Stamford-Norwalk PMSA, CT	Y	42030 FQ	51360 AW	59630 TQ	CTBLS	10/01-12/01
	Waterbury PMSA, CT	Y	38050 FQ	47610 AW	56960 TQ	CTBLS	10/01-12/01
	Delaware	Y	27930 FQ	45170 AW	65140 TQ	DEBLS	10/01-12/01
	Wilmington-Newark PMSA, DE-MD	Y	30730 FQ	45250 AW	63680 TQ	DEBLS	10/01-12/01
	Washington PMSA, DC-MD-VA-WV	Y	33280 FQ	50620 AW	70340 TQ	DCBLS	10/01-12/01

AAW	Average annual wage	**AOH**	Average offered, high	**ASH**	Average starting, high	**H**	Hourly	**M**	Monthly	**S**	Special: hourly and annual
AE	Average entry wage	**AOL**	Average offered, low	**ASL**	Average starting, low	**HI**	Highest wage paid	**MTC**	Median total compensation	**TQ**	Third quartile wage
AEX	Average experienced wage	**APH**	Average pay, high range	**AW**	Average wage paid	**HR**	High end range	**MW**	Median wage paid	**W**	Weekly
AO	Average offered	**APL**	Average pay, low range	**FQ**	First quartile wage	**LR**	Low end range	**SQ**	Second quartile wage	**Y**	Yearly

Occupation/Type/Industry	Location	Per	Low	Mid	High	Source	Date
Police and Sheriff's Patrol Officer	Florida	Y	27660 FQ	42750 AW	58800 TQ	FLBLS	10/01-12/01
	Daytona Beach MSA, FL	Y	23050 FQ	32600 AW	44620 TQ	FLBLS	10/01-12/01
	Fort Lauderdale PMSA, FL	Y	38390 FQ	49810 AW	62300 TQ	FLBLS	10/01-12/01
	Fort Myers-Cape Coral MSA, FL	Y	25960 FQ	36120 AW	46820 TQ	FLBLS	10/01-12/01
	Fort Pierce-Port St. Lucie MSA, FL	Y	25990 FQ	37680 AW	51670 TQ	FLBLS	10/01-12/01
	Fort Walton Beach MSA, FL	Y	22370 FQ	30620 AW	42470 TQ	FLBLS	10/01-12/01
	Gainesville MSA, FL	Y	26430 FQ	37300 AW	51660 TQ	FLBLS	10/01-12/01
	Lakeland-Winter Haven MSA, FL	Y	25330 FQ	34990 AW	45320 TQ	FLBLS	10/01-12/01
	Melbourne-Titusville-Palm Bay MSA, FL	Y	26010 FQ	35550 AW	45430 TQ	FLBLS	10/01-12/01
	Miami PMSA, FL	Y	35950 FQ	48540 AW	63570 TQ	FLBLS	10/01-12/01
	Naples MSA, FL	Y	27420 FQ	38340 AW	50870 TQ	FLBLS	10/01-12/01
	Orlando MSA, FL	Y	28600 FQ	40230 AW	56090 TQ	FLBLS	10/01-12/01
	Pensacola MSA, FL	Y	23860 FQ	35390 AW	47950 TQ	FLBLS	10/01-12/01
	Sarasota-Bradenton MSA, FL	Y	26200 FQ	39710 AW	56120 TQ	FLBLS	10/01-12/01
	Tallahassee MSA, FL	Y	27770 FQ	36860 AW	46340 TQ	FLBLS	10/01-12/01
	Tampa-St. Petersburg-Clearwater MSA, FL	Y	30650 FQ	44500 AW	58730 TQ	FLBLS	10/01-12/01
	West Palm Beach-Boca Raton MSA, FL	Y	32360 FQ	46960 AW	65170 TQ	FLBLS	10/01-12/01
	Georgia	Y	21630 FQ	32150 AW	44580 TQ	GABLS	10/01-12/01
	Atlanta MSA, GA	Y	26080 FQ	36370 AW	46890 TQ	GABLS	10/01-12/01
	Augusta-Aiken MSA, GA-SC	Y	20740 FQ	29710 AW	41170 TQ	GABLS	10/01-12/01
	Macon MSA, GA	Y	20570 FQ	28270 AW	36690 TQ	GABLS	10/01-12/01
	Savannah MSA, GA	Y	24780 FQ	33960 AW	44560 TQ	GABLS	10/01-12/01
	Hawaii	Y	29520 FQ	37160 AW	44550 TQ	HIBLS	10/01-12/01
	Honolulu MSA, HI	Y	29330 FQ	36980 AW	44580 TQ	HIBLS	10/01-12/01
	Idaho	Y	22720 FQ	32980 AW	47000 TQ	IDBLS	10/01-12/01
	Boise City MSA, ID	Y	27830 FQ	40990 AW	55390 TQ	IDBLS	10/01-12/01
	Illinois	Y	23100 FQ	42310 AW	62230 TQ	ILBLS	10/01-12/01
	Champaign-Urbana MSA, IL	Y	28290 FQ	44030 AW	62480 TQ	ILBLS	10/01-12/01
	Chicago PMSA, IL	Y	26320 FQ	44370 AW	63520 TQ	ILBLS	10/01-12/01
	Peoria-Pekin MSA, IL	Y	19760 FQ	39950 AW	61290 TQ	ILBLS	10/01-12/01
	Rockford MSA, IL	Y	25000 FQ	42380 AW	60710 TQ	ILBLS	10/01-12/01
	Springfield MSA, IL	Y	24530 FQ	45870 AW	73400 TQ	ILBLS	10/01-12/01
	Indiana	Y	24710 FQ	34090 AW	44150 TQ	INBLS	10/01-12/01
	Elkhart-Goshen MSA, IN	Y	27090 FQ	33550 AW	42200 TQ	INBLS	10/01-12/01
	Evansville-Henderson MSA, IN-KY	Y	22950 FQ	30530 AW	42420 TQ	INBLS	10/01-12/01
	Fort Wayne MSA, IN	Y	27080 FQ	34590 AW	43520 TQ	INBLS	10/01-12/01
	Gary PMSA, IN	Y	30440 FQ	38190 AW	46250 TQ	INBLS	10/01-12/01
	Indianapolis MSA, IN	Y	25740 FQ	34980 AW	44710 TQ	INBLS	10/01-12/01
	Lafayette MSA, IN	Y	26610 FQ	36200 AW	45290 TQ	INBLS	10/01-12/01
	South Bend MSA, IN	Y	26460 FQ	35520 AW	44220 TQ	INBLS	10/01-12/01
	Iowa	Y	24400 FQ	37210 AW	51700 TQ	IABLS	10/01-12/01
	Cedar Rapids MSA, IA	Y	30940 FQ	40030 AW	46930 TQ	IABLS	10/01-12/01
	Davenport-Moline-Rock Island MSA, IA-IL	Y	26290 FQ	42340 AW	56830 TQ	IABLS	10/01-12/01
	Des Moines MSA, IA	Y	31040 FQ	44760 AW	59820 TQ	IABLS	10/01-12/01
	Kansas	Y	20700 FQ	31900 AW	44920 TQ	KSBLS	10/01-12/01
	Topeka MSA, KS	Y	25980 FQ	36220 AW	45280 TQ	KSBLS	10/01-12/01
	Wichita MSA, KS	Y	21780 FQ	31220 AW	42060 TQ	KSBLS	10/01-12/01
	Kentucky	Y	20170 FQ	31590 AW	45220 TQ	KYBLS	10/01-12/01
	Lexington MSA, KY	Y	22840 FQ	31420 AW	37680 TQ	KYBLS	10/01-12/01
	Louisville MSA, KY-IN	Y	22390 FQ	35180 AW	50180 TQ	KYBLS	10/01-12/01
	Louisiana	Y	15010 FQ	24760 AW	34870 TQ	LABLS	10/01-12/01
	Baton Rouge MSA, LA	Y	20290 FQ	28940 AW	37220 TQ	LABLS	10/01-12/01
	Houma MSA, LA	Y	20290 FQ	25180 AW	31140 TQ	LABLS	10/01-12/01
	Lafayette MSA, LA	Y	13010 FQ	28370 AW	42790 TQ	LABLS	10/01-12/01
	Lake Charles MSA, LA	Y	15670 FQ	24130 AW	35990 TQ	LABLS	10/01-12/01
	New Orleans MSA, LA	Y	14980 FQ	24760 AW	32310 TQ	LABLS	10/01-12/01
	Maine	Y	18050 FQ	29700 AW	41810 TQ	MEBLS	10/01-12/01
	Portland MSA, ME	Y	26220 FQ	34420 AW	43220 TQ	MEBLS	10/01-12/01
	Maryland	Y	30380 FQ	44290 AW	60740 TQ	MDBLS	10/01-12/01
	Baltimore PMSA, MD	Y	30210 FQ	43680 AW	57390 TQ	MDBLS	10/01-12/01
	Massachusetts	Y	27050 FQ	44320 AW	66220 TQ	MABLS	10/01-12/01
	Boston PMSA, MA-NH	Y	27200 FQ	47660 AW	69270 TQ	MABLS	10/01-12/01
	Brockton PMSA, MA	Y	27050 FQ	42990 AW	63380 TQ	MABLS	10/01-12/01
	Lawrence PMSA, MA-NH	Y	26500 FQ	41810 AW	56500 TQ	MABLS	10/01-12/01

AAW	Average annual wage	**AOH**	Average offered, high	**ASH**	Average starting, high	**H**	Hourly	**M**	Monthly	**S**	Special: hourly and annual
AE	Average entry wage	**AOL**	Average offered, low	**ASL**	Average starting, low	**HI**	Highest wage paid	**MTC**	Median total compensation	**TQ**	Third quartile wage
AEX	Average experienced wage	**APH**	Average pay, high range	**AW**	Average wage paid	**HR**	High end range	**MW**	Median wage paid	**W**	Weekly
AO	Average offered	**APL**	Average pay, low range	**FQ**	First quartile wage	**LR**	Low end range	**SQ**	Second quartile wage	**Y**	Yearly

Occupation/Type/Industry	Location	Per	Low	Mid	High	Source	Date
Police and Sheriff's Patrol Officer	Lowell PMSA, MA-NH	Y	34650 FQ	42660 AW	53350 TQ	MABLS	10/01-12/01
	New Bedford PMSA, MA	Y	30980 FQ	42330 AW	60480 TQ	MABLS	10/01-12/01
	Springfield MSA, MA	Y	27850 FQ	38220 AW	51410 TQ	MABLS	10/01-12/01
	Worcester PMSA, MA-CT	Y	26400 FQ	42250 AW	58180 TQ	MABLS	10/01-12/01
	Michigan	Y	29610 FQ	41830 AW	54880 TQ	MIBLS	10/01-12/01
	Ann Arbor PMSA, MI	Y	33390 FQ	43050 AW	55130 TQ	MIBLS	10/01-12/01
	Detroit PMSA, MI	Y	30670 FQ	43620 AW	55600 TQ	MIBLS	10/01-12/01
	Flint PMSA, MI	Y	26520 FQ	39430 AW	51940 TQ	MIBLS	10/01-12/01
	Grand Rapids-Muskegon-Holland MSA, MI	Y	29840 FQ	43020 AW	55680 TQ	MIBLS	10/01-12/01
	Kalamazoo-Battle Creek MSA, MI	Y	30850 FQ	42980 AW	55270 TQ	MIBLS	10/01-12/01
	Lansing-East Lansing MSA, MI	Y	30030 FQ	42050 AW	54960 TQ	MIBLS	10/01-12/01
	Saginaw-Bay City-Midland MSA, MI	Y	30130 FQ	40570 AW	51610 TQ	MIBLS	10/01-12/01
	Minnesota	Y	27150 FQ	41990 AW	56100 TQ	MNBLS	10/01-12/01
	Duluth-Superior MSA, MN-WI	Y	33500 FQ	40990 AW	48000 TQ	MNBLS	10/01-12/01
	Minneapolis-St. Paul MSA, MN-WI	Y	34380 FQ	46880 AW	58110 TQ	MNBLS	10/01-12/01
	St. Cloud MSA, MN	Y	26680 FQ	38160 AW	49790 TQ	MNBLS	10/01-12/01
	Mississippi	Y	14860 FQ	25260 AW	34490 TQ	MSBLS	10/01-12/01
	Biloxi-Gulfport-Pascagoula MSA, MS	Y	17670 FQ	28260 AW	37640 TQ	MSBLS	10/01-12/01
	Jackson MSA, MS	Y	20660 FQ	28060 AW	36330 TQ	MSBLS	10/01-12/01
	Missouri	Y	15870 FQ	28570 AW	44850 TQ	MOBLS	10/01-12/01
	Kansas City MSA, MO-KS	Y	16410 FQ	32370 AW	49570 TQ	MOBLS	10/01-12/01
	St. Louis MSA, MO-IL	Y	18390 FQ	30850 AW	47100 TQ	MOBLS	10/01-12/01
	Springfield MSA, MO	Y	17750 FQ	23480 AW	29190 TQ	MOBLS	10/01-12/01
	Montana	Y	22280 FQ	32230 AW	43930 TQ	MTBLS	10/01-12/01
	Nebraska	Y	22090 FQ	36650 AW	55350 TQ	NEBLS	10/01-12/01
	Nevada	Y	35750 FQ	48480 AW	59940 TQ	NVBLS	10/01-12/01
	Reno MSA, NV	Y	34780 FQ	47000 AW	57990 TQ	NVBLS	10/01-12/01
	New Hampshire	Y	23510 FQ	36100 AW	49620 TQ	NHBLS	10/01-12/01
	Nashua PMSA, NH	Y	33220 FQ	44630 AW	56170 TQ	NHBLS	10/01-12/01
	Portsmouth-Rochester PMSA, NH-ME	Y	26110 FQ	36450 AW	48010 TQ	NHBLS	10/01-12/01
	New Jersey	Y	34210 FQ	58200 AW	82050 TQ	NJBLS	10/01-12/01
	Atlantic-Cape May PMSA, NJ	Y	35760 FQ	52230 AW	68710 TQ	NJBLS	10/01-12/01
	Bergen-Passaic PMSA, NJ	Y	40850 FQ	67970 AW	90900 TQ	NJBLS	10/01-12/01
	Jersey City PMSA, NJ	Y	33420 FQ	59930 AW	85730 TQ	NJBLS	10/01-12/01
	Middlesex-Somerset-Hunterdon PMSA, NJ	Y	37490 FQ	59030 AW	77150 TQ	NJBLS	10/01-12/01
	Monmouth-Ocean PMSA, NJ	Y	28800 FQ	58540 AW	86630 TQ	NJBLS	10/01-12/01
	Newark PMSA, NJ	Y	32520 FQ	55800 AW	74960 TQ	NJBLS	10/01-12/01
	Trenton PMSA, NJ	Y	43270 FQ	58820 AW	71510 TQ	NJBLS	10/01-12/01
	New Mexico	Y	21860 FQ	32930 AW	44470 TQ	NMBLS	10/01-12/01
	Albuquerque MSA, NM	Y	28210 FQ	37360 AW	46150 TQ	NMBLS	10/01-12/01
	Las Cruces MSA, NM	Y	26480 FQ	35580 AW	45970 TQ	NMBLS	10/01-12/01
	New York	Y	30790 FQ	49130 AW	67670 TQ	NYBLS	10/01-12/01
	Albany-Schenectady-Troy MSA, NY	Y	29390 FQ	43040 AW	55260 TQ	NYBLS	10/01-12/01
	Binghamton MSA, NY	Y	24110 FQ	46960 AW	78210 TQ	NYBLS	10/01-12/01
	Buffalo-Niagara Falls MSA, NY	Y	27550 FQ	43940 AW	57530 TQ	NYBLS	10/01-12/01
	Dutchess County PMSA, NY	Y	21260 FQ	38770 AW	55250 TQ	NYBLS	10/01-12/01
	Nassau-Suffolk PMSA, NY	Y	42330 FQ	66990 AW	88400 TQ	NYBLS	10/01-12/01
	Newburgh PMSA, NY-PA	Y	26640 FQ	41290 AW	55510 TQ	NYBLS	10/01-12/01
	Rochester MSA, NY	Y	28080 FQ	42410 AW	55800 TQ	NYBLS	10/01-12/01
	Syracuse MSA, NY	Y	25630 FQ	39780 AW	54720 TQ	NYBLS	10/01-12/01
	Utica-Rome MSA, NY	Y	20660 FQ	33360 AW	45680 TQ	NYBLS	10/01-12/01
	North Carolina	Y	22060 FQ	32590 AW	47940 TQ	NCBLS	10/01-12/01
	Asheville MSA, NC	Y	20490 FQ	31590 AW	46410 TQ	NCBLS	10/01-12/01
	Charlotte-Gastonia-Rock Hill MSA, NC-SC	Y	25390 FQ	36440 AW	52410 TQ	NCBLS	10/01-12/01
	Fayetteville MSA, NC	Y	24210 FQ	31070 AW	37860 TQ	NCBLS	10/01-12/01
	Greensboro-Winston-Salem-High Point MSA, NC	Y	25390 FQ	35460 AW	47650 TQ	NCBLS	10/01-12/01
	Hickory-Morganton-Lenoir MSA, NC	Y	21330 FQ	29370 AW	43280 TQ	NCBLS	10/01-12/01
	Raleigh-Durham-Chapel Hill MSA, NC	Y	24800 FQ	34970 AW	49160 TQ	NCBLS	10/01-12/01
	Wilmington MSA, NC	Y	24330 FQ	31310 AW	36570 TQ	NCBLS	10/01-12/01

AAW	Average annual wage	**AOH**	Average offered, high	**ASH**	Average starting, high	**H**	Hourly	**M**	Monthly	**S**	Special: hourly and annual
AE	Average entry wage	**AOL**	Average offered, low	**ASL**	Average starting, low	**HI**	Highest wage paid	**MTC**	Median total compensation	**TQ**	Third quartile wage
AEX	Average experienced wage	**APH**	Average pay, high range	**AW**	Average wage paid	**HR**	High end range	**MW**	Median wage paid	**W**	Weekly
AO	Average offered	**APL**	Average pay, low range	**FQ**	First quartile wage	**LR**	Low end range	**SQ**	Second quartile wage	**Y**	Yearly

Occupation/Type/Industry	Location	Per	Low	Mid	High	Source	Date
Police and Sheriff's Patrol Officer	North Dakota	Y	20310 FQ	30410 AW	42570 TQ	NDBLS	10/01-12/01
	Fargo-Moorhead MSA, ND-MN	Y	28380 FQ	37160 AW	45770 TQ	NDBLS	10/01-12/01
	Ohio	Y	21840 FQ	39490 AW	55180 TQ	OHBLS	10/01-12/01
	Akron PMSA, OH	Y	25540 FQ	38920 AW	47760 TQ	OHBLS	10/01-12/01
	Canton-Massillon MSA, OH	Y	17210 FQ	35600 AW	49930 TQ	OHBLS	10/01-12/01
	Cincinnati PMSA, OH-KY-IN	Y	30980 FQ	43240 AW	56260 TQ	OHBLS	10/01-12/01
	Cleveland-Lorain-Elyria PMSA, OH	Y	24990 FQ	41710 AW	54670 TQ	OHBLS	10/01-12/01
	Columbus MSA, OH	Y	17120 FQ	41630 AW	58610 TQ	OHBLS	10/01-12/01
	Dayton-Springfield MSA, OH	Y	31570 FQ	42720 AW	54710 TQ	OHBLS	10/01-12/01
	Hamilton-Middletown PMSA, OH	Y	30960 FQ	40850 AW	48260 TQ	OHBLS	10/01-12/01
	Mansfield MSA, OH	Y	22330 FQ	35890 AW	47220 TQ	OHBLS	10/01-12/01
	Toledo MSA, OH	Y	28600 FQ	39980 AW	53920 TQ	OHBLS	10/01-12/01
	Youngstown-Warren MSA, OH	Y	19610 FQ	33330 AW	47260 TQ	OHBLS	10/01-12/01
	Oklahoma	Y	16630 FQ	29290 AW	46650 TQ	OKBLS	10/01-12/01
	Oklahoma City MSA, OK	Y	22350 FQ	37550 AW	54780 TQ	OKBLS	10/01-12/01
	Tulsa MSA, OK	Y	19140 FQ	28020 AW	36540 TQ	OKBLS	10/01-12/01
	Oregon	Y	27990 FQ	42950 AW	59790 TQ	ORBLS	10/01-12/01
	Eugene-Springfield MSA, OR	Y	32110 FQ	46050 AW	56130 TQ	ORBLS	10/01-12/01
	Medford-Ashland MSA, OR	Y	26720 FQ	39340 AW	54990 TQ	ORBLS	10/01-12/01
	Portland-Vancouver PMSA, OR-WA	Y	34640 FQ	49410 AW	65550 TQ	ORBLS	10/01-12/01
	Salem PMSA, OR	Y	24690 FQ	39530 AW	59990 TQ	ORBLS	10/01-12/01
	Pennsylvania	Y	24350 FQ	43200 AW	60990 TQ	PABLS	10/01-12/01
	Allentown-Bethlehem-Easton MSA, PA	Y	14320 FQ	38400 AW	56400 TQ	PABLS	10/01-12/01
	Erie MSA, PA	Y	29720 FQ	45510 AW	65940 TQ	PABLS	10/01-12/01
	Harrisburg-Lebanon-Carlisle MSA, PA	Y	30510 FQ	50480 AW	69670 TQ	PABLS	10/01-12/01
	Johnstown MSA, PA	Y	13270 FQ	32230 AW	52980 TQ	PABLS	10/01-12/01
	Lancaster MSA, PA	Y	30340 FQ	44550 AW	63540 TQ	PABLS	10/01-12/01
	Philadelphia PMSA, PA-NJ	Y	37050 FQ	46780 AW	60930 TQ	PABLS	10/01-12/01
	Pittsburgh MSA, PA	Y	21580 FQ	43800 AW	68350 TQ	PABLS	10/01-12/01
	Reading MSA, PA	Y	25750 FQ	40090 AW	55830 TQ	PABLS	10/01-12/01
	Scranton-Wilkes-Barre-Hazleton MSA, PA	Y	14870 FQ	33860 AW	53870 TQ	PABLS	10/01-12/01
	York MSA, PA	Y	32770 FQ	45720 AW	58570 TQ	PABLS	10/01-12/01
	Rhode Island	Y	32520 FQ	43240 AW	55120 TQ	RIBLS	10/01-12/01
	Providence-Fall River-Warwick MSA, RI-MA	Y	33040 FQ	43610 AW	55760 TQ	RIBLS	10/01-12/01
	South Carolina	Y	21390 FQ	30510 AW	42360 TQ	SCBLS	10/01-12/01
	Charleston-North Charleston MSA, SC	Y	21330 FQ	30680 AW	43150 TQ	SCBLS	10/01-12/01
	Columbia MSA, SC	Y	23860 FQ	33110 AW	46860 TQ	SCBLS	10/01-12/01
	Greenville-Spartanburg-Anderson MSA, SC	Y	23760 FQ	31590 AW	41390 TQ	SCBLS	10/01-12/01
	Myrtle Beach MSA, SC	Y	24350 FQ	30860 AW	38010 TQ	SCBLS	10/01-12/01
	South Dakota	Y	17990 FQ	28720 AW	42090 TQ	SDBLS	10/01-12/01
	Tennessee	Y	22020 FQ	32330 AW	44330 TQ	TNBLS	10/01-12/01
	Chattanooga MSA, TN-GA	Y	24250 FQ	32500 AW	44010 TQ	TNBLS	10/01-12/01
	Clarksville-Hopkinsville MSA, TN-KY	Y	24090 FQ	30570 AW	39690 TQ	TNBLS	10/01-12/01
	Johnson City-Kingsport-Bristol MSA, TN-VA	Y	23610 FQ	30510 AW	41360 TQ	TNBLS	10/01-12/01
	Knoxville MSA, TN	Y	20760 FQ	30260 AW	37880 TQ	TNBLS	10/01-12/01
	Memphis MSA, TN-AR-MS	Y	24910 FQ	36700 AW	46320 TQ	TNBLS	10/01-12/01
	Nashville MSA, TN	Y	24220 FQ	32610 AW	43630 TQ	TNBLS	10/01-12/01
	Texas	Y	26930 FQ	39990 AW	54620 TQ	TXBLS	10/01-12/01
	Austin-San Marcos MSA, TX	Y	30340 FQ	40010 AW	49330 TQ	TXBLS	10/01-12/01
	Beaumont-Port Arthur MSA, TX	Y	31170 FQ	39400 AW	48150 TQ	TXBLS	10/01-12/01
	Brazoria PMSA, TX	Y	21730 FQ	32150 AW	42850 TQ	TXBLS	10/01-12/01
	Brownsville-Harlingen-San Benito MSA, TX	Y	24970 FQ	37720 AW	49160 TQ	TXBLS	10/01-12/01
	Corpus Christi MSA, TX	Y	24240 FQ	45320 AW	58930 TQ	TXBLS	10/01-12/01
	Dallas PMSA, TX	Y	31620 FQ	46530 AW	62620 TQ	TXBLS	10/01-12/01
	El Paso MSA, TX	Y	30120 FQ	37220 AW	46740 TQ	TXBLS	10/01-12/01
	Fort Worth-Arlington PMSA, TX	Y	30010 FQ	41700 AW	54820 TQ	TXBLS	10/01-12/01

AAW	Average annual wage	**AOH**	Average offered, high	**ASH**	Average starting, high	**H**	Hourly	**M**	Monthly	**S**	Special: hourly and annual
AE	Average entry wage	**AOL**	Average offered, low	**ASL**	Average starting, low	**HI**	Highest wage paid	**MTC**	Median total compensation	**TQ**	Third quartile wage
AEX	Average experienced wage	**APH**	Average pay, high range	**AW**	Average wage paid	**HR**	High end range	**MW**	Median wage paid	**W**	Weekly
AO	Average offered	**APL**	Average pay, low range	**FQ**	First quartile wage	**LR**	Low end range	**SQ**	Second quartile wage	**Y**	Yearly

Occupation/Type/Industry	Location	Per	Low	Mid	High	Source	Date
Police and Sheriff's Patrol Officer	Galveston-Texas City PMSA, TX	Y	30120 FQ	39550 AW	48380 TQ	TXBLS	10/01-12/01
	Houston PMSA, TX	Y	30730 FQ	41940 AW	53620 TQ	TXBLS	10/01-12/01
	Killeen-Temple MSA, TX	Y	26920 FQ	35070 AW	44850 TQ	TXBLS	10/01-12/01
	Laredo MSA, TX	Y	32310 FQ	40320 AW	48810 TQ	TXBLS	10/01-12/01
	Longview-Marshall MSA, TX	Y	20040 FQ	29210 AW	40860 TQ	TXBLS	10/01-12/01
	McAllen-Edinburg-Mission MSA, TX	Y	22360 FQ	34180 AW	45840 TQ	TXBLS	10/01-12/01
	Odessa-Midland MSA, TX	Y	30300 FQ	37150 AW	45750 TQ	TXBLS	10/01-12/01
	San Antonio MSA, TX	Y	25800 FQ	40020 AW	56360 TQ	TXBLS	10/01-12/01
	Tyler MSA, TX	Y	30530 FQ	39710 AW	47860 TQ	TXBLS	10/01-12/01
	Waco MSA, TX	Y	19570 FQ	27610 AW	39540 TQ	TXBLS	10/01-12/01
	Utah	Y	25500 FQ	35690 AW	46130 TQ	UTBLS	10/01-12/01
	Provo-Orem MSA, UT	Y	25980 FQ	35150 AW	46280 TQ	UTBLS	10/01-12/01
	Salt Lake City-Ogden MSA, UT	Y	29000 FQ	37940 AW	46740 TQ	UTBLS	10/01-12/01
	Vermont	Y	19580 FQ	32360 AW	46700 TQ	VTBLS	10/01-12/01
	Burlington MSA, VT	Y	17140 FQ	32480 AW	47090 TQ	VTBLS	10/01-12/01
	Virginia	Y	25460 FQ	38750 AW	57970 TQ	VABLS	10/01-12/01
	Lynchburg MSA, VA	Y	24770 FQ	32300 AW	43520 TQ	VABLS	10/01-12/01
	Norfolk-Virginia Beach-Newport News MSA, VA-NC	Y	25660 FQ	35760 AW	47710 TQ	VABLS	10/01-12/01
	Richmond-Petersburg MSA, VA	Y	25760 FQ	37420 AW	57320 TQ	VABLS	10/01-12/01
	Washington	Y	36870 FQ	49390 AW	63120 TQ	WABLS	10/01-12/01
	Bremerton PMSA, WA	Y	30570 FQ	47250 AW	60890 TQ	WABLS	10/01-12/01
	Olympia PMSA, WA	Y	29620 FQ	47590 AW	65150 TQ	WABLS	10/01-12/01
	Richland-Kennewick-Pasco MSA, WA	Y	38690 FQ	48000 AW	57110 TQ	WABLS	10/01-12/01
	Seattle-Bellevue-Everett PMSA, WA	Y	40570 FQ	52430 AW	67160 TQ	WABLS	10/01-12/01
	Spokane MSA, WA	Y	39700 FQ	50010 AW	59500 TQ	WABLS	10/01-12/01
	Tacoma PMSA, WA	Y	36690 FQ	49170 AW	61840 TQ	WABLS	10/01-12/01
	Yakima MSA, WA	Y	29300 FQ	42990 AW	58270 TQ	WABLS	10/01-12/01
	West Virginia	Y	19580 FQ	28000 AW	37010 TQ	WVBLS	10/01-12/01
	Charleston MSA, WV	Y	23980 FQ	32110 AW	41980 TQ	WVBLS	10/01-12/01
	Huntington-Ashland MSA, WV-KY-OH	Y	14830 FQ	26920 AW	39940 TQ	WVBLS	10/01-12/01
	Wisconsin	Y	27480 FQ	40530 AW	53980 TQ	WIBLS	10/01-12/01
	Appleton-Oshkosh-Neenah MSA, WI	Y	24040 FQ	39690 AW	53040 TQ	WIBLS	10/01-12/01
	Green Bay MSA, WI	Y	38430 FQ	43390 AW	50290 TQ	WIBLS	10/01-12/01
	Madison MSA, WI	Y	35670 FQ	44270 AW	55900 TQ	WIBLS	10/01-12/01
	Milwaukee-Waukesha PMSA, WI	Y	34380 FQ	44750 AW	56730 TQ	WIBLS	10/01-12/01
	Racine PMSA, WI	Y	34950 FQ	46320 AW	57190 TQ	WIBLS	10/01-12/01
	Wyoming	Y	24520 FQ	32870 AW	42870 TQ	WYBLS	10/01-12/01
	Cheyenne MSA, WY	Y	25490 FQ	31860 AW	37260 TQ	WYBLS	10/01-12/01
	Puerto Rico	Y	13760 FQ	19510 AW	24820 TQ	PRBLS	10/01-12/01
Police, Fire, and Ambulance Dispatcher	Alabama	H	7.44 FQ	11.21 AW	16.02 TQ	ALBLS	10/01-12/01
	Birmingham MSA, AL	H	6.54 FQ	12.42 AW	18.20 TQ	ALBLS	10/01-12/01
	Huntsville MSA, AL	H	9.47 FQ	11.79 AW	13.97 TQ	ALBLS	10/01-12/01
	Mobile MSA, AL	H	8.18 FQ	11.63 AW	15.16 TQ	ALBLS	10/01-12/01
	Montgomery MSA, AL	H	8.43 FQ	11.78 AW	16.07 TQ	ALBLS	10/01-12/01
	Alaska	H	13.05 FQ	17.75 AW	24.55 TQ	AKBLS	10/01-12/01
	Arizona	H	8.64 FQ	14.10 AW	20.12 TQ	AZBLS	10/01-12/01
	Phoenix-Mesa MSA, AZ	H	11.77 FQ	16.36 AW	21.45 TQ	AZBLS	10/01-12/01
	Tucson MSA, AZ	H	7.47 FQ	10.21 AW	13.32 TQ	AZBLS	10/01-12/01
	Arkansas	H	6.75 FQ	9.31 AW	12.34 TQ	ARBLS	10/01-12/01
	Fayetteville-Springdale-Rogers MSA, AR	H	9.32 FQ	11.71 AW	15.12 TQ	ARBLS	10/01-12/01
	Fort Smith MSA, AR-OK	H	6.42 FQ	8.25 AW	10.59 TQ	ARBLS	10/01-12/01
	Little Rock-North Little Rock MSA, AR	H	7.35 FQ	9.59 AW	13.07 TQ	ARBLS	10/01-12/01
	California	H	11.02 FQ	18.04 AW	24.72 TQ	CABLS	10/01-12/01
	Bakersfield MSA, CA	H	7.15 FQ	10.69 AW	16.74 TQ	CABLS	10/01-12/01
	Chico-Paradise MSA, CA	H	12.49 FQ	15.58 AW	18.56 TQ	CABLS	10/01-12/01
	Fresno MSA, CA	H	10.49 FQ	16.34 AW	22.95 TQ	CABLS	10/01-12/01

AAW	Average annual wage	**AOH**	Average offered, high	**ASH**	Average starting, high	**H**	Hourly	**M**	Monthly	**S**	Special: hourly and annual
AE	Average entry wage	**AOL**	Average offered, low	**ASL**	Average starting, low	**HI**	Highest wage paid	**MTC**	Median total compensation	**TQ**	Third quartile wage
AEX	Average experienced wage	**APH**	Average pay, high range	**AW**	Average wage paid	**HR**	High end range	**MW**	Median wage paid	**W**	Weekly
AO	Average offered	**APL**	Average pay, low range	**FQ**	First quartile wage	**LR**	Low end range	**SQ**	Second quartile wage	**Y**	Yearly

Occupation/Type/Industry	Location	Per	Low	Mid	High	Source	Date
Police, Fire, and Ambulance Dispatcher	Los Angeles-Long Beach PMSA, CA	H	15.02 FQ	19.53 AW	23.22 TQ	CABLS	10/01-12/01
	Merced MSA, CA	H	9.29 FQ	14.63 AW	20.71 TQ	CABLS	10/01-12/01
	Oakland PMSA, CA	H	11.34 FQ	19.71 AW	27.85 TQ	CABLS	10/01-12/01
	Orange County PMSA, CA	H	15.84 FQ	21.32 AW	27.29 TQ	CABLS	10/01-12/01
	Riverside-San Bernardino PMSA, CA	H	13.51 FQ	16.61 AW	21.03 TQ	CABLS	10/01-12/01
	Sacramento PMSA, CA	H	14.88 FQ	19.67 AW	24.81 TQ	CABLS	10/01-12/01
	San Diego MSA, CA	H	13.80 FQ	19.44 AW	23.17 TQ	CABLS	10/01-12/01
	San Francisco PMSA, CA	H	12.88 FQ	19.77 AW	26.09 TQ	CABLS	10/01-12/01
	San Jose PMSA, CA	H	13.60 FQ	20.77 AW	29.07 TQ	CABLS	10/01-12/01
	San Luis Obispo-Atascadero-Paso Robles MSA, CA	H	14.47 FQ	17.71 AW	22.70 TQ	CABLS	10/01-12/01
	Santa Barbara-Santa Maria-Lompoc MSA, CA	H	13.95 FQ	17.45 AW	21.01 TQ	CABLS	10/01-12/01
	Santa Rosa PMSA, CA	H	15.90 FQ	21.23 AW	27.66 TQ	CABLS	10/01-12/01
	Stockton-Lodi MSA, CA	H	13.56 FQ	17.86 AW	23.47 TQ	CABLS	10/01-12/01
	Vallejo-Fairfield-Napa PMSA, CA	H	15.19 FQ	23.13 AW	31.43 TQ	CABLS	10/01-12/01
	Ventura PMSA, CA	H	11.53 FQ	16.44 AW	22.52 TQ	CABLS	10/01-12/01
	Visalia-Tulare-Porterville MSA, CA	H	8.83 FQ	16.06 AW	22.70 TQ	CABLS	10/01-12/01
	Colorado	H	10.46 FQ	15.44 AW	21.04 TQ	COBLS	10/01-12/01
	Boulder-Longmont PMSA, CO	H	12.69 FQ	16.40 AW	20.48 TQ	COBLS	10/01-12/01
	Denver PMSA, CO	H	12.45 FQ	16.85 AW	22.12 TQ	COBLS	10/01-12/01
	Fort Collins-Loveland MSA, CO	H	11.06 FQ	15.93 AW	22.23 TQ	COBLS	10/01-12/01
	Connecticut	H	10.52 FQ	15.46 AW	20.93 TQ	CTBLS	10/01-12/01
	Bridgeport PMSA, CT	H	7.67 FQ	12.79 AW	16.71 TQ	CTBLS	10/01-12/01
	Danbury PMSA, CT	H	12.33 FQ	16.08 AW	20.77 TQ	CTBLS	10/01-12/01
	Hartford MSA, CT	H	10.08 FQ	15.72 AW	21.03 TQ	CTBLS	10/01-12/01
	New Haven-Meriden PMSA, CT	H	11.32 FQ	15.39 AW	20.82 TQ	CTBLS	10/01-12/01
	New London-Norwich MSA, CT-RI	H	9.49 FQ	15.52 AW	21.22 TQ	CTBLS	10/01-12/01
	Stamford-Norwalk PMSA, CT	H	12.99 FQ	17.94 AW	22.95 TQ	CTBLS	10/01-12/01
	Waterbury PMSA, CT	H	11.09 FQ	16.27 AW	22.11 TQ	CTBLS	10/01-12/01
	Delaware	H	9.11 FQ	14.34 AW	20.12 TQ	DEBLS	10/01-12/01
	Wilmington-Newark PMSA, DE-MD	H	9.26 FQ	14.60 AW	20.45 TQ	DEBLS	10/01-12/01
	Washington PMSA, DC-MD-VA-WV	H	10.35 FQ	15.26 AW	22.04 TQ	DCBLS	10/01-12/01
	Florida	H	9.33 FQ	12.89 AW	17.73 TQ	FLBLS	10/01-12/01
	Daytona Beach MSA, FL	H	9.04 FQ	11.58 AW	15.29 TQ	FLBLS	10/01-12/01
	Fort Lauderdale PMSA, FL	H	9.70 FQ	13.88 AW	19.12 TQ	FLBLS	10/01-12/01
	Fort Myers-Cape Coral MSA, FL	H	10.41 FQ	13.53 AW	17.46 TQ	FLBLS	10/01-12/01
	Fort Pierce-Port St. Lucie MSA, FL	H	7.58 FQ	12.20 AW	17.44 TQ	FLBLS	10/01-12/01
	Fort Walton Beach MSA, FL	H	7.98 FQ	10.54 AW	13.34 TQ	FLBLS	10/01-12/01
	Jacksonville MSA, FL	H	9.91 FQ	12.99 AW	16.72 TQ	FLBLS	10/01-12/01
	Lakeland-Winter Haven MSA, FL	H	9.42 FQ	11.54 AW	14.10 TQ	FLBLS	10/01-12/01
	Melbourne-Titusville-Palm Bay MSA, FL	H	9.27 FQ	11.68 AW	14.11 TQ	FLBLS	10/01-12/01
	Miami PMSA, FL	H	9.41 FQ	13.93 AW	19.91 TQ	FLBLS	10/01-12/01
	Orlando MSA, FL	H	9.64 FQ	12.91 AW	17.69 TQ	FLBLS	10/01-12/01
	Pensacola MSA, FL	H	9.22 FQ	10.88 AW	13.48 TQ	FLBLS	10/01-12/01
	Sarasota-Bradenton MSA, FL	H	9.68 FQ	12.57 AW	16.51 TQ	FLBLS	10/01-12/01
	Tallahassee MSA, FL	H	8.91 FQ	10.97 AW	13.52 TQ	FLBLS	10/01-12/01
	Tampa-St. Petersburg-Clearwater MSA, FL	H	9.77 FQ	14.10 AW	19.56 TQ	FLBLS	10/01-12/01
	West Palm Beach-Boca Raton MSA, FL	H	10.30 FQ	14.35 AW	20.31 TQ	FLBLS	10/01-12/01
	Georgia	H	7.76 FQ	11.00 AW	14.84 TQ	GABLS	10/01-12/01
	Atlanta MSA, GA	H	9.58 FQ	12.42 AW	16.23 TQ	GABLS	10/01-12/01
	Augusta-Aiken MSA, GA-SC	H	7.98 FQ	11.03 AW	13.45 TQ	GABLS	10/01-12/01
	Columbus MSA, GA-AL	H	6.40 FQ	9.52 AW	12.51 TQ	GABLS	10/01-12/01
	Macon MSA, GA	H	8.13 FQ	10.57 AW	14.29 TQ	GABLS	10/01-12/01
	Savannah MSA, GA	H	8.77 FQ	11.11 AW	14.83 TQ	GABLS	10/01-12/01
	Hawaii	H	11.34 FQ	14.92 AW	19.26 TQ	HIBLS	10/01-12/01

AAW	Average annual wage	**AOH**	Average offered, high	**ASH**	Average starting, high	**H**	Hourly	**M**	Monthly	**S**	Special: hourly and annual
AE	Average entry wage	**AOL**	Average offered, low	**ASL**	Average starting, low	**HI**	Highest wage paid	**MTC**	Median total compensation	**TQ**	Third quartile wage
AEX	Average experienced wage	**APH**	Average pay, high range	**AW**	Average wage paid	**HR**	High end range	**MW**	Median wage paid	**W**	Weekly
AO	Average offered	**APL**	Average pay, low range	**FQ**	First quartile wage	**LR**	Low end range	**SQ**	Second quartile wage	**Y**	Yearly

Occupation/Type/Industry	Location	Per	Low	Mid	High	Source	Date
Police, Fire, and Ambulance Dispatcher	Honolulu MSA, HI	H	11.54 FQ	15.10 AW	19.79 TQ	HIBLS	10/01-12/01
	Idaho	H	9.69 FQ	12.97 AW	17.03 TQ	IDBLS	10/01-12/01
	Boise City MSA, ID	H	11.06 FQ	14.45 AW	18.65 TQ	IDBLS	10/01-12/01
	Illinois	H	8.32 FQ	13.96 AW	20.65 TQ	ILBLS	10/01-12/01
	Chicago PMSA, IL	H	9.76 FQ	14.94 AW	21.32 TQ	ILBLS	10/01-12/01
	Peoria-Pekin MSA, IL	H	7.89 FQ	13.92 AW	20.68 TQ	ILBLS	10/01-12/01
	Rockford MSA, IL	H	9.85 FQ	15.98 AW	21.63 TQ	ILBLS	10/01-12/01
	Springfield MSA, IL	H	6.23 FQ	11.86 AW	18.50 TQ	ILBLS	10/01-12/01
	Indiana	H	8.22 FQ	11.67 AW	15.83 TQ	INBLS	10/01-12/01
	Elkhart-Goshen MSA, IN	H	9.63 FQ	12.84 AW	16.53 TQ	INBLS	10/01-12/01
	Evansville-Henderson MSA, IN-KY	H	9.08 FQ	12.18 AW	16.22 TQ	INBLS	10/01-12/01
	Fort Wayne MSA, IN	H	9.10 FQ	12.29 AW	16.03 TQ	INBLS	10/01-12/01
	Gary PMSA, IN	H	6.15 FQ	10.91 AW	15.98 TQ	INBLS	10/01-12/01
	Indianapolis MSA, IN	H	9.88 FQ	13.31 AW	16.91 TQ	INBLS	10/01-12/01
	Lafayette MSA, IN	H	9.29 FQ	11.96 AW	14.56 TQ	INBLS	10/01-12/01
	South Bend MSA, IN	H	8.89 FQ	11.84 AW	15.59 TQ	INBLS	10/01-12/01
	Iowa	H	9.38 FQ	12.90 AW	18.21 TQ	IABLS	10/01-12/01
	Davenport-Moline-Rock Island MSA, IA-IL	H	9.47 FQ	14.42 AW	20.17 TQ	IABLS	10/01-12/01
	Des Moines MSA, IA	H	12.47 FQ	16.61 AW	20.64 TQ	IABLS	10/01-12/01
	Kansas	H	7.66 FQ	10.79 AW	14.90 TQ	KSBLS	10/01-12/01
	Wichita MSA, KS	H	8.59 FQ	12.55 AW	19.51 TQ	KSBLS	10/01-12/01
	Kentucky	H	7.03 FQ	11.20 AW	16.35 TQ	KYBLS	10/01-12/01
	Lexington MSA, KY	H	8.95 FQ	12.02 AW	16.20 TQ	KYBLS	10/01-12/01
	Louisville MSA, KY-IN	H	8.37 FQ	12.17 AW	15.30 TQ	KYBLS	10/01-12/01
	Louisiana	H	6.37 FQ	9.37 AW	13.08 TQ	LABLS	10/01-12/01
	Baton Rouge MSA, LA	H	7.99 FQ	10.50 AW	13.51 TQ	LABLS	10/01-12/01
	Houma MSA, LA	H	6.65 FQ	9.01 AW	11.36 TQ	LABLS	10/01-12/01
	Lafayette MSA, LA	H	6.41 FQ	9.96 AW	13.88 TQ	LABLS	10/01-12/01
	Lake Charles MSA, LA	H	6.34 FQ	9.21 AW	11.68 TQ	LABLS	10/01-12/01
	New Orleans MSA, LA	H	6.78 FQ	10.17 AW	15.01 TQ	LABLS	10/01-12/01
	Shreveport-Bossier City MSA, LA	H	7.06 FQ	8.96 AW	11.97 TQ	LABLS	10/01-12/01
	Maine	H	8.00 FQ	11.96 AW	16.02 TQ	MEBLS	10/01-12/01
	Portland MSA, ME	H	9.40 FQ	12.72 AW	16.33 TQ	MEBLS	10/01-12/01
	Maryland	H	11.07 FQ	14.59 AW	20.23 TQ	MDBLS	10/01-12/01
	Baltimore PMSA, MD	H	10.98 FQ	14.25 AW	18.68 TQ	MDBLS	10/01-12/01
	Massachusetts	H	9.39 FQ	13.95 AW	18.37 TQ	MABLS	10/01-12/01
	Boston PMSA, MA-NH	H	10.09 FQ	14.82 AW	19.65 TQ	MABLS	10/01-12/01
	Brockton PMSA, MA	H	8.97 FQ	13.53 AW	17.95 TQ	MABLS	10/01-12/01
	Lawrence PMSA, MA-NH	H	8.83 FQ	12.62 AW	16.78 TQ	MABLS	10/01-12/01
	Lowell PMSA, MA-NH	H	9.71 FQ	14.41 AW	17.65 TQ	MABLS	10/01-12/01
	New Bedford PMSA, MA	H	9.74 FQ	13.40 AW	17.35 TQ	MABLS	10/01-12/01
	Springfield MSA, MA	H	9.59 FQ	12.80 AW	16.85 TQ	MABLS	10/01-12/01
	Worcester PMSA, MA-CT	H	9.41 FQ	13.68 AW	17.43 TQ	MABLS	10/01-12/01
	Michigan	H	9.86 FQ	14.71 AW	20.44 TQ	MIBLS	10/01-12/01
	Ann Arbor PMSA, MI	H	11.03 FQ	14.32 AW	18.59 TQ	MIBLS	10/01-12/01
	Detroit PMSA, MI	H	10.67 FQ	16.17 AW	21.25 TQ	MIBLS	10/01-12/01
	Grand Rapids-Muskegon-Holland MSA, MI	H	11.04 FQ	15.40 AW	20.42 TQ	MIBLS	10/01-12/01
	Kalamazoo-Battle Creek MSA, MI	H	10.60 FQ	15.20 AW	20.16 TQ	MIBLS	10/01-12/01
	Lansing-East Lansing MSA, MI	H	14.76 FQ	18.63 AW	22.49 TQ	MIBLS	10/01-12/01
	Saginaw-Bay City-Midland MSA, MI	H	9.77 FQ	15.45 AW	20.33 TQ	MIBLS	10/01-12/01
	Minnesota	H	10.93 FQ	15.63 AW	20.82 TQ	MNBLS	10/01-12/01
	Duluth-Superior MSA, MN-WI	H	6.62 FQ	14.43 AW	18.50 TQ	MNBLS	10/01-12/01
	Minneapolis-St. Paul MSA, MN-WI	H	13.27 FQ	17.56 AW	22.21 TQ	MNBLS	10/01-12/01
	St. Cloud MSA, MN	H	9.29 FQ	13.67 AW	17.72 TQ	MNBLS	10/01-12/01
	Mississippi	H	6.26 FQ	9.16 AW	13.04 TQ	MSBLS	10/01-12/01
	Biloxi-Gulfport-Pascagoula MSA, MS	H	7.38 FQ	10.55 AW	13.59 TQ	MSBLS	10/01-12/01
	Jackson MSA, MS	H	8.19 FQ	11.39 AW	14.43 TQ	MSBLS	10/01-12/01
	Missouri	H	6.67 FQ	11.65 AW	17.53 TQ	MOBLS	10/01-12/01
	Kansas City MSA, MO-KS	H	9.63 FQ	14.26 AW	20.15 TQ	MOBLS	10/01-12/01
	St. Louis MSA, MO-IL	H	8.74 FQ	12.90 AW	17.86 TQ	MOBLS	10/01-12/01
	Springfield MSA, MO	H	8.38 FQ	12.44 AW	17.66 TQ	MOBLS	10/01-12/01
	Montana	H	7.88 FQ	10.92 AW	15.23 TQ	MTBLS	10/01-12/01
	Nebraska	H	8.36 FQ	11.67 AW	15.97 TQ	NEBLS	10/01-12/01

AAW	Average annual wage	**AOH**	Average offered, high	**ASH**	Average starting, high	**H**	Hourly	**M**	Monthly	**S**	Special: hourly and annual
AE	Average entry wage	**AOL**	Average offered, low	**ASL**	Average starting, low	**HI**	Highest wage paid	**MTC**	Median total compensation	**TQ**	Third quartile wage
AEX	Average experienced wage	**APH**	Average pay, high range	**AW**	Average wage paid	**HR**	High end range	**MW**	Median wage paid	**W**	Weekly
AO	Average offered	**APL**	Average pay, low range	**FQ**	First quartile wage	**LR**	Low end range	**SQ**	Second quartile wage	**Y**	Yearly

Occupation/Type/Industry	Location	Per	Low	Mid	High	Source	Date
Police, Fire, and Ambulance Dispatcher	Lincoln MSA, NE	H	9.59 FQ	13.45 AW	19.55 TQ	NEBLS	10/01-12/01
	Omaha MSA, NE-IA	H	10.16 FQ	13.33 AW	17.35 TQ	NEBLS	10/01-12/01
	Nevada	H	11.96 FQ	16.94 AW	22.47 TQ	NVBLS	10/01-12/01
	Las Vegas MSA, NV-AZ	H	8.72 FQ	15.07 AW	22.93 TQ	NVBLS	10/01-12/01
	New Hampshire	H	9.65 FQ	12.85 AW	16.72 TQ	NHBLS	10/01-12/01
	Manchester PMSA, NH	H	9.79 FQ	13.69 AW	18.10 TQ	NHBLS	10/01-12/01
	Nashua PMSA, NH	H	11.15 FQ	14.96 AW	20.05 TQ	NHBLS	10/01-12/01
	Portsmouth-Rochester PMSA, NH-ME	H	11.19 FQ	13.79 AW	17.44 TQ	NHBLS	10/01-12/01
	New Jersey	H	10.05 FQ	14.93 AW	20.71 TQ	NJBLS	10/01-12/01
	Atlantic-Cape May PMSA, NJ	H	10.16 FQ	15.00 AW	20.51 TQ	NJBLS	10/01-12/01
	Bergen-Passaic PMSA, NJ	H	9.00 FQ	12.98 AW	18.17 TQ	NJBLS	10/01-12/01
	Jersey City PMSA, NJ	H	9.44 FQ	14.76 AW	21.34 TQ	NJBLS	10/01-12/01
	Middlesex-Somerset-Hunterdon PMSA, NJ	H	10.16 FQ	14.67 AW	19.06 TQ	NJBLS	10/01-12/01
	Monmouth-Ocean PMSA, NJ	H	9.46 FQ	14.09 AW	20.60 TQ	NJBLS	10/01-12/01
	Newark PMSA, NJ	H	11.81 FQ	15.41 AW	19.84 TQ	NJBLS	10/01-12/01
	Trenton PMSA, NJ	H	12.85 FQ	17.14 AW	22.37 TQ	NJBLS	10/01-12/01
	New Mexico	H	7.28 FQ	10.19 AW	13.92 TQ	NMBLS	10/01-12/01
	Albuquerque MSA, NM	H	8.59 FQ	11.18 AW	14.10 TQ	NMBLS	10/01-12/01
	New York	H	9.36 FQ	14.86 AW	21.12 TQ	NYBLS	10/01-12/01
	Albany-Schenectady-Troy MSA, NY	H	9.72 FQ	15.14 AW	21.19 TQ	NYBLS	10/01-12/01
	Binghamton MSA, NY	H	10.03 FQ	13.83 AW	17.54 TQ	NYBLS	10/01-12/01
	Buffalo-Niagara Falls MSA, NY	H	6.99 FQ	12.50 AW	17.67 TQ	NYBLS	10/01-12/01
	Dutchess County PMSA, NY	H	10.00 FQ	14.91 AW	19.33 TQ	NYBLS	10/01-12/01
	Nassau-Suffolk PMSA, NY	H	9.64 FQ	15.95 AW	21.94 TQ	NYBLS	10/01-12/01
	Newburgh PMSA, NY-PA	H	10.22 FQ	14.60 AW	19.76 TQ	NYBLS	10/01-12/01
	Rochester MSA, NY	H	9.82 FQ	15.15 AW	20.87 TQ	NYBLS	10/01-12/01
	Utica-Rome MSA, NY	H	7.88 FQ	12.80 AW	21.60 TQ	NYBLS	10/01-12/01
	North Carolina	H	7.56 FQ	11.61 AW	15.91 TQ	NCBLS	10/01-12/01
	Asheville MSA, NC	H	9.72 FQ	12.38 AW	15.00 TQ	NCBLS	10/01-12/01
	Charlotte-Gastonia-Rock Hill MSA, NC-SC	H	9.99 FQ	13.35 AW	17.45 TQ	NCBLS	10/01-12/01
	Fayetteville MSA, NC	H	9.97 FQ	12.41 AW	15.25 TQ	NCBLS	10/01-12/01
	Greensboro-Winston-Salem-High Point MSA, NC	H	10.65 FQ	13.82 AW	17.57 TQ	NCBLS	10/01-12/01
	Hickory-Morganton-Lenoir MSA, NC	H	7.74 FQ	11.24 AW	14.24 TQ	NCBLS	10/01-12/01
	Raleigh-Durham-Chapel Hill MSA, NC	H	10.09 FQ	13.49 AW	17.71 TQ	NCBLS	10/01-12/01
	North Dakota	H	7.89 FQ	11.42 AW	16.01 TQ	NDBLS	10/01-12/01
	Fargo-Moorhead MSA, ND-MN	H	10.32 FQ	14.61 AW	19.78 TQ	NDBLS	10/01-12/01
	Ohio	H	9.26 FQ	13.70 AW	18.30 TQ	OHBLS	10/01-12/01
	Akron PMSA, OH	H	6.59 FQ	12.32 AW	17.62 TQ	OHBLS	10/01-12/01
	Canton-Massillon MSA, OH	H	9.07 FQ	11.64 AW	16.41 TQ	OHBLS	10/01-12/01
	Cincinnati PMSA, OH-KY-IN	H	9.36 FQ	14.94 AW	20.50 TQ	OHBLS	10/01-12/01
	Cleveland-Lorain-Elyria PMSA, OH	H	11.25 FQ	14.57 AW	18.26 TQ	OHBLS	10/01-12/01
	Columbus MSA, OH	H	11.20 FQ	15.11 AW	19.45 TQ	OHBLS	10/01-12/01
	Dayton-Springfield MSA, OH	H	10.92 FQ	14.57 AW	18.43 TQ	OHBLS	10/01-12/01
	Hamilton-Middletown PMSA, OH	H	12.58 FQ	15.24 AW	17.71 TQ	OHBLS	10/01-12/01
	Mansfield MSA, OH	H	9.41 FQ	11.96 AW	15.27 TQ	OHBLS	10/01-12/01
	Toledo MSA, OH	H	9.10 FQ	14.10 AW	19.19 TQ	OHBLS	10/01-12/01
	Youngstown-Warren MSA, OH	H	7.69 FQ	11.64 AW	16.00 TQ	OHBLS	10/01-12/01
	Oklahoma	H	6.23 FQ	9.37 AW	13.93 TQ	OKBLS	10/01-12/01
	Oklahoma City MSA, OK	H	7.04 FQ	11.41 AW	17.19 TQ	OKBLS	10/01-12/01
	Tulsa MSA, OK	H	7.52 FQ	11.53 AW	16.13 TQ	OKBLS	10/01-12/01
	Oregon	H	10.97 FQ	15.99 AW	22.45 TQ	ORBLS	10/01-12/01
	Eugene-Springfield MSA, OR	H	11.21 FQ	16.36 AW	20.88 TQ	ORBLS	10/01-12/01
	Medford-Ashland MSA, OR	H	10.37 FQ	14.67 AW	18.73 TQ	ORBLS	10/01-12/01
	Portland-Vancouver PMSA, OR-WA	H	13.84 FQ	19.17 AW	25.72 TQ	ORBLS	10/01-12/01
	Pennsylvania	H	8.47 FQ	14.04 AW	20.32 TQ	PABLS	10/01-12/01
	Allentown-Bethlehem-Easton MSA, PA	H	8.97 FQ	13.85 AW	17.71 TQ	PABLS	10/01-12/01
	Erie MSA, PA	H	9.50 FQ	13.81 AW	20.27 TQ	PABLS	10/01-12/01

AAW	Average annual wage	**AOH**	Average offered, high	**ASH**	Average starting, high	**H**	Hourly	**M**	Monthly	**S**	Special: hourly and annual
AE	Average entry wage	**AOL**	Average offered, low	**ASL**	Average starting, low	**HI**	Highest wage paid	**MTC**	Median total compensation	**TQ**	Third quartile wage
AEX	Average experienced wage	**APH**	Average pay, high range	**AW**	Average wage paid	**HR**	High end range	**MW**	Median wage paid	**W**	Weekly
AO	Average offered	**APL**	Average pay, low range	**FQ**	First quartile wage	**LR**	Low end range	**SQ**	Second quartile wage	**Y**	Yearly

Occupation/Type/Industry	Location	Per	Low	Mid	High	Source	Date
Police, Fire, and Ambulance Dispatcher							
	Harrisburg-Lebanon-Carlisle MSA, PA	H	10.22 FQ	14.64 AW	20.29 TQ	PABLS	10/01-12/01
	Philadelphia PMSA, PA-NJ	H	10.48 FQ	15.68 AW	21.22 TQ	PABLS	10/01-12/01
	Pittsburgh MSA, PA	H	7.58 FQ	13.53 AW	20.73 TQ	PABLS	10/01-12/01
	Reading MSA, PA	H	9.46 FQ	12.05 AW	15.12 TQ	PABLS	10/01-12/01
	Scranton-Wilkes-Barre-Hazleton MSA, PA	H	6.29 FQ	11.07 AW	16.58 TQ	PABLS	10/01-12/01
	Rhode Island	H	11.45 FQ	16.40 AW	21.57 TQ	RIBLS	10/01-12/01
	Providence-Fall River-Warwick MSA, RI-MA	H	11.28 FQ	15.93 AW	21.22 TQ	RIBLS	10/01-12/01
	South Carolina	H	8.44 FQ	11.25 AW	14.29 TQ	SCBLS	10/01-12/01
	Charleston-North Charleston MSA, SC	H	8.58 FQ	10.59 AW	13.42 TQ	SCBLS	10/01-12/01
	Columbia MSA, SC	H	6.39 FQ	10.22 AW	13.65 TQ	SCBLS	10/01-12/01
	Greenville-Spartanburg-Anderson MSA, SC	H	9.97 FQ	12.44 AW	15.54 TQ	SCBLS	10/01-12/01
	South Dakota	H	7.69 FQ	10.24 AW	13.72 TQ	SDBLS	10/01-12/01
	Tennessee	H	8.07 FQ	11.86 AW	17.86 TQ	TNBLS	10/01-12/01
	Chattanooga MSA, TN-GA	H	7.58 FQ	10.69 AW	13.19 TQ	TNBLS	10/01-12/01
	Clarksville-Hopkinsville MSA, TN-KY	H	7.73 FQ	12.01 AW	17.03 TQ	TNBLS	10/01-12/01
	Johnson City-Kingsport-Bristol MSA, TN-VA	H	6.36 FQ	10.54 AW	14.25 TQ	TNBLS	10/01-12/01
	Knoxville MSA, TN	H	8.50 FQ	12.09 AW	18.14 TQ	TNBLS	10/01-12/01
	Memphis MSA, TN-AR-MS	H	9.05 FQ	15.14 AW	22.12 TQ	TNBLS	10/01-12/01
	Nashville MSA, TN	H	9.37 FQ	12.98 AW	17.59 TQ	TNBLS	10/01-12/01
	Texas	H	8.05 FQ	12.16 AW	16.91 TQ	TXBLS	10/01-12/01
	Austin-San Marcos MSA, TX	H	10.16 FQ	14.71 AW	20.11 TQ	TXBLS	10/01-12/01
	Beaumont-Port Arthur MSA, TX	H	8.45 FQ	12.05 AW	16.10 TQ	TXBLS	10/01-12/01
	Brazoria PMSA, TX	H	8.69 FQ	11.44 AW	14.16 TQ	TXBLS	10/01-12/01
	Brownsville-Harlingen-San Benito MSA, TX	H	8.13 FQ	10.47 AW	13.55 TQ	TXBLS	10/01-12/01
	Corpus Christi MSA, TX	H	7.11 FQ	10.37 AW	14.11 TQ	TXBLS	10/01-12/01
	Dallas PMSA, TX	H	9.86 FQ	14.26 AW	19.44 TQ	TXBLS	10/01-12/01
	El Paso MSA, TX	H	8.05 FQ	12.39 AW	14.62 TQ	TXBLS	10/01-12/01
	Fort Worth-Arlington PMSA, TX	H	9.84 FQ	13.15 AW	17.00 TQ	TXBLS	10/01-12/01
	Galveston-Texas City PMSA, TX	H	8.11 FQ	13.03 AW	17.21 TQ	TXBLS	10/01-12/01
	Houston PMSA, TX	H	8.93 FQ	12.98 AW	17.05 TQ	TXBLS	10/01-12/01
	Laredo MSA, TX	H	11.44 FQ	12.85 AW	15.08 TQ	TXBLS	10/01-12/01
	Longview-Marshall MSA, TX	H	7.87 FQ	9.69 AW	11.51 TQ	TXBLS	10/01-12/01
	McAllen-Edinburg-Mission MSA, TX	H	6.54 FQ	9.57 AW	12.89 TQ	TXBLS	10/01-12/01
	Odessa-Midland MSA, TX	H	9.65 FQ	11.84 AW	13.78 TQ	TXBLS	10/01-12/01
	San Antonio MSA, TX	H	9.37 FQ	11.67 AW	13.76 TQ	TXBLS	10/01-12/01
	Tyler MSA, TX	H	8.88 FQ	11.01 AW	13.85 TQ	TXBLS	10/01-12/01
	Waco MSA, TX	H	7.55 FQ	9.67 AW	12.43 TQ	TXBLS	10/01-12/01
	Utah	H	10.01 FQ	13.43 AW	17.70 TQ	UTBLS	10/01-12/01
	Provo-Orem MSA, UT	H	9.87 FQ	13.04 AW	16.96 TQ	UTBLS	10/01-12/01
	Salt Lake City-Ogden MSA, UT	H	9.98 FQ	13.96 AW	19.04 TQ	UTBLS	10/01-12/01
	Vermont	H	10.06 FQ	13.51 AW	17.20 TQ	VTBLS	10/01-12/01
	Burlington MSA, VT	H	11.15 FQ	13.84 AW	16.96 TQ	VTBLS	10/01-12/01
	Virginia	H	9.14 FQ	13.03 AW	18.78 TQ	VABLS	10/01-12/01
	Lynchburg MSA, VA	H	9.26 FQ	10.73 AW	13.18 TQ	VABLS	10/01-12/01
	Norfolk-Virginia Beach-Newport News MSA, VA-NC	H	9.42 FQ	13.35 AW	19.60 TQ	VABLS	10/01-12/01
	Richmond-Petersburg MSA, VA	H	10.97 FQ	13.95 AW	17.76 TQ	VABLS	10/01-12/01
	Roanoke MSA, VA	H	10.43 FQ	14.03 AW	18.05 TQ	VABLS	10/01-12/01
	Washington	H	12.32 FQ	16.71 AW	21.96 TQ	WABLS	10/01-12/01
	Seattle-Bellevue-Everett PMSA, WA	H	12.19 FQ	17.12 AW	22.57 TQ	WABLS	10/01-12/01
	Tacoma PMSA, WA	H	13.93 FQ	17.51 AW	21.23 TQ	WABLS	10/01-12/01
	Yakima MSA, WA	H	8.03 FQ	13.37 AW	18.20 TQ	WABLS	10/01-12/01
	West Virginia	H	5.99 FQ	8.29 AW	11.02 TQ	WVBLS	10/01-12/01
	Charleston MSA, WV	H	7.13 FQ	9.40 AW	12.02 TQ	WVBLS	10/01-12/01

AAW	Average annual wage	**AOH**	Average offered, high	**ASH**	Average starting, high	**H**	Hourly	**M**	Monthly	**S**	Special: hourly and annual
AE	Average entry wage	**AOL**	Average offered, low	**ASL**	Average starting, low	**HI**	Highest wage paid	**MTC**	Median total compensation	**TQ**	Third quartile wage
AEX	Average experienced wage	**APH**	Average pay, high range	**AW**	Average wage paid	**HR**	High end range	**MW**	Median wage paid	**W**	Weekly
AO	Average offered	**APL**	Average pay, low range	**FQ**	First quartile wage	**LR**	Low end range	**SQ**	Second quartile wage	**Y**	Yearly

Occupation/Type/Industry	Location	Per	Low	Mid	High	Source	Date
Police, Fire, and Ambulance Dispatcher	Huntington-Ashland MSA, WV-KY-OH	H	6.43 FQ	9.78 AW	15.37 TQ	WVBLS	10/01-12/01
	Wisconsin	H	11.43 FQ	15.23 AW	20.10 TQ	WIBLS	10/01-12/01
	Appleton-Oshkosh-Neenah MSA, WI	H	11.99 FQ	14.47 AW	16.95 TQ	WIBLS	10/01-12/01
	Green Bay MSA, WI	H	14.83 FQ	17.20 AW	21.20 TQ	WIBLS	10/01-12/01
	Madison MSA, WI	H	13.51 FQ	15.76 AW	19.19 TQ	WIBLS	10/01-12/01
	Milwaukee-Waukesha PMSA, WI	H	11.31 FQ	15.94 AW	21.44 TQ	WIBLS	10/01-12/01
	Racine PMSA, WI	H	11.94 FQ	16.90 AW	21.79 TQ	WIBLS	10/01-12/01
	Wyoming	H	9.39 FQ	11.87 AW	14.95 TQ	WYBLS	10/01-12/01
	Cheyenne MSA, WY	H	9.19 FQ	12.03 AW	16.06 TQ	WYBLS	10/01-12/01
	Puerto Rico	H	5.70 FQ	7.38 AW	10.26 TQ	PRBLS	10/01-12/01
	Virgin Islands	H	7.28 FQ	9.56 AW	12.96 TQ	VIBLS	10/01-12/01
Police Officer	United States	Y		39790 MW		OOH2	1/99-1/00
Federal government	United States	Y		37760 MW		OOH2	1/99-1/00
Local government	United States	Y		39710 MW		OOH2	1/99-1/00
State government	United States	Y		44400 MW		OOH2	1/99-1/00
Police Officer G-4							
Federal Government	San Francisco-Oakland-San Jose CMSA, CA	Y	33516 AE			OPM7	2003
Federal Government	Washington-Baltimore CMSA, DC-MD-VA-WV	Y	29542 AE			OPM5	2003
Federal Government	St. Louis MSA, MO-IL	Y	26400 AE			OPM2	2003
Federal Government	New York-Northern New Jersey-Long Island CMSA, NY-NJ-CT-PA	Y	30380 AE			OPM6	2003
Federal Government	Philadelphia-Wilmington-Atlantic City CMSA, PA-NJ-DE-MD	Y	28704 AE			OPM4	2003
Federal Government	Dallas-Fort Worth CMSA, TX	Y	27028 AE			OPM3	2003
Police Officer G-5							
Federal Government	Los Angeles-Riverside-Orange County CMSA, CA	Y	33991 AE			OPM6	2003
Federal Government	San Diego MSA, CA	Y	32116 AE			OPM4	2003
Federal Government	Kansas City MSA, MO-KS	Y	29537 AE			OPM2	2003
Federal Government	Portland-Salem CMSA, OR-WA	Y	30240 AE			OPM3	2003
Police Officer G-6							
Federal Government	Denver-Boulder-Greeley CMSA, CO	Y	35798 AE			OPM4	2003
Federal Government	Atlanta MSA, GA	Y	32924 AE			OPM2	2003
Police Officer G-7							
Federal Government	Boston-Worcester-Lawrence CMSA, MA-NH-ME-CT-RI	Y	39781 AE			OPM4	2003
Federal Government	Cleveland-Akron CMSA, OH	Y	36587 AE			OPM2	2003
Federal Government	Seattle-Tacoma-Bremerton CMSA, WA	Y	37458 AE			OPM3	2003
Police Officer G-8							
Federal Government	Chicago-Gary-Kenosha CMSA, IL-IN-WI	Y	42449 AE			OPM4	2003
Federal Government	Cincinnati-Hamilton CMSA, OH-KY-IN	Y	40198 AE			OPM3	2003
Police Officer G-9							
Federal Government	Miami-Fort Lauderdale CMSA, FL	Y	42623 AE			OPM3	2003
Federal Government	Detroit-Ann Arbor-Flint CMSA, MI	Y	45109 AE			OPM4	2003
Police Officer G-10							
Federal Government	Houston-Galveston-Brazoria CMSA, TX	Y	47720 AE			OPM4	2003
Police Patrol Officer	United States	Y	34556 AE			SCJS	1/99-1/00
250,000 to 349,999 population	United States	Y	35095 AE			SCJS	1/99-1/00

AAW Average annual wage; AE Average entry wage; AEX Average experienced wage; AO Average offered; AOH Average offered, high; AOL Average offered, low; APH Average pay, high range; APL Average pay, low range; ASH Average starting, high; ASL Average starting, low; AW Average wage paid; FQ First quartile wage; H Hourly; HI Highest wage paid; HR High end range; LR Low end range; M Monthly; MTC Median total compensation; MW Median wage paid; SQ Second quartile wage; S Special: hourly and annual; TQ Third quartile wage; W Weekly; Y Yearly

Occupation/Type/Industry	Location	Per	Low	Mid	High	Source	Date
Police Patrol Officer							
350,000 to 499,999 population	United States	Y	34476 AE			SCJS	1/99-1/00
500,000 to 999,999 population	United States	Y	34454 AE			SCJS	1/99-1/00
1,000,000 or more population	United States	Y	34153 AE			SCJS	1/99-1/00
Police Sergeant	United States	Y	50541 AE			SCJS	1/99-1/00
250,000 to 349,000 population	United States	Y	52298 AE			SCJS	1/99-1/00
350,000 to 499,000 population	United States	Y	48718 AE			SCJS	1/99-1/00
500,000 to 999,999 population	United States	Y	51265 AE			SCJS	1/99-1/00
1,000,000 or more population	United States	Y	49726 AE			SCJS	1/99-1/00
Political Science Teacher							
Postsecondary	Alabama	Y	28800 FQ	54100 AW	85210 TQ	ALBLS	10/01-12/01
Postsecondary	Arkansas	Y	28730 FQ	51990 AW	84250 TQ	ARBLS	10/01-12/01
Postsecondary	California	Y	45010 FQ	72630 AW	108070 TQ	CABLS	10/01-12/01
Postsecondary	Colorado	Y	33040 FQ	57170 AW	92850 TQ	COBLS	10/01-12/01
Postsecondary	District of Columbia	Y	43040 FQ	63170 AW	89500 TQ	DCBLS	10/01-12/01
Postsecondary	Florida	Y	37580 FQ	63710 AW	102740 TQ	FLBLS	10/01-12/01
Postsecondary	Georgia	Y	34730 FQ	56830 AW	85490 TQ	GABLS	10/01-12/01
Postsecondary	Hawaii	Y	38580 FQ	65070 AW	93270 TQ	HIBLS	10/01-12/01
Postsecondary	Illinois	Y	22840 FQ	55370 AW	91190 TQ	ILBLS	10/01-12/01
Postsecondary	Indiana	Y	31210 FQ	60300 AW	100960 TQ	INBLS	10/01-12/01
Postsecondary	Iowa	Y	35190 FQ	65080 AW	104930 TQ	IABLS	10/01-12/01
Postsecondary	Kansas	Y	21780 FQ	48960 AW	81680 TQ	KSBLS	10/01-12/01
Postsecondary	Kentucky	Y	36810 FQ	60920 AW	90370 TQ	KYBLS	10/01-12/01
Postsecondary	Louisiana	Y	32400 FQ	55450 AW	89070 TQ	LABLS	10/01-12/01
Postsecondary	Maine	Y	32720 FQ	53590 AW	73150 TQ	MEBLS	10/01-12/01
Postsecondary	Maryland	Y	37200 FQ	69530 AW	120020 TQ	MDBLS	10/01-12/01
Postsecondary	Massachusetts	Y	39870 FQ	66280 AW	108300 TQ	MABLS	10/01-12/01
Postsecondary	Michigan	Y	31510 FQ	60590 AW	96930 TQ	MIBLS	10/01-12/01
Postsecondary	Minnesota	Y	37820 FQ	64060 AW	110160 TQ	MNBLS	10/01-12/01
Postsecondary	Mississippi	Y	27110 FQ	47990 AW	68810 TQ	MSBLS	10/01-12/01
Postsecondary	Missouri	Y	27590 FQ	52100 AW	74240 TQ	MOBLS	10/01-12/01
Postsecondary	Nebraska	Y	38070 FQ	55820 AW	73360 TQ	NEBLS	10/01-12/01
Postsecondary	Nevada	Y	24700 FQ	55150 AW	92500 TQ	NVBLS	10/01-12/01
Postsecondary	New Hampshire	Y	37900 FQ	55750 AW	82550 TQ	NHBLS	10/01-12/01
Postsecondary	New Jersey	Y	38170 FQ	67390 AW	106220 TQ	NJBLS	10/01-12/01
Postsecondary	New York	Y	40770 FQ	69850 AW	109350 TQ	NYBLS	10/01-12/01
Postsecondary	North Carolina	Y	32050 FQ	52460 AW	83330 TQ	NCBLS	10/01-12/01
Postsecondary	Ohio	Y	29020 FQ	51710 AW	78000 TQ	OHBLS	10/01-12/01
Postsecondary	Oklahoma	Y	25510 FQ	39250 AW	57910 TQ	OKBLS	10/01-12/01
Postsecondary	Oregon	Y	36390 FQ	63220 AW	96470 TQ	ORBLS	10/01-12/01
Postsecondary	Pennsylvania	Y	27920 FQ	60210 AW	101740 TQ	PABLS	10/01-12/01
Postsecondary	Rhode Island	Y	35990 FQ	63450 AW	92450 TQ	RIBLS	10/01-12/01
Postsecondary	South Carolina	Y	34090 FQ	50570 AW	72150 TQ	SCBLS	10/01-12/01
Postsecondary	South Dakota	Y	37190 FQ	54010 AW	82460 TQ	SDBLS	10/01-12/01
Postsecondary	Tennessee	Y	29040 FQ	59780 AW	95020 TQ	TNBLS	10/01-12/01
Postsecondary	Texas	Y	31640 FQ	57920 AW	92630 TQ	TXBLS	10/01-12/01
Postsecondary	Utah	Y	40540 FQ	71830 AW	104040 TQ	UTBLS	10/01-12/01
Postsecondary	Vermont	Y	37250 FQ	53290 AW	77310 TQ	VTBLS	10/01-12/01
Postsecondary	Virginia	Y	34650 FQ	61550 AW	107160 TQ	VABLS	10/01-12/01
Postsecondary	Washington	Y	32450 FQ	65530 AW	110690 TQ	WABLS	10/01-12/01
Postsecondary	West Virginia	Y	34560 FQ	57010 AW	80020 TQ	WVBLS	10/01-12/01
Postsecondary	Wisconsin	Y	30030 FQ	54390 AW	87820 TQ	WIBLS	10/01-12/01
Postsecondary	Puerto Rico	Y	27440 FQ	47900 AW	82490 TQ	PRBLS	10/01-12/01
Political Scientist	California	Y	25210 FQ	54050 AW	99640 TQ	CABLS	10/01-12/01
	Connecticut	Y	33700 FQ	72510 AW		CTBLS	10/01-12/01
	District of Columbia	Y	48450 FQ	84010 AW	115900 TQ	DCBLS	10/01-12/01
	Florida	Y	37490 FQ	80600 AW		FLBLS	10/01-12/01
	Maryland	Y	34030 FQ	70370 AW	114100 TQ	MDBLS	10/01-12/01
	New York	Y	21030 FQ	69230 AW		NYBLS	10/01-12/01
	Virginia	Y	51850 FQ	77130 AW	111630 TQ	VABLS	10/01-12/01
Postal Service Clerk	Alabama	H	15.68 FQ	18.42 AW	20.97 TQ	ALBLS	10/01-12/01
	Alaska	H	15.96 FQ	18.50 AW	20.98 TQ	AKBLS	10/01-12/01
	Arizona	H	15.38 FQ	18.33 AW	20.96 TQ	AZBLS	10/01-12/01
	Arkansas	H	14.77 FQ	18.02 AW	20.90 TQ	ARBLS	10/01-12/01
	California	H	15.48 FQ	18.37 AW	20.97 TQ	CABLS	10/01-12/01
	Colorado	H	15.22 FQ	18.27 AW	20.95 TQ	COBLS	10/01-12/01
	Connecticut	H	15.98 FQ	18.52 AW	20.99 TQ	CTBLS	10/01-12/01
	Delaware	H	14.89 FQ	18.17 AW	21.00 TQ	DEBLS	10/01-12/01
	Florida	H	16.34 FQ	18.59 AW	21.00 TQ	FLBLS	10/01-12/01

AAW Average annual wage; **AE** Average entry wage; **AEX** Average experienced wage; **AO** Average offered; **AOH** Average offered, high; **AOL** Average offered, low; **APH** Average pay, high range; **APL** Average pay, low range; **ASH** Average starting, high; **ASL** Average starting, low; **AW** Average wage paid; **FQ** First quartile wage; **H** Hourly; **HI** Highest wage paid; **HR** High end range; **LR** Low end range; **M** Monthly; **MTC** Median total compensation; **MW** Median wage paid; **SQ** Second quartile wage; **S** Special: hourly and annual; **TQ** Third quartile wage; **W** Weekly; **Y** Yearly

Occupation/Type/Industry	Location	Per	Low	Mid	High	Source	Date
Postal Service Clerk	Georgia	H	14.86 FQ	18.05 AW	20.90 TQ	GABLS	10/01-12/01
	Hawaii	H	15.15 FQ	18.25 AW	20.95 TQ	HIBLS	10/01-12/01
	Idaho	H	14.79 FQ	18.01 AW	20.89 TQ	IDBLS	10/01-12/01
	Illinois	H	16.19 FQ	18.55 AW	20.99 TQ	ILBLS	10/01-12/01
	Indiana	H	15.93 FQ	18.49 AW	20.97 TQ	INBLS	10/01-12/01
	Iowa	H	17.10 FQ	18.75 AW	21.01 TQ	IABLS	10/01-12/01
	Kansas	H	15.30 FQ	18.30 AW	20.95 TQ	KSBLS	10/01-12/01
	Kentucky	H	15.15 FQ	18.22 AW	20.93 TQ	KYBLS	10/01-12/01
	Louisiana	H	15.51 FQ	18.37 AW	20.96 TQ	LABLS	10/01-12/01
	Maine	H	14.89 FQ	18.08 AW	20.91 TQ	MEBLS	10/01-12/01
	Maryland	H	16.02 FQ	18.52 AW	20.98 TQ	MDBLS	10/01-12/01
	Massachusetts	H	16.07 FQ	18.52 AW	20.99 TQ	MABLS	10/01-12/01
	Michigan	H	15.28 FQ	18.30 AW	20.95 TQ	MIBLS	10/01-12/01
	Minnesota	H	17.15 FQ	18.81 AW	21.03 TQ	MNBLS	10/01-12/01
	Mississippi	H	14.89 FQ	18.07 AW	20.91 TQ	MSBLS	10/01-12/01
	Missouri	H	16.11 FQ	18.57 AW	21.02 TQ	MOBLS	10/01-12/01
	Montana	H	15.36 FQ	18.31 AW	20.95 TQ	MTBLS	10/01-12/01
	Nebraska	H	15.19 FQ	18.24 AW	20.93 TQ	NEBLS	10/01-12/01
	Nevada	H	15.12 FQ	18.20 AW	20.93 TQ	NVBLS	10/01-12/01
	New Hampshire	H	15.58 FQ	18.39 AW	20.96 TQ	NHBLS	10/01-12/01
	New Jersey	H	15.32 FQ	18.31 AW	20.95 TQ	NJBLS	10/01-12/01
	New Mexico	H	15.74 FQ	18.44 AW	20.97 TQ	NMBLS	10/01-12/01
	New York	H	15.30 FQ	18.30 AW	20.95 TQ	NYBLS	10/01-12/01
	North Carolina	H	15.45 FQ	18.37 AW	20.97 TQ	NCBLS	10/01-12/01
	North Dakota	H	15.31 FQ	18.30 AW	20.94 TQ	NDBLS	10/01-12/01
	Ohio	H	15.93 FQ	18.48 AW	20.99 TQ	OHBLS	10/01-12/01
	Oklahoma	H	17.11 FQ	18.76 AW	21.01 TQ	OKBLS	10/01-12/01
	Oregon	H	15.31 FQ	18.30 AW	20.94 TQ	ORBLS	10/01-12/01
	Pennsylvania	H	15.57 FQ	18.40 AW	20.97 TQ	PABLS	10/01-12/01
	Rhode Island	H	16.51 FQ	18.60 AW	20.99 TQ	RIBLS	10/01-12/01
	South Carolina	H	15.77 FQ	18.45 AW	20.97 TQ	SCBLS	10/01-12/01
	South Dakota	H	15.12 FQ	18.20 AW	20.93 TQ	SDBLS	10/01-12/01
	Tennessee	H	16.08 FQ	18.54 AW	20.99 TQ	TNBLS	10/01-12/01
	Texas	H	15.31 FQ	18.31 AW	20.95 TQ	TXBLS	10/01-12/01
	Utah	H	15.01 FQ	18.14 AW	20.91 TQ	UTBLS	10/01-12/01
	Vermont	H	15.12 FQ	18.21 AW	20.93 TQ	VTBLS	10/01-12/01
	Virginia	H	15.43 FQ	18.36 AW	20.97 TQ	VABLS	10/01-12/01
	Washington	H	14.58 FQ	17.96 AW	20.91 TQ	WABLS	10/01-12/01
	West Virginia	H	14.78 FQ	17.98 AW	20.88 TQ	WVBLS	10/01-12/01
	Wisconsin	H	15.18 FQ	18.24 AW	20.94 TQ	WIBLS	10/01-12/01
	Wyoming	H	14.79 FQ	17.99 AW	20.88 TQ	WYBLS	10/01-12/01
Postal Service Mail Carrier	Alabama	H	14.07 FQ	17.85 AW	22.02 TQ	ALBLS	10/01-12/01
	Birmingham MSA, AL	H	14.04 FQ	17.78 AW	21.24 TQ	ALBLS	10/01-12/01
	Montgomery MSA, AL	H	14.27 FQ	17.78 AW	21.19 TQ	ALBLS	10/01-12/01
	Alaska	H	17.02 FQ	18.68 AW	21.03 TQ	AKBLS	10/01-12/01
	Arizona	H	14.91 FQ	18.22 AW	21.04 TQ	AZBLS	10/01-12/01
	Phoenix-Mesa MSA, AZ	H	15.03 FQ	18.26 AW	21.02 TQ	AZBLS	10/01-12/01
	Arkansas	H	14.10 FQ	17.74 AW	21.29 TQ	ARBLS	10/01-12/01
	Fort Smith MSA, AR-OK	H	14.37 FQ	18.08 AW	21.37 TQ	ARBLS	10/01-12/01
	Little Rock-North Little Rock MSA, AR	H	14.51 FQ	18.06 AW	21.08 TQ	ARBLS	10/01-12/01
	California	H	15.84 FQ	18.53 AW	21.05 TQ	CABLS	10/01-12/01
	Riverside-San Bernardino PMSA, CA	H	15.44 FQ	18.56 AW	21.17 TQ	CABLS	10/01-12/01
	Sacramento PMSA, CA	H	14.79 FQ	18.17 AW	21.05 TQ	CABLS	10/01-12/01
	San Francisco PMSA, CA	H	16.63 FQ	18.62 AW	20.99 TQ	CABLS	10/01-12/01
	Colorado	H	14.76 FQ	18.19 AW	21.03 TQ	COBLS	10/01-12/01
	Denver PMSA, CO	H	15.45 FQ	18.40 AW	21.01 TQ	COBLS	10/01-12/01
	Connecticut	H	15.14 FQ	18.52 AW	21.23 TQ	CTBLS	10/01-12/01
	Bridgeport PMSA, CT	H	17.09 FQ	18.84 AW	21.12 TQ	CTBLS	10/01-12/01
	Danbury PMSA, CT	H	13.96 FQ	18.26 AW	21.45 TQ	CTBLS	10/01-12/01
	Hartford MSA, CT	H	14.91 FQ	18.44 AW	21.24 TQ	CTBLS	10/01-12/01
	New Haven-Meriden PMSA, CT	H	16.71 FQ	18.69 AW	21.11 TQ	CTBLS	10/01-12/01
	New London-Norwich MSA, CT-RI	H	14.98 FQ	18.53 AW	21.31 TQ	CTBLS	10/01-12/01
	Stamford-Norwalk PMSA, CT	H	16.04 FQ	18.58 AW	21.05 TQ	CTBLS	10/01-12/01
	Waterbury PMSA, CT	H	15.06 FQ	18.47 AW	21.22 TQ	CTBLS	10/01-12/01
	Delaware	H	14.57 FQ	18.16 AW	21.23 TQ	DEBLS	10/01-12/01
	Washington PMSA, DC-MD-VA-WV	H	15.53 FQ	18.55 AW	21.15 TQ	DCBLS	10/01-12/01
	Florida	H	14.99 FQ	18.47 AW	21.25 TQ	FLBLS	10/01-12/01

AAW	Average annual wage	**AOH**	Average offered, high	**ASH**	Average starting, high	**H**	Hourly	**M**	Monthly	**S**	Special: hourly and annual
AE	Average entry wage	**AOL**	Average offered, low	**ASL**	Average starting, low	**HI**	Highest wage paid	**MTC**	Median total compensation	**TQ**	Third quartile wage
AEX	Average experienced wage	**APH**	Average pay, high range	**AW**	Average wage paid	**HR**	High end range	**MW**	Median wage paid	**W**	Weekly
AO	Average offered	**APL**	Average pay, low range	**FQ**	First quartile wage	**LR**	Low end range	**SQ**	Second quartile wage	**Y**	Yearly

Occupation/Type/Industry	Location	Per	Low	Mid	High	Source	Date
Postal Service Mail Carrier	Jacksonville MSA, FL	H	14.83 FQ	18.43 AW	21.32 TQ	FLBLS	10/01-12/01
	Orlando MSA, FL	H	15.07 FQ	18.45 AW	21.21 TQ	FLBLS	10/01-12/01
	Tampa-St. Petersburg-Clearwater MSA, FL	H	14.77 FQ	18.35 AW	21.25 TQ	FLBLS	10/01-12/01
	Georgia	H	14.02 FQ	17.75 AW	21.27 TQ	GABLS	10/01-12/01
	Atlanta MSA, GA	H	14.07 FQ	17.79 AW	21.13 TQ	GABLS	10/01-12/01
	Augusta-Aiken MSA, GA-SC	H	14.35 FQ	17.93 AW	21.21 TQ	GABLS	10/01-12/01
	Columbus MSA, GA-AL	H	14.73 FQ	18.16 AW	21.08 TQ	GABLS	10/01-12/01
	Macon MSA, GA	H	14.22 FQ	17.79 AW	21.10 TQ	GABLS	10/01-12/01
	Savannah MSA, GA	H	14.33 FQ	18.01 AW	21.28 TQ	GABLS	10/01-12/01
	Hawaii	H	16.80 FQ	18.72 AW	21.08 TQ	HIBLS	10/01-12/01
	Idaho	H	13.92 FQ	17.61 AW	21.12 TQ	IDBLS	10/01-12/01
	Illinois	H	15.11 FQ	18.39 AW	21.13 TQ	ILBLS	10/01-12/01
	Chicago PMSA, IL	H	15.81 FQ	18.55 AW	21.06 TQ	ILBLS	10/01-12/01
	Peoria-Pekin MSA, IL	H	15.08 FQ	18.40 AW	21.15 TQ	ILBLS	10/01-12/01
	Rockford MSA, IL	H	14.83 FQ	18.41 AW	21.31 TQ	ILBLS	10/01-12/01
	Indiana	H	14.36 FQ	18.10 AW	21.24 TQ	INBLS	10/01-12/01
	Evansville-Henderson MSA, IN-KY	H	14.47 FQ	18.10 AW	21.10 TQ	INBLS	10/01-12/01
	Fort Wayne MSA, IN	H	14.56 FQ	18.22 AW	21.22 TQ	INBLS	10/01-12/01
	Indianapolis MSA, IN	H	14.60 FQ	18.22 AW	21.14 TQ	INBLS	10/01-12/01
	Iowa	H	14.41 FQ	18.00 AW	21.19 TQ	IABLS	10/01-12/01
	Davenport-Moline-Rock Island MSA, IA-IL	H	14.88 FQ	18.26 AW	21.08 TQ	IABLS	10/01-12/01
	Des Moines MSA, IA	H	14.90 FQ	18.33 AW	21.14 TQ	IABLS	10/01-12/01
	Kansas	H	14.29 FQ	17.89 AW	21.08 TQ	KSBLS	10/01-12/01
	Wichita MSA, KS	H	14.46 FQ	18.09 AW	21.03 TQ	KSBLS	10/01-12/01
	Kentucky	H	14.18 FQ	17.91 AW	21.31 TQ	KYBLS	10/01-12/01
	Lexington MSA, KY	H	15.10 FQ	18.41 AW	21.15 TQ	KYBLS	10/01-12/01
	Louisville MSA, KY-IN	H	14.62 FQ	18.20 AW	21.14 TQ	KYBLS	10/01-12/01
	Louisiana	H	14.43 FQ	18.05 AW	21.13 TQ	LABLS	10/01-12/01
	Baton Rouge MSA, LA	H	14.08 FQ	17.72 AW	20.98 TQ	LABLS	10/01-12/01
	Lafayette MSA, LA	H	14.35 FQ	17.90 AW	21.18 TQ	LABLS	10/01-12/01
	New Orleans MSA, LA	H	16.39 FQ	18.66 AW	21.09 TQ	LABLS	10/01-12/01
	Shreveport-Bossier City MSA, LA	H	14.71 FQ	18.17 AW	21.07 TQ	LABLS	10/01-12/01
	Maine	H	13.46 FQ	17.40 AW	21.08 TQ	MEBLS	10/01-12/01
	Portland MSA, ME	H	14.46 FQ	18.11 AW	21.10 TQ	MEBLS	10/01-12/01
	Maryland	H	14.92 FQ	18.40 AW	21.17 TQ	MDBLS	10/01-12/01
	Baltimore PMSA, MD	H	14.73 FQ	18.33 AW	21.14 TQ	MDBLS	10/01-12/01
	Massachusetts	H	15.45 FQ	18.51 AW	21.12 TQ	MABLS	10/01-12/01
	Boston PMSA, MA-NH	H	15.98 FQ	18.57 AW	21.06 TQ	MABLS	10/01-12/01
	Brockton PMSA, MA	H	14.93 FQ	18.49 AW	21.31 TQ	MABLS	10/01-12/01
	Lawrence PMSA, MA-NH	H	14.26 FQ	18.13 AW	21.24 TQ	MABLS	10/01-12/01
	Lowell PMSA, MA-NH	H	15.04 FQ	18.47 AW	21.20 TQ	MABLS	10/01-12/01
	New Bedford PMSA, MA	H	15.38 FQ	18.46 AW	21.09 TQ	MABLS	10/01-12/01
	Springfield MSA, MA	H	15.66 FQ	18.60 AW	21.18 TQ	MABLS	10/01-12/01
	Worcester PMSA, MA-CT	H	14.97 FQ	18.48 AW	21.24 TQ	MABLS	10/01-12/01
	Michigan	H	14.41 FQ	18.09 AW	21.11 TQ	MIBLS	10/01-12/01
	Ann Arbor PMSA, MI	H	13.81 FQ	17.72 AW	21.27 TQ	MIBLS	10/01-12/01
	Detroit PMSA, MI	H	15.75 FQ	18.50 AW	21.03 TQ	MIBLS	10/01-12/01
	Grand Rapids-Muskegon-Holland MSA, MI	H	13.78 FQ	17.89 AW	21.16 TQ	MIBLS	10/01-12/01
	Kalamazoo-Battle Creek MSA, MI	H	14.18 FQ	18.05 AW	21.13 TQ	MIBLS	10/01-12/01
	Lansing-East Lansing MSA, MI	H	14.53 FQ	18.26 AW	21.25 TQ	MIBLS	10/01-12/01
	Saginaw-Bay City-Midland MSA, MI	H	14.62 FQ	18.17 AW	21.13 TQ	MIBLS	10/01-12/01
	Minnesota	H	14.25 FQ	18.03 AW	21.19 TQ	MNBLS	10/01-12/01
	Minneapolis-St. Paul MSA, MN-WI	H	14.51 FQ	18.19 AW	21.09 TQ	MNBLS	10/01-12/01
	Mississippi	H	13.86 FQ	17.65 AW	22.91 TQ	MSBLS	10/01-12/01
	Biloxi-Gulfport-Pascagoula MSA, MS	H	14.19 FQ	17.69 AW	21.11 TQ	MSBLS	10/01-12/01
	Jackson MSA, MS	H	13.79 FQ	17.59 AW	21.44 TQ	MSBLS	10/01-12/01
	Missouri	H	14.40 FQ	17.98 AW	21.11 TQ	MOBLS	10/01-12/01
	Kansas City MSA, MO-KS	H	14.85 FQ	18.22 AW	21.04 TQ	MOBLS	10/01-12/01
	St. Louis MSA, MO-IL	H	15.08 FQ	18.32 AW	21.09 TQ	MOBLS	10/01-12/01
	Springfield MSA, MO	H	14.23 FQ	17.79 AW	21.11 TQ	MOBLS	10/01-12/01
	Montana	H	14.08 FQ	17.72 AW	21.06 TQ	MTBLS	10/01-12/01
	Nebraska	H	14.45 FQ	17.97 AW	21.12 TQ	NEBLS	10/01-12/01
	Omaha MSA, NE-IA	H	15.34 FQ	18.48 AW	21.12 TQ	NEBLS	10/01-12/01

AAW	Average annual wage	**AOH**	Average offered, high	**ASH**	Average starting, high	**H**	Hourly	**M**	Monthly	**S**	Special: hourly and annual
AE	Average entry wage	**AOL**	Average offered, low	**ASL**	Average starting, low	**HI**	Highest wage paid	**MTC**	Median total compensation	**TQ**	Third quartile wage
AEX	Average experienced wage	**APH**	Average pay, high range	**AW**	Average wage paid	**HR**	High end range	**MW**	Median wage paid	**W**	Weekly
AO	Average offered	**APL**	Average pay, low range	**FQ**	First quartile wage	**LR**	Low end range	**SQ**	Second quartile wage	**Y**	Yearly

Occupation/Type/Industry	Location	Per	Low	Mid	High	Source	Date
Postal Service Mail Carrier	Nevada	H	15.38 FQ	18.36 AW	20.99 TQ	NVBLS	10/01-12/01
	Las Vegas MSA, NV-AZ	H	15.54 FQ	18.41 AW	20.99 TQ	NVBLS	10/01-12/01
	New Hampshire	H	13.60 FQ	17.81 AW	21.31 TQ	NHBLS	10/01-12/01
	Manchester PMSA, NH	H	15.14 FQ	18.67 AW	21.39 TQ	NHBLS	10/01-12/01
	Nashua PMSA, NH	H	14.02 FQ	18.09 AW	21.20 TQ	NHBLS	10/01-12/01
	Portsmouth-Rochester PMSA, NH-ME	H	13.84 FQ	17.94 AW	21.24 TQ	NHBLS	10/01-12/01
	New Jersey	H	15.25 FQ	18.46 AW	21.14 TQ	NJBLS	10/01-12/01
	Middlesex-Somerset-Hunterdon PMSA, NJ	H	15.06 FQ	18.47 AW	21.22 TQ	NJBLS	10/01-12/01
	Newark PMSA, NJ	H	15.11 FQ	18.44 AW	21.16 TQ	NJBLS	10/01-12/01
	New Mexico	H	14.95 FQ	18.35 AW	21.12 TQ	NMBLS	10/01-12/01
	Albuquerque MSA, NM	H	15.39 FQ	18.45 AW	21.07 TQ	NMBLS	10/01-12/01
	New York	H	15.07 FQ	18.33 AW	21.07 TQ	NYBLS	10/01-12/01
	Albany-Schenectady-Troy MSA, NY	H	13.99 FQ	18.05 AW	21.24 TQ	NYBLS	10/01-12/01
	New York PMSA, NY	H	15.96 FQ	18.52 AW	21.00 TQ	NYBLS	10/01-12/01
	Rochester MSA, NY	H	14.94 FQ	18.29 AW	21.13 TQ	NYBLS	10/01-12/01
	Syracuse MSA, NY	H	13.94 FQ	17.90 AW	21.17 TQ	NYBLS	10/01-12/01
	North Carolina	H	13.76 FQ	17.59 AW	21.22 TQ	NCBLS	10/01-12/01
	Charlotte-Gastonia-Rock Hill MSA, NC-SC	H	13.65 FQ	17.55 AW	21.15 TQ	NCBLS	10/01-12/01
	Greensboro-Winston-Salem-High Point MSA, NC	H	13.99 FQ	17.80 AW	21.17 TQ	NCBLS	10/01-12/01
	Hickory-Morganton-Lenoir MSA, NC	H	13.96 FQ	17.82 AW	21.75 TQ	NCBLS	10/01-12/01
	Raleigh-Durham-Chapel Hill MSA, NC	H	13.58 FQ	17.49 AW	21.04 TQ	NCBLS	10/01-12/01
	North Dakota	H	14.36 FQ	17.92 AW	21.24 TQ	NDBLS	10/01-12/01
	Ohio	H	14.80 FQ	18.29 AW	21.16 TQ	OHBLS	10/01-12/01
	Cincinnati PMSA, OH-KY-IN	H	14.82 FQ	18.28 AW	21.12 TQ	OHBLS	10/01-12/01
	Cleveland-Lorain-Elyria PMSA, OH	H	17.10 FQ	18.82 AW	21.11 TQ	OHBLS	10/01-12/01
	Columbus MSA, OH	H	14.53 FQ	18.10 AW	21.16 TQ	OHBLS	10/01-12/01
	Dayton-Springfield MSA, OH	H	15.85 FQ	18.58 AW	21.09 TQ	OHBLS	10/01-12/01
	Toledo MSA, OH	H	15.09 FQ	18.35 AW	21.07 TQ	OHBLS	10/01-12/01
	Youngstown-Warren MSA, OH	H	14.59 FQ	18.17 AW	21.10 TQ	OHBLS	10/01-12/01
	Oklahoma	H	14.05 FQ	17.98 AW	21.32 TQ	OKBLS	10/01-12/01
	Oklahoma City MSA, OK	H	14.59 FQ	18.28 AW	21.25 TQ	OKBLS	10/01-12/01
	Tulsa MSA, OK	H	14.52 FQ	18.18 AW	21.15 TQ	OKBLS	10/01-12/01
	Oregon	H	14.90 FQ	18.32 AW	21.12 TQ	ORBLS	10/01-12/01
	Portland-Vancouver PMSA, OR-WA	H	15.06 FQ	18.36 AW	21.08 TQ	ORBLS	10/01-12/01
	Pennsylvania	H	14.68 FQ	18.29 AW	21.20 TQ	PABLS	10/01-12/01
	Allentown-Bethlehem-Easton MSA, PA	H	14.59 FQ	18.33 AW	21.27 TQ	PABLS	10/01-12/01
	Harrisburg-Lebanon-Carlisle MSA, PA	H	14.57 FQ	18.43 AW	21.43 TQ	PABLS	10/01-12/01
	Philadelphia PMSA, PA-NJ	H	15.73 FQ	18.53 AW	21.08 TQ	PABLS	10/01-12/01
	Pittsburgh MSA, PA	H	14.92 FQ	18.30 AW	21.09 TQ	PABLS	10/01-12/01
	Scranton-Wilkes-Barre-Hazleton MSA, PA	H	14.61 FQ	18.26 AW	21.22 TQ	PABLS	10/01-12/01
	Rhode Island	H	15.68 FQ	18.59 AW	21.14 TQ	RIBLS	10/01-12/01
	Providence-Fall River-Warwick MSA, RI-MA	H	16.24 FQ	18.69 AW	21.14 TQ	RIBLS	10/01-12/01
	South Carolina	H	14.08 FQ	17.73 AW	21.28 TQ	SCBLS	10/01-12/01
	Charleston-North Charleston MSA, SC	H	13.91 FQ	17.78 AW	21.31 TQ	SCBLS	10/01-12/01
	Greenville-Spartanburg-Anderson MSA, SC	H	14.24 FQ	17.81 AW	21.15 TQ	SCBLS	10/01-12/01
	South Dakota	H	14.29 FQ	17.80 AW	21.19 TQ	SDBLS	10/01-12/01
	Tennessee	H	14.08 FQ	18.02 AW	22.45 TQ	TNBLS	10/01-12/01
	Chattanooga MSA, TN-GA	H	14.28 FQ	18.24 AW	22.17 TQ	TNBLS	10/01-12/01
	Johnson City-Kingsport-Bristol MSA, TN-VA	H	14.23 FQ	18.12 AW	23.25 TQ	TNBLS	10/01-12/01
	Knoxville MSA, TN	H	14.30 FQ	18.08 AW	22.28 TQ	TNBLS	10/01-12/01
	Memphis MSA, TN-AR-MS	H	14.47 FQ	18.21 AW	21.22 TQ	TNBLS	10/01-12/01
	Nashville MSA, TN	H	14.05 FQ	18.00 AW	21.42 TQ	TNBLS	10/01-12/01
	Texas	H	14.55 FQ	18.16 AW	21.17 TQ	TXBLS	10/01-12/01
	Austin-San Marcos MSA, TX	H	14.16 FQ	17.95 AW	21.14 TQ	TXBLS	10/01-12/01
	Beaumont-Port Arthur MSA, TX	H	15.13 FQ	18.34 AW	21.11 TQ	TXBLS	10/01-12/01

AAW	Average annual wage	**AOH**	Average offered, high	**ASH**	Average starting, high	**H**	Hourly	**M**	Monthly	**S**	Special: hourly and annual
AE	Average entry wage	**AOL**	Average offered, low	**ASL**	Average starting, low	**HI**	Highest wage paid	**MTC**	Median total compensation	**TQ**	Third quartile wage
AEX	Average experienced wage	**APH**	Average pay, high range	**AW**	Average wage paid	**HR**	High end range	**MW**	Median wage paid	**W**	Weekly
AO	Average offered	**APL**	Average pay, low range	**FQ**	First quartile wage	**LR**	Low end range	**SQ**	Second quartile wage	**Y**	Yearly

Occupation/Type/Industry	Location	Per	Low	Mid	High	Source	Date
Postal Service Mail Carrier	Dallas PMSA, TX	H	14.52 FQ	18.07 AW	21.11 TQ	TXBLS	10/01-12/01
	Fort Worth-Arlington PMSA, TX	H	14.16 FQ	18.11 AW	21.27 TQ	TXBLS	10/01-12/01
	Houston PMSA, TX	H	15.58 FQ	18.51 AW	21.11 TQ	TXBLS	10/01-12/01
	Longview-Marshall MSA, TX	H	14.33 FQ	17.99 AW	21.44 TQ	TXBLS	10/01-12/01
	San Antonio MSA, TX	H	15.02 FQ	18.42 AW	21.18 TQ	TXBLS	10/01-12/01
	Utah	H	14.66 FQ	18.17 AW	21.07 TQ	UTBLS	10/01-12/01
	Salt Lake City-Ogden MSA, UT	H	15.11 FQ	18.36 AW	21.07 TQ	UTBLS	10/01-12/01
	Vermont	H	12.83 FQ	17.33 AW	21.42 TQ	VTBLS	10/01-12/01
	Burlington MSA, VT	H	14.11 FQ	18.12 AW	21.39 TQ	VTBLS	10/01-12/01
	Virginia	H	14.47 FQ	18.18 AW	21.26 TQ	VABLS	10/01-12/01
	Lynchburg MSA, VA	H	14.02 FQ	17.79 AW	21.32 TQ	VABLS	10/01-12/01
	Norfolk-Virginia Beach-Newport News MSA, VA-NC	H	15.69 FQ	18.54 AW	21.08 TQ	VABLS	10/01-12/01
	Richmond-Petersburg MSA, VA	H	14.46 FQ	18.18 AW	21.28 TQ	VABLS	10/01-12/01
	Roanoke MSA, VA	H	15.26 FQ	18.52 AW	21.19 TQ	VABLS	10/01-12/01
	Washington	H	14.86 FQ	18.22 AW	21.06 TQ	WABLS	10/01-12/01
	Seattle-Bellevue-Everett PMSA, WA	H	15.44 FQ	18.41 AW	21.02 TQ	WABLS	10/01-12/01
	West Virginia	H	14.08 FQ	17.84 AW	21.22 TQ	WVBLS	10/01-12/01
	Huntington-Ashland MSA, WV-KY-OH	H	14.09 FQ	17.79 AW	21.25 TQ	WVBLS	10/01-12/01
	Wisconsin	H	14.23 FQ	17.88 AW	21.17 TQ	WIBLS	10/01-12/01
	Appleton-Oshkosh-Neenah MSA, WI	H	14.53 FQ	18.04 AW	21.12 TQ	WIBLS	10/01-12/01
	Milwaukee-Waukesha PMSA, WI	H	15.34 FQ	18.40 AW	21.06 TQ	WIBLS	10/01-12/01
	Wyoming	H	15.31 FQ	18.36 AW	21.02 TQ	WYBLS	10/01-12/01
Postal Service Mail Sorter, Processor, and Processing Machine Operator	Alabama	H	7.60 FQ	14.78 AW	20.50 TQ	ALBLS	10/01-12/01
	Alaska	H	8.44 FQ	13.30 AW	19.97 TQ	AKBLS	10/01-12/01
	Arizona	H	11.40 FQ	15.63 AW	20.49 TQ	AZBLS	10/01-12/01
	Arkansas	H	8.54 FQ	13.74 AW	20.05 TQ	ARBLS	10/01-12/01
	California	H	9.95 FQ	15.71 AW	20.66 TQ	CABLS	10/01-12/01
	Colorado	H	11.11 FQ	14.96 AW	20.38 TQ	COBLS	10/01-12/01
	Connecticut	H	11.33 FQ	16.39 AW	20.74 TQ	CTBLS	10/01-12/01
	Delaware	H	11.12 FQ	15.12 AW	20.43 TQ	DEBLS	10/01-12/01
	Florida	H	8.50 FQ	14.99 AW	20.60 TQ	FLBLS	10/01-12/01
	Georgia	H	9.29 FQ	15.07 AW	20.48 TQ	GABLS	10/01-12/01
	Hawaii	H	7.28 FQ	14.12 AW	20.56 TQ	HIBLS	10/01-12/01
	Idaho	H	8.56 FQ	13.52 AW	20.04 TQ	IDBLS	10/01-12/01
	Illinois	H	9.54 FQ	15.58 AW	20.64 TQ	ILBLS	10/01-12/01
	Indiana	H	10.58 FQ	15.51 AW	20.47 TQ	INBLS	10/01-12/01
	Iowa	H	8.92 FQ	15.01 AW	20.57 TQ	IABLS	10/01-12/01
	Kansas	H	8.78 FQ	15.03 AW	20.58 TQ	KSBLS	10/01-12/01
	Kentucky	H	8.87 FQ	14.00 AW	20.14 TQ	KYBLS	10/01-12/01
	Louisiana	H	8.74 FQ	15.33 AW	20.57 TQ	LABLS	10/01-12/01
	Maine	H	9.35 FQ	14.88 AW	20.38 TQ	MEBLS	10/01-12/01
	Maryland	H	9.53 FQ	16.17 AW	20.78 TQ	MDBLS	10/01-12/01
	Massachusetts	H	11.61 FQ	16.46 AW	20.75 TQ	MABLS	10/01-12/01
	Michigan	H	9.18 FQ	14.82 AW	20.40 TQ	MIBLS	10/01-12/01
	Minnesota	H	11.23 FQ	15.76 AW	20.56 TQ	MNBLS	10/01-12/01
	Mississippi	H	7.46 FQ	14.15 AW	20.38 TQ	MSBLS	10/01-12/01
	Missouri	H	9.15 FQ	15.32 AW	20.61 TQ	MOBLS	10/01-12/01
	Montana	H	8.06 FQ	12.60 AW	19.41 TQ	MTBLS	10/01-12/01
	Nebraska	H	9.07 FQ	14.67 AW	20.33 TQ	NEBLS	10/01-12/01
	Nevada	H	8.99 FQ	14.31 AW	20.38 TQ	NVBLS	10/01-12/01
	New Hampshire	H	11.01 FQ	14.15 AW	20.01 TQ	NHBLS	10/01-12/01
	New Jersey	H	10.15 FQ	16.51 AW	20.80 TQ	NJBLS	10/01-12/01
	New Mexico	H	9.40 FQ	14.00 AW	19.94 TQ	NMBLS	10/01-12/01
	New York	H	9.48 FQ	15.90 AW	20.72 TQ	NYBLS	10/01-12/01
	North Carolina	H	11.00 FQ	15.27 AW	20.42 TQ	NCBLS	10/01-12/01
	North Dakota	H	8.14 FQ	13.19 AW	19.80 TQ	NDBLS	10/01-12/01
	Ohio	H	9.53 FQ	15.24 AW	20.54 TQ	OHBLS	10/01-12/01
	Oklahoma	H	8.84 FQ	14.68 AW	20.44 TQ	OKBLS	10/01-12/01
	Oregon	H	11.23 FQ	15.48 AW	20.44 TQ	ORBLS	10/01-12/01
	Pennsylvania	H	9.38 FQ	15.73 AW	20.71 TQ	PABLS	10/01-12/01

AAW	Average annual wage	**AOH**	Average offered, high	**ASH**	Average starting, high	**H**	Hourly	**M**	Monthly	**S**	Special: hourly and annual
AE	Average entry wage	**AOL**	Average offered, low	**ASL**	Average starting, low	**HI**	Highest wage paid	**MTC**	Median total compensation	**TQ**	Third quartile wage
AEX	Average experienced wage	**APH**	Average pay, high range	**AW**	Average wage paid	**HR**	High end range	**MW**	Median wage paid	**W**	Weekly
AO	Average offered	**APL**	Average pay, low range	**FQ**	First quartile wage	**LR**	Low end range	**SQ**	Second quartile wage	**Y**	Yearly

Occupation/Type/Industry	Location	Per	Low	Mid	High	Source	Date
Postal Service Mail Sorter, Processor, and Processing Machine Operator	Rhode Island	H	11.37 FQ	15.60 AW	20.55 TQ	RIBLS	10/01-12/01
	South Carolina	H	8.93 FQ	13.82 AW	20.18 TQ	SCBLS	10/01-12/01
	South Dakota	H	7.78 FQ	13.29 AW	20.01 TQ	SDBLS	10/01-12/01
	Tennessee	H	9.59 FQ	15.95 AW	20.66 TQ	TNBLS	10/01-12/01
	Texas	H	9.99 FQ	16.16 AW	20.68 TQ	TXBLS	10/01-12/01
	Utah	H	8.92 FQ	14.38 AW	20.37 TQ	UTBLS	10/01-12/01
	Vermont	H	8.75 FQ	14.22 AW	20.21 TQ	VTBLS	10/01-12/01
	Virginia	H	11.09 FQ	16.07 AW	20.70 TQ	VABLS	10/01-12/01
	Washington	H	11.00 FQ	14.76 AW	20.24 TQ	WABLS	10/01-12/01
	West Virginia	H	8.27 FQ	13.22 AW	19.85 TQ	WVBLS	10/01-12/01
	Wisconsin	H	9.23 FQ	15.02 AW	20.48 TQ	WIBLS	10/01-12/01
	Wyoming	H	7.18 FQ	11.74 AW	19.48 TQ	WYBLS	10/01-12/01
Postmaster and Mail Superintendent	Alabama	Y	35930 FQ	47210 AW	64980 TQ	ALBLS	10/01-12/01
	Alaska	Y	22310 FQ	38190 AW	54610 TQ	AKBLS	10/01-12/01
	Arizona	Y	37070 FQ	49490 AW	67110 TQ	AZBLS	10/01-12/01
	Arkansas	Y	30200 FQ	43160 AW	58620 TQ	ARBLS	10/01-12/01
	California	Y	37050 FQ	53300 AW	73130 TQ	CABLS	10/01-12/01
	Colorado	Y	31540 FQ	45630 AW	64750 TQ	COBLS	10/01-12/01
	Connecticut	Y	38340 FQ	52980 AW	69670 TQ	CTBLS	10/01-12/01
	Delaware	Y	37760 FQ	53290 AW	70180 TQ	DEBLS	10/01-12/01
	Florida	Y	39180 FQ	55850 AW	71750 TQ	FLBLS	10/01-12/01
	Georgia	Y	37100 FQ	50080 AW	67780 TQ	GABLS	10/01-12/01
	Hawaii	Y	36220 FQ	49190 AW	67400 TQ	HIBLS	10/01-12/01
	Idaho	Y	32660 FQ	44730 AW	63490 TQ	IDBLS	10/01-12/01
	Illinois	Y	35470 FQ	46620 AW	65950 TQ	ILBLS	10/01-12/01
	Indiana	Y	35440 FQ	46520 AW	65400 TQ	INBLS	10/01-12/01
	Iowa	Y	31730 FQ	42830 AW	56500 TQ	IABLS	10/01-12/01
	Kansas	Y	27820 FQ	41930 AW	58920 TQ	KSBLS	10/01-12/01
	Kentucky	Y	29290 FQ	42830 AW	59680 TQ	KYBLS	10/01-12/01
	Louisiana	Y	36480 FQ	48220 AW	66320 TQ	LABLS	10/01-12/01
	Maine	Y	35370 FQ	44700 AW	59760 TQ	MEBLS	10/01-12/01
	Maryland	Y	36320 FQ	49100 AW	67310 TQ	MDBLS	10/01-12/01
	Massachusetts	Y	39100 FQ	54340 AW	69740 TQ	MABLS	10/01-12/01
	Michigan	Y	36810 FQ	49500 AW	67180 TQ	MIBLS	10/01-12/01
	Minnesota	Y	35530 FQ	45530 AW	62950 TQ	MNBLS	10/01-12/01
	Mississippi	Y	36550 FQ	47270 AW	64580 TQ	MSBLS	10/01-12/01
	Missouri	Y	29790 FQ	43560 AW	61980 TQ	MOBLS	10/01-12/01
	Montana	Y	28210 FQ	40430 AW	55510 TQ	MTBLS	10/01-12/01
	Nebraska	Y	33520 FQ	42530 AW	55540 TQ	NEBLS	10/01-12/01
	Nevada	Y	31560 FQ	45840 AW	66170 TQ	NVBLS	10/01-12/01
	New Hampshire	Y	37120 FQ	49040 AW	66530 TQ	NHBLS	10/01-12/01
	New Jersey	Y	40430 FQ	56500 AW	70720 TQ	NJBLS	10/01-12/01
	New Mexico	Y	27890 FQ	41200 AW	58020 TQ	NMBLS	10/01-12/01
	New York	Y	36700 FQ	49010 AW	66860 TQ	NYBLS	10/01-12/01
	North Carolina	Y	37380 FQ	49900 AW	67480 TQ	NCBLS	10/01-12/01
	North Dakota	Y	24700 FQ	38100 AW	50560 TQ	NDBLS	10/01-12/01
	Ohio	Y	35960 FQ	47750 AW	66150 TQ	OHBLS	10/01-12/01
	Oklahoma	Y	31990 FQ	44190 AW	61580 TQ	OKBLS	10/01-12/01
	Oregon	Y	33110 FQ	46620 AW	66460 TQ	ORBLS	10/01-12/01
	Pennsylvania	Y	35810 FQ	46710 AW	64970 TQ	PABLS	10/01-12/01
	Rhode Island	Y	38020 FQ	53390 AW	70250 TQ	RIBLS	10/01-12/01
	South Carolina	Y	36820 FQ	49750 AW	67380 TQ	SCBLS	10/01-12/01
	South Dakota	Y	29600 FQ	39820 AW	52440 TQ	SDBLS	10/01-12/01
	Tennessee	Y	36710 FQ	49250 AW	66870 TQ	TNBLS	10/01-12/01
	Texas	Y	33770 FQ	47010 AW	66380 TQ	TXBLS	10/01-12/01
	Utah	Y	35770 FQ	47380 AW	66650 TQ	UTBLS	10/01-12/01
	Vermont	Y	35610 FQ	43830 AW	58990 TQ	VTBLS	10/01-12/01
	Virginia	Y	33870 FQ	45780 AW	64020 TQ	VABLS	10/01-12/01
	Washington	Y	34330 FQ	48010 AW	67510 TQ	WABLS	10/01-12/01
	West Virginia	Y	31510 FQ	41810 AW	55490 TQ	WVBLS	10/01-12/01
	Wisconsin	Y	36320 FQ	47610 AW	64850 TQ	WIBLS	10/01-12/01
	Wyoming	Y	26570 FQ	40620 AW	59250 TQ	WYBLS	10/01-12/01
Pourer and Caster							
Metal	Alabama	H	8.24 FQ	13.44 AW	18.66 TQ	ALBLS	10/01-12/01
Metal	Birmingham MSA, AL	H	11.59 FQ	16.03 AW	21.32 TQ	ALBLS	10/01-12/01
Metal	Montgomery MSA, AL	H	11.13 FQ	12.87 AW	15.76 TQ	ALBLS	10/01-12/01
Metal	Arizona	H	9.66 FQ	13.17 AW	17.12 TQ	AZBLS	10/01-12/01

AAW	Average annual wage	AOH	Average offered, high	ASH	Average starting, high	H	Hourly	M	Monthly	S	Special: hourly and annual
AE	Average entry wage	AOL	Average offered, low	ASL	Average starting, low	HI	Highest wage paid	MTC	Median total compensation	TQ	Third quartile wage
AEX	Average experienced wage	APH	Average pay, high range	AW	Average wage paid	HR	High end range	MW	Median wage paid	W	Weekly
AO	Average offered	APL	Average pay, low range	FQ	First quartile wage	LR	Low end range	SQ	Second quartile wage	Y	Yearly

Occupation/Type/Industry	Location	Per	Low	Mid	High	Source	Date
Pourer and Caster							
Metal	Phoenix-Mesa MSA, AZ	H	9.58 FQ	12.27 AW	16.23 TQ	AZBLS	10/01-12/01
Metal	Arkansas	H	9.67 FQ	14.01 AW	17.49 TQ	ARBLS	10/01-12/01
Metal	California	H	7.39 FQ	11.54 AW	17.27 TQ	CABLS	10/01-12/01
Metal	Los Angeles-Long Beach PMSA, CA	H	6.93 FQ	10.28 AW	13.41 TQ	CABLS	10/01-12/01
Metal	Oakland PMSA, CA	H	7.55 FQ	15.40 AW	23.74 TQ	CABLS	10/01-12/01
Metal	Riverside-San Bernardino PMSA, CA	H	7.98 FQ	11.96 AW	20.42 TQ	CABLS	10/01-12/01
Metal	Colorado	H	9.39 FQ	12.68 AW	17.35 TQ	COBLS	10/01-12/01
Metal	Connecticut	H	9.36 FQ	12.63 AW	16.63 TQ	CTBLS	10/01-12/01
Metal	Florida	H	7.93 FQ	11.41 AW	16.23 TQ	FLBLS	10/01-12/01
Metal	Tampa-St. Petersburg-Clearwater MSA, FL	H	7.91 FQ	12.39 AW	16.97 TQ	FLBLS	10/01-12/01
Metal	Georgia	H	9.85 FQ	14.30 AW	21.14 TQ	GABLS	10/01-12/01
Metal	Illinois	H	9.31 FQ	12.82 AW	16.84 TQ	ILBLS	10/01-12/01
Metal	Chicago PMSA, IL	H	9.45 FQ	12.60 AW	16.50 TQ	ILBLS	10/01-12/01
Metal	Peoria-Pekin MSA, IL	H	9.27 FQ	15.81 AW	26.51 TQ	ILBLS	10/01-12/01
Metal	Indiana	H	9.45 FQ	15.24 AW	23.25 TQ	INBLS	10/01-12/01
Metal	Evansville-Henderson MSA, IN-KY	H	10.17 FQ	16.31 AW	21.93 TQ	INBLS	10/01-12/01
Metal	Fort Wayne MSA, IN	H	9.81 FQ	12.82 AW	15.92 TQ	INBLS	10/01-12/01
Metal	Indianapolis MSA, IN	H	9.06 FQ	12.18 AW	16.85 TQ	INBLS	10/01-12/01
Metal	South Bend MSA, IN	H	9.52 FQ	15.74 AW	24.99 TQ	INBLS	10/01-12/01
Metal	Iowa	H	9.82 FQ	13.20 AW	17.99 TQ	IABLS	10/01-12/01
Metal	Kansas	H	8.05 FQ	11.81 AW	16.19 TQ	KSBLS	10/01-12/01
Metal	Kentucky	H	10.50 FQ	14.39 AW	19.92 TQ	KYBLS	10/01-12/01
Metal	Louisiana	H	6.65 FQ	11.15 AW	16.12 TQ	LABLS	10/01-12/01
Metal	Baltimore PMSA, MD	H	12.36 FQ	18.08 AW	25.04 TQ	MDBLS	10/01-12/01
Metal	Massachusetts	H	9.43 FQ	13.53 AW	18.67 TQ	MABLS	10/01-12/01
Metal	Michigan	H	9.92 FQ	15.01 AW	24.05 TQ	MIBLS	10/01-12/01
Metal	Ann Arbor PMSA, MI	H	10.27 FQ	12.81 AW	16.27 TQ	MIBLS	10/01-12/01
Metal	Detroit PMSA, MI	H	10.45 FQ	15.31 AW	21.34 TQ	MIBLS	10/01-12/01
Metal	Grand Rapids-Muskegon-Holland MSA, MI	H	9.25 FQ	11.76 AW	15.51 TQ	MIBLS	10/01-12/01
Metal	Saginaw-Bay City-Midland MSA, MI	H	14.66 FQ	23.22 AW	27.55 TQ	MIBLS	10/01-12/01
Metal	Minnesota	H	10.52 FQ	13.92 AW	17.31 TQ	MNBLS	10/01-12/01
Metal	Minneapolis-St. Paul MSA, MN-WI	H	12.22 FQ	15.02 AW	17.68 TQ	MNBLS	10/01-12/01
Metal	Missouri	H	8.71 FQ	12.18 AW	16.72 TQ	MOBLS	10/01-12/01
Metal	St. Louis MSA, MO-IL	H	9.34 FQ	12.81 AW	16.59 TQ	MOBLS	10/01-12/01
Metal	Nebraska	H	9.61 FQ	12.93 AW	16.75 TQ	NEBLS	10/01-12/01
Metal	New Hampshire	H	10.07 FQ	13.92 AW	19.53 TQ	NHBLS	10/01-12/01
Metal	Nashua PMSA, NH	H	10.64 FQ	12.94 AW	16.09 TQ	NHBLS	10/01-12/01
Metal	New Jersey	H	9.41 FQ	14.69 AW	24.67 TQ	NJBLS	10/01-12/01
Metal	Newark PMSA, NJ	H	8.91 FQ	11.65 AW	15.54 TQ	NJBLS	10/01-12/01
Metal	New York	H	7.47 FQ	14.12 AW	21.33 TQ	NYBLS	10/01-12/01
Metal	Syracuse MSA, NY	H	7.81 FQ	15.11 AW	21.88 TQ	NYBLS	10/01-12/01
Metal	North Carolina	H	7.81 FQ	12.51 AW	17.55 TQ	NCBLS	10/01-12/01
Metal	Ohio	H	9.89 FQ	14.96 AW	21.24 TQ	OHBLS	10/01-12/01
Metal	Akron PMSA, OH	H	11.29 FQ	14.16 AW	17.27 TQ	OHBLS	10/01-12/01
Metal	Canton-Massillon MSA, OH	H	8.97 FQ	13.21 AW	19.53 TQ	OHBLS	10/01-12/01
Metal	Cincinnati PMSA, OH-KY-IN	H	10.88 FQ	14.80 AW	19.59 TQ	OHBLS	10/01-12/01
Metal	Cleveland-Lorain-Elyria PMSA, OH	H	10.88 FQ	16.45 AW	24.31 TQ	OHBLS	10/01-12/01
Metal	Columbus MSA, OH	H	10.35 FQ	15.22 AW	22.34 TQ	OHBLS	10/01-12/01
Metal	Dayton-Springfield MSA, OH	H	8.94 FQ	12.48 AW	16.36 TQ	OHBLS	10/01-12/01
Metal	Mansfield MSA, OH	H	10.44 FQ	13.91 AW	17.75 TQ	OHBLS	10/01-12/01
Metal	Oklahoma	H	9.01 FQ	13.99 AW	21.72 TQ	OKBLS	10/01-12/01
Metal	Oregon	H	9.20 FQ	15.43 AW	21.60 TQ	ORBLS	10/01-12/01
Metal	Portland-Vancouver PMSA, OR-WA	H	10.69 FQ	15.39 AW	21.24 TQ	ORBLS	10/01-12/01
Metal	Pennsylvania	H	10.79 FQ	14.30 AW	18.97 TQ	PABLS	10/01-12/01
Metal	Allentown-Bethlehem-Easton MSA, PA	H	11.08 FQ	13.53 AW	17.42 TQ	PABLS	10/01-12/01
Metal	Harrisburg-Lebanon-Carlisle MSA, PA	H	12.08 FQ	17.58 AW	24.74 TQ	PABLS	10/01-12/01
Metal	Lancaster MSA, PA	H	10.31 FQ	12.62 AW	15.18 TQ	PABLS	10/01-12/01
Metal	Philadelphia PMSA, PA-NJ	H	10.08 FQ	14.25 AW	18.76 TQ	PABLS	10/01-12/01
Metal	Pittsburgh MSA, PA	H	11.15 FQ	14.68 AW	19.06 TQ	PABLS	10/01-12/01
Metal	Reading MSA, PA	H	10.87 FQ	14.17 AW	17.61 TQ	PABLS	10/01-12/01

AAW Average annual wage **AOH** Average offered, high **ASH** Average starting, high **H** Hourly **M** Monthly **S** Special: hourly and annual
AE Average entry wage **AOL** Average offered, low **ASL** Average starting, low **HI** Highest wage paid **MTC** Median total compensation **TQ** Third quartile wage
AEX Average experienced wage **APH** Average pay, high range **AW** Average wage paid **HR** High end range **MW** Median wage paid **W** Weekly
AO Average offered **APL** Average pay, low range **FQ** First quartile wage **LR** Low end range **SQ** Second quartile wage **Y** Yearly

Occupation/Type/Industry	Location	Per	Low	Mid	High	Source	Date
Pourer and Caster							
Metal	Rhode Island	H	8.78 FQ	13.31 AW	19.66 TQ	RIBLS	10/01-12/01
Metal	Providence-Fall River-Warwick MSA, RI-MA	H	8.76 FQ	13.44 AW	19.94 TQ	RIBLS	10/01-12/01
Metal	South Carolina	H	9.55 FQ	13.84 AW	20.18 TQ	SCBLS	10/01-12/01
Metal	Tennessee	H	8.55 FQ	14.17 AW	20.91 TQ	TNBLS	10/01-12/01
Metal	Texas	H	8.37 FQ	14.16 AW	20.68 TQ	TXBLS	10/01-12/01
Metal	Dallas PMSA, TX	H	8.45 FQ	14.76 AW	23.63 TQ	TXBLS	10/01-12/01
Metal	Houston PMSA, TX	H	7.59 FQ	12.38 AW	16.76 TQ	TXBLS	10/01-12/01
Metal	Utah	H	9.89 FQ	13.92 AW	19.68 TQ	UTBLS	10/01-12/01
Metal	Provo-Orem MSA, UT	H	10.81 FQ	14.82 AW	22.68 TQ	UTBLS	10/01-12/01
Metal	Virginia	H	8.48 FQ	12.84 AW	17.49 TQ	VABLS	10/01-12/01
Metal	Washington	H	10.27 FQ	15.95 AW	22.71 TQ	WABLS	10/01-12/01
Metal	Seattle-Bellevue-Everett PMSA, WA	H	10.11 FQ	16.82 AW	25.67 TQ	WABLS	10/01-12/01
Metal	West Virginia	H	11.78 FQ	15.42 AW	19.88 TQ	WVBLS	10/01-12/01
Metal	Huntington-Ashland MSA, WV-KY-OH	H	13.55 FQ	18.56 AW	22.58 TQ	WVBLS	10/01-12/01
Metal	Wisconsin	H	10.25 FQ	14.07 AW	17.88 TQ	WIBLS	10/01-12/01
Metal	Milwaukee-Waukesha PMSA, WI	H	9.11 FQ	12.84 AW	17.86 TQ	WIBLS	10/01-12/01
Power Distributor and Dispatcher	Alabama	H	19.43 FQ	28.99 AW	38.62 TQ	ALBLS	10/01-12/01
	Alaska	H	20.14 FQ	32.80 AW	50.62 TQ	AKBLS	10/01-12/01
	Anchorage MSA, AK	H	24.08 FQ	33.26 AW	42.68 TQ	AKBLS	10/01-12/01
	Arizona	H	23.84 FQ	29.66 AW	36.61 TQ	AZBLS	10/01-12/01
	Tucson MSA, AZ	H	17.48 FQ	28.50 AW	40.95 TQ	AZBLS	10/01-12/01
	Arkansas	H	17.52 FQ	24.74 AW	33.29 TQ	ARBLS	10/01-12/01
	Little Rock-North Little Rock MSA, AR	H	18.23 FQ	25.40 AW	37.36 TQ	ARBLS	10/01-12/01
	California	H	21.01 FQ	31.19 AW	42.38 TQ	CABLS	10/01-12/01
	Los Angeles-Long Beach PMSA, CA	H	23.85 FQ	35.50 AW	51.08 TQ	CABLS	10/01-12/01
	Riverside-San Bernardino PMSA, CA	H	21.02 FQ	26.73 AW	33.47 TQ	CABLS	10/01-12/01
	Sacramento PMSA, CA	H	24.09 FQ	34.31 AW	42.36 TQ	CABLS	10/01-12/01
	Colorado	H	22.83 FQ	26.85 AW	34.08 TQ	COBLS	10/01-12/01
	Fort Collins-Loveland MSA, CO	H	17.04 FQ	24.96 AW	32.26 TQ	COBLS	10/01-12/01
	Connecticut	H	20.85 FQ	27.19 AW	33.73 TQ	CTBLS	10/01-12/01
	New London-Norwich MSA, CT-RI	H	21.58 FQ	27.17 AW	33.55 TQ	CTBLS	10/01-12/01
	Delaware	H	17.22 FQ	20.73 AW	22.98 TQ	DEBLS	10/01-12/01
	Washington PMSA, DC-MD-VA-WV	H	16.83 FQ	24.35 AW	32.69 TQ	DCBLS	10/01-12/01
	Florida	H	11.50 FQ	23.32 AW	34.75 TQ	FLBLS	10/01-12/01
	Orlando MSA, FL	H	16.07 FQ	24.53 AW	33.95 TQ	FLBLS	10/01-12/01
	Tampa-St. Petersburg-Clearwater MSA, FL	H	10.63 FQ	22.83 AW	34.17 TQ	FLBLS	10/01-12/01
	Georgia	H	17.95 FQ	26.97 AW	40.53 TQ	GABLS	10/01-12/01
	Atlanta MSA, GA	H	18.67 FQ	28.46 AW	42.16 TQ	GABLS	10/01-12/01
	Illinois	H	8.63 FQ	26.78 AW	47.43 TQ	ILBLS	10/01-12/01
	Chicago PMSA, IL	H	8.53 FQ	27.85 AW	52.36 TQ	ILBLS	10/01-12/01
	Rockford MSA, IL	H	7.19 FQ	17.14 AW	33.22 TQ	ILBLS	10/01-12/01
	Indiana	H	13.96 FQ	22.74 AW	31.00 TQ	INBLS	10/01-12/01
	Evansville-Henderson MSA, IN-KY	H	10.97 FQ	21.22 AW	29.62 TQ	INBLS	10/01-12/01
	Iowa	H	19.25 FQ	27.05 AW	35.26 TQ	IABLS	10/01-12/01
	Kansas	H	12.64 FQ	22.22 AW	29.35 TQ	KSBLS	10/01-12/01
	Kentucky	H	20.31 FQ	27.41 AW	37.84 TQ	KYBLS	10/01-12/01
	Louisiana	H	13.73 FQ	25.00 AW	35.52 TQ	LABLS	10/01-12/01
	Maine	H	17.39 FQ	22.59 AW	29.43 TQ	MEBLS	10/01-12/01
	Maryland	H	15.20 FQ	23.61 AW	32.45 TQ	MDBLS	10/01-12/01
	Massachusetts	H	15.76 FQ	24.63 AW	33.83 TQ	MABLS	10/01-12/01
	Boston PMSA, MA-NH	H	18.65 FQ	25.11 AW	33.10 TQ	MABLS	10/01-12/01
	Worcester PMSA, MA-CT	H	15.32 FQ	24.33 AW	35.10 TQ	MABLS	10/01-12/01
	Michigan	H	15.97 FQ	23.81 AW	32.29 TQ	MIBLS	10/01-12/01
	Detroit PMSA, MI	H	18.78 FQ	27.44 AW	36.50 TQ	MIBLS	10/01-12/01
	Minnesota	H	19.09 FQ	25.87 AW	34.84 TQ	MNBLS	10/01-12/01
	Duluth-Superior MSA, MN-WI	H	18.72 FQ	25.31 AW	40.82 TQ	MNBLS	10/01-12/01
	Minneapolis-St. Paul MSA, MN-WI	H	20.44 FQ	28.75 AW	36.73 TQ	MNBLS	10/01-12/01
	Mississippi	H	9.07 FQ	15.40 AW	21.45 TQ	MSBLS	10/01-12/01

AAW	Average annual wage	**AOH**	Average offered, high	**ASH**	Average starting, high	**H**	Hourly	**M**	Monthly	**S**	Special: hourly and annual
AE	Average entry wage	**AOL**	Average offered, low	**ASL**	Average starting, low	**HI**	Highest wage paid	**MTC**	Median total compensation	**TQ**	Third quartile wage
AEX	Average experienced wage	**APH**	Average pay, high range	**AW**	Average wage paid	**HR**	High end range	**MW**	Median wage paid	**W**	Weekly
AO	Average offered	**APL**	Average pay, low range	**FQ**	First quartile wage	**LR**	Low end range	**SQ**	Second quartile wage	**Y**	Yearly

Occupation/Type/Industry	Location	Per	Low	Mid	High	Source	Date
Power Distributor and Dispatcher	Missouri	H	10.35 FQ	23.38 AW	33.29 TQ	MOBLS	10/01-12/01
	St. Louis MSA, MO-IL	H	19.74 FQ	26.35 AW	34.35 TQ	MOBLS	10/01-12/01
	Nebraska	H	17.91 FQ	28.47 AW	35.75 TQ	NEBLS	10/01-12/01
	Nevada	H	21.61 FQ	29.09 AW	34.69 TQ	NVBLS	10/01-12/01
	Las Vegas MSA, NV-AZ	H	22.01 FQ	29.70 AW	34.87 TQ	NVBLS	10/01-12/01
	New Jersey	H	21.52 FQ	28.09 AW	36.92 TQ	NJBLS	10/01-12/01
	New York	H	12.86 FQ	29.27 AW	44.70 TQ	NYBLS	10/01-12/01
	Albany-Schenectady-Troy MSA, NY	H	27.30 FQ	35.21 AW	49.13 TQ	NYBLS	10/01-12/01
	Syracuse MSA, NY	H	13.00 FQ	30.23 AW	47.44 TQ	NYBLS	10/01-12/01
	North Carolina	H	11.44 FQ	17.75 AW	26.55 TQ	NCBLS	10/01-12/01
	Charlotte-Gastonia-Rock Hill MSA, NC-SC	H	18.02 FQ	24.66 AW	31.10 TQ	NCBLS	10/01-12/01
	North Dakota	H	14.51 FQ	24.11 AW	33.23 TQ	NDBLS	10/01-12/01
	Ohio	H	17.80 FQ	20.86 AW	26.58 TQ	OHBLS	10/01-12/01
	Cincinnati PMSA, OH-KY-IN	H	17.64 FQ	25.09 AW	35.05 TQ	OHBLS	10/01-12/01
	Cleveland-Lorain-Elyria PMSA, OH	H	15.60 FQ	22.54 AW	27.98 TQ	OHBLS	10/01-12/01
	Columbus MSA, OH	H	16.62 FQ	21.75 AW	28.06 TQ	OHBLS	10/01-12/01
	Oklahoma	H	10.06 FQ	19.33 AW	29.39 TQ	OKBLS	10/01-12/01
	Oklahoma City MSA, OK	H	20.66 FQ	24.93 AW	31.93 TQ	OKBLS	10/01-12/01
	Oregon	H	21.20 FQ	29.10 AW	34.70 TQ	ORBLS	10/01-12/01
	Eugene-Springfield MSA, OR	H	20.84 FQ	33.02 AW	45.01 TQ	ORBLS	10/01-12/01
	Portland-Vancouver PMSA, OR-WA	H	18.99 FQ	27.67 AW	38.14 TQ	ORBLS	10/01-12/01
	Pennsylvania	H	18.00 FQ	26.60 AW	36.78 TQ	PABLS	10/01-12/01
	Philadelphia PMSA, PA-NJ	H	24.11 FQ	30.54 AW	37.06 TQ	PABLS	10/01-12/01
	Pittsburgh MSA, PA	H	15.84 FQ	25.49 AW	38.65 TQ	PABLS	10/01-12/01
	South Carolina	H	13.21 FQ	21.36 AW	28.50 TQ	SCBLS	10/01-12/01
	South Dakota	H	12.28 FQ	21.58 AW	32.22 TQ	SDBLS	10/01-12/01
	Tennessee	H	18.14 FQ	22.70 AW	32.23 TQ	TNBLS	10/01-12/01
	Johnson City-Kingsport-Bristol MSA, TN-VA	H	18.56 FQ	21.88 AW	31.12 TQ	TNBLS	10/01-12/01
	Nashville MSA, TN	H	18.18 FQ	26.16 AW	34.19 TQ	TNBLS	10/01-12/01
	Texas	H	12.69 FQ	22.22 AW	29.85 TQ	TXBLS	10/01-12/01
	Corpus Christi MSA, TX	H	22.72 FQ	24.26 AW	27.78 TQ	TXBLS	10/01-12/01
	Houston PMSA, TX	H	7.41 FQ	24.00 AW	34.48 TQ	TXBLS	10/01-12/01
	Utah	H	16.14 FQ	23.99 AW	29.15 TQ	UTBLS	10/01-12/01
	Vermont	H	20.21 FQ	26.15 AW	33.90 TQ	VTBLS	10/01-12/01
	Virginia	H	18.82 FQ	23.97 AW	31.61 TQ	VABLS	10/01-12/01
	Richmond-Petersburg MSA, VA	H	19.17 FQ	24.88 AW	33.07 TQ	VABLS	10/01-12/01
	Washington	H	19.45 FQ	28.51 AW	37.52 TQ	WABLS	10/01-12/01
	Richland-Kennewick-Pasco MSA, WA	H	23.60 FQ	28.58 AW	33.91 TQ	WABLS	10/01-12/01
	Seattle-Bellevue-Everett PMSA, WA	H	19.95 FQ	28.49 AW	36.09 TQ	WABLS	10/01-12/01
	West Virginia	H	16.74 FQ	22.92 AW	33.31 TQ	WVBLS	10/01-12/01
	Wisconsin	H	18.39 FQ	27.19 AW	38.43 TQ	WIBLS	10/01-12/01
	Wyoming	H	18.57 FQ	22.24 AW	28.82 TQ	WYBLS	10/01-12/01
Power Plant Operator	Mobile MSA, AL	H	16.22 FQ	23.95 AW	35.40 TQ	ALBLS	10/01-12/01
	Alaska	H	15.02 FQ	26.66 AW	37.14 TQ	AKBLS	10/01-12/01
	Arizona	H	17.43 FQ	25.72 AW	34.75 TQ	AZBLS	10/01-12/01
	Phoenix-Mesa MSA, AZ	H	18.62 FQ	26.36 AW	35.12 TQ	AZBLS	10/01-12/01
	Arkansas	H	19.48 FQ	24.67 AW	29.19 TQ	ARBLS	10/01-12/01
	Little Rock-North Little Rock MSA, AR	H	18.56 FQ	23.46 AW	27.63 TQ	ARBLS	10/01-12/01
	California	H	17.60 FQ	25.12 AW	33.20 TQ	CABLS	10/01-12/01
	Bakersfield MSA, CA	H	14.97 FQ	23.70 AW	32.69 TQ	CABLS	10/01-12/01
	Chico-Paradise MSA, CA	H	18.75 FQ	28.66 AW	34.35 TQ	CABLS	10/01-12/01
	Fresno MSA, CA	H	17.85 FQ	21.62 AW	26.32 TQ	CABLS	10/01-12/01
	Los Angeles-Long Beach PMSA, CA	H	19.36 FQ	26.40 AW	33.23 TQ	CABLS	10/01-12/01
	Oakland PMSA, CA	H	19.06 FQ	25.26 AW	32.71 TQ	CABLS	10/01-12/01
	Redding MSA, CA	H	14.83 FQ	23.47 AW	33.04 TQ	CABLS	10/01-12/01
	Riverside-San Bernardino PMSA, CA	H	16.10 FQ	23.30 AW	30.61 TQ	CABLS	10/01-12/01
	Sacramento PMSA, CA	H	19.60 FQ	28.75 AW	37.98 TQ	CABLS	10/01-12/01
	San Jose PMSA, CA	H	16.50 FQ	22.27 AW	28.44 TQ	CABLS	10/01-12/01
	Stockton-Lodi MSA, CA	H	19.09 FQ	25.19 AW	32.47 TQ	CABLS	10/01-12/01
	Colorado	H	15.78 FQ	22.97 AW	28.56 TQ	COBLS	10/01-12/01
	Connecticut	H	18.27 FQ	24.75 AW	32.91 TQ	CTBLS	10/01-12/01

AAW Average annual wage **AOH** Average offered, high **ASH** Average starting, high **H** Hourly **M** Monthly **S** Special: hourly and annual
AE Average entry wage **AOL** Average offered, low **ASL** Average starting, low **HI** Highest wage paid **MTC** Median total compensation **TQ** Third quartile wage
AEX Average experienced wage **APH** Average pay, high range **AW** Average wage paid **HR** High end range **MW** Median wage paid **W** Weekly
AO Average offered **APL** Average pay, low range **FQ** First quartile wage **LR** Low end range **SQ** Second quartile wage **Y** Yearly

Occupation/Type/Industry	Location	Per	Low	Mid	High	Source	Date
Power Plant Operator	New London-Norwich MSA, CT-RI	H	17.91 FQ	23.85 AW	31.62 TQ	CTBLS	10/01-12/01
	Washington PMSA, DC-MD-VA-WV	H	14.88 FQ	22.71 AW	30.67 TQ	DCBLS	10/01-12/01
	Florida	H	14.91 FQ	21.98 AW	29.24 TQ	FLBLS	10/01-12/01
	West Palm Beach-Boca Raton MSA, FL	H	15.33 FQ	20.09 AW	26.34 TQ	FLBLS	10/01-12/01
	Georgia	H	15.38 FQ	23.07 AW	33.42 TQ	GABLS	10/01-12/01
	Atlanta MSA, GA	H	11.84 FQ	22.49 AW	33.69 TQ	GABLS	10/01-12/01
	Columbus MSA, GA-AL	H	14.64 FQ	20.04 AW	26.10 TQ	GABLS	10/01-12/01
	Macon MSA, GA	H	14.59 FQ	24.94 AW	35.25 TQ	GABLS	10/01-12/01
	Savannah MSA, GA	H	14.04 FQ	21.64 AW	27.11 TQ	GABLS	10/01-12/01
	Hawaii	H	19.07 FQ	25.72 AW	33.17 TQ	HIBLS	10/01-12/01
	Honolulu MSA, HI	H	19.98 FQ	26.34 AW	33.02 TQ	HIBLS	10/01-12/01
	Idaho	H	16.13 FQ	26.73 AW	34.17 TQ	IDBLS	10/01-12/01
	Boise City MSA, ID	H	10.36 FQ	23.04 AW	32.80 TQ	IDBLS	10/01-12/01
	Illinois	H	14.94 FQ	23.81 AW	32.94 TQ	ILBLS	10/01-12/01
	Chicago PMSA, IL	H	14.51 FQ	23.39 AW	32.41 TQ	ILBLS	10/01-12/01
	Indiana	H	17.83 FQ	23.50 AW	28.31 TQ	INBLS	10/01-12/01
	Fort Wayne MSA, IN	H	14.99 FQ	21.99 AW	27.42 TQ	INBLS	10/01-12/01
	Gary PMSA, IN	H	18.65 FQ	25.57 AW	32.17 TQ	INBLS	10/01-12/01
	Indianapolis MSA, IN	H	18.63 FQ	23.87 AW	28.18 TQ	INBLS	10/01-12/01
	Iowa	H	13.56 FQ	20.97 AW	28.61 TQ	IABLS	10/01-12/01
	Cedar Rapids MSA, IA	H	18.39 FQ	23.34 AW	27.13 TQ	IABLS	10/01-12/01
	Davenport-Moline-Rock Island MSA, IA-IL	H	17.34 FQ	25.50 AW	33.80 TQ	IABLS	10/01-12/01
	Kansas	H	10.03 FQ	19.38 AW	27.78 TQ	KSBLS	10/01-12/01
	Topeka MSA, KS	H	16.39 FQ	22.91 AW	28.37 TQ	KSBLS	10/01-12/01
	Wichita MSA, KS	H	9.02 FQ	16.50 AW	26.85 TQ	KSBLS	10/01-12/01
	Kentucky	H	14.53 FQ	20.81 AW	27.06 TQ	KYBLS	10/01-12/01
	Louisiana	H	12.38 FQ	19.74 AW	28.83 TQ	LABLS	10/01-12/01
	Lafayette MSA, LA	H	11.67 FQ	16.22 AW	22.45 TQ	LABLS	10/01-12/01
	New Orleans MSA, LA	H	14.12 FQ	21.44 AW	29.44 TQ	LABLS	10/01-12/01
	Maine	H	15.22 FQ	20.99 AW	26.81 TQ	MEBLS	10/01-12/01
	Maryland	H	18.20 FQ	24.34 AW	31.99 TQ	MDBLS	10/01-12/01
	Massachusetts	H	15.34 FQ	22.25 AW	30.64 TQ	MABLS	10/01-12/01
	Boston PMSA, MA-NH	H	15.78 FQ	22.08 AW	29.41 TQ	MABLS	10/01-12/01
	Lowell PMSA, MA-NH	H	14.46 FQ	20.97 AW	29.21 TQ	MABLS	10/01-12/01
	Springfield MSA, MA	H	17.56 FQ	25.08 AW	33.79 TQ	MABLS	10/01-12/01
	Worcester PMSA, MA-CT	H	18.07 FQ	22.88 AW	28.87 TQ	MABLS	10/01-12/01
	Michigan	H	15.83 FQ	22.99 AW	31.98 TQ	MIBLS	10/01-12/01
	Ann Arbor PMSA, MI	H	18.46 FQ	28.80 AW	40.66 TQ	MIBLS	10/01-12/01
	Detroit PMSA, MI	H	18.32 FQ	23.93 AW	31.17 TQ	MIBLS	10/01-12/01
	Grand Rapids-Muskegon-Holland MSA, MI	H	15.59 FQ	21.79 AW	29.26 TQ	MIBLS	10/01-12/01
	Kalamazoo-Battle Creek MSA, MI	H	15.04 FQ	20.01 AW	25.56 TQ	MIBLS	10/01-12/01
	Lansing-East Lansing MSA, MI	H	15.33 FQ	21.62 AW	31.15 TQ	MIBLS	10/01-12/01
	Minnesota	H	18.68 FQ	24.44 AW	32.05 TQ	MNBLS	10/01-12/01
	Duluth-Superior MSA, MN-WI	H	18.33 FQ	24.72 AW	33.92 TQ	MNBLS	10/01-12/01
	Minneapolis-St. Paul MSA, MN-WI	H	19.82 FQ	25.58 AW	33.07 TQ	MNBLS	10/01-12/01
	Missouri	H	11.10 FQ	21.88 AW	32.80 TQ	MOBLS	10/01-12/01
	Kansas City MSA, MO-KS	H	17.58 FQ	24.02 AW	32.97 TQ	MOBLS	10/01-12/01
	St. Louis MSA, MO-IL	H	17.45 FQ	24.78 AW	33.53 TQ	MOBLS	10/01-12/01
	Montana	H	16.00 FQ	24.21 AW	32.57 TQ	MTBLS	10/01-12/01
	Nebraska	H	12.54 FQ	20.56 AW	27.86 TQ	NEBLS	10/01-12/01
	Lincoln MSA, NE	H	14.72 FQ	17.80 AW	21.71 TQ	NEBLS	10/01-12/01
	Nevada	H	14.33 FQ	23.58 AW	33.11 TQ	NVBLS	10/01-12/01
	New Hampshire	H	13.31 FQ	18.11 AW	23.57 TQ	NHBLS	10/01-12/01
	Manchester PMSA, NH	H	13.81 FQ	16.09 AW	19.83 TQ	NHBLS	10/01-12/01
	New Jersey	H	18.85 FQ	26.43 AW	34.23 TQ	NJBLS	10/01-12/01
	Atlantic-Cape May PMSA, NJ	H	17.84 FQ	25.44 AW	33.94 TQ	NJBLS	10/01-12/01
	Bergen-Passaic PMSA, NJ	H	18.69 FQ	25.65 AW	33.72 TQ	NJBLS	10/01-12/01
	Middlesex-Somerset-Hunterdon PMSA, NJ	H	18.14 FQ	25.90 AW	33.53 TQ	NJBLS	10/01-12/01
	Monmouth-Ocean PMSA, NJ	H	21.60 FQ	28.89 AW	35.07 TQ	NJBLS	10/01-12/01
	Newark PMSA, NJ	H	20.34 FQ	27.19 AW	34.29 TQ	NJBLS	10/01-12/01
	Trenton PMSA, NJ	H	18.83 FQ	24.87 AW	32.55 TQ	NJBLS	10/01-12/01
	New Mexico	H	18.37 FQ	23.61 AW	28.97 TQ	NMBLS	10/01-12/01
	New York	H	16.99 FQ	26.51 AW	34.56 TQ	NYBLS	10/01-12/01

AAW	Average annual wage	AOH	Average offered, high	ASH	Average starting, high	H	Hourly	M	Monthly	S	Special: hourly and annual
AE	Average entry wage	AOL	Average offered, low	ASL	Average starting, low	HI	Highest wage paid	MTC	Median total compensation	TQ	Third quartile wage
AEX	Average experienced wage	APH	Average pay, high range	AW	Average wage paid	HR	High end range	MW	Median wage paid	W	Weekly
AO	Average offered	APL	Average pay, low range	FQ	First quartile wage	LR	Low end range	SQ	Second quartile wage	Y	Yearly

Occupation/Type/Industry	Location	Per	Low	Mid	High	Source	Date
Power Plant Operator	Albany-Schenectady-Troy MSA, NY	H	18.94 FQ	24.69 AW	32.15 TQ	NYBLS	10/01-12/01
	Buffalo-Niagara Falls MSA, NY	H	17.92 FQ	24.59 AW	32.84 TQ	NYBLS	10/01-12/01
	Dutchess County PMSA, NY	H	17.78 FQ	25.61 AW	34.60 TQ	NYBLS	10/01-12/01
	Nassau-Suffolk PMSA, NY	H	16.48 FQ	26.81 AW	35.50 TQ	NYBLS	10/01-12/01
	New York PMSA, NY	H	21.96 FQ	29.52 AW	34.91 TQ	NYBLS	10/01-12/01
	Syracuse MSA, NY	H	17.08 FQ	24.93 AW	33.60 TQ	NYBLS	10/01-12/01
	North Carolina	H	15.26 FQ	23.44 AW	29.12 TQ	NCBLS	10/01-12/01
	Asheville MSA, NC	H	15.27 FQ	22.63 AW	28.18 TQ	NCBLS	10/01-12/01
	Charlotte-Gastonia-Rock Hill MSA, NC-SC	H	18.47 FQ	24.20 AW	28.73 TQ	NCBLS	10/01-12/01
	Wilmington MSA, NC	H	17.25 FQ	23.38 AW	30.61 TQ	NCBLS	10/01-12/01
	North Dakota	H	18.19 FQ	24.46 AW	32.28 TQ	NDBLS	10/01-12/01
	Ohio	H	16.13 FQ	22.18 AW	27.87 TQ	OHBLS	10/01-12/01
	Cincinnati PMSA, OH-KY-IN	H	18.77 FQ	24.23 AW	30.78 TQ	OHBLS	10/01-12/01
	Cleveland-Lorain-Elyria PMSA, OH	H	17.94 FQ	23.03 AW	27.69 TQ	OHBLS	10/01-12/01
	Toledo MSA, OH	H	19.05 FQ	24.11 AW	28.87 TQ	OHBLS	10/01-12/01
	Oklahoma	H	15.48 FQ	22.36 AW	27.74 TQ	OKBLS	10/01-12/01
	Oklahoma City MSA, OK	H	14.02 FQ	21.84 AW	27.24 TQ	OKBLS	10/01-12/01
	Tulsa MSA, OK	H	17.69 FQ	22.51 AW	26.82 TQ	OKBLS	10/01-12/01
	Oregon	H	15.87 FQ	23.02 AW	31.34 TQ	ORBLS	10/01-12/01
	Pennsylvania	H	14.78 FQ	22.85 AW	31.28 TQ	PABLS	10/01-12/01
	Philadelphia PMSA, PA-NJ	H	17.04 FQ	25.40 AW	33.92 TQ	PABLS	10/01-12/01
	Pittsburgh MSA, PA	H	13.46 FQ	20.77 AW	27.11 TQ	PABLS	10/01-12/01
	Reading MSA, PA	H	15.80 FQ	22.23 AW	28.59 TQ	PABLS	10/01-12/01
	Scranton-Wilkes-Barre-Hazleton MSA, PA	H	17.57 FQ	26.71 AW	37.20 TQ	PABLS	10/01-12/01
	Rhode Island	H	14.68 FQ	22.17 AW	29.16 TQ	RIBLS	10/01-12/01
	Providence-Fall River-Warwick MSA, RI-MA	H	14.80 FQ	22.56 AW	29.47 TQ	RIBLS	10/01-12/01
	South Carolina	H	12.74 FQ	18.93 AW	25.48 TQ	SCBLS	10/01-12/01
	Tennessee	H	11.17 FQ	18.50 AW	26.09 TQ	TNBLS	10/01-12/01
	Nashville MSA, TN	H	14.50 FQ	19.88 AW	25.76 TQ	TNBLS	10/01-12/01
	Texas	H	14.34 FQ	22.58 AW	28.40 TQ	TXBLS	10/01-12/01
	Beaumont-Port Arthur MSA, TX	H	20.42 FQ	23.90 AW	27.80 TQ	TXBLS	10/01-12/01
	Corpus Christi MSA, TX	H	18.51 FQ	21.92 AW	26.96 TQ	TXBLS	10/01-12/01
	Dallas PMSA, TX	H	14.33 FQ	20.53 AW	28.23 TQ	TXBLS	10/01-12/01
	Houston PMSA, TX	H	11.67 FQ	20.13 AW	28.86 TQ	TXBLS	10/01-12/01
	Utah	H	16.20 FQ	23.35 AW	31.84 TQ	UTBLS	10/01-12/01
	Provo-Orem MSA, UT	H	13.57 FQ	18.05 AW	23.37 TQ	UTBLS	10/01-12/01
	Salt Lake City-Ogden MSA, UT	H	17.30 FQ	23.18 AW	28.43 TQ	UTBLS	10/01-12/01
	Vermont	H	15.36 FQ	21.72 AW	27.37 TQ	VTBLS	10/01-12/01
	Virginia	H	11.62 FQ	17.32 AW	27.15 TQ	VABLS	10/01-12/01
	Norfolk-Virginia Beach-Newport News MSA, VA-NC	H	13.87 FQ	18.04 AW	24.76 TQ	VABLS	10/01-12/01
	Richmond-Petersburg MSA, VA	H	11.81 FQ	16.80 AW	26.96 TQ	VABLS	10/01-12/01
	Washington	H	16.39 FQ	26.43 AW	34.80 TQ	WABLS	10/01-12/01
	Seattle-Bellevue-Everett PMSA, WA	H	15.09 FQ	29.94 AW		WABLS	10/01-12/01
	Tacoma PMSA, WA	H	13.95 FQ	22.53 AW	28.20 TQ	WABLS	10/01-12/01
	West Virginia	H	15.71 FQ	21.62 AW	27.19 TQ	WVBLS	10/01-12/01
	Huntington-Ashland MSA, WV-KY-OH	H	18.17 FQ	22.29 AW	26.38 TQ	WVBLS	10/01-12/01
	Wisconsin	H	12.37 FQ	20.43 AW	28.06 TQ	WIBLS	10/01-12/01
	Wyoming	H	19.66 FQ	24.42 AW	28.83 TQ	WYBLS	10/01-12/01
	Puerto Rico	H	11.11 FQ	14.83 AW	21.14 TQ	PRBLS	10/01-12/01
	Guam	H	11.55 FQ	16.06 AW	20.69 TQ	GUBLS	10/01-12/01
Prepress Technician and Worker	Alabama	H	7.02 FQ	13.30 AW	21.73 TQ	ALBLS	10/01-12/01
	Alaska	H	9.51 FQ	16.94 AW	27.70 TQ	AKBLS	10/01-12/01
	Arizona	H	9.45 FQ	14.60 AW	21.21 TQ	AZBLS	10/01-12/01
	Arkansas	H	7.20 FQ	11.71 AW	18.23 TQ	ARBLS	10/01-12/01
	California	H	8.34 FQ	16.62 AW	26.81 TQ	CABLS	10/01-12/01
	Colorado	H	9.80 FQ	15.89 AW	21.83 TQ	COBLS	10/01-12/01
	Connecticut	H	10.95 FQ	16.45 AW	22.28 TQ	CTBLS	10/01-12/01
	Delaware	H	11.38 FQ	16.18 AW	20.96 TQ	DEBLS	10/01-12/01
	District of Columbia	H	13.42 FQ	23.61 AW	32.31 TQ	DCBLS	10/01-12/01

AAW	Average annual wage	**AOH**	Average offered, high	**ASH**	Average starting, high	**H**	Hourly	**M**	Monthly	**S**	Special: hourly and annual
AE	Average entry wage	**AOL**	Average offered, low	**ASL**	Average starting, low	**HI**	Highest wage paid	**MTC**	Median total compensation	**TQ**	Third quartile wage
AEX	Average experienced wage	**APH**	Average pay, high range	**AW**	Average wage paid	**HR**	High end range	**MW**	Median wage paid	**W**	Weekly
AO	Average offered	**APL**	Average pay, low range	**FQ**	First quartile wage	**LR**	Low end range	**SQ**	Second quartile wage	**Y**	Yearly

Occupation/Type/Industry	Location	Per	Low	Mid	High	Source	Date
Prepress Technician and Worker	Florida	H	8.21 FQ	13.46 AW	19.65 TQ	FLBLS	10/01-12/01
	Georgia	H	7.90 FQ	14.39 AW	22.01 TQ	GABLS	10/01-12/01
	Hawaii	H	9.62 FQ	15.78 AW	24.17 TQ	HIBLS	10/01-12/01
	Idaho	H	8.86 FQ	13.53 AW	19.66 TQ	IDBLS	10/01-12/01
	Illinois	H	7.96 FQ	17.02 AW	25.91 TQ	ILBLS	10/01-12/01
	Indiana	H	9.44 FQ	14.74 AW	20.58 TQ	INBLS	10/01-12/01
	Iowa	H	7.67 FQ	12.77 AW	19.11 TQ	IABLS	10/01-12/01
	Kansas	H	8.22 FQ	14.21 AW	20.80 TQ	KSBLS	10/01-12/01
	Kentucky	H	7.25 FQ	13.80 AW	23.23 TQ	KYBLS	10/01-12/01
	Louisiana	H	7.45 FQ	12.71 AW	18.40 TQ	LABLS	10/01-12/01
	Maine	H	9.46 FQ	13.66 AW	19.29 TQ	MEBLS	10/01-12/01
	Maryland	H	9.11 FQ	15.83 AW	24.75 TQ	MDBLS	10/01-12/01
	Massachusetts	H	10.50 FQ	16.96 AW	24.66 TQ	MABLS	10/01-12/01
	Michigan	H	9.36 FQ	15.73 AW	22.28 TQ	MIBLS	10/01-12/01
	Minnesota	H	9.68 FQ	17.01 AW	26.00 TQ	MNBLS	10/01-12/01
	Mississippi	H	7.42 FQ	11.38 AW	16.37 TQ	MSBLS	10/01-12/01
	Missouri	H	7.73 FQ	14.13 AW	23.24 TQ	MOBLS	10/01-12/01
	Montana	H	8.65 FQ	12.69 AW	19.06 TQ	MTBLS	10/01-12/01
	Nebraska	H	8.89 FQ	13.07 AW	18.75 TQ	NEBLS	10/01-12/01
	Nevada	H	9.57 FQ	15.08 AW	20.70 TQ	NVBLS	10/01-12/01
	New Hampshire	H	10.24 FQ	15.74 AW	22.82 TQ	NHBLS	10/01-12/01
	New Jersey	H	10.79 FQ	18.92 AW	27.28 TQ	NJBLS	10/01-12/01
	New Mexico	H	8.13 FQ	14.61 AW	25.06 TQ	NMBLS	10/01-12/01
	New York	H	9.45 FQ	17.81 AW	27.05 TQ	NYBLS	10/01-12/01
	North Carolina	H	8.80 FQ	13.91 AW	20.33 TQ	NCBLS	10/01-12/01
	North Dakota	H	6.80 FQ	10.64 AW	14.89 TQ	NDBLS	10/01-12/01
	Ohio	H	8.20 FQ	15.10 AW	22.18 TQ	OHBLS	10/01-12/01
	Oklahoma	H	7.18 FQ	12.76 AW	19.25 TQ	OKBLS	10/01-12/01
	Oregon	H	9.63 FQ	17.80 AW	26.49 TQ	ORBLS	10/01-12/01
	Pennsylvania	H	9.09 FQ	15.31 AW	22.09 TQ	PABLS	10/01-12/01
	Rhode Island	H	11.26 FQ	18.78 AW	26.19 TQ	RIBLS	10/01-12/01
	South Carolina	H	7.65 FQ	12.30 AW	17.49 TQ	SCBLS	10/01-12/01
	South Dakota	H	8.55 FQ	11.54 AW	16.36 TQ	SDBLS	10/01-12/01
	Tennessee	H	8.75 FQ	14.46 AW	20.75 TQ	TNBLS	10/01-12/01
	Texas	H	7.33 FQ	14.51 AW	22.26 TQ	TXBLS	10/01-12/01
	Utah	H	6.81 FQ	12.48 AW	19.06 TQ	UTBLS	10/01-12/01
	Vermont	H	10.64 FQ	15.01 AW	21.09 TQ	VTBLS	10/01-12/01
	Virginia	H	8.28 FQ	14.71 AW	21.61 TQ	VABLS	10/01-12/01
	Washington	H	10.17 FQ	17.39 AW	26.11 TQ	WABLS	10/01-12/01
	West Virginia	H	7.39 FQ	11.73 AW	17.54 TQ	WVBLS	10/01-12/01
	Wisconsin	H	9.45 FQ	16.10 AW	24.59 TQ	WIBLS	10/01-12/01
	Wyoming	H	5.93 FQ	9.34 AW	13.77 TQ	WYBLS	10/01-12/01
	Puerto Rico	H	6.98 FQ	10.98 AW	18.76 TQ	PRBLS	10/01-12/01
Preschool Teacher							
Except Special Education	Alabama	Y	12020 FQ	16150 AW	21290 TQ	ALBLS	10/01-12/01
Except Special Education	Alaska	Y	14730 FQ	23810 AW	35930 TQ	AKBLS	10/01-12/01
Except Special Education	Arizona	Y	12180 FQ	20610 AW	34660 TQ	AZBLS	10/01-12/01
Except Special Education	Arkansas	Y	12050 FQ	17750 AW	27070 TQ	ARBLS	10/01-12/01
Except Special Education	California	Y	15040 FQ	23050 AW	34610 TQ	CABLS	10/01-12/01
Except Special Education	Colorado	Y	14370 FQ	20880 AW	27970 TQ	COBLS	10/01-12/01
Except Special Education	Connecticut	Y	15190 FQ	23130 AW	34780 TQ	CTBLS	10/01-12/01
Except Special Education	Delaware	Y	13440 FQ	19710 AW	29430 TQ	DEBLS	10/01-12/01
Except Special Education	District of Columbia	Y	18370 FQ	28270 AW	43490 TQ	DCBLS	10/01-12/01
Except Special Education	Florida	Y	13190 FQ	19960 AW	28200 TQ	FLBLS	10/01-12/01
Except Special Education	Georgia	Y	12610 FQ	19420 AW	29660 TQ	GABLS	10/01-12/01
Except Special Education	Hawaii	Y	14830 FQ	21540 AW	29570 TQ	HIBLS	10/01-12/01
Except Special Education	Idaho	Y	11810 FQ	15400 AW	21230 TQ	IDBLS	10/01-12/01
Except Special Education	Illinois	Y	14050 FQ	20270 AW	27950 TQ	ILBLS	10/01-12/01
Except Special Education	Indiana	Y	12150 FQ	17450 AW	24770 TQ	INBLS	10/01-12/01
Except Special Education	Iowa	Y	12120 FQ	17590 AW	25510 TQ	IABLS	10/01-12/01
Except Special Education	Kansas	Y	13590 FQ	20260 AW	28670 TQ	KSBLS	10/01-12/01
Except Special Education	Kentucky	Y	12390 FQ	19330 AW	31360 TQ	KYBLS	10/01-12/01
Except Special Education	Louisiana	Y	12170 FQ	19670 AW	31180 TQ	LABLS	10/01-12/01
Except Special Education	Maine	Y	15290 FQ	20750 AW	27570 TQ	MEBLS	10/01-12/01
Except Special Education	Maryland	Y	14710 FQ	22220 AW	32960 TQ	MDBLS	10/01-12/01
Except Special Education	Massachusetts	Y	16610 FQ	23580 AW	32450 TQ	MABLS	10/01-12/01
Except Special Education	Michigan	Y	14680 FQ	22490 AW	33540 TQ	MIBLS	10/01-12/01
Except Special Education	Minnesota	Y	15230 FQ	24290 AW	36720 TQ	MNBLS	10/01-12/01
Except Special Education	Mississippi	Y	11900 FQ	17650 AW	27000 TQ	MSBLS	10/01-12/01
Except Special Education	Missouri	Y	12360 FQ	19890 AW	33230 TQ	MOBLS	10/01-12/01
Except Special Education	Montana	Y	12050 FQ	18310 AW	24520 TQ	MTBLS	10/01-12/01
Except Special Education	Nebraska	Y	12430 FQ	18640 AW	28380 TQ	NEBLS	10/01-12/01

AAW	Average annual wage	AOH	Average offered, high	ASH	Average starting, high	H	Hourly	M	Monthly	S	Special: hourly and annual
AE	Average entry wage	AOL	Average offered, low	ASL	Average starting, low	HI	Highest wage paid	MTC	Median total compensation	TQ	Third quartile wage
AEX	Average experienced wage	APH	Average pay, high range	AW	Average wage paid	HR	High end range	MW	Median wage paid	W	Weekly
AO	Average offered	APL	Average pay, low range	FQ	First quartile wage	LR	Low end range	SQ	Second quartile wage	Y	Yearly

Occupation/Type/Industry	Location	Per	Low	Mid	High	Source	Date
Preschool Teacher							
Except Special Education	Nevada	Y	13100 FQ	17920 AW	23700 TQ	NVBLS	10/01-12/01
Except Special Education	New Hampshire	Y	13940 FQ	19450 AW	26540 TQ	NHBLS	10/01-12/01
Except Special Education	New Jersey	Y	15780 FQ	24630 AW	36180 TQ	NJBLS	10/01-12/01
Except Special Education	New Mexico	Y	12040 FQ	17720 AW	28140 TQ	NMBLS	10/01-12/01
Except Special Education	New York	Y	14240 FQ	24180 AW	37240 TQ	NYBLS	10/01-12/01
Except Special Education	North Carolina	Y	12270 FQ	17440 AW	23640 TQ	NCBLS	10/01-12/01
Except Special Education	North Dakota	Y	11800 FQ	16040 AW	22470 TQ	NDBLS	10/01-12/01
Except Special Education	Ohio	Y	12490 FQ	18860 AW	26930 TQ	OHBLS	10/01-12/01
Except Special Education	Oklahoma	Y	12430 FQ	18700 AW	29930 TQ	OKBLS	10/01-12/01
Except Special Education	Oregon	Y	15600 FQ	22070 AW	29840 TQ	ORBLS	10/01-12/01
Except Special Education	Pennsylvania	Y	13430 FQ	21620 AW	32990 TQ	PABLS	10/01-12/01
Except Special Education	Rhode Island	Y	16130 FQ	25130 AW	34280 TQ	RIBLS	10/01-12/01
Except Special Education	South Carolina	Y	11950 FQ	18970 AW	34740 TQ	SCBLS	10/01-12/01
Except Special Education	South Dakota	Y	15900 FQ	21580 AW	28890 TQ	SDBLS	10/01-12/01
Except Special Education	Tennessee	Y	11980 FQ	16030 AW	21130 TQ	TNBLS	10/01-12/01
Except Special Education	Texas	Y	12450 FQ	20310 AW	36260 TQ	TXBLS	10/01-12/01
Except Special Education	Utah	Y	14480 FQ	19510 AW	27490 TQ	UTBLS	10/01-12/01
Except Special Education	Vermont	Y	15450 FQ	25310 AW	41820 TQ	VTBLS	10/01-12/01
Except Special Education	Virginia	Y	12690 FQ	21580 AW	36010 TQ	VABLS	10/01-12/01
Except Special Education	Washington	Y	15140 FQ	22330 AW	33500 TQ	WABLS	10/01-12/01
Except Special Education	West Virginia	Y	11890 FQ	18300 AW	31010 TQ	WVBLS	10/01-12/01
Except Special Education	Wisconsin	Y	14100 FQ	19630 AW	27800 TQ	WIBLS	10/01-12/01
Except Special Education	Wyoming	Y	11900 FQ	17700 AW	27010 TQ	WYBLS	10/01-12/01
Except Special Education	Puerto Rico	Y	12270 FQ	16660 AW	21840 TQ	PRBLS	10/01-12/01
Except Special Education	Virgin Islands	Y	15450 FQ	19740 AW	25460 TQ	VIBLS	10/01-12/01
Except Special Education	Guam	Y	12340 FQ	18600 AW	26960 TQ	GUBLS	10/01-12/01
President and CEO							
Home Care	United States	Y			83967 HI	HCM	1/01-1/02
Marketing, Medical	United States	Y		189000 AW		MM&M	1/01-1/02
Presser							
Textile, Garment, and Related Material	Alabama	H	5.87 FQ	7.91 AW	10.79 TQ	ALBLS	10/01-12/01
Textile, Garment, and Related Material	Alaska	H	7.07 FQ	9.77 AW	14.89 TQ	AKBLS	10/01-12/01
Textile, Garment, and Related Material	Arizona	H	5.82 FQ	7.61 AW	10.41 TQ	AZBLS	10/01-12/01
Textile, Garment, and Related Material	Arkansas	H	5.84 FQ	7.82 AW	10.47 TQ	ARBLS	10/01-12/01
Textile, Garment, and Related Material	California	H	6.58 FQ	8.58 AW	10.98 TQ	CABLS	10/01-12/01
Textile, Garment, and Related Material	Colorado	H	6.33 FQ	8.74 AW	10.98 TQ	COBLS	10/01-12/01
Textile, Garment, and Related Material	Connecticut	H	7.01 FQ	9.03 AW	11.86 TQ	CTBLS	10/01-12/01
Textile, Garment, and Related Material	Delaware	H	6.55 FQ	8.04 AW	10.30 TQ	DEBLS	10/01-12/01
Textile, Garment, and Related Material	District of Columbia	H	6.64 FQ	7.65 AW	8.97 TQ	DCBLS	10/01-12/01
Textile, Garment, and Related Material	Florida	H	5.86 FQ	7.99 AW	10.48 TQ	FLBLS	10/01-12/01
Textile, Garment, and Related Material	Georgia	H	5.85 FQ	7.95 AW	10.57 TQ	GABLS	10/01-12/01
Textile, Garment, and Related Material	Hawaii	H	5.95 FQ	7.97 AW	10.65 TQ	HIBLS	10/01-12/01
Textile, Garment, and Related Material	Idaho	H	5.79 FQ	7.20 AW	8.68 TQ	IDBLS	10/01-12/01
Textile, Garment, and Related Material	Illinois	H	5.86 FQ	8.33 AW	11.62 TQ	ILBLS	10/01-12/01
Textile, Garment, and Related Material	Indiana	H	6.46 FQ	8.75 AW	12.11 TQ	INBLS	10/01-12/01
Textile, Garment, and Related Material	Iowa	H	5.77 FQ	7.79 AW	10.40 TQ	IABLS	10/01-12/01
Textile, Garment, and Related Material	Kansas	H	6.08 FQ	8.25 AW	10.63 TQ	KSBLS	10/01-12/01
Textile, Garment, and Related Material	Kentucky	H	5.72 FQ	8.15 AW	11.56 TQ	KYBLS	10/01-12/01
Textile, Garment, and Related Material	Louisiana	H	5.64 FQ	7.32 AW	9.88 TQ	LABLS	10/01-12/01
Textile, Garment, and Related Material	Maine	H	6.34 FQ	8.90 AW	11.47 TQ	MEBLS	10/01-12/01
Textile, Garment, and Related Material	Maryland	H	6.00 FQ	8.09 AW	10.51 TQ	MDBLS	10/01-12/01
Textile, Garment, and Related Material	Massachusetts	H	7.15 FQ	9.30 AW	12.08 TQ	MABLS	10/01-12/01
Textile, Garment, and Related Material	Michigan	H	6.32 FQ	8.44 AW	10.66 TQ	MIBLS	10/01-12/01
Textile, Garment, and Related Material	Minnesota	H	7.63 FQ	9.79 AW	12.32 TQ	MNBLS	10/01-12/01
Textile, Garment, and Related Material	Mississippi	H	5.61 FQ	7.08 AW	8.95 TQ	MSBLS	10/01-12/01
Textile, Garment, and Related Material	Missouri	H	5.95 FQ	8.08 AW	11.68 TQ	MOBLS	10/01-12/01
Textile, Garment, and Related Material	Montana	H	5.91 FQ	7.54 AW	8.94 TQ	MTBLS	10/01-12/01
Textile, Garment, and Related Material	Nebraska	H	6.21 FQ	7.93 AW	10.01 TQ	NEBLS	10/01-12/01
Textile, Garment, and Related Material	Nevada	H	6.37 FQ	8.50 AW	12.20 TQ	NVBLS	10/01-12/01
Textile, Garment, and Related Material	New Hampshire	H	7.03 FQ	8.95 AW	11.62 TQ	NHBLS	10/01-12/01
Textile, Garment, and Related Material	New Jersey	H	6.00 FQ	9.31 AW	13.31 TQ	NJBLS	10/01-12/01
Textile, Garment, and Related Material	New Mexico	H	5.56 FQ	6.52 AW	8.10 TQ	NMBLS	10/01-12/01
Textile, Garment, and Related Material	New York	H	6.08 FQ	9.11 AW	12.67 TQ	NYBLS	10/01-12/01
Textile, Garment, and Related Material	North Carolina	H	6.11 FQ	8.48 AW	11.01 TQ	NCBLS	10/01-12/01
Textile, Garment, and Related Material	North Dakota	H	5.88 FQ	7.33 AW	9.05 TQ	NDBLS	10/01-12/01
Textile, Garment, and Related Material	Ohio	H	6.25 FQ	8.24 AW	10.68 TQ	OHBLS	10/01-12/01
Textile, Garment, and Related Material	Oklahoma	H	5.67 FQ	6.74 AW	8.44 TQ	OKBLS	10/01-12/01
Textile, Garment, and Related Material	Oregon	H	7.33 FQ	9.16 AW	11.01 TQ	ORBLS	10/01-12/01
Textile, Garment, and Related Material	Pennsylvania	H	6.33 FQ	8.96 AW	12.15 TQ	PABLS	10/01-12/01
Textile, Garment, and Related Material	Rhode Island	H	7.71 FQ	9.53 AW	11.12 TQ	RIBLS	10/01-12/01

AAW Average annual wage **AE** Average entry wage **AEX** Average experienced wage **AO** Average offered **AOH** Average offered, high **AOL** Average offered, low **APH** Average pay, high range **APL** Average pay, low range **ASH** Average starting, high **ASL** Average starting, low **AW** Average wage paid **FQ** First quartile wage **H** Hourly **HI** Highest wage paid **HR** High end range **LR** Low end range **M** Monthly **MTC** Median total compensation **MW** Median wage paid **SQ** Second quartile wage **S** Special: hourly and annual **TQ** Third quartile wage **W** Weekly **Y** Yearly

Occupation/Type/Industry	Location	Per	Low	Mid	High	Source	Date
Presser							
Textile, Garment, and Related Material	South Carolina	H	6.12 FQ	9.63 AW	15.30 TQ	SCBLS	10/01-12/01
Textile, Garment, and Related Material	South Dakota	H	6.11 FQ	7.73 AW	9.44 TQ	SDBLS	10/01-12/01
Textile, Garment, and Related Material	Tennessee	H	6.06 FQ	7.60 AW	9.08 TQ	TNBLS	10/01-12/01
Textile, Garment, and Related Material	Texas	H	5.60 FQ	7.43 AW	10.74 TQ	TXBLS	10/01-12/01
Textile, Garment, and Related Material	Utah	H	5.65 FQ	6.96 AW	8.61 TQ	UTBLS	10/01-12/01
Textile, Garment, and Related Material	Vermont	H	6.49 FQ	8.16 AW	10.45 TQ	VTBLS	10/01-12/01
Textile, Garment, and Related Material	Virginia	H	6.12 FQ	8.58 AW	11.93 TQ	VABLS	10/01-12/01
Textile, Garment, and Related Material	Washington	H	7.18 FQ	9.40 AW	11.05 TQ	WABLS	10/01-12/01
Textile, Garment, and Related Material	West Virginia	H	5.61 FQ	7.19 AW	10.13 TQ	WVBLS	10/01-12/01
Textile, Garment, and Related Material	Wisconsin	H	6.96 FQ	8.62 AW	10.96 TQ	WIBLS	10/01-12/01
Textile, Garment, and Related Material	Wyoming	H	5.73 FQ	6.84 AW	8.51 TQ	WYBLS	10/01-12/01
Textile, Garment, and Related Material	Puerto Rico	H	5.54 FQ	6.27 AW	7.32 TQ	PRBLS	10/01-12/01
Priest							
Roman Catholic	United States	Y	12936 AOL		15483 HI	OOH8	1999-2000
Printing Machine Operator	Alabama	H	7.46 FQ	12.09 AW	18.93 TQ	ALBLS	10/01-12/01
	Alaska	H	11.44 FQ	17.13 AW	22.22 TQ	AKBLS	10/01-12/01
	Arizona	H	8.82 FQ	14.51 AW	20.86 TQ	AZBLS	10/01-12/01
	Arkansas	H	7.66 FQ	12.45 AW	19.23 TQ	ARBLS	10/01-12/01
	California	H	7.42 FQ	14.42 AW	23.08 TQ	CABLS	10/01-12/01
	Colorado	H	9.28 FQ	15.56 AW	24.04 TQ	COBLS	10/01-12/01
	Connecticut	H	9.34 FQ	15.65 AW	22.44 TQ	CTBLS	10/01-12/01
	Delaware	H	7.43 FQ	14.06 AW	23.43 TQ	DEBLS	10/01-12/01
	District of Columbia	H	9.90 FQ	21.80 AW	36.41 TQ	DCBLS	10/01-12/01
	Florida	H	7.76 FQ	13.02 AW	20.25 TQ	FLBLS	10/01-12/01
	Georgia	H	8.66 FQ	14.30 AW	21.89 TQ	GABLS	10/01-12/01
	Hawaii	H	6.06 FQ	12.84 AW	22.27 TQ	HIBLS	10/01-12/01
	Idaho	H	8.70 FQ	13.90 AW	20.58 TQ	IDBLS	10/01-12/01
	Illinois	H	8.11 FQ	14.33 AW	21.67 TQ	ILBLS	10/01-12/01
	Indiana	H	8.81 FQ	14.35 AW	20.94 TQ	INBLS	10/01-12/01
	Iowa	H	8.49 FQ	13.86 AW	21.37 TQ	IABLS	10/01-12/01
	Kansas	H	8.59 FQ	13.64 AW	19.98 TQ	KSBLS	10/01-12/01
	Kentucky	H	8.84 FQ	14.13 AW	20.39 TQ	KYBLS	10/01-12/01
	Louisiana	H	7.36 FQ	11.82 AW	16.83 TQ	LABLS	10/01-12/01
	Maine	H	8.53 FQ	12.87 AW	18.07 TQ	MEBLS	10/01-12/01
	Maryland	H	8.73 FQ	15.27 AW	23.21 TQ	MDBLS	10/01-12/01
	Massachusetts	H	10.17 FQ	16.11 AW	23.56 TQ	MABLS	10/01-12/01
	Michigan	H	9.41 FQ	15.69 AW	21.55 TQ	MIBLS	10/01-12/01
	Minnesota	H	10.68 FQ	16.46 AW	23.97 TQ	MNBLS	10/01-12/01
	Mississippi	H	7.78 FQ	11.99 AW	16.95 TQ	MSBLS	10/01-12/01
	Missouri	H	8.40 FQ	16.22 AW	26.18 TQ	MOBLS	10/01-12/01
	Montana	H	7.88 FQ	12.01 AW	15.77 TQ	MTBLS	10/01-12/01
	Nebraska	H	8.65 FQ	13.37 AW	20.02 TQ	NEBLS	10/01-12/01
	Nevada	H	9.52 FQ	14.32 AW	20.49 TQ	NVBLS	10/01-12/01
	New Hampshire	H	9.11 FQ	14.05 AW	20.53 TQ	NHBLS	10/01-12/01
	New Jersey	H	7.81 FQ	16.61 AW	26.13 TQ	NJBLS	10/01-12/01
	New Mexico	H	6.49 FQ	10.67 AW	16.15 TQ	NMBLS	10/01-12/01
	New York	H	8.45 FQ	16.89 AW	26.81 TQ	NYBLS	10/01-12/01
	North Carolina	H	8.22 FQ	13.69 AW	20.43 TQ	NCBLS	10/01-12/01
	North Dakota	H	7.20 FQ	11.61 AW	19.30 TQ	NDBLS	10/01-12/01
	Ohio	H	8.48 FQ	14.31 AW	20.75 TQ	OHBLS	10/01-12/01
	Oklahoma	H	7.34 FQ	12.04 AW	17.52 TQ	OKBLS	10/01-12/01
	Oregon	H	9.19 FQ	15.68 AW	24.06 TQ	ORBLS	10/01-12/01
	Pennsylvania	H	8.66 FQ	14.81 AW	21.76 TQ	PABLS	10/01-12/01
	Rhode Island	H	9.35 FQ	17.44 AW	26.60 TQ	RIBLS	10/01-12/01
	South Carolina	H	8.89 FQ	13.28 AW	18.16 TQ	SCBLS	10/01-12/01
	South Dakota	H	8.85 FQ	12.20 AW	16.92 TQ	SDBLS	10/01-12/01
	Tennessee	H	9.09 FQ	13.97 AW	20.13 TQ	TNBLS	10/01-12/01
	Texas	H	7.26 FQ	13.55 AW	21.25 TQ	TXBLS	10/01-12/01
	Utah	H	8.42 FQ	13.30 AW	19.37 TQ	UTBLS	10/01-12/01
	Vermont	H	9.46 FQ	13.93 AW	19.77 TQ	VTBLS	10/01-12/01
	Virginia	H	8.29 FQ	14.53 AW	22.15 TQ	VABLS	10/01-12/01
	Washington	H	9.64 FQ	16.60 AW	24.47 TQ	WABLS	10/01-12/01
	West Virginia	H	7.30 FQ	11.50 AW	18.08 TQ	WVBLS	10/01-12/01
	Wisconsin	H	9.25 FQ	15.79 AW	24.80 TQ	WIBLS	10/01-12/01
	Wyoming	H	8.17 FQ	12.56 AW	17.46 TQ	WYBLS	10/01-12/01
	Puerto Rico	H	5.92 FQ	9.63 AW	15.84 TQ	PRBLS	10/01-12/01
	Guam	H	7.48 FQ	11.10 AW	17.01 TQ	GUBLS	10/01-12/01
Private Detective and Investigator	Alabama	Y	13190 FQ	26740 AW	47460 TQ	ALBLS	10/01-12/01
	Birmingham MSA, AL	Y	12640 FQ	23600 AW	48610 TQ	ALBLS	10/01-12/01

AAW	Average annual wage	AOH	Average offered, high	ASH	Average starting, high	H	Hourly	M	Monthly	S	Special: hourly and annual
AE	Average entry wage	AOL	Average offered, low	ASL	Average starting, low	HI	Highest wage paid	MTC	Median total compensation	TQ	Third quartile wage
AEX	Average experienced wage	APH	Average pay, high range	AW	Average wage paid	HR	High end range	MW	Median wage paid	W	Weekly
AO	Average offered	APL	Average pay, low range	FQ	First quartile wage	LR	Low end range	SQ	Second quartile wage	Y	Yearly

Occupation/Type/Industry	Location	Per	Low	Mid	High	Source	Date
Private Detective and Investigator	Mobile MSA, AL	Y	12440 FQ	27110 AW	57560 TQ	ALBLS	10/01-12/01
	Alaska	Y	20640 FQ	28700 AW	40300 TQ	AKBLS	10/01-12/01
	Arizona	Y	16820 FQ	34360 AW	64070 TQ	AZBLS	10/01-12/01
	Phoenix-Mesa MSA, AZ	Y	17580 FQ	31510 AW	51420 TQ	AZBLS	10/01-12/01
	Tucson MSA, AZ	Y	15790 FQ	29940 AW	51890 TQ	AZBLS	10/01-12/01
	Arkansas	Y	16340 FQ	28010 AW	41710 TQ	ARBLS	10/01-12/01
	California	Y	19250 FQ	34060 AW	54490 TQ	CABLS	10/01-12/01
	Fresno MSA, CA	Y	13900 FQ	18820 AW	25190 TQ	CABLS	10/01-12/01
	Los Angeles-Long Beach PMSA, CA	Y	19940 FQ	33920 AW	49850 TQ	CABLS	10/01-12/01
	Oakland PMSA, CA	Y	18170 FQ	32440 AW	59460 TQ	CABLS	10/01-12/01
	Orange County PMSA, CA	Y	19360 FQ	29070 AW	42350 TQ	CABLS	10/01-12/01
	Riverside-San Bernardino PMSA, CA	Y	20800 FQ	38770 AW	58170 TQ	CABLS	10/01-12/01
	Sacramento PMSA, CA	Y	18860 FQ	25760 AW	40370 TQ	CABLS	10/01-12/01
	San Diego MSA, CA	Y	21550 FQ	40390 AW	56590 TQ	CABLS	10/01-12/01
	San Francisco PMSA, CA	Y	23820 FQ	45730 AW	80920 TQ	CABLS	10/01-12/01
	San Jose PMSA, CA	Y	16780 FQ	34960 AW	62230 TQ	CABLS	10/01-12/01
	Stockton-Lodi MSA, CA	Y	14900 FQ	22310 AW	36030 TQ	CABLS	10/01-12/01
	Vallejo-Fairfield-Napa PMSA, CA	Y	15770 FQ	26950 AW	43470 TQ	CABLS	10/01-12/01
	Colorado	Y	18010 FQ	36900 AW	58670 TQ	COBLS	10/01-12/01
	Colorado Springs MSA, CO	Y	16590 FQ	24300 AW	33000 TQ	COBLS	10/01-12/01
	Denver PMSA, CO	Y	20160 FQ	40720 AW	61220 TQ	COBLS	10/01-12/01
	Connecticut	Y	19740 FQ	33170 AW	58250 TQ	CTBLS	10/01-12/01
	Hartford MSA, CT	Y	20610 FQ	38000 AW	59960 TQ	CTBLS	10/01-12/01
	Delaware	Y	18650 FQ	33090 AW	57570 TQ	DEBLS	10/01-12/01
	Wilmington-Newark PMSA, DE-MD	Y	20030 FQ	34540 AW	60180 TQ	DEBLS	10/01-12/01
	District of Columbia	Y	24670 FQ	30210 AW	30270 TQ	DCBLS	10/01-12/01
	Washington PMSA, DC-MD-VA-WV	Y	16040 FQ	29240 AW	49990 TQ	DCBLS	10/01-12/01
	Florida	Y	18490 FQ	31120 AW	45600 TQ	FLBLS	10/01-12/01
	Daytona Beach MSA, FL	Y	15940 FQ	26440 AW	39620 TQ	FLBLS	10/01-12/01
	Fort Lauderdale PMSA, FL	Y	19110 FQ	39110 AW	61410 TQ	FLBLS	10/01-12/01
	Fort Myers-Cape Coral MSA, FL	Y	21140 FQ	38150 AW	67930 TQ	FLBLS	10/01-12/01
	Fort Walton Beach MSA, FL	Y	23510 FQ	27480 AW	31680 TQ	FLBLS	10/01-12/01
	Gainesville MSA, FL	Y	17250 FQ	29070 AW	42850 TQ	FLBLS	10/01-12/01
	Jacksonville MSA, FL	Y	16060 FQ	31680 AW	55920 TQ	FLBLS	10/01-12/01
	Lakeland-Winter Haven MSA, FL	Y	22470 FQ	29380 AW	36420 TQ	FLBLS	10/01-12/01
	Melbourne-Titusville-Palm Bay MSA, FL	Y	19920 FQ	33030 AW	44830 TQ	FLBLS	10/01-12/01
	Miami PMSA, FL	Y	18000 FQ	33130 AW	47360 TQ	FLBLS	10/01-12/01
	Ocala MSA, FL	Y	18510 FQ	22650 AW	27990 TQ	FLBLS	10/01-12/01
	Orlando MSA, FL	Y	18670 FQ	31830 AW	48770 TQ	FLBLS	10/01-12/01
	Pensacola MSA, FL	Y	16310 FQ	31190 AW	55060 TQ	FLBLS	10/01-12/01
	Sarasota-Bradenton MSA, FL	Y	17230 FQ	31110 AW	51700 TQ	FLBLS	10/01-12/01
	Tallahassee MSA, FL	Y	21260 FQ	33390 AW	48300 TQ	FLBLS	10/01-12/01
	Tampa-St. Petersburg-Clearwater MSA, FL	Y	19230 FQ	27580 AW	35340 TQ	FLBLS	10/01-12/01
	West Palm Beach-Boca Raton MSA, FL	Y	19850 FQ	31180 AW	45900 TQ	FLBLS	10/01-12/01
	Georgia	Y	20730 FQ	37240 AW	57740 TQ	GABLS	10/01-12/01
	Atlanta MSA, GA	Y	21850 FQ	42410 AW	66280 TQ	GABLS	10/01-12/01
	Columbus MSA, GA-AL	Y	18800 FQ	26690 AW	34760 TQ	GABLS	10/01-12/01
	Hawaii	Y	16680 FQ	24700 AW	30010 TQ	HIBLS	10/01-12/01
	Honolulu MSA, HI	Y	16880 FQ	27520 AW	46670 TQ	HIBLS	10/01-12/01
	Idaho	Y	15550 FQ	28570 AW	52600 TQ	IDBLS	10/01-12/01
	Illinois	Y	22600 FQ	39590 AW	63780 TQ	ILBLS	10/01-12/01
	Champaign-Urbana MSA, IL	Y	17490 FQ	35780 AW	61670 TQ	ILBLS	10/01-12/01
	Chicago PMSA, IL	Y	24090 FQ	40100 AW	62380 TQ	ILBLS	10/01-12/01
	Springfield MSA, IL	Y	18890 FQ	47420 AW	84870 TQ	ILBLS	10/01-12/01
	Indiana	Y	15120 FQ	24200 AW	39740 TQ	INBLS	10/01-12/01
	Gary PMSA, IN	Y	11270 FQ	17870 AW	32530 TQ	INBLS	10/01-12/01
	Indianapolis MSA, IN	Y	16400 FQ	30320 AW	51530 TQ	INBLS	10/01-12/01
	South Bend MSA, IN	Y	15100 FQ	19490 AW	26200 TQ	INBLS	10/01-12/01
	Iowa	Y	15880 FQ	28710 AW	57220 TQ	IABLS	10/01-12/01
	Des Moines MSA, IA	Y	22500 FQ	41760 AW	71730 TQ	IABLS	10/01-12/01
	Kansas	Y	17930 FQ	31450 AW	44990 TQ	KSBLS	10/01-12/01
	Wichita MSA, KS	Y	16730 FQ	30790 AW	60320 TQ	KSBLS	10/01-12/01

AAW	Average annual wage	**AOH**	Average offered, high	**ASH**	Average starting, high	**H**	Hourly	**M**	Monthly	**S**	Special: hourly and annual
AE	Average entry wage	**AOL**	Average offered, low	**ASL**	Average starting, low	**HI**	Highest wage paid	**MTC**	Median total compensation	**TQ**	Third quartile wage
AEX	Average experienced wage	**APH**	Average pay, high range	**AW**	Average wage paid	**HR**	High end range	**MW**	Median wage paid	**W**	Weekly
AO	Average offered	**APL**	Average pay, low range	**FQ**	First quartile wage	**LR**	Low end range	**SQ**	Second quartile wage	**Y**	Yearly

Occupation/Type/Industry	Location	Per	Low	Mid	High	Source	Date
Private Detective and Investigator	Kentucky	Y	13710 FQ	25190 AW	40880 TQ	KYBLS	10/01-12/01
	Louisville MSA, KY-IN	Y	16230 FQ	25420 AW	39720 TQ	KYBLS	10/01-12/01
	Louisiana	Y	17780 FQ	26650 AW	40970 TQ	LABLS	10/01-12/01
	Baton Rouge MSA, LA	Y	18620 FQ	28380 AW	44020 TQ	LABLS	10/01-12/01
	Lafayette MSA, LA	Y	20330 FQ	26730 AW	35660 TQ	LABLS	10/01-12/01
	New Orleans MSA, LA	Y	17940 FQ	28460 AW	42660 TQ	LABLS	10/01-12/01
	Shreveport-Bossier City MSA, LA	Y	15800 FQ	22930 AW	32810 TQ	LABLS	10/01-12/01
	Maine	Y	20230 FQ	31710 AW	44160 TQ	MEBLS	10/01-12/01
	Portland MSA, ME	Y	22690 FQ	33100 AW	43240 TQ	MEBLS	10/01-12/01
	Maryland	Y	13140 FQ	28550 AW	48270 TQ	MDBLS	10/01-12/01
	Baltimore PMSA, MD	Y	12940 FQ	30860 AW	56840 TQ	MDBLS	10/01-12/01
	Massachusetts	Y	19140 FQ	35020 AW	47810 TQ	MABLS	10/01-12/01
	Boston PMSA, MA-NH	Y	20520 FQ	38450 AW	48880 TQ	MABLS	10/01-12/01
	Worcester PMSA, MA-CT	Y	14860 FQ	22470 AW	33080 TQ	MABLS	10/01-12/01
	Michigan	Y	16650 FQ	26050 AW	38560 TQ	MIBLS	10/01-12/01
	Ann Arbor PMSA, MI	Y	19700 FQ	27930 AW	34950 TQ	MIBLS	10/01-12/01
	Detroit PMSA, MI	Y	19170 FQ	28260 AW	44220 TQ	MIBLS	10/01-12/01
	Flint PMSA, MI	Y	19310 FQ	27320 AW	35160 TQ	MIBLS	10/01-12/01
	Grand Rapids-Muskegon-Holland MSA, MI	Y	16280 FQ	25920 AW	45180 TQ	MIBLS	10/01-12/01
	Lansing-East Lansing MSA, MI	Y	18680 FQ	25540 AW	40070 TQ	MIBLS	10/01-12/01
	Saginaw-Bay City-Midland MSA, MI	Y	19640 FQ	27920 AW	36240 TQ	MIBLS	10/01-12/01
	Minnesota	Y	17550 FQ	28380 AW	48670 TQ	MNBLS	10/01-12/01
	Minneapolis-St. Paul MSA, MN-WI	Y	18400 FQ	29680 AW	51100 TQ	MNBLS	10/01-12/01
	Mississippi	Y	12570 FQ	24870 AW	42800 TQ	MSBLS	10/01-12/01
	Jackson MSA, MS	Y	18150 FQ	29750 AW	43610 TQ	MSBLS	10/01-12/01
	Missouri	Y	16580 FQ	28270 AW	50770 TQ	MOBLS	10/01-12/01
	Kansas City MSA, MO-KS	Y	20560 FQ	34230 AW	51930 TQ	MOBLS	10/01-12/01
	St. Louis MSA, MO-IL	Y	16840 FQ	31440 AW	62580 TQ	MOBLS	10/01-12/01
	Springfield MSA, MO	Y	16050 FQ	27820 AW	48270 TQ	MOBLS	10/01-12/01
	Montana	Y	15040 FQ	20040 AW	27100 TQ	MTBLS	10/01-12/01
	Nevada	Y	14340 FQ	31570 AW	48590 TQ	NVBLS	10/01-12/01
	Las Vegas MSA, NV-AZ	Y	20160 FQ	34760 AW	49450 TQ	NVBLS	10/01-12/01
	Reno MSA, NV	Y	12450 FQ	24730 AW	41680 TQ	NVBLS	10/01-12/01
	New Hampshire	Y	21550 FQ	29970 AW	36210 TQ	NHBLS	10/01-12/01
	Portsmouth-Rochester PMSA, NH-ME	Y	22170 FQ	30760 AW	36160 TQ	NHBLS	10/01-12/01
	New Jersey	Y	20750 FQ	45410 AW	70420 TQ	NJBLS	10/01-12/01
	Atlantic-Cape May PMSA, NJ	Y	21910 FQ	38110 AW	55280 TQ	NJBLS	10/01-12/01
	Bergen-Passaic PMSA, NJ	Y	18090 FQ	46470 AW	84950 TQ	NJBLS	10/01-12/01
	Middlesex-Somerset-Hunterdon PMSA, NJ	Y	14160 FQ	30390 AW	59780 TQ	NJBLS	10/01-12/01
	Newark PMSA, NJ	Y	23650 FQ	51060 AW	74000 TQ	NJBLS	10/01-12/01
	Trenton PMSA, NJ	Y	35650 FQ	43510 AW	56280 TQ	NJBLS	10/01-12/01
	New Mexico	Y	14470 FQ	22290 AW	33950 TQ	NMBLS	10/01-12/01
	Albuquerque MSA, NM	Y	16620 FQ	23410 AW	33910 TQ	NMBLS	10/01-12/01
	New York	Y	17290 FQ	35890 AW	61590 TQ	NYBLS	10/01-12/01
	Albany-Schenectady-Troy MSA, NY	Y	16120 FQ	34100 AW	56910 TQ	NYBLS	10/01-12/01
	Buffalo-Niagara Falls MSA, NY	Y	15660 FQ	25770 AW	44500 TQ	NYBLS	10/01-12/01
	Nassau-Suffolk PMSA, NY	Y	19130 FQ	40480 AW	70000 TQ	NYBLS	10/01-12/01
	New York PMSA, NY	Y	18810 FQ	39810 AW	61170 TQ	NYBLS	10/01-12/01
	Newburgh PMSA, NY-PA	Y	19970 FQ	35420 AW	51140 TQ	NYBLS	10/01-12/01
	Rochester MSA, NY	Y	15500 FQ	24440 AW	42540 TQ	NYBLS	10/01-12/01
	Syracuse MSA, NY	Y	17920 FQ	26280 AW	48950 TQ	NYBLS	10/01-12/01
	North Carolina	Y	17100 FQ	28740 AW	45800 TQ	NCBLS	10/01-12/01
	Charlotte-Gastonia-Rock Hill MSA, NC-SC	Y	17700 FQ	35720 AW	49080 TQ	NCBLS	10/01-12/01
	North Dakota	Y	15590 FQ	26500 AW	42880 TQ	NDBLS	10/01-12/01
	Ohio	Y	18940 FQ	32780 AW	51230 TQ	OHBLS	10/01-12/01
	Akron PMSA, OH	Y	18160 FQ	23870 AW	29340 TQ	OHBLS	10/01-12/01
	Cincinnati PMSA, OH-KY-IN	Y	18660 FQ	33350 AW	43800 TQ	OHBLS	10/01-12/01
	Cleveland-Lorain-Elyria PMSA, OH	Y	18420 FQ	35530 AW	57320 TQ	OHBLS	10/01-12/01
	Columbus MSA, OH	Y	19260 FQ	34150 AW	60970 TQ	OHBLS	10/01-12/01
	Dayton-Springfield MSA, OH	Y	17200 FQ	24560 AW	32520 TQ	OHBLS	10/01-12/01
	Hamilton-Middletown PMSA, OH	Y	16460 FQ	22040 AW	28640 TQ	OHBLS	10/01-12/01

AAW	Average annual wage	**AOH**	Average offered, high	**ASH**	Average starting, high	**H**	Hourly	**M**	Monthly	**S**	Special: hourly and annual
AE	Average entry wage	**AOL**	Average offered, low	**ASL**	Average starting, low	**HI**	Highest wage paid	**MTC**	Median total compensation	**TQ**	Third quartile wage
AEX	Average experienced wage	**APH**	Average pay, high range	**AW**	Average wage paid	**HR**	High end range	**MW**	Median wage paid	**W**	Weekly
AO	Average offered	**APL**	Average pay, low range	**FQ**	First quartile wage	**LR**	Low end range	**SQ**	Second quartile wage	**Y**	Yearly

Occupation/Type/Industry	Location	Per	Low	Mid	High	Source	Date
Private Detective and Investigator	Toledo MSA, OH	Y	18560 FQ	22970 AW	29600 TQ	OHBLS	10/01-12/01
	Youngstown-Warren MSA, OH	Y	17960 FQ	19940 AW	22090 TQ	OHBLS	10/01-12/01
	Oklahoma	Y	16630 FQ	30930 AW	45330 TQ	OKBLS	10/01-12/01
	Tulsa MSA, OK	Y	15290 FQ	24380 AW	50110 TQ	OKBLS	10/01-12/01
	Oregon	Y	19720 FQ	28440 AW	42950 TQ	ORBLS	10/01-12/01
	Portland-Vancouver PMSA, OR-WA	Y	19930 FQ	27660 AW	37860 TQ	ORBLS	10/01-12/01
	Salem PMSA, OR	Y	19000 FQ	34740 AW	55150 TQ	ORBLS	10/01-12/01
	Pennsylvania	Y	17380 FQ	32540 AW	64070 TQ	PABLS	10/01-12/01
	Allentown-Bethlehem-Easton MSA, PA	Y	20810 FQ	36810 AW	64130 TQ	PABLS	10/01-12/01
	Harrisburg-Lebanon-Carlisle MSA, PA	Y	18430 FQ	40760 AW	72120 TQ	PABLS	10/01-12/01
	Philadelphia PMSA, PA-NJ	Y	18120 FQ	33760 AW	65440 TQ	PABLS	10/01-12/01
	Pittsburgh MSA, PA	Y	17830 FQ	34150 AW	66950 TQ	PABLS	10/01-12/01
	Rhode Island	Y	19330 FQ	27260 AW	36480 TQ	RIBLS	10/01-12/01
	Providence-Fall River-Warwick MSA, RI-MA	Y	18550 FQ	26360 AW	36520 TQ	RIBLS	10/01-12/01
	South Carolina	Y	18500 FQ	29050 AW	44420 TQ	SCBLS	10/01-12/01
	Charleston-North Charleston MSA, SC	Y	18480 FQ	23590 AW	29210 TQ	SCBLS	10/01-12/01
	Columbia MSA, SC	Y	24260 FQ	30950 AW	43170 TQ	SCBLS	10/01-12/01
	Greenville-Spartanburg-Anderson MSA, SC	Y	16390 FQ	28730 AW	67420 TQ	SCBLS	10/01-12/01
	Tennessee	Y	19570 FQ	32150 AW	56260 TQ	TNBLS	10/01-12/01
	Knoxville MSA, TN	Y	19740 FQ	40420 AW	66190 TQ	TNBLS	10/01-12/01
	Memphis MSA, TN-AR-MS	Y	13870 FQ	27790 AW	43280 TQ	TNBLS	10/01-12/01
	Nashville MSA, TN	Y	20210 FQ	32560 AW	51150 TQ	TNBLS	10/01-12/01
	Texas	Y	17220 FQ	34070 AW	53650 TQ	TXBLS	10/01-12/01
	Amarillo MSA, TX	Y	14530 FQ	27240 AW	41610 TQ	TXBLS	10/01-12/01
	Corpus Christi MSA, TX	Y	18200 FQ	32600 AW	49510 TQ	TXBLS	10/01-12/01
	Dallas PMSA, TX	Y	21170 FQ	42810 AW	70250 TQ	TXBLS	10/01-12/01
	El Paso MSA, TX	Y	16790 FQ	28950 AW	43540 TQ	TXBLS	10/01-12/01
	Fort Worth-Arlington PMSA, TX	Y	20060 FQ	31490 AW	44010 TQ	TXBLS	10/01-12/01
	Houston PMSA, TX	Y	15800 FQ	29390 AW	44760 TQ	TXBLS	10/01-12/01
	Longview-Marshall MSA, TX	Y	15250 FQ	29160 AW	46180 TQ	TXBLS	10/01-12/01
	McAllen-Edinburg-Mission MSA, TX	Y	19710 FQ	32010 AW	50930 TQ	TXBLS	10/01-12/01
	San Antonio MSA, TX	Y	16930 FQ	31310 AW	51410 TQ	TXBLS	10/01-12/01
	Utah	Y	15710 FQ	27120 AW	45940 TQ	UTBLS	10/01-12/01
	Salt Lake City-Ogden MSA, UT	Y	15510 FQ	25390 AW	42250 TQ	UTBLS	10/01-12/01
	Vermont	Y	19120 FQ	25170 AW	35590 TQ	VTBLS	10/01-12/01
	Virginia	Y	16160 FQ	32830 AW	61110 TQ	VABLS	10/01-12/01
	Norfolk-Virginia Beach-Newport News MSA, VA-NC	Y	17140 FQ	24820 AW	34120 TQ	VABLS	10/01-12/01
	Washington	Y	20140 FQ	44730 AW	70390 TQ	WABLS	10/01-12/01
	Seattle-Bellevue-Everett PMSA, WA	Y	21010 FQ	45660 AW	69850 TQ	WABLS	10/01-12/01
	Spokane MSA, WA	Y	17760 FQ	44950 AW	93030 TQ	WABLS	10/01-12/01
	Yakima MSA, WA	Y	48410 FQ	51240 AW	59730 TQ	WABLS	10/01-12/01
	West Virginia	Y	22710 FQ	26400 AW	28190 TQ	WVBLS	10/01-12/01
	Charleston MSA, WV	Y	23480 FQ	36380 AW	62500 TQ	WVBLS	10/01-12/01
	Wisconsin	Y	15690 FQ	25070 AW	42160 TQ	WIBLS	10/01-12/01
	Green Bay MSA, WI	Y	15150 FQ	18030 AW	22490 TQ	WIBLS	10/01-12/01
	Milwaukee-Waukesha PMSA, WI	Y	15500 FQ	21350 AW	31120 TQ	WIBLS	10/01-12/01
	Puerto Rico	Y	11950 FQ	19630 AW	30770 TQ	PRBLS	10/01-12/01
Probation Officer and Correctional Treatment Specialist	Alabama	Y	19680 FQ	33460 AW	49350 TQ	ALBLS	10/01-12/01
	Alaska	Y	30920 FQ	43070 AW	56020 TQ	AKBLS	10/01-12/01
	Arizona	Y	22450 FQ	32510 AW	43680 TQ	AZBLS	10/01-12/01
	Phoenix-Mesa MSA, AZ	Y	29350 FQ	36320 AW	46090 TQ	AZBLS	10/01-12/01
	Arkansas	Y	22570 FQ	28560 AW	38950 TQ	ARBLS	10/01-12/01
	Fayetteville-Springdale-Rogers MSA, AR	Y	19190 FQ	26640 AW	36440 TQ	ARBLS	10/01-12/01
	Little Rock-North Little Rock MSA, AR	Y	23360 FQ	32000 AW	44590 TQ	ARBLS	10/01-12/01

AAW	Average annual wage	**AOH**	Average offered, high	**ASH**	Average starting, high	**H**	Hourly	**M**	Monthly	**S**	Special: hourly and annual
AE	Average entry wage	**AOL**	Average offered, low	**ASL**	Average starting, low	**HI**	Highest wage paid	**MTC**	Median total compensation	**TQ**	Third quartile wage
AEX	Average experienced wage	**APH**	Average pay, high range	**AW**	Average wage paid	**HR**	High end range	**MW**	Median wage paid	**W**	Weekly
AO	Average offered	**APL**	Average pay, low range	**FQ**	First quartile wage	**LR**	Low end range	**SQ**	Second quartile wage	**Y**	Yearly

Occupation/Type/Industry	Location	Per	Low	Mid	High	Source	Date
Probation Officer and Correctional Treatment Specialist	California	Y	35120 FQ	54890 AW	77490 TQ	CABLS	10/01-12/01
	Oakland PMSA, CA	Y	51160 FQ	66130 AW	85150 TQ	CABLS	10/01-12/01
	Sacramento PMSA, CA	Y	38960 FQ	65290 AW	87020 TQ	CABLS	10/01-12/01
	San Francisco PMSA, CA	Y	50320 FQ	66710 AW	87220 TQ	CABLS	10/01-12/01
	Colorado	Y	31260 FQ	48010 AW	66850 TQ	COBLS	10/01-12/01
	Boulder-Longmont PMSA, CO	Y	31760 FQ	47280 AW	65760 TQ	COBLS	10/01-12/01
	Colorado Springs MSA, CO	Y	30780 FQ	50600 AW	68440 TQ	COBLS	10/01-12/01
	Denver PMSA, CO	Y	31540 FQ	48570 AW	67620 TQ	COBLS	10/01-12/01
	Connecticut	Y	32350 FQ	46320 AW	60110 TQ	CTBLS	10/01-12/01
	Washington PMSA, DC-MD-VA-WV	Y	31810 FQ	44890 AW	60120 TQ	DCBLS	10/01-12/01
	Florida	Y	24910 FQ	33860 AW	44140 TQ	FLBLS	10/01-12/01
	Daytona Beach MSA, FL	Y	25400 FQ	32770 AW	42320 TQ	FLBLS	10/01-12/01
	Fort Lauderdale PMSA, FL	Y	25500 FQ	34850 AW	43690 TQ	FLBLS	10/01-12/01
	Fort Walton Beach MSA, FL	Y	24370 FQ	31760 AW	42370 TQ	FLBLS	10/01-12/01
	Jacksonville MSA, FL	Y	25020 FQ	33880 AW	43800 TQ	FLBLS	10/01-12/01
	Lakeland-Winter Haven MSA, FL	Y	24620 FQ	32050 AW	42150 TQ	FLBLS	10/01-12/01
	Miami PMSA, FL	Y	25060 FQ	35180 AW	45920 TQ	FLBLS	10/01-12/01
	Orlando MSA, FL	Y	24570 FQ	32170 AW	41980 TQ	FLBLS	10/01-12/01
	Pensacola MSA, FL	Y	24840 FQ	33020 AW	43380 TQ	FLBLS	10/01-12/01
	Sarasota-Bradenton MSA, FL	Y	20240 FQ	31040 AW	43330 TQ	FLBLS	10/01-12/01
	Tallahassee MSA, FL	Y	26010 FQ	38230 AW	58320 TQ	FLBLS	10/01-12/01
	Tampa-St. Petersburg-Clearwater MSA, FL	Y	25100 FQ	33250 AW	43730 TQ	FLBLS	10/01-12/01
	West Palm Beach-Boca Raton MSA, FL	Y	24060 FQ	33910 AW	44560 TQ	FLBLS	10/01-12/01
	Georgia	Y	23390 FQ	32870 AW	46390 TQ	GABLS	10/01-12/01
	Atlanta MSA, GA	Y	23680 FQ	33490 AW	49440 TQ	GABLS	10/01-12/01
	Augusta-Aiken MSA, GA-SC	Y	19300 FQ	27340 AW	38880 TQ	GABLS	10/01-12/01
	Columbus MSA, GA-AL	Y	20740 FQ	31580 AW	43140 TQ	GABLS	10/01-12/01
	Macon MSA, GA	Y	20990 FQ	29680 AW	41190 TQ	GABLS	10/01-12/01
	Hawaii	Y	36590 FQ	44950 AW	55880 TQ	HIBLS	10/01-12/01
	Idaho	Y	25770 FQ	33950 AW	42980 TQ	IDBLS	10/01-12/01
	Boise City MSA, ID	Y	27630 FQ	34590 AW	42880 TQ	IDBLS	10/01-12/01
	Illinois	Y	30790 FQ	41720 AW	52910 TQ	ILBLS	10/01-12/01
	Chicago PMSA, IL	Y	31540 FQ	41560 AW	49900 TQ	ILBLS	10/01-12/01
	Springfield MSA, IL	Y	29320 FQ	41150 AW	53900 TQ	ILBLS	10/01-12/01
	Indiana	Y	19410 FQ	29100 AW	41900 TQ	INBLS	10/01-12/01
	Fort Wayne MSA, IN	Y	19780 FQ	34110 AW	46670 TQ	INBLS	10/01-12/01
	Iowa	Y	29060 FQ	38100 AW	51340 TQ	IABLS	10/01-12/01
	Kansas	Y	22940 FQ	31070 AW	41230 TQ	KSBLS	10/01-12/01
	Wichita MSA, KS	Y	23530 FQ	31610 AW	40790 TQ	KSBLS	10/01-12/01
	Kentucky	Y	25520 FQ	36190 AW	53130 TQ	KYBLS	10/01-12/01
	Louisiana	Y	23720 FQ	34500 AW	49410 TQ	LABLS	10/01-12/01
	Baton Rouge MSA, LA	Y	24570 FQ	36440 AW	51220 TQ	LABLS	10/01-12/01
	Houma MSA, LA	Y	24480 FQ	35050 AW	46400 TQ	LABLS	10/01-12/01
	Lafayette MSA, LA	Y	23590 FQ	32190 AW	43810 TQ	LABLS	10/01-12/01
	Maine	Y	23700 FQ	29530 AW	40160 TQ	MEBLS	10/01-12/01
	Portland MSA, ME	Y	23690 FQ	28250 AW	37290 TQ	MEBLS	10/01-12/01
	Michigan	Y	36070 FQ	47120 AW	56970 TQ	MIBLS	10/01-12/01
	Detroit PMSA, MI	Y	35920 FQ	47390 AW	58120 TQ	MIBLS	10/01-12/01
	Grand Rapids-Muskegon-Holland MSA, MI	Y	39280 FQ	49320 AW	57740 TQ	MIBLS	10/01-12/01
	Kalamazoo-Battle Creek MSA, MI	Y	38290 FQ	48370 AW	57680 TQ	MIBLS	10/01-12/01
	Minnesota	Y	32150 FQ	50700 AW	72420 TQ	MNBLS	10/01-12/01
	Mississippi	Y	18610 FQ	23900 AW	32020 TQ	MSBLS	10/01-12/01
	Kansas City MSA, MO-KS	Y	22160 FQ	32260 AW	44260 TQ	MOBLS	10/01-12/01
	St. Louis MSA, MO-IL	Y	22550 FQ	41850 AW	57760 TQ	MOBLS	10/01-12/01
	Montana	Y	24050 FQ	32830 AW	43210 TQ	MTBLS	10/01-12/01
	Nebraska	Y	18630 FQ	26840 AW	37020 TQ	NEBLS	10/01-12/01
	Lincoln MSA, NE	Y	20410 FQ	29670 AW	38940 TQ	NEBLS	10/01-12/01
	Omaha MSA, NE-IA	Y	27210 FQ	34900 AW	44220 TQ	NEBLS	10/01-12/01
	Nevada	Y	35860 FQ	49320 AW	68810 TQ	NVBLS	10/01-12/01
	Las Vegas MSA, NV-AZ	Y	21940 FQ	43210 AW	67110 TQ	NVBLS	10/01-12/01
	New Hampshire	Y	29460 FQ	37110 AW	44450 TQ	NHBLS	10/01-12/01
	New Mexico	Y	23520 FQ	31020 AW	42100 TQ	NMBLS	10/01-12/01
	New York	Y	35330 FQ	50270 AW	68000 TQ	NYBLS	10/01-12/01

AAW	Average annual wage	**AOH**	Average offered, high	**ASH**	Average starting, high	**H**	Hourly	**M**	Monthly	**S**	Special: hourly and annual
AE	Average entry wage	**AOL**	Average offered, low	**ASL**	Average starting, low	**HI**	Highest wage paid	**MTC**	Median total compensation	**TQ**	Third quartile wage
AEX	Average experienced wage	**APH**	Average pay, high range	**AW**	Average wage paid	**HR**	High end range	**MW**	Median wage paid	**W**	Weekly
AO	Average offered	**APL**	Average pay, low range	**FQ**	First quartile wage	**LR**	Low end range	**SQ**	Second quartile wage	**Y**	Yearly

Occupation/Type/Industry	Location	Per	Low	Mid	High	Source	Date
Probation Officer and Correctional Treatment Specialist	Albany-Schenectady-Troy MSA, NY	Y	36750 FQ	50820 AW	67930 TQ	NYBLS	10/01-12/01
	Buffalo-Niagara Falls MSA, NY	Y	32980 FQ	50510 AW	65620 TQ	NYBLS	10/01-12/01
	New York PMSA, NY	Y	37440 FQ	51740 AW	68630 TQ	NYBLS	10/01-12/01
	Rochester MSA, NY	Y	27870 FQ	43340 AW	59900 TQ	NYBLS	10/01-12/01
	Utica-Rome MSA, NY	Y	34890 FQ	49710 AW	64570 TQ	NYBLS	10/01-12/01
	North Carolina	Y	24940 FQ	32120 AW	41240 TQ	NCBLS	10/01-12/01
	Charlotte-Gastonia-Rock Hill MSA, NC-SC	Y	22640 FQ	31080 AW	40970 TQ	NCBLS	10/01-12/01
	Fayetteville MSA, NC	Y	25450 FQ	32340 AW	40980 TQ	NCBLS	10/01-12/01
	Greensboro-Winston-Salem-High Point MSA, NC	Y	25080 FQ	32010 AW	40970 TQ	NCBLS	10/01-12/01
	North Dakota	Y	23470 FQ	31870 AW	42460 TQ	NDBLS	10/01-12/01
	Ohio	Y	25330 FQ	39070 AW	54150 TQ	OHBLS	10/01-12/01
	Akron PMSA, OH	Y	26040 FQ	39610 AW	53990 TQ	OHBLS	10/01-12/01
	Canton-Massillon MSA, OH	Y	25930 FQ	37740 AW	51960 TQ	OHBLS	10/01-12/01
	Cleveland-Lorain-Elyria PMSA, OH	Y	27380 FQ	40450 AW	55800 TQ	OHBLS	10/01-12/01
	Columbus MSA, OH	Y	29460 FQ	43500 AW	55790 TQ	OHBLS	10/01-12/01
	Toledo MSA, OH	Y	22870 FQ	32800 AW	46520 TQ	OHBLS	10/01-12/01
	Oklahoma	Y	23240 FQ	31550 AW	41620 TQ	OKBLS	10/01-12/01
	Oregon	Y	32280 FQ	43550 AW	55540 TQ	ORBLS	10/01-12/01
	Pennsylvania	Y	25170 FQ	37770 AW	54630 TQ	PABLS	10/01-12/01
	Pittsburgh MSA, PA	Y	31420 FQ	45730 AW	63470 TQ	PABLS	10/01-12/01
	Providence-Fall River-Warwick MSA, RI-MA	Y	41450 FQ	57270 AW	72470 TQ	RIBLS	10/01-12/01
	South Carolina	Y	19810 FQ	28410 AW	39010 TQ	SCBLS	10/01-12/01
	Charleston-North Charleston MSA, SC	Y	19460 FQ	29420 AW	43320 TQ	SCBLS	10/01-12/01
	Greenville-Spartanburg-Anderson MSA, SC	Y	19280 FQ	25930 AW	34240 TQ	SCBLS	10/01-12/01
	South Dakota	Y	22770 FQ	29740 AW	35420 TQ	SDBLS	10/01-12/01
	Tennessee	Y	23360 FQ	32040 AW	44020 TQ	TNBLS	10/01-12/01
	Chattanooga MSA, TN-GA	Y	23080 FQ	32080 AW	45710 TQ	TNBLS	10/01-12/01
	Johnson City-Kingsport-Bristol MSA, TN-VA	Y	28080 FQ	37050 AW	52200 TQ	TNBLS	10/01-12/01
	Memphis MSA, TN-AR-MS	Y	23140 FQ	29460 AW	38680 TQ	TNBLS	10/01-12/01
	Texas	Y	26110 FQ	32400 AW	41240 TQ	TXBLS	10/01-12/01
	Dallas PMSA, TX	Y	26970 FQ	32880 AW	41300 TQ	TXBLS	10/01-12/01
	Fort Worth-Arlington PMSA, TX	Y	26700 FQ	33810 AW	43780 TQ	TXBLS	10/01-12/01
	Longview-Marshall MSA, TX	Y	27170 FQ	34750 AW	44210 TQ	TXBLS	10/01-12/01
	Utah	Y	23310 FQ	31750 AW	42170 TQ	UTBLS	10/01-12/01
	Salt Lake City-Ogden MSA, UT	Y	23450 FQ	31930 AW	42310 TQ	UTBLS	10/01-12/01
	Virginia	Y	28610 FQ	39590 AW	54890 TQ	VABLS	10/01-12/01
	Norfolk-Virginia Beach-Newport News MSA, VA-NC	Y	29020 FQ	37890 AW	51750 TQ	VABLS	10/01-12/01
	Richmond-Petersburg MSA, VA	Y	27990 FQ	36220 AW	47700 TQ	VABLS	10/01-12/01
	Washington	Y	31240 FQ	41840 AW	54090 TQ	WABLS	10/01-12/01
	Bremerton PMSA, WA	Y	37380 FQ	47580 AW	59200 TQ	WABLS	10/01-12/01
	Olympia PMSA, WA	Y	36140 FQ	42280 AW	52790 TQ	WABLS	10/01-12/01
	Seattle-Bellevue-Everett PMSA, WA	Y	33730 FQ	43810 AW	55670 TQ	WABLS	10/01-12/01
	Spokane MSA, WA	Y	20820 FQ	40020 AW	53810 TQ	WABLS	10/01-12/01
	Tacoma PMSA, WA	Y	25740 FQ	37620 AW	51220 TQ	WABLS	10/01-12/01
	West Virginia	Y	18910 FQ	24650 AW	29120 TQ	WVBLS	10/01-12/01
	Wisconsin	Y	25270 FQ	35940 AW	44540 TQ	WIBLS	10/01-12/01
	Wyoming	Y	16430 FQ	21860 AW	28840 TQ	WYBLS	10/01-12/01
Procurement Clerk	Alabama	H	8.29 FQ	13.26 AW	17.93 TQ	ALBLS	10/01-12/01
	Alaska	H	12.80 FQ	18.12 AW	25.09 TQ	AKBLS	10/01-12/01
	Arizona	H	8.98 FQ	13.34 AW	17.64 TQ	AZBLS	10/01-12/01
	Arkansas	H	8.20 FQ	11.38 AW	15.59 TQ	ARBLS	10/01-12/01
	California	H	10.11 FQ	15.92 AW	21.93 TQ	CABLS	10/01-12/01
	Colorado	H	9.25 FQ	14.26 AW	19.87 TQ	COBLS	10/01-12/01
	Connecticut	H	10.83 FQ	16.20 AW	21.94 TQ	CTBLS	10/01-12/01

AAW Average annual wage | AE Average entry wage | AEX Average experienced wage | AO Average offered | AOH Average offered, high | AOL Average offered, low | APH Average pay, high range | APL Average pay, low range | ASH Average starting, high | ASL Average starting, low | AW Average wage paid | FQ First quartile wage | H Hourly | HI Highest wage paid | HR High end range | LR Low end range | M Monthly | MTC Median total compensation | MW Median wage paid | SQ Second quartile wage | S Special: hourly and annual | TQ Third quartile wage | W Weekly | Y Yearly

Occupation/Type/Industry	Location	Per	Low	Mid	High	Source	Date
Procurement Clerk	Delaware	H	9.93 FQ	15.07 AW	21.32 TQ	DEBLS	10/01-12/01
	District of Columbia	H	12.17 FQ	16.32 AW	20.78 TQ	DCBLS	10/01-12/01
	Florida	H	8.14 FQ	12.66 AW	18.00 TQ	FLBLS	10/01-12/01
	Georgia	H	9.29 FQ	13.56 AW	18.07 TQ	GABLS	10/01-12/01
	Hawaii	H	11.08 FQ	15.86 AW	20.63 TQ	HIBLS	10/01-12/01
	Idaho	H	7.57 FQ	12.84 AW	18.36 TQ	IDBLS	10/01-12/01
	Illinois	H	9.23 FQ	14.79 AW	20.50 TQ	ILBLS	10/01-12/01
	Indiana	H	8.06 FQ	12.62 AW	17.93 TQ	INBLS	10/01-12/01
	Iowa	H	8.93 FQ	12.55 AW	17.61 TQ	IABLS	10/01-12/01
	Kansas	H	7.84 FQ	13.28 AW	20.19 TQ	KSBLS	10/01-12/01
	Kentucky	H	8.78 FQ	13.17 AW	17.64 TQ	KYBLS	10/01-12/01
	Louisiana	H	7.55 FQ	12.82 AW	19.20 TQ	LABLS	10/01-12/01
	Maine	H	9.98 FQ	14.49 AW	19.82 TQ	MEBLS	10/01-12/01
	Maryland	H	10.23 FQ	15.28 AW	20.55 TQ	MDBLS	10/01-12/01
	Massachusetts	H	9.76 FQ	15.35 AW	21.71 TQ	MABLS	10/01-12/01
	Michigan	H	9.60 FQ	15.64 AW	20.83 TQ	MIBLS	10/01-12/01
	Minnesota	H	9.26 FQ	13.49 AW	17.80 TQ	MNBLS	10/01-12/01
	Mississippi	H	8.24 FQ	12.80 AW	17.10 TQ	MSBLS	10/01-12/01
	Missouri	H	8.67 FQ	13.51 AW	19.89 TQ	MOBLS	10/01-12/01
	Montana	H	7.98 FQ	12.57 AW	17.28 TQ	MTBLS	10/01-12/01
	Nebraska	H	8.65 FQ	13.22 AW	18.71 TQ	NEBLS	10/01-12/01
	Nevada	H	9.05 FQ	13.94 AW	19.44 TQ	NVBLS	10/01-12/01
	New Hampshire	H	8.96 FQ	13.70 AW	19.65 TQ	NHBLS	10/01-12/01
	New Jersey	H	10.22 FQ	15.38 AW	21.02 TQ	NJBLS	10/01-12/01
	New Mexico	H	9.67 FQ	15.43 AW	21.52 TQ	NMBLS	10/01-12/01
	New York	H	8.14 FQ	14.40 AW	21.05 TQ	NYBLS	10/01-12/01
	North Carolina	H	8.15 FQ	13.07 AW	17.64 TQ	NCBLS	10/01-12/01
	North Dakota	H	8.45 FQ	12.70 AW	18.50 TQ	NDBLS	10/01-12/01
	Ohio	H	9.40 FQ	13.79 AW	18.85 TQ	OHBLS	10/01-12/01
	Oklahoma	H	9.13 FQ	13.93 AW	19.47 TQ	OKBLS	10/01-12/01
	Oregon	H	10.21 FQ	14.77 AW	20.05 TQ	ORBLS	10/01-12/01
	Pennsylvania	H	9.20 FQ	14.29 AW	19.83 TQ	PABLS	10/01-12/01
	Rhode Island	H	9.30 FQ	13.30 AW	20.16 TQ	RIBLS	10/01-12/01
	South Carolina	H	8.91 FQ	13.46 AW	17.79 TQ	SCBLS	10/01-12/01
	South Dakota	H	8.22 FQ	11.56 AW	15.77 TQ	SDBLS	10/01-12/01
	Tennessee	H	8.07 FQ	12.49 AW	17.13 TQ	TNBLS	10/01-12/01
	Texas	H	8.50 FQ	14.10 AW	20.63 TQ	TXBLS	10/01-12/01
	Utah	H	8.50 FQ	13.84 AW	19.10 TQ	UTBLS	10/01-12/01
	Vermont	H	9.18 FQ	12.87 AW	16.85 TQ	VTBLS	10/01-12/01
	Virginia	H	9.98 FQ	14.63 AW	20.20 TQ	VABLS	10/01-12/01
	Washington	H	9.95 FQ	14.80 AW	20.45 TQ	WABLS	10/01-12/01
	West Virginia	H	8.17 FQ	13.37 AW	19.01 TQ	WVBLS	10/01-12/01
	Wisconsin	H	9.22 FQ	13.36 AW	18.23 TQ	WIBLS	10/01-12/01
	Wyoming	H	9.69 FQ	14.47 AW	19.75 TQ	WYBLS	10/01-12/01
	Puerto Rico	H	6.19 FQ	10.24 AW	16.24 TQ	PRBLS	10/01-12/01
	Guam	H	7.10 FQ	13.98 AW	20.15 TQ	GUBLS	10/01-12/01
Producer and Director	Alabama	Y	18740 FQ	43180 AW	82590 TQ	ALBLS	10/01-12/01
	Birmingham MSA, AL	Y	21460 FQ	47470 AW	86780 TQ	ALBLS	10/01-12/01
	Huntsville MSA, AL	Y	23500 FQ	49720 AW	88710 TQ	ALBLS	10/01-12/01
	Mobile MSA, AL	Y	21090 FQ	49480 AW	88520 TQ	ALBLS	10/01-12/01
	Montgomery MSA, AL	Y	16190 FQ	38520 AW	69450 TQ	ALBLS	10/01-12/01
	Alaska	Y	24440 FQ	33870 AW	46270 TQ	AKBLS	10/01-12/01
	Anchorage MSA, AK	Y	28710 FQ	35740 AW	49110 TQ	AKBLS	10/01-12/01
	Arizona	Y	22590 FQ	56120 AW	109220 TQ	AZBLS	10/01-12/01
	Phoenix-Mesa MSA, AZ	Y	27540 FQ	62530 AW	117350 TQ	AZBLS	10/01-12/01
	Tucson MSA, AZ	Y	20680 FQ	37650 AW	66230 TQ	AZBLS	10/01-12/01
	Arkansas	Y	17990 FQ	35760 AW	55380 TQ	ARBLS	10/01-12/01
	Fayetteville-Springdale-Rogers MSA, AR	Y	16500 FQ	31520 AW	59470 TQ	ARBLS	10/01-12/01
	Little Rock-North Little Rock MSA, AR	Y	20710 FQ	41000 AW	60900 TQ	ARBLS	10/01-12/01
	California	Y	33420 FQ	87300 AW		CABLS	10/01-12/01
	Bakersfield MSA, CA	Y	28790 FQ	54030 AW	84880 TQ	CABLS	10/01-12/01
	Fresno MSA, CA	Y	20210 FQ	38840 AW	60730 TQ	CABLS	10/01-12/01
	Oakland PMSA, CA	Y	29510 FQ	44920 AW	75000 TQ	CABLS	10/01-12/01
	Orange County PMSA, CA	Y	16170 FQ	48880 AW	104860 TQ	CABLS	10/01-12/01
	Riverside-San Bernardino PMSA, CA	Y	22300 FQ	46090 AW	70450 TQ	CABLS	10/01-12/01
	Sacramento PMSA, CA	Y	30660 FQ	55320 AW	81960 TQ	CABLS	10/01-12/01
	Salinas MSA, CA	Y	33910 FQ	64810 AW		CABLS	10/01-12/01
	San Diego MSA, CA	Y	25590 FQ	55240 AW	105210 TQ	CABLS	10/01-12/01
	San Francisco PMSA, CA	Y	32930 FQ	75760 AW		CABLS	10/01-12/01

AAW Average annual wage	**AOH** Average offered, high	**ASH** Average starting, high	**H** Hourly	**M** Monthly	**S** Special: hourly and annual
AE Average entry wage	**AOL** Average offered, low	**ASL** Average starting, low	**HI** Highest wage paid	**MTC** Median total compensation	**TQ** Third quartile wage
AEX Average experienced wage	**APH** Average pay, high range	**AW** Average wage paid	**HR** High end range	**MW** Median wage paid	**W** Weekly
AO Average offered	**APL** Average pay, low range	**FQ** First quartile wage	**LR** Low end range	**SQ** Second quartile wage	**Y** Yearly

Occupation/Type/Industry	Location	Per	Low	Mid	High	Source	Date
Producer and Director	San Jose PMSA, CA	Y	25160 FQ	45810 AW	76300 TQ	CABLS	10/01-12/01
	San Luis Obispo-Atascadero-Paso Robles MSA, CA	Y	19690 FQ	28810 AW	36090 TQ	CABLS	10/01-12/01
	Santa Barbara-Santa Maria-Lompoc MSA, CA	Y	21450 FQ	71080 AW		CABLS	10/01-12/01
	Ventura PMSA, CA	Y	29060 FQ	82760 AW		CABLS	10/01-12/01
	Colorado	Y	27820 FQ	55590 AW	97980 TQ	COBLS	10/01-12/01
	Boulder-Longmont PMSA, CO	Y	25370 FQ	40590 AW	60590 TQ	COBLS	10/01-12/01
	Colorado Springs MSA, CO	Y	25430 FQ	62020 AW	132170 TQ	COBLS	10/01-12/01
	Denver PMSA, CO	Y	31800 FQ	57580 AW	98990 TQ	COBLS	10/01-12/01
	Connecticut	Y	31420 FQ	61870 AW	112120 TQ	CTBLS	10/01-12/01
	Bridgeport PMSA, CT	Y	29600 FQ	51370 AW	85510 TQ	CTBLS	10/01-12/01
	Hartford MSA, CT	Y	30270 FQ	54240 AW	87040 TQ	CTBLS	10/01-12/01
	New Haven-Meriden PMSA, CT	Y	35140 FQ	50720 AW	70660 TQ	CTBLS	10/01-12/01
	Stamford-Norwalk PMSA, CT	Y	41560 FQ	86940 AW		CTBLS	10/01-12/01
	Delaware	Y	28100 FQ	47340 AW	71610 TQ	DEBLS	10/01-12/01
	Wilmington-Newark PMSA, DE-MD	Y	28100 FQ	47340 AW	71610 TQ	DEBLS	10/01-12/01
	District of Columbia	Y	25460 FQ	51550 AW	81770 TQ	DCBLS	10/01-12/01
	Washington PMSA, DC-MD-VA-WV	Y	26060 FQ	51480 AW	81140 TQ	DCBLS	10/01-12/01
	Florida	Y	24260 FQ	52750 AW	103980 TQ	FLBLS	10/01-12/01
	Fort Lauderdale PMSA, FL	Y	25240 FQ	42030 AW	65350 TQ	FLBLS	10/01-12/01
	Fort Myers-Cape Coral MSA, FL	Y	14480 FQ	41640 AW	82150 TQ	FLBLS	10/01-12/01
	Gainesville MSA, FL	Y	16780 FQ	29490 AW	44740 TQ	FLBLS	10/01-12/01
	Jacksonville MSA, FL	Y	20430 FQ	37450 AW	57690 TQ	FLBLS	10/01-12/01
	Miami PMSA, FL	Y	30120 FQ	64670 AW	124270 TQ	FLBLS	10/01-12/01
	Orlando MSA, FL	Y	27700 FQ	52300 AW	87790 TQ	FLBLS	10/01-12/01
	Pensacola MSA, FL	Y	24700 FQ	39890 AW	69170 TQ	FLBLS	10/01-12/01
	Sarasota-Bradenton MSA, FL	Y	17810 FQ	43130 AW	83290 TQ	FLBLS	10/01-12/01
	Tallahassee MSA, FL	Y	19070 FQ	36870 AW	76560 TQ	FLBLS	10/01-12/01
	Tampa-St. Petersburg-Clearwater MSA, FL	Y	24330 FQ	52450 AW	87250 TQ	FLBLS	10/01-12/01
	Georgia	Y	25400 FQ	51390 AW	83030 TQ	GABLS	10/01-12/01
	Atlanta MSA, GA	Y	28190 FQ	53390 AW	85380 TQ	GABLS	10/01-12/01
	Macon MSA, GA	Y	26610 FQ	42470 AW	63500 TQ	GABLS	10/01-12/01
	Hawaii	Y	24750 FQ	47020 AW	77440 TQ	HIBLS	10/01-12/01
	Honolulu MSA, HI	Y	24650 FQ	45250 AW	71230 TQ	HIBLS	10/01-12/01
	Idaho	Y	23330 FQ	32950 AW	46170 TQ	IDBLS	10/01-12/01
	Boise City MSA, ID	Y	23130 FQ	32640 AW	46920 TQ	IDBLS	10/01-12/01
	Illinois	Y	24480 FQ	51840 AW	90460 TQ	ILBLS	10/01-12/01
	Chicago PMSA, IL	Y	25300 FQ	53730 AW	92670 TQ	ILBLS	10/01-12/01
	Indiana	Y	22760 FQ	43570 AW	75220 TQ	INBLS	10/01-12/01
	Evansville-Henderson MSA, IN-KY	Y	13380 FQ	29610 AW	48790 TQ	INBLS	10/01-12/01
	Fort Wayne MSA, IN	Y	22970 FQ	33250 AW	48340 TQ	INBLS	10/01-12/01
	Indianapolis MSA, IN	Y	25440 FQ	43170 AW	68090 TQ	INBLS	10/01-12/01
	Lafayette MSA, IN	Y	19970 FQ	41850 AW	80440 TQ	INBLS	10/01-12/01
	South Bend MSA, IN	Y	19890 FQ	45150 AW	73200 TQ	INBLS	10/01-12/01
	Iowa	Y	18460 FQ	39040 AW	65620 TQ	IABLS	10/01-12/01
	Cedar Rapids MSA, IA	Y	16270 FQ	25280 AW	33810 TQ	IABLS	10/01-12/01
	Davenport-Moline-Rock Island MSA, IA-IL	Y	24270 FQ	42280 AW	61730 TQ	IABLS	10/01-12/01
	Des Moines MSA, IA	Y	25300 FQ	45800 AW	67690 TQ	IABLS	10/01-12/01
	Kansas	Y	22760 FQ	46620 AW	81710 TQ	KSBLS	10/01-12/01
	Topeka MSA, KS	Y	21150 FQ	37420 AW	59720 TQ	KSBLS	10/01-12/01
	Wichita MSA, KS	Y	27020 FQ	52150 AW	88230 TQ	KSBLS	10/01-12/01
	Kentucky	Y	18340 FQ	32190 AW	50550 TQ	KYBLS	10/01-12/01
	Lexington MSA, KY	Y	20980 FQ	35100 AW	52540 TQ	KYBLS	10/01-12/01
	Louisville MSA, KY-IN	Y	18300 FQ	32810 AW	53410 TQ	KYBLS	10/01-12/01
	Louisiana	Y	12400 FQ	32060 AW	64160 TQ	LABLS	10/01-12/01
	Baton Rouge MSA, LA	Y	12080 FQ	19540 AW	40210 TQ	LABLS	10/01-12/01
	New Orleans MSA, LA	Y	28590 FQ	57290 AW	107070 TQ	LABLS	10/01-12/01
	Shreveport-Bossier City MSA, LA	Y	19710 FQ	40450 AW	62890 TQ	LABLS	10/01-12/01
	Maine	Y	18760 FQ	33190 AW	51960 TQ	MEBLS	10/01-12/01
	Portland MSA, ME	Y	20450 FQ	34870 AW	57550 TQ	MEBLS	10/01-12/01
	Maryland	Y	23730 FQ	50210 AW	81410 TQ	MDBLS	10/01-12/01
	Baltimore PMSA, MD	Y	25550 FQ	52230 AW	85750 TQ	MDBLS	10/01-12/01
	Massachusetts	Y	24890 FQ	49300 AW	83170 TQ	MABLS	10/01-12/01

AAW Average annual wage; **AE** Average entry wage; **AEX** Average experienced wage; **AO** Average offered; **AOH** Average offered, high; **AOL** Average offered, low; **APH** Average pay, high range; **APL** Average pay, low range; **ASH** Average starting, high; **ASL** Average starting, low; **AW** Average wage paid; **FQ** First quartile wage; **H** Hourly; **HI** Highest wage paid; **HR** High end range; **LR** Low end range; **M** Monthly; **MTC** Median total compensation; **MW** Median wage paid; **SQ** Second quartile wage; **S** Special: hourly and annual; **TQ** Third quartile wage; **W** Weekly; **Y** Yearly

Occupation/Type/Industry	Location	Per	Low	Mid	High	Source	Date
Producer and Director	Boston PMSA, MA-NH	Y	27700 FQ	51480 AW	84180 TQ	MABLS	10/01-12/01
	Springfield MSA, MA	Y	19780 FQ	39560 AW	68060 TQ	MABLS	10/01-12/01
	Michigan	Y	27930 FQ	54050 AW	89820 TQ	MIBLS	10/01-12/01
	Ann Arbor PMSA, MI	Y	29550 FQ	49270 AW	80540 TQ	MIBLS	10/01-12/01
	Detroit PMSA, MI	Y	32020 FQ	59860 AW	99330 TQ	MIBLS	10/01-12/01
	Grand Rapids-Muskegon-Holland MSA, MI	Y	25760 FQ	50800 AW	88800 TQ	MIBLS	10/01-12/01
	Kalamazoo-Battle Creek MSA, MI	Y	26510 FQ	45310 AW	59240 TQ	MIBLS	10/01-12/01
	Lansing-East Lansing MSA, MI	Y	23180 FQ	40540 AW	57270 TQ	MIBLS	10/01-12/01
	Minnesota	Y	21270 FQ	44960 AW	75430 TQ	MNBLS	10/01-12/01
	Duluth-Superior MSA, MN-WI	Y	16870 FQ	32650 AW	53150 TQ	MNBLS	10/01-12/01
	Minneapolis-St. Paul MSA, MN-WI	Y	24560 FQ	49450 AW	84820 TQ	MNBLS	10/01-12/01
	Mississippi	Y	20910 FQ	32440 AW	44910 TQ	MSBLS	10/01-12/01
	Jackson MSA, MS	Y	19710 FQ	30740 AW	44580 TQ	MSBLS	10/01-12/01
	Missouri	Y	17750 FQ	39940 AW	76950 TQ	MOBLS	10/01-12/01
	Kansas City MSA, MO-KS	Y	16630 FQ	36500 AW	68000 TQ	MOBLS	10/01-12/01
	St. Louis MSA, MO-IL	Y	28330 FQ	48280 AW	84590 TQ	MOBLS	10/01-12/01
	Springfield MSA, MO	Y	12070 FQ	28980 AW	62390 TQ	MOBLS	10/01-12/01
	Montana	Y	17580 FQ	36000 AW	58330 TQ	MTBLS	10/01-12/01
	Nebraska	Y	21100 FQ	43970 AW	69680 TQ	NEBLS	10/01-12/01
	Lincoln MSA, NE	Y	21560 FQ	39360 AW	56430 TQ	NEBLS	10/01-12/01
	Omaha MSA, NE-IA	Y	22580 FQ	48120 AW	86580 TQ	NEBLS	10/01-12/01
	Nevada	Y	23790 FQ	47230 AW	81050 TQ	NVBLS	10/01-12/01
	Las Vegas MSA, NV-AZ	Y	26900 FQ	48780 AW	81230 TQ	NVBLS	10/01-12/01
	Reno MSA, NV	Y	18830 FQ	31360 AW	56400 TQ	NVBLS	10/01-12/01
	New Hampshire	Y	22530 FQ	35390 AW	50000 TQ	NHBLS	10/01-12/01
	Manchester PMSA, NH	Y	29540 FQ	36360 AW	44080 TQ	NHBLS	10/01-12/01
	Portsmouth-Rochester PMSA, NH-ME	Y	22700 FQ	31410 AW	42560 TQ	NHBLS	10/01-12/01
	New Jersey	Y	27440 FQ	70450 AW	130450 TQ	NJBLS	10/01-12/01
	Jersey City PMSA, NJ	Y	24960 FQ	59540 AW	125390 TQ	NJBLS	10/01-12/01
	Newark PMSA, NJ	Y	36190 FQ	73490 AW	122840 TQ	NJBLS	10/01-12/01
	Trenton PMSA, NJ	Y	21200 FQ	51210 AW	85290 TQ	NJBLS	10/01-12/01
	New Mexico	Y	14840 FQ	28830 AW	46210 TQ	NMBLS	10/01-12/01
	Albuquerque MSA, NM	Y	15070 FQ	35470 AW	54130 TQ	NMBLS	10/01-12/01
	New York	Y	22990 FQ	53090 AW	105440 TQ	NYBLS	10/01-12/01
	Albany-Schenectady-Troy MSA, NY	Y	23040 FQ	43230 AW	71020 TQ	NYBLS	10/01-12/01
	Binghamton MSA, NY	Y	19380 FQ	38790 AW	52340 TQ	NYBLS	10/01-12/01
	Buffalo-Niagara Falls MSA, NY	Y	22910 FQ	39890 AW	56100 TQ	NYBLS	10/01-12/01
	Nassau-Suffolk PMSA, NY	Y	32480 FQ	64730 AW	135240 TQ	NYBLS	10/01-12/01
	New York PMSA, NY	Y	23290 FQ	54250 AW	106880 TQ	NYBLS	10/01-12/01
	Rochester MSA, NY	Y	12330 FQ	34210 AW	66000 TQ	NYBLS	10/01-12/01
	Syracuse MSA, NY	Y	26160 FQ	59680 AW		NYBLS	10/01-12/01
	North Carolina	Y	20990 FQ	42680 AW	69870 TQ	NCBLS	10/01-12/01
	Charlotte-Gastonia-Rock Hill MSA, NC-SC	Y	28660 FQ	50210 AW	82120 TQ	NCBLS	10/01-12/01
	Greensboro-Winston-Salem-High Point MSA, NC	Y	20350 FQ	42160 AW	72720 TQ	NCBLS	10/01-12/01
	Raleigh-Durham-Chapel Hill MSA, NC	Y	26560 FQ	44470 AW	59980 TQ	NCBLS	10/01-12/01
	Wilmington MSA, NC	Y	18950 FQ	31960 AW	54740 TQ	NCBLS	10/01-12/01
	North Dakota	Y	20030 FQ	38730 AW	63950 TQ	NDBLS	10/01-12/01
	Ohio	Y	20720 FQ	41700 AW	69110 TQ	OHBLS	10/01-12/01
	Akron PMSA, OH	Y	13120 FQ	35130 AW	57150 TQ	OHBLS	10/01-12/01
	Cincinnati PMSA, OH-KY-IN	Y	24240 FQ	44370 AW	74240 TQ	OHBLS	10/01-12/01
	Cleveland-Lorain-Elyria PMSA, OH	Y	17450 FQ	44220 AW	76510 TQ	OHBLS	10/01-12/01
	Columbus MSA, OH	Y	27450 FQ	48440 AW	72750 TQ	OHBLS	10/01-12/01
	Dayton-Springfield MSA, OH	Y	18840 FQ	36660 AW	57800 TQ	OHBLS	10/01-12/01
	Toledo MSA, OH	Y	21460 FQ	34250 AW	52500 TQ	OHBLS	10/01-12/01
	Youngstown-Warren MSA, OH	Y	20380 FQ	31640 AW	42740 TQ	OHBLS	10/01-12/01
	Oklahoma	Y	18260 FQ	38790 AW	55650 TQ	OKBLS	10/01-12/01
	Oklahoma City MSA, OK	Y	18890 FQ	44330 AW	71550 TQ	OKBLS	10/01-12/01
	Tulsa MSA, OK	Y	17700 FQ	36390 AW	49270 TQ	OKBLS	10/01-12/01
	Oregon	Y	21170 FQ	54610 AW	92750 TQ	ORBLS	10/01-12/01
	Eugene-Springfield MSA, OR	Y	17800 FQ	37790 AW	56270 TQ	ORBLS	10/01-12/01
	Portland-Vancouver PMSA, OR-WA	Y	21310 FQ	58320 AW		ORBLS	10/01-12/01

AAW Average annual wage; **AE** Average entry wage; **AEX** Average experienced wage; **AO** Average offered; **AOH** Average offered, high; **AOL** Average offered, low; **APH** Average pay, high range; **APL** Average pay, low range; **ASH** Average starting, high; **ASL** Average starting, low; **AW** Average wage paid; **FQ** First quartile wage; **H** Hourly; **HI** Highest wage paid; **HR** High end range; **LR** Low end range; **M** Monthly; **MTC** Median total compensation; **MW** Median wage paid; **SQ** Second quartile wage; **S** Special: hourly and annual; **TQ** Third quartile wage; **W** Weekly; **Y** Yearly

Occupation/Type/Industry	Location	Per	Low	Mid	High	Source	Date
Producer and Director	Pennsylvania	Y	19130 FQ	42550 AW	73900 TQ	PABLS	10/01-12/01
	Allentown-Bethlehem-Easton MSA, PA	Y	24240 FQ	41170 AW	69930 TQ	PABLS	10/01-12/01
	Erie MSA, PA	Y	16200 FQ	25300 AW	39100 TQ	PABLS	10/01-12/01
	Harrisburg-Lebanon-Carlisle MSA, PA	Y	19530 FQ	35000 AW	56170 TQ	PABLS	10/01-12/01
	Lancaster MSA, PA	Y	19360 FQ	38710 AW	69000 TQ	PABLS	10/01-12/01
	Philadelphia PMSA, PA-NJ	Y	25310 FQ	61430 AW	112710 TQ	PABLS	10/01-12/01
	Pittsburgh MSA, PA	Y	18190 FQ	37350 AW	61690 TQ	PABLS	10/01-12/01
	Scranton-Wilkes-Barre-Hazleton MSA, PA	Y	14560 FQ	28680 AW	44710 TQ	PABLS	10/01-12/01
	Rhode Island	Y	23840 FQ	47950 AW	85280 TQ	RIBLS	10/01-12/01
	Providence-Fall River-Warwick MSA, RI-MA	Y	21180 FQ	45690 AW	76720 TQ	RIBLS	10/01-12/01
	South Carolina	Y	20850 FQ	38620 AW	67500 TQ	SCBLS	10/01-12/01
	Charleston-North Charleston MSA, SC	Y	19550 FQ	37790 AW	67520 TQ	SCBLS	10/01-12/01
	Columbia MSA, SC	Y	20430 FQ	33080 AW	49360 TQ	SCBLS	10/01-12/01
	Greenville-Spartanburg-Anderson MSA, SC	Y	24910 FQ	35720 AW	46320 TQ	SCBLS	10/01-12/01
	South Dakota	Y	22900 FQ	36300 AW	52930 TQ	SDBLS	10/01-12/01
	Sioux Falls MSA, SD	Y	28990 FQ	40800 AW	55780 TQ	SDBLS	10/01-12/01
	Tennessee	Y	22680 FQ	47240 AW	84550 TQ	TNBLS	10/01-12/01
	Chattanooga MSA, TN-GA	Y	21310 FQ	30620 AW	42050 TQ	TNBLS	10/01-12/01
	Johnson City-Kingsport-Bristol MSA, TN-VA	Y	19170 FQ	33580 AW	47970 TQ	TNBLS	10/01-12/01
	Knoxville MSA, TN	Y	27140 FQ	59370 AW	101340 TQ	TNBLS	10/01-12/01
	Memphis MSA, TN-AR-MS	Y	19890 FQ	37810 AW	67270 TQ	TNBLS	10/01-12/01
	Nashville MSA, TN	Y	23340 FQ	46650 AW	84050 TQ	TNBLS	10/01-12/01
	Texas	Y	17980 FQ	42560 AW	84810 TQ	TXBLS	10/01-12/01
	Amarillo MSA, TX	Y	13330 FQ	25560 AW	45890 TQ	TXBLS	10/01-12/01
	Austin-San Marcos MSA, TX	Y	23200 FQ	43160 AW	79420 TQ	TXBLS	10/01-12/01
	Corpus Christi MSA, TX	Y	20320 FQ	35450 AW	58450 TQ	TXBLS	10/01-12/01
	Dallas PMSA, TX	Y	28250 FQ	48950 AW	97220 TQ	TXBLS	10/01-12/01
	El Paso MSA, TX	Y	25120 FQ	43610 AW	63770 TQ	TXBLS	10/01-12/01
	Fort Worth-Arlington PMSA, TX	Y	19140 FQ	40820 AW	71280 TQ	TXBLS	10/01-12/01
	Houston PMSA, TX	Y	21030 FQ	47590 AW	98290 TQ	TXBLS	10/01-12/01
	McAllen-Edinburg-Mission MSA, TX	Y	19040 FQ	30540 AW	43920 TQ	TXBLS	10/01-12/01
	San Antonio MSA, TX	Y	12210 FQ	35220 AW	65520 TQ	TXBLS	10/01-12/01
	Utah	Y	18970 FQ	44980 AW	96920 TQ	UTBLS	10/01-12/01
	Salt Lake City-Ogden MSA, UT	Y	18770 FQ	40740 AW	73120 TQ	UTBLS	10/01-12/01
	Vermont	Y	18480 FQ	45240 AW	70080 TQ	VTBLS	10/01-12/01
	Burlington MSA, VT	Y	18840 FQ	42660 AW	68880 TQ	VTBLS	10/01-12/01
	Virginia	Y	19260 FQ	41940 AW	69900 TQ	VABLS	10/01-12/01
	Norfolk-Virginia Beach-Newport News MSA, VA-NC	Y	17030 FQ	36130 AW	58360 TQ	VABLS	10/01-12/01
	Richmond-Petersburg MSA, VA	Y	25990 FQ	38840 AW	55120 TQ	VABLS	10/01-12/01
	Roanoke MSA, VA	Y	18430 FQ	29580 AW	47040 TQ	VABLS	10/01-12/01
	Washington	Y	27070 FQ	58080 AW	92420 TQ	WABLS	10/01-12/01
	Seattle-Bellevue-Everett PMSA, WA	Y	35770 FQ	65490 AW	98660 TQ	WABLS	10/01-12/01
	Spokane MSA, WA	Y	23680 FQ	36060 AW	56290 TQ	WABLS	10/01-12/01
	West Virginia	Y	19500 FQ	39000 AW	62490 TQ	WVBLS	10/01-12/01
	Charleston MSA, WV	Y	25380 FQ	38590 AW	53290 TQ	WVBLS	10/01-12/01
	Huntington-Ashland MSA, WV-KY-OH	Y	19790 FQ	33980 AW	52330 TQ	WVBLS	10/01-12/01
	Wisconsin	Y	19340 FQ	39600 AW	66660 TQ	WIBLS	10/01-12/01
	Green Bay MSA, WI	Y	23120 FQ	35100 AW	53420 TQ	WIBLS	10/01-12/01
	Madison MSA, WI	Y	25820 FQ	46090 AW	81800 TQ	WIBLS	10/01-12/01
	Milwaukee-Waukesha PMSA, WI	Y	17800 FQ	38550 AW	65080 TQ	WIBLS	10/01-12/01
	Puerto Rico	Y	16980 FQ	37060 AW	70220 TQ	PRBLS	10/01-12/01
Product Engineer Quality Control	United States	Y			120000 HI	ASQ	1/00-1/01

AAW	Average annual wage	**AOH**	Average offered, high	**ASH**	Average starting, high	**H**	Hourly	**M**	Monthly	**S**	Special: hourly and annual
AE	Average entry wage	**AOL**	Average offered, low	**ASL**	Average starting, low	**HI**	Highest wage paid	**MTC**	Median total compensation	**TQ**	Third quartile wage
AEX	Average experienced wage	**APH**	Average pay, high range	**AW**	Average wage paid	**HR**	High end range	**MW**	Median wage paid	**W**	Weekly
AO	Average offered	**APL**	Average pay, low range	**FQ**	First quartile wage	**LR**	Low end range	**SQ**	Second quartile wage	**Y**	Yearly

Occupation/Type/Industry	Location	Per	Low	Mid	High	Source	Date
Production, Planning, and Expediting Clerk	Alabama	H	6.33 FQ	13.47 AW	21.45 TQ	ALBLS	10/01-12/01
	Alaska	H	11.57 FQ	21.31 AW	35.77 TQ	AKBLS	10/01-12/01
	Arizona	H	6.97 FQ	13.94 AW	22.48 TQ	AZBLS	10/01-12/01
	Arkansas	H	7.25 FQ	13.00 AW	20.08 TQ	ARBLS	10/01-12/01
	California	H	9.76 FQ	17.16 AW	27.04 TQ	CABLS	10/01-12/01
	Colorado	H	10.76 FQ	17.01 AW	23.19 TQ	COBLS	10/01-12/01
	Connecticut	H	11.51 FQ	18.74 AW	26.84 TQ	CTBLS	10/01-12/01
	Delaware	H	8.26 FQ	16.82 AW	27.24 TQ	DEBLS	10/01-12/01
	District of Columbia	H	10.61 FQ	17.56 AW	25.80 TQ	DCBLS	10/01-12/01
	Florida	H	8.53 FQ	14.10 AW	20.84 TQ	FLBLS	10/01-12/01
	Georgia	H	9.55 FQ	15.85 AW	22.96 TQ	GABLS	10/01-12/01
	Hawaii	H	10.69 FQ	17.46 AW	26.27 TQ	HIBLS	10/01-12/01
	Idaho	H	10.29 FQ	16.29 AW	21.82 TQ	IDBLS	10/01-12/01
	Illinois	H	6.93 FQ	15.18 AW	24.76 TQ	ILBLS	10/01-12/01
	Indiana	H	9.27 FQ	16.71 AW	25.27 TQ	INBLS	10/01-12/01
	Iowa	H	8.95 FQ	14.64 AW	21.54 TQ	IABLS	10/01-12/01
	Kansas	H	9.67 FQ	16.15 AW	23.47 TQ	KSBLS	10/01-12/01
	Kentucky	H	9.65 FQ	15.25 AW	21.88 TQ	KYBLS	10/01-12/01
	Louisiana	H	6.62 FQ	15.24 AW	25.91 TQ	LABLS	10/01-12/01
	Maine	H	11.01 FQ	18.20 AW	26.06 TQ	MEBLS	10/01-12/01
	Maryland	H	9.76 FQ	16.57 AW	24.24 TQ	MDBLS	10/01-12/01
	Massachusetts	H	11.20 FQ	19.13 AW	28.33 TQ	MABLS	10/01-12/01
	Michigan	H	10.52 FQ	17.76 AW	26.23 TQ	MIBLS	10/01-12/01
	Minnesota	H	9.88 FQ	16.61 AW	23.83 TQ	MNBLS	10/01-12/01
	Mississippi	H	8.56 FQ	14.95 AW	22.78 TQ	MSBLS	10/01-12/01
	Missouri	H	9.64 FQ	16.54 AW	25.88 TQ	MOBLS	10/01-12/01
	Montana	H	8.23 FQ	14.75 AW	21.93 TQ	MTBLS	10/01-12/01
	Nebraska	H	8.61 FQ	14.01 AW	20.71 TQ	NEBLS	10/01-12/01
	Nevada	H	9.47 FQ	14.70 AW	21.35 TQ	NVBLS	10/01-12/01
	New Hampshire	H	10.60 FQ	17.24 AW	25.77 TQ	NHBLS	10/01-12/01
	New Jersey	H	9.46 FQ	17.26 AW	26.42 TQ	NJBLS	10/01-12/01
	New Mexico	H	9.63 FQ	14.56 AW	21.04 TQ	NMBLS	10/01-12/01
	New York	H	9.80 FQ	18.34 AW	28.00 TQ	NYBLS	10/01-12/01
	North Carolina	H	9.07 FQ	15.76 AW	24.77 TQ	NCBLS	10/01-12/01
	North Dakota	H	9.88 FQ	15.55 AW	23.37 TQ	NDBLS	10/01-12/01
	Ohio	H	10.28 FQ	16.62 AW	24.70 TQ	OHBLS	10/01-12/01
	Oklahoma	H	8.46 FQ	15.79 AW	23.28 TQ	OKBLS	10/01-12/01
	Oregon	H	11.24 FQ	16.80 AW	22.12 TQ	ORBLS	10/01-12/01
	Pennsylvania	H	9.55 FQ	16.29 AW	24.00 TQ	PABLS	10/01-12/01
	Rhode Island	H	10.30 FQ	16.30 AW	23.21 TQ	RIBLS	10/01-12/01
	South Carolina	H	7.89 FQ	14.13 AW	21.53 TQ	SCBLS	10/01-12/01
	South Dakota	H	9.36 FQ	12.98 AW	17.83 TQ	SDBLS	10/01-12/01
	Tennessee	H	8.85 FQ	15.17 AW	23.17 TQ	TNBLS	10/01-12/01
	Texas	H	8.50 FQ	15.88 AW	25.27 TQ	TXBLS	10/01-12/01
	Utah	H	7.96 FQ	14.98 AW	23.37 TQ	UTBLS	10/01-12/01
	Vermont	H	10.23 FQ	15.65 AW	21.56 TQ	VTBLS	10/01-12/01
	Virginia	H	9.59 FQ	16.44 AW	25.36 TQ	VABLS	10/01-12/01
	Washington	H	11.39 FQ	17.78 AW	25.75 TQ	WABLS	10/01-12/01
	West Virginia	H	9.60 FQ	15.87 AW	22.36 TQ	WVBLS	10/01-12/01
	Wisconsin	H	10.55 FQ	16.92 AW	24.84 TQ	WIBLS	10/01-12/01
	Wyoming	H	7.13 FQ	14.80 AW	24.44 TQ	WYBLS	10/01-12/01
	Puerto Rico	H	6.12 FQ	11.93 AW	20.04 TQ	PRBLS	10/01-12/01
	Guam	H	7.46 FQ	15.07 AW	30.74 TQ	GUBLS	10/01-12/01
Production Worker	United States	H		19.86 AW		ELNEWS	1/99-1/00
Programmer/Analyst							
Level 1	United States	Y	34535 LR			IOMA2	1/99-1/00
Level 1	Border States	Y	46983 LR			IOMA2	1/99-1/00
Level 1	Middle Atlantic	Y	37250 LR			IOMA2	1/99-1/00
Level 1	New England	Y	37911 LR			IOMA2	1/99-1/00
Level 1	Southeast	Y	31618 LR			IOMA2	1/99-1/00
Level 5	United States	Y	51032 LR			IOMA2	1/99-1/00
Level 5	Middle Atlantic	Y	50354 LR			IOMA2	1/99-1/00
Level 5	New England	Y	51410 LR			IOMA2	1/99-1/00
Level 5	Southeast	Y	50121 LR			IOMA2	1/99-1/00
Project Manager	San Diego, CA	Y		50000 AW		SDBJ	1/01-1/02
Proofreader and Copy Marker	Alabama	H	7.10 FQ	11.03 AW	16.27 TQ	ALBLS	10/01-12/01
	Birmingham MSA, AL	H	7.59 FQ	12.14 AW	17.04 TQ	ALBLS	10/01-12/01
	Mobile MSA, AL	H	7.27 FQ	10.80 AW	16.31 TQ	ALBLS	10/01-12/01

AAW	Average annual wage	**AOH**	Average offered, high	**ASH**	Average starting, high	**H**	Hourly	**M**	Monthly	**S**	Special: hourly and annual
AE	Average entry wage	**AOL**	Average offered, low	**ASL**	Average starting, low	**HI**	Highest wage paid	**MTC**	Median total compensation	**TQ**	Third quartile wage
AEX	Average experienced wage	**APH**	Average pay, high range	**AW**	Average wage paid	**HR**	High end range	**MW**	Median wage paid	**W**	Weekly
AO	Average offered	**APL**	Average pay, low range	**FQ**	First quartile wage	**LR**	Low end range	**SQ**	Second quartile wage	**Y**	Yearly

Occupation/Type/Industry	Location	Per	Low	Mid	High	Source	Date
Proofreader and Copy Marker	Arizona	H	6.09 FQ	10.08 AW	14.58 TQ	AZBLS	10/01-12/01
	Phoenix-Mesa MSA, AZ	H	6.15 FQ	10.53 AW	16.32 TQ	AZBLS	10/01-12/01
	Little Rock-North Little Rock MSA, AR	H	7.75 FQ	12.83 AW	19.69 TQ	ARBLS	10/01-12/01
	California	H	7.99 FQ	12.24 AW	18.61 TQ	CABLS	10/01-12/01
	Chico-Paradise MSA, CA	H	8.77 FQ	9.83 AW	10.74 TQ	CABLS	10/01-12/01
	Los Angeles-Long Beach PMSA, CA	H	8.13 FQ	12.83 AW	19.48 TQ	CABLS	10/01-12/01
	Oakland PMSA, CA	H	8.01 FQ	12.32 AW	19.53 TQ	CABLS	10/01-12/01
	Orange County PMSA, CA	H	8.60 FQ	13.63 AW	20.71 TQ	CABLS	10/01-12/01
	Riverside-San Bernardino PMSA, CA	H	6.87 FQ	9.87 AW	13.55 TQ	CABLS	10/01-12/01
	Sacramento PMSA, CA	H	8.48 FQ	14.20 AW	21.90 TQ	CABLS	10/01-12/01
	Salinas MSA, CA	H	7.65 FQ	12.68 AW	16.60 TQ	CABLS	10/01-12/01
	San Diego MSA, CA	H	8.36 FQ	11.51 AW	15.92 TQ	CABLS	10/01-12/01
	San Jose PMSA, CA	H	9.52 FQ	11.60 AW	14.51 TQ	CABLS	10/01-12/01
	San Luis Obispo-Atascadero-Paso Robles MSA, CA	H	8.08 FQ	12.09 AW	17.49 TQ	CABLS	10/01-12/01
	Ventura PMSA, CA	H	7.77 FQ	11.30 AW	17.63 TQ	CABLS	10/01-12/01
	Colorado	H	8.12 FQ	12.29 AW	17.49 TQ	COBLS	10/01-12/01
	Colorado Springs MSA, CO	H	7.91 FQ	12.07 AW	17.17 TQ	COBLS	10/01-12/01
	Denver PMSA, CO	H	8.87 FQ	12.81 AW	17.91 TQ	COBLS	10/01-12/01
	Connecticut	H	9.58 FQ	13.68 AW	17.91 TQ	CTBLS	10/01-12/01
	Bridgeport PMSA, CT	H	8.56 FQ	14.04 AW	18.45 TQ	CTBLS	10/01-12/01
	Hartford MSA, CT	H	9.65 FQ	13.43 AW	17.28 TQ	CTBLS	10/01-12/01
	New Haven-Meriden PMSA, CT	H	9.88 FQ	13.82 AW	17.81 TQ	CTBLS	10/01-12/01
	Delaware	H	7.26 FQ	11.09 AW	16.81 TQ	DEBLS	10/01-12/01
	Wilmington-Newark PMSA, DE-MD	H	7.33 FQ	11.31 AW	16.95 TQ	DEBLS	10/01-12/01
	District of Columbia	H	8.73 FQ	13.70 AW	20.18 TQ	DCBLS	10/01-12/01
	Washington PMSA, DC-MD-VA-WV	H	9.14 FQ	13.38 AW	18.46 TQ	DCBLS	10/01-12/01
	Florida	H	7.56 FQ	11.06 AW	16.37 TQ	FLBLS	10/01-12/01
	Fort Lauderdale PMSA, FL	H	7.37 FQ	8.59 AW	10.72 TQ	FLBLS	10/01-12/01
	Jacksonville MSA, FL	H	8.21 FQ	12.85 AW	17.76 TQ	FLBLS	10/01-12/01
	Melbourne-Titusville-Palm Bay MSA, FL	H	7.27 FQ	9.70 AW	11.33 TQ	FLBLS	10/01-12/01
	Miami PMSA, FL	H	9.36 FQ	13.71 AW	17.86 TQ	FLBLS	10/01-12/01
	Naples MSA, FL	H	5.92 FQ	9.20 AW	11.49 TQ	FLBLS	10/01-12/01
	Orlando MSA, FL	H	8.12 FQ	11.89 AW	16.65 TQ	FLBLS	10/01-12/01
	Sarasota-Bradenton MSA, FL	H	7.62 FQ	10.80 AW	15.92 TQ	FLBLS	10/01-12/01
	Tallahassee MSA, FL	H	6.71 FQ	9.76 AW	11.88 TQ	FLBLS	10/01-12/01
	Tampa-St. Petersburg-Clearwater MSA, FL	H	7.96 FQ	12.33 AW	17.28 TQ	FLBLS	10/01-12/01
	West Palm Beach-Boca Raton MSA, FL	H	8.86 FQ	11.66 AW	13.93 TQ	FLBLS	10/01-12/01
	Georgia	H	8.06 FQ	12.19 AW	17.30 TQ	GABLS	10/01-12/01
	Atlanta MSA, GA	H	8.63 FQ	12.51 AW	17.61 TQ	GABLS	10/01-12/01
	Hawaii	H	8.22 FQ	11.85 AW	16.83 TQ	HIBLS	10/01-12/01
	Honolulu MSA, HI	H	8.20 FQ	11.61 AW	16.49 TQ	HIBLS	10/01-12/01
	Idaho	H	6.32 FQ	10.87 AW	16.53 TQ	IDBLS	10/01-12/01
	Boise City MSA, ID	H	7.82 FQ	10.07 AW	13.88 TQ	IDBLS	10/01-12/01
	Illinois	H	8.01 FQ	12.65 AW	19.15 TQ	ILBLS	10/01-12/01
	Chicago PMSA, IL	H	8.39 FQ	13.02 AW	19.81 TQ	ILBLS	10/01-12/01
	Indiana	H	6.22 FQ	10.42 AW	14.49 TQ	INBLS	10/01-12/01
	Indianapolis MSA, IN	H	6.56 FQ	11.03 AW	14.37 TQ	INBLS	10/01-12/01
	Iowa	H	6.94 FQ	10.34 AW	13.47 TQ	IABLS	10/01-12/01
	Des Moines MSA, IA	H	7.14 FQ	11.54 AW	16.23 TQ	IABLS	10/01-12/01
	Kansas	H	6.37 FQ	10.61 AW	14.55 TQ	KSBLS	10/01-12/01
	Kentucky	H	5.99 FQ	9.27 AW	12.38 TQ	KYBLS	10/01-12/01
	Louisiana	H	6.22 FQ	9.71 AW	13.41 TQ	LABLS	10/01-12/01
	Baton Rouge MSA, LA	H	6.08 FQ	9.77 AW	13.54 TQ	LABLS	10/01-12/01
	Maine	H	7.00 FQ	11.00 AW	16.27 TQ	MEBLS	10/01-12/01
	Maryland	H	8.22 FQ	13.01 AW	17.72 TQ	MDBLS	10/01-12/01
	Baltimore PMSA, MD	H	8.27 FQ	13.05 AW	17.19 TQ	MDBLS	10/01-12/01
	Massachusetts	H	7.00 FQ	13.14 AW	20.90 TQ	MABLS	10/01-12/01
	Boston PMSA, MA-NH	H	6.93 FQ	12.57 AW	20.67 TQ	MABLS	10/01-12/01
	Lawrence PMSA, MA-NH	H	13.05 FQ	18.59 AW	21.89 TQ	MABLS	10/01-12/01
	Springfield MSA, MA	H	9.01 FQ	12.53 AW	16.26 TQ	MABLS	10/01-12/01
	Michigan	H	7.56 FQ	11.92 AW	17.71 TQ	MIBLS	10/01-12/01
	Ann Arbor PMSA, MI	H	8.23 FQ	11.92 AW	16.41 TQ	MIBLS	10/01-12/01

AAW	Average annual wage	**AOH**	Average offered, high	**ASH**	Average starting, high	**H**	Hourly	**M**	Monthly	**S**	Special: hourly and annual
AE	Average entry wage	**AOL**	Average offered, low	**ASL**	Average starting, low	**HI**	Highest wage paid	**MTC**	Median total compensation	**TQ**	Third quartile wage
AEX	Average experienced wage	**APH**	Average pay, high range	**AW**	Average wage paid	**HR**	High end range	**MW**	Median wage paid	**W**	Weekly
AO	Average offered	**APL**	Average pay, low range	**FQ**	First quartile wage	**LR**	Low end range	**SQ**	Second quartile wage	**Y**	Yearly

Occupation/Type/Industry	Location	Per	Low	Mid	High	Source	Date
Proofreader and Copy Marker	Detroit PMSA, MI	H	8.05 FQ	13.04 AW	19.27 TQ	MIBLS	10/01-12/01
	Grand Rapids-Muskegon-Holland MSA, MI	H	6.63 FQ	10.15 AW	13.92 TQ	MIBLS	10/01-12/01
	Kalamazoo-Battle Creek MSA, MI	H	11.81 FQ	14.96 AW	17.99 TQ	MIBLS	10/01-12/01
	Saginaw-Bay City-Midland MSA, MI	H	7.75 FQ	10.88 AW	17.01 TQ	MIBLS	10/01-12/01
	Mississippi	H	7.15 FQ	10.87 AW	16.00 TQ	MSBLS	10/01-12/01
	Missouri	H	7.11 FQ	12.12 AW	19.05 TQ	MOBLS	10/01-12/01
	Kansas City MSA, MO-KS	H	7.53 FQ	12.06 AW	16.91 TQ	MOBLS	10/01-12/01
	St. Louis MSA, MO-IL	H	7.74 FQ	13.13 AW	20.24 TQ	MOBLS	10/01-12/01
	Nebraska	H	6.67 FQ	11.46 AW	17.12 TQ	NEBLS	10/01-12/01
	Omaha MSA, NE-IA	H	7.35 FQ	11.33 AW	16.86 TQ	NEBLS	10/01-12/01
	Nevada	H	7.31 FQ	9.74 AW	13.58 TQ	NVBLS	10/01-12/01
	New Hampshire	H	8.74 FQ	11.89 AW	16.11 TQ	NHBLS	10/01-12/01
	New Jersey	H	9.72 FQ	17.46 AW	34.73 TQ	NJBLS	10/01-12/01
	Bergen-Passaic PMSA, NJ	H	10.92 FQ	21.19 AW	41.83 TQ	NJBLS	10/01-12/01
	Jersey City PMSA, NJ	H	6.52 FQ	18.36 AW	33.57 TQ	NJBLS	10/01-12/01
	Middlesex-Somerset-Hunterdon PMSA, NJ	H	8.96 FQ	15.32 AW	25.62 TQ	NJBLS	10/01-12/01
	Monmouth-Ocean PMSA, NJ	H	9.67 FQ	17.11 AW	38.25 TQ	NJBLS	10/01-12/01
	Newark PMSA, NJ	H	9.56 FQ	15.03 AW	22.50 TQ	NJBLS	10/01-12/01
	Trenton PMSA, NJ	H	10.06 FQ	14.75 AW	21.04 TQ	NJBLS	10/01-12/01
	New Mexico	H	6.55 FQ	11.03 AW	14.30 TQ	NMBLS	10/01-12/01
	New York	H	8.98 FQ	15.51 AW	24.00 TQ	NYBLS	10/01-12/01
	Albany-Schenectady-Troy MSA, NY	H	9.09 FQ	14.35 AW	24.91 TQ	NYBLS	10/01-12/01
	Buffalo-Niagara Falls MSA, NY	H	7.51 FQ	10.67 AW	15.83 TQ	NYBLS	10/01-12/01
	Nassau-Suffolk PMSA, NY	H	8.01 FQ	15.51 AW	25.90 TQ	NYBLS	10/01-12/01
	New York PMSA, NY	H	10.52 FQ	16.38 AW	24.41 TQ	NYBLS	10/01-12/01
	Rochester MSA, NY	H	7.68 FQ	11.56 AW	17.87 TQ	NYBLS	10/01-12/01
	North Carolina	H	8.69 FQ	12.82 AW	18.00 TQ	NCBLS	10/01-12/01
	Greensboro-Winston-Salem-High Point MSA, NC	H	6.78 FQ	11.86 AW	16.77 TQ	NCBLS	10/01-12/01
	Raleigh-Durham-Chapel Hill MSA, NC	H	8.88 FQ	13.08 AW	18.03 TQ	NCBLS	10/01-12/01
	North Dakota	H	6.34 FQ	8.44 AW	10.60 TQ	NDBLS	10/01-12/01
	Ohio	H	7.09 FQ	11.39 AW	16.43 TQ	OHBLS	10/01-12/01
	Canton-Massillon MSA, OH	H	6.26 FQ	11.91 AW	16.94 TQ	OHBLS	10/01-12/01
	Cincinnati PMSA, OH-KY-IN	H	7.72 FQ	11.67 AW	16.61 TQ	OHBLS	10/01-12/01
	Cleveland-Lorain-Elyria PMSA, OH	H	6.74 FQ	10.81 AW	15.30 TQ	OHBLS	10/01-12/01
	Columbus MSA, OH	H	9.24 FQ	12.86 AW	16.98 TQ	OHBLS	10/01-12/01
	Dayton-Springfield MSA, OH	H	7.05 FQ	11.80 AW	17.31 TQ	OHBLS	10/01-12/01
	Toledo MSA, OH	H	7.59 FQ	11.82 AW	18.78 TQ	OHBLS	10/01-12/01
	Oklahoma	H	6.24 FQ	10.14 AW	16.37 TQ	OKBLS	10/01-12/01
	Oklahoma City MSA, OK	H	6.30 FQ	9.63 AW	14.02 TQ	OKBLS	10/01-12/01
	Tulsa MSA, OK	H	6.37 FQ	10.38 AW	15.51 TQ	OKBLS	10/01-12/01
	Oregon	H	7.28 FQ	11.60 AW	16.54 TQ	ORBLS	10/01-12/01
	Portland-Vancouver PMSA, OR-WA	H	7.34 FQ	11.48 AW	16.37 TQ	ORBLS	10/01-12/01
	Pennsylvania	H	7.59 FQ	12.89 AW	19.82 TQ	PABLS	10/01-12/01
	Harrisburg-Lebanon-Carlisle MSA, PA	H	6.69 FQ	10.72 AW	15.79 TQ	PABLS	10/01-12/01
	Philadelphia PMSA, PA-NJ	H	9.30 FQ	15.02 AW	22.37 TQ	PABLS	10/01-12/01
	Pittsburgh MSA, PA	H	7.43 FQ	10.45 AW	15.02 TQ	PABLS	10/01-12/01
	York MSA, PA	H	8.16 FQ	12.16 AW	16.49 TQ	PABLS	10/01-12/01
	South Carolina	H	7.33 FQ	10.59 AW	15.81 TQ	SCBLS	10/01-12/01
	South Dakota	H	5.80 FQ	7.89 AW	10.89 TQ	SDBLS	10/01-12/01
	Tennessee	H	7.21 FQ	12.43 AW	16.51 TQ	TNBLS	10/01-12/01
	Nashville MSA, TN	H	9.11 FQ	13.71 AW	16.60 TQ	TNBLS	10/01-12/01
	Texas	H	6.36 FQ	10.79 AW	17.51 TQ	TXBLS	10/01-12/01
	Austin-San Marcos MSA, TX	H	8.03 FQ	12.85 AW	17.12 TQ	TXBLS	10/01-12/01
	Beaumont-Port Arthur MSA, TX	H	7.68 FQ	9.32 AW	11.25 TQ	TXBLS	10/01-12/01
	Dallas PMSA, TX	H	6.63 FQ	11.57 AW	19.51 TQ	TXBLS	10/01-12/01
	Fort Worth-Arlington PMSA, TX	H	7.82 FQ	13.92 AW	22.62 TQ	TXBLS	10/01-12/01
	Houston PMSA, TX	H	6.46 FQ	10.32 AW	15.15 TQ	TXBLS	10/01-12/01
	San Antonio MSA, TX	H	6.19 FQ	9.77 AW	11.79 TQ	TXBLS	10/01-12/01
	Utah	H	7.35 FQ	10.18 AW	13.81 TQ	UTBLS	10/01-12/01

AAW Average annual wage; **AE** Average entry wage; **AEX** Average experienced wage; **AO** Average offered; **AOH** Average offered, high; **AOL** Average offered, low; **APH** Average pay, high range; **APL** Average pay, low range; **ASH** Average starting, high; **ASL** Average starting, low; **AW** Average wage paid; **FQ** First quartile wage; **H** Hourly; **HI** Highest wage paid; **HR** High end range; **LR** Low end range; **M** Monthly; **MTC** Median total compensation; **MW** Median wage paid; **SQ** Second quartile wage; **S** Special: hourly and annual; **TQ** Third quartile wage; **W** Weekly; **Y** Yearly

Occupation/Type/Industry	Location	Per	Low	Mid	High	Source	Date
Proofreader and Copy Marker	Provo-Orem MSA, UT	H	7.28 FQ	10.16 AW	14.20 TQ	UTBLS	10/01-12/01
	Salt Lake City-Ogden MSA, UT	H	7.28 FQ	10.38 AW	13.87 TQ	UTBLS	10/01-12/01
	Vermont	H	9.15 FQ	12.59 AW	16.58 TQ	VTBLS	10/01-12/01
	Virginia	H	8.16 FQ	12.31 AW	16.58 TQ	VABLS	10/01-12/01
	Norfolk-Virginia Beach-Newport News MSA, VA-NC	H	7.42 FQ	10.53 AW	14.79 TQ	VABLS	10/01-12/01
	Richmond-Petersburg MSA, VA	H	8.42 FQ	12.53 AW	17.09 TQ	VABLS	10/01-12/01
	Washington	H	7.88 FQ	12.31 AW	19.60 TQ	WABLS	10/01-12/01
	West Virginia	H	6.28 FQ	9.88 AW	15.26 TQ	WVBLS	10/01-12/01
	Wisconsin	H	7.30 FQ	11.75 AW	18.77 TQ	WIBLS	10/01-12/01
	Green Bay MSA, WI	H	7.95 FQ	11.82 AW	16.76 TQ	WIBLS	10/01-12/01
	Madison MSA, WI	H	7.19 FQ	11.52 AW	18.42 TQ	WIBLS	10/01-12/01
	Milwaukee-Waukesha PMSA, WI	H	7.22 FQ	12.92 AW	20.77 TQ	WIBLS	10/01-12/01
	Wyoming	H	8.12 FQ	10.21 AW	12.98 TQ	WYBLS	10/01-12/01
	Puerto Rico	H	8.10 FQ	12.61 AW	16.79 TQ	PRBLS	10/01-12/01
Property, Real Estate, and Community Association Manager	Alabama	Y	15480 FQ	36290 AW	57150 TQ	ALBLS	10/01-12/01
	Birmingham MSA, AL	Y	24500 FQ	43230 AW	66070 TQ	ALBLS	10/01-12/01
	Huntsville MSA, AL	Y	20110 FQ	30270 AW	44390 TQ	ALBLS	10/01-12/01
	Mobile MSA, AL	Y	21490 FQ	41140 AW	55900 TQ	ALBLS	10/01-12/01
	Montgomery MSA, AL	Y	16060 FQ	40930 AW	72460 TQ	ALBLS	10/01-12/01
	Alaska	Y	15040 FQ	39920 AW	68020 TQ	AKBLS	10/01-12/01
	Anchorage MSA, AK	Y	20680 FQ	43340 AW	69410 TQ	AKBLS	10/01-12/01
	Arizona	Y	18560 FQ	39970 AW	57300 TQ	AZBLS	10/01-12/01
	Phoenix-Mesa MSA, AZ	Y	19900 FQ	41550 AW	57820 TQ	AZBLS	10/01-12/01
	Tucson MSA, AZ	Y	16010 FQ	34830 AW	51060 TQ	AZBLS	10/01-12/01
	Arkansas	Y	14110 FQ	28560 AW	53050 TQ	ARBLS	10/01-12/01
	Fayetteville-Springdale-Rogers MSA, AR	Y	14970 FQ	29240 AW	65500 TQ	ARBLS	10/01-12/01
	Fort Smith MSA, AR-OK	Y	13890 FQ	34030 AW	85890 TQ	ARBLS	10/01-12/01
	Little Rock-North Little Rock MSA, AR	Y	14680 FQ	28970 AW	48810 TQ	ARBLS	10/01-12/01
	California	Y	13990 FQ	41760 AW	92640 TQ	CABLS	10/01-12/01
	Bakersfield MSA, CA	Y	14900 FQ	34840 AW	71540 TQ	CABLS	10/01-12/01
	Chico-Paradise MSA, CA	Y	14300 FQ	29450 AW	64720 TQ	CABLS	10/01-12/01
	Fresno MSA, CA	Y	13370 FQ	26610 AW	47570 TQ	CABLS	10/01-12/01
	Los Angeles-Long Beach PMSA, CA	Y	13970 FQ	36780 AW	76730 TQ	CABLS	10/01-12/01
	Merced MSA, CA	Y	13230 FQ	16860 AW	25450 TQ	CABLS	10/01-12/01
	Modesto MSA, CA	Y	14480 FQ	30240 AW	55300 TQ	CABLS	10/01-12/01
	Oakland PMSA, CA	Y	16570 FQ	42560 AW	79360 TQ	CABLS	10/01-12/01
	Orange County PMSA, CA	Y	25680 FQ	52860 AW	102900 TQ	CABLS	10/01-12/01
	Riverside-San Bernardino PMSA, CA	Y	13480 FQ	32100 AW	64600 TQ	CABLS	10/01-12/01
	Sacramento PMSA, CA	Y	13370 FQ	35060 AW	80490 TQ	CABLS	10/01-12/01
	Salinas MSA, CA	Y	19610 FQ	38250 AW	70370 TQ	CABLS	10/01-12/01
	San Diego MSA, CA	Y	17550 FQ	54910 AW	108330 TQ	CABLS	10/01-12/01
	San Francisco PMSA, CA	Y	13450 FQ	41720 AW	96630 TQ	CABLS	10/01-12/01
	San Jose PMSA, CA	Y	18020 FQ	41270 AW	88200 TQ	CABLS	10/01-12/01
	San Luis Obispo-Atascadero-Paso Robles MSA, CA	Y	16300 FQ	26440 AW	40760 TQ	CABLS	10/01-12/01
	Santa Barbara-Santa Maria-Lompoc MSA, CA	Y	18540 FQ	46110 AW	90430 TQ	CABLS	10/01-12/01
	Santa Cruz-Watsonville PMSA, CA	Y	26890 FQ	44170 AW	80890 TQ	CABLS	10/01-12/01
	Stockton-Lodi MSA, CA	Y	13410 FQ	27720 AW	56140 TQ	CABLS	10/01-12/01
	Vallejo-Fairfield-Napa PMSA, CA	Y	20190 FQ	44800 AW	83210 TQ	CABLS	10/01-12/01
	Ventura PMSA, CA	Y	20310 FQ	52380 AW	106260 TQ	CABLS	10/01-12/01
	Visalia-Tulare-Porterville MSA, CA	Y	15680 FQ	42340 AW	77810 TQ	CABLS	10/01-12/01
	Colorado	Y	22340 FQ	43150 AW	75390 TQ	COBLS	10/01-12/01
	Boulder-Longmont PMSA, CO	Y	24870 FQ	42940 AW	76520 TQ	COBLS	10/01-12/01
	Colorado Springs MSA, CO	Y	19300 FQ	35260 AW	54970 TQ	COBLS	10/01-12/01
	Denver PMSA, CO	Y	22890 FQ	44590 AW	80640 TQ	COBLS	10/01-12/01

AAW	Average annual wage	**AOH**	Average offered, high	**ASH**	Average starting, high	**H**	Hourly	**M**	Monthly	**S**	Special: hourly and annual
AE	Average entry wage	**AOL**	Average offered, low	**ASL**	Average starting, low	**HI**	Highest wage paid	**MTC**	Median total compensation	**TQ**	Third quartile wage
AEX	Average experienced wage	**APH**	Average pay, high range	**AW**	Average wage paid	**HR**	High end range	**MW**	Median wage paid	**W**	Weekly
AO	Average offered	**APL**	Average pay, low range	**FQ**	First quartile wage	**LR**	Low end range	**SQ**	Second quartile wage	**Y**	Yearly

Occupation/Type/Industry	Location	Per	Low	Mid	High	Source	Date
Property, Real Estate, and Community Association Manager	Fort Collins-Loveland MSA, CO	Y	21400 FQ	42790 AW	84400 TQ	COBLS	10/01-12/01
	Greeley PMSA, CO	Y	19900 FQ	42370 AW	79950 TQ	COBLS	10/01-12/01
	Connecticut	Y	31190 FQ	58870 AW	102770 TQ	CTBLS	10/01-12/01
	Bridgeport PMSA, CT	Y	31590 FQ	55190 AW	110660 TQ	CTBLS	10/01-12/01
	Danbury PMSA, CT	Y	21860 FQ	51460 AW	85740 TQ	CTBLS	10/01-12/01
	Hartford MSA, CT	Y	31740 FQ	55970 AW	87550 TQ	CTBLS	10/01-12/01
	New Haven-Meriden PMSA, CT	Y	26890 FQ	56990 AW	88320 TQ	CTBLS	10/01-12/01
	New London-Norwich MSA, CT-RI	Y	25920 FQ	50770 AW	100650 TQ	CTBLS	10/01-12/01
	Stamford-Norwalk PMSA, CT	Y	39760 FQ	78770 AW		CTBLS	10/01-12/01
	Waterbury PMSA, CT	Y	34270 FQ	53090 AW	103320 TQ	CTBLS	10/01-12/01
	Delaware	Y	24650 FQ	42450 AW	68820 TQ	DEBLS	10/01-12/01
	Wilmington-Newark PMSA, DE-MD	Y	24700 FQ	41350 AW	65940 TQ	DEBLS	10/01-12/01
	District of Columbia	Y	23590 FQ	49430 AW	91370 TQ	DCBLS	10/01-12/01
	Washington PMSA, DC-MD-VA-WV	Y	24080 FQ	51680 AW	91270 TQ	DCBLS	10/01-12/01
	Florida	Y	18380 FQ	40840 AW	76340 TQ	FLBLS	10/01-12/01
	Daytona Beach MSA, FL	Y	18080 FQ	31720 AW	49940 TQ	FLBLS	10/01-12/01
	Fort Lauderdale PMSA, FL	Y	26600 FQ	59850 AW	88640 TQ	FLBLS	10/01-12/01
	Fort Myers-Cape Coral MSA, FL	Y	23290 FQ	35940 AW	52000 TQ	FLBLS	10/01-12/01
	Fort Pierce-Port St. Lucie MSA, FL	Y	14490 FQ	39570 AW	78130 TQ	FLBLS	10/01-12/01
	Fort Walton Beach MSA, FL	Y	20470 FQ	33280 AW	53310 TQ	FLBLS	10/01-12/01
	Gainesville MSA, FL	Y	19610 FQ	39120 AW	68150 TQ	FLBLS	10/01-12/01
	Jacksonville MSA, FL	Y	14980 FQ	40890 AW	83070 TQ	FLBLS	10/01-12/01
	Lakeland-Winter Haven MSA, FL	Y	13300 FQ	31830 AW	57620 TQ	FLBLS	10/01-12/01
	Melbourne-Titusville-Palm Bay MSA, FL	Y	19410 FQ	36360 AW	62850 TQ	FLBLS	10/01-12/01
	Miami PMSA, FL	Y	13320 FQ	35530 AW	65380 TQ	FLBLS	10/01-12/01
	Naples MSA, FL	Y	24400 FQ	49360 AW	72750 TQ	FLBLS	10/01-12/01
	Ocala MSA, FL	Y	12570 FQ	43950 AW	101850 TQ	FLBLS	10/01-12/01
	Orlando MSA, FL	Y	15630 FQ	40270 AW	77170 TQ	FLBLS	10/01-12/01
	Pensacola MSA, FL	Y	18780 FQ	37830 AW	58740 TQ	FLBLS	10/01-12/01
	Sarasota-Bradenton MSA, FL	Y	16000 FQ	34010 AW	54140 TQ	FLBLS	10/01-12/01
	Tallahassee MSA, FL	Y	19860 FQ	48050 AW	86000 TQ	FLBLS	10/01-12/01
	Tampa-St. Petersburg-Clearwater MSA, FL	Y	20190 FQ	36800 AW	59380 TQ	FLBLS	10/01-12/01
	West Palm Beach-Boca Raton MSA, FL	Y	26780 FQ	45340 AW	73860 TQ	FLBLS	10/01-12/01
	Georgia	Y	28610 FQ	47830 AW	82510 TQ	GABLS	10/01-12/01
	Atlanta MSA, GA	Y	29410 FQ	49680 AW	93020 TQ	GABLS	10/01-12/01
	Augusta-Aiken MSA, GA-SC	Y	21250 FQ	39050 AW	65040 TQ	GABLS	10/01-12/01
	Columbus MSA, GA-AL	Y	15150 FQ	38800 AW	69210 TQ	GABLS	10/01-12/01
	Macon MSA, GA	Y	24320 FQ	37750 AW	53210 TQ	GABLS	10/01-12/01
	Savannah MSA, GA	Y	25940 FQ	40840 AW	59280 TQ	GABLS	10/01-12/01
	Hawaii	Y	31990 FQ	55480 AW	97910 TQ	HIBLS	10/01-12/01
	Honolulu MSA, HI	Y	33500 FQ	58110 AW	100580 TQ	HIBLS	10/01-12/01
	Idaho	Y	13630 FQ	48720 AW		IDBLS	10/01-12/01
	Illinois	Y	22180 FQ	53310 AW	105180 TQ	ILBLS	10/01-12/01
	Champaign-Urbana MSA, IL	Y	14490 FQ	39110 AW	77370 TQ	ILBLS	10/01-12/01
	Chicago PMSA, IL	Y	22340 FQ	55190 AW	110350 TQ	ILBLS	10/01-12/01
	Peoria-Pekin MSA, IL	Y	29320 FQ	42940 AW	55940 TQ	ILBLS	10/01-12/01
	Rockford MSA, IL	Y	30020 FQ	42160 AW	60520 TQ	ILBLS	10/01-12/01
	Indiana	Y	18960 FQ	37710 AW	58330 TQ	INBLS	10/01-12/01
	Evansville-Henderson MSA, IN-KY	Y	19940 FQ	31300 AW	47050 TQ	INBLS	10/01-12/01
	Fort Wayne MSA, IN	Y	17810 FQ	39430 AW	93960 TQ	INBLS	10/01-12/01
	Gary PMSA, IN	Y	20450 FQ	39020 AW	55050 TQ	INBLS	10/01-12/01
	Indianapolis MSA, IN	Y	25970 FQ	42490 AW	67760 TQ	INBLS	10/01-12/01
	Lafayette MSA, IN	Y	19470 FQ	35910 AW	44390 TQ	INBLS	10/01-12/01
	South Bend MSA, IN	Y	14020 FQ	28520 AW	45010 TQ	INBLS	10/01-12/01
	Iowa	Y	14030 FQ	41590 AW	83610 TQ	IABLS	10/01-12/01
	Cedar Rapids MSA, IA	Y	23800 FQ	35120 AW	55300 TQ	IABLS	10/01-12/01
	Davenport-Moline-Rock Island MSA, IA-IL	Y	21400 FQ	37590 AW	70150 TQ	IABLS	10/01-12/01

AAW	Average annual wage	AOH	Average offered, high	ASH	Average starting, high	H	Hourly	M	Monthly	S	Special: hourly and annual
AE	Average entry wage	AOL	Average offered, low	ASL	Average starting, low	HI	Highest wage paid	MTC	Median total compensation	TQ	Third quartile wage
AEX	Average experienced wage	APH	Average pay, high range	AW	Average wage paid	HR	High end range	MW	Median wage paid	W	Weekly
AO	Average offered	APL	Average pay, low range	FQ	First quartile wage	LR	Low end range	SQ	Second quartile wage	Y	Yearly

Occupation/Type/Industry	Location	Per	Low	Mid	High	Source	Date
Property, Real Estate, and Community Association Manager	Des Moines MSA, IA	Y	12820 FQ	46850 AW	88600 TQ	IABLS	10/01-12/01
	Kansas	Y	18710 FQ	58890 AW	129770 TQ	KSBLS	10/01-12/01
	Topeka MSA, KS	Y	13700 FQ	49530 AW	92620 TQ	KSBLS	10/01-12/01
	Wichita MSA, KS	Y	19350 FQ	35950 AW	55950 TQ	KSBLS	10/01-12/01
	Kentucky	Y	15520 FQ	33340 AW	59060 TQ	KYBLS	10/01-12/01
	Lexington MSA, KY	Y	19140 FQ	28330 AW	43880 TQ	KYBLS	10/01-12/01
	Louisville MSA, KY-IN	Y	15870 FQ	35940 AW	58550 TQ	KYBLS	10/01-12/01
	Louisiana	Y	13530 FQ	30270 AW	51450 TQ	LABLS	10/01-12/01
	Baton Rouge MSA, LA	Y	17160 FQ	30410 AW	47280 TQ	LABLS	10/01-12/01
	Houma MSA, LA	Y	12350 FQ	36160 AW	78440 TQ	LABLS	10/01-12/01
	Lafayette MSA, LA	Y	12530 FQ	30690 AW	50690 TQ	LABLS	10/01-12/01
	New Orleans MSA, LA	Y	16540 FQ	35810 AW	64620 TQ	LABLS	10/01-12/01
	Shreveport-Bossier City MSA, LA	Y	13700 FQ	22270 AW	30660 TQ	LABLS	10/01-12/01
	Maine	Y	19820 FQ	37380 AW	64070 TQ	MEBLS	10/01-12/01
	Portland MSA, ME	Y	24320 FQ	41630 AW	57980 TQ	MEBLS	10/01-12/01
	Maryland	Y	20060 FQ	45350 AW	84140 TQ	MDBLS	10/01-12/01
	Baltimore PMSA, MD	Y	19560 FQ	41040 AW	71460 TQ	MDBLS	10/01-12/01
	Massachusetts	Y	30060 FQ	51320 AW	77670 TQ	MABLS	10/01-12/01
	Boston PMSA, MA-NH	Y	34070 FQ	53300 AW	80780 TQ	MABLS	10/01-12/01
	Brockton PMSA, MA	Y	21860 FQ	38220 AW	56960 TQ	MABLS	10/01-12/01
	Lawrence PMSA, MA-NH	Y	26500 FQ	51430 AW	84920 TQ	MABLS	10/01-12/01
	Lowell PMSA, MA-NH	Y	34570 FQ	52140 AW	86830 TQ	MABLS	10/01-12/01
	Springfield MSA, MA	Y	24260 FQ	40970 AW	62720 TQ	MABLS	10/01-12/01
	Worcester PMSA, MA-CT	Y	34860 FQ	61360 AW	117760 TQ	MABLS	10/01-12/01
	Michigan	Y	22950 FQ	50060 AW	89670 TQ	MIBLS	10/01-12/01
	Ann Arbor PMSA, MI	Y	29570 FQ	42540 AW	67110 TQ	MIBLS	10/01-12/01
	Detroit PMSA, MI	Y	24470 FQ	54430 AW	114200 TQ	MIBLS	10/01-12/01
	Flint PMSA, MI	Y	19120 FQ	38660 AW	64600 TQ	MIBLS	10/01-12/01
	Grand Rapids-Muskegon-Holland MSA, MI	Y	23420 FQ	43470 AW	65680 TQ	MIBLS	10/01-12/01
	Kalamazoo-Battle Creek MSA, MI	Y	22800 FQ	41960 AW	64150 TQ	MIBLS	10/01-12/01
	Lansing-East Lansing MSA, MI	Y	15750 FQ	42350 AW	103070 TQ	MIBLS	10/01-12/01
	Minnesota	Y	22030 FQ	45820 AW	80480 TQ	MNBLS	10/01-12/01
	Duluth-Superior MSA, MN-WI	Y	13900 FQ	32220 AW	57320 TQ	MNBLS	10/01-12/01
	Minneapolis-St. Paul MSA, MN-WI	Y	22110 FQ	48440 AW	87250 TQ	MNBLS	10/01-12/01
	St. Cloud MSA, MN	Y	25960 FQ	37510 AW	54380 TQ	MNBLS	10/01-12/01
	Mississippi	Y	14380 FQ	32200 AW	72400 TQ	MSBLS	10/01-12/01
	Biloxi-Gulfport-Pascagoula MSA, MS	Y	18650 FQ	31940 AW	44280 TQ	MSBLS	10/01-12/01
	Jackson MSA, MS	Y	15450 FQ	32970 AW	69620 TQ	MSBLS	10/01-12/01
	Missouri	Y	14610 FQ	35980 AW	69710 TQ	MOBLS	10/01-12/01
	Kansas City MSA, MO-KS	Y	18480 FQ	61140 AW	130260 TQ	MOBLS	10/01-12/01
	St. Louis MSA, MO-IL	Y	16430 FQ	37890 AW	68670 TQ	MOBLS	10/01-12/01
	Springfield MSA, MO	Y	12980 FQ	28840 AW	81700 TQ	MOBLS	10/01-12/01
	Montana	Y	17730 FQ	51230 AW	84020 TQ	MTBLS	10/01-12/01
	Billings MSA, MT	Y	12800 FQ	37260 AW	73720 TQ	MTBLS	10/01-12/01
	Nebraska	Y	15590 FQ	37890 AW	72930 TQ	NEBLS	10/01-12/01
	Lincoln MSA, NE	Y	15170 FQ	37460 AW	57880 TQ	NEBLS	10/01-12/01
	Omaha MSA, NE-IA	Y	16380 FQ	38720 AW	72050 TQ	NEBLS	10/01-12/01
	Nevada	Y	19830 FQ	52380 AW		NVBLS	10/01-12/01
	Las Vegas MSA, NV-AZ	Y	19360 FQ	55170 AW		NVBLS	10/01-12/01
	Reno MSA, NV	Y	19880 FQ	37550 AW	65890 TQ	NVBLS	10/01-12/01
	New Hampshire	Y	21830 FQ	49050 AW	94220 TQ	NHBLS	10/01-12/01
	Manchester PMSA, NH	Y	28380 FQ	53080 AW	101440 TQ	NHBLS	10/01-12/01
	Nashua PMSA, NH	Y	27340 FQ	43670 AW	56490 TQ	NHBLS	10/01-12/01
	Portsmouth-Rochester PMSA, NH-ME	Y	14500 FQ	61580 AW	142530 TQ	NHBLS	10/01-12/01
	New Jersey	Y	29260 FQ	56200 AW	93410 TQ	NJBLS	10/01-12/01
	Atlantic-Cape May PMSA, NJ	Y	21620 FQ	47430 AW	79870 TQ	NJBLS	10/01-12/01
	Bergen-Passaic PMSA, NJ	Y	31320 FQ	54630 AW	89460 TQ	NJBLS	10/01-12/01
	Jersey City PMSA, NJ	Y	38860 FQ	66150 AW	113940 TQ	NJBLS	10/01-12/01
	Middlesex-Somerset-Hunterdon PMSA, NJ	Y	35770 FQ	55590 AW	82950 TQ	NJBLS	10/01-12/01
	Monmouth-Ocean PMSA, NJ	Y	25930 FQ	53500 AW	106090 TQ	NJBLS	10/01-12/01
	Newark PMSA, NJ	Y	29840 FQ	57350 AW	91010 TQ	NJBLS	10/01-12/01
	Trenton PMSA, NJ	Y	30190 FQ	50190 AW	85100 TQ	NJBLS	10/01-12/01
	New Mexico	Y	18430 FQ	37960 AW	58420 TQ	NMBLS	10/01-12/01

AAW Average annual wage; AE Average entry wage; AEX Average experienced wage; AO Average offered; AOH Average offered, high; AOL Average offered, low; APH Average pay, high range; APL Average pay, low range; ASH Average starting, high; ASL Average starting, low; AW Average wage paid; FQ First quartile wage; H Hourly; HI Highest wage paid; HR High end range; LR Low end range; M Monthly; MTC Median total compensation; MW Median wage paid; SQ Second quartile wage; S Special: hourly and annual; TQ Third quartile wage; W Weekly; Y Yearly

Occupation/Type/Industry	Location	Per	Low	Mid	High	Source	Date
Property, Real Estate, and Community Association Manager	Albuquerque MSA, NM	Y	23240 FQ	37130 AW	56510 TQ	NMBLS	10/01-12/01
	Las Cruces MSA, NM	Y	20200 FQ	39350 AW	68300 TQ	NMBLS	10/01-12/01
	New York	Y	29060 FQ	59350 AW	112630 TQ	NYBLS	10/01-12/01
	Albany-Schenectady-Troy MSA, NY	Y	25790 FQ	48130 AW	85400 TQ	NYBLS	10/01-12/01
	Binghamton MSA, NY	Y	22370 FQ	54230 AW	94960 TQ	NYBLS	10/01-12/01
	Buffalo-Niagara Falls MSA, NY	Y	26410 FQ	54850 AW	97510 TQ	NYBLS	10/01-12/01
	Dutchess County PMSA, NY	Y	29820 FQ	42960 AW	58690 TQ	NYBLS	10/01-12/01
	Nassau-Suffolk PMSA, NY	Y	37610 FQ	82890 AW		NYBLS	10/01-12/01
	New York PMSA, NY	Y	29830 FQ	59880 AW	112490 TQ	NYBLS	10/01-12/01
	Newburgh PMSA, NY-PA	Y	26060 FQ	47740 AW	78460 TQ	NYBLS	10/01-12/01
	Rochester MSA, NY	Y	30280 FQ	52730 AW	88790 TQ	NYBLS	10/01-12/01
	Syracuse MSA, NY	Y	19820 FQ	42140 AW	72170 TQ	NYBLS	10/01-12/01
	Utica-Rome MSA, NY	Y	19040 FQ	41160 AW	56220 TQ	NYBLS	10/01-12/01
	North Carolina	Y	21670 FQ	43920 AW	72160 TQ	NCBLS	10/01-12/01
	Asheville MSA, NC	Y	23900 FQ	42860 AW	72930 TQ	NCBLS	10/01-12/01
	Charlotte-Gastonia-Rock Hill MSA, NC-SC	Y	20310 FQ	46320 AW	86560 TQ	NCBLS	10/01-12/01
	Fayetteville MSA, NC	Y	24240 FQ	42580 AW	80490 TQ	NCBLS	10/01-12/01
	Greensboro-Winston-Salem-High Point MSA, NC	Y	24080 FQ	42930 AW	62900 TQ	NCBLS	10/01-12/01
	Hickory-Morganton-Lenoir MSA, NC	Y	27750 FQ	67220 AW	92820 TQ	NCBLS	10/01-12/01
	Raleigh-Durham-Chapel Hill MSA, NC	Y	21710 FQ	40960 AW	68890 TQ	NCBLS	10/01-12/01
	Wilmington MSA, NC	Y	20580 FQ	40400 AW	69560 TQ	NCBLS	10/01-12/01
	North Dakota	Y	13170 FQ	30680 AW	55060 TQ	NDBLS	10/01-12/01
	Fargo-Moorhead MSA, ND-MN	Y	14520 FQ	31210 AW	55360 TQ	NDBLS	10/01-12/01
	Ohio	Y	20380 FQ	46700 AW	89840 TQ	OHBLS	10/01-12/01
	Akron PMSA, OH	Y	30570 FQ	59990 AW	108450 TQ	OHBLS	10/01-12/01
	Canton-Massillon MSA, OH	Y	19930 FQ	39420 AW	92830 TQ	OHBLS	10/01-12/01
	Cincinnati PMSA, OH-KY-IN	Y	22110 FQ	43310 AW	75610 TQ	OHBLS	10/01-12/01
	Cleveland-Lorain-Elyria PMSA, OH	Y	22560 FQ	51970 AW	91940 TQ	OHBLS	10/01-12/01
	Columbus MSA, OH	Y	21680 FQ	42020 AW	83530 TQ	OHBLS	10/01-12/01
	Dayton-Springfield MSA, OH	Y	27730 FQ	56330 AW	132540 TQ	OHBLS	10/01-12/01
	Hamilton-Middletown PMSA, OH	Y	20120 FQ	36870 AW	73350 TQ	OHBLS	10/01-12/01
	Toledo MSA, OH	Y	27840 FQ	57060 AW	92550 TQ	OHBLS	10/01-12/01
	Youngstown-Warren MSA, OH	Y	13100 FQ	37170 AW	100080 TQ	OHBLS	10/01-12/01
	Oklahoma	Y	14210 FQ	31080 AW	57200 TQ	OKBLS	10/01-12/01
	Oklahoma City MSA, OK	Y	17700 FQ	28160 AW	53850 TQ	OKBLS	10/01-12/01
	Tulsa MSA, OK	Y	19240 FQ	37760 AW	70280 TQ	OKBLS	10/01-12/01
	Oregon	Y	14080 FQ	31630 AW	66680 TQ	ORBLS	10/01-12/01
	Eugene-Springfield MSA, OR	Y	14080 FQ	26980 AW	53260 TQ	ORBLS	10/01-12/01
	Medford-Ashland MSA, OR	Y	13930 FQ	27380 AW	40760 TQ	ORBLS	10/01-12/01
	Portland-Vancouver PMSA, OR-WA	Y	14260 FQ	34570 AW	76360 TQ	ORBLS	10/01-12/01
	Salem PMSA, OR	Y	14000 FQ	20320 AW	28600 TQ	ORBLS	10/01-12/01
	Pennsylvania	Y	22910 FQ	46220 AW	81650 TQ	PABLS	10/01-12/01
	Allentown-Bethlehem-Easton MSA, PA	Y	29290 FQ	48190 AW	88260 TQ	PABLS	10/01-12/01
	Erie MSA, PA	Y	33720 FQ	43140 AW	64430 TQ	PABLS	10/01-12/01
	Harrisburg-Lebanon-Carlisle MSA, PA	Y	20310 FQ	30720 AW	51020 TQ	PABLS	10/01-12/01
	Johnstown MSA, PA	Y	24190 FQ	44650 AW	82820 TQ	PABLS	10/01-12/01
	Lancaster MSA, PA	Y	24440 FQ	35970 AW	50440 TQ	PABLS	10/01-12/01
	Philadelphia PMSA, PA-NJ	Y	27860 FQ	53460 AW	88400 TQ	PABLS	10/01-12/01
	Pittsburgh MSA, PA	Y	23510 FQ	45710 AW	78280 TQ	PABLS	10/01-12/01
	Reading MSA, PA	Y	29960 FQ	45820 AW	60130 TQ	PABLS	10/01-12/01
	Scranton-Wilkes-Barre-Hazleton MSA, PA	Y	26550 FQ	42250 AW	56240 TQ	PABLS	10/01-12/01
	York MSA, PA	Y	19870 FQ	34640 AW	54750 TQ	PABLS	10/01-12/01
	Rhode Island	Y	31270 FQ	62250 AW	112020 TQ	RIBLS	10/01-12/01
	Providence-Fall River-Warwick MSA, RI-MA	Y	25740 FQ	59440 AW	110060 TQ	RIBLS	10/01-12/01
	South Carolina	Y	21380 FQ	41720 AW	63910 TQ	SCBLS	10/01-12/01

AAW Average annual wage · AE Average entry wage · AEX Average experienced wage · AO Average offered · AOH Average offered, high · AOL Average offered, low · APH Average pay, high range · APL Average pay, low range · ASH Average starting, high · ASL Average starting, low · AW Average wage paid · FQ First quartile wage · H Hourly · HI Highest wage paid · HR High end range · LR Low end range · M Monthly · MTC Median total compensation · MW Median wage paid · SQ Second quartile wage · S Special: hourly and annual · TQ Third quartile wage · W Weekly · Y Yearly

Occupation/Type/Industry	Location	Per	Low	Mid	High	Source	Date
Property, Real Estate, and Community Association Manager	Charleston-North Charleston MSA, SC	Y	21820 FQ	37730 AW	54120 TQ	SCBLS	10/01-12/01
	Columbia MSA, SC	Y	22810 FQ	43730 AW	70890 TQ	SCBLS	10/01-12/01
	Greenville-Spartanburg-Anderson MSA, SC	Y	28080 FQ	41010 AW	57020 TQ	SCBLS	10/01-12/01
	Myrtle Beach MSA, SC	Y	23330 FQ	46280 AW	74020 TQ	SCBLS	10/01-12/01
	South Dakota	Y	21500 FQ	32110 AW	47800 TQ	SDBLS	10/01-12/01
	Sioux Falls MSA, SD	Y	24090 FQ	32610 AW	45660 TQ	SDBLS	10/01-12/01
	Tennessee	Y	15310 FQ	41380 AW	71920 TQ	TNBLS	10/01-12/01
	Chattanooga MSA, TN-GA	Y	11740 FQ	34760 AW	68130 TQ	TNBLS	10/01-12/01
	Clarksville-Hopkinsville MSA, TN-KY	Y	13160 FQ	26110 AW	40330 TQ	TNBLS	10/01-12/01
	Johnson City-Kingsport-Bristol MSA, TN-VA	Y	15020 FQ	31480 AW	62430 TQ	TNBLS	10/01-12/01
	Knoxville MSA, TN	Y	20280 FQ	40870 AW	59210 TQ	TNBLS	10/01-12/01
	Memphis MSA, TN-AR-MS	Y	15880 FQ	38910 AW	81210 TQ	TNBLS	10/01-12/01
	Nashville MSA, TN	Y	22260 FQ	50130 AW	75910 TQ	TNBLS	10/01-12/01
	Texas	Y	19100 FQ	41130 AW	71480 TQ	TXBLS	10/01-12/01
	Amarillo MSA, TX	Y	17160 FQ	36740 AW	64940 TQ	TXBLS	10/01-12/01
	Austin-San Marcos MSA, TX	Y	18720 FQ	44100 AW	70040 TQ	TXBLS	10/01-12/01
	Beaumont-Port Arthur MSA, TX	Y	12790 FQ	28080 AW	44650 TQ	TXBLS	10/01-12/01
	Brazoria PMSA, TX	Y	11670 FQ	22610 AW	36540 TQ	TXBLS	10/01-12/01
	Brownsville-Harlingen-San Benito MSA, TX	Y	15800 FQ	34020 AW	59720 TQ	TXBLS	10/01-12/01
	Corpus Christi MSA, TX	Y	12870 FQ	37780 AW	69490 TQ	TXBLS	10/01-12/01
	Dallas PMSA, TX	Y	23900 FQ	44160 AW	79690 TQ	TXBLS	10/01-12/01
	El Paso MSA, TX	Y	15350 FQ	40640 AW	71010 TQ	TXBLS	10/01-12/01
	Fort Worth-Arlington PMSA, TX	Y	23020 FQ	42090 AW	63090 TQ	TXBLS	10/01-12/01
	Galveston-Texas City PMSA, TX	Y	22520 FQ	43040 AW	67990 TQ	TXBLS	10/01-12/01
	Houston PMSA, TX	Y	20310 FQ	41310 AW	75680 TQ	TXBLS	10/01-12/01
	Killeen-Temple MSA, TX	Y	11980 FQ	27960 AW	45350 TQ	TXBLS	10/01-12/01
	Laredo MSA, TX	Y	15690 FQ	30340 AW	63340 TQ	TXBLS	10/01-12/01
	Longview-Marshall MSA, TX	Y	19180 FQ	33020 AW	55590 TQ	TXBLS	10/01-12/01
	Lubbock MSA, TX	Y	12080 FQ	22960 AW	46200 TQ	TXBLS	10/01-12/01
	McAllen-Edinburg-Mission MSA, TX	Y	16430 FQ	45180 AW	88990 TQ	TXBLS	10/01-12/01
	Odessa-Midland MSA, TX	Y	15090 FQ	32500 AW	53420 TQ	TXBLS	10/01-12/01
	San Antonio MSA, TX	Y	19410 FQ	43680 AW	70820 TQ	TXBLS	10/01-12/01
	Tyler MSA, TX	Y	19410 FQ	33530 AW	58910 TQ	TXBLS	10/01-12/01
	Waco MSA, TX	Y	14260 FQ	31780 AW	66550 TQ	TXBLS	10/01-12/01
	Utah	Y	12710 FQ	33540 AW	66840 TQ	UTBLS	10/01-12/01
	Provo-Orem MSA, UT	Y	16980 FQ	44130 AW	73330 TQ	UTBLS	10/01-12/01
	Salt Lake City-Ogden MSA, UT	Y	12430 FQ	30020 AW	52010 TQ	UTBLS	10/01-12/01
	Vermont	Y	36090 FQ	60840 AW	97560 TQ	VTBLS	10/01-12/01
	Virginia	Y	22810 FQ	41880 AW	67780 TQ	VABLS	10/01-12/01
	Lynchburg MSA, VA	Y	16720 FQ	32690 AW	44420 TQ	VABLS	10/01-12/01
	Norfolk-Virginia Beach-Newport News MSA, VA-NC	Y	24110 FQ	37880 AW	57690 TQ	VABLS	10/01-12/01
	Richmond-Petersburg MSA, VA	Y	20360 FQ	37200 AW	55570 TQ	VABLS	10/01-12/01
	Roanoke MSA, VA	Y	19680 FQ	33930 AW	46280 TQ	VABLS	10/01-12/01
	Washington	Y	23370 FQ	58480 AW	105480 TQ	WABLS	10/01-12/01
	Bremerton PMSA, WA	Y	37970 FQ	73490 AW		WABLS	10/01-12/01
	Seattle-Bellevue-Everett PMSA, WA	Y	22300 FQ	64520 AW	112200 TQ	WABLS	10/01-12/01
	Spokane MSA, WA	Y	24310 FQ	33880 AW	60580 TQ	WABLS	10/01-12/01
	Tacoma PMSA, WA	Y	32190 FQ	48220 AW	71510 TQ	WABLS	10/01-12/01
	West Virginia	Y	13490 FQ	30670 AW	57780 TQ	WVBLS	10/01-12/01
	Charleston MSA, WV	Y	11430 FQ	25730 AW	50880 TQ	WVBLS	10/01-12/01
	Huntington-Ashland MSA, WV-KY-OH	Y	15790 FQ	35880 AW	74400 TQ	WVBLS	10/01-12/01
	Wisconsin	Y	14760 FQ	41620 AW	76590 TQ	WIBLS	10/01-12/01
	Appleton-Oshkosh-Neenah MSA, WI	Y	38120 FQ	49660 AW	67090 TQ	WIBLS	10/01-12/01
	Green Bay MSA, WI	Y	19830 FQ	39080 AW	58450 TQ	WIBLS	10/01-12/01

AAW	Average annual wage	AOH	Average offered, high	ASH	Average starting, high	H	Hourly	M	Monthly	S	Special: hourly and annual
AE	Average entry wage	AOL	Average offered, low	ASL	Average starting, low	HI	Highest wage paid	MTC	Median total compensation	TQ	Third quartile wage
AEX	Average experienced wage	APH	Average pay, high range	AW	Average wage paid	HR	High end range	MW	Median wage paid	W	Weekly
AO	Average offered	APL	Average pay, low range	FQ	First quartile wage	LR	Low end range	SQ	Second quartile wage	Y	Yearly

Occupation/Type/Industry	Location	Per	Low	Mid	High	Source	Date
Property, Real Estate, and Community Association Manager	Madison MSA, WI	Y	15100 FQ	27380 AW	52890 TQ	WIBLS	10/01-12/01
	Milwaukee-Waukesha PMSA, WI	Y	22280 FQ	49990 AW	106930 TQ	WIBLS	10/01-12/01
	Wyoming	Y	16420 FQ	28880 AW	38670 TQ	WYBLS	10/01-12/01
	Puerto Rico	Y	15180 FQ	27920 AW	49240 TQ	PRBLS	10/01-12/01
	Virgin Islands	Y	30640 FQ	55260 AW	125420 TQ	VIBLS	10/01-12/01
	Guam	Y	13960 FQ	40860 AW	63050 TQ	GUBLS	10/01-12/01
Psychiatric Aide	Alabama	H	6.07 FQ	8.01 AW	10.53 TQ	ALBLS	10/01-12/01
	Arizona	H	7.53 FQ	9.62 AW	11.48 TQ	AZBLS	10/01-12/01
	Arkansas	H	5.99 FQ	8.00 AW	10.37 TQ	ARBLS	10/01-12/01
	California	H	8.67 FQ	11.10 AW	14.22 TQ	CABLS	10/01-12/01
	Colorado	H	7.97 FQ	10.67 AW	13.94 TQ	COBLS	10/01-12/01
	Connecticut	H	8.75 FQ	12.34 AW	16.33 TQ	CTBLS	10/01-12/01
	Delaware	H	8.75 FQ	10.83 AW	13.09 TQ	DEBLS	10/01-12/01
	Florida	H	8.14 FQ	10.93 AW	14.38 TQ	FLBLS	10/01-12/01
	Georgia	H	7.38 FQ	10.57 AW	14.47 TQ	GABLS	10/01-12/01
	Idaho	H	6.53 FQ	10.13 AW	14.21 TQ	IDBLS	10/01-12/01
	Illinois	H	6.45 FQ	11.27 AW	16.44 TQ	ILBLS	10/01-12/01
	Indiana	H	8.58 FQ	10.80 AW	13.67 TQ	INBLS	10/01-12/01
	Iowa	H	8.76 FQ	12.11 AW	16.63 TQ	IABLS	10/01-12/01
	Kansas	H	6.72 FQ	8.97 AW	12.22 TQ	KSBLS	10/01-12/01
	Kentucky	H	7.53 FQ	9.65 AW	12.12 TQ	KYBLS	10/01-12/01
	Louisiana	H	5.83 FQ	8.13 AW	10.76 TQ	LABLS	10/01-12/01
	Maine	H	9.35 FQ	11.04 AW	13.59 TQ	MEBLS	10/01-12/01
	Maryland	H	8.43 FQ	11.23 AW	13.59 TQ	MDBLS	10/01-12/01
	Massachusetts	H	10.92 FQ	13.54 AW	16.53 TQ	MABLS	10/01-12/01
	Michigan	H	8.73 FQ	13.67 AW	18.66 TQ	MIBLS	10/01-12/01
	Minnesota	H	9.27 FQ	12.24 AW	16.44 TQ	MNBLS	10/01-12/01
	Mississippi	H	6.35 FQ	8.74 AW	12.78 TQ	MSBLS	10/01-12/01
	Missouri	H	7.26 FQ	9.82 AW	13.12 TQ	MOBLS	10/01-12/01
	Montana	H	8.16 FQ	10.65 AW	15.28 TQ	MTBLS	10/01-12/01
	Nebraska	H	8.87 FQ	10.01 AW	11.32 TQ	NEBLS	10/01-12/01
	New Hampshire	H	9.23 FQ	11.09 AW	13.39 TQ	NHBLS	10/01-12/01
	New Jersey	H	9.23 FQ	12.59 AW	16.53 TQ	NJBLS	10/01-12/01
	New Mexico	H	5.41 FQ	7.07 AW	10.16 TQ	NMBLS	10/01-12/01
	New York	H	10.90 FQ	14.24 AW	17.23 TQ	NYBLS	10/01-12/01
	North Carolina	H	7.19 FQ	9.97 AW	13.10 TQ	NCBLS	10/01-12/01
	North Dakota	H	7.84 FQ	9.89 AW	11.97 TQ	NDBLS	10/01-12/01
	Ohio	H	7.92 FQ	13.32 AW	19.46 TQ	OHBLS	10/01-12/01
	Oklahoma	H	6.94 FQ	9.54 AW	12.77 TQ	OKBLS	10/01-12/01
	Oregon	H	8.01 FQ	12.37 AW	16.50 TQ	ORBLS	10/01-12/01
	Pennsylvania	H	9.24 FQ	13.10 AW	16.83 TQ	PABLS	10/01-12/01
	Rhode Island	H	8.76 FQ	12.81 AW	16.75 TQ	RIBLS	10/01-12/01
	South Carolina	H	7.23 FQ	8.92 AW	11.49 TQ	SCBLS	10/01-12/01
	South Dakota	H	6.75 FQ	10.57 AW	13.84 TQ	SDBLS	10/01-12/01
	Tennessee	H	7.26 FQ	10.11 AW	13.57 TQ	TNBLS	10/01-12/01
	Texas	H	7.15 FQ	9.19 AW	11.71 TQ	TXBLS	10/01-12/01
	Utah	H	7.49 FQ	9.60 AW	12.11 TQ	UTBLS	10/01-12/01
	Vermont	H	9.02 FQ	10.26 AW	11.99 TQ	VTBLS	10/01-12/01
	Virginia	H	8.12 FQ	10.74 AW	13.55 TQ	VABLS	10/01-12/01
	Washington	H	8.74 FQ	13.86 AW	17.28 TQ	WABLS	10/01-12/01
	West Virginia	H	5.88 FQ	7.54 AW	9.56 TQ	WVBLS	10/01-12/01
	Wisconsin	H	7.18 FQ	10.14 AW	13.35 TQ	WIBLS	10/01-12/01
	Wyoming	H	5.56 FQ	6.89 AW	8.22 TQ	WYBLS	10/01-12/01
	Puerto Rico	H	5.39 FQ	6.70 AW	8.28 TQ	PRBLS	10/01-12/01
Psychiatric Technician	Alabama	Y	13130 FQ	19230 AW	26780 TQ	ALBLS	10/01-12/01
	Arizona	Y	17440 FQ	22250 AW	27540 TQ	AZBLS	10/01-12/01
	Arkansas	Y	14690 FQ	18600 AW	24890 TQ	ARBLS	10/01-12/01
	California	Y	27220 FQ	36670 AW	45550 TQ	CABLS	10/01-12/01
	Colorado	Y	21550 FQ	29470 AW	36180 TQ	COBLS	10/01-12/01
	Connecticut	Y	29570 FQ	42360 AW	54340 TQ	CTBLS	10/01-12/01
	Delaware	Y	20300 FQ	29060 AW	42670 TQ	DEBLS	10/01-12/01
	District of Columbia	Y	19810 FQ	32480 AW	42760 TQ	DCBLS	10/01-12/01
	Florida	Y	15770 FQ	21430 AW	27810 TQ	FLBLS	10/01-12/01
	Georgia	Y	16400 FQ	24570 AW	35030 TQ	GABLS	10/01-12/01
	Idaho	Y	16340 FQ	22260 AW	31300 TQ	IDBLS	10/01-12/01
	Illinois	Y	19470 FQ	27400 AW	34700 TQ	ILBLS	10/01-12/01
	Indiana	Y	18250 FQ	23690 AW	29860 TQ	INBLS	10/01-12/01

AAW	Average annual wage	AOH	Average offered, high	ASH	Average starting, high	H	Hourly	M	Monthly	S	Special: hourly and annual
AE	Average entry wage	AOL	Average offered, low	ASL	Average starting, low	HI	Highest wage paid	MTC	Median total compensation	TQ	Third quartile wage
AEX	Average experienced wage	APH	Average pay, high range	AW	Average wage paid	HR	High end range	MW	Median wage paid	W	Weekly
AO	Average offered	APL	Average pay, low range	FQ	First quartile wage	LR	Low end range	SQ	Second quartile wage	Y	Yearly

Occupation/Type/Industry	Location	Per	Low	Mid	High	Source	Date
Psychiatric Technician	Iowa	Y	15660 FQ	21430 AW	27630 TQ	IABLS	10/01-12/01
	Kansas	Y	19160 FQ	25340 AW	31270 TQ	KSBLS	10/01-12/01
	Kentucky	Y	14700 FQ	18630 AW	23080 TQ	KYBLS	10/01-12/01
	Louisiana	Y	13350 FQ	17860 AW	22800 TQ	LABLS	10/01-12/01
	Maine	Y	17740 FQ	23180 AW	30510 TQ	MEBLS	10/01-12/01
	Maryland	Y	15010 FQ	23170 AW	33380 TQ	MDBLS	10/01-12/01
	Massachusetts	Y	19280 FQ	27830 AW	39290 TQ	MABLS	10/01-12/01
	Michigan	Y	23050 FQ	28010 AW	34730 TQ	MIBLS	10/01-12/01
	Minnesota	Y	18490 FQ	28340 AW	40630 TQ	MNBLS	10/01-12/01
	Mississippi	Y	13710 FQ	17510 AW	22000 TQ	MSBLS	10/01-12/01
	Nebraska	Y	16140 FQ	21310 AW	27160 TQ	NEBLS	10/01-12/01
	New Jersey	Y	20530 FQ	33200 AW	45410 TQ	NJBLS	10/01-12/01
	New Mexico	Y	14730 FQ	19010 AW	25160 TQ	NMBLS	10/01-12/01
	New York	Y	19760 FQ	28430 AW	41540 TQ	NYBLS	10/01-12/01
	North Carolina	Y	17340 FQ	24930 AW	34920 TQ	NCBLS	10/01-12/01
	North Dakota	Y	17910 FQ	24650 AW	40330 TQ	NDBLS	10/01-12/01
	Ohio	Y	16730 FQ	23710 AW	31770 TQ	OHBLS	10/01-12/01
	Oklahoma	Y	15200 FQ	22780 AW	34510 TQ	OKBLS	10/01-12/01
	Oregon	Y	24120 FQ	31960 AW	41120 TQ	ORBLS	10/01-12/01
	Pennsylvania	Y	16030 FQ	25840 AW	38680 TQ	PABLS	10/01-12/01
	Rhode Island	Y	29500 FQ	35190 AW	43730 TQ	RIBLS	10/01-12/01
	South Carolina	Y	15390 FQ	20070 AW	25580 TQ	SCBLS	10/01-12/01
	South Dakota	Y	18920 FQ	23810 AW	28180 TQ	SDBLS	10/01-12/01
	Tennessee	Y	14710 FQ	19520 AW	26630 TQ	TNBLS	10/01-12/01
	Texas	Y	15700 FQ	20360 AW	28420 TQ	TXBLS	10/01-12/01
	Utah	Y	16170 FQ	20180 AW	25330 TQ	UTBLS	10/01-12/01
	Vermont	Y	18920 FQ	30050 AW	43160 TQ	VTBLS	10/01-12/01
	Virginia	Y	18500 FQ	23390 AW	30580 TQ	VABLS	10/01-12/01
	Washington	Y	24440 FQ	30950 AW	37530 TQ	WABLS	10/01-12/01
	West Virginia	Y	15360 FQ	23620 AW	37420 TQ	WVBLS	10/01-12/01
	Wisconsin	Y	18810 FQ	28910 AW	42320 TQ	WIBLS	10/01-12/01
	Puerto Rico	Y	13390 FQ	19840 AW	31010 TQ	PRBLS	10/01-12/01
Psychiatrist	Alabama	Y	48500 FQ	112960 AW		ALBLS	10/01-12/01
	Alaska	Y	87350 FQ	130950 AW		AKBLS	10/01-12/01
	Arizona	Y	97790 FQ	128920 AW		AZBLS	10/01-12/01
	Phoenix-Mesa MSA, AZ	Y	118770 FQ	136930 AW		AZBLS	10/01-12/01
	Tucson MSA, AZ	Y	36650 FQ	100380 AW		AZBLS	10/01-12/01
	Arkansas	Y	54600 FQ	104300 AW		ARBLS	10/01-12/01
	Fayetteville-Springdale-Rogers MSA, AR	Y	84750 FQ	104380 AW	130150 TQ	ARBLS	10/01-12/01
	Little Rock-North Little Rock MSA, AR	Y	51800 FQ	94650 AW		ARBLS	10/01-12/01
	California	Y	68240 FQ	114120 AW		CABLS	10/01-12/01
	Fresno MSA, CA	Y	20570 FQ	101360 AW		CABLS	10/01-12/01
	Los Angeles-Long Beach PMSA, CA	Y	95690 FQ	113250 AW		CABLS	10/01-12/01
	Oakland PMSA, CA	Y	19390 FQ	85170 AW		CABLS	10/01-12/01
	Orange County PMSA, CA	Y	58980 FQ	116970 AW		CABLS	10/01-12/01
	Riverside-San Bernardino PMSA, CA	Y	102230 FQ	122890 AW		CABLS	10/01-12/01
	Sacramento PMSA, CA	Y	52160 FQ	111970 AW		CABLS	10/01-12/01
	San Diego MSA, CA	Y	72890 FQ	110930 AW		CABLS	10/01-12/01
	San Francisco PMSA, CA	Y	82630 FQ	116430 AW		CABLS	10/01-12/01
	San Jose PMSA, CA	Y	21200 FQ	106120 AW		CABLS	10/01-12/01
	San Luis Obispo-Atascadero-Paso Robles MSA, CA	Y	121090 FQ	132040 AW		CABLS	10/01-12/01
	Vallejo-Fairfield-Napa PMSA, CA	Y	101970 FQ	129190 AW		CABLS	10/01-12/01
	Colorado	Y	80610 FQ	123000 AW		COBLS	10/01-12/01
	Denver PMSA, CO	Y	91770 FQ	123650 AW		COBLS	10/01-12/01
	Connecticut	Y	38750 FQ	106860 AW		CTBLS	10/01-12/01
	Hartford MSA, CT	Y	41840 FQ	105890 AW		CTBLS	10/01-12/01
	New Haven-Meriden PMSA, CT	Y	28970 FQ	76190 AW		CTBLS	10/01-12/01
	Stamford-Norwalk PMSA, CT	Y	45040 FQ	121770 AW		CTBLS	10/01-12/01
	Waterbury PMSA, CT	Y	96660 FQ	128100 AW		CTBLS	10/01-12/01
	Delaware	Y	48130 FQ	96560 AW		DEBLS	10/01-12/01
	Wilmington-Newark PMSA, DE-MD	Y	47990 FQ	100210 AW		DEBLS	10/01-12/01
	Washington PMSA, DC-MD-VA-WV	Y	49820 FQ	93940 AW		DCBLS	10/01-12/01
	Florida	Y	62940 FQ	117030 AW		FLBLS	10/01-12/01

AAW	Average annual wage	**AOH**	Average offered, high	**ASH**	Average starting, high	**H**	Hourly	**M**	Monthly	**S**	Special: hourly and annual
AE	Average entry wage	**AOL**	Average offered, low	**ASL**	Average starting, low	**HI**	Highest wage paid	**MTC**	Median total compensation	**TQ**	Third quartile wage
AEX	Average experienced wage	**APH**	Average pay, high range	**AW**	Average wage paid	**HR**	High end range	**MW**	Median wage paid	**W**	Weekly
AO	Average offered	**APL**	Average pay, low range	**FQ**	First quartile wage	**LR**	Low end range	**SQ**	Second quartile wage	**Y**	Yearly

Occupation/Type/Industry	Location	Per	Low	Mid	High	Source	Date
Psychiatrist	Miami PMSA, FL	Y	62590 FQ	108850 AW		FLBLS	10/01-12/01
	Tampa-St. Petersburg-Clearwater MSA, FL	Y	52620 FQ	107630 AW		FLBLS	10/01-12/01
	West Palm Beach-Boca Raton MSA, FL	Y	84650 FQ	121170 AW		FLBLS	10/01-12/01
	Georgia	Y	71520 FQ	118700 AW		GABLS	10/01-12/01
	Atlanta MSA, GA	Y	53690 FQ	113270 AW		GABLS	10/01-12/01
	Hawaii	Y	40210 FQ	69290 AW	122940 TQ	HIBLS	10/01-12/01
	Honolulu MSA, HI	Y	39900 FQ	62830 AW	122920 TQ	HIBLS	10/01-12/01
	Idaho	Y	76500 FQ	124020 AW		IDBLS	10/01-12/01
	Illinois	Y	33130 FQ	88290 AW		ILBLS	10/01-12/01
	Chicago PMSA, IL	Y	32380 FQ	80360 AW	129920 TQ	ILBLS	10/01-12/01
	Indiana	Y	68090 FQ	123720 AW		INBLS	10/01-12/01
	Gary PMSA, IN	Y	32420 FQ	91010 AW		INBLS	10/01-12/01
	Indianapolis MSA, IN	Y	120410 FQ	133160 AW		INBLS	10/01-12/01
	Iowa	Y	44700 FQ	118010 AW		IABLS	10/01-12/01
	Kansas	Y	97100 FQ	131500 AW		KSBLS	10/01-12/01
	Topeka MSA, KS	Y	117610 FQ	130480 AW		KSBLS	10/01-12/01
	Kentucky	Y	45940 FQ	124300 AW		KYBLS	10/01-12/01
	Louisville MSA, KY-IN	Y	40200 FQ	97860 AW		KYBLS	10/01-12/01
	Maine	Y	117940 FQ	132260 AW		MEBLS	10/01-12/01
	Maryland	Y	71160 FQ	117900 AW		MDBLS	10/01-12/01
	Baltimore PMSA, MD	Y	70870 FQ	117880 AW		MDBLS	10/01-12/01
	Massachusetts	Y	81810 FQ	120420 AW		MABLS	10/01-12/01
	Boston PMSA, MA-NH	Y	80690 FQ	117730 AW		MABLS	10/01-12/01
	Lawrence PMSA, MA-NH	Y	69450 FQ	101210 AW	133860 TQ	MABLS	10/01-12/01
	Springfield MSA, MA	Y	74000 FQ	119880 AW		MABLS	10/01-12/01
	Michigan	Y	70900 FQ	126120 AW		MIBLS	10/01-12/01
	Ann Arbor PMSA, MI	Y	76550 FQ	126480 AW		MIBLS	10/01-12/01
	Detroit PMSA, MI	Y	120770 FQ	135850 AW		MIBLS	10/01-12/01
	Grand Rapids-Muskegon-Holland MSA, MI	Y	107190 FQ	126830 AW		MIBLS	10/01-12/01
	Lansing-East Lansing MSA, MI	Y	61480 FQ	80720 AW	137100 TQ	MIBLS	10/01-12/01
	Minnesota	Y	36090 FQ	92200 AW		MNBLS	10/01-12/01
	Duluth-Superior MSA, MN-WI	Y	119870 FQ	131220 AW		MNBLS	10/01-12/01
	Minneapolis-St. Paul MSA, MN-WI	Y	33650 FQ	71700 AW	129940 TQ	MNBLS	10/01-12/01
	Missouri	Y	44090 FQ	116830 AW		MOBLS	10/01-12/01
	Kansas City MSA, MO-KS	Y	40660 FQ	120370 AW		MOBLS	10/01-12/01
	St. Louis MSA, MO-IL	Y	54030 FQ	120070 AW		MOBLS	10/01-12/01
	Nebraska	Y	34540 FQ	97160 AW		NEBLS	10/01-12/01
	Omaha MSA, NE-IA	Y	35330 FQ	85330 AW	143750 TQ	NEBLS	10/01-12/01
	Nevada	Y	116890 FQ	132790 AW		NVBLS	10/01-12/01
	Las Vegas MSA, NV-AZ	Y	112550 FQ	133040 AW		NVBLS	10/01-12/01
	New Hampshire	Y	106030 FQ	124210 AW	144250 TQ	NHBLS	10/01-12/01
	Portsmouth-Rochester PMSA, NH-ME	Y	118480 FQ	128070 AW	143010 TQ	NHBLS	10/01-12/01
	New Jersey	Y	106100 FQ	131300 AW		NJBLS	10/01-12/01
	Bergen-Passaic PMSA, NJ	Y	102970 FQ	127280 AW		NJBLS	10/01-12/01
	Middlesex-Somerset-Hunterdon PMSA, NJ	Y	96660 FQ	128670 AW		NJBLS	10/01-12/01
	Monmouth-Ocean PMSA, NJ	Y	120270 FQ	134790 AW		NJBLS	10/01-12/01
	Newark PMSA, NJ	Y	101700 FQ	129480 AW		NJBLS	10/01-12/01
	Trenton PMSA, NJ	Y	116700 FQ	131870 AW		NJBLS	10/01-12/01
	New Mexico	Y	72580 FQ	121880 AW		NMBLS	10/01-12/01
	New York	Y	69940 FQ	114220 AW		NYBLS	10/01-12/01
	Albany-Schenectady-Troy MSA, NY	Y	103860 FQ	128550 AW		NYBLS	10/01-12/01
	Binghamton MSA, NY	Y	99310 FQ	118380 AW		NYBLS	10/01-12/01
	Buffalo-Niagara Falls MSA, NY	Y	96480 FQ	116420 AW		NYBLS	10/01-12/01
	Nassau-Suffolk PMSA, NY	Y	83280 FQ	115510 AW		NYBLS	10/01-12/01
	New York PMSA, NY	Y	71160 FQ	114420 AW		NYBLS	10/01-12/01
	Newburgh PMSA, NY-PA	Y	92470 FQ	120820 AW		NYBLS	10/01-12/01
	Rochester MSA, NY	Y	79530 FQ	116630 AW		NYBLS	10/01-12/01
	Syracuse MSA, NY	Y	59460 FQ	94910 AW	140190 TQ	NYBLS	10/01-12/01
	Utica-Rome MSA, NY	Y	97980 FQ	112920 AW	141220 TQ	NYBLS	10/01-12/01
	North Carolina	Y	48350 FQ	117030 AW		NCBLS	10/01-12/01
	Charlotte-Gastonia-Rock Hill MSA, NC-SC	Y	46820 FQ	104940 AW		NCBLS	10/01-12/01
	Greensboro-Winston-Salem-High Point MSA, NC	Y	84120 FQ	129670 AW		NCBLS	10/01-12/01

AAW	Average annual wage	**AOH**	Average offered, high	**ASH**	Average starting, high	**H**	Hourly	**M**	Monthly	**S**	Special: hourly and annual
AE	Average entry wage	**AOL**	Average offered, low	**ASL**	Average starting, low	**HI**	Highest wage paid	**MTC**	Median total compensation	**TQ**	Third quartile wage
AEX	Average experienced wage	**APH**	Average pay, high range	**AW**	Average wage paid	**HR**	High end range	**MW**	Median wage paid	**W**	Weekly
AO	Average offered	**APL**	Average pay, low range	**FQ**	First quartile wage	**LR**	Low end range	**SQ**	Second quartile wage	**Y**	Yearly

Occupation/Type/Industry	Location	Per	Low	Mid	High	Source	Date
Psychiatrist	Raleigh-Durham-Chapel Hill MSA, NC	Y	76100 FQ	104370 AW		NCBLS	10/01-12/01
	North Dakota	Y	123250 FQ	136610 AW		NDBLS	10/01-12/01
	Ohio	Y	85130 FQ	126410 AW		OHBLS	10/01-12/01
	Akron PMSA, OH	Y	107330 FQ	129840 AW		OHBLS	10/01-12/01
	Canton-Massillon MSA, OH	Y	74840 FQ	116760 AW		OHBLS	10/01-12/01
	Cincinnati PMSA, OH-KY-IN	Y	105080 FQ	129270 AW		OHBLS	10/01-12/01
	Cleveland-Lorain-Elyria PMSA, OH	Y	111560 FQ	131210 AW		OHBLS	10/01-12/01
	Columbus MSA, OH	Y	55430 FQ	122710 AW		OHBLS	10/01-12/01
	Dayton-Springfield MSA, OH	Y	97540 FQ	131040 AW		OHBLS	10/01-12/01
	Toledo MSA, OH	Y	80890 FQ	131160 AW		OHBLS	10/01-12/01
	Oklahoma	Y	47350 FQ	116290 AW		OKBLS	10/01-12/01
	Tulsa MSA, OK	Y	88720 FQ	131930 AW		OKBLS	10/01-12/01
	Oregon	Y	99870 FQ	131280 AW		ORBLS	10/01-12/01
	Portland-Vancouver PMSA, OR-WA	Y	116250 FQ	135430 AW		ORBLS	10/01-12/01
	Pennsylvania	Y	62990 FQ	122920 AW		PABLS	10/01-12/01
	Harrisburg-Lebanon-Carlisle MSA, PA	Y	102860 FQ	125170 AW		PABLS	10/01-12/01
	Philadelphia PMSA, PA-NJ	Y	95970 FQ	129520 AW		PABLS	10/01-12/01
	Pittsburgh MSA, PA	Y	48310 FQ	116120 AW		PABLS	10/01-12/01
	Scranton-Wilkes-Barre-Hazleton MSA, PA	Y	52880 FQ	115920 AW		PABLS	10/01-12/01
	Rhode Island	Y	93420 FQ	124130 AW		RIBLS	10/01-12/01
	Providence-Fall River-Warwick MSA, RI-MA	Y	88270 FQ	123750 AW		RIBLS	10/01-12/01
	South Carolina	Y	75060 FQ	94700 AW	131480 TQ	SCBLS	10/01-12/01
	Tennessee	Y	116070 FQ	128600 AW		TNBLS	10/01-12/01
	Knoxville MSA, TN	Y	118930 FQ	130640 AW		TNBLS	10/01-12/01
	Memphis MSA, TN-AR-MS	Y	40960 FQ	114520 AW		TNBLS	10/01-12/01
	Nashville MSA, TN	Y	108830 FQ	133810 AW		TNBLS	10/01-12/01
	Texas	Y	51820 FQ	116260 AW		TXBLS	10/01-12/01
	Austin-San Marcos MSA, TX	Y	92110 FQ	119320 AW		TXBLS	10/01-12/01
	Dallas PMSA, TX	Y	71140 FQ	113180 AW		TXBLS	10/01-12/01
	Fort Worth-Arlington PMSA, TX	Y	39150 FQ	101100 AW		TXBLS	10/01-12/01
	Houston PMSA, TX	Y	51110 FQ	119860 AW		TXBLS	10/01-12/01
	San Antonio MSA, TX	Y	82300 FQ	119330 AW	145330 TQ	TXBLS	10/01-12/01
	Utah	Y	50850 FQ	113140 AW		UTBLS	10/01-12/01
	Provo-Orem MSA, UT	Y	125120 FQ	133450 AW		UTBLS	10/01-12/01
	Salt Lake City-Ogden MSA, UT	Y	36070 FQ	98270 AW	144880 TQ	UTBLS	10/01-12/01
	Vermont	Y	39590 FQ	79900 AW		VTBLS	10/01-12/01
	Burlington MSA, VT	Y	38010 FQ	68330 AW	131770 TQ	VTBLS	10/01-12/01
	Virginia	Y	75640 FQ	111970 AW		VABLS	10/01-12/01
	Norfolk-Virginia Beach-Newport News MSA, VA-NC	Y	86660 FQ	122050 AW		VABLS	10/01-12/01
	Washington	Y	43010 FQ	105130 AW		WABLS	10/01-12/01
	Seattle-Bellevue-Everett PMSA, WA	Y	41550 FQ	100870 AW		WABLS	10/01-12/01
	Spokane MSA, WA	Y	44150 FQ	106560 AW		WABLS	10/01-12/01
	Tacoma PMSA, WA	Y	42770 FQ	102660 AW		WABLS	10/01-12/01
	West Virginia	Y	92660 FQ	129740 AW		WVBLS	10/01-12/01
	Huntington-Ashland MSA, WV-KY-OH	Y	64870 FQ	116270 AW		WVBLS	10/01-12/01
	Wisconsin	Y	23200 FQ	85520 AW		WIBLS	10/01-12/01
	Green Bay MSA, WI	Y	46570 FQ	94040 AW		WIBLS	10/01-12/01
	Milwaukee-Waukesha PMSA, WI	Y	21940 FQ	72700 AW		WIBLS	10/01-12/01
	Racine PMSA, WI	Y	32190 FQ	93520 AW		WIBLS	10/01-12/01
	Puerto Rico	Y	60480 FQ	96340 AW		PRBLS	10/01-12/01
Psychology Teacher							
Postsecondary	Alabama	Y	20610 FQ	49330 AW	85430 TQ	ALBLS	10/01-12/01
Postsecondary	Birmingham MSA, AL	Y	27270 FQ	61320 AW	112210 TQ	ALBLS	10/01-12/01
Postsecondary	Alaska	Y	23250 FQ	47600 AW	78960 TQ	AKBLS	10/01-12/01
Postsecondary	Arkansas	Y	21320 FQ	40220 AW	64600 TQ	ARBLS	10/01-12/01
Postsecondary	California	Y	34900 FQ	66410 AW	105860 TQ	CABLS	10/01-12/01
Postsecondary	Los Angeles-Long Beach PMSA, CA	Y	41370 FQ	67840 AW	107580 TQ	CABLS	10/01-12/01
Postsecondary	Orange County PMSA, CA	Y	35940 FQ	64520 AW	97310 TQ	CABLS	10/01-12/01

AAW Average annual wage; AE Average entry wage; AEX Average experienced wage; AO Average offered; AOH Average offered, high; AOL Average offered, low; APH Average pay, high range; APL Average pay, low range; ASH Average starting, high; ASL Average starting, low; AW Average wage paid; FQ First quartile wage; H Hourly; HI Highest wage paid; HR High end range; LR Low end range; M Monthly; MTC Median total compensation; MW Median wage paid; SQ Second quartile wage; S Special: hourly and annual; TQ Third quartile wage; W Weekly; Y Yearly

Occupation/Type/Industry	Location	Per	Low	Mid	High	Source	Date
Psychology Teacher							
Postsecondary	Riverside-San Bernardino PMSA, CA	Y	39510 FQ	62390 AW	96370 TQ	CABLS	10/01-12/01
Postsecondary	San Diego MSA, CA	Y	25820 FQ	63390 AW	92480 TQ	CABLS	10/01-12/01
Postsecondary	San Francisco PMSA, CA	Y	51960 FQ	77620 AW	114570 TQ	CABLS	10/01-12/01
Postsecondary	San Jose PMSA, CA	Y	48980 FQ	74770 AW	110580 TQ	CABLS	10/01-12/01
Postsecondary	Santa Cruz-Watsonville PMSA, CA	Y	37700 FQ	63140 AW	95040 TQ	CABLS	10/01-12/01
Postsecondary	Colorado	Y	29450 FQ	53340 AW	86220 TQ	COBLS	10/01-12/01
Postsecondary	Denver PMSA, CO	Y	32460 FQ	59720 AW	94120 TQ	COBLS	10/01-12/01
Postsecondary	Connecticut	Y	34640 FQ	64110 AW	99890 TQ	CTBLS	10/01-12/01
Postsecondary	Bridgeport PMSA, CT	Y	38600 FQ	65230 AW	93300 TQ	CTBLS	10/01-12/01
Postsecondary	New Haven-Meriden PMSA, CT	Y	31490 FQ	59310 AW	94030 TQ	CTBLS	10/01-12/01
Postsecondary	Delaware	Y	22570 FQ	69080 AW	101400 TQ	DEBLS	10/01-12/01
Postsecondary	Wilmington-Newark PMSA, DE-MD	Y	34350 FQ	69770 AW	109370 TQ	DEBLS	10/01-12/01
Postsecondary	District of Columbia	Y	34570 FQ	61470 AW	91610 TQ	DCBLS	10/01-12/01
Postsecondary	Washington PMSA, DC-MD-VA-WV	Y	31320 FQ	59710 AW	94410 TQ	DCBLS	10/01-12/01
Postsecondary	Florida	Y	36240 FQ	62590 AW	103730 TQ	FLBLS	10/01-12/01
Postsecondary	Fort Lauderdale PMSA, FL	Y	45140 FQ	57610 AW	76650 TQ	FLBLS	10/01-12/01
Postsecondary	Gainesville MSA, FL	Y	42910 FQ	72110 AW	114820 TQ	FLBLS	10/01-12/01
Postsecondary	Jacksonville MSA, FL	Y	33510 FQ	55720 AW	88290 TQ	FLBLS	10/01-12/01
Postsecondary	Miami PMSA, FL	Y	39380 FQ	63030 AW	96230 TQ	FLBLS	10/01-12/01
Postsecondary	Orlando MSA, FL	Y	26570 FQ	60420 AW	107960 TQ	FLBLS	10/01-12/01
Postsecondary	Pensacola MSA, FL	Y	36940 FQ	64950 AW	109190 TQ	FLBLS	10/01-12/01
Postsecondary	Tallahassee MSA, FL	Y	44760 FQ	70040 AW	109450 TQ	FLBLS	10/01-12/01
Postsecondary	Tampa-St. Petersburg-Clearwater MSA, FL	Y	37400 FQ	61000 AW	104950 TQ	FLBLS	10/01-12/01
Postsecondary	West Palm Beach-Boca Raton MSA, FL	Y	31680 FQ	68790 AW	114130 TQ	FLBLS	10/01-12/01
Postsecondary	Georgia	Y	38650 FQ	59650 AW	86740 TQ	GABLS	10/01-12/01
Postsecondary	Atlanta MSA, GA	Y	41260 FQ	62950 AW	93450 TQ	GABLS	10/01-12/01
Postsecondary	Hawaii	Y	36440 FQ	60030 AW	91560 TQ	HIBLS	10/01-12/01
Postsecondary	Honolulu MSA, HI	Y	37520 FQ	62250 AW	93500 TQ	HIBLS	10/01-12/01
Postsecondary	Illinois	Y	24310 FQ	62880 AW	104210 TQ	ILBLS	10/01-12/01
Postsecondary	Champaign-Urbana MSA, IL	Y	14900 FQ	58400 AW	94030 TQ	ILBLS	10/01-12/01
Postsecondary	Chicago PMSA, IL	Y	28640 FQ	67970 AW	120260 TQ	ILBLS	10/01-12/01
Postsecondary	Indiana	Y	29870 FQ	53790 AW	86400 TQ	INBLS	10/01-12/01
Postsecondary	South Bend MSA, IN	Y	30680 FQ	50850 AW	71660 TQ	INBLS	10/01-12/01
Postsecondary	Iowa	Y	32990 FQ	62430 AW	107900 TQ	IABLS	10/01-12/01
Postsecondary	Des Moines MSA, IA	Y	33250 FQ	53570 AW	73730 TQ	IABLS	10/01-12/01
Postsecondary	Kansas	Y	16040 FQ	34880 AW	57410 TQ	KSBLS	10/01-12/01
Postsecondary	Kentucky	Y	29250 FQ	55070 AW	86890 TQ	KYBLS	10/01-12/01
Postsecondary	Louisville MSA, KY-IN	Y	33560 FQ	60270 AW	89110 TQ	KYBLS	10/01-12/01
Postsecondary	Louisiana	Y	17950 FQ	59920 AW	108110 TQ	LABLS	10/01-12/01
Postsecondary	New Orleans MSA, LA	Y	16390 FQ	66390 AW	111630 TQ	LABLS	10/01-12/01
Postsecondary	Maine	Y	38390 FQ	53980 AW	72490 TQ	MEBLS	10/01-12/01
Postsecondary	Maryland	Y	34700 FQ	60750 AW	97220 TQ	MDBLS	10/01-12/01
Postsecondary	Baltimore PMSA, MD	Y	33680 FQ	58990 AW	92510 TQ	MDBLS	10/01-12/01
Postsecondary	Massachusetts	Y	34690 FQ	61490 AW	106070 TQ	MABLS	10/01-12/01
Postsecondary	Boston PMSA, MA-NH	Y	34500 FQ	65010 AW	116070 TQ	MABLS	10/01-12/01
Postsecondary	Brockton PMSA, MA	Y	29790 FQ	46710 AW	68570 TQ	MABLS	10/01-12/01
Postsecondary	Springfield MSA, MA	Y	33490 FQ	55710 AW	80320 TQ	MABLS	10/01-12/01
Postsecondary	Worcester PMSA, MA-CT	Y	39160 FQ	60680 AW	86310 TQ	MABLS	10/01-12/01
Postsecondary	Michigan	Y	27370 FQ	54470 AW	86470 TQ	MIBLS	10/01-12/01
Postsecondary	Ann Arbor PMSA, MI	Y	25920 FQ	50210 AW	71160 TQ	MIBLS	10/01-12/01
Postsecondary	Detroit PMSA, MI	Y	24540 FQ	44430 AW	71360 TQ	MIBLS	10/01-12/01
Postsecondary	Minnesota	Y	33470 FQ	58020 AW	90340 TQ	MNBLS	10/01-12/01
Postsecondary	Duluth-Superior MSA, MN-WI	Y	39900 FQ	54270 AW	72730 TQ	MNBLS	10/01-12/01
Postsecondary	Minneapolis-St. Paul MSA, MN-WI	Y	38050 FQ	64320 AW	103760 TQ	MNBLS	10/01-12/01
Postsecondary	Mississippi	Y	31860 FQ	47980 AW	66760 TQ	MSBLS	10/01-12/01
Postsecondary	Jackson MSA, MS	Y	13380 FQ	36030 AW	55790 TQ	MSBLS	10/01-12/01
Postsecondary	Missouri	Y	25640 FQ	49430 AW	75030 TQ	MOBLS	10/01-12/01
Postsecondary	Kansas City MSA, MO-KS	Y	26450 FQ	44330 AW	67460 TQ	MOBLS	10/01-12/01
Postsecondary	St. Louis MSA, MO-IL	Y	22430 FQ	50160 AW	84720 TQ	MOBLS	10/01-12/01
Postsecondary	Springfield MSA, MO	Y	39350 FQ	54210 AW	75110 TQ	MOBLS	10/01-12/01
Postsecondary	Montana	Y	28430 FQ	54820 AW	87340 TQ	MTBLS	10/01-12/01
Postsecondary	Nebraska	Y	28820 FQ	50710 AW	74350 TQ	NEBLS	10/01-12/01
Postsecondary	Lincoln MSA, NE	Y	41940 FQ	61220 AW	92850 TQ	NEBLS	10/01-12/01

AAW	Average annual wage	**AOH**	Average offered, high	**ASH**	Average starting, high	**H**	Hourly	**M**	Monthly	**S**	Special: hourly and annual
AE	Average entry wage	**AOL**	Average offered, low	**ASL**	Average starting, low	**HI**	Highest wage paid	**MTC**	Median total compensation	**TQ**	Third quartile wage
AEX	Average experienced wage	**APH**	Average pay, high range	**AW**	Average wage paid	**HR**	High end range	**MW**	Median wage paid	**W**	Weekly
AO	Average offered	**APL**	Average pay, low range	**FQ**	First quartile wage	**LR**	Low end range	**SQ**	Second quartile wage	**Y**	Yearly

Occupation/Type/Industry	Location	Per	Low	Mid	High	Source	Date
Psychology Teacher							
Postsecondary	Omaha MSA, NE-IA	Y	35240 FQ	49260 AW	71160 TQ	NEBLS	10/01-12/01
Postsecondary	Nevada	Y	23600 FQ	52990 AW	91030 TQ	NVBLS	10/01-12/01
Postsecondary	Las Vegas MSA, NV-AZ	Y	22400 FQ	43180 AW	72100 TQ	NVBLS	10/01-12/01
Postsecondary	New Hampshire	Y	36760 FQ	55860 AW	81300 TQ	NHBLS	10/01-12/01
Postsecondary	Manchester PMSA, NH	Y	36710 FQ	45230 AW	55600 TQ	NHBLS	10/01-12/01
Postsecondary	New Jersey	Y	33160 FQ	67500 AW	104410 TQ	NJBLS	10/01-12/01
Postsecondary	Jersey City PMSA, NJ	Y	41950 FQ	76510 AW	115490 TQ	NJBLS	10/01-12/01
Postsecondary	Monmouth-Ocean PMSA, NJ	Y	33570 FQ	62380 AW	93890 TQ	NJBLS	10/01-12/01
Postsecondary	Newark PMSA, NJ	Y	23040 FQ	61920 AW	98250 TQ	NJBLS	10/01-12/01
Postsecondary	New Mexico	Y	28680 FQ	47200 AW	68190 TQ	NMBLS	10/01-12/01
Postsecondary	New York	Y	36860 FQ	59190 AW	100300 TQ	NYBLS	10/01-12/01
Postsecondary	Albany-Schenectady-Troy MSA, NY	Y	39530 FQ	58950 AW	89620 TQ	NYBLS	10/01-12/01
Postsecondary	Dutchess County PMSA, NY	Y	37500 FQ	58910 AW	98700 TQ	NYBLS	10/01-12/01
Postsecondary	Nassau-Suffolk PMSA, NY	Y	32320 FQ	60810 AW	95440 TQ	NYBLS	10/01-12/01
Postsecondary	New York PMSA, NY	Y	37870 FQ	58440 AW	99170 TQ	NYBLS	10/01-12/01
Postsecondary	Rochester MSA, NY	Y	25280 FQ	50440 AW	75090 TQ	NYBLS	10/01-12/01
Postsecondary	Utica-Rome MSA, NY	Y	24310 FQ	48990 AW	72290 TQ	NYBLS	10/01-12/01
Postsecondary	North Carolina	Y	33330 FQ	51290 AW	74390 TQ	NCBLS	10/01-12/01
Postsecondary	Asheville MSA, NC	Y	39940 FQ	54580 AW	70810 TQ	NCBLS	10/01-12/01
Postsecondary	Charlotte-Gastonia-Rock Hill MSA, NC-SC	Y	33700 FQ	51530 AW	73220 TQ	NCBLS	10/01-12/01
Postsecondary	Greensboro-Winston-Salem-High Point MSA, NC	Y	36910 FQ	52130 AW	71840 TQ	NCBLS	10/01-12/01
Postsecondary	Raleigh-Durham-Chapel Hill MSA, NC	Y	33970 FQ	52000 AW	78370 TQ	NCBLS	10/01-12/01
Postsecondary	Wilmington MSA, NC	Y	40830 FQ	59340 AW	86630 TQ	NCBLS	10/01-12/01
Postsecondary	North Dakota	Y	24090 FQ	44830 AW	66170 TQ	NDBLS	10/01-12/01
Postsecondary	Fargo-Moorhead MSA, ND-MN	Y	29610 FQ	51920 AW	75930 TQ	NDBLS	10/01-12/01
Postsecondary	Ohio	Y	28130 FQ	55330 AW	85450 TQ	OHBLS	10/01-12/01
Postsecondary	Cincinnati PMSA, OH-KY-IN	Y	34290 FQ	60200 AW	97500 TQ	OHBLS	10/01-12/01
Postsecondary	Cleveland-Lorain-Elyria PMSA, OH	Y	35840 FQ	61980 AW	96570 TQ	OHBLS	10/01-12/01
Postsecondary	Columbus MSA, OH	Y	39830 FQ	54770 AW	72970 TQ	OHBLS	10/01-12/01
Postsecondary	Dayton-Springfield MSA, OH	Y	18490 FQ	50290 AW	80740 TQ	OHBLS	10/01-12/01
Postsecondary	Toledo MSA, OH	Y	34860 FQ	61140 AW	87890 TQ	OHBLS	10/01-12/01
Postsecondary	Oklahoma	Y	24260 FQ	41100 AW	64210 TQ	OKBLS	10/01-12/01
Postsecondary	Oklahoma City MSA, OK	Y	24570 FQ	40810 AW	65950 TQ	OKBLS	10/01-12/01
Postsecondary	Oregon	Y	33740 FQ	62910 AW	90560 TQ	ORBLS	10/01-12/01
Postsecondary	Portland-Vancouver PMSA, OR-WA	Y	30550 FQ	58080 AW	86990 TQ	ORBLS	10/01-12/01
Postsecondary	Pennsylvania	Y	28690 FQ	64590 AW	120510 TQ	PABLS	10/01-12/01
Postsecondary	Allentown-Bethlehem-Easton MSA, PA	Y	30710 FQ	48130 AW	68060 TQ	PABLS	10/01-12/01
Postsecondary	Philadelphia PMSA, PA-NJ	Y	28890 FQ	67780 AW	127810 TQ	PABLS	10/01-12/01
Postsecondary	Pittsburgh MSA, PA	Y	25950 FQ	63400 AW	125010 TQ	PABLS	10/01-12/01
Postsecondary	Reading MSA, PA	Y	26180 FQ	57170 AW	89460 TQ	PABLS	10/01-12/01
Postsecondary	Scranton-Wilkes-Barre-Hazleton MSA, PA	Y	35410 FQ	56490 AW	85090 TQ	PABLS	10/01-12/01
Postsecondary	Rhode Island	Y	35340 FQ	61010 AW	91340 TQ	RIBLS	10/01-12/01
Postsecondary	South Carolina	Y	25500 FQ	46090 AW	68370 TQ	SCBLS	10/01-12/01
Postsecondary	Greenville-Spartanburg-Anderson MSA, SC	Y	27980 FQ	49030 AW	75330 TQ	SCBLS	10/01-12/01
Postsecondary	South Dakota	Y	28750 FQ	47810 AW	71340 TQ	SDBLS	10/01-12/01
Postsecondary	Tennessee	Y	31100 FQ	55050 AW	85750 TQ	TNBLS	10/01-12/01
Postsecondary	Chattanooga MSA, TN-GA	Y	30470 FQ	47460 AW	62060 TQ	TNBLS	10/01-12/01
Postsecondary	Johnson City-Kingsport-Bristol MSA, TN-VA	Y	22000 FQ	60000 AW	126070 TQ	TNBLS	10/01-12/01
Postsecondary	Knoxville MSA, TN	Y	31980 FQ	50210 AW	76600 TQ	TNBLS	10/01-12/01
Postsecondary	Memphis MSA, TN-AR-MS	Y	36430 FQ	61240 AW	93630 TQ	TNBLS	10/01-12/01
Postsecondary	Nashville MSA, TN	Y	36220 FQ	57040 AW	84290 TQ	TNBLS	10/01-12/01
Postsecondary	Texas	Y	24210 FQ	53400 AW	80440 TQ	TXBLS	10/01-12/01
Postsecondary	Austin-San Marcos MSA, TX	Y	37600 FQ	57850 AW	75590 TQ	TXBLS	10/01-12/01
Postsecondary	Dallas PMSA, TX	Y	19740 FQ	55150 AW	106530 TQ	TXBLS	10/01-12/01
Postsecondary	Fort Worth-Arlington PMSA, TX	Y	26570 FQ	55980 AW	80570 TQ	TXBLS	10/01-12/01
Postsecondary	Houston PMSA, TX	Y	39400 FQ	62040 AW	110900 TQ	TXBLS	10/01-12/01
Postsecondary	San Antonio MSA, TX	Y	30700 FQ	54180 AW	81040 TQ	TXBLS	10/01-12/01
Postsecondary	Utah	Y	39130 FQ	60900 AW	94450 TQ	UTBLS	10/01-12/01

AAW	Average annual wage	**AOH**	Average offered, high	**ASH**	Average starting, high	**H**	Hourly	**M**	Monthly	**S**	Special: hourly and annual
AE	Average entry wage	**AOL**	Average offered, low	**ASL**	Average starting, low	**HI**	Highest wage paid	**MTC**	Median total compensation	**TQ**	Third quartile wage
AEX	Average experienced wage	**APH**	Average pay, high range	**AW**	Average wage paid	**HR**	High end range	**MW**	Median wage paid	**W**	Weekly
AO	Average offered	**APL**	Average pay, low range	**FQ**	First quartile wage	**LR**	Low end range	**SQ**	Second quartile wage	**Y**	Yearly

Occupation/Type/Industry	Location	Per	Low	Mid	High	Source	Date
Psychology Teacher							
Postsecondary	Salt Lake City-Ogden MSA, UT	Y	38560 FQ	58290 AW	101950 TQ	UTBLS	10/01-12/01
Postsecondary	Vermont	Y	36090 FQ	57090 AW	89160 TQ	VTBLS	10/01-12/01
Postsecondary	Burlington MSA, VT	Y	34320 FQ	61960 AW	99950 TQ	VTBLS	10/01-12/01
Postsecondary	Virginia	Y	23760 FQ	53460 AW	88740 TQ	VABLS	10/01-12/01
Postsecondary	Norfolk-Virginia Beach-Newport News MSA, VA-NC	Y	40100 FQ	62080 AW	88630 TQ	VABLS	10/01-12/01
Postsecondary	Richmond-Petersburg MSA, VA	Y	17260 FQ	47530 AW	84540 TQ	VABLS	10/01-12/01
Postsecondary	Roanoke MSA, VA	Y	33010 FQ	56350 AW	90950 TQ	VABLS	10/01-12/01
Postsecondary	Washington	Y	25830 FQ	53590 AW	85060 TQ	WABLS	10/01-12/01
Postsecondary	Seattle-Bellevue-Everett PMSA, WA	Y	32520 FQ	60810 AW	93630 TQ	WABLS	10/01-12/01
Postsecondary	Tacoma PMSA, WA	Y	30020 FQ	54550 AW	85640 TQ	WABLS	10/01-12/01
Postsecondary	West Virginia	Y	26560 FQ	53380 AW	83350 TQ	WVBLS	10/01-12/01
Postsecondary	Wisconsin	Y	27580 FQ	46720 AW	69860 TQ	WIBLS	10/01-12/01
Postsecondary	Appleton-Oshkosh-Neenah MSA, WI	Y	25760 FQ	47250 AW	65520 TQ	WIBLS	10/01-12/01
Postsecondary	Milwaukee-Waukesha PMSA, WI	Y	19560 FQ	39710 AW	62880 TQ	WIBLS	10/01-12/01
Postsecondary	Wyoming	Y	40640 FQ	58330 AW	82090 TQ	WYBLS	10/01-12/01
Postsecondary	Puerto Rico	Y	25040 FQ	50740 AW	93840 TQ	PRBLS	10/01-12/01
Public Relations Manager	Alabama	Y	25250 FQ	47750 AW	82350 TQ	ALBLS	10/01-12/01
	Birmingham MSA, AL	Y	24240 FQ	49490 AW	88680 TQ	ALBLS	10/01-12/01
	Huntsville MSA, AL	Y	27670 FQ	56530 AW	89570 TQ	ALBLS	10/01-12/01
	Mobile MSA, AL	Y	26420 FQ	41440 AW	62620 TQ	ALBLS	10/01-12/01
	Montgomery MSA, AL	Y	26400 FQ	49690 AW	84520 TQ	ALBLS	10/01-12/01
	Alaska	Y	29000 FQ	71610 AW		AKBLS	10/01-12/01
	Anchorage MSA, AK	Y	36970 FQ	79910 AW		AKBLS	10/01-12/01
	Arizona	Y	30440 FQ	59560 AW	95190 TQ	AZBLS	10/01-12/01
	Phoenix-Mesa MSA, AZ	Y	29710 FQ	61940 AW	99330 TQ	AZBLS	10/01-12/01
	Tucson MSA, AZ	Y	31680 FQ	53480 AW	82660 TQ	AZBLS	10/01-12/01
	Arkansas	Y	27720 FQ	52160 AW	88950 TQ	ARBLS	10/01-12/01
	Fayetteville-Springdale-Rogers MSA, AR	Y	26560 FQ	55680 AW	103560 TQ	ARBLS	10/01-12/01
	Little Rock-North Little Rock MSA, AR	Y	29820 FQ	57710 AW	102710 TQ	ARBLS	10/01-12/01
	California	Y	39480 FQ	73510 AW	120610 TQ	CABLS	10/01-12/01
	Bakersfield MSA, CA	Y	45120 FQ	75690 AW	138840 TQ	CABLS	10/01-12/01
	Fresno MSA, CA	Y	35650 FQ	68750 AW	118030 TQ	CABLS	10/01-12/01
	Los Angeles-Long Beach PMSA, CA	Y	45050 FQ	71530 AW	110700 TQ	CABLS	10/01-12/01
	Modesto MSA, CA	Y	34200 FQ	58220 AW	87760 TQ	CABLS	10/01-12/01
	Oakland PMSA, CA	Y	39250 FQ	81580 AW	137510 TQ	CABLS	10/01-12/01
	Orange County PMSA, CA	Y	41010 FQ	78500 AW		CABLS	10/01-12/01
	Riverside-San Bernardino PMSA, CA	Y	33310 FQ	55940 AW	86050 TQ	CABLS	10/01-12/01
	Sacramento PMSA, CA	Y	32470 FQ	80490 AW		CABLS	10/01-12/01
	Salinas MSA, CA	Y	32790 FQ	60300 AW	92170 TQ	CABLS	10/01-12/01
	San Diego MSA, CA	Y	35430 FQ	64480 AW	95790 TQ	CABLS	10/01-12/01
	San Francisco PMSA, CA	Y	42780 FQ	77650 AW	117890 TQ	CABLS	10/01-12/01
	San Jose PMSA, CA	Y	52850 FQ	88660 AW	145170 TQ	CABLS	10/01-12/01
	Santa Barbara-Santa Maria-Lompoc MSA, CA	Y	31860 FQ	52260 AW	79320 TQ	CABLS	10/01-12/01
	Santa Cruz-Watsonville PMSA, CA	Y	23660 FQ	69330 AW	133360 TQ	CABLS	10/01-12/01
	Santa Rosa PMSA, CA	Y	35240 FQ	64870 AW	100530 TQ	CABLS	10/01-12/01
	Stockton-Lodi MSA, CA	Y	36000 FQ	66760 AW	111810 TQ	CABLS	10/01-12/01
	Vallejo-Fairfield-Napa PMSA, CA	Y	43020 FQ	74660 AW		CABLS	10/01-12/01
	Ventura PMSA, CA	Y	27200 FQ	55780 AW	86990 TQ	CABLS	10/01-12/01
	Colorado	Y	29510 FQ	67420 AW	131920 TQ	COBLS	10/01-12/01
	Boulder-Longmont PMSA, CO	Y	31250 FQ	89700 AW	142090 TQ	COBLS	10/01-12/01
	Colorado Springs MSA, CO	Y	29910 FQ	74560 AW		COBLS	10/01-12/01
	Denver PMSA, CO	Y	29520 FQ	63200 AW	109410 TQ	COBLS	10/01-12/01
	Fort Collins-Loveland MSA, CO	Y	26420 FQ	45790 AW	80100 TQ	COBLS	10/01-12/01
	Greeley PMSA, CO	Y	23640 FQ	65140 AW	97130 TQ	COBLS	10/01-12/01
	Connecticut	Y	41260 FQ	74140 AW	124740 TQ	CTBLS	10/01-12/01
	Bridgeport PMSA, CT	Y	46290 FQ	86230 AW		CTBLS	10/01-12/01

AAW	Average annual wage	**AOH**	Average offered, high	**ASH**	Average starting, high	**H**	Hourly	**M**	Monthly	**S**	Special: hourly and annual
AE	Average entry wage	**AOL**	Average offered, low	**ASL**	Average starting, low	**HI**	Highest wage paid	**MTC**	Median total compensation	**TQ**	Third quartile wage
AEX	Average experienced wage	**APH**	Average pay, high range	**AW**	Average wage paid	**HR**	High end range	**MW**	Median wage paid	**W**	Weekly
AO	Average offered	**APL**	Average pay, low range	**FQ**	First quartile wage	**LR**	Low end range	**SQ**	Second quartile wage	**Y**	Yearly

Occupation/Type/Industry	Location	Per	Low	Mid	High	Source	Date
Public Relations Manager	Hartford MSA, CT	Y	41590 FQ	70860 AW	113290 TQ	CTBLS	10/01-12/01
	New Haven-Meriden PMSA, CT	Y	39910 FQ	67570 AW	106830 TQ	CTBLS	10/01-12/01
	New London-Norwich MSA, CT-RI	Y	52320 FQ	88480 AW	141420 TQ	CTBLS	10/01-12/01
	Stamford-Norwalk PMSA, CT	Y	41460 FQ	79850 AW	137170 TQ	CTBLS	10/01-12/01
	Delaware	Y	33260 FQ	64030 AW	111280 TQ	DEBLS	10/01-12/01
	Wilmington-Newark PMSA, DE-MD	Y	33780 FQ	63550 AW	108460 TQ	DEBLS	10/01-12/01
	District of Columbia	Y	44900 FQ	74930 AW	123700 TQ	DCBLS	10/01-12/01
	Washington PMSA, DC-MD-VA-WV	Y	41640 FQ	74380 AW	116560 TQ	DCBLS	10/01-12/01
	Florida	Y	36270 FQ	71780 AW	136010 TQ	FLBLS	10/01-12/01
	Daytona Beach MSA, FL	Y	33950 FQ	63850 AW	108370 TQ	FLBLS	10/01-12/01
	Fort Lauderdale PMSA, FL	Y	40660 FQ	80260 AW		FLBLS	10/01-12/01
	Fort Myers-Cape Coral MSA, FL	Y	31440 FQ	64400 AW	134180 TQ	FLBLS	10/01-12/01
	Fort Pierce-Port St. Lucie MSA, FL	Y	39610 FQ	57650 AW	89820 TQ	FLBLS	10/01-12/01
	Gainesville MSA, FL	Y	43350 FQ	62990 AW	88600 TQ	FLBLS	10/01-12/01
	Jacksonville MSA, FL	Y	37930 FQ	63380 AW	92050 TQ	FLBLS	10/01-12/01
	Lakeland-Winter Haven MSA, FL	Y	35330 FQ	57920 AW	91690 TQ	FLBLS	10/01-12/01
	Melbourne-Titusville-Palm Bay MSA, FL	Y	31730 FQ	56590 AW	95800 TQ	FLBLS	10/01-12/01
	Miami PMSA, FL	Y	38270 FQ	70160 AW	110370 TQ	FLBLS	10/01-12/01
	Naples MSA, FL	Y	39760 FQ	70030 AW	110440 TQ	FLBLS	10/01-12/01
	Orlando MSA, FL	Y	36980 FQ	66480 AW	114260 TQ	FLBLS	10/01-12/01
	Pensacola MSA, FL	Y	28300 FQ	51360 AW	86940 TQ	FLBLS	10/01-12/01
	Sarasota-Bradenton MSA, FL	Y	34480 FQ	65800 AW	109720 TQ	FLBLS	10/01-12/01
	Tallahassee MSA, FL	Y	50810 FQ	94400 AW		FLBLS	10/01-12/01
	Tampa-St. Petersburg-Clearwater MSA, FL	Y	28780 FQ	64300 AW	121770 TQ	FLBLS	10/01-12/01
	West Palm Beach-Boca Raton MSA, FL	Y	32550 FQ	86030 AW		FLBLS	10/01-12/01
	Georgia	Y	31300 FQ	61040 AW	107220 TQ	GABLS	10/01-12/01
	Atlanta MSA, GA	Y	31560 FQ	63850 AW	111820 TQ	GABLS	10/01-12/01
	Augusta-Aiken MSA, GA-SC	Y	27080 FQ	62460 AW	97270 TQ	GABLS	10/01-12/01
	Macon MSA, GA	Y	31100 FQ	53590 AW	82780 TQ	GABLS	10/01-12/01
	Hawaii	Y	36800 FQ	53300 AW	79750 TQ	HIBLS	10/01-12/01
	Honolulu MSA, HI	Y	37010 FQ	52810 AW	79730 TQ	HIBLS	10/01-12/01
	Idaho	Y	24860 FQ	45280 AW	74980 TQ	IDBLS	10/01-12/01
	Boise City MSA, ID	Y	30590 FQ	49390 AW	78230 TQ	IDBLS	10/01-12/01
	Illinois	Y	27060 FQ	62440 AW	121630 TQ	ILBLS	10/01-12/01
	Champaign-Urbana MSA, IL	Y	25950 FQ	53530 AW	94520 TQ	ILBLS	10/01-12/01
	Chicago PMSA, IL	Y	32210 FQ	68200 AW	130940 TQ	ILBLS	10/01-12/01
	Peoria-Pekin MSA, IL	Y	20110 FQ	41490 AW	67120 TQ	ILBLS	10/01-12/01
	Rockford MSA, IL	Y	28580 FQ	50710 AW	79730 TQ	ILBLS	10/01-12/01
	Springfield MSA, IL	Y	32850 FQ	54900 AW	81420 TQ	ILBLS	10/01-12/01
	Indiana	Y	26790 FQ	50230 AW	83120 TQ	INBLS	10/01-12/01
	Evansville-Henderson MSA, IN-KY	Y	29520 FQ	42570 AW	69780 TQ	INBLS	10/01-12/01
	Fort Wayne MSA, IN	Y	25090 FQ	40100 AW	62140 TQ	INBLS	10/01-12/01
	Gary PMSA, IN	Y	26790 FQ	55580 AW	85480 TQ	INBLS	10/01-12/01
	Indianapolis MSA, IN	Y	30850 FQ	57400 AW	92350 TQ	INBLS	10/01-12/01
	South Bend MSA, IN	Y	28610 FQ	44800 AW	67130 TQ	INBLS	10/01-12/01
	Iowa	Y	26340 FQ	53050 AW	92060 TQ	IABLS	10/01-12/01
	Davenport-Moline-Rock Island MSA, IA-IL	Y	24830 FQ	51200 AW	88950 TQ	IABLS	10/01-12/01
	Des Moines MSA, IA	Y	31260 FQ	59850 AW	111050 TQ	IABLS	10/01-12/01
	Kansas	Y	29770 FQ	58850 AW	105270 TQ	KSBLS	10/01-12/01
	Topeka MSA, KS	Y	31690 FQ	57570 AW	88140 TQ	KSBLS	10/01-12/01
	Wichita MSA, KS	Y	29540 FQ	56910 AW	102880 TQ	KSBLS	10/01-12/01
	Kentucky	Y	30070 FQ	54370 AW	86040 TQ	KYBLS	10/01-12/01
	Lexington MSA, KY	Y	29420 FQ	56760 AW	94990 TQ	KYBLS	10/01-12/01
	Louisville MSA, KY-IN	Y	33600 FQ	55360 AW	86000 TQ	KYBLS	10/01-12/01
	Louisiana	Y	25440 FQ	49010 AW	82170 TQ	LABLS	10/01-12/01
	Baton Rouge MSA, LA	Y	30010 FQ	51920 AW	84160 TQ	LABLS	10/01-12/01
	Lafayette MSA, LA	Y	20000 FQ	36140 AW	62400 TQ	LABLS	10/01-12/01
	Lake Charles MSA, LA	Y	24880 FQ	49250 AW	92630 TQ	LABLS	10/01-12/01
	New Orleans MSA, LA	Y	21120 FQ	45370 AW	72580 TQ	LABLS	10/01-12/01

AAW	Average annual wage	**AOH**	Average offered, high	**ASH**	Average starting, high	**H**	Hourly	**M**	Monthly	**S**	Special: hourly and annual
AE	Average entry wage	**AOL**	Average offered, low	**ASL**	Average starting, low	**HI**	Highest wage paid	**MTC**	Median total compensation	**TQ**	Third quartile wage
AEX	Average experienced wage	**APH**	Average pay, high range	**AW**	Average wage paid	**HR**	High end range	**MW**	Median wage paid	**W**	Weekly
AO	Average offered	**APL**	Average pay, low range	**FQ**	First quartile wage	**LR**	Low end range	**SQ**	Second quartile wage	**Y**	Yearly

Occupation/Type/Industry	Location	Per	Low	Mid	High	Source	Date
Public Relations Manager	Shreveport-Bossier City MSA, LA	Y	26140 FQ	51900 AW	88030 TQ	LABLS	10/01-12/01
	Maine	Y	28630 FQ	48390 AW	76010 TQ	MEBLS	10/01-12/01
	Portland MSA, ME	Y	30020 FQ	51310 AW	91550 TQ	MEBLS	10/01-12/01
	Maryland	Y	37670 FQ	64730 AW	104740 TQ	MDBLS	10/01-12/01
	Baltimore PMSA, MD	Y	36840 FQ	61200 AW	96190 TQ	MDBLS	10/01-12/01
	Massachusetts	Y	39730 FQ	60920 AW	95710 TQ	MABLS	10/01-12/01
	Boston PMSA, MA-NH	Y	44830 FQ	61690 AW	96440 TQ	MABLS	10/01-12/01
	Brockton PMSA, MA	Y	44770 FQ	72860 AW	125250 TQ	MABLS	10/01-12/01
	Lawrence PMSA, MA-NH	Y	33140 FQ	64380 AW	88510 TQ	MABLS	10/01-12/01
	Lowell PMSA, MA-NH	Y	23880 FQ	44020 AW	80430 TQ	MABLS	10/01-12/01
	Springfield MSA, MA	Y	32880 FQ	56590 AW	97340 TQ	MABLS	10/01-12/01
	Worcester PMSA, MA-CT	Y	31590 FQ	62150 AW	120700 TQ	MABLS	10/01-12/01
	Michigan	Y	38780 FQ	72380 AW	129640 TQ	MIBLS	10/01-12/01
	Ann Arbor PMSA, MI	Y	33740 FQ	83150 AW	135250 TQ	MIBLS	10/01-12/01
	Detroit PMSA, MI	Y	45560 FQ	78460 AW		MIBLS	10/01-12/01
	Grand Rapids-Muskegon-Holland MSA, MI	Y	38330 FQ	66840 AW	111990 TQ	MIBLS	10/01-12/01
	Kalamazoo-Battle Creek MSA, MI	Y	32930 FQ	61090 AW	93710 TQ	MIBLS	10/01-12/01
	Lansing-East Lansing MSA, MI	Y	35170 FQ	64870 AW	110500 TQ	MIBLS	10/01-12/01
	Minnesota	Y	42370 FQ	68670 AW	110710 TQ	MNBLS	10/01-12/01
	Minneapolis-St. Paul MSA, MN-WI	Y	44220 FQ	69440 AW	112170 TQ	MNBLS	10/01-12/01
	Mississippi	Y	23650 FQ	40890 AW	66520 TQ	MSBLS	10/01-12/01
	Biloxi-Gulfport-Pascagoula MSA, MS	Y	22460 FQ	46810 AW	87610 TQ	MSBLS	10/01-12/01
	Jackson MSA, MS	Y	24400 FQ	37920 AW	56880 TQ	MSBLS	10/01-12/01
	Missouri	Y	29690 FQ	56610 AW	91280 TQ	MOBLS	10/01-12/01
	Kansas City MSA, MO-KS	Y	33040 FQ	62930 AW	100980 TQ	MOBLS	10/01-12/01
	St. Louis MSA, MO-IL	Y	31750 FQ	61260 AW	101370 TQ	MOBLS	10/01-12/01
	Springfield MSA, MO	Y	23030 FQ	48420 AW	89200 TQ	MOBLS	10/01-12/01
	Montana	Y	20160 FQ	39360 AW	67340 TQ	MTBLS	10/01-12/01
	Billings MSA, MT	Y	18730 FQ	37300 AW	63740 TQ	MTBLS	10/01-12/01
	Nebraska	Y	29020 FQ	55460 AW	85410 TQ	NEBLS	10/01-12/01
	Lincoln MSA, NE	Y	33850 FQ	57930 AW	76730 TQ	NEBLS	10/01-12/01
	Omaha MSA, NE-IA	Y	28210 FQ	54960 AW	90100 TQ	NEBLS	10/01-12/01
	Nevada	Y	29800 FQ	62740 AW	107240 TQ	NVBLS	10/01-12/01
	Las Vegas MSA, NV-AZ	Y	29770 FQ	63880 AW	109980 TQ	NVBLS	10/01-12/01
	Reno MSA, NV	Y	31970 FQ	61770 AW	90270 TQ	NVBLS	10/01-12/01
	New Hampshire	Y	34810 FQ	60450 AW	94920 TQ	NHBLS	10/01-12/01
	Manchester PMSA, NH	Y	31520 FQ	58300 AW	91030 TQ	NHBLS	10/01-12/01
	Nashua PMSA, NH	Y	39810 FQ	76450 AW	114350 TQ	NHBLS	10/01-12/01
	Portsmouth-Rochester PMSA, NH-ME	Y	40900 FQ	62760 AW	88170 TQ	NHBLS	10/01-12/01
	New Jersey	Y	43940 FQ	82230 AW	134250 TQ	NJBLS	10/01-12/01
	Atlantic-Cape May PMSA, NJ	Y	43580 FQ	77420 AW	121930 TQ	NJBLS	10/01-12/01
	Bergen-Passaic PMSA, NJ	Y	48410 FQ	80990 AW	129980 TQ	NJBLS	10/01-12/01
	Jersey City PMSA, NJ	Y	45560 FQ	84260 AW	143530 TQ	NJBLS	10/01-12/01
	Middlesex-Somerset-Hunterdon PMSA, NJ	Y	42650 FQ	82370 AW	134340 TQ	NJBLS	10/01-12/01
	Monmouth-Ocean PMSA, NJ	Y	39680 FQ	70520 AW	120800 TQ	NJBLS	10/01-12/01
	Newark PMSA, NJ	Y	42480 FQ	86770 AW	145210 TQ	NJBLS	10/01-12/01
	Trenton PMSA, NJ	Y	56180 FQ	85920 AW	124410 TQ	NJBLS	10/01-12/01
	New Mexico	Y	29510 FQ	55620 AW	92280 TQ	NMBLS	10/01-12/01
	Albuquerque MSA, NM	Y	31190 FQ	56640 AW	90280 TQ	NMBLS	10/01-12/01
	New York	Y	42410 FQ	81430 AW		NYBLS	10/01-12/01
	Albany-Schenectady-Troy MSA, NY	Y	34070 FQ	70460 AW	117620 TQ	NYBLS	10/01-12/01
	Buffalo-Niagara Falls MSA, NY	Y	32650 FQ	59400 AW	101160 TQ	NYBLS	10/01-12/01
	Dutchess County PMSA, NY	Y	42370 FQ	63650 AW	87050 TQ	NYBLS	10/01-12/01
	Nassau-Suffolk PMSA, NY	Y	40760 FQ	77370 AW		NYBLS	10/01-12/01
	New York PMSA, NY	Y	46180 FQ	87500 AW		NYBLS	10/01-12/01
	Rochester MSA, NY	Y	36600 FQ	66950 AW	107110 TQ	NYBLS	10/01-12/01
	Syracuse MSA, NY	Y	36820 FQ	62420 AW	96480 TQ	NYBLS	10/01-12/01
	Utica-Rome MSA, NY	Y	36690 FQ	61810 AW	110320 TQ	NYBLS	10/01-12/01
	North Carolina	Y	26870 FQ	56120 AW	95940 TQ	NCBLS	10/01-12/01
	Asheville MSA, NC	Y	29080 FQ	45130 AW	69280 TQ	NCBLS	10/01-12/01
	Charlotte-Gastonia-Rock Hill MSA, NC-SC	Y	33210 FQ	66880 AW	133980 TQ	NCBLS	10/01-12/01
	Fayetteville MSA, NC	Y	26420 FQ	49440 AW	84960 TQ	NCBLS	10/01-12/01

AAW Average annual wage; **AE** Average entry wage; **AEX** Average experienced wage; **AO** Average offered; **AOH** Average offered, high; **AOL** Average offered, low; **APH** Average pay, high range; **APL** Average pay, low range; **ASH** Average starting, high; **ASL** Average starting, low; **AW** Average wage paid; **FQ** First quartile wage; **H** Hourly; **HI** Highest wage paid; **HR** High end range; **LR** Low end range; **M** Monthly; **MTC** Median total compensation; **MW** Median wage paid; **SQ** Second quartile wage; **S** Special: hourly and annual; **TQ** Third quartile wage; **W** Weekly; **Y** Yearly

Occupation/Type/Industry	Location	Per	Low	Mid	High	Source	Date
Public Relations Manager	Greensboro-Winston-Salem-High Point MSA, NC	Y	25180 FQ	61090 AW	99450 TQ	NCBLS	10/01-12/01
	Hickory-Morganton-Lenoir MSA, NC	Y	26680 FQ	47420 AW	74950 TQ	NCBLS	10/01-12/01
	Raleigh-Durham-Chapel Hill MSA, NC	Y	29010 FQ	55820 AW	96430 TQ	NCBLS	10/01-12/01
	Wilmington MSA, NC	Y	29590 FQ	49950 AW	75140 TQ	NCBLS	10/01-12/01
	North Dakota	Y	23530 FQ	42810 AW	73650 TQ	NDBLS	10/01-12/01
	Fargo-Moorhead MSA, ND-MN	Y	28320 FQ	55610 AW	87240 TQ	NDBLS	10/01-12/01
	Ohio	Y	30910 FQ	58680 AW	96690 TQ	OHBLS	10/01-12/01
	Akron PMSA, OH	Y	31890 FQ	61670 AW	98150 TQ	OHBLS	10/01-12/01
	Canton-Massillon MSA, OH	Y	28290 FQ	51050 AW	83350 TQ	OHBLS	10/01-12/01
	Cincinnati PMSA, OH-KY-IN	Y	32670 FQ	58160 AW	91510 TQ	OHBLS	10/01-12/01
	Cleveland-Lorain-Elyria PMSA, OH	Y	32340 FQ	68260 AW		OHBLS	10/01-12/01
	Columbus MSA, OH	Y	32510 FQ	56330 AW	90550 TQ	OHBLS	10/01-12/01
	Dayton-Springfield MSA, OH	Y	29670 FQ	56410 AW	86550 TQ	OHBLS	10/01-12/01
	Toledo MSA, OH	Y	29190 FQ	58250 AW	91690 TQ	OHBLS	10/01-12/01
	Youngstown-Warren MSA, OH	Y	26090 FQ	42780 AW	72300 TQ	OHBLS	10/01-12/01
	Oklahoma	Y	25900 FQ	46350 AW	72830 TQ	OKBLS	10/01-12/01
	Oklahoma City MSA, OK	Y	24710 FQ	47060 AW	72380 TQ	OKBLS	10/01-12/01
	Tulsa MSA, OK	Y	26240 FQ	47570 AW	80410 TQ	OKBLS	10/01-12/01
	Oregon	Y	33860 FQ	65840 AW	109270 TQ	ORBLS	10/01-12/01
	Eugene-Springfield MSA, OR	Y	25570 FQ	58240 AW	91710 TQ	ORBLS	10/01-12/01
	Portland-Vancouver PMSA, OR-WA	Y	38930 FQ	71490 AW	118340 TQ	ORBLS	10/01-12/01
	Salem PMSA, OR	Y	21380 FQ	45590 AW	68020 TQ	ORBLS	10/01-12/01
	Pennsylvania	Y	30270 FQ	56800 AW	93840 TQ	PABLS	10/01-12/01
	Allentown-Bethlehem-Easton MSA, PA	Y	29370 FQ	52980 AW	85170 TQ	PABLS	10/01-12/01
	Erie MSA, PA	Y	22300 FQ	43610 AW	70920 TQ	PABLS	10/01-12/01
	Harrisburg-Lebanon-Carlisle MSA, PA	Y	32620 FQ	61190 AW	102970 TQ	PABLS	10/01-12/01
	Lancaster MSA, PA	Y	27010 FQ	43810 AW	67220 TQ	PABLS	10/01-12/01
	Philadelphia PMSA, PA-NJ	Y	37270 FQ	64720 AW	107140 TQ	PABLS	10/01-12/01
	Pittsburgh MSA, PA	Y	31440 FQ	55290 AW	87780 TQ	PABLS	10/01-12/01
	Reading MSA, PA	Y	27790 FQ	49500 AW	70950 TQ	PABLS	10/01-12/01
	Scranton-Wilkes-Barre-Hazleton MSA, PA	Y	22820 FQ	46760 AW	69780 TQ	PABLS	10/01-12/01
	York MSA, PA	Y	26320 FQ	43510 AW	72870 TQ	PABLS	10/01-12/01
	Rhode Island	Y	40580 FQ	79020 AW	136350 TQ	RIBLS	10/01-12/01
	Providence-Fall River-Warwick MSA, RI-MA	Y	36140 FQ	74900 AW	132910 TQ	RIBLS	10/01-12/01
	South Carolina	Y	28040 FQ	48140 AW	79540 TQ	SCBLS	10/01-12/01
	Charleston-North Charleston MSA, SC	Y	29910 FQ	47440 AW	78380 TQ	SCBLS	10/01-12/01
	Columbia MSA, SC	Y	27840 FQ	44340 AW	67400 TQ	SCBLS	10/01-12/01
	Greenville-Spartanburg-Anderson MSA, SC	Y	28540 FQ	48970 AW	79240 TQ	SCBLS	10/01-12/01
	Myrtle Beach MSA, SC	Y	25450 FQ	42810 AW	59210 TQ	SCBLS	10/01-12/01
	South Dakota	Y	47230 FQ	65050 AW	88920 TQ	SDBLS	10/01-12/01
	Sioux Falls MSA, SD	Y	48680 FQ	65940 AW	93760 TQ	SDBLS	10/01-12/01
	Tennessee	Y	23650 FQ	49880 AW	85670 TQ	TNBLS	10/01-12/01
	Chattanooga MSA, TN-GA	Y	25960 FQ	40010 AW	61090 TQ	TNBLS	10/01-12/01
	Johnson City-Kingsport-Bristol MSA, TN-VA	Y	17780 FQ	34330 AW	57940 TQ	TNBLS	10/01-12/01
	Knoxville MSA, TN	Y	26390 FQ	57150 AW	114170 TQ	TNBLS	10/01-12/01
	Memphis MSA, TN-AR-MS	Y	24910 FQ	55000 AW	101990 TQ	TNBLS	10/01-12/01
	Nashville MSA, TN	Y	32000 FQ	54640 AW	86170 TQ	TNBLS	10/01-12/01
	Texas	Y	25990 FQ	58080 AW	98400 TQ	TXBLS	10/01-12/01
	Amarillo MSA, TX	Y	24040 FQ	49440 AW	76690 TQ	TXBLS	10/01-12/01
	Austin-San Marcos MSA, TX	Y	30260 FQ	59980 AW	96890 TQ	TXBLS	10/01-12/01
	Beaumont-Port Arthur MSA, TX	Y	28800 FQ	53340 AW	96890 TQ	TXBLS	10/01-12/01
	Corpus Christi MSA, TX	Y	29310 FQ	55660 AW	96570 TQ	TXBLS	10/01-12/01
	Dallas PMSA, TX	Y	35100 FQ	70040 AW	113000 TQ	TXBLS	10/01-12/01
	El Paso MSA, TX	Y	31750 FQ	59310 AW	107500 TQ	TXBLS	10/01-12/01
	Fort Worth-Arlington PMSA, TX	Y	27980 FQ	63000 AW	121220 TQ	TXBLS	10/01-12/01
	Galveston-Texas City PMSA, TX	Y	22050 FQ	39270 AW	68720 TQ	TXBLS	10/01-12/01

AAW	Average annual wage	**AOH**	Average offered, high	**ASH**	Average starting, high	**H**	Hourly	**M**	Monthly	**S**	Special: hourly and annual
AE	Average entry wage	**AOL**	Average offered, low	**ASL**	Average starting, low	**HI**	Highest wage paid	**MTC**	Median total compensation	**TQ**	Third quartile wage
AEX	Average experienced wage	**APH**	Average pay, high range	**AW**	Average wage paid	**HR**	High end range	**MW**	Median wage paid	**W**	Weekly
AO	Average offered	**APL**	Average pay, low range	**FQ**	First quartile wage	**LR**	Low end range	**SQ**	Second quartile wage	**Y**	Yearly

Occupation/Type/Industry	Location	Per	Low	Mid	High	Source	Date
Public Relations Manager	Houston PMSA, TX	Y	20950 FQ	52170 AW	90470 TQ	TXBLS	10/01-12/01
	Longview-Marshall MSA, TX	Y	30010 FQ	73280 AW	124030 TQ	TXBLS	10/01-12/01
	Lubbock MSA, TX	Y	20560 FQ	45890 AW	71920 TQ	TXBLS	10/01-12/01
	McAllen-Edinburg-Mission MSA, TX	Y	17280 FQ	44610 AW	76340 TQ	TXBLS	10/01-12/01
	Odessa-Midland MSA, TX	Y	29840 FQ	47890 AW	84040 TQ	TXBLS	10/01-12/01
	San Antonio MSA, TX	Y	31000 FQ	60260 AW	97260 TQ	TXBLS	10/01-12/01
	Waco MSA, TX	Y	26190 FQ	48870 AW	82100 TQ	TXBLS	10/01-12/01
	Utah	Y	31340 FQ	60240 AW	95340 TQ	UTBLS	10/01-12/01
	Provo-Orem MSA, UT	Y	26320 FQ	62330 AW	93430 TQ	UTBLS	10/01-12/01
	Salt Lake City-Ogden MSA, UT	Y	36230 FQ	62750 AW	99160 TQ	UTBLS	10/01-12/01
	Vermont	Y	39640 FQ	65590 AW	105770 TQ	VTBLS	10/01-12/01
	Burlington MSA, VT	Y	38140 FQ	79790 AW		VTBLS	10/01-12/01
	Virginia	Y	33200 FQ	71510 AW	115340 TQ	VABLS	10/01-12/01
	Norfolk-Virginia Beach-Newport News MSA, VA-NC	Y	32490 FQ	64170 AW	90810 TQ	VABLS	10/01-12/01
	Richmond-Petersburg MSA, VA	Y	33700 FQ	62730 AW	102740 TQ	VABLS	10/01-12/01
	Roanoke MSA, VA	Y	28920 FQ	56000 AW	91590 TQ	VABLS	10/01-12/01
	Washington	Y	40640 FQ	74270 AW	122180 TQ	WABLS	10/01-12/01
	Seattle-Bellevue-Everett PMSA, WA	Y	40950 FQ	77470 AW	130730 TQ	WABLS	10/01-12/01
	Spokane MSA, WA	Y	48290 FQ	75470 AW	130040 TQ	WABLS	10/01-12/01
	Tacoma PMSA, WA	Y	39160 FQ	68070 AW	102660 TQ	WABLS	10/01-12/01
	Yakima MSA, WA	Y	40490 FQ	63970 AW	91050 TQ	WABLS	10/01-12/01
	West Virginia	Y	26710 FQ	48170 AW	79090 TQ	WVBLS	10/01-12/01
	Charleston MSA, WV	Y	29230 FQ	51080 AW	81090 TQ	WVBLS	10/01-12/01
	Wisconsin	Y	26270 FQ	51960 AW	89910 TQ	WIBLS	10/01-12/01
	Appleton-Oshkosh-Neenah MSA, WI	Y	13880 FQ	46740 AW	73360 TQ	WIBLS	10/01-12/01
	Green Bay MSA, WI	Y	29500 FQ	56380 AW	91660 TQ	WIBLS	10/01-12/01
	Madison MSA, WI	Y	29320 FQ	48790 AW	78710 TQ	WIBLS	10/01-12/01
	Milwaukee-Waukesha PMSA, WI	Y	27170 FQ	54210 AW	104600 TQ	WIBLS	10/01-12/01
	Wyoming	Y	24360 FQ	51380 AW	96350 TQ	WYBLS	10/01-12/01
	Puerto Rico	Y	23120 FQ	37550 AW	66910 TQ	PRBLS	10/01-12/01
Public Relations Professional	Orange County, CA	Y		69190 AW		PRW	2001-2002
	San Francisco, CA	Y		82000 AW		PR	1/00-1/01
	San Jose, CA	Y		86000 AW		PR	1/00-1/01
	San Jose, CA	Y		90560 AW		PRW	2001-2002
	Denver, CO	Y		55680 AW		PRW	2001-2002
	Washington, DC	Y		65000 AW		PR	1/00-1/01
	Boston, MA	Y		65000 AW		PR	1/00-1/01
	Kansas City, MO	Y		77710 AW		PRW	2001-2002
	New York, NY	Y		71000 AW		PR	1/00-1/01
	Dallas, TX	Y		62920 AW		PRW	2001-2002
Public Relations Specialist	Midwest	Y		63000 AW		WW	1/00-1/01
	Northeast	Y		65000 AW		WW	1/00-1/01
	Alabama	Y	20220 FQ	38060 AW	60080 TQ	ALBLS	10/01-12/01
	Birmingham MSA, AL	Y	24600 FQ	41020 AW	62830 TQ	ALBLS	10/01-12/01
	Huntsville MSA, AL	Y	25820 FQ	41370 AW	61310 TQ	ALBLS	10/01-12/01
	Mobile MSA, AL	Y	22860 FQ	38510 AW	62730 TQ	ALBLS	10/01-12/01
	Montgomery MSA, AL	Y	19480 FQ	33370 AW	54160 TQ	ALBLS	10/01-12/01
	Alaska	Y	30880 FQ	49890 AW	72750 TQ	AKBLS	10/01-12/01
	Anchorage MSA, AK	Y	29120 FQ	50370 AW	84600 TQ	AKBLS	10/01-12/01
	Arizona	Y	23520 FQ	39740 AW	61590 TQ	AZBLS	10/01-12/01
	Phoenix-Mesa MSA, AZ	Y	23310 FQ	39640 AW	60960 TQ	AZBLS	10/01-12/01
	Tucson MSA, AZ	Y	24010 FQ	39840 AW	63490 TQ	AZBLS	10/01-12/01
	Arkansas	Y	18080 FQ	32040 AW	49340 TQ	ARBLS	10/01-12/01
	Fayetteville-Springdale-Rogers MSA, AR	Y	19750 FQ	32130 AW	48730 TQ	ARBLS	10/01-12/01
	Fort Smith MSA, AR-OK	Y	18430 FQ	31600 AW	47250 TQ	ARBLS	10/01-12/01
	Little Rock-North Little Rock MSA, AR	Y	21130 FQ	34720 AW	53680 TQ	ARBLS	10/01-12/01
	California	Y	28040 FQ	54340 AW	93720 TQ	CABLS	10/01-12/01
	Bakersfield MSA, CA	Y	23950 FQ	45710 AW	68580 TQ	CABLS	10/01-12/01
	Chico-Paradise MSA, CA	Y	14400 FQ	34500 AW	61470 TQ	CABLS	10/01-12/01
	Fresno MSA, CA	Y	21160 FQ	42520 AW	63500 TQ	CABLS	10/01-12/01

AAW	Average annual wage	**AOH**	Average offered, high	**ASH**	Average starting, high	**H**	Hourly	**M**	Monthly	**S**	Special: hourly and annual
AE	Average entry wage	**AOL**	Average offered, low	**ASL**	Average starting, low	**HI**	Highest wage paid	**MTC**	Median total compensation	**TQ**	Third quartile wage
AEX	Average experienced wage	**APH**	Average pay, high range	**AW**	Average wage paid	**HR**	High end range	**MW**	Median wage paid	**W**	Weekly
AO	Average offered	**APL**	Average pay, low range	**FQ**	First quartile wage	**LR**	Low end range	**SQ**	Second quartile wage	**Y**	Yearly

Occupation/Type/Industry	Location	Per	Low	Mid	High	Source	Date
Public Relations Specialist	Los Angeles-Long Beach PMSA, CA	Y	28780 FQ	50300 AW	71610 TQ	CABLS	10/01-12/01
	Merced MSA, CA	Y	26630 FQ	44940 AW	66510 TQ	CABLS	10/01-12/01
	Modesto MSA, CA	Y	13580 FQ	33360 AW	55880 TQ	CABLS	10/01-12/01
	Oakland PMSA, CA	Y	30080 FQ	52820 AW	84690 TQ	CABLS	10/01-12/01
	Orange County PMSA, CA	Y	25350 FQ	43970 AW	69390 TQ	CABLS	10/01-12/01
	Redding MSA, CA	Y	27260 FQ	45060 AW	64150 TQ	CABLS	10/01-12/01
	Riverside-San Bernardino PMSA, CA	Y	18510 FQ	41280 AW	61630 TQ	CABLS	10/01-12/01
	Sacramento PMSA, CA	Y	34430 FQ	60400 AW	89960 TQ	CABLS	10/01-12/01
	Salinas MSA, CA	Y	24770 FQ	44800 AW	71300 TQ	CABLS	10/01-12/01
	San Diego MSA, CA	Y	29860 FQ	52210 AW	73800 TQ	CABLS	10/01-12/01
	San Francisco PMSA, CA	Y	35390 FQ	70500 AW	109960 TQ	CABLS	10/01-12/01
	San Jose PMSA, CA	Y	34900 FQ	68690 AW		CABLS	10/01-12/01
	San Luis Obispo-Atascadero-Paso Robles MSA, CA	Y	25250 FQ	40670 AW	57650 TQ	CABLS	10/01-12/01
	Santa Barbara-Santa Maria-Lompoc MSA, CA	Y	23450 FQ	41090 AW	55930 TQ	CABLS	10/01-12/01
	Santa Cruz-Watsonville PMSA, CA	Y	30200 FQ	48020 AW	70510 TQ	CABLS	10/01-12/01
	Santa Rosa PMSA, CA	Y	18040 FQ	41260 AW	66790 TQ	CABLS	10/01-12/01
	Stockton-Lodi MSA, CA	Y	22260 FQ	42270 AW	61180 TQ	CABLS	10/01-12/01
	Vallejo-Fairfield-Napa PMSA, CA	Y	32120 FQ	48430 AW	67160 TQ	CABLS	10/01-12/01
	Ventura PMSA, CA	Y	30110 FQ	45610 AW	63940 TQ	CABLS	10/01-12/01
	Visalia-Tulare-Porterville MSA, CA	Y	19420 FQ	37120 AW	63900 TQ	CABLS	10/01-12/01
	Colorado	Y	24420 FQ	45140 AW	71620 TQ	COBLS	10/01-12/01
	Boulder-Longmont PMSA, CO	Y	27730 FQ	50050 AW	71420 TQ	COBLS	10/01-12/01
	Colorado Springs MSA, CO	Y	15590 FQ	36010 AW	67180 TQ	COBLS	10/01-12/01
	Denver PMSA, CO	Y	29980 FQ	44980 AW	67660 TQ	COBLS	10/01-12/01
	Fort Collins-Loveland MSA, CO	Y	32250 FQ	65210 AW	105510 TQ	COBLS	10/01-12/01
	Greeley PMSA, CO	Y	31450 FQ	50160 AW	69250 TQ	COBLS	10/01-12/01
	Connecticut	Y	30700 FQ	49120 AW	73370 TQ	CTBLS	10/01-12/01
	Bridgeport PMSA, CT	Y	31360 FQ	49120 AW	72940 TQ	CTBLS	10/01-12/01
	Danbury PMSA, CT	Y	29400 FQ	50970 AW	77760 TQ	CTBLS	10/01-12/01
	Hartford MSA, CT	Y	30930 FQ	50000 AW	75990 TQ	CTBLS	10/01-12/01
	New Haven-Meriden PMSA, CT	Y	30410 FQ	43680 AW	59450 TQ	CTBLS	10/01-12/01
	New London-Norwich MSA, CT-RI	Y	29410 FQ	44150 AW	58510 TQ	CTBLS	10/01-12/01
	Stamford-Norwalk PMSA, CT	Y	30230 FQ	50170 AW	75820 TQ	CTBLS	10/01-12/01
	Delaware	Y	14530 FQ	36040 AW	56990 TQ	DEBLS	10/01-12/01
	Wilmington-Newark PMSA, DE-MD	Y	14220 FQ	34070 AW	55390 TQ	DEBLS	10/01-12/01
	District of Columbia	Y	27930 FQ	54600 AW	87060 TQ	DCBLS	10/01-12/01
	Washington PMSA, DC-MD-VA-WV	Y	29020 FQ	54010 AW	84970 TQ	DCBLS	10/01-12/01
	Florida	Y	22480 FQ	39870 AW	63340 TQ	FLBLS	10/01-12/01
	Daytona Beach MSA, FL	Y	24130 FQ	36960 AW	54600 TQ	FLBLS	10/01-12/01
	Fort Lauderdale PMSA, FL	Y	20580 FQ	39790 AW	63630 TQ	FLBLS	10/01-12/01
	Fort Myers-Cape Coral MSA, FL	Y	22440 FQ	35070 AW	54910 TQ	FLBLS	10/01-12/01
	Fort Pierce-Port St. Lucie MSA, FL	Y	23560 FQ	42420 AW	70500 TQ	FLBLS	10/01-12/01
	Fort Walton Beach MSA, FL	Y	22070 FQ	34590 AW	55270 TQ	FLBLS	10/01-12/01
	Gainesville MSA, FL	Y	23060 FQ	35250 AW	55330 TQ	FLBLS	10/01-12/01
	Jacksonville MSA, FL	Y	23530 FQ	41150 AW	62620 TQ	FLBLS	10/01-12/01
	Lakeland-Winter Haven MSA, FL	Y	21080 FQ	41800 AW	69970 TQ	FLBLS	10/01-12/01
	Melbourne-Titusville-Palm Bay MSA, FL	Y	20700 FQ	33930 AW	56720 TQ	FLBLS	10/01-12/01
	Miami PMSA, FL	Y	23710 FQ	39090 AW	60080 TQ	FLBLS	10/01-12/01
	Naples MSA, FL	Y	22410 FQ	34360 AW	53250 TQ	FLBLS	10/01-12/01
	Ocala MSA, FL	Y	26220 FQ	40690 AW	62230 TQ	FLBLS	10/01-12/01
	Orlando MSA, FL	Y	26820 FQ	43150 AW	63780 TQ	FLBLS	10/01-12/01
	Pensacola MSA, FL	Y	20730 FQ	37760 AW	61320 TQ	FLBLS	10/01-12/01
	Sarasota-Bradenton MSA, FL	Y	25770 FQ	39780 AW	59680 TQ	FLBLS	10/01-12/01
	Tallahassee MSA, FL	Y	24330 FQ	47690 AW	81400 TQ	FLBLS	10/01-12/01
	Tampa-St. Petersburg-Clearwater MSA, FL	Y	20340 FQ	37920 AW	63430 TQ	FLBLS	10/01-12/01

AAW	Average annual wage	**AOH**	Average offered, high	**ASH**	Average starting, high	**H**	Hourly	**M**	Monthly	**S**	Special: hourly and annual
AE	Average entry wage	**AOL**	Average offered, low	**ASL**	Average starting, low	**HI**	Highest wage paid	**MTC**	Median total compensation	**TQ**	Third quartile wage
AEX	Average experienced wage	**APH**	Average pay, high range	**AW**	Average wage paid	**HR**	High end range	**MW**	Median wage paid	**W**	Weekly
AO	Average offered	**APL**	Average pay, low range	**FQ**	First quartile wage	**LR**	Low end range	**SQ**	Second quartile wage	**Y**	Yearly

Occupation/Type/Industry	Location	Per	Low	Mid	High	Source	Date
Public Relations Specialist	West Palm Beach-Boca Raton MSA, FL	Y	25010 FQ	39570 AW	58490 TQ	FLBLS	10/01-12/01
	Georgia	Y	23660 FQ	40340 AW	62620 TQ	GABLS	10/01-12/01
	Atlanta MSA, GA	Y	23800 FQ	41550 AW	67620 TQ	GABLS	10/01-12/01
	Augusta-Aiken MSA, GA-SC	Y	24100 FQ	49830 AW	83810 TQ	GABLS	10/01-12/01
	Columbus MSA, GA-AL	Y	25470 FQ	39620 AW	56460 TQ	GABLS	10/01-12/01
	Macon MSA, GA	Y	26470 FQ	39150 AW	54860 TQ	GABLS	10/01-12/01
	Savannah MSA, GA	Y	25960 FQ	37200 AW	51160 TQ	GABLS	10/01-12/01
	Hawaii	Y	25000 FQ	38920 AW	58270 TQ	HIBLS	10/01-12/01
	Honolulu MSA, HI	Y	24850 FQ	38880 AW	57840 TQ	HIBLS	10/01-12/01
	Idaho	Y	24630 FQ	41530 AW	60470 TQ	IDBLS	10/01-12/01
	Boise City MSA, ID	Y	25650 FQ	41320 AW	56960 TQ	IDBLS	10/01-12/01
	Illinois	Y	21700 FQ	39570 AW	61210 TQ	ILBLS	10/01-12/01
	Champaign-Urbana MSA, IL	Y	21520 FQ	41700 AW	67870 TQ	ILBLS	10/01-12/01
	Chicago PMSA, IL	Y	21900 FQ	39810 AW	62790 TQ	ILBLS	10/01-12/01
	Peoria-Pekin MSA, IL	Y	20850 FQ	39090 AW	61050 TQ	ILBLS	10/01-12/01
	Rockford MSA, IL	Y	23580 FQ	40370 AW	58880 TQ	ILBLS	10/01-12/01
	Springfield MSA, IL	Y	32290 FQ	40700 AW	46330 TQ	ILBLS	10/01-12/01
	Indiana	Y	21980 FQ	36910 AW	57870 TQ	INBLS	10/01-12/01
	Elkhart-Goshen MSA, IN	Y	20550 FQ	42910 AW	67610 TQ	INBLS	10/01-12/01
	Evansville-Henderson MSA, IN-KY	Y	19100 FQ	34860 AW	57100 TQ	INBLS	10/01-12/01
	Fort Wayne MSA, IN	Y	23350 FQ	39160 AW	57170 TQ	INBLS	10/01-12/01
	Gary PMSA, IN	Y	17530 FQ	40470 AW	64330 TQ	INBLS	10/01-12/01
	Indianapolis MSA, IN	Y	25240 FQ	37560 AW	57240 TQ	INBLS	10/01-12/01
	Lafayette MSA, IN	Y	19480 FQ	30310 AW	44080 TQ	INBLS	10/01-12/01
	South Bend MSA, IN	Y	25660 FQ	38040 AW	61020 TQ	INBLS	10/01-12/01
	Iowa	Y	22850 FQ	36600 AW	54220 TQ	IABLS	10/01-12/01
	Cedar Rapids MSA, IA	Y	21760 FQ	33510 AW	48850 TQ	IABLS	10/01-12/01
	Davenport-Moline-Rock Island MSA, IA-IL	Y	13730 FQ	33450 AW	56960 TQ	IABLS	10/01-12/01
	Des Moines MSA, IA	Y	24180 FQ	38780 AW	59240 TQ	IABLS	10/01-12/01
	Kansas	Y	23640 FQ	37640 AW	56570 TQ	KSBLS	10/01-12/01
	Topeka MSA, KS	Y	29230 FQ	44490 AW	67540 TQ	KSBLS	10/01-12/01
	Wichita MSA, KS	Y	23510 FQ	36850 AW	54030 TQ	KSBLS	10/01-12/01
	Kentucky	Y	22090 FQ	37720 AW	55770 TQ	KYBLS	10/01-12/01
	Lexington MSA, KY	Y	24160 FQ	40070 AW	66230 TQ	KYBLS	10/01-12/01
	Louisville MSA, KY-IN	Y	21620 FQ	36590 AW	53860 TQ	KYBLS	10/01-12/01
	Louisiana	Y	20610 FQ	37070 AW	62480 TQ	LABLS	10/01-12/01
	Baton Rouge MSA, LA	Y	22680 FQ	32340 AW	46070 TQ	LABLS	10/01-12/01
	Houma MSA, LA	Y	13520 FQ	38110 AW	55490 TQ	LABLS	10/01-12/01
	Lafayette MSA, LA	Y	18530 FQ	32360 AW	47470 TQ	LABLS	10/01-12/01
	Lake Charles MSA, LA	Y	22750 FQ	37810 AW	58010 TQ	LABLS	10/01-12/01
	New Orleans MSA, LA	Y	20170 FQ	40140 AW	69010 TQ	LABLS	10/01-12/01
	Shreveport-Bossier City MSA, LA	Y	18270 FQ	34800 AW	67240 TQ	LABLS	10/01-12/01
	Maine	Y	24490 FQ	39540 AW	59850 TQ	MEBLS	10/01-12/01
	Portland MSA, ME	Y	24280 FQ	38230 AW	55760 TQ	MEBLS	10/01-12/01
	Maryland	Y	26810 FQ	49990 AW	81120 TQ	MDBLS	10/01-12/01
	Baltimore PMSA, MD	Y	24050 FQ	43870 AW	69830 TQ	MDBLS	10/01-12/01
	Massachusetts	Y	26820 FQ	45130 AW	68640 TQ	MABLS	10/01-12/01
	Boston PMSA, MA-NH	Y	27440 FQ	46190 AW	71180 TQ	MABLS	10/01-12/01
	Brockton PMSA, MA	Y	31860 FQ	42780 AW	57010 TQ	MABLS	10/01-12/01
	Lawrence PMSA, MA-NH	Y	29270 FQ	43290 AW	61780 TQ	MABLS	10/01-12/01
	Lowell PMSA, MA-NH	Y	25290 FQ	43260 AW	70180 TQ	MABLS	10/01-12/01
	Springfield MSA, MA	Y	26280 FQ	40190 AW	57520 TQ	MABLS	10/01-12/01
	Worcester PMSA, MA-CT	Y	25820 FQ	41670 AW	61900 TQ	MABLS	10/01-12/01
	Michigan	Y	27170 FQ	48040 AW	76250 TQ	MIBLS	10/01-12/01
	Ann Arbor PMSA, MI	Y	25280 FQ	42250 AW	67220 TQ	MIBLS	10/01-12/01
	Detroit PMSA, MI	Y	28880 FQ	52240 AW	86730 TQ	MIBLS	10/01-12/01
	Flint PMSA, MI	Y	25000 FQ	44450 AW	74190 TQ	MIBLS	10/01-12/01
	Grand Rapids-Muskegon-Holland MSA, MI	Y	25420 FQ	47610 AW	79310 TQ	MIBLS	10/01-12/01
	Kalamazoo-Battle Creek MSA, MI	Y	26810 FQ	44250 AW	71010 TQ	MIBLS	10/01-12/01
	Lansing-East Lansing MSA, MI	Y	31700 FQ	54110 AW	87480 TQ	MIBLS	10/01-12/01
	Saginaw-Bay City-Midland MSA, MI	Y	23300 FQ	43340 AW	70490 TQ	MIBLS	10/01-12/01
	Minnesota	Y	28420 FQ	46870 AW	72810 TQ	MNBLS	10/01-12/01
	Duluth-Superior MSA, MN-WI	Y	27210 FQ	43340 AW	62560 TQ	MNBLS	10/01-12/01
	Minneapolis-St. Paul MSA, MN-WI	Y	30090 FQ	48480 AW	73240 TQ	MNBLS	10/01-12/01

AAW	Average annual wage	**AOH**	Average offered, high	**ASH**	Average starting, high	**H**	Hourly	**M**	Monthly	**S**	Special: hourly and annual
AE	Average entry wage	**AOL**	Average offered, low	**ASL**	Average starting, low	**HI**	Highest wage paid	**MTC**	Median total compensation	**TQ**	Third quartile wage
AEX	Average experienced wage	**APH**	Average pay, high range	**AW**	Average wage paid	**HR**	High end range	**MW**	Median wage paid	**W**	Weekly
AO	Average offered	**APL**	Average pay, low range	**FQ**	First quartile wage	**LR**	Low end range	**SQ**	Second quartile wage	**Y**	Yearly

Occupation/Type/Industry	Location	Per	Low	Mid	High	Source	Date
Public Relations Specialist	St. Cloud MSA, MN	Y	26440 FQ	39860 AW	54950 TQ	MNBLS	10/01-12/01
	Mississippi	Y	19000 FQ	35760 AW	56270 TQ	MSBLS	10/01-12/01
	Biloxi-Gulfport-Pascagoula MSA, MS	Y	23900 FQ	41950 AW	65000 TQ	MSBLS	10/01-12/01
	Jackson MSA, MS	Y	22140 FQ	37480 AW	58910 TQ	MSBLS	10/01-12/01
	Missouri	Y	20040 FQ	39600 AW	65310 TQ	MOBLS	10/01-12/01
	Kansas City MSA, MO-KS	Y	23680 FQ	39100 AW	64960 TQ	MOBLS	10/01-12/01
	St. Louis MSA, MO-IL	Y	21970 FQ	42890 AW	69100 TQ	MOBLS	10/01-12/01
	Springfield MSA, MO	Y	13690 FQ	30790 AW	48240 TQ	MOBLS	10/01-12/01
	Montana	Y	18920 FQ	37590 AW	61010 TQ	MTBLS	10/01-12/01
	Nebraska	Y	23620 FQ	40620 AW	63580 TQ	NEBLS	10/01-12/01
	Lincoln MSA, NE	Y	24750 FQ	35420 AW	49950 TQ	NEBLS	10/01-12/01
	Omaha MSA, NE-IA	Y	26710 FQ	44560 AW	66940 TQ	NEBLS	10/01-12/01
	Nevada	Y	26360 FQ	41980 AW	61350 TQ	NVBLS	10/01-12/01
	Las Vegas MSA, NV-AZ	Y	28300 FQ	41150 AW	59910 TQ	NVBLS	10/01-12/01
	Reno MSA, NV	Y	23230 FQ	45030 AW	65190 TQ	NVBLS	10/01-12/01
	New Hampshire	Y	28360 FQ	39760 AW	56780 TQ	NHBLS	10/01-12/01
	Manchester PMSA, NH	Y	29260 FQ	40720 AW	56420 TQ	NHBLS	10/01-12/01
	Nashua PMSA, NH	Y	26150 FQ	47300 AW	74030 TQ	NHBLS	10/01-12/01
	Portsmouth-Rochester PMSA, NH-ME	Y	26170 FQ	40040 AW	56080 TQ	NHBLS	10/01-12/01
	New Jersey	Y	24120 FQ	48080 AW	77930 TQ	NJBLS	10/01-12/01
	Atlantic-Cape May PMSA, NJ	Y	28260 FQ	41580 AW	60120 TQ	NJBLS	10/01-12/01
	Bergen-Passaic PMSA, NJ	Y	27960 FQ	50250 AW	79550 TQ	NJBLS	10/01-12/01
	Jersey City PMSA, NJ	Y	20820 FQ	45790 AW	69970 TQ	NJBLS	10/01-12/01
	Middlesex-Somerset-Hunterdon PMSA, NJ	Y	25410 FQ	49500 AW	81770 TQ	NJBLS	10/01-12/01
	Monmouth-Ocean PMSA, NJ	Y	20280 FQ	34800 AW	57870 TQ	NJBLS	10/01-12/01
	Newark PMSA, NJ	Y	25890 FQ	52820 AW	85950 TQ	NJBLS	10/01-12/01
	Trenton PMSA, NJ	Y	30070 FQ	52820 AW	81290 TQ	NJBLS	10/01-12/01
	New Mexico	Y	24440 FQ	40810 AW	63500 TQ	NMBLS	10/01-12/01
	Albuquerque MSA, NM	Y	25450 FQ	41880 AW	66730 TQ	NMBLS	10/01-12/01
	Las Cruces MSA, NM	Y	22700 FQ	36040 AW	52950 TQ	NMBLS	10/01-12/01
	New York	Y	26140 FQ	52710 AW	91660 TQ	NYBLS	10/01-12/01
	Albany-Schenectady-Troy MSA, NY	Y	21570 FQ	50650 AW	89990 TQ	NYBLS	10/01-12/01
	Binghamton MSA, NY	Y	20690 FQ	36210 AW	57690 TQ	NYBLS	10/01-12/01
	Buffalo-Niagara Falls MSA, NY	Y	22920 FQ	37180 AW	58240 TQ	NYBLS	10/01-12/01
	Dutchess County PMSA, NY	Y	23250 FQ	37800 AW	55890 TQ	NYBLS	10/01-12/01
	Nassau-Suffolk PMSA, NY	Y	23590 FQ	45870 AW	76200 TQ	NYBLS	10/01-12/01
	New York PMSA, NY	Y	30190 FQ	57410 AW	97870 TQ	NYBLS	10/01-12/01
	Newburgh PMSA, NY-PA	Y	23310 FQ	39690 AW	56020 TQ	NYBLS	10/01-12/01
	Rochester MSA, NY	Y	24530 FQ	44100 AW	74850 TQ	NYBLS	10/01-12/01
	Syracuse MSA, NY	Y	20950 FQ	36900 AW	60550 TQ	NYBLS	10/01-12/01
	Utica-Rome MSA, NY	Y	17830 FQ	32920 AW	52820 TQ	NYBLS	10/01-12/01
	North Carolina	Y	23680 FQ	41570 AW	66690 TQ	NCBLS	10/01-12/01
	Asheville MSA, NC	Y	23320 FQ	42180 AW	65690 TQ	NCBLS	10/01-12/01
	Charlotte-Gastonia-Rock Hill MSA, NC-SC	Y	22030 FQ	41450 AW	68500 TQ	NCBLS	10/01-12/01
	Fayetteville MSA, NC	Y	22540 FQ	36720 AW	55560 TQ	NCBLS	10/01-12/01
	Greensboro-Winston-Salem-High Point MSA, NC	Y	22250 FQ	36180 AW	54250 TQ	NCBLS	10/01-12/01
	Hickory-Morganton-Lenoir MSA, NC	Y	14740 FQ	33730 AW	47920 TQ	NCBLS	10/01-12/01
	Raleigh-Durham-Chapel Hill MSA, NC	Y	29040 FQ	47290 AW	75940 TQ	NCBLS	10/01-12/01
	Wilmington MSA, NC	Y	24530 FQ	34840 AW	52360 TQ	NCBLS	10/01-12/01
	North Dakota	Y	23000 FQ	38860 AW	77130 TQ	NDBLS	10/01-12/01
	Fargo-Moorhead MSA, ND-MN	Y	22960 FQ	33780 AW	50050 TQ	NDBLS	10/01-12/01
	Ohio	Y	24120 FQ	42330 AW	67200 TQ	OHBLS	10/01-12/01
	Akron PMSA, OH	Y	22350 FQ	42190 AW	61410 TQ	OHBLS	10/01-12/01
	Canton-Massillon MSA, OH	Y	29610 FQ	45060 AW	68450 TQ	OHBLS	10/01-12/01
	Cincinnati PMSA, OH-KY-IN	Y	26150 FQ	43100 AW	63840 TQ	OHBLS	10/01-12/01
	Cleveland-Lorain-Elyria PMSA, OH	Y	22440 FQ	42900 AW	68830 TQ	OHBLS	10/01-12/01
	Columbus MSA, OH	Y	25910 FQ	44600 AW	73130 TQ	OHBLS	10/01-12/01
	Dayton-Springfield MSA, OH	Y	26090 FQ	41780 AW	62620 TQ	OHBLS	10/01-12/01
	Hamilton-Middletown PMSA, OH	Y	26850 FQ	43520 AW	71620 TQ	OHBLS	10/01-12/01
	Toledo MSA, OH	Y	21550 FQ	37340 AW	55950 TQ	OHBLS	10/01-12/01

AAW Average annual wage	**AOH** Average offered, high	**ASH** Average starting, high	**H** Hourly	**M** Monthly	**S** Special: hourly and annual
AE Average entry wage	**AOL** Average offered, low	**ASL** Average starting, low	**HI** Highest wage paid	**MTC** Median total compensation	**TQ** Third quartile wage
AEX Average experienced wage	**APH** Average pay, high range	**AW** Average wage paid	**HR** High end range	**MW** Median wage paid	**W** Weekly
AO Average offered	**APL** Average pay, low range	**FQ** First quartile wage	**LR** Low end range	**SQ** Second quartile wage	**Y** Yearly

Occupation/Type/Industry	Location	Per	Low	Mid	High	Source	Date
Public Relations Specialist	Youngstown-Warren MSA, OH	Y	25550 FQ	39780 AW	58050 TQ	OHBLS	10/01-12/01
	Oklahoma	Y	19110 FQ	33900 AW	52030 TQ	OKBLS	10/01-12/01
	Oklahoma City MSA, OK	Y	23680 FQ	39670 AW	55450 TQ	OKBLS	10/01-12/01
	Tulsa MSA, OK	Y	17940 FQ	30750 AW	43220 TQ	OKBLS	10/01-12/01
	Oregon	Y	24720 FQ	44710 AW	68830 TQ	ORBLS	10/01-12/01
	Eugene-Springfield MSA, OR	Y	26340 FQ	40960 AW	58450 TQ	ORBLS	10/01-12/01
	Portland-Vancouver PMSA, OR-WA	Y	24830 FQ	45510 AW	68730 TQ	ORBLS	10/01-12/01
	Salem PMSA, OR	Y	28710 FQ	51680 AW	95770 TQ	ORBLS	10/01-12/01
	Pennsylvania	Y	21720 FQ	43440 AW	73970 TQ	PABLS	10/01-12/01
	Allentown-Bethlehem-Easton MSA, PA	Y	22510 FQ	36220 AW	59820 TQ	PABLS	10/01-12/01
	Erie MSA, PA	Y	15760 FQ	30990 AW	53180 TQ	PABLS	10/01-12/01
	Harrisburg-Lebanon-Carlisle MSA, PA	Y	28930 FQ	45430 AW	70780 TQ	PABLS	10/01-12/01
	Johnstown MSA, PA	Y	19910 FQ	37830 AW	68360 TQ	PABLS	10/01-12/01
	Lancaster MSA, PA	Y	18040 FQ	32930 AW	44990 TQ	PABLS	10/01-12/01
	Philadelphia PMSA, PA-NJ	Y	24080 FQ	49380 AW	84650 TQ	PABLS	10/01-12/01
	Pittsburgh MSA, PA	Y	19290 FQ	37450 AW	58040 TQ	PABLS	10/01-12/01
	Reading MSA, PA	Y	16740 FQ	41240 AW	70260 TQ	PABLS	10/01-12/01
	Scranton-Wilkes-Barre-Hazleton MSA, PA	Y	17920 FQ	34170 AW	54560 TQ	PABLS	10/01-12/01
	York MSA, PA	Y	23800 FQ	37770 AW	54890 TQ	PABLS	10/01-12/01
	Rhode Island	Y	26640 FQ	43780 AW	64810 TQ	RIBLS	10/01-12/01
	Providence-Fall River-Warwick MSA, RI-MA	Y	25850 FQ	43250 AW	64180 TQ	RIBLS	10/01-12/01
	South Carolina	Y	19240 FQ	34610 AW	56700 TQ	SCBLS	10/01-12/01
	Charleston-North Charleston MSA, SC	Y	20200 FQ	35350 AW	58250 TQ	SCBLS	10/01-12/01
	Columbia MSA, SC	Y	24470 FQ	37180 AW	56130 TQ	SCBLS	10/01-12/01
	Greenville-Spartanburg-Anderson MSA, SC	Y	22800 FQ	36800 AW	52610 TQ	SCBLS	10/01-12/01
	Myrtle Beach MSA, SC	Y	23190 FQ	35640 AW	64090 TQ	SCBLS	10/01-12/01
	South Dakota	Y	21710 FQ	32210 AW	45660 TQ	SDBLS	10/01-12/01
	Sioux Falls MSA, SD	Y	20640 FQ	32400 AW	47810 TQ	SDBLS	10/01-12/01
	Tennessee	Y	20730 FQ	37690 AW	61860 TQ	TNBLS	10/01-12/01
	Chattanooga MSA, TN-GA	Y	20480 FQ	34630 AW	51140 TQ	TNBLS	10/01-12/01
	Clarksville-Hopkinsville MSA, TN-KY	Y	16270 FQ	32450 AW	47980 TQ	TNBLS	10/01-12/01
	Johnson City-Kingsport-Bristol MSA, TN-VA	Y	18970 FQ	35570 AW	54660 TQ	TNBLS	10/01-12/01
	Knoxville MSA, TN	Y	18370 FQ	29360 AW	46310 TQ	TNBLS	10/01-12/01
	Memphis MSA, TN-AR-MS	Y	22120 FQ	40690 AW	66840 TQ	TNBLS	10/01-12/01
	Nashville MSA, TN	Y	24900 FQ	41270 AW	64600 TQ	TNBLS	10/01-12/01
	Texas	Y	24290 FQ	45070 AW	71560 TQ	TXBLS	10/01-12/01
	Amarillo MSA, TX	Y	20970 FQ	34430 AW	53970 TQ	TXBLS	10/01-12/01
	Austin-San Marcos MSA, TX	Y	25260 FQ	49160 AW	70760 TQ	TXBLS	10/01-12/01
	Brownsville-Harlingen-San Benito MSA, TX	Y	17700 FQ	41200 AW	70770 TQ	TXBLS	10/01-12/01
	Corpus Christi MSA, TX	Y	25790 FQ	41930 AW	66170 TQ	TXBLS	10/01-12/01
	Dallas PMSA, TX	Y	25770 FQ	47820 AW	80660 TQ	TXBLS	10/01-12/01
	El Paso MSA, TX	Y	14660 FQ	35080 AW	57990 TQ	TXBLS	10/01-12/01
	Fort Worth-Arlington PMSA, TX	Y	27310 FQ	46010 AW	72670 TQ	TXBLS	10/01-12/01
	Galveston-Texas City PMSA, TX	Y	21970 FQ	37580 AW	64070 TQ	TXBLS	10/01-12/01
	Houston PMSA, TX	Y	28240 FQ	47570 AW	72730 TQ	TXBLS	10/01-12/01
	Killeen-Temple MSA, TX	Y	22950 FQ	34220 AW	50690 TQ	TXBLS	10/01-12/01
	Laredo MSA, TX	Y	25600 FQ	40110 AW	58040 TQ	TXBLS	10/01-12/01
	Lubbock MSA, TX	Y	19880 FQ	32620 AW	48930 TQ	TXBLS	10/01-12/01
	McAllen-Edinburg-Mission MSA, TX	Y	21630 FQ	34960 AW	51670 TQ	TXBLS	10/01-12/01
	Odessa-Midland MSA, TX	Y	19960 FQ	32450 AW	50060 TQ	TXBLS	10/01-12/01
	San Antonio MSA, TX	Y	25140 FQ	41190 AW	59780 TQ	TXBLS	10/01-12/01
	Tyler MSA, TX	Y	23680 FQ	38630 AW	60520 TQ	TXBLS	10/01-12/01
	Waco MSA, TX	Y	22530 FQ	43360 AW	69470 TQ	TXBLS	10/01-12/01
	Utah	Y	25470 FQ	41020 AW	59350 TQ	UTBLS	10/01-12/01
	Provo-Orem MSA, UT	Y	25680 FQ	41780 AW	57760 TQ	UTBLS	10/01-12/01
	Salt Lake City-Ogden MSA, UT	Y	25330 FQ	40410 AW	58390 TQ	UTBLS	10/01-12/01
	Vermont	Y	27140 FQ	42980 AW	71410 TQ	VTBLS	10/01-12/01
	Burlington MSA, VT	Y	26380 FQ	41210 AW	62950 TQ	VTBLS	10/01-12/01

AAW	Average annual wage	**AOH**	Average offered, high	**ASH**	Average starting, high	**H**	Hourly	**M**	Monthly	**S**	Special: hourly and annual
AE	Average entry wage	**AOL**	Average offered, low	**ASL**	Average starting, low	**HI**	Highest wage paid	**MTC**	Median total compensation	**TQ**	Third quartile wage
AEX	Average experienced wage	**APH**	Average pay, high range	**AW**	Average wage paid	**HR**	High end range	**MW**	Median wage paid	**W**	Weekly
AO	Average offered	**APL**	Average pay, low range	**FQ**	First quartile wage	**LR**	Low end range	**SQ**	Second quartile wage	**Y**	Yearly

Occupation/Type/Industry	Location	Per	Low	Mid	High	Source	Date
Public Relations Specialist	Virginia	Y	25530 FQ	46470 AW	71280 TQ	VABLS	10/01-12/01
	Lynchburg MSA, VA	Y	23420 FQ	38090 AW	62810 TQ	VABLS	10/01-12/01
	Norfolk-Virginia Beach-Newport News MSA, VA-NC	Y	23700 FQ	42660 AW	68980 TQ	VABLS	10/01-12/01
	Richmond-Petersburg MSA, VA	Y	26720 FQ	44220 AW	67480 TQ	VABLS	10/01-12/01
	Roanoke MSA, VA	Y	24530 FQ	38440 AW	58060 TQ	VABLS	10/01-12/01
	Washington	Y	29450 FQ	53350 AW	88670 TQ	WABLS	10/01-12/01
	Bremerton PMSA, WA	Y	25460 FQ	43640 AW	67340 TQ	WABLS	10/01-12/01
	Olympia PMSA, WA	Y	34130 FQ	54090 AW	84920 TQ	WABLS	10/01-12/01
	Richland-Kennewick-Pasco MSA, WA	Y	30460 FQ	47600 AW	73530 TQ	WABLS	10/01-12/01
	Seattle-Bellevue-Everett PMSA, WA	Y	31430 FQ	57940 AW	94760 TQ	WABLS	10/01-12/01
	Spokane MSA, WA	Y	25470 FQ	45570 AW	69380 TQ	WABLS	10/01-12/01
	Tacoma PMSA, WA	Y	29160 FQ	46080 AW	69050 TQ	WABLS	10/01-12/01
	Yakima MSA, WA	Y	26780 FQ	49410 AW	87620 TQ	WABLS	10/01-12/01
	West Virginia	Y	20470 FQ	37340 AW	63510 TQ	WVBLS	10/01-12/01
	Charleston MSA, WV	Y	23440 FQ	36650 AW	56910 TQ	WVBLS	10/01-12/01
	Huntington-Ashland MSA, WV-KY-OH	Y	20130 FQ	35270 AW	56060 TQ	WVBLS	10/01-12/01
	Wisconsin	Y	12700 FQ	34080 AW	60570 TQ	WIBLS	10/01-12/01
	Appleton-Oshkosh-Neenah MSA, WI	Y	12540 FQ	29730 AW	48280 TQ	WIBLS	10/01-12/01
	Green Bay MSA, WI	Y	12250 FQ	28660 AW	49610 TQ	WIBLS	10/01-12/01
	Madison MSA, WI	Y	13910 FQ	41750 AW	68970 TQ	WIBLS	10/01-12/01
	Milwaukee-Waukesha PMSA, WI	Y	12650 FQ	34440 AW	60180 TQ	WIBLS	10/01-12/01
	Wyoming	Y	24570 FQ	41790 AW	61460 TQ	WYBLS	10/01-12/01
	Cheyenne MSA, WY	Y	23520 FQ	34980 AW	48170 TQ	WYBLS	10/01-12/01
	Puerto Rico	Y	14240 FQ	25790 AW	43220 TQ	PRBLS	10/01-12/01
Public Transportation Professional							
Sound Transit	Tacoma, WA	Y		63180 AW		NTT	1/01-1/02
Publisher							
Marketing, Medical	United States	Y		123500 AW		MM&M	1/01-1/02
Pump Operator							
Except Wellhead Pumper	Alabama	H	12.45 FQ	20.87 AW	27.27 TQ	ALBLS	10/01-12/01
Except Wellhead Pumper	Alaska	H	11.74 FQ	27.70 AW	50.15 TQ	AKBLS	10/01-12/01
Except Wellhead Pumper	Arkansas	H	6.37 FQ	12.01 AW	16.97 TQ	ARBLS	10/01-12/01
Except Wellhead Pumper	California	H	9.95 FQ	18.55 AW	27.63 TQ	CABLS	10/01-12/01
Except Wellhead Pumper	Colorado	H	8.51 FQ	13.25 AW	20.17 TQ	COBLS	10/01-12/01
Except Wellhead Pumper	Florida	H	10.64 FQ	17.27 AW	23.39 TQ	FLBLS	10/01-12/01
Except Wellhead Pumper	Georgia	H	9.56 FQ	14.36 AW	17.77 TQ	GABLS	10/01-12/01
Except Wellhead Pumper	Idaho	H	10.93 FQ	15.19 AW	21.46 TQ	IDBLS	10/01-12/01
Except Wellhead Pumper	Illinois	H	8.05 FQ	16.44 AW	29.01 TQ	ILBLS	10/01-12/01
Except Wellhead Pumper	Indiana	H	8.55 FQ	14.10 AW	21.27 TQ	INBLS	10/01-12/01
Except Wellhead Pumper	Iowa	H	9.31 FQ	15.18 AW	21.08 TQ	IABLS	10/01-12/01
Except Wellhead Pumper	Kansas	H	9.40 FQ	20.02 AW	33.44 TQ	KSBLS	10/01-12/01
Except Wellhead Pumper	Kentucky	H	11.38 FQ	17.62 AW	21.92 TQ	KYBLS	10/01-12/01
Except Wellhead Pumper	Louisiana	H	10.43 FQ	19.25 AW	27.50 TQ	LABLS	10/01-12/01
Except Wellhead Pumper	Maryland	H	11.63 FQ	18.94 AW	25.74 TQ	MDBLS	10/01-12/01
Except Wellhead Pumper	Massachusetts	H	9.48 FQ	20.05 AW	28.59 TQ	MABLS	10/01-12/01
Except Wellhead Pumper	Michigan	H	9.99 FQ	16.49 AW	24.72 TQ	MIBLS	10/01-12/01
Except Wellhead Pumper	Minnesota	H	9.46 FQ	15.55 AW	25.29 TQ	MNBLS	10/01-12/01
Except Wellhead Pumper	Mississippi	H	10.81 FQ	14.68 AW	18.26 TQ	MSBLS	10/01-12/01
Except Wellhead Pumper	Missouri	H	10.16 FQ	15.04 AW	22.57 TQ	MOBLS	10/01-12/01
Except Wellhead Pumper	Montana	H	9.86 FQ	14.84 AW	24.10 TQ	MTBLS	10/01-12/01
Except Wellhead Pumper	Nebraska	H	9.49 FQ	14.31 AW	20.14 TQ	NEBLS	10/01-12/01
Except Wellhead Pumper	Nevada	H	7.64 FQ	10.93 AW	15.49 TQ	NVBLS	10/01-12/01
Except Wellhead Pumper	New Jersey	H	10.51 FQ	28.74 AW	54.10 TQ	NJBLS	10/01-12/01
Except Wellhead Pumper	New Mexico	H	6.60 FQ	14.53 AW	25.76 TQ	NMBLS	10/01-12/01
Except Wellhead Pumper	New York	H	8.84 FQ	13.08 AW	20.63 TQ	NYBLS	10/01-12/01
Except Wellhead Pumper	North Carolina	H	8.54 FQ	11.81 AW	16.21 TQ	NCBLS	10/01-12/01
Except Wellhead Pumper	North Dakota	H	7.20 FQ	18.16 AW	27.32 TQ	NDBLS	10/01-12/01
Except Wellhead Pumper	Ohio	H	6.94 FQ	17.95 AW	35.36 TQ	OHBLS	10/01-12/01
Except Wellhead Pumper	Oklahoma	H	5.73 FQ	12.11 AW	23.76 TQ	OKBLS	10/01-12/01
Except Wellhead Pumper	Oregon	H	11.58 FQ	18.43 AW	27.09 TQ	ORBLS	10/01-12/01

AAW	Average annual wage	**AOH**	Average offered, high	**ASH**	Average starting, high	**H**	Hourly	**M**	Monthly	**S**	Special: hourly and annual
AE	Average entry wage	**AOL**	Average offered, low	**ASL**	Average starting, low	**HI**	Highest wage paid	**MTC**	Median total compensation	**TQ**	Third quartile wage
AEX	Average experienced wage	**APH**	Average pay, high range	**AW**	Average wage paid	**HR**	High end range	**MW**	Median wage paid	**W**	Weekly
AO	Average offered	**APL**	Average pay, low range	**FQ**	First quartile wage	**LR**	Low end range	**SQ**	Second quartile wage	**Y**	Yearly

Occupation/Type/Industry	Location	Per	Low	Mid	High	Source	Date
Pump Operator							
Except Wellhead Pumper	Pennsylvania	H	9.37 FQ	14.72 AW	22.48 TQ	PABLS	10/01-12/01
Except Wellhead Pumper	South Carolina	H	7.60 FQ	9.91 AW	14.30 TQ	SCBLS	10/01-12/01
Except Wellhead Pumper	Tennessee	H	8.88 FQ	14.33 AW	25.46 TQ	TNBLS	10/01-12/01
Except Wellhead Pumper	Texas	H	9.85 FQ	20.28 AW	27.70 TQ	TXBLS	10/01-12/01
Except Wellhead Pumper	Washington	H	13.28 FQ	20.44 AW	29.91 TQ	WABLS	10/01-12/01
Except Wellhead Pumper	West Virginia	H	11.74 FQ	15.38 AW	20.72 TQ	WVBLS	10/01-12/01
Except Wellhead Pumper	Wisconsin	H	10.27 FQ	17.05 AW	27.27 TQ	WIBLS	10/01-12/01
Except Wellhead Pumper	Wyoming	H	17.20 FQ	20.85 AW	26.97 TQ	WYBLS	10/01-12/01
Except Wellhead Pumper	Puerto Rico	H	5.53 FQ	10.72 AW	20.99 TQ	PRBLS	10/01-12/01
Purchasing Agent							
Except Wholesale, Retail, and Farm	Alabama	Y	24900 FQ	46170 AW	71340 TQ	ALBLS	10/01-12/01
Except Wholesale, Retail, and Farm	Birmingham MSA, AL	Y	25020 FQ	46340 AW	77080 TQ	ALBLS	10/01-12/01
Except Wholesale, Retail, and Farm	Huntsville MSA, AL	Y	32230 FQ	54740 AW	78090 TQ	ALBLS	10/01-12/01
Except Wholesale, Retail, and Farm	Mobile MSA, AL	Y	22770 FQ	37690 AW	59760 TQ	ALBLS	10/01-12/01
Except Wholesale, Retail, and Farm	Montgomery MSA, AL	Y	25980 FQ	41260 AW	60050 TQ	ALBLS	10/01-12/01
Except Wholesale, Retail, and Farm	Alaska	Y	30470 FQ	51310 AW	81390 TQ	AKBLS	10/01-12/01
Except Wholesale, Retail, and Farm	Anchorage MSA, AK	Y	30370 FQ	51180 AW	79400 TQ	AKBLS	10/01-12/01
Except Wholesale, Retail, and Farm	Arizona	Y	25830 FQ	44670 AW	68960 TQ	AZBLS	10/01-12/01
Except Wholesale, Retail, and Farm	Phoenix-Mesa MSA, AZ	Y	26970 FQ	45980 AW	70070 TQ	AZBLS	10/01-12/01
Except Wholesale, Retail, and Farm	Tucson MSA, AZ	Y	22430 FQ	40540 AW	62550 TQ	AZBLS	10/01-12/01
Except Wholesale, Retail, and Farm	Arkansas	Y	23360 FQ	40100 AW	63220 TQ	ARBLS	10/01-12/01
Except Wholesale, Retail, and Farm	Fayetteville-Springdale-Rogers MSA, AR	Y	22750 FQ	36640 AW	52220 TQ	ARBLS	10/01-12/01
Except Wholesale, Retail, and Farm	Fort Smith MSA, AR-OK	Y	27660 FQ	42490 AW	62180 TQ	ARBLS	10/01-12/01
Except Wholesale, Retail, and Farm	Little Rock-North Little Rock MSA, AR	Y	24340 FQ	39190 AW	56150 TQ	ARBLS	10/01-12/01
Except Wholesale, Retail, and Farm	California	Y	28630 FQ	48980 AW	73100 TQ	CABLS	10/01-12/01
Except Wholesale, Retail, and Farm	Bakersfield MSA, CA	Y	30510 FQ	55330 AW	83890 TQ	CABLS	10/01-12/01
Except Wholesale, Retail, and Farm	Chico-Paradise MSA, CA	Y	22530 FQ	32180 AW	44010 TQ	CABLS	10/01-12/01
Except Wholesale, Retail, and Farm	Fresno MSA, CA	Y	23120 FQ	36780 AW	54970 TQ	CABLS	10/01-12/01
Except Wholesale, Retail, and Farm	Los Angeles-Long Beach PMSA, CA	Y	26920 FQ	48970 AW	73620 TQ	CABLS	10/01-12/01
Except Wholesale, Retail, and Farm	Merced MSA, CA	Y	26640 FQ	44940 AW	68820 TQ	CABLS	10/01-12/01
Except Wholesale, Retail, and Farm	Modesto MSA, CA	Y	24840 FQ	40540 AW	58110 TQ	CABLS	10/01-12/01
Except Wholesale, Retail, and Farm	Oakland PMSA, CA	Y	32210 FQ	52310 AW	75990 TQ	CABLS	10/01-12/01
Except Wholesale, Retail, and Farm	Orange County PMSA, CA	Y	29000 FQ	46530 AW	70360 TQ	CABLS	10/01-12/01
Except Wholesale, Retail, and Farm	Redding MSA, CA	Y	28330 FQ	40760 AW	60260 TQ	CABLS	10/01-12/01
Except Wholesale, Retail, and Farm	Riverside-San Bernardino PMSA, CA	Y	25020 FQ	40280 AW	60760 TQ	CABLS	10/01-12/01
Except Wholesale, Retail, and Farm	Sacramento PMSA, CA	Y	29530 FQ	44980 AW	65610 TQ	CABLS	10/01-12/01
Except Wholesale, Retail, and Farm	Salinas MSA, CA	Y	30080 FQ	46320 AW	67040 TQ	CABLS	10/01-12/01
Except Wholesale, Retail, and Farm	San Diego MSA, CA	Y	28140 FQ	48220 AW	70560 TQ	CABLS	10/01-12/01
Except Wholesale, Retail, and Farm	San Francisco PMSA, CA	Y	32470 FQ	51860 AW	74410 TQ	CABLS	10/01-12/01
Except Wholesale, Retail, and Farm	San Jose PMSA, CA	Y	37240 FQ	58710 AW	85570 TQ	CABLS	10/01-12/01
Except Wholesale, Retail, and Farm	San Luis Obispo-Atascadero-Paso Robles MSA, CA	Y	24190 FQ	43020 AW	60760 TQ	CABLS	10/01-12/01
Except Wholesale, Retail, and Farm	Santa Barbara-Santa Maria-Lompoc MSA, CA	Y	27730 FQ	48400 AW	69360 TQ	CABLS	10/01-12/01
Except Wholesale, Retail, and Farm	Santa Cruz-Watsonville PMSA, CA	Y	32140 FQ	46750 AW	65060 TQ	CABLS	10/01-12/01
Except Wholesale, Retail, and Farm	Santa Rosa PMSA, CA	Y	29810 FQ	46520 AW	67160 TQ	CABLS	10/01-12/01
Except Wholesale, Retail, and Farm	Stockton-Lodi MSA, CA	Y	27920 FQ	46220 AW	71610 TQ	CABLS	10/01-12/01
Except Wholesale, Retail, and Farm	Vallejo-Fairfield-Napa PMSA, CA	Y	31050 FQ	45800 AW	65900 TQ	CABLS	10/01-12/01
Except Wholesale, Retail, and Farm	Ventura PMSA, CA	Y	28970 FQ	46580 AW	69020 TQ	CABLS	10/01-12/01
Except Wholesale, Retail, and Farm	Visalia-Tulare-Porterville MSA, CA	Y	23850 FQ	38690 AW	54600 TQ	CABLS	10/01-12/01
Except Wholesale, Retail, and Farm	Colorado	Y	30090 FQ	47160 AW	69220 TQ	COBLS	10/01-12/01
Except Wholesale, Retail, and Farm	Boulder-Longmont PMSA, CO	Y	32780 FQ	49570 AW	70660 TQ	COBLS	10/01-12/01
Except Wholesale, Retail, and Farm	Colorado Springs MSA, CO	Y	31120 FQ	46910 AW	67130 TQ	COBLS	10/01-12/01
Except Wholesale, Retail, and Farm	Denver PMSA, CO	Y	30660 FQ	48110 AW	70660 TQ	COBLS	10/01-12/01
Except Wholesale, Retail, and Farm	Fort Collins-Loveland MSA, CO	Y	30420 FQ	46030 AW	67240 TQ	COBLS	10/01-12/01
Except Wholesale, Retail, and Farm	Greeley PMSA, CO	Y	29470 FQ	46200 AW	66380 TQ	COBLS	10/01-12/01
Except Wholesale, Retail, and Farm	Connecticut	Y	30760 FQ	49600 AW	70910 TQ	CTBLS	10/01-12/01
Except Wholesale, Retail, and Farm	Bridgeport PMSA, CT	Y	32400 FQ	50190 AW	71180 TQ	CTBLS	10/01-12/01
Except Wholesale, Retail, and Farm	Danbury PMSA, CT	Y	29800 FQ	48110 AW	70250 TQ	CTBLS	10/01-12/01
Except Wholesale, Retail, and Farm	Hartford MSA, CT	Y	30780 FQ	48730 AW	70150 TQ	CTBLS	10/01-12/01
Except Wholesale, Retail, and Farm	New Haven-Meriden PMSA, CT	Y	28850 FQ	46940 AW	65900 TQ	CTBLS	10/01-12/01

AAW	Average annual wage	**AOH**	Average offered, high	**ASH**	Average starting, high	**H**	Hourly	**M**	Monthly	**S**	Special: hourly and annual
AE	Average entry wage	**AOL**	Average offered, low	**ASL**	Average starting, low	**HI**	Highest wage paid	**MTC**	Median total compensation	**TQ**	Third quartile wage
AEX	Average experienced wage	**APH**	Average pay, high range	**AW**	Average wage paid	**HR**	High end range	**MW**	Median wage paid	**W**	Weekly
AO	Average offered	**APL**	Average pay, low range	**FQ**	First quartile wage	**LR**	Low end range	**SQ**	Second quartile wage	**Y**	Yearly

Occupation/Type/Industry	Location	Per	Low	Mid	High	Source	Date
Purchasing Agent							
Except Wholesale, Retail, and Farm	New London-Norwich MSA, CT-RI	Y	34440 FQ	52420 AW	70790 TQ	CTBLS	10/01-12/01
Except Wholesale, Retail, and Farm	Stamford-Norwalk PMSA, CT	Y	34480 FQ	54890 AW	78850 TQ	CTBLS	10/01-12/01
Except Wholesale, Retail, and Farm	Waterbury PMSA, CT	Y	30580 FQ	50940 AW	79690 TQ	CTBLS	10/01-12/01
Except Wholesale, Retail, and Farm	Delaware	Y	29030 FQ	48090 AW	73590 TQ	DEBLS	10/01-12/01
Except Wholesale, Retail, and Farm	Wilmington-Newark PMSA, DE-MD	Y	30540 FQ	49590 AW	76430 TQ	DEBLS	10/01-12/01
Except Wholesale, Retail, and Farm	District of Columbia	Y	36420 FQ	62800 AW	89430 TQ	DCBLS	10/01-12/01
Except Wholesale, Retail, and Farm	Washington PMSA, DC-MD-VA-WV	Y	35340 FQ	59200 AW	87040 TQ	DCBLS	10/01-12/01
Except Wholesale, Retail, and Farm	Florida	Y	24710 FQ	40370 AW	61620 TQ	FLBLS	10/01-12/01
Except Wholesale, Retail, and Farm	Daytona Beach MSA, FL	Y	25400 FQ	38010 AW	53960 TQ	FLBLS	10/01-12/01
Except Wholesale, Retail, and Farm	Fort Lauderdale PMSA, FL	Y	25330 FQ	40060 AW	58970 TQ	FLBLS	10/01-12/01
Except Wholesale, Retail, and Farm	Fort Myers-Cape Coral MSA, FL	Y	24100 FQ	39070 AW	66430 TQ	FLBLS	10/01-12/01
Except Wholesale, Retail, and Farm	Fort Pierce-Port St. Lucie MSA, FL	Y	21610 FQ	36030 AW	54640 TQ	FLBLS	10/01-12/01
Except Wholesale, Retail, and Farm	Fort Walton Beach MSA, FL	Y	26580 FQ	48030 AW	69300 TQ	FLBLS	10/01-12/01
Except Wholesale, Retail, and Farm	Gainesville MSA, FL	Y	25030 FQ	37440 AW	56750 TQ	FLBLS	10/01-12/01
Except Wholesale, Retail, and Farm	Jacksonville MSA, FL	Y	24520 FQ	40410 AW	61340 TQ	FLBLS	10/01-12/01
Except Wholesale, Retail, and Farm	Lakeland-Winter Haven MSA, FL	Y	24440 FQ	39580 AW	57780 TQ	FLBLS	10/01-12/01
Except Wholesale, Retail, and Farm	Melbourne-Titusville-Palm Bay MSA, FL	Y	23140 FQ	42370 AW	66960 TQ	FLBLS	10/01-12/01
Except Wholesale, Retail, and Farm	Miami PMSA, FL	Y	24920 FQ	38940 AW	56920 TQ	FLBLS	10/01-12/01
Except Wholesale, Retail, and Farm	Naples MSA, FL	Y	25010 FQ	38490 AW	55450 TQ	FLBLS	10/01-12/01
Except Wholesale, Retail, and Farm	Ocala MSA, FL	Y	20530 FQ	33920 AW	50850 TQ	FLBLS	10/01-12/01
Except Wholesale, Retail, and Farm	Orlando MSA, FL	Y	25190 FQ	41360 AW	63340 TQ	FLBLS	10/01-12/01
Except Wholesale, Retail, and Farm	Pensacola MSA, FL	Y	21500 FQ	38130 AW	62190 TQ	FLBLS	10/01-12/01
Except Wholesale, Retail, and Farm	Sarasota-Bradenton MSA, FL	Y	24130 FQ	39830 AW	58360 TQ	FLBLS	10/01-12/01
Except Wholesale, Retail, and Farm	Tallahassee MSA, FL	Y	24570 FQ	41130 AW	67090 TQ	FLBLS	10/01-12/01
Except Wholesale, Retail, and Farm	Tampa-St. Petersburg-Clearwater MSA, FL	Y	26510 FQ	41410 AW	62900 TQ	FLBLS	10/01-12/01
Except Wholesale, Retail, and Farm	West Palm Beach-Boca Raton MSA, FL	Y	26300 FQ	41820 AW	61690 TQ	FLBLS	10/01-12/01
Except Wholesale, Retail, and Farm	Georgia	Y	27160 FQ	43890 AW	65770 TQ	GABLS	10/01-12/01
Except Wholesale, Retail, and Farm	Atlanta MSA, GA	Y	28450 FQ	46350 AW	69030 TQ	GABLS	10/01-12/01
Except Wholesale, Retail, and Farm	Augusta-Aiken MSA, GA-SC	Y	22720 FQ	54040 AW	88710 TQ	GABLS	10/01-12/01
Except Wholesale, Retail, and Farm	Columbus MSA, GA-AL	Y	24720 FQ	38870 AW	56290 TQ	GABLS	10/01-12/01
Except Wholesale, Retail, and Farm	Macon MSA, GA	Y	30520 FQ	48450 AW	67530 TQ	GABLS	10/01-12/01
Except Wholesale, Retail, and Farm	Savannah MSA, GA	Y	26840 FQ	41820 AW	58330 TQ	GABLS	10/01-12/01
Except Wholesale, Retail, and Farm	Hawaii	Y	29190 FQ	47270 AW	70980 TQ	HIBLS	10/01-12/01
Except Wholesale, Retail, and Farm	Honolulu MSA, HI	Y	29620 FQ	48730 AW	72450 TQ	HIBLS	10/01-12/01
Except Wholesale, Retail, and Farm	Idaho	Y	25770 FQ	43070 AW	65490 TQ	IDBLS	10/01-12/01
Except Wholesale, Retail, and Farm	Boise City MSA, ID	Y	27790 FQ	45030 AW	67310 TQ	IDBLS	10/01-12/01
Except Wholesale, Retail, and Farm	Illinois	Y	27830 FQ	46420 AW	69520 TQ	ILBLS	10/01-12/01
Except Wholesale, Retail, and Farm	Champaign-Urbana MSA, IL	Y	26290 FQ	35770 AW	51100 TQ	ILBLS	10/01-12/01
Except Wholesale, Retail, and Farm	Chicago PMSA, IL	Y	28930 FQ	46900 AW	69350 TQ	ILBLS	10/01-12/01
Except Wholesale, Retail, and Farm	Peoria-Pekin MSA, IL	Y	29600 FQ	53110 AW	87600 TQ	ILBLS	10/01-12/01
Except Wholesale, Retail, and Farm	Rockford MSA, IL	Y	28360 FQ	45720 AW	68870 TQ	ILBLS	10/01-12/01
Except Wholesale, Retail, and Farm	Springfield MSA, IL	Y	24920 FQ	41090 AW	55580 TQ	ILBLS	10/01-12/01
Except Wholesale, Retail, and Farm	Indiana	Y	24270 FQ	40730 AW	62460 TQ	INBLS	10/01-12/01
Except Wholesale, Retail, and Farm	Elkhart-Goshen MSA, IN	Y	26910 FQ	42880 AW	64150 TQ	INBLS	10/01-12/01
Except Wholesale, Retail, and Farm	Evansville-Henderson MSA, IN-KY	Y	23220 FQ	36860 AW	55480 TQ	INBLS	10/01-12/01
Except Wholesale, Retail, and Farm	Fort Wayne MSA, IN	Y	26220 FQ	44330 AW	69110 TQ	INBLS	10/01-12/01
Except Wholesale, Retail, and Farm	Gary PMSA, IN	Y	21300 FQ	41700 AW	72560 TQ	INBLS	10/01-12/01
Except Wholesale, Retail, and Farm	Indianapolis MSA, IN	Y	24120 FQ	39440 AW	58970 TQ	INBLS	10/01-12/01
Except Wholesale, Retail, and Farm	Lafayette MSA, IN	Y	27600 FQ	41810 AW	57200 TQ	INBLS	10/01-12/01
Except Wholesale, Retail, and Farm	South Bend MSA, IN	Y	26430 FQ	47040 AW	72090 TQ	INBLS	10/01-12/01
Except Wholesale, Retail, and Farm	Iowa	Y	23250 FQ	38860 AW	58020 TQ	IABLS	10/01-12/01
Except Wholesale, Retail, and Farm	Cedar Rapids MSA, IA	Y	31870 FQ	47230 AW	67050 TQ	IABLS	10/01-12/01
Except Wholesale, Retail, and Farm	Davenport-Moline-Rock Island MSA, IA-IL	Y	29850 FQ	51620 AW	71740 TQ	IABLS	10/01-12/01
Except Wholesale, Retail, and Farm	Des Moines MSA, IA	Y	25620 FQ	38840 AW	55720 TQ	IABLS	10/01-12/01
Except Wholesale, Retail, and Farm	Kansas	Y	24570 FQ	42740 AW	62720 TQ	KSBLS	10/01-12/01
Except Wholesale, Retail, and Farm	Topeka MSA, KS	Y	28720 FQ	41320 AW	61720 TQ	KSBLS	10/01-12/01
Except Wholesale, Retail, and Farm	Wichita MSA, KS	Y	31560 FQ	47290 AW	65310 TQ	KSBLS	10/01-12/01
Except Wholesale, Retail, and Farm	Kentucky	Y	24480 FQ	42890 AW	66400 TQ	KYBLS	10/01-12/01
Except Wholesale, Retail, and Farm	Lexington MSA, KY	Y	26780 FQ	44540 AW	66460 TQ	KYBLS	10/01-12/01
Except Wholesale, Retail, and Farm	Louisville MSA, KY-IN	Y	25910 FQ	45850 AW	73870 TQ	KYBLS	10/01-12/01

AAW Average annual wage; AE Average entry wage; AEX Average experienced wage; AO Average offered; AOH Average offered, high; AOL Average offered, low; APH Average pay, high range; APL Average pay, low range; ASH Average starting, high; ASL Average starting, low; AW Average wage paid; FQ First quartile wage; H Hourly; HI Highest wage paid; HR High end range; LR Low end range; M Monthly; MTC Median total compensation; MW Median wage paid; SQ Second quartile wage; S Special: hourly and annual; TQ Third quartile wage; W Weekly; Y Yearly

Occupation/Type/Industry	Location	Per	Low	Mid	High	Source	Date
Purchasing Agent							
Except Wholesale, Retail, and Farm	Louisiana	Y	22900 FQ	39690 AW	60540 TQ	LABLS	10/01-12/01
Except Wholesale, Retail, and Farm	Baton Rouge MSA, LA	Y	21990 FQ	39060 AW	60800 TQ	LABLS	10/01-12/01
Except Wholesale, Retail, and Farm	Houma MSA, LA	Y	23960 FQ	35160 AW	48750 TQ	LABLS	10/01-12/01
Except Wholesale, Retail, and Farm	Lafayette MSA, LA	Y	23110 FQ	35180 AW	54360 TQ	LABLS	10/01-12/01
Except Wholesale, Retail, and Farm	Lake Charles MSA, LA	Y	21180 FQ	38540 AW	55960 TQ	LABLS	10/01-12/01
Except Wholesale, Retail, and Farm	New Orleans MSA, LA	Y	23870 FQ	42580 AW	66990 TQ	LABLS	10/01-12/01
Except Wholesale, Retail, and Farm	Shreveport-Bossier City MSA, LA	Y	22700 FQ	40300 AW	57020 TQ	LABLS	10/01-12/01
Except Wholesale, Retail, and Farm	Maine	Y	24670 FQ	39460 AW	56950 TQ	MEBLS	10/01-12/01
Except Wholesale, Retail, and Farm	Portland MSA, ME	Y	25100 FQ	38280 AW	56120 TQ	MEBLS	10/01-12/01
Except Wholesale, Retail, and Farm	Maryland	Y	29780 FQ	50330 AW	77230 TQ	MDBLS	10/01-12/01
Except Wholesale, Retail, and Farm	Baltimore PMSA, MD	Y	28750 FQ	45970 AW	70040 TQ	MDBLS	10/01-12/01
Except Wholesale, Retail, and Farm	Massachusetts	Y	30620 FQ	48260 AW	69660 TQ	MABLS	10/01-12/01
Except Wholesale, Retail, and Farm	Boston PMSA, MA-NH	Y	32420 FQ	50040 AW	70910 TQ	MABLS	10/01-12/01
Except Wholesale, Retail, and Farm	Brockton PMSA, MA	Y	30840 FQ	44670 AW	65550 TQ	MABLS	10/01-12/01
Except Wholesale, Retail, and Farm	Lawrence PMSA, MA-NH	Y	30580 FQ	45130 AW	65050 TQ	MABLS	10/01-12/01
Except Wholesale, Retail, and Farm	Lowell PMSA, MA-NH	Y	29990 FQ	49170 AW	69150 TQ	MABLS	10/01-12/01
Except Wholesale, Retail, and Farm	New Bedford PMSA, MA	Y	25670 FQ	40910 AW	64020 TQ	MABLS	10/01-12/01
Except Wholesale, Retail, and Farm	Springfield MSA, MA	Y	29260 FQ	44000 AW	60970 TQ	MABLS	10/01-12/01
Except Wholesale, Retail, and Farm	Worcester PMSA, MA-CT	Y	28230 FQ	44120 AW	61610 TQ	MABLS	10/01-12/01
Except Wholesale, Retail, and Farm	Michigan	Y	29140 FQ	51860 AW	82680 TQ	MIBLS	10/01-12/01
Except Wholesale, Retail, and Farm	Ann Arbor PMSA, MI	Y	30600 FQ	51970 AW	83200 TQ	MIBLS	10/01-12/01
Except Wholesale, Retail, and Farm	Detroit PMSA, MI	Y	30480 FQ	57150 AW	87550 TQ	MIBLS	10/01-12/01
Except Wholesale, Retail, and Farm	Flint PMSA, MI	Y	30920 FQ	56700 AW	88930 TQ	MIBLS	10/01-12/01
Except Wholesale, Retail, and Farm	Grand Rapids-Muskegon-Holland MSA, MI	Y	28710 FQ	44120 AW	63110 TQ	MIBLS	10/01-12/01
Except Wholesale, Retail, and Farm	Kalamazoo-Battle Creek MSA, MI	Y	30350 FQ	48890 AW	72010 TQ	MIBLS	10/01-12/01
Except Wholesale, Retail, and Farm	Lansing-East Lansing MSA, MI	Y	30420 FQ	43520 AW	59060 TQ	MIBLS	10/01-12/01
Except Wholesale, Retail, and Farm	Saginaw-Bay City-Midland MSA, MI	Y	25890 FQ	48980 AW	85450 TQ	MIBLS	10/01-12/01
Except Wholesale, Retail, and Farm	Minnesota	Y	30120 FQ	45060 AW	63570 TQ	MNBLS	10/01-12/01
Except Wholesale, Retail, and Farm	Duluth-Superior MSA, MN-WI	Y	25310 FQ	39160 AW	57510 TQ	MNBLS	10/01-12/01
Except Wholesale, Retail, and Farm	Minneapolis-St. Paul MSA, MN-WI	Y	31780 FQ	46880 AW	65380 TQ	MNBLS	10/01-12/01
Except Wholesale, Retail, and Farm	St. Cloud MSA, MN	Y	25800 FQ	36930 AW	52230 TQ	MNBLS	10/01-12/01
Except Wholesale, Retail, and Farm	Mississippi	Y	23330 FQ	47990 AW	100510 TQ	MSBLS	10/01-12/01
Except Wholesale, Retail, and Farm	Biloxi-Gulfport-Pascagoula MSA, MS	Y	22000 FQ	39390 AW	60760 TQ	MSBLS	10/01-12/01
Except Wholesale, Retail, and Farm	Jackson MSA, MS	Y	22550 FQ	35140 AW	48620 TQ	MSBLS	10/01-12/01
Except Wholesale, Retail, and Farm	Missouri	Y	25340 FQ	43040 AW	64940 TQ	MOBLS	10/01-12/01
Except Wholesale, Retail, and Farm	Kansas City MSA, MO-KS	Y	25920 FQ	44040 AW	65870 TQ	MOBLS	10/01-12/01
Except Wholesale, Retail, and Farm	St. Louis MSA, MO-IL	Y	28120 FQ	46370 AW	68470 TQ	MOBLS	10/01-12/01
Except Wholesale, Retail, and Farm	Springfield MSA, MO	Y	21720 FQ	35730 AW	55860 TQ	MOBLS	10/01-12/01
Except Wholesale, Retail, and Farm	Montana	Y	22050 FQ	37450 AW	55670 TQ	MTBLS	10/01-12/01
Except Wholesale, Retail, and Farm	Billings MSA, MT	Y	28360 FQ	41280 AW	64270 TQ	MTBLS	10/01-12/01
Except Wholesale, Retail, and Farm	Nebraska	Y	24640 FQ	40590 AW	63960 TQ	NEBLS	10/01-12/01
Except Wholesale, Retail, and Farm	Lincoln MSA, NE	Y	24540 FQ	40170 AW	56010 TQ	NEBLS	10/01-12/01
Except Wholesale, Retail, and Farm	Omaha MSA, NE-IA	Y	25970 FQ	41440 AW	62790 TQ	NEBLS	10/01-12/01
Except Wholesale, Retail, and Farm	Nevada	Y	25980 FQ	40370 AW	57130 TQ	NVBLS	10/01-12/01
Except Wholesale, Retail, and Farm	Las Vegas MSA, NV-AZ	Y	25900 FQ	41130 AW	59190 TQ	NVBLS	10/01-12/01
Except Wholesale, Retail, and Farm	Reno MSA, NV	Y	25080 FQ	37860 AW	53810 TQ	NVBLS	10/01-12/01
Except Wholesale, Retail, and Farm	New Hampshire	Y	28340 FQ	42790 AW	60320 TQ	NHBLS	10/01-12/01
Except Wholesale, Retail, and Farm	Manchester PMSA, NH	Y	29390 FQ	43940 AW	60130 TQ	NHBLS	10/01-12/01
Except Wholesale, Retail, and Farm	Nashua PMSA, NH	Y	32100 FQ	45870 AW	66240 TQ	NHBLS	10/01-12/01
Except Wholesale, Retail, and Farm	Portsmouth-Rochester PMSA, NH-ME	Y	28840 FQ	42770 AW	56490 TQ	NHBLS	10/01-12/01
Except Wholesale, Retail, and Farm	New Jersey	Y	31500 FQ	52660 AW	79690 TQ	NJBLS	10/01-12/01
Except Wholesale, Retail, and Farm	Atlantic-Cape May PMSA, NJ	Y	28070 FQ	49070 AW	78340 TQ	NJBLS	10/01-12/01
Except Wholesale, Retail, and Farm	Bergen-Passaic PMSA, NJ	Y	30490 FQ	54260 AW	84770 TQ	NJBLS	10/01-12/01
Except Wholesale, Retail, and Farm	Jersey City PMSA, NJ	Y	29110 FQ	49940 AW	74030 TQ	NJBLS	10/01-12/01
Except Wholesale, Retail, and Farm	Middlesex-Somerset-Hunterdon PMSA, NJ	Y	34570 FQ	54660 AW	82770 TQ	NJBLS	10/01-12/01
Except Wholesale, Retail, and Farm	Monmouth-Ocean PMSA, NJ	Y	30400 FQ	55390 AW	83110 TQ	NJBLS	10/01-12/01
Except Wholesale, Retail, and Farm	Newark PMSA, NJ	Y	33770 FQ	53220 AW	79630 TQ	NJBLS	10/01-12/01
Except Wholesale, Retail, and Farm	Trenton PMSA, NJ	Y	33300 FQ	49500 AW	68660 TQ	NJBLS	10/01-12/01
Except Wholesale, Retail, and Farm	New Mexico	Y	26380 FQ	44080 AW	68280 TQ	NMBLS	10/01-12/01
Except Wholesale, Retail, and Farm	Albuquerque MSA, NM	Y	28090 FQ	45950 AW	69020 TQ	NMBLS	10/01-12/01
Except Wholesale, Retail, and Farm	Las Cruces MSA, NM	Y	24350 FQ	40000 AW	62680 TQ	NMBLS	10/01-12/01
Except Wholesale, Retail, and Farm	New York	Y	28430 FQ	47400 AW	70910 TQ	NYBLS	10/01-12/01

AAW	Average annual wage	**AOH**	Average offered, high	**ASH**	Average starting, high	**H**	Hourly	**M**	Monthly	**S**	Special: hourly and annual
AE	Average entry wage	**AOL**	Average offered, low	**ASL**	Average starting, low	**HI**	Highest wage paid	**MTC**	Median total compensation	**TQ**	Third quartile wage
AEX	Average experienced wage	**APH**	Average pay, high range	**AW**	Average wage paid	**HR**	High end range	**MW**	Median wage paid	**W**	Weekly
AO	Average offered	**APL**	Average pay, low range	**FQ**	First quartile wage	**LR**	Low end range	**SQ**	Second quartile wage	**Y**	Yearly

Occupation/Type/Industry	Location	Per	Low	Mid	High	Source	Date
Purchasing Agent							
Except Wholesale, Retail, and Farm	Albany-Schenectady-Troy MSA, NY	Y	26770 FQ	43690 AW	64390 TQ	NYBLS	10/01-12/01
Except Wholesale, Retail, and Farm	Binghamton MSA, NY	Y	28770 FQ	47610 AW	70230 TQ	NYBLS	10/01-12/01
Except Wholesale, Retail, and Farm	Buffalo-Niagara Falls MSA, NY	Y	25600 FQ	42500 AW	60720 TQ	NYBLS	10/01-12/01
Except Wholesale, Retail, and Farm	Nassau-Suffolk PMSA, NY	Y	30070 FQ	49390 AW	72090 TQ	NYBLS	10/01-12/01
Except Wholesale, Retail, and Farm	New York PMSA, NY	Y	30170 FQ	49740 AW	76210 TQ	NYBLS	10/01-12/01
Except Wholesale, Retail, and Farm	Newburgh PMSA, NY-PA	Y	31190 FQ	43530 AW	55930 TQ	NYBLS	10/01-12/01
Except Wholesale, Retail, and Farm	Rochester MSA, NY	Y	28530 FQ	44340 AW	63980 TQ	NYBLS	10/01-12/01
Except Wholesale, Retail, and Farm	Syracuse MSA, NY	Y	26500 FQ	43090 AW	61080 TQ	NYBLS	10/01-12/01
Except Wholesale, Retail, and Farm	Utica-Rome MSA, NY	Y	24640 FQ	43030 AW	69140 TQ	NYBLS	10/01-12/01
Except Wholesale, Retail, and Farm	North Carolina	Y	25890 FQ	43910 AW	67650 TQ	NCBLS	10/01-12/01
Except Wholesale, Retail, and Farm	Asheville MSA, NC	Y	24270 FQ	40030 AW	61180 TQ	NCBLS	10/01-12/01
Except Wholesale, Retail, and Farm	Charlotte-Gastonia-Rock Hill MSA, NC-SC	Y	28180 FQ	45660 AW	68770 TQ	NCBLS	10/01-12/01
Except Wholesale, Retail, and Farm	Fayetteville MSA, NC	Y	26540 FQ	41350 AW	59420 TQ	NCBLS	10/01-12/01
Except Wholesale, Retail, and Farm	Greensboro-Winston-Salem-High Point MSA, NC	Y	25850 FQ	42600 AW	65670 TQ	NCBLS	10/01-12/01
Except Wholesale, Retail, and Farm	Hickory-Morganton-Lenoir MSA, NC	Y	24260 FQ	39650 AW	57300 TQ	NCBLS	10/01-12/01
Except Wholesale, Retail, and Farm	Raleigh-Durham-Chapel Hill MSA, NC	Y	29860 FQ	49840 AW	76610 TQ	NCBLS	10/01-12/01
Except Wholesale, Retail, and Farm	Wilmington MSA, NC	Y	23810 FQ	37300 AW	54920 TQ	NCBLS	10/01-12/01
Except Wholesale, Retail, and Farm	North Dakota	Y	22040 FQ	37750 AW	55680 TQ	NDBLS	10/01-12/01
Except Wholesale, Retail, and Farm	Fargo-Moorhead MSA, ND-MN	Y	22160 FQ	34760 AW	50420 TQ	NDBLS	10/01-12/01
Except Wholesale, Retail, and Farm	Ohio	Y	26920 FQ	44720 AW	68230 TQ	OHBLS	10/01-12/01
Except Wholesale, Retail, and Farm	Akron PMSA, OH	Y	27480 FQ	44300 AW	65970 TQ	OHBLS	10/01-12/01
Except Wholesale, Retail, and Farm	Canton-Massillon MSA, OH	Y	23200 FQ	38160 AW	57620 TQ	OHBLS	10/01-12/01
Except Wholesale, Retail, and Farm	Cincinnati PMSA, OH-KY-IN	Y	27180 FQ	46860 AW	70220 TQ	OHBLS	10/01-12/01
Except Wholesale, Retail, and Farm	Cleveland-Lorain-Elyria PMSA, OH	Y	27950 FQ	45590 AW	70940 TQ	OHBLS	10/01-12/01
Except Wholesale, Retail, and Farm	Columbus MSA, OH	Y	29280 FQ	43850 AW	62080 TQ	OHBLS	10/01-12/01
Except Wholesale, Retail, and Farm	Dayton-Springfield MSA, OH	Y	30530 FQ	52130 AW	76320 TQ	OHBLS	10/01-12/01
Except Wholesale, Retail, and Farm	Hamilton-Middletown PMSA, OH	Y	29580 FQ	43910 AW	60790 TQ	OHBLS	10/01-12/01
Except Wholesale, Retail, and Farm	Mansfield MSA, OH	Y	24900 FQ	39530 AW	57640 TQ	OHBLS	10/01-12/01
Except Wholesale, Retail, and Farm	Toledo MSA, OH	Y	24740 FQ	41100 AW	62830 TQ	OHBLS	10/01-12/01
Except Wholesale, Retail, and Farm	Youngstown-Warren MSA, OH	Y	25150 FQ	43410 AW	69750 TQ	OHBLS	10/01-12/01
Except Wholesale, Retail, and Farm	Oklahoma	Y	22660 FQ	39660 AW	61610 TQ	OKBLS	10/01-12/01
Except Wholesale, Retail, and Farm	Oklahoma City MSA, OK	Y	25380 FQ	43090 AW	65350 TQ	OKBLS	10/01-12/01
Except Wholesale, Retail, and Farm	Tulsa MSA, OK	Y	21870 FQ	38790 AW	58020 TQ	OKBLS	10/01-12/01
Except Wholesale, Retail, and Farm	Oregon	Y	25900 FQ	42230 AW	63000 TQ	ORBLS	10/01-12/01
Except Wholesale, Retail, and Farm	Eugene-Springfield MSA, OR	Y	25410 FQ	36850 AW	52890 TQ	ORBLS	10/01-12/01
Except Wholesale, Retail, and Farm	Medford-Ashland MSA, OR	Y	23910 FQ	37650 AW	54850 TQ	ORBLS	10/01-12/01
Except Wholesale, Retail, and Farm	Portland-Vancouver PMSA, OR-WA	Y	27350 FQ	44650 AW	66280 TQ	ORBLS	10/01-12/01
Except Wholesale, Retail, and Farm	Salem PMSA, OR	Y	26550 FQ	39830 AW	55920 TQ	ORBLS	10/01-12/01
Except Wholesale, Retail, and Farm	Pennsylvania	Y	25760 FQ	44880 AW	68040 TQ	PABLS	10/01-12/01
Except Wholesale, Retail, and Farm	Allentown-Bethlehem-Easton MSA, PA	Y	27470 FQ	44900 AW	62610 TQ	PABLS	10/01-12/01
Except Wholesale, Retail, and Farm	Erie MSA, PA	Y	22110 FQ	39260 AW	64040 TQ	PABLS	10/01-12/01
Except Wholesale, Retail, and Farm	Harrisburg-Lebanon-Carlisle MSA, PA	Y	28200 FQ	48310 AW	71490 TQ	PABLS	10/01-12/01
Except Wholesale, Retail, and Farm	Johnstown MSA, PA	Y	23780 FQ	38020 AW	54980 TQ	PABLS	10/01-12/01
Except Wholesale, Retail, and Farm	Lancaster MSA, PA	Y	27350 FQ	41120 AW	58510 TQ	PABLS	10/01-12/01
Except Wholesale, Retail, and Farm	Philadelphia PMSA, PA-NJ	Y	28990 FQ	48760 AW	70690 TQ	PABLS	10/01-12/01
Except Wholesale, Retail, and Farm	Pittsburgh MSA, PA	Y	26880 FQ	44780 AW	67970 TQ	PABLS	10/01-12/01
Except Wholesale, Retail, and Farm	Reading MSA, PA	Y	26590 FQ	45250 AW	69260 TQ	PABLS	10/01-12/01
Except Wholesale, Retail, and Farm	Scranton-Wilkes-Barre-Hazleton MSA, PA	Y	22110 FQ	35240 AW	51860 TQ	PABLS	10/01-12/01
Except Wholesale, Retail, and Farm	York MSA, PA	Y	24250 FQ	42580 AW	65790 TQ	PABLS	10/01-12/01
Except Wholesale, Retail, and Farm	Rhode Island	Y	29120 FQ	44950 AW	67020 TQ	RIBLS	10/01-12/01
Except Wholesale, Retail, and Farm	Providence-Fall River-Warwick MSA, RI-MA	Y	27960 FQ	43860 AW	66140 TQ	RIBLS	10/01-12/01
Except Wholesale, Retail, and Farm	South Carolina	Y	25370 FQ	44100 AW	70670 TQ	SCBLS	10/01-12/01
Except Wholesale, Retail, and Farm	Charleston-North Charleston MSA, SC	Y	26160 FQ	46720 AW	71310 TQ	SCBLS	10/01-12/01
Except Wholesale, Retail, and Farm	Columbia MSA, SC	Y	24110 FQ	38120 AW	56460 TQ	SCBLS	10/01-12/01
Except Wholesale, Retail, and Farm	Greenville-Spartanburg-Anderson MSA, SC	Y	25280 FQ	42580 AW	66200 TQ	SCBLS	10/01-12/01

AAW Average annual wage · AE Average entry wage · AEX Average experienced wage · AO Average offered · AOH Average offered, high · AOL Average offered, low · APH Average pay, high range · APL Average pay, low range · ASH Average starting, high · ASL Average starting, low · AW Average wage paid · FQ First quartile wage · H Hourly · HI Highest wage paid · HR High end range · LR Low end range · M Monthly · MTC Median total compensation · MW Median wage paid · SQ Second quartile wage · S Special: hourly and annual · TQ Third quartile wage · W Weekly · Y Yearly

Occupation/Type/Industry	Location	Per	Low	Mid	High	Source	Date
Purchasing Agent							
Except Wholesale, Retail, and Farm	Myrtle Beach MSA, SC	Y	23630 FQ	35390 AW	53510 TQ	SCBLS	10/01-12/01
Except Wholesale, Retail, and Farm	South Dakota	Y	26450 FQ	38240 AW	53370 TQ	SDBLS	10/01-12/01
Except Wholesale, Retail, and Farm	Sioux Falls MSA, SD	Y	25640 FQ	37320 AW	52770 TQ	SDBLS	10/01-12/01
Except Wholesale, Retail, and Farm	Tennessee	Y	23710 FQ	41360 AW	62850 TQ	TNBLS	10/01-12/01
Except Wholesale, Retail, and Farm	Chattanooga MSA, TN-GA	Y	24950 FQ	47190 AW	79370 TQ	TNBLS	10/01-12/01
Except Wholesale, Retail, and Farm	Clarksville-Hopkinsville MSA, TN-KY	Y	25810 FQ	41240 AW	58230 TQ	TNBLS	10/01-12/01
Except Wholesale, Retail, and Farm	Johnson City-Kingsport-Bristol MSA, TN-VA	Y	20630 FQ	36920 AW	55670 TQ	TNBLS	10/01-12/01
Except Wholesale, Retail, and Farm	Knoxville MSA, TN	Y	24770 FQ	44010 AW	69930 TQ	TNBLS	10/01-12/01
Except Wholesale, Retail, and Farm	Memphis MSA, TN-AR-MS	Y	24180 FQ	41000 AW	60810 TQ	TNBLS	10/01-12/01
Except Wholesale, Retail, and Farm	Nashville MSA, TN	Y	23790 FQ	42310 AW	62130 TQ	TNBLS	10/01-12/01
Except Wholesale, Retail, and Farm	Texas	Y	25160 FQ	44310 AW	70030 TQ	TXBLS	10/01-12/01
Except Wholesale, Retail, and Farm	Amarillo MSA, TX	Y	23190 FQ	33890 AW	46840 TQ	TXBLS	10/01-12/01
Except Wholesale, Retail, and Farm	Austin-San Marcos MSA, TX	Y	28550 FQ	51360 AW	96630 TQ	TXBLS	10/01-12/01
Except Wholesale, Retail, and Farm	Beaumont-Port Arthur MSA, TX	Y	16500 FQ	36980 AW	63940 TQ	TXBLS	10/01-12/01
Except Wholesale, Retail, and Farm	Brazoria PMSA, TX	Y	24370 FQ	38860 AW	57570 TQ	TXBLS	10/01-12/01
Except Wholesale, Retail, and Farm	Brownsville-Harlingen-San Benito MSA, TX	Y	22430 FQ	33820 AW	45830 TQ	TXBLS	10/01-12/01
Except Wholesale, Retail, and Farm	Corpus Christi MSA, TX	Y	23280 FQ	42220 AW	71540 TQ	TXBLS	10/01-12/01
Except Wholesale, Retail, and Farm	Dallas PMSA, TX	Y	25650 FQ	43860 AW	68400 TQ	TXBLS	10/01-12/01
Except Wholesale, Retail, and Farm	El Paso MSA, TX	Y	21920 FQ	34470 AW	52530 TQ	TXBLS	10/01-12/01
Except Wholesale, Retail, and Farm	Fort Worth-Arlington PMSA, TX	Y	28410 FQ	47790 AW	74000 TQ	TXBLS	10/01-12/01
Except Wholesale, Retail, and Farm	Galveston-Texas City PMSA, TX	Y	25180 FQ	40570 AW	64180 TQ	TXBLS	10/01-12/01
Except Wholesale, Retail, and Farm	Houston PMSA, TX	Y	26180 FQ	46660 AW	73410 TQ	TXBLS	10/01-12/01
Except Wholesale, Retail, and Farm	Killeen-Temple MSA, TX	Y	26770 FQ	42150 AW	62370 TQ	TXBLS	10/01-12/01
Except Wholesale, Retail, and Farm	Laredo MSA, TX	Y	19010 FQ	31950 AW	56320 TQ	TXBLS	10/01-12/01
Except Wholesale, Retail, and Farm	Longview-Marshall MSA, TX	Y	24370 FQ	38760 AW	55360 TQ	TXBLS	10/01-12/01
Except Wholesale, Retail, and Farm	Lubbock MSA, TX	Y	22860 FQ	37260 AW	54010 TQ	TXBLS	10/01-12/01
Except Wholesale, Retail, and Farm	McAllen-Edinburg-Mission MSA, TX	Y	15790 FQ	34390 AW	60040 TQ	TXBLS	10/01-12/01
Except Wholesale, Retail, and Farm	Odessa-Midland MSA, TX	Y	23740 FQ	45320 AW	77090 TQ	TXBLS	10/01-12/01
Except Wholesale, Retail, and Farm	San Antonio MSA, TX	Y	25360 FQ	42620 AW	64980 TQ	TXBLS	10/01-12/01
Except Wholesale, Retail, and Farm	Tyler MSA, TX	Y	24710 FQ	42000 AW	59810 TQ	TXBLS	10/01-12/01
Except Wholesale, Retail, and Farm	Waco MSA, TX	Y	21830 FQ	38410 AW	59320 TQ	TXBLS	10/01-12/01
Except Wholesale, Retail, and Farm	Utah	Y	27320 FQ	44110 AW	64880 TQ	UTBLS	10/01-12/01
Except Wholesale, Retail, and Farm	Provo-Orem MSA, UT	Y	23780 FQ	38370 AW	54150 TQ	UTBLS	10/01-12/01
Except Wholesale, Retail, and Farm	Salt Lake City-Ogden MSA, UT	Y	28050 FQ	44500 AW	64730 TQ	UTBLS	10/01-12/01
Except Wholesale, Retail, and Farm	Vermont	Y	29430 FQ	47530 AW	72310 TQ	VTBLS	10/01-12/01
Except Wholesale, Retail, and Farm	Burlington MSA, VT	Y	31580 FQ	49150 AW	70580 TQ	VTBLS	10/01-12/01
Except Wholesale, Retail, and Farm	Virginia	Y	29490 FQ	50530 AW	78640 TQ	VABLS	10/01-12/01
Except Wholesale, Retail, and Farm	Lynchburg MSA, VA	Y	27290 FQ	40790 AW	62550 TQ	VABLS	10/01-12/01
Except Wholesale, Retail, and Farm	Norfolk-Virginia Beach-Newport News MSA, VA-NC	Y	28350 FQ	44950 AW	67450 TQ	VABLS	10/01-12/01
Except Wholesale, Retail, and Farm	Richmond-Petersburg MSA, VA	Y	29980 FQ	46180 AW	68180 TQ	VABLS	10/01-12/01
Except Wholesale, Retail, and Farm	Roanoke MSA, VA	Y	23100 FQ	38600 AW	56400 TQ	VABLS	10/01-12/01
Except Wholesale, Retail, and Farm	Washington	Y	30790 FQ	48750 AW	71040 TQ	WABLS	10/01-12/01
Except Wholesale, Retail, and Farm	Bremerton PMSA, WA	Y	29760 FQ	45600 AW	67570 TQ	WABLS	10/01-12/01
Except Wholesale, Retail, and Farm	Olympia PMSA, WA	Y	33260 FQ	44860 AW	58780 TQ	WABLS	10/01-12/01
Except Wholesale, Retail, and Farm	Richland-Kennewick-Pasco MSA, WA	Y	30460 FQ	52320 AW	77450 TQ	WABLS	10/01-12/01
Except Wholesale, Retail, and Farm	Seattle-Bellevue-Everett PMSA, WA	Y	32670 FQ	51340 AW	73960 TQ	WABLS	10/01-12/01
Except Wholesale, Retail, and Farm	Spokane MSA, WA	Y	26200 FQ	43080 AW	61410 TQ	WABLS	10/01-12/01
Except Wholesale, Retail, and Farm	Tacoma PMSA, WA	Y	29280 FQ	46200 AW	68740 TQ	WABLS	10/01-12/01
Except Wholesale, Retail, and Farm	Yakima MSA, WA	Y	24090 FQ	41780 AW	64010 TQ	WABLS	10/01-12/01
Except Wholesale, Retail, and Farm	West Virginia	Y	18770 FQ	37390 AW	60340 TQ	WVBLS	10/01-12/01
Except Wholesale, Retail, and Farm	Charleston MSA, WV	Y	22130 FQ	41840 AW	68650 TQ	WVBLS	10/01-12/01
Except Wholesale, Retail, and Farm	Huntington-Ashland MSA, WV-KY-OH	Y	23420 FQ	41930 AW	61270 TQ	WVBLS	10/01-12/01
Except Wholesale, Retail, and Farm	Wisconsin	Y	25650 FQ	42990 AW	65310 TQ	WIBLS	10/01-12/01
Except Wholesale, Retail, and Farm	Appleton-Oshkosh-Neenah MSA, WI	Y	24680 FQ	42810 AW	68870 TQ	WIBLS	10/01-12/01
Except Wholesale, Retail, and Farm	Green Bay MSA, WI	Y	26570 FQ	44050 AW	66520 TQ	WIBLS	10/01-12/01
Except Wholesale, Retail, and Farm	Madison MSA, WI	Y	26890 FQ	40880 AW	55970 TQ	WIBLS	10/01-12/01

AAW Average annual wage **AOH** Average offered, high **ASH** Average starting, high **H** Hourly **M** Monthly **S** Special: hourly and annual
AE Average entry wage **AOL** Average offered, low **ASL** Average starting, low **HI** Highest wage paid **MTC** Median total compensation **TQ** Third quartile wage
AEX Average experienced wage **APH** Average pay, high range **AW** Average wage paid **HR** High end range **MW** Median wage paid **W** Weekly
AO Average offered **APL** Average pay, low range **FQ** First quartile wage **LR** Low end range **SQ** Second quartile wage **Y** Yearly

Occupation/Type/Industry	Location	Per	Low	Mid	High	Source	Date
Purchasing Agent							
Except Wholesale, Retail, and Farm	Milwaukee-Waukesha PMSA, WI	Y	28880 FQ	47130 AW	70040 TQ	WIBLS	10/01-12/01
Except Wholesale, Retail, and Farm	Racine PMSA, WI	Y	23510 FQ	40960 AW	59370 TQ	WIBLS	10/01-12/01
Except Wholesale, Retail, and Farm	Wyoming	Y	23460 FQ	39510 AW	59680 TQ	WYBLS	10/01-12/01
Except Wholesale, Retail, and Farm	Cheyenne MSA, WY	Y	28290 FQ	39120 AW	52280 TQ	WYBLS	10/01-12/01
Except Wholesale, Retail, and Farm	Puerto Rico	Y	14830 FQ	27970 AW	48190 TQ	PRBLS	10/01-12/01
Except Wholesale, Retail, and Farm	Virgin Islands	Y	19530 FQ	31120 AW	46960 TQ	VIBLS	10/01-12/01
Except Wholesale, Retail, and Farm	Guam	Y	18340 FQ	35640 AW	60590 TQ	GUBLS	10/01-12/01
Purchasing Agent and Buyer							
Farm Product	Alabama	Y	18000 FQ	39960 AW	67230 TQ	ALBLS	10/01-12/01
Farm Product	Arizona	Y	24770 FQ	50120 AW	107380 TQ	AZBLS	10/01-12/01
Farm Product	Phoenix-Mesa MSA, AZ	Y	27530 FQ	52560 AW	108920 TQ	AZBLS	10/01-12/01
Farm Product	Arkansas	Y	25510 FQ	41550 AW	56790 TQ	ARBLS	10/01-12/01
Farm Product	Little Rock-North Little Rock MSA, AR	Y	21860 FQ	33110 AW	42610 TQ	ARBLS	10/01-12/01
Farm Product	California	Y	24120 FQ	49910 AW	86780 TQ	CABLS	10/01-12/01
Farm Product	Fresno MSA, CA	Y	16130 FQ	45910 AW	102050 TQ	CABLS	10/01-12/01
Farm Product	Los Angeles-Long Beach PMSA, CA	Y	33020 FQ	53300 AW	80350 TQ	CABLS	10/01-12/01
Farm Product	Oakland PMSA, CA	Y	21410 FQ	47690 AW	77700 TQ	CABLS	10/01-12/01
Farm Product	Orange County PMSA, CA	Y	27370 FQ	49720 AW	85890 TQ	CABLS	10/01-12/01
Farm Product	Riverside-San Bernardino PMSA, CA	Y	22130 FQ	45980 AW	94440 TQ	CABLS	10/01-12/01
Farm Product	Sacramento PMSA, CA	Y	22840 FQ	49350 AW	74560 TQ	CABLS	10/01-12/01
Farm Product	San Diego MSA, CA	Y	34600 FQ	47510 AW	68890 TQ	CABLS	10/01-12/01
Farm Product	San Francisco PMSA, CA	Y	17410 FQ	56040 AW	101770 TQ	CABLS	10/01-12/01
Farm Product	San Jose PMSA, CA	Y	25030 FQ	65700 AW		CABLS	10/01-12/01
Farm Product	Stockton-Lodi MSA, CA	Y	31780 FQ	48200 AW	69100 TQ	CABLS	10/01-12/01
Farm Product	Visalia-Tulare-Porterville MSA, CA	Y	28220 FQ	44580 AW	63600 TQ	CABLS	10/01-12/01
Farm Product	Colorado	Y	24250 FQ	42430 AW	66870 TQ	COBLS	10/01-12/01
Farm Product	Denver PMSA, CO	Y	26240 FQ	46700 AW	68660 TQ	COBLS	10/01-12/01
Farm Product	Connecticut	Y	32030 FQ	67500 AW	121140 TQ	CTBLS	10/01-12/01
Farm Product	Delaware	Y	22510 FQ	42770 AW	72650 TQ	DEBLS	10/01-12/01
Farm Product	Wilmington-Newark PMSA, DE-MD	Y	22650 FQ	46720 AW	74810 TQ	DEBLS	10/01-12/01
Farm Product	District of Columbia	Y	40990 FQ	69120 AW	108600 TQ	DCBLS	10/01-12/01
Farm Product	Washington PMSA, DC-MD-VA-WV	Y	26680 FQ	59540 AW	109290 TQ	DCBLS	10/01-12/01
Farm Product	Florida	Y	19600 FQ	43340 AW	86840 TQ	FLBLS	10/01-12/01
Farm Product	Daytona Beach MSA, FL	Y	24000 FQ	40430 AW	54730 TQ	FLBLS	10/01-12/01
Farm Product	Fort Lauderdale PMSA, FL	Y	36870 FQ	64650 AW	93880 TQ	FLBLS	10/01-12/01
Farm Product	Jacksonville MSA, FL	Y	26840 FQ	50550 AW	88670 TQ	FLBLS	10/01-12/01
Farm Product	Miami PMSA, FL	Y	20000 FQ	30510 AW	43090 TQ	FLBLS	10/01-12/01
Farm Product	Orlando MSA, FL	Y	27420 FQ	40870 AW	72680 TQ	FLBLS	10/01-12/01
Farm Product	Sarasota-Bradenton MSA, FL	Y	23210 FQ	39830 AW	60770 TQ	FLBLS	10/01-12/01
Farm Product	Tampa-St. Petersburg-Clearwater MSA, FL	Y	20050 FQ	47780 AW	103010 TQ	FLBLS	10/01-12/01
Farm Product	West Palm Beach-Boca Raton MSA, FL	Y	31690 FQ	72020 AW	96680 TQ	FLBLS	10/01-12/01
Farm Product	Georgia	Y	24090 FQ	59760 AW		GABLS	10/01-12/01
Farm Product	Atlanta MSA, GA	Y	29500 FQ	68890 AW		GABLS	10/01-12/01
Farm Product	Hawaii	Y	28770 FQ	32130 AW	34940 TQ	HIBLS	10/01-12/01
Farm Product	Honolulu MSA, HI	Y	28810 FQ	31630 AW	34830 TQ	HIBLS	10/01-12/01
Farm Product	Idaho	Y	15650 FQ	37530 AW	60520 TQ	IDBLS	10/01-12/01
Farm Product	Boise City MSA, ID	Y	26760 FQ	37350 AW	54110 TQ	IDBLS	10/01-12/01
Farm Product	Illinois	Y	24550 FQ	42910 AW	66640 TQ	ILBLS	10/01-12/01
Farm Product	Chicago PMSA, IL	Y	27850 FQ	46030 AW	69930 TQ	ILBLS	10/01-12/01
Farm Product	Indiana	Y	24490 FQ	42880 AW	58320 TQ	INBLS	10/01-12/01
Farm Product	Elkhart-Goshen MSA, IN	Y	31480 FQ	46650 AW	59620 TQ	INBLS	10/01-12/01
Farm Product	Evansville-Henderson MSA, IN-KY	Y	22880 FQ	46760 AW	72410 TQ	INBLS	10/01-12/01
Farm Product	Fort Wayne MSA, IN	Y	31890 FQ	45890 AW	57280 TQ	INBLS	10/01-12/01
Farm Product	Indianapolis MSA, IN	Y	27210 FQ	46230 AW	57620 TQ	INBLS	10/01-12/01
Farm Product	South Bend MSA, IN	Y	24490 FQ	35560 AW	46040 TQ	INBLS	10/01-12/01
Farm Product	Iowa	Y	23090 FQ	44780 AW	68980 TQ	IABLS	10/01-12/01
Farm Product	Des Moines MSA, IA	Y	29200 FQ	49770 AW	82510 TQ	IABLS	10/01-12/01
Farm Product	Kansas	Y	26090 FQ	42260 AW	57750 TQ	KSBLS	10/01-12/01
Farm Product	Kentucky	Y	21430 FQ	33880 AW	46010 TQ	KYBLS	10/01-12/01
Farm Product	Lexington MSA, KY	Y	23240 FQ	33130 AW	43430 TQ	KYBLS	10/01-12/01
Farm Product	Louisville MSA, KY-IN	Y	23240 FQ	38590 AW	55340 TQ	KYBLS	10/01-12/01

AAW Average annual wage · **AE** Average entry wage · **AEX** Average experienced wage · **AO** Average offered · **AOH** Average offered, high · **AOL** Average offered, low · **APH** Average pay, high range · **APL** Average pay, low range · **ASH** Average starting, high · **ASL** Average starting, low · **AW** Average wage paid · **FQ** First quartile wage · **H** Hourly · **HI** Highest wage paid · **HR** High end range · **LR** Low end range · **M** Monthly · **MTC** Median total compensation · **MW** Median wage paid · **SQ** Second quartile wage · **S** Special: hourly and annual · **TQ** Third quartile wage · **W** Weekly · **Y** Yearly

Occupation/Type/Industry	Location	Per	Low	Mid	High	Source	Date
Purchasing Agent and Buyer							
Farm Product	Louisiana	Y	18360 FQ	31140 AW	48210 TQ	LABLS	10/01-12/01
Farm Product	New Orleans MSA, LA	Y	17570 FQ	29140 AW	50300 TQ	LABLS	10/01-12/01
Farm Product	Maine	Y	22210 FQ	38690 AW	56170 TQ	MEBLS	10/01-12/01
Farm Product	Maryland	Y	26080 FQ	46110 AW	72660 TQ	MDBLS	10/01-12/01
Farm Product	Baltimore PMSA, MD	Y	30870 FQ	43460 AW	64020 TQ	MDBLS	10/01-12/01
Farm Product	Massachusetts	Y	24930 FQ	44850 AW	73130 TQ	MABLS	10/01-12/01
Farm Product	Boston PMSA, MA-NH	Y	29290 FQ	50410 AW	76930 TQ	MABLS	10/01-12/01
Farm Product	Michigan	Y	22780 FQ	45890 AW	81940 TQ	MIBLS	10/01-12/01
Farm Product	Ann Arbor PMSA, MI	Y	24140 FQ	34450 AW	47900 TQ	MIBLS	10/01-12/01
Farm Product	Detroit PMSA, MI	Y	34320 FQ	59750 AW	92630 TQ	MIBLS	10/01-12/01
Farm Product	Grand Rapids-Muskegon-Holland MSA, MI	Y	18170 FQ	50160 AW	76690 TQ	MIBLS	10/01-12/01
Farm Product	Kalamazoo-Battle Creek MSA, MI	Y	16420 FQ	41400 AW	58110 TQ	MIBLS	10/01-12/01
Farm Product	Minnesota	Y	28120 FQ	49750 AW	82140 TQ	MNBLS	10/01-12/01
Farm Product	Minneapolis-St. Paul MSA, MN-WI	Y	30060 FQ	51420 AW	83260 TQ	MNBLS	10/01-12/01
Farm Product	Mississippi	Y	24210 FQ	36200 AW	52620 TQ	MSBLS	10/01-12/01
Farm Product	Jackson MSA, MS	Y	30400 FQ	34840 AW	37900 TQ	MSBLS	10/01-12/01
Farm Product	Missouri	Y	20490 FQ	39460 AW	78720 TQ	MOBLS	10/01-12/01
Farm Product	Kansas City MSA, MO-KS	Y	30850 FQ	48900 AW	73740 TQ	MOBLS	10/01-12/01
Farm Product	St. Louis MSA, MO-IL	Y	27480 FQ	44790 AW	78040 TQ	MOBLS	10/01-12/01
Farm Product	Springfield MSA, MO	Y	14890 FQ	29360 AW	45900 TQ	MOBLS	10/01-12/01
Farm Product	Montana	Y	23730 FQ	40240 AW	62160 TQ	MTBLS	10/01-12/01
Farm Product	Nebraska	Y	25970 FQ	46620 AW	77470 TQ	NEBLS	10/01-12/01
Farm Product	Omaha MSA, NE-IA	Y	31520 FQ	57010 AW	92080 TQ	NEBLS	10/01-12/01
Farm Product	Nevada	Y	24850 FQ	39470 AW	58430 TQ	NVBLS	10/01-12/01
Farm Product	Las Vegas MSA, NV-AZ	Y	25670 FQ	39630 AW	59440 TQ	NVBLS	10/01-12/01
Farm Product	New Jersey	Y	27210 FQ	58250 AW	116650 TQ	NJBLS	10/01-12/01
Farm Product	Bergen-Passaic PMSA, NJ	Y	33800 FQ	77350 AW	137200 TQ	NJBLS	10/01-12/01
Farm Product	Middlesex-Somerset-Hunterdon PMSA, NJ	Y	21970 FQ	46910 AW	98600 TQ	NJBLS	10/01-12/01
Farm Product	Newark PMSA, NJ	Y	32510 FQ	69360 AW	130100 TQ	NJBLS	10/01-12/01
Farm Product	New Mexico	Y	12930 FQ	30500 AW	57390 TQ	NMBLS	10/01-12/01
Farm Product	Albuquerque MSA, NM	Y	12540 FQ	30110 AW	56050 TQ	NMBLS	10/01-12/01
Farm Product	New York	Y	26900 FQ	50050 AW	89050 TQ	NYBLS	10/01-12/01
Farm Product	Buffalo-Niagara Falls MSA, NY	Y	26390 FQ	45970 AW	82660 TQ	NYBLS	10/01-12/01
Farm Product	Nassau-Suffolk PMSA, NY	Y	32150 FQ	51560 AW	81160 TQ	NYBLS	10/01-12/01
Farm Product	New York PMSA, NY	Y	21860 FQ	53350 AW	113050 TQ	NYBLS	10/01-12/01
Farm Product	Syracuse MSA, NY	Y	22740 FQ	36170 AW	45530 TQ	NYBLS	10/01-12/01
Farm Product	North Carolina	Y	22530 FQ	46100 AW	95420 TQ	NCBLS	10/01-12/01
Farm Product	Charlotte-Gastonia-Rock Hill MSA, NC-SC	Y	18000 FQ	43760 AW	74250 TQ	NCBLS	10/01-12/01
Farm Product	Greensboro-Winston-Salem-High Point MSA, NC	Y	30970 FQ	46940 AW	67560 TQ	NCBLS	10/01-12/01
Farm Product	Raleigh-Durham-Chapel Hill MSA, NC	Y	28900 FQ	62010 AW	122130 TQ	NCBLS	10/01-12/01
Farm Product	North Dakota	Y	30900 FQ	47420 AW	67470 TQ	NDBLS	10/01-12/01
Farm Product	Fargo-Moorhead MSA, ND-MN	Y	32280 FQ	50660 AW	70480 TQ	NDBLS	10/01-12/01
Farm Product	Ohio	Y	22190 FQ	41740 AW	62510 TQ	OHBLS	10/01-12/01
Farm Product	Canton-Massillon MSA, OH	Y	18150 FQ	38070 AW	55690 TQ	OHBLS	10/01-12/01
Farm Product	Cincinnati PMSA, OH-KY-IN	Y	27060 FQ	47170 AW	68890 TQ	OHBLS	10/01-12/01
Farm Product	Cleveland-Lorain-Elyria PMSA, OH	Y	22710 FQ	39220 AW	65460 TQ	OHBLS	10/01-12/01
Farm Product	Columbus MSA, OH	Y	20520 FQ	42370 AW	61520 TQ	OHBLS	10/01-12/01
Farm Product	Toledo MSA, OH	Y	26720 FQ	47710 AW	73170 TQ	OHBLS	10/01-12/01
Farm Product	Oklahoma	Y	17360 FQ	36660 AW	56100 TQ	OKBLS	10/01-12/01
Farm Product	Oklahoma City MSA, OK	Y	16140 FQ	34820 AW	54870 TQ	OKBLS	10/01-12/01
Farm Product	Tulsa MSA, OK	Y	24380 FQ	38140 AW	54710 TQ	OKBLS	10/01-12/01
Farm Product	Oregon	Y	30130 FQ	48030 AW	77800 TQ	ORBLS	10/01-12/01
Farm Product	Portland-Vancouver PMSA, OR-WA	Y	28950 FQ	52680 AW	89470 TQ	ORBLS	10/01-12/01
Farm Product	Pennsylvania	Y	24310 FQ	46700 AW	100930 TQ	PABLS	10/01-12/01
Farm Product	Philadelphia PMSA, PA-NJ	Y	24730 FQ	45780 AW	82400 TQ	PABLS	10/01-12/01
Farm Product	Pittsburgh MSA, PA	Y	25350 FQ	66130 AW	142680 TQ	PABLS	10/01-12/01
Farm Product	Reading MSA, PA	Y	26020 FQ	36330 AW	47600 TQ	PABLS	10/01-12/01
Farm Product	Rhode Island	Y	30930 FQ	51630 AW	85570 TQ	RIBLS	10/01-12/01
Farm Product	Providence-Fall River-Warwick MSA, RI-MA	Y	31990 FQ	52370 AW	87170 TQ	RIBLS	10/01-12/01

AAW	Average annual wage	**AOH**	Average offered, high	**ASH**	Average starting, high	**H**	Hourly	**M**	Monthly	**S**	Special: hourly and annual
AE	Average entry wage	**AOL**	Average offered, low	**ASL**	Average starting, low	**HI**	Highest wage paid	**MTC**	Median total compensation	**TQ**	Third quartile wage
AEX	Average experienced wage	**APH**	Average pay, high range	**AW**	Average wage paid	**HR**	High end range	**MW**	Median wage paid	**W**	Weekly
AO	Average offered	**APL**	Average pay, low range	**FQ**	First quartile wage	**LR**	Low end range	**SQ**	Second quartile wage	**Y**	Yearly

Occupation/Type/Industry	Location	Per	Low	Mid	High	Source	Date
Purchasing Agent and Buyer							
Farm Product	South Carolina	Y	25550 FQ	45470 AW	86380 TQ	SCBLS	10/01-12/01
Farm Product	Columbia MSA, SC	Y	29920 FQ	57160 AW	92340 TQ	SCBLS	10/01-12/01
Farm Product	South Dakota	Y	29980 FQ	39810 AW	53490 TQ	SDBLS	10/01-12/01
Farm Product	Tennessee	Y	21670 FQ	43680 AW	69490 TQ	TNBLS	10/01-12/01
Farm Product	Memphis MSA, TN-AR-MS	Y	24170 FQ	54120 AW	76210 TQ	TNBLS	10/01-12/01
Farm Product	Nashville MSA, TN	Y	21330 FQ	46380 AW	70120 TQ	TNBLS	10/01-12/01
Farm Product	Texas	Y	21270 FQ	48890 AW	90330 TQ	TXBLS	10/01-12/01
Farm Product	Amarillo MSA, TX	Y	28510 FQ	50240 AW	81510 TQ	TXBLS	10/01-12/01
Farm Product	Austin-San Marcos MSA, TX	Y	18090 FQ	64770 AW	110500 TQ	TXBLS	10/01-12/01
Farm Product	Dallas PMSA, TX	Y	25610 FQ	53250 AW	96400 TQ	TXBLS	10/01-12/01
Farm Product	Fort Worth-Arlington PMSA, TX	Y	21260 FQ	41960 AW	63090 TQ	TXBLS	10/01-12/01
Farm Product	Houston PMSA, TX	Y	28410 FQ	54380 AW	105700 TQ	TXBLS	10/01-12/01
Farm Product	Lubbock MSA, TX	Y	36130 FQ	70500 AW	94290 TQ	TXBLS	10/01-12/01
Farm Product	San Antonio MSA, TX	Y	26320 FQ	47460 AW	83850 TQ	TXBLS	10/01-12/01
Farm Product	Utah	Y	18270 FQ	38150 AW	56760 TQ	UTBLS	10/01-12/01
Farm Product	Salt Lake City-Ogden MSA, UT	Y	21000 FQ	37180 AW	54060 TQ	UTBLS	10/01-12/01
Farm Product	Vermont	Y	20540 FQ	51940 AW	103110 TQ	VTBLS	10/01-12/01
Farm Product	Virginia	Y	24620 FQ	41130 AW	62780 TQ	VABLS	10/01-12/01
Farm Product	Norfolk-Virginia Beach-Newport News MSA, VA-NC	Y	20500 FQ	40030 AW	68720 TQ	VABLS	10/01-12/01
Farm Product	Richmond-Petersburg MSA, VA	Y	29370 FQ	46810 AW	69000 TQ	VABLS	10/01-12/01
Farm Product	Washington	Y	20810 FQ	41110 AW	62700 TQ	WABLS	10/01-12/01
Farm Product	Seattle-Bellevue-Everett PMSA, WA	Y	21140 FQ	40940 AW	59040 TQ	WABLS	10/01-12/01
Farm Product	Spokane MSA, WA	Y	21710 FQ	35880 AW	48040 TQ	WABLS	10/01-12/01
Farm Product	Yakima MSA, WA	Y	33830 FQ	54040 AW	71430 TQ	WABLS	10/01-12/01
Farm Product	West Virginia	Y	25550 FQ	36080 AW	54000 TQ	WVBLS	10/01-12/01
Farm Product	Wisconsin	Y	23290 FQ	39670 AW	63260 TQ	WIBLS	10/01-12/01
Farm Product	Milwaukee-Waukesha PMSA, WI	Y	16300 FQ	47420 AW	90630 TQ	WIBLS	10/01-12/01
Farm Product	Puerto Rico	Y	14080 FQ	27270 AW	48800 TQ	PRBLS	10/01-12/01
Purchasing Manager	Alabama	Y	24530 FQ	52680 AW	89390 TQ	ALBLS	10/01-12/01
	Birmingham MSA, AL	Y	30860 FQ	55100 AW	88940 TQ	ALBLS	10/01-12/01
	Huntsville MSA, AL	Y	30400 FQ	66140 AW	105060 TQ	ALBLS	10/01-12/01
	Mobile MSA, AL	Y	21200 FQ	46560 AW	81140 TQ	ALBLS	10/01-12/01
	Montgomery MSA, AL	Y	22310 FQ	48760 AW	80530 TQ	ALBLS	10/01-12/01
	Alaska	Y	30980 FQ	59260 AW	91210 TQ	AKBLS	10/01-12/01
	Anchorage MSA, AK	Y	34140 FQ	65010 AW	105150 TQ	AKBLS	10/01-12/01
	Arizona	Y	31300 FQ	56470 AW	88160 TQ	AZBLS	10/01-12/01
	Phoenix-Mesa MSA, AZ	Y	31960 FQ	58080 AW	89420 TQ	AZBLS	10/01-12/01
	Tucson MSA, AZ	Y	28000 FQ	49640 AW	76390 TQ	AZBLS	10/01-12/01
	Arkansas	Y	25430 FQ	50280 AW	81820 TQ	ARBLS	10/01-12/01
	Fayetteville-Springdale-Rogers MSA, AR	Y	24850 FQ	52690 AW	83780 TQ	ARBLS	10/01-12/01
	Fort Smith MSA, AR-OK	Y	29930 FQ	52110 AW	83060 TQ	ARBLS	10/01-12/01
	Little Rock-North Little Rock MSA, AR	Y	30260 FQ	52650 AW	85010 TQ	ARBLS	10/01-12/01
	California	Y	37700 FQ	70590 AW	115020 TQ	CABLS	10/01-12/01
	Bakersfield MSA, CA	Y	32160 FQ	72080 AW	120220 TQ	CABLS	10/01-12/01
	Chico-Paradise MSA, CA	Y	31520 FQ	53730 AW	79630 TQ	CABLS	10/01-12/01
	Fresno MSA, CA	Y	30810 FQ	55000 AW	85050 TQ	CABLS	10/01-12/01
	Los Angeles-Long Beach PMSA, CA	Y	38980 FQ	71870 AW	134590 TQ	CABLS	10/01-12/01
	Merced MSA, CA	Y	31030 FQ	56490 AW	89320 TQ	CABLS	10/01-12/01
	Modesto MSA, CA	Y	35420 FQ	62800 AW	94450 TQ	CABLS	10/01-12/01
	Oakland PMSA, CA	Y	41260 FQ	70630 AW	108310 TQ	CABLS	10/01-12/01
	Orange County PMSA, CA	Y	40970 FQ	76090 AW	126530 TQ	CABLS	10/01-12/01
	Riverside-San Bernardino PMSA, CA	Y	32290 FQ	60830 AW	97030 TQ	CABLS	10/01-12/01
	Sacramento PMSA, CA	Y	35710 FQ	62280 AW	90600 TQ	CABLS	10/01-12/01
	Salinas MSA, CA	Y	32270 FQ	61920 AW	101700 TQ	CABLS	10/01-12/01
	San Diego MSA, CA	Y	36670 FQ	68120 AW	105490 TQ	CABLS	10/01-12/01
	San Francisco PMSA, CA	Y	31100 FQ	63560 AW	105640 TQ	CABLS	10/01-12/01
	San Jose PMSA, CA	Y	49380 FQ	82740 AW	128490 TQ	CABLS	10/01-12/01
	San Luis Obispo-Atascadero-Paso Robles MSA, CA	Y	39490 FQ	65070 AW	107050 TQ	CABLS	10/01-12/01

AAW Average annual wage · **AE** Average entry wage · **AEX** Average experienced wage · **AO** Average offered · **AOH** Average offered, high · **AOL** Average offered, low · **APH** Average pay, high range · **APL** Average pay, low range · **ASH** Average starting, high · **ASL** Average starting, low · **AW** Average wage paid · **FQ** First quartile wage · **H** Hourly · **HI** Highest wage paid · **HR** High end range · **LR** Low end range · **M** Monthly · **MTC** Median total compensation · **MW** Median wage paid · **SQ** Second quartile wage · **S** Special: hourly and annual · **TQ** Third quartile wage · **W** Weekly · **Y** Yearly

Occupation/Type/Industry	Location	Per	Low	Mid	High	Source	Date
Purchasing Manager	Santa Barbara-Santa Maria-Lompoc MSA, CA	Y	33100 FQ	63100 AW	95850 TQ	CABLS	10/01-12/01
	Santa Cruz-Watsonville PMSA, CA	Y	39750 FQ	72460 AW	111580 TQ	CABLS	10/01-12/01
	Santa Rosa PMSA, CA	Y	34790 FQ	65030 AW	105330 TQ	CABLS	10/01-12/01
	Stockton-Lodi MSA, CA	Y	36630 FQ	64910 AW	108420 TQ	CABLS	10/01-12/01
	Vallejo-Fairfield-Napa PMSA, CA	Y	31290 FQ	69410 AW	111730 TQ	CABLS	10/01-12/01
	Ventura PMSA, CA	Y	40130 FQ	70180 AW	103560 TQ	CABLS	10/01-12/01
	Visalia-Tulare-Porterville MSA, CA	Y	33490 FQ	71710 AW	127760 TQ	CABLS	10/01-12/01
	Colorado	Y	34320 FQ	63460 AW	104210 TQ	COBLS	10/01-12/01
	Boulder-Longmont PMSA, CO	Y	54060 FQ	87900 AW	132460 TQ	COBLS	10/01-12/01
	Colorado Springs MSA, CO	Y	39010 FQ	67800 AW	100600 TQ	COBLS	10/01-12/01
	Denver PMSA, CO	Y	34140 FQ	59790 AW	96360 TQ	COBLS	10/01-12/01
	Fort Collins-Loveland MSA, CO	Y	27840 FQ	66080 AW	107890 TQ	COBLS	10/01-12/01
	Greeley PMSA, CO	Y	39000 FQ	64300 AW	96960 TQ	COBLS	10/01-12/01
	Connecticut	Y	38870 FQ	69540 AW	111830 TQ	CTBLS	10/01-12/01
	Bridgeport PMSA, CT	Y	41230 FQ	69570 AW	110510 TQ	CTBLS	10/01-12/01
	Danbury PMSA, CT	Y	37920 FQ	63490 AW	96430 TQ	CTBLS	10/01-12/01
	Hartford MSA, CT	Y	47620 FQ	76660 AW	120070 TQ	CTBLS	10/01-12/01
	New Haven-Meriden PMSA, CT	Y	26920 FQ	54820 AW	88560 TQ	CTBLS	10/01-12/01
	New London-Norwich MSA, CT-RI	Y	41130 FQ	71940 AW	122030 TQ	CTBLS	10/01-12/01
	Stamford-Norwalk PMSA, CT	Y	39670 FQ	71610 AW	118910 TQ	CTBLS	10/01-12/01
	Waterbury PMSA, CT	Y	48970 FQ	67680 AW	93810 TQ	CTBLS	10/01-12/01
	Delaware	Y	30150 FQ	56800 AW	89860 TQ	DEBLS	10/01-12/01
	Wilmington-Newark PMSA, DE-MD	Y	31240 FQ	59350 AW	94180 TQ	DEBLS	10/01-12/01
	District of Columbia	Y	45100 FQ	78020 AW	108970 TQ	DCBLS	10/01-12/01
	Washington PMSA, DC-MD-VA-WV	Y	39520 FQ	70870 AW	107120 TQ	DCBLS	10/01-12/01
	Florida	Y	28580 FQ	54540 AW	90500 TQ	FLBLS	10/01-12/01
	Daytona Beach MSA, FL	Y	29990 FQ	44990 AW	74420 TQ	FLBLS	10/01-12/01
	Fort Lauderdale PMSA, FL	Y	30110 FQ	60050 AW	101980 TQ	FLBLS	10/01-12/01
	Fort Myers-Cape Coral MSA, FL	Y	28350 FQ	48510 AW	80960 TQ	FLBLS	10/01-12/01
	Fort Pierce-Port St. Lucie MSA, FL	Y	27440 FQ	45110 AW	72100 TQ	FLBLS	10/01-12/01
	Fort Walton Beach MSA, FL	Y	26340 FQ	57820 AW	89660 TQ	FLBLS	10/01-12/01
	Gainesville MSA, FL	Y	22060 FQ	49070 AW	72190 TQ	FLBLS	10/01-12/01
	Jacksonville MSA, FL	Y	29830 FQ	51150 AW	81340 TQ	FLBLS	10/01-12/01
	Lakeland-Winter Haven MSA, FL	Y	28810 FQ	50700 AW	84040 TQ	FLBLS	10/01-12/01
	Melbourne-Titusville-Palm Bay MSA, FL	Y	30600 FQ	61960 AW	101800 TQ	FLBLS	10/01-12/01
	Miami PMSA, FL	Y	29440 FQ	53840 AW	91130 TQ	FLBLS	10/01-12/01
	Naples MSA, FL	Y	27380 FQ	50230 AW	75860 TQ	FLBLS	10/01-12/01
	Ocala MSA, FL	Y	28330 FQ	58080 AW	104730 TQ	FLBLS	10/01-12/01
	Orlando MSA, FL	Y	29270 FQ	56270 AW	93330 TQ	FLBLS	10/01-12/01
	Pensacola MSA, FL	Y	28750 FQ	50830 AW	83950 TQ	FLBLS	10/01-12/01
	Sarasota-Bradenton MSA, FL	Y	29030 FQ	55410 AW	98290 TQ	FLBLS	10/01-12/01
	Tallahassee MSA, FL	Y	33120 FQ	55850 AW	89670 TQ	FLBLS	10/01-12/01
	Tampa-St. Petersburg-Clearwater MSA, FL	Y	27490 FQ	55040 AW	87400 TQ	FLBLS	10/01-12/01
	West Palm Beach-Boca Raton MSA, FL	Y	28570 FQ	57140 AW	99530 TQ	FLBLS	10/01-12/01
	Georgia	Y	37850 FQ	66950 AW	118420 TQ	GABLS	10/01-12/01
	Atlanta MSA, GA	Y	39560 FQ	71920 AW	128730 TQ	GABLS	10/01-12/01
	Augusta-Aiken MSA, GA-SC	Y	32770 FQ	63040 AW	95630 TQ	GABLS	10/01-12/01
	Columbus MSA, GA-AL	Y	32930 FQ	56400 AW	89370 TQ	GABLS	10/01-12/01
	Macon MSA, GA	Y	33040 FQ	64100 AW	102370 TQ	GABLS	10/01-12/01
	Savannah MSA, GA	Y	39670 FQ	58290 AW	73140 TQ	GABLS	10/01-12/01
	Hawaii	Y	30740 FQ	63130 AW	102750 TQ	HIBLS	10/01-12/01
	Honolulu MSA, HI	Y	35800 FQ	67490 AW	108450 TQ	HIBLS	10/01-12/01
	Idaho	Y	24380 FQ	54530 AW	92800 TQ	IDBLS	10/01-12/01
	Boise City MSA, ID	Y	30710 FQ	60580 AW	99430 TQ	IDBLS	10/01-12/01
	Illinois	Y	30380 FQ	57860 AW	93060 TQ	ILBLS	10/01-12/01
	Champaign-Urbana MSA, IL	Y	14970 FQ	50760 AW	93240 TQ	ILBLS	10/01-12/01
	Chicago PMSA, IL	Y	31620 FQ	58900 AW	93710 TQ	ILBLS	10/01-12/01

AAW Average annual wage	**AOH** Average offered, high	**ASH** Average starting, high	**H** Hourly	**M** Monthly	**S** Special: hourly and annual
AE Average entry wage	**AOL** Average offered, low	**ASL** Average starting, low	**HI** Highest wage paid	**MTC** Median total compensation	**TQ** Third quartile wage
AEX Average experienced wage	**APH** Average pay, high range	**AW** Average wage paid	**HR** High end range	**MW** Median wage paid	**W** Weekly
AO Average offered	**APL** Average pay, low range	**FQ** First quartile wage	**LR** Low end range	**SQ** Second quartile wage	**Y** Yearly

Occupation/Type/Industry	Location	Per	Low	Mid	High	Source	Date
Purchasing Manager	Peoria-Pekin MSA, IL	Y	28710 FQ	64430 AW	116320 TQ	ILBLS	10/01-12/01
	Rockford MSA, IL	Y	27590 FQ	54920 AW	85720 TQ	ILBLS	10/01-12/01
	Springfield MSA, IL	Y	31350 FQ	60770 AW	102190 TQ	ILBLS	10/01-12/01
	Indiana	Y	31520 FQ	56760 AW	89460 TQ	INBLS	10/01-12/01
	Elkhart-Goshen MSA, IN	Y	33200 FQ	54080 AW	75370 TQ	INBLS	10/01-12/01
	Evansville-Henderson MSA, IN-KY	Y	26190 FQ	50990 AW	85660 TQ	INBLS	10/01-12/01
	Fort Wayne MSA, IN	Y	32550 FQ	54800 AW	85240 TQ	INBLS	10/01-12/01
	Gary PMSA, IN	Y	30170 FQ	51670 AW	83050 TQ	INBLS	10/01-12/01
	Indianapolis MSA, IN	Y	38380 FQ	63750 AW	105700 TQ	INBLS	10/01-12/01
	Lafayette MSA, IN	Y	35140 FQ	62870 AW	91970 TQ	INBLS	10/01-12/01
	South Bend MSA, IN	Y	30600 FQ	54490 AW	96320 TQ	INBLS	10/01-12/01
	Iowa	Y	23120 FQ	52540 AW	85820 TQ	IABLS	10/01-12/01
	Cedar Rapids MSA, IA	Y	26000 FQ	74490 AW		IABLS	10/01-12/01
	Davenport-Moline-Rock Island MSA, IA-IL	Y	22760 FQ	52650 AW	92250 TQ	IABLS	10/01-12/01
	Des Moines MSA, IA	Y	22060 FQ	49140 AW	81580 TQ	IABLS	10/01-12/01
	Kansas	Y	29940 FQ	59080 AW	92640 TQ	KSBLS	10/01-12/01
	Topeka MSA, KS	Y	29330 FQ	66500 AW	115320 TQ	KSBLS	10/01-12/01
	Wichita MSA, KS	Y	33640 FQ	65850 AW	96670 TQ	KSBLS	10/01-12/01
	Kentucky	Y	25750 FQ	52440 AW	85210 TQ	KYBLS	10/01-12/01
	Lexington MSA, KY	Y	29060 FQ	54860 AW	80610 TQ	KYBLS	10/01-12/01
	Louisville MSA, KY-IN	Y	27080 FQ	55670 AW	90820 TQ	KYBLS	10/01-12/01
	Louisiana	Y	24270 FQ	46970 AW	77970 TQ	LABLS	10/01-12/01
	Baton Rouge MSA, LA	Y	24510 FQ	47110 AW	74430 TQ	LABLS	10/01-12/01
	Houma MSA, LA	Y	22190 FQ	51220 AW	86000 TQ	LABLS	10/01-12/01
	Lafayette MSA, LA	Y	20850 FQ	45500 AW	86470 TQ	LABLS	10/01-12/01
	Lake Charles MSA, LA	Y	22400 FQ	43000 AW	74120 TQ	LABLS	10/01-12/01
	New Orleans MSA, LA	Y	25510 FQ	47550 AW	84580 TQ	LABLS	10/01-12/01
	Shreveport-Bossier City MSA, LA	Y	21780 FQ	50250 AW	79230 TQ	LABLS	10/01-12/01
	Maine	Y	25690 FQ	50190 AW	83780 TQ	MEBLS	10/01-12/01
	Portland MSA, ME	Y	29790 FQ	65810 AW	110540 TQ	MEBLS	10/01-12/01
	Maryland	Y	32240 FQ	62320 AW	101310 TQ	MDBLS	10/01-12/01
	Baltimore PMSA, MD	Y	31050 FQ	62220 AW	103750 TQ	MDBLS	10/01-12/01
	Massachusetts	Y	38040 FQ	68410 AW	107480 TQ	MABLS	10/01-12/01
	Boston PMSA, MA-NH	Y	41170 FQ	72360 AW	110260 TQ	MABLS	10/01-12/01
	Brockton PMSA, MA	Y	40750 FQ	70260 AW	109540 TQ	MABLS	10/01-12/01
	Lawrence PMSA, MA-NH	Y	35470 FQ	66270 AW	110930 TQ	MABLS	10/01-12/01
	Lowell PMSA, MA-NH	Y	38470 FQ	64260 AW	90200 TQ	MABLS	10/01-12/01
	New Bedford PMSA, MA	Y	25830 FQ	54770 AW	91460 TQ	MABLS	10/01-12/01
	Springfield MSA, MA	Y	31700 FQ	57900 AW	93700 TQ	MABLS	10/01-12/01
	Worcester PMSA, MA-CT	Y	38810 FQ	66530 AW	105760 TQ	MABLS	10/01-12/01
	Michigan	Y	39440 FQ	74770 AW	122110 TQ	MIBLS	10/01-12/01
	Ann Arbor PMSA, MI	Y	34020 FQ	72640 AW	131130 TQ	MIBLS	10/01-12/01
	Detroit PMSA, MI	Y	43350 FQ	81420 AW	137400 TQ	MIBLS	10/01-12/01
	Flint PMSA, MI	Y	38020 FQ	68860 AW	110130 TQ	MIBLS	10/01-12/01
	Grand Rapids-Muskegon-Holland MSA, MI	Y	46110 FQ	72050 AW	109800 TQ	MIBLS	10/01-12/01
	Kalamazoo-Battle Creek MSA, MI	Y	37260 FQ	72630 AW	110830 TQ	MIBLS	10/01-12/01
	Lansing-East Lansing MSA, MI	Y	31970 FQ	58760 AW	92400 TQ	MIBLS	10/01-12/01
	Saginaw-Bay City-Midland MSA, MI	Y	23170 FQ	60530 AW	102900 TQ	MIBLS	10/01-12/01
	Minnesota	Y	39990 FQ	67230 AW	99760 TQ	MNBLS	10/01-12/01
	Duluth-Superior MSA, MN-WI	Y	35840 FQ	61820 AW	93060 TQ	MNBLS	10/01-12/01
	Minneapolis-St. Paul MSA, MN-WI	Y	41360 FQ	69360 AW	104450 TQ	MNBLS	10/01-12/01
	St. Cloud MSA, MN	Y	38880 FQ	56520 AW	77070 TQ	MNBLS	10/01-12/01
	Mississippi	Y	23770 FQ	46450 AW	75320 TQ	MSBLS	10/01-12/01
	Biloxi-Gulfport-Pascagoula MSA, MS	Y	26400 FQ	52420 AW	76510 TQ	MSBLS	10/01-12/01
	Jackson MSA, MS	Y	23250 FQ	46680 AW	80840 TQ	MSBLS	10/01-12/01
	Missouri	Y	27410 FQ	54950 AW	90520 TQ	MOBLS	10/01-12/01
	Kansas City MSA, MO-KS	Y	31510 FQ	60110 AW	95280 TQ	MOBLS	10/01-12/01
	St. Louis MSA, MO-IL	Y	29100 FQ	56180 AW	92600 TQ	MOBLS	10/01-12/01
	Springfield MSA, MO	Y	29160 FQ	50540 AW	75100 TQ	MOBLS	10/01-12/01
	Montana	Y	22120 FQ	42410 AW	70410 TQ	MTBLS	10/01-12/01
	Billings MSA, MT	Y	26600 FQ	45060 AW	69440 TQ	MTBLS	10/01-12/01
	Nebraska	Y	26040 FQ	54450 AW	94610 TQ	NEBLS	10/01-12/01
	Lincoln MSA, NE	Y	26430 FQ	46350 AW	76420 TQ	NEBLS	10/01-12/01
	Omaha MSA, NE-IA	Y	28220 FQ	60810 AW	101940 TQ	NEBLS	10/01-12/01

AAW Average annual wage; **AE** Average entry wage; **AEX** Average experienced wage; **AO** Average offered; **AOH** Average offered, high; **AOL** Average offered, low; **APH** Average pay, high range; **APL** Average pay, low range; **ASH** Average starting, high; **ASL** Average starting, low; **AW** Average wage paid; **FQ** First quartile wage; **H** Hourly; **HI** Highest wage paid; **HR** High end range; **LR** Low end range; **M** Monthly; **MTC** Median total compensation; **MW** Median wage paid; **SQ** Second quartile wage; **S** Special: hourly and annual; **TQ** Third quartile wage; **W** Weekly; **Y** Yearly

Occupation/Type/Industry	Location	Per	Low	Mid	High	Source	Date
Purchasing Manager	Nevada	Y	32220 FQ	60120 AW	98110 TQ	NVBLS	10/01-12/01
	Las Vegas MSA, NV-AZ	Y	31790 FQ	60440 AW	100710 TQ	NVBLS	10/01-12/01
	Reno MSA, NV	Y	31220 FQ	59670 AW	92500 TQ	NVBLS	10/01-12/01
	New Hampshire	Y	30780 FQ	60540 AW	92800 TQ	NHBLS	10/01-12/01
	Manchester PMSA, NH	Y	30860 FQ	53830 AW	81010 TQ	NHBLS	10/01-12/01
	Nashua PMSA, NH	Y	39600 FQ	68260 AW	104680 TQ	NHBLS	10/01-12/01
	Portsmouth-Rochester PMSA, NH-ME	Y	28510 FQ	64470 AW	101020 TQ	NHBLS	10/01-12/01
	New Jersey	Y	50620 FQ	83670 AW	133740 TQ	NJBLS	10/01-12/01
	Atlantic-Cape May PMSA, NJ	Y	48690 FQ	72980 AW	101360 TQ	NJBLS	10/01-12/01
	Bergen-Passaic PMSA, NJ	Y	51360 FQ	91290 AW		NJBLS	10/01-12/01
	Jersey City PMSA, NJ	Y	48610 FQ	78500 AW	135430 TQ	NJBLS	10/01-12/01
	Middlesex-Somerset-Hunterdon PMSA, NJ	Y	58170 FQ	84200 AW	121030 TQ	NJBLS	10/01-12/01
	Monmouth-Ocean PMSA, NJ	Y	41870 FQ	77830 AW	114200 TQ	NJBLS	10/01-12/01
	Newark PMSA, NJ	Y	50800 FQ	83840 AW	122790 TQ	NJBLS	10/01-12/01
	Trenton PMSA, NJ	Y	47660 FQ	70230 AW	107720 TQ	NJBLS	10/01-12/01
	New Mexico	Y	26000 FQ	50620 AW	86230 TQ	NMBLS	10/01-12/01
	Albuquerque MSA, NM	Y	26750 FQ	56490 AW	89990 TQ	NMBLS	10/01-12/01
	Las Cruces MSA, NM	Y	27720 FQ	48760 AW	75840 TQ	NMBLS	10/01-12/01
	New York	Y	38330 FQ	71130 AW	124210 TQ	NYBLS	10/01-12/01
	Albany-Schenectady-Troy MSA, NY	Y	34880 FQ	63820 AW	95160 TQ	NYBLS	10/01-12/01
	Binghamton MSA, NY	Y	24560 FQ	67440 AW	109360 TQ	NYBLS	10/01-12/01
	Buffalo-Niagara Falls MSA, NY	Y	36770 FQ	58530 AW	88400 TQ	NYBLS	10/01-12/01
	Dutchess County PMSA, NY	Y	32520 FQ	74740 AW	120650 TQ	NYBLS	10/01-12/01
	Nassau-Suffolk PMSA, NY	Y	46830 FQ	70970 AW	110970 TQ	NYBLS	10/01-12/01
	New York PMSA, NY	Y	40910 FQ	77870 AW		NYBLS	10/01-12/01
	Newburgh PMSA, NY-PA	Y	40830 FQ	62490 AW	84570 TQ	NYBLS	10/01-12/01
	Rochester MSA, NY	Y	37280 FQ	64110 AW	99650 TQ	NYBLS	10/01-12/01
	Syracuse MSA, NY	Y	31350 FQ	64330 AW	104130 TQ	NYBLS	10/01-12/01
	Utica-Rome MSA, NY	Y	36470 FQ	62150 AW	88830 TQ	NYBLS	10/01-12/01
	North Carolina	Y	28280 FQ	56970 AW	96040 TQ	NCBLS	10/01-12/01
	Asheville MSA, NC	Y	25630 FQ	48380 AW	76750 TQ	NCBLS	10/01-12/01
	Charlotte-Gastonia-Rock Hill MSA, NC-SC	Y	31290 FQ	60410 AW	103350 TQ	NCBLS	10/01-12/01
	Fayetteville MSA, NC	Y	23880 FQ	42730 AW	73950 TQ	NCBLS	10/01-12/01
	Greensboro-Winston-Salem-High Point MSA, NC	Y	30330 FQ	56010 AW	92180 TQ	NCBLS	10/01-12/01
	Hickory-Morganton-Lenoir MSA, NC	Y	26900 FQ	53810 AW	103510 TQ	NCBLS	10/01-12/01
	Raleigh-Durham-Chapel Hill MSA, NC	Y	26720 FQ	59380 AW	101650 TQ	NCBLS	10/01-12/01
	Wilmington MSA, NC	Y	26960 FQ	55790 AW	106280 TQ	NCBLS	10/01-12/01
	North Dakota	Y	23540 FQ	43430 AW	78510 TQ	NDBLS	10/01-12/01
	Fargo-Moorhead MSA, ND-MN	Y	25880 FQ	50270 AW	93920 TQ	NDBLS	10/01-12/01
	Ohio	Y	30840 FQ	58590 AW	90960 TQ	OHBLS	10/01-12/01
	Akron PMSA, OH	Y	28210 FQ	60310 AW	94270 TQ	OHBLS	10/01-12/01
	Canton-Massillon MSA, OH	Y	22430 FQ	47870 AW	81520 TQ	OHBLS	10/01-12/01
	Cincinnati PMSA, OH-KY-IN	Y	31900 FQ	61090 AW	97170 TQ	OHBLS	10/01-12/01
	Cleveland-Lorain-Elyria PMSA, OH	Y	37910 FQ	61160 AW	92240 TQ	OHBLS	10/01-12/01
	Columbus MSA, OH	Y	33930 FQ	59360 AW	89240 TQ	OHBLS	10/01-12/01
	Dayton-Springfield MSA, OH	Y	31950 FQ	63170 AW	98600 TQ	OHBLS	10/01-12/01
	Hamilton-Middletown PMSA, OH	Y	26150 FQ	51820 AW	73580 TQ	OHBLS	10/01-12/01
	Mansfield MSA, OH	Y	25880 FQ	54220 AW	84190 TQ	OHBLS	10/01-12/01
	Toledo MSA, OH	Y	26550 FQ	54170 AW	90040 TQ	OHBLS	10/01-12/01
	Youngstown-Warren MSA, OH	Y	24960 FQ	57900 AW	114730 TQ	OHBLS	10/01-12/01
	Oklahoma	Y	26730 FQ	52350 AW	85890 TQ	OKBLS	10/01-12/01
	Oklahoma City MSA, OK	Y	28720 FQ	53130 AW	86390 TQ	OKBLS	10/01-12/01
	Tulsa MSA, OK	Y	30270 FQ	58440 AW	91320 TQ	OKBLS	10/01-12/01
	Oregon	Y	38000 FQ	64730 AW	94670 TQ	ORBLS	10/01-12/01
	Eugene-Springfield MSA, OR	Y	29810 FQ	60620 AW	110370 TQ	ORBLS	10/01-12/01
	Portland-Vancouver PMSA, OR-WA	Y	39950 FQ	66710 AW	96120 TQ	ORBLS	10/01-12/01
	Salem PMSA, OR	Y	36460 FQ	52920 AW	84940 TQ	ORBLS	10/01-12/01
	Pennsylvania	Y	32100 FQ	59480 AW	92190 TQ	PABLS	10/01-12/01
	Allentown-Bethlehem-Easton MSA, PA	Y	32940 FQ	52870 AW	78970 TQ	PABLS	10/01-12/01

AAW	Average annual wage	**AOH**	Average offered, high	**ASH**	Average starting, high	**H**	Hourly	**M**	Monthly	**S**	Special: hourly and annual
AE	Average entry wage	**AOL**	Average offered, low	**ASL**	Average starting, low	**HI**	Highest wage paid	**MTC**	Median total compensation	**TQ**	Third quartile wage
AEX	Average experienced wage	**APH**	Average pay, high range	**AW**	Average wage paid	**HR**	High end range	**MW**	Median wage paid	**W**	Weekly
AO	Average offered	**APL**	Average pay, low range	**FQ**	First quartile wage	**LR**	Low end range	**SQ**	Second quartile wage	**Y**	Yearly

Occupation/Type/Industry	Location	Per	Low	Mid	High	Source	Date
Purchasing Manager	Erie MSA, PA	Y	31400 FQ	54630 AW	74290 TQ	PABLS	10/01-12/01
	Harrisburg-Lebanon-Carlisle MSA, PA	Y	38540 FQ	60580 AW	88160 TQ	PABLS	10/01-12/01
	Johnstown MSA, PA	Y	30210 FQ	50100 AW	69230 TQ	PABLS	10/01-12/01
	Lancaster MSA, PA	Y	37650 FQ	57480 AW	86860 TQ	PABLS	10/01-12/01
	Philadelphia PMSA, PA-NJ	Y	36550 FQ	66810 AW	106350 TQ	PABLS	10/01-12/01
	Pittsburgh MSA, PA	Y	30530 FQ	59330 AW	95300 TQ	PABLS	10/01-12/01
	Reading MSA, PA	Y	33280 FQ	57700 AW	88750 TQ	PABLS	10/01-12/01
	Scranton-Wilkes-Barre-Hazleton MSA, PA	Y	26420 FQ	48440 AW	72840 TQ	PABLS	10/01-12/01
	York MSA, PA	Y	35720 FQ	60710 AW	86500 TQ	PABLS	10/01-12/01
	Rhode Island	Y	35910 FQ	70710 AW	109510 TQ	RIBLS	10/01-12/01
	Providence-Fall River-Warwick MSA, RI-MA	Y	36600 FQ	63410 AW	100600 TQ	RIBLS	10/01-12/01
	South Carolina	Y	24540 FQ	51610 AW	88770 TQ	SCBLS	10/01-12/01
	Charleston-North Charleston MSA, SC	Y	22690 FQ	53790 AW	89210 TQ	SCBLS	10/01-12/01
	Columbia MSA, SC	Y	24100 FQ	46590 AW	79880 TQ	SCBLS	10/01-12/01
	Greenville-Spartanburg-Anderson MSA, SC	Y	24730 FQ	50210 AW	83160 TQ	SCBLS	10/01-12/01
	Myrtle Beach MSA, SC	Y	23930 FQ	46070 AW	70560 TQ	SCBLS	10/01-12/01
	South Dakota	Y	41350 FQ	66720 AW	95690 TQ	SDBLS	10/01-12/01
	Sioux Falls MSA, SD	Y	47130 FQ	65370 AW	90200 TQ	SDBLS	10/01-12/01
	Tennessee	Y	25950 FQ	54320 AW	92040 TQ	TNBLS	10/01-12/01
	Chattanooga MSA, TN-GA	Y	21120 FQ	47670 AW	74160 TQ	TNBLS	10/01-12/01
	Clarksville-Hopkinsville MSA, TN-KY	Y	22820 FQ	52200 AW	75670 TQ	TNBLS	10/01-12/01
	Johnson City-Kingsport-Bristol MSA, TN-VA	Y	25180 FQ	51800 AW	89540 TQ	TNBLS	10/01-12/01
	Knoxville MSA, TN	Y	28760 FQ	61180 AW	103780 TQ	TNBLS	10/01-12/01
	Memphis MSA, TN-AR-MS	Y	24710 FQ	50990 AW	86650 TQ	TNBLS	10/01-12/01
	Nashville MSA, TN	Y	28710 FQ	58890 AW	96750 TQ	TNBLS	10/01-12/01
	Texas	Y	28610 FQ	55750 AW	91820 TQ	TXBLS	10/01-12/01
	Amarillo MSA, TX	Y	27540 FQ	50530 AW	89960 TQ	TXBLS	10/01-12/01
	Austin-San Marcos MSA, TX	Y	31690 FQ	57920 AW	88820 TQ	TXBLS	10/01-12/01
	Beaumont-Port Arthur MSA, TX	Y	22420 FQ	54140 AW	88510 TQ	TXBLS	10/01-12/01
	Brazoria PMSA, TX	Y	32100 FQ	51370 AW	81410 TQ	TXBLS	10/01-12/01
	Brownsville-Harlingen-San Benito MSA, TX	Y	19400 FQ	39570 AW	66570 TQ	TXBLS	10/01-12/01
	Corpus Christi MSA, TX	Y	26650 FQ	50220 AW	78590 TQ	TXBLS	10/01-12/01
	Dallas PMSA, TX	Y	31370 FQ	60900 AW	101380 TQ	TXBLS	10/01-12/01
	El Paso MSA, TX	Y	23770 FQ	49420 AW	78540 TQ	TXBLS	10/01-12/01
	Fort Worth-Arlington PMSA, TX	Y	30450 FQ	55530 AW	90080 TQ	TXBLS	10/01-12/01
	Galveston-Texas City PMSA, TX	Y	25470 FQ	52570 AW	110460 TQ	TXBLS	10/01-12/01
	Houston PMSA, TX	Y	30830 FQ	58280 AW	98710 TQ	TXBLS	10/01-12/01
	Killeen-Temple MSA, TX	Y	17650 FQ	48130 AW	84890 TQ	TXBLS	10/01-12/01
	Laredo MSA, TX	Y	27220 FQ	50770 AW	77810 TQ	TXBLS	10/01-12/01
	Longview-Marshall MSA, TX	Y	22140 FQ	50060 AW	82440 TQ	TXBLS	10/01-12/01
	Lubbock MSA, TX	Y	23630 FQ	47160 AW	82660 TQ	TXBLS	10/01-12/01
	McAllen-Edinburg-Mission MSA, TX	Y	14120 FQ	51420 AW	94740 TQ	TXBLS	10/01-12/01
	Odessa-Midland MSA, TX	Y	31970 FQ	57240 AW	86790 TQ	TXBLS	10/01-12/01
	San Antonio MSA, TX	Y	29160 FQ	53100 AW	87410 TQ	TXBLS	10/01-12/01
	Tyler MSA, TX	Y	22320 FQ	44100 AW	74450 TQ	TXBLS	10/01-12/01
	Waco MSA, TX	Y	22160 FQ	47350 AW	76060 TQ	TXBLS	10/01-12/01
	Utah	Y	28950 FQ	54620 AW	90760 TQ	UTBLS	10/01-12/01
	Provo-Orem MSA, UT	Y	26170 FQ	50910 AW	76050 TQ	UTBLS	10/01-12/01
	Salt Lake City-Ogden MSA, UT	Y	30780 FQ	56830 AW	97440 TQ	UTBLS	10/01-12/01
	Vermont	Y	41800 FQ	69590 AW	106470 TQ	VTBLS	10/01-12/01
	Burlington MSA, VT	Y	50620 FQ	77470 AW	108900 TQ	VTBLS	10/01-12/01
	Virginia	Y	33780 FQ	65100 AW	103970 TQ	VABLS	10/01-12/01
	Lynchburg MSA, VA	Y	36860 FQ	58440 AW	92440 TQ	VABLS	10/01-12/01
	Norfolk-Virginia Beach-Newport News MSA, VA-NC	Y	34780 FQ	62020 AW	92430 TQ	VABLS	10/01-12/01
	Richmond-Petersburg MSA, VA	Y	31830 FQ	61930 AW	93260 TQ	VABLS	10/01-12/01
	Roanoke MSA, VA	Y	30720 FQ	54280 AW	84840 TQ	VABLS	10/01-12/01

AAW Average annual wage; **AE** Average entry wage; **AEX** Average experienced wage; **AO** Average offered; **AOH** Average offered, high; **AOL** Average offered, low; **APH** Average pay, high range; **APL** Average pay, low range; **ASH** Average starting, high; **ASL** Average starting, low; **AW** Average wage paid; **FQ** First quartile wage; **H** Hourly; **HI** Highest wage paid; **HR** High end range; **LR** Low end range; **M** Monthly; **MTC** Median total compensation; **MW** Median wage paid; **SQ** Second quartile wage; **S** Special: hourly and annual; **TQ** Third quartile wage; **W** Weekly; **Y** Yearly

Occupation/Type/Industry	Location	Per	Low	Mid	High	Source	Date
Purchasing Manager	Washington	Y	39100 FQ	69270 AW	106780 TQ	WABLS	10/01-12/01
	Bremerton PMSA, WA	Y	37500 FQ	63930 AW	90920 TQ	WABLS	10/01-12/01
	Richland-Kennewick-Pasco MSA, WA	Y	46610 FQ	70100 AW	101450 TQ	WABLS	10/01-12/01
	Seattle-Bellevue-Everett PMSA, WA	Y	41560 FQ	72970 AW	110430 TQ	WABLS	10/01-12/01
	Spokane MSA, WA	Y	26130 FQ	51960 AW	81580 TQ	WABLS	10/01-12/01
	Tacoma PMSA, WA	Y	28330 FQ	58860 AW	92600 TQ	WABLS	10/01-12/01
	West Virginia	Y	24520 FQ	48540 AW	83300 TQ	WVBLS	10/01-12/01
	Charleston MSA, WV	Y	26510 FQ	47370 AW	82500 TQ	WVBLS	10/01-12/01
	Huntington-Ashland MSA, WV-KY-OH	Y	26070 FQ	45930 AW	66920 TQ	WVBLS	10/01-12/01
	Wisconsin	Y	27400 FQ	55160 AW	87520 TQ	WIBLS	10/01-12/01
	Appleton-Oshkosh-Neenah MSA, WI	Y	32890 FQ	58880 AW	92450 TQ	WIBLS	10/01-12/01
	Green Bay MSA, WI	Y	33470 FQ	61080 AW	97480 TQ	WIBLS	10/01-12/01
	Madison MSA, WI	Y	29130 FQ	55320 AW	86490 TQ	WIBLS	10/01-12/01
	Milwaukee-Waukesha PMSA, WI	Y	33300 FQ	61270 AW	91000 TQ	WIBLS	10/01-12/01
	Racine PMSA, WI	Y	29550 FQ	55960 AW	74760 TQ	WIBLS	10/01-12/01
	Wyoming	Y	24490 FQ	46490 AW	79900 TQ	WYBLS	10/01-12/01
	Puerto Rico	Y	26190 FQ	52570 AW	94730 TQ	PRBLS	10/01-12/01
	Virgin Islands	Y	31090 FQ	47630 AW	69650 TQ	VIBLS	10/01-12/01
	Guam	Y	23270 FQ	36980 AW	59230 TQ	GUBLS	10/01-12/01
Quality Control Analyst	United States	Y			120000 HI	ASQ	1/00-1/01
Quality Control Associate	United States	Y			122000 HI	ASQ	1/00-1/01
Quality Control Coordinator	United States	Y			105000 HI	ASQ	1/00-1/01
Quality Control Director	United States	Y			175000 HI	ASQ	1/00-1/01
Quality Control Executive							
Apparel Industry	United States	Y		140000 MW		BOB1	1/01-1/02
Apparel Industry	Los Angeles, CA	Y		190000 AW		BOB1	1/01-1/02
Apparel Industry	New Jersey	Y		175000 AW		BOB1	1/01-1/02
Apparel Industry	New York, NY	Y		240000 AW		BOB1	1/01-1/02
Apparel Industry	Tennessee	Y		105000 AW		BOB1	1/01-1/02
Quality Control Inspector	United States	Y			100000 HI	ASQ	1/00-1/01
Quality Control Manager	United States	Y			190000 HI	ASQ	1/00-1/01
Quality Control Specialist	United States	Y			145000 HI	ASQ	1/00-1/01
Quality Control Supervisor	United States	Y			108000 HI	ASQ	1/00-1/01
Quality Engineer							
Quality Control	United States	Y			150000 HI	ASQ	1/00-1/01
Radiation Therapist	Alabama	Y	31620 FQ	47030 AW	62330 TQ	ALBLS	10/01-12/01
	Arizona	Y	29100 FQ	43450 AW	55920 TQ	AZBLS	10/01-12/01
	Arkansas	Y	36120 FQ	46600 AW	59300 TQ	ARBLS	10/01-12/01
	California	Y	39370 FQ	59880 AW	81540 TQ	CABLS	10/01-12/01
	Colorado	Y	44920 FQ	55300 AW	70410 TQ	COBLS	10/01-12/01
	Connecticut	Y	30880 FQ	41980 AW	56080 TQ	CTBLS	10/01-12/01
	District of Columbia	Y	36890 FQ	49190 AW	62570 TQ	DCBLS	10/01-12/01
	Florida	Y	36720 FQ	49130 AW	66380 TQ	FLBLS	10/01-12/01
	Georgia	Y	36780 FQ	68620 AW		GABLS	10/01-12/01
	Idaho	Y	37320 FQ	51680 AW	67150 TQ	IDBLS	10/01-12/01
	Illinois	Y	31580 FQ	49700 AW	70230 TQ	ILBLS	10/01-12/01
	Indiana	Y	32670 FQ	69160 AW		INBLS	10/01-12/01
	Kansas	Y	34540 FQ	60470 AW	139290 TQ	KSBLS	10/01-12/01
	Kentucky	Y	29990 FQ	45730 AW	63750 TQ	KYBLS	10/01-12/01
	Louisiana	Y	31840 FQ	45580 AW	59700 TQ	LABLS	10/01-12/01
	Maine	Y	31470 FQ	41910 AW	56370 TQ	MEBLS	10/01-12/01
	Maryland	Y	38280 FQ	60240 AW		MDBLS	10/01-12/01
	Massachusetts	Y	37930 FQ	56040 AW	76100 TQ	MABLS	10/01-12/01
	Michigan	Y	31880 FQ	47630 AW	64030 TQ	MIBLS	10/01-12/01
	Minnesota	Y	34300 FQ	46320 AW	63910 TQ	MNBLS	10/01-12/01
	Mississippi	Y	38440 FQ	55800 AW	73660 TQ	MSBLS	10/01-12/01
	Missouri	Y	33280 FQ	45330 AW	59780 TQ	MOBLS	10/01-12/01
	Montana	Y	23550 FQ	43050 AW	58170 TQ	MTBLS	10/01-12/01

AAW	Average annual wage	**AOH**	Average offered, high	**ASH**	Average starting, high	**H**	Hourly	**M**	Monthly	**S**	Special: hourly and annual
AE	Average entry wage	**AOL**	Average offered, low	**ASL**	Average starting, low	**HI**	Highest wage paid	**MTC**	Median total compensation	**TQ**	Third quartile wage
AEX	Average experienced wage	**APH**	Average pay, high range	**AW**	Average wage paid	**HR**	High end range	**MW**	Median wage paid	**W**	Weekly
AO	Average offered	**APL**	Average pay, low range	**FQ**	First quartile wage	**LR**	Low end range	**SQ**	Second quartile wage	**Y**	Yearly

Occupation/Type/Industry	Location	Per	Low	Mid	High	Source	Date
Radiation Therapist	Nebraska	Y	35310 FQ	46530 AW	60490 TQ	NEBLS	10/01-12/01
	Nevada	Y	37070 FQ	47500 AW	56090 TQ	NVBLS	10/01-12/01
	New Hampshire	Y	36820 FQ	50170 AW	71060 TQ	NHBLS	10/01-12/01
	New Jersey	Y	38750 FQ	55270 AW	73830 TQ	NJBLS	10/01-12/01
	New Mexico	Y	39360 FQ	50490 AW	67550 TQ	NMBLS	10/01-12/01
	New York	Y	37090 FQ	57080 AW	81140 TQ	NYBLS	10/01-12/01
	North Carolina	Y	30600 FQ	46260 AW	62920 TQ	NCBLS	10/01-12/01
	Ohio	Y	37600 FQ	48380 AW	61000 TQ	OHBLS	10/01-12/01
	Oklahoma	Y	30300 FQ	45200 AW	64140 TQ	OKBLS	10/01-12/01
	Oregon	Y	38290 FQ	51330 AW	67570 TQ	ORBLS	10/01-12/01
	Pennsylvania	Y	37440 FQ	49650 AW	61010 TQ	PABLS	10/01-12/01
	South Carolina	Y	33550 FQ	45020 AW	57860 TQ	SCBLS	10/01-12/01
	Tennessee	Y	36570 FQ	50830 AW	70430 TQ	TNBLS	10/01-12/01
	Texas	Y	36120 FQ	51620 AW	70150 TQ	TXBLS	10/01-12/01
	Utah	Y	46030 FQ	59170 AW	71600 TQ	UTBLS	10/01-12/01
	Virginia	Y	32650 FQ	48460 AW	68250 TQ	VABLS	10/01-12/01
	Washington	Y	47840 FQ	62180 AW	76960 TQ	WABLS	10/01-12/01
	West Virginia	Y	32080 FQ	46030 AW	60950 TQ	WVBLS	10/01-12/01
	Wisconsin	Y	36170 FQ	49380 AW	65370 TQ	WIBLS	10/01-12/01
	Wyoming	Y	29270 FQ	40700 AW	58310 TQ	WYBLS	10/01-12/01
	Puerto Rico	Y	17790 FQ	42140 AW		PRBLS	10/01-12/01
Radio Mechanic	Alabama	H	7.32 FQ	11.80 AW	18.62 TQ	ALBLS	10/01-12/01
	Arizona	H	10.44 FQ	23.79 AW	33.21 TQ	AZBLS	10/01-12/01
	Colorado	H	9.75 FQ	21.84 AW	33.66 TQ	COBLS	10/01-12/01
	Connecticut	H	9.95 FQ	15.44 AW	20.95 TQ	CTBLS	10/01-12/01
	Florida	H	10.64 FQ	17.45 AW	25.09 TQ	FLBLS	10/01-12/01
	Georgia	H	9.47 FQ	18.63 AW	32.60 TQ	GABLS	10/01-12/01
	Hawaii	H	9.65 FQ	17.35 AW	24.96 TQ	HIBLS	10/01-12/01
	Illinois	H	9.52 FQ	17.93 AW	26.86 TQ	ILBLS	10/01-12/01
	Indiana	H	10.51 FQ	17.11 AW	26.07 TQ	INBLS	10/01-12/01
	Iowa	H	9.05 FQ	10.77 AW	14.85 TQ	IABLS	10/01-12/01
	Kansas	H	11.86 FQ	16.16 AW	21.47 TQ	KSBLS	10/01-12/01
	Louisiana	H	5.85 FQ	12.98 AW	18.94 TQ	LABLS	10/01-12/01
	Maine	H	7.72 FQ	14.46 AW	21.81 TQ	MEBLS	10/01-12/01
	Maryland	H	9.21 FQ	15.51 AW	21.24 TQ	MDBLS	10/01-12/01
	Massachusetts	H	8.34 FQ	17.85 AW	23.05 TQ	MABLS	10/01-12/01
	Michigan	H	11.86 FQ	18.58 AW	23.02 TQ	MIBLS	10/01-12/01
	Minnesota	H	11.96 FQ	19.17 AW	27.88 TQ	MNBLS	10/01-12/01
	Mississippi	H	7.01 FQ	15.55 AW	23.93 TQ	MSBLS	10/01-12/01
	Missouri	H	11.08 FQ	16.07 AW	23.93 TQ	MOBLS	10/01-12/01
	Nebraska	H	11.51 FQ	14.23 AW	17.40 TQ	NEBLS	10/01-12/01
	Nevada	H	8.80 FQ	18.36 AW	25.60 TQ	NVBLS	10/01-12/01
	New Hampshire	H	9.57 FQ	16.02 AW	22.59 TQ	NHBLS	10/01-12/01
	New Jersey	H	8.74 FQ	15.89 AW	23.90 TQ	NJBLS	10/01-12/01
	New Mexico	H	7.50 FQ	11.87 AW	22.45 TQ	NMBLS	10/01-12/01
	New York	H	10.96 FQ	18.77 AW	28.91 TQ	NYBLS	10/01-12/01
	North Carolina	H	8.64 FQ	15.05 AW	20.71 TQ	NCBLS	10/01-12/01
	Ohio	H	11.59 FQ	17.19 AW	22.56 TQ	OHBLS	10/01-12/01
	Oklahoma	H	8.47 FQ	15.25 AW	25.06 TQ	OKBLS	10/01-12/01
	Oregon	H	10.43 FQ	15.95 AW	23.00 TQ	ORBLS	10/01-12/01
	Pennsylvania	H	11.03 FQ	19.00 AW	27.63 TQ	PABLS	10/01-12/01
	South Carolina	H	12.50 FQ	19.43 AW	27.95 TQ	SCBLS	10/01-12/01
	South Dakota	H	10.23 FQ	13.94 AW	17.90 TQ	SDBLS	10/01-12/01
	Tennessee	H	10.09 FQ	18.48 AW	26.99 TQ	TNBLS	10/01-12/01
	Texas	H	10.68 FQ	17.50 AW	25.52 TQ	TXBLS	10/01-12/01
	Utah	H	12.20 FQ	19.93 AW	30.30 TQ	UTBLS	10/01-12/01
	Virginia	H	11.61 FQ	16.32 AW	21.45 TQ	VABLS	10/01-12/01
	Washington	H	15.24 FQ	23.58 AW	33.35 TQ	WABLS	10/01-12/01
	Wisconsin	H	7.72 FQ	15.59 AW	24.20 TQ	WIBLS	10/01-12/01
	Wyoming	H	9.08 FQ	11.87 AW	15.98 TQ	WYBLS	10/01-12/01
Radio Operator	Alabama	Y	15780 FQ	25320 AW	33580 TQ	ALBLS	10/01-12/01
	Alaska	Y	18990 FQ	30180 AW	41960 TQ	AKBLS	10/01-12/01
	California	Y	15880 FQ	40550 AW	70960 TQ	CABLS	10/01-12/01
	Delaware	Y	24410 FQ	30190 AW	34950 TQ	DEBLS	10/01-12/01
	Florida	Y	14850 FQ	29500 AW	45230 TQ	FLBLS	10/01-12/01
	Georgia	Y	20960 FQ	31670 AW	45050 TQ	GABLS	10/01-12/01
	Illinois	Y	18270 FQ	25850 AW	40010 TQ	ILBLS	10/01-12/01
	Iowa	Y	15710 FQ	20930 AW	34090 TQ	IABLS	10/01-12/01
	Louisiana	Y	19760 FQ	27690 AW	40330 TQ	LABLS	10/01-12/01
	Michigan	Y	29460 FQ	38960 AW	50460 TQ	MIBLS	10/01-12/01
	Minnesota	Y	25100 FQ	36760 AW	47700 TQ	MNBLS	10/01-12/01

AAW Average annual wage **AE** Average entry wage **AEX** Average experienced wage **AO** Average offered
AOH Average offered, high **AOL** Average offered, low **APH** Average pay, high range **APL** Average pay, low range
ASH Average starting, high **ASL** Average starting, low **AW** Average wage paid **FQ** First quartile wage
H Hourly **HI** Highest wage paid **HR** High end range **LR** Low end range
M Monthly **MTC** Median total compensation **MW** Median wage paid **SQ** Second quartile wage
S Special: hourly and annual **TQ** Third quartile wage **W** Weekly **Y** Yearly

Occupation/Type/Industry	Location	Per	Low	Mid	High	Source	Date
Radio Operator	Mississippi	Y	14680 FQ	25150 AW	36460 TQ	MSBLS	10/01-12/01
	Nevada	Y	25960 FQ	43510 AW	60680 TQ	NVBLS	10/01-12/01
	New York	Y	23910 FQ	40870 AW	72130 TQ	NYBLS	10/01-12/01
	North Carolina	Y	24930 FQ	32780 AW	42290 TQ	NCBLS	10/01-12/01
	Ohio	Y	15110 FQ	28780 AW	35070 TQ	OHBLS	10/01-12/01
	Pennsylvania	Y	14260 FQ	28070 AW	43530 TQ	PABLS	10/01-12/01
	South Carolina	Y	12160 FQ	21680 AW	33640 TQ	SCBLS	10/01-12/01
	Tennessee	Y	15170 FQ	30180 AW	43120 TQ	TNBLS	10/01-12/01
	Texas	Y	16570 FQ	31940 AW	47850 TQ	TXBLS	10/01-12/01
	Puerto Rico	Y	12180 FQ	15220 AW	17620 TQ	PRBLS	10/01-12/01
Radiologic Technologist	United States	Y		44021 AW		BWIRE	1/01-1/02
Radiologic Technologist and Technician	Alabama	Y	24490 FQ	35240 AW	48200 TQ	ALBLS	10/01-12/01
	Alaska	Y	37080 FQ	46110 AW	56850 TQ	AKBLS	10/01-12/01
	Arizona	Y	24490 FQ	37360 AW	52240 TQ	AZBLS	10/01-12/01
	Arkansas	Y	22840 FQ	31910 AW	45250 TQ	ARBLS	10/01-12/01
	California	Y	31640 FQ	45610 AW	62800 TQ	CABLS	10/01-12/01
	Colorado	Y	27960 FQ	38930 AW	52000 TQ	COBLS	10/01-12/01
	Connecticut	Y	32580 FQ	43990 AW	56450 TQ	CTBLS	10/01-12/01
	Delaware	Y	30580 FQ	41690 AW	54480 TQ	DEBLS	10/01-12/01
	District of Columbia	Y	31440 FQ	44490 AW	62750 TQ	DCBLS	10/01-12/01
	Florida	Y	24250 FQ	35060 AW	47130 TQ	FLBLS	10/01-12/01
	Georgia	Y	25500 FQ	36040 AW	47870 TQ	GABLS	10/01-12/01
	Hawaii	Y	36600 FQ	44650 AW	56340 TQ	HIBLS	10/01-12/01
	Idaho	Y	28160 FQ	37590 AW	48280 TQ	IDBLS	10/01-12/01
	Illinois	Y	25180 FQ	37030 AW	51960 TQ	ILBLS	10/01-12/01
	Indiana	Y	26910 FQ	35950 AW	46010 TQ	INBLS	10/01-12/01
	Iowa	Y	21690 FQ	31920 AW	43500 TQ	IABLS	10/01-12/01
	Kansas	Y	24280 FQ	33520 AW	43890 TQ	KSBLS	10/01-12/01
	Kentucky	Y	24900 FQ	34700 AW	45750 TQ	KYBLS	10/01-12/01
	Louisiana	Y	23180 FQ	32590 AW	43090 TQ	LABLS	10/01-12/01
	Maine	Y	27510 FQ	36640 AW	47150 TQ	MEBLS	10/01-12/01
	Maryland	Y	35040 FQ	45850 AW	57810 TQ	MDBLS	10/01-12/01
	Massachusetts	Y	32470 FQ	46140 AW	63100 TQ	MABLS	10/01-12/01
	Michigan	Y	27340 FQ	37590 AW	48980 TQ	MIBLS	10/01-12/01
	Minnesota	Y	29390 FQ	40730 AW	55800 TQ	MNBLS	10/01-12/01
	Mississippi	Y	22480 FQ	33030 AW	43870 TQ	MSBLS	10/01-12/01
	Missouri	Y	24380 FQ	35740 AW	46800 TQ	MOBLS	10/01-12/01
	Montana	Y	24420 FQ	32630 AW	43180 TQ	MTBLS	10/01-12/01
	Nebraska	Y	23210 FQ	32840 AW	44720 TQ	NEBLS	10/01-12/01
	Nevada	Y	33100 FQ	44080 AW	56180 TQ	NVBLS	10/01-12/01
	New Hampshire	Y	30000 FQ	39930 AW	53010 TQ	NHBLS	10/01-12/01
	New Jersey	Y	32580 FQ	45640 AW	58890 TQ	NJBLS	10/01-12/01
	New Mexico	Y	28250 FQ	36980 AW	46230 TQ	NMBLS	10/01-12/01
	New York	Y	29960 FQ	44550 AW	60030 TQ	NYBLS	10/01-12/01
	North Carolina	Y	26470 FQ	37940 AW	51180 TQ	NCBLS	10/01-12/01
	North Dakota	Y	24460 FQ	34390 AW	43430 TQ	NDBLS	10/01-12/01
	Ohio	Y	26530 FQ	35370 AW	44690 TQ	OHBLS	10/01-12/01
	Oklahoma	Y	23360 FQ	33830 AW	47410 TQ	OKBLS	10/01-12/01
	Oregon	Y	31320 FQ	43000 AW	55240 TQ	ORBLS	10/01-12/01
	Pennsylvania	Y	25210 FQ	34570 AW	45470 TQ	PABLS	10/01-12/01
	Rhode Island	Y	32140 FQ	42810 AW	55550 TQ	RIBLS	10/01-12/01
	South Carolina	Y	28580 FQ	42150 AW	61390 TQ	SCBLS	10/01-12/01
	South Dakota	Y	25880 FQ	35250 AW	45230 TQ	SDBLS	10/01-12/01
	Tennessee	Y	25610 FQ	42250 AW	52920 TQ	TNBLS	10/01-12/01
	Texas	Y	25490 FQ	36020 AW	47510 TQ	TXBLS	10/01-12/01
	Utah	Y	27310 FQ	35860 AW	47800 TQ	UTBLS	10/01-12/01
	Vermont	Y	27050 FQ	37770 AW	50160 TQ	VTBLS	10/01-12/01
	Virginia	Y	26810 FQ	38330 AW	53220 TQ	VABLS	10/01-12/01
	Washington	Y	32190 FQ	43540 AW	56500 TQ	WABLS	10/01-12/01
	West Virginia	Y	24500 FQ	31170 AW	39060 TQ	WVBLS	10/01-12/01
	Wisconsin	Y	27250 FQ	37120 AW	49600 TQ	WIBLS	10/01-12/01
	Wyoming	Y	21380 FQ	36070 AW	53600 TQ	WYBLS	10/01-12/01
	Puerto Rico	Y	11960 FQ	17100 AW	24140 TQ	PRBLS	10/01-12/01
	Guam	Y	22320 FQ	33230 AW	50430 TQ	GUBLS	10/01-12/01
Radiologist	United States	Y		267466 AW		BWIRE	1/01-1/02
Radiology Administrator	United States	Y		69561 AW		BWIRE	1/01-1/02
Rail Car Repairer	Alabama	H	13.63 FQ	18.92 AW	22.32 TQ	ALBLS	10/01-12/01

AAW	Average annual wage	AOH	Average offered, high	ASH	Average starting, high	H	Hourly	M	Monthly	S	Special: hourly and annual
AE	Average entry wage	AOL	Average offered, low	ASL	Average starting, low	HI	Highest wage paid	MTC	Median total compensation	TQ	Third quartile wage
AEX	Average experienced wage	APH	Average pay, high range	AW	Average wage paid	HR	High end range	MW	Median wage paid	W	Weekly
AO	Average offered	APL	Average pay, low range	FQ	First quartile wage	LR	Low end range	SQ	Second quartile wage	Y	Yearly

Occupation/Type/Industry	Location	Per	Low	Mid	High	Source	Date
Rail Car Repairer	Arkansas	H	10.00 FQ	16.36 AW	21.26 TQ	ARBLS	10/01-12/01
	California	H	11.52 FQ	17.42 AW	21.26 TQ	CABLS	10/01-12/01
	Colorado	H	10.26 FQ	17.01 AW	21.86 TQ	COBLS	10/01-12/01
	Connecticut	H	10.54 FQ	16.60 AW	23.63 TQ	CTBLS	10/01-12/01
	Florida	H	10.06 FQ	14.24 AW	18.47 TQ	FLBLS	10/01-12/01
	Georgia	H	9.67 FQ	14.17 AW	20.87 TQ	GABLS	10/01-12/01
	Illinois	H	13.66 FQ	18.59 AW	22.43 TQ	ILBLS	10/01-12/01
	Indiana	H	13.92 FQ	18.47 AW	21.72 TQ	INBLS	10/01-12/01
	Iowa	H	12.13 FQ	18.69 AW	25.75 TQ	IABLS	10/01-12/01
	Kansas	H	11.48 FQ	17.49 AW	22.64 TQ	KSBLS	10/01-12/01
	Kentucky	H	14.13 FQ	17.58 AW	21.49 TQ	KYBLS	10/01-12/01
	Louisiana	H	17.23 FQ	19.35 AW	21.93 TQ	LABLS	10/01-12/01
	Maryland	H	17.06 FQ	19.51 AW	23.87 TQ	MDBLS	10/01-12/01
	Michigan	H	12.84 FQ	18.19 AW	22.01 TQ	MIBLS	10/01-12/01
	Minnesota	H	10.49 FQ	15.44 AW	20.80 TQ	MNBLS	10/01-12/01
	Missouri	H	12.74 FQ	17.96 AW	21.80 TQ	MOBLS	10/01-12/01
	New Jersey	H	20.40 FQ	25.98 AW	31.58 TQ	NJBLS	10/01-12/01
	New York	H	14.74 FQ	20.30 AW	26.05 TQ	NYBLS	10/01-12/01
	North Carolina	H	7.41 FQ	10.09 AW	13.50 TQ	NCBLS	10/01-12/01
	North Dakota	H	14.90 FQ	19.71 AW	25.48 TQ	NDBLS	10/01-12/01
	Ohio	H	11.87 FQ	16.98 AW	21.13 TQ	OHBLS	10/01-12/01
	Oklahoma	H	12.36 FQ	18.80 AW	23.93 TQ	OKBLS	10/01-12/01
	Oregon	H	10.68 FQ	15.53 AW	20.54 TQ	ORBLS	10/01-12/01
	Pennsylvania	H	10.71 FQ	18.00 AW	23.50 TQ	PABLS	10/01-12/01
	South Carolina	H	10.93 FQ	16.41 AW	21.48 TQ	SCBLS	10/01-12/01
	Tennessee	H	10.87 FQ	14.60 AW	20.94 TQ	TNBLS	10/01-12/01
	Texas	H	11.47 FQ	16.66 AW	21.14 TQ	TXBLS	10/01-12/01
	Utah	H	17.88 FQ	20.80 AW	25.32 TQ	UTBLS	10/01-12/01
	Virginia	H	16.56 FQ	19.25 AW	22.27 TQ	VABLS	10/01-12/01
	Washington	H	9.66 FQ	13.51 AW	19.25 TQ	WABLS	10/01-12/01
Rail-Track Laying and Maintenance Equipment Operator	Alabama	H	8.02 FQ	14.57 AW	21.47 TQ	ALBLS	10/01-12/01
	Arizona	H	9.37 FQ	16.72 AW	26.01 TQ	AZBLS	10/01-12/01
	Arkansas	H	10.55 FQ	15.65 AW	20.63 TQ	ARBLS	10/01-12/01
	California	H	12.14 FQ	16.77 AW	22.76 TQ	CABLS	10/01-12/01
	Florida	H	9.22 FQ	12.79 AW	19.25 TQ	FLBLS	10/01-12/01
	Georgia	H	9.38 FQ	13.54 AW	17.59 TQ	GABLS	10/01-12/01
	Illinois	H	12.64 FQ	16.99 AW	21.69 TQ	ILBLS	10/01-12/01
	Indiana	H	14.12 FQ	16.72 AW	21.14 TQ	INBLS	10/01-12/01
	Kansas	H	10.68 FQ	16.34 AW	21.61 TQ	KSBLS	10/01-12/01
	Kentucky	H	13.70 FQ	17.68 AW	22.89 TQ	KYBLS	10/01-12/01
	Louisiana	H	7.94 FQ	14.64 AW	20.41 TQ	LABLS	10/01-12/01
	Maine	H	12.46 FQ	15.98 AW	20.12 TQ	MEBLS	10/01-12/01
	Maryland	H	14.19 FQ	19.14 AW	25.68 TQ	MDBLS	10/01-12/01
	Michigan	H	10.02 FQ	13.99 AW	17.33 TQ	MIBLS	10/01-12/01
	Minnesota	H	13.62 FQ	17.58 AW	23.54 TQ	MNBLS	10/01-12/01
	Missouri	H	12.36 FQ	17.17 AW	23.41 TQ	MOBLS	10/01-12/01
	Montana	H	8.08 FQ	12.86 AW	18.17 TQ	MTBLS	10/01-12/01
	New Jersey	H	13.39 FQ	20.41 AW	27.58 TQ	NJBLS	10/01-12/01
	New Mexico	H	13.58 FQ	16.31 AW	20.53 TQ	NMBLS	10/01-12/01
	New York	H	12.47 FQ	21.11 AW	26.44 TQ	NYBLS	10/01-12/01
	North Carolina	H	8.62 FQ	13.63 AW	20.68 TQ	NCBLS	10/01-12/01
	North Dakota	H	10.35 FQ	17.71 AW	24.70 TQ	NDBLS	10/01-12/01
	Ohio	H	11.85 FQ	16.72 AW	22.69 TQ	OHBLS	10/01-12/01
	Oklahoma	H	6.50 FQ	13.48 AW	19.13 TQ	OKBLS	10/01-12/01
	Oregon	H	6.67 FQ	14.02 AW	20.26 TQ	ORBLS	10/01-12/01
	Pennsylvania	H	11.79 FQ	16.95 AW	21.62 TQ	PABLS	10/01-12/01
	South Carolina	H	13.00 FQ	18.25 AW	24.82 TQ	SCBLS	10/01-12/01
	Tennessee	H	11.26 FQ	15.61 AW	21.63 TQ	TNBLS	10/01-12/01
	Texas	H	7.50 FQ	12.19 AW	18.91 TQ	TXBLS	10/01-12/01
	Virginia	H	14.11 FQ	17.60 AW	22.39 TQ	VABLS	10/01-12/01
	Washington	H	9.42 FQ	16.20 AW	25.07 TQ	WABLS	10/01-12/01
	West Virginia	H	12.02 FQ	17.18 AW	21.94 TQ	WVBLS	10/01-12/01
Rail Yard Engineer, Dinkey Operator, and Hostler	Alabama	H	12.97 FQ	21.61 AW	46.13 TQ	ALBLS	10/01-12/01
	Arkansas	H	9.91 FQ	19.67 AW	39.88 TQ	ARBLS	10/01-12/01
	California	H	11.23 FQ	15.75 AW	20.41 TQ	CABLS	10/01-12/01
	Colorado	H	14.31 FQ	19.90 AW	27.55 TQ	COBLS	10/01-12/01
	Georgia	H	10.93 FQ	17.83 AW	22.67 TQ	GABLS	10/01-12/01

AAW Average annual wage	**AOH** Average offered, high	**ASH** Average starting, high	**H** Hourly	**M** Monthly	**S** Special: hourly and annual
AE Average entry wage	**AOL** Average offered, low	**ASL** Average starting, low	**HI** Highest wage paid	**MTC** Median total compensation	**TQ** Third quartile wage
AEX Average experienced wage	**APH** Average pay, high range	**AW** Average wage paid	**HR** High end range	**MW** Median wage paid	**W** Weekly
AO Average offered	**APL** Average pay, low range	**FQ** First quartile wage	**LR** Low end range	**SQ** Second quartile wage	**Y** Yearly

Occupation/Type/Industry	Location	Per	Low	Mid	High	Source	Date
Rail Yard Engineer, Dinkey Operator, and Hostler	Illinois	H	13.92 FQ	19.33 AW	24.30 TQ	ILBLS	10/01-12/01
	Indiana	H	16.07 FQ	20.33 AW	23.60 TQ	INBLS	10/01-12/01
	Iowa	H	11.69 FQ	13.09 AW	14.46 TQ	IABLS	10/01-12/01
	Kentucky	H	12.26 FQ	16.80 AW	21.89 TQ	KYBLS	10/01-12/01
	Louisiana	H	15.16 FQ	26.64 AW	52.52 TQ	LABLS	10/01-12/01
	Maryland	H	13.38 FQ	19.72 AW	24.49 TQ	MDBLS	10/01-12/01
	Michigan	H	14.94 FQ	20.12 AW	23.85 TQ	MIBLS	10/01-12/01
	Missouri	H	13.07 FQ	17.61 AW	22.07 TQ	MOBLS	10/01-12/01
	Nebraska	H	9.08 FQ	17.53 AW	26.00 TQ	NEBLS	10/01-12/01
	New Jersey	H	12.30 FQ	16.67 AW	21.31 TQ	NJBLS	10/01-12/01
	New York	H	14.74 FQ	20.58 AW	26.04 TQ	NYBLS	10/01-12/01
	Ohio	H	12.97 FQ	18.49 AW	22.38 TQ	OHBLS	10/01-12/01
	Oregon	H	13.42 FQ	17.62 AW	20.42 TQ	ORBLS	10/01-12/01
	Pennsylvania	H	17.56 FQ	19.43 AW	21.99 TQ	PABLS	10/01-12/01
	South Carolina	H	14.33 FQ	20.09 AW	24.65 TQ	SCBLS	10/01-12/01
	Tennessee	H	9.80 FQ	27.64 AW	54.35 TQ	TNBLS	10/01-12/01
	Utah	H	14.18 FQ	17.56 AW	21.27 TQ	UTBLS	10/01-12/01
	Virginia	H	14.74 FQ	19.72 AW	24.56 TQ	VABLS	10/01-12/01
	Washington	H	13.99 FQ	21.65 AW	29.08 TQ	WABLS	10/01-12/01
	West Virginia	H	14.55 FQ	19.17 AW	24.03 TQ	WVBLS	10/01-12/01
Railroad Brake, Signal, and Switch Operator	Alabama	H	14.05 FQ	22.67 AW	33.16 TQ	ALBLS	10/01-12/01
	California	H	15.74 FQ	24.90 AW	35.83 TQ	CABLS	10/01-12/01
	Connecticut	H	13.25 FQ	20.08 AW	27.18 TQ	CTBLS	10/01-12/01
	Florida	H	12.48 FQ	20.69 AW	31.64 TQ	FLBLS	10/01-12/01
	Georgia	H	12.77 FQ	21.50 AW	28.77 TQ	GABLS	10/01-12/01
	Idaho	H	13.01 FQ	20.16 AW	27.63 TQ	IDBLS	10/01-12/01
	Illinois	H	13.97 FQ	23.03 AW	34.54 TQ	ILBLS	10/01-12/01
	Indiana	H	12.73 FQ	20.81 AW	31.38 TQ	INBLS	10/01-12/01
	Iowa	H	11.95 FQ	18.30 AW	32.20 TQ	IABLS	10/01-12/01
	Kansas	H	12.47 FQ	20.90 AW	32.32 TQ	KSBLS	10/01-12/01
	Kentucky	H	14.05 FQ	23.98 AW	35.38 TQ	KYBLS	10/01-12/01
	Louisiana	H	18.01 FQ	27.47 AW	38.16 TQ	LABLS	10/01-12/01
	Michigan	H	15.42 FQ	24.37 AW	35.04 TQ	MIBLS	10/01-12/01
	Mississippi	H	15.32 FQ	26.48 AW	39.55 TQ	MSBLS	10/01-12/01
	Montana	H	12.34 FQ	21.56 AW	34.30 TQ	MTBLS	10/01-12/01
	New Jersey	H	23.18 FQ	25.72 AW	30.39 TQ	NJBLS	10/01-12/01
	New Mexico	H	13.03 FQ	23.08 AW	35.17 TQ	NMBLS	10/01-12/01
	New York	H	13.01 FQ	20.93 AW	27.97 TQ	NYBLS	10/01-12/01
	North Carolina	H	9.35 FQ	13.94 AW	17.00 TQ	NCBLS	10/01-12/01
	Ohio	H	14.07 FQ	22.73 AW	33.47 TQ	OHBLS	10/01-12/01
	Oklahoma	H	8.01 FQ	14.44 AW	29.89 TQ	OKBLS	10/01-12/01
	Oregon	H	15.33 FQ	23.95 AW	34.62 TQ	ORBLS	10/01-12/01
	Pennsylvania	H	11.96 FQ	16.85 AW	21.82 TQ	PABLS	10/01-12/01
	South Carolina	H	12.56 FQ	21.77 AW	31.24 TQ	SCBLS	10/01-12/01
	Tennessee	H	11.28 FQ	16.73 AW	31.04 TQ	TNBLS	10/01-12/01
	Texas	H	13.96 FQ	23.50 AW	35.31 TQ	TXBLS	10/01-12/01
	Virginia	H	15.74 FQ	25.46 AW	36.56 TQ	VABLS	10/01-12/01
	Washington	H	13.37 FQ	20.86 AW	31.62 TQ	WABLS	10/01-12/01
	West Virginia	H	13.08 FQ	23.38 AW	35.27 TQ	WVBLS	10/01-12/01
Railroad Conductor and Yardmaster	Alabama	H	16.33 FQ	24.58 AW	35.87 TQ	ALBLS	10/01-12/01
	Arkansas	H	12.18 FQ	21.85 AW	32.20 TQ	ARBLS	10/01-12/01
	California	H	15.05 FQ	22.50 AW	33.48 TQ	CABLS	10/01-12/01
	Colorado	H	14.91 FQ	22.42 AW	36.98 TQ	COBLS	10/01-12/01
	Connecticut	H	15.07 FQ	20.32 AW	27.20 TQ	CTBLS	10/01-12/01
	Florida	H	11.44 FQ	17.95 AW	22.19 TQ	FLBLS	10/01-12/01
	Georgia	H	16.99 FQ	24.06 AW	33.24 TQ	GABLS	10/01-12/01
	Idaho	H	14.71 FQ	21.61 AW	28.93 TQ	IDBLS	10/01-12/01
	Illinois	H	15.00 FQ	22.58 AW	35.32 TQ	ILBLS	10/01-12/01
	Indiana	H	16.88 FQ	24.61 AW	34.48 TQ	INBLS	10/01-12/01
	Iowa	H	15.15 FQ	22.61 AW	32.02 TQ	IABLS	10/01-12/01
	Kansas	H	14.75 FQ	21.98 AW	32.55 TQ	KSBLS	10/01-12/01
	Kentucky	H	14.89 FQ	23.29 AW	36.08 TQ	KYBLS	10/01-12/01
	Louisiana	H	15.43 FQ	28.65 AW	43.66 TQ	LABLS	10/01-12/01
	Maryland	H	15.14 FQ	21.92 AW	32.17 TQ	MDBLS	10/01-12/01
	Michigan	H	14.79 FQ	22.12 AW	32.74 TQ	MIBLS	10/01-12/01
	Minnesota	H	18.49 FQ	28.28 AW	40.50 TQ	MNBLS	10/01-12/01
	Mississippi	H	12.18 FQ	19.09 AW	34.40 TQ	MSBLS	10/01-12/01

AAW	Average annual wage	**AOH**	Average offered, high	**ASH**	Average starting, high	**H**	Hourly	**M**	Monthly	**S**	Special: hourly and annual
AE	Average entry wage	**AOL**	Average offered, low	**ASL**	Average starting, low	**HI**	Highest wage paid	**MTC**	Median total compensation	**TQ**	Third quartile wage
AEX	Average experienced wage	**APH**	Average pay, high range	**AW**	Average wage paid	**HR**	High end range	**MW**	Median wage paid	**W**	Weekly
AO	Average offered	**APL**	Average pay, low range	**FQ**	First quartile wage	**LR**	Low end range	**SQ**	Second quartile wage	**Y**	Yearly

Occupation/Type/Industry	Location	Per	Low	Mid	High	Source	Date
Railroad Conductor and Yardmaster	Missouri	H	14.74 FQ	22.88 AW	38.66 TQ	MOBLS	10/01-12/01
	Nevada	H	14.54 FQ	22.79 AW	39.78 TQ	NVBLS	10/01-12/01
	New Jersey	H	12.99 FQ	24.11 AW	31.65 TQ	NJBLS	10/01-12/01
	New York	H	15.14 FQ	20.96 AW	30.89 TQ	NYBLS	10/01-12/01
	North Carolina	H	14.06 FQ	18.19 AW	22.19 TQ	NCBLS	10/01-12/01
	Ohio	H	14.22 FQ	20.01 AW	28.53 TQ	OHBLS	10/01-12/01
	Oklahoma	H	15.67 FQ	22.06 AW	29.40 TQ	OKBLS	10/01-12/01
	Oregon	H	15.20 FQ	23.68 AW	33.82 TQ	ORBLS	10/01-12/01
	Pennsylvania	H	15.09 FQ	19.06 AW	22.39 TQ	PABLS	10/01-12/01
	South Carolina	H	15.44 FQ	20.20 AW	25.61 TQ	SCBLS	10/01-12/01
	Tennessee	H	16.08 FQ	26.67 AW	40.82 TQ	TNBLS	10/01-12/01
	Texas	H	13.31 FQ	20.31 AW	32.78 TQ	TXBLS	10/01-12/01
	Utah	H	16.44 FQ	22.27 AW	29.25 TQ	UTBLS	10/01-12/01
	Virginia	H	15.24 FQ	23.58 AW	34.42 TQ	VABLS	10/01-12/01
	Washington	H	14.55 FQ	22.69 AW	39.38 TQ	WABLS	10/01-12/01
	West Virginia	H	14.99 FQ	23.61 AW	36.60 TQ	WVBLS	10/01-12/01
	Wisconsin	H	15.92 FQ	23.00 AW	32.58 TQ	WIBLS	10/01-12/01
Real Estate Broker	Alabama	Y	17380 FQ	54090 AW	91110 TQ	ALBLS	10/01-12/01
	Birmingham MSA, AL	Y	15660 FQ	58910 AW		ALBLS	10/01-12/01
	Mobile MSA, AL	Y	17560 FQ	56690 AW	71620 TQ	ALBLS	10/01-12/01
	Tucson MSA, AZ	Y	14550 FQ	42200 AW	82870 TQ	AZBLS	10/01-12/01
	Arkansas	Y	12670 FQ	36090 AW	55500 TQ	ARBLS	10/01-12/01
	Little Rock-North Little Rock MSA, AR	Y	23260 FQ	40400 AW	55740 TQ	ARBLS	10/01-12/01
	California	Y	23170 FQ	85320 AW		CABLS	10/01-12/01
	Bakersfield MSA, CA	Y	19600 FQ	89900 AW	115720 TQ	CABLS	10/01-12/01
	Los Angeles-Long Beach PMSA, CA	Y	38380 FQ	94730 AW		CABLS	10/01-12/01
	Orange County PMSA, CA	Y	24670 FQ	67070 AW		CABLS	10/01-12/01
	Riverside-San Bernardino PMSA, CA	Y	30510 FQ	76540 AW		CABLS	10/01-12/01
	Sacramento PMSA, CA	Y	40800 FQ	78600 AW		CABLS	10/01-12/01
	San Diego MSA, CA	Y	17870 FQ	72930 AW		CABLS	10/01-12/01
	San Jose PMSA, CA	Y	37890 FQ	94360 AW		CABLS	10/01-12/01
	Santa Rosa PMSA, CA	Y	24190 FQ	77630 AW		CABLS	10/01-12/01
	Stockton-Lodi MSA, CA	Y	14860 FQ	56480 AW		CABLS	10/01-12/01
	Vallejo-Fairfield-Napa PMSA, CA	Y	29510 FQ	36000 AW	35890 TQ	CABLS	10/01-12/01
	Ventura PMSA, CA	Y	42890 FQ	77340 AW		CABLS	10/01-12/01
	Colorado	Y	23240 FQ	53690 AW	117250 TQ	COBLS	10/01-12/01
	Boulder-Longmont PMSA, CO	Y	21140 FQ	66620 AW	89510 TQ	COBLS	10/01-12/01
	Colorado Springs MSA, CO	Y	12230 FQ	48880 AW	123990 TQ	COBLS	10/01-12/01
	Denver PMSA, CO	Y	23690 FQ	52650 AW	114980 TQ	COBLS	10/01-12/01
	Connecticut	Y	31890 FQ	85640 AW		CTBLS	10/01-12/01
	Hartford MSA, CT	Y	48420 FQ	110240 AW		CTBLS	10/01-12/01
	New Haven-Meriden PMSA, CT	Y	20670 FQ	63780 AW	143470 TQ	CTBLS	10/01-12/01
	New London-Norwich MSA, CT-RI	Y	39980 FQ	65430 AW	99170 TQ	CTBLS	10/01-12/01
	Stamford-Norwalk PMSA, CT	Y	22110 FQ	62850 AW	120320 TQ	CTBLS	10/01-12/01
	Delaware	Y	19490 FQ	63470 AW	121680 TQ	DEBLS	10/01-12/01
	Wilmington-Newark PMSA, DE-MD	Y	22180 FQ	66610 AW	122320 TQ	DEBLS	10/01-12/01
	District of Columbia	Y	21480 FQ	103820 AW		DCBLS	10/01-12/01
	Washington PMSA, DC-MD-VA-WV	Y	19980 FQ	76690 AW		DCBLS	10/01-12/01
	Florida	Y	12820 FQ	64420 AW		FLBLS	10/01-12/01
	Fort Lauderdale PMSA, FL	Y	45360 FQ	84690 AW		FLBLS	10/01-12/01
	Fort Myers-Cape Coral MSA, FL	Y	27730 FQ	99670 AW		FLBLS	10/01-12/01
	Jacksonville MSA, FL	Y	13130 FQ	73140 AW		FLBLS	10/01-12/01
	Lakeland-Winter Haven MSA, FL	Y	29810 FQ	41620 AW	71110 TQ	FLBLS	10/01-12/01
	Melbourne-Titusville-Palm Bay MSA, FL	Y	40610 FQ	123180 AW		FLBLS	10/01-12/01
	Miami PMSA, FL	Y	32790 FQ	109580 AW		FLBLS	10/01-12/01
	Ocala MSA, FL	Y	22320 FQ	39330 AW	72070 TQ	FLBLS	10/01-12/01
	Orlando MSA, FL	Y	29770 FQ	55410 AW	128340 TQ	FLBLS	10/01-12/01
	Tallahassee MSA, FL	Y	38110 FQ	54070 AW	70900 TQ	FLBLS	10/01-12/01

AAW Average annual wage **AE** Average entry wage **AEX** Average experienced wage **AO** Average offered **AOH** Average offered, high **AOL** Average offered, low **APH** Average pay, high range **APL** Average pay, low range **ASH** Average starting, high **ASL** Average starting, low **AW** Average wage paid **FQ** First quartile wage **H** Hourly **HI** Highest wage paid **HR** High end range **LR** Low end range **M** Monthly **MTC** Median total compensation **MW** Median wage paid **SQ** Second quartile wage **S** Special: hourly and annual **TQ** Third quartile wage **W** Weekly **Y** Yearly

Occupation/Type/Industry	Location	Per	Low	Mid	High	Source	Date
Real Estate Broker	Tampa-St. Petersburg-Clearwater MSA, FL	Y	58220 FQ	64390 AW	72280 TQ	FLBLS	10/01-12/01
	Georgia	Y	38550 FQ	68040 AW	106560 TQ	GABLS	10/01-12/01
	Atlanta MSA, GA	Y	56770 FQ	70220 AW	105270 TQ	GABLS	10/01-12/01
	Hawaii	Y	75770 FQ	107800 AW		HIBLS	10/01-12/01
	Honolulu MSA, HI	Y	56970 FQ	130640 AW		HIBLS	10/01-12/01
	Idaho	Y	19610 FQ	30470 AW	58210 TQ	IDBLS	10/01-12/01
	Illinois	Y	23210 FQ	64550 AW		ILBLS	10/01-12/01
	Peoria-Pekin MSA, IL	Y	14180 FQ	51790 AW	89430 TQ	ILBLS	10/01-12/01
	Rockford MSA, IL	Y	60600 FQ	67610 AW	75950 TQ	ILBLS	10/01-12/01
	Indiana	Y	23080 FQ	55420 AW	89730 TQ	INBLS	10/01-12/01
	Fort Wayne MSA, IN	Y	42580 FQ	56060 AW	84990 TQ	INBLS	10/01-12/01
	Gary PMSA, IN	Y	40160 FQ	60190 AW	70560 TQ	INBLS	10/01-12/01
	Indianapolis MSA, IN	Y	23200 FQ	74260 AW		INBLS	10/01-12/01
	Iowa	Y	21030 FQ	46770 AW	84350 TQ	IABLS	10/01-12/01
	Cedar Rapids MSA, IA	Y	15200 FQ	53590 AW	122260 TQ	IABLS	10/01-12/01
	Des Moines MSA, IA	Y	21950 FQ	40930 AW	68200 TQ	IABLS	10/01-12/01
	Kansas	Y	13550 FQ	60040 AW	119890 TQ	KSBLS	10/01-12/01
	Wichita MSA, KS	Y	11930 FQ	63300 AW	133480 TQ	KSBLS	10/01-12/01
	Kentucky	Y	15750 FQ	36510 AW	59830 TQ	KYBLS	10/01-12/01
	Louisville MSA, KY-IN	Y	18400 FQ	46380 AW	91040 TQ	KYBLS	10/01-12/01
	Maine	Y	34990 FQ	72990 AW	137000 TQ	MEBLS	10/01-12/01
	Portland MSA, ME	Y	59750 FQ	66760 AW	72430 TQ	MEBLS	10/01-12/01
	Baltimore PMSA, MD	Y	31090 FQ	69190 AW	89180 TQ	MDBLS	10/01-12/01
	Massachusetts	Y	28780 FQ	83300 AW		MABLS	10/01-12/01
	Boston PMSA, MA-NH	Y	37070 FQ	93390 AW		MABLS	10/01-12/01
	Michigan	Y	21850 FQ	58600 AW		MIBLS	10/01-12/01
	Kalamazoo-Battle Creek MSA, MI	Y	39400 FQ	115040 AW		MIBLS	10/01-12/01
	Lansing-East Lansing MSA, MI	Y	45570 FQ	62700 AW	90110 TQ	MIBLS	10/01-12/01
	Minnesota	Y	20820 FQ	51920 AW		MNBLS	10/01-12/01
	Minneapolis-St. Paul MSA, MN-WI	Y	20430 FQ	60700 AW		MNBLS	10/01-12/01
	Mississippi	Y	24050 FQ	47240 AW	70940 TQ	MSBLS	10/01-12/01
	Missouri	Y	12600 FQ	62710 AW	121770 TQ	MOBLS	10/01-12/01
	Kansas City MSA, MO-KS	Y	44830 FQ	61870 AW	128970 TQ	MOBLS	10/01-12/01
	St. Louis MSA, MO-IL	Y	12600 FQ	68160 AW	119430 TQ	MOBLS	10/01-12/01
	Springfield MSA, MO	Y	12830 FQ	18840 AW	30610 TQ	MOBLS	10/01-12/01
	Montana	Y	75080 FQ	83060 AW	92200 TQ	MTBLS	10/01-12/01
	Nebraska	Y	13060 FQ	31970 AW	54580 TQ	NEBLS	10/01-12/01
	Omaha MSA, NE-IA	Y	28180 FQ	40140 AW	68900 TQ	NEBLS	10/01-12/01
	Nevada	Y	30870 FQ	42390 AW	50650 TQ	NVBLS	10/01-12/01
	Las Vegas MSA, NV-AZ	Y	29870 FQ	44160 AW	45840 TQ	NVBLS	10/01-12/01
	New Hampshire	Y	13750 FQ	72550 AW		NHBLS	10/01-12/01
	New Jersey	Y	29240 FQ	67380 AW	129140 TQ	NJBLS	10/01-12/01
	Bergen-Passaic PMSA, NJ	Y	46140 FQ	63160 AW	121080 TQ	NJBLS	10/01-12/01
	Middlesex-Somerset-Hunterdon PMSA, NJ	Y	48040 FQ	89370 AW	116250 TQ	NJBLS	10/01-12/01
	Monmouth-Ocean PMSA, NJ	Y	13960 FQ	61430 AW	125590 TQ	NJBLS	10/01-12/01
	Newark PMSA, NJ	Y	22270 FQ	76210 AW	121090 TQ	NJBLS	10/01-12/01
	New Mexico	Y	12090 FQ	42150 AW	110800 TQ	NMBLS	10/01-12/01
	Albuquerque MSA, NM	Y	18740 FQ	47670 AW	117710 TQ	NMBLS	10/01-12/01
	New York	Y	20950 FQ	58140 AW		NYBLS	10/01-12/01
	Nassau-Suffolk PMSA, NY	Y	23600 FQ	65670 AW		NYBLS	10/01-12/01
	New York PMSA, NY	Y	22480 FQ	57660 AW		NYBLS	10/01-12/01
	North Carolina	Y	21660 FQ	49130 AW	108500 TQ	NCBLS	10/01-12/01
	Charlotte-Gastonia-Rock Hill MSA, NC-SC	Y	27010 FQ	75440 AW		NCBLS	10/01-12/01
	Greensboro-Winston-Salem-High Point MSA, NC	Y	22640 FQ	32630 AW	55970 TQ	NCBLS	10/01-12/01
	Hickory-Morganton-Lenoir MSA, NC	Y	23250 FQ	36260 AW	81020 TQ	NCBLS	10/01-12/01
	Raleigh-Durham-Chapel Hill MSA, NC	Y	27120 FQ	39580 AW	46840 TQ	NCBLS	10/01-12/01
	Ohio	Y	15720 FQ	53580 AW	124240 TQ	OHBLS	10/01-12/01
	Akron PMSA, OH	Y	22820 FQ	55970 AW		OHBLS	10/01-12/01
	Cincinnati PMSA, OH-KY-IN	Y	16100 FQ	73030 AW		OHBLS	10/01-12/01
	Cleveland-Lorain-Elyria PMSA, OH	Y	28980 FQ	63090 AW	121760 TQ	OHBLS	10/01-12/01
	Dayton-Springfield MSA, OH	Y	24320 FQ	36030 AW	81260 TQ	OHBLS	10/01-12/01
	Toledo MSA, OH	Y	13000 FQ	67340 AW		OHBLS	10/01-12/01
	Oklahoma	Y	14200 FQ	75030 AW		OKBLS	10/01-12/01

AAW	Average annual wage	**AOH**	Average offered, high	**ASH**	Average starting, high	**H**	Hourly	**M**	Monthly	**S**	Special: hourly and annual
AE	Average entry wage	**AOL**	Average offered, low	**ASL**	Average starting, low	**HI**	Highest wage paid	**MTC**	Median total compensation	**TQ**	Third quartile wage
AEX	Average experienced wage	**APH**	Average pay, high range	**AW**	Average wage paid	**HR**	High end range	**MW**	Median wage paid	**W**	Weekly
AO	Average offered	**APL**	Average pay, low range	**FQ**	First quartile wage	**LR**	Low end range	**SQ**	Second quartile wage	**Y**	Yearly

Occupation/Type/Industry	Location	Per	Low	Mid	High	Source	Date
Real Estate Broker	Oregon	Y	22130 FQ	52710 AW	108580 TQ	ORBLS	10/01-12/01
	Medford-Ashland MSA, OR	Y	14760 FQ	31250 AW	47470 TQ	ORBLS	10/01-12/01
	Portland-Vancouver PMSA, OR-WA	Y	35480 FQ	74130 AW		ORBLS	10/01-12/01
	Pennsylvania	Y	17880 FQ	53790 AW	119380 TQ	PABLS	10/01-12/01
	Philadelphia PMSA, PA-NJ	Y	22190 FQ	73580 AW		PABLS	10/01-12/01
	Pittsburgh MSA, PA	Y	21000 FQ	51280 AW	109140 TQ	PABLS	10/01-12/01
	Rhode Island	Y	30660 FQ	77090 AW		RIBLS	10/01-12/01
	Providence-Fall River-Warwick MSA, RI-MA	Y	31910 FQ	78220 AW		RIBLS	10/01-12/01
	South Carolina	Y	20920 FQ	60900 AW	90810 TQ	SCBLS	10/01-12/01
	Charleston-North Charleston MSA, SC	Y	37710 FQ	57630 AW	88950 TQ	SCBLS	10/01-12/01
	Greenville-Spartanburg-Anderson MSA, SC	Y	17190 FQ	64130 AW	90610 TQ	SCBLS	10/01-12/01
	Myrtle Beach MSA, SC	Y	20490 FQ	49700 AW	74430 TQ	SCBLS	10/01-12/01
	South Dakota	Y	19450 FQ	26270 AW	48860 TQ	SDBLS	10/01-12/01
	Tennessee	Y	23640 FQ	76540 AW		TNBLS	10/01-12/01
	Johnson City-Kingsport-Bristol MSA, TN-VA	Y	15190 FQ	46850 AW	129500 TQ	TNBLS	10/01-12/01
	Knoxville MSA, TN	Y	22430 FQ	53730 AW	95870 TQ	TNBLS	10/01-12/01
	Memphis MSA, TN-AR-MS	Y	38540 FQ	110150 AW		TNBLS	10/01-12/01
	Nashville MSA, TN	Y	47100 FQ	89640 AW		TNBLS	10/01-12/01
	Texas	Y	13020 FQ	46860 AW	118570 TQ	TXBLS	10/01-12/01
	Austin-San Marcos MSA, TX	Y	15320 FQ	38540 AW	81280 TQ	TXBLS	10/01-12/01
	Dallas PMSA, TX	Y	13610 FQ	52030 AW	126490 TQ	TXBLS	10/01-12/01
	McAllen-Edinburg-Mission MSA, TX	Y	37160 FQ	42850 AW	56880 TQ	TXBLS	10/01-12/01
	San Antonio MSA, TX	Y	18730 FQ	42670 AW	55130 TQ	TXBLS	10/01-12/01
	Utah	Y	21590 FQ	64780 AW	139870 TQ	UTBLS	10/01-12/01
	Salt Lake City-Ogden MSA, UT	Y	21020 FQ	57450 AW	98010 TQ	UTBLS	10/01-12/01
	Vermont	Y	38370 FQ	52540 AW	74860 TQ	VTBLS	10/01-12/01
	Virginia	Y	18380 FQ	51180 AW	138920 TQ	VABLS	10/01-12/01
	Norfolk-Virginia Beach-Newport News MSA, VA-NC	Y	20200 FQ	38990 AW	72280 TQ	VABLS	10/01-12/01
	Richmond-Petersburg MSA, VA	Y	22820 FQ	46130 AW	56060 TQ	VABLS	10/01-12/01
	Washington	Y	31930 FQ	72840 AW	144850 TQ	WABLS	10/01-12/01
	Seattle-Bellevue-Everett PMSA, WA	Y	51320 FQ	91360 AW		WABLS	10/01-12/01
	Spokane MSA, WA	Y	50310 FQ	73950 AW	89510 TQ	WABLS	10/01-12/01
	West Virginia	Y	12990 FQ	47870 AW	105430 TQ	WVBLS	10/01-12/01
	Wisconsin	Y	19060 FQ	78510 AW	143850 TQ	WIBLS	10/01-12/01
	Milwaukee-Waukesha PMSA, WI	Y	20350 FQ	94040 AW		WIBLS	10/01-12/01
Real Estate Executive	Southeast	Y		316900 AW		WW	1/00-1/01
	West	Y		250000 AW		WW	1/00-1/01
Real Estate Sales Agent	Alabama	Y	17060 FQ	37370 AW	80130 TQ	ALBLS	10/01-12/01
	Birmingham MSA, AL	Y	19460 FQ	31240 AW	36200 TQ	ALBLS	10/01-12/01
	Huntsville MSA, AL	Y	29340 FQ	35930 AW	51310 TQ	ALBLS	10/01-12/01
	Montgomery MSA, AL	Y	17490 FQ	40590 AW	62530 TQ	ALBLS	10/01-12/01
	Alaska	Y	30870 FQ	51990 AW	73260 TQ	AKBLS	10/01-12/01
	Anchorage MSA, AK	Y	31630 FQ	53610 AW	81560 TQ	AKBLS	10/01-12/01
	Arizona	Y	16990 FQ	41030 AW	96640 TQ	AZBLS	10/01-12/01
	Phoenix-Mesa MSA, AZ	Y	17070 FQ	41420 AW	101230 TQ	AZBLS	10/01-12/01
	Tucson MSA, AZ	Y	13850 FQ	38910 AW	82450 TQ	AZBLS	10/01-12/01
	Arkansas	Y	12200 FQ	25950 AW	47140 TQ	ARBLS	10/01-12/01
	Fayetteville-Springdale-Rogers MSA, AR	Y	22850 FQ	36530 AW	52890 TQ	ARBLS	10/01-12/01
	Fort Smith MSA, AR-OK	Y	19050 FQ	34960 AW	55910 TQ	ARBLS	10/01-12/01
	Little Rock-North Little Rock MSA, AR	Y	12620 FQ	26960 AW	54040 TQ	ARBLS	10/01-12/01
	California	Y	14160 FQ	40100 AW	89190 TQ	CABLS	10/01-12/01
	Bakersfield MSA, CA	Y	15840 FQ	50920 AW		CABLS	10/01-12/01
	Chico-Paradise MSA, CA	Y	15010 FQ	20880 AW	28210 TQ	CABLS	10/01-12/01
	Los Angeles-Long Beach PMSA, CA	Y	13890 FQ	34390 AW	79760 TQ	CABLS	10/01-12/01
	Merced MSA, CA	Y	14090 FQ	40240 AW	58890 TQ	CABLS	10/01-12/01
	Modesto MSA, CA	Y	16120 FQ	30140 AW	53760 TQ	CABLS	10/01-12/01

AAW	Average annual wage	AOH	Average offered, high	ASH	Average starting, high	H	Hourly	M	Monthly	S	Special: hourly and annual
AE	Average entry wage	AOL	Average offered, low	ASL	Average starting, low	HI	Highest wage paid	MTC	Median total compensation	TQ	Third quartile wage
AEX	Average experienced wage	APH	Average pay, high range	AW	Average wage paid	HR	High end range	MW	Median wage paid	W	Weekly
AO	Average offered	APL	Average pay, low range	FQ	First quartile wage	LR	Low end range	SQ	Second quartile wage	Y	Yearly

Occupation/Type/Industry	Location	Per	Low	Mid	High	Source	Date
Real Estate Sales Agent	Oakland PMSA, CA	Y	14100 FQ	40330 AW	69550 TQ	CABLS	10/01-12/01
	Orange County PMSA, CA	Y	13760 FQ	40170 AW	101650 TQ	CABLS	10/01-12/01
	Riverside-San Bernardino PMSA, CA	Y	19090 FQ	37630 AW	75520 TQ	CABLS	10/01-12/01
	Sacramento PMSA, CA	Y	18650 FQ	59150 AW	113770 TQ	CABLS	10/01-12/01
	Salinas MSA, CA	Y	17400 FQ	36740 AW	68580 TQ	CABLS	10/01-12/01
	San Diego MSA, CA	Y	13890 FQ	29790 AW	55400 TQ	CABLS	10/01-12/01
	San Francisco PMSA, CA	Y	13730 FQ	40650 AW	84470 TQ	CABLS	10/01-12/01
	San Jose PMSA, CA	Y	14060 FQ	44540 AW	92480 TQ	CABLS	10/01-12/01
	San Luis Obispo-Atascadero-Paso Robles MSA, CA	Y	13740 FQ	64120 AW		CABLS	10/01-12/01
	Santa Barbara-Santa Maria-Lompoc MSA, CA	Y	16640 FQ	34000 AW	57500 TQ	CABLS	10/01-12/01
	Santa Cruz-Watsonville PMSA, CA	Y	31480 FQ	44170 AW	53370 TQ	CABLS	10/01-12/01
	Santa Rosa PMSA, CA	Y	14210 FQ	45260 AW	121870 TQ	CABLS	10/01-12/01
	Stockton-Lodi MSA, CA	Y	24230 FQ	55910 AW	104010 TQ	CABLS	10/01-12/01
	Vallejo-Fairfield-Napa PMSA, CA	Y	26470 FQ	67850 AW	93060 TQ	CABLS	10/01-12/01
	Ventura PMSA, CA	Y	32330 FQ	55690 AW	70040 TQ	CABLS	10/01-12/01
	Visalia-Tulare-Porterville MSA, CA	Y	15560 FQ	26120 AW	48220 TQ	CABLS	10/01-12/01
	Colorado	Y	20670 FQ	45390 AW	89330 TQ	COBLS	10/01-12/01
	Boulder-Longmont PMSA, CO	Y	22350 FQ	38970 AW	68150 TQ	COBLS	10/01-12/01
	Colorado Springs MSA, CO	Y	14780 FQ	37540 AW	83800 TQ	COBLS	10/01-12/01
	Denver PMSA, CO	Y	22320 FQ	48770 AW	106150 TQ	COBLS	10/01-12/01
	Fort Collins-Loveland MSA, CO	Y	21690 FQ	45170 AW	100250 TQ	COBLS	10/01-12/01
	Connecticut	Y	24530 FQ	42560 AW	63510 TQ	CTBLS	10/01-12/01
	Bridgeport PMSA, CT	Y	24670 FQ	35980 AW	51190 TQ	CTBLS	10/01-12/01
	Danbury PMSA, CT	Y	28280 FQ	54860 AW		CTBLS	10/01-12/01
	Hartford MSA, CT	Y	24510 FQ	48950 AW	68790 TQ	CTBLS	10/01-12/01
	New Haven-Meriden PMSA, CT	Y	23140 FQ	35300 AW	43570 TQ	CTBLS	10/01-12/01
	New London-Norwich MSA, CT-RI	Y	14320 FQ	30950 AW	43820 TQ	CTBLS	10/01-12/01
	Stamford-Norwalk PMSA, CT	Y	33730 FQ	61590 AW	102000 TQ	CTBLS	10/01-12/01
	Delaware	Y	18620 FQ	32740 AW	54890 TQ	DEBLS	10/01-12/01
	Wilmington-Newark PMSA, DE-MD	Y	18830 FQ	33450 AW	57550 TQ	DEBLS	10/01-12/01
	District of Columbia	Y	19560 FQ	50580 AW	83750 TQ	DCBLS	10/01-12/01
	Washington PMSA, DC-MD-VA-WV	Y	17930 FQ	39030 AW	75670 TQ	DCBLS	10/01-12/01
	Florida	Y	16640 FQ	38670 AW	86280 TQ	FLBLS	10/01-12/01
	Daytona Beach MSA, FL	Y	16650 FQ	37450 AW	54480 TQ	FLBLS	10/01-12/01
	Fort Lauderdale PMSA, FL	Y	16530 FQ	35510 AW	62690 TQ	FLBLS	10/01-12/01
	Fort Myers-Cape Coral MSA, FL	Y	17870 FQ	66410 AW	140500 TQ	FLBLS	10/01-12/01
	Fort Pierce-Port St. Lucie MSA, FL	Y	17060 FQ	44940 AW	78680 TQ	FLBLS	10/01-12/01
	Fort Walton Beach MSA, FL	Y	11450 FQ	17220 AW	27770 TQ	FLBLS	10/01-12/01
	Jacksonville MSA, FL	Y	16180 FQ	44340 AW	100660 TQ	FLBLS	10/01-12/01
	Lakeland-Winter Haven MSA, FL	Y	17140 FQ	44910 AW	83320 TQ	FLBLS	10/01-12/01
	Melbourne-Titusville-Palm Bay MSA, FL	Y	13850 FQ	24730 AW	31900 TQ	FLBLS	10/01-12/01
	Miami PMSA, FL	Y	15860 FQ	49460 AW	111410 TQ	FLBLS	10/01-12/01
	Naples MSA, FL	Y	19820 FQ	74830 AW		FLBLS	10/01-12/01
	Ocala MSA, FL	Y	11810 FQ	27240 AW	48530 TQ	FLBLS	10/01-12/01
	Orlando MSA, FL	Y	20290 FQ	34550 AW	70780 TQ	FLBLS	10/01-12/01
	Pensacola MSA, FL	Y	17310 FQ	40980 AW	67820 TQ	FLBLS	10/01-12/01
	Sarasota-Bradenton MSA, FL	Y	18870 FQ	27740 AW	48540 TQ	FLBLS	10/01-12/01
	Tallahassee MSA, FL	Y	21070 FQ	52090 AW	82170 TQ	FLBLS	10/01-12/01
	Tampa-St. Petersburg-Clearwater MSA, FL	Y	17520 FQ	34730 AW	57600 TQ	FLBLS	10/01-12/01
	West Palm Beach-Boca Raton MSA, FL	Y	20740 FQ	63670 AW	142470 TQ	FLBLS	10/01-12/01
	Georgia	Y	14290 FQ	30430 AW	55530 TQ	GABLS	10/01-12/01
	Atlanta MSA, GA	Y	14160 FQ	30720 AW	67190 TQ	GABLS	10/01-12/01
	Augusta-Aiken MSA, GA-SC	Y	14180 FQ	32620 AW	72230 TQ	GABLS	10/01-12/01
	Columbus MSA, GA-AL	Y	14860 FQ	26310 AW	32810 TQ	GABLS	10/01-12/01
	Macon MSA, GA	Y	17360 FQ	30270 AW	44520 TQ	GABLS	10/01-12/01

AAW	Average annual wage	AOH	Average offered, high	ASH	Average starting, high	H	Hourly	M	Monthly	S	Special: hourly and annual
AE	Average entry wage	AOL	Average offered, low	ASL	Average starting, low	HI	Highest wage paid	MTC	Median total compensation	TQ	Third quartile wage
AEX	Average experienced wage	APH	Average pay, high range	AW	Average wage paid	HR	High end range	MW	Median wage paid	W	Weekly
AO	Average offered	APL	Average pay, low range	FQ	First quartile wage	LR	Low end range	SQ	Second quartile wage	Y	Yearly

Occupation/Type/Industry	Location	Per	Low	Mid	High	Source	Date
Real Estate Sales Agent	Savannah MSA, GA	Y	20600 FQ	35160 AW	54550 TQ	GABLS	10/01-12/01
	Hawaii	Y	36580 FQ	83700 AW	143770 TQ	HIBLS	10/01-12/01
	Honolulu MSA, HI	Y	26150 FQ	64150 AW		HIBLS	10/01-12/01
	Idaho	Y	14860 FQ	28820 AW	55270 TQ	IDBLS	10/01-12/01
	Boise City MSA, ID	Y	18930 FQ	35760 AW	65510 TQ	IDBLS	10/01-12/01
	Illinois	Y	11770 FQ	26910 AW	56190 TQ	ILBLS	10/01-12/01
	Champaign-Urbana MSA, IL	Y	14400 FQ	30570 AW	41760 TQ	ILBLS	10/01-12/01
	Chicago PMSA, IL	Y	11690 FQ	25710 AW	53760 TQ	ILBLS	10/01-12/01
	Rockford MSA, IL	Y	25590 FQ	40400 AW	68710 TQ	ILBLS	10/01-12/01
	Springfield MSA, IL	Y	20240 FQ	30210 AW	45550 TQ	ILBLS	10/01-12/01
	Indiana	Y	13150 FQ	37540 AW	70400 TQ	INBLS	10/01-12/01
	Evansville-Henderson MSA, IN-KY	Y	12790 FQ	31730 AW	57910 TQ	INBLS	10/01-12/01
	Fort Wayne MSA, IN	Y	13200 FQ	29380 AW	43930 TQ	INBLS	10/01-12/01
	Gary PMSA, IN	Y	16610 FQ	53600 AW	87520 TQ	INBLS	10/01-12/01
	Indianapolis MSA, IN	Y	13510 FQ	41800 AW	70600 TQ	INBLS	10/01-12/01
	Lafayette MSA, IN	Y	14800 FQ	19330 AW	26010 TQ	INBLS	10/01-12/01
	South Bend MSA, IN	Y	17910 FQ	29180 AW	36190 TQ	INBLS	10/01-12/01
	Iowa	Y	11890 FQ	26500 AW	53180 TQ	IABLS	10/01-12/01
	Cedar Rapids MSA, IA	Y	11440 FQ	21170 AW	54140 TQ	IABLS	10/01-12/01
	Davenport-Moline-Rock Island MSA, IA-IL	Y	15980 FQ	45970 AW	80030 TQ	IABLS	10/01-12/01
	Des Moines MSA, IA	Y	20940 FQ	35460 AW	70010 TQ	IABLS	10/01-12/01
	Kansas	Y	12050 FQ	27330 AW	48020 TQ	KSBLS	10/01-12/01
	Topeka MSA, KS	Y	12020 FQ	28980 AW	55780 TQ	KSBLS	10/01-12/01
	Wichita MSA, KS	Y	16630 FQ	40680 AW	116980 TQ	KSBLS	10/01-12/01
	Kentucky	Y	14940 FQ	30690 AW	53760 TQ	KYBLS	10/01-12/01
	Lexington MSA, KY	Y	15580 FQ	26800 AW	42210 TQ	KYBLS	10/01-12/01
	Louisville MSA, KY-IN	Y	15110 FQ	31280 AW	53850 TQ	KYBLS	10/01-12/01
	Louisiana	Y	14330 FQ	35920 AW	54830 TQ	LABLS	10/01-12/01
	Baton Rouge MSA, LA	Y	21600 FQ	43570 AW	55080 TQ	LABLS	10/01-12/01
	New Orleans MSA, LA	Y	20770 FQ	49560 AW	97270 TQ	LABLS	10/01-12/01
	Shreveport-Bossier City MSA, LA	Y	12950 FQ	20870 AW	40430 TQ	LABLS	10/01-12/01
	Maine	Y	14690 FQ	27680 AW	49100 TQ	MEBLS	10/01-12/01
	Portland MSA, ME	Y	19740 FQ	45050 AW	87700 TQ	MEBLS	10/01-12/01
	Maryland	Y	12430 FQ	33540 AW	55630 TQ	MDBLS	10/01-12/01
	Baltimore PMSA, MD	Y	11910 FQ	30820 AW	54430 TQ	MDBLS	10/01-12/01
	Massachusetts	Y	22950 FQ	43280 AW	69570 TQ	MABLS	10/01-12/01
	Boston PMSA, MA-NH	Y	31340 FQ	46530 AW	73850 TQ	MABLS	10/01-12/01
	Brockton PMSA, MA	Y	25420 FQ	55780 AW	73200 TQ	MABLS	10/01-12/01
	Lawrence PMSA, MA-NH	Y	18770 FQ	30610 AW	42800 TQ	MABLS	10/01-12/01
	Springfield MSA, MA	Y	14210 FQ	70270 AW		MABLS	10/01-12/01
	Worcester PMSA, MA-CT	Y	24000 FQ	33060 AW	43810 TQ	MABLS	10/01-12/01
	Michigan	Y	19190 FQ	37300 AW	61880 TQ	MIBLS	10/01-12/01
	Ann Arbor PMSA, MI	Y	19780 FQ	71190 AW		MIBLS	10/01-12/01
	Detroit PMSA, MI	Y	21530 FQ	33270 AW	42980 TQ	MIBLS	10/01-12/01
	Flint PMSA, MI	Y	16000 FQ	28440 AW	43080 TQ	MIBLS	10/01-12/01
	Grand Rapids-Muskegon-Holland MSA, MI	Y	15540 FQ	35380 AW	58360 TQ	MIBLS	10/01-12/01
	Kalamazoo-Battle Creek MSA, MI	Y	24840 FQ	41750 AW	88320 TQ	MIBLS	10/01-12/01
	Lansing-East Lansing MSA, MI	Y	17010 FQ	39060 AW	56160 TQ	MIBLS	10/01-12/01
	Saginaw-Bay City-Midland MSA, MI	Y	25270 FQ	48770 AW	98490 TQ	MIBLS	10/01-12/01
	Minnesota	Y	22700 FQ	53350 AW	87010 TQ	MNBLS	10/01-12/01
	Duluth-Superior MSA, MN-WI	Y	23730 FQ	38760 AW	66860 TQ	MNBLS	10/01-12/01
	Minneapolis-St. Paul MSA, MN-WI	Y	22480 FQ	56720 AW	87830 TQ	MNBLS	10/01-12/01
	Mississippi	Y	11820 FQ	32290 AW	64810 TQ	MSBLS	10/01-12/01
	Biloxi-Gulfport-Pascagoula MSA, MS	Y	11820 FQ	22870 AW	38980 TQ	MSBLS	10/01-12/01
	Jackson MSA, MS	Y	12310 FQ	55370 AW	135310 TQ	MSBLS	10/01-12/01
	Missouri	Y	15980 FQ	36240 AW	75140 TQ	MOBLS	10/01-12/01
	Kansas City MSA, MO-KS	Y	16590 FQ	34140 AW	75690 TQ	MOBLS	10/01-12/01
	St. Louis MSA, MO-IL	Y	18960 FQ	43180 AW	86890 TQ	MOBLS	10/01-12/01
	Springfield MSA, MO	Y	22400 FQ	24670 AW	27640 TQ	MOBLS	10/01-12/01
	Montana	Y	15090 FQ	28790 AW	60260 TQ	MTBLS	10/01-12/01
	Nebraska	Y	13280 FQ	29200 AW	53130 TQ	NEBLS	10/01-12/01
	Lincoln MSA, NE	Y	19060 FQ	44900 AW	87800 TQ	NEBLS	10/01-12/01
	Omaha MSA, NE-IA	Y	15870 FQ	32470 AW	56190 TQ	NEBLS	10/01-12/01
	Nevada	Y	19310 FQ	45830 AW	89590 TQ	NVBLS	10/01-12/01

AAW Average annual wage **AOH** Average offered, high **ASH** Average starting, high **H** Hourly **M** Monthly **S** Special: hourly and annual
AE Average entry wage **AOL** Average offered, low **ASL** Average starting, low **HI** Highest wage paid **MTC** Median total compensation **TQ** Third quartile wage
AEX Average experienced wage **APH** Average pay, high range **AW** Average wage paid **HR** High end range **MW** Median wage paid **W** Weekly
AO Average offered **APL** Average pay, low range **FQ** First quartile wage **LR** Low end range **SQ** Second quartile wage **Y** Yearly

Occupation/Type/Industry	Location	Per	Low	Mid	High	Source	Date
Real Estate Sales Agent	Las Vegas MSA, NV-AZ	Y	19300 FQ	44670 AW	93100 TQ	NVBLS	10/01-12/01
	Reno MSA, NV	Y	15240 FQ	46430 AW	84100 TQ	NVBLS	10/01-12/01
	New Hampshire	Y	12110 FQ	32880 AW	80920 TQ	NHBLS	10/01-12/01
	Manchester PMSA, NH	Y	26930 FQ	55570 AW	91850 TQ	NHBLS	10/01-12/01
	Nashua PMSA, NH	Y	11420 FQ	16150 AW	27840 TQ	NHBLS	10/01-12/01
	Portsmouth-Rochester PMSA, NH-ME	Y	12070 FQ	22650 AW	35150 TQ	NHBLS	10/01-12/01
	New Jersey	Y	21570 FQ	41860 AW	68980 TQ	NJBLS	10/01-12/01
	Atlantic-Cape May PMSA, NJ	Y	22770 FQ	39220 AW	65560 TQ	NJBLS	10/01-12/01
	Bergen-Passaic PMSA, NJ	Y	31660 FQ	65420 AW	120810 TQ	NJBLS	10/01-12/01
	Jersey City PMSA, NJ	Y	24700 FQ	34940 AW	44450 TQ	NJBLS	10/01-12/01
	Middlesex-Somerset-Hunterdon PMSA, NJ	Y	28800 FQ	34430 AW	42190 TQ	NJBLS	10/01-12/01
	Monmouth-Ocean PMSA, NJ	Y	18670 FQ	44680 AW	75570 TQ	NJBLS	10/01-12/01
	Newark PMSA, NJ	Y	21010 FQ	40900 AW	62150 TQ	NJBLS	10/01-12/01
	Trenton PMSA, NJ	Y	24470 FQ	58920 AW	106500 TQ	NJBLS	10/01-12/01
	New Mexico	Y	12600 FQ	31310 AW	56920 TQ	NMBLS	10/01-12/01
	Albuquerque MSA, NM	Y	17560 FQ	33750 AW	56690 TQ	NMBLS	10/01-12/01
	Las Cruces MSA, NM	Y	12210 FQ	22940 AW	38410 TQ	NMBLS	10/01-12/01
	New York	Y	15900 FQ	43660 AW	90560 TQ	NYBLS	10/01-12/01
	Albany-Schenectady-Troy MSA, NY	Y	15890 FQ	29050 AW	57730 TQ	NYBLS	10/01-12/01
	Buffalo-Niagara Falls MSA, NY	Y	12770 FQ	31010 AW	62650 TQ	NYBLS	10/01-12/01
	Dutchess County PMSA, NY	Y	18670 FQ	31160 AW	56180 TQ	NYBLS	10/01-12/01
	Nassau-Suffolk PMSA, NY	Y	11660 FQ	30730 AW	45670 TQ	NYBLS	10/01-12/01
	New York PMSA, NY	Y	18970 FQ	48410 AW	95990 TQ	NYBLS	10/01-12/01
	Newburgh PMSA, NY-PA	Y	12190 FQ	42950 AW		NYBLS	10/01-12/01
	Rochester MSA, NY	Y	12860 FQ	36900 AW	56190 TQ	NYBLS	10/01-12/01
	Syracuse MSA, NY	Y	19750 FQ	49290 AW		NYBLS	10/01-12/01
	North Carolina	Y	19210 FQ	36830 AW	67900 TQ	NCBLS	10/01-12/01
	Asheville MSA, NC	Y	21590 FQ	35990 AW	56500 TQ	NCBLS	10/01-12/01
	Charlotte-Gastonia-Rock Hill MSA, NC-SC	Y	21150 FQ	55920 AW		NCBLS	10/01-12/01
	Fayetteville MSA, NC	Y	17000 FQ	24660 AW	32100 TQ	NCBLS	10/01-12/01
	Greensboro-Winston-Salem-High Point MSA, NC	Y	20310 FQ	35110 AW	56230 TQ	NCBLS	10/01-12/01
	Hickory-Morganton-Lenoir MSA, NC	Y	18770 FQ	39290 AW	80000 TQ	NCBLS	10/01-12/01
	Raleigh-Durham-Chapel Hill MSA, NC	Y	18920 FQ	29540 AW	52340 TQ	NCBLS	10/01-12/01
	North Dakota	Y	13050 FQ	36640 AW	64310 TQ	NDBLS	10/01-12/01
	Fargo-Moorhead MSA, ND-MN	Y	12900 FQ	40650 AW	82090 TQ	NDBLS	10/01-12/01
	Ohio	Y	18950 FQ	46750 AW	85180 TQ	OHBLS	10/01-12/01
	Akron PMSA, OH	Y	18060 FQ	36250 AW	76430 TQ	OHBLS	10/01-12/01
	Canton-Massillon MSA, OH	Y	22950 FQ	42430 AW	72120 TQ	OHBLS	10/01-12/01
	Cincinnati PMSA, OH-KY-IN	Y	16950 FQ	43070 AW	86290 TQ	OHBLS	10/01-12/01
	Cleveland-Lorain-Elyria PMSA, OH	Y	19290 FQ	58810 AW	89780 TQ	OHBLS	10/01-12/01
	Columbus MSA, OH	Y	18340 FQ	37400 AW	61080 TQ	OHBLS	10/01-12/01
	Hamilton-Middletown PMSA, OH	Y	17870 FQ	54610 AW	141790 TQ	OHBLS	10/01-12/01
	Toledo MSA, OH	Y	19590 FQ	32910 AW	47340 TQ	OHBLS	10/01-12/01
	Youngstown-Warren MSA, OH	Y	45640 FQ	61080 AW	79410 TQ	OHBLS	10/01-12/01
	Oklahoma	Y	12700 FQ	30640 AW	66350 TQ	OKBLS	10/01-12/01
	Oklahoma City MSA, OK	Y	12970 FQ	36180 AW	70190 TQ	OKBLS	10/01-12/01
	Tulsa MSA, OK	Y	14720 FQ	23970 AW	42940 TQ	OKBLS	10/01-12/01
	Oregon	Y	15550 FQ	44210 AW	120590 TQ	ORBLS	10/01-12/01
	Portland-Vancouver PMSA, OR-WA	Y	18930 FQ	55320 AW	134430 TQ	ORBLS	10/01-12/01
	Salem PMSA, OR	Y	14830 FQ	21440 AW	19870 TQ	ORBLS	10/01-12/01
	Pennsylvania	Y	18200 FQ	40620 AW	67160 TQ	PABLS	10/01-12/01
	Allentown-Bethlehem-Easton MSA, PA	Y	17770 FQ	37760 AW	87480 TQ	PABLS	10/01-12/01
	Erie MSA, PA	Y	17410 FQ	26980 AW	45020 TQ	PABLS	10/01-12/01
	Harrisburg-Lebanon-Carlisle MSA, PA	Y	17720 FQ	38580 AW	74450 TQ	PABLS	10/01-12/01
	Philadelphia PMSA, PA-NJ	Y	23670 FQ	44300 AW	68050 TQ	PABLS	10/01-12/01
	Pittsburgh MSA, PA	Y	13880 FQ	32120 AW	55480 TQ	PABLS	10/01-12/01
	Reading MSA, PA	Y	15540 FQ	25430 AW	42650 TQ	PABLS	10/01-12/01

AAW	Average annual wage	**AOH**	Average offered, high	**ASH**	Average starting, high	**H**	Hourly	**M**	Monthly	**S**	Special: hourly and annual
AE	Average entry wage	**AOL**	Average offered, low	**ASL**	Average starting, low	**HI**	Highest wage paid	**MTC**	Median total compensation	**TQ**	Third quartile wage
AEX	Average experienced wage	**APH**	Average pay, high range	**AW**	Average wage paid	**HR**	High end range	**MW**	Median wage paid	**W**	Weekly
AO	Average offered	**APL**	Average pay, low range	**FQ**	First quartile wage	**LR**	Low end range	**SQ**	Second quartile wage	**Y**	Yearly

Occupation/Type/Industry	Location	Per	Low	Mid	High	Source	Date
Real Estate Sales Agent	Scranton-Wilkes-Barre-Hazleton MSA, PA	Y	13720 FQ	50030 AW	84490 TQ	PABLS	10/01-12/01
	York MSA, PA	Y	12990 FQ	27400 AW	42890 TQ	PABLS	10/01-12/01
	Rhode Island	Y	18560 FQ	32220 AW	54630 TQ	RIBLS	10/01-12/01
	Providence-Fall River-Warwick MSA, RI-MA	Y	16250 FQ	27270 AW	46820 TQ	RIBLS	10/01-12/01
	South Carolina	Y	19840 FQ	70760 AW		SCBLS	10/01-12/01
	Charleston-North Charleston MSA, SC	Y	34520 FQ	101270 AW		SCBLS	10/01-12/01
	Columbia MSA, SC	Y	17190 FQ	33200 AW	46120 TQ	SCBLS	10/01-12/01
	Greenville-Spartanburg-Anderson MSA, SC	Y	18920 FQ	32720 AW	44480 TQ	SCBLS	10/01-12/01
	Myrtle Beach MSA, SC	Y	19510 FQ	55260 AW	131100 TQ	SCBLS	10/01-12/01
	South Dakota	Y	30690 FQ	60020 AW	89100 TQ	SDBLS	10/01-12/01
	Tennessee	Y	19220 FQ	31160 AW	56910 TQ	TNBLS	10/01-12/01
	Chattanooga MSA, TN-GA	Y	18400 FQ	43800 AW	83240 TQ	TNBLS	10/01-12/01
	Johnson City-Kingsport-Bristol MSA, TN-VA	Y	13290 FQ	25380 AW	47260 TQ	TNBLS	10/01-12/01
	Knoxville MSA, TN	Y	13470 FQ	38210 AW	85090 TQ	TNBLS	10/01-12/01
	Memphis MSA, TN-AR-MS	Y	15020 FQ	41130 AW	68140 TQ	TNBLS	10/01-12/01
	Nashville MSA, TN	Y	19460 FQ	29150 AW	45270 TQ	TNBLS	10/01-12/01
	Texas	Y	14070 FQ	35860 AW	76530 TQ	TXBLS	10/01-12/01
	Amarillo MSA, TX	Y	13070 FQ	22230 AW	27540 TQ	TXBLS	10/01-12/01
	Austin-San Marcos MSA, TX	Y	15800 FQ	43520 AW	69660 TQ	TXBLS	10/01-12/01
	Brownsville-Harlingen-San Benito MSA, TX	Y	13160 FQ	22120 AW	33540 TQ	TXBLS	10/01-12/01
	Corpus Christi MSA, TX	Y	13630 FQ	34050 AW	67810 TQ	TXBLS	10/01-12/01
	Dallas PMSA, TX	Y	13220 FQ	35250 AW	79490 TQ	TXBLS	10/01-12/01
	El Paso MSA, TX	Y	11350 FQ	15600 AW	19620 TQ	TXBLS	10/01-12/01
	Fort Worth-Arlington PMSA, TX	Y	13410 FQ	34600 AW	70190 TQ	TXBLS	10/01-12/01
	Galveston-Texas City PMSA, TX	Y	16560 FQ	41050 AW	85860 TQ	TXBLS	10/01-12/01
	Houston PMSA, TX	Y	15820 FQ	40640 AW	90310 TQ	TXBLS	10/01-12/01
	Killeen-Temple MSA, TX	Y	12200 FQ	20010 AW	33980 TQ	TXBLS	10/01-12/01
	Laredo MSA, TX	Y	15140 FQ	44040 AW	83400 TQ	TXBLS	10/01-12/01
	Lubbock MSA, TX	Y	12390 FQ	25220 AW	50540 TQ	TXBLS	10/01-12/01
	McAllen-Edinburg-Mission MSA, TX	Y	14290 FQ	24110 AW	28460 TQ	TXBLS	10/01-12/01
	Odessa-Midland MSA, TX	Y	11820 FQ	30320 AW	71470 TQ	TXBLS	10/01-12/01
	San Antonio MSA, TX	Y	16020 FQ	37060 AW	56470 TQ	TXBLS	10/01-12/01
	Waco MSA, TX	Y	17720 FQ	32240 AW	78400 TQ	TXBLS	10/01-12/01
	Utah	Y	18010 FQ	36510 AW	70110 TQ	UTBLS	10/01-12/01
	Provo-Orem MSA, UT	Y	17270 FQ	57210 AW	121220 TQ	UTBLS	10/01-12/01
	Salt Lake City-Ogden MSA, UT	Y	18290 FQ	28720 AW	54950 TQ	UTBLS	10/01-12/01
	Vermont	Y	30630 FQ	48730 AW	67960 TQ	VTBLS	10/01-12/01
	Burlington MSA, VT	Y	30740 FQ	52180 AW	124110 TQ	VTBLS	10/01-12/01
	Virginia	Y	15650 FQ	31890 AW	63220 TQ	VABLS	10/01-12/01
	Lynchburg MSA, VA	Y	14490 FQ	24450 AW	39890 TQ	VABLS	10/01-12/01
	Norfolk-Virginia Beach-Newport News MSA, VA-NC	Y	15280 FQ	31760 AW	62290 TQ	VABLS	10/01-12/01
	Richmond-Petersburg MSA, VA	Y	15510 FQ	27400 AW	46210 TQ	VABLS	10/01-12/01
	Roanoke MSA, VA	Y	15070 FQ	26780 AW	51460 TQ	VABLS	10/01-12/01
	Washington	Y	20420 FQ	45460 AW	76150 TQ	WABLS	10/01-12/01
	Bremerton PMSA, WA	Y	27000 FQ	38710 AW	58100 TQ	WABLS	10/01-12/01
	Olympia PMSA, WA	Y	25160 FQ	45580 AW	69210 TQ	WABLS	10/01-12/01
	Seattle-Bellevue-Everett PMSA, WA	Y	20780 FQ	47240 AW	81900 TQ	WABLS	10/01-12/01
	Spokane MSA, WA	Y	22530 FQ	39890 AW	53290 TQ	WABLS	10/01-12/01
	Tacoma PMSA, WA	Y	16120 FQ	35290 AW	57490 TQ	WABLS	10/01-12/01
	West Virginia	Y	13460 FQ	32170 AW	54160 TQ	WVBLS	10/01-12/01
	Charleston MSA, WV	Y	16040 FQ	28630 AW	42950 TQ	WVBLS	10/01-12/01
	Huntington-Ashland MSA, WV-KY-OH	Y	14770 FQ	33430 AW	54490 TQ	WVBLS	10/01-12/01
	Wisconsin	Y	19520 FQ	43790 AW	73420 TQ	WIBLS	10/01-12/01
	Appleton-Oshkosh-Neenah MSA, WI	Y	14800 FQ	21790 AW	28880 TQ	WIBLS	10/01-12/01
	Green Bay MSA, WI	Y	21060 FQ	41980 AW	57110 TQ	WIBLS	10/01-12/01
	Madison MSA, WI	Y	27820 FQ	51490 AW	74920 TQ	WIBLS	10/01-12/01

AAW	Average annual wage	**AOH**	Average offered, high	**ASH**	Average starting, high	**H**	Hourly	**M**	Monthly	**S**	Special: hourly and annual
AE	Average entry wage	**AOL**	Average offered, low	**ASL**	Average starting, low	**HI**	Highest wage paid	**MTC**	Median total compensation	**TQ**	Third quartile wage
AEX	Average experienced wage	**APH**	Average pay, high range	**AW**	Average wage paid	**HR**	High end range	**MW**	Median wage paid	**W**	Weekly
AO	Average offered	**APL**	Average pay, low range	**FQ**	First quartile wage	**LR**	Low end range	**SQ**	Second quartile wage	**Y**	Yearly

Occupation/Type/Industry	Location	Per	Low	Mid	High	Source	Date
Real Estate Sales Agent	Milwaukee-Waukesha PMSA, WI	Y	22600 FQ	48450 AW	78920 TQ	WIBLS	10/01-12/01
	Wyoming	Y	18810 FQ	43100 AW	72290 TQ	WYBLS	10/01-12/01
	Puerto Rico	Y	15220 FQ	36460 AW	69080 TQ	PRBLS	10/01-12/01
Receptionist	United States	Y		19450 AW		USATOD4	1/00-1/01
Receptionist and Information Clerk	Alabama	H	6.13 FQ	8.96 AW	12.77 TQ	ALBLS	10/01-12/01
	Birmingham MSA, AL	H	6.38 FQ	9.89 AW	14.61 TQ	ALBLS	10/01-12/01
	Huntsville MSA, AL	H	7.09 FQ	9.48 AW	13.78 TQ	ALBLS	10/01-12/01
	Mobile MSA, AL	H	6.00 FQ	8.30 AW	10.89 TQ	ALBLS	10/01-12/01
	Montgomery MSA, AL	H	6.11 FQ	8.59 AW	11.64 TQ	ALBLS	10/01-12/01
	Alaska	H	7.64 FQ	11.35 AW	16.14 TQ	AKBLS	10/01-12/01
	Anchorage MSA, AK	H	7.78 FQ	11.31 AW	15.16 TQ	AKBLS	10/01-12/01
	Arizona	H	6.93 FQ	9.80 AW	13.18 TQ	AZBLS	10/01-12/01
	Phoenix-Mesa MSA, AZ	H	7.13 FQ	10.01 AW	13.32 TQ	AZBLS	10/01-12/01
	Tucson MSA, AZ	H	6.97 FQ	9.75 AW	13.16 TQ	AZBLS	10/01-12/01
	Arkansas	H	6.36 FQ	8.66 AW	11.03 TQ	ARBLS	10/01-12/01
	Fayetteville-Springdale-Rogers MSA, AR	H	6.74 FQ	8.54 AW	10.82 TQ	ARBLS	10/01-12/01
	Fort Smith MSA, AR-OK	H	6.68 FQ	8.54 AW	10.77 TQ	ARBLS	10/01-12/01
	Little Rock-North Little Rock MSA, AR	H	6.83 FQ	9.35 AW	12.37 TQ	ARBLS	10/01-12/01
	California	H	7.14 FQ	11.20 AW	16.24 TQ	CABLS	10/01-12/01
	Bakersfield MSA, CA	H	6.83 FQ	9.85 AW	14.46 TQ	CABLS	10/01-12/01
	Chico-Paradise MSA, CA	H	6.81 FQ	10.30 AW	15.87 TQ	CABLS	10/01-12/01
	Fresno MSA, CA	H	7.07 FQ	9.68 AW	12.85 TQ	CABLS	10/01-12/01
	Los Angeles-Long Beach PMSA, CA	H	7.25 FQ	11.22 AW	16.01 TQ	CABLS	10/01-12/01
	Merced MSA, CA	H	7.08 FQ	9.36 AW	12.91 TQ	CABLS	10/01-12/01
	Modesto MSA, CA	H	7.00 FQ	9.50 AW	12.95 TQ	CABLS	10/01-12/01
	Oakland PMSA, CA	H	7.32 FQ	12.22 AW	17.25 TQ	CABLS	10/01-12/01
	Orange County PMSA, CA	H	6.73 FQ	10.47 AW	14.72 TQ	CABLS	10/01-12/01
	Redding MSA, CA	H	6.63 FQ	10.80 AW	16.41 TQ	CABLS	10/01-12/01
	Riverside-San Bernardino PMSA, CA	H	6.77 FQ	9.73 AW	13.70 TQ	CABLS	10/01-12/01
	Sacramento PMSA, CA	H	7.46 FQ	11.46 AW	15.97 TQ	CABLS	10/01-12/01
	Salinas MSA, CA	H	7.52 FQ	10.97 AW	15.32 TQ	CABLS	10/01-12/01
	San Diego MSA, CA	H	7.43 FQ	11.79 AW	16.78 TQ	CABLS	10/01-12/01
	San Francisco PMSA, CA	H	7.79 FQ	12.98 AW	17.81 TQ	CABLS	10/01-12/01
	San Jose PMSA, CA	H	8.30 FQ	13.22 AW	18.32 TQ	CABLS	10/01-12/01
	San Luis Obispo-Atascadero-Paso Robles MSA, CA	H	7.08 FQ	11.05 AW	16.29 TQ	CABLS	10/01-12/01
	Santa Barbara-Santa Maria-Lompoc MSA, CA	H	7.35 FQ	10.64 AW	14.06 TQ	CABLS	10/01-12/01
	Santa Cruz-Watsonville PMSA, CA	H	8.06 FQ	12.38 AW	17.56 TQ	CABLS	10/01-12/01
	Santa Rosa PMSA, CA	H	8.36 FQ	12.88 AW	19.39 TQ	CABLS	10/01-12/01
	Stockton-Lodi MSA, CA	H	6.89 FQ	10.41 AW	14.24 TQ	CABLS	10/01-12/01
	Vallejo-Fairfield-Napa PMSA, CA	H	7.10 FQ	10.74 AW	15.10 TQ	CABLS	10/01-12/01
	Ventura PMSA, CA	H	7.20 FQ	10.81 AW	14.72 TQ	CABLS	10/01-12/01
	Visalia-Tulare-Porterville MSA, CA	H	6.71 FQ	9.19 AW	12.47 TQ	CABLS	10/01-12/01
	Colorado	H	7.38 FQ	11.02 AW	15.48 TQ	COBLS	10/01-12/01
	Boulder-Longmont PMSA, CO	H	7.92 FQ	10.61 AW	14.03 TQ	COBLS	10/01-12/01
	Colorado Springs MSA, CO	H	7.32 FQ	10.50 AW	14.87 TQ	COBLS	10/01-12/01
	Denver PMSA, CO	H	7.64 FQ	11.70 AW	16.40 TQ	COBLS	10/01-12/01
	Fort Collins-Loveland MSA, CO	H	7.39 FQ	10.62 AW	14.89 TQ	COBLS	10/01-12/01
	Greeley PMSA, CO	H	7.30 FQ	9.58 AW	12.24 TQ	COBLS	10/01-12/01
	Connecticut	H	7.90 FQ	11.83 AW	16.38 TQ	CTBLS	10/01-12/01
	Bridgeport PMSA, CT	H	8.90 FQ	12.45 AW	16.54 TQ	CTBLS	10/01-12/01
	Danbury PMSA, CT	H	7.90 FQ	11.75 AW	16.06 TQ	CTBLS	10/01-12/01
	Hartford MSA, CT	H	7.30 FQ	11.02 AW	15.17 TQ	CTBLS	10/01-12/01
	New Haven-Meriden PMSA, CT	H	8.50 FQ	11.60 AW	15.88 TQ	CTBLS	10/01-12/01
	New London-Norwich MSA, CT-RI	H	7.68 FQ	10.72 AW	14.14 TQ	CTBLS	10/01-12/01
	Stamford-Norwalk PMSA, CT	H	9.82 FQ	14.24 AW	18.48 TQ	CTBLS	10/01-12/01
	Waterbury PMSA, CT	H	7.15 FQ	11.04 AW	14.57 TQ	CTBLS	10/01-12/01

AAW	Average annual wage	**AOH**	Average offered, high	**ASH**	Average starting, high	**H**	Hourly	**M**	Monthly	**S**	Special: hourly and annual
AE	Average entry wage	**AOL**	Average offered, low	**ASL**	Average starting, low	**HI**	Highest wage paid	**MTC**	Median total compensation	**TQ**	Third quartile wage
AEX	Average experienced wage	**APH**	Average pay, high range	**AW**	Average wage paid	**HR**	High end range	**MW**	Median wage paid	**W**	Weekly
AO	Average offered	**APL**	Average pay, low range	**FQ**	First quartile wage	**LR**	Low end range	**SQ**	Second quartile wage	**Y**	Yearly

Occupation/Type/Industry	Location	Per	Low	Mid	High	Source	Date
Receptionist and Information Clerk	Delaware	H	7.44 FQ	10.68 AW	14.12 TQ	DEBLS	10/01-12/01
	Wilmington-Newark PMSA, DE-MD	H	7.64 FQ	10.99 AW	14.41 TQ	DEBLS	10/01-12/01
	District of Columbia	H	8.64 FQ	12.60 AW	16.72 TQ	DCBLS	10/01-12/01
	Washington PMSA, DC-MD-VA-WV	H	7.43 FQ	11.58 AW	16.31 TQ	DCBLS	10/01-12/01
	Florida	H	6.57 FQ	9.47 AW	12.82 TQ	FLBLS	10/01-12/01
	Daytona Beach MSA, FL	H	6.46 FQ	8.79 AW	12.27 TQ	FLBLS	10/01-12/01
	Fort Lauderdale PMSA, FL	H	7.29 FQ	10.32 AW	13.59 TQ	FLBLS	10/01-12/01
	Fort Myers-Cape Coral MSA, FL	H	7.09 FQ	9.24 AW	11.63 TQ	FLBLS	10/01-12/01
	Fort Pierce-Port St. Lucie MSA, FL	H	6.58 FQ	9.47 AW	12.59 TQ	FLBLS	10/01-12/01
	Fort Walton Beach MSA, FL	H	6.37 FQ	8.85 AW	12.84 TQ	FLBLS	10/01-12/01
	Gainesville MSA, FL	H	6.15 FQ	9.10 AW	12.29 TQ	FLBLS	10/01-12/01
	Jacksonville MSA, FL	H	6.99 FQ	9.65 AW	12.86 TQ	FLBLS	10/01-12/01
	Lakeland-Winter Haven MSA, FL	H	6.41 FQ	8.90 AW	11.78 TQ	FLBLS	10/01-12/01
	Melbourne-Titusville-Palm Bay MSA, FL	H	6.02 FQ	8.50 AW	11.36 TQ	FLBLS	10/01-12/01
	Miami PMSA, FL	H	6.73 FQ	9.62 AW	12.98 TQ	FLBLS	10/01-12/01
	Naples MSA, FL	H	6.35 FQ	10.07 AW	13.84 TQ	FLBLS	10/01-12/01
	Ocala MSA, FL	H	6.37 FQ	8.86 AW	11.18 TQ	FLBLS	10/01-12/01
	Orlando MSA, FL	H	7.11 FQ	9.70 AW	13.03 TQ	FLBLS	10/01-12/01
	Pensacola MSA, FL	H	6.24 FQ	8.46 AW	10.99 TQ	FLBLS	10/01-12/01
	Sarasota-Bradenton MSA, FL	H	6.31 FQ	9.68 AW	12.90 TQ	FLBLS	10/01-12/01
	Tallahassee MSA, FL	H	6.11 FQ	8.71 AW	11.83 TQ	FLBLS	10/01-12/01
	Tampa-St. Petersburg-Clearwater MSA, FL	H	6.38 FQ	9.30 AW	12.65 TQ	FLBLS	10/01-12/01
	West Palm Beach-Boca Raton MSA, FL	H	6.72 FQ	9.92 AW	13.23 TQ	FLBLS	10/01-12/01
	Georgia	H	6.63 FQ	9.60 AW	13.49 TQ	GABLS	10/01-12/01
	Atlanta MSA, GA	H	6.95 FQ	9.98 AW	13.84 TQ	GABLS	10/01-12/01
	Augusta-Aiken MSA, GA-SC	H	6.80 FQ	9.45 AW	13.05 TQ	GABLS	10/01-12/01
	Columbus MSA, GA-AL	H	6.92 FQ	8.86 AW	11.44 TQ	GABLS	10/01-12/01
	Macon MSA, GA	H	6.08 FQ	9.16 AW	12.93 TQ	GABLS	10/01-12/01
	Savannah MSA, GA	H	6.66 FQ	9.02 AW	11.81 TQ	GABLS	10/01-12/01
	Hawaii	H	7.36 FQ	11.03 AW	14.45 TQ	HIBLS	10/01-12/01
	Honolulu MSA, HI	H	7.38 FQ	11.24 AW	14.68 TQ	HIBLS	10/01-12/01
	Idaho	H	6.62 FQ	9.76 AW	13.54 TQ	IDBLS	10/01-12/01
	Boise City MSA, ID	H	7.09 FQ	10.56 AW	14.70 TQ	IDBLS	10/01-12/01
	Illinois	H	6.82 FQ	10.28 AW	14.48 TQ	ILBLS	10/01-12/01
	Champaign-Urbana MSA, IL	H	5.94 FQ	8.38 AW	10.86 TQ	ILBLS	10/01-12/01
	Chicago PMSA, IL	H	7.14 FQ	10.71 AW	15.06 TQ	ILBLS	10/01-12/01
	Peoria-Pekin MSA, IL	H	6.07 FQ	9.03 AW	12.64 TQ	ILBLS	10/01-12/01
	Rockford MSA, IL	H	6.95 FQ	9.47 AW	12.06 TQ	ILBLS	10/01-12/01
	Springfield MSA, IL	H	5.90 FQ	9.09 AW	13.16 TQ	ILBLS	10/01-12/01
	Indiana	H	6.53 FQ	9.55 AW	13.13 TQ	INBLS	10/01-12/01
	Elkhart-Goshen MSA, IN	H	7.61 FQ	10.28 AW	13.32 TQ	INBLS	10/01-12/01
	Evansville-Henderson MSA, IN-KY	H	5.86 FQ	8.63 AW	11.61 TQ	INBLS	10/01-12/01
	Fort Wayne MSA, IN	H	7.23 FQ	10.12 AW	14.01 TQ	INBLS	10/01-12/01
	Gary PMSA, IN	H	5.98 FQ	9.19 AW	13.92 TQ	INBLS	10/01-12/01
	Indianapolis MSA, IN	H	7.17 FQ	10.18 AW	13.57 TQ	INBLS	10/01-12/01
	Lafayette MSA, IN	H	6.13 FQ	8.68 AW	11.46 TQ	INBLS	10/01-12/01
	South Bend MSA, IN	H	6.46 FQ	9.12 AW	12.21 TQ	INBLS	10/01-12/01
	Iowa	H	6.50 FQ	9.56 AW	13.24 TQ	IABLS	10/01-12/01
	Cedar Rapids MSA, IA	H	7.19 FQ	9.73 AW	12.85 TQ	IABLS	10/01-12/01
	Davenport-Moline-Rock Island MSA, IA-IL	H	6.48 FQ	9.14 AW	12.51 TQ	IABLS	10/01-12/01
	Des Moines MSA, IA	H	6.95 FQ	10.45 AW	14.45 TQ	IABLS	10/01-12/01
	Kansas	H	6.56 FQ	9.40 AW	12.60 TQ	KSBLS	10/01-12/01
	Topeka MSA, KS	H	6.26 FQ	9.05 AW	12.37 TQ	KSBLS	10/01-12/01
	Wichita MSA, KS	H	7.17 FQ	9.61 AW	11.68 TQ	KSBLS	10/01-12/01
	Kentucky	H	6.29 FQ	9.30 AW	12.71 TQ	KYBLS	10/01-12/01
	Lexington MSA, KY	H	6.35 FQ	9.53 AW	13.22 TQ	KYBLS	10/01-12/01
	Louisville MSA, KY-IN	H	7.08 FQ	9.96 AW	13.12 TQ	KYBLS	10/01-12/01
	Louisiana	H	6.33 FQ	8.71 AW	11.57 TQ	LABLS	10/01-12/01
	Baton Rouge MSA, LA	H	6.68 FQ	8.70 AW	11.47 TQ	LABLS	10/01-12/01
	Houma MSA, LA	H	6.07 FQ	8.24 AW	10.67 TQ	LABLS	10/01-12/01
	Lafayette MSA, LA	H	6.37 FQ	8.86 AW	12.66 TQ	LABLS	10/01-12/01

AAW Average annual wage	**AOH** Average offered, high	**ASH** Average starting, high	**H** Hourly	**M** Monthly	**S** Special: hourly and annual
AE Average entry wage	**AOL** Average offered, low	**ASL** Average starting, low	**HI** Highest wage paid	**MTC** Median total compensation	**TQ** Third quartile wage
AEX Average experienced wage	**APH** Average pay, high range	**AW** Average wage paid	**HR** High end range	**MW** Median wage paid	**W** Weekly
AO Average offered	**APL** Average pay, low range	**FQ** First quartile wage	**LR** Low end range	**SQ** Second quartile wage	**Y** Yearly

Occupation/Type/Industry	Location	Per	Low	Mid	High	Source	Date
Receptionist and Information Clerk	Lake Charles MSA, LA	H	6.13 FQ	8.65 AW	10.89 TQ	LABLS	10/01-12/01
	New Orleans MSA, LA	H	6.44 FQ	9.05 AW	12.07 TQ	LABLS	10/01-12/01
	Shreveport-Bossier City MSA, LA	H	6.62 FQ	8.55 AW	11.50 TQ	LABLS	10/01-12/01
	Maine	H	6.57 FQ	9.44 AW	12.63 TQ	MEBLS	10/01-12/01
	Portland MSA, ME	H	8.08 FQ	10.47 AW	13.22 TQ	MEBLS	10/01-12/01
	Maryland	H	6.85 FQ	10.69 AW	15.48 TQ	MDBLS	10/01-12/01
	Baltimore PMSA, MD	H	6.57 FQ	10.57 AW	15.39 TQ	MDBLS	10/01-12/01
	Massachusetts	H	7.74 FQ	11.43 AW	15.92 TQ	MABLS	10/01-12/01
	Boston PMSA, MA-NH	H	8.17 FQ	11.92 AW	16.64 TQ	MABLS	10/01-12/01
	Brockton PMSA, MA	H	7.56 FQ	10.34 AW	14.06 TQ	MABLS	10/01-12/01
	Lawrence PMSA, MA-NH	H	7.80 FQ	10.47 AW	13.73 TQ	MABLS	10/01-12/01
	Lowell PMSA, MA-NH	H	8.98 FQ	12.37 AW	16.95 TQ	MABLS	10/01-12/01
	New Bedford PMSA, MA	H	7.03 FQ	9.38 AW	12.81 TQ	MABLS	10/01-12/01
	Springfield MSA, MA	H	7.71 FQ	11.02 AW	14.63 TQ	MABLS	10/01-12/01
	Worcester PMSA, MA-CT	H	7.42 FQ	10.58 AW	13.78 TQ	MABLS	10/01-12/01
	Michigan	H	7.38 FQ	10.82 AW	14.91 TQ	MIBLS	10/01-12/01
	Ann Arbor PMSA, MI	H	6.96 FQ	10.76 AW	14.01 TQ	MIBLS	10/01-12/01
	Detroit PMSA, MI	H	7.96 FQ	11.58 AW	16.06 TQ	MIBLS	10/01-12/01
	Flint PMSA, MI	H	7.19 FQ	10.06 AW	13.56 TQ	MIBLS	10/01-12/01
	Grand Rapids-Muskegon-Holland MSA, MI	H	7.53 FQ	10.40 AW	13.48 TQ	MIBLS	10/01-12/01
	Kalamazoo-Battle Creek MSA, MI	H	6.67 FQ	9.48 AW	13.08 TQ	MIBLS	10/01-12/01
	Lansing-East Lansing MSA, MI	H	7.15 FQ	10.49 AW	15.27 TQ	MIBLS	10/01-12/01
	Saginaw-Bay City-Midland MSA, MI	H	6.74 FQ	9.43 AW	12.42 TQ	MIBLS	10/01-12/01
	Minnesota	H	7.21 FQ	10.84 AW	14.36 TQ	MNBLS	10/01-12/01
	Duluth-Superior MSA, MN-WI	H	5.85 FQ	8.93 AW	12.82 TQ	MNBLS	10/01-12/01
	Minneapolis-St. Paul MSA, MN-WI	H	7.38 FQ	11.20 AW	14.89 TQ	MNBLS	10/01-12/01
	St. Cloud MSA, MN	H	7.04 FQ	9.49 AW	12.60 TQ	MNBLS	10/01-12/01
	Mississippi	H	6.26 FQ	8.82 AW	11.18 TQ	MSBLS	10/01-12/01
	Biloxi-Gulfport-Pascagoula MSA, MS	H	6.30 FQ	8.83 AW	10.89 TQ	MSBLS	10/01-12/01
	Jackson MSA, MS	H	6.78 FQ	9.28 AW	11.88 TQ	MSBLS	10/01-12/01
	Missouri	H	6.73 FQ	9.59 AW	13.08 TQ	MOBLS	10/01-12/01
	Kansas City MSA, MO-KS	H	7.63 FQ	10.47 AW	13.71 TQ	MOBLS	10/01-12/01
	St. Louis MSA, MO-IL	H	6.80 FQ	9.78 AW	13.19 TQ	MOBLS	10/01-12/01
	Springfield MSA, MO	H	6.42 FQ	8.67 AW	11.56 TQ	MOBLS	10/01-12/01
	Montana	H	6.30 FQ	8.76 AW	11.41 TQ	MTBLS	10/01-12/01
	Billings MSA, MT	H	6.25 FQ	9.15 AW	12.70 TQ	MTBLS	10/01-12/01
	Nebraska	H	6.53 FQ	9.48 AW	13.12 TQ	NEBLS	10/01-12/01
	Lincoln MSA, NE	H	7.38 FQ	9.94 AW	13.04 TQ	NEBLS	10/01-12/01
	Omaha MSA, NE-IA	H	6.98 FQ	10.07 AW	13.92 TQ	NEBLS	10/01-12/01
	Nevada	H	7.36 FQ	10.80 AW	15.79 TQ	NVBLS	10/01-12/01
	Las Vegas MSA, NV-AZ	H	7.12 FQ	10.81 AW	16.52 TQ	NVBLS	10/01-12/01
	Reno MSA, NV	H	7.84 FQ	10.83 AW	15.41 TQ	NVBLS	10/01-12/01
	New Hampshire	H	7.79 FQ	10.40 AW	13.43 TQ	NHBLS	10/01-12/01
	Manchester PMSA, NH	H	7.29 FQ	10.41 AW	13.57 TQ	NHBLS	10/01-12/01
	Nashua PMSA, NH	H	7.92 FQ	10.73 AW	13.86 TQ	NHBLS	10/01-12/01
	Portsmouth-Rochester PMSA, NH-ME	H	8.47 FQ	10.67 AW	13.41 TQ	NHBLS	10/01-12/01
	New Jersey	H	7.34 FQ	11.02 AW	15.56 TQ	NJBLS	10/01-12/01
	Atlantic-Cape May PMSA, NJ	H	6.38 FQ	9.56 AW	13.34 TQ	NJBLS	10/01-12/01
	Bergen-Passaic PMSA, NJ	H	7.33 FQ	11.37 AW	16.00 TQ	NJBLS	10/01-12/01
	Jersey City PMSA, NJ	H	7.62 FQ	11.11 AW	15.19 TQ	NJBLS	10/01-12/01
	Middlesex-Somerset-Hunterdon PMSA, NJ	H	7.36 FQ	11.02 AW	15.25 TQ	NJBLS	10/01-12/01
	Monmouth-Ocean PMSA, NJ	H	6.76 FQ	10.01 AW	13.48 TQ	NJBLS	10/01-12/01
	Newark PMSA, NJ	H	7.24 FQ	11.14 AW	16.10 TQ	NJBLS	10/01-12/01
	Trenton PMSA, NJ	H	7.88 FQ	11.82 AW	16.85 TQ	NJBLS	10/01-12/01
	New Mexico	H	6.20 FQ	8.84 AW	11.56 TQ	NMBLS	10/01-12/01
	Albuquerque MSA, NM	H	6.28 FQ	8.92 AW	11.53 TQ	NMBLS	10/01-12/01
	Las Cruces MSA, NM	H	5.93 FQ	7.88 AW	10.50 TQ	NMBLS	10/01-12/01
	New York	H	7.06 FQ	11.73 AW	17.45 TQ	NYBLS	10/01-12/01
	Albany-Schenectady-Troy MSA, NY	H	7.18 FQ	10.24 AW	14.18 TQ	NYBLS	10/01-12/01
	Binghamton MSA, NY	H	5.99 FQ	8.96 AW	12.69 TQ	NYBLS	10/01-12/01
	Buffalo-Niagara Falls MSA, NY	H	6.26 FQ	9.72 AW	13.20 TQ	NYBLS	10/01-12/01

AAW	Average annual wage	AOH	Average offered, high	ASH	Average starting, high	H	Hourly	M	Monthly	S	Special: hourly and annual
AE	Average entry wage	AOL	Average offered, low	ASL	Average starting, low	HI	Highest wage paid	MTC	Median total compensation	TQ	Third quartile wage
AEX	Average experienced wage	APH	Average pay, high range	AW	Average wage paid	HR	High end range	MW	Median wage paid	W	Weekly
AO	Average offered	APL	Average pay, low range	FQ	First quartile wage	LR	Low end range	SQ	Second quartile wage	Y	Yearly

Occupation/Type/Industry	Location	Per	Low	Mid	High	Source	Date
Receptionist and Information Clerk	Dutchess County PMSA, NY	H	7.10 FQ	10.43 AW	13.87 TQ	NYBLS	10/01-12/01
	Nassau-Suffolk PMSA, NY	H	7.92 FQ	12.11 AW	17.08 TQ	NYBLS	10/01-12/01
	New York PMSA, NY	H	7.22 FQ	12.68 AW	18.71 TQ	NYBLS	10/01-12/01
	Newburgh PMSA, NY-PA	H	7.34 FQ	10.78 AW	15.09 TQ	NYBLS	10/01-12/01
	Rochester MSA, NY	H	6.74 FQ	10.28 AW	14.25 TQ	NYBLS	10/01-12/01
	Syracuse MSA, NY	H	7.14 FQ	10.16 AW	13.34 TQ	NYBLS	10/01-12/01
	Utica-Rome MSA, NY	H	6.19 FQ	9.37 AW	13.13 TQ	NYBLS	10/01-12/01
	North Carolina	H	6.99 FQ	9.91 AW	13.39 TQ	NCBLS	10/01-12/01
	Asheville MSA, NC	H	7.22 FQ	9.55 AW	12.54 TQ	NCBLS	10/01-12/01
	Charlotte-Gastonia-Rock Hill MSA, NC-SC	H	7.30 FQ	10.67 AW	14.17 TQ	NCBLS	10/01-12/01
	Fayetteville MSA, NC	H	6.06 FQ	8.78 AW	10.94 TQ	NCBLS	10/01-12/01
	Greensboro-Winston-Salem-High Point MSA, NC	H	7.15 FQ	10.13 AW	13.48 TQ	NCBLS	10/01-12/01
	Hickory-Morganton-Lenoir MSA, NC	H	7.48 FQ	10.22 AW	13.11 TQ	NCBLS	10/01-12/01
	Raleigh-Durham-Chapel Hill MSA, NC	H	7.52 FQ	10.54 AW	13.83 TQ	NCBLS	10/01-12/01
	Wilmington MSA, NC	H	6.73 FQ	10.13 AW	18.02 TQ	NCBLS	10/01-12/01
	North Dakota	H	6.33 FQ	8.98 AW	11.77 TQ	NDBLS	10/01-12/01
	Fargo-Moorhead MSA, ND-MN	H	6.36 FQ	9.31 AW	12.46 TQ	NDBLS	10/01-12/01
	Ohio	H	6.55 FQ	9.63 AW	13.14 TQ	OHBLS	10/01-12/01
	Akron PMSA, OH	H	6.88 FQ	9.48 AW	12.61 TQ	OHBLS	10/01-12/01
	Canton-Massillon MSA, OH	H	6.83 FQ	9.31 AW	12.02 TQ	OHBLS	10/01-12/01
	Cincinnati PMSA, OH-KY-IN	H	7.04 FQ	10.27 AW	13.67 TQ	OHBLS	10/01-12/01
	Cleveland-Lorain-Elyria PMSA, OH	H	6.14 FQ	9.64 AW	13.75 TQ	OHBLS	10/01-12/01
	Columbus MSA, OH	H	7.14 FQ	9.91 AW	13.17 TQ	OHBLS	10/01-12/01
	Dayton-Springfield MSA, OH	H	6.60 FQ	9.62 AW	12.59 TQ	OHBLS	10/01-12/01
	Hamilton-Middletown PMSA, OH	H	6.96 FQ	10.03 AW	13.40 TQ	OHBLS	10/01-12/01
	Mansfield MSA, OH	H	7.03 FQ	9.52 AW	13.12 TQ	OHBLS	10/01-12/01
	Toledo MSA, OH	H	7.17 FQ	9.48 AW	12.48 TQ	OHBLS	10/01-12/01
	Youngstown-Warren MSA, OH	H	6.55 FQ	9.36 AW	13.15 TQ	OHBLS	10/01-12/01
	Oklahoma	H	6.42 FQ	9.32 AW	13.06 TQ	OKBLS	10/01-12/01
	Oklahoma City MSA, OK	H	6.83 FQ	9.99 AW	13.85 TQ	OKBLS	10/01-12/01
	Tulsa MSA, OK	H	7.12 FQ	9.43 AW	12.38 TQ	OKBLS	10/01-12/01
	Oregon	H	7.71 FQ	10.50 AW	13.59 TQ	ORBLS	10/01-12/01
	Eugene-Springfield MSA, OR	H	7.79 FQ	10.66 AW	13.76 TQ	ORBLS	10/01-12/01
	Medford-Ashland MSA, OR	H	7.43 FQ	9.90 AW	12.83 TQ	ORBLS	10/01-12/01
	Portland-Vancouver PMSA, OR-WA	H	7.74 FQ	10.74 AW	13.94 TQ	ORBLS	10/01-12/01
	Salem PMSA, OR	H	7.59 FQ	10.13 AW	13.17 TQ	ORBLS	10/01-12/01
	Pennsylvania	H	6.68 FQ	10.05 AW	13.53 TQ	PABLS	10/01-12/01
	Allentown-Bethlehem-Easton MSA, PA	H	6.42 FQ	10.05 AW	14.66 TQ	PABLS	10/01-12/01
	Erie MSA, PA	H	6.29 FQ	8.50 AW	11.28 TQ	PABLS	10/01-12/01
	Harrisburg-Lebanon-Carlisle MSA, PA	H	6.44 FQ	9.77 AW	13.42 TQ	PABLS	10/01-12/01
	Johnstown MSA, PA	H	6.14 FQ	8.62 AW	11.65 TQ	PABLS	10/01-12/01
	Lancaster MSA, PA	H	7.31 FQ	9.75 AW	12.73 TQ	PABLS	10/01-12/01
	Philadelphia PMSA, PA-NJ	H	7.59 FQ	11.11 AW	15.02 TQ	PABLS	10/01-12/01
	Pittsburgh MSA, PA	H	6.39 FQ	9.76 AW	13.21 TQ	PABLS	10/01-12/01
	Reading MSA, PA	H	7.14 FQ	10.72 AW	15.59 TQ	PABLS	10/01-12/01
	Scranton-Wilkes-Barre-Hazleton MSA, PA	H	6.60 FQ	9.09 AW	11.84 TQ	PABLS	10/01-12/01
	York MSA, PA	H	6.82 FQ	9.34 AW	12.25 TQ	PABLS	10/01-12/01
	Rhode Island	H	7.36 FQ	10.83 AW	15.64 TQ	RIBLS	10/01-12/01
	Providence-Fall River-Warwick MSA, RI-MA	H	7.20 FQ	10.79 AW	15.90 TQ	RIBLS	10/01-12/01
	South Carolina	H	6.98 FQ	9.83 AW	13.42 TQ	SCBLS	10/01-12/01
	Charleston-North Charleston MSA, SC	H	6.86 FQ	9.27 AW	12.24 TQ	SCBLS	10/01-12/01
	Columbia MSA, SC	H	7.21 FQ	10.36 AW	17.42 TQ	SCBLS	10/01-12/01
	Greenville-Spartanburg-Anderson MSA, SC	H	7.22 FQ	10.02 AW	13.31 TQ	SCBLS	10/01-12/01
	Myrtle Beach MSA, SC	H	7.21 FQ	9.17 AW	11.32 TQ	SCBLS	10/01-12/01
	South Dakota	H	6.75 FQ	8.62 AW	10.97 TQ	SDBLS	10/01-12/01
	Sioux Falls MSA, SD	H	7.06 FQ	9.25 AW	11.69 TQ	SDBLS	10/01-12/01
	Tennessee	H	6.81 FQ	9.67 AW	13.08 TQ	TNBLS	10/01-12/01

AAW	Average annual wage	**AOH**	Average offered, high	**ASH**	Average starting, high	**H**	Hourly	**M**	Monthly	**S**	Special: hourly and annual
AE	Average entry wage	**AOL**	Average offered, low	**ASL**	Average starting, low	**HI**	Highest wage paid	**MTC**	Median total compensation	**TQ**	Third quartile wage
AEX	Average experienced wage	**APH**	Average pay, high range	**AW**	Average wage paid	**HR**	High end range	**MW**	Median wage paid	**W**	Weekly
AO	Average offered	**APL**	Average pay, low range	**FQ**	First quartile wage	**LR**	Low end range	**SQ**	Second quartile wage	**Y**	Yearly

Occupation/Type/Industry	Location	Per	Low	Mid	High	Source	Date
Receptionist and Information Clerk	Chattanooga MSA, TN-GA	H	6.35 FQ	9.42 AW	12.56 TQ	TNBLS	10/01-12/01
	Clarksville-Hopkinsville MSA, TN-KY	H	5.80 FQ	8.20 AW	11.34 TQ	TNBLS	10/01-12/01
	Johnson City-Kingsport-Bristol MSA, TN-VA	H	6.54 FQ	9.27 AW	12.19 TQ	TNBLS	10/01-12/01
	Knoxville MSA, TN	H	7.05 FQ	9.53 AW	12.52 TQ	TNBLS	10/01-12/01
	Memphis MSA, TN-AR-MS	H	7.22 FQ	9.86 AW	13.01 TQ	TNBLS	10/01-12/01
	Nashville MSA, TN	H	7.50 FQ	10.66 AW	14.55 TQ	TNBLS	10/01-12/01
	Texas	H	6.44 FQ	9.76 AW	13.63 TQ	TXBLS	10/01-12/01
	Amarillo MSA, TX	H	6.23 FQ	9.12 AW	13.24 TQ	TXBLS	10/01-12/01
	Austin-San Marcos MSA, TX	H	7.40 FQ	10.94 AW	14.93 TQ	TXBLS	10/01-12/01
	Beaumont-Port Arthur MSA, TX	H	6.48 FQ	8.53 AW	10.75 TQ	TXBLS	10/01-12/01
	Brazoria PMSA, TX	H	6.15 FQ	8.48 AW	10.79 TQ	TXBLS	10/01-12/01
	Brownsville-Harlingen-San Benito MSA, TX	H	5.79 FQ	7.68 AW	10.26 TQ	TXBLS	10/01-12/01
	Corpus Christi MSA, TX	H	6.20 FQ	8.46 AW	11.09 TQ	TXBLS	10/01-12/01
	Dallas PMSA, TX	H	7.62 FQ	10.72 AW	14.11 TQ	TXBLS	10/01-12/01
	El Paso MSA, TX	H	5.75 FQ	7.92 AW	10.44 TQ	TXBLS	10/01-12/01
	Fort Worth-Arlington PMSA, TX	H	7.50 FQ	10.86 AW	15.27 TQ	TXBLS	10/01-12/01
	Galveston-Texas City PMSA, TX	H	6.11 FQ	9.06 AW	12.57 TQ	TXBLS	10/01-12/01
	Houston PMSA, TX	H	6.28 FQ	10.28 AW	14.61 TQ	TXBLS	10/01-12/01
	Killeen-Temple MSA, TX	H	6.07 FQ	8.52 AW	11.51 TQ	TXBLS	10/01-12/01
	Laredo MSA, TX	H	5.88 FQ	7.97 AW	10.75 TQ	TXBLS	10/01-12/01
	Longview-Marshall MSA, TX	H	6.17 FQ	8.59 AW	11.61 TQ	TXBLS	10/01-12/01
	Lubbock MSA, TX	H	6.39 FQ	8.54 AW	11.37 TQ	TXBLS	10/01-12/01
	McAllen-Edinburg-Mission MSA, TX	H	6.12 FQ	8.16 AW	10.42 TQ	TXBLS	10/01-12/01
	Odessa-Midland MSA, TX	H	5.93 FQ	8.21 AW	11.26 TQ	TXBLS	10/01-12/01
	San Antonio MSA, TX	H	7.09 FQ	9.08 AW	11.61 TQ	TXBLS	10/01-12/01
	Tyler MSA, TX	H	6.48 FQ	9.10 AW	11.55 TQ	TXBLS	10/01-12/01
	Waco MSA, TX	H	6.31 FQ	9.08 AW	12.77 TQ	TXBLS	10/01-12/01
	Utah	H	6.99 FQ	9.49 AW	12.49 TQ	UTBLS	10/01-12/01
	Provo-Orem MSA, UT	H	6.83 FQ	8.81 AW	11.46 TQ	UTBLS	10/01-12/01
	Salt Lake City-Ogden MSA, UT	H	7.48 FQ	9.89 AW	12.95 TQ	UTBLS	10/01-12/01
	Vermont	H	6.80 FQ	9.85 AW	13.21 TQ	VTBLS	10/01-12/01
	Burlington MSA, VT	H	7.04 FQ	10.41 AW	13.70 TQ	VTBLS	10/01-12/01
	Virginia	H	6.53 FQ	9.98 AW	14.29 TQ	VABLS	10/01-12/01
	Lynchburg MSA, VA	H	6.36 FQ	9.34 AW	14.08 TQ	VABLS	10/01-12/01
	Norfolk-Virginia Beach-Newport News MSA, VA-NC	H	6.05 FQ	8.54 AW	11.38 TQ	VABLS	10/01-12/01
	Richmond-Petersburg MSA, VA	H	6.48 FQ	9.51 AW	13.01 TQ	VABLS	10/01-12/01
	Roanoke MSA, VA	H	6.46 FQ	8.69 AW	11.40 TQ	VABLS	10/01-12/01
	Washington	H	7.35 FQ	10.93 AW	14.86 TQ	WABLS	10/01-12/01
	Bremerton PMSA, WA	H	7.82 FQ	10.18 AW	12.95 TQ	WABLS	10/01-12/01
	Olympia PMSA, WA	H	7.27 FQ	9.68 AW	12.80 TQ	WABLS	10/01-12/01
	Richland-Kennewick-Pasco MSA, WA	H	7.52 FQ	10.32 AW	13.15 TQ	WABLS	10/01-12/01
	Seattle-Bellevue-Everett PMSA, WA	H	7.41 FQ	11.70 AW	16.13 TQ	WABLS	10/01-12/01
	Spokane MSA, WA	H	7.15 FQ	9.56 AW	12.30 TQ	WABLS	10/01-12/01
	Tacoma PMSA, WA	H	7.74 FQ	10.84 AW	14.19 TQ	WABLS	10/01-12/01
	Yakima MSA, WA	H	7.34 FQ	10.38 AW	13.74 TQ	WABLS	10/01-12/01
	West Virginia	H	6.04 FQ	8.32 AW	10.84 TQ	WVBLS	10/01-12/01
	Charleston MSA, WV	H	6.54 FQ	8.46 AW	10.53 TQ	WVBLS	10/01-12/01
	Huntington-Ashland MSA, WV-KY-OH	H	5.97 FQ	8.74 AW	11.79 TQ	WVBLS	10/01-12/01
	Wisconsin	H	7.30 FQ	10.06 AW	13.36 TQ	WIBLS	10/01-12/01
	Appleton-Oshkosh-Neenah MSA, WI	H	7.46 FQ	10.11 AW	13.66 TQ	WIBLS	10/01-12/01
	Green Bay MSA, WI	H	7.25 FQ	10.29 AW	13.87 TQ	WIBLS	10/01-12/01
	Madison MSA, WI	H	7.69 FQ	10.53 AW	13.68 TQ	WIBLS	10/01-12/01
	Milwaukee-Waukesha PMSA, WI	H	7.59 FQ	10.44 AW	13.52 TQ	WIBLS	10/01-12/01
	Racine PMSA, WI	H	7.49 FQ	10.40 AW	14.25 TQ	WIBLS	10/01-12/01
	Wyoming	H	6.06 FQ	8.54 AW	11.02 TQ	WYBLS	10/01-12/01

AAW Average annual wage **AE** Average entry wage **AEX** Average experienced wage **AO** Average offered **AOH** Average offered, high **AOL** Average offered, low **APH** Average pay, high range **APL** Average pay, low range **ASH** Average starting, high **ASL** Average starting, low **AW** Average wage paid **FQ** First quartile wage **H** Hourly **HI** Highest wage paid **HR** High end range **LR** Low end range **M** Monthly **MTC** Median total compensation **MW** Median wage paid **SQ** Second quartile wage **S** Special: hourly and annual **TQ** Third quartile wage **W** Weekly **Y** Yearly

Occupation/Type/Industry	Location	Per	Low	Mid	High	Source	Date
Receptionist and Information Clerk	Cheyenne MSA, WY	H	6.66 FQ	8.45 AW	10.83 TQ	WYBLS	10/01-12/01
	Puerto Rico	H	5.67 FQ	7.18 AW	9.63 TQ	PRBLS	10/01-12/01
	Virgin Islands	H	6.06 FQ	8.24 AW	10.60 TQ	VIBLS	10/01-12/01
	Guam	H	5.81 FQ	8.20 AW	11.47 TQ	GUBLS	10/01-12/01
Recreation and Fitness Studies Teacher							
Postsecondary	Alabama	Y	18100 FQ	40750 AW	66650 TQ	ALBLS	10/01-12/01
Postsecondary	Arkansas	Y	21010 FQ	36940 AW	56220 TQ	ARBLS	10/01-12/01
Postsecondary	California	Y	31890 FQ	62010 AW	100170 TQ	CABLS	10/01-12/01
Postsecondary	Colorado	Y	25640 FQ	43100 AW	62040 TQ	COBLS	10/01-12/01
Postsecondary	Connecticut	Y	24120 FQ	51430 AW	84450 TQ	CTBLS	10/01-12/01
Postsecondary	District of Columbia	Y	30770 FQ	54310 AW	79530 TQ	DCBLS	10/01-12/01
Postsecondary	Florida	Y	16500 FQ	51570 AW	93770 TQ	FLBLS	10/01-12/01
Postsecondary	Georgia	Y	22520 FQ	44100 AW	69980 TQ	GABLS	10/01-12/01
Postsecondary	Idaho	Y	15570 FQ	26550 AW	54970 TQ	IDBLS	10/01-12/01
Postsecondary	Illinois	Y	17120 FQ	44770 AW	70280 TQ	ILBLS	10/01-12/01
Postsecondary	Indiana	Y	22940 FQ	48360 AW	75890 TQ	INBLS	10/01-12/01
Postsecondary	Iowa	Y	34430 FQ	57590 AW	91080 TQ	IABLS	10/01-12/01
Postsecondary	Kansas	Y	16730 FQ	32930 AW	53390 TQ	KSBLS	10/01-12/01
Postsecondary	Kentucky	Y	23890 FQ	44080 AW	69040 TQ	KYBLS	10/01-12/01
Postsecondary	Louisiana	Y	14050 FQ	35840 AW	63630 TQ	LABLS	10/01-12/01
Postsecondary	Maine	Y	28960 FQ	49500 AW	76560 TQ	MEBLS	10/01-12/01
Postsecondary	Maryland	Y	16280 FQ	43480 AW	82490 TQ	MDBLS	10/01-12/01
Postsecondary	Massachusetts	Y	15790 FQ	36640 AW	63660 TQ	MABLS	10/01-12/01
Postsecondary	Michigan	Y	26550 FQ	48480 AW	82460 TQ	MIBLS	10/01-12/01
Postsecondary	Minnesota	Y	25890 FQ	45960 AW	68940 TQ	MNBLS	10/01-12/01
Postsecondary	Mississippi	Y	13470 FQ	41280 AW	58130 TQ	MSBLS	10/01-12/01
Postsecondary	Missouri	Y	22010 FQ	42380 AW	66460 TQ	MOBLS	10/01-12/01
Postsecondary	Nebraska	Y	12900 FQ	30980 AW	50330 TQ	NEBLS	10/01-12/01
Postsecondary	New Hampshire	Y	29130 FQ	48910 AW	68800 TQ	NHBLS	10/01-12/01
Postsecondary	New Jersey	Y	28400 FQ	49320 AW	81880 TQ	NJBLS	10/01-12/01
Postsecondary	New Mexico	Y	16830 FQ	30090 AW	44940 TQ	NMBLS	10/01-12/01
Postsecondary	New York	Y	28560 FQ	49870 AW	79510 TQ	NYBLS	10/01-12/01
Postsecondary	North Carolina	Y	29800 FQ	45190 AW	60740 TQ	NCBLS	10/01-12/01
Postsecondary	North Dakota	Y	19960 FQ	33020 AW	45330 TQ	NDBLS	10/01-12/01
Postsecondary	Ohio	Y	22430 FQ	39590 AW	58250 TQ	OHBLS	10/01-12/01
Postsecondary	Oklahoma	Y	23390 FQ	36150 AW	54320 TQ	OKBLS	10/01-12/01
Postsecondary	Oregon	Y	24150 FQ	50750 AW	85160 TQ	ORBLS	10/01-12/01
Postsecondary	Pennsylvania	Y	14500 FQ	41550 AW	69750 TQ	PABLS	10/01-12/01
Postsecondary	Rhode Island	Y	17540 FQ	45190 AW	71640 TQ	RIBLS	10/01-12/01
Postsecondary	South Carolina	Y	25180 FQ	47620 AW	71470 TQ	SCBLS	10/01-12/01
Postsecondary	South Dakota	Y	30720 FQ	43760 AW	60400 TQ	SDBLS	10/01-12/01
Postsecondary	Tennessee	Y	20740 FQ	40290 AW	61050 TQ	TNBLS	10/01-12/01
Postsecondary	Texas	Y	19760 FQ	44890 AW	70110 TQ	TXBLS	10/01-12/01
Postsecondary	Utah	Y	30920 FQ	49540 AW	76330 TQ	UTBLS	10/01-12/01
Postsecondary	Virginia	Y	23580 FQ	47660 AW	80070 TQ	VABLS	10/01-12/01
Postsecondary	Washington	Y	25190 FQ	40860 AW	61340 TQ	WABLS	10/01-12/01
Postsecondary	West Virginia	Y	32800 FQ	50740 AW	74930 TQ	WVBLS	10/01-12/01
Postsecondary	Wisconsin	Y	27290 FQ	42350 AW	60720 TQ	WIBLS	10/01-12/01
Postsecondary	Wyoming	Y	26820 FQ	38240 AW	53830 TQ	WYBLS	10/01-12/01
Postsecondary	Puerto Rico	Y	26600 FQ	46130 AW	73800 TQ	PRBLS	10/01-12/01
Recreation Worker	Alabama	H	5.78 FQ	8.71 AW	13.17 TQ	ALBLS	10/01-12/01
	Birmingham MSA, AL	H	5.89 FQ	8.62 AW	12.88 TQ	ALBLS	10/01-12/01
	Huntsville MSA, AL	H	6.10 FQ	9.24 AW	13.74 TQ	ALBLS	10/01-12/01
	Mobile MSA, AL	H	5.82 FQ	9.05 AW	13.45 TQ	ALBLS	10/01-12/01
	Montgomery MSA, AL	H	5.80 FQ	8.60 AW	10.74 TQ	ALBLS	10/01-12/01
	Alaska	H	6.83 FQ	11.05 AW	18.09 TQ	AKBLS	10/01-12/01
	Arizona	H	6.22 FQ	11.38 AW	18.71 TQ	AZBLS	10/01-12/01
	Phoenix-Mesa MSA, AZ	H	6.64 FQ	12.63 AW	22.02 TQ	AZBLS	10/01-12/01
	Tucson MSA, AZ	H	5.80 FQ	8.86 AW	13.85 TQ	AZBLS	10/01-12/01
	Arkansas	H	5.84 FQ	8.13 AW	11.07 TQ	ARBLS	10/01-12/01
	Fayetteville-Springdale-Rogers MSA, AR	H	5.98 FQ	8.50 AW	10.57 TQ	ARBLS	10/01-12/01
	Fort Smith MSA, AR-OK	H	5.99 FQ	8.85 AW	11.49 TQ	ARBLS	10/01-12/01
	Little Rock-North Little Rock MSA, AR	H	5.88 FQ	8.32 AW	12.13 TQ	ARBLS	10/01-12/01
	California	H	6.65 FQ	9.89 AW	14.59 TQ	CABLS	10/01-12/01
	Bakersfield MSA, CA	H	6.40 FQ	8.11 AW	11.27 TQ	CABLS	10/01-12/01
	Chico-Paradise MSA, CA	H	6.53 FQ	8.28 AW	10.63 TQ	CABLS	10/01-12/01

AAW	Average annual wage	AOH	Average offered, high	ASH	Average starting, high	H	Hourly	M	Monthly	S	Special: hourly and annual
AE	Average entry wage	AOL	Average offered, low	ASL	Average starting, low	HI	Highest wage paid	MTC	Median total compensation	TQ	Third quartile wage
AEX	Average experienced wage	APH	Average pay, high range	AW	Average wage paid	HR	High end range	MW	Median wage paid	W	Weekly
AO	Average offered	APL	Average pay, low range	FQ	First quartile wage	LR	Low end range	SQ	Second quartile wage	Y	Yearly

Occupation/Type/Industry	Location	Per	Low	Mid	High	Source	Date
Recreation Worker	Los Angeles-Long Beach PMSA, CA	H	6.78 FQ	9.76 AW	13.46 TQ	CABLS	10/01-12/01
	Merced MSA, CA	H	6.38 FQ	7.31 AW	9.00 TQ	CABLS	10/01-12/01
	Modesto MSA, CA	H	6.43 FQ	9.20 AW	14.73 TQ	CABLS	10/01-12/01
	Oakland PMSA, CA	H	6.94 FQ	11.13 AW	15.83 TQ	CABLS	10/01-12/01
	Orange County PMSA, CA	H	6.54 FQ	9.98 AW	14.79 TQ	CABLS	10/01-12/01
	Redding MSA, CA	H	6.61 FQ	9.40 AW	11.81 TQ	CABLS	10/01-12/01
	Riverside-San Bernardino PMSA, CA	H	6.70 FQ	8.99 AW	11.57 TQ	CABLS	10/01-12/01
	Sacramento PMSA, CA	H	6.59 FQ	9.24 AW	13.51 TQ	CABLS	10/01-12/01
	Salinas MSA, CA	H	6.79 FQ	9.72 AW	13.65 TQ	CABLS	10/01-12/01
	San Diego MSA, CA	H	6.66 FQ	8.96 AW	11.64 TQ	CABLS	10/01-12/01
	San Francisco PMSA, CA	H	7.28 FQ	11.91 AW	17.64 TQ	CABLS	10/01-12/01
	San Jose PMSA, CA	H	7.09 FQ	12.80 AW	21.89 TQ	CABLS	10/01-12/01
	San Luis Obispo-Atascadero-Paso Robles MSA, CA	H	6.34 FQ	7.82 AW	10.73 TQ	CABLS	10/01-12/01
	Santa Barbara-Santa Maria-Lompoc MSA, CA	H	6.56 FQ	10.01 AW	15.78 TQ	CABLS	10/01-12/01
	Santa Cruz-Watsonville PMSA, CA	H	7.03 FQ	10.16 AW	14.14 TQ	CABLS	10/01-12/01
	Santa Rosa PMSA, CA	H	6.82 FQ	9.97 AW	14.49 TQ	CABLS	10/01-12/01
	Stockton-Lodi MSA, CA	H	6.56 FQ	10.14 AW	14.64 TQ	CABLS	10/01-12/01
	Vallejo-Fairfield-Napa PMSA, CA	H	6.90 FQ	10.16 AW	14.46 TQ	CABLS	10/01-12/01
	Ventura PMSA, CA	H	6.40 FQ	8.24 AW	11.38 TQ	CABLS	10/01-12/01
	Visalia-Tulare-Porterville MSA, CA	H	6.48 FQ	8.60 AW	11.90 TQ	CABLS	10/01-12/01
	Colorado	H	6.26 FQ	10.00 AW	15.56 TQ	COBLS	10/01-12/01
	Boulder-Longmont PMSA, CO	H	6.13 FQ	10.62 AW	16.10 TQ	COBLS	10/01-12/01
	Colorado Springs MSA, CO	H	7.18 FQ	11.02 AW	16.07 TQ	COBLS	10/01-12/01
	Denver PMSA, CO	H	7.03 FQ	10.61 AW	16.63 TQ	COBLS	10/01-12/01
	Fort Collins-Loveland MSA, CO	H	6.00 FQ	8.60 AW	12.78 TQ	COBLS	10/01-12/01
	Greeley PMSA, CO	H	7.32 FQ	8.77 AW	10.78 TQ	COBLS	10/01-12/01
	Connecticut	H	7.02 FQ	11.10 AW	17.31 TQ	CTBLS	10/01-12/01
	Bridgeport PMSA, CT	H	6.64 FQ	10.43 AW	17.27 TQ	CTBLS	10/01-12/01
	Danbury PMSA, CT	H	7.24 FQ	13.20 AW	22.54 TQ	CTBLS	10/01-12/01
	Hartford MSA, CT	H	6.74 FQ	11.13 AW	16.96 TQ	CTBLS	10/01-12/01
	New Haven-Meriden PMSA, CT	H	8.07 FQ	11.82 AW	19.61 TQ	CTBLS	10/01-12/01
	New London-Norwich MSA, CT-RI	H	7.23 FQ	9.53 AW	14.16 TQ	CTBLS	10/01-12/01
	Stamford-Norwalk PMSA, CT	H	7.45 FQ	12.24 AW	20.68 TQ	CTBLS	10/01-12/01
	Waterbury PMSA, CT	H	7.29 FQ	11.83 AW	17.02 TQ	CTBLS	10/01-12/01
	Delaware	H	7.10 FQ	8.92 AW	12.18 TQ	DEBLS	10/01-12/01
	Wilmington-Newark PMSA, DE-MD	H	7.00 FQ	9.23 AW	12.75 TQ	DEBLS	10/01-12/01
	District of Columbia	H	7.05 FQ	13.16 AW	23.77 TQ	DCBLS	10/01-12/01
	Washington PMSA, DC-MD-VA-WV	H	6.63 FQ	10.49 AW	17.23 TQ	DCBLS	10/01-12/01
	Florida	H	5.96 FQ	9.34 AW	14.12 TQ	FLBLS	10/01-12/01
	Daytona Beach MSA, FL	H	6.13 FQ	8.87 AW	12.23 TQ	FLBLS	10/01-12/01
	Fort Lauderdale PMSA, FL	H	6.37 FQ	10.39 AW	15.85 TQ	FLBLS	10/01-12/01
	Fort Myers-Cape Coral MSA, FL	H	7.68 FQ	10.74 AW	14.15 TQ	FLBLS	10/01-12/01
	Fort Pierce-Port St. Lucie MSA, FL	H	5.82 FQ	8.33 AW	11.70 TQ	FLBLS	10/01-12/01
	Fort Walton Beach MSA, FL	H	6.45 FQ	9.22 AW	13.58 TQ	FLBLS	10/01-12/01
	Gainesville MSA, FL	H	5.70 FQ	7.85 AW	11.61 TQ	FLBLS	10/01-12/01
	Lakeland-Winter Haven MSA, FL	H	5.78 FQ	9.03 AW	13.61 TQ	FLBLS	10/01-12/01
	Melbourne-Titusville-Palm Bay MSA, FL	H	5.75 FQ	7.94 AW	11.14 TQ	FLBLS	10/01-12/01
	Miami PMSA, FL	H	5.65 FQ	9.30 AW	16.44 TQ	FLBLS	10/01-12/01
	Naples MSA, FL	H	6.21 FQ	8.92 AW	12.90 TQ	FLBLS	10/01-12/01
	Ocala MSA, FL	H	5.47 FQ	7.37 AW	10.39 TQ	FLBLS	10/01-12/01
	Orlando MSA, FL	H	6.10 FQ	9.49 AW	15.15 TQ	FLBLS	10/01-12/01
	Pensacola MSA, FL	H	5.85 FQ	8.76 AW	13.66 TQ	FLBLS	10/01-12/01
	Sarasota-Bradenton MSA, FL	H	6.34 FQ	8.78 AW	11.09 TQ	FLBLS	10/01-12/01
	Tallahassee MSA, FL	H	6.35 FQ	10.03 AW	14.28 TQ	FLBLS	10/01-12/01
	Tampa-St. Petersburg-Clearwater MSA, FL	H	6.15 FQ	10.05 AW	15.42 TQ	FLBLS	10/01-12/01

AAW	Average annual wage	AOH	Average offered, high	ASH	Average starting, high	H	Hourly	M	Monthly	S	Special: hourly and annual
AE	Average entry wage	AOL	Average offered, low	ASL	Average starting, low	HI	Highest wage paid	MTC	Median total compensation	TQ	Third quartile wage
AEX	Average experienced wage	APH	Average pay, high range	AW	Average wage paid	HR	High end range	MW	Median wage paid	W	Weekly
AO	Average offered	APL	Average pay, low range	FQ	First quartile wage	LR	Low end range	SQ	Second quartile wage	Y	Yearly

Occupation/Type/Industry	Location	Per	Low	Mid	High	Source	Date
Recreation Worker	West Palm Beach-Boca Raton MSA, FL	H	5.99 FQ	8.74 AW	12.50 TQ	FLBLS	10/01-12/01
	Georgia	H	5.84 FQ	8.90 AW	14.25 TQ	GABLS	10/01-12/01
	Atlanta MSA, GA	H	5.86 FQ	8.67 AW	13.64 TQ	GABLS	10/01-12/01
	Augusta-Aiken MSA, GA-SC	H	6.83 FQ	11.33 AW	16.71 TQ	GABLS	10/01-12/01
	Columbus MSA, GA-AL	H	6.03 FQ	8.93 AW	14.62 TQ	GABLS	10/01-12/01
	Macon MSA, GA	H	6.05 FQ	9.88 AW	15.77 TQ	GABLS	10/01-12/01
	Savannah MSA, GA	H	6.21 FQ	9.21 AW	12.82 TQ	GABLS	10/01-12/01
	Hawaii	H	7.11 FQ	11.15 AW	17.93 TQ	HIBLS	10/01-12/01
	Honolulu MSA, HI	H	7.11 FQ	11.04 AW	18.60 TQ	HIBLS	10/01-12/01
	Idaho	H	6.29 FQ	9.68 AW	14.48 TQ	IDBLS	10/01-12/01
	Boise City MSA, ID	H	6.82 FQ	10.54 AW	15.09 TQ	IDBLS	10/01-12/01
	Illinois	H	6.00 FQ	10.99 AW	18.38 TQ	ILBLS	10/01-12/01
	Champaign-Urbana MSA, IL	H	6.79 FQ	14.24 AW	19.43 TQ	ILBLS	10/01-12/01
	Chicago PMSA, IL	H	6.34 FQ	11.26 AW	18.04 TQ	ILBLS	10/01-12/01
	Peoria-Pekin MSA, IL	H	5.78 FQ	8.99 AW	16.34 TQ	ILBLS	10/01-12/01
	Springfield MSA, IL	H	5.62 FQ	8.06 AW	14.30 TQ	ILBLS	10/01-12/01
	Indiana	H	5.87 FQ	8.77 AW	13.27 TQ	INBLS	10/01-12/01
	Elkhart-Goshen MSA, IN	H	6.58 FQ	9.52 AW	13.71 TQ	INBLS	10/01-12/01
	Evansville-Henderson MSA, IN-KY	H	5.84 FQ	8.74 AW	12.52 TQ	INBLS	10/01-12/01
	Fort Wayne MSA, IN	H	6.70 FQ	9.92 AW	13.11 TQ	INBLS	10/01-12/01
	Gary PMSA, IN	H	5.68 FQ	7.38 AW	10.47 TQ	INBLS	10/01-12/01
	Indianapolis MSA, IN	H	6.91 FQ	10.29 AW	15.44 TQ	INBLS	10/01-12/01
	Lafayette MSA, IN	H	5.85 FQ	7.95 AW	12.09 TQ	INBLS	10/01-12/01
	South Bend MSA, IN	H	6.05 FQ	8.25 AW	11.89 TQ	INBLS	10/01-12/01
	Iowa	H	5.74 FQ	8.16 AW	12.01 TQ	IABLS	10/01-12/01
	Davenport-Moline-Rock Island MSA, IA-IL	H	5.79 FQ	9.49 AW	16.40 TQ	IABLS	10/01-12/01
	Des Moines MSA, IA	H	5.99 FQ	8.62 AW	12.65 TQ	IABLS	10/01-12/01
	Kansas	H	6.31 FQ	9.64 AW	14.52 TQ	KSBLS	10/01-12/01
	Topeka MSA, KS	H	6.10 FQ	8.64 AW	11.68 TQ	KSBLS	10/01-12/01
	Wichita MSA, KS	H	5.94 FQ	8.91 AW	13.33 TQ	KSBLS	10/01-12/01
	Kentucky	H	6.99 FQ	14.09 AW	21.19 TQ	KYBLS	10/01-12/01
	Lexington MSA, KY	H	5.95 FQ	10.55 AW	16.69 TQ	KYBLS	10/01-12/01
	Louisville MSA, KY-IN	H	10.23 FQ	15.57 AW	21.71 TQ	KYBLS	10/01-12/01
	Louisiana	H	5.77 FQ	7.79 AW	11.29 TQ	LABLS	10/01-12/01
	Baton Rouge MSA, LA	H	5.86 FQ	7.51 AW	9.51 TQ	LABLS	10/01-12/01
	Houma MSA, LA	H	5.73 FQ	7.10 AW	8.85 TQ	LABLS	10/01-12/01
	Lafayette MSA, LA	H	5.70 FQ	7.77 AW	12.79 TQ	LABLS	10/01-12/01
	Lake Charles MSA, LA	H	5.68 FQ	8.46 AW	13.59 TQ	LABLS	10/01-12/01
	New Orleans MSA, LA	H	5.75 FQ	8.09 AW	11.63 TQ	LABLS	10/01-12/01
	Shreveport-Bossier City MSA, LA	H	5.89 FQ	9.46 AW	15.91 TQ	LABLS	10/01-12/01
	Maine	H	6.21 FQ	9.53 AW	13.48 TQ	MEBLS	10/01-12/01
	Portland MSA, ME	H	5.87 FQ	10.21 AW	15.61 TQ	MEBLS	10/01-12/01
	Maryland	H	6.28 FQ	9.52 AW	13.92 TQ	MDBLS	10/01-12/01
	Baltimore PMSA, MD	H	6.15 FQ	9.22 AW	13.71 TQ	MDBLS	10/01-12/01
	Massachusetts	H	6.92 FQ	10.21 AW	15.88 TQ	MABLS	10/01-12/01
	Boston PMSA, MA-NH	H	7.06 FQ	10.45 AW	16.01 TQ	MABLS	10/01-12/01
	Lawrence PMSA, MA-NH	H	7.03 FQ	10.40 AW	15.14 TQ	MABLS	10/01-12/01
	New Bedford PMSA, MA	H	6.81 FQ	9.15 AW	14.04 TQ	MABLS	10/01-12/01
	Springfield MSA, MA	H	6.90 FQ	10.70 AW	16.87 TQ	MABLS	10/01-12/01
	Worcester PMSA, MA-CT	H	6.93 FQ	9.57 AW	14.75 TQ	MABLS	10/01-12/01
	Michigan	H	5.97 FQ	9.46 AW	14.17 TQ	MIBLS	10/01-12/01
	Detroit PMSA, MI	H	6.17 FQ	9.82 AW	14.50 TQ	MIBLS	10/01-12/01
	Flint PMSA, MI	H	5.93 FQ	9.10 AW	14.48 TQ	MIBLS	10/01-12/01
	Grand Rapids-Muskegon-Holland MSA, MI	H	6.94 FQ	10.01 AW	14.63 TQ	MIBLS	10/01-12/01
	Kalamazoo-Battle Creek MSA, MI	H	5.94 FQ	9.43 AW	14.88 TQ	MIBLS	10/01-12/01
	Lansing-East Lansing MSA, MI	H	7.55 FQ	13.23 AW	23.43 TQ	MIBLS	10/01-12/01
	Saginaw-Bay City-Midland MSA, MI	H	5.83 FQ	8.57 AW	12.58 TQ	MIBLS	10/01-12/01
	Minnesota	H	6.52 FQ	10.89 AW	16.89 TQ	MNBLS	10/01-12/01
	Duluth-Superior MSA, MN-WI	H	5.83 FQ	8.87 AW	13.02 TQ	MNBLS	10/01-12/01
	Minneapolis-St. Paul MSA, MN-WI	H	7.17 FQ	12.24 AW	20.01 TQ	MNBLS	10/01-12/01
	St. Cloud MSA, MN	H	5.99 FQ	9.02 AW	13.53 TQ	MNBLS	10/01-12/01
	Mississippi	H	5.73 FQ	8.87 AW	13.89 TQ	MSBLS	10/01-12/01
	Jackson MSA, MS	H	6.22 FQ	10.89 AW	14.58 TQ	MSBLS	10/01-12/01
	Missouri	H	5.96 FQ	9.41 AW	14.47 TQ	MOBLS	10/01-12/01

AAW	Average annual wage	**AOH**	Average offered, high	**ASH**	Average starting, high	**H**	Hourly	**M**	Monthly	**S**	Special: hourly and annual
AE	Average entry wage	**AOL**	Average offered, low	**ASL**	Average starting, low	**HI**	Highest wage paid	**MTC**	Median total compensation	**TQ**	Third quartile wage
AEX	Average experienced wage	**APH**	Average pay, high range	**AW**	Average wage paid	**HR**	High end range	**MW**	Median wage paid	**W**	Weekly
AO	Average offered	**APL**	Average pay, low range	**FQ**	First quartile wage	**LR**	Low end range	**SQ**	Second quartile wage	**Y**	Yearly

Occupation/Type/Industry	Location	Per	Low	Mid	High	Source	Date
Recreation Worker	Kansas City MSA, MO-KS	H	7.34 FQ	10.60 AW	15.65 TQ	MOBLS	10/01-12/01
	St. Louis MSA, MO-IL	H	5.93 FQ	9.23 AW	14.28 TQ	MOBLS	10/01-12/01
	Springfield MSA, MO	H	6.80 FQ	9.57 AW	14.96 TQ	MOBLS	10/01-12/01
	Montana	H	6.15 FQ	9.13 AW	13.37 TQ	MTBLS	10/01-12/01
	Nebraska	H	5.80 FQ	8.03 AW	11.79 TQ	NEBLS	10/01-12/01
	Lincoln MSA, NE	H	6.14 FQ	9.64 AW	13.96 TQ	NEBLS	10/01-12/01
	Omaha MSA, NE-IA	H	5.92 FQ	8.27 AW	11.96 TQ	NEBLS	10/01-12/01
	Nevada	H	6.10 FQ	9.66 AW	14.92 TQ	NVBLS	10/01-12/01
	Las Vegas MSA, NV-AZ	H	6.04 FQ	10.26 AW	17.49 TQ	NVBLS	10/01-12/01
	New Hampshire	H	6.20 FQ	9.91 AW	15.11 TQ	NHBLS	10/01-12/01
	Manchester PMSA, NH	H	6.79 FQ	9.18 AW	13.18 TQ	NHBLS	10/01-12/01
	Nashua PMSA, NH	H	7.36 FQ	11.10 AW	16.00 TQ	NHBLS	10/01-12/01
	Portsmouth-Rochester PMSA, NH-ME	H	7.45 FQ	11.05 AW	17.81 TQ	NHBLS	10/01-12/01
	New Jersey	H	6.09 FQ	10.08 AW	16.54 TQ	NJBLS	10/01-12/01
	Atlantic-Cape May PMSA, NJ	H	6.38 FQ	9.64 AW	14.40 TQ	NJBLS	10/01-12/01
	Bergen-Passaic PMSA, NJ	H	5.99 FQ	9.68 AW	16.00 TQ	NJBLS	10/01-12/01
	Middlesex-Somerset-Hunterdon PMSA, NJ	H	6.14 FQ	9.67 AW	15.44 TQ	NJBLS	10/01-12/01
	Monmouth-Ocean PMSA, NJ	H	6.04 FQ	9.94 AW	16.41 TQ	NJBLS	10/01-12/01
	Newark PMSA, NJ	H	5.97 FQ	10.16 AW	16.77 TQ	NJBLS	10/01-12/01
	Trenton PMSA, NJ	H	5.93 FQ	9.49 AW	15.44 TQ	NJBLS	10/01-12/01
	New Mexico	H	5.94 FQ	8.52 AW	12.40 TQ	NMBLS	10/01-12/01
	Albuquerque MSA, NM	H	6.02 FQ	8.56 AW	12.41 TQ	NMBLS	10/01-12/01
	Las Cruces MSA, NM	H	5.73 FQ	8.04 AW	11.62 TQ	NMBLS	10/01-12/01
	New York	H	5.88 FQ	9.56 AW	15.61 TQ	NYBLS	10/01-12/01
	Albany-Schenectady-Troy MSA, NY	H	5.95 FQ	8.57 AW	12.40 TQ	NYBLS	10/01-12/01
	Binghamton MSA, NY	H	5.53 FQ	7.27 AW	9.14 TQ	NYBLS	10/01-12/01
	Buffalo-Niagara Falls MSA, NY	H	5.87 FQ	7.90 AW	10.38 TQ	NYBLS	10/01-12/01
	Dutchess County PMSA, NY	H	5.97 FQ	9.75 AW	16.71 TQ	NYBLS	10/01-12/01
	Nassau-Suffolk PMSA, NY	H	5.77 FQ	9.73 AW	16.00 TQ	NYBLS	10/01-12/01
	New York PMSA, NY	H	6.20 FQ	10.39 AW	16.70 TQ	NYBLS	10/01-12/01
	Newburgh PMSA, NY-PA	H	5.64 FQ	10.20 AW	16.64 TQ	NYBLS	10/01-12/01
	Rochester MSA, NY	H	6.06 FQ	9.78 AW	14.99 TQ	NYBLS	10/01-12/01
	Syracuse MSA, NY	H	5.68 FQ	8.91 AW	13.76 TQ	NYBLS	10/01-12/01
	Utica-Rome MSA, NY	H	5.70 FQ	9.50 AW	17.28 TQ	NYBLS	10/01-12/01
	North Carolina	H	5.93 FQ	9.24 AW	15.10 TQ	NCBLS	10/01-12/01
	Asheville MSA, NC	H	6.52 FQ	10.07 AW	14.59 TQ	NCBLS	10/01-12/01
	Charlotte-Gastonia-Rock Hill MSA, NC-SC	H	5.90 FQ	10.42 AW	16.95 TQ	NCBLS	10/01-12/01
	Fayetteville MSA, NC	H	5.86 FQ	10.79 AW	17.18 TQ	NCBLS	10/01-12/01
	Greensboro-Winston-Salem-High Point MSA, NC	H	5.83 FQ	8.26 AW	13.50 TQ	NCBLS	10/01-12/01
	Hickory-Morganton-Lenoir MSA, NC	H	5.87 FQ	9.90 AW	15.55 TQ	NCBLS	10/01-12/01
	Raleigh-Durham-Chapel Hill MSA, NC	H	6.11 FQ	9.17 AW	14.18 TQ	NCBLS	10/01-12/01
	Wilmington MSA, NC	H	6.29 FQ	10.56 AW	17.31 TQ	NCBLS	10/01-12/01
	North Dakota	H	5.70 FQ	7.94 AW	10.96 TQ	NDBLS	10/01-12/01
	Fargo-Moorhead MSA, ND-MN	H	6.09 FQ	10.25 AW	17.27 TQ	NDBLS	10/01-12/01
	Ohio	H	5.97 FQ	8.93 AW	12.73 TQ	OHBLS	10/01-12/01
	Akron PMSA, OH	H	6.52 FQ	9.08 AW	11.15 TQ	OHBLS	10/01-12/01
	Canton-Massillon MSA, OH	H	5.81 FQ	7.81 AW	10.74 TQ	OHBLS	10/01-12/01
	Cincinnati PMSA, OH-KY-IN	H	6.00 FQ	8.76 AW	12.19 TQ	OHBLS	10/01-12/01
	Cleveland-Lorain-Elyria PMSA, OH	H	6.37 FQ	9.52 AW	13.48 TQ	OHBLS	10/01-12/01
	Columbus MSA, OH	H	5.77 FQ	8.96 AW	13.98 TQ	OHBLS	10/01-12/01
	Dayton-Springfield MSA, OH	H	6.20 FQ	9.50 AW	13.94 TQ	OHBLS	10/01-12/01
	Hamilton-Middletown PMSA, OH	H	6.34 FQ	9.88 AW	13.89 TQ	OHBLS	10/01-12/01
	Mansfield MSA, OH	H	5.70 FQ	7.94 AW	11.30 TQ	OHBLS	10/01-12/01
	Toledo MSA, OH	H	5.71 FQ	8.71 AW	13.25 TQ	OHBLS	10/01-12/01
	Youngstown-Warren MSA, OH	H	5.92 FQ	8.38 AW	11.49 TQ	OHBLS	10/01-12/01
	Oklahoma	H	5.90 FQ	8.18 AW	11.63 TQ	OKBLS	10/01-12/01
	Oklahoma City MSA, OK	H	5.90 FQ	7.95 AW	11.10 TQ	OKBLS	10/01-12/01
	Tulsa MSA, OK	H	5.98 FQ	8.70 AW	13.45 TQ	OKBLS	10/01-12/01
	Oregon	H	7.11 FQ	10.85 AW	17.63 TQ	ORBLS	10/01-12/01
	Eugene-Springfield MSA, OR	H	7.14 FQ	9.49 AW	13.27 TQ	ORBLS	10/01-12/01
	Medford-Ashland MSA, OR	H	7.22 FQ	10.23 AW	14.97 TQ	ORBLS	10/01-12/01

AAW	Average annual wage	**AOH**	Average offered, high	**ASH**	Average starting, high	**H**	Hourly	**M**	Monthly	**S**	Special: hourly and annual
AE	Average entry wage	**AOL**	Average offered, low	**ASL**	Average starting, low	**HI**	Highest wage paid	**MTC**	Median total compensation	**TQ**	Third quartile wage
AEX	Average experienced wage	**APH**	Average pay, high range	**AW**	Average wage paid	**HR**	High end range	**MW**	Median wage paid	**W**	Weekly
AO	Average offered	**APL**	Average pay, low range	**FQ**	First quartile wage	**LR**	Low end range	**SQ**	Second quartile wage	**Y**	Yearly

Occupation/Type/Industry	Location	Per	Low	Mid	High	Source	Date
Recreation Worker	Portland-Vancouver PMSA, OR-WA	H	7.31 FQ	12.40 AW	20.01 TQ	ORBLS	10/01-12/01
	Salem PMSA, OR	H	6.60 FQ	8.94 AW	12.73 TQ	ORBLS	10/01-12/01
	Pennsylvania	H	5.90 FQ	9.72 AW	16.18 TQ	PABLS	10/01-12/01
	Allentown-Bethlehem-Easton MSA, PA	H	5.80 FQ	8.79 AW	13.53 TQ	PABLS	10/01-12/01
	Erie MSA, PA	H	5.58 FQ	7.91 AW	14.04 TQ	PABLS	10/01-12/01
	Harrisburg-Lebanon-Carlisle MSA, PA	H	6.07 FQ	9.33 AW	13.79 TQ	PABLS	10/01-12/01
	Johnstown MSA, PA	H	5.72 FQ	7.51 AW	9.82 TQ	PABLS	10/01-12/01
	Lancaster MSA, PA	H	7.35 FQ	10.17 AW	13.60 TQ	PABLS	10/01-12/01
	Philadelphia PMSA, PA-NJ	H	6.41 FQ	11.70 AW	19.40 TQ	PABLS	10/01-12/01
	Pittsburgh MSA, PA	H	5.86 FQ	8.34 AW	12.15 TQ	PABLS	10/01-12/01
	Reading MSA, PA	H	5.82 FQ	8.85 AW	13.01 TQ	PABLS	10/01-12/01
	Scranton-Wilkes-Barre-Hazleton MSA, PA	H	5.65 FQ	7.92 AW	11.33 TQ	PABLS	10/01-12/01
	York MSA, PA	H	5.63 FQ	8.01 AW	12.68 TQ	PABLS	10/01-12/01
	Rhode Island	H	6.56 FQ	8.96 AW	13.22 TQ	RIBLS	10/01-12/01
	Providence-Fall River-Warwick MSA, RI-MA	H	6.64 FQ	8.76 AW	13.10 TQ	RIBLS	10/01-12/01
	South Carolina	H	5.76 FQ	8.55 AW	12.99 TQ	SCBLS	10/01-12/01
	Charleston-North Charleston MSA, SC	H	5.61 FQ	8.30 AW	12.93 TQ	SCBLS	10/01-12/01
	Columbia MSA, SC	H	6.24 FQ	9.02 AW	12.44 TQ	SCBLS	10/01-12/01
	Greenville-Spartanburg-Anderson MSA, SC	H	5.71 FQ	7.40 AW	10.34 TQ	SCBLS	10/01-12/01
	Myrtle Beach MSA, SC	H	6.48 FQ	10.52 AW	16.83 TQ	SCBLS	10/01-12/01
	South Dakota	H	6.31 FQ	9.28 AW	12.96 TQ	SDBLS	10/01-12/01
	Sioux Falls MSA, SD	H	7.26 FQ	9.40 AW	13.18 TQ	SDBLS	10/01-12/01
	Tennessee	H	5.89 FQ	9.18 AW	13.79 TQ	TNBLS	10/01-12/01
	Chattanooga MSA, TN-GA	H	5.68 FQ	8.25 AW	12.82 TQ	TNBLS	10/01-12/01
	Clarksville-Hopkinsville MSA, TN-KY	H	5.93 FQ	9.17 AW	14.93 TQ	TNBLS	10/01-12/01
	Johnson City-Kingsport-Bristol MSA, TN-VA	H	6.12 FQ	9.70 AW	15.78 TQ	TNBLS	10/01-12/01
	Knoxville MSA, TN	H	6.46 FQ	11.16 AW	16.45 TQ	TNBLS	10/01-12/01
	Memphis MSA, TN-AR-MS	H	5.90 FQ	9.25 AW	15.55 TQ	TNBLS	10/01-12/01
	Nashville MSA, TN	H	5.95 FQ	9.07 AW	13.31 TQ	TNBLS	10/01-12/01
	Texas	H	5.88 FQ	9.08 AW	13.72 TQ	TXBLS	10/01-12/01
	Amarillo MSA, TX	H	5.74 FQ	8.84 AW	14.45 TQ	TXBLS	10/01-12/01
	Austin-San Marcos MSA, TX	H	6.61 FQ	10.41 AW	15.61 TQ	TXBLS	10/01-12/01
	Beaumont-Port Arthur MSA, TX	H	5.77 FQ	9.02 AW	13.63 TQ	TXBLS	10/01-12/01
	Brazoria PMSA, TX	H	5.73 FQ	9.08 AW	14.41 TQ	TXBLS	10/01-12/01
	Brownsville-Harlingen-San Benito MSA, TX	H	6.15 FQ	9.39 AW	12.62 TQ	TXBLS	10/01-12/01
	Corpus Christi MSA, TX	H	5.75 FQ	8.14 AW	12.06 TQ	TXBLS	10/01-12/01
	Dallas PMSA, TX	H	5.95 FQ	9.40 AW	14.76 TQ	TXBLS	10/01-12/01
	El Paso MSA, TX	H	5.79 FQ	8.50 AW	13.71 TQ	TXBLS	10/01-12/01
	Fort Worth-Arlington PMSA, TX	H	6.34 FQ	10.91 AW	18.66 TQ	TXBLS	10/01-12/01
	Galveston-Texas City PMSA, TX	H	5.79 FQ	8.25 AW	11.14 TQ	TXBLS	10/01-12/01
	Houston PMSA, TX	H	6.12 FQ	9.10 AW	12.54 TQ	TXBLS	10/01-12/01
	Killeen-Temple MSA, TX	H	6.02 FQ	10.70 AW	16.59 TQ	TXBLS	10/01-12/01
	Laredo MSA, TX	H	5.86 FQ	9.33 AW	13.25 TQ	TXBLS	10/01-12/01
	Longview-Marshall MSA, TX	H	5.90 FQ	8.24 AW	11.87 TQ	TXBLS	10/01-12/01
	Lubbock MSA, TX	H	5.95 FQ	8.86 AW	12.23 TQ	TXBLS	10/01-12/01
	McAllen-Edinburg-Mission MSA, TX	H	5.89 FQ	8.91 AW	14.36 TQ	TXBLS	10/01-12/01
	Odessa-Midland MSA, TX	H	5.69 FQ	8.52 AW	14.08 TQ	TXBLS	10/01-12/01
	San Antonio MSA, TX	H	5.88 FQ	8.35 AW	11.82 TQ	TXBLS	10/01-12/01
	Tyler MSA, TX	H	6.22 FQ	9.16 AW	12.28 TQ	TXBLS	10/01-12/01
	Waco MSA, TX	H	5.57 FQ	9.09 AW	17.26 TQ	TXBLS	10/01-12/01
	Utah	H	5.79 FQ	8.65 AW	13.17 TQ	UTBLS	10/01-12/01
	Provo-Orem MSA, UT	H	6.06 FQ	8.61 AW	11.40 TQ	UTBLS	10/01-12/01
	Vermont	H	6.50 FQ	9.41 AW	14.03 TQ	VTBLS	10/01-12/01
	Burlington MSA, VT	H	6.50 FQ	9.02 AW	13.76 TQ	VTBLS	10/01-12/01
	Virginia	H	6.22 FQ	10.14 AW	16.44 TQ	VABLS	10/01-12/01
	Lynchburg MSA, VA	H	6.27 FQ	9.64 AW	15.15 TQ	VABLS	10/01-12/01

AAW	Average annual wage	**AOH**	Average offered, high	**ASH**	Average starting, high	**H**	Hourly	**M**	Monthly	**S**	Special: hourly and annual
AE	Average entry wage	**AOL**	Average offered, low	**ASL**	Average starting, low	**HI**	Highest wage paid	**MTC**	Median total compensation	**TQ**	Third quartile wage
AEX	Average experienced wage	**APH**	Average pay, high range	**AW**	Average wage paid	**HR**	High end range	**MW**	Median wage paid	**W**	Weekly
AO	Average offered	**APL**	Average pay, low range	**FQ**	First quartile wage	**LR**	Low end range	**SQ**	Second quartile wage	**Y**	Yearly

Occupation/Type/Industry	Location	Per	Low	Mid	High	Source	Date
Recreation Worker	Norfolk-Virginia Beach-Newport News MSA, VA-NC	H	5.96 FQ	9.10 AW	15.35 TQ	VABLS	10/01-12/01
	Richmond-Petersburg MSA, VA	H	6.41 FQ	9.07 AW	13.21 TQ	VABLS	10/01-12/01
	Roanoke MSA, VA	H	6.02 FQ	9.57 AW	16.09 TQ	VABLS	10/01-12/01
	Washington	H	7.18 FQ	11.15 AW	16.92 TQ	WABLS	10/01-12/01
	Bremerton PMSA, WA	H	7.04 FQ	10.29 AW	15.42 TQ	WABLS	10/01-12/01
	Olympia PMSA, WA	H	6.93 FQ	11.25 AW	19.50 TQ	WABLS	10/01-12/01
	Seattle-Bellevue-Everett PMSA, WA	H	7.83 FQ	11.63 AW	16.33 TQ	WABLS	10/01-12/01
	Spokane MSA, WA	H	6.95 FQ	9.81 AW	15.21 TQ	WABLS	10/01-12/01
	Tacoma PMSA, WA	H	7.81 FQ	14.11 AW	21.79 TQ	WABLS	10/01-12/01
	Yakima MSA, WA	H	7.11 FQ	11.31 AW	19.20 TQ	WABLS	10/01-12/01
	West Virginia	H	5.72 FQ	8.19 AW	11.80 TQ	WVBLS	10/01-12/01
	Charleston MSA, WV	H	5.68 FQ	8.29 AW	11.62 TQ	WVBLS	10/01-12/01
	Huntington-Ashland MSA, WV-KY-OH	H	5.60 FQ	8.70 AW	14.96 TQ	WVBLS	10/01-12/01
	Wisconsin	H	5.95 FQ	8.99 AW	13.87 TQ	WIBLS	10/01-12/01
	Appleton-Oshkosh-Neenah MSA, WI	H	5.84 FQ	9.01 AW	14.41 TQ	WIBLS	10/01-12/01
	Green Bay MSA, WI	H	7.07 FQ	10.10 AW	13.60 TQ	WIBLS	10/01-12/01
	Madison MSA, WI	H	8.03 FQ	11.25 AW	16.92 TQ	WIBLS	10/01-12/01
	Milwaukee-Waukesha PMSA, WI	H	6.17 FQ	9.08 AW	13.59 TQ	WIBLS	10/01-12/01
	Racine PMSA, WI	H	6.13 FQ	8.85 AW	11.41 TQ	WIBLS	10/01-12/01
	Wyoming	H	5.66 FQ	8.45 AW	13.12 TQ	WYBLS	10/01-12/01
	Cheyenne MSA, WY	H	6.21 FQ	9.17 AW	14.53 TQ	WYBLS	10/01-12/01
	Puerto Rico	H	5.63 FQ	6.99 AW	8.64 TQ	PRBLS	10/01-12/01
	Virgin Islands	H	5.79 FQ	8.20 AW	10.89 TQ	VIBLS	10/01-12/01
	Guam	H	5.57 FQ	7.28 AW	10.94 TQ	GUBLS	10/01-12/01
Recreational Therapist	Alabama	Y	19220 FQ	29440 AW	43630 TQ	ALBLS	10/01-12/01
	Arizona	Y	16870 FQ	28630 AW	39860 TQ	AZBLS	10/01-12/01
	Arkansas	Y	15910 FQ	24690 AW	37210 TQ	ARBLS	10/01-12/01
	California	Y	18330 FQ	35050 AW	51120 TQ	CABLS	10/01-12/01
	Colorado	Y	17190 FQ	27820 AW	42050 TQ	COBLS	10/01-12/01
	Connecticut	Y	25460 FQ	37960 AW	55820 TQ	CTBLS	10/01-12/01
	Delaware	Y	24180 FQ	30840 AW	40180 TQ	DEBLS	10/01-12/01
	District of Columbia	Y	25570 FQ	45880 AW	66160 TQ	DCBLS	10/01-12/01
	Florida	Y	17740 FQ	30650 AW	43790 TQ	FLBLS	10/01-12/01
	Georgia	Y	21390 FQ	31270 AW	43840 TQ	GABLS	10/01-12/01
	Hawaii	Y	23910 FQ	36780 AW	47460 TQ	HIBLS	10/01-12/01
	Idaho	Y	17420 FQ	31900 AW	45470 TQ	IDBLS	10/01-12/01
	Illinois	Y	13780 FQ	26850 AW	43770 TQ	ILBLS	10/01-12/01
	Indiana	Y	16350 FQ	25310 AW	36290 TQ	INBLS	10/01-12/01
	Iowa	Y	16110 FQ	24780 AW	37540 TQ	IABLS	10/01-12/01
	Kansas	Y	16570 FQ	28710 AW	42020 TQ	KSBLS	10/01-12/01
	Kentucky	Y	16680 FQ	25070 AW	34340 TQ	KYBLS	10/01-12/01
	Louisiana	Y	14770 FQ	27050 AW	38480 TQ	LABLS	10/01-12/01
	Maine	Y	16420 FQ	26890 AW	39820 TQ	MEBLS	10/01-12/01
	Maryland	Y	17380 FQ	32280 AW	45480 TQ	MDBLS	10/01-12/01
	Massachusetts	Y	19490 FQ	30700 AW	44050 TQ	MABLS	10/01-12/01
	Michigan	Y	20610 FQ	33450 AW	46020 TQ	MIBLS	10/01-12/01
	Minnesota	Y	22470 FQ	33840 AW	46860 TQ	MNBLS	10/01-12/01
	Mississippi	Y	17570 FQ	26140 AW	34240 TQ	MSBLS	10/01-12/01
	Missouri	Y	17300 FQ	27970 AW	37740 TQ	MOBLS	10/01-12/01
	Montana	Y	13070 FQ	23810 AW	43150 TQ	MTBLS	10/01-12/01
	Nebraska	Y	15600 FQ	24340 AW	34850 TQ	NEBLS	10/01-12/01
	New Hampshire	Y	18830 FQ	27970 AW	36490 TQ	NHBLS	10/01-12/01
	New Jersey	Y	20430 FQ	32980 AW	45590 TQ	NJBLS	10/01-12/01
	New Mexico	Y	21740 FQ	33210 AW	45990 TQ	NMBLS	10/01-12/01
	New York	Y	23980 FQ	37900 AW	51590 TQ	NYBLS	10/01-12/01
	North Carolina	Y	19890 FQ	30010 AW	42340 TQ	NCBLS	10/01-12/01
	North Dakota	Y	16430 FQ	28430 AW	38070 TQ	NDBLS	10/01-12/01
	Ohio	Y	20020 FQ	31400 AW	44650 TQ	OHBLS	10/01-12/01
	Oklahoma	Y	15110 FQ	29510 AW	44690 TQ	OKBLS	10/01-12/01
	Oregon	Y	21470 FQ	35290 AW	48170 TQ	ORBLS	10/01-12/01
	Pennsylvania	Y	18000 FQ	30480 AW	49120 TQ	PABLS	10/01-12/01
	Rhode Island	Y	23080 FQ	35050 AW	52230 TQ	RIBLS	10/01-12/01
	South Carolina	Y	13910 FQ	29320 AW	51050 TQ	SCBLS	10/01-12/01
	South Dakota	Y	18570 FQ	31770 AW	43760 TQ	SDBLS	10/01-12/01
	Tennessee	Y	18370 FQ	27150 AW	36930 TQ	TNBLS	10/01-12/01

AAW	Average annual wage	**AOH**	Average offered, high	**ASH**	Average starting, high	**H**	Hourly	**M**	Monthly	**S**	Special: hourly and annual
AE	Average entry wage	**AOL**	Average offered, low	**ASL**	Average starting, low	**HI**	Highest wage paid	**MTC**	Median total compensation	**TQ**	Third quartile wage
AEX	Average experienced wage	**APH**	Average pay, high range	**AW**	Average wage paid	**HR**	High end range	**MW**	Median wage paid	**W**	Weekly
AO	Average offered	**APL**	Average pay, low range	**FQ**	First quartile wage	**LR**	Low end range	**SQ**	Second quartile wage	**Y**	Yearly

Occupation/Type/Industry	Location	Per	Low	Mid	High	Source	Date
Recreational Therapist	Texas	Y	15970 FQ	26370 AW	39280 TQ	TXBLS	10/01-12/01
	Utah	Y	15740 FQ	27580 AW	40650 TQ	UTBLS	10/01-12/01
	Virginia	Y	21680 FQ	29800 AW	39760 TQ	VABLS	10/01-12/01
	Washington	Y	31240 FQ	40280 AW	49890 TQ	WABLS	10/01-12/01
	West Virginia	Y	17370 FQ	25720 AW	34970 TQ	WVBLS	10/01-12/01
	Wisconsin	Y	17650 FQ	28620 AW	41210 TQ	WIBLS	10/01-12/01
	Wyoming	Y	14100 FQ	24960 AW	42560 TQ	WYBLS	10/01-12/01
	Puerto Rico	Y	17030 FQ	30210 AW	47410 TQ	PRBLS	10/01-12/01
Recreational Vehicle Service Technician	Alabama	H	9.45 FQ	13.40 AW	17.74 TQ	ALBLS	10/01-12/01
	Alaska	H	6.90 FQ	15.27 AW	23.56 TQ	AKBLS	10/01-12/01
	Arizona	H	8.33 FQ	14.40 AW	22.19 TQ	AZBLS	10/01-12/01
	Arkansas	H	8.59 FQ	12.44 AW	18.01 TQ	ARBLS	10/01-12/01
	California	H	9.05 FQ	14.91 AW	22.50 TQ	CABLS	10/01-12/01
	Colorado	H	9.23 FQ	16.05 AW	24.54 TQ	COBLS	10/01-12/01
	Connecticut	H	9.35 FQ	13.38 AW	20.06 TQ	CTBLS	10/01-12/01
	Florida	H	7.79 FQ	13.66 AW	21.42 TQ	FLBLS	10/01-12/01
	Georgia	H	8.97 FQ	12.85 AW	18.71 TQ	GABLS	10/01-12/01
	Idaho	H	9.19 FQ	13.55 AW	17.37 TQ	IDBLS	10/01-12/01
	Illinois	H	7.56 FQ	11.18 AW	16.13 TQ	ILBLS	10/01-12/01
	Indiana	H	9.34 FQ	13.11 AW	17.60 TQ	INBLS	10/01-12/01
	Iowa	H	8.70 FQ	12.41 AW	17.84 TQ	IABLS	10/01-12/01
	Kansas	H	7.31 FQ	11.10 AW	16.35 TQ	KSBLS	10/01-12/01
	Kentucky	H	7.32 FQ	12.66 AW	19.16 TQ	KYBLS	10/01-12/01
	Louisiana	H	8.14 FQ	12.21 AW	16.62 TQ	LABLS	10/01-12/01
	Maine	H	9.73 FQ	14.26 AW	18.90 TQ	MEBLS	10/01-12/01
	Maryland	H	8.06 FQ	11.71 AW	16.51 TQ	MDBLS	10/01-12/01
	Massachusetts	H	9.47 FQ	15.04 AW	21.34 TQ	MABLS	10/01-12/01
	Michigan	H	8.79 FQ	13.26 AW	18.87 TQ	MIBLS	10/01-12/01
	Minnesota	H	9.84 FQ	13.76 AW	18.88 TQ	MNBLS	10/01-12/01
	Mississippi	H	8.94 FQ	11.86 AW	16.33 TQ	MSBLS	10/01-12/01
	Missouri	H	8.49 FQ	11.54 AW	15.73 TQ	MOBLS	10/01-12/01
	Montana	H	8.70 FQ	13.04 AW	17.90 TQ	MTBLS	10/01-12/01
	Nebraska	H	6.84 FQ	10.66 AW	15.53 TQ	NEBLS	10/01-12/01
	Nevada	H	10.21 FQ	16.02 AW	21.96 TQ	NVBLS	10/01-12/01
	New Hampshire	H	8.01 FQ	12.81 AW	17.30 TQ	NHBLS	10/01-12/01
	New Jersey	H	7.55 FQ	11.57 AW	16.22 TQ	NJBLS	10/01-12/01
	New Mexico	H	9.19 FQ	14.09 AW	20.64 TQ	NMBLS	10/01-12/01
	New York	H	7.62 FQ	11.48 AW	16.26 TQ	NYBLS	10/01-12/01
	North Carolina	H	8.41 FQ	13.13 AW	18.43 TQ	NCBLS	10/01-12/01
	North Dakota	H	7.64 FQ	11.28 AW	16.75 TQ	NDBLS	10/01-12/01
	Ohio	H	8.01 FQ	12.10 AW	17.41 TQ	OHBLS	10/01-12/01
	Oklahoma	H	9.37 FQ	13.38 AW	17.40 TQ	OKBLS	10/01-12/01
	Oregon	H	10.08 FQ	15.02 AW	21.01 TQ	ORBLS	10/01-12/01
	Pennsylvania	H	7.76 FQ	12.07 AW	17.06 TQ	PABLS	10/01-12/01
	Rhode Island	H	9.98 FQ	14.33 AW	19.23 TQ	RIBLS	10/01-12/01
	South Carolina	H	9.00 FQ	12.15 AW	18.38 TQ	SCBLS	10/01-12/01
	South Dakota	H	7.08 FQ	11.24 AW	15.97 TQ	SDBLS	10/01-12/01
	Tennessee	H	7.74 FQ	11.90 AW	16.27 TQ	TNBLS	10/01-12/01
	Texas	H	7.67 FQ	13.11 AW	20.86 TQ	TXBLS	10/01-12/01
	Utah	H	9.64 FQ	14.53 AW	20.29 TQ	UTBLS	10/01-12/01
	Vermont	H	8.90 FQ	11.99 AW	14.82 TQ	VTBLS	10/01-12/01
	Virginia	H	8.89 FQ	13.85 AW	23.34 TQ	VABLS	10/01-12/01
	Washington	H	10.84 FQ	15.69 AW	20.16 TQ	WABLS	10/01-12/01
	West Virginia	H	6.65 FQ	9.53 AW	12.25 TQ	WVBLS	10/01-12/01
	Wisconsin	H	8.54 FQ	12.59 AW	17.03 TQ	WIBLS	10/01-12/01
	Wyoming	H	6.17 FQ	10.55 AW	16.07 TQ	WYBLS	10/01-12/01
Refractory Materials Repairer							
Except Brickmason	Alabama	H	11.69 FQ	15.00 AW	20.75 TQ	ALBLS	10/01-12/01
Except Brickmason	Arkansas	H	9.72 FQ	18.08 AW	33.87 TQ	ARBLS	10/01-12/01
Except Brickmason	California	H	14.98 FQ	21.70 AW	38.21 TQ	CABLS	10/01-12/01
Except Brickmason	Florida	H	13.23 FQ	17.73 AW	20.96 TQ	FLBLS	10/01-12/01
Except Brickmason	Georgia	H	10.06 FQ	14.74 AW	21.09 TQ	GABLS	10/01-12/01
Except Brickmason	Illinois	H	11.58 FQ	17.57 AW	24.50 TQ	ILBLS	10/01-12/01
Except Brickmason	Indiana	H	12.52 FQ	17.34 AW	24.60 TQ	INBLS	10/01-12/01
Except Brickmason	Iowa	H	11.48 FQ	15.38 AW	21.03 TQ	IABLS	10/01-12/01
Except Brickmason	Kentucky	H	12.23 FQ	18.20 AW	22.20 TQ	KYBLS	10/01-12/01
Except Brickmason	Michigan	H	9.55 FQ	13.53 AW	19.55 TQ	MIBLS	10/01-12/01
Except Brickmason	Missouri	H	14.35 FQ	17.66 AW	21.95 TQ	MOBLS	10/01-12/01
Except Brickmason	New Jersey	H	14.66 FQ	21.11 AW	27.82 TQ	NJBLS	10/01-12/01

AAW	Average annual wage	**AOH**	Average offered, high	**ASH**	Average starting, high	**H**	Hourly	**M**	Monthly	**S**	Special: hourly and annual
AE	Average entry wage	**AOL**	Average offered, low	**ASL**	Average starting, low	**HI**	Highest wage paid	**MTC**	Median total compensation	**TQ**	Third quartile wage
AEX	Average experienced wage	**APH**	Average pay, high range	**AW**	Average wage paid	**HR**	High end range	**MW**	Median wage paid	**W**	Weekly
AO	Average offered	**APL**	Average pay, low range	**FQ**	First quartile wage	**LR**	Low end range	**SQ**	Second quartile wage	**Y**	Yearly

Occupation/Type/Industry	Location	Per	Low	Mid	High	Source	Date
Refractory Materials Repairer							
Except Brickmason	Ohio	H	12.08 FQ	17.64 AW	22.25 TQ	OHBLS	10/01-12/01
Except Brickmason	Oklahoma	H	11.15 FQ	14.87 AW	20.04 TQ	OKBLS	10/01-12/01
Except Brickmason	Pennsylvania	H	12.33 FQ	17.43 AW	21.87 TQ	PABLS	10/01-12/01
Except Brickmason	South Carolina	H	7.68 FQ	14.94 AW	21.47 TQ	SCBLS	10/01-12/01
Except Brickmason	Tennessee	H	11.36 FQ	16.26 AW	20.88 TQ	TNBLS	10/01-12/01
Except Brickmason	Texas	H	12.01 FQ	16.20 AW	21.44 TQ	TXBLS	10/01-12/01
Except Brickmason	Virginia	H	7.48 FQ	14.09 AW	21.72 TQ	VABLS	10/01-12/01
Except Brickmason	Washington	H	16.19 FQ	21.71 AW	31.21 TQ	WABLS	10/01-12/01
Except Brickmason	Wisconsin	H	9.84 FQ	15.06 AW	21.04 TQ	WIBLS	10/01-12/01
Refuse and Recyclable Material Collector	Alabama	H	7.20 FQ	9.65 AW	13.22 TQ	ALBLS	10/01-12/01
	Birmingham MSA, AL	H	7.61 FQ	9.56 AW	11.65 TQ	ALBLS	10/01-12/01
	Mobile MSA, AL	H	7.40 FQ	10.17 AW	13.84 TQ	ALBLS	10/01-12/01
	Montgomery MSA, AL	H	7.24 FQ	13.10 AW	19.83 TQ	ALBLS	10/01-12/01
	Alaska	H	6.99 FQ	15.99 AW	26.35 TQ	AKBLS	10/01-12/01
	Anchorage MSA, AK	H	6.45 FQ	14.49 AW	26.06 TQ	AKBLS	10/01-12/01
	Arizona	H	8.71 FQ	14.69 AW	21.23 TQ	AZBLS	10/01-12/01
	Phoenix-Mesa MSA, AZ	H	9.68 FQ	15.61 AW	22.17 TQ	AZBLS	10/01-12/01
	Tucson MSA, AZ	H	6.97 FQ	11.24 AW	16.83 TQ	AZBLS	10/01-12/01
	Arkansas	H	5.60 FQ	8.43 AW	12.87 TQ	ARBLS	10/01-12/01
	Fayetteville-Springdale-Rogers MSA, AR	H	7.65 FQ	9.72 AW	11.82 TQ	ARBLS	10/01-12/01
	Fort Smith MSA, AR-OK	H	6.07 FQ	10.05 AW	13.80 TQ	ARBLS	10/01-12/01
	Little Rock-North Little Rock MSA, AR	H	8.21 FQ	12.55 AW	18.00 TQ	ARBLS	10/01-12/01
	California	H	8.94 FQ	16.19 AW	22.81 TQ	CABLS	10/01-12/01
	Bakersfield MSA, CA	H	7.27 FQ	12.98 AW	16.55 TQ	CABLS	10/01-12/01
	Los Angeles-Long Beach PMSA, CA	H	8.84 FQ	14.62 AW	21.48 TQ	CABLS	10/01-12/01
	Modesto MSA, CA	H	8.84 FQ	13.60 AW	16.48 TQ	CABLS	10/01-12/01
	Oakland PMSA, CA	H	10.74 FQ	17.09 AW	23.80 TQ	CABLS	10/01-12/01
	Orange County PMSA, CA	H	6.73 FQ	14.40 AW	22.31 TQ	CABLS	10/01-12/01
	Riverside-San Bernardino PMSA, CA	H	9.76 FQ	15.32 AW	22.91 TQ	CABLS	10/01-12/01
	Sacramento PMSA, CA	H	8.36 FQ	15.70 AW	21.84 TQ	CABLS	10/01-12/01
	Salinas MSA, CA	H	10.02 FQ	14.50 AW	17.85 TQ	CABLS	10/01-12/01
	San Diego MSA, CA	H	6.84 FQ	15.28 AW	22.30 TQ	CABLS	10/01-12/01
	San Francisco PMSA, CA	H	6.88 FQ	19.48 AW	27.32 TQ	CABLS	10/01-12/01
	San Jose PMSA, CA	H	17.49 FQ	20.23 AW	23.23 TQ	CABLS	10/01-12/01
	San Luis Obispo-Atascadero-Paso Robles MSA, CA	H	8.15 FQ	13.90 AW	20.95 TQ	CABLS	10/01-12/01
	Santa Barbara-Santa Maria-Lompoc MSA, CA	H	11.77 FQ	17.47 AW	23.49 TQ	CABLS	10/01-12/01
	Santa Rosa PMSA, CA	H	10.20 FQ	16.69 AW	22.80 TQ	CABLS	10/01-12/01
	Stockton-Lodi MSA, CA	H	9.48 FQ	15.05 AW	19.94 TQ	CABLS	10/01-12/01
	Vallejo-Fairfield-Napa PMSA, CA	H	9.93 FQ	16.81 AW	22.25 TQ	CABLS	10/01-12/01
	Ventura PMSA, CA	H	6.67 FQ	14.25 AW	17.65 TQ	CABLS	10/01-12/01
	Visalia-Tulare-Porterville MSA, CA	H	10.87 FQ	16.19 AW	21.69 TQ	CABLS	10/01-12/01
	Colorado	H	8.53 FQ	12.84 AW	18.38 TQ	COBLS	10/01-12/01
	Boulder-Longmont PMSA, CO	H	9.76 FQ	12.45 AW	15.56 TQ	COBLS	10/01-12/01
	Denver PMSA, CO	H	7.52 FQ	13.37 AW	22.01 TQ	COBLS	10/01-12/01
	Fort Collins-Loveland MSA, CO	H	9.81 FQ	12.76 AW	16.19 TQ	COBLS	10/01-12/01
	Greeley PMSA, CO	H	7.96 FQ	13.33 AW	17.06 TQ	COBLS	10/01-12/01
	Connecticut	H	9.07 FQ	14.16 AW	19.67 TQ	CTBLS	10/01-12/01
	Bridgeport PMSA, CT	H	10.69 FQ	15.45 AW	19.90 TQ	CTBLS	10/01-12/01
	Danbury PMSA, CT	H	9.88 FQ	13.53 AW	17.00 TQ	CTBLS	10/01-12/01
	Hartford MSA, CT	H	7.12 FQ	12.83 AW	20.70 TQ	CTBLS	10/01-12/01
	New Haven-Meriden PMSA, CT	H	9.58 FQ	14.90 AW	18.75 TQ	CTBLS	10/01-12/01
	New London-Norwich MSA, CT-RI	H	9.91 FQ	14.37 AW	19.86 TQ	CTBLS	10/01-12/01
	Stamford-Norwalk PMSA, CT	H	11.16 FQ	16.11 AW	19.56 TQ	CTBLS	10/01-12/01
	Delaware	H	9.10 FQ	13.86 AW	17.85 TQ	DEBLS	10/01-12/01
	Wilmington-Newark PMSA, DE-MD	H	10.73 FQ	14.65 AW	18.07 TQ	DEBLS	10/01-12/01
	District of Columbia	H	7.23 FQ	8.43 AW	8.77 TQ	DCBLS	10/01-12/01

AAW	Average annual wage	AOH	Average offered, high	ASH	Average starting, high	H	Hourly	M	Monthly	S	Special: hourly and annual
AE	Average entry wage	AOL	Average offered, low	ASL	Average starting, low	HI	Highest wage paid	MTC	Median total compensation	TQ	Third quartile wage
AEX	Average experienced wage	APH	Average pay, high range	AW	Average wage paid	HR	High end range	MW	Median wage paid	W	Weekly
AO	Average offered	APL	Average pay, low range	FQ	First quartile wage	LR	Low end range	SQ	Second quartile wage	Y	Yearly

Occupation/Type/Industry	Location	Per	Low	Mid	High	Source	Date
Refuse and Recyclable Material Collector	Washington PMSA, DC-MD-VA-WV	H	6.86 FQ	11.70 AW	17.35 TQ	DCBLS	10/01-12/01
	Fort Lauderdale PMSA, FL	H	5.70 FQ	10.37 AW	16.64 TQ	FLBLS	10/01-12/01
	Fort Myers-Cape Coral MSA, FL	H	5.49 FQ	9.51 AW	16.26 TQ	FLBLS	10/01-12/01
	Fort Walton Beach MSA, FL	H	6.01 FQ	8.72 AW	12.22 TQ	FLBLS	10/01-12/01
	Gainesville MSA, FL	H	5.40 FQ	7.79 AW	12.95 TQ	FLBLS	10/01-12/01
	Jacksonville MSA, FL	H	5.91 FQ	9.92 AW	13.86 TQ	FLBLS	10/01-12/01
	Lakeland-Winter Haven MSA, FL	H	6.79 FQ	11.01 AW	15.07 TQ	FLBLS	10/01-12/01
	Miami PMSA, FL	H	5.66 FQ	11.57 AW	17.62 TQ	FLBLS	10/01-12/01
	Naples MSA, FL	H	5.68 FQ	9.97 AW	15.82 TQ	FLBLS	10/01-12/01
	Ocala MSA, FL	H	8.65 FQ	10.50 AW	13.09 TQ	FLBLS	10/01-12/01
	Orlando MSA, FL	H	5.46 FQ	9.03 AW	15.06 TQ	FLBLS	10/01-12/01
	Pensacola MSA, FL	H	6.59 FQ	10.03 AW	14.57 TQ	FLBLS	10/01-12/01
	Sarasota-Bradenton MSA, FL	H	5.82 FQ	10.39 AW	15.89 TQ	FLBLS	10/01-12/01
	Tampa-St. Petersburg-Clearwater MSA, FL	H	5.34 FQ	6.70 AW	8.45 TQ	FLBLS	10/01-12/01
	West Palm Beach-Boca Raton MSA, FL	H	5.47 FQ	7.96 AW	12.36 TQ	FLBLS	10/01-12/01
	Georgia	H	6.56 FQ	11.06 AW	16.34 TQ	GABLS	10/01-12/01
	Atlanta MSA, GA	H	8.00 FQ	12.47 AW	17.22 TQ	GABLS	10/01-12/01
	Augusta-Aiken MSA, GA-SC	H	6.56 FQ	11.75 AW	16.93 TQ	GABLS	10/01-12/01
	Columbus MSA, GA-AL	H	7.19 FQ	12.97 AW	23.79 TQ	GABLS	10/01-12/01
	Macon MSA, GA	H	5.87 FQ	9.12 AW	13.74 TQ	GABLS	10/01-12/01
	Savannah MSA, GA	H	7.71 FQ	9.79 AW	11.47 TQ	GABLS	10/01-12/01
	Hawaii	H	10.92 FQ	12.53 AW	15.37 TQ	HIBLS	10/01-12/01
	Honolulu MSA, HI	H	10.92 FQ	12.55 AW	15.79 TQ	HIBLS	10/01-12/01
	Idaho	H	7.86 FQ	12.12 AW	16.63 TQ	IDBLS	10/01-12/01
	Boise City MSA, ID	H	7.25 FQ	11.27 AW	17.50 TQ	IDBLS	10/01-12/01
	Illinois	H	9.11 FQ	15.24 AW	21.26 TQ	ILBLS	10/01-12/01
	Champaign-Urbana MSA, IL	H	8.11 FQ	13.63 AW	20.52 TQ	ILBLS	10/01-12/01
	Chicago PMSA, IL	H	10.05 FQ	16.42 AW	21.54 TQ	ILBLS	10/01-12/01
	Peoria-Pekin MSA, IL	H	9.09 FQ	12.54 AW	17.62 TQ	ILBLS	10/01-12/01
	Rockford MSA, IL	H	7.61 FQ	13.78 AW	21.38 TQ	ILBLS	10/01-12/01
	Indiana	H	6.32 FQ	11.99 AW	17.63 TQ	INBLS	10/01-12/01
	Evansville-Henderson MSA, IN-KY	H	7.77 FQ	11.19 AW	16.09 TQ	INBLS	10/01-12/01
	Fort Wayne MSA, IN	H	9.14 FQ	15.00 AW	23.20 TQ	INBLS	10/01-12/01
	Gary PMSA, IN	H	9.62 FQ	14.54 AW	20.04 TQ	INBLS	10/01-12/01
	Indianapolis MSA, IN	H	5.53 FQ	11.34 AW	22.46 TQ	INBLS	10/01-12/01
	Lafayette MSA, IN	H	8.22 FQ	12.09 AW	16.37 TQ	INBLS	10/01-12/01
	Iowa	H	7.87 FQ	12.80 AW	18.17 TQ	IABLS	10/01-12/01
	Davenport-Moline-Rock Island MSA, IA-IL	H	7.89 FQ	13.52 AW	18.74 TQ	IABLS	10/01-12/01
	Des Moines MSA, IA	H	12.34 FQ	15.85 AW	20.49 TQ	IABLS	10/01-12/01
	Kansas	H	6.99 FQ	11.55 AW	19.83 TQ	KSBLS	10/01-12/01
	Kentucky	H	6.59 FQ	9.40 AW	12.66 TQ	KYBLS	10/01-12/01
	Lexington MSA, KY	H	7.32 FQ	9.08 AW	11.32 TQ	KYBLS	10/01-12/01
	Louisville MSA, KY-IN	H	6.99 FQ	9.92 AW	13.30 TQ	KYBLS	10/01-12/01
	Louisiana	H	5.75 FQ	7.86 AW	11.00 TQ	LABLS	10/01-12/01
	Baton Rouge MSA, LA	H	5.66 FQ	7.32 AW	10.25 TQ	LABLS	10/01-12/01
	Houma MSA, LA	H	5.58 FQ	6.48 AW	8.18 TQ	LABLS	10/01-12/01
	Lafayette MSA, LA	H	6.15 FQ	9.05 AW	13.15 TQ	LABLS	10/01-12/01
	New Orleans MSA, LA	H	6.26 FQ	9.28 AW	12.27 TQ	LABLS	10/01-12/01
	Maine	H	7.54 FQ	10.36 AW	13.48 TQ	MEBLS	10/01-12/01
	Portland MSA, ME	H	8.88 FQ	10.76 AW	13.64 TQ	MEBLS	10/01-12/01
	Maryland	H	8.17 FQ	12.21 AW	17.24 TQ	MDBLS	10/01-12/01
	Baltimore PMSA, MD	H	8.70 FQ	11.90 AW	17.58 TQ	MDBLS	10/01-12/01
	Massachusetts	H	8.16 FQ	14.77 AW	20.88 TQ	MABLS	10/01-12/01
	Boston PMSA, MA-NH	H	7.02 FQ	14.98 AW	21.34 TQ	MABLS	10/01-12/01
	Lawrence PMSA, MA-NH	H	10.34 FQ	14.54 AW	21.76 TQ	MABLS	10/01-12/01
	Springfield MSA, MA	H	11.78 FQ	15.74 AW	21.18 TQ	MABLS	10/01-12/01
	Worcester PMSA, MA-CT	H	7.35 FQ	12.63 AW	19.27 TQ	MABLS	10/01-12/01
	Michigan	H	8.56 FQ	13.29 AW	18.13 TQ	MIBLS	10/01-12/01
	Ann Arbor PMSA, MI	H	6.67 FQ	16.99 AW	27.40 TQ	MIBLS	10/01-12/01
	Detroit PMSA, MI	H	8.25 FQ	12.85 AW	16.63 TQ	MIBLS	10/01-12/01
	Grand Rapids-Muskegon-Holland MSA, MI	H	9.91 FQ	14.27 AW	20.32 TQ	MIBLS	10/01-12/01
	Kalamazoo-Battle Creek MSA, MI	H	7.38 FQ	13.15 AW	21.38 TQ	MIBLS	10/01-12/01

AAW Average annual wage	**AOH** Average offered, high	**ASH** Average starting, high	**H** Hourly	**M** Monthly	**S** Special: hourly and annual
AE Average entry wage	**AOL** Average offered, low	**ASL** Average starting, low	**HI** Highest wage paid	**MTC** Median total compensation	**TQ** Third quartile wage
AEX Average experienced wage	**APH** Average pay, high range	**AW** Average wage paid	**HR** High end range	**MW** Median wage paid	**W** Weekly
AO Average offered	**APL** Average pay, low range	**FQ** First quartile wage	**LR** Low end range	**SQ** Second quartile wage	**Y** Yearly

Occupation/Type/Industry	Location	Per	Low	Mid	High	Source	Date
Refuse and Recyclable Material Collector	Lansing-East Lansing MSA, MI	H	9.44 FQ	12.93 AW	16.83 TQ	MIBLS	10/01-12/01
	Saginaw-Bay City-Midland MSA, MI	H	11.58 FQ	13.37 AW	16.51 TQ	MIBLS	10/01-12/01
	Minnesota	H	9.80 FQ	14.30 AW	20.49 TQ	MNBLS	10/01-12/01
	Duluth-Superior MSA, MN-WI	H	11.13 FQ	13.55 AW	17.72 TQ	MNBLS	10/01-12/01
	Minneapolis-St. Paul MSA, MN-WI	H	9.87 FQ	14.91 AW	21.28 TQ	MNBLS	10/01-12/01
	St. Cloud MSA, MN	H	8.97 FQ	13.24 AW	17.42 TQ	MNBLS	10/01-12/01
	Mississippi	H	6.00 FQ	8.72 AW	11.75 TQ	MSBLS	10/01-12/01
	Biloxi-Gulfport-Pascagoula MSA, MS	H	8.56 FQ	9.61 AW	11.09 TQ	MSBLS	10/01-12/01
	Missouri	H	7.91 FQ	11.91 AW	18.93 TQ	MOBLS	10/01-12/01
	Kansas City MSA, MO-KS	H	7.22 FQ	13.68 AW	22.68 TQ	MOBLS	10/01-12/01
	St. Louis MSA, MO-IL	H	8.87 FQ	12.61 AW	20.33 TQ	MOBLS	10/01-12/01
	Springfield MSA, MO	H	8.30 FQ	13.76 AW	21.27 TQ	MOBLS	10/01-12/01
	Montana	H	6.23 FQ	11.61 AW	16.10 TQ	MTBLS	10/01-12/01
	Billings MSA, MT	H	8.30 FQ	12.17 AW	15.73 TQ	MTBLS	10/01-12/01
	Nebraska	H	6.17 FQ	9.04 AW	12.31 TQ	NEBLS	10/01-12/01
	Lincoln MSA, NE	H	8.86 FQ	12.17 AW	17.39 TQ	NEBLS	10/01-12/01
	Nevada	H	6.61 FQ	11.98 AW	17.18 TQ	NVBLS	10/01-12/01
	Las Vegas MSA, NV-AZ	H	6.14 FQ	10.87 AW	16.50 TQ	NVBLS	10/01-12/01
	Reno MSA, NV	H	10.85 FQ	14.87 AW	18.62 TQ	NVBLS	10/01-12/01
	New Hampshire	H	7.65 FQ	13.13 AW	21.24 TQ	NHBLS	10/01-12/01
	Portsmouth-Rochester PMSA, NH-ME	H	9.69 FQ	15.47 AW	22.24 TQ	NHBLS	10/01-12/01
	New Jersey	H	6.71 FQ	14.53 AW	22.04 TQ	NJBLS	10/01-12/01
	Atlantic-Cape May PMSA, NJ	H	6.03 FQ	11.79 AW	17.85 TQ	NJBLS	10/01-12/01
	Bergen-Passaic PMSA, NJ	H	7.99 FQ	15.04 AW	25.23 TQ	NJBLS	10/01-12/01
	Jersey City PMSA, NJ	H	8.19 FQ	13.24 AW	17.55 TQ	NJBLS	10/01-12/01
	Middlesex-Somerset-Hunterdon PMSA, NJ	H	9.70 FQ	15.46 AW	21.94 TQ	NJBLS	10/01-12/01
	Monmouth-Ocean PMSA, NJ	H	9.27 FQ	15.23 AW	21.89 TQ	NJBLS	10/01-12/01
	Newark PMSA, NJ	H	5.69 FQ	12.42 AW	21.17 TQ	NJBLS	10/01-12/01
	Trenton PMSA, NJ	H	12.27 FQ	18.56 AW	22.39 TQ	NJBLS	10/01-12/01
	New Mexico	H	6.74 FQ	10.27 AW	14.25 TQ	NMBLS	10/01-12/01
	Albuquerque MSA, NM	H	8.94 FQ	12.62 AW	16.78 TQ	NMBLS	10/01-12/01
	New York	H	11.66 FQ	17.92 AW	23.18 TQ	NYBLS	10/01-12/01
	Albany-Schenectady-Troy MSA, NY	H	9.83 FQ	13.22 AW	16.94 TQ	NYBLS	10/01-12/01
	Binghamton MSA, NY	H	7.41 FQ	10.06 AW	14.15 TQ	NYBLS	10/01-12/01
	Buffalo-Niagara Falls MSA, NY	H	9.93 FQ	14.07 AW	18.87 TQ	NYBLS	10/01-12/01
	Dutchess County PMSA, NY	H	7.96 FQ	11.67 AW	15.21 TQ	NYBLS	10/01-12/01
	Nassau-Suffolk PMSA, NY	H	11.80 FQ	18.28 AW	26.08 TQ	NYBLS	10/01-12/01
	Newburgh PMSA, NY-PA	H	7.36 FQ	13.05 AW	16.90 TQ	NYBLS	10/01-12/01
	Rochester MSA, NY	H	6.41 FQ	11.89 AW	16.85 TQ	NYBLS	10/01-12/01
	Syracuse MSA, NY	H	9.65 FQ	13.49 AW	20.23 TQ	NYBLS	10/01-12/01
	Utica-Rome MSA, NY	H	5.79 FQ	11.28 AW	15.27 TQ	NYBLS	10/01-12/01
	North Carolina	H	7.15 FQ	9.68 AW	13.39 TQ	NCBLS	10/01-12/01
	Asheville MSA, NC	H	7.26 FQ	9.71 AW	12.25 TQ	NCBLS	10/01-12/01
	Charlotte-Gastonia-Rock Hill MSA, NC-SC	H	7.23 FQ	9.20 AW	11.76 TQ	NCBLS	10/01-12/01
	Fayetteville MSA, NC	H	7.48 FQ	8.72 AW	10.94 TQ	NCBLS	10/01-12/01
	Greensboro-Winston-Salem-High Point MSA, NC	H	7.43 FQ	11.11 AW	16.09 TQ	NCBLS	10/01-12/01
	Hickory-Morganton-Lenoir MSA, NC	H	6.98 FQ	10.22 AW	13.97 TQ	NCBLS	10/01-12/01
	Raleigh-Durham-Chapel Hill MSA, NC	H	8.13 FQ	11.68 AW	16.34 TQ	NCBLS	10/01-12/01
	Wilmington MSA, NC	H	9.13 FQ	11.55 AW	14.71 TQ	NCBLS	10/01-12/01
	North Dakota	H	6.54 FQ	10.37 AW	15.72 TQ	NDBLS	10/01-12/01
	Fargo-Moorhead MSA, ND-MN	H	10.38 FQ	13.70 AW	17.30 TQ	NDBLS	10/01-12/01
	Ohio	H	6.63 FQ	12.77 AW	17.73 TQ	OHBLS	10/01-12/01
	Akron PMSA, OH	H	8.63 FQ	12.98 AW	19.02 TQ	OHBLS	10/01-12/01
	Canton-Massillon MSA, OH	H	9.43 FQ	14.26 AW	20.03 TQ	OHBLS	10/01-12/01
	Cincinnati PMSA, OH-KY-IN	H	7.64 FQ	13.14 AW	18.73 TQ	OHBLS	10/01-12/01
	Cleveland-Lorain-Elyria PMSA, OH	H	9.69 FQ	14.11 AW	18.40 TQ	OHBLS	10/01-12/01
	Columbus MSA, OH	H	7.77 FQ	13.94 AW	18.09 TQ	OHBLS	10/01-12/01
	Dayton-Springfield MSA, OH	H	10.25 FQ	14.49 AW	19.96 TQ	OHBLS	10/01-12/01

AAW Average annual wage; **AE** Average entry wage; **AEX** Average experienced wage; **AO** Average offered; **AOH** Average offered, high; **AOL** Average offered, low; **APH** Average pay, high range; **APL** Average pay, low range; **ASH** Average starting, high; **ASL** Average starting, low; **AW** Average wage paid; **FQ** First quartile wage; **H** Hourly; **HI** Highest wage paid; **HR** High end range; **LR** Low end range; **M** Monthly; **MTC** Median total compensation; **MW** Median wage paid; **SQ** Second quartile wage; **S** Special: hourly and annual; **TQ** Third quartile wage; **W** Weekly; **Y** Yearly

Occupation/Type/Industry	Location	Per	Low	Mid	High	Source	Date
Refuse and Recyclable Material Collector	Toledo MSA, OH	H	10.43 FQ	13.69 AW	17.41 TQ	OHBLS	10/01-12/01
	Youngstown-Warren MSA, OH	H	7.51 FQ	12.01 AW	15.99 TQ	OHBLS	10/01-12/01
	Oklahoma	H	5.93 FQ	8.66 AW	12.82 TQ	OKBLS	10/01-12/01
	Oklahoma City MSA, OK	H	5.86 FQ	8.17 AW	12.78 TQ	OKBLS	10/01-12/01
	Tulsa MSA, OK	H	6.88 FQ	10.77 AW	16.44 TQ	OKBLS	10/01-12/01
	Oregon	H	9.74 FQ	14.49 AW	20.12 TQ	ORBLS	10/01-12/01
	Medford-Ashland MSA, OR	H	9.80 FQ	15.36 AW	18.11 TQ	ORBLS	10/01-12/01
	Portland-Vancouver PMSA, OR-WA	H	9.39 FQ	14.47 AW	20.27 TQ	ORBLS	10/01-12/01
	Salem PMSA, OR	H	9.85 FQ	15.52 AW	18.42 TQ	ORBLS	10/01-12/01
	Pennsylvania	H	7.54 FQ	13.06 AW	20.04 TQ	PABLS	10/01-12/01
	Allentown-Bethlehem-Easton MSA, PA	H	7.84 FQ	12.34 AW	18.78 TQ	PABLS	10/01-12/01
	Erie MSA, PA	H	9.54 FQ	11.04 AW	13.61 TQ	PABLS	10/01-12/01
	Harrisburg-Lebanon-Carlisle MSA, PA	H	6.27 FQ	10.07 AW	15.27 TQ	PABLS	10/01-12/01
	Johnstown MSA, PA	H	8.14 FQ	11.54 AW	15.14 TQ	PABLS	10/01-12/01
	Philadelphia PMSA, PA-NJ	H	7.03 FQ	14.67 AW	22.30 TQ	PABLS	10/01-12/01
	Pittsburgh MSA, PA	H	9.30 FQ	14.82 AW	21.37 TQ	PABLS	10/01-12/01
	Reading MSA, PA	H	10.33 FQ	14.40 AW	19.06 TQ	PABLS	10/01-12/01
	Scranton-Wilkes-Barre-Hazleton MSA, PA	H	6.76 FQ	11.21 AW	16.81 TQ	PABLS	10/01-12/01
	Rhode Island	H	10.07 FQ	15.39 AW	19.74 TQ	RIBLS	10/01-12/01
	Providence-Fall River-Warwick MSA, RI-MA	H	10.06 FQ	15.11 AW	19.19 TQ	RIBLS	10/01-12/01
	South Carolina	H	6.15 FQ	9.26 AW	12.86 TQ	SCBLS	10/01-12/01
	Charleston-North Charleston MSA, SC	H	7.61 FQ	10.11 AW	13.19 TQ	SCBLS	10/01-12/01
	Columbia MSA, SC	H	6.05 FQ	9.14 AW	14.00 TQ	SCBLS	10/01-12/01
	Greenville-Spartanburg-Anderson MSA, SC	H	7.92 FQ	10.07 AW	12.45 TQ	SCBLS	10/01-12/01
	South Dakota	H	5.92 FQ	8.83 AW	12.61 TQ	SDBLS	10/01-12/01
	Tennessee	H	6.63 FQ	10.51 AW	14.29 TQ	TNBLS	10/01-12/01
	Chattanooga MSA, TN-GA	H	7.72 FQ	11.53 AW	16.40 TQ	TNBLS	10/01-12/01
	Johnson City-Kingsport-Bristol MSA, TN-VA	H	7.88 FQ	11.85 AW	17.11 TQ	TNBLS	10/01-12/01
	Knoxville MSA, TN	H	9.04 FQ	11.51 AW	13.85 TQ	TNBLS	10/01-12/01
	Memphis MSA, TN-AR-MS	H	6.48 FQ	9.94 AW	13.89 TQ	TNBLS	10/01-12/01
	Nashville MSA, TN	H	7.30 FQ	10.67 AW	14.04 TQ	TNBLS	10/01-12/01
	Texas	H	7.15 FQ	10.90 AW	15.74 TQ	TXBLS	10/01-12/01
	Beaumont-Port Arthur MSA, TX	H	5.50 FQ	9.64 AW	16.05 TQ	TXBLS	10/01-12/01
	Brownsville-Harlingen-San Benito MSA, TX	H	7.23 FQ	9.65 AW	13.28 TQ	TXBLS	10/01-12/01
	Corpus Christi MSA, TX	H	5.90 FQ	8.54 AW	14.78 TQ	TXBLS	10/01-12/01
	Dallas PMSA, TX	H	7.71 FQ	11.16 AW	15.70 TQ	TXBLS	10/01-12/01
	El Paso MSA, TX	H	5.77 FQ	9.40 AW	15.05 TQ	TXBLS	10/01-12/01
	Fort Worth-Arlington PMSA, TX	H	6.48 FQ	9.39 AW	12.71 TQ	TXBLS	10/01-12/01
	Houston PMSA, TX	H	7.82 FQ	11.82 AW	17.29 TQ	TXBLS	10/01-12/01
	Laredo MSA, TX	H	6.46 FQ	7.90 AW	9.55 TQ	TXBLS	10/01-12/01
	Lubbock MSA, TX	H	9.36 FQ	12.50 AW	19.10 TQ	TXBLS	10/01-12/01
	McAllen-Edinburg-Mission MSA, TX	H	7.51 FQ	10.09 AW	13.68 TQ	TXBLS	10/01-12/01
	Tyler MSA, TX	H	7.39 FQ	9.83 AW	12.89 TQ	TXBLS	10/01-12/01
	Utah	H	8.20 FQ	14.63 AW	22.55 TQ	UTBLS	10/01-12/01
	Salt Lake City-Ogden MSA, UT	H	8.11 FQ	15.32 AW	24.86 TQ	UTBLS	10/01-12/01
	Vermont	H	7.46 FQ	10.89 AW	14.13 TQ	VTBLS	10/01-12/01
	Virginia	H	6.70 FQ	11.00 AW	16.77 TQ	VABLS	10/01-12/01
	Lynchburg MSA, VA	H	9.20 FQ	12.19 AW	18.09 TQ	VABLS	10/01-12/01
	Norfolk-Virginia Beach-Newport News MSA, VA-NC	H	7.38 FQ	11.98 AW	17.26 TQ	VABLS	10/01-12/01
	Richmond-Petersburg MSA, VA	H	7.72 FQ	11.34 AW	16.31 TQ	VABLS	10/01-12/01
	Roanoke MSA, VA	H	7.73 FQ	10.03 AW	12.94 TQ	VABLS	10/01-12/01
	Washington	H	8.95 FQ	16.83 AW	23.00 TQ	WABLS	10/01-12/01
	Bremerton PMSA, WA	H	11.90 FQ	17.75 AW	22.44 TQ	WABLS	10/01-12/01
	Olympia PMSA, WA	H	12.18 FQ	17.27 AW	21.57 TQ	WABLS	10/01-12/01

AAW Average annual wage **AE** Average entry wage **AEX** Average experienced wage **AO** Average offered **AOH** Average offered, high **AOL** Average offered, low **APH** Average pay, high range **APL** Average pay, low range **ASH** Average starting, high **ASL** Average starting, low **AW** Average wage paid **FQ** First quartile wage **H** Hourly **HI** Highest wage paid **HR** High end range **LR** Low end range **M** Monthly **MTC** Median total compensation **MW** Median wage paid **SQ** Second quartile wage **S** Special: hourly and annual **TQ** Third quartile wage **W** Weekly **Y** Yearly

Occupation/Type/Industry	Location	Per	Low	Mid	High	Source	Date
Refuse and Recyclable Material Collector	Seattle-Bellevue-Everett PMSA, WA	H	9.19 FQ	19.55 AW	25.74 TQ	WABLS	10/01-12/01
	Tacoma PMSA, WA	H	13.56 FQ	18.72 AW	24.75 TQ	WABLS	10/01-12/01
	West Virginia	H	5.82 FQ	8.70 AW	12.51 TQ	WVBLS	10/01-12/01
	Charleston MSA, WV	H	5.98 FQ	8.59 AW	11.28 TQ	WVBLS	10/01-12/01
	Huntington-Ashland MSA, WV-KY-OH	H	7.01 FQ	9.83 AW	12.38 TQ	WVBLS	10/01-12/01
	Wisconsin	H	6.79 FQ	12.84 AW	17.68 TQ	WIBLS	10/01-12/01
	Appleton-Oshkosh-Neenah MSA, WI	H	10.95 FQ	14.36 AW	19.43 TQ	WIBLS	10/01-12/01
	Green Bay MSA, WI	H	14.73 FQ	16.94 AW	20.66 TQ	WIBLS	10/01-12/01
	Madison MSA, WI	H	11.30 FQ	15.37 AW	18.68 TQ	WIBLS	10/01-12/01
	Milwaukee-Waukesha PMSA, WI	H	5.89 FQ	13.08 AW	20.48 TQ	WIBLS	10/01-12/01
	Racine PMSA, WI	H	11.41 FQ	16.68 AW	21.44 TQ	WIBLS	10/01-12/01
	Wyoming	H	8.66 FQ	11.66 AW	16.02 TQ	WYBLS	10/01-12/01
	Puerto Rico	H	5.68 FQ	7.19 AW	9.99 TQ	PRBLS	10/01-12/01
	Virgin Islands	H	6.08 FQ	7.89 AW	10.05 TQ	VIBLS	10/01-12/01
Registered Nurse	United States	Y	39600 ASL	43500 AW	53000 ASH	USATOD3	1/01-1/02
	Alabama	Y	30410 FQ	42510 AW	56270 TQ	ALBLS	10/01-12/01
	Birmingham MSA, AL	Y	32940 FQ	45610 AW	57840 TQ	ALBLS	10/01-12/01
	Mobile MSA, AL	Y	31760 FQ	42390 AW	55000 TQ	ALBLS	10/01-12/01
	Montgomery MSA, AL	Y	31780 FQ	43280 AW	57370 TQ	ALBLS	10/01-12/01
	Alaska	Y	39150 FQ	54620 AW	72060 TQ	AKBLS	10/01-12/01
	Anchorage MSA, AK	Y	40980 FQ	56760 AW	73110 TQ	AKBLS	10/01-12/01
	Arizona	Y	35590 FQ	47480 AW	64160 TQ	AZBLS	10/01-12/01
	Phoenix-Mesa MSA, AZ	Y	36550 FQ	48750 AW	66310 TQ	AZBLS	10/01-12/01
	Tucson MSA, AZ	Y	33090 FQ	46220 AW	60710 TQ	AZBLS	10/01-12/01
	Arkansas	Y	27170 FQ	39630 AW	54720 TQ	ARBLS	10/01-12/01
	Fayetteville-Springdale-Rogers MSA, AR	Y	27610 FQ	38580 AW	50450 TQ	ARBLS	10/01-12/01
	Fort Smith MSA, AR-OK	Y	26910 FQ	38290 AW	53210 TQ	ARBLS	10/01-12/01
	Little Rock-North Little Rock MSA, AR	Y	29700 FQ	44440 AW	59960 TQ	ARBLS	10/01-12/01
	California	Y	41770 FQ	57940 AW	76400 TQ	CABLS	10/01-12/01
	Bakersfield MSA, CA	Y	42200 FQ	55960 AW	70930 TQ	CABLS	10/01-12/01
	Chico-Paradise MSA, CA	Y	39300 FQ	49080 AW	59560 TQ	CABLS	10/01-12/01
	Fresno MSA, CA	Y	39370 FQ	56760 AW	79250 TQ	CABLS	10/01-12/01
	Los Angeles-Long Beach PMSA, CA	Y	40880 FQ	55860 AW	71640 TQ	CABLS	10/01-12/01
	Merced MSA, CA	Y	33530 FQ	48940 AW	66480 TQ	CABLS	10/01-12/01
	Modesto MSA, CA	Y	41630 FQ	55940 AW	72210 TQ	CABLS	10/01-12/01
	Oakland PMSA, CA	Y	55600 FQ	71560 AW	91580 TQ	CABLS	10/01-12/01
	Orange County PMSA, CA	Y	40710 FQ	54220 AW	70140 TQ	CABLS	10/01-12/01
	Redding MSA, CA	Y	36900 FQ	48270 AW	66470 TQ	CABLS	10/01-12/01
	Riverside-San Bernardino PMSA, CA	Y	42510 FQ	57050 AW	73510 TQ	CABLS	10/01-12/01
	Sacramento PMSA, CA	Y	44780 FQ	58700 AW	76480 TQ	CABLS	10/01-12/01
	Salinas MSA, CA	Y	42490 FQ	60660 AW	84200 TQ	CABLS	10/01-12/01
	San Diego MSA, CA	Y	39650 FQ	54340 AW	71060 TQ	CABLS	10/01-12/01
	San Francisco PMSA, CA	Y	49180 FQ	66390 AW	87080 TQ	CABLS	10/01-12/01
	San Jose PMSA, CA	Y	48240 FQ	65750 AW	87800 TQ	CABLS	10/01-12/01
	San Luis Obispo-Atascadero-Paso Robles MSA, CA	Y	38800 FQ	50260 AW	60300 TQ	CABLS	10/01-12/01
	Santa Barbara-Santa Maria-Lompoc MSA, CA	Y	40960 FQ	51340 AW	63610 TQ	CABLS	10/01-12/01
	Santa Cruz-Watsonville PMSA, CA	Y	41490 FQ	56260 AW	71430 TQ	CABLS	10/01-12/01
	Santa Rosa PMSA, CA	Y	41830 FQ	57550 AW	73680 TQ	CABLS	10/01-12/01
	Stockton-Lodi MSA, CA	Y	45750 FQ	57520 AW	70160 TQ	CABLS	10/01-12/01
	Vallejo-Fairfield-Napa PMSA, CA	Y	43760 FQ	55400 AW	71570 TQ	CABLS	10/01-12/01
	Ventura PMSA, CA	Y	38330 FQ	56550 AW	77820 TQ	CABLS	10/01-12/01
	Visalia-Tulare-Porterville MSA, CA	Y	42340 FQ	55380 AW	70100 TQ	CABLS	10/01-12/01
	Colorado	Y	33980 FQ	47390 AW	62660 TQ	COBLS	10/01-12/01
	Boulder-Longmont PMSA, CO	Y	36700 FQ	47450 AW	58390 TQ	COBLS	10/01-12/01
	Colorado Springs MSA, CO	Y	29690 FQ	42570 AW	56150 TQ	COBLS	10/01-12/01
	Denver PMSA, CO	Y	36700 FQ	50400 AW	67460 TQ	COBLS	10/01-12/01

AAW Average annual wage · **AE** Average entry wage · **AEX** Average experienced wage · **AO** Average offered · **AOH** Average offered, high · **AOL** Average offered, low · **APH** Average pay, high range · **APL** Average pay, low range · **ASH** Average starting, high · **ASL** Average starting, low · **AW** Average wage paid · **FQ** First quartile wage · **H** Hourly · **HI** Highest wage paid · **HR** High end range · **LR** Low end range · **M** Monthly · **MTC** Median total compensation · **MW** Median wage paid · **SQ** Second quartile wage · **S** Special: hourly and annual · **TQ** Third quartile wage · **W** Weekly · **Y** Yearly

Occupation/Type/Industry	Location	Per	Low	Mid	High	Source	Date
Registered Nurse	Fort Collins-Loveland MSA, CO	Y	35050 FQ	45540 AW	57140 TQ	COBLS	10/01-12/01
	Greeley PMSA, CO	Y	32790 FQ	42430 AW	54680 TQ	COBLS	10/01-12/01
	Connecticut	Y	39450 FQ	53150 AW	69840 TQ	CTBLS	10/01-12/01
	Bridgeport PMSA, CT	Y	41420 FQ	53330 AW	69630 TQ	CTBLS	10/01-12/01
	Danbury PMSA, CT	Y	38420 FQ	54610 AW	69900 TQ	CTBLS	10/01-12/01
	Hartford MSA, CT	Y	39880 FQ	53700 AW	70170 TQ	CTBLS	10/01-12/01
	New Haven-Meriden PMSA, CT	Y	42800 FQ	56340 AW	72040 TQ	CTBLS	10/01-12/01
	New London-Norwich MSA, CT-RI	Y	38100 FQ	49980 AW	62590 TQ	CTBLS	10/01-12/01
	Stamford-Norwalk PMSA, CT	Y	38110 FQ	50560 AW	67320 TQ	CTBLS	10/01-12/01
	Waterbury PMSA, CT	Y	34750 FQ	48930 AW	61310 TQ	CTBLS	10/01-12/01
	Delaware	Y	38710 FQ	52860 AW	70620 TQ	DEBLS	10/01-12/01
	Wilmington-Newark PMSA, DE-MD	Y	39370 FQ	54200 AW	71130 TQ	DEBLS	10/01-12/01
	District of Columbia	Y	38160 FQ	53700 AW	71690 TQ	DCBLS	10/01-12/01
	Washington PMSA, DC-MD-VA-WV	Y	37270 FQ	55550 AW	76890 TQ	DCBLS	10/01-12/01
	Florida	Y	33130 FQ	45370 AW	59010 TQ	FLBLS	10/01-12/01
	Daytona Beach MSA, FL	Y	19970 FQ	37840 AW	53430 TQ	FLBLS	10/01-12/01
	Fort Lauderdale PMSA, FL	Y	35490 FQ	47030 AW	60020 TQ	FLBLS	10/01-12/01
	Fort Myers-Cape Coral MSA, FL	Y	31980 FQ	41560 AW	53480 TQ	FLBLS	10/01-12/01
	Fort Pierce-Port St. Lucie MSA, FL	Y	32480 FQ	45370 AW	59970 TQ	FLBLS	10/01-12/01
	Fort Walton Beach MSA, FL	Y	29480 FQ	37730 AW	45690 TQ	FLBLS	10/01-12/01
	Gainesville MSA, FL	Y	33280 FQ	46220 AW	61090 TQ	FLBLS	10/01-12/01
	Jacksonville MSA, FL	Y	34520 FQ	46790 AW	64600 TQ	FLBLS	10/01-12/01
	Lakeland-Winter Haven MSA, FL	Y	33350 FQ	43720 AW	56840 TQ	FLBLS	10/01-12/01
	Melbourne-Titusville-Palm Bay MSA, FL	Y	31750 FQ	43020 AW	56640 TQ	FLBLS	10/01-12/01
	Miami PMSA, FL	Y	37720 FQ	49710 AW	64250 TQ	FLBLS	10/01-12/01
	Ocala MSA, FL	Y	31580 FQ	43220 AW	55360 TQ	FLBLS	10/01-12/01
	Orlando MSA, FL	Y	33590 FQ	44350 AW	56750 TQ	FLBLS	10/01-12/01
	Pensacola MSA, FL	Y	28840 FQ	42390 AW	59120 TQ	FLBLS	10/01-12/01
	Sarasota-Bradenton MSA, FL	Y	32940 FQ	43730 AW	55620 TQ	FLBLS	10/01-12/01
	Tallahassee MSA, FL	Y	32450 FQ	53130 AW	100870 TQ	FLBLS	10/01-12/01
	Tampa-St. Petersburg-Clearwater MSA, FL	Y	32720 FQ	43850 AW	55750 TQ	FLBLS	10/01-12/01
	West Palm Beach-Boca Raton MSA, FL	Y	35780 FQ	47480 AW	59910 TQ	FLBLS	10/01-12/01
	Georgia	Y	32870 FQ	45420 AW	58300 TQ	GABLS	10/01-12/01
	Atlanta MSA, GA	Y	34570 FQ	47340 AW	60100 TQ	GABLS	10/01-12/01
	Augusta-Aiken MSA, GA-SC	Y	34040 FQ	46030 AW	57840 TQ	GABLS	10/01-12/01
	Columbus MSA, GA-AL	Y	36370 FQ	46380 AW	59020 TQ	GABLS	10/01-12/01
	Macon MSA, GA	Y	31930 FQ	43340 AW	56170 TQ	GABLS	10/01-12/01
	Savannah MSA, GA	Y	32260 FQ	45250 AW	62180 TQ	GABLS	10/01-12/01
	Hawaii	Y	41950 FQ	56370 AW	70960 TQ	HIBLS	10/01-12/01
	Honolulu MSA, HI	Y	43630 FQ	57670 AW	71270 TQ	HIBLS	10/01-12/01
	Idaho	Y	32290 FQ	44990 AW	57330 TQ	IDBLS	10/01-12/01
	Boise City MSA, ID	Y	35720 FQ	47410 AW	58150 TQ	IDBLS	10/01-12/01
	Illinois	Y	31710 FQ	46840 AW	63820 TQ	ILBLS	10/01-12/01
	Champaign-Urbana MSA, IL	Y	27060 FQ	39870 AW	57120 TQ	ILBLS	10/01-12/01
	Chicago PMSA, IL	Y	35540 FQ	50190 AW	67740 TQ	ILBLS	10/01-12/01
	Peoria-Pekin MSA, IL	Y	31760 FQ	42360 AW	55890 TQ	ILBLS	10/01-12/01
	Rockford MSA, IL	Y	31730 FQ	42040 AW	54490 TQ	ILBLS	10/01-12/01
	Springfield MSA, IL	Y	34480 FQ	45850 AW	57520 TQ	ILBLS	10/01-12/01
	Indiana	Y	30380 FQ	42350 AW	55930 TQ	INBLS	10/01-12/01
	Elkhart-Goshen MSA, IN	Y	35540 FQ	46650 AW	58660 TQ	INBLS	10/01-12/01
	Evansville-Henderson MSA, IN-KY	Y	30700 FQ	37930 AW	46200 TQ	INBLS	10/01-12/01
	Fort Wayne MSA, IN	Y	31340 FQ	41060 AW	53310 TQ	INBLS	10/01-12/01
	Gary PMSA, IN	Y	24770 FQ	38790 AW	53770 TQ	INBLS	10/01-12/01
	Indianapolis MSA, IN	Y	35440 FQ	46480 AW	58550 TQ	INBLS	10/01-12/01
	Lafayette MSA, IN	Y	32200 FQ	43290 AW	60250 TQ	INBLS	10/01-12/01
	South Bend MSA, IN	Y	32710 FQ	42250 AW	52880 TQ	INBLS	10/01-12/01
	Iowa	Y	29300 FQ	39130 AW	52390 TQ	IABLS	10/01-12/01
	Cedar Rapids MSA, IA	Y	29490 FQ	38960 AW	47540 TQ	IABLS	10/01-12/01
	Davenport-Moline-Rock Island MSA, IA-IL	Y	27590 FQ	36050 AW	48650 TQ	IABLS	10/01-12/01

AAW Average annual wage **AOH** Average offered, high **ASH** Average starting, high **H** Hourly **M** Monthly **S** Special: hourly and annual
AE Average entry wage **AOL** Average offered, low **ASL** Average starting, low **HI** Highest wage paid **MTC** Median total compensation **TQ** Third quartile wage
AEX Average experienced wage **APH** Average pay, high range **AW** Average wage paid **HR** High end range **MW** Median wage paid **W** Weekly
AO Average offered **APL** Average pay, low range **FQ** First quartile wage **LR** Low end range **SQ** Second quartile wage **Y** Yearly

Occupation/Type/Industry	Location	Per	Low	Mid	High	Source	Date
Registered Nurse	Des Moines MSA, IA	Y	31140 FQ	41690 AW	55690 TQ	IABLS	10/01-12/01
	Kansas	Y	29830 FQ	40330 AW	54140 TQ	KSBLS	10/01-12/01
	Topeka MSA, KS	Y	31730 FQ	41260 AW	52300 TQ	KSBLS	10/01-12/01
	Wichita MSA, KS	Y	29370 FQ	39350 AW	48500 TQ	KSBLS	10/01-12/01
	Kentucky	Y	30710 FQ	42200 AW	55930 TQ	KYBLS	10/01-12/01
	Lexington MSA, KY	Y	31500 FQ	42910 AW	56610 TQ	KYBLS	10/01-12/01
	Louisville MSA, KY-IN	Y	33700 FQ	45700 AW	57230 TQ	KYBLS	10/01-12/01
	Louisiana	Y	30850 FQ	44100 AW	57960 TQ	LABLS	10/01-12/01
	Baton Rouge MSA, LA	Y	31070 FQ	41370 AW	53160 TQ	LABLS	10/01-12/01
	Houma MSA, LA	Y	30720 FQ	42280 AW	56080 TQ	LABLS	10/01-12/01
	Lafayette MSA, LA	Y	32230 FQ	44010 AW	57290 TQ	LABLS	10/01-12/01
	Lake Charles MSA, LA	Y	22820 FQ	39640 AW	53190 TQ	LABLS	10/01-12/01
	New Orleans MSA, LA	Y	35080 FQ	47470 AW	61060 TQ	LABLS	10/01-12/01
	Shreveport-Bossier City MSA, LA	Y	26320 FQ	42420 AW	58650 TQ	LABLS	10/01-12/01
	Maine	Y	32380 FQ	45080 AW	59720 TQ	MEBLS	10/01-12/01
	Portland MSA, ME	Y	33000 FQ	46330 AW	65620 TQ	MEBLS	10/01-12/01
	Maryland	Y	37830 FQ	56770 AW	75790 TQ	MDBLS	10/01-12/01
	Baltimore PMSA, MD	Y	38060 FQ	56190 AW	73060 TQ	MDBLS	10/01-12/01
	Massachusetts	Y	36780 FQ	52550 AW	73500 TQ	MABLS	10/01-12/01
	Boston PMSA, MA-NH	Y	36910 FQ	54700 AW	76990 TQ	MABLS	10/01-12/01
	Brockton PMSA, MA	Y	34630 FQ	48730 AW	63380 TQ	MABLS	10/01-12/01
	Lawrence PMSA, MA-NH	Y	35880 FQ	46780 AW	57550 TQ	MABLS	10/01-12/01
	Lowell PMSA, MA-NH	Y	37120 FQ	51610 AW	68870 TQ	MABLS	10/01-12/01
	New Bedford PMSA, MA	Y	36960 FQ	47220 AW	67430 TQ	MABLS	10/01-12/01
	Springfield MSA, MA	Y	37250 FQ	50350 AW	67470 TQ	MABLS	10/01-12/01
	Worcester PMSA, MA-CT	Y	38240 FQ	50040 AW	65100 TQ	MABLS	10/01-12/01
	Michigan	Y	36250 FQ	48510 AW	59700 TQ	MIBLS	10/01-12/01
	Ann Arbor PMSA, MI	Y	30850 FQ	43200 AW	55720 TQ	MIBLS	10/01-12/01
	Detroit PMSA, MI	Y	40070 FQ	52180 AW	61210 TQ	MIBLS	10/01-12/01
	Flint PMSA, MI	Y	39140 FQ	54770 AW	95350 TQ	MIBLS	10/01-12/01
	Grand Rapids-Muskegon-Holland MSA, MI	Y	37190 FQ	46760 AW	57670 TQ	MIBLS	10/01-12/01
	Kalamazoo-Battle Creek MSA, MI	Y	35410 FQ	47030 AW	57360 TQ	MIBLS	10/01-12/01
	Lansing-East Lansing MSA, MI	Y	37650 FQ	44840 AW	56110 TQ	MIBLS	10/01-12/01
	Saginaw-Bay City-Midland MSA, MI	Y	36270 FQ	46400 AW	57440 TQ	MIBLS	10/01-12/01
	Minnesota	Y	37190 FQ	50360 AW	67220 TQ	MNBLS	10/01-12/01
	Duluth-Superior MSA, MN-WI	Y	34440 FQ	43880 AW	55850 TQ	MNBLS	10/01-12/01
	Minneapolis-St. Paul MSA, MN-WI	Y	38380 FQ	52180 AW	69650 TQ	MNBLS	10/01-12/01
	Mississippi	Y	27590 FQ	41290 AW	57660 TQ	MSBLS	10/01-12/01
	Biloxi-Gulfport-Pascagoula MSA, MS	Y	29760 FQ	42830 AW	58270 TQ	MSBLS	10/01-12/01
	Jackson MSA, MS	Y	24770 FQ	40360 AW	58780 TQ	MSBLS	10/01-12/01
	Missouri	Y	30590 FQ	43350 AW	57410 TQ	MOBLS	10/01-12/01
	Kansas City MSA, MO-KS	Y	32630 FQ	46140 AW	60770 TQ	MOBLS	10/01-12/01
	St. Louis MSA, MO-IL	Y	31530 FQ	43940 AW	57580 TQ	MOBLS	10/01-12/01
	Springfield MSA, MO	Y	29040 FQ	39280 AW	52040 TQ	MOBLS	10/01-12/01
	Montana	Y	30290 FQ	40360 AW	53070 TQ	MTBLS	10/01-12/01
	Billings MSA, MT	Y	30700 FQ	39790 AW	52260 TQ	MTBLS	10/01-12/01
	Nebraska	Y	30230 FQ	41250 AW	54670 TQ	NEBLS	10/01-12/01
	Lincoln MSA, NE	Y	30820 FQ	42040 AW	55880 TQ	NEBLS	10/01-12/01
	Omaha MSA, NE-IA	Y	31430 FQ	43340 AW	55770 TQ	NEBLS	10/01-12/01
	Nevada	Y	38430 FQ	52860 AW	69910 TQ	NVBLS	10/01-12/01
	Las Vegas MSA, NV-AZ	Y	39130 FQ	52340 AW	67870 TQ	NVBLS	10/01-12/01
	Reno MSA, NV	Y	36700 FQ	55020 AW	81720 TQ	NVBLS	10/01-12/01
	New Hampshire	Y	31610 FQ	44400 AW	57560 TQ	NHBLS	10/01-12/01
	Manchester PMSA, NH	Y	34560 FQ	46520 AW	59290 TQ	NHBLS	10/01-12/01
	Nashua PMSA, NH	Y	33100 FQ	46050 AW	60750 TQ	NHBLS	10/01-12/01
	Portsmouth-Rochester PMSA, NH-ME	Y	32470 FQ	48290 AW	60510 TQ	NHBLS	10/01-12/01
	New Jersey	Y	40110 FQ	53870 AW	70350 TQ	NJBLS	10/01-12/01
	Atlantic-Cape May PMSA, NJ	Y	39690 FQ	51620 AW	61630 TQ	NJBLS	10/01-12/01
	Bergen-Passaic PMSA, NJ	Y	40310 FQ	57510 AW	75140 TQ	NJBLS	10/01-12/01
	Jersey City PMSA, NJ	Y	42140 FQ	53910 AW	68500 TQ	NJBLS	10/01-12/01
	Middlesex-Somerset-Hunterdon PMSA, NJ	Y	42280 FQ	53150 AW	67200 TQ	NJBLS	10/01-12/01
	Monmouth-Ocean PMSA, NJ	Y	40000 FQ	53340 AW	69330 TQ	NJBLS	10/01-12/01
	Newark PMSA, NJ	Y	39940 FQ	53460 AW	69620 TQ	NJBLS	10/01-12/01
	Trenton PMSA, NJ	Y	39020 FQ	53450 AW	70230 TQ	NJBLS	10/01-12/01

AAW Average annual wage; **AE** Average entry wage; **AEX** Average experienced wage; **AO** Average offered; **AOH** Average offered, high; **AOL** Average offered, low; **APH** Average pay, high range; **APL** Average pay, low range; **ASH** Average starting, high; **ASL** Average starting, low; **AW** Average wage paid; **FQ** First quartile wage; **H** Hourly; **HI** Highest wage paid; **HR** High end range; **LR** Low end range; **M** Monthly; **MTC** Median total compensation; **MW** Median wage paid; **SQ** Second quartile wage; **S** Special: hourly and annual; **TQ** Third quartile wage; **W** Weekly; **Y** Yearly

Occupation/Type/Industry	Location	Per	Low	Mid	High	Source	Date
Registered Nurse	New Mexico	Y	32390 FQ	45220 AW	58530 TQ	NMBLS	10/01-12/01
	Albuquerque MSA, NM	Y	36070 FQ	47990 AW	60620 TQ	NMBLS	10/01-12/01
	Las Cruces MSA, NM	Y	31950 FQ	42900 AW	57610 TQ	NMBLS	10/01-12/01
	New York	Y	33830 FQ	53470 AW	76690 TQ	NYBLS	10/01-12/01
	Albany-Schenectady-Troy MSA, NY	Y	31590 FQ	44240 AW	58620 TQ	NYBLS	10/01-12/01
	Binghamton MSA, NY	Y	29140 FQ	40470 AW	57820 TQ	NYBLS	10/01-12/01
	Buffalo-Niagara Falls MSA, NY	Y	30240 FQ	43960 AW	59360 TQ	NYBLS	10/01-12/01
	Dutchess County PMSA, NY	Y	29000 FQ	42880 AW	56950 TQ	NYBLS	10/01-12/01
	Nassau-Suffolk PMSA, NY	Y	37210 FQ	57670 AW	77850 TQ	NYBLS	10/01-12/01
	New York PMSA, NY	Y	45120 FQ	60940 AW	84400 TQ	NYBLS	10/01-12/01
	Newburgh PMSA, NY-PA	Y	35940 FQ	50580 AW	68020 TQ	NYBLS	10/01-12/01
	Rochester MSA, NY	Y	30730 FQ	42650 AW	56230 TQ	NYBLS	10/01-12/01
	Syracuse MSA, NY	Y	29030 FQ	41050 AW	56770 TQ	NYBLS	10/01-12/01
	Utica-Rome MSA, NY	Y	31030 FQ	41970 AW	54590 TQ	NYBLS	10/01-12/01
	North Carolina	Y	33230 FQ	45090 AW	57330 TQ	NCBLS	10/01-12/01
	Asheville MSA, NC	Y	31750 FQ	46930 AW	67030 TQ	NCBLS	10/01-12/01
	Charlotte-Gastonia-Rock Hill MSA, NC-SC	Y	33610 FQ	45760 AW	58650 TQ	NCBLS	10/01-12/01
	Fayetteville MSA, NC	Y	34110 FQ	45160 AW	57220 TQ	NCBLS	10/01-12/01
	Greensboro-Winston-Salem-High Point MSA, NC	Y	35000 FQ	45340 AW	57210 TQ	NCBLS	10/01-12/01
	Hickory-Morganton-Lenoir MSA, NC	Y	34050 FQ	46230 AW	57620 TQ	NCBLS	10/01-12/01
	Raleigh-Durham-Chapel Hill MSA, NC	Y	35020 FQ	47090 AW	58430 TQ	NCBLS	10/01-12/01
	North Dakota	Y	30490 FQ	41760 AW	55710 TQ	NDBLS	10/01-12/01
	Fargo-Moorhead MSA, ND-MN	Y	31900 FQ	43210 AW	57040 TQ	NDBLS	10/01-12/01
	Ohio	Y	33430 FQ	45300 AW	58080 TQ	OHBLS	10/01-12/01
	Akron PMSA, OH	Y	33300 FQ	47350 AW	58820 TQ	OHBLS	10/01-12/01
	Canton-Massillon MSA, OH	Y	33360 FQ	44750 AW	56820 TQ	OHBLS	10/01-12/01
	Cincinnati PMSA, OH-KY-IN	Y	34020 FQ	45340 AW	57590 TQ	OHBLS	10/01-12/01
	Cleveland-Lorain-Elyria PMSA, OH	Y	38730 FQ	49090 AW	61010 TQ	OHBLS	10/01-12/01
	Columbus MSA, OH	Y	32870 FQ	45330 AW	58590 TQ	OHBLS	10/01-12/01
	Dayton-Springfield MSA, OH	Y	33400 FQ	44550 AW	56710 TQ	OHBLS	10/01-12/01
	Hamilton-Middletown PMSA, OH	Y	32990 FQ	42940 AW	54600 TQ	OHBLS	10/01-12/01
	Toledo MSA, OH	Y	34850 FQ	43930 AW	54680 TQ	OHBLS	10/01-12/01
	Youngstown-Warren MSA, OH	Y	32530 FQ	43650 AW	55400 TQ	OHBLS	10/01-12/01
	Oklahoma	Y	30440 FQ	41740 AW	55490 TQ	OKBLS	10/01-12/01
	Oklahoma City MSA, OK	Y	30570 FQ	42250 AW	56050 TQ	OKBLS	10/01-12/01
	Tulsa MSA, OK	Y	31070 FQ	43190 AW	56530 TQ	OKBLS	10/01-12/01
	Oregon	Y	37980 FQ	50610 AW	65550 TQ	ORBLS	10/01-12/01
	Medford-Ashland MSA, OR	Y	36390 FQ	47010 AW	60090 TQ	ORBLS	10/01-12/01
	Portland-Vancouver PMSA, OR-WA	Y	40070 FQ	52550 AW	67650 TQ	ORBLS	10/01-12/01
	Salem PMSA, OR	Y	39850 FQ	49660 AW	59200 TQ	ORBLS	10/01-12/01
	Pennsylvania	Y	32500 FQ	46430 AW	60540 TQ	PABLS	10/01-12/01
	Allentown-Bethlehem-Easton MSA, PA	Y	37300 FQ	54110 AW	70520 TQ	PABLS	10/01-12/01
	Erie MSA, PA	Y	30070 FQ	38210 AW	50050 TQ	PABLS	10/01-12/01
	Harrisburg-Lebanon-Carlisle MSA, PA	Y	34080 FQ	45980 AW	57580 TQ	PABLS	10/01-12/01
	Johnstown MSA, PA	Y	29240 FQ	40580 AW	52220 TQ	PABLS	10/01-12/01
	Lancaster MSA, PA	Y	30680 FQ	43280 AW	56410 TQ	PABLS	10/01-12/01
	Philadelphia PMSA, PA-NJ	Y	38870 FQ	51780 AW	67760 TQ	PABLS	10/01-12/01
	Pittsburgh MSA, PA	Y	31420 FQ	43320 AW	57890 TQ	PABLS	10/01-12/01
	Reading MSA, PA	Y	28530 FQ	44450 AW	56370 TQ	PABLS	10/01-12/01
	Scranton-Wilkes-Barre-Hazleton MSA, PA	Y	29740 FQ	39730 AW	52030 TQ	PABLS	10/01-12/01
	York MSA, PA	Y	32580 FQ	49140 AW	78050 TQ	PABLS	10/01-12/01
	Rhode Island	Y	38060 FQ	50550 AW	66530 TQ	RIBLS	10/01-12/01
	Providence-Fall River-Warwick MSA, RI-MA	Y	37010 FQ	49320 AW	65590 TQ	RIBLS	10/01-12/01
	South Carolina	Y	32500 FQ	46960 AW	65830 TQ	SCBLS	10/01-12/01
	Charleston-North Charleston MSA, SC	Y	31450 FQ	48020 AW	71080 TQ	SCBLS	10/01-12/01
	Columbia MSA, SC	Y	32610 FQ	45340 AW	60530 TQ	SCBLS	10/01-12/01

AAW	Average annual wage	**AOH**	Average offered, high	**ASH**	Average starting, high	**H**	Hourly	**M**	Monthly	**S**	Special: hourly and annual
AE	Average entry wage	**AOL**	Average offered, low	**ASL**	Average starting, low	**HI**	Highest wage paid	**MTC**	Median total compensation	**TQ**	Third quartile wage
AEX	Average experienced wage	**APH**	Average pay, high range	**AW**	Average wage paid	**HR**	High end range	**MW**	Median wage paid	**W**	Weekly
AO	Average offered	**APL**	Average pay, low range	**FQ**	First quartile wage	**LR**	Low end range	**SQ**	Second quartile wage	**Y**	Yearly

Occupation/Type/Industry	Location	Per	Low	Mid	High	Source	Date
Registered Nurse	Greenville-Spartanburg-Anderson MSA, SC	Y	33900 FQ	50120 AW	69930 TQ	SCBLS	10/01-12/01
	Myrtle Beach MSA, SC	Y	30190 FQ	40500 AW	54260 TQ	SCBLS	10/01-12/01
	South Dakota	Y	29880 FQ	39630 AW	53010 TQ	SDBLS	10/01-12/01
	Sioux Falls MSA, SD	Y	30960 FQ	41590 AW	54960 TQ	SDBLS	10/01-12/01
	Tennessee	Y	31570 FQ	46130 AW	63800 TQ	TNBLS	10/01-12/01
	Chattanooga MSA, TN-GA	Y	31350 FQ	42460 AW	54350 TQ	TNBLS	10/01-12/01
	Clarksville-Hopkinsville MSA, TN-KY	Y	30740 FQ	45590 AW	64250 TQ	TNBLS	10/01-12/01
	Johnson City-Kingsport-Bristol MSA, TN-VA	Y	27210 FQ	41640 AW	55410 TQ	TNBLS	10/01-12/01
	Knoxville MSA, TN	Y	31250 FQ	40780 AW	53080 TQ	TNBLS	10/01-12/01
	Memphis MSA, TN-AR-MS	Y	32440 FQ	43820 AW	55420 TQ	TNBLS	10/01-12/01
	Nashville MSA, TN	Y	34420 FQ	54380 AW	73080 TQ	TNBLS	10/01-12/01
	Texas	Y	33390 FQ	46360 AW	61340 TQ	TXBLS	10/01-12/01
	Amarillo MSA, TX	Y	31160 FQ	40810 AW	54500 TQ	TXBLS	10/01-12/01
	Austin-San Marcos MSA, TX	Y	33480 FQ	44910 AW	57760 TQ	TXBLS	10/01-12/01
	Beaumont-Port Arthur MSA, TX	Y	32540 FQ	42670 AW	55610 TQ	TXBLS	10/01-12/01
	Brazoria PMSA, TX	Y	31740 FQ	43090 AW	59210 TQ	TXBLS	10/01-12/01
	Brownsville-Harlingen-San Benito MSA, TX	Y	27660 FQ	44000 AW	60800 TQ	TXBLS	10/01-12/01
	Corpus Christi MSA, TX	Y	32210 FQ	43640 AW	58680 TQ	TXBLS	10/01-12/01
	Dallas PMSA, TX	Y	35830 FQ	47120 AW	62740 TQ	TXBLS	10/01-12/01
	El Paso MSA, TX	Y	30400 FQ	43270 AW	59940 TQ	TXBLS	10/01-12/01
	Fort Worth-Arlington PMSA, TX	Y	35740 FQ	48290 AW	66260 TQ	TXBLS	10/01-12/01
	Houston PMSA, TX	Y	37030 FQ	50900 AW	69040 TQ	TXBLS	10/01-12/01
	Killeen-Temple MSA, TX	Y	31920 FQ	42820 AW	56360 TQ	TXBLS	10/01-12/01
	Laredo MSA, TX	Y	20150 FQ	42330 AW	60150 TQ	TXBLS	10/01-12/01
	Longview-Marshall MSA, TX	Y	32350 FQ	41390 AW	52770 TQ	TXBLS	10/01-12/01
	Lubbock MSA, TX	Y	31980 FQ	44890 AW	59940 TQ	TXBLS	10/01-12/01
	McAllen-Edinburg-Mission MSA, TX	Y	37820 FQ	51790 AW	73400 TQ	TXBLS	10/01-12/01
	Odessa-Midland MSA, TX	Y	35670 FQ	45880 AW	56430 TQ	TXBLS	10/01-12/01
	San Antonio MSA, TX	Y	32390 FQ	45210 AW	61120 TQ	TXBLS	10/01-12/01
	Tyler MSA, TX	Y	32820 FQ	45500 AW	58780 TQ	TXBLS	10/01-12/01
	Waco MSA, TX	Y	31920 FQ	44740 AW	64580 TQ	TXBLS	10/01-12/01
	Utah	Y	34070 FQ	45760 AW	58820 TQ	UTBLS	10/01-12/01
	Provo-Orem MSA, UT	Y	33940 FQ	43640 AW	55950 TQ	UTBLS	10/01-12/01
	Salt Lake City-Ogden MSA, UT	Y	35700 FQ	47120 AW	59900 TQ	UTBLS	10/01-12/01
	Vermont	Y	32540 FQ	44160 AW	56950 TQ	VTBLS	10/01-12/01
	Virginia	Y	32220 FQ	46020 AW	62820 TQ	VABLS	10/01-12/01
	Lynchburg MSA, VA	Y	30550 FQ	42770 AW	59290 TQ	VABLS	10/01-12/01
	Norfolk-Virginia Beach-Newport News MSA, VA-NC	Y	32030 FQ	43930 AW	56560 TQ	VABLS	10/01-12/01
	Richmond-Petersburg MSA, VA	Y	33170 FQ	45910 AW	60860 TQ	VABLS	10/01-12/01
	Roanoke MSA, VA	Y	31670 FQ	43260 AW	57060 TQ	VABLS	10/01-12/01
	Washington	Y	38370 FQ	52200 AW	69520 TQ	WABLS	10/01-12/01
	Bremerton PMSA, WA	Y	39040 FQ	51340 AW	66860 TQ	WABLS	10/01-12/01
	Richland-Kennewick-Pasco MSA, WA	Y	36790 FQ	47010 AW	60220 TQ	WABLS	10/01-12/01
	Seattle-Bellevue-Everett PMSA, WA	Y	40590 FQ	55400 AW	71790 TQ	WABLS	10/01-12/01
	Spokane MSA, WA	Y	35580 FQ	46670 AW	57870 TQ	WABLS	10/01-12/01
	Tacoma PMSA, WA	Y	40690 FQ	54230 AW	69560 TQ	WABLS	10/01-12/01
	Yakima MSA, WA	Y	36110 FQ	47630 AW	62810 TQ	WABLS	10/01-12/01
	West Virginia	Y	29340 FQ	40620 AW	54170 TQ	WVBLS	10/01-12/01
	Charleston MSA, WV	Y	31570 FQ	47180 AW	88190 TQ	WVBLS	10/01-12/01
	Huntington-Ashland MSA, WV-KY-OH	Y	30490 FQ	41740 AW	56150 TQ	WVBLS	10/01-12/01
	Wisconsin	Y	35130 FQ	46750 AW	60890 TQ	WIBLS	10/01-12/01
	Appleton-Oshkosh-Neenah MSA, WI	Y	30690 FQ	41500 AW	54520 TQ	WIBLS	10/01-12/01
	Green Bay MSA, WI	Y	35040 FQ	45340 AW	57090 TQ	WIBLS	10/01-12/01
	Madison MSA, WI	Y	37470 FQ	48170 AW	61370 TQ	WIBLS	10/01-12/01
	Milwaukee-Waukesha PMSA, WI	Y	37070 FQ	49810 AW	67540 TQ	WIBLS	10/01-12/01
	Racine PMSA, WI	Y	36780 FQ	45350 AW	55780 TQ	WIBLS	10/01-12/01

AAW Average annual wage; **AE** Average entry wage; **AEX** Average experienced wage; **AO** Average offered; **AOH** Average offered, high; **AOL** Average offered, low; **APH** Average pay, high range; **APL** Average pay, low range; **ASH** Average starting, high; **ASL** Average starting, low; **AW** Average wage paid; **FQ** First quartile wage; **H** Hourly; **HI** Highest wage paid; **HR** High end range; **LR** Low end range; **M** Monthly; **MTC** Median total compensation; **MW** Median wage paid; **SQ** Second quartile wage; **S** Special: hourly and annual; **TQ** Third quartile wage; **W** Weekly; **Y** Yearly

Occupation/Type/Industry	Location	Per	Low	Mid	High	Source	Date
Registered Nurse	Wyoming	Y	28640 FQ	39590 AW	52350 TQ	WYBLS	10/01-12/01
	Cheyenne MSA, WY	Y	28870 FQ	39620 AW	50280 TQ	WYBLS	10/01-12/01
	Puerto Rico	Y	14560 FQ	21610 AW	30810 TQ	PRBLS	10/01-12/01
	Virgin Islands	Y	30420 FQ	42530 AW	57550 TQ	VIBLS	10/01-12/01
	Guam	Y	28140 FQ	39970 AW	53700 TQ	GUBLS	10/01-12/01
Rehabilitation Counselor	Alabama	Y	15460 FQ	27690 AW	45910 TQ	ALBLS	10/01-12/01
	Alaska	Y	24490 FQ	32290 AW	44450 TQ	AKBLS	10/01-12/01
	Arizona	Y	15890 FQ	26540 AW	42100 TQ	AZBLS	10/01-12/01
	Arkansas	Y	20110 FQ	32330 AW	50420 TQ	ARBLS	10/01-12/01
	California	Y	15740 FQ	29900 AW	47930 TQ	CABLS	10/01-12/01
	Colorado	Y	16220 FQ	26780 AW	47140 TQ	COBLS	10/01-12/01
	Connecticut	Y	22940 FQ	35110 AW	54760 TQ	CTBLS	10/01-12/01
	Delaware	Y	19390 FQ	27610 AW	35110 TQ	DEBLS	10/01-12/01
	District of Columbia	Y	15930 FQ	30040 AW	50330 TQ	DCBLS	10/01-12/01
	Florida	Y	16270 FQ	30930 AW	58390 TQ	FLBLS	10/01-12/01
	Georgia	Y	21890 FQ	33560 AW	49740 TQ	GABLS	10/01-12/01
	Hawaii	Y	16380 FQ	34980 AW	52500 TQ	HIBLS	10/01-12/01
	Idaho	Y	16610 FQ	32210 AW	47310 TQ	IDBLS	10/01-12/01
	Illinois	Y	15880 FQ	28070 AW	48130 TQ	ILBLS	10/01-12/01
	Indiana	Y	16660 FQ	26140 AW	35320 TQ	INBLS	10/01-12/01
	Iowa	Y	17070 FQ	26670 AW	39990 TQ	IABLS	10/01-12/01
	Kansas	Y	15160 FQ	21330 AW	30290 TQ	KSBLS	10/01-12/01
	Kentucky	Y	17110 FQ	28440 AW	47700 TQ	KYBLS	10/01-12/01
	Louisiana	Y	16270 FQ	29970 AW	43440 TQ	LABLS	10/01-12/01
	Maine	Y	18100 FQ	22990 AW	29630 TQ	MEBLS	10/01-12/01
	Maryland	Y	15440 FQ	21490 AW	28750 TQ	MDBLS	10/01-12/01
	Massachusetts	Y	18710 FQ	30550 AW	51440 TQ	MABLS	10/01-12/01
	Michigan	Y	19470 FQ	40650 AW	63520 TQ	MIBLS	10/01-12/01
	Minnesota	Y	18510 FQ	31360 AW	50000 TQ	MNBLS	10/01-12/01
	Mississippi	Y	23100 FQ	52340 AW	94260 TQ	MSBLS	10/01-12/01
	Montana	Y	13550 FQ	24780 AW	37200 TQ	MTBLS	10/01-12/01
	Nebraska	Y	16370 FQ	23690 AW	32750 TQ	NEBLS	10/01-12/01
	Nevada	Y	15390 FQ	28700 AW	51920 TQ	NVBLS	10/01-12/01
	New Hampshire	Y	16220 FQ	23470 AW	35850 TQ	NHBLS	10/01-12/01
	New Jersey	Y	17230 FQ	25520 AW	35630 TQ	NJBLS	10/01-12/01
	New Mexico	Y	13260 FQ	20570 AW	32560 TQ	NMBLS	10/01-12/01
	New York	Y	17770 FQ	30420 AW	44650 TQ	NYBLS	10/01-12/01
	North Carolina	Y	15610 FQ	25250 AW	38710 TQ	NCBLS	10/01-12/01
	North Dakota	Y	15990 FQ	23720 AW	33930 TQ	NDBLS	10/01-12/01
	Ohio	Y	21190 FQ	38770 AW	63460 TQ	OHBLS	10/01-12/01
	Oklahoma	Y	12550 FQ	18060 AW	25960 TQ	OKBLS	10/01-12/01
	Oregon	Y	18280 FQ	26150 AW	41410 TQ	ORBLS	10/01-12/01
	Pennsylvania	Y	17530 FQ	28570 AW	45700 TQ	PABLS	10/01-12/01
	Rhode Island	Y	17100 FQ	33310 AW	59830 TQ	RIBLS	10/01-12/01
	South Carolina	Y	15890 FQ	26120 AW	41140 TQ	SCBLS	10/01-12/01
	South Dakota	Y	20270 FQ	35190 AW	58640 TQ	SDBLS	10/01-12/01
	Tennessee	Y	15430 FQ	21630 AW	31640 TQ	TNBLS	10/01-12/01
	Texas	Y	15540 FQ	27840 AW	40350 TQ	TXBLS	10/01-12/01
	Utah	Y	15450 FQ	29090 AW	44800 TQ	UTBLS	10/01-12/01
	Vermont	Y	21490 FQ	31260 AW	41230 TQ	VTBLS	10/01-12/01
	Virginia	Y	18370 FQ	26990 AW	38800 TQ	VABLS	10/01-12/01
	Washington	Y	19320 FQ	29740 AW	44290 TQ	WABLS	10/01-12/01
	West Virginia	Y	17920 FQ	31200 AW	44950 TQ	WVBLS	10/01-12/01
	Wisconsin	Y	15400 FQ	25230 AW	42130 TQ	WIBLS	10/01-12/01
	Wyoming	Y	15410 FQ	25150 AW	43660 TQ	WYBLS	10/01-12/01
	Puerto Rico	Y	14290 FQ	26180 AW	43600 TQ	PRBLS	10/01-12/01
	Virgin Islands	Y	28860 FQ	45530 AW	65590 TQ	VIBLS	10/01-12/01
Reinforcing Iron and Rebar Worker	Alabama	H	9.29 FQ	14.18 AW	20.34 TQ	ALBLS	10/01-12/01
	Arizona	H	9.11 FQ	14.52 AW	20.74 TQ	AZBLS	10/01-12/01
	Arkansas	H	9.78 FQ	14.48 AW	19.85 TQ	ARBLS	10/01-12/01
	California	H	11.74 FQ	21.04 AW	31.51 TQ	CABLS	10/01-12/01
	Colorado	H	9.15 FQ	13.42 AW	21.22 TQ	COBLS	10/01-12/01
	Connecticut	H	16.19 FQ	23.07 AW	28.42 TQ	CTBLS	10/01-12/01
	Delaware	H	7.23 FQ	22.31 AW	28.60 TQ	DEBLS	10/01-12/01
	Florida	H	10.62 FQ	14.38 AW	18.13 TQ	FLBLS	10/01-12/01
	Georgia	H	11.67 FQ	15.45 AW	23.86 TQ	GABLS	10/01-12/01
	Idaho	H	11.56 FQ	15.58 AW	21.65 TQ	IDBLS	10/01-12/01
	Illinois	H	13.86 FQ	24.99 AW	33.93 TQ	ILBLS	10/01-12/01
	Indiana	H	12.87 FQ	23.41 AW	31.31 TQ	INBLS	10/01-12/01

AAW	Average annual wage	AOH	Average offered, high	ASH	Average starting, high	H	Hourly	M	Monthly	S	Special: hourly and annual
AE	Average entry wage	AOL	Average offered, low	ASL	Average starting, low	HI	Highest wage paid	MTC	Median total compensation	TQ	Third quartile wage
AEX	Average experienced wage	APH	Average pay, high range	AW	Average wage paid	HR	High end range	MW	Median wage paid	W	Weekly
AO	Average offered	APL	Average pay, low range	FQ	First quartile wage	LR	Low end range	SQ	Second quartile wage	Y	Yearly

Occupation/Type/Industry	Location	Per	Low	Mid	High	Source	Date
Reinforcing Iron and Rebar Worker	Iowa	H	11.24 FQ	17.23 AW	23.79 TQ	IABLS	10/01-12/01
	Kansas	H	9.11 FQ	16.52 AW	25.09 TQ	KSBLS	10/01-12/01
	Kentucky	H	14.94 FQ	21.48 AW	28.16 TQ	KYBLS	10/01-12/01
	Louisiana	H	9.63 FQ	15.20 AW	20.27 TQ	LABLS	10/01-12/01
	Maryland	H	14.70 FQ	21.54 AW	27.97 TQ	MDBLS	10/01-12/01
	Massachusetts	H	10.61 FQ	26.33 AW	42.22 TQ	MABLS	10/01-12/01
	Michigan	H	9.18 FQ	19.24 AW	27.71 TQ	MIBLS	10/01-12/01
	Minnesota	H	15.65 FQ	22.97 AW	27.97 TQ	MNBLS	10/01-12/01
	Mississippi	H	7.34 FQ	12.09 AW	17.32 TQ	MSBLS	10/01-12/01
	Missouri	H	10.13 FQ	21.72 AW	28.90 TQ	MOBLS	10/01-12/01
	Montana	H	18.67 FQ	21.62 AW	27.46 TQ	MTBLS	10/01-12/01
	Nebraska	H	6.54 FQ	13.66 AW	22.47 TQ	NEBLS	10/01-12/01
	Nevada	H	7.89 FQ	19.48 AW	29.45 TQ	NVBLS	10/01-12/01
	New Jersey	H	22.49 FQ	27.80 AW	34.04 TQ	NJBLS	10/01-12/01
	New Mexico	H	8.14 FQ	17.29 AW	27.52 TQ	NMBLS	10/01-12/01
	New York	H	14.19 FQ	28.15 AW	43.00 TQ	NYBLS	10/01-12/01
	North Carolina	H	8.49 FQ	13.91 AW	20.24 TQ	NCBLS	10/01-12/01
	North Dakota	H	10.21 FQ	15.27 AW	20.42 TQ	NDBLS	10/01-12/01
	Ohio	H	19.55 FQ	24.95 AW	32.38 TQ	OHBLS	10/01-12/01
	Oklahoma	H	10.18 FQ	16.29 AW	21.86 TQ	OKBLS	10/01-12/01
	Oregon	H	15.82 FQ	24.68 AW	30.10 TQ	ORBLS	10/01-12/01
	Pennsylvania	H	11.72 FQ	21.62 AW	32.53 TQ	PABLS	10/01-12/01
	Rhode Island	H	22.59 FQ	24.66 AW	27.81 TQ	RIBLS	10/01-12/01
	South Carolina	H	9.31 FQ	14.95 AW	20.99 TQ	SCBLS	10/01-12/01
	Tennessee	H	12.14 FQ	18.65 AW	25.13 TQ	TNBLS	10/01-12/01
	Texas	H	8.91 FQ	12.10 AW	16.91 TQ	TXBLS	10/01-12/01
	Utah	H	9.37 FQ	12.61 AW	16.58 TQ	UTBLS	10/01-12/01
	Virginia	H	11.88 FQ	17.51 AW	22.06 TQ	VABLS	10/01-12/01
	Washington	H	20.17 FQ	25.52 AW	32.03 TQ	WABLS	10/01-12/01
	West Virginia	H	17.89 FQ	23.74 AW	30.17 TQ	WVBLS	10/01-12/01
	Wisconsin	H	11.19 FQ	22.71 AW	28.92 TQ	WIBLS	10/01-12/01
	Puerto Rico	H	5.77 FQ	7.06 AW	8.37 TQ	PRBLS	10/01-12/01
	Guam	H	9.35 FQ	10.67 AW	12.87 TQ	GUBLS	10/01-12/01
Reliability Engineer							
Quality Control	United States	Y			123000 HI	ASQ	1/00-1/01
Research Manager							
Marketing, Medical	United States	Y		83000 AW		MM&M	1/01-1/02
Reservation and Transportation Ticket Agent and Travel Clerk	Alabama	H	8.92 FQ	13.36 AW	22.17 TQ	ALBLS	10/01-12/01
	Alaska	H	9.34 FQ	13.39 AW	20.49 TQ	AKBLS	10/01-12/01
	Arizona	H	7.54 FQ	11.51 AW	17.64 TQ	AZBLS	10/01-12/01
	California	H	8.36 FQ	13.52 AW	21.57 TQ	CABLS	10/01-12/01
	Colorado	H	8.73 FQ	12.58 AW	18.62 TQ	COBLS	10/01-12/01
	Connecticut	H	7.72 FQ	12.76 AW	21.28 TQ	CTBLS	10/01-12/01
	Delaware	H	7.94 FQ	13.98 AW	19.55 TQ	DEBLS	10/01-12/01
	District of Columbia	H	7.33 FQ	12.82 AW	20.13 TQ	DCBLS	10/01-12/01
	Florida	H	7.38 FQ	12.43 AW	21.81 TQ	FLBLS	10/01-12/01
	Hawaii	H	8.13 FQ	14.16 AW	21.61 TQ	HIBLS	10/01-12/01
	Idaho	H	7.65 FQ	11.56 AW	19.38 TQ	IDBLS	10/01-12/01
	Illinois	H	8.44 FQ	15.39 AW	21.84 TQ	ILBLS	10/01-12/01
	Indiana	H	7.52 FQ	12.10 AW	20.06 TQ	INBLS	10/01-12/01
	Iowa	H	7.21 FQ	11.64 AW	20.52 TQ	IABLS	10/01-12/01
	Kansas	H	7.09 FQ	10.41 AW	15.75 TQ	KSBLS	10/01-12/01
	Louisiana	H	7.18 FQ	12.76 AW	21.31 TQ	LABLS	10/01-12/01
	Maine	H	7.95 FQ	10.95 AW	14.55 TQ	MEBLS	10/01-12/01
	Maryland	H	8.53 FQ	11.87 AW	15.64 TQ	MDBLS	10/01-12/01
	Massachusetts	H	9.26 FQ	14.97 AW	24.27 TQ	MABLS	10/01-12/01
	Michigan	H	8.62 FQ	15.55 AW	22.15 TQ	MIBLS	10/01-12/01
	Minnesota	H	9.27 FQ	14.11 AW	20.87 TQ	MNBLS	10/01-12/01
	Mississippi	H	7.03 FQ	9.84 AW	14.65 TQ	MSBLS	10/01-12/01
	Missouri	H	7.61 FQ	11.70 AW	18.61 TQ	MOBLS	10/01-12/01
	Montana	H	7.27 FQ	12.34 AW	20.95 TQ	MTBLS	10/01-12/01
	Nevada	H	7.71 FQ	11.45 AW	15.84 TQ	NVBLS	10/01-12/01
	New Hampshire	H	7.24 FQ	11.69 AW	23.46 TQ	NHBLS	10/01-12/01
	New Jersey	H	7.46 FQ	11.96 AW	19.58 TQ	NJBLS	10/01-12/01
	New York	H	9.77 FQ	16.58 AW	22.52 TQ	NYBLS	10/01-12/01
	North Carolina	H	6.18 FQ	11.86 AW	19.74 TQ	NCBLS	10/01-12/01
	North Dakota	H	7.36 FQ	10.90 AW	19.06 TQ	NDBLS	10/01-12/01

AAW Average annual wage; **AE** Average entry wage; **AEX** Average experienced wage; **AO** Average offered; **AOH** Average offered, high; **AOL** Average offered, low; **APH** Average pay, high range; **APL** Average pay, low range; **ASH** Average starting, high; **ASL** Average starting, low; **AW** Average wage paid; **FQ** First quartile wage; **H** Hourly; **HI** Highest wage paid; **HR** High end range; **LR** Low end range; **M** Monthly; **MTC** Median total compensation; **MW** Median wage paid; **SQ** Second quartile wage; **S** Special: hourly and annual; **TQ** Third quartile wage; **W** Weekly; **Y** Yearly

Occupation/Type/Industry	Location	Per	Low	Mid	High	Source	Date
Reservation and Transportation Ticket Agent and Travel Clerk	Ohio	H	7.87 FQ	13.34 AW	20.56 TQ	OHBLS	10/01-12/01
	Oregon	H	7.73 FQ	10.82 AW	15.29 TQ	ORBLS	10/01-12/01
	Pennsylvania	H	7.78 FQ	13.81 AW	21.78 TQ	PABLS	10/01-12/01
	Rhode Island	H	8.18 FQ	14.78 AW	25.94 TQ	RIBLS	10/01-12/01
	South Carolina	H	8.01 FQ	12.03 AW	19.40 TQ	SCBLS	10/01-12/01
	Tennessee	H	7.78 FQ	14.27 AW	22.09 TQ	TNBLS	10/01-12/01
	Texas	H	7.89 FQ	12.36 AW	19.77 TQ	TXBLS	10/01-12/01
	Utah	H	7.57 FQ	12.72 AW	23.23 TQ	UTBLS	10/01-12/01
	Vermont	H	7.58 FQ	13.24 AW	21.68 TQ	VTBLS	10/01-12/01
	Virginia	H	8.33 FQ	14.41 AW	22.24 TQ	VABLS	10/01-12/01
	Washington	H	8.39 FQ	13.35 AW	20.85 TQ	WABLS	10/01-12/01
	West Virginia	H	7.74 FQ	10.06 AW	12.77 TQ	WVBLS	10/01-12/01
	Wisconsin	H	7.31 FQ	12.35 AW	20.27 TQ	WIBLS	10/01-12/01
	Wyoming	H	7.34 FQ	8.87 AW	11.07 TQ	WYBLS	10/01-12/01
	Puerto Rico	H	6.02 FQ	11.94 AW	21.19 TQ	PRBLS	10/01-12/01
	Virgin Islands	H	7.17 FQ	9.47 AW	12.14 TQ	VIBLS	10/01-12/01
	Guam	H	6.78 FQ	11.89 AW	17.99 TQ	GUBLS	10/01-12/01
Residential Advisor	Alabama	H	5.98 FQ	8.74 AW	12.82 TQ	ALBLS	10/01-12/01
	Alaska	H	9.37 FQ	15.07 AW	24.21 TQ	AKBLS	10/01-12/01
	Arizona	H	7.27 FQ	11.77 AW	17.40 TQ	AZBLS	10/01-12/01
	Arkansas	H	6.12 FQ	8.42 AW	10.88 TQ	ARBLS	10/01-12/01
	California	H	6.88 FQ	11.66 AW	16.92 TQ	CABLS	10/01-12/01
	Colorado	H	7.26 FQ	9.96 AW	13.75 TQ	COBLS	10/01-12/01
	Connecticut	H	9.48 FQ	12.78 AW	17.49 TQ	CTBLS	10/01-12/01
	Delaware	H	6.71 FQ	9.64 AW	13.99 TQ	DEBLS	10/01-12/01
	District of Columbia	H	7.67 FQ	9.86 AW	12.21 TQ	DCBLS	10/01-12/01
	Florida	H	6.59 FQ	9.39 AW	13.03 TQ	FLBLS	10/01-12/01
	Georgia	H	6.49 FQ	8.82 AW	11.45 TQ	GABLS	10/01-12/01
	Hawaii	H	6.65 FQ	12.06 AW	19.61 TQ	HIBLS	10/01-12/01
	Idaho	H	5.89 FQ	9.20 AW	12.73 TQ	IDBLS	10/01-12/01
	Illinois	H	6.81 FQ	12.97 AW	20.34 TQ	ILBLS	10/01-12/01
	Indiana	H	7.01 FQ	9.84 AW	13.31 TQ	INBLS	10/01-12/01
	Iowa	H	7.28 FQ	10.06 AW	13.53 TQ	IABLS	10/01-12/01
	Kansas	H	6.07 FQ	8.26 AW	11.22 TQ	KSBLS	10/01-12/01
	Kentucky	H	6.63 FQ	9.05 AW	12.06 TQ	KYBLS	10/01-12/01
	Louisiana	H	5.76 FQ	8.23 AW	11.19 TQ	LABLS	10/01-12/01
	Maine	H	6.43 FQ	9.99 AW	13.64 TQ	MEBLS	10/01-12/01
	Maryland	H	7.63 FQ	12.23 AW	19.02 TQ	MDBLS	10/01-12/01
	Massachusetts	H	8.60 FQ	10.83 AW	15.04 TQ	MABLS	10/01-12/01
	Michigan	H	8.10 FQ	13.12 AW	19.64 TQ	MIBLS	10/01-12/01
	Minnesota	H	9.07 FQ	12.98 AW	16.99 TQ	MNBLS	10/01-12/01
	Mississippi	H	6.52 FQ	9.37 AW	13.19 TQ	MSBLS	10/01-12/01
	Missouri	H	6.21 FQ	9.64 AW	13.92 TQ	MOBLS	10/01-12/01
	Montana	H	6.52 FQ	11.06 AW	16.69 TQ	MTBLS	10/01-12/01
	Nebraska	H	9.04 FQ	15.68 AW	21.07 TQ	NEBLS	10/01-12/01
	New Hampshire	H	6.59 FQ	9.72 AW	13.98 TQ	NHBLS	10/01-12/01
	New Jersey	H	8.68 FQ	13.05 AW	19.80 TQ	NJBLS	10/01-12/01
	New Mexico	H	7.00 FQ	9.89 AW	13.43 TQ	NMBLS	10/01-12/01
	New York	H	9.27 FQ	13.16 AW	17.74 TQ	NYBLS	10/01-12/01
	North Carolina	H	6.39 FQ	10.43 AW	14.95 TQ	NCBLS	10/01-12/01
	North Dakota	H	6.83 FQ	10.07 AW	13.13 TQ	NDBLS	10/01-12/01
	Ohio	H	7.01 FQ	9.91 AW	13.54 TQ	OHBLS	10/01-12/01
	Oklahoma	H	5.73 FQ	8.11 AW	10.97 TQ	OKBLS	10/01-12/01
	Oregon	H	7.52 FQ	10.36 AW	14.12 TQ	ORBLS	10/01-12/01
	Pennsylvania	H	7.05 FQ	9.03 AW	10.90 TQ	PABLS	10/01-12/01
	Rhode Island	H	6.85 FQ	12.91 AW	19.80 TQ	RIBLS	10/01-12/01
	South Carolina	H	7.41 FQ	11.86 AW	17.37 TQ	SCBLS	10/01-12/01
	South Dakota	H	6.94 FQ	8.47 AW	10.60 TQ	SDBLS	10/01-12/01
	Tennessee	H	5.83 FQ	9.13 AW	13.17 TQ	TNBLS	10/01-12/01
	Texas	H	6.18 FQ	9.62 AW	13.38 TQ	TXBLS	10/01-12/01
	Utah	H	7.10 FQ	9.28 AW	12.85 TQ	UTBLS	10/01-12/01
	Vermont	H	6.64 FQ	11.15 AW	16.52 TQ	VTBLS	10/01-12/01
	Virginia	H	6.40 FQ	10.72 AW	14.82 TQ	VABLS	10/01-12/01
	Washington	H	6.90 FQ	11.54 AW	17.69 TQ	WABLS	10/01-12/01
	West Virginia	H	5.93 FQ	10.16 AW	14.29 TQ	WVBLS	10/01-12/01
	Wisconsin	H	6.45 FQ	10.38 AW	15.39 TQ	WIBLS	10/01-12/01
	Wyoming	H	7.00 FQ	8.79 AW	11.75 TQ	WYBLS	10/01-12/01
	Puerto Rico	H	5.61 FQ	7.53 AW	10.45 TQ	PRBLS	10/01-12/01
Respiratory Therapist	Alabama	Y	25830 FQ	35260 AW	45030 TQ	ALBLS	10/01-12/01

AAW	Average annual wage	AOH	Average offered, high	ASH	Average starting, high	H	Hourly	M	Monthly	S	Special: hourly and annual
AE	Average entry wage	AOL	Average offered, low	ASL	Average starting, low	HI	Highest wage paid	MTC	Median total compensation	TQ	Third quartile wage
AEX	Average experienced wage	APH	Average pay, high range	AW	Average wage paid	HR	High end range	MW	Median wage paid	W	Weekly
AO	Average offered	APL	Average pay, low range	FQ	First quartile wage	LR	Low end range	SQ	Second quartile wage	Y	Yearly

Occupation/Type/Industry	Location	Per	Low	Mid	High	Source	Date
Respiratory Therapist	Alaska	Y	39400 FQ	47940 AW	57720 TQ	AKBLS	10/01-12/01
	Arizona	Y	28160 FQ	35740 AW	44800 TQ	AZBLS	10/01-12/01
	Arkansas	Y	24650 FQ	34290 AW	44830 TQ	ARBLS	10/01-12/01
	California	Y	33950 FQ	44940 AW	58820 TQ	CABLS	10/01-12/01
	Colorado	Y	29000 FQ	37650 AW	46340 TQ	COBLS	10/01-12/01
	Connecticut	Y	36990 FQ	45690 AW	56920 TQ	CTBLS	10/01-12/01
	Delaware	Y	32750 FQ	49320 AW	68490 TQ	DEBLS	10/01-12/01
	District of Columbia	Y	31780 FQ	48650 AW	80810 TQ	DCBLS	10/01-12/01
	Florida	Y	30540 FQ	39320 AW	48680 TQ	FLBLS	10/01-12/01
	Georgia	Y	29170 FQ	37980 AW	47480 TQ	GABLS	10/01-12/01
	Hawaii	Y	32960 FQ	46010 AW	56680 TQ	HIBLS	10/01-12/01
	Idaho	Y	27540 FQ	36190 AW	46340 TQ	IDBLS	10/01-12/01
	Illinois	Y	26910 FQ	38080 AW	51620 TQ	ILBLS	10/01-12/01
	Indiana	Y	30700 FQ	39050 AW	48210 TQ	INBLS	10/01-12/01
	Iowa	Y	27030 FQ	35730 AW	44710 TQ	IABLS	10/01-12/01
	Kansas	Y	25390 FQ	35430 AW	45200 TQ	KSBLS	10/01-12/01
	Kentucky	Y	25940 FQ	34410 AW	43950 TQ	KYBLS	10/01-12/01
	Louisiana	Y	27690 FQ	36140 AW	45270 TQ	LABLS	10/01-12/01
	Maine	Y	30620 FQ	39340 AW	47680 TQ	MEBLS	10/01-12/01
	Maryland	Y	36090 FQ	47520 AW	58640 TQ	MDBLS	10/01-12/01
	Massachusetts	Y	34480 FQ	44070 AW	55610 TQ	MABLS	10/01-12/01
	Michigan	Y	31080 FQ	39210 AW	47410 TQ	MIBLS	10/01-12/01
	Minnesota	Y	32410 FQ	43780 AW	56460 TQ	MNBLS	10/01-12/01
	Mississippi	Y	23750 FQ	32780 AW	43600 TQ	MSBLS	10/01-12/01
	Missouri	Y	26620 FQ	37500 AW	49080 TQ	MOBLS	10/01-12/01
	Montana	Y	25440 FQ	33780 AW	43380 TQ	MTBLS	10/01-12/01
	Nebraska	Y	30390 FQ	38140 AW	46980 TQ	NEBLS	10/01-12/01
	Nevada	Y	32300 FQ	40810 AW	50900 TQ	NVBLS	10/01-12/01
	New Hampshire	Y	33420 FQ	41700 AW	52100 TQ	NHBLS	10/01-12/01
	New Jersey	Y	38040 FQ	46250 AW	56450 TQ	NJBLS	10/01-12/01
	New Mexico	Y	27880 FQ	36720 AW	45580 TQ	NMBLS	10/01-12/01
	New York	Y	32880 FQ	45450 AW	58710 TQ	NYBLS	10/01-12/01
	North Carolina	Y	30630 FQ	39210 AW	49880 TQ	NCBLS	10/01-12/01
	North Dakota	Y	27340 FQ	34840 AW	44360 TQ	NDBLS	10/01-12/01
	Ohio	Y	29830 FQ	37900 AW	46070 TQ	OHBLS	10/01-12/01
	Oklahoma	Y	13670 FQ	31040 AW	44860 TQ	OKBLS	10/01-12/01
	Oregon	Y	32020 FQ	39940 AW	47610 TQ	ORBLS	10/01-12/01
	Pennsylvania	Y	29400 FQ	38560 AW	48220 TQ	PABLS	10/01-12/01
	Rhode Island	Y	33650 FQ	42000 AW	52860 TQ	RIBLS	10/01-12/01
	South Carolina	Y	30630 FQ	41450 AW	54620 TQ	SCBLS	10/01-12/01
	South Dakota	Y	29050 FQ	36740 AW	45120 TQ	SDBLS	10/01-12/01
	Tennessee	Y	25950 FQ	35010 AW	44320 TQ	TNBLS	10/01-12/01
	Texas	Y	27650 FQ	36540 AW	45950 TQ	TXBLS	10/01-12/01
	Utah	Y	31330 FQ	41110 AW	49000 TQ	UTBLS	10/01-12/01
	Virginia	Y	28620 FQ	39970 AW	52780 TQ	VABLS	10/01-12/01
	Washington	Y	35720 FQ	43190 AW	53670 TQ	WABLS	10/01-12/01
	West Virginia	Y	25930 FQ	33990 AW	43610 TQ	WVBLS	10/01-12/01
	Wisconsin	Y	30640 FQ	39420 AW	49300 TQ	WIBLS	10/01-12/01
	Wyoming	Y	25470 FQ	31800 AW	36980 TQ	WYBLS	10/01-12/01
	Puerto Rico	Y	12490 FQ	17790 AW	22880 TQ	PRBLS	10/01-12/01
Respiratory Therapy Technician	Alabama	Y	17740 FQ	29090 AW	41850 TQ	ALBLS	10/01-12/01
	Arizona	Y	20390 FQ	28880 AW	38840 TQ	AZBLS	10/01-12/01
	Arkansas	Y	16660 FQ	27680 AW	36860 TQ	ARBLS	10/01-12/01
	California	Y	31140 FQ	40960 AW	52880 TQ	CABLS	10/01-12/01
	Colorado	Y	17550 FQ	31000 AW	43800 TQ	COBLS	10/01-12/01
	Connecticut	Y	31260 FQ	39620 AW	49030 TQ	CTBLS	10/01-12/01
	District of Columbia	Y	28870 FQ	37260 AW	46370 TQ	DCBLS	10/01-12/01
	Florida	Y	27080 FQ	33250 AW	40450 TQ	FLBLS	10/01-12/01
	Georgia	Y	23560 FQ	33240 AW	45170 TQ	GABLS	10/01-12/01
	Hawaii	Y	26270 FQ	38890 AW	51960 TQ	HIBLS	10/01-12/01
	Idaho	Y	23980 FQ	38470 AW	66900 TQ	IDBLS	10/01-12/01
	Illinois	Y	18890 FQ	32760 AW	53790 TQ	ILBLS	10/01-12/01
	Indiana	Y	29250 FQ	35970 AW	44280 TQ	INBLS	10/01-12/01
	Iowa	Y	20710 FQ	28120 AW	35570 TQ	IABLS	10/01-12/01
	Kansas	Y	18630 FQ	30910 AW	43120 TQ	KSBLS	10/01-12/01
	Kentucky	Y	22010 FQ	28810 AW	36660 TQ	KYBLS	10/01-12/01
	Louisiana	Y	22660 FQ	31790 AW	42140 TQ	LABLS	10/01-12/01
	Maine	Y	26980 FQ	33460 AW	41930 TQ	MEBLS	10/01-12/01
	Massachusetts	Y	22360 FQ	36420 AW	48110 TQ	MABLS	10/01-12/01
	Michigan	Y	21380 FQ	30830 AW	40700 TQ	MIBLS	10/01-12/01
	Minnesota	Y	24600 FQ	31860 AW	40180 TQ	MNBLS	10/01-12/01
	Mississippi	Y	20130 FQ	28290 AW	36240 TQ	MSBLS	10/01-12/01

AAW	Average annual wage	AOH	Average offered, high	ASH	Average starting, high	H	Hourly	M	Monthly	S	Special: hourly and annual
AE	Average entry wage	AOL	Average offered, low	ASL	Average starting, low	HI	Highest wage paid	MTC	Median total compensation	TQ	Third quartile wage
AEX	Average experienced wage	APH	Average pay, high range	AW	Average wage paid	HR	High end range	MW	Median wage paid	W	Weekly
AO	Average offered	APL	Average pay, low range	FQ	First quartile wage	LR	Low end range	SQ	Second quartile wage	Y	Yearly

Occupation/Type/Industry	Location	Per	Low	Mid	High	Source	Date
Respiratory Therapy Technician	Missouri	Y	19630 FQ	28610 AW	36040 TQ	MOBLS	10/01-12/01
	Montana	Y	18650 FQ	31540 AW	43920 TQ	MTBLS	10/01-12/01
	Nebraska	Y	21160 FQ	31110 AW	40320 TQ	NEBLS	10/01-12/01
	Nevada	Y	31130 FQ	41260 AW	56160 TQ	NVBLS	10/01-12/01
	New Jersey	Y	29850 FQ	42770 AW	56350 TQ	NJBLS	10/01-12/01
	New Mexico	Y	21090 FQ	30740 AW	40550 TQ	NMBLS	10/01-12/01
	New York	Y	25990 FQ	37260 AW	51010 TQ	NYBLS	10/01-12/01
	North Carolina	Y	21670 FQ	31910 AW	43610 TQ	NCBLS	10/01-12/01
	Ohio	Y	25080 FQ	34240 AW	44210 TQ	OHBLS	10/01-12/01
	Oklahoma	Y	18250 FQ	29800 AW	42130 TQ	OKBLS	10/01-12/01
	Oregon	Y	31000 FQ	40040 AW	51920 TQ	ORBLS	10/01-12/01
	Pennsylvania	Y	23060 FQ	33610 AW	44870 TQ	PABLS	10/01-12/01
	South Carolina	Y	27120 FQ	36180 AW	44690 TQ	SCBLS	10/01-12/01
	Tennessee	Y	23980 FQ	32290 AW	42670 TQ	TNBLS	10/01-12/01
	Texas	Y	20200 FQ	31040 AW	41830 TQ	TXBLS	10/01-12/01
	Utah	Y	20880 FQ	32550 AW	44060 TQ	UTBLS	10/01-12/01
	Vermont	Y	19630 FQ	29950 AW	42360 TQ	VTBLS	10/01-12/01
	Virginia	Y	22390 FQ	32440 AW	43690 TQ	VABLS	10/01-12/01
	Washington	Y	30290 FQ	41020 AW	53420 TQ	WABLS	10/01-12/01
	West Virginia	Y	23090 FQ	32560 AW	45660 TQ	WVBLS	10/01-12/01
	Wisconsin	Y	26110 FQ	35470 AW	44610 TQ	WIBLS	10/01-12/01
	Wyoming	Y	25970 FQ	37100 AW	44980 TQ	WYBLS	10/01-12/01
	Puerto Rico	Y	11780 FQ	15920 AW	24570 TQ	PRBLS	10/01-12/01
Retail Salesperson	Alabama	Y	11990 FQ	20010 AW	33700 TQ	ALBLS	10/01-12/01
	Birmingham MSA, AL	Y	12340 FQ	22060 AW	40480 TQ	ALBLS	10/01-12/01
	Huntsville MSA, AL	Y	11980 FQ	20050 AW	31960 TQ	ALBLS	10/01-12/01
	Mobile MSA, AL	Y	11980 FQ	20350 AW	33580 TQ	ALBLS	10/01-12/01
	Montgomery MSA, AL	Y	11990 FQ	21830 AW	37170 TQ	ALBLS	10/01-12/01
	Alaska	Y	15350 FQ	24750 AW	36550 TQ	AKBLS	10/01-12/01
	Anchorage MSA, AK	Y	15620 FQ	26140 AW	39800 TQ	AKBLS	10/01-12/01
	Arizona	Y	12330 FQ	22000 AW	35930 TQ	AZBLS	10/01-12/01
	Phoenix-Mesa MSA, AZ	Y	12590 FQ	22580 AW	36200 TQ	AZBLS	10/01-12/01
	Tucson MSA, AZ	Y	12020 FQ	21650 AW	38450 TQ	AZBLS	10/01-12/01
	Arkansas	Y	11920 FQ	18030 AW	27450 TQ	ARBLS	10/01-12/01
	Fayetteville-Springdale-Rogers MSA, AR	Y	12100 FQ	18880 AW	28270 TQ	ARBLS	10/01-12/01
	Fort Smith MSA, AR-OK	Y	11920 FQ	18480 AW	29780 TQ	ARBLS	10/01-12/01
	Little Rock-North Little Rock MSA, AR	Y	12020 FQ	18410 AW	27350 TQ	ARBLS	10/01-12/01
	California	Y	13800 FQ	22370 AW	36040 TQ	CABLS	10/01-12/01
	Bakersfield MSA, CA	Y	13460 FQ	20100 AW	34190 TQ	CABLS	10/01-12/01
	Chico-Paradise MSA, CA	Y	13520 FQ	19230 AW	27900 TQ	CABLS	10/01-12/01
	Fresno MSA, CA	Y	13510 FQ	21160 AW	36900 TQ	CABLS	10/01-12/01
	Los Angeles-Long Beach PMSA, CA	Y	13670 FQ	21740 AW	34940 TQ	CABLS	10/01-12/01
	Merced MSA, CA	Y	13550 FQ	20720 AW	35550 TQ	CABLS	10/01-12/01
	Modesto MSA, CA	Y	13520 FQ	20930 AW	33990 TQ	CABLS	10/01-12/01
	Oakland PMSA, CA	Y	14520 FQ	24310 AW	41010 TQ	CABLS	10/01-12/01
	Orange County PMSA, CA	Y	13990 FQ	22790 AW	35870 TQ	CABLS	10/01-12/01
	Redding MSA, CA	Y	13740 FQ	20250 AW	32260 TQ	CABLS	10/01-12/01
	Riverside-San Bernardino PMSA, CA	Y	13620 FQ	21600 AW	34880 TQ	CABLS	10/01-12/01
	Sacramento PMSA, CA	Y	13570 FQ	21430 AW	34560 TQ	CABLS	10/01-12/01
	Salinas MSA, CA	Y	13860 FQ	22550 AW	35870 TQ	CABLS	10/01-12/01
	San Diego MSA, CA	Y	13820 FQ	22720 AW	37120 TQ	CABLS	10/01-12/01
	San Francisco PMSA, CA	Y	14580 FQ	25040 AW	41620 TQ	CABLS	10/01-12/01
	San Jose PMSA, CA	Y	14640 FQ	24170 AW	39070 TQ	CABLS	10/01-12/01
	San Luis Obispo-Atascadero-Paso Robles MSA, CA	Y	13460 FQ	19970 AW	32820 TQ	CABLS	10/01-12/01
	Santa Barbara-Santa Maria-Lompoc MSA, CA	Y	13880 FQ	21250 AW	32340 TQ	CABLS	10/01-12/01
	Santa Cruz-Watsonville PMSA, CA	Y	13990 FQ	20860 AW	28550 TQ	CABLS	10/01-12/01
	Santa Rosa PMSA, CA	Y	14460 FQ	23010 AW	35000 TQ	CABLS	10/01-12/01
	Stockton-Lodi MSA, CA	Y	13570 FQ	21910 AW	37240 TQ	CABLS	10/01-12/01
	Vallejo-Fairfield-Napa PMSA, CA	Y	13760 FQ	21900 AW	35570 TQ	CABLS	10/01-12/01
	Ventura PMSA, CA	Y	14040 FQ	23390 AW	36120 TQ	CABLS	10/01-12/01
	Visalia-Tulare-Porterville MSA, CA	Y	13540 FQ	19970 AW	31570 TQ	CABLS	10/01-12/01
	Colorado	Y	13270 FQ	23030 AW	37800 TQ	COBLS	10/01-12/01
	Boulder-Longmont PMSA, CO	Y	12820 FQ	21150 AW	33350 TQ	COBLS	10/01-12/01

AAW	Average annual wage	**AOH**	Average offered, high	**ASH**	Average starting, high	**H**	Hourly	**M**	Monthly	**S**	Special: hourly and annual
AE	Average entry wage	**AOL**	Average offered, low	**ASL**	Average starting, low	**HI**	Highest wage paid	**MTC**	Median total compensation	**TQ**	Third quartile wage
AEX	Average experienced wage	**APH**	Average pay, high range	**AW**	Average wage paid	**HR**	High end range	**MW**	Median wage paid	**W**	Weekly
AO	Average offered	**APL**	Average pay, low range	**FQ**	First quartile wage	**LR**	Low end range	**SQ**	Second quartile wage	**Y**	Yearly

Occupation/Type/Industry	Location	Per	Low	Mid	High	Source	Date
Retail Salesperson	Colorado Springs MSA, CO	Y	12490 FQ	21470 AW	35100 TQ	COBLS	10/01-12/01
	Denver PMSA, CO	Y	14480 FQ	24690 AW	41580 TQ	COBLS	10/01-12/01
	Fort Collins-Loveland MSA, CO	Y	12990 FQ	21530 AW	33690 TQ	COBLS	10/01-12/01
	Greeley PMSA, CO	Y	12670 FQ	22370 AW	37230 TQ	COBLS	10/01-12/01
	Connecticut	Y	14120 FQ	23450 AW	39690 TQ	CTBLS	10/01-12/01
	Bridgeport PMSA, CT	Y	13960 FQ	23220 AW	40010 TQ	CTBLS	10/01-12/01
	Danbury PMSA, CT	Y	14100 FQ	23810 AW	42300 TQ	CTBLS	10/01-12/01
	Hartford MSA, CT	Y	14020 FQ	22380 AW	36170 TQ	CTBLS	10/01-12/01
	New Haven-Meriden PMSA, CT	Y	14120 FQ	22020 AW	34560 TQ	CTBLS	10/01-12/01
	New London-Norwich MSA, CT-RI	Y	14190 FQ	23500 AW	41230 TQ	CTBLS	10/01-12/01
	Stamford-Norwalk PMSA, CT	Y	14900 FQ	28570 AW	53440 TQ	CTBLS	10/01-12/01
	Waterbury PMSA, CT	Y	13970 FQ	22650 AW	37590 TQ	CTBLS	10/01-12/01
	Delaware	Y	13690 FQ	21110 AW	34240 TQ	DEBLS	10/01-12/01
	Wilmington-Newark PMSA, DE-MD	Y	13630 FQ	21530 AW	34920 TQ	DEBLS	10/01-12/01
	District of Columbia	Y	14490 FQ	21580 AW	34850 TQ	DCBLS	10/01-12/01
	Washington PMSA, DC-MD-VA-WV	Y	12930 FQ	21830 AW	35450 TQ	DCBLS	10/01-12/01
	Florida	Y	12240 FQ	20430 AW	33720 TQ	FLBLS	10/01-12/01
	Daytona Beach MSA, FL	Y	12290 FQ	20680 AW	33400 TQ	FLBLS	10/01-12/01
	Fort Lauderdale PMSA, FL	Y	12410 FQ	21380 AW	37270 TQ	FLBLS	10/01-12/01
	Fort Myers-Cape Coral MSA, FL	Y	12830 FQ	23340 AW	40600 TQ	FLBLS	10/01-12/01
	Fort Pierce-Port St. Lucie MSA, FL	Y	12520 FQ	21500 AW	35330 TQ	FLBLS	10/01-12/01
	Fort Walton Beach MSA, FL	Y	12300 FQ	19050 AW	28680 TQ	FLBLS	10/01-12/01
	Gainesville MSA, FL	Y	11980 FQ	19440 AW	32540 TQ	FLBLS	10/01-12/01
	Jacksonville MSA, FL	Y	12300 FQ	20240 AW	35070 TQ	FLBLS	10/01-12/01
	Lakeland-Winter Haven MSA, FL	Y	12190 FQ	19510 AW	30590 TQ	FLBLS	10/01-12/01
	Melbourne-Titusville-Palm Bay MSA, FL	Y	12120 FQ	19320 AW	29370 TQ	FLBLS	10/01-12/01
	Miami PMSA, FL	Y	12250 FQ	19390 AW	29550 TQ	FLBLS	10/01-12/01
	Naples MSA, FL	Y	14060 FQ	23300 AW	37690 TQ	FLBLS	10/01-12/01
	Ocala MSA, FL	Y	12110 FQ	19440 AW	32820 TQ	FLBLS	10/01-12/01
	Orlando MSA, FL	Y	12030 FQ	19230 AW	30480 TQ	FLBLS	10/01-12/01
	Pensacola MSA, FL	Y	11910 FQ	18400 AW	28580 TQ	FLBLS	10/01-12/01
	Sarasota-Bradenton MSA, FL	Y	12560 FQ	21100 AW	34440 TQ	FLBLS	10/01-12/01
	Tallahassee MSA, FL	Y	11820 FQ	18460 AW	27270 TQ	FLBLS	10/01-12/01
	Tampa-St. Petersburg-Clearwater MSA, FL	Y	12270 FQ	20950 AW	34770 TQ	FLBLS	10/01-12/01
	West Palm Beach-Boca Raton MSA, FL	Y	12630 FQ	23890 AW	40620 TQ	FLBLS	10/01-12/01
	Georgia	Y	12300 FQ	20690 AW	34440 TQ	GABLS	10/01-12/01
	Atlanta MSA, GA	Y	12670 FQ	21720 AW	36430 TQ	GABLS	10/01-12/01
	Augusta-Aiken MSA, GA-SC	Y	11950 FQ	19230 AW	29530 TQ	GABLS	10/01-12/01
	Columbus MSA, GA-AL	Y	11900 FQ	19190 AW	28670 TQ	GABLS	10/01-12/01
	Macon MSA, GA	Y	12000 FQ	20800 AW	34780 TQ	GABLS	10/01-12/01
	Savannah MSA, GA	Y	12050 FQ	18530 AW	30010 TQ	GABLS	10/01-12/01
	Hawaii	Y	12810 FQ	20490 AW	29930 TQ	HIBLS	10/01-12/01
	Honolulu MSA, HI	Y	12680 FQ	20390 AW	29780 TQ	HIBLS	10/01-12/01
	Idaho	Y	12210 FQ	20250 AW	32520 TQ	IDBLS	10/01-12/01
	Boise City MSA, ID	Y	12390 FQ	19930 AW	29820 TQ	IDBLS	10/01-12/01
	Illinois	Y	12360 FQ	21330 AW	36260 TQ	ILBLS	10/01-12/01
	Champaign-Urbana MSA, IL	Y	11960 FQ	17800 AW	25990 TQ	ILBLS	10/01-12/01
	Chicago PMSA, IL	Y	12750 FQ	22590 AW	41320 TQ	ILBLS	10/01-12/01
	Peoria-Pekin MSA, IL	Y	11770 FQ	19550 AW	33970 TQ	ILBLS	10/01-12/01
	Rockford MSA, IL	Y	12610 FQ	20620 AW	34310 TQ	ILBLS	10/01-12/01
	Springfield MSA, IL	Y	12430 FQ	19390 AW	30800 TQ	ILBLS	10/01-12/01
	Indiana	Y	12200 FQ	20680 AW	34650 TQ	INBLS	10/01-12/01
	Elkhart-Goshen MSA, IN	Y	12220 FQ	21060 AW	38600 TQ	INBLS	10/01-12/01
	Evansville-Henderson MSA, IN-KY	Y	12160 FQ	21950 AW	40070 TQ	INBLS	10/01-12/01
	Fort Wayne MSA, IN	Y	12180 FQ	20550 AW	34330 TQ	INBLS	10/01-12/01
	Gary PMSA, IN	Y	11980 FQ	20200 AW	35590 TQ	INBLS	10/01-12/01
	Indianapolis MSA, IN	Y	12960 FQ	22550 AW	37740 TQ	INBLS	10/01-12/01
	Lafayette MSA, IN	Y	12090 FQ	19310 AW	30410 TQ	INBLS	10/01-12/01
	South Bend MSA, IN	Y	12300 FQ	20070 AW	32890 TQ	INBLS	10/01-12/01
	Iowa	Y	12050 FQ	20100 AW	33410 TQ	IABLS	10/01-12/01

AAW Average annual wage **AOH** Average offered, high **ASH** Average starting, high **H** Hourly **M** Monthly **S** Special: hourly and annual
AE Average entry wage **AOL** Average offered, low **ASL** Average starting, low **HI** Highest wage paid **MTC** Median total compensation **TQ** Third quartile wage
AEX Average experienced wage **APH** Average pay, high range **AW** Average wage paid **HR** High end range **MW** Median wage paid **W** Weekly
AO Average offered **APL** Average pay, low range **FQ** First quartile wage **LR** Low end range **SQ** Second quartile wage **Y** Yearly

Occupation/Type/Industry	Location	Per	Low	Mid	High	Source	Date
Retail Salesperson	Cedar Rapids MSA, IA	Y	12040 FQ	21400 AW	36810 TQ	IABLS	10/01-12/01
	Davenport-Moline-Rock Island MSA, IA-IL	Y	12250 FQ	19550 AW	31470 TQ	IABLS	10/01-12/01
	Des Moines MSA, IA	Y	12590 FQ	23480 AW	40850 TQ	IABLS	10/01-12/01
	Kansas	Y	11990 FQ	19430 AW	30850 TQ	KSBLS	10/01-12/01
	Topeka MSA, KS	Y	12040 FQ	20670 AW	36860 TQ	KSBLS	10/01-12/01
	Wichita MSA, KS	Y	11890 FQ	20370 AW	33910 TQ	KSBLS	10/01-12/01
	Kentucky	Y	12030 FQ	19100 AW	30180 TQ	KYBLS	10/01-12/01
	Lexington MSA, KY	Y	12340 FQ	19780 AW	32260 TQ	KYBLS	10/01-12/01
	Louisville MSA, KY-IN	Y	12750 FQ	21630 AW	35330 TQ	KYBLS	10/01-12/01
	Louisiana	Y	11860 FQ	18900 AW	30910 TQ	LABLS	10/01-12/01
	Baton Rouge MSA, LA	Y	11990 FQ	19020 AW	30850 TQ	LABLS	10/01-12/01
	Houma MSA, LA	Y	11840 FQ	18430 AW	31470 TQ	LABLS	10/01-12/01
	Lafayette MSA, LA	Y	11890 FQ	18510 AW	29390 TQ	LABLS	10/01-12/01
	Lake Charles MSA, LA	Y	11940 FQ	20670 AW	37410 TQ	LABLS	10/01-12/01
	New Orleans MSA, LA	Y	11790 FQ	18610 AW	30390 TQ	LABLS	10/01-12/01
	Shreveport-Bossier City MSA, LA	Y	11850 FQ	19700 AW	33140 TQ	LABLS	10/01-12/01
	Maine	Y	12540 FQ	19670 AW	28820 TQ	MEBLS	10/01-12/01
	Portland MSA, ME	Y	13220 FQ	20120 AW	28680 TQ	MEBLS	10/01-12/01
	Maryland	Y	12120 FQ	20730 AW	35100 TQ	MDBLS	10/01-12/01
	Baltimore PMSA, MD	Y	12020 FQ	20210 AW	33880 TQ	MDBLS	10/01-12/01
	Massachusetts	Y	14420 FQ	22610 AW	34570 TQ	MABLS	10/01-12/01
	Boston PMSA, MA-NH	Y	14540 FQ	23590 AW	36020 TQ	MABLS	10/01-12/01
	Brockton PMSA, MA	Y	14450 FQ	22600 AW	36860 TQ	MABLS	10/01-12/01
	Lawrence PMSA, MA-NH	Y	14070 FQ	21940 AW	34890 TQ	MABLS	10/01-12/01
	Lowell PMSA, MA-NH	Y	14540 FQ	22950 AW	35650 TQ	MABLS	10/01-12/01
	New Bedford PMSA, MA	Y	14250 FQ	20160 AW	30560 TQ	MABLS	10/01-12/01
	Springfield MSA, MA	Y	14240 FQ	19620 AW	29000 TQ	MABLS	10/01-12/01
	Worcester PMSA, MA-CT	Y	14370 FQ	21880 AW	34260 TQ	MABLS	10/01-12/01
	Michigan	Y	12520 FQ	21350 AW	34900 TQ	MIBLS	10/01-12/01
	Ann Arbor PMSA, MI	Y	13340 FQ	21880 AW	34580 TQ	MIBLS	10/01-12/01
	Detroit PMSA, MI	Y	12730 FQ	22410 AW	36220 TQ	MIBLS	10/01-12/01
	Flint PMSA, MI	Y	11940 FQ	19170 AW	29540 TQ	MIBLS	10/01-12/01
	Grand Rapids-Muskegon-Holland MSA, MI	Y	12940 FQ	22080 AW	37900 TQ	MIBLS	10/01-12/01
	Kalamazoo-Battle Creek MSA, MI	Y	12320 FQ	19140 AW	28850 TQ	MIBLS	10/01-12/01
	Lansing-East Lansing MSA, MI	Y	12480 FQ	19950 AW	32330 TQ	MIBLS	10/01-12/01
	Saginaw-Bay City-Midland MSA, MI	Y	11920 FQ	18030 AW	29020 TQ	MIBLS	10/01-12/01
	Minnesota	Y	12830 FQ	20790 AW	32270 TQ	MNBLS	10/01-12/01
	Duluth-Superior MSA, MN-WI	Y	11970 FQ	18450 AW	27300 TQ	MNBLS	10/01-12/01
	Minneapolis-St. Paul MSA, MN-WI	Y	13960 FQ	21950 AW	33720 TQ	MNBLS	10/01-12/01
	St. Cloud MSA, MN	Y	12110 FQ	19560 AW	30790 TQ	MNBLS	10/01-12/01
	Mississippi	Y	11900 FQ	18370 AW	27510 TQ	MSBLS	10/01-12/01
	Biloxi-Gulfport-Pascagoula MSA, MS	Y	11990 FQ	18710 AW	27770 TQ	MSBLS	10/01-12/01
	Jackson MSA, MS	Y	12380 FQ	21350 AW	35400 TQ	MSBLS	10/01-12/01
	Missouri	Y	12240 FQ	20250 AW	31990 TQ	MOBLS	10/01-12/01
	Kansas City MSA, MO-KS	Y	12600 FQ	21310 AW	35180 TQ	MOBLS	10/01-12/01
	St. Louis MSA, MO-IL	Y	12320 FQ	20620 AW	31280 TQ	MOBLS	10/01-12/01
	Springfield MSA, MO	Y	12190 FQ	20960 AW	35280 TQ	MOBLS	10/01-12/01
	Montana	Y	11940 FQ	18960 AW	30440 TQ	MTBLS	10/01-12/01
	Billings MSA, MT	Y	12130 FQ	20580 AW	34680 TQ	MTBLS	10/01-12/01
	Nebraska	Y	12140 FQ	20030 AW	32450 TQ	NEBLS	10/01-12/01
	Lincoln MSA, NE	Y	12180 FQ	19870 AW	31480 TQ	NEBLS	10/01-12/01
	Omaha MSA, NE-IA	Y	12440 FQ	21020 AW	33530 TQ	NEBLS	10/01-12/01
	Nevada	Y	12850 FQ	22380 AW	38010 TQ	NVBLS	10/01-12/01
	Las Vegas MSA, NV-AZ	Y	12880 FQ	22610 AW	39080 TQ	NVBLS	10/01-12/01
	Reno MSA, NV	Y	12920 FQ	22540 AW	37540 TQ	NVBLS	10/01-12/01
	New Hampshire	Y	12950 FQ	21110 AW	33400 TQ	NHBLS	10/01-12/01
	Manchester PMSA, NH	Y	12890 FQ	24910 AW	46220 TQ	NHBLS	10/01-12/01
	Nashua PMSA, NH	Y	14450 FQ	21520 AW	32650 TQ	NHBLS	10/01-12/01
	Portsmouth-Rochester PMSA, NH-ME	Y	13400 FQ	20600 AW	32060 TQ	NHBLS	10/01-12/01
	New Jersey	Y	12680 FQ	22570 AW	37100 TQ	NJBLS	10/01-12/01
	Atlantic-Cape May PMSA, NJ	Y	12470 FQ	20510 AW	32120 TQ	NJBLS	10/01-12/01
	Bergen-Passaic PMSA, NJ	Y	13350 FQ	24350 AW	42860 TQ	NJBLS	10/01-12/01
	Jersey City PMSA, NJ	Y	12230 FQ	20270 AW	30520 TQ	NJBLS	10/01-12/01

AAW	Average annual wage	**AOH**	Average offered, high	**ASH**	Average starting, high	**H**	Hourly	**M**	Monthly	**S**	Special: hourly and annual
AE	Average entry wage	**AOL**	Average offered, low	**ASL**	Average starting, low	**HI**	Highest wage paid	**MTC**	Median total compensation	**TQ**	Third quartile wage
AEX	Average experienced wage	**APH**	Average pay, high range	**AW**	Average wage paid	**HR**	High end range	**MW**	Median wage paid	**W**	Weekly
AO	Average offered	**APL**	Average pay, low range	**FQ**	First quartile wage	**LR**	Low end range	**SQ**	Second quartile wage	**Y**	Yearly

Occupation/Type/Industry	Location	Per	Low	Mid	High	Source	Date
Retail Salesperson	Middlesex-Somerset-Hunterdon PMSA, NJ	Y	13070 FQ	23570 AW	38330 TQ	NJBLS	10/01-12/01
	Monmouth-Ocean PMSA, NJ	Y	12510 FQ	21770 AW	36080 TQ	NJBLS	10/01-12/01
	Newark PMSA, NJ	Y	12910 FQ	23480 AW	38650 TQ	NJBLS	10/01-12/01
	Trenton PMSA, NJ	Y	12910 FQ	21820 AW	34500 TQ	NJBLS	10/01-12/01
	New Mexico	Y	12020 FQ	19110 AW	29860 TQ	NMBLS	10/01-12/01
	Albuquerque MSA, NM	Y	12110 FQ	19570 AW	31650 TQ	NMBLS	10/01-12/01
	Las Cruces MSA, NM	Y	11810 FQ	18850 AW	33860 TQ	NMBLS	10/01-12/01
	New York	Y	12070 FQ	20440 AW	34470 TQ	NYBLS	10/01-12/01
	Albany-Schenectady-Troy MSA, NY	Y	12070 FQ	19220 AW	30280 TQ	NYBLS	10/01-12/01
	Binghamton MSA, NY	Y	12000 FQ	18380 AW	27970 TQ	NYBLS	10/01-12/01
	Buffalo-Niagara Falls MSA, NY	Y	11830 FQ	18140 AW	29010 TQ	NYBLS	10/01-12/01
	Dutchess County PMSA, NY	Y	12450 FQ	20480 AW	33600 TQ	NYBLS	10/01-12/01
	Nassau-Suffolk PMSA, NY	Y	12750 FQ	22600 AW	39670 TQ	NYBLS	10/01-12/01
	New York PMSA, NY	Y	12040 FQ	21090 AW	36130 TQ	NYBLS	10/01-12/01
	Newburgh PMSA, NY-PA	Y	12260 FQ	18720 AW	27710 TQ	NYBLS	10/01-12/01
	Rochester MSA, NY	Y	11950 FQ	19250 AW	30990 TQ	NYBLS	10/01-12/01
	Syracuse MSA, NY	Y	11790 FQ	17030 AW	26430 TQ	NYBLS	10/01-12/01
	Utica-Rome MSA, NY	Y	11850 FQ	17830 AW	27790 TQ	NYBLS	10/01-12/01
	North Carolina	Y	12350 FQ	20320 AW	32290 TQ	NCBLS	10/01-12/01
	Asheville MSA, NC	Y	12470 FQ	19950 AW	29110 TQ	NCBLS	10/01-12/01
	Charlotte-Gastonia-Rock Hill MSA, NC-SC	Y	12670 FQ	21420 AW	35010 TQ	NCBLS	10/01-12/01
	Fayetteville MSA, NC	Y	12070 FQ	19450 AW	31770 TQ	NCBLS	10/01-12/01
	Greensboro-Winston-Salem-High Point MSA, NC	Y	12630 FQ	21470 AW	33770 TQ	NCBLS	10/01-12/01
	Hickory-Morganton-Lenoir MSA, NC	Y	12080 FQ	21030 AW	35080 TQ	NCBLS	10/01-12/01
	Raleigh-Durham-Chapel Hill MSA, NC	Y	12840 FQ	19790 AW	29300 TQ	NCBLS	10/01-12/01
	Wilmington MSA, NC	Y	12370 FQ	20250 AW	31740 TQ	NCBLS	10/01-12/01
	North Dakota	Y	12000 FQ	18670 AW	30400 TQ	NDBLS	10/01-12/01
	Fargo-Moorhead MSA, ND-MN	Y	12120 FQ	20140 AW	33230 TQ	NDBLS	10/01-12/01
	Ohio	Y	12120 FQ	20140 AW	32690 TQ	OHBLS	10/01-12/01
	Akron PMSA, OH	Y	12080 FQ	20300 AW	32990 TQ	OHBLS	10/01-12/01
	Canton-Massillon MSA, OH	Y	11880 FQ	18790 AW	30980 TQ	OHBLS	10/01-12/01
	Cincinnati PMSA, OH-KY-IN	Y	12200 FQ	21340 AW	35690 TQ	OHBLS	10/01-12/01
	Cleveland-Lorain-Elyria PMSA, OH	Y	12160 FQ	20080 AW	32170 TQ	OHBLS	10/01-12/01
	Columbus MSA, OH	Y	12700 FQ	20780 AW	32890 TQ	OHBLS	10/01-12/01
	Dayton-Springfield MSA, OH	Y	12090 FQ	20640 AW	32550 TQ	OHBLS	10/01-12/01
	Hamilton-Middletown PMSA, OH	Y	12540 FQ	20560 AW	32770 TQ	OHBLS	10/01-12/01
	Mansfield MSA, OH	Y	11870 FQ	18620 AW	28500 TQ	OHBLS	10/01-12/01
	Toledo MSA, OH	Y	12150 FQ	20470 AW	33110 TQ	OHBLS	10/01-12/01
	Youngstown-Warren MSA, OH	Y	11850 FQ	18420 AW	28350 TQ	OHBLS	10/01-12/01
	Oklahoma	Y	11960 FQ	19700 AW	31800 TQ	OKBLS	10/01-12/01
	Oklahoma City MSA, OK	Y	12050 FQ	20450 AW	33390 TQ	OKBLS	10/01-12/01
	Tulsa MSA, OK	Y	12160 FQ	20710 AW	33760 TQ	OKBLS	10/01-12/01
	Oregon	Y	14700 FQ	22340 AW	35020 TQ	ORBLS	10/01-12/01
	Eugene-Springfield MSA, OR	Y	14600 FQ	21700 AW	34710 TQ	ORBLS	10/01-12/01
	Medford-Ashland MSA, OR	Y	14610 FQ	21450 AW	31380 TQ	ORBLS	10/01-12/01
	Portland-Vancouver PMSA, OR-WA	Y	14960 FQ	23310 AW	36650 TQ	ORBLS	10/01-12/01
	Salem PMSA, OR	Y	14580 FQ	21910 AW	35480 TQ	ORBLS	10/01-12/01
	Pennsylvania	Y	12130 FQ	19340 AW	30320 TQ	PABLS	10/01-12/01
	Allentown-Bethlehem-Easton MSA, PA	Y	12260 FQ	20210 AW	32760 TQ	PABLS	10/01-12/01
	Erie MSA, PA	Y	11960 FQ	18570 AW	29550 TQ	PABLS	10/01-12/01
	Harrisburg-Lebanon-Carlisle MSA, PA	Y	12190 FQ	19020 AW	29830 TQ	PABLS	10/01-12/01
	Johnstown MSA, PA	Y	11860 FQ	18160 AW	27940 TQ	PABLS	10/01-12/01
	Lancaster MSA, PA	Y	12300 FQ	19490 AW	29270 TQ	PABLS	10/01-12/01
	Philadelphia PMSA, PA-NJ	Y	12420 FQ	21040 AW	35030 TQ	PABLS	10/01-12/01
	Pittsburgh MSA, PA	Y	12110 FQ	18450 AW	28200 TQ	PABLS	10/01-12/01
	Reading MSA, PA	Y	12100 FQ	19040 AW	30480 TQ	PABLS	10/01-12/01
	Scranton-Wilkes-Barre-Hazleton MSA, PA	Y	11920 FQ	18050 AW	28210 TQ	PABLS	10/01-12/01
	York MSA, PA	Y	12120 FQ	19340 AW	28520 TQ	PABLS	10/01-12/01

AAW	Average annual wage	**AOH**	Average offered, high	**ASH**	Average starting, high	**H**	Hourly	**M**	Monthly	**S**	Special: hourly and annual
AE	Average entry wage	**AOL**	Average offered, low	**ASL**	Average starting, low	**HI**	Highest wage paid	**MTC**	Median total compensation	**TQ**	Third quartile wage
AEX	Average experienced wage	**APH**	Average pay, high range	**AW**	Average wage paid	**HR**	High end range	**MW**	Median wage paid	**W**	Weekly
AO	Average offered	**APL**	Average pay, low range	**FQ**	First quartile wage	**LR**	Low end range	**SQ**	Second quartile wage	**Y**	Yearly

Occupation/Type/Industry	Location	Per	Low	Mid	High	Source	Date
Retail Salesperson	Rhode Island	Y	13720 FQ	21800 AW	35200 TQ	RIBLS	10/01-12/01
	Providence-Fall River-Warwick MSA, RI-MA	Y	13990 FQ	21370 AW	34280 TQ	RIBLS	10/01-12/01
	South Carolina	Y	12310 FQ	20420 AW	33230 TQ	SCBLS	10/01-12/01
	Charleston-North Charleston MSA, SC	Y	12640 FQ	21470 AW	34820 TQ	SCBLS	10/01-12/01
	Columbia MSA, SC	Y	12390 FQ	20980 AW	33220 TQ	SCBLS	10/01-12/01
	Greenville-Spartanburg-Anderson MSA, SC	Y	12260 FQ	20080 AW	33080 TQ	SCBLS	10/01-12/01
	Myrtle Beach MSA, SC	Y	12530 FQ	20050 AW	32840 TQ	SCBLS	10/01-12/01
	South Dakota	Y	12250 FQ	18620 AW	28130 TQ	SDBLS	10/01-12/01
	Sioux Falls MSA, SD	Y	12520 FQ	19140 AW	28380 TQ	SDBLS	10/01-12/01
	Tennessee	Y	12270 FQ	21190 AW	35120 TQ	TNBLS	10/01-12/01
	Chattanooga MSA, TN-GA	Y	12010 FQ	21060 AW	37440 TQ	TNBLS	10/01-12/01
	Clarksville-Hopkinsville MSA, TN-KY	Y	11900 FQ	19360 AW	31570 TQ	TNBLS	10/01-12/01
	Johnson City-Kingsport-Bristol MSA, TN-VA	Y	11940 FQ	18690 AW	30120 TQ	TNBLS	10/01-12/01
	Knoxville MSA, TN	Y	12610 FQ	21430 AW	35500 TQ	TNBLS	10/01-12/01
	Memphis MSA, TN-AR-MS	Y	12500 FQ	23750 AW	43190 TQ	TNBLS	10/01-12/01
	Nashville MSA, TN	Y	12840 FQ	21710 AW	34000 TQ	TNBLS	10/01-12/01
	Texas	Y	12070 FQ	20490 AW	34040 TQ	TXBLS	10/01-12/01
	Amarillo MSA, TX	Y	11900 FQ	20160 AW	34780 TQ	TXBLS	10/01-12/01
	Austin-San Marcos MSA, TX	Y	13010 FQ	23170 AW	36460 TQ	TXBLS	10/01-12/01
	Beaumont-Port Arthur MSA, TX	Y	11860 FQ	20180 AW	35160 TQ	TXBLS	10/01-12/01
	Brazoria PMSA, TX	Y	12000 FQ	20820 AW	34210 TQ	TXBLS	10/01-12/01
	Brownsville-Harlingen-San Benito MSA, TX	Y	11620 FQ	16240 AW	22930 TQ	TXBLS	10/01-12/01
	Corpus Christi MSA, TX	Y	11990 FQ	19160 AW	29630 TQ	TXBLS	10/01-12/01
	Dallas PMSA, TX	Y	12420 FQ	21210 AW	34290 TQ	TXBLS	10/01-12/01
	El Paso MSA, TX	Y	11700 FQ	16800 AW	24570 TQ	TXBLS	10/01-12/01
	Fort Worth-Arlington PMSA, TX	Y	12460 FQ	21530 AW	35360 TQ	TXBLS	10/01-12/01
	Galveston-Texas City PMSA, TX	Y	11820 FQ	19150 AW	29710 TQ	TXBLS	10/01-12/01
	Houston PMSA, TX	Y	12020 FQ	20700 AW	35350 TQ	TXBLS	10/01-12/01
	Killeen-Temple MSA, TX	Y	12000 FQ	20860 AW	37930 TQ	TXBLS	10/01-12/01
	Laredo MSA, TX	Y	11690 FQ	16070 AW	23540 TQ	TXBLS	10/01-12/01
	Longview-Marshall MSA, TX	Y	11800 FQ	18790 AW	32450 TQ	TXBLS	10/01-12/01
	Lubbock MSA, TX	Y	11930 FQ	20290 AW	34590 TQ	TXBLS	10/01-12/01
	McAllen-Edinburg-Mission MSA, TX	Y	11720 FQ	17610 AW	26970 TQ	TXBLS	10/01-12/01
	Odessa-Midland MSA, TX	Y	11880 FQ	19540 AW	32770 TQ	TXBLS	10/01-12/01
	San Antonio MSA, TX	Y	12210 FQ	20600 AW	35310 TQ	TXBLS	10/01-12/01
	Tyler MSA, TX	Y	12080 FQ	19890 AW	34330 TQ	TXBLS	10/01-12/01
	Waco MSA, TX	Y	12140 FQ	19260 AW	29280 TQ	TXBLS	10/01-12/01
	Utah	Y	12450 FQ	20140 AW	30550 TQ	UTBLS	10/01-12/01
	Provo-Orem MSA, UT	Y	12420 FQ	19470 AW	28800 TQ	UTBLS	10/01-12/01
	Salt Lake City-Ogden MSA, UT	Y	12620 FQ	20800 AW	32160 TQ	UTBLS	10/01-12/01
	Vermont	Y	14130 FQ	22260 AW	34520 TQ	VTBLS	10/01-12/01
	Burlington MSA, VT	Y	13920 FQ	21030 AW	33140 TQ	VTBLS	10/01-12/01
	Virginia	Y	12310 FQ	19990 AW	30800 TQ	VABLS	10/01-12/01
	Lynchburg MSA, VA	Y	11860 FQ	18200 AW	27730 TQ	VABLS	10/01-12/01
	Norfolk-Virginia Beach-Newport News MSA, VA-NC	Y	12030 FQ	18920 AW	28630 TQ	VABLS	10/01-12/01
	Richmond-Petersburg MSA, VA	Y	12400 FQ	20000 AW	29960 TQ	VABLS	10/01-12/01
	Roanoke MSA, VA	Y	12350 FQ	18800 AW	27520 TQ	VABLS	10/01-12/01
	Washington	Y	14710 FQ	25060 AW	40920 TQ	WABLS	10/01-12/01
	Bremerton PMSA, WA	Y	14510 FQ	22860 AW	35280 TQ	WABLS	10/01-12/01
	Olympia PMSA, WA	Y	15170 FQ	25690 AW	41150 TQ	WABLS	10/01-12/01
	Richland-Kennewick-Pasco MSA, WA	Y	14330 FQ	22110 AW	35540 TQ	WABLS	10/01-12/01
	Seattle-Bellevue-Everett PMSA, WA	Y	14940 FQ	26420 AW	43600 TQ	WABLS	10/01-12/01
	Spokane MSA, WA	Y	14570 FQ	23280 AW	37560 TQ	WABLS	10/01-12/01
	Tacoma PMSA, WA	Y	14730 FQ	26700 AW	44120 TQ	WABLS	10/01-12/01
	Yakima MSA, WA	Y	14420 FQ	21570 AW	34260 TQ	WABLS	10/01-12/01
	West Virginia	Y	11710 FQ	16930 AW	25610 TQ	WVBLS	10/01-12/01

AAW	Average annual wage	AOH	Average offered, high	ASH	Average starting, high	H	Hourly	M	Monthly	S	Special: hourly and annual
AE	Average entry wage	AOL	Average offered, low	ASL	Average starting, low	HI	Highest wage paid	MTC	Median total compensation	TQ	Third quartile wage
AEX	Average experienced wage	APH	Average pay, high range	AW	Average wage paid	HR	High end range	MW	Median wage paid	W	Weekly
AO	Average offered	APL	Average pay, low range	FQ	First quartile wage	LR	Low end range	SQ	Second quartile wage	Y	Yearly

Occupation/Type/Industry	Location	Per	Low	Mid	High	Source	Date
Retail Salesperson	Charleston MSA, WV	Y	11870 FQ	18790 AW	31950 TQ	WVBLS	10/01-12/01
	Huntington-Ashland MSA, WV-KY-OH	Y	11650 FQ	16100 AW	23220 TQ	WVBLS	10/01-12/01
	Wisconsin	Y	12390 FQ	20450 AW	33040 TQ	WIBLS	10/01-12/01
	Appleton-Oshkosh-Neenah MSA, WI	Y	12410 FQ	21620 AW	37430 TQ	WIBLS	10/01-12/01
	Green Bay MSA, WI	Y	13300 FQ	21830 AW	36640 TQ	WIBLS	10/01-12/01
	Madison MSA, WI	Y	12980 FQ	21300 AW	34280 TQ	WIBLS	10/01-12/01
	Milwaukee-Waukesha PMSA, WI	Y	12480 FQ	21030 AW	34780 TQ	WIBLS	10/01-12/01
	Racine PMSA, WI	Y	12100 FQ	19260 AW	30310 TQ	WIBLS	10/01-12/01
	Wyoming	Y	11920 FQ	18130 AW	27750 TQ	WYBLS	10/01-12/01
	Cheyenne MSA, WY	Y	11900 FQ	18250 AW	29560 TQ	WYBLS	10/01-12/01
	Puerto Rico	Y	11440 FQ	14050 AW	17100 TQ	PRBLS	10/01-12/01
	Virgin Islands	Y	12040 FQ	17900 AW	26280 TQ	VIBLS	10/01-12/01
	Guam	Y	11680 FQ	15840 AW	21730 TQ	GUBLS	10/01-12/01
Rigger	Alabama	H	11.26 FQ	17.76 AW	26.46 TQ	ALBLS	10/01-12/01
	Arizona	H	9.11 FQ	15.95 AW	25.81 TQ	AZBLS	10/01-12/01
	Arkansas	H	7.97 FQ	10.43 AW	15.28 TQ	ARBLS	10/01-12/01
	California	H	10.18 FQ	18.17 AW	28.34 TQ	CABLS	10/01-12/01
	Connecticut	H	14.38 FQ	19.01 AW	25.55 TQ	CTBLS	10/01-12/01
	Delaware	H	7.83 FQ	16.35 AW	26.79 TQ	DEBLS	10/01-12/01
	Florida	H	7.91 FQ	12.75 AW	18.86 TQ	FLBLS	10/01-12/01
	Georgia	H	10.27 FQ	16.37 AW	21.15 TQ	GABLS	10/01-12/01
	Hawaii	H	15.80 FQ	22.36 AW	28.30 TQ	HIBLS	10/01-12/01
	Illinois	H	9.01 FQ	18.58 AW	27.02 TQ	ILBLS	10/01-12/01
	Indiana	H	9.71 FQ	16.70 AW	22.52 TQ	INBLS	10/01-12/01
	Kansas	H	9.12 FQ	22.31 AW	33.43 TQ	KSBLS	10/01-12/01
	Kentucky	H	13.65 FQ	21.10 AW	34.46 TQ	KYBLS	10/01-12/01
	Louisiana	H	8.63 FQ	12.78 AW	16.75 TQ	LABLS	10/01-12/01
	Maine	H	13.27 FQ	16.93 AW	20.98 TQ	MEBLS	10/01-12/01
	Maryland	H	11.20 FQ	16.73 AW	22.05 TQ	MDBLS	10/01-12/01
	Massachusetts	H	13.81 FQ	16.84 AW	22.32 TQ	MABLS	10/01-12/01
	Michigan	H	9.32 FQ	17.35 AW	24.65 TQ	MIBLS	10/01-12/01
	Minnesota	H	9.86 FQ	19.50 AW	32.26 TQ	MNBLS	10/01-12/01
	Mississippi	H	8.56 FQ	13.29 AW	19.46 TQ	MSBLS	10/01-12/01
	Missouri	H	10.03 FQ	20.19 AW	22.82 TQ	MOBLS	10/01-12/01
	New Jersey	H	9.61 FQ	14.77 AW	21.01 TQ	NJBLS	10/01-12/01
	New Mexico	H	11.46 FQ	12.84 AW	14.58 TQ	NMBLS	10/01-12/01
	New York	H	12.12 FQ	17.66 AW	25.22 TQ	NYBLS	10/01-12/01
	North Carolina	H	7.93 FQ	15.00 AW	21.49 TQ	NCBLS	10/01-12/01
	Ohio	H	9.76 FQ	16.27 AW	24.22 TQ	OHBLS	10/01-12/01
	Oklahoma	H	10.31 FQ	19.00 AW	26.47 TQ	OKBLS	10/01-12/01
	Oregon	H	11.12 FQ	17.73 AW	25.85 TQ	ORBLS	10/01-12/01
	Pennsylvania	H	9.27 FQ	14.69 AW	20.53 TQ	PABLS	10/01-12/01
	Rhode Island	H	9.63 FQ	17.25 AW	23.94 TQ	RIBLS	10/01-12/01
	South Carolina	H	10.38 FQ	18.34 AW	33.74 TQ	SCBLS	10/01-12/01
	Tennessee	H	6.32 FQ	15.12 AW	20.77 TQ	TNBLS	10/01-12/01
	Texas	H	9.57 FQ	15.39 AW	21.00 TQ	TXBLS	10/01-12/01
	Utah	H	10.02 FQ	14.99 AW	22.55 TQ	UTBLS	10/01-12/01
	Virginia	H	13.10 FQ	16.63 AW	20.43 TQ	VABLS	10/01-12/01
	Washington	H	14.54 FQ	20.88 AW	26.46 TQ	WABLS	10/01-12/01
	West Virginia	H	13.17 FQ	20.01 AW	25.67 TQ	WVBLS	10/01-12/01
	Wisconsin	H	11.38 FQ	23.01 AW	37.26 TQ	WIBLS	10/01-12/01
	Puerto Rico	H	5.79 FQ	8.98 AW	14.01 TQ	PRBLS	10/01-12/01
	Virgin Islands	H	13.93 FQ	15.24 AW	17.07 TQ	VIBLS	10/01-12/01
Risk Manager							
Environment	United States	Y		62603 AW		SAFEDIR	2001
Environment	Midwest	Y		60944 AW		SAFEDIR	2001
Environment	Northeast	Y		67286 AW		SAFEDIR	2001
Environment	South	Y		62250 AW		SAFEDIR	2001
Environment	West	Y		71500 AW		SAFEDIR	2001
Insurance	United States	Y		124947 AW		WW	1/00-1/01
River Pilot							
Mississippi River	Louisiana	Y		321000 AW		TPNO	1/00-1/00
Rock Splitter							
Quarry	Arizona	H	10.84 FQ	12.63 AW	14.21 TQ	AZBLS	10/01-12/01
Quarry	California	H	6.96 FQ	9.91 AW	16.67 TQ	CABLS	10/01-12/01
Quarry	Colorado	H	10.16 FQ	13.97 AW	18.11 TQ	COBLS	10/01-12/01

AAW	Average annual wage	**AOH**	Average offered, high	**ASH**	Average starting, high	**H**	Hourly	**M**	Monthly	**S**	Special: hourly and annual
AE	Average entry wage	**AOL**	Average offered, low	**ASL**	Average starting, low	**HI**	Highest wage paid	**MTC**	Median total compensation	**TQ**	Third quartile wage
AEX	Average experienced wage	**APH**	Average pay, high range	**AW**	Average wage paid	**HR**	High end range	**MW**	Median wage paid	**W**	Weekly
AO	Average offered	**APL**	Average pay, low range	**FQ**	First quartile wage	**LR**	Low end range	**SQ**	Second quartile wage	**Y**	Yearly

Occupation/Type/Industry	Location	Per	Low	Mid	High	Source	Date
Rock Splitter							
Quarry	Georgia	H	8.82 FQ	12.05 AW	14.30 TQ	GABLS	10/01-12/01
Quarry	Idaho	H	8.93 FQ	11.75 AW	15.87 TQ	IDBLS	10/01-12/01
Quarry	Illinois	H	10.64 FQ	19.69 AW	31.62 TQ	ILBLS	10/01-12/01
Quarry	Indiana	H	12.13 FQ	15.43 AW	17.59 TQ	INBLS	10/01-12/01
Quarry	Iowa	H	8.28 FQ	13.56 AW	17.15 TQ	IABLS	10/01-12/01
Quarry	Kansas	H	8.69 FQ	11.74 AW	15.22 TQ	KSBLS	10/01-12/01
Quarry	Maryland	H	8.09 FQ	11.32 AW	15.52 TQ	MDBLS	10/01-12/01
Quarry	Missouri	H	9.70 FQ	17.96 AW	31.43 TQ	MOBLS	10/01-12/01
Quarry	Montana	H	7.29 FQ	9.80 AW	13.90 TQ	MTBLS	10/01-12/01
Quarry	New York	H	6.18 FQ	9.93 AW	13.45 TQ	NYBLS	10/01-12/01
Quarry	Ohio	H	8.93 FQ	16.75 AW	27.98 TQ	OHBLS	10/01-12/01
Quarry	Oklahoma	H	10.37 FQ	17.30 AW	33.65 TQ	OKBLS	10/01-12/01
Quarry	Pennsylvania	H	9.28 FQ	13.98 AW	20.27 TQ	PABLS	10/01-12/01
Quarry	South Carolina	H	8.65 FQ	11.43 AW	15.28 TQ	SCBLS	10/01-12/01
Quarry	Tennessee	H	8.73 FQ	11.15 AW	14.05 TQ	TNBLS	10/01-12/01
Quarry	Texas	H	7.20 FQ	12.68 AW	18.99 TQ	TXBLS	10/01-12/01
Quarry	Utah	H	7.45 FQ	12.25 AW	18.17 TQ	UTBLS	10/01-12/01
Quarry	Vermont	H	10.11 FQ	13.28 AW	17.15 TQ	VTBLS	10/01-12/01
Quarry	Virginia	H	8.29 FQ	22.44 AW	33.91 TQ	VABLS	10/01-12/01
Quarry	Wisconsin	H	9.57 FQ	12.53 AW	16.95 TQ	WIBLS	10/01-12/01
Rolling Machine Setter, Operator, and Tender							
Metals and Plastics	Alabama	H	9.12 FQ	13.79 AW	20.64 TQ	ALBLS	10/01-12/01
Metals and Plastics	Birmingham MSA, AL	H	11.40 FQ	17.01 AW	23.98 TQ	ALBLS	10/01-12/01
Metals and Plastics	Mobile MSA, AL	H	7.46 FQ	12.75 AW	16.84 TQ	ALBLS	10/01-12/01
Metals and Plastics	Arizona	H	6.28 FQ	10.15 AW	15.06 TQ	AZBLS	10/01-12/01
Metals and Plastics	Phoenix-Mesa MSA, AZ	H	6.19 FQ	9.96 AW	14.45 TQ	AZBLS	10/01-12/01
Metals and Plastics	Arkansas	H	7.49 FQ	12.19 AW	16.75 TQ	ARBLS	10/01-12/01
Metals and Plastics	Little Rock-North Little Rock MSA, AR	H	7.03 FQ	10.40 AW	14.33 TQ	ARBLS	10/01-12/01
Metals and Plastics	California	H	6.72 FQ	11.31 AW	17.67 TQ	CABLS	10/01-12/01
Metals and Plastics	Bakersfield MSA, CA	H	9.67 FQ	13.67 AW	16.90 TQ	CABLS	10/01-12/01
Metals and Plastics	Los Angeles-Long Beach PMSA, CA	H	6.66 FQ	10.17 AW	15.33 TQ	CABLS	10/01-12/01
Metals and Plastics	Oakland PMSA, CA	H	7.86 FQ	12.84 AW	17.74 TQ	CABLS	10/01-12/01
Metals and Plastics	Orange County PMSA, CA	H	6.49 FQ	9.33 AW	13.15 TQ	CABLS	10/01-12/01
Metals and Plastics	Riverside-San Bernardino PMSA, CA	H	8.23 FQ	15.33 AW	24.37 TQ	CABLS	10/01-12/01
Metals and Plastics	Sacramento PMSA, CA	H	7.19 FQ	9.03 AW	11.25 TQ	CABLS	10/01-12/01
Metals and Plastics	San Diego MSA, CA	H	6.61 FQ	10.20 AW	16.16 TQ	CABLS	10/01-12/01
Metals and Plastics	San Francisco PMSA, CA	H	7.59 FQ	13.08 AW	20.87 TQ	CABLS	10/01-12/01
Metals and Plastics	San Jose PMSA, CA	H	8.36 FQ	12.98 AW	18.12 TQ	CABLS	10/01-12/01
Metals and Plastics	Stockton-Lodi MSA, CA	H	11.40 FQ	16.19 AW	20.85 TQ	CABLS	10/01-12/01
Metals and Plastics	Ventura PMSA, CA	H	7.03 FQ	10.41 AW	14.76 TQ	CABLS	10/01-12/01
Metals and Plastics	Visalia-Tulare-Porterville MSA, CA	H	7.62 FQ	11.42 AW	15.71 TQ	CABLS	10/01-12/01
Metals and Plastics	Colorado	H	9.45 FQ	13.87 AW	19.04 TQ	COBLS	10/01-12/01
Metals and Plastics	Denver PMSA, CO	H	9.23 FQ	12.35 AW	16.55 TQ	COBLS	10/01-12/01
Metals and Plastics	Connecticut	H	11.27 FQ	17.20 AW	25.27 TQ	CTBLS	10/01-12/01
Metals and Plastics	Bridgeport PMSA, CT	H	10.15 FQ	15.67 AW	20.56 TQ	CTBLS	10/01-12/01
Metals and Plastics	Hartford MSA, CT	H	12.75 FQ	18.83 AW	28.31 TQ	CTBLS	10/01-12/01
Metals and Plastics	New Haven-Meriden PMSA, CT	H	10.67 FQ	16.84 AW	24.95 TQ	CTBLS	10/01-12/01
Metals and Plastics	Waterbury PMSA, CT	H	9.57 FQ	13.37 AW	16.69 TQ	CTBLS	10/01-12/01
Metals and Plastics	Delaware	H	8.18 FQ	16.60 AW	29.73 TQ	DEBLS	10/01-12/01
Metals and Plastics	Wilmington-Newark PMSA, DE-MD	H	8.65 FQ	17.23 AW	30.25 TQ	DEBLS	10/01-12/01
Metals and Plastics	Washington PMSA, DC-MD-VA-WV	H	7.23 FQ	10.09 AW	14.47 TQ	DCBLS	10/01-12/01
Metals and Plastics	Florida	H	7.40 FQ	10.29 AW	14.61 TQ	FLBLS	10/01-12/01
Metals and Plastics	Fort Lauderdale PMSA, FL	H	7.70 FQ	11.17 AW	16.03 TQ	FLBLS	10/01-12/01
Metals and Plastics	Jacksonville MSA, FL	H	7.26 FQ	9.71 AW	12.86 TQ	FLBLS	10/01-12/01
Metals and Plastics	Miami PMSA, FL	H	7.77 FQ	10.52 AW	13.99 TQ	FLBLS	10/01-12/01
Metals and Plastics	Orlando MSA, FL	H	8.75 FQ	12.85 AW	19.78 TQ	FLBLS	10/01-12/01
Metals and Plastics	Tampa-St. Petersburg-Clearwater MSA, FL	H	6.32 FQ	8.93 AW	10.99 TQ	FLBLS	10/01-12/01
Metals and Plastics	Georgia	H	8.80 FQ	12.28 AW	16.39 TQ	GABLS	10/01-12/01
Metals and Plastics	Atlanta MSA, GA	H	8.14 FQ	11.90 AW	16.07 TQ	GABLS	10/01-12/01
Metals and Plastics	Illinois	H	10.75 FQ	14.15 AW	17.40 TQ	ILBLS	10/01-12/01
Metals and Plastics	Chicago PMSA, IL	H	11.05 FQ	14.04 AW	17.19 TQ	ILBLS	10/01-12/01

AAW Average annual wage; **AE** Average entry wage; **AEX** Average experienced wage; **AO** Average offered; **AOH** Average offered, high; **AOL** Average offered, low; **APH** Average pay, high range; **APL** Average pay, low range; **ASH** Average starting, high; **ASL** Average starting, low; **AW** Average wage paid; **FQ** First quartile wage; **H** Hourly; **HI** Highest wage paid; **HR** High end range; **LR** Low end range; **M** Monthly; **MTC** Median total compensation; **MW** Median wage paid; **SQ** Second quartile wage; **S** Special: hourly and annual; **TQ** Third quartile wage; **W** Weekly; **Y** Yearly

Occupation/Type/Industry	Location	Per	Low	Mid	High	Source	Date
Rolling Machine Setter, Operator, and Tender							
Metals and Plastics	Peoria-Pekin MSA, IL	H	10.54 FQ	13.75 AW	18.68 TQ	ILBLS	10/01-12/01
Metals and Plastics	Rockford MSA, IL	H	12.72 FQ	15.65 AW	19.27 TQ	ILBLS	10/01-12/01
Metals and Plastics	Indiana	H	9.15 FQ	14.70 AW	23.57 TQ	INBLS	10/01-12/01
Metals and Plastics	Elkhart-Goshen MSA, IN	H	9.24 FQ	11.14 AW	13.76 TQ	INBLS	10/01-12/01
Metals and Plastics	Fort Wayne MSA, IN	H	8.19 FQ	12.69 AW	23.42 TQ	INBLS	10/01-12/01
Metals and Plastics	Indianapolis MSA, IN	H	7.78 FQ	13.22 AW	18.05 TQ	INBLS	10/01-12/01
Metals and Plastics	South Bend MSA, IN	H	9.31 FQ	12.85 AW	19.74 TQ	INBLS	10/01-12/01
Metals and Plastics	Iowa	H	9.00 FQ	13.66 AW	18.76 TQ	IABLS	10/01-12/01
Metals and Plastics	Davenport-Moline-Rock Island MSA, IA-IL	H	8.12 FQ	12.53 AW	16.95 TQ	IABLS	10/01-12/01
Metals and Plastics	Kentucky	H	9.11 FQ	16.35 AW	22.05 TQ	KYBLS	10/01-12/01
Metals and Plastics	Lexington MSA, KY	H	9.42 FQ	15.58 AW	20.85 TQ	KYBLS	10/01-12/01
Metals and Plastics	Louisville MSA, KY-IN	H	8.79 FQ	15.60 AW	21.91 TQ	KYBLS	10/01-12/01
Metals and Plastics	Louisiana	H	8.27 FQ	12.66 AW	17.36 TQ	LABLS	10/01-12/01
Metals and Plastics	New Orleans MSA, LA	H	8.72 FQ	15.45 AW	21.91 TQ	LABLS	10/01-12/01
Metals and Plastics	Maine	H	11.10 FQ	14.18 AW	17.03 TQ	MEBLS	10/01-12/01
Metals and Plastics	Maryland	H	9.03 FQ	15.92 AW	23.48 TQ	MDBLS	10/01-12/01
Metals and Plastics	Baltimore PMSA, MD	H	10.09 FQ	16.32 AW	23.76 TQ	MDBLS	10/01-12/01
Metals and Plastics	Massachusetts	H	7.73 FQ	13.36 AW	19.21 TQ	MABLS	10/01-12/01
Metals and Plastics	Boston PMSA, MA-NH	H	8.07 FQ	14.04 AW	18.96 TQ	MABLS	10/01-12/01
Metals and Plastics	Lowell PMSA, MA-NH	H	7.75 FQ	10.79 AW	15.26 TQ	MABLS	10/01-12/01
Metals and Plastics	Springfield MSA, MA	H	9.87 FQ	14.31 AW	17.96 TQ	MABLS	10/01-12/01
Metals and Plastics	Worcester PMSA, MA-CT	H	6.99 FQ	9.74 AW	16.47 TQ	MABLS	10/01-12/01
Metals and Plastics	Michigan	H	9.40 FQ	12.96 AW	17.18 TQ	MIBLS	10/01-12/01
Metals and Plastics	Ann Arbor PMSA, MI	H	9.41 FQ	13.99 AW	22.89 TQ	MIBLS	10/01-12/01
Metals and Plastics	Detroit PMSA, MI	H	8.85 FQ	12.45 AW	18.24 TQ	MIBLS	10/01-12/01
Metals and Plastics	Grand Rapids-Muskegon-Holland MSA, MI	H	10.14 FQ	13.23 AW	16.95 TQ	MIBLS	10/01-12/01
Metals and Plastics	Minnesota	H	8.61 FQ	14.06 AW	20.16 TQ	MNBLS	10/01-12/01
Metals and Plastics	Minneapolis-St. Paul MSA, MN-WI	H	8.03 FQ	13.77 AW	20.34 TQ	MNBLS	10/01-12/01
Metals and Plastics	Mississippi	H	8.22 FQ	11.02 AW	13.72 TQ	MSBLS	10/01-12/01
Metals and Plastics	Missouri	H	6.00 FQ	10.73 AW	16.98 TQ	MOBLS	10/01-12/01
Metals and Plastics	St. Louis MSA, MO-IL	H	6.11 FQ	10.85 AW	16.15 TQ	MOBLS	10/01-12/01
Metals and Plastics	Springfield MSA, MO	H	8.71 FQ	11.81 AW	15.55 TQ	MOBLS	10/01-12/01
Metals and Plastics	Nebraska	H	8.88 FQ	13.13 AW	20.48 TQ	NEBLS	10/01-12/01
Metals and Plastics	Nevada	H	7.54 FQ	11.02 AW	15.85 TQ	NVBLS	10/01-12/01
Metals and Plastics	Las Vegas MSA, NV-AZ	H	7.34 FQ	10.86 AW	15.71 TQ	NVBLS	10/01-12/01
Metals and Plastics	Reno MSA, NV	H	8.26 FQ	11.85 AW	16.68 TQ	NVBLS	10/01-12/01
Metals and Plastics	Manchester PMSA, NH	H	9.06 FQ	13.14 AW	19.17 TQ	NHBLS	10/01-12/01
Metals and Plastics	New Jersey	H	8.63 FQ	14.90 AW	22.05 TQ	NJBLS	10/01-12/01
Metals and Plastics	Middlesex-Somerset-Hunterdon PMSA, NJ	H	8.64 FQ	15.88 AW	24.24 TQ	NJBLS	10/01-12/01
Metals and Plastics	Monmouth-Ocean PMSA, NJ	H	8.27 FQ	16.15 AW	21.47 TQ	NJBLS	10/01-12/01
Metals and Plastics	Newark PMSA, NJ	H	11.25 FQ	14.89 AW	21.48 TQ	NJBLS	10/01-12/01
Metals and Plastics	Trenton PMSA, NJ	H	8.05 FQ	10.87 AW	16.48 TQ	NJBLS	10/01-12/01
Metals and Plastics	New York	H	8.73 FQ	14.29 AW	21.23 TQ	NYBLS	10/01-12/01
Metals and Plastics	Buffalo-Niagara Falls MSA, NY	H	11.43 FQ	17.01 AW	25.14 TQ	NYBLS	10/01-12/01
Metals and Plastics	Nassau-Suffolk PMSA, NY	H	7.63 FQ	12.38 AW	17.28 TQ	NYBLS	10/01-12/01
Metals and Plastics	New York PMSA, NY	H	7.82 FQ	11.81 AW	16.74 TQ	NYBLS	10/01-12/01
Metals and Plastics	Rochester MSA, NY	H	9.59 FQ	13.50 AW	18.12 TQ	NYBLS	10/01-12/01
Metals and Plastics	Syracuse MSA, NY	H	14.37 FQ	18.37 AW	22.18 TQ	NYBLS	10/01-12/01
Metals and Plastics	North Carolina	H	8.16 FQ	13.28 AW	19.16 TQ	NCBLS	10/01-12/01
Metals and Plastics	Charlotte-Gastonia-Rock Hill MSA, NC-SC	H	7.84 FQ	13.58 AW	20.53 TQ	NCBLS	10/01-12/01
Metals and Plastics	Greensboro-Winston-Salem-High Point MSA, NC	H	9.42 FQ	14.46 AW	24.12 TQ	NCBLS	10/01-12/01
Metals and Plastics	Raleigh-Durham-Chapel Hill MSA, NC	H	9.40 FQ	13.18 AW	16.95 TQ	NCBLS	10/01-12/01
Metals and Plastics	North Dakota	H	8.92 FQ	11.73 AW	15.97 TQ	NDBLS	10/01-12/01
Metals and Plastics	Ohio	H	9.45 FQ	14.26 AW	20.24 TQ	OHBLS	10/01-12/01
Metals and Plastics	Akron PMSA, OH	H	9.12 FQ	11.58 AW	14.71 TQ	OHBLS	10/01-12/01
Metals and Plastics	Canton-Massillon MSA, OH	H	9.03 FQ	15.21 AW	22.32 TQ	OHBLS	10/01-12/01
Metals and Plastics	Cincinnati PMSA, OH-KY-IN	H	7.34 FQ	13.46 AW	20.32 TQ	OHBLS	10/01-12/01
Metals and Plastics	Cleveland-Lorain-Elyria PMSA, OH	H	9.39 FQ	15.02 AW	21.04 TQ	OHBLS	10/01-12/01
Metals and Plastics	Columbus MSA, OH	H	9.05 FQ	11.99 AW	16.86 TQ	OHBLS	10/01-12/01
Metals and Plastics	Hamilton-Middletown PMSA, OH	H	9.45 FQ	11.86 AW	16.05 TQ	OHBLS	10/01-12/01

AAW Average annual wage	**AOH** Average offered, high	**ASH** Average starting, high	**H** Hourly	**M** Monthly	**S** Special: hourly and annual
AE Average entry wage	**AOL** Average offered, low	**ASL** Average starting, low	**HI** Highest wage paid	**MTC** Median total compensation	**TQ** Third quartile wage
AEX Average experienced wage	**APH** Average pay, high range	**AW** Average wage paid	**HR** High end range	**MW** Median wage paid	**W** Weekly
AO Average offered	**APL** Average pay, low range	**FQ** First quartile wage	**LR** Low end range	**SQ** Second quartile wage	**Y** Yearly

Occupation/Type/Industry	Location	Per	Low	Mid	High	Source	Date
Rolling Machine Setter, Operator, and Tender							
Metals and Plastics	Mansfield MSA, OH	H	11.35 FQ	13.68 AW	17.14 TQ	OHBLS	10/01-12/01
Metals and Plastics	Toledo MSA, OH	H	9.46 FQ	14.01 AW	20.70 TQ	OHBLS	10/01-12/01
Metals and Plastics	Youngstown-Warren MSA, OH	H	11.05 FQ	15.69 AW	20.63 TQ	OHBLS	10/01-12/01
Metals and Plastics	Oklahoma	H	7.49 FQ	10.58 AW	15.19 TQ	OKBLS	10/01-12/01
Metals and Plastics	Oklahoma City MSA, OK	H	7.76 FQ	11.67 AW	16.12 TQ	OKBLS	10/01-12/01
Metals and Plastics	Tulsa MSA, OK	H	7.39 FQ	9.42 AW	12.94 TQ	OKBLS	10/01-12/01
Metals and Plastics	Oregon	H	7.92 FQ	17.95 AW	27.76 TQ	ORBLS	10/01-12/01
Metals and Plastics	Eugene-Springfield MSA, OR	H	9.30 FQ	12.24 AW	16.79 TQ	ORBLS	10/01-12/01
Metals and Plastics	Portland-Vancouver PMSA, OR-WA	H	7.86 FQ	18.27 AW	27.87 TQ	ORBLS	10/01-12/01
Metals and Plastics	Pennsylvania	H	9.21 FQ	14.69 AW	20.03 TQ	PABLS	10/01-12/01
Metals and Plastics	Allentown-Bethlehem-Easton MSA, PA	H	8.36 FQ	13.31 AW	17.12 TQ	PABLS	10/01-12/01
Metals and Plastics	Erie MSA, PA	H	7.48 FQ	10.97 AW	15.76 TQ	PABLS	10/01-12/01
Metals and Plastics	Harrisburg-Lebanon-Carlisle MSA, PA	H	6.48 FQ	13.91 AW	19.89 TQ	PABLS	10/01-12/01
Metals and Plastics	Philadelphia PMSA, PA-NJ	H	9.04 FQ	15.05 AW	20.17 TQ	PABLS	10/01-12/01
Metals and Plastics	Pittsburgh MSA, PA	H	9.61 FQ	14.97 AW	20.41 TQ	PABLS	10/01-12/01
Metals and Plastics	Reading MSA, PA	H	12.04 FQ	16.62 AW	22.34 TQ	PABLS	10/01-12/01
Metals and Plastics	Rhode Island	H	8.05 FQ	13.02 AW	20.48 TQ	RIBLS	10/01-12/01
Metals and Plastics	Providence-Fall River-Warwick MSA, RI-MA	H	7.70 FQ	12.59 AW	19.67 TQ	RIBLS	10/01-12/01
Metals and Plastics	South Carolina	H	9.18 FQ	14.42 AW	20.88 TQ	SCBLS	10/01-12/01
Metals and Plastics	Greenville-Spartanburg-Anderson MSA, SC	H	8.10 FQ	14.43 AW	25.57 TQ	SCBLS	10/01-12/01
Metals and Plastics	South Dakota	H	7.66 FQ	10.61 AW	16.82 TQ	SDBLS	10/01-12/01
Metals and Plastics	Sioux Falls MSA, SD	H	7.59 FQ	11.26 AW	18.72 TQ	SDBLS	10/01-12/01
Metals and Plastics	Tennessee	H	8.75 FQ	14.13 AW	17.80 TQ	TNBLS	10/01-12/01
Metals and Plastics	Chattanooga MSA, TN-GA	H	9.84 FQ	12.47 AW	14.37 TQ	TNBLS	10/01-12/01
Metals and Plastics	Memphis MSA, TN-AR-MS	H	9.74 FQ	13.04 AW	18.96 TQ	TNBLS	10/01-12/01
Metals and Plastics	Nashville MSA, TN	H	7.78 FQ	13.14 AW	17.64 TQ	TNBLS	10/01-12/01
Metals and Plastics	Texas	H	6.82 FQ	11.03 AW	16.31 TQ	TXBLS	10/01-12/01
Metals and Plastics	Austin-San Marcos MSA, TX	H	6.66 FQ	10.02 AW	14.38 TQ	TXBLS	10/01-12/01
Metals and Plastics	Dallas PMSA, TX	H	6.08 FQ	9.66 AW	13.63 TQ	TXBLS	10/01-12/01
Metals and Plastics	El Paso MSA, TX	H	6.21 FQ	10.13 AW	14.76 TQ	TXBLS	10/01-12/01
Metals and Plastics	Fort Worth-Arlington PMSA, TX	H	9.37 FQ	12.24 AW	18.13 TQ	TXBLS	10/01-12/01
Metals and Plastics	Houston PMSA, TX	H	7.85 FQ	11.81 AW	17.22 TQ	TXBLS	10/01-12/01
Metals and Plastics	Longview-Marshall MSA, TX	H	5.87 FQ	9.35 AW	15.30 TQ	TXBLS	10/01-12/01
Metals and Plastics	San Antonio MSA, TX	H	7.73 FQ	10.89 AW	15.57 TQ	TXBLS	10/01-12/01
Metals and Plastics	Waco MSA, TX	H	5.83 FQ	7.91 AW	11.05 TQ	TXBLS	10/01-12/01
Metals and Plastics	Utah	H	7.66 FQ	13.74 AW	20.63 TQ	UTBLS	10/01-12/01
Metals and Plastics	Provo-Orem MSA, UT	H	6.32 FQ	9.19 AW	14.20 TQ	UTBLS	10/01-12/01
Metals and Plastics	Vermont	H	9.30 FQ	13.03 AW	19.43 TQ	VTBLS	10/01-12/01
Metals and Plastics	Virginia	H	9.02 FQ	14.07 AW	23.13 TQ	VABLS	10/01-12/01
Metals and Plastics	Norfolk-Virginia Beach-Newport News MSA, VA-NC	H	9.61 FQ	18.62 AW	26.06 TQ	VABLS	10/01-12/01
Metals and Plastics	Richmond-Petersburg MSA, VA	H	10.04 FQ	13.74 AW	17.73 TQ	VABLS	10/01-12/01
Metals and Plastics	Washington	H	11.44 FQ	20.39 AW	27.77 TQ	WABLS	10/01-12/01
Metals and Plastics	Seattle-Bellevue-Everett PMSA, WA	H	12.19 FQ	20.70 AW	27.59 TQ	WABLS	10/01-12/01
Metals and Plastics	Spokane MSA, WA	H	11.14 FQ	20.13 AW	27.90 TQ	WABLS	10/01-12/01
Metals and Plastics	West Virginia	H	11.49 FQ	17.08 AW	22.49 TQ	WVBLS	10/01-12/01
Metals and Plastics	Huntington-Ashland MSA, WV-KY-OH	H	13.95 FQ	17.09 AW	20.74 TQ	WVBLS	10/01-12/01
Metals and Plastics	Wisconsin	H	8.98 FQ	14.40 AW	20.32 TQ	WIBLS	10/01-12/01
Metals and Plastics	Milwaukee-Waukesha PMSA, WI	H	10.51 FQ	15.77 AW	20.69 TQ	WIBLS	10/01-12/01
Metals and Plastics	Puerto Rico	H	6.12 FQ	12.42 AW	21.51 TQ	PRBLS	10/01-12/01
Roof Bolter							
Mining	Colorado	H	10.11 FQ	17.55 AW	25.19 TQ	COBLS	10/01-12/01
Mining	Illinois	H	17.70 FQ	19.91 AW	22.39 TQ	ILBLS	10/01-12/01
Mining	Indiana	H	14.93 FQ	16.97 AW	19.31 TQ	INBLS	10/01-12/01
Mining	Kentucky	H	12.24 FQ	15.35 AW	19.66 TQ	KYBLS	10/01-12/01
Mining	Ohio	H	15.18 FQ	19.32 AW	22.39 TQ	OHBLS	10/01-12/01
Mining	Pennsylvania	H	17.38 FQ	20.95 AW	26.07 TQ	PABLS	10/01-12/01
Mining	Tennessee	H	11.89 FQ	14.98 AW	18.52 TQ	TNBLS	10/01-12/01

AAW Average annual wage; AE Average entry wage; AEX Average experienced wage; AO Average offered; AOH Average offered, high; AOL Average offered, low; APH Average pay, high range; APL Average pay, low range; ASH Average starting, high; ASL Average starting, low; AW Average wage paid; FQ First quartile wage; H Hourly; HI Highest wage paid; HR High end range; LR Low end range; M Monthly; MTC Median total compensation; MW Median wage paid; SQ Second quartile wage; S Special: hourly and annual; TQ Third quartile wage; W Weekly; Y Yearly

Occupation/Type/Industry	Location	Per	Low	Mid	High	Source	Date
Roof Bolter							
Mining	Utah	H	14.41 FQ	19.00 AW	25.10 TQ	UTBLS	10/01-12/01
Mining	Virginia	H	13.29 FQ	18.47 AW	23.09 TQ	VABLS	10/01-12/01
Mining	West Virginia	H	14.44 FQ	18.75 AW	21.78 TQ	WVBLS	10/01-12/01
Roofer	Alabama	H	7.88 FQ	11.91 AW	17.11 TQ	ALBLS	10/01-12/01
	Birmingham MSA, AL	H	8.43 FQ	13.44 AW	19.51 TQ	ALBLS	10/01-12/01
	Huntsville MSA, AL	H	8.72 FQ	9.83 AW	11.18 TQ	ALBLS	10/01-12/01
	Mobile MSA, AL	H	7.45 FQ	10.90 AW	15.27 TQ	ALBLS	10/01-12/01
	Montgomery MSA, AL	H	9.69 FQ	12.55 AW	16.61 TQ	ALBLS	10/01-12/01
	Alaska	H	14.78 FQ	23.25 AW	37.67 TQ	AKBLS	10/01-12/01
	Anchorage MSA, AK	H	13.94 FQ	21.20 AW	30.83 TQ	AKBLS	10/01-12/01
	Arizona	H	7.87 FQ	13.25 AW	19.34 TQ	AZBLS	10/01-12/01
	Phoenix-Mesa MSA, AZ	H	7.36 FQ	13.38 AW	19.88 TQ	AZBLS	10/01-12/01
	Tucson MSA, AZ	H	8.19 FQ	13.22 AW	19.48 TQ	AZBLS	10/01-12/01
	Arkansas	H	8.55 FQ	12.45 AW	17.12 TQ	ARBLS	10/01-12/01
	Little Rock-North Little Rock MSA, AR	H	9.25 FQ	13.60 AW	18.35 TQ	ARBLS	10/01-12/01
	California	H	9.66 FQ	17.15 AW	25.78 TQ	CABLS	10/01-12/01
	Bakersfield MSA, CA	H	7.26 FQ	12.60 AW	20.06 TQ	CABLS	10/01-12/01
	Chico-Paradise MSA, CA	H	10.08 FQ	15.23 AW	23.40 TQ	CABLS	10/01-12/01
	Fresno MSA, CA	H	10.39 FQ	18.34 AW	26.51 TQ	CABLS	10/01-12/01
	Los Angeles-Long Beach PMSA, CA	H	9.46 FQ	16.20 AW	23.95 TQ	CABLS	10/01-12/01
	Merced MSA, CA	H	9.59 FQ	15.65 AW	20.88 TQ	CABLS	10/01-12/01
	Modesto MSA, CA	H	9.28 FQ	15.74 AW	24.27 TQ	CABLS	10/01-12/01
	Oakland PMSA, CA	H	11.31 FQ	19.67 AW	27.25 TQ	CABLS	10/01-12/01
	Orange County PMSA, CA	H	7.65 FQ	15.01 AW	26.26 TQ	CABLS	10/01-12/01
	Redding MSA, CA	H	9.33 FQ	14.37 AW	21.04 TQ	CABLS	10/01-12/01
	Riverside-San Bernardino PMSA, CA	H	10.21 FQ	14.88 AW	21.45 TQ	CABLS	10/01-12/01
	Sacramento PMSA, CA	H	10.78 FQ	17.72 AW	26.18 TQ	CABLS	10/01-12/01
	Salinas MSA, CA	H	14.05 FQ	18.66 AW	23.54 TQ	CABLS	10/01-12/01
	San Diego MSA, CA	H	10.35 FQ	18.27 AW	23.18 TQ	CABLS	10/01-12/01
	San Francisco PMSA, CA	H	11.19 FQ	20.36 AW	29.67 TQ	CABLS	10/01-12/01
	San Jose PMSA, CA	H	12.92 FQ	21.08 AW	28.50 TQ	CABLS	10/01-12/01
	San Luis Obispo-Atascadero-Paso Robles MSA, CA	H	8.26 FQ	14.48 AW	22.84 TQ	CABLS	10/01-12/01
	Santa Barbara-Santa Maria-Lompoc MSA, CA	H	8.52 FQ	14.23 AW	20.57 TQ	CABLS	10/01-12/01
	Santa Cruz-Watsonville PMSA, CA	H	13.06 FQ	18.17 AW	25.29 TQ	CABLS	10/01-12/01
	Santa Rosa PMSA, CA	H	11.12 FQ	18.71 AW	25.78 TQ	CABLS	10/01-12/01
	Stockton-Lodi MSA, CA	H	11.65 FQ	16.82 AW	21.96 TQ	CABLS	10/01-12/01
	Vallejo-Fairfield-Napa PMSA, CA	H	9.38 FQ	17.60 AW	25.07 TQ	CABLS	10/01-12/01
	Ventura PMSA, CA	H	8.07 FQ	12.49 AW	17.77 TQ	CABLS	10/01-12/01
	Visalia-Tulare-Porterville MSA, CA	H	7.99 FQ	11.42 AW	15.04 TQ	CABLS	10/01-12/01
	Colorado	H	9.75 FQ	14.15 AW	18.95 TQ	COBLS	10/01-12/01
	Boulder-Longmont PMSA, CO	H	10.53 FQ	13.93 AW	17.57 TQ	COBLS	10/01-12/01
	Colorado Springs MSA, CO	H	9.83 FQ	14.41 AW	19.75 TQ	COBLS	10/01-12/01
	Denver PMSA, CO	H	10.92 FQ	14.52 AW	18.10 TQ	COBLS	10/01-12/01
	Fort Collins-Loveland MSA, CO	H	7.37 FQ	11.40 AW	16.96 TQ	COBLS	10/01-12/01
	Greeley PMSA, CO	H	8.73 FQ	13.17 AW	19.87 TQ	COBLS	10/01-12/01
	Connecticut	H	9.11 FQ	18.66 AW	27.01 TQ	CTBLS	10/01-12/01
	Hartford MSA, CT	H	8.25 FQ	19.22 AW	27.25 TQ	CTBLS	10/01-12/01
	New Haven-Meriden PMSA, CT	H	11.27 FQ	17.74 AW	25.22 TQ	CTBLS	10/01-12/01
	New London-Norwich MSA, CT-RI	H	9.38 FQ	13.07 AW	19.99 TQ	CTBLS	10/01-12/01
	Stamford-Norwalk PMSA, CT	H	7.66 FQ	19.76 AW	29.22 TQ	CTBLS	10/01-12/01
	Waterbury PMSA, CT	H	14.64 FQ	18.03 AW	21.59 TQ	CTBLS	10/01-12/01
	Delaware	H	9.38 FQ	14.16 AW	19.48 TQ	DEBLS	10/01-12/01
	Wilmington-Newark PMSA, DE-MD	H	10.68 FQ	14.91 AW	19.87 TQ	DEBLS	10/01-12/01
	District of Columbia	H	9.18 FQ	12.86 AW	20.22 TQ	DCBLS	10/01-12/01
	Washington PMSA, DC-MD-VA-WV	H	10.92 FQ	15.40 AW	20.82 TQ	DCBLS	10/01-12/01
	Florida	H	8.81 FQ	13.09 AW	17.76 TQ	FLBLS	10/01-12/01
	Daytona Beach MSA, FL	H	7.42 FQ	12.01 AW	17.13 TQ	FLBLS	10/01-12/01
	Fort Lauderdale PMSA, FL	H	10.07 FQ	15.42 AW	19.91 TQ	FLBLS	10/01-12/01

AAW Average annual wage **AOH** Average offered, high **ASH** Average starting, high **H** Hourly **M** Monthly **S** Special: hourly and annual
AE Average entry wage **AOL** Average offered, low **ASL** Average starting, low **HI** Highest wage paid **MTC** Median total compensation **TQ** Third quartile wage
AEX Average experienced wage **APH** Average pay, high range **AW** Average wage paid **HR** High end range **MW** Median wage paid **W** Weekly
AO Average offered **APL** Average pay, low range **FQ** First quartile wage **LR** Low end range **SQ** Second quartile wage **Y** Yearly

Occupation/Type/Industry	Location	Per	Low	Mid	High	Source	Date
Roofer	Fort Myers-Cape Coral MSA, FL	H	10.87 FQ	14.17 AW	17.15 TQ	FLBLS	10/01-12/01
	Fort Pierce-Port St. Lucie MSA, FL	H	6.54 FQ	11.80 AW	18.14 TQ	FLBLS	10/01-12/01
	Gainesville MSA, FL	H	9.33 FQ	12.41 AW	16.35 TQ	FLBLS	10/01-12/01
	Jacksonville MSA, FL	H	10.29 FQ	13.50 AW	19.40 TQ	FLBLS	10/01-12/01
	Lakeland-Winter Haven MSA, FL	H	8.60 FQ	13.99 AW	18.90 TQ	FLBLS	10/01-12/01
	Melbourne-Titusville-Palm Bay MSA, FL	H	8.42 FQ	12.23 AW	19.04 TQ	FLBLS	10/01-12/01
	Miami PMSA, FL	H	7.32 FQ	10.04 AW	13.92 TQ	FLBLS	10/01-12/01
	Naples MSA, FL	H	9.40 FQ	18.05 AW	30.72 TQ	FLBLS	10/01-12/01
	Ocala MSA, FL	H	8.78 FQ	12.34 AW	16.18 TQ	FLBLS	10/01-12/01
	Orlando MSA, FL	H	9.24 FQ	13.36 AW	17.69 TQ	FLBLS	10/01-12/01
	Pensacola MSA, FL	H	8.02 FQ	10.89 AW	13.49 TQ	FLBLS	10/01-12/01
	Sarasota-Bradenton MSA, FL	H	10.31 FQ	13.42 AW	16.94 TQ	FLBLS	10/01-12/01
	Tallahassee MSA, FL	H	9.29 FQ	11.42 AW	16.36 TQ	FLBLS	10/01-12/01
	Tampa-St. Petersburg-Clearwater MSA, FL	H	9.16 FQ	13.22 AW	18.09 TQ	FLBLS	10/01-12/01
	West Palm Beach-Boca Raton MSA, FL	H	8.85 FQ	12.48 AW	16.96 TQ	FLBLS	10/01-12/01
	Georgia	H	8.47 FQ	12.64 AW	17.57 TQ	GABLS	10/01-12/01
	Atlanta MSA, GA	H	8.88 FQ	13.17 AW	18.06 TQ	GABLS	10/01-12/01
	Augusta-Aiken MSA, GA-SC	H	7.38 FQ	10.56 AW	15.90 TQ	GABLS	10/01-12/01
	Macon MSA, GA	H	5.51 FQ	9.24 AW	16.43 TQ	GABLS	10/01-12/01
	Savannah MSA, GA	H	7.59 FQ	11.02 AW	16.93 TQ	GABLS	10/01-12/01
	Hawaii	H	9.87 FQ	18.40 AW	27.40 TQ	HIBLS	10/01-12/01
	Honolulu MSA, HI	H	9.36 FQ	17.79 AW	27.33 TQ	HIBLS	10/01-12/01
	Idaho	H	7.97 FQ	13.00 AW	17.61 TQ	IDBLS	10/01-12/01
	Boise City MSA, ID	H	7.90 FQ	12.60 AW	17.27 TQ	IDBLS	10/01-12/01
	Illinois	H	11.27 FQ	22.42 AW	34.19 TQ	ILBLS	10/01-12/01
	Champaign-Urbana MSA, IL	H	13.50 FQ	23.01 AW	28.58 TQ	ILBLS	10/01-12/01
	Chicago PMSA, IL	H	14.19 FQ	24.27 AW	35.24 TQ	ILBLS	10/01-12/01
	Peoria-Pekin MSA, IL	H	9.52 FQ	17.39 AW	25.70 TQ	ILBLS	10/01-12/01
	Rockford MSA, IL	H	7.11 FQ	14.93 AW	26.15 TQ	ILBLS	10/01-12/01
	Indiana	H	9.22 FQ	15.81 AW	25.67 TQ	INBLS	10/01-12/01
	Elkhart-Goshen MSA, IN	H	9.35 FQ	13.38 AW	20.49 TQ	INBLS	10/01-12/01
	Evansville-Henderson MSA, IN-KY	H	9.53 FQ	15.91 AW	22.77 TQ	INBLS	10/01-12/01
	Fort Wayne MSA, IN	H	10.78 FQ	15.19 AW	21.63 TQ	INBLS	10/01-12/01
	Gary PMSA, IN	H	17.54 FQ	25.12 AW	33.42 TQ	INBLS	10/01-12/01
	Indianapolis MSA, IN	H	8.49 FQ	13.48 AW	20.55 TQ	INBLS	10/01-12/01
	Lafayette MSA, IN	H	6.56 FQ	14.88 AW	21.98 TQ	INBLS	10/01-12/01
	South Bend MSA, IN	H	9.14 FQ	16.32 AW	25.81 TQ	INBLS	10/01-12/01
	Iowa	H	8.83 FQ	13.29 AW	18.99 TQ	IABLS	10/01-12/01
	Cedar Rapids MSA, IA	H	9.90 FQ	14.59 AW	19.99 TQ	IABLS	10/01-12/01
	Davenport-Moline-Rock Island MSA, IA-IL	H	9.22 FQ	14.66 AW	21.55 TQ	IABLS	10/01-12/01
	Des Moines MSA, IA	H	10.35 FQ	15.06 AW	20.40 TQ	IABLS	10/01-12/01
	Kansas	H	8.53 FQ	13.33 AW	20.80 TQ	KSBLS	10/01-12/01
	Topeka MSA, KS	H	9.18 FQ	12.79 AW	20.00 TQ	KSBLS	10/01-12/01
	Wichita MSA, KS	H	9.72 FQ	13.07 AW	16.79 TQ	KSBLS	10/01-12/01
	Kentucky	H	9.52 FQ	13.75 AW	19.01 TQ	KYBLS	10/01-12/01
	Lexington MSA, KY	H	9.98 FQ	12.96 AW	16.57 TQ	KYBLS	10/01-12/01
	Louisville MSA, KY-IN	H	9.82 FQ	13.98 AW	18.08 TQ	KYBLS	10/01-12/01
	Louisiana	H	7.63 FQ	11.52 AW	16.11 TQ	LABLS	10/01-12/01
	Baton Rouge MSA, LA	H	7.95 FQ	13.02 AW	19.70 TQ	LABLS	10/01-12/01
	Lafayette MSA, LA	H	7.29 FQ	10.64 AW	16.46 TQ	LABLS	10/01-12/01
	New Orleans MSA, LA	H	7.67 FQ	11.53 AW	15.99 TQ	LABLS	10/01-12/01
	Shreveport-Bossier City MSA, LA	H	8.29 FQ	11.18 AW	15.03 TQ	LABLS	10/01-12/01
	Maine	H	8.79 FQ	11.73 AW	15.89 TQ	MEBLS	10/01-12/01
	Portland MSA, ME	H	8.50 FQ	11.71 AW	15.56 TQ	MEBLS	10/01-12/01
	Maryland	H	9.74 FQ	14.97 AW	20.49 TQ	MDBLS	10/01-12/01
	Baltimore PMSA, MD	H	9.42 FQ	14.46 AW	19.61 TQ	MDBLS	10/01-12/01
	Massachusetts	H	11.71 FQ	18.57 AW	26.39 TQ	MABLS	10/01-12/01
	Boston PMSA, MA-NH	H	11.97 FQ	19.65 AW	27.00 TQ	MABLS	10/01-12/01
	Brockton PMSA, MA	H	12.51 FQ	17.39 AW	22.62 TQ	MABLS	10/01-12/01
	Lawrence PMSA, MA-NH	H	11.85 FQ	17.74 AW	23.23 TQ	MABLS	10/01-12/01
	Lowell PMSA, MA-NH	H	13.38 FQ	18.72 AW	22.29 TQ	MABLS	10/01-12/01
	Springfield MSA, MA	H	12.42 FQ	18.26 AW	25.48 TQ	MABLS	10/01-12/01
	Worcester PMSA, MA-CT	H	10.88 FQ	18.23 AW	26.37 TQ	MABLS	10/01-12/01

AAW Average annual wage	**AOH** Average offered, high	**ASH** Average starting, high	**H** Hourly	**M** Monthly	**S** Special: hourly and annual
AE Average entry wage	**AOL** Average offered, low	**ASL** Average starting, low	**HI** Highest wage paid	**MTC** Median total compensation	**TQ** Third quartile wage
AEX Average experienced wage	**APH** Average pay, high range	**AW** Average wage paid	**HR** High end range	**MW** Median wage paid	**W** Weekly
AO Average offered	**APL** Average pay, low range	**FQ** First quartile wage	**LR** Low end range	**SQ** Second quartile wage	**Y** Yearly

Occupation/Type/Industry	Location	Per	Low	Mid	High	Source	Date
Roofer	Michigan	H	9.20 FQ	16.69 AW	26.19 TQ	MIBLS	10/01-12/01
	Ann Arbor PMSA, MI	H	11.58 FQ	18.73 AW	26.00 TQ	MIBLS	10/01-12/01
	Detroit PMSA, MI	H	13.90 FQ	21.69 AW	27.59 TQ	MIBLS	10/01-12/01
	Grand Rapids-Muskegon-Holland MSA, MI	H	8.50 FQ	12.13 AW	16.26 TQ	MIBLS	10/01-12/01
	Kalamazoo-Battle Creek MSA, MI	H	6.56 FQ	12.44 AW	20.10 TQ	MIBLS	10/01-12/01
	Lansing-East Lansing MSA, MI	H	9.46 FQ	13.79 AW	19.83 TQ	MIBLS	10/01-12/01
	Saginaw-Bay City-Midland MSA, MI	H	8.05 FQ	13.52 AW	20.56 TQ	MIBLS	10/01-12/01
	Minnesota	H	10.29 FQ	18.06 AW	26.99 TQ	MNBLS	10/01-12/01
	Duluth-Superior MSA, MN-WI	H	8.74 FQ	13.70 AW	24.02 TQ	MNBLS	10/01-12/01
	Minneapolis-St. Paul MSA, MN-WI	H	13.45 FQ	20.44 AW	27.44 TQ	MNBLS	10/01-12/01
	St. Cloud MSA, MN	H	13.31 FQ	21.29 AW	31.72 TQ	MNBLS	10/01-12/01
	Mississippi	H	7.42 FQ	10.39 AW	14.45 TQ	MSBLS	10/01-12/01
	Biloxi-Gulfport-Pascagoula MSA, MS	H	8.34 FQ	11.67 AW	17.14 TQ	MSBLS	10/01-12/01
	Jackson MSA, MS	H	8.14 FQ	10.89 AW	14.18 TQ	MSBLS	10/01-12/01
	Missouri	H	10.66 FQ	17.38 AW	26.05 TQ	MOBLS	10/01-12/01
	Kansas City MSA, MO-KS	H	11.87 FQ	17.72 AW	26.51 TQ	MOBLS	10/01-12/01
	St. Louis MSA, MO-IL	H	12.30 FQ	19.67 AW	26.83 TQ	MOBLS	10/01-12/01
	Springfield MSA, MO	H	5.99 FQ	11.50 AW	16.89 TQ	MOBLS	10/01-12/01
	Montana	H	11.19 FQ	15.25 AW	20.15 TQ	MTBLS	10/01-12/01
	Billings MSA, MT	H	11.11 FQ	14.96 AW	18.69 TQ	MTBLS	10/01-12/01
	Nebraska	H	9.16 FQ	12.76 AW	17.14 TQ	NEBLS	10/01-12/01
	Lincoln MSA, NE	H	9.53 FQ	12.32 AW	15.96 TQ	NEBLS	10/01-12/01
	Omaha MSA, NE-IA	H	9.47 FQ	13.04 AW	17.18 TQ	NEBLS	10/01-12/01
	Nevada	H	12.22 FQ	22.85 AW	34.10 TQ	NVBLS	10/01-12/01
	Las Vegas MSA, NV-AZ	H	11.57 FQ	23.85 AW	34.67 TQ	NVBLS	10/01-12/01
	Reno MSA, NV	H	12.48 FQ	18.39 AW	25.04 TQ	NVBLS	10/01-12/01
	New Hampshire	H	9.34 FQ	14.07 AW	19.94 TQ	NHBLS	10/01-12/01
	Nashua PMSA, NH	H	13.57 FQ	16.56 AW	20.44 TQ	NHBLS	10/01-12/01
	Portsmouth-Rochester PMSA, NH-ME	H	9.35 FQ	13.42 AW	17.31 TQ	NHBLS	10/01-12/01
	New Jersey	H	11.71 FQ	22.83 AW	34.33 TQ	NJBLS	10/01-12/01
	Atlantic-Cape May PMSA, NJ	H	15.51 FQ	22.45 AW	28.18 TQ	NJBLS	10/01-12/01
	Bergen-Passaic PMSA, NJ	H	15.12 FQ	23.13 AW	30.01 TQ	NJBLS	10/01-12/01
	Jersey City PMSA, NJ	H	9.42 FQ	16.42 AW	28.23 TQ	NJBLS	10/01-12/01
	Middlesex-Somerset-Hunterdon PMSA, NJ	H	13.67 FQ	22.68 AW	33.25 TQ	NJBLS	10/01-12/01
	Monmouth-Ocean PMSA, NJ	H	15.02 FQ	26.03 AW	41.40 TQ	NJBLS	10/01-12/01
	Newark PMSA, NJ	H	9.79 FQ	18.73 AW	31.44 TQ	NJBLS	10/01-12/01
	Trenton PMSA, NJ	H	8.68 FQ	18.75 AW	26.77 TQ	NJBLS	10/01-12/01
	New Mexico	H	7.79 FQ	11.35 AW	16.36 TQ	NMBLS	10/01-12/01
	Albuquerque MSA, NM	H	9.24 FQ	12.14 AW	16.82 TQ	NMBLS	10/01-12/01
	Las Cruces MSA, NM	H	6.83 FQ	9.98 AW	13.29 TQ	NMBLS	10/01-12/01
	New York	H	9.13 FQ	17.15 AW	29.47 TQ	NYBLS	10/01-12/01
	Albany-Schenectady-Troy MSA, NY	H	11.44 FQ	15.43 AW	21.06 TQ	NYBLS	10/01-12/01
	Binghamton MSA, NY	H	9.41 FQ	15.58 AW	21.04 TQ	NYBLS	10/01-12/01
	Buffalo-Niagara Falls MSA, NY	H	10.16 FQ	13.81 AW	20.91 TQ	NYBLS	10/01-12/01
	Dutchess County PMSA, NY	H	11.43 FQ	14.77 AW	18.13 TQ	NYBLS	10/01-12/01
	Nassau-Suffolk PMSA, NY	H	13.33 FQ	25.47 AW	39.12 TQ	NYBLS	10/01-12/01
	New York PMSA, NY	H	6.70 FQ	15.00 AW	27.80 TQ	NYBLS	10/01-12/01
	Newburgh PMSA, NY-PA	H	11.82 FQ	15.76 AW	21.13 TQ	NYBLS	10/01-12/01
	Rochester MSA, NY	H	9.80 FQ	18.35 AW	26.26 TQ	NYBLS	10/01-12/01
	Syracuse MSA, NY	H	6.34 FQ	13.56 AW	21.32 TQ	NYBLS	10/01-12/01
	Utica-Rome MSA, NY	H	5.78 FQ	12.48 AW	21.82 TQ	NYBLS	10/01-12/01
	North Carolina	H	8.16 FQ	11.71 AW	16.32 TQ	NCBLS	10/01-12/01
	Asheville MSA, NC	H	8.15 FQ	11.10 AW	14.01 TQ	NCBLS	10/01-12/01
	Charlotte-Gastonia-Rock Hill MSA, NC-SC	H	7.83 FQ	11.25 AW	15.76 TQ	NCBLS	10/01-12/01
	Fayetteville MSA, NC	H	8.12 FQ	13.06 AW	21.26 TQ	NCBLS	10/01-12/01
	Greensboro-Winston-Salem-High Point MSA, NC	H	9.13 FQ	12.75 AW	17.44 TQ	NCBLS	10/01-12/01
	Hickory-Morganton-Lenoir MSA, NC	H	9.01 FQ	11.67 AW	14.15 TQ	NCBLS	10/01-12/01
	Raleigh-Durham-Chapel Hill MSA, NC	H	8.86 FQ	12.24 AW	16.20 TQ	NCBLS	10/01-12/01
	Wilmington MSA, NC	H	9.37 FQ	13.06 AW	18.74 TQ	NCBLS	10/01-12/01

AAW	Average annual wage	**AOH**	Average offered, high	**ASH**	Average starting, high	**H**	Hourly	**M**	Monthly	**S**	Special: hourly and annual
AE	Average entry wage	**AOL**	Average offered, low	**ASL**	Average starting, low	**HI**	Highest wage paid	**MTC**	Median total compensation	**TQ**	Third quartile wage
AEX	Average experienced wage	**APH**	Average pay, high range	**AW**	Average wage paid	**HR**	High end range	**MW**	Median wage paid	**W**	Weekly
AO	Average offered	**APL**	Average pay, low range	**FQ**	First quartile wage	**LR**	Low end range	**SQ**	Second quartile wage	**Y**	Yearly

Occupation/Type/Industry	Location	Per	Low	Mid	High	Source	Date
Roofer	North Dakota	H	8.95 FQ	11.70 AW	15.58 TQ	NDBLS	10/01-12/01
	Fargo-Moorhead MSA, ND-MN	H	9.42 FQ	13.10 AW	17.28 TQ	NDBLS	10/01-12/01
	Ohio	H	10.16 FQ	16.47 AW	24.26 TQ	OHBLS	10/01-12/01
	Akron PMSA, OH	H	9.08 FQ	14.86 AW	20.95 TQ	OHBLS	10/01-12/01
	Canton-Massillon MSA, OH	H	12.82 FQ	18.89 AW	22.67 TQ	OHBLS	10/01-12/01
	Cincinnati PMSA, OH-KY-IN	H	9.86 FQ	16.84 AW	25.90 TQ	OHBLS	10/01-12/01
	Cleveland-Lorain-Elyria PMSA, OH	H	11.75 FQ	17.97 AW	25.99 TQ	OHBLS	10/01-12/01
	Columbus MSA, OH	H	11.80 FQ	16.01 AW	21.31 TQ	OHBLS	10/01-12/01
	Dayton-Springfield MSA, OH	H	12.22 FQ	17.96 AW	22.14 TQ	OHBLS	10/01-12/01
	Mansfield MSA, OH	H	9.13 FQ	14.09 AW	19.62 TQ	OHBLS	10/01-12/01
	Toledo MSA, OH	H	11.40 FQ	17.51 AW	26.03 TQ	OHBLS	10/01-12/01
	Youngstown-Warren MSA, OH	H	12.12 FQ	19.50 AW	26.40 TQ	OHBLS	10/01-12/01
	Oklahoma	H	7.57 FQ	12.54 AW	18.21 TQ	OKBLS	10/01-12/01
	Oklahoma City MSA, OK	H	8.29 FQ	14.13 AW	22.83 TQ	OKBLS	10/01-12/01
	Tulsa MSA, OK	H	9.01 FQ	12.07 AW	16.55 TQ	OKBLS	10/01-12/01
	Oregon	H	9.95 FQ	16.87 AW	26.69 TQ	ORBLS	10/01-12/01
	Eugene-Springfield MSA, OR	H	9.16 FQ	14.10 AW	20.67 TQ	ORBLS	10/01-12/01
	Medford-Ashland MSA, OR	H	8.40 FQ	13.00 AW	16.56 TQ	ORBLS	10/01-12/01
	Portland-Vancouver PMSA, OR-WA	H	10.47 FQ	18.74 AW	27.91 TQ	ORBLS	10/01-12/01
	Salem PMSA, OR	H	10.37 FQ	18.20 AW	27.09 TQ	ORBLS	10/01-12/01
	Pennsylvania	H	8.54 FQ	14.93 AW	23.25 TQ	PABLS	10/01-12/01
	Allentown-Bethlehem-Easton MSA, PA	H	8.03 FQ	14.70 AW	21.92 TQ	PABLS	10/01-12/01
	Erie MSA, PA	H	10.28 FQ	17.36 AW	22.46 TQ	PABLS	10/01-12/01
	Harrisburg-Lebanon-Carlisle MSA, PA	H	9.88 FQ	15.94 AW	25.61 TQ	PABLS	10/01-12/01
	Lancaster MSA, PA	H	9.76 FQ	16.23 AW	21.46 TQ	PABLS	10/01-12/01
	Philadelphia PMSA, PA-NJ	H	6.46 FQ	19.93 AW	33.56 TQ	PABLS	10/01-12/01
	Pittsburgh MSA, PA	H	9.14 FQ	14.56 AW	21.73 TQ	PABLS	10/01-12/01
	Reading MSA, PA	H	11.94 FQ	18.54 AW	26.71 TQ	PABLS	10/01-12/01
	Scranton-Wilkes-Barre-Hazleton MSA, PA	H	11.09 FQ	13.91 AW	19.32 TQ	PABLS	10/01-12/01
	York MSA, PA	H	9.11 FQ	14.89 AW	20.69 TQ	PABLS	10/01-12/01
	Rhode Island	H	11.03 FQ	16.73 AW	23.02 TQ	RIBLS	10/01-12/01
	Providence-Fall River-Warwick MSA, RI-MA	H	11.18 FQ	16.77 AW	23.18 TQ	RIBLS	10/01-12/01
	South Carolina	H	6.54 FQ	10.29 AW	14.44 TQ	SCBLS	10/01-12/01
	Charleston-North Charleston MSA, SC	H	7.98 FQ	11.51 AW	16.68 TQ	SCBLS	10/01-12/01
	Columbia MSA, SC	H	7.86 FQ	10.72 AW	14.28 TQ	SCBLS	10/01-12/01
	Greenville-Spartanburg-Anderson MSA, SC	H	6.00 FQ	9.07 AW	13.37 TQ	SCBLS	10/01-12/01
	Myrtle Beach MSA, SC	H	6.85 FQ	10.47 AW	14.77 TQ	SCBLS	10/01-12/01
	South Dakota	H	8.22 FQ	10.93 AW	14.16 TQ	SDBLS	10/01-12/01
	Sioux Falls MSA, SD	H	8.87 FQ	11.18 AW	14.12 TQ	SDBLS	10/01-12/01
	Tennessee	H	9.12 FQ	13.02 AW	17.19 TQ	TNBLS	10/01-12/01
	Chattanooga MSA, TN-GA	H	10.83 FQ	13.85 AW	17.79 TQ	TNBLS	10/01-12/01
	Johnson City-Kingsport-Bristol MSA, TN-VA	H	7.82 FQ	10.62 AW	14.05 TQ	TNBLS	10/01-12/01
	Knoxville MSA, TN	H	10.07 FQ	12.94 AW	16.62 TQ	TNBLS	10/01-12/01
	Memphis MSA, TN-AR-MS	H	9.36 FQ	13.39 AW	17.71 TQ	TNBLS	10/01-12/01
	Nashville MSA, TN	H	11.77 FQ	14.63 AW	17.76 TQ	TNBLS	10/01-12/01
	Texas	H	7.92 FQ	12.25 AW	17.49 TQ	TXBLS	10/01-12/01
	Amarillo MSA, TX	H	7.00 FQ	10.77 AW	15.79 TQ	TXBLS	10/01-12/01
	Austin-San Marcos MSA, TX	H	6.41 FQ	15.80 AW	22.53 TQ	TXBLS	10/01-12/01
	Beaumont-Port Arthur MSA, TX	H	8.46 FQ	15.49 AW	21.32 TQ	TXBLS	10/01-12/01
	Brazoria PMSA, TX	H	8.49 FQ	12.74 AW	17.83 TQ	TXBLS	10/01-12/01
	Brownsville-Harlingen-San Benito MSA, TX	H	5.85 FQ	8.41 AW	11.48 TQ	TXBLS	10/01-12/01
	Corpus Christi MSA, TX	H	7.47 FQ	10.52 AW	15.06 TQ	TXBLS	10/01-12/01
	Dallas PMSA, TX	H	9.74 FQ	13.97 AW	17.56 TQ	TXBLS	10/01-12/01
	El Paso MSA, TX	H	6.35 FQ	8.39 AW	10.46 TQ	TXBLS	10/01-12/01
	Fort Worth-Arlington PMSA, TX	H	8.95 FQ	12.34 AW	16.26 TQ	TXBLS	10/01-12/01
	Galveston-Texas City PMSA, TX	H	8.71 FQ	12.72 AW	17.72 TQ	TXBLS	10/01-12/01
	Houston PMSA, TX	H	8.73 FQ	12.51 AW	17.76 TQ	TXBLS	10/01-12/01
	Killeen-Temple MSA, TX	H	8.11 FQ	11.81 AW	15.23 TQ	TXBLS	10/01-12/01

AAW	Average annual wage	**AOH**	Average offered, high	**ASH**	Average starting, high	**H**	Hourly	**M**	Monthly	**S**	Special: hourly and annual
AE	Average entry wage	**AOL**	Average offered, low	**ASL**	Average starting, low	**HI**	Highest wage paid	**MTC**	Median total compensation	**TQ**	Third quartile wage
AEX	Average experienced wage	**APH**	Average pay, high range	**AW**	Average wage paid	**HR**	High end range	**MW**	Median wage paid	**W**	Weekly
AO	Average offered	**APL**	Average pay, low range	**FQ**	First quartile wage	**LR**	Low end range	**SQ**	Second quartile wage	**Y**	Yearly

Occupation/Type/Industry	Location	Per	Low	Mid	High	Source	Date
Roofer	Laredo MSA, TX	H	6.26 FQ	9.22 AW	13.07 TQ	TXBLS	10/01-12/01
	Longview-Marshall MSA, TX	H	8.02 FQ	10.22 AW	13.52 TQ	TXBLS	10/01-12/01
	Lubbock MSA, TX	H	7.92 FQ	11.69 AW	18.62 TQ	TXBLS	10/01-12/01
	McAllen-Edinburg-Mission MSA, TX	H	6.33 FQ	8.41 AW	10.61 TQ	TXBLS	10/01-12/01
	Odessa-Midland MSA, TX	H	6.91 FQ	13.51 AW	23.80 TQ	TXBLS	10/01-12/01
	San Antonio MSA, TX	H	8.45 FQ	11.84 AW	16.75 TQ	TXBLS	10/01-12/01
	Tyler MSA, TX	H	7.14 FQ	9.65 AW	13.36 TQ	TXBLS	10/01-12/01
	Waco MSA, TX	H	7.36 FQ	10.76 AW	15.37 TQ	TXBLS	10/01-12/01
	Utah	H	7.21 FQ	12.37 AW	18.20 TQ	UTBLS	10/01-12/01
	Provo-Orem MSA, UT	H	9.20 FQ	12.29 AW	17.51 TQ	UTBLS	10/01-12/01
	Salt Lake City-Ogden MSA, UT	H	6.87 FQ	12.30 AW	18.70 TQ	UTBLS	10/01-12/01
	Vermont	H	10.13 FQ	12.92 AW	16.55 TQ	VTBLS	10/01-12/01
	Burlington MSA, VT	H	10.16 FQ	13.33 AW	16.95 TQ	VTBLS	10/01-12/01
	Virginia	H	9.43 FQ	13.53 AW	18.23 TQ	VABLS	10/01-12/01
	Lynchburg MSA, VA	H	10.26 FQ	13.17 AW	16.64 TQ	VABLS	10/01-12/01
	Norfolk-Virginia Beach-Newport News MSA, VA-NC	H	9.65 FQ	12.94 AW	17.40 TQ	VABLS	10/01-12/01
	Richmond-Petersburg MSA, VA	H	10.06 FQ	13.65 AW	17.49 TQ	VABLS	10/01-12/01
	Roanoke MSA, VA	H	10.17 FQ	13.42 AW	16.62 TQ	VABLS	10/01-12/01
	Washington	H	8.72 FQ	17.59 AW	27.01 TQ	WABLS	10/01-12/01
	Bremerton PMSA, WA	H	12.94 FQ	16.00 AW	18.10 TQ	WABLS	10/01-12/01
	Olympia PMSA, WA	H	7.68 FQ	14.05 AW	25.13 TQ	WABLS	10/01-12/01
	Seattle-Bellevue-Everett PMSA, WA	H	12.27 FQ	19.80 AW	29.16 TQ	WABLS	10/01-12/01
	Spokane MSA, WA	H	9.45 FQ	18.09 AW	27.78 TQ	WABLS	10/01-12/01
	Tacoma PMSA, WA	H	6.96 FQ	16.43 AW	26.17 TQ	WABLS	10/01-12/01
	Yakima MSA, WA	H	9.09 FQ	17.10 AW	24.22 TQ	WABLS	10/01-12/01
	West Virginia	H	7.17 FQ	11.27 AW	19.61 TQ	WVBLS	10/01-12/01
	Charleston MSA, WV	H	7.75 FQ	11.35 AW	16.23 TQ	WVBLS	10/01-12/01
	Huntington-Ashland MSA, WV-KY-OH	H	6.90 FQ	13.26 AW	22.21 TQ	WVBLS	10/01-12/01
	Wisconsin	H	9.88 FQ	15.56 AW	22.53 TQ	WIBLS	10/01-12/01
	Appleton-Oshkosh-Neenah MSA, WI	H	11.02 FQ	15.74 AW	20.95 TQ	WIBLS	10/01-12/01
	Madison MSA, WI	H	9.60 FQ	14.73 AW	20.82 TQ	WIBLS	10/01-12/01
	Milwaukee-Waukesha PMSA, WI	H	10.67 FQ	16.82 AW	25.25 TQ	WIBLS	10/01-12/01
	Wyoming	H	9.40 FQ	13.68 AW	17.65 TQ	WYBLS	10/01-12/01
	Cheyenne MSA, WY	H	11.24 FQ	14.93 AW	17.76 TQ	WYBLS	10/01-12/01
	Virgin Islands	H	11.40 FQ	13.73 AW	16.49 TQ	VIBLS	10/01-12/01
	Guam	H	7.77 FQ	11.24 AW	15.72 TQ	GUBLS	10/01-12/01
Rotary Drill Operator							
Oil and Gas	Alabama	H	9.90 FQ	14.82 AW	21.05 TQ	ALBLS	10/01-12/01
Oil and Gas	Arkansas	H	12.23 FQ	15.15 AW	18.75 TQ	ARBLS	10/01-12/01
Oil and Gas	California	H	14.58 FQ	19.06 AW	24.61 TQ	CABLS	10/01-12/01
Oil and Gas	Colorado	H	11.84 FQ	19.18 AW	23.17 TQ	COBLS	10/01-12/01
Oil and Gas	Illinois	H	9.48 FQ	13.35 AW	20.14 TQ	ILBLS	10/01-12/01
Oil and Gas	Kansas	H	11.66 FQ	15.79 AW	23.28 TQ	KSBLS	10/01-12/01
Oil and Gas	Kentucky	H	7.15 FQ	10.59 AW	16.03 TQ	KYBLS	10/01-12/01
Oil and Gas	Louisiana	H	13.76 FQ	22.93 AW	47.24 TQ	LABLS	10/01-12/01
Oil and Gas	Michigan	H	11.57 FQ	15.64 AW	18.88 TQ	MIBLS	10/01-12/01
Oil and Gas	New Mexico	H	14.18 FQ	20.11 AW	26.03 TQ	NMBLS	10/01-12/01
Oil and Gas	New York	H	9.64 FQ	18.28 AW	26.38 TQ	NYBLS	10/01-12/01
Oil and Gas	North Carolina	H	9.89 FQ	14.38 AW	19.59 TQ	NCBLS	10/01-12/01
Oil and Gas	Ohio	H	6.52 FQ	11.21 AW	15.34 TQ	OHBLS	10/01-12/01
Oil and Gas	Oklahoma	H	9.76 FQ	14.46 AW	21.27 TQ	OKBLS	10/01-12/01
Oil and Gas	Pennsylvania	H	10.88 FQ	15.29 AW	24.51 TQ	PABLS	10/01-12/01
Oil and Gas	Tennessee	H	11.46 FQ	12.93 AW	13.91 TQ	TNBLS	10/01-12/01
Oil and Gas	Texas	H	10.18 FQ	16.68 AW	27.10 TQ	TXBLS	10/01-12/01
Oil and Gas	Utah	H	14.75 FQ	17.77 AW	21.56 TQ	UTBLS	10/01-12/01
Oil and Gas	Virginia	H	12.12 FQ	17.43 AW	24.97 TQ	VABLS	10/01-12/01
Oil and Gas	West Virginia	H	11.73 FQ	14.91 AW	16.99 TQ	WVBLS	10/01-12/01
Oil and Gas	Wyoming	H	14.33 FQ	18.89 AW	22.88 TQ	WYBLS	10/01-12/01
Roustabout							
Oil and Gas	Alabama	H	7.64 FQ	11.61 AW	17.02 TQ	ALBLS	10/01-12/01
Oil and Gas	Alaska	H	8.86 FQ	15.23 AW	22.68 TQ	AKBLS	10/01-12/01
Oil and Gas	Arkansas	H	10.74 FQ	13.26 AW	18.69 TQ	ARBLS	10/01-12/01

AAW	Average annual wage	AOH	Average offered, high	ASH	Average starting, high	H	Hourly	M	Monthly	S	Special: hourly and annual
AE	Average entry wage	AOL	Average offered, low	ASL	Average starting, low	HI	Highest wage paid	MTC	Median total compensation	TQ	Third quartile wage
AEX	Average experienced wage	APH	Average pay, high range	AW	Average wage paid	HR	High end range	MW	Median wage paid	W	Weekly
AO	Average offered	APL	Average pay, low range	FQ	First quartile wage	LR	Low end range	SQ	Second quartile wage	Y	Yearly

Occupation/Type/Industry	Location	Per	Low	Mid	High	Source	Date
Roustabout							
Oil and Gas	California	H	9.71 FQ	15.42 AW	22.32 TQ	CABLS	10/01-12/01
Oil and Gas	Colorado	H	8.87 FQ	12.21 AW	16.63 TQ	COBLS	10/01-12/01
Oil and Gas	Illinois	H	7.70 FQ	10.49 AW	14.90 TQ	ILBLS	10/01-12/01
Oil and Gas	Indiana	H	7.71 FQ	12.30 AW	19.29 TQ	INBLS	10/01-12/01
Oil and Gas	Kansas	H	8.78 FQ	12.92 AW	17.25 TQ	KSBLS	10/01-12/01
Oil and Gas	Kentucky	H	7.79 FQ	15.67 AW	31.94 TQ	KYBLS	10/01-12/01
Oil and Gas	Louisiana	H	7.50 FQ	11.33 AW	16.41 TQ	LABLS	10/01-12/01
Oil and Gas	Michigan	H	9.14 FQ	13.45 AW	18.30 TQ	MIBLS	10/01-12/01
Oil and Gas	Mississippi	H	7.32 FQ	11.14 AW	16.12 TQ	MSBLS	10/01-12/01
Oil and Gas	Montana	H	9.10 FQ	14.94 AW	20.40 TQ	MTBLS	10/01-12/01
Oil and Gas	New Mexico	H	6.08 FQ	11.71 AW	16.94 TQ	NMBLS	10/01-12/01
Oil and Gas	North Dakota	H	7.50 FQ	12.49 AW	20.06 TQ	NDBLS	10/01-12/01
Oil and Gas	Ohio	H	6.92 FQ	9.23 AW	12.93 TQ	OHBLS	10/01-12/01
Oil and Gas	Oklahoma	H	8.05 FQ	11.81 AW	16.31 TQ	OKBLS	10/01-12/01
Oil and Gas	Pennsylvania	H	8.79 FQ	13.86 AW	29.50 TQ	PABLS	10/01-12/01
Oil and Gas	Texas	H	7.14 FQ	10.33 AW	16.69 TQ	TXBLS	10/01-12/01
Oil and Gas	Utah	H	7.92 FQ	12.12 AW	17.69 TQ	UTBLS	10/01-12/01
Oil and Gas	Virginia	H	7.51 FQ	11.50 AW	15.62 TQ	VABLS	10/01-12/01
Oil and Gas	West Virginia	H	5.87 FQ	9.88 AW	18.57 TQ	WVBLS	10/01-12/01
Oil and Gas	Wyoming	H	8.66 FQ	12.39 AW	16.92 TQ	WYBLS	10/01-12/01
Safety Director							
Environment	United States	Y		54000-60000 AW		SAFEDIR	2001
Safety Manager							
Environment	United States	Y		59405 AW		SAFEDIR	2001
Environment	Midwest	Y		59895 AW		SAFEDIR	2001
Environment	Northeast	Y		59448 AW		SAFEDIR	2001
Environment	South	Y		58728 AW		SAFEDIR	2001
Environment	West	Y		63334 AW		SAFEDIR	2001
Safety Trainer							
Environment	United States	Y		49315 AW		SAFEDIR	2001
Environment	Midwest	Y		65000 AW		SAFEDIR	2001
Environment	South	Y		38550 AW		SAFEDIR	2001
Environment	West	Y		46333 AW		SAFEDIR	2001
Sailor and Marine Oiler	Alabama	H	7.37 FQ	9.57 AW	13.06 TQ	ALBLS	10/01-12/01
	Alaska	H	11.86 FQ	17.33 AW	23.03 TQ	AKBLS	10/01-12/01
	Arkansas	H	7.68 FQ	9.93 AW	12.99 TQ	ARBLS	10/01-12/01
	California	H	6.97 FQ	16.58 AW	22.76 TQ	CABLS	10/01-12/01
	Connecticut	H	7.61 FQ	13.15 AW	20.22 TQ	CTBLS	10/01-12/01
	Florida	H	6.41 FQ	13.97 AW	21.42 TQ	FLBLS	10/01-12/01
	Georgia	H	10.70 FQ	13.66 AW	16.78 TQ	GABLS	10/01-12/01
	Hawaii	H	7.94 FQ	14.31 AW	21.84 TQ	HIBLS	10/01-12/01
	Illinois	H	9.43 FQ	13.18 AW	17.96 TQ	ILBLS	10/01-12/01
	Indiana	H	9.46 FQ	15.02 AW	21.19 TQ	INBLS	10/01-12/01
	Iowa	H	7.44 FQ	10.93 AW	16.50 TQ	IABLS	10/01-12/01
	Kentucky	H	9.49 FQ	15.56 AW	21.25 TQ	KYBLS	10/01-12/01
	Louisiana	H	7.51 FQ	13.47 AW	22.30 TQ	LABLS	10/01-12/01
	Maine	H	7.45 FQ	11.55 AW	18.14 TQ	MEBLS	10/01-12/01
	Maryland	H	6.13 FQ	10.38 AW	14.12 TQ	MDBLS	10/01-12/01
	Michigan	H	6.37 FQ	14.39 AW	21.20 TQ	MIBLS	10/01-12/01
	Minnesota	H	13.12 FQ	18.35 AW	22.96 TQ	MNBLS	10/01-12/01
	Mississippi	H	7.82 FQ	12.26 AW	16.65 TQ	MSBLS	10/01-12/01
	Missouri	H	6.92 FQ	11.34 AW	15.15 TQ	MOBLS	10/01-12/01
	New Jersey	H	7.52 FQ	13.48 AW	22.96 TQ	NJBLS	10/01-12/01
	New York	H	10.05 FQ	16.68 AW	24.77 TQ	NYBLS	10/01-12/01
	North Carolina	H	10.96 FQ	13.36 AW	16.58 TQ	NCBLS	10/01-12/01
	Ohio	H	10.20 FQ	16.06 AW	22.31 TQ	OHBLS	10/01-12/01
	Oregon	H	7.62 FQ	15.80 AW	22.45 TQ	ORBLS	10/01-12/01
	Pennsylvania	H	7.11 FQ	12.33 AW	18.47 TQ	PABLS	10/01-12/01
	Rhode Island	H	7.44 FQ	10.57 AW	13.46 TQ	RIBLS	10/01-12/01
	South Carolina	H	8.09 FQ	11.84 AW	16.65 TQ	SCBLS	10/01-12/01
	Tennessee	H	10.29 FQ	17.03 AW	25.19 TQ	TNBLS	10/01-12/01
	Texas	H	6.35 FQ	12.07 AW	18.54 TQ	TXBLS	10/01-12/01
	Virginia	H	10.88 FQ	16.87 AW	25.39 TQ	VABLS	10/01-12/01
	Washington	H	8.07 FQ	16.66 AW	22.24 TQ	WABLS	10/01-12/01
	West Virginia	H	10.64 FQ	15.89 AW	22.04 TQ	WVBLS	10/01-12/01
	Wisconsin	H	7.09 FQ	11.67 AW	18.37 TQ	WIBLS	10/01-12/01
	Virgin Islands	H	6.05 FQ	8.06 AW	10.44 TQ	VIBLS	10/01-12/01

AAW Average annual wage **AE** Average entry wage **AEX** Average experienced wage **AO** Average offered **AOH** Average offered, high **AOL** Average offered, low **APH** Average pay, high range **APL** Average pay, low range **ASH** Average starting, high **ASL** Average starting, low **AW** Average wage paid **FQ** First quartile wage **H** Hourly **HI** Highest wage paid **HR** High end range **LR** Low end range **M** Monthly **MTC** Median total compensation **MW** Median wage paid **SQ** Second quartile wage **S** Special: hourly and annual **TQ** Third quartile wage **W** Weekly **Y** Yearly

Occupation/Type/Industry	Location	Per	Low	Mid	High	Source	Date
Sales Director							
Marketing, Medical	United States	Y		120200 AW		MM&M	1/01-1/02
Sales Engineer	Alabama	Y	32100 FQ	54010 AW	84030 TQ	ALBLS	10/01-12/01
	Arizona	Y	30250 FQ	62210 AW	102140 TQ	AZBLS	10/01-12/01
	Arkansas	Y	35160 FQ	51940 AW	79550 TQ	ARBLS	10/01-12/01
	California	Y	42890 FQ	72830 AW	113990 TQ	CABLS	10/01-12/01
	Colorado	Y	37520 FQ	67050 AW	108160 TQ	COBLS	10/01-12/01
	Connecticut	Y	45730 FQ	71020 AW	105120 TQ	CTBLS	10/01-12/01
	Delaware	Y	39890 FQ	63120 AW	91020 TQ	DEBLS	10/01-12/01
	Florida	Y	32700 FQ	62690 AW	106220 TQ	FLBLS	10/01-12/01
	Georgia	Y	38530 FQ	67180 AW	101170 TQ	GABLS	10/01-12/01
	Hawaii	Y	37070 FQ	52360 AW	83110 TQ	HIBLS	10/01-12/01
	Idaho	Y	39800 FQ	65120 AW	104300 TQ	IDBLS	10/01-12/01
	Illinois	Y	34590 FQ	58830 AW	97320 TQ	ILBLS	10/01-12/01
	Indiana	Y	38920 FQ	63910 AW	97200 TQ	INBLS	10/01-12/01
	Iowa	Y	36440 FQ	58390 AW	88060 TQ	IABLS	10/01-12/01
	Kansas	Y	36230 FQ	64200 AW	89460 TQ	KSBLS	10/01-12/01
	Kentucky	Y	30660 FQ	57810 AW	89950 TQ	KYBLS	10/01-12/01
	Louisiana	Y	22900 FQ	47370 AW	75000 TQ	LABLS	10/01-12/01
	Maine	Y	38740 FQ	68200 AW	135210 TQ	MEBLS	10/01-12/01
	Maryland	Y	28280 FQ	55880 AW	99420 TQ	MDBLS	10/01-12/01
	Massachusetts	Y	42620 FQ	77540 AW	131570 TQ	MABLS	10/01-12/01
	Michigan	Y	41350 FQ	70190 AW	112410 TQ	MIBLS	10/01-12/01
	Minnesota	Y	35580 FQ	61540 AW	90640 TQ	MNBLS	10/01-12/01
	Mississippi	Y	30930 FQ	52290 AW	83730 TQ	MSBLS	10/01-12/01
	Missouri	Y	36580 FQ	60330 AW	91650 TQ	MOBLS	10/01-12/01
	Montana	Y	31930 FQ	61240 AW	106730 TQ	MTBLS	10/01-12/01
	Nebraska	Y	29620 FQ	59640 AW	116050 TQ	NEBLS	10/01-12/01
	Nevada	Y	35110 FQ	61530 AW	102630 TQ	NVBLS	10/01-12/01
	New Hampshire	Y	36710 FQ	57510 AW	82470 TQ	NHBLS	10/01-12/01
	New Jersey	Y	40460 FQ	67210 AW	101000 TQ	NJBLS	10/01-12/01
	New Mexico	Y	34580 FQ	61030 AW	101170 TQ	NMBLS	10/01-12/01
	New York	Y	37430 FQ	63640 AW	100730 TQ	NYBLS	10/01-12/01
	North Carolina	Y	28420 FQ	59260 AW	94550 TQ	NCBLS	10/01-12/01
	North Dakota	Y	19760 FQ	44400 AW	78480 TQ	NDBLS	10/01-12/01
	Ohio	Y	28510 FQ	58990 AW	92160 TQ	OHBLS	10/01-12/01
	Oklahoma	Y	23210 FQ	53330 AW	90100 TQ	OKBLS	10/01-12/01
	Oregon	Y	47850 FQ	75590 AW	111590 TQ	ORBLS	10/01-12/01
	Pennsylvania	Y	34260 FQ	59790 AW	89200 TQ	PABLS	10/01-12/01
	Rhode Island	Y	32580 FQ	53680 AW	77930 TQ	RIBLS	10/01-12/01
	South Carolina	Y	33050 FQ	64220 AW	94550 TQ	SCBLS	10/01-12/01
	South Dakota	Y	39250 FQ	57630 AW	72830 TQ	SDBLS	10/01-12/01
	Tennessee	Y	30930 FQ	56670 AW	89070 TQ	TNBLS	10/01-12/01
	Texas	Y	38020 FQ	63520 AW	90270 TQ	TXBLS	10/01-12/01
	Utah	Y	27620 FQ	59090 AW	112340 TQ	UTBLS	10/01-12/01
	Vermont	Y	31110 FQ	56060 AW	81600 TQ	VTBLS	10/01-12/01
	Virginia	Y	34820 FQ	57200 AW	89090 TQ	VABLS	10/01-12/01
	Washington	Y	38970 FQ	67450 AW	102530 TQ	WABLS	10/01-12/01
	West Virginia	Y	28730 FQ	45810 AW	70980 TQ	WVBLS	10/01-12/01
	Wisconsin	Y	36590 FQ	61390 AW	89900 TQ	WIBLS	10/01-12/01
	Wyoming	Y	44770 FQ	91890 AW	140920 TQ	WYBLS	10/01-12/01
	Puerto Rico	Y	27270 FQ	46510 AW	72420 TQ	PRBLS	10/01-12/01
Sales Executive	United States	Y		87178 AW		SMM	1/01-1/02
Sales Manager	South	Y		78500 AW		WW	1/00-1/01
	Southeast	Y		90800 AW		WW	1/00-1/01
	Alabama	Y	29190 FQ	60470 AW	108630 TQ	ALBLS	10/01-12/01
	Birmingham MSA, AL	Y	29800 FQ	69910 AW	121120 TQ	ALBLS	10/01-12/01
	Huntsville MSA, AL	Y	32660 FQ	71730 AW		ALBLS	10/01-12/01
	Mobile MSA, AL	Y	31760 FQ	60050 AW	100710 TQ	ALBLS	10/01-12/01
	Montgomery MSA, AL	Y	26320 FQ	64560 AW	107550 TQ	ALBLS	10/01-12/01
	Alaska	Y	31580 FQ	66730 AW	128300 TQ	AKBLS	10/01-12/01
	Anchorage MSA, AK	Y	32700 FQ	71230 AW		AKBLS	10/01-12/01
	Arizona	Y	32800 FQ	67680 AW	115860 TQ	AZBLS	10/01-12/01
	Phoenix-Mesa MSA, AZ	Y	34650 FQ	69040 AW	115840 TQ	AZBLS	10/01-12/01
	Tucson MSA, AZ	Y	29110 FQ	60550 AW	114250 TQ	AZBLS	10/01-12/01
	Arkansas	Y	37390 FQ	69020 AW	111130 TQ	ARBLS	10/01-12/01
	Fayetteville-Springdale-Rogers MSA, AR	Y	29850 FQ	57060 AW	105200 TQ	ARBLS	10/01-12/01
	Fort Smith MSA, AR-OK	Y	39720 FQ	69650 AW	118080 TQ	ARBLS	10/01-12/01

AAW	Average annual wage	AOH	Average offered, high	ASH	Average starting, high	H	Hourly	M	Monthly	S	Special: hourly and annual
AE	Average entry wage	AOL	Average offered, low	ASL	Average starting, low	HI	Highest wage paid	MTC	Median total compensation	TQ	Third quartile wage
AEX	Average experienced wage	APH	Average pay, high range	AW	Average wage paid	HR	High end range	MW	Median wage paid	W	Weekly
AO	Average offered	APL	Average pay, low range	FQ	First quartile wage	LR	Low end range	SQ	Second quartile wage	Y	Yearly

Occupation/Type/Industry	Location	Per	Low	Mid	High	Source	Date
Sales Manager	Little Rock-North Little Rock MSA, AR	Y	40110 FQ	74780 AW	113900 TQ	ARBLS	10/01-12/01
	California	Y	43110 FQ	86430 AW		CABLS	10/01-12/01
	Bakersfield MSA, CA	Y	44360 FQ	78750 AW	144580 TQ	CABLS	10/01-12/01
	Chico-Paradise MSA, CA	Y	37750 FQ	74420 AW	137610 TQ	CABLS	10/01-12/01
	Fresno MSA, CA	Y	35030 FQ	67320 AW	108360 TQ	CABLS	10/01-12/01
	Los Angeles-Long Beach PMSA, CA	Y	42290 FQ	83720 AW		CABLS	10/01-12/01
	Merced MSA, CA	Y	44720 FQ	91790 AW		CABLS	10/01-12/01
	Modesto MSA, CA	Y	37690 FQ	72360 AW	124650 TQ	CABLS	10/01-12/01
	Oakland PMSA, CA	Y	47790 FQ	91230 AW		CABLS	10/01-12/01
	Orange County PMSA, CA	Y	45170 FQ	89270 AW		CABLS	10/01-12/01
	Redding MSA, CA	Y	42330 FQ	75050 AW	120110 TQ	CABLS	10/01-12/01
	Riverside-San Bernardino PMSA, CA	Y	41480 FQ	78280 AW		CABLS	10/01-12/01
	Sacramento PMSA, CA	Y	42690 FQ	80020 AW	144430 TQ	CABLS	10/01-12/01
	Salinas MSA, CA	Y	44630 FQ	82880 AW		CABLS	10/01-12/01
	San Diego MSA, CA	Y	39440 FQ	79870 AW	141400 TQ	CABLS	10/01-12/01
	San Francisco PMSA, CA	Y	45770 FQ	89620 AW		CABLS	10/01-12/01
	San Jose PMSA, CA	Y	51010 FQ	102990 AW		CABLS	10/01-12/01
	San Luis Obispo-Atascadero-Paso Robles MSA, CA	Y	39200 FQ	69530 AW	114190 TQ	CABLS	10/01-12/01
	Santa Barbara-Santa Maria-Lompoc MSA, CA	Y	36210 FQ	79160 AW		CABLS	10/01-12/01
	Santa Cruz-Watsonville PMSA, CA	Y	48520 FQ	85600 AW		CABLS	10/01-12/01
	Santa Rosa PMSA, CA	Y	43420 FQ	88600 AW		CABLS	10/01-12/01
	Stockton-Lodi MSA, CA	Y	41790 FQ	73270 AW	122860 TQ	CABLS	10/01-12/01
	Vallejo-Fairfield-Napa PMSA, CA	Y	42490 FQ	75970 AW	115150 TQ	CABLS	10/01-12/01
	Ventura PMSA, CA	Y	46820 FQ	88100 AW		CABLS	10/01-12/01
	Visalia-Tulare-Porterville MSA, CA	Y	37170 FQ	71710 AW	118850 TQ	CABLS	10/01-12/01
	Colorado	Y	39550 FQ	81590 AW		COBLS	10/01-12/01
	Boulder-Longmont PMSA, CO	Y	52860 FQ	96240 AW		COBLS	10/01-12/01
	Colorado Springs MSA, CO	Y	40720 FQ	84860 AW		COBLS	10/01-12/01
	Denver PMSA, CO	Y	41320 FQ	81980 AW		COBLS	10/01-12/01
	Fort Collins-Loveland MSA, CO	Y	40440 FQ	83320 AW		COBLS	10/01-12/01
	Greeley PMSA, CO	Y	31510 FQ	63200 AW	119060 TQ	COBLS	10/01-12/01
	Connecticut	Y	46600 FQ	91370 AW		CTBLS	10/01-12/01
	Bridgeport PMSA, CT	Y	49860 FQ	90070 AW		CTBLS	10/01-12/01
	Danbury PMSA, CT	Y	41520 FQ	85090 AW		CTBLS	10/01-12/01
	Hartford MSA, CT	Y	52010 FQ	91460 AW		CTBLS	10/01-12/01
	New Haven-Meriden PMSA, CT	Y	40270 FQ	89370 AW		CTBLS	10/01-12/01
	New London-Norwich MSA, CT-RI	Y	38850 FQ	82620 AW		CTBLS	10/01-12/01
	Stamford-Norwalk PMSA, CT	Y	51500 FQ	100880 AW		CTBLS	10/01-12/01
	Waterbury PMSA, CT	Y	35010 FQ	73910 AW	119610 TQ	CTBLS	10/01-12/01
	Delaware	Y	29090 FQ	68720 AW	130180 TQ	DEBLS	10/01-12/01
	Wilmington-Newark PMSA, DE-MD	Y	33830 FQ	74680 AW	139060 TQ	DEBLS	10/01-12/01
	District of Columbia	Y	27520 FQ	63990 AW	126100 TQ	DCBLS	10/01-12/01
	Washington PMSA, DC-MD-VA-WV	Y	35620 FQ	73280 AW	135670 TQ	DCBLS	10/01-12/01
	Florida	Y	32200 FQ	72420 AW	135090 TQ	FLBLS	10/01-12/01
	Daytona Beach MSA, FL	Y	18760 FQ	61470 AW	121560 TQ	FLBLS	10/01-12/01
	Fort Lauderdale PMSA, FL	Y	34170 FQ	74840 AW	137790 TQ	FLBLS	10/01-12/01
	Fort Myers-Cape Coral MSA, FL	Y	27880 FQ	69460 AW	128910 TQ	FLBLS	10/01-12/01
	Fort Pierce-Port St. Lucie MSA, FL	Y	29030 FQ	56760 AW	113040 TQ	FLBLS	10/01-12/01
	Fort Walton Beach MSA, FL	Y	23470 FQ	51750 AW	93530 TQ	FLBLS	10/01-12/01
	Gainesville MSA, FL	Y	26190 FQ	76690 AW		FLBLS	10/01-12/01
	Jacksonville MSA, FL	Y	34290 FQ	76190 AW	137470 TQ	FLBLS	10/01-12/01
	Lakeland-Winter Haven MSA, FL	Y	26120 FQ	67920 AW	116810 TQ	FLBLS	10/01-12/01
	Melbourne-Titusville-Palm Bay MSA, FL	Y	32030 FQ	72790 AW		FLBLS	10/01-12/01
	Miami PMSA, FL	Y	36100 FQ	75510 AW		FLBLS	10/01-12/01
	Naples MSA, FL	Y	32150 FQ	67230 AW		FLBLS	10/01-12/01

AAW	Average annual wage	**AOH**	Average offered, high	**ASH**	Average starting, high	**H**	Hourly	**M**	Monthly	**S**	Special: hourly and annual
AE	Average entry wage	**AOL**	Average offered, low	**ASL**	Average starting, low	**HI**	Highest wage paid	**MTC**	Median total compensation	**TQ**	Third quartile wage
AEX	Average experienced wage	**APH**	Average pay, high range	**AW**	Average wage paid	**HR**	High end range	**MW**	Median wage paid	**W**	Weekly
AO	Average offered	**APL**	Average pay, low range	**FQ**	First quartile wage	**LR**	Low end range	**SQ**	Second quartile wage	**Y**	Yearly

Occupation/Type/Industry	Location	Per	Low	Mid	High	Source	Date
Sales Manager	Ocala MSA, FL	Y	24650 FQ	67090 AW	122070 TQ	FLBLS	10/01-12/01
	Orlando MSA, FL	Y	30540 FQ	70450 AW	127300 TQ	FLBLS	10/01-12/01
	Pensacola MSA, FL	Y	27420 FQ	65420 AW	119080 TQ	FLBLS	10/01-12/01
	Sarasota-Bradenton MSA, FL	Y	27840 FQ	64060 AW	126190 TQ	FLBLS	10/01-12/01
	Tallahassee MSA, FL	Y	23990 FQ	66820 AW	117250 TQ	FLBLS	10/01-12/01
	Tampa-St. Petersburg-Clearwater MSA, FL	Y	32920 FQ	70570 AW	130200 TQ	FLBLS	10/01-12/01
	West Palm Beach-Boca Raton MSA, FL	Y	42170 FQ	83880 AW		FLBLS	10/01-12/01
	Georgia	Y	40140 FQ	80880 AW		GABLS	10/01-12/01
	Atlanta MSA, GA	Y	41080 FQ	82130 AW		GABLS	10/01-12/01
	Augusta-Aiken MSA, GA-SC	Y	30140 FQ	61260 AW	95560 TQ	GABLS	10/01-12/01
	Columbus MSA, GA-AL	Y	39740 FQ	78250 AW	141660 TQ	GABLS	10/01-12/01
	Macon MSA, GA	Y	32700 FQ	65230 AW	114560 TQ	GABLS	10/01-12/01
	Savannah MSA, GA	Y	38970 FQ	76640 AW	116600 TQ	GABLS	10/01-12/01
	Hawaii	Y	37540 FQ	66150 AW	105500 TQ	HIBLS	10/01-12/01
	Honolulu MSA, HI	Y	37960 FQ	68160 AW	108990 TQ	HIBLS	10/01-12/01
	Idaho	Y	29230 FQ	61370 AW	97320 TQ	IDBLS	10/01-12/01
	Boise City MSA, ID	Y	32560 FQ	65140 AW	106860 TQ	IDBLS	10/01-12/01
	Illinois	Y	35100 FQ	73460 AW	126780 TQ	ILBLS	10/01-12/01
	Champaign-Urbana MSA, IL	Y	19770 FQ	55780 AW	94070 TQ	ILBLS	10/01-12/01
	Chicago PMSA, IL	Y	37810 FQ	76570 AW	133600 TQ	ILBLS	10/01-12/01
	Peoria-Pekin MSA, IL	Y	30130 FQ	65080 AW	116860 TQ	ILBLS	10/01-12/01
	Rockford MSA, IL	Y	27150 FQ	61030 AW	99220 TQ	ILBLS	10/01-12/01
	Springfield MSA, IL	Y	23670 FQ	62700 AW	117470 TQ	ILBLS	10/01-12/01
	Indiana	Y	37270 FQ	71810 AW	118660 TQ	INBLS	10/01-12/01
	Elkhart-Goshen MSA, IN	Y	44030 FQ	80300 AW	117890 TQ	INBLS	10/01-12/01
	Evansville-Henderson MSA, IN-KY	Y	37280 FQ	71460 AW	121290 TQ	INBLS	10/01-12/01
	Fort Wayne MSA, IN	Y	40780 FQ	73120 AW	112540 TQ	INBLS	10/01-12/01
	Gary PMSA, IN	Y	38250 FQ	67720 AW	111990 TQ	INBLS	10/01-12/01
	Indianapolis MSA, IN	Y	35890 FQ	74710 AW	137810 TQ	INBLS	10/01-12/01
	Lafayette MSA, IN	Y	34310 FQ	72420 AW	119530 TQ	INBLS	10/01-12/01
	South Bend MSA, IN	Y	40970 FQ	74410 AW	128010 TQ	INBLS	10/01-12/01
	Iowa	Y	24550 FQ	57150 AW	102590 TQ	IABLS	10/01-12/01
	Cedar Rapids MSA, IA	Y	33150 FQ	68260 AW	117410 TQ	IABLS	10/01-12/01
	Davenport-Moline-Rock Island MSA, IA-IL	Y	28070 FQ	59120 AW	103370 TQ	IABLS	10/01-12/01
	Des Moines MSA, IA	Y	22040 FQ	58650 AW	109590 TQ	IABLS	10/01-12/01
	Kansas	Y	37680 FQ	72480 AW	122360 TQ	KSBLS	10/01-12/01
	Topeka MSA, KS	Y	34760 FQ	69960 AW	114620 TQ	KSBLS	10/01-12/01
	Wichita MSA, KS	Y	36490 FQ	65920 AW	110420 TQ	KSBLS	10/01-12/01
	Kentucky	Y	34320 FQ	66150 AW	113420 TQ	KYBLS	10/01-12/01
	Lexington MSA, KY	Y	33250 FQ	64720 AW	114570 TQ	KYBLS	10/01-12/01
	Louisville MSA, KY-IN	Y	33990 FQ	69660 AW	124160 TQ	KYBLS	10/01-12/01
	Louisiana	Y	28260 FQ	58080 AW	102540 TQ	LABLS	10/01-12/01
	Baton Rouge MSA, LA	Y	24870 FQ	58410 AW	118740 TQ	LABLS	10/01-12/01
	Houma MSA, LA	Y	34880 FQ	63290 AW	104770 TQ	LABLS	10/01-12/01
	Lafayette MSA, LA	Y	34190 FQ	65990 AW	100550 TQ	LABLS	10/01-12/01
	Lake Charles MSA, LA	Y	28870 FQ	63330 AW	108090 TQ	LABLS	10/01-12/01
	New Orleans MSA, LA	Y	28650 FQ	52680 AW	86680 TQ	LABLS	10/01-12/01
	Shreveport-Bossier City MSA, LA	Y	25400 FQ	57590 AW	104590 TQ	LABLS	10/01-12/01
	Maine	Y	33470 FQ	63120 AW	103870 TQ	MEBLS	10/01-12/01
	Portland MSA, ME	Y	36490 FQ	67620 AW	113010 TQ	MEBLS	10/01-12/01
	Maryland	Y	36680 FQ	72940 AW	129340 TQ	MDBLS	10/01-12/01
	Baltimore PMSA, MD	Y	35070 FQ	72500 AW	127190 TQ	MDBLS	10/01-12/01
	Massachusetts	Y	45610 FQ	89910 AW		MABLS	10/01-12/01
	Boston PMSA, MA-NH	Y	47450 FQ	94230 AW		MABLS	10/01-12/01
	Brockton PMSA, MA	Y	47050 FQ	89090 AW		MABLS	10/01-12/01
	Lawrence PMSA, MA-NH	Y	41990 FQ	84020 AW		MABLS	10/01-12/01
	Lowell PMSA, MA-NH	Y	51580 FQ	90940 AW	141510 TQ	MABLS	10/01-12/01
	New Bedford PMSA, MA	Y	40670 FQ	70480 AW	118740 TQ	MABLS	10/01-12/01
	Springfield MSA, MA	Y	42850 FQ	79140 AW	131650 TQ	MABLS	10/01-12/01
	Worcester PMSA, MA-CT	Y	45010 FQ	82510 AW	124780 TQ	MABLS	10/01-12/01
	Michigan	Y	40070 FQ	85900 AW		MIBLS	10/01-12/01
	Ann Arbor PMSA, MI	Y	43090 FQ	81650 AW		MIBLS	10/01-12/01
	Detroit PMSA, MI	Y	43730 FQ	92280 AW		MIBLS	10/01-12/01
	Flint PMSA, MI	Y	48620 FQ	95380 AW		MIBLS	10/01-12/01
	Grand Rapids-Muskegon-Holland MSA, MI	Y	46430 FQ	88020 AW	144800 TQ	MIBLS	10/01-12/01

AAW	Average annual wage	AOH	Average offered, high	ASH	Average starting, high	H	Hourly	M	Monthly	S	Special: hourly and annual
AE	Average entry wage	AOL	Average offered, low	ASL	Average starting, low	HI	Highest wage paid	MTC	Median total compensation	TQ	Third quartile wage
AEX	Average experienced wage	APH	Average pay, high range	AW	Average wage paid	HR	High end range	MW	Median wage paid	W	Weekly
AO	Average offered	APL	Average pay, low range	FQ	First quartile wage	LR	Low end range	SQ	Second quartile wage	Y	Yearly

Occupation/Type/Industry	Location	Per	Low	Mid	High	Source	Date
Sales Manager	Kalamazoo-Battle Creek MSA, MI	Y	37080 FQ	84420 AW		MIBLS	10/01-12/01
	Lansing-East Lansing MSA, MI	Y	31100 FQ	64090 AW	113960 TQ	MIBLS	10/01-12/01
	Saginaw-Bay City-Midland MSA, MI	Y	40640 FQ	79060 AW	134430 TQ	MIBLS	10/01-12/01
	Minnesota	Y	47730 FQ	87320 AW		MNBLS	10/01-12/01
	Duluth-Superior MSA, MN-WI	Y	28150 FQ	76370 AW	135250 TQ	MNBLS	10/01-12/01
	Minneapolis-St. Paul MSA, MN-WI	Y	50380 FQ	89160 AW		MNBLS	10/01-12/01
	St. Cloud MSA, MN	Y	48350 FQ	80110 AW	135980 TQ	MNBLS	10/01-12/01
	Mississippi	Y	28950 FQ	61300 AW	106930 TQ	MSBLS	10/01-12/01
	Biloxi-Gulfport-Pascagoula MSA, MS	Y	26820 FQ	50700 AW	76750 TQ	MSBLS	10/01-12/01
	Jackson MSA, MS	Y	27800 FQ	67470 AW	125280 TQ	MSBLS	10/01-12/01
	Missouri	Y	37340 FQ	73390 AW	128370 TQ	MOBLS	10/01-12/01
	Kansas City MSA, MO-KS	Y	42260 FQ	78160 AW	135510 TQ	MOBLS	10/01-12/01
	St. Louis MSA, MO-IL	Y	39080 FQ	76610 AW	133810 TQ	MOBLS	10/01-12/01
	Springfield MSA, MO	Y	38440 FQ	66280 AW	112820 TQ	MOBLS	10/01-12/01
	Montana	Y	25160 FQ	54390 AW	90350 TQ	MTBLS	10/01-12/01
	Billings MSA, MT	Y	25950 FQ	52590 AW	96220 TQ	MTBLS	10/01-12/01
	Nebraska	Y	25880 FQ	61880 AW	109650 TQ	NEBLS	10/01-12/01
	Lincoln MSA, NE	Y	33740 FQ	62290 AW	95150 TQ	NEBLS	10/01-12/01
	Omaha MSA, NE-IA	Y	24010 FQ	63150 AW	111820 TQ	NEBLS	10/01-12/01
	Nevada	Y	34500 FQ	69720 AW	133690 TQ	NVBLS	10/01-12/01
	Las Vegas MSA, NV-AZ	Y	34730 FQ	69440 AW	132580 TQ	NVBLS	10/01-12/01
	Reno MSA, NV	Y	31670 FQ	68300 AW	137050 TQ	NVBLS	10/01-12/01
	New Hampshire	Y	38440 FQ	77770 AW	132360 TQ	NHBLS	10/01-12/01
	Manchester PMSA, NH	Y	38940 FQ	76660 AW	128270 TQ	NHBLS	10/01-12/01
	Nashua PMSA, NH	Y	40990 FQ	81850 AW	136370 TQ	NHBLS	10/01-12/01
	Portsmouth-Rochester PMSA, NH-ME	Y	37810 FQ	77850 AW	140770 TQ	NHBLS	10/01-12/01
	New Jersey	Y	47850 FQ	94030 AW		NJBLS	10/01-12/01
	Atlantic-Cape May PMSA, NJ	Y	37260 FQ	65450 AW	108330 TQ	NJBLS	10/01-12/01
	Bergen-Passaic PMSA, NJ	Y	43730 FQ	93240 AW		NJBLS	10/01-12/01
	Jersey City PMSA, NJ	Y	46710 FQ	93230 AW		NJBLS	10/01-12/01
	Middlesex-Somerset-Hunterdon PMSA, NJ	Y	49330 FQ	95380 AW		NJBLS	10/01-12/01
	Monmouth-Ocean PMSA, NJ	Y	48220 FQ	90100 AW		NJBLS	10/01-12/01
	Newark PMSA, NJ	Y	52920 FQ	98040 AW		NJBLS	10/01-12/01
	Trenton PMSA, NJ	Y	51000 FQ	91640 AW		NJBLS	10/01-12/01
	New Mexico	Y	25460 FQ	54140 AW	92070 TQ	NMBLS	10/01-12/01
	Albuquerque MSA, NM	Y	30780 FQ	58300 AW	105900 TQ	NMBLS	10/01-12/01
	Las Cruces MSA, NM	Y	21740 FQ	53110 AW	106530 TQ	NMBLS	10/01-12/01
	New York	Y	51900 FQ	98180 AW		NYBLS	10/01-12/01
	Albany-Schenectady-Troy MSA, NY	Y	41930 FQ	81680 AW	134730 TQ	NYBLS	10/01-12/01
	Binghamton MSA, NY	Y	40080 FQ	69450 AW	113810 TQ	NYBLS	10/01-12/01
	Buffalo-Niagara Falls MSA, NY	Y	41550 FQ	78460 AW	135960 TQ	NYBLS	10/01-12/01
	Dutchess County PMSA, NY	Y	42540 FQ	87710 AW		NYBLS	10/01-12/01
	Nassau-Suffolk PMSA, NY	Y	54370 FQ	96890 AW		NYBLS	10/01-12/01
	New York PMSA, NY	Y	59130 FQ	105070 AW		NYBLS	10/01-12/01
	Newburgh PMSA, NY-PA	Y	48140 FQ	90950 AW		NYBLS	10/01-12/01
	Rochester MSA, NY	Y	45130 FQ	89420 AW		NYBLS	10/01-12/01
	Syracuse MSA, NY	Y	47950 FQ	85750 AW		NYBLS	10/01-12/01
	Utica-Rome MSA, NY	Y	37520 FQ	73830 AW	123340 TQ	NYBLS	10/01-12/01
	North Carolina	Y	34040 FQ	75900 AW	143570 TQ	NCBLS	10/01-12/01
	Asheville MSA, NC	Y	28750 FQ	68730 AW	128880 TQ	NCBLS	10/01-12/01
	Charlotte-Gastonia-Rock Hill MSA, NC-SC	Y	35560 FQ	76520 AW	141890 TQ	NCBLS	10/01-12/01
	Fayetteville MSA, NC	Y	34270 FQ	69100 AW	118860 TQ	NCBLS	10/01-12/01
	Greensboro-Winston-Salem-High Point MSA, NC	Y	35360 FQ	74930 AW	137410 TQ	NCBLS	10/01-12/01
	Hickory-Morganton-Lenoir MSA, NC	Y	28170 FQ	67370 AW	125550 TQ	NCBLS	10/01-12/01
	Raleigh-Durham-Chapel Hill MSA, NC	Y	34320 FQ	75780 AW	137940 TQ	NCBLS	10/01-12/01
	Wilmington MSA, NC	Y	37640 FQ	72240 AW	124380 TQ	NCBLS	10/01-12/01
	North Dakota	Y	28270 FQ	58560 AW	92440 TQ	NDBLS	10/01-12/01
	Fargo-Moorhead MSA, ND-MN	Y	35940 FQ	63270 AW	94480 TQ	NDBLS	10/01-12/01
	Ohio	Y	34780 FQ	72880 AW	128290 TQ	OHBLS	10/01-12/01

AAW Average annual wage **AOH** Average offered, high **ASH** Average starting, high **H** Hourly **M** Monthly **S** Special: hourly and annual
AE Average entry wage **AOL** Average offered, low **ASL** Average starting, low **HI** Highest wage paid **MTC** Median total compensation **TQ** Third quartile wage
AEX Average experienced wage **APH** Average pay, high range **AW** Average wage paid **HR** High end range **MW** Median wage paid **W** Weekly
AO Average offered **APL** Average pay, low range **FQ** First quartile wage **LR** Low end range **SQ** Second quartile wage **Y** Yearly

Occupation/Type/Industry	Location	Per	Low	Mid	High	Source	Date
Sales Manager	Akron PMSA, OH	Y	37640 FQ	73870 AW	120360 TQ	OHBLS	10/01-12/01
	Canton-Massillon MSA, OH	Y	33600 FQ	65830 AW	108150 TQ	OHBLS	10/01-12/01
	Cincinnati PMSA, OH-KY-IN	Y	35520 FQ	73690 AW	126450 TQ	OHBLS	10/01-12/01
	Cleveland-Lorain-Elyria PMSA, OH	Y	36920 FQ	77210 AW	140220 TQ	OHBLS	10/01-12/01
	Columbus MSA, OH	Y	36670 FQ	73950 AW	136640 TQ	OHBLS	10/01-12/01
	Dayton-Springfield MSA, OH	Y	31800 FQ	70880 AW	130330 TQ	OHBLS	10/01-12/01
	Hamilton-Middletown PMSA, OH	Y	31850 FQ	67940 AW	113880 TQ	OHBLS	10/01-12/01
	Mansfield MSA, OH	Y	37400 FQ	67450 AW	107770 TQ	OHBLS	10/01-12/01
	Toledo MSA, OH	Y	36180 FQ	76070 AW	134090 TQ	OHBLS	10/01-12/01
	Youngstown-Warren MSA, OH	Y	38360 FQ	72200 AW	128210 TQ	OHBLS	10/01-12/01
	Oklahoma	Y	27300 FQ	63270 AW	121350 TQ	OKBLS	10/01-12/01
	Oklahoma City MSA, OK	Y	28270 FQ	59940 AW	103590 TQ	OKBLS	10/01-12/01
	Tulsa MSA, OK	Y	35080 FQ	76300 AW	134530 TQ	OKBLS	10/01-12/01
	Oregon	Y	43370 FQ	82410 AW		ORBLS	10/01-12/01
	Eugene-Springfield MSA, OR	Y	34650 FQ	71780 AW	135200 TQ	ORBLS	10/01-12/01
	Medford-Ashland MSA, OR	Y	42320 FQ	71380 AW	110240 TQ	ORBLS	10/01-12/01
	Portland-Vancouver PMSA, OR-WA	Y	46750 FQ	86260 AW		ORBLS	10/01-12/01
	Salem PMSA, OR	Y	38410 FQ	72780 AW	129850 TQ	ORBLS	10/01-12/01
	Pennsylvania	Y	35400 FQ	74510 AW	130670 TQ	PABLS	10/01-12/01
	Allentown-Bethlehem-Easton MSA, PA	Y	38640 FQ	69150 AW	112750 TQ	PABLS	10/01-12/01
	Erie MSA, PA	Y	36950 FQ	65650 AW	103330 TQ	PABLS	10/01-12/01
	Harrisburg-Lebanon-Carlisle MSA, PA	Y	36100 FQ	78530 AW	138630 TQ	PABLS	10/01-12/01
	Johnstown MSA, PA	Y	25190 FQ	57730 AW	88130 TQ	PABLS	10/01-12/01
	Lancaster MSA, PA	Y	36910 FQ	68820 AW	118090 TQ	PABLS	10/01-12/01
	Philadelphia PMSA, PA-NJ	Y	42310 FQ	84000 AW		PABLS	10/01-12/01
	Pittsburgh MSA, PA	Y	34670 FQ	75550 AW	120340 TQ	PABLS	10/01-12/01
	Reading MSA, PA	Y	35940 FQ	70720 AW	120390 TQ	PABLS	10/01-12/01
	Scranton-Wilkes-Barre-Hazleton MSA, PA	Y	28420 FQ	58720 AW	92970 TQ	PABLS	10/01-12/01
	York MSA, PA	Y	25970 FQ	62960 AW	109540 TQ	PABLS	10/01-12/01
	Rhode Island	Y	39790 FQ	83720 AW		RIBLS	10/01-12/01
	Providence-Fall River-Warwick MSA, RI-MA	Y	39000 FQ	80020 AW	142280 TQ	RIBLS	10/01-12/01
	South Carolina	Y	29770 FQ	63050 AW	110460 TQ	SCBLS	10/01-12/01
	Charleston-North Charleston MSA, SC	Y	27310 FQ	56200 AW	96310 TQ	SCBLS	10/01-12/01
	Columbia MSA, SC	Y	36210 FQ	70510 AW	111280 TQ	SCBLS	10/01-12/01
	Greenville-Spartanburg-Anderson MSA, SC	Y	30650 FQ	67470 AW	119060 TQ	SCBLS	10/01-12/01
	Myrtle Beach MSA, SC	Y	29480 FQ	48530 AW	81620 TQ	SCBLS	10/01-12/01
	South Dakota	Y	50110 FQ	83250 AW	137380 TQ	SDBLS	10/01-12/01
	Sioux Falls MSA, SD	Y	49420 FQ	79380 AW	117290 TQ	SDBLS	10/01-12/01
	Tennessee	Y	31310 FQ	65420 AW	113910 TQ	TNBLS	10/01-12/01
	Chattanooga MSA, TN-GA	Y	27440 FQ	58140 AW	104170 TQ	TNBLS	10/01-12/01
	Clarksville-Hopkinsville MSA, TN-KY	Y	24670 FQ	59960 AW	106530 TQ	TNBLS	10/01-12/01
	Johnson City-Kingsport-Bristol MSA, TN-VA	Y	25270 FQ	55900 AW	92770 TQ	TNBLS	10/01-12/01
	Knoxville MSA, TN	Y	29150 FQ	63970 AW	117940 TQ	TNBLS	10/01-12/01
	Memphis MSA, TN-AR-MS	Y	33730 FQ	70640 AW	133550 TQ	TNBLS	10/01-12/01
	Nashville MSA, TN	Y	35330 FQ	67200 AW	111770 TQ	TNBLS	10/01-12/01
	Texas	Y	34760 FQ	74990 AW	140600 TQ	TXBLS	10/01-12/01
	Amarillo MSA, TX	Y	31630 FQ	54030 AW	93720 TQ	TXBLS	10/01-12/01
	Austin-San Marcos MSA, TX	Y	37780 FQ	85220 AW		TXBLS	10/01-12/01
	Beaumont-Port Arthur MSA, TX	Y	25400 FQ	64610 AW	115540 TQ	TXBLS	10/01-12/01
	Brazoria PMSA, TX	Y	39240 FQ	72910 AW	123220 TQ	TXBLS	10/01-12/01
	Brownsville-Harlingen-San Benito MSA, TX	Y	19300 FQ	55070 AW	103090 TQ	TXBLS	10/01-12/01
	Corpus Christi MSA, TX	Y	29640 FQ	58350 AW	95860 TQ	TXBLS	10/01-12/01
	Dallas PMSA, TX	Y	41250 FQ	84490 AW		TXBLS	10/01-12/01
	El Paso MSA, TX	Y	24280 FQ	60220 AW	112440 TQ	TXBLS	10/01-12/01
	Fort Worth-Arlington PMSA, TX	Y	34230 FQ	71350 AW	118990 TQ	TXBLS	10/01-12/01
	Galveston-Texas City PMSA, TX	Y	33420 FQ	69710 AW	139750 TQ	TXBLS	10/01-12/01
	Houston PMSA, TX	Y	34860 FQ	72890 AW	127670 TQ	TXBLS	10/01-12/01

AAW	Average annual wage	AOH	Average offered, high	ASH	Average starting, high	H	Hourly	M	Monthly	S	Special: hourly and annual
AE	Average entry wage	AOL	Average offered, low	ASL	Average starting, low	HI	Highest wage paid	MTC	Median total compensation	TQ	Third quartile wage
AEX	Average experienced wage	APH	Average pay, high range	AW	Average wage paid	HR	High end range	MW	Median wage paid	W	Weekly
AO	Average offered	APL	Average pay, low range	FQ	First quartile wage	LR	Low end range	SQ	Second quartile wage	Y	Yearly

Occupation/Type/Industry	Location	Per	Low	Mid	High	Source	Date
Sales Manager	Killeen-Temple MSA, TX	Y	23300 FQ	65170 AW	124970 TQ	TXBLS	10/01-12/01
	Laredo MSA, TX	Y	25390 FQ	59050 AW	106350 TQ	TXBLS	10/01-12/01
	Longview-Marshall MSA, TX	Y	26310 FQ	56680 AW	95250 TQ	TXBLS	10/01-12/01
	Lubbock MSA, TX	Y	26040 FQ	62670 AW	108300 TQ	TXBLS	10/01-12/01
	McAllen-Edinburg-Mission MSA, TX	Y	25050 FQ	63560 AW	125320 TQ	TXBLS	10/01-12/01
	Odessa-Midland MSA, TX	Y	28270 FQ	62150 AW	113600 TQ	TXBLS	10/01-12/01
	San Antonio MSA, TX	Y	31030 FQ	64830 AW	116740 TQ	TXBLS	10/01-12/01
	Tyler MSA, TX	Y	31120 FQ	64180 AW	115100 TQ	TXBLS	10/01-12/01
	Waco MSA, TX	Y	27860 FQ	58910 AW	110390 TQ	TXBLS	10/01-12/01
	Utah	Y	30760 FQ	61910 AW	107920 TQ	UTBLS	10/01-12/01
	Provo-Orem MSA, UT	Y	30810 FQ	59200 AW	100790 TQ	UTBLS	10/01-12/01
	Salt Lake City-Ogden MSA, UT	Y	31620 FQ	63800 AW	110130 TQ	UTBLS	10/01-12/01
	Vermont	Y	42550 FQ	79550 AW	133570 TQ	VTBLS	10/01-12/01
	Burlington MSA, VT	Y	41610 FQ	79690 AW	131270 TQ	VTBLS	10/01-12/01
	Virginia	Y	31190 FQ	70420 AW	135550 TQ	VABLS	10/01-12/01
	Lynchburg MSA, VA	Y	16640 FQ	59910 AW	110330 TQ	VABLS	10/01-12/01
	Norfolk-Virginia Beach-Newport News MSA, VA-NC	Y	35430 FQ	70800 AW	136890 TQ	VABLS	10/01-12/01
	Richmond-Petersburg MSA, VA	Y	24530 FQ	66730 AW	133120 TQ	VABLS	10/01-12/01
	Roanoke MSA, VA	Y	37240 FQ	66400 AW	111700 TQ	VABLS	10/01-12/01
	Washington	Y	46000 FQ	84820 AW		WABLS	10/01-12/01
	Bremerton PMSA, WA	Y	35550 FQ	70310 AW	117040 TQ	WABLS	10/01-12/01
	Olympia PMSA, WA	Y	49790 FQ	79050 AW	114240 TQ	WABLS	10/01-12/01
	Richland-Kennewick-Pasco MSA, WA	Y	48040 FQ	80980 AW		WABLS	10/01-12/01
	Seattle-Bellevue-Everett PMSA, WA	Y	47760 FQ	87660 AW		WABLS	10/01-12/01
	Spokane MSA, WA	Y	42190 FQ	77330 AW		WABLS	10/01-12/01
	Tacoma PMSA, WA	Y	41800 FQ	78060 AW		WABLS	10/01-12/01
	Yakima MSA, WA	Y	47220 FQ	69930 AW	111920 TQ	WABLS	10/01-12/01
	West Virginia	Y	25940 FQ	58430 AW	107420 TQ	WVBLS	10/01-12/01
	Charleston MSA, WV	Y	32050 FQ	68460 AW	110570 TQ	WVBLS	10/01-12/01
	Huntington-Ashland MSA, WV-KY-OH	Y	31380 FQ	60310 AW	107480 TQ	WVBLS	10/01-12/01
	Wisconsin	Y	33750 FQ	69510 AW	115510 TQ	WIBLS	10/01-12/01
	Appleton-Oshkosh-Neenah MSA, WI	Y	36680 FQ	63110 AW	99220 TQ	WIBLS	10/01-12/01
	Green Bay MSA, WI	Y	40120 FQ	75370 AW	121420 TQ	WIBLS	10/01-12/01
	Madison MSA, WI	Y	40300 FQ	71320 AW	112900 TQ	WIBLS	10/01-12/01
	Milwaukee-Waukesha PMSA, WI	Y	33950 FQ	73640 AW	119110 TQ	WIBLS	10/01-12/01
	Racine PMSA, WI	Y	40200 FQ	70370 AW	102720 TQ	WIBLS	10/01-12/01
	Wyoming	Y	25150 FQ	55110 AW	99640 TQ	WYBLS	10/01-12/01
	Cheyenne MSA, WY	Y	30100 FQ	61300 AW	107260 TQ	WYBLS	10/01-12/01
	Puerto Rico	Y	28500 FQ	52980 AW	89030 TQ	PRBLS	10/01-12/01
	Virgin Islands	Y	30270 FQ	46850 AW	68080 TQ	VIBLS	10/01-12/01
	Guam	Y	22660 FQ	42710 AW	69330 TQ	GUBLS	10/01-12/01
Sales Representative	United States	Y		54452 AW		SMM	1/01-1/02
Mid-Level	United States	Y		49144 AW		SMM	1/01-1/02
Wholesale and Manufacturing	Alabama	Y	19320 FQ	46230 AW	83060 TQ	ALBLS	10/01-12/01
Wholesale and Manufacturing	Birmingham MSA, AL	Y	22710 FQ	49590 AW	76160 TQ	ALBLS	10/01-12/01
Wholesale and Manufacturing	Huntsville MSA, AL	Y	20720 FQ	51180 AW	90210 TQ	ALBLS	10/01-12/01
Wholesale and Manufacturing	Mobile MSA, AL	Y	18710 FQ	38920 AW	65940 TQ	ALBLS	10/01-12/01
Wholesale and Manufacturing	Montgomery MSA, AL	Y	19300 FQ	43160 AW	75410 TQ	ALBLS	10/01-12/01
Wholesale and Manufacturing	Alaska	Y	23690 FQ	42970 AW	61900 TQ	AKBLS	10/01-12/01
Wholesale and Manufacturing	Anchorage MSA, AK	Y	25490 FQ	45860 AW	66830 TQ	AKBLS	10/01-12/01
Wholesale and Manufacturing	Arizona	Y	20490 FQ	40980 AW	68340 TQ	AZBLS	10/01-12/01
Wholesale and Manufacturing	Phoenix-Mesa MSA, AZ	Y	21190 FQ	42040 AW	69770 TQ	AZBLS	10/01-12/01
Wholesale and Manufacturing	Tucson MSA, AZ	Y	18750 FQ	36070 AW	59360 TQ	AZBLS	10/01-12/01
Wholesale and Manufacturing	Arkansas	Y	18990 FQ	44090 AW	84820 TQ	ARBLS	10/01-12/01
Wholesale and Manufacturing	Fayetteville-Springdale-Rogers MSA, AR	Y	18770 FQ	59370 AW		ARBLS	10/01-12/01
Wholesale and Manufacturing	Fort Smith MSA, AR-OK	Y	16040 FQ	35880 AW	57250 TQ	ARBLS	10/01-12/01
Wholesale and Manufacturing	Little Rock-North Little Rock MSA, AR	Y	20420 FQ	40410 AW	67320 TQ	ARBLS	10/01-12/01
Wholesale and Manufacturing	California	Y	22410 FQ	50480 AW	90200 TQ	CABLS	10/01-12/01
Wholesale and Manufacturing	Bakersfield MSA, CA	Y	24440 FQ	46830 AW	78210 TQ	CABLS	10/01-12/01
Wholesale and Manufacturing	Chico-Paradise MSA, CA	Y	20910 FQ	39790 AW	59260 TQ	CABLS	10/01-12/01

AAW	Average annual wage	**AOH**	Average offered, high	**ASH**	Average starting, high	**H**	Hourly	**M**	Monthly	**S**	Special: hourly and annual
AE	Average entry wage	**AOL**	Average offered, low	**ASL**	Average starting, low	**HI**	Highest wage paid	**MTC**	Median total compensation	**TQ**	Third quartile wage
AEX	Average experienced wage	**APH**	Average pay, high range	**AW**	Average wage paid	**HR**	High end range	**MW**	Median wage paid	**W**	Weekly
AO	Average offered	**APL**	Average pay, low range	**FQ**	First quartile wage	**LR**	Low end range	**SQ**	Second quartile wage	**Y**	Yearly

Occupation/Type/Industry	Location	Per	Low	Mid	High	Source	Date
Sales Representative							
Wholesale and Manufacturing	Fresno MSA, CA	Y	23090 FQ	49790 AW	90530 TQ	CABLS	10/01-12/01
Wholesale and Manufacturing	Los Angeles-Long Beach PMSA, CA	Y	20780 FQ	46810 AW	82610 TQ	CABLS	10/01-12/01
Wholesale and Manufacturing	Merced MSA, CA	Y	26300 FQ	43960 AW	66130 TQ	CABLS	10/01-12/01
Wholesale and Manufacturing	Modesto MSA, CA	Y	24180 FQ	45020 AW	73670 TQ	CABLS	10/01-12/01
Wholesale and Manufacturing	Oakland PMSA, CA	Y	27780 FQ	55980 AW	97620 TQ	CABLS	10/01-12/01
Wholesale and Manufacturing	Orange County PMSA, CA	Y	23640 FQ	55500 AW	108580 TQ	CABLS	10/01-12/01
Wholesale and Manufacturing	Redding MSA, CA	Y	19140 FQ	36640 AW	56710 TQ	CABLS	10/01-12/01
Wholesale and Manufacturing	Riverside-San Bernardino PMSA, CA	Y	21340 FQ	46150 AW	83280 TQ	CABLS	10/01-12/01
Wholesale and Manufacturing	Sacramento PMSA, CA	Y	22530 FQ	45560 AW	73520 TQ	CABLS	10/01-12/01
Wholesale and Manufacturing	Salinas MSA, CA	Y	30580 FQ	63430 AW	138430 TQ	CABLS	10/01-12/01
Wholesale and Manufacturing	San Diego MSA, CA	Y	24100 FQ	48960 AW	83880 TQ	CABLS	10/01-12/01
Wholesale and Manufacturing	San Francisco PMSA, CA	Y	24120 FQ	54700 AW	98070 TQ	CABLS	10/01-12/01
Wholesale and Manufacturing	San Jose PMSA, CA	Y	27570 FQ	63510 AW	114540 TQ	CABLS	10/01-12/01
Wholesale and Manufacturing	San Luis Obispo-Atascadero-Paso Robles MSA, CA	Y	16200 FQ	36790 AW	65670 TQ	CABLS	10/01-12/01
Wholesale and Manufacturing	Santa Barbara-Santa Maria-Lompoc MSA, CA	Y	22460 FQ	45980 AW	79660 TQ	CABLS	10/01-12/01
Wholesale and Manufacturing	Santa Cruz-Watsonville PMSA, CA	Y	22780 FQ	46410 AW	82950 TQ	CABLS	10/01-12/01
Wholesale and Manufacturing	Santa Rosa PMSA, CA	Y	24850 FQ	46620 AW	80280 TQ	CABLS	10/01-12/01
Wholesale and Manufacturing	Stockton-Lodi MSA, CA	Y	20900 FQ	45740 AW	76310 TQ	CABLS	10/01-12/01
Wholesale and Manufacturing	Vallejo-Fairfield-Napa PMSA, CA	Y	26130 FQ	47100 AW	78540 TQ	CABLS	10/01-12/01
Wholesale and Manufacturing	Ventura PMSA, CA	Y	22910 FQ	50020 AW	90290 TQ	CABLS	10/01-12/01
Wholesale and Manufacturing	Visalia-Tulare-Porterville MSA, CA	Y	25890 FQ	44750 AW	69840 TQ	CABLS	10/01-12/01
Wholesale and Manufacturing	Colorado	Y	24430 FQ	48960 AW	79950 TQ	COBLS	10/01-12/01
Wholesale and Manufacturing	Boulder-Longmont PMSA, CO	Y	22760 FQ	44610 AW	77480 TQ	COBLS	10/01-12/01
Wholesale and Manufacturing	Colorado Springs MSA, CO	Y	22400 FQ	43120 AW	71660 TQ	COBLS	10/01-12/01
Wholesale and Manufacturing	Denver PMSA, CO	Y	27850 FQ	52120 AW	83380 TQ	COBLS	10/01-12/01
Wholesale and Manufacturing	Fort Collins-Loveland MSA, CO	Y	21780 FQ	45390 AW	75790 TQ	COBLS	10/01-12/01
Wholesale and Manufacturing	Greeley PMSA, CO	Y	22600 FQ	44260 AW	78370 TQ	COBLS	10/01-12/01
Wholesale and Manufacturing	Connecticut	Y	27980 FQ	59880 AW	111930 TQ	CTBLS	10/01-12/01
Wholesale and Manufacturing	Bridgeport PMSA, CT	Y	26870 FQ	58180 AW	101140 TQ	CTBLS	10/01-12/01
Wholesale and Manufacturing	Danbury PMSA, CT	Y	25580 FQ	62270 AW	139900 TQ	CTBLS	10/01-12/01
Wholesale and Manufacturing	Hartford MSA, CT	Y	30130 FQ	55050 AW	87450 TQ	CTBLS	10/01-12/01
Wholesale and Manufacturing	New Haven-Meriden PMSA, CT	Y	28290 FQ	56490 AW	96650 TQ	CTBLS	10/01-12/01
Wholesale and Manufacturing	New London-Norwich MSA, CT-RI	Y	19730 FQ	46720 AW	79910 TQ	CTBLS	10/01-12/01
Wholesale and Manufacturing	Stamford-Norwalk PMSA, CT	Y	31220 FQ	71510 AW		CTBLS	10/01-12/01
Wholesale and Manufacturing	Waterbury PMSA, CT	Y	29590 FQ	50510 AW	76740 TQ	CTBLS	10/01-12/01
Wholesale and Manufacturing	Delaware	Y	23220 FQ	48570 AW	83280 TQ	DEBLS	10/01-12/01
Wholesale and Manufacturing	Wilmington-Newark PMSA, DE-MD	Y	26060 FQ	49760 AW	82520 TQ	DEBLS	10/01-12/01
Wholesale and Manufacturing	District of Columbia	Y	18090 FQ	49010 AW	94200 TQ	DCBLS	10/01-12/01
Wholesale and Manufacturing	Washington PMSA, DC-MD-VA-WV	Y	23220 FQ	51750 AW	93270 TQ	DCBLS	10/01-12/01
Wholesale and Manufacturing	Florida	Y	19440 FQ	45340 AW	83240 TQ	FLBLS	10/01-12/01
Wholesale and Manufacturing	Daytona Beach MSA, FL	Y	18580 FQ	37180 AW	59540 TQ	FLBLS	10/01-12/01
Wholesale and Manufacturing	Fort Lauderdale PMSA, FL	Y	19550 FQ	49010 AW	89200 TQ	FLBLS	10/01-12/01
Wholesale and Manufacturing	Fort Myers-Cape Coral MSA, FL	Y	19550 FQ	47990 AW	94680 TQ	FLBLS	10/01-12/01
Wholesale and Manufacturing	Fort Pierce-Port St. Lucie MSA, FL	Y	20660 FQ	44500 AW	80120 TQ	FLBLS	10/01-12/01
Wholesale and Manufacturing	Fort Walton Beach MSA, FL	Y	15940 FQ	36440 AW	64780 TQ	FLBLS	10/01-12/01
Wholesale and Manufacturing	Gainesville MSA, FL	Y	20270 FQ	42020 AW	73020 TQ	FLBLS	10/01-12/01
Wholesale and Manufacturing	Jacksonville MSA, FL	Y	20550 FQ	42890 AW	69820 TQ	FLBLS	10/01-12/01
Wholesale and Manufacturing	Lakeland-Winter Haven MSA, FL	Y	20170 FQ	44350 AW	78140 TQ	FLBLS	10/01-12/01
Wholesale and Manufacturing	Melbourne-Titusville-Palm Bay MSA, FL	Y	13130 FQ	44050 AW	111860 TQ	FLBLS	10/01-12/01
Wholesale and Manufacturing	Miami PMSA, FL	Y	19020 FQ	41940 AW	75950 TQ	FLBLS	10/01-12/01
Wholesale and Manufacturing	Naples MSA, FL	Y	23330 FQ	49620 AW	90610 TQ	FLBLS	10/01-12/01
Wholesale and Manufacturing	Ocala MSA, FL	Y	16500 FQ	37040 AW	65230 TQ	FLBLS	10/01-12/01
Wholesale and Manufacturing	Orlando MSA, FL	Y	21770 FQ	51330 AW	98320 TQ	FLBLS	10/01-12/01
Wholesale and Manufacturing	Pensacola MSA, FL	Y	16650 FQ	40350 AW	71850 TQ	FLBLS	10/01-12/01
Wholesale and Manufacturing	Sarasota-Bradenton MSA, FL	Y	19870 FQ	40500 AW	70760 TQ	FLBLS	10/01-12/01

AAW	Average annual wage	**AOH**	Average offered, high	**ASH**	Average starting, high	**H**	Hourly	**M**	Monthly	**S**	Special: hourly and annual
AE	Average entry wage	**AOL**	Average offered, low	**ASL**	Average starting, low	**HI**	Highest wage paid	**MTC**	Median total compensation	**TQ**	Third quartile wage
AEX	Average experienced wage	**APH**	Average pay, high range	**AW**	Average wage paid	**HR**	High end range	**MW**	Median wage paid	**W**	Weekly
AO	Average offered	**APL**	Average pay, low range	**FQ**	First quartile wage	**LR**	Low end range	**SQ**	Second quartile wage	**Y**	Yearly

Occupation/Type/Industry	Location	Per	Low	Mid	High	Source	Date
Sales Representative							
Wholesale and Manufacturing	Tallahassee MSA, FL	Y	17840 FQ	36320 AW	67350 TQ	FLBLS	10/01-12/01
Wholesale and Manufacturing	Tampa-St. Petersburg-Clearwater MSA, FL	Y	18690 FQ	46730 AW	92290 TQ	FLBLS	10/01-12/01
Wholesale and Manufacturing	West Palm Beach-Boca Raton MSA, FL	Y	22700 FQ	48720 AW	90510 TQ	FLBLS	10/01-12/01
Wholesale and Manufacturing	Georgia	Y	23560 FQ	48910 AW	88870 TQ	GABLS	10/01-12/01
Wholesale and Manufacturing	Atlanta MSA, GA	Y	24330 FQ	50160 AW	91900 TQ	GABLS	10/01-12/01
Wholesale and Manufacturing	Augusta-Aiken MSA, GA-SC	Y	23120 FQ	44150 AW	78590 TQ	GABLS	10/01-12/01
Wholesale and Manufacturing	Columbus MSA, GA-AL	Y	19660 FQ	38660 AW	65390 TQ	GABLS	10/01-12/01
Wholesale and Manufacturing	Macon MSA, GA	Y	18330 FQ	41090 AW	74000 TQ	GABLS	10/01-12/01
Wholesale and Manufacturing	Savannah MSA, GA	Y	22430 FQ	43480 AW	68240 TQ	GABLS	10/01-12/01
Wholesale and Manufacturing	Hawaii	Y	18420 FQ	38290 AW	59500 TQ	HIBLS	10/01-12/01
Wholesale and Manufacturing	Honolulu MSA, HI	Y	18860 FQ	38950 AW	59670 TQ	HIBLS	10/01-12/01
Wholesale and Manufacturing	Idaho	Y	19430 FQ	37190 AW	59070 TQ	IDBLS	10/01-12/01
Wholesale and Manufacturing	Boise City MSA, ID	Y	19660 FQ	40550 AW	72160 TQ	IDBLS	10/01-12/01
Wholesale and Manufacturing	Illinois	Y	21910 FQ	45260 AW	76630 TQ	ILBLS	10/01-12/01
Wholesale and Manufacturing	Champaign-Urbana MSA, IL	Y	16380 FQ	37910 AW	67630 TQ	ILBLS	10/01-12/01
Wholesale and Manufacturing	Chicago PMSA, IL	Y	24070 FQ	47170 AW	79200 TQ	ILBLS	10/01-12/01
Wholesale and Manufacturing	Peoria-Pekin MSA, IL	Y	21270 FQ	42340 AW	66580 TQ	ILBLS	10/01-12/01
Wholesale and Manufacturing	Rockford MSA, IL	Y	22860 FQ	48760 AW	73500 TQ	ILBLS	10/01-12/01
Wholesale and Manufacturing	Springfield MSA, IL	Y	21930 FQ	43230 AW	75730 TQ	ILBLS	10/01-12/01
Wholesale and Manufacturing	Indiana	Y	23670 FQ	46910 AW	79570 TQ	INBLS	10/01-12/01
Wholesale and Manufacturing	Elkhart-Goshen MSA, IN	Y	25760 FQ	51080 AW	82240 TQ	INBLS	10/01-12/01
Wholesale and Manufacturing	Evansville-Henderson MSA, IN-KY	Y	20960 FQ	40070 AW	65220 TQ	INBLS	10/01-12/01
Wholesale and Manufacturing	Fort Wayne MSA, IN	Y	24060 FQ	46210 AW	82150 TQ	INBLS	10/01-12/01
Wholesale and Manufacturing	Gary PMSA, IN	Y	22830 FQ	45010 AW	77220 TQ	INBLS	10/01-12/01
Wholesale and Manufacturing	Indianapolis MSA, IN	Y	25670 FQ	49080 AW	82160 TQ	INBLS	10/01-12/01
Wholesale and Manufacturing	Lafayette MSA, IN	Y	21030 FQ	41090 AW	67930 TQ	INBLS	10/01-12/01
Wholesale and Manufacturing	South Bend MSA, IN	Y	20770 FQ	44600 AW	73240 TQ	INBLS	10/01-12/01
Wholesale and Manufacturing	Iowa	Y	19920 FQ	44410 AW	78780 TQ	IABLS	10/01-12/01
Wholesale and Manufacturing	Cedar Rapids MSA, IA	Y	19380 FQ	45810 AW	81320 TQ	IABLS	10/01-12/01
Wholesale and Manufacturing	Davenport-Moline-Rock Island MSA, IA-IL	Y	16760 FQ	40150 AW	69170 TQ	IABLS	10/01-12/01
Wholesale and Manufacturing	Des Moines MSA, IA	Y	19200 FQ	53000 AW	102400 TQ	IABLS	10/01-12/01
Wholesale and Manufacturing	Kansas	Y	22770 FQ	47300 AW	81990 TQ	KSBLS	10/01-12/01
Wholesale and Manufacturing	Topeka MSA, KS	Y	24200 FQ	43150 AW	68170 TQ	KSBLS	10/01-12/01
Wholesale and Manufacturing	Wichita MSA, KS	Y	20680 FQ	46320 AW	84310 TQ	KSBLS	10/01-12/01
Wholesale and Manufacturing	Kentucky	Y	20940 FQ	43100 AW	74430 TQ	KYBLS	10/01-12/01
Wholesale and Manufacturing	Lexington MSA, KY	Y	24180 FQ	43080 AW	68430 TQ	KYBLS	10/01-12/01
Wholesale and Manufacturing	Louisville MSA, KY-IN	Y	23540 FQ	44690 AW	77960 TQ	KYBLS	10/01-12/01
Wholesale and Manufacturing	Louisiana	Y	19130 FQ	39920 AW	66600 TQ	LABLS	10/01-12/01
Wholesale and Manufacturing	Baton Rouge MSA, LA	Y	22060 FQ	42640 AW	69460 TQ	LABLS	10/01-12/01
Wholesale and Manufacturing	Houma MSA, LA	Y	21040 FQ	39710 AW	64420 TQ	LABLS	10/01-12/01
Wholesale and Manufacturing	Lafayette MSA, LA	Y	19110 FQ	41070 AW	70650 TQ	LABLS	10/01-12/01
Wholesale and Manufacturing	Lake Charles MSA, LA	Y	20420 FQ	44860 AW	75900 TQ	LABLS	10/01-12/01
Wholesale and Manufacturing	New Orleans MSA, LA	Y	20750 FQ	40930 AW	65800 TQ	LABLS	10/01-12/01
Wholesale and Manufacturing	Shreveport-Bossier City MSA, LA	Y	18210 FQ	35120 AW	57170 TQ	LABLS	10/01-12/01
Wholesale and Manufacturing	Maine	Y	20060 FQ	45070 AW	81280 TQ	MEBLS	10/01-12/01
Wholesale and Manufacturing	Portland MSA, ME	Y	25630 FQ	46760 AW	74160 TQ	MEBLS	10/01-12/01
Wholesale and Manufacturing	Maryland	Y	21220 FQ	48780 AW	87470 TQ	MDBLS	10/01-12/01
Wholesale and Manufacturing	Baltimore PMSA, MD	Y	19570 FQ	47270 AW	85900 TQ	MDBLS	10/01-12/01
Wholesale and Manufacturing	Massachusetts	Y	25220 FQ	54040 AW	94930 TQ	MABLS	10/01-12/01
Wholesale and Manufacturing	Boston PMSA, MA-NH	Y	25100 FQ	56950 AW	109770 TQ	MABLS	10/01-12/01
Wholesale and Manufacturing	Brockton PMSA, MA	Y	22730 FQ	46010 AW	73940 TQ	MABLS	10/01-12/01
Wholesale and Manufacturing	Lawrence PMSA, MA-NH	Y	25360 FQ	51270 AW	91410 TQ	MABLS	10/01-12/01
Wholesale and Manufacturing	Lowell PMSA, MA-NH	Y	30080 FQ	55730 AW	90400 TQ	MABLS	10/01-12/01
Wholesale and Manufacturing	New Bedford PMSA, MA	Y	23110 FQ	46430 AW	84970 TQ	MABLS	10/01-12/01
Wholesale and Manufacturing	Springfield MSA, MA	Y	20040 FQ	47310 AW	81040 TQ	MABLS	10/01-12/01
Wholesale and Manufacturing	Worcester PMSA, MA-CT	Y	28080 FQ	50250 AW	76590 TQ	MABLS	10/01-12/01
Wholesale and Manufacturing	Michigan	Y	23440 FQ	51610 AW	89200 TQ	MIBLS	10/01-12/01
Wholesale and Manufacturing	Ann Arbor PMSA, MI	Y	25140 FQ	52140 AW	84550 TQ	MIBLS	10/01-12/01
Wholesale and Manufacturing	Detroit PMSA, MI	Y	26210 FQ	56920 AW	97480 TQ	MIBLS	10/01-12/01
Wholesale and Manufacturing	Flint PMSA, MI	Y	21420 FQ	46030 AW	84270 TQ	MIBLS	10/01-12/01
Wholesale and Manufacturing	Grand Rapids-Muskegon-Holland MSA, MI	Y	20960 FQ	49060 AW	83800 TQ	MIBLS	10/01-12/01
Wholesale and Manufacturing	Kalamazoo-Battle Creek MSA, MI	Y	24990 FQ	51840 AW	90150 TQ	MIBLS	10/01-12/01
Wholesale and Manufacturing	Lansing-East Lansing MSA, MI	Y	26520 FQ	52120 AW	86090 TQ	MIBLS	10/01-12/01

AAW Average annual wage **AOH** Average offered, high **ASH** Average starting, high **H** Hourly **M** Monthly **S** Special: hourly and annual
AE Average entry wage **AOL** Average offered, low **ASL** Average starting, low **HI** Highest wage paid **MTC** Median total compensation **TQ** Third quartile wage
AEX Average experienced wage **APH** Average pay, high range **AW** Average wage paid **HR** High end range **MW** Median wage paid **W** Weekly
AO Average offered **APL** Average pay, low range **FQ** First quartile wage **LR** Low end range **SQ** Second quartile wage **Y** Yearly

Occupation/Type/Industry	Location	Per	Low	Mid	High	Source	Date
Sales Representative							
Wholesale and Manufacturing	Saginaw-Bay City-Midland MSA, MI	Y	24440 FQ	51090 AW	83480 TQ	MIBLS	10/01-12/01
Wholesale and Manufacturing	Minnesota	Y	26960 FQ	54960 AW	91420 TQ	MNBLS	10/01-12/01
Wholesale and Manufacturing	Duluth-Superior MSA, MN-WI	Y	23230 FQ	41230 AW	62400 TQ	MNBLS	10/01-12/01
Wholesale and Manufacturing	Minneapolis-St. Paul MSA, MN-WI	Y	29330 FQ	57930 AW	97740 TQ	MNBLS	10/01-12/01
Wholesale and Manufacturing	St. Cloud MSA, MN	Y	25200 FQ	46980 AW	79070 TQ	MNBLS	10/01-12/01
Wholesale and Manufacturing	Mississippi	Y	20290 FQ	37620 AW	61740 TQ	MSBLS	10/01-12/01
Wholesale and Manufacturing	Biloxi-Gulfport-Pascagoula MSA, MS	Y	14490 FQ	30650 AW	51190 TQ	MSBLS	10/01-12/01
Wholesale and Manufacturing	Jackson MSA, MS	Y	23750 FQ	38410 AW	58060 TQ	MSBLS	10/01-12/01
Wholesale and Manufacturing	Missouri	Y	18990 FQ	45190 AW	79650 TQ	MOBLS	10/01-12/01
Wholesale and Manufacturing	Kansas City MSA, MO-KS	Y	20900 FQ	48850 AW	84120 TQ	MOBLS	10/01-12/01
Wholesale and Manufacturing	St. Louis MSA, MO-IL	Y	21080 FQ	47840 AW	84150 TQ	MOBLS	10/01-12/01
Wholesale and Manufacturing	Springfield MSA, MO	Y	19210 FQ	37810 AW	62600 TQ	MOBLS	10/01-12/01
Wholesale and Manufacturing	Montana	Y	19010 FQ	37120 AW	55540 TQ	MTBLS	10/01-12/01
Wholesale and Manufacturing	Billings MSA, MT	Y	21670 FQ	37820 AW	55860 TQ	MTBLS	10/01-12/01
Wholesale and Manufacturing	Nebraska	Y	18650 FQ	40090 AW	69670 TQ	NEBLS	10/01-12/01
Wholesale and Manufacturing	Lincoln MSA, NE	Y	14030 FQ	41510 AW	78960 TQ	NEBLS	10/01-12/01
Wholesale and Manufacturing	Omaha MSA, NE-IA	Y	23370 FQ	46340 AW	75790 TQ	NEBLS	10/01-12/01
Wholesale and Manufacturing	Nevada	Y	21860 FQ	45520 AW	77120 TQ	NVBLS	10/01-12/01
Wholesale and Manufacturing	Las Vegas MSA, NV-AZ	Y	21560 FQ	46540 AW	79540 TQ	NVBLS	10/01-12/01
Wholesale and Manufacturing	Reno MSA, NV	Y	21490 FQ	42870 AW	70310 TQ	NVBLS	10/01-12/01
Wholesale and Manufacturing	New Hampshire	Y	24220 FQ	48510 AW	81470 TQ	NHBLS	10/01-12/01
Wholesale and Manufacturing	Manchester PMSA, NH	Y	28120 FQ	48710 AW	73770 TQ	NHBLS	10/01-12/01
Wholesale and Manufacturing	Nashua PMSA, NH	Y	20390 FQ	46850 AW	85630 TQ	NHBLS	10/01-12/01
Wholesale and Manufacturing	Portsmouth-Rochester PMSA, NH-ME	Y	24170 FQ	47170 AW	79300 TQ	NHBLS	10/01-12/01
Wholesale and Manufacturing	New Jersey	Y	25290 FQ	56310 AW	100350 TQ	NJBLS	10/01-12/01
Wholesale and Manufacturing	Atlantic-Cape May PMSA, NJ	Y	17890 FQ	45130 AW	75540 TQ	NJBLS	10/01-12/01
Wholesale and Manufacturing	Bergen-Passaic PMSA, NJ	Y	22890 FQ	55730 AW	108880 TQ	NJBLS	10/01-12/01
Wholesale and Manufacturing	Jersey City PMSA, NJ	Y	30810 FQ	67890 AW		NJBLS	10/01-12/01
Wholesale and Manufacturing	Middlesex-Somerset-Hunterdon PMSA, NJ	Y	29140 FQ	57720 AW	95760 TQ	NJBLS	10/01-12/01
Wholesale and Manufacturing	Monmouth-Ocean PMSA, NJ	Y	24970 FQ	49080 AW	85560 TQ	NJBLS	10/01-12/01
Wholesale and Manufacturing	Newark PMSA, NJ	Y	28270 FQ	58320 AW	106050 TQ	NJBLS	10/01-12/01
Wholesale and Manufacturing	Trenton PMSA, NJ	Y	24320 FQ	51990 AW	88280 TQ	NJBLS	10/01-12/01
Wholesale and Manufacturing	New Mexico	Y	17180 FQ	37540 AW	63230 TQ	NMBLS	10/01-12/01
Wholesale and Manufacturing	Albuquerque MSA, NM	Y	21320 FQ	40950 AW	66750 TQ	NMBLS	10/01-12/01
Wholesale and Manufacturing	Las Cruces MSA, NM	Y	14510 FQ	27000 AW	49970 TQ	NMBLS	10/01-12/01
Wholesale and Manufacturing	New York	Y	24910 FQ	55090 AW	106510 TQ	NYBLS	10/01-12/01
Wholesale and Manufacturing	Albany-Schenectady-Troy MSA, NY	Y	25620 FQ	46150 AW	75350 TQ	NYBLS	10/01-12/01
Wholesale and Manufacturing	Binghamton MSA, NY	Y	22070 FQ	41390 AW	66730 TQ	NYBLS	10/01-12/01
Wholesale and Manufacturing	Buffalo-Niagara Falls MSA, NY	Y	21760 FQ	45900 AW	81160 TQ	NYBLS	10/01-12/01
Wholesale and Manufacturing	Dutchess County PMSA, NY	Y	24910 FQ	47260 AW	76750 TQ	NYBLS	10/01-12/01
Wholesale and Manufacturing	Nassau-Suffolk PMSA, NY	Y	25810 FQ	56280 AW	116510 TQ	NYBLS	10/01-12/01
Wholesale and Manufacturing	New York PMSA, NY	Y	25280 FQ	59480 AW	120090 TQ	NYBLS	10/01-12/01
Wholesale and Manufacturing	Newburgh PMSA, NY-PA	Y	25630 FQ	53110 AW	87330 TQ	NYBLS	10/01-12/01
Wholesale and Manufacturing	Rochester MSA, NY	Y	24570 FQ	48130 AW	83750 TQ	NYBLS	10/01-12/01
Wholesale and Manufacturing	Syracuse MSA, NY	Y	23790 FQ	44870 AW	77650 TQ	NYBLS	10/01-12/01
Wholesale and Manufacturing	Utica-Rome MSA, NY	Y	21070 FQ	43240 AW	71020 TQ	NYBLS	10/01-12/01
Wholesale and Manufacturing	North Carolina	Y	20730 FQ	45640 AW	81370 TQ	NCBLS	10/01-12/01
Wholesale and Manufacturing	Asheville MSA, NC	Y	20750 FQ	38680 AW	70130 TQ	NCBLS	10/01-12/01
Wholesale and Manufacturing	Charlotte-Gastonia-Rock Hill MSA, NC-SC	Y	20800 FQ	44640 AW	78670 TQ	NCBLS	10/01-12/01
Wholesale and Manufacturing	Fayetteville MSA, NC	Y	14530 FQ	34470 AW	55880 TQ	NCBLS	10/01-12/01
Wholesale and Manufacturing	Greensboro-Winston-Salem-High Point MSA, NC	Y	25640 FQ	53450 AW	90310 TQ	NCBLS	10/01-12/01
Wholesale and Manufacturing	Hickory-Morganton-Lenoir MSA, NC	Y	19640 FQ	48330 AW	98740 TQ	NCBLS	10/01-12/01
Wholesale and Manufacturing	Raleigh-Durham-Chapel Hill MSA, NC	Y	22020 FQ	44810 AW	72590 TQ	NCBLS	10/01-12/01
Wholesale and Manufacturing	Wilmington MSA, NC	Y	20240 FQ	51830 AW		NCBLS	10/01-12/01
Wholesale and Manufacturing	North Dakota	Y	21580 FQ	39650 AW	65510 TQ	NDBLS	10/01-12/01
Wholesale and Manufacturing	Fargo-Moorhead MSA, ND-MN	Y	22840 FQ	40720 AW	66500 TQ	NDBLS	10/01-12/01
Wholesale and Manufacturing	Ohio	Y	21630 FQ	49360 AW	87840 TQ	OHBLS	10/01-12/01
Wholesale and Manufacturing	Akron PMSA, OH	Y	20470 FQ	46900 AW	85740 TQ	OHBLS	10/01-12/01
Wholesale and Manufacturing	Canton-Massillon MSA, OH	Y	23320 FQ	44510 AW	71070 TQ	OHBLS	10/01-12/01

AAW	Average annual wage	**AOH**	Average offered, high	**ASH**	Average starting, high	**H**	Hourly	**M**	Monthly	**S**	Special: hourly and annual
AE	Average entry wage	**AOL**	Average offered, low	**ASL**	Average starting, low	**HI**	Highest wage paid	**MTC**	Median total compensation	**TQ**	Third quartile wage
AEX	Average experienced wage	**APH**	Average pay, high range	**AW**	Average wage paid	**HR**	High end range	**MW**	Median wage paid	**W**	Weekly
AO	Average offered	**APL**	Average pay, low range	**FQ**	First quartile wage	**LR**	Low end range	**SQ**	Second quartile wage	**Y**	Yearly

Occupation/Type/Industry	Location	Per	Low	Mid	High	Source	Date
Sales Representative							
Wholesale and Manufacturing	Cincinnati PMSA, OH-KY-IN	Y	24790 FQ	53450 AW	92100 TQ	OHBLS	10/01-12/01
Wholesale and Manufacturing	Cleveland-Lorain-Elyria PMSA, OH	Y	20560 FQ	50680 AW	91080 TQ	OHBLS	10/01-12/01
Wholesale and Manufacturing	Columbus MSA, OH	Y	21530 FQ	48830 AW	89270 TQ	OHBLS	10/01-12/01
Wholesale and Manufacturing	Dayton-Springfield MSA, OH	Y	21280 FQ	46490 AW	82260 TQ	OHBLS	10/01-12/01
Wholesale and Manufacturing	Hamilton-Middletown PMSA, OH	Y	25410 FQ	51200 AW	81130 TQ	OHBLS	10/01-12/01
Wholesale and Manufacturing	Mansfield MSA, OH	Y	20360 FQ	38370 AW	60980 TQ	OHBLS	10/01-12/01
Wholesale and Manufacturing	Toledo MSA, OH	Y	24100 FQ	48470 AW	85530 TQ	OHBLS	10/01-12/01
Wholesale and Manufacturing	Youngstown-Warren MSA, OH	Y	19680 FQ	42160 AW	69930 TQ	OHBLS	10/01-12/01
Wholesale and Manufacturing	Oklahoma	Y	19680 FQ	40150 AW	65690 TQ	OKBLS	10/01-12/01
Wholesale and Manufacturing	Oklahoma City MSA, OK	Y	18780 FQ	39400 AW	65500 TQ	OKBLS	10/01-12/01
Wholesale and Manufacturing	Tulsa MSA, OK	Y	22880 FQ	42940 AW	69190 TQ	OKBLS	10/01-12/01
Wholesale and Manufacturing	Oregon	Y	24030 FQ	47480 AW	80040 TQ	ORBLS	10/01-12/01
Wholesale and Manufacturing	Eugene-Springfield MSA, OR	Y	21060 FQ	41620 AW	76070 TQ	ORBLS	10/01-12/01
Wholesale and Manufacturing	Medford-Ashland MSA, OR	Y	19070 FQ	35100 AW	56160 TQ	ORBLS	10/01-12/01
Wholesale and Manufacturing	Portland-Vancouver PMSA, OR-WA	Y	25640 FQ	49520 AW	83770 TQ	ORBLS	10/01-12/01
Wholesale and Manufacturing	Salem PMSA, OR	Y	21470 FQ	45720 AW	79350 TQ	ORBLS	10/01-12/01
Wholesale and Manufacturing	Pennsylvania	Y	23000 FQ	47030 AW	81110 TQ	PABLS	10/01-12/01
Wholesale and Manufacturing	Allentown-Bethlehem-Easton MSA, PA	Y	25150 FQ	42670 AW	67920 TQ	PABLS	10/01-12/01
Wholesale and Manufacturing	Erie MSA, PA	Y	19720 FQ	41790 AW	69540 TQ	PABLS	10/01-12/01
Wholesale and Manufacturing	Harrisburg-Lebanon-Carlisle MSA, PA	Y	20910 FQ	43950 AW	73520 TQ	PABLS	10/01-12/01
Wholesale and Manufacturing	Johnstown MSA, PA	Y	16010 FQ	33540 AW	54820 TQ	PABLS	10/01-12/01
Wholesale and Manufacturing	Lancaster MSA, PA	Y	19340 FQ	45780 AW	82550 TQ	PABLS	10/01-12/01
Wholesale and Manufacturing	Philadelphia PMSA, PA-NJ	Y	25510 FQ	52240 AW	87850 TQ	PABLS	10/01-12/01
Wholesale and Manufacturing	Pittsburgh MSA, PA	Y	22020 FQ	43630 AW	70230 TQ	PABLS	10/01-12/01
Wholesale and Manufacturing	Reading MSA, PA	Y	24480 FQ	47530 AW	80400 TQ	PABLS	10/01-12/01
Wholesale and Manufacturing	Scranton-Wilkes-Barre-Hazleton MSA, PA	Y	21470 FQ	39830 AW	66010 TQ	PABLS	10/01-12/01
Wholesale and Manufacturing	York MSA, PA	Y	24750 FQ	50330 AW	84910 TQ	PABLS	10/01-12/01
Wholesale and Manufacturing	Rhode Island	Y	23560 FQ	47190 AW	82480 TQ	RIBLS	10/01-12/01
Wholesale and Manufacturing	Providence-Fall River-Warwick MSA, RI-MA	Y	23750 FQ	46160 AW	78420 TQ	RIBLS	10/01-12/01
Wholesale and Manufacturing	South Carolina	Y	20120 FQ	45530 AW	83530 TQ	SCBLS	10/01-12/01
Wholesale and Manufacturing	Charleston-North Charleston MSA, SC	Y	19470 FQ	39270 AW	64060 TQ	SCBLS	10/01-12/01
Wholesale and Manufacturing	Columbia MSA, SC	Y	18350 FQ	42200 AW	76180 TQ	SCBLS	10/01-12/01
Wholesale and Manufacturing	Greenville-Spartanburg-Anderson MSA, SC	Y	21630 FQ	51040 AW	99640 TQ	SCBLS	10/01-12/01
Wholesale and Manufacturing	Myrtle Beach MSA, SC	Y	19310 FQ	34550 AW	52560 TQ	SCBLS	10/01-12/01
Wholesale and Manufacturing	South Dakota	Y	21920 FQ	38760 AW	58830 TQ	SDBLS	10/01-12/01
Wholesale and Manufacturing	Sioux Falls MSA, SD	Y	24930 FQ	40990 AW	63590 TQ	SDBLS	10/01-12/01
Wholesale and Manufacturing	Tennessee	Y	22200 FQ	45830 AW	78890 TQ	TNBLS	10/01-12/01
Wholesale and Manufacturing	Chattanooga MSA, TN-GA	Y	19430 FQ	41720 AW	68220 TQ	TNBLS	10/01-12/01
Wholesale and Manufacturing	Clarksville-Hopkinsville MSA, TN-KY	Y	20430 FQ	40100 AW	66240 TQ	TNBLS	10/01-12/01
Wholesale and Manufacturing	Johnson City-Kingsport-Bristol MSA, TN-VA	Y	15730 FQ	34260 AW	60820 TQ	TNBLS	10/01-12/01
Wholesale and Manufacturing	Knoxville MSA, TN	Y	22580 FQ	46340 AW	77340 TQ	TNBLS	10/01-12/01
Wholesale and Manufacturing	Memphis MSA, TN-AR-MS	Y	21180 FQ	45540 AW	77120 TQ	TNBLS	10/01-12/01
Wholesale and Manufacturing	Nashville MSA, TN	Y	23960 FQ	46050 AW	80560 TQ	TNBLS	10/01-12/01
Wholesale and Manufacturing	Texas	Y	20540 FQ	45940 AW	78680 TQ	TXBLS	10/01-12/01
Wholesale and Manufacturing	Amarillo MSA, TX	Y	17070 FQ	35900 AW	62510 TQ	TXBLS	10/01-12/01
Wholesale and Manufacturing	Austin-San Marcos MSA, TX	Y	20010 FQ	39880 AW	71210 TQ	TXBLS	10/01-12/01
Wholesale and Manufacturing	Beaumont-Port Arthur MSA, TX	Y	17690 FQ	38020 AW	62050 TQ	TXBLS	10/01-12/01
Wholesale and Manufacturing	Brazoria PMSA, TX	Y	22520 FQ	48320 AW	85010 TQ	TXBLS	10/01-12/01
Wholesale and Manufacturing	Brownsville-Harlingen-San Benito MSA, TX	Y	17740 FQ	46880 AW		TXBLS	10/01-12/01
Wholesale and Manufacturing	Corpus Christi MSA, TX	Y	22960 FQ	40080 AW	57780 TQ	TXBLS	10/01-12/01
Wholesale and Manufacturing	Dallas PMSA, TX	Y	22490 FQ	48880 AW	82540 TQ	TXBLS	10/01-12/01
Wholesale and Manufacturing	El Paso MSA, TX	Y	15700 FQ	38090 AW	64880 TQ	TXBLS	10/01-12/01
Wholesale and Manufacturing	Fort Worth-Arlington PMSA, TX	Y	22650 FQ	46210 AW	78160 TQ	TXBLS	10/01-12/01
Wholesale and Manufacturing	Galveston-Texas City PMSA, TX	Y	15630 FQ	35940 AW	73680 TQ	TXBLS	10/01-12/01
Wholesale and Manufacturing	Houston PMSA, TX	Y	23890 FQ	51440 AW	93920 TQ	TXBLS	10/01-12/01
Wholesale and Manufacturing	Killeen-Temple MSA, TX	Y	18210 FQ	38190 AW	57210 TQ	TXBLS	10/01-12/01

AAW	Average annual wage	AOH	Average offered, high	ASH	Average starting, high	H	Hourly	M	Monthly	S	Special: hourly and annual
AE	Average entry wage	AOL	Average offered, low	ASL	Average starting, low	HI	Highest wage paid	MTC	Median total compensation	TQ	Third quartile wage
AEX	Average experienced wage	APH	Average pay, high range	AW	Average wage paid	HR	High end range	MW	Median wage paid	W	Weekly
AO	Average offered	APL	Average pay, low range	FQ	First quartile wage	LR	Low end range	SQ	Second quartile wage	Y	Yearly

Occupation/Type/Industry	Location	Per	Low	Mid	High	Source	Date
Sales Representative							
Wholesale and Manufacturing	Laredo MSA, TX	Y	16160 FQ	39490 AW	70190 TQ	TXBLS	10/01-12/01
Wholesale and Manufacturing	Longview-Marshall MSA, TX	Y	20840 FQ	42770 AW	70860 TQ	TXBLS	10/01-12/01
Wholesale and Manufacturing	Lubbock MSA, TX	Y	18550 FQ	42120 AW	71510 TQ	TXBLS	10/01-12/01
Wholesale and Manufacturing	McAllen-Edinburg-Mission MSA, TX	Y	13630 FQ	37370 AW	71720 TQ	TXBLS	10/01-12/01
Wholesale and Manufacturing	Odessa-Midland MSA, TX	Y	15640 FQ	40520 AW	66590 TQ	TXBLS	10/01-12/01
Wholesale and Manufacturing	San Antonio MSA, TX	Y	18890 FQ	36680 AW	57780 TQ	TXBLS	10/01-12/01
Wholesale and Manufacturing	Tyler MSA, TX	Y	20230 FQ	46060 AW	73150 TQ	TXBLS	10/01-12/01
Wholesale and Manufacturing	Waco MSA, TX	Y	17270 FQ	39620 AW	68630 TQ	TXBLS	10/01-12/01
Wholesale and Manufacturing	Utah	Y	22740 FQ	46180 AW	76210 TQ	UTBLS	10/01-12/01
Wholesale and Manufacturing	Provo-Orem MSA, UT	Y	19610 FQ	43290 AW	79940 TQ	UTBLS	10/01-12/01
Wholesale and Manufacturing	Salt Lake City-Ogden MSA, UT	Y	23890 FQ	47610 AW	77730 TQ	UTBLS	10/01-12/01
Wholesale and Manufacturing	Vermont	Y	26060 FQ	46810 AW	72060 TQ	VTBLS	10/01-12/01
Wholesale and Manufacturing	Burlington MSA, VT	Y	28310 FQ	47040 AW	71880 TQ	VTBLS	10/01-12/01
Wholesale and Manufacturing	Virginia	Y	19980 FQ	46180 AW	83410 TQ	VABLS	10/01-12/01
Wholesale and Manufacturing	Lynchburg MSA, VA	Y	21240 FQ	53910 AW	121980 TQ	VABLS	10/01-12/01
Wholesale and Manufacturing	Norfolk-Virginia Beach-Newport News MSA, VA-NC	Y	20380 FQ	42210 AW	73630 TQ	VABLS	10/01-12/01
Wholesale and Manufacturing	Richmond-Petersburg MSA, VA	Y	20980 FQ	48730 AW	82460 TQ	VABLS	10/01-12/01
Wholesale and Manufacturing	Roanoke MSA, VA	Y	22570 FQ	42530 AW	71020 TQ	VABLS	10/01-12/01
Wholesale and Manufacturing	Washington	Y	24390 FQ	46780 AW	78000 TQ	WABLS	10/01-12/01
Wholesale and Manufacturing	Bremerton PMSA, WA	Y	15840 FQ	42390 AW	82100 TQ	WABLS	10/01-12/01
Wholesale and Manufacturing	Olympia PMSA, WA	Y	21870 FQ	41040 AW	67810 TQ	WABLS	10/01-12/01
Wholesale and Manufacturing	Richland-Kennewick-Pasco MSA, WA	Y	22140 FQ	38430 AW	60130 TQ	WABLS	10/01-12/01
Wholesale and Manufacturing	Seattle-Bellevue-Everett PMSA, WA	Y	25300 FQ	48720 AW	81240 TQ	WABLS	10/01-12/01
Wholesale and Manufacturing	Spokane MSA, WA	Y	23360 FQ	38970 AW	59060 TQ	WABLS	10/01-12/01
Wholesale and Manufacturing	Tacoma PMSA, WA	Y	22890 FQ	40600 AW	66320 TQ	WABLS	10/01-12/01
Wholesale and Manufacturing	Yakima MSA, WA	Y	29060 FQ	55000 AW	104700 TQ	WABLS	10/01-12/01
Wholesale and Manufacturing	West Virginia	Y	18480 FQ	36500 AW	61160 TQ	WVBLS	10/01-12/01
Wholesale and Manufacturing	Charleston MSA, WV	Y	19360 FQ	36340 AW	60190 TQ	WVBLS	10/01-12/01
Wholesale and Manufacturing	Huntington-Ashland MSA, WV-KY-OH	Y	18020 FQ	34500 AW	57320 TQ	WVBLS	10/01-12/01
Wholesale and Manufacturing	Wisconsin	Y	23120 FQ	49240 AW	85210 TQ	WIBLS	10/01-12/01
Wholesale and Manufacturing	Appleton-Oshkosh-Neenah MSA, WI	Y	25100 FQ	48140 AW	78900 TQ	WIBLS	10/01-12/01
Wholesale and Manufacturing	Green Bay MSA, WI	Y	22480 FQ	45710 AW	78430 TQ	WIBLS	10/01-12/01
Wholesale and Manufacturing	Madison MSA, WI	Y	26050 FQ	49260 AW	77720 TQ	WIBLS	10/01-12/01
Wholesale and Manufacturing	Milwaukee-Waukesha PMSA, WI	Y	26650 FQ	55100 AW	90830 TQ	WIBLS	10/01-12/01
Wholesale and Manufacturing	Racine PMSA, WI	Y	20920 FQ	47960 AW	82290 TQ	WIBLS	10/01-12/01
Wholesale and Manufacturing	Wyoming	Y	18830 FQ	35780 AW	55430 TQ	WYBLS	10/01-12/01
Wholesale and Manufacturing	Cheyenne MSA, WY	Y	20260 FQ	34900 AW	56270 TQ	WYBLS	10/01-12/01
Wholesale and Manufacturing	Puerto Rico	Y	12870 FQ	27080 AW	49370 TQ	PRBLS	10/01-12/01
Wholesale and Manufacturing	Virgin Islands	Y	19110 FQ	26630 AW	35430 TQ	VIBLS	10/01-12/01
Wholesale and Manufacturing	Guam	Y	13700 FQ	22100 AW	33150 TQ	GUBLS	10/01-12/01
Wholesale and Manufacturing, Technical and Scientific Product	Alabama	Y	29490 FQ	59180 AW	100350 TQ	ALBLS	10/01-12/01
Wholesale and Manufacturing, Technical and Scientific Product	Birmingham MSA, AL	Y	30580 FQ	56490 AW	97980 TQ	ALBLS	10/01-12/01
Wholesale and Manufacturing, Technical and Scientific Product	Huntsville MSA, AL	Y	25770 FQ	51320 AW	83470 TQ	ALBLS	10/01-12/01
Wholesale and Manufacturing, Technical and Scientific Product	Mobile MSA, AL	Y	27130 FQ	49080 AW	70970 TQ	ALBLS	10/01-12/01
Wholesale and Manufacturing, Technical and Scientific Product	Montgomery MSA, AL	Y	26490 FQ	46290 AW	77970 TQ	ALBLS	10/01-12/01
Wholesale and Manufacturing, Technical and Scientific Product	Alaska	Y	26610 FQ	47180 AW	73490 TQ	AKBLS	10/01-12/01
Wholesale and Manufacturing, Technical and Scientific Product	Anchorage MSA, AK	Y	26120 FQ	46480 AW	72500 TQ	AKBLS	10/01-12/01
Wholesale and Manufacturing, Technical and Scientific Product	Arizona	Y	24860 FQ	50640 AW	85980 TQ	AZBLS	10/01-12/01
Wholesale and Manufacturing, Technical and Scientific Product	Phoenix-Mesa MSA, AZ	Y	24980 FQ	50400 AW	85610 TQ	AZBLS	10/01-12/01
Wholesale and Manufacturing, Technical and Scientific Product	Tucson MSA, AZ	Y	26120 FQ	55050 AW	87680 TQ	AZBLS	10/01-12/01

AAW	Average annual wage	AOH	Average offered, high	ASH	Average starting, high	H	Hourly	M	Monthly	S	Special: hourly and annual
AE	Average entry wage	AOL	Average offered, low	ASL	Average starting, low	HI	Highest wage paid	MTC	Median total compensation	TQ	Third quartile wage
AEX	Average experienced wage	APH	Average pay, high range	AW	Average wage paid	HR	High end range	MW	Median wage paid	W	Weekly
AO	Average offered	APL	Average pay, low range	FQ	First quartile wage	LR	Low end range	SQ	Second quartile wage	Y	Yearly

Occupation/Type/Industry	Location	Per	Low	Mid	High	Source	Date
Sales Representative							
Wholesale and Manufacturing, Technical and Scientific Product	Arkansas	Y	25760 FQ	48220 AW	81100 TQ	ARBLS	10/01-12/01
Wholesale and Manufacturing, Technical and Scientific Product	Fayetteville-Springdale-Rogers MSA, AR	Y	17150 FQ	37620 AW	77730 TQ	ARBLS	10/01-12/01
Wholesale and Manufacturing, Technical and Scientific Product	Fort Smith MSA, AR-OK	Y	30830 FQ	60500 AW	95830 TQ	ARBLS	10/01-12/01
Wholesale and Manufacturing, Technical and Scientific Product	Little Rock-North Little Rock MSA, AR	Y	25980 FQ	47580 AW	81130 TQ	ARBLS	10/01-12/01
Wholesale and Manufacturing, Technical and Scientific Product	California	Y	30730 FQ	69730 AW	119360 TQ	CABLS	10/01-12/01
Wholesale and Manufacturing, Technical and Scientific Product	Bakersfield MSA, CA	Y	27880 FQ	51500 AW	76410 TQ	CABLS	10/01-12/01
Wholesale and Manufacturing, Technical and Scientific Product	Fresno MSA, CA	Y	24310 FQ	47180 AW	91340 TQ	CABLS	10/01-12/01
Wholesale and Manufacturing, Technical and Scientific Product	Los Angeles-Long Beach PMSA, CA	Y	27290 FQ	65470 AW	115830 TQ	CABLS	10/01-12/01
Wholesale and Manufacturing, Technical and Scientific Product	Modesto MSA, CA	Y	29670 FQ	61030 AW	95260 TQ	CABLS	10/01-12/01
Wholesale and Manufacturing, Technical and Scientific Product	Oakland PMSA, CA	Y	32390 FQ	69380 AW	125790 TQ	CABLS	10/01-12/01
Wholesale and Manufacturing, Technical and Scientific Product	Orange County PMSA, CA	Y	32240 FQ	66370 AW	112190 TQ	CABLS	10/01-12/01
Wholesale and Manufacturing, Technical and Scientific Product	Riverside-San Bernardino PMSA, CA	Y	30830 FQ	58950 AW	90560 TQ	CABLS	10/01-12/01
Wholesale and Manufacturing, Technical and Scientific Product	Sacramento PMSA, CA	Y	35660 FQ	71280 AW	112670 TQ	CABLS	10/01-12/01
Wholesale and Manufacturing, Technical and Scientific Product	Salinas MSA, CA	Y	46180 FQ	66540 AW	99340 TQ	CABLS	10/01-12/01
Wholesale and Manufacturing, Technical and Scientific Product	San Diego MSA, CA	Y	22860 FQ	57290 AW	90380 TQ	CABLS	10/01-12/01
Wholesale and Manufacturing, Technical and Scientific Product	San Francisco PMSA, CA	Y	32640 FQ	86280 AW		CABLS	10/01-12/01
Wholesale and Manufacturing, Technical and Scientific Product	San Jose PMSA, CA	Y	41380 FQ	81150 AW	139620 TQ	CABLS	10/01-12/01
Wholesale and Manufacturing, Technical and Scientific Product	San Luis Obispo-Atascadero-Paso Robles MSA, CA	Y	28650 FQ	62990 AW		CABLS	10/01-12/01
Wholesale and Manufacturing, Technical and Scientific Product	Santa Barbara-Santa Maria-Lompoc MSA, CA	Y	29400 FQ	63730 AW	129870 TQ	CABLS	10/01-12/01
Wholesale and Manufacturing, Technical and Scientific Product	Santa Cruz-Watsonville PMSA, CA	Y	27130 FQ	61410 AW	114280 TQ	CABLS	10/01-12/01
Wholesale and Manufacturing, Technical and Scientific Product	Santa Rosa PMSA, CA	Y	39730 FQ	75130 AW	129590 TQ	CABLS	10/01-12/01
Wholesale and Manufacturing, Technical and Scientific Product	Stockton-Lodi MSA, CA	Y	30960 FQ	51650 AW	86770 TQ	CABLS	10/01-12/01
Wholesale and Manufacturing, Technical and Scientific Product	Vallejo-Fairfield-Napa PMSA, CA	Y	35330 FQ	61150 AW	106380 TQ	CABLS	10/01-12/01
Wholesale and Manufacturing, Technical and Scientific Product	Ventura PMSA, CA	Y	35460 FQ	68550 AW	133800 TQ	CABLS	10/01-12/01
Wholesale and Manufacturing, Technical and Scientific Product	Visalia-Tulare-Porterville MSA, CA	Y	30730 FQ	47400 AW	76270 TQ	CABLS	10/01-12/01
Wholesale and Manufacturing, Technical and Scientific Product	Colorado	Y	33050 FQ	66740 AW	118490 TQ	COBLS	10/01-12/01
Wholesale and Manufacturing, Technical and Scientific Product	Boulder-Longmont PMSA, CO	Y	34470 FQ	63660 AW	113000 TQ	COBLS	10/01-12/01
Wholesale and Manufacturing, Technical and Scientific Product	Colorado Springs MSA, CO	Y	35030 FQ	65730 AW	107740 TQ	COBLS	10/01-12/01
Wholesale and Manufacturing, Technical and Scientific Product	Denver PMSA, CO	Y	33310 FQ	69280 AW	121670 TQ	COBLS	10/01-12/01
Wholesale and Manufacturing, Technical and Scientific Product	Fort Collins-Loveland MSA, CO	Y	33970 FQ	55600 AW	79550 TQ	COBLS	10/01-12/01

AAW	Average annual wage	AOH	Average offered, high	ASH	Average starting, high	H	Hourly	M	Monthly	S	Special: hourly and annual
AE	Average entry wage	AOL	Average offered, low	ASL	Average starting, low	HI	Highest wage paid	MTC	Median total compensation	TQ	Third quartile wage
AEX	Average experienced wage	APH	Average pay, high range	AW	Average wage paid	HR	High end range	MW	Median wage paid	W	Weekly
AO	Average offered	APL	Average pay, low range	FQ	First quartile wage	LR	Low end range	SQ	Second quartile wage	Y	Yearly

Occupation/Type/Industry	Location	Per	Low	Mid	High	Source	Date
Sales Representative							
Wholesale and Manufacturing, Technical and Scientific Product	Greeley PMSA, CO	Y	20720 FQ	46210 AW	75790 TQ	COBLS	10/01-12/01
Wholesale and Manufacturing, Technical and Scientific Product	Connecticut	Y	37670 FQ	71900 AW	118280 TQ	CTBLS	10/01-12/01
Wholesale and Manufacturing, Technical and Scientific Product	Bridgeport PMSA, CT	Y	38550 FQ	80200 AW		CTBLS	10/01-12/01
Wholesale and Manufacturing, Technical and Scientific Product	Danbury PMSA, CT	Y	35940 FQ	71710 AW	139250 TQ	CTBLS	10/01-12/01
Wholesale and Manufacturing, Technical and Scientific Product	Hartford MSA, CT	Y	31040 FQ	65830 AW	105470 TQ	CTBLS	10/01-12/01
Wholesale and Manufacturing, Technical and Scientific Product	New Haven-Meriden PMSA, CT	Y	35740 FQ	71050 AW	136490 TQ	CTBLS	10/01-12/01
Wholesale and Manufacturing, Technical and Scientific Product	New London-Norwich MSA, CT-RI	Y	33780 FQ	62180 AW	102570 TQ	CTBLS	10/01-12/01
Wholesale and Manufacturing, Technical and Scientific Product	Stamford-Norwalk PMSA, CT	Y	38680 FQ	69330 AW	110000 TQ	CTBLS	10/01-12/01
Wholesale and Manufacturing, Technical and Scientific Product	Waterbury PMSA, CT	Y	37500 FQ	67350 AW	113890 TQ	CTBLS	10/01-12/01
Wholesale and Manufacturing, Technical and Scientific Product	Delaware	Y	23640 FQ	54890 AW	85400 TQ	DEBLS	10/01-12/01
Wholesale and Manufacturing, Technical and Scientific Product	Wilmington-Newark PMSA, DE-MD	Y	22380 FQ	55940 AW	87080 TQ	DEBLS	10/01-12/01
Wholesale and Manufacturing, Technical and Scientific Product	District of Columbia	Y	13450 FQ	46950 AW	88670 TQ	DCBLS	10/01-12/01
Wholesale and Manufacturing, Technical and Scientific Product	Washington PMSA, DC-MD-VA-WV	Y	33480 FQ	72510 AW	119780 TQ	DCBLS	10/01-12/01
Wholesale and Manufacturing, Technical and Scientific Product	Florida	Y	25040 FQ	53730 AW	100700 TQ	FLBLS	10/01-12/01
Wholesale and Manufacturing, Technical and Scientific Product	Daytona Beach MSA, FL	Y	19800 FQ	35180 AW	56880 TQ	FLBLS	10/01-12/01
Wholesale and Manufacturing, Technical and Scientific Product	Fort Lauderdale PMSA, FL	Y	24880 FQ	53050 AW	104160 TQ	FLBLS	10/01-12/01
Wholesale and Manufacturing, Technical and Scientific Product	Fort Myers-Cape Coral MSA, FL	Y	20820 FQ	41700 AW	78910 TQ	FLBLS	10/01-12/01
Wholesale and Manufacturing, Technical and Scientific Product	Fort Pierce-Port St. Lucie MSA, FL	Y	26180 FQ	42840 AW	63800 TQ	FLBLS	10/01-12/01
Wholesale and Manufacturing, Technical and Scientific Product	Fort Walton Beach MSA, FL	Y	13820 FQ	38810 AW	75050 TQ	FLBLS	10/01-12/01
Wholesale and Manufacturing, Technical and Scientific Product	Gainesville MSA, FL	Y	25250 FQ	39330 AW	49940 TQ	FLBLS	10/01-12/01
Wholesale and Manufacturing, Technical and Scientific Product	Jacksonville MSA, FL	Y	25990 FQ	48410 AW	84420 TQ	FLBLS	10/01-12/01
Wholesale and Manufacturing, Technical and Scientific Product	Lakeland-Winter Haven MSA, FL	Y	23680 FQ	48780 AW	85200 TQ	FLBLS	10/01-12/01
Wholesale and Manufacturing, Technical and Scientific Product	Melbourne-Titusville-Palm Bay MSA, FL	Y	23520 FQ	53030 AW	100160 TQ	FLBLS	10/01-12/01
Wholesale and Manufacturing, Technical and Scientific Product	Miami PMSA, FL	Y	24730 FQ	49970 AW	99750 TQ	FLBLS	10/01-12/01
Wholesale and Manufacturing, Technical and Scientific Product	Naples MSA, FL	Y	25810 FQ	45810 AW	68600 TQ	FLBLS	10/01-12/01
Wholesale and Manufacturing, Technical and Scientific Product	Ocala MSA, FL	Y	24660 FQ	52390 AW	102420 TQ	FLBLS	10/01-12/01
Wholesale and Manufacturing, Technical and Scientific Product	Orlando MSA, FL	Y	25740 FQ	56770 AW	94720 TQ	FLBLS	10/01-12/01
Wholesale and Manufacturing, Technical and Scientific Product	Sarasota-Bradenton MSA, FL	Y	21220 FQ	44510 AW	86660 TQ	FLBLS	10/01-12/01
Wholesale and Manufacturing, Technical and Scientific Product	Tallahassee MSA, FL	Y	26550 FQ	70100 AW	133860 TQ	FLBLS	10/01-12/01
Wholesale and Manufacturing, Technical and Scientific Product	Tampa-St. Petersburg-Clearwater MSA, FL	Y	27910 FQ	63360 AW	116210 TQ	FLBLS	10/01-12/01

AAW	Average annual wage	AOH	Average offered, high	ASH	Average starting, high	H	Hourly	M	Monthly	S	Special: hourly and annual
AE	Average entry wage	AOL	Average offered, low	ASL	Average starting, low	HI	Highest wage paid	MTC	Median total compensation	TQ	Third quartile wage
AEX	Average experienced wage	APH	Average pay, high range	AW	Average wage paid	HR	High end range	MW	Median wage paid	W	Weekly
AO	Average offered	APL	Average pay, low range	FQ	First quartile wage	LR	Low end range	SQ	Second quartile wage	Y	Yearly

Occupation/Type/Industry	Location	Per	Low	Mid	High	Source	Date
Sales Representative							
Wholesale and Manufacturing, Technical and Scientific Product	West Palm Beach-Boca Raton MSA, FL	Y	27960 FQ	54250 AW	102310 TQ	FLBLS	10/01-12/01
Wholesale and Manufacturing, Technical and Scientific Product	Georgia	Y	33840 FQ	57680 AW	95750 TQ	GABLS	10/01-12/01
Wholesale and Manufacturing, Technical and Scientific Product	Atlanta MSA, GA	Y	34980 FQ	58060 AW	95380 TQ	GABLS	10/01-12/01
Wholesale and Manufacturing, Technical and Scientific Product	Columbus MSA, GA-AL	Y	25260 FQ	48150 AW	86900 TQ	GABLS	10/01-12/01
Wholesale and Manufacturing, Technical and Scientific Product	Macon MSA, GA	Y	25540 FQ	52020 AW	89900 TQ	GABLS	10/01-12/01
Wholesale and Manufacturing, Technical and Scientific Product	Savannah MSA, GA	Y	35520 FQ	57560 AW	101960 TQ	GABLS	10/01-12/01
Wholesale and Manufacturing, Technical and Scientific Product	Hawaii	Y	28570 FQ	47200 AW	73040 TQ	HIBLS	10/01-12/01
Wholesale and Manufacturing, Technical and Scientific Product	Honolulu MSA, HI	Y	29780 FQ	48410 AW	76410 TQ	HIBLS	10/01-12/01
Wholesale and Manufacturing, Technical and Scientific Product	Idaho	Y	17700 FQ	45560 AW	77310 TQ	IDBLS	10/01-12/01
Wholesale and Manufacturing, Technical and Scientific Product	Boise City MSA, ID	Y	16150 FQ	48670 AW	82020 TQ	IDBLS	10/01-12/01
Wholesale and Manufacturing, Technical and Scientific Product	Illinois	Y	22020 FQ	54560 AW	92230 TQ	ILBLS	10/01-12/01
Wholesale and Manufacturing, Technical and Scientific Product	Champaign-Urbana MSA, IL	Y	26450 FQ	53810 AW	84980 TQ	ILBLS	10/01-12/01
Wholesale and Manufacturing, Technical and Scientific Product	Chicago PMSA, IL	Y	21480 FQ	55720 AW	94880 TQ	ILBLS	10/01-12/01
Wholesale and Manufacturing, Technical and Scientific Product	Peoria-Pekin MSA, IL	Y	18340 FQ	38140 AW	65670 TQ	ILBLS	10/01-12/01
Wholesale and Manufacturing, Technical and Scientific Product	Rockford MSA, IL	Y	18320 FQ	53480 AW	86970 TQ	ILBLS	10/01-12/01
Wholesale and Manufacturing, Technical and Scientific Product	Springfield MSA, IL	Y	29650 FQ	49350 AW	80290 TQ	ILBLS	10/01-12/01
Wholesale and Manufacturing, Technical and Scientific Product	Indiana	Y	29170 FQ	57830 AW	100790 TQ	INBLS	10/01-12/01
Wholesale and Manufacturing, Technical and Scientific Product	Elkhart-Goshen MSA, IN	Y	24360 FQ	59280 AW	130630 TQ	INBLS	10/01-12/01
Wholesale and Manufacturing, Technical and Scientific Product	Evansville-Henderson MSA, IN-KY	Y	30210 FQ	59110 AW	105910 TQ	INBLS	10/01-12/01
Wholesale and Manufacturing, Technical and Scientific Product	Fort Wayne MSA, IN	Y	27550 FQ	51020 AW	86010 TQ	INBLS	10/01-12/01
Wholesale and Manufacturing, Technical and Scientific Product	Gary PMSA, IN	Y	31120 FQ	69920 AW		INBLS	10/01-12/01
Wholesale and Manufacturing, Technical and Scientific Product	Indianapolis MSA, IN	Y	29890 FQ	60260 AW	119760 TQ	INBLS	10/01-12/01
Wholesale and Manufacturing, Technical and Scientific Product	Lafayette MSA, IN	Y	28080 FQ	57620 AW	91680 TQ	INBLS	10/01-12/01
Wholesale and Manufacturing, Technical and Scientific Product	South Bend MSA, IN	Y	25250 FQ	50750 AW	86070 TQ	INBLS	10/01-12/01
Wholesale and Manufacturing, Technical and Scientific Product	Iowa	Y	22690 FQ	45200 AW	77070 TQ	IABLS	10/01-12/01
Wholesale and Manufacturing, Technical and Scientific Product	Cedar Rapids MSA, IA	Y	23080 FQ	53200 AW	91730 TQ	IABLS	10/01-12/01
Wholesale and Manufacturing, Technical and Scientific Product	Davenport-Moline-Rock Island MSA, IA-IL	Y	22690 FQ	44480 AW	77990 TQ	IABLS	10/01-12/01
Wholesale and Manufacturing, Technical and Scientific Product	Des Moines MSA, IA	Y	24380 FQ	47410 AW	78060 TQ	IABLS	10/01-12/01
Wholesale and Manufacturing, Technical and Scientific Product	Kansas	Y	34730 FQ	68890 AW		KSBLS	10/01-12/01
Wholesale and Manufacturing, Technical and Scientific Product	Topeka MSA, KS	Y	36500 FQ	60080 AW	91000 TQ	KSBLS	10/01-12/01
Wholesale and Manufacturing, Technical and Scientific Product	Wichita MSA, KS	Y	32650 FQ	65940 AW	115010 TQ	KSBLS	10/01-12/01
Wholesale and Manufacturing, Technical and Scientific Product	Kentucky	Y	27040 FQ	63190 AW	112710 TQ	KYBLS	10/01-12/01
Wholesale and Manufacturing, Technical and Scientific Product	Lexington MSA, KY	Y	30340 FQ	62740 AW	105220 TQ	KYBLS	10/01-12/01

AAW	Average annual wage	AOH	Average offered, high	ASH	Average starting, high	H	Hourly	M	Monthly	S	Special: hourly and annual
AE	Average entry wage	AOL	Average offered, low	ASL	Average starting, low	HI	Highest wage paid	MTC	Median total compensation	TQ	Third quartile wage
AEX	Average experienced wage	APH	Average pay, high range	AW	Average wage paid	HR	High end range	MW	Median wage paid	W	Weekly
AO	Average offered	APL	Average pay, low range	FQ	First quartile wage	LR	Low end range	SQ	Second quartile wage	Y	Yearly

Occupation/Type/Industry	Location	Per	Low	Mid	High	Source	Date
Sales Representative							
Wholesale and Manufacturing, Technical and Scientific Product	Louisville MSA, KY-IN	Y	25420 FQ	60140 AW	122410 TQ	KYBLS	10/01-12/01
Wholesale and Manufacturing, Technical and Scientific Product	Louisiana	Y	23850 FQ	50610 AW	84130 TQ	LABLS	10/01-12/01
Wholesale and Manufacturing, Technical and Scientific Product	Baton Rouge MSA, LA	Y	26120 FQ	55260 AW	104350 TQ	LABLS	10/01-12/01
Wholesale and Manufacturing, Technical and Scientific Product	Houma MSA, LA	Y	26590 FQ	46750 AW	68810 TQ	LABLS	10/01-12/01
Wholesale and Manufacturing, Technical and Scientific Product	Lafayette MSA, LA	Y	26390 FQ	50570 AW	81340 TQ	LABLS	10/01-12/01
Wholesale and Manufacturing, Technical and Scientific Product	Lake Charles MSA, LA	Y	25430 FQ	39040 AW	46350 TQ	LABLS	10/01-12/01
Wholesale and Manufacturing, Technical and Scientific Product	New Orleans MSA, LA	Y	22110 FQ	55410 AW	115750 TQ	LABLS	10/01-12/01
Wholesale and Manufacturing, Technical and Scientific Product	Shreveport-Bossier City MSA, LA	Y	16290 FQ	40580 AW	71100 TQ	LABLS	10/01-12/01
Wholesale and Manufacturing, Technical and Scientific Product	Maine	Y	30200 FQ	60250 AW	105970 TQ	MEBLS	10/01-12/01
Wholesale and Manufacturing, Technical and Scientific Product	Portland MSA, ME	Y	29920 FQ	55590 AW	87150 TQ	MEBLS	10/01-12/01
Wholesale and Manufacturing, Technical and Scientific Product	Maryland	Y	31730 FQ	79250 AW		MDBLS	10/01-12/01
Wholesale and Manufacturing, Technical and Scientific Product	Baltimore PMSA, MD	Y	27860 FQ	77500 AW		MDBLS	10/01-12/01
Wholesale and Manufacturing, Technical and Scientific Product	Massachusetts	Y	31600 FQ	62360 AW	97120 TQ	MABLS	10/01-12/01
Wholesale and Manufacturing, Technical and Scientific Product	Boston PMSA, MA-NH	Y	32100 FQ	62640 AW	98430 TQ	MABLS	10/01-12/01
Wholesale and Manufacturing, Technical and Scientific Product	Brockton PMSA, MA	Y	20410 FQ	46220 AW	72900 TQ	MABLS	10/01-12/01
Wholesale and Manufacturing, Technical and Scientific Product	Lawrence PMSA, MA-NH	Y	35280 FQ	59260 AW	90800 TQ	MABLS	10/01-12/01
Wholesale and Manufacturing, Technical and Scientific Product	Lowell PMSA, MA-NH	Y	38700 FQ	70150 AW	96270 TQ	MABLS	10/01-12/01
Wholesale and Manufacturing, Technical and Scientific Product	New Bedford PMSA, MA	Y	22430 FQ	44890 AW	66210 TQ	MABLS	10/01-12/01
Wholesale and Manufacturing, Technical and Scientific Product	Springfield MSA, MA	Y	29680 FQ	52830 AW	86240 TQ	MABLS	10/01-12/01
Wholesale and Manufacturing, Technical and Scientific Product	Worcester PMSA, MA-CT	Y	31050 FQ	61220 AW	105100 TQ	MABLS	10/01-12/01
Wholesale and Manufacturing, Technical and Scientific Product	Michigan	Y	32330 FQ	70470 AW	127770 TQ	MIBLS	10/01-12/01
Wholesale and Manufacturing, Technical and Scientific Product	Ann Arbor PMSA, MI	Y	44250 FQ	77510 AW	121860 TQ	MIBLS	10/01-12/01
Wholesale and Manufacturing, Technical and Scientific Product	Detroit PMSA, MI	Y	39040 FQ	77300 AW	133410 TQ	MIBLS	10/01-12/01
Wholesale and Manufacturing, Technical and Scientific Product	Flint PMSA, MI	Y	28560 FQ	54130 AW	86710 TQ	MIBLS	10/01-12/01
Wholesale and Manufacturing, Technical and Scientific Product	Grand Rapids-Muskegon-Holland MSA, MI	Y	19790 FQ	51140 AW	94950 TQ	MIBLS	10/01-12/01
Wholesale and Manufacturing, Technical and Scientific Product	Kalamazoo-Battle Creek MSA, MI	Y	33020 FQ	87640 AW	142770 TQ	MIBLS	10/01-12/01
Wholesale and Manufacturing, Technical and Scientific Product	Lansing-East Lansing MSA, MI	Y	28050 FQ	57800 AW	88800 TQ	MIBLS	10/01-12/01
Wholesale and Manufacturing, Technical and Scientific Product	Saginaw-Bay City-Midland MSA, MI	Y	23000 FQ	52040 AW	80920 TQ	MIBLS	10/01-12/01
Wholesale and Manufacturing, Technical and Scientific Product	Minnesota	Y	31450 FQ	65660 AW	112070 TQ	MNBLS	10/01-12/01
Wholesale and Manufacturing, Technical and Scientific Product	Duluth-Superior MSA, MN-WI	Y	24000 FQ	40030 AW	67200 TQ	MNBLS	10/01-12/01
Wholesale and Manufacturing, Technical and Scientific Product	Minneapolis-St. Paul MSA, MN-WI	Y	32560 FQ	66680 AW	111750 TQ	MNBLS	10/01-12/01
Wholesale and Manufacturing, Technical and Scientific Product	St. Cloud MSA, MN	Y	32060 FQ	88140 AW	139380 TQ	MNBLS	10/01-12/01

AAW Average annual wage; AE Average entry wage; AEX Average experienced wage; AO Average offered; AOH Average offered, high; AOL Average offered, low; APH Average pay, high range; APL Average pay, low range; ASH Average starting, high; ASL Average starting, low; AW Average wage paid; FQ First quartile wage; H Hourly; HI Highest wage paid; HR High end range; LR Low end range; M Monthly; MTC Median total compensation; MW Median wage paid; SQ Second quartile wage; S Special: hourly and annual; TQ Third quartile wage; W Weekly; Y Yearly

Occupation/Type/Industry	Location	Per	Low	Mid	High	Source	Date
Sales Representative							
Wholesale and Manufacturing, Technical and Scientific Product	Mississippi	Y	21220 FQ	53770 AW	105520 TQ	MSBLS	10/01-12/01
Wholesale and Manufacturing, Technical and Scientific Product	Biloxi-Gulfport-Pascagoula MSA, MS	Y	20950 FQ	51800 AW	74700 TQ	MSBLS	10/01-12/01
Wholesale and Manufacturing, Technical and Scientific Product	Jackson MSA, MS	Y	24650 FQ	43310 AW	67390 TQ	MSBLS	10/01-12/01
Wholesale and Manufacturing, Technical and Scientific Product	Missouri	Y	26240 FQ	55710 AW	95910 TQ	MOBLS	10/01-12/01
Wholesale and Manufacturing, Technical and Scientific Product	Kansas City MSA, MO-KS	Y	28060 FQ	64040 AW		MOBLS	10/01-12/01
Wholesale and Manufacturing, Technical and Scientific Product	St. Louis MSA, MO-IL	Y	28880 FQ	55790 AW	88530 TQ	MOBLS	10/01-12/01
Wholesale and Manufacturing, Technical and Scientific Product	Springfield MSA, MO	Y	22130 FQ	54720 AW	105810 TQ	MOBLS	10/01-12/01
Wholesale and Manufacturing, Technical and Scientific Product	Montana	Y	18870 FQ	56890 AW	130770 TQ	MTBLS	10/01-12/01
Wholesale and Manufacturing, Technical and Scientific Product	Billings MSA, MT	Y	19610 FQ	38680 AW	57040 TQ	MTBLS	10/01-12/01
Wholesale and Manufacturing, Technical and Scientific Product	Nebraska	Y	26870 FQ	50340 AW	80720 TQ	NEBLS	10/01-12/01
Wholesale and Manufacturing, Technical and Scientific Product	Lincoln MSA, NE	Y	26800 FQ	51970 AW	101280 TQ	NEBLS	10/01-12/01
Wholesale and Manufacturing, Technical and Scientific Product	Omaha MSA, NE-IA	Y	26010 FQ	51210 AW	82180 TQ	NEBLS	10/01-12/01
Wholesale and Manufacturing, Technical and Scientific Product	Nevada	Y	30450 FQ	55250 AW	89110 TQ	NVBLS	10/01-12/01
Wholesale and Manufacturing, Technical and Scientific Product	Las Vegas MSA, NV-AZ	Y	30090 FQ	52530 AW	78370 TQ	NVBLS	10/01-12/01
Wholesale and Manufacturing, Technical and Scientific Product	Reno MSA, NV	Y	27700 FQ	55860 AW	89690 TQ	NVBLS	10/01-12/01
Wholesale and Manufacturing, Technical and Scientific Product	New Hampshire	Y	26510 FQ	61630 AW	108040 TQ	NHBLS	10/01-12/01
Wholesale and Manufacturing, Technical and Scientific Product	Manchester PMSA, NH	Y	24990 FQ	59380 AW	107280 TQ	NHBLS	10/01-12/01
Wholesale and Manufacturing, Technical and Scientific Product	Nashua PMSA, NH	Y	24260 FQ	58800 AW	130630 TQ	NHBLS	10/01-12/01
Wholesale and Manufacturing, Technical and Scientific Product	Portsmouth-Rochester PMSA, NH-ME	Y	26460 FQ	56020 AW	88510 TQ	NHBLS	10/01-12/01
Wholesale and Manufacturing, Technical and Scientific Product	New Jersey	Y	35050 FQ	70730 AW	119910 TQ	NJBLS	10/01-12/01
Wholesale and Manufacturing, Technical and Scientific Product	Atlantic-Cape May PMSA, NJ	Y	28280 FQ	50590 AW	89540 TQ	NJBLS	10/01-12/01
Wholesale and Manufacturing, Technical and Scientific Product	Bergen-Passaic PMSA, NJ	Y	37290 FQ	78200 AW	144330 TQ	NJBLS	10/01-12/01
Wholesale and Manufacturing, Technical and Scientific Product	Jersey City PMSA, NJ	Y	39190 FQ	76610 AW	137400 TQ	NJBLS	10/01-12/01
Wholesale and Manufacturing, Technical and Scientific Product	Middlesex-Somerset-Hunterdon PMSA, NJ	Y	33490 FQ	72690 AW	119150 TQ	NJBLS	10/01-12/01
Wholesale and Manufacturing, Technical and Scientific Product	Monmouth-Ocean PMSA, NJ	Y	35320 FQ	64810 AW	113940 TQ	NJBLS	10/01-12/01
Wholesale and Manufacturing, Technical and Scientific Product	Newark PMSA, NJ	Y	40030 FQ	68120 AW	97560 TQ	NJBLS	10/01-12/01
Wholesale and Manufacturing, Technical and Scientific Product	Trenton PMSA, NJ	Y	47310 FQ	103640 AW		NJBLS	10/01-12/01
Wholesale and Manufacturing, Technical and Scientific Product	New Mexico	Y	23300 FQ	50170 AW	93840 TQ	NMBLS	10/01-12/01
Wholesale and Manufacturing, Technical and Scientific Product	Albuquerque MSA, NM	Y	21730 FQ	49300 AW	96760 TQ	NMBLS	10/01-12/01
Wholesale and Manufacturing, Technical and Scientific Product	Las Cruces MSA, NM	Y	16090 FQ	38570 AW	55310 TQ	NMBLS	10/01-12/01
Wholesale and Manufacturing, Technical and Scientific Product	New York	Y	29830 FQ	67220 AW	125960 TQ	NYBLS	10/01-12/01
Wholesale and Manufacturing, Technical and Scientific Product	Albany-Schenectady-Troy MSA, NY	Y	25290 FQ	55350 AW	91260 TQ	NYBLS	10/01-12/01
Wholesale and Manufacturing, Technical and Scientific Product	Binghamton MSA, NY	Y	16120 FQ	44900 AW	86130 TQ	NYBLS	10/01-12/01

AAW Average annual wage; AE Average entry wage; AEX Average experienced wage; AO Average offered; AOH Average offered, high; AOL Average offered, low; APH Average pay, high range; APL Average pay, low range; ASH Average starting, high; ASL Average starting, low; AW Average wage paid; FQ First quartile wage; H Hourly; HI Highest wage paid; HR High end range; LR Low end range; M Monthly; MTC Median total compensation; MW Median wage paid; SQ Second quartile wage; S Special: hourly and annual; TQ Third quartile wage; W Weekly; Y Yearly

Occupation/Type/Industry	Location	Per	Low	Mid	High	Source	Date
Sales Representative							
Wholesale and Manufacturing, Technical and Scientific Product	Buffalo-Niagara Falls MSA, NY	Y	26580 FQ	48990 AW	76140 TQ	NYBLS	10/01-12/01
Wholesale and Manufacturing, Technical and Scientific Product	Dutchess County PMSA, NY	Y	29210 FQ	64110 AW	106770 TQ	NYBLS	10/01-12/01
Wholesale and Manufacturing, Technical and Scientific Product	Nassau-Suffolk PMSA, NY	Y	29730 FQ	59540 AW	99560 TQ	NYBLS	10/01-12/01
Wholesale and Manufacturing, Technical and Scientific Product	New York PMSA, NY	Y	36990 FQ	81110 AW		NYBLS	10/01-12/01
Wholesale and Manufacturing, Technical and Scientific Product	Newburgh PMSA, NY-PA	Y	25960 FQ	44980 AW	69770 TQ	NYBLS	10/01-12/01
Wholesale and Manufacturing, Technical and Scientific Product	Rochester MSA, NY	Y	28790 FQ	59350 AW	90810 TQ	NYBLS	10/01-12/01
Wholesale and Manufacturing, Technical and Scientific Product	Syracuse MSA, NY	Y	27940 FQ	57380 AW	97360 TQ	NYBLS	10/01-12/01
Wholesale and Manufacturing, Technical and Scientific Product	Utica-Rome MSA, NY	Y	28170 FQ	40200 AW	64920 TQ	NYBLS	10/01-12/01
Wholesale and Manufacturing, Technical and Scientific Product	North Carolina	Y	26800 FQ	50830 AW	87040 TQ	NCBLS	10/01-12/01
Wholesale and Manufacturing, Technical and Scientific Product	Asheville MSA, NC	Y	22740 FQ	41090 AW	69820 TQ	NCBLS	10/01-12/01
Wholesale and Manufacturing, Technical and Scientific Product	Charlotte-Gastonia-Rock Hill MSA, NC-SC	Y	28870 FQ	54340 AW	89240 TQ	NCBLS	10/01-12/01
Wholesale and Manufacturing, Technical and Scientific Product	Fayetteville MSA, NC	Y	22200 FQ	36680 AW	62180 TQ	NCBLS	10/01-12/01
Wholesale and Manufacturing, Technical and Scientific Product	Greensboro-Winston-Salem-High Point MSA, NC	Y	29090 FQ	53400 AW	88430 TQ	NCBLS	10/01-12/01
Wholesale and Manufacturing, Technical and Scientific Product	Hickory-Morganton-Lenoir MSA, NC	Y	26030 FQ	48260 AW	78310 TQ	NCBLS	10/01-12/01
Wholesale and Manufacturing, Technical and Scientific Product	Raleigh-Durham-Chapel Hill MSA, NC	Y	26690 FQ	48060 AW	80700 TQ	NCBLS	10/01-12/01
Wholesale and Manufacturing, Technical and Scientific Product	Wilmington MSA, NC	Y	24130 FQ	37610 AW	54150 TQ	NCBLS	10/01-12/01
Wholesale and Manufacturing, Technical and Scientific Product	North Dakota	Y	23270 FQ	47010 AW	83500 TQ	NDBLS	10/01-12/01
Wholesale and Manufacturing, Technical and Scientific Product	Fargo-Moorhead MSA, ND-MN	Y	23580 FQ	47430 AW	84250 TQ	NDBLS	10/01-12/01
Wholesale and Manufacturing, Technical and Scientific Product	Ohio	Y	28630 FQ	60270 AW	103910 TQ	OHBLS	10/01-12/01
Wholesale and Manufacturing, Technical and Scientific Product	Akron PMSA, OH	Y	32610 FQ	62900 AW	110890 TQ	OHBLS	10/01-12/01
Wholesale and Manufacturing, Technical and Scientific Product	Canton-Massillon MSA, OH	Y	28580 FQ	56630 AW	87580 TQ	OHBLS	10/01-12/01
Wholesale and Manufacturing, Technical and Scientific Product	Cincinnati PMSA, OH-KY-IN	Y	30780 FQ	65860 AW	113920 TQ	OHBLS	10/01-12/01
Wholesale and Manufacturing, Technical and Scientific Product	Cleveland-Lorain-Elyria PMSA, OH	Y	30530 FQ	59170 AW	92650 TQ	OHBLS	10/01-12/01
Wholesale and Manufacturing, Technical and Scientific Product	Columbus MSA, OH	Y	26400 FQ	60440 AW	111080 TQ	OHBLS	10/01-12/01
Wholesale and Manufacturing, Technical and Scientific Product	Dayton-Springfield MSA, OH	Y	28140 FQ	56110 AW	96010 TQ	OHBLS	10/01-12/01
Wholesale and Manufacturing, Technical and Scientific Product	Hamilton-Middletown PMSA, OH	Y	27020 FQ	55880 AW	88510 TQ	OHBLS	10/01-12/01
Wholesale and Manufacturing, Technical and Scientific Product	Mansfield MSA, OH	Y	14080 FQ	48090 AW	94020 TQ	OHBLS	10/01-12/01
Wholesale and Manufacturing, Technical and Scientific Product	Toledo MSA, OH	Y	31110 FQ	59380 AW	96450 TQ	OHBLS	10/01-12/01
Wholesale and Manufacturing, Technical and Scientific Product	Youngstown-Warren MSA, OH	Y	21110 FQ	53110 AW	95720 TQ	OHBLS	10/01-12/01
Wholesale and Manufacturing, Technical and Scientific Product	Oklahoma	Y	25560 FQ	52890 AW	93540 TQ	OKBLS	10/01-12/01
Wholesale and Manufacturing, Technical and Scientific Product	Oklahoma City MSA, OK	Y	23970 FQ	51920 AW	91540 TQ	OKBLS	10/01-12/01

AAW	Average annual wage	**AOH**	Average offered, high	**ASH**	Average starting, high	**H**	Hourly	**M**	Monthly	**S**	Special: hourly and annual
AE	Average entry wage	**AOL**	Average offered, low	**ASL**	Average starting, low	**HI**	Highest wage paid	**MTC**	Median total compensation	**TQ**	Third quartile wage
AEX	Average experienced wage	**APH**	Average pay, high range	**AW**	Average wage paid	**HR**	High end range	**MW**	Median wage paid	**W**	Weekly
AO	Average offered	**APL**	Average pay, low range	**FQ**	First quartile wage	**LR**	Low end range	**SQ**	Second quartile wage	**Y**	Yearly

Occupation/Type/Industry	Location	Per	Low	Mid	High	Source	Date
Sales Representative							
Wholesale and Manufacturing, Technical and Scientific Product	Tulsa MSA, OK	Y	27590 FQ	54370 AW	89040 TQ	OKBLS	10/01-12/01
Wholesale and Manufacturing, Technical and Scientific Product	Oregon	Y	25740 FQ	53050 AW	87410 TQ	ORBLS	10/01-12/01
Wholesale and Manufacturing, Technical and Scientific Product	Eugene-Springfield MSA, OR	Y	28610 FQ	52310 AW	79150 TQ	ORBLS	10/01-12/01
Wholesale and Manufacturing, Technical and Scientific Product	Medford-Ashland MSA, OR	Y	24660 FQ	39270 AW	74950 TQ	ORBLS	10/01-12/01
Wholesale and Manufacturing, Technical and Scientific Product	Portland-Vancouver PMSA, OR-WA	Y	25550 FQ	54720 AW	89350 TQ	ORBLS	10/01-12/01
Wholesale and Manufacturing, Technical and Scientific Product	Salem PMSA, OR	Y	24130 FQ	44280 AW	89060 TQ	ORBLS	10/01-12/01
Wholesale and Manufacturing, Technical and Scientific Product	Pennsylvania	Y	30950 FQ	64730 AW	111310 TQ	PABLS	10/01-12/01
Wholesale and Manufacturing, Technical and Scientific Product	Allentown-Bethlehem-Easton MSA, PA	Y	28400 FQ	48280 AW	72190 TQ	PABLS	10/01-12/01
Wholesale and Manufacturing, Technical and Scientific Product	Erie MSA, PA	Y	29000 FQ	47000 AW	64750 TQ	PABLS	10/01-12/01
Wholesale and Manufacturing, Technical and Scientific Product	Harrisburg-Lebanon-Carlisle MSA, PA	Y	32350 FQ	58730 AW	89750 TQ	PABLS	10/01-12/01
Wholesale and Manufacturing, Technical and Scientific Product	Johnstown MSA, PA	Y	26820 FQ	58620 AW	91330 TQ	PABLS	10/01-12/01
Wholesale and Manufacturing, Technical and Scientific Product	Lancaster MSA, PA	Y	30710 FQ	55800 AW	85890 TQ	PABLS	10/01-12/01
Wholesale and Manufacturing, Technical and Scientific Product	Philadelphia PMSA, PA-NJ	Y	32620 FQ	70710 AW	125720 TQ	PABLS	10/01-12/01
Wholesale and Manufacturing, Technical and Scientific Product	Pittsburgh MSA, PA	Y	27190 FQ	58610 AW	92960 TQ	PABLS	10/01-12/01
Wholesale and Manufacturing, Technical and Scientific Product	Reading MSA, PA	Y	28200 FQ	56770 AW	93910 TQ	PABLS	10/01-12/01
Wholesale and Manufacturing, Technical and Scientific Product	Scranton-Wilkes-Barre-Hazleton MSA, PA	Y	25030 FQ	47720 AW	76500 TQ	PABLS	10/01-12/01
Wholesale and Manufacturing, Technical and Scientific Product	York MSA, PA	Y	28300 FQ	49190 AW	72420 TQ	PABLS	10/01-12/01
Wholesale and Manufacturing, Technical and Scientific Product	Rhode Island	Y	31160 FQ	58490 AW	90540 TQ	RIBLS	10/01-12/01
Wholesale and Manufacturing, Technical and Scientific Product	Providence-Fall River-Warwick MSA, RI-MA	Y	30890 FQ	58250 AW	89760 TQ	RIBLS	10/01-12/01
Wholesale and Manufacturing, Technical and Scientific Product	South Carolina	Y	26800 FQ	53840 AW	88640 TQ	SCBLS	10/01-12/01
Wholesale and Manufacturing, Technical and Scientific Product	Charleston-North Charleston MSA, SC	Y	27070 FQ	50580 AW	76200 TQ	SCBLS	10/01-12/01
Wholesale and Manufacturing, Technical and Scientific Product	Columbia MSA, SC	Y	25240 FQ	45260 AW	66810 TQ	SCBLS	10/01-12/01
Wholesale and Manufacturing, Technical and Scientific Product	Greenville-Spartanburg-Anderson MSA, SC	Y	24090 FQ	51160 AW	87660 TQ	SCBLS	10/01-12/01
Wholesale and Manufacturing, Technical and Scientific Product	Myrtle Beach MSA, SC	Y	24290 FQ	46260 AW	70950 TQ	SCBLS	10/01-12/01
Wholesale and Manufacturing, Technical and Scientific Product	South Dakota	Y	29220 FQ	60450 AW	98990 TQ	SDBLS	10/01-12/01
Wholesale and Manufacturing, Technical and Scientific Product	Sioux Falls MSA, SD	Y	26610 FQ	68640 AW	132140 TQ	SDBLS	10/01-12/01
Wholesale and Manufacturing, Technical and Scientific Product	Tennessee	Y	27520 FQ	60180 AW	121160 TQ	TNBLS	10/01-12/01
Wholesale and Manufacturing, Technical and Scientific Product	Chattanooga MSA, TN-GA	Y	25530 FQ	44660 AW	66560 TQ	TNBLS	10/01-12/01
Wholesale and Manufacturing, Technical and Scientific Product	Clarksville-Hopkinsville MSA, TN-KY	Y	16270 FQ	46350 AW	90300 TQ	TNBLS	10/01-12/01
Wholesale and Manufacturing, Technical and Scientific Product	Johnson City-Kingsport-Bristol MSA, TN-VA	Y	23000 FQ	47480 AW	72510 TQ	TNBLS	10/01-12/01

AAW Average annual wage **AE** Average entry wage **AEX** Average experienced wage **AO** Average offered **AOH** Average offered, high **AOL** Average offered, low **APH** Average pay, high range **APL** Average pay, low range **ASH** Average starting, high **ASL** Average starting, low **AW** Average wage paid **FQ** First quartile wage **H** Hourly **HI** Highest wage paid **HR** High end range **LR** Low end range **M** Monthly **MTC** Median total compensation **MW** Median wage paid **SQ** Second quartile wage **S** Special: hourly and annual **TQ** Third quartile wage **W** Weekly **Y** Yearly

Occupation/Type/Industry	Location	Per	Low	Mid	High	Source	Date
Sales Representative							
Wholesale and Manufacturing, Technical and Scientific Product	Knoxville MSA, TN	Y	22050 FQ	45180 AW	73740 TQ	TNBLS	10/01-12/01
Wholesale and Manufacturing, Technical and Scientific Product	Memphis MSA, TN-AR-MS	Y	26610 FQ	69890 AW	134520 TQ	TNBLS	10/01-12/01
Wholesale and Manufacturing, Technical and Scientific Product	Nashville MSA, TN	Y	28890 FQ	63050 AW	124930 TQ	TNBLS	10/01-12/01
Wholesale and Manufacturing, Technical and Scientific Product	Texas	Y	25310 FQ	55890 AW	94900 TQ	TXBLS	10/01-12/01
Wholesale and Manufacturing, Technical and Scientific Product	Amarillo MSA, TX	Y	28730 FQ	54580 AW	84520 TQ	TXBLS	10/01-12/01
Wholesale and Manufacturing, Technical and Scientific Product	Austin-San Marcos MSA, TX	Y	34280 FQ	66840 AW	116840 TQ	TXBLS	10/01-12/01
Wholesale and Manufacturing, Technical and Scientific Product	Beaumont-Port Arthur MSA, TX	Y	16690 FQ	49090 AW	99590 TQ	TXBLS	10/01-12/01
Wholesale and Manufacturing, Technical and Scientific Product	Brazoria PMSA, TX	Y	21690 FQ	50100 AW	90380 TQ	TXBLS	10/01-12/01
Wholesale and Manufacturing, Technical and Scientific Product	Brownsville-Harlingen-San Benito MSA, TX	Y	22860 FQ	45640 AW	76180 TQ	TXBLS	10/01-12/01
Wholesale and Manufacturing, Technical and Scientific Product	Corpus Christi MSA, TX	Y	26830 FQ	51600 AW	86410 TQ	TXBLS	10/01-12/01
Wholesale and Manufacturing, Technical and Scientific Product	Dallas PMSA, TX	Y	30070 FQ	59500 AW	96420 TQ	TXBLS	10/01-12/01
Wholesale and Manufacturing, Technical and Scientific Product	El Paso MSA, TX	Y	20320 FQ	54740 AW	114980 TQ	TXBLS	10/01-12/01
Wholesale and Manufacturing, Technical and Scientific Product	Fort Worth-Arlington PMSA, TX	Y	23160 FQ	41770 AW	76870 TQ	TXBLS	10/01-12/01
Wholesale and Manufacturing, Technical and Scientific Product	Houston PMSA, TX	Y	27440 FQ	56860 AW	92730 TQ	TXBLS	10/01-12/01
Wholesale and Manufacturing, Technical and Scientific Product	Killeen-Temple MSA, TX	Y	20150 FQ	51890 AW	88550 TQ	TXBLS	10/01-12/01
Wholesale and Manufacturing, Technical and Scientific Product	Laredo MSA, TX	Y	15070 FQ	37990 AW	73700 TQ	TXBLS	10/01-12/01
Wholesale and Manufacturing, Technical and Scientific Product	Longview-Marshall MSA, TX	Y	19250 FQ	42270 AW	66770 TQ	TXBLS	10/01-12/01
Wholesale and Manufacturing, Technical and Scientific Product	Lubbock MSA, TX	Y	20100 FQ	48350 AW	90110 TQ	TXBLS	10/01-12/01
Wholesale and Manufacturing, Technical and Scientific Product	McAllen-Edinburg-Mission MSA, TX	Y	19480 FQ	42940 AW	97950 TQ	TXBLS	10/01-12/01
Wholesale and Manufacturing, Technical and Scientific Product	Odessa-Midland MSA, TX	Y	30000 FQ	53280 AW	89090 TQ	TXBLS	10/01-12/01
Wholesale and Manufacturing, Technical and Scientific Product	San Antonio MSA, TX	Y	18630 FQ	46260 AW	84630 TQ	TXBLS	10/01-12/01
Wholesale and Manufacturing, Technical and Scientific Product	Tyler MSA, TX	Y	21700 FQ	54090 AW	89050 TQ	TXBLS	10/01-12/01
Wholesale and Manufacturing, Technical and Scientific Product	Waco MSA, TX	Y	24400 FQ	56310 AW	88760 TQ	TXBLS	10/01-12/01
Wholesale and Manufacturing, Technical and Scientific Product	Utah	Y	30360 FQ	57690 AW	90540 TQ	UTBLS	10/01-12/01
Wholesale and Manufacturing, Technical and Scientific Product	Provo-Orem MSA, UT	Y	28520 FQ	63580 AW	95950 TQ	UTBLS	10/01-12/01
Wholesale and Manufacturing, Technical and Scientific Product	Salt Lake City-Ogden MSA, UT	Y	31220 FQ	57920 AW	89480 TQ	UTBLS	10/01-12/01
Wholesale and Manufacturing, Technical and Scientific Product	Vermont	Y	25200 FQ	54010 AW	89900 TQ	VTBLS	10/01-12/01
Wholesale and Manufacturing, Technical and Scientific Product	Burlington MSA, VT	Y	22260 FQ	54180 AW	91580 TQ	VTBLS	10/01-12/01
Wholesale and Manufacturing, Technical and Scientific Product	Virginia	Y	29930 FQ	61900 AW	103670 TQ	VABLS	10/01-12/01
Wholesale and Manufacturing, Technical and Scientific Product	Lynchburg MSA, VA	Y	30570 FQ	63690 AW	94410 TQ	VABLS	10/01-12/01
Wholesale and Manufacturing, Technical and Scientific Product	Norfolk-Virginia Beach-Newport News MSA, VA-NC	Y	23910 FQ	52920 AW	95580 TQ	VABLS	10/01-12/01

AAW	Average annual wage	**AOH**	Average offered, high	**ASH**	Average starting, high	**H**	Hourly	**M**	Monthly	**S**	Special: hourly and annual
AE	Average entry wage	**AOL**	Average offered, low	**ASL**	Average starting, low	**HI**	Highest wage paid	**MTC**	Median total compensation	**TQ**	Third quartile wage
AEX	Average experienced wage	**APH**	Average pay, high range	**AW**	Average wage paid	**HR**	High end range	**MW**	Median wage paid	**W**	Weekly
AO	Average offered	**APL**	Average pay, low range	**FQ**	First quartile wage	**LR**	Low end range	**SQ**	Second quartile wage	**Y**	Yearly

Occupation/Type/Industry	Location	Per	Low	Mid	High	Source	Date
Sales Representative							
Wholesale and Manufacturing, Technical and Scientific Product	Richmond-Petersburg MSA, VA	Y	28840 FQ	52360 AW	85780 TQ	VABLS	10/01-12/01
Wholesale and Manufacturing, Technical and Scientific Product	Roanoke MSA, VA	Y	26390 FQ	62120 AW		VABLS	10/01-12/01
Wholesale and Manufacturing, Technical and Scientific Product	Washington	Y	35710 FQ	61130 AW	92910 TQ	WABLS	10/01-12/01
Wholesale and Manufacturing, Technical and Scientific Product	Bremerton PMSA, WA	Y	24810 FQ	67940 AW	92690 TQ	WABLS	10/01-12/01
Wholesale and Manufacturing, Technical and Scientific Product	Olympia PMSA, WA	Y	33990 FQ	74090 AW	115570 TQ	WABLS	10/01-12/01
Wholesale and Manufacturing, Technical and Scientific Product	Richland-Kennewick-Pasco MSA, WA	Y	27860 FQ	54810 AW	89910 TQ	WABLS	10/01-12/01
Wholesale and Manufacturing, Technical and Scientific Product	Seattle-Bellevue-Everett PMSA, WA	Y	40190 FQ	62990 AW	94150 TQ	WABLS	10/01-12/01
Wholesale and Manufacturing, Technical and Scientific Product	Spokane MSA, WA	Y	24210 FQ	44700 AW	66620 TQ	WABLS	10/01-12/01
Wholesale and Manufacturing, Technical and Scientific Product	Tacoma PMSA, WA	Y	18760 FQ	54000 AW	90760 TQ	WABLS	10/01-12/01
Wholesale and Manufacturing, Technical and Scientific Product	Yakima MSA, WA	Y	35950 FQ	64170 AW	124800 TQ	WABLS	10/01-12/01
Wholesale and Manufacturing, Technical and Scientific Product	West Virginia	Y	24480 FQ	45750 AW	70310 TQ	WVBLS	10/01-12/01
Wholesale and Manufacturing, Technical and Scientific Product	Charleston MSA, WV	Y	17880 FQ	42760 AW	78540 TQ	WVBLS	10/01-12/01
Wholesale and Manufacturing, Technical and Scientific Product	Huntington-Ashland MSA, WV-KY-OH	Y	24940 FQ	52070 AW	88480 TQ	WVBLS	10/01-12/01
Wholesale and Manufacturing, Technical and Scientific Product	Wisconsin	Y	31890 FQ	63890 AW	117010 TQ	WIBLS	10/01-12/01
Wholesale and Manufacturing, Technical and Scientific Product	Appleton-Oshkosh-Neenah MSA, WI	Y	27020 FQ	49570 AW	75440 TQ	WIBLS	10/01-12/01
Wholesale and Manufacturing, Technical and Scientific Product	Green Bay MSA, WI	Y	31160 FQ	61270 AW	94360 TQ	WIBLS	10/01-12/01
Wholesale and Manufacturing, Technical and Scientific Product	Madison MSA, WI	Y	29070 FQ	49240 AW	82520 TQ	WIBLS	10/01-12/01
Wholesale and Manufacturing, Technical and Scientific Product	Milwaukee-Waukesha PMSA, WI	Y	34270 FQ	73800 AW		WIBLS	10/01-12/01
Wholesale and Manufacturing, Technical and Scientific Product	Racine PMSA, WI	Y	31380 FQ	57060 AW	81160 TQ	WIBLS	10/01-12/01
Wholesale and Manufacturing, Technical and Scientific Product	Wyoming	Y	24740 FQ	62130 AW	104550 TQ	WYBLS	10/01-12/01
Wholesale and Manufacturing, Technical and Scientific Product	Cheyenne MSA, WY	Y	18810 FQ	55180 AW	92560 TQ	WYBLS	10/01-12/01
Wholesale and Manufacturing, Technical and Scientific Product	Puerto Rico	Y	19720 FQ	39540 AW	64870 TQ	PRBLS	10/01-12/01
Wholesale and Manufacturing, Technical and Scientific Product	Virgin Islands	Y	19500 FQ	32670 AW	67120 TQ	VIBLS	10/01-12/01
Wholesale and Manufacturing, Technical and Scientific Product	Guam	Y	18020 FQ	42280 AW	82780 TQ	GUBLS	10/01-12/01
Salesperson							
Hardware Store	United States	H		9.81 AW		DIYR	1/01-1/02
Sawing Machine Setter, Operator, and Tender, Wood	Alabama	H	6.28 FQ	9.80 AW	14.05 TQ	ALBLS	10/01-12/01
	Birmingham MSA, AL	H	6.72 FQ	9.66 AW	13.15 TQ	ALBLS	10/01-12/01
	Huntsville MSA, AL	H	7.62 FQ	11.72 AW	16.64 TQ	ALBLS	10/01-12/01
	Mobile MSA, AL	H	5.86 FQ	8.59 AW	12.54 TQ	ALBLS	10/01-12/01
	Montgomery MSA, AL	H	6.84 FQ	9.83 AW	13.47 TQ	ALBLS	10/01-12/01
	Alaska	H	9.23 FQ	14.32 AW	20.17 TQ	AKBLS	10/01-12/01
	Arizona	H	6.96 FQ	9.89 AW	14.30 TQ	AZBLS	10/01-12/01
	Phoenix-Mesa MSA, AZ	H	7.01 FQ	9.77 AW	14.06 TQ	AZBLS	10/01-12/01
	Tucson MSA, AZ	H	6.01 FQ	9.78 AW	14.00 TQ	AZBLS	10/01-12/01
	Arkansas	H	6.71 FQ	10.00 AW	13.73 TQ	ARBLS	10/01-12/01
	Little Rock-North Little Rock MSA, AR	H	7.69 FQ	11.14 AW	14.18 TQ	ARBLS	10/01-12/01

AAW	Average annual wage	**AOH**	Average offered, high	**ASH**	Average starting, high	**H**	Hourly	**M**	Monthly	**S**	Special: hourly and annual
AE	Average entry wage	**AOL**	Average offered, low	**ASL**	Average starting, low	**HI**	Highest wage paid	**MTC**	Median total compensation	**TQ**	Third quartile wage
AEX	Average experienced wage	**APH**	Average pay, high range	**AW**	Average wage paid	**HR**	High end range	**MW**	Median wage paid	**W**	Weekly
AO	Average offered	**APL**	Average pay, low range	**FQ**	First quartile wage	**LR**	Low end range	**SQ**	Second quartile wage	**Y**	Yearly

Occupation/Type/Industry	Location	Per	Low	Mid	High	Source	Date
Sawing Machine Setter, Operator, and Tender, Wood	California	H	6.81 FQ	11.07 AW	16.58 TQ	CABLS	10/01-12/01
	Fresno MSA, CA	H	6.39 FQ	8.40 AW	11.66 TQ	CABLS	10/01-12/01
	Los Angeles-Long Beach PMSA, CA	H	7.23 FQ	10.49 AW	13.99 TQ	CABLS	10/01-12/01
	Modesto MSA, CA	H	7.78 FQ	10.01 AW	12.68 TQ	CABLS	10/01-12/01
	Oakland PMSA, CA	H	6.75 FQ	12.22 AW	19.08 TQ	CABLS	10/01-12/01
	Riverside-San Bernardino PMSA, CA	H	6.78 FQ	10.15 AW	14.00 TQ	CABLS	10/01-12/01
	Sacramento PMSA, CA	H	6.74 FQ	11.15 AW	16.18 TQ	CABLS	10/01-12/01
	San Diego MSA, CA	H	6.66 FQ	10.52 AW	14.03 TQ	CABLS	10/01-12/01
	San Francisco PMSA, CA	H	9.23 FQ	13.35 AW	16.90 TQ	CABLS	10/01-12/01
	San Jose PMSA, CA	H	9.45 FQ	13.32 AW	21.83 TQ	CABLS	10/01-12/01
	Santa Rosa PMSA, CA	H	9.80 FQ	13.02 AW	17.55 TQ	CABLS	10/01-12/01
	Stockton-Lodi MSA, CA	H	7.85 FQ	10.73 AW	13.49 TQ	CABLS	10/01-12/01
	Visalia-Tulare-Porterville MSA, CA	H	8.74 FQ	10.92 AW	13.98 TQ	CABLS	10/01-12/01
	Colorado	H	8.64 FQ	11.33 AW	15.31 TQ	COBLS	10/01-12/01
	Boulder-Longmont PMSA, CO	H	10.16 FQ	13.17 AW	16.59 TQ	COBLS	10/01-12/01
	Denver PMSA, CO	H	9.31 FQ	11.40 AW	14.88 TQ	COBLS	10/01-12/01
	Connecticut	H	9.51 FQ	14.33 AW	19.99 TQ	CTBLS	10/01-12/01
	Hartford MSA, CT	H	9.90 FQ	14.01 AW	17.98 TQ	CTBLS	10/01-12/01
	Washington PMSA, DC-MD-VA-WV	H	7.27 FQ	10.96 AW	17.89 TQ	DCBLS	10/01-12/01
	Florida	H	7.00 FQ	9.95 AW	13.43 TQ	FLBLS	10/01-12/01
	Daytona Beach MSA, FL	H	7.92 FQ	10.14 AW	12.78 TQ	FLBLS	10/01-12/01
	Fort Lauderdale PMSA, FL	H	7.35 FQ	11.87 AW	16.53 TQ	FLBLS	10/01-12/01
	Jacksonville MSA, FL	H	8.13 FQ	10.88 AW	14.67 TQ	FLBLS	10/01-12/01
	Melbourne-Titusville-Palm Bay MSA, FL	H	7.63 FQ	9.53 AW	11.36 TQ	FLBLS	10/01-12/01
	Miami PMSA, FL	H	6.75 FQ	9.79 AW	13.78 TQ	FLBLS	10/01-12/01
	Orlando MSA, FL	H	5.85 FQ	8.45 AW	11.60 TQ	FLBLS	10/01-12/01
	Sarasota-Bradenton MSA, FL	H	6.76 FQ	9.57 AW	11.33 TQ	FLBLS	10/01-12/01
	Tallahassee MSA, FL	H	7.45 FQ	11.36 AW	16.99 TQ	FLBLS	10/01-12/01
	Tampa-St. Petersburg-Clearwater MSA, FL	H	7.20 FQ	10.24 AW	13.85 TQ	FLBLS	10/01-12/01
	West Palm Beach-Boca Raton MSA, FL	H	8.08 FQ	11.41 AW	13.88 TQ	FLBLS	10/01-12/01
	Georgia	H	7.03 FQ	10.28 AW	14.22 TQ	GABLS	10/01-12/01
	Atlanta MSA, GA	H	7.44 FQ	11.58 AW	20.34 TQ	GABLS	10/01-12/01
	Augusta-Aiken MSA, GA-SC	H	6.81 FQ	10.03 AW	13.43 TQ	GABLS	10/01-12/01
	Columbus MSA, GA-AL	H	7.18 FQ	10.42 AW	13.44 TQ	GABLS	10/01-12/01
	Idaho	H	7.26 FQ	14.60 AW	21.42 TQ	IDBLS	10/01-12/01
	Boise City MSA, ID	H	7.84 FQ	10.84 AW	15.81 TQ	IDBLS	10/01-12/01
	Illinois	H	7.61 FQ	11.35 AW	15.61 TQ	ILBLS	10/01-12/01
	Champaign-Urbana MSA, IL	H	9.29 FQ	10.80 AW	13.41 TQ	ILBLS	10/01-12/01
	Chicago PMSA, IL	H	7.40 FQ	10.89 AW	15.14 TQ	ILBLS	10/01-12/01
	Indiana	H	7.36 FQ	11.36 AW	17.92 TQ	INBLS	10/01-12/01
	Elkhart-Goshen MSA, IN	H	7.19 FQ	10.24 AW	13.66 TQ	INBLS	10/01-12/01
	Evansville-Henderson MSA, IN-KY	H	7.00 FQ	10.00 AW	13.46 TQ	INBLS	10/01-12/01
	Fort Wayne MSA, IN	H	7.08 FQ	10.73 AW	15.27 TQ	INBLS	10/01-12/01
	Gary PMSA, IN	H	6.38 FQ	10.46 AW	14.07 TQ	INBLS	10/01-12/01
	Indianapolis MSA, IN	H	8.77 FQ	12.26 AW	16.35 TQ	INBLS	10/01-12/01
	Davenport-Moline-Rock Island MSA, IA-IL	H	8.70 FQ	12.71 AW	17.57 TQ	IABLS	10/01-12/01
	Kansas	H	6.47 FQ	8.85 AW	11.42 TQ	KSBLS	10/01-12/01
	Wichita MSA, KS	H	6.82 FQ	8.50 AW	10.55 TQ	KSBLS	10/01-12/01
	Kentucky	H	6.74 FQ	9.59 AW	13.10 TQ	KYBLS	10/01-12/01
	Louisville MSA, KY-IN	H	7.30 FQ	9.92 AW	13.98 TQ	KYBLS	10/01-12/01
	Louisiana	H	7.27 FQ	10.98 AW	14.96 TQ	LABLS	10/01-12/01
	New Orleans MSA, LA	H	6.41 FQ	11.20 AW	17.21 TQ	LABLS	10/01-12/01
	Maine	H	7.64 FQ	10.54 AW	13.74 TQ	MEBLS	10/01-12/01
	Portland MSA, ME	H	7.83 FQ	11.81 AW	18.40 TQ	MEBLS	10/01-12/01
	Maryland	H	7.96 FQ	11.72 AW	16.63 TQ	MDBLS	10/01-12/01
	Baltimore PMSA, MD	H	8.65 FQ	12.45 AW	16.68 TQ	MDBLS	10/01-12/01
	Massachusetts	H	9.45 FQ	13.48 AW	18.85 TQ	MABLS	10/01-12/01
	Boston PMSA, MA-NH	H	9.95 FQ	14.99 AW	20.89 TQ	MABLS	10/01-12/01
	Worcester PMSA, MA-CT	H	9.48 FQ	12.44 AW	16.24 TQ	MABLS	10/01-12/01
	Michigan	H	7.69 FQ	10.67 AW	13.73 TQ	MIBLS	10/01-12/01
	Ann Arbor PMSA, MI	H	5.42 FQ	9.14 AW	16.03 TQ	MIBLS	10/01-12/01
	Detroit PMSA, MI	H	7.90 FQ	10.69 AW	14.00 TQ	MIBLS	10/01-12/01

AAW	Average annual wage	AOH	Average offered, high	ASH	Average starting, high	H	Hourly	M	Monthly	S	Special: hourly and annual
AE	Average entry wage	AOL	Average offered, low	ASL	Average starting, low	HI	Highest wage paid	MTC	Median total compensation	TQ	Third quartile wage
AEX	Average experienced wage	APH	Average pay, high range	AW	Average wage paid	HR	High end range	MW	Median wage paid	W	Weekly
AO	Average offered	APL	Average pay, low range	FQ	First quartile wage	LR	Low end range	SQ	Second quartile wage	Y	Yearly

Occupation/Type/Industry	Location	Per	Low	Mid	High	Source	Date
Sawing Machine Setter, Operator, and Tender, Wood	Saginaw-Bay City-Midland MSA, MI	H	7.95 FQ	10.76 AW	13.95 TQ	MIBLS	10/01-12/01
	Minnesota	H	9.08 FQ	12.44 AW	16.55 TQ	MNBLS	10/01-12/01
	Duluth-Superior MSA, MN-WI	H	9.42 FQ	12.25 AW	16.75 TQ	MNBLS	10/01-12/01
	Minneapolis-St. Paul MSA, MN-WI	H	9.14 FQ	13.02 AW	16.90 TQ	MNBLS	10/01-12/01
	Mississippi	H	7.36 FQ	10.25 AW	13.37 TQ	MSBLS	10/01-12/01
	Jackson MSA, MS	H	7.52 FQ	9.96 AW	13.18 TQ	MSBLS	10/01-12/01
	Missouri	H	6.91 FQ	10.06 AW	13.44 TQ	MOBLS	10/01-12/01
	Kansas City MSA, MO-KS	H	6.17 FQ	9.53 AW	13.05 TQ	MOBLS	10/01-12/01
	St. Louis MSA, MO-IL	H	5.93 FQ	10.59 AW	15.95 TQ	MOBLS	10/01-12/01
	Springfield MSA, MO	H	7.48 FQ	9.15 AW	12.21 TQ	MOBLS	10/01-12/01
	Montana	H	7.65 FQ	11.48 AW	15.84 TQ	MTBLS	10/01-12/01
	Nebraska	H	7.83 FQ	10.10 AW	14.08 TQ	NEBLS	10/01-12/01
	Omaha MSA, NE-IA	H	7.61 FQ	10.00 AW	13.48 TQ	NEBLS	10/01-12/01
	Nevada	H	6.70 FQ	10.25 AW	13.98 TQ	NVBLS	10/01-12/01
	Las Vegas MSA, NV-AZ	H	6.61 FQ	10.38 AW	14.07 TQ	NVBLS	10/01-12/01
	New Hampshire	H	8.03 FQ	11.45 AW	16.31 TQ	NHBLS	10/01-12/01
	New Jersey	H	7.36 FQ	12.23 AW	22.69 TQ	NJBLS	10/01-12/01
	Atlantic-Cape May PMSA, NJ	H	7.46 FQ	8.61 AW	10.70 TQ	NJBLS	10/01-12/01
	Middlesex-Somerset-Hunterdon PMSA, NJ	H	9.37 FQ	16.27 AW	24.54 TQ	NJBLS	10/01-12/01
	Monmouth-Ocean PMSA, NJ	H	7.14 FQ	11.33 AW	19.19 TQ	NJBLS	10/01-12/01
	Newark PMSA, NJ	H	6.70 FQ	9.61 AW	14.23 TQ	NJBLS	10/01-12/01
	New Mexico	H	6.65 FQ	8.81 AW	10.79 TQ	NMBLS	10/01-12/01
	Albuquerque MSA, NM	H	6.65 FQ	9.00 AW	10.97 TQ	NMBLS	10/01-12/01
	New York	H	6.82 FQ	10.99 AW	16.25 TQ	NYBLS	10/01-12/01
	Albany-Schenectady-Troy MSA, NY	H	8.81 FQ	11.74 AW	15.79 TQ	NYBLS	10/01-12/01
	Binghamton MSA, NY	H	8.66 FQ	10.60 AW	13.94 TQ	NYBLS	10/01-12/01
	Buffalo-Niagara Falls MSA, NY	H	8.01 FQ	9.79 AW	11.34 TQ	NYBLS	10/01-12/01
	Nassau-Suffolk PMSA, NY	H	5.68 FQ	9.80 AW	17.22 TQ	NYBLS	10/01-12/01
	New York PMSA, NY	H	6.34 FQ	12.76 AW	20.65 TQ	NYBLS	10/01-12/01
	Rochester MSA, NY	H	6.33 FQ	11.26 AW	16.59 TQ	NYBLS	10/01-12/01
	Syracuse MSA, NY	H	8.73 FQ	12.34 AW	17.36 TQ	NYBLS	10/01-12/01
	Utica-Rome MSA, NY	H	6.44 FQ	10.59 AW	15.90 TQ	NYBLS	10/01-12/01
	North Carolina	H	7.55 FQ	10.91 AW	14.79 TQ	NCBLS	10/01-12/01
	Charlotte-Gastonia-Rock Hill MSA, NC-SC	H	7.38 FQ	9.90 AW	13.49 TQ	NCBLS	10/01-12/01
	Greensboro-Winston-Salem-High Point MSA, NC	H	7.83 FQ	10.98 AW	13.97 TQ	NCBLS	10/01-12/01
	Hickory-Morganton-Lenoir MSA, NC	H	8.39 FQ	11.80 AW	16.34 TQ	NCBLS	10/01-12/01
	Raleigh-Durham-Chapel Hill MSA, NC	H	6.94 FQ	9.61 AW	15.24 TQ	NCBLS	10/01-12/01
	North Dakota	H	7.64 FQ	10.31 AW	13.52 TQ	NDBLS	10/01-12/01
	Fargo-Moorhead MSA, ND-MN	H	8.87 FQ	11.17 AW	13.87 TQ	NDBLS	10/01-12/01
	Ohio	H	7.53 FQ	11.01 AW	15.06 TQ	OHBLS	10/01-12/01
	Cincinnati PMSA, OH-KY-IN	H	7.42 FQ	10.25 AW	13.45 TQ	OHBLS	10/01-12/01
	Cleveland-Lorain-Elyria PMSA, OH	H	8.36 FQ	12.84 AW	16.92 TQ	OHBLS	10/01-12/01
	Columbus MSA, OH	H	9.50 FQ	12.15 AW	15.69 TQ	OHBLS	10/01-12/01
	Dayton-Springfield MSA, OH	H	7.43 FQ	9.65 AW	12.87 TQ	OHBLS	10/01-12/01
	Toledo MSA, OH	H	7.82 FQ	11.39 AW	14.19 TQ	OHBLS	10/01-12/01
	Youngstown-Warren MSA, OH	H	7.08 FQ	10.22 AW	13.93 TQ	OHBLS	10/01-12/01
	Oklahoma	H	6.47 FQ	11.53 AW	17.38 TQ	OKBLS	10/01-12/01
	Oklahoma City MSA, OK	H	5.53 FQ	8.38 AW	12.10 TQ	OKBLS	10/01-12/01
	Tulsa MSA, OK	H	7.38 FQ	15.26 AW	26.72 TQ	OKBLS	10/01-12/01
	Oregon	H	9.41 FQ	13.02 AW	16.95 TQ	ORBLS	10/01-12/01
	Eugene-Springfield MSA, OR	H	9.64 FQ	13.22 AW	17.00 TQ	ORBLS	10/01-12/01
	Medford-Ashland MSA, OR	H	10.48 FQ	14.40 AW	16.95 TQ	ORBLS	10/01-12/01
	Portland-Vancouver PMSA, OR-WA	H	8.48 FQ	12.95 AW	17.54 TQ	ORBLS	10/01-12/01
	Salem PMSA, OR	H	8.06 FQ	11.56 AW	15.70 TQ	ORBLS	10/01-12/01
	Pennsylvania	H	7.68 FQ	11.01 AW	14.51 TQ	PABLS	10/01-12/01
	Erie MSA, PA	H	8.49 FQ	12.44 AW	17.92 TQ	PABLS	10/01-12/01
	Harrisburg-Lebanon-Carlisle MSA, PA	H	7.91 FQ	10.27 AW	12.93 TQ	PABLS	10/01-12/01
	Johnstown MSA, PA	H	7.24 FQ	9.49 AW	12.67 TQ	PABLS	10/01-12/01

AAW	Average annual wage	AOH	Average offered, high	ASH	Average starting, high	H	Hourly	M	Monthly	S	Special: hourly and annual
AE	Average entry wage	AOL	Average offered, low	ASL	Average starting, low	HI	Highest wage paid	MTC	Median total compensation	TQ	Third quartile wage
AEX	Average experienced wage	APH	Average pay, high range	AW	Average wage paid	HR	High end range	MW	Median wage paid	W	Weekly
AO	Average offered	APL	Average pay, low range	FQ	First quartile wage	LR	Low end range	SQ	Second quartile wage	Y	Yearly

Occupation/Type/Industry	Location	Per	Low	Mid	High	Source	Date
Sawing Machine Setter, Operator, and Tender, Wood	Lancaster MSA, PA	H	8.96 FQ	11.90 AW	14.74 TQ	PABLS	10/01-12/01
	Philadelphia PMSA, PA-NJ	H	7.51 FQ	12.78 AW	24.13 TQ	PABLS	10/01-12/01
	Pittsburgh MSA, PA	H	6.65 FQ	10.09 AW	15.62 TQ	PABLS	10/01-12/01
	Scranton-Wilkes-Barre-Hazleton MSA, PA	H	7.66 FQ	11.12 AW	13.99 TQ	PABLS	10/01-12/01
	York MSA, PA	H	8.50 FQ	11.83 AW	15.86 TQ	PABLS	10/01-12/01
	Rhode Island	H	7.53 FQ	10.35 AW	13.54 TQ	RIBLS	10/01-12/01
	Providence-Fall River-Warwick MSA, RI-MA	H	7.94 FQ	11.84 AW	19.66 TQ	RIBLS	10/01-12/01
	South Carolina	H	7.07 FQ	10.08 AW	13.95 TQ	SCBLS	10/01-12/01
	Charleston-North Charleston MSA, SC	H	8.09 FQ	12.42 AW	16.85 TQ	SCBLS	10/01-12/01
	Greenville-Spartanburg-Anderson MSA, SC	H	9.03 FQ	11.44 AW	14.40 TQ	SCBLS	10/01-12/01
	South Dakota	H	8.11 FQ	11.20 AW	15.00 TQ	SDBLS	10/01-12/01
	Sioux Falls MSA, SD	H	8.75 FQ	10.82 AW	13.42 TQ	SDBLS	10/01-12/01
	Tennessee	H	7.04 FQ	10.29 AW	14.70 TQ	TNBLS	10/01-12/01
	Johnson City-Kingsport-Bristol MSA, TN-VA	H	7.69 FQ	11.49 AW	16.12 TQ	TNBLS	10/01-12/01
	Knoxville MSA, TN	H	8.72 FQ	11.57 AW	16.31 TQ	TNBLS	10/01-12/01
	Memphis MSA, TN-AR-MS	H	7.43 FQ	10.65 AW	15.05 TQ	TNBLS	10/01-12/01
	Nashville MSA, TN	H	7.87 FQ	12.04 AW	16.53 TQ	TNBLS	10/01-12/01
	Texas	H	6.10 FQ	9.04 AW	12.78 TQ	TXBLS	10/01-12/01
	Austin-San Marcos MSA, TX	H	7.44 FQ	9.06 AW	10.99 TQ	TXBLS	10/01-12/01
	Beaumont-Port Arthur MSA, TX	H	8.29 FQ	12.45 AW	16.40 TQ	TXBLS	10/01-12/01
	Brownsville-Harlingen-San Benito MSA, TX	H	5.86 FQ	7.10 AW	8.43 TQ	TXBLS	10/01-12/01
	Dallas PMSA, TX	H	6.17 FQ	9.20 AW	12.42 TQ	TXBLS	10/01-12/01
	Fort Worth-Arlington PMSA, TX	H	6.10 FQ	9.15 AW	12.66 TQ	TXBLS	10/01-12/01
	Houston PMSA, TX	H	5.95 FQ	8.07 AW	10.99 TQ	TXBLS	10/01-12/01
	San Antonio MSA, TX	H	6.47 FQ	9.00 AW	12.29 TQ	TXBLS	10/01-12/01
	Utah	H	6.76 FQ	10.16 AW	14.98 TQ	UTBLS	10/01-12/01
	Provo-Orem MSA, UT	H	7.14 FQ	8.94 AW	11.92 TQ	UTBLS	10/01-12/01
	Salt Lake City-Ogden MSA, UT	H	6.42 FQ	10.10 AW	13.87 TQ	UTBLS	10/01-12/01
	Vermont	H	7.94 FQ	11.55 AW	16.12 TQ	VTBLS	10/01-12/01
	Virginia	H	7.20 FQ	10.90 AW	15.77 TQ	VABLS	10/01-12/01
	Lynchburg MSA, VA	H	5.89 FQ	10.93 AW	18.14 TQ	VABLS	10/01-12/01
	Norfolk-Virginia Beach-Newport News MSA, VA-NC	H	7.37 FQ	10.14 AW	14.82 TQ	VABLS	10/01-12/01
	Richmond-Petersburg MSA, VA	H	7.19 FQ	10.64 AW	16.23 TQ	VABLS	10/01-12/01
	Washington	H	9.08 FQ	14.21 AW	20.35 TQ	WABLS	10/01-12/01
	Seattle-Bellevue-Everett PMSA, WA	H	10.34 FQ	16.18 AW	23.82 TQ	WABLS	10/01-12/01
	Tacoma PMSA, WA	H	8.91 FQ	11.42 AW	14.40 TQ	WABLS	10/01-12/01
	West Virginia	H	6.14 FQ	10.06 AW	14.90 TQ	WVBLS	10/01-12/01
	Wisconsin	H	7.69 FQ	10.85 AW	14.95 TQ	WIBLS	10/01-12/01
	Appleton-Oshkosh-Neenah MSA, WI	H	7.86 FQ	11.08 AW	16.25 TQ	WIBLS	10/01-12/01
	Green Bay MSA, WI	H	7.80 FQ	11.71 AW	16.47 TQ	WIBLS	10/01-12/01
	Madison MSA, WI	H	10.43 FQ	13.64 AW	17.15 TQ	WIBLS	10/01-12/01
	Milwaukee-Waukesha PMSA, WI	H	8.28 FQ	12.70 AW	17.04 TQ	WIBLS	10/01-12/01
	Wyoming	H	8.04 FQ	13.08 AW	20.36 TQ	WYBLS	10/01-12/01
	Puerto Rico	H	5.55 FQ	6.49 AW	8.03 TQ	PRBLS	10/01-12/01
Secondary School Teacher							
Except Special and Vocational Education	Alabama	Y	30750 FQ	39640 AW	50610 TQ	ALBLS	10/01-12/01
Except Special and Vocational Education	Alaska	Y	32330 FQ	48440 AW	67990 TQ	AKBLS	10/01-12/01
Except Special and Vocational Education	Arizona	Y	24650 FQ	39960 AW	59500 TQ	AZBLS	10/01-12/01
Except Special and Vocational Education	Arkansas	Y	25100 FQ	35370 AW	47370 TQ	ARBLS	10/01-12/01
Except Special and Vocational Education	California	Y	35190 FQ	52330 AW	71890 TQ	CABLS	10/01-12/01
Except Special and Vocational Education	Colorado	Y	26710 FQ	42370 AW	64360 TQ	COBLS	10/01-12/01
Except Special and Vocational Education	Connecticut	Y	30480 FQ	52560 AW	73180 TQ	CTBLS	10/01-12/01
Except Special and Vocational Education	Delaware	Y	32790 FQ	54900 AW	80640 TQ	DEBLS	10/01-12/01
Except Special and Vocational Education	District of Columbia	Y	13510 FQ	44750 AW	78910 TQ	DCBLS	10/01-12/01
Except Special and Vocational Education	Florida	Y	28320 FQ	42210 AW	60100 TQ	FLBLS	10/01-12/01

AAW	Average annual wage	AOH	Average offered, high	ASH	Average starting, high	H	Hourly	M	Monthly	S	Special: hourly and annual
AE	Average entry wage	AOL	Average offered, low	ASL	Average starting, low	HI	Highest wage paid	MTC	Median total compensation	TQ	Third quartile wage
AEX	Average experienced wage	APH	Average pay, high range	AW	Average wage paid	HR	High end range	MW	Median wage paid	W	Weekly
AO	Average offered	APL	Average pay, low range	FQ	First quartile wage	LR	Low end range	SQ	Second quartile wage	Y	Yearly

Occupation/Type/Industry	Location	Per	Low	Mid	High	Source	Date
Secondary School Teacher							
Except Special and Vocational Education	Georgia	Y	29690 FQ	44100 AW	58470 TQ	GABLS	10/01-12/01
Except Special and Vocational Education	Hawaii	Y	29740 FQ	42530 AW	58650 TQ	HIBLS	10/01-12/01
Except Special and Vocational Education	Idaho	Y	30650 FQ	37590 AW	44870 TQ	IDBLS	10/01-12/01
Except Special and Vocational Education	Illinois	Y	33000 FQ	52070 AW	79640 TQ	ILBLS	10/01-12/01
Except Special and Vocational Education	Indiana	Y	28220 FQ	44620 AW	60760 TQ	INBLS	10/01-12/01
Except Special and Vocational Education	Iowa	Y	21370 FQ	35890 AW	52850 TQ	IABLS	10/01-12/01
Except Special and Vocational Education	Kansas	Y	24410 FQ	35330 AW	46120 TQ	KSBLS	10/01-12/01
Except Special and Vocational Education	Kentucky	Y	27200 FQ	39790 AW	53800 TQ	KYBLS	10/01-12/01
Except Special and Vocational Education	Louisiana	Y	25140 FQ	34410 AW	44600 TQ	LABLS	10/01-12/01
Except Special and Vocational Education	Maine	Y	25720 FQ	39080 AW	52940 TQ	MEBLS	10/01-12/01
Except Special and Vocational Education	Maryland	Y	30060 FQ	46050 AW	66270 TQ	MDBLS	10/01-12/01
Except Special and Vocational Education	Massachusetts	Y	28070 FQ	46780 AW	65650 TQ	MABLS	10/01-12/01
Except Special and Vocational Education	Michigan	Y	28840 FQ	47380 AW	69160 TQ	MIBLS	10/01-12/01
Except Special and Vocational Education	Minnesota	Y	28260 FQ	42530 AW	59960 TQ	MNBLS	10/01-12/01
Except Special and Vocational Education	Mississippi	Y	23930 FQ	32940 AW	44530 TQ	MSBLS	10/01-12/01
Except Special and Vocational Education	Missouri	Y	21290 FQ	35610 AW	54710 TQ	MOBLS	10/01-12/01
Except Special and Vocational Education	Montana	Y	19840 FQ	30340 AW	43880 TQ	MTBLS	10/01-12/01
Except Special and Vocational Education	Nebraska	Y	24670 FQ	37800 AW	53130 TQ	NEBLS	10/01-12/01
Except Special and Vocational Education	New Hampshire	Y	25960 FQ	39100 AW	54820 TQ	NHBLS	10/01-12/01
Except Special and Vocational Education	New Jersey	Y	32930 FQ	55240 AW	81380 TQ	NJBLS	10/01-12/01
Except Special and Vocational Education	New Mexico	Y	25930 FQ	36960 AW	51660 TQ	NMBLS	10/01-12/01
Except Special and Vocational Education	New York	Y	30650 FQ	58780 AW	96290 TQ	NYBLS	10/01-12/01
Except Special and Vocational Education	North Carolina	Y	26080 FQ	38770 AW	53660 TQ	NCBLS	10/01-12/01
Except Special and Vocational Education	North Dakota	Y	22760 FQ	31710 AW	43690 TQ	NDBLS	10/01-12/01
Except Special and Vocational Education	Ohio	Y	27670 FQ	43310 AW	61030 TQ	OHBLS	10/01-12/01
Except Special and Vocational Education	Oklahoma	Y	22390 FQ	33590 AW	44670 TQ	OKBLS	10/01-12/01
Except Special and Vocational Education	Oregon	Y	29940 FQ	43130 AW	58810 TQ	ORBLS	10/01-12/01
Except Special and Vocational Education	Pennsylvania	Y	26920 FQ	47360 AW	69590 TQ	PABLS	10/01-12/01
Except Special and Vocational Education	Rhode Island	Y	33420 FQ	50760 AW	68090 TQ	RIBLS	10/01-12/01
Except Special and Vocational Education	South Carolina	Y	27510 FQ	38700 AW	53330 TQ	SCBLS	10/01-12/01
Except Special and Vocational Education	South Dakota	Y	22830 FQ	32090 AW	44620 TQ	SDBLS	10/01-12/01
Except Special and Vocational Education	Tennessee	Y	26360 FQ	36810 AW	48210 TQ	TNBLS	10/01-12/01
Except Special and Vocational Education	Texas	Y	30170 FQ	41700 AW	56170 TQ	TXBLS	10/01-12/01
Except Special and Vocational Education	Utah	Y	27910 FQ	44610 AW	66320 TQ	UTBLS	10/01-12/01
Except Special and Vocational Education	Vermont	Y	28070 FQ	41320 AW	56060 TQ	VTBLS	10/01-12/01
Except Special and Vocational Education	Virginia	Y	28370 FQ	43550 AW	62350 TQ	VABLS	10/01-12/01
Except Special and Vocational Education	Washington	Y	28420 FQ	43200 AW	57030 TQ	WABLS	10/01-12/01
Except Special and Vocational Education	West Virginia	Y	29200 FQ	37170 AW	45280 TQ	WVBLS	10/01-12/01
Except Special and Vocational Education	Wisconsin	Y	26160 FQ	42210 AW	58830 TQ	WIBLS	10/01-12/01
Except Special and Vocational Education	Wyoming	Y	26320 FQ	37500 AW	48360 TQ	WYBLS	10/01-12/01
Except Special and Vocational Education	Puerto Rico	Y	18980 FQ	23010 AW	27700 TQ	PRBLS	10/01-12/01
Except Special and Vocational Education	Virgin Islands	Y	23980 FQ	36770 AW	55090 TQ	VIBLS	10/01-12/01
Except Special and Vocational Education	Guam	Y	18620 FQ	33260 AW	46250 TQ	GUBLS	10/01-12/01
Secret Shopper	United States	H		10.00-20.00 AW		MC	1/01-1/01
Secretary	United States	Y		22550 AW		USATOD4	1/00-1/01
Except Legal, Medical, and Executive	Alabama	H	6.41 FQ	10.26 AW	15.13 TQ	ALBLS	10/01-12/01
Except Legal, Medical, and Executive	Birmingham MSA, AL	H	6.97 FQ	10.99 AW	15.83 TQ	ALBLS	10/01-12/01
Except Legal, Medical, and Executive	Huntsville MSA, AL	H	6.38 FQ	11.19 AW	16.69 TQ	ALBLS	10/01-12/01
Except Legal, Medical, and Executive	Mobile MSA, AL	H	6.42 FQ	10.40 AW	14.60 TQ	ALBLS	10/01-12/01
Except Legal, Medical, and Executive	Montgomery MSA, AL	H	6.76 FQ	10.79 AW	16.01 TQ	ALBLS	10/01-12/01
Except Legal, Medical, and Executive	Alaska	H	8.91 FQ	14.50 AW	21.01 TQ	AKBLS	10/01-12/01
Except Legal, Medical, and Executive	Anchorage MSA, AK	H	7.99 FQ	13.59 AW	20.39 TQ	AKBLS	10/01-12/01
Except Legal, Medical, and Executive	Arizona	H	8.02 FQ	11.93 AW	16.73 TQ	AZBLS	10/01-12/01
Except Legal, Medical, and Executive	Phoenix-Mesa MSA, AZ	H	8.53 FQ	12.45 AW	17.29 TQ	AZBLS	10/01-12/01
Except Legal, Medical, and Executive	Tucson MSA, AZ	H	7.58 FQ	10.92 AW	14.92 TQ	AZBLS	10/01-12/01
Except Legal, Medical, and Executive	Arkansas	H	6.70 FQ	9.65 AW	13.29 TQ	ARBLS	10/01-12/01
Except Legal, Medical, and Executive	Fayetteville-Springdale-Rogers MSA, AR	H	7.07 FQ	10.06 AW	13.35 TQ	ARBLS	10/01-12/01
Except Legal, Medical, and Executive	Fort Smith MSA, AR-OK	H	6.76 FQ	9.70 AW	13.47 TQ	ARBLS	10/01-12/01
Except Legal, Medical, and Executive	Little Rock-North Little Rock MSA, AR	H	7.42 FQ	10.56 AW	14.46 TQ	ARBLS	10/01-12/01
Except Legal, Medical, and Executive	California	H	8.98 FQ	14.25 AW	20.61 TQ	CABLS	10/01-12/01
Except Legal, Medical, and Executive	Bakersfield MSA, CA	H	8.42 FQ	13.05 AW	18.21 TQ	CABLS	10/01-12/01
Except Legal, Medical, and Executive	Chico-Paradise MSA, CA	H	7.94 FQ	11.01 AW	15.17 TQ	CABLS	10/01-12/01
Except Legal, Medical, and Executive	Fresno MSA, CA	H	7.32 FQ	11.92 AW	16.87 TQ	CABLS	10/01-12/01
Except Legal, Medical, and Executive	Los Angeles-Long Beach PMSA, CA	H	9.57 FQ	14.73 AW	20.96 TQ	CABLS	10/01-12/01
Except Legal, Medical, and Executive	Merced MSA, CA	H	7.17 FQ	11.19 AW	16.12 TQ	CABLS	10/01-12/01
Except Legal, Medical, and Executive	Modesto MSA, CA	H	7.66 FQ	12.40 AW	19.69 TQ	CABLS	10/01-12/01

AAW	Average annual wage	**AOH**	Average offered, high	**ASH**	Average starting, high	**H**	Hourly	**M**	Monthly	**S**	Special: hourly and annual
AE	Average entry wage	**AOL**	Average offered, low	**ASL**	Average starting, low	**HI**	Highest wage paid	**MTC**	Median total compensation	**TQ**	Third quartile wage
AEX	Average experienced wage	**APH**	Average pay, high range	**AW**	Average wage paid	**HR**	High end range	**MW**	Median wage paid	**W**	Weekly
AO	Average offered	**APL**	Average pay, low range	**FQ**	First quartile wage	**LR**	Low end range	**SQ**	Second quartile wage	**Y**	Yearly

Occupation/Type/Industry	Location	Per	Low	Mid	High	Source	Date
Secretary							
Except Legal, Medical, and Executive	Oakland PMSA, CA	H	10.55 FQ	16.10 AW	22.18 TQ	CABLS	10/01-12/01
Except Legal, Medical, and Executive	Orange County PMSA, CA	H	9.50 FQ	14.27 AW	20.39 TQ	CABLS	10/01-12/01
Except Legal, Medical, and Executive	Redding MSA, CA	H	8.06 FQ	11.60 AW	16.10 TQ	CABLS	10/01-12/01
Except Legal, Medical, and Executive	Riverside-San Bernardino PMSA, CA	H	8.92 FQ	13.28 AW	18.22 TQ	CABLS	10/01-12/01
Except Legal, Medical, and Executive	Sacramento PMSA, CA	H	9.24 FQ	13.39 AW	17.59 TQ	CABLS	10/01-12/01
Except Legal, Medical, and Executive	Salinas MSA, CA	H	8.80 FQ	13.89 AW	20.40 TQ	CABLS	10/01-12/01
Except Legal, Medical, and Executive	San Diego MSA, CA	H	8.23 FQ	13.48 AW	19.60 TQ	CABLS	10/01-12/01
Except Legal, Medical, and Executive	San Francisco PMSA, CA	H	10.43 FQ	16.81 AW	23.57 TQ	CABLS	10/01-12/01
Except Legal, Medical, and Executive	San Jose PMSA, CA	H	9.87 FQ	16.97 AW	23.18 TQ	CABLS	10/01-12/01
Except Legal, Medical, and Executive	San Luis Obispo-Atascadero-Paso Robles MSA, CA	H	6.99 FQ	11.99 AW	17.34 TQ	CABLS	10/01-12/01
Except Legal, Medical, and Executive	Santa Barbara-Santa Maria-Lompoc MSA, CA	H	9.34 FQ	14.20 AW	18.83 TQ	CABLS	10/01-12/01
Except Legal, Medical, and Executive	Santa Cruz-Watsonville PMSA, CA	H	7.52 FQ	12.73 AW	17.71 TQ	CABLS	10/01-12/01
Except Legal, Medical, and Executive	Santa Rosa PMSA, CA	H	9.19 FQ	14.32 AW	22.19 TQ	CABLS	10/01-12/01
Except Legal, Medical, and Executive	Stockton-Lodi MSA, CA	H	7.38 FQ	12.26 AW	17.32 TQ	CABLS	10/01-12/01
Except Legal, Medical, and Executive	Vallejo-Fairfield-Napa PMSA, CA	H	8.43 FQ	13.18 AW	17.43 TQ	CABLS	10/01-12/01
Except Legal, Medical, and Executive	Ventura PMSA, CA	H	9.30 FQ	13.50 AW	18.69 TQ	CABLS	10/01-12/01
Except Legal, Medical, and Executive	Visalia-Tulare-Porterville MSA, CA	H	6.99 FQ	11.79 AW	16.64 TQ	CABLS	10/01-12/01
Except Legal, Medical, and Executive	Colorado	H	8.19 FQ	13.00 AW	18.12 TQ	COBLS	10/01-12/01
Except Legal, Medical, and Executive	Boulder-Longmont PMSA, CO	H	9.55 FQ	13.78 AW	19.23 TQ	COBLS	10/01-12/01
Except Legal, Medical, and Executive	Colorado Springs MSA, CO	H	9.12 FQ	12.88 AW	17.16 TQ	COBLS	10/01-12/01
Except Legal, Medical, and Executive	Denver PMSA, CO	H	9.31 FQ	14.18 AW	19.39 TQ	COBLS	10/01-12/01
Except Legal, Medical, and Executive	Fort Collins-Loveland MSA, CO	H	7.04 FQ	11.03 AW	15.91 TQ	COBLS	10/01-12/01
Except Legal, Medical, and Executive	Greeley PMSA, CO	H	8.01 FQ	12.09 AW	19.07 TQ	COBLS	10/01-12/01
Except Legal, Medical, and Executive	Connecticut	H	9.18 FQ	14.40 AW	20.41 TQ	CTBLS	10/01-12/01
Except Legal, Medical, and Executive	Bridgeport PMSA, CT	H	9.16 FQ	14.47 AW	21.01 TQ	CTBLS	10/01-12/01
Except Legal, Medical, and Executive	Danbury PMSA, CT	H	9.62 FQ	14.69 AW	20.94 TQ	CTBLS	10/01-12/01
Except Legal, Medical, and Executive	Hartford MSA, CT	H	9.27 FQ	14.57 AW	20.44 TQ	CTBLS	10/01-12/01
Except Legal, Medical, and Executive	New Haven-Meriden PMSA, CT	H	9.30 FQ	14.34 AW	20.32 TQ	CTBLS	10/01-12/01
Except Legal, Medical, and Executive	New London-Norwich MSA, CT-RI	H	7.30 FQ	12.98 AW	18.42 TQ	CTBLS	10/01-12/01
Except Legal, Medical, and Executive	Stamford-Norwalk PMSA, CT	H	9.73 FQ	15.13 AW	20.96 TQ	CTBLS	10/01-12/01
Except Legal, Medical, and Executive	Waterbury PMSA, CT	H	9.27 FQ	13.97 AW	19.49 TQ	CTBLS	10/01-12/01
Except Legal, Medical, and Executive	Delaware	H	7.31 FQ	13.00 AW	19.23 TQ	DEBLS	10/01-12/01
Except Legal, Medical, and Executive	Wilmington-Newark PMSA, DE-MD	H	7.38 FQ	13.34 AW	19.61 TQ	DEBLS	10/01-12/01
Except Legal, Medical, and Executive	District of Columbia	H	11.85 FQ	16.76 AW	22.07 TQ	DCBLS	10/01-12/01
Except Legal, Medical, and Executive	Washington PMSA, DC-MD-VA-WV	H	9.27 FQ	14.89 AW	20.90 TQ	DCBLS	10/01-12/01
Except Legal, Medical, and Executive	Florida	H	7.57 FQ	11.59 AW	16.16 TQ	FLBLS	10/01-12/01
Except Legal, Medical, and Executive	Daytona Beach MSA, FL	H	7.08 FQ	10.89 AW	16.01 TQ	FLBLS	10/01-12/01
Except Legal, Medical, and Executive	Fort Lauderdale PMSA, FL	H	6.83 FQ	11.65 AW	16.47 TQ	FLBLS	10/01-12/01
Except Legal, Medical, and Executive	Fort Myers-Cape Coral MSA, FL	H	7.59 FQ	10.75 AW	14.42 TQ	FLBLS	10/01-12/01
Except Legal, Medical, and Executive	Fort Pierce-Port St. Lucie MSA, FL	H	7.99 FQ	11.26 AW	14.87 TQ	FLBLS	10/01-12/01
Except Legal, Medical, and Executive	Fort Walton Beach MSA, FL	H	7.54 FQ	11.84 AW	16.51 TQ	FLBLS	10/01-12/01
Except Legal, Medical, and Executive	Gainesville MSA, FL	H	7.32 FQ	11.02 AW	15.38 TQ	FLBLS	10/01-12/01
Except Legal, Medical, and Executive	Jacksonville MSA, FL	H	8.11 FQ	11.54 AW	15.62 TQ	FLBLS	10/01-12/01
Except Legal, Medical, and Executive	Lakeland-Winter Haven MSA, FL	H	7.22 FQ	11.06 AW	15.47 TQ	FLBLS	10/01-12/01
Except Legal, Medical, and Executive	Melbourne-Titusville-Palm Bay MSA, FL	H	7.26 FQ	11.43 AW	16.53 TQ	FLBLS	10/01-12/01
Except Legal, Medical, and Executive	Miami PMSA, FL	H	7.48 FQ	12.09 AW	16.60 TQ	FLBLS	10/01-12/01
Except Legal, Medical, and Executive	Naples MSA, FL	H	7.90 FQ	11.44 AW	15.17 TQ	FLBLS	10/01-12/01
Except Legal, Medical, and Executive	Ocala MSA, FL	H	6.95 FQ	10.79 AW	14.32 TQ	FLBLS	10/01-12/01
Except Legal, Medical, and Executive	Orlando MSA, FL	H	8.55 FQ	12.41 AW	17.33 TQ	FLBLS	10/01-12/01
Except Legal, Medical, and Executive	Pensacola MSA, FL	H	6.40 FQ	10.82 AW	16.41 TQ	FLBLS	10/01-12/01
Except Legal, Medical, and Executive	Sarasota-Bradenton MSA, FL	H	7.32 FQ	11.28 AW	14.42 TQ	FLBLS	10/01-12/01
Except Legal, Medical, and Executive	Tallahassee MSA, FL	H	7.92 FQ	12.23 AW	19.85 TQ	FLBLS	10/01-12/01
Except Legal, Medical, and Executive	Tampa-St. Petersburg-Clearwater MSA, FL	H	8.48 FQ	11.83 AW	15.80 TQ	FLBLS	10/01-12/01
Except Legal, Medical, and Executive	West Palm Beach-Boca Raton MSA, FL	H	6.67 FQ	11.55 AW	16.44 TQ	FLBLS	10/01-12/01

AAW	Average annual wage	AOH	Average offered, high	ASH	Average starting, high	H	Hourly	M	Monthly	S	Special: hourly and annual
AE	Average entry wage	AOL	Average offered, low	ASL	Average starting, low	HI	Highest wage paid	MTC	Median total compensation	TQ	Third quartile wage
AEX	Average experienced wage	APH	Average pay, high range	AW	Average wage paid	HR	High end range	MW	Median wage paid	W	Weekly
AO	Average offered	APL	Average pay, low range	FQ	First quartile wage	LR	Low end range	SQ	Second quartile wage	Y	Yearly

Occupation/Type/Industry	Location	Per	Low	Mid	High	Source	Date
Secretary							
Except Legal, Medical, and Executive	Georgia	H	7.30 FQ	11.64 AW	16.62 TQ	GABLS	10/01-12/01
Except Legal, Medical, and Executive	Atlanta MSA, GA	H	8.20 FQ	12.70 AW	17.59 TQ	GABLS	10/01-12/01
Except Legal, Medical, and Executive	Augusta-Aiken MSA, GA-SC	H	7.20 FQ	11.00 AW	15.12 TQ	GABLS	10/01-12/01
Except Legal, Medical, and Executive	Columbus MSA, GA-AL	H	7.42 FQ	10.44 AW	14.80 TQ	GABLS	10/01-12/01
Except Legal, Medical, and Executive	Macon MSA, GA	H	7.64 FQ	11.41 AW	15.90 TQ	GABLS	10/01-12/01
Except Legal, Medical, and Executive	Savannah MSA, GA	H	6.44 FQ	10.96 AW	15.29 TQ	GABLS	10/01-12/01
Except Legal, Medical, and Executive	Hawaii	H	9.82 FQ	14.60 AW	20.19 TQ	HIBLS	10/01-12/01
Except Legal, Medical, and Executive	Honolulu MSA, HI	H	10.03 FQ	14.88 AW	20.45 TQ	HIBLS	10/01-12/01
Except Legal, Medical, and Executive	Idaho	H	6.67 FQ	10.39 AW	14.62 TQ	IDBLS	10/01-12/01
Except Legal, Medical, and Executive	Boise City MSA, ID	H	7.89 FQ	11.54 AW	16.32 TQ	IDBLS	10/01-12/01
Except Legal, Medical, and Executive	Illinois	H	7.61 FQ	13.12 AW	19.57 TQ	ILBLS	10/01-12/01
Except Legal, Medical, and Executive	Champaign-Urbana MSA, IL	H	7.43 FQ	12.37 AW	17.60 TQ	ILBLS	10/01-12/01
Except Legal, Medical, and Executive	Chicago PMSA, IL	H	9.00 FQ	14.46 AW	20.96 TQ	ILBLS	10/01-12/01
Except Legal, Medical, and Executive	Peoria-Pekin MSA, IL	H	7.33 FQ	11.04 AW	15.56 TQ	ILBLS	10/01-12/01
Except Legal, Medical, and Executive	Rockford MSA, IL	H	8.12 FQ	11.51 AW	15.87 TQ	ILBLS	10/01-12/01
Except Legal, Medical, and Executive	Springfield MSA, IL	H	8.05 FQ	12.80 AW	18.39 TQ	ILBLS	10/01-12/01
Except Legal, Medical, and Executive	Indiana	H	7.79 FQ	11.22 AW	15.06 TQ	INBLS	10/01-12/01
Except Legal, Medical, and Executive	Elkhart-Goshen MSA, IN	H	8.30 FQ	11.39 AW	14.67 TQ	INBLS	10/01-12/01
Except Legal, Medical, and Executive	Evansville-Henderson MSA, IN-KY	H	7.23 FQ	10.56 AW	14.10 TQ	INBLS	10/01-12/01
Except Legal, Medical, and Executive	Fort Wayne MSA, IN	H	7.67 FQ	11.43 AW	15.04 TQ	INBLS	10/01-12/01
Except Legal, Medical, and Executive	Gary PMSA, IN	H	7.24 FQ	11.21 AW	16.12 TQ	INBLS	10/01-12/01
Except Legal, Medical, and Executive	Indianapolis MSA, IN	H	8.49 FQ	11.91 AW	15.99 TQ	INBLS	10/01-12/01
Except Legal, Medical, and Executive	Lafayette MSA, IN	H	9.38 FQ	11.99 AW	14.38 TQ	INBLS	10/01-12/01
Except Legal, Medical, and Executive	South Bend MSA, IN	H	9.06 FQ	11.46 AW	13.96 TQ	INBLS	10/01-12/01
Except Legal, Medical, and Executive	Iowa	H	7.22 FQ	11.19 AW	16.03 TQ	IABLS	10/01-12/01
Except Legal, Medical, and Executive	Cedar Rapids MSA, IA	H	6.88 FQ	10.51 AW	14.16 TQ	IABLS	10/01-12/01
Except Legal, Medical, and Executive	Davenport-Moline-Rock Island MSA, IA-IL	H	6.85 FQ	11.21 AW	16.12 TQ	IABLS	10/01-12/01
Except Legal, Medical, and Executive	Des Moines MSA, IA	H	8.54 FQ	12.12 AW	16.32 TQ	IABLS	10/01-12/01
Except Legal, Medical, and Executive	Kansas	H	7.28 FQ	10.67 AW	14.88 TQ	KSBLS	10/01-12/01
Except Legal, Medical, and Executive	Topeka MSA, KS	H	7.80 FQ	11.08 AW	15.37 TQ	KSBLS	10/01-12/01
Except Legal, Medical, and Executive	Wichita MSA, KS	H	7.45 FQ	10.89 AW	15.24 TQ	KSBLS	10/01-12/01
Except Legal, Medical, and Executive	Kentucky	H	6.82 FQ	10.66 AW	15.34 TQ	KYBLS	10/01-12/01
Except Legal, Medical, and Executive	Lexington MSA, KY	H	7.63 FQ	11.35 AW	15.69 TQ	KYBLS	10/01-12/01
Except Legal, Medical, and Executive	Louisville MSA, KY-IN	H	7.53 FQ	11.36 AW	15.76 TQ	KYBLS	10/01-12/01
Except Legal, Medical, and Executive	Louisiana	H	6.53 FQ	10.11 AW	13.95 TQ	LABLS	10/01-12/01
Except Legal, Medical, and Executive	Baton Rouge MSA, LA	H	7.28 FQ	10.56 AW	14.52 TQ	LABLS	10/01-12/01
Except Legal, Medical, and Executive	Houma MSA, LA	H	6.99 FQ	10.33 AW	14.01 TQ	LABLS	10/01-12/01
Except Legal, Medical, and Executive	Lafayette MSA, LA	H	6.39 FQ	9.59 AW	13.46 TQ	LABLS	10/01-12/01
Except Legal, Medical, and Executive	Lake Charles MSA, LA	H	6.41 FQ	9.55 AW	13.08 TQ	LABLS	10/01-12/01
Except Legal, Medical, and Executive	New Orleans MSA, LA	H	7.07 FQ	10.66 AW	13.96 TQ	LABLS	10/01-12/01
Except Legal, Medical, and Executive	Shreveport-Bossier City MSA, LA	H	6.27 FQ	10.16 AW	15.00 TQ	LABLS	10/01-12/01
Except Legal, Medical, and Executive	Maine	H	7.52 FQ	11.00 AW	14.93 TQ	MEBLS	10/01-12/01
Except Legal, Medical, and Executive	Portland MSA, ME	H	8.09 FQ	11.84 AW	16.13 TQ	MEBLS	10/01-12/01
Except Legal, Medical, and Executive	Maryland	H	8.01 FQ	12.73 AW	17.88 TQ	MDBLS	10/01-12/01
Except Legal, Medical, and Executive	Baltimore PMSA, MD	H	8.52 FQ	12.65 AW	16.88 TQ	MDBLS	10/01-12/01
Except Legal, Medical, and Executive	Massachusetts	H	9.22 FQ	14.08 AW	19.84 TQ	MABLS	10/01-12/01
Except Legal, Medical, and Executive	Boston PMSA, MA-NH	H	9.62 FQ	14.72 AW	20.46 TQ	MABLS	10/01-12/01
Except Legal, Medical, and Executive	Brockton PMSA, MA	H	8.56 FQ	13.78 AW	20.27 TQ	MABLS	10/01-12/01
Except Legal, Medical, and Executive	Lawrence PMSA, MA-NH	H	9.26 FQ	13.31 AW	17.90 TQ	MABLS	10/01-12/01
Except Legal, Medical, and Executive	Lowell PMSA, MA-NH	H	9.60 FQ	14.27 AW	19.85 TQ	MABLS	10/01-12/01
Except Legal, Medical, and Executive	New Bedford PMSA, MA	H	8.17 FQ	12.17 AW	17.82 TQ	MABLS	10/01-12/01
Except Legal, Medical, and Executive	Springfield MSA, MA	H	7.58 FQ	13.06 AW	18.64 TQ	MABLS	10/01-12/01
Except Legal, Medical, and Executive	Worcester PMSA, MA-CT	H	8.91 FQ	12.56 AW	16.92 TQ	MABLS	10/01-12/01
Except Legal, Medical, and Executive	Michigan	H	7.98 FQ	12.88 AW	18.76 TQ	MIBLS	10/01-12/01
Except Legal, Medical, and Executive	Ann Arbor PMSA, MI	H	8.68 FQ	13.53 AW	19.31 TQ	MIBLS	10/01-12/01
Except Legal, Medical, and Executive	Detroit PMSA, MI	H	8.87 FQ	14.03 AW	19.95 TQ	MIBLS	10/01-12/01
Except Legal, Medical, and Executive	Flint PMSA, MI	H	7.01 FQ	12.12 AW	17.34 TQ	MIBLS	10/01-12/01
Except Legal, Medical, and Executive	Grand Rapids-Muskegon-Holland MSA, MI	H	8.26 FQ	12.12 AW	17.00 TQ	MIBLS	10/01-12/01
Except Legal, Medical, and Executive	Kalamazoo-Battle Creek MSA, MI	H	7.51 FQ	12.16 AW	17.53 TQ	MIBLS	10/01-12/01
Except Legal, Medical, and Executive	Lansing-East Lansing MSA, MI	H	9.04 FQ	14.00 AW	19.62 TQ	MIBLS	10/01-12/01
Except Legal, Medical, and Executive	Saginaw-Bay City-Midland MSA, MI	H	6.64 FQ	10.45 AW	15.01 TQ	MIBLS	10/01-12/01
Except Legal, Medical, and Executive	Minnesota	H	9.76 FQ	14.05 AW	18.41 TQ	MNBLS	10/01-12/01
Except Legal, Medical, and Executive	Duluth-Superior MSA, MN-WI	H	8.29 FQ	12.59 AW	17.44 TQ	MNBLS	10/01-12/01
Except Legal, Medical, and Executive	Minneapolis-St. Paul MSA, MN-WI	H	10.64 FQ	14.72 AW	19.55 TQ	MNBLS	10/01-12/01

AAW	Average annual wage	**AOH**	Average offered, high	**ASH**	Average starting, high	**H**	Hourly	**M**	Monthly	**S**	Special: hourly and annual
AE	Average entry wage	**AOL**	Average offered, low	**ASL**	Average starting, low	**HI**	Highest wage paid	**MTC**	Median total compensation	**TQ**	Third quartile wage
AEX	Average experienced wage	**APH**	Average pay, high range	**AW**	Average wage paid	**HR**	High end range	**MW**	Median wage paid	**W**	Weekly
AO	Average offered	**APL**	Average pay, low range	**FQ**	First quartile wage	**LR**	Low end range	**SQ**	Second quartile wage	**Y**	Yearly

Occupation/Type/Industry	Location	Per	Low	Mid	High	Source	Date
Secretary							
Except Legal, Medical, and Executive	St. Cloud MSA, MN	H	8.96 FQ	11.97 AW	16.42 TQ	MNBLS	10/01-12/01
Except Legal, Medical, and Executive	Mississippi	H	6.59 FQ	10.15 AW	13.93 TQ	MSBLS	10/01-12/01
Except Legal, Medical, and Executive	Biloxi-Gulfport-Pascagoula MSA, MS	H	6.45 FQ	10.66 AW	15.48 TQ	MSBLS	10/01-12/01
Except Legal, Medical, and Executive	Jackson MSA, MS	H	7.10 FQ	11.41 AW	15.76 TQ	MSBLS	10/01-12/01
Except Legal, Medical, and Executive	Missouri	H	7.13 FQ	11.32 AW	16.49 TQ	MOBLS	10/01-12/01
Except Legal, Medical, and Executive	Kansas City MSA, MO-KS	H	7.91 FQ	12.04 AW	16.71 TQ	MOBLS	10/01-12/01
Except Legal, Medical, and Executive	St. Louis MSA, MO-IL	H	7.49 FQ	12.01 AW	17.18 TQ	MOBLS	10/01-12/01
Except Legal, Medical, and Executive	Springfield MSA, MO	H	7.11 FQ	10.16 AW	13.93 TQ	MOBLS	10/01-12/01
Except Legal, Medical, and Executive	Montana	H	6.53 FQ	9.67 AW	13.28 TQ	MTBLS	10/01-12/01
Except Legal, Medical, and Executive	Billings MSA, MT	H	6.97 FQ	10.10 AW	13.84 TQ	MTBLS	10/01-12/01
Except Legal, Medical, and Executive	Nebraska	H	6.81 FQ	10.37 AW	14.55 TQ	NEBLS	10/01-12/01
Except Legal, Medical, and Executive	Lincoln MSA, NE	H	7.65 FQ	11.07 AW	15.38 TQ	NEBLS	10/01-12/01
Except Legal, Medical, and Executive	Omaha MSA, NE-IA	H	8.17 FQ	11.76 AW	16.05 TQ	NEBLS	10/01-12/01
Except Legal, Medical, and Executive	Nevada	H	8.92 FQ	13.26 AW	18.45 TQ	NVBLS	10/01-12/01
Except Legal, Medical, and Executive	Las Vegas MSA, NV-AZ	H	8.78 FQ	13.17 AW	18.91 TQ	NVBLS	10/01-12/01
Except Legal, Medical, and Executive	Reno MSA, NV	H	8.98 FQ	12.93 AW	17.52 TQ	NVBLS	10/01-12/01
Except Legal, Medical, and Executive	New Hampshire	H	8.26 FQ	11.73 AW	16.17 TQ	NHBLS	10/01-12/01
Except Legal, Medical, and Executive	Manchester PMSA, NH	H	8.63 FQ	12.07 AW	16.89 TQ	NHBLS	10/01-12/01
Except Legal, Medical, and Executive	Nashua PMSA, NH	H	7.45 FQ	12.01 AW	17.06 TQ	NHBLS	10/01-12/01
Except Legal, Medical, and Executive	Portsmouth-Rochester PMSA, NH-ME	H	9.12 FQ	12.23 AW	16.37 TQ	NHBLS	10/01-12/01
Except Legal, Medical, and Executive	New Jersey	H	10.15 FQ	15.52 AW	21.42 TQ	NJBLS	10/01-12/01
Except Legal, Medical, and Executive	Atlantic-Cape May PMSA, NJ	H	9.09 FQ	13.86 AW	19.90 TQ	NJBLS	10/01-12/01
Except Legal, Medical, and Executive	Bergen-Passaic PMSA, NJ	H	10.21 FQ	15.76 AW	21.52 TQ	NJBLS	10/01-12/01
Except Legal, Medical, and Executive	Jersey City PMSA, NJ	H	8.63 FQ	15.84 AW	23.17 TQ	NJBLS	10/01-12/01
Except Legal, Medical, and Executive	Middlesex-Somerset-Hunterdon PMSA, NJ	H	11.04 FQ	16.22 AW	21.77 TQ	NJBLS	10/01-12/01
Except Legal, Medical, and Executive	Monmouth-Ocean PMSA, NJ	H	9.45 FQ	14.51 AW	20.50 TQ	NJBLS	10/01-12/01
Except Legal, Medical, and Executive	Newark PMSA, NJ	H	11.03 FQ	15.93 AW	21.82 TQ	NJBLS	10/01-12/01
Except Legal, Medical, and Executive	Trenton PMSA, NJ	H	10.02 FQ	15.99 AW	21.90 TQ	NJBLS	10/01-12/01
Except Legal, Medical, and Executive	New Mexico	H	7.07 FQ	10.85 AW	15.71 TQ	NMBLS	10/01-12/01
Except Legal, Medical, and Executive	Albuquerque MSA, NM	H	7.48 FQ	11.26 AW	15.93 TQ	NMBLS	10/01-12/01
Except Legal, Medical, and Executive	Las Cruces MSA, NM	H	6.69 FQ	10.10 AW	14.36 TQ	NMBLS	10/01-12/01
Except Legal, Medical, and Executive	New York	H	8.05 FQ	13.83 AW	21.08 TQ	NYBLS	10/01-12/01
Except Legal, Medical, and Executive	Albany-Schenectady-Troy MSA, NY	H	9.68 FQ	14.54 AW	20.71 TQ	NYBLS	10/01-12/01
Except Legal, Medical, and Executive	Binghamton MSA, NY	H	7.15 FQ	11.07 AW	16.57 TQ	NYBLS	10/01-12/01
Except Legal, Medical, and Executive	Buffalo-Niagara Falls MSA, NY	H	7.74 FQ	11.93 AW	16.67 TQ	NYBLS	10/01-12/01
Except Legal, Medical, and Executive	Dutchess County PMSA, NY	H	8.43 FQ	12.94 AW	18.24 TQ	NYBLS	10/01-12/01
Except Legal, Medical, and Executive	Nassau-Suffolk PMSA, NY	H	7.28 FQ	13.70 AW	20.86 TQ	NYBLS	10/01-12/01
Except Legal, Medical, and Executive	New York PMSA, NY	H	8.94 FQ	14.92 AW	22.86 TQ	NYBLS	10/01-12/01
Except Legal, Medical, and Executive	Newburgh PMSA, NY-PA	H	7.98 FQ	12.02 AW	16.80 TQ	NYBLS	10/01-12/01
Except Legal, Medical, and Executive	Rochester MSA, NY	H	7.23 FQ	12.25 AW	17.87 TQ	NYBLS	10/01-12/01
Except Legal, Medical, and Executive	Syracuse MSA, NY	H	8.11 FQ	11.74 AW	16.70 TQ	NYBLS	10/01-12/01
Except Legal, Medical, and Executive	Utica-Rome MSA, NY	H	6.85 FQ	10.87 AW	15.91 TQ	NYBLS	10/01-12/01
Except Legal, Medical, and Executive	North Carolina	H	7.41 FQ	11.35 AW	16.04 TQ	NCBLS	10/01-12/01
Except Legal, Medical, and Executive	Asheville MSA, NC	H	7.23 FQ	10.67 AW	14.71 TQ	NCBLS	10/01-12/01
Except Legal, Medical, and Executive	Charlotte-Gastonia-Rock Hill MSA, NC-SC	H	8.28 FQ	12.07 AW	16.64 TQ	NCBLS	10/01-12/01
Except Legal, Medical, and Executive	Fayetteville MSA, NC	H	7.24 FQ	11.05 AW	16.04 TQ	NCBLS	10/01-12/01
Except Legal, Medical, and Executive	Greensboro-Winston-Salem-High Point MSA, NC	H	8.00 FQ	11.74 AW	15.85 TQ	NCBLS	10/01-12/01
Except Legal, Medical, and Executive	Hickory-Morganton-Lenoir MSA, NC	H	6.76 FQ	10.59 AW	14.17 TQ	NCBLS	10/01-12/01
Except Legal, Medical, and Executive	Raleigh-Durham-Chapel Hill MSA, NC	H	7.49 FQ	12.00 AW	16.92 TQ	NCBLS	10/01-12/01
Except Legal, Medical, and Executive	Wilmington MSA, NC	H	8.40 FQ	10.83 AW	13.76 TQ	NCBLS	10/01-12/01
Except Legal, Medical, and Executive	North Dakota	H	6.65 FQ	10.09 AW	13.99 TQ	NDBLS	10/01-12/01
Except Legal, Medical, and Executive	Fargo-Moorhead MSA, ND-MN	H	7.89 FQ	11.21 AW	15.43 TQ	NDBLS	10/01-12/01
Except Legal, Medical, and Executive	Ohio	H	7.47 FQ	11.72 AW	16.40 TQ	OHBLS	10/01-12/01
Except Legal, Medical, and Executive	Akron PMSA, OH	H	8.01 FQ	11.76 AW	16.34 TQ	OHBLS	10/01-12/01
Except Legal, Medical, and Executive	Canton-Massillon MSA, OH	H	6.94 FQ	10.88 AW	15.66 TQ	OHBLS	10/01-12/01
Except Legal, Medical, and Executive	Cincinnati PMSA, OH-KY-IN	H	7.71 FQ	12.20 AW	16.69 TQ	OHBLS	10/01-12/01
Except Legal, Medical, and Executive	Cleveland-Lorain-Elyria PMSA, OH	H	7.21 FQ	12.25 AW	16.93 TQ	OHBLS	10/01-12/01
Except Legal, Medical, and Executive	Columbus MSA, OH	H	8.91 FQ	12.64 AW	16.87 TQ	OHBLS	10/01-12/01
Except Legal, Medical, and Executive	Dayton-Springfield MSA, OH	H	7.61 FQ	11.63 AW	16.28 TQ	OHBLS	10/01-12/01

AAW	Average annual wage	AOH	Average offered, high	ASH	Average starting, high	H	Hourly	M	Monthly	S	Special: hourly and annual
AE	Average entry wage	AOL	Average offered, low	ASL	Average starting, low	HI	Highest wage paid	MTC	Median total compensation	TQ	Third quartile wage
AEX	Average experienced wage	APH	Average pay, high range	AW	Average wage paid	HR	High end range	MW	Median wage paid	W	Weekly
AO	Average offered	APL	Average pay, low range	FQ	First quartile wage	LR	Low end range	SQ	Second quartile wage	Y	Yearly

Occupation/Type/Industry	Location	Per	Low	Mid	High	Source	Date
Secretary							
Except Legal, Medical, and Executive	Hamilton-Middletown PMSA, OH	H	8.51 FQ	11.97 AW	16.19 TQ	OHBLS	10/01-12/01
Except Legal, Medical, and Executive	Mansfield MSA, OH	H	7.33 FQ	10.38 AW	14.20 TQ	OHBLS	10/01-12/01
Except Legal, Medical, and Executive	Toledo MSA, OH	H	8.56 FQ	12.05 AW	16.55 TQ	OHBLS	10/01-12/01
Except Legal, Medical, and Executive	Youngstown-Warren MSA, OH	H	6.92 FQ	10.26 AW	14.52 TQ	OHBLS	10/01-12/01
Except Legal, Medical, and Executive	Oklahoma	H	6.41 FQ	10.07 AW	14.44 TQ	OKBLS	10/01-12/01
Except Legal, Medical, and Executive	Oklahoma City MSA, OK	H	6.87 FQ	10.58 AW	14.65 TQ	OKBLS	10/01-12/01
Except Legal, Medical, and Executive	Tulsa MSA, OK	H	7.20 FQ	11.16 AW	15.92 TQ	OKBLS	10/01-12/01
Except Legal, Medical, and Executive	Oregon	H	8.93 FQ	12.64 AW	16.81 TQ	ORBLS	10/01-12/01
Except Legal, Medical, and Executive	Eugene-Springfield MSA, OR	H	8.19 FQ	11.67 AW	15.77 TQ	ORBLS	10/01-12/01
Except Legal, Medical, and Executive	Medford-Ashland MSA, OR	H	7.40 FQ	10.77 AW	15.01 TQ	ORBLS	10/01-12/01
Except Legal, Medical, and Executive	Portland-Vancouver PMSA, OR-WA	H	9.58 FQ	13.49 AW	17.49 TQ	ORBLS	10/01-12/01
Except Legal, Medical, and Executive	Salem PMSA, OR	H	8.67 FQ	12.27 AW	16.38 TQ	ORBLS	10/01-12/01
Except Legal, Medical, and Executive	Pennsylvania	H	6.70 FQ	11.45 AW	16.88 TQ	PABLS	10/01-12/01
Except Legal, Medical, and Executive	Allentown-Bethlehem-Easton MSA, PA	H	7.35 FQ	11.29 AW	15.95 TQ	PABLS	10/01-12/01
Except Legal, Medical, and Executive	Erie MSA, PA	H	6.44 FQ	10.45 AW	15.07 TQ	PABLS	10/01-12/01
Except Legal, Medical, and Executive	Harrisburg-Lebanon-Carlisle MSA, PA	H	7.70 FQ	12.27 AW	17.33 TQ	PABLS	10/01-12/01
Except Legal, Medical, and Executive	Johnstown MSA, PA	H	6.19 FQ	9.44 AW	13.21 TQ	PABLS	10/01-12/01
Except Legal, Medical, and Executive	Lancaster MSA, PA	H	8.32 FQ	11.53 AW	15.51 TQ	PABLS	10/01-12/01
Except Legal, Medical, and Executive	Philadelphia PMSA, PA-NJ	H	8.68 FQ	13.61 AW	19.38 TQ	PABLS	10/01-12/01
Except Legal, Medical, and Executive	Pittsburgh MSA, PA	H	6.18 FQ	10.65 AW	15.81 TQ	PABLS	10/01-12/01
Except Legal, Medical, and Executive	Reading MSA, PA	H	7.38 FQ	11.38 AW	16.17 TQ	PABLS	10/01-12/01
Except Legal, Medical, and Executive	Scranton-Wilkes-Barre-Hazleton MSA, PA	H	6.15 FQ	9.56 AW	13.95 TQ	PABLS	10/01-12/01
Except Legal, Medical, and Executive	York MSA, PA	H	7.64 FQ	11.19 AW	14.88 TQ	PABLS	10/01-12/01
Except Legal, Medical, and Executive	Rhode Island	H	8.46 FQ	12.90 AW	17.47 TQ	RIBLS	10/01-12/01
Except Legal, Medical, and Executive	Providence-Fall River-Warwick MSA, RI-MA	H	8.39 FQ	12.70 AW	17.44 TQ	RIBLS	10/01-12/01
Except Legal, Medical, and Executive	South Carolina	H	7.36 FQ	10.89 AW	15.27 TQ	SCBLS	10/01-12/01
Except Legal, Medical, and Executive	Charleston-North Charleston MSA, SC	H	7.43 FQ	11.14 AW	15.79 TQ	SCBLS	10/01-12/01
Except Legal, Medical, and Executive	Columbia MSA, SC	H	7.56 FQ	11.22 AW	15.70 TQ	SCBLS	10/01-12/01
Except Legal, Medical, and Executive	Greenville-Spartanburg-Anderson MSA, SC	H	7.74 FQ	11.17 AW	15.30 TQ	SCBLS	10/01-12/01
Except Legal, Medical, and Executive	Myrtle Beach MSA, SC	H	7.42 FQ	10.64 AW	15.13 TQ	SCBLS	10/01-12/01
Except Legal, Medical, and Executive	South Dakota	H	7.43 FQ	9.88 AW	12.86 TQ	SDBLS	10/01-12/01
Except Legal, Medical, and Executive	Sioux Falls MSA, SD	H	8.63 FQ	10.84 AW	13.50 TQ	SDBLS	10/01-12/01
Except Legal, Medical, and Executive	Tennessee	H	6.71 FQ	10.88 AW	16.06 TQ	TNBLS	10/01-12/01
Except Legal, Medical, and Executive	Chattanooga MSA, TN-GA	H	7.20 FQ	10.95 AW	15.29 TQ	TNBLS	10/01-12/01
Except Legal, Medical, and Executive	Clarksville-Hopkinsville MSA, TN-KY	H	6.77 FQ	10.15 AW	14.48 TQ	TNBLS	10/01-12/01
Except Legal, Medical, and Executive	Johnson City-Kingsport-Bristol MSA, TN-VA	H	6.54 FQ	9.86 AW	14.40 TQ	TNBLS	10/01-12/01
Except Legal, Medical, and Executive	Knoxville MSA, TN	H	6.15 FQ	10.14 AW	15.75 TQ	TNBLS	10/01-12/01
Except Legal, Medical, and Executive	Memphis MSA, TN-AR-MS	H	7.48 FQ	11.70 AW	16.99 TQ	TNBLS	10/01-12/01
Except Legal, Medical, and Executive	Nashville MSA, TN	H	7.56 FQ	12.06 AW	17.09 TQ	TNBLS	10/01-12/01
Except Legal, Medical, and Executive	Texas	H	6.93 FQ	11.42 AW	16.73 TQ	TXBLS	10/01-12/01
Except Legal, Medical, and Executive	Amarillo MSA, TX	H	7.05 FQ	10.46 AW	14.92 TQ	TXBLS	10/01-12/01
Except Legal, Medical, and Executive	Austin-San Marcos MSA, TX	H	7.42 FQ	11.90 AW	16.77 TQ	TXBLS	10/01-12/01
Except Legal, Medical, and Executive	Beaumont-Port Arthur MSA, TX	H	6.57 FQ	10.36 AW	14.99 TQ	TXBLS	10/01-12/01
Except Legal, Medical, and Executive	Brazoria PMSA, TX	H	7.22 FQ	10.74 AW	14.70 TQ	TXBLS	10/01-12/01
Except Legal, Medical, and Executive	Brownsville-Harlingen-San Benito MSA, TX	H	5.96 FQ	9.65 AW	14.00 TQ	TXBLS	10/01-12/01
Except Legal, Medical, and Executive	Corpus Christi MSA, TX	H	7.27 FQ	10.86 AW	15.68 TQ	TXBLS	10/01-12/01
Except Legal, Medical, and Executive	Dallas PMSA, TX	H	7.80 FQ	13.01 AW	18.27 TQ	TXBLS	10/01-12/01
Except Legal, Medical, and Executive	El Paso MSA, TX	H	6.20 FQ	10.15 AW	14.21 TQ	TXBLS	10/01-12/01
Except Legal, Medical, and Executive	Fort Worth-Arlington PMSA, TX	H	7.53 FQ	12.03 AW	16.98 TQ	TXBLS	10/01-12/01
Except Legal, Medical, and Executive	Galveston-Texas City PMSA, TX	H	6.73 FQ	11.12 AW	15.84 TQ	TXBLS	10/01-12/01
Except Legal, Medical, and Executive	Houston PMSA, TX	H	7.75 FQ	12.69 AW	17.90 TQ	TXBLS	10/01-12/01
Except Legal, Medical, and Executive	Killeen-Temple MSA, TX	H	6.42 FQ	9.70 AW	13.66 TQ	TXBLS	10/01-12/01
Except Legal, Medical, and Executive	Laredo MSA, TX	H	5.99 FQ	9.51 AW	14.25 TQ	TXBLS	10/01-12/01
Except Legal, Medical, and Executive	Longview-Marshall MSA, TX	H	6.30 FQ	9.23 AW	12.84 TQ	TXBLS	10/01-12/01
Except Legal, Medical, and Executive	Lubbock MSA, TX	H	6.43 FQ	9.43 AW	13.29 TQ	TXBLS	10/01-12/01
Except Legal, Medical, and Executive	McAllen-Edinburg-Mission MSA, TX	H	6.32 FQ	9.65 AW	13.11 TQ	TXBLS	10/01-12/01

AAW	Average annual wage	**AOH**	Average offered, high	**ASH**	Average starting, high	**H**	Hourly	**M**	Monthly	**S**	Special: hourly and annual
AE	Average entry wage	**AOL**	Average offered, low	**ASL**	Average starting, low	**HI**	Highest wage paid	**MTC**	Median total compensation	**TQ**	Third quartile wage
AEX	Average experienced wage	**APH**	Average pay, high range	**AW**	Average wage paid	**HR**	High end range	**MW**	Median wage paid	**W**	Weekly
AO	Average offered	**APL**	Average pay, low range	**FQ**	First quartile wage	**LR**	Low end range	**SQ**	Second quartile wage	**Y**	Yearly

Occupation/Type/Industry	Location	Per	Low	Mid	High	Source	Date
Secretary							
Except Legal, Medical, and Executive	Odessa-Midland MSA, TX	H	7.02 FQ	11.29 AW	15.38 TQ	TXBLS	10/01-12/01
Except Legal, Medical, and Executive	San Antonio MSA, TX	H	7.21 FQ	10.78 AW	15.58 TQ	TXBLS	10/01-12/01
Except Legal, Medical, and Executive	Tyler MSA, TX	H	6.78 FQ	10.34 AW	13.80 TQ	TXBLS	10/01-12/01
Except Legal, Medical, and Executive	Waco MSA, TX	H	6.51 FQ	10.01 AW	13.84 TQ	TXBLS	10/01-12/01
Except Legal, Medical, and Executive	Utah	H	7.81 FQ	11.22 AW	15.55 TQ	UTBLS	10/01-12/01
Except Legal, Medical, and Executive	Provo-Orem MSA, UT	H	6.14 FQ	10.13 AW	14.29 TQ	UTBLS	10/01-12/01
Except Legal, Medical, and Executive	Salt Lake City-Ogden MSA, UT	H	8.76 FQ	11.70 AW	16.16 TQ	UTBLS	10/01-12/01
Except Legal, Medical, and Executive	Vermont	H	8.63 FQ	11.41 AW	14.65 TQ	VTBLS	10/01-12/01
Except Legal, Medical, and Executive	Burlington MSA, VT	H	9.17 FQ	11.96 AW	15.47 TQ	VTBLS	10/01-12/01
Except Legal, Medical, and Executive	Virginia	H	7.41 FQ	12.56 AW	18.31 TQ	VABLS	10/01-12/01
Except Legal, Medical, and Executive	Lynchburg MSA, VA	H	7.38 FQ	10.57 AW	14.85 TQ	VABLS	10/01-12/01
Except Legal, Medical, and Executive	Norfolk-Virginia Beach-Newport News MSA, VA-NC	H	6.93 FQ	11.10 AW	16.35 TQ	VABLS	10/01-12/01
Except Legal, Medical, and Executive	Richmond-Petersburg MSA, VA	H	9.07 FQ	13.03 AW	17.51 TQ	VABLS	10/01-12/01
Except Legal, Medical, and Executive	Roanoke MSA, VA	H	6.96 FQ	13.71 AW	16.74 TQ	VABLS	10/01-12/01
Except Legal, Medical, and Executive	Washington	H	9.71 FQ	14.06 AW	18.98 TQ	WABLS	10/01-12/01
Except Legal, Medical, and Executive	Bremerton PMSA, WA	H	9.53 FQ	13.80 AW	19.30 TQ	WABLS	10/01-12/01
Except Legal, Medical, and Executive	Olympia PMSA, WA	H	11.27 FQ	15.26 AW	20.01 TQ	WABLS	10/01-12/01
Except Legal, Medical, and Executive	Richland-Kennewick-Pasco MSA, WA	H	9.52 FQ	13.17 AW	16.99 TQ	WABLS	10/01-12/01
Except Legal, Medical, and Executive	Seattle-Bellevue-Everett PMSA, WA	H	10.83 FQ	14.98 AW	20.03 TQ	WABLS	10/01-12/01
Except Legal, Medical, and Executive	Spokane MSA, WA	H	8.03 FQ	12.43 AW	17.21 TQ	WABLS	10/01-12/01
Except Legal, Medical, and Executive	Tacoma PMSA, WA	H	8.13 FQ	13.56 AW	18.27 TQ	WABLS	10/01-12/01
Except Legal, Medical, and Executive	Yakima MSA, WA	H	9.32 FQ	13.32 AW	17.47 TQ	WABLS	10/01-12/01
Except Legal, Medical, and Executive	West Virginia	H	6.33 FQ	9.76 AW	13.85 TQ	WVBLS	10/01-12/01
Except Legal, Medical, and Executive	Charleston MSA, WV	H	7.20 FQ	10.53 AW	14.87 TQ	WVBLS	10/01-12/01
Except Legal, Medical, and Executive	Huntington-Ashland MSA, WV-KY-OH	H	6.36 FQ	9.78 AW	13.72 TQ	WVBLS	10/01-12/01
Except Legal, Medical, and Executive	Wisconsin	H	7.98 FQ	11.73 AW	16.08 TQ	WIBLS	10/01-12/01
Except Legal, Medical, and Executive	Appleton-Oshkosh-Neenah MSA, WI	H	8.59 FQ	11.57 AW	15.73 TQ	WIBLS	10/01-12/01
Except Legal, Medical, and Executive	Green Bay MSA, WI	H	8.80 FQ	12.16 AW	17.08 TQ	WIBLS	10/01-12/01
Except Legal, Medical, and Executive	Milwaukee-Waukesha PMSA, WI	H	9.14 FQ	12.54 AW	16.68 TQ	WIBLS	10/01-12/01
Except Legal, Medical, and Executive	Racine PMSA, WI	H	6.96 FQ	10.93 AW	15.43 TQ	WIBLS	10/01-12/01
Except Legal, Medical, and Executive	Wyoming	H	6.75 FQ	9.99 AW	13.48 TQ	WYBLS	10/01-12/01
Except Legal, Medical, and Executive	Cheyenne MSA, WY	H	7.49 FQ	10.73 AW	14.21 TQ	WYBLS	10/01-12/01
Except Legal, Medical, and Executive	Puerto Rico	H	5.66 FQ	7.94 AW	11.31 TQ	PRBLS	10/01-12/01
Except Legal, Medical, and Executive	Virgin Islands	H	7.74 FQ	10.20 AW	13.18 TQ	VIBLS	10/01-12/01
Except Legal, Medical, and Executive	Guam	H	6.48 FQ	11.20 AW	16.37 TQ	GUBLS	10/01-12/01
Securities, Commodities, and Financial Services Sales Agent	United States	Y		56080 MW		OOH5	1999-2000
	Alabama	Y	24690 FQ	76260 AW		ALBLS	10/01-12/01
	Birmingham MSA, AL	Y	25790 FQ	67540 AW		ALBLS	10/01-12/01
	Huntsville MSA, AL	Y	31230 FQ	85380 AW		ALBLS	10/01-12/01
	Mobile MSA, AL	Y	12710 FQ	55290 AW		ALBLS	10/01-12/01
	Montgomery MSA, AL	Y	30410 FQ	102630 AW		ALBLS	10/01-12/01
	Alaska	Y	31510 FQ	73090 AW		AKBLS	10/01-12/01
	Anchorage MSA, AK	Y	36710 FQ	78530 AW		AKBLS	10/01-12/01
	Arizona	Y	22500 FQ	55100 AW	136250 TQ	AZBLS	10/01-12/01
	Phoenix-Mesa MSA, AZ	Y	21970 FQ	51250 AW	126200 TQ	AZBLS	10/01-12/01
	Tucson MSA, AZ	Y	36260 FQ	90180 AW	141150 TQ	AZBLS	10/01-12/01
	Arkansas	Y	25540 FQ	61980 AW		ARBLS	10/01-12/01
	Fayetteville-Springdale-Rogers MSA, AR	Y	28690 FQ	59300 AW	119100 TQ	ARBLS	10/01-12/01
	Fort Smith MSA, AR-OK	Y	21560 FQ	75600 AW		ARBLS	10/01-12/01
	Little Rock-North Little Rock MSA, AR	Y	25690 FQ	61280 AW		ARBLS	10/01-12/01
	California	Y	29070 FQ	75140 AW		CABLS	10/01-12/01
	Bakersfield MSA, CA	Y	25680 FQ	56250 AW	93730 TQ	CABLS	10/01-12/01
	Chico-Paradise MSA, CA	Y	23040 FQ	61270 AW	121850 TQ	CABLS	10/01-12/01
	Fresno MSA, CA	Y	25890 FQ	70200 AW		CABLS	10/01-12/01
	Los Angeles-Long Beach PMSA, CA	Y	26790 FQ	70560 AW		CABLS	10/01-12/01
	Modesto MSA, CA	Y	30080 FQ	71970 AW	126490 TQ	CABLS	10/01-12/01
	Oakland PMSA, CA	Y	31470 FQ	68850 AW		CABLS	10/01-12/01

AAW	Average annual wage	AOH	Average offered, high	ASH	Average starting, high	H	Hourly	M	Monthly	S	Special: hourly and annual
AE	Average entry wage	AOL	Average offered, low	ASL	Average starting, low	HI	Highest wage paid	MTC	Median total compensation	TQ	Third quartile wage
AEX	Average experienced wage	APH	Average pay, high range	AW	Average wage paid	HR	High end range	MW	Median wage paid	W	Weekly
AO	Average offered	APL	Average pay, low range	FQ	First quartile wage	LR	Low end range	SQ	Second quartile wage	Y	Yearly

Occupation/Type/Industry	Location	Per	Low	Mid	High	Source	Date
Securities, Commodities, and Financial Services Sales Agent	Orange County PMSA, CA	Y	24380 FQ	66140 AW	142040 TQ	CABLS	10/01-12/01
	Redding MSA, CA	Y	28090 FQ	53550 AW	89300 TQ	CABLS	10/01-12/01
	Riverside-San Bernardino PMSA, CA	Y	24100 FQ	56200 AW		CABLS	10/01-12/01
	Sacramento PMSA, CA	Y	25920 FQ	58400 AW		CABLS	10/01-12/01
	Salinas MSA, CA	Y	27250 FQ	69900 AW		CABLS	10/01-12/01
	San Diego MSA, CA	Y	31820 FQ	66020 AW		CABLS	10/01-12/01
	San Francisco PMSA, CA	Y	39290 FQ	91290 AW		CABLS	10/01-12/01
	San Jose PMSA, CA	Y	27440 FQ	84560 AW		CABLS	10/01-12/01
	San Luis Obispo-Atascadero-Paso Robles MSA, CA	Y	40520 FQ	79060 AW		CABLS	10/01-12/01
	Santa Barbara-Santa Maria-Lompoc MSA, CA	Y	34440 FQ	75740 AW		CABLS	10/01-12/01
	Santa Cruz-Watsonville PMSA, CA	Y	37820 FQ	71930 AW		CABLS	10/01-12/01
	Santa Rosa PMSA, CA	Y	29210 FQ	74490 AW		CABLS	10/01-12/01
	Stockton-Lodi MSA, CA	Y	24530 FQ	55030 AW	115950 TQ	CABLS	10/01-12/01
	Vallejo-Fairfield-Napa PMSA, CA	Y	23480 FQ	44060 AW	86170 TQ	CABLS	10/01-12/01
	Ventura PMSA, CA	Y	24620 FQ	70090 AW		CABLS	10/01-12/01
	Visalia-Tulare-Porterville MSA, CA	Y	21520 FQ	55050 AW	100680 TQ	CABLS	10/01-12/01
	Colorado	Y	26790 FQ	55440 AW	112570 TQ	COBLS	10/01-12/01
	Boulder-Longmont PMSA, CO	Y	26110 FQ	72800 AW		COBLS	10/01-12/01
	Colorado Springs MSA, CO	Y	24580 FQ	52730 AW	140550 TQ	COBLS	10/01-12/01
	Denver PMSA, CO	Y	27420 FQ	53520 AW	100400 TQ	COBLS	10/01-12/01
	Fort Collins-Loveland MSA, CO	Y	24630 FQ	57920 AW	112740 TQ	COBLS	10/01-12/01
	Greeley PMSA, CO	Y	13600 FQ	57060 AW	113570 TQ	COBLS	10/01-12/01
	Connecticut	Y	33630 FQ	92350 AW		CTBLS	10/01-12/01
	Bridgeport PMSA, CT	Y	30520 FQ	67570 AW		CTBLS	10/01-12/01
	Danbury PMSA, CT	Y	22110 FQ	69850 AW		CTBLS	10/01-12/01
	Hartford MSA, CT	Y	26390 FQ	71620 AW		CTBLS	10/01-12/01
	New Haven-Meriden PMSA, CT	Y	39460 FQ	78770 AW		CTBLS	10/01-12/01
	Stamford-Norwalk PMSA, CT	Y	49330 FQ	110470 AW		CTBLS	10/01-12/01
	Waterbury PMSA, CT	Y	28690 FQ	82440 AW		CTBLS	10/01-12/01
	Delaware	Y	27670 FQ	79250 AW		DEBLS	10/01-12/01
	Wilmington-Newark PMSA, DE-MD	Y	27720 FQ	79350 AW		DEBLS	10/01-12/01
	District of Columbia	Y	31870 FQ	80070 AW		DCBLS	10/01-12/01
	Washington PMSA, DC-MD-VA-WV	Y	24310 FQ	57760 AW	122850 TQ	DCBLS	10/01-12/01
	Florida	Y	25790 FQ	68030 AW		FLBLS	10/01-12/01
	Daytona Beach MSA, FL	Y	33860 FQ	103650 AW		FLBLS	10/01-12/01
	Fort Lauderdale PMSA, FL	Y	26540 FQ	80440 AW		FLBLS	10/01-12/01
	Fort Myers-Cape Coral MSA, FL	Y	24100 FQ	72390 AW		FLBLS	10/01-12/01
	Fort Pierce-Port St. Lucie MSA, FL	Y	25740 FQ	68340 AW		FLBLS	10/01-12/01
	Fort Walton Beach MSA, FL	Y	21660 FQ	48360 AW	119850 TQ	FLBLS	10/01-12/01
	Gainesville MSA, FL	Y	24990 FQ	60830 AW	117040 TQ	FLBLS	10/01-12/01
	Jacksonville MSA, FL	Y	31230 FQ	69140 AW	130630 TQ	FLBLS	10/01-12/01
	Lakeland-Winter Haven MSA, FL	Y	33970 FQ	101240 AW		FLBLS	10/01-12/01
	Melbourne-Titusville-Palm Bay MSA, FL	Y	25010 FQ	76270 AW		FLBLS	10/01-12/01
	Miami PMSA, FL	Y	26020 FQ	71900 AW		FLBLS	10/01-12/01
	Naples MSA, FL	Y	25610 FQ	57330 AW	118240 TQ	FLBLS	10/01-12/01
	Ocala MSA, FL	Y	26430 FQ	68830 AW	137790 TQ	FLBLS	10/01-12/01
	Orlando MSA, FL	Y	25580 FQ	59510 AW	113280 TQ	FLBLS	10/01-12/01
	Pensacola MSA, FL	Y	23220 FQ	67890 AW		FLBLS	10/01-12/01
	Sarasota-Bradenton MSA, FL	Y	26120 FQ	60890 AW	141460 TQ	FLBLS	10/01-12/01
	Tallahassee MSA, FL	Y	23550 FQ	67390 AW		FLBLS	10/01-12/01
	Tampa-St. Petersburg-Clearwater MSA, FL	Y	23290 FQ	48980 AW	89020 TQ	FLBLS	10/01-12/01
	West Palm Beach-Boca Raton MSA, FL	Y	28200 FQ	90790 AW		FLBLS	10/01-12/01
	Georgia	Y	27750 FQ	60420 AW	137230 TQ	GABLS	10/01-12/01
	Atlanta MSA, GA	Y	29620 FQ	62300 AW	141940 TQ	GABLS	10/01-12/01
	Augusta-Aiken MSA, GA-SC	Y	27140 FQ	64240 AW	135450 TQ	GABLS	10/01-12/01

AAW	Average annual wage	**AOH**	Average offered, high	**ASH**	Average starting, high	**H**	Hourly	**M**	Monthly	**S**	Special: hourly and annual
AE	Average entry wage	**AOL**	Average offered, low	**ASL**	Average starting, low	**HI**	Highest wage paid	**MTC**	Median total compensation	**TQ**	Third quartile wage
AEX	Average experienced wage	**APH**	Average pay, high range	**AW**	Average wage paid	**HR**	High end range	**MW**	Median wage paid	**W**	Weekly
AO	Average offered	**APL**	Average pay, low range	**FQ**	First quartile wage	**LR**	Low end range	**SQ**	Second quartile wage	**Y**	Yearly

Occupation/Type/Industry	Location	Per	Low	Mid	High	Source	Date
Securities, Commodities, and Financial Services Sales Agent	Columbus MSA, GA-AL	Y	22620 FQ	53580 AW		GABLS	10/01-12/01
	Macon MSA, GA	Y	23860 FQ	47190 AW	115510 TQ	GABLS	10/01-12/01
	Savannah MSA, GA	Y	23330 FQ	39260 AW	100110 TQ	GABLS	10/01-12/01
	Hawaii	Y	24550 FQ	56610 AW		HIBLS	10/01-12/01
	Honolulu MSA, HI	Y	25010 FQ	57110 AW		HIBLS	10/01-12/01
	Idaho	Y	23730 FQ	66740 AW		IDBLS	10/01-12/01
	Boise City MSA, ID	Y	28700 FQ	78190 AW		IDBLS	10/01-12/01
	Illinois	Y	27710 FQ	76640 AW		ILBLS	10/01-12/01
	Champaign-Urbana MSA, IL	Y	25920 FQ	59650 AW		ILBLS	10/01-12/01
	Chicago PMSA, IL	Y	28240 FQ	76980 AW		ILBLS	10/01-12/01
	Peoria-Pekin MSA, IL	Y	25080 FQ	57690 AW		ILBLS	10/01-12/01
	Springfield MSA, IL	Y	35420 FQ	81330 AW	139440 TQ	ILBLS	10/01-12/01
	Indiana	Y	22590 FQ	61320 AW		INBLS	10/01-12/01
	Elkhart-Goshen MSA, IN	Y	25870 FQ	48990 AW	73840 TQ	INBLS	10/01-12/01
	Evansville-Henderson MSA, IN-KY	Y	23260 FQ	67990 AW		INBLS	10/01-12/01
	Fort Wayne MSA, IN	Y	21710 FQ	55090 AW	108760 TQ	INBLS	10/01-12/01
	Gary PMSA, IN	Y	26550 FQ	63220 AW		INBLS	10/01-12/01
	Indianapolis MSA, IN	Y	28330 FQ	60580 AW	114890 TQ	INBLS	10/01-12/01
	Lafayette MSA, IN	Y	21010 FQ	58040 AW	88440 TQ	INBLS	10/01-12/01
	South Bend MSA, IN	Y	22730 FQ	65780 AW		INBLS	10/01-12/01
	Iowa	Y	21890 FQ	57270 AW	118280 TQ	IABLS	10/01-12/01
	Cedar Rapids MSA, IA	Y	20080 FQ	60220 AW	126520 TQ	IABLS	10/01-12/01
	Davenport-Moline-Rock Island MSA, IA-IL	Y	13990 FQ	75840 AW		IABLS	10/01-12/01
	Des Moines MSA, IA	Y	22780 FQ	54090 AW	88950 TQ	IABLS	10/01-12/01
	Kansas	Y	27720 FQ	74080 AW		KSBLS	10/01-12/01
	Topeka MSA, KS	Y	33980 FQ	75800 AW		KSBLS	10/01-12/01
	Wichita MSA, KS	Y	26260 FQ	75170 AW		KSBLS	10/01-12/01
	Kentucky	Y	22600 FQ	56540 AW	119250 TQ	KYBLS	10/01-12/01
	Lexington MSA, KY	Y	20730 FQ	51420 AW	92090 TQ	KYBLS	10/01-12/01
	Louisville MSA, KY-IN	Y	23880 FQ	50950 AW	106160 TQ	KYBLS	10/01-12/01
	Louisiana	Y	27650 FQ	69410 AW		LABLS	10/01-12/01
	Baton Rouge MSA, LA	Y	26480 FQ	77660 AW		LABLS	10/01-12/01
	Lafayette MSA, LA	Y	23770 FQ	65000 AW		LABLS	10/01-12/01
	Lake Charles MSA, LA	Y	37060 FQ	56230 AW	88640 TQ	LABLS	10/01-12/01
	New Orleans MSA, LA	Y	36900 FQ	66430 AW	110560 TQ	LABLS	10/01-12/01
	Shreveport-Bossier City MSA, LA	Y	22720 FQ	65090 AW		LABLS	10/01-12/01
	Maine	Y	27350 FQ	71410 AW		MEBLS	10/01-12/01
	Portland MSA, ME	Y	28560 FQ	73080 AW		MEBLS	10/01-12/01
	Maryland	Y	24090 FQ	46530 AW	89040 TQ	MDBLS	10/01-12/01
	Baltimore PMSA, MD	Y	24720 FQ	46300 AW	87400 TQ	MDBLS	10/01-12/01
	Massachusetts	Y	24530 FQ	67140 AW		MABLS	10/01-12/01
	Boston PMSA, MA-NH	Y	24030 FQ	68180 AW		MABLS	10/01-12/01
	Brockton PMSA, MA	Y	28700 FQ	40730 AW	58020 TQ	MABLS	10/01-12/01
	Lawrence PMSA, MA-NH	Y	29370 FQ	51890 AW	126050 TQ	MABLS	10/01-12/01
	New Bedford PMSA, MA	Y	16010 FQ	40010 AW	73510 TQ	MABLS	10/01-12/01
	Springfield MSA, MA	Y	28410 FQ	43600 AW	74540 TQ	MABLS	10/01-12/01
	Worcester PMSA, MA-CT	Y	30130 FQ	63010 AW	125250 TQ	MABLS	10/01-12/01
	Michigan	Y	24870 FQ	61430 AW		MIBLS	10/01-12/01
	Ann Arbor PMSA, MI	Y	27850 FQ	70960 AW	144890 TQ	MIBLS	10/01-12/01
	Detroit PMSA, MI	Y	26730 FQ	62940 AW		MIBLS	10/01-12/01
	Flint PMSA, MI	Y	29380 FQ	80160 AW		MIBLS	10/01-12/01
	Grand Rapids-Muskegon-Holland MSA, MI	Y	25780 FQ	71950 AW		MIBLS	10/01-12/01
	Kalamazoo-Battle Creek MSA, MI	Y	22210 FQ	55980 AW	121600 TQ	MIBLS	10/01-12/01
	Lansing-East Lansing MSA, MI	Y	25330 FQ	55560 AW	89540 TQ	MIBLS	10/01-12/01
	Saginaw-Bay City-Midland MSA, MI	Y	17410 FQ	44500 AW	81750 TQ	MIBLS	10/01-12/01
	Minnesota	Y	34370 FQ	84030 AW		MNBLS	10/01-12/01
	Duluth-Superior MSA, MN-WI	Y	30160 FQ	82900 AW		MNBLS	10/01-12/01
	Minneapolis-St. Paul MSA, MN-WI	Y	36130 FQ	87630 AW		MNBLS	10/01-12/01
	St. Cloud MSA, MN	Y	29410 FQ	72580 AW		MNBLS	10/01-12/01
	Mississippi	Y	21810 FQ	66550 AW		MSBLS	10/01-12/01
	Biloxi-Gulfport-Pascagoula MSA, MS	Y	11860 FQ	35460 AW	82130 TQ	MSBLS	10/01-12/01
	Jackson MSA, MS	Y	30560 FQ	80600 AW		MSBLS	10/01-12/01
	Missouri	Y	22250 FQ	54980 AW	138580 TQ	MOBLS	10/01-12/01

AAW Average annual wage; **AE** Average entry wage; **AEX** Average experienced wage; **AO** Average offered; **AOH** Average offered, high; **AOL** Average offered, low; **APH** Average pay, high range; **APL** Average pay, low range; **ASH** Average starting, high; **ASL** Average starting, low; **AW** Average wage paid; **FQ** First quartile wage; **H** Hourly; **HI** Highest wage paid; **HR** High end range; **LR** Low end range; **M** Monthly; **MTC** Median total compensation; **MW** Median wage paid; **SQ** Second quartile wage; **S** Special: hourly and annual; **TQ** Third quartile wage; **W** Weekly; **Y** Yearly

Occupation/Type/Industry	Location	Per	Low	Mid	High	Source	Date
Securities, Commodities, and Financial Services Sales Agent	Kansas City MSA, MO-KS	Y	25160 FQ	71130 AW		MOBLS	10/01-12/01
	St. Louis MSA, MO-IL	Y	22950 FQ	52540 AW	130430 TQ	MOBLS	10/01-12/01
	Springfield MSA, MO	Y	14840 FQ	44890 AW	87390 TQ	MOBLS	10/01-12/01
	Montana	Y	25890 FQ	76280 AW		MTBLS	10/01-12/01
	Billings MSA, MT	Y	25340 FQ	69210 AW		MTBLS	10/01-12/01
	Nebraska	Y	23330 FQ	59490 AW		NEBLS	10/01-12/01
	Lincoln MSA, NE	Y	21120 FQ	66760 AW		NEBLS	10/01-12/01
	Omaha MSA, NE-IA	Y	23580 FQ	55360 AW		NEBLS	10/01-12/01
	Nevada	Y	25410 FQ	62940 AW	144520 TQ	NVBLS	10/01-12/01
	Las Vegas MSA, NV-AZ	Y	28960 FQ	61170 AW	116750 TQ	NVBLS	10/01-12/01
	Reno MSA, NV	Y	23180 FQ	65270 AW		NVBLS	10/01-12/01
	New Hampshire	Y	27350 FQ	55160 AW	97790 TQ	NHBLS	10/01-12/01
	Manchester PMSA, NH	Y	24030 FQ	44710 AW	71210 TQ	NHBLS	10/01-12/01
	Portsmouth-Rochester PMSA, NH-ME	Y	22460 FQ	48560 AW	103170 TQ	NHBLS	10/01-12/01
	New Jersey	Y	31680 FQ	70180 AW		NJBLS	10/01-12/01
	Atlantic-Cape May PMSA, NJ	Y	31920 FQ	83300 AW		NJBLS	10/01-12/01
	Bergen-Passaic PMSA, NJ	Y	29880 FQ	69770 AW	120360 TQ	NJBLS	10/01-12/01
	Jersey City PMSA, NJ	Y	33650 FQ	67930 AW		NJBLS	10/01-12/01
	Middlesex-Somerset-Hunterdon PMSA, NJ	Y	37000 FQ	66970 AW	105360 TQ	NJBLS	10/01-12/01
	Monmouth-Ocean PMSA, NJ	Y	23920 FQ	82500 AW		NJBLS	10/01-12/01
	Newark PMSA, NJ	Y	33700 FQ	77620 AW		NJBLS	10/01-12/01
	Trenton PMSA, NJ	Y	28800 FQ	69820 AW		NJBLS	10/01-12/01
	New Mexico	Y	25440 FQ	52530 AW	111900 TQ	NMBLS	10/01-12/01
	Albuquerque MSA, NM	Y	25260 FQ	50820 AW	106250 TQ	NMBLS	10/01-12/01
	New York	Y	35340 FQ	103730 AW		NYBLS	10/01-12/01
	Albany-Schenectady-Troy MSA, NY	Y	31150 FQ	51860 AW	95910 TQ	NYBLS	10/01-12/01
	Binghamton MSA, NY	Y	34480 FQ	98290 AW		NYBLS	10/01-12/01
	Buffalo-Niagara Falls MSA, NY	Y	21140 FQ	71420 AW		NYBLS	10/01-12/01
	Dutchess County PMSA, NY	Y	30230 FQ	82850 AW		NYBLS	10/01-12/01
	Nassau-Suffolk PMSA, NY	Y	25500 FQ	76770 AW		NYBLS	10/01-12/01
	New York PMSA, NY	Y	42030 FQ	107540 AW		NYBLS	10/01-12/01
	Newburgh PMSA, NY-PA	Y	18210 FQ	61950 AW		NYBLS	10/01-12/01
	Rochester MSA, NY	Y	23660 FQ	79240 AW		NYBLS	10/01-12/01
	Syracuse MSA, NY	Y	31440 FQ	80220 AW		NYBLS	10/01-12/01
	Utica-Rome MSA, NY	Y	17740 FQ	77340 AW		NYBLS	10/01-12/01
	North Carolina	Y	24730 FQ	73640 AW		NCBLS	10/01-12/01
	Asheville MSA, NC	Y	22430 FQ	64710 AW		NCBLS	10/01-12/01
	Charlotte-Gastonia-Rock Hill MSA, NC-SC	Y	27600 FQ	81830 AW		NCBLS	10/01-12/01
	Fayetteville MSA, NC	Y	26160 FQ	65750 AW		NCBLS	10/01-12/01
	Greensboro-Winston-Salem-High Point MSA, NC	Y	26460 FQ	74450 AW		NCBLS	10/01-12/01
	Hickory-Morganton-Lenoir MSA, NC	Y	25390 FQ	88640 AW		NCBLS	10/01-12/01
	Raleigh-Durham-Chapel Hill MSA, NC	Y	21100 FQ	72270 AW		NCBLS	10/01-12/01
	Wilmington MSA, NC	Y	23160 FQ	67190 AW		NCBLS	10/01-12/01
	North Dakota	Y	24260 FQ	66410 AW		NDBLS	10/01-12/01
	Fargo-Moorhead MSA, ND-MN	Y	24720 FQ	66160 AW		NDBLS	10/01-12/01
	Ohio	Y	22080 FQ	62970 AW		OHBLS	10/01-12/01
	Akron PMSA, OH	Y	19890 FQ	39930 AW	70060 TQ	OHBLS	10/01-12/01
	Canton-Massillon MSA, OH	Y	30080 FQ	68290 AW		OHBLS	10/01-12/01
	Cincinnati PMSA, OH-KY-IN	Y	31010 FQ	67480 AW		OHBLS	10/01-12/01
	Cleveland-Lorain-Elyria PMSA, OH	Y	20690 FQ	65380 AW		OHBLS	10/01-12/01
	Columbus MSA, OH	Y	23070 FQ	59140 AW		OHBLS	10/01-12/01
	Dayton-Springfield MSA, OH	Y	24500 FQ	62460 AW		OHBLS	10/01-12/01
	Hamilton-Middletown PMSA, OH	Y	22400 FQ	58580 AW	107280 TQ	OHBLS	10/01-12/01
	Toledo MSA, OH	Y	26500 FQ	82250 AW		OHBLS	10/01-12/01
	Youngstown-Warren MSA, OH	Y	23860 FQ	60430 AW		OHBLS	10/01-12/01
	Oklahoma	Y	23970 FQ	64760 AW		OKBLS	10/01-12/01
	Oklahoma City MSA, OK	Y	21990 FQ	70230 AW		OKBLS	10/01-12/01
	Tulsa MSA, OK	Y	25350 FQ	57790 AW	113530 TQ	OKBLS	10/01-12/01
	Oregon	Y	23520 FQ	58760 AW		ORBLS	10/01-12/01
	Eugene-Springfield MSA, OR	Y	31820 FQ	79120 AW		ORBLS	10/01-12/01

AAW	Average annual wage	**AOH**	Average offered, high	**ASH**	Average starting, high	**H**	Hourly	**M**	Monthly	**S**	Special: hourly and annual
AE	Average entry wage	**AOL**	Average offered, low	**ASL**	Average starting, low	**HI**	Highest wage paid	**MTC**	Median total compensation	**TQ**	Third quartile wage
AEX	Average experienced wage	**APH**	Average pay, high range	**AW**	Average wage paid	**HR**	High end range	**MW**	Median wage paid	**W**	Weekly
AO	Average offered	**APL**	Average pay, low range	**FQ**	First quartile wage	**LR**	Low end range	**SQ**	Second quartile wage	**Y**	Yearly

Occupation/Type/Industry	Location	Per	Low	Mid	High	Source	Date
Securities, Commodities, and Financial Services Sales Agent	Medford-Ashland MSA, OR	Y	21960 FQ	45430 AW	67810 TQ	ORBLS	10/01-12/01
	Portland-Vancouver PMSA, OR-WA	Y	23780 FQ	55490 AW	125540 TQ	ORBLS	10/01-12/01
	Salem PMSA, OR	Y	23710 FQ	70040 AW		ORBLS	10/01-12/01
	Pennsylvania	Y	22240 FQ	50850 AW	117680 TQ	PABLS	10/01-12/01
	Allentown-Bethlehem-Easton MSA, PA	Y	22590 FQ	55890 AW		PABLS	10/01-12/01
	Erie MSA, PA	Y	21790 FQ	46820 AW	100960 TQ	PABLS	10/01-12/01
	Harrisburg-Lebanon-Carlisle MSA, PA	Y	17940 FQ	52100 AW		PABLS	10/01-12/01
	Johnstown MSA, PA	Y	22550 FQ	50260 AW	97730 TQ	PABLS	10/01-12/01
	Lancaster MSA, PA	Y	19600 FQ	44700 AW	92750 TQ	PABLS	10/01-12/01
	Philadelphia PMSA, PA-NJ	Y	23380 FQ	51270 AW	115870 TQ	PABLS	10/01-12/01
	Pittsburgh MSA, PA	Y	29970 FQ	56150 AW	123450 TQ	PABLS	10/01-12/01
	Reading MSA, PA	Y	20440 FQ	49420 AW	132180 TQ	PABLS	10/01-12/01
	Scranton-Wilkes-Barre-Hazleton MSA, PA	Y	12550 FQ	41590 AW		PABLS	10/01-12/01
	York MSA, PA	Y	22700 FQ	38830 AW	66200 TQ	PABLS	10/01-12/01
	Rhode Island	Y	23830 FQ	61950 AW		RIBLS	10/01-12/01
	Providence-Fall River-Warwick MSA, RI-MA	Y	23890 FQ	61850 AW		RIBLS	10/01-12/01
	South Carolina	Y	25190 FQ	52930 AW	106800 TQ	SCBLS	10/01-12/01
	Charleston-North Charleston MSA, SC	Y	21450 FQ	56120 AW	133950 TQ	SCBLS	10/01-12/01
	Columbia MSA, SC	Y	32620 FQ	50040 AW	80770 TQ	SCBLS	10/01-12/01
	Greenville-Spartanburg-Anderson MSA, SC	Y	23440 FQ	60030 AW		SCBLS	10/01-12/01
	Myrtle Beach MSA, SC	Y	25320 FQ	35610 AW	53360 TQ	SCBLS	10/01-12/01
	South Dakota	Y	50380 FQ	90390 AW		SDBLS	10/01-12/01
	Sioux Falls MSA, SD	Y	49570 FQ	86160 AW		SDBLS	10/01-12/01
	Tennessee	Y	22690 FQ	77500 AW		TNBLS	10/01-12/01
	Chattanooga MSA, TN-GA	Y	21260 FQ	82570 AW		TNBLS	10/01-12/01
	Johnson City-Kingsport-Bristol MSA, TN-VA	Y	29170 FQ	83430 AW		TNBLS	10/01-12/01
	Knoxville MSA, TN	Y	46070 FQ	106420 AW		TNBLS	10/01-12/01
	Memphis MSA, TN-AR-MS	Y	28320 FQ	80070 AW		TNBLS	10/01-12/01
	Nashville MSA, TN	Y	19260 FQ	70340 AW		TNBLS	10/01-12/01
	Texas	Y	20440 FQ	57460 AW	141240 TQ	TXBLS	10/01-12/01
	Amarillo MSA, TX	Y	22040 FQ	72030 AW		TXBLS	10/01-12/01
	Austin-San Marcos MSA, TX	Y	27800 FQ	74550 AW		TXBLS	10/01-12/01
	Beaumont-Port Arthur MSA, TX	Y	19760 FQ	61370 AW		TXBLS	10/01-12/01
	Brazoria PMSA, TX	Y	24180 FQ	78260 AW		TXBLS	10/01-12/01
	Brownsville-Harlingen-San Benito MSA, TX	Y	29960 FQ	51850 AW	88650 TQ	TXBLS	10/01-12/01
	Corpus Christi MSA, TX	Y	16960 FQ	64360 AW		TXBLS	10/01-12/01
	Dallas PMSA, TX	Y	22230 FQ	44660 AW	85170 TQ	TXBLS	10/01-12/01
	El Paso MSA, TX	Y	30340 FQ	76640 AW		TXBLS	10/01-12/01
	Fort Worth-Arlington PMSA, TX	Y	19440 FQ	43080 AW	101450 TQ	TXBLS	10/01-12/01
	Galveston-Texas City PMSA, TX	Y	29270 FQ	77800 AW		TXBLS	10/01-12/01
	Houston PMSA, TX	Y	21020 FQ	70290 AW		TXBLS	10/01-12/01
	Killeen-Temple MSA, TX	Y	18830 FQ	84370 AW		TXBLS	10/01-12/01
	Longview-Marshall MSA, TX	Y	20470 FQ	74970 AW		TXBLS	10/01-12/01
	Lubbock MSA, TX	Y	25260 FQ	63910 AW	137480 TQ	TXBLS	10/01-12/01
	McAllen-Edinburg-Mission MSA, TX	Y	14390 FQ	50870 AW	96370 TQ	TXBLS	10/01-12/01
	Odessa-Midland MSA, TX	Y	17460 FQ	49600 AW	89410 TQ	TXBLS	10/01-12/01
	San Antonio MSA, TX	Y	13420 FQ	43620 AW	96570 TQ	TXBLS	10/01-12/01
	Tyler MSA, TX	Y	30760 FQ	67620 AW		TXBLS	10/01-12/01
	Waco MSA, TX	Y	28770 FQ	74270 AW		TXBLS	10/01-12/01
	Utah	Y	28860 FQ	62070 AW		UTBLS	10/01-12/01
	Provo-Orem MSA, UT	Y	25600 FQ	43210 AW	47450 TQ	UTBLS	10/01-12/01
	Salt Lake City-Ogden MSA, UT	Y	29000 FQ	65690 AW		UTBLS	10/01-12/01
	Vermont	Y	23060 FQ	54310 AW	120250 TQ	VTBLS	10/01-12/01
	Burlington MSA, VT	Y	26500 FQ	52030 AW	109820 TQ	VTBLS	10/01-12/01
	Virginia	Y	25580 FQ	71200 AW		VABLS	10/01-12/01
	Lynchburg MSA, VA	Y	25400 FQ	74300 AW		VABLS	10/01-12/01

AAW	Average annual wage	AOH	Average offered, high	ASH	Average starting, high	H	Hourly	M	Monthly	S	Special: hourly and annual
AE	Average entry wage	AOL	Average offered, low	ASL	Average starting, low	HI	Highest wage paid	MTC	Median total compensation	TQ	Third quartile wage
AEX	Average experienced wage	APH	Average pay, high range	AW	Average wage paid	HR	High end range	MW	Median wage paid	W	Weekly
AO	Average offered	APL	Average pay, low range	FQ	First quartile wage	LR	Low end range	SQ	Second quartile wage	Y	Yearly

Occupation/Type/Industry	Location	Per	Low	Mid	High	Source	Date
Securities, Commodities, and Financial Services Sales Agent	Norfolk-Virginia Beach-Newport News MSA, VA-NC	Y	23140 FQ	68360 AW		VABLS	10/01-12/01
	Richmond-Petersburg MSA, VA	Y	26580 FQ	78670 AW		VABLS	10/01-12/01
	Roanoke MSA, VA	Y	26670 FQ	68450 AW		VABLS	10/01-12/01
	Washington	Y	30490 FQ	72000 AW		WABLS	10/01-12/01
	Olympia PMSA, WA	Y	20260 FQ	57830 AW	138010 TQ	WABLS	10/01-12/01
	Richland-Kennewick-Pasco MSA, WA	Y	30590 FQ	65750 AW	109070 TQ	WABLS	10/01-12/01
	Seattle-Bellevue-Everett PMSA, WA	Y	31240 FQ	70810 AW		WABLS	10/01-12/01
	Spokane MSA, WA	Y	32470 FQ	72550 AW		WABLS	10/01-12/01
	Tacoma PMSA, WA	Y	28200 FQ	86120 AW		WABLS	10/01-12/01
	Yakima MSA, WA	Y	41060 FQ	84160 AW		WABLS	10/01-12/01
	West Virginia	Y	19230 FQ	53580 AW	134570 TQ	WVBLS	10/01-12/01
	Charleston MSA, WV	Y	17650 FQ	52670 AW	136520 TQ	WVBLS	10/01-12/01
	Huntington-Ashland MSA, WV-KY-OH	Y	21500 FQ	62010 AW		WVBLS	10/01-12/01
	Wisconsin	Y	25870 FQ	72120 AW	138980 TQ	WIBLS	10/01-12/01
	Appleton-Oshkosh-Neenah MSA, WI	Y	35210 FQ	84670 AW	144830 TQ	WIBLS	10/01-12/01
	Green Bay MSA, WI	Y	26260 FQ	55750 AW	101050 TQ	WIBLS	10/01-12/01
	Madison MSA, WI	Y	28260 FQ	67090 AW	140430 TQ	WIBLS	10/01-12/01
	Milwaukee-Waukesha PMSA, WI	Y	24980 FQ	76220 AW	138740 TQ	WIBLS	10/01-12/01
	Wyoming	Y	24070 FQ	73970 AW		WYBLS	10/01-12/01
	Puerto Rico	Y	15340 FQ	36050 AW	72030 TQ	PRBLS	10/01-12/01
Mortgage Bankers and Brokers	United States	Y		69550 MW		OOH5	1999-2000
Personal Credit Institutions	United States	Y		37690 MW		OOH5	1999-2000
Securities and Commodities Services	United States	Y		71260 MW		OOH5	1999-2000
Securities Brokers and Dealers	United States	Y		69550 MW		OOH5	1999-2000
Security Administrator	United States	Y		60500-84250 AW		WW	1/00-1/01
Security and Fire Alarm Systems Installer	Alabama	H	8.97 FQ	13.82 AW	20.86 TQ	ALBLS	10/01-12/01
	Alaska	H	6.49 FQ	15.16 AW	24.16 TQ	AKBLS	10/01-12/01
	Arizona	H	10.98 FQ	13.75 AW	16.89 TQ	AZBLS	10/01-12/01
	Arkansas	H	6.06 FQ	11.77 AW	17.24 TQ	ARBLS	10/01-12/01
	California	H	8.74 FQ	15.44 AW	23.81 TQ	CABLS	10/01-12/01
	Colorado	H	9.91 FQ	16.62 AW	22.57 TQ	COBLS	10/01-12/01
	Connecticut	H	13.31 FQ	18.74 AW	25.34 TQ	CTBLS	10/01-12/01
	Delaware	H	11.16 FQ	19.28 AW	27.05 TQ	DEBLS	10/01-12/01
	District of Columbia	H	10.40 FQ	16.14 AW	22.09 TQ	DCBLS	10/01-12/01
	Florida	H	9.38 FQ	14.76 AW	20.83 TQ	FLBLS	10/01-12/01
	Georgia	H	9.12 FQ	15.05 AW	21.14 TQ	GABLS	10/01-12/01
	Hawaii	H	12.15 FQ	16.58 AW	24.03 TQ	HIBLS	10/01-12/01
	Illinois	H	12.43 FQ	28.54 AW	43.44 TQ	ILBLS	10/01-12/01
	Indiana	H	8.39 FQ	15.48 AW	21.86 TQ	INBLS	10/01-12/01
	Iowa	H	9.73 FQ	15.75 AW	23.76 TQ	IABLS	10/01-12/01
	Kansas	H	8.87 FQ	12.10 AW	17.36 TQ	KSBLS	10/01-12/01
	Kentucky	H	9.29 FQ	13.58 AW	20.72 TQ	KYBLS	10/01-12/01
	Louisiana	H	9.63 FQ	13.81 AW	18.89 TQ	LABLS	10/01-12/01
	Maine	H	11.51 FQ	15.60 AW	18.27 TQ	MEBLS	10/01-12/01
	Maryland	H	12.39 FQ	18.58 AW	24.66 TQ	MDBLS	10/01-12/01
	Massachusetts	H	10.45 FQ	17.78 AW	27.70 TQ	MABLS	10/01-12/01
	Michigan	H	10.16 FQ	18.38 AW	25.95 TQ	MIBLS	10/01-12/01
	Minnesota	H	11.18 FQ	19.73 AW	28.94 TQ	MNBLS	10/01-12/01
	Mississippi	H	8.14 FQ	12.48 AW	18.89 TQ	MSBLS	10/01-12/01
	Missouri	H	9.92 FQ	13.54 AW	18.28 TQ	MOBLS	10/01-12/01
	Montana	H	10.24 FQ	16.78 AW	24.18 TQ	MTBLS	10/01-12/01
	Nevada	H	11.70 FQ	16.95 AW	24.04 TQ	NVBLS	10/01-12/01
	New Hampshire	H	11.49 FQ	15.70 AW	21.20 TQ	NHBLS	10/01-12/01
	New Jersey	H	11.81 FQ	17.60 AW	25.20 TQ	NJBLS	10/01-12/01
	New Mexico	H	9.82 FQ	13.17 AW	16.57 TQ	NMBLS	10/01-12/01
	New York	H	11.48 FQ	18.08 AW	25.96 TQ	NYBLS	10/01-12/01
	North Carolina	H	11.19 FQ	15.10 AW	20.12 TQ	NCBLS	10/01-12/01
	North Dakota	H	11.96 FQ	15.79 AW	20.53 TQ	NDBLS	10/01-12/01
	Ohio	H	9.55 FQ	15.07 AW	22.64 TQ	OHBLS	10/01-12/01

AAW	Average annual wage	**AOH**	Average offered, high	**ASH**	Average starting, high	**H**	Hourly	**M**	Monthly	**S**	Special: hourly and annual
AE	Average entry wage	**AOL**	Average offered, low	**ASL**	Average starting, low	**HI**	Highest wage paid	**MTC**	Median total compensation	**TQ**	Third quartile wage
AEX	Average experienced wage	**APH**	Average pay, high range	**AW**	Average wage paid	**HR**	High end range	**MW**	Median wage paid	**W**	Weekly
AO	Average offered	**APL**	Average pay, low range	**FQ**	First quartile wage	**LR**	Low end range	**SQ**	Second quartile wage	**Y**	Yearly

Occupation/Type/Industry	Location	Per	Low	Mid	High	Source	Date
Security and Fire Alarm Systems							
Installer	Oklahoma	H	6.46 FQ	11.79 AW	19.57 TQ	OKBLS	10/01-12/01
	Oregon	H	11.01 FQ	17.15 AW	24.01 TQ	ORBLS	10/01-12/01
	Pennsylvania	H	7.75 FQ	13.98 AW	21.47 TQ	PABLS	10/01-12/01
	Rhode Island	H	7.60 FQ	13.59 AW	21.00 TQ	RIBLS	10/01-12/01
	South Carolina	H	8.91 FQ	15.66 AW	24.82 TQ	SCBLS	10/01-12/01
	Tennessee	H	8.06 FQ	11.23 AW	15.98 TQ	TNBLS	10/01-12/01
	Texas	H	7.61 FQ	12.47 AW	18.30 TQ	TXBLS	10/01-12/01
	Utah	H	12.39 FQ	19.43 AW	30.38 TQ	UTBLS	10/01-12/01
	Vermont	H	11.41 FQ	16.37 AW	22.24 TQ	VTBLS	10/01-12/01
	Virginia	H	10.61 FQ	15.01 AW	20.95 TQ	VABLS	10/01-12/01
	Washington	H	11.73 FQ	17.79 AW	25.34 TQ	WABLS	10/01-12/01
	West Virginia	H	11.61 FQ	16.11 AW	21.72 TQ	WVBLS	10/01-12/01
	Wisconsin	H	8.73 FQ	16.28 AW	26.14 TQ	WIBLS	10/01-12/01
	Puerto Rico	H	6.17 FQ	9.38 AW	15.82 TQ	PRBLS	10/01-12/01
Security Director							
All locations - national and international	United States	Y		90539 AW		SAFEDIR1	1/01-1/02
All locations in a region	United States	Y		68522 AW		SAFEDIR1	1/02-1/02
All locations in the United States	United States	Y		87258 AW		SAFEDIR1	1/02-1/02
One location and building	United States	Y		54300 AW		SAFEDIR1	1/01-1/02
One location and several buildings	United States	Y		55907 AW		SAFEDIR1	1/01-1/02
Several locations	United States	Y		57437 AW		SAFEDIR1	1/01-1/02
Security Guard	United States	Y		17570 MW		OOH12	1999-2000
	Alabama	Y	12050 FQ	17650 AW	26220 TQ	ALBLS	10/01-12/01
	Birmingham MSA, AL	Y	12410 FQ	17570 AW	23020 TQ	ALBLS	10/01-12/01
	Huntsville MSA, AL	Y	13060 FQ	22040 AW	37930 TQ	ALBLS	10/01-12/01
	Mobile MSA, AL	Y	11510 FQ	14720 AW	20460 TQ	ALBLS	10/01-12/01
	Montgomery MSA, AL	Y	12420 FQ	19030 AW	32150 TQ	ALBLS	10/01-12/01
	Alaska	Y	18040 FQ	27540 AW	42700 TQ	AKBLS	10/01-12/01
	Anchorage MSA, AK	Y	17240 FQ	26530 AW	41940 TQ	AKBLS	10/01-12/01
	Arizona	Y	13230 FQ	20180 AW	29950 TQ	AZBLS	10/01-12/01
	Phoenix-Mesa MSA, AZ	Y	13950 FQ	20500 AW	30240 TQ	AZBLS	10/01-12/01
	Tucson MSA, AZ	Y	12360 FQ	19810 AW	31650 TQ	AZBLS	10/01-12/01
	Arkansas	Y	12280 FQ	18840 AW	28910 TQ	ARBLS	10/01-12/01
	Fayetteville-Springdale-Rogers MSA, AR	Y	12950 FQ	21310 AW	32840 TQ	ARBLS	10/01-12/01
	Fort Smith MSA, AR-OK	Y	12230 FQ	17640 AW	25390 TQ	ARBLS	10/01-12/01
	Little Rock-North Little Rock MSA, AR	Y	12150 FQ	17770 AW	26090 TQ	ARBLS	10/01-12/01
	California	Y	14550 FQ	20290 AW	28390 TQ	CABLS	10/01-12/01
	Bakersfield MSA, CA	Y	13610 FQ	21910 AW	40110 TQ	CABLS	10/01-12/01
	Chico-Paradise MSA, CA	Y	13440 FQ	18920 AW	27720 TQ	CABLS	10/01-12/01
	Fresno MSA, CA	Y	13440 FQ	17430 AW	25180 TQ	CABLS	10/01-12/01
	Los Angeles-Long Beach PMSA, CA	Y	14670 FQ	19260 AW	27190 TQ	CABLS	10/01-12/01
	Merced MSA, CA	Y	14300 FQ	19910 AW	27260 TQ	CABLS	10/01-12/01
	Modesto MSA, CA	Y	13630 FQ	17480 AW	25240 TQ	CABLS	10/01-12/01
	Oakland PMSA, CA	Y	17160 FQ	22740 AW	31010 TQ	CABLS	10/01-12/01
	Orange County PMSA, CA	Y	14730 FQ	20400 AW	27990 TQ	CABLS	10/01-12/01
	Redding MSA, CA	Y	14180 FQ	20710 AW	28730 TQ	CABLS	10/01-12/01
	Riverside-San Bernardino PMSA, CA	Y	13530 FQ	18580 AW	26910 TQ	CABLS	10/01-12/01
	Sacramento PMSA, CA	Y	15580 FQ	19380 AW	23200 TQ	CABLS	10/01-12/01
	Salinas MSA, CA	Y	14450 FQ	18580 AW	25320 TQ	CABLS	10/01-12/01
	San Diego MSA, CA	Y	14180 FQ	18980 AW	25070 TQ	CABLS	10/01-12/01
	San Francisco PMSA, CA	Y	16350 FQ	24080 AW	31560 TQ	CABLS	10/01-12/01
	San Jose PMSA, CA	Y	14810 FQ	24280 AW	33670 TQ	CABLS	10/01-12/01
	San Luis Obispo-Atascadero-Paso Robles MSA, CA	Y	13680 FQ	28880 AW	47030 TQ	CABLS	10/01-12/01
	Santa Barbara-Santa Maria-Lompoc MSA, CA	Y	13830 FQ	19700 AW	26280 TQ	CABLS	10/01-12/01
	Santa Cruz-Watsonville PMSA, CA	Y	14760 FQ	20540 AW	28640 TQ	CABLS	10/01-12/01
	Santa Rosa PMSA, CA	Y	15850 FQ	22140 AW	29810 TQ	CABLS	10/01-12/01
	Stockton-Lodi MSA, CA	Y	13830 FQ	19460 AW	31530 TQ	CABLS	10/01-12/01
	Vallejo-Fairfield-Napa PMSA, CA	Y	17000 FQ	26190 AW	38260 TQ	CABLS	10/01-12/01
	Ventura PMSA, CA	Y	14120 FQ	19200 AW	28240 TQ	CABLS	10/01-12/01
	Visalia-Tulare-Porterville MSA, CA	Y	13590 FQ	20010 AW	28710 TQ	CABLS	10/01-12/01

AAW	Average annual wage	AOH	Average offered, high	ASH	Average starting, high	H	Hourly	M	Monthly	S	Special: hourly and annual
AE	Average entry wage	AOL	Average offered, low	ASL	Average starting, low	HI	Highest wage paid	MTC	Median total compensation	TQ	Third quartile wage
AEX	Average experienced wage	APH	Average pay, high range	AW	Average wage paid	HR	High end range	MW	Median wage paid	W	Weekly
AO	Average offered	APL	Average pay, low range	FQ	First quartile wage	LR	Low end range	SQ	Second quartile wage	Y	Yearly

Occupation/Type/Industry	Location	Per	Low	Mid	High	Source	Date
Security Guard	Colorado	Y	16860 FQ	23950 AW	38210 TQ	COBLS	10/01-12/01
	Boulder-Longmont PMSA, CO	Y	14980 FQ	23470 AW	30450 TQ	COBLS	10/01-12/01
	Colorado Springs MSA, CO	Y	14410 FQ	19160 AW	25530 TQ	COBLS	10/01-12/01
	Denver PMSA, CO	Y	18600 FQ	25050 AW	40730 TQ	COBLS	10/01-12/01
	Fort Collins-Loveland MSA, CO	Y	16810 FQ	22630 AW	30740 TQ	COBLS	10/01-12/01
	Greeley PMSA, CO	Y	15830 FQ	22720 AW	29740 TQ	COBLS	10/01-12/01
	Connecticut	Y	15390 FQ	21680 AW	30570 TQ	CTBLS	10/01-12/01
	Bridgeport PMSA, CT	Y	15630 FQ	22260 AW	30500 TQ	CTBLS	10/01-12/01
	Danbury PMSA, CT	Y	15890 FQ	24270 AW	34960 TQ	CTBLS	10/01-12/01
	Hartford MSA, CT	Y	15610 FQ	21680 AW	30910 TQ	CTBLS	10/01-12/01
	New Haven-Meriden PMSA, CT	Y	14230 FQ	20160 AW	29680 TQ	CTBLS	10/01-12/01
	Stamford-Norwalk PMSA, CT	Y	15640 FQ	21570 AW	29440 TQ	CTBLS	10/01-12/01
	Waterbury PMSA, CT	Y	17870 FQ	24660 AW	30270 TQ	CTBLS	10/01-12/01
	Delaware	Y	14940 FQ	21240 AW	31010 TQ	DEBLS	10/01-12/01
	Wilmington-Newark PMSA, DE-MD	Y	14870 FQ	21200 AW	31130 TQ	DEBLS	10/01-12/01
	District of Columbia	Y	15670 FQ	23730 AW	32840 TQ	DCBLS	10/01-12/01
	Washington PMSA, DC-MD-VA-WV	Y	14540 FQ	24130 AW	35300 TQ	DCBLS	10/01-12/01
	Florida	Y	12720 FQ	18380 AW	25730 TQ	FLBLS	10/01-12/01
	Daytona Beach MSA, FL	Y	12080 FQ	16170 AW	21270 TQ	FLBLS	10/01-12/01
	Fort Lauderdale PMSA, FL	Y	12830 FQ	18490 AW	26180 TQ	FLBLS	10/01-12/01
	Fort Myers-Cape Coral MSA, FL	Y	12180 FQ	16340 AW	21570 TQ	FLBLS	10/01-12/01
	Fort Pierce-Port St. Lucie MSA, FL	Y	12340 FQ	19730 AW	31340 TQ	FLBLS	10/01-12/01
	Fort Walton Beach MSA, FL	Y	12000 FQ	16040 AW	20760 TQ	FLBLS	10/01-12/01
	Gainesville MSA, FL	Y	12370 FQ	18080 AW	28380 TQ	FLBLS	10/01-12/01
	Jacksonville MSA, FL	Y	13780 FQ	18350 AW	23110 TQ	FLBLS	10/01-12/01
	Lakeland-Winter Haven MSA, FL	Y	12500 FQ	19990 AW	34050 TQ	FLBLS	10/01-12/01
	Melbourne-Titusville-Palm Bay MSA, FL	Y	14130 FQ	24370 AW	35500 TQ	FLBLS	10/01-12/01
	Miami PMSA, FL	Y	12330 FQ	17000 AW	22670 TQ	FLBLS	10/01-12/01
	Naples MSA, FL	Y	15520 FQ	20860 AW	26260 TQ	FLBLS	10/01-12/01
	Ocala MSA, FL	Y	11980 FQ	16930 AW	22120 TQ	FLBLS	10/01-12/01
	Orlando MSA, FL	Y	14120 FQ	18980 AW	25700 TQ	FLBLS	10/01-12/01
	Pensacola MSA, FL	Y	12730 FQ	18780 AW	30940 TQ	FLBLS	10/01-12/01
	Sarasota-Bradenton MSA, FL	Y	13200 FQ	19010 AW	25480 TQ	FLBLS	10/01-12/01
	Tallahassee MSA, FL	Y	11720 FQ	20410 AW	36700 TQ	FLBLS	10/01-12/01
	Tampa-St. Petersburg-Clearwater MSA, FL	Y	12390 FQ	17070 AW	22350 TQ	FLBLS	10/01-12/01
	West Palm Beach-Boca Raton MSA, FL	Y	14620 FQ	20480 AW	27200 TQ	FLBLS	10/01-12/01
	Georgia	Y	12500 FQ	18910 AW	27820 TQ	GABLS	10/01-12/01
	Atlanta MSA, GA	Y	12780 FQ	19200 AW	27730 TQ	GABLS	10/01-12/01
	Augusta-Aiken MSA, GA-SC	Y	12250 FQ	23450 AW	40710 TQ	GABLS	10/01-12/01
	Columbus MSA, GA-AL	Y	12360 FQ	18100 AW	23900 TQ	GABLS	10/01-12/01
	Macon MSA, GA	Y	12140 FQ	17560 AW	30080 TQ	GABLS	10/01-12/01
	Savannah MSA, GA	Y	12070 FQ	18750 AW	31680 TQ	GABLS	10/01-12/01
	Hawaii	Y	14050 FQ	20750 AW	30610 TQ	HIBLS	10/01-12/01
	Honolulu MSA, HI	Y	13980 FQ	20350 AW	30360 TQ	HIBLS	10/01-12/01
	Idaho	Y	13770 FQ	19550 AW	29270 TQ	IDBLS	10/01-12/01
	Boise City MSA, ID	Y	15230 FQ	19540 AW	26390 TQ	IDBLS	10/01-12/01
	Illinois	Y	14690 FQ	21400 AW	30360 TQ	ILBLS	10/01-12/01
	Chicago PMSA, IL	Y	15040 FQ	21470 AW	29830 TQ	ILBLS	10/01-12/01
	Peoria-Pekin MSA, IL	Y	14900 FQ	26570 AW	48330 TQ	ILBLS	10/01-12/01
	Rockford MSA, IL	Y	13570 FQ	23680 AW	48750 TQ	ILBLS	10/01-12/01
	Springfield MSA, IL	Y	12560 FQ	20270 AW	33140 TQ	ILBLS	10/01-12/01
	Indiana	Y	13040 FQ	20070 AW	30730 TQ	INBLS	10/01-12/01
	Elkhart-Goshen MSA, IN	Y	14600 FQ	19050 AW	25080 TQ	INBLS	10/01-12/01
	Evansville-Henderson MSA, IN-KY	Y	12390 FQ	19080 AW	32600 TQ	INBLS	10/01-12/01
	Fort Wayne MSA, IN	Y	13200 FQ	21270 AW	35240 TQ	INBLS	10/01-12/01
	Gary PMSA, IN	Y	11630 FQ	16860 AW	25340 TQ	INBLS	10/01-12/01
	Indianapolis MSA, IN	Y	15110 FQ	20440 AW	28980 TQ	INBLS	10/01-12/01
	Lafayette MSA, IN	Y	14490 FQ	28640 AW	51770 TQ	INBLS	10/01-12/01
	South Bend MSA, IN	Y	12370 FQ	23800 AW	42740 TQ	INBLS	10/01-12/01
	Iowa	Y	12720 FQ	19440 AW	28640 TQ	IABLS	10/01-12/01

AAW	Average annual wage	**AOH**	Average offered, high	**ASH**	Average starting, high	**H**	Hourly	**M**	Monthly	**S**	Special: hourly and annual
AE	Average entry wage	**AOL**	Average offered, low	**ASL**	Average starting, low	**HI**	Highest wage paid	**MTC**	Median total compensation	**TQ**	Third quartile wage
AEX	Average experienced wage	**APH**	Average pay, high range	**AW**	Average wage paid	**HR**	High end range	**MW**	Median wage paid	**W**	Weekly
AO	Average offered	**APL**	Average pay, low range	**FQ**	First quartile wage	**LR**	Low end range	**SQ**	Second quartile wage	**Y**	Yearly

Occupation/Type/Industry	Location	Per	Low	Mid	High	Source	Date
Security Guard	Davenport-Moline-Rock Island MSA, IA-IL	Y	11850 FQ	19130 AW	32710 TQ	IABLS	10/01-12/01
	Des Moines MSA, IA	Y	14480 FQ	20160 AW	28020 TQ	IABLS	10/01-12/01
	Kansas	Y	13000 FQ	20760 AW	33450 TQ	KSBLS	10/01-12/01
	Topeka MSA, KS	Y	13600 FQ	22560 AW	33830 TQ	KSBLS	10/01-12/01
	Wichita MSA, KS	Y	13080 FQ	22580 AW	38310 TQ	KSBLS	10/01-12/01
	Kentucky	Y	12280 FQ	18160 AW	26170 TQ	KYBLS	10/01-12/01
	Lexington MSA, KY	Y	13700 FQ	20180 AW	29190 TQ	KYBLS	10/01-12/01
	Louisville MSA, KY-IN	Y	13310 FQ	20080 AW	33000 TQ	KYBLS	10/01-12/01
	Louisiana	Y	11820 FQ	16800 AW	24310 TQ	LABLS	10/01-12/01
	Baton Rouge MSA, LA	Y	11780 FQ	17340 AW	29970 TQ	LABLS	10/01-12/01
	Houma MSA, LA	Y	11750 FQ	16460 AW	23040 TQ	LABLS	10/01-12/01
	Lafayette MSA, LA	Y	11990 FQ	17230 AW	22530 TQ	LABLS	10/01-12/01
	Lake Charles MSA, LA	Y	11920 FQ	18020 AW	27560 TQ	LABLS	10/01-12/01
	New Orleans MSA, LA	Y	11800 FQ	16350 AW	22580 TQ	LABLS	10/01-12/01
	Shreveport-Bossier City MSA, LA	Y	12290 FQ	18350 AW	29540 TQ	LABLS	10/01-12/01
	Maine	Y	13450 FQ	19000 AW	25940 TQ	MEBLS	10/01-12/01
	Portland MSA, ME	Y	15050 FQ	19260 AW	23680 TQ	MEBLS	10/01-12/01
	Maryland	Y	15030 FQ	24080 AW	37320 TQ	MDBLS	10/01-12/01
	Baltimore PMSA, MD	Y	14920 FQ	22070 AW	34430 TQ	MDBLS	10/01-12/01
	Massachusetts	Y	15570 FQ	21760 AW	29240 TQ	MABLS	10/01-12/01
	Boston PMSA, MA-NH	Y	15770 FQ	21590 AW	28490 TQ	MABLS	10/01-12/01
	Brockton PMSA, MA	Y	15870 FQ	22660 AW	31220 TQ	MABLS	10/01-12/01
	Lawrence PMSA, MA-NH	Y	15960 FQ	23490 AW	34060 TQ	MABLS	10/01-12/01
	New Bedford PMSA, MA	Y	14950 FQ	20980 AW	30720 TQ	MABLS	10/01-12/01
	Springfield MSA, MA	Y	14770 FQ	20380 AW	28660 TQ	MABLS	10/01-12/01
	Worcester PMSA, MA-CT	Y	14680 FQ	21490 AW	29760 TQ	MABLS	10/01-12/01
	Michigan	Y	14920 FQ	21250 AW	29770 TQ	MIBLS	10/01-12/01
	Ann Arbor PMSA, MI	Y	16100 FQ	23890 AW	32880 TQ	MIBLS	10/01-12/01
	Detroit PMSA, MI	Y	15670 FQ	21560 AW	30110 TQ	MIBLS	10/01-12/01
	Flint PMSA, MI	Y	14270 FQ	21240 AW	28980 TQ	MIBLS	10/01-12/01
	Grand Rapids-Muskegon-Holland MSA, MI	Y	14810 FQ	21860 AW	28590 TQ	MIBLS	10/01-12/01
	Kalamazoo-Battle Creek MSA, MI	Y	13690 FQ	23190 AW	38640 TQ	MIBLS	10/01-12/01
	Lansing-East Lansing MSA, MI	Y	13800 FQ	19050 AW	23940 TQ	MIBLS	10/01-12/01
	Saginaw-Bay City-Midland MSA, MI	Y	11940 FQ	18580 AW	26000 TQ	MIBLS	10/01-12/01
	Minnesota	Y	15880 FQ	22990 AW	32350 TQ	MNBLS	10/01-12/01
	Duluth-Superior MSA, MN-WI	Y	15170 FQ	19260 AW	26640 TQ	MNBLS	10/01-12/01
	Minneapolis-St. Paul MSA, MN-WI	Y	16470 FQ	23070 AW	31020 TQ	MNBLS	10/01-12/01
	St. Cloud MSA, MN	Y	12370 FQ	19670 AW	28200 TQ	MNBLS	10/01-12/01
	Mississippi	Y	11630 FQ	15920 AW	22990 TQ	MSBLS	10/01-12/01
	Biloxi-Gulfport-Pascagoula MSA, MS	Y	12720 FQ	18130 AW	26710 TQ	MSBLS	10/01-12/01
	Jackson MSA, MS	Y	11630 FQ	15310 AW	22140 TQ	MSBLS	10/01-12/01
	Missouri	Y	13850 FQ	21840 AW	34170 TQ	MOBLS	10/01-12/01
	Kansas City MSA, MO-KS	Y	16080 FQ	23460 AW	36170 TQ	MOBLS	10/01-12/01
	St. Louis MSA, MO-IL	Y	13420 FQ	21150 AW	33450 TQ	MOBLS	10/01-12/01
	Springfield MSA, MO	Y	12010 FQ	17390 AW	24600 TQ	MOBLS	10/01-12/01
	Montana	Y	12050 FQ	17230 AW	25400 TQ	MTBLS	10/01-12/01
	Billings MSA, MT	Y	13120 FQ	17450 AW	22060 TQ	MTBLS	10/01-12/01
	Nebraska	Y	13210 FQ	20920 AW	33240 TQ	NEBLS	10/01-12/01
	Lincoln MSA, NE	Y	13200 FQ	21350 AW	33620 TQ	NEBLS	10/01-12/01
	Omaha MSA, NE-IA	Y	15160 FQ	22140 AW	34280 TQ	NEBLS	10/01-12/01
	Nevada	Y	13490 FQ	21090 AW	30780 TQ	NVBLS	10/01-12/01
	Las Vegas MSA, NV-AZ	Y	13180 FQ	21300 AW	31680 TQ	NVBLS	10/01-12/01
	Reno MSA, NV	Y	15180 FQ	19520 AW	25140 TQ	NVBLS	10/01-12/01
	New Hampshire	Y	15920 FQ	21190 AW	27790 TQ	NHBLS	10/01-12/01
	Manchester PMSA, NH	Y	15950 FQ	19660 AW	23680 TQ	NHBLS	10/01-12/01
	Nashua PMSA, NH	Y	15980 FQ	22500 AW	29730 TQ	NHBLS	10/01-12/01
	Portsmouth-Rochester PMSA, NH-ME	Y	12850 FQ	19750 AW	27390 TQ	NHBLS	10/01-12/01
	New Jersey	Y	14380 FQ	21400 AW	31710 TQ	NJBLS	10/01-12/01
	Atlantic-Cape May PMSA, NJ	Y	14830 FQ	21520 AW	28730 TQ	NJBLS	10/01-12/01
	Bergen-Passaic PMSA, NJ	Y	14950 FQ	21170 AW	30800 TQ	NJBLS	10/01-12/01
	Jersey City PMSA, NJ	Y	13270 FQ	25620 AW	44500 TQ	NJBLS	10/01-12/01
	Middlesex-Somerset-Hunterdon PMSA, NJ	Y	14060 FQ	20570 AW	28860 TQ	NJBLS	10/01-12/01
	Monmouth-Ocean PMSA, NJ	Y	13700 FQ	20360 AW	27870 TQ	NJBLS	10/01-12/01

AAW	Average annual wage	AOH	Average offered, high	ASH	Average starting, high	H	Hourly	M	Monthly	S	Special: hourly and annual
AE	Average entry wage	AOL	Average offered, low	ASL	Average starting, low	HI	Highest wage paid	MTC	Median total compensation	TQ	Third quartile wage
AEX	Average experienced wage	APH	Average pay, high range	AW	Average wage paid	HR	High end range	MW	Median wage paid	W	Weekly
AO	Average offered	APL	Average pay, low range	FQ	First quartile wage	LR	Low end range	SQ	Second quartile wage	Y	Yearly

Occupation/Type/Industry	Location	Per	Low	Mid	High	Source	Date
Security Guard	Newark PMSA, NJ	Y	14480 FQ	20360 AW	28610 TQ	NJBLS	10/01-12/01
	Trenton PMSA, NJ	Y	15210 FQ	25760 AW	41360 TQ	NJBLS	10/01-12/01
	New Mexico	Y	12860 FQ	18480 AW	25560 TQ	NMBLS	10/01-12/01
	Albuquerque MSA, NM	Y	13090 FQ	18410 AW	25630 TQ	NMBLS	10/01-12/01
	Las Cruces MSA, NM	Y	12040 FQ	20360 AW	27280 TQ	NMBLS	10/01-12/01
	New York	Y	12850 FQ	21600 AW	34510 TQ	NYBLS	10/01-12/01
	Albany-Schenectady-Troy MSA, NY	Y	12150 FQ	19400 AW	29560 TQ	NYBLS	10/01-12/01
	Binghamton MSA, NY	Y	14710 FQ	23200 AW	39830 TQ	NYBLS	10/01-12/01
	Buffalo-Niagara Falls MSA, NY	Y	11950 FQ	17820 AW	27520 TQ	NYBLS	10/01-12/01
	Dutchess County PMSA, NY	Y	13530 FQ	21530 AW	32740 TQ	NYBLS	10/01-12/01
	Nassau-Suffolk PMSA, NY	Y	15170 FQ	22740 AW	34240 TQ	NYBLS	10/01-12/01
	New York PMSA, NY	Y	12710 FQ	21600 AW	34570 TQ	NYBLS	10/01-12/01
	Newburgh PMSA, NY-PA	Y	15990 FQ	25220 AW	41990 TQ	NYBLS	10/01-12/01
	Rochester MSA, NY	Y	12990 FQ	20750 AW	32560 TQ	NYBLS	10/01-12/01
	Syracuse MSA, NY	Y	15660 FQ	22010 AW	33880 TQ	NYBLS	10/01-12/01
	Utica-Rome MSA, NY	Y	13120 FQ	29380 AW	46810 TQ	NYBLS	10/01-12/01
	North Carolina	Y	13440 FQ	20970 AW	31880 TQ	NCBLS	10/01-12/01
	Asheville MSA, NC	Y	11990 FQ	17400 AW	26690 TQ	NCBLS	10/01-12/01
	Charlotte-Gastonia-Rock Hill MSA, NC-SC	Y	15520 FQ	22910 AW	36990 TQ	NCBLS	10/01-12/01
	Fayetteville MSA, NC	Y	11560 FQ	16910 AW	27310 TQ	NCBLS	10/01-12/01
	Greensboro-Winston-Salem-High Point MSA, NC	Y	15210 FQ	21940 AW	33130 TQ	NCBLS	10/01-12/01
	Hickory-Morganton-Lenoir MSA, NC	Y	12050 FQ	17330 AW	23180 TQ	NCBLS	10/01-12/01
	Raleigh-Durham-Chapel Hill MSA, NC	Y	15930 FQ	22500 AW	30060 TQ	NCBLS	10/01-12/01
	Wilmington MSA, NC	Y	11970 FQ	19530 AW	36460 TQ	NCBLS	10/01-12/01
	North Dakota	Y	11850 FQ	17530 AW	24370 TQ	NDBLS	10/01-12/01
	Fargo-Moorhead MSA, ND-MN	Y	11980 FQ	16700 AW	22860 TQ	NDBLS	10/01-12/01
	Ohio	Y	13210 FQ	20980 AW	33850 TQ	OHBLS	10/01-12/01
	Akron PMSA, OH	Y	12800 FQ	22330 AW	40180 TQ	OHBLS	10/01-12/01
	Canton-Massillon MSA, OH	Y	11930 FQ	16300 AW	23040 TQ	OHBLS	10/01-12/01
	Cincinnati PMSA, OH-KY-IN	Y	14580 FQ	20710 AW	32180 TQ	OHBLS	10/01-12/01
	Cleveland-Lorain-Elyria PMSA, OH	Y	14730 FQ	22670 AW	37230 TQ	OHBLS	10/01-12/01
	Columbus MSA, OH	Y	13400 FQ	20500 AW	28110 TQ	OHBLS	10/01-12/01
	Dayton-Springfield MSA, OH	Y	13080 FQ	19710 AW	26900 TQ	OHBLS	10/01-12/01
	Hamilton-Middletown PMSA, OH	Y	15220 FQ	24560 AW	35130 TQ	OHBLS	10/01-12/01
	Toledo MSA, OH	Y	12320 FQ	21140 AW	34480 TQ	OHBLS	10/01-12/01
	Youngstown-Warren MSA, OH	Y	12180 FQ	20070 AW	39170 TQ	OHBLS	10/01-12/01
	Oklahoma	Y	14300 FQ	20800 AW	30100 TQ	OKBLS	10/01-12/01
	Oklahoma City MSA, OK	Y	14480 FQ	22410 AW	31610 TQ	OKBLS	10/01-12/01
	Tulsa MSA, OK	Y	14540 FQ	19580 AW	28370 TQ	OKBLS	10/01-12/01
	Oregon	Y	14910 FQ	20120 AW	27440 TQ	ORBLS	10/01-12/01
	Eugene-Springfield MSA, OR	Y	14520 FQ	18920 AW	23200 TQ	ORBLS	10/01-12/01
	Portland-Vancouver PMSA, OR-WA	Y	15060 FQ	20460 AW	27750 TQ	ORBLS	10/01-12/01
	Salem PMSA, OR	Y	15740 FQ	21210 AW	29850 TQ	ORBLS	10/01-12/01
	Pennsylvania	Y	12510 FQ	19140 AW	27450 TQ	PABLS	10/01-12/01
	Allentown-Bethlehem-Easton MSA, PA	Y	14880 FQ	19460 AW	26300 TQ	PABLS	10/01-12/01
	Erie MSA, PA	Y	11800 FQ	17560 AW	28470 TQ	PABLS	10/01-12/01
	Harrisburg-Lebanon-Carlisle MSA, PA	Y	12980 FQ	19250 AW	26380 TQ	PABLS	10/01-12/01
	Johnstown MSA, PA	Y	11420 FQ	15400 AW	23810 TQ	PABLS	10/01-12/01
	Lancaster MSA, PA	Y	15150 FQ	20400 AW	26820 TQ	PABLS	10/01-12/01
	Philadelphia PMSA, PA-NJ	Y	13290 FQ	20490 AW	29010 TQ	PABLS	10/01-12/01
	Pittsburgh MSA, PA	Y	12010 FQ	17640 AW	25540 TQ	PABLS	10/01-12/01
	Reading MSA, PA	Y	14240 FQ	19310 AW	26750 TQ	PABLS	10/01-12/01
	Scranton-Wilkes-Barre-Hazleton MSA, PA	Y	12280 FQ	19550 AW	30290 TQ	PABLS	10/01-12/01
	Rhode Island	Y	14050 FQ	20350 AW	31410 TQ	RIBLS	10/01-12/01
	Providence-Fall River-Warwick MSA, RI-MA	Y	14100 FQ	20080 AW	31150 TQ	RIBLS	10/01-12/01
	South Carolina	Y	12930 FQ	19720 AW	31830 TQ	SCBLS	10/01-12/01
	Charleston-North Charleston MSA, SC	Y	13260 FQ	16930 AW	21630 TQ	SCBLS	10/01-12/01

AAW	Average annual wage	**AOH**	Average offered, high	**ASH**	Average starting, high	**H**	Hourly	**M**	Monthly	**S**	Special: hourly and annual
AE	Average entry wage	**AOL**	Average offered, low	**ASL**	Average starting, low	**HI**	Highest wage paid	**MTC**	Median total compensation	**TQ**	Third quartile wage
AEX	Average experienced wage	**APH**	Average pay, high range	**AW**	Average wage paid	**HR**	High end range	**MW**	Median wage paid	**W**	Weekly
AO	Average offered	**APL**	Average pay, low range	**FQ**	First quartile wage	**LR**	Low end range	**SQ**	Second quartile wage	**Y**	Yearly

Occupation/Type/Industry	Location	Per	Low	Mid	High	Source	Date
Security Guard	Columbia MSA, SC	Y	13470 FQ	18080 AW	26210 TQ	SCBLS	10/01-12/01
	Greenville-Spartanburg-Anderson MSA, SC	Y	12670 FQ	18170 AW	26840 TQ	SCBLS	10/01-12/01
	Myrtle Beach MSA, SC	Y	14860 FQ	19320 AW	25600 TQ	SCBLS	10/01-12/01
	South Dakota	Y	14920 FQ	19100 AW	25540 TQ	SDBLS	10/01-12/01
	Sioux Falls MSA, SD	Y	15190 FQ	20550 AW	27730 TQ	SDBLS	10/01-12/01
	Tennessee	Y	12670 FQ	20330 AW	32640 TQ	TNBLS	10/01-12/01
	Chattanooga MSA, TN-GA	Y	11900 FQ	18150 AW	26680 TQ	TNBLS	10/01-12/01
	Clarksville-Hopkinsville MSA, TN-KY	Y	11910 FQ	14880 AW	20750 TQ	TNBLS	10/01-12/01
	Johnson City-Kingsport-Bristol MSA, TN-VA	Y	12060 FQ	17690 AW	26350 TQ	TNBLS	10/01-12/01
	Knoxville MSA, TN	Y	12670 FQ	20020 AW	30940 TQ	TNBLS	10/01-12/01
	Memphis MSA, TN-AR-MS	Y	12690 FQ	19610 AW	27430 TQ	TNBLS	10/01-12/01
	Nashville MSA, TN	Y	14270 FQ	24080 AW	43430 TQ	TNBLS	10/01-12/01
	Texas	Y	12510 FQ	19360 AW	29120 TQ	TXBLS	10/01-12/01
	Amarillo MSA, TX	Y	11740 FQ	16680 AW	26740 TQ	TXBLS	10/01-12/01
	Austin-San Marcos MSA, TX	Y	14430 FQ	21650 AW	32460 TQ	TXBLS	10/01-12/01
	Beaumont-Port Arthur MSA, TX	Y	11760 FQ	17860 AW	27830 TQ	TXBLS	10/01-12/01
	Brazoria PMSA, TX	Y	13820 FQ	18670 AW	26200 TQ	TXBLS	10/01-12/01
	Brownsville-Harlingen-San Benito MSA, TX	Y	11390 FQ	15490 AW	21550 TQ	TXBLS	10/01-12/01
	Corpus Christi MSA, TX	Y	11240 FQ	14690 AW	20100 TQ	TXBLS	10/01-12/01
	Dallas PMSA, TX	Y	14560 FQ	20950 AW	28370 TQ	TXBLS	10/01-12/01
	El Paso MSA, TX	Y	11880 FQ	18250 AW	29520 TQ	TXBLS	10/01-12/01
	Fort Worth-Arlington PMSA, TX	Y	15270 FQ	22260 AW	39750 TQ	TXBLS	10/01-12/01
	Galveston-Texas City PMSA, TX	Y	13610 FQ	22030 AW	34510 TQ	TXBLS	10/01-12/01
	Houston PMSA, TX	Y	13030 FQ	18760 AW	26110 TQ	TXBLS	10/01-12/01
	Killeen-Temple MSA, TX	Y	12090 FQ	16380 AW	25510 TQ	TXBLS	10/01-12/01
	Laredo MSA, TX	Y	11660 FQ	15710 AW	23430 TQ	TXBLS	10/01-12/01
	Longview-Marshall MSA, TX	Y	12120 FQ	18600 AW	32740 TQ	TXBLS	10/01-12/01
	Lubbock MSA, TX	Y	12120 FQ	18060 AW	29350 TQ	TXBLS	10/01-12/01
	McAllen-Edinburg-Mission MSA, TX	Y	12110 FQ	17080 AW	25890 TQ	TXBLS	10/01-12/01
	Odessa-Midland MSA, TX	Y	12180 FQ	18800 AW	31760 TQ	TXBLS	10/01-12/01
	San Antonio MSA, TX	Y	12030 FQ	16930 AW	25800 TQ	TXBLS	10/01-12/01
	Tyler MSA, TX	Y	12010 FQ	18870 AW	33310 TQ	TXBLS	10/01-12/01
	Waco MSA, TX	Y	11850 FQ	18500 AW	30110 TQ	TXBLS	10/01-12/01
	Utah	Y	15560 FQ	22140 AW	32440 TQ	UTBLS	10/01-12/01
	Provo-Orem MSA, UT	Y	14940 FQ	20840 AW	28620 TQ	UTBLS	10/01-12/01
	Salt Lake City-Ogden MSA, UT	Y	15620 FQ	21940 AW	32020 TQ	UTBLS	10/01-12/01
	Vermont	Y	13860 FQ	20540 AW	32580 TQ	VTBLS	10/01-12/01
	Burlington MSA, VT	Y	13900 FQ	19860 AW	28340 TQ	VTBLS	10/01-12/01
	Virginia	Y	12860 FQ	20500 AW	30540 TQ	VABLS	10/01-12/01
	Lynchburg MSA, VA	Y	12470 FQ	26900 AW	44380 TQ	VABLS	10/01-12/01
	Norfolk-Virginia Beach-Newport News MSA, VA-NC	Y	12260 FQ	18600 AW	27770 TQ	VABLS	10/01-12/01
	Richmond-Petersburg MSA, VA	Y	13630 FQ	19990 AW	28850 TQ	VABLS	10/01-12/01
	Roanoke MSA, VA	Y	14170 FQ	20050 AW	27420 TQ	VABLS	10/01-12/01
	Washington	Y	15320 FQ	22740 AW	31920 TQ	WABLS	10/01-12/01
	Bremerton PMSA, WA	Y	16080 FQ	23910 AW	34800 TQ	WABLS	10/01-12/01
	Olympia PMSA, WA	Y	14730 FQ	20150 AW	28160 TQ	WABLS	10/01-12/01
	Richland-Kennewick-Pasco MSA, WA	Y	21980 FQ	39090 AW	55460 TQ	WABLS	10/01-12/01
	Seattle-Bellevue-Everett PMSA, WA	Y	16100 FQ	22640 AW	30550 TQ	WABLS	10/01-12/01
	Spokane MSA, WA	Y	14870 FQ	22160 AW	30500 TQ	WABLS	10/01-12/01
	Tacoma PMSA, WA	Y	14970 FQ	22660 AW	32820 TQ	WABLS	10/01-12/01
	Yakima MSA, WA	Y	16330 FQ	25860 AW	38090 TQ	WABLS	10/01-12/01
	West Virginia	Y	11960 FQ	16800 AW	24320 TQ	WVBLS	10/01-12/01
	Charleston MSA, WV	Y	11700 FQ	15820 AW	21660 TQ	WVBLS	10/01-12/01
	Huntington-Ashland MSA, WV-KY-OH	Y	11700 FQ	15100 AW	21900 TQ	WVBLS	10/01-12/01
	Wisconsin	Y	15120 FQ	19640 AW	26130 TQ	WIBLS	10/01-12/01
	Appleton-Oshkosh-Neenah MSA, WI	Y	15290 FQ	21460 AW	31470 TQ	WIBLS	10/01-12/01

AAW	Average annual wage	**AOH**	Average offered, high	**ASH**	Average starting, high	**H**	Hourly	**M**	Monthly	**S**	Special: hourly and annual
AE	Average entry wage	**AOL**	Average offered, low	**ASL**	Average starting, low	**HI**	Highest wage paid	**MTC**	Median total compensation	**TQ**	Third quartile wage
AEX	Average experienced wage	**APH**	Average pay, high range	**AW**	Average wage paid	**HR**	High end range	**MW**	Median wage paid	**W**	Weekly
AO	Average offered	**APL**	Average pay, low range	**FQ**	First quartile wage	**LR**	Low end range	**SQ**	Second quartile wage	**Y**	Yearly

Occupation/Type/Industry	Location	Per	Low	Mid	High	Source	Date
Security Guard	Green Bay MSA, WI	Y	14260 FQ	19520 AW	26990 TQ	WIBLS	10/01-12/01
	Madison MSA, WI	Y	15340 FQ	20860 AW	28680 TQ	WIBLS	10/01-12/01
	Milwaukee-Waukesha PMSA, WI	Y	15370 FQ	19260 AW	23180 TQ	WIBLS	10/01-12/01
	Racine PMSA, WI	Y	15560 FQ	23420 AW	36170 TQ	WIBLS	10/01-12/01
	Wyoming	Y	13870 FQ	19460 AW	26550 TQ	WYBLS	10/01-12/01
	Cheyenne MSA, WY	Y	15540 FQ	21700 AW	27080 TQ	WYBLS	10/01-12/01
	Puerto Rico	Y	11460 FQ	13050 AW	14610 TQ	PRBLS	10/01-12/01
	Virgin Islands	Y	11860 FQ	15570 AW	21820 TQ	VIBLS	10/01-12/01
	Guam	Y	11520 FQ	13500 AW	16560 TQ	GUBLS	10/01-12/01
Armed, For-profit organization	United States	S		14.82 MW	31600 AAW	IOMA3	1/02-1/02
Armed, For-profit organization	North Central	S		14.19 MW	29900 AAW	IOMA3	1/02-1/02
Armed, For-profit organization	Northeast	S		18.27 MW	37300 AAW	IOMA3	1/02-1/02
Armed, For-profit organization	South Central	S		14.43 MW	29600 AAW	IOMA3	1/02-1/02
Armed, For-profit organization	Southeast	S		14.24 MW	30100 AAW	IOMA3	1/02-1/02
Armed, For-profit organization	West	S		16.98 MW	31400 AAW	IOMA3	1/02-1/02
Armed, Not-for-profit organization	United States	S		14.57 MW	30000 AAW	IOMA3	1/02-1/02
Armed, Not-for-profit organization	North Central	S		13.42 MW	29200 AAW	IOMA3	1/02-1/02
Armed, Not-for-profit organization	Northeast	S		16.93 MW	35600 AAW	IOMA3	1/02-1/02
Armed, Not-for-profit organization	South Central	S		13.59 MW	28300 AAW	IOMA3	1/02-1/02
Armed, Not-for-profit organization	Southeast	S		13.13 MW	28000 AAW	IOMA3	1/02-1/02
Armed, Not-for-profit organization	West	S		16.06 MW	35600 AAW	IOMA3	1/02-1/02
Eating and Drinking Establishments	United States	Y		15870 MW		OOH12	1999-2000
Elementary and Secondary School	United States	Y		22240 MW		OOH12	1999-2000
Federal Government	United States	Y		28960 MW		OOH12	2000-2001
Federal Government	United States	Y	21950-27190 AE			OOH12	1999-2000
Hospital	United States	Y		22260 MW		OOH12	1999-2000
Hotel and Motel	United States	Y		20230 MW		OOH12	1999-2000
Miscellaneous Business Services	United States	Y		16830 MW		OOH12	1999-2000
Unarmed, For-profit organization	United States	S		12.07 MW	26100 AAW	IOMA3	1/02-1/02
Unarmed, For-profit organization	North Central	S		12.29 MW	26200 AAW	IOMA3	1/02-1/02
Unarmed, For-profit organization	Northeast	S		13.45 MW	27700 AAW	IOMA3	1/02-1/02
Unarmed, For-profit organization	South Central	S		12.36 MW	26200 AAW	IOMA3	1/02-1/02
Unarmed, For-profit organization	Southeast	S		12.00 MW	25000 AAW	IOMA3	1/02-1/02
Unarmed, For-profit organization	West	S		11.65 MW	24700 AAW	IOMA3	1/02-1/02
Unarmed, Not-for-profit organization	United States	S		11.93 MW	25400 AAW	IOMA3	1/02-1/02
Unarmed, Not-for-profit organization	North Central	S		12.29 MW	25600 AAW	IOMA3	1/02-1/02
Unarmed, Not-for-profit organization	Northeast	S		13.17 MW	28500 AAW	IOMA3	1/02-1/02
Unarmed, Not-for-profit organization	South Central	S		11.04 MW	22900 AAW	IOMA3	1/02-1/02
Unarmed, Not-for-profit organization	Southeast	S		10.63 MW	22600 AAW	IOMA3	1/02-1/02
Unarmed, Not-for-profit organization	West	S		15.87 MW	30700 AAW	IOMA3	1/02-1/02
Security/Loss Prevention Director and Vice President	Los Angeles-Long Beach-San Diego MSA, CA	Y			90650 HI	IOMA	1/01-1/02
	San Jose, CA	Y			112000 HI	IOMA	1/01-1/02
	Georgia	Y		42000 AW		IOMA	1/01-1/02
	Chicago, IL	Y			77000 HI	IOMA	1/01-1/02
	Oklahoma	Y		30000 AW		IOMA	1/01-1/02
	Texas	Y		36250 AW		IOMA	1/01-1/02
1,500 and more employees	Southeast	Y		66300 AW		IOMA	1/01-1/02
2,000-7,500 employees	United States	Y		70900 AW		IOMA	1/01-1/02
2,000-7,500 employees	Northeast	Y		76300 AW		IOMA	1/01-1/02
2,000-7,500 employees	West	Y		75000 AW		IOMA	1/01-1/02
7,500 or more employees	United States	Y		70800 AW		IOMA	1/01-1/02
7,500 or more employees	Northeast	Y		76700 AW		IOMA	1/01-1/02
Nonprofit organization, Fewer than 3,000 employees	Northeast	Y		65600 AW		IOMA	1/01-1/02
Segmental Paver	Arizona	H	6.58 FQ	12.09 AW	16.16 TQ	AZBLS	10/01-12/01
	California	H	13.79 FQ	20.54 AW	27.06 TQ	CABLS	10/01-12/01
	Connecticut	H	10.53 FQ	13.61 AW	16.98 TQ	CTBLS	10/01-12/01
	Georgia	H	8.24 FQ	12.04 AW	16.83 TQ	GABLS	10/01-12/01
	Illinois	H	6.58 FQ	11.75 AW	17.54 TQ	ILBLS	10/01-12/01
	Michigan	H	6.02 FQ	12.06 AW	20.86 TQ	MIBLS	10/01-12/01
	Mississippi	H	7.59 FQ	9.92 AW	12.85 TQ	MSBLS	10/01-12/01
	Ohio	H	8.91 FQ	11.79 AW	14.03 TQ	OHBLS	10/01-12/01
	Pennsylvania	H	10.10 FQ	13.97 AW	22.30 TQ	PABLS	10/01-12/01
	South Carolina	H	7.73 FQ	10.56 AW	14.81 TQ	SCBLS	10/01-12/01
	Tennessee	H	7.90 FQ	11.00 AW	14.34 TQ	TNBLS	10/01-12/01
	Texas	H	6.54 FQ	9.83 AW	14.86 TQ	TXBLS	10/01-12/01

AAW	Average annual wage	**AOH**	Average offered, high	**ASH**	Average starting, high	**H**	Hourly	**M**	Monthly	**S**	Special: hourly and annual
AE	Average entry wage	**AOL**	Average offered, low	**ASL**	Average starting, low	**HI**	Highest wage paid	**MTC**	Median total compensation	**TQ**	Third quartile wage
AEX	Average experienced wage	**APH**	Average pay, high range	**AW**	Average wage paid	**HR**	High end range	**MW**	Median wage paid	**W**	Weekly
AO	Average offered	**APL**	Average pay, low range	**FQ**	First quartile wage	**LR**	Low end range	**SQ**	Second quartile wage	**Y**	Yearly

Occupation/Type/Industry	Location	Per	Low	Mid	High	Source	Date
Segmental Paver	Virginia	H	12.11 FQ	14.83 AW	17.68 TQ	VABLS	10/01-12/01
Self-Enrichment Education Teacher	Alabama	Y	14820 FQ	25700 AW	43070 TQ	ALBLS	10/01-12/01
	Alaska	Y	23800 FQ	34540 AW	51940 TQ	AKBLS	10/01-12/01
	Arizona	Y	14740 FQ	33590 AW	55730 TQ	AZBLS	10/01-12/01
	Arkansas	Y	12670 FQ	25090 AW	44300 TQ	ARBLS	10/01-12/01
	California	Y	17510 FQ	34650 AW	57530 TQ	CABLS	10/01-12/01
	Colorado	Y	14710 FQ	28560 AW	45140 TQ	COBLS	10/01-12/01
	Connecticut	Y	20090 FQ	36640 AW	60160 TQ	CTBLS	10/01-12/01
	Delaware	Y	20200 FQ	39620 AW	66170 TQ	DEBLS	10/01-12/01
	District of Columbia	Y	15370 FQ	29870 AW	49310 TQ	DCBLS	10/01-12/01
	Florida	Y	13920 FQ	28930 AW	53730 TQ	FLBLS	10/01-12/01
	Georgia	Y	15570 FQ	27620 AW	46380 TQ	GABLS	10/01-12/01
	Hawaii	Y	13610 FQ	31890 AW	47490 TQ	HIBLS	10/01-12/01
	Idaho	Y	13440 FQ	24020 AW	42960 TQ	IDBLS	10/01-12/01
	Illinois	Y	13190 FQ	26880 AW	45630 TQ	ILBLS	10/01-12/01
	Indiana	Y	13000 FQ	24680 AW	42300 TQ	INBLS	10/01-12/01
	Iowa	Y	11860 FQ	24740 AW	50450 TQ	IABLS	10/01-12/01
	Kansas	Y	17780 FQ	33550 AW	54310 TQ	KSBLS	10/01-12/01
	Kentucky	Y	13690 FQ	30070 AW	61970 TQ	KYBLS	10/01-12/01
	Louisiana	Y	12570 FQ	28970 AW	45000 TQ	LABLS	10/01-12/01
	Maine	Y	15740 FQ	28460 AW	48890 TQ	MEBLS	10/01-12/01
	Maryland	Y	15270 FQ	29530 AW	53940 TQ	MDBLS	10/01-12/01
	Massachusetts	Y	21070 FQ	37720 AW	61760 TQ	MABLS	10/01-12/01
	Michigan	Y	15800 FQ	32070 AW	51850 TQ	MIBLS	10/01-12/01
	Minnesota	Y	18140 FQ	32950 AW	52350 TQ	MNBLS	10/01-12/01
	Mississippi	Y	14680 FQ	25030 AW	36330 TQ	MSBLS	10/01-12/01
	Missouri	Y	14780 FQ	28040 AW	47210 TQ	MOBLS	10/01-12/01
	Montana	Y	17160 FQ	27150 AW	44150 TQ	MTBLS	10/01-12/01
	Nebraska	Y	11990 FQ	22670 AW	40360 TQ	NEBLS	10/01-12/01
	Nevada	Y	20240 FQ	35880 AW	56010 TQ	NVBLS	10/01-12/01
	New Hampshire	Y	19610 FQ	36540 AW	56070 TQ	NHBLS	10/01-12/01
	New Jersey	Y	18370 FQ	39520 AW	61150 TQ	NJBLS	10/01-12/01
	New Mexico	Y	17980 FQ	31940 AW	55430 TQ	NMBLS	10/01-12/01
	New York	Y	16930 FQ	38190 AW	68360 TQ	NYBLS	10/01-12/01
	North Carolina	Y	13880 FQ	31050 AW	50170 TQ	NCBLS	10/01-12/01
	North Dakota	Y	12790 FQ	20180 AW	29580 TQ	NDBLS	10/01-12/01
	Ohio	Y	15670 FQ	27090 AW	43670 TQ	OHBLS	10/01-12/01
	Oklahoma	Y	12980 FQ	31200 AW	53350 TQ	OKBLS	10/01-12/01
	Oregon	Y	16070 FQ	28890 AW	43530 TQ	ORBLS	10/01-12/01
	Pennsylvania	Y	12560 FQ	27440 AW	48350 TQ	PABLS	10/01-12/01
	Rhode Island	Y	14040 FQ	36630 AW	68750 TQ	RIBLS	10/01-12/01
	South Carolina	Y	16270 FQ	28240 AW	36530 TQ	SCBLS	10/01-12/01
	South Dakota	Y	15650 FQ	21420 AW	28520 TQ	SDBLS	10/01-12/01
	Tennessee	Y	16190 FQ	27830 AW	41290 TQ	TNBLS	10/01-12/01
	Texas	Y	14320 FQ	38050 AW	78570 TQ	TXBLS	10/01-12/01
	Utah	Y	15330 FQ	24310 AW	36830 TQ	UTBLS	10/01-12/01
	Vermont	Y	22480 FQ	35990 AW	50870 TQ	VTBLS	10/01-12/01
	Virginia	Y	16960 FQ	33300 AW	51900 TQ	VABLS	10/01-12/01
	Washington	Y	21430 FQ	38710 AW	57440 TQ	WABLS	10/01-12/01
	West Virginia	Y	12100 FQ	21320 AW	35790 TQ	WVBLS	10/01-12/01
	Wisconsin	Y	15670 FQ	27020 AW	43500 TQ	WIBLS	10/01-12/01
	Wyoming	Y	16320 FQ	29390 AW	52290 TQ	WYBLS	10/01-12/01
	Puerto Rico	Y	14040 FQ	18870 AW	25140 TQ	PRBLS	10/01-12/01
Semiconductor Processor	Arizona	H	9.65 FQ	13.25 AW	16.65 TQ	AZBLS	10/01-12/01
	California	H	7.76 FQ	12.96 AW	19.54 TQ	CABLS	10/01-12/01
	Los Angeles-Long Beach PMSA, CA	H	6.80 FQ	11.13 AW	17.33 TQ	CABLS	10/01-12/01
	Oakland PMSA, CA	H	9.01 FQ	12.71 AW	16.92 TQ	CABLS	10/01-12/01
	Orange County PMSA, CA	H	7.28 FQ	12.03 AW	17.18 TQ	CABLS	10/01-12/01
	San Jose PMSA, CA	H	8.96 FQ	14.12 AW	21.16 TQ	CABLS	10/01-12/01
	Ventura PMSA, CA	H	7.51 FQ	12.85 AW	19.44 TQ	CABLS	10/01-12/01
	Fort Collins-Loveland MSA, CO	H	7.84 FQ	12.29 AW	18.82 TQ	COBLS	10/01-12/01
	Connecticut	H	9.87 FQ	14.63 AW	20.95 TQ	CTBLS	10/01-12/01
	Florida	H	7.38 FQ	11.06 AW	15.96 TQ	FLBLS	10/01-12/01
	Illinois	H	9.27 FQ	14.01 AW	20.67 TQ	ILBLS	10/01-12/01
	Chicago PMSA, IL	H	9.26 FQ	13.54 AW	18.93 TQ	ILBLS	10/01-12/01
	Massachusetts	H	9.71 FQ	14.04 AW	19.97 TQ	MABLS	10/01-12/01
	Michigan	H	9.16 FQ	13.54 AW	19.58 TQ	MIBLS	10/01-12/01

AAW	Average annual wage	**AOH**	Average offered, high	**ASH**	Average starting, high	**H**	Hourly	**M**	Monthly	**S**	Special: hourly and annual
AE	Average entry wage	**AOL**	Average offered, low	**ASL**	Average starting, low	**HI**	Highest wage paid	**MTC**	Median total compensation	**TQ**	Third quartile wage
AEX	Average experienced wage	**APH**	Average pay, high range	**AW**	Average wage paid	**HR**	High end range	**MW**	Median wage paid	**W**	Weekly
AO	Average offered	**APL**	Average pay, low range	**FQ**	First quartile wage	**LR**	Low end range	**SQ**	Second quartile wage	**Y**	Yearly

Occupation/Type/Industry	Location	Per	Low	Mid	High	Source	Date
Semiconductor Processor	Minnesota	H	9.62 FQ	12.67 AW	16.46 TQ	MNBLS	10/01-12/01
	Minneapolis-St. Paul MSA, MN-WI	H	9.62 FQ	12.67 AW	16.46 TQ	MNBLS	10/01-12/01
	New Hampshire	H	9.68 FQ	13.47 AW	17.61 TQ	NHBLS	10/01-12/01
	New Jersey	H	9.66 FQ	13.42 AW	18.14 TQ	NJBLS	10/01-12/01
	Middlesex-Somerset-Hunterdon PMSA, NJ	H	9.42 FQ	12.61 AW	16.96 TQ	NJBLS	10/01-12/01
	Newark PMSA, NJ	H	10.98 FQ	14.67 AW	19.58 TQ	NJBLS	10/01-12/01
	New Mexico	H	10.28 FQ	14.37 AW	19.51 TQ	NMBLS	10/01-12/01
	Albuquerque MSA, NM	H	10.33 FQ	14.39 AW	19.53 TQ	NMBLS	10/01-12/01
	New York	H	9.37 FQ	15.56 AW	23.14 TQ	NYBLS	10/01-12/01
	Oregon	H	9.26 FQ	13.18 AW	18.36 TQ	ORBLS	10/01-12/01
	Portland-Vancouver PMSA, OR-WA	H	9.40 FQ	13.43 AW	18.77 TQ	ORBLS	10/01-12/01
	Pennsylvania	H	9.76 FQ	13.33 AW	17.33 TQ	PABLS	10/01-12/01
	Philadelphia PMSA, PA-NJ	H	9.68 FQ	13.98 AW	19.47 TQ	PABLS	10/01-12/01
	Texas	H	9.56 FQ	14.42 AW	21.04 TQ	TXBLS	10/01-12/01
	Austin-San Marcos MSA, TX	H	9.97 FQ	14.11 AW	17.24 TQ	TXBLS	10/01-12/01
	Virginia	H	9.26 FQ	13.36 AW	19.68 TQ	VABLS	10/01-12/01
	Seattle-Bellevue-Everett PMSA, WA	H	10.59 FQ	15.34 AW	21.81 TQ	WABLS	10/01-12/01
Senior Architect							
Web Design	United States	Y		69593 AW		DFMAR	1/01-1/02
Senior Designer	Phoenix, AZ	Y		46300 AW		TBJ	1/00-1/01
Senior Information Technology Manager							
Aerospace	United States	Y		141056 AW		INFO2	1/00-1/01
Federal Government	United States	Y		85000 AW		INFO2	1/00-1/01
Finance and Banking	United States	Y		138128 AW		INFO2	1/00-1/01
Insurance, Real Estate, Legal fields	United States	Y		104910 AW		INFO2	1/00-1/01
Manufacturing, Computer-related	United States	Y		120268 AW		INFO2	1/00-1/01
Publishing	United States	Y		107250 AW		INFO2	1/00-1/01
Research and Development	United States	Y		105700 AW		INFO2	1/00-1/01
State/Local Government	United States	Y		79638 AW		INFO2	1/00-1/01
Telecommunications	United States	Y		118000 AW		INFO2	1/00-1/01
Transportation and Utilities	United States	Y		115700 AW		INFO2	1/00-1/01
Senior Internet/Intranet Developer							
Internet and E-Commerce	United States	Y		68750-94250 AW		IW	1/00-1/01
Separating, Filtering, Clarifying, Precipitating, and Still Machine Setter, Operator, and Tender	Alabama	H	8.05 FQ	12.04 AW	18.08 TQ	ALBLS	10/01-12/01
	Birmingham MSA, AL	H	9.11 FQ	11.63 AW	16.97 TQ	ALBLS	10/01-12/01
	Mobile MSA, AL	H	7.89 FQ	14.62 AW	22.69 TQ	ALBLS	10/01-12/01
	Montgomery MSA, AL	H	7.51 FQ	9.82 AW	14.04 TQ	ALBLS	10/01-12/01
	Alaska	H	13.17 FQ	19.10 AW	22.14 TQ	AKBLS	10/01-12/01
	Arizona	H	8.53 FQ	15.27 AW	21.12 TQ	AZBLS	10/01-12/01
	Phoenix-Mesa MSA, AZ	H	7.72 FQ	11.54 AW	16.11 TQ	AZBLS	10/01-12/01
	Tucson MSA, AZ	H	12.67 FQ	17.47 AW	21.51 TQ	AZBLS	10/01-12/01
	Arkansas	H	9.10 FQ	13.21 AW	16.70 TQ	ARBLS	10/01-12/01
	California	H	8.01 FQ	14.09 AW	21.03 TQ	CABLS	10/01-12/01
	Bakersfield MSA, CA	H	12.31 FQ	18.70 AW	22.13 TQ	CABLS	10/01-12/01
	Chico-Paradise MSA, CA	H	6.65 FQ	11.74 AW	19.32 TQ	CABLS	10/01-12/01
	Fresno MSA, CA	H	7.59 FQ	12.34 AW	17.03 TQ	CABLS	10/01-12/01
	Los Angeles-Long Beach PMSA, CA	H	10.05 FQ	15.70 AW	22.95 TQ	CABLS	10/01-12/01
	Merced MSA, CA	H	7.63 FQ	11.41 AW	17.27 TQ	CABLS	10/01-12/01
	Modesto MSA, CA	H	6.39 FQ	10.70 AW	18.43 TQ	CABLS	10/01-12/01
	Oakland PMSA, CA	H	9.18 FQ	15.80 AW	21.69 TQ	CABLS	10/01-12/01
	Orange County PMSA, CA	H	6.43 FQ	10.30 AW	18.03 TQ	CABLS	10/01-12/01
	Riverside-San Bernardino PMSA, CA	H	9.37 FQ	15.11 AW	22.60 TQ	CABLS	10/01-12/01
	Sacramento PMSA, CA	H	7.27 FQ	10.19 AW	13.84 TQ	CABLS	10/01-12/01
	Salinas MSA, CA	H	9.05 FQ	13.11 AW	19.28 TQ	CABLS	10/01-12/01
	San Diego MSA, CA	H	8.73 FQ	15.66 AW	20.80 TQ	CABLS	10/01-12/01
	San Francisco PMSA, CA	H	10.71 FQ	23.98 AW	35.21 TQ	CABLS	10/01-12/01

AAW Average annual wage **AE** Average entry wage **AEX** Average experienced wage **AO** Average offered **AOH** Average offered, high **AOL** Average offered, low **APH** Average pay, high range **APL** Average pay, low range **ASH** Average starting, high **ASL** Average starting, low **AW** Average wage paid **FQ** First quartile wage **H** Hourly **HI** Highest wage paid **HR** High end range **LR** Low end range **M** Monthly **MTC** Median total compensation **MW** Median wage paid **SQ** Second quartile wage **S** Special: hourly and annual **TQ** Third quartile wage **W** Weekly **Y** Yearly

Occupation/Type/Industry	Location	Per	Low	Mid	High	Source	Date
Separating, Filtering, Clarifying, Precipitating, and Still Machine Setter, Operator, and Tender	San Jose PMSA, CA	H	9.85 FQ	15.80 AW	23.44 TQ	CABLS	10/01-12/01
	Santa Barbara-Santa Maria-Lompoc MSA, CA	H	11.45 FQ	14.42 AW	18.85 TQ	CABLS	10/01-12/01
	Santa Cruz-Watsonville PMSA, CA	H	6.45 FQ	11.45 AW	18.73 TQ	CABLS	10/01-12/01
	Santa Rosa PMSA, CA	H	9.21 FQ	13.95 AW	20.54 TQ	CABLS	10/01-12/01
	Stockton-Lodi MSA, CA	H	12.45 FQ	18.17 AW	30.16 TQ	CABLS	10/01-12/01
	Vallejo-Fairfield-Napa PMSA, CA	H	11.29 FQ	14.98 AW	19.84 TQ	CABLS	10/01-12/01
	Visalia-Tulare-Porterville MSA, CA	H	6.97 FQ	11.58 AW	17.15 TQ	CABLS	10/01-12/01
	Colorado	H	6.69 FQ	12.76 AW	19.36 TQ	COBLS	10/01-12/01
	Denver PMSA, CO	H	6.66 FQ	12.68 AW	19.76 TQ	COBLS	10/01-12/01
	Fort Collins-Loveland MSA, CO	H	5.87 FQ	12.45 AW	16.69 TQ	COBLS	10/01-12/01
	Connecticut	H	11.11 FQ	14.50 AW	17.47 TQ	CTBLS	10/01-12/01
	Delaware	H	9.32 FQ	14.98 AW	22.23 TQ	DEBLS	10/01-12/01
	Wilmington-Newark PMSA, DE-MD	H	9.34 FQ	15.21 AW	22.24 TQ	DEBLS	10/01-12/01
	Washington PMSA, DC-MD-VA-WV	H	10.23 FQ	16.82 AW	25.13 TQ	DCBLS	10/01-12/01
	Florida	H	7.73 FQ	11.17 AW	15.26 TQ	FLBLS	10/01-12/01
	Jacksonville MSA, FL	H	11.12 FQ	12.76 AW	15.55 TQ	FLBLS	10/01-12/01
	Lakeland-Winter Haven MSA, FL	H	7.81 FQ	11.50 AW	16.85 TQ	FLBLS	10/01-12/01
	Miami PMSA, FL	H	7.98 FQ	11.03 AW	15.28 TQ	FLBLS	10/01-12/01
	Orlando MSA, FL	H	7.60 FQ	9.68 AW	12.63 TQ	FLBLS	10/01-12/01
	Pensacola MSA, FL	H	7.80 FQ	10.73 AW	15.35 TQ	FLBLS	10/01-12/01
	Tampa-St. Petersburg-Clearwater MSA, FL	H	9.24 FQ	12.53 AW	16.44 TQ	FLBLS	10/01-12/01
	Georgia	H	8.00 FQ	15.07 AW	24.15 TQ	GABLS	10/01-12/01
	Atlanta MSA, GA	H	7.57 FQ	11.08 AW	17.92 TQ	GABLS	10/01-12/01
	Hawaii	H	7.20 FQ	10.64 AW	15.00 TQ	HIBLS	10/01-12/01
	Idaho	H	9.10 FQ	12.42 AW	16.35 TQ	IDBLS	10/01-12/01
	Boise City MSA, ID	H	11.18 FQ	13.20 AW	16.18 TQ	IDBLS	10/01-12/01
	Illinois	H	9.29 FQ	14.58 AW	19.68 TQ	ILBLS	10/01-12/01
	Chicago PMSA, IL	H	9.24 FQ	14.20 AW	17.36 TQ	ILBLS	10/01-12/01
	Indiana	H	12.43 FQ	18.64 AW	25.48 TQ	INBLS	10/01-12/01
	Fort Wayne MSA, IN	H	12.81 FQ	16.74 AW	24.32 TQ	INBLS	10/01-12/01
	Gary PMSA, IN	H	14.41 FQ	18.33 AW	22.37 TQ	INBLS	10/01-12/01
	Iowa	H	11.20 FQ	15.91 AW	21.15 TQ	IABLS	10/01-12/01
	Kansas	H	7.54 FQ	10.94 AW	14.78 TQ	KSBLS	10/01-12/01
	Kentucky	H	9.36 FQ	14.45 AW	22.34 TQ	KYBLS	10/01-12/01
	Louisville MSA, KY-IN	H	10.66 FQ	16.24 AW	26.28 TQ	KYBLS	10/01-12/01
	Louisiana	H	6.43 FQ	15.38 AW	28.66 TQ	LABLS	10/01-12/01
	Baton Rouge MSA, LA	H	10.79 FQ	14.79 AW	17.96 TQ	LABLS	10/01-12/01
	Lafayette MSA, LA	H	6.42 FQ	9.87 AW	13.35 TQ	LABLS	10/01-12/01
	Shreveport-Bossier City MSA, LA	H	6.56 FQ	11.20 AW	13.62 TQ	LABLS	10/01-12/01
	Maine	H	11.29 FQ	15.60 AW	21.00 TQ	MEBLS	10/01-12/01
	Portland MSA, ME	H	8.53 FQ	12.31 AW	15.90 TQ	MEBLS	10/01-12/01
	Maryland	H	9.72 FQ	15.07 AW	20.94 TQ	MDBLS	10/01-12/01
	Baltimore PMSA, MD	H	10.94 FQ	15.83 AW	21.23 TQ	MDBLS	10/01-12/01
	Massachusetts	H	9.42 FQ	14.26 AW	18.45 TQ	MABLS	10/01-12/01
	Boston PMSA, MA-NH	H	10.20 FQ	15.03 AW	20.10 TQ	MABLS	10/01-12/01
	Lawrence PMSA, MA-NH	H	11.76 FQ	14.03 AW	17.46 TQ	MABLS	10/01-12/01
	Michigan	H	8.65 FQ	14.56 AW	19.94 TQ	MIBLS	10/01-12/01
	Detroit PMSA, MI	H	8.54 FQ	15.44 AW	21.18 TQ	MIBLS	10/01-12/01
	Grand Rapids-Muskegon-Holland MSA, MI	H	7.51 FQ	12.77 AW	17.21 TQ	MIBLS	10/01-12/01
	Kalamazoo-Battle Creek MSA, MI	H	8.96 FQ	14.59 AW	19.01 TQ	MIBLS	10/01-12/01
	Minnesota	H	9.28 FQ	12.86 AW	16.68 TQ	MNBLS	10/01-12/01
	Minneapolis-St. Paul MSA, MN-WI	H	11.19 FQ	13.54 AW	16.68 TQ	MNBLS	10/01-12/01
	Mississippi	H	5.90 FQ	8.86 AW	12.90 TQ	MSBLS	10/01-12/01
	Missouri	H	9.03 FQ	12.93 AW	17.24 TQ	MOBLS	10/01-12/01
	Kansas City MSA, MO-KS	H	9.83 FQ	13.82 AW	17.55 TQ	MOBLS	10/01-12/01
	St. Louis MSA, MO-IL	H	8.97 FQ	13.07 AW	17.61 TQ	MOBLS	10/01-12/01
	Montana	H	8.62 FQ	13.63 AW	20.38 TQ	MTBLS	10/01-12/01

AAW Average annual wage; AE Average entry wage; AEX Average experienced wage; AO Average offered; AOH Average offered, high; AOL Average offered, low; APH Average pay, high range; APL Average pay, low range; ASH Average starting, high; ASL Average starting, low; AW Average wage paid; FQ First quartile wage; H Hourly; HI Highest wage paid; HR High end range; LR Low end range; M Monthly; MTC Median total compensation; MW Median wage paid; SQ Second quartile wage; S Special: hourly and annual; TQ Third quartile wage; W Weekly; Y Yearly

Occupation/Type/Industry	Location	Per	Low	Mid	High	Source	Date
Separating, Filtering, Clarifying, Precipitating, and Still Machine Setter, Operator, and Tender	Nebraska	H	7.57 FQ	10.96 AW	15.44 TQ	NEBLS	10/01-12/01
	Omaha MSA, NE-IA	H	7.09 FQ	11.03 AW	16.50 TQ	NEBLS	10/01-12/01
	Nevada	H	11.07 FQ	17.42 AW	22.35 TQ	NVBLS	10/01-12/01
	New Hampshire	H	10.22 FQ	15.91 AW	19.36 TQ	NHBLS	10/01-12/01
	New Jersey	H	9.25 FQ	16.33 AW	24.80 TQ	NJBLS	10/01-12/01
	Bergen-Passaic PMSA, NJ	H	10.85 FQ	20.62 AW	26.36 TQ	NJBLS	10/01-12/01
	Middlesex-Somerset-Hunterdon PMSA, NJ	H	10.06 FQ	15.25 AW	20.96 TQ	NJBLS	10/01-12/01
	Newark PMSA, NJ	H	9.60 FQ	17.13 AW	25.06 TQ	NJBLS	10/01-12/01
	New Mexico	H	11.28 FQ	15.02 AW	20.69 TQ	NMBLS	10/01-12/01
	Albuquerque MSA, NM	H	11.47 FQ	15.05 AW	20.81 TQ	NMBLS	10/01-12/01
	New York	H	7.64 FQ	12.60 AW	18.87 TQ	NYBLS	10/01-12/01
	Buffalo-Niagara Falls MSA, NY	H	13.37 FQ	15.73 AW	19.10 TQ	NYBLS	10/01-12/01
	Nassau-Suffolk PMSA, NY	H	7.10 FQ	10.43 AW	17.23 TQ	NYBLS	10/01-12/01
	New York PMSA, NY	H	7.30 FQ	8.98 AW	11.86 TQ	NYBLS	10/01-12/01
	Rochester MSA, NY	H	8.85 FQ	13.91 AW	20.94 TQ	NYBLS	10/01-12/01
	Syracuse MSA, NY	H	7.71 FQ	14.34 AW	21.68 TQ	NYBLS	10/01-12/01
	North Carolina	H	8.53 FQ	14.39 AW	20.99 TQ	NCBLS	10/01-12/01
	Greensboro-Winston-Salem-High Point MSA, NC	H	7.71 FQ	11.02 AW	15.35 TQ	NCBLS	10/01-12/01
	North Dakota	H	8.25 FQ	12.11 AW	17.55 TQ	NDBLS	10/01-12/01
	Ohio	H	9.12 FQ	13.73 AW	19.41 TQ	OHBLS	10/01-12/01
	Akron PMSA, OH	H	5.63 FQ	10.65 AW	18.83 TQ	OHBLS	10/01-12/01
	Canton-Massillon MSA, OH	H	10.12 FQ	14.38 AW	17.37 TQ	OHBLS	10/01-12/01
	Cincinnati PMSA, OH-KY-IN	H	9.22 FQ	13.78 AW	20.44 TQ	OHBLS	10/01-12/01
	Cleveland-Lorain-Elyria PMSA, OH	H	7.66 FQ	13.64 AW	17.58 TQ	OHBLS	10/01-12/01
	Columbus MSA, OH	H	9.03 FQ	12.87 AW	18.17 TQ	OHBLS	10/01-12/01
	Oklahoma	H	7.32 FQ	13.81 AW	20.47 TQ	OKBLS	10/01-12/01
	Oklahoma City MSA, OK	H	7.57 FQ	11.24 AW	14.72 TQ	OKBLS	10/01-12/01
	Oregon	H	8.47 FQ	14.39 AW	21.37 TQ	ORBLS	10/01-12/01
	Eugene-Springfield MSA, OR	H	7.68 FQ	13.16 AW	22.54 TQ	ORBLS	10/01-12/01
	Portland-Vancouver PMSA, OR-WA	H	9.61 FQ	15.02 AW	20.95 TQ	ORBLS	10/01-12/01
	Salem PMSA, OR	H	8.26 FQ	13.00 AW	17.98 TQ	ORBLS	10/01-12/01
	Pennsylvania	H	11.84 FQ	15.19 AW	17.83 TQ	PABLS	10/01-12/01
	Allentown-Bethlehem-Easton MSA, PA	H	11.93 FQ	15.16 AW	18.40 TQ	PABLS	10/01-12/01
	Harrisburg-Lebanon-Carlisle MSA, PA	H	11.52 FQ	15.10 AW	21.60 TQ	PABLS	10/01-12/01
	Lancaster MSA, PA	H	12.12 FQ	14.63 AW	16.84 TQ	PABLS	10/01-12/01
	Philadelphia PMSA, PA-NJ	H	11.44 FQ	15.22 AW	17.99 TQ	PABLS	10/01-12/01
	Pittsburgh MSA, PA	H	10.58 FQ	15.49 AW	20.72 TQ	PABLS	10/01-12/01
	Reading MSA, PA	H	11.39 FQ	14.74 AW	17.55 TQ	PABLS	10/01-12/01
	York MSA, PA	H	11.70 FQ	14.49 AW	16.89 TQ	PABLS	10/01-12/01
	Rhode Island	H	7.71 FQ	15.69 AW	21.80 TQ	RIBLS	10/01-12/01
	Providence-Fall River-Warwick MSA, RI-MA	H	7.76 FQ	15.84 AW	21.83 TQ	RIBLS	10/01-12/01
	South Carolina	H	9.46 FQ	13.83 AW	20.25 TQ	SCBLS	10/01-12/01
	Greenville-Spartanburg-Anderson MSA, SC	H	9.61 FQ	12.98 AW	17.06 TQ	SCBLS	10/01-12/01
	South Dakota	H	8.27 FQ	12.17 AW	18.00 TQ	SDBLS	10/01-12/01
	Tennessee	H	9.36 FQ	15.30 AW	22.56 TQ	TNBLS	10/01-12/01
	Johnson City-Kingsport-Bristol MSA, TN-VA	H	10.16 FQ	16.34 AW	24.77 TQ	TNBLS	10/01-12/01
	Memphis MSA, TN-AR-MS	H	7.67 FQ	13.69 AW	18.95 TQ	TNBLS	10/01-12/01
	Nashville MSA, TN	H	9.64 FQ	13.32 AW	18.47 TQ	TNBLS	10/01-12/01
	Texas	H	8.03 FQ	17.43 AW	26.86 TQ	TXBLS	10/01-12/01
	Austin-San Marcos MSA, TX	H	7.56 FQ	10.79 AW	18.21 TQ	TXBLS	10/01-12/01
	Beaumont-Port Arthur MSA, TX	H	8.60 FQ	18.27 AW	26.41 TQ	TXBLS	10/01-12/01
	Brazoria PMSA, TX	H	8.83 FQ	11.66 AW	18.37 TQ	TXBLS	10/01-12/01
	Dallas PMSA, TX	H	8.87 FQ	16.05 AW	24.63 TQ	TXBLS	10/01-12/01
	Fort Worth-Arlington PMSA, TX	H	7.69 FQ	16.61 AW	25.97 TQ	TXBLS	10/01-12/01
	Houston PMSA, TX	H	10.28 FQ	19.49 AW	27.21 TQ	TXBLS	10/01-12/01
	Utah	H	9.50 FQ	17.06 AW	22.04 TQ	UTBLS	10/01-12/01
	Salt Lake City-Ogden MSA, UT	H	13.83 FQ	18.91 AW	22.24 TQ	UTBLS	10/01-12/01

AAW	Average annual wage	**AOH**	Average offered, high	**ASH**	Average starting, high	**H**	Hourly	**M**	Monthly	**S**	Special: hourly and annual
AE	Average entry wage	**AOL**	Average offered, low	**ASL**	Average starting, low	**HI**	Highest wage paid	**MTC**	Median total compensation	**TQ**	Third quartile wage
AEX	Average experienced wage	**APH**	Average pay, high range	**AW**	Average wage paid	**HR**	High end range	**MW**	Median wage paid	**W**	Weekly
AO	Average offered	**APL**	Average pay, low range	**FQ**	First quartile wage	**LR**	Low end range	**SQ**	Second quartile wage	**Y**	Yearly

Occupation/Type/Industry	Location	Per	Low	Mid	High	Source	Date
Separating, Filtering, Clarifying, Precipitating, and Still Machine Setter, Operator, and Tender	Vermont	H	8.11 FQ	11.78 AW	16.26 TQ	VTBLS	10/01-12/01
	Virginia	H	7.47 FQ	16.99 AW	26.51 TQ	VABLS	10/01-12/01
	Richmond-Petersburg MSA, VA	H	8.26 FQ	14.84 AW	22.46 TQ	VABLS	10/01-12/01
	Washington	H	9.88 FQ	15.04 AW	20.83 TQ	WABLS	10/01-12/01
	Richland-Kennewick-Pasco MSA, WA	H	11.92 FQ	15.56 AW	18.68 TQ	WABLS	10/01-12/01
	Seattle-Bellevue-Everett PMSA, WA	H	11.56 FQ	16.05 AW	21.81 TQ	WABLS	10/01-12/01
	Tacoma PMSA, WA	H	12.87 FQ	18.49 AW	21.80 TQ	WABLS	10/01-12/01
	Yakima MSA, WA	H	9.31 FQ	14.04 AW	17.00 TQ	WABLS	10/01-12/01
	Wisconsin	H	10.01 FQ	14.56 AW	19.99 TQ	WIBLS	10/01-12/01
	Appleton-Oshkosh-Neenah MSA, WI	H	11.72 FQ	15.08 AW	18.18 TQ	WIBLS	10/01-12/01
	Green Bay MSA, WI	H	8.87 FQ	12.30 AW	16.16 TQ	WIBLS	10/01-12/01
	Madison MSA, WI	H	9.54 FQ	12.91 AW	17.20 TQ	WIBLS	10/01-12/01
	Milwaukee-Waukesha PMSA, WI	H	11.19 FQ	17.05 AW	25.88 TQ	WIBLS	10/01-12/01
	Wyoming	H	9.31 FQ	19.04 AW	26.83 TQ	WYBLS	10/01-12/01
	Puerto Rico	H	6.30 FQ	9.65 AW	14.63 TQ	PRBLS	10/01-12/01
	Virgin Islands	H	6.17 FQ	9.65 AW	13.04 TQ	VIBLS	10/01-12/01
Septic Tank Service and Sewer Pipe Cleaner	Alabama	H	6.19 FQ	9.17 AW	14.51 TQ	ALBLS	10/01-12/01
	Alaska	H	6.81 FQ	15.70 AW	20.64 TQ	AKBLS	10/01-12/01
	Arizona	H	7.59 FQ	13.30 AW	21.29 TQ	AZBLS	10/01-12/01
	Phoenix-Mesa MSA, AZ	H	10.01 FQ	15.86 AW	24.05 TQ	AZBLS	10/01-12/01
	Arkansas	H	8.56 FQ	11.05 AW	16.25 TQ	ARBLS	10/01-12/01
	Fort Smith MSA, AR-OK	H	8.82 FQ	10.59 AW	12.99 TQ	ARBLS	10/01-12/01
	California	H	9.37 FQ	17.49 AW	27.16 TQ	CABLS	10/01-12/01
	Chico-Paradise MSA, CA	H	13.68 FQ	16.14 AW	20.27 TQ	CABLS	10/01-12/01
	Oakland PMSA, CA	H	15.31 FQ	21.83 AW	26.44 TQ	CABLS	10/01-12/01
	Riverside-San Bernardino PMSA, CA	H	11.47 FQ	17.85 AW	29.53 TQ	CABLS	10/01-12/01
	Salinas MSA, CA	H	11.13 FQ	16.71 AW	24.31 TQ	CABLS	10/01-12/01
	Colorado	H	9.58 FQ	14.84 AW	22.04 TQ	COBLS	10/01-12/01
	Colorado Springs MSA, CO	H	7.40 FQ	15.99 AW	26.62 TQ	COBLS	10/01-12/01
	Connecticut	H	10.86 FQ	16.12 AW	20.97 TQ	CTBLS	10/01-12/01
	New London-Norwich MSA, CT-RI	H	12.64 FQ	15.65 AW	18.18 TQ	CTBLS	10/01-12/01
	Stamford-Norwalk PMSA, CT	H	11.42 FQ	17.80 AW	22.88 TQ	CTBLS	10/01-12/01
	Delaware	H	9.45 FQ	13.10 AW	17.87 TQ	DEBLS	10/01-12/01
	Washington PMSA, DC-MD-VA-WV	H	9.01 FQ	14.24 AW	18.60 TQ	DCBLS	10/01-12/01
	Florida	H	6.51 FQ	11.09 AW	15.86 TQ	FLBLS	10/01-12/01
	Jacksonville MSA, FL	H	10.85 FQ	12.13 AW	13.63 TQ	FLBLS	10/01-12/01
	Orlando MSA, FL	H	9.67 FQ	12.33 AW	16.13 TQ	FLBLS	10/01-12/01
	Pensacola MSA, FL	H	8.75 FQ	11.80 AW	16.69 TQ	FLBLS	10/01-12/01
	Sarasota-Bradenton MSA, FL	H	10.53 FQ	13.62 AW	16.55 TQ	FLBLS	10/01-12/01
	Tampa-St. Petersburg-Clearwater MSA, FL	H	5.85 FQ	9.50 AW	15.81 TQ	FLBLS	10/01-12/01
	Georgia	H	8.62 FQ	13.83 AW	18.61 TQ	GABLS	10/01-12/01
	Idaho	H	7.06 FQ	16.98 AW	25.55 TQ	IDBLS	10/01-12/01
	Illinois	H	12.05 FQ	17.08 AW	21.57 TQ	ILBLS	10/01-12/01
	Chicago PMSA, IL	H	12.72 FQ	15.57 AW	19.18 TQ	ILBLS	10/01-12/01
	Rockford MSA, IL	H	13.54 FQ	18.12 AW	21.76 TQ	ILBLS	10/01-12/01
	Indiana	H	6.11 FQ	12.05 AW	16.96 TQ	INBLS	10/01-12/01
	Gary PMSA, IN	H	6.58 FQ	11.48 AW	15.40 TQ	INBLS	10/01-12/01
	Indianapolis MSA, IN	H	11.06 FQ	14.39 AW	17.95 TQ	INBLS	10/01-12/01
	Iowa	H	9.55 FQ	13.75 AW	17.63 TQ	IABLS	10/01-12/01
	Kansas	H	9.67 FQ	14.12 AW	20.73 TQ	KSBLS	10/01-12/01
	Kentucky	H	5.83 FQ	13.38 AW	21.31 TQ	KYBLS	10/01-12/01
	Louisville MSA, KY-IN	H	5.81 FQ	13.67 AW	21.26 TQ	KYBLS	10/01-12/01
	Louisiana	H	8.60 FQ	13.99 AW	18.74 TQ	LABLS	10/01-12/01
	New Orleans MSA, LA	H	9.60 FQ	14.77 AW	19.34 TQ	LABLS	10/01-12/01
	Maine	H	10.07 FQ	15.56 AW	21.68 TQ	MEBLS	10/01-12/01
	Maryland	H	11.28 FQ	15.80 AW	20.61 TQ	MDBLS	10/01-12/01
	Baltimore PMSA, MD	H	12.07 FQ	17.23 AW	21.01 TQ	MDBLS	10/01-12/01
	Massachusetts	H	11.45 FQ	15.15 AW	20.43 TQ	MABLS	10/01-12/01

AAW	Average annual wage	**AOH**	Average offered, high	**ASH**	Average starting, high	**H**	Hourly	**M**	Monthly	**S**	Special: hourly and annual
AE	Average entry wage	**AOL**	Average offered, low	**ASL**	Average starting, low	**HI**	Highest wage paid	**MTC**	Median total compensation	**TQ**	Third quartile wage
AEX	Average experienced wage	**APH**	Average pay, high range	**AW**	Average wage paid	**HR**	High end range	**MW**	Median wage paid	**W**	Weekly
AO	Average offered	**APL**	Average pay, low range	**FQ**	First quartile wage	**LR**	Low end range	**SQ**	Second quartile wage	**Y**	Yearly

Occupation/Type/Industry	Location	Per	Low	Mid	High	Source	Date
Septic Tank Service and Sewer Pipe Cleaner	Boston PMSA, MA-NH	H	11.68 FQ	14.82 AW	17.82 TQ	MABLS	10/01-12/01
	Michigan	H	7.55 FQ	11.06 AW	16.01 TQ	MIBLS	10/01-12/01
	Detroit PMSA, MI	H	7.63 FQ	11.44 AW	17.58 TQ	MIBLS	10/01-12/01
	Grand Rapids-Muskegon-Holland MSA, MI	H	9.30 FQ	11.85 AW	14.75 TQ	MIBLS	10/01-12/01
	Kalamazoo-Battle Creek MSA, MI	H	7.24 FQ	9.12 AW	14.48 TQ	MIBLS	10/01-12/01
	Minnesota	H	11.24 FQ	16.85 AW	28.66 TQ	MNBLS	10/01-12/01
	Minneapolis-St. Paul MSA, MN-WI	H	12.25 FQ	17.89 AW	29.95 TQ	MNBLS	10/01-12/01
	Missouri	H	8.95 FQ	12.69 AW	17.53 TQ	MOBLS	10/01-12/01
	Kansas City MSA, MO-KS	H	8.83 FQ	11.36 AW	17.08 TQ	MOBLS	10/01-12/01
	St. Louis MSA, MO-IL	H	11.75 FQ	15.47 AW	21.17 TQ	MOBLS	10/01-12/01
	Nebraska	H	10.47 FQ	13.90 AW	22.31 TQ	NEBLS	10/01-12/01
	Nevada	H	14.08 FQ	15.91 AW	17.57 TQ	NVBLS	10/01-12/01
	Las Vegas MSA, NV-AZ	H	7.69 FQ	13.30 AW	17.24 TQ	NVBLS	10/01-12/01
	New Hampshire	H	9.24 FQ	14.96 AW	19.46 TQ	NHBLS	10/01-12/01
	New Jersey	H	11.72 FQ	15.80 AW	21.29 TQ	NJBLS	10/01-12/01
	Monmouth-Ocean PMSA, NJ	H	11.36 FQ	14.59 AW	17.40 TQ	NJBLS	10/01-12/01
	Newark PMSA, NJ	H	11.51 FQ	15.30 AW	21.42 TQ	NJBLS	10/01-12/01
	Trenton PMSA, NJ	H	11.65 FQ	15.78 AW	21.38 TQ	NJBLS	10/01-12/01
	New Mexico	H	6.96 FQ	11.59 AW	17.15 TQ	NMBLS	10/01-12/01
	Albuquerque MSA, NM	H	7.08 FQ	11.91 AW	17.57 TQ	NMBLS	10/01-12/01
	New York	H	8.88 FQ	18.96 AW	35.84 TQ	NYBLS	10/01-12/01
	Albany-Schenectady-Troy MSA, NY	H	7.42 FQ	11.35 AW	13.48 TQ	NYBLS	10/01-12/01
	Buffalo-Niagara Falls MSA, NY	H	11.48 FQ	17.57 AW	25.43 TQ	NYBLS	10/01-12/01
	Nassau-Suffolk PMSA, NY	H	8.94 FQ	14.02 AW	21.96 TQ	NYBLS	10/01-12/01
	North Carolina	H	6.17 FQ	9.90 AW	13.79 TQ	NCBLS	10/01-12/01
	Charlotte-Gastonia-Rock Hill MSA, NC-SC	H	9.62 FQ	12.50 AW	16.24 TQ	NCBLS	10/01-12/01
	Ohio	H	7.68 FQ	12.64 AW	17.98 TQ	OHBLS	10/01-12/01
	Canton-Massillon MSA, OH	H	6.86 FQ	12.91 AW	19.66 TQ	OHBLS	10/01-12/01
	Cincinnati PMSA, OH-KY-IN	H	8.79 FQ	13.32 AW	19.32 TQ	OHBLS	10/01-12/01
	Cleveland-Lorain-Elyria PMSA, OH	H	11.94 FQ	15.25 AW	18.82 TQ	OHBLS	10/01-12/01
	Columbus MSA, OH	H	8.41 FQ	11.35 AW	16.05 TQ	OHBLS	10/01-12/01
	Toledo MSA, OH	H	7.21 FQ	9.37 AW	14.30 TQ	OHBLS	10/01-12/01
	Oklahoma	H	9.50 FQ	13.92 AW	18.28 TQ	OKBLS	10/01-12/01
	Pennsylvania	H	6.84 FQ	13.13 AW	18.92 TQ	PABLS	10/01-12/01
	Philadelphia PMSA, PA-NJ	H	10.22 FQ	15.56 AW	21.76 TQ	PABLS	10/01-12/01
	Pittsburgh MSA, PA	H	11.41 FQ	12.96 AW	13.92 TQ	PABLS	10/01-12/01
	Rhode Island	H	9.90 FQ	16.42 AW	22.05 TQ	RIBLS	10/01-12/01
	Providence-Fall River-Warwick MSA, RI-MA	H	9.97 FQ	16.12 AW	21.96 TQ	RIBLS	10/01-12/01
	South Carolina	H	6.84 FQ	12.42 AW	17.54 TQ	SCBLS	10/01-12/01
	Greenville-Spartanburg-Anderson MSA, SC	H	6.41 FQ	11.62 AW	17.21 TQ	SCBLS	10/01-12/01
	South Dakota	H	7.20 FQ	10.44 AW	15.89 TQ	SDBLS	10/01-12/01
	Texas	H	6.00 FQ	11.02 AW	17.03 TQ	TXBLS	10/01-12/01
	Odessa-Midland MSA, TX	H	8.58 FQ	11.12 AW	13.92 TQ	TXBLS	10/01-12/01
	Utah	H	11.09 FQ	13.86 AW	17.41 TQ	UTBLS	10/01-12/01
	Vermont	H	7.84 FQ	11.19 AW	13.89 TQ	VTBLS	10/01-12/01
	Virginia	H	6.02 FQ	12.02 AW	17.78 TQ	VABLS	10/01-12/01
	Norfolk-Virginia Beach-Newport News MSA, VA-NC	H	7.19 FQ	13.25 AW	20.50 TQ	VABLS	10/01-12/01
	Washington	H	9.57 FQ	17.29 AW	25.32 TQ	WABLS	10/01-12/01
	Seattle-Bellevue-Everett PMSA, WA	H	9.91 FQ	18.92 AW	27.37 TQ	WABLS	10/01-12/01
	West Virginia	H	5.69 FQ	8.81 AW	14.95 TQ	WVBLS	10/01-12/01
	Wisconsin	H	10.94 FQ	14.99 AW	18.01 TQ	WIBLS	10/01-12/01
	Appleton-Oshkosh-Neenah MSA, WI	H	9.76 FQ	12.69 AW	16.19 TQ	WIBLS	10/01-12/01
	Green Bay MSA, WI	H	13.03 FQ	23.01 AW	28.58 TQ	WIBLS	10/01-12/01
	Wyoming	H	8.88 FQ	11.54 AW	16.47 TQ	WYBLS	10/01-12/01
Service Station Attendant	Alabama	H	6.02 FQ	8.02 AW	10.48 TQ	ALBLS	10/01-12/01
	Alaska	H	6.44 FQ	10.14 AW	16.17 TQ	AKBLS	10/01-12/01
	Arizona	H	5.88 FQ	8.34 AW	11.62 TQ	AZBLS	10/01-12/01

AAW	Average annual wage	**AOH**	Average offered, high	**ASH**	Average starting, high	**H**	Hourly	**M**	Monthly	**S**	Special: hourly and annual
AE	Average entry wage	**AOL**	Average offered, low	**ASL**	Average starting, low	**HI**	Highest wage paid	**MTC**	Median total compensation	**TQ**	Third quartile wage
AEX	Average experienced wage	**APH**	Average pay, high range	**AW**	Average wage paid	**HR**	High end range	**MW**	Median wage paid	**W**	Weekly
AO	Average offered	**APL**	Average pay, low range	**FQ**	First quartile wage	**LR**	Low end range	**SQ**	Second quartile wage	**Y**	Yearly

Occupation/Type/Industry	Location	Per	Low	Mid	High	Source	Date
Service Station Attendant	Arkansas	H	5.98 FQ	8.53 AW	11.36 TQ	ARBLS	10/01-12/01
	California	H	6.59 FQ	9.34 AW	14.53 TQ	CABLS	10/01-12/01
	Colorado	H	6.47 FQ	9.58 AW	13.78 TQ	COBLS	10/01-12/01
	Connecticut	H	6.73 FQ	8.40 AW	10.51 TQ	CTBLS	10/01-12/01
	Delaware	H	6.77 FQ	9.36 AW	13.63 TQ	DEBLS	10/01-12/01
	Florida	H	5.91 FQ	8.48 AW	12.44 TQ	FLBLS	10/01-12/01
	Georgia	H	5.85 FQ	7.88 AW	10.60 TQ	GABLS	10/01-12/01
	Hawaii	H	5.76 FQ	7.91 AW	11.02 TQ	HIBLS	10/01-12/01
	Idaho	H	5.93 FQ	8.20 AW	11.17 TQ	IDBLS	10/01-12/01
	Illinois	H	5.75 FQ	8.86 AW	16.05 TQ	ILBLS	10/01-12/01
	Indiana	H	5.75 FQ	7.75 AW	10.35 TQ	INBLS	10/01-12/01
	Iowa	H	5.83 FQ	7.92 AW	10.57 TQ	IABLS	10/01-12/01
	Kansas	H	6.14 FQ	8.23 AW	10.68 TQ	KSBLS	10/01-12/01
	Kentucky	H	5.69 FQ	7.72 AW	11.40 TQ	KYBLS	10/01-12/01
	Louisiana	H	5.74 FQ	7.64 AW	11.04 TQ	LABLS	10/01-12/01
	Maine	H	5.69 FQ	7.11 AW	9.34 TQ	MEBLS	10/01-12/01
	Maryland	H	5.78 FQ	8.14 AW	11.50 TQ	MDBLS	10/01-12/01
	Massachusetts	H	7.00 FQ	8.86 AW	11.29 TQ	MABLS	10/01-12/01
	Michigan	H	6.23 FQ	8.60 AW	12.62 TQ	MIBLS	10/01-12/01
	Minnesota	H	7.02 FQ	8.93 AW	11.90 TQ	MNBLS	10/01-12/01
	Mississippi	H	6.46 FQ	8.82 AW	10.87 TQ	MSBLS	10/01-12/01
	Missouri	H	5.84 FQ	9.08 AW	13.76 TQ	MOBLS	10/01-12/01
	Montana	H	5.55 FQ	7.22 AW	10.57 TQ	MTBLS	10/01-12/01
	Nebraska	H	6.36 FQ	8.43 AW	10.91 TQ	NEBLS	10/01-12/01
	Nevada	H	6.01 FQ	8.93 AW	13.13 TQ	NVBLS	10/01-12/01
	New Hampshire	H	6.13 FQ	8.27 AW	10.62 TQ	NHBLS	10/01-12/01
	New Jersey	H	5.83 FQ	7.54 AW	9.96 TQ	NJBLS	10/01-12/01
	New Mexico	H	5.66 FQ	7.55 AW	11.26 TQ	NMBLS	10/01-12/01
	New York	H	5.71 FQ	7.07 AW	8.86 TQ	NYBLS	10/01-12/01
	North Carolina	H	6.10 FQ	9.13 AW	13.39 TQ	NCBLS	10/01-12/01
	North Dakota	H	6.24 FQ	8.61 AW	11.23 TQ	NDBLS	10/01-12/01
	Ohio	H	5.89 FQ	8.17 AW	10.74 TQ	OHBLS	10/01-12/01
	Oklahoma	H	5.75 FQ	7.50 AW	10.22 TQ	OKBLS	10/01-12/01
	Oregon	H	6.88 FQ	8.01 AW	9.14 TQ	ORBLS	10/01-12/01
	Pennsylvania	H	5.74 FQ	7.27 AW	9.80 TQ	PABLS	10/01-12/01
	Rhode Island	H	6.67 FQ	7.97 AW	9.65 TQ	RIBLS	10/01-12/01
	South Carolina	H	6.05 FQ	8.15 AW	10.69 TQ	SCBLS	10/01-12/01
	South Dakota	H	6.01 FQ	7.65 AW	9.75 TQ	SDBLS	10/01-12/01
	Tennessee	H	6.05 FQ	8.61 AW	12.39 TQ	TNBLS	10/01-12/01
	Texas	H	5.99 FQ	8.85 AW	11.64 TQ	TXBLS	10/01-12/01
	Utah	H	6.04 FQ	8.98 AW	13.53 TQ	UTBLS	10/01-12/01
	Vermont	H	6.57 FQ	8.62 AW	11.08 TQ	VTBLS	10/01-12/01
	Virginia	H	5.78 FQ	7.97 AW	11.11 TQ	VABLS	10/01-12/01
	Washington	H	6.90 FQ	9.17 AW	12.82 TQ	WABLS	10/01-12/01
	West Virginia	H	5.54 FQ	6.80 AW	9.56 TQ	WVBLS	10/01-12/01
	Wisconsin	H	6.73 FQ	8.60 AW	10.62 TQ	WIBLS	10/01-12/01
	Wyoming	H	5.74 FQ	7.47 AW	9.59 TQ	WYBLS	10/01-12/01
	Puerto Rico	H	5.65 FQ	6.34 AW	7.22 TQ	PRBLS	10/01-12/01
	Virgin Islands	H	5.56 FQ	6.28 AW	7.32 TQ	VIBLS	10/01-12/01
	Guam	H	5.49 FQ	6.31 AW	7.76 TQ	GUBLS	10/01-12/01
Service Unit Operator							
Oil, Gas, and Mining	Alabama	H	8.06 FQ	11.94 AW	17.41 TQ	ALBLS	10/01-12/01
Oil, Gas, and Mining	Arkansas	H	9.75 FQ	14.72 AW	26.10 TQ	ARBLS	10/01-12/01
Oil, Gas, and Mining	California	H	12.54 FQ	19.51 AW	27.50 TQ	CABLS	10/01-12/01
Oil, Gas, and Mining	Colorado	H	11.44 FQ	14.74 AW	19.87 TQ	COBLS	10/01-12/01
Oil, Gas, and Mining	Illinois	H	7.74 FQ	11.80 AW	19.84 TQ	ILBLS	10/01-12/01
Oil, Gas, and Mining	Kansas	H	9.09 FQ	12.68 AW	19.59 TQ	KSBLS	10/01-12/01
Oil, Gas, and Mining	Kentucky	H	7.99 FQ	10.33 AW	11.78 TQ	KYBLS	10/01-12/01
Oil, Gas, and Mining	Louisiana	H	8.93 FQ	15.20 AW	22.29 TQ	LABLS	10/01-12/01
Oil, Gas, and Mining	Michigan	H	12.49 FQ	15.47 AW	18.97 TQ	MIBLS	10/01-12/01
Oil, Gas, and Mining	Mississippi	H	9.10 FQ	13.38 AW	18.20 TQ	MSBLS	10/01-12/01
Oil, Gas, and Mining	Montana	H	11.87 FQ	14.61 AW	17.62 TQ	MTBLS	10/01-12/01
Oil, Gas, and Mining	New Mexico	H	8.82 FQ	14.64 AW	20.72 TQ	NMBLS	10/01-12/01
Oil, Gas, and Mining	New York	H	8.08 FQ	18.14 AW	25.91 TQ	NYBLS	10/01-12/01
Oil, Gas, and Mining	North Dakota	H	9.49 FQ	12.78 AW	17.09 TQ	NDBLS	10/01-12/01
Oil, Gas, and Mining	Ohio	H	8.10 FQ	12.63 AW	16.96 TQ	OHBLS	10/01-12/01
Oil, Gas, and Mining	Oklahoma	H	10.18 FQ	17.98 AW	26.58 TQ	OKBLS	10/01-12/01
Oil, Gas, and Mining	Pennsylvania	H	8.88 FQ	11.63 AW	16.30 TQ	PABLS	10/01-12/01
Oil, Gas, and Mining	Texas	H	8.74 FQ	13.04 AW	20.49 TQ	TXBLS	10/01-12/01
Oil, Gas, and Mining	Utah	H	11.57 FQ	14.64 AW	20.77 TQ	UTBLS	10/01-12/01
Oil, Gas, and Mining	West Virginia	H	8.51 FQ	16.45 AW	31.22 TQ	WVBLS	10/01-12/01
Oil, Gas, and Mining	Wyoming	H	12.37 FQ	16.86 AW	22.46 TQ	WYBLS	10/01-12/01

AAW	Average annual wage	AOH	Average offered, high	ASH	Average starting, high	H	Hourly	M	Monthly	S	Special: hourly and annual
AE	Average entry wage	AOL	Average offered, low	ASL	Average starting, low	HI	Highest wage paid	MTC	Median total compensation	TQ	Third quartile wage
AEX	Average experienced wage	APH	Average pay, high range	AW	Average wage paid	HR	High end range	MW	Median wage paid	W	Weekly
AO	Average offered	APL	Average pay, low range	FQ	First quartile wage	LR	Low end range	SQ	Second quartile wage	Y	Yearly

Occupation/Type/Industry	Location	Per	Low	Mid	High	Source	Date
Set and Exhibit Designer	Arizona	Y	16880 FQ	28310 AW	42760 TQ	AZBLS	10/01-12/01
	California	Y	20160 FQ	44640 AW	70450 TQ	CABLS	10/01-12/01
	Colorado	Y	21600 FQ	36810 AW	60050 TQ	COBLS	10/01-12/01
	Connecticut	Y	23180 FQ	40180 AW	75160 TQ	CTBLS	10/01-12/01
	District of Columbia	Y	24710 FQ	47510 AW	68870 TQ	DCBLS	10/01-12/01
	Florida	Y	16540 FQ	27190 AW	39990 TQ	FLBLS	10/01-12/01
	Georgia	Y	19280 FQ	30410 AW	44270 TQ	GABLS	10/01-12/01
	Illinois	Y	23700 FQ	37960 AW	48260 TQ	ILBLS	10/01-12/01
	Indiana	Y	18660 FQ	31730 AW	52210 TQ	INBLS	10/01-12/01
	Kansas	Y	12750 FQ	26020 AW	41690 TQ	KSBLS	10/01-12/01
	Kentucky	Y	11730 FQ	21460 AW	34930 TQ	KYBLS	10/01-12/01
	Louisiana	Y	21680 FQ	31800 AW	42620 TQ	LABLS	10/01-12/01
	Maryland	Y	19690 FQ	40770 AW	66430 TQ	MDBLS	10/01-12/01
	Massachusetts	Y	26690 FQ	36100 AW	44700 TQ	MABLS	10/01-12/01
	Michigan	Y	17520 FQ	36280 AW	66930 TQ	MIBLS	10/01-12/01
	Minnesota	Y	25740 FQ	38220 AW	63360 TQ	MNBLS	10/01-12/01
	Missouri	Y	22600 FQ	41110 AW	63900 TQ	MOBLS	10/01-12/01
	New Jersey	Y	25050 FQ	47530 AW	70450 TQ	NJBLS	10/01-12/01
	New Mexico	Y	12980 FQ	26710 AW	45530 TQ	NMBLS	10/01-12/01
	New York	Y	12410 FQ	32660 AW	62090 TQ	NYBLS	10/01-12/01
	North Carolina	Y	18690 FQ	29990 AW	45450 TQ	NCBLS	10/01-12/01
	Ohio	Y	21890 FQ	37680 AW	49650 TQ	OHBLS	10/01-12/01
	Oregon	Y	19710 FQ	30660 AW	42270 TQ	ORBLS	10/01-12/01
	Pennsylvania	Y	21470 FQ	37310 AW	53910 TQ	PABLS	10/01-12/01
	South Carolina	Y	23020 FQ	28090 AW	35070 TQ	SCBLS	10/01-12/01
	Tennessee	Y	21580 FQ	31540 AW	42390 TQ	TNBLS	10/01-12/01
	Texas	Y	21040 FQ	32510 AW	45210 TQ	TXBLS	10/01-12/01
	Utah	Y	15770 FQ	26620 AW	44830 TQ	UTBLS	10/01-12/01
	Virginia	Y	21550 FQ	35880 AW	53710 TQ	VABLS	10/01-12/01
	Washington	Y	17880 FQ	32880 AW	50980 TQ	WABLS	10/01-12/01
	West Virginia	Y	11630 FQ	23610 AW	60460 TQ	WVBLS	10/01-12/01
	Wisconsin	Y	14360 FQ	25610 AW	38750 TQ	WIBLS	10/01-12/01
Sewer							
Hand	Alabama	H	7.86 FQ	9.73 AW	11.14 TQ	ALBLS	10/01-12/01
Hand	Arizona	H	6.03 FQ	8.68 AW	17.93 TQ	AZBLS	10/01-12/01
Hand	Arkansas	H	6.23 FQ	8.56 AW	10.95 TQ	ARBLS	10/01-12/01
Hand	California	H	6.70 FQ	9.09 AW	12.79 TQ	CABLS	10/01-12/01
Hand	Colorado	H	7.37 FQ	8.61 AW	10.75 TQ	COBLS	10/01-12/01
Hand	Connecticut	H	7.07 FQ	10.86 AW	14.21 TQ	CTBLS	10/01-12/01
Hand	Delaware	H	7.21 FQ	8.16 AW	8.80 TQ	DEBLS	10/01-12/01
Hand	Florida	H	6.04 FQ	8.86 AW	12.96 TQ	FLBLS	10/01-12/01
Hand	Georgia	H	7.67 FQ	10.61 AW	13.88 TQ	GABLS	10/01-12/01
Hand	Illinois	H	6.97 FQ	10.10 AW	13.46 TQ	ILBLS	10/01-12/01
Hand	Indiana	H	7.49 FQ	9.74 AW	12.29 TQ	INBLS	10/01-12/01
Hand	Iowa	H	7.35 FQ	9.64 AW	13.20 TQ	IABLS	10/01-12/01
Hand	Kansas	H	5.82 FQ	8.01 AW	11.29 TQ	KSBLS	10/01-12/01
Hand	Kentucky	H	5.99 FQ	8.11 AW	10.77 TQ	KYBLS	10/01-12/01
Hand	Louisiana	H	5.50 FQ	7.29 AW	9.95 TQ	LABLS	10/01-12/01
Hand	Maine	H	7.77 FQ	10.78 AW	14.37 TQ	MEBLS	10/01-12/01
Hand	Maryland	H	5.81 FQ	7.84 AW	10.38 TQ	MDBLS	10/01-12/01
Hand	Massachusetts	H	7.12 FQ	9.93 AW	13.78 TQ	MABLS	10/01-12/01
Hand	Michigan	H	6.82 FQ	9.33 AW	11.61 TQ	MIBLS	10/01-12/01
Hand	Minnesota	H	6.50 FQ	10.21 AW	15.72 TQ	MNBLS	10/01-12/01
Hand	Missouri	H	5.71 FQ	8.74 AW	12.73 TQ	MOBLS	10/01-12/01
Hand	Montana	H	5.98 FQ	8.39 AW	13.50 TQ	MTBLS	10/01-12/01
Hand	Nevada	H	7.09 FQ	11.03 AW	15.04 TQ	NVBLS	10/01-12/01
Hand	New Jersey	H	5.94 FQ	9.43 AW	14.50 TQ	NJBLS	10/01-12/01
Hand	New Mexico	H	5.66 FQ	7.65 AW	9.81 TQ	NMBLS	10/01-12/01
Hand	New York	H	5.80 FQ	10.95 AW	19.87 TQ	NYBLS	10/01-12/01
Hand	North Carolina	H	6.25 FQ	9.42 AW	13.42 TQ	NCBLS	10/01-12/01
Hand	Ohio	H	6.34 FQ	9.56 AW	13.62 TQ	OHBLS	10/01-12/01
Hand	Oklahoma	H	7.39 FQ	9.74 AW	12.48 TQ	OKBLS	10/01-12/01
Hand	Oregon	H	6.89 FQ	9.12 AW	13.46 TQ	ORBLS	10/01-12/01
Hand	Pennsylvania	H	6.83 FQ	8.83 AW	12.03 TQ	PABLS	10/01-12/01
Hand	Rhode Island	H	7.26 FQ	10.70 AW	17.77 TQ	RIBLS	10/01-12/01
Hand	South Carolina	H	5.72 FQ	7.56 AW	10.63 TQ	SCBLS	10/01-12/01
Hand	Tennessee	H	6.14 FQ	8.47 AW	11.16 TQ	TNBLS	10/01-12/01
Hand	Texas	H	5.54 FQ	7.11 AW	9.92 TQ	TXBLS	10/01-12/01
Hand	Utah	H	5.75 FQ	7.15 AW	8.99 TQ	UTBLS	10/01-12/01
Hand	Vermont	H	6.51 FQ	7.93 AW	10.31 TQ	VTBLS	10/01-12/01
Hand	Virginia	H	6.69 FQ	8.87 AW	11.74 TQ	VABLS	10/01-12/01
Hand	Washington	H	8.54 FQ	12.46 AW	17.92 TQ	WABLS	10/01-12/01

AAW Average annual wage **AOH** Average offered, high **ASH** Average starting, high **H** Hourly **M** Monthly **S** Special: hourly and annual
AE Average entry wage **AOL** Average offered, low **ASL** Average starting, low **HI** Highest wage paid **MTC** Median total compensation **TQ** Third quartile wage
AEX Average experienced wage **APH** Average pay, high range **AW** Average wage paid **HR** High end range **MW** Median wage paid **W** Weekly
AO Average offered **APL** Average pay, low range **FQ** First quartile wage **LR** Low end range **SQ** Second quartile wage **Y** Yearly

Occupation/Type/Industry	Location	Per	Low	Mid	High	Source	Date
Sewer							
Hand	Wisconsin	H	6.79 FQ	9.00 AW	11.02 TQ	WIBLS	10/01-12/01
Hand	Puerto Rico	H	5.61 FQ	6.80 AW	8.26 TQ	PRBLS	10/01-12/01
Sewing Machine Operator	Alabama	H	5.80 FQ	8.05 AW	11.22 TQ	ALBLS	10/01-12/01
	Birmingham MSA, AL	H	5.88 FQ	7.70 AW	10.68 TQ	ALBLS	10/01-12/01
	Huntsville MSA, AL	H	5.66 FQ	7.71 AW	10.59 TQ	ALBLS	10/01-12/01
	Mobile MSA, AL	H	5.79 FQ	7.61 AW	9.88 TQ	ALBLS	10/01-12/01
	Montgomery MSA, AL	H	5.64 FQ	7.70 AW	10.63 TQ	ALBLS	10/01-12/01
	Alaska	H	9.02 FQ	12.33 AW	16.48 TQ	AKBLS	10/01-12/01
	Anchorage MSA, AK	H	9.00 FQ	12.14 AW	16.38 TQ	AKBLS	10/01-12/01
	Arizona	H	6.16 FQ	8.77 AW	12.38 TQ	AZBLS	10/01-12/01
	Phoenix-Mesa MSA, AZ	H	6.78 FQ	9.05 AW	12.52 TQ	AZBLS	10/01-12/01
	Tucson MSA, AZ	H	5.72 FQ	8.59 AW	12.99 TQ	AZBLS	10/01-12/01
	Arkansas	H	5.90 FQ	8.04 AW	10.83 TQ	ARBLS	10/01-12/01
	Fayetteville-Springdale-Rogers MSA, AR	H	6.81 FQ	8.38 AW	10.47 TQ	ARBLS	10/01-12/01
	Little Rock-North Little Rock MSA, AR	H	6.67 FQ	8.96 AW	11.17 TQ	ARBLS	10/01-12/01
	California	H	6.43 FQ	7.95 AW	10.45 TQ	CABLS	10/01-12/01
	Bakersfield MSA, CA	H	6.92 FQ	7.92 AW	8.44 TQ	CABLS	10/01-12/01
	Chico-Paradise MSA, CA	H	6.71 FQ	8.41 AW	10.73 TQ	CABLS	10/01-12/01
	Fresno MSA, CA	H	6.44 FQ	7.99 AW	10.52 TQ	CABLS	10/01-12/01
	Los Angeles-Long Beach PMSA, CA	H	6.42 FQ	7.72 AW	9.82 TQ	CABLS	10/01-12/01
	Modesto MSA, CA	H	7.51 FQ	9.30 AW	11.07 TQ	CABLS	10/01-12/01
	Oakland PMSA, CA	H	6.43 FQ	9.03 AW	13.67 TQ	CABLS	10/01-12/01
	Orange County PMSA, CA	H	6.53 FQ	8.12 AW	10.65 TQ	CABLS	10/01-12/01
	Redding MSA, CA	H	7.07 FQ	8.41 AW	10.51 TQ	CABLS	10/01-12/01
	Riverside-San Bernardino PMSA, CA	H	6.54 FQ	8.94 AW	12.86 TQ	CABLS	10/01-12/01
	Sacramento PMSA, CA	H	6.71 FQ	8.36 AW	11.52 TQ	CABLS	10/01-12/01
	San Diego MSA, CA	H	6.44 FQ	8.04 AW	10.76 TQ	CABLS	10/01-12/01
	San Francisco PMSA, CA	H	6.38 FQ	8.54 AW	12.70 TQ	CABLS	10/01-12/01
	San Jose PMSA, CA	H	6.79 FQ	10.69 AW	16.75 TQ	CABLS	10/01-12/01
	San Luis Obispo-Atascadero-Paso Robles MSA, CA	H	7.17 FQ	10.16 AW	13.59 TQ	CABLS	10/01-12/01
	Santa Barbara-Santa Maria-Lompoc MSA, CA	H	6.88 FQ	10.87 AW	17.42 TQ	CABLS	10/01-12/01
	Santa Cruz-Watsonville PMSA, CA	H	6.76 FQ	9.39 AW	13.67 TQ	CABLS	10/01-12/01
	Santa Rosa PMSA, CA	H	6.64 FQ	8.84 AW	12.19 TQ	CABLS	10/01-12/01
	Stockton-Lodi MSA, CA	H	6.57 FQ	8.53 AW	10.92 TQ	CABLS	10/01-12/01
	Vallejo-Fairfield-Napa PMSA, CA	H	6.97 FQ	10.25 AW	13.56 TQ	CABLS	10/01-12/01
	Ventura PMSA, CA	H	6.45 FQ	8.13 AW	10.88 TQ	CABLS	10/01-12/01
	Colorado	H	6.96 FQ	9.34 AW	12.86 TQ	COBLS	10/01-12/01
	Colorado Springs MSA, CO	H	7.20 FQ	9.90 AW	13.89 TQ	COBLS	10/01-12/01
	Denver PMSA, CO	H	6.58 FQ	9.17 AW	12.57 TQ	COBLS	10/01-12/01
	Connecticut	H	7.10 FQ	9.74 AW	13.60 TQ	CTBLS	10/01-12/01
	Bridgeport PMSA, CT	H	6.94 FQ	9.37 AW	12.50 TQ	CTBLS	10/01-12/01
	Hartford MSA, CT	H	7.01 FQ	9.48 AW	13.32 TQ	CTBLS	10/01-12/01
	New Haven-Meriden PMSA, CT	H	7.35 FQ	9.95 AW	14.89 TQ	CTBLS	10/01-12/01
	New London-Norwich MSA, CT-RI	H	7.65 FQ	10.73 AW	15.32 TQ	CTBLS	10/01-12/01
	Stamford-Norwalk PMSA, CT	H	7.46 FQ	10.00 AW	13.28 TQ	CTBLS	10/01-12/01
	Waterbury PMSA, CT	H	7.91 FQ	10.48 AW	13.80 TQ	CTBLS	10/01-12/01
	Delaware	H	8.51 FQ	12.52 AW	16.34 TQ	DEBLS	10/01-12/01
	Wilmington-Newark PMSA, DE-MD	H	8.73 FQ	13.08 AW	16.48 TQ	DEBLS	10/01-12/01
	Washington PMSA, DC-MD-VA-WV	H	7.79 FQ	11.07 AW	13.27 TQ	DCBLS	10/01-12/01
	Florida	H	5.77 FQ	7.77 AW	10.59 TQ	FLBLS	10/01-12/01
	Daytona Beach MSA, FL	H	6.33 FQ	9.15 AW	13.01 TQ	FLBLS	10/01-12/01
	Fort Lauderdale PMSA, FL	H	6.28 FQ	8.98 AW	12.53 TQ	FLBLS	10/01-12/01
	Fort Myers-Cape Coral MSA, FL	H	6.26 FQ	8.82 AW	11.35 TQ	FLBLS	10/01-12/01
	Fort Pierce-Port St. Lucie MSA, FL	H	5.59 FQ	8.05 AW	10.72 TQ	FLBLS	10/01-12/01
	Jacksonville MSA, FL	H	7.35 FQ	9.42 AW	12.68 TQ	FLBLS	10/01-12/01
	Lakeland-Winter Haven MSA, FL	H	5.76 FQ	7.33 AW	8.68 TQ	FLBLS	10/01-12/01

AAW	Average annual wage	**AOH**	Average offered, high	**ASH**	Average starting, high	**H**	Hourly	**M**	Monthly	**S**	Special: hourly and annual
AE	Average entry wage	**AOL**	Average offered, low	**ASL**	Average starting, low	**HI**	Highest wage paid	**MTC**	Median total compensation	**TQ**	Third quartile wage
AEX	Average experienced wage	**APH**	Average pay, high range	**AW**	Average wage paid	**HR**	High end range	**MW**	Median wage paid	**W**	Weekly
AO	Average offered	**APL**	Average pay, low range	**FQ**	First quartile wage	**LR**	Low end range	**SQ**	Second quartile wage	**Y**	Yearly

Occupation/Type/Industry	Location	Per	Low	Mid	High	Source	Date
Sewing Machine Operator	Melbourne-Titusville-Palm Bay MSA, FL	H	6.52 FQ	9.57 AW	13.39 TQ	FLBLS	10/01-12/01
	Miami PMSA, FL	H	5.64 FQ	6.97 AW	9.02 TQ	FLBLS	10/01-12/01
	Naples MSA, FL	H	6.18 FQ	8.06 AW	10.58 TQ	FLBLS	10/01-12/01
	Ocala MSA, FL	H	6.88 FQ	8.34 AW	10.49 TQ	FLBLS	10/01-12/01
	Orlando MSA, FL	H	7.13 FQ	9.75 AW	12.92 TQ	FLBLS	10/01-12/01
	Pensacola MSA, FL	H	6.22 FQ	7.97 AW	10.09 TQ	FLBLS	10/01-12/01
	Sarasota-Bradenton MSA, FL	H	7.37 FQ	9.89 AW	13.02 TQ	FLBLS	10/01-12/01
	Tampa-St. Petersburg-Clearwater MSA, FL	H	6.05 FQ	8.02 AW	10.48 TQ	FLBLS	10/01-12/01
	West Palm Beach-Boca Raton MSA, FL	H	6.18 FQ	8.91 AW	12.71 TQ	FLBLS	10/01-12/01
	Georgia	H	5.92 FQ	8.50 AW	12.11 TQ	GABLS	10/01-12/01
	Atlanta MSA, GA	H	6.44 FQ	8.91 AW	11.42 TQ	GABLS	10/01-12/01
	Columbus MSA, GA-AL	H	7.22 FQ	10.50 AW	13.47 TQ	GABLS	10/01-12/01
	Macon MSA, GA	H	7.21 FQ	10.39 AW	15.82 TQ	GABLS	10/01-12/01
	Hawaii	H	5.66 FQ	7.08 AW	9.59 TQ	HIBLS	10/01-12/01
	Honolulu MSA, HI	H	5.65 FQ	6.93 AW	9.05 TQ	HIBLS	10/01-12/01
	Idaho	H	5.99 FQ	8.36 AW	11.46 TQ	IDBLS	10/01-12/01
	Boise City MSA, ID	H	6.48 FQ	8.62 AW	11.51 TQ	IDBLS	10/01-12/01
	Illinois	H	5.91 FQ	8.84 AW	12.12 TQ	ILBLS	10/01-12/01
	Chicago PMSA, IL	H	5.80 FQ	8.92 AW	12.62 TQ	ILBLS	10/01-12/01
	Peoria-Pekin MSA, IL	H	7.22 FQ	8.13 AW	9.15 TQ	ILBLS	10/01-12/01
	Rockford MSA, IL	H	7.39 FQ	9.09 AW	11.90 TQ	ILBLS	10/01-12/01
	Indiana	H	6.57 FQ	9.77 AW	13.76 TQ	INBLS	10/01-12/01
	Elkhart-Goshen MSA, IN	H	6.66 FQ	10.95 AW	15.03 TQ	INBLS	10/01-12/01
	Fort Wayne MSA, IN	H	7.20 FQ	9.15 AW	12.07 TQ	INBLS	10/01-12/01
	Gary PMSA, IN	H	5.75 FQ	8.06 AW	11.20 TQ	INBLS	10/01-12/01
	Indianapolis MSA, IN	H	7.60 FQ	10.57 AW	14.48 TQ	INBLS	10/01-12/01
	South Bend MSA, IN	H	7.08 FQ	8.11 AW	9.75 TQ	INBLS	10/01-12/01
	Iowa	H	6.17 FQ	9.10 AW	12.70 TQ	IABLS	10/01-12/01
	Cedar Rapids MSA, IA	H	7.27 FQ	9.31 AW	11.75 TQ	IABLS	10/01-12/01
	Des Moines MSA, IA	H	7.42 FQ	9.21 AW	10.91 TQ	IABLS	10/01-12/01
	Kansas	H	6.08 FQ	8.95 AW	12.58 TQ	KSBLS	10/01-12/01
	Wichita MSA, KS	H	5.73 FQ	8.90 AW	15.53 TQ	KSBLS	10/01-12/01
	Kentucky	H	6.14 FQ	8.86 AW	11.96 TQ	KYBLS	10/01-12/01
	Lexington MSA, KY	H	6.46 FQ	9.90 AW	13.62 TQ	KYBLS	10/01-12/01
	Louisville MSA, KY-IN	H	7.46 FQ	9.87 AW	12.95 TQ	KYBLS	10/01-12/01
	Louisiana	H	5.60 FQ	7.30 AW	10.85 TQ	LABLS	10/01-12/01
	Baton Rouge MSA, LA	H	5.76 FQ	7.59 AW	10.86 TQ	LABLS	10/01-12/01
	Lafayette MSA, LA	H	5.55 FQ	7.96 AW	13.16 TQ	LABLS	10/01-12/01
	New Orleans MSA, LA	H	5.69 FQ	7.72 AW	10.54 TQ	LABLS	10/01-12/01
	Shreveport-Bossier City MSA, LA	H	6.13 FQ	9.50 AW	13.53 TQ	LABLS	10/01-12/01
	Maine	H	6.14 FQ	8.80 AW	12.15 TQ	MEBLS	10/01-12/01
	Maryland	H	7.07 FQ	10.34 AW	13.13 TQ	MDBLS	10/01-12/01
	Baltimore PMSA, MD	H	6.85 FQ	9.25 AW	12.49 TQ	MDBLS	10/01-12/01
	Massachusetts	H	7.10 FQ	9.37 AW	12.73 TQ	MABLS	10/01-12/01
	Boston PMSA, MA-NH	H	7.06 FQ	9.51 AW	13.25 TQ	MABLS	10/01-12/01
	Brockton PMSA, MA	H	7.09 FQ	9.58 AW	14.04 TQ	MABLS	10/01-12/01
	Lawrence PMSA, MA-NH	H	7.30 FQ	10.19 AW	13.82 TQ	MABLS	10/01-12/01
	Lowell PMSA, MA-NH	H	7.17 FQ	11.86 AW	19.87 TQ	MABLS	10/01-12/01
	New Bedford PMSA, MA	H	7.02 FQ	8.77 AW	11.03 TQ	MABLS	10/01-12/01
	Springfield MSA, MA	H	7.06 FQ	9.38 AW	12.43 TQ	MABLS	10/01-12/01
	Worcester PMSA, MA-CT	H	7.21 FQ	9.69 AW	13.45 TQ	MABLS	10/01-12/01
	Michigan	H	7.66 FQ	11.96 AW	19.92 TQ	MIBLS	10/01-12/01
	Ann Arbor PMSA, MI	H	7.00 FQ	9.59 AW	12.83 TQ	MIBLS	10/01-12/01
	Detroit PMSA, MI	H	7.68 FQ	13.26 AW	26.15 TQ	MIBLS	10/01-12/01
	Flint PMSA, MI	H	7.31 FQ	8.75 AW	10.49 TQ	MIBLS	10/01-12/01
	Grand Rapids-Muskegon-Holland MSA, MI	H	9.11 FQ	11.41 AW	14.28 TQ	MIBLS	10/01-12/01
	Kalamazoo-Battle Creek MSA, MI	H	7.60 FQ	10.65 AW	13.67 TQ	MIBLS	10/01-12/01
	Lansing-East Lansing MSA, MI	H	6.67 FQ	10.75 AW	15.73 TQ	MIBLS	10/01-12/01
	Saginaw-Bay City-Midland MSA, MI	H	5.83 FQ	8.22 AW	12.20 TQ	MIBLS	10/01-12/01
	Minnesota	H	7.25 FQ	9.96 AW	13.30 TQ	MNBLS	10/01-12/01
	Duluth-Superior MSA, MN-WI	H	6.09 FQ	8.70 AW	12.04 TQ	MNBLS	10/01-12/01
	Minneapolis-St. Paul MSA, MN-WI	H	7.66 FQ	10.43 AW	13.53 TQ	MNBLS	10/01-12/01
	St. Cloud MSA, MN	H	7.44 FQ	9.90 AW	12.74 TQ	MNBLS	10/01-12/01
	Mississippi	H	5.91 FQ	9.14 AW	13.11 TQ	MSBLS	10/01-12/01

AAW Average annual wage **AE** Average entry wage **AEX** Average experienced wage **AO** Average offered **AOH** Average offered, high **AOL** Average offered, low **APH** Average pay, high range **APL** Average pay, low range **ASH** Average starting, high **ASL** Average starting, low **AW** Average wage paid **FQ** First quartile wage **H** Hourly **HI** Highest wage paid **HR** High end range **LR** Low end range **M** Monthly **MTC** Median total compensation **MW** Median wage paid **SQ** Second quartile wage **S** Special: hourly and annual **TQ** Third quartile wage **W** Weekly **Y** Yearly

Occupation/Type/Industry	Location	Per	Low	Mid	High	Source	Date
Sewing Machine Operator	Jackson MSA, MS	H	6.09 FQ	9.24 AW	13.53 TQ	MSBLS	10/01-12/01
	Missouri	H	6.08 FQ	8.54 AW	11.85 TQ	MOBLS	10/01-12/01
	Kansas City MSA, MO-KS	H	6.80 FQ	8.98 AW	11.56 TQ	MOBLS	10/01-12/01
	St. Louis MSA, MO-IL	H	6.09 FQ	8.42 AW	10.97 TQ	MOBLS	10/01-12/01
	Springfield MSA, MO	H	6.28 FQ	9.30 AW	12.43 TQ	MOBLS	10/01-12/01
	Montana	H	5.85 FQ	8.09 AW	10.73 TQ	MTBLS	10/01-12/01
	Billings MSA, MT	H	6.83 FQ	8.32 AW	10.36 TQ	MTBLS	10/01-12/01
	Nebraska	H	6.25 FQ	8.48 AW	10.78 TQ	NEBLS	10/01-12/01
	Lincoln MSA, NE	H	7.28 FQ	8.72 AW	10.75 TQ	NEBLS	10/01-12/01
	Omaha MSA, NE-IA	H	6.72 FQ	8.86 AW	10.83 TQ	NEBLS	10/01-12/01
	Nevada	H	6.42 FQ	9.03 AW	11.94 TQ	NVBLS	10/01-12/01
	Las Vegas MSA, NV-AZ	H	6.17 FQ	9.10 AW	12.41 TQ	NVBLS	10/01-12/01
	Reno MSA, NV	H	7.03 FQ	8.76 AW	10.96 TQ	NVBLS	10/01-12/01
	New Hampshire	H	7.28 FQ	9.62 AW	12.86 TQ	NHBLS	10/01-12/01
	Manchester PMSA, NH	H	7.71 FQ	9.81 AW	12.49 TQ	NHBLS	10/01-12/01
	Nashua PMSA, NH	H	8.27 FQ	10.53 AW	13.40 TQ	NHBLS	10/01-12/01
	Portsmouth-Rochester PMSA, NH-ME	H	8.81 FQ	11.27 AW	14.55 TQ	NHBLS	10/01-12/01
	New Jersey	H	5.85 FQ	8.45 AW	11.71 TQ	NJBLS	10/01-12/01
	Atlantic-Cape May PMSA, NJ	H	7.33 FQ	10.16 AW	15.09 TQ	NJBLS	10/01-12/01
	Bergen-Passaic PMSA, NJ	H	5.81 FQ	8.32 AW	11.39 TQ	NJBLS	10/01-12/01
	Jersey City PMSA, NJ	H	5.70 FQ	8.05 AW	11.34 TQ	NJBLS	10/01-12/01
	Middlesex-Somerset-Hunterdon PMSA, NJ	H	5.68 FQ	7.90 AW	11.42 TQ	NJBLS	10/01-12/01
	Newark PMSA, NJ	H	5.98 FQ	8.66 AW	11.43 TQ	NJBLS	10/01-12/01
	Trenton PMSA, NJ	H	6.81 FQ	9.22 AW	12.36 TQ	NJBLS	10/01-12/01
	New Mexico	H	6.06 FQ	8.26 AW	10.80 TQ	NMBLS	10/01-12/01
	Albuquerque MSA, NM	H	6.87 FQ	8.73 AW	11.20 TQ	NMBLS	10/01-12/01
	New York	H	5.72 FQ	8.62 AW	13.90 TQ	NYBLS	10/01-12/01
	Albany-Schenectady-Troy MSA, NY	H	6.21 FQ	10.03 AW	18.00 TQ	NYBLS	10/01-12/01
	Binghamton MSA, NY	H	6.76 FQ	9.55 AW	13.14 TQ	NYBLS	10/01-12/01
	Buffalo-Niagara Falls MSA, NY	H	7.22 FQ	10.99 AW	15.75 TQ	NYBLS	10/01-12/01
	Nassau-Suffolk PMSA, NY	H	6.78 FQ	10.03 AW	15.33 TQ	NYBLS	10/01-12/01
	New York PMSA, NY	H	5.67 FQ	8.39 AW	13.81 TQ	NYBLS	10/01-12/01
	Newburgh PMSA, NY-PA	H	5.63 FQ	8.72 AW	14.34 TQ	NYBLS	10/01-12/01
	Syracuse MSA, NY	H	7.33 FQ	9.22 AW	11.19 TQ	NYBLS	10/01-12/01
	Utica-Rome MSA, NY	H	5.93 FQ	9.09 AW	13.08 TQ	NYBLS	10/01-12/01
	North Carolina	H	6.39 FQ	9.77 AW	13.88 TQ	NCBLS	10/01-12/01
	Asheville MSA, NC	H	7.02 FQ	9.19 AW	11.73 TQ	NCBLS	10/01-12/01
	Charlotte-Gastonia-Rock Hill MSA, NC-SC	H	6.01 FQ	9.04 AW	12.80 TQ	NCBLS	10/01-12/01
	Greensboro-Winston-Salem-High Point MSA, NC	H	7.47 FQ	10.69 AW	14.36 TQ	NCBLS	10/01-12/01
	Hickory-Morganton-Lenoir MSA, NC	H	7.87 FQ	12.13 AW	17.10 TQ	NCBLS	10/01-12/01
	Raleigh-Durham-Chapel Hill MSA, NC	H	6.34 FQ	8.83 AW	11.87 TQ	NCBLS	10/01-12/01
	Wilmington MSA, NC	H	5.68 FQ	8.32 AW	11.96 TQ	NCBLS	10/01-12/01
	North Dakota	H	6.82 FQ	9.10 AW	12.61 TQ	NDBLS	10/01-12/01
	Fargo-Moorhead MSA, ND-MN	H	6.91 FQ	9.57 AW	13.18 TQ	NDBLS	10/01-12/01
	Ohio	H	7.21 FQ	9.82 AW	13.22 TQ	OHBLS	10/01-12/01
	Akron PMSA, OH	H	7.48 FQ	9.38 AW	11.11 TQ	OHBLS	10/01-12/01
	Canton-Massillon MSA, OH	H	7.01 FQ	8.55 AW	10.69 TQ	OHBLS	10/01-12/01
	Cincinnati PMSA, OH-KY-IN	H	7.47 FQ	9.86 AW	12.74 TQ	OHBLS	10/01-12/01
	Cleveland-Lorain-Elyria PMSA, OH	H	7.23 FQ	9.74 AW	12.96 TQ	OHBLS	10/01-12/01
	Columbus MSA, OH	H	7.28 FQ	11.07 AW	16.81 TQ	OHBLS	10/01-12/01
	Dayton-Springfield MSA, OH	H	7.31 FQ	10.07 AW	13.15 TQ	OHBLS	10/01-12/01
	Hamilton-Middletown PMSA, OH	H	7.49 FQ	11.24 AW	14.03 TQ	OHBLS	10/01-12/01
	Toledo MSA, OH	H	7.60 FQ	9.71 AW	12.39 TQ	OHBLS	10/01-12/01
	Youngstown-Warren MSA, OH	H	6.89 FQ	8.84 AW	10.64 TQ	OHBLS	10/01-12/01
	Oklahoma	H	6.03 FQ	8.47 AW	11.30 TQ	OKBLS	10/01-12/01
	Oklahoma City MSA, OK	H	5.80 FQ	7.74 AW	10.81 TQ	OKBLS	10/01-12/01
	Tulsa MSA, OK	H	5.87 FQ	8.02 AW	11.00 TQ	OKBLS	10/01-12/01
	Oregon	H	7.06 FQ	9.03 AW	11.50 TQ	ORBLS	10/01-12/01
	Eugene-Springfield MSA, OR	H	7.41 FQ	9.08 AW	11.01 TQ	ORBLS	10/01-12/01
	Medford-Ashland MSA, OR	H	7.48 FQ	9.30 AW	11.38 TQ	ORBLS	10/01-12/01

AAW	Average annual wage	AOH	Average offered, high	ASH	Average starting, high	H	Hourly	M	Monthly	S	Special: hourly and annual
AE	Average entry wage	AOL	Average offered, low	ASL	Average starting, low	HI	Highest wage paid	MTC	Median total compensation	TQ	Third quartile wage
AEX	Average experienced wage	APH	Average pay, high range	AW	Average wage paid	HR	High end range	MW	Median wage paid	W	Weekly
AO	Average offered	APL	Average pay, low range	FQ	First quartile wage	LR	Low end range	SQ	Second quartile wage	Y	Yearly

Occupation/Type/Industry	Location	Per	Low	Mid	High	Source	Date
Sewing Machine Operator	Portland-Vancouver PMSA, OR-WA	H	6.97 FQ	8.92 AW	11.39 TQ	ORBLS	10/01-12/01
	Salem PMSA, OR	H	7.15 FQ	9.09 AW	11.98 TQ	ORBLS	10/01-12/01
	Pennsylvania	H	6.06 FQ	8.56 AW	11.49 TQ	PABLS	10/01-12/01
	Allentown-Bethlehem-Easton MSA, PA	H	6.50 FQ	8.20 AW	10.38 TQ	PABLS	10/01-12/01
	Harrisburg-Lebanon-Carlisle MSA, PA	H	6.09 FQ	8.90 AW	12.73 TQ	PABLS	10/01-12/01
	Johnstown MSA, PA	H	6.07 FQ	8.35 AW	10.86 TQ	PABLS	10/01-12/01
	Lancaster MSA, PA	H	6.13 FQ	8.69 AW	12.05 TQ	PABLS	10/01-12/01
	Philadelphia PMSA, PA-NJ	H	6.57 FQ	9.52 AW	13.52 TQ	PABLS	10/01-12/01
	Pittsburgh MSA, PA	H	5.84 FQ	8.58 AW	11.53 TQ	PABLS	10/01-12/01
	Reading MSA, PA	H	6.02 FQ	8.77 AW	12.37 TQ	PABLS	10/01-12/01
	Scranton-Wilkes-Barre-Hazleton MSA, PA	H	5.96 FQ	8.25 AW	11.48 TQ	PABLS	10/01-12/01
	York MSA, PA	H	7.08 FQ	8.93 AW	11.14 TQ	PABLS	10/01-12/01
	Rhode Island	H	6.79 FQ	9.52 AW	12.66 TQ	RIBLS	10/01-12/01
	Providence-Fall River-Warwick MSA, RI-MA	H	7.04 FQ	9.16 AW	11.85 TQ	RIBLS	10/01-12/01
	South Carolina	H	5.93 FQ	8.53 AW	11.80 TQ	SCBLS	10/01-12/01
	Columbia MSA, SC	H	6.07 FQ	8.73 AW	12.38 TQ	SCBLS	10/01-12/01
	Greenville-Spartanburg-Anderson MSA, SC	H	5.91 FQ	8.43 AW	11.88 TQ	SCBLS	10/01-12/01
	Myrtle Beach MSA, SC	H	6.87 FQ	9.60 AW	15.21 TQ	SCBLS	10/01-12/01
	South Dakota	H	6.97 FQ	8.48 AW	10.86 TQ	SDBLS	10/01-12/01
	Sioux Falls MSA, SD	H	7.33 FQ	9.84 AW	12.75 TQ	SDBLS	10/01-12/01
	Tennessee	H	5.95 FQ	8.42 AW	11.38 TQ	TNBLS	10/01-12/01
	Chattanooga MSA, TN-GA	H	6.10 FQ	8.44 AW	11.30 TQ	TNBLS	10/01-12/01
	Clarksville-Hopkinsville MSA, TN-KY	H	6.19 FQ	8.82 AW	11.07 TQ	TNBLS	10/01-12/01
	Johnson City-Kingsport-Bristol MSA, TN-VA	H	5.68 FQ	7.51 AW	10.06 TQ	TNBLS	10/01-12/01
	Knoxville MSA, TN	H	5.86 FQ	8.88 AW	12.95 TQ	TNBLS	10/01-12/01
	Memphis MSA, TN-AR-MS	H	6.40 FQ	9.20 AW	11.88 TQ	TNBLS	10/01-12/01
	Nashville MSA, TN	H	6.38 FQ	9.48 AW	12.68 TQ	TNBLS	10/01-12/01
	Texas	H	5.86 FQ	8.33 AW	11.89 TQ	TXBLS	10/01-12/01
	Austin-San Marcos MSA, TX	H	6.04 FQ	9.19 AW	14.13 TQ	TXBLS	10/01-12/01
	Beaumont-Port Arthur MSA, TX	H	5.77 FQ	8.32 AW	11.37 TQ	TXBLS	10/01-12/01
	Brownsville-Harlingen-San Benito MSA, TX	H	6.76 FQ	9.99 AW	12.76 TQ	TXBLS	10/01-12/01
	Corpus Christi MSA, TX	H	5.75 FQ	8.02 AW	11.23 TQ	TXBLS	10/01-12/01
	Dallas PMSA, TX	H	5.99 FQ	8.25 AW	11.11 TQ	TXBLS	10/01-12/01
	El Paso MSA, TX	H	6.43 FQ	8.92 AW	12.33 TQ	TXBLS	10/01-12/01
	Fort Worth-Arlington PMSA, TX	H	5.61 FQ	7.26 AW	10.12 TQ	TXBLS	10/01-12/01
	Houston PMSA, TX	H	5.85 FQ	8.21 AW	11.11 TQ	TXBLS	10/01-12/01
	Killeen-Temple MSA, TX	H	6.39 FQ	8.37 AW	10.75 TQ	TXBLS	10/01-12/01
	Longview-Marshall MSA, TX	H	5.54 FQ	6.53 AW	8.45 TQ	TXBLS	10/01-12/01
	Lubbock MSA, TX	H	6.65 FQ	9.11 AW	12.07 TQ	TXBLS	10/01-12/01
	McAllen-Edinburg-Mission MSA, TX	H	6.13 FQ	7.93 AW	10.10 TQ	TXBLS	10/01-12/01
	Odessa-Midland MSA, TX	H	5.67 FQ	6.77 AW	8.42 TQ	TXBLS	10/01-12/01
	San Antonio MSA, TX	H	5.83 FQ	8.86 AW	13.36 TQ	TXBLS	10/01-12/01
	Tyler MSA, TX	H	5.71 FQ	7.38 AW	8.87 TQ	TXBLS	10/01-12/01
	Waco MSA, TX	H	5.62 FQ	6.76 AW	8.63 TQ	TXBLS	10/01-12/01
	Utah	H	6.70 FQ	9.71 AW	13.21 TQ	UTBLS	10/01-12/01
	Provo-Orem MSA, UT	H	5.65 FQ	7.43 AW	10.54 TQ	UTBLS	10/01-12/01
	Salt Lake City-Ogden MSA, UT	H	7.09 FQ	9.73 AW	13.01 TQ	UTBLS	10/01-12/01
	Vermont	H	7.12 FQ	9.50 AW	12.76 TQ	VTBLS	10/01-12/01
	Burlington MSA, VT	H	7.30 FQ	9.26 AW	11.45 TQ	VTBLS	10/01-12/01
	Virginia	H	5.87 FQ	7.93 AW	10.57 TQ	VABLS	10/01-12/01
	Lynchburg MSA, VA	H	5.63 FQ	7.78 AW	11.01 TQ	VABLS	10/01-12/01
	Norfolk-Virginia Beach-Newport News MSA, VA-NC	H	6.05 FQ	8.48 AW	10.87 TQ	VABLS	10/01-12/01
	Richmond-Petersburg MSA, VA	H	5.99 FQ	7.98 AW	10.52 TQ	VABLS	10/01-12/01
	Roanoke MSA, VA	H	6.24 FQ	8.41 AW	11.02 TQ	VABLS	10/01-12/01
	Washington	H	6.94 FQ	9.37 AW	12.97 TQ	WABLS	10/01-12/01
	Bremerton PMSA, WA	H	7.44 FQ	9.71 AW	12.56 TQ	WABLS	10/01-12/01

AAW	Average annual wage	**AOH**	Average offered, high	**ASH**	Average starting, high	**H**	Hourly	**M**	Monthly	**S**	Special: hourly and annual
AE	Average entry wage	**AOL**	Average offered, low	**ASL**	Average starting, low	**HI**	Highest wage paid	**MTC**	Median total compensation	**TQ**	Third quartile wage
AEX	Average experienced wage	**APH**	Average pay, high range	**AW**	Average wage paid	**HR**	High end range	**MW**	Median wage paid	**W**	Weekly
AO	Average offered	**APL**	Average pay, low range	**FQ**	First quartile wage	**LR**	Low end range	**SQ**	Second quartile wage	**Y**	Yearly

Occupation/Type/Industry	Location	Per	Low	Mid	High	Source	Date
Sewing Machine Operator	Seattle-Bellevue-Everett PMSA, WA	H	7.17 FQ	9.61 AW	13.17 TQ	WABLS	10/01-12/01
	Spokane MSA, WA	H	6.73 FQ	7.99 AW	10.18 TQ	WABLS	10/01-12/01
	Tacoma PMSA, WA	H	6.97 FQ	9.21 AW	11.67 TQ	WABLS	10/01-12/01
	Yakima MSA, WA	H	7.38 FQ	9.99 AW	13.56 TQ	WABLS	10/01-12/01
	West Virginia	H	5.70 FQ	8.21 AW	13.56 TQ	WVBLS	10/01-12/01
	Charleston MSA, WV	H	5.85 FQ	8.06 AW	12.23 TQ	WVBLS	10/01-12/01
	Huntington-Ashland MSA, WV-KY-OH	H	5.81 FQ	7.97 AW	10.73 TQ	WVBLS	10/01-12/01
	Wisconsin	H	7.02 FQ	9.95 AW	13.51 TQ	WIBLS	10/01-12/01
	Appleton-Oshkosh-Neenah MSA, WI	H	6.07 FQ	9.69 AW	14.82 TQ	WIBLS	10/01-12/01
	Green Bay MSA, WI	H	7.20 FQ	9.62 AW	12.77 TQ	WIBLS	10/01-12/01
	Madison MSA, WI	H	9.04 FQ	10.69 AW	13.39 TQ	WIBLS	10/01-12/01
	Milwaukee-Waukesha PMSA, WI	H	7.16 FQ	9.98 AW	13.71 TQ	WIBLS	10/01-12/01
	Racine PMSA, WI	H	6.24 FQ	9.42 AW	13.23 TQ	WIBLS	10/01-12/01
	Wyoming	H	5.77 FQ	7.84 AW	10.42 TQ	WYBLS	10/01-12/01
	Puerto Rico	H	5.53 FQ	6.08 AW	6.95 TQ	PRBLS	10/01-12/01
Shampooer	Alabama	H	5.65 FQ	6.94 AW	8.45 TQ	ALBLS	10/01-12/01
	Arizona	H	5.65 FQ	7.23 AW	9.79 TQ	AZBLS	10/01-12/01
	California	H	6.41 FQ	7.54 AW	9.41 TQ	CABLS	10/01-12/01
	Connecticut	H	6.56 FQ	8.72 AW	12.94 TQ	CTBLS	10/01-12/01
	Delaware	H	6.76 FQ	7.67 AW	8.64 TQ	DEBLS	10/01-12/01
	District of Columbia	H	6.83 FQ	9.48 AW	12.82 TQ	DCBLS	10/01-12/01
	Florida	H	5.54 FQ	6.69 AW	9.02 TQ	FLBLS	10/01-12/01
	Georgia	H	5.54 FQ	6.19 AW	6.98 TQ	GABLS	10/01-12/01
	Hawaii	H	5.55 FQ	6.37 AW	6.94 TQ	HIBLS	10/01-12/01
	Illinois	H	5.72 FQ	7.20 AW	10.14 TQ	ILBLS	10/01-12/01
	Indiana	H	5.49 FQ	6.33 AW	7.61 TQ	INBLS	10/01-12/01
	Kansas	H	5.77 FQ	6.63 AW	8.16 TQ	KSBLS	10/01-12/01
	Kentucky	H	5.81 FQ	7.19 AW	8.78 TQ	KYBLS	10/01-12/01
	Louisiana	H	5.74 FQ	6.53 AW	7.90 TQ	LABLS	10/01-12/01
	Maryland	H	5.42 FQ	6.07 AW	6.95 TQ	MDBLS	10/01-12/01
	Massachusetts	H	6.86 FQ	8.57 AW	11.05 TQ	MABLS	10/01-12/01
	Michigan	H	5.67 FQ	6.87 AW	8.48 TQ	MIBLS	10/01-12/01
	Missouri	H	5.98 FQ	7.91 AW	10.39 TQ	MOBLS	10/01-12/01
	New Jersey	H	5.66 FQ	7.15 AW	9.07 TQ	NJBLS	10/01-12/01
	New York	H	5.93 FQ	7.83 AW	9.84 TQ	NYBLS	10/01-12/01
	North Carolina	H	5.83 FQ	7.59 AW	10.05 TQ	NCBLS	10/01-12/01
	Ohio	H	5.82 FQ	7.44 AW	8.95 TQ	OHBLS	10/01-12/01
	Pennsylvania	H	5.51 FQ	6.33 AW	7.65 TQ	PABLS	10/01-12/01
	Tennessee	H	5.41 FQ	6.46 AW	8.89 TQ	TNBLS	10/01-12/01
	Texas	H	5.62 FQ	7.37 AW	10.32 TQ	TXBLS	10/01-12/01
	Virginia	H	5.49 FQ	7.12 AW	10.06 TQ	VABLS	10/01-12/01
	Wisconsin	H	5.99 FQ	10.16 AW	15.25 TQ	WIBLS	10/01-12/01
	Puerto Rico	H	5.59 FQ	6.22 AW	7.01 TQ	PRBLS	10/01-12/01
Sheet Metal Worker	Alabama	H	8.58 FQ	13.04 AW	19.35 TQ	ALBLS	10/01-12/01
	Birmingham MSA, AL	H	8.85 FQ	12.94 AW	19.24 TQ	ALBLS	10/01-12/01
	Huntsville MSA, AL	H	8.15 FQ	12.83 AW	17.61 TQ	ALBLS	10/01-12/01
	Mobile MSA, AL	H	7.46 FQ	13.06 AW	19.68 TQ	ALBLS	10/01-12/01
	Montgomery MSA, AL	H	7.27 FQ	12.20 AW	18.25 TQ	ALBLS	10/01-12/01
	Alaska	H	11.55 FQ	23.91 AW	34.85 TQ	AKBLS	10/01-12/01
	Anchorage MSA, AK	H	10.83 FQ	21.14 AW	33.08 TQ	AKBLS	10/01-12/01
	Arizona	H	7.99 FQ	13.72 AW	21.35 TQ	AZBLS	10/01-12/01
	Phoenix-Mesa MSA, AZ	H	8.52 FQ	14.81 AW	22.90 TQ	AZBLS	10/01-12/01
	Tucson MSA, AZ	H	7.54 FQ	11.43 AW	18.66 TQ	AZBLS	10/01-12/01
	Arkansas	H	8.93 FQ	13.67 AW	20.34 TQ	ARBLS	10/01-12/01
	Fayetteville-Springdale-Rogers MSA, AR	H	9.85 FQ	12.18 AW	14.84 TQ	ARBLS	10/01-12/01
	Fort Smith MSA, AR-OK	II	10.07 FQ	13.26 AW	16.65 TQ	ARBLS	10/01-12/01
	Little Rock-North Little Rock MSA, AR	H	8.35 FQ	13.33 AW	19.67 TQ	ARBLS	10/01-12/01
	California	H	9.16 FQ	19.71 AW	33.18 TQ	CABLS	10/01-12/01
	Bakersfield MSA, CA	H	10.77 FQ	17.69 AW	25.14 TQ	CABLS	10/01-12/01
	Chico-Paradise MSA, CA	H	10.13 FQ	13.64 AW	17.02 TQ	CABLS	10/01-12/01
	Fresno MSA, CA	H	8.04 FQ	16.91 AW	27.09 TQ	CABLS	10/01-12/01
	Los Angeles-Long Beach PMSA, CA	H	8.06 FQ	16.73 AW	30.59 TQ	CABLS	10/01-12/01
	Merced MSA, CA	H	8.40 FQ	17.67 AW	38.21 TQ	CABLS	10/01-12/01
	Modesto MSA, CA	H	8.64 FQ	15.84 AW	25.48 TQ	CABLS	10/01-12/01

AAW	Average annual wage	**AOH**	Average offered, high	**ASH**	Average starting, high	**H**	Hourly	**M**	Monthly	**S**	Special: hourly and annual
AE	Average entry wage	**AOL**	Average offered, low	**ASL**	Average starting, low	**HI**	Highest wage paid	**MTC**	Median total compensation	**TQ**	Third quartile wage
AEX	Average experienced wage	**APH**	Average pay, high range	**AW**	Average wage paid	**HR**	High end range	**MW**	Median wage paid	**W**	Weekly
AO	Average offered	**APL**	Average pay, low range	**FQ**	First quartile wage	**LR**	Low end range	**SQ**	Second quartile wage	**Y**	Yearly

Occupation/Type/Industry	Location	Per	Low	Mid	High	Source	Date
Sheet Metal Worker	Oakland PMSA, CA	H	10.68 FQ	21.55 AW	37.44 TQ	CABLS	10/01-12/01
	Orange County PMSA, CA	H	7.55 FQ	16.81 AW	30.07 TQ	CABLS	10/01-12/01
	Redding MSA, CA	H	9.69 FQ	15.88 AW	22.22 TQ	CABLS	10/01-12/01
	Riverside-San Bernardino PMSA, CA	H	8.96 FQ	20.19 AW	32.90 TQ	CABLS	10/01-12/01
	Sacramento PMSA, CA	H	10.46 FQ	21.57 AW	32.85 TQ	CABLS	10/01-12/01
	Salinas MSA, CA	H	14.68 FQ	22.22 AW	31.92 TQ	CABLS	10/01-12/01
	San Diego MSA, CA	H	11.14 FQ	18.20 AW	26.10 TQ	CABLS	10/01-12/01
	San Francisco PMSA, CA	H	13.73 FQ	26.45 AW	41.39 TQ	CABLS	10/01-12/01
	San Jose PMSA, CA	H	13.93 FQ	28.04 AW	42.48 TQ	CABLS	10/01-12/01
	San Luis Obispo-Atascadero-Paso Robles MSA, CA	H	8.33 FQ	14.37 AW	21.15 TQ	CABLS	10/01-12/01
	Santa Barbara-Santa Maria-Lompoc MSA, CA	H	10.01 FQ	19.11 AW	28.23 TQ	CABLS	10/01-12/01
	Santa Cruz-Watsonville PMSA, CA	H	7.95 FQ	18.42 AW	33.76 TQ	CABLS	10/01-12/01
	Santa Rosa PMSA, CA	H	7.95 FQ	18.95 AW	31.86 TQ	CABLS	10/01-12/01
	Stockton-Lodi MSA, CA	H	10.91 FQ	20.73 AW	30.20 TQ	CABLS	10/01-12/01
	Vallejo-Fairfield-Napa PMSA, CA	H	8.79 FQ	20.87 AW	32.85 TQ	CABLS	10/01-12/01
	Ventura PMSA, CA	H	7.52 FQ	13.89 AW	25.50 TQ	CABLS	10/01-12/01
	Visalia-Tulare-Porterville MSA, CA	H	8.67 FQ	14.66 AW	21.42 TQ	CABLS	10/01-12/01
	Colorado	H	10.01 FQ	16.89 AW	26.14 TQ	COBLS	10/01-12/01
	Boulder-Longmont PMSA, CO	H	10.82 FQ	17.45 AW	25.18 TQ	COBLS	10/01-12/01
	Colorado Springs MSA, CO	H	10.02 FQ	15.69 AW	25.08 TQ	COBLS	10/01-12/01
	Denver PMSA, CO	H	10.16 FQ	17.74 AW	27.03 TQ	COBLS	10/01-12/01
	Fort Collins-Loveland MSA, CO	H	10.59 FQ	16.91 AW	26.87 TQ	COBLS	10/01-12/01
	Greeley PMSA, CO	H	10.97 FQ	16.80 AW	25.04 TQ	COBLS	10/01-12/01
	Connecticut	H	11.76 FQ	19.15 AW	26.92 TQ	CTBLS	10/01-12/01
	Bridgeport PMSA, CT	H	11.34 FQ	17.81 AW	26.11 TQ	CTBLS	10/01-12/01
	Danbury PMSA, CT	H	11.57 FQ	19.35 AW	30.54 TQ	CTBLS	10/01-12/01
	Hartford MSA, CT	H	11.74 FQ	19.44 AW	26.96 TQ	CTBLS	10/01-12/01
	New Haven-Meriden PMSA, CT	H	13.70 FQ	20.99 AW	27.33 TQ	CTBLS	10/01-12/01
	New London-Norwich MSA, CT-RI	H	10.58 FQ	16.55 AW	23.26 TQ	CTBLS	10/01-12/01
	Stamford-Norwalk PMSA, CT	H	12.79 FQ	19.13 AW	26.83 TQ	CTBLS	10/01-12/01
	Waterbury PMSA, CT	H	11.86 FQ	18.00 AW	27.67 TQ	CTBLS	10/01-12/01
	Delaware	H	11.41 FQ	18.57 AW	25.52 TQ	DEBLS	10/01-12/01
	Wilmington-Newark PMSA, DE-MD	H	12.22 FQ	19.36 AW	26.13 TQ	DEBLS	10/01-12/01
	District of Columbia	H	10.71 FQ	19.39 AW	28.71 TQ	DCBLS	10/01-12/01
	Washington PMSA, DC-MD-VA-WV	H	10.78 FQ	18.11 AW	26.97 TQ	DCBLS	10/01-12/01
	Florida	H	8.80 FQ	14.18 AW	20.55 TQ	FLBLS	10/01-12/01
	Daytona Beach MSA, FL	H	9.36 FQ	13.17 AW	17.18 TQ	FLBLS	10/01-12/01
	Fort Lauderdale PMSA, FL	H	9.88 FQ	14.05 AW	18.95 TQ	FLBLS	10/01-12/01
	Fort Myers-Cape Coral MSA, FL	H	9.84 FQ	13.94 AW	19.07 TQ	FLBLS	10/01-12/01
	Fort Pierce-Port St. Lucie MSA, FL	H	6.23 FQ	11.93 AW	17.11 TQ	FLBLS	10/01-12/01
	Gainesville MSA, FL	H	8.14 FQ	13.86 AW	20.66 TQ	FLBLS	10/01-12/01
	Jacksonville MSA, FL	H	8.44 FQ	15.20 AW	21.43 TQ	FLBLS	10/01-12/01
	Lakeland-Winter Haven MSA, FL	H	8.28 FQ	13.41 AW	18.58 TQ	FLBLS	10/01-12/01
	Melbourne-Titusville-Palm Bay MSA, FL	H	9.11 FQ	13.76 AW	19.65 TQ	FLBLS	10/01-12/01
	Miami PMSA, FL	H	7.65 FQ	14.87 AW	21.21 TQ	FLBLS	10/01-12/01
	Naples MSA, FL	H	11.22 FQ	15.07 AW	20.81 TQ	FLBLS	10/01-12/01
	Ocala MSA, FL	H	7.94 FQ	10.99 AW	13.84 TQ	FLBLS	10/01-12/01
	Orlando MSA, FL	H	9.72 FQ	15.68 AW	21.67 TQ	FLBLS	10/01-12/01
	Pensacola MSA, FL	H	10.55 FQ	14.55 AW	20.52 TQ	FLBLS	10/01-12/01
	Sarasota-Bradenton MSA, FL	H	7.27 FQ	13.19 AW	21.64 TQ	FLBLS	10/01-12/01
	Tallahassee MSA, FL	H	8.84 FQ	11.33 AW	14.88 TQ	FLBLS	10/01-12/01
	Tampa-St. Petersburg-Clearwater MSA, FL	H	9.51 FQ	13.59 AW	17.49 TQ	FLBLS	10/01-12/01
	West Palm Beach-Boca Raton MSA, FL	H	9.62 FQ	15.14 AW	21.05 TQ	FLBLS	10/01-12/01
	Georgia	H	8.98 FQ	14.61 AW	21.31 TQ	GABLS	10/01-12/01
	Atlanta MSA, GA	H	10.35 FQ	16.21 AW	24.21 TQ	GABLS	10/01-12/01

AAW Average annual wage **AE** Average entry wage **AEX** Average experienced wage **AO** Average offered **AOH** Average offered, high **AOL** Average offered, low **APH** Average pay, high range **APL** Average pay, low range **ASH** Average starting, high **ASL** Average starting, low **AW** Average wage paid **FQ** First quartile wage **H** Hourly **HI** Highest wage paid **HR** High end range **LR** Low end range **M** Monthly **MTC** Median total compensation **MW** Median wage paid **SQ** Second quartile wage **S** Special: hourly and annual **TQ** Third quartile wage **W** Weekly **Y** Yearly

Occupation/Type/Industry	Location	Per	Low	Mid	High	Source	Date
Sheet Metal Worker	Augusta-Aiken MSA, GA-SC	H	9.31 FQ	14.63 AW	21.83 TQ	GABLS	10/01-12/01
	Columbus MSA, GA-AL	H	9.71 FQ	13.51 AW	17.46 TQ	GABLS	10/01-12/01
	Macon MSA, GA	H	12.32 FQ	16.80 AW	20.73 TQ	GABLS	10/01-12/01
	Savannah MSA, GA	H	9.58 FQ	14.02 AW	19.43 TQ	GABLS	10/01-12/01
	Hawaii	H	14.65 FQ	24.96 AW	33.91 TQ	HIBLS	10/01-12/01
	Honolulu MSA, HI	H	15.04 FQ	25.75 AW	34.11 TQ	HIBLS	10/01-12/01
	Idaho	H	7.93 FQ	13.99 AW	21.75 TQ	IDBLS	10/01-12/01
	Boise City MSA, ID	H	7.90 FQ	14.18 AW	23.61 TQ	IDBLS	10/01-12/01
	Illinois	H	10.93 FQ	22.70 AW	34.11 TQ	ILBLS	10/01-12/01
	Champaign-Urbana MSA, IL	H	12.53 FQ	20.52 AW	27.67 TQ	ILBLS	10/01-12/01
	Chicago PMSA, IL	H	12.76 FQ	24.89 AW	34.74 TQ	ILBLS	10/01-12/01
	Peoria-Pekin MSA, IL	H	17.85 FQ	22.98 AW	27.57 TQ	ILBLS	10/01-12/01
	Rockford MSA, IL	H	9.47 FQ	21.26 AW	30.92 TQ	ILBLS	10/01-12/01
	Springfield MSA, IL	H	11.05 FQ	20.74 AW	27.08 TQ	ILBLS	10/01-12/01
	Indiana	H	10.17 FQ	18.63 AW	27.52 TQ	INBLS	10/01-12/01
	Elkhart-Goshen MSA, IN	H	7.95 FQ	20.33 AW	31.69 TQ	INBLS	10/01-12/01
	Evansville-Henderson MSA, IN-KY	H	11.77 FQ	19.87 AW	27.22 TQ	INBLS	10/01-12/01
	Fort Wayne MSA, IN	H	7.23 FQ	15.12 AW	26.19 TQ	INBLS	10/01-12/01
	Gary PMSA, IN	H	9.92 FQ	18.77 AW	28.74 TQ	INBLS	10/01-12/01
	Indianapolis MSA, IN	H	11.94 FQ	18.84 AW	27.16 TQ	INBLS	10/01-12/01
	Lafayette MSA, IN	H	11.71 FQ	20.28 AW	26.63 TQ	INBLS	10/01-12/01
	South Bend MSA, IN	H	10.05 FQ	21.12 AW	27.08 TQ	INBLS	10/01-12/01
	Iowa	H	10.26 FQ	17.76 AW	26.74 TQ	IABLS	10/01-12/01
	Cedar Rapids MSA, IA	H	13.48 FQ	21.73 AW	28.76 TQ	IABLS	10/01-12/01
	Davenport-Moline-Rock Island MSA, IA-IL	H	8.38 FQ	16.84 AW	26.85 TQ	IABLS	10/01-12/01
	Des Moines MSA, IA	H	10.44 FQ	19.39 AW	27.33 TQ	IABLS	10/01-12/01
	Kansas	H	10.15 FQ	17.76 AW	28.94 TQ	KSBLS	10/01-12/01
	Topeka MSA, KS	H	10.29 FQ	19.70 AW	31.74 TQ	KSBLS	10/01-12/01
	Wichita MSA, KS	H	10.50 FQ	16.00 AW	22.23 TQ	KSBLS	10/01-12/01
	Kentucky	H	8.97 FQ	14.75 AW	25.06 TQ	KYBLS	10/01-12/01
	Lexington MSA, KY	H	9.22 FQ	13.85 AW	18.81 TQ	KYBLS	10/01-12/01
	Louisville MSA, KY-IN	H	10.26 FQ	17.54 AW	27.03 TQ	KYBLS	10/01-12/01
	Louisiana	H	8.86 FQ	13.65 AW	19.72 TQ	LABLS	10/01-12/01
	Baton Rouge MSA, LA	H	9.60 FQ	14.80 AW	21.66 TQ	LABLS	10/01-12/01
	Houma MSA, LA	H	8.83 FQ	16.10 AW	28.94 TQ	LABLS	10/01-12/01
	Lafayette MSA, LA	H	7.97 FQ	10.88 AW	15.79 TQ	LABLS	10/01-12/01
	Lake Charles MSA, LA	H	7.77 FQ	12.53 AW	16.97 TQ	LABLS	10/01-12/01
	New Orleans MSA, LA	H	9.67 FQ	13.69 AW	18.34 TQ	LABLS	10/01-12/01
	Shreveport-Bossier City MSA, LA	H	8.85 FQ	14.25 AW	21.55 TQ	LABLS	10/01-12/01
	Maine	H	9.88 FQ	15.52 AW	20.34 TQ	MEBLS	10/01-12/01
	Portland MSA, ME	H	10.66 FQ	18.00 AW	31.45 TQ	MEBLS	10/01-12/01
	Maryland	H	9.79 FQ	17.16 AW	26.23 TQ	MDBLS	10/01-12/01
	Baltimore PMSA, MD	H	8.43 FQ	15.06 AW	22.08 TQ	MDBLS	10/01-12/01
	Massachusetts	H	11.66 FQ	21.47 AW	35.46 TQ	MABLS	10/01-12/01
	Boston PMSA, MA-NH	H	12.40 FQ	24.33 AW	39.67 TQ	MABLS	10/01-12/01
	Brockton PMSA, MA	H	11.00 FQ	19.19 AW	28.14 TQ	MABLS	10/01-12/01
	Lawrence PMSA, MA-NH	H	11.28 FQ	18.40 AW	26.09 TQ	MABLS	10/01-12/01
	Lowell PMSA, MA-NH	H	12.95 FQ	22.56 AW	34.49 TQ	MABLS	10/01-12/01
	Springfield MSA, MA	H	12.73 FQ	19.14 AW	26.14 TQ	MABLS	10/01-12/01
	Worcester PMSA, MA-CT	H	11.42 FQ	19.21 AW	26.56 TQ	MABLS	10/01-12/01
	Michigan	H	11.58 FQ	21.81 AW	31.40 TQ	MIBLS	10/01-12/01
	Ann Arbor PMSA, MI	H	12.87 FQ	23.89 AW	33.88 TQ	MIBLS	10/01-12/01
	Detroit PMSA, MI	H	14.41 FQ	22.88 AW	31.42 TQ	MIBLS	10/01-12/01
	Flint PMSA, MI	H	17.18 FQ	25.61 AW	33.79 TQ	MIBLS	10/01-12/01
	Grand Rapids-Muskegon-Holland MSA, MI	H	11.00 FQ	20.06 AW	28.51 TQ	MIBLS	10/01-12/01
	Kalamazoo-Battle Creek MSA, MI	H	13.57 FQ	22.53 AW	28.45 TQ	MIBLS	10/01-12/01
	Lansing-East Lansing MSA, MI	H	9.99 FQ	23.31 AW	34.03 TQ	MIBLS	10/01-12/01
	Saginaw-Bay City-Midland MSA, MI	H	9.14 FQ	19.44 AW	29.96 TQ	MIBLS	10/01-12/01
	Minnesota	H	11.83 FQ	21.49 AW	32.23 TQ	MNBLS	10/01-12/01
	Duluth-Superior MSA, MN-WI	H	10.82 FQ	19.89 AW	28.22 TQ	MNBLS	10/01-12/01
	Minneapolis-St. Paul MSA, MN-WI	H	14.38 FQ	23.07 AW	33.01 TQ	MNBLS	10/01-12/01
	St. Cloud MSA, MN	H	10.41 FQ	20.48 AW	26.78 TQ	MNBLS	10/01-12/01
	Mississippi	H	7.74 FQ	12.23 AW	17.68 TQ	MSBLS	10/01-12/01
	Biloxi-Gulfport-Pascagoula MSA, MS	H	10.13 FQ	14.62 AW	18.11 TQ	MSBLS	10/01-12/01

AAW Average annual wage; **AE** Average entry wage; **AEX** Average experienced wage; **AO** Average offered; **AOH** Average offered, high; **AOL** Average offered, low; **APH** Average pay, high range; **APL** Average pay, low range; **ASH** Average starting, high; **ASL** Average starting, low; **AW** Average wage paid; **FQ** First quartile wage; **H** Hourly; **HI** Highest wage paid; **HR** High end range; **LR** Low end range; **M** Monthly; **MTC** Median total compensation; **MW** Median wage paid; **SQ** Second quartile wage; **S** Special: hourly and annual; **TQ** Third quartile wage; **W** Weekly; **Y** Yearly

Occupation/Type/Industry	Location	Per	Low	Mid	High	Source	Date
Sheet Metal Worker	Jackson MSA, MS	H	8.13 FQ	12.21 AW	17.56 TQ	MSBLS	10/01-12/01
	Missouri	H	10.29 FQ	20.12 AW	30.93 TQ	MOBLS	10/01-12/01
	Kansas City MSA, MO-KS	H	12.21 FQ	21.96 AW	32.96 TQ	MOBLS	10/01-12/01
	St. Louis MSA, MO-IL	H	6.74 FQ	21.67 AW	31.91 TQ	MOBLS	10/01-12/01
	Springfield MSA, MO	H	9.49 FQ	16.06 AW	29.56 TQ	MOBLS	10/01-12/01
	Montana	H	10.26 FQ	17.64 AW	25.02 TQ	MTBLS	10/01-12/01
	Nebraska	H	9.47 FQ	15.66 AW	25.97 TQ	NEBLS	10/01-12/01
	Lincoln MSA, NE	H	9.44 FQ	13.08 AW	19.09 TQ	NEBLS	10/01-12/01
	Omaha MSA, NE-IA	H	10.23 FQ	19.42 AW	27.83 TQ	NEBLS	10/01-12/01
	Nevada	H	11.25 FQ	20.71 AW	32.96 TQ	NVBLS	10/01-12/01
	Las Vegas MSA, NV-AZ	H	11.28 FQ	21.98 AW	33.71 TQ	NVBLS	10/01-12/01
	Reno MSA, NV	H	10.79 FQ	20.11 AW	30.69 TQ	NVBLS	10/01-12/01
	New Hampshire	H	10.28 FQ	15.56 AW	21.69 TQ	NHBLS	10/01-12/01
	Manchester PMSA, NH	H	11.52 FQ	16.25 AW	21.81 TQ	NHBLS	10/01-12/01
	Nashua PMSA, NH	H	9.59 FQ	13.66 AW	18.15 TQ	NHBLS	10/01-12/01
	Portsmouth-Rochester PMSA, NH-ME	H	10.57 FQ	15.64 AW	21.04 TQ	NHBLS	10/01-12/01
	New Jersey	H	11.05 FQ	23.01 AW	35.27 TQ	NJBLS	10/01-12/01
	Atlantic-Cape May PMSA, NJ	H	16.33 FQ	27.94 AW	34.79 TQ	NJBLS	10/01-12/01
	Bergen-Passaic PMSA, NJ	H	12.57 FQ	25.16 AW	34.58 TQ	NJBLS	10/01-12/01
	Middlesex-Somerset-Hunterdon PMSA, NJ	H	10.76 FQ	20.45 AW	33.37 TQ	NJBLS	10/01-12/01
	Monmouth-Ocean PMSA, NJ	H	11.18 FQ	17.85 AW	29.77 TQ	NJBLS	10/01-12/01
	Newark PMSA, NJ	H	10.76 FQ	23.85 AW	43.69 TQ	NJBLS	10/01-12/01
	New Mexico	H	7.99 FQ	13.13 AW	20.73 TQ	NMBLS	10/01-12/01
	Albuquerque MSA, NM	H	7.90 FQ	12.79 AW	20.74 TQ	NMBLS	10/01-12/01
	Las Cruces MSA, NM	H	8.59 FQ	14.42 AW	24.32 TQ	NMBLS	10/01-12/01
	New York	H	8.44 FQ	22.16 AW	39.40 TQ	NYBLS	10/01-12/01
	Albany-Schenectady-Troy MSA, NY	H	11.98 FQ	15.76 AW	21.03 TQ	NYBLS	10/01-12/01
	Binghamton MSA, NY	H	9.45 FQ	18.08 AW	31.49 TQ	NYBLS	10/01-12/01
	Buffalo-Niagara Falls MSA, NY	H	8.55 FQ	17.59 AW	27.37 TQ	NYBLS	10/01-12/01
	Nassau-Suffolk PMSA, NY	H	6.60 FQ	22.40 AW	41.69 TQ	NYBLS	10/01-12/01
	New York PMSA, NY	H	10.81 FQ	27.77 AW	42.25 TQ	NYBLS	10/01-12/01
	Newburgh PMSA, NY-PA	H	11.42 FQ	19.02 AW	26.76 TQ	NYBLS	10/01-12/01
	Rochester MSA, NY	H	11.93 FQ	19.58 AW	27.15 TQ	NYBLS	10/01-12/01
	Syracuse MSA, NY	H	10.76 FQ	17.87 AW	26.36 TQ	NYBLS	10/01-12/01
	Utica-Rome MSA, NY	H	9.08 FQ	13.49 AW	21.41 TQ	NYBLS	10/01-12/01
	North Carolina	H	9.10 FQ	13.68 AW	19.99 TQ	NCBLS	10/01-12/01
	Asheville MSA, NC	H	8.36 FQ	12.99 AW	17.13 TQ	NCBLS	10/01-12/01
	Charlotte-Gastonia-Rock Hill MSA, NC-SC	H	8.89 FQ	14.24 AW	20.68 TQ	NCBLS	10/01-12/01
	Fayetteville MSA, NC	H	8.21 FQ	12.00 AW	16.91 TQ	NCBLS	10/01-12/01
	Greensboro-Winston-Salem-High Point MSA, NC	H	9.75 FQ	15.23 AW	22.44 TQ	NCBLS	10/01-12/01
	Hickory-Morganton-Lenoir MSA, NC	H	9.06 FQ	12.59 AW	16.84 TQ	NCBLS	10/01-12/01
	Raleigh-Durham-Chapel Hill MSA, NC	H	10.91 FQ	13.82 AW	19.81 TQ	NCBLS	10/01-12/01
	Wilmington MSA, NC	H	9.11 FQ	12.75 AW	17.14 TQ	NCBLS	10/01-12/01
	North Dakota	H	10.14 FQ	15.32 AW	20.91 TQ	NDBLS	10/01-12/01
	Fargo-Moorhead MSA, ND-MN	H	10.06 FQ	16.00 AW	21.65 TQ	NDBLS	10/01-12/01
	Ohio	H	9.84 FQ	17.88 AW	26.93 TQ	OHBLS	10/01-12/01
	Akron PMSA, OH	H	9.72 FQ	18.26 AW	27.33 TQ	OHBLS	10/01-12/01
	Canton-Massillon MSA, OH	H	6.94 FQ	15.40 AW	26.49 TQ	OHBLS	10/01-12/01
	Cincinnati PMSA, OH-KY-IN	H	9.31 FQ	15.75 AW	25.21 TQ	OHBLS	10/01-12/01
	Cleveland-Lorain-Elyria PMSA, OH	H	9.49 FQ	17.82 AW	26.59 TQ	OHBLS	10/01-12/01
	Columbus MSA, OH	H	11.25 FQ	17.87 AW	26.46 TQ	OHBLS	10/01-12/01
	Dayton-Springfield MSA, OH	H	11.17 FQ	19.94 AW	29.29 TQ	OHBLS	10/01-12/01
	Hamilton-Middletown PMSA, OH	H	9.74 FQ	16.89 AW	25.73 TQ	OHBLS	10/01-12/01
	Mansfield MSA, OH	H	10.58 FQ	18.48 AW	24.92 TQ	OHBLS	10/01-12/01
	Toledo MSA, OH	H	11.63 FQ	20.89 AW	28.03 TQ	OHBLS	10/01-12/01
	Youngstown-Warren MSA, OH	H	12.48 FQ	22.37 AW	29.64 TQ	OHBLS	10/01-12/01
	Oklahoma	H	9.14 FQ	16.33 AW	23.63 TQ	OKBLS	10/01-12/01
	Oklahoma City MSA, OK	H	11.40 FQ	17.74 AW	23.20 TQ	OKBLS	10/01-12/01
	Tulsa MSA, OK	H	9.36 FQ	16.11 AW	25.45 TQ	OKBLS	10/01-12/01
	Oregon	H	10.28 FQ	17.99 AW	27.37 TQ	ORBLS	10/01-12/01
	Eugene-Springfield MSA, OR	H	10.49 FQ	17.99 AW	25.96 TQ	ORBLS	10/01-12/01

AAW	Average annual wage	**AOH**	Average offered, high	**ASH**	Average starting, high	**H**	Hourly	**M**	Monthly	**S**	Special: hourly and annual
AE	Average entry wage	**AOL**	Average offered, low	**ASL**	Average starting, low	**HI**	Highest wage paid	**MTC**	Median total compensation	**TQ**	Third quartile wage
AEX	Average experienced wage	**APH**	Average pay, high range	**AW**	Average wage paid	**HR**	High end range	**MW**	Median wage paid	**W**	Weekly
AO	Average offered	**APL**	Average pay, low range	**FQ**	First quartile wage	**LR**	Low end range	**SQ**	Second quartile wage	**Y**	Yearly

Occupation/Type/Industry	Location	Per	Low	Mid	High	Source	Date
Sheet Metal Worker	Medford-Ashland MSA, OR	H	9.71 FQ	14.48 AW	20.68 TQ	ORBLS	10/01-12/01
	Portland-Vancouver PMSA, OR-WA	H	10.93 FQ	19.41 AW	30.18 TQ	ORBLS	10/01-12/01
	Salem PMSA, OR	H	10.73 FQ	17.26 AW	24.69 TQ	ORBLS	10/01-12/01
	Pennsylvania	H	10.40 FQ	18.14 AW	26.74 TQ	PABLS	10/01-12/01
	Allentown-Bethlehem-Easton MSA, PA	H	12.06 FQ	19.93 AW	26.41 TQ	PABLS	10/01-12/01
	Erie MSA, PA	H	12.85 FQ	21.86 AW	31.64 TQ	PABLS	10/01-12/01
	Harrisburg-Lebanon-Carlisle MSA, PA	H	11.14 FQ	20.28 AW	28.14 TQ	PABLS	10/01-12/01
	Johnstown MSA, PA	H	10.52 FQ	16.19 AW	24.99 TQ	PABLS	10/01-12/01
	Lancaster MSA, PA	H	11.03 FQ	17.53 AW	26.04 TQ	PABLS	10/01-12/01
	Philadelphia PMSA, PA-NJ	H	10.02 FQ	19.03 AW	29.39 TQ	PABLS	10/01-12/01
	Pittsburgh MSA, PA	H	10.88 FQ	18.88 AW	27.23 TQ	PABLS	10/01-12/01
	Reading MSA, PA	H	12.16 FQ	19.91 AW	27.63 TQ	PABLS	10/01-12/01
	Scranton-Wilkes-Barre-Hazleton MSA, PA	H	10.43 FQ	17.47 AW	24.62 TQ	PABLS	10/01-12/01
	York MSA, PA	H	11.55 FQ	16.97 AW	23.45 TQ	PABLS	10/01-12/01
	Rhode Island	H	10.89 FQ	19.26 AW	27.98 TQ	RIBLS	10/01-12/01
	Providence-Fall River-Warwick MSA, RI-MA	H	10.16 FQ	17.97 AW	27.32 TQ	RIBLS	10/01-12/01
	South Carolina	H	9.25 FQ	13.39 AW	18.48 TQ	SCBLS	10/01-12/01
	Charleston-North Charleston MSA, SC	H	9.61 FQ	13.44 AW	17.74 TQ	SCBLS	10/01-12/01
	Columbia MSA, SC	H	9.00 FQ	12.85 AW	17.05 TQ	SCBLS	10/01-12/01
	Greenville-Spartanburg-Anderson MSA, SC	H	9.22 FQ	13.31 AW	17.43 TQ	SCBLS	10/01-12/01
	Myrtle Beach MSA, SC	H	8.13 FQ	11.58 AW	17.29 TQ	SCBLS	10/01-12/01
	South Dakota	H	8.65 FQ	12.47 AW	17.52 TQ	SDBLS	10/01-12/01
	Sioux Falls MSA, SD	H	9.01 FQ	12.05 AW	16.23 TQ	SDBLS	10/01-12/01
	Tennessee	H	9.19 FQ	14.99 AW	22.17 TQ	TNBLS	10/01-12/01
	Chattanooga MSA, TN-GA	H	9.74 FQ	15.37 AW	20.79 TQ	TNBLS	10/01-12/01
	Clarksville-Hopkinsville MSA, TN-KY	H	9.06 FQ	14.58 AW	21.17 TQ	TNBLS	10/01-12/01
	Johnson City-Kingsport-Bristol MSA, TN-VA	H	7.66 FQ	11.84 AW	16.87 TQ	TNBLS	10/01-12/01
	Knoxville MSA, TN	H	10.11 FQ	14.93 AW	21.33 TQ	TNBLS	10/01-12/01
	Memphis MSA, TN-AR-MS	H	9.03 FQ	15.73 AW	26.52 TQ	TNBLS	10/01-12/01
	Nashville MSA, TN	H	9.95 FQ	15.96 AW	23.53 TQ	TNBLS	10/01-12/01
	Texas	H	7.98 FQ	13.39 AW	20.93 TQ	TXBLS	10/01-12/01
	Amarillo MSA, TX	H	7.76 FQ	12.57 AW	18.63 TQ	TXBLS	10/01-12/01
	Austin-San Marcos MSA, TX	H	9.45 FQ	16.59 AW	25.08 TQ	TXBLS	10/01-12/01
	Beaumont-Port Arthur MSA, TX	H	9.23 FQ	18.59 AW	37.99 TQ	TXBLS	10/01-12/01
	Brazoria PMSA, TX	H	7.46 FQ	13.38 AW	17.97 TQ	TXBLS	10/01-12/01
	Brownsville-Harlingen-San Benito MSA, TX	H	6.41 FQ	10.25 AW	15.70 TQ	TXBLS	10/01-12/01
	Corpus Christi MSA, TX	H	8.80 FQ	16.02 AW	21.42 TQ	TXBLS	10/01-12/01
	Dallas PMSA, TX	H	9.40 FQ	13.26 AW	20.34 TQ	TXBLS	10/01-12/01
	El Paso MSA, TX	H	6.86 FQ	10.69 AW	16.77 TQ	TXBLS	10/01-12/01
	Fort Worth-Arlington PMSA, TX	H	7.76 FQ	13.64 AW	20.04 TQ	TXBLS	10/01-12/01
	Galveston-Texas City PMSA, TX	H	9.99 FQ	16.03 AW	20.50 TQ	TXBLS	10/01-12/01
	Houston PMSA, TX	H	7.77 FQ	13.50 AW	20.89 TQ	TXBLS	10/01-12/01
	Killeen-Temple MSA, TX	H	7.99 FQ	12.13 AW	18.06 TQ	TXBLS	10/01-12/01
	Laredo MSA, TX	H	6.67 FQ	10.33 AW	14.40 TQ	TXBLS	10/01-12/01
	Longview-Marshall MSA, TX	H	8.46 FQ	11.76 AW	16.65 TQ	TXBLS	10/01-12/01
	Lubbock MSA, TX	H	8.77 FQ	13.62 AW	20.73 TQ	TXBLS	10/01-12/01
	McAllen-Edinburg-Mission MSA, TX	H	5.67 FQ	7.98 AW	9.96 TQ	TXBLS	10/01-12/01
	Odessa-Midland MSA, TX	H	8.23 FQ	12.37 AW	16.73 TQ	TXBLS	10/01-12/01
	San Antonio MSA, TX	H	7.95 FQ	13.25 AW	21.25 TQ	TXBLS	10/01-12/01
	Tyler MSA, TX	H	8.16 FQ	12.71 AW	20.33 TQ	TXBLS	10/01-12/01
	Waco MSA, TX	H	8.69 FQ	13.09 AW	19.55 TQ	TXBLS	10/01-12/01
	Utah	H	7.99 FQ	15.49 AW	23.42 TQ	UTBLS	10/01-12/01
	Provo-Orem MSA, UT	H	10.53 FQ	15.81 AW	21.92 TQ	UTBLS	10/01-12/01
	Salt Lake City-Ogden MSA, UT	H	7.86 FQ	15.50 AW	23.86 TQ	UTBLS	10/01-12/01
	Vermont	H	9.77 FQ	14.87 AW	21.13 TQ	VTBLS	10/01-12/01
	Burlington MSA, VT	H	10.70 FQ	16.07 AW	22.69 TQ	VTBLS	10/01-12/01
	Virginia	H	9.68 FQ	14.82 AW	20.55 TQ	VABLS	10/01-12/01

AAW Average annual wage; **AE** Average entry wage; **AEX** Average experienced wage; **AO** Average offered; **AOH** Average offered, high; **AOL** Average offered, low; **APH** Average pay, high range; **APL** Average pay, low range; **ASH** Average starting, high; **ASL** Average starting, low; **AW** Average wage paid; **FQ** First quartile wage; **H** Hourly; **HI** Highest wage paid; **HR** High end range; **LR** Low end range; **M** Monthly; **MTC** Median total compensation; **MW** Median wage paid; **SQ** Second quartile wage; **S** Special: hourly and annual; **TQ** Third quartile wage; **W** Weekly; **Y** Yearly

Occupation/Type/Industry	Location	Per	Low	Mid	High	Source	Date
Sheet Metal Worker	Lynchburg MSA, VA	H	9.43 FQ	12.99 AW	16.72 TQ	VABLS	10/01-12/01
	Norfolk-Virginia Beach-Newport News MSA, VA-NC	H	9.33 FQ	15.19 AW	19.24 TQ	VABLS	10/01-12/01
	Richmond-Petersburg MSA, VA	H	10.67 FQ	14.11 AW	19.18 TQ	VABLS	10/01-12/01
	Roanoke MSA, VA	H	8.68 FQ	11.97 AW	15.84 TQ	VABLS	10/01-12/01
	Washington	H	11.05 FQ	20.66 AW	33.24 TQ	WABLS	10/01-12/01
	Bremerton PMSA, WA	H	14.03 FQ	22.37 AW	30.40 TQ	WABLS	10/01-12/01
	Olympia PMSA, WA	H	12.57 FQ	20.84 AW	32.53 TQ	WABLS	10/01-12/01
	Richland-Kennewick-Pasco MSA, WA	H	11.06 FQ	21.73 AW	33.05 TQ	WABLS	10/01-12/01
	Seattle-Bellevue-Everett PMSA, WA	H	12.17 FQ	21.88 AW	34.12 TQ	WABLS	10/01-12/01
	Spokane MSA, WA	H	8.64 FQ	12.67 AW	20.35 TQ	WABLS	10/01-12/01
	Tacoma PMSA, WA	H	12.38 FQ	20.97 AW	32.43 TQ	WABLS	10/01-12/01
	Yakima MSA, WA	H	9.85 FQ	16.97 AW	25.71 TQ	WABLS	10/01-12/01
	West Virginia	H	8.48 FQ	17.62 AW	27.29 TQ	WVBLS	10/01-12/01
	Charleston MSA, WV	H	9.01 FQ	18.07 AW	27.28 TQ	WVBLS	10/01-12/01
	Huntington-Ashland MSA, WV-KY-OH	H	9.74 FQ	18.41 AW	27.64 TQ	WVBLS	10/01-12/01
	Wisconsin	H	10.50 FQ	18.26 AW	27.97 TQ	WIBLS	10/01-12/01
	Appleton-Oshkosh-Neenah MSA, WI	H	10.72 FQ	17.75 AW	25.24 TQ	WIBLS	10/01-12/01
	Green Bay MSA, WI	H	12.08 FQ	20.69 AW	31.21 TQ	WIBLS	10/01-12/01
	Madison MSA, WI	H	10.78 FQ	20.68 AW	32.18 TQ	WIBLS	10/01-12/01
	Milwaukee-Waukesha PMSA, WI	H	10.79 FQ	19.05 AW	28.00 TQ	WIBLS	10/01-12/01
	Racine PMSA, WI	H	11.51 FQ	19.49 AW	34.13 TQ	WIBLS	10/01-12/01
	Wyoming	H	9.70 FQ	17.45 AW	25.35 TQ	WYBLS	10/01-12/01
	Cheyenne MSA, WY	H	8.60 FQ	14.78 AW	22.46 TQ	WYBLS	10/01-12/01
	Puerto Rico	H	5.47 FQ	7.82 AW	12.74 TQ	PRBLS	10/01-12/01
	Guam	H	9.42 FQ	12.80 AW	16.79 TQ	GUBLS	10/01-12/01
Ship Engineer	Connecticut	H	12.61 FQ	21.75 AW	32.18 TQ	CTBLS	10/01-12/01
	Florida	H	16.04 FQ	25.53 AW	35.12 TQ	FLBLS	10/01-12/01
	Hawaii	H	12.05 FQ	20.97 AW	32.00 TQ	HIBLS	10/01-12/01
	Illinois	H	17.68 FQ	26.52 AW	36.22 TQ	ILBLS	10/01-12/01
	Indiana	H	16.09 FQ	23.69 AW	33.05 TQ	INBLS	10/01-12/01
	Kentucky	H	9.91 FQ	24.31 AW	34.71 TQ	KYBLS	10/01-12/01
	Louisiana	H	10.78 FQ	23.17 AW	37.55 TQ	LABLS	10/01-12/01
	Maryland	H	14.19 FQ	23.92 AW	42.83 TQ	MDBLS	10/01-12/01
	Mississippi	H	14.48 FQ	20.67 AW	30.18 TQ	MSBLS	10/01-12/01
	New Jersey	H	18.16 FQ	30.29 AW	49.93 TQ	NJBLS	10/01-12/01
	North Carolina	H	14.01 FQ	16.48 AW	20.31 TQ	NCBLS	10/01-12/01
	Ohio	H	18.49 FQ	26.04 AW	39.47 TQ	OHBLS	10/01-12/01
	Oregon	H	11.74 FQ	22.50 AW	33.19 TQ	ORBLS	10/01-12/01
	Pennsylvania	H	13.98 FQ	27.94 AW	47.01 TQ	PABLS	10/01-12/01
	South Carolina	H	7.56 FQ	18.11 AW	41.36 TQ	SCBLS	10/01-12/01
	Tennessee	H	15.54 FQ	21.73 AW	27.97 TQ	TNBLS	10/01-12/01
	Texas	H	14.75 FQ	26.18 AW	39.18 TQ	TXBLS	10/01-12/01
	Virginia	H	12.13 FQ	23.52 AW	45.50 TQ	VABLS	10/01-12/01
	Washington	H	17.03 FQ	26.48 AW	39.88 TQ	WABLS	10/01-12/01
	West Virginia	H	18.59 FQ	22.93 AW	28.63 TQ	WVBLS	10/01-12/01
Shipping, Receiving, and Traffic Clerk	Alabama	H	7.07 FQ	10.73 AW	15.96 TQ	ALBLS	10/01-12/01
	Alaska	H	8.05 FQ	13.19 AW	20.51 TQ	AKBLS	10/01-12/01
	Arizona	H	6.77 FQ	10.23 AW	15.08 TQ	AZBLS	10/01-12/01
	Arkansas	H	7.21 FQ	10.63 AW	15.20 TQ	ARBLS	10/01-12/01
	California	H	7.24 FQ	11.76 AW	17.55 TQ	CABLS	10/01-12/01
	Colorado	H	7.81 FQ	11.90 AW	16.70 TQ	COBLS	10/01-12/01
	Connecticut	H	8.54 FQ	13.08 AW	18.08 TQ	CTBLS	10/01-12/01
	Delaware	H	7.22 FQ	10.16 AW	15.15 TQ	DEBLS	10/01-12/01
	District of Columbia	H	9.28 FQ	13.98 AW	20.20 TQ	DCBLS	10/01-12/01
	Florida	H	7.10 FQ	10.54 AW	15.07 TQ	FLBLS	10/01-12/01
	Georgia	H	7.58 FQ	11.31 AW	15.95 TQ	GABLS	10/01-12/01
	Hawaii	H	7.30 FQ	13.24 AW	20.27 TQ	HIBLS	10/01-12/01
	Idaho	H	6.95 FQ	10.52 AW	15.01 TQ	IDBLS	10/01-12/01
	Illinois	H	7.59 FQ	12.17 AW	17.70 TQ	ILBLS	10/01-12/01
	Indiana	H	7.56 FQ	11.38 AW	16.13 TQ	INBLS	10/01-12/01
	Iowa	H	6.77 FQ	10.85 AW	15.97 TQ	IABLS	10/01-12/01

AAW	Average annual wage	**AOH**	Average offered, high	**ASH**	Average starting, high	**H**	Hourly	**M**	Monthly	**S**	Special: hourly and annual
AE	Average entry wage	**AOL**	Average offered, low	**ASL**	Average starting, low	**HI**	Highest wage paid	**MTC**	Median total compensation	**TQ**	Third quartile wage
AEX	Average experienced wage	**APH**	Average pay, high range	**AW**	Average wage paid	**HR**	High end range	**MW**	Median wage paid	**W**	Weekly
AO	Average offered	**APL**	Average pay, low range	**FQ**	First quartile wage	**LR**	Low end range	**SQ**	Second quartile wage	**Y**	Yearly

Occupation/Type/Industry	Location	Per	Low	Mid	High	Source	Date
Shipping, Receiving, and Traffic Clerk	Kansas	H	7.43 FQ	12.73 AW	23.16 TQ	KSBLS	10/01-12/01
	Kentucky	H	7.49 FQ	11.32 AW	16.25 TQ	KYBLS	10/01-12/01
	Louisiana	H	6.48 FQ	10.87 AW	16.62 TQ	LABLS	10/01-12/01
	Maine	H	7.42 FQ	10.84 AW	15.23 TQ	MEBLS	10/01-12/01
	Maryland	H	7.31 FQ	12.25 AW	18.83 TQ	MDBLS	10/01-12/01
	Massachusetts	H	8.41 FQ	12.75 AW	17.90 TQ	MABLS	10/01-12/01
	Michigan	H	7.89 FQ	13.03 AW	20.35 TQ	MIBLS	10/01-12/01
	Minnesota	H	8.15 FQ	12.49 AW	17.56 TQ	MNBLS	10/01-12/01
	Mississippi	H	6.49 FQ	9.97 AW	13.98 TQ	MSBLS	10/01-12/01
	Missouri	H	7.39 FQ	11.22 AW	16.40 TQ	MOBLS	10/01-12/01
	Montana	H	7.04 FQ	9.86 AW	13.74 TQ	MTBLS	10/01-12/01
	Nebraska	H	6.60 FQ	10.35 AW	14.74 TQ	NEBLS	10/01-12/01
	Nevada	H	7.36 FQ	11.25 AW	16.62 TQ	NVBLS	10/01-12/01
	New Hampshire	H	8.23 FQ	11.86 AW	16.46 TQ	NHBLS	10/01-12/01
	New Jersey	H	7.42 FQ	12.80 AW	19.69 TQ	NJBLS	10/01-12/01
	New Mexico	H	6.65 FQ	10.14 AW	14.77 TQ	NMBLS	10/01-12/01
	New York	H	7.12 FQ	11.86 AW	17.83 TQ	NYBLS	10/01-12/01
	North Carolina	H	7.71 FQ	11.27 AW	15.86 TQ	NCBLS	10/01-12/01
	North Dakota	H	6.96 FQ	10.60 AW	15.29 TQ	NDBLS	10/01-12/01
	Ohio	H	7.57 FQ	11.78 AW	16.91 TQ	OHBLS	10/01-12/01
	Oklahoma	H	6.49 FQ	10.35 AW	15.41 TQ	OKBLS	10/01-12/01
	Oregon	H	7.93 FQ	11.97 AW	16.99 TQ	ORBLS	10/01-12/01
	Pennsylvania	H	7.24 FQ	11.81 AW	17.15 TQ	PABLS	10/01-12/01
	Rhode Island	H	7.62 FQ	11.66 AW	16.78 TQ	RIBLS	10/01-12/01
	South Carolina	H	7.35 FQ	10.94 AW	15.62 TQ	SCBLS	10/01-12/01
	South Dakota	H	7.53 FQ	10.55 AW	13.98 TQ	SDBLS	10/01-12/01
	Tennessee	H	7.54 FQ	11.27 AW	16.04 TQ	TNBLS	10/01-12/01
	Texas	H	7.02 FQ	11.09 AW	16.52 TQ	TXBLS	10/01-12/01
	Utah	H	7.62 FQ	11.23 AW	15.60 TQ	UTBLS	10/01-12/01
	Vermont	H	7.50 FQ	11.06 AW	15.23 TQ	VTBLS	10/01-12/01
	Virginia	H	7.05 FQ	11.12 AW	16.46 TQ	VABLS	10/01-12/01
	Washington	H	8.44 FQ	13.52 AW	21.03 TQ	WABLS	10/01-12/01
	West Virginia	H	6.06 FQ	10.88 AW	18.09 TQ	WVBLS	10/01-12/01
	Wisconsin	H	7.98 FQ	12.01 AW	16.81 TQ	WIBLS	10/01-12/01
	Wyoming	H	6.74 FQ	10.62 AW	16.12 TQ	WYBLS	10/01-12/01
	Puerto Rico	H	5.82 FQ	8.53 AW	13.20 TQ	PRBLS	10/01-12/01
	Virgin Islands	H	6.23 FQ	9.18 AW	13.89 TQ	VIBLS	10/01-12/01
	Guam	H	6.45 FQ	10.80 AW	16.42 TQ	GUBLS	10/01-12/01
Shoe and Leather Worker and Repairer	Alabama	H	6.37 FQ	8.53 AW	11.25 TQ	ALBLS	10/01-12/01
	Arizona	H	5.72 FQ	7.91 AW	10.70 TQ	AZBLS	10/01-12/01
	Arkansas	H	5.84 FQ	7.87 AW	10.48 TQ	ARBLS	10/01-12/01
	California	H	6.53 FQ	9.02 AW	12.16 TQ	CABLS	10/01-12/01
	Colorado	H	7.99 FQ	11.02 AW	14.14 TQ	COBLS	10/01-12/01
	Florida	H	5.78 FQ	8.43 AW	12.95 TQ	FLBLS	10/01-12/01
	Georgia	H	6.46 FQ	9.06 AW	12.09 TQ	GABLS	10/01-12/01
	Illinois	H	7.17 FQ	11.14 AW	15.18 TQ	ILBLS	10/01-12/01
	Indiana	H	6.15 FQ	10.74 AW	15.67 TQ	INBLS	10/01-12/01
	Iowa	H	6.07 FQ	9.47 AW	13.32 TQ	IABLS	10/01-12/01
	Kansas	H	6.36 FQ	8.98 AW	11.05 TQ	KSBLS	10/01-12/01
	Kentucky	H	5.97 FQ	8.37 AW	12.56 TQ	KYBLS	10/01-12/01
	Louisiana	H	6.05 FQ	7.77 AW	9.63 TQ	LABLS	10/01-12/01
	Maine	H	6.34 FQ	8.86 AW	11.59 TQ	MEBLS	10/01-12/01
	Maryland	H	7.23 FQ	9.53 AW	11.43 TQ	MDBLS	10/01-12/01
	Massachusetts	H	7.20 FQ	11.17 AW	14.05 TQ	MABLS	10/01-12/01
	Missouri	H	6.12 FQ	9.88 AW	13.91 TQ	MOBLS	10/01-12/01
	Nevada	H	5.97 FQ	8.92 AW	13.50 TQ	NVBLS	10/01-12/01
	New Hampshire	H	5.85 FQ	7.47 AW	10.58 TQ	NHBLS	10/01-12/01
	New Jersey	H	5.61 FQ	8.51 AW	13.19 TQ	NJBLS	10/01-12/01
	New Mexico	H	5.99 FQ	9.61 AW	13.45 TQ	NMBLS	10/01-12/01
	New York	H	6.06 FQ	9.18 AW	13.71 TQ	NYBLS	10/01-12/01
	North Carolina	H	6.39 FQ	8.76 AW	11.50 TQ	NCBLS	10/01-12/01
	Ohio	H	6.50 FQ	10.03 AW	16.04 TQ	OHBLS	10/01-12/01
	Oklahoma	H	5.74 FQ	7.28 AW	10.11 TQ	OKBLS	10/01-12/01
	Oregon	H	7.69 FQ	10.90 AW	14.14 TQ	ORBLS	10/01-12/01
	Pennsylvania	H	6.84 FQ	11.46 AW	16.63 TQ	PABLS	10/01-12/01
	South Carolina	H	5.98 FQ	9.41 AW	13.41 TQ	SCBLS	10/01-12/01
	Tennessee	H	6.37 FQ	8.46 AW	11.02 TQ	TNBLS	10/01-12/01
	Texas	H	5.93 FQ	8.46 AW	12.34 TQ	TXBLS	10/01-12/01
	Utah	H	8.64 FQ	10.60 AW	13.49 TQ	UTBLS	10/01-12/01

AAW	Average annual wage	**AOH**	Average offered, high	**ASH**	Average starting, high	**H**	Hourly	**M**	Monthly	**S**	Special: hourly and annual
AE	Average entry wage	**AOL**	Average offered, low	**ASL**	Average starting, low	**HI**	Highest wage paid	**MTC**	Median total compensation	**TQ**	Third quartile wage
AEX	Average experienced wage	**APH**	Average pay, high range	**AW**	Average wage paid	**HR**	High end range	**MW**	Median wage paid	**W**	Weekly
AO	Average offered	**APL**	Average pay, low range	**FQ**	First quartile wage	**LR**	Low end range	**SQ**	Second quartile wage	**Y**	Yearly

Occupation/Type/Industry	Location	Per	Low	Mid	High	Source	Date
Shoe and Leather Worker and Repairer	Virginia	H	7.05 FQ	10.43 AW	14.78 TQ	VABLS	10/01-12/01
	Washington	H	7.38 FQ	10.34 AW	13.73 TQ	WABLS	10/01-12/01
	Wyoming	H	5.89 FQ	11.72 AW	20.76 TQ	WYBLS	10/01-12/01
	Puerto Rico	H	5.45 FQ	6.28 AW	7.48 TQ	PRBLS	10/01-12/01
Shoe Machine Operator and Tender	California	H	6.72 FQ	8.44 AW	10.37 TQ	CABLS	10/01-12/01
	Los Angeles-Long Beach PMSA, CA	H	6.63 FQ	7.96 AW	9.76 TQ	CABLS	10/01-12/01
	Maine	H	7.09 FQ	9.24 AW	12.19 TQ	MEBLS	10/01-12/01
	Massachusetts	H	7.59 FQ	10.21 AW	14.44 TQ	MABLS	10/01-12/01
	Boston PMSA, MA-NH	H	7.82 FQ	11.41 AW	16.25 TQ	MABLS	10/01-12/01
	Brockton PMSA, MA	H	7.55 FQ	10.45 AW	15.84 TQ	MABLS	10/01-12/01
	Missouri	H	6.77 FQ	9.51 AW	11.28 TQ	MOBLS	10/01-12/01
	St. Louis MSA, MO-IL	H	8.13 FQ	10.04 AW	11.94 TQ	MOBLS	10/01-12/01
	New York	H	7.23 FQ	9.00 AW	11.35 TQ	NYBLS	10/01-12/01
	New York PMSA, NY	H	7.15 FQ	7.94 AW	8.70 TQ	NYBLS	10/01-12/01
	Tennessee	H	5.80 FQ	7.73 AW	10.57 TQ	TNBLS	10/01-12/01
	Texas	H	5.97 FQ	8.43 AW	11.42 TQ	TXBLS	10/01-12/01
	Wisconsin	H	6.95 FQ	9.81 AW	13.36 TQ	WIBLS	10/01-12/01
	Milwaukee-Waukesha PMSA, WI	H	6.46 FQ	9.68 AW	13.44 TQ	WIBLS	10/01-12/01
Shuttle Car Operator	Colorado	H	13.76 FQ	17.28 AW	24.15 TQ	COBLS	10/01-12/01
	Illinois	H	17.00 FQ	19.52 AW	22.27 TQ	ILBLS	10/01-12/01
	Kentucky	H	12.15 FQ	14.65 AW	17.45 TQ	KYBLS	10/01-12/01
	Pennsylvania	H	16.48 FQ	20.04 AW	25.15 TQ	PABLS	10/01-12/01
	Virginia	H	12.90 FQ	18.02 AW	22.14 TQ	VABLS	10/01-12/01
	West Virginia	H	17.42 FQ	19.36 AW	21.75 TQ	WVBLS	10/01-12/01
Signal and Track Switch Repairer	Arkansas	H	14.14 FQ	19.25 AW	25.26 TQ	ARBLS	10/01-12/01
	Colorado	H	15.07 FQ	19.31 AW	24.67 TQ	COBLS	10/01-12/01
	Connecticut	H	18.38 FQ	21.30 AW	26.16 TQ	CTBLS	10/01-12/01
	Florida	H	8.88 FQ	14.37 AW	20.64 TQ	FLBLS	10/01-12/01
	Georgia	H	16.57 FQ	20.56 AW	23.88 TQ	GABLS	10/01-12/01
	Illinois	H	17.26 FQ	19.86 AW	23.79 TQ	ILBLS	10/01-12/01
	Indiana	H	17.24 FQ	20.46 AW	26.20 TQ	INBLS	10/01-12/01
	Kansas	H	17.31 FQ	21.23 AW	26.87 TQ	KSBLS	10/01-12/01
	Louisiana	H	16.23 FQ	20.61 AW	26.45 TQ	LABLS	10/01-12/01
	Michigan	H	17.31 FQ	20.76 AW	26.08 TQ	MIBLS	10/01-12/01
	Minnesota	H	17.32 FQ	21.18 AW	27.42 TQ	MNBLS	10/01-12/01
	Mississippi	H	17.08 FQ	20.97 AW	26.52 TQ	MSBLS	10/01-12/01
	Missouri	H	17.89 FQ	20.64 AW	25.59 TQ	MOBLS	10/01-12/01
	New Jersey	H	19.03 FQ	24.62 AW	29.34 TQ	NJBLS	10/01-12/01
	North Carolina	H	15.06 FQ	18.99 AW	22.91 TQ	NCBLS	10/01-12/01
	Ohio	H	17.26 FQ	21.13 AW	27.07 TQ	OHBLS	10/01-12/01
	Pennsylvania	H	17.44 FQ	20.26 AW	25.02 TQ	PABLS	10/01-12/01
	South Carolina	H	15.12 FQ	19.11 AW	25.02 TQ	SCBLS	10/01-12/01
	Tennessee	H	11.61 FQ	15.88 AW	20.68 TQ	TNBLS	10/01-12/01
	Texas	H	17.14 FQ	20.58 AW	26.60 TQ	TXBLS	10/01-12/01
	Washington	H	11.47 FQ	18.53 AW	24.49 TQ	WABLS	10/01-12/01
	Wisconsin	H	16.54 FQ	19.90 AW	25.11 TQ	WIBLS	10/01-12/01
Skin Care Specialist	Alabama	H	5.85 FQ	9.05 AW	13.33 TQ	ALBLS	10/01-12/01
	Arizona	H	6.48 FQ	13.47 AW	26.17 TQ	AZBLS	10/01-12/01
	California	H	6.67 FQ	13.30 AW	21.58 TQ	CABLS	10/01-12/01
	Colorado	H	5.66 FQ	8.64 AW	13.10 TQ	COBLS	10/01-12/01
	Connecticut	H	6.88 FQ	11.28 AW	15.59 TQ	CTBLS	10/01-12/01
	District of Columbia	H	10.49 FQ	17.72 AW	27.78 TQ	DCBLS	10/01-12/01
	Florida	H	6.11 FQ	10.51 AW	16.45 TQ	FLBLS	10/01-12/01
	Georgia	H	6.27 FQ	9.32 AW	13.49 TQ	GABLS	10/01-12/01
	Hawaii	H	7.20 FQ	13.50 AW	20.58 TQ	HIBLS	10/01-12/01
	Illinois	H	6.46 FQ	13.28 AW	19.89 TQ	ILBLS	10/01-12/01
	Indiana	H	6.39 FQ	10.41 AW	15.78 TQ	INBLS	10/01-12/01
	Iowa	H	6.06 FQ	8.98 AW	13.20 TQ	IABLS	10/01-12/01
	Kansas	H	8.91 FQ	12.98 AW	14.49 TQ	KSBLS	10/01-12/01
	Kentucky	H	6.76 FQ	11.02 AW	13.95 TQ	KYBLS	10/01-12/01
	Louisiana	H	6.01 FQ	9.90 AW	16.64 TQ	LABLS	10/01-12/01
	Maryland	H	6.53 FQ	10.47 AW	18.67 TQ	MDBLS	10/01-12/01
	Massachusetts	H	6.92 FQ	10.44 AW	15.96 TQ	MABLS	10/01-12/01
	Michigan	H	6.23 FQ	10.19 AW	15.03 TQ	MIBLS	10/01-12/01

AAW	Average annual wage	**AOH**	Average offered, high	**ASH**	Average starting, high	**H**	Hourly	**M**	Monthly	**S**	Special: hourly and annual
AE	Average entry wage	**AOL**	Average offered, low	**ASL**	Average starting, low	**HI**	Highest wage paid	**MTC**	Median total compensation	**TQ**	Third quartile wage
AEX	Average experienced wage	**APH**	Average pay, high range	**AW**	Average wage paid	**HR**	High end range	**MW**	Median wage paid	**W**	Weekly
AO	Average offered	**APL**	Average pay, low range	**FQ**	First quartile wage	**LR**	Low end range	**SQ**	Second quartile wage	**Y**	Yearly

Occupation/Type/Industry	Location	Per	Low	Mid	High	Source	Date
Skin Care Specialist	Minnesota	H	7.24 FQ	12.81 AW	20.08 TQ	MNBLS	10/01-12/01
	Mississippi	H	5.71 FQ	7.82 AW	11.99 TQ	MSBLS	10/01-12/01
	Missouri	H	6.22 FQ	12.44 AW	22.15 TQ	MOBLS	10/01-12/01
	Nebraska	H	5.97 FQ	11.07 AW	18.70 TQ	NEBLS	10/01-12/01
	Nevada	H	6.71 FQ	13.89 AW	32.49 TQ	NVBLS	10/01-12/01
	New Hampshire	H	6.24 FQ	12.09 AW	19.44 TQ	NHBLS	10/01-12/01
	New Jersey	H	7.11 FQ	11.95 AW	20.32 TQ	NJBLS	10/01-12/01
	New Mexico	H	5.72 FQ	8.26 AW	12.12 TQ	NMBLS	10/01-12/01
	New York	H	6.43 FQ	15.16 AW	26.33 TQ	NYBLS	10/01-12/01
	North Carolina	H	7.14 FQ	12.44 AW	21.55 TQ	NCBLS	10/01-12/01
	Ohio	H	6.84 FQ	11.98 AW	17.57 TQ	OHBLS	10/01-12/01
	Oklahoma	H	5.92 FQ	9.48 AW	18.77 TQ	OKBLS	10/01-12/01
	Oregon	H	7.23 FQ	12.49 AW	17.47 TQ	ORBLS	10/01-12/01
	Pennsylvania	H	6.16 FQ	11.36 AW	19.32 TQ	PABLS	10/01-12/01
	Rhode Island	H	7.60 FQ	11.23 AW	18.22 TQ	RIBLS	10/01-12/01
	South Carolina	H	5.79 FQ	7.23 AW	9.71 TQ	SCBLS	10/01-12/01
	Tennessee	H	7.60 FQ	12.20 AW	22.49 TQ	TNBLS	10/01-12/01
	Texas	H	6.28 FQ	13.04 AW	28.82 TQ	TXBLS	10/01-12/01
	Utah	H	6.86 FQ	15.80 AW	21.25 TQ	UTBLS	10/01-12/01
	Virginia	H	6.20 FQ	11.80 AW	22.62 TQ	VABLS	10/01-12/01
	Washington	H	7.50 FQ	15.59 AW	28.44 TQ	WABLS	10/01-12/01
	Wisconsin	H	5.91 FQ	10.21 AW	16.46 TQ	WIBLS	10/01-12/01
	Puerto Rico	H	6.49 FQ	8.02 AW	10.44 TQ	PRBLS	10/01-12/01
Sky Cap							
Airport	United States	Y	13200 ASL		25200 ASH	AEAC	1/99-1/99
Slaughterer and Meat Packer	Alabama	H	6.30 FQ	7.89 AW	9.99 TQ	ALBLS	10/01-12/01
	Arizona	H	7.36 FQ	9.13 AW	11.15 TQ	AZBLS	10/01-12/01
	Phoenix-Mesa MSA, AZ	H	7.37 FQ	9.12 AW	11.15 TQ	AZBLS	10/01-12/01
	Arkansas	H	7.05 FQ	8.55 AW	10.69 TQ	ARBLS	10/01-12/01
	Fayetteville-Springdale-Rogers MSA, AR	H	7.17 FQ	8.73 AW	10.88 TQ	ARBLS	10/01-12/01
	Little Rock-North Little Rock MSA, AR	H	7.23 FQ	8.35 AW	10.18 TQ	ARBLS	10/01-12/01
	California	H	6.63 FQ	10.52 AW	18.63 TQ	CABLS	10/01-12/01
	Los Angeles-Long Beach PMSA, CA	H	6.50 FQ	10.20 AW	16.37 TQ	CABLS	10/01-12/01
	Merced MSA, CA	H	6.59 FQ	8.31 AW	10.70 TQ	CABLS	10/01-12/01
	Oakland PMSA, CA	H	8.41 FQ	11.01 AW	15.55 TQ	CABLS	10/01-12/01
	Santa Rosa PMSA, CA	H	6.73 FQ	8.69 AW	11.04 TQ	CABLS	10/01-12/01
	Denver PMSA, CO	H	6.35 FQ	9.58 AW	13.16 TQ	COBLS	10/01-12/01
	Florida	H	6.39 FQ	8.79 AW	12.12 TQ	FLBLS	10/01-12/01
	Miami PMSA, FL	H	5.68 FQ	7.47 AW	9.97 TQ	FLBLS	10/01-12/01
	Georgia	H	6.98 FQ	7.92 AW	9.00 TQ	GABLS	10/01-12/01
	Atlanta MSA, GA	H	7.39 FQ	8.22 AW	9.13 TQ	GABLS	10/01-12/01
	Hawaii	H	5.77 FQ	8.27 AW	11.83 TQ	HIBLS	10/01-12/01
	Idaho	H	8.37 FQ	10.14 AW	12.20 TQ	IDBLS	10/01-12/01
	Illinois	H	7.66 FQ	10.69 AW	13.74 TQ	ILBLS	10/01-12/01
	Chicago PMSA, IL	H	7.59 FQ	11.00 AW	13.94 TQ	ILBLS	10/01-12/01
	Indiana	H	7.50 FQ	10.04 AW	13.20 TQ	INBLS	10/01-12/01
	Iowa	H	8.08 FQ	10.13 AW	12.36 TQ	IABLS	10/01-12/01
	Kansas	H	8.83 FQ	10.21 AW	12.51 TQ	KSBLS	10/01-12/01
	Louisiana	H	5.84 FQ	7.91 AW	10.90 TQ	LABLS	10/01-12/01
	Lafayette MSA, LA	H	5.65 FQ	7.26 AW	9.96 TQ	LABLS	10/01-12/01
	New Orleans MSA, LA	H	6.90 FQ	9.02 AW	13.09 TQ	LABLS	10/01-12/01
	Maryland	H	6.09 FQ	8.61 AW	11.22 TQ	MDBLS	10/01-12/01
	Baltimore PMSA, MD	H	5.99 FQ	8.37 AW	10.94 TQ	MDBLS	10/01-12/01
	Massachusetts	H	7.13 FQ	10.81 AW	15.64 TQ	MABLS	10/01-12/01
	Michigan	H	7.18 FQ	9.81 AW	12.80 TQ	MIBLS	10/01-12/01
	Detroit PMSA, MI	H	6.42 FQ	9.13 AW	11.38 TQ	MIBLS	10/01-12/01
	Grand Rapids-Muskegon-Holland MSA, MI	H	8.30 FQ	10.33 AW	12.84 TQ	MIBLS	10/01-12/01
	Minnesota	H	7.81 FQ	10.06 AW	12.62 TQ	MNBLS	10/01-12/01
	Minneapolis-St. Paul MSA, MN-WI	H	7.62 FQ	9.91 AW	11.51 TQ	MNBLS	10/01-12/01
	Mississippi	H	6.91 FQ	9.04 AW	11.25 TQ	MSBLS	10/01-12/01
	Biloxi-Gulfport-Pascagoula MSA, MS	H	5.93 FQ	7.51 AW	9.18 TQ	MSBLS	10/01-12/01
	Missouri	H	7.49 FQ	9.13 AW	11.22 TQ	MOBLS	10/01-12/01
	Kansas City MSA, MO-KS	H	6.10 FQ	9.75 AW	13.91 TQ	MOBLS	10/01-12/01
	St. Louis MSA, MO-IL	H	7.41 FQ	9.97 AW	12.78 TQ	MOBLS	10/01-12/01
	Montana	H	6.91 FQ	9.95 AW	13.34 TQ	MTBLS	10/01-12/01

AAW	Average annual wage	**AOH**	Average offered, high	**ASH**	Average starting, high	**H**	Hourly	**M**	Monthly	**S**	Special: hourly and annual
AE	Average entry wage	**AOL**	Average offered, low	**ASL**	Average starting, low	**HI**	Highest wage paid	**MTC**	Median total compensation	**TQ**	Third quartile wage
AEX	Average experienced wage	**APH**	Average pay, high range	**AW**	Average wage paid	**HR**	High end range	**MW**	Median wage paid	**W**	Weekly
AO	Average offered	**APL**	Average pay, low range	**FQ**	First quartile wage	**LR**	Low end range	**SQ**	Second quartile wage	**Y**	Yearly

Occupation/Type/Industry	Location	Per	Low	Mid	High	Source	Date
Slaughterer and Meat Packer	Nebraska	H	8.45 FQ	10.17 AW	12.35 TQ	NEBLS	10/01-12/01
	Omaha MSA, NE-IA	H	8.39 FQ	10.20 AW	12.50 TQ	NEBLS	10/01-12/01
	New Jersey	H	6.16 FQ	8.31 AW	10.81 TQ	NJBLS	10/01-12/01
	Newark PMSA, NJ	H	7.39 FQ	9.03 AW	12.34 TQ	NJBLS	10/01-12/01
	New Mexico	H	6.06 FQ	8.11 AW	10.46 TQ	NMBLS	10/01-12/01
	New York	H	7.19 FQ	10.20 AW	13.42 TQ	NYBLS	10/01-12/01
	New York PMSA, NY	H	6.23 FQ	9.89 AW	14.94 TQ	NYBLS	10/01-12/01
	North Carolina	H	7.14 FQ	8.27 AW	9.99 TQ	NCBLS	10/01-12/01
	Greensboro-Winston-Salem-High Point MSA, NC	H	6.19 FQ	7.82 AW	9.69 TQ	NCBLS	10/01-12/01
	Raleigh-Durham-Chapel Hill MSA, NC	H	7.10 FQ	8.05 AW	9.55 TQ	NCBLS	10/01-12/01
	North Dakota	H	6.40 FQ	9.07 AW	11.80 TQ	NDBLS	10/01-12/01
	Ohio	H	7.42 FQ	10.52 AW	14.34 TQ	OHBLS	10/01-12/01
	Cincinnati PMSA, OH-KY-IN	H	8.83 FQ	11.25 AW	13.71 TQ	OHBLS	10/01-12/01
	Dayton-Springfield MSA, OH	H	7.56 FQ	9.82 AW	13.39 TQ	OHBLS	10/01-12/01
	Oregon	H	7.63 FQ	11.17 AW	15.74 TQ	ORBLS	10/01-12/01
	Portland-Vancouver PMSA, OR-WA	H	8.80 FQ	13.33 AW	17.47 TQ	ORBLS	10/01-12/01
	Pennsylvania	H	8.01 FQ	10.91 AW	13.77 TQ	PABLS	10/01-12/01
	Harrisburg-Lebanon-Carlisle MSA, PA	H	7.32 FQ	10.21 AW	13.96 TQ	PABLS	10/01-12/01
	Philadelphia PMSA, PA-NJ	H	7.47 FQ	10.37 AW	13.73 TQ	PABLS	10/01-12/01
	Greenville-Spartanburg-Anderson MSA, SC	H	6.77 FQ	7.83 AW	8.43 TQ	SCBLS	10/01-12/01
	Tennessee	H	5.63 FQ	9.39 AW	15.22 TQ	TNBLS	10/01-12/01
	Chattanooga MSA, TN-GA	H	5.54 FQ	9.33 AW	17.46 TQ	TNBLS	10/01-12/01
	Texas	H	6.00 FQ	8.81 AW	11.67 TQ	TXBLS	10/01-12/01
	Austin-San Marcos MSA, TX	H	7.41 FQ	10.19 AW	14.07 TQ	TXBLS	10/01-12/01
	Dallas PMSA, TX	H	5.97 FQ	7.87 AW	9.93 TQ	TXBLS	10/01-12/01
	Fort Worth-Arlington PMSA, TX	H	5.82 FQ	8.22 AW	10.73 TQ	TXBLS	10/01-12/01
	Houston PMSA, TX	H	5.97 FQ	8.70 AW	11.17 TQ	TXBLS	10/01-12/01
	McAllen-Edinburg-Mission MSA, TX	H	5.50 FQ	6.14 AW	6.94 TQ	TXBLS	10/01-12/01
	Salt Lake City-Ogden MSA, UT	H	9.71 FQ	12.46 AW	15.45 TQ	UTBLS	10/01-12/01
	Virginia	H	7.68 FQ	9.54 AW	11.06 TQ	VABLS	10/01-12/01
	Norfolk-Virginia Beach-Newport News MSA, VA-NC	H	7.62 FQ	9.50 AW	11.01 TQ	VABLS	10/01-12/01
	Washington	H	7.26 FQ	10.09 AW	14.23 TQ	WABLS	10/01-12/01
	Seattle-Bellevue-Everett PMSA, WA	H	11.42 FQ	15.21 AW	24.15 TQ	WABLS	10/01-12/01
	West Virginia	H	5.69 FQ	7.49 AW	10.88 TQ	WVBLS	10/01-12/01
	Wisconsin	H	8.06 FQ	10.02 AW	12.49 TQ	WIBLS	10/01-12/01
	Madison MSA, WI	H	7.56 FQ	9.35 AW	10.92 TQ	WIBLS	10/01-12/01
	Wyoming	H	5.79 FQ	6.78 AW	8.59 TQ	WYBLS	10/01-12/01
Slot Key Person	Arizona	H	7.83 FQ	11.55 AW	16.41 TQ	AZBLS	10/01-12/01
	California	H	6.92 FQ	12.61 AW	22.32 TQ	CABLS	10/01-12/01
	Colorado	H	8.08 FQ	12.26 AW	16.66 TQ	COBLS	10/01-12/01
	Florida	H	8.03 FQ	13.78 AW	20.94 TQ	FLBLS	10/01-12/01
	Georgia	H	7.57 FQ	10.75 AW	15.80 TQ	GABLS	10/01-12/01
	Illinois	H	7.61 FQ	12.31 AW	20.23 TQ	ILBLS	10/01-12/01
	Indiana	H	7.70 FQ	10.81 AW	15.64 TQ	INBLS	10/01-12/01
	Iowa	H	7.42 FQ	10.07 AW	14.76 TQ	IABLS	10/01-12/01
	Louisiana	H	7.03 FQ	9.73 AW	13.82 TQ	LABLS	10/01-12/01
	Mississippi	H	7.48 FQ	11.24 AW	16.78 TQ	MSBLS	10/01-12/01
	Missouri	H	8.64 FQ	12.69 AW	17.95 TQ	MOBLS	10/01-12/01
	Nevada	H	7.42 FQ	11.45 AW	15.87 TQ	NVBLS	10/01-12/01
	New Jersey	H	7.86 FQ	13.18 AW	20.67 TQ	NJBLS	10/01-12/01
	New Mexico	H	7.04 FQ	8.52 AW	10.63 TQ	NMBLS	10/01-12/01
	New York	H	7.43 FQ	12.04 AW	18.81 TQ	NYBLS	10/01-12/01
	Oklahoma	H	5.86 FQ	8.48 AW	12.50 TQ	OKBLS	10/01-12/01
	Texas	H	8.05 FQ	12.93 AW	19.61 TQ	TXBLS	10/01-12/01
	Washington	H	7.56 FQ	11.89 AW	19.98 TQ	WABLS	10/01-12/01
	West Virginia	H	7.88 FQ	13.29 AW	20.58 TQ	WVBLS	10/01-12/01
	Puerto Rico	H	5.52 FQ	7.81 AW	11.20 TQ	PRBLS	10/01-12/01
Social and Community Service Manager	Alabama	Y	21170 FQ	36470 AW	60350 TQ	ALBLS	10/01-12/01

AAW Average annual wage; AE Average entry wage; AEX Average experienced wage; AO Average offered; AOH Average offered, high; AOL Average offered, low; APH Average pay, high range; APL Average pay, low range; ASH Average starting, high; ASL Average starting, low; AW Average wage paid; FQ First quartile wage; H Hourly; HI Highest wage paid; HR High end range; LR Low end range; M Monthly; MTC Median total compensation; MW Median wage paid; SQ Second quartile wage; S Special: hourly and annual; TQ Third quartile wage; W Weekly; Y Yearly

Occupation/Type/Industry	Location	Per	Low	Mid	High	Source	Date
Social and Community Service Manager	Alaska	Y	25860 FQ	45550 AW	70510 TQ	AKBLS	10/01-12/01
	Arizona	Y	24160 FQ	42630 AW	62950 TQ	AZBLS	10/01-12/01
	Arkansas	Y	20890 FQ	38680 AW	56240 TQ	ARBLS	10/01-12/01
	California	Y	29190 FQ	51800 AW	82880 TQ	CABLS	10/01-12/01
	Colorado	Y	24660 FQ	43000 AW	66820 TQ	COBLS	10/01-12/01
	Connecticut	Y	31970 FQ	52320 AW	74110 TQ	CTBLS	10/01-12/01
	Delaware	Y	27080 FQ	46010 AW	68540 TQ	DEBLS	10/01-12/01
	District of Columbia	Y	25300 FQ	52490 AW	84660 TQ	DCBLS	10/01-12/01
	Florida	Y	28030 FQ	46730 AW	71280 TQ	FLBLS	10/01-12/01
	Hawaii	Y	30650 FQ	45590 AW	67030 TQ	HIBLS	10/01-12/01
	Idaho	Y	16170 FQ	39230 AW	64330 TQ	IDBLS	10/01-12/01
	Illinois	Y	24010 FQ	42080 AW	65300 TQ	ILBLS	10/01-12/01
	Indiana	Y	23380 FQ	36790 AW	54880 TQ	INBLS	10/01-12/01
	Iowa	Y	20540 FQ	38560 AW	60290 TQ	IABLS	10/01-12/01
	Kansas	Y	24030 FQ	40980 AW	63720 TQ	KSBLS	10/01-12/01
	Kentucky	Y	24360 FQ	42330 AW	66090 TQ	KYBLS	10/01-12/01
	Louisiana	Y	21560 FQ	40580 AW	62760 TQ	LABLS	10/01-12/01
	Maine	Y	25300 FQ	40080 AW	56140 TQ	MEBLS	10/01-12/01
	Maryland	Y	18730 FQ	35330 AW	61760 TQ	MDBLS	10/01-12/01
	Massachusetts	Y	28340 FQ	43190 AW	62980 TQ	MABLS	10/01-12/01
	Michigan	Y	26890 FQ	51020 AW	82440 TQ	MIBLS	10/01-12/01
	Minnesota	Y	31550 FQ	48890 AW	71730 TQ	MNBLS	10/01-12/01
	Mississippi	Y	23710 FQ	36700 AW	53810 TQ	MSBLS	10/01-12/01
	Missouri	Y	21160 FQ	35420 AW	52750 TQ	MOBLS	10/01-12/01
	Montana	Y	18030 FQ	33220 AW	51780 TQ	MTBLS	10/01-12/01
	Nebraska	Y	20320 FQ	38580 AW	60630 TQ	NEBLS	10/01-12/01
	Nevada	Y	31420 FQ	57440 AW	88710 TQ	NVBLS	10/01-12/01
	New Hampshire	Y	21140 FQ	37890 AW	57580 TQ	NHBLS	10/01-12/01
	New Jersey	Y	33150 FQ	57640 AW	90350 TQ	NJBLS	10/01-12/01
	New Mexico	Y	25590 FQ	39670 AW	55430 TQ	NMBLS	10/01-12/01
	New York	Y	31310 FQ	54540 AW	83990 TQ	NYBLS	10/01-12/01
	North Carolina	Y	25830 FQ	43330 AW	65350 TQ	NCBLS	10/01-12/01
	North Dakota	Y	21050 FQ	35140 AW	49710 TQ	NDBLS	10/01-12/01
	Ohio	Y	25290 FQ	43160 AW	66950 TQ	OHBLS	10/01-12/01
	Oklahoma	Y	16370 FQ	32300 AW	51710 TQ	OKBLS	10/01-12/01
	Oregon	Y	26970 FQ	44150 AW	68470 TQ	ORBLS	10/01-12/01
	Pennsylvania	Y	21790 FQ	44460 AW	71730 TQ	PABLS	10/01-12/01
	Rhode Island	Y	28720 FQ	50620 AW	83990 TQ	RIBLS	10/01-12/01
	South Carolina	Y	19930 FQ	38030 AW	67630 TQ	SCBLS	10/01-12/01
	South Dakota	Y	33090 FQ	45700 AW	61370 TQ	SDBLS	10/01-12/01
	Tennessee	Y	21950 FQ	37980 AW	58120 TQ	TNBLS	10/01-12/01
	Texas	Y	23630 FQ	40430 AW	61240 TQ	TXBLS	10/01-12/01
	Utah	Y	25830 FQ	45530 AW	69170 TQ	UTBLS	10/01-12/01
	Vermont	Y	34960 FQ	53570 AW	71170 TQ	VTBLS	10/01-12/01
	Virginia	Y	29350 FQ	51070 AW	79920 TQ	VABLS	10/01-12/01
	Washington	Y	34260 FQ	60340 AW	89180 TQ	WABLS	10/01-12/01
	West Virginia	Y	18850 FQ	33660 AW	51900 TQ	WVBLS	10/01-12/01
	Wisconsin	Y	24760 FQ	41370 AW	63520 TQ	WIBLS	10/01-12/01
	Wyoming	Y	23320 FQ	39100 AW	62870 TQ	WYBLS	10/01-12/01
	Puerto Rico	Y	23370 FQ	35310 AW	54230 TQ	PRBLS	10/01-12/01
Social and Human Service Assistant	United States	Y		22330 MW		OOH11	1999-2000
	United States	Y		18500-25760 AW		FREEP1	1/00-1/00
	Alabama	Y	13880 FQ	24980 AW	39650 TQ	ALBLS	10/01-12/01
	Birmingham MSA, AL	Y	15950 FQ	25380 AW	39320 TQ	ALBLS	10/01-12/01
	Huntsville MSA, AL	Y	12630 FQ	22450 AW	36140 TQ	ALBLS	10/01-12/01
	Mobile MSA, AL	Y	12610 FQ	22630 AW	38290 TQ	ALBLS	10/01-12/01
	Montgomery MSA, AL	Y	13990 FQ	26280 AW	39320 TQ	ALBLS	10/01-12/01
	Alaska	Y	19960 FQ	28000 AW	41000 TQ	AKBLS	10/01-12/01
	Anchorage MSA, AK	Y	20020 FQ	25480 AW	31750 TQ	AKBLS	10/01-12/01
	Arizona	Y	15940 FQ	24550 AW	35100 TQ	AZBLS	10/01-12/01
	Phoenix-Mesa MSA, AZ	Y	17340 FQ	26200 AW	37160 TQ	AZBLS	10/01-12/01
	Tucson MSA, AZ	Y	12920 FQ	20290 AW	27410 TQ	AZBLS	10/01-12/01
	Arkansas	Y	14350 FQ	20680 AW	29520 TQ	ARBLS	10/01-12/01
	Fayetteville-Springdale-Rogers MSA, AR	Y	16540 FQ	22440 AW	27750 TQ	ARBLS	10/01-12/01
	Fort Smith MSA, AR-OK	Y	12030 FQ	19180 AW	31450 TQ	ARBLS	10/01-12/01
	Little Rock-North Little Rock MSA, AR	Y	14660 FQ	20170 AW	27400 TQ	ARBLS	10/01-12/01

AAW	Average annual wage	AOH	Average offered, high	ASH	Average starting, high	H	Hourly	M	Monthly	S	Special: hourly and annual
AE	Average entry wage	AOL	Average offered, low	ASL	Average starting, low	HI	Highest wage paid	MTC	Median total compensation	TQ	Third quartile wage
AEX	Average experienced wage	APH	Average pay, high range	AW	Average wage paid	HR	High end range	MW	Median wage paid	W	Weekly
AO	Average offered	APL	Average pay, low range	FQ	First quartile wage	LR	Low end range	SQ	Second quartile wage	Y	Yearly

Occupation/Type/Industry	Location	Per	Low	Mid	High	Source	Date
Social and Human Service Assistant	California	Y	16640 FQ	28370 AW	44420 TQ	CABLS	10/01-12/01
	Bakersfield MSA, CA	Y	16720 FQ	29930 AW	58280 TQ	CABLS	10/01-12/01
	Chico-Paradise MSA, CA	Y	19750 FQ	34160 AW	48100 TQ	CABLS	10/01-12/01
	Fresno MSA, CA	Y	15140 FQ	26820 AW	51340 TQ	CABLS	10/01-12/01
	Los Angeles-Long Beach PMSA, CA	Y	16550 FQ	27360 AW	40470 TQ	CABLS	10/01-12/01
	Merced MSA, CA	Y	13900 FQ	19110 AW	28110 TQ	CABLS	10/01-12/01
	Modesto MSA, CA	Y	16700 FQ	28170 AW	43260 TQ	CABLS	10/01-12/01
	Oakland PMSA, CA	Y	23890 FQ	34160 AW	49300 TQ	CABLS	10/01-12/01
	Orange County PMSA, CA	Y	18970 FQ	32070 AW	51710 TQ	CABLS	10/01-12/01
	Redding MSA, CA	Y	18650 FQ	30660 AW	45810 TQ	CABLS	10/01-12/01
	Riverside-San Bernardino PMSA, CA	Y	17240 FQ	27600 AW	42590 TQ	CABLS	10/01-12/01
	Sacramento PMSA, CA	Y	14400 FQ	27340 AW	38700 TQ	CABLS	10/01-12/01
	Salinas MSA, CA	Y	16380 FQ	23680 AW	32860 TQ	CABLS	10/01-12/01
	San Diego MSA, CA	Y	14760 FQ	24420 AW	38120 TQ	CABLS	10/01-12/01
	San Francisco PMSA, CA	Y	19300 FQ	29880 AW	44210 TQ	CABLS	10/01-12/01
	San Jose PMSA, CA	Y	22040 FQ	35640 AW	54640 TQ	CABLS	10/01-12/01
	Santa Barbara-Santa Maria-Lompoc MSA, CA	Y	18630 FQ	27310 AW	47340 TQ	CABLS	10/01-12/01
	Santa Cruz-Watsonville PMSA, CA	Y	19910 FQ	26170 AW	34300 TQ	CABLS	10/01-12/01
	Santa Rosa PMSA, CA	Y	19160 FQ	30310 AW	46340 TQ	CABLS	10/01-12/01
	Stockton-Lodi MSA, CA	Y	18180 FQ	31790 AW	52920 TQ	CABLS	10/01-12/01
	Vallejo-Fairfield-Napa PMSA, CA	Y	17550 FQ	27130 AW	42670 TQ	CABLS	10/01-12/01
	Ventura PMSA, CA	Y	15190 FQ	22630 AW	37010 TQ	CABLS	10/01-12/01
	Visalia-Tulare-Porterville MSA, CA	Y	13980 FQ	29390 AW	46020 TQ	CABLS	10/01-12/01
	Colorado	Y	16620 FQ	26010 AW	36990 TQ	COBLS	10/01-12/01
	Boulder-Longmont PMSA, CO	Y	17820 FQ	24720 AW	36430 TQ	COBLS	10/01-12/01
	Colorado Springs MSA, CO	Y	19330 FQ	25660 AW	33950 TQ	COBLS	10/01-12/01
	Denver PMSA, CO	Y	17330 FQ	26780 AW	36830 TQ	COBLS	10/01-12/01
	Fort Collins-Loveland MSA, CO	Y	16080 FQ	28690 AW	44310 TQ	COBLS	10/01-12/01
	Greeley PMSA, CO	Y	15870 FQ	24010 AW	34880 TQ	COBLS	10/01-12/01
	Connecticut	Y	19900 FQ	32830 AW	45260 TQ	CTBLS	10/01-12/01
	Bridgeport PMSA, CT	Y	19840 FQ	32320 AW	44300 TQ	CTBLS	10/01-12/01
	Danbury PMSA, CT	Y	23570 FQ	33670 AW	44040 TQ	CTBLS	10/01-12/01
	Hartford MSA, CT	Y	21800 FQ	34930 AW	50350 TQ	CTBLS	10/01-12/01
	New Haven-Meriden PMSA, CT	Y	16540 FQ	29160 AW	44180 TQ	CTBLS	10/01-12/01
	New London-Norwich MSA, CT-RI	Y	20310 FQ	31830 AW	44080 TQ	CTBLS	10/01-12/01
	Stamford-Norwalk PMSA, CT	Y	19570 FQ	30830 AW	44640 TQ	CTBLS	10/01-12/01
	Delaware	Y	13860 FQ	23250 AW	31430 TQ	DEBLS	10/01-12/01
	Wilmington-Newark PMSA, DE-MD	Y	13750 FQ	24090 AW	32190 TQ	DEBLS	10/01-12/01
	District of Columbia	Y	24240 FQ	37410 AW	54410 TQ	DCBLS	10/01-12/01
	Washington PMSA, DC-MD-VA-WV	Y	19320 FQ	31820 AW	48270 TQ	DCBLS	10/01-12/01
	Florida	Y	14650 FQ	21500 AW	29990 TQ	FLBLS	10/01-12/01
	Daytona Beach MSA, FL	Y	13070 FQ	19800 AW	30630 TQ	FLBLS	10/01-12/01
	Fort Lauderdale PMSA, FL	Y	14460 FQ	22280 AW	33320 TQ	FLBLS	10/01-12/01
	Fort Myers-Cape Coral MSA, FL	Y	15040 FQ	23120 AW	35170 TQ	FLBLS	10/01-12/01
	Fort Pierce-Port St. Lucie MSA, FL	Y	14540 FQ	18580 AW	23800 TQ	FLBLS	10/01-12/01
	Fort Walton Beach MSA, FL	Y	13160 FQ	19340 AW	28130 TQ	FLBLS	10/01-12/01
	Gainesville MSA, FL	Y	15010 FQ	20530 AW	27800 TQ	FLBLS	10/01-12/01
	Jacksonville MSA, FL	Y	14600 FQ	20810 AW	29790 TQ	FLBLS	10/01-12/01
	Lakeland-Winter Haven MSA, FL	Y	13410 FQ	21650 AW	33100 TQ	FLBLS	10/01-12/01
	Melbourne-Titusville-Palm Bay MSA, FL	Y	15650 FQ	22850 AW	31750 TQ	FLBLS	10/01-12/01
	Miami PMSA, FL	Y	13300 FQ	22050 AW	28810 TQ	FLBLS	10/01-12/01
	Naples MSA, FL	Y	15470 FQ	19890 AW	27430 TQ	FLBLS	10/01-12/01
	Ocala MSA, FL	Y	15670 FQ	22740 AW	34030 TQ	FLBLS	10/01-12/01
	Orlando MSA, FL	Y	15830 FQ	22690 AW	30250 TQ	FLBLS	10/01-12/01
	Pensacola MSA, FL	Y	14660 FQ	21680 AW	28490 TQ	FLBLS	10/01-12/01
	Sarasota-Bradenton MSA, FL	Y	14340 FQ	20420 AW	30780 TQ	FLBLS	10/01-12/01

AAW	Average annual wage	AOH	Average offered, high	ASH	Average starting, high	H	Hourly	M	Monthly	S	Special: hourly and annual
AE	Average entry wage	AOL	Average offered, low	ASL	Average starting, low	HI	Highest wage paid	MTC	Median total compensation	TQ	Third quartile wage
AEX	Average experienced wage	APH	Average pay, high range	AW	Average wage paid	HR	High end range	MW	Median wage paid	W	Weekly
AO	Average offered	APL	Average pay, low range	FQ	First quartile wage	LR	Low end range	SQ	Second quartile wage	Y	Yearly

Occupation/Type/Industry	Location	Per	Low	Mid	High	Source	Date
Social and Human Service Assistant	Tallahassee MSA, FL	Y	14240 FQ	19120 AW	27610 TQ	FLBLS	10/01-12/01
	Tampa-St. Petersburg-Clearwater MSA, FL	Y	15360 FQ	21590 AW	30180 TQ	FLBLS	10/01-12/01
	West Palm Beach-Boca Raton MSA, FL	Y	15250 FQ	23900 AW	39480 TQ	FLBLS	10/01-12/01
	Georgia	Y	14170 FQ	21370 AW	30620 TQ	GABLS	10/01-12/01
	Atlanta MSA, GA	Y	14260 FQ	22490 AW	32540 TQ	GABLS	10/01-12/01
	Augusta-Aiken MSA, GA-SC	Y	12950 FQ	22090 AW	33020 TQ	GABLS	10/01-12/01
	Columbus MSA, GA-AL	Y	13030 FQ	19260 AW	27380 TQ	GABLS	10/01-12/01
	Macon MSA, GA	Y	12720 FQ	17940 AW	24710 TQ	GABLS	10/01-12/01
	Savannah MSA, GA	Y	14220 FQ	19870 AW	28430 TQ	GABLS	10/01-12/01
	Hawaii	Y	17890 FQ	24710 AW	32980 TQ	HIBLS	10/01-12/01
	Honolulu MSA, HI	Y	16720 FQ	24870 AW	34730 TQ	HIBLS	10/01-12/01
	Idaho	Y	13740 FQ	20440 AW	29970 TQ	IDBLS	10/01-12/01
	Boise City MSA, ID	Y	14630 FQ	20140 AW	28260 TQ	IDBLS	10/01-12/01
	Illinois	Y	14910 FQ	24120 AW	36260 TQ	ILBLS	10/01-12/01
	Champaign-Urbana MSA, IL	Y	16500 FQ	24260 AW	35110 TQ	ILBLS	10/01-12/01
	Chicago PMSA, IL	Y	15430 FQ	24970 AW	37750 TQ	ILBLS	10/01-12/01
	Peoria-Pekin MSA, IL	Y	13630 FQ	25170 AW	39930 TQ	ILBLS	10/01-12/01
	Rockford MSA, IL	Y	14290 FQ	22090 AW	30180 TQ	ILBLS	10/01-12/01
	Springfield MSA, IL	Y	18980 FQ	29330 AW	49900 TQ	ILBLS	10/01-12/01
	Indiana	Y	15710 FQ	23260 AW	32960 TQ	INBLS	10/01-12/01
	Elkhart-Goshen MSA, IN	Y	17610 FQ	23650 AW	33380 TQ	INBLS	10/01-12/01
	Evansville-Henderson MSA, IN-KY	Y	17520 FQ	25650 AW	40990 TQ	INBLS	10/01-12/01
	Fort Wayne MSA, IN	Y	17890 FQ	24760 AW	33120 TQ	INBLS	10/01-12/01
	Gary PMSA, IN	Y	14740 FQ	20990 AW	29090 TQ	INBLS	10/01-12/01
	Indianapolis MSA, IN	Y	18720 FQ	26490 AW	36260 TQ	INBLS	10/01-12/01
	Lafayette MSA, IN	Y	13690 FQ	21450 AW	30220 TQ	INBLS	10/01-12/01
	South Bend MSA, IN	Y	18620 FQ	25050 AW	32620 TQ	INBLS	10/01-12/01
	Iowa	Y	14760 FQ	23660 AW	33990 TQ	IABLS	10/01-12/01
	Cedar Rapids MSA, IA	Y	12610 FQ	21140 AW	34100 TQ	IABLS	10/01-12/01
	Davenport-Moline-Rock Island MSA, IA-IL	Y	13090 FQ	23670 AW	35990 TQ	IABLS	10/01-12/01
	Des Moines MSA, IA	Y	16450 FQ	25410 AW	36500 TQ	IABLS	10/01-12/01
	Kansas	Y	14720 FQ	22040 AW	29260 TQ	KSBLS	10/01-12/01
	Topeka MSA, KS	Y	14070 FQ	23870 AW	32190 TQ	KSBLS	10/01-12/01
	Wichita MSA, KS	Y	15260 FQ	22590 AW	29790 TQ	KSBLS	10/01-12/01
	Kentucky	Y	14480 FQ	21590 AW	31480 TQ	KYBLS	10/01-12/01
	Lexington MSA, KY	Y	13980 FQ	21690 AW	32250 TQ	KYBLS	10/01-12/01
	Louisville MSA, KY-IN	Y	16480 FQ	24600 AW	34040 TQ	KYBLS	10/01-12/01
	Louisiana	Y	12550 FQ	19280 AW	27240 TQ	LABLS	10/01-12/01
	Baton Rouge MSA, LA	Y	15510 FQ	20630 AW	27800 TQ	LABLS	10/01-12/01
	Houma MSA, LA	Y	13210 FQ	20880 AW	27690 TQ	LABLS	10/01-12/01
	Lafayette MSA, LA	Y	12020 FQ	19880 AW	27730 TQ	LABLS	10/01-12/01
	Lake Charles MSA, LA	Y	14330 FQ	21190 AW	29310 TQ	LABLS	10/01-12/01
	New Orleans MSA, LA	Y	12480 FQ	19120 AW	27520 TQ	LABLS	10/01-12/01
	Shreveport-Bossier City MSA, LA	Y	12220 FQ	17570 AW	24190 TQ	LABLS	10/01-12/01
	Maine	Y	17020 FQ	23640 AW	31520 TQ	MEBLS	10/01-12/01
	Portland MSA, ME	Y	18800 FQ	23010 AW	28870 TQ	MEBLS	10/01-12/01
	Maryland	Y	15130 FQ	22710 AW	35090 TQ	MDBLS	10/01-12/01
	Baltimore PMSA, MD	Y	14970 FQ	21470 AW	31550 TQ	MDBLS	10/01-12/01
	Massachusetts	Y	18200 FQ	27000 AW	43380 TQ	MABLS	10/01-12/01
	Boston PMSA, MA-NH	Y	18710 FQ	28020 AW	44240 TQ	MABLS	10/01-12/01
	Brockton PMSA, MA	Y	18890 FQ	25850 AW	35830 TQ	MABLS	10/01-12/01
	Lawrence PMSA, MA-NH	Y	18640 FQ	27210 AW	44510 TQ	MABLS	10/01-12/01
	Lowell PMSA, MA-NH	Y	18510 FQ	29010 AW	45380 TQ	MABLS	10/01-12/01
	New Bedford PMSA, MA	Y	17000 FQ	26820 AW	46300 TQ	MABLS	10/01-12/01
	Springfield MSA, MA	Y	19210 FQ	29360 AW	49410 TQ	MABLS	10/01-12/01
	Worcester PMSA, MA-CT	Y	16950 FQ	25270 AW	39300 TQ	MABLS	10/01-12/01
	Michigan	Y	15110 FQ	24450 AW	36690 TQ	MIBLS	10/01-12/01
	Ann Arbor PMSA, MI	Y	15960 FQ	25800 AW	38650 TQ	MIBLS	10/01-12/01
	Detroit PMSA, MI	Y	14510 FQ	24610 AW	38470 TQ	MIBLS	10/01-12/01
	Flint PMSA, MI	Y	14920 FQ	22150 AW	33240 TQ	MIBLS	10/01-12/01
	Grand Rapids-Muskegon-Holland MSA, MI	Y	16000 FQ	24240 AW	36710 TQ	MIBLS	10/01-12/01
	Kalamazoo-Battle Creek MSA, MI	Y	14340 FQ	24130 AW	35470 TQ	MIBLS	10/01-12/01
	Lansing-East Lansing MSA, MI	Y	14890 FQ	26600 AW	42300 TQ	MIBLS	10/01-12/01

AAW	Average annual wage	**AOH**	Average offered, high	**ASH**	Average starting, high	**H**	Hourly	**M**	Monthly	**S**	Special: hourly and annual
AE	Average entry wage	**AOL**	Average offered, low	**ASL**	Average starting, low	**HI**	Highest wage paid	**MTC**	Median total compensation	**TQ**	Third quartile wage
AEX	Average experienced wage	**APH**	Average pay, high range	**AW**	Average wage paid	**HR**	High end range	**MW**	Median wage paid	**W**	Weekly
AO	Average offered	**APL**	Average pay, low range	**FQ**	First quartile wage	**LR**	Low end range	**SQ**	Second quartile wage	**Y**	Yearly

Occupation/Type/Industry	Location	Per	Low	Mid	High	Source	Date
Social and Human Service Assistant	Saginaw-Bay City-Midland MSA, MI	Y	17980 FQ	24680 AW	33080 TQ	MIBLS	10/01-12/01
	Minnesota	Y	17030 FQ	25920 AW	36300 TQ	MNBLS	10/01-12/01
	Duluth-Superior MSA, MN-WI	Y	13890 FQ	20270 AW	32310 TQ	MNBLS	10/01-12/01
	Minneapolis-St. Paul MSA, MN-WI	Y	18880 FQ	27420 AW	39160 TQ	MNBLS	10/01-12/01
	St. Cloud MSA, MN	Y	14680 FQ	21210 AW	31080 TQ	MNBLS	10/01-12/01
	Mississippi	Y	13210 FQ	20160 AW	27910 TQ	MSBLS	10/01-12/01
	Biloxi-Gulfport-Pascagoula MSA, MS	Y	14250 FQ	20280 AW	27550 TQ	MSBLS	10/01-12/01
	Jackson MSA, MS	Y	12460 FQ	19020 AW	28640 TQ	MSBLS	10/01-12/01
	Missouri	Y	15350 FQ	21870 AW	32020 TQ	MOBLS	10/01-12/01
	Kansas City MSA, MO-KS	Y	17020 FQ	24920 AW	33270 TQ	MOBLS	10/01-12/01
	St. Louis MSA, MO-IL	Y	15540 FQ	21410 AW	30180 TQ	MOBLS	10/01-12/01
	Springfield MSA, MO	Y	15210 FQ	18840 AW	23410 TQ	MOBLS	10/01-12/01
	Montana	Y	14160 FQ	21430 AW	29190 TQ	MTBLS	10/01-12/01
	Billings MSA, MT	Y	13020 FQ	20660 AW	38840 TQ	MTBLS	10/01-12/01
	Nebraska	Y	14790 FQ	21790 AW	32630 TQ	NEBLS	10/01-12/01
	Lincoln MSA, NE	Y	15270 FQ	21600 AW	31380 TQ	NEBLS	10/01-12/01
	Omaha MSA, NE-IA	Y	15500 FQ	22210 AW	32520 TQ	NEBLS	10/01-12/01
	Nevada	Y	15720 FQ	25230 AW	36710 TQ	NVBLS	10/01-12/01
	Las Vegas MSA, NV-AZ	Y	15750 FQ	23610 AW	33750 TQ	NVBLS	10/01-12/01
	Reno MSA, NV	Y	24640 FQ	33220 AW	43050 TQ	NVBLS	10/01-12/01
	New Hampshire	Y	15090 FQ	20610 AW	27430 TQ	NHBLS	10/01-12/01
	Manchester PMSA, NH	Y	16380 FQ	22240 AW	28970 TQ	NHBLS	10/01-12/01
	Nashua PMSA, NH	Y	15800 FQ	21200 AW	28590 TQ	NHBLS	10/01-12/01
	Portsmouth-Rochester PMSA, NH-ME	Y	18150 FQ	22960 AW	29450 TQ	NHBLS	10/01-12/01
	New Jersey	Y	17520 FQ	26500 AW	38390 TQ	NJBLS	10/01-12/01
	Bergen-Passaic PMSA, NJ	Y	18490 FQ	28650 AW	42310 TQ	NJBLS	10/01-12/01
	Jersey City PMSA, NJ	Y	13480 FQ	25610 AW	42680 TQ	NJBLS	10/01-12/01
	Monmouth-Ocean PMSA, NJ	Y	17700 FQ	25100 AW	38310 TQ	NJBLS	10/01-12/01
	Newark PMSA, NJ	Y	17950 FQ	24750 AW	35410 TQ	NJBLS	10/01-12/01
	Trenton PMSA, NJ	Y	16110 FQ	29020 AW	43080 TQ	NJBLS	10/01-12/01
	New Mexico	Y	14870 FQ	21530 AW	29180 TQ	NMBLS	10/01-12/01
	Albuquerque MSA, NM	Y	17920 FQ	24000 AW	30260 TQ	NMBLS	10/01-12/01
	Las Cruces MSA, NM	Y	12730 FQ	18720 AW	25690 TQ	NMBLS	10/01-12/01
	New York	Y	14390 FQ	27530 AW	42110 TQ	NYBLS	10/01-12/01
	Albany-Schenectady-Troy MSA, NY	Y	15910 FQ	26830 AW	42730 TQ	NYBLS	10/01-12/01
	Binghamton MSA, NY	Y	13870 FQ	25950 AW	42390 TQ	NYBLS	10/01-12/01
	Buffalo-Niagara Falls MSA, NY	Y	16890 FQ	28870 AW	40840 TQ	NYBLS	10/01-12/01
	Dutchess County PMSA, NY	Y	19500 FQ	30960 AW	44880 TQ	NYBLS	10/01-12/01
	Nassau-Suffolk PMSA, NY	Y	18810 FQ	30940 AW	44830 TQ	NYBLS	10/01-12/01
	New York PMSA, NY	Y	13300 FQ	27270 AW	42160 TQ	NYBLS	10/01-12/01
	Newburgh PMSA, NY-PA	Y	20020 FQ	29860 AW	42650 TQ	NYBLS	10/01-12/01
	Rochester MSA, NY	Y	18410 FQ	27100 AW	39490 TQ	NYBLS	10/01-12/01
	Syracuse MSA, NY	Y	13920 FQ	25520 AW	42350 TQ	NYBLS	10/01-12/01
	Utica-Rome MSA, NY	Y	18820 FQ	24630 AW	34740 TQ	NYBLS	10/01-12/01
	North Carolina	Y	16150 FQ	23540 AW	33050 TQ	NCBLS	10/01-12/01
	Asheville MSA, NC	Y	15660 FQ	23610 AW	30640 TQ	NCBLS	10/01-12/01
	Charlotte-Gastonia-Rock Hill MSA, NC-SC	Y	16170 FQ	24310 AW	34780 TQ	NCBLS	10/01-12/01
	Fayetteville MSA, NC	Y	15530 FQ	23300 AW	36030 TQ	NCBLS	10/01-12/01
	Greensboro-Winston-Salem-High Point MSA, NC	Y	14500 FQ	21980 AW	29680 TQ	NCBLS	10/01-12/01
	Hickory-Morganton-Lenoir MSA, NC	Y	19180 FQ	27840 AW	40970 TQ	NCBLS	10/01-12/01
	Raleigh-Durham-Chapel Hill MSA, NC	Y	16110 FQ	23080 AW	32170 TQ	NCBLS	10/01-12/01
	Wilmington MSA, NC	Y	16200 FQ	22960 AW	30990 TQ	NCBLS	10/01-12/01
	North Dakota	Y	14640 FQ	21300 AW	31430 TQ	NDBLS	10/01-12/01
	Fargo-Moorhead MSA, ND-MN	Y	12970 FQ	21650 AW	33610 TQ	NDBLS	10/01-12/01
	Ohio	Y	15640 FQ	23900 AW	33860 TQ	OHBLS	10/01-12/01
	Akron PMSA, OH	Y	16340 FQ	23980 AW	34010 TQ	OHBLS	10/01-12/01
	Canton-Massillon MSA, OH	Y	15800 FQ	24310 AW	35020 TQ	OHBLS	10/01-12/01
	Cincinnati PMSA, OH-KY-IN	Y	15540 FQ	23190 AW	32210 TQ	OHBLS	10/01-12/01
	Cleveland-Lorain-Elyria PMSA, OH	Y	15630 FQ	23040 AW	32050 TQ	OHBLS	10/01-12/01

AAW Average annual wage; **AE** Average entry wage; **AEX** Average experienced wage; **AO** Average offered; **AOH** Average offered, high; **AOL** Average offered, low; **APH** Average pay, high range; **APL** Average pay, low range; **ASH** Average starting, high; **ASL** Average starting, low; **AW** Average wage paid; **FQ** First quartile wage; **H** Hourly; **HI** Highest wage paid; **HR** High end range; **LR** Low end range; **M** Monthly; **MTC** Median total compensation; **MW** Median wage paid; **SQ** Second quartile wage; **S** Special: hourly and annual; **TQ** Third quartile wage; **W** Weekly; **Y** Yearly

Occupation/Type/Industry	Location	Per	Low	Mid	High	Source	Date
Social and Human Service Assistant	Columbus MSA, OH	Y	15000 FQ	25920 AW	36950 TQ	OHBLS	10/01-12/01
	Dayton-Springfield MSA, OH	Y	15760 FQ	23250 AW	30340 TQ	OHBLS	10/01-12/01
	Hamilton-Middletown PMSA, OH	Y	14460 FQ	19610 AW	27330 TQ	OHBLS	10/01-12/01
	Mansfield MSA, OH	Y	16520 FQ	23070 AW	30440 TQ	OHBLS	10/01-12/01
	Toledo MSA, OH	Y	19510 FQ	25780 AW	34770 TQ	OHBLS	10/01-12/01
	Youngstown-Warren MSA, OH	Y	15070 FQ	23340 AW	35090 TQ	OHBLS	10/01-12/01
	Oklahoma	Y	13010 FQ	22930 AW	33400 TQ	OKBLS	10/01-12/01
	Tulsa MSA, OK	Y	15280 FQ	25140 AW	34350 TQ	OKBLS	10/01-12/01
	Oregon	Y	16670 FQ	25590 AW	35170 TQ	ORBLS	10/01-12/01
	Eugene-Springfield MSA, OR	Y	15680 FQ	24100 AW	35610 TQ	ORBLS	10/01-12/01
	Medford-Ashland MSA, OR	Y	16570 FQ	23540 AW	32540 TQ	ORBLS	10/01-12/01
	Portland-Vancouver PMSA, OR-WA	Y	16990 FQ	25550 AW	35280 TQ	ORBLS	10/01-12/01
	Pennsylvania	Y	14550 FQ	22560 AW	32400 TQ	PABLS	10/01-12/01
	Allentown-Bethlehem-Easton MSA, PA	Y	12770 FQ	22940 AW	34420 TQ	PABLS	10/01-12/01
	Erie MSA, PA	Y	15980 FQ	19690 AW	23390 TQ	PABLS	10/01-12/01
	Harrisburg-Lebanon-Carlisle MSA, PA	Y	15500 FQ	24120 AW	36650 TQ	PABLS	10/01-12/01
	Lancaster MSA, PA	Y	15990 FQ	23620 AW	34800 TQ	PABLS	10/01-12/01
	Philadelphia PMSA, PA-NJ	Y	15070 FQ	23440 AW	34570 TQ	PABLS	10/01-12/01
	Pittsburgh MSA, PA	Y	12840 FQ	21420 AW	31540 TQ	PABLS	10/01-12/01
	Reading MSA, PA	Y	16420 FQ	22350 AW	29910 TQ	PABLS	10/01-12/01
	Scranton-Wilkes-Barre-Hazleton MSA, PA	Y	16580 FQ	25220 AW	34060 TQ	PABLS	10/01-12/01
	York MSA, PA	Y	15220 FQ	20640 AW	27160 TQ	PABLS	10/01-12/01
	Rhode Island	Y	17320 FQ	25970 AW	38010 TQ	RIBLS	10/01-12/01
	Providence-Fall River-Warwick MSA, RI-MA	Y	17730 FQ	24780 AW	35260 TQ	RIBLS	10/01-12/01
	South Carolina	Y	14880 FQ	22590 AW	32740 TQ	SCBLS	10/01-12/01
	Charleston-North Charleston MSA, SC	Y	12000 FQ	19800 AW	31190 TQ	SCBLS	10/01-12/01
	Columbia MSA, SC	Y	15780 FQ	23290 AW	29720 TQ	SCBLS	10/01-12/01
	Greenville-Spartanburg-Anderson MSA, SC	Y	14710 FQ	26000 AW	42920 TQ	SCBLS	10/01-12/01
	South Dakota	Y	14710 FQ	19040 AW	24900 TQ	SDBLS	10/01-12/01
	Sioux Falls MSA, SD	Y	14840 FQ	17900 AW	22640 TQ	SDBLS	10/01-12/01
	Tennessee	Y	13260 FQ	23130 AW	36390 TQ	TNBLS	10/01-12/01
	Chattanooga MSA, TN-GA	Y	15600 FQ	26400 AW	41030 TQ	TNBLS	10/01-12/01
	Clarksville-Hopkinsville MSA, TN-KY	Y	14830 FQ	20420 AW	26910 TQ	TNBLS	10/01-12/01
	Johnson City-Kingsport-Bristol MSA, TN-VA	Y	11900 FQ	18400 AW	32830 TQ	TNBLS	10/01-12/01
	Knoxville MSA, TN	Y	13870 FQ	23700 AW	36110 TQ	TNBLS	10/01-12/01
	Memphis MSA, TN-AR-MS	Y	13330 FQ	24210 AW	35860 TQ	TNBLS	10/01-12/01
	Nashville MSA, TN	Y	15980 FQ	27190 AW	42040 TQ	TNBLS	10/01-12/01
	Texas	Y	14160 FQ	23270 AW	35460 TQ	TXBLS	10/01-12/01
	Austin-San Marcos MSA, TX	Y	13350 FQ	23910 AW	34340 TQ	TXBLS	10/01-12/01
	Beaumont-Port Arthur MSA, TX	Y	13150 FQ	25380 AW	45260 TQ	TXBLS	10/01-12/01
	Brazoria PMSA, TX	Y	14740 FQ	22690 AW	34890 TQ	TXBLS	10/01-12/01
	Brownsville-Harlingen-San Benito MSA, TX	Y	14750 FQ	18540 AW	22110 TQ	TXBLS	10/01-12/01
	Corpus Christi MSA, TX	Y	15500 FQ	21370 AW	29080 TQ	TXBLS	10/01-12/01
	Dallas PMSA, TX	Y	20250 FQ	32240 AW	52680 TQ	TXBLS	10/01-12/01
	El Paso MSA, TX	Y	12360 FQ	19590 AW	28200 TQ	TXBLS	10/01-12/01
	Fort Worth-Arlington PMSA, TX	Y	13630 FQ	22410 AW	31630 TQ	TXBLS	10/01-12/01
	Galveston-Texas City PMSA, TX	Y	14990 FQ	21050 AW	29070 TQ	TXBLS	10/01-12/01
	Houston PMSA, TX	Y	14860 FQ	24660 AW	34650 TQ	TXBLS	10/01-12/01
	Killeen-Temple MSA, TX	Y	15440 FQ	18760 AW	26850 TQ	TXBLS	10/01-12/01
	Laredo MSA, TX	Y	17080 FQ	26390 AW	34810 TQ	TXBLS	10/01-12/01
	Longview-Marshall MSA, TX	Y	11980 FQ	16690 AW	23040 TQ	TXBLS	10/01-12/01
	McAllen-Edinburg-Mission MSA, TX	Y	14560 FQ	19810 AW	25900 TQ	TXBLS	10/01-12/01
	Odessa-Midland MSA, TX	Y	11850 FQ	19670 AW	29980 TQ	TXBLS	10/01-12/01
	San Antonio MSA, TX	Y	17090 FQ	25470 AW	37690 TQ	TXBLS	10/01-12/01
	Waco MSA, TX	Y	15180 FQ	20920 AW	27990 TQ	TXBLS	10/01-12/01
	Utah	Y	14710 FQ	21800 AW	32840 TQ	UTBLS	10/01-12/01

AAW Average annual wage **AOH** Average offered, high **ASH** Average starting, high **H** Hourly **M** Monthly **S** Special: hourly and annual
AE Average entry wage **AOL** Average offered, low **ASL** Average starting, low **HI** Highest wage paid **MTC** Median total compensation **TQ** Third quartile wage
AEX Average experienced wage **APH** Average pay, high range **AW** Average wage paid **HR** High end range **MW** Median wage paid **W** Weekly
AO Average offered **APL** Average pay, low range **FQ** First quartile wage **LR** Low end range **SQ** Second quartile wage **Y** Yearly

Occupation/Type/Industry	Location	Per	Low	Mid	High	Source	Date
Social and Human Service Assistant	Provo-Orem MSA, UT	Y	15450 FQ	22390 AW	32720 TQ	UTBLS	10/01-12/01
	Salt Lake City-Ogden MSA, UT	Y	15390 FQ	22910 AW	34100 TQ	UTBLS	10/01-12/01
	Vermont	Y	17880 FQ	25250 AW	36460 TQ	VTBLS	10/01-12/01
	Burlington MSA, VT	Y	19320 FQ	28380 AW	40620 TQ	VTBLS	10/01-12/01
	Virginia	Y	15380 FQ	23050 AW	31250 TQ	VABLS	10/01-12/01
	Lynchburg MSA, VA	Y	14130 FQ	20460 AW	26630 TQ	VABLS	10/01-12/01
	Norfolk-Virginia Beach-Newport News MSA, VA-NC	Y	13820 FQ	21640 AW	29310 TQ	VABLS	10/01-12/01
	Richmond-Petersburg MSA, VA	Y	15550 FQ	21780 AW	28130 TQ	VABLS	10/01-12/01
	Roanoke MSA, VA	Y	17180 FQ	21410 AW	24190 TQ	VABLS	10/01-12/01
	Washington	Y	16510 FQ	24830 AW	33680 TQ	WABLS	10/01-12/01
	Bremerton PMSA, WA	Y	16100 FQ	22570 AW	31550 TQ	WABLS	10/01-12/01
	Olympia PMSA, WA	Y	15110 FQ	24280 AW	33500 TQ	WABLS	10/01-12/01
	Richland-Kennewick-Pasco MSA, WA	Y	15750 FQ	26190 AW	37170 TQ	WABLS	10/01-12/01
	Seattle-Bellevue-Everett PMSA, WA	Y	21130 FQ	27110 AW	34280 TQ	WABLS	10/01-12/01
	Spokane MSA, WA	Y	15870 FQ	23090 AW	32650 TQ	WABLS	10/01-12/01
	Tacoma PMSA, WA	Y	14460 FQ	21640 AW	32830 TQ	WABLS	10/01-12/01
	Yakima MSA, WA	Y	15520 FQ	22410 AW	32320 TQ	WABLS	10/01-12/01
	West Virginia	Y	12180 FQ	17290 AW	23280 TQ	WVBLS	10/01-12/01
	Charleston MSA, WV	Y	12400 FQ	17300 AW	23780 TQ	WVBLS	10/01-12/01
	Huntington-Ashland MSA, WV-KY-OH	Y	12940 FQ	20700 AW	31040 TQ	WVBLS	10/01-12/01
	Wisconsin	Y	16550 FQ	24810 AW	35350 TQ	WIBLS	10/01-12/01
	Appleton-Oshkosh-Neenah MSA, WI	Y	17560 FQ	24110 AW	34670 TQ	WIBLS	10/01-12/01
	Green Bay MSA, WI	Y	16680 FQ	28200 AW	43150 TQ	WIBLS	10/01-12/01
	Madison MSA, WI	Y	18980 FQ	25980 AW	37940 TQ	WIBLS	10/01-12/01
	Milwaukee-Waukesha PMSA, WI	Y	18380 FQ	24690 AW	34180 TQ	WIBLS	10/01-12/01
	Racine PMSA, WI	Y	15540 FQ	20760 AW	28380 TQ	WIBLS	10/01-12/01
	Wyoming	Y	14600 FQ	19060 AW	27080 TQ	WYBLS	10/01-12/01
	Puerto Rico	Y	11980 FQ	15550 AW	20200 TQ	PRBLS	10/01-12/01
	Virgin Islands	Y	14960 FQ	19770 AW	26390 TQ	VIBLS	10/01-12/01
Individual and Family Services	United States	Y		21350 MW		OOH11	1999-2000
Local Government, Except Education and Hospitals	United States	Y		25320 MW		OOH11	1999-2000
Residential Care	United States	Y		19880 MW		OOH11	1999-2000
Social Services	United States	Y		21820 MW		OOH11	1999-2000
State Government, Except Education and Hospitals	United States	Y		27130 MW		OOH11	1999-2000
Social Work Teacher							
Postsecondary	Alabama	Y	15120 FQ	42970 AW	58120 TQ	ALBLS	10/01-12/01
Postsecondary	California	Y	34640 FQ	57070 AW	91370 TQ	CABLS	10/01-12/01
Postsecondary	Colorado	Y	32160 FQ	55020 AW	92960 TQ	COBLS	10/01-12/01
Postsecondary	District of Columbia	Y	37250 FQ	60610 AW	84760 TQ	DCBLS	10/01-12/01
Postsecondary	Florida	Y	35140 FQ	63040 AW	103310 TQ	FLBLS	10/01-12/01
Postsecondary	Georgia	Y	43040 FQ	58760 AW	81180 TQ	GABLS	10/01-12/01
Postsecondary	Illinois	Y	26190 FQ	57170 AW	89530 TQ	ILBLS	10/01-12/01
Postsecondary	Indiana	Y	21940 FQ	48020 AW	72280 TQ	INBLS	10/01-12/01
Postsecondary	Iowa	Y	30360 FQ	60130 AW	110070 TQ	IABLS	10/01-12/01
Postsecondary	Kansas	Y	30260 FQ	49230 AW	77440 TQ	KSBLS	10/01-12/01
Postsecondary	Kentucky	Y	32990 FQ	51910 AW	78380 TQ	KYBLS	10/01-12/01
Postsecondary	Louisiana	Y	18620 FQ	45420 AW	78910 TQ	LABLS	10/01-12/01
Postsecondary	Maine	Y	32080 FQ	49400 AW	71430 TQ	MEBLS	10/01-12/01
Postsecondary	Maryland	Y	31980 FQ	52390 AW	85050 TQ	MDBLS	10/01-12/01
Postsecondary	Massachusetts	Y	30580 FQ	52410 AW	76050 TQ	MABLS	10/01-12/01
Postsecondary	Michigan	Y	31260 FQ	54500 AW	85850 TQ	MIBLS	10/01-12/01
Postsecondary	Minnesota	Y	38030 FQ	55540 AW	75050 TQ	MNBLS	10/01-12/01
Postsecondary	Mississippi	Y	37650 FQ	49380 AW	68560 TQ	MSBLS	10/01-12/01
Postsecondary	Missouri	Y	32000 FQ	51670 AW	73460 TQ	MOBLS	10/01-12/01
Postsecondary	Montana	Y	30030 FQ	45040 AW	67450 TQ	MTBLS	10/01-12/01
Postsecondary	Nebraska	Y	35950 FQ	54470 AW	70150 TQ	NEBLS	10/01-12/01
Postsecondary	New Hampshire	Y	22540 FQ	41460 AW	61580 TQ	NHBLS	10/01-12/01
Postsecondary	New Jersey	Y	35180 FQ	56700 AW	87760 TQ	NJBLS	10/01-12/01
Postsecondary	New York	Y	32740 FQ	51100 AW	74190 TQ	NYBLS	10/01-12/01

AAW	Average annual wage	**AOH**	Average offered, high	**ASH**	Average starting, high	**H**	Hourly	**M**	Monthly	**S**	Special: hourly and annual
AE	Average entry wage	**AOL**	Average offered, low	**ASL**	Average starting, low	**HI**	Highest wage paid	**MTC**	Median total compensation	**TQ**	Third quartile wage
AEX	Average experienced wage	**APH**	Average pay, high range	**AW**	Average wage paid	**HR**	High end range	**MW**	Median wage paid	**W**	Weekly
AO	Average offered	**APL**	Average pay, low range	**FQ**	First quartile wage	**LR**	Low end range	**SQ**	Second quartile wage	**Y**	Yearly

Occupation/Type/Industry	Location	Per	Low	Mid	High	Source	Date
Social Work Teacher							
Postsecondary	North Carolina	Y	35880 FQ	50030 AW	70610 TQ	NCBLS	10/01-12/01
Postsecondary	North Dakota	Y	22370 FQ	38950 AW	55690 TQ	NDBLS	10/01-12/01
Postsecondary	Ohio	Y	21710 FQ	45460 AW	72150 TQ	OHBLS	10/01-12/01
Postsecondary	Oklahoma	Y	21860 FQ	35780 AW	45360 TQ	OKBLS	10/01-12/01
Postsecondary	Oregon	Y	28190 FQ	59440 AW	95030 TQ	ORBLS	10/01-12/01
Postsecondary	Pennsylvania	Y	33770 FQ	53620 AW	79770 TQ	PABLS	10/01-12/01
Postsecondary	Rhode Island	Y	32940 FQ	49690 AW	76620 TQ	RIBLS	10/01-12/01
Postsecondary	South Carolina	Y	30480 FQ	50660 AW	82610 TQ	SCBLS	10/01-12/01
Postsecondary	South Dakota	Y	32150 FQ	44670 AW	57440 TQ	SDBLS	10/01-12/01
Postsecondary	Tennessee	Y	30420 FQ	50490 AW	71530 TQ	TNBLS	10/01-12/01
Postsecondary	Texas	Y	28410 FQ	49360 AW	73040 TQ	TXBLS	10/01-12/01
Postsecondary	Vermont	Y	28520 FQ	40460 AW	55300 TQ	VTBLS	10/01-12/01
Postsecondary	Virginia	Y	33590 FQ	67610 AW	109230 TQ	VABLS	10/01-12/01
Postsecondary	Washington	Y	26280 FQ	62690 AW	113030 TQ	WABLS	10/01-12/01
Postsecondary	West Virginia	Y	34770 FQ	56910 AW	90100 TQ	WVBLS	10/01-12/01
Postsecondary	Wisconsin	Y	28330 FQ	47580 AW	70860 TQ	WIBLS	10/01-12/01
Postsecondary	Puerto Rico	Y	27150 FQ	44050 AW	71740 TQ	PRBLS	10/01-12/01
Sociologist	California	Y	17060 FQ	47940 AW	73140 TQ	CABLS	10/01-12/01
	District of Columbia	Y	38450 FQ	74830 AW	126360 TQ	DCBLS	10/01-12/01
	Illinois	Y	25770 FQ	49660 AW	80660 TQ	ILBLS	10/01-12/01
	Chicago PMSA, IL	Y	25710 FQ	49420 AW	81040 TQ	ILBLS	10/01-12/01
	New Jersey	Y	31400 FQ	49200 AW	83960 TQ	NJBLS	10/01-12/01
	New York	Y	18390 FQ	58980 AW	100270 TQ	NYBLS	10/01-12/01
	New York PMSA, NY	Y	17530 FQ	59530 AW	106220 TQ	NYBLS	10/01-12/01
	North Carolina	Y	29770 FQ	49350 AW	73190 TQ	NCBLS	10/01-12/01
	Raleigh-Durham-Chapel Hill MSA, NC	Y	29390 FQ	51000 AW	77390 TQ	NCBLS	10/01-12/01
	Oklahoma	Y	30070 FQ	45680 AW	56200 TQ	OKBLS	10/01-12/01
	Pennsylvania	Y	31810 FQ	54570 AW	89100 TQ	PABLS	10/01-12/01
	Philadelphia PMSA, PA-NJ	Y	31960 FQ	50220 AW	83470 TQ	PABLS	10/01-12/01
	Texas	Y	16710 FQ	45960 AW	79990 TQ	TXBLS	10/01-12/01
	Washington	Y	44520 FQ	74450 AW	121810 TQ	WABLS	10/01-12/01
	Seattle-Bellevue-Everett PMSA, WA	Y	44290 FQ	74430 AW	122000 TQ	WABLS	10/01-12/01
Sociology Teacher							
Postsecondary	Alabama	Y	24750 FQ	55110 AW	98740 TQ	ALBLS	10/01-12/01
Postsecondary	Birmingham MSA, AL	Y	38300 FQ	59820 AW	105360 TQ	ALBLS	10/01-12/01
Postsecondary	Arkansas	Y	28130 FQ	48850 AW	71150 TQ	ARBLS	10/01-12/01
Postsecondary	California	Y	37780 FQ	68520 AW	110820 TQ	CABLS	10/01-12/01
Postsecondary	Los Angeles-Long Beach PMSA, CA	Y	38540 FQ	64520 AW	94820 TQ	CABLS	10/01-12/01
Postsecondary	Orange County PMSA, CA	Y	34150 FQ	63630 AW	100560 TQ	CABLS	10/01-12/01
Postsecondary	Riverside-San Bernardino PMSA, CA	Y	36810 FQ	65750 AW	107600 TQ	CABLS	10/01-12/01
Postsecondary	San Francisco PMSA, CA	Y	49290 FQ	90100 AW	119830 TQ	CABLS	10/01-12/01
Postsecondary	Colorado	Y	30810 FQ	55440 AW	89720 TQ	COBLS	10/01-12/01
Postsecondary	Denver PMSA, CO	Y	31630 FQ	57840 AW	93690 TQ	COBLS	10/01-12/01
Postsecondary	Connecticut	Y	36100 FQ	56940 AW	86340 TQ	CTBLS	10/01-12/01
Postsecondary	Hartford MSA, CT	Y	35550 FQ	56070 AW	88140 TQ	CTBLS	10/01-12/01
Postsecondary	District of Columbia	Y	45890 FQ	67800 AW	89010 TQ	DCBLS	10/01-12/01
Postsecondary	Washington PMSA, DC-MD-VA-WV	Y	38460 FQ	66780 AW	96180 TQ	DCBLS	10/01-12/01
Postsecondary	Florida	Y	22360 FQ	56270 AW	94280 TQ	FLBLS	10/01-12/01
Postsecondary	Fort Lauderdale PMSA, FL	Y	14200 FQ	45730 AW	79720 TQ	FLBLS	10/01-12/01
Postsecondary	Gainesville MSA, FL	Y	40560 FQ	65570 AW	104140 TQ	FLBLS	10/01-12/01
Postsecondary	Miami PMSA, FL	Y	44070 FQ	70120 AW	105040 TQ	FLBLS	10/01-12/01
Postsecondary	Orlando MSA, FL	Y	26960 FQ	52600 AW	87830 TQ	FLBLS	10/01-12/01
Postsecondary	Tallahassee MSA, FL	Y	40370 FQ	69410 AW	113940 TQ	FLBLS	10/01-12/01
Postsecondary	Tampa-St. Petersburg-Clearwater MSA, FL	Y	18300 FQ	46880 AW	73970 TQ	FLBLS	10/01-12/01
Postsecondary	Georgia	Y	38310 FQ	54290 AW	82190 TQ	GABLS	10/01-12/01
Postsecondary	Atlanta MSA, GA	Y	38740 FQ	53150 AW	77570 TQ	GABLS	10/01-12/01
Postsecondary	Hawaii	Y	29970 FQ	56220 AW	87940 TQ	HIBLS	10/01-12/01
Postsecondary	Honolulu MSA, HI	Y	29130 FQ	57150 AW	88930 TQ	HIBLS	10/01-12/01
Postsecondary	Illinois	Y	23190 FQ	54620 AW	90740 TQ	ILBLS	10/01-12/01
Postsecondary	Chicago PMSA, IL	Y	21620 FQ	56980 AW	94950 TQ	ILBLS	10/01-12/01
Postsecondary	Indiana	Y	23670 FQ	51380 AW	82910 TQ	INBLS	10/01-12/01
Postsecondary	South Bend MSA, IN	Y	28090 FQ	41540 AW	55510 TQ	INBLS	10/01-12/01
Postsecondary	Iowa	Y	36770 FQ	57310 AW	84730 TQ	IABLS	10/01-12/01
Postsecondary	Kansas	Y	18640 FQ	43750 AW	71320 TQ	KSBLS	10/01-12/01

AAW	Average annual wage	AOH	Average offered, high	ASH	Average starting, high	H	Hourly	M	Monthly	S	Special: hourly and annual
AE	Average entry wage	AOL	Average offered, low	ASL	Average starting, low	HI	Highest wage paid	MTC	Median total compensation	TQ	Third quartile wage
AEX	Average experienced wage	APH	Average pay, high range	AW	Average wage paid	HR	High end range	MW	Median wage paid	W	Weekly
AO	Average offered	APL	Average pay, low range	FQ	First quartile wage	LR	Low end range	SQ	Second quartile wage	Y	Yearly

Occupation/Type/Industry	Location	Per	Low	Mid	High	Source	Date
Sociology Teacher							
Postsecondary	Kentucky	Y	27830 FQ	47040 AW	72100 TQ	KYBLS	10/01-12/01
Postsecondary	Louisiana	Y	22450 FQ	47380 AW	73250 TQ	LABLS	10/01-12/01
Postsecondary	New Orleans MSA, LA	Y	24460 FQ	48370 AW	74680 TQ	LABLS	10/01-12/01
Postsecondary	Maine	Y	30970 FQ	50750 AW	69930 TQ	MEBLS	10/01-12/01
Postsecondary	Maryland	Y	33530 FQ	56050 AW	89210 TQ	MDBLS	10/01-12/01
Postsecondary	Massachusetts	Y	29310 FQ	53690 AW	80690 TQ	MABLS	10/01-12/01
Postsecondary	Boston PMSA, MA-NH	Y	29240 FQ	54090 AW	81510 TQ	MABLS	10/01-12/01
Postsecondary	Springfield MSA, MA	Y	21460 FQ	50930 AW	77410 TQ	MABLS	10/01-12/01
Postsecondary	Worcester PMSA, MA-CT	Y	35130 FQ	56420 AW	83640 TQ	MABLS	10/01-12/01
Postsecondary	Michigan	Y	30260 FQ	51620 AW	82320 TQ	MIBLS	10/01-12/01
Postsecondary	Ann Arbor PMSA, MI	Y	30840 FQ	45800 AW	67250 TQ	MIBLS	10/01-12/01
Postsecondary	Detroit PMSA, MI	Y	23830 FQ	38720 AW	60770 TQ	MIBLS	10/01-12/01
Postsecondary	Minnesota	Y	33690 FQ	56190 AW	85100 TQ	MNBLS	10/01-12/01
Postsecondary	Minneapolis-St. Paul MSA, MN-WI	Y	34460 FQ	58750 AW	91990 TQ	MNBLS	10/01-12/01
Postsecondary	Mississippi	Y	23510 FQ	41760 AW	57670 TQ	MSBLS	10/01-12/01
Postsecondary	Missouri	Y	24890 FQ	44680 AW	67360 TQ	MOBLS	10/01-12/01
Postsecondary	Kansas City MSA, MO-KS	Y	27890 FQ	48350 AW	68150 TQ	MOBLS	10/01-12/01
Postsecondary	St. Louis MSA, MO-IL	Y	24600 FQ	44700 AW	69690 TQ	MOBLS	10/01-12/01
Postsecondary	Montana	Y	24740 FQ	49290 AW	82510 TQ	MTBLS	10/01-12/01
Postsecondary	Nebraska	Y	30420 FQ	47230 AW	67290 TQ	NEBLS	10/01-12/01
Postsecondary	Omaha MSA, NE-IA	Y	30770 FQ	44840 AW	64750 TQ	NEBLS	10/01-12/01
Postsecondary	Nevada	Y	23990 FQ	45080 AW	75470 TQ	NVBLS	10/01-12/01
Postsecondary	Las Vegas MSA, NV-AZ	Y	23860 FQ	42810 AW	74120 TQ	NVBLS	10/01-12/01
Postsecondary	New Hampshire	Y	30770 FQ	48340 AW	77490 TQ	NHBLS	10/01-12/01
Postsecondary	New Jersey	Y	29970 FQ	61100 AW	95870 TQ	NJBLS	10/01-12/01
Postsecondary	Bergen-Passaic PMSA, NJ	Y	33610 FQ	69830 AW	108350 TQ	NJBLS	10/01-12/01
Postsecondary	Jersey City PMSA, NJ	Y	31980 FQ	58470 AW	92080 TQ	NJBLS	10/01-12/01
Postsecondary	Newark PMSA, NJ	Y	21140 FQ	49980 AW	87060 TQ	NJBLS	10/01-12/01
Postsecondary	New Mexico	Y	33100 FQ	50590 AW	69750 TQ	NMBLS	10/01-12/01
Postsecondary	New York	Y	36720 FQ	65840 AW	105700 TQ	NYBLS	10/01-12/01
Postsecondary	Albany-Schenectady-Troy MSA, NY	Y	37190 FQ	53500 AW	86300 TQ	NYBLS	10/01-12/01
Postsecondary	New York PMSA, NY	Y	41650 FQ	71640 AW	108060 TQ	NYBLS	10/01-12/01
Postsecondary	North Carolina	Y	29850 FQ	46290 AW	66370 TQ	NCBLS	10/01-12/01
Postsecondary	Asheville MSA, NC	Y	32380 FQ	45450 AW	60010 TQ	NCBLS	10/01-12/01
Postsecondary	Charlotte-Gastonia-Rock Hill MSA, NC-SC	Y	27770 FQ	43830 AW	58140 TQ	NCBLS	10/01-12/01
Postsecondary	Greensboro-Winston-Salem-High Point MSA, NC	Y	34360 FQ	51700 AW	82900 TQ	NCBLS	10/01-12/01
Postsecondary	Raleigh-Durham-Chapel Hill MSA, NC	Y	30510 FQ	48010 AW	70150 TQ	NCBLS	10/01-12/01
Postsecondary	North Dakota	Y	29940 FQ	47740 AW	67560 TQ	NDBLS	10/01-12/01
Postsecondary	Ohio	Y	26350 FQ	47950 AW	72600 TQ	OHBLS	10/01-12/01
Postsecondary	Cincinnati PMSA, OH-KY-IN	Y	31290 FQ	52250 AW	81640 TQ	OHBLS	10/01-12/01
Postsecondary	Cleveland-Lorain-Elyria PMSA, OH	Y	30090 FQ	47750 AW	69810 TQ	OHBLS	10/01-12/01
Postsecondary	Columbus MSA, OH	Y	27350 FQ	45530 AW	71870 TQ	OHBLS	10/01-12/01
Postsecondary	Dayton-Springfield MSA, OH	Y	20900 FQ	42960 AW	66440 TQ	OHBLS	10/01-12/01
Postsecondary	Toledo MSA, OH	Y	21580 FQ	49200 AW	73990 TQ	OHBLS	10/01-12/01
Postsecondary	Youngstown-Warren MSA, OH	Y	37340 FQ	58810 AW	96750 TQ	OHBLS	10/01-12/01
Postsecondary	Oklahoma	Y	29510 FQ	39420 AW	57790 TQ	OKBLS	10/01-12/01
Postsecondary	Oklahoma City MSA, OK	Y	29440 FQ	39070 AW	58290 TQ	OKBLS	10/01-12/01
Postsecondary	Oregon	Y	32370 FQ	59460 AW	88090 TQ	ORBLS	10/01-12/01
Postsecondary	Portland-Vancouver PMSA, OR-WA	Y	29550 FQ	57100 AW	87490 TQ	ORBLS	10/01-12/01
Postsecondary	Pennsylvania	Y	26320 FQ	61070 AW	121610 TQ	PABLS	10/01-12/01
Postsecondary	Allentown-Bethlehem-Easton MSA, PA	Y	26880 FQ	44660 AW	67980 TQ	PABLS	10/01-12/01
Postsecondary	Philadelphia PMSA, PA-NJ	Y	25700 FQ	64210 AW	128540 TQ	PABLS	10/01-12/01
Postsecondary	Pittsburgh MSA, PA	Y	25100 FQ	56030 AW	119210 TQ	PABLS	10/01-12/01
Postsecondary	Scranton-Wilkes-Barre-Hazleton MSA, PA	Y	32450 FQ	57450 AW	86090 TQ	PABLS	10/01-12/01
Postsecondary	Rhode Island	Y	45770 FQ	63840 AW	89610 TQ	RIBLS	10/01-12/01
Postsecondary	South Carolina	Y	20340 FQ	43270 AW	68010 TQ	SCBLS	10/01-12/01
Postsecondary	Greenville-Spartanburg-Anderson MSA, SC	Y	20130 FQ	44540 AW	70570 TQ	SCBLS	10/01-12/01
Postsecondary	South Dakota	Y	31660 FQ	48360 AW	70230 TQ	SDBLS	10/01-12/01
Postsecondary	Tennessee	Y	29250 FQ	49630 AW	75840 TQ	TNBLS	10/01-12/01
Postsecondary	Memphis MSA, TN-AR-MS	Y	23950 FQ	44920 AW	69930 TQ	TNBLS	10/01-12/01
Postsecondary	Nashville MSA, TN	Y	36100 FQ	55550 AW	90590 TQ	TNBLS	10/01-12/01

AAW	Average annual wage	**AOH**	Average offered, high	**ASH**	Average starting, high	**H**	Hourly	**M**	Monthly	**S**	Special: hourly and annual
AE	Average entry wage	**AOL**	Average offered, low	**ASL**	Average starting, low	**HI**	Highest wage paid	**MTC**	Median total compensation	**TQ**	Third quartile wage
AEX	Average experienced wage	**APH**	Average pay, high range	**AW**	Average wage paid	**HR**	High end range	**MW**	Median wage paid	**W**	Weekly
AO	Average offered	**APL**	Average pay, low range	**FQ**	First quartile wage	**LR**	Low end range	**SQ**	Second quartile wage	**Y**	Yearly

Occupation/Type/Industry	Location	Per	Low	Mid	High	Source	Date
Sociology Teacher							
Postsecondary	Texas	Y	20450 FQ	54950 AW	98010 TQ	TXBLS	10/01-12/01
Postsecondary	Austin-San Marcos MSA, TX	Y	22560 FQ	62130 AW	118460 TQ	TXBLS	10/01-12/01
Postsecondary	Dallas PMSA, TX	Y	21250 FQ	72350 AW		TXBLS	10/01-12/01
Postsecondary	Fort Worth-Arlington PMSA, TX	Y	16120 FQ	45640 AW	83580 TQ	TXBLS	10/01-12/01
Postsecondary	Houston PMSA, TX	Y	37840 FQ	58320 AW	86320 TQ	TXBLS	10/01-12/01
Postsecondary	San Antonio MSA, TX	Y	31290 FQ	58480 AW	90580 TQ	TXBLS	10/01-12/01
Postsecondary	Utah	Y	37120 FQ	63460 AW	107490 TQ	UTBLS	10/01-12/01
Postsecondary	Vermont	Y	38510 FQ	49050 AW	61260 TQ	VTBLS	10/01-12/01
Postsecondary	Burlington MSA, VT	Y	34270 FQ	50940 AW	65090 TQ	VTBLS	10/01-12/01
Postsecondary	Virginia	Y	25170 FQ	55220 AW	91720 TQ	VABLS	10/01-12/01
Postsecondary	Norfolk-Virginia Beach-Newport News MSA, VA-NC	Y	38780 FQ	58350 AW	87290 TQ	VABLS	10/01-12/01
Postsecondary	Richmond-Petersburg MSA, VA	Y	14340 FQ	49700 AW	93440 TQ	VABLS	10/01-12/01
Postsecondary	Washington	Y	28740 FQ	52660 AW	86850 TQ	WABLS	10/01-12/01
Postsecondary	Seattle-Bellevue-Everett PMSA, WA	Y	31410 FQ	58330 AW	108660 TQ	WABLS	10/01-12/01
Postsecondary	Tacoma PMSA, WA	Y	29470 FQ	53240 AW	84990 TQ	WABLS	10/01-12/01
Postsecondary	West Virginia	Y	28140 FQ	53290 AW	77390 TQ	WVBLS	10/01-12/01
Postsecondary	Wisconsin	Y	28250 FQ	50220 AW	73680 TQ	WIBLS	10/01-12/01
Postsecondary	Milwaukee-Waukesha PMSA, WI	Y	22980 FQ	43660 AW	71530 TQ	WIBLS	10/01-12/01
Postsecondary	Puerto Rico	Y	27610 FQ	50410 AW	85550 TQ	PRBLS	10/01-12/01
Software and Computer Services Professional	San Diego, CA	Y		79360 AW		SDBJ1	1/99-1/00
Software Engineer	San Diego, CA	Y		83000 AW		SDBJ	1/01-1/02
Software Quality Engineer							
Quality Control	United States	Y			130000 HI	ASQ	1/00-1/01
Sound Engineering Technician	Alabama	Y	15210 FQ	30130 AW	44540 TQ	ALBLS	10/01-12/01
	Arizona	Y	18130 FQ	35320 AW	68060 TQ	AZBLS	10/01-12/01
	Arkansas	Y	12870 FQ	23440 AW	35130 TQ	ARBLS	10/01-12/01
	California	Y	18850 FQ	44820 AW	79800 TQ	CABLS	10/01-12/01
	Colorado	Y	19180 FQ	36230 AW	57040 TQ	COBLS	10/01-12/01
	Connecticut	Y	18860 FQ	32220 AW	54210 TQ	CTBLS	10/01-12/01
	Delaware	Y	19060 FQ	28040 AW	45510 TQ	DEBLS	10/01-12/01
	District of Columbia	Y	33550 FQ	45690 AW	58380 TQ	DCBLS	10/01-12/01
	Florida	Y	17880 FQ	32770 AW	60450 TQ	FLBLS	10/01-12/01
	Georgia	Y	16270 FQ	33350 AW	45210 TQ	GABLS	10/01-12/01
	Hawaii	Y	13960 FQ	33710 AW	53460 TQ	HIBLS	10/01-12/01
	Illinois	Y	21400 FQ	47520 AW	98410 TQ	ILBLS	10/01-12/01
	Indiana	Y	21260 FQ	37450 AW	49060 TQ	INBLS	10/01-12/01
	Iowa	Y	12980 FQ	20910 AW	33150 TQ	IABLS	10/01-12/01
	Kansas	Y	15880 FQ	36350 AW	64010 TQ	KSBLS	10/01-12/01
	Louisiana	Y	16380 FQ	32190 AW	51210 TQ	LABLS	10/01-12/01
	Maine	Y	17770 FQ	31060 AW	44500 TQ	MEBLS	10/01-12/01
	Maryland	Y	16610 FQ	43560 AW	87620 TQ	MDBLS	10/01-12/01
	Massachusetts	Y	20960 FQ	36280 AW	64550 TQ	MABLS	10/01-12/01
	Michigan	Y	30990 FQ	49090 AW	80790 TQ	MIBLS	10/01-12/01
	Minnesota	Y	20770 FQ	35840 AW	51430 TQ	MNBLS	10/01-12/01
	Mississippi	Y	21390 FQ	35310 AW	45220 TQ	MSBLS	10/01-12/01
	Missouri	Y	21300 FQ	36890 AW	54950 TQ	MOBLS	10/01-12/01
	Nebraska	Y	20780 FQ	40300 AW	83130 TQ	NEBLS	10/01-12/01
	Nevada	Y	24730 FQ	45260 AW	57870 TQ	NVBLS	10/01-12/01
	New Jersey	Y	20100 FQ	43790 AW	74390 TQ	NJBLS	10/01-12/01
	New York	Y	20660 FQ	68520 AW	142820 TQ	NYBLS	10/01-12/01
	North Carolina	Y	18380 FQ	28010 AW	42660 TQ	NCBLS	10/01-12/01
	Ohio	Y	18110 FQ	34870 AW	57030 TQ	OHBLS	10/01-12/01
	Oklahoma	Y	15870 FQ	30930 AW	47490 TQ	OKBLS	10/01-12/01
	Oregon	Y	16520 FQ	38440 AW	63460 TQ	ORBLS	10/01-12/01
	Pennsylvania	Y	16280 FQ	29360 AW	50950 TQ	PABLS	10/01-12/01
	South Carolina	Y	15960 FQ	41610 AW	83180 TQ	SCBLS	10/01-12/01
	Tennessee	Y	13390 FQ	31140 AW	50200 TQ	TNBLS	10/01-12/01
	Texas	Y	15410 FQ	33390 AW	65220 TQ	TXBLS	10/01-12/01
	Utah	Y	12400 FQ	21610 AW	37870 TQ	UTBLS	10/01-12/01
	Vermont	Y	19480 FQ	40300 AW	69850 TQ	VTBLS	10/01-12/01
	Virginia	Y	19130 FQ	40290 AW	65830 TQ	VABLS	10/01-12/01

AAW	Average annual wage	**AOH**	Average offered, high	**ASH**	Average starting, high	**H**	Hourly	**M**	Monthly	**S**	Special: hourly and annual
AE	Average entry wage	**AOL**	Average offered, low	**ASL**	Average starting, low	**HI**	Highest wage paid	**MTC**	Median total compensation	**TQ**	Third quartile wage
AEX	Average experienced wage	**APH**	Average pay, high range	**AW**	Average wage paid	**HR**	High end range	**MW**	Median wage paid	**W**	Weekly
AO	Average offered	**APL**	Average pay, low range	**FQ**	First quartile wage	**LR**	Low end range	**SQ**	Second quartile wage	**Y**	Yearly

Occupation/Type/Industry	Location	Per	Low	Mid	High	Source	Date
Sound Engineering Technician	Washington	Y	28450 FQ	52680 AW	87050 TQ	WABLS	10/01-12/01
	Wisconsin	Y	28930 FQ	53180 AW	68990 TQ	WIBLS	10/01-12/01
	Puerto Rico	Y	11660 FQ	19660 AW	35390 TQ	PRBLS	10/01-12/01
Sourcing Professional							
Apparel Industry	United States	Y	120000 AOL	188596 AW	350000 HI	BOB	1/00-1/01
Special Education Teacher							
Middle School	Alabama	Y	31300 FQ	39580 AW	47380 TQ	ALBLS	10/01-12/01
Middle School	Birmingham MSA, AL	Y	31140 FQ	39720 AW	47770 TQ	ALBLS	10/01-12/01
Middle School	Huntsville MSA, AL	Y	37480 FQ	44280 AW	53920 TQ	ALBLS	10/01-12/01
Middle School	Alaska	Y	38040 FQ	52680 AW	70730 TQ	AKBLS	10/01-12/01
Middle School	Arizona	Y	24280 FQ	33490 AW	47360 TQ	AZBLS	10/01-12/01
Middle School	Phoenix-Mesa MSA, AZ	Y	26490 FQ	35300 AW	50510 TQ	AZBLS	10/01-12/01
Middle School	Tucson MSA, AZ	Y	26510 FQ	33850 AW	43980 TQ	AZBLS	10/01-12/01
Middle School	Arkansas	Y	26380 FQ	34330 AW	43540 TQ	ARBLS	10/01-12/01
Middle School	Fayetteville-Springdale-Rogers MSA, AR	Y	27160 FQ	36320 AW	47910 TQ	ARBLS	10/01-12/01
Middle School	Little Rock-North Little Rock MSA, AR	Y	25310 FQ	32900 AW	43460 TQ	ARBLS	10/01-12/01
Middle School	California	Y	35430 FQ	51120 AW	69690 TQ	CABLS	10/01-12/01
Middle School	Bakersfield MSA, CA	Y	33910 FQ	48360 AW	68020 TQ	CABLS	10/01-12/01
Middle School	Chico-Paradise MSA, CA	Y	34310 FQ	50730 AW	70780 TQ	CABLS	10/01-12/01
Middle School	Fresno MSA, CA	Y	33830 FQ	49730 AW	69560 TQ	CABLS	10/01-12/01
Middle School	Los Angeles-Long Beach PMSA, CA	Y	37980 FQ	53110 AW	69300 TQ	CABLS	10/01-12/01
Middle School	Merced MSA, CA	Y	38100 FQ	53760 AW	71310 TQ	CABLS	10/01-12/01
Middle School	Modesto MSA, CA	Y	34520 FQ	55560 AW	72010 TQ	CABLS	10/01-12/01
Middle School	Oakland PMSA, CA	Y	35780 FQ	51570 AW	70230 TQ	CABLS	10/01-12/01
Middle School	Orange County PMSA, CA	Y	39120 FQ	53740 AW	71130 TQ	CABLS	10/01-12/01
Middle School	Riverside-San Bernardino PMSA, CA	Y	33310 FQ	50770 AW	71560 TQ	CABLS	10/01-12/01
Middle School	Sacramento PMSA, CA	Y	34740 FQ	51310 AW	70710 TQ	CABLS	10/01-12/01
Middle School	Salinas MSA, CA	Y	35680 FQ	50550 AW	69070 TQ	CABLS	10/01-12/01
Middle School	San Diego MSA, CA	Y	36930 FQ	51350 AW	69280 TQ	CABLS	10/01-12/01
Middle School	San Francisco PMSA, CA	Y	40370 FQ	51380 AW	65510 TQ	CABLS	10/01-12/01
Middle School	San Jose PMSA, CA	Y	34480 FQ	50660 AW	70040 TQ	CABLS	10/01-12/01
Middle School	San Luis Obispo-Atascadero-Paso Robles MSA, CA	Y	38060 FQ	51600 AW	69340 TQ	CABLS	10/01-12/01
Middle School	Santa Rosa PMSA, CA	Y	38530 FQ	48190 AW	60470 TQ	CABLS	10/01-12/01
Middle School	Stockton-Lodi MSA, CA	Y	36690 FQ	49960 AW	66510 TQ	CABLS	10/01-12/01
Middle School	Visalia-Tulare-Porterville MSA, CA	Y	34960 FQ	51890 AW	71400 TQ	CABLS	10/01-12/01
Middle School	Colorado	Y	28690 FQ	41390 AW	56460 TQ	COBLS	10/01-12/01
Middle School	Colorado Springs MSA, CO	Y	27530 FQ	37760 AW	50890 TQ	COBLS	10/01-12/01
Middle School	Denver PMSA, CO	Y	30400 FQ	43050 AW	56830 TQ	COBLS	10/01-12/01
Middle School	Greeley PMSA, CO	Y	25370 FQ	36880 AW	52240 TQ	COBLS	10/01-12/01
Middle School	Connecticut	Y	34190 FQ	52830 AW	71500 TQ	CTBLS	10/01-12/01
Middle School	Bridgeport PMSA, CT	Y	34370 FQ	53050 AW	71350 TQ	CTBLS	10/01-12/01
Middle School	Danbury PMSA, CT	Y	34330 FQ	55320 AW	72860 TQ	CTBLS	10/01-12/01
Middle School	Hartford MSA, CT	Y	34180 FQ	52570 AW	71040 TQ	CTBLS	10/01-12/01
Middle School	New Haven-Meriden PMSA, CT	Y	34310 FQ	51850 AW	70380 TQ	CTBLS	10/01-12/01
Middle School	New London-Norwich MSA, CT-RI	Y	33960 FQ	51180 AW	69520 TQ	CTBLS	10/01-12/01
Middle School	Stamford-Norwalk PMSA, CT	Y	35520 FQ	56390 AW	78820 TQ	CTBLS	10/01-12/01
Middle School	Waterbury PMSA, CT	Y	37080 FQ	55210 AW	73430 TQ	CTBLS	10/01-12/01
Middle School	Delaware	Y	33310 FQ	50190 AW	70180 TQ	DEBLS	10/01-12/01
Middle School	Wilmington-Newark PMSA, DE-MD	Y	33540 FQ	50110 AW	70510 TQ	DEBLS	10/01-12/01
Middle School	District of Columbia	Y	48790 FQ	77740 AW	94440 TQ	DCBLS	10/01-12/01
Middle School	Washington PMSA, DC-MD-VA-WV	Y	28590 FQ	46190 AW	77890 TQ	DCBLS	10/01-12/01
Middle School	Florida	Y	25110 FQ	37480 AW	49920 TQ	FLBLS	10/01-12/01
Middle School	Gainesville MSA, FL	Y	24020 FQ	38150 AW	55380 TQ	FLBLS	10/01-12/01
Middle School	Jacksonville MSA, FL	Y	30830 FQ	40850 AW	54240 TQ	FLBLS	10/01-12/01
Middle School	Pensacola MSA, FL	Y	24220 FQ	36390 AW	50680 TQ	FLBLS	10/01-12/01
Middle School	West Palm Beach-Boca Raton MSA, FL	Y	25840 FQ	38930 AW	51840 TQ	FLBLS	10/01-12/01
Middle School	Georgia	Y	32380 FQ	43860 AW	57210 TQ	GABLS	10/01-12/01
Middle School	Atlanta MSA, GA	Y	36460 FQ	44960 AW	57400 TQ	GABLS	10/01-12/01
Middle School	Augusta-Aiken MSA, GA-SC	Y	30470 FQ	41610 AW	55610 TQ	GABLS	10/01-12/01
Middle School	Columbus MSA, GA-AL	Y	32490 FQ	42240 AW	54100 TQ	GABLS	10/01-12/01

AAW Average annual wage	**AOH** Average offered, high	**ASH** Average starting, high	**H** Hourly	**M** Monthly	**S** Special: hourly and annual
AE Average entry wage	**AOL** Average offered, low	**ASL** Average starting, low	**HI** Highest wage paid	**MTC** Median total compensation	**TQ** Third quartile wage
AEX Average experienced wage	**APH** Average pay, high range	**AW** Average wage paid	**HR** High end range	**MW** Median wage paid	**W** Weekly
AO Average offered	**APL** Average pay, low range	**FQ** First quartile wage	**LR** Low end range	**SQ** Second quartile wage	**Y** Yearly

Occupation/Type/Industry	Location	Per	Low	Mid	High	Source	Date
Special Education Teacher							
Middle School	Macon MSA, GA	Y	31300 FQ	43560 AW	56960 TQ	GABLS	10/01-12/01
Middle School	Hawaii	Y	22760 FQ	35060 AW	49730 TQ	HIBLS	10/01-12/01
Middle School	Honolulu MSA, HI	Y	22120 FQ	35150 AW	50420 TQ	HIBLS	10/01-12/01
Middle School	Illinois	Y	26190 FQ	42260 AW	63360 TQ	ILBLS	10/01-12/01
Middle School	Champaign-Urbana MSA, IL	Y	25160 FQ	38850 AW	58690 TQ	ILBLS	10/01-12/01
Middle School	Chicago PMSA, IL	Y	30120 FQ	48040 AW	70080 TQ	ILBLS	10/01-12/01
Middle School	Peoria-Pekin MSA, IL	Y	28200 FQ	41840 AW	56020 TQ	ILBLS	10/01-12/01
Middle School	Rockford MSA, IL	Y	31490 FQ	46080 AW	65320 TQ	ILBLS	10/01-12/01
Middle School	Indiana	Y	29790 FQ	44350 AW	58990 TQ	INBLS	10/01-12/01
Middle School	Elkhart-Goshen MSA, IN	Y	29520 FQ	42360 AW	57010 TQ	INBLS	10/01-12/01
Middle School	Fort Wayne MSA, IN	Y	26680 FQ	40600 AW	55320 TQ	INBLS	10/01-12/01
Middle School	Gary PMSA, IN	Y	31740 FQ	42940 AW	55800 TQ	INBLS	10/01-12/01
Middle School	Indianapolis MSA, IN	Y	32860 FQ	50730 AW	71750 TQ	INBLS	10/01-12/01
Middle School	Lafayette MSA, IN	Y	30670 FQ	40340 AW	53510 TQ	INBLS	10/01-12/01
Middle School	Iowa	Y	24730 FQ	35660 AW	49210 TQ	IABLS	10/01-12/01
Middle School	Cedar Rapids MSA, IA	Y	30510 FQ	40710 AW	53930 TQ	IABLS	10/01-12/01
Middle School	Davenport-Moline-Rock Island MSA, IA-IL	Y	30900 FQ	41840 AW	57410 TQ	IABLS	10/01-12/01
Middle School	Des Moines MSA, IA	Y	24540 FQ	36720 AW	47880 TQ	IABLS	10/01-12/01
Middle School	Kansas	Y	26470 FQ	35900 AW	46320 TQ	KSBLS	10/01-12/01
Middle School	Wichita MSA, KS	Y	26150 FQ	35540 AW	45670 TQ	KSBLS	10/01-12/01
Middle School	Kentucky	Y	25560 FQ	38030 AW	53110 TQ	KYBLS	10/01-12/01
Middle School	Louisiana	Y	25470 FQ	32140 AW	40050 TQ	LABLS	10/01-12/01
Middle School	New Orleans MSA, LA	Y	25220 FQ	32380 AW	42050 TQ	LABLS	10/01-12/01
Middle School	Maine	Y	24700 FQ	35330 AW	48860 TQ	MEBLS	10/01-12/01
Middle School	Portland MSA, ME	Y	28690 FQ	40780 AW	55100 TQ	MEBLS	10/01-12/01
Middle School	Maryland	Y	29200 FQ	44530 AW	64040 TQ	MDBLS	10/01-12/01
Middle School	Baltimore PMSA, MD	Y	33890 FQ	53390 AW	78170 TQ	MDBLS	10/01-12/01
Middle School	Massachusetts	Y	28040 FQ	43400 AW	59310 TQ	MABLS	10/01-12/01
Middle School	Boston PMSA, MA-NH	Y	25040 FQ	42350 AW	59240 TQ	MABLS	10/01-12/01
Middle School	Brockton PMSA, MA	Y	31730 FQ	46700 AW	64450 TQ	MABLS	10/01-12/01
Middle School	Lawrence PMSA, MA-NH	Y	26360 FQ	43070 AW	59270 TQ	MABLS	10/01-12/01
Middle School	Lowell PMSA, MA-NH	Y	30000 FQ	46330 AW	59310 TQ	MABLS	10/01-12/01
Middle School	Springfield MSA, MA	Y	32700 FQ	49490 AW	77470 TQ	MABLS	10/01-12/01
Middle School	Worcester PMSA, MA-CT	Y	32420 FQ	45130 AW	58630 TQ	MABLS	10/01-12/01
Middle School	Michigan	Y	30290 FQ	47160 AW	67210 TQ	MIBLS	10/01-12/01
Middle School	Ann Arbor PMSA, MI	Y	31890 FQ	51510 AW	71200 TQ	MIBLS	10/01-12/01
Middle School	Detroit PMSA, MI	Y	30700 FQ	47610 AW	68760 TQ	MIBLS	10/01-12/01
Middle School	Flint PMSA, MI	Y	26310 FQ	43670 AW	65420 TQ	MIBLS	10/01-12/01
Middle School	Grand Rapids-Muskegon-Holland MSA, MI	Y	31570 FQ	47880 AW	63640 TQ	MIBLS	10/01-12/01
Middle School	Kalamazoo-Battle Creek MSA, MI	Y	25680 FQ	43310 AW	61180 TQ	MIBLS	10/01-12/01
Middle School	Lansing-East Lansing MSA, MI	Y	29220 FQ	45330 AW	64940 TQ	MIBLS	10/01-12/01
Middle School	Saginaw-Bay City-Midland MSA, MI	Y	30320 FQ	54320 AW	110150 TQ	MIBLS	10/01-12/01
Middle School	Minnesota	Y	28080 FQ	40690 AW	58150 TQ	MNBLS	10/01-12/01
Middle School	Duluth-Superior MSA, MN-WI	Y	30180 FQ	43280 AW	55210 TQ	MNBLS	10/01-12/01
Middle School	Minneapolis-St. Paul MSA, MN-WI	Y	28970 FQ	41920 AW	61180 TQ	MNBLS	10/01-12/01
Middle School	St. Cloud MSA, MN	Y	25710 FQ	39020 AW	56580 TQ	MNBLS	10/01-12/01
Middle School	Mississippi	Y	24730 FQ	33090 AW	43990 TQ	MSBLS	10/01-12/01
Middle School	Biloxi-Gulfport-Pascagoula MSA, MS	Y	25830 FQ	33510 AW	43370 TQ	MSBLS	10/01-12/01
Middle School	Jackson MSA, MS	Y	24670 FQ	34220 AW	45240 TQ	MSBLS	10/01-12/01
Middle School	Missouri	Y	24700 FQ	33620 AW	45670 TQ	MOBLS	10/01-12/01
Middle School	Kansas City MSA, MO-KS	Y	26270 FQ	37370 AW	51550 TQ	MOBLS	10/01-12/01
Middle School	St. Louis MSA, MO-IL	Y	26170 FQ	36140 AW	49570 TQ	MOBLS	10/01-12/01
Middle School	Springfield MSA, MO	Y	25130 FQ	32960 AW	43850 TQ	MOBLS	10/01-12/01
Middle School	Montana	Y	24660 FQ	33430 AW	45910 TQ	MTBLS	10/01-12/01
Middle School	Nebraska	Y	24240 FQ	35310 AW	49850 TQ	NEBLS	10/01-12/01
Middle School	Omaha MSA, NE-IA	Y	26800 FQ	39960 AW	54290 TQ	NEBLS	10/01-12/01
Middle School	New Hampshire	Y	26230 FQ	36860 AW	50590 TQ	NHBLS	10/01-12/01
Middle School	Manchester PMSA, NH	Y	23890 FQ	32040 AW	45230 TQ	NHBLS	10/01-12/01
Middle School	Nashua PMSA, NH	Y	28390 FQ	39400 AW	53440 TQ	NHBLS	10/01-12/01
Middle School	Portsmouth-Rochester PMSA, NH-ME	Y	26450 FQ	37860 AW	52060 TQ	NHBLS	10/01-12/01
Middle School	New Jersey	Y	32010 FQ	50460 AW	76630 TQ	NJBLS	10/01-12/01
Middle School	Atlantic-Cape May PMSA, NJ	Y	29280 FQ	47300 AW	69280 TQ	NJBLS	10/01-12/01
Middle School	Bergen-Passaic PMSA, NJ	Y	35980 FQ	55510 AW	84210 TQ	NJBLS	10/01-12/01

AAW	Average annual wage	**AOH**	Average offered, high	**ASH**	Average starting, high	**H**	Hourly	**M**	Monthly	**S**	Special: hourly and annual
AE	Average entry wage	**AOL**	Average offered, low	**ASL**	Average starting, low	**HI**	Highest wage paid	**MTC**	Median total compensation	**TQ**	Third quartile wage
AEX	Average experienced wage	**APH**	Average pay, high range	**AW**	Average wage paid	**HR**	High end range	**MW**	Median wage paid	**W**	Weekly
AO	Average offered	**APL**	Average pay, low range	**FQ**	First quartile wage	**LR**	Low end range	**SQ**	Second quartile wage	**Y**	Yearly

Special Education Teacher

Occupation/Type/Industry	Location	Per	Low	Mid	High	Source	Date
Middle School	Middlesex-Somerset-Hunterdon PMSA, NJ	Y	29780 FQ	46180 AW	67950 TQ	NJBLS	10/01-12/01
Middle School	Monmouth-Ocean PMSA, NJ	Y	31210 FQ	47090 AW	68300 TQ	NJBLS	10/01-12/01
Middle School	Newark PMSA, NJ	Y	32990 FQ	50140 AW	73550 TQ	NJBLS	10/01-12/01
Middle School	Trenton PMSA, NJ	Y	28030 FQ	47690 AW	71140 TQ	NJBLS	10/01-12/01
Middle School	New Mexico	Y	26560 FQ	37180 AW	51010 TQ	NMBLS	10/01-12/01
Middle School	New York	Y	33240 FQ	61080 AW	101450 TQ	NYBLS	10/01-12/01
Middle School	Albany-Schenectady-Troy MSA, NY	Y	27780 FQ	46000 AW	67580 TQ	NYBLS	10/01-12/01
Middle School	Binghamton MSA, NY	Y	32670 FQ	46020 AW	64750 TQ	NYBLS	10/01-12/01
Middle School	Buffalo-Niagara Falls MSA, NY	Y	36480 FQ	48610 AW	64050 TQ	NYBLS	10/01-12/01
Middle School	Dutchess County PMSA, NY	Y	31760 FQ	51070 AW	74760 TQ	NYBLS	10/01-12/01
Middle School	Nassau-Suffolk PMSA, NY	Y	37880 FQ	61420 AW	88010 TQ	NYBLS	10/01-12/01
Middle School	Newburgh PMSA, NY-PA	Y	36100 FQ	54020 AW	77270 TQ	NYBLS	10/01-12/01
Middle School	Rochester MSA, NY	Y	27780 FQ	42030 AW	62690 TQ	NYBLS	10/01-12/01
Middle School	Syracuse MSA, NY	Y	34110 FQ	42400 AW	53910 TQ	NYBLS	10/01-12/01
Middle School	Utica-Rome MSA, NY	Y	27580 FQ	44690 AW	63840 TQ	NYBLS	10/01-12/01
Middle School	North Carolina	Y	24330 FQ	35190 AW	47390 TQ	NCBLS	10/01-12/01
Middle School	Charlotte-Gastonia-Rock Hill MSA, NC-SC	Y	25620 FQ	37240 AW	52310 TQ	NCBLS	10/01-12/01
Middle School	Fayetteville MSA, NC	Y	25440 FQ	34470 AW	45410 TQ	NCBLS	10/01-12/01
Middle School	Greensboro-Winston-Salem-High Point MSA, NC	Y	24730 FQ	32790 AW	45700 TQ	NCBLS	10/01-12/01
Middle School	Hickory-Morganton-Lenoir MSA, NC	Y	21640 FQ	30470 AW	42250 TQ	NCBLS	10/01-12/01
Middle School	Raleigh-Durham-Chapel Hill MSA, NC	Y	27960 FQ	42240 AW	57150 TQ	NCBLS	10/01-12/01
Middle School	Wilmington MSA, NC	Y	26750 FQ	36360 AW	46450 TQ	NCBLS	10/01-12/01
Middle School	Ohio	Y	28820 FQ	42740 AW	58010 TQ	OHBLS	10/01-12/01
Middle School	Akron PMSA, OH	Y	30550 FQ	42420 AW	56520 TQ	OHBLS	10/01-12/01
Middle School	Canton-Massillon MSA, OH	Y	29570 FQ	42710 AW	57070 TQ	OHBLS	10/01-12/01
Middle School	Cincinnati PMSA, OH-KY-IN	Y	27650 FQ	41510 AW	57160 TQ	OHBLS	10/01-12/01
Middle School	Cleveland-Lorain-Elyria PMSA, OH	Y	31410 FQ	48020 AW	67100 TQ	OHBLS	10/01-12/01
Middle School	Columbus MSA, OH	Y	30590 FQ	44200 AW	59970 TQ	OHBLS	10/01-12/01
Middle School	Dayton-Springfield MSA, OH	Y	29220 FQ	41940 AW	57100 TQ	OHBLS	10/01-12/01
Middle School	Hamilton-Middletown PMSA, OH	Y	31910 FQ	44320 AW	56530 TQ	OHBLS	10/01-12/01
Middle School	Mansfield MSA, OH	Y	30400 FQ	41230 AW	55680 TQ	OHBLS	10/01-12/01
Middle School	Toledo MSA, OH	Y	29010 FQ	41430 AW	55930 TQ	OHBLS	10/01-12/01
Middle School	Youngstown-Warren MSA, OH	Y	26580 FQ	38740 AW	53130 TQ	OHBLS	10/01-12/01
Middle School	Oklahoma	Y	28300 FQ	35380 AW	44530 TQ	OKBLS	10/01-12/01
Middle School	Oklahoma City MSA, OK	Y	28650 FQ	37200 AW	47530 TQ	OKBLS	10/01-12/01
Middle School	Tulsa MSA, OK	Y	27680 FQ	33780 AW	42320 TQ	OKBLS	10/01-12/01
Middle School	Oregon	Y	30090 FQ	39120 AW	54490 TQ	ORBLS	10/01-12/01
Middle School	Eugene-Springfield MSA, OR	Y	33310 FQ	43020 AW	54740 TQ	ORBLS	10/01-12/01
Middle School	Medford-Ashland MSA, OR	Y	31070 FQ	39240 AW	50840 TQ	ORBLS	10/01-12/01
Middle School	Portland-Vancouver PMSA, OR-WA	Y	30160 FQ	40640 AW	56960 TQ	ORBLS	10/01-12/01
Middle School	Salem PMSA, OR	Y	31150 FQ	41910 AW	55840 TQ	ORBLS	10/01-12/01
Middle School	Pennsylvania	Y	30920 FQ	48940 AW	73470 TQ	PABLS	10/01-12/01
Middle School	Allentown-Bethlehem-Easton MSA, PA	Y	29420 FQ	44670 AW	62940 TQ	PABLS	10/01-12/01
Middle School	Erie MSA, PA	Y	31880 FQ	45620 AW	59270 TQ	PABLS	10/01-12/01
Middle School	Harrisburg-Lebanon-Carlisle MSA, PA	Y	33000 FQ	42770 AW	55280 TQ	PABLS	10/01-12/01
Middle School	Johnstown MSA, PA	Y	35630 FQ	49910 AW	65600 TQ	PABLS	10/01-12/01
Middle School	Lancaster MSA, PA	Y	33750 FQ	44510 AW	57580 TQ	PABLS	10/01-12/01
Middle School	Philadelphia PMSA, PA-NJ	Y	31580 FQ	48160 AW	70330 TQ	PABLS	10/01-12/01
Middle School	Pittsburgh MSA, PA	Y	29190 FQ	55190 AW	92150 TQ	PABLS	10/01-12/01
Middle School	Reading MSA, PA	Y	29960 FQ	48120 AW	72540 TQ	PABLS	10/01-12/01
Middle School	Scranton-Wilkes-Barre-Hazleton MSA, PA	Y	29030 FQ	47810 AW	65620 TQ	PABLS	10/01-12/01
Middle School	York MSA, PA	Y	29700 FQ	45440 AW	65870 TQ	PABLS	10/01-12/01
Middle School	Rhode Island	Y	34300 FQ	48840 AW	64760 TQ	RIBLS	10/01-12/01
Middle School	Providence-Fall River-Warwick MSA, RI-MA	Y	31790 FQ	46830 AW	60110 TQ	RIBLS	10/01-12/01
Middle School	South Carolina	Y	28000 FQ	39260 AW	53600 TQ	SCBLS	10/01-12/01
Middle School	Charleston-North Charleston MSA, SC	Y	27430 FQ	40270 AW	52470 TQ	SCBLS	10/01-12/01

AAW	Average annual wage	AOH	Average offered, high	ASH	Average starting, high	H	Hourly	M	Monthly	S	Special: hourly and annual
AE	Average entry wage	AOL	Average offered, low	ASL	Average starting, low	HI	Highest wage paid	MTC	Median total compensation	TQ	Third quartile wage
AEX	Average experienced wage	APH	Average pay, high range	AW	Average wage paid	HR	High end range	MW	Median wage paid	W	Weekly
AO	Average offered	APL	Average pay, low range	FQ	First quartile wage	LR	Low end range	SQ	Second quartile wage	Y	Yearly

Occupation/Type/Industry	Location	Per	Low	Mid	High	Source	Date
Special Education Teacher							
Middle School	Columbia MSA, SC	Y	23520 FQ	39730 AW	55120 TQ	SCBLS	10/01-12/01
Middle School	Greenville-Spartanburg-Anderson MSA, SC	Y	26940 FQ	39840 AW	55220 TQ	SCBLS	10/01-12/01
Middle School	South Dakota	Y	23680 FQ	31030 AW	42000 TQ	SDBLS	10/01-12/01
Middle School	Tennessee	Y	28740 FQ	37230 AW	45070 TQ	TNBLS	10/01-12/01
Middle School	Chattanooga MSA, TN-GA	Y	28460 FQ	40510 AW	55530 TQ	TNBLS	10/01-12/01
Middle School	Johnson City-Kingsport-Bristol MSA, TN-VA	Y	28110 FQ	42360 AW	65200 TQ	TNBLS	10/01-12/01
Middle School	Knoxville MSA, TN	Y	29630 FQ	38510 AW	52230 TQ	TNBLS	10/01-12/01
Middle School	Memphis MSA, TN-AR-MS	Y	26600 FQ	35250 AW	43730 TQ	TNBLS	10/01-12/01
Middle School	Nashville MSA, TN	Y	30510 FQ	37810 AW	43840 TQ	TNBLS	10/01-12/01
Middle School	Texas	Y	29200 FQ	39080 AW	52320 TQ	TXBLS	10/01-12/01
Middle School	Austin-San Marcos MSA, TX	Y	29610 FQ	38430 AW	50230 TQ	TXBLS	10/01-12/01
Middle School	Beaumont-Port Arthur MSA, TX	Y	29010 FQ	38340 AW	50560 TQ	TXBLS	10/01-12/01
Middle School	Brazoria PMSA, TX	Y	29920 FQ	39220 AW	51210 TQ	TXBLS	10/01-12/01
Middle School	Brownsville-Harlingen-San Benito MSA, TX	Y	31190 FQ	42160 AW	55350 TQ	TXBLS	10/01-12/01
Middle School	Corpus Christi MSA, TX	Y	28930 FQ	44050 AW	57430 TQ	TXBLS	10/01-12/01
Middle School	Dallas PMSA, TX	Y	29620 FQ	38980 AW	51300 TQ	TXBLS	10/01-12/01
Middle School	El Paso MSA, TX	Y	30190 FQ	37300 AW	45960 TQ	TXBLS	10/01-12/01
Middle School	Fort Worth-Arlington PMSA, TX	Y	29920 FQ	43780 AW	74140 TQ	TXBLS	10/01-12/01
Middle School	Houston PMSA, TX	Y	30940 FQ	40340 AW	53710 TQ	TXBLS	10/01-12/01
Middle School	Killeen-Temple MSA, TX	Y	25790 FQ	35590 AW	47900 TQ	TXBLS	10/01-12/01
Middle School	Laredo MSA, TX	Y	29160 FQ	39210 AW	52420 TQ	TXBLS	10/01-12/01
Middle School	Longview-Marshall MSA, TX	Y	24520 FQ	35550 AW	45240 TQ	TXBLS	10/01-12/01
Middle School	McAllen-Edinburg-Mission MSA, TX	Y	29170 FQ	39020 AW	51810 TQ	TXBLS	10/01-12/01
Middle School	San Antonio MSA, TX	Y	31850 FQ	42400 AW	56120 TQ	TXBLS	10/01-12/01
Middle School	Waco MSA, TX	Y	25520 FQ	34390 AW	44430 TQ	TXBLS	10/01-12/01
Middle School	Utah	Y	24450 FQ	37120 AW	51090 TQ	UTBLS	10/01-12/01
Middle School	Salt Lake City-Ogden MSA, UT	Y	26390 FQ	38580 AW	50460 TQ	UTBLS	10/01-12/01
Middle School	Vermont	Y	29270 FQ	40420 AW	56040 TQ	VTBLS	10/01-12/01
Middle School	Burlington MSA, VT	Y	28560 FQ	44260 AW	59440 TQ	VTBLS	10/01-12/01
Middle School	Virginia	Y	28080 FQ	39410 AW	54470 TQ	VABLS	10/01-12/01
Middle School	Lynchburg MSA, VA	Y	26020 FQ	38200 AW	52370 TQ	VABLS	10/01-12/01
Middle School	Norfolk-Virginia Beach-Newport News MSA, VA-NC	Y	28830 FQ	35930 AW	45600 TQ	VABLS	10/01-12/01
Middle School	Richmond-Petersburg MSA, VA	Y	34860 FQ	44370 AW	55940 TQ	VABLS	10/01-12/01
Middle School	Washington	Y	28110 FQ	41320 AW	55930 TQ	WABLS	10/01-12/01
Middle School	Bremerton PMSA, WA	Y	29270 FQ	41650 AW	55250 TQ	WABLS	10/01-12/01
Middle School	Olympia PMSA, WA	Y	27670 FQ	41920 AW	56150 TQ	WABLS	10/01-12/01
Middle School	Richland-Kennewick-Pasco MSA, WA	Y	28460 FQ	40760 AW	55140 TQ	WABLS	10/01-12/01
Middle School	Seattle-Bellevue-Everett PMSA, WA	Y	28170 FQ	40180 AW	55170 TQ	WABLS	10/01-12/01
Middle School	Spokane MSA, WA	Y	26050 FQ	39860 AW	56100 TQ	WABLS	10/01-12/01
Middle School	Tacoma PMSA, WA	Y	27050 FQ	40890 AW	55930 TQ	WABLS	10/01-12/01
Middle School	Yakima MSA, WA	Y	30060 FQ	40690 AW	54590 TQ	WABLS	10/01-12/01
Middle School	West Virginia	Y	27300 FQ	35560 AW	44160 TQ	WVBLS	10/01-12/01
Middle School	Huntington-Ashland MSA, WV-KY-OH	Y	26710 FQ	36190 AW	46700 TQ	WVBLS	10/01-12/01
Middle School	Wisconsin	Y	26320 FQ	39240 AW	55470 TQ	WIBLS	10/01-12/01
Middle School	Appleton-Oshkosh-Neenah MSA, WI	Y	20400 FQ	32590 AW	49650 TQ	WIBLS	10/01-12/01
Middle School	Madison MSA, WI	Y	25840 FQ	39070 AW	58990 TQ	WIBLS	10/01-12/01
Middle School	Milwaukee-Waukesha PMSA, WI	Y	30190 FQ	43240 AW	63770 TQ	WIBLS	10/01-12/01
Middle School	Wyoming	Y	25760 FQ	36020 AW	45890 TQ	WYBLS	10/01-12/01
Middle School	Puerto Rico	Y	18530 FQ	21270 AW	24420 TQ	PRBLS	10/01-12/01
Preschool, K-12	United States	Y		39700 AW		FREEP1	1/00-1/00
Preschool, K-12	Alabama	Y	14880 FQ	34570 AW	44810 TQ	ALBLS	10/01-12/01
Preschool, K-12	Birmingham MSA, AL	Y	12180 FQ	21810 AW	41290 TQ	ALBLS	10/01-12/01
Preschool, K-12	Huntsville MSA, AL	Y	32520 FQ	40840 AW	50740 TQ	ALBLS	10/01-12/01
Preschool, K-12	Mobile MSA, AL	Y	30820 FQ	37360 AW	49370 TQ	ALBLS	10/01-12/01
Preschool, K-12	Montgomery MSA, AL	Y	21260 FQ	34280 AW	44830 TQ	ALBLS	10/01-12/01
Preschool, K-12	Alaska	Y	35190 FQ	50670 AW	69340 TQ	AKBLS	10/01-12/01

AAW Average annual wage; **AE** Average entry wage; **AEX** Average experienced wage; **AO** Average offered; **AOH** Average offered, high; **AOL** Average offered, low; **APH** Average pay, high range; **APL** Average pay, low range; **ASH** Average starting, high; **ASL** Average starting, low; **AW** Average wage paid; **FQ** First quartile wage; **H** Hourly; **HI** Highest wage paid; **HR** High end range; **LR** Low end range; **M** Monthly; **MTC** Median total compensation; **MW** Median wage paid; **SQ** Second quartile wage; **S** Special: hourly and annual; **TQ** Third quartile wage; **W** Weekly; **Y** Yearly

Occupation/Type/Industry	Location	Per	Low	Mid	High	Source	Date
Special Education Teacher							
Preschool, K-12	Arizona	Y	21190 FQ	35350 AW	55370 TQ	AZBLS	10/01-12/01
Preschool, K-12	Phoenix-Mesa MSA, AZ	Y	21350 FQ	36400 AW	56980 TQ	AZBLS	10/01-12/01
Preschool, K-12	Tucson MSA, AZ	Y	19920 FQ	34310 AW	59390 TQ	AZBLS	10/01-12/01
Preschool, K-12	Arkansas	Y	25690 FQ	33750 AW	42640 TQ	ARBLS	10/01-12/01
Preschool, K-12	Fayetteville-Springdale-Rogers MSA, AR	Y	19860 FQ	30950 AW	42690 TQ	ARBLS	10/01-12/01
Preschool, K-12	Fort Smith MSA, AR-OK	Y	28460 FQ	35390 AW	44590 TQ	ARBLS	10/01-12/01
Preschool, K-12	Little Rock-North Little Rock MSA, AR	Y	24160 FQ	35270 AW	47540 TQ	ARBLS	10/01-12/01
Preschool, K-12	California	Y	33760 FQ	51200 AW	70620 TQ	CABLS	10/01-12/01
Preschool, K-12	Bakersfield MSA, CA	Y	38630 FQ	53890 AW	72440 TQ	CABLS	10/01-12/01
Preschool, K-12	Chico-Paradise MSA, CA	Y	34310 FQ	53670 AW	71160 TQ	CABLS	10/01-12/01
Preschool, K-12	Fresno MSA, CA	Y	16710 FQ	40900 AW	65760 TQ	CABLS	10/01-12/01
Preschool, K-12	Los Angeles-Long Beach PMSA, CA	Y	36440 FQ	51000 AW	69040 TQ	CABLS	10/01-12/01
Preschool, K-12	Merced MSA, CA	Y	33950 FQ	49770 AW	69780 TQ	CABLS	10/01-12/01
Preschool, K-12	Modesto MSA, CA	Y	37000 FQ	56770 AW	75980 TQ	CABLS	10/01-12/01
Preschool, K-12	Oakland PMSA, CA	Y	29090 FQ	47130 AW	66800 TQ	CABLS	10/01-12/01
Preschool, K-12	Orange County PMSA, CA	Y	36490 FQ	55380 AW	76640 TQ	CABLS	10/01-12/01
Preschool, K-12	Redding MSA, CA	Y	15940 FQ	40300 AW	59980 TQ	CABLS	10/01-12/01
Preschool, K-12	Riverside-San Bernardino PMSA, CA	Y	35100 FQ	52710 AW	72860 TQ	CABLS	10/01-12/01
Preschool, K-12	Sacramento PMSA, CA	Y	32400 FQ	51620 AW	72820 TQ	CABLS	10/01-12/01
Preschool, K-12	Salinas MSA, CA	Y	32560 FQ	49960 AW	71120 TQ	CABLS	10/01-12/01
Preschool, K-12	San Diego MSA, CA	Y	27400 FQ	54270 AW	87780 TQ	CABLS	10/01-12/01
Preschool, K-12	San Francisco PMSA, CA	Y	35300 FQ	54530 AW	74120 TQ	CABLS	10/01-12/01
Preschool, K-12	San Jose PMSA, CA	Y	25670 FQ	41100 AW	63330 TQ	CABLS	10/01-12/01
Preschool, K-12	San Luis Obispo-Atascadero-Paso Robles MSA, CA	Y	36340 FQ	50760 AW	67650 TQ	CABLS	10/01-12/01
Preschool, K-12	Santa Barbara-Santa Maria-Lompoc MSA, CA	Y	41660 FQ	59900 AW	75140 TQ	CABLS	10/01-12/01
Preschool, K-12	Santa Rosa PMSA, CA	Y	34210 FQ	47090 AW	58610 TQ	CABLS	10/01-12/01
Preschool, K-12	Stockton-Lodi MSA, CA	Y	33270 FQ	50730 AW	71800 TQ	CABLS	10/01-12/01
Preschool, K-12	Vallejo-Fairfield-Napa PMSA, CA	Y	41980 FQ	56630 AW	72490 TQ	CABLS	10/01-12/01
Preschool, K-12	Ventura PMSA, CA	Y	39060 FQ	65700 AW		CABLS	10/01-12/01
Preschool, K-12	Colorado	Y	28640 FQ	43480 AW	63330 TQ	COBLS	10/01-12/01
Preschool, K-12	Boulder-Longmont PMSA, CO	Y	25670 FQ	37680 AW	58150 TQ	COBLS	10/01-12/01
Preschool, K-12	Colorado Springs MSA, CO	Y	27620 FQ	41700 AW	58900 TQ	COBLS	10/01-12/01
Preschool, K-12	Denver PMSA, CO	Y	30570 FQ	46110 AW	66100 TQ	COBLS	10/01-12/01
Preschool, K-12	Fort Collins-Loveland MSA, CO	Y	29190 FQ	42810 AW	59470 TQ	COBLS	10/01-12/01
Preschool, K-12	Greeley PMSA, CO	Y	26320 FQ	39410 AW	56060 TQ	COBLS	10/01-12/01
Preschool, K-12	Connecticut	Y	33460 FQ	52340 AW	71580 TQ	CTBLS	10/01-12/01
Preschool, K-12	Bridgeport PMSA, CT	Y	33150 FQ	49860 AW	69620 TQ	CTBLS	10/01-12/01
Preschool, K-12	Danbury PMSA, CT	Y	34910 FQ	52210 AW	69900 TQ	CTBLS	10/01-12/01
Preschool, K-12	Hartford MSA, CT	Y	32060 FQ	51510 AW	71060 TQ	CTBLS	10/01-12/01
Preschool, K-12	New Haven-Meriden PMSA, CT	Y	33030 FQ	52600 AW	71760 TQ	CTBLS	10/01-12/01
Preschool, K-12	New London-Norwich MSA, CT-RI	Y	34850 FQ	53670 AW	70990 TQ	CTBLS	10/01-12/01
Preschool, K-12	Stamford-Norwalk PMSA, CT	Y	40390 FQ	59240 AW	85810 TQ	CTBLS	10/01-12/01
Preschool, K-12	Waterbury PMSA, CT	Y	38320 FQ	56780 AW	74830 TQ	CTBLS	10/01-12/01
Preschool, K-12	Delaware	Y	31950 FQ	52610 AW	76240 TQ	DEBLS	10/01-12/01
Preschool, K-12	Wilmington-Newark PMSA, DE-MD	Y	31390 FQ	51940 AW	75440 TQ	DEBLS	10/01-12/01
Preschool, K-12	District of Columbia	Y	34050 FQ	60640 AW	76910 TQ	DCBLS	10/01-12/01
Preschool, K-12	Washington PMSA, DC-MD-VA-WV	Y	33170 FQ	49670 AW	70010 TQ	DCBLS	10/01-12/01
Preschool, K-12	Florida	Y	27900 FQ	42170 AW	59190 TQ	FLBLS	10/01-12/01
Preschool, K-12	Daytona Beach MSA, FL	Y	25790 FQ	45450 AW	60310 TQ	FLBLS	10/01-12/01
Preschool, K-12	Fort Lauderdale PMSA, FL	Y	29040 FQ	36390 AW	50370 TQ	FLBLS	10/01-12/01
Preschool, K-12	Fort Myers-Cape Coral MSA, FL	Y	30490 FQ	41450 AW	56650 TQ	FLBLS	10/01-12/01
Preschool, K-12	Jacksonville MSA, FL	Y	38770 FQ	48350 AW	60170 TQ	FLBLS	10/01-12/01
Preschool, K-12	Orlando MSA, FL	Y	26950 FQ	39030 AW	56200 TQ	FLBLS	10/01-12/01
Preschool, K-12	Sarasota-Bradenton MSA, FL	Y	18860 FQ	32350 AW	52920 TQ	FLBLS	10/01-12/01
Preschool, K-12	Tampa-St. Petersburg-Clearwater MSA, FL	Y	32950 FQ	44290 AW	60480 TQ	FLBLS	10/01-12/01
Preschool, K-12	Georgia	Y	31940 FQ	44110 AW	58020 TQ	GABLS	10/01-12/01
Preschool, K-12	Atlanta MSA, GA	Y	33030 FQ	45700 AW	59360 TQ	GABLS	10/01-12/01

AAW	Average annual wage	**AOH**	Average offered, high	**ASH**	Average starting, high	**H**	Hourly	**M**	Monthly	**S**	Special: hourly and annual
AE	Average entry wage	**AOL**	Average offered, low	**ASL**	Average starting, low	**HI**	Highest wage paid	**MTC**	Median total compensation	**TQ**	Third quartile wage
AEX	Average experienced wage	**APH**	Average pay, high range	**AW**	Average wage paid	**HR**	High end range	**MW**	Median wage paid	**W**	Weekly
AO	Average offered	**APL**	Average pay, low range	**FQ**	First quartile wage	**LR**	Low end range	**SQ**	Second quartile wage	**Y**	Yearly

Occupation/Type/Industry	Location	Per	Low	Mid	High	Source	Date
Special Education Teacher							
Preschool, K-12	Augusta-Aiken MSA, GA-SC	Y	30360 FQ	41270 AW	54720 TQ	GABLS	10/01-12/01
Preschool, K-12	Columbus MSA, GA-AL	Y	35840 FQ	46480 AW	57740 TQ	GABLS	10/01-12/01
Preschool, K-12	Macon MSA, GA	Y	32270 FQ	43230 AW	55770 TQ	GABLS	10/01-12/01
Preschool, K-12	Savannah MSA, GA	Y	31300 FQ	40100 AW	50450 TQ	GABLS	10/01-12/01
Preschool, K-12	Hawaii	Y	23510 FQ	36900 AW	54030 TQ	HIBLS	10/01-12/01
Preschool, K-12	Honolulu MSA, HI	Y	22550 FQ	37710 AW	55890 TQ	HIBLS	10/01-12/01
Preschool, K-12	Illinois	Y	25230 FQ	41070 AW	61590 TQ	ILBLS	10/01-12/01
Preschool, K-12	Champaign-Urbana MSA, IL	Y	26570 FQ	41260 AW	62950 TQ	ILBLS	10/01-12/01
Preschool, K-12	Chicago PMSA, IL	Y	29630 FQ	45830 AW	68480 TQ	ILBLS	10/01-12/01
Preschool, K-12	Peoria-Pekin MSA, IL	Y	28010 FQ	41750 AW	60070 TQ	ILBLS	10/01-12/01
Preschool, K-12	Springfield MSA, IL	Y	25730 FQ	37380 AW	52800 TQ	ILBLS	10/01-12/01
Preschool, K-12	Indiana	Y	30150 FQ	43220 AW	57900 TQ	INBLS	10/01-12/01
Preschool, K-12	Elkhart-Goshen MSA, IN	Y	30580 FQ	42820 AW	56220 TQ	INBLS	10/01-12/01
Preschool, K-12	Evansville-Henderson MSA, IN-KY	Y	31200 FQ	44130 AW	56670 TQ	INBLS	10/01-12/01
Preschool, K-12	Fort Wayne MSA, IN	Y	26960 FQ	39270 AW	55850 TQ	INBLS	10/01-12/01
Preschool, K-12	Gary PMSA, IN	Y	32310 FQ	45510 AW	58310 TQ	INBLS	10/01-12/01
Preschool, K-12	Indianapolis MSA, IN	Y	31520 FQ	46030 AW	65710 TQ	INBLS	10/01-12/01
Preschool, K-12	Lafayette MSA, IN	Y	29570 FQ	36860 AW	47950 TQ	INBLS	10/01-12/01
Preschool, K-12	Iowa	Y	24770 FQ	34320 AW	45970 TQ	IABLS	10/01-12/01
Preschool, K-12	Cedar Rapids MSA, IA	Y	24580 FQ	33520 AW	47990 TQ	IABLS	10/01-12/01
Preschool, K-12	Davenport-Moline-Rock Island MSA, IA-IL	Y	28890 FQ	42460 AW	57630 TQ	IABLS	10/01-12/01
Preschool, K-12	Des Moines MSA, IA	Y	13220 FQ	29240 AW	40230 TQ	IABLS	10/01-12/01
Preschool, K-12	Kansas	Y	25540 FQ	36110 AW	47780 TQ	KSBLS	10/01-12/01
Preschool, K-12	Topeka MSA, KS	Y	28390 FQ	39000 AW	53010 TQ	KSBLS	10/01-12/01
Preschool, K-12	Wichita MSA, KS	Y	25130 FQ	36100 AW	47370 TQ	KSBLS	10/01-12/01
Preschool, K-12	Kentucky	Y	25470 FQ	37470 AW	52090 TQ	KYBLS	10/01-12/01
Preschool, K-12	Lexington MSA, KY	Y	25440 FQ	37160 AW	50850 TQ	KYBLS	10/01-12/01
Preschool, K-12	Louisville MSA, KY-IN	Y	27690 FQ	44100 AW	57100 TQ	KYBLS	10/01-12/01
Preschool, K-12	Louisiana	Y	21260 FQ	30800 AW	41940 TQ	LABLS	10/01-12/01
Preschool, K-12	Baton Rouge MSA, LA	Y	24700 FQ	33800 AW	43900 TQ	LABLS	10/01-12/01
Preschool, K-12	Maine	Y	25060 FQ	37420 AW	49640 TQ	MEBLS	10/01-12/01
Preschool, K-12	Portland MSA, ME	Y	30250 FQ	43330 AW	56210 TQ	MEBLS	10/01-12/01
Preschool, K-12	Maryland	Y	32430 FQ	51100 AW	72030 TQ	MDBLS	10/01-12/01
Preschool, K-12	Baltimore PMSA, MD	Y	32180 FQ	53820 AW	80150 TQ	MDBLS	10/01-12/01
Preschool, K-12	Massachusetts	Y	24830 FQ	43110 AW	59970 TQ	MABLS	10/01-12/01
Preschool, K-12	Boston PMSA, MA-NH	Y	25100 FQ	43350 AW	60900 TQ	MABLS	10/01-12/01
Preschool, K-12	Brockton PMSA, MA	Y	18910 FQ	33680 AW	58120 TQ	MABLS	10/01-12/01
Preschool, K-12	Lawrence PMSA, MA-NH	Y	25960 FQ	43430 AW	61170 TQ	MABLS	10/01-12/01
Preschool, K-12	Lowell PMSA, MA-NH	Y	32360 FQ	46240 AW	58640 TQ	MABLS	10/01-12/01
Preschool, K-12	New Bedford PMSA, MA	Y	23860 FQ	41990 AW	58940 TQ	MABLS	10/01-12/01
Preschool, K-12	Springfield MSA, MA	Y	29380 FQ	45590 AW	64060 TQ	MABLS	10/01-12/01
Preschool, K-12	Worcester PMSA, MA-CT	Y	32710 FQ	45050 AW	58660 TQ	MABLS	10/01-12/01
Preschool, K-12	Michigan	Y	30770 FQ	49820 AW	70240 TQ	MIBLS	10/01-12/01
Preschool, K-12	Ann Arbor PMSA, MI	Y	33710 FQ	56620 AW	73140 TQ	MIBLS	10/01-12/01
Preschool, K-12	Detroit PMSA, MI	Y	32790 FQ	55500 AW	77630 TQ	MIBLS	10/01-12/01
Preschool, K-12	Flint PMSA, MI	Y	32730 FQ	51380 AW	71810 TQ	MIBLS	10/01-12/01
Preschool, K-12	Grand Rapids-Muskegon-Holland MSA, MI	Y	27790 FQ	42540 AW	61180 TQ	MIBLS	10/01-12/01
Preschool, K-12	Kalamazoo-Battle Creek MSA, MI	Y	29530 FQ	45530 AW	56760 TQ	MIBLS	10/01-12/01
Preschool, K-12	Lansing-East Lansing MSA, MI	Y	33400 FQ	50430 AW	63630 TQ	MIBLS	10/01-12/01
Preschool, K-12	Saginaw-Bay City-Midland MSA, MI	Y	30570 FQ	43190 AW	64570 TQ	MIBLS	10/01-12/01
Preschool, K-12	Minnesota	Y	29460 FQ	43200 AW	59210 TQ	MNBLS	10/01-12/01
Preschool, K-12	Duluth-Superior MSA, MN-WI	Y	17480 FQ	38480 AW	55320 TQ	MNBLS	10/01-12/01
Preschool, K-12	Minneapolis-St. Paul MSA, MN-WI	Y	30650 FQ	45060 AW	63550 TQ	MNBLS	10/01-12/01
Preschool, K-12	St. Cloud MSA, MN	Y	34180 FQ	44540 AW	56670 TQ	MNBLS	10/01-12/01
Preschool, K-12	Mississippi	Y	25090 FQ	32850 AW	43130 TQ	MSBLS	10/01-12/01
Preschool, K-12	Biloxi-Gulfport-Pascagoula MSA, MS	Y	26200 FQ	32860 AW	40870 TQ	MSBLS	10/01-12/01
Preschool, K-12	Jackson MSA, MS	Y	19020 FQ	29870 AW	42210 TQ	MSBLS	10/01-12/01
Preschool, K-12	Missouri	Y	19400 FQ	31930 AW	46330 TQ	MOBLS	10/01-12/01
Preschool, K-12	Kansas City MSA, MO-KS	Y	25500 FQ	36570 AW	51810 TQ	MOBLS	10/01-12/01
Preschool, K-12	St. Louis MSA, MO-IL	Y	19050 FQ	33510 AW	52160 TQ	MOBLS	10/01-12/01
Preschool, K-12	Springfield MSA, MO	Y	20500 FQ	30230 AW	42620 TQ	MOBLS	10/01-12/01
Preschool, K-12	Montana	Y	20490 FQ	32520 AW	46100 TQ	MTBLS	10/01-12/01
Preschool, K-12	Nebraska	Y	24030 FQ	37200 AW	52960 TQ	NEBLS	10/01-12/01
Preschool, K-12	Lincoln MSA, NE	Y	24780 FQ	35260 AW	50840 TQ	NEBLS	10/01-12/01

AAW	Average annual wage	**AOH**	Average offered, high	**ASH**	Average starting, high	**H**	Hourly	**M**	Monthly	**S**	Special: hourly and annual
AE	Average entry wage	**AOL**	Average offered, low	**ASL**	Average starting, low	**HI**	Highest wage paid	**MTC**	Median total compensation	**TQ**	Third quartile wage
AEX	Average experienced wage	**APH**	Average pay, high range	**AW**	Average wage paid	**HR**	High end range	**MW**	Median wage paid	**W**	Weekly
AO	Average offered	**APL**	Average pay, low range	**FQ**	First quartile wage	**LR**	Low end range	**SQ**	Second quartile wage	**Y**	Yearly

Occupation/Type/Industry	Location	Per	Low	Mid	High	Source	Date
Special Education Teacher							
Preschool, K-12	Omaha MSA, NE-IA	Y	22900 FQ	40330 AW	59860 TQ	NEBLS	10/01-12/01
Preschool, K-12	New Hampshire	Y	26180 FQ	37380 AW	52920 TQ	NHBLS	10/01-12/01
Preschool, K-12	Nashua PMSA, NH	Y	28470 FQ	41070 AW	55740 TQ	NHBLS	10/01-12/01
Preschool, K-12	Portsmouth-Rochester PMSA, NH-ME	Y	27520 FQ	40320 AW	55580 TQ	NHBLS	10/01-12/01
Preschool, K-12	New Jersey	Y	31040 FQ	47400 AW	71150 TQ	NJBLS	10/01-12/01
Preschool, K-12	Atlantic-Cape May PMSA, NJ	Y	31730 FQ	47490 AW	71480 TQ	NJBLS	10/01-12/01
Preschool, K-12	Bergen-Passaic PMSA, NJ	Y	27260 FQ	48220 AW	81010 TQ	NJBLS	10/01-12/01
Preschool, K-12	Middlesex-Somerset-Hunterdon PMSA, NJ	Y	32560 FQ	46670 AW	67690 TQ	NJBLS	10/01-12/01
Preschool, K-12	Monmouth-Ocean PMSA, NJ	Y	29320 FQ	43350 AW	67220 TQ	NJBLS	10/01-12/01
Preschool, K-12	Newark PMSA, NJ	Y	35980 FQ	47650 AW	68610 TQ	NJBLS	10/01-12/01
Preschool, K-12	Trenton PMSA, NJ	Y	24130 FQ	46500 AW	69390 TQ	NJBLS	10/01-12/01
Preschool, K-12	New Mexico	Y	25470 FQ	37020 AW	54380 TQ	NMBLS	10/01-12/01
Preschool, K-12	Albuquerque MSA, NM	Y	25180 FQ	33560 AW	46380 TQ	NMBLS	10/01-12/01
Preschool, K-12	Las Cruces MSA, NM	Y	25580 FQ	31720 AW	38950 TQ	NMBLS	10/01-12/01
Preschool, K-12	New York	Y	33250 FQ	63000 AW	105330 TQ	NYBLS	10/01-12/01
Preschool, K-12	Albany-Schenectady-Troy MSA, NY	Y	26230 FQ	43320 AW	64890 TQ	NYBLS	10/01-12/01
Preschool, K-12	Binghamton MSA, NY	Y	32780 FQ	44790 AW	57050 TQ	NYBLS	10/01-12/01
Preschool, K-12	Buffalo-Niagara Falls MSA, NY	Y	33990 FQ	51840 AW	70280 TQ	NYBLS	10/01-12/01
Preschool, K-12	Dutchess County PMSA, NY	Y	32050 FQ	60030 AW	100730 TQ	NYBLS	10/01-12/01
Preschool, K-12	Nassau-Suffolk PMSA, NY	Y	35020 FQ	60210 AW	91780 TQ	NYBLS	10/01-12/01
Preschool, K-12	Newburgh PMSA, NY-PA	Y	33340 FQ	50040 AW	70190 TQ	NYBLS	10/01-12/01
Preschool, K-12	Rochester MSA, NY	Y	31820 FQ	46040 AW	65850 TQ	NYBLS	10/01-12/01
Preschool, K-12	Syracuse MSA, NY	Y	35400 FQ	44690 AW	55970 TQ	NYBLS	10/01-12/01
Preschool, K-12	Utica-Rome MSA, NY	Y	26180 FQ	40910 AW	58590 TQ	NYBLS	10/01-12/01
Preschool, K-12	North Carolina	Y	26250 FQ	37250 AW	48520 TQ	NCBLS	10/01-12/01
Preschool, K-12	Asheville MSA, NC	Y	27550 FQ	39330 AW	49800 TQ	NCBLS	10/01-12/01
Preschool, K-12	Charlotte-Gastonia-Rock Hill MSA, NC-SC	Y	28690 FQ	38620 AW	51910 TQ	NCBLS	10/01-12/01
Preschool, K-12	Fayetteville MSA, NC	Y	24450 FQ	35190 AW	46990 TQ	NCBLS	10/01-12/01
Preschool, K-12	Greensboro-Winston-Salem-High Point MSA, NC	Y	26240 FQ	39280 AW	54450 TQ	NCBLS	10/01-12/01
Preschool, K-12	Hickory-Morganton-Lenoir MSA, NC	Y	24520 FQ	37460 AW	49460 TQ	NCBLS	10/01-12/01
Preschool, K-12	Raleigh-Durham-Chapel Hill MSA, NC	Y	29030 FQ	40200 AW	52490 TQ	NCBLS	10/01-12/01
Preschool, K-12	Wilmington MSA, NC	Y	25190 FQ	34960 AW	44240 TQ	NCBLS	10/01-12/01
Preschool, K-12	North Dakota	Y	23650 FQ	33170 AW	44120 TQ	NDBLS	10/01-12/01
Preschool, K-12	Fargo-Moorhead MSA, ND-MN	Y	25590 FQ	38000 AW	51290 TQ	NDBLS	10/01-12/01
Preschool, K-12	Ohio	Y	28070 FQ	42680 AW	58650 TQ	OHBLS	10/01-12/01
Preschool, K-12	Akron PMSA, OH	Y	30960 FQ	44780 AW	58350 TQ	OHBLS	10/01-12/01
Preschool, K-12	Canton-Massillon MSA, OH	Y	27810 FQ	41500 AW	57250 TQ	OHBLS	10/01-12/01
Preschool, K-12	Cincinnati PMSA, OH-KY-IN	Y	29400 FQ	43320 AW	59170 TQ	OHBLS	10/01-12/01
Preschool, K-12	Cleveland-Lorain-Elyria PMSA, OH	Y	30650 FQ	49220 AW	70090 TQ	OHBLS	10/01-12/01
Preschool, K-12	Columbus MSA, OH	Y	26860 FQ	42040 AW	58330 TQ	OHBLS	10/01-12/01
Preschool, K-12	Dayton-Springfield MSA, OH	Y	22830 FQ	39720 AW	57500 TQ	OHBLS	10/01-12/01
Preschool, K-12	Hamilton-Middletown PMSA, OH	Y	30260 FQ	42460 AW	55760 TQ	OHBLS	10/01-12/01
Preschool, K-12	Mansfield MSA, OH	Y	23130 FQ	36690 AW	52640 TQ	OHBLS	10/01-12/01
Preschool, K-12	Toledo MSA, OH	Y	30010 FQ	41470 AW	55740 TQ	OHBLS	10/01-12/01
Preschool, K-12	Youngstown-Warren MSA, OH	Y	28000 FQ	39860 AW	53920 TQ	OHBLS	10/01-12/01
Preschool, K-12	Oklahoma	Y	26530 FQ	34540 AW	43980 TQ	OKBLS	10/01-12/01
Preschool, K-12	Oklahoma City MSA, OK	Y	25860 FQ	34040 AW	44060 TQ	OKBLS	10/01-12/01
Preschool, K-12	Tulsa MSA, OK	Y	25740 FQ	33840 AW	43850 TQ	OKBLS	10/01-12/01
Preschool, K-12	Oregon	Y	30610 FQ	42900 AW	58370 TQ	ORBLS	10/01-12/01
Preschool, K-12	Eugene-Springfield MSA, OR	Y	31430 FQ	43750 AW	56030 TQ	ORBLS	10/01-12/01
Preschool, K-12	Medford-Ashland MSA, OR	Y	32120 FQ	46850 AW	62340 TQ	ORBLS	10/01-12/01
Preschool, K-12	Portland-Vancouver PMSA, OR-WA	Y	30380 FQ	44450 AW	64390 TQ	ORBLS	10/01-12/01
Preschool, K-12	Salem PMSA, OR	Y	30540 FQ	44290 AW	57650 TQ	ORBLS	10/01-12/01
Preschool, K-12	Pennsylvania	Y	30410 FQ	47900 AW	70170 TQ	PABLS	10/01-12/01
Preschool, K-12	Allentown-Bethlehem-Easton MSA, PA	Y	33910 FQ	51470 AW	73140 TQ	PABLS	10/01-12/01
Preschool, K-12	Erie MSA, PA	Y	32670 FQ	43530 AW	56960 TQ	PABLS	10/01-12/01
Preschool, K-12	Harrisburg-Lebanon-Carlisle MSA, PA	Y	34630 FQ	47360 AW	59170 TQ	PABLS	10/01-12/01

AAW	Average annual wage	AOH	Average offered, high	ASH	Average starting, high	H	Hourly	M	Monthly	S	Special: hourly and annual
AE	Average entry wage	AOL	Average offered, low	ASL	Average starting, low	HI	Highest wage paid	MTC	Median total compensation	TQ	Third quartile wage
AEX	Average experienced wage	APH	Average pay, high range	AW	Average wage paid	HR	High end range	MW	Median wage paid	W	Weekly
AO	Average offered	APL	Average pay, low range	FQ	First quartile wage	LR	Low end range	SQ	Second quartile wage	Y	Yearly

Occupation/Type/Industry	Location	Per	Low	Mid	High	Source	Date
Special Education Teacher							
Preschool, K-12	Johnstown MSA, PA	Y	33590 FQ	48900 AW	67260 TQ	PABLS	10/01-12/01
Preschool, K-12	Lancaster MSA, PA	Y	33510 FQ	46540 AW	57990 TQ	PABLS	10/01-12/01
Preschool, K-12	Philadelphia PMSA, PA-NJ	Y	30300 FQ	49900 AW	74030 TQ	PABLS	10/01-12/01
Preschool, K-12	Pittsburgh MSA, PA	Y	25560 FQ	47660 AW	72500 TQ	PABLS	10/01-12/01
Preschool, K-12	Reading MSA, PA	Y	33140 FQ	50110 AW	72380 TQ	PABLS	10/01-12/01
Preschool, K-12	Scranton-Wilkes-Barre-Hazleton MSA, PA	Y	32090 FQ	51030 AW	69130 TQ	PABLS	10/01-12/01
Preschool, K-12	York MSA, PA	Y	31390 FQ	45940 AW	64830 TQ	PABLS	10/01-12/01
Preschool, K-12	Rhode Island	Y	26400 FQ	45240 AW	64600 TQ	RIBLS	10/01-12/01
Preschool, K-12	Providence-Fall River-Warwick MSA, RI-MA	Y	27460 FQ	44820 AW	63790 TQ	RIBLS	10/01-12/01
Preschool, K-12	South Carolina	Y	27200 FQ	39290 AW	54080 TQ	SCBLS	10/01-12/01
Preschool, K-12	Charleston-North Charleston MSA, SC	Y	25130 FQ	36350 AW	49190 TQ	SCBLS	10/01-12/01
Preschool, K-12	Columbia MSA, SC	Y	24160 FQ	39700 AW	58030 TQ	SCBLS	10/01-12/01
Preschool, K-12	Greenville-Spartanburg-Anderson MSA, SC	Y	27780 FQ	41050 AW	54640 TQ	SCBLS	10/01-12/01
Preschool, K-12	South Dakota	Y	23220 FQ	31070 AW	41580 TQ	SDBLS	10/01-12/01
Preschool, K-12	Sioux Falls MSA, SD	Y	22560 FQ	30770 AW	42600 TQ	SDBLS	10/01-12/01
Preschool, K-12	Tennessee	Y	25360 FQ	34060 AW	44210 TQ	TNBLS	10/01-12/01
Preschool, K-12	Chattanooga MSA, TN-GA	Y	16780 FQ	33060 AW	47620 TQ	TNBLS	10/01-12/01
Preschool, K-12	Johnson City-Kingsport-Bristol MSA, TN-VA	Y	24990 FQ	33220 AW	43010 TQ	TNBLS	10/01-12/01
Preschool, K-12	Knoxville MSA, TN	Y	29160 FQ	36650 AW	45970 TQ	TNBLS	10/01-12/01
Preschool, K-12	Memphis MSA, TN-AR-MS	Y	24590 FQ	33770 AW	43770 TQ	TNBLS	10/01-12/01
Preschool, K-12	Nashville MSA, TN	Y	25120 FQ	34430 AW	44980 TQ	TNBLS	10/01-12/01
Preschool, K-12	Texas	Y	29300 FQ	38610 AW	51910 TQ	TXBLS	10/01-12/01
Preschool, K-12	Austin-San Marcos MSA, TX	Y	30450 FQ	39010 AW	50170 TQ	TXBLS	10/01-12/01
Preschool, K-12	Beaumont-Port Arthur MSA, TX	Y	29410 FQ	37050 AW	45960 TQ	TXBLS	10/01-12/01
Preschool, K-12	Brazoria PMSA, TX	Y	30290 FQ	39300 AW	50370 TQ	TXBLS	10/01-12/01
Preschool, K-12	Dallas PMSA, TX	Y	29400 FQ	38280 AW	51440 TQ	TXBLS	10/01-12/01
Preschool, K-12	El Paso MSA, TX	Y	29330 FQ	34980 AW	45470 TQ	TXBLS	10/01-12/01
Preschool, K-12	Fort Worth-Arlington PMSA, TX	Y	31160 FQ	42360 AW	55580 TQ	TXBLS	10/01-12/01
Preschool, K-12	Houston PMSA, TX	Y	30650 FQ	39530 AW	52570 TQ	TXBLS	10/01-12/01
Preschool, K-12	Killeen-Temple MSA, TX	Y	18030 FQ	36080 AW	55930 TQ	TXBLS	10/01-12/01
Preschool, K-12	Laredo MSA, TX	Y	30010 FQ	41610 AW	55070 TQ	TXBLS	10/01-12/01
Preschool, K-12	Longview-Marshall MSA, TX	Y	26190 FQ	34840 AW	44390 TQ	TXBLS	10/01-12/01
Preschool, K-12	McAllen-Edinburg-Mission MSA, TX	Y	13470 FQ	34900 AW	51310 TQ	TXBLS	10/01-12/01
Preschool, K-12	Odessa-Midland MSA, TX	Y	30070 FQ	37580 AW	48090 TQ	TXBLS	10/01-12/01
Preschool, K-12	San Antonio MSA, TX	Y	31430 FQ	42680 AW	57030 TQ	TXBLS	10/01-12/01
Preschool, K-12	Tyler MSA, TX	Y	22870 FQ	31680 AW	42250 TQ	TXBLS	10/01-12/01
Preschool, K-12	Waco MSA, TX	Y	26260 FQ	37040 AW	46140 TQ	TXBLS	10/01-12/01
Preschool, K-12	Utah	Y	25490 FQ	36990 AW	51720 TQ	UTBLS	10/01-12/01
Preschool, K-12	Provo-Orem MSA, UT	Y	30430 FQ	38080 AW	51230 TQ	UTBLS	10/01-12/01
Preschool, K-12	Salt Lake City-Ogden MSA, UT	Y	24340 FQ	37080 AW	52580 TQ	UTBLS	10/01-12/01
Preschool, K-12	Vermont	Y	28150 FQ	40800 AW	55230 TQ	VTBLS	10/01-12/01
Preschool, K-12	Burlington MSA, VT	Y	29510 FQ	44890 AW	59100 TQ	VTBLS	10/01-12/01
Preschool, K-12	Virginia	Y	29890 FQ	43520 AW	63740 TQ	VABLS	10/01-12/01
Preschool, K-12	Lynchburg MSA, VA	Y	30120 FQ	43410 AW	61030 TQ	VABLS	10/01-12/01
Preschool, K-12	Norfolk-Virginia Beach-Newport News MSA, VA-NC	Y	29520 FQ	37230 AW	49470 TQ	VABLS	10/01-12/01
Preschool, K-12	Richmond-Petersburg MSA, VA	Y	33200 FQ	44750 AW	60040 TQ	VABLS	10/01-12/01
Preschool, K-12	Washington	Y	29390 FQ	43280 AW	57190 TQ	WABLS	10/01-12/01
Preschool, K-12	Bremerton PMSA, WA	Y	30430 FQ	41980 AW	55120 TQ	WABLS	10/01-12/01
Preschool, K-12	Olympia PMSA, WA	Y	30360 FQ	44360 AW	57530 TQ	WABLS	10/01-12/01
Preschool, K-12	Richland-Kennewick-Pasco MSA, WA	Y	27720 FQ	41180 AW	55840 TQ	WABLS	10/01-12/01
Preschool, K-12	Seattle-Bellevue-Everett PMSA, WA	Y	28920 FQ	43390 AW	57970 TQ	WABLS	10/01-12/01
Preschool, K-12	Spokane MSA, WA	Y	26740 FQ	39910 AW	53960 TQ	WABLS	10/01-12/01
Preschool, K-12	Tacoma PMSA, WA	Y	28200 FQ	41820 AW	55960 TQ	WABLS	10/01-12/01
Preschool, K-12	Yakima MSA, WA	Y	30780 FQ	42240 AW	54880 TQ	WABLS	10/01-12/01
Preschool, K-12	West Virginia	Y	27800 FQ	35880 AW	44210 TQ	WVBLS	10/01-12/01
Preschool, K-12	Huntington-Ashland MSA, WV-KY-OH	Y	27230 FQ	36560 AW	46360 TQ	WVBLS	10/01-12/01

AAW	Average annual wage	**AOH**	Average offered, high	**ASH**	Average starting, high	**H**	Hourly	**M**	Monthly	**S**	Special: hourly and annual
AE	Average entry wage	**AOL**	Average offered, low	**ASL**	Average starting, low	**HI**	Highest wage paid	**MTC**	Median total compensation	**TQ**	Third quartile wage
AEX	Average experienced wage	**APH**	Average pay, high range	**AW**	Average wage paid	**HR**	High end range	**MW**	Median wage paid	**W**	Weekly
AO	Average offered	**APL**	Average pay, low range	**FQ**	First quartile wage	**LR**	Low end range	**SQ**	Second quartile wage	**Y**	Yearly

Occupation/Type/Industry	Location	Per	Low	Mid	High	Source	Date
Special Education Teacher							
Preschool, K-12	Wisconsin	Y	25430 FQ	41560 AW	59540 TQ	WIBLS	10/01-12/01
Preschool, K-12	Appleton-Oshkosh-Neenah MSA, WI	Y	28080 FQ	38760 AW	52710 TQ	WIBLS	10/01-12/01
Preschool, K-12	Green Bay MSA, WI	Y	30080 FQ	48530 AW	76440 TQ	WIBLS	10/01-12/01
Preschool, K-12	Madison MSA, WI	Y	29420 FQ	45100 AW	68640 TQ	WIBLS	10/01-12/01
Preschool, K-12	Milwaukee-Waukesha PMSA, WI	Y	27130 FQ	44010 AW	63010 TQ	WIBLS	10/01-12/01
Preschool, K-12	Racine PMSA, WI	Y	30020 FQ	42650 AW	59040 TQ	WIBLS	10/01-12/01
Preschool, K-12	Wyoming	Y	26170 FQ	35800 AW	46360 TQ	WYBLS	10/01-12/01
Preschool, K-12	Puerto Rico	Y	19030 FQ	22040 AW	26370 TQ	PRBLS	10/01-12/01
Secondary School	Alabama	Y	31330 FQ	38860 AW	46020 TQ	ALBLS	10/01-12/01
Secondary School	Birmingham MSA, AL	Y	27620 FQ	37220 AW	46060 TQ	ALBLS	10/01-12/01
Secondary School	Huntsville MSA, AL	Y	29910 FQ	38200 AW	46230 TQ	ALBLS	10/01-12/01
Secondary School	Montgomery MSA, AL	Y	31730 FQ	38940 AW	46220 TQ	ALBLS	10/01-12/01
Secondary School	Alaska	Y	36730 FQ	50640 AW	68060 TQ	AKBLS	10/01-12/01
Secondary School	Arizona	Y	22310 FQ	40410 AW	66140 TQ	AZBLS	10/01-12/01
Secondary School	Phoenix-Mesa MSA, AZ	Y	23120 FQ	44390 AW	70860 TQ	AZBLS	10/01-12/01
Secondary School	Tucson MSA, AZ	Y	20010 FQ	30670 AW	44350 TQ	AZBLS	10/01-12/01
Secondary School	Arkansas	Y	26280 FQ	34890 AW	45820 TQ	ARBLS	10/01-12/01
Secondary School	Fayetteville-Springdale-Rogers MSA, AR	Y	27340 FQ	37510 AW	51220 TQ	ARBLS	10/01-12/01
Secondary School	Fort Smith MSA, AR-OK	Y	27150 FQ	36750 AW	49330 TQ	ARBLS	10/01-12/01
Secondary School	Little Rock-North Little Rock MSA, AR	Y	24800 FQ	33900 AW	45590 TQ	ARBLS	10/01-12/01
Secondary School	California	Y	36440 FQ	54590 AW	72920 TQ	CABLS	10/01-12/01
Secondary School	Bakersfield MSA, CA	Y	35120 FQ	52200 AW	71690 TQ	CABLS	10/01-12/01
Secondary School	Chico-Paradise MSA, CA	Y	33500 FQ	50480 AW	70980 TQ	CABLS	10/01-12/01
Secondary School	Fresno MSA, CA	Y	35950 FQ	53080 AW	73240 TQ	CABLS	10/01-12/01
Secondary School	Los Angeles-Long Beach PMSA, CA	Y	37830 FQ	56640 AW	72740 TQ	CABLS	10/01-12/01
Secondary School	Modesto MSA, CA	Y	35430 FQ	53460 AW	69340 TQ	CABLS	10/01-12/01
Secondary School	Oakland PMSA, CA	Y	37090 FQ	53170 AW	71090 TQ	CABLS	10/01-12/01
Secondary School	Orange County PMSA, CA	Y	36740 FQ	55990 AW	77240 TQ	CABLS	10/01-12/01
Secondary School	Redding MSA, CA	Y	36760 FQ	51540 AW	69430 TQ	CABLS	10/01-12/01
Secondary School	Riverside-San Bernardino PMSA, CA	Y	35220 FQ	53970 AW	73510 TQ	CABLS	10/01-12/01
Secondary School	Sacramento PMSA, CA	Y	27680 FQ	48450 AW	71420 TQ	CABLS	10/01-12/01
Secondary School	Salinas MSA, CA	Y	36140 FQ	49950 AW	70190 TQ	CABLS	10/01-12/01
Secondary School	San Diego MSA, CA	Y	38440 FQ	54290 AW	72470 TQ	CABLS	10/01-12/01
Secondary School	San Jose PMSA, CA	Y	36140 FQ	56770 AW	80100 TQ	CABLS	10/01-12/01
Secondary School	San Luis Obispo-Atascadero-Paso Robles MSA, CA	Y	36310 FQ	51620 AW	70560 TQ	CABLS	10/01-12/01
Secondary School	Santa Barbara-Santa Maria-Lompoc MSA, CA	Y	34380 FQ	50070 AW	71220 TQ	CABLS	10/01-12/01
Secondary School	Santa Rosa PMSA, CA	Y	35210 FQ	52350 AW	69950 TQ	CABLS	10/01-12/01
Secondary School	Stockton-Lodi MSA, CA	Y	32470 FQ	49090 AW	68850 TQ	CABLS	10/01-12/01
Secondary School	Vallejo-Fairfield-Napa PMSA, CA	Y	48430 FQ	63430 AW	89240 TQ	CABLS	10/01-12/01
Secondary School	Ventura PMSA, CA	Y	35710 FQ	53900 AW	73350 TQ	CABLS	10/01-12/01
Secondary School	Visalia-Tulare-Porterville MSA, CA	Y	37310 FQ	51370 AW	69510 TQ	CABLS	10/01-12/01
Secondary School	Colorado	Y	28470 FQ	44040 AW	63680 TQ	COBLS	10/01-12/01
Secondary School	Colorado Springs MSA, CO	Y	28870 FQ	42630 AW	57000 TQ	COBLS	10/01-12/01
Secondary School	Denver PMSA, CO	Y	29280 FQ	46650 AW	66640 TQ	COBLS	10/01-12/01
Secondary School	Greeley PMSA, CO	Y	25550 FQ	38950 AW	55750 TQ	COBLS	10/01-12/01
Secondary School	Connecticut	Y	34750 FQ	56380 AW	74150 TQ	CTBLS	10/01-12/01
Secondary School	Bridgeport PMSA, CT	Y	38160 FQ	56700 AW	72910 TQ	CTBLS	10/01-12/01
Secondary School	Danbury PMSA, CT	Y	36740 FQ	57450 AW	82540 TQ	CTBLS	10/01-12/01
Secondary School	Hartford MSA, CT	Y	31770 FQ	53160 AW	71650 TQ	CTBLS	10/01-12/01
Secondary School	New Haven-Meriden PMSA, CT	Y	36970 FQ	57650 AW	73660 TQ	CTBLS	10/01-12/01
Secondary School	New London-Norwich MSA, CT-RI	Y	37190 FQ	54910 AW	70120 TQ	CTBLS	10/01-12/01
Secondary School	Stamford-Norwalk PMSA, CT	Y	38120 FQ	63340 AW	87600 TQ	CTBLS	10/01-12/01
Secondary School	Waterbury PMSA, CT	Y	43170 FQ	63020 AW	77760 TQ	CTBLS	10/01-12/01
Secondary School	Delaware	Y	35980 FQ	55960 AW	78160 TQ	DEBLS	10/01-12/01
Secondary School	Wilmington-Newark PMSA, DE-MD	Y	35570 FQ	56640 AW	77780 TQ	DEBLS	10/01-12/01
Secondary School	Washington PMSA, DC-MD-VA-WV	Y	25660 FQ	44660 AW	69410 TQ	DCBLS	10/01-12/01
Secondary School	Florida	Y	28550 FQ	42600 AW	59240 TQ	FLBLS	10/01-12/01

AAW	Average annual wage	**AOH**	Average offered, high	**ASH**	Average starting, high	**H**	Hourly	**M**	Monthly	**S**	Special: hourly and annual
AE	Average entry wage	**AOL**	Average offered, low	**ASL**	Average starting, low	**HI**	Highest wage paid	**MTC**	Median total compensation	**TQ**	Third quartile wage
AEX	Average experienced wage	**APH**	Average pay, high range	**AW**	Average wage paid	**HR**	High end range	**MW**	Median wage paid	**W**	Weekly
AO	Average offered	**APL**	Average pay, low range	**FQ**	First quartile wage	**LR**	Low end range	**SQ**	Second quartile wage	**Y**	Yearly

Occupation/Type/Industry	Location	Per	Low	Mid	High	Source	Date
Special Education Teacher							
Secondary School	Fort Myers-Cape Coral MSA, FL	Y	33910 FQ	44580 AW	59280 TQ	FLBLS	10/01-12/01
Secondary School	Jacksonville MSA, FL	Y	20190 FQ	43660 AW	73230 TQ	FLBLS	10/01-12/01
Secondary School	Georgia	Y	30490 FQ	43860 AW	57400 TQ	GABLS	10/01-12/01
Secondary School	Atlanta MSA, GA	Y	31180 FQ	45250 AW	57820 TQ	GABLS	10/01-12/01
Secondary School	Augusta-Aiken MSA, GA-SC	Y	29690 FQ	40960 AW	54260 TQ	GABLS	10/01-12/01
Secondary School	Columbus MSA, GA-AL	Y	34870 FQ	46300 AW	58230 TQ	GABLS	10/01-12/01
Secondary School	Macon MSA, GA	Y	34420 FQ	46670 AW	58110 TQ	GABLS	10/01-12/01
Secondary School	Hawaii	Y	22630 FQ	35010 AW	49900 TQ	HIBLS	10/01-12/01
Secondary School	Illinois	Y	30170 FQ	50860 AW	81580 TQ	ILBLS	10/01-12/01
Secondary School	Champaign-Urbana MSA, IL	Y	28720 FQ	49410 AW	84000 TQ	ILBLS	10/01-12/01
Secondary School	Chicago PMSA, IL	Y	36710 FQ	59390 AW	88220 TQ	ILBLS	10/01-12/01
Secondary School	Peoria-Pekin MSA, IL	Y	30610 FQ	45500 AW	65460 TQ	ILBLS	10/01-12/01
Secondary School	Rockford MSA, IL	Y	27030 FQ	42440 AW	62390 TQ	ILBLS	10/01-12/01
Secondary School	Springfield MSA, IL	Y	28710 FQ	41990 AW	56620 TQ	ILBLS	10/01-12/01
Secondary School	Indiana	Y	31690 FQ	46970 AW	61060 TQ	INBLS	10/01-12/01
Secondary School	Elkhart-Goshen MSA, IN	Y	29900 FQ	42600 AW	57690 TQ	INBLS	10/01-12/01
Secondary School	Fort Wayne MSA, IN	Y	30490 FQ	45000 AW	57860 TQ	INBLS	10/01-12/01
Secondary School	Gary PMSA, IN	Y	32060 FQ	45260 AW	58300 TQ	INBLS	10/01-12/01
Secondary School	Indianapolis MSA, IN	Y	34230 FQ	51270 AW	70770 TQ	INBLS	10/01-12/01
Secondary School	Lafayette MSA, IN	Y	30190 FQ	40810 AW	53750 TQ	INBLS	10/01-12/01
Secondary School	Iowa	Y	22410 FQ	34330 AW	49800 TQ	IABLS	10/01-12/01
Secondary School	Davenport-Moline-Rock Island MSA, IA-IL	Y	30120 FQ	42550 AW	59220 TQ	IABLS	10/01-12/01
Secondary School	Des Moines MSA, IA	Y	12520 FQ	34150 AW	55970 TQ	IABLS	10/01-12/01
Secondary School	Kansas	Y	27920 FQ	37780 AW	49520 TQ	KSBLS	10/01-12/01
Secondary School	Wichita MSA, KS	Y	30760 FQ	39410 AW	49630 TQ	KSBLS	10/01-12/01
Secondary School	Kentucky	Y	27470 FQ	39850 AW	53910 TQ	KYBLS	10/01-12/01
Secondary School	Louisiana	Y	27920 FQ	38420 AW	47430 TQ	LABLS	10/01-12/01
Secondary School	Baton Rouge MSA, LA	Y	32000 FQ	41240 AW	48080 TQ	LABLS	10/01-12/01
Secondary School	Lafayette MSA, LA	Y	32580 FQ	42080 AW	52250 TQ	LABLS	10/01-12/01
Secondary School	New Orleans MSA, LA	Y	27460 FQ	39340 AW	46470 TQ	LABLS	10/01-12/01
Secondary School	Maine	Y	25270 FQ	38100 AW	52960 TQ	MEBLS	10/01-12/01
Secondary School	Portland MSA, ME	Y	27680 FQ	41630 AW	55430 TQ	MEBLS	10/01-12/01
Secondary School	Maryland	Y	28460 FQ	42160 AW	60400 TQ	MDBLS	10/01-12/01
Secondary School	Baltimore PMSA, MD	Y	27490 FQ	39760 AW	56050 TQ	MDBLS	10/01-12/01
Secondary School	Massachusetts	Y	25630 FQ	43700 AW	62610 TQ	MABLS	10/01-12/01
Secondary School	Boston PMSA, MA-NH	Y	29260 FQ	44740 AW	64000 TQ	MABLS	10/01-12/01
Secondary School	Brockton PMSA, MA	Y	29800 FQ	45820 AW	64990 TQ	MABLS	10/01-12/01
Secondary School	Lawrence PMSA, MA-NH	Y	25460 FQ	42480 AW	64660 TQ	MABLS	10/01-12/01
Secondary School	Lowell PMSA, MA-NH	Y	39220 FQ	54390 AW	69580 TQ	MABLS	10/01-12/01
Secondary School	New Bedford PMSA, MA	Y	31080 FQ	46230 AW	59510 TQ	MABLS	10/01-12/01
Secondary School	Springfield MSA, MA	Y	19700 FQ	33700 AW	56770 TQ	MABLS	10/01-12/01
Secondary School	Worcester PMSA, MA-CT	Y	32230 FQ	43440 AW	55450 TQ	MABLS	10/01-12/01
Secondary School	Michigan	Y	32770 FQ	52610 AW	70190 TQ	MIBLS	10/01-12/01
Secondary School	Ann Arbor PMSA, MI	Y	45020 FQ	56460 AW	72540 TQ	MIBLS	10/01-12/01
Secondary School	Detroit PMSA, MI	Y	31700 FQ	55090 AW	71610 TQ	MIBLS	10/01-12/01
Secondary School	Flint PMSA, MI	Y	28290 FQ	49070 AW	69050 TQ	MIBLS	10/01-12/01
Secondary School	Grand Rapids-Muskegon-Holland MSA, MI	Y	33180 FQ	53240 AW	69600 TQ	MIBLS	10/01-12/01
Secondary School	Kalamazoo-Battle Creek MSA, MI	Y	29520 FQ	46930 AW	64240 TQ	MIBLS	10/01-12/01
Secondary School	Lansing-East Lansing MSA, MI	Y	34070 FQ	50950 AW	70340 TQ	MIBLS	10/01-12/01
Secondary School	Saginaw-Bay City-Midland MSA, MI	Y	38210 FQ	58870 AW	77070 TQ	MIBLS	10/01-12/01
Secondary School	Minnesota	Y	29130 FQ	41710 AW	57570 TQ	MNBLS	10/01-12/01
Secondary School	Duluth-Superior MSA, MN-WI	Y	30920 FQ	43750 AW	56390 TQ	MNBLS	10/01-12/01
Secondary School	Minneapolis-St. Paul MSA, MN-WI	Y	30200 FQ	43550 AW	61000 TQ	MNBLS	10/01-12/01
Secondary School	St. Cloud MSA, MN	Y	28670 FQ	40220 AW	56680 TQ	MNBLS	10/01-12/01
Secondary School	Mississippi	Y	24660 FQ	33060 AW	43930 TQ	MSBLS	10/01-12/01
Secondary School	Biloxi-Gulfport-Pascagoula MSA, MS	Y	25040 FQ	32290 AW	42610 TQ	MSBLS	10/01-12/01
Secondary School	Jackson MSA, MS	Y	23390 FQ	32080 AW	43800 TQ	MSBLS	10/01-12/01
Secondary School	Missouri	Y	23370 FQ	33860 AW	47930 TQ	MOBLS	10/01-12/01
Secondary School	Kansas City MSA, MO-KS	Y	24560 FQ	37230 AW	53580 TQ	MOBLS	10/01-12/01
Secondary School	St. Louis MSA, MO-IL	Y	28500 FQ	38870 AW	54600 TQ	MOBLS	10/01-12/01
Secondary School	Springfield MSA, MO	Y	23870 FQ	31340 AW	42740 TQ	MOBLS	10/01-12/01
Secondary School	Montana	Y	21550 FQ	33300 AW	44770 TQ	MTBLS	10/01-12/01
Secondary School	Billings MSA, MT	Y	26120 FQ	33260 AW	41290 TQ	MTBLS	10/01-12/01
Secondary School	Nebraska	Y	24920 FQ	36690 AW	51500 TQ	NEBLS	10/01-12/01

AAW	Average annual wage	**AOH**	Average offered, high	**ASH**	Average starting, high	**H**	Hourly	**M**	Monthly	**S**	Special: hourly and annual
AE	Average entry wage	**AOL**	Average offered, low	**ASL**	Average starting, low	**HI**	Highest wage paid	**MTC**	Median total compensation	**TQ**	Third quartile wage
AEX	Average experienced wage	**APH**	Average pay, high range	**AW**	Average wage paid	**HR**	High end range	**MW**	Median wage paid	**W**	Weekly
AO	Average offered	**APL**	Average pay, low range	**FQ**	First quartile wage	**LR**	Low end range	**SQ**	Second quartile wage	**Y**	Yearly

Occupation/Type/Industry	Location	Per	Low	Mid	High	Source	Date
Special Education Teacher							
Secondary School	Lincoln MSA, NE	Y	25420 FQ	36110 AW	49190 TQ	NEBLS	10/01-12/01
Secondary School	Omaha MSA, NE-IA	Y	22780 FQ	38710 AW	56920 TQ	NEBLS	10/01-12/01
Secondary School	New Hampshire	Y	24710 FQ	34320 AW	50700 TQ	NHBLS	10/01-12/01
Secondary School	Manchester PMSA, NH	Y	25130 FQ	39160 AW	55080 TQ	NHBLS	10/01-12/01
Secondary School	Nashua PMSA, NH	Y	25550 FQ	37080 AW	50780 TQ	NHBLS	10/01-12/01
Secondary School	Portsmouth-Rochester PMSA, NH-ME	Y	25700 FQ	37330 AW	52740 TQ	NHBLS	10/01-12/01
Secondary School	New Jersey	Y	33920 FQ	51890 AW	73940 TQ	NJBLS	10/01-12/01
Secondary School	Atlantic-Cape May PMSA, NJ	Y	36170 FQ	57350 AW	84820 TQ	NJBLS	10/01-12/01
Secondary School	Bergen-Passaic PMSA, NJ	Y	36370 FQ	54120 AW	82250 TQ	NJBLS	10/01-12/01
Secondary School	Jersey City PMSA, NJ	Y	36530 FQ	60940 AW	87790 TQ	NJBLS	10/01-12/01
Secondary School	Middlesex-Somerset-Hunterdon PMSA, NJ	Y	33480 FQ	53740 AW	75300 TQ	NJBLS	10/01-12/01
Secondary School	Monmouth-Ocean PMSA, NJ	Y	31570 FQ	47970 AW	69570 TQ	NJBLS	10/01-12/01
Secondary School	Newark PMSA, NJ	Y	36600 FQ	52890 AW	71760 TQ	NJBLS	10/01-12/01
Secondary School	Trenton PMSA, NJ	Y	35480 FQ	51500 AW	72000 TQ	NJBLS	10/01-12/01
Secondary School	New Mexico	Y	28440 FQ	36900 AW	50740 TQ	NMBLS	10/01-12/01
Secondary School	Las Cruces MSA, NM	Y	30660 FQ	43880 AW	55460 TQ	NMBLS	10/01-12/01
Secondary School	New York	Y	32770 FQ	61440 AW	100900 TQ	NYBLS	10/01-12/01
Secondary School	Albany-Schenectady-Troy MSA, NY	Y	26620 FQ	44500 AW	66700 TQ	NYBLS	10/01-12/01
Secondary School	Binghamton MSA, NY	Y	32660 FQ	45620 AW	60450 TQ	NYBLS	10/01-12/01
Secondary School	Buffalo-Niagara Falls MSA, NY	Y	35370 FQ	52610 AW	73920 TQ	NYBLS	10/01-12/01
Secondary School	Dutchess County PMSA, NY	Y	23920 FQ	42090 AW	74480 TQ	NYBLS	10/01-12/01
Secondary School	Nassau-Suffolk PMSA, NY	Y	40380 FQ	67330 AW	95240 TQ	NYBLS	10/01-12/01
Secondary School	Newburgh PMSA, NY-PA	Y	36010 FQ	53610 AW	72880 TQ	NYBLS	10/01-12/01
Secondary School	Rochester MSA, NY	Y	30460 FQ	47870 AW	73860 TQ	NYBLS	10/01-12/01
Secondary School	Syracuse MSA, NY	Y	35140 FQ	44040 AW	56810 TQ	NYBLS	10/01-12/01
Secondary School	Utica-Rome MSA, NY	Y	29910 FQ	51560 AW	88420 TQ	NYBLS	10/01-12/01
Secondary School	North Carolina	Y	25910 FQ	37620 AW	51010 TQ	NCBLS	10/01-12/01
Secondary School	Asheville MSA, NC	Y	29740 FQ	39530 AW	52110 TQ	NCBLS	10/01-12/01
Secondary School	Charlotte-Gastonia-Rock Hill MSA, NC-SC	Y	27360 FQ	39940 AW	54100 TQ	NCBLS	10/01-12/01
Secondary School	Fayetteville MSA, NC	Y	25170 FQ	36150 AW	50360 TQ	NCBLS	10/01-12/01
Secondary School	Greensboro-Winston-Salem-High Point MSA, NC	Y	25730 FQ	36440 AW	49440 TQ	NCBLS	10/01-12/01
Secondary School	Hickory-Morganton-Lenoir MSA, NC	Y	26180 FQ	37570 AW	45660 TQ	NCBLS	10/01-12/01
Secondary School	Raleigh-Durham-Chapel Hill MSA, NC	Y	28890 FQ	40870 AW	57480 TQ	NCBLS	10/01-12/01
Secondary School	Wilmington MSA, NC	Y	26200 FQ	36220 AW	47280 TQ	NCBLS	10/01-12/01
Secondary School	North Dakota	Y	23900 FQ	31710 AW	43210 TQ	NDBLS	10/01-12/01
Secondary School	Fargo-Moorhead MSA, ND-MN	Y	25640 FQ	36350 AW	47900 TQ	NDBLS	10/01-12/01
Secondary School	Ohio	Y	27370 FQ	42930 AW	59380 TQ	OHBLS	10/01-12/01
Secondary School	Akron PMSA, OH	Y	32000 FQ	45640 AW	60330 TQ	OHBLS	10/01-12/01
Secondary School	Canton-Massillon MSA, OH	Y	27900 FQ	42750 AW	57820 TQ	OHBLS	10/01-12/01
Secondary School	Cincinnati PMSA, OH-KY-IN	Y	19330 FQ	38840 AW	58070 TQ	OHBLS	10/01-12/01
Secondary School	Cleveland-Lorain-Elyria PMSA, OH	Y	28040 FQ	46260 AW	67010 TQ	OHBLS	10/01-12/01
Secondary School	Columbus MSA, OH	Y	32310 FQ	46170 AW	61740 TQ	OHBLS	10/01-12/01
Secondary School	Dayton-Springfield MSA, OH	Y	30930 FQ	44010 AW	56930 TQ	OHBLS	10/01-12/01
Secondary School	Hamilton-Middletown PMSA, OH	Y	32500 FQ	44910 AW	56270 TQ	OHBLS	10/01-12/01
Secondary School	Mansfield MSA, OH	Y	26570 FQ	38690 AW	53990 TQ	OHBLS	10/01-12/01
Secondary School	Toledo MSA, OH	Y	28150 FQ	41860 AW	56750 TQ	OHBLS	10/01-12/01
Secondary School	Youngstown-Warren MSA, OH	Y	21380 FQ	36800 AW	53210 TQ	OHBLS	10/01-12/01
Secondary School	Oklahoma	Y	28020 FQ	35710 AW	44690 TQ	OKBLS	10/01-12/01
Secondary School	Oklahoma City MSA, OK	Y	26290 FQ	35340 AW	44970 TQ	OKBLS	10/01-12/01
Secondary School	Tulsa MSA, OK	Y	28410 FQ	36450 AW	46410 TQ	OKBLS	10/01-12/01
Secondary School	Oregon	Y	30460 FQ	43030 AW	60230 TQ	ORBLS	10/01-12/01
Secondary School	Eugene-Springfield MSA, OR	Y	30950 FQ	43640 AW	55630 TQ	ORBLS	10/01-12/01
Secondary School	Medford-Ashland MSA, OR	Y	30360 FQ	44240 AW	61910 TQ	ORBLS	10/01-12/01
Secondary School	Portland-Vancouver PMSA, OR-WA	Y	30440 FQ	44050 AW	62770 TQ	ORBLS	10/01-12/01
Secondary School	Salem PMSA, OR	Y	31940 FQ	42430 AW	55620 TQ	ORBLS	10/01-12/01
Secondary School	Pennsylvania	Y	29190 FQ	46100 AW	66900 TQ	PABLS	10/01-12/01
Secondary School	Allentown-Bethlehem-Easton MSA, PA	Y	30710 FQ	46050 AW	65580 TQ	PABLS	10/01-12/01
Secondary School	Erie MSA, PA	Y	31980 FQ	44870 AW	60140 TQ	PABLS	10/01-12/01

AAW	Average annual wage	**AOH**	Average offered, high	**ASH**	Average starting, high	**H**	Hourly	**M**	Monthly	**S**	Special: hourly and annual
AE	Average entry wage	**AOL**	Average offered, low	**ASL**	Average starting, low	**HI**	Highest wage paid	**MTC**	Median total compensation	**TQ**	Third quartile wage
AEX	Average experienced wage	**APH**	Average pay, high range	**AW**	Average wage paid	**HR**	High end range	**MW**	Median wage paid	**W**	Weekly
AO	Average offered	**APL**	Average pay, low range	**FQ**	First quartile wage	**LR**	Low end range	**SQ**	Second quartile wage	**Y**	Yearly

Occupation/Type/Industry	Location	Per	Low	Mid	High	Source	Date
Special Education Teacher							
Secondary School	Harrisburg-Lebanon-Carlisle MSA, PA	Y	32880 FQ	45870 AW	58530 TQ	PABLS	10/01-12/01
Secondary School	Johnstown MSA, PA	Y	32250 FQ	45480 AW	58740 TQ	PABLS	10/01-12/01
Secondary School	Lancaster MSA, PA	Y	32100 FQ	45380 AW	56400 TQ	PABLS	10/01-12/01
Secondary School	Philadelphia PMSA, PA-NJ	Y	31310 FQ	48580 AW	73340 TQ	PABLS	10/01-12/01
Secondary School	Pittsburgh MSA, PA	Y	26810 FQ	46820 AW	70270 TQ	PABLS	10/01-12/01
Secondary School	Reading MSA, PA	Y	32310 FQ	48280 AW	67030 TQ	PABLS	10/01-12/01
Secondary School	Scranton-Wilkes-Barre-Hazleton MSA, PA	Y	31500 FQ	49270 AW	68060 TQ	PABLS	10/01-12/01
Secondary School	York MSA, PA	Y	29820 FQ	44670 AW	64420 TQ	PABLS	10/01-12/01
Secondary School	Rhode Island	Y	33470 FQ	51750 AW	69620 TQ	RIBLS	10/01-12/01
Secondary School	Providence-Fall River-Warwick MSA, RI-MA	Y	33030 FQ	50710 AW	69090 TQ	RIBLS	10/01-12/01
Secondary School	South Carolina	Y	28240 FQ	39640 AW	51980 TQ	SCBLS	10/01-12/01
Secondary School	Charleston-North Charleston MSA, SC	Y	29990 FQ	39840 AW	45580 TQ	SCBLS	10/01-12/01
Secondary School	Columbia MSA, SC	Y	31140 FQ	40590 AW	51070 TQ	SCBLS	10/01-12/01
Secondary School	Greenville-Spartanburg-Anderson MSA, SC	Y	25480 FQ	37700 AW	50940 TQ	SCBLS	10/01-12/01
Secondary School	South Dakota	Y	24590 FQ	32570 AW	43250 TQ	SDBLS	10/01-12/01
Secondary School	Tennessee	Y	28130 FQ	36910 AW	49080 TQ	TNBLS	10/01-12/01
Secondary School	Chattanooga MSA, TN-GA	Y	27630 FQ	37530 AW	51260 TQ	TNBLS	10/01-12/01
Secondary School	Johnson City-Kingsport-Bristol MSA, TN-VA	Y	25620 FQ	35350 AW	45820 TQ	TNBLS	10/01-12/01
Secondary School	Knoxville MSA, TN	Y	29930 FQ	40380 AW	54210 TQ	TNBLS	10/01-12/01
Secondary School	Memphis MSA, TN-AR-MS	Y	28740 FQ	39210 AW	55030 TQ	TNBLS	10/01-12/01
Secondary School	Nashville MSA, TN	Y	29000 FQ	35840 AW	44340 TQ	TNBLS	10/01-12/01
Secondary School	Texas	Y	28960 FQ	39880 AW	53890 TQ	TXBLS	10/01-12/01
Secondary School	Austin-San Marcos MSA, TX	Y	28240 FQ	37910 AW	50130 TQ	TXBLS	10/01-12/01
Secondary School	Beaumont-Port Arthur MSA, TX	Y	29860 FQ	39670 AW	53060 TQ	TXBLS	10/01-12/01
Secondary School	Brazoria PMSA, TX	Y	30090 FQ	40470 AW	53280 TQ	TXBLS	10/01-12/01
Secondary School	Brownsville-Harlingen-San Benito MSA, TX	Y	34610 FQ	42840 AW	53730 TQ	TXBLS	10/01-12/01
Secondary School	Dallas PMSA, TX	Y	25270 FQ	37990 AW	51780 TQ	TXBLS	10/01-12/01
Secondary School	Fort Worth-Arlington PMSA, TX	Y	31720 FQ	44210 AW	57990 TQ	TXBLS	10/01-12/01
Secondary School	Houston PMSA, TX	Y	30880 FQ	42300 AW	56280 TQ	TXBLS	10/01-12/01
Secondary School	Killeen-Temple MSA, TX	Y	26200 FQ	37740 AW	54010 TQ	TXBLS	10/01-12/01
Secondary School	Laredo MSA, TX	Y	30010 FQ	41960 AW	55160 TQ	TXBLS	10/01-12/01
Secondary School	Longview-Marshall MSA, TX	Y	27540 FQ	37620 AW	45910 TQ	TXBLS	10/01-12/01
Secondary School	McAllen-Edinburg-Mission MSA, TX	Y	30200 FQ	41130 AW	54580 TQ	TXBLS	10/01-12/01
Secondary School	Odessa-Midland MSA, TX	Y	29560 FQ	36780 AW	50460 TQ	TXBLS	10/01-12/01
Secondary School	San Antonio MSA, TX	Y	31370 FQ	42810 AW	57090 TQ	TXBLS	10/01-12/01
Secondary School	Waco MSA, TX	Y	26710 FQ	38430 AW	49450 TQ	TXBLS	10/01-12/01
Secondary School	Utah	Y	26440 FQ	41410 AW	56380 TQ	UTBLS	10/01-12/01
Secondary School	Provo-Orem MSA, UT	Y	29290 FQ	44050 AW	56140 TQ	UTBLS	10/01-12/01
Secondary School	Salt Lake City-Ogden MSA, UT	Y	27390 FQ	42280 AW	57000 TQ	UTBLS	10/01-12/01
Secondary School	Vermont	Y	26520 FQ	41070 AW	56410 TQ	VTBLS	10/01-12/01
Secondary School	Burlington MSA, VT	Y	29860 FQ	43780 AW	58180 TQ	VTBLS	10/01-12/01
Secondary School	Virginia	Y	27660 FQ	41460 AW	60800 TQ	VABLS	10/01-12/01
Secondary School	Lynchburg MSA, VA	Y	25210 FQ	38520 AW	55790 TQ	VABLS	10/01-12/01
Secondary School	Norfolk-Virginia Beach-Newport News MSA, VA-NC	Y	29030 FQ	36940 AW	49700 TQ	VABLS	10/01-12/01
Secondary School	Richmond-Petersburg MSA, VA	Y	35660 FQ	45130 AW	58610 TQ	VABLS	10/01-12/01
Secondary School	Washington	Y	28550 FQ	42970 AW	56840 TQ	WABLS	10/01-12/01
Secondary School	Bremerton PMSA, WA	Y	28220 FQ	40080 AW	54260 TQ	WABLS	10/01-12/01
Secondary School	Olympia PMSA, WA	Y	28850 FQ	42410 AW	56610 TQ	WABLS	10/01-12/01
Secondary School	Richland-Kennewick-Pasco MSA, WA	Y	28790 FQ	42910 AW	56700 TQ	WABLS	10/01-12/01
Secondary School	Seattle-Bellevue-Everett PMSA, WA	Y	27010 FQ	42380 AW	57400 TQ	WABLS	10/01-12/01
Secondary School	Spokane MSA, WA	Y	32910 FQ	46580 AW	58130 TQ	WABLS	10/01-12/01
Secondary School	Tacoma PMSA, WA	Y	29190 FQ	43580 AW	56940 TQ	WABLS	10/01-12/01
Secondary School	Yakima MSA, WA	Y	26370 FQ	40180 AW	55390 TQ	WABLS	10/01-12/01
Secondary School	West Virginia	Y	27370 FQ	35750 AW	44320 TQ	WVBLS	10/01-12/01

AAW Average annual wage, **AE** Average entry wage, **AEX** Average experienced wage, **AO** Average offered, **AOH** Average offered, high, **AOL** Average offered, low, **APH** Average pay, high range, **APL** Average pay, low range, **ASH** Average starting, high, **ASL** Average starting, low, **AW** Average wage paid, **FQ** First quartile wage, **H** Hourly, **HI** Highest wage paid, **HR** High end range, **LR** Low end range, **M** Monthly, **MTC** Median total compensation, **MW** Median wage paid, **SQ** Second quartile wage, **S** Special: hourly and annual, **TQ** Third quartile wage, **W** Weekly, **Y** Yearly

Occupation/Type/Industry	Location	Per	Low	Mid	High	Source	Date
Special Education Teacher							
Secondary School	Huntington-Ashland MSA, WV-KY-OH	Y	27530 FQ	37290 AW	48400 TQ	WVBLS	10/01-12/01
Secondary School	Wisconsin	Y	29470 FQ	42800 AW	57350 TQ	WIBLS	10/01-12/01
Secondary School	Appleton-Oshkosh-Neenah MSA, WI	Y	31630 FQ	45150 AW	58610 TQ	WIBLS	10/01-12/01
Secondary School	Madison MSA, WI	Y	27990 FQ	40790 AW	55880 TQ	WIBLS	10/01-12/01
Secondary School	Milwaukee-Waukesha PMSA, WI	Y	30780 FQ	45800 AW	60510 TQ	WIBLS	10/01-12/01
Secondary School	Wyoming	Y	25260 FQ	34010 AW	44280 TQ	WYBLS	10/01-12/01
Specifications Writer							
Web Design	United States	Y		60216 AW		DFMAR	1/01-1/02
Speech-Language Pathologist	United States	Y		39700 AW		FREEP1	1/00-1/00
	Alabama	Y	29850 FQ	46350 AW	69290 TQ	ALBLS	10/01-12/01
	Alaska	Y	40620 FQ	56320 AW	72770 TQ	AKBLS	10/01-12/01
	Arizona	Y	25980 FQ	45280 AW	70300 TQ	AZBLS	10/01-12/01
	Arkansas	Y	29160 FQ	41770 AW	57690 TQ	ARBLS	10/01-12/01
	California	Y	39120 FQ	58860 AW	80800 TQ	CABLS	10/01-12/01
	Colorado	Y	33550 FQ	49420 AW	67260 TQ	COBLS	10/01-12/01
	Connecticut	Y	39400 FQ	59060 AW	78790 TQ	CTBLS	10/01-12/01
	Delaware	Y	38310 FQ	59590 AW	83800 TQ	DEBLS	10/01-12/01
	District of Columbia	Y	32710 FQ	52550 AW	76850 TQ	DCBLS	10/01-12/01
	Florida	Y	31770 FQ	49650 AW	69410 TQ	FLBLS	10/01-12/01
	Georgia	Y	34920 FQ	51300 AW	74590 TQ	GABLS	10/01-12/01
	Hawaii	Y	38100 FQ	48770 AW	58970 TQ	HIBLS	10/01-12/01
	Idaho	Y	32480 FQ	44520 AW	57050 TQ	IDBLS	10/01-12/01
	Illinois	Y	31000 FQ	48840 AW	71730 TQ	ILBLS	10/01-12/01
	Indiana	Y	30870 FQ	47650 AW	68100 TQ	INBLS	10/01-12/01
	Iowa	Y	31660 FQ	46050 AW	59380 TQ	IABLS	10/01-12/01
	Kansas	Y	30190 FQ	43690 AW	60850 TQ	KSBLS	10/01-12/01
	Kentucky	Y	30470 FQ	44370 AW	59510 TQ	KYBLS	10/01-12/01
	Louisiana	Y	34650 FQ	51430 AW	73520 TQ	LABLS	10/01-12/01
	Maine	Y	30410 FQ	43210 AW	57560 TQ	MEBLS	10/01-12/01
	Maryland	Y	36400 FQ	56140 AW	84880 TQ	MDBLS	10/01-12/01
	Massachusetts	Y	28090 FQ	53010 AW	80850 TQ	MABLS	10/01-12/01
	Michigan	Y	36940 FQ	53290 AW	73370 TQ	MIBLS	10/01-12/01
	Minnesota	Y	32470 FQ	46010 AW	60190 TQ	MNBLS	10/01-12/01
	Mississippi	Y	27230 FQ	41570 AW	59700 TQ	MSBLS	10/01-12/01
	Missouri	Y	26260 FQ	49930 AW	77110 TQ	MOBLS	10/01-12/01
	Montana	Y	27770 FQ	45420 AW	60770 TQ	MTBLS	10/01-12/01
	Nebraska	Y	26700 FQ	40940 AW	58940 TQ	NEBLS	10/01-12/01
	Nevada	Y	42290 FQ	63430 AW	89020 TQ	NVBLS	10/01-12/01
	New Hampshire	Y	35930 FQ	52330 AW	71820 TQ	NHBLS	10/01-12/01
	New Jersey	Y	38650 FQ	58170 AW	83040 TQ	NJBLS	10/01-12/01
	New Mexico	Y	29720 FQ	45130 AW	66300 TQ	NMBLS	10/01-12/01
	New York	Y	35410 FQ	52620 AW	74300 TQ	NYBLS	10/01-12/01
	North Carolina	Y	34490 FQ	49970 AW	68860 TQ	NCBLS	10/01-12/01
	North Dakota	Y	26280 FQ	36700 AW	47870 TQ	NDBLS	10/01-12/01
	Ohio	Y	34990 FQ	52140 AW	72400 TQ	OHBLS	10/01-12/01
	Oklahoma	Y	28750 FQ	45900 AW	66340 TQ	OKBLS	10/01-12/01
	Oregon	Y	35290 FQ	49240 AW	60780 TQ	ORBLS	10/01-12/01
	Pennsylvania	Y	36240 FQ	54000 AW	74110 TQ	PABLS	10/01-12/01
	Rhode Island	Y	37240 FQ	54890 AW	74160 TQ	RIBLS	10/01-12/01
	South Carolina	Y	25980 FQ	49660 AW	77120 TQ	SCBLS	10/01-12/01
	South Dakota	Y	27390 FQ	37180 AW	50810 TQ	SDBLS	10/01-12/01
	Tennessee	Y	30340 FQ	45340 AW	65250 TQ	TNBLS	10/01-12/01
	Texas	Y	30870 FQ	45280 AW	61140 TQ	TXBLS	10/01-12/01
	Utah	Y	26850 FQ	43820 AW	63480 TQ	UTBLS	10/01-12/01
	Vermont	Y	32020 FQ	46990 AW	64010 TQ	VTBLS	10/01-12/01
	Virginia	Y	30030 FQ	47510 AW	67830 TQ	VABLS	10/01-12/01
	Washington	Y	34520 FQ	50410 AW	69300 TQ	WABLS	10/01-12/01
	West Virginia	Y	30960 FQ	42560 AW	57580 TQ	WVBLS	10/01-12/01
	Wisconsin	Y	32950 FQ	48040 AW	61430 TQ	WIBLS	10/01-12/01
	Wyoming	Y	30040 FQ	43230 AW	57460 TQ	WYBLS	10/01-12/01
	Puerto Rico	Y	14690 FQ	28540 AW	50060 TQ	PRBLS	10/01-12/01
Staff Member							
Community College	United States	Y		52490 AW		MSW	1/99-1/00
Stationary Engineer and Boiler Operator	Alabama	H	10.07 FQ	18.32 AW	27.80 TQ	ALBLS	10/01-12/01

AAW	Average annual wage	**AOH**	Average offered, high	**ASH**	Average starting, high	**H**	Hourly	**M**	Monthly	**S**	Special: hourly and annual
AE	Average entry wage	**AOL**	Average offered, low	**ASL**	Average starting, low	**HI**	Highest wage paid	**MTC**	Median total compensation	**TQ**	Third quartile wage
AEX	Average experienced wage	**APH**	Average pay, high range	**AW**	Average wage paid	**HR**	High end range	**MW**	Median wage paid	**W**	Weekly
AO	Average offered	**APL**	Average pay, low range	**FQ**	First quartile wage	**LR**	Low end range	**SQ**	Second quartile wage	**Y**	Yearly

Occupation/Type/Industry	Location	Per	Low	Mid	High	Source	Date
Stationary Engineer and Boiler Operator	Alaska	H	20.09 FQ	26.53 AW	33.51 TQ	AKBLS	10/01-12/01
	Arizona	H	10.63 FQ	19.83 AW	28.47 TQ	AZBLS	10/01-12/01
	Arkansas	H	11.08 FQ	16.63 AW	24.57 TQ	ARBLS	10/01-12/01
	California	H	14.26 FQ	23.79 AW	33.08 TQ	CABLS	10/01-12/01
	Colorado	H	12.79 FQ	20.16 AW	26.76 TQ	COBLS	10/01-12/01
	Connecticut	H	14.73 FQ	20.71 AW	28.44 TQ	CTBLS	10/01-12/01
	Delaware	H	15.91 FQ	23.02 AW	32.93 TQ	DEBLS	10/01-12/01
	District of Columbia	H	16.14 FQ	22.89 AW	29.21 TQ	DCBLS	10/01-12/01
	Florida	H	10.53 FQ	16.01 AW	23.70 TQ	FLBLS	10/01-12/01
	Georgia	H	10.88 FQ	18.81 AW	27.26 TQ	GABLS	10/01-12/01
	Hawaii	H	11.42 FQ	17.60 AW	30.46 TQ	HIBLS	10/01-12/01
	Idaho	H	11.08 FQ	16.21 AW	21.53 TQ	IDBLS	10/01-12/01
	Illinois	H	12.67 FQ	23.44 AW	32.84 TQ	ILBLS	10/01-12/01
	Indiana	H	10.08 FQ	18.84 AW	31.48 TQ	INBLS	10/01-12/01
	Iowa	H	12.59 FQ	18.17 AW	23.49 TQ	IABLS	10/01-12/01
	Kansas	H	11.41 FQ	18.68 AW	27.27 TQ	KSBLS	10/01-12/01
	Kentucky	H	10.88 FQ	18.78 AW	27.73 TQ	KYBLS	10/01-12/01
	Louisiana	H	9.87 FQ	17.47 AW	26.25 TQ	LABLS	10/01-12/01
	Maine	H	10.66 FQ	17.79 AW	26.14 TQ	MEBLS	10/01-12/01
	Maryland	H	14.31 FQ	20.86 AW	28.21 TQ	MDBLS	10/01-12/01
	Massachusetts	H	13.75 FQ	19.76 AW	27.80 TQ	MABLS	10/01-12/01
	Michigan	H	16.88 FQ	24.06 AW	32.48 TQ	MIBLS	10/01-12/01
	Minnesota	H	14.35 FQ	20.17 AW	26.74 TQ	MNBLS	10/01-12/01
	Mississippi	H	10.93 FQ	18.71 AW	27.03 TQ	MSBLS	10/01-12/01
	Missouri	H	12.81 FQ	18.96 AW	25.44 TQ	MOBLS	10/01-12/01
	Montana	H	11.34 FQ	17.12 AW	25.11 TQ	MTBLS	10/01-12/01
	Nebraska	H	12.32 FQ	16.57 AW	21.43 TQ	NEBLS	10/01-12/01
	Nevada	H	11.32 FQ	19.90 AW	26.86 TQ	NVBLS	10/01-12/01
	New Hampshire	H	12.44 FQ	17.44 AW	22.29 TQ	NHBLS	10/01-12/01
	New Jersey	H	14.69 FQ	20.40 AW	26.87 TQ	NJBLS	10/01-12/01
	New Mexico	H	10.22 FQ	17.24 AW	25.92 TQ	NMBLS	10/01 12/01
	New York	H	14.79 FQ	23.42 AW	34.22 TQ	NYBLS	10/01-12/01
	North Carolina	H	9.70 FQ	16.95 AW	26.55 TQ	NCBLS	10/01-12/01
	North Dakota	H	11.09 FQ	16.02 AW	22.37 TQ	NDBLS	10/01-12/01
	Ohio	H	13.38 FQ	18.74 AW	25.91 TQ	OHBLS	10/01-12/01
	Oklahoma	H	11.32 FQ	17.54 AW	24.69 TQ	OKBLS	10/01-12/01
	Oregon	H	12.21 FQ	17.98 AW	25.41 TQ	ORBLS	10/01-12/01
	Pennsylvania	H	13.46 FQ	20.59 AW	31.26 TQ	PABLS	10/01-12/01
	Rhode Island	H	12.87 FQ	19.20 AW	25.83 TQ	RIBLS	10/01-12/01
	South Carolina	H	10.88 FQ	20.56 AW	34.26 TQ	SCBLS	10/01-12/01
	South Dakota	H	8.46 FQ	13.59 AW	19.65 TQ	SDBLS	10/01-12/01
	Tennessee	H	10.85 FQ	17.73 AW	25.07 TQ	TNBLS	10/01-12/01
	Texas	H	10.35 FQ	18.27 AW	27.06 TQ	TXBLS	10/01-12/01
	Utah	H	11.24 FQ	18.24 AW	23.82 TQ	UTBLS	10/01-12/01
	Vermont	H	9.05 FQ	14.77 AW	20.85 TQ	VTBLS	10/01-12/01
	Virginia	H	10.01 FQ	17.76 AW	26.28 TQ	VABLS	10/01-12/01
	Washington	H	15.31 FQ	21.49 AW	28.12 TQ	WABLS	10/01-12/01
	West Virginia	H	10.84 FQ	18.93 AW	26.23 TQ	WVBLS	10/01-12/01
	Wisconsin	H	12.43 FQ	18.10 AW	25.53 TQ	WIBLS	10/01-12/01
	Wyoming	H	11.35 FQ	18.75 AW	25.93 TQ	WYBLS	10/01-12/01
	Puerto Rico	H	6.85 FQ	12.08 AW	19.10 TQ	PRBLS	10/01-12/01
	Virgin Islands	H	10.86 FQ	17.35 AW	30.21 TQ	VIBLS	10/01-12/01
Statistical Assistant	Alabama	H	7.82 FQ	12.69 AW	19.13 TQ	ALBLS	10/01-12/01
	Alaska	H	11.80 FQ	17.40 AW	22.95 TQ	AKBLS	10/01-12/01
	Arizona	H	9.09 FQ	13.12 AW	18.96 TQ	AZBLS	10/01-12/01
	Arkansas	H	6.83 FQ	9.63 AW	13.44 TQ	ARBLS	10/01-12/01
	California	H	12.19 FQ	16.36 AW	22.06 TQ	CABLS	10/01-12/01
	Colorado	H	12.85 FQ	17.50 AW	21.96 TQ	COBLS	10/01-12/01
	Connecticut	H	11.96 FQ	21.18 AW	33.81 TQ	CTBLS	10/01-12/01
	Delaware	H	8.83 FQ	17.69 AW	25.78 TQ	DEBLS	10/01-12/01
	District of Columbia	H	10.10 FQ	17.41 AW	22.79 TQ	DCBLS	10/01-12/01
	Florida	H	8.27 FQ	12.27 AW	17.19 TQ	FLBLS	10/01-12/01
	Georgia	H	8.97 FQ	12.24 AW	16.74 TQ	GABLS	10/01-12/01
	Hawaii	H	9.35 FQ	13.79 AW	20.36 TQ	HIBLS	10/01-12/01
	Idaho	H	10.91 FQ	16.70 AW	21.41 TQ	IDBLS	10/01-12/01
	Illinois	H	10.70 FQ	16.87 AW	22.29 TQ	ILBLS	10/01-12/01
	Indiana	H	9.37 FQ	12.94 AW	16.76 TQ	INBLS	10/01-12/01
	Iowa	H	8.78 FQ	11.37 AW	18.19 TQ	IABLS	10/01-12/01
	Kansas	H	11.24 FQ	16.16 AW	27.24 TQ	KSBLS	10/01-12/01
	Kentucky	H	8.10 FQ	13.37 AW	20.52 TQ	KYBLS	10/01-12/01

AAW Average annual wage **AOH** Average offered, high **ASH** Average starting, high **H** Hourly **M** Monthly **S** Special: hourly and annual
AE Average entry wage **AOL** Average offered, low **ASL** Average starting, low **HI** Highest wage paid **MTC** Median total compensation **TQ** Third quartile wage
AEX Average experienced wage **APH** Average pay, high range **AW** Average wage paid **HR** High end range **MW** Median wage paid **W** Weekly
AO Average offered **APL** Average pay, low range **FQ** First quartile wage **LR** Low end range **SQ** Second quartile wage **Y** Yearly

Occupation/Type/Industry	Location	Per	Low	Mid	High	Source	Date
Statistical Assistant	Louisiana	H	9.57 FQ	15.64 AW	23.32 TQ	LABLS	10/01-12/01
	Maine	H	11.60 FQ	19.07 AW	33.10 TQ	MEBLS	10/01-12/01
	Maryland	H	11.33 FQ	16.64 AW	22.39 TQ	MDBLS	10/01-12/01
	Massachusetts	H	9.99 FQ	15.15 AW	20.81 TQ	MABLS	10/01-12/01
	Michigan	H	7.84 FQ	15.43 AW	21.60 TQ	MIBLS	10/01-12/01
	Minnesota	H	11.87 FQ	17.02 AW	21.10 TQ	MNBLS	10/01-12/01
	Missouri	H	10.17 FQ	18.58 AW	32.97 TQ	MOBLS	10/01-12/01
	Nebraska	H	9.26 FQ	13.85 AW	20.78 TQ	NEBLS	10/01-12/01
	Nevada	H	8.98 FQ	14.17 AW	20.39 TQ	NVBLS	10/01-12/01
	New Hampshire	H	9.10 FQ	14.42 AW	22.33 TQ	NHBLS	10/01-12/01
	New Jersey	H	8.57 FQ	17.29 AW	25.62 TQ	NJBLS	10/01-12/01
	New Mexico	H	11.57 FQ	17.72 AW	21.76 TQ	NMBLS	10/01-12/01
	New York	H	10.57 FQ	17.37 AW	22.65 TQ	NYBLS	10/01-12/01
	North Carolina	H	11.01 FQ	15.30 AW	20.97 TQ	NCBLS	10/01-12/01
	North Dakota	H	9.58 FQ	14.26 AW	20.92 TQ	NDBLS	10/01-12/01
	Ohio	H	8.95 FQ	12.99 AW	18.28 TQ	OHBLS	10/01-12/01
	Oklahoma	H	7.66 FQ	11.44 AW	16.24 TQ	OKBLS	10/01-12/01
	Oregon	H	10.18 FQ	15.14 AW	20.38 TQ	ORBLS	10/01-12/01
	Pennsylvania	H	8.96 FQ	14.63 AW	21.38 TQ	PABLS	10/01-12/01
	Rhode Island	H	10.38 FQ	15.02 AW	20.06 TQ	RIBLS	10/01-12/01
	South Carolina	H	10.51 FQ	18.22 AW	31.20 TQ	SCBLS	10/01-12/01
	South Dakota	H	8.44 FQ	11.03 AW	14.84 TQ	SDBLS	10/01-12/01
	Tennessee	H	10.26 FQ	15.88 AW	24.70 TQ	TNBLS	10/01-12/01
	Texas	H	10.00 FQ	16.68 AW	22.88 TQ	TXBLS	10/01-12/01
	Utah	H	7.29 FQ	11.77 AW	17.69 TQ	UTBLS	10/01-12/01
	Vermont	H	9.91 FQ	14.47 AW	20.67 TQ	VTBLS	10/01-12/01
	Virginia	H	9.35 FQ	13.53 AW	19.18 TQ	VABLS	10/01-12/01
	Washington	H	12.10 FQ	16.99 AW	21.52 TQ	WABLS	10/01-12/01
	West Virginia	H	8.47 FQ	13.63 AW	19.68 TQ	WVBLS	10/01-12/01
	Wisconsin	H	9.88 FQ	15.02 AW	20.67 TQ	WIBLS	10/01-12/01
	Puerto Rico	H	5.72 FQ	8.58 AW	13.44 TQ	PRBLS	10/01-12/01
Statistician	Alabama	Y	24850 FQ	43410 AW	64460 TQ	ALBLS	10/01-12/01
	Birmingham MSA, AL	Y	28280 FQ	43690 AW	69410 TQ	ALBLS	10/01-12/01
	Montgomery MSA, AL	Y	21220 FQ	36720 AW	56610 TQ	ALBLS	10/01-12/01
	Alaska	Y	44620 FQ	59440 AW	80520 TQ	AKBLS	10/01-12/01
	Arizona	Y	31150 FQ	49610 AW	78410 TQ	AZBLS	10/01-12/01
	Phoenix-Mesa MSA, AZ	Y	31010 FQ	50040 AW	79380 TQ	AZBLS	10/01-12/01
	Arkansas	Y	25760 FQ	46830 AW	73770 TQ	ARBLS	10/01-12/01
	Little Rock-North Little Rock MSA, AR	Y	25800 FQ	42110 AW	61140 TQ	ARBLS	10/01-12/01
	California	Y	25640 FQ	67120 AW	92320 TQ	CABLS	10/01-12/01
	Los Angeles-Long Beach PMSA, CA	Y	45520 FQ	77630 AW	104490 TQ	CABLS	10/01-12/01
	Oakland PMSA, CA	Y	45020 FQ	64130 AW	103860 TQ	CABLS	10/01-12/01
	Orange County PMSA, CA	Y	45780 FQ	70230 AW	89090 TQ	CABLS	10/01-12/01
	Riverside-San Bernardino PMSA, CA	Y	37350 FQ	61100 AW	85450 TQ	CABLS	10/01-12/01
	Sacramento PMSA, CA	Y	40310 FQ	58580 AW	82190 TQ	CABLS	10/01-12/01
	San Diego MSA, CA	Y	35710 FQ	60590 AW	93560 TQ	CABLS	10/01-12/01
	San Francisco PMSA, CA	Y	58260 FQ	77010 AW	93540 TQ	CABLS	10/01-12/01
	San Jose PMSA, CA	Y	48560 FQ	73130 AW	130020 TQ	CABLS	10/01-12/01
	Colorado	Y	38220 FQ	57940 AW	85070 TQ	COBLS	10/01-12/01
	Denver PMSA, CO	Y	38130 FQ	56150 AW	78030 TQ	COBLS	10/01-12/01
	Connecticut	Y	40890 FQ	80400 AW	134980 TQ	CTBLS	10/01-12/01
	Hartford MSA, CT	Y	37440 FQ	51300 AW	71880 TQ	CTBLS	10/01-12/01
	New Haven-Meriden PMSA, CT	Y	59250 FQ	87820 AW	134290 TQ	CTBLS	10/01-12/01
	Delaware	Y	35560 FQ	72590 AW	111280 TQ	DEBLS	10/01-12/01
	Wilmington-Newark PMSA, DE-MD	Y	41450 FQ	76280 AW	111840 TQ	DEBLS	10/01-12/01
	District of Columbia	Y	47570 FQ	73200 AW	103900 TQ	DCBLS	10/01-12/01
	Washington PMSA, DC-MD-VA-WV	Y	40720 FQ	68600 AW	101810 TQ	DCBLS	10/01-12/01
	Florida	Y	24710 FQ	41720 AW	66670 TQ	FLBLS	10/01-12/01
	Fort Lauderdale PMSA, FL	Y	29500 FQ	49160 AW	65260 TQ	FLBLS	10/01-12/01
	Gainesville MSA, FL	Y	27120 FQ	37370 AW	51550 TQ	FLBLS	10/01-12/01
	Jacksonville MSA, FL	Y	17700 FQ	40280 AW	59380 TQ	FLBLS	10/01-12/01
	Melbourne-Titusville-Palm Bay MSA, FL	Y	26070 FQ	39230 AW	60280 TQ	FLBLS	10/01-12/01
	Miami PMSA, FL	Y	28940 FQ	44390 AW	72120 TQ	FLBLS	10/01-12/01
	Orlando MSA, FL	Y	27110 FQ	41480 AW	58910 TQ	FLBLS	10/01-12/01
	Pensacola MSA, FL	Y	16410 FQ	26560 AW	34710 TQ	FLBLS	10/01-12/01

AAW	Average annual wage	**AOH**	Average offered, high	**ASH**	Average starting, high	**H**	Hourly	**M**	Monthly	**S**	Special: hourly and annual
AE	Average entry wage	**AOL**	Average offered, low	**ASL**	Average starting, low	**HI**	Highest wage paid	**MTC**	Median total compensation	**TQ**	Third quartile wage
AEX	Average experienced wage	**APH**	Average pay, high range	**AW**	Average wage paid	**HR**	High end range	**MW**	Median wage paid	**W**	Weekly
AO	Average offered	**APL**	Average pay, low range	**FQ**	First quartile wage	**LR**	Low end range	**SQ**	Second quartile wage	**Y**	Yearly

Occupation/Type/Industry	Location	Per	Low	Mid	High	Source	Date
Statistician	Tallahassee MSA, FL	Y	24460 FQ	44380 AW	81530 TQ	FLBLS	10/01-12/01
	Tampa-St. Petersburg-Clearwater MSA, FL	Y	24930 FQ	44010 AW	69830 TQ	FLBLS	10/01-12/01
	Georgia	Y	32120 FQ	53900 AW	83530 TQ	GABLS	10/01-12/01
	Atlanta MSA, GA	Y	32400 FQ	55430 AW	85410 TQ	GABLS	10/01-12/01
	Hawaii	Y	31180 FQ	43010 AW	56270 TQ	HIBLS	10/01-12/01
	Honolulu MSA, HI	Y	31060 FQ	42900 AW	56250 TQ	HIBLS	10/01-12/01
	Idaho	Y	32740 FQ	55940 AW	85290 TQ	IDBLS	10/01-12/01
	Boise City MSA, ID	Y	31490 FQ	49660 AW	68980 TQ	IDBLS	10/01-12/01
	Illinois	Y	31470 FQ	58530 AW	91650 TQ	ILBLS	10/01-12/01
	Chicago PMSA, IL	Y	33250 FQ	61790 AW	94660 TQ	ILBLS	10/01-12/01
	Rockford MSA, IL	Y	30220 FQ	45530 AW	73420 TQ	ILBLS	10/01-12/01
	Indiana	Y	28580 FQ	53280 AW	82360 TQ	INBLS	10/01-12/01
	Iowa	Y	29130 FQ	53390 AW	91460 TQ	IABLS	10/01-12/01
	Kansas	Y	31270 FQ	47620 AW	66960 TQ	KSBLS	10/01-12/01
	Kentucky	Y	25090 FQ	41080 AW	66480 TQ	KYBLS	10/01-12/01
	Louisville MSA, KY-IN	Y	33250 FQ	50000 AW	69820 TQ	KYBLS	10/01-12/01
	Louisiana	Y	25580 FQ	59770 AW	89630 TQ	LABLS	10/01-12/01
	Baton Rouge MSA, LA	Y	24060 FQ	59020 AW	98910 TQ	LABLS	10/01-12/01
	Maine	Y	28610 FQ	45510 AW	64420 TQ	MEBLS	10/01-12/01
	Portland MSA, ME	Y	38000 FQ	49770 AW	65650 TQ	MEBLS	10/01-12/01
	Maryland	Y	39450 FQ	65870 AW	99240 TQ	MDBLS	10/01-12/01
	Baltimore PMSA, MD	Y	26800 FQ	55710 AW	87810 TQ	MDBLS	10/01-12/01
	Massachusetts	Y	33310 FQ	57050 AW	86460 TQ	MABLS	10/01-12/01
	Boston PMSA, MA-NH	Y	33290 FQ	56970 AW	85950 TQ	MABLS	10/01-12/01
	Michigan	Y	36290 FQ	51990 AW	72790 TQ	MIBLS	10/01-12/01
	Ann Arbor PMSA, MI	Y	37100 FQ	54960 AW	71560 TQ	MIBLS	10/01-12/01
	Detroit PMSA, MI	Y	36160 FQ	51050 AW	76730 TQ	MIBLS	10/01-12/01
	Minnesota	Y	34150 FQ	57910 AW	86940 TQ	MNBLS	10/01-12/01
	Minneapolis-St. Paul MSA, MN-WI	Y	33220 FQ	55880 AW	84910 TQ	MNBLS	10/01-12/01
	Mississippi	Y	15140 FQ	27280 AW	50550 TQ	MSBLS	10/01-12/01
	Jackson MSA, MS	Y	16070 FQ	27970 AW	43520 TQ	MSBLS	10/01-12/01
	Missouri	Y	29580 FQ	47330 AW	74430 TQ	MOBLS	10/01-12/01
	Kansas City MSA, MO-KS	Y	30120 FQ	50710 AW	71590 TQ	MOBLS	10/01-12/01
	St. Louis MSA, MO-IL	Y	28400 FQ	51110 AW	86330 TQ	MOBLS	10/01-12/01
	Montana	Y	35110 FQ	50300 AW	75330 TQ	MTBLS	10/01-12/01
	Nebraska	Y	26320 FQ	45610 AW	73510 TQ	NEBLS	10/01-12/01
	Lincoln MSA, NE	Y	25810 FQ	46540 AW	78560 TQ	NEBLS	10/01-12/01
	Omaha MSA, NE-IA	Y	27720 FQ	43690 AW	67120 TQ	NEBLS	10/01-12/01
	Nevada	Y	32690 FQ	47930 AW	71330 TQ	NVBLS	10/01-12/01
	New Hampshire	Y	26210 FQ	42490 AW	68500 TQ	NHBLS	10/01-12/01
	New Jersey	Y	35410 FQ	59680 AW	103720 TQ	NJBLS	10/01-12/01
	Bergen-Passaic PMSA, NJ	Y	49160 FQ	54210 AW	60670 TQ	NJBLS	10/01-12/01
	Middlesex-Somerset-Hunterdon PMSA, NJ	Y	31700 FQ	72160 AW	119020 TQ	NJBLS	10/01-12/01
	Newark PMSA, NJ	Y	33160 FQ	54370 AW	97200 TQ	NJBLS	10/01-12/01
	Trenton PMSA, NJ	Y	40310 FQ	61170 AW	87360 TQ	NJBLS	10/01-12/01
	New Mexico	Y	24210 FQ	65970 AW	118690 TQ	NMBLS	10/01-12/01
	New York	Y	23870 FQ	53920 AW	97240 TQ	NYBLS	10/01-12/01
	Albany-Schenectady-Troy MSA, NY	Y	31870 FQ	60090 AW	92130 TQ	NYBLS	10/01-12/01
	Buffalo-Niagara Falls MSA, NY	Y	30270 FQ	53270 AW	107930 TQ	NYBLS	10/01-12/01
	Nassau-Suffolk PMSA, NY	Y	29960 FQ	40740 AW	63090 TQ	NYBLS	10/01-12/01
	New York PMSA, NY	Y	20820 FQ	56320 AW	100770 TQ	NYBLS	10/01-12/01
	Rochester MSA, NY	Y	25390 FQ	51980 AW	75360 TQ	NYBLS	10/01-12/01
	North Carolina	Y	35890 FQ	60680 AW	94130 TQ	NCBLS	10/01-12/01
	Greensboro-Winston-Salem-High Point MSA, NC	Y	32790 FQ	52830 AW	78720 TQ	NCBLS	10/01-12/01
	Raleigh-Durham-Chapel Hill MSA, NC	Y	37550 FQ	63520 AW	100520 TQ	NCBLS	10/01-12/01
	North Dakota	Y	29550 FQ	44730 AW	66000 TQ	NDBLS	10/01-12/01
	Ohio	Y	25710 FQ	48250 AW	74460 TQ	OHBLS	10/01-12/01
	Cincinnati PMSA, OH-KY-IN	Y	26450 FQ	51200 AW	86210 TQ	OHBLS	10/01-12/01
	Cleveland-Lorain-Elyria PMSA, OH	Y	33880 FQ	52090 AW	72620 TQ	OHBLS	10/01-12/01
	Columbus MSA, OH	Y	23710 FQ	39540 AW	65260 TQ	OHBLS	10/01-12/01
	Toledo MSA, OH	Y	35390 FQ	53910 AW	74240 TQ	OHBLS	10/01-12/01
	Oklahoma	Y	24450 FQ	31580 AW	45560 TQ	OKBLS	10/01-12/01
	Oklahoma City MSA, OK	Y	24610 FQ	30930 AW	44750 TQ	OKBLS	10/01-12/01
	Oregon	Y	32140 FQ	46740 AW	65460 TQ	ORBLS	10/01-12/01

AAW	Average annual wage	**AOH**	Average offered, high	**ASH**	Average starting, high	**H**	Hourly	**M**	Monthly	**S**	Special: hourly and annual
AE	Average entry wage	**AOL**	Average offered, low	**ASL**	Average starting, low	**HI**	Highest wage paid	**MTC**	Median total compensation	**TQ**	Third quartile wage
AEX	Average experienced wage	**APH**	Average pay, high range	**AW**	Average wage paid	**HR**	High end range	**MW**	Median wage paid	**W**	Weekly
AO	Average offered	**APL**	Average pay, low range	**FQ**	First quartile wage	**LR**	Low end range	**SQ**	Second quartile wage	**Y**	Yearly

Occupation/Type/Industry	Location	Per	Low	Mid	High	Source	Date
Statistician	Eugene-Springfield MSA, OR	Y	31450 FQ	41060 AW	47840 TQ	ORBLS	10/01-12/01
	Portland-Vancouver PMSA, OR-WA	Y	35300 FQ	51440 AW	72690 TQ	ORBLS	10/01-12/01
	Pennsylvania	Y	23910 FQ	59700 AW	110220 TQ	PABLS	10/01-12/01
	Philadelphia PMSA, PA-NJ	Y	18920 FQ	61390 AW	112620 TQ	PABLS	10/01-12/01
	Pittsburgh MSA, PA	Y	27340 FQ	64170 AW	122370 TQ	PABLS	10/01-12/01
	Rhode Island	Y	34440 FQ	51490 AW	75320 TQ	RIBLS	10/01-12/01
	Providence-Fall River-Warwick MSA, RI-MA	Y	34210 FQ	50840 AW	75060 TQ	RIBLS	10/01-12/01
	South Carolina	Y	28780 FQ	42730 AW	58610 TQ	SCBLS	10/01-12/01
	Tennessee	Y	24290 FQ	41030 AW	65700 TQ	TNBLS	10/01-12/01
	Nashville MSA, TN	Y	23240 FQ	38380 AW	60330 TQ	TNBLS	10/01-12/01
	Texas	Y	28410 FQ	46710 AW	77580 TQ	TXBLS	10/01-12/01
	Dallas PMSA, TX	Y	31630 FQ	49330 AW	80830 TQ	TXBLS	10/01-12/01
	Houston PMSA, TX	Y	29200 FQ	52060 AW	86080 TQ	TXBLS	10/01-12/01
	San Antonio MSA, TX	Y	29940 FQ	54760 AW	86300 TQ	TXBLS	10/01-12/01
	Utah	Y	23430 FQ	37560 AW	56440 TQ	UTBLS	10/01-12/01
	Vermont	Y	30110 FQ	39620 AW	52730 TQ	VTBLS	10/01-12/01
	Virginia	Y	28340 FQ	51220 AW	80390 TQ	VABLS	10/01-12/01
	Norfolk-Virginia Beach-Newport News MSA, VA-NC	Y	15840 FQ	28630 AW	44640 TQ	VABLS	10/01-12/01
	Richmond-Petersburg MSA, VA	Y	30560 FQ	51720 AW	75730 TQ	VABLS	10/01-12/01
	Washington	Y	34750 FQ	53870 AW	80110 TQ	WABLS	10/01-12/01
	Olympia PMSA, WA	Y	31470 FQ	44800 AW	63650 TQ	WABLS	10/01-12/01
	Seattle-Bellevue-Everett PMSA, WA	Y	38290 FQ	56990 AW	85070 TQ	WABLS	10/01-12/01
	West Virginia	Y	36340 FQ	60780 AW	88770 TQ	WVBLS	10/01-12/01
	Wisconsin	Y	32930 FQ	53310 AW	77770 TQ	WIBLS	10/01-12/01
	Madison MSA, WI	Y	31120 FQ	53790 AW	85810 TQ	WIBLS	10/01-12/01
	Milwaukee-Waukesha PMSA, WI	Y	37480 FQ	59020 AW	92070 TQ	WIBLS	10/01-12/01
	Puerto Rico	Y	14860 FQ	21350 AW	30740 TQ	PRBLS	10/01-12/01
Stock Clerk and Order Filler	Alabama	H	5.94 FQ	9.09 AW	13.76 TQ	ALBLS	10/01-12/01
	Alaska	H	7.87 FQ	12.78 AW	20.15 TQ	AKBLS	10/01-12/01
	Arizona	H	6.28 FQ	10.20 AW	16.79 TQ	AZBLS	10/01-12/01
	Arkansas	H	5.93 FQ	9.11 AW	13.67 TQ	ARBLS	10/01-12/01
	California	H	6.84 FQ	11.32 AW	18.46 TQ	CABLS	10/01-12/01
	Colorado	H	7.20 FQ	11.69 AW	17.89 TQ	COBLS	10/01-12/01
	Connecticut	H	7.22 FQ	11.36 AW	18.31 TQ	CTBLS	10/01-12/01
	Delaware	H	7.00 FQ	11.61 AW	17.65 TQ	DEBLS	10/01-12/01
	District of Columbia	H	7.48 FQ	12.93 AW	20.40 TQ	DCBLS	10/01-12/01
	Florida	H	6.38 FQ	9.46 AW	13.79 TQ	FLBLS	10/01-12/01
	Georgia	H	6.57 FQ	10.20 AW	15.36 TQ	GABLS	10/01-12/01
	Hawaii	H	6.76 FQ	11.19 AW	17.16 TQ	HIBLS	10/01-12/01
	Idaho	H	6.14 FQ	9.88 AW	17.02 TQ	IDBLS	10/01-12/01
	Illinois	H	6.26 FQ	10.23 AW	17.01 TQ	ILBLS	10/01-12/01
	Indiana	H	6.12 FQ	9.71 AW	14.87 TQ	INBLS	10/01-12/01
	Iowa	H	5.95 FQ	9.62 AW	16.01 TQ	IABLS	10/01-12/01
	Kansas	H	6.19 FQ	10.17 AW	16.55 TQ	KSBLS	10/01-12/01
	Kentucky	H	6.08 FQ	9.84 AW	15.28 TQ	KYBLS	10/01-12/01
	Louisiana	H	5.78 FQ	8.76 AW	13.78 TQ	LABLS	10/01-12/01
	Maine	H	6.62 FQ	9.99 AW	14.60 TQ	MEBLS	10/01-12/01
	Maryland	H	6.77 FQ	10.41 AW	16.14 TQ	MDBLS	10/01-12/01
	Massachusetts	H	7.33 FQ	11.25 AW	17.76 TQ	MABLS	10/01-12/01
	Michigan	H	6.57 FQ	11.15 AW	18.47 TQ	MIBLS	10/01-12/01
	Minnesota	H	6.54 FQ	10.84 AW	17.50 TQ	MNBLS	10/01-12/01
	Mississippi	H	5.86 FQ	8.70 AW	12.73 TQ	MSBLS	10/01-12/01
	Missouri	H	6.30 FQ	10.46 AW	17.30 TQ	MOBLS	10/01-12/01
	Montana	H	5.99 FQ	9.87 AW	17.14 TQ	MTBLS	10/01-12/01
	Nebraska	H	6.29 FQ	9.69 AW	14.74 TQ	NEBLS	10/01-12/01
	Nevada	H	6.89 FQ	10.92 AW	16.91 TQ	NVBLS	10/01-12/01
	New Hampshire	H	7.13 FQ	10.35 AW	15.19 TQ	NHBLS	10/01-12/01
	New Jersey	H	6.56 FQ	11.50 AW	19.08 TQ	NJBLS	10/01-12/01
	New Mexico	H	6.10 FQ	9.80 AW	15.96 TQ	NMBLS	10/01-12/01
	New York	H	6.11 FQ	10.60 AW	18.56 TQ	NYBLS	10/01-12/01
	North Carolina	H	6.42 FQ	9.75 AW	13.87 TQ	NCBLS	10/01-12/01
	North Dakota	H	6.00 FQ	9.31 AW	14.60 TQ	NDBLS	10/01-12/01
	Ohio	H	6.13 FQ	10.14 AW	16.18 TQ	OHBLS	10/01-12/01
	Oklahoma	H	5.94 FQ	9.47 AW	15.80 TQ	OKBLS	10/01-12/01
	Oregon	H	7.56 FQ	11.36 AW	16.92 TQ	ORBLS	10/01-12/01

AAW	Average annual wage	AOH	Average offered, high	ASH	Average starting, high	H	Hourly	M	Monthly	S	Special: hourly and annual
AE	Average entry wage	AOL	Average offered, low	ASL	Average starting, low	HI	Highest wage paid	MTC	Median total compensation	TQ	Third quartile wage
AEX	Average experienced wage	APH	Average pay, high range	AW	Average wage paid	HR	High end range	MW	Median wage paid	W	Weekly
AO	Average offered	APL	Average pay, low range	FQ	First quartile wage	LR	Low end range	SQ	Second quartile wage	Y	Yearly

Occupation/Type/Industry	Location	Per	Low	Mid	High	Source	Date
Stock Clerk and Order Filler	Pennsylvania	H	6.04 FQ	9.98 AW	16.88 TQ	PABLS	10/01-12/01
	Rhode Island	H	6.80 FQ	10.29 AW	17.14 TQ	RIBLS	10/01-12/01
	South Carolina	H	6.24 FQ	9.57 AW	13.93 TQ	SCBLS	10/01-12/01
	South Dakota	H	5.82 FQ	8.55 AW	13.18 TQ	SDBLS	10/01-12/01
	Tennessee	H	6.18 FQ	9.49 AW	13.86 TQ	TNBLS	10/01-12/01
	Texas	H	6.25 FQ	10.12 AW	16.55 TQ	TXBLS	10/01-12/01
	Utah	H	6.81 FQ	10.11 AW	13.86 TQ	UTBLS	10/01-12/01
	Vermont	H	6.63 FQ	9.72 AW	14.13 TQ	VTBLS	10/01-12/01
	Virginia	H	6.37 FQ	9.93 AW	15.28 TQ	VABLS	10/01-12/01
	Washington	H	7.27 FQ	11.64 AW	17.97 TQ	WABLS	10/01-12/01
	West Virginia	H	5.84 FQ	9.28 AW	14.73 TQ	WVBLS	10/01-12/01
	Wisconsin	H	6.20 FQ	9.97 AW	15.93 TQ	WIBLS	10/01-12/01
	Wyoming	H	6.15 FQ	10.13 AW	18.04 TQ	WYBLS	10/01-12/01
	Puerto Rico	H	5.60 FQ	7.24 AW	10.25 TQ	PRBLS	10/01-12/01
	Virgin Islands	H	5.74 FQ	7.97 AW	11.45 TQ	VIBLS	10/01-12/01
	Guam	H	5.74 FQ	8.49 AW	13.49 TQ	GUBLS	10/01-12/01
Stock Person							
Hardware Store	United States	H		7.50 AW		DIYR	1/01-1/02
Stonemason	Alabama	H	7.16 FQ	11.19 AW	16.28 TQ	ALBLS	10/01-12/01
	Arizona	H	8.70 FQ	12.87 AW	18.75 TQ	AZBLS	10/01-12/01
	Phoenix-Mesa MSA, AZ	H	8.89 FQ	12.49 AW	16.55 TQ	AZBLS	10/01-12/01
	Tucson MSA, AZ	H	6.65 FQ	14.18 AW	20.78 TQ	AZBLS	10/01-12/01
	Arkansas	H	7.23 FQ	8.72 AW	11.97 TQ	ARBLS	10/01-12/01
	California	H	12.10 FQ	18.30 AW	26.13 TQ	CABLS	10/01-12/01
	Los Angeles-Long Beach PMSA, CA	H	11.19 FQ	17.68 AW	24.99 TQ	CABLS	10/01-12/01
	Orange County PMSA, CA	H	12.25 FQ	19.97 AW	30.10 TQ	CABLS	10/01-12/01
	Sacramento PMSA, CA	H	13.87 FQ	15.34 AW	16.84 TQ	CABLS	10/01-12/01
	Salinas MSA, CA	H	10.35 FQ	18.48 AW	27.33 TQ	CABLS	10/01-12/01
	Santa Rosa PMSA, CA	H	8.62 FQ	18.67 AW	26.37 TQ	CABLS	10/01-12/01
	Colorado	H	12.47 FQ	18.50 AW	25.46 TQ	COBLS	10/01-12/01
	Denver PMSA, CO	H	12.14 FQ	19.66 AW	26.77 TQ	COBLS	10/01-12/01
	Connecticut	H	10.30 FQ	18.49 AW	26.54 TQ	CTBLS	10/01-12/01
	Hartford MSA, CT	H	16.30 FQ	23.61 AW	27.63 TQ	CTBLS	10/01-12/01
	Stamford-Norwalk PMSA, CT	H	10.10 FQ	17.91 AW	26.66 TQ	CTBLS	10/01-12/01
	Delaware	H	10.13 FQ	12.64 AW	16.54 TQ	DEBLS	10/01-12/01
	Washington PMSA, DC-MD-VA-WV	H	10.32 FQ	17.90 AW	24.17 TQ	DCBLS	10/01-12/01
	Florida	H	11.05 FQ	17.77 AW	24.89 TQ	FLBLS	10/01-12/01
	Georgia	H	7.97 FQ	14.30 AW	20.90 TQ	GABLS	10/01-12/01
	Atlanta MSA, GA	H	14.97 FQ	18.51 AW	22.24 TQ	GABLS	10/01-12/01
	Hawaii	H	20.41 FQ	25.26 AW	30.07 TQ	HIBLS	10/01-12/01
	Idaho	H	17.06 FQ	18.92 AW	22.06 TQ	IDBLS	10/01-12/01
	Illinois	H	13.14 FQ	24.26 AW	41.06 TQ	ILBLS	10/01-12/01
	Chicago PMSA, IL	H	10.50 FQ	25.81 AW	33.51 TQ	ILBLS	10/01-12/01
	Indiana	H	9.75 FQ	15.18 AW	20.41 TQ	INBLS	10/01-12/01
	Iowa	H	10.01 FQ	12.49 AW	14.36 TQ	IABLS	10/01-12/01
	Kentucky	H	10.67 FQ	16.81 AW	23.54 TQ	KYBLS	10/01-12/01
	Lexington MSA, KY	H	9.77 FQ	18.08 AW	22.56 TQ	KYBLS	10/01-12/01
	Louisiana	H	9.00 FQ	11.85 AW	17.46 TQ	LABLS	10/01-12/01
	Maine	H	12.09 FQ	16.27 AW	21.49 TQ	MEBLS	10/01-12/01
	Maryland	H	12.33 FQ	17.00 AW	22.19 TQ	MDBLS	10/01-12/01
	Baltimore PMSA, MD	H	14.84 FQ	18.43 AW	22.32 TQ	MDBLS	10/01-12/01
	Massachusetts	H	13.55 FQ	21.25 AW	31.79 TQ	MABLS	10/01-12/01
	Boston PMSA, MA-NH	H	12.72 FQ	19.37 AW	29.01 TQ	MABLS	10/01-12/01
	Michigan	H	9.54 FQ	13.53 AW	19.15 TQ	MIBLS	10/01-12/01
	Detroit PMSA, MI	H	9.17 FQ	10.30 AW	11.74 TQ	MIBLS	10/01-12/01
	Minnesota	H	12.68 FQ	15.73 AW	17.99 TQ	MNBLS	10/01-12/01
	Mississippi	H	8.87 FQ	9.94 AW	11.03 TQ	MSBLS	10/01-12/01
	Missouri	H	9.26 FQ	12.97 AW	20.28 TQ	MOBLS	10/01-12/01
	Montana	H	9.34 FQ	16.70 AW	22.33 TQ	MTBLS	10/01-12/01
	Billings MSA, MT	H	9.04 FQ	15.30 AW	22.16 TQ	MTBLS	10/01-12/01
	Nebraska	H	7.92 FQ	14.14 AW	21.83 TQ	NEBLS	10/01-12/01
	Omaha MSA, NE-IA	H	9.40 FQ	16.72 AW	28.57 TQ	NEBLS	10/01-12/01
	Nevada	H	13.96 FQ	16.91 AW	24.39 TQ	NVBLS	10/01-12/01
	Las Vegas MSA, NV-AZ	H	13.93 FQ	16.42 AW	20.98 TQ	NVBLS	10/01-12/01
	New Hampshire	H	11.21 FQ	16.43 AW	24.29 TQ	NHBLS	10/01-12/01
	New Jersey	H	7.60 FQ	16.12 AW	24.38 TQ	NJBLS	10/01-12/01
	Bergen-Passaic PMSA, NJ	H	14.49 FQ	18.67 AW	25.99 TQ	NJBLS	10/01-12/01
	New Mexico	H	7.76 FQ	10.55 AW	13.70 TQ	NMBLS	10/01-12/01
	New York	H	17.20 FQ	22.95 AW	32.10 TQ	NYBLS	10/01-12/01

AAW	Average annual wage	**AOH**	Average offered, high	**ASH**	Average starting, high	**H**	Hourly	**M**	Monthly	**S**	Special: hourly and annual
AE	Average entry wage	**AOL**	Average offered, low	**ASL**	Average starting, low	**HI**	Highest wage paid	**MTC**	Median total compensation	**TQ**	Third quartile wage
AEX	Average experienced wage	**APH**	Average pay, high range	**AW**	Average wage paid	**HR**	High end range	**MW**	Median wage paid	**W**	Weekly
AO	Average offered	**APL**	Average pay, low range	**FQ**	First quartile wage	**LR**	Low end range	**SQ**	Second quartile wage	**Y**	Yearly

Occupation/Type/Industry	Location	Per	Low	Mid	High	Source	Date
Stonemason	New York PMSA, NY	H	17.67 FQ	23.42 AW	32.19 TQ	NYBLS	10/01-12/01
	North Carolina	H	9.34 FQ	14.29 AW	19.97 TQ	NCBLS	10/01-12/01
	Ohio	H	9.16 FQ	14.81 AW	21.58 TQ	OHBLS	10/01-12/01
	Cleveland-Lorain-Elyria PMSA, OH	H	11.09 FQ	18.36 AW	22.58 TQ	OHBLS	10/01-12/01
	Oregon	H	10.85 FQ	16.95 AW	26.31 TQ	ORBLS	10/01-12/01
	Pennsylvania	H	9.02 FQ	19.37 AW	34.47 TQ	PABLS	10/01-12/01
	Philadelphia PMSA, PA-NJ	H	13.14 FQ	24.50 AW	40.93 TQ	PABLS	10/01-12/01
	Rhode Island	H	6.48 FQ	16.32 AW	26.41 TQ	RIBLS	10/01-12/01
	Providence-Fall River-Warwick MSA, RI-MA	H	6.47 FQ	16.50 AW	26.21 TQ	RIBLS	10/01-12/01
	South Carolina	H	10.11 FQ	14.95 AW	21.41 TQ	SCBLS	10/01-12/01
	Tennessee	H	11.14 FQ	15.07 AW	20.87 TQ	TNBLS	10/01-12/01
	Texas	H	9.05 FQ	12.15 AW	18.70 TQ	TXBLS	10/01-12/01
	Utah	H	11.44 FQ	20.31 AW	37.64 TQ	UTBLS	10/01-12/01
	Vermont	H	13.88 FQ	21.54 AW	26.90 TQ	VTBLS	10/01-12/01
	Virginia	H	9.43 FQ	15.46 AW	21.70 TQ	VABLS	10/01-12/01
	Washington	H	10.22 FQ	21.41 AW	33.23 TQ	WABLS	10/01-12/01
	Seattle-Bellevue-Everett PMSA, WA	H	16.06 FQ	24.11 AW	34.06 TQ	WABLS	10/01-12/01
	Wisconsin	H	10.80 FQ	15.66 AW	21.24 TQ	WIBLS	10/01-12/01
	Milwaukee-Waukesha PMSA, WI	H	12.32 FQ	17.45 AW	30.11 TQ	WIBLS	10/01-12/01
	Puerto Rico	H	5.80 FQ	8.39 AW	11.06 TQ	PRBLS	10/01-12/01
	Virgin Islands	H	12.78 FQ	15.40 AW	17.60 TQ	VIBLS	10/01-12/01
Store Manager							
Convenience Store	United States	Y			28800 MW	BEVA	1/01-1/02
Structural Iron and Steel Worker	Alabama	H	11.73 FQ	16.66 AW	21.90 TQ	ALBLS	10/01-12/01
	Birmingham MSA, AL	H	12.32 FQ	16.99 AW	22.09 TQ	ALBLS	10/01-12/01
	Mobile MSA, AL	H	8.86 FQ	15.64 AW	21.06 TQ	ALBLS	10/01-12/01
	Montgomery MSA, AL	H	15.32 FQ	19.48 AW	22.59 TQ	ALBLS	10/01-12/01
	Alaska	H	14.57 FQ	26.05 AW	37.95 TQ	AKBLS	10/01-12/01
	Anchorage MSA, AK	H	14.17 FQ	24.37 AW	33.44 TQ	AKBLS	10/01-12/01
	Arizona	H	11.20 FQ	15.77 AW	21.44 TQ	AZBLS	10/01-12/01
	Phoenix-Mesa MSA, AZ	H	11.80 FQ	16.08 AW	21.43 TQ	AZBLS	10/01-12/01
	Tucson MSA, AZ	H	10.99 FQ	16.00 AW	21.37 TQ	AZBLS	10/01-12/01
	Arkansas	H	9.74 FQ	13.33 AW	17.09 TQ	ARBLS	10/01-12/01
	Little Rock-North Little Rock MSA, AR	H	10.10 FQ	13.92 AW	17.55 TQ	ARBLS	10/01-12/01
	California	H	11.84 FQ	22.55 AW	33.28 TQ	CABLS	10/01-12/01
	Bakersfield MSA, CA	H	11.21 FQ	18.35 AW	30.09 TQ	CABLS	10/01-12/01
	Fresno MSA, CA	H	11.58 FQ	14.85 AW	20.11 TQ	CABLS	10/01-12/01
	Los Angeles-Long Beach PMSA, CA	H	11.68 FQ	21.70 AW	31.62 TQ	CABLS	10/01-12/01
	Modesto MSA, CA	H	12.21 FQ	18.79 AW	29.60 TQ	CABLS	10/01-12/01
	Oakland PMSA, CA	H	14.51 FQ	25.72 AW	34.75 TQ	CABLS	10/01-12/01
	Orange County PMSA, CA	H	15.26 FQ	23.58 AW	32.30 TQ	CABLS	10/01-12/01
	Riverside-San Bernardino PMSA, CA	H	16.79 FQ	26.88 AW	34.04 TQ	CABLS	10/01-12/01
	Sacramento PMSA, CA	H	12.51 FQ	21.15 AW	32.17 TQ	CABLS	10/01-12/01
	San Diego MSA, CA	H	14.80 FQ	23.62 AW	33.10 TQ	CABLS	10/01-12/01
	San Francisco PMSA, CA	H	10.02 FQ	19.31 AW	30.27 TQ	CABLS	10/01-12/01
	San Jose PMSA, CA	H	11.84 FQ	21.92 AW	34.61 TQ	CABLS	10/01-12/01
	San Luis Obispo-Atascadero-Paso Robles MSA, CA	H	12.45 FQ	20.02 AW	27.88 TQ	CABLS	10/01-12/01
	Vallejo-Fairfield-Napa PMSA, CA	H	18.86 FQ	27.34 AW	33.61 TQ	CABLS	10/01-12/01
	Visalia-Tulare-Porterville MSA, CA	H	11.32 FQ	18.35 AW	31.80 TQ	CABLS	10/01-12/01
	Colorado	H	11.98 FQ	17.99 AW	23.16 TQ	COBLS	10/01-12/01
	Colorado Springs MSA, CO	H	11.42 FQ	13.40 AW	17.06 TQ	COBLS	10/01-12/01
	Denver PMSA, CO	H	15.14 FQ	19.47 AW	22.60 TQ	COBLS	10/01-12/01
	Connecticut	H	17.06 FQ	24.38 AW	31.45 TQ	CTBLS	10/01-12/01
	Hartford MSA, CT	H	20.20 FQ	25.42 AW	31.55 TQ	CTBLS	10/01-12/01
	New Haven-Meriden PMSA, CT	H	18.85 FQ	24.91 AW	31.27 TQ	CTBLS	10/01-12/01
	Delaware	H	12.13 FQ	18.68 AW	25.59 TQ	DEBLS	10/01-12/01
	Wilmington-Newark PMSA, DE-MD	H	14.00 FQ	19.56 AW	26.40 TQ	DEBLS	10/01-12/01
	Washington PMSA, DC-MD-VA-WV	H	11.51 FQ	16.58 AW	22.11 TQ	DCBLS	10/01-12/01

AAW	Average annual wage	**AOH**	Average offered, high	**ASH**	Average starting, high	**H**	Hourly	**M**	Monthly	**S**	Special: hourly and annual
AE	Average entry wage	**AOL**	Average offered, low	**ASL**	Average starting, low	**HI**	Highest wage paid	**MTC**	Median total compensation	**TQ**	Third quartile wage
AEX	Average experienced wage	**APH**	Average pay, high range	**AW**	Average wage paid	**HR**	High end range	**MW**	Median wage paid	**W**	Weekly
AO	Average offered	**APL**	Average pay, low range	**FQ**	First quartile wage	**LR**	Low end range	**SQ**	Second quartile wage	**Y**	Yearly

Occupation/Type/Industry	Location	Per	Low	Mid	High	Source	Date
Structural Iron and Steel Worker	Florida	H	11.03 FQ	17.16 AW	21.97 TQ	FLBLS	10/01-12/01
	Fort Lauderdale PMSA, FL	H	9.52 FQ	14.66 AW	18.92 TQ	FLBLS	10/01-12/01
	Fort Myers-Cape Coral MSA, FL	H	8.56 FQ	14.24 AW	20.13 TQ	FLBLS	10/01-12/01
	Jacksonville MSA, FL	H	12.03 FQ	16.91 AW	22.00 TQ	FLBLS	10/01-12/01
	Lakeland-Winter Haven MSA, FL	H	12.89 FQ	16.05 AW	19.83 TQ	FLBLS	10/01-12/01
	Melbourne-Titusville-Palm Bay MSA, FL	H	14.41 FQ	18.80 AW	22.43 TQ	FLBLS	10/01-12/01
	Miami PMSA, FL	H	12.90 FQ	17.96 AW	21.61 TQ	FLBLS	10/01-12/01
	Orlando MSA, FL	H	14.85 FQ	20.47 AW	28.88 TQ	FLBLS	10/01-12/01
	Sarasota-Bradenton MSA, FL	H	8.51 FQ	11.53 AW	16.02 TQ	FLBLS	10/01-12/01
	Tampa-St. Petersburg-Clearwater MSA, FL	H	9.89 FQ	16.75 AW	21.71 TQ	FLBLS	10/01-12/01
	West Palm Beach-Boca Raton MSA, FL	H	10.96 FQ	17.72 AW	22.33 TQ	FLBLS	10/01-12/01
	Georgia	H	11.76 FQ	17.68 AW	25.62 TQ	GABLS	10/01-12/01
	Atlanta MSA, GA	H	11.90 FQ	18.62 AW	26.78 TQ	GABLS	10/01-12/01
	Savannah MSA, GA	H	13.95 FQ	15.87 AW	18.83 TQ	GABLS	10/01-12/01
	Hawaii	H	20.36 FQ	24.87 AW	29.24 TQ	HIBLS	10/01-12/01
	Honolulu MSA, HI	H	20.03 FQ	24.84 AW	29.23 TQ	HIBLS	10/01-12/01
	Idaho	H	11.74 FQ	17.44 AW	21.86 TQ	IDBLS	10/01-12/01
	Boise City MSA, ID	H	9.74 FQ	15.57 AW	20.95 TQ	IDBLS	10/01-12/01
	Illinois	H	13.41 FQ	23.92 AW	33.50 TQ	ILBLS	10/01-12/01
	Chicago PMSA, IL	H	6.64 FQ	24.62 AW	34.24 TQ	ILBLS	10/01-12/01
	Peoria-Pekin MSA, IL	H	16.66 FQ	21.48 AW	27.27 TQ	ILBLS	10/01-12/01
	Indiana	H	13.58 FQ	20.84 AW	27.64 TQ	INBLS	10/01-12/01
	Evansville-Henderson MSA, IN-KY	H	15.95 FQ	20.98 AW	26.18 TQ	INBLS	10/01-12/01
	Fort Wayne MSA, IN	H	14.16 FQ	17.78 AW	21.78 TQ	INBLS	10/01-12/01
	Gary PMSA, IN	H	11.40 FQ	21.89 AW	31.90 TQ	INBLS	10/01-12/01
	Indianapolis MSA, IN	H	15.35 FQ	22.08 AW	27.47 TQ	INBLS	10/01-12/01
	South Bend MSA, IN	H	14.93 FQ	21.48 AW	26.71 TQ	INBLS	10/01-12/01
	Iowa	H	10.93 FQ	16.54 AW	22.08 TQ	IABLS	10/01-12/01
	Cedar Rapids MSA, IA	H	18.60 FQ	20.96 AW	22.80 TQ	IABLS	10/01-12/01
	Davenport-Moline-Rock Island MSA, IA-IL	H	15.48 FQ	21.17 AW	26.68 TQ	IABLS	10/01-12/01
	Des Moines MSA, IA	H	17.19 FQ	19.10 AW	21.42 TQ	IABLS	10/01-12/01
	Kansas	H	10.51 FQ	16.95 AW	23.80 TQ	KSBLS	10/01-12/01
	Wichita MSA, KS	H	9.77 FQ	14.90 AW	21.01 TQ	KSBLS	10/01-12/01
	Kentucky	H	10.64 FQ	18.24 AW	26.44 TQ	KYBLS	10/01-12/01
	Lexington MSA, KY	H	12.26 FQ	18.21 AW	23.75 TQ	KYBLS	10/01-12/01
	Louisville MSA, KY-IN	H	11.16 FQ	18.76 AW	26.12 TQ	KYBLS	10/01-12/01
	Louisiana	H	9.28 FQ	14.92 AW	19.97 TQ	LABLS	10/01-12/01
	Houma MSA, LA	H	9.84 FQ	14.64 AW	17.94 TQ	LABLS	10/01-12/01
	Lafayette MSA, LA	H	8.70 FQ	13.76 AW	23.71 TQ	LABLS	10/01-12/01
	Lake Charles MSA, LA	H	7.74 FQ	13.11 AW	19.26 TQ	LABLS	10/01-12/01
	New Orleans MSA, LA	H	9.04 FQ	14.51 AW	20.40 TQ	LABLS	10/01-12/01
	Shreveport-Bossier City MSA, LA	H	12.07 FQ	14.96 AW	17.89 TQ	LABLS	10/01-12/01
	Maine	H	11.26 FQ	15.74 AW	21.23 TQ	MEBLS	10/01-12/01
	Maryland	H	11.64 FQ	18.58 AW	27.35 TQ	MDBLS	10/01-12/01
	Baltimore PMSA, MD	H	12.21 FQ	20.83 AW	28.28 TQ	MDBLS	10/01-12/01
	Massachusetts	H	15.28 FQ	24.30 AW	32.74 TQ	MABLS	10/01-12/01
	Boston PMSA, MA-NH	H	17.58 FQ	24.86 AW	32.84 TQ	MABLS	10/01-12/01
	Brockton PMSA, MA	H	23.63 FQ	25.55 AW	28.76 TQ	MABLS	10/01-12/01
	Lawrence PMSA, MA-NH	H	20.67 FQ	25.12 AW	29.54 TQ	MABLS	10/01-12/01
	Springfield MSA, MA	H	9.27 FQ	13.55 AW	19.98 TQ	MABLS	10/01-12/01
	Michigan	H	14.36 FQ	23.13 AW	29.31 TQ	MIBLS	10/01-12/01
	Ann Arbor PMSA, MI	H	18.84 FQ	26.44 AW	34.20 TQ	MIBLS	10/01-12/01
	Detroit PMSA, MI	H	15.73 FQ	23.62 AW	28.58 TQ	MIBLS	10/01-12/01
	Flint PMSA, MI	H	13.99 FQ	24.16 AW	31.88 TQ	MIBLS	10/01-12/01
	Grand Rapids-Muskegon-Holland MSA, MI	H	11.45 FQ	17.62 AW	26.99 TQ	MIBLS	10/01-12/01
	Minnesota	H	19.84 FQ	26.54 AW	33.34 TQ	MNBLS	10/01-12/01
	Duluth-Superior MSA, MN-WI	H	11.55 FQ	17.21 AW	28.89 TQ	MNBLS	10/01-12/01
	Minneapolis-St. Paul MSA, MN-WI	H	22.92 FQ	27.57 AW	33.51 TQ	MNBLS	10/01-12/01
	Mississippi	H	7.47 FQ	13.30 AW	19.47 TQ	MSBLS	10/01-12/01
	Biloxi-Gulfport-Pascagoula MSA, MS	H	12.00 FQ	16.26 AW	20.52 TQ	MSBLS	10/01-12/01
	Jackson MSA, MS	H	12.62 FQ	16.00 AW	19.58 TQ	MSBLS	10/01-12/01

AAW	Average annual wage	AOH	Average offered, high	ASH	Average starting, high	H	Hourly	M	Monthly	S	Special: hourly and annual
AE	Average entry wage	AOL	Average offered, low	ASL	Average starting, low	HI	Highest wage paid	MTC	Median total compensation	TQ	Third quartile wage
AEX	Average experienced wage	APH	Average pay, high range	AW	Average wage paid	HR	High end range	MW	Median wage paid	W	Weekly
AO	Average offered	APL	Average pay, low range	FQ	First quartile wage	LR	Low end range	SQ	Second quartile wage	Y	Yearly

Occupation/Type/Industry	Location	Per	Low	Mid	High	Source	Date
Structural Iron and Steel Worker	Missouri	H	11.70 FQ	20.26 AW	27.17 TQ	MOBLS	10/01-12/01
	Kansas City MSA, MO-KS	H	17.33 FQ	20.65 AW	25.68 TQ	MOBLS	10/01-12/01
	St. Louis MSA, MO-IL	H	16.31 FQ	23.32 AW	28.99 TQ	MOBLS	10/01-12/01
	Springfield MSA, MO	H	13.43 FQ	19.36 AW	22.60 TQ	MOBLS	10/01-12/01
	Nebraska	H	12.10 FQ	18.99 AW	23.16 TQ	NEBLS	10/01-12/01
	Lincoln MSA, NE	H	12.29 FQ	18.90 AW	26.21 TQ	NEBLS	10/01-12/01
	Omaha MSA, NE-IA	H	15.37 FQ	20.81 AW	29.25 TQ	NEBLS	10/01-12/01
	Nevada	H	10.57 FQ	21.20 AW	31.49 TQ	NVBLS	10/01-12/01
	Las Vegas MSA, NV-AZ	H	10.31 FQ	20.61 AW	29.68 TQ	NVBLS	10/01-12/01
	Reno MSA, NV	H	11.50 FQ	22.23 AW	30.42 TQ	NVBLS	10/01-12/01
	New Hampshire	H	13.24 FQ	17.63 AW	23.19 TQ	NHBLS	10/01-12/01
	New Jersey	H	18.19 FQ	28.61 AW	36.43 TQ	NJBLS	10/01-12/01
	Atlantic-Cape May PMSA, NJ	H	21.68 FQ	26.98 AW	33.48 TQ	NJBLS	10/01-12/01
	Bergen-Passaic PMSA, NJ	H	23.99 FQ	31.22 AW	40.84 TQ	NJBLS	10/01-12/01
	Jersey City PMSA, NJ	H	22.40 FQ	28.44 AW	33.85 TQ	NJBLS	10/01-12/01
	Middlesex-Somerset-Hunterdon PMSA, NJ	H	23.50 FQ	28.05 AW	34.12 TQ	NJBLS	10/01-12/01
	Monmouth-Ocean PMSA, NJ	H	26.48 FQ	32.30 AW	36.67 TQ	NJBLS	10/01-12/01
	Newark PMSA, NJ	H	15.48 FQ	22.23 AW	30.90 TQ	NJBLS	10/01-12/01
	Trenton PMSA, NJ	H	12.48 FQ	28.54 AW	36.20 TQ	NJBLS	10/01-12/01
	New Mexico	H	8.85 FQ	15.56 AW	22.18 TQ	NMBLS	10/01-12/01
	Albuquerque MSA, NM	H	8.98 FQ	15.64 AW	22.59 TQ	NMBLS	10/01-12/01
	New York	H	19.69 FQ	30.54 AW	38.89 TQ	NYBLS	10/01-12/01
	Albany-Schenectady-Troy MSA, NY	H	19.12 FQ	30.14 AW	40.60 TQ	NYBLS	10/01-12/01
	Buffalo-Niagara Falls MSA, NY	H	18.49 FQ	23.87 AW	31.69 TQ	NYBLS	10/01-12/01
	Nassau-Suffolk PMSA, NY	H	20.34 FQ	32.93 AW	42.14 TQ	NYBLS	10/01-12/01
	New York PMSA, NY	H	28.52 FQ	31.78 AW	36.94 TQ	NYBLS	10/01-12/01
	Newburgh PMSA, NY-PA	H	19.81 FQ	34.56 AW	43.22 TQ	NYBLS	10/01-12/01
	Rochester MSA, NY	H	13.05 FQ	21.34 AW	31.37 TQ	NYBLS	10/01-12/01
	Syracuse MSA, NY	H	13.47 FQ	24.33 AW	35.92 TQ	NYBLS	10/01-12/01
	Utica-Rome MSA, NY	H	18.65 FQ	23.76 AW	28.69 TQ	NYBLS	10/01-12/01
	North Carolina	H	9.40 FQ	14.49 AW	19.23 TQ	NCBLS	10/01-12/01
	Charlotte-Gastonia-Rock Hill MSA, NC-SC	H	11.30 FQ	14.68 AW	19.95 TQ	NCBLS	10/01-12/01
	Fayetteville MSA, NC	H	9.33 FQ	12.32 AW	16.26 TQ	NCBLS	10/01-12/01
	Greensboro-Winston-Salem-High Point MSA, NC	H	14.23 FQ	17.37 AW	26.05 TQ	NCBLS	10/01-12/01
	Hickory-Morganton-Lenoir MSA, NC	H	10.61 FQ	13.60 AW	16.99 TQ	NCBLS	10/01-12/01
	Raleigh-Durham-Chapel Hill MSA, NC	H	8.04 FQ	11.41 AW	16.41 TQ	NCBLS	10/01-12/01
	Wilmington MSA, NC	H	9.03 FQ	11.63 AW	16.35 TQ	NCBLS	10/01-12/01
	North Dakota	H	11.23 FQ	16.69 AW	21.94 TQ	NDBLS	10/01-12/01
	Fargo-Moorhead MSA, ND-MN	H	10.98 FQ	15.00 AW	20.08 TQ	NDBLS	10/01-12/01
	Ohio	H	13.25 FQ	21.34 AW	27.73 TQ	OHBLS	10/01-12/01
	Canton-Massillon MSA, OH	H	15.02 FQ	20.45 AW	25.93 TQ	OHBLS	10/01-12/01
	Cincinnati PMSA, OH-KY-IN	H	15.33 FQ	21.65 AW	26.92 TQ	OHBLS	10/01-12/01
	Cleveland-Lorain-Elyria PMSA, OH	H	16.83 FQ	23.76 AW	28.90 TQ	OHBLS	10/01-12/01
	Columbus MSA, OH	H	11.94 FQ	18.14 AW	26.57 TQ	OHBLS	10/01-12/01
	Dayton-Springfield MSA, OH	H	10.65 FQ	17.08 AW	24.31 TQ	OHBLS	10/01-12/01
	Toledo MSA, OH	H	18.45 FQ	23.67 AW	27.74 TQ	OHBLS	10/01-12/01
	Youngstown-Warren MSA, OH	H	19.06 FQ	23.98 AW	28.10 TQ	OHBLS	10/01-12/01
	Oklahoma	H	9.12 FQ	13.73 AW	20.55 TQ	OKBLS	10/01-12/01
	Oklahoma City MSA, OK	H	12.05 FQ	16.71 AW	21.33 TQ	OKBLS	10/01-12/01
	Tulsa MSA, OK	H	9.14 FQ	12.63 AW	20.78 TQ	OKBLS	10/01-12/01
	Oregon	H	14.50 FQ	21.63 AW	29.38 TQ	ORBLS	10/01-12/01
	Portland-Vancouver PMSA, OR-WA	H	15.07 FQ	21.69 AW	29.03 TQ	ORBLS	10/01-12/01
	Pennsylvania	H	12.31 FQ	21.63 AW	29.76 TQ	PABLS	10/01-12/01
	Allentown-Bethlehem-Easton MSA, PA	H	14.00 FQ	20.98 AW	27.34 TQ	PABLS	10/01-12/01
	Harrisburg-Lebanon-Carlisle MSA, PA	H	11.45 FQ	16.57 AW	24.59 TQ	PABLS	10/01-12/01
	Lancaster MSA, PA	H	10.47 FQ	14.48 AW	18.03 TQ	PABLS	10/01-12/01
	Philadelphia PMSA, PA-NJ	H	14.97 FQ	27.82 AW	39.13 TQ	PABLS	10/01-12/01
	Pittsburgh MSA, PA	H	13.89 FQ	21.95 AW	28.23 TQ	PABLS	10/01-12/01
	Reading MSA, PA	H	14.34 FQ	20.89 AW	28.18 TQ	PABLS	10/01-12/01

AAW	Average annual wage	**AOH**	Average offered, high	**ASH**	Average starting, high	**H**	Hourly	**M**	Monthly	**S**	Special: hourly and annual
AE	Average entry wage	**AOL**	Average offered, low	**ASL**	Average starting, low	**HI**	Highest wage paid	**MTC**	Median total compensation	**TQ**	Third quartile wage
AEX	Average experienced wage	**APH**	Average pay, high range	**AW**	Average wage paid	**HR**	High end range	**MW**	Median wage paid	**W**	Weekly
AO	Average offered	**APL**	Average pay, low range	**FQ**	First quartile wage	**LR**	Low end range	**SQ**	Second quartile wage	**Y**	Yearly

Occupation/Type/Industry	Location	Per	Low	Mid	High	Source	Date
Structural Iron and Steel Worker	Scranton-Wilkes-Barre-Hazleton MSA, PA	H	15.34 FQ	22.02 AW	26.56 TQ	PABLS	10/01-12/01
	York MSA, PA	H	10.10 FQ	14.88 AW	20.61 TQ	PABLS	10/01-12/01
	Rhode Island	H	12.19 FQ	19.06 AW	27.22 TQ	RIBLS	10/01-12/01
	Providence-Fall River-Warwick MSA, RI-MA	H	12.26 FQ	18.81 AW	27.06 TQ	RIBLS	10/01-12/01
	South Carolina	H	11.34 FQ	15.98 AW	21.53 TQ	SCBLS	10/01-12/01
	Charleston-North Charleston MSA, SC	H	9.61 FQ	16.05 AW	26.06 TQ	SCBLS	10/01-12/01
	Columbia MSA, SC	H	10.22 FQ	14.25 AW	17.74 TQ	SCBLS	10/01-12/01
	Greenville-Spartanburg-Anderson MSA, SC	H	10.85 FQ	15.05 AW	17.89 TQ	SCBLS	10/01-12/01
	South Dakota	H	8.59 FQ	11.86 AW	16.91 TQ	SDBLS	10/01-12/01
	Sioux Falls MSA, SD	H	9.62 FQ	13.38 AW	18.26 TQ	SDBLS	10/01-12/01
	Tennessee	H	9.61 FQ	14.51 AW	20.85 TQ	TNBLS	10/01-12/01
	Johnson City-Kingsport-Bristol MSA, TN-VA	H	8.87 FQ	12.32 AW	17.39 TQ	TNBLS	10/01-12/01
	Knoxville MSA, TN	H	9.89 FQ	14.63 AW	20.96 TQ	TNBLS	10/01-12/01
	Memphis MSA, TN-AR-MS	H	12.50 FQ	17.25 AW	21.78 TQ	TNBLS	10/01-12/01
	Nashville MSA, TN	H	11.59 FQ	17.69 AW	21.74 TQ	TNBLS	10/01-12/01
	Texas	H	7.68 FQ	13.03 AW	19.34 TQ	TXBLS	10/01-12/01
	Beaumont-Port Arthur MSA, TX	H	9.46 FQ	14.61 AW	21.12 TQ	TXBLS	10/01-12/01
	Brazoria PMSA, TX	H	9.70 FQ	14.60 AW	19.99 TQ	TXBLS	10/01-12/01
	Corpus Christi MSA, TX	H	7.57 FQ	11.58 AW	17.15 TQ	TXBLS	10/01-12/01
	Dallas PMSA, TX	H	7.75 FQ	13.71 AW	20.09 TQ	TXBLS	10/01-12/01
	El Paso MSA, TX	H	8.07 FQ	11.32 AW	13.92 TQ	TXBLS	10/01-12/01
	Fort Worth-Arlington PMSA, TX	H	9.16 FQ	14.62 AW	21.04 TQ	TXBLS	10/01-12/01
	Houston PMSA, TX	H	7.40 FQ	12.88 AW	19.24 TQ	TXBLS	10/01-12/01
	Longview-Marshall MSA, TX	H	7.85 FQ	13.38 AW	19.98 TQ	TXBLS	10/01-12/01
	McAllen-Edinburg-Mission MSA, TX	H	5.91 FQ	9.33 AW	16.55 TQ	TXBLS	10/01-12/01
	Odessa-Midland MSA, TX	H	7.97 FQ	11.50 AW	17.46 TQ	TXBLS	10/01-12/01
	San Antonio MSA, TX	H	7.94 FQ	11.49 AW	16.56 TQ	TXBLS	10/01-12/01
	Waco MSA, TX	H	12.10 FQ	17.51 AW	21.01 TQ	TXBLS	10/01-12/01
	Utah	H	10.30 FQ	17.87 AW	22.30 TQ	UTBLS	10/01-12/01
	Provo-Orem MSA, UT	H	9.26 FQ	15.18 AW	22.70 TQ	UTBLS	10/01-12/01
	Salt Lake City-Ogden MSA, UT	H	15.27 FQ	19.33 AW	22.21 TQ	UTBLS	10/01-12/01
	Virginia	H	11.63 FQ	16.16 AW	21.36 TQ	VABLS	10/01-12/01
	Norfolk-Virginia Beach-Newport News MSA, VA-NC	H	10.37 FQ	14.64 AW	17.98 TQ	VABLS	10/01-12/01
	Richmond-Petersburg MSA, VA	H	12.50 FQ	17.38 AW	22.05 TQ	VABLS	10/01-12/01
	Washington	H	15.37 FQ	22.82 AW	30.48 TQ	WABLS	10/01-12/01
	Richland-Kennewick-Pasco MSA, WA	H	16.21 FQ	22.00 AW	26.68 TQ	WABLS	10/01-12/01
	Seattle-Bellevue-Everett PMSA, WA	H	17.66 FQ	24.77 AW	32.59 TQ	WABLS	10/01-12/01
	Tacoma PMSA, WA	H	12.21 FQ	22.99 AW	29.93 TQ	WABLS	10/01-12/01
	West Virginia	H	10.80 FQ	17.50 AW	23.15 TQ	WVBLS	10/01-12/01
	Charleston MSA, WV	H	11.09 FQ	16.64 AW	22.00 TQ	WVBLS	10/01-12/01
	Huntington-Ashland MSA, WV-KY-OH	H	8.41 FQ	13.46 AW	20.04 TQ	WVBLS	10/01-12/01
	Wisconsin	H	14.00 FQ	23.18 AW	33.17 TQ	WIBLS	10/01-12/01
	Green Bay MSA, WI	H	14.61 FQ	18.91 AW	22.42 TQ	WIBLS	10/01-12/01
	Madison MSA, WI	H	16.41 FQ	25.05 AW	32.68 TQ	WIBLS	10/01-12/01
	Milwaukee-Waukesha PMSA, WI	H	14.65 FQ	24.32 AW	33.78 TQ	WIBLS	10/01-12/01
	Wyoming	H	9.37 FQ	15.86 AW	22.32 TQ	WYBLS	10/01-12/01
	Puerto Rico	H	5.58 FQ	6.77 AW	8.38 TQ	PRBLS	10/01-12/01
	Virgin Islands	H	11.63 FQ	14.58 AW	20.21 TQ	VIBLS	10/01-12/01
	Guam	H	9.09 FQ	10.77 AW	13.18 TQ	GUBLS	10/01-12/01
Structural Metal Fabricator and Fitter	Alabama	H	9.43 FQ	14.31 AW	19.73 TQ	ALBLS	10/01-12/01
	Birmingham MSA, AL	H	10.52 FQ	14.59 AW	17.78 TQ	ALBLS	10/01-12/01
	Mobile MSA, AL	H	9.73 FQ	14.65 AW	20.41 TQ	ALBLS	10/01-12/01
	Montgomery MSA, AL	H	8.62 FQ	12.90 AW	17.78 TQ	ALBLS	10/01-12/01
	Arizona	H	9.58 FQ	13.92 AW	18.76 TQ	AZBLS	10/01-12/01

AAW Average annual wage; **AE** Average entry wage; **AEX** Average experienced wage; **AO** Average offered; **AOH** Average offered, high; **AOL** Average offered, low; **APH** Average pay, high range; **APL** Average pay, low range; **ASH** Average starting, high; **ASL** Average starting, low; **AW** Average wage paid; **FQ** First quartile wage; **H** Hourly; **HI** Highest wage paid; **HR** High end range; **LR** Low end range; **M** Monthly; **MTC** Median total compensation; **MW** Median wage paid; **SQ** Second quartile wage; **S** Special: hourly and annual; **TQ** Third quartile wage; **W** Weekly; **Y** Yearly

Occupation/Type/Industry	Location	Per	Low	Mid	High	Source	Date
Structural Metal Fabricator and Fitter	Phoenix-Mesa MSA, AZ	H	9.90 FQ	14.49 AW	20.13 TQ	AZBLS	10/01-12/01
	Tucson MSA, AZ	H	9.50 FQ	13.22 AW	17.64 TQ	AZBLS	10/01-12/01
	Arkansas	H	9.05 FQ	12.52 AW	16.69 TQ	ARBLS	10/01-12/01
	Fort Smith MSA, AR-OK	H	11.54 FQ	14.17 AW	16.54 TQ	ARBLS	10/01-12/01
	Little Rock-North Little Rock MSA, AR	H	9.06 FQ	11.71 AW	16.10 TQ	ARBLS	10/01-12/01
	California	H	8.05 FQ	13.87 AW	20.45 TQ	CABLS	10/01-12/01
	Bakersfield MSA, CA	H	14.17 FQ	21.28 AW	31.59 TQ	CABLS	10/01-12/01
	Chico-Paradise MSA, CA	H	9.31 FQ	12.26 AW	15.66 TQ	CABLS	10/01-12/01
	Fresno MSA, CA	H	8.79 FQ	11.17 AW	13.60 TQ	CABLS	10/01-12/01
	Los Angeles-Long Beach PMSA, CA	H	8.75 FQ	13.66 AW	20.17 TQ	CABLS	10/01-12/01
	Modesto MSA, CA	H	9.47 FQ	15.11 AW	20.99 TQ	CABLS	10/01-12/01
	Oakland PMSA, CA	H	8.36 FQ	15.21 AW	21.66 TQ	CABLS	10/01-12/01
	Orange County PMSA, CA	H	6.73 FQ	11.60 AW	19.45 TQ	CABLS	10/01-12/01
	Riverside-San Bernardino PMSA, CA	H	7.88 FQ	13.05 AW	18.23 TQ	CABLS	10/01-12/01
	Sacramento PMSA, CA	H	7.65 FQ	12.90 AW	18.68 TQ	CABLS	10/01-12/01
	Salinas MSA, CA	H	6.42 FQ	12.66 AW	23.49 TQ	CABLS	10/01-12/01
	San Diego MSA, CA	H	7.95 FQ	13.48 AW	19.00 TQ	CABLS	10/01-12/01
	San Francisco PMSA, CA	H	9.87 FQ	15.79 AW	22.31 TQ	CABLS	10/01-12/01
	San Jose PMSA, CA	H	7.31 FQ	15.91 AW	24.72 TQ	CABLS	10/01-12/01
	Santa Barbara-Santa Maria-Lompoc MSA, CA	H	6.55 FQ	12.18 AW	20.90 TQ	CABLS	10/01-12/01
	Santa Rosa PMSA, CA	H	11.63 FQ	16.45 AW	21.80 TQ	CABLS	10/01-12/01
	Stockton-Lodi MSA, CA	H	9.66 FQ	15.64 AW	20.93 TQ	CABLS	10/01-12/01
	Vallejo-Fairfield-Napa PMSA, CA	H	9.59 FQ	16.77 AW	21.34 TQ	CABLS	10/01-12/01
	Ventura PMSA, CA	H	9.63 FQ	14.04 AW	18.02 TQ	CABLS	10/01-12/01
	Visalia-Tulare-Porterville MSA, CA	H	7.91 FQ	11.79 AW	17.19 TQ	CABLS	10/01-12/01
	Colorado	H	9.23 FQ	14.65 AW	22.42 TQ	COBLS	10/01-12/01
	Colorado Springs MSA, CO	H	10.09 FQ	13.25 AW	19.81 TQ	COBLS	10/01-12/01
	Denver PMSA, CO	H	9.84 FQ	16.48 AW	25.55 TQ	COBLS	10/01-12/01
	Greeley PMSA, CO	H	6.18 FQ	11.70 AW	21.06 TQ	COBLS	10/01-12/01
	Connecticut	H	11.52 FQ	17.39 AW	22.35 TQ	CTBLS	10/01-12/01
	Bridgeport PMSA, CT	H	9.38 FQ	15.77 AW	21.57 TQ	CTBLS	10/01-12/01
	Hartford MSA, CT	H	12.13 FQ	17.80 AW	22.85 TQ	CTBLS	10/01-12/01
	New Haven-Meriden PMSA, CT	H	11.59 FQ	17.41 AW	22.69 TQ	CTBLS	10/01-12/01
	New London-Norwich MSA, CT-RI	H	13.89 FQ	17.44 AW	20.86 TQ	CTBLS	10/01-12/01
	Waterbury PMSA, CT	H	12.56 FQ	16.16 AW	20.17 TQ	CTBLS	10/01-12/01
	Delaware	H	9.89 FQ	14.44 AW	20.11 TQ	DEBLS	10/01-12/01
	Wilmington-Newark PMSA, DE-MD	H	10.45 FQ	14.99 AW	20.42 TQ	DEBLS	10/01-12/01
	Washington PMSA, DC-MD-VA-WV	H	10.12 FQ	14.69 AW	19.79 TQ	DCBLS	10/01-12/01
	Florida	H	8.87 FQ	12.18 AW	16.35 TQ	FLBLS	10/01-12/01
	Daytona Beach MSA, FL	H	6.75 FQ	12.37 AW	17.36 TQ	FLBLS	10/01-12/01
	Fort Lauderdale PMSA, FL	H	9.10 FQ	13.65 AW	17.56 TQ	FLBLS	10/01-12/01
	Fort Myers-Cape Coral MSA, FL	H	7.77 FQ	10.85 AW	14.32 TQ	FLBLS	10/01-12/01
	Gainesville MSA, FL	H	9.36 FQ	13.54 AW	19.21 TQ	FLBLS	10/01-12/01
	Jacksonville MSA, FL	H	9.42 FQ	12.91 AW	16.56 TQ	FLBLS	10/01-12/01
	Lakeland-Winter Haven MSA, FL	H	8.90 FQ	12.90 AW	17.13 TQ	FLBLS	10/01-12/01
	Melbourne-Titusville-Palm Bay MSA, FL	H	9.27 FQ	12.93 AW	17.27 TQ	FLBLS	10/01-12/01
	Miami PMSA, FL	H	6.60 FQ	11.18 AW	15.60 TQ	FLBLS	10/01-12/01
	Naples MSA, FL	H	10.47 FQ	14.29 AW	17.44 TQ	FLBLS	10/01-12/01
	Orlando MSA, FL	H	9.30 FQ	11.71 AW	16.05 TQ	FLBLS	10/01-12/01
	Pensacola MSA, FL	H	8.58 FQ	12.41 AW	16.90 TQ	FLBLS	10/01-12/01
	Sarasota-Bradenton MSA, FL	H	9.48 FQ	11.45 AW	14.23 TQ	FLBLS	10/01-12/01
	Tampa-St. Petersburg-Clearwater MSA, FL	H	8.21 FQ	12.28 AW	16.26 TQ	FLBLS	10/01-12/01
	West Palm Beach-Boca Raton MSA, FL	H	9.40 FQ	12.54 AW	14.84 TQ	FLBLS	10/01-12/01
	Georgia	H	9.43 FQ	13.19 AW	17.32 TQ	GABLS	10/01-12/01
	Atlanta MSA, GA	H	9.22 FQ	12.88 AW	17.46 TQ	GABLS	10/01-12/01
	Augusta-Aiken MSA, GA-SC	H	7.62 FQ	13.01 AW	17.40 TQ	GABLS	10/01-12/01

AAW Average annual wage **AE** Average entry wage **AEX** Average experienced wage **AO** Average offered **AOH** Average offered, high **AOL** Average offered, low **APH** Average pay, high range **APL** Average pay, low range **ASH** Average starting, high **ASL** Average starting, low **AW** Average wage paid **FQ** First quartile wage **H** Hourly **HI** Highest wage paid **HR** High end range **LR** Low end range **M** Monthly **MTC** Median total compensation **MW** Median wage paid **SQ** Second quartile wage **S** Special: hourly and annual **TQ** Third quartile wage **W** Weekly **Y** Yearly

Occupation/Type/Industry	Location	Per	Low	Mid	High	Source	Date
Structural Metal Fabricator and Fitter	Columbus MSA, GA-AL	H	8.86 FQ	12.19 AW	16.96 TQ	GABLS	10/01-12/01
	Macon MSA, GA	H	9.29 FQ	14.65 AW	21.71 TQ	GABLS	10/01-12/01
	Hawaii	H	12.43 FQ	22.50 AW	30.95 TQ	HIBLS	10/01-12/01
	Honolulu MSA, HI	H	12.16 FQ	22.41 AW	31.26 TQ	HIBLS	10/01-12/01
	Idaho	H	8.21 FQ	12.65 AW	17.20 TQ	IDBLS	10/01-12/01
	Boise City MSA, ID	H	11.07 FQ	14.00 AW	18.36 TQ	IDBLS	10/01-12/01
	Illinois	H	9.00 FQ	15.25 AW	22.27 TQ	ILBLS	10/01-12/01
	Chicago PMSA, IL	H	9.18 FQ	16.60 AW	27.78 TQ	ILBLS	10/01-12/01
	Peoria-Pekin MSA, IL	H	9.28 FQ	13.67 AW	19.33 TQ	ILBLS	10/01-12/01
	Rockford MSA, IL	H	10.17 FQ	14.89 AW	21.58 TQ	ILBLS	10/01-12/01
	Indiana	H	8.33 FQ	13.11 AW	19.26 TQ	INBLS	10/01-12/01
	Elkhart-Goshen MSA, IN	H	7.99 FQ	12.58 AW	17.33 TQ	INBLS	10/01-12/01
	Evansville-Henderson MSA, IN-KY	H	8.46 FQ	13.01 AW	17.19 TQ	INBLS	10/01-12/01
	Fort Wayne MSA, IN	H	9.63 FQ	16.17 AW	25.58 TQ	INBLS	10/01-12/01
	Gary PMSA, IN	H	6.81 FQ	12.85 AW	19.64 TQ	INBLS	10/01-12/01
	Indianapolis MSA, IN	H	9.02 FQ	13.41 AW	19.95 TQ	INBLS	10/01-12/01
	South Bend MSA, IN	H	9.30 FQ	11.58 AW	13.87 TQ	INBLS	10/01-12/01
	Iowa	H	9.34 FQ	13.52 AW	19.20 TQ	IABLS	10/01-12/01
	Cedar Rapids MSA, IA	H	9.52 FQ	13.45 AW	17.15 TQ	IABLS	10/01-12/01
	Davenport-Moline-Rock Island MSA, IA-IL	H	7.50 FQ	11.25 AW	16.04 TQ	IABLS	10/01-12/01
	Des Moines MSA, IA	H	10.54 FQ	14.10 AW	17.59 TQ	IABLS	10/01-12/01
	Kansas	H	8.92 FQ	13.81 AW	19.81 TQ	KSBLS	10/01-12/01
	Wichita MSA, KS	H	9.15 FQ	14.47 AW	20.51 TQ	KSBLS	10/01-12/01
	Kentucky	H	9.24 FQ	12.75 AW	16.70 TQ	KYBLS	10/01-12/01
	Lexington MSA, KY	H	8.87 FQ	12.24 AW	16.20 TQ	KYBLS	10/01-12/01
	Louisville MSA, KY-IN	H	10.37 FQ	13.22 AW	17.08 TQ	KYBLS	10/01-12/01
	Louisiana	H	9.76 FQ	14.81 AW	20.45 TQ	LABLS	10/01-12/01
	Baton Rouge MSA, LA	H	9.17 FQ	15.46 AW	26.96 TQ	LABLS	10/01-12/01
	Houma MSA, LA	H	11.81 FQ	16.04 AW	20.67 TQ	LABLS	10/01-12/01
	Lafayette MSA, LA	H	8.58 FQ	12.49 AW	16.51 TQ	LABLS	10/01-12/01
	Lake Charles MSA, LA	H	6.77 FQ	17.30 AW	28.91 TQ	LABLS	10/01-12/01
	New Orleans MSA, LA	H	10.32 FQ	15.27 AW	20.87 TQ	LABLS	10/01-12/01
	Shreveport-Bossier City MSA, LA	H	10.12 FQ	13.09 AW	17.60 TQ	LABLS	10/01-12/01
	Maryland	H	10.33 FQ	15.46 AW	21.06 TQ	MDBLS	10/01-12/01
	Baltimore PMSA, MD	H	10.16 FQ	15.33 AW	20.99 TQ	MDBLS	10/01-12/01
	Massachusetts	H	11.22 FQ	17.69 AW	24.86 TQ	MABLS	10/01-12/01
	Boston PMSA, MA-NH	H	11.82 FQ	16.83 AW	21.43 TQ	MABLS	10/01-12/01
	Lawrence PMSA, MA-NH	H	11.94 FQ	19.89 AW	30.36 TQ	MABLS	10/01-12/01
	Lowell PMSA, MA-NH	H	11.92 FQ	17.80 AW	22.48 TQ	MABLS	10/01-12/01
	Springfield MSA, MA	H	12.29 FQ	17.06 AW	22.82 TQ	MABLS	10/01-12/01
	Worcester PMSA, MA-CT	H	11.24 FQ	15.60 AW	21.35 TQ	MABLS	10/01-12/01
	Michigan	H	10.51 FQ	19.69 AW	33.62 TQ	MIBLS	10/01-12/01
	Ann Arbor PMSA, MI	H	9.31 FQ	14.51 AW	20.63 TQ	MIBLS	10/01-12/01
	Detroit PMSA, MI	H	12.98 FQ	24.02 AW	35.48 TQ	MIBLS	10/01-12/01
	Grand Rapids-Muskegon-Holland MSA, MI	H	10.16 FQ	15.15 AW	21.00 TQ	MIBLS	10/01-12/01
	Kalamazoo-Battle Creek MSA, MI	H	10.68 FQ	13.71 AW	20.38 TQ	MIBLS	10/01-12/01
	Saginaw-Bay City-Midland MSA, MI	H	8.59 FQ	12.75 AW	19.62 TQ	MIBLS	10/01-12/01
	Minnesota	H	9.90 FQ	14.62 AW	19.43 TQ	MNBLS	10/01-12/01
	Duluth-Superior MSA, MN-WI	H	11.38 FQ	17.49 AW	27.67 TQ	MNBLS	10/01-12/01
	Minneapolis-St. Paul MSA, MN-WI	H	10.26 FQ	14.73 AW	19.06 TQ	MNBLS	10/01-12/01
	St. Cloud MSA, MN	H	12.44 FQ	18.05 AW	31.64 TQ	MNBLS	10/01-12/01
	Mississippi	H	8.63 FQ	11.92 AW	15.94 TQ	MSBLS	10/01-12/01
	Biloxi-Gulfport-Pascagoula MSA, MS	H	10.17 FQ	14.62 AW	18.42 TQ	MSBLS	10/01-12/01
	Missouri	H	9.14 FQ	13.65 AW	17.65 TQ	MOBLS	10/01-12/01
	Kansas City MSA, MO-KS	H	9.80 FQ	14.67 AW	19.52 TQ	MOBLS	10/01-12/01
	St. Louis MSA, MO-IL	H	10.36 FQ	15.05 AW	22.63 TQ	MOBLS	10/01-12/01
	Springfield MSA, MO	H	9.52 FQ	12.87 AW	16.70 TQ	MOBLS	10/01-12/01
	Montana	H	8.12 FQ	12.54 AW	16.49 TQ	MTBLS	10/01-12/01
	Billings MSA, MT	H	9.21 FQ	13.32 AW	16.75 TQ	MTBLS	10/01-12/01
	Nebraska	H	8.71 FQ	11.69 AW	14.50 TQ	NEBLS	10/01-12/01
	Lincoln MSA, NE	H	9.90 FQ	12.96 AW	16.49 TQ	NEBLS	10/01-12/01
	Omaha MSA, NE-IA	H	8.34 FQ	12.09 AW	17.05 TQ	NEBLS	10/01-12/01
	Nevada	H	9.05 FQ	15.09 AW	25.37 TQ	NVBLS	10/01-12/01

AAW Average annual wage; **AE** Average entry wage; **AEX** Average experienced wage; **AO** Average offered; **AOH** Average offered, high; **AOL** Average offered, low; **APH** Average pay, high range; **APL** Average pay, low range; **ASH** Average starting, high; **ASL** Average starting, low; **AW** Average wage paid; **FQ** First quartile wage; **H** Hourly; **HI** Highest wage paid; **HR** High end range; **LR** Low end range; **M** Monthly; **MTC** Median total compensation; **MW** Median wage paid; **SQ** Second quartile wage; **S** Special: hourly and annual; **TQ** Third quartile wage; **W** Weekly; **Y** Yearly

Occupation/Type/Industry	Location	Per	Low	Mid	High	Source	Date
Structural Metal Fabricator and Fitter	Las Vegas MSA, NV-AZ	H	9.17 FQ	16.88 AW	26.88 TQ	NVBLS	10/01-12/01
	New Hampshire	H	9.90 FQ	14.27 AW	19.62 TQ	NHBLS	10/01-12/01
	Manchester PMSA, NH	H	9.27 FQ	13.82 AW	17.55 TQ	NHBLS	10/01-12/01
	Portsmouth-Rochester PMSA, NH-ME	H	12.84 FQ	18.08 AW	22.39 TQ	NHBLS	10/01-12/01
	New Jersey	H	9.78 FQ	15.63 AW	23.24 TQ	NJBLS	10/01-12/01
	Bergen-Passaic PMSA, NJ	H	9.62 FQ	17.50 AW	27.99 TQ	NJBLS	10/01-12/01
	Jersey City PMSA, NJ	H	10.24 FQ	17.49 AW	30.57 TQ	NJBLS	10/01-12/01
	Middlesex-Somerset-Hunterdon PMSA, NJ	H	9.27 FQ	14.32 AW	19.76 TQ	NJBLS	10/01-12/01
	Monmouth-Ocean PMSA, NJ	H	9.22 FQ	13.35 AW	19.96 TQ	NJBLS	10/01-12/01
	Newark PMSA, NJ	H	10.50 FQ	14.31 AW	17.51 TQ	NJBLS	10/01-12/01
	Trenton PMSA, NJ	H	12.51 FQ	19.77 AW	30.95 TQ	NJBLS	10/01-12/01
	New Mexico	H	8.87 FQ	11.49 AW	16.08 TQ	NMBLS	10/01-12/01
	Albuquerque MSA, NM	H	8.98 FQ	10.98 AW	15.21 TQ	NMBLS	10/01-12/01
	New York	H	9.22 FQ	16.17 AW	26.85 TQ	NYBLS	10/01-12/01
	Albany-Schenectady-Troy MSA, NY	H	11.10 FQ	15.46 AW	21.01 TQ	NYBLS	10/01-12/01
	Buffalo-Niagara Falls MSA, NY	H	8.75 FQ	12.91 AW	17.60 TQ	NYBLS	10/01-12/01
	Nassau-Suffolk PMSA, NY	H	8.87 FQ	15.77 AW	23.80 TQ	NYBLS	10/01-12/01
	New York PMSA, NY	H	8.20 FQ	20.37 AW	36.23 TQ	NYBLS	10/01-12/01
	Rochester MSA, NY	H	9.89 FQ	13.23 AW	18.82 TQ	NYBLS	10/01-12/01
	Syracuse MSA, NY	H	9.93 FQ	13.94 AW	19.02 TQ	NYBLS	10/01-12/01
	Utica-Rome MSA, NY	H	8.47 FQ	12.76 AW	16.67 TQ	NYBLS	10/01-12/01
	North Carolina	H	9.41 FQ	13.55 AW	18.94 TQ	NCBLS	10/01-12/01
	Asheville MSA, NC	H	9.51 FQ	13.59 AW	17.57 TQ	NCBLS	10/01-12/01
	Charlotte-Gastonia-Rock Hill MSA, NC-SC	H	10.11 FQ	15.43 AW	21.10 TQ	NCBLS	10/01-12/01
	Greensboro-Winston-Salem-High Point MSA, NC	H	9.49 FQ	12.80 AW	17.30 TQ	NCBLS	10/01-12/01
	Hickory-Morganton-Lenoir MSA, NC	H	9.22 FQ	13.49 AW	23.65 TQ	NCBLS	10/01-12/01
	Raleigh-Durham-Chapel Hill MSA, NC	H	9.49 FQ	13.79 AW	19.56 TQ	NCBLS	10/01-12/01
	North Dakota	H	9.58 FQ	12.00 AW	14.32 TQ	NDBLS	10/01-12/01
	Fargo-Moorhead MSA, ND-MN	H	10.47 FQ	11.86 AW	13.36 TQ	NDBLS	10/01-12/01
	Ohio	H	10.10 FQ	14.57 AW	18.30 TQ	OHBLS	10/01-12/01
	Akron PMSA, OH	H	11.98 FQ	15.28 AW	17.93 TQ	OHBLS	10/01-12/01
	Canton-Massillon MSA, OH	H	9.13 FQ	12.50 AW	16.65 TQ	OHBLS	10/01-12/01
	Cincinnati PMSA, OH-KY-IN	H	10.15 FQ	14.26 AW	17.64 TQ	OHBLS	10/01-12/01
	Cleveland-Lorain-Elyria PMSA, OH	H	11.34 FQ	14.56 AW	17.53 TQ	OHBLS	10/01-12/01
	Columbus MSA, OH	H	9.31 FQ	13.72 AW	17.53 TQ	OHBLS	10/01-12/01
	Dayton-Springfield MSA, OH	H	9.67 FQ	14.58 AW	21.43 TQ	OHBLS	10/01-12/01
	Hamilton-Middletown PMSA, OH	H	9.86 FQ	14.35 AW	20.17 TQ	OHBLS	10/01-12/01
	Mansfield MSA, OH	H	9.79 FQ	13.46 AW	16.82 TQ	OHBLS	10/01-12/01
	Toledo MSA, OH	H	11.64 FQ	15.18 AW	18.98 TQ	OHBLS	10/01-12/01
	Youngstown-Warren MSA, OH	H	9.22 FQ	15.68 AW	21.84 TQ	OHBLS	10/01-12/01
	Oklahoma	H	8.09 FQ	12.20 AW	16.60 TQ	OKBLS	10/01-12/01
	Oklahoma City MSA, OK	H	8.84 FQ	11.92 AW	15.84 TQ	OKBLS	10/01-12/01
	Tulsa MSA, OK	H	8.91 FQ	13.73 AW	17.93 TQ	OKBLS	10/01-12/01
	Oregon	H	9.66 FQ	15.44 AW	24.88 TQ	ORBLS	10/01-12/01
	Eugene-Springfield MSA, OR	H	9.20 FQ	12.75 AW	16.74 TQ	ORBLS	10/01-12/01
	Medford-Ashland MSA, OR	H	9.50 FQ	14.27 AW	19.61 TQ	ORBLS	10/01-12/01
	Portland-Vancouver PMSA, OR-WA	H	10.45 FQ	16.44 AW	24.81 TQ	ORBLS	10/01-12/01
	Salem PMSA, OR	H	8.99 FQ	17.11 AW	28.90 TQ	ORBLS	10/01-12/01
	Pennsylvania	H	9.89 FQ	14.47 AW	19.29 TQ	PABLS	10/01-12/01
	Allentown-Bethlehem-Easton MSA, PA	H	9.08 FQ	14.79 AW	19.93 TQ	PABLS	10/01-12/01
	Erie MSA, PA	H	10.01 FQ	13.34 AW	16.91 TQ	PABLS	10/01-12/01
	Harrisburg-Lebanon-Carlisle MSA, PA	H	11.54 FQ	15.71 AW	20.44 TQ	PABLS	10/01-12/01
	Johnstown MSA, PA	H	9.93 FQ	14.20 AW	17.46 TQ	PABLS	10/01-12/01
	Lancaster MSA, PA	H	10.85 FQ	14.26 AW	17.27 TQ	PABLS	10/01-12/01
	Philadelphia PMSA, PA-NJ	H	10.62 FQ	15.92 AW	22.84 TQ	PABLS	10/01-12/01
	Pittsburgh MSA, PA	H	10.05 FQ	14.74 AW	20.45 TQ	PABLS	10/01-12/01
	Reading MSA, PA	H	11.90 FQ	15.41 AW	19.91 TQ	PABLS	10/01-12/01

AAW Average annual wage **AOH** Average offered, high **ASH** Average starting, high **H** Hourly **M** Monthly **S** Special: hourly and annual
AE Average entry wage **AOL** Average offered, low **ASL** Average starting, low **HI** Highest wage paid **MTC** Median total compensation **TQ** Third quartile wage
AEX Average experienced wage **APH** Average pay, high range **AW** Average wage paid **HR** High end range **MW** Median wage paid **W** Weekly
AO Average offered **APL** Average pay, low range **FQ** First quartile wage **LR** Low end range **SQ** Second quartile wage **Y** Yearly

Occupation/Type/Industry	Location	Per	Low	Mid	High	Source	Date
Structural Metal Fabricator and Fitter	Scranton-Wilkes-Barre-Hazleton MSA, PA	H	7.57 FQ	10.52 AW	14.44 TQ	PABLS	10/01-12/01
	York MSA, PA	H	11.60 FQ	14.95 AW	17.72 TQ	PABLS	10/01-12/01
	Rhode Island	H	9.81 FQ	13.90 AW	18.78 TQ	RIBLS	10/01-12/01
	Providence-Fall River-Warwick MSA, RI-MA	H	10.05 FQ	16.04 AW	25.69 TQ	RIBLS	10/01-12/01
	South Carolina	H	8.98 FQ	12.96 AW	16.96 TQ	SCBLS	10/01-12/01
	Charleston-North Charleston MSA, SC	H	8.15 FQ	11.10 AW	14.99 TQ	SCBLS	10/01-12/01
	Columbia MSA, SC	H	8.04 FQ	11.24 AW	15.40 TQ	SCBLS	10/01-12/01
	Greenville-Spartanburg-Anderson MSA, SC	H	10.23 FQ	13.49 AW	16.89 TQ	SCBLS	10/01-12/01
	South Dakota	H	9.35 FQ	12.30 AW	17.43 TQ	SDBLS	10/01-12/01
	Sioux Falls MSA, SD	H	8.86 FQ	13.22 AW	18.86 TQ	SDBLS	10/01-12/01
	Tennessee	H	8.90 FQ	12.42 AW	16.79 TQ	TNBLS	10/01-12/01
	Chattanooga MSA, TN-GA	H	9.80 FQ	13.37 AW	17.15 TQ	TNBLS	10/01-12/01
	Johnson City-Kingsport-Bristol MSA, TN-VA	H	11.40 FQ	13.20 AW	16.00 TQ	TNBLS	10/01-12/01
	Knoxville MSA, TN	H	9.36 FQ	12.37 AW	16.51 TQ	TNBLS	10/01-12/01
	Memphis MSA, TN-AR-MS	H	7.90 FQ	12.01 AW	17.62 TQ	TNBLS	10/01-12/01
	Nashville MSA, TN	H	9.73 FQ	13.30 AW	17.01 TQ	TNBLS	10/01-12/01
	Texas	H	7.14 FQ	11.64 AW	16.67 TQ	TXBLS	10/01-12/01
	Austin-San Marcos MSA, TX	H	7.60 FQ	10.82 AW	14.84 TQ	TXBLS	10/01-12/01
	Beaumont-Port Arthur MSA, TX	H	8.65 FQ	13.50 AW	17.74 TQ	TXBLS	10/01-12/01
	Brazoria PMSA, TX	H	12.71 FQ	17.85 AW	22.22 TQ	TXBLS	10/01-12/01
	Brownsville-Harlingen-San Benito MSA, TX	H	7.55 FQ	9.37 AW	12.26 TQ	TXBLS	10/01-12/01
	Corpus Christi MSA, TX	H	8.52 FQ	12.21 AW	16.10 TQ	TXBLS	10/01-12/01
	Dallas PMSA, TX	H	6.37 FQ	11.25 AW	16.26 TQ	TXBLS	10/01-12/01
	El Paso MSA, TX	H	5.83 FQ	8.16 AW	11.39 TQ	TXBLS	10/01-12/01
	Fort Worth-Arlington PMSA, TX	H	6.19 FQ	10.80 AW	15.77 TQ	TXBLS	10/01-12/01
	Houston PMSA, TX	H	8.96 FQ	12.39 AW	17.52 TQ	TXBLS	10/01-12/01
	Killeen-Temple MSA, TX	H	7.42 FQ	11.29 AW	16.19 TQ	TXBLS	10/01-12/01
	Lubbock MSA, TX	H	8.78 FQ	11.30 AW	14.34 TQ	TXBLS	10/01-12/01
	McAllen-Edinburg-Mission MSA, TX	H	5.93 FQ	8.86 AW	13.07 TQ	TXBLS	10/01-12/01
	San Antonio MSA, TX	H	7.94 FQ	11.23 AW	15.02 TQ	TXBLS	10/01-12/01
	Utah	H	8.89 FQ	13.33 AW	18.41 TQ	UTBLS	10/01-12/01
	Provo-Orem MSA, UT	H	8.42 FQ	12.29 AW	17.63 TQ	UTBLS	10/01-12/01
	Salt Lake City-Ogden MSA, UT	H	9.82 FQ	13.98 AW	18.28 TQ	UTBLS	10/01-12/01
	Virginia	H	9.88 FQ	14.49 AW	18.20 TQ	VABLS	10/01-12/01
	Lynchburg MSA, VA	H	9.63 FQ	12.55 AW	15.98 TQ	VABLS	10/01-12/01
	Richmond-Petersburg MSA, VA	H	10.33 FQ	15.16 AW	20.31 TQ	VABLS	10/01-12/01
	Roanoke MSA, VA	H	7.92 FQ	11.39 AW	16.72 TQ	VABLS	10/01-12/01
	Washington	H	10.14 FQ	16.93 AW	24.93 TQ	WABLS	10/01-12/01
	Seattle-Bellevue-Everett PMSA, WA	H	9.56 FQ	14.61 AW	21.81 TQ	WABLS	10/01-12/01
	West Virginia	H	9.56 FQ	12.46 AW	16.14 TQ	WVBLS	10/01-12/01
	Huntington-Ashland MSA, WV-KY-OH	H	9.32 FQ	12.57 AW	16.24 TQ	WVBLS	10/01-12/01
	Wisconsin	H	9.92 FQ	14.92 AW	20.47 TQ	WIBLS	10/01-12/01
	Appleton-Oshkosh-Neenah MSA, WI	H	10.85 FQ	15.57 AW	20.80 TQ	WIBLS	10/01-12/01
	Madison MSA, WI	H	8.86 FQ	14.05 AW	19.57 TQ	WIBLS	10/01-12/01
	Milwaukee-Waukesha PMSA, WI	H	9.99 FQ	15.78 AW	21.87 TQ	WIBLS	10/01-12/01
	Racine PMSA, WI	H	10.96 FQ	15.23 AW	21.17 TQ	WIBLS	10/01-12/01
	Wyoming	H	9.00 FQ	12.56 AW	16.93 TQ	WYBLS	10/01-12/01
	Puerto Rico	H	5.49 FQ	7.56 AW	11.92 TQ	PRBLS	10/01-12/01
Substance Abuse and Behavioral Disorder Counselor	Alabama	Y	16060 FQ	29630 AW	41470 TQ	ALBLS	10/01-12/01
	Alaska	Y	25560 FQ	35730 AW	48180 TQ	AKBLS	10/01-12/01
	Arizona	Y	15860 FQ	27500 AW	43800 TQ	AZBLS	10/01-12/01
	Arkansas	Y	15080 FQ	22910 AW	32970 TQ	ARBLS	10/01-12/01
	California	Y	17380 FQ	29310 AW	41970 TQ	CABLS	10/01-12/01
	Colorado	Y	20230 FQ	29880 AW	43160 TQ	COBLS	10/01-12/01

AAW	Average annual wage	**AOH**	Average offered, high	**ASH**	Average starting, high	**H**	Hourly	**M**	Monthly	**S**	Special: hourly and annual
AE	Average entry wage	**AOL**	Average offered, low	**ASL**	Average starting, low	**HI**	Highest wage paid	**MTC**	Median total compensation	**TQ**	Third quartile wage
AEX	Average experienced wage	**APH**	Average pay, high range	**AW**	Average wage paid	**HR**	High end range	**MW**	Median wage paid	**W**	Weekly
AO	Average offered	**APL**	Average pay, low range	**FQ**	First quartile wage	**LR**	Low end range	**SQ**	Second quartile wage	**Y**	Yearly

Occupation/Type/Industry	Location	Per	Low	Mid	High	Source	Date
Substance Abuse and Behavioral Disorder Counselor	Connecticut	Y	24250 FQ	36190 AW	51990 TQ	CTBLS	10/01-12/01
	Delaware	Y	24180 FQ	34910 AW	46270 TQ	DEBLS	10/01-12/01
	District of Columbia	Y	19380 FQ	31200 AW	42710 TQ	DCBLS	10/01-12/01
	Florida	Y	19040 FQ	29770 AW	41660 TQ	FLBLS	10/01-12/01
	Georgia	Y	19210 FQ	29030 AW	39840 TQ	GABLS	10/01-12/01
	Hawaii	Y	21530 FQ	35680 AW	53010 TQ	HIBLS	10/01-12/01
	Idaho	Y	20700 FQ	31340 AW	42820 TQ	IDBLS	10/01-12/01
	Illinois	Y	18680 FQ	28870 AW	41210 TQ	ILBLS	10/01-12/01
	Indiana	Y	18260 FQ	29850 AW	43720 TQ	INBLS	10/01-12/01
	Iowa	Y	19010 FQ	30630 AW	44530 TQ	IABLS	10/01-12/01
	Kansas	Y	17960 FQ	29670 AW	40890 TQ	KSBLS	10/01-12/01
	Kentucky	Y	18440 FQ	28650 AW	43120 TQ	KYBLS	10/01-12/01
	Louisiana	Y	20860 FQ	30520 AW	41490 TQ	LABLS	10/01-12/01
	Maine	Y	22860 FQ	32700 AW	44340 TQ	MEBLS	10/01-12/01
	Maryland	Y	24680 FQ	35160 AW	46960 TQ	MDBLS	10/01-12/01
	Massachusetts	Y	21190 FQ	30740 AW	43700 TQ	MABLS	10/01-12/01
	Michigan	Y	21220 FQ	32500 AW	46280 TQ	MIBLS	10/01-12/01
	Minnesota	Y	24960 FQ	33860 AW	44710 TQ	MNBLS	10/01-12/01
	Mississippi	Y	17020 FQ	26980 AW	39800 TQ	MSBLS	10/01-12/01
	Missouri	Y	17960 FQ	28840 AW	42760 TQ	MOBLS	10/01-12/01
	Montana	Y	15720 FQ	26930 AW	36600 TQ	MTBLS	10/01-12/01
	Nebraska	Y	18380 FQ	27690 AW	39620 TQ	NEBLS	10/01-12/01
	Nevada	Y	17700 FQ	29530 AW	42700 TQ	NVBLS	10/01-12/01
	New Hampshire	Y	13490 FQ	26660 AW	38220 TQ	NHBLS	10/01-12/01
	New Jersey	Y	20230 FQ	34020 AW	52160 TQ	NJBLS	10/01-12/01
	New Mexico	Y	19560 FQ	30050 AW	42580 TQ	NMBLS	10/01-12/01
	New York	Y	24130 FQ	37620 AW	52670 TQ	NYBLS	10/01-12/01
	North Carolina	Y	21490 FQ	31810 AW	43300 TQ	NCBLS	10/01-12/01
	North Dakota	Y	27280 FQ	35350 AW	46380 TQ	NDBLS	10/01-12/01
	Ohio	Y	21450 FQ	31180 AW	43290 TQ	OHBLS	10/01-12/01
	Oklahoma	Y	15890 FQ	27280 AW	41400 TQ	OKBLS	10/01-12/01
	Oregon	Y	15480 FQ	28170 AW	43240 TQ	ORBLS	10/01-12/01
	Pennsylvania	Y	21160 FQ	33190 AW	47500 TQ	PABLS	10/01-12/01
	Rhode Island	Y	20660 FQ	26930 AW	35820 TQ	RIBLS	10/01-12/01
	South Carolina	Y	18860 FQ	31320 AW	45750 TQ	SCBLS	10/01-12/01
	South Dakota	Y	20270 FQ	29390 AW	42290 TQ	SDBLS	10/01-12/01
	Tennessee	Y	14600 FQ	25920 AW	38850 TQ	TNBLS	10/01-12/01
	Texas	Y	20000 FQ	27540 AW	36600 TQ	TXBLS	10/01-12/01
	Utah	Y	15990 FQ	27620 AW	40590 TQ	UTBLS	10/01-12/01
	Vermont	Y	25020 FQ	34180 AW	44250 TQ	VTBLS	10/01-12/01
	Virginia	Y	22550 FQ	37140 AW	56080 TQ	VABLS	10/01-12/01
	Washington	Y	20420 FQ	30190 AW	39800 TQ	WABLS	10/01-12/01
	West Virginia	Y	21530 FQ	30310 AW	42760 TQ	WVBLS	10/01-12/01
	Wisconsin	Y	25200 FQ	43720 AW	83100 TQ	WIBLS	10/01-12/01
	Wyoming	Y	17500 FQ	29970 AW	43940 TQ	WYBLS	10/01-12/01
	Puerto Rico	Y	13530 FQ	22070 AW	33870 TQ	PRBLS	10/01-12/01
Subway and Streetcar Operator	California	H	15.46 FQ	19.60 AW	24.83 TQ	CABLS	10/01-12/01
	Florida	H	5.95 FQ	9.33 AW	14.69 TQ	FLBLS	10/01-12/01
	Virginia	H	9.03 FQ	16.24 AW	25.91 TQ	VABLS	10/01-12/01
Surgeon	Alabama	Y		143320 AW		ALBLS	10/01-12/01
	Birmingham MSA, AL	Y		# AW		ALBLS	10/01-12/01
	Montgomery MSA, AL	Y	124980 FQ	134640 AW		ALBLS	10/01-12/01
	Arizona	Y	142050 FQ	143030 AW		AZBLS	10/01-12/01
	Phoenix-Mesa MSA, AZ	Y	127150 FQ	138790 AW		AZBLS	10/01-12/01
	Tucson MSA, AZ	Y		143350 AW		AZBLS	10/01-12/01
	Arkansas	Y		144400 AW		ARBLS	10/01-12/01
	California	Y	97890 FQ	133820 AW		CABLS	10/01-12/01
	Bakersfield MSA, CA	Y	116460 FQ	127810 AW	144910 TQ	CABLS	10/01-12/01
	Los Angeles-Long Beach PMSA, CA	Y	99200 FQ	127920 AW		CABLS	10/01-12/01
	Oakland PMSA, CA	Y	78790 FQ	100700 AW		CABLS	10/01-12/01
	Orange County PMSA, CA	Y	104550 FQ	127810 AW		CABLS	10/01-12/01
	Riverside-San Bernardino PMSA, CA	Y	116350 FQ	134200 AW		CABLS	10/01-12/01
	Sacramento PMSA, CA	Y		144500 AW		CABLS	10/01-12/01
	Salinas MSA, CA	Y	59340 FQ	124760 AW		CABLS	10/01-12/01
	San Diego MSA, CA	Y	127290 FQ	140770 AW		CABLS	10/01-12/01
	San Jose PMSA, CA	Y	111520 FQ	134440 AW		CABLS	10/01-12/01

AAW	Average annual wage	AOH	Average offered, high	ASH	Average starting, high	H	Hourly	M	Monthly	S	Special: hourly and annual
AE	Average entry wage	AOL	Average offered, low	ASL	Average starting, low	HI	Highest wage paid	MTC	Median total compensation	TQ	Third quartile wage
AEX	Average experienced wage	APH	Average pay, high range	AW	Average wage paid	HR	High end range	MW	Median wage paid	W	Weekly
AO	Average offered	APL	Average pay, low range	FQ	First quartile wage	LR	Low end range	SQ	Second quartile wage	Y	Yearly

Occupation/Type/Industry	Location	Per	Low	Mid	High	Source	Date
Surgeon	San Luis Obispo-Atascadero-Paso Robles MSA, CA	Y	120050 FQ	136210 AW		CABLS	10/01-12/01
	Santa Barbara-Santa Maria-Lompoc MSA, CA	Y	78220 FQ	111500 AW		CABLS	10/01-12/01
	Santa Cruz-Watsonville PMSA, CA	Y	122980 FQ	139180 AW		CABLS	10/01-12/01
	Santa Rosa PMSA, CA	Y	72480 FQ	123430 AW		CABLS	10/01-12/01
	Vallejo-Fairfield-Napa PMSA, CA	Y	91100 FQ	120290 AW	145280 TQ	CABLS	10/01-12/01
	Ventura PMSA, CA	Y		141810 AW		CABLS	10/01-12/01
	Colorado	Y		141870 AW		COBLS	10/01-12/01
	Denver PMSA, CO	Y		141950 AW		COBLS	10/01-12/01
	Connecticut	Y	42550 FQ	128700 AW		CTBLS	10/01-12/01
	Danbury PMSA, CT	Y	39670 FQ	119030 AW		CTBLS	10/01-12/01
	Hartford MSA, CT	Y	39460 FQ	119190 AW		CTBLS	10/01-12/01
	New Haven-Meriden PMSA, CT	Y		143960 AW		CTBLS	10/01-12/01
	New London-Norwich MSA, CT-RI	Y		141510 AW		CTBLS	10/01-12/01
	Stamford-Norwalk PMSA, CT	Y		144760 AW		CTBLS	10/01-12/01
	Delaware	Y	124260 FQ	138020 AW		DEBLS	10/01-12/01
	Wilmington-Newark PMSA, DE-MD	Y	77050 FQ	121360 AW		DEBLS	10/01-12/01
	District of Columbia	Y	54930 FQ	93370 AW		DCBLS	10/01-12/01
	Washington PMSA, DC-MD-VA-WV	Y	75710 FQ	117910 AW		DCBLS	10/01-12/01
	Florida	Y	79140 FQ	127110 AW		FLBLS	10/01-12/01
	Daytona Beach MSA, FL	Y	98420 FQ	130960 AW		FLBLS	10/01-12/01
	Fort Lauderdale PMSA, FL	Y	73900 FQ	88390 AW		FLBLS	10/01-12/01
	Fort Myers-Cape Coral MSA, FL	Y	141770 FQ	143610 AW		FLBLS	10/01-12/01
	Jacksonville MSA, FL	Y	106690 FQ	135380 AW		FLBLS	10/01-12/01
	Lakeland-Winter Haven MSA, FL	Y		142720 AW		FLBLS	10/01-12/01
	Orlando MSA, FL	Y		144600 AW		FLBLS	10/01-12/01
	Pensacola MSA, FL	Y	101280 FQ	129670 AW		FLBLS	10/01-12/01
	Tallahassee MSA, FL	Y	138570 FQ	143100 AW		FLBLS	10/01-12/01
	Tampa-St. Petersburg-Clearwater MSA, FL	Y		143970 AW		FLBLS	10/01-12/01
	Georgia	Y		143600 AW		GABLS	10/01-12/01
	Atlanta MSA, GA	Y	133660 FQ	141330 AW		GABLS	10/01-12/01
	Augusta-Aiken MSA, GA-SC	Y		143590 AW		GABLS	10/01-12/01
	Macon MSA, GA	Y		144420 AW		GABLS	10/01-12/01
	Hawaii	Y	42460 FQ	115160 AW		HIBLS	10/01-12/01
	Honolulu MSA, HI	Y	42430 FQ	114890 AW		HIBLS	10/01-12/01
	Idaho	Y		141950 AW		IDBLS	10/01-12/01
	Illinois	Y	89680 FQ	130110 AW		ILBLS	10/01-12/01
	Chicago PMSA, IL	Y	111100 FQ	134850 AW		ILBLS	10/01-12/01
	Peoria-Pekin MSA, IL	Y		143600 AW		ILBLS	10/01-12/01
	Indiana	Y		138200 AW		INBLS	10/01-12/01
	Indianapolis MSA, IN	Y	66770 FQ	131740 AW		INBLS	10/01-12/01
	Iowa	Y		145140 AW		IABLS	10/01-12/01
	Davenport-Moline-Rock Island MSA, IA-IL	Y		144260 AW		IABLS	10/01-12/01
	Kansas	Y	140670 FQ	142730 AW		KSBLS	10/01-12/01
	Topeka MSA, KS	Y		145340 AW		KSBLS	10/01-12/01
	Wichita MSA, KS	Y	121280 FQ	137400 AW		KSBLS	10/01-12/01
	Kentucky	Y	97420 FQ	130060 AW		KYBLS	10/01-12/01
	Louisville MSA, KY-IN	Y		142780 AW		KYBLS	10/01-12/01
	Louisiana	Y		144510 AW		LABLS	10/01-12/01
	Baton Rouge MSA, LA	Y	137140 FQ	143030 AW		LABLS	10/01-12/01
	Lafayette MSA, LA	Y		144840 AW		LABLS	10/01-12/01
	Maine	Y		144910 AW		MEBLS	10/01-12/01
	Portland MSA, ME	Y		145270 AW		MEBLS	10/01-12/01
	Maryland	Y	140960 FQ	141740 AW		MDBLS	10/01-12/01
	Baltimore PMSA, MD	Y	135130 FQ	141630 AW		MDBLS	10/01-12/01
	Massachusetts	Y		141540 AW		MABLS	10/01-12/01
	Boston PMSA, MA-NH	Y		141290 AW		MABLS	10/01-12/01
	Michigan	Y	140910 FQ	142720 AW		MIBLS	10/01-12/01
	Detroit PMSA, MI	Y		145110 AW		MIBLS	10/01-12/01
	Grand Rapids-Muskegon-Holland MSA, MI	Y	137640 FQ	142600 AW		MIBLS	10/01-12/01

AAW	Average annual wage	**AOH**	Average offered, high	**ASH**	Average starting, high	**H**	Hourly	**M**	Monthly	**S**	Special: hourly and annual
AE	Average entry wage	**AOL**	Average offered, low	**ASL**	Average starting, low	**HI**	Highest wage paid	**MTC**	Median total compensation	**TQ**	Third quartile wage
AEX	Average experienced wage	**APH**	Average pay, high range	**AW**	Average wage paid	**HR**	High end range	**MW**	Median wage paid	**W**	Weekly
AO	Average offered	**APL**	Average pay, low range	**FQ**	First quartile wage	**LR**	Low end range	**SQ**	Second quartile wage	**Y**	Yearly

Occupation/Type/Industry	Location	Per	Low	Mid	High	Source	Date
Surgeon	Kalamazoo-Battle Creek MSA, MI	Y		144570 AW		MIBLS	10/01-12/01
	Lansing-East Lansing MSA, MI	Y		142030 AW		MIBLS	10/01-12/01
	Minnesota	Y		143130 AW		MNBLS	10/01-12/01
	Minneapolis-St. Paul MSA, MN-WI	Y		142290 AW		MNBLS	10/01-12/01
	Mississippi	Y	69870 FQ	120520 AW		MSBLS	10/01-12/01
	Missouri	Y		143550 AW		MOBLS	10/01-12/01
	Kansas City MSA, MO-KS	Y		144700 AW		MOBLS	10/01-12/01
	St. Louis MSA, MO-IL	Y	129070 FQ	139110 AW		MOBLS	10/01-12/01
	Montana	Y	93340 FQ	132730 AW		MTBLS	10/01-12/01
	Nebraska	Y		144500 AW		NEBLS	10/01-12/01
	Lincoln MSA, NE	Y		144410 AW		NEBLS	10/01-12/01
	Omaha MSA, NE-IA	Y	140430 FQ	143400 AW		NEBLS	10/01-12/01
	New Hampshire	Y		145180 AW		NHBLS	10/01-12/01
	New Jersey	Y	116300 FQ	137210 AW		NJBLS	10/01-12/01
	Atlantic-Cape May PMSA, NJ	Y	103160 FQ	129580 AW		NJBLS	10/01-12/01
	Newark PMSA, NJ	Y	119570 FQ	136940 AW		NJBLS	10/01-12/01
	Trenton PMSA, NJ	Y	44330 FQ	132620 AW		NJBLS	10/01-12/01
	New Mexico	Y	120850 FQ	135680 AW		NMBLS	10/01-12/01
	Albuquerque MSA, NM	Y	118920 FQ	131210 AW		NMBLS	10/01-12/01
	New York	Y	126700 FQ	138760 AW		NYBLS	10/01-12/01
	Buffalo-Niagara Falls MSA, NY	Y	122430 FQ	138630 AW		NYBLS	10/01-12/01
	Nassau-Suffolk PMSA, NY	Y		143300 AW		NYBLS	10/01-12/01
	New York PMSA, NY	Y	113790 FQ	135830 AW		NYBLS	10/01-12/01
	Rochester MSA, NY	Y	128360 FQ	140850 AW		NYBLS	10/01-12/01
	Syracuse MSA, NY	Y		144530 AW		NYBLS	10/01-12/01
	Utica-Rome MSA, NY	Y		# AW		NYBLS	10/01-12/01
	North Carolina	Y		142240 AW		NCBLS	10/01-12/01
	Asheville MSA, NC	Y		144180 AW		NCBLS	10/01-12/01
	Charlotte-Gastonia-Rock Hill MSA, NC-SC	Y	116340 FQ	139720 AW		NCBLS	10/01-12/01
	Greensboro-Winston-Salem-High Point MSA, NC	Y		145380 AW		NCBLS	10/01-12/01
	North Dakota	Y		145260 AW		NDBLS	10/01-12/01
	Ohio	Y		141930 AW		OHBLS	10/01-12/01
	Canton-Massillon MSA, OH	Y		# AW		OHBLS	10/01-12/01
	Cincinnati PMSA, OH-KY-IN	Y	102810 FQ	135350 AW		OHBLS	10/01-12/01
	Cleveland-Lorain-Elyria PMSA, OH	Y	99170 FQ	127880 AW		OHBLS	10/01-12/01
	Columbus MSA, OH	Y		142440 AW		OHBLS	10/01-12/01
	Mansfield MSA, OH	Y		144700 AW		OHBLS	10/01-12/01
	Youngstown-Warren MSA, OH	Y	42580 FQ	126890 AW		OHBLS	10/01-12/01
	Oklahoma	Y		144960 AW		OKBLS	10/01-12/01
	Oregon	Y		144440 AW		ORBLS	10/01-12/01
	Portland-Vancouver PMSA, OR-WA	Y		144200 AW		ORBLS	10/01-12/01
	Pennsylvania	Y	128040 FQ	139840 AW		PABLS	10/01-12/01
	Johnstown MSA, PA	Y	118810 FQ	140260 AW		PABLS	10/01-12/01
	Lancaster MSA, PA	Y	120910 FQ	140270 AW		PABLS	10/01-12/01
	Philadelphia PMSA, PA-NJ	Y	126460 FQ	138230 AW		PABLS	10/01-12/01
	Pittsburgh MSA, PA	Y	126000 FQ	141170 AW		PABLS	10/01-12/01
	Reading MSA, PA	Y		144640 AW		PABLS	10/01-12/01
	Scranton-Wilkes-Barre-Hazleton MSA, PA	Y		# AW		PABLS	10/01-12/01
	York MSA, PA	Y	75780 FQ	136520 AW		PABLS	10/01-12/01
	Rhode Island	Y	84950 FQ	125380 AW		RIBLS	10/01-12/01
	Providence-Fall River-Warwick MSA, RI-MA	Y	84330 FQ	125090 AW		RIBLS	10/01-12/01
	South Carolina	Y	123010 FQ	140440 AW		SCBLS	10/01-12/01
	Greenville-Spartanburg-Anderson MSA, SC	Y		145010 AW		SCBLS	10/01-12/01
	South Dakota	Y		143960 AW		SDBLS	10/01-12/01
	Tennessee	Y	131260 FQ	139070 AW		TNBLS	10/01-12/01
	Johnson City-Kingsport-Bristol MSA, TN-VA	Y	117270 FQ	139080 AW		TNBLS	10/01-12/01
	Memphis MSA, TN-AR-MS	Y		145440 AW		TNBLS	10/01-12/01
	Nashville MSA, TN	Y	124670 FQ	137320 AW		TNBLS	10/01-12/01
	Texas	Y	45750 FQ	128550 AW		TXBLS	10/01-12/01
	Austin-San Marcos MSA, TX	Y		140470 AW		TXBLS	10/01-12/01
	Dallas PMSA, TX	Y	41450 FQ	97180 AW		TXBLS	10/01-12/01

AAW	Average annual wage	**AOH**	Average offered, high	**ASH**	Average starting, high	**H**	Hourly	**M**	Monthly	**S**	Special: hourly and annual
AE	Average entry wage	**AOL**	Average offered, low	**ASL**	Average starting, low	**HI**	Highest wage paid	**MTC**	Median total compensation	**TQ**	Third quartile wage
AEX	Average experienced wage	**APH**	Average pay, high range	**AW**	Average wage paid	**HR**	High end range	**MW**	Median wage paid	**W**	Weekly
AO	Average offered	**APL**	Average pay, low range	**FQ**	First quartile wage	**LR**	Low end range	**SQ**	Second quartile wage	**Y**	Yearly

Occupation/Type/Industry	Location	Per	Low	Mid	High	Source	Date
Surgeon	Fort Worth-Arlington PMSA, TX	Y	30270 FQ	99240 AW		TXBLS	10/01-12/01
	Tyler MSA, TX	Y		144740 AW		TXBLS	10/01-12/01
	Utah	Y	83140 FQ	133170 AW		UTBLS	10/01-12/01
	Vermont	Y	119670 FQ	134960 AW		VTBLS	10/01-12/01
	Virginia	Y	91950 FQ	132930 AW		VABLS	10/01-12/01
	Lynchburg MSA, VA	Y		144130 AW		VABLS	10/01-12/01
	Norfolk-Virginia Beach-Newport News MSA, VA-NC	Y	117510 FQ	137450 AW		VABLS	10/01-12/01
	Roanoke MSA, VA	Y	38200 FQ	119650 AW		VABLS	10/01-12/01
	Washington	Y	43780 FQ	123370 AW		WABLS	10/01-12/01
	Seattle-Bellevue-Everett PMSA, WA	Y	39750 FQ	111870 AW		WABLS	10/01-12/01
	West Virginia	Y	128150 FQ	140770 AW		WVBLS	10/01-12/01
	Huntington-Ashland MSA, WV-KY-OH	Y	122070 FQ	137330 AW		WVBLS	10/01-12/01
	Wisconsin	Y	131380 FQ	141390 AW		WIBLS	10/01-12/01
	Milwaukee-Waukesha PMSA, WI	Y	130590 FQ	141740 AW		WIBLS	10/01-12/01
	Wyoming	Y	145530 FQ	142590 AW		WYBLS	10/01-12/01
	Puerto Rico	Y	46040 FQ	93520 AW		PRBLS	10/01-12/01
Surgical Technologist	Alabama	Y	17770 FQ	26780 AW	39150 TQ	ALBLS	10/01-12/01
	Birmingham MSA, AL	Y	18220 FQ	25920 AW	34290 TQ	ALBLS	10/01-12/01
	Mobile MSA, AL	Y	16260 FQ	23000 AW	29730 TQ	ALBLS	10/01-12/01
	Montgomery MSA, AL	Y	17080 FQ	28260 AW	43920 TQ	ALBLS	10/01-12/01
	Alaska	Y	29930 FQ	36590 AW	44580 TQ	AKBLS	10/01-12/01
	Arizona	Y	22460 FQ	32620 AW	42310 TQ	AZBLS	10/01-12/01
	Phoenix-Mesa MSA, AZ	Y	23370 FQ	30950 AW	41110 TQ	AZBLS	10/01-12/01
	Tucson MSA, AZ	Y	20200 FQ	38220 AW	70880 TQ	AZBLS	10/01-12/01
	Arkansas	Y	17100 FQ	24490 AW	33390 TQ	ARBLS	10/01-12/01
	Fayetteville-Springdale-Rogers MSA, AR	Y	15900 FQ	22170 AW	30780 TQ	ARBLS	10/01-12/01
	Fort Smith MSA, AR-OK	Y	16310 FQ	24000 AW	33220 TQ	ARBLS	10/01-12/01
	California	Y	25010 FQ	35230 AW	46010 TQ	CABLS	10/01-12/01
	Bakersfield MSA, CA	Y	24680 FQ	33050 AW	43350 TQ	CABLS	10/01-12/01
	Fresno MSA, CA	Y	22150 FQ	33690 AW	45730 TQ	CABLS	10/01-12/01
	Los Angeles-Long Beach PMSA, CA	Y	24760 FQ	34760 AW	45130 TQ	CABLS	10/01-12/01
	Modesto MSA, CA	Y	25970 FQ	34970 AW	45970 TQ	CABLS	10/01-12/01
	Oakland PMSA, CA	Y	31980 FQ	44670 AW	59920 TQ	CABLS	10/01-12/01
	Orange County PMSA, CA	Y	26780 FQ	35070 AW	45680 TQ	CABLS	10/01-12/01
	Redding MSA, CA	Y	22890 FQ	34560 AW	43340 TQ	CABLS	10/01-12/01
	Riverside-San Bernardino PMSA, CA	Y	24270 FQ	31580 AW	40860 TQ	CABLS	10/01-12/01
	Sacramento PMSA, CA	Y	22610 FQ	32760 AW	41280 TQ	CABLS	10/01-12/01
	San Diego MSA, CA	Y	26680 FQ	36480 AW	46820 TQ	CABLS	10/01-12/01
	San Francisco PMSA, CA	Y	27440 FQ	38940 AW	52350 TQ	CABLS	10/01-12/01
	San Jose PMSA, CA	Y	28390 FQ	38600 AW	50000 TQ	CABLS	10/01-12/01
	San Luis Obispo-Atascadero-Paso Robles MSA, CA	Y	20060 FQ	27930 AW	36060 TQ	CABLS	10/01-12/01
	Santa Barbara-Santa Maria-Lompoc MSA, CA	Y	28360 FQ	34470 AW	42540 TQ	CABLS	10/01-12/01
	Santa Cruz-Watsonville PMSA, CA	Y	35760 FQ	42430 AW	53160 TQ	CABLS	10/01-12/01
	Santa Rosa PMSA, CA	Y	26000 FQ	35800 AW	45930 TQ	CABLS	10/01-12/01
	Stockton-Lodi MSA, CA	Y	23230 FQ	30530 AW	41190 TQ	CABLS	10/01-12/01
	Vallejo-Fairfield-Napa PMSA, CA	Y	26030 FQ	36540 AW	49670 TQ	CABLS	10/01-12/01
	Ventura PMSA, CA	Y	24680 FQ	33850 AW	47900 TQ	CABLS	10/01-12/01
	Colorado	Y	21610 FQ	30710 AW	41960 TQ	COBLS	10/01-12/01
	Boulder-Longmont PMSA, CO	Y	21190 FQ	33890 AW	45530 TQ	COBLS	10/01-12/01
	Colorado Springs MSA, CO	Y	23720 FQ	30070 AW	37820 TQ	COBLS	10/01-12/01
	Denver PMSA, CO	Y	21730 FQ	30940 AW	41650 TQ	COBLS	10/01-12/01
	Greeley PMSA, CO	Y	21820 FQ	26990 AW	34240 TQ	COBLS	10/01-12/01
	Connecticut	Y	27140 FQ	36820 AW	46840 TQ	CTBLS	10/01-12/01
	Bridgeport PMSA, CT	Y	30610 FQ	39260 AW	51410 TQ	CTBLS	10/01-12/01
	Hartford MSA, CT	Y	29150 FQ	37480 AW	46250 TQ	CTBLS	10/01-12/01
	New London-Norwich MSA, CT-RI	Y	25270 FQ	34070 AW	43970 TQ	CTBLS	10/01-12/01
	Delaware	Y	21580 FQ	33060 AW	48980 TQ	DEBLS	10/01-12/01
	District of Columbia	Y	22940 FQ	34200 AW	47940 TQ	DCBLS	10/01-12/01

AAW	Average annual wage	AOH	Average offered, high	ASH	Average starting, high	H	Hourly	M	Monthly	S	Special: hourly and annual
AE	Average entry wage	AOL	Average offered, low	ASL	Average starting, low	HI	Highest wage paid	MTC	Median total compensation	TQ	Third quartile wage
AEX	Average experienced wage	APH	Average pay, high range	AW	Average wage paid	HR	High end range	MW	Median wage paid	W	Weekly
AO	Average offered	APL	Average pay, low range	FQ	First quartile wage	LR	Low end range	SQ	Second quartile wage	Y	Yearly

Occupation/Type/Industry	Location	Per	Low	Mid	High	Source	Date
Surgical Technologist	Washington PMSA, DC-MD-VA-WV	Y	24390 FQ	36860 AW	52340 TQ	DCBLS	10/01-12/01
	Florida	Y	21020 FQ	29050 AW	37440 TQ	FLBLS	10/01-12/01
	Fort Lauderdale PMSA, FL	Y	24530 FQ	32090 AW	41240 TQ	FLBLS	10/01-12/01
	Fort Walton Beach MSA, FL	Y	20170 FQ	25960 AW	32320 TQ	FLBLS	10/01-12/01
	Jacksonville MSA, FL	Y	20690 FQ	28550 AW	36440 TQ	FLBLS	10/01-12/01
	Lakeland-Winter Haven MSA, FL	Y	23310 FQ	29390 AW	35430 TQ	FLBLS	10/01-12/01
	Miami PMSA, FL	Y	22330 FQ	30470 AW	40220 TQ	FLBLS	10/01-12/01
	Naples MSA, FL	Y	25780 FQ	37970 AW	51530 TQ	FLBLS	10/01-12/01
	Ocala MSA, FL	Y	23720 FQ	35350 AW	66720 TQ	FLBLS	10/01-12/01
	Orlando MSA, FL	Y	22620 FQ	27890 AW	34890 TQ	FLBLS	10/01-12/01
	Pensacola MSA, FL	Y	20500 FQ	29540 AW	37680 TQ	FLBLS	10/01-12/01
	Sarasota-Bradenton MSA, FL	Y	21080 FQ	28870 AW	35660 TQ	FLBLS	10/01-12/01
	Tampa-St. Petersburg-Clearwater MSA, FL	Y	19730 FQ	27020 AW	35490 TQ	FLBLS	10/01-12/01
	West Palm Beach-Boca Raton MSA, FL	Y	21550 FQ	31520 AW	43390 TQ	FLBLS	10/01-12/01
	Georgia	Y	19680 FQ	27110 AW	36680 TQ	GABLS	10/01-12/01
	Atlanta MSA, GA	Y	19890 FQ	26780 AW	35780 TQ	GABLS	10/01-12/01
	Augusta-Aiken MSA, GA-SC	Y	23220 FQ	34440 AW	52020 TQ	GABLS	10/01-12/01
	Macon MSA, GA	Y	17800 FQ	24890 AW	34330 TQ	GABLS	10/01-12/01
	Savannah MSA, GA	Y	19980 FQ	27830 AW	38310 TQ	GABLS	10/01-12/01
	Hawaii	Y	24400 FQ	33350 AW	43890 TQ	HIBLS	10/01-12/01
	Honolulu MSA, HI	Y	24760 FQ	33600 AW	44160 TQ	HIBLS	10/01-12/01
	Idaho	Y	22900 FQ	33480 AW	44120 TQ	IDBLS	10/01-12/01
	Illinois	Y	21700 FQ	31760 AW	43190 TQ	ILBLS	10/01-12/01
	Champaign-Urbana MSA, IL	Y	21730 FQ	33140 AW	44630 TQ	ILBLS	10/01-12/01
	Chicago PMSA, IL	Y	22500 FQ	32470 AW	43890 TQ	ILBLS	10/01-12/01
	Peoria-Pekin MSA, IL	Y	23330 FQ	30860 AW	40280 TQ	ILBLS	10/01-12/01
	Indiana	Y	24210 FQ	32370 AW	40930 TQ	INBLS	10/01-12/01
	Elkhart-Goshen MSA, IN	Y	28630 FQ	35880 AW	44670 TQ	INBLS	10/01-12/01
	Evansville-Henderson MSA, IN-KY	Y	25750 FQ	40820 AW	69030 TQ	INBLS	10/01-12/01
	Fort Wayne MSA, IN	Y	23520 FQ	30630 AW	37370 TQ	INBLS	10/01-12/01
	Gary PMSA, IN	Y	23480 FQ	30960 AW	37750 TQ	INBLS	10/01-12/01
	Indianapolis MSA, IN	Y	25130 FQ	32530 AW	41670 TQ	INBLS	10/01-12/01
	South Bend MSA, IN	Y	25230 FQ	32290 AW	40100 TQ	INBLS	10/01-12/01
	Iowa	Y	19960 FQ	27320 AW	35730 TQ	IABLS	10/01-12/01
	Davenport-Moline-Rock Island MSA, IA-IL	Y	21530 FQ	29370 AW	36080 TQ	IABLS	10/01-12/01
	Kansas	Y	19490 FQ	26670 AW	34570 TQ	KSBLS	10/01-12/01
	Topeka MSA, KS	Y	22990 FQ	29090 AW	36110 TQ	KSBLS	10/01-12/01
	Wichita MSA, KS	Y	23130 FQ	27330 AW	31840 TQ	KSBLS	10/01-12/01
	Kentucky	Y	21480 FQ	28810 AW	35560 TQ	KYBLS	10/01-12/01
	Lexington MSA, KY	Y	22650 FQ	30070 AW	38050 TQ	KYBLS	10/01-12/01
	Louisville MSA, KY-IN	Y	24730 FQ	30720 AW	35980 TQ	KYBLS	10/01-12/01
	Louisiana	Y	18990 FQ	25930 AW	34390 TQ	LABLS	10/01-12/01
	Baton Rouge MSA, LA	Y	19350 FQ	25470 AW	33690 TQ	LABLS	10/01-12/01
	Houma MSA, LA	Y	20900 FQ	29180 AW	42070 TQ	LABLS	10/01-12/01
	Lafayette MSA, LA	Y	18800 FQ	26270 AW	34880 TQ	LABLS	10/01-12/01
	Lake Charles MSA, LA	Y	17720 FQ	25040 AW	34050 TQ	LABLS	10/01-12/01
	New Orleans MSA, LA	Y	19030 FQ	25650 AW	33640 TQ	LABLS	10/01-12/01
	Shreveport-Bossier City MSA, LA	Y	19120 FQ	26080 AW	34320 TQ	LABLS	10/01-12/01
	Maine	Y	20270 FQ	28380 AW	37360 TQ	MEBLS	10/01-12/01
	Portland MSA, ME	Y	20120 FQ	27830 AW	36050 TQ	MEBLS	10/01-12/01
	Maryland	Y	26970 FQ	37320 AW	49560 TQ	MDBLS	10/01-12/01
	Baltimore PMSA, MD	Y	27620 FQ	35430 AW	44210 TQ	MDBLS	10/01-12/01
	Massachusetts	Y	25920 FQ	35000 AW	45160 TQ	MABLS	10/01-12/01
	Boston PMSA, MA-NH	Y	26780 FQ	35320 AW	45050 TQ	MABLS	10/01-12/01
	Brockton PMSA, MA	Y	29500 FQ	37340 AW	45380 TQ	MABLS	10/01-12/01
	Lawrence PMSA, MA-NH	Y	20810 FQ	33720 AW	45300 TQ	MABLS	10/01-12/01
	Springfield MSA, MA	Y	23430 FQ	32070 AW	42730 TQ	MABLS	10/01-12/01
	Worcester PMSA, MA-CT	Y	25660 FQ	33490 AW	43360 TQ	MABLS	10/01-12/01
	Michigan	Y	24470 FQ	31720 AW	39870 TQ	MIBLS	10/01-12/01
	Ann Arbor PMSA, MI	Y	24560 FQ	30590 AW	36870 TQ	MIBLS	10/01-12/01
	Detroit PMSA, MI	Y	25930 FQ	32940 AW	41270 TQ	MIBLS	10/01-12/01
	Flint PMSA, MI	Y	26550 FQ	31850 AW	37290 TQ	MIBLS	10/01-12/01
	Grand Rapids-Muskegon-Holland MSA, MI	Y	24190 FQ	29140 AW	37310 TQ	MIBLS	10/01-12/01

AAW Average annual wage; AE Average entry wage; AEX Average experienced wage; AO Average offered; AOH Average offered, high; AOL Average offered, low; APH Average pay, high range; APL Average pay, low range; ASH Average starting, high; ASL Average starting, low; AW Average wage paid; FQ First quartile wage; H Hourly; HI Highest wage paid; HR High end range; LR Low end range; M Monthly; MTC Median total compensation; MW Median wage paid; SQ Second quartile wage; S Special: hourly and annual; TQ Third quartile wage; W Weekly; Y Yearly

Occupation/Type/Industry	Location	Per	Low	Mid	High	Source	Date
Surgical Technologist	Kalamazoo-Battle Creek MSA, MI	Y	24820 FQ	32870 AW	43210 TQ	MIBLS	10/01-12/01
	Lansing-East Lansing MSA, MI	Y	23980 FQ	31860 AW	41320 TQ	MIBLS	10/01-12/01
	Minnesota	Y	27310 FQ	36130 AW	44290 TQ	MNBLS	10/01-12/01
	Duluth-Superior MSA, MN-WI	Y	27420 FQ	42000 AW	66260 TQ	MNBLS	10/01-12/01
	Minneapolis-St. Paul MSA, MN-WI	Y	28340 FQ	36410 AW	44440 TQ	MNBLS	10/01-12/01
	Mississippi	Y	14170 FQ	22490 AW	30280 TQ	MSBLS	10/01-12/01
	Biloxi-Gulfport-Pascagoula MSA, MS	Y	16990 FQ	25660 AW	35050 TQ	MSBLS	10/01-12/01
	Jackson MSA, MS	Y	19420 FQ	24900 AW	32040 TQ	MSBLS	10/01-12/01
	Missouri	Y	19830 FQ	28630 AW	37580 TQ	MOBLS	10/01-12/01
	Kansas City MSA, MO-KS	Y	19050 FQ	30060 AW	41510 TQ	MOBLS	10/01-12/01
	St. Louis MSA, MO-IL	Y	20640 FQ	28930 AW	36810 TQ	MOBLS	10/01-12/01
	Montana	Y	22380 FQ	29750 AW	36680 TQ	MTBLS	10/01-12/01
	Billings MSA, MT	Y	23260 FQ	31080 AW	36280 TQ	MTBLS	10/01-12/01
	Nebraska	Y	21420 FQ	28570 AW	35550 TQ	NEBLS	10/01-12/01
	Omaha MSA, NE-IA	Y	23300 FQ	29640 AW	36040 TQ	NEBLS	10/01-12/01
	Nevada	Y	26870 FQ	35570 AW	44910 TQ	NVBLS	10/01-12/01
	Las Vegas MSA, NV-AZ	Y	25850 FQ	35650 AW	45640 TQ	NVBLS	10/01-12/01
	Reno MSA, NV	Y	28780 FQ	34480 AW	43420 TQ	NVBLS	10/01-12/01
	New Hampshire	Y	24800 FQ	31460 AW	37730 TQ	NHBLS	10/01-12/01
	Manchester PMSA, NH	Y	27190 FQ	32310 AW	38810 TQ	NHBLS	10/01-12/01
	Portsmouth-Rochester PMSA, NH-ME	Y	25650 FQ	32930 AW	41090 TQ	NHBLS	10/01-12/01
	New Jersey	Y	25090 FQ	35240 AW	46830 TQ	NJBLS	10/01-12/01
	Bergen-Passaic PMSA, NJ	Y	25730 FQ	38050 AW	53150 TQ	NJBLS	10/01-12/01
	Jersey City PMSA, NJ	Y	23340 FQ	34570 AW	45260 TQ	NJBLS	10/01-12/01
	Middlesex-Somerset-Hunterdon PMSA, NJ	Y	24390 FQ	33890 AW	45020 TQ	NJBLS	10/01-12/01
	Monmouth-Ocean PMSA, NJ	Y	27980 FQ	38030 AW	48670 TQ	NJBLS	10/01-12/01
	Newark PMSA, NJ	Y	23850 FQ	35940 AW	48260 TQ	NJBLS	10/01-12/01
	New Mexico	Y	16410 FQ	25170 AW	34610 TQ	NMBLS	10/01-12/01
	New York	Y	24240 FQ	30430 AW	41670 TQ	NYBLS	10/01-12/01
	Albany-Schenectady-Troy MSA, NY	Y	20150 FQ	28370 AW	39830 TQ	NYBLS	10/01-12/01
	Buffalo-Niagara Falls MSA, NY	Y	25010 FQ	29920 AW	34850 TQ	NYBLS	10/01-12/01
	Nassau-Suffolk PMSA, NY	Y	25150 FQ	34900 AW	45070 TQ	NYBLS	10/01-12/01
	New York PMSA, NY	Y	24740 FQ	30600 AW	41430 TQ	NYBLS	10/01-12/01
	Newburgh PMSA, NY-PA	Y	25810 FQ	38840 AW	55200 TQ	NYBLS	10/01-12/01
	Rochester MSA, NY	Y	22790 FQ	28140 AW	35850 TQ	NYBLS	10/01-12/01
	Syracuse MSA, NY	Y	22610 FQ	30040 AW	39990 TQ	NYBLS	10/01-12/01
	Utica-Rome MSA, NY	Y	20270 FQ	26880 AW	34290 TQ	NYBLS	10/01-12/01
	North Carolina	Y	21580 FQ	29990 AW	38170 TQ	NCBLS	10/01-12/01
	Charlotte-Gastonia-Rock Hill MSA, NC-SC	Y	22400 FQ	32240 AW	43370 TQ	NCBLS	10/01-12/01
	Fayetteville MSA, NC	Y	22470 FQ	30850 AW	42150 TQ	NCBLS	10/01-12/01
	Greensboro-Winston-Salem-High Point MSA, NC	Y	21770 FQ	30700 AW	41720 TQ	NCBLS	10/01-12/01
	Raleigh-Durham-Chapel Hill MSA, NC	Y	23450 FQ	30080 AW	36890 TQ	NCBLS	10/01-12/01
	North Dakota	Y	20020 FQ	26570 AW	34690 TQ	NDBLS	10/01-12/01
	Fargo-Moorhead MSA, ND-MN	Y	20000 FQ	25520 AW	33560 TQ	NDBLS	10/01-12/01
	Ohio	Y	21620 FQ	29660 AW	36840 TQ	OHBLS	10/01-12/01
	Akron PMSA, OH	Y	20530 FQ	28360 AW	36240 TQ	OHBLS	10/01-12/01
	Canton-Massillon MSA, OH	Y	22300 FQ	31940 AW	46690 TQ	OHBLS	10/01-12/01
	Cincinnati PMSA, OH-KY-IN	Y	21820 FQ	29690 AW	36660 TQ	OHBLS	10/01-12/01
	Cleveland-Lorain-Elyria PMSA, OH	Y	23290 FQ	31420 AW	37810 TQ	OHBLS	10/01-12/01
	Columbus MSA, OH	Y	20790 FQ	28170 AW	35650 TQ	OHBLS	10/01-12/01
	Dayton-Springfield MSA, OH	Y	22520 FQ	30560 AW	36660 TQ	OHBLS	10/01-12/01
	Hamilton-Middletown PMSA, OH	Y	23260 FQ	29370 AW	36240 TQ	OHBLS	10/01-12/01
	Toledo MSA, OH	Y	24060 FQ	31190 AW	37900 TQ	OHBLS	10/01-12/01
	Youngstown-Warren MSA, OH	Y	22460 FQ	28930 AW	36540 TQ	OHBLS	10/01-12/01
	Oklahoma	Y	18950 FQ	27130 AW	35490 TQ	OKBLS	10/01-12/01
	Oklahoma City MSA, OK	Y	19920 FQ	28750 AW	36750 TQ	OKBLS	10/01-12/01
	Tulsa MSA, OK	Y	19600 FQ	28030 AW	36350 TQ	OKBLS	10/01-12/01
	Oregon	Y	27440 FQ	34660 AW	43160 TQ	ORBLS	10/01-12/01
	Medford-Ashland MSA, OR	Y	26330 FQ	34110 AW	43000 TQ	ORBLS	10/01-12/01

AAW	Average annual wage	AOH	Average offered, high	ASH	Average starting, high	H	Hourly	M	Monthly	S	Special: hourly and annual
AE	Average entry wage	AOL	Average offered, low	ASL	Average starting, low	HI	Highest wage paid	MTC	Median total compensation	TQ	Third quartile wage
AEX	Average experienced wage	APH	Average pay, high range	AW	Average wage paid	HR	High end range	MW	Median wage paid	W	Weekly
AO	Average offered	APL	Average pay, low range	FQ	First quartile wage	LR	Low end range	SQ	Second quartile wage	Y	Yearly

Occupation/Type/Industry	Location	Per	Low	Mid	High	Source	Date
Surgical Technologist	Portland-Vancouver PMSA, OR-WA	Y	28310 FQ	35370 AW	43630 TQ	ORBLS	10/01-12/01
	Salem PMSA, OR	Y	29740 FQ	34430 AW	40740 TQ	ORBLS	10/01-12/01
	Pennsylvania	Y	19580 FQ	27480 AW	35590 TQ	PABLS	10/01-12/01
	Allentown-Bethlehem-Easton MSA, PA	Y	22430 FQ	28640 AW	35300 TQ	PABLS	10/01-12/01
	Erie MSA, PA	Y	21810 FQ	29310 AW	36710 TQ	PABLS	10/01-12/01
	Harrisburg-Lebanon-Carlisle MSA, PA	Y	23360 FQ	30160 AW	38160 TQ	PABLS	10/01-12/01
	Johnstown MSA, PA	Y	20370 FQ	26350 AW	33430 TQ	PABLS	10/01-12/01
	Lancaster MSA, PA	Y	21970 FQ	29410 AW	36860 TQ	PABLS	10/01-12/01
	Philadelphia PMSA, PA-NJ	Y	18960 FQ	27080 AW	35780 TQ	PABLS	10/01-12/01
	Pittsburgh MSA, PA	Y	23980 FQ	29340 AW	35990 TQ	PABLS	10/01-12/01
	Reading MSA, PA	Y	21010 FQ	28170 AW	35070 TQ	PABLS	10/01-12/01
	Scranton-Wilkes-Barre-Hazleton MSA, PA	Y	21080 FQ	28450 AW	35750 TQ	PABLS	10/01-12/01
	Rhode Island	Y	25970 FQ	35010 AW	44190 TQ	RIBLS	10/01-12/01
	Providence-Fall River-Warwick MSA, RI-MA	Y	25610 FQ	34980 AW	44340 TQ	RIBLS	10/01-12/01
	South Carolina	Y	20690 FQ	28210 AW	35300 TQ	SCBLS	10/01-12/01
	Charleston-North Charleston MSA, SC	Y	19660 FQ	27700 AW	34800 TQ	SCBLS	10/01-12/01
	Columbia MSA, SC	Y	20650 FQ	28440 AW	36320 TQ	SCBLS	10/01-12/01
	Greenville-Spartanburg-Anderson MSA, SC	Y	21650 FQ	29240 AW	37910 TQ	SCBLS	10/01-12/01
	Myrtle Beach MSA, SC	Y	22440 FQ	28070 AW	35040 TQ	SCBLS	10/01-12/01
	South Dakota	Y	20510 FQ	27630 AW	36540 TQ	SDBLS	10/01-12/01
	Tennessee	Y	20540 FQ	30740 AW	42900 TQ	TNBLS	10/01-12/01
	Johnson City-Kingsport-Bristol MSA, TN-VA	Y	20980 FQ	30540 AW	48340 TQ	TNBLS	10/01-12/01
	Knoxville MSA, TN	Y	19890 FQ	29250 AW	39600 TQ	TNBLS	10/01-12/01
	Memphis MSA, TN-AR-MS	Y	24310 FQ	31560 AW	40520 TQ	TNBLS	10/01-12/01
	Nashville MSA, TN	Y	22890 FQ	32720 AW	45520 TQ	TNBLS	10/01-12/01
	Texas	Y	18920 FQ	27360 AW	36140 TQ	TXBLS	10/01-12/01
	Austin-San Marcos MSA, TX	Y	21100 FQ	30450 AW	39410 TQ	TXBLS	10/01-12/01
	Beaumont-Port Arthur MSA, TX	Y	20810 FQ	29590 AW	37090 TQ	TXBLS	10/01-12/01
	Brownsville-Harlingen-San Benito MSA, TX	Y	18460 FQ	23360 AW	32340 TQ	TXBLS	10/01-12/01
	Corpus Christi MSA, TX	Y	20830 FQ	27340 AW	35150 TQ	TXBLS	10/01-12/01
	Dallas PMSA, TX	Y	18690 FQ	27280 AW	35960 TQ	TXBLS	10/01-12/01
	El Paso MSA, TX	Y	19030 FQ	24470 AW	30730 TQ	TXBLS	10/01-12/01
	Fort Worth-Arlington PMSA, TX	Y	17810 FQ	26840 AW	36610 TQ	TXBLS	10/01-12/01
	Houston PMSA, TX	Y	19190 FQ	28170 AW	36670 TQ	TXBLS	10/01-12/01
	Longview-Marshall MSA, TX	Y	17720 FQ	26320 AW	35260 TQ	TXBLS	10/01-12/01
	Lubbock MSA, TX	Y	19520 FQ	29210 AW	36320 TQ	TXBLS	10/01-12/01
	McAllen-Edinburg-Mission MSA, TX	Y	19270 FQ	27240 AW	35730 TQ	TXBLS	10/01-12/01
	Odessa-Midland MSA, TX	Y	18850 FQ	27490 AW	34360 TQ	TXBLS	10/01-12/01
	San Antonio MSA, TX	Y	18470 FQ	24980 AW	34060 TQ	TXBLS	10/01-12/01
	Tyler MSA, TX	Y	22540 FQ	28600 AW	34440 TQ	TXBLS	10/01-12/01
	Utah	Y	19710 FQ	28420 AW	39810 TQ	UTBLS	10/01-12/01
	Provo-Orem MSA, UT	Y	25630 FQ	32110 AW	39230 TQ	UTBLS	10/01-12/01
	Salt Lake City-Ogden MSA, UT	Y	19320 FQ	28540 AW	40570 TQ	UTBLS	10/01-12/01
	Virginia	Y	23070 FQ	31440 AW	42660 TQ	VABLS	10/01-12/01
	Norfolk-Virginia Beach-Newport News MSA, VA-NC	Y	23360 FQ	31030 AW	43610 TQ	VABLS	10/01-12/01
	Richmond-Petersburg MSA, VA	Y	22960 FQ	31260 AW	42540 TQ	VABLS	10/01-12/01
	Washington	Y	25710 FQ	34100 AW	43250 TQ	WABLS	10/01-12/01
	Bremerton PMSA, WA	Y	30090 FQ	34780 AW	41720 TQ	WABLS	10/01-12/01
	Richland-Kennewick-Pasco MSA, WA	Y	26040 FQ	33430 AW	44220 TQ	WABLS	10/01-12/01
	Seattle-Bellevue-Everett PMSA, WA	Y	25980 FQ	35550 AW	44950 TQ	WABLS	10/01-12/01
	Spokane MSA, WA	Y	25090 FQ	33990 AW	42780 TQ	WABLS	10/01-12/01
	Yakima MSA, WA	Y	29260 FQ	33400 AW	39230 TQ	WABLS	10/01-12/01
	West Virginia	Y	18880 FQ	26210 AW	35050 TQ	WVBLS	10/01-12/01
	Charleston MSA, WV	Y	18910 FQ	25940 AW	34070 TQ	WVBLS	10/01-12/01

AAW Average annual wage **AE** Average entry wage **AEX** Average experienced wage **AO** Average offered **AOH** Average offered, high **AOL** Average offered, low **APH** Average pay, high range **APL** Average pay, low range **ASH** Average starting, high **ASL** Average starting, low **AW** Average wage paid **FQ** First quartile wage **H** Hourly **HI** Highest wage paid **HR** High end range **LR** Low end range **M** Monthly **MTC** Median total compensation **MW** Median wage paid **SQ** Second quartile wage **S** Special: hourly and annual **TQ** Third quartile wage **W** Weekly **Y** Yearly

Occupation/Type/Industry	Location	Per	Low	Mid	High	Source	Date
Surgical Technologist	Huntington-Ashland MSA, WV-KY-OH	Y	20150 FQ	28170 AW	35990 TQ	WVBLS	10/01-12/01
	Wisconsin	Y	24750 FQ	32900 AW	43570 TQ	WIBLS	10/01-12/01
	Appleton-Oshkosh-Neenah MSA, WI	Y	25410 FQ	36030 AW	51950 TQ	WIBLS	10/01-12/01
	Green Bay MSA, WI	Y	24560 FQ	32460 AW	43710 TQ	WIBLS	10/01-12/01
	Madison MSA, WI	Y	26960 FQ	34480 AW	44100 TQ	WIBLS	10/01-12/01
	Milwaukee-Waukesha PMSA, WI	Y	26000 FQ	34530 AW	44200 TQ	WIBLS	10/01-12/01
	Wyoming	Y	19140 FQ	27110 AW	37320 TQ	WYBLS	10/01-12/01
	Puerto Rico	Y	11960 FQ	14900 AW	19550 TQ	PRBLS	10/01-12/01
Survey Researcher	Alabama	Y	14010 FQ	26050 AW	49070 TQ	ALBLS	10/01-12/01
	Arizona	Y	14410 FQ	22720 AW	40080 TQ	AZBLS	10/01-12/01
	California	Y	16280 FQ	47330 AW	85150 TQ	CABLS	10/01-12/01
	Colorado	Y	16030 FQ	26340 AW	42990 TQ	COBLS	10/01-12/01
	Connecticut	Y	29290 FQ	41020 AW	68440 TQ	CTBLS	10/01-12/01
	District of Columbia	Y	27050 FQ	51060 AW	88420 TQ	DCBLS	10/01-12/01
	Florida	Y	18530 FQ	29050 AW	38670 TQ	FLBLS	10/01-12/01
	Georgia	Y	16910 FQ	20760 AW	23700 TQ	GABLS	10/01-12/01
	Hawaii	Y	12810 FQ	22540 AW	36410 TQ	HIBLS	10/01-12/01
	Idaho	Y	11450 FQ	19970 AW	38210 TQ	IDBLS	10/01-12/01
	Illinois	Y	15840 FQ	27990 AW	55650 TQ	ILBLS	10/01-12/01
	Indiana	Y	16100 FQ	30760 AW	58910 TQ	INBLS	10/01-12/01
	Iowa	Y	15780 FQ	19010 AW	22470 TQ	IABLS	10/01-12/01
	Kansas	Y	15160 FQ	29990 AW	46920 TQ	KSBLS	10/01-12/01
	Maryland	Y	22300 FQ	33360 AW	46850 TQ	MDBLS	10/01-12/01
	Massachusetts	Y	18800 FQ	36470 AW	53980 TQ	MABLS	10/01-12/01
	Michigan	Y	15550 FQ	26670 AW	47880 TQ	MIBLS	10/01-12/01
	Minnesota	Y	18020 FQ	32390 AW	51180 TQ	MNBLS	10/01-12/01
	Missouri	Y	15380 FQ	27430 AW	38220 TQ	MOBLS	10/01-12/01
	Nevada	Y	15710 FQ	17700 AW	20620 TQ	NVBLS	10/01-12/01
	New Jersey	Y	28340 FQ	50230 AW	87360 TQ	NJBLS	10/01-12/01
	New Mexico	Y	12500 FQ	28020 AW	62450 TQ	NMBLS	10/01-12/01
	New York	Y	24220 FQ	49400 AW	76760 TQ	NYBLS	10/01-12/01
	North Carolina	Y	16120 FQ	33770 AW	63040 TQ	NCBLS	10/01-12/01
	Ohio	Y	15810 FQ	25690 AW	48060 TQ	OHBLS	10/01-12/01
	Oklahoma	Y	30740 FQ	34630 AW	37660 TQ	OKBLS	10/01-12/01
	Oregon	Y	25540 FQ	49350 AW	83950 TQ	ORBLS	10/01-12/01
	Pennsylvania	Y	14680 FQ	26880 AW	47930 TQ	PABLS	10/01-12/01
	Rhode Island	Y	18810 FQ	46280 AW	81910 TQ	RIBLS	10/01-12/01
	Tennessee	Y	12410 FQ	23440 AW	43110 TQ	TNBLS	10/01-12/01
	Texas	Y	17260 FQ	29810 AW	52840 TQ	TXBLS	10/01-12/01
	Utah	Y	16340 FQ	21080 AW	26620 TQ	UTBLS	10/01-12/01
	Vermont	Y	31020 FQ	42660 AW	62510 TQ	VTBLS	10/01-12/01
	Washington	Y	14880 FQ	24580 AW	42020 TQ	WABLS	10/01-12/01
	West Virginia	Y	12400 FQ	19920 AW	38150 TQ	WVBLS	10/01-12/01
	Wisconsin	Y	13980 FQ	31840 AW	44800 TQ	WIBLS	10/01-12/01
Surveying and Mapping Technician	Alabama	Y	15250 FQ	26560 AW	41830 TQ	ALBLS	10/01-12/01
	Alaska	Y	30050 FQ	42420 AW	60710 TQ	AKBLS	10/01-12/01
	Arizona	Y	23560 FQ	38120 AW	56580 TQ	AZBLS	10/01-12/01
	Arkansas	Y	17240 FQ	25410 AW	38870 TQ	ARBLS	10/01-12/01
	California	Y	24330 FQ	44750 AW	65980 TQ	CABLS	10/01-12/01
	Colorado	Y	23040 FQ	36650 AW	49440 TQ	COBLS	10/01-12/01
	Connecticut	Y	21050 FQ	36560 AW	51390 TQ	CTBLS	10/01-12/01
	Delaware	Y	20220 FQ	33070 AW	37800 TQ	DEBLS	10/01-12/01
	Florida	Y	17050 FQ	25980 AW	38700 TQ	FLBLS	10/01-12/01
	Georgia	Y	15570 FQ	26200 AW	40670 TQ	GABLS	10/01-12/01
	Hawaii	Y	19400 FQ	31840 AW	47490 TQ	HIBLS	10/01-12/01
	Idaho	Y	20620 FQ	31430 AW	44410 TQ	IDBLS	10/01-12/01
	Illinois	Y	18950 FQ	29700 AW	42780 TQ	ILBLS	10/01-12/01
	Indiana	Y	20060 FQ	27610 AW	36840 TQ	INBLS	10/01-12/01
	Iowa	Y	22580 FQ	33960 AW	48430 TQ	IABLS	10/01-12/01
	Kansas	Y	17910 FQ	29740 AW	43250 TQ	KSBLS	10/01-12/01
	Kentucky	Y	17740 FQ	30230 AW	47500 TQ	KYBLS	10/01-12/01
	Louisiana	Y	18800 FQ	29800 AW	44340 TQ	LABLS	10/01-12/01
	Maine	Y	17430 FQ	29980 AW	43160 TQ	MEBLS	10/01-12/01
	Maryland	Y	19510 FQ	31140 AW	46330 TQ	MDBLS	10/01-12/01
	Massachusetts	Y	21670 FQ	35850 AW	52750 TQ	MABLS	10/01-12/01
	Michigan	Y	18460 FQ	28380 AW	41270 TQ	MIBLS	10/01-12/01

AAW	Average annual wage	AOH	Average offered, high	ASH	Average starting, high	H	Hourly	M	Monthly	S	Special: hourly and annual
AE	Average entry wage	AOL	Average offered, low	ASL	Average starting, low	HI	Highest wage paid	MTC	Median total compensation	TQ	Third quartile wage
AEX	Average experienced wage	APH	Average pay, high range	AW	Average wage paid	HR	High end range	MW	Median wage paid	W	Weekly
AO	Average offered	APL	Average pay, low range	FQ	First quartile wage	LR	Low end range	SQ	Second quartile wage	Y	Yearly

Occupation/Type/Industry	Location	Per	Low	Mid	High	Source	Date
Surveying and Mapping Technician	Minnesota	Y	19650 FQ	33290 AW	50580 TQ	MNBLS	10/01-12/01
	Mississippi	Y	16120 FQ	26100 AW	41750 TQ	MSBLS	10/01-12/01
	Missouri	Y	22120 FQ	35110 AW	49780 TQ	MOBLS	10/01-12/01
	Montana	Y	19120 FQ	32140 AW	46300 TQ	MTBLS	10/01-12/01
	Nebraska	Y	17740 FQ	26050 AW	37250 TQ	NEBLS	10/01-12/01
	Nevada	Y	23790 FQ	40300 AW	57320 TQ	NVBLS	10/01-12/01
	New Hampshire	Y	19640 FQ	26120 AW	34320 TQ	NHBLS	10/01-12/01
	New Jersey	Y	20430 FQ	34940 AW	54220 TQ	NJBLS	10/01-12/01
	New Mexico	Y	19790 FQ	33350 AW	49050 TQ	NMBLS	10/01-12/01
	New York	Y	19750 FQ	30690 AW	47830 TQ	NYBLS	10/01-12/01
	North Carolina	Y	19610 FQ	26850 AW	35640 TQ	NCBLS	10/01-12/01
	North Dakota	Y	16330 FQ	26280 AW	41530 TQ	NDBLS	10/01-12/01
	Ohio	Y	19040 FQ	30080 AW	43460 TQ	OHBLS	10/01-12/01
	Oklahoma	Y	16260 FQ	33000 AW	53020 TQ	OKBLS	10/01-12/01
	Oregon	Y	24720 FQ	35150 AW	47470 TQ	ORBLS	10/01-12/01
	Pennsylvania	Y	18350 FQ	33630 AW	52130 TQ	PABLS	10/01-12/01
	Rhode Island	Y	16330 FQ	31780 AW	44500 TQ	RIBLS	10/01-12/01
	South Carolina	Y	18520 FQ	29370 AW	46170 TQ	SCBLS	10/01-12/01
	South Dakota	Y	19930 FQ	27700 AW	39320 TQ	SDBLS	10/01-12/01
	Tennessee	Y	16110 FQ	26130 AW	36350 TQ	TNBLS	10/01-12/01
	Texas	Y	16320 FQ	28480 AW	44120 TQ	TXBLS	10/01-12/01
	Utah	Y	20290 FQ	28980 AW	39290 TQ	UTBLS	10/01-12/01
	Vermont	Y	18080 FQ	27490 AW	37810 TQ	VTBLS	10/01-12/01
	Virginia	Y	19780 FQ	32380 AW	48050 TQ	VABLS	10/01-12/01
	Washington	Y	22670 FQ	35000 AW	50460 TQ	WABLS	10/01-12/01
	West Virginia	Y	14960 FQ	26780 AW	40390 TQ	WVBLS	10/01-12/01
	Wisconsin	Y	20260 FQ	30010 AW	40840 TQ	WIBLS	10/01-12/01
	Wyoming	Y	15710 FQ	27070 AW	43030 TQ	WYBLS	10/01-12/01
	Puerto Rico	Y	12680 FQ	19170 AW	27030 TQ	PRBLS	10/01-12/01
Surveyor	Alabama	Y	16510 FQ	29530 AW	43990 TQ	ALBLS	10/01-12/01
	Birmingham MSA, AL	Y	19380 FQ	30820 AW	43470 TQ	ALBLS	10/01-12/01
	Huntsville MSA, AL	Y	18480 FQ	29010 AW	42540 TQ	ALBLS	10/01-12/01
	Mobile MSA, AL	Y	15620 FQ	24470 AW	42840 TQ	ALBLS	10/01-12/01
	Alaska	Y	38080 FQ	59180 AW	95870 TQ	AKBLS	10/01-12/01
	Anchorage MSA, AK	Y	37820 FQ	56180 AW	79170 TQ	AKBLS	10/01-12/01
	Arizona	Y	22000 FQ	38570 AW	59760 TQ	AZBLS	10/01-12/01
	Phoenix-Mesa MSA, AZ	Y	22150 FQ	38710 AW	60090 TQ	AZBLS	10/01-12/01
	Tucson MSA, AZ	Y	20020 FQ	37190 AW	61560 TQ	AZBLS	10/01-12/01
	Arkansas	Y	18170 FQ	30790 AW	47700 TQ	ARBLS	10/01-12/01
	Fayetteville-Springdale-Rogers MSA, AR	Y	18500 FQ	23980 AW	34830 TQ	ARBLS	10/01-12/01
	Little Rock-North Little Rock MSA, AR	Y	20230 FQ	35500 AW	53380 TQ	ARBLS	10/01-12/01
	California	Y	37160 FQ	57850 AW	74090 TQ	CABLS	10/01-12/01
	Bakersfield MSA, CA	Y	28830 FQ	48370 AW	71450 TQ	CABLS	10/01-12/01
	Fresno MSA, CA	Y	30120 FQ	49950 AW	69470 TQ	CABLS	10/01-12/01
	Los Angeles-Long Beach PMSA, CA	Y	43890 FQ	60170 AW	73830 TQ	CABLS	10/01-12/01
	Oakland PMSA, CA	Y	49560 FQ	61030 AW	72320 TQ	CABLS	10/01-12/01
	Orange County PMSA, CA	Y	33210 FQ	56510 AW	78400 TQ	CABLS	10/01-12/01
	Redding MSA, CA	Y	43920 FQ	59550 AW	70830 TQ	CABLS	10/01-12/01
	Riverside-San Bernardino PMSA, CA	Y	29710 FQ	54510 AW	77290 TQ	CABLS	10/01-12/01
	Sacramento PMSA, CA	Y	44770 FQ	64050 AW	87110 TQ	CABLS	10/01-12/01
	Salinas MSA, CA	Y	56990 FQ	63100 AW	71170 TQ	CABLS	10/01-12/01
	San Diego MSA, CA	Y	32340 FQ	53630 AW	73350 TQ	CABLS	10/01-12/01
	San Francisco PMSA, CA	Y	32760 FQ	55190 AW	76400 TQ	CABLS	10/01-12/01
	San Jose PMSA, CA	Y	47200 FQ	57450 AW	69750 TQ	CABLS	10/01-12/01
	San Luis Obispo-Atascadero-Paso Robles MSA, CA	Y	39440 FQ	55000 AW	71020 TQ	CABLS	10/01-12/01
	Santa Rosa PMSA, CA	Y	34580 FQ	55060 AW	100940 TQ	CABLS	10/01-12/01
	Stockton-Lodi MSA, CA	Y	34720 FQ	54920 AW	75780 TQ	CABLS	10/01-12/01
	Vallejo-Fairfield-Napa PMSA, CA	Y	47010 FQ	60240 AW	73840 TQ	CABLS	10/01-12/01
	Ventura PMSA, CA	Y	38910 FQ	54550 AW	72580 TQ	CABLS	10/01-12/01
	Colorado	Y	29140 FQ	40960 AW	56090 TQ	COBLS	10/01-12/01
	Boulder-Longmont PMSA, CO	Y	22990 FQ	37910 AW	52550 TQ	COBLS	10/01-12/01
	Colorado Springs MSA, CO	Y	27580 FQ	42060 AW	61650 TQ	COBLS	10/01-12/01
	Denver PMSA, CO	Y	29790 FQ	40590 AW	55000 TQ	COBLS	10/01-12/01

AAW	Average annual wage	**AOH**	Average offered, high	**ASH**	Average starting, high	**H**	Hourly	**M**	Monthly	**S**	Special: hourly and annual
AE	Average entry wage	**AOL**	Average offered, low	**ASL**	Average starting, low	**HI**	Highest wage paid	**MTC**	Median total compensation	**TQ**	Third quartile wage
AEX	Average experienced wage	**APH**	Average pay, high range	**AW**	Average wage paid	**HR**	High end range	**MW**	Median wage paid	**W**	Weekly
AO	Average offered	**APL**	Average pay, low range	**FQ**	First quartile wage	**LR**	Low end range	**SQ**	Second quartile wage	**Y**	Yearly

Occupation/Type/Industry	Location	Per	Low	Mid	High	Source	Date
Surveyor	Fort Collins-Loveland MSA, CO	Y	23340 FQ	36250 AW	54460 TQ	COBLS	10/01-12/01
	Greeley PMSA, CO	Y	31190 FQ	42720 AW	64330 TQ	COBLS	10/01-12/01
	Connecticut	Y	29220 FQ	43440 AW	56290 TQ	CTBLS	10/01-12/01
	Bridgeport PMSA, CT	Y	25810 FQ	46220 AW	58300 TQ	CTBLS	10/01-12/01
	Danbury PMSA, CT	Y	29370 FQ	40390 AW	51810 TQ	CTBLS	10/01-12/01
	Hartford MSA, CT	Y	27840 FQ	43250 AW	56680 TQ	CTBLS	10/01-12/01
	New Haven-Meriden PMSA, CT	Y	30260 FQ	43610 AW	56190 TQ	CTBLS	10/01-12/01
	New London-Norwich MSA, CT-RI	Y	28580 FQ	40790 AW	54220 TQ	CTBLS	10/01-12/01
	Waterbury PMSA, CT	Y	31530 FQ	37410 AW	45610 TQ	CTBLS	10/01-12/01
	Delaware	Y	22330 FQ	38980 AW	61340 TQ	DEBLS	10/01-12/01
	Wilmington-Newark PMSA, DE-MD	Y	23840 FQ	43510 AW	74340 TQ	DEBLS	10/01-12/01
	District of Columbia	Y	26480 FQ	49730 AW	71370 TQ	DCBLS	10/01-12/01
	Washington PMSA, DC-MD-VA-WV	Y	20830 FQ	39320 AW	61850 TQ	DCBLS	10/01-12/01
	Florida	Y	26710 FQ	45340 AW	69710 TQ	FLBLS	10/01-12/01
	Daytona Beach MSA, FL	Y	31780 FQ	43160 AW	59530 TQ	FLBLS	10/01-12/01
	Fort Lauderdale PMSA, FL	Y	39810 FQ	55360 AW	75430 TQ	FLBLS	10/01-12/01
	Fort Myers-Cape Coral MSA, FL	Y	26540 FQ	47850 AW	72070 TQ	FLBLS	10/01-12/01
	Fort Pierce-Port St. Lucie MSA, FL	Y	30350 FQ	40820 AW	54440 TQ	FLBLS	10/01-12/01
	Fort Walton Beach MSA, FL	Y	22050 FQ	39610 AW	57040 TQ	FLBLS	10/01-12/01
	Gainesville MSA, FL	Y	29290 FQ	55440 AW	88760 TQ	FLBLS	10/01-12/01
	Jacksonville MSA, FL	Y	28220 FQ	46700 AW	73920 TQ	FLBLS	10/01-12/01
	Lakeland-Winter Haven MSA, FL	Y	17080 FQ	35780 AW	57970 TQ	FLBLS	10/01-12/01
	Melbourne-Titusville-Palm Bay MSA, FL	Y	22280 FQ	40490 AW	70580 TQ	FLBLS	10/01-12/01
	Miami PMSA, FL	Y	33180 FQ	57320 AW	82780 TQ	FLBLS	10/01-12/01
	Naples MSA, FL	Y	20950 FQ	47740 AW	82550 TQ	FLBLS	10/01-12/01
	Ocala MSA, FL	Y	19640 FQ	29890 AW	45120 TQ	FLBLS	10/01-12/01
	Orlando MSA, FL	Y	28700 FQ	38680 AW	54960 TQ	FLBLS	10/01-12/01
	Pensacola MSA, FL	Y	23730 FQ	39210 AW	63540 TQ	FLBLS	10/01-12/01
	Sarasota-Bradenton MSA, FL	Y	26690 FQ	45890 AW	60950 TQ	FLBLS	10/01-12/01
	Tallahassee MSA, FL	Y	32020 FQ	58300 AW	108270 TQ	FLBLS	10/01-12/01
	Tampa-St. Petersburg-Clearwater MSA, FL	Y	25250 FQ	39650 AW	60760 TQ	FLBLS	10/01-12/01
	West Palm Beach-Boca Raton MSA, FL	Y	31160 FQ	47620 AW	70030 TQ	FLBLS	10/01-12/01
	Georgia	Y	19780 FQ	35300 AW	60060 TQ	GABLS	10/01-12/01
	Atlanta MSA, GA	Y	19800 FQ	36270 AW	62260 TQ	GABLS	10/01-12/01
	Macon MSA, GA	Y	24670 FQ	37320 AW	63420 TQ	GABLS	10/01-12/01
	Savannah MSA, GA	Y	20000 FQ	26500 AW	32660 TQ	GABLS	10/01-12/01
	Hawaii	Y	22130 FQ	41450 AW	66150 TQ	HIBLS	10/01-12/01
	Honolulu MSA, HI	Y	21650 FQ	41490 AW	68330 TQ	HIBLS	10/01-12/01
	Idaho	Y	31190 FQ	43030 AW	57250 TQ	IDBLS	10/01-12/01
	Boise City MSA, ID	Y	30400 FQ	43290 AW	58780 TQ	IDBLS	10/01-12/01
	Illinois	Y	30910 FQ	45300 AW	56520 TQ	ILBLS	10/01-12/01
	Chicago PMSA, IL	Y	36750 FQ	47120 AW	55960 TQ	ILBLS	10/01-12/01
	Peoria-Pekin MSA, IL	Y	19340 FQ	40740 AW	58470 TQ	ILBLS	10/01-12/01
	Rockford MSA, IL	Y	37690 FQ	58730 AW	103680 TQ	ILBLS	10/01-12/01
	Springfield MSA, IL	Y	26650 FQ	42160 AW	61900 TQ	ILBLS	10/01-12/01
	Indiana	Y	23550 FQ	35740 AW	51100 TQ	INBLS	10/01-12/01
	Evansville-Henderson MSA, IN-KY	Y	19200 FQ	33960 AW	51880 TQ	INBLS	10/01-12/01
	Fort Wayne MSA, IN	Y	32580 FQ	56840 AW	85810 TQ	INBLS	10/01-12/01
	Gary PMSA, IN	Y	18140 FQ	35160 AW	56230 TQ	INBLS	10/01-12/01
	Indianapolis MSA, IN	Y	26660 FQ	34340 AW	44000 TQ	INBLS	10/01-12/01
	Iowa	Y	28750 FQ	42070 AW	59300 TQ	IABLS	10/01-12/01
	Des Moines MSA, IA	Y	28550 FQ	44120 AW	70200 TQ	IABLS	10/01-12/01
	Kansas	Y	21010 FQ	34760 AW	47040 TQ	KSBLS	10/01-12/01
	Topeka MSA, KS	Y	29840 FQ	39960 AW	47550 TQ	KSBLS	10/01-12/01
	Kentucky	Y	19030 FQ	34110 AW	53410 TQ	KYBLS	10/01-12/01
	Lexington MSA, KY	Y	24290 FQ	34470 AW	49560 TQ	KYBLS	10/01-12/01
	Louisville MSA, KY-IN	Y	27500 FQ	44720 AW	60570 TQ	KYBLS	10/01-12/01
	Louisiana	Y	19370 FQ	37180 AW	60330 TQ	LABLS	10/01-12/01
	Baton Rouge MSA, LA	Y	20820 FQ	38900 AW	59020 TQ	LABLS	10/01-12/01
	Lafayette MSA, LA	Y	21470 FQ	42360 AW	66960 TQ	LABLS	10/01-12/01

AAW Average annual wage; **AE** Average entry wage; **AEX** Average experienced wage; **AO** Average offered; **AOH** Average offered, high; **AOL** Average offered, low; **APH** Average pay, high range; **APL** Average pay, low range; **ASH** Average starting, high; **ASL** Average starting, low; **AW** Average wage paid; **FQ** First quartile wage; **H** Hourly; **HI** Highest wage paid; **HR** High end range; **LR** Low end range; **M** Monthly; **MTC** Median total compensation; **MW** Median wage paid; **SQ** Second quartile wage; **S** Special: hourly and annual; **TQ** Third quartile wage; **W** Weekly; **Y** Yearly

Occupation/Type/Industry	Location	Per	Low	Mid	High	Source	Date
Surveyor	Lake Charles MSA, LA	Y	16290 FQ	28890 AW	41550 TQ	LABLS	10/01-12/01
	New Orleans MSA, LA	Y	19680 FQ	37720 AW	63380 TQ	LABLS	10/01-12/01
	Shreveport-Bossier City MSA, LA	Y	14960 FQ	31380 AW	60820 TQ	LABLS	10/01-12/01
	Maine	Y	28760 FQ	38470 AW	46780 TQ	MEBLS	10/01-12/01
	Maryland	Y	21710 FQ	38130 AW	55820 TQ	MDBLS	10/01-12/01
	Baltimore PMSA, MD	Y	24410 FQ	39130 AW	52970 TQ	MDBLS	10/01-12/01
	Massachusetts	Y	26320 FQ	43480 AW	68970 TQ	MABLS	10/01-12/01
	Boston PMSA, MA-NH	Y	27550 FQ	42510 AW	66120 TQ	MABLS	10/01-12/01
	Brockton PMSA, MA	Y	36070 FQ	64360 AW	86690 TQ	MABLS	10/01-12/01
	Lawrence PMSA, MA-NH	Y	23110 FQ	34620 AW	46300 TQ	MABLS	10/01-12/01
	Worcester PMSA, MA-CT	Y	30340 FQ	46280 AW	68960 TQ	MABLS	10/01-12/01
	Michigan	Y	25540 FQ	45430 AW	66150 TQ	MIBLS	10/01-12/01
	Ann Arbor PMSA, MI	Y	22790 FQ	34930 AW	48950 TQ	MIBLS	10/01-12/01
	Detroit PMSA, MI	Y	29730 FQ	53410 AW	71490 TQ	MIBLS	10/01-12/01
	Flint PMSA, MI	Y	24450 FQ	41040 AW	57370 TQ	MIBLS	10/01-12/01
	Grand Rapids-Muskegon-Holland MSA, MI	Y	21880 FQ	39030 AW	56720 TQ	MIBLS	10/01-12/01
	Kalamazoo-Battle Creek MSA, MI	Y	29920 FQ	41600 AW	54910 TQ	MIBLS	10/01-12/01
	Lansing-East Lansing MSA, MI	Y	24670 FQ	39760 AW	59030 TQ	MIBLS	10/01-12/01
	Saginaw-Bay City-Midland MSA, MI	Y	25730 FQ	39810 AW	55140 TQ	MIBLS	10/01-12/01
	Minnesota	Y	30890 FQ	44420 AW	61840 TQ	MNBLS	10/01-12/01
	Duluth-Superior MSA, MN-WI	Y	23880 FQ	39190 AW	57710 TQ	MNBLS	10/01-12/01
	Minneapolis-St. Paul MSA, MN-WI	Y	33500 FQ	44980 AW	61860 TQ	MNBLS	10/01-12/01
	Mississippi	Y	16990 FQ	30940 AW	47260 TQ	MSBLS	10/01-12/01
	Biloxi-Gulfport-Pascagoula MSA, MS	Y	15240 FQ	25890 AW	43690 TQ	MSBLS	10/01-12/01
	Jackson MSA, MS	Y	20690 FQ	32920 AW	44110 TQ	MSBLS	10/01-12/01
	Missouri	Y	23640 FQ	39750 AW	57420 TQ	MOBLS	10/01-12/01
	Kansas City MSA, MO-KS	Y	25830 FQ	39340 AW	56530 TQ	MOBLS	10/01-12/01
	St. Louis MSA, MO-IL	Y	24330 FQ	42070 AW	65670 TQ	MOBLS	10/01-12/01
	Springfield MSA, MO	Y	17840 FQ	32000 AW	46270 TQ	MOBLS	10/01-12/01
	Montana	Y	26030 FQ	39030 AW	55510 TQ	MTBLS	10/01-12/01
	Nebraska	Y	20980 FQ	34690 AW	48320 TQ	NEBLS	10/01-12/01
	Lincoln MSA, NE	Y	25870 FQ	36190 AW	48830 TQ	NEBLS	10/01-12/01
	Omaha MSA, NE-IA	Y	24390 FQ	36080 AW	50560 TQ	NEBLS	10/01-12/01
	Nevada	Y	24880 FQ	45030 AW	75150 TQ	NVBLS	10/01-12/01
	Las Vegas MSA, NV-AZ	Y	23710 FQ	44090 AW	75230 TQ	NVBLS	10/01-12/01
	Reno MSA, NV	Y	35440 FQ	53150 AW	74910 TQ	NVBLS	10/01-12/01
	New Hampshire	Y	26020 FQ	38330 AW	53570 TQ	NHBLS	10/01-12/01
	Nashua PMSA, NH	Y	26540 FQ	41020 AW	56700 TQ	NHBLS	10/01-12/01
	Portsmouth-Rochester PMSA, NH-ME	Y	28910 FQ	38160 AW	52320 TQ	NHBLS	10/01-12/01
	New Jersey	Y	35280 FQ	52150 AW	71580 TQ	NJBLS	10/01-12/01
	Atlantic-Cape May PMSA, NJ	Y	47850 FQ	59530 AW	71840 TQ	NJBLS	10/01-12/01
	Bergen-Passaic PMSA, NJ	Y	42190 FQ	54410 AW	73680 TQ	NJBLS	10/01-12/01
	Middlesex-Somerset-Hunterdon PMSA, NJ	Y	33230 FQ	51580 AW	72310 TQ	NJBLS	10/01-12/01
	Monmouth-Ocean PMSA, NJ	Y	25770 FQ	56010 AW	102660 TQ	NJBLS	10/01-12/01
	Newark PMSA, NJ	Y	38310 FQ	51980 AW	64550 TQ	NJBLS	10/01-12/01
	Trenton PMSA, NJ	Y	32290 FQ	50190 AW	76590 TQ	NJBLS	10/01-12/01
	New Mexico	Y	21000 FQ	44050 AW	69760 TQ	NMBLS	10/01-12/01
	Albuquerque MSA, NM	Y	25270 FQ	46810 AW	70690 TQ	NMBLS	10/01-12/01
	New York	Y	27290 FQ	45870 AW	67170 TQ	NYBLS	10/01-12/01
	Albany-Schenectady-Troy MSA, NY	Y	35920 FQ	55530 AW	81440 TQ	NYBLS	10/01-12/01
	Buffalo-Niagara Falls MSA, NY	Y	26030 FQ	46390 AW	66640 TQ	NYBLS	10/01-12/01
	Nassau-Suffolk PMSA, NY	Y	41570 FQ	57810 AW	80190 TQ	NYBLS	10/01-12/01
	New York PMSA, NY	Y	28210 FQ	46570 AW	68500 TQ	NYBLS	10/01-12/01
	Newburgh PMSA, NY-PA	Y	24930 FQ	30630 AW	43250 TQ	NYBLS	10/01-12/01
	Rochester MSA, NY	Y	32450 FQ	47850 AW	58020 TQ	NYBLS	10/01-12/01
	Syracuse MSA, NY	Y	27280 FQ	43610 AW	65780 TQ	NYBLS	10/01-12/01
	Utica-Rome MSA, NY	Y	44800 FQ	49710 AW	56640 TQ	NYBLS	10/01-12/01
	North Carolina	Y	22070 FQ	39320 AW	64640 TQ	NCBLS	10/01-12/01
	Charlotte-Gastonia-Rock Hill MSA, NC-SC	Y	22840 FQ	39010 AW	58700 TQ	NCBLS	10/01-12/01
	Greensboro-Winston-Salem-High Point MSA, NC	Y	21620 FQ	34230 AW	50690 TQ	NCBLS	10/01-12/01

AAW	Average annual wage	**AOH**	Average offered, high	**ASH**	Average starting, high	**H**	Hourly	**M**	Monthly	**S**	Special: hourly and annual
AE	Average entry wage	**AOL**	Average offered, low	**ASL**	Average starting, low	**HI**	Highest wage paid	**MTC**	Median total compensation	**TQ**	Third quartile wage
AEX	Average experienced wage	**APH**	Average pay, high range	**AW**	Average wage paid	**HR**	High end range	**MW**	Median wage paid	**W**	Weekly
AO	Average offered	**APL**	Average pay, low range	**FQ**	First quartile wage	**LR**	Low end range	**SQ**	Second quartile wage	**Y**	Yearly

Occupation/Type/Industry	Location	Per	Low	Mid	High	Source	Date
Surveyor	Hickory-Morganton-Lenoir MSA, NC	Y	27160 FQ	60840 AW	88220 TQ	NCBLS	10/01-12/01
	Raleigh-Durham-Chapel Hill MSA, NC	Y	35450 FQ	49220 AW	68770 TQ	NCBLS	10/01-12/01
	Wilmington MSA, NC	Y	17390 FQ	33160 AW	47570 TQ	NCBLS	10/01-12/01
	North Dakota	Y	19970 FQ	35900 AW	59060 TQ	NDBLS	10/01-12/01
	Fargo-Moorhead MSA, ND-MN	Y	20540 FQ	37450 AW	67800 TQ	NDBLS	10/01-12/01
	Ohio	Y	20790 FQ	37350 AW	57420 TQ	OHBLS	10/01-12/01
	Akron PMSA, OH	Y	20650 FQ	34840 AW	54340 TQ	OHBLS	10/01-12/01
	Canton-Massillon MSA, OH	Y	20220 FQ	27990 AW	37340 TQ	OHBLS	10/01-12/01
	Cincinnati PMSA, OH-KY-IN	Y	24590 FQ	43620 AW	61250 TQ	OHBLS	10/01-12/01
	Cleveland-Lorain-Elyria PMSA, OH	Y	22900 FQ	38570 AW	57220 TQ	OHBLS	10/01-12/01
	Columbus MSA, OH	Y	20210 FQ	36250 AW	55690 TQ	OHBLS	10/01-12/01
	Dayton-Springfield MSA, OH	Y	31200 FQ	42040 AW	55280 TQ	OHBLS	10/01-12/01
	Toledo MSA, OH	Y	18680 FQ	38390 AW	68330 TQ	OHBLS	10/01-12/01
	Youngstown-Warren MSA, OH	Y	19350 FQ	32330 AW	54180 TQ	OHBLS	10/01-12/01
	Oklahoma	Y	14410 FQ	32930 AW	56870 TQ	OKBLS	10/01-12/01
	Oklahoma City MSA, OK	Y	14380 FQ	31780 AW	55060 TQ	OKBLS	10/01-12/01
	Tulsa MSA, OK	Y	13200 FQ	38650 AW	76690 TQ	OKBLS	10/01-12/01
	Oregon	Y	34330 FQ	48180 AW	67690 TQ	ORBLS	10/01-12/01
	Eugene-Springfield MSA, OR	Y	27160 FQ	51070 AW	70410 TQ	ORBLS	10/01-12/01
	Medford-Ashland MSA, OR	Y	14890 FQ	38800 AW	58580 TQ	ORBLS	10/01-12/01
	Portland-Vancouver PMSA, OR-WA	Y	36260 FQ	53450 AW	71480 TQ	ORBLS	10/01-12/01
	Salem PMSA, OR	Y	33440 FQ	48930 AW	66610 TQ	ORBLS	10/01-12/01
	Pennsylvania	Y	20840 FQ	38560 AW	56170 TQ	PABLS	10/01-12/01
	Allentown-Bethlehem-Easton MSA, PA	Y	30740 FQ	41060 AW	55220 TQ	PABLS	10/01-12/01
	Harrisburg-Lebanon-Carlisle MSA, PA	Y	25840 FQ	39040 AW	53270 TQ	PABLS	10/01-12/01
	Johnstown MSA, PA	Y	21340 FQ	35160 AW	51460 TQ	PABLS	10/01-12/01
	Lancaster MSA, PA	Y	23760 FQ	36060 AW	54310 TQ	PABLS	10/01-12/01
	Philadelphia PMSA, PA-NJ	Y	23380 FQ	43910 AW	59430 TQ	PABLS	10/01-12/01
	Pittsburgh MSA, PA	Y	25390 FQ	40080 AW	54630 TQ	PABLS	10/01-12/01
	Scranton-Wilkes-Barre-Hazleton MSA, PA	Y	28320 FQ	42000 AW	66960 TQ	PABLS	10/01-12/01
	York MSA, PA	Y	24540 FQ	38980 AW	53900 TQ	PABLS	10/01-12/01
	Rhode Island	Y	25000 FQ	40930 AW	62210 TQ	RIBLS	10/01-12/01
	Providence-Fall River-Warwick MSA, RI-MA	Y	23920 FQ	40730 AW	62970 TQ	RIBLS	10/01-12/01
	South Carolina	Y	18690 FQ	35080 AW	55430 TQ	SCBLS	10/01-12/01
	Charleston-North Charleston MSA, SC	Y	21540 FQ	35760 AW	52130 TQ	SCBLS	10/01-12/01
	Columbia MSA, SC	Y	19490 FQ	34670 AW	51780 TQ	SCBLS	10/01-12/01
	Greenville-Spartanburg-Anderson MSA, SC	Y	19840 FQ	32710 AW	49970 TQ	SCBLS	10/01-12/01
	Myrtle Beach MSA, SC	Y	16070 FQ	27890 AW	48370 TQ	SCBLS	10/01-12/01
	South Dakota	Y	21630 FQ	34110 AW	50000 TQ	SDBLS	10/01-12/01
	Tennessee	Y	18130 FQ	29270 AW	46870 TQ	TNBLS	10/01-12/01
	Chattanooga MSA, TN-GA	Y	19260 FQ	32290 AW	48020 TQ	TNBLS	10/01-12/01
	Johnson City-Kingsport-Bristol MSA, TN-VA	Y	19980 FQ	25620 AW	31580 TQ	TNBLS	10/01-12/01
	Knoxville MSA, TN	Y	16680 FQ	27130 AW	41140 TQ	TNBLS	10/01-12/01
	Memphis MSA, TN-AR-MS	Y	21030 FQ	33910 AW	47280 TQ	TNBLS	10/01-12/01
	Nashville MSA, TN	Y	21450 FQ	36390 AW	55100 TQ	TNBLS	10/01-12/01
	Texas	Y	18820 FQ	33830 AW	57190 TQ	TXBLS	10/01-12/01
	Amarillo MSA, TX	Y	18560 FQ	34270 AW	47560 TQ	TXBLS	10/01-12/01
	Austin-San Marcos MSA, TX	Y	18620 FQ	34700 AW	54870 TQ	TXBLS	10/01-12/01
	Beaumont-Port Arthur MSA, TX	Y	18210 FQ	31170 AW	45750 TQ	TXBLS	10/01-12/01
	Brownsville-Harlingen-San Benito MSA, TX	Y	30010 FQ	36120 AW	49720 TQ	TXBLS	10/01-12/01
	Dallas PMSA, TX	Y	22840 FQ	29810 AW	46900 TQ	TXBLS	10/01-12/01
	El Paso MSA, TX	Y	17250 FQ	44260 AW	137050 TQ	TXBLS	10/01-12/01
	Fort Worth-Arlington PMSA, TX	Y	17540 FQ	37220 AW	60230 TQ	TXBLS	10/01-12/01
	Galveston-Texas City PMSA, TX	Y	20190 FQ	30600 AW	37440 TQ	TXBLS	10/01-12/01
	Houston PMSA, TX	Y	18930 FQ	37430 AW	68740 TQ	TXBLS	10/01-12/01
	Killeen-Temple MSA, TX	Y	13670 FQ	29520 AW	48900 TQ	TXBLS	10/01-12/01

AAW	Average annual wage	AOH	Average offered, high	ASH	Average starting, high	H	Hourly	M	Monthly	S	Special: hourly and annual
AE	Average entry wage	AOL	Average offered, low	ASL	Average starting, low	HI	Highest wage paid	MTC	Median total compensation	TQ	Third quartile wage
AEX	Average experienced wage	APH	Average pay, high range	AW	Average wage paid	HR	High end range	MW	Median wage paid	W	Weekly
AO	Average offered	APL	Average pay, low range	FQ	First quartile wage	LR	Low end range	SQ	Second quartile wage	Y	Yearly

Occupation/Type/Industry	Location	Per	Low	Mid	High	Source	Date
Surveyor	McAllen-Edinburg-Mission MSA, TX	Y	13250 FQ	29870 AW	65500 TQ	TXBLS	10/01-12/01
	Odessa-Midland MSA, TX	Y	12160 FQ	24920 AW	40950 TQ	TXBLS	10/01-12/01
	San Antonio MSA, TX	Y	19190 FQ	31420 AW	59100 TQ	TXBLS	10/01-12/01
	Tyler MSA, TX	Y	16850 FQ	35780 AW	64360 TQ	TXBLS	10/01-12/01
	Utah	Y	17030 FQ	36950 AW	56110 TQ	UTBLS	10/01-12/01
	Provo-Orem MSA, UT	Y	23920 FQ	34340 AW	50210 TQ	UTBLS	10/01-12/01
	Salt Lake City-Ogden MSA, UT	Y	16390 FQ	38790 AW	56710 TQ	UTBLS	10/01-12/01
	Vermont	Y	19850 FQ	34120 AW	47580 TQ	VTBLS	10/01-12/01
	Virginia	Y	19270 FQ	37520 AW	58520 TQ	VABLS	10/01-12/01
	Norfolk-Virginia Beach-Newport News MSA, VA-NC	Y	24490 FQ	47600 AW	102060 TQ	VABLS	10/01-12/01
	Richmond-Petersburg MSA, VA	Y	16710 FQ	31190 AW	53880 TQ	VABLS	10/01-12/01
	Washington	Y	33580 FQ	54750 AW	90530 TQ	WABLS	10/01-12/01
	Olympia PMSA, WA	Y	39370 FQ	52290 AW	64940 TQ	WABLS	10/01-12/01
	Seattle-Bellevue-Everett PMSA, WA	Y	36770 FQ	60360 AW	115320 TQ	WABLS	10/01-12/01
	Tacoma PMSA, WA	Y	33470 FQ	46690 AW	66040 TQ	WABLS	10/01-12/01
	Yakima MSA, WA	Y	29480 FQ	37840 AW	53620 TQ	WABLS	10/01-12/01
	West Virginia	Y	18270 FQ	36210 AW	64210 TQ	WVBLS	10/01-12/01
	Charleston MSA, WV	Y	25770 FQ	47960 AW	68550 TQ	WVBLS	10/01-12/01
	Huntington-Ashland MSA, WV-KY-OH	Y	15100 FQ	30640 AW	47730 TQ	WVBLS	10/01-12/01
	Wisconsin	Y	24710 FQ	40380 AW	55350 TQ	WIBLS	10/01-12/01
	Appleton-Oshkosh-Neenah MSA, WI	Y	36720 FQ	42540 AW	53820 TQ	WIBLS	10/01-12/01
	Green Bay MSA, WI	Y	28370 FQ	41620 AW	56080 TQ	WIBLS	10/01-12/01
	Madison MSA, WI	Y	24960 FQ	40140 AW	54690 TQ	WIBLS	10/01-12/01
	Milwaukee-Waukesha PMSA, WI	Y	25670 FQ	41880 AW	56770 TQ	WIBLS	10/01-12/01
	Wyoming	Y	35600 FQ	47780 AW	56700 TQ	WYBLS	10/01-12/01
	Puerto Rico	Y	17980 FQ	26730 AW	38570 TQ	PRBLS	10/01-12/01
Surveyor/Inspector							
Nursing Homes, State agency	Missouri	Y		35000 AW		STLOUPD	2002
Switchboard Operator							
Including Answering Service	Alabama	H	6.17 FQ	8.83 AW	12.15 TQ	ALBLS	10/01-12/01
Including Answering Service	Alaska	H	8.88 FQ	12.96 AW	17.55 TQ	AKBLS	10/01-12/01
Including Answering Service	Arizona	H	7.28 FQ	10.22 AW	13.47 TQ	AZBLS	10/01-12/01
Including Answering Service	Arkansas	H	6.36 FQ	8.73 AW	11.51 TQ	ARBLS	10/01-12/01
Including Answering Service	California	H	7.51 FQ	11.37 AW	16.10 TQ	CABLS	10/01-12/01
Including Answering Service	Colorado	H	7.31 FQ	10.86 AW	14.00 TQ	COBLS	10/01-12/01
Including Answering Service	Connecticut	H	8.84 FQ	12.21 AW	16.69 TQ	CTBLS	10/01-12/01
Including Answering Service	Delaware	H	7.44 FQ	10.60 AW	14.30 TQ	DEBLS	10/01-12/01
Including Answering Service	District of Columbia	H	8.76 FQ	11.55 AW	15.71 TQ	DCBLS	10/01-12/01
Including Answering Service	Florida	H	6.30 FQ	9.09 AW	12.36 TQ	FLBLS	10/01-12/01
Including Answering Service	Georgia	H	7.31 FQ	9.93 AW	13.04 TQ	GABLS	10/01-12/01
Including Answering Service	Hawaii	H	9.30 FQ	12.44 AW	16.46 TQ	HIBLS	10/01-12/01
Including Answering Service	Idaho	H	6.57 FQ	9.27 AW	12.02 TQ	IDBLS	10/01-12/01
Including Answering Service	Illinois	H	7.19 FQ	10.57 AW	14.29 TQ	ILBLS	10/01-12/01
Including Answering Service	Indiana	H	7.27 FQ	9.95 AW	13.14 TQ	INBLS	10/01-12/01
Including Answering Service	Iowa	H	7.26 FQ	10.03 AW	13.30 TQ	IABLS	10/01-12/01
Including Answering Service	Kansas	H	7.06 FQ	9.84 AW	14.41 TQ	KSBLS	10/01-12/01
Including Answering Service	Kentucky	H	6.93 FQ	9.44 AW	12.58 TQ	KYBLS	10/01-12/01
Including Answering Service	Louisiana	H	6.18 FQ	8.40 AW	11.43 TQ	LABLS	10/01-12/01
Including Answering Service	Maine	H	7.43 FQ	10.01 AW	13.13 TQ	MEBLS	10/01-12/01
Including Answering Service	Maryland	H	7.54 FQ	10.76 AW	15.17 TQ	MDBLS	10/01-12/01
Including Answering Service	Massachusetts	H	8.28 FQ	11.83 AW	16.03 TQ	MABLS	10/01-12/01
Including Answering Service	Michigan	H	7.76 FQ	11.38 AW	16.18 TQ	MIBLS	10/01-12/01
Including Answering Service	Minnesota	H	7.85 FQ	11.14 AW	14.46 TQ	MNBLS	10/01-12/01
Including Answering Service	Mississippi	H	6.14 FQ	9.03 AW	11.89 TQ	MSBLS	10/01-12/01
Including Answering Service	Missouri	H	7.05 FQ	9.90 AW	13.34 TQ	MOBLS	10/01-12/01
Including Answering Service	Montana	H	6.75 FQ	8.69 AW	11.18 TQ	MTBLS	10/01-12/01
Including Answering Service	Nebraska	H	7.43 FQ	10.00 AW	13.19 TQ	NEBLS	10/01-12/01
Including Answering Service	Nevada	H	6.60 FQ	10.38 AW	14.16 TQ	NVBLS	10/01-12/01
Including Answering Service	New Hampshire	H	7.68 FQ	10.55 AW	13.87 TQ	NHBLS	10/01-12/01
Including Answering Service	New Jersey	H	7.55 FQ	11.64 AW	16.44 TQ	NJBLS	10/01-12/01
Including Answering Service	New Mexico	H	6.21 FQ	9.19 AW	12.61 TQ	NMBLS	10/01-12/01
Including Answering Service	New York	H	7.36 FQ	11.62 AW	17.26 TQ	NYBLS	10/01-12/01

AAW	Average annual wage	**AOH**	Average offered, high	**ASH**	Average starting, high	**H**	Hourly	**M**	Monthly	**S**	Special: hourly and annual
AE	Average entry wage	**AOL**	Average offered, low	**ASL**	Average starting, low	**HI**	Highest wage paid	**MTC**	Median total compensation	**TQ**	Third quartile wage
AEX	Average experienced wage	**APH**	Average pay, high range	**AW**	Average wage paid	**HR**	High end range	**MW**	Median wage paid	**W**	Weekly
AO	Average offered	**APL**	Average pay, low range	**FQ**	First quartile wage	**LR**	Low end range	**SQ**	Second quartile wage	**Y**	Yearly

Occupation/Type/Industry	Location	Per	Low	Mid	High	Source	Date
Switchboard Operator							
Including Answering Service	North Carolina	H	7.54 FQ	10.13 AW	13.18 TQ	NCBLS	10/01-12/01
Including Answering Service	North Dakota	H	7.12 FQ	9.21 AW	11.55 TQ	NDBLS	10/01-12/01
Including Answering Service	Ohio	H	7.38 FQ	10.35 AW	13.74 TQ	OHBLS	10/01-12/01
Including Answering Service	Oklahoma	H	6.17 FQ	9.41 AW	13.99 TQ	OKBLS	10/01-12/01
Including Answering Service	Oregon	H	7.84 FQ	10.78 AW	14.17 TQ	ORBLS	10/01-12/01
Including Answering Service	Pennsylvania	H	6.38 FQ	9.80 AW	13.49 TQ	PABLS	10/01-12/01
Including Answering Service	Rhode Island	H	7.60 FQ	10.84 AW	14.18 TQ	RIBLS	10/01-12/01
Including Answering Service	South Carolina	H	6.71 FQ	9.28 AW	12.51 TQ	SCBLS	10/01-12/01
Including Answering Service	South Dakota	H	7.54 FQ	9.81 AW	12.65 TQ	SDBLS	10/01-12/01
Including Answering Service	Tennessee	H	7.27 FQ	10.03 AW	13.38 TQ	TNBLS	10/01-12/01
Including Answering Service	Texas	H	5.99 FQ	9.31 AW	13.48 TQ	TXBLS	10/01-12/01
Including Answering Service	Utah	H	7.10 FQ	9.54 AW	12.67 TQ	UTBLS	10/01-12/01
Including Answering Service	Vermont	H	7.57 FQ	9.93 AW	13.03 TQ	VTBLS	10/01-12/01
Including Answering Service	Virginia	H	7.01 FQ	9.49 AW	12.86 TQ	VABLS	10/01-12/01
Including Answering Service	Washington	H	7.89 FQ	11.22 AW	14.55 TQ	WABLS	10/01-12/01
Including Answering Service	West Virginia	H	5.89 FQ	8.10 AW	10.99 TQ	WVBLS	10/01-12/01
Including Answering Service	Wisconsin	H	7.46 FQ	10.06 AW	13.21 TQ	WIBLS	10/01-12/01
Including Answering Service	Wyoming	H	6.11 FQ	8.35 AW	11.02 TQ	WYBLS	10/01-12/01
Including Answering Service	Puerto Rico	H	5.64 FQ	7.16 AW	10.13 TQ	PRBLS	10/01-12/01
Including Answering Service	Virgin Islands	H	6.86 FQ	8.43 AW	10.64 TQ	VIBLS	10/01-12/01
Including Answering Service	Guam	H	5.88 FQ	8.50 AW	12.69 TQ	GUBLS	10/01-12/01
Systems Architect	United States	Y		77500-108250 AW		IW	1/00-1/01
Tailor, Dressmaker, and Custom Sewer	Alabama	H	6.52 FQ	8.59 AW	11.09 TQ	ALBLS	10/01-12/01
	Birmingham MSA, AL	H	7.02 FQ	8.52 AW	10.74 TQ	ALBLS	10/01-12/01
	Huntsville MSA, AL	H	5.43 FQ	7.47 AW	10.79 TQ	ALBLS	10/01-12/01
	Mobile MSA, AL	H	6.86 FQ	8.99 AW	11.88 TQ	ALBLS	10/01-12/01
	Montgomery MSA, AL	H	7.48 FQ	9.69 AW	12.80 TQ	ALBLS	10/01-12/01
	Alaska	H	9.04 FQ	12.31 AW	17.09 TQ	AKBLS	10/01-12/01
	Anchorage MSA, AK	H	9.07 FQ	12.33 AW	17.10 TQ	AKBLS	10/01-12/01
	Arizona	H	8.45 FQ	12.81 AW	19.21 TQ	AZBLS	10/01-12/01
	Phoenix-Mesa MSA, AZ	H	9.39 FQ	13.56 AW	20.49 TQ	AZBLS	10/01-12/01
	Tucson MSA, AZ	H	7.10 FQ	9.16 AW	12.41 TQ	AZBLS	10/01-12/01
	Arkansas	H	5.84 FQ	7.96 AW	11.32 TQ	ARBLS	10/01-12/01
	Fayetteville-Springdale-Rogers MSA, AR	H	5.76 FQ	6.55 AW	8.12 TQ	ARBLS	10/01-12/01
	Little Rock-North Little Rock MSA, AR	H	5.96 FQ	8.97 AW	12.75 TQ	ARBLS	10/01-12/01
	California	H	7.50 FQ	13.19 AW	18.85 TQ	CABLS	10/01-12/01
	Los Angeles-Long Beach PMSA, CA	H	7.50 FQ	12.83 AW	17.67 TQ	CABLS	10/01-12/01
	Oakland PMSA, CA	H	10.86 FQ	16.62 AW	20.96 TQ	CABLS	10/01-12/01
	Orange County PMSA, CA	H	8.67 FQ	14.55 AW	21.49 TQ	CABLS	10/01-12/01
	Riverside-San Bernardino PMSA, CA	H	7.60 FQ	11.11 AW	15.43 TQ	CABLS	10/01-12/01
	Sacramento PMSA, CA	H	7.47 FQ	11.73 AW	17.21 TQ	CABLS	10/01-12/01
	San Diego MSA, CA	H	6.67 FQ	12.25 AW	18.16 TQ	CABLS	10/01-12/01
	San Francisco PMSA, CA	H	6.65 FQ	14.30 AW	21.67 TQ	CABLS	10/01-12/01
	San Jose PMSA, CA	H	10.98 FQ	13.33 AW	17.19 TQ	CABLS	10/01-12/01
	Vallejo-Fairfield-Napa PMSA, CA	H	6.93 FQ	8.28 AW	9.11 TQ	CABLS	10/01-12/01
	Ventura PMSA, CA	H	7.62 FQ	11.87 AW	17.91 TQ	CABLS	10/01-12/01
	Visalia-Tulare-Porterville MSA, CA	H	7.48 FQ	9.76 AW	12.45 TQ	CABLS	10/01-12/01
	Colorado	H	7.39 FQ	13.61 AW	20.97 TQ	COBLS	10/01-12/01
	Boulder-Longmont PMSA, CO	H	7.32 FQ	11.75 AW	20.13 TQ	COBLS	10/01-12/01
	Denver PMSA, CO	H	7.62 FQ	14.43 AW	21.17 TQ	COBLS	10/01-12/01
	Connecticut	H	8.20 FQ	12.95 AW	18.92 TQ	CTBLS	10/01-12/01
	Hartford MSA, CT	H	9.05 FQ	13.01 AW	17.65 TQ	CTBLS	10/01-12/01
	New Haven-Meriden PMSA, CT	H	8.99 FQ	13.72 AW	19.54 TQ	CTBLS	10/01-12/01
	Stamford-Norwalk PMSA, CT	H	8.21 FQ	13.55 AW	20.42 TQ	CTBLS	10/01-12/01
	Delaware	H	7.81 FQ	12.08 AW	17.08 TQ	DEBLS	10/01-12/01
	Wilmington-Newark PMSA, DE-MD	H	8.48 FQ	12.89 AW	17.71 TQ	DEBLS	10/01-12/01
	District of Columbia	H	7.69 FQ	11.99 AW	18.50 TQ	DCBLS	10/01-12/01
	Washington PMSA, DC-MD-VA-WV	H	7.24 FQ	11.88 AW	16.61 TQ	DCBLS	10/01-12/01

AAW	Average annual wage	AOH	Average offered, high	ASH	Average starting, high	H	Hourly	M	Monthly	S	Special: hourly and annual
AE	Average entry wage	AOL	Average offered, low	ASL	Average starting, low	HI	Highest wage paid	MTC	Median total compensation	TQ	Third quartile wage
AEX	Average experienced wage	APH	Average pay, high range	AW	Average wage paid	HR	High end range	MW	Median wage paid	W	Weekly
AO	Average offered	APL	Average pay, low range	FQ	First quartile wage	LR	Low end range	SQ	Second quartile wage	Y	Yearly

Occupation/Type/Industry	Location	Per	Low	Mid	High	Source	Date
Tailor, Dressmaker, and Custom Sewer	Florida	H	5.99 FQ	10.34 AW	16.24 TQ	FLBLS	10/01-12/01
	Fort Lauderdale PMSA, FL	H	5.52 FQ	8.62 AW	13.94 TQ	FLBLS	10/01-12/01
	Fort Myers-Cape Coral MSA, FL	H	5.86 FQ	9.06 AW	11.82 TQ	FLBLS	10/01-12/01
	Jacksonville MSA, FL	H	6.94 FQ	9.83 AW	14.32 TQ	FLBLS	10/01-12/01
	Melbourne-Titusville-Palm Bay MSA, FL	H	7.58 FQ	13.40 AW	16.50 TQ	FLBLS	10/01-12/01
	Miami PMSA, FL	H	8.10 FQ	11.94 AW	16.90 TQ	FLBLS	10/01-12/01
	Orlando MSA, FL	H	5.48 FQ	7.87 AW	11.60 TQ	FLBLS	10/01-12/01
	Pensacola MSA, FL	H	6.20 FQ	8.43 AW	11.98 TQ	FLBLS	10/01-12/01
	Sarasota-Bradenton MSA, FL	H	6.85 FQ	9.45 AW	12.66 TQ	FLBLS	10/01-12/01
	Tampa-St. Petersburg-Clearwater MSA, FL	H	7.55 FQ	11.97 AW	20.95 TQ	FLBLS	10/01-12/01
	West Palm Beach-Boca Raton MSA, FL	H	7.65 FQ	11.93 AW	17.16 TQ	FLBLS	10/01-12/01
	Georgia	H	6.97 FQ	10.31 AW	14.53 TQ	GABLS	10/01-12/01
	Atlanta MSA, GA	H	8.06 FQ	11.48 AW	14.98 TQ	GABLS	10/01-12/01
	Augusta-Aiken MSA, GA-SC	H	6.43 FQ	9.89 AW	14.10 TQ	GABLS	10/01-12/01
	Macon MSA, GA	H	6.52 FQ	8.66 AW	10.63 TQ	GABLS	10/01-12/01
	Hawaii	H	7.53 FQ	11.15 AW	17.63 TQ	HIBLS	10/01-12/01
	Honolulu MSA, HI	H	7.53 FQ	11.12 AW	18.75 TQ	HIBLS	10/01-12/01
	Idaho	H	5.94 FQ	9.18 AW	12.61 TQ	IDBLS	10/01-12/01
	Boise City MSA, ID	H	8.98 FQ	10.27 AW	12.68 TQ	IDBLS	10/01-12/01
	Illinois	H	7.06 FQ	10.49 AW	14.32 TQ	ILBLS	10/01-12/01
	Chicago PMSA, IL	H	7.15 FQ	10.76 AW	15.17 TQ	ILBLS	10/01-12/01
	Indiana	H	6.79 FQ	10.26 AW	14.71 TQ	INBLS	10/01-12/01
	Evansville-Henderson MSA, IN-KY	H	7.57 FQ	9.76 AW	13.10 TQ	INBLS	10/01-12/01
	Indianapolis MSA, IN	H	7.74 FQ	11.92 AW	14.54 TQ	INBLS	10/01-12/01
	Lafayette MSA, IN	H	7.21 FQ	12.87 AW	16.44 TQ	INBLS	10/01-12/01
	Iowa	H	6.24 FQ	9.16 AW	11.55 TQ	IABLS	10/01-12/01
	Cedar Rapids MSA, IA	H	7.63 FQ	9.42 AW	11.28 TQ	IABLS	10/01-12/01
	Davenport-Moline-Rock Island MSA, IA-IL	H	6.56 FQ	9.20 AW	12.42 TQ	IABLS	10/01-12/01
	Des Moines MSA, IA	H	7.75 FQ	10.68 AW	14.18 TQ	IABLS	10/01-12/01
	Kansas	H	6.31 FQ	9.14 AW	10.93 TQ	KSBLS	10/01-12/01
	Wichita MSA, KS	H	8.23 FQ	9.53 AW	10.66 TQ	KSBLS	10/01-12/01
	Kentucky	H	6.39 FQ	9.02 AW	12.37 TQ	KYBLS	10/01-12/01
	Lexington MSA, KY	H	7.24 FQ	8.96 AW	11.03 TQ	KYBLS	10/01-12/01
	Louisville MSA, KY-IN	H	7.07 FQ	9.90 AW	13.09 TQ	KYBLS	10/01-12/01
	Louisiana	H	7.01 FQ	8.50 AW	10.29 TQ	LABLS	10/01-12/01
	Baton Rouge MSA, LA	H	6.08 FQ	9.07 AW	12.89 TQ	LABLS	10/01-12/01
	Lafayette MSA, LA	H	6.35 FQ	7.84 AW	8.98 TQ	LABLS	10/01-12/01
	New Orleans MSA, LA	H	7.34 FQ	8.65 AW	10.13 TQ	LABLS	10/01-12/01
	Shreveport-Bossier City MSA, LA	H	6.48 FQ	8.27 AW	10.66 TQ	LABLS	10/01-12/01
	Maine	H	7.46 FQ	10.84 AW	15.51 TQ	MEBLS	10/01-12/01
	Portland MSA, ME	H	8.02 FQ	11.42 AW	16.11 TQ	MEBLS	10/01-12/01
	Maryland	H	7.35 FQ	10.85 AW	15.26 TQ	MDBLS	10/01-12/01
	Baltimore PMSA, MD	H	7.32 FQ	10.35 AW	14.17 TQ	MDBLS	10/01-12/01
	Massachusetts	H	8.86 FQ	14.94 AW	21.04 TQ	MABLS	10/01-12/01
	Boston PMSA, MA-NH	H	9.64 FQ	15.99 AW	21.80 TQ	MABLS	10/01-12/01
	Springfield MSA, MA	H	6.75 FQ	9.77 AW	12.58 TQ	MABLS	10/01-12/01
	Worcester PMSA, MA-CT	H	8.34 FQ	11.31 AW	15.65 TQ	MABLS	10/01-12/01
	Michigan	H	6.61 FQ	10.40 AW	16.24 TQ	MIBLS	10/01-12/01
	Ann Arbor PMSA, MI	H	6.61 FQ	11.36 AW	16.82 TQ	MIBLS	10/01-12/01
	Detroit PMSA, MI	H	6.29 FQ	10.73 AW	17.05 TQ	MIBLS	10/01-12/01
	Flint PMSA, MI	H	6.50 FQ	9.16 AW	13.10 TQ	MIBLS	10/01-12/01
	Grand Rapids-Muskegon-Holland MSA, MI	H	7.23 FQ	10.53 AW	15.27 TQ	MIBLS	10/01-12/01
	Kalamazoo-Battle Creek MSA, MI	H	7.41 FQ	10.59 AW	15.63 TQ	MIBLS	10/01-12/01
	Lansing-East Lansing MSA, MI	H	8.69 FQ	10.12 AW	12.68 TQ	MIBLS	10/01-12/01
	Minnesota	H	6.85 FQ	12.38 AW	17.31 TQ	MNBLS	10/01-12/01
	Minneapolis-St. Paul MSA, MN-WI	H	9.51 FQ	13.60 AW	17.54 TQ	MNBLS	10/01-12/01
	Mississippi	H	6.85 FQ	9.56 AW	13.09 TQ	MSBLS	10/01-12/01
	Biloxi-Gulfport-Pascagoula MSA, MS	H	7.11 FQ	8.74 AW	10.91 TQ	MSBLS	10/01-12/01
	Jackson MSA, MS	H	7.77 FQ	11.49 AW	14.46 TQ	MSBLS	10/01-12/01
	Missouri	H	6.16 FQ	10.21 AW	16.14 TQ	MOBLS	10/01-12/01

AAW	Average annual wage	AOH	Average offered, high	ASH	Average starting, high	H	Hourly	M	Monthly	S	Special: hourly and annual
AE	Average entry wage	AOL	Average offered, low	ASL	Average starting, low	HI	Highest wage paid	MTC	Median total compensation	TQ	Third quartile wage
AEX	Average experienced wage	APH	Average pay, high range	AW	Average wage paid	HR	High end range	MW	Median wage paid	W	Weekly
AO	Average offered	APL	Average pay, low range	FQ	First quartile wage	LR	Low end range	SQ	Second quartile wage	Y	Yearly

Occupation/Type/Industry	Location	Per	Low	Mid	High	Source	Date
Tailor, Dressmaker, and Custom Sewer	Kansas City MSA, MO-KS	H	7.15 FQ	10.78 AW	15.46 TQ	MOBLS	10/01-12/01
	St. Louis MSA, MO-IL	H	7.42 FQ	10.30 AW	13.34 TQ	MOBLS	10/01-12/01
	Montana	H	7.08 FQ	8.30 AW	9.99 TQ	MTBLS	10/01-12/01
	Nebraska	H	6.35 FQ	10.48 AW	14.32 TQ	NEBLS	10/01-12/01
	Omaha MSA, NE-IA	H	7.56 FQ	11.27 AW	14.75 TQ	NEBLS	10/01-12/01
	Nevada	H	8.32 FQ	11.37 AW	16.19 TQ	NVBLS	10/01-12/01
	Las Vegas MSA, NV-AZ	H	8.45 FQ	11.58 AW	16.88 TQ	NVBLS	10/01-12/01
	Reno MSA, NV	H	8.19 FQ	10.10 AW	12.06 TQ	NVBLS	10/01-12/01
	New Hampshire	H	8.97 FQ	12.46 AW	16.81 TQ	NHBLS	10/01-12/01
	New Jersey	H	8.88 FQ	13.78 AW	19.79 TQ	NJBLS	10/01-12/01
	Atlantic-Cape May PMSA, NJ	H	9.20 FQ	18.61 AW	27.25 TQ	NJBLS	10/01-12/01
	Bergen-Passaic PMSA, NJ	H	8.89 FQ	14.25 AW	21.96 TQ	NJBLS	10/01-12/01
	Jersey City PMSA, NJ	H	9.01 FQ	13.62 AW	19.40 TQ	NJBLS	10/01-12/01
	Middlesex-Somerset-Hunterdon PMSA, NJ	H	9.75 FQ	13.83 AW	18.26 TQ	NJBLS	10/01-12/01
	Monmouth-Ocean PMSA, NJ	H	10.85 FQ	15.82 AW	26.67 TQ	NJBLS	10/01-12/01
	Newark PMSA, NJ	H	8.69 FQ	12.49 AW	17.50 TQ	NJBLS	10/01-12/01
	New Mexico	H	7.56 FQ	10.94 AW	14.09 TQ	NMBLS	10/01-12/01
	Albuquerque MSA, NM	H	8.21 FQ	11.22 AW	13.95 TQ	NMBLS	10/01-12/01
	New York	H	6.87 FQ	14.11 AW	21.51 TQ	NYBLS	10/01-12/01
	Albany-Schenectady-Troy MSA, NY	H	7.85 FQ	13.41 AW	20.78 TQ	NYBLS	10/01-12/01
	Buffalo-Niagara Falls MSA, NY	H	6.72 FQ	9.57 AW	13.86 TQ	NYBLS	10/01-12/01
	Dutchess County PMSA, NY	H	8.39 FQ	13.62 AW	17.15 TQ	NYBLS	10/01-12/01
	Nassau-Suffolk PMSA, NY	H	7.42 FQ	11.68 AW	18.35 TQ	NYBLS	10/01-12/01
	New York PMSA, NY	H	6.68 FQ	15.38 AW	22.27 TQ	NYBLS	10/01-12/01
	Newburgh PMSA, NY-PA	H	6.27 FQ	10.87 AW	18.19 TQ	NYBLS	10/01-12/01
	Rochester MSA, NY	H	6.22 FQ	10.59 AW	16.72 TQ	NYBLS	10/01-12/01
	Syracuse MSA, NY	H	7.09 FQ	10.51 AW	13.75 TQ	NYBLS	10/01-12/01
	North Carolina	H	6.11 FQ	10.17 AW	14.99 TQ	NCBLS	10/01-12/01
	Charlotte-Gastonia-Rock Hill MSA, NC-SC	H	6.95 FQ	10.62 AW	14.63 TQ	NCBLS	10/01-12/01
	Greensboro-Winston-Salem-High Point MSA, NC	H	6.94 FQ	9.61 AW	12.78 TQ	NCBLS	10/01-12/01
	Hickory-Morganton-Lenoir MSA, NC	H	6.28 FQ	8.69 AW	10.89 TQ	NCBLS	10/01-12/01
	Raleigh-Durham-Chapel Hill MSA, NC	H	8.74 FQ	11.98 AW	15.96 TQ	NCBLS	10/01-12/01
	Wilmington MSA, NC	H	5.80 FQ	10.60 AW	15.59 TQ	NCBLS	10/01-12/01
	North Dakota	H	6.01 FQ	10.45 AW	17.29 TQ	NDBLS	10/01-12/01
	Ohio	H	7.13 FQ	10.99 AW	15.67 TQ	OHBLS	10/01-12/01
	Akron PMSA, OH	H	9.58 FQ	12.91 AW	17.09 TQ	OHBLS	10/01-12/01
	Canton-Massillon MSA, OH	H	5.95 FQ	8.60 AW	13.05 TQ	OHBLS	10/01-12/01
	Cincinnati PMSA, OH-KY-IN	H	7.65 FQ	11.74 AW	18.86 TQ	OHBLS	10/01-12/01
	Cleveland-Lorain-Elyria PMSA, OH	H	8.38 FQ	12.28 AW	17.11 TQ	OHBLS	10/01-12/01
	Columbus MSA, OH	H	9.26 FQ	11.58 AW	15.66 TQ	OHBLS	10/01-12/01
	Dayton-Springfield MSA, OH	H	7.41 FQ	10.23 AW	13.92 TQ	OHBLS	10/01-12/01
	Toledo MSA, OH	H	5.99 FQ	10.27 AW	15.29 TQ	OHBLS	10/01-12/01
	Youngstown-Warren MSA, OH	H	6.91 FQ	10.07 AW	13.76 TQ	OHBLS	10/01-12/01
	Oklahoma	H	6.20 FQ	9.23 AW	12.68 TQ	OKBLS	10/01-12/01
	Oklahoma City MSA, OK	H	6.31 FQ	9.64 AW	13.10 TQ	OKBLS	10/01-12/01
	Tulsa MSA, OK	H	7.12 FQ	9.60 AW	12.60 TQ	OKBLS	10/01-12/01
	Oregon	H	8.79 FQ	12.77 AW	17.16 TQ	ORBLS	10/01-12/01
	Portland-Vancouver PMSA, OR-WA	H	8.89 FQ	12.95 AW	17.28 TQ	ORBLS	10/01-12/01
	Pennsylvania	H	7.10 FQ	12.30 AW	19.12 TQ	PABLS	10/01-12/01
	Allentown-Bethlehem-Easton MSA, PA	H	7.12 FQ	10.49 AW	15.08 TQ	PABLS	10/01-12/01
	Harrisburg-Lebanon-Carlisle MSA, PA	H	8.18 FQ	12.84 AW	17.84 TQ	PABLS	10/01-12/01
	Lancaster MSA, PA	H	9.00 FQ	11.54 AW	15.88 TQ	PABLS	10/01-12/01
	Philadelphia PMSA, PA-NJ	H	7.72 FQ	14.32 AW	20.21 TQ	PABLS	10/01-12/01
	Pittsburgh MSA, PA	H	7.40 FQ	10.29 AW	14.09 TQ	PABLS	10/01-12/01
	Scranton-Wilkes-Barre-Hazleton MSA, PA	H	7.62 FQ	10.28 AW	13.80 TQ	PABLS	10/01-12/01
	Rhode Island	H	8.39 FQ	12.78 AW	17.20 TQ	RIBLS	10/01-12/01
	Providence-Fall River-Warwick MSA, RI-MA	H	8.17 FQ	12.66 AW	17.41 TQ	RIBLS	10/01-12/01
	South Carolina	H	6.44 FQ	8.90 AW	13.52 TQ	SCBLS	10/01-12/01

AAW	Average annual wage	**AOH**	Average offered, high	**ASH**	Average starting, high	**H**	Hourly	**M**	Monthly	**S**	Special: hourly and annual
AE	Average entry wage	**AOL**	Average offered, low	**ASL**	Average starting, low	**HI**	Highest wage paid	**MTC**	Median total compensation	**TQ**	Third quartile wage
AEX	Average experienced wage	**APH**	Average pay, high range	**AW**	Average wage paid	**HR**	High end range	**MW**	Median wage paid	**W**	Weekly
AO	Average offered	**APL**	Average pay, low range	**FQ**	First quartile wage	**LR**	Low end range	**SQ**	Second quartile wage	**Y**	Yearly

Occupation/Type/Industry	Location	Per	Low	Mid	High	Source	Date
Tailor, Dressmaker, and Custom Sewer	Charleston-North Charleston MSA, SC	H	5.95 FQ	8.22 AW	12.76 TQ	SCBLS	10/01-12/01
	South Dakota	H	7.18 FQ	8.24 AW	9.90 TQ	SDBLS	10/01-12/01
	Tennessee	H	6.97 FQ	9.98 AW	15.00 TQ	TNBLS	10/01-12/01
	Knoxville MSA, TN	H	7.28 FQ	10.70 AW	16.45 TQ	TNBLS	10/01-12/01
	Memphis MSA, TN-AR-MS	H	6.94 FQ	9.72 AW	14.05 TQ	TNBLS	10/01-12/01
	Nashville MSA, TN	H	7.71 FQ	10.62 AW	15.50 TQ	TNBLS	10/01-12/01
	Texas	H	6.09 FQ	9.96 AW	15.28 TQ	TXBLS	10/01-12/01
	Austin-San Marcos MSA, TX	H	7.15 FQ	10.52 AW	16.85 TQ	TXBLS	10/01-12/01
	Dallas PMSA, TX	H	6.00 FQ	11.07 AW	17.24 TQ	TXBLS	10/01-12/01
	El Paso MSA, TX	H	5.74 FQ	8.67 AW	13.15 TQ	TXBLS	10/01-12/01
	Fort Worth-Arlington PMSA, TX	H	6.26 FQ	9.16 AW	14.78 TQ	TXBLS	10/01-12/01
	Houston PMSA, TX	H	6.45 FQ	11.39 AW	16.68 TQ	TXBLS	10/01-12/01
	Laredo MSA, TX	H	5.57 FQ	6.81 AW	9.08 TQ	TXBLS	10/01-12/01
	McAllen-Edinburg-Mission MSA, TX	H	5.75 FQ	7.39 AW	11.11 TQ	TXBLS	10/01-12/01
	San Antonio MSA, TX	H	7.15 FQ	9.42 AW	13.40 TQ	TXBLS	10/01-12/01
	Tyler MSA, TX	H	6.41 FQ	11.76 AW	19.00 TQ	TXBLS	10/01-12/01
	Utah	H	7.46 FQ	11.83 AW	16.45 TQ	UTBLS	10/01-12/01
	Salt Lake City-Ogden MSA, UT	H	8.77 FQ	12.52 AW	17.06 TQ	UTBLS	10/01-12/01
	Virginia	H	5.59 FQ	9.01 AW	13.56 TQ	VABLS	10/01-12/01
	Lynchburg MSA, VA	H	5.58 FQ	7.24 AW	11.19 TQ	VABLS	10/01-12/01
	Norfolk-Virginia Beach-Newport News MSA, VA-NC	H	5.40 FQ	7.42 AW	10.76 TQ	VABLS	10/01-12/01
	Richmond-Petersburg MSA, VA	H	9.06 FQ	12.05 AW	16.04 TQ	VABLS	10/01-12/01
	Washington	H	7.87 FQ	11.80 AW	15.44 TQ	WABLS	10/01-12/01
	Seattle-Bellevue-Everett PMSA, WA	H	9.76 FQ	13.11 AW	16.20 TQ	WABLS	10/01-12/01
	Tacoma PMSA, WA	H	7.84 FQ	12.23 AW	16.87 TQ	WABLS	10/01-12/01
	West Virginia	H	5.67 FQ	8.46 AW	12.54 TQ	WVBLS	10/01-12/01
	Charleston MSA, WV	H	5.74 FQ	9.02 AW	13.04 TQ	WVBLS	10/01-12/01
	Wisconsin	H	7.45 FQ	10.55 AW	15.00 TQ	WIBLS	10/01-12/01
	Appleton-Oshkosh-Neenah MSA, WI	H	7.56 FQ	10.58 AW	13.53 TQ	WIBLS	10/01-12/01
	Madison MSA, WI	H	7.18 FQ	10.21 AW	16.47 TQ	WIBLS	10/01-12/01
	Milwaukee-Waukesha PMSA, WI	H	8.06 FQ	12.54 AW	17.68 TQ	WIBLS	10/01-12/01
	Wyoming	H	5.88 FQ	7.55 AW	10.19 TQ	WYBLS	10/01-12/01
	Puerto Rico	H	5.57 FQ	6.55 AW	7.28 TQ	PRBLS	10/01-12/01
Tank Car, Truck, and Ship Loader	Alabama	H	8.13 FQ	14.62 AW	20.74 TQ	ALBLS	10/01-12/01
	Mobile MSA, AL	H	7.93 FQ	14.46 AW	20.69 TQ	ALBLS	10/01-12/01
	Arkansas	H	8.37 FQ	12.84 AW	20.10 TQ	ARBLS	10/01-12/01
	California	H	10.38 FQ	16.37 AW	25.65 TQ	CABLS	10/01-12/01
	Los Angeles-Long Beach PMSA, CA	H	11.01 FQ	18.19 AW	27.61 TQ	CABLS	10/01-12/01
	Modesto MSA, CA	H	11.70 FQ	12.99 AW	14.44 TQ	CABLS	10/01-12/01
	Oakland PMSA, CA	H	9.79 FQ	17.26 AW	30.89 TQ	CABLS	10/01-12/01
	Orange County PMSA, CA	H	11.19 FQ	14.94 AW	18.46 TQ	CABLS	10/01-12/01
	Riverside-San Bernardino PMSA, CA	H	10.79 FQ	15.40 AW	20.18 TQ	CABLS	10/01-12/01
	Stockton-Lodi MSA, CA	H	9.87 FQ	13.67 AW	19.44 TQ	CABLS	10/01-12/01
	Colorado	H	9.31 FQ	14.63 AW	24.68 TQ	COBLS	10/01-12/01
	Denver PMSA, CO	H	9.14 FQ	15.56 AW	25.85 TQ	COBLS	10/01-12/01
	Delaware	H	8.74 FQ	13.69 AW	23.50 TQ	DEBLS	10/01-12/01
	Wilmington-Newark PMSA, DE-MD	H	9.61 FQ	16.34 AW	25.38 TQ	DEBLS	10/01-12/01
	Florida	H	9.66 FQ	19.51 AW	28.11 TQ	FLBLS	10/01-12/01
	Jacksonville MSA, FL	H	12.63 FQ	22.91 AW	28.45 TQ	FLBLS	10/01-12/01
	Lakeland-Winter Haven MSA, FL	H	7.27 FQ	11.45 AW	14.45 TQ	FLBLS	10/01-12/01
	Orlando MSA, FL	H	10.57 FQ	13.76 AW	17.52 TQ	FLBLS	10/01-12/01
	Pensacola MSA, FL	H	10.16 FQ	15.23 AW	21.10 TQ	FLBLS	10/01-12/01
	Tampa-St. Petersburg-Clearwater MSA, FL	H	9.22 FQ	12.90 AW	18.89 TQ	FLBLS	10/01-12/01
	Georgia	H	8.96 FQ	15.33 AW	26.17 TQ	GABLS	10/01-12/01

AAW Average annual wage · AE Average entry wage · AEX Average experienced wage · AO Average offered · AOH Average offered, high · AOL Average offered, low · APH Average pay, high range · APL Average pay, low range · ASH Average starting, high · ASL Average starting, low · AW Average wage paid · FQ First quartile wage · H Hourly · HI Highest wage paid · HR High end range · LR Low end range · M Monthly · MTC Median total compensation · MW Median wage paid · SQ Second quartile wage · S Special: hourly and annual · TQ Third quartile wage · W Weekly · Y Yearly

Occupation/Type/Industry	Location	Per	Low	Mid	High	Source	Date
Tank Car, Truck, and Ship Loader	Atlanta MSA, GA	H	7.00 FQ	14.33 AW	21.05 TQ	GABLS	10/01-12/01
	Augusta-Aiken MSA, GA-SC	H	18.38 FQ	22.75 AW	27.41 TQ	GABLS	10/01-12/01
	Savannah MSA, GA	H	9.56 FQ	19.05 AW	29.11 TQ	GABLS	10/01-12/01
	Idaho	H	11.76 FQ	13.79 AW	16.40 TQ	IDBLS	10/01-12/01
	Illinois	H	13.60 FQ	17.46 AW	21.12 TQ	ILBLS	10/01-12/01
	Chicago PMSA, IL	H	14.04 FQ	17.61 AW	21.13 TQ	ILBLS	10/01-12/01
	Indiana	H	11.06 FQ	16.47 AW	21.87 TQ	INBLS	10/01-12/01
	Evansville-Henderson MSA, IN-KY	H	10.39 FQ	16.01 AW	21.74 TQ	INBLS	10/01-12/01
	Indianapolis MSA, IN	H	10.94 FQ	16.26 AW	23.62 TQ	INBLS	10/01-12/01
	Iowa	H	9.23 FQ	12.71 AW	17.43 TQ	IABLS	10/01-12/01
	Des Moines MSA, IA	H	7.95 FQ	10.26 AW	13.31 TQ	IABLS	10/01-12/01
	Kansas	H	8.20 FQ	12.31 AW	16.08 TQ	KSBLS	10/01-12/01
	Kentucky	H	10.66 FQ	15.23 AW	22.13 TQ	KYBLS	10/01-12/01
	Louisville MSA, KY-IN	H	11.27 FQ	17.16 AW	22.42 TQ	KYBLS	10/01-12/01
	Louisiana	H	9.52 FQ	13.57 AW	20.29 TQ	LABLS	10/01-12/01
	Baton Rouge MSA, LA	H	10.22 FQ	14.87 AW	20.18 TQ	LABLS	10/01-12/01
	New Orleans MSA, LA	H	9.60 FQ	13.48 AW	19.65 TQ	LABLS	10/01-12/01
	Maryland	H	8.57 FQ	16.19 AW	27.15 TQ	MDBLS	10/01-12/01
	Baltimore PMSA, MD	H	9.24 FQ	17.01 AW	27.78 TQ	MDBLS	10/01-12/01
	Massachusetts	H	8.76 FQ	15.63 AW	29.66 TQ	MABLS	10/01-12/01
	Boston PMSA, MA-NH	H	8.13 FQ	17.25 AW	38.50 TQ	MABLS	10/01-12/01
	Michigan	H	9.33 FQ	15.38 AW	23.41 TQ	MIBLS	10/01-12/01
	Detroit PMSA, MI	H	9.24 FQ	13.28 AW	17.44 TQ	MIBLS	10/01-12/01
	Minnesota	H	9.02 FQ	14.77 AW	23.87 TQ	MNBLS	10/01-12/01
	Minneapolis-St. Paul MSA, MN-WI	H	9.32 FQ	15.93 AW	26.11 TQ	MNBLS	10/01-12/01
	Mississippi	H	9.03 FQ	13.60 AW	21.30 TQ	MSBLS	10/01-12/01
	Missouri	H	9.11 FQ	13.41 AW	19.75 TQ	MOBLS	10/01-12/01
	Kansas City MSA, MO-KS	H	10.44 FQ	12.73 AW	14.43 TQ	MOBLS	10/01-12/01
	St. Louis MSA, MO-IL	H	11.00 FQ	15.98 AW	21.53 TQ	MOBLS	10/01-12/01
	Montana	H	5.60 FQ	10.78 AW	16.10 TQ	MTBLS	10/01-12/01
	Nebraska	H	9.91 FQ	14.12 AW	19.06 TQ	NEBLS	10/01-12/01
	Nevada	H	10.08 FQ	13.98 AW	19.39 TQ	NVBLS	10/01-12/01
	Las Vegas MSA, NV-AZ	H	10.21 FQ	14.82 AW	20.34 TQ	NVBLS	10/01-12/01
	New Hampshire	H	10.85 FQ	14.53 AW	20.59 TQ	NHBLS	10/01-12/01
	New Jersey	H	9.94 FQ	17.35 AW	25.96 TQ	NJBLS	10/01-12/01
	Middlesex-Somerset-Hunterdon PMSA, NJ	H	8.56 FQ	18.66 AW	26.77 TQ	NJBLS	10/01-12/01
	Newark PMSA, NJ	H	10.06 FQ	16.18 AW	25.84 TQ	NJBLS	10/01-12/01
	Buffalo-Niagara Falls MSA, NY	H	13.05 FQ	19.86 AW	26.54 TQ	NYBLS	10/01-12/01
	North Carolina	H	8.38 FQ	12.53 AW	18.69 TQ	NCBLS	10/01-12/01
	Charlotte-Gastonia-Rock Hill MSA, NC-SC	H	7.87 FQ	12.77 AW	20.45 TQ	NCBLS	10/01-12/01
	Greensboro-Winston-Salem-High Point MSA, NC	H	9.42 FQ	12.24 AW	16.02 TQ	NCBLS	10/01-12/01
	Ohio	H	11.60 FQ	16.31 AW	22.25 TQ	OHBLS	10/01-12/01
	Cincinnati PMSA, OH-KY-IN	H	10.57 FQ	14.36 AW	19.57 TQ	OHBLS	10/01-12/01
	Columbus MSA, OH	H	12.01 FQ	16.11 AW	20.95 TQ	OHBLS	10/01-12/01
	Toledo MSA, OH	H	12.04 FQ	16.68 AW	21.83 TQ	OHBLS	10/01-12/01
	Oregon	H	11.34 FQ	18.58 AW	32.38 TQ	ORBLS	10/01-12/01
	Portland-Vancouver PMSA, OR-WA	H	11.66 FQ	19.57 AW	32.99 TQ	ORBLS	10/01-12/01
	Pennsylvania	H	10.11 FQ	17.07 AW	27.11 TQ	PABLS	10/01-12/01
	Philadelphia PMSA, PA-NJ	H	10.08 FQ	18.81 AW	28.10 TQ	PABLS	10/01-12/01
	Pittsburgh MSA, PA	H	11.70 FQ	14.58 AW	17.72 TQ	PABLS	10/01-12/01
	South Carolina	H	9.48 FQ	14.75 AW	20.43 TQ	SCBLS	10/01-12/01
	Tennessee	H	8.59 FQ	12.77 AW	19.51 TQ	TNBLS	10/01-12/01
	Memphis MSA, TN-AR-MS	H	11.36 FQ	13.45 AW	16.32 TQ	TNBLS	10/01-12/01
	Texas	H	7.31 FQ	17.19 AW	28.97 TQ	TXBLS	10/01-12/01
	Beaumont-Port Arthur MSA, TX	H	8.14 FQ	14.62 AW	25.28 TQ	TXBLS	10/01-12/01
	Dallas PMSA, TX	H	7.62 FQ	15.96 AW	25.33 TQ	TXBLS	10/01-12/01
	El Paso MSA, TX	H	6.26 FQ	13.80 AW	25.78 TQ	TXBLS	10/01-12/01
	Fort Worth-Arlington PMSA, TX	H	8.61 FQ	13.25 AW	21.90 TQ	TXBLS	10/01-12/01
	Galveston-Texas City PMSA, TX	H	11.12 FQ	20.78 AW	26.52 TQ	TXBLS	10/01-12/01
	Houston PMSA, TX	H	8.61 FQ	21.57 AW	32.56 TQ	TXBLS	10/01-12/01

AAW	Average annual wage	AOH	Average offered, high	ASH	Average starting, high	H	Hourly	M	Monthly	S	Special: hourly and annual
AE	Average entry wage	AOL	Average offered, low	ASL	Average starting, low	HI	Highest wage paid	MTC	Median total compensation	TQ	Third quartile wage
AEX	Average experienced wage	APH	Average pay, high range	AW	Average wage paid	HR	High end range	MW	Median wage paid	W	Weekly
AO	Average offered	APL	Average pay, low range	FQ	First quartile wage	LR	Low end range	SQ	Second quartile wage	Y	Yearly

Occupation/Type/Industry	Location	Per	Low	Mid	High	Source	Date
Tank Car, Truck, and Ship Loader	McAllen-Edinburg-Mission MSA, TX	H	5.92 FQ	10.86 AW	22.96 TQ	TXBLS	10/01-12/01
	Utah	H	10.83 FQ	14.52 AW	19.65 TQ	UTBLS	10/01-12/01
	Salt Lake City-Ogden MSA, UT	H	11.31 FQ	14.62 AW	19.21 TQ	UTBLS	10/01-12/01
	Virginia	H	10.08 FQ	15.61 AW	24.94 TQ	VABLS	10/01-12/01
	Richmond-Petersburg MSA, VA	H	10.83 FQ	14.73 AW	21.71 TQ	VABLS	10/01-12/01
	Washington	H	11.44 FQ	21.38 AW	33.11 TQ	WABLS	10/01-12/01
	Seattle-Bellevue-Everett PMSA, WA	H	11.45 FQ	20.56 AW	32.74 TQ	WABLS	10/01-12/01
	West Virginia	H	8.01 FQ	15.98 AW	24.92 TQ	WVBLS	10/01-12/01
	Huntington-Ashland MSA, WV-KY-OH	H	11.39 FQ	15.29 AW	21.94 TQ	WVBLS	10/01-12/01
	Wisconsin	H	9.09 FQ	12.64 AW	16.22 TQ	WIBLS	10/01-12/01
	Wyoming	H	10.12 FQ	19.03 AW	26.35 TQ	WYBLS	10/01-12/01
Taper	Alabama	H	9.22 FQ	13.48 AW	17.90 TQ	ALBLS	10/01-12/01
	Arizona	H	9.50 FQ	14.45 AW	18.40 TQ	AZBLS	10/01-12/01
	California	H	11.14 FQ	19.50 AW	27.52 TQ	CABLS	10/01-12/01
	Colorado	H	11.57 FQ	16.81 AW	23.09 TQ	COBLS	10/01-12/01
	Connecticut	H	17.79 FQ	21.56 AW	26.95 TQ	CTBLS	10/01-12/01
	Delaware	H	11.32 FQ	17.85 AW	26.29 TQ	DEBLS	10/01-12/01
	Florida	H	11.08 FQ	15.27 AW	20.13 TQ	FLBLS	10/01-12/01
	Georgia	H	11.37 FQ	14.66 AW	20.20 TQ	GABLS	10/01-12/01
	Hawaii	H	19.03 FQ	29.09 AW	35.42 TQ	HIBLS	10/01-12/01
	Idaho	H	11.23 FQ	17.88 AW	27.05 TQ	IDBLS	10/01-12/01
	Illinois	H	7.34 FQ	22.47 AW	33.22 TQ	ILBLS	10/01-12/01
	Indiana	H	8.68 FQ	16.86 AW	24.01 TQ	INBLS	10/01-12/01
	Iowa	H	6.93 FQ	17.00 AW	26.42 TQ	IABLS	10/01-12/01
	Kansas	H	13.90 FQ	19.35 AW	25.50 TQ	KSBLS	10/01-12/01
	Kentucky	H	11.71 FQ	15.51 AW	20.66 TQ	KYBLS	10/01-12/01
	Louisiana	H	9.50 FQ	11.54 AW	13.74 TQ	LABLS	10/01-12/01
	Maine	H	10.76 FQ	15.35 AW	18.30 TQ	MEBLS	10/01-12/01
	Maryland	H	13.74 FQ	16.14 AW	18.96 TQ	MDBLS	10/01-12/01
	Massachusetts	H	16.85 FQ	26.75 AW	35.00 TQ	MABLS	10/01-12/01
	Michigan	H	11.74 FQ	19.79 AW	27.26 TQ	MIBLS	10/01-12/01
	Minnesota	H	12.81 FQ	21.24 AW	27.23 TQ	MNBLS	10/01-12/01
	Mississippi	H	8.00 FQ	12.82 AW	17.86 TQ	MSBLS	10/01-12/01
	Missouri	H	13.65 FQ	22.24 AW	28.95 TQ	MOBLS	10/01-12/01
	Montana	H	12.41 FQ	16.26 AW	21.11 TQ	MTBLS	10/01-12/01
	Nebraska	H	9.33 FQ	16.21 AW	22.30 TQ	NEBLS	10/01-12/01
	Nevada	H	11.15 FQ	18.57 AW	27.29 TQ	NVBLS	10/01-12/01
	New Hampshire	H	10.83 FQ	17.51 AW	27.17 TQ	NHBLS	10/01-12/01
	New Jersey	H	27.48 FQ	29.92 AW	34.22 TQ	NJBLS	10/01-12/01
	New Mexico	H	10.63 FQ	13.70 AW	17.79 TQ	NMBLS	10/01-12/01
	New York	H	9.43 FQ	21.47 AW	33.72 TQ	NYBLS	10/01-12/01
	North Carolina	H	10.58 FQ	13.21 AW	16.64 TQ	NCBLS	10/01-12/01
	North Dakota	H	9.48 FQ	14.03 AW	20.35 TQ	NDBLS	10/01-12/01
	Ohio	H	11.15 FQ	16.98 AW	24.18 TQ	OHBLS	10/01-12/01
	Oklahoma	H	13.52 FQ	14.95 AW	16.89 TQ	OKBLS	10/01-12/01
	Oregon	H	13.99 FQ	19.86 AW	29.03 TQ	ORBLS	10/01-12/01
	Pennsylvania	H	12.73 FQ	19.52 AW	28.88 TQ	PABLS	10/01-12/01
	Rhode Island	H	14.59 FQ	20.43 AW	27.06 TQ	RIBLS	10/01-12/01
	South Carolina	H	10.99 FQ	16.80 AW	26.10 TQ	SCBLS	10/01-12/01
	Tennessee	H	11.97 FQ	14.96 AW	17.51 TQ	TNBLS	10/01-12/01
	Texas	H	7.98 FQ	11.22 AW	14.62 TQ	TXBLS	10/01-12/01
	Utah	H	11.35 FQ	16.96 AW	21.44 TQ	UTBLS	10/01-12/01
	Vermont	H	14.31 FQ	17.74 AW	22.62 TQ	VTBLS	10/01-12/01
	Virginia	H	11.21 FQ	16.58 AW	23.87 TQ	VABLS	10/01-12/01
	Washington	H	16.50 FQ	23.45 AW	29.19 TQ	WABLS	10/01-12/01
	West Virginia	H	8.37 FQ	16.36 AW	25.21 TQ	WVBLS	10/01-12/01
	Wisconsin	H	14.76 FQ	21.35 AW	27.12 TQ	WIBLS	10/01-12/01
	Wyoming	H	12.16 FQ	15.93 AW	20.45 TQ	WYBLS	10/01-12/01
Tax Examiner, Collector, and Revenue Agent	Alabama	Y	16340 FQ	39320 AW	64860 TQ	ALBLS	10/01-12/01
	Alaska	Y	32250 FQ	57480 AW	85690 TQ	AKBLS	10/01-12/01
	Arizona	Y	28970 FQ	47240 AW	69390 TQ	AZBLS	10/01-12/01
	Arkansas	Y	16600 FQ	32400 AW	55210 TQ	ARBLS	10/01-12/01
	California	Y	30930 FQ	51050 AW	74690 TQ	CABLS	10/01-12/01

AAW	Average annual wage	AOH	Average offered, high	ASH	Average starting, high	H	Hourly	M	Monthly	S	Special: hourly and annual
AE	Average entry wage	AOL	Average offered, low	ASL	Average starting, low	HI	Highest wage paid	MTC	Median total compensation	TQ	Third quartile wage
AEX	Average experienced wage	APH	Average pay, high range	AW	Average wage paid	HR	High end range	MW	Median wage paid	W	Weekly
AO	Average offered	APL	Average pay, low range	FQ	First quartile wage	LR	Low end range	SQ	Second quartile wage	Y	Yearly

Occupation/Type/Industry	Location	Per	Low	Mid	High	Source	Date
Tax Examiner, Collector, and Revenue Agent	Colorado	Y	31090 FQ	50140 AW	77800 TQ	COBLS	10/01-12/01
	Connecticut	Y	30520 FQ	53930 AW	80560 TQ	CTBLS	10/01-12/01
	Delaware	Y	32640 FQ	56430 AW	84470 TQ	DEBLS	10/01-12/01
	Florida	Y	26560 FQ	56050 AW	82410 TQ	FLBLS	10/01-12/01
	Georgia	Y	22960 FQ	38900 AW	62250 TQ	GABLS	10/01-12/01
	Hawaii	Y	34830 FQ	55010 AW	82200 TQ	HIBLS	10/01-12/01
	Idaho	Y	20050 FQ	37580 AW	63320 TQ	IDBLS	10/01-12/01
	Illinois	Y	34610 FQ	53060 AW	77410 TQ	ILBLS	10/01-12/01
	Indiana	Y	20590 FQ	40160 AW	69070 TQ	INBLS	10/01-12/01
	Iowa	Y	28750 FQ	46700 AW	69900 TQ	IABLS	10/01-12/01
	Kansas	Y	24870 FQ	40460 AW	64930 TQ	KSBLS	10/01-12/01
	Kentucky	Y	23320 FQ	35630 AW	54310 TQ	KYBLS	10/01-12/01
	Louisiana	Y	22040 FQ	41850 AW	67910 TQ	LABLS	10/01-12/01
	Maine	Y	21170 FQ	35910 AW	56870 TQ	MEBLS	10/01-12/01
	Maryland	Y	31250 FQ	48350 AW	74800 TQ	MDBLS	10/01-12/01
	Massachusetts	Y	29050 FQ	49370 AW	74080 TQ	MABLS	10/01-12/01
	Michigan	Y	29460 FQ	49910 AW	75310 TQ	MIBLS	10/01-12/01
	Minnesota	Y	32090 FQ	51160 AW	71490 TQ	MNBLS	10/01-12/01
	Mississippi	Y	15980 FQ	32310 AW	57340 TQ	MSBLS	10/01-12/01
	Missouri	Y	18990 FQ	39630 AW	69770 TQ	MOBLS	10/01-12/01
	Montana	Y	18890 FQ	40350 AW	67190 TQ	MTBLS	10/01-12/01
	Nebraska	Y	23600 FQ	45100 AW	70690 TQ	NEBLS	10/01-12/01
	Nevada	Y	33380 FQ	48520 AW	70220 TQ	NVBLS	10/01-12/01
	New Hampshire	Y	15910 FQ	36160 AW	61170 TQ	NHBLS	10/01-12/01
	New Jersey	Y	32820 FQ	53370 AW	79480 TQ	NJBLS	10/01-12/01
	New Mexico	Y	20660 FQ	34360 AW	56450 TQ	NMBLS	10/01-12/01
	New York	Y	27800 FQ	48090 AW	75580 TQ	NYBLS	10/01-12/01
	North Carolina	Y	22370 FQ	38810 AW	63270 TQ	NCBLS	10/01-12/01
	North Dakota	Y	19760 FQ	40660 AW	65820 TQ	NDBLS	10/01-12/01
	Ohio	Y	24930 FQ	46190 AW	71410 TQ	OHBLS	10/01-12/01
	Oklahoma	Y	18750 FQ	37300 AW	67300 TQ	OKBLS	10/01-12/01
	Oregon	Y	23850 FQ	41270 AW	67880 TQ	ORBLS	10/01-12/01
	Pennsylvania	Y	12860 FQ	32950 AW	60160 TQ	PABLS	10/01-12/01
	Rhode Island	Y	30820 FQ	50040 AW	74380 TQ	RIBLS	10/01-12/01
	South Carolina	Y	20020 FQ	43090 AW	68210 TQ	SCBLS	10/01-12/01
	South Dakota	Y	20590 FQ	31210 AW	55480 TQ	SDBLS	10/01-12/01
	Tennessee	Y	22900 FQ	36820 AW	62320 TQ	TNBLS	10/01-12/01
	Texas	Y	22750 FQ	45000 AW	74070 TQ	TXBLS	10/01-12/01
	Utah	Y	24850 FQ	34320 AW	43970 TQ	UTBLS	10/01-12/01
	Vermont	Y	25780 FQ	40910 AW	63270 TQ	VTBLS	10/01-12/01
	Virginia	Y	24660 FQ	43760 AW	68280 TQ	VABLS	10/01-12/01
	Washington	Y	31950 FQ	48200 AW	68140 TQ	WABLS	10/01-12/01
	West Virginia	Y	16410 FQ	33120 AW	64310 TQ	WVBLS	10/01-12/01
	Wisconsin	Y	24270 FQ	45610 AW	71840 TQ	WIBLS	10/01-12/01
	Wyoming	Y	22090 FQ	42240 AW	64860 TQ	WYBLS	10/01-12/01
	Puerto Rico	Y	14250 FQ	25270 AW	44980 TQ	PRBLS	10/01-12/01
Tax Preparer	Alabama	Y	14720 FQ	23520 AW	40770 TQ	ALBLS	10/01-12/01
	Huntsville MSA, AL	Y	14940 FQ	16790 AW	18040 TQ	ALBLS	10/01-12/01
	Montgomery MSA, AL	Y	21020 FQ	29780 AW	43940 TQ	ALBLS	10/01-12/01
	Alaska	Y	19300 FQ	28600 AW	42180 TQ	AKBLS	10/01-12/01
	Arizona	Y	14610 FQ	27270 AW	43470 TQ	AZBLS	10/01-12/01
	Phoenix-Mesa MSA, AZ	Y	14720 FQ	25810 AW	39720 TQ	AZBLS	10/01-12/01
	Arkansas	Y	12690 FQ	20860 AW	33820 TQ	ARBLS	10/01-12/01
	Little Rock-North Little Rock MSA, AR	Y	22880 FQ	29270 AW	41780 TQ	ARBLS	10/01-12/01
	California	Y	13880 FQ	38700 AW	84430 TQ	CABLS	10/01-12/01
	Bakersfield MSA, CA	Y	28500 FQ	34390 AW	42710 TQ	CABLS	10/01-12/01
	Los Angeles-Long Beach PMSA, CA	Y	19560 FQ	47190 AW	81760 TQ	CABLS	10/01-12/01
	Oakland PMSA, CA	Y	13310 FQ	20730 AW	42780 TQ	CABLS	10/01-12/01
	Redding MSA, CA	Y	20510 FQ	33070 AW	43150 TQ	CABLS	10/01-12/01
	San Diego MSA, CA	Y	15500 FQ	25320 AW	36280 TQ	CABLS	10/01-12/01
	San Francisco PMSA, CA	Y	13990 FQ	53520 AW	119630 TQ	CABLS	10/01-12/01
	San Jose PMSA, CA	Y	15370 FQ	37500 AW	78780 TQ	CABLS	10/01-12/01
	Santa Barbara-Santa Maria-Lompoc MSA, CA	Y	28680 FQ	47560 AW	70090 TQ	CABLS	10/01-12/01
	Santa Cruz-Watsonville PMSA, CA	Y	20130 FQ	28260 AW	36410 TQ	CABLS	10/01-12/01
	Santa Rosa PMSA, CA	Y	15490 FQ	27210 AW	39080 TQ	CABLS	10/01-12/01

AAW Average annual wage; AE Average entry wage; AEX Average experienced wage; AO Average offered; AOH Average offered, high; AOL Average offered, low; APH Average pay, high range; APL Average pay, low range; ASH Average starting, high; ASL Average starting, low; AW Average wage paid; FQ First quartile wage; H Hourly; HI Highest wage paid; HR High end range; LR Low end range; M Monthly; MTC Median total compensation; MW Median wage paid; SQ Second quartile wage; S Special: hourly and annual; TQ Third quartile wage; W Weekly; Y Yearly

Occupation/Type/Industry	Location	Per	Low	Mid	High	Source	Date
Tax Preparer	Visalia-Tulare-Porterville MSA, CA	Y	17760 FQ	37930 AW	76360 TQ	CABLS	10/01-12/01
	Colorado	Y	15110 FQ	30480 AW	50560 TQ	COBLS	10/01-12/01
	Boulder-Longmont PMSA, CO	Y	15720 FQ	26610 AW	45440 TQ	COBLS	10/01-12/01
	Denver PMSA, CO	Y	13810 FQ	30790 AW	55720 TQ	COBLS	10/01-12/01
	Connecticut	Y	17960 FQ	36670 AW	55330 TQ	CTBLS	10/01-12/01
	Danbury PMSA, CT	Y	25110 FQ	46550 AW	70880 TQ	CTBLS	10/01-12/01
	Hartford MSA, CT	Y	21450 FQ	33070 AW	43460 TQ	CTBLS	10/01-12/01
	New Haven-Meriden PMSA, CT	Y	16030 FQ	29520 AW	48280 TQ	CTBLS	10/01-12/01
	Stamford-Norwalk PMSA, CT	Y	28830 FQ	48850 AW	75010 TQ	CTBLS	10/01-12/01
	Delaware	Y	15980 FQ	29740 AW	45720 TQ	DEBLS	10/01-12/01
	Wilmington-Newark PMSA, DE-MD	Y	17890 FQ	30960 AW	62890 TQ	DEBLS	10/01-12/01
	Washington PMSA, DC-MD-VA-WV	Y	14900 FQ	36990 AW	62380 TQ	DCBLS	10/01-12/01
	Florida	Y	14840 FQ	23600 AW	34670 TQ	FLBLS	10/01-12/01
	Daytona Beach MSA, FL	Y	23640 FQ	27020 AW	28940 TQ	FLBLS	10/01-12/01
	Fort Lauderdale PMSA, FL	Y	12790 FQ	16730 AW	21890 TQ	FLBLS	10/01-12/01
	Fort Pierce-Port St. Lucie MSA, FL	Y	11610 FQ	17970 AW	34370 TQ	FLBLS	10/01-12/01
	Fort Walton Beach MSA, FL	Y	13940 FQ	21190 AW	28110 TQ	FLBLS	10/01-12/01
	Jacksonville MSA, FL	Y	15420 FQ	22060 AW	38550 TQ	FLBLS	10/01-12/01
	Lakeland-Winter Haven MSA, FL	Y	12270 FQ	16660 AW	18800 TQ	FLBLS	10/01-12/01
	Melbourne-Titusville-Palm Bay MSA, FL	Y	14810 FQ	21630 AW	34430 TQ	FLBLS	10/01-12/01
	Miami PMSA, FL	Y	18380 FQ	26360 AW	34460 TQ	FLBLS	10/01-12/01
	Naples MSA, FL	Y	12010 FQ	23830 AW	43260 TQ	FLBLS	10/01-12/01
	Orlando MSA, FL	Y	18350 FQ	27800 AW	51140 TQ	FLBLS	10/01-12/01
	Pensacola MSA, FL	Y	15470 FQ	27130 AW	35600 TQ	FLBLS	10/01-12/01
	Sarasota-Bradenton MSA, FL	Y	15070 FQ	29570 AW	57370 TQ	FLBLS	10/01-12/01
	Tallahassee MSA, FL	Y	11920 FQ	18560 AW	18350 TQ	FLBLS	10/01-12/01
	Tampa-St. Petersburg-Clearwater MSA, FL	Y	19830 FQ	30660 AW	51000 TQ	FLBLS	10/01-12/01
	West Palm Beach-Boca Raton MSA, FL	Y	15770 FQ	23700 AW	35230 TQ	FLBLS	10/01-12/01
	Georgia	Y	13400 FQ	26810 AW	42120 TQ	GABLS	10/01-12/01
	Atlanta MSA, GA	Y	12710 FQ	28220 AW	45290 TQ	GABLS	10/01-12/01
	Augusta-Aiken MSA, GA-SC	Y	13340 FQ	29230 AW	60890 TQ	GABLS	10/01-12/01
	Hawaii	Y	14040 FQ	27350 AW	43650 TQ	HIBLS	10/01-12/01
	Idaho	Y	15410 FQ	26140 AW	43370 TQ	IDBLS	10/01-12/01
	Illinois	Y	17390 FQ	36140 AW	58400 TQ	ILBLS	10/01-12/01
	Chicago PMSA, IL	Y	19830 FQ	36600 AW	59420 TQ	ILBLS	10/01-12/01
	Peoria-Pekin MSA, IL	Y	33030 FQ	44060 AW	55500 TQ	ILBLS	10/01-12/01
	Indiana	Y	15440 FQ	29290 AW	44350 TQ	INBLS	10/01-12/01
	Evansville-Henderson MSA, IN-KY	Y	16860 FQ	30380 AW	42310 TQ	INBLS	10/01-12/01
	Fort Wayne MSA, IN	Y	22580 FQ	40250 AW	58390 TQ	INBLS	10/01-12/01
	Indianapolis MSA, IN	Y	23680 FQ	34890 AW	53640 TQ	INBLS	10/01-12/01
	South Bend MSA, IN	Y	12650 FQ	27120 AW	43760 TQ	INBLS	10/01-12/01
	Iowa	Y	12250 FQ	22770 AW	31730 TQ	IABLS	10/01-12/01
	Des Moines MSA, IA	Y	12430 FQ	28890 AW	55100 TQ	IABLS	10/01-12/01
	Kansas	Y	15300 FQ	25990 AW	40100 TQ	KSBLS	10/01-12/01
	Wichita MSA, KS	Y	29660 FQ	37520 AW	49350 TQ	KSBLS	10/01-12/01
	Kentucky	Y	14090 FQ	22940 AW	37770 TQ	KYBLS	10/01-12/01
	Louisville MSA, KY-IN	Y	17220 FQ	26000 AW	38260 TQ	KYBLS	10/01-12/01
	Louisiana	Y	12870 FQ	22290 AW	37680 TQ	LABLS	10/01-12/01
	New Orleans MSA, LA	Y	13610 FQ	24220 AW	40500 TQ	LABLS	10/01-12/01
	Shreveport-Bossier City MSA, LA	Y	15330 FQ	23580 AW	37600 TQ	LABLS	10/01-12/01
	Maine	Y	16840 FQ	28380 AW	39310 TQ	MEBLS	10/01-12/01
	Maryland	Y	19660 FQ	39490 AW	59090 TQ	MDBLS	10/01-12/01
	Baltimore PMSA, MD	Y	28730 FQ	45100 AW	71200 TQ	MDBLS	10/01-12/01
	Massachusetts	Y	24520 FQ	53340 AW	85330 TQ	MABLS	10/01-12/01
	Boston PMSA, MA-NH	Y	38390 FQ	61690 AW	87620 TQ	MABLS	10/01-12/01
	Worcester PMSA, MA-CT	Y	14630 FQ	25330 AW	42600 TQ	MABLS	10/01-12/01
	Michigan	Y	19090 FQ	33180 AW	53190 TQ	MIBLS	10/01-12/01
	Detroit PMSA, MI	Y	20110 FQ	34100 AW	54600 TQ	MIBLS	10/01-12/01
	Grand Rapids-Muskegon-Holland MSA, MI	Y	19410 FQ	35830 AW	53070 TQ	MIBLS	10/01-12/01
	Minnesota	Y	16990 FQ	37810 AW	66060 TQ	MNBLS	10/01-12/01

AAW	Average annual wage	AOH	Average offered, high	ASH	Average starting, high	H	Hourly	M	Monthly	S	Special: hourly and annual
AE	Average entry wage	AOL	Average offered, low	ASL	Average starting, low	HI	Highest wage paid	MTC	Median total compensation	TQ	Third quartile wage
AEX	Average experienced wage	APH	Average pay, high range	AW	Average wage paid	HR	High end range	MW	Median wage paid	W	Weekly
AO	Average offered	APL	Average pay, low range	FQ	First quartile wage	LR	Low end range	SQ	Second quartile wage	Y	Yearly

Occupation/Type/Industry	Location	Per	Low	Mid	High	Source	Date
Tax Preparer	Minneapolis-St. Paul MSA, MN-WI	Y	16910 FQ	39350 AW	69320 TQ	MNBLS	10/01-12/01
	Mississippi	Y	12620 FQ	22200 AW	40610 TQ	MSBLS	10/01-12/01
	Jackson MSA, MS	Y	13850 FQ	37980 AW	57940 TQ	MSBLS	10/01-12/01
	Missouri	Y	18490 FQ	38150 AW	59300 TQ	MOBLS	10/01-12/01
	Kansas City MSA, MO-KS	Y	16180 FQ	33470 AW	54450 TQ	MOBLS	10/01-12/01
	St. Louis MSA, MO-IL	Y	18500 FQ	42660 AW	67650 TQ	MOBLS	10/01-12/01
	Springfield MSA, MO	Y	19700 FQ	39600 AW	59520 TQ	MOBLS	10/01-12/01
	Montana	Y	24420 FQ	27190 AW	29740 TQ	MTBLS	10/01-12/01
	Nebraska	Y	15300 FQ	29190 AW	44100 TQ	NEBLS	10/01-12/01
	Nevada	Y	18530 FQ	27060 AW	46900 TQ	NVBLS	10/01-12/01
	New Hampshire	Y	14450 FQ	29020 AW	44430 TQ	NHBLS	10/01-12/01
	Portsmouth-Rochester PMSA, NH-ME	Y	13720 FQ	25940 AW	47570 TQ	NHBLS	10/01-12/01
	New Jersey	Y	19620 FQ	43360 AW	78390 TQ	NJBLS	10/01-12/01
	Bergen-Passaic PMSA, NJ	Y	14440 FQ	30310 AW	56890 TQ	NJBLS	10/01-12/01
	Middlesex-Somerset-Hunterdon PMSA, NJ	Y	24410 FQ	43470 AW	72120 TQ	NJBLS	10/01-12/01
	Monmouth-Ocean PMSA, NJ	Y	35700 FQ	68130 AW	89680 TQ	NJBLS	10/01-12/01
	Newark PMSA, NJ	Y	27180 FQ	46960 AW	79190 TQ	NJBLS	10/01-12/01
	New Mexico	Y	18040 FQ	27860 AW	35990 TQ	NMBLS	10/01-12/01
	New York	Y	14530 FQ	32340 AW	55310 TQ	NYBLS	10/01-12/01
	Albany-Schenectady-Troy MSA, NY	Y	16980 FQ	28810 AW	38670 TQ	NYBLS	10/01-12/01
	Binghamton MSA, NY	Y	18470 FQ	22520 AW	32030 TQ	NYBLS	10/01-12/01
	Buffalo-Niagara Falls MSA, NY	Y	11190 FQ	20010 AW	43110 TQ	NYBLS	10/01-12/01
	Dutchess County PMSA, NY	Y	14220 FQ	25410 AW	42920 TQ	NYBLS	10/01-12/01
	Nassau-Suffolk PMSA, NY	Y	13600 FQ	47130 AW	95380 TQ	NYBLS	10/01-12/01
	New York PMSA, NY	Y	18220 FQ	34830 AW	56240 TQ	NYBLS	10/01-12/01
	Rochester MSA, NY	Y	11660 FQ	20990 AW	36990 TQ	NYBLS	10/01-12/01
	Syracuse MSA, NY	Y	14360 FQ	31350 AW	46940 TQ	NYBLS	10/01-12/01
	Utica-Rome MSA, NY	Y	11940 FQ	14420 AW	19990 TQ	NYBLS	10/01-12/01
	North Carolina	Y	17060 FQ	34680 AW	56550 TQ	NCBLS	10/01-12/01
	Asheville MSA, NC	Y	19560 FQ	22740 AW	24960 TQ	NCBLS	10/01-12/01
	Charlotte-Gastonia-Rock Hill MSA, NC-SC	Y	23470 FQ	46950 AW	99830 TQ	NCBLS	10/01-12/01
	Greensboro-Winston-Salem-High Point MSA, NC	Y	27840 FQ	47200 AW	58640 TQ	NCBLS	10/01-12/01
	Hickory-Morganton-Lenoir MSA, NC	Y	14650 FQ	23660 AW	34480 TQ	NCBLS	10/01-12/01
	Raleigh-Durham-Chapel Hill MSA, NC	Y	15000 FQ	20080 AW	29120 TQ	NCBLS	10/01-12/01
	Ohio	Y	19150 FQ	33730 AW	51830 TQ	OHBLS	10/01-12/01
	Akron PMSA, OH	Y	23550 FQ	35490 AW	52820 TQ	OHBLS	10/01-12/01
	Canton-Massillon MSA, OH	Y	27100 FQ	40440 AW	56370 TQ	OHBLS	10/01-12/01
	Cincinnati PMSA, OH-KY-IN	Y	18300 FQ	30020 AW	44440 TQ	OHBLS	10/01-12/01
	Cleveland-Lorain-Elyria PMSA, OH	Y	26480 FQ	37370 AW	58210 TQ	OHBLS	10/01-12/01
	Columbus MSA, OH	Y	23820 FQ	29110 AW	36190 TQ	OHBLS	10/01-12/01
	Dayton-Springfield MSA, OH	Y	26740 FQ	36530 AW	47760 TQ	OHBLS	10/01-12/01
	Toledo MSA, OH	Y	16440 FQ	42130 AW	73140 TQ	OHBLS	10/01-12/01
	Youngstown-Warren MSA, OH	Y	23270 FQ	28760 AW	35460 TQ	OHBLS	10/01-12/01
	Oklahoma	Y	15390 FQ	33260 AW	56950 TQ	OKBLS	10/01-12/01
	Tulsa MSA, OK	Y	19410 FQ	43260 AW	67800 TQ	OKBLS	10/01-12/01
	Oregon	Y	19560 FQ	29570 AW	40530 TQ	ORBLS	10/01-12/01
	Eugene-Springfield MSA, OR	Y	19570 FQ	24920 AW	34820 TQ	ORBLS	10/01-12/01
	Medford-Ashland MSA, OR	Y	18330 FQ	33880 AW	55970 TQ	ORBLS	10/01-12/01
	Portland-Vancouver PMSA, OR-WA	Y	19360 FQ	28880 AW	35300 TQ	ORBLS	10/01-12/01
	Salem PMSA, OR	Y	25530 FQ	32210 AW	37040 TQ	ORBLS	10/01-12/01
	Pennsylvania	Y	13370 FQ	38150 AW	85050 TQ	PABLS	10/01-12/01
	Lancaster MSA, PA	Y	25950 FQ	38870 AW	59270 TQ	PABLS	10/01-12/01
	Philadelphia PMSA, PA-NJ	Y	19990 FQ	47140 AW	99650 TQ	PABLS	10/01-12/01
	Pittsburgh MSA, PA	Y	12720 FQ	48000 AW	105330 TQ	PABLS	10/01-12/01
	Rhode Island	Y	13640 FQ	19850 AW	26580 TQ	RIBLS	10/01-12/01
	Providence-Fall River-Warwick MSA, RI-MA	Y	13660 FQ	20450 AW	25480 TQ	RIBLS	10/01-12/01
	South Carolina	Y	13630 FQ	26980 AW	47080 TQ	SCBLS	10/01-12/01
	Charleston-North Charleston MSA, SC	Y	16110 FQ	26500 AW	46170 TQ	SCBLS	10/01-12/01
	Columbia MSA, SC	Y	11570 FQ	16100 AW	23620 TQ	SCBLS	10/01-12/01

AAW	Average annual wage	**AOH**	Average offered, high	**ASH**	Average starting, high	**H**	Hourly	**M**	Monthly	**S**	Special: hourly and annual
AE	Average entry wage	**AOL**	Average offered, low	**ASL**	Average starting, low	**HI**	Highest wage paid	**MTC**	Median total compensation	**TQ**	Third quartile wage
AEX	Average experienced wage	**APH**	Average pay, high range	**AW**	Average wage paid	**HR**	High end range	**MW**	Median wage paid	**W**	Weekly
AO	Average offered	**APL**	Average pay, low range	**FQ**	First quartile wage	**LR**	Low end range	**SQ**	Second quartile wage	**Y**	Yearly

Occupation/Type/Industry	Location	Per	Low	Mid	High	Source	Date
Tax Preparer	Greenville-Spartanburg-Anderson MSA, SC	Y	14440 FQ	26600 AW	46960 TQ	SCBLS	10/01-12/01
	Myrtle Beach MSA, SC	Y	16770 FQ	29330 AW	50830 TQ	SCBLS	10/01-12/01
	South Dakota	Y	19110 FQ	25010 AW	35470 TQ	SDBLS	10/01-12/01
	Sioux Falls MSA, SD	Y	24980 FQ	30500 AW	40130 TQ	SDBLS	10/01-12/01
	Tennessee	Y	15120 FQ	34300 AW	53290 TQ	TNBLS	10/01-12/01
	Clarksville-Hopkinsville MSA, TN-KY	Y	14710 FQ	17890 AW	21750 TQ	TNBLS	10/01-12/01
	Johnson City-Kingsport-Bristol MSA, TN-VA	Y	15630 FQ	20250 AW	25000 TQ	TNBLS	10/01-12/01
	Knoxville MSA, TN	Y	13330 FQ	35010 AW	56590 TQ	TNBLS	10/01-12/01
	Memphis MSA, TN-AR-MS	Y	19390 FQ	38050 AW	67160 TQ	TNBLS	10/01-12/01
	Nashville MSA, TN	Y	16730 FQ	36860 AW	52780 TQ	TNBLS	10/01-12/01
	Texas	Y	14330 FQ	27930 AW	44560 TQ	TXBLS	10/01-12/01
	Austin-San Marcos MSA, TX	Y	16080 FQ	26190 AW	42650 TQ	TXBLS	10/01-12/01
	Brownsville-Harlingen-San Benito MSA, TX	Y	11930 FQ	16070 AW	31730 TQ	TXBLS	10/01-12/01
	Dallas PMSA, TX	Y	17420 FQ	34020 AW	55880 TQ	TXBLS	10/01-12/01
	Fort Worth-Arlington PMSA, TX	Y	23000 FQ	31250 AW	41660 TQ	TXBLS	10/01-12/01
	Houston PMSA, TX	Y	23310 FQ	34330 AW	44000 TQ	TXBLS	10/01-12/01
	Killeen-Temple MSA, TX	Y	14840 FQ	16500 AW	18180 TQ	TXBLS	10/01-12/01
	Lubbock MSA, TX	Y	11610 FQ	17550 AW	34030 TQ	TXBLS	10/01-12/01
	McAllen-Edinburg-Mission MSA, TX	Y	12090 FQ	20100 AW	38010 TQ	TXBLS	10/01-12/01
	San Antonio MSA, TX	Y	18880 FQ	32110 AW	52630 TQ	TXBLS	10/01-12/01
	Waco MSA, TX	Y	18480 FQ	28770 AW	48440 TQ	TXBLS	10/01-12/01
	Utah	Y	19210 FQ	46550 AW	103100 TQ	UTBLS	10/01-12/01
	Salt Lake City-Ogden MSA, UT	Y	19520 FQ	50810 AW	107530 TQ	UTBLS	10/01-12/01
	Vermont	Y	22570 FQ	30310 AW	43780 TQ	VTBLS	10/01-12/01
	Virginia	Y	13760 FQ	26140 AW	47720 TQ	VABLS	10/01-12/01
	Norfolk-Virginia Beach-Newport News MSA, VA-NC	Y	13160 FQ	19170 AW	29290 TQ	VABLS	10/01-12/01
	Richmond-Petersburg MSA, VA	Y	15040 FQ	29030 AW	41520 TQ	VABLS	10/01-12/01
	Washington	Y	17190 FQ	35690 AW	61440 TQ	WABLS	10/01-12/01
	Seattle-Bellevue-Everett PMSA, WA	Y	17400 FQ	36720 AW	66380 TQ	WABLS	10/01-12/01
	West Virginia	Y	14240 FQ	19980 AW	37480 TQ	WVBLS	10/01-12/01
	Huntington-Ashland MSA, WV-KY-OH	Y	13810 FQ	20000 AW	32370 TQ	WVBLS	10/01-12/01
	Wisconsin	Y	17820 FQ	33020 AW	52120 TQ	WIBLS	10/01-12/01
	Madison MSA, WI	Y	25150 FQ	37760 AW	55980 TQ	WIBLS	10/01-12/01
	Puerto Rico	Y	27740 FQ	36330 AW	56510 TQ	PRBLS	10/01-12/01
	Guam	Y	11090 FQ	15110 AW	13980 TQ	GUBLS	10/01-12/01
Taxi Driver and Chauffeur	Alabama	H	5.94 FQ	8.56 AW	13.39 TQ	ALBLS	10/01-12/01
	Birmingham MSA, AL	H	5.78 FQ	8.75 AW	14.70 TQ	ALBLS	10/01-12/01
	Huntsville MSA, AL	H	6.86 FQ	7.89 AW	9.74 TQ	ALBLS	10/01-12/01
	Mobile MSA, AL	H	5.73 FQ	7.11 AW	8.58 TQ	ALBLS	10/01-12/01
	Montgomery MSA, AL	H	5.98 FQ	9.52 AW	14.36 TQ	ALBLS	10/01-12/01
	Alaska	H	7.37 FQ	10.96 AW	16.35 TQ	AKBLS	10/01-12/01
	Anchorage MSA, AK	H	7.34 FQ	10.39 AW	15.26 TQ	AKBLS	10/01-12/01
	Arizona	H	6.31 FQ	9.19 AW	12.56 TQ	AZBLS	10/01-12/01
	Phoenix-Mesa MSA, AZ	H	6.96 FQ	9.50 AW	12.61 TQ	AZBLS	10/01-12/01
	Tucson MSA, AZ	H	6.16 FQ	8.97 AW	12.83 TQ	AZBLS	10/01-12/01
	Arkansas	H	5.64 FQ	7.22 AW	10.06 TQ	ARBLS	10/01-12/01
	Little Rock-North Little Rock MSA, AR	H	5.77 FQ	7.26 AW	10.45 TQ	ARBLS	10/01-12/01
	California	H	6.78 FQ	10.69 AW	16.40 TQ	CABLS	10/01-12/01
	Bakersfield MSA, CA	H	6.59 FQ	9.04 AW	10.88 TQ	CABLS	10/01-12/01
	Chico-Paradise MSA, CA	H	6.85 FQ	9.93 AW	14.83 TQ	CABLS	10/01-12/01
	Fresno MSA, CA	H	6.74 FQ	10.36 AW	14.33 TQ	CABLS	10/01-12/01
	Los Angeles-Long Beach PMSA, CA	H	6.57 FQ	10.35 AW	15.86 TQ	CABLS	10/01-12/01
	Oakland PMSA, CA	H	7.19 FQ	10.23 AW	16.21 TQ	CABLS	10/01-12/01
	Orange County PMSA, CA	H	7.00 FQ	11.71 AW	16.45 TQ	CABLS	10/01-12/01
	Riverside-San Bernardino PMSA, CA	H	7.02 FQ	10.06 AW	14.80 TQ	CABLS	10/01-12/01
	Sacramento PMSA, CA	H	6.50 FQ	8.47 AW	10.58 TQ	CABLS	10/01-12/01
	Salinas MSA, CA	H	6.44 FQ	11.51 AW	23.96 TQ	CABLS	10/01-12/01

AAW	Average annual wage	AOH	Average offered, high	ASH	Average starting, high	H	Hourly	M	Monthly	S	Special: hourly and annual
AE	Average entry wage	AOL	Average offered, low	ASL	Average starting, low	HI	Highest wage paid	MTC	Median total compensation	TQ	Third quartile wage
AEX	Average experienced wage	APH	Average pay, high range	AW	Average wage paid	HR	High end range	MW	Median wage paid	W	Weekly
AO	Average offered	APL	Average pay, low range	FQ	First quartile wage	LR	Low end range	SQ	Second quartile wage	Y	Yearly

Occupation/Type/Industry	Location	Per	Low	Mid	High	Source	Date
Taxi Driver and Chauffeur	San Diego MSA, CA	H	6.72 FQ	9.30 AW	13.91 TQ	CABLS	10/01-12/01
	San Francisco PMSA, CA	H	7.74 FQ	12.60 AW	20.81 TQ	CABLS	10/01-12/01
	San Jose PMSA, CA	H	8.06 FQ	12.52 AW	16.73 TQ	CABLS	10/01-12/01
	San Luis Obispo-Atascadero-Paso Robles MSA, CA	H	8.60 FQ	15.43 AW	26.87 TQ	CABLS	10/01-12/01
	Santa Barbara-Santa Maria-Lompoc MSA, CA	H	6.81 FQ	11.21 AW	18.65 TQ	CABLS	10/01-12/01
	Santa Cruz-Watsonville PMSA, CA	H	8.42 FQ	9.87 AW	11.34 TQ	CABLS	10/01-12/01
	Santa Rosa PMSA, CA	H	7.91 FQ	11.57 AW	15.73 TQ	CABLS	10/01-12/01
	Stockton-Lodi MSA, CA	H	7.91 FQ	10.82 AW	15.41 TQ	CABLS	10/01-12/01
	Vallejo-Fairfield-Napa PMSA, CA	H	6.43 FQ	8.99 AW	13.43 TQ	CABLS	10/01-12/01
	Ventura PMSA, CA	H	7.20 FQ	10.56 AW	17.11 TQ	CABLS	10/01-12/01
	Visalia-Tulare-Porterville MSA, CA	H	6.56 FQ	10.36 AW	13.50 TQ	CABLS	10/01-12/01
	Colorado	H	6.59 FQ	9.56 AW	13.10 TQ	COBLS	10/01-12/01
	Boulder-Longmont PMSA, CO	H	6.35 FQ	8.40 AW	10.93 TQ	COBLS	10/01-12/01
	Colorado Springs MSA, CO	H	5.73 FQ	7.52 AW	10.29 TQ	COBLS	10/01-12/01
	Denver PMSA, CO	H	7.42 FQ	9.95 AW	12.88 TQ	COBLS	10/01-12/01
	Fort Collins-Loveland MSA, CO	H	6.96 FQ	8.14 AW	10.06 TQ	COBLS	10/01-12/01
	Greeley PMSA, CO	H	7.22 FQ	10.39 AW	15.33 TQ	COBLS	10/01-12/01
	Connecticut	H	7.22 FQ	12.63 AW	20.39 TQ	CTBLS	10/01-12/01
	Bridgeport PMSA, CT	H	6.60 FQ	10.45 AW	16.58 TQ	CTBLS	10/01-12/01
	Danbury PMSA, CT	H	6.76 FQ	12.82 AW	17.64 TQ	CTBLS	10/01-12/01
	Hartford MSA, CT	H	7.44 FQ	10.03 AW	12.42 TQ	CTBLS	10/01-12/01
	New Haven-Meriden PMSA, CT	H	8.59 FQ	13.38 AW	18.47 TQ	CTBLS	10/01-12/01
	New London-Norwich MSA, CT-RI	H	7.02 FQ	9.39 AW	12.86 TQ	CTBLS	10/01-12/01
	Stamford-Norwalk PMSA, CT	H	8.77 FQ	16.72 AW	22.61 TQ	CTBLS	10/01-12/01
	Waterbury PMSA, CT	H	7.03 FQ	11.05 AW	18.01 TQ	CTBLS	10/01-12/01
	Delaware	H	7.11 FQ	10.54 AW	15.71 TQ	DEBLS	10/01-12/01
	Wilmington-Newark PMSA, DE-MD	H	7.57 FQ	11.32 AW	16.39 TQ	DEBLS	10/01-12/01
	District of Columbia	H	6.93 FQ	11.30 AW	16.29 TQ	DCBLS	10/01-12/01
	Washington PMSA, DC-MD-VA-WV	H	7.05 FQ	10.99 AW	15.91 TQ	DCBLS	10/01-12/01
	Florida	H	5.57 FQ	7.53 AW	10.50 TQ	FLBLS	10/01-12/01
	Daytona Beach MSA, FL	H	5.50 FQ	6.73 AW	8.62 TQ	FLBLS	10/01-12/01
	Fort Lauderdale PMSA, FL	H	7.04 FQ	9.29 AW	12.91 TQ	FLBLS	10/01-12/01
	Fort Myers-Cape Coral MSA, FL	H	6.74 FQ	8.43 AW	10.44 TQ	FLBLS	10/01-12/01
	Fort Pierce-Port St. Lucie MSA, FL	H	5.77 FQ	7.89 AW	11.15 TQ	FLBLS	10/01-12/01
	Gainesville MSA, FL	H	6.05 FQ	7.83 AW	9.71 TQ	FLBLS	10/01-12/01
	Jacksonville MSA, FL	H	5.71 FQ	7.97 AW	10.75 TQ	FLBLS	10/01-12/01
	Melbourne-Titusville-Palm Bay MSA, FL	H	5.47 FQ	7.09 AW	10.55 TQ	FLBLS	10/01-12/01
	Miami PMSA, FL	H	5.71 FQ	8.10 AW	10.75 TQ	FLBLS	10/01-12/01
	Naples MSA, FL	H	5.76 FQ	7.77 AW	10.21 TQ	FLBLS	10/01-12/01
	Ocala MSA, FL	H	5.65 FQ	7.84 AW	10.85 TQ	FLBLS	10/01-12/01
	Orlando MSA, FL	H	5.66 FQ	7.36 AW	10.16 TQ	FLBLS	10/01-12/01
	Pensacola MSA, FL	H	5.63 FQ	6.74 AW	8.55 TQ	FLBLS	10/01-12/01
	Sarasota-Bradenton MSA, FL	H	5.43 FQ	6.72 AW	8.38 TQ	FLBLS	10/01-12/01
	Tampa-St. Petersburg-Clearwater MSA, FL	H	5.43 FQ	6.89 AW	9.33 TQ	FLBLS	10/01-12/01
	West Palm Beach-Boca Raton MSA, FL	H	5.67 FQ	8.04 AW	12.41 TQ	FLBLS	10/01-12/01
	Georgia	H	5.89 FQ	8.29 AW	11.23 TQ	GABLS	10/01-12/01
	Atlanta MSA, GA	H	6.41 FQ	8.87 AW	11.67 TQ	GABLS	10/01-12/01
	Augusta-Aiken MSA, GA-SC	H	5.67 FQ	7.26 AW	10.89 TQ	GABLS	10/01-12/01
	Columbus MSA, GA-AL	H	5.83 FQ	7.43 AW	9.77 TQ	GABLS	10/01-12/01
	Macon MSA, GA	H	5.54 FQ	7.10 AW	10.46 TQ	GABLS	10/01-12/01
	Savannah MSA, GA	H	5.56 FQ	6.40 AW	7.85 TQ	GABLS	10/01-12/01
	Hawaii	H	6.39 FQ	9.85 AW	14.13 TQ	HIBLS	10/01-12/01
	Honolulu MSA, HI	H	6.11 FQ	8.97 AW	12.74 TQ	HIBLS	10/01-12/01
	Idaho	H	6.04 FQ	8.38 AW	11.71 TQ	IDBLS	10/01-12/01
	Boise City MSA, ID	H	6.29 FQ	9.13 AW	13.04 TQ	IDBLS	10/01-12/01
	Illinois	H	6.76 FQ	10.53 AW	16.61 TQ	ILBLS	10/01-12/01
	Champaign-Urbana MSA, IL	H	5.65 FQ	7.36 AW	10.04 TQ	ILBLS	10/01-12/01

AAW	Average annual wage	AOH	Average offered, high	ASH	Average starting, high	H	Hourly	M	Monthly	S	Special: hourly and annual
AE	Average entry wage	AOL	Average offered, low	ASL	Average starting, low	HI	Highest wage paid	MTC	Median total compensation	TQ	Third quartile wage
AEX	Average experienced wage	APH	Average pay, high range	AW	Average wage paid	HR	High end range	MW	Median wage paid	W	Weekly
AO	Average offered	APL	Average pay, low range	FQ	First quartile wage	LR	Low end range	SQ	Second quartile wage	Y	Yearly

Occupation/Type/Industry	Location	Per	Low	Mid	High	Source	Date
Taxi Driver and Chauffeur	Chicago PMSA, IL	H	7.31 FQ	10.96 AW	17.01 TQ	ILBLS	10/01-12/01
	Peoria-Pekin MSA, IL	H	5.91 FQ	9.38 AW	14.69 TQ	ILBLS	10/01-12/01
	Rockford MSA, IL	H	7.05 FQ	9.70 AW	12.57 TQ	ILBLS	10/01-12/01
	Springfield MSA, IL	H	6.25 FQ	8.26 AW	10.89 TQ	ILBLS	10/01-12/01
	Indiana	H	5.88 FQ	8.46 AW	11.41 TQ	INBLS	10/01-12/01
	Evansville-Henderson MSA, IN-KY	H	5.77 FQ	7.87 AW	10.25 TQ	INBLS	10/01-12/01
	Fort Wayne MSA, IN	H	6.07 FQ	8.20 AW	10.59 TQ	INBLS	10/01-12/01
	Gary PMSA, IN	H	6.01 FQ	8.79 AW	12.66 TQ	INBLS	10/01-12/01
	Indianapolis MSA, IN	H	6.11 FQ	8.95 AW	11.70 TQ	INBLS	10/01-12/01
	Lafayette MSA, IN	H	5.80 FQ	8.92 AW	13.38 TQ	INBLS	10/01-12/01
	South Bend MSA, IN	H	5.81 FQ	9.49 AW	14.00 TQ	INBLS	10/01-12/01
	Iowa	H	5.75 FQ	8.59 AW	11.95 TQ	IABLS	10/01-12/01
	Cedar Rapids MSA, IA	H	6.98 FQ	9.01 AW	12.40 TQ	IABLS	10/01-12/01
	Davenport-Moline-Rock Island MSA, IA-IL	H	5.89 FQ	8.52 AW	11.81 TQ	IABLS	10/01-12/01
	Des Moines MSA, IA	H	5.61 FQ	9.85 AW	11.52 TQ	IABLS	10/01-12/01
	Kansas	H	5.70 FQ	7.95 AW	11.16 TQ	KSBLS	10/01-12/01
	Topeka MSA, KS	H	5.71 FQ	7.39 AW	9.88 TQ	KSBLS	10/01-12/01
	Wichita MSA, KS	H	5.61 FQ	7.11 AW	9.24 TQ	KSBLS	10/01-12/01
	Kentucky	H	5.91 FQ	8.55 AW	11.77 TQ	KYBLS	10/01-12/01
	Lexington MSA, KY	H	5.77 FQ	8.17 AW	13.05 TQ	KYBLS	10/01-12/01
	Louisville MSA, KY-IN	H	6.32 FQ	9.71 AW	17.91 TQ	KYBLS	10/01-12/01
	Louisiana	H	5.70 FQ	8.07 AW	12.20 TQ	LABLS	10/01-12/01
	Baton Rouge MSA, LA	H	5.79 FQ	7.60 AW	10.32 TQ	LABLS	10/01-12/01
	Houma MSA, LA	H	5.60 FQ	6.90 AW	8.78 TQ	LABLS	10/01-12/01
	Lafayette MSA, LA	H	5.76 FQ	7.82 AW	12.10 TQ	LABLS	10/01-12/01
	Lake Charles MSA, LA	H	5.60 FQ	7.38 AW	10.37 TQ	LABLS	10/01-12/01
	New Orleans MSA, LA	H	5.74 FQ	8.01 AW	11.57 TQ	LABLS	10/01-12/01
	Shreveport-Bossier City MSA, LA	H	7.35 FQ	9.90 AW	15.87 TQ	LABLS	10/01-12/01
	Maine	H	6.18 FQ	8.63 AW	12.15 TQ	MEBLS	10/01-12/01
	Portland MSA, ME	H	6.31 FQ	8.76 AW	12.58 TQ	MEBLS	10/01-12/01
	Maryland	H	6.65 FQ	9.81 AW	13.73 TQ	MDBLS	10/01-12/01
	Baltimore PMSA, MD	H	6.52 FQ	9.67 AW	13.60 TQ	MDBLS	10/01-12/01
	Massachusetts	H	7.08 FQ	10.11 AW	14.02 TQ	MABLS	10/01-12/01
	Boston PMSA, MA-NH	H	7.12 FQ	10.35 AW	14.41 TQ	MABLS	10/01-12/01
	Brockton PMSA, MA	H	6.95 FQ	8.82 AW	11.41 TQ	MABLS	10/01-12/01
	Lawrence PMSA, MA-NH	H	7.34 FQ	9.66 AW	12.45 TQ	MABLS	10/01-12/01
	Lowell PMSA, MA-NH	H	7.75 FQ	10.86 AW	14.03 TQ	MABLS	10/01-12/01
	New Bedford PMSA, MA	H	7.20 FQ	9.09 AW	11.51 TQ	MABLS	10/01-12/01
	Worcester PMSA, MA-CT	H	6.99 FQ	9.42 AW	12.44 TQ	MABLS	10/01-12/01
	Michigan	H	6.40 FQ	9.70 AW	13.43 TQ	MIBLS	10/01-12/01
	Ann Arbor PMSA, MI	H	8.03 FQ	11.47 AW	16.23 TQ	MIBLS	10/01-12/01
	Detroit PMSA, MI	H	6.99 FQ	10.19 AW	13.65 TQ	MIBLS	10/01-12/01
	Flint PMSA, MI	H	6.16 FQ	11.78 AW	25.66 TQ	MIBLS	10/01-12/01
	Grand Rapids-Muskegon-Holland MSA, MI	H	6.09 FQ	8.63 AW	11.76 TQ	MIBLS	10/01-12/01
	Kalamazoo-Battle Creek MSA, MI	H	5.65 FQ	8.18 AW	10.90 TQ	MIBLS	10/01-12/01
	Lansing-East Lansing MSA, MI	H	5.38 FQ	6.48 AW	8.45 TQ	MIBLS	10/01-12/01
	Saginaw-Bay City-Midland MSA, MI	H	5.63 FQ	7.64 AW	9.98 TQ	MIBLS	10/01-12/01
	Minnesota	H	7.07 FQ	9.48 AW	12.45 TQ	MNBLS	10/01-12/01
	Duluth-Superior MSA, MN-WI	H	5.94 FQ	8.88 AW	11.18 TQ	MNBLS	10/01-12/01
	Minneapolis-St. Paul MSA, MN-WI	H	7.44 FQ	9.71 AW	12.59 TQ	MNBLS	10/01-12/01
	Mississippi	H	6.09 FQ	8.17 AW	10.41 TQ	MSBLS	10/01-12/01
	Biloxi-Gulfport-Pascagoula MSA, MS	H	6.49 FQ	8.07 AW	10.07 TQ	MSBLS	10/01-12/01
	Jackson MSA, MS	H	6.50 FQ	8.29 AW	10.37 TQ	MSBLS	10/01-12/01
	Missouri	H	6.04 FQ	8.86 AW	12.17 TQ	MOBLS	10/01-12/01
	Kansas City MSA, MO-KS	H	6.17 FQ	8.67 AW	10.69 TQ	MOBLS	10/01-12/01
	St. Louis MSA, MO-IL	H	6.29 FQ	9.64 AW	14.95 TQ	MOBLS	10/01-12/01
	Springfield MSA, MO	H	6.02 FQ	8.13 AW	11.71 TQ	MOBLS	10/01-12/01
	Montana	H	5.79 FQ	9.47 AW	21.90 TQ	MTBLS	10/01-12/01
	Billings MSA, MT	H	5.59 FQ	6.83 AW	9.79 TQ	MTBLS	10/01-12/01
	Nebraska	H	5.81 FQ	8.04 AW	10.72 TQ	NEBLS	10/01-12/01
	Lincoln MSA, NE	H	6.09 FQ	7.82 AW	9.81 TQ	NEBLS	10/01-12/01
	Omaha MSA, NE-IA	H	6.17 FQ	8.87 AW	11.08 TQ	NEBLS	10/01-12/01
	Nevada	H	6.94 FQ	11.27 AW	15.69 TQ	NVBLS	10/01-12/01
	Las Vegas MSA, NV-AZ	H	7.00 FQ	11.41 AW	15.84 TQ	NVBLS	10/01-12/01

AAW Average annual wage **AOH** Average offered, high **ASH** Average starting, high **H** Hourly **M** Monthly **S** Special: hourly and annual
AE Average entry wage **AOL** Average offered, low **ASL** Average starting, low **HI** Highest wage paid **MTC** Median total compensation **TQ** Third quartile wage
AEX Average experienced wage **APH** Average pay, high range **AW** Average wage paid **HR** High end range **MW** Median wage paid **W** Weekly
AO Average offered **APL** Average pay, low range **FQ** First quartile wage **LR** Low end range **SQ** Second quartile wage **Y** Yearly

Occupation/Type/Industry	Location	Per	Low	Mid	High	Source	Date
Taxi Driver and Chauffeur	Reno MSA, NV	H	6.76 FQ	10.11 AW	14.00 TQ	NVBLS	10/01-12/01
	New Hampshire	H	6.26 FQ	9.02 AW	12.37 TQ	NHBLS	10/01-12/01
	Manchester PMSA, NH	H	7.50 FQ	9.86 AW	13.15 TQ	NHBLS	10/01-12/01
	Nashua PMSA, NH	H	5.78 FQ	8.51 AW	11.50 TQ	NHBLS	10/01-12/01
	Portsmouth-Rochester PMSA, NH-ME	H	6.10 FQ	9.20 AW	12.75 TQ	NHBLS	10/01-12/01
	New Jersey	H	6.41 FQ	10.89 AW	16.46 TQ	NJBLS	10/01-12/01
	Atlantic-Cape May PMSA, NJ	H	5.72 FQ	7.88 AW	11.42 TQ	NJBLS	10/01-12/01
	Bergen-Passaic PMSA, NJ	H	6.78 FQ	12.52 AW	21.01 TQ	NJBLS	10/01-12/01
	Jersey City PMSA, NJ	H	6.92 FQ	10.28 AW	14.00 TQ	NJBLS	10/01-12/01
	Middlesex-Somerset-Hunterdon PMSA, NJ	H	7.19 FQ	10.36 AW	13.62 TQ	NJBLS	10/01-12/01
	Monmouth-Ocean PMSA, NJ	H	6.16 FQ	11.75 AW	19.00 TQ	NJBLS	10/01-12/01
	Newark PMSA, NJ	H	6.89 FQ	11.79 AW	20.07 TQ	NJBLS	10/01-12/01
	New Mexico	H	6.00 FQ	8.82 AW	12.59 TQ	NMBLS	10/01-12/01
	Albuquerque MSA, NM	H	6.49 FQ	9.57 AW	12.83 TQ	NMBLS	10/01-12/01
	Las Cruces MSA, NM	H	5.89 FQ	7.34 AW	8.78 TQ	NMBLS	10/01-12/01
	New York	H	6.21 FQ	11.00 AW	18.71 TQ	NYBLS	10/01-12/01
	Albany-Schenectady-Troy MSA, NY	H	5.89 FQ	8.55 AW	12.86 TQ	NYBLS	10/01-12/01
	Binghamton MSA, NY	H	6.00 FQ	7.74 AW	9.72 TQ	NYBLS	10/01-12/01
	Buffalo-Niagara Falls MSA, NY	H	5.74 FQ	8.40 AW	13.41 TQ	NYBLS	10/01-12/01
	Dutchess County PMSA, NY	H	8.83 FQ	13.25 AW	17.09 TQ	NYBLS	10/01-12/01
	Nassau-Suffolk PMSA, NY	H	6.06 FQ	9.30 AW	13.40 TQ	NYBLS	10/01-12/01
	New York PMSA, NY	H	6.85 FQ	12.46 AW	20.91 TQ	NYBLS	10/01-12/01
	Newburgh PMSA, NY-PA	H	6.02 FQ	9.54 AW	14.63 TQ	NYBLS	10/01-12/01
	Rochester MSA, NY	H	6.86 FQ	10.37 AW	14.42 TQ	NYBLS	10/01-12/01
	Syracuse MSA, NY	H	5.60 FQ	6.89 AW	9.43 TQ	NYBLS	10/01-12/01
	Utica-Rome MSA, NY	H	5.77 FQ	7.45 AW	9.86 TQ	NYBLS	10/01-12/01
	North Carolina	H	6.00 FQ	8.48 AW	11.67 TQ	NCBLS	10/01-12/01
	Asheville MSA, NC	H	5.84 FQ	7.28 AW	8.98 TQ	NCBLS	10/01-12/01
	Charlotte-Gastonia-Rock Hill MSA, NC-SC	H	6.17 FQ	8.89 AW	12.29 TQ	NCBLS	10/01-12/01
	Fayetteville MSA, NC	H	6.02 FQ	7.79 AW	9.99 TQ	NCBLS	10/01-12/01
	Greensboro-Winston-Salem-High Point MSA, NC	H	5.91 FQ	8.16 AW	10.83 TQ	NCBLS	10/01-12/01
	Hickory-Morganton-Lenoir MSA, NC	H	5.97 FQ	8.32 AW	12.19 TQ	NCBLS	10/01-12/01
	Raleigh-Durham-Chapel Hill MSA, NC	H	5.97 FQ	8.80 AW	12.45 TQ	NCBLS	10/01-12/01
	Wilmington MSA, NC	H	6.38 FQ	10.79 AW	13.69 TQ	NCBLS	10/01-12/01
	North Dakota	H	5.56 FQ	7.02 AW	8.58 TQ	NDBLS	10/01-12/01
	Fargo-Moorhead MSA, ND-MN	H	5.60 FQ	7.32 AW	8.73 TQ	NDBLS	10/01-12/01
	Ohio	H	6.12 FQ	8.58 AW	11.63 TQ	OHBLS	10/01-12/01
	Akron PMSA, OH	H	5.61 FQ	7.50 AW	8.84 TQ	OHBLS	10/01-12/01
	Canton-Massillon MSA, OH	H	5.90 FQ	7.87 AW	10.48 TQ	OHBLS	10/01-12/01
	Cincinnati PMSA, OH-KY-IN	H	6.33 FQ	8.74 AW	11.36 TQ	OHBLS	10/01-12/01
	Cleveland-Lorain-Elyria PMSA, OH	H	7.01 FQ	9.54 AW	13.22 TQ	OHBLS	10/01-12/01
	Columbus MSA, OH	H	6.03 FQ	7.78 AW	10.26 TQ	OHBLS	10/01-12/01
	Dayton-Springfield MSA, OH	H	6.07 FQ	9.18 AW	10.93 TQ	OHBLS	10/01-12/01
	Hamilton-Middletown PMSA, OH	H	7.35 FQ	9.16 AW	10.79 TQ	OHBLS	10/01-12/01
	Toledo MSA, OH	H	6.68 FQ	9.84 AW	15.23 TQ	OHBLS	10/01-12/01
	Youngstown-Warren MSA, OH	H	5.77 FQ	7.48 AW	10.52 TQ	OHBLS	10/01-12/01
	Oklahoma	H	5.80 FQ	7.83 AW	10.27 TQ	OKBLS	10/01-12/01
	Oklahoma City MSA, OK	H	6.57 FQ	8.32 AW	10.43 TQ	OKBLS	10/01-12/01
	Tulsa MSA, OK	H	5.72 FQ	7.62 AW	10.16 TQ	OKBLS	10/01-12/01
	Oregon	H	6.86 FQ	8.62 AW	11.10 TQ	ORBLS	10/01-12/01
	Eugene-Springfield MSA, OR	H	7.06 FQ	8.66 AW	10.55 TQ	ORBLS	10/01-12/01
	Medford-Ashland MSA, OR	H	7.09 FQ	8.97 AW	10.75 TQ	ORBLS	10/01-12/01
	Portland-Vancouver PMSA, OR-WA	H	6.85 FQ	8.52 AW	10.94 TQ	ORBLS	10/01-12/01
	Salem PMSA, OR	H	7.29 FQ	10.03 AW	13.94 TQ	ORBLS	10/01-12/01
	Pennsylvania	H	5.71 FQ	8.34 AW	12.57 TQ	PABLS	10/01-12/01
	Allentown-Bethlehem-Easton MSA, PA	H	5.93 FQ	9.10 AW	13.20 TQ	PABLS	10/01-12/01
	Erie MSA, PA	H	5.46 FQ	7.57 AW	10.40 TQ	PABLS	10/01-12/01
	Harrisburg-Lebanon-Carlisle MSA, PA	H	6.00 FQ	8.30 AW	11.99 TQ	PABLS	10/01-12/01

AAW	Average annual wage	AOH	Average offered, high	ASH	Average starting, high	H	Hourly	M	Monthly	S	Special: hourly and annual
AE	Average entry wage	AOL	Average offered, low	ASL	Average starting, low	HI	Highest wage paid	MTC	Median total compensation	TQ	Third quartile wage
AEX	Average experienced wage	APH	Average pay, high range	AW	Average wage paid	HR	High end range	MW	Median wage paid	W	Weekly
AO	Average offered	APL	Average pay, low range	FQ	First quartile wage	LR	Low end range	SQ	Second quartile wage	Y	Yearly

Occupation/Type/Industry	Location	Per	Low	Mid	High	Source	Date
Taxi Driver and Chauffeur	Johnstown MSA, PA	H	5.41 FQ	6.52 AW	8.46 TQ	PABLS	10/01-12/01
	Lancaster MSA, PA	H	5.93 FQ	8.50 AW	12.75 TQ	PABLS	10/01-12/01
	Philadelphia PMSA, PA-NJ	H	5.77 FQ	9.08 AW	14.28 TQ	PABLS	10/01-12/01
	Pittsburgh MSA, PA	H	5.71 FQ	7.85 AW	11.91 TQ	PABLS	10/01-12/01
	Reading MSA, PA	H	6.06 FQ	8.60 AW	12.62 TQ	PABLS	10/01-12/01
	Scranton-Wilkes-Barre-Hazleton MSA, PA	H	5.75 FQ	7.56 AW	9.72 TQ	PABLS	10/01-12/01
	Rhode Island	H	6.66 FQ	9.45 AW	14.64 TQ	RIBLS	10/01-12/01
	Providence-Fall River-Warwick MSA, RI-MA	H	6.73 FQ	9.29 AW	14.64 TQ	RIBLS	10/01-12/01
	South Carolina	H	5.70 FQ	7.63 AW	10.56 TQ	SCBLS	10/01-12/01
	Charleston-North Charleston MSA, SC	H	5.70 FQ	7.36 AW	10.05 TQ	SCBLS	10/01-12/01
	Columbia MSA, SC	H	6.14 FQ	8.93 AW	13.35 TQ	SCBLS	10/01-12/01
	Greenville-Spartanburg-Anderson MSA, SC	H	5.73 FQ	7.45 AW	10.53 TQ	SCBLS	10/01-12/01
	Myrtle Beach MSA, SC	H	5.45 FQ	6.20 AW	6.93 TQ	SCBLS	10/01-12/01
	South Dakota	H	6.99 FQ	8.85 AW	11.09 TQ	SDBLS	10/01-12/01
	Sioux Falls MSA, SD	H	6.94 FQ	8.66 AW	10.66 TQ	SDBLS	10/01-12/01
	Tennessee	H	5.80 FQ	7.93 AW	10.70 TQ	TNBLS	10/01-12/01
	Chattanooga MSA, TN-GA	H	5.43 FQ	6.64 AW	8.57 TQ	TNBLS	10/01-12/01
	Clarksville-Hopkinsville MSA, TN-KY	H	6.30 FQ	8.63 AW	10.83 TQ	TNBLS	10/01-12/01
	Johnson City-Kingsport-Bristol MSA, TN-VA	H	5.80 FQ	7.47 AW	10.00 TQ	TNBLS	10/01-12/01
	Knoxville MSA, TN	H	5.88 FQ	8.55 AW	13.09 TQ	TNBLS	10/01-12/01
	Memphis MSA, TN-AR-MS	H	5.90 FQ	8.49 AW	12.02 TQ	TNBLS	10/01-12/01
	Nashville MSA, TN	H	6.24 FQ	8.36 AW	10.77 TQ	TNBLS	10/01-12/01
	Texas	H	5.82 FQ	8.78 AW	13.60 TQ	TXBLS	10/01-12/01
	Amarillo MSA, TX	H	5.71 FQ	8.12 AW	11.76 TQ	TXBLS	10/01-12/01
	Austin-San Marcos MSA, TX	H	6.65 FQ	10.95 AW	17.07 TQ	TXBLS	10/01-12/01
	Beaumont-Port Arthur MSA, TX	H	5.72 FQ	7.44 AW	10.14 TQ	TXBLS	10/01-12/01
	Brownsville-Harlingen-San Benito MSA, TX	H	5.41 FQ	6.54 AW	8.58 TQ	TXBLS	10/01-12/01
	Corpus Christi MSA, TX	H	5.57 FQ	7.89 AW	10.84 TQ	TXBLS	10/01-12/01
	Dallas PMSA, TX	H	5.87 FQ	8.52 AW	12.64 TQ	TXBLS	10/01-12/01
	El Paso MSA, TX	H	5.75 FQ	12.57 AW	26.41 TQ	TXBLS	10/01-12/01
	Fort Worth-Arlington PMSA, TX	H	6.30 FQ	9.61 AW	13.76 TQ	TXBLS	10/01-12/01
	Galveston-Texas City PMSA, TX	H	6.24 FQ	8.57 AW	10.69 TQ	TXBLS	10/01-12/01
	Houston PMSA, TX	H	5.73 FQ	7.68 AW	10.82 TQ	TXBLS	10/01-12/01
	Laredo MSA, TX	H	5.72 FQ	6.70 AW	8.43 TQ	TXBLS	10/01-12/01
	Lubbock MSA, TX	H	5.88 FQ	9.18 AW	17.86 TQ	TXBLS	10/01-12/01
	McAllen-Edinburg-Mission MSA, TX	H	5.61 FQ	6.65 AW	8.30 TQ	TXBLS	10/01-12/01
	Odessa-Midland MSA, TX	H	5.71 FQ	7.55 AW	10.25 TQ	TXBLS	10/01-12/01
	San Antonio MSA, TX	H	6.20 FQ	10.17 AW	15.73 TQ	TXBLS	10/01-12/01
	Tyler MSA, TX	H	5.82 FQ	7.79 AW	10.38 TQ	TXBLS	10/01-12/01
	Waco MSA, TX	H	5.59 FQ	7.08 AW	9.97 TQ	TXBLS	10/01-12/01
	Utah	H	6.46 FQ	12.35 AW	31.49 TQ	UTBLS	10/01-12/01
	Provo-Orem MSA, UT	H	6.64 FQ	9.40 AW	11.15 TQ	UTBLS	10/01-12/01
	Salt Lake City-Ogden MSA, UT	H	6.37 FQ	15.32 AW	34.05 TQ	UTBLS	10/01-12/01
	Vermont	H	6.46 FQ	8.42 AW	10.91 TQ	VTBLS	10/01-12/01
	Burlington MSA, VT	H	6.99 FQ	9.14 AW	11.57 TQ	VTBLS	10/01-12/01
	Virginia	H	5.99 FQ	9.70 AW	14.31 TQ	VABLS	10/01-12/01
	Lynchburg MSA, VA	H	5.82 FQ	8.36 AW	13.00 TQ	VABLS	10/01-12/01
	Norfolk-Virginia Beach-Newport News MSA, VA-NC	H	6.13 FQ	10.29 AW	16.12 TQ	VABLS	10/01-12/01
	Richmond-Petersburg MSA, VA	H	6.23 FQ	9.81 AW	13.74 TQ	VABLS	10/01-12/01
	Roanoke MSA, VA	H	6.06 FQ	7.50 AW	8.59 TQ	VABLS	10/01-12/01
	Washington	H	7.09 FQ	9.58 AW	14.07 TQ	WABLS	10/01-12/01
	Bremerton PMSA, WA	H	6.73 FQ	9.02 AW	11.28 TQ	WABLS	10/01-12/01
	Olympia PMSA, WA	H	7.84 FQ	11.61 AW	14.18 TQ	WABLS	10/01-12/01
	Seattle-Bellevue-Everett PMSA, WA	H	7.10 FQ	9.22 AW	13.12 TQ	WABLS	10/01-12/01
	Spokane MSA, WA	H	7.46 FQ	12.92 AW	17.20 TQ	WABLS	10/01-12/01
	Tacoma PMSA, WA	H	6.75 FQ	8.37 AW	10.51 TQ	WABLS	10/01-12/01

AAW	Average annual wage	**AOH**	Average offered, high	**ASH**	Average starting, high	**H**	Hourly	**M**	Monthly	**S**	Special: hourly and annual
AE	Average entry wage	**AOL**	Average offered, low	**ASL**	Average starting, low	**HI**	Highest wage paid	**MTC**	Median total compensation	**TQ**	Third quartile wage
AEX	Average experienced wage	**APH**	Average pay, high range	**AW**	Average wage paid	**HR**	High end range	**MW**	Median wage paid	**W**	Weekly
AO	Average offered	**APL**	Average pay, low range	**FQ**	First quartile wage	**LR**	Low end range	**SQ**	Second quartile wage	**Y**	Yearly

Occupation/Type/Industry	Location	Per	Low	Mid	High	Source	Date
Taxi Driver and Chauffeur	West Virginia	H	5.61 FQ	6.97 AW	8.55 TQ	WVBLS	10/01-12/01
	Charleston MSA, WV	H	5.57 FQ	7.00 AW	8.37 TQ	WVBLS	10/01-12/01
	Huntington-Ashland MSA, WV-KY-OH	H	5.78 FQ	6.85 AW	8.29 TQ	WVBLS	10/01-12/01
	Wisconsin	H	6.49 FQ	8.73 AW	11.11 TQ	WIBLS	10/01-12/01
	Appleton-Oshkosh-Neenah MSA, WI	H	6.20 FQ	7.92 AW	10.02 TQ	WIBLS	10/01-12/01
	Green Bay MSA, WI	H	5.77 FQ	8.46 AW	13.38 TQ	WIBLS	10/01-12/01
	Madison MSA, WI	H	7.26 FQ	9.25 AW	13.68 TQ	WIBLS	10/01-12/01
	Milwaukee-Waukesha PMSA, WI	H	6.89 FQ	9.15 AW	11.46 TQ	WIBLS	10/01-12/01
	Racine PMSA, WI	H	7.37 FQ	8.98 AW	11.14 TQ	WIBLS	10/01-12/01
	Wyoming	H	5.71 FQ	7.30 AW	8.91 TQ	WYBLS	10/01-12/01
	Cheyenne MSA, WY	H	5.77 FQ	7.32 AW	9.29 TQ	WYBLS	10/01-12/01
	Puerto Rico	H	5.63 FQ	9.26 AW	22.54 TQ	PRBLS	10/01-12/01
	Virgin Islands	H	6.95 FQ	8.66 AW	10.97 TQ	VIBLS	10/01-12/01
	Guam	H	5.88 FQ	7.60 AW	9.38 TQ	GUBLS	10/01-12/01
Teacher	United States	Y	27989 AE	41820 AW		DIG	1/99-1/00
	Alabama	Y	29790 AE	36689 AW		DIG	1/99-1/00
	Alaska	Y	33676 AE	46481 AW		DIG	1/99-1/00
	Arizona	Y	25613 AE	34824 AW		DIG	1/99-1/00
	Arkansas	Y	22599 AE	33691 AW		DIG	1/99-1/00
	California	Y	32190 AE	47680 AW		DIG	1/99-1/00
	Colorado	Y	24875 AE	38073 AW		DIG	1/99-1/00
	Connecticut	Y	30466 AE	52410 AW		DIG	1/99-1/00
	Delaware	Y	30945 AE	44435 AW		DIG	1/99-1/00
	District of Columbia	Y	30850 AE	48304 AW		DIG	1/99-1/00
	Florida	Y	25132 AE	36722 AW		DIG	1/99-1/00
	Georgia	Y	30402 AE	41122 AW		DIG	1/99-1/00
	Hawaii	Y	29204 AE	41292 AW		DIG	1/99-1/00
	Idaho	Y	20915 AE	35155 AW		DIG	1/99-1/00
	Illinois	Y	30151 AE	46480 AW		DIG	1/99-1/00
	Collinsville, IL	Y	33262 AE	52028 AW	65855 HI	BND	1/01-1/02
	Mascoutah, IL	Y	32645 AE			BND	1/01-1/02
	Indiana	Y	26553 AE	41855 AW		DIG	1/99-1/00
	Iowa	Y	25275 AE	35678 AW		DIG	1/99-1/00
	Kansas	Y	25252 AE	36282 AW		DIG	1/99-1/00
	Kentucky	Y	24753 AE	36255 AW		DIG	1/99-1/00
	Louisiana	Y	25738 AE	33109 AW		DIG	1/99-1/00
	Maine	Y	22942 AE	35561 AW		DIG	1/99-1/00
	Maryland	Y	28612 AE	43720 AW		DIG	1/99-1/00
	Massachusetts	Y	30330 AE	46955 AW		DIG	1/99-1/00
	Michigan	Y	28545 AE	48729 AW		DIG	1/99-1/00
	Minnesota	Y	25666 AE	40678 AW		DIG	1/99-1/00
	Mississippi	Y	23040 AE	31897 AW		DIG	1/99-1/00
	Missouri	Y	25977 AE	35660 AW		DIG	1/99-1/00
	Montana	Y	20969 AE	32121 AW		DIG	1/99-1/00
	Nebraska	Y	22923 AE	33237 AW		DIG	1/99-1/00
	Nevada	Y	28734 AE	43083 AW		DIG	1/99-1/00
	New Hampshire	Y	24650 AE	37734 AW		DIG	1/99-1/00
	New Jersey	Y	30480 AE	50878 AW		DIG	1/99-1/00
	New Mexico	Y	25042 AE	32713 AW		DIG	1/99-1/00
	New York	Y	31910 AE	51020 AW		DIG	1/99-1/00
	North Carolina	Y	27968 AE	39404 AW		DIG	1/99-1/00
	North Dakota	Y	20422 AE	29863 AW		DIG	1/99-1/00
	Ohio	Y	23597 AE	41713 AW		DIG	1/99-1/00
	Oklahoma	Y	24025 AE	29525 AW		DIG	1/99-1/00
	Oregon	Y	29733 AE	45103 AW		DIG	1/99-1/00
	Pennsylvania	Y	30185 AE	48321 AW		DIG	1/99-1/00
	Rhode Island	Y	27286 AE	48138 AW		DIG	1/99-1/00
	South Carolina	Y	25215 AE	36081 AW		DIG	1/99-1/00
	South Dakota	Y	21889 AE	29072 AW		DIG	1/99-1/00
	Tennessee	Y	27228 AE	36328 AW		DIG	1/99-1/00
	Texas	Y	28400 AE	37567 AW		DIG	1/99-1/00
	Utah	Y	23273 AE	34946 AW		DIG	1/99-1/00
	Vermont	Y	25791 AE	36402 AW		DIG	1/99-1/00
	Virginia	Y	26783 AE	38992 AW		DIG	1/99-1/00
	Washington	Y	26514 AE	41047 AW		DIG	1/99-1/00
	West Virginia	Y	23829 AE	35011 AW		DIG	1/99-1/00
	Wisconsin	Y	25344 AE	39897 AW		DIG	1/99-1/00
	Wyoming	Y	24168 AE	34188 AW		DIG	1/99-1/00

AAW	Average annual wage	**AOH**	Average offered, high	**ASH**	Average starting, high	**H**	Hourly	**M**	Monthly	**S**	Special: hourly and annual
AE	Average entry wage	**AOL**	Average offered, low	**ASL**	Average starting, low	**HI**	Highest wage paid	**MTC**	Median total compensation	**TQ**	Third quartile wage
AEX	Average experienced wage	**APH**	Average pay, high range	**AW**	Average wage paid	**HR**	High end range	**MW**	Median wage paid	**W**	Weekly
AO	Average offered	**APL**	Average pay, low range	**FQ**	First quartile wage	**LR**	Low end range	**SQ**	Second quartile wage	**Y**	Yearly

Occupation/Type/Industry	Location	Per	Low	Mid	High	Source	Date
Teacher							
Adult Literacy and Remedial and Self Enrichment Education	United States	H		16.12 MW		OOH9	1999-2000
Public School	United States	Y		40582 AW		NEA	1/98-1/99
Public School	Alabama	Y		35820 AW		NEA	1/98-1/99
Public School	Alaska	Y		46845 AW		NEA	1/98-1/99
Public School	Arizona	Y		35025 AW		NEA	1/98-1/99
Public School	Arkansas	Y		32350 AW		NEA	1/98-1/99
Public School	California	Y		45400 AW		NEA	1/98-1/99
Public School	Colorado	Y		38025 AW		NEA	1/98-1/99
Public School	Connecticut	Y		51584 AW		NEA	1/98-1/99
Public School	Delaware	Y		43164 AW		NEA	1/98-1/99
Public School	District of Columbia	Y		47150 AW		NEA	1/98-1/99
Public School	Florida	Y		35916 AW		NEA	1/98-1/99
Public School	Georgia	Y		39675 AW		NEA	1/98-1/99
Public School	Hawaii	Y		40377 AW		NEA	1/98-1/99
Public School	Idaho	Y		34063 AW		NEA	1/98-1/99
Public School	Illinois	Y		45569 AW		NEA	1/98-1/99
Public School	Indiana	Y		41163 AW		NEA	1/98-1/99
Public School	Iowa	Y		34927 AW		NEA	1/98-1/99
Public School	Kansas	Y		37405 AW		NEA	1/98-1/99
Public School	Kentucky	Y		35526 AW		NEA	1/98-1/99
Public School	Louisiana	Y		32510 AW		NEA	1/98-1/99
Public School	Maine	Y		34906 AW		NEA	1/98-1/99
Public School	Maryland	Y		42526 AW		NEA	1/98-1/99
Public School	Massachusetts	Y		45075 AW		NEA	1/98-1/99
Public School	Michigan	Y		48207 AW		NEA	1/98-1/99
Public School	Minnesota	Y		39458 AW		NEA	1/98-1/99
Public School	Mississippi	Y		29530 AW		NEA	1/98-1/99
Public School	Missouri	Y		34746 AW		NEA	1/98-1/99
Public School	Montana	Y		31356 AW		NEA	1/98-1/99
Public School	Nebraska	Y		32880 AW		NEA	1/98-1/99
Public School	Nevada	Y		38883 AW		NEA	1/98-1/99
Public School	New Hampshire	Y		37405 AW		NEA	1/98-1/99
Public School	New Jersey	Y		51193 AW		NEA	1/98-1/99
Public School	New Mexico	Y		32398 AW		NEA	1/98-1/99
Public School	New York	Y		49437 AW		NEA	1/98-1/99
Public School	North Carolina	Y		36098 AW		NEA	1/98-1/99
Public School	North Dakota	Y		28976 AW		NEA	1/98-1/99
Public School	Ohio	Y		40566 AW		NEA	1/98-1/99
Public School	Oklahoma	Y		31149 AW		NEA	1/98-1/99
Public School	Oregon	Y		42833 AW		NEA	1/98-1/99
Public School	Pennsylvania	Y		48457 AW		NEA	1/98-1/99
Public School	Rhode Island	Y		45650 AW		NEA	1/98-1/99
Public School	South Carolina	Y		34506 AW		NEA	1/98-1/99
Public School	South Dakota	Y		28552 AW		NEA	1/98-1/99
Public School	Tennessee	Y		36500 AW		NEA	1/98-1/99
Public School	Texas	Y		35041 AW		NEA	1/98-1/99
Public School	Utah	Y		32950 AW		NEA	1/98-1/99
Public School	Vermont	Y		36800 AW		NEA	1/98-1/99
Public School	Virginia	Y		37475 AW		NEA	1/98-1/99
Public School	Washington	Y		38692 AW		NEA	1/98-1/99
Public School	West Virginia	Y		34244 AW		NEA	1/98-1/99
Public School	Wisconsin	Y		40657 AW		NEA	1/98-1/99
Public School	Wyoming	Y		33500 AW		NEA	1/98-1/99
Self-Enrichment Education	United States	H		13.44 MW		OOH9	1999-2000
Teacher Assistant	Alabama	Y	11720 FQ	14500 AW	18110 TQ	ALBLS	10/01-12/01
	Alaska	Y	17320 FQ	27940 AW	39820 TQ	AKBLS	10/01-12/01
	Arizona	Y	12450 FQ	17620 AW	23940 TQ	AZBLS	10/01-12/01
	Arkansas	Y	11720 FQ	13680 AW	16960 TQ	ARBLS	10/01-12/01
	California	Y	14280 FQ	22720 AW	31560 TQ	CABLS	10/01-12/01
	Colorado	Y	13690 FQ	19340 AW	26230 TQ	COBLS	10/01-12/01
	Connecticut	Y	15060 FQ	22770 AW	32080 TQ	CTBLS	10/01-12/01
	Delaware	Y	13920 FQ	21040 AW	31160 TQ	DEBLS	10/01-12/01
	District of Columbia	Y	15190 FQ	28140 AW	45400 TQ	DCBLS	10/01-12/01
	Florida	Y	12290 FQ	16860 AW	23050 TQ	FLBLS	10/01-12/01
	Georgia	Y	11880 FQ	15690 AW	21190 TQ	GABLS	10/01-12/01
	Hawaii	Y	13690 FQ	19560 AW	24720 TQ	HIBLS	10/01-12/01
	Idaho	Y	14030 FQ	18480 AW	22510 TQ	IDBLS	10/01-12/01
	Illinois	Y	12830 FQ	19790 AW	28150 TQ	ILBLS	10/01-12/01
	Indiana	Y	12670 FQ	18010 AW	23770 TQ	INBLS	10/01-12/01
	Iowa	Y	12210 FQ	16740 AW	22430 TQ	IABLS	10/01-12/01

AAW	Average annual wage	**AOH**	Average offered, high	**ASH**	Average starting, high	**H**	Hourly	**M**	Monthly	**S**	Special: hourly and annual
AE	Average entry wage	**AOL**	Average offered, low	**ASL**	Average starting, low	**HI**	Highest wage paid	**MTC**	Median total compensation	**TQ**	Third quartile wage
AEX	Average experienced wage	**APH**	Average pay, high range	**AW**	Average wage paid	**HR**	High end range	**MW**	Median wage paid	**W**	Weekly
AO	Average offered	**APL**	Average pay, low range	**FQ**	First quartile wage	**LR**	Low end range	**SQ**	Second quartile wage	**Y**	Yearly

Occupation/Type/Industry	Location	Per	Low	Mid	High	Source	Date
Teacher Assistant	Kansas	Y	12380 FQ	16940 AW	22380 TQ	KSBLS	10/01-12/01
	Kentucky	Y	13120 FQ	18610 AW	25820 TQ	KYBLS	10/01-12/01
	Louisiana	Y	11650 FQ	13950 AW	17330 TQ	LABLS	10/01-12/01
	Maine	Y	15540 FQ	22330 AW	30440 TQ	MEBLS	10/01-12/01
	Maryland	Y	12630 FQ	18960 AW	27030 TQ	MDBLS	10/01-12/01
	Massachusetts	Y	14360 FQ	20760 AW	29260 TQ	MABLS	10/01-12/01
	Michigan	Y	14080 FQ	22110 AW	31380 TQ	MIBLS	10/01-12/01
	Minnesota	Y	13490 FQ	21980 AW	32050 TQ	MNBLS	10/01-12/01
	Mississippi	Y	11770 FQ	13790 AW	17370 TQ	MSBLS	10/01-12/01
	Missouri	Y	12040 FQ	16090 AW	22620 TQ	MOBLS	10/01-12/01
	Montana	Y	12430 FQ	16600 AW	21630 TQ	MTBLS	10/01-12/01
	Nebraska	Y	12280 FQ	15940 AW	20580 TQ	NEBLS	10/01-12/01
	Nevada	Y	17680 FQ	24350 AW	29390 TQ	NVBLS	10/01-12/01
	New Hampshire	Y	13150 FQ	18520 AW	24160 TQ	NHBLS	10/01-12/01
	New Jersey	Y	12220 FQ	18910 AW	28150 TQ	NJBLS	10/01-12/01
	New Mexico	Y	11540 FQ	14550 AW	20100 TQ	NMBLS	10/01-12/01
	New York	Y	13170 FQ	22780 AW	35350 TQ	NYBLS	10/01-12/01
	North Carolina	Y	13770 FQ	17630 AW	22360 TQ	NCBLS	10/01-12/01
	North Dakota	Y	13130 FQ	18100 AW	23680 TQ	NDBLS	10/01-12/01
	Ohio	Y	13470 FQ	21220 AW	29020 TQ	OHBLS	10/01-12/01
	Oklahoma	Y	11620 FQ	14310 AW	18800 TQ	OKBLS	10/01-12/01
	Oregon	Y	16030 FQ	22580 AW	29730 TQ	ORBLS	10/01-12/01
	Pennsylvania	Y	12370 FQ	17690 AW	24130 TQ	PABLS	10/01-12/01
	Rhode Island	Y	13990 FQ	21170 AW	31180 TQ	RIBLS	10/01-12/01
	South Carolina	Y	11810 FQ	15280 AW	19480 TQ	SCBLS	10/01-12/01
	South Dakota	Y	14250 FQ	18900 AW	24830 TQ	SDBLS	10/01-12/01
	Tennessee	Y	11700 FQ	14290 AW	18020 TQ	TNBLS	10/01-12/01
	Texas	Y	11810 FQ	15790 AW	21430 TQ	TXBLS	10/01-12/01
	Utah	Y	13340 FQ	18680 AW	25140 TQ	UTBLS	10/01-12/01
	Vermont	Y	14030 FQ	18750 AW	23720 TQ	VTBLS	10/01-12/01
	Virginia	Y	11880 FQ	18070 AW	25250 TQ	VABLS	10/01-12/01
	Washington	Y	16500 FQ	22320 AW	27900 TQ	WABLS	10/01-12/01
	West Virginia	Y	14000 FQ	19200 AW	25290 TQ	WVBLS	10/01-12/01
	Wisconsin	Y	13350 FQ	19890 AW	27660 TQ	WIBLS	10/01-12/01
	Wyoming	Y	12280 FQ	16340 AW	21610 TQ	WYBLS	10/01-12/01
	Puerto Rico	Y	11370 FQ	13260 AW	16340 TQ	PRBLS	10/01-12/01
	Virgin Islands	Y	14810 FQ	17740 AW	22070 TQ	VIBLS	10/01-12/01
	Guam	Y	14610 FQ	20090 AW	26840 TQ	GUBLS	10/01-12/01
Team Assembler	Alabama	H	7.19 FQ	10.60 AW	15.59 TQ	ALBLS	10/01-12/01
	Alaska	H	7.56 FQ	12.42 AW	18.18 TQ	AKBLS	10/01-12/01
	Arizona	H	6.44 FQ	10.11 AW	14.37 TQ	AZBLS	10/01-12/01
	Arkansas	H	7.05 FQ	10.06 AW	14.01 TQ	ARBLS	10/01-12/01
	California	H	6.86 FQ	10.87 AW	16.68 TQ	CABLS	10/01-12/01
	Colorado	H	7.66 FQ	10.98 AW	15.00 TQ	COBLS	10/01-12/01
	Connecticut	H	7.54 FQ	12.47 AW	17.92 TQ	CTBLS	10/01-12/01
	Delaware	H	7.75 FQ	11.55 AW	16.23 TQ	DEBLS	10/01-12/01
	Florida	H	6.65 FQ	9.83 AW	13.96 TQ	FLBLS	10/01-12/01
	Georgia	H	7.37 FQ	10.81 AW	15.14 TQ	GABLS	10/01-12/01
	Hawaii	H	7.31 FQ	10.68 AW	14.36 TQ	HIBLS	10/01-12/01
	Idaho	H	7.32 FQ	10.91 AW	14.28 TQ	IDBLS	10/01-12/01
	Illinois	H	7.47 FQ	12.43 AW	19.74 TQ	ILBLS	10/01-12/01
	Indiana	H	8.00 FQ	12.31 AW	17.27 TQ	INBLS	10/01-12/01
	Iowa	H	8.22 FQ	12.92 AW	19.76 TQ	IABLS	10/01-12/01
	Kansas	H	7.35 FQ	11.62 AW	17.37 TQ	KSBLS	10/01-12/01
	Kentucky	H	7.87 FQ	15.42 AW	25.31 TQ	KYBLS	10/01-12/01
	Louisiana	H	6.79 FQ	11.49 AW	18.81 TQ	LABLS	10/01-12/01
	Maine	H	6.90 FQ	10.03 AW	13.57 TQ	MEBLS	10/01-12/01
	Maryland	H	7.11 FQ	11.00 AW	16.98 TQ	MDBLS	10/01-12/01
	Massachusetts	H	7.64 FQ	12.14 AW	18.12 TQ	MABLS	10/01-12/01
	Michigan	H	8.16 FQ	14.19 AW	24.83 TQ	MIBLS	10/01-12/01
	Minnesota	H	8.35 FQ	12.26 AW	16.93 TQ	MNBLS	10/01-12/01
	Mississippi	H	6.27 FQ	9.41 AW	13.09 TQ	MSBLS	10/01-12/01
	Missouri	H	7.32 FQ	12.38 AW	23.56 TQ	MOBLS	10/01-12/01
	Montana	H	7.28 FQ	10.30 AW	13.74 TQ	MTBLS	10/01-12/01
	Nebraska	H	7.92 FQ	11.80 AW	16.62 TQ	NEBLS	10/01-12/01
	Nevada	H	7.15 FQ	10.52 AW	15.54 TQ	NVBLS	10/01-12/01
	New Hampshire	H	8.00 FQ	11.55 AW	16.13 TQ	NHBLS	10/01-12/01
	New Jersey	H	7.16 FQ	12.02 AW	18.73 TQ	NJBLS	10/01-12/01
	New Mexico	H	7.23 FQ	10.97 AW	15.32 TQ	NMBLS	10/01-12/01
	New York	H	6.26 FQ	10.54 AW	16.41 TQ	NYBLS	10/01-12/01
	North Carolina	H	7.58 FQ	11.21 AW	15.92 TQ	NCBLS	10/01-12/01
	North Dakota	H	7.55 FQ	10.83 AW	16.31 TQ	NDBLS	10/01-12/01

AAW	Average annual wage	**AOH**	Average offered, high	**ASH**	Average starting, high	**H**	Hourly	**M**	Monthly	**S**	Special: hourly and annual
AE	Average entry wage	**AOL**	Average offered, low	**ASL**	Average starting, low	**HI**	Highest wage paid	**MTC**	Median total compensation	**TQ**	Third quartile wage
AEX	Average experienced wage	**APH**	Average pay, high range	**AW**	Average wage paid	**HR**	High end range	**MW**	Median wage paid	**W**	Weekly
AO	Average offered	**APL**	Average pay, low range	**FQ**	First quartile wage	**LR**	Low end range	**SQ**	Second quartile wage	**Y**	Yearly

Occupation/Type/Industry	Location	Per	Low	Mid	High	Source	Date
Team Assembler	Ohio	H	7.92 FQ	12.43 AW	17.62 TQ	OHBLS	10/01-12/01
	Oklahoma	H	7.08 FQ	11.64 AW	20.10 TQ	OKBLS	10/01-12/01
	Oregon	H	7.67 FQ	10.96 AW	15.49 TQ	ORBLS	10/01-12/01
	Pennsylvania	H	7.40 FQ	11.26 AW	16.42 TQ	PABLS	10/01-12/01
	Rhode Island	H	6.88 FQ	9.82 AW	14.09 TQ	RIBLS	10/01-12/01
	South Carolina	H	8.22 FQ	13.07 AW	23.02 TQ	SCBLS	10/01-12/01
	South Dakota	H	7.23 FQ	9.36 AW	12.01 TQ	SDBLS	10/01-12/01
	Tennessee	H	7.90 FQ	11.96 AW	16.40 TQ	TNBLS	10/01-12/01
	Texas	H	6.48 FQ	9.82 AW	14.07 TQ	TXBLS	10/01-12/01
	Utah	H	7.54 FQ	10.57 AW	14.06 TQ	UTBLS	10/01-12/01
	Vermont	H	7.07 FQ	10.97 AW	16.81 TQ	VTBLS	10/01-12/01
	Virginia	H	7.52 FQ	11.19 AW	15.54 TQ	VABLS	10/01-12/01
	Washington	H	8.03 FQ	12.10 AW	17.51 TQ	WABLS	10/01-12/01
	West Virginia	H	6.73 FQ	9.78 AW	13.57 TQ	WVBLS	10/01-12/01
	Wisconsin	H	7.78 FQ	12.09 AW	16.97 TQ	WIBLS	10/01-12/01
	Wyoming	H	6.52 FQ	10.29 AW	15.92 TQ	WYBLS	10/01-12/01
	Puerto Rico	H	5.70 FQ	7.67 AW	10.39 TQ	PRBLS	10/01-12/01
	Guam	H	7.41 FQ	10.10 AW	14.42 TQ	GUBLS	10/01-12/01
Technical Writer	Alabama	Y	22280 FQ	41090 AW	57850 TQ	ALBLS	10/01-12/01
	Birmingham MSA, AL	Y	21530 FQ	41360 AW	64150 TQ	ALBLS	10/01-12/01
	Huntsville MSA, AL	Y	28990 FQ	43240 AW	58330 TQ	ALBLS	10/01-12/01
	Mobile MSA, AL	Y	24120 FQ	40450 AW	56100 TQ	ALBLS	10/01-12/01
	Montgomery MSA, AL	Y	20970 FQ	37110 AW	53050 TQ	ALBLS	10/01-12/01
	Arizona	Y	23980 FQ	46360 AW	70130 TQ	AZBLS	10/01-12/01
	Phoenix-Mesa MSA, AZ	Y	23290 FQ	46260 AW	70490 TQ	AZBLS	10/01-12/01
	Tucson MSA, AZ	Y	25830 FQ	45770 AW	69590 TQ	AZBLS	10/01-12/01
	Arkansas	Y	26580 FQ	44020 AW	63430 TQ	ARBLS	10/01-12/01
	Fayetteville-Springdale-Rogers MSA, AR	Y	30700 FQ	45610 AW	64740 TQ	ARBLS	10/01-12/01
	Little Rock-North Little Rock MSA, AR	Y	27310 FQ	44650 AW	58630 TQ	ARBLS	10/01-12/01
	California	Y	34860 FQ	61350 AW	91980 TQ	CABLS	10/01-12/01
	Bakersfield MSA, CA	Y	38920 FQ	57410 AW	77930 TQ	CABLS	10/01-12/01
	Fresno MSA, CA	Y	36630 FQ	58450 AW	95770 TQ	CABLS	10/01-12/01
	Los Angeles-Long Beach PMSA, CA	Y	44870 FQ	58040 AW	73060 TQ	CABLS	10/01-12/01
	Oakland PMSA, CA	Y	40860 FQ	63110 AW	93270 TQ	CABLS	10/01-12/01
	Orange County PMSA, CA	Y	39030 FQ	59850 AW	84100 TQ	CABLS	10/01-12/01
	Riverside-San Bernardino PMSA, CA	Y	24730 FQ	42910 AW	78700 TQ	CABLS	10/01-12/01
	Sacramento PMSA, CA	Y	19240 FQ	35720 AW	67140 TQ	CABLS	10/01-12/01
	San Diego MSA, CA	Y	36850 FQ	53580 AW	74050 TQ	CABLS	10/01-12/01
	San Francisco PMSA, CA	Y	46710 FQ	74650 AW	112790 TQ	CABLS	10/01-12/01
	San Jose PMSA, CA	Y	42720 FQ	71230 AW	110650 TQ	CABLS	10/01-12/01
	San Luis Obispo-Atascadero-Paso Robles MSA, CA	Y	29650 FQ	52380 AW	86800 TQ	CABLS	10/01-12/01
	Santa Barbara-Santa Maria-Lompoc MSA, CA	Y	33380 FQ	53730 AW	80400 TQ	CABLS	10/01-12/01
	Santa Cruz-Watsonville PMSA, CA	Y	42600 FQ	66590 AW	101040 TQ	CABLS	10/01-12/01
	Santa Rosa PMSA, CA	Y	41130 FQ	65290 AW	101600 TQ	CABLS	10/01-12/01
	Ventura PMSA, CA	Y	36030 FQ	54130 AW	70850 TQ	CABLS	10/01-12/01
	Colorado	Y	33110 FQ	49920 AW	67600 TQ	COBLS	10/01-12/01
	Boulder-Longmont PMSA, CO	Y	29840 FQ	52590 AW	73490 TQ	COBLS	10/01-12/01
	Colorado Springs MSA, CO	Y	31320 FQ	48320 AW	69270 TQ	COBLS	10/01-12/01
	Denver PMSA, CO	Y	35380 FQ	49850 AW	64730 TQ	COBLS	10/01-12/01
	Fort Collins-Loveland MSA, CO	Y	32290 FQ	52870 AW	69890 TQ	COBLS	10/01-12/01
	Connecticut	Y	36260 FQ	52270 AW	72900 TQ	CTBLS	10/01-12/01
	Bridgeport PMSA, CT	Y	36650 FQ	50290 AW	68090 TQ	CTBLS	10/01-12/01
	Danbury PMSA, CT	Y	32460 FQ	44900 AW	59810 TQ	CTBLS	10/01-12/01
	Hartford MSA, CT	Y	35090 FQ	52160 AW	73090 TQ	CTBLS	10/01-12/01
	New Haven-Meriden PMSA, CT	Y	38250 FQ	54720 AW	73350 TQ	CTBLS	10/01-12/01
	Stamford-Norwalk PMSA, CT	Y	40340 FQ	58460 AW	77220 TQ	CTBLS	10/01-12/01
	Delaware	Y	30170 FQ	49540 AW	75380 TQ	DEBLS	10/01-12/01
	Wilmington-Newark PMSA, DE-MD	Y	30610 FQ	50260 AW	74970 TQ	DEBLS	10/01-12/01
	District of Columbia	Y	31640 FQ	53950 AW	79160 TQ	DCBLS	10/01-12/01
	Washington PMSA, DC-MD-VA-WV	Y	28500 FQ	52160 AW	77270 TQ	DCBLS	10/01-12/01
	Florida	Y	26050 FQ	41350 AW	58260 TQ	FLBLS	10/01-12/01

AAW Average annual wage	**AOH** Average offered, high	**ASH** Average starting, high	**H** Hourly	**M** Monthly	**S** Special: hourly and annual
AE Average entry wage	**AOL** Average offered, low	**ASL** Average starting, low	**HI** Highest wage paid	**MTC** Median total compensation	**TQ** Third quartile wage
AEX Average experienced wage	**APH** Average pay, high range	**AW** Average wage paid	**HR** High end range	**MW** Median wage paid	**W** Weekly
AO Average offered	**APL** Average pay, low range	**FQ** First quartile wage	**LR** Low end range	**SQ** Second quartile wage	**Y** Yearly

Occupation/Type/Industry	Location	Per	Low	Mid	High	Source	Date
Technical Writer	Fort Lauderdale PMSA, FL	Y	32630 FQ	46920 AW	63960 TQ	FLBLS	10/01-12/01
	Fort Walton Beach MSA, FL	Y	24090 FQ	35670 AW	45380 TQ	FLBLS	10/01-12/01
	Gainesville MSA, FL	Y	27020 FQ	38580 AW	51580 TQ	FLBLS	10/01-12/01
	Jacksonville MSA, FL	Y	29010 FQ	38210 AW	53050 TQ	FLBLS	10/01-12/01
	Melbourne-Titusville-Palm Bay MSA, FL	Y	28550 FQ	42960 AW	63700 TQ	FLBLS	10/01-12/01
	Miami PMSA, FL	Y	26440 FQ	42640 AW	57840 TQ	FLBLS	10/01-12/01
	Orlando MSA, FL	Y	23220 FQ	37910 AW	59990 TQ	FLBLS	10/01-12/01
	Pensacola MSA, FL	Y	31400 FQ	39680 AW	48090 TQ	FLBLS	10/01-12/01
	Sarasota-Bradenton MSA, FL	Y	31160 FQ	40570 AW	53370 TQ	FLBLS	10/01-12/01
	Tampa-St. Petersburg-Clearwater MSA, FL	Y	28640 FQ	42710 AW	58270 TQ	FLBLS	10/01-12/01
	West Palm Beach-Boca Raton MSA, FL	Y	29400 FQ	45600 AW	61080 TQ	FLBLS	10/01-12/01
	Georgia	Y	27680 FQ	50480 AW	78620 TQ	GABLS	10/01-12/01
	Atlanta MSA, GA	Y	32280 FQ	53910 AW	81370 TQ	GABLS	10/01-12/01
	Columbus MSA, GA-AL	Y	33070 FQ	48390 AW	70010 TQ	GABLS	10/01-12/01
	Macon MSA, GA	Y	21500 FQ	40670 AW	64810 TQ	GABLS	10/01-12/01
	Savannah MSA, GA	Y	24530 FQ	39560 AW	52460 TQ	GABLS	10/01-12/01
	Hawaii	Y	25640 FQ	44720 AW	60680 TQ	HIBLS	10/01-12/01
	Honolulu MSA, HI	Y	29190 FQ	46710 AW	60340 TQ	HIBLS	10/01-12/01
	Idaho	Y	31470 FQ	44820 AW	59280 TQ	IDBLS	10/01-12/01
	Boise City MSA, ID	Y	30780 FQ	39260 AW	51960 TQ	IDBLS	10/01-12/01
	Illinois	Y	29430 FQ	48920 AW	73970 TQ	ILBLS	10/01-12/01
	Chicago PMSA, IL	Y	30020 FQ	50530 AW	78220 TQ	ILBLS	10/01-12/01
	Rockford MSA, IL	Y	30550 FQ	44720 AW	58070 TQ	ILBLS	10/01-12/01
	Indiana	Y	28050 FQ	46790 AW	70170 TQ	INBLS	10/01-12/01
	Fort Wayne MSA, IN	Y	30330 FQ	46120 AW	66160 TQ	INBLS	10/01-12/01
	Indianapolis MSA, IN	Y	27530 FQ	51070 AW	87580 TQ	INBLS	10/01-12/01
	Iowa	Y	23480 FQ	38550 AW	57350 TQ	IABLS	10/01-12/01
	Davenport-Moline-Rock Island MSA, IA-IL	Y	30670 FQ	45120 AW	64910 TQ	IABLS	10/01-12/01
	Des Moines MSA, IA	Y	25840 FQ	40330 AW	61130 TQ	IABLS	10/01-12/01
	Kansas	Y	29610 FQ	44200 AW	61160 TQ	KSBLS	10/01-12/01
	Wichita MSA, KS	Y	31980 FQ	44150 AW	56160 TQ	KSBLS	10/01-12/01
	Kentucky	Y	31510 FQ	47030 AW	66700 TQ	KYBLS	10/01-12/01
	Lexington MSA, KY	Y	31390 FQ	49080 AW	70460 TQ	KYBLS	10/01-12/01
	Louisville MSA, KY-IN	Y	33620 FQ	47960 AW	66930 TQ	KYBLS	10/01-12/01
	Louisiana	Y	18260 FQ	36670 AW	55170 TQ	LABLS	10/01-12/01
	Maine	Y	30880 FQ	47800 AW	72890 TQ	MEBLS	10/01-12/01
	Maryland	Y	34630 FQ	55670 AW	84190 TQ	MDBLS	10/01-12/01
	Baltimore PMSA, MD	Y	34140 FQ	52550 AW	71920 TQ	MDBLS	10/01-12/01
	Massachusetts	Y	38860 FQ	60150 AW	87120 TQ	MABLS	10/01-12/01
	Boston PMSA, MA-NH	Y	39320 FQ	59940 AW	86920 TQ	MABLS	10/01-12/01
	Lawrence PMSA, MA-NH	Y	37490 FQ	64270 AW	90310 TQ	MABLS	10/01-12/01
	Lowell PMSA, MA-NH	Y	40190 FQ	62570 AW	87150 TQ	MABLS	10/01-12/01
	Worcester PMSA, MA-CT	Y	39200 FQ	59280 AW	83970 TQ	MABLS	10/01-12/01
	Michigan	Y	31780 FQ	48130 AW	68710 TQ	MIBLS	10/01-12/01
	Ann Arbor PMSA, MI	Y	30400 FQ	47040 AW	66990 TQ	MIBLS	10/01-12/01
	Detroit PMSA, MI	Y	31950 FQ	51050 AW	73370 TQ	MIBLS	10/01-12/01
	Flint PMSA, MI	Y	35560 FQ	41280 AW	48140 TQ	MIBLS	10/01-12/01
	Grand Rapids-Muskegon-Holland MSA, MI	Y	29240 FQ	42140 AW	58380 TQ	MIBLS	10/01-12/01
	Kalamazoo-Battle Creek MSA, MI	Y	31030 FQ	41700 AW	55570 TQ	MIBLS	10/01-12/01
	Minnesota	Y	33640 FQ	51040 AW	70220 TQ	MNBLS	10/01-12/01
	Duluth-Superior MSA, MN-WI	Y	18760 FQ	33580 AW	56210 TQ	MNBLS	10/01-12/01
	Minneapolis-St. Paul MSA, MN-WI	Y	36270 FQ	52840 AW	70990 TQ	MNBLS	10/01-12/01
	Mississippi	Y	24690 FQ	39540 AW	54500 TQ	MSBLS	10/01-12/01
	Missouri	Y	25210 FQ	42220 AW	64110 TQ	MOBLS	10/01-12/01
	Kansas City MSA, MO-KS	Y	29420 FQ	45730 AW	68280 TQ	MOBLS	10/01-12/01
	St. Louis MSA, MO-IL	Y	26420 FQ	42480 AW	63480 TQ	MOBLS	10/01-12/01
	Montana	Y	25410 FQ	42400 AW	66720 TQ	MTBLS	10/01-12/01
	Nebraska	Y	26360 FQ	41480 AW	61870 TQ	NEBLS	10/01-12/01
	Omaha MSA, NE-IA	Y	28410 FQ	41550 AW	58550 TQ	NEBLS	10/01-12/01
	Nevada	Y	29860 FQ	43590 AW	58880 TQ	NVBLS	10/01-12/01
	Las Vegas MSA, NV-AZ	Y	30260 FQ	45040 AW	59080 TQ	NVBLS	10/01-12/01
	Reno MSA, NV	Y	30110 FQ	41630 AW	63120 TQ	NVBLS	10/01-12/01
	New Hampshire	Y	35700 FQ	55950 AW	88510 TQ	NHBLS	10/01-12/01
	Manchester PMSA, NH	Y	35290 FQ	61500 AW	91390 TQ	NHBLS	10/01-12/01
	Nashua PMSA, NH	Y	38950 FQ	60780 AW	88760 TQ	NHBLS	10/01-12/01

AAW	Average annual wage	**AOH**	Average offered, high	**ASH**	Average starting, high	**H**	Hourly	**M**	Monthly	**S**	Special: hourly and annual
AE	Average entry wage	**AOL**	Average offered, low	**ASL**	Average starting, low	**HI**	Highest wage paid	**MTC**	Median total compensation	**TQ**	Third quartile wage
AEX	Average experienced wage	**APH**	Average pay, high range	**AW**	Average wage paid	**HR**	High end range	**MW**	Median wage paid	**W**	Weekly
AO	Average offered	**APL**	Average pay, low range	**FQ**	First quartile wage	**LR**	Low end range	**SQ**	Second quartile wage	**Y**	Yearly

Occupation/Type/Industry	Location	Per	Low	Mid	High	Source	Date
Technical Writer	Portsmouth-Rochester PMSA, NH-ME	Y	28390 FQ	46150 AW	65740 TQ	NHBLS	10/01-12/01
	New Jersey	Y	37200 FQ	60760 AW	100450 TQ	NJBLS	10/01-12/01
	Atlantic-Cape May PMSA, NJ	Y	25550 FQ	47400 AW	71390 TQ	NJBLS	10/01-12/01
	Bergen-Passaic PMSA, NJ	Y	36940 FQ	60490 AW	96490 TQ	NJBLS	10/01-12/01
	Jersey City PMSA, NJ	Y	38750 FQ	56750 AW	82320 TQ	NJBLS	10/01-12/01
	Middlesex-Somerset-Hunterdon PMSA, NJ	Y	38740 FQ	68630 AW	113330 TQ	NJBLS	10/01-12/01
	Monmouth-Ocean PMSA, NJ	Y	37790 FQ	63460 AW	104320 TQ	NJBLS	10/01-12/01
	Newark PMSA, NJ	Y	36530 FQ	60870 AW	98200 TQ	NJBLS	10/01-12/01
	Trenton PMSA, NJ	Y	37940 FQ	58640 AW	87750 TQ	NJBLS	10/01-12/01
	New Mexico	Y	29590 FQ	46520 AW	61180 TQ	NMBLS	10/01-12/01
	Albuquerque MSA, NM	Y	30430 FQ	47340 AW	62440 TQ	NMBLS	10/01-12/01
	New York	Y	32180 FQ	55770 AW	89190 TQ	NYBLS	10/01-12/01
	Albany-Schenectady-Troy MSA, NY	Y	30610 FQ	46170 AW	65530 TQ	NYBLS	10/01-12/01
	Binghamton MSA, NY	Y	29260 FQ	43680 AW	59820 TQ	NYBLS	10/01-12/01
	Buffalo-Niagara Falls MSA, NY	Y	24430 FQ	43110 AW	65310 TQ	NYBLS	10/01-12/01
	Nassau-Suffolk PMSA, NY	Y	35350 FQ	63070 AW	100570 TQ	NYBLS	10/01-12/01
	New York PMSA, NY	Y	36180 FQ	61010 AW	94990 TQ	NYBLS	10/01-12/01
	Rochester MSA, NY	Y	32440 FQ	49180 AW	68510 TQ	NYBLS	10/01-12/01
	Syracuse MSA, NY	Y	27110 FQ	45420 AW	70140 TQ	NYBLS	10/01-12/01
	North Carolina	Y	32690 FQ	53170 AW	74340 TQ	NCBLS	10/01-12/01
	Charlotte-Gastonia-Rock Hill MSA, NC-SC	Y	33480 FQ	47650 AW	65220 TQ	NCBLS	10/01-12/01
	Greensboro-Winston-Salem-High Point MSA, NC	Y	33510 FQ	53860 AW	72880 TQ	NCBLS	10/01-12/01
	Raleigh-Durham-Chapel Hill MSA, NC	Y	37150 FQ	57550 AW	81820 TQ	NCBLS	10/01-12/01
	North Dakota	Y	25180 FQ	38650 AW	55230 TQ	NDBLS	10/01-12/01
	Fargo-Moorhead MSA, ND-MN	Y	25340 FQ	38960 AW	54820 TQ	NDBLS	10/01-12/01
	Ohio	Y	25040 FQ	43250 AW	60620 TQ	OHBLS	10/01-12/01
	Akron PMSA, OH	Y	28290 FQ	46590 AW	68040 TQ	OHBLS	10/01-12/01
	Cincinnati PMSA, OH-KY-IN	Y	29390 FQ	47670 AW	66100 TQ	OHBLS	10/01-12/01
	Cleveland-Lorain-Elyria PMSA, OH	Y	22080 FQ	38940 AW	55960 TQ	OHBLS	10/01-12/01
	Columbus MSA, OH	Y	22960 FQ	45850 AW	62090 TQ	OHBLS	10/01-12/01
	Dayton-Springfield MSA, OH	Y	24610 FQ	37110 AW	54310 TQ	OHBLS	10/01-12/01
	Hamilton-Middletown PMSA, OH	Y	25470 FQ	48890 AW	130980 TQ	OHBLS	10/01-12/01
	Toledo MSA, OH	Y	33020 FQ	47300 AW	59200 TQ	OHBLS	10/01-12/01
	Oklahoma	Y	24880 FQ	39050 AW	53800 TQ	OKBLS	10/01-12/01
	Oklahoma City MSA, OK	Y	26280 FQ	38400 AW	50570 TQ	OKBLS	10/01-12/01
	Tulsa MSA, OK	Y	24010 FQ	42300 AW	60330 TQ	OKBLS	10/01-12/01
	Oregon	Y	28950 FQ	50310 AW	75870 TQ	ORBLS	10/01-12/01
	Eugene-Springfield MSA, OR	Y	25230 FQ	37800 AW	54260 TQ	ORBLS	10/01-12/01
	Portland-Vancouver PMSA, OR-WA	Y	30790 FQ	53080 AW	78110 TQ	ORBLS	10/01-12/01
	Pennsylvania	Y	28290 FQ	46190 AW	69900 TQ	PABLS	10/01-12/01
	Allentown-Bethlehem-Easton MSA, PA	Y	26480 FQ	42470 AW	58150 TQ	PABLS	10/01-12/01
	Harrisburg-Lebanon-Carlisle MSA, PA	Y	23010 FQ	41830 AW	58200 TQ	PABLS	10/01-12/01
	Lancaster MSA, PA	Y	30540 FQ	48700 AW	69440 TQ	PABLS	10/01-12/01
	Philadelphia PMSA, PA-NJ	Y	31260 FQ	52210 AW	79010 TQ	PABLS	10/01-12/01
	Pittsburgh MSA, PA	Y	27830 FQ	41710 AW	57670 TQ	PABLS	10/01-12/01
	Scranton-Wilkes-Barre-Hazleton MSA, PA	Y	23970 FQ	42500 AW	64570 TQ	PABLS	10/01-12/01
	Rhode Island	Y	33790 FQ	49720 AW	70280 TQ	RIBLS	10/01-12/01
	Providence-Fall River-Warwick MSA, RI-MA	Y	31960 FQ	52200 AW	80470 TQ	RIBLS	10/01-12/01
	South Carolina	Y	29590 FQ	45210 AW	66140 TQ	SCBLS	10/01-12/01
	Charleston-North Charleston MSA, SC	Y	25540 FQ	40820 AW	59470 TQ	SCBLS	10/01-12/01
	Greenville-Spartanburg-Anderson MSA, SC	Y	31160 FQ	42760 AW	57440 TQ	SCBLS	10/01-12/01
	South Dakota	Y	22800 FQ	34950 AW	45290 TQ	SDBLS	10/01-12/01
	Tennessee	Y	17180 FQ	41040 AW	64020 TQ	TNBLS	10/01-12/01
	Knoxville MSA, TN	Y	30020 FQ	48330 AW	69060 TQ	TNBLS	10/01-12/01
	Memphis MSA, TN-AR-MS	Y	24440 FQ	42820 AW	62520 TQ	TNBLS	10/01-12/01

AAW	Average annual wage	AOH	Average offered, high	ASH	Average starting, high	H	Hourly	M	Monthly	S	Special: hourly and annual
AE	Average entry wage	AOL	Average offered, low	ASL	Average starting, low	HI	Highest wage paid	MTC	Median total compensation	TQ	Third quartile wage
AEX	Average experienced wage	APH	Average pay, high range	AW	Average wage paid	HR	High end range	MW	Median wage paid	W	Weekly
AO	Average offered	APL	Average pay, low range	FQ	First quartile wage	LR	Low end range	SQ	Second quartile wage	Y	Yearly

Occupation/Type/Industry	Location	Per	Low	Mid	High	Source	Date
Technical Writer	Nashville MSA, TN	Y	26600 FQ	45480 AW	64360 TQ	TNBLS	10/01-12/01
	Texas	Y	29480 FQ	48430 AW	71510 TQ	TXBLS	10/01-12/01
	Austin-San Marcos MSA, TX	Y	31710 FQ	51750 AW	71550 TQ	TXBLS	10/01-12/01
	Brazoria PMSA, TX	Y	24090 FQ	32510 AW	53350 TQ	TXBLS	10/01-12/01
	Dallas PMSA, TX	Y	33640 FQ	53860 AW	78920 TQ	TXBLS	10/01-12/01
	El Paso MSA, TX	Y	24100 FQ	45000 AW	63860 TQ	TXBLS	10/01-12/01
	Fort Worth-Arlington PMSA, TX	Y	34240 FQ	52390 AW	73880 TQ	TXBLS	10/01-12/01
	Houston PMSA, TX	Y	29400 FQ	45410 AW	67940 TQ	TXBLS	10/01-12/01
	Killeen-Temple MSA, TX	Y	16510 FQ	32720 AW	49920 TQ	TXBLS	10/01-12/01
	San Antonio MSA, TX	Y	28180 FQ	43980 AW	66870 TQ	TXBLS	10/01-12/01
	Utah	Y	28910 FQ	45900 AW	67450 TQ	UTBLS	10/01-12/01
	Provo-Orem MSA, UT	Y	29730 FQ	46050 AW	66380 TQ	UTBLS	10/01-12/01
	Salt Lake City-Ogden MSA, UT	Y	28960 FQ	46430 AW	69200 TQ	UTBLS	10/01-12/01
	Vermont	Y	24410 FQ	39890 AW	66930 TQ	VTBLS	10/01-12/01
	Burlington MSA, VT	Y	24410 FQ	39620 AW	64050 TQ	VTBLS	10/01-12/01
	Virginia	Y	25810 FQ	48290 AW	71230 TQ	VABLS	10/01-12/01
	Lynchburg MSA, VA	Y	20420 FQ	35950 AW	62400 TQ	VABLS	10/01-12/01
	Norfolk-Virginia Beach-Newport News MSA, VA-NC	Y	26790 FQ	42760 AW	60130 TQ	VABLS	10/01-12/01
	Richmond-Petersburg MSA, VA	Y	32720 FQ	48230 AW	63410 TQ	VABLS	10/01-12/01
	Roanoke MSA, VA	Y	27710 FQ	48550 AW	70980 TQ	VABLS	10/01-12/01
	Washington	Y	38010 FQ	61550 AW	87120 TQ	WABLS	10/01-12/01
	Richland-Kennewick-Pasco MSA, WA	Y	32780 FQ	50640 AW	71160 TQ	WABLS	10/01-12/01
	Seattle-Bellevue-Everett PMSA, WA	Y	40470 FQ	63340 AW	88010 TQ	WABLS	10/01-12/01
	Spokane MSA, WA	Y	27550 FQ	43650 AW	65100 TQ	WABLS	10/01-12/01
	West Virginia	Y	24820 FQ	43710 AW	56440 TQ	WVBLS	10/01-12/01
	Wisconsin	Y	31520 FQ	51270 AW	80710 TQ	WIBLS	10/01-12/01
	Appleton-Oshkosh-Neenah MSA, WI	Y	31120 FQ	46620 AW	59790 TQ	WIBLS	10/01-12/01
	Green Bay MSA, WI	Y	30350 FQ	40110 AW	44960 TQ	WIBLS	10/01-12/01
	Madison MSA, WI	Y	32920 FQ	45230 AW	58650 TQ	WIBLS	10/01-12/01
	Milwaukee-Waukesha PMSA, WI	Y	35600 FQ	50590 AW	71510 TQ	WIBLS	10/01-12/01
	Puerto Rico	Y	20000 FQ	35900 AW	52930 TQ	PRBLS	10/01-12/01
Technical Writer and Programmer	Puget Sound, WA	Y		50000 AW	65000 HR	PSBJ	1/99-1/00
Technician							
Quality Control	United States	Y			120000 HI	ASQ	1/00-1/01
Telecommunications Equipment Installer and Repairer							
Except Line Installer	Alabama	H	10.05 FQ	18.62 AW	26.06 TQ	ALBLS	10/01-12/01
Except Line Installer	Alaska	H	16.96 FQ	27.79 AW	35.84 TQ	AKBLS	10/01-12/01
Except Line Installer	Arizona	H	12.81 FQ	21.35 AW	27.48 TQ	AZBLS	10/01-12/01
Except Line Installer	Arkansas	H	11.71 FQ	19.75 AW	26.46 TQ	ARBLS	10/01-12/01
Except Line Installer	California	H	13.32 FQ	21.30 AW	27.34 TQ	CABLS	10/01-12/01
Except Line Installer	Colorado	H	16.19 FQ	22.89 AW	28.26 TQ	COBLS	10/01-12/01
Except Line Installer	Connecticut	H	11.71 FQ	20.83 AW	28.26 TQ	CTBLS	10/01-12/01
Except Line Installer	Delaware	H	9.82 FQ	18.21 AW	25.86 TQ	DEBLS	10/01-12/01
Except Line Installer	Florida	H	12.05 FQ	18.99 AW	26.13 TQ	FLBLS	10/01-12/01
Except Line Installer	Georgia	H	13.58 FQ	19.89 AW	25.89 TQ	GABLS	10/01-12/01
Except Line Installer	Hawaii	H	16.26 FQ	22.16 AW	27.62 TQ	HIBLS	10/01-12/01
Except Line Installer	Idaho	H	12.50 FQ	21.53 AW	27.08 TQ	IDBLS	10/01-12/01
Except Line Installer	Illinois	H	14.95 FQ	21.30 AW	26.63 TQ	ILBLS	10/01-12/01
Except Line Installer	Indiana	H	14.45 FQ	20.23 AW	26.10 TQ	INBLS	10/01-12/01
Except Line Installer	Iowa	H	11.90 FQ	20.72 AW	27.02 TQ	IABLS	10/01-12/01
Except Line Installer	Kansas	H	11.86 FQ	20.14 AW	26.99 TQ	KSBLS	10/01-12/01
Except Line Installer	Kentucky	H	11.48 FQ	18.86 AW	25.86 TQ	KYBLS	10/01-12/01
Except Line Installer	Louisiana	H	12.09 FQ	18.39 AW	24.65 TQ	LABLS	10/01-12/01
Except Line Installer	Maine	H	11.60 FQ	21.76 AW	30.41 TQ	MEBLS	10/01-12/01
Except Line Installer	Maryland	H	16.05 FQ	23.28 AW	29.83 TQ	MDBLS	10/01-12/01
Except Line Installer	Massachusetts	H	15.57 FQ	25.94 AW	35.07 TQ	MABLS	10/01-12/01
Except Line Installer	Michigan	H	13.06 FQ	20.05 AW	26.29 TQ	MIBLS	10/01-12/01

AAW	Average annual wage	**AOH**	Average offered, high	**ASH**	Average starting, high	**H**	Hourly	**M**	Monthly	**S**	Special: hourly and annual
AE	Average entry wage	**AOL**	Average offered, low	**ASL**	Average starting, low	**HI**	Highest wage paid	**MTC**	Median total compensation	**TQ**	Third quartile wage
AEX	Average experienced wage	**APH**	Average pay, high range	**AW**	Average wage paid	**HR**	High end range	**MW**	Median wage paid	**W**	Weekly
AO	Average offered	**APL**	Average pay, low range	**FQ**	First quartile wage	**LR**	Low end range	**SQ**	Second quartile wage	**Y**	Yearly

Occupation/Type/Industry	Location	Per	Low	Mid	High	Source	Date
Telecommunications Equipment Installer and Repairer							
Except Line Installer	Minnesota	H	18.15 FQ	23.09 AW	27.30 TQ	MNBLS	10/01-12/01
Except Line Installer	Mississippi	H	9.29 FQ	16.36 AW	24.60 TQ	MSBLS	10/01-12/01
Except Line Installer	Missouri	H	11.89 FQ	20.02 AW	26.86 TQ	MOBLS	10/01-12/01
Except Line Installer	Montana	H	9.59 FQ	19.04 AW	26.96 TQ	MTBLS	10/01-12/01
Except Line Installer	Nebraska	H	12.13 FQ	20.34 AW	26.76 TQ	NEBLS	10/01-12/01
Except Line Installer	Nevada	H	11.59 FQ	19.84 AW	26.97 TQ	NVBLS	10/01-12/01
Except Line Installer	New Hampshire	H	15.10 FQ	23.80 AW	29.98 TQ	NHBLS	10/01-12/01
Except Line Installer	New Jersey	H	17.88 FQ	24.23 AW	30.57 TQ	NJBLS	10/01-12/01
Except Line Installer	New Mexico	H	12.54 FQ	22.43 AW	33.76 TQ	NMBLS	10/01-12/01
Except Line Installer	New York	H	17.34 FQ	25.61 AW	33.30 TQ	NYBLS	10/01-12/01
Except Line Installer	North Carolina	H	14.06 FQ	20.29 AW	26.70 TQ	NCBLS	10/01-12/01
Except Line Installer	North Dakota	H	16.33 FQ	20.44 AW	25.09 TQ	NDBLS	10/01-12/01
Except Line Installer	Ohio	H	12.36 FQ	19.40 AW	25.81 TQ	OHBLS	10/01-12/01
Except Line Installer	Oklahoma	H	15.03 FQ	21.46 AW	27.38 TQ	OKBLS	10/01-12/01
Except Line Installer	Oregon	H	14.21 FQ	21.84 AW	27.03 TQ	ORBLS	10/01-12/01
Except Line Installer	Pennsylvania	H	12.90 FQ	20.94 AW	26.97 TQ	PABLS	10/01-12/01
Except Line Installer	Rhode Island	H	12.08 FQ	23.72 AW	33.50 TQ	RIBLS	10/01-12/01
Except Line Installer	South Carolina	H	11.91 FQ	16.76 AW	22.76 TQ	SCBLS	10/01-12/01
Except Line Installer	South Dakota	H	14.50 FQ	20.51 AW	26.41 TQ	SDBLS	10/01-12/01
Except Line Installer	Tennessee	H	13.10 FQ	19.61 AW	25.70 TQ	TNBLS	10/01-12/01
Except Line Installer	Texas	H	10.31 FQ	19.25 AW	27.18 TQ	TXBLS	10/01-12/01
Except Line Installer	Utah	H	16.10 FQ	22.75 AW	27.37 TQ	UTBLS	10/01-12/01
Except Line Installer	Vermont	H	14.16 FQ	21.75 AW	29.21 TQ	VTBLS	10/01-12/01
Except Line Installer	Virginia	H	12.27 FQ	21.07 AW	27.46 TQ	VABLS	10/01-12/01
Except Line Installer	Washington	H	15.85 FQ	22.74 AW	27.61 TQ	WABLS	10/01-12/01
Except Line Installer	West Virginia	H	12.46 FQ	21.85 AW	28.88 TQ	WVBLS	10/01-12/01
Except Line Installer	Wisconsin	H	11.40 FQ	18.34 AW	25.91 TQ	WIBLS	10/01-12/01
Except Line Installer	Wyoming	H	12.55 FQ	20.53 AW	26.69 TQ	WYBLS	10/01-12/01
Except Line Installer	Puerto Rico	H	8.22 FQ	15.77 AW	26.05 TQ	PRBLS	10/01-12/01
Except Line Installer	Virgin Islands	H	12.22 FQ	16.32 AW	20.73 TQ	VIBLS	10/01-12/01
Except Line Installer	Guam	H	14.71 FQ	23.86 AW	33.31 TQ	GUBLS	10/01-12/01
Telecommunications Line Installer and Repairer	Alabama	H	8.90 FQ	15.39 AW	21.86 TQ	ALBLS	10/01-12/01
	Birmingham MSA, AL	H	9.14 FQ	14.27 AW	20.57 TQ	ALBLS	10/01-12/01
	Huntsville MSA, AL	H	9.78 FQ	16.92 AW	22.31 TQ	ALBLS	10/01-12/01
	Mobile MSA, AL	H	9.03 FQ	15.64 AW	21.80 TQ	ALBLS	10/01-12/01
	Montgomery MSA, AL	H	7.80 FQ	12.59 AW	20.47 TQ	ALBLS	10/01-12/01
	Alaska	H	12.38 FQ	22.04 AW	34.35 TQ	AKBLS	10/01-12/01
	Anchorage MSA, AK	H	13.11 FQ	23.99 AW	35.52 TQ	AKBLS	10/01-12/01
	Arizona	H	9.13 FQ	14.38 AW	21.43 TQ	AZBLS	10/01-12/01
	Phoenix-Mesa MSA, AZ	H	9.13 FQ	14.38 AW	21.38 TQ	AZBLS	10/01-12/01
	Tucson MSA, AZ	H	9.03 FQ	13.89 AW	21.31 TQ	AZBLS	10/01-12/01
	Arkansas	H	8.64 FQ	14.45 AW	24.69 TQ	ARBLS	10/01-12/01
	Fort Smith MSA, AR-OK	H	10.14 FQ	20.50 AW	26.44 TQ	ARBLS	10/01-12/01
	Little Rock-North Little Rock MSA, AR	H	9.12 FQ	12.59 AW	21.91 TQ	ARBLS	10/01-12/01
	California	H	11.98 FQ	20.90 AW	27.47 TQ	CABLS	10/01-12/01
	Bakersfield MSA, CA	H	10.41 FQ	22.00 AW	27.63 TQ	CABLS	10/01-12/01
	Fresno MSA, CA	H	18.37 FQ	23.17 AW	27.65 TQ	CABLS	10/01-12/01
	Los Angeles-Long Beach PMSA, CA	H	10.99 FQ	20.14 AW	27.52 TQ	CABLS	10/01-12/01
	Oakland PMSA, CA	H	15.29 FQ	23.01 AW	31.11 TQ	CABLS	10/01-12/01
	Orange County PMSA, CA	H	11.65 FQ	20.62 AW	27.31 TQ	CABLS	10/01-12/01
	Redding MSA, CA	H	10.22 FQ	19.34 AW	26.20 TQ	CABLS	10/01-12/01
	Riverside-San Bernardino PMSA, CA	H	14.29 FQ	21.45 AW	27.78 TQ	CABLS	10/01-12/01
	Sacramento PMSA, CA	H	12.49 FQ	19.45 AW	26.75 TQ	CABLS	10/01-12/01
	Salinas MSA, CA	H	21.66 FQ	23.60 AW	26.95 TQ	CABLS	10/01-12/01
	San Diego MSA, CA	H	9.89 FQ	19.76 AW	26.75 TQ	CABLS	10/01-12/01
	San Francisco PMSA, CA	H	12.82 FQ	20.90 AW	27.91 TQ	CABLS	10/01-12/01
	San Jose PMSA, CA	H	15.39 FQ	22.26 AW	27.73 TQ	CABLS	10/01-12/01
	San Luis Obispo-Atascadero-Paso Robles MSA, CA	H	14.05 FQ	22.05 AW	28.02 TQ	CABLS	10/01-12/01
	Santa Rosa PMSA, CA	H	17.28 FQ	23.40 AW	28.26 TQ	CABLS	10/01-12/01
	Stockton-Lodi MSA, CA	H	13.80 FQ	20.97 AW	26.47 TQ	CABLS	10/01-12/01
	Vallejo-Fairfield-Napa PMSA, CA	H	9.32 FQ	18.76 AW	27.03 TQ	CABLS	10/01-12/01
	Ventura PMSA, CA	H	13.13 FQ	20.15 AW	27.23 TQ	CABLS	10/01-12/01

AAW	Average annual wage	AOH	Average offered, high	ASH	Average starting, high	H	Hourly	M	Monthly	S	Special: hourly and annual
AE	Average entry wage	AOL	Average offered, low	ASL	Average starting, low	HI	Highest wage paid	MTC	Median total compensation	TQ	Third quartile wage
AEX	Average experienced wage	APH	Average pay, high range	AW	Average wage paid	HR	High end range	MW	Median wage paid	W	Weekly
AO	Average offered	APL	Average pay, low range	FQ	First quartile wage	LR	Low end range	SQ	Second quartile wage	Y	Yearly

Occupation/Type/Industry	Location	Per	Low	Mid	High	Source	Date
Telecommunications Line Installer and Repairer	Visalia-Tulare-Porterville MSA, CA	H	13.77 FQ	20.72 AW	27.20 TQ	CABLS	10/01-12/01
	Colorado	H	10.42 FQ	16.25 AW	23.95 TQ	COBLS	10/01-12/01
	Boulder-Longmont PMSA, CO	H	9.71 FQ	16.26 AW	29.02 TQ	COBLS	10/01-12/01
	Colorado Springs MSA, CO	H	10.84 FQ	18.02 AW	35.17 TQ	COBLS	10/01-12/01
	Denver PMSA, CO	H	10.38 FQ	15.56 AW	21.47 TQ	COBLS	10/01-12/01
	Fort Collins-Loveland MSA, CO	H	12.08 FQ	15.87 AW	21.00 TQ	COBLS	10/01-12/01
	Connecticut	H	10.29 FQ	18.29 AW	27.17 TQ	CTBLS	10/01-12/01
	Bridgeport PMSA, CT	H	10.86 FQ	18.73 AW	27.27 TQ	CTBLS	10/01-12/01
	Danbury PMSA, CT	H	9.58 FQ	14.95 AW	21.23 TQ	CTBLS	10/01-12/01
	Hartford MSA, CT	H	10.14 FQ	18.37 AW	27.77 TQ	CTBLS	10/01-12/01
	New Haven-Meriden PMSA, CT	H	13.87 FQ	21.10 AW	27.79 TQ	CTBLS	10/01-12/01
	New London-Norwich MSA, CT-RI	H	8.72 FQ	11.93 AW	16.14 TQ	CTBLS	10/01-12/01
	Delaware	H	10.98 FQ	19.56 AW	27.12 TQ	DEBLS	10/01-12/01
	Wilmington-Newark PMSA, DE-MD	H	10.20 FQ	17.82 AW	26.21 TQ	DEBLS	10/01-12/01
	Washington PMSA, DC-MD-VA-WV	H	9.55 FQ	17.69 AW	27.26 TQ	DCBLS	10/01-12/01
	Florida	H	9.30 FQ	17.42 AW	26.57 TQ	FLBLS	10/01-12/01
	Fort Lauderdale PMSA, FL	H	8.93 FQ	14.00 AW	20.84 TQ	FLBLS	10/01-12/01
	Fort Myers-Cape Coral MSA, FL	H	10.17 FQ	13.23 AW	19.15 TQ	FLBLS	10/01-12/01
	Fort Pierce-Port St. Lucie MSA, FL	H	13.38 FQ	18.81 AW	22.65 TQ	FLBLS	10/01-12/01
	Fort Walton Beach MSA, FL	H	7.57 FQ	11.25 AW	19.18 TQ	FLBLS	10/01-12/01
	Jacksonville MSA, FL	H	8.77 FQ	15.87 AW	21.57 TQ	FLBLS	10/01-12/01
	Lakeland-Winter Haven MSA, FL	H	8.27 FQ	16.71 AW	21.19 TQ	FLBLS	10/01-12/01
	Melbourne-Titusville-Palm Bay MSA, FL	H	8.42 FQ	16.43 AW	22.31 TQ	FLBLS	10/01-12/01
	Miami PMSA, FL	H	10.66 FQ	17.49 AW	22.25 TQ	FLBLS	10/01-12/01
	Ocala MSA, FL	H	8.38 FQ	17.28 AW	21.19 TQ	FLBLS	10/01-12/01
	Orlando MSA, FL	H	8.85 FQ	15.16 AW	22.69 TQ	FLBLS	10/01-12/01
	Pensacola MSA, FL	H	6.27 FQ	11.18 AW	19.20 TQ	FLBLS	10/01-12/01
	Sarasota-Bradenton MSA, FL	H	9.97 FQ	16.45 AW	21.22 TQ	FLBLS	10/01-12/01
	Tallahassee MSA, FL	H	9.75 FQ	15.14 AW	21.33 TQ	FLBLS	10/01-12/01
	Tampa-St. Petersburg-Clearwater MSA, FL	H	12.18 FQ	24.61 AW	38.22 TQ	FLBLS	10/01-12/01
	West Palm Beach-Boca Raton MSA, FL	H	10.73 FQ	15.12 AW	20.83 TQ	FLBLS	10/01-12/01
	Georgia	H	10.89 FQ	16.88 AW	23.12 TQ	GABLS	10/01-12/01
	Atlanta MSA, GA	H	12.51 FQ	17.63 AW	23.95 TQ	GABLS	10/01-12/01
	Augusta-Aiken MSA, GA-SC	H	10.23 FQ	15.48 AW	20.66 TQ	GABLS	10/01-12/01
	Columbus MSA, GA-AL	H	10.25 FQ	16.11 AW	22.28 TQ	GABLS	10/01-12/01
	Macon MSA, GA	H	9.15 FQ	14.66 AW	23.12 TQ	GABLS	10/01-12/01
	Savannah MSA, GA	H	9.15 FQ	14.17 AW	21.34 TQ	GABLS	10/01-12/01
	Hawaii	H	14.31 FQ	21.11 AW	27.20 TQ	HIBLS	10/01-12/01
	Honolulu MSA, HI	H	14.61 FQ	20.41 AW	27.59 TQ	HIBLS	10/01-12/01
	Idaho	H	10.47 FQ	17.37 AW	26.06 TQ	IDBLS	10/01-12/01
	Boise City MSA, ID	H	10.77 FQ	16.44 AW	25.37 TQ	IDBLS	10/01-12/01
	Illinois	H	13.06 FQ	20.73 AW	27.11 TQ	ILBLS	10/01-12/01
	Chicago PMSA, IL	H	12.95 FQ	21.67 AW	27.56 TQ	ILBLS	10/01-12/01
	Peoria-Pekin MSA, IL	H	15.53 FQ	21.69 AW	27.64 TQ	ILBLS	10/01-12/01
	Rockford MSA, IL	H	17.67 FQ	21.51 AW	27.92 TQ	ILBLS	10/01-12/01
	Springfield MSA, IL	H	10.17 FQ	18.54 AW	26.33 TQ	ILBLS	10/01-12/01
	Indiana	H	10.36 FQ	17.27 AW	25.14 TQ	INBLS	10/01-12/01
	Evansville-Henderson MSA, IN-KY	H	10.03 FQ	18.73 AW	27.50 TQ	INBLS	10/01-12/01
	Fort Wayne MSA, IN	H	10.32 FQ	16.97 AW	24.47 TQ	INBLS	10/01-12/01
	Gary PMSA, IN	H	17.80 FQ	22.37 AW	26.98 TQ	INBLS	10/01-12/01
	Indianapolis MSA, IN	H	9.60 FQ	13.61 AW	19.14 TQ	INBLS	10/01-12/01
	Lafayette MSA, IN	H	15.42 FQ	19.03 AW	22.08 TQ	INBLS	10/01-12/01
	Iowa	H	9.59 FQ	15.96 AW	24.76 TQ	IABLS	10/01-12/01
	Davenport-Moline-Rock Island MSA, IA-IL	H	11.00 FQ	19.62 AW	26.20 TQ	IABLS	10/01-12/01
	Des Moines MSA, IA	H	9.35 FQ	15.32 AW	23.80 TQ	IABLS	10/01-12/01
	Kansas	H	13.26 FQ	22.09 AW	28.00 TQ	KSBLS	10/01-12/01
	Topeka MSA, KS	H	15.78 FQ	23.44 AW	28.17 TQ	KSBLS	10/01-12/01

AAW	Average annual wage	AOH	Average offered, high	ASH	Average starting, high	H	Hourly	M	Monthly	S	Special: hourly and annual
AE	Average entry wage	AOL	Average offered, low	ASL	Average starting, low	HI	Highest wage paid	MTC	Median total compensation	TQ	Third quartile wage
AEX	Average experienced wage	APH	Average pay, high range	AW	Average wage paid	HR	High end range	MW	Median wage paid	W	Weekly
AO	Average offered	APL	Average pay, low range	FQ	First quartile wage	LR	Low end range	SQ	Second quartile wage	Y	Yearly

Occupation/Type/Industry	Location	Per	Low	Mid	High	Source	Date
Telecommunications Line Installer and Repairer	Wichita MSA, KS	H	16.27 FQ	23.31 AW	28.01 TQ	KSBLS	10/01-12/01
	Kentucky	H	9.67 FQ	16.01 AW	21.81 TQ	KYBLS	10/01-12/01
	Lexington MSA, KY	H	10.46 FQ	17.34 AW	21.59 TQ	KYBLS	10/01-12/01
	Louisville MSA, KY-IN	H	9.66 FQ	15.42 AW	22.03 TQ	KYBLS	10/01-12/01
	Louisiana	H	9.42 FQ	17.29 AW	27.18 TQ	LABLS	10/01-12/01
	Baton Rouge MSA, LA	H	10.87 FQ	16.23 AW	22.51 TQ	LABLS	10/01-12/01
	Lafayette MSA, LA	H	9.54 FQ	22.01 AW	44.39 TQ	LABLS	10/01-12/01
	Lake Charles MSA, LA	H	9.26 FQ	15.23 AW	21.88 TQ	LABLS	10/01-12/01
	New Orleans MSA, LA	H	8.96 FQ	18.01 AW	33.23 TQ	LABLS	10/01-12/01
	Shreveport-Bossier City MSA, LA	H	9.55 FQ	15.87 AW	21.53 TQ	LABLS	10/01-12/01
	Maine	H	10.37 FQ	19.09 AW	32.03 TQ	MEBLS	10/01-12/01
	Maryland	H	9.63 FQ	15.53 AW	21.98 TQ	MDBLS	10/01-12/01
	Baltimore PMSA, MD	H	9.62 FQ	14.93 AW	21.37 TQ	MDBLS	10/01-12/01
	Massachusetts	H	14.11 FQ	23.67 AW	32.38 TQ	MABLS	10/01-12/01
	Boston PMSA, MA-NH	H	16.15 FQ	25.36 AW	33.16 TQ	MABLS	10/01-12/01
	Brockton PMSA, MA	H	12.78 FQ	24.76 AW	33.04 TQ	MABLS	10/01-12/01
	Lawrence PMSA, MA-NH	H	12.66 FQ	22.81 AW	30.75 TQ	MABLS	10/01-12/01
	Lowell PMSA, MA-NH	H	10.11 FQ	18.30 AW	27.01 TQ	MABLS	10/01-12/01
	Springfield MSA, MA	H	10.87 FQ	19.49 AW	29.04 TQ	MABLS	10/01-12/01
	Worcester PMSA, MA-CT	H	13.36 FQ	22.58 AW	33.78 TQ	MABLS	10/01-12/01
	Michigan	H	6.93 FQ	14.34 AW	21.99 TQ	MIBLS	10/01-12/01
	Detroit PMSA, MI	H	6.23 FQ	13.38 AW	22.11 TQ	MIBLS	10/01-12/01
	Grand Rapids-Muskegon-Holland MSA, MI	H	10.17 FQ	14.92 AW	21.94 TQ	MIBLS	10/01-12/01
	Kalamazoo-Battle Creek MSA, MI	H	13.63 FQ	16.10 AW	20.93 TQ	MIBLS	10/01-12/01
	Lansing-East Lansing MSA, MI	H	10.07 FQ	16.55 AW	22.10 TQ	MIBLS	10/01-12/01
	Saginaw-Bay City-Midland MSA, MI	H	8.89 FQ	14.17 AW	19.59 TQ	MIBLS	10/01-12/01
	Minnesota	H	10.40 FQ	16.36 AW	24.37 TQ	MNBLS	10/01-12/01
	Duluth-Superior MSA, MN-WI	H	11.65 FQ	17.73 AW	25.49 TQ	MNBLS	10/01-12/01
	Minneapolis-St. Paul MSA, MN-WI	H	10.94 FQ	16.50 AW	24.04 TQ	MNBLS	10/01-12/01
	St. Cloud MSA, MN	H	10.21 FQ	15.29 AW	21.77 TQ	MNBLS	10/01-12/01
	Mississippi	H	9.03 FQ	15.00 AW	25.26 TQ	MSBLS	10/01-12/01
	Biloxi-Gulfport-Pascagoula MSA, MS	H	9.75 FQ	15.32 AW	23.23 TQ	MSBLS	10/01-12/01
	Jackson MSA, MS	H	8.89 FQ	14.43 AW	25.45 TQ	MSBLS	10/01-12/01
	Missouri	H	10.41 FQ	18.12 AW	26.57 TQ	MOBLS	10/01-12/01
	Kansas City MSA, MO-KS	H	11.46 FQ	20.92 AW	28.02 TQ	MOBLS	10/01-12/01
	St. Louis MSA, MO-IL	H	10.81 FQ	17.93 AW	26.53 TQ	MOBLS	10/01-12/01
	Springfield MSA, MO	H	10.17 FQ	21.92 AW	28.02 TQ	MOBLS	10/01-12/01
	Montana	H	9.51 FQ	17.27 AW	26.46 TQ	MTBLS	10/01-12/01
	Billings MSA, MT	H	10.73 FQ	15.74 AW	22.52 TQ	MTBLS	10/01-12/01
	Nebraska	H	9.70 FQ	17.33 AW	26.74 TQ	NEBLS	10/01-12/01
	Lincoln MSA, NE	H	8.62 FQ	17.25 AW	25.81 TQ	NEBLS	10/01-12/01
	Omaha MSA, NE-IA	H	10.04 FQ	17.13 AW	27.05 TQ	NEBLS	10/01-12/01
	Nevada	H	12.40 FQ	18.68 AW	26.89 TQ	NVBLS	10/01-12/01
	Las Vegas MSA, NV-AZ	H	12.66 FQ	19.05 AW	27.20 TQ	NVBLS	10/01-12/01
	Reno MSA, NV	H	11.82 FQ	16.85 AW	24.98 TQ	NVBLS	10/01-12/01
	New Hampshire	H	10.95 FQ	18.87 AW	27.66 TQ	NHBLS	10/01-12/01
	Nashua PMSA, NH	H	12.01 FQ	21.32 AW	29.38 TQ	NHBLS	10/01-12/01
	New Jersey	H	11.10 FQ	19.25 AW	27.61 TQ	NJBLS	10/01-12/01
	Bergen-Passaic PMSA, NJ	H	9.64 FQ	16.35 AW	22.34 TQ	NJBLS	10/01-12/01
	Jersey City PMSA, NJ	H	10.03 FQ	15.72 AW	23.21 TQ	NJBLS	10/01-12/01
	Middlesex-Somerset-Hunterdon PMSA, NJ	H	9.32 FQ	14.38 AW	20.68 TQ	NJBLS	10/01-12/01
	Monmouth-Ocean PMSA, NJ	H	10.79 FQ	15.07 AW	21.05 TQ	NJBLS	10/01-12/01
	Newark PMSA, NJ	H	13.83 FQ	22.43 AW	28.85 TQ	NJBLS	10/01-12/01
	New Mexico	H	9.66 FQ	14.62 AW	22.80 TQ	NMBLS	10/01-12/01
	Albuquerque MSA, NM	H	9.87 FQ	15.12 AW	24.51 TQ	NMBLS	10/01-12/01
	New York	H	14.82 FQ	23.44 AW	28.86 TQ	NYBLS	10/01-12/01
	Albany-Schenectady-Troy MSA, NY	H	10.20 FQ	20.07 AW	27.91 TQ	NYBLS	10/01-12/01
	Binghamton MSA, NY	H	10.51 FQ	19.95 AW	27.39 TQ	NYBLS	10/01-12/01
	Buffalo-Niagara Falls MSA, NY	H	9.44 FQ	21.23 AW	27.73 TQ	NYBLS	10/01-12/01
	Dutchess County PMSA, NY	H	21.72 FQ	24.55 AW	30.62 TQ	NYBLS	10/01-12/01
	Nassau-Suffolk PMSA, NY	H	21.55 FQ	25.97 AW	32.72 TQ	NYBLS	10/01-12/01
	New York PMSA, NY	H	15.94 FQ	23.64 AW	28.58 TQ	NYBLS	10/01-12/01

AAW	Average annual wage	**AOH**	Average offered, high	**ASH**	Average starting, high	**H**	Hourly	**M**	Monthly	**S**	Special: hourly and annual
AE	Average entry wage	**AOL**	Average offered, low	**ASL**	Average starting, low	**HI**	Highest wage paid	**MTC**	Median total compensation	**TQ**	Third quartile wage
AEX	Average experienced wage	**APH**	Average pay, high range	**AW**	Average wage paid	**HR**	High end range	**MW**	Median wage paid	**W**	Weekly
AO	Average offered	**APL**	Average pay, low range	**FQ**	First quartile wage	**LR**	Low end range	**SQ**	Second quartile wage	**Y**	Yearly

Occupation/Type/Industry	Location	Per	Low	Mid	High	Source	Date
Telecommunications Line Installer and Repairer	Newburgh PMSA, NY-PA	H	10.53 FQ	21.22 AW	27.25 TQ	NYBLS	10/01-12/01
	Rochester MSA, NY	H	14.65 FQ	22.88 AW	28.26 TQ	NYBLS	10/01-12/01
	Syracuse MSA, NY	H	13.42 FQ	22.69 AW	27.70 TQ	NYBLS	10/01-12/01
	Utica-Rome MSA, NY	H	16.66 FQ	23.83 AW	28.83 TQ	NYBLS	10/01-12/01
	North Carolina	H	10.22 FQ	16.15 AW	22.53 TQ	NCBLS	10/01-12/01
	Asheville MSA, NC	H	8.61 FQ	13.53 AW	19.92 TQ	NCBLS	10/01-12/01
	Charlotte-Gastonia-Rock Hill MSA, NC-SC	H	10.33 FQ	15.89 AW	22.12 TQ	NCBLS	10/01-12/01
	Fayetteville MSA, NC	H	9.37 FQ	18.97 AW	27.58 TQ	NCBLS	10/01-12/01
	Greensboro-Winston-Salem-High Point MSA, NC	H	11.10 FQ	18.29 AW	26.34 TQ	NCBLS	10/01-12/01
	Hickory-Morganton-Lenoir MSA, NC	H	8.85 FQ	15.34 AW	21.91 TQ	NCBLS	10/01-12/01
	Raleigh-Durham-Chapel Hill MSA, NC	H	11.48 FQ	16.24 AW	21.67 TQ	NCBLS	10/01-12/01
	North Dakota	H	8.29 FQ	15.64 AW	22.10 TQ	NDBLS	10/01-12/01
	Fargo-Moorhead MSA, ND-MN	H	8.75 FQ	15.60 AW	21.89 TQ	NDBLS	10/01-12/01
	Ohio	H	10.22 FQ	16.29 AW	23.49 TQ	OHBLS	10/01-12/01
	Akron PMSA, OH	H	11.32 FQ	19.17 AW	28.48 TQ	OHBLS	10/01-12/01
	Canton-Massillon MSA, OH	H	10.42 FQ	18.25 AW	26.78 TQ	OHBLS	10/01-12/01
	Cincinnati PMSA, OH-KY-IN	H	10.09 FQ	16.58 AW	24.14 TQ	OHBLS	10/01-12/01
	Cleveland-Lorain-Elyria PMSA, OH	H	9.97 FQ	15.52 AW	21.40 TQ	OHBLS	10/01-12/01
	Columbus MSA, OH	H	10.54 FQ	15.25 AW	22.38 TQ	OHBLS	10/01-12/01
	Dayton-Springfield MSA, OH	H	10.60 FQ	17.92 AW	27.61 TQ	OHBLS	10/01-12/01
	Hamilton-Middletown PMSA, OH	H	12.54 FQ	22.53 AW	33.81 TQ	OHBLS	10/01-12/01
	Toledo MSA, OH	H	9.86 FQ	15.19 AW	21.25 TQ	OHBLS	10/01-12/01
	Youngstown-Warren MSA, OH	H	9.26 FQ	14.56 AW	20.60 TQ	OHBLS	10/01-12/01
	Oklahoma	H	9.08 FQ	17.75 AW	26.33 TQ	OKBLS	10/01-12/01
	Oklahoma City MSA, OK	H	8.45 FQ	17.67 AW	26.27 TQ	OKBLS	10/01-12/01
	Tulsa MSA, OK	H	10.02 FQ	17.47 AW	26.23 TQ	OKBLS	10/01-12/01
	Oregon	H	11.08 FQ	18.40 AW	26.69 TQ	ORBLS	10/01-12/01
	Eugene-Springfield MSA, OR	H	11.52 FQ	18.90 AW	26.29 TQ	ORBLS	10/01-12/01
	Medford-Ashland MSA, OR	H	10.98 FQ	21.18 AW	32.24 TQ	ORBLS	10/01-12/01
	Portland-Vancouver PMSA, OR-WA	H	11.03 FQ	17.72 AW	25.95 TQ	ORBLS	10/01-12/01
	Salem PMSA, OR	H	10.12 FQ	20.33 AW	28.20 TQ	ORBLS	10/01-12/01
	Pennsylvania	H	11.32 FQ	18.21 AW	25.68 TQ	PABLS	10/01-12/01
	Allentown-Bethlehem-Easton MSA, PA	H	12.08 FQ	20.53 AW	28.47 TQ	PABLS	10/01-12/01
	Erie MSA, PA	H	12.06 FQ	17.59 AW	21.35 TQ	PABLS	10/01-12/01
	Harrisburg-Lebanon-Carlisle MSA, PA	H	12.12 FQ	16.85 AW	24.12 TQ	PABLS	10/01-12/01
	Johnstown MSA, PA	H	7.31 FQ	15.44 AW	21.82 TQ	PABLS	10/01-12/01
	Lancaster MSA, PA	H	7.63 FQ	14.72 AW	22.88 TQ	PABLS	10/01-12/01
	Philadelphia PMSA, PA-NJ	H	11.85 FQ	18.71 AW	25.78 TQ	PABLS	10/01-12/01
	Pittsburgh MSA, PA	H	11.60 FQ	17.83 AW	25.24 TQ	PABLS	10/01-12/01
	Reading MSA, PA	H	10.45 FQ	17.76 AW	26.21 TQ	PABLS	10/01-12/01
	Scranton-Wilkes-Barre-Hazleton MSA, PA	H	10.78 FQ	20.20 AW	27.61 TQ	PABLS	10/01-12/01
	York MSA, PA	H	9.86 FQ	16.72 AW	24.09 TQ	PABLS	10/01-12/01
	Rhode Island	H	11.68 FQ	21.67 AW	30.85 TQ	RIBLS	10/01-12/01
	Providence-Fall River-Warwick MSA, RI-MA	H	12.15 FQ	22.13 AW	31.39 TQ	RIBLS	10/01-12/01
	South Carolina	H	9.82 FQ	15.91 AW	21.72 TQ	SCBLS	10/01-12/01
	Charleston-North Charleston MSA, SC	H	10.48 FQ	15.28 AW	19.49 TQ	SCBLS	10/01-12/01
	Columbia MSA, SC	H	9.25 FQ	16.41 AW	21.61 TQ	SCBLS	10/01-12/01
	Greenville-Spartanburg-Anderson MSA, SC	H	9.22 FQ	13.46 AW	20.53 TQ	SCBLS	10/01-12/01
	Myrtle Beach MSA, SC	H	12.77 FQ	18.83 AW	24.98 TQ	SCBLS	10/01-12/01
	South Dakota	H	9.99 FQ	16.16 AW	24.85 TQ	SDBLS	10/01-12/01
	Sioux Falls MSA, SD	H	9.41 FQ	15.61 AW	25.34 TQ	SDBLS	10/01-12/01
	Tennessee	H	9.92 FQ	16.83 AW	23.92 TQ	TNBLS	10/01-12/01
	Chattanooga MSA, TN-GA	H	10.19 FQ	15.53 AW	21.06 TQ	TNBLS	10/01-12/01
	Johnson City-Kingsport-Bristol MSA, TN-VA	H	7.84 FQ	15.26 AW	21.95 TQ	TNBLS	10/01-12/01
	Knoxville MSA, TN	H	10.67 FQ	16.61 AW	22.16 TQ	TNBLS	10/01-12/01
	Memphis MSA, TN-AR-MS	H	9.71 FQ	15.46 AW	22.52 TQ	TNBLS	10/01-12/01

AAW	Average annual wage	**AOH**	Average offered, high	**ASH**	Average starting, high	**H**	Hourly	**M**	Monthly	**S**	Special: hourly and annual
AE	Average entry wage	**AOL**	Average offered, low	**ASL**	Average starting, low	**HI**	Highest wage paid	**MTC**	Median total compensation	**TQ**	Third quartile wage
AEX	Average experienced wage	**APH**	Average pay, high range	**AW**	Average wage paid	**HR**	High end range	**MW**	Median wage paid	**W**	Weekly
AO	Average offered	**APL**	Average pay, low range	**FQ**	First quartile wage	**LR**	Low end range	**SQ**	Second quartile wage	**Y**	Yearly

Occupation/Type/Industry	Location	Per	Low	Mid	High	Source	Date
Telecommunications Line Installer and Repairer	Nashville MSA, TN	H	9.71 FQ	18.08 AW	26.04 TQ	TNBLS	10/01-12/01
	Texas	H	9.81 FQ	18.27 AW	26.69 TQ	TXBLS	10/01-12/01
	Amarillo MSA, TX	H	20.83 FQ	24.49 AW	28.56 TQ	TXBLS	10/01-12/01
	Austin-San Marcos MSA, TX	H	10.11 FQ	18.09 AW	26.13 TQ	TXBLS	10/01-12/01
	Beaumont-Port Arthur MSA, TX	H	9.80 FQ	17.41 AW	26.40 TQ	TXBLS	10/01-12/01
	Brazoria PMSA, TX	H	9.09 FQ	16.39 AW	25.77 TQ	TXBLS	10/01-12/01
	Brownsville-Harlingen-San Benito MSA, TX	H	21.98 FQ	24.03 AW	26.92 TQ	TXBLS	10/01-12/01
	Corpus Christi MSA, TX	H	10.97 FQ	13.58 AW	22.29 TQ	TXBLS	10/01-12/01
	Dallas PMSA, TX	H	9.22 FQ	16.80 AW	32.44 TQ	TXBLS	10/01-12/01
	El Paso MSA, TX	H	13.62 FQ	20.66 AW	26.65 TQ	TXBLS	10/01-12/01
	Fort Worth-Arlington PMSA, TX	H	10.82 FQ	17.52 AW	26.38 TQ	TXBLS	10/01-12/01
	Galveston-Texas City PMSA, TX	H	15.21 FQ	22.94 AW	27.13 TQ	TXBLS	10/01-12/01
	Houston PMSA, TX	H	9.33 FQ	16.39 AW	25.77 TQ	TXBLS	10/01-12/01
	Killeen-Temple MSA, TX	H	17.25 FQ	21.48 AW	27.09 TQ	TXBLS	10/01-12/01
	Longview-Marshall MSA, TX	H	9.90 FQ	18.98 AW	26.49 TQ	TXBLS	10/01-12/01
	Lubbock MSA, TX	H	9.03 FQ	16.39 AW	25.78 TQ	TXBLS	10/01-12/01
	McAllen-Edinburg-Mission MSA, TX	H	12.76 FQ	19.81 AW	26.89 TQ	TXBLS	10/01-12/01
	Odessa-Midland MSA, TX	H	9.57 FQ	20.62 AW	27.59 TQ	TXBLS	10/01-12/01
	San Antonio MSA, TX	H	9.64 FQ	16.61 AW	25.23 TQ	TXBLS	10/01-12/01
	Tyler MSA, TX	H	8.82 FQ	16.00 AW	26.85 TQ	TXBLS	10/01-12/01
	Waco MSA, TX	H	8.88 FQ	19.90 AW	26.68 TQ	TXBLS	10/01-12/01
	Utah	H	8.97 FQ	14.43 AW	21.09 TQ	UTBLS	10/01-12/01
	Provo-Orem MSA, UT	H	11.88 FQ	15.60 AW	22.45 TQ	UTBLS	10/01-12/01
	Salt Lake City-Ogden MSA, UT	H	10.57 FQ	15.22 AW	20.96 TQ	UTBLS	10/01-12/01
	Vermont	H	10.06 FQ	16.10 AW	25.92 TQ	VTBLS	10/01-12/01
	Burlington MSA, VT	H	9.57 FQ	12.41 AW	16.04 TQ	VTBLS	10/01-12/01
	Virginia	H	9.39 FQ	16.25 AW	25.96 TQ	VABLS	10/01-12/01
	Lynchburg MSA, VA	H	9.54 FQ	15.53 AW	23.98 TQ	VABLS	10/01-12/01
	Norfolk-Virginia Beach-Newport News MSA, VA-NC	H	7.71 FQ	13.23 AW	19.91 TQ	VABLS	10/01-12/01
	Richmond-Petersburg MSA, VA	H	9.69 FQ	14.94 AW	23.39 TQ	VABLS	10/01-12/01
	Roanoke MSA, VA	H	9.59 FQ	14.55 AW	20.60 TQ	VABLS	10/01-12/01
	Washington	H	9.52 FQ	17.41 AW	26.17 TQ	WABLS	10/01-12/01
	Bremerton PMSA, WA	H	10.30 FQ	15.06 AW	22.21 TQ	WABLS	10/01-12/01
	Olympia PMSA, WA	H	8.68 FQ	18.01 AW	26.82 TQ	WABLS	10/01-12/01
	Seattle-Bellevue-Everett PMSA, WA	H	9.70 FQ	18.06 AW	26.51 TQ	WABLS	10/01-12/01
	Spokane MSA, WA	H	7.17 FQ	16.00 AW	26.39 TQ	WABLS	10/01-12/01
	Tacoma PMSA, WA	H	11.29 FQ	17.14 AW	25.75 TQ	WABLS	10/01-12/01
	West Virginia	H	8.39 FQ	13.28 AW	19.50 TQ	WVBLS	10/01-12/01
	Charleston MSA, WV	H	9.10 FQ	13.80 AW	19.02 TQ	WVBLS	10/01-12/01
	Huntington-Ashland MSA, WV-KY-OH	H	9.65 FQ	14.23 AW	19.84 TQ	WVBLS	10/01-12/01
	Wisconsin	H	7.43 FQ	16.29 AW	25.71 TQ	WIBLS	10/01-12/01
	Madison MSA, WI	H	5.55 FQ	8.15 AW	17.21 TQ	WIBLS	10/01-12/01
	Milwaukee-Waukesha PMSA, WI	H	9.83 FQ	16.55 AW	25.19 TQ	WIBLS	10/01-12/01
	Racine PMSA, WI	H	9.16 FQ	17.78 AW	27.75 TQ	WIBLS	10/01-12/01
	Wyoming	H	6.95 FQ	18.20 AW	30.36 TQ	WYBLS	10/01-12/01
	Cheyenne MSA, WY	H	6.44 FQ	16.32 AW	25.44 TQ	WYBLS	10/01-12/01
	Puerto Rico	H	7.39 FQ	11.63 AW	17.05 TQ	PRBLS	10/01-12/01
Telemarketer	Alabama	Y	13320 FQ	16860 AW	20210 TQ	ALBLS	10/01-12/01
	Birmingham MSA, AL	Y	12110 FQ	17140 AW	22360 TQ	ALBLS	10/01-12/01
	Huntsville MSA, AL	Y	14220 FQ	16740 AW	17660 TQ	ALBLS	10/01-12/01
	Mobile MSA, AL	Y	14410 FQ	16120 AW	17970 TQ	ALBLS	10/01-12/01
	Montgomery MSA, AL	Y	13980 FQ	16720 AW	18750 TQ	ALBLS	10/01-12/01
	Alaska	Y	13150 FQ	18040 AW	22350 TQ	AKBLS	10/01-12/01
	Anchorage MSA, AK	Y	13960 FQ	19890 AW	23580 TQ	AKBLS	10/01-12/01
	Arizona	Y	13440 FQ	22150 AW	36390 TQ	AZBLS	10/01-12/01
	Phoenix-Mesa MSA, AZ	Y	13320 FQ	22650 AW	38230 TQ	AZBLS	10/01-12/01
	Tucson MSA, AZ	Y	14540 FQ	17690 AW	23320 TQ	AZBLS	10/01-12/01
	Arkansas	Y	12660 FQ	17650 AW	24610 TQ	ARBLS	10/01-12/01

AAW Average annual wage; **AE** Average entry wage; **AEX** Average experienced wage; **AO** Average offered; **AOH** Average offered, high; **AOL** Average offered, low; **APH** Average pay, high range; **APL** Average pay, low range; **ASH** Average starting, high; **ASL** Average starting, low; **AW** Average wage paid; **FQ** First quartile wage; **H** Hourly; **HI** Highest wage paid; **HR** High end range; **LR** Low end range; **M** Monthly; **MTC** Median total compensation; **MW** Median wage paid; **SQ** Second quartile wage; **S** Special: hourly and annual; **TQ** Third quartile wage; **W** Weekly; **Y** Yearly

Occupation/Type/Industry	Location	Per	Low	Mid	High	Source	Date
Telemarketer	Fayetteville-Springdale-Rogers MSA, AR	Y	14850 FQ	17670 AW	21510 TQ	ARBLS	10/01-12/01
	Little Rock-North Little Rock MSA, AR	Y	13130 FQ	18670 AW	28730 TQ	ARBLS	10/01-12/01
	California	Y	14150 FQ	24940 AW	41020 TQ	CABLS	10/01-12/01
	Bakersfield MSA, CA	Y	13610 FQ	18160 AW	25690 TQ	CABLS	10/01-12/01
	Chico-Paradise MSA, CA	Y	14700 FQ	25430 AW	48490 TQ	CABLS	10/01-12/01
	Fresno MSA, CA	Y	13920 FQ	21730 AW	33440 TQ	CABLS	10/01-12/01
	Los Angeles-Long Beach PMSA, CA	Y	13750 FQ	22230 AW	33740 TQ	CABLS	10/01-12/01
	Modesto MSA, CA	Y	14210 FQ	23150 AW	37640 TQ	CABLS	10/01-12/01
	Oakland PMSA, CA	Y	15360 FQ	27370 AW	47030 TQ	CABLS	10/01-12/01
	Orange County PMSA, CA	Y	15460 FQ	25450 AW	41000 TQ	CABLS	10/01-12/01
	Riverside-San Bernardino PMSA, CA	Y	14920 FQ	29810 AW	43050 TQ	CABLS	10/01-12/01
	Sacramento PMSA, CA	Y	14180 FQ	20880 AW	29610 TQ	CABLS	10/01-12/01
	Salinas MSA, CA	Y	13300 FQ	17910 AW	26300 TQ	CABLS	10/01-12/01
	San Diego MSA, CA	Y	14410 FQ	23110 AW	34380 TQ	CABLS	10/01-12/01
	San Francisco PMSA, CA	Y	13800 FQ	24780 AW	44260 TQ	CABLS	10/01-12/01
	San Jose PMSA, CA	Y	14910 FQ	42000 AW	84270 TQ	CABLS	10/01-12/01
	San Luis Obispo-Atascadero-Paso Robles MSA, CA	Y	13760 FQ	20040 AW	26820 TQ	CABLS	10/01-12/01
	Santa Barbara-Santa Maria-Lompoc MSA, CA	Y	13530 FQ	22540 AW	34940 TQ	CABLS	10/01-12/01
	Santa Cruz-Watsonville PMSA, CA	Y	15570 FQ	26720 AW	48190 TQ	CABLS	10/01-12/01
	Santa Rosa PMSA, CA	Y	14210 FQ	21240 AW	29610 TQ	CABLS	10/01-12/01
	Vallejo-Fairfield-Napa PMSA, CA	Y	18420 FQ	38650 AW	75780 TQ	CABLS	10/01-12/01
	Ventura PMSA, CA	Y	19390 FQ	28060 AW	41660 TQ	CABLS	10/01-12/01
	Visalia-Tulare-Porterville MSA, CA	Y	15480 FQ	20980 AW	32020 TQ	CABLS	10/01-12/01
	Colorado	Y	13320 FQ	21060 AW	31110 TQ	COBLS	10/01-12/01
	Boulder-Longmont PMSA, CO	Y	15820 FQ	24900 AW	39110 TQ	COBLS	10/01-12/01
	Colorado Springs MSA, CO	Y	12220 FQ	17550 AW	24970 TQ	COBLS	10/01-12/01
	Denver PMSA, CO	Y	13380 FQ	22550 AW	33850 TQ	COBLS	10/01-12/01
	Fort Collins-Loveland MSA, CO	Y	15080 FQ	17710 AW	22000 TQ	COBLS	10/01-12/01
	Greeley PMSA, CO	Y	15170 FQ	22010 AW	30720 TQ	COBLS	10/01-12/01
	Connecticut	Y	14110 FQ	27360 AW	44750 TQ	CTBLS	10/01-12/01
	Bridgeport PMSA, CT	Y	13630 FQ	20670 AW	32240 TQ	CTBLS	10/01-12/01
	Danbury PMSA, CT	Y	17660 FQ	26150 AW	40410 TQ	CTBLS	10/01-12/01
	Hartford MSA, CT	Y	14100 FQ	24330 AW	37990 TQ	CTBLS	10/01-12/01
	New Haven-Meriden PMSA, CT	Y	14800 FQ	22830 AW	36130 TQ	CTBLS	10/01-12/01
	New London-Norwich MSA, CT-RI	Y	15480 FQ	26120 AW	41520 TQ	CTBLS	10/01-12/01
	Stamford-Norwalk PMSA, CT	Y	15360 FQ	46440 AW	87280 TQ	CTBLS	10/01-12/01
	Waterbury PMSA, CT	Y	13680 FQ	22870 AW	31780 TQ	CTBLS	10/01-12/01
	Delaware	Y	15320 FQ	20730 AW	27760 TQ	DEBLS	10/01-12/01
	Wilmington-Newark PMSA, DE-MD	Y	15470 FQ	21050 AW	27790 TQ	DEBLS	10/01-12/01
	District of Columbia	Y	13570 FQ	19620 AW	28960 TQ	DCBLS	10/01-12/01
	Washington PMSA, DC-MD-VA-WV	Y	13140 FQ	22600 AW	37970 TQ	DCBLS	10/01-12/01
	Florida	Y	14950 FQ	24540 AW	39220 TQ	FLBLS	10/01-12/01
	Daytona Beach MSA, FL	Y	12140 FQ	17830 AW	27960 TQ	FLBLS	10/01-12/01
	Fort Lauderdale PMSA, FL	Y	15150 FQ	21450 AW	27390 TQ	FLBLS	10/01-12/01
	Fort Myers-Cape Coral MSA, FL	Y	15680 FQ	31610 AW	53320 TQ	FLBLS	10/01-12/01
	Fort Pierce-Port St. Lucie MSA, FL	Y	12530 FQ	17490 AW	25260 TQ	FLBLS	10/01-12/01
	Fort Walton Beach MSA, FL	Y	12330 FQ	18190 AW	26300 TQ	FLBLS	10/01-12/01
	Gainesville MSA, FL	Y	11610 FQ	19830 AW	38270 TQ	FLBLS	10/01-12/01
	Jacksonville MSA, FL	Y	15260 FQ	25540 AW	42850 TQ	FLBLS	10/01-12/01
	Lakeland-Winter Haven MSA, FL	Y	15260 FQ	22290 AW	32450 TQ	FLBLS	10/01-12/01
	Melbourne-Titusville-Palm Bay MSA, FL	Y	14900 FQ	18770 AW	22080 TQ	FLBLS	10/01-12/01
	Miami PMSA, FL	Y	15870 FQ	24590 AW	35880 TQ	FLBLS	10/01-12/01
	Naples MSA, FL	Y	15270 FQ	20070 AW	27040 TQ	FLBLS	10/01-12/01
	Ocala MSA, FL	Y	17360 FQ	24520 AW	27990 TQ	FLBLS	10/01-12/01

AAW	Average annual wage	**AOH**	Average offered, high	**ASH**	Average starting, high	**H**	Hourly	**M**	Monthly	**S**	Special: hourly and annual
AE	Average entry wage	**AOL**	Average offered, low	**ASL**	Average starting, low	**HI**	Highest wage paid	**MTC**	Median total compensation	**TQ**	Third quartile wage
AEX	Average experienced wage	**APH**	Average pay, high range	**AW**	Average wage paid	**HR**	High end range	**MW**	Median wage paid	**W**	Weekly
AO	Average offered	**APL**	Average pay, low range	**FQ**	First quartile wage	**LR**	Low end range	**SQ**	Second quartile wage	**Y**	Yearly

Occupation/Type/Industry	Location	Per	Low	Mid	High	Source	Date
Telemarketer	Orlando MSA, FL	Y	13970 FQ	22140 AW	34030 TQ	FLBLS	10/01-12/01
	Pensacola MSA, FL	Y	12230 FQ	16210 AW	19040 TQ	FLBLS	10/01-12/01
	Sarasota-Bradenton MSA, FL	Y	15730 FQ	26400 AW	42090 TQ	FLBLS	10/01-12/01
	Tallahassee MSA, FL	Y	11880 FQ	21940 AW	46200 TQ	FLBLS	10/01-12/01
	Tampa-St. Petersburg-Clearwater MSA, FL	Y	17150 FQ	27960 AW	43060 TQ	FLBLS	10/01-12/01
	West Palm Beach-Boca Raton MSA, FL	Y	12620 FQ	29310 AW	77930 TQ	FLBLS	10/01-12/01
	Georgia	Y	14210 FQ	21350 AW	30060 TQ	GABLS	10/01-12/01
	Atlanta MSA, GA	Y	14820 FQ	22770 AW	34220 TQ	GABLS	10/01-12/01
	Columbus MSA, GA-AL	Y	12450 FQ	19130 AW	28640 TQ	GABLS	10/01-12/01
	Macon MSA, GA	Y	13040 FQ	20700 AW	28120 TQ	GABLS	10/01-12/01
	Savannah MSA, GA	Y	15880 FQ	20480 AW	23630 TQ	GABLS	10/01-12/01
	Hawaii	Y	13310 FQ	18780 AW	26800 TQ	HIBLS	10/01-12/01
	Honolulu MSA, HI	Y	13740 FQ	19110 AW	27370 TQ	HIBLS	10/01-12/01
	Idaho	Y	13930 FQ	18800 AW	23420 TQ	IDBLS	10/01-12/01
	Boise City MSA, ID	Y	16080 FQ	20080 AW	22980 TQ	IDBLS	10/01-12/01
	Illinois	Y	14790 FQ	21100 AW	29610 TQ	ILBLS	10/01-12/01
	Champaign-Urbana MSA, IL	Y	14660 FQ	21150 AW	30350 TQ	ILBLS	10/01-12/01
	Chicago PMSA, IL	Y	15020 FQ	21450 AW	29840 TQ	ILBLS	10/01-12/01
	Peoria-Pekin MSA, IL	Y	12610 FQ	17260 AW	23920 TQ	ILBLS	10/01-12/01
	Rockford MSA, IL	Y	12590 FQ	18110 AW	26050 TQ	ILBLS	10/01-12/01
	Springfield MSA, IL	Y	12290 FQ	18650 AW	27950 TQ	ILBLS	10/01-12/01
	Indiana	Y	14830 FQ	20640 AW	27520 TQ	INBLS	10/01-12/01
	Elkhart-Goshen MSA, IN	Y	12310 FQ	19930 AW	28640 TQ	INBLS	10/01-12/01
	Evansville-Henderson MSA, IN-KY	Y	14940 FQ	19330 AW	25730 TQ	INBLS	10/01-12/01
	Fort Wayne MSA, IN	Y	22230 FQ	29090 AW	42260 TQ	INBLS	10/01-12/01
	Indianapolis MSA, IN	Y	15800 FQ	20300 AW	23810 TQ	INBLS	10/01-12/01
	Lafayette MSA, IN	Y	12010 FQ	17500 AW	24670 TQ	INBLS	10/01-12/01
	South Bend MSA, IN	Y	13970 FQ	20800 AW	27600 TQ	INBLS	10/01-12/01
	Iowa	Y	12250 FQ	17310 AW	22790 TQ	IABLS	10/01-12/01
	Cedar Rapids MSA, IA	Y	14160 FQ	19970 AW	25540 TQ	IABLS	10/01-12/01
	Davenport-Moline-Rock Island MSA, IA-IL	Y	13500 FQ	18170 AW	26050 TQ	IABLS	10/01-12/01
	Des Moines MSA, IA	Y	12500 FQ	19050 AW	26070 TQ	IABLS	10/01-12/01
	Kansas	Y	12930 FQ	20520 AW	28580 TQ	KSBLS	10/01-12/01
	Topeka MSA, KS	Y	15640 FQ	25750 AW	40080 TQ	KSBLS	10/01-12/01
	Wichita MSA, KS	Y	11690 FQ	17810 AW	24290 TQ	KSBLS	10/01-12/01
	Kentucky	Y	14110 FQ	18640 AW	25870 TQ	KYBLS	10/01-12/01
	Lexington MSA, KY	Y	13640 FQ	24270 AW	39830 TQ	KYBLS	10/01-12/01
	Louisville MSA, KY-IN	Y	13710 FQ	18750 AW	25530 TQ	KYBLS	10/01-12/01
	Louisiana	Y	11670 FQ	20560 AW	31000 TQ	LABLS	10/01-12/01
	Lafayette MSA, LA	Y	14290 FQ	17680 AW	21980 TQ	LABLS	10/01-12/01
	Lake Charles MSA, LA	Y	11660 FQ	21360 AW	41890 TQ	LABLS	10/01-12/01
	New Orleans MSA, LA	Y	14290 FQ	32950 AW	86630 TQ	LABLS	10/01-12/01
	Shreveport-Bossier City MSA, LA	Y	11660 FQ	15440 AW	18480 TQ	LABLS	10/01-12/01
	Maine	Y	13330 FQ	23170 AW	36870 TQ	MEBLS	10/01-12/01
	Portland MSA, ME	Y	16940 FQ	28950 AW	42620 TQ	MEBLS	10/01-12/01
	Maryland	Y	14730 FQ	22830 AW	35690 TQ	MDBLS	10/01-12/01
	Baltimore PMSA, MD	Y	15310 FQ	22510 AW	31370 TQ	MDBLS	10/01-12/01
	Massachusetts	Y	15680 FQ	28470 AW	45620 TQ	MABLS	10/01-12/01
	Boston PMSA, MA-NH	Y	15680 FQ	29200 AW	46560 TQ	MABLS	10/01-12/01
	Lawrence PMSA, MA-NH	Y	18660 FQ	25540 AW	36500 TQ	MABLS	10/01-12/01
	Lowell PMSA, MA-NH	Y	18070 FQ	36280 AW	66290 TQ	MABLS	10/01-12/01
	New Bedford PMSA, MA	Y	14590 FQ	26120 AW	41620 TQ	MABLS	10/01-12/01
	Springfield MSA, MA	Y	17880 FQ	25070 AW	36190 TQ	MABLS	10/01-12/01
	Worcester PMSA, MA-CT	Y	15110 FQ	24090 AW	34860 TQ	MABLS	10/01-12/01
	Michigan	Y	13620 FQ	23110 AW	36630 TQ	MIBLS	10/01-12/01
	Ann Arbor PMSA, MI	Y	13130 FQ	21390 AW	33600 TQ	MIBLS	10/01-12/01
	Detroit PMSA, MI	Y	13190 FQ	23510 AW	36660 TQ	MIBLS	10/01-12/01
	Flint PMSA, MI	Y	12270 FQ	20290 AW	32970 TQ	MIBLS	10/01-12/01
	Grand Rapids-Muskegon-Holland MSA, MI	Y	16180 FQ	24600 AW	38400 TQ	MIBLS	10/01-12/01
	Kalamazoo-Battle Creek MSA, MI	Y	16470 FQ	26350 AW	44720 TQ	MIBLS	10/01-12/01
	Lansing-East Lansing MSA, MI	Y	14410 FQ	21380 AW	34370 TQ	MIBLS	10/01-12/01
	Saginaw-Bay City-Midland MSA, MI	Y	12530 FQ	22120 AW	35880 TQ	MIBLS	10/01-12/01
	Minnesota	Y	14530 FQ	23280 AW	36540 TQ	MNBLS	10/01-12/01
	Duluth-Superior MSA, MN-WI	Y	15020 FQ	18650 AW	22280 TQ	MNBLS	10/01-12/01

AAW	Average annual wage	AOH	Average offered, high	ASH	Average starting, high	H	Hourly	M	Monthly	S	Special: hourly and annual
AE	Average entry wage	AOL	Average offered, low	ASL	Average starting, low	HI	Highest wage paid	MTC	Median total compensation	TQ	Third quartile wage
AEX	Average experienced wage	APH	Average pay, high range	AW	Average wage paid	HR	High end range	MW	Median wage paid	W	Weekly
AO	Average offered	APL	Average pay, low range	FQ	First quartile wage	LR	Low end range	SQ	Second quartile wage	Y	Yearly

Occupation/Type/Industry	Location	Per	Low	Mid	High	Source	Date
Telemarketer	Minneapolis-St. Paul MSA, MN-WI	Y	15400 FQ	24740 AW	40530 TQ	MNBLS	10/01-12/01
	Mississippi	Y	12390 FQ	22030 AW	41430 TQ	MSBLS	10/01-12/01
	Jackson MSA, MS	Y	12240 FQ	25240 AW	51400 TQ	MSBLS	10/01-12/01
	Missouri	Y	12980 FQ	20470 AW	33200 TQ	MOBLS	10/01-12/01
	Kansas City MSA, MO-KS	Y	14950 FQ	22710 AW	35150 TQ	MOBLS	10/01-12/01
	St. Louis MSA, MO-IL	Y	12680 FQ	21700 AW	34690 TQ	MOBLS	10/01-12/01
	Springfield MSA, MO	Y	14540 FQ	17360 AW	20420 TQ	MOBLS	10/01-12/01
	Montana	Y	11700 FQ	15270 AW	18670 TQ	MTBLS	10/01-12/01
	Nebraska	Y	12880 FQ	18140 AW	24470 TQ	NEBLS	10/01-12/01
	Lincoln MSA, NE	Y	11770 FQ	16870 AW	24910 TQ	NEBLS	10/01-12/01
	Omaha MSA, NE-IA	Y	13530 FQ	18780 AW	25530 TQ	NEBLS	10/01-12/01
	Nevada	Y	14780 FQ	24670 AW	39560 TQ	NVBLS	10/01-12/01
	Las Vegas MSA, NV-AZ	Y	14560 FQ	24150 AW	39020 TQ	NVBLS	10/01-12/01
	Reno MSA, NV	Y	17150 FQ	24950 AW	35300 TQ	NVBLS	10/01-12/01
	New Hampshire	Y	13690 FQ	23300 AW	34050 TQ	NHBLS	10/01-12/01
	Manchester PMSA, NH	Y	12380 FQ	22700 AW	41560 TQ	NHBLS	10/01-12/01
	Nashua PMSA, NH	Y	17910 FQ	28060 AW	43140 TQ	NHBLS	10/01-12/01
	Portsmouth-Rochester PMSA, NH-ME	Y	13820 FQ	24170 AW	33970 TQ	NHBLS	10/01-12/01
	New Jersey	Y	14760 FQ	24600 AW	37540 TQ	NJBLS	10/01-12/01
	Bergen-Passaic PMSA, NJ	Y	14840 FQ	25710 AW	41590 TQ	NJBLS	10/01-12/01
	Jersey City PMSA, NJ	Y	12930 FQ	21100 AW	34500 TQ	NJBLS	10/01-12/01
	Middlesex-Somerset-Hunterdon PMSA, NJ	Y	14330 FQ	22010 AW	29870 TQ	NJBLS	10/01-12/01
	Monmouth-Ocean PMSA, NJ	Y	15130 FQ	28910 AW	52810 TQ	NJBLS	10/01-12/01
	Newark PMSA, NJ	Y	15620 FQ	26800 AW	37520 TQ	NJBLS	10/01-12/01
	Trenton PMSA, NJ	Y	19190 FQ	30640 AW	43810 TQ	NJBLS	10/01-12/01
	New Mexico	Y	11760 FQ	18290 AW	26940 TQ	NMBLS	10/01-12/01
	Albuquerque MSA, NM	Y	13840 FQ	21060 AW	27720 TQ	NMBLS	10/01-12/01
	Las Cruces MSA, NM	Y	11280 FQ	12570 AW	14090 TQ	NMBLS	10/01-12/01
	New York	Y	14050 FQ	23270 AW	34940 TQ	NYBLS	10/01-12/01
	Albany-Schenectady-Troy MSA, NY	Y	14670 FQ	22040 AW	33060 TQ	NYBLS	10/01-12/01
	Buffalo-Niagara Falls MSA, NY	Y	12890 FQ	20740 AW	34080 TQ	NYBLS	10/01-12/01
	Dutchess County PMSA, NY	Y	13090 FQ	22940 AW	32480 TQ	NYBLS	10/01-12/01
	Nassau-Suffolk PMSA, NY	Y	15830 FQ	24170 AW	29680 TQ	NYBLS	10/01-12/01
	New York PMSA, NY	Y	13630 FQ	23760 AW	38160 TQ	NYBLS	10/01-12/01
	Newburgh PMSA, NY-PA	Y	11910 FQ	20990 AW	35930 TQ	NYBLS	10/01-12/01
	Rochester MSA, NY	Y	14750 FQ	20540 AW	27960 TQ	NYBLS	10/01-12/01
	Syracuse MSA, NY	Y	12450 FQ	21370 AW	38640 TQ	NYBLS	10/01-12/01
	Utica-Rome MSA, NY	Y	12410 FQ	20430 AW	28110 TQ	NYBLS	10/01-12/01
	North Carolina	Y	14560 FQ	22540 AW	29510 TQ	NCBLS	10/01-12/01
	Asheville MSA, NC	Y	13490 FQ	19020 AW	26200 TQ	NCBLS	10/01-12/01
	Charlotte-Gastonia-Rock Hill MSA, NC-SC	Y	15350 FQ	23070 AW	27940 TQ	NCBLS	10/01-12/01
	Greensboro-Winston-Salem-High Point MSA, NC	Y	15240 FQ	22300 AW	33320 TQ	NCBLS	10/01-12/01
	Hickory-Morganton-Lenoir MSA, NC	Y	14900 FQ	18300 AW	23120 TQ	NCBLS	10/01-12/01
	Raleigh-Durham-Chapel Hill MSA, NC	Y	17850 FQ	27220 AW	41790 TQ	NCBLS	10/01-12/01
	Wilmington MSA, NC	Y	14660 FQ	23600 AW	46840 TQ	NCBLS	10/01-12/01
	North Dakota	Y	13090 FQ	17150 AW	22530 TQ	NDBLS	10/01-12/01
	Fargo-Moorhead MSA, ND-MN	Y	12920 FQ	17740 AW	23950 TQ	NDBLS	10/01-12/01
	Ohio	Y	14020 FQ	20660 AW	29750 TQ	OHBLS	10/01-12/01
	Akron PMSA, OH	Y	15170 FQ	20490 AW	27660 TQ	OHBLS	10/01-12/01
	Canton-Massillon MSA, OH	Y	12100 FQ	18490 AW	25980 TQ	OHBLS	10/01-12/01
	Cincinnati PMSA, OH-KY-IN	Y	15020 FQ	21110 AW	30950 TQ	OHBLS	10/01-12/01
	Cleveland-Lorain-Elyria PMSA, OH	Y	14710 FQ	21160 AW	29990 TQ	OHBLS	10/01-12/01
	Columbus MSA, OH	Y	13430 FQ	20970 AW	31650 TQ	OHBLS	10/01-12/01
	Dayton-Springfield MSA, OH	Y	14520 FQ	23860 AW	35640 TQ	OHBLS	10/01-12/01
	Hamilton-Middletown PMSA, OH	Y	12320 FQ	19410 AW	27900 TQ	OHBLS	10/01-12/01
	Mansfield MSA, OH	Y	13800 FQ	17530 AW	22330 TQ	OHBLS	10/01-12/01
	Toledo MSA, OH	Y	13950 FQ	21920 AW	27860 TQ	OHBLS	10/01-12/01
	Youngstown-Warren MSA, OH	Y	11870 FQ	16920 AW	24710 TQ	OHBLS	10/01-12/01
	Oklahoma	Y	12120 FQ	16260 AW	21390 TQ	OKBLS	10/01-12/01
	Oklahoma City MSA, OK	Y	12650 FQ	16540 AW	20130 TQ	OKBLS	10/01-12/01

AAW Average annual wage; AE Average entry wage; AEX Average experienced wage; AO Average offered; AOH Average offered, high; AOL Average offered, low; APH Average pay, high range; APL Average pay, low range; ASH Average starting, high; ASL Average starting, low; AW Average wage paid; FQ First quartile wage; H Hourly; HI Highest wage paid; HR High end range; LR Low end range; M Monthly; MTC Median total compensation; MW Median wage paid; SQ Second quartile wage; S Special: hourly and annual; TQ Third quartile wage; W Weekly; Y Yearly

Occupation/Type/Industry	Location	Per	Low	Mid	High	Source	Date
Telemarketer	Tulsa MSA, OK	Y	12040 FQ	16370 AW	22030 TQ	OKBLS	10/01-12/01
	Oregon	Y	14750 FQ	20480 AW	27990 TQ	ORBLS	10/01-12/01
	Eugene-Springfield MSA, OR	Y	15310 FQ	23570 AW	35830 TQ	ORBLS	10/01-12/01
	Medford-Ashland MSA, OR	Y	14130 FQ	16090 AW	18100 TQ	ORBLS	10/01-12/01
	Portland-Vancouver PMSA, OR-WA	Y	15070 FQ	21520 AW	29170 TQ	ORBLS	10/01-12/01
	Salem PMSA, OR	Y	14070 FQ	16410 AW	20790 TQ	ORBLS	10/01-12/01
	Pennsylvania	Y	13580 FQ	19980 AW	28200 TQ	PABLS	10/01-12/01
	Allentown-Bethlehem-Easton MSA, PA	Y	13760 FQ	18570 AW	22760 TQ	PABLS	10/01-12/01
	Erie MSA, PA	Y	12370 FQ	18690 AW	28620 TQ	PABLS	10/01-12/01
	Harrisburg-Lebanon-Carlisle MSA, PA	Y	12610 FQ	19480 AW	29660 TQ	PABLS	10/01-12/01
	Lancaster MSA, PA	Y	13540 FQ	19500 AW	25290 TQ	PABLS	10/01-12/01
	Philadelphia PMSA, PA-NJ	Y	14460 FQ	20920 AW	30190 TQ	PABLS	10/01-12/01
	Pittsburgh MSA, PA	Y	14050 FQ	21420 AW	31480 TQ	PABLS	10/01-12/01
	Reading MSA, PA	Y	13090 FQ	22400 AW	35080 TQ	PABLS	10/01-12/01
	Scranton-Wilkes-Barre-Hazleton MSA, PA	Y	11990 FQ	15860 AW	18590 TQ	PABLS	10/01-12/01
	York MSA, PA	Y	12600 FQ	21590 AW	40270 TQ	PABLS	10/01-12/01
	Rhode Island	Y	16040 FQ	23160 AW	36150 TQ	RIBLS	10/01-12/01
	Providence-Fall River-Warwick MSA, RI-MA	Y	15950 FQ	23140 AW	36100 TQ	RIBLS	10/01-12/01
	South Carolina	Y	14110 FQ	20500 AW	28730 TQ	SCBLS	10/01-12/01
	Charleston-North Charleston MSA, SC	Y	12670 FQ	17030 AW	22290 TQ	SCBLS	10/01-12/01
	Greenville-Spartanburg-Anderson MSA, SC	Y	14340 FQ	19480 AW	27940 TQ	SCBLS	10/01-12/01
	Myrtle Beach MSA, SC	Y	12110 FQ	17880 AW	26700 TQ	SCBLS	10/01-12/01
	South Dakota	Y	12760 FQ	18170 AW	25060 TQ	SDBLS	10/01-12/01
	Sioux Falls MSA, SD	Y	13690 FQ	19340 AW	27640 TQ	SDBLS	10/01-12/01
	Tennessee	Y	14530 FQ	21040 AW	36490 TQ	TNBLS	10/01-12/01
	Clarksville-Hopkinsville MSA, TN-KY	Y	15050 FQ	19830 AW	27290 TQ	TNBLS	10/01-12/01
	Johnson City-Kingsport-Bristol MSA, TN-VA	Y	14620 FQ	17770 AW	24710 TQ	TNBLS	10/01-12/01
	Memphis MSA, TN-AR-MS	Y	14510 FQ	18920 AW	26880 TQ	TNBLS	10/01-12/01
	Nashville MSA, TN	Y	15760 FQ	24760 AW	40530 TQ	TNBLS	10/01-12/01
	Texas	Y	12960 FQ	20590 AW	32710 TQ	TXBLS	10/01-12/01
	Amarillo MSA, TX	Y	12210 FQ	16120 AW	20830 TQ	TXBLS	10/01-12/01
	Austin-San Marcos MSA, TX	Y	14270 FQ	20320 AW	28700 TQ	TXBLS	10/01-12/01
	Beaumont-Port Arthur MSA, TX	Y	11830 FQ	20440 AW	30050 TQ	TXBLS	10/01-12/01
	Corpus Christi MSA, TX	Y	11420 FQ	14800 AW	20300 TQ	TXBLS	10/01-12/01
	Dallas PMSA, TX	Y	15280 FQ	27220 AW	45720 TQ	TXBLS	10/01-12/01
	Fort Worth-Arlington PMSA, TX	Y	15020 FQ	18610 AW	23000 TQ	TXBLS	10/01-12/01
	Houston PMSA, TX	Y	14200 FQ	20110 AW	26200 TQ	TXBLS	10/01-12/01
	Killeen-Temple MSA, TX	Y	12890 FQ	16600 AW	20840 TQ	TXBLS	10/01-12/01
	Longview-Marshall MSA, TX	Y	14280 FQ	16490 AW	18580 TQ	TXBLS	10/01-12/01
	McAllen-Edinburg-Mission MSA, TX	Y	12500 FQ	19590 AW	27350 TQ	TXBLS	10/01-12/01
	San Antonio MSA, TX	Y	11950 FQ	16780 AW	26620 TQ	TXBLS	10/01-12/01
	Utah	Y	15590 FQ	21860 AW	27320 TQ	UTBLS	10/01-12/01
	Salt Lake City-Ogden MSA, UT	Y	16980 FQ	21840 AW	26860 TQ	UTBLS	10/01-12/01
	Vermont	Y	14060 FQ	27140 AW	44540 TQ	VTBLS	10/01-12/01
	Burlington MSA, VT	Y	13600 FQ	25350 AW	45580 TQ	VTBLS	10/01-12/01
	Virginia	Y	12130 FQ	20770 AW	33850 TQ	VABLS	10/01-12/01
	Norfolk-Virginia Beach-Newport News MSA, VA-NC	Y	11870 FQ	18310 AW	29520 TQ	VABLS	10/01-12/01
	Richmond-Petersburg MSA, VA	Y	16980 FQ	24670 AW	34710 TQ	VABLS	10/01-12/01
	Roanoke MSA, VA	Y	11690 FQ	19160 AW	31070 TQ	VABLS	10/01-12/01
	Washington	Y	14280 FQ	24590 AW	43030 TQ	WABLS	10/01-12/01
	Bremerton PMSA, WA	Y	14040 FQ	15940 AW	18350 TQ	WABLS	10/01-12/01
	Olympia PMSA, WA	Y	14330 FQ	25900 AW	43770 TQ	WABLS	10/01-12/01
	Richland-Kennewick-Pasco MSA, WA	Y	14010 FQ	21600 AW	39670 TQ	WABLS	10/01-12/01
	Seattle-Bellevue-Everett PMSA, WA	Y	14260 FQ	25790 AW	43630 TQ	WABLS	10/01-12/01

AAW	Average annual wage	**AOH**	Average offered, high	**ASH**	Average starting, high	**H**	Hourly	**M**	Monthly	**S**	Special: hourly and annual
AE	Average entry wage	**AOL**	Average offered, low	**ASL**	Average starting, low	**HI**	Highest wage paid	**MTC**	Median total compensation	**TQ**	Third quartile wage
AEX	Average experienced wage	**APH**	Average pay, high range	**AW**	Average wage paid	**HR**	High end range	**MW**	Median wage paid	**W**	Weekly
AO	Average offered	**APL**	Average pay, low range	**FQ**	First quartile wage	**LR**	Low end range	**SQ**	Second quartile wage	**Y**	Yearly

Occupation/Type/Industry	Location	Per	Low	Mid	High	Source	Date
Telemarketer	Spokane MSA, WA	Y	14750 FQ	19740 AW	29320 TQ	WABLS	10/01-12/01
	Tacoma PMSA, WA	Y	14180 FQ	18330 AW	25260 TQ	WABLS	10/01-12/01
	West Virginia	Y	14110 FQ	17990 AW	24030 TQ	WVBLS	10/01-12/01
	Charleston MSA, WV	Y	14780 FQ	19820 AW	27600 TQ	WVBLS	10/01-12/01
	Huntington-Ashland MSA, WV-KY-OH	Y	12590 FQ	16790 AW	23130 TQ	WVBLS	10/01-12/01
	Wisconsin	Y	14420 FQ	20930 AW	28680 TQ	WIBLS	10/01-12/01
	Appleton-Oshkosh-Neenah MSA, WI	Y	14990 FQ	21770 AW	35680 TQ	WIBLS	10/01-12/01
	Green Bay MSA, WI	Y	16240 FQ	32560 AW	56820 TQ	WIBLS	10/01-12/01
	Madison MSA, WI	Y	12970 FQ	18040 AW	24840 TQ	WIBLS	10/01-12/01
	Milwaukee-Waukesha PMSA, WI	Y	16150 FQ	22760 AW	29310 TQ	WIBLS	10/01-12/01
	Racine PMSA, WI	Y	14780 FQ	21710 AW	32960 TQ	WIBLS	10/01-12/01
	Wyoming	Y	12350 FQ	15900 AW	18630 TQ	WYBLS	10/01-12/01
	Puerto Rico	Y	11340 FQ	14680 AW	20440 TQ	PRBLS	10/01-12/01
Telephone Operator	Alabama	H	7.59 FQ	10.99 AW	15.48 TQ	ALBLS	10/01-12/01
	Anchorage MSA, AK	H	10.64 FQ	15.26 AW	18.14 TQ	AKBLS	10/01-12/01
	Arizona	H	7.30 FQ	12.86 AW	17.92 TQ	AZBLS	10/01-12/01
	California	H	8.54 FQ	13.67 AW	20.32 TQ	CABLS	10/01-12/01
	Oakland PMSA, CA	H	8.88 FQ	13.44 AW	20.14 TQ	CABLS	10/01-12/01
	Orange County PMSA, CA	H	7.99 FQ	16.53 AW	21.70 TQ	CABLS	10/01-12/01
	Riverside-San Bernardino PMSA, CA	H	7.53 FQ	13.24 AW	20.85 TQ	CABLS	10/01-12/01
	San Diego MSA, CA	H	8.86 FQ	12.81 AW	19.36 TQ	CABLS	10/01-12/01
	Colorado	H	6.73 FQ	11.04 AW	15.36 TQ	COBLS	10/01-12/01
	Denver PMSA, CO	H	6.46 FQ	10.35 AW	13.92 TQ	COBLS	10/01-12/01
	Connecticut	H	7.35 FQ	10.58 AW	16.02 TQ	CTBLS	10/01-12/01
	Bridgeport PMSA, CT	H	8.99 FQ	14.66 AW	20.82 TQ	CTBLS	10/01-12/01
	Delaware	H	6.61 FQ	10.78 AW	14.28 TQ	DEBLS	10/01-12/01
	Wilmington-Newark PMSA, DE-MD	H	6.45 FQ	9.92 AW	13.19 TQ	DEBLS	10/01-12/01
	Washington PMSA, DC-MD-VA-WV	H	7.56 FQ	16.29 AW	24.24 TQ	DCBLS	10/01-12/01
	Florida	H	6.62 FQ	12.28 AW	18.12 TQ	FLBLS	10/01-12/01
	Orlando MSA, FL	H	14.20 FQ	15.75 AW	18.00 TQ	FLBLS	10/01-12/01
	Tampa-St. Petersburg-Clearwater MSA, FL	H	6.30 FQ	10.87 AW	17.42 TQ	FLBLS	10/01-12/01
	West Palm Beach-Boca Raton MSA, FL	H	15.05 FQ	19.07 AW	22.31 TQ	FLBLS	10/01-12/01
	Georgia	H	6.60 FQ	12.25 AW	19.92 TQ	GABLS	10/01-12/01
	Atlanta MSA, GA	H	6.18 FQ	13.13 AW	20.42 TQ	GABLS	10/01-12/01
	Hawaii	H	11.89 FQ	14.40 AW	18.08 TQ	HIBLS	10/01-12/01
	Honolulu MSA, HI	H	11.86 FQ	14.80 AW	19.70 TQ	HIBLS	10/01-12/01
	Idaho	H	8.51 FQ	13.45 AW	19.02 TQ	IDBLS	10/01-12/01
	Boise City MSA, ID	H	9.18 FQ	12.43 AW	19.56 TQ	IDBLS	10/01-12/01
	Illinois	H	10.82 FQ	14.75 AW	17.52 TQ	ILBLS	10/01-12/01
	Chicago PMSA, IL	H	10.50 FQ	14.71 AW	17.50 TQ	ILBLS	10/01-12/01
	Indiana	H	7.44 FQ	12.76 AW	19.61 TQ	INBLS	10/01-12/01
	Indianapolis MSA, IN	H	7.15 FQ	11.16 AW	19.36 TQ	INBLS	10/01-12/01
	Iowa	H	7.62 FQ	12.28 AW	17.77 TQ	IABLS	10/01-12/01
	Kansas	H	7.28 FQ	10.48 AW	15.80 TQ	KSBLS	10/01-12/01
	Louisiana	H	6.92 FQ	12.24 AW	17.55 TQ	LABLS	10/01-12/01
	Maryland	H	9.94 FQ	16.84 AW	21.00 TQ	MDBLS	10/01-12/01
	Massachusetts	H	8.98 FQ	15.28 AW	20.83 TQ	MABLS	10/01-12/01
	Boston PMSA, MA-NH	H	9.38 FQ	15.36 AW	20.71 TQ	MABLS	10/01-12/01
	Michigan	H	10.86 FQ	16.48 AW	21.08 TQ	MIBLS	10/01-12/01
	Detroit PMSA, MI	H	11.23 FQ	16.93 AW	21.46 TQ	MIBLS	10/01-12/01
	Minnesota	H	6.90 FQ	12.55 AW	18.95 TQ	MNBLS	10/01-12/01
	Minneapolis-St. Paul MSA, MN-WI	H	6.60 FQ	12.24 AW	19.50 TQ	MNBLS	10/01-12/01
	Missouri	H	8.69 FQ	12.99 AW	18.44 TQ	MOBLS	10/01-12/01
	Kansas City MSA, MO-KS	H	8.98 FQ	15.55 AW	20.62 TQ	MOBLS	10/01-12/01
	St. Louis MSA, MO-IL	H	8.65 FQ	12.72 AW	17.03 TQ	MOBLS	10/01-12/01
	Nebraska	H	6.66 FQ	9.69 AW	13.37 TQ	NEBLS	10/01-12/01
	Omaha MSA, NE-IA	H	6.65 FQ	8.72 AW	11.75 TQ	NEBLS	10/01-12/01
	Nevada	H	8.85 FQ	11.30 AW	16.27 TQ	NVBLS	10/01-12/01
	New Jersey	H	9.29 FQ	14.58 AW	20.82 TQ	NJBLS	10/01-12/01
	Bergen-Passaic PMSA, NJ	H	9.71 FQ	16.95 AW	21.74 TQ	NJBLS	10/01-12/01
	Middlesex-Somerset-Hunterdon PMSA, NJ	H	9.34 FQ	14.44 AW	20.46 TQ	NJBLS	10/01-12/01
	Newark PMSA, NJ	H	9.60 FQ	15.04 AW	21.39 TQ	NJBLS	10/01-12/01

AAW	Average annual wage	AOH	Average offered, high	ASH	Average starting, high	H	Hourly	M	Monthly	S	Special: hourly and annual
AE	Average entry wage	AOL	Average offered, low	ASL	Average starting, low	HI	Highest wage paid	MTC	Median total compensation	TQ	Third quartile wage
AEX	Average experienced wage	APH	Average pay, high range	AW	Average wage paid	HR	High end range	MW	Median wage paid	W	Weekly
AO	Average offered	APL	Average pay, low range	FQ	First quartile wage	LR	Low end range	SQ	Second quartile wage	Y	Yearly

Occupation/Type/Industry	Location	Per	Low	Mid	High	Source	Date
Telephone Operator	New Mexico	H	6.05 FQ	8.77 AW	12.31 TQ	NMBLS	10/01-12/01
	Albuquerque MSA, NM	H	8.49 FQ	10.43 AW	13.30 TQ	NMBLS	10/01-12/01
	New York	H	8.27 FQ	16.13 AW	23.19 TQ	NYBLS	10/01-12/01
	Albany-Schenectady-Troy MSA, NY	H	10.98 FQ	14.70 AW	19.81 TQ	NYBLS	10/01-12/01
	Nassau-Suffolk PMSA, NY	H	7.45 FQ	13.55 AW	21.09 TQ	NYBLS	10/01-12/01
	New York PMSA, NY	H	8.19 FQ	17.50 AW	24.06 TQ	NYBLS	10/01-12/01
	North Carolina	H	7.75 FQ	13.49 AW	19.19 TQ	NCBLS	10/01-12/01
	Charlotte-Gastonia-Rock Hill MSA, NC-SC	H	9.28 FQ	14.67 AW	20.69 TQ	NCBLS	10/01-12/01
	Raleigh-Durham-Chapel Hill MSA, NC	H	7.18 FQ	11.91 AW	17.64 TQ	NCBLS	10/01-12/01
	Ohio	H	9.24 FQ	15.06 AW	20.93 TQ	OHBLS	10/01-12/01
	Cleveland-Lorain-Elyria PMSA, OH	H	10.05 FQ	17.28 AW	22.35 TQ	OHBLS	10/01-12/01
	Oklahoma	H	6.78 FQ	13.27 AW	17.88 TQ	OKBLS	10/01-12/01
	Pennsylvania	H	8.55 FQ	13.86 AW	20.42 TQ	PABLS	10/01-12/01
	Rhode Island	H	9.03 FQ	13.85 AW	20.37 TQ	RIBLS	10/01-12/01
	Providence-Fall River-Warwick MSA, RI-MA	H	9.17 FQ	14.99 AW	20.72 TQ	RIBLS	10/01-12/01
	Charleston-North Charleston MSA, SC	H	9.53 FQ	12.55 AW	15.43 TQ	SCBLS	10/01-12/01
	Memphis MSA, TN-AR-MS	H	7.15 FQ	9.08 AW	12.08 TQ	TNBLS	10/01-12/01
	Texas	H	11.78 FQ	16.39 AW	20.69 TQ	TXBLS	10/01-12/01
	Austin-San Marcos MSA, TX	H	11.33 FQ	16.52 AW	20.84 TQ	TXBLS	10/01-12/01
	Dallas PMSA, TX	H	11.92 FQ	15.98 AW	20.52 TQ	TXBLS	10/01-12/01
	Fort Worth-Arlington PMSA, TX	H	14.89 FQ	16.13 AW	18.10 TQ	TXBLS	10/01-12/01
	Houston PMSA, TX	H	15.14 FQ	18.23 AW	20.97 TQ	TXBLS	10/01-12/01
	San Antonio MSA, TX	H	14.86 FQ	17.05 AW	21.08 TQ	TXBLS	10/01-12/01
	Virginia	H	7.76 FQ	16.43 AW	25.19 TQ	VABLS	10/01-12/01
	Richmond-Petersburg MSA, VA	H	8.35 FQ	18.08 AW	28.21 TQ	VABLS	10/01-12/01
	Washington	H	10.84 FQ	13.49 AW	16.80 TQ	WABLS	10/01-12/01
	Seattle-Bellevue-Everett PMSA, WA	H	11.84 FQ	13.87 AW	17.04 TQ	WABLS	10/01-12/01
	West Virginia	H	8.79 FQ	14.04 AW	20.92 TQ	WVBLS	10/01-12/01
	Wisconsin	H	7.73 FQ	12.98 AW	18.12 TQ	WIBLS	10/01-12/01
	Madison MSA, WI	H	7.40 FQ	11.07 AW	19.12 TQ	WIBLS	10/01-12/01
	Milwaukee-Waukesha PMSA, WI	H	10.34 FQ	15.16 AW	18.84 TQ	WIBLS	10/01-12/01
Television-Audience Member	United States	H		7.00-25.00 AW		MC	1/01-1/01
Teller	Alabama	H	6.69 FQ	8.60 AW	11.04 TQ	ALBLS	10/01-12/01
	Birmingham MSA, AL	H	6.68 FQ	8.62 AW	10.88 TQ	ALBLS	10/01-12/01
	Huntsville MSA, AL	H	7.40 FQ	9.33 AW	11.60 TQ	ALBLS	10/01-12/01
	Mobile MSA, AL	H	7.11 FQ	8.48 AW	10.52 TQ	ALBLS	10/01-12/01
	Montgomery MSA, AL	H	6.91 FQ	8.40 AW	10.78 TQ	ALBLS	10/01-12/01
	Alaska	H	9.15 FQ	11.47 AW	14.73 TQ	AKBLS	10/01-12/01
	Anchorage MSA, AK	H	9.24 FQ	11.75 AW	15.22 TQ	AKBLS	10/01-12/01
	Arizona	H	8.38 FQ	10.43 AW	13.13 TQ	AZBLS	10/01-12/01
	Phoenix-Mesa MSA, AZ	H	8.24 FQ	10.59 AW	13.34 TQ	AZBLS	10/01-12/01
	Tucson MSA, AZ	H	8.64 FQ	10.27 AW	12.82 TQ	AZBLS	10/01-12/01
	Arkansas	H	6.49 FQ	8.79 AW	11.50 TQ	ARBLS	10/01-12/01
	Fayetteville-Springdale-Rogers MSA, AR	H	7.45 FQ	9.31 AW	11.60 TQ	ARBLS	10/01-12/01
	Fort Smith MSA, AR-OK	H	6.32 FQ	8.36 AW	10.71 TQ	ARBLS	10/01-12/01
	Little Rock-North Little Rock MSA, AR	H	7.41 FQ	10.07 AW	13.00 TQ	ARBLS	10/01-12/01
	California	H	8.12 FQ	10.42 AW	13.44 TQ	CABLS	10/01-12/01
	Bakersfield MSA, CA	H	7.54 FQ	9.60 AW	12.28 TQ	CABLS	10/01-12/01
	Chico-Paradise MSA, CA	H	7.68 FQ	9.89 AW	12.60 TQ	CABLS	10/01-12/01
	Fresno MSA, CA	H	7.75 FQ	10.04 AW	13.01 TQ	CABLS	10/01-12/01
	Los Angeles-Long Beach PMSA, CA	H	8.09 FQ	10.39 AW	13.63 TQ	CABLS	10/01-12/01
	Merced MSA, CA	H	7.75 FQ	9.85 AW	12.67 TQ	CABLS	10/01-12/01
	Modesto MSA, CA	H	7.58 FQ	9.72 AW	12.45 TQ	CABLS	10/01-12/01
	Oakland PMSA, CA	H	8.70 FQ	10.53 AW	13.35 TQ	CABLS	10/01-12/01
	Orange County PMSA, CA	H	8.67 FQ	10.60 AW	13.56 TQ	CABLS	10/01-12/01
	Redding MSA, CA	H	7.50 FQ	10.73 AW	14.88 TQ	CABLS	10/01-12/01

AAW Average annual wage **AE** Average entry wage **AEX** Average experienced wage **AO** Average offered **AOH** Average offered, high **AOL** Average offered, low **APH** Average pay, high range **APL** Average pay, low range **ASH** Average starting, high **ASL** Average starting, low **AW** Average wage paid **FQ** First quartile wage **H** Hourly **HI** Highest wage paid **HR** High end range **LR** Low end range **M** Monthly **MTC** Median total compensation **MW** Median wage paid **SQ** Second quartile wage **S** Special: hourly and annual **TQ** Third quartile wage **W** Weekly **Y** Yearly

Occupation/Type/Industry	Location	Per	Low	Mid	High	Source	Date
Teller	Riverside-San Bernardino PMSA, CA	H	7.77 FQ	10.04 AW	12.87 TQ	CABLS	10/01-12/01
	Sacramento PMSA, CA	H	8.28 FQ	10.24 AW	13.08 TQ	CABLS	10/01-12/01
	Salinas MSA, CA	H	8.51 FQ	10.92 AW	14.37 TQ	CABLS	10/01-12/01
	San Diego MSA, CA	H	7.84 FQ	10.18 AW	12.97 TQ	CABLS	10/01-12/01
	San Francisco PMSA, CA	H	8.17 FQ	11.24 AW	14.43 TQ	CABLS	10/01-12/01
	San Jose PMSA, CA	H	9.08 FQ	11.66 AW	15.59 TQ	CABLS	10/01-12/01
	San Luis Obispo-Atascadero-Paso Robles MSA, CA	H	7.36 FQ	10.26 AW	13.86 TQ	CABLS	10/01-12/01
	Santa Barbara-Santa Maria-Lompoc MSA, CA	H	7.93 FQ	10.38 AW	13.44 TQ	CABLS	10/01-12/01
	Santa Cruz-Watsonville PMSA, CA	H	8.74 FQ	10.45 AW	12.98 TQ	CABLS	10/01-12/01
	Santa Rosa PMSA, CA	H	8.86 FQ	11.03 AW	14.38 TQ	CABLS	10/01-12/01
	Stockton-Lodi MSA, CA	H	7.70 FQ	10.02 AW	12.78 TQ	CABLS	10/01-12/01
	Vallejo-Fairfield-Napa PMSA, CA	H	7.73 FQ	10.04 AW	13.02 TQ	CABLS	10/01-12/01
	Ventura PMSA, CA	H	8.73 FQ	10.46 AW	12.95 TQ	CABLS	10/01-12/01
	Visalia-Tulare-Porterville MSA, CA	H	7.46 FQ	9.72 AW	12.83 TQ	CABLS	10/01-12/01
	Colorado	H	7.93 FQ	10.36 AW	13.31 TQ	COBLS	10/01-12/01
	Boulder-Longmont PMSA, CO	H	9.13 FQ	11.04 AW	13.33 TQ	COBLS	10/01-12/01
	Colorado Springs MSA, CO	H	7.66 FQ	9.37 AW	11.13 TQ	COBLS	10/01-12/01
	Denver PMSA, CO	H	9.12 FQ	11.14 AW	14.00 TQ	COBLS	10/01-12/01
	Fort Collins-Loveland MSA, CO	H	7.70 FQ	9.63 AW	11.76 TQ	COBLS	10/01-12/01
	Greeley PMSA, CO	H	7.82 FQ	10.01 AW	12.92 TQ	COBLS	10/01-12/01
	Connecticut	H	8.94 FQ	11.31 AW	14.59 TQ	CTBLS	10/01-12/01
	Bridgeport PMSA, CT	H	9.27 FQ	11.71 AW	14.53 TQ	CTBLS	10/01-12/01
	Danbury PMSA, CT	H	10.07 FQ	12.30 AW	15.06 TQ	CTBLS	10/01-12/01
	Hartford MSA, CT	H	8.75 FQ	10.67 AW	13.27 TQ	CTBLS	10/01-12/01
	New Haven-Meriden PMSA, CT	H	9.05 FQ	11.40 AW	14.85 TQ	CTBLS	10/01-12/01
	New London-Norwich MSA, CT-RI	H	8.88 FQ	11.35 AW	16.07 TQ	CTBLS	10/01-12/01
	Stamford-Norwalk PMSA, CT	H	9.34 FQ	12.03 AW	15.62 TQ	CTBLS	10/01-12/01
	Waterbury PMSA, CT	H	8.73 FQ	11.35 AW	15.04 TQ	CTBLS	10/01-12/01
	Delaware	H	7.33 FQ	10.28 AW	13.50 TQ	DEBLS	10/01-12/01
	Wilmington-Newark PMSA, DE-MD	H	7.27 FQ	10.40 AW	13.56 TQ	DEBLS	10/01-12/01
	District of Columbia	H	9.11 FQ	12.10 AW	16.08 TQ	DCBLS	10/01-12/01
	Washington PMSA, DC-MD-VA-WV	H	8.04 FQ	10.53 AW	13.56 TQ	DCBLS	10/01-12/01
	Florida	H	7.50 FQ	9.72 AW	12.50 TQ	FLBLS	10/01-12/01
	Daytona Beach MSA, FL	H	7.14 FQ	9.66 AW	12.80 TQ	FLBLS	10/01-12/01
	Fort Lauderdale PMSA, FL	H	8.60 FQ	10.13 AW	12.55 TQ	FLBLS	10/01-12/01
	Fort Myers-Cape Coral MSA, FL	H	8.51 FQ	10.39 AW	13.23 TQ	FLBLS	10/01-12/01
	Fort Pierce-Port St. Lucie MSA, FL	H	7.72 FQ	10.12 AW	13.21 TQ	FLBLS	10/01-12/01
	Fort Walton Beach MSA, FL	H	7.14 FQ	9.05 AW	11.05 TQ	FLBLS	10/01-12/01
	Gainesville MSA, FL	H	7.05 FQ	9.00 AW	11.10 TQ	FLBLS	10/01-12/01
	Jacksonville MSA, FL	H	7.73 FQ	10.12 AW	12.95 TQ	FLBLS	10/01-12/01
	Lakeland-Winter Haven MSA, FL	H	7.45 FQ	9.59 AW	12.12 TQ	FLBLS	10/01-12/01
	Melbourne-Titusville-Palm Bay MSA, FL	H	7.47 FQ	9.66 AW	12.00 TQ	FLBLS	10/01-12/01
	Miami PMSA, FL	H	7.60 FQ	10.14 AW	13.19 TQ	FLBLS	10/01-12/01
	Naples MSA, FL	H	8.35 FQ	10.26 AW	12.72 TQ	FLBLS	10/01-12/01
	Ocala MSA, FL	H	7.39 FQ	9.23 AW	11.39 TQ	FLBLS	10/01-12/01
	Orlando MSA, FL	H	7.52 FQ	9.50 AW	11.98 TQ	FLBLS	10/01-12/01
	Pensacola MSA, FL	H	7.13 FQ	8.96 AW	11.22 TQ	FLBLS	10/01-12/01
	Sarasota-Bradenton MSA, FL	H	7.71 FQ	10.14 AW	13.08 TQ	FLBLS	10/01-12/01
	Tallahassee MSA, FL	H	7.32 FQ	9.28 AW	11.19 TQ	FLBLS	10/01-12/01
	Tampa-St. Petersburg-Clearwater MSA, FL	H	7.68 FQ	9.76 AW	12.44 TQ	FLBLS	10/01-12/01
	West Palm Beach-Boca Raton MSA, FL	H	7.51 FQ	9.61 AW	12.21 TQ	FLBLS	10/01-12/01
	Georgia	H	6.70 FQ	9.48 AW	12.51 TQ	GABLS	10/01-12/01
	Atlanta MSA, GA	H	8.68 FQ	10.51 AW	13.04 TQ	GABLS	10/01-12/01
	Augusta-Aiken MSA, GA-SC	H	7.21 FQ	9.25 AW	11.51 TQ	GABLS	10/01-12/01
	Columbus MSA, GA-AL	H	6.92 FQ	8.60 AW	10.98 TQ	GABLS	10/01-12/01

AAW	Average annual wage	AOH	Average offered, high	ASH	Average starting, high	H	Hourly	M	Monthly	S	Special: hourly and annual
AE	Average entry wage	AOL	Average offered, low	ASL	Average starting, low	HI	Highest wage paid	MTC	Median total compensation	TQ	Third quartile wage
AEX	Average experienced wage	APH	Average pay, high range	AW	Average wage paid	HR	High end range	MW	Median wage paid	W	Weekly
AO	Average offered	APL	Average pay, low range	FQ	First quartile wage	LR	Low end range	SQ	Second quartile wage	Y	Yearly

Occupation/Type/Industry	Location	Per	Low	Mid	High	Source	Date
Teller	Macon MSA, GA	H	7.35 FQ	9.60 AW	11.70 TQ	GABLS	10/01-12/01
	Savannah MSA, GA	H	7.83 FQ	10.33 AW	13.65 TQ	GABLS	10/01-12/01
	Hawaii	H	7.53 FQ	9.96 AW	13.19 TQ	HIBLS	10/01-12/01
	Honolulu MSA, HI	H	7.51 FQ	9.95 AW	13.28 TQ	HIBLS	10/01-12/01
	Idaho	H	7.25 FQ	9.27 AW	12.04 TQ	IDBLS	10/01-12/01
	Boise City MSA, ID	H	7.37 FQ	9.39 AW	12.02 TQ	IDBLS	10/01-12/01
	Illinois	H	7.05 FQ	9.71 AW	13.03 TQ	ILBLS	10/01-12/01
	Champaign-Urbana MSA, IL	H	6.38 FQ	8.19 AW	10.21 TQ	ILBLS	10/01-12/01
	Chicago PMSA, IL	H	7.63 FQ	10.31 AW	13.34 TQ	ILBLS	10/01-12/01
	Peoria-Pekin MSA, IL	H	6.82 FQ	8.33 AW	10.47 TQ	ILBLS	10/01-12/01
	Rockford MSA, IL	H	7.05 FQ	8.72 AW	11.28 TQ	ILBLS	10/01-12/01
	Springfield MSA, IL	H	6.74 FQ	8.50 AW	10.65 TQ	ILBLS	10/01-12/01
	Indiana	H	7.10 FQ	9.00 AW	11.11 TQ	INBLS	10/01-12/01
	Elkhart-Goshen MSA, IN	H	7.23 FQ	9.13 AW	11.49 TQ	INBLS	10/01-12/01
	Evansville-Henderson MSA, IN-KY	H	7.01 FQ	8.89 AW	10.87 TQ	INBLS	10/01-12/01
	Fort Wayne MSA, IN	H	7.51 FQ	9.22 AW	10.83 TQ	INBLS	10/01-12/01
	Gary PMSA, IN	H	7.29 FQ	8.95 AW	10.73 TQ	INBLS	10/01-12/01
	Indianapolis MSA, IN	H	6.80 FQ	9.41 AW	12.25 TQ	INBLS	10/01-12/01
	Lafayette MSA, IN	H	6.75 FQ	8.47 AW	10.87 TQ	INBLS	10/01-12/01
	South Bend MSA, IN	H	6.90 FQ	9.16 AW	11.29 TQ	INBLS	10/01-12/01
	Iowa	H	7.20 FQ	9.33 AW	11.74 TQ	IABLS	10/01-12/01
	Cedar Rapids MSA, IA	H	8.68 FQ	10.17 AW	12.53 TQ	IABLS	10/01-12/01
	Davenport-Moline-Rock Island MSA, IA-IL	H	7.00 FQ	9.36 AW	12.64 TQ	IABLS	10/01-12/01
	Des Moines MSA, IA	H	8.69 FQ	10.22 AW	12.62 TQ	IABLS	10/01-12/01
	Kansas	H	6.62 FQ	9.10 AW	12.08 TQ	KSBLS	10/01-12/01
	Topeka MSA, KS	H	7.61 FQ	9.23 AW	10.69 TQ	KSBLS	10/01-12/01
	Wichita MSA, KS	H	7.37 FQ	9.58 AW	12.49 TQ	KSBLS	10/01-12/01
	Kentucky	H	6.82 FQ	8.92 AW	11.30 TQ	KYBLS	10/01-12/01
	Lexington MSA, KY	H	7.27 FQ	9.20 AW	12.30 TQ	KYBLS	10/01-12/01
	Louisville MSA, KY-IN	H	7.57 FQ	9.38 AW	11.25 TQ	KYBLS	10/01-12/01
	Louisiana	H	6.73 FQ	8.77 AW	11.59 TQ	LABLS	10/01-12/01
	Baton Rouge MSA, LA	H	6.87 FQ	8.88 AW	11.49 TQ	LABLS	10/01-12/01
	Houma MSA, LA	H	6.77 FQ	8.25 AW	10.41 TQ	LABLS	10/01-12/01
	Lafayette MSA, LA	H	5.97 FQ	7.86 AW	10.19 TQ	LABLS	10/01-12/01
	Lake Charles MSA, LA	H	7.04 FQ	8.58 AW	11.59 TQ	LABLS	10/01-12/01
	New Orleans MSA, LA	H	7.01 FQ	9.03 AW	11.95 TQ	LABLS	10/01-12/01
	Shreveport-Bossier City MSA, LA	H	7.15 FQ	10.29 AW	13.67 TQ	LABLS	10/01-12/01
	Maine	H	7.30 FQ	9.09 AW	11.20 TQ	MEBLS	10/01-12/01
	Portland MSA, ME	H	7.59 FQ	9.11 AW	11.09 TQ	MEBLS	10/01-12/01
	Maryland	H	7.38 FQ	9.95 AW	13.09 TQ	MDBLS	10/01-12/01
	Baltimore PMSA, MD	H	7.51 FQ	9.91 AW	12.85 TQ	MDBLS	10/01-12/01
	Massachusetts	H	8.58 FQ	10.57 AW	13.46 TQ	MABLS	10/01-12/01
	Boston PMSA, MA-NH	H	8.80 FQ	10.80 AW	13.78 TQ	MABLS	10/01-12/01
	Brockton PMSA, MA	H	8.75 FQ	10.56 AW	13.49 TQ	MABLS	10/01-12/01
	Lawrence PMSA, MA-NH	H	8.56 FQ	10.46 AW	13.33 TQ	MABLS	10/01-12/01
	Lowell PMSA, MA-NH	H	7.99 FQ	10.39 AW	13.25 TQ	MABLS	10/01-12/01
	New Bedford PMSA, MA	H	7.55 FQ	9.69 AW	12.36 TQ	MABLS	10/01-12/01
	Springfield MSA, MA	H	8.40 FQ	10.10 AW	12.61 TQ	MABLS	10/01-12/01
	Worcester PMSA, MA-CT	H	7.86 FQ	10.02 AW	12.73 TQ	MABLS	10/01-12/01
	Michigan	H	7.26 FQ	9.86 AW	13.05 TQ	MIBLS	10/01-12/01
	Ann Arbor PMSA, MI	H	7.99 FQ	9.99 AW	12.75 TQ	MIBLS	10/01-12/01
	Detroit PMSA, MI	H	7.42 FQ	10.18 AW	13.18 TQ	MIBLS	10/01-12/01
	Flint PMSA, MI	H	7.47 FQ	10.40 AW	15.44 TQ	MIBLS	10/01-12/01
	Grand Rapids-Muskegon-Holland MSA, MI	H	7.37 FQ	9.44 AW	12.03 TQ	MIBLS	10/01-12/01
	Kalamazoo-Battle Creek MSA, MI	H	7.52 FQ	9.44 AW	11.22 TQ	MIBLS	10/01-12/01
	Lansing-East Lansing MSA, MI	H	6.69 FQ	9.94 AW	13.08 TQ	MIBLS	10/01-12/01
	Saginaw-Bay City-Midland MSA, MI	H	7.10 FQ	11.26 AW	19.81 TQ	MIBLS	10/01-12/01
	Minnesota	H	7.49 FQ	9.58 AW	12.12 TQ	MNBLS	10/01-12/01
	Duluth-Superior MSA, MN-WI	H	7.16 FQ	8.65 AW	10.82 TQ	MNBLS	10/01-12/01
	Minneapolis-St. Paul MSA, MN-WI	H	8.67 FQ	10.34 AW	12.72 TQ	MNBLS	10/01-12/01
	St. Cloud MSA, MN	H	6.85 FQ	9.04 AW	11.98 TQ	MNBLS	10/01-12/01
	Mississippi	H	7.13 FQ	9.73 AW	13.29 TQ	MSBLS	10/01-12/01
	Biloxi-Gulfport-Pascagoula MSA, MS	H	6.54 FQ	8.53 AW	10.66 TQ	MSBLS	10/01-12/01
	Missouri	H	6.51 FQ	8.88 AW	11.83 TQ	MOBLS	10/01-12/01

AAW	Average annual wage	**AOH**	Average offered, high	**ASH**	Average starting, high	**H**	Hourly	**M**	Monthly	**S**	Special: hourly and annual
AE	Average entry wage	**AOL**	Average offered, low	**ASL**	Average starting, low	**HI**	Highest wage paid	**MTC**	Median total compensation	**TQ**	Third quartile wage
AEX	Average experienced wage	**APH**	Average pay, high range	**AW**	Average wage paid	**HR**	High end range	**MW**	Median wage paid	**W**	Weekly
AO	Average offered	**APL**	Average pay, low range	**FQ**	First quartile wage	**LR**	Low end range	**SQ**	Second quartile wage	**Y**	Yearly

Occupation/Type/Industry	Location	Per	Low	Mid	High	Source	Date
Teller	Kansas City MSA, MO-KS	H	7.65 FQ	9.73 AW	12.26 TQ	MOBLS	10/01-12/01
	St. Louis MSA, MO-IL	H	7.51 FQ	9.70 AW	12.70 TQ	MOBLS	10/01-12/01
	Springfield MSA, MO	H	6.41 FQ	8.70 AW	12.40 TQ	MOBLS	10/01-12/01
	Montana	H	6.58 FQ	8.36 AW	10.48 TQ	MTBLS	10/01-12/01
	Billings MSA, MT	H	7.13 FQ	8.65 AW	10.62 TQ	MTBLS	10/01-12/01
	Nebraska	H	7.16 FQ	9.05 AW	11.14 TQ	NEBLS	10/01-12/01
	Lincoln MSA, NE	H	6.98 FQ	8.64 AW	10.75 TQ	NEBLS	10/01-12/01
	Omaha MSA, NE-IA	H	7.24 FQ	9.28 AW	12.08 TQ	NEBLS	10/01-12/01
	Nevada	H	8.55 FQ	10.68 AW	13.48 TQ	NVBLS	10/01-12/01
	Las Vegas MSA, NV-AZ	H	8.32 FQ	10.61 AW	13.38 TQ	NVBLS	10/01-12/01
	Reno MSA, NV	H	8.56 FQ	10.55 AW	13.26 TQ	NVBLS	10/01-12/01
	New Hampshire	H	7.38 FQ	9.37 AW	11.41 TQ	NHBLS	10/01-12/01
	Manchester PMSA, NH	H	7.71 FQ	9.67 AW	11.63 TQ	NHBLS	10/01-12/01
	Nashua PMSA, NH	H	6.76 FQ	9.48 AW	11.85 TQ	NHBLS	10/01-12/01
	Portsmouth-Rochester PMSA, NH-ME	H	8.55 FQ	9.93 AW	11.53 TQ	NHBLS	10/01-12/01
	New Jersey	H	7.31 FQ	9.69 AW	12.80 TQ	NJBLS	10/01-12/01
	Atlantic-Cape May PMSA, NJ	H	7.55 FQ	9.69 AW	11.93 TQ	NJBLS	10/01-12/01
	Bergen-Passaic PMSA, NJ	H	7.75 FQ	9.96 AW	12.86 TQ	NJBLS	10/01-12/01
	Jersey City PMSA, NJ	H	7.34 FQ	9.62 AW	12.64 TQ	NJBLS	10/01-12/01
	Middlesex-Somerset-Hunterdon PMSA, NJ	H	7.31 FQ	9.55 AW	12.75 TQ	NJBLS	10/01-12/01
	Monmouth-Ocean PMSA, NJ	H	7.81 FQ	10.38 AW	13.79 TQ	NJBLS	10/01-12/01
	Newark PMSA, NJ	H	7.09 FQ	9.77 AW	13.12 TQ	NJBLS	10/01-12/01
	Trenton PMSA, NJ	H	6.50 FQ	9.87 AW	12.90 TQ	NJBLS	10/01-12/01
	New Mexico	H	6.57 FQ	8.84 AW	11.42 TQ	NMBLS	10/01-12/01
	Albuquerque MSA, NM	H	7.07 FQ	9.24 AW	11.79 TQ	NMBLS	10/01-12/01
	Las Cruces MSA, NM	H	6.15 FQ	8.42 AW	10.96 TQ	NMBLS	10/01-12/01
	New York	H	7.09 FQ	10.03 AW	13.49 TQ	NYBLS	10/01-12/01
	Albany-Schenectady-Troy MSA, NY	H	7.84 FQ	9.59 AW	11.09 TQ	NYBLS	10/01-12/01
	Binghamton MSA, NY	H	7.08 FQ	8.90 AW	11.37 TQ	NYBLS	10/01-12/01
	Buffalo-Niagara Falls MSA, NY	H	6.45 FQ	9.16 AW	12.21 TQ	NYBLS	10/01-12/01
	Dutchess County PMSA, NY	H	7.22 FQ	9.82 AW	13.52 TQ	NYBLS	10/01-12/01
	Nassau-Suffolk PMSA, NY	H	6.32 FQ	9.97 AW	13.41 TQ	NYBLS	10/01-12/01
	New York PMSA, NY	H	7.43 FQ	10.65 AW	14.01 TQ	NYBLS	10/01-12/01
	Newburgh PMSA, NY-PA	H	6.55 FQ	8.72 AW	11.95 TQ	NYBLS	10/01-12/01
	Rochester MSA, NY	H	7.24 FQ	9.16 AW	11.93 TQ	NYBLS	10/01-12/01
	Syracuse MSA, NY	H	6.89 FQ	8.75 AW	11.19 TQ	NYBLS	10/01-12/01
	Utica-Rome MSA, NY	H	7.36 FQ	9.36 AW	12.29 TQ	NYBLS	10/01-12/01
	North Carolina	H	7.20 FQ	9.91 AW	13.03 TQ	NCBLS	10/01-12/01
	Asheville MSA, NC	H	7.32 FQ	9.75 AW	12.84 TQ	NCBLS	10/01-12/01
	Charlotte-Gastonia-Rock Hill MSA, NC-SC	H	7.02 FQ	10.13 AW	13.08 TQ	NCBLS	10/01-12/01
	Fayetteville MSA, NC	H	7.02 FQ	8.84 AW	10.85 TQ	NCBLS	10/01-12/01
	Greensboro-Winston-Salem-High Point MSA, NC	H	7.50 FQ	10.44 AW	13.34 TQ	NCBLS	10/01-12/01
	Hickory-Morganton-Lenoir MSA, NC	H	7.32 FQ	9.18 AW	11.09 TQ	NCBLS	10/01-12/01
	Raleigh-Durham-Chapel Hill MSA, NC	H	8.42 FQ	10.93 AW	15.09 TQ	NCBLS	10/01-12/01
	Wilmington MSA, NC	H	7.39 FQ	10.14 AW	13.18 TQ	NCBLS	10/01-12/01
	North Dakota	H	6.75 FQ	8.66 AW	10.73 TQ	NDBLS	10/01-12/01
	Fargo-Moorhead MSA, ND-MN	H	7.13 FQ	9.11 AW	11.08 TQ	NDBLS	10/01-12/01
	Ohio	H	7.03 FQ	9.15 AW	11.75 TQ	OHBLS	10/01-12/01
	Akron PMSA, OH	H	7.73 FQ	9.86 AW	12.47 TQ	OHBLS	10/01-12/01
	Canton-Massillon MSA, OH	H	7.84 FQ	9.85 AW	11.66 TQ	OHBLS	10/01-12/01
	Cincinnati PMSA, OH-KY-IN	H	7.52 FQ	9.79 AW	12.63 TQ	OHBLS	10/01-12/01
	Cleveland-Lorain-Elyria PMSA, OH	H	7.15 FQ	9.42 AW	12.35 TQ	OHBLS	10/01-12/01
	Columbus MSA, OH	H	7.53 FQ	9.97 AW	12.90 TQ	OHBLS	10/01-12/01
	Dayton-Springfield MSA, OH	H	6.40 FQ	8.71 AW	11.17 TQ	OHBLS	10/01-12/01
	Hamilton-Middletown PMSA, OH	H	7.07 FQ	8.56 AW	10.54 TQ	OHBLS	10/01-12/01
	Mansfield MSA, OH	H	6.13 FQ	8.29 AW	10.63 TQ	OHBLS	10/01-12/01
	Toledo MSA, OH	H	7.37 FQ	9.34 AW	11.70 TQ	OHBLS	10/01-12/01
	Youngstown-Warren MSA, OH	H	6.92 FQ	8.79 AW	11.85 TQ	OHBLS	10/01-12/01
	Oklahoma	H	6.34 FQ	8.76 AW	11.22 TQ	OKBLS	10/01-12/01
	Oklahoma City MSA, OK	H	7.45 FQ	9.35 AW	11.71 TQ	OKBLS	10/01-12/01
	Tulsa MSA, OK	H	7.45 FQ	9.44 AW	11.32 TQ	OKBLS	10/01-12/01

AAW	Average annual wage	**AOH**	Average offered, high	**ASH**	Average starting, high	**H**	Hourly	**M**	Monthly	**S**	Special: hourly and annual
AE	Average entry wage	**AOL**	Average offered, low	**ASL**	Average starting, low	**HI**	Highest wage paid	**MTC**	Median total compensation	**TQ**	Third quartile wage
AEX	Average experienced wage	**APH**	Average pay, high range	**AW**	Average wage paid	**HR**	High end range	**MW**	Median wage paid	**W**	Weekly
AO	Average offered	**APL**	Average pay, low range	**FQ**	First quartile wage	**LR**	Low end range	**SQ**	Second quartile wage	**Y**	Yearly

Occupation/Type/Industry	Location	Per	Low	Mid	High	Source	Date
Teller	Oregon	H	7.60 FQ	9.69 AW	12.18 TQ	ORBLS	10/01-12/01
	Eugene-Springfield MSA, OR	H	7.85 FQ	9.71 AW	11.66 TQ	ORBLS	10/01-12/01
	Medford-Ashland MSA, OR	H	7.21 FQ	9.18 AW	11.55 TQ	ORBLS	10/01-12/01
	Portland-Vancouver PMSA, OR-WA	H	7.96 FQ	10.00 AW	12.64 TQ	ORBLS	10/01-12/01
	Salem PMSA, OR	H	7.26 FQ	9.40 AW	11.53 TQ	ORBLS	10/01-12/01
	Pennsylvania	H	7.02 FQ	9.72 AW	13.11 TQ	PABLS	10/01-12/01
	Allentown-Bethlehem-Easton MSA, PA	H	6.15 FQ	9.19 AW	11.51 TQ	PABLS	10/01-12/01
	Erie MSA, PA	H	6.78 FQ	8.74 AW	11.27 TQ	PABLS	10/01-12/01
	Harrisburg-Lebanon-Carlisle MSA, PA	H	7.56 FQ	9.48 AW	11.08 TQ	PABLS	10/01-12/01
	Johnstown MSA, PA	H	6.79 FQ	9.06 AW	12.24 TQ	PABLS	10/01-12/01
	Lancaster MSA, PA	H	6.16 FQ	8.96 AW	12.06 TQ	PABLS	10/01-12/01
	Philadelphia PMSA, PA-NJ	H	7.49 FQ	10.24 AW	13.07 TQ	PABLS	10/01-12/01
	Pittsburgh MSA, PA	H	7.07 FQ	10.47 AW	14.64 TQ	PABLS	10/01-12/01
	Reading MSA, PA	H	7.78 FQ	9.88 AW	12.83 TQ	PABLS	10/01-12/01
	Scranton-Wilkes-Barre-Hazleton MSA, PA	H	5.79 FQ	7.71 AW	10.03 TQ	PABLS	10/01-12/01
	York MSA, PA	H	7.25 FQ	9.06 AW	11.03 TQ	PABLS	10/01-12/01
	Rhode Island	H	8.60 FQ	10.81 AW	13.32 TQ	RIBLS	10/01-12/01
	Providence-Fall River-Warwick MSA, RI-MA	H	8.38 FQ	10.57 AW	13.18 TQ	RIBLS	10/01-12/01
	South Carolina	H	7.60 FQ	9.93 AW	12.95 TQ	SCBLS	10/01-12/01
	Charleston-North Charleston MSA, SC	H	7.45 FQ	9.93 AW	13.16 TQ	SCBLS	10/01-12/01
	Columbia MSA, SC	H	7.81 FQ	10.21 AW	13.37 TQ	SCBLS	10/01-12/01
	Greenville-Spartanburg-Anderson MSA, SC	H	8.00 FQ	10.54 AW	13.33 TQ	SCBLS	10/01-12/01
	Myrtle Beach MSA, SC	H	7.68 FQ	9.76 AW	12.34 TQ	SCBLS	10/01-12/01
	South Dakota	H	7.13 FQ	8.61 AW	10.66 TQ	SDBLS	10/01-12/01
	Sioux Falls MSA, SD	H	7.29 FQ	8.80 AW	10.71 TQ	SDBLS	10/01-12/01
	Tennessee	H	6.97 FQ	9.19 AW	12.01 TQ	TNBLS	10/01-12/01
	Chattanooga MSA, TN-GA	H	7.17 FQ	9.37 AW	12.06 TQ	TNBLS	10/01-12/01
	Clarksville-Hopkinsville MSA, TN-KY	H	7.22 FQ	8.77 AW	10.84 TQ	TNBLS	10/01-12/01
	Johnson City-Kingsport-Bristol MSA, TN-VA	H	7.01 FQ	8.88 AW	11.40 TQ	TNBLS	10/01-12/01
	Knoxville MSA, TN	H	7.00 FQ	9.10 AW	11.54 TQ	TNBLS	10/01-12/01
	Memphis MSA, TN-AR-MS	H	7.65 FQ	10.02 AW	12.91 TQ	TNBLS	10/01-12/01
	Nashville MSA, TN	H	7.55 FQ	10.17 AW	13.09 TQ	TNBLS	10/01-12/01
	Texas	H	7.06 FQ	9.45 AW	12.30 TQ	TXBLS	10/01-12/01
	Amarillo MSA, TX	H	6.50 FQ	8.32 AW	10.76 TQ	TXBLS	10/01-12/01
	Austin-San Marcos MSA, TX	H	7.91 FQ	9.83 AW	11.97 TQ	TXBLS	10/01-12/01
	Beaumont-Port Arthur MSA, TX	H	7.42 FQ	10.07 AW	13.58 TQ	TXBLS	10/01-12/01
	Brazoria PMSA, TX	H	6.18 FQ	8.64 AW	10.99 TQ	TXBLS	10/01-12/01
	Brownsville-Harlingen-San Benito MSA, TX	H	5.81 FQ	7.70 AW	10.34 TQ	TXBLS	10/01-12/01
	Corpus Christi MSA, TX	H	7.54 FQ	10.09 AW	13.44 TQ	TXBLS	10/01-12/01
	Dallas PMSA, TX	H	7.75 FQ	10.59 AW	13.29 TQ	TXBLS	10/01-12/01
	El Paso MSA, TX	H	5.98 FQ	7.93 AW	10.45 TQ	TXBLS	10/01-12/01
	Fort Worth-Arlington PMSA, TX	H	7.64 FQ	9.56 AW	11.28 TQ	TXBLS	10/01-12/01
	Galveston-Texas City PMSA, TX	H	7.37 FQ	9.30 AW	11.85 TQ	TXBLS	10/01-12/01
	Houston PMSA, TX	H	7.37 FQ	9.82 AW	12.51 TQ	TXBLS	10/01-12/01
	Killeen-Temple MSA, TX	H	6.12 FQ	8.38 AW	10.71 TQ	TXBLS	10/01-12/01
	Laredo MSA, TX	H	6.68 FQ	9.03 AW	11.57 TQ	TXBLS	10/01-12/01
	Longview-Marshall MSA, TX	H	7.05 FQ	8.81 AW	10.86 TQ	TXBLS	10/01-12/01
	Lubbock MSA, TX	H	6.34 FQ	8.17 AW	10.71 TQ	TXBLS	10/01-12/01
	McAllen-Edinburg-Mission MSA, TX	H	6.38 FQ	8.59 AW	11.12 TQ	TXBLS	10/01-12/01
	Odessa-Midland MSA, TX	H	6.65 FQ	8.43 AW	10.75 TQ	TXBLS	10/01-12/01
	San Antonio MSA, TX	H	7.39 FQ	9.45 AW	11.69 TQ	TXBLS	10/01-12/01
	Tyler MSA, TX	H	7.35 FQ	9.45 AW	11.90 TQ	TXBLS	10/01-12/01
	Waco MSA, TX	H	7.11 FQ	8.72 AW	10.96 TQ	TXBLS	10/01-12/01
	Utah	H	7.36 FQ	9.21 AW	11.01 TQ	UTBLS	10/01-12/01
	Provo-Orem MSA, UT	H	7.13 FQ	8.99 AW	11.13 TQ	UTBLS	10/01-12/01
	Salt Lake City-Ogden MSA, UT	H	7.46 FQ	9.37 AW	11.03 TQ	UTBLS	10/01-12/01
	Vermont	H	7.12 FQ	9.62 AW	12.65 TQ	VTBLS	10/01-12/01

AAW Average annual wage **AOH** Average offered, high **ASH** Average starting, high **H** Hourly **M** Monthly **S** Special: hourly and annual
AE Average entry wage **AOL** Average offered, low **ASL** Average starting, low **HI** Highest wage paid **MTC** Median total compensation **TQ** Third quartile wage
AEX Average experienced wage **APH** Average pay, high range **AW** Average wage paid **HR** High end range **MW** Median wage paid **W** Weekly
AO Average offered **APL** Average pay, low range **FQ** First quartile wage **LR** Low end range **SQ** Second quartile wage **Y** Yearly

Occupation/Type/Industry	Location	Per	Low	Mid	High	Source	Date
Teller	Burlington MSA, VT	H	6.74 FQ	9.25 AW	12.48 TQ	VTBLS	10/01-12/01
	Virginia	H	7.42 FQ	9.80 AW	12.80 TQ	VABLS	10/01-12/01
	Lynchburg MSA, VA	H	7.42 FQ	10.52 AW	14.97 TQ	VABLS	10/01-12/01
	Norfolk-Virginia Beach-Newport News MSA, VA-NC	H	7.38 FQ	9.30 AW	11.62 TQ	VABLS	10/01-12/01
	Richmond-Petersburg MSA, VA	H	7.80 FQ	10.06 AW	12.85 TQ	VABLS	10/01-12/01
	Roanoke MSA, VA	H	7.42 FQ	9.38 AW	11.90 TQ	VABLS	10/01-12/01
	Washington	H	8.28 FQ	10.41 AW	13.16 TQ	WABLS	10/01-12/01
	Bremerton PMSA, WA	H	8.10 FQ	10.08 AW	12.67 TQ	WABLS	10/01-12/01
	Olympia PMSA, WA	H	8.70 FQ	10.09 AW	12.10 TQ	WABLS	10/01-12/01
	Richland-Kennewick-Pasco MSA, WA	H	7.08 FQ	9.58 AW	13.35 TQ	WABLS	10/01-12/01
	Seattle-Bellevue-Everett PMSA, WA	H	8.93 FQ	10.76 AW	13.19 TQ	WABLS	10/01-12/01
	Spokane MSA, WA	H	6.75 FQ	9.52 AW	12.41 TQ	WABLS	10/01-12/01
	Tacoma PMSA, WA	H	7.87 FQ	10.60 AW	14.52 TQ	WABLS	10/01-12/01
	Yakima MSA, WA	H	7.54 FQ	9.54 AW	11.55 TQ	WABLS	10/01-12/01
	West Virginia	H	5.96 FQ	8.26 AW	11.01 TQ	WVBLS	10/01-12/01
	Charleston MSA, WV	H	5.98 FQ	8.13 AW	10.76 TQ	WVBLS	10/01-12/01
	Huntington-Ashland MSA, WV-KY-OH	H	6.00 FQ	8.14 AW	10.70 TQ	WVBLS	10/01-12/01
	Wisconsin	H	7.28 FQ	9.39 AW	12.02 TQ	WIBLS	10/01-12/01
	Appleton-Oshkosh-Neenah MSA, WI	H	7.38 FQ	9.29 AW	11.55 TQ	WIBLS	10/01-12/01
	Green Bay MSA, WI	H	7.80 FQ	10.35 AW	14.36 TQ	WIBLS	10/01-12/01
	Madison MSA, WI	H	7.41 FQ	9.52 AW	12.42 TQ	WIBLS	10/01-12/01
	Milwaukee-Waukesha PMSA, WI	H	7.51 FQ	9.76 AW	12.67 TQ	WIBLS	10/01-12/01
	Racine PMSA, WI	H	7.23 FQ	9.34 AW	12.13 TQ	WIBLS	10/01-12/01
	Wyoming	H	6.57 FQ	8.69 AW	11.02 TQ	WYBLS	10/01-12/01
	Cheyenne MSA, WY	H	7.09 FQ	8.50 AW	10.58 TQ	WYBLS	10/01-12/01
	Puerto Rico	H	5.55 FQ	6.65 AW	8.53 TQ	PRBLS	10/01-12/01
	Virgin Islands	H	7.21 FQ	8.51 AW	10.67 TQ	VIBLS	10/01-12/01
	Guam	H	7.05 FQ	9.19 AW	12.78 TQ	GUBLS	10/01-12/01
Terrazzo Worker and Finisher	Alabama	H	7.37 FQ	10.09 AW	13.42 TQ	ALBLS	10/01-12/01
	Arizona	H	7.84 FQ	12.93 AW	20.10 TQ	AZBLS	10/01-12/01
	California	H	8.24 FQ	14.17 AW	23.43 TQ	CABLS	10/01-12/01
	Florida	H	7.83 FQ	13.18 AW	17.56 TQ	FLBLS	10/01-12/01
	Georgia	H	8.98 FQ	12.20 AW	16.69 TQ	GABLS	10/01-12/01
	Illinois	H	18.05 FQ	21.75 AW	26.85 TQ	ILBLS	10/01-12/01
	Indiana	H	18.42 FQ	22.05 AW	26.20 TQ	INBLS	10/01-12/01
	Kentucky	H	11.78 FQ	12.76 AW	14.24 TQ	KYBLS	10/01-12/01
	Maryland	H	11.09 FQ	13.08 AW	16.74 TQ	MDBLS	10/01-12/01
	Massachusetts	H	15.14 FQ	22.11 AW	32.59 TQ	MABLS	10/01-12/01
	Michigan	H	8.99 FQ	14.69 AW	21.32 TQ	MIBLS	10/01-12/01
	Minnesota	H	15.37 FQ	21.37 AW	28.21 TQ	MNBLS	10/01-12/01
	Mississippi	H	8.97 FQ	20.94 AW	57.07 TQ	MSBLS	10/01-12/01
	Nevada	H	14.05 FQ	15.77 AW	17.51 TQ	NVBLS	10/01-12/01
	New York	H	9.65 FQ	20.26 AW	33.96 TQ	NYBLS	10/01-12/01
	Ohio	H	12.56 FQ	18.35 AW	25.95 TQ	OHBLS	10/01-12/01
	Pennsylvania	H	6.08 FQ	18.57 AW	26.46 TQ	PABLS	10/01-12/01
	South Carolina	H	7.48 FQ	10.52 AW	15.26 TQ	SCBLS	10/01-12/01
	Tennessee	H	9.71 FQ	13.70 AW	18.33 TQ	TNBLS	10/01-12/01
	Texas	H	8.79 FQ	11.31 AW	17.68 TQ	TXBLS	10/01-12/01
	Washington	H	7.63 FQ	16.99 AW	23.07 TQ	WABLS	10/01-12/01
	Wisconsin	H	11.12 FQ	18.37 AW	27.31 TQ	WIBLS	10/01-12/01
Textile Bleaching and Dyeing Machine Operator and Tender	Alabama	H	8.19 FQ	9.91 AW	11.75 TQ	ALBLS	10/01-12/01
	California	H	6.42 FQ	8.37 AW	11.72 TQ	CABLS	10/01-12/01
	Los Angeles-Long Beach PMSA, CA	H	6.37 FQ	7.67 AW	10.32 TQ	CABLS	10/01-12/01
	Orange County PMSA, CA	H	6.60 FQ	9.55 AW	13.24 TQ	CABLS	10/01-12/01
	San Francisco PMSA, CA	H	6.80 FQ	8.84 AW	12.21 TQ	CABLS	10/01-12/01
	Connecticut	H	9.26 FQ	12.29 AW	16.88 TQ	CTBLS	10/01-12/01
	Hartford MSA, CT	H	9.44 FQ	12.65 AW	17.17 TQ	CTBLS	10/01-12/01
	New London-Norwich MSA, CT-RI	H	9.95 FQ	12.86 AW	16.97 TQ	CTBLS	10/01-12/01
	Florida	H	6.00 FQ	8.66 AW	11.70 TQ	FLBLS	10/01-12/01

AAW Average annual wage; AE Average entry wage; AEX Average experienced wage; AO Average offered; AOH Average offered, high; AOL Average offered, low; APH Average pay, high range; APL Average pay, low range; ASH Average starting, high; ASL Average starting, low; AW Average wage paid; FQ First quartile wage; H Hourly; HI Highest wage paid; HR High end range; LR Low end range; M Monthly; MTC Median total compensation; MW Median wage paid; SQ Second quartile wage; S Special: hourly and annual; TQ Third quartile wage; W Weekly; Y Yearly

Occupation/Type/Industry	Location	Per	Low	Mid	High	Source	Date
Textile Bleaching and Dyeing Machine Operator and Tender	Miami PMSA, FL	H	6.81 FQ	9.95 AW	14.05 TQ	FLBLS	10/01-12/01
	Georgia	H	7.33 FQ	9.61 AW	12.63 TQ	GABLS	10/01-12/01
	Atlanta MSA, GA	H	7.12 FQ	8.99 AW	12.12 TQ	GABLS	10/01-12/01
	Augusta-Aiken MSA, GA-SC	H	6.02 FQ	9.66 AW	13.15 TQ	GABLS	10/01-12/01
	Illinois	H	5.86 FQ	8.74 AW	12.60 TQ	ILBLS	10/01-12/01
	Chicago PMSA, IL	H	6.18 FQ	9.85 AW	13.16 TQ	ILBLS	10/01-12/01
	Indiana	H	5.74 FQ	8.80 AW	10.77 TQ	INBLS	10/01-12/01
	Indianapolis MSA, IN	H	5.68 FQ	7.33 AW	9.75 TQ	INBLS	10/01-12/01
	Kentucky	H	6.04 FQ	8.45 AW	11.22 TQ	KYBLS	10/01-12/01
	Maine	H	9.25 FQ	11.49 AW	14.15 TQ	MEBLS	10/01-12/01
	Massachusetts	H	9.06 FQ	12.04 AW	13.99 TQ	MABLS	10/01-12/01
	Boston PMSA, MA-NH	H	7.04 FQ	10.98 AW	15.62 TQ	MABLS	10/01-12/01
	New Bedford PMSA, MA	H	9.96 FQ	12.13 AW	14.02 TQ	MABLS	10/01-12/01
	Michigan	H	6.03 FQ	8.64 AW	12.13 TQ	MIBLS	10/01-12/01
	Mississippi	H	6.88 FQ	9.19 AW	11.96 TQ	MSBLS	10/01-12/01
	Nevada	H	5.69 FQ	7.38 AW	9.49 TQ	NVBLS	10/01-12/01
	Las Vegas MSA, NV-AZ	H	5.70 FQ	7.50 AW	9.80 TQ	NVBLS	10/01-12/01
	New Hampshire	H	8.27 FQ	11.21 AW	14.89 TQ	NHBLS	10/01-12/01
	New Jersey	H	6.22 FQ	12.43 AW	21.33 TQ	NJBLS	10/01-12/01
	Bergen-Passaic PMSA, NJ	H	8.12 FQ	14.39 AW	23.83 TQ	NJBLS	10/01-12/01
	Jersey City PMSA, NJ	H	6.43 FQ	12.07 AW	22.74 TQ	NJBLS	10/01-12/01
	New York	H	5.94 FQ	9.63 AW	14.54 TQ	NYBLS	10/01-12/01
	Albany-Schenectady-Troy MSA, NY	H	8.09 FQ	11.33 AW	17.09 TQ	NYBLS	10/01-12/01
	New York PMSA, NY	H	5.76 FQ	9.04 AW	16.19 TQ	NYBLS	10/01-12/01
	North Carolina	H	7.18 FQ	10.08 AW	13.19 TQ	NCBLS	10/01-12/01
	Charlotte-Gastonia-Rock Hill MSA, NC-SC	H	7.99 FQ	10.70 AW	13.57 TQ	NCBLS	10/01-12/01
	Greensboro-Winston-Salem-High Point MSA, NC	H	6.61 FQ	9.90 AW	13.21 TQ	NCBLS	10/01-12/01
	Hickory-Morganton-Lenoir MSA, NC	H	7.33 FQ	9.94 AW	13.22 TQ	NCBLS	10/01-12/01
	Ohio	H	6.13 FQ	8.61 AW	11.70 TQ	OHBLS	10/01-12/01
	Dayton-Springfield MSA, OH	H	6.95 FQ	8.85 AW	10.97 TQ	OHBLS	10/01-12/01
	Portland-Vancouver PMSA, OR-WA	H	7.38 FQ	10.52 AW	13.94 TQ	ORBLS	10/01-12/01
	Pennsylvania	H	7.36 FQ	10.74 AW	15.12 TQ	PABLS	10/01-12/01
	Allentown-Bethlehem-Easton MSA, PA	H	7.48 FQ	9.62 AW	12.40 TQ	PABLS	10/01-12/01
	Philadelphia PMSA, PA-NJ	H	6.56 FQ	9.67 AW	13.26 TQ	PABLS	10/01-12/01
	Scranton-Wilkes-Barre-Hazleton MSA, PA	H	6.22 FQ	11.17 AW	16.26 TQ	PABLS	10/01-12/01
	Rhode Island	H	6.94 FQ	11.74 AW	16.28 TQ	RIBLS	10/01-12/01
	Providence-Fall River-Warwick MSA, RI-MA	H	7.73 FQ	11.85 AW	14.33 TQ	RIBLS	10/01-12/01
	South Carolina	H	8.13 FQ	10.82 AW	13.61 TQ	SCBLS	10/01-12/01
	Greenville-Spartanburg-Anderson MSA, SC	H	9.13 FQ	11.18 AW	13.90 TQ	SCBLS	10/01-12/01
	Tennessee	H	7.99 FQ	10.44 AW	13.26 TQ	TNBLS	10/01-12/01
	Vermont	H	9.32 FQ	10.49 AW	11.46 TQ	VTBLS	10/01-12/01
	Virginia	H	8.35 FQ	10.92 AW	13.39 TQ	VABLS	10/01-12/01
	Washington	H	7.51 FQ	9.61 AW	11.89 TQ	WABLS	10/01-12/01
	Wisconsin	H	6.53 FQ	9.39 AW	12.13 TQ	WIBLS	10/01-12/01
	Milwaukee-Waukesha PMSA, WI	H	6.26 FQ	9.35 AW	13.10 TQ	WIBLS	10/01-12/01
	Puerto Rico	H	5.76 FQ	7.06 AW	8.34 TQ	PRBLS	10/01-12/01
Textile Cutting Machine Setter, Operator, and Tender	Alabama	H	6.60 FQ	9.45 AW	11.83 TQ	ALBLS	10/01-12/01
	Phoenix-Mesa MSA, AZ	H	6.91 FQ	7.73 AW	8.45 TQ	AZBLS	10/01-12/01
	Tucson MSA, AZ	H	6.50 FQ	8.42 AW	10.78 TQ	AZBLS	10/01-12/01
	Arkansas	H	7.03 FQ	9.31 AW	12.02 TQ	ARBLS	10/01-12/01
	California	H	6.52 FQ	8.85 AW	12.87 TQ	CABLS	10/01-12/01
	Los Angeles-Long Beach PMSA, CA	H	6.44 FQ	9.10 AW	13.08 TQ	CABLS	10/01-12/01
	Orange County PMSA, CA	H	6.60 FQ	7.84 AW	9.56 TQ	CABLS	10/01-12/01
	Riverside-San Bernardino PMSA, CA	H	7.62 FQ	12.28 AW	17.00 TQ	CABLS	10/01-12/01
	San Diego MSA, CA	H	6.80 FQ	9.46 AW	12.77 TQ	CABLS	10/01-12/01
	San Francisco PMSA, CA	H	7.08 FQ	10.20 AW	13.94 TQ	CABLS	10/01-12/01
	Ventura PMSA, CA	H	6.81 FQ	9.62 AW	12.67 TQ	CABLS	10/01-12/01

AAW	Average annual wage	**AOH**	Average offered, high	**ASH**	Average starting, high	**H**	Hourly	**M**	Monthly	**S**	Special: hourly and annual
AE	Average entry wage	**AOL**	Average offered, low	**ASL**	Average starting, low	**HI**	Highest wage paid	**MTC**	Median total compensation	**TQ**	Third quartile wage
AEX	Average experienced wage	**APH**	Average pay, high range	**AW**	Average wage paid	**HR**	High end range	**MW**	Median wage paid	**W**	Weekly
AO	Average offered	**APL**	Average pay, low range	**FQ**	First quartile wage	**LR**	Low end range	**SQ**	Second quartile wage	**Y**	Yearly

Occupation/Type/Industry	Location	Per	Low	Mid	High	Source	Date
Textile Cutting Machine Setter, Operator, and Tender	Colorado	H	7.28 FQ	10.34 AW	15.69 TQ	COBLS	10/01-12/01
	Denver PMSA, CO	H	8.32 FQ	11.27 AW	17.14 TQ	COBLS	10/01-12/01
	Connecticut	H	7.28 FQ	10.18 AW	13.76 TQ	CTBLS	10/01-12/01
	Hartford MSA, CT	H	7.12 FQ	9.62 AW	12.39 TQ	CTBLS	10/01-12/01
	Washington PMSA, DC-MD-VA-WV	H	7.01 FQ	10.15 AW	14.94 TQ	DCBLS	10/01-12/01
	Florida	H	6.14 FQ	8.91 AW	12.89 TQ	FLBLS	10/01-12/01
	Fort Lauderdale PMSA, FL	H	6.51 FQ	9.29 AW	13.41 TQ	FLBLS	10/01-12/01
	Lakeland-Winter Haven MSA, FL	H	7.22 FQ	8.28 AW	9.87 TQ	FLBLS	10/01-12/01
	Miami PMSA, FL	H	5.97 FQ	8.74 AW	12.83 TQ	FLBLS	10/01-12/01
	Tampa-St. Petersburg-Clearwater MSA, FL	H	6.23 FQ	8.77 AW	11.68 TQ	FLBLS	10/01-12/01
	Georgia	H	6.75 FQ	9.50 AW	13.05 TQ	GABLS	10/01-12/01
	Atlanta MSA, GA	H	6.46 FQ	9.11 AW	12.87 TQ	GABLS	10/01-12/01
	Columbus MSA, GA-AL	H	7.69 FQ	10.78 AW	13.78 TQ	GABLS	10/01-12/01
	Hawaii	H	6.40 FQ	8.33 AW	10.59 TQ	HIBLS	10/01-12/01
	Honolulu MSA, HI	H	6.40 FQ	8.33 AW	10.59 TQ	HIBLS	10/01-12/01
	Illinois	H	7.15 FQ	9.94 AW	13.45 TQ	ILBLS	10/01-12/01
	Chicago PMSA, IL	H	7.12 FQ	10.03 AW	13.74 TQ	ILBLS	10/01-12/01
	Indiana	H	7.96 FQ	11.90 AW	16.63 TQ	INBLS	10/01-12/01
	Elkhart-Goshen MSA, IN	H	8.80 FQ	11.41 AW	13.60 TQ	INBLS	10/01-12/01
	Fort Wayne MSA, IN	H	9.10 FQ	11.82 AW	14.93 TQ	INBLS	10/01-12/01
	Indianapolis MSA, IN	H	8.23 FQ	10.59 AW	13.56 TQ	INBLS	10/01-12/01
	Iowa	H	6.13 FQ	9.58 AW	13.74 TQ	IABLS	10/01-12/01
	Kansas	H	7.42 FQ	11.58 AW	17.21 TQ	KSBLS	10/01-12/01
	Kentucky	H	6.92 FQ	8.98 AW	13.19 TQ	KYBLS	10/01-12/01
	Louisville MSA, KY-IN	H	6.92 FQ	7.85 AW	8.48 TQ	KYBLS	10/01-12/01
	Maine	H	6.66 FQ	10.18 AW	13.11 TQ	MEBLS	10/01-12/01
	Maryland	H	7.32 FQ	10.98 AW	16.75 TQ	MDBLS	10/01-12/01
	Baltimore PMSA, MD	H	7.40 FQ	10.55 AW	16.07 TQ	MDBLS	10/01-12/01
	Massachusetts	H	7.92 FQ	11.30 AW	15.47 TQ	MABLS	10/01-12/01
	Boston PMSA, MA-NH	H	7.36 FQ	11.54 AW	16.29 TQ	MABLS	10/01-12/01
	New Bedford PMSA, MA	H	7.34 FQ	10.39 AW	16.42 TQ	MABLS	10/01-12/01
	Springfield MSA, MA	H	8.93 FQ	11.91 AW	15.92 TQ	MABLS	10/01-12/01
	Michigan	H	7.77 FQ	12.31 AW	20.73 TQ	MIBLS	10/01-12/01
	Detroit PMSA, MI	H	7.96 FQ	13.23 AW	21.69 TQ	MIBLS	10/01-12/01
	Grand Rapids-Muskegon-Holland MSA, MI	H	9.15 FQ	13.06 AW	18.19 TQ	MIBLS	10/01-12/01
	Minnesota	H	7.49 FQ	10.00 AW	13.32 TQ	MNBLS	10/01-12/01
	Minneapolis-St. Paul MSA, MN-WI	H	7.48 FQ	10.05 AW	13.65 TQ	MNBLS	10/01-12/01
	Mississippi	H	6.91 FQ	10.21 AW	13.21 TQ	MSBLS	10/01-12/01
	Missouri	H	6.08 FQ	9.58 AW	15.79 TQ	MOBLS	10/01-12/01
	Kansas City MSA, MO-KS	H	7.60 FQ	10.25 AW	13.35 TQ	MOBLS	10/01-12/01
	St. Louis MSA, MO-IL	H	5.78 FQ	7.84 AW	10.80 TQ	MOBLS	10/01-12/01
	Montana	H	6.55 FQ	10.15 AW	13.42 TQ	MTBLS	10/01-12/01
	Nebraska	H	8.20 FQ	11.46 AW	19.45 TQ	NEBLS	10/01-12/01
	Omaha MSA, NE-IA	H	6.11 FQ	9.07 AW	11.08 TQ	NEBLS	10/01-12/01
	New Hampshire	H	8.93 FQ	11.48 AW	16.32 TQ	NHBLS	10/01-12/01
	Portsmouth-Rochester PMSA, NH-ME	H	8.22 FQ	10.43 AW	13.48 TQ	NHBLS	10/01-12/01
	New Jersey	H	6.64 FQ	11.09 AW	16.67 TQ	NJBLS	10/01-12/01
	Bergen-Passaic PMSA, NJ	H	6.51 FQ	11.19 AW	16.60 TQ	NJBLS	10/01-12/01
	Jersey City PMSA, NJ	H	6.14 FQ	11.37 AW	19.18 TQ	NJBLS	10/01-12/01
	Middlesex-Somerset-Hunterdon PMSA, NJ	H	6.32 FQ	10.55 AW	15.48 TQ	NJBLS	10/01-12/01
	Monmouth-Ocean PMSA, NJ	H	7.57 FQ	10.17 AW	14.67 TQ	NJBLS	10/01-12/01
	Newark PMSA, NJ	H	7.05 FQ	11.06 AW	16.72 TQ	NJBLS	10/01-12/01
	New York	H	6.07 FQ	10.00 AW	15.62 TQ	NYBLS	10/01-12/01
	Albany-Schenectady-Troy MSA, NY	H	7.70 FQ	10.15 AW	12.94 TQ	NYBLS	10/01-12/01
	Buffalo-Niagara Falls MSA, NY	H	7.69 FQ	11.74 AW	16.98 TQ	NYBLS	10/01-12/01
	Nassau-Suffolk PMSA, NY	H	6.76 FQ	11.18 AW	15.86 TQ	NYBLS	10/01-12/01
	New York PMSA, NY	H	5.93 FQ	9.87 AW	15.92 TQ	NYBLS	10/01-12/01
	North Carolina	H	7.16 FQ	10.78 AW	16.16 TQ	NCBLS	10/01-12/01
	Asheville MSA, NC	H	6.13 FQ	8.67 AW	10.78 TQ	NCBLS	10/01-12/01
	Charlotte-Gastonia-Rock Hill MSA, NC-SC	H	7.23 FQ	9.47 AW	13.75 TQ	NCBLS	10/01-12/01

AAW	Average annual wage	**AOH**	Average offered, high	**ASH**	Average starting, high	**H**	Hourly	**M**	Monthly	**S**	Special: hourly and annual
AE	Average entry wage	**AOL**	Average offered, low	**ASL**	Average starting, low	**HI**	Highest wage paid	**MTC**	Median total compensation	**TQ**	Third quartile wage
AEX	Average experienced wage	**APH**	Average pay, high range	**AW**	Average wage paid	**HR**	High end range	**MW**	Median wage paid	**W**	Weekly
AO	Average offered	**APL**	Average pay, low range	**FQ**	First quartile wage	**LR**	Low end range	**SQ**	Second quartile wage	**Y**	Yearly

Occupation/Type/Industry	Location	Per	Low	Mid	High	Source	Date
Textile Cutting Machine Setter, Operator, and Tender	Greensboro-Winston-Salem-High Point MSA, NC	H	6.83 FQ	11.86 AW	16.98 TQ	NCBLS	10/01-12/01
	Hickory-Morganton-Lenoir MSA, NC	H	9.18 FQ	13.24 AW	18.74 TQ	NCBLS	10/01-12/01
	Raleigh-Durham-Chapel Hill MSA, NC	H	6.86 FQ	8.92 AW	12.25 TQ	NCBLS	10/01-12/01
	Ohio	H	7.83 FQ	11.28 AW	15.88 TQ	OHBLS	10/01-12/01
	Canton-Massillon MSA, OH	H	6.47 FQ	10.96 AW	16.13 TQ	OHBLS	10/01-12/01
	Cincinnati PMSA, OH-KY-IN	H	7.11 FQ	11.09 AW	14.60 TQ	OHBLS	10/01-12/01
	Cleveland-Lorain-Elyria PMSA, OH	H	7.92 FQ	11.15 AW	15.16 TQ	OHBLS	10/01-12/01
	Dayton-Springfield MSA, OH	H	7.84 FQ	10.48 AW	14.28 TQ	OHBLS	10/01-12/01
	Oklahoma	H	6.22 FQ	9.08 AW	12.71 TQ	OKBLS	10/01-12/01
	Tulsa MSA, OK	H	6.35 FQ	9.48 AW	12.93 TQ	OKBLS	10/01-12/01
	Oregon	H	7.65 FQ	10.39 AW	13.48 TQ	ORBLS	10/01-12/01
	Portland-Vancouver PMSA, OR-WA	H	7.69 FQ	10.42 AW	13.59 TQ	ORBLS	10/01-12/01
	Pennsylvania	H	7.22 FQ	10.50 AW	15.08 TQ	PABLS	10/01-12/01
	Allentown-Bethlehem-Easton MSA, PA	H	7.65 FQ	11.21 AW	14.11 TQ	PABLS	10/01-12/01
	Lancaster MSA, PA	H	7.18 FQ	11.22 AW	17.13 TQ	PABLS	10/01-12/01
	Philadelphia PMSA, PA-NJ	H	7.65 FQ	11.14 AW	16.34 TQ	PABLS	10/01-12/01
	Pittsburgh MSA, PA	H	7.04 FQ	10.12 AW	14.31 TQ	PABLS	10/01-12/01
	Reading MSA, PA	H	5.88 FQ	8.42 AW	11.79 TQ	PABLS	10/01-12/01
	Scranton-Wilkes-Barre-Hazleton MSA, PA	H	6.85 FQ	10.45 AW	15.41 TQ	PABLS	10/01-12/01
	Rhode Island	H	7.60 FQ	10.64 AW	13.23 TQ	RIBLS	10/01-12/01
	Providence-Fall River-Warwick MSA, RI-MA	H	8.23 FQ	11.23 AW	13.88 TQ	RIBLS	10/01-12/01
	South Carolina	H	7.88 FQ	10.66 AW	13.78 TQ	SCBLS	10/01-12/01
	Columbia MSA, SC	H	8.68 FQ	9.82 AW	11.09 TQ	SCBLS	10/01-12/01
	Greenville-Spartanburg-Anderson MSA, SC	H	7.89 FQ	10.98 AW	14.07 TQ	SCBLS	10/01-12/01
	Tennessee	H	7.34 FQ	10.08 AW	13.44 TQ	TNBLS	10/01-12/01
	Johnson City-Kingsport-Bristol MSA, TN-VA	H	7.34 FQ	9.43 AW	13.16 TQ	TNBLS	10/01-12/01
	Knoxville MSA, TN	H	7.99 FQ	10.47 AW	13.51 TQ	TNBLS	10/01-12/01
	Nashville MSA, TN	H	7.42 FQ	11.42 AW	15.47 TQ	TNBLS	10/01-12/01
	Texas	H	6.06 FQ	8.74 AW	11.89 TQ	TXBLS	10/01-12/01
	Dallas PMSA, TX	H	7.40 FQ	10.36 AW	13.91 TQ	TXBLS	10/01-12/01
	El Paso MSA, TX	H	5.96 FQ	8.23 AW	10.84 TQ	TXBLS	10/01-12/01
	Fort Worth-Arlington PMSA, TX	H	6.08 FQ	8.55 AW	12.09 TQ	TXBLS	10/01-12/01
	Houston PMSA, TX	H	6.04 FQ	8.53 AW	12.49 TQ	TXBLS	10/01-12/01
	McAllen-Edinburg-Mission MSA, TX	H	6.13 FQ	7.55 AW	9.28 TQ	TXBLS	10/01-12/01
	San Antonio MSA, TX	H	6.09 FQ	8.40 AW	10.80 TQ	TXBLS	10/01-12/01
	Utah	H	6.95 FQ	10.11 AW	15.73 TQ	UTBLS	10/01-12/01
	Salt Lake City-Ogden MSA, UT	H	6.74 FQ	9.26 AW	14.85 TQ	UTBLS	10/01-12/01
	Vermont	H	8.87 FQ	11.12 AW	15.24 TQ	VTBLS	10/01-12/01
	Virginia	H	7.40 FQ	10.13 AW	13.43 TQ	VABLS	10/01-12/01
	Norfolk-Virginia Beach-Newport News MSA, VA-NC	H	6.25 FQ	7.88 AW	9.56 TQ	VABLS	10/01-12/01
	Richmond-Petersburg MSA, VA	H	6.54 FQ	8.43 AW	11.12 TQ	VABLS	10/01-12/01
	Washington	H	7.51 FQ	10.72 AW	13.74 TQ	WABLS	10/01-12/01
	Seattle-Bellevue-Everett PMSA, WA	H	7.77 FQ	10.91 AW	13.82 TQ	WABLS	10/01-12/01
	West Virginia	H	7.12 FQ	10.02 AW	13.77 TQ	WVBLS	10/01-12/01
	Wisconsin	H	7.34 FQ	11.33 AW	18.58 TQ	WIBLS	10/01-12/01
	Milwaukee-Waukesha PMSA, WI	H	7.01 FQ	11.44 AW	14.03 TQ	WIBLS	10/01-12/01
	Puerto Rico	H	5.55 FQ	6.47 AW	8.06 TQ	PRBLS	10/01-12/01
Textile Knitting and Weaving Machine Setter, Operator, and Tender	Alabama	H	7.92 FQ	10.30 AW	13.19 TQ	ALBLS	10/01-12/01
	Arkansas	H	7.46 FQ	11.65 AW	16.60 TQ	ARBLS	10/01-12/01

AAW	Average annual wage	**AOH**	Average offered, high	**ASH**	Average starting, high	**H**	Hourly	**M**	Monthly	**S**	Special: hourly and annual
AE	Average entry wage	**AOL**	Average offered, low	**ASL**	Average starting, low	**HI**	Highest wage paid	**MTC**	Median total compensation	**TQ**	Third quartile wage
AEX	Average experienced wage	**APH**	Average pay, high range	**AW**	Average wage paid	**HR**	High end range	**MW**	Median wage paid	**W**	Weekly
AO	Average offered	**APL**	Average pay, low range	**FQ**	First quartile wage	**LR**	Low end range	**SQ**	Second quartile wage	**Y**	Yearly

Occupation/Type/Industry	Location	Per	Low	Mid	High	Source	Date
Textile Knitting and Weaving Machine Setter, Operator, and Tender	California	H	6.42 FQ	7.97 AW	10.69 TQ	CABLS	10/01-12/01
	Los Angeles-Long Beach PMSA, CA	H	6.42 FQ	7.86 AW	10.35 TQ	CABLS	10/01-12/01
	Oakland PMSA, CA	H	6.48 FQ	9.01 AW	13.08 TQ	CABLS	10/01-12/01
	Orange County PMSA, CA	H	6.38 FQ	7.84 AW	10.67 TQ	CABLS	10/01-12/01
	Riverside-San Bernardino PMSA, CA	H	6.52 FQ	9.23 AW	12.55 TQ	CABLS	10/01-12/01
	San Diego MSA, CA	H	6.44 FQ	8.29 AW	10.93 TQ	CABLS	10/01-12/01
	Colorado	H	7.17 FQ	11.83 AW	16.21 TQ	COBLS	10/01-12/01
	Denver PMSA, CO	H	10.77 FQ	13.80 AW	16.47 TQ	COBLS	10/01-12/01
	Connecticut	H	7.98 FQ	12.29 AW	16.51 TQ	CTBLS	10/01-12/01
	Delaware	H	8.23 FQ	11.66 AW	14.70 TQ	DEBLS	10/01-12/01
	Washington PMSA, DC-MD-VA-WV	H	6.75 FQ	8.22 AW	10.43 TQ	DCBLS	10/01-12/01
	Florida	H	6.28 FQ	9.75 AW	13.73 TQ	FLBLS	10/01-12/01
	Miami PMSA, FL	H	5.82 FQ	8.18 AW	11.34 TQ	FLBLS	10/01-12/01
	Georgia	H	9.13 FQ	11.74 AW	15.30 TQ	GABLS	10/01-12/01
	Atlanta MSA, GA	H	8.94 FQ	11.66 AW	15.13 TQ	GABLS	10/01-12/01
	Augusta-Aiken MSA, GA-SC	H	8.94 FQ	10.74 AW	13.04 TQ	GABLS	10/01-12/01
	Columbus MSA, GA-AL	H	8.65 FQ	11.42 AW	14.28 TQ	GABLS	10/01-12/01
	Illinois	H	7.77 FQ	11.63 AW	14.17 TQ	ILBLS	10/01-12/01
	Chicago PMSA, IL	H	7.91 FQ	11.78 AW	13.97 TQ	ILBLS	10/01-12/01
	Indiana	H	6.59 FQ	11.49 AW	15.37 TQ	INBLS	10/01-12/01
	Kentucky	H	8.59 FQ	11.64 AW	14.08 TQ	KYBLS	10/01-12/01
	Lexington MSA, KY	H	6.14 FQ	8.54 AW	10.96 TQ	KYBLS	10/01-12/01
	Maine	H	8.65 FQ	11.32 AW	13.69 TQ	MEBLS	10/01-12/01
	Maryland	H	7.63 FQ	10.85 AW	13.64 TQ	MDBLS	10/01-12/01
	Massachusetts	H	9.18 FQ	11.61 AW	13.87 TQ	MABLS	10/01-12/01
	Boston PMSA, MA-NH	H	8.53 FQ	10.27 AW	12.59 TQ	MABLS	10/01-12/01
	New Bedford PMSA, MA	H	9.31 FQ	11.80 AW	13.99 TQ	MABLS	10/01-12/01
	Worcester PMSA, MA-CT	H	9.80 FQ	12.66 AW	14.94 TQ	MABLS	10/01-12/01
	Michigan	H	8.82 FQ	15.28 AW	25.91 TQ	MIBLS	10/01-12/01
	Grand Rapids-Muskegon-Holland MSA, MI	H	9.28 FQ	16.09 AW	25.64 TQ	MIBLS	10/01-12/01
	Minnesota	H	7.53 FQ	10.58 AW	15.71 TQ	MNBLS	10/01-12/01
	Minneapolis-St. Paul MSA, MN-WI	H	8.91 FQ	12.35 AW	17.41 TQ	MNBLS	10/01-12/01
	Mississippi	H	7.39 FQ	9.84 AW	13.13 TQ	MSBLS	10/01-12/01
	Missouri	H	6.05 FQ	9.45 AW	13.41 TQ	MOBLS	10/01-12/01
	St. Louis MSA, MO-IL	H	5.78 FQ	9.19 AW	14.24 TQ	MOBLS	10/01-12/01
	New Hampshire	H	9.34 FQ	12.67 AW	16.47 TQ	NHBLS	10/01-12/01
	Nashua PMSA, NH	H	9.15 FQ	12.43 AW	16.04 TQ	NHBLS	10/01-12/01
	Portsmouth-Rochester PMSA, NH-ME	H	9.43 FQ	12.17 AW	15.31 TQ	NHBLS	10/01-12/01
	New Jersey	H	7.06 FQ	10.98 AW	15.20 TQ	NJBLS	10/01-12/01
	Bergen-Passaic PMSA, NJ	H	7.20 FQ	10.68 AW	13.70 TQ	NJBLS	10/01-12/01
	Jersey City PMSA, NJ	H	7.44 FQ	10.67 AW	16.35 TQ	NJBLS	10/01-12/01
	Newark PMSA, NJ	H	6.45 FQ	10.70 AW	15.75 TQ	NJBLS	10/01-12/01
	New York	H	7.23 FQ	10.43 AW	18.57 TQ	NYBLS	10/01-12/01
	Albany-Schenectady-Troy MSA, NY	H	7.39 FQ	15.41 AW	21.45 TQ	NYBLS	10/01-12/01
	Buffalo-Niagara Falls MSA, NY	H	7.44 FQ	12.05 AW	20.47 TQ	NYBLS	10/01-12/01
	Nassau-Suffolk PMSA, NY	H	5.97 FQ	10.33 AW	16.77 TQ	NYBLS	10/01-12/01
	New York PMSA, NY	H	7.22 FQ	9.21 AW	12.98 TQ	NYBLS	10/01-12/01
	North Carolina	H	7.86 FQ	10.82 AW	13.81 TQ	NCBLS	10/01-12/01
	Asheville MSA, NC	H	8.85 FQ	11.58 AW	16.59 TQ	NCBLS	10/01-12/01
	Charlotte-Gastonia-Rock Hill MSA, NC-SC	H	7.58 FQ	10.29 AW	13.43 TQ	NCBLS	10/01-12/01
	Greensboro-Winston-Salem-High Point MSA, NC	H	7.98 FQ	11.09 AW	13.84 TQ	NCBLS	10/01-12/01
	Hickory-Morganton-Lenoir MSA, NC	H	6.51 FQ	10.35 AW	14.17 TQ	NCBLS	10/01-12/01
	Raleigh-Durham-Chapel Hill MSA, NC	H	7.21 FQ	11.53 AW	16.53 TQ	NCBLS	10/01-12/01
	Ohio	H	8.89 FQ	12.51 AW	16.89 TQ	OHBLS	10/01-12/01
	Portland-Vancouver PMSA, OR-WA	H	8.10 FQ	13.97 AW	20.85 TQ	ORBLS	10/01-12/01
	Pennsylvania	H	7.73 FQ	11.64 AW	16.08 TQ	PABLS	10/01-12/01

AAW	Average annual wage	**AOH**	Average offered, high	**ASH**	Average starting, high	**H**	Hourly	**M**	Monthly	**S**	Special: hourly and annual
AE	Average entry wage	**AOL**	Average offered, low	**ASL**	Average starting, low	**HI**	Highest wage paid	**MTC**	Median total compensation	**TQ**	Third quartile wage
AEX	Average experienced wage	**APH**	Average pay, high range	**AW**	Average wage paid	**HR**	High end range	**MW**	Median wage paid	**W**	Weekly
AO	Average offered	**APL**	Average pay, low range	**FQ**	First quartile wage	**LR**	Low end range	**SQ**	Second quartile wage	**Y**	Yearly

Occupation/Type/Industry	Location	Per	Low	Mid	High	Source	Date
Textile Knitting and Weaving Machine Setter, Operator, and Tender	Allentown-Bethlehem-Easton MSA, PA	H	8.94 FQ	11.02 AW	13.51 TQ	PABLS	10/01-12/01
	Harrisburg-Lebanon-Carlisle MSA, PA	H	7.68 FQ	12.10 AW	16.77 TQ	PABLS	10/01-12/01
	Lancaster MSA, PA	H	7.99 FQ	10.22 AW	13.19 TQ	PABLS	10/01-12/01
	Philadelphia PMSA, PA-NJ	H	8.10 FQ	12.38 AW	16.42 TQ	PABLS	10/01-12/01
	Pittsburgh MSA, PA	H	7.20 FQ	11.24 AW	16.45 TQ	PABLS	10/01-12/01
	Reading MSA, PA	H	9.33 FQ	13.09 AW	17.17 TQ	PABLS	10/01-12/01
	Scranton-Wilkes-Barre-Hazleton MSA, PA	H	8.13 FQ	11.01 AW	13.87 TQ	PABLS	10/01-12/01
	Rhode Island	H	6.66 FQ	8.97 AW	12.74 TQ	RIBLS	10/01-12/01
	Providence-Fall River-Warwick MSA, RI-MA	H	6.86 FQ	10.24 AW	13.74 TQ	RIBLS	10/01-12/01
	South Carolina	H	9.34 FQ	11.82 AW	13.98 TQ	SCBLS	10/01-12/01
	Charleston-North Charleston MSA, SC	H	10.97 FQ	13.05 AW	16.91 TQ	SCBLS	10/01-12/01
	Greenville-Spartanburg-Anderson MSA, SC	H	9.51 FQ	11.99 AW	13.99 TQ	SCBLS	10/01-12/01
	Tennessee	H	7.67 FQ	9.93 AW	12.70 TQ	TNBLS	10/01-12/01
	Johnson City-Kingsport-Bristol MSA, TN-VA	H	7.61 FQ	9.48 AW	11.43 TQ	TNBLS	10/01-12/01
	Texas	H	7.03 FQ	10.85 AW	14.24 TQ	TXBLS	10/01-12/01
	Dallas PMSA, TX	H	6.36 FQ	9.04 AW	13.32 TQ	TXBLS	10/01-12/01
	El Paso MSA, TX	H	5.97 FQ	11.04 AW	15.52 TQ	TXBLS	10/01-12/01
	Houston PMSA, TX	H	5.38 FQ	6.54 AW	8.24 TQ	TXBLS	10/01-12/01
	San Antonio MSA, TX	H	9.49 FQ	11.67 AW	14.91 TQ	TXBLS	10/01-12/01
	Vermont	H	7.98 FQ	10.36 AW	12.99 TQ	VTBLS	10/01-12/01
	Virginia	H	8.33 FQ	10.96 AW	13.38 TQ	VABLS	10/01-12/01
	Washington	H	8.31 FQ	13.36 AW	20.41 TQ	WABLS	10/01-12/01
	Seattle-Bellevue-Everett PMSA, WA	H	8.09 FQ	11.38 AW	15.13 TQ	WABLS	10/01-12/01
	West Virginia	H	9.09 FQ	11.71 AW	13.98 TQ	WVBLS	10/01-12/01
	Wisconsin	H	7.81 FQ	11.50 AW	19.35 TQ	WIBLS	10/01-12/01
	Milwaukee-Waukesha PMSA, WI	H	8.57 FQ	10.33 AW	13.20 TQ	WIBLS	10/01-12/01
	Puerto Rico	H	5.60 FQ	7.65 AW	10.47 TQ	PRBLS	10/01-12/01
Textile Winding, Twisting, and Drawing Out Machine Setter, Operator, and Tender	Alabama	H	7.92 FQ	10.09 AW	12.70 TQ	ALBLS	10/01-12/01
	California	H	6.49 FQ	8.96 AW	12.46 TQ	CABLS	10/01-12/01
	Los Angeles-Long Beach PMSA, CA	H	6.60 FQ	9.31 AW	12.84 TQ	CABLS	10/01-12/01
	Orange County PMSA, CA	H	6.38 FQ	8.06 AW	11.12 TQ	CABLS	10/01-12/01
	Colorado	H	6.82 FQ	9.25 AW	12.78 TQ	COBLS	10/01-12/01
	New London-Norwich MSA, CT-RI	H	6.68 FQ	8.18 AW	10.50 TQ	CTBLS	10/01-12/01
	Delaware	H	9.74 FQ	15.86 AW	22.40 TQ	DEBLS	10/01-12/01
	Florida	H	6.98 FQ	10.97 AW	16.52 TQ	FLBLS	10/01-12/01
	Miami PMSA, FL	H	6.66 FQ	9.84 AW	13.46 TQ	FLBLS	10/01-12/01
	Georgia	H	8.94 FQ	10.52 AW	12.95 TQ	GABLS	10/01-12/01
	Atlanta MSA, GA	H	8.17 FQ	10.85 AW	13.54 TQ	GABLS	10/01-12/01
	Augusta-Aiken MSA, GA-SC	H	8.70 FQ	9.71 AW	10.71 TQ	GABLS	10/01-12/01
	Columbus MSA, GA-AL	H	9.19 FQ	10.48 AW	12.74 TQ	GABLS	10/01-12/01
	Illinois	H	7.38 FQ	9.54 AW	12.32 TQ	ILBLS	10/01-12/01
	Chicago PMSA, IL	H	7.38 FQ	9.54 AW	12.33 TQ	ILBLS	10/01-12/01
	Indiana	H	7.99 FQ	10.42 AW	13.31 TQ	INBLS	10/01-12/01
	Kansas	H	9.23 FQ	13.53 AW	16.75 TQ	KSBLS	10/01-12/01
	Kentucky	H	6.34 FQ	9.54 AW	11.64 TQ	KYBLS	10/01-12/01
	Maine	H	8.90 FQ	10.80 AW	13.41 TQ	MEBLS	10/01-12/01
	Massachusetts	H	8.11 FQ	10.82 AW	13.88 TQ	MABLS	10/01-12/01
	New Bedford PMSA, MA	H	8.50 FQ	10.37 AW	12.91 TQ	MABLS	10/01-12/01
	Springfield MSA, MA	H	7.81 FQ	10.63 AW	13.91 TQ	MABLS	10/01-12/01
	Worcester PMSA, MA-CT	H	9.13 FQ	10.44 AW	12.69 TQ	MABLS	10/01-12/01
	Michigan	H	7.26 FQ	9.80 AW	12.92 TQ	MIBLS	10/01-12/01
	Detroit PMSA, MI	H	7.26 FQ	8.78 AW	10.82 TQ	MIBLS	10/01-12/01
	Saginaw-Bay City-Midland MSA, MI	H	7.26 FQ	9.83 AW	12.99 TQ	MIBLS	10/01-12/01
	Minnesota	H	8.36 FQ	11.44 AW	14.05 TQ	MNBLS	10/01-12/01

AAW	Average annual wage	**AOH**	Average offered, high	**ASH**	Average starting, high	**H**	Hourly	**M**	Monthly	**S**	Special: hourly and annual
AE	Average entry wage	**AOL**	Average offered, low	**ASL**	Average starting, low	**HI**	Highest wage paid	**MTC**	Median total compensation	**TQ**	Third quartile wage
AEX	Average experienced wage	**APH**	Average pay, high range	**AW**	Average wage paid	**HR**	High end range	**MW**	Median wage paid	**W**	Weekly
AO	Average offered	**APL**	Average pay, low range	**FQ**	First quartile wage	**LR**	Low end range	**SQ**	Second quartile wage	**Y**	Yearly

Occupation/Type/Industry	Location	Per	Low	Mid	High	Source	Date
Textile Winding, Twisting, and Drawing Out Machine Setter, Operator, and Tender	Mississippi	H	7.03 FQ	9.33 AW	13.10 TQ	MSBLS	10/01-12/01
	Biloxi-Gulfport-Pascagoula MSA, MS	H	7.81 FQ	10.86 AW	19.67 TQ	MSBLS	10/01-12/01
	Missouri	H	5.94 FQ	9.46 AW	13.66 TQ	MOBLS	10/01-12/01
	New Hampshire	H	9.27 FQ	11.71 AW	14.50 TQ	NHBLS	10/01-12/01
	New Jersey	H	6.11 FQ	9.81 AW	13.82 TQ	NJBLS	10/01-12/01
	Bergen-Passaic PMSA, NJ	H	7.28 FQ	11.02 AW	14.24 TQ	NJBLS	10/01-12/01
	Jersey City PMSA, NJ	H	6.74 FQ	9.76 AW	13.25 TQ	NJBLS	10/01-12/01
	Middlesex-Somerset-Hunterdon PMSA, NJ	H	5.76 FQ	8.18 AW	12.29 TQ	NJBLS	10/01-12/01
	Newark PMSA, NJ	H	5.57 FQ	7.32 AW	10.82 TQ	NJBLS	10/01-12/01
	New York	H	6.89 FQ	10.31 AW	14.74 TQ	NYBLS	10/01-12/01
	Albany-Schenectady-Troy MSA, NY	H	8.72 FQ	12.92 AW	19.64 TQ	NYBLS	10/01-12/01
	Buffalo-Niagara Falls MSA, NY	H	8.89 FQ	13.86 AW	20.97 TQ	NYBLS	10/01-12/01
	New York PMSA, NY	H	6.92 FQ	9.26 AW	11.42 TQ	NYBLS	10/01-12/01
	North Carolina	H	8.11 FQ	10.19 AW	12.84 TQ	NCBLS	10/01-12/01
	Charlotte-Gastonia-Rock Hill MSA, NC-SC	H	7.78 FQ	9.60 AW	11.23 TQ	NCBLS	10/01-12/01
	Greensboro-Winston-Salem-High Point MSA, NC	H	8.06 FQ	10.74 AW	13.27 TQ	NCBLS	10/01-12/01
	Hickory-Morganton-Lenoir MSA, NC	H	7.91 FQ	10.45 AW	13.91 TQ	NCBLS	10/01-12/01
	Raleigh-Durham-Chapel Hill MSA, NC	H	8.30 FQ	11.25 AW	16.12 TQ	NCBLS	10/01-12/01
	Ohio	H	8.27 FQ	11.61 AW	14.63 TQ	OHBLS	10/01-12/01
	Cincinnati PMSA, OH-KY-IN	H	7.04 FQ	11.25 AW	14.24 TQ	OHBLS	10/01-12/01
	Pennsylvania	H	6.59 FQ	9.29 AW	12.81 TQ	PABLS	10/01-12/01
	Allentown-Bethlehem-Easton MSA, PA	H	7.42 FQ	9.62 AW	12.49 TQ	PABLS	10/01-12/01
	Philadelphia PMSA, PA-NJ	H	6.00 FQ	8.92 AW	12.59 TQ	PABLS	10/01-12/01
	Pittsburgh MSA, PA	H	6.09 FQ	8.94 AW	12.81 TQ	PABLS	10/01-12/01
	Scranton-Wilkes-Barre-Hazleton MSA, PA	H	7.35 FQ	8.66 AW	10.48 TQ	PABLS	10/01-12/01
	Rhode Island	H	6.74 FQ	8.65 AW	11.62 TQ	RIBLS	10/01-12/01
	Providence-Fall River-Warwick MSA, RI-MA	H	7.21 FQ	10.23 AW	13.53 TQ	RIBLS	10/01-12/01
	South Carolina	H	8.74 FQ	10.50 AW	13.37 TQ	SCBLS	10/01-12/01
	Charleston-North Charleston MSA, SC	H	8.80 FQ	10.95 AW	14.16 TQ	SCBLS	10/01-12/01
	Columbia MSA, SC	H	9.13 FQ	12.49 AW	18.88 TQ	SCBLS	10/01-12/01
	Greenville-Spartanburg-Anderson MSA, SC	H	8.82 FQ	10.60 AW	13.39 TQ	SCBLS	10/01-12/01
	Tennessee	H	8.87 FQ	10.80 AW	14.24 TQ	TNBLS	10/01-12/01
	Chattanooga MSA, TN-GA	H	8.91 FQ	11.07 AW	13.46 TQ	TNBLS	10/01-12/01
	Johnson City-Kingsport-Bristol MSA, TN-VA	H	9.10 FQ	10.54 AW	12.65 TQ	TNBLS	10/01-12/01
	Texas	H	7.50 FQ	9.76 AW	12.64 TQ	TXBLS	10/01-12/01
	Dallas PMSA, TX	H	7.32 FQ	9.09 AW	11.19 TQ	TXBLS	10/01-12/01
	Virginia	H	8.87 FQ	14.24 AW	24.57 TQ	VABLS	10/01-12/01
	Washington	H	7.78 FQ	10.16 AW	13.11 TQ	WABLS	10/01-12/01
	Seattle-Bellevue-Everett PMSA, WA	H	9.11 FQ	10.25 AW	11.47 TQ	WABLS	10/01-12/01
	Wisconsin	H	7.60 FQ	11.31 AW	16.46 TQ	WIBLS	10/01-12/01
	Milwaukee-Waukesha PMSA, WI	H	8.79 FQ	12.16 AW	15.96 TQ	WIBLS	10/01-12/01
	Puerto Rico	H	7.90 FQ	10.62 AW	15.37 TQ	PRBLS	10/01-12/01
Tile and Marble Setter	Alabama	H	7.56 FQ	12.80 AW	18.94 TQ	ALBLS	10/01-12/01
	Birmingham MSA, AL	H	7.79 FQ	12.32 AW	18.11 TQ	ALBLS	10/01-12/01
	Mobile MSA, AL	H	10.32 FQ	18.55 AW	32.25 TQ	ALBLS	10/01-12/01
	Arizona	H	8.79 FQ	14.22 AW	20.84 TQ	AZBLS	10/01-12/01
	Phoenix-Mesa MSA, AZ	H	9.76 FQ	15.13 AW	21.30 TQ	AZBLS	10/01-12/01
	Arkansas	H	6.72 FQ	11.20 AW	16.03 TQ	ARBLS	10/01-12/01
	California	H	11.74 FQ	19.49 AW	29.05 TQ	CABLS	10/01-12/01
	Bakersfield MSA, CA	H	9.79 FQ	15.43 AW	21.82 TQ	CABLS	10/01-12/01
	Fresno MSA, CA	H	11.69 FQ	18.66 AW	27.96 TQ	CABLS	10/01-12/01
	Los Angeles-Long Beach PMSA, CA	H	10.87 FQ	18.44 AW	27.54 TQ	CABLS	10/01-12/01

AAW	Average annual wage	AOH	Average offered, high	ASH	Average starting, high	H	Hourly	M	Monthly	S	Special: hourly and annual
AE	Average entry wage	AOL	Average offered, low	ASL	Average starting, low	HI	Highest wage paid	MTC	Median total compensation	TQ	Third quartile wage
AEX	Average experienced wage	APH	Average pay, high range	AW	Average wage paid	HR	High end range	MW	Median wage paid	W	Weekly
AO	Average offered	APL	Average pay, low range	FQ	First quartile wage	LR	Low end range	SQ	Second quartile wage	Y	Yearly

Occupation/Type/Industry	Location	Per	Low	Mid	High	Source	Date
Tile and Marble Setter	Modesto MSA, CA	H	12.72 FQ	18.67 AW	22.05 TQ	CABLS	10/01-12/01
	Oakland PMSA, CA	H	15.60 FQ	23.58 AW	36.42 TQ	CABLS	10/01-12/01
	Orange County PMSA, CA	H	10.30 FQ	15.64 AW	26.68 TQ	CABLS	10/01-12/01
	Riverside-San Bernardino PMSA, CA	H	12.71 FQ	19.46 AW	26.85 TQ	CABLS	10/01-12/01
	Sacramento PMSA, CA	H	14.60 FQ	23.13 AW	33.85 TQ	CABLS	10/01-12/01
	Salinas MSA, CA	H	10.09 FQ	24.66 AW	35.49 TQ	CABLS	10/01-12/01
	San Diego MSA, CA	H	14.06 FQ	21.60 AW	28.10 TQ	CABLS	10/01-12/01
	San Francisco PMSA, CA	H	12.69 FQ	18.77 AW	28.44 TQ	CABLS	10/01-12/01
	San Jose PMSA, CA	H	12.92 FQ	19.56 AW	30.58 TQ	CABLS	10/01-12/01
	Santa Barbara-Santa Maria-Lompoc MSA, CA	H	17.31 FQ	23.45 AW	29.45 TQ	CABLS	10/01-12/01
	Santa Cruz-Watsonville PMSA, CA	H	12.58 FQ	20.33 AW	31.89 TQ	CABLS	10/01-12/01
	Santa Rosa PMSA, CA	H	18.10 FQ	24.10 AW	28.60 TQ	CABLS	10/01-12/01
	Stockton-Lodi MSA, CA	H	11.61 FQ	14.07 AW	18.43 TQ	CABLS	10/01-12/01
	Vallejo-Fairfield-Napa PMSA, CA	H	17.41 FQ	26.08 AW	34.89 TQ	CABLS	10/01-12/01
	Ventura PMSA, CA	H	16.30 FQ	23.26 AW	32.70 TQ	CABLS	10/01-12/01
	Visalia-Tulare-Porterville MSA, CA	H	8.98 FQ	17.51 AW	26.45 TQ	CABLS	10/01-12/01
	Colorado	H	11.08 FQ	20.77 AW	59.03 TQ	COBLS	10/01-12/01
	Denver PMSA, CO	H	14.33 FQ	22.92 AW	61.91 TQ	COBLS	10/01-12/01
	Connecticut	H	15.88 FQ	21.71 AW	27.03 TQ	CTBLS	10/01-12/01
	Hartford MSA, CT	H	17.83 FQ	22.64 AW	27.21 TQ	CTBLS	10/01-12/01
	New Haven-Meriden PMSA, CT	H	17.08 FQ	21.38 AW	27.02 TQ	CTBLS	10/01-12/01
	Delaware	H	17.03 FQ	18.69 AW	21.07 TQ	DEBLS	10/01-12/01
	Washington PMSA, DC-MD-VA-WV	H	10.91 FQ	15.16 AW	21.46 TQ	DCBLS	10/01-12/01
	Florida	H	7.92 FQ	15.39 AW	24.35 TQ	FLBLS	10/01-12/01
	Daytona Beach MSA, FL	H	11.40 FQ	13.16 AW	16.14 TQ	FLBLS	10/01-12/01
	Fort Lauderdale PMSA, FL	H	14.83 FQ	20.55 AW	26.96 TQ	FLBLS	10/01-12/01
	Fort Myers-Cape Coral MSA, FL	H	11.13 FQ	16.91 AW	30.33 TQ	FLBLS	10/01-12/01
	Jacksonville MSA, FL	H	7.92 FQ	14.73 AW	20.48 TQ	FLBLS	10/01-12/01
	Melbourne-Titusville-Palm Bay MSA, FL	H	12.15 FQ	17.04 AW	25.66 TQ	FLBLS	10/01-12/01
	Miami PMSA, FL	H	7.26 FQ	10.90 AW	18.47 TQ	FLBLS	10/01-12/01
	Naples MSA, FL	H	8.93 FQ	19.68 AW	31.48 TQ	FLBLS	10/01-12/01
	Orlando MSA, FL	H	5.87 FQ	11.97 AW	17.56 TQ	FLBLS	10/01-12/01
	Pensacola MSA, FL	H	11.38 FQ	14.12 AW	16.56 TQ	FLBLS	10/01-12/01
	Sarasota-Bradenton MSA, FL	H	10.98 FQ	19.65 AW	33.26 TQ	FLBLS	10/01-12/01
	Tampa-St. Petersburg-Clearwater MSA, FL	H	9.94 FQ	15.75 AW	21.82 TQ	FLBLS	10/01-12/01
	West Palm Beach-Boca Raton MSA, FL	H	6.90 FQ	16.13 AW	25.18 TQ	FLBLS	10/01-12/01
	Georgia	H	9.39 FQ	14.71 AW	21.19 TQ	GABLS	10/01-12/01
	Atlanta MSA, GA	H	9.75 FQ	15.98 AW	21.93 TQ	GABLS	10/01-12/01
	Hawaii	H	14.43 FQ	24.82 AW	39.91 TQ	HIBLS	10/01-12/01
	Honolulu MSA, HI	H	13.95 FQ	28.01 AW	43.72 TQ	HIBLS	10/01-12/01
	Idaho	H	6.00 FQ	12.58 AW	20.41 TQ	IDBLS	10/01-12/01
	Illinois	H	10.57 FQ	21.12 AW	29.24 TQ	ILBLS	10/01-12/01
	Champaign-Urbana MSA, IL	H	17.47 FQ	19.42 AW	21.44 TQ	ILBLS	10/01-12/01
	Chicago PMSA, IL	H	10.14 FQ	21.58 AW	31.37 TQ	ILBLS	10/01-12/01
	Indiana	H	14.15 FQ	20.47 AW	25.98 TQ	INBLS	10/01-12/01
	Evansville-Henderson MSA, IN-KY	H	18.44 FQ	21.88 AW	26.13 TQ	INBLS	10/01-12/01
	Iowa	H	7.98 FQ	16.69 AW	24.13 TQ	IABLS	10/01-12/01
	Kansas	H	9.45 FQ	15.04 AW	22.00 TQ	KSBLS	10/01-12/01
	Wichita MSA, KS	H	9.23 FQ	13.81 AW	20.84 TQ	KSBLS	10/01-12/01
	Kentucky	H	13.94 FQ	20.57 AW	36.04 TQ	KYBLS	10/01-12/01
	Louisville MSA, KY-IN	H	10.20 FQ	17.93 AW	22.53 TQ	KYBLS	10/01-12/01
	Louisiana	H	6.33 FQ	12.99 AW	20.20 TQ	LABLS	10/01-12/01
	Baton Rouge MSA, LA	H	5.82 FQ	11.37 AW	19.37 TQ	LABLS	10/01-12/01
	New Orleans MSA, LA	H	10.38 FQ	15.52 AW	21.22 TQ	LABLS	10/01-12/01
	Maine	H	10.83 FQ	18.82 AW	28.73 TQ	MEBLS	10/01-12/01
	Portland MSA, ME	H	13.01 FQ	22.72 AW	32.16 TQ	MEBLS	10/01-12/01
	Maryland	H	10.08 FQ	17.24 AW	26.14 TQ	MDBLS	10/01-12/01
	Baltimore PMSA, MD	H	16.15 FQ	26.81 AW	41.34 TQ	MDBLS	10/01-12/01
	Massachusetts	H	15.53 FQ	24.65 AW	32.66 TQ	MABLS	10/01-12/01
	Boston PMSA, MA-NH	H	23.62 FQ	28.46 AW	33.49 TQ	MABLS	10/01-12/01

AAW	Average annual wage	**AOH**	Average offered, high	**ASH**	Average starting, high	**H**	Hourly	**M**	Monthly	**S**	Special: hourly and annual
AE	Average entry wage	**AOL**	Average offered, low	**ASL**	Average starting, low	**HI**	Highest wage paid	**MTC**	Median total compensation	**TQ**	Third quartile wage
AEX	Average experienced wage	**APH**	Average pay, high range	**AW**	Average wage paid	**HR**	High end range	**MW**	Median wage paid	**W**	Weekly
AO	Average offered	**APL**	Average pay, low range	**FQ**	First quartile wage	**LR**	Low end range	**SQ**	Second quartile wage	**Y**	Yearly

Occupation/Type/Industry	Location	Per	Low	Mid	High	Source	Date
Tile and Marble Setter	Lawrence PMSA, MA-NH	H	20.26 FQ	28.79 AW	33.92 TQ	MABLS	10/01-12/01
	Michigan	H	12.89 FQ	19.41 AW	27.30 TQ	MIBLS	10/01-12/01
	Detroit PMSA, MI	H	15.77 FQ	23.30 AW	28.05 TQ	MIBLS	10/01-12/01
	Grand Rapids-Muskegon-Holland MSA, MI	H	17.48 FQ	19.30 AW	21.69 TQ	MIBLS	10/01-12/01
	Minnesota	H	14.68 FQ	20.26 AW	26.59 TQ	MNBLS	10/01-12/01
	Minneapolis-St. Paul MSA, MN-WI	H	14.83 FQ	20.28 AW	26.55 TQ	MNBLS	10/01-12/01
	Mississippi	H	9.04 FQ	12.85 AW	17.37 TQ	MSBLS	10/01-12/01
	Missouri	H	12.13 FQ	20.75 AW	27.22 TQ	MOBLS	10/01-12/01
	Kansas City MSA, MO-KS	H	15.07 FQ	21.93 AW	28.07 TQ	MOBLS	10/01-12/01
	St. Louis MSA, MO-IL	H	17.33 FQ	20.67 AW	26.00 TQ	MOBLS	10/01-12/01
	Montana	H	12.06 FQ	15.81 AW	21.78 TQ	MTBLS	10/01-12/01
	Nebraska	H	10.22 FQ	18.04 AW	26.56 TQ	NEBLS	10/01-12/01
	Omaha MSA, NE-IA	H	10.28 FQ	18.27 AW	26.94 TQ	NEBLS	10/01-12/01
	Nevada	H	13.11 FQ	20.00 AW	26.76 TQ	NVBLS	10/01-12/01
	Las Vegas MSA, NV-AZ	H	12.82 FQ	20.07 AW	26.75 TQ	NVBLS	10/01-12/01
	Reno MSA, NV	H	11.87 FQ	19.22 AW	27.05 TQ	NVBLS	10/01-12/01
	New Hampshire	H	19.34 FQ	28.22 AW	34.33 TQ	NHBLS	10/01-12/01
	New Jersey	H	9.36 FQ	20.40 AW	33.27 TQ	NJBLS	10/01-12/01
	Bergen-Passaic PMSA, NJ	H	8.87 FQ	12.07 AW	17.42 TQ	NJBLS	10/01-12/01
	Jersey City PMSA, NJ	H	16.56 FQ	25.14 AW	28.90 TQ	NJBLS	10/01-12/01
	New Mexico	H	9.15 FQ	13.72 AW	19.89 TQ	NMBLS	10/01-12/01
	Albuquerque MSA, NM	H	11.22 FQ	14.30 AW	19.87 TQ	NMBLS	10/01-12/01
	New York	H	11.90 FQ	20.75 AW	32.20 TQ	NYBLS	10/01-12/01
	Albany-Schenectady-Troy MSA, NY	H	16.02 FQ	21.58 AW	30.37 TQ	NYBLS	10/01-12/01
	Binghamton MSA, NY	H	15.27 FQ	18.94 AW	22.10 TQ	NYBLS	10/01-12/01
	Buffalo-Niagara Falls MSA, NY	H	11.15 FQ	17.39 AW	25.28 TQ	NYBLS	10/01-12/01
	Nassau-Suffolk PMSA, NY	H	10.15 FQ	19.76 AW	34.21 TQ	NYBLS	10/01-12/01
	New York PMSA, NY	H	12.60 FQ	21.93 AW	32.82 TQ	NYBLS	10/01-12/01
	Syracuse MSA, NY	H	15.72 FQ	18.92 AW	21.78 TQ	NYBLS	10/01-12/01
	North Carolina	H	9.26 FQ	15.51 AW	21.57 TQ	NCBLS	10/01-12/01
	Charlotte-Gastonia-Rock Hill MSA, NC-SC	H	11.98 FQ	17.67 AW	21.88 TQ	NCBLS	10/01-12/01
	Greensboro-Winston-Salem-High Point MSA, NC	H	6.57 FQ	11.67 AW	18.24 TQ	NCBLS	10/01-12/01
	Ohio	H	11.58 FQ	17.25 AW	25.00 TQ	OHBLS	10/01-12/01
	Cincinnati PMSA, OH-KY-IN	H	12.64 FQ	20.28 AW	38.36 TQ	OHBLS	10/01-12/01
	Cleveland-Lorain-Elyria PMSA, OH	H	11.24 FQ	17.78 AW	24.56 TQ	OHBLS	10/01-12/01
	Dayton-Springfield MSA, OH	H	8.10 FQ	21.56 AW	27.54 TQ	OHBLS	10/01-12/01
	Oklahoma	H	8.50 FQ	13.47 AW	21.46 TQ	OKBLS	10/01-12/01
	Oklahoma City MSA, OK	H	7.54 FQ	12.16 AW	18.51 TQ	OKBLS	10/01-12/01
	Tulsa MSA, OK	H	9.99 FQ	18.33 AW	22.58 TQ	OKBLS	10/01-12/01
	Oregon	H	11.23 FQ	15.76 AW	22.30 TQ	ORBLS	10/01-12/01
	Eugene-Springfield MSA, OR	H	14.30 FQ	20.89 AW	31.42 TQ	ORBLS	10/01-12/01
	Portland-Vancouver PMSA, OR-WA	H	11.25 FQ	14.49 AW	19.31 TQ	ORBLS	10/01-12/01
	Pennsylvania	H	11.34 FQ	19.35 AW	28.32 TQ	PABLS	10/01-12/01
	Lancaster MSA, PA	H	14.15 FQ	19.62 AW	26.61 TQ	PABLS	10/01-12/01
	Philadelphia PMSA, PA-NJ	H	11.62 FQ	20.57 AW	30.76 TQ	PABLS	10/01-12/01
	Pittsburgh MSA, PA	H	10.14 FQ	16.91 AW	25.03 TQ	PABLS	10/01-12/01
	York MSA, PA	H	11.85 FQ	16.39 AW	20.68 TQ	PABLS	10/01-12/01
	South Carolina	H	10.12 FQ	13.67 AW	18.39 TQ	SCBLS	10/01-12/01
	Columbia MSA, SC	H	10.08 FQ	12.46 AW	13.99 TQ	SCBLS	10/01-12/01
	Tennessee	H	9.75 FQ	15.66 AW	21.24 TQ	TNBLS	10/01-12/01
	Chattanooga MSA, TN-GA	H	7.67 FQ	12.22 AW	18.51 TQ	TNBLS	10/01-12/01
	Knoxville MSA, TN	H	11.80 FQ	15.26 AW	20.09 TQ	TNBLS	10/01-12/01
	Memphis MSA, TN-AR-MS	H	9.95 FQ	16.61 AW	27.94 TQ	TNBLS	10/01-12/01
	Texas	H	6.33 FQ	12.37 AW	19.23 TQ	TXBLS	10/01-12/01
	Dallas PMSA, TX	H	10.41 FQ	15.99 AW	20.97 TQ	TXBLS	10/01-12/01
	Fort Worth-Arlington PMSA, TX	H	8.85 FQ	10.05 AW	11.34 TQ	TXBLS	10/01-12/01
	Houston PMSA, TX	H	6.46 FQ	13.98 AW	21.64 TQ	TXBLS	10/01-12/01
	McAllen-Edinburg-Mission MSA, TX	H	5.78 FQ	6.66 AW	8.32 TQ	TXBLS	10/01-12/01
	San Antonio MSA, TX	H	10.83 FQ	13.89 AW	16.84 TQ	TXBLS	10/01-12/01
	Utah	H	9.52 FQ	17.15 AW	22.88 TQ	UTBLS	10/01-12/01
	Salt Lake City-Ogden MSA, UT	H	9.56 FQ	17.64 AW	22.91 TQ	UTBLS	10/01-12/01

AAW	Average annual wage	AOH	Average offered, high	ASH	Average starting, high	H	Hourly	M	Monthly	S	Special: hourly and annual
AE	Average entry wage	AOL	Average offered, low	ASL	Average starting, low	HI	Highest wage paid	MTC	Median total compensation	TQ	Third quartile wage
AEX	Average experienced wage	APH	Average pay, high range	AW	Average wage paid	HR	High end range	MW	Median wage paid	W	Weekly
AO	Average offered	APL	Average pay, low range	FQ	First quartile wage	LR	Low end range	SQ	Second quartile wage	Y	Yearly

Occupation/Type/Industry	Location	Per	Low	Mid	High	Source	Date
Tile and Marble Setter	Virginia	H	10.73 FQ	16.01 AW	23.69 TQ	VABLS	10/01-12/01
	Norfolk-Virginia Beach-Newport News MSA, VA-NC	H	12.11 FQ	18.04 AW	27.05 TQ	VABLS	10/01-12/01
	Richmond-Petersburg MSA, VA	H	11.47 FQ	18.32 AW	22.73 TQ	VABLS	10/01-12/01
	Washington	H	15.69 FQ	22.37 AW	29.02 TQ	WABLS	10/01-12/01
	Bremerton PMSA, WA	H	18.14 FQ	23.56 AW	27.44 TQ	WABLS	10/01-12/01
	Seattle-Bellevue-Everett PMSA, WA	H	16.40 FQ	22.73 AW	29.01 TQ	WABLS	10/01-12/01
	Tacoma PMSA, WA	H	18.79 FQ	20.90 AW	22.89 TQ	WABLS	10/01-12/01
	West Virginia	H	11.14 FQ	14.82 AW	27.39 TQ	WVBLS	10/01-12/01
	Wisconsin	H	11.06 FQ	18.94 AW	27.24 TQ	WIBLS	10/01-12/01
	Green Bay MSA, WI	H	13.20 FQ	21.08 AW	27.30 TQ	WIBLS	10/01-12/01
	Madison MSA, WI	H	18.60 FQ	23.41 AW	28.11 TQ	WIBLS	10/01-12/01
	Puerto Rico	H	6.25 FQ	12.75 AW	23.70 TQ	PRBLS	10/01-12/01
Timing Device Assembler, Adjuster, and Calibrator	California	H	8.40 FQ	12.72 AW	21.32 TQ	CABLS	10/01-12/01
	Connecticut	H	10.38 FQ	14.83 AW	19.53 TQ	CTBLS	10/01-12/01
	Florida	H	7.59 FQ	10.20 AW	14.56 TQ	FLBLS	10/01-12/01
	Georgia	H	7.41 FQ	10.92 AW	18.47 TQ	GABLS	10/01-12/01
	Illinois	H	8.81 FQ	12.39 AW	16.11 TQ	ILBLS	10/01-12/01
	Indiana	H	9.17 FQ	12.61 AW	17.44 TQ	INBLS	10/01-12/01
	Massachusetts	H	7.61 FQ	11.29 AW	16.73 TQ	MABLS	10/01-12/01
	Minnesota	H	9.23 FQ	12.44 AW	15.57 TQ	MNBLS	10/01-12/01
	Mississippi	H	8.94 FQ	11.73 AW	16.62 TQ	MSBLS	10/01-12/01
	Missouri	H	8.17 FQ	18.87 AW	42.45 TQ	MOBLS	10/01-12/01
	New Hampshire	H	8.67 FQ	11.71 AW	14.43 TQ	NHBLS	10/01-12/01
	New Mexico	H	7.93 FQ	13.76 AW	22.55 TQ	NMBLS	10/01-12/01
	New York	H	8.76 FQ	12.15 AW	16.95 TQ	NYBLS	10/01-12/01
	Ohio	H	8.52 FQ	12.80 AW	19.75 TQ	OHBLS	10/01-12/01
	Pennsylvania	H	8.16 FQ	12.08 AW	16.72 TQ	PABLS	10/01-12/01
	Texas	H	8.91 FQ	12.44 AW	17.89 TQ	TXBLS	10/01-12/01
	Virginia	H	8.60 FQ	12.87 AW	16.77 TQ	VABLS	10/01-12/01
	Washington	H	8.37 FQ	12.18 AW	15.80 TQ	WABLS	10/01-12/01
	Wisconsin	H	9.00 FQ	13.37 AW	20.41 TQ	WIBLS	10/01-12/01
	Virgin Islands	H	6.31 FQ	8.24 AW	10.47 TQ	VIBLS	10/01-12/01
Tire Builder	Arizona	H	7.37 FQ	9.00 AW	11.11 TQ	AZBLS	10/01-12/01
	Arkansas	H	12.04 FQ	18.89 AW	27.33 TQ	ARBLS	10/01-12/01
	California	H	9.30 FQ	15.57 AW	21.67 TQ	CABLS	10/01-12/01
	Florida	H	8.52 FQ	11.52 AW	16.95 TQ	FLBLS	10/01-12/01
	Georgia	H	7.70 FQ	9.98 AW	12.74 TQ	GABLS	10/01-12/01
	Illinois	H	11.45 FQ	17.48 AW	21.47 TQ	ILBLS	10/01-12/01
	Iowa	H	11.72 FQ	17.11 AW	21.65 TQ	IABLS	10/01-12/01
	Kansas	H	10.48 FQ	18.74 AW	27.57 TQ	KSBLS	10/01-12/01
	Missouri	H	9.30 FQ	15.14 AW	21.36 TQ	MOBLS	10/01-12/01
	Nebraska	H	6.01 FQ	9.84 AW	13.20 TQ	NEBLS	10/01-12/01
	New Jersey	H	9.00 FQ	10.84 AW	13.61 TQ	NJBLS	10/01-12/01
	North Carolina	H	8.42 FQ	14.65 AW	21.39 TQ	NCBLS	10/01-12/01
	Ohio	H	7.72 FQ	15.60 AW	21.90 TQ	OHBLS	10/01-12/01
	Pennsylvania	H	8.05 FQ	14.61 AW	25.92 TQ	PABLS	10/01-12/01
	Tennessee	H	11.77 FQ	18.12 AW	26.49 TQ	TNBLS	10/01-12/01
	Virginia	H	11.24 FQ	18.96 AW	27.04 TQ	VABLS	10/01-12/01
	Wisconsin	H	8.48 FQ	10.34 AW	12.86 TQ	WIBLS	10/01-12/01
	Puerto Rico	H	5.56 FQ	9.20 AW	16.15 TQ	PRBLS	10/01-12/01
Tire Repairer and Changer	Alabama	H	6.50 FQ	8.87 AW	11.96 TQ	ALBLS	10/01-12/01
	Birmingham MSA, AL	H	7.16 FQ	9.30 AW	12.88 TQ	ALBLS	10/01-12/01
	Huntsville MSA, AL	H	7.46 FQ	8.44 AW	10.06 TQ	ALBLS	10/01-12/01
	Mobile MSA, AL	H	5.73 FQ	7.96 AW	11.49 TQ	ALBLS	10/01-12/01
	Montgomery MSA, AL	H	6.70 FQ	8.32 AW	10.24 TQ	ALBLS	10/01-12/01
	Alaska	H	8.39 FQ	12.23 AW	16.63 TQ	AKBLS	10/01-12/01
	Anchorage MSA, AK	H	8.98 FQ	11.86 AW	16.02 TQ	AKBLS	10/01-12/01
	Arizona	H	6.62 FQ	9.25 AW	12.23 TQ	AZBLS	10/01-12/01
	Phoenix-Mesa MSA, AZ	H	6.72 FQ	9.51 AW	12.44 TQ	AZBLS	10/01-12/01
	Tucson MSA, AZ	H	7.05 FQ	8.76 AW	11.47 TQ	AZBLS	10/01-12/01
	Arkansas	H	5.79 FQ	8.39 AW	11.16 TQ	ARBLS	10/01-12/01
	Fayetteville-Springdale-Rogers MSA, AR	H	7.35 FQ	9.94 AW	12.86 TQ	ARBLS	10/01-12/01
	Fort Smith MSA, AR-OK	H	6.14 FQ	8.29 AW	10.63 TQ	ARBLS	10/01-12/01

AAW	Average annual wage	**AOH**	Average offered, high	**ASH**	Average starting, high	**H**	Hourly	**M**	Monthly	**S**	Special: hourly and annual
AE	Average entry wage	**AOL**	Average offered, low	**ASL**	Average starting, low	**HI**	Highest wage paid	**MTC**	Median total compensation	**TQ**	Third quartile wage
AEX	Average experienced wage	**APH**	Average pay, high range	**AW**	Average wage paid	**HR**	High end range	**MW**	Median wage paid	**W**	Weekly
AO	Average offered	**APL**	Average pay, low range	**FQ**	First quartile wage	**LR**	Low end range	**SQ**	Second quartile wage	**Y**	Yearly

Occupation/Type/Industry	Location	Per	Low	Mid	High	Source	Date
Tire Repairer and Changer	Little Rock-North Little Rock MSA, AR	H	5.50 FQ	7.86 AW	11.30 TQ	ARBLS	10/01-12/01
	California	H	7.43 FQ	10.85 AW	16.04 TQ	CABLS	10/01-12/01
	Bakersfield MSA, CA	H	6.66 FQ	10.40 AW	14.33 TQ	CABLS	10/01-12/01
	Chico-Paradise MSA, CA	H	7.36 FQ	9.95 AW	13.11 TQ	CABLS	10/01-12/01
	Fresno MSA, CA	H	6.74 FQ	10.27 AW	14.27 TQ	CABLS	10/01-12/01
	Los Angeles-Long Beach PMSA, CA	H	7.39 FQ	11.03 AW	16.88 TQ	CABLS	10/01-12/01
	Merced MSA, CA	H	8.22 FQ	10.35 AW	14.61 TQ	CABLS	10/01-12/01
	Modesto MSA, CA	H	7.67 FQ	11.20 AW	13.88 TQ	CABLS	10/01-12/01
	Oakland PMSA, CA	H	8.83 FQ	11.33 AW	16.04 TQ	CABLS	10/01-12/01
	Orange County PMSA, CA	H	8.31 FQ	14.52 AW	24.23 TQ	CABLS	10/01-12/01
	Redding MSA, CA	H	8.55 FQ	11.67 AW	16.35 TQ	CABLS	10/01-12/01
	Riverside-San Bernardino PMSA, CA	H	7.79 FQ	11.50 AW	14.73 TQ	CABLS	10/01-12/01
	Sacramento PMSA, CA	H	7.60 FQ	9.67 AW	11.19 TQ	CABLS	10/01-12/01
	Salinas MSA, CA	H	7.71 FQ	11.25 AW	14.17 TQ	CABLS	10/01-12/01
	San Diego MSA, CA	H	7.41 FQ	9.23 AW	11.17 TQ	CABLS	10/01-12/01
	San Francisco PMSA, CA	H	9.50 FQ	12.64 AW	16.82 TQ	CABLS	10/01-12/01
	San Jose PMSA, CA	H	7.00 FQ	8.97 AW	12.36 TQ	CABLS	10/01-12/01
	San Luis Obispo-Atascadero-Paso Robles MSA, CA	H	7.23 FQ	8.60 AW	10.26 TQ	CABLS	10/01-12/01
	Santa Barbara-Santa Maria-Lompoc MSA, CA	H	7.29 FQ	10.64 AW	16.69 TQ	CABLS	10/01-12/01
	Santa Cruz-Watsonville PMSA, CA	H	7.32 FQ	9.67 AW	13.49 TQ	CABLS	10/01-12/01
	Santa Rosa PMSA, CA	H	8.60 FQ	11.66 AW	15.02 TQ	CABLS	10/01-12/01
	Stockton-Lodi MSA, CA	H	7.16 FQ	8.70 AW	10.74 TQ	CABLS	10/01-12/01
	Vallejo-Fairfield-Napa PMSA, CA	H	7.43 FQ	9.57 AW	13.28 TQ	CABLS	10/01-12/01
	Ventura PMSA, CA	H	7.44 FQ	10.57 AW	15.40 TQ	CABLS	10/01-12/01
	Visalia-Tulare-Porterville MSA, CA	H	6.92 FQ	8.65 AW	10.72 TQ	CABLS	10/01-12/01
	Colorado	H	7.46 FQ	9.51 AW	11.23 TQ	COBLS	10/01-12/01
	Boulder-Longmont PMSA, CO	H	7.37 FQ	9.84 AW	12.65 TQ	COBLS	10/01-12/01
	Colorado Springs MSA, CO	H	8.48 FQ	10.56 AW	14.59 TQ	COBLS	10/01-12/01
	Denver PMSA, CO	H	7.66 FQ	9.51 AW	11.00 TQ	COBLS	10/01-12/01
	Fort Collins-Loveland MSA, CO	H	8.32 FQ	9.95 AW	12.32 TQ	COBLS	10/01-12/01
	Greeley PMSA, CO	H	6.76 FQ	9.02 AW	11.04 TQ	COBLS	10/01-12/01
	Connecticut	H	6.65 FQ	9.42 AW	13.32 TQ	CTBLS	10/01-12/01
	Bridgeport PMSA, CT	H	6.65 FQ	8.55 AW	11.02 TQ	CTBLS	10/01-12/01
	Danbury PMSA, CT	H	6.94 FQ	10.08 AW	14.47 TQ	CTBLS	10/01-12/01
	Hartford MSA, CT	H	6.54 FQ	8.24 AW	11.14 TQ	CTBLS	10/01-12/01
	New Haven-Meriden PMSA, CT	H	6.68 FQ	9.92 AW	14.89 TQ	CTBLS	10/01-12/01
	Stamford-Norwalk PMSA, CT	H	7.33 FQ	8.75 AW	10.81 TQ	CTBLS	10/01-12/01
	Waterbury PMSA, CT	H	8.91 FQ	11.21 AW	13.57 TQ	CTBLS	10/01-12/01
	Delaware	H	6.93 FQ	8.56 AW	10.60 TQ	DEBLS	10/01-12/01
	Wilmington-Newark PMSA, DE-MD	H	6.94 FQ	8.38 AW	10.10 TQ	DEBLS	10/01-12/01
	Washington PMSA, DC-MD-VA-WV	H	7.26 FQ	10.48 AW	15.77 TQ	DCBLS	10/01-12/01
	Florida	H	7.29 FQ	9.97 AW	13.42 TQ	FLBLS	10/01-12/01
	Daytona Beach MSA, FL	H	6.88 FQ	9.06 AW	11.26 TQ	FLBLS	10/01-12/01
	Fort Lauderdale PMSA, FL	H	7.15 FQ	10.40 AW	17.50 TQ	FLBLS	10/01-12/01
	Fort Myers-Cape Coral MSA, FL	H	7.29 FQ	10.42 AW	15.75 TQ	FLBLS	10/01-12/01
	Fort Pierce-Port St. Lucie MSA, FL	H	6.80 FQ	11.37 AW	16.29 TQ	FLBLS	10/01-12/01
	Fort Walton Beach MSA, FL	H	7.21 FQ	8.91 AW	10.81 TQ	FLBLS	10/01-12/01
	Gainesville MSA, FL	H	6.23 FQ	8.65 AW	11.00 TQ	FLBLS	10/01-12/01
	Jacksonville MSA, FL	H	8.57 FQ	10.46 AW	13.90 TQ	FLBLS	10/01-12/01
	Lakeland-Winter Haven MSA, FL	H	6.13 FQ	9.07 AW	12.67 TQ	FLBLS	10/01-12/01
	Melbourne-Titusville-Palm Bay MSA, FL	H	7.37 FQ	10.45 AW	14.39 TQ	FLBLS	10/01-12/01
	Miami PMSA, FL	H	6.54 FQ	9.44 AW	12.90 TQ	FLBLS	10/01-12/01
	Naples MSA, FL	H	7.34 FQ	10.66 AW	13.86 TQ	FLBLS	10/01-12/01
	Ocala MSA, FL	H	6.51 FQ	9.69 AW	13.52 TQ	FLBLS	10/01-12/01
	Orlando MSA, FL	H	8.10 FQ	9.94 AW	11.17 TQ	FLBLS	10/01-12/01
	Pensacola MSA, FL	H	7.52 FQ	9.07 AW	10.48 TQ	FLBLS	10/01-12/01

AAW Average annual wage; AE Average entry wage; AEX Average experienced wage; AO Average offered; AOH Average offered, high; AOL Average offered, low; APH Average pay, high range; APL Average pay, low range; ASH Average starting, high; ASL Average starting, low; AW Average wage paid; FQ First quartile wage; H Hourly; HI Highest wage paid; HR High end range; LR Low end range; M Monthly; MTC Median total compensation; MW Median wage paid; SQ Second quartile wage; S Special: hourly and annual; TQ Third quartile wage; W Weekly; Y Yearly

Occupation/Type/Industry	Location	Per	Low	Mid	High	Source	Date
Tire Repairer and Changer	Sarasota-Bradenton MSA, FL	H	7.73 FQ	9.90 AW	12.71 TQ	FLBLS	10/01-12/01
	Tallahassee MSA, FL	H	7.57 FQ	12.30 AW	19.62 TQ	FLBLS	10/01-12/01
	Tampa-St. Petersburg-Clearwater MSA, FL	H	7.66 FQ	9.74 AW	11.99 TQ	FLBLS	10/01-12/01
	West Palm Beach-Boca Raton MSA, FL	H	7.69 FQ	12.13 AW	17.39 TQ	FLBLS	10/01-12/01
	Georgia	H	7.47 FQ	10.63 AW	14.68 TQ	GABLS	10/01-12/01
	Atlanta MSA, GA	H	8.38 FQ	11.12 AW	14.30 TQ	GABLS	10/01-12/01
	Augusta-Aiken MSA, GA-SC	H	5.78 FQ	8.43 AW	13.15 TQ	GABLS	10/01-12/01
	Columbus MSA, GA-AL	H	7.25 FQ	10.07 AW	15.21 TQ	GABLS	10/01-12/01
	Macon MSA, GA	H	7.37 FQ	9.35 AW	10.94 TQ	GABLS	10/01-12/01
	Savannah MSA, GA	H	6.64 FQ	8.65 AW	12.42 TQ	GABLS	10/01-12/01
	Hawaii	H	7.49 FQ	11.37 AW	16.45 TQ	HIBLS	10/01-12/01
	Honolulu MSA, HI	H	7.54 FQ	11.58 AW	16.76 TQ	HIBLS	10/01-12/01
	Idaho	H	7.16 FQ	10.81 AW	15.14 TQ	IDBLS	10/01-12/01
	Boise City MSA, ID	H	7.18 FQ	11.02 AW	15.80 TQ	IDBLS	10/01-12/01
	Illinois	H	6.56 FQ	9.85 AW	13.16 TQ	ILBLS	10/01-12/01
	Chicago PMSA, IL	H	6.57 FQ	10.43 AW	15.21 TQ	ILBLS	10/01-12/01
	Peoria-Pekin MSA, IL	H	8.03 FQ	13.24 AW	20.28 TQ	ILBLS	10/01-12/01
	Rockford MSA, IL	H	7.68 FQ	9.98 AW	12.71 TQ	ILBLS	10/01-12/01
	Springfield MSA, IL	H	6.04 FQ	8.61 AW	12.19 TQ	ILBLS	10/01-12/01
	Indiana	H	7.10 FQ	10.14 AW	15.17 TQ	INBLS	10/01-12/01
	Elkhart-Goshen MSA, IN	H	7.29 FQ	11.81 AW	17.15 TQ	INBLS	10/01-12/01
	Evansville-Henderson MSA, IN-KY	H	6.50 FQ	8.19 AW	10.57 TQ	INBLS	10/01-12/01
	Fort Wayne MSA, IN	H	6.76 FQ	10.06 AW	16.54 TQ	INBLS	10/01-12/01
	Gary PMSA, IN	H	7.37 FQ	11.70 AW	16.25 TQ	INBLS	10/01-12/01
	Indianapolis MSA, IN	H	8.68 FQ	11.65 AW	15.10 TQ	INBLS	10/01-12/01
	Lafayette MSA, IN	H	6.59 FQ	8.88 AW	11.11 TQ	INBLS	10/01-12/01
	South Bend MSA, IN	H	7.37 FQ	9.72 AW	13.45 TQ	INBLS	10/01-12/01
	Iowa	H	6.89 FQ	9.47 AW	13.82 TQ	IABLS	10/01-12/01
	Cedar Rapids MSA, IA	H	5.92 FQ	9.12 AW	13.35 TQ	IABLS	10/01-12/01
	Davenport-Moline-Rock Island MSA, IA-IL	H	7.86 FQ	11.97 AW	18.68 TQ	IABLS	10/01-12/01
	Des Moines MSA, IA	H	7.59 FQ	9.42 AW	12.11 TQ	IABLS	10/01-12/01
	Kansas	H	7.39 FQ	10.05 AW	13.30 TQ	KSBLS	10/01-12/01
	Topeka MSA, KS	H	7.11 FQ	9.35 AW	12.66 TQ	KSBLS	10/01-12/01
	Wichita MSA, KS	H	7.49 FQ	9.33 AW	11.46 TQ	KSBLS	10/01-12/01
	Kentucky	H	6.82 FQ	9.38 AW	12.83 TQ	KYBLS	10/01-12/01
	Lexington MSA, KY	H	7.34 FQ	9.99 AW	13.71 TQ	KYBLS	10/01-12/01
	Louisville MSA, KY-IN	H	7.29 FQ	9.92 AW	13.49 TQ	KYBLS	10/01-12/01
	Louisiana	H	5.85 FQ	8.41 AW	11.71 TQ	LABLS	10/01-12/01
	Baton Rouge MSA, LA	H	5.82 FQ	7.72 AW	11.35 TQ	LABLS	10/01-12/01
	Houma MSA, LA	H	6.81 FQ	8.34 AW	10.46 TQ	LABLS	10/01-12/01
	Lafayette MSA, LA	H	6.21 FQ	12.54 AW	22.28 TQ	LABLS	10/01-12/01
	New Orleans MSA, LA	H	5.81 FQ	8.23 AW	11.14 TQ	LABLS	10/01-12/01
	Shreveport-Bossier City MSA, LA	H	6.12 FQ	8.45 AW	10.81 TQ	LABLS	10/01-12/01
	Maine	H	6.19 FQ	8.98 AW	11.51 TQ	MEBLS	10/01-12/01
	Portland MSA, ME	H	7.40 FQ	9.59 AW	11.14 TQ	MEBLS	10/01-12/01
	Maryland	H	6.94 FQ	9.36 AW	12.80 TQ	MDBLS	10/01-12/01
	Baltimore PMSA, MD	H	7.05 FQ	9.25 AW	12.78 TQ	MDBLS	10/01-12/01
	Massachusetts	H	7.81 FQ	11.38 AW	16.13 TQ	MABLS	10/01-12/01
	Boston PMSA, MA-NH	H	8.89 FQ	12.18 AW	16.44 TQ	MABLS	10/01-12/01
	Brockton PMSA, MA	H	8.60 FQ	11.22 AW	15.49 TQ	MABLS	10/01-12/01
	Lawrence PMSA, MA-NH	H	7.15 FQ	9.57 AW	13.43 TQ	MABLS	10/01-12/01
	New Bedford PMSA, MA	H	7.46 FQ	9.53 AW	13.84 TQ	MABLS	10/01-12/01
	Springfield MSA, MA	H	6.92 FQ	10.87 AW	15.87 TQ	MABLS	10/01-12/01
	Worcester PMSA, MA-CT	H	6.98 FQ	9.62 AW	12.89 TQ	MABLS	10/01-12/01
	Michigan	H	7.43 FQ	11.39 AW	15.86 TQ	MIBLS	10/01-12/01
	Ann Arbor PMSA, MI	H	8.29 FQ	10.77 AW	13.87 TQ	MIBLS	10/01-12/01
	Detroit PMSA, MI	H	7.62 FQ	10.58 AW	16.47 TQ	MIBLS	10/01-12/01
	Flint PMSA, MI	H	7.59 FQ	9.57 AW	12.19 TQ	MIBLS	10/01-12/01
	Grand Rapids-Muskegon-Holland MSA, MI	H	8.29 FQ	16.48 AW	43.02 TQ	MIBLS	10/01-12/01
	Kalamazoo-Battle Creek MSA, MI	H	7.02 FQ	11.06 AW	14.05 TQ	MIBLS	10/01-12/01
	Lansing-East Lansing MSA, MI	H	6.97 FQ	9.52 AW	11.57 TQ	MIBLS	10/01-12/01
	Saginaw-Bay City-Midland MSA, MI	H	7.44 FQ	9.98 AW	13.99 TQ	MIBLS	10/01-12/01
	Minnesota	H	7.16 FQ	9.77 AW	13.21 TQ	MNBLS	10/01-12/01
	Duluth-Superior MSA, MN-WI	H	7.48 FQ	10.52 AW	15.90 TQ	MNBLS	10/01-12/01

AAW Average annual wage; **AE** Average entry wage; **AEX** Average experienced wage; **AO** Average offered; **AOH** Average offered, high; **AOL** Average offered, low; **APH** Average pay, high range; **APL** Average pay, low range; **ASH** Average starting, high; **ASL** Average starting, low; **AW** Average wage paid; **FQ** First quartile wage; **H** Hourly; **HI** Highest wage paid; **HR** High end range; **LR** Low end range; **M** Monthly; **MTC** Median total compensation; **MW** Median wage paid; **SQ** Second quartile wage; **S** Special: hourly and annual; **TQ** Third quartile wage; **W** Weekly; **Y** Yearly

Occupation/Type/Industry	Location	Per	Low	Mid	High	Source	Date
Tire Repairer and Changer	Minneapolis-St. Paul MSA, MN-WI	H	7.50 FQ	9.90 AW	13.09 TQ	MNBLS	10/01-12/01
	St. Cloud MSA, MN	H	7.54 FQ	9.54 AW	12.22 TQ	MNBLS	10/01-12/01
	Mississippi	H	5.84 FQ	7.99 AW	10.68 TQ	MSBLS	10/01-12/01
	Biloxi-Gulfport-Pascagoula MSA, MS	H	5.59 FQ	7.14 AW	9.82 TQ	MSBLS	10/01-12/01
	Jackson MSA, MS	H	6.04 FQ	7.94 AW	10.61 TQ	MSBLS	10/01-12/01
	Missouri	H	7.14 FQ	9.51 AW	13.10 TQ	MOBLS	10/01-12/01
	Kansas City MSA, MO-KS	H	5.89 FQ	9.07 AW	12.65 TQ	MOBLS	10/01-12/01
	St. Louis MSA, MO-IL	H	7.24 FQ	9.34 AW	12.38 TQ	MOBLS	10/01-12/01
	Springfield MSA, MO	H	7.59 FQ	10.08 AW	13.80 TQ	MOBLS	10/01-12/01
	Montana	H	6.89 FQ	10.05 AW	15.52 TQ	MTBLS	10/01-12/01
	Billings MSA, MT	H	7.30 FQ	9.15 AW	13.02 TQ	MTBLS	10/01-12/01
	Nebraska	H	6.97 FQ	9.71 AW	13.07 TQ	NEBLS	10/01-12/01
	Omaha MSA, NE-IA	H	7.05 FQ	9.41 AW	12.90 TQ	NEBLS	10/01-12/01
	Nevada	H	7.22 FQ	11.18 AW	16.69 TQ	NVBLS	10/01-12/01
	Las Vegas MSA, NV-AZ	H	6.87 FQ	9.77 AW	14.14 TQ	NVBLS	10/01-12/01
	Reno MSA, NV	H	9.20 FQ	13.20 AW	16.83 TQ	NVBLS	10/01-12/01
	New Hampshire	H	7.46 FQ	9.49 AW	11.87 TQ	NHBLS	10/01-12/01
	Nashua PMSA, NH	H	8.39 FQ	9.62 AW	10.91 TQ	NHBLS	10/01-12/01
	Portsmouth-Rochester PMSA, NH-ME	H	7.28 FQ	9.54 AW	13.14 TQ	NHBLS	10/01-12/01
	New Jersey	H	7.54 FQ	11.73 AW	17.12 TQ	NJBLS	10/01-12/01
	Bergen-Passaic PMSA, NJ	H	7.86 FQ	11.64 AW	14.83 TQ	NJBLS	10/01-12/01
	Jersey City PMSA, NJ	H	8.11 FQ	13.44 AW	19.32 TQ	NJBLS	10/01-12/01
	Middlesex-Somerset-Hunterdon PMSA, NJ	H	7.56 FQ	12.64 AW	18.41 TQ	NJBLS	10/01-12/01
	Monmouth-Ocean PMSA, NJ	H	7.45 FQ	10.48 AW	13.91 TQ	NJBLS	10/01-12/01
	Newark PMSA, NJ	H	7.15 FQ	10.88 AW	16.47 TQ	NJBLS	10/01-12/01
	Trenton PMSA, NJ	H	9.01 FQ	11.97 AW	15.42 TQ	NJBLS	10/01-12/01
	New Mexico	H	6.18 FQ	8.82 AW	11.32 TQ	NMBLS	10/01-12/01
	Albuquerque MSA, NM	H	7.15 FQ	9.79 AW	13.86 TQ	NMBLS	10/01-12/01
	Las Cruces MSA, NM	H	6.26 FQ	8.55 AW	11.19 TQ	NMBLS	10/01-12/01
	New York	H	7.52 FQ	12.43 AW	18.02 TQ	NYBLS	10/01-12/01
	Albany-Schenectady-Troy MSA, NY	H	8.60 FQ	12.86 AW	16.90 TQ	NYBLS	10/01-12/01
	Binghamton MSA, NY	H	7.32 FQ	9.47 AW	12.89 TQ	NYBLS	10/01-12/01
	Dutchess County PMSA, NY	H	7.32 FQ	10.55 AW	20.25 TQ	NYBLS	10/01-12/01
	Nassau-Suffolk PMSA, NY	H	7.49 FQ	10.37 AW	14.61 TQ	NYBLS	10/01-12/01
	New York PMSA, NY	H	7.80 FQ	12.95 AW	16.55 TQ	NYBLS	10/01-12/01
	Newburgh PMSA, NY-PA	H	7.46 FQ	11.89 AW	16.60 TQ	NYBLS	10/01-12/01
	Rochester MSA, NY	H	6.35 FQ	10.33 AW	15.66 TQ	NYBLS	10/01-12/01
	Syracuse MSA, NY	H	6.97 FQ	11.39 AW	16.10 TQ	NYBLS	10/01-12/01
	North Carolina	H	7.10 FQ	11.01 AW	22.76 TQ	NCBLS	10/01-12/01
	Asheville MSA, NC	H	7.30 FQ	10.44 AW	16.67 TQ	NCBLS	10/01-12/01
	Charlotte-Gastonia-Rock Hill MSA, NC-SC	H	6.88 FQ	11.04 AW	16.12 TQ	NCBLS	10/01-12/01
	Fayetteville MSA, NC	H	6.83 FQ	8.34 AW	10.58 TQ	NCBLS	10/01-12/01
	Greensboro-Winston-Salem-High Point MSA, NC	H	7.08 FQ	14.26 AW	26.58 TQ	NCBLS	10/01-12/01
	Hickory-Morganton-Lenoir MSA, NC	H	7.58 FQ	9.49 AW	11.55 TQ	NCBLS	10/01-12/01
	Raleigh-Durham-Chapel Hill MSA, NC	H	7.74 FQ	9.89 AW	12.37 TQ	NCBLS	10/01-12/01
	North Dakota	H	7.02 FQ	9.88 AW	13.43 TQ	NDBLS	10/01-12/01
	Fargo-Moorhead MSA, ND-MN	H	6.82 FQ	9.44 AW	13.07 TQ	NDBLS	10/01-12/01
	Ohio	H	7.05 FQ	9.92 AW	13.65 TQ	OHBLS	10/01-12/01
	Akron PMSA, OH	H	7.44 FQ	9.69 AW	12.94 TQ	OHBLS	10/01-12/01
	Canton-Massillon MSA, OH	H	6.36 FQ	9.70 AW	12.61 TQ	OHBLS	10/01-12/01
	Cincinnati PMSA, OH-KY-IN	H	7.12 FQ	9.15 AW	12.51 TQ	OHBLS	10/01-12/01
	Cleveland-Lorain-Elyria PMSA, OH	H	6.41 FQ	10.05 AW	17.87 TQ	OHBLS	10/01-12/01
	Columbus MSA, OH	H	7.24 FQ	8.70 AW	10.97 TQ	OHBLS	10/01-12/01
	Dayton-Springfield MSA, OH	H	8.62 FQ	11.43 AW	13.18 TQ	OHBLS	10/01-12/01
	Hamilton-Middletown PMSA, OH	H	7.77 FQ	11.51 AW	16.13 TQ	OHBLS	10/01-12/01
	Mansfield MSA, OH	H	7.13 FQ	9.16 AW	13.34 TQ	OHBLS	10/01-12/01
	Toledo MSA, OH	H	7.30 FQ	12.51 AW	18.24 TQ	OHBLS	10/01-12/01
	Youngstown-Warren MSA, OH	H	5.69 FQ	8.28 AW	10.82 TQ	OHBLS	10/01-12/01
	Oklahoma	H	6.81 FQ	8.35 AW	10.64 TQ	OKBLS	10/01-12/01
	Oklahoma City MSA, OK	H	7.13 FQ	8.52 AW	10.73 TQ	OKBLS	10/01-12/01

AAW	Average annual wage	**AOH**	Average offered, high	**ASH**	Average starting, high	**H**	Hourly	**M**	Monthly	**S**	Special: hourly and annual
AE	Average entry wage	**AOL**	Average offered, low	**ASL**	Average starting, low	**HI**	Highest wage paid	**MTC**	Median total compensation	**TQ**	Third quartile wage
AEX	Average experienced wage	**APH**	Average pay, high range	**AW**	Average wage paid	**HR**	High end range	**MW**	Median wage paid	**W**	Weekly
AO	Average offered	**APL**	Average pay, low range	**FQ**	First quartile wage	**LR**	Low end range	**SQ**	Second quartile wage	**Y**	Yearly

Occupation/Type/Industry	Location	Per	Low	Mid	High	Source	Date
Tire Repairer and Changer	Tulsa MSA, OK	H	6.89 FQ	8.39 AW	10.65 TQ	OKBLS	10/01-12/01
	Oregon	H	8.83 FQ	12.37 AW	16.48 TQ	ORBLS	10/01-12/01
	Eugene-Springfield MSA, OR	H	8.81 FQ	12.46 AW	16.56 TQ	ORBLS	10/01-12/01
	Medford-Ashland MSA, OR	H	9.09 FQ	12.99 AW	17.49 TQ	ORBLS	10/01-12/01
	Portland-Vancouver PMSA, OR-WA	H	8.04 FQ	12.19 AW	16.66 TQ	ORBLS	10/01-12/01
	Salem PMSA, OR	H	7.89 FQ	11.80 AW	16.60 TQ	ORBLS	10/01-12/01
	Pennsylvania	H	6.88 FQ	9.82 AW	13.49 TQ	PABLS	10/01-12/01
	Allentown-Bethlehem-Easton MSA, PA	H	7.56 FQ	9.83 AW	12.77 TQ	PABLS	10/01-12/01
	Erie MSA, PA	H	6.77 FQ	8.55 AW	10.96 TQ	PABLS	10/01-12/01
	Harrisburg-Lebanon-Carlisle MSA, PA	H	7.59 FQ	10.30 AW	13.41 TQ	PABLS	10/01-12/01
	Johnstown MSA, PA	H	6.77 FQ	8.88 AW	11.21 TQ	PABLS	10/01-12/01
	Philadelphia PMSA, PA-NJ	H	6.91 FQ	9.72 AW	13.60 TQ	PABLS	10/01-12/01
	Pittsburgh MSA, PA	H	7.62 FQ	10.66 AW	14.15 TQ	PABLS	10/01-12/01
	Reading MSA, PA	H	5.80 FQ	9.24 AW	14.42 TQ	PABLS	10/01-12/01
	York MSA, PA	H	6.31 FQ	9.93 AW	13.68 TQ	PABLS	10/01-12/01
	Rhode Island	H	7.10 FQ	9.54 AW	13.55 TQ	RIBLS	10/01-12/01
	Providence-Fall River-Warwick MSA, RI-MA	H	7.18 FQ	9.34 AW	13.11 TQ	RIBLS	10/01-12/01
	South Carolina	H	7.32 FQ	10.12 AW	14.53 TQ	SCBLS	10/01-12/01
	Charleston-North Charleston MSA, SC	H	7.47 FQ	9.44 AW	11.05 TQ	SCBLS	10/01-12/01
	Columbia MSA, SC	H	7.19 FQ	9.45 AW	12.79 TQ	SCBLS	10/01-12/01
	Greenville-Spartanburg-Anderson MSA, SC	H	8.00 FQ	11.88 AW	16.78 TQ	SCBLS	10/01-12/01
	Myrtle Beach MSA, SC	H	7.35 FQ	8.55 AW	10.49 TQ	SCBLS	10/01-12/01
	South Dakota	H	7.17 FQ	8.93 AW	11.12 TQ	SDBLS	10/01-12/01
	Sioux Falls MSA, SD	H	7.39 FQ	10.12 AW	15.06 TQ	SDBLS	10/01-12/01
	Tennessee	H	7.06 FQ	10.12 AW	13.46 TQ	TNBLS	10/01-12/01
	Chattanooga MSA, TN-GA	H	7.09 FQ	9.43 AW	12.89 TQ	TNBLS	10/01-12/01
	Johnson City-Kingsport-Bristol MSA, TN-VA	H	6.65 FQ	8.80 AW	11.43 TQ	TNBLS	10/01-12/01
	Knoxville MSA, TN	H	7.32 FQ	9.63 AW	11.42 TQ	TNBLS	10/01-12/01
	Memphis MSA, TN-AR-MS	H	7.14 FQ	9.07 AW	12.18 TQ	TNBLS	10/01-12/01
	Nashville MSA, TN	H	8.28 FQ	10.89 AW	13.63 TQ	TNBLS	10/01-12/01
	Texas	H	6.61 FQ	9.62 AW	13.23 TQ	TXBLS	10/01-12/01
	Amarillo MSA, TX	H	7.10 FQ	10.90 AW	18.07 TQ	TXBLS	10/01-12/01
	Austin-San Marcos MSA, TX	H	8.71 FQ	11.58 AW	15.92 TQ	TXBLS	10/01-12/01
	Brazoria PMSA, TX	H	7.12 FQ	8.88 AW	10.85 TQ	TXBLS	10/01-12/01
	Brownsville-Harlingen-San Benito MSA, TX	H	6.06 FQ	8.27 AW	10.90 TQ	TXBLS	10/01-12/01
	Corpus Christi MSA, TX	H	5.92 FQ	8.17 AW	12.19 TQ	TXBLS	10/01-12/01
	Dallas PMSA, TX	H	7.67 FQ	10.20 AW	11.58 TQ	TXBLS	10/01-12/01
	El Paso MSA, TX	H	6.18 FQ	10.77 AW	14.72 TQ	TXBLS	10/01-12/01
	Fort Worth-Arlington PMSA, TX	H	7.52 FQ	9.41 AW	11.35 TQ	TXBLS	10/01-12/01
	Galveston-Texas City PMSA, TX	H	7.82 FQ	9.99 AW	12.63 TQ	TXBLS	10/01-12/01
	Houston PMSA, TX	H	7.12 FQ	10.34 AW	16.02 TQ	TXBLS	10/01-12/01
	Killeen-Temple MSA, TX	H	7.07 FQ	9.71 AW	12.52 TQ	TXBLS	10/01-12/01
	Laredo MSA, TX	H	6.46 FQ	9.03 AW	11.44 TQ	TXBLS	10/01-12/01
	Longview-Marshall MSA, TX	H	5.50 FQ	7.80 AW	10.93 TQ	TXBLS	10/01-12/01
	Lubbock MSA, TX	H	7.35 FQ	8.88 AW	11.04 TQ	TXBLS	10/01-12/01
	McAllen-Edinburg-Mission MSA, TX	H	6.10 FQ	10.38 AW	14.08 TQ	TXBLS	10/01-12/01
	Odessa-Midland MSA, TX	H	6.03 FQ	8.32 AW	11.77 TQ	TXBLS	10/01-12/01
	San Antonio MSA, TX	H	6.28 FQ	8.80 AW	10.98 TQ	TXBLS	10/01-12/01
	Tyler MSA, TX	H	7.42 FQ	9.11 AW	11.18 TQ	TXBLS	10/01-12/01
	Waco MSA, TX	H	6.89 FQ	9.52 AW	13.06 TQ	TXBLS	10/01-12/01
	Utah	H	6.06 FQ	8.71 AW	12.42 TQ	UTBLS	10/01-12/01
	Provo-Orem MSA, UT	H	6.05 FQ	8.19 AW	11.47 TQ	UTBLS	10/01-12/01
	Salt Lake City-Ogden MSA, UT	H	6.27 FQ	9.06 AW	12.82 TQ	UTBLS	10/01-12/01
	Vermont	H	7.32 FQ	9.99 AW	14.61 TQ	VTBLS	10/01-12/01
	Burlington MSA, VT	H	7.70 FQ	10.61 AW	14.72 TQ	VTBLS	10/01-12/01
	Virginia	H	6.51 FQ	10.00 AW	14.31 TQ	VABLS	10/01-12/01
	Norfolk-Virginia Beach-Newport News MSA, VA-NC	H	5.89 FQ	8.83 AW	13.85 TQ	VABLS	10/01-12/01

AAW	Average annual wage	**AOH**	Average offered, high	**ASH**	Average starting, high	**H**	Hourly	**M**	Monthly	**S**	Special: hourly and annual
AE	Average entry wage	**AOL**	Average offered, low	**ASL**	Average starting, low	**HI**	Highest wage paid	**MTC**	Median total compensation	**TQ**	Third quartile wage
AEX	Average experienced wage	**APH**	Average pay, high range	**AW**	Average wage paid	**HR**	High end range	**MW**	Median wage paid	**W**	Weekly
AO	Average offered	**APL**	Average pay, low range	**FQ**	First quartile wage	**LR**	Low end range	**SQ**	Second quartile wage	**Y**	Yearly

Occupation/Type/Industry	Location	Per	Low	Mid	High	Source	Date
Tire Repairer and Changer	Richmond-Petersburg MSA, VA	H	7.00 FQ	10.39 AW	14.32 TQ	VABLS	10/01-12/01
	Roanoke MSA, VA	H	7.06 FQ	8.46 AW	10.57 TQ	VABLS	10/01-12/01
	Washington	H	7.38 FQ	11.10 AW	16.35 TQ	WABLS	10/01-12/01
	Bremerton PMSA, WA	H	7.14 FQ	10.35 AW	15.57 TQ	WABLS	10/01-12/01
	Olympia PMSA, WA	H	8.86 FQ	11.59 AW	16.87 TQ	WABLS	10/01-12/01
	Seattle-Bellevue-Everett PMSA, WA	H	7.17 FQ	10.40 AW	15.42 TQ	WABLS	10/01-12/01
	Spokane MSA, WA	H	7.98 FQ	10.47 AW	14.54 TQ	WABLS	10/01-12/01
	Tacoma PMSA, WA	H	8.85 FQ	15.29 AW	26.33 TQ	WABLS	10/01-12/01
	Yakima MSA, WA	H	7.25 FQ	9.38 AW	11.18 TQ	WABLS	10/01-12/01
	West Virginia	H	6.07 FQ	8.52 AW	11.05 TQ	WVBLS	10/01-12/01
	Charleston MSA, WV	H	6.31 FQ	8.93 AW	11.35 TQ	WVBLS	10/01-12/01
	Huntington-Ashland MSA, WV-KY-OH	H	5.86 FQ	7.36 AW	8.82 TQ	WVBLS	10/01-12/01
	Wisconsin	H	7.40 FQ	10.74 AW	15.14 TQ	WIBLS	10/01-12/01
	Appleton-Oshkosh-Neenah MSA, WI	H	6.62 FQ	8.70 AW	11.09 TQ	WIBLS	10/01-12/01
	Green Bay MSA, WI	H	7.46 FQ	10.84 AW	17.27 TQ	WIBLS	10/01-12/01
	Madison MSA, WI	H	7.96 FQ	10.20 AW	12.50 TQ	WIBLS	10/01-12/01
	Milwaukee-Waukesha PMSA, WI	H	7.65 FQ	11.87 AW	19.20 TQ	WIBLS	10/01-12/01
	Racine PMSA, WI	H	6.22 FQ	8.73 AW	12.10 TQ	WIBLS	10/01-12/01
	Wyoming	H	5.73 FQ	8.87 AW	14.47 TQ	WYBLS	10/01-12/01
	Cheyenne MSA, WY	H	5.63 FQ	7.05 AW	9.74 TQ	WYBLS	10/01-12/01
	Puerto Rico	H	5.53 FQ	6.47 AW	8.03 TQ	PRBLS	10/01-12/01
	Virgin Islands	H	6.17 FQ	8.37 AW	10.58 TQ	VIBLS	10/01-12/01
	Guam	H	5.67 FQ	7.54 AW	10.65 TQ	GUBLS	10/01-12/01
Title Examiner, Abstractor, and Searcher	Alabama	Y	18490 FQ	26150 AW	34720 TQ	ALBLS	10/01-12/01
	Birmingham MSA, AL	Y	18340 FQ	25680 AW	33720 TQ	ALBLS	10/01-12/01
	Mobile MSA, AL	Y	20640 FQ	29400 AW	39410 TQ	ALBLS	10/01-12/01
	Montgomery MSA, AL	Y	18340 FQ	25030 AW	28810 TQ	ALBLS	10/01-12/01
	Alaska	Y	27640 FQ	41070 AW	54340 TQ	AKBLS	10/01-12/01
	Anchorage MSA, AK	Y	26210 FQ	38460 AW	50610 TQ	AKBLS	10/01-12/01
	Arizona	Y	19870 FQ	29840 AW	44480 TQ	AZBLS	10/01-12/01
	Phoenix-Mesa MSA, AZ	Y	19800 FQ	29650 AW	44180 TQ	AZBLS	10/01-12/01
	Tucson MSA, AZ	Y	22650 FQ	31800 AW	46880 TQ	AZBLS	10/01-12/01
	Arkansas	Y	17190 FQ	25450 AW	35680 TQ	ARBLS	10/01-12/01
	Fayetteville-Springdale-Rogers MSA, AR	Y	16810 FQ	24080 AW	32870 TQ	ARBLS	10/01-12/01
	Fort Smith MSA, AR-OK	Y	17530 FQ	31700 AW	47270 TQ	ARBLS	10/01-12/01
	Little Rock-North Little Rock MSA, AR	Y	18660 FQ	28080 AW	40180 TQ	ARBLS	10/01-12/01
	California	Y	26830 FQ	48130 AW	75580 TQ	CABLS	10/01-12/01
	Fresno MSA, CA	Y	23700 FQ	45850 AW	71170 TQ	CABLS	10/01-12/01
	Los Angeles-Long Beach PMSA, CA	Y	26660 FQ	42570 AW	64820 TQ	CABLS	10/01-12/01
	Modesto MSA, CA	Y	28250 FQ	43660 AW	57780 TQ	CABLS	10/01-12/01
	Oakland PMSA, CA	Y	29430 FQ	52930 AW	72880 TQ	CABLS	10/01-12/01
	Orange County PMSA, CA	Y	26750 FQ	49660 AW	79470 TQ	CABLS	10/01-12/01
	Redding MSA, CA	Y	27050 FQ	43850 AW	64420 TQ	CABLS	10/01-12/01
	Riverside-San Bernardino PMSA, CA	Y	25500 FQ	51340 AW	73600 TQ	CABLS	10/01-12/01
	Sacramento PMSA, CA	Y	29520 FQ	54820 AW	91020 TQ	CABLS	10/01-12/01
	Salinas MSA, CA	Y	28410 FQ	43730 AW	56890 TQ	CABLS	10/01-12/01
	San Diego MSA, CA	Y	27740 FQ	48570 AW	70520 TQ	CABLS	10/01-12/01
	San Francisco PMSA, CA	Y	28460 FQ	53420 AW	92410 TQ	CABLS	10/01-12/01
	San Jose PMSA, CA	Y	28510 FQ	52180 AW	90470 TQ	CABLS	10/01-12/01
	San Luis Obispo-Atascadero-Paso Robles MSA, CA	Y	32050 FQ	48130 AW	58270 TQ	CABLS	10/01-12/01
	Santa Rosa PMSA, CA	Y	29000 FQ	43670 AW	61780 TQ	CABLS	10/01-12/01
	Stockton-Lodi MSA, CA	Y	30090 FQ	51690 AW	79890 TQ	CABLS	10/01-12/01
	Vallejo-Fairfield-Napa PMSA, CA	Y	33160 FQ	52670 AW	77340 TQ	CABLS	10/01-12/01
	Ventura PMSA, CA	Y	26350 FQ	52370 AW	91040 TQ	CABLS	10/01-12/01
	Visalia-Tulare-Porterville MSA, CA	Y	29160 FQ	46300 AW	69680 TQ	CABLS	10/01-12/01
	Colorado	Y	19950 FQ	31580 AW	45280 TQ	COBLS	10/01-12/01
	Boulder-Longmont PMSA, CO	Y	25000 FQ	30500 AW	42720 TQ	COBLS	10/01-12/01
	Colorado Springs MSA, CO	Y	16700 FQ	27120 AW	40440 TQ	COBLS	10/01-12/01

AAW	Average annual wage	**AOH**	Average offered, high	**ASH**	Average starting, high	**H**	Hourly	**M**	Monthly	**S**	Special: hourly and annual
AE	Average entry wage	**AOL**	Average offered, low	**ASL**	Average starting, low	**HI**	Highest wage paid	**MTC**	Median total compensation	**TQ**	Third quartile wage
AEX	Average experienced wage	**APH**	Average pay, high range	**AW**	Average wage paid	**HR**	High end range	**MW**	Median wage paid	**W**	Weekly
AO	Average offered	**APL**	Average pay, low range	**FQ**	First quartile wage	**LR**	Low end range	**SQ**	Second quartile wage	**Y**	Yearly

Occupation/Type/Industry	Location	Per	Low	Mid	High	Source	Date
Title Examiner, Abstractor, and Searcher	Denver PMSA, CO	Y	17100 FQ	36090 AW	57770 TQ	COBLS	10/01-12/01
	Fort Collins-Loveland MSA, CO	Y	18530 FQ	31020 AW	44630 TQ	COBLS	10/01-12/01
	Greeley PMSA, CO	Y	20840 FQ	37270 AW	59060 TQ	COBLS	10/01-12/01
	Connecticut	Y	25480 FQ	39550 AW	58690 TQ	CTBLS	10/01-12/01
	Hartford MSA, CT	Y	29660 FQ	38770 AW	47860 TQ	CTBLS	10/01-12/01
	Delaware	Y	20110 FQ	31130 AW	43800 TQ	DEBLS	10/01-12/01
	Wilmington-Newark PMSA, DE-MD	Y	20260 FQ	30400 AW	41680 TQ	DEBLS	10/01-12/01
	District of Columbia	Y	25420 FQ	39550 AW	57230 TQ	DCBLS	10/01-12/01
	Washington PMSA, DC-MD-VA-WV	Y	21470 FQ	34660 AW	51730 TQ	DCBLS	10/01-12/01
	Florida	Y	21580 FQ	35830 AW	53200 TQ	FLBLS	10/01-12/01
	Daytona Beach MSA, FL	Y	25010 FQ	33190 AW	43890 TQ	FLBLS	10/01-12/01
	Fort Lauderdale PMSA, FL	Y	21960 FQ	38110 AW	53810 TQ	FLBLS	10/01-12/01
	Fort Myers-Cape Coral MSA, FL	Y	21170 FQ	38040 AW	55170 TQ	FLBLS	10/01-12/01
	Fort Pierce-Port St. Lucie MSA, FL	Y	22570 FQ	32570 AW	45520 TQ	FLBLS	10/01-12/01
	Jacksonville MSA, FL	Y	22430 FQ	34190 AW	51510 TQ	FLBLS	10/01-12/01
	Lakeland-Winter Haven MSA, FL	Y	20340 FQ	41820 AW	47140 TQ	FLBLS	10/01-12/01
	Melbourne-Titusville-Palm Bay MSA, FL	Y	20800 FQ	31710 AW	42510 TQ	FLBLS	10/01-12/01
	Miami PMSA, FL	Y	21740 FQ	39660 AW	69890 TQ	FLBLS	10/01-12/01
	Naples MSA, FL	Y	19720 FQ	40280 AW	55940 TQ	FLBLS	10/01-12/01
	Ocala MSA, FL	Y	21430 FQ	31230 AW	42240 TQ	FLBLS	10/01-12/01
	Orlando MSA, FL	Y	20730 FQ	33900 AW	51500 TQ	FLBLS	10/01-12/01
	Pensacola MSA, FL	Y	20670 FQ	31140 AW	43730 TQ	FLBLS	10/01-12/01
	Sarasota-Bradenton MSA, FL	Y	24090 FQ	41820 AW	70750 TQ	FLBLS	10/01-12/01
	Tallahassee MSA, FL	Y	24750 FQ	33390 AW	39560 TQ	FLBLS	10/01-12/01
	Tampa-St. Petersburg-Clearwater MSA, FL	Y	21150 FQ	35390 AW	53490 TQ	FLBLS	10/01-12/01
	West Palm Beach-Boca Raton MSA, FL	Y	28130 FQ	41900 AW	64670 TQ	FLBLS	10/01-12/01
	Georgia	Y	18960 FQ	34210 AW	55660 TQ	GABLS	10/01-12/01
	Atlanta MSA, GA	Y	24830 FQ	41630 AW	62140 TQ	GABLS	10/01-12/01
	Savannah MSA, GA	Y	18810 FQ	21740 AW	24030 TQ	GABLS	10/01-12/01
	Hawaii	Y	23010 FQ	35360 AW	46890 TQ	HIBLS	10/01-12/01
	Honolulu MSA, HI	Y	22780 FQ	35220 AW	46810 TQ	HIBLS	10/01-12/01
	Idaho	Y	17900 FQ	31610 AW	51920 TQ	IDBLS	10/01-12/01
	Boise City MSA, ID	Y	20210 FQ	34270 AW	55390 TQ	IDBLS	10/01-12/01
	Illinois	Y	18310 FQ	31280 AW	48600 TQ	ILBLS	10/01-12/01
	Chicago PMSA, IL	Y	19310 FQ	33110 AW	50210 TQ	ILBLS	10/01-12/01
	Peoria-Pekin MSA, IL	Y	16600 FQ	23980 AW	31580 TQ	ILBLS	10/01-12/01
	Indiana	Y	18360 FQ	28360 AW	41900 TQ	INBLS	10/01-12/01
	Evansville-Henderson MSA, IN-KY	Y	16650 FQ	24710 AW	35960 TQ	INBLS	10/01-12/01
	Fort Wayne MSA, IN	Y	16800 FQ	23180 AW	32370 TQ	INBLS	10/01-12/01
	Gary PMSA, IN	Y	19250 FQ	28700 AW	43450 TQ	INBLS	10/01-12/01
	Indianapolis MSA, IN	Y	19980 FQ	34500 AW	61280 TQ	INBLS	10/01-12/01
	Iowa	Y	15560 FQ	25840 AW	40950 TQ	IABLS	10/01-12/01
	Davenport-Moline-Rock Island MSA, IA-IL	Y	17630 FQ	28830 AW	46110 TQ	IABLS	10/01-12/01
	Des Moines MSA, IA	Y	19630 FQ	29910 AW	50220 TQ	IABLS	10/01-12/01
	Kansas	Y	18630 FQ	34300 AW	55120 TQ	KSBLS	10/01-12/01
	Wichita MSA, KS	Y	19100 FQ	36240 AW	58570 TQ	KSBLS	10/01-12/01
	Kentucky	Y	18330 FQ	27280 AW	40620 TQ	KYBLS	10/01-12/01
	Lexington MSA, KY	Y	18170 FQ	21890 AW	28630 TQ	KYBLS	10/01-12/01
	Louisville MSA, KY-IN	Y	19010 FQ	30860 AW	45450 TQ	KYBLS	10/01-12/01
	Louisiana	Y	15560 FQ	27480 AW	40970 TQ	LABLS	10/01-12/01
	Baton Rouge MSA, LA	Y	20770 FQ	29260 AW	36030 TQ	LABLS	10/01-12/01
	New Orleans MSA, LA	Y	17080 FQ	27980 AW	41630 TQ	LABLS	10/01-12/01
	Maine	Y	24300 FQ	33550 AW	44350 TQ	MEBLS	10/01-12/01
	Portland MSA, ME	Y	24610 FQ	34320 AW	45120 TQ	MEBLS	10/01-12/01
	Maryland	Y	20900 FQ	32290 AW	46470 TQ	MDBLS	10/01-12/01
	Baltimore PMSA, MD	Y	21010 FQ	31400 AW	43940 TQ	MDBLS	10/01-12/01
	Massachusetts	Y	22520 FQ	41710 AW	57390 TQ	MABLS	10/01-12/01
	Boston PMSA, MA-NH	Y	22310 FQ	44730 AW	73570 TQ	MABLS	10/01-12/01
	Michigan	Y	19240 FQ	31420 AW	44120 TQ	MIBLS	10/01-12/01
	Detroit PMSA, MI	Y	19430 FQ	31340 AW	43430 TQ	MIBLS	10/01-12/01

AAW	Average annual wage	AOH	Average offered, high	ASH	Average starting, high	H	Hourly	M	Monthly	S	Special: hourly and annual
AE	Average entry wage	AOL	Average offered, low	ASL	Average starting, low	HI	Highest wage paid	MTC	Median total compensation	TQ	Third quartile wage
AEX	Average experienced wage	APH	Average pay, high range	AW	Average wage paid	HR	High end range	MW	Median wage paid	W	Weekly
AO	Average offered	APL	Average pay, low range	FQ	First quartile wage	LR	Low end range	SQ	Second quartile wage	Y	Yearly

Occupation/Type/Industry	Location	Per	Low	Mid	High	Source	Date
Title Examiner, Abstractor, and Searcher	Flint PMSA, MI	Y	18730 FQ	33470 AW	43500 TQ	MIBLS	10/01-12/01
	Grand Rapids-Muskegon-Holland MSA, MI	Y	24230 FQ	34850 AW	50290 TQ	MIBLS	10/01-12/01
	Saginaw-Bay City-Midland MSA, MI	Y	19880 FQ	33560 AW	42510 TQ	MIBLS	10/01-12/01
	Minnesota	Y	20740 FQ	34960 AW	56160 TQ	MNBLS	10/01-12/01
	Minneapolis-St. Paul MSA, MN-WI	Y	25010 FQ	39880 AW	64660 TQ	MNBLS	10/01-12/01
	Mississippi	Y	18890 FQ	29280 AW	42660 TQ	MSBLS	10/01-12/01
	Jackson MSA, MS	Y	20960 FQ	29810 AW	42530 TQ	MSBLS	10/01-12/01
	Missouri	Y	15740 FQ	25700 AW	36830 TQ	MOBLS	10/01-12/01
	Kansas City MSA, MO-KS	Y	20820 FQ	33830 AW	44560 TQ	MOBLS	10/01-12/01
	St. Louis MSA, MO-IL	Y	20990 FQ	29840 AW	41500 TQ	MOBLS	10/01-12/01
	Springfield MSA, MO	Y	19400 FQ	24640 AW	34190 TQ	MOBLS	10/01-12/01
	Montana	Y	13730 FQ	25250 AW	36210 TQ	MTBLS	10/01-12/01
	Nebraska	Y	19440 FQ	29420 AW	40250 TQ	NEBLS	10/01-12/01
	Lincoln MSA, NE	Y	20080 FQ	31760 AW	43710 TQ	NEBLS	10/01-12/01
	Omaha MSA, NE-IA	Y	20670 FQ	28450 AW	35320 TQ	NEBLS	10/01-12/01
	Nevada	Y	24270 FQ	42000 AW	69210 TQ	NVBLS	10/01-12/01
	Las Vegas MSA, NV-AZ	Y	23690 FQ	39240 AW	61300 TQ	NVBLS	10/01-12/01
	Reno MSA, NV	Y	35030 FQ	55190 AW	85860 TQ	NVBLS	10/01-12/01
	New Hampshire	Y	18890 FQ	29120 AW	42930 TQ	NHBLS	10/01-12/01
	Manchester PMSA, NH	Y	20210 FQ	30550 AW	43240 TQ	NHBLS	10/01-12/01
	New Jersey	Y	25350 FQ	43640 AW	66360 TQ	NJBLS	10/01-12/01
	Atlantic-Cape May PMSA, NJ	Y	21880 FQ	35730 AW	37940 TQ	NJBLS	10/01-12/01
	Bergen-Passaic PMSA, NJ	Y	35970 FQ	52360 AW	69500 TQ	NJBLS	10/01-12/01
	Middlesex-Somerset-Hunterdon PMSA, NJ	Y	27350 FQ	43720 AW	67450 TQ	NJBLS	10/01-12/01
	Monmouth-Ocean PMSA, NJ	Y	24310 FQ	42510 AW	70120 TQ	NJBLS	10/01-12/01
	Newark PMSA, NJ	Y	25440 FQ	41940 AW	59890 TQ	NJBLS	10/01-12/01
	Trenton PMSA, NJ	Y	23310 FQ	35450 AW	52540 TQ	NJBLS	10/01-12/01
	New Mexico	Y	15760 FQ	25860 AW	40050 TQ	NMBLS	10/01-12/01
	Albuquerque MSA, NM	Y	14370 FQ	29800 AW	43390 TQ	NMBLS	10/01-12/01
	Las Cruces MSA, NM	Y	19500 FQ	27720 AW	51190 TQ	NMBLS	10/01-12/01
	New York	Y	19150 FQ	35910 AW	62500 TQ	NYBLS	10/01-12/01
	Albany-Schenectady-Troy MSA, NY	Y	20120 FQ	33030 AW	48750 TQ	NYBLS	10/01-12/01
	Buffalo-Niagara Falls MSA, NY	Y	17480 FQ	31140 AW	48690 TQ	NYBLS	10/01-12/01
	Nassau-Suffolk PMSA, NY	Y	19430 FQ	36980 AW	71980 TQ	NYBLS	10/01-12/01
	New York PMSA, NY	Y	18690 FQ	40450 AW	80860 TQ	NYBLS	10/01-12/01
	Rochester MSA, NY	Y	20820 FQ	32540 AW	42440 TQ	NYBLS	10/01-12/01
	Syracuse MSA, NY	Y	22620 FQ	32280 AW	44030 TQ	NYBLS	10/01-12/01
	North Carolina	Y	18970 FQ	27640 AW	38650 TQ	NCBLS	10/01-12/01
	Charlotte-Gastonia-Rock Hill MSA, NC-SC	Y	19830 FQ	26040 AW	34000 TQ	NCBLS	10/01-12/01
	Hickory-Morganton-Lenoir MSA, NC	Y	23500 FQ	28510 AW	34990 TQ	NCBLS	10/01-12/01
	Raleigh-Durham-Chapel Hill MSA, NC	Y	13970 FQ	30120 AW	42960 TQ	NCBLS	10/01-12/01
	North Dakota	Y	14970 FQ	27270 AW	46610 TQ	NDBLS	10/01-12/01
	Ohio	Y	20250 FQ	32530 AW	49430 TQ	OHBLS	10/01-12/01
	Akron PMSA, OH	Y	18440 FQ	32240 AW	48360 TQ	OHBLS	10/01-12/01
	Canton-Massillon MSA, OH	Y	19650 FQ	26370 AW	33400 TQ	OHBLS	10/01-12/01
	Cincinnati PMSA, OH-KY-IN	Y	22690 FQ	34630 AW	53860 TQ	OHBLS	10/01-12/01
	Cleveland-Lorain-Elyria PMSA, OH	Y	22710 FQ	33550 AW	49860 TQ	OHBLS	10/01-12/01
	Columbus MSA, OH	Y	27570 FQ	39530 AW	53630 TQ	OHBLS	10/01-12/01
	Dayton-Springfield MSA, OH	Y	16860 FQ	28220 AW	43860 TQ	OHBLS	10/01-12/01
	Mansfield MSA, OH	Y	18970 FQ	30150 AW	45220 TQ	OHBLS	10/01-12/01
	Toledo MSA, OH	Y	22810 FQ	33510 AW	45290 TQ	OHBLS	10/01-12/01
	Youngstown-Warren MSA, OH	Y	17620 FQ	25930 AW	35660 TQ	OHBLS	10/01-12/01
	Oklahoma	Y	16040 FQ	32340 AW	57980 TQ	OKBLS	10/01-12/01
	Oklahoma City MSA, OK	Y	24380 FQ	43560 AW	72330 TQ	OKBLS	10/01-12/01
	Tulsa MSA, OK	Y	21830 FQ	38540 AW	56400 TQ	OKBLS	10/01-12/01
	Oregon	Y	26390 FQ	42730 AW	66690 TQ	ORBLS	10/01-12/01
	Eugene-Springfield MSA, OR	Y	31220 FQ	40450 AW	60150 TQ	ORBLS	10/01-12/01
	Portland-Vancouver PMSA, OR-WA	Y	28150 FQ	45380 AW	74890 TQ	ORBLS	10/01-12/01
	Salem PMSA, OR	Y	24190 FQ	40870 AW	62660 TQ	ORBLS	10/01-12/01
	Pennsylvania	Y	18640 FQ	30100 AW	43870 TQ	PABLS	10/01-12/01

AAW	Average annual wage	AOH	Average offered, high	ASH	Average starting, high	H	Hourly	M	Monthly	S	Special: hourly and annual
AE	Average entry wage	AOL	Average offered, low	ASL	Average starting, low	HI	Highest wage paid	MTC	Median total compensation	TQ	Third quartile wage
AEX	Average experienced wage	APH	Average pay, high range	AW	Average wage paid	HR	High end range	MW	Median wage paid	W	Weekly
AO	Average offered	APL	Average pay, low range	FQ	First quartile wage	LR	Low end range	SQ	Second quartile wage	Y	Yearly

Occupation/Type/Industry	Location	Per	Low	Mid	High	Source	Date
Title Examiner, Abstractor, and Searcher							
	Allentown-Bethlehem-Easton MSA, PA	Y	13450 FQ	35450 AW	47710 TQ	PABLS	10/01-12/01
	Harrisburg-Lebanon-Carlisle MSA, PA	Y	17800 FQ	28430 AW	40920 TQ	PABLS	10/01-12/01
	Lancaster MSA, PA	Y	21910 FQ	32370 AW	44650 TQ	PABLS	10/01-12/01
	Philadelphia PMSA, PA-NJ	Y	21750 FQ	32980 AW	47300 TQ	PABLS	10/01-12/01
	Pittsburgh MSA, PA	Y	19740 FQ	28280 AW	38980 TQ	PABLS	10/01-12/01
	Scranton-Wilkes-Barre-Hazleton MSA, PA	Y	19160 FQ	23400 AW	27890 TQ	PABLS	10/01-12/01
	York MSA, PA	Y	19800 FQ	28690 AW	35540 TQ	PABLS	10/01-12/01
	Rhode Island	Y	19080 FQ	33400 AW	53310 TQ	RIBLS	10/01-12/01
	Providence-Fall River-Warwick MSA, RI-MA	Y	19220 FQ	33650 AW	53030 TQ	RIBLS	10/01-12/01
	South Carolina	Y	18930 FQ	25450 AW	39150 TQ	SCBLS	10/01-12/01
	Greenville-Spartanburg-Anderson MSA, SC	Y	19110 FQ	24150 AW	30990 TQ	SCBLS	10/01-12/01
	Myrtle Beach MSA, SC	Y	18440 FQ	21660 AW	27260 TQ	SCBLS	10/01-12/01
	South Dakota	Y	18930 FQ	25420 AW	35010 TQ	SDBLS	10/01-12/01
	Sioux Falls MSA, SD	Y	20320 FQ	27500 AW	37560 TQ	SDBLS	10/01-12/01
	Tennessee	Y	16020 FQ	32280 AW	45020 TQ	TNBLS	10/01-12/01
	Chattanooga MSA, TN-GA	Y	19620 FQ	32330 AW	44310 TQ	TNBLS	10/01-12/01
	Knoxville MSA, TN	Y	19280 FQ	33230 AW	51960 TQ	TNBLS	10/01-12/01
	Memphis MSA, TN-AR-MS	Y	21410 FQ	45820 AW	110620 TQ	TNBLS	10/01-12/01
	Nashville MSA, TN	Y	28390 FQ	35310 AW	44230 TQ	TNBLS	10/01-12/01
	Texas	Y	18580 FQ	36850 AW	58660 TQ	TXBLS	10/01-12/01
	Amarillo MSA, TX	Y	14280 FQ	25070 AW	41470 TQ	TXBLS	10/01-12/01
	Austin-San Marcos MSA, TX	Y	15270 FQ	31460 AW	52060 TQ	TXBLS	10/01-12/01
	Beaumont-Port Arthur MSA, TX	Y	22040 FQ	43310 AW	79070 TQ	TXBLS	10/01-12/01
	Dallas PMSA, TX	Y	24930 FQ	49790 AW	88840 TQ	TXBLS	10/01-12/01
	Fort Worth-Arlington PMSA, TX	Y	22230 FQ	38780 AW	59740 TQ	TXBLS	10/01-12/01
	Galveston-Texas City PMSA, TX	Y	21770 FQ	30810 AW	36180 TQ	TXBLS	10/01-12/01
	Houston PMSA, TX	Y	21760 FQ	37510 AW	57150 TQ	TXBLS	10/01-12/01
	Killeen-Temple MSA, TX	Y	13150 FQ	23110 AW	41440 TQ	TXBLS	10/01-12/01
	Laredo MSA, TX	Y	15630 FQ	23630 AW	33070 TQ	TXBLS	10/01-12/01
	Lubbock MSA, TX	Y	17750 FQ	32950 AW	51690 TQ	TXBLS	10/01-12/01
	McAllen-Edinburg-Mission MSA, TX	Y	18460 FQ	30980 AW	47510 TQ	TXBLS	10/01-12/01
	Odessa-Midland MSA, TX	Y	16300 FQ	34470 AW	78840 TQ	TXBLS	10/01-12/01
	San Antonio MSA, TX	Y	18610 FQ	35120 AW	55670 TQ	TXBLS	10/01-12/01
	Tyler MSA, TX	Y	17050 FQ	28360 AW	41680 TQ	TXBLS	10/01-12/01
	Utah	Y	23450 FQ	42900 AW	65070 TQ	UTBLS	10/01-12/01
	Provo-Orem MSA, UT	Y	23030 FQ	34490 AW	57510 TQ	UTBLS	10/01-12/01
	Salt Lake City-Ogden MSA, UT	Y	23970 FQ	43340 AW	65930 TQ	UTBLS	10/01-12/01
	Virginia	Y	18870 FQ	30830 AW	45320 TQ	VABLS	10/01-12/01
	Norfolk-Virginia Beach-Newport News MSA, VA-NC	Y	16750 FQ	25930 AW	34730 TQ	VABLS	10/01-12/01
	Richmond-Petersburg MSA, VA	Y	19710 FQ	31980 AW	46200 TQ	VABLS	10/01-12/01
	Roanoke MSA, VA	Y	17060 FQ	29940 AW	40060 TQ	VABLS	10/01-12/01
	Washington	Y	23010 FQ	36940 AW	53570 TQ	WABLS	10/01-12/01
	Seattle-Bellevue-Everett PMSA, WA	Y	27110 FQ	41330 AW	58110 TQ	WABLS	10/01-12/01
	Spokane MSA, WA	Y	20830 FQ	34110 AW	48180 TQ	WABLS	10/01-12/01
	Tacoma PMSA, WA	Y	21240 FQ	32590 AW	44150 TQ	WABLS	10/01-12/01
	Yakima MSA, WA	Y	19510 FQ	29560 AW	43110 TQ	WABLS	10/01-12/01
	West Virginia	Y	19600 FQ	29970 AW	41500 TQ	WVBLS	10/01-12/01
	Wisconsin	Y	20230 FQ	30190 AW	40960 TQ	WIBLS	10/01-12/01
	Appleton-Oshkosh-Neenah MSA, WI	Y	23210 FQ	31880 AW	39770 TQ	WIBLS	10/01-12/01
	Green Bay MSA, WI	Y	19420 FQ	28340 AW	36990 TQ	WIBLS	10/01-12/01
	Madison MSA, WI	Y	21520 FQ	33070 AW	48340 TQ	WIBLS	10/01-12/01
	Milwaukee-Waukesha PMSA, WI	Y	23690 FQ	33370 AW	45070 TQ	WIBLS	10/01-12/01
	Racine PMSA, WI	Y	21450 FQ	34110 AW	44190 TQ	WIBLS	10/01-12/01
	Wyoming	Y	16400 FQ	26080 AW	38540 TQ	WYBLS	10/01-12/01
	Puerto Rico	Y	14220 FQ	23230 AW	37840 TQ	PRBLS	10/01-12/01

AAW Average annual wage **AOH** Average offered, high **ASH** Average starting, high **H** Hourly **M** Monthly **S** Special: hourly and annual
AE Average entry wage **AOL** Average offered, low **ASL** Average starting, low **HI** Highest wage paid **MTC** Median total compensation **TQ** Third quartile wage
AEX Average experienced wage **APH** Average pay, high range **AW** Average wage paid **HR** High end range **MW** Median wage paid **W** Weekly
AO Average offered **APL** Average pay, low range **FQ** First quartile wage **LR** Low end range **SQ** Second quartile wage **Y** Yearly

Occupation/Type/Industry	Location	Per	Low	Mid	High	Source	Date
Tool and Die Maker	Alabama	H	11.90 FQ	19.18 AW	27.95 TQ	ALBLS	10/01-12/01
	Birmingham MSA, AL	H	14.23 FQ	17.67 AW	22.69 TQ	ALBLS	10/01-12/01
	Huntsville MSA, AL	H	12.72 FQ	22.41 AW	32.70 TQ	ALBLS	10/01-12/01
	Mobile MSA, AL	H	9.59 FQ	17.91 AW	30.94 TQ	ALBLS	10/01-12/01
	Montgomery MSA, AL	H	12.92 FQ	17.22 AW	23.17 TQ	ALBLS	10/01-12/01
	Arizona	H	12.35 FQ	19.85 AW	27.60 TQ	AZBLS	10/01-12/01
	Phoenix-Mesa MSA, AZ	H	14.66 FQ	20.86 AW	28.25 TQ	AZBLS	10/01-12/01
	Tucson MSA, AZ	H	9.05 FQ	17.77 AW	26.09 TQ	AZBLS	10/01-12/01
	Arkansas	H	11.69 FQ	16.41 AW	21.47 TQ	ARBLS	10/01-12/01
	Fayetteville-Springdale-Rogers MSA, AR	H	12.65 FQ	16.06 AW	20.59 TQ	ARBLS	10/01-12/01
	Fort Smith MSA, AR-OK	H	10.22 FQ	14.79 AW	18.84 TQ	ARBLS	10/01-12/01
	Little Rock-North Little Rock MSA, AR	H	15.00 FQ	18.58 AW	21.89 TQ	ARBLS	10/01-12/01
	California	H	11.14 FQ	20.76 AW	29.24 TQ	CABLS	10/01-12/01
	Fresno MSA, CA	H	14.91 FQ	20.06 AW	26.99 TQ	CABLS	10/01-12/01
	Los Angeles-Long Beach PMSA, CA	H	9.32 FQ	18.96 AW	27.92 TQ	CABLS	10/01-12/01
	Modesto MSA, CA	H	8.21 FQ	17.12 AW	26.09 TQ	CABLS	10/01-12/01
	Oakland PMSA, CA	H	17.40 FQ	26.40 AW	33.68 TQ	CABLS	10/01-12/01
	Orange County PMSA, CA	H	11.38 FQ	20.29 AW	28.19 TQ	CABLS	10/01-12/01
	Riverside-San Bernardino PMSA, CA	H	13.57 FQ	21.70 AW	30.44 TQ	CABLS	10/01-12/01
	Sacramento PMSA, CA	H	10.86 FQ	18.37 AW	25.71 TQ	CABLS	10/01-12/01
	San Diego MSA, CA	H	14.14 FQ	21.59 AW	27.60 TQ	CABLS	10/01-12/01
	San Francisco PMSA, CA	H	14.38 FQ	21.45 AW	30.81 TQ	CABLS	10/01-12/01
	San Jose PMSA, CA	H	17.01 FQ	24.84 AW	33.93 TQ	CABLS	10/01-12/01
	San Luis Obispo-Atascadero-Paso Robles MSA, CA	H	12.70 FQ	21.93 AW	29.37 TQ	CABLS	10/01-12/01
	Santa Barbara-Santa Maria-Lompoc MSA, CA	H	9.65 FQ	19.21 AW	26.49 TQ	CABLS	10/01-12/01
	Santa Rosa PMSA, CA	H	16.77 FQ	23.73 AW	33.04 TQ	CABLS	10/01-12/01
	Stockton-Lodi MSA, CA	H	10.01 FQ	20.18 AW	26.91 TQ	CABLS	10/01-12/01
	Ventura PMSA, CA	H	10.91 FQ	19.58 AW	27.07 TQ	CABLS	10/01-12/01
	Colorado	H	14.56 FQ	20.29 AW	26.78 TQ	COBLS	10/01-12/01
	Boulder-Longmont PMSA, CO	H	15.55 FQ	21.71 AW	27.15 TQ	COBLS	10/01-12/01
	Colorado Springs MSA, CO	H	15.05 FQ	19.90 AW	24.90 TQ	COBLS	10/01-12/01
	Denver PMSA, CO	H	14.78 FQ	20.34 AW	26.94 TQ	COBLS	10/01-12/01
	Fort Collins-Loveland MSA, CO	H	13.23 FQ	19.48 AW	25.81 TQ	COBLS	10/01-12/01
	Greeley PMSA, CO	H	15.55 FQ	22.17 AW	28.39 TQ	COBLS	10/01-12/01
	Connecticut	H	15.31 FQ	21.14 AW	27.53 TQ	CTBLS	10/01-12/01
	Bridgeport PMSA, CT	H	15.67 FQ	21.29 AW	26.80 TQ	CTBLS	10/01-12/01
	Danbury PMSA, CT	H	13.96 FQ	20.88 AW	28.96 TQ	CTBLS	10/01-12/01
	Hartford MSA, CT	H	15.61 FQ	20.89 AW	26.95 TQ	CTBLS	10/01-12/01
	New Haven-Meriden PMSA, CT	H	14.49 FQ	20.11 AW	26.29 TQ	CTBLS	10/01-12/01
	New London-Norwich MSA, CT-RI	H	14.27 FQ	18.59 AW	22.09 TQ	CTBLS	10/01-12/01
	Stamford-Norwalk PMSA, CT	H	19.14 FQ	25.66 AW	33.11 TQ	CTBLS	10/01-12/01
	Waterbury PMSA, CT	H	15.12 FQ	22.13 AW	29.35 TQ	CTBLS	10/01-12/01
	Washington PMSA, DC-MD-VA-WV	H	12.94 FQ	18.06 AW	27.70 TQ	DCBLS	10/01-12/01
	Florida	H	9.60 FQ	16.32 AW	22.51 TQ	FLBLS	10/01-12/01
	Daytona Beach MSA, FL	H	10.33 FQ	16.46 AW	22.25 TQ	FLBLS	10/01-12/01
	Fort Lauderdale PMSA, FL	H	12.00 FQ	17.59 AW	24.84 TQ	FLBLS	10/01-12/01
	Jacksonville MSA, FL	H	9.58 FQ	15.76 AW	22.10 TQ	FLBLS	10/01-12/01
	Lakeland-Winter Haven MSA, FL	H	6.40 FQ	13.67 AW	17.70 TQ	FLBLS	10/01-12/01
	Melbourne-Titusville-Palm Bay MSA, FL	H	9.90 FQ	14.33 AW	20.11 TQ	FLBLS	10/01-12/01
	Miami PMSA, FL	H	7.67 FQ	15.46 AW	22.96 TQ	FLBLS	10/01-12/01
	Orlando MSA, FL	H	9.59 FQ	15.35 AW	21.30 TQ	FLBLS	10/01-12/01
	Sarasota-Bradenton MSA, FL	H	12.65 FQ	20.94 AW	36.59 TQ	FLBLS	10/01-12/01
	Tampa-St. Petersburg-Clearwater MSA, FL	H	9.50 FQ	16.67 AW	24.23 TQ	FLBLS	10/01-12/01
	West Palm Beach-Boca Raton MSA, FL	H	15.77 FQ	19.64 AW	22.59 TQ	FLBLS	10/01-12/01
	Georgia	H	11.71 FQ	17.95 AW	26.40 TQ	GABLS	10/01-12/01
	Atlanta MSA, GA	H	12.13 FQ	19.73 AW	31.38 TQ	GABLS	10/01-12/01
	Augusta-Aiken MSA, GA-SC	H	13.73 FQ	17.75 AW	24.37 TQ	GABLS	10/01-12/01
	Columbus MSA, GA-AL	H	11.66 FQ	15.65 AW	20.70 TQ	GABLS	10/01-12/01

AAW	Average annual wage	AOH	Average offered, high	ASH	Average starting, high	H	Hourly	M	Monthly	S	Special: hourly and annual
AE	Average entry wage	AOL	Average offered, low	ASL	Average starting, low	HI	Highest wage paid	MTC	Median total compensation	TQ	Third quartile wage
AEX	Average experienced wage	APH	Average pay, high range	AW	Average wage paid	HR	High end range	MW	Median wage paid	W	Weekly
AO	Average offered	APL	Average pay, low range	FQ	First quartile wage	LR	Low end range	SQ	Second quartile wage	Y	Yearly

Occupation/Type/Industry	Location	Per	Low	Mid	High	Source	Date
Tool and Die Maker	Macon MSA, GA	H	17.09 FQ	19.73 AW	24.17 TQ	GABLS	10/01-12/01
	Idaho	H	8.30 FQ	16.93 AW	25.87 TQ	IDBLS	10/01-12/01
	Boise City MSA, ID	H	8.48 FQ	18.56 AW	26.87 TQ	IDBLS	10/01-12/01
	Illinois	H	12.71 FQ	20.58 AW	27.95 TQ	ILBLS	10/01-12/01
	Chicago PMSA, IL	H	13.23 FQ	21.16 AW	27.83 TQ	ILBLS	10/01-12/01
	Peoria-Pekin MSA, IL	H	12.53 FQ	21.16 AW	28.12 TQ	ILBLS	10/01-12/01
	Rockford MSA, IL	H	10.28 FQ	19.91 AW	33.40 TQ	ILBLS	10/01-12/01
	Indiana	H	13.19 FQ	20.95 AW	31.98 TQ	INBLS	10/01-12/01
	Elkhart-Goshen MSA, IN	H	12.45 FQ	17.54 AW	22.17 TQ	INBLS	10/01-12/01
	Evansville-Henderson MSA, IN-KY	H	13.27 FQ	18.70 AW	26.13 TQ	INBLS	10/01-12/01
	Fort Wayne MSA, IN	H	12.01 FQ	18.63 AW	26.59 TQ	INBLS	10/01-12/01
	Gary PMSA, IN	H	11.15 FQ	18.20 AW	29.07 TQ	INBLS	10/01-12/01
	Indianapolis MSA, IN	H	13.53 FQ	24.96 AW	34.17 TQ	INBLS	10/01-12/01
	Lafayette MSA, IN	H	13.56 FQ	20.02 AW	26.57 TQ	INBLS	10/01-12/01
	South Bend MSA, IN	H	13.64 FQ	18.79 AW	23.93 TQ	INBLS	10/01-12/01
	Iowa	H	11.72 FQ	18.00 AW	24.85 TQ	IABLS	10/01-12/01
	Cedar Rapids MSA, IA	H	16.05 FQ	20.78 AW	26.54 TQ	IABLS	10/01-12/01
	Davenport-Moline-Rock Island MSA, IA-IL	H	13.72 FQ	18.20 AW	22.84 TQ	IABLS	10/01-12/01
	Des Moines MSA, IA	H	13.25 FQ	17.72 AW	25.07 TQ	IABLS	10/01-12/01
	Kansas	H	13.24 FQ	21.42 AW	29.84 TQ	KSBLS	10/01-12/01
	Wichita MSA, KS	H	14.66 FQ	22.22 AW	28.28 TQ	KSBLS	10/01-12/01
	Kentucky	H	12.41 FQ	18.75 AW	26.52 TQ	KYBLS	10/01-12/01
	Lexington MSA, KY	H	13.19 FQ	19.83 AW	26.54 TQ	KYBLS	10/01-12/01
	Louisville MSA, KY-IN	H	13.37 FQ	20.38 AW	27.75 TQ	KYBLS	10/01-12/01
	Louisiana	H	10.50 FQ	18.75 AW	30.37 TQ	LABLS	10/01-12/01
	New Orleans MSA, LA	H	13.99 FQ	18.42 AW	23.26 TQ	LABLS	10/01-12/01
	Maine	H	15.08 FQ	19.74 AW	23.21 TQ	MEBLS	10/01-12/01
	Portland MSA, ME	H	13.37 FQ	18.12 AW	21.91 TQ	MEBLS	10/01-12/01
	Maryland	H	13.61 FQ	20.30 AW	29.87 TQ	MDBLS	10/01-12/01
	Baltimore PMSA, MD	H	12.98 FQ	22.00 AW	33.61 TQ	MDBLS	10/01-12/01
	Massachusetts	H	13.34 FQ	19.40 AW	26.92 TQ	MABLS	10/01-12/01
	Boston PMSA, MA-NH	H	13.22 FQ	19.14 AW	26.20 TQ	MABLS	10/01-12/01
	Brockton PMSA, MA	H	10.95 FQ	17.84 AW	23.13 TQ	MABLS	10/01-12/01
	Lawrence PMSA, MA-NH	H	16.36 FQ	22.69 AW	27.99 TQ	MABLS	10/01-12/01
	Lowell PMSA, MA-NH	H	13.82 FQ	18.57 AW	25.85 TQ	MABLS	10/01-12/01
	Springfield MSA, MA	H	12.93 FQ	18.01 AW	22.48 TQ	MABLS	10/01-12/01
	Worcester PMSA, MA-CT	H	14.51 FQ	18.75 AW	24.13 TQ	MABLS	10/01-12/01
	Michigan	H	15.46 FQ	24.01 AW	33.56 TQ	MIBLS	10/01-12/01
	Ann Arbor PMSA, MI	H	17.35 FQ	24.43 AW	32.02 TQ	MIBLS	10/01-12/01
	Detroit PMSA, MI	H	17.03 FQ	25.32 AW	33.94 TQ	MIBLS	10/01-12/01
	Flint PMSA, MI	H	23.29 FQ	29.47 AW	35.30 TQ	MIBLS	10/01-12/01
	Grand Rapids-Muskegon-Holland MSA, MI	H	15.30 FQ	23.33 AW	32.83 TQ	MIBLS	10/01-12/01
	Kalamazoo-Battle Creek MSA, MI	H	14.60 FQ	22.71 AW	34.02 TQ	MIBLS	10/01-12/01
	Lansing-East Lansing MSA, MI	H	12.56 FQ	20.61 AW	29.06 TQ	MIBLS	10/01-12/01
	Saginaw-Bay City-Midland MSA, MI	H	13.18 FQ	25.02 AW	34.52 TQ	MIBLS	10/01-12/01
	Minnesota	H	14.58 FQ	22.14 AW	29.00 TQ	MNBLS	10/01-12/01
	Minneapolis-St. Paul MSA, MN-WI	H	17.04 FQ	23.75 AW	32.92 TQ	MNBLS	10/01-12/01
	Mississippi	H	9.61 FQ	14.50 AW	19.70 TQ	MSBLS	10/01-12/01
	Jackson MSA, MS	H	11.30 FQ	15.23 AW	20.62 TQ	MSBLS	10/01-12/01
	Missouri	H	11.81 FQ	19.79 AW	27.91 TQ	MOBLS	10/01-12/01
	Kansas City MSA, MO-KS	H	13.57 FQ	21.00 AW	29.96 TQ	MOBLS	10/01-12/01
	St. Louis MSA, MO-IL	H	14.00 FQ	22.38 AW	30.80 TQ	MOBLS	10/01-12/01
	Springfield MSA, MO	H	15.31 FQ	20.75 AW	26.95 TQ	MOBLS	10/01-12/01
	Nebraska	H	11.29 FQ	16.65 AW	22.43 TQ	NEBLS	10/01-12/01
	Omaha MSA, NE-IA	H	14.81 FQ	18.64 AW	22.58 TQ	NEBLS	10/01-12/01
	Nevada	H	8.73 FQ	18.11 AW	23.13 TQ	NVBLS	10/01-12/01
	Las Vegas MSA, NV-AZ	H	13.44 FQ	19.64 AW	26.61 TQ	NVBLS	10/01-12/01
	Reno MSA, NV	H	7.32 FQ	16.51 AW	23.33 TQ	NVBLS	10/01-12/01
	New Hampshire	H	12.02 FQ	17.27 AW	24.48 TQ	NHBLS	10/01-12/01
	Manchester PMSA, NH	H	14.85 FQ	21.17 AW	26.86 TQ	NHBLS	10/01-12/01
	Nashua PMSA, NH	H	14.87 FQ	20.63 AW	26.80 TQ	NHBLS	10/01-12/01
	Portsmouth-Rochester PMSA, NH-ME	H	14.81 FQ	19.83 AW	25.92 TQ	NHBLS	10/01-12/01
	New Jersey	H	11.38 FQ	20.55 AW	28.17 TQ	NJBLS	10/01-12/01
	Bergen-Passaic PMSA, NJ	H	9.22 FQ	17.64 AW	26.47 TQ	NJBLS	10/01-12/01
	Jersey City PMSA, NJ	H	9.10 FQ	15.19 AW	23.92 TQ	NJBLS	10/01-12/01

AAW	Average annual wage	AOH	Average offered, high	ASH	Average starting, high	H	Hourly	M	Monthly	S	Special: hourly and annual
AE	Average entry wage	AOL	Average offered, low	ASL	Average starting, low	HI	Highest wage paid	MTC	Median total compensation	TQ	Third quartile wage
AEX	Average experienced wage	APH	Average pay, high range	AW	Average wage paid	HR	High end range	MW	Median wage paid	W	Weekly
AO	Average offered	APL	Average pay, low range	FQ	First quartile wage	LR	Low end range	SQ	Second quartile wage	Y	Yearly

Occupation/Type/Industry	Location	Per	Low	Mid	High	Source	Date
Tool and Die Maker	Middlesex-Somerset-Hunterdon PMSA, NJ	H	17.28 FQ	22.56 AW	27.88 TQ	NJBLS	10/01-12/01
	Monmouth-Ocean PMSA, NJ	H	11.63 FQ	19.86 AW	26.91 TQ	NJBLS	10/01-12/01
	Newark PMSA, NJ	H	12.84 FQ	22.15 AW	31.25 TQ	NJBLS	10/01-12/01
	Trenton PMSA, NJ	H	6.65 FQ	17.72 AW	25.07 TQ	NJBLS	10/01-12/01
	New Mexico	H	6.42 FQ	16.86 AW	26.40 TQ	NMBLS	10/01-12/01
	Albuquerque MSA, NM	H	11.73 FQ	20.02 AW	27.15 TQ	NMBLS	10/01-12/01
	Las Cruces MSA, NM	H	5.69 FQ	11.34 AW	20.29 TQ	NMBLS	10/01-12/01
	New York	H	9.90 FQ	18.35 AW	27.02 TQ	NYBLS	10/01-12/01
	Albany-Schenectady-Troy MSA, NY	H	12.24 FQ	19.15 AW	26.02 TQ	NYBLS	10/01-12/01
	Binghamton MSA, NY	H	11.95 FQ	17.35 AW	24.82 TQ	NYBLS	10/01-12/01
	Buffalo-Niagara Falls MSA, NY	H	13.60 FQ	21.42 AW	28.04 TQ	NYBLS	10/01-12/01
	Nassau-Suffolk PMSA, NY	H	8.48 FQ	19.98 AW	31.84 TQ	NYBLS	10/01-12/01
	New York PMSA, NY	H	7.03 FQ	15.87 AW	26.55 TQ	NYBLS	10/01-12/01
	Rochester MSA, NY	H	12.13 FQ	19.02 AW	26.86 TQ	NYBLS	10/01-12/01
	Syracuse MSA, NY	H	10.23 FQ	18.35 AW	25.46 TQ	NYBLS	10/01-12/01
	Utica-Rome MSA, NY	H	8.58 FQ	14.36 AW	20.97 TQ	NYBLS	10/01-12/01
	North Carolina	H	12.46 FQ	18.23 AW	23.24 TQ	NCBLS	10/01-12/01
	Asheville MSA, NC	H	14.04 FQ	17.79 AW	21.74 TQ	NCBLS	10/01-12/01
	Charlotte-Gastonia-Rock Hill MSA, NC-SC	H	13.61 FQ	18.75 AW	24.15 TQ	NCBLS	10/01-12/01
	Fayetteville MSA, NC	H	14.21 FQ	19.52 AW	24.64 TQ	NCBLS	10/01-12/01
	Greensboro-Winston-Salem-High Point MSA, NC	H	12.34 FQ	18.19 AW	22.53 TQ	NCBLS	10/01-12/01
	Hickory-Morganton-Lenoir MSA, NC	H	11.66 FQ	17.30 AW	25.69 TQ	NCBLS	10/01-12/01
	Raleigh-Durham-Chapel Hill MSA, NC	H	12.45 FQ	18.38 AW	22.46 TQ	NCBLS	10/01-12/01
	North Dakota	H	13.36 FQ	19.10 AW	22.88 TQ	NDBLS	10/01-12/01
	Fargo-Moorhead MSA, ND-MN	H	12.97 FQ	17.95 AW	22.41 TQ	NDBLS	10/01-12/01
	Ohio	H	13.63 FQ	21.12 AW	31.73 TQ	OHBLS	10/01-12/01
	Akron PMSA, OH	H	13.78 FQ	19.73 AW	26.69 TQ	OHBLS	10/01-12/01
	Canton-Massillon MSA, OH	H	13.68 FQ	19.14 AW	29.31 TQ	OHBLS	10/01-12/01
	Cincinnati PMSA, OH-KY-IN	H	13.76 FQ	19.90 AW	27.54 TQ	OHBLS	10/01-12/01
	Cleveland-Lorain-Elyria PMSA, OH	H	14.23 FQ	21.26 AW	28.30 TQ	OHBLS	10/01-12/01
	Columbus MSA, OH	H	12.68 FQ	18.04 AW	26.43 TQ	OHBLS	10/01-12/01
	Dayton-Springfield MSA, OH	H	14.46 FQ	23.23 AW	33.90 TQ	OHBLS	10/01-12/01
	Hamilton-Middletown PMSA, OH	H	11.54 FQ	19.24 AW	26.97 TQ	OHBLS	10/01-12/01
	Toledo MSA, OH	H	14.73 FQ	23.97 AW	33.89 TQ	OHBLS	10/01-12/01
	Oklahoma	H	14.31 FQ	20.60 AW	28.79 TQ	OKBLS	10/01-12/01
	Oklahoma City MSA, OK	H	15.23 FQ	24.63 AW	34.82 TQ	OKBLS	10/01-12/01
	Tulsa MSA, OK	H	14.49 FQ	19.90 AW	25.99 TQ	OKBLS	10/01-12/01
	Oregon	H	15.50 FQ	21.81 AW	27.93 TQ	ORBLS	10/01-12/01
	Eugene-Springfield MSA, OR	H	14.92 FQ	18.94 AW	26.79 TQ	ORBLS	10/01-12/01
	Portland-Vancouver PMSA, OR-WA	H	16.17 FQ	22.33 AW	28.03 TQ	ORBLS	10/01-12/01
	Pennsylvania	H	12.53 FQ	18.72 AW	25.70 TQ	PABLS	10/01-12/01
	Allentown-Bethlehem-Easton MSA, PA	H	12.68 FQ	17.42 AW	23.93 TQ	PABLS	10/01-12/01
	Erie MSA, PA	H	12.79 FQ	19.65 AW	26.01 TQ	PABLS	10/01-12/01
	Harrisburg-Lebanon-Carlisle MSA, PA	H	12.12 FQ	16.23 AW	21.14 TQ	PABLS	10/01-12/01
	Johnstown MSA, PA	H	11.57 FQ	16.19 AW	21.36 TQ	PABLS	10/01-12/01
	Lancaster MSA, PA	H	14.36 FQ	19.92 AW	26.49 TQ	PABLS	10/01-12/01
	Philadelphia PMSA, PA-NJ	H	14.13 FQ	19.21 AW	25.55 TQ	PABLS	10/01-12/01
	Pittsburgh MSA, PA	H	10.76 FQ	19.33 AW	33.04 TQ	PABLS	10/01-12/01
	Reading MSA, PA	H	15.10 FQ	19.65 AW	26.69 TQ	PABLS	10/01-12/01
	Scranton-Wilkes-Barre-Hazleton MSA, PA	H	11.69 FQ	16.54 AW	23.82 TQ	PABLS	10/01-12/01
	York MSA, PA	H	14.33 FQ	18.50 AW	22.29 TQ	PABLS	10/01-12/01
	Rhode Island	H	13.15 FQ	19.46 AW	26.57 TQ	RIBLS	10/01-12/01
	Providence-Fall River-Warwick MSA, RI-MA	H	13.06 FQ	19.59 AW	26.90 TQ	RIBLS	10/01-12/01
	South Carolina	H	12.71 FQ	18.35 AW	24.01 TQ	SCBLS	10/01-12/01
	Charleston-North Charleston MSA, SC	H	9.64 FQ	15.12 AW	29.75 TQ	SCBLS	10/01-12/01
	Columbia MSA, SC	H	11.96 FQ	19.99 AW	26.78 TQ	SCBLS	10/01-12/01

AAW	Average annual wage	**AOH**	Average offered, high	**ASH**	Average starting, high	**H**	Hourly	**M**	Monthly	**S**	Special: hourly and annual
AE	Average entry wage	**AOL**	Average offered, low	**ASL**	Average starting, low	**HI**	Highest wage paid	**MTC**	Median total compensation	**TQ**	Third quartile wage
AEX	Average experienced wage	**APH**	Average pay, high range	**AW**	Average wage paid	**HR**	High end range	**MW**	Median wage paid	**W**	Weekly
AO	Average offered	**APL**	Average pay, low range	**FQ**	First quartile wage	**LR**	Low end range	**SQ**	Second quartile wage	**Y**	Yearly

Occupation/Type/Industry	Location	Per	Low	Mid	High	Source	Date
Tool and Die Maker	Greenville-Spartanburg-Anderson MSA, SC	H	13.68 FQ	19.13 AW	24.99 TQ	SCBLS	10/01-12/01
	South Dakota	H	11.68 FQ	15.86 AW	21.63 TQ	SDBLS	10/01-12/01
	Sioux Falls MSA, SD	H	13.41 FQ	18.50 AW	25.06 TQ	SDBLS	10/01-12/01
	Tennessee	H	12.01 FQ	17.42 AW	24.20 TQ	TNBLS	10/01-12/01
	Chattanooga MSA, TN-GA	H	11.19 FQ	14.81 AW	18.08 TQ	TNBLS	10/01-12/01
	Clarksville-Hopkinsville MSA, TN-KY	H	17.02 FQ	19.67 AW	22.97 TQ	TNBLS	10/01-12/01
	Johnson City-Kingsport-Bristol MSA, TN-VA	H	10.88 FQ	15.94 AW	21.13 TQ	TNBLS	10/01-12/01
	Knoxville MSA, TN	H	11.75 FQ	16.04 AW	21.92 TQ	TNBLS	10/01-12/01
	Memphis MSA, TN-AR-MS	H	12.19 FQ	17.16 AW	22.00 TQ	TNBLS	10/01-12/01
	Nashville MSA, TN	H	11.88 FQ	17.21 AW	22.55 TQ	TNBLS	10/01-12/01
	Texas	H	8.93 FQ	17.26 AW	25.80 TQ	TXBLS	10/01-12/01
	Austin-San Marcos MSA, TX	H	8.53 FQ	18.53 AW	28.14 TQ	TXBLS	10/01-12/01
	Brownsville-Harlingen-San Benito MSA, TX	H	7.47 FQ	15.14 AW	21.89 TQ	TXBLS	10/01-12/01
	Dallas PMSA, TX	H	8.20 FQ	16.44 AW	22.91 TQ	TXBLS	10/01-12/01
	El Paso MSA, TX	H	10.36 FQ	16.81 AW	24.06 TQ	TXBLS	10/01-12/01
	Fort Worth-Arlington PMSA, TX	H	11.49 FQ	20.30 AW	31.18 TQ	TXBLS	10/01-12/01
	Houston PMSA, TX	H	10.43 FQ	17.43 AW	22.38 TQ	TXBLS	10/01-12/01
	Killeen-Temple MSA, TX	H	10.55 FQ	18.09 AW	26.25 TQ	TXBLS	10/01-12/01
	Longview-Marshall MSA, TX	H	12.08 FQ	16.96 AW	21.56 TQ	TXBLS	10/01-12/01
	McAllen-Edinburg-Mission MSA, TX	H	8.76 FQ	13.58 AW	17.67 TQ	TXBLS	10/01-12/01
	Utah	H	11.15 FQ	17.76 AW	24.46 TQ	UTBLS	10/01-12/01
	Salt Lake City-Ogden MSA, UT	H	11.39 FQ	17.91 AW	24.62 TQ	UTBLS	10/01-12/01
	Vermont	H	10.90 FQ	17.71 AW	24.90 TQ	VTBLS	10/01-12/01
	Virginia	H	11.68 FQ	17.93 AW	24.40 TQ	VABLS	10/01-12/01
	Lynchburg MSA, VA	H	8.95 FQ	17.28 AW	22.49 TQ	VABLS	10/01-12/01
	Norfolk-Virginia Beach-Newport News MSA, VA-NC	H	13.92 FQ	19.53 AW	26.56 TQ	VABLS	10/01-12/01
	Richmond-Petersburg MSA, VA	H	10.25 FQ	17.23 AW	25.34 TQ	VABLS	10/01-12/01
	Roanoke MSA, VA	H	13.75 FQ	17.95 AW	22.68 TQ	VABLS	10/01-12/01
	Washington	H	14.15 FQ	22.42 AW	28.31 TQ	WABLS	10/01-12/01
	Seattle-Bellevue-Everett PMSA, WA	H	14.79 FQ	23.08 AW	28.74 TQ	WABLS	10/01-12/01
	Spokane MSA, WA	H	11.83 FQ	18.55 AW	26.97 TQ	WABLS	10/01-12/01
	Tacoma PMSA, WA	H	16.88 FQ	22.90 AW	28.60 TQ	WABLS	10/01-12/01
	West Virginia	H	9.44 FQ	14.68 AW	21.01 TQ	WVBLS	10/01-12/01
	Wisconsin	H	13.68 FQ	20.20 AW	27.31 TQ	WIBLS	10/01-12/01
	Appleton-Oshkosh-Neenah MSA, WI	H	16.00 FQ	21.12 AW	27.26 TQ	WIBLS	10/01-12/01
	Green Bay MSA, WI	H	15.28 FQ	18.79 AW	21.83 TQ	WIBLS	10/01-12/01
	Madison MSA, WI	H	12.48 FQ	19.31 AW	25.16 TQ	WIBLS	10/01-12/01
	Milwaukee-Waukesha PMSA, WI	H	14.00 FQ	21.34 AW	28.41 TQ	WIBLS	10/01-12/01
	Racine PMSA, WI	H	13.78 FQ	19.29 AW	25.71 TQ	WIBLS	10/01-12/01
	Puerto Rico	H	7.61 FQ	12.11 AW	16.45 TQ	PRBLS	10/01-12/01
Tool Grinder, Filer, and Sharpener	Alabama	H	7.37 FQ	12.03 AW	18.09 TQ	ALBLS	10/01-12/01
	Birmingham MSA, AL	H	7.03 FQ	10.97 AW	19.42 TQ	ALBLS	10/01-12/01
	Mobile MSA, AL	H	7.02 FQ	10.18 AW	16.87 TQ	ALBLS	10/01-12/01
	Arizona	H	9.29 FQ	14.52 AW	21.96 TQ	AZBLS	10/01-12/01
	Phoenix-Mesa MSA, AZ	H	9.23 FQ	14.69 AW	22.46 TQ	AZBLS	10/01-12/01
	Tucson MSA, AZ	H	9.58 FQ	14.08 AW	21.16 TQ	AZBLS	10/01-12/01
	Arkansas	H	8.94 FQ	12.53 AW	16.55 TQ	ARBLS	10/01-12/01
	Fayetteville-Springdale-Rogers MSA, AR	H	8.30 FQ	12.13 AW	15.79 TQ	ARBLS	10/01-12/01
	Little Rock-North Little Rock MSA, AR	H	8.71 FQ	12.73 AW	16.92 TQ	ARBLS	10/01-12/01
	California	H	7.36 FQ	12.45 AW	19.84 TQ	CABLS	10/01-12/01
	Los Angeles-Long Beach PMSA, CA	H	7.00 FQ	11.58 AW	19.80 TQ	CABLS	10/01-12/01
	Modesto MSA, CA	H	7.22 FQ	11.82 AW	17.03 TQ	CABLS	10/01-12/01
	Oakland PMSA, CA	H	9.86 FQ	17.18 AW	23.15 TQ	CABLS	10/01-12/01
	Orange County PMSA, CA	H	7.94 FQ	14.15 AW	21.32 TQ	CABLS	10/01-12/01

AAW	Average annual wage	AOH	Average offered, high	ASH	Average starting, high	H	Hourly	M	Monthly	S	Special: hourly and annual
AE	Average entry wage	AOL	Average offered, low	ASL	Average starting, low	HI	Highest wage paid	MTC	Median total compensation	TQ	Third quartile wage
AEX	Average experienced wage	APH	Average pay, high range	AW	Average wage paid	HR	High end range	MW	Median wage paid	W	Weekly
AO	Average offered	APL	Average pay, low range	FQ	First quartile wage	LR	Low end range	SQ	Second quartile wage	Y	Yearly

Occupation/Type/Industry	Location	Per	Low	Mid	High	Source	Date
Tool Grinder, Filer, and Sharpener	Riverside-San Bernardino PMSA, CA	H	7.74 FQ	12.27 AW	18.90 TQ	CABLS	10/01-12/01
	Sacramento PMSA, CA	H	8.26 FQ	12.95 AW	18.48 TQ	CABLS	10/01-12/01
	San Diego MSA, CA	H	7.39 FQ	12.35 AW	17.67 TQ	CABLS	10/01-12/01
	San Jose PMSA, CA	H	6.50 FQ	11.93 AW	17.00 TQ	CABLS	10/01-12/01
	Stockton-Lodi MSA, CA	H	7.77 FQ	11.47 AW	15.77 TQ	CABLS	10/01-12/01
	Ventura PMSA, CA	H	7.24 FQ	10.45 AW	15.92 TQ	CABLS	10/01-12/01
	Colorado	H	8.03 FQ	12.76 AW	18.64 TQ	COBLS	10/01-12/01
	Denver PMSA, CO	H	8.91 FQ	14.00 AW	19.97 TQ	COBLS	10/01-12/01
	Connecticut	H	8.55 FQ	14.97 AW	20.64 TQ	CTBLS	10/01-12/01
	Bridgeport PMSA, CT	H	10.98 FQ	15.98 AW	20.90 TQ	CTBLS	10/01-12/01
	Hartford MSA, CT	H	10.03 FQ	15.37 AW	20.70 TQ	CTBLS	10/01-12/01
	New Haven-Meriden PMSA, CT	H	9.53 FQ	14.12 AW	17.85 TQ	CTBLS	10/01-12/01
	Waterbury PMSA, CT	H	7.60 FQ	12.91 AW	18.38 TQ	CTBLS	10/01-12/01
	Florida	H	7.41 FQ	12.23 AW	18.63 TQ	FLBLS	10/01-12/01
	Fort Lauderdale PMSA, FL	H	8.52 FQ	14.68 AW	21.30 TQ	FLBLS	10/01-12/01
	Miami PMSA, FL	H	7.29 FQ	10.61 AW	16.32 TQ	FLBLS	10/01-12/01
	Orlando MSA, FL	H	9.90 FQ	15.35 AW	21.85 TQ	FLBLS	10/01-12/01
	Tampa-St. Petersburg-Clearwater MSA, FL	H	7.97 FQ	11.87 AW	16.88 TQ	FLBLS	10/01-12/01
	Georgia	H	9.61 FQ	12.92 AW	16.77 TQ	GABLS	10/01-12/01
	Atlanta MSA, GA	H	9.39 FQ	13.12 AW	18.29 TQ	GABLS	10/01-12/01
	Macon MSA, GA	H	10.14 FQ	12.87 AW	15.43 TQ	GABLS	10/01-12/01
	Idaho	H	6.57 FQ	13.29 AW	17.55 TQ	IDBLS	10/01-12/01
	Boise City MSA, ID	H	6.08 FQ	11.08 AW	15.71 TQ	IDBLS	10/01-12/01
	Illinois	H	8.91 FQ	14.49 AW	20.99 TQ	ILBLS	10/01-12/01
	Chicago PMSA, IL	H	9.48 FQ	14.61 AW	20.41 TQ	ILBLS	10/01-12/01
	Peoria-Pekin MSA, IL	H	7.80 FQ	15.92 AW	27.13 TQ	ILBLS	10/01-12/01
	Rockford MSA, IL	H	9.33 FQ	15.97 AW	24.87 TQ	ILBLS	10/01-12/01
	Indiana	H	10.20 FQ	17.71 AW	26.46 TQ	INBLS	10/01-12/01
	Elkhart-Goshen MSA, IN	H	9.70 FQ	16.11 AW	21.27 TQ	INBLS	10/01-12/01
	Fort Wayne MSA, IN	H	13.64 FQ	17.98 AW	21.85 TQ	INBLS	10/01-12/01
	Gary PMSA, IN	H	12.74 FQ	19.65 AW	27.77 TQ	INBLS	10/01-12/01
	Indianapolis MSA, IN	H	9.76 FQ	20.48 AW	32.84 TQ	INBLS	10/01-12/01
	Lafayette MSA, IN	H	5.63 FQ	11.94 AW	18.66 TQ	INBLS	10/01-12/01
	South Bend MSA, IN	H	9.68 FQ	15.51 AW	20.62 TQ	INBLS	10/01-12/01
	Iowa	H	9.37 FQ	15.38 AW	24.85 TQ	IABLS	10/01-12/01
	Cedar Rapids MSA, IA	H	8.27 FQ	11.99 AW	16.73 TQ	IABLS	10/01-12/01
	Davenport-Moline-Rock Island MSA, IA-IL	H	9.60 FQ	13.38 AW	19.08 TQ	IABLS	10/01-12/01
	Kansas	H	10.05 FQ	16.91 AW	26.02 TQ	KSBLS	10/01-12/01
	Wichita MSA, KS	H	10.39 FQ	19.24 AW	27.63 TQ	KSBLS	10/01-12/01
	Kentucky	H	10.37 FQ	13.95 AW	19.49 TQ	KYBLS	10/01-12/01
	Lexington MSA, KY	H	7.90 FQ	13.15 AW	19.57 TQ	KYBLS	10/01-12/01
	Louisville MSA, KY-IN	H	9.79 FQ	15.29 AW	20.99 TQ	KYBLS	10/01-12/01
	Louisiana	H	7.54 FQ	13.33 AW	21.30 TQ	LABLS	10/01-12/01
	Baton Rouge MSA, LA	H	7.60 FQ	11.37 AW	16.51 TQ	LABLS	10/01-12/01
	Maine	H	9.47 FQ	12.85 AW	17.14 TQ	MEBLS	10/01-12/01
	Maryland	H	9.15 FQ	15.58 AW	24.71 TQ	MDBLS	10/01-12/01
	Baltimore PMSA, MD	H	8.96 FQ	15.29 AW	24.38 TQ	MDBLS	10/01-12/01
	Massachusetts	H	10.22 FQ	14.92 AW	20.50 TQ	MABLS	10/01-12/01
	Boston PMSA, MA-NH	H	10.19 FQ	16.22 AW	24.52 TQ	MABLS	10/01-12/01
	Springfield MSA, MA	H	9.67 FQ	14.47 AW	18.20 TQ	MABLS	10/01-12/01
	Worcester PMSA, MA-CT	H	10.45 FQ	13.97 AW	16.81 TQ	MABLS	10/01-12/01
	Michigan	H	10.65 FQ	18.76 AW	27.83 TQ	MIBLS	10/01-12/01
	Ann Arbor PMSA, MI	H	11.28 FQ	18.19 AW	27.36 TQ	MIBLS	10/01-12/01
	Detroit PMSA, MI	H	10.16 FQ	19.64 AW	28.25 TQ	MIBLS	10/01-12/01
	Grand Rapids-Muskegon-Holland MSA, MI	H	11.49 FQ	17.18 AW	24.31 TQ	MIBLS	10/01-12/01
	Kalamazoo-Battle Creek MSA, MI	H	11.90 FQ	21.43 AW	29.90 TQ	MIBLS	10/01-12/01
	Lansing-East Lansing MSA, MI	H	11.49 FQ	16.47 AW	20.93 TQ	MIBLS	10/01-12/01
	Saginaw-Bay City-Midland MSA, MI	H	13.19 FQ	19.41 AW	26.66 TQ	MIBLS	10/01-12/01
	Minnesota	H	11.33 FQ	15.67 AW	21.37 TQ	MNBLS	10/01-12/01
	Minneapolis-St. Paul MSA, MN-WI	H	12.28 FQ	16.88 AW	22.75 TQ	MNBLS	10/01-12/01
	Mississippi	H	10.07 FQ	14.83 AW	17.98 TQ	MSBLS	10/01-12/01
	Missouri	H	8.60 FQ	13.24 AW	18.29 TQ	MOBLS	10/01-12/01
	Kansas City MSA, MO-KS	H	8.82 FQ	12.38 AW	17.39 TQ	MOBLS	10/01-12/01

AAW	Average annual wage	**AOH**	Average offered, high	**ASH**	Average starting, high	**H**	Hourly	**M**	Monthly	**S**	Special: hourly and annual
AE	Average entry wage	**AOL**	Average offered, low	**ASL**	Average starting, low	**HI**	Highest wage paid	**MTC**	Median total compensation	**TQ**	Third quartile wage
AEX	Average experienced wage	**APH**	Average pay, high range	**AW**	Average wage paid	**HR**	High end range	**MW**	Median wage paid	**W**	Weekly
AO	Average offered	**APL**	Average pay, low range	**FQ**	First quartile wage	**LR**	Low end range	**SQ**	Second quartile wage	**Y**	Yearly

Occupation/Type/Industry	Location	Per	Low	Mid	High	Source	Date
Tool Grinder, Filer, and Sharpener	St. Louis MSA, MO-IL	H	9.25 FQ	14.65 AW	22.97 TQ	MOBLS	10/01-12/01
	Montana	H	9.62 FQ	14.69 AW	20.52 TQ	MTBLS	10/01-12/01
	Omaha MSA, NE-IA	H	9.81 FQ	14.41 AW	21.48 TQ	NEBLS	10/01-12/01
	New Hampshire	H	9.41 FQ	13.40 AW	17.78 TQ	NHBLS	10/01-12/01
	New Jersey	H	8.16 FQ	13.66 AW	20.08 TQ	NJBLS	10/01-12/01
	Bergen-Passaic PMSA, NJ	H	7.94 FQ	13.04 AW	21.38 TQ	NJBLS	10/01-12/01
	Middlesex-Somerset-Hunterdon PMSA, NJ	H	8.51 FQ	14.61 AW	19.95 TQ	NJBLS	10/01-12/01
	Newark PMSA, NJ	H	8.22 FQ	13.53 AW	19.88 TQ	NJBLS	10/01-12/01
	New Mexico	H	6.95 FQ	10.87 AW	14.17 TQ	NMBLS	10/01-12/01
	Albuquerque MSA, NM	H	6.80 FQ	11.35 AW	14.29 TQ	NMBLS	10/01-12/01
	New York	H	8.51 FQ	15.07 AW	21.31 TQ	NYBLS	10/01-12/01
	Albany-Schenectady-Troy MSA, NY	H	6.93 FQ	13.81 AW	20.65 TQ	NYBLS	10/01-12/01
	Buffalo-Niagara Falls MSA, NY	H	10.47 FQ	16.42 AW	21.99 TQ	NYBLS	10/01-12/01
	Nassau-Suffolk PMSA, NY	H	9.56 FQ	14.63 AW	18.07 TQ	NYBLS	10/01-12/01
	New York PMSA, NY	H	6.96 FQ	14.95 AW	30.81 TQ	NYBLS	10/01-12/01
	Rochester MSA, NY	H	12.33 FQ	18.34 AW	21.79 TQ	NYBLS	10/01-12/01
	Utica-Rome MSA, NY	H	8.85 FQ	12.62 AW	16.47 TQ	NYBLS	10/01-12/01
	North Carolina	H	9.06 FQ	13.82 AW	19.97 TQ	NCBLS	10/01-12/01
	Asheville MSA, NC	H	12.12 FQ	15.46 AW	17.95 TQ	NCBLS	10/01-12/01
	Charlotte-Gastonia-Rock Hill MSA, NC-SC	H	9.25 FQ	14.00 AW	20.62 TQ	NCBLS	10/01-12/01
	Greensboro-Winston-Salem-High Point MSA, NC	H	7.92 FQ	12.69 AW	18.57 TQ	NCBLS	10/01-12/01
	Hickory-Morganton-Lenoir MSA, NC	H	9.47 FQ	12.42 AW	16.16 TQ	NCBLS	10/01-12/01
	Raleigh-Durham-Chapel Hill MSA, NC	H	10.06 FQ	15.20 AW	20.56 TQ	NCBLS	10/01-12/01
	Ohio	H	9.27 FQ	14.62 AW	21.51 TQ	OHBLS	10/01-12/01
	Akron PMSA, OH	H	8.79 FQ	13.80 AW	18.40 TQ	OHBLS	10/01-12/01
	Canton-Massillon MSA, OH	H	9.12 FQ	10.82 AW	13.75 TQ	OHBLS	10/01-12/01
	Cincinnati PMSA, OH-KY-IN	H	9.28 FQ	12.57 AW	18.09 TQ	OHBLS	10/01-12/01
	Cleveland-Lorain-Elyria PMSA, OH	H	9.08 FQ	14.82 AW	21.12 TQ	OHBLS	10/01-12/01
	Columbus MSA, OH	H	9.49 FQ	13.36 AW	19.31 TQ	OHBLS	10/01-12/01
	Mansfield MSA, OH	H	9.04 FQ	12.82 AW	17.18 TQ	OHBLS	10/01-12/01
	Toledo MSA, OH	H	6.25 FQ	12.44 AW	19.98 TQ	OHBLS	10/01-12/01
	Youngstown-Warren MSA, OH	H	8.07 FQ	13.61 AW	19.06 TQ	OHBLS	10/01-12/01
	Oklahoma	H	6.93 FQ	11.36 AW	17.38 TQ	OKBLS	10/01-12/01
	Oklahoma City MSA, OK	H	8.59 FQ	14.40 AW	22.40 TQ	OKBLS	10/01-12/01
	Oregon	H	10.14 FQ	16.11 AW	22.34 TQ	ORBLS	10/01-12/01
	Eugene-Springfield MSA, OR	H	10.15 FQ	14.69 AW	20.16 TQ	ORBLS	10/01-12/01
	Portland-Vancouver PMSA, OR-WA	H	9.03 FQ	15.87 AW	25.27 TQ	ORBLS	10/01-12/01
	Pennsylvania	H	9.39 FQ	14.50 AW	21.24 TQ	PABLS	10/01-12/01
	Allentown-Bethlehem-Easton MSA, PA	H	8.95 FQ	12.59 AW	19.93 TQ	PABLS	10/01-12/01
	Erie MSA, PA	H	9.02 FQ	14.07 AW	20.06 TQ	PABLS	10/01-12/01
	Lancaster MSA, PA	H	9.34 FQ	12.96 AW	19.13 TQ	PABLS	10/01-12/01
	Philadelphia PMSA, PA-NJ	H	8.32 FQ	14.61 AW	21.46 TQ	PABLS	10/01-12/01
	Pittsburgh MSA, PA	H	9.82 FQ	15.46 AW	21.97 TQ	PABLS	10/01-12/01
	Scranton-Wilkes-Barre-Hazleton MSA, PA	H	7.44 FQ	13.28 AW	16.99 TQ	PABLS	10/01-12/01
	Rhode Island	H	8.95 FQ	12.63 AW	17.77 TQ	RIBLS	10/01-12/01
	Providence-Fall River-Warwick MSA, RI-MA	H	9.26 FQ	13.11 AW	18.44 TQ	RIBLS	10/01-12/01
	South Carolina	H	9.18 FQ	12.97 AW	17.75 TQ	SCBLS	10/01-12/01
	Greenville-Spartanburg-Anderson MSA, SC	H	9.23 FQ	15.05 AW	25.72 TQ	SCBLS	10/01-12/01
	South Dakota	H	9.31 FQ	11.66 AW	14.15 TQ	SDBLS	10/01-12/01
	Tennessee	H	8.25 FQ	11.90 AW	16.53 TQ	TNBLS	10/01-12/01
	Chattanooga MSA, TN-GA	H	9.80 FQ	12.85 AW	16.48 TQ	TNBLS	10/01-12/01
	Johnson City-Kingsport-Bristol MSA, TN-VA	H	7.46 FQ	11.59 AW	16.75 TQ	TNBLS	10/01-12/01
	Knoxville MSA, TN	H	10.31 FQ	13.70 AW	17.17 TQ	TNBLS	10/01-12/01
	Memphis MSA, TN-AR-MS	H	9.03 FQ	10.60 AW	13.32 TQ	TNBLS	10/01-12/01
	Nashville MSA, TN	H	10.76 FQ	12.97 AW	18.87 TQ	TNBLS	10/01-12/01
	Texas	H	7.61 FQ	13.47 AW	21.95 TQ	TXBLS	10/01-12/01
	Austin-San Marcos MSA, TX	H	7.86 FQ	16.88 AW	27.89 TQ	TXBLS	10/01-12/01

AAW	Average annual wage	**AOH**	Average offered, high	**ASH**	Average starting, high	**H**	Hourly	**M**	Monthly	**S**	Special: hourly and annual
AE	Average entry wage	**AOL**	Average offered, low	**ASL**	Average starting, low	**HI**	Highest wage paid	**MTC**	Median total compensation	**TQ**	Third quartile wage
AEX	Average experienced wage	**APH**	Average pay, high range	**AW**	Average wage paid	**HR**	High end range	**MW**	Median wage paid	**W**	Weekly
AO	Average offered	**APL**	Average pay, low range	**FQ**	First quartile wage	**LR**	Low end range	**SQ**	Second quartile wage	**Y**	Yearly

Occupation/Type/Industry	Location	Per	Low	Mid	High	Source	Date
Tool Grinder, Filer, and Sharpener	Dallas PMSA, TX	H	7.62 FQ	13.08 AW	22.16 TQ	TXBLS	10/01-12/01
	Fort Worth-Arlington PMSA, TX	H	7.52 FQ	15.06 AW	25.47 TQ	TXBLS	10/01-12/01
	Houston PMSA, TX	H	7.48 FQ	13.37 AW	21.40 TQ	TXBLS	10/01-12/01
	Utah	H	9.17 FQ	14.40 AW	20.14 TQ	UTBLS	10/01-12/01
	Salt Lake City-Ogden MSA, UT	H	9.32 FQ	14.77 AW	20.28 TQ	UTBLS	10/01-12/01
	Vermont	H	9.39 FQ	13.01 AW	18.66 TQ	VTBLS	10/01-12/01
	Virginia	H	8.67 FQ	12.84 AW	17.26 TQ	VABLS	10/01-12/01
	Lynchburg MSA, VA	H	9.33 FQ	14.44 AW	17.97 TQ	VABLS	10/01-12/01
	Norfolk-Virginia Beach-Newport News MSA, VA-NC	H	8.23 FQ	13.19 AW	20.20 TQ	VABLS	10/01-12/01
	Washington	H	9.52 FQ	16.28 AW	24.36 TQ	WABLS	10/01-12/01
	Seattle-Bellevue-Everett PMSA, WA	H	9.46 FQ	17.23 AW	27.11 TQ	WABLS	10/01-12/01
	Tacoma PMSA, WA	H	7.95 FQ	13.14 AW	19.20 TQ	WABLS	10/01-12/01
	West Virginia	H	7.61 FQ	11.19 AW	16.49 TQ	WVBLS	10/01-12/01
	Wisconsin	H	10.62 FQ	16.60 AW	24.83 TQ	WIBLS	10/01-12/01
	Appleton-Oshkosh-Neenah MSA, WI	H	9.82 FQ	13.97 AW	22.12 TQ	WIBLS	10/01-12/01
	Milwaukee-Waukesha PMSA, WI	H	12.98 FQ	19.08 AW	26.43 TQ	WIBLS	10/01-12/01
	Racine PMSA, WI	H	9.77 FQ	16.28 AW	24.49 TQ	WIBLS	10/01-12/01
	Puerto Rico	H	6.20 FQ	10.11 AW	13.54 TQ	PRBLS	10/01-12/01
Tour Guide and Escort	Alabama	H	5.58 FQ	7.23 AW	9.98 TQ	ALBLS	10/01-12/01
	Alaska	H	7.03 FQ	12.04 AW	18.88 TQ	AKBLS	10/01-12/01
	Arizona	H	5.82 FQ	10.48 AW	16.28 TQ	AZBLS	10/01-12/01
	Arkansas	H	5.66 FQ	7.91 AW	11.83 TQ	ARBLS	10/01-12/01
	California	H	6.85 FQ	11.57 AW	17.74 TQ	CABLS	10/01-12/01
	Colorado	H	7.59 FQ	12.35 AW	16.70 TQ	COBLS	10/01-12/01
	Connecticut	H	6.65 FQ	8.38 AW	10.98 TQ	CTBLS	10/01-12/01
	District of Columbia	H	6.79 FQ	14.57 AW	24.64 TQ	DCBLS	10/01-12/01
	Florida	H	7.16 FQ	10.16 AW	13.52 TQ	FLBLS	10/01-12/01
	Georgia	H	7.07 FQ	10.09 AW	12.92 TQ	GABLS	10/01-12/01
	Hawaii	H	6.21 FQ	12.27 AW	26.07 TQ	HIBLS	10/01-12/01
	Idaho	H	7.52 FQ	14.07 AW	30.76 TQ	IDBLS	10/01-12/01
	Illinois	H	6.30 FQ	9.42 AW	14.62 TQ	ILBLS	10/01-12/01
	Indiana	H	6.05 FQ	8.71 AW	11.25 TQ	INBLS	10/01-12/01
	Iowa	H	5.85 FQ	8.38 AW	12.02 TQ	IABLS	10/01-12/01
	Kansas	H	5.70 FQ	7.71 AW	10.35 TQ	KSBLS	10/01-12/01
	Kentucky	H	5.79 FQ	8.07 AW	10.61 TQ	KYBLS	10/01-12/01
	Louisiana	H	5.59 FQ	7.75 AW	11.56 TQ	LABLS	10/01-12/01
	Maine	H	5.51 FQ	7.48 AW	10.52 TQ	MEBLS	10/01-12/01
	Maryland	H	6.28 FQ	12.15 AW	17.88 TQ	MDBLS	10/01-12/01
	Massachusetts	H	7.04 FQ	9.42 AW	11.81 TQ	MABLS	10/01-12/01
	Michigan	H	6.23 FQ	11.01 AW	18.99 TQ	MIBLS	10/01-12/01
	Minnesota	H	7.52 FQ	11.11 AW	15.93 TQ	MNBLS	10/01-12/01
	Mississippi	H	5.81 FQ	7.89 AW	10.64 TQ	MSBLS	10/01-12/01
	Missouri	H	5.74 FQ	8.06 AW	11.66 TQ	MOBLS	10/01-12/01
	Montana	H	6.01 FQ	7.35 AW	8.62 TQ	MTBLS	10/01-12/01
	Nebraska	H	5.88 FQ	7.87 AW	11.47 TQ	NEBLS	10/01-12/01
	Nevada	H	9.32 FQ	11.86 AW	15.20 TQ	NVBLS	10/01-12/01
	New Hampshire	H	6.21 FQ	8.59 AW	11.79 TQ	NHBLS	10/01-12/01
	New Jersey	H	6.81 FQ	8.91 AW	11.94 TQ	NJBLS	10/01-12/01
	New Mexico	H	6.99 FQ	8.96 AW	11.17 TQ	NMBLS	10/01-12/01
	New York	H	6.11 FQ	10.15 AW	14.04 TQ	NYBLS	10/01-12/01
	North Carolina	H	6.52 FQ	8.10 AW	10.06 TQ	NCBLS	10/01-12/01
	North Dakota	H	5.68 FQ	7.10 AW	9.51 TQ	NDBLS	10/01-12/01
	Ohio	H	5.80 FQ	8.41 AW	12.52 TQ	OHBLS	10/01-12/01
	Oklahoma	H	5.44 FQ	7.44 AW	11.96 TQ	OKBLS	10/01-12/01
	Oregon	H	6.97 FQ	10.21 AW	14.99 TQ	ORBLS	10/01-12/01
	Pennsylvania	H	5.73 FQ	7.34 AW	10.25 TQ	PABLS	10/01-12/01
	South Carolina	H	5.76 FQ	8.65 AW	15.35 TQ	SCBLS	10/01-12/01
	South Dakota	H	5.82 FQ	7.56 AW	9.53 TQ	SDBLS	10/01-12/01
	Tennessee	H	5.91 FQ	8.67 AW	11.90 TQ	TNBLS	10/01-12/01
	Texas	H	5.71 FQ	8.51 AW	13.00 TQ	TXBLS	10/01-12/01
	Utah	H	6.73 FQ	9.86 AW	15.82 TQ	UTBLS	10/01-12/01
	Vermont	H	6.39 FQ	7.26 AW	8.48 TQ	VTBLS	10/01-12/01
	Virginia	H	5.73 FQ	8.17 AW	12.29 TQ	VABLS	10/01-12/01

AAW Average annual wage; AE Average entry wage; AEX Average experienced wage; AO Average offered; AOH Average offered, high; AOL Average offered, low; APH Average pay, high range; APL Average pay, low range; ASH Average starting, high; ASL Average starting, low; AW Average wage paid; FQ First quartile wage; H Hourly; HI Highest wage paid; HR High end range; LR Low end range; M Monthly; MTC Median total compensation; MW Median wage paid; SQ Second quartile wage; S Special: hourly and annual; TQ Third quartile wage; W Weekly; Y Yearly

Occupation/Type/Industry	Location	Per	Low	Mid	High	Source	Date
Tour Guide and Escort	Washington	H	7.82 FQ	10.94 AW	15.14 TQ	WABLS	10/01-12/01
	West Virginia	H	5.67 FQ	7.58 AW	10.73 TQ	WVBLS	10/01-12/01
	Wisconsin	H	5.81 FQ	8.12 AW	11.46 TQ	WIBLS	10/01-12/01
	Wyoming	H	6.89 FQ	9.82 AW	11.39 TQ	WYBLS	10/01-12/01
	Puerto Rico	H	5.76 FQ	7.90 AW	10.41 TQ	PRBLS	10/01-12/01
	Virgin Islands	H	7.08 FQ	9.28 AW	12.19 TQ	VIBLS	10/01-12/01
	Guam	H	6.88 FQ	14.07 AW	35.36 TQ	GUBLS	10/01-12/01
Tow-Truck Driver							
City government	Boston, MA	Y		33968 Y		BGLOBE	9/25/02
Traffic Technician	Alabama	H	8.91 FQ	14.12 AW	22.41 TQ	ALBLS	10/01-12/01
	Arizona	H	14.69 FQ	21.39 AW	29.36 TQ	AZBLS	10/01-12/01
	Phoenix-Mesa MSA, AZ	H	15.18 FQ	22.05 AW	29.44 TQ	AZBLS	10/01-12/01
	California	H	16.16 FQ	23.68 AW	33.39 TQ	CABLS	10/01-12/01
	Los Angeles-Long Beach PMSA, CA	H	15.62 FQ	22.22 AW	31.47 TQ	CABLS	10/01-12/01
	Oakland PMSA, CA	H	18.42 FQ	24.26 AW	33.71 TQ	CABLS	10/01-12/01
	Colorado	H	12.59 FQ	19.12 AW	27.13 TQ	COBLS	10/01-12/01
	Denver PMSA, CO	H	13.63 FQ	21.02 AW	28.76 TQ	COBLS	10/01-12/01
	Connecticut	H	12.08 FQ	22.40 AW	34.04 TQ	CTBLS	10/01-12/01
	Washington PMSA, DC-MD-VA-WV	H	13.34 FQ	20.41 AW	27.57 TQ	DCBLS	10/01-12/01
	Florida	H	9.80 FQ	15.26 AW	20.94 TQ	FLBLS	10/01-12/01
	Tampa-St. Petersburg-Clearwater MSA, FL	H	12.09 FQ	18.45 AW	32.42 TQ	FLBLS	10/01-12/01
	Georgia	H	9.26 FQ	14.18 AW	20.44 TQ	GABLS	10/01-12/01
	Atlanta MSA, GA	H	9.57 FQ	14.49 AW	20.94 TQ	GABLS	10/01-12/01
	Idaho	H	9.36 FQ	12.13 AW	15.55 TQ	IDBLS	10/01-12/01
	Illinois	H	7.23 FQ	16.01 AW	25.40 TQ	ILBLS	10/01-12/01
	Chicago PMSA, IL	H	6.30 FQ	15.10 AW	25.24 TQ	ILBLS	10/01-12/01
	Indiana	H	11.19 FQ	16.26 AW	24.15 TQ	INBLS	10/01-12/01
	Iowa	H	11.87 FQ	17.53 AW	24.66 TQ	IABLS	10/01-12/01
	Kansas	H	11.14 FQ	16.52 AW	22.70 TQ	KSBLS	10/01-12/01
	Louisiana	H	9.45 FQ	14.23 AW	21.15 TQ	LABLS	10/01-12/01
	Maryland	H	12.18 FQ	18.67 AW	26.38 TQ	MDBLS	10/01-12/01
	Baltimore PMSA, MD	H	11.77 FQ	17.19 AW	23.80 TQ	MDBLS	10/01-12/01
	Massachusetts	H	15.37 FQ	24.51 AW	39.66 TQ	MABLS	10/01-12/01
	Boston PMSA, MA-NH	H	15.36 FQ	24.75 AW	39.90 TQ	MABLS	10/01-12/01
	Michigan	H	12.97 FQ	19.46 AW	26.49 TQ	MIBLS	10/01-12/01
	Mississippi	H	8.18 FQ	11.90 AW	17.44 TQ	MSBLS	10/01-12/01
	Missouri	H	11.42 FQ	17.03 AW	25.50 TQ	MOBLS	10/01-12/01
	Nevada	H	10.68 FQ	21.87 AW	30.66 TQ	NVBLS	10/01-12/01
	Las Vegas MSA, NV-AZ	H	21.55 FQ	26.64 AW	32.87 TQ	NVBLS	10/01-12/01
	New Jersey	H	10.16 FQ	18.23 AW	30.13 TQ	NJBLS	10/01-12/01
	New Mexico	H	8.71 FQ	13.35 AW	17.56 TQ	NMBLS	10/01-12/01
	Nassau-Suffolk PMSA, NY	H	16.09 FQ	25.43 AW	39.92 TQ	NYBLS	10/01-12/01
	North Carolina	H	10.72 FQ	15.15 AW	21.04 TQ	NCBLS	10/01-12/01
	Ohio	H	12.04 FQ	17.16 AW	21.90 TQ	OHBLS	10/01-12/01
	Oklahoma	H	8.25 FQ	14.36 AW	21.01 TQ	OKBLS	10/01-12/01
	Oklahoma City MSA, OK	H	8.00 FQ	13.73 AW	20.77 TQ	OKBLS	10/01-12/01
	Oregon	H	10.24 FQ	16.62 AW	25.43 TQ	ORBLS	10/01-12/01
	Portland-Vancouver PMSA, OR-WA	H	9.95 FQ	16.94 AW	26.77 TQ	ORBLS	10/01-12/01
	Pennsylvania	H	13.31 FQ	21.60 AW	31.03 TQ	PABLS	10/01-12/01
	Tennessee	H	9.42 FQ	14.32 AW	20.96 TQ	TNBLS	10/01-12/01
	Knoxville MSA, TN	H	7.87 FQ	12.90 AW	17.83 TQ	TNBLS	10/01-12/01
	Memphis MSA, TN-AR-MS	H	10.23 FQ	17.79 AW	27.67 TQ	TNBLS	10/01-12/01
	Nashville MSA, TN	H	9.77 FQ	15.28 AW	22.27 TQ	TNBLS	10/01-12/01
	Texas	H	6.15 FQ	12.03 AW	19.04 TQ	TXBLS	10/01-12/01
	Dallas PMSA, TX	H	11.41 FQ	14.83 AW	19.11 TQ	TXBLS	10/01-12/01
	El Paso MSA, TX	H	6.55 FQ	12.30 AW	20.20 TQ	TXBLS	10/01-12/01
	Houston PMSA, TX	H	6.54 FQ	14.27 AW	22.01 TQ	TXBLS	10/01-12/01
	Utah	H	8.89 FQ	11.80 AW	16.95 TQ	UTBLS	10/01-12/01
	Salt Lake City-Ogden MSA, UT	H	8.92 FQ	12.42 AW	19.36 TQ	UTBLS	10/01-12/01
	Virginia	H	9.71 FQ	17.52 AW	26.64 TQ	VABLS	10/01-12/01
	Washington	H	15.52 FQ	22.38 AW	29.76 TQ	WABLS	10/01-12/01
	Seattle-Bellevue-Everett PMSA, WA	H	21.00 FQ	25.55 AW	31.63 TQ	WABLS	10/01-12/01
	West Virginia	H	9.20 FQ	16.52 AW	20.94 TQ	WVBLS	10/01-12/01

AAW	Average annual wage	**AOH**	Average offered, high	**ASH**	Average starting, high	**H**	Hourly	**M**	Monthly	**S**	Special: hourly and annual
AE	Average entry wage	**AOL**	Average offered, low	**ASL**	Average starting, low	**HI**	Highest wage paid	**MTC**	Median total compensation	**TQ**	Third quartile wage
AEX	Average experienced wage	**APH**	Average pay, high range	**AW**	Average wage paid	**HR**	High end range	**MW**	Median wage paid	**W**	Weekly
AO	Average offered	**APL**	Average pay, low range	**FQ**	First quartile wage	**LR**	Low end range	**SQ**	Second quartile wage	**Y**	Yearly

Occupation/Type/Industry	Location	Per	Low	Mid	High	Source	Date
Training and Development Specialist	Alabama	Y	20240 FQ	38660 AW	60600 TQ	ALBLS	10/01-12/01
	Alaska	Y	27290 FQ	50740 AW	82240 TQ	AKBLS	10/01-12/01
	Arizona	Y	24080 FQ	41050 AW	63330 TQ	AZBLS	10/01-12/01
	Arkansas	Y	18110 FQ	36870 AW	66160 TQ	ARBLS	10/01-12/01
	California	Y	26730 FQ	49940 AW	76480 TQ	CABLS	10/01-12/01
	Colorado	Y	26450 FQ	44330 AW	69030 TQ	COBLS	10/01-12/01
	Connecticut	Y	27740 FQ	50390 AW	73730 TQ	CTBLS	10/01-12/01
	Delaware	Y	24450 FQ	43120 AW	65290 TQ	DEBLS	10/01-12/01
	District of Columbia	Y	29420 FQ	52350 AW	81840 TQ	DCBLS	10/01-12/01
	Florida	Y	22830 FQ	38350 AW	57900 TQ	FLBLS	10/01-12/01
	Georgia	Y	25180 FQ	46510 AW	69880 TQ	GABLS	10/01-12/01
	Hawaii	Y	23290 FQ	46410 AW	76740 TQ	HIBLS	10/01-12/01
	Idaho	Y	25270 FQ	42290 AW	62920 TQ	IDBLS	10/01-12/01
	Illinois	Y	24410 FQ	48470 AW	76660 TQ	ILBLS	10/01-12/01
	Indiana	Y	22040 FQ	39100 AW	60240 TQ	INBLS	10/01-12/01
	Iowa	Y	20350 FQ	39050 AW	62160 TQ	IABLS	10/01-12/01
	Kansas	Y	22070 FQ	40740 AW	65690 TQ	KSBLS	10/01-12/01
	Kentucky	Y	23440 FQ	40010 AW	58750 TQ	KYBLS	10/01-12/01
	Louisiana	Y	17030 FQ	37190 AW	65470 TQ	LABLS	10/01-12/01
	Maine	Y	24260 FQ	38430 AW	55690 TQ	MEBLS	10/01-12/01
	Maryland	Y	24740 FQ	44410 AW	68740 TQ	MDBLS	10/01-12/01
	Massachusetts	Y	30370 FQ	54370 AW	91780 TQ	MABLS	10/01-12/01
	Michigan	Y	25860 FQ	52970 AW	84370 TQ	MIBLS	10/01-12/01
	Minnesota	Y	26410 FQ	43530 AW	63680 TQ	MNBLS	10/01-12/01
	Mississippi	Y	20770 FQ	36520 AW	56510 TQ	MSBLS	10/01-12/01
	Missouri	Y	22140 FQ	40700 AW	63780 TQ	MOBLS	10/01-12/01
	Montana	Y	20680 FQ	33700 AW	51100 TQ	MTBLS	10/01-12/01
	Nebraska	Y	20670 FQ	38120 AW	61830 TQ	NEBLS	10/01-12/01
	Nevada	Y	24000 FQ	43870 AW	67440 TQ	NVBLS	10/01-12/01
	New Hampshire	Y	27820 FQ	48800 AW	73670 TQ	NHBLS	10/01-12/01
	New Jersey	Y	29470 FQ	51180 AW	76950 TQ	NJBLS	10/01-12/01
	New Mexico	Y	24920 FQ	41190 AW	61750 TQ	NMBLS	10/01-12/01
	New York	Y	26750 FQ	50790 AW	80070 TQ	NYBLS	10/01-12/01
	North Carolina	Y	24010 FQ	44290 AW	70600 TQ	NCBLS	10/01-12/01
	North Dakota	Y	20940 FQ	34590 AW	55460 TQ	NDBLS	10/01-12/01
	Ohio	Y	23370 FQ	42910 AW	67450 TQ	OHBLS	10/01-12/01
	Oklahoma	Y	18890 FQ	36420 AW	59150 TQ	OKBLS	10/01-12/01
	Oregon	Y	25780 FQ	44620 AW	67150 TQ	ORBLS	10/01-12/01
	Pennsylvania	Y	24730 FQ	43650 AW	69110 TQ	PABLS	10/01-12/01
	Rhode Island	Y	28280 FQ	44920 AW	70220 TQ	RIBLS	10/01-12/01
	South Carolina	Y	22960 FQ	39070 AW	59370 TQ	SCBLS	10/01-12/01
	South Dakota	Y	24030 FQ	34140 AW	46750 TQ	SDBLS	10/01-12/01
	Tennessee	Y	20620 FQ	40550 AW	62800 TQ	TNBLS	10/01-12/01
	Texas	Y	24210 FQ	44490 AW	69620 TQ	TXBLS	10/01-12/01
	Utah	Y	19370 FQ	38060 AW	59270 TQ	UTBLS	10/01-12/01
	Vermont	Y	28790 FQ	45180 AW	66740 TQ	VTBLS	10/01-12/01
	Virginia	Y	26700 FQ	45760 AW	70050 TQ	VABLS	10/01-12/01
	Washington	Y	28410 FQ	50380 AW	82920 TQ	WABLS	10/01-12/01
	West Virginia	Y	17740 FQ	37870 AW	65150 TQ	WVBLS	10/01-12/01
	Wisconsin	Y	21230 FQ	39250 AW	61720 TQ	WIBLS	10/01-12/01
	Wyoming	Y	17930 FQ	37580 AW	60370 TQ	WYBLS	10/01-12/01
	Puerto Rico	Y	15310 FQ	29200 AW	47040 TQ	PRBLS	10/01-12/01
	Virgin Islands	Y	23820 FQ	30870 AW	40420 TQ	VIBLS	10/01-12/01
Training Professional	Central	Y		62539 AW		TRAIN	1/01-1/02
	East North Central	Y		66087 AW		TRAIN	1/01-1/02
	Northeast	Y		72158 AW		TRAIN	1/01-1/02
	Pacific	Y		74555 AW		TRAIN	1/01-1/02
	Southeast	Y		67409 AW		TRAIN	1/01-1/02
	West Central	Y		61235 AW		TRAIN	1/01-1/02
Transit and Railroad Police	California	Y	20940 FQ	46750 AW	75230 TQ	CABLS	10/01-12/01
	Georgia	Y	27030 FQ	39520 AW	56640 TQ	GABLS	10/01-12/01
	Illinois	Y	24990 FQ	44800 AW	66870 TQ	ILBLS	10/01-12/01
	Louisiana	Y	35410 FQ	50450 AW	72600 TQ	LABLS	10/01-12/01
	Maine	Y	29180 FQ	42620 AW	58050 TQ	MEBLS	10/01-12/01
	Maryland	Y	23970 FQ	32720 AW	55330 TQ	MDBLS	10/01-12/01
	Minnesota	Y	37350 FQ	49600 AW	58510 TQ	MNBLS	10/01-12/01
	Mississippi	Y	19590 FQ	28210 AW	42050 TQ	MSBLS	10/01-12/01
	Missouri	Y	37040 FQ	49290 AW	67000 TQ	MOBLS	10/01-12/01
	Ohio	Y	27460 FQ	39930 AW	54140 TQ	OHBLS	10/01-12/01

AAW	Average annual wage	**AOH**	Average offered, high	**ASH**	Average starting, high	**H**	Hourly	**M**	Monthly	**S**	Special: hourly and annual
AE	Average entry wage	**AOL**	Average offered, low	**ASL**	Average starting, low	**HI**	Highest wage paid	**MTC**	Median total compensation	**TQ**	Third quartile wage
AEX	Average experienced wage	**APH**	Average pay, high range	**AW**	Average wage paid	**HR**	High end range	**MW**	Median wage paid	**W**	Weekly
AO	Average offered	**APL**	Average pay, low range	**FQ**	First quartile wage	**LR**	Low end range	**SQ**	Second quartile wage	**Y**	Yearly

Occupation/Type/Industry	Location	Per	Low	Mid	High	Source	Date
Transit and Railroad Police	Oregon	Y	23170 FQ	41280 AW	60430 TQ	ORBLS	10/01-12/01
	South Carolina	Y	20010 FQ	30310 AW	53080 TQ	SCBLS	10/01-12/01
	Texas	Y	21790 FQ	37040 AW	50010 TQ	TXBLS	10/01-12/01
	Virginia	Y	29940 FQ	42730 AW	60160 TQ	VABLS	10/01-12/01
	Wisconsin	Y	27130 FQ	42640 AW	61720 TQ	WIBLS	10/01-12/01
Translator							
Arabic languages, Government employers (FBI)	United States	H		27.00-38.00 AW		NYT2	1/00-1/01
Arabic languages, Private-sector employers	United States	H		150.00-220.00 AW		NYT2	1/00-1/01
Transportation Attendant							
Except Flight Attendant and Baggage	Arizona	H	6.79 FQ	8.85 AW	12.60 TQ	AZBLS	10/01-12/01
Except Flight Attendant and Baggage	Arkansas	H	5.92 FQ	7.96 AW	11.22 TQ	ARBLS	10/01-12/01
Except Flight Attendant and Baggage	California	H	7.15 FQ	11.52 AW	16.82 TQ	CABLS	10/01-12/01
Except Flight Attendant and Baggage	Colorado	H	5.99 FQ	8.02 AW	11.35 TQ	COBLS	10/01-12/01
Except Flight Attendant and Baggage	Connecticut	H	6.75 FQ	9.57 AW	11.42 TQ	CTBLS	10/01-12/01
Except Flight Attendant and Baggage	Delaware	H	6.88 FQ	9.28 AW	12.81 TQ	DEBLS	10/01-12/01
Except Flight Attendant and Baggage	Florida	H	5.71 FQ	8.65 AW	12.70 TQ	FLBLS	10/01-12/01
Except Flight Attendant and Baggage	Georgia	H	5.63 FQ	10.20 AW	17.13 TQ	GABLS	10/01-12/01
Except Flight Attendant and Baggage	Hawaii	H	6.16 FQ	9.53 AW	13.42 TQ	HIBLS	10/01-12/01
Except Flight Attendant and Baggage	Illinois	H	6.40 FQ	10.18 AW	15.50 TQ	ILBLS	10/01-12/01
Except Flight Attendant and Baggage	Indiana	H	6.62 FQ	13.68 AW	19.44 TQ	INBLS	10/01-12/01
Except Flight Attendant and Baggage	Louisiana	H	5.59 FQ	7.13 AW	12.02 TQ	LABLS	10/01-12/01
Except Flight Attendant and Baggage	Maine	H	7.65 FQ	9.50 AW	10.94 TQ	MEBLS	10/01-12/01
Except Flight Attendant and Baggage	Maryland	H	7.64 FQ	14.93 AW	20.90 TQ	MDBLS	10/01-12/01
Except Flight Attendant and Baggage	Massachusetts	H	6.85 FQ	9.56 AW	17.31 TQ	MABLS	10/01-12/01
Except Flight Attendant and Baggage	Michigan	H	6.87 FQ	10.17 AW	12.68 TQ	MIBLS	10/01-12/01
Except Flight Attendant and Baggage	Minnesota	H	8.47 FQ	13.14 AW	17.00 TQ	MNBLS	10/01-12/01
Except Flight Attendant and Baggage	Missouri	H	6.14 FQ	9.82 AW	16.09 TQ	MOBLS	10/01-12/01
Except Flight Attendant and Baggage	Montana	H	6.22 FQ	11.96 AW	18.29 TQ	MTBLS	10/01-12/01
Except Flight Attendant and Baggage	New Jersey	H	5.72 FQ	7.35 AW	8.82 TQ	NJBLS	10/01-12/01
Except Flight Attendant and Baggage	New Mexico	H	6.96 FQ	9.30 AW	11.21 TQ	NMBLS	10/01-12/01
Except Flight Attendant and Baggage	New York	H	6.67 FQ	9.95 AW	15.56 TQ	NYBLS	10/01-12/01
Except Flight Attendant and Baggage	North Carolina	H	6.52 FQ	11.98 AW	18.95 TQ	NCBLS	10/01-12/01
Except Flight Attendant and Baggage	Ohio	H	5.93 FQ	7.60 AW	10.24 TQ	OHBLS	10/01-12/01
Except Flight Attendant and Baggage	Oklahoma	H	6.42 FQ	8.34 AW	10.75 TQ	OKBLS	10/01-12/01
Except Flight Attendant and Baggage	Pennsylvania	H	6.16 FQ	9.43 AW	13.43 TQ	PABLS	10/01-12/01
Except Flight Attendant and Baggage	South Carolina	H	7.23 FQ	9.55 AW	13.56 TQ	SCBLS	10/01-12/01
Except Flight Attendant and Baggage	Tennessee	H	5.65 FQ	8.02 AW	11.74 TQ	TNBLS	10/01-12/01
Except Flight Attendant and Baggage	Texas	H	5.66 FQ	8.59 AW	14.17 TQ	TXBLS	10/01-12/01
Except Flight Attendant and Baggage	Utah	H	5.93 FQ	8.59 AW	12.93 TQ	UTBLS	10/01-12/01
Except Flight Attendant and Baggage	Virginia	H	5.63 FQ	10.54 AW	16.68 TQ	VABLS	10/01-12/01
Except Flight Attendant and Baggage	Washington	H	7.14 FQ	11.85 AW	16.60 TQ	WABLS	10/01-12/01
Except Flight Attendant and Baggage	Wisconsin	H	5.55 FQ	7.83 AW	10.62 TQ	WIBLS	10/01-12/01
Except Flight Attendant and Baggage	Puerto Rico	H	5.45 FQ	6.81 AW	8.76 TQ	PRBLS	10/01-12/01
Transportation Inspector	Alabama	H	9.28 FQ	21.85 AW	35.72 TQ	ALBLS	10/01-12/01
	Alaska	H	19.02 FQ	28.75 AW	39.55 TQ	AKBLS	10/01-12/01
	Arizona	H	13.73 FQ	23.31 AW	37.88 TQ	AZBLS	10/01-12/01
	Arkansas	H	13.07 FQ	21.65 AW	33.81 TQ	ARBLS	10/01-12/01
	California	H	14.87 FQ	25.15 AW	37.63 TQ	CABLS	10/01-12/01
	Colorado	H	13.14 FQ	23.43 AW	39.16 TQ	COBLS	10/01-12/01
	Connecticut	H	9.59 FQ	21.78 AW	32.12 TQ	CTBLS	10/01-12/01
	Florida	H	8.39 FQ	20.54 AW	37.07 TQ	FLBLS	10/01-12/01
	Georgia	H	9.65 FQ	24.94 AW	35.64 TQ	GABLS	10/01-12/01
	Hawaii	H	14.96 FQ	24.26 AW	36.35 TQ	HIBLS	10/01-12/01
	Illinois	H	8.46 FQ	19.33 AW	32.79 TQ	ILBLS	10/01-12/01
	Indiana	H	14.24 FQ	22.79 AW	32.01 TQ	INBLS	10/01-12/01
	Iowa	H	13.92 FQ	25.38 AW	37.23 TQ	IABLS	10/01-12/01
	Kentucky	H	7.81 FQ	17.43 AW	32.82 TQ	KYBLS	10/01-12/01
	Louisiana	H	9.65 FQ	17.90 AW	29.61 TQ	LABLS	10/01-12/01
	Maine	H	13.98 FQ	26.77 AW	40.90 TQ	MEBLS	10/01-12/01
	Maryland	H	13.79 FQ	21.40 AW	33.25 TQ	MDBLS	10/01-12/01
	Michigan	H	8.77 FQ	22.96 AW	37.75 TQ	MIBLS	10/01-12/01
	Minnesota	H	9.28 FQ	17.51 AW	35.03 TQ	MNBLS	10/01-12/01
	Mississippi	H	10.17 FQ	19.78 AW	30.95 TQ	MSBLS	10/01-12/01
	Missouri	H	11.17 FQ	22.42 AW	36.97 TQ	MOBLS	10/01-12/01
	Montana	H	14.53 FQ	28.34 AW	40.78 TQ	MTBLS	10/01-12/01
	Nevada	H	14.70 FQ	25.94 AW	40.57 TQ	NVBLS	10/01-12/01
	New Hampshire	H	13.55 FQ	16.78 AW	20.70 TQ	NHBLS	10/01-12/01

AAW	Average annual wage	AOH	Average offered, high	ASH	Average starting, high	H	Hourly	M	Monthly	S	Special: hourly and annual
AE	Average entry wage	AOL	Average offered, low	ASL	Average starting, low	HI	Highest wage paid	MTC	Median total compensation	TQ	Third quartile wage
AEX	Average experienced wage	APH	Average pay, high range	AW	Average wage paid	HR	High end range	MW	Median wage paid	W	Weekly
AO	Average offered	APL	Average pay, low range	FQ	First quartile wage	LR	Low end range	SQ	Second quartile wage	Y	Yearly

Occupation/Type/Industry	Location	Per	Low	Mid	High	Source	Date
Transportation Inspector	New Jersey	H	15.89 FQ	24.01 AW	30.35 TQ	NJBLS	10/01-12/01
	New Mexico	H	11.34 FQ	17.55 AW	28.82 TQ	NMBLS	10/01-12/01
	North Carolina	H	8.47 FQ	19.13 AW	32.65 TQ	NCBLS	10/01-12/01
	North Dakota	H	13.19 FQ	20.05 AW	32.10 TQ	NDBLS	10/01-12/01
	Ohio	H	7.94 FQ	17.37 AW	30.72 TQ	OHBLS	10/01-12/01
	Oklahoma	H	10.74 FQ	27.73 AW	43.05 TQ	OKBLS	10/01-12/01
	Oregon	H	13.74 FQ	20.95 AW	32.97 TQ	ORBLS	10/01-12/01
	Pennsylvania	H	6.55 FQ	21.70 AW	34.31 TQ	PABLS	10/01-12/01
	South Carolina	H	7.41 FQ	14.05 AW	27.91 TQ	SCBLS	10/01-12/01
	South Dakota	H	11.05 FQ	16.23 AW	28.53 TQ	SDBLS	10/01-12/01
	Tennessee	H	11.84 FQ	21.97 AW	36.09 TQ	TNBLS	10/01-12/01
	Texas	H	9.00 FQ	21.34 AW	35.58 TQ	TXBLS	10/01-12/01
	Utah	H	11.89 FQ	20.43 AW	35.08 TQ	UTBLS	10/01-12/01
	Virginia	H	13.50 FQ	22.37 AW	35.62 TQ	VABLS	10/01-12/01
	Washington	H	18.19 FQ	25.16 AW	33.23 TQ	WABLS	10/01-12/01
	West Virginia	H	11.11 FQ	18.69 AW	29.10 TQ	WVBLS	10/01-12/01
	Wisconsin	H	11.58 FQ	22.44 AW	34.49 TQ	WIBLS	10/01-12/01
	Wyoming	H	14.47 FQ	21.14 AW	31.42 TQ	WYBLS	10/01-12/01
	Puerto Rico	H	8.14 FQ	18.96 AW	33.59 TQ	PRBLS	10/01-12/01
Transportation Manager							
Environment	United States	Y		58500 AW		SAFEDIR	2001
Environment	Midwest	Y		56750 AW		SAFEDIR	2001
Environment	Northeast	Y		60000 AW		SAFEDIR	2001
Environment	South	Y		59167 AW		SAFEDIR	2001
Environment	West	Y		55800 AW		SAFEDIR	2001
Transportation, Storage, and Distribution Manager	Alabama	Y	28620 FQ	50080 AW	76620 TQ	ALBLS	10/01-12/01
	Birmingham MSA, AL	Y	30500 FQ	48660 AW	73360 TQ	ALBLS	10/01-12/01
	Huntsville MSA, AL	Y	25270 FQ	48080 AW	79850 TQ	ALBLS	10/01-12/01
	Mobile MSA, AL	Y	29340 FQ	51200 AW	82170 TQ	ALBLS	10/01-12/01
	Montgomery MSA, AL	Y	30660 FQ	54010 AW	81650 TQ	ALBLS	10/01-12/01
	Alaska	Y	35920 FQ	65820 AW	109810 TQ	AKBLS	10/01-12/01
	Anchorage MSA, AK	Y	28450 FQ	55710 AW	86570 TQ	AKBLS	10/01-12/01
	Arizona	Y	33780 FQ	57950 AW	91730 TQ	AZBLS	10/01-12/01
	Phoenix-Mesa MSA, AZ	Y	33730 FQ	58240 AW	93600 TQ	AZBLS	10/01-12/01
	Tucson MSA, AZ	Y	37980 FQ	62060 AW	92500 TQ	AZBLS	10/01-12/01
	Arkansas	Y	31460 FQ	62000 AW	99340 TQ	ARBLS	10/01-12/01
	Fayetteville-Springdale-Rogers MSA, AR	Y	26380 FQ	61150 AW		ARBLS	10/01-12/01
	Fort Smith MSA, AR-OK	Y	26200 FQ	48060 AW	69410 TQ	ARBLS	10/01-12/01
	Little Rock-North Little Rock MSA, AR	Y	39760 FQ	66380 AW	110420 TQ	ARBLS	10/01-12/01
	California	Y	37610 FQ	64380 AW	97610 TQ	CABLS	10/01-12/01
	Bakersfield MSA, CA	Y	35330 FQ	61820 AW	91550 TQ	CABLS	10/01-12/01
	Chico-Paradise MSA, CA	Y	28830 FQ	59110 AW	91050 TQ	CABLS	10/01-12/01
	Fresno MSA, CA	Y	35420 FQ	62050 AW	93550 TQ	CABLS	10/01-12/01
	Los Angeles-Long Beach PMSA, CA	Y	36480 FQ	64730 AW	99380 TQ	CABLS	10/01-12/01
	Merced MSA, CA	Y	41670 FQ	65110 AW	94230 TQ	CABLS	10/01-12/01
	Modesto MSA, CA	Y	18220 FQ	49360 AW	74100 TQ	CABLS	10/01-12/01
	Oakland PMSA, CA	Y	42800 FQ	68110 AW	103490 TQ	CABLS	10/01-12/01
	Orange County PMSA, CA	Y	40830 FQ	71050 AW	132510 TQ	CABLS	10/01-12/01
	Redding MSA, CA	Y	41400 FQ	60280 AW	81510 TQ	CABLS	10/01-12/01
	Riverside-San Bernardino PMSA, CA	Y	38530 FQ	62860 AW	91290 TQ	CABLS	10/01-12/01
	Sacramento PMSA, CA	Y	36230 FQ	59600 AW	90580 TQ	CABLS	10/01-12/01
	Salinas MSA, CA	Y	40130 FQ	66960 AW	113120 TQ	CABLS	10/01-12/01
	San Diego MSA, CA	Y	33070 FQ	60080 AW	93120 TQ	CABLS	10/01-12/01
	San Francisco PMSA, CA	Y	38900 FQ	63270 AW	93030 TQ	CABLS	10/01-12/01
	San Jose PMSA, CA	Y	43680 FQ	71350 AW	111930 TQ	CABLS	10/01-12/01
	San Luis Obispo-Atascadero-Paso Robles MSA, CA	Y	35110 FQ	57570 AW	88450 TQ	CABLS	10/01-12/01
	Santa Barbara-Santa Maria-Lompoc MSA, CA	Y	30070 FQ	59050 AW	88630 TQ	CABLS	10/01-12/01
	Santa Cruz-Watsonville PMSA, CA	Y	40570 FQ	61560 AW	96720 TQ	CABLS	10/01-12/01
	Santa Rosa PMSA, CA	Y	42210 FQ	63770 AW	95280 TQ	CABLS	10/01-12/01
	Stockton-Lodi MSA, CA	Y	37590 FQ	57450 AW	85270 TQ	CABLS	10/01-12/01
	Vallejo-Fairfield-Napa PMSA, CA	Y	40070 FQ	62890 AW	92580 TQ	CABLS	10/01-12/01

AAW	Average annual wage	AOH	Average offered, high	ASH	Average starting, high	H	Hourly	M	Monthly	S	Special: hourly and annual
AE	Average entry wage	AOL	Average offered, low	ASL	Average starting, low	HI	Highest wage paid	MTC	Median total compensation	TQ	Third quartile wage
AEX	Average experienced wage	APH	Average pay, high range	AW	Average wage paid	HR	High end range	MW	Median wage paid	W	Weekly
AO	Average offered	APL	Average pay, low range	FQ	First quartile wage	LR	Low end range	SQ	Second quartile wage	Y	Yearly

Occupation/Type/Industry	Location	Per	Low	Mid	High	Source	Date
Transportation, Storage, and Distribution Manager	Ventura PMSA, CA	Y	39400 FQ	63610 AW	100200 TQ	CABLS	10/01-12/01
	Visalia-Tulare-Porterville MSA, CA	Y	31670 FQ	51910 AW	76930 TQ	CABLS	10/01-12/01
	Colorado	Y	28710 FQ	60580 AW	96140 TQ	COBLS	10/01-12/01
	Boulder-Longmont PMSA, CO	Y	38870 FQ	65170 AW	106280 TQ	COBLS	10/01-12/01
	Colorado Springs MSA, CO	Y	36590 FQ	73620 AW	116480 TQ	COBLS	10/01-12/01
	Denver PMSA, CO	Y	29570 FQ	59910 AW	92060 TQ	COBLS	10/01-12/01
	Fort Collins-Loveland MSA, CO	Y	38780 FQ	69430 AW	114570 TQ	COBLS	10/01-12/01
	Greeley PMSA, CO	Y	30890 FQ	53310 AW	80040 TQ	COBLS	10/01-12/01
	Connecticut	Y	41520 FQ	72600 AW	119260 TQ	CTBLS	10/01-12/01
	Bridgeport PMSA, CT	Y	37580 FQ	69460 AW	116410 TQ	CTBLS	10/01-12/01
	Danbury PMSA, CT	Y	38250 FQ	69030 AW	111330 TQ	CTBLS	10/01-12/01
	Hartford MSA, CT	Y	44850 FQ	76740 AW	131490 TQ	CTBLS	10/01-12/01
	New Haven-Meriden PMSA, CT	Y	41420 FQ	62620 AW	98810 TQ	CTBLS	10/01-12/01
	New London-Norwich MSA, CT-RI	Y	36810 FQ	66590 AW	115390 TQ	CTBLS	10/01-12/01
	Stamford-Norwalk PMSA, CT	Y	45210 FQ	80420 AW	143190 TQ	CTBLS	10/01-12/01
	Waterbury PMSA, CT	Y	40220 FQ	66040 AW	102150 TQ	CTBLS	10/01-12/01
	Delaware	Y	36160 FQ	62080 AW	91880 TQ	DEBLS	10/01-12/01
	Wilmington-Newark PMSA, DE-MD	Y	41160 FQ	63660 AW	92090 TQ	DEBLS	10/01-12/01
	District of Columbia	Y	48200 FQ	80220 AW	112730 TQ	DCBLS	10/01-12/01
	Washington PMSA, DC-MD-VA-WV	Y	35080 FQ	68490 AW	108090 TQ	DCBLS	10/01-12/01
	Florida	Y	33390 FQ	62300 AW	99850 TQ	FLBLS	10/01-12/01
	Daytona Beach MSA, FL	Y	29150 FQ	53470 AW	83790 TQ	FLBLS	10/01-12/01
	Fort Lauderdale PMSA, FL	Y	35200 FQ	69010 AW	116310 TQ	FLBLS	10/01-12/01
	Fort Myers-Cape Coral MSA, FL	Y	28610 FQ	53750 AW	92260 TQ	FLBLS	10/01-12/01
	Fort Pierce-Port St. Lucie MSA, FL	Y	31320 FQ	52370 AW	80290 TQ	FLBLS	10/01-12/01
	Fort Walton Beach MSA, FL	Y	27010 FQ	50240 AW	72410 TQ	FLBLS	10/01-12/01
	Gainesville MSA, FL	Y	35290 FQ	63370 AW	95230 TQ	FLBLS	10/01-12/01
	Jacksonville MSA, FL	Y	33820 FQ	59620 AW	94160 TQ	FLBLS	10/01-12/01
	Lakeland-Winter Haven MSA, FL	Y	31430 FQ	56540 AW	92300 TQ	FLBLS	10/01-12/01
	Melbourne-Titusville-Palm Bay MSA, FL	Y	35470 FQ	57590 AW	81720 TQ	FLBLS	10/01-12/01
	Miami PMSA, FL	Y	33410 FQ	62080 AW	98400 TQ	FLBLS	10/01-12/01
	Naples MSA, FL	Y	36780 FQ	62510 AW	87880 TQ	FLBLS	10/01-12/01
	Ocala MSA, FL	Y	31400 FQ	67920 AW	114400 TQ	FLBLS	10/01-12/01
	Orlando MSA, FL	Y	35900 FQ	62490 AW	103030 TQ	FLBLS	10/01-12/01
	Pensacola MSA, FL	Y	27720 FQ	59480 AW	97620 TQ	FLBLS	10/01-12/01
	Sarasota-Bradenton MSA, FL	Y	33930 FQ	60440 AW	97810 TQ	FLBLS	10/01-12/01
	Tallahassee MSA, FL	Y	35990 FQ	70930 AW	113380 TQ	FLBLS	10/01-12/01
	Tampa-St. Petersburg-Clearwater MSA, FL	Y	36360 FQ	66090 AW	105020 TQ	FLBLS	10/01-12/01
	West Palm Beach-Boca Raton MSA, FL	Y	33150 FQ	64220 AW	104800 TQ	FLBLS	10/01-12/01
	Georgia	Y	36220 FQ	61600 AW	92510 TQ	GABLS	10/01-12/01
	Atlanta MSA, GA	Y	40330 FQ	66840 AW	99110 TQ	GABLS	10/01-12/01
	Columbus MSA, GA-AL	Y	24330 FQ	43970 AW	66390 TQ	GABLS	10/01-12/01
	Macon MSA, GA	Y	36380 FQ	55560 AW	83140 TQ	GABLS	10/01-12/01
	Savannah MSA, GA	Y	35940 FQ	58770 AW	83010 TQ	GABLS	10/01-12/01
	Hawaii	Y	35790 FQ	58900 AW	87960 TQ	HIBLS	10/01-12/01
	Honolulu MSA, HI	Y	38770 FQ	61280 AW	89500 TQ	HIBLS	10/01-12/01
	Idaho	Y	27830 FQ	55400 AW	90490 TQ	IDBLS	10/01-12/01
	Boise City MSA, ID	Y	22130 FQ	62900 AW	108290 TQ	IDBLS	10/01-12/01
	Illinois	Y	32890 FQ	57050 AW	87580 TQ	ILBLS	10/01-12/01
	Champaign-Urbana MSA, IL	Y	38650 FQ	61840 AW	89450 TQ	ILBLS	10/01-12/01
	Chicago PMSA, IL	Y	34910 FQ	57510 AW	87760 TQ	ILBLS	10/01-12/01
	Peoria-Pekin MSA, IL	Y	30540 FQ	52570 AW	73720 TQ	ILBLS	10/01-12/01
	Rockford MSA, IL	Y	20170 FQ	47760 AW	80440 TQ	ILBLS	10/01-12/01
	Indiana	Y	33880 FQ	57720 AW	87050 TQ	INBLS	10/01-12/01
	Elkhart-Goshen MSA, IN	Y	31710 FQ	49960 AW	71140 TQ	INBLS	10/01-12/01
	Evansville-Henderson MSA, IN-KY	Y	36330 FQ	56200 AW	74460 TQ	INBLS	10/01-12/01
	Fort Wayne MSA, IN	Y	38420 FQ	60640 AW	91450 TQ	INBLS	10/01-12/01
	Gary PMSA, IN	Y	31060 FQ	56580 AW	84780 TQ	INBLS	10/01-12/01

AAW	Average annual wage	AOH	Average offered, high	ASH	Average starting, high	H	Hourly	M	Monthly	S	Special: hourly and annual
AE	Average entry wage	AOL	Average offered, low	ASL	Average starting, low	HI	Highest wage paid	MTC	Median total compensation	TQ	Third quartile wage
AEX	Average experienced wage	APH	Average pay, high range	AW	Average wage paid	HR	High end range	MW	Median wage paid	W	Weekly
AO	Average offered	APL	Average pay, low range	FQ	First quartile wage	LR	Low end range	SQ	Second quartile wage	Y	Yearly

Occupation/Type/Industry	Location	Per	Low	Mid	High	Source	Date
Transportation, Storage, and Distribution Manager	Indianapolis MSA, IN	Y	36440 FQ	60400 AW	88950 TQ	INBLS	10/01-12/01
	Lafayette MSA, IN	Y	37790 FQ	67060 AW	103020 TQ	INBLS	10/01-12/01
	South Bend MSA, IN	Y	33580 FQ	59380 AW	92090 TQ	INBLS	10/01-12/01
	Iowa	Y	30540 FQ	55940 AW	86850 TQ	IABLS	10/01-12/01
	Cedar Rapids MSA, IA	Y	34940 FQ	62890 AW	91320 TQ	IABLS	10/01-12/01
	Davenport-Moline-Rock Island MSA, IA-IL	Y	33390 FQ	60810 AW	92140 TQ	IABLS	10/01-12/01
	Des Moines MSA, IA	Y	29890 FQ	55380 AW	86590 TQ	IABLS	10/01-12/01
	Kansas	Y	31600 FQ	58610 AW	93280 TQ	KSBLS	10/01-12/01
	Topeka MSA, KS	Y	37930 FQ	68060 AW	92840 TQ	KSBLS	10/01-12/01
	Wichita MSA, KS	Y	35550 FQ	57100 AW	88830 TQ	KSBLS	10/01-12/01
	Kentucky	Y	31580 FQ	54980 AW	85070 TQ	KYBLS	10/01-12/01
	Lexington MSA, KY	Y	33030 FQ	58060 AW	89170 TQ	KYBLS	10/01-12/01
	Louisville MSA, KY-IN	Y	31540 FQ	56110 AW	87780 TQ	KYBLS	10/01-12/01
	Louisiana	Y	27340 FQ	50360 AW	80470 TQ	LABLS	10/01-12/01
	Baton Rouge MSA, LA	Y	26660 FQ	48920 AW	73570 TQ	LABLS	10/01-12/01
	Houma MSA, LA	Y	28650 FQ	50810 AW	81120 TQ	LABLS	10/01-12/01
	Lafayette MSA, LA	Y	22850 FQ	45270 AW	73770 TQ	LABLS	10/01-12/01
	Lake Charles MSA, LA	Y	34140 FQ	59040 AW	95710 TQ	LABLS	10/01-12/01
	New Orleans MSA, LA	Y	29830 FQ	49420 AW	77600 TQ	LABLS	10/01-12/01
	Shreveport-Bossier City MSA, LA	Y	22080 FQ	50670 AW	90660 TQ	LABLS	10/01-12/01
	Maine	Y	26700 FQ	47450 AW	71600 TQ	MEBLS	10/01-12/01
	Portland MSA, ME	Y	31920 FQ	51970 AW	74030 TQ	MEBLS	10/01-12/01
	Maryland	Y	33940 FQ	63320 AW	100370 TQ	MDBLS	10/01-12/01
	Baltimore PMSA, MD	Y	35210 FQ	59100 AW	90060 TQ	MDBLS	10/01-12/01
	Massachusetts	Y	35490 FQ	61830 AW	92890 TQ	MABLS	10/01-12/01
	Boston PMSA, MA-NH	Y	38300 FQ	64600 AW	96960 TQ	MABLS	10/01-12/01
	Brockton PMSA, MA	Y	39950 FQ	59940 AW	89080 TQ	MABLS	10/01-12/01
	Lawrence PMSA, MA-NH	Y	34230 FQ	59810 AW	86060 TQ	MABLS	10/01-12/01
	Lowell PMSA, MA-NH	Y	32520 FQ	53770 AW	74460 TQ	MABLS	10/01-12/01
	New Bedford PMSA, MA	Y	38930 FQ	56350 AW	76220 TQ	MABLS	10/01-12/01
	Springfield MSA, MA	Y	35090 FQ	60650 AW	100040 TQ	MABLS	10/01-12/01
	Worcester PMSA, MA-CT	Y	33320 FQ	60050 AW	88560 TQ	MABLS	10/01-12/01
	Michigan	Y	43000 FQ	69860 AW	105400 TQ	MIBLS	10/01-12/01
	Ann Arbor PMSA, MI	Y	45000 FQ	70610 AW	92420 TQ	MIBLS	10/01-12/01
	Detroit PMSA, MI	Y	45960 FQ	72450 AW	109100 TQ	MIBLS	10/01-12/01
	Flint PMSA, MI	Y	46930 FQ	71910 AW	94550 TQ	MIBLS	10/01-12/01
	Grand Rapids-Muskegon-Holland MSA, MI	Y	44720 FQ	70170 AW	103000 TQ	MIBLS	10/01-12/01
	Kalamazoo-Battle Creek MSA, MI	Y	40960 FQ	69690 AW	114110 TQ	MIBLS	10/01-12/01
	Lansing-East Lansing MSA, MI	Y	41090 FQ	61560 AW	88310 TQ	MIBLS	10/01-12/01
	Saginaw-Bay City-Midland MSA, MI	Y	45500 FQ	77940 AW	119050 TQ	MIBLS	10/01-12/01
	Minnesota	Y	39960 FQ	65050 AW	93950 TQ	MNBLS	10/01-12/01
	Duluth-Superior MSA, MN-WI	Y	32600 FQ	58540 AW	98390 TQ	MNBLS	10/01-12/01
	Minneapolis-St. Paul MSA, MN-WI	Y	40290 FQ	66030 AW	96680 TQ	MNBLS	10/01-12/01
	St. Cloud MSA, MN	Y	45180 FQ	57690 AW	73520 TQ	MNBLS	10/01-12/01
	Mississippi	Y	25140 FQ	43300 AW	69880 TQ	MSBLS	10/01-12/01
	Biloxi-Gulfport-Pascagoula MSA, MS	Y	21700 FQ	43760 AW	73200 TQ	MSBLS	10/01-12/01
	Jackson MSA, MS	Y	26120 FQ	47230 AW	76260 TQ	MSBLS	10/01-12/01
	Missouri	Y	30190 FQ	56970 AW	91620 TQ	MOBLS	10/01-12/01
	Kansas City MSA, MO-KS	Y	33660 FQ	60170 AW	98750 TQ	MOBLS	10/01-12/01
	St. Louis MSA, MO-IL	Y	36770 FQ	62720 AW	100860 TQ	MOBLS	10/01-12/01
	Springfield MSA, MO	Y	34220 FQ	62350 AW	91310 TQ	MOBLS	10/01-12/01
	Montana	Y	26320 FQ	51810 AW	85480 TQ	MTBLS	10/01-12/01
	Billings MSA, MT	Y	28420 FQ	49620 AW	70590 TQ	MTBLS	10/01-12/01
	Nebraska	Y	31260 FQ	65140 AW	105330 TQ	NEBLS	10/01-12/01
	Lincoln MSA, NE	Y	29720 FQ	49670 AW	73210 TQ	NEBLS	10/01-12/01
	Omaha MSA, NE-IA	Y	33710 FQ	58950 AW	92500 TQ	NEBLS	10/01-12/01
	Nevada	Y	34620 FQ	56580 AW	85920 TQ	NVBLS	10/01-12/01
	Las Vegas MSA, NV-AZ	Y	33010 FQ	56910 AW	88450 TQ	NVBLS	10/01-12/01
	Reno MSA, NV	Y	35360 FQ	55940 AW	80230 TQ	NVBLS	10/01-12/01
	New Hampshire	Y	32990 FQ	59250 AW	91020 TQ	NHBLS	10/01-12/01
	Manchester PMSA, NH	Y	33590 FQ	55170 AW	83930 TQ	NHBLS	10/01-12/01
	Nashua PMSA, NH	Y	29840 FQ	63180 AW	95960 TQ	NHBLS	10/01-12/01
	Portsmouth-Rochester PMSA, NH-ME	Y	32060 FQ	57870 AW	93600 TQ	NHBLS	10/01-12/01

AAW	Average annual wage	**AOH**	Average offered, high	**ASH**	Average starting, high	**H**	Hourly	**M**	Monthly	**S**	Special: hourly and annual
AE	Average entry wage	**AOL**	Average offered, low	**ASL**	Average starting, low	**HI**	Highest wage paid	**MTC**	Median total compensation	**TQ**	Third quartile wage
AEX	Average experienced wage	**APH**	Average pay, high range	**AW**	Average wage paid	**HR**	High end range	**MW**	Median wage paid	**W**	Weekly
AO	Average offered	**APL**	Average pay, low range	**FQ**	First quartile wage	**LR**	Low end range	**SQ**	Second quartile wage	**Y**	Yearly

Occupation/Type/Industry	Location	Per	Low	Mid	High	Source	Date
Transportation, Storage, and Distribution Manager	New Jersey	Y	48890 FQ	75630 AW	113580 TQ	NJBLS	10/01-12/01
	Atlantic-Cape May PMSA, NJ	Y	40730 FQ	66530 AW	93420 TQ	NJBLS	10/01-12/01
	Bergen-Passaic PMSA, NJ	Y	48640 FQ	76000 AW	129290 TQ	NJBLS	10/01-12/01
	Jersey City PMSA, NJ	Y	48840 FQ	79390 AW	122020 TQ	NJBLS	10/01-12/01
	Middlesex-Somerset-Hunterdon PMSA, NJ	Y	47870 FQ	76410 AW	114530 TQ	NJBLS	10/01-12/01
	Monmouth-Ocean PMSA, NJ	Y	47980 FQ	71200 AW	98060 TQ	NJBLS	10/01-12/01
	Newark PMSA, NJ	Y	50750 FQ	75530 AW	111050 TQ	NJBLS	10/01-12/01
	Trenton PMSA, NJ	Y	59060 FQ	77640 AW	92640 TQ	NJBLS	10/01-12/01
	New Mexico	Y	17300 FQ	49880 AW	94770 TQ	NMBLS	10/01-12/01
	Albuquerque MSA, NM	Y	28940 FQ	59950 AW	99810 TQ	NMBLS	10/01-12/01
	New York	Y	42720 FQ	74910 AW	127490 TQ	NYBLS	10/01-12/01
	Albany-Schenectady-Troy MSA, NY	Y	39920 FQ	70280 AW	103920 TQ	NYBLS	10/01-12/01
	Binghamton MSA, NY	Y	31790 FQ	61680 AW	105170 TQ	NYBLS	10/01-12/01
	Buffalo-Niagara Falls MSA, NY	Y	39340 FQ	64800 AW	92200 TQ	NYBLS	10/01-12/01
	Dutchess County PMSA, NY	Y	33580 FQ	64350 AW	122220 TQ	NYBLS	10/01-12/01
	Nassau-Suffolk PMSA, NY	Y	46060 FQ	78880 AW	135530 TQ	NYBLS	10/01-12/01
	New York PMSA, NY	Y	45330 FQ	79260 AW	144970 TQ	NYBLS	10/01-12/01
	Newburgh PMSA, NY-PA	Y	41560 FQ	69970 AW	112460 TQ	NYBLS	10/01-12/01
	Rochester MSA, NY	Y	39700 FQ	62820 AW	91260 TQ	NYBLS	10/01-12/01
	Syracuse MSA, NY	Y	35700 FQ	63410 AW	93150 TQ	NYBLS	10/01-12/01
	Utica-Rome MSA, NY	Y	33820 FQ	63490 AW	104430 TQ	NYBLS	10/01-12/01
	North Carolina	Y	32440 FQ	57860 AW	91700 TQ	NCBLS	10/01-12/01
	Asheville MSA, NC	Y	30110 FQ	46710 AW	58410 TQ	NCBLS	10/01-12/01
	Charlotte-Gastonia-Rock Hill MSA, NC-SC	Y	37150 FQ	63830 AW	104910 TQ	NCBLS	10/01-12/01
	Fayetteville MSA, NC	Y	28260 FQ	48990 AW	76500 TQ	NCBLS	10/01-12/01
	Greensboro-Winston-Salem-High Point MSA, NC	Y	33150 FQ	57370 AW	88000 TQ	NCBLS	10/01-12/01
	Hickory-Morganton-Lenoir MSA, NC	Y	30810 FQ	52500 AW	85090 TQ	NCBLS	10/01-12/01
	Raleigh-Durham-Chapel Hill MSA, NC	Y	36270 FQ	65610 AW	106850 TQ	NCBLS	10/01-12/01
	Wilmington MSA, NC	Y	28150 FQ	53550 AW	85230 TQ	NCBLS	10/01-12/01
	North Dakota	Y	25430 FQ	45750 AW	68120 TQ	NDBLS	10/01-12/01
	Fargo-Moorhead MSA, ND-MN	Y	29150 FQ	49620 AW	73340 TQ	NDBLS	10/01-12/01
	Ohio	Y	32250 FQ	57060 AW	87740 TQ	OHBLS	10/01-12/01
	Akron PMSA, OH	Y	36840 FQ	60910 AW	94200 TQ	OHBLS	10/01-12/01
	Canton-Massillon MSA, OH	Y	32990 FQ	54330 AW	84370 TQ	OHBLS	10/01-12/01
	Cincinnati PMSA, OH-KY-IN	Y	33110 FQ	57150 AW	86860 TQ	OHBLS	10/01-12/01
	Cleveland-Lorain-Elyria PMSA, OH	Y	35920 FQ	58940 AW	87790 TQ	OHBLS	10/01-12/01
	Columbus MSA, OH	Y	33260 FQ	62740 AW	108130 TQ	OHBLS	10/01-12/01
	Dayton-Springfield MSA, OH	Y	35010 FQ	57460 AW	86200 TQ	OHBLS	10/01-12/01
	Hamilton-Middletown PMSA, OH	Y	36800 FQ	56480 AW	75920 TQ	OHBLS	10/01-12/01
	Mansfield MSA, OH	Y	34350 FQ	55360 AW	85670 TQ	OHBLS	10/01-12/01
	Toledo MSA, OH	Y	34820 FQ	56070 AW	78530 TQ	OHBLS	10/01-12/01
	Youngstown-Warren MSA, OH	Y	30680 FQ	55690 AW	82550 TQ	OHBLS	10/01-12/01
	Oklahoma	Y	24370 FQ	53510 AW	86440 TQ	OKBLS	10/01-12/01
	Oklahoma City MSA, OK	Y	26090 FQ	56230 AW	93380 TQ	OKBLS	10/01-12/01
	Tulsa MSA, OK	Y	29470 FQ	55910 AW	85570 TQ	OKBLS	10/01-12/01
	Oregon	Y	37390 FQ	61620 AW	92160 TQ	ORBLS	10/01-12/01
	Eugene-Springfield MSA, OR	Y	36000 FQ	54510 AW	81720 TQ	ORBLS	10/01-12/01
	Medford-Ashland MSA, OR	Y	43560 FQ	63560 AW	84510 TQ	ORBLS	10/01-12/01
	Portland-Vancouver PMSA, OR-WA	Y	36130 FQ	61780 AW	94530 TQ	ORBLS	10/01-12/01
	Salem PMSA, OR	Y	39920 FQ	58900 AW	80730 TQ	ORBLS	10/01-12/01
	Pennsylvania	Y	34370 FQ	61970 AW	95460 TQ	PABLS	10/01-12/01
	Allentown-Bethlehem-Easton MSA, PA	Y	34600 FQ	63040 AW	95850 TQ	PABLS	10/01-12/01
	Erie MSA, PA	Y	30220 FQ	51220 AW	76810 TQ	PABLS	10/01-12/01
	Harrisburg-Lebanon-Carlisle MSA, PA	Y	33460 FQ	64510 AW	104290 TQ	PABLS	10/01-12/01
	Johnstown MSA, PA	Y	24450 FQ	56740 AW	108040 TQ	PABLS	10/01-12/01
	Lancaster MSA, PA	Y	33710 FQ	65470 AW	107600 TQ	PABLS	10/01-12/01
	Philadelphia PMSA, PA-NJ	Y	43010 FQ	68830 AW	101970 TQ	PABLS	10/01-12/01
	Pittsburgh MSA, PA	Y	30160 FQ	53490 AW	88630 TQ	PABLS	10/01-12/01

AAW	Average annual wage	**AOH**	Average offered, high	**ASH**	Average starting, high	**H**	Hourly	**M**	Monthly	**S**	Special: hourly and annual
AE	Average entry wage	**AOL**	Average offered, low	**ASL**	Average starting, low	**HI**	Highest wage paid	**MTC**	Median total compensation	**TQ**	Third quartile wage
AEX	Average experienced wage	**APH**	Average pay, high range	**AW**	Average wage paid	**HR**	High end range	**MW**	Median wage paid	**W**	Weekly
AO	Average offered	**APL**	Average pay, low range	**FQ**	First quartile wage	**LR**	Low end range	**SQ**	Second quartile wage	**Y**	Yearly

Occupation/Type/Industry	Location	Per	Low	Mid	High	Source	Date
Transportation, Storage, and Distribution Manager	Reading MSA, PA	Y	37840 FQ	57630 AW	84970 TQ	PABLS	10/01-12/01
	Scranton-Wilkes-Barre-Hazleton MSA, PA	Y	34160 FQ	55880 AW	83670 TQ	PABLS	10/01-12/01
	York MSA, PA	Y	37160 FQ	55750 AW	80430 TQ	PABLS	10/01-12/01
	Rhode Island	Y	41980 FQ	71280 AW	108510 TQ	RIBLS	10/01-12/01
	Providence-Fall River-Warwick MSA, RI-MA	Y	35660 FQ	66740 AW	106630 TQ	RIBLS	10/01-12/01
	South Carolina	Y	27870 FQ	58960 AW	97630 TQ	SCBLS	10/01-12/01
	Charleston-North Charleston MSA, SC	Y	30290 FQ	50890 AW	78470 TQ	SCBLS	10/01-12/01
	Columbia MSA, SC	Y	31850 FQ	62740 AW		SCBLS	10/01-12/01
	Greenville-Spartanburg-Anderson MSA, SC	Y	30080 FQ	49870 AW	80180 TQ	SCBLS	10/01-12/01
	Myrtle Beach MSA, SC	Y	16760 FQ	45350 AW	85160 TQ	SCBLS	10/01-12/01
	South Dakota	Y	40080 FQ	60200 AW	87130 TQ	SDBLS	10/01-12/01
	Sioux Falls MSA, SD	Y	39300 FQ	60180 AW	89140 TQ	SDBLS	10/01-12/01
	Tennessee	Y	28940 FQ	53970 AW	85060 TQ	TNBLS	10/01-12/01
	Chattanooga MSA, TN-GA	Y	29840 FQ	58500 AW	89380 TQ	TNBLS	10/01-12/01
	Clarksville-Hopkinsville MSA, TN-KY	Y	31210 FQ	46490 AW	72720 TQ	TNBLS	10/01-12/01
	Johnson City-Kingsport-Bristol MSA, TN-VA	Y	29460 FQ	50960 AW	77830 TQ	TNBLS	10/01-12/01
	Knoxville MSA, TN	Y	27360 FQ	49770 AW	74820 TQ	TNBLS	10/01-12/01
	Memphis MSA, TN-AR-MS	Y	34630 FQ	63330 AW	107240 TQ	TNBLS	10/01-12/01
	Nashville MSA, TN	Y	27040 FQ	50210 AW	71250 TQ	TNBLS	10/01-12/01
	Texas	Y	30390 FQ	59400 AW	97570 TQ	TXBLS	10/01-12/01
	Amarillo MSA, TX	Y	25460 FQ	50580 AW	88440 TQ	TXBLS	10/01-12/01
	Austin-San Marcos MSA, TX	Y	31530 FQ	56970 AW	92110 TQ	TXBLS	10/01-12/01
	Beaumont-Port Arthur MSA, TX	Y	36480 FQ	66230 AW	107060 TQ	TXBLS	10/01-12/01
	Brazoria PMSA, TX	Y	40110 FQ	61630 AW	87290 TQ	TXBLS	10/01-12/01
	Brownsville-Harlingen-San Benito MSA, TX	Y	26870 FQ	51010 AW	78350 TQ	TXBLS	10/01-12/01
	Corpus Christi MSA, TX	Y	31070 FQ	53590 AW	81670 TQ	TXBLS	10/01-12/01
	Dallas PMSA, TX	Y	34580 FQ	65860 AW	131110 TQ	TXBLS	10/01-12/01
	El Paso MSA, TX	Y	20490 FQ	42010 AW	71850 TQ	TXBLS	10/01-12/01
	Fort Worth-Arlington PMSA, TX	Y	29930 FQ	64950 AW	112160 TQ	TXBLS	10/01-12/01
	Galveston-Texas City PMSA, TX	Y	30970 FQ	62950 AW	126560 TQ	TXBLS	10/01-12/01
	Houston PMSA, TX	Y	36100 FQ	64760 AW	97690 TQ	TXBLS	10/01-12/01
	Killeen-Temple MSA, TX	Y	32130 FQ	51580 AW	73320 TQ	TXBLS	10/01-12/01
	Laredo MSA, TX	Y	23730 FQ	44290 AW	64710 TQ	TXBLS	10/01-12/01
	Longview-Marshall MSA, TX	Y	31490 FQ	57340 AW	92460 TQ	TXBLS	10/01-12/01
	Lubbock MSA, TX	Y	20840 FQ	49390 AW	74460 TQ	TXBLS	10/01-12/01
	McAllen-Edinburg-Mission MSA, TX	Y	29210 FQ	57270 AW	94280 TQ	TXBLS	10/01-12/01
	Odessa-Midland MSA, TX	Y	30300 FQ	54050 AW	80420 TQ	TXBLS	10/01-12/01
	San Antonio MSA, TX	Y	25610 FQ	49470 AW	81260 TQ	TXBLS	10/01-12/01
	Waco MSA, TX	Y	23040 FQ	51400 AW	91850 TQ	TXBLS	10/01-12/01
	Utah	Y	32930 FQ	56630 AW	87200 TQ	UTBLS	10/01-12/01
	Provo-Orem MSA, UT	Y	24850 FQ	47220 AW	67970 TQ	UTBLS	10/01-12/01
	Salt Lake City-Ogden MSA, UT	Y	35500 FQ	58360 AW	88440 TQ	UTBLS	10/01-12/01
	Vermont	Y	46530 FQ	74340 AW	137300 TQ	VTBLS	10/01-12/01
	Burlington MSA, VT	Y	49150 FQ	72570 AW	117680 TQ	VTBLS	10/01-12/01
	Virginia	Y	32290 FQ	58650 AW	90770 TQ	VABLS	10/01-12/01
	Lynchburg MSA, VA	Y	24880 FQ	43990 AW	69460 TQ	VABLS	10/01-12/01
	Norfolk-Virginia Beach-Newport News MSA, VA-NC	Y	27850 FQ	54400 AW	83900 TQ	VABLS	10/01-12/01
	Richmond-Petersburg MSA, VA	Y	38570 FQ	58300 AW	85460 TQ	VABLS	10/01-12/01
	Roanoke MSA, VA	Y	35240 FQ	58400 AW	87230 TQ	VABLS	10/01-12/01
	Washington	Y	41870 FQ	69680 AW	108370 TQ	WABLS	10/01-12/01
	Bremerton PMSA, WA	Y	39330 FQ	57900 AW	84730 TQ	WABLS	10/01-12/01
	Olympia PMSA, WA	Y	35220 FQ	62880 AW	93350 TQ	WABLS	10/01-12/01
	Seattle-Bellevue-Everett PMSA, WA	Y	40240 FQ	71320 AW	125930 TQ	WABLS	10/01-12/01
	Spokane MSA, WA	Y	39790 FQ	57960 AW	81220 TQ	WABLS	10/01-12/01
	Tacoma PMSA, WA	Y	44420 FQ	66380 AW	92000 TQ	WABLS	10/01-12/01

AAW Average annual wage **AE** Average entry wage **AEX** Average experienced wage **AO** Average offered **AOH** Average offered, high **AOL** Average offered, low **APH** Average pay, high range **APL** Average pay, low range **ASH** Average starting, high **ASL** Average starting, low **AW** Average wage paid **FQ** First quartile wage **H** Hourly **HI** Highest wage paid **HR** High end range **LR** Low end range **M** Monthly **MTC** Median total compensation **MW** Median wage paid **SQ** Second quartile wage **S** Special: hourly and annual **TQ** Third quartile wage **W** Weekly **Y** Yearly

Occupation/Type/Industry	Location	Per	Low	Mid	High	Source	Date
Transportation, Storage, and Distribution Manager	Yakima MSA, WA	Y	34710 FQ	53210 AW	73400 TQ	WABLS	10/01-12/01
	West Virginia	Y	29840 FQ	53720 AW	83120 TQ	WVBLS	10/01-12/01
	Charleston MSA, WV	Y	28910 FQ	52480 AW	83260 TQ	WVBLS	10/01-12/01
	Huntington-Ashland MSA, WV-KY-OH	Y	23620 FQ	53710 AW	83680 TQ	WVBLS	10/01-12/01
	Wisconsin	Y	32440 FQ	57160 AW	87290 TQ	WIBLS	10/01-12/01
	Appleton-Oshkosh-Neenah MSA, WI	Y	35350 FQ	59560 AW	88860 TQ	WIBLS	10/01-12/01
	Green Bay MSA, WI	Y	32490 FQ	60300 AW	89320 TQ	WIBLS	10/01-12/01
	Madison MSA, WI	Y	32120 FQ	54520 AW	85130 TQ	WIBLS	10/01-12/01
	Milwaukee-Waukesha PMSA, WI	Y	36880 FQ	59290 AW	88390 TQ	WIBLS	10/01-12/01
	Racine PMSA, WI	Y	39710 FQ	67340 AW	110310 TQ	WIBLS	10/01-12/01
	Wyoming	Y	28510 FQ	57810 AW	87940 TQ	WYBLS	10/01-12/01
	Cheyenne MSA, WY	Y	28250 FQ	50960 AW	74720 TQ	WYBLS	10/01-12/01
	Puerto Rico	Y	26890 FQ	50190 AW	81860 TQ	PRBLS	10/01-12/01
	Virgin Islands	Y	33230 FQ	49880 AW	67160 TQ	VIBLS	10/01-12/01
	Guam	Y	25090 FQ	46960 AW	77170 TQ	GUBLS	10/01-12/01
Travel Agent	Alabama	Y	17920 FQ	26320 AW	36070 TQ	ALBLS	10/01-12/01
	Birmingham MSA, AL	Y	20090 FQ	28330 AW	35790 TQ	ALBLS	10/01-12/01
	Huntsville MSA, AL	Y	18360 FQ	23630 AW	32350 TQ	ALBLS	10/01-12/01
	Mobile MSA, AL	Y	18270 FQ	33180 AW	57020 TQ	ALBLS	10/01-12/01
	Montgomery MSA, AL	Y	16510 FQ	25610 AW	36280 TQ	ALBLS	10/01-12/01
	Alaska	Y	18150 FQ	25130 AW	35770 TQ	AKBLS	10/01-12/01
	Anchorage MSA, AK	Y	18550 FQ	25120 AW	34480 TQ	AKBLS	10/01-12/01
	Arizona	Y	15140 FQ	21960 AW	30420 TQ	AZBLS	10/01-12/01
	Phoenix-Mesa MSA, AZ	Y	15320 FQ	21640 AW	28860 TQ	AZBLS	10/01-12/01
	Tucson MSA, AZ	Y	12840 FQ	28800 AW	44300 TQ	AZBLS	10/01-12/01
	Arkansas	Y	15320 FQ	21530 AW	29260 TQ	ARBLS	10/01-12/01
	Fayetteville-Springdale-Rogers MSA, AR	Y	15070 FQ	22000 AW	29940 TQ	ARBLS	10/01-12/01
	Fort Smith MSA, AR-OK	Y	16560 FQ	21900 AW	28610 TQ	ARBLS	10/01-12/01
	Little Rock-North Little Rock MSA, AR	Y	15930 FQ	22450 AW	32670 TQ	ARBLS	10/01-12/01
	California	Y	14080 FQ	29000 AW	43840 TQ	CABLS	10/01-12/01
	Bakersfield MSA, CA	Y	13540 FQ	21140 AW	30090 TQ	CABLS	10/01-12/01
	Fresno MSA, CA	Y	14050 FQ	23700 AW	35140 TQ	CABLS	10/01-12/01
	Los Angeles-Long Beach PMSA, CA	Y	13560 FQ	28120 AW	44260 TQ	CABLS	10/01-12/01
	Modesto MSA, CA	Y	16990 FQ	22270 AW	28210 TQ	CABLS	10/01-12/01
	Oakland PMSA, CA	Y	13860 FQ	29680 AW	43980 TQ	CABLS	10/01-12/01
	Orange County PMSA, CA	Y	22920 FQ	31440 AW	42180 TQ	CABLS	10/01-12/01
	Riverside-San Bernardino PMSA, CA	Y	14510 FQ	25500 AW	35530 TQ	CABLS	10/01-12/01
	Sacramento PMSA, CA	Y	16630 FQ	25170 AW	34950 TQ	CABLS	10/01-12/01
	Salinas MSA, CA	Y	14240 FQ	27820 AW	46120 TQ	CABLS	10/01-12/01
	San Diego MSA, CA	Y	17310 FQ	25430 AW	36340 TQ	CABLS	10/01-12/01
	San Francisco PMSA, CA	Y	18340 FQ	33930 AW	47720 TQ	CABLS	10/01-12/01
	San Jose PMSA, CA	Y	19260 FQ	33450 AW	51200 TQ	CABLS	10/01-12/01
	San Luis Obispo-Atascadero-Paso Robles MSA, CA	Y	16260 FQ	24660 AW	34950 TQ	CABLS	10/01-12/01
	Santa Barbara-Santa Maria-Lompoc MSA, CA	Y	13830 FQ	25170 AW	36610 TQ	CABLS	10/01-12/01
	Santa Cruz-Watsonville PMSA, CA	Y	14690 FQ	22460 AW	29750 TQ	CABLS	10/01-12/01
	Santa Rosa PMSA, CA	Y	19060 FQ	27510 AW	39090 TQ	CABLS	10/01-12/01
	Stockton-Lodi MSA, CA	Y	14600 FQ	27220 AW	44510 TQ	CABLS	10/01-12/01
	Vallejo-Fairfield-Napa PMSA, CA	Y	15440 FQ	24120 AW	34910 TQ	CABLS	10/01-12/01
	Ventura PMSA, CA	Y	20140 FQ	31050 AW	42320 TQ	CABLS	10/01-12/01
	Visalia-Tulare-Porterville MSA, CA	Y	13380 FQ	18350 AW	26710 TQ	CABLS	10/01-12/01
	Colorado	Y	16520 FQ	25190 AW	35080 TQ	COBLS	10/01-12/01
	Boulder-Longmont PMSA, CO	Y	19030 FQ	26740 AW	35550 TQ	COBLS	10/01-12/01
	Colorado Springs MSA, CO	Y	15890 FQ	23430 AW	33810 TQ	COBLS	10/01-12/01
	Denver PMSA, CO	Y	17370 FQ	25970 AW	34990 TQ	COBLS	10/01-12/01
	Fort Collins-Loveland MSA, CO	Y	14480 FQ	24350 AW	35790 TQ	COBLS	10/01-12/01
	Connecticut	Y	19120 FQ	30120 AW	44050 TQ	CTBLS	10/01-12/01
	Bridgeport PMSA, CT	Y	18260 FQ	31870 AW	52740 TQ	CTBLS	10/01-12/01

AAW	Average annual wage	**AOH**	Average offered, high	**ASH**	Average starting, high	**H**	Hourly	**M**	Monthly	**S**	Special: hourly and annual
AE	Average entry wage	**AOL**	Average offered, low	**ASL**	Average starting, low	**HI**	Highest wage paid	**MTC**	Median total compensation	**TQ**	Third quartile wage
AEX	Average experienced wage	**APH**	Average pay, high range	**AW**	Average wage paid	**HR**	High end range	**MW**	Median wage paid	**W**	Weekly
AO	Average offered	**APL**	Average pay, low range	**FQ**	First quartile wage	**LR**	Low end range	**SQ**	Second quartile wage	**Y**	Yearly

Occupation/Type/Industry	Location	Per	Low	Mid	High	Source	Date
Travel Agent	Danbury PMSA, CT	Y	15920 FQ	28060 AW	41940 TQ	CTBLS	10/01-12/01
	Hartford MSA, CT	Y	18950 FQ	26930 AW	36880 TQ	CTBLS	10/01-12/01
	New Haven-Meriden PMSA, CT	Y	19360 FQ	28130 AW	37780 TQ	CTBLS	10/01-12/01
	New London-Norwich MSA, CT-RI	Y	19620 FQ	25590 AW	33630 TQ	CTBLS	10/01-12/01
	Stamford-Norwalk PMSA, CT	Y	21770 FQ	38400 AW	52970 TQ	CTBLS	10/01-12/01
	Waterbury PMSA, CT	Y	19500 FQ	27650 AW	41850 TQ	CTBLS	10/01-12/01
	Delaware	Y	18930 FQ	27100 AW	39850 TQ	DEBLS	10/01-12/01
	Wilmington-Newark PMSA, DE-MD	Y	17230 FQ	26340 AW	40650 TQ	DEBLS	10/01-12/01
	District of Columbia	Y	20940 FQ	29520 AW	38620 TQ	DCBLS	10/01-12/01
	Washington PMSA, DC-MD-VA-WV	Y	16060 FQ	28690 AW	43710 TQ	DCBLS	10/01-12/01
	Florida	Y	16160 FQ	26790 AW	37690 TQ	FLBLS	10/01-12/01
	Daytona Beach MSA, FL	Y	17780 FQ	24150 AW	28950 TQ	FLBLS	10/01-12/01
	Fort Lauderdale PMSA, FL	Y	15970 FQ	27640 AW	44830 TQ	FLBLS	10/01-12/01
	Fort Myers-Cape Coral MSA, FL	Y	15450 FQ	24450 AW	38300 TQ	FLBLS	10/01-12/01
	Fort Pierce-Port St. Lucie MSA, FL	Y	15690 FQ	23890 AW	33770 TQ	FLBLS	10/01-12/01
	Fort Walton Beach MSA, FL	Y	12820 FQ	19820 AW	27670 TQ	FLBLS	10/01-12/01
	Gainesville MSA, FL	Y	16060 FQ	22510 AW	30690 TQ	FLBLS	10/01-12/01
	Jacksonville MSA, FL	Y	19770 FQ	27130 AW	35150 TQ	FLBLS	10/01-12/01
	Lakeland-Winter Haven MSA, FL	Y	15750 FQ	22730 AW	31030 TQ	FLBLS	10/01-12/01
	Melbourne-Titusville-Palm Bay MSA, FL	Y	15790 FQ	24180 AW	34860 TQ	FLBLS	10/01-12/01
	Miami PMSA, FL	Y	14740 FQ	27980 AW	52060 TQ	FLBLS	10/01-12/01
	Naples MSA, FL	Y	14040 FQ	29810 AW	50470 TQ	FLBLS	10/01-12/01
	Orlando MSA, FL	Y	15620 FQ	23730 AW	32810 TQ	FLBLS	10/01-12/01
	Sarasota-Bradenton MSA, FL	Y	12340 FQ	20370 AW	30500 TQ	FLBLS	10/01-12/01
	Tallahassee MSA, FL	Y	21570 FQ	26670 AW	32830 TQ	FLBLS	10/01-12/01
	Tampa-St. Petersburg-Clearwater MSA, FL	Y	20890 FQ	28730 AW	39800 TQ	FLBLS	10/01-12/01
	West Palm Beach-Boca Raton MSA, FL	Y	20900 FQ	30530 AW	37410 TQ	FLBLS	10/01-12/01
	Georgia	Y	18150 FQ	27180 AW	38770 TQ	GABLS	10/01-12/01
	Atlanta MSA, GA	Y	19660 FQ	28300 AW	40210 TQ	GABLS	10/01-12/01
	Augusta-Aiken MSA, GA-SC	Y	19530 FQ	24200 AW	28810 TQ	GABLS	10/01-12/01
	Savannah MSA, GA	Y	19900 FQ	26760 AW	39950 TQ	GABLS	10/01-12/01
	Hawaii	Y	17620 FQ	25190 AW	34420 TQ	HIBLS	10/01-12/01
	Honolulu MSA, HI	Y	16760 FQ	23660 AW	33260 TQ	HIBLS	10/01-12/01
	Idaho	Y	16100 FQ	25630 AW	35910 TQ	IDBLS	10/01-12/01
	Boise City MSA, ID	Y	16640 FQ	26620 AW	36290 TQ	IDBLS	10/01-12/01
	Illinois	Y	15590 FQ	28760 AW	43290 TQ	ILBLS	10/01-12/01
	Champaign-Urbana MSA, IL	Y	18880 FQ	25980 AW	36380 TQ	ILBLS	10/01-12/01
	Chicago PMSA, IL	Y	15820 FQ	29570 AW	43590 TQ	ILBLS	10/01-12/01
	Peoria-Pekin MSA, IL	Y	14880 FQ	23180 AW	37220 TQ	ILBLS	10/01-12/01
	Rockford MSA, IL	Y	14830 FQ	22220 AW	32420 TQ	ILBLS	10/01-12/01
	Springfield MSA, IL	Y	17120 FQ	25920 AW	36750 TQ	ILBLS	10/01-12/01
	Indiana	Y	15210 FQ	25020 AW	35370 TQ	INBLS	10/01-12/01
	Evansville-Henderson MSA, IN-KY	Y	15060 FQ	22470 AW	31560 TQ	INBLS	10/01-12/01
	Fort Wayne MSA, IN	Y	16220 FQ	22380 AW	30380 TQ	INBLS	10/01-12/01
	Gary PMSA, IN	Y	12480 FQ	16700 AW	22380 TQ	INBLS	10/01-12/01
	Indianapolis MSA, IN	Y	20280 FQ	28820 AW	36030 TQ	INBLS	10/01-12/01
	Lafayette MSA, IN	Y	15330 FQ	20260 AW	25920 TQ	INBLS	10/01-12/01
	South Bend MSA, IN	Y	16530 FQ	28120 AW	41120 TQ	INBLS	10/01-12/01
	Iowa	Y	13310 FQ	23130 AW	34200 TQ	IABLS	10/01-12/01
	Cedar Rapids MSA, IA	Y	21220 FQ	30060 AW	35410 TQ	IABLS	10/01-12/01
	Davenport-Moline-Rock Island MSA, IA-IL	Y	13080 FQ	19890 AW	29900 TQ	IABLS	10/01-12/01
	Des Moines MSA, IA	Y	14540 FQ	25720 AW	35390 TQ	IABLS	10/01-12/01
	Kansas	Y	18970 FQ	26680 AW	38430 TQ	KSBLS	10/01-12/01
	Topeka MSA, KS	Y	18160 FQ	25400 AW	34980 TQ	KSBLS	10/01-12/01
	Wichita MSA, KS	Y	18840 FQ	25680 AW	36780 TQ	KSBLS	10/01-12/01
	Kentucky	Y	15910 FQ	23230 AW	33330 TQ	KYBLS	10/01-12/01
	Lexington MSA, KY	Y	18880 FQ	23210 AW	31400 TQ	KYBLS	10/01-12/01
	Louisville MSA, KY-IN	Y	16380 FQ	23750 AW	32150 TQ	KYBLS	10/01-12/01
	Louisiana	Y	13530 FQ	22410 AW	34430 TQ	LABLS	10/01-12/01
	Baton Rouge MSA, LA	Y	11950 FQ	19730 AW	32570 TQ	LABLS	10/01-12/01

AAW	Average annual wage	**AOH**	Average offered, high	**ASH**	Average starting, high	**H**	Hourly	**M**	Monthly	**S**	Special: hourly and annual
AE	Average entry wage	**AOL**	Average offered, low	**ASL**	Average starting, low	**HI**	Highest wage paid	**MTC**	Median total compensation	**TQ**	Third quartile wage
AEX	Average experienced wage	**APH**	Average pay, high range	**AW**	Average wage paid	**HR**	High end range	**MW**	Median wage paid	**W**	Weekly
AO	Average offered	**APL**	Average pay, low range	**FQ**	First quartile wage	**LR**	Low end range	**SQ**	Second quartile wage	**Y**	Yearly

Occupation/Type/Industry	Location	Per	Low	Mid	High	Source	Date
Travel Agent	Lafayette MSA, LA	Y	14300 FQ	28630 AW	55380 TQ	LABLS	10/01-12/01
	New Orleans MSA, LA	Y	14430 FQ	21900 AW	33860 TQ	LABLS	10/01-12/01
	Shreveport-Bossier City MSA, LA	Y	12990 FQ	19560 AW	27840 TQ	LABLS	10/01-12/01
	Maine	Y	16620 FQ	25550 AW	34080 TQ	MEBLS	10/01-12/01
	Portland MSA, ME	Y	22930 FQ	28390 AW	34660 TQ	MEBLS	10/01-12/01
	Maryland	Y	13580 FQ	26550 AW	41070 TQ	MDBLS	10/01-12/01
	Baltimore PMSA, MD	Y	13860 FQ	24640 AW	35990 TQ	MDBLS	10/01-12/01
	Massachusetts	Y	18340 FQ	28920 AW	39830 TQ	MABLS	10/01-12/01
	Boston PMSA, MA-NH	Y	18830 FQ	29740 AW	40810 TQ	MABLS	10/01-12/01
	Brockton PMSA, MA	Y	16880 FQ	25890 AW	35360 TQ	MABLS	10/01-12/01
	Lawrence PMSA, MA-NH	Y	15830 FQ	28650 AW	51550 TQ	MABLS	10/01-12/01
	Lowell PMSA, MA-NH	Y	18390 FQ	27010 AW	36350 TQ	MABLS	10/01-12/01
	New Bedford PMSA, MA	Y	14270 FQ	22480 AW	35860 TQ	MABLS	10/01-12/01
	Springfield MSA, MA	Y	14190 FQ	24090 AW	34320 TQ	MABLS	10/01-12/01
	Worcester PMSA, MA-CT	Y	18660 FQ	26270 AW	34530 TQ	MABLS	10/01-12/01
	Michigan	Y	15810 FQ	23970 AW	33030 TQ	MIBLS	10/01-12/01
	Ann Arbor PMSA, MI	Y	19130 FQ	23760 AW	30790 TQ	MIBLS	10/01-12/01
	Detroit PMSA, MI	Y	17990 FQ	25220 AW	33770 TQ	MIBLS	10/01-12/01
	Flint PMSA, MI	Y	15750 FQ	21830 AW	30110 TQ	MIBLS	10/01-12/01
	Grand Rapids-Muskegon-Holland MSA, MI	Y	12940 FQ	21430 AW	33260 TQ	MIBLS	10/01-12/01
	Kalamazoo-Battle Creek MSA, MI	Y	18940 FQ	24050 AW	29590 TQ	MIBLS	10/01-12/01
	Lansing-East Lansing MSA, MI	Y	18160 FQ	24540 AW	32310 TQ	MIBLS	10/01-12/01
	Saginaw-Bay City-Midland MSA, MI	Y	14460 FQ	21710 AW	28730 TQ	MIBLS	10/01-12/01
	Minnesota	Y	17080 FQ	26060 AW	35650 TQ	MNBLS	10/01-12/01
	Duluth-Superior MSA, MN-WI	Y	12940 FQ	18060 AW	22580 TQ	MNBLS	10/01-12/01
	Minneapolis-St. Paul MSA, MN-WI	Y	18080 FQ	26760 AW	36010 TQ	MNBLS	10/01-12/01
	St. Cloud MSA, MN	Y	18140 FQ	23700 AW	33200 TQ	MNBLS	10/01-12/01
	Mississippi	Y	15640 FQ	23230 AW	29150 TQ	MSBLS	10/01-12/01
	Biloxi-Gulfport-Pascagoula MSA, MS	Y	18460 FQ	22160 AW	27850 TQ	MSBLS	10/01-12/01
	Missouri	Y	14450 FQ	24410 AW	33180 TQ	MOBLS	10/01-12/01
	Kansas City MSA, MO-KS	Y	18540 FQ	24000 AW	34510 TQ	MOBLS	10/01-12/01
	St. Louis MSA, MO-IL	Y	13770 FQ	26420 AW	34540 TQ	MOBLS	10/01-12/01
	Springfield MSA, MO	Y	13140 FQ	22910 AW	34190 TQ	MOBLS	10/01-12/01
	Montana	Y	14920 FQ	21680 AW	28530 TQ	MTBLS	10/01-12/01
	Billings MSA, MT	Y	14430 FQ	17370 AW	21840 TQ	MTBLS	10/01-12/01
	Nebraska	Y	18480 FQ	26550 AW	35360 TQ	NEBLS	10/01-12/01
	Lincoln MSA, NE	Y	18290 FQ	25190 AW	36580 TQ	NEBLS	10/01-12/01
	Omaha MSA, NE-IA	Y	19300 FQ	27890 AW	35700 TQ	NEBLS	10/01-12/01
	Nevada	Y	15970 FQ	45500 AW		NVBLS	10/01-12/01
	Las Vegas MSA, NV-AZ	Y	15990 FQ	47820 AW		NVBLS	10/01-12/01
	Reno MSA, NV	Y	14970 FQ	26820 AW	42640 TQ	NVBLS	10/01-12/01
	New Hampshire	Y	18940 FQ	27980 AW	41460 TQ	NHBLS	10/01-12/01
	Manchester PMSA, NH	Y	18890 FQ	27650 AW	37060 TQ	NHBLS	10/01-12/01
	Nashua PMSA, NH	Y	19440 FQ	29980 AW	43350 TQ	NHBLS	10/01-12/01
	Portsmouth-Rochester PMSA, NH-ME	Y	20890 FQ	31480 AW	51290 TQ	NHBLS	10/01-12/01
	New Jersey	Y	17480 FQ	29440 AW	43540 TQ	NJBLS	10/01-12/01
	Atlantic-Cape May PMSA, NJ	Y	19600 FQ	28510 AW	35960 TQ	NJBLS	10/01-12/01
	Bergen-Passaic PMSA, NJ	Y	18600 FQ	32100 AW	51710 TQ	NJBLS	10/01-12/01
	Jersey City PMSA, NJ	Y	15930 FQ	28710 AW	42060 TQ	NJBLS	10/01-12/01
	Middlesex-Somerset-Hunterdon PMSA, NJ	Y	19840 FQ	29250 AW	36690 TQ	NJBLS	10/01-12/01
	Monmouth-Ocean PMSA, NJ	Y	14490 FQ	26970 AW	40090 TQ	NJBLS	10/01-12/01
	Newark PMSA, NJ	Y	16500 FQ	28940 AW	42190 TQ	NJBLS	10/01-12/01
	Trenton PMSA, NJ	Y	13020 FQ	27840 AW	39610 TQ	NJBLS	10/01-12/01
	New Mexico	Y	15360 FQ	22210 AW	31690 TQ	NMBLS	10/01-12/01
	Albuquerque MSA, NM	Y	15890 FQ	21280 AW	27780 TQ	NMBLS	10/01-12/01
	New York	Y	14590 FQ	29520 AW	47820 TQ	NYBLS	10/01-12/01
	Albany-Schenectady-Troy MSA, NY	Y	17450 FQ	25200 AW	34920 TQ	NYBLS	10/01-12/01
	Binghamton MSA, NY	Y	18990 FQ	24390 AW	32890 TQ	NYBLS	10/01-12/01
	Buffalo-Niagara Falls MSA, NY	Y	14880 FQ	24740 AW	33630 TQ	NYBLS	10/01-12/01
	Dutchess County PMSA, NY	Y	14300 FQ	19450 AW	27640 TQ	NYBLS	10/01-12/01
	Nassau-Suffolk PMSA, NY	Y	12520 FQ	27250 AW	40080 TQ	NYBLS	10/01-12/01
	New York PMSA, NY	Y	15770 FQ	31790 AW	52920 TQ	NYBLS	10/01-12/01

Occupation/Type/Industry	Location	Per	Low	Mid	High	Source	Date
Travel Agent	Newburgh PMSA, NY-PA	Y	16890 FQ	25250 AW	35820 TQ	NYBLS	10/01-12/01
	Rochester MSA, NY	Y	13970 FQ	26830 AW	35890 TQ	NYBLS	10/01-12/01
	Syracuse MSA, NY	Y	23300 FQ	29800 AW	37610 TQ	NYBLS	10/01-12/01
	Utica-Rome MSA, NY	Y	15260 FQ	22800 AW	31670 TQ	NYBLS	10/01-12/01
	North Carolina	Y	13730 FQ	27380 AW	40870 TQ	NCBLS	10/01-12/01
	Asheville MSA, NC	Y	12520 FQ	23750 AW	39700 TQ	NCBLS	10/01-12/01
	Charlotte-Gastonia-Rock Hill MSA, NC-SC	Y	18580 FQ	31080 AW	52420 TQ	NCBLS	10/01-12/01
	Fayetteville MSA, NC	Y	15900 FQ	21620 AW	27760 TQ	NCBLS	10/01-12/01
	Greensboro-Winston-Salem-High Point MSA, NC	Y	11700 FQ	24230 AW	40000 TQ	NCBLS	10/01-12/01
	Raleigh-Durham-Chapel Hill MSA, NC	Y	20210 FQ	28740 AW	38180 TQ	NCBLS	10/01-12/01
	North Dakota	Y	16490 FQ	25420 AW	39990 TQ	NDBLS	10/01-12/01
	Fargo-Moorhead MSA, ND-MN	Y	17620 FQ	27990 AW	41930 TQ	NDBLS	10/01-12/01
	Ohio	Y	16470 FQ	25700 AW	35350 TQ	OHBLS	10/01-12/01
	Akron PMSA, OH	Y	16130 FQ	26540 AW	35520 TQ	OHBLS	10/01-12/01
	Canton-Massillon MSA, OH	Y	15830 FQ	22890 AW	31590 TQ	OHBLS	10/01-12/01
	Cincinnati PMSA, OH-KY-IN	Y	17610 FQ	25470 AW	35470 TQ	OHBLS	10/01-12/01
	Cleveland-Lorain-Elyria PMSA, OH	Y	17160 FQ	25320 AW	33750 TQ	OHBLS	10/01-12/01
	Columbus MSA, OH	Y	13940 FQ	26120 AW	35210 TQ	OHBLS	10/01-12/01
	Dayton-Springfield MSA, OH	Y	15940 FQ	25870 AW	40970 TQ	OHBLS	10/01-12/01
	Hamilton-Middletown PMSA, OH	Y	16600 FQ	22040 AW	29000 TQ	OHBLS	10/01-12/01
	Toledo MSA, OH	Y	13370 FQ	23250 AW	31180 TQ	OHBLS	10/01-12/01
	Youngstown-Warren MSA, OH	Y	16340 FQ	25000 AW	36830 TQ	OHBLS	10/01-12/01
	Oklahoma	Y	15140 FQ	22910 AW	34010 TQ	OKBLS	10/01-12/01
	Oklahoma City MSA, OK	Y	14670 FQ	21540 AW	28140 TQ	OKBLS	10/01-12/01
	Oregon	Y	15830 FQ	25110 AW	36740 TQ	ORBLS	10/01-12/01
	Eugene-Springfield MSA, OR	Y	17810 FQ	26890 AW	39680 TQ	ORBLS	10/01-12/01
	Portland-Vancouver PMSA, OR-WA	Y	17060 FQ	25700 AW	37350 TQ	ORBLS	10/01-12/01
	Salem PMSA, OR	Y	19210 FQ	25590 AW	32050 TQ	ORBLS	10/01-12/01
	Pennsylvania	Y	14920 FQ	27130 AW	40870 TQ	PABLS	10/01-12/01
	Allentown-Bethlehem-Easton MSA, PA	Y	17400 FQ	28710 AW	41620 TQ	PABLS	10/01-12/01
	Erie MSA, PA	Y	15050 FQ	22850 AW	33790 TQ	PABLS	10/01-12/01
	Harrisburg-Lebanon-Carlisle MSA, PA	Y	18000 FQ	24790 AW	34390 TQ	PABLS	10/01-12/01
	Lancaster MSA, PA	Y	16610 FQ	29430 AW	37140 TQ	PABLS	10/01-12/01
	Philadelphia PMSA, PA-NJ	Y	14480 FQ	28740 AW	43990 TQ	PABLS	10/01-12/01
	Pittsburgh MSA, PA	Y	15490 FQ	26900 AW	42310 TQ	PABLS	10/01-12/01
	Reading MSA, PA	Y	16120 FQ	25690 AW	34330 TQ	PABLS	10/01-12/01
	Scranton-Wilkes-Barre-Hazleton MSA, PA	Y	15660 FQ	24590 AW	34400 TQ	PABLS	10/01-12/01
	York MSA, PA	Y	14210 FQ	24940 AW	34520 TQ	PABLS	10/01-12/01
	Rhode Island	Y	16640 FQ	25270 AW	36320 TQ	RIBLS	10/01-12/01
	Providence-Fall River-Warwick MSA, RI-MA	Y	16530 FQ	25070 AW	36590 TQ	RIBLS	10/01-12/01
	South Carolina	Y	14660 FQ	24120 AW	34800 TQ	SCBLS	10/01-12/01
	Charleston-North Charleston MSA, SC	Y	14780 FQ	21480 AW	33310 TQ	SCBLS	10/01-12/01
	Columbia MSA, SC	Y	16540 FQ	27440 AW	38780 TQ	SCBLS	10/01-12/01
	Greenville-Spartanburg-Anderson MSA, SC	Y	15450 FQ	28740 AW	42910 TQ	SCBLS	10/01-12/01
	Myrtle Beach MSA, SC	Y	12640 FQ	20510 AW	32220 TQ	SCBLS	10/01-12/01
	South Dakota	Y	15480 FQ	19580 AW	25150 TQ	SDBLS	10/01-12/01
	Sioux Falls MSA, SD	Y	15240 FQ	20120 AW	27760 TQ	SDBLS	10/01-12/01
	Tennessee	Y	15400 FQ	24450 AW	34620 TQ	TNBLS	10/01-12/01
	Chattanooga MSA, TN-GA	Y	15140 FQ	22830 AW	31430 TQ	TNBLS	10/01-12/01
	Johnson City-Kingsport-Bristol MSA, TN-VA	Y	13900 FQ	22820 AW	35080 TQ	TNBLS	10/01-12/01
	Knoxville MSA, TN	Y	12770 FQ	19850 AW	28540 TQ	TNBLS	10/01-12/01
	Memphis MSA, TN-AR-MS	Y	17060 FQ	29720 AW	41900 TQ	TNBLS	10/01-12/01
	Nashville MSA, TN	Y	16990 FQ	24870 AW	33120 TQ	TNBLS	10/01-12/01
	Texas	Y	17500 FQ	28380 AW	40620 TQ	TXBLS	10/01-12/01
	Austin-San Marcos MSA, TX	Y	11780 FQ	23780 AW	39140 TQ	TXBLS	10/01-12/01
	Corpus Christi MSA, TX	Y	19210 FQ	28570 AW	43470 TQ	TXBLS	10/01-12/01
	Dallas PMSA, TX	Y	24180 FQ	31440 AW	38080 TQ	TXBLS	10/01-12/01
	El Paso MSA, TX	Y	14830 FQ	21390 AW	27830 TQ	TXBLS	10/01-12/01

AAW	Average annual wage	AOH	Average offered, high	ASH	Average starting, high	H	Hourly	M	Monthly	S	Special: hourly and annual
AE	Average entry wage	AOL	Average offered, low	ASL	Average starting, low	HI	Highest wage paid	MTC	Median total compensation	TQ	Third quartile wage
AEX	Average experienced wage	APH	Average pay, high range	AW	Average wage paid	HR	High end range	MW	Median wage paid	W	Weekly
AO	Average offered	APL	Average pay, low range	FQ	First quartile wage	LR	Low end range	SQ	Second quartile wage	Y	Yearly

Occupation/Type/Industry	Location	Per	Low	Mid	High	Source	Date
Travel Agent	Fort Worth-Arlington PMSA, TX	Y	14510 FQ	26100 AW	45380 TQ	TXBLS	10/01-12/01
	Galveston-Texas City PMSA, TX	Y	16180 FQ	30280 AW	50950 TQ	TXBLS	10/01-12/01
	Longview-Marshall MSA, TX	Y	14250 FQ	23030 AW	28120 TQ	TXBLS	10/01-12/01
	McAllen-Edinburg-Mission MSA, TX	Y	15610 FQ	23180 AW	34400 TQ	TXBLS	10/01-12/01
	Odessa-Midland MSA, TX	Y	12580 FQ	20450 AW	28040 TQ	TXBLS	10/01-12/01
	San Antonio MSA, TX	Y	18850 FQ	24620 AW	33340 TQ	TXBLS	10/01-12/01
	Utah	Y	15080 FQ	25420 AW	35070 TQ	UTBLS	10/01-12/01
	Provo-Orem MSA, UT	Y	17360 FQ	25700 AW	34840 TQ	UTBLS	10/01-12/01
	Salt Lake City-Ogden MSA, UT	Y	14900 FQ	24790 AW	34710 TQ	UTBLS	10/01-12/01
	Vermont	Y	19040 FQ	26500 AW	34190 TQ	VTBLS	10/01-12/01
	Burlington MSA, VT	Y	24170 FQ	29890 AW	34880 TQ	VTBLS	10/01-12/01
	Virginia	Y	15830 FQ	26540 AW	42160 TQ	VABLS	10/01-12/01
	Lynchburg MSA, VA	Y	13510 FQ	25510 AW	41830 TQ	VABLS	10/01-12/01
	Norfolk-Virginia Beach-Newport News MSA, VA-NC	Y	15490 FQ	23750 AW	34910 TQ	VABLS	10/01-12/01
	Richmond-Petersburg MSA, VA	Y	17960 FQ	23480 AW	33270 TQ	VABLS	10/01-12/01
	Washington	Y	18170 FQ	27850 AW	40660 TQ	WABLS	10/01-12/01
	Bremerton PMSA, WA	Y	14520 FQ	23500 AW	43010 TQ	WABLS	10/01-12/01
	Olympia PMSA, WA	Y	15520 FQ	23440 AW	35740 TQ	WABLS	10/01-12/01
	Richland-Kennewick-Pasco MSA, WA	Y	16430 FQ	23080 AW	30570 TQ	WABLS	10/01-12/01
	Seattle-Bellevue-Everett PMSA, WA	Y	19770 FQ	28730 AW	40030 TQ	WABLS	10/01-12/01
	Spokane MSA, WA	Y	16020 FQ	30780 AW	53370 TQ	WABLS	10/01-12/01
	Tacoma PMSA, WA	Y	19350 FQ	26250 AW	35140 TQ	WABLS	10/01-12/01
	West Virginia	Y	14850 FQ	21620 AW	28860 TQ	WVBLS	10/01-12/01
	Charleston MSA, WV	Y	18080 FQ	23060 AW	29790 TQ	WVBLS	10/01-12/01
	Wisconsin	Y	17690 FQ	24820 AW	29860 TQ	WIBLS	10/01-12/01
	Appleton-Oshkosh-Neenah MSA, WI	Y	18510 FQ	25940 AW	34630 TQ	WIBLS	10/01-12/01
	Green Bay MSA, WI	Y	15190 FQ	25190 AW	29960 TQ	WIBLS	10/01-12/01
	Madison MSA, WI	Y	15440 FQ	21880 AW	31960 TQ	WIBLS	10/01-12/01
	Milwaukee-Waukesha PMSA, WI	Y	22500 FQ	26610 AW	29050 TQ	WIBLS	10/01-12/01
	Puerto Rico	Y	11820 FQ	16330 AW	22010 TQ	PRBLS	10/01-12/01
	Virgin Islands	Y	15370 FQ	20750 AW	28580 TQ	VIBLS	10/01-12/01
	Guam	Y	13030 FQ	21930 AW	32030 TQ	GUBLS	10/01-12/01
Travel Buyer	United States	Y		62600 AW		IOMA1	1/01-1/02
Travel Guide	Arizona	H	7.67 FQ	11.84 AW	17.21 TQ	AZBLS	10/01-12/01
	California	H	7.84 FQ	18.85 AW	43.58 TQ	CABLS	10/01-12/01
	Los Angeles-Long Beach PMSA, CA	H	7.30 FQ	12.37 AW	14.92 TQ	CABLS	10/01-12/01
	Oakland PMSA, CA	H	17.01 FQ	24.41 AW	35.17 TQ	CABLS	10/01-12/01
	San Francisco PMSA, CA	H	10.00 FQ	14.30 AW	20.95 TQ	CABLS	10/01-12/01
	Colorado	H	7.65 FQ	12.31 AW	16.61 TQ	COBLS	10/01-12/01
	Denver PMSA, CO	H	11.35 FQ	14.42 AW	16.91 TQ	COBLS	10/01-12/01
	Washington PMSA, DC-MD-VA-WV	H	9.93 FQ	16.44 AW	23.27 TQ	DCBLS	10/01-12/01
	Florida	H	9.06 FQ	12.93 AW	18.26 TQ	FLBLS	10/01-12/01
	Fort Lauderdale PMSA, FL	H	9.39 FQ	14.10 AW	22.82 TQ	FLBLS	10/01-12/01
	Miami PMSA, FL	H	8.93 FQ	12.30 AW	16.74 TQ	FLBLS	10/01-12/01
	Orlando MSA, FL	H	9.12 FQ	12.07 AW	16.30 TQ	FLBLS	10/01-12/01
	Georgia	H	7.91 FQ	14.24 AW	19.82 TQ	GABLS	10/01-12/01
	Atlanta MSA, GA	H	8.06 FQ	14.28 AW	19.52 TQ	GABLS	10/01-12/01
	Hawaii	H	6.51 FQ	12.13 AW	18.44 TQ	HIBLS	10/01-12/01
	Honolulu MSA, HI	H	7.72 FQ	11.72 AW	16.60 TQ	HIBLS	10/01-12/01
	Illinois	H	9.25 FQ	14.64 AW	24.69 TQ	ILBLS	10/01-12/01
	Chicago PMSA, IL	H	9.26 FQ	14.83 AW	25.81 TQ	ILBLS	10/01-12/01
	Indiana	H	7.41 FQ	11.02 AW	16.24 TQ	INBLS	10/01-12/01
	Iowa	H	5.92 FQ	9.37 AW	13.70 TQ	IABLS	10/01-12/01
	Kansas	H	9.09 FQ	10.31 AW	11.15 TQ	KSBLS	10/01-12/01
	Wichita MSA, KS	H	9.07 FQ	10.16 AW	10.99 TQ	KSBLS	10/01-12/01
	Kentucky	H	7.26 FQ	9.45 AW	13.48 TQ	KYBLS	10/01-12/01
	Louisiana	H	7.23 FQ	12.49 AW	18.57 TQ	LABLS	10/01-12/01
	New Orleans MSA, LA	H	8.45 FQ	13.49 AW	21.72 TQ	LABLS	10/01-12/01

AAW	Average annual wage	**AOH**	Average offered, high	**ASH**	Average starting, high	**H**	Hourly	**M**	Monthly	**S**	Special: hourly and annual
AE	Average entry wage	**AOL**	Average offered, low	**ASL**	Average starting, low	**HI**	Highest wage paid	**MTC**	Median total compensation	**TQ**	Third quartile wage
AEX	Average experienced wage	**APH**	Average pay, high range	**AW**	Average wage paid	**HR**	High end range	**MW**	Median wage paid	**W**	Weekly
AO	Average offered	**APL**	Average pay, low range	**FQ**	First quartile wage	**LR**	Low end range	**SQ**	Second quartile wage	**Y**	Yearly

Occupation/Type/Industry	Location	Per	Low	Mid	High	Source	Date
Travel Guide	Massachusetts	H	12.90 FQ	18.42 AW	22.54 TQ	MABLS	10/01-12/01
	Boston PMSA, MA-NH	H	15.27 FQ	18.56 AW	21.48 TQ	MABLS	10/01-12/01
	Michigan	H	8.14 FQ	13.27 AW	18.78 TQ	MIBLS	10/01-12/01
	Missouri	H	9.43 FQ	12.35 AW	16.70 TQ	MOBLS	10/01-12/01
	Montana	H	9.29 FQ	14.22 AW	21.29 TQ	MTBLS	10/01-12/01
	Nebraska	H	9.76 FQ	16.73 AW	31.26 TQ	NEBLS	10/01-12/01
	Nevada	H	11.21 FQ	12.77 AW	14.02 TQ	NVBLS	10/01-12/01
	New Jersey	H	8.87 FQ	14.00 AW	18.78 TQ	NJBLS	10/01-12/01
	New York	H	8.41 FQ	25.27 AW	46.47 TQ	NYBLS	10/01-12/01
	New York PMSA, NY	H	11.75 FQ	26.38 AW	49.13 TQ	NYBLS	10/01-12/01
	North Carolina	H	9.40 FQ	15.15 AW	27.26 TQ	NCBLS	10/01-12/01
	Charlotte-Gastonia-Rock Hill MSA, NC-SC	H	8.54 FQ	13.31 AW	17.33 TQ	NCBLS	10/01-12/01
	Hickory-Morganton-Lenoir MSA, NC	H	9.46 FQ	11.97 AW	16.28 TQ	NCBLS	10/01-12/01
	Raleigh-Durham-Chapel Hill MSA, NC	H	9.86 FQ	17.17 AW	30.51 TQ	NCBLS	10/01-12/01
	Ohio	H	6.55 FQ	12.31 AW	17.36 TQ	OHBLS	10/01-12/01
	Oklahoma	H	9.71 FQ	14.24 AW	16.95 TQ	OKBLS	10/01-12/01
	Tulsa MSA, OK	H	10.03 FQ	14.45 AW	16.92 TQ	OKBLS	10/01-12/01
	Pennsylvania	H	7.99 FQ	13.41 AW	17.43 TQ	PABLS	10/01-12/01
	Philadelphia PMSA, PA-NJ	H	12.02 FQ	15.27 AW	17.90 TQ	PABLS	10/01-12/01
	Pittsburgh MSA, PA	H	7.58 FQ	9.91 AW	13.64 TQ	PABLS	10/01-12/01
	South Carolina	H	6.58 FQ	11.80 AW	19.53 TQ	SCBLS	10/01-12/01
	Texas	H	6.73 FQ	18.10 AW	31.41 TQ	TXBLS	10/01-12/01
	Utah	H	10.97 FQ	13.76 AW	16.74 TQ	UTBLS	10/01-12/01
	Salt Lake City-Ogden MSA, UT	H	9.57 FQ	14.25 AW	16.90 TQ	UTBLS	10/01-12/01
	Vermont	H	14.17 FQ	19.03 AW	27.85 TQ	VTBLS	10/01-12/01
	Virginia	H	5.73 FQ	11.86 AW	17.05 TQ	VABLS	10/01-12/01
	Norfolk-Virginia Beach-Newport News MSA, VA-NC	H	10.84 FQ	14.97 AW	19.23 TQ	VABLS	10/01-12/01
	Washington	H	9.34 FQ	14.66 AW	22.19 TQ	WABLS	10/01-12/01
	Tacoma PMSA, WA	H	9.16 FQ	15.34 AW	26.66 TQ	WABLS	10/01-12/01
	Wisconsin	H	8.74 FQ	14.19 AW	18.07 TQ	WIBLS	10/01-12/01
Travel Manager	United States	Y		74400 AW		BTN	1/01-1/02
	United States	Y		68500 AW		IOMA1	1/01-1/02
Tree Trimmer and Pruner	Alabama	H	8.93 FQ	11.88 AW	15.79 TQ	ALBLS	10/01-12/01
	Arizona	H	7.17 FQ	10.51 AW	14.43 TQ	AZBLS	10/01-12/01
	Arkansas	H	7.93 FQ	11.47 AW	15.32 TQ	ARBLS	10/01-12/01
	California	H	8.01 FQ	12.77 AW	18.79 TQ	CABLS	10/01-12/01
	Colorado	H	8.77 FQ	12.88 AW	18.92 TQ	COBLS	10/01-12/01
	Connecticut	H	9.96 FQ	13.91 AW	19.12 TQ	CTBLS	10/01-12/01
	Delaware	H	9.06 FQ	15.00 AW	21.34 TQ	DEBLS	10/01-12/01
	District of Columbia	H	8.83 FQ	17.96 AW	25.77 TQ	DCBLS	10/01-12/01
	Florida	H	6.88 FQ	10.22 AW	13.66 TQ	FLBLS	10/01-12/01
	Georgia	H	7.84 FQ	11.13 AW	16.06 TQ	GABLS	10/01-12/01
	Hawaii	H	8.99 FQ	13.31 AW	19.53 TQ	HIBLS	10/01-12/01
	Idaho	H	8.26 FQ	11.74 AW	19.27 TQ	IDBLS	10/01-12/01
	Illinois	H	9.08 FQ	13.42 AW	19.54 TQ	ILBLS	10/01-12/01
	Indiana	H	6.35 FQ	13.26 AW	20.89 TQ	INBLS	10/01-12/01
	Kansas	H	8.04 FQ	14.67 AW	22.24 TQ	KSBLS	10/01-12/01
	Kentucky	H	7.33 FQ	9.54 AW	13.11 TQ	KYBLS	10/01-12/01
	Louisiana	H	6.10 FQ	10.81 AW	16.48 TQ	LABLS	10/01-12/01
	Maine	H	7.79 FQ	12.92 AW	20.24 TQ	MEBLS	10/01-12/01
	Maryland	H	8.93 FQ	13.23 AW	18.84 TQ	MDBLS	10/01-12/01
	Massachusetts	H	8.98 FQ	15.00 AW	22.01 TQ	MABLS	10/01-12/01
	Michigan	H	7.07 FQ	10.68 AW	17.74 TQ	MIBLS	10/01-12/01
	Minnesota	H	9.19 FQ	12.81 AW	17.07 TQ	MNBLS	10/01-12/01
	Mississippi	H	7.41 FQ	9.94 AW	13.39 TQ	MSBLS	10/01-12/01
	Missouri	H	8.94 FQ	13.51 AW	20.18 TQ	MOBLS	10/01-12/01
	Nebraska	H	8.24 FQ	12.18 AW	18.10 TQ	NEBLS	10/01-12/01
	Nevada	H	9.43 FQ	12.34 AW	16.81 TQ	NVBLS	10/01-12/01
	New Hampshire	H	9.00 FQ	11.63 AW	14.50 TQ	NHBLS	10/01-12/01
	New Jersey	H	11.34 FQ	15.54 AW	22.90 TQ	NJBLS	10/01-12/01
	New Mexico	H	7.30 FQ	11.97 AW	18.10 TQ	NMBLS	10/01-12/01
	New York	H	10.15 FQ	19.42 AW	28.71 TQ	NYBLS	10/01-12/01
	North Carolina	H	8.37 FQ	11.47 AW	14.75 TQ	NCBLS	10/01-12/01
	Ohio	H	7.84 FQ	13.04 AW	18.08 TQ	OHBLS	10/01-12/01
	Oklahoma	H	7.53 FQ	10.06 AW	13.28 TQ	OKBLS	10/01-12/01

AAW	Average annual wage	**AOH**	Average offered, high	**ASH**	Average starting, high	**H**	Hourly	**M**	Monthly	**S**	Special: hourly and annual
AE	Average entry wage	**AOL**	Average offered, low	**ASL**	Average starting, low	**HI**	Highest wage paid	**MTC**	Median total compensation	**TQ**	Third quartile wage
AEX	Average experienced wage	**APH**	Average pay, high range	**AW**	Average wage paid	**HR**	High end range	**MW**	Median wage paid	**W**	Weekly
AO	Average offered	**APL**	Average pay, low range	**FQ**	First quartile wage	**LR**	Low end range	**SQ**	Second quartile wage	**Y**	Yearly

Occupation/Type/Industry	Location	Per	Low	Mid	High	Source	Date
Tree Trimmer and Pruner	Oregon	H	10.07 FQ	15.57 AW	21.88 TQ	ORBLS	10/01-12/01
	Pennsylvania	H	9.58 FQ	15.13 AW	23.17 TQ	PABLS	10/01-12/01
	South Carolina	H	5.53 FQ	9.30 AW	13.97 TQ	SCBLS	10/01-12/01
	South Dakota	H	7.48 FQ	9.90 AW	13.17 TQ	SDBLS	10/01-12/01
	Tennessee	H	6.19 FQ	8.99 AW	12.35 TQ	TNBLS	10/01-12/01
	Texas	H	6.81 FQ	9.29 AW	12.85 TQ	TXBLS	10/01-12/01
	Utah	H	9.02 FQ	10.82 AW	13.85 TQ	UTBLS	10/01-12/01
	Vermont	H	8.23 FQ	11.16 AW	14.86 TQ	VTBLS	10/01-12/01
	Virginia	H	7.73 FQ	11.43 AW	16.62 TQ	VABLS	10/01-12/01
	West Virginia	H	8.06 FQ	12.87 AW	18.28 TQ	WVBLS	10/01-12/01
	Wisconsin	H	10.95 FQ	15.81 AW	19.78 TQ	WIBLS	10/01-12/01
	Wyoming	H	7.59 FQ	10.24 AW	15.73 TQ	WYBLS	10/01-12/01
Trial Judge	Indiana	Y		90000 MW		ABA	1/00-1/01
	New Jersey	Y		137165 MW		ABA	1/00-1/01
	New Mexico	Y		81593 MW		ABA	1/00-1/01
	Oregon	Y		90420 MW		ABA	1/00-1/01
	Wyoming	Y		83700 MW		ABA	1/00-1/01
Truck Driver							
Heavy and Tractor-Trailer	Alabama	H	8.78 FQ	15.18 AW	22.37 TQ	ALBLS	10/01-12/01
Heavy and Tractor-Trailer	Birmingham MSA, AL	H	9.59 FQ	17.02 AW	23.34 TQ	ALBLS	10/01-12/01
Heavy and Tractor-Trailer	Huntsville MSA, AL	H	9.69 FQ	15.36 AW	23.36 TQ	ALBLS	10/01-12/01
Heavy and Tractor-Trailer	Mobile MSA, AL	H	8.37 FQ	14.63 AW	22.81 TQ	ALBLS	10/01-12/01
Heavy and Tractor-Trailer	Montgomery MSA, AL	H	9.18 FQ	14.96 AW	21.75 TQ	ALBLS	10/01-12/01
Heavy and Tractor-Trailer	Alaska	H	12.71 FQ	20.19 AW	28.95 TQ	AKBLS	10/01-12/01
Heavy and Tractor-Trailer	Anchorage MSA, AK	H	12.13 FQ	18.73 AW	27.23 TQ	AKBLS	10/01-12/01
Heavy and Tractor-Trailer	Arizona	H	10.45 FQ	15.77 AW	22.89 TQ	AZBLS	10/01-12/01
Heavy and Tractor-Trailer	Phoenix-Mesa MSA, AZ	H	10.81 FQ	16.24 AW	23.93 TQ	AZBLS	10/01-12/01
Heavy and Tractor-Trailer	Tucson MSA, AZ	H	9.80 FQ	14.80 AW	20.08 TQ	AZBLS	10/01-12/01
Heavy and Tractor-Trailer	Arkansas	H	8.53 FQ	15.09 AW	24.25 TQ	ARBLS	10/01-12/01
Heavy and Tractor-Trailer	Fayetteville-Springdale-Rogers MSA, AR	H	8.42 FQ	16.24 AW	26.85 TQ	ARBLS	10/01-12/01
Heavy and Tractor-Trailer	Fort Smith MSA, AR-OK	H	8.71 FQ	14.74 AW	20.03 TQ	ARBLS	10/01-12/01
Heavy and Tractor-Trailer	Little Rock-North Little Rock MSA, AR	H	8.54 FQ	15.60 AW	26.14 TQ	ARBLS	10/01-12/01
Heavy and Tractor-Trailer	California	H	11.34 FQ	16.75 AW	22.19 TQ	CABLS	10/01-12/01
Heavy and Tractor-Trailer	Bakersfield MSA, CA	H	9.91 FQ	15.92 AW	21.74 TQ	CABLS	10/01-12/01
Heavy and Tractor-Trailer	Chico-Paradise MSA, CA	H	8.46 FQ	13.02 AW	18.76 TQ	CABLS	10/01-12/01
Heavy and Tractor-Trailer	Fresno MSA, CA	H	10.56 FQ	15.98 AW	22.97 TQ	CABLS	10/01-12/01
Heavy and Tractor-Trailer	Los Angeles-Long Beach PMSA, CA	H	11.67 FQ	16.56 AW	21.59 TQ	CABLS	10/01-12/01
Heavy and Tractor-Trailer	Merced MSA, CA	H	9.96 FQ	15.46 AW	23.28 TQ	CABLS	10/01-12/01
Heavy and Tractor-Trailer	Modesto MSA, CA	H	9.98 FQ	14.57 AW	20.28 TQ	CABLS	10/01-12/01
Heavy and Tractor-Trailer	Oakland PMSA, CA	H	13.28 FQ	18.82 AW	26.79 TQ	CABLS	10/01-12/01
Heavy and Tractor-Trailer	Orange County PMSA, CA	H	11.92 FQ	16.78 AW	21.64 TQ	CABLS	10/01-12/01
Heavy and Tractor-Trailer	Redding MSA, CA	H	10.51 FQ	14.72 AW	20.96 TQ	CABLS	10/01-12/01
Heavy and Tractor-Trailer	Riverside-San Bernardino PMSA, CA	H	12.05 FQ	17.49 AW	22.85 TQ	CABLS	10/01-12/01
Heavy and Tractor-Trailer	Sacramento PMSA, CA	H	11.73 FQ	17.83 AW	27.39 TQ	CABLS	10/01-12/01
Heavy and Tractor-Trailer	Salinas MSA, CA	H	9.43 FQ	15.14 AW	21.45 TQ	CABLS	10/01-12/01
Heavy and Tractor-Trailer	San Diego MSA, CA	H	11.46 FQ	15.83 AW	21.00 TQ	CABLS	10/01-12/01
Heavy and Tractor-Trailer	San Francisco PMSA, CA	H	12.83 FQ	18.34 AW	23.58 TQ	CABLS	10/01-12/01
Heavy and Tractor-Trailer	San Jose PMSA, CA	H	14.51 FQ	18.57 AW	22.53 TQ	CABLS	10/01-12/01
Heavy and Tractor-Trailer	San Luis Obispo-Atascadero-Paso Robles MSA, CA	H	10.25 FQ	15.50 AW	21.37 TQ	CABLS	10/01-12/01
Heavy and Tractor-Trailer	Santa Barbara-Santa Maria-Lompoc MSA, CA	H	10.49 FQ	15.18 AW	20.99 TQ	CABLS	10/01-12/01
Heavy and Tractor-Trailer	Santa Cruz-Watsonville PMSA, CA	H	11.40 FQ	16.86 AW	22.19 TQ	CABLS	10/01-12/01
Heavy and Tractor-Trailer	Santa Rosa PMSA, CA	H	12.31 FQ	17.63 AW	24.49 TQ	CABLS	10/01-12/01
Heavy and Tractor-Trailer	Stockton-Lodi MSA, CA	H	9.78 FQ	17.08 AW	28.66 TQ	CABLS	10/01-12/01
Heavy and Tractor-Trailer	Vallejo-Fairfield-Napa PMSA, CA	H	11.78 FQ	17.70 AW	22.53 TQ	CABLS	10/01-12/01
Heavy and Tractor-Trailer	Ventura PMSA, CA	H	11.09 FQ	16.72 AW	21.93 TQ	CABLS	10/01-12/01
Heavy and Tractor-Trailer	Visalia-Tulare-Porterville MSA, CA	H	9.64 FQ	14.68 AW	20.77 TQ	CABLS	10/01-12/01
Heavy and Tractor-Trailer	Colorado	H	10.85 FQ	15.65 AW	21.40 TQ	COBLS	10/01-12/01
Heavy and Tractor-Trailer	Boulder-Longmont PMSA, CO	H	11.20 FQ	15.21 AW	20.49 TQ	COBLS	10/01-12/01
Heavy and Tractor-Trailer	Colorado Springs MSA, CO	H	10.26 FQ	14.57 AW	20.62 TQ	COBLS	10/01-12/01
Heavy and Tractor-Trailer	Denver PMSA, CO	H	11.72 FQ	16.56 AW	21.81 TQ	COBLS	10/01-12/01
Heavy and Tractor-Trailer	Fort Collins-Loveland MSA, CO	H	9.53 FQ	15.37 AW	23.31 TQ	COBLS	10/01-12/01

AAW	Average annual wage	**AOH**	Average offered, high	**ASH**	Average starting, high	**H**	Hourly	**M**	Monthly	**S**	Special: hourly and annual
AE	Average entry wage	**AOL**	Average offered, low	**ASL**	Average starting, low	**HI**	Highest wage paid	**MTC**	Median total compensation	**TQ**	Third quartile wage
AEX	Average experienced wage	**APH**	Average pay, high range	**AW**	Average wage paid	**HR**	High end range	**MW**	Median wage paid	**W**	Weekly
AO	Average offered	**APL**	Average pay, low range	**FQ**	First quartile wage	**LR**	Low end range	**SQ**	Second quartile wage	**Y**	Yearly

Occupation/Type/Industry	Location	Per	Low	Mid	High	Source	Date
Truck Driver							
Heavy and Tractor-Trailer	Greeley PMSA, CO	H	10.34 FQ	14.52 AW	19.29 TQ	COBLS	10/01-12/01
Heavy and Tractor-Trailer	Connecticut	H	11.85 FQ	17.71 AW	22.44 TQ	CTBLS	10/01-12/01
Heavy and Tractor-Trailer	Danbury PMSA, CT	H	12.12 FQ	17.00 AW	21.65 TQ	CTBLS	10/01-12/01
Heavy and Tractor-Trailer	Hartford MSA, CT	H	11.99 FQ	16.78 AW	22.03 TQ	CTBLS	10/01-12/01
Heavy and Tractor-Trailer	New Haven-Meriden PMSA, CT	H	11.62 FQ	17.14 AW	22.32 TQ	CTBLS	10/01-12/01
Heavy and Tractor-Trailer	New London-Norwich MSA, CT-RI	H	11.33 FQ	15.41 AW	20.16 TQ	CTBLS	10/01-12/01
Heavy and Tractor-Trailer	Stamford-Norwalk PMSA, CT	H	12.61 FQ	19.08 AW	23.39 TQ	CTBLS	10/01-12/01
Heavy and Tractor-Trailer	Waterbury PMSA, CT	H	11.95 FQ	17.58 AW	24.46 TQ	CTBLS	10/01-12/01
Heavy and Tractor-Trailer	Delaware	H	10.52 FQ	15.37 AW	20.85 TQ	DEBLS	10/01-12/01
Heavy and Tractor-Trailer	Wilmington-Newark PMSA, DE-MD	H	11.94 FQ	15.82 AW	20.74 TQ	DEBLS	10/01-12/01
Heavy and Tractor-Trailer	District of Columbia	H	11.44 FQ	15.11 AW	19.91 TQ	DCBLS	10/01-12/01
Heavy and Tractor-Trailer	Washington PMSA, DC-MD-VA-WV	H	11.47 FQ	16.62 AW	22.97 TQ	DCBLS	10/01-12/01
Heavy and Tractor-Trailer	Florida	H	9.11 FQ	14.72 AW	22.35 TQ	FLBLS	10/01-12/01
Heavy and Tractor-Trailer	Daytona Beach MSA, FL	H	9.09 FQ	14.76 AW	25.16 TQ	FLBLS	10/01-12/01
Heavy and Tractor-Trailer	Fort Lauderdale PMSA, FL	H	9.33 FQ	13.71 AW	19.07 TQ	FLBLS	10/01-12/01
Heavy and Tractor-Trailer	Fort Myers-Cape Coral MSA, FL	H	10.11 FQ	14.61 AW	20.47 TQ	FLBLS	10/01-12/01
Heavy and Tractor-Trailer	Fort Pierce-Port St. Lucie MSA, FL	H	9.17 FQ	17.25 AW	27.98 TQ	FLBLS	10/01-12/01
Heavy and Tractor-Trailer	Fort Walton Beach MSA, FL	H	8.15 FQ	10.21 AW	12.08 TQ	FLBLS	10/01-12/01
Heavy and Tractor-Trailer	Gainesville MSA, FL	H	9.17 FQ	23.07 AW	44.10 TQ	FLBLS	10/01-12/01
Heavy and Tractor-Trailer	Jacksonville MSA, FL	H	9.58 FQ	16.31 AW	23.98 TQ	FLBLS	10/01-12/01
Heavy and Tractor-Trailer	Lakeland-Winter Haven MSA, FL	H	9.04 FQ	15.03 AW	24.02 TQ	FLBLS	10/01-12/01
Heavy and Tractor-Trailer	Melbourne-Titusville-Palm Bay MSA, FL	H	9.14 FQ	13.67 AW	19.87 TQ	FLBLS	10/01-12/01
Heavy and Tractor-Trailer	Miami PMSA, FL	H	9.13 FQ	14.73 AW	22.04 TQ	FLBLS	10/01-12/01
Heavy and Tractor-Trailer	Naples MSA, FL	H	9.40 FQ	14.05 AW	21.30 TQ	FLBLS	10/01-12/01
Heavy and Tractor-Trailer	Ocala MSA, FL	H	9.55 FQ	16.63 AW	27.09 TQ	FLBLS	10/01-12/01
Heavy and Tractor-Trailer	Orlando MSA, FL	H	9.91 FQ	16.28 AW	25.21 TQ	FLBLS	10/01-12/01
Heavy and Tractor-Trailer	Pensacola MSA, FL	H	6.88 FQ	12.38 AW	20.08 TQ	FLBLS	10/01-12/01
Heavy and Tractor-Trailer	Sarasota-Bradenton MSA, FL	H	8.53 FQ	12.43 AW	17.44 TQ	FLBLS	10/01-12/01
Heavy and Tractor-Trailer	Tallahassee MSA, FL	H	8.48 FQ	12.96 AW	18.54 TQ	FLBLS	10/01-12/01
Heavy and Tractor-Trailer	Tampa-St. Petersburg-Clearwater MSA, FL	H	9.37 FQ	13.58 AW	19.53 TQ	FLBLS	10/01-12/01
Heavy and Tractor-Trailer	West Palm Beach-Boca Raton MSA, FL	H	9.30 FQ	14.30 AW	21.38 TQ	FLBLS	10/01-12/01
Heavy and Tractor-Trailer	Georgia	H	10.63 FQ	17.01 AW	24.60 TQ	GABLS	10/01-12/01
Heavy and Tractor-Trailer	Atlanta MSA, GA	H	11.77 FQ	18.73 AW	26.84 TQ	GABLS	10/01-12/01
Heavy and Tractor-Trailer	Augusta-Aiken MSA, GA-SC	H	9.37 FQ	15.74 AW	25.09 TQ	GABLS	10/01-12/01
Heavy and Tractor-Trailer	Columbus MSA, GA-AL	H	9.73 FQ	14.21 AW	20.27 TQ	GABLS	10/01-12/01
Heavy and Tractor-Trailer	Macon MSA, GA	H	9.10 FQ	15.57 AW	23.03 TQ	GABLS	10/01-12/01
Heavy and Tractor-Trailer	Savannah MSA, GA	H	9.16 FQ	14.97 AW	22.55 TQ	GABLS	10/01-12/01
Heavy and Tractor-Trailer	Hawaii	H	10.00 FQ	16.05 AW	25.44 TQ	HIBLS	10/01-12/01
Heavy and Tractor-Trailer	Honolulu MSA, HI	H	10.08 FQ	16.36 AW	25.82 TQ	HIBLS	10/01-12/01
Heavy and Tractor-Trailer	Idaho	H	8.26 FQ	14.84 AW	21.37 TQ	IDBLS	10/01-12/01
Heavy and Tractor-Trailer	Boise City MSA, ID	H	9.89 FQ	15.06 AW	21.05 TQ	IDBLS	10/01-12/01
Heavy and Tractor-Trailer	Illinois	H	11.37 FQ	17.72 AW	23.89 TQ	ILBLS	10/01-12/01
Heavy and Tractor-Trailer	Champaign-Urbana MSA, IL	H	11.60 FQ	19.90 AW	28.50 TQ	ILBLS	10/01-12/01
Heavy and Tractor-Trailer	Chicago PMSA, IL	H	13.56 FQ	18.87 AW	24.58 TQ	ILBLS	10/01-12/01
Heavy and Tractor-Trailer	Peoria-Pekin MSA, IL	H	11.11 FQ	17.23 AW	25.60 TQ	ILBLS	10/01-12/01
Heavy and Tractor-Trailer	Rockford MSA, IL	H	11.54 FQ	17.25 AW	23.41 TQ	ILBLS	10/01-12/01
Heavy and Tractor-Trailer	Springfield MSA, IL	H	9.69 FQ	17.57 AW	26.83 TQ	ILBLS	10/01-12/01
Heavy and Tractor-Trailer	Indiana	H	10.30 FQ	16.76 AW	24.03 TQ	INBLS	10/01-12/01
Heavy and Tractor-Trailer	Elkhart-Goshen MSA, IN	H	11.88 FQ	16.39 AW	21.68 TQ	INBLS	10/01-12/01
Heavy and Tractor-Trailer	Evansville-Henderson MSA, IN-KY	H	10.76 FQ	14.53 AW	20.30 TQ	INBLS	10/01-12/01
Heavy and Tractor-Trailer	Fort Wayne MSA, IN	H	10.78 FQ	17.80 AW	25.91 TQ	INBLS	10/01-12/01
Heavy and Tractor-Trailer	Gary PMSA, IN	H	12.36 FQ	19.11 AW	26.89 TQ	INBLS	10/01-12/01
Heavy and Tractor-Trailer	Indianapolis MSA, IN	H	10.05 FQ	16.93 AW	23.84 TQ	INBLS	10/01-12/01
Heavy and Tractor-Trailer	Lafayette MSA, IN	H	9.91 FQ	16.24 AW	21.73 TQ	INBLS	10/01-12/01
Heavy and Tractor-Trailer	South Bend MSA, IN	H	10.33 FQ	16.45 AW	21.46 TQ	INBLS	10/01-12/01
Heavy and Tractor-Trailer	Iowa	H	8.57 FQ	15.03 AW	21.71 TQ	IABLS	10/01-12/01
Heavy and Tractor-Trailer	Cedar Rapids MSA, IA	H	12.60 FQ	18.20 AW	22.31 TQ	IABLS	10/01-12/01
Heavy and Tractor-Trailer	Davenport-Moline-Rock Island MSA, IA-IL	H	8.31 FQ	15.57 AW	22.52 TQ	IABLS	10/01-12/01
Heavy and Tractor-Trailer	Des Moines MSA, IA	H	10.58 FQ	16.18 AW	22.73 TQ	IABLS	10/01-12/01

AAW	Average annual wage	AOH	Average offered, high	ASH	Average starting, high	H	Hourly	M	Monthly	S	Special: hourly and annual
AE	Average entry wage	AOL	Average offered, low	ASL	Average starting, low	HI	Highest wage paid	MTC	Median total compensation	TQ	Third quartile wage
AEX	Average experienced wage	APH	Average pay, high range	AW	Average wage paid	HR	High end range	MW	Median wage paid	W	Weekly
AO	Average offered	APL	Average pay, low range	FQ	First quartile wage	LR	Low end range	SQ	Second quartile wage	Y	Yearly

Occupation/Type/Industry	Location	Per	Low	Mid	High	Source	Date
Truck Driver							
Heavy and Tractor-Trailer	Kansas	H	9.62 FQ	15.69 AW	22.23 TQ	KSBLS	10/01-12/01
Heavy and Tractor-Trailer	Topeka MSA, KS	H	9.36 FQ	14.70 AW	20.49 TQ	KSBLS	10/01-12/01
Heavy and Tractor-Trailer	Wichita MSA, KS	H	10.08 FQ	14.85 AW	20.58 TQ	KSBLS	10/01-12/01
Heavy and Tractor-Trailer	Kentucky	H	9.39 FQ	14.94 AW	22.23 TQ	KYBLS	10/01-12/01
Heavy and Tractor-Trailer	Lexington MSA, KY	H	10.16 FQ	18.40 AW	29.61 TQ	KYBLS	10/01-12/01
Heavy and Tractor-Trailer	Louisville MSA, KY-IN	H	10.28 FQ	15.90 AW	22.32 TQ	KYBLS	10/01-12/01
Heavy and Tractor-Trailer	Louisiana	H	8.64 FQ	14.00 AW	21.01 TQ	LABLS	10/01-12/01
Heavy and Tractor-Trailer	Baton Rouge MSA, LA	H	8.83 FQ	15.39 AW	21.99 TQ	LABLS	10/01-12/01
Heavy and Tractor-Trailer	Houma MSA, LA	H	7.81 FQ	11.89 AW	18.04 TQ	LABLS	10/01-12/01
Heavy and Tractor-Trailer	Lafayette MSA, LA	H	8.32 FQ	14.01 AW	21.87 TQ	LABLS	10/01-12/01
Heavy and Tractor-Trailer	Lake Charles MSA, LA	H	9.61 FQ	13.59 AW	18.04 TQ	LABLS	10/01-12/01
Heavy and Tractor-Trailer	New Orleans MSA, LA	H	9.34 FQ	13.92 AW	20.21 TQ	LABLS	10/01-12/01
Heavy and Tractor-Trailer	Shreveport-Bossier City MSA, LA	H	9.24 FQ	15.10 AW	22.33 TQ	LABLS	10/01-12/01
Heavy and Tractor-Trailer	Maine	H	9.11 FQ	13.74 AW	21.68 TQ	MEBLS	10/01-12/01
Heavy and Tractor-Trailer	Portland MSA, ME	H	10.53 FQ	15.10 AW	23.50 TQ	MEBLS	10/01-12/01
Heavy and Tractor-Trailer	Maryland	H	10.74 FQ	16.21 AW	23.38 TQ	MDBLS	10/01-12/01
Heavy and Tractor-Trailer	Baltimore PMSA, MD	H	10.65 FQ	16.32 AW	22.98 TQ	MDBLS	10/01-12/01
Heavy and Tractor-Trailer	Massachusetts	H	12.53 FQ	18.09 AW	25.02 TQ	MABLS	10/01-12/01
Heavy and Tractor-Trailer	Boston PMSA, MA-NH	H	13.70 FQ	18.73 AW	25.45 TQ	MABLS	10/01-12/01
Heavy and Tractor-Trailer	Brockton PMSA, MA	H	13.15 FQ	18.18 AW	25.77 TQ	MABLS	10/01-12/01
Heavy and Tractor-Trailer	Lawrence PMSA, MA-NH	H	11.91 FQ	17.01 AW	23.68 TQ	MABLS	10/01-12/01
Heavy and Tractor-Trailer	Lowell PMSA, MA-NH	H	13.01 FQ	19.46 AW	26.58 TQ	MABLS	10/01-12/01
Heavy and Tractor-Trailer	New Bedford PMSA, MA	H	10.35 FQ	15.87 AW	24.16 TQ	MABLS	10/01-12/01
Heavy and Tractor-Trailer	Springfield MSA, MA	H	9.13 FQ	16.06 AW	21.91 TQ	MABLS	10/01-12/01
Heavy and Tractor-Trailer	Worcester PMSA, MA-CT	H	13.52 FQ	18.26 AW	24.63 TQ	MABLS	10/01-12/01
Heavy and Tractor-Trailer	Michigan	H	11.43 FQ	16.34 AW	22.50 TQ	MIBLS	10/01-12/01
Heavy and Tractor-Trailer	Ann Arbor PMSA, MI	H	10.24 FQ	17.00 AW	22.67 TQ	MIBLS	10/01-12/01
Heavy and Tractor-Trailer	Detroit PMSA, MI	H	12.70 FQ	17.37 AW	24.08 TQ	MIBLS	10/01-12/01
Heavy and Tractor-Trailer	Flint PMSA, MI	H	10.77 FQ	16.77 AW	23.13 TQ	MIBLS	10/01-12/01
Heavy and Tractor-Trailer	Grand Rapids-Muskegon-Holland MSA, MI	H	11.57 FQ	15.93 AW	21.48 TQ	MIBLS	10/01-12/01
Heavy and Tractor-Trailer	Kalamazoo-Battle Creek MSA, MI	H	11.16 FQ	15.33 AW	20.45 TQ	MIBLS	10/01-12/01
Heavy and Tractor-Trailer	Lansing-East Lansing MSA, MI	H	12.12 FQ	17.97 AW	24.93 TQ	MIBLS	10/01-12/01
Heavy and Tractor-Trailer	Saginaw-Bay City-Midland MSA, MI	H	7.22 FQ	13.05 AW	19.28 TQ	MIBLS	10/01-12/01
Heavy and Tractor-Trailer	Minnesota	H	10.98 FQ	16.99 AW	23.70 TQ	MNBLS	10/01-12/01
Heavy and Tractor-Trailer	Duluth-Superior MSA, MN-WI	H	9.94 FQ	15.20 AW	21.06 TQ	MNBLS	10/01-12/01
Heavy and Tractor-Trailer	Minneapolis-St. Paul MSA, MN-WI	H	13.45 FQ	18.54 AW	25.11 TQ	MNBLS	10/01-12/01
Heavy and Tractor-Trailer	St. Cloud MSA, MN	H	11.04 FQ	16.95 AW	22.22 TQ	MNBLS	10/01-12/01
Heavy and Tractor-Trailer	Mississippi	H	8.09 FQ	15.01 AW	23.02 TQ	MSBLS	10/01-12/01
Heavy and Tractor-Trailer	Biloxi-Gulfport-Pascagoula MSA, MS	H	8.99 FQ	13.07 AW	19.03 TQ	MSBLS	10/01-12/01
Heavy and Tractor-Trailer	Missouri	H	9.68 FQ	17.00 AW	24.40 TQ	MOBLS	10/01-12/01
Heavy and Tractor-Trailer	Kansas City MSA, MO-KS	H	11.56 FQ	17.45 AW	23.52 TQ	MOBLS	10/01-12/01
Heavy and Tractor-Trailer	St. Louis MSA, MO-IL	H	11.08 FQ	18.21 AW	27.01 TQ	MOBLS	10/01-12/01
Heavy and Tractor-Trailer	Springfield MSA, MO	H	9.31 FQ	16.28 AW	23.95 TQ	MOBLS	10/01-12/01
Heavy and Tractor-Trailer	Montana	H	8.59 FQ	15.33 AW	24.67 TQ	MTBLS	10/01-12/01
Heavy and Tractor-Trailer	Billings MSA, MT	H	7.82 FQ	13.77 AW	21.49 TQ	MTBLS	10/01-12/01
Heavy and Tractor-Trailer	Nebraska	H	9.51 FQ	15.75 AW	23.38 TQ	NEBLS	10/01-12/01
Heavy and Tractor-Trailer	Lincoln MSA, NE	H	9.36 FQ	13.88 AW	18.26 TQ	NEBLS	10/01-12/01
Heavy and Tractor-Trailer	Omaha MSA, NE-IA	H	10.37 FQ	17.07 AW	25.15 TQ	NEBLS	10/01-12/01
Heavy and Tractor-Trailer	Nevada	H	10.92 FQ	16.56 AW	22.35 TQ	NVBLS	10/01-12/01
Heavy and Tractor-Trailer	Las Vegas MSA, NV-AZ	H	10.29 FQ	16.29 AW	23.08 TQ	NVBLS	10/01-12/01
Heavy and Tractor-Trailer	Reno MSA, NV	H	12.76 FQ	17.00 AW	22.15 TQ	NVBLS	10/01-12/01
Heavy and Tractor-Trailer	New Hampshire	H	10.64 FQ	14.84 AW	20.43 TQ	NHBLS	10/01-12/01
Heavy and Tractor-Trailer	Manchester PMSA, NH	H	11.82 FQ	15.85 AW	20.96 TQ	NHBLS	10/01-12/01
Heavy and Tractor-Trailer	Nashua PMSA, NH	H	11.77 FQ	14.83 AW	18.15 TQ	NHBLS	10/01-12/01
Heavy and Tractor-Trailer	Portsmouth-Rochester PMSA, NH-ME	H	10.34 FQ	15.40 AW	22.65 TQ	NHBLS	10/01-12/01
Heavy and Tractor-Trailer	New Jersey	H	12.13 FQ	17.73 AW	23.57 TQ	NJBLS	10/01-12/01
Heavy and Tractor-Trailer	Atlantic-Cape May PMSA, NJ	H	9.51 FQ	16.16 AW	22.99 TQ	NJBLS	10/01-12/01
Heavy and Tractor-Trailer	Bergen-Passaic PMSA, NJ	H	11.96 FQ	17.83 AW	24.67 TQ	NJBLS	10/01-12/01
Heavy and Tractor-Trailer	Jersey City PMSA, NJ	H	12.54 FQ	17.71 AW	22.20 TQ	NJBLS	10/01-12/01
Heavy and Tractor-Trailer	Middlesex-Somerset-Hunterdon PMSA, NJ	H	14.07 FQ	19.34 AW	26.49 TQ	NJBLS	10/01-12/01
Heavy and Tractor-Trailer	Monmouth-Ocean PMSA, NJ	H	10.19 FQ	16.43 AW	22.23 TQ	NJBLS	10/01-12/01
Heavy and Tractor-Trailer	Newark PMSA, NJ	H	12.21 FQ	17.93 AW	23.95 TQ	NJBLS	10/01-12/01
Heavy and Tractor-Trailer	Trenton PMSA, NJ	H	13.03 FQ	18.47 AW	24.66 TQ	NJBLS	10/01-12/01

AAW	Average annual wage	**AOH**	Average offered, high	**ASH**	Average starting, high	**H**	Hourly	**M**	Monthly	**S**	Special: hourly and annual
AE	Average entry wage	**AOL**	Average offered, low	**ASL**	Average starting, low	**HI**	Highest wage paid	**MTC**	Median total compensation	**TQ**	Third quartile wage
AEX	Average experienced wage	**APH**	Average pay, high range	**AW**	Average wage paid	**HR**	High end range	**MW**	Median wage paid	**W**	Weekly
AO	Average offered	**APL**	Average pay, low range	**FQ**	First quartile wage	**LR**	Low end range	**SQ**	Second quartile wage	**Y**	Yearly

Occupation/Type/Industry	Location	Per	Low	Mid	High	Source	Date
Truck Driver							
Heavy and Tractor-Trailer	New Mexico	H	8.89 FQ	14.14 AW	21.19 TQ	NMBLS	10/01-12/01
Heavy and Tractor-Trailer	Albuquerque MSA, NM	H	9.90 FQ	15.25 AW	21.78 TQ	NMBLS	10/01-12/01
Heavy and Tractor-Trailer	New York	H	10.50 FQ	17.64 AW	27.20 TQ	NYBLS	10/01-12/01
Heavy and Tractor-Trailer	Albany-Schenectady-Troy MSA, NY	H	9.93 FQ	16.78 AW	25.74 TQ	NYBLS	10/01-12/01
Heavy and Tractor-Trailer	Binghamton MSA, NY	H	9.77 FQ	16.16 AW	26.18 TQ	NYBLS	10/01-12/01
Heavy and Tractor-Trailer	Buffalo-Niagara Falls MSA, NY	H	10.39 FQ	17.40 AW	26.05 TQ	NYBLS	10/01-12/01
Heavy and Tractor-Trailer	Dutchess County PMSA, NY	H	11.20 FQ	16.40 AW	22.19 TQ	NYBLS	10/01-12/01
Heavy and Tractor-Trailer	Nassau-Suffolk PMSA, NY	H	11.53 FQ	19.19 AW	28.91 TQ	NYBLS	10/01-12/01
Heavy and Tractor-Trailer	New York PMSA, NY	H	11.18 FQ	19.59 AW	34.78 TQ	NYBLS	10/01-12/01
Heavy and Tractor-Trailer	Newburgh PMSA, NY-PA	H	11.55 FQ	18.28 AW	25.98 TQ	NYBLS	10/01-12/01
Heavy and Tractor-Trailer	Rochester MSA, NY	H	10.02 FQ	15.20 AW	20.87 TQ	NYBLS	10/01-12/01
Heavy and Tractor-Trailer	Syracuse MSA, NY	H	10.81 FQ	16.95 AW	25.05 TQ	NYBLS	10/01-12/01
Heavy and Tractor-Trailer	Utica-Rome MSA, NY	H	9.21 FQ	14.28 AW	23.36 TQ	NYBLS	10/01-12/01
Heavy and Tractor-Trailer	North Carolina	H	9.91 FQ	15.75 AW	22.63 TQ	NCBLS	10/01-12/01
Heavy and Tractor-Trailer	Asheville MSA, NC	H	10.38 FQ	15.88 AW	21.37 TQ	NCBLS	10/01-12/01
Heavy and Tractor-Trailer	Charlotte-Gastonia-Rock Hill MSA, NC-SC	H	11.31 FQ	16.94 AW	24.63 TQ	NCBLS	10/01-12/01
Heavy and Tractor-Trailer	Fayetteville MSA, NC	H	9.67 FQ	14.40 AW	20.22 TQ	NCBLS	10/01-12/01
Heavy and Tractor-Trailer	Greensboro-Winston-Salem-High Point MSA, NC	H	10.50 FQ	16.27 AW	21.82 TQ	NCBLS	10/01-12/01
Heavy and Tractor-Trailer	Hickory-Morganton-Lenoir MSA, NC	H	11.01 FQ	15.75 AW	22.77 TQ	NCBLS	10/01-12/01
Heavy and Tractor-Trailer	Raleigh-Durham-Chapel Hill MSA, NC	H	9.06 FQ	14.20 AW	20.48 TQ	NCBLS	10/01-12/01
Heavy and Tractor-Trailer	Wilmington MSA, NC	H	8.96 FQ	14.21 AW	22.95 TQ	NCBLS	10/01-12/01
Heavy and Tractor-Trailer	North Dakota	H	9.42 FQ	14.35 AW	21.17 TQ	NDBLS	10/01-12/01
Heavy and Tractor-Trailer	Fargo-Moorhead MSA, ND-MN	H	9.91 FQ	15.74 AW	21.72 TQ	NDBLS	10/01-12/01
Heavy and Tractor-Trailer	Ohio	H	10.72 FQ	16.51 AW	23.63 TQ	OHBLS	10/01-12/01
Heavy and Tractor-Trailer	Akron PMSA, OH	H	11.15 FQ	16.87 AW	24.22 TQ	OHBLS	10/01-12/01
Heavy and Tractor-Trailer	Canton-Massillon MSA, OH	H	9.46 FQ	15.39 AW	22.87 TQ	OHBLS	10/01-12/01
Heavy and Tractor-Trailer	Cincinnati PMSA, OH-KY-IN	H	10.19 FQ	16.13 AW	24.04 TQ	OHBLS	10/01-12/01
Heavy and Tractor-Trailer	Cleveland-Lorain-Elyria PMSA, OH	H	11.76 FQ	17.95 AW	25.57 TQ	OHBLS	10/01-12/01
Heavy and Tractor-Trailer	Columbus MSA, OH	H	11.62 FQ	16.40 AW	22.29 TQ	OHBLS	10/01-12/01
Heavy and Tractor-Trailer	Dayton-Springfield MSA, OH	H	11.73 FQ	18.31 AW	28.10 TQ	OHBLS	10/01-12/01
Heavy and Tractor-Trailer	Hamilton-Middletown PMSA, OH	H	9.97 FQ	15.23 AW	21.16 TQ	OHBLS	10/01-12/01
Heavy and Tractor-Trailer	Mansfield MSA, OH	H	8.75 FQ	13.83 AW	20.34 TQ	OHBLS	10/01-12/01
Heavy and Tractor-Trailer	Toledo MSA, OH	H	11.88 FQ	17.57 AW	24.22 TQ	OHBLS	10/01-12/01
Heavy and Tractor-Trailer	Youngstown-Warren MSA, OH	H	9.74 FQ	15.28 AW	21.81 TQ	OHBLS	10/01-12/01
Heavy and Tractor-Trailer	Oklahoma	H	8.96 FQ	14.61 AW	22.16 TQ	OKBLS	10/01-12/01
Heavy and Tractor-Trailer	Oklahoma City MSA, OK	H	9.26 FQ	15.28 AW	24.65 TQ	OKBLS	10/01-12/01
Heavy and Tractor-Trailer	Tulsa MSA, OK	H	10.11 FQ	15.45 AW	21.63 TQ	OKBLS	10/01-12/01
Heavy and Tractor-Trailer	Oregon	H	11.13 FQ	15.83 AW	21.25 TQ	ORBLS	10/01-12/01
Heavy and Tractor-Trailer	Eugene-Springfield MSA, OR	H	10.78 FQ	14.95 AW	20.61 TQ	ORBLS	10/01-12/01
Heavy and Tractor-Trailer	Medford-Ashland MSA, OR	H	11.19 FQ	14.55 AW	20.18 TQ	ORBLS	10/01-12/01
Heavy and Tractor-Trailer	Portland-Vancouver PMSA, OR-WA	H	11.89 FQ	16.67 AW	21.52 TQ	ORBLS	10/01-12/01
Heavy and Tractor-Trailer	Salem PMSA, OR	H	10.21 FQ	14.58 AW	18.75 TQ	ORBLS	10/01-12/01
Heavy and Tractor-Trailer	Pennsylvania	H	10.84 FQ	17.03 AW	24.83 TQ	PABLS	10/01-12/01
Heavy and Tractor-Trailer	Allentown-Bethlehem-Easton MSA, PA	H	11.65 FQ	16.46 AW	22.07 TQ	PABLS	10/01-12/01
Heavy and Tractor-Trailer	Erie MSA, PA	H	10.13 FQ	16.11 AW	23.49 TQ	PABLS	10/01-12/01
Heavy and Tractor-Trailer	Harrisburg-Lebanon-Carlisle MSA, PA	H	11.97 FQ	20.24 AW	31.90 TQ	PABLS	10/01-12/01
Heavy and Tractor-Trailer	Johnstown MSA, PA	H	7.84 FQ	12.86 AW	17.61 TQ	PABLS	10/01-12/01
Heavy and Tractor-Trailer	Lancaster MSA, PA	H	11.71 FQ	16.07 AW	22.98 TQ	PABLS	10/01-12/01
Heavy and Tractor-Trailer	Philadelphia PMSA, PA-NJ	H	12.08 FQ	17.79 AW	24.88 TQ	PABLS	10/01-12/01
Heavy and Tractor-Trailer	Pittsburgh MSA, PA	H	11.27 FQ	17.57 AW	25.71 TQ	PABLS	10/01-12/01
Heavy and Tractor-Trailer	Reading MSA, PA	H	10.34 FQ	15.47 AW	22.33 TQ	PABLS	10/01-12/01
Heavy and Tractor-Trailer	Scranton-Wilkes-Barre-Hazleton MSA, PA	H	11.40 FQ	17.16 AW	22.28 TQ	PABLS	10/01-12/01
Heavy and Tractor-Trailer	York MSA, PA	H	9.92 FQ	16.19 AW	23.10 TQ	PABLS	10/01-12/01
Heavy and Tractor-Trailer	Rhode Island	H	11.45 FQ	15.55 AW	20.94 TQ	RIBLS	10/01-12/01
Heavy and Tractor-Trailer	Providence-Fall River-Warwick MSA, RI-MA	H	11.46 FQ	15.58 AW	21.07 TQ	RIBLS	10/01-12/01
Heavy and Tractor-Trailer	South Carolina	H	10.06 FQ	16.12 AW	24.12 TQ	SCBLS	10/01-12/01

AAW	Average annual wage	AOH	Average offered, high	ASH	Average starting, high	H	Hourly	M	Monthly	S	Special: hourly and annual
AE	Average entry wage	AOL	Average offered, low	ASL	Average starting, low	HI	Highest wage paid	MTC	Median total compensation	TQ	Third quartile wage
AEX	Average experienced wage	APH	Average pay, high range	AW	Average wage paid	HR	High end range	MW	Median wage paid	W	Weekly
AO	Average offered	APL	Average pay, low range	FQ	First quartile wage	LR	Low end range	SQ	Second quartile wage	Y	Yearly

Occupation/Type/Industry	Location	Per	Low	Mid	High	Source	Date
Truck Driver							
Heavy and Tractor-Trailer	Charleston-North Charleston MSA, SC	H	10.04 FQ	16.03 AW	23.38 TQ	SCBLS	10/01-12/01
Heavy and Tractor-Trailer	Columbia MSA, SC	H	9.86 FQ	15.98 AW	23.74 TQ	SCBLS	10/01-12/01
Heavy and Tractor-Trailer	Greenville-Spartanburg-Anderson MSA, SC	H	11.44 FQ	17.50 AW	26.08 TQ	SCBLS	10/01-12/01
Heavy and Tractor-Trailer	Myrtle Beach MSA, SC	H	9.26 FQ	13.35 AW	20.28 TQ	SCBLS	10/01-12/01
Heavy and Tractor-Trailer	South Dakota	H	9.60 FQ	14.80 AW	21.59 TQ	SDBLS	10/01-12/01
Heavy and Tractor-Trailer	Sioux Falls MSA, SD	H	9.89 FQ	16.17 AW	23.04 TQ	SDBLS	10/01-12/01
Heavy and Tractor-Trailer	Tennessee	H	9.74 FQ	16.58 AW	23.47 TQ	TNBLS	10/01-12/01
Heavy and Tractor-Trailer	Chattanooga MSA, TN-GA	H	13.21 FQ	18.50 AW	24.33 TQ	TNBLS	10/01-12/01
Heavy and Tractor-Trailer	Clarksville-Hopkinsville MSA, TN-KY	H	9.16 FQ	13.73 AW	21.13 TQ	TNBLS	10/01-12/01
Heavy and Tractor-Trailer	Johnson City-Kingsport-Bristol MSA, TN-VA	H	8.85 FQ	13.72 AW	21.79 TQ	TNBLS	10/01-12/01
Heavy and Tractor-Trailer	Knoxville MSA, TN	H	9.53 FQ	16.40 AW	25.09 TQ	TNBLS	10/01-12/01
Heavy and Tractor-Trailer	Memphis MSA, TN-AR-MS	H	11.40 FQ	16.46 AW	21.71 TQ	TNBLS	10/01-12/01
Heavy and Tractor-Trailer	Nashville MSA, TN	H	11.34 FQ	17.57 AW	25.08 TQ	TNBLS	10/01-12/01
Heavy and Tractor-Trailer	Texas	H	8.84 FQ	14.87 AW	22.29 TQ	TXBLS	10/01-12/01
Heavy and Tractor-Trailer	Amarillo MSA, TX	H	7.64 FQ	14.84 AW	28.54 TQ	TXBLS	10/01-12/01
Heavy and Tractor-Trailer	Austin-San Marcos MSA, TX	H	9.31 FQ	14.18 AW	20.88 TQ	TXBLS	10/01-12/01
Heavy and Tractor-Trailer	Beaumont-Port Arthur MSA, TX	H	8.96 FQ	13.40 AW	18.59 TQ	TXBLS	10/01-12/01
Heavy and Tractor-Trailer	Brazoria PMSA, TX	H	9.70 FQ	15.87 AW	22.77 TQ	TXBLS	10/01-12/01
Heavy and Tractor-Trailer	Brownsville-Harlingen-San Benito MSA, TX	H	6.87 FQ	11.95 AW	17.67 TQ	TXBLS	10/01-12/01
Heavy and Tractor-Trailer	Corpus Christi MSA, TX	H	8.14 FQ	13.27 AW	20.23 TQ	TXBLS	10/01-12/01
Heavy and Tractor-Trailer	Dallas PMSA, TX	H	10.05 FQ	16.96 AW	23.25 TQ	TXBLS	10/01-12/01
Heavy and Tractor-Trailer	El Paso MSA, TX	H	8.65 FQ	12.95 AW	19.39 TQ	TXBLS	10/01-12/01
Heavy and Tractor-Trailer	Fort Worth-Arlington PMSA, TX	H	9.91 FQ	16.15 AW	25.29 TQ	TXBLS	10/01-12/01
Heavy and Tractor-Trailer	Galveston-Texas City PMSA, TX	H	9.51 FQ	14.00 AW	20.08 TQ	TXBLS	10/01-12/01
Heavy and Tractor-Trailer	Houston PMSA, TX	H	9.35 FQ	14.57 AW	21.57 TQ	TXBLS	10/01-12/01
Heavy and Tractor-Trailer	Killeen-Temple MSA, TX	H	8.21 FQ	13.64 AW	19.70 TQ	TXBLS	10/01-12/01
Heavy and Tractor-Trailer	Laredo MSA, TX	H	8.03 FQ	15.11 AW	21.62 TQ	TXBLS	10/01-12/01
Heavy and Tractor-Trailer	Longview-Marshall MSA, TX	H	7.85 FQ	12.76 AW	20.02 TQ	TXBLS	10/01-12/01
Heavy and Tractor-Trailer	Lubbock MSA, TX	H	8.10 FQ	13.27 AW	20.74 TQ	TXBLS	10/01-12/01
Heavy and Tractor-Trailer	McAllen-Edinburg-Mission MSA, TX	H	7.27 FQ	13.71 AW	21.95 TQ	TXBLS	10/01-12/01
Heavy and Tractor-Trailer	Odessa-Midland MSA, TX	H	7.01 FQ	13.17 AW	19.87 TQ	TXBLS	10/01-12/01
Heavy and Tractor-Trailer	San Antonio MSA, TX	H	6.66 FQ	13.56 AW	23.53 TQ	TXBLS	10/01-12/01
Heavy and Tractor-Trailer	Tyler MSA, TX	H	9.20 FQ	14.33 AW	20.74 TQ	TXBLS	10/01-12/01
Heavy and Tractor-Trailer	Waco MSA, TX	H	9.48 FQ	15.54 AW	26.18 TQ	TXBLS	10/01-12/01
Heavy and Tractor-Trailer	Utah	H	11.48 FQ	17.26 AW	24.65 TQ	UTBLS	10/01-12/01
Heavy and Tractor-Trailer	Provo-Orem MSA, UT	H	11.80 FQ	16.81 AW	23.70 TQ	UTBLS	10/01-12/01
Heavy and Tractor-Trailer	Salt Lake City-Ogden MSA, UT	H	12.20 FQ	17.72 AW	24.43 TQ	UTBLS	10/01-12/01
Heavy and Tractor-Trailer	Vermont	H	9.64 FQ	14.38 AW	20.88 TQ	VTBLS	10/01-12/01
Heavy and Tractor-Trailer	Burlington MSA, VT	H	9.50 FQ	14.96 AW	23.75 TQ	VTBLS	10/01-12/01
Heavy and Tractor-Trailer	Virginia	H	9.39 FQ	15.50 AW	22.16 TQ	VABLS	10/01-12/01
Heavy and Tractor-Trailer	Lynchburg MSA, VA	H	9.01 FQ	12.85 AW	18.92 TQ	VABLS	10/01-12/01
Heavy and Tractor-Trailer	Norfolk-Virginia Beach-Newport News MSA, VA-NC	H	9.35 FQ	14.64 AW	22.31 TQ	VABLS	10/01-12/01
Heavy and Tractor-Trailer	Richmond-Petersburg MSA, VA	H	10.47 FQ	17.56 AW	27.71 TQ	VABLS	10/01-12/01
Heavy and Tractor-Trailer	Roanoke MSA, VA	H	9.80 FQ	16.00 AW	22.33 TQ	VABLS	10/01-12/01
Heavy and Tractor-Trailer	Washington	H	11.68 FQ	17.03 AW	22.77 TQ	WABLS	10/01-12/01
Heavy and Tractor-Trailer	Bremerton PMSA, WA	H	10.37 FQ	16.55 AW	21.61 TQ	WABLS	10/01-12/01
Heavy and Tractor-Trailer	Olympia PMSA, WA	H	11.27 FQ	15.32 AW	20.64 TQ	WABLS	10/01-12/01
Heavy and Tractor-Trailer	Richland-Kennewick-Pasco MSA, WA	H	10.63 FQ	16.51 AW	21.03 TQ	WABLS	10/01-12/01
Heavy and Tractor-Trailer	Seattle-Bellevue-Everett PMSA, WA	H	12.37 FQ	18.28 AW	24.71 TQ	WABLS	10/01-12/01
Heavy and Tractor-Trailer	Spokane MSA, WA	H	11.52 FQ	16.49 AW	22.26 TQ	WABLS	10/01-12/01
Heavy and Tractor-Trailer	Tacoma PMSA, WA	H	13.15 FQ	18.22 AW	24.05 TQ	WABLS	10/01-12/01
Heavy and Tractor-Trailer	Yakima MSA, WA	H	11.38 FQ	15.35 AW	20.94 TQ	WABLS	10/01-12/01
Heavy and Tractor-Trailer	West Virginia	H	8.18 FQ	13.70 AW	21.29 TQ	WVBLS	10/01-12/01
Heavy and Tractor-Trailer	Charleston MSA, WV	H	9.66 FQ	14.78 AW	21.05 TQ	WVBLS	10/01-12/01
Heavy and Tractor-Trailer	Huntington-Ashland MSA, WV-KY-OH	H	8.85 FQ	13.58 AW	20.13 TQ	WVBLS	10/01-12/01

AAW Average annual wage **AE** Average entry wage **AEX** Average experienced wage **AO** Average offered **AOH** Average offered, high **AOL** Average offered, low **APH** Average pay, high range **APL** Average pay, low range **ASH** Average starting, high **ASL** Average starting, low **AW** Average wage paid **FQ** First quartile wage **H** Hourly **HI** Highest wage paid **HR** High end range **LR** Low end range **M** Monthly **MTC** Median total compensation **MW** Median wage paid **SQ** Second quartile wage **S** Special: hourly and annual **TQ** Third quartile wage **W** Weekly **Y** Yearly

Occupation/Type/Industry	Location	Per	Low	Mid	High	Source	Date
Truck Driver							
Heavy and Tractor-Trailer	Wisconsin	H	11.17 FQ	17.15 AW	25.03 TQ	WIBLS	10/01-12/01
Heavy and Tractor-Trailer	Appleton-Oshkosh-Neenah MSA, WI	H	11.45 FQ	16.99 AW	24.61 TQ	WIBLS	10/01-12/01
Heavy and Tractor-Trailer	Green Bay MSA, WI	H	11.99 FQ	19.06 AW	26.84 TQ	WIBLS	10/01-12/01
Heavy and Tractor-Trailer	Madison MSA, WI	H	12.35 FQ	17.83 AW	26.08 TQ	WIBLS	10/01-12/01
Heavy and Tractor-Trailer	Milwaukee-Waukesha PMSA, WI	H	11.86 FQ	17.67 AW	24.36 TQ	WIBLS	10/01-12/01
Heavy and Tractor-Trailer	Racine PMSA, WI	H	11.56 FQ	17.30 AW	23.55 TQ	WIBLS	10/01-12/01
Heavy and Tractor-Trailer	Wyoming	H	10.07 FQ	14.69 AW	21.21 TQ	WYBLS	10/01-12/01
Heavy and Tractor-Trailer	Cheyenne MSA, WY	H	10.77 FQ	14.48 AW	20.16 TQ	WYBLS	10/01-12/01
Heavy and Tractor-Trailer	Puerto Rico	H	5.63 FQ	8.05 AW	11.08 TQ	PRBLS	10/01-12/01
Heavy and Tractor-Trailer	Virgin Islands	H	8.23 FQ	11.64 AW	16.60 TQ	VIBLS	10/01-12/01
Heavy and Tractor-Trailer	Guam	H	7.64 FQ	11.38 AW	16.31 TQ	GUBLS	10/01-12/01
Light or Delivery Service	Alabama	H	6.45 FQ	12.05 AW	22.98 TQ	ALBLS	10/01-12/01
Light or Delivery Service	Birmingham MSA, AL	H	7.46 FQ	12.77 AW	23.02 TQ	ALBLS	10/01-12/01
Light or Delivery Service	Huntsville MSA, AL	H	6.26 FQ	11.37 AW	20.52 TQ	ALBLS	10/01-12/01
Light or Delivery Service	Mobile MSA, AL	H	6.26 FQ	10.66 AW	16.96 TQ	ALBLS	10/01-12/01
Light or Delivery Service	Montgomery MSA, AL	H	6.96 FQ	12.59 AW	24.79 TQ	ALBLS	10/01-12/01
Light or Delivery Service	Alaska	H	9.05 FQ	13.58 AW	19.20 TQ	AKBLS	10/01-12/01
Light or Delivery Service	Anchorage MSA, AK	H	9.15 FQ	13.48 AW	19.02 TQ	AKBLS	10/01-12/01
Light or Delivery Service	Arizona	H	7.02 FQ	12.38 AW	22.07 TQ	AZBLS	10/01-12/01
Light or Delivery Service	Phoenix-Mesa MSA, AZ	H	7.42 FQ	12.68 AW	21.89 TQ	AZBLS	10/01-12/01
Light or Delivery Service	Tucson MSA, AZ	H	6.13 FQ	11.19 AW	22.03 TQ	AZBLS	10/01-12/01
Light or Delivery Service	Arkansas	H	6.05 FQ	10.96 AW	20.75 TQ	ARBLS	10/01-12/01
Light or Delivery Service	Fayetteville-Springdale-Rogers MSA, AR	H	6.25 FQ	11.04 AW	17.82 TQ	ARBLS	10/01-12/01
Light or Delivery Service	Fort Smith MSA, AR-OK	H	5.84 FQ	10.47 AW	23.02 TQ	ARBLS	10/01-12/01
Light or Delivery Service	Little Rock-North Little Rock MSA, AR	H	7.16 FQ	12.12 AW	21.38 TQ	ARBLS	10/01-12/01
Light or Delivery Service	California	H	7.13 FQ	12.21 AW	18.75 TQ	CABLS	10/01-12/01
Light or Delivery Service	Bakersfield MSA, CA	H	7.17 FQ	12.09 AW	18.41 TQ	CABLS	10/01-12/01
Light or Delivery Service	Chico-Paradise MSA, CA	H	6.79 FQ	10.96 AW	16.39 TQ	CABLS	10/01-12/01
Light or Delivery Service	Fresno MSA, CA	H	6.94 FQ	11.51 AW	17.63 TQ	CABLS	10/01-12/01
Light or Delivery Service	Los Angeles-Long Beach PMSA, CA	H	6.91 FQ	11.83 AW	18.56 TQ	CABLS	10/01-12/01
Light or Delivery Service	Merced MSA, CA	H	6.91 FQ	11.20 AW	15.12 TQ	CABLS	10/01-12/01
Light or Delivery Service	Modesto MSA, CA	H	7.79 FQ	12.14 AW	17.23 TQ	CABLS	10/01-12/01
Light or Delivery Service	Oakland PMSA, CA	H	7.90 FQ	13.16 AW	19.06 TQ	CABLS	10/01-12/01
Light or Delivery Service	Orange County PMSA, CA	H	7.04 FQ	12.85 AW	20.10 TQ	CABLS	10/01-12/01
Light or Delivery Service	Redding MSA, CA	H	6.65 FQ	11.68 AW	19.21 TQ	CABLS	10/01-12/01
Light or Delivery Service	Riverside-San Bernardino PMSA, CA	H	7.03 FQ	11.70 AW	19.39 TQ	CABLS	10/01-12/01
Light or Delivery Service	Sacramento PMSA, CA	H	6.94 FQ	11.73 AW	16.88 TQ	CABLS	10/01-12/01
Light or Delivery Service	Salinas MSA, CA	H	7.09 FQ	11.65 AW	17.64 TQ	CABLS	10/01-12/01
Light or Delivery Service	San Diego MSA, CA	H	7.11 FQ	11.47 AW	17.32 TQ	CABLS	10/01-12/01
Light or Delivery Service	San Francisco PMSA, CA	H	8.22 FQ	13.14 AW	18.93 TQ	CABLS	10/01-12/01
Light or Delivery Service	San Jose PMSA, CA	H	8.71 FQ	12.92 AW	19.42 TQ	CABLS	10/01-12/01
Light or Delivery Service	San Luis Obispo-Atascadero-Paso Robles MSA, CA	H	7.13 FQ	11.49 AW	17.20 TQ	CABLS	10/01-12/01
Light or Delivery Service	Santa Barbara-Santa Maria-Lompoc MSA, CA	H	7.10 FQ	11.34 AW	16.82 TQ	CABLS	10/01-12/01
Light or Delivery Service	Santa Cruz-Watsonville PMSA, CA	H	8.86 FQ	12.34 AW	16.65 TQ	CABLS	10/01-12/01
Light or Delivery Service	Santa Rosa PMSA, CA	H	7.95 FQ	12.02 AW	17.24 TQ	CABLS	10/01-12/01
Light or Delivery Service	Stockton-Lodi MSA, CA	H	6.85 FQ	12.49 AW	18.19 TQ	CABLS	10/01-12/01
Light or Delivery Service	Vallejo-Fairfield-Napa PMSA, CA	H	7.48 FQ	12.44 AW	17.94 TQ	CABLS	10/01-12/01
Light or Delivery Service	Ventura PMSA, CA	H	7.41 FQ	11.36 AW	16.34 TQ	CABLS	10/01-12/01
Light or Delivery Service	Visalia-Tulare-Porterville MSA, CA	H	6.84 FQ	13.34 AW	21.17 TQ	CABLS	10/01-12/01
Light or Delivery Service	Colorado	H	7.71 FQ	13.13 AW	20.41 TQ	COBLS	10/01-12/01
Light or Delivery Service	Boulder-Longmont PMSA, CO	H	8.00 FQ	13.30 AW	22.58 TQ	COBLS	10/01-12/01
Light or Delivery Service	Colorado Springs MSA, CO	H	7.67 FQ	12.22 AW	19.95 TQ	COBLS	10/01-12/01
Light or Delivery Service	Denver PMSA, CO	H	7.87 FQ	13.14 AW	18.96 TQ	COBLS	10/01-12/01
Light or Delivery Service	Fort Collins-Loveland MSA, CO	H	6.76 FQ	11.84 AW	20.50 TQ	COBLS	10/01-12/01
Light or Delivery Service	Greeley PMSA, CO	H	7.62 FQ	13.14 AW	21.42 TQ	COBLS	10/01-12/01
Light or Delivery Service	Connecticut	H	7.13 FQ	13.05 AW	20.32 TQ	CTBLS	10/01-12/01
Light or Delivery Service	Bridgeport PMSA, CT	H	7.54 FQ	13.48 AW	20.55 TQ	CTBLS	10/01-12/01
Light or Delivery Service	Danbury PMSA, CT	H	8.54 FQ	13.97 AW	21.07 TQ	CTBLS	10/01-12/01
Light or Delivery Service	Hartford MSA, CT	H	6.72 FQ	12.86 AW	20.58 TQ	CTBLS	10/01-12/01

AAW	Average annual wage	**AOH**	Average offered, high	**ASH**	Average starting, high	**H**	Hourly	**M**	Monthly	**S**	Special: hourly and annual
AE	Average entry wage	**AOL**	Average offered, low	**ASL**	Average starting, low	**HI**	Highest wage paid	**MTC**	Median total compensation	**TQ**	Third quartile wage
AEX	Average experienced wage	**APH**	Average pay, high range	**AW**	Average wage paid	**HR**	High end range	**MW**	Median wage paid	**W**	Weekly
AO	Average offered	**APL**	Average pay, low range	**FQ**	First quartile wage	**LR**	Low end range	**SQ**	Second quartile wage	**Y**	Yearly

Occupation/Type/Industry	Location	Per	Low	Mid	High	Source	Date
Truck Driver							
Light or Delivery Service	New Haven-Meriden PMSA, CT	H	7.70 FQ	13.60 AW	21.04 TQ	CTBLS	10/01-12/01
Light or Delivery Service	New London-Norwich MSA, CT-RI	H	6.96 FQ	12.88 AW	21.17 TQ	CTBLS	10/01-12/01
Light or Delivery Service	Stamford-Norwalk PMSA, CT	H	7.16 FQ	12.30 AW	16.90 TQ	CTBLS	10/01-12/01
Light or Delivery Service	Waterbury PMSA, CT	H	7.21 FQ	12.93 AW	20.27 TQ	CTBLS	10/01-12/01
Light or Delivery Service	Delaware	H	7.49 FQ	13.04 AW	20.26 TQ	DEBLS	10/01-12/01
Light or Delivery Service	Wilmington-Newark PMSA, DE-MD	H	8.35 FQ	13.59 AW	20.59 TQ	DEBLS	10/01-12/01
Light or Delivery Service	District of Columbia	H	6.88 FQ	12.88 AW	22.60 TQ	DCBLS	10/01-12/01
Light or Delivery Service	Washington PMSA, DC-MD-VA-WV	H	6.95 FQ	12.78 AW	21.39 TQ	DCBLS	10/01-12/01
Light or Delivery Service	Florida	H	6.56 FQ	11.40 AW	18.38 TQ	FLBLS	10/01-12/01
Light or Delivery Service	Daytona Beach MSA, FL	H	6.23 FQ	10.51 AW	16.79 TQ	FLBLS	10/01-12/01
Light or Delivery Service	Fort Lauderdale PMSA, FL	H	7.08 FQ	11.33 AW	16.81 TQ	FLBLS	10/01-12/01
Light or Delivery Service	Fort Myers-Cape Coral MSA, FL	H	7.07 FQ	11.77 AW	18.81 TQ	FLBLS	10/01-12/01
Light or Delivery Service	Fort Pierce-Port St. Lucie MSA, FL	H	6.87 FQ	11.82 AW	21.02 TQ	FLBLS	10/01-12/01
Light or Delivery Service	Fort Walton Beach MSA, FL	H	7.09 FQ	11.10 AW	17.20 TQ	FLBLS	10/01-12/01
Light or Delivery Service	Gainesville MSA, FL	H	6.15 FQ	12.31 AW	25.10 TQ	FLBLS	10/01-12/01
Light or Delivery Service	Jacksonville MSA, FL	H	6.47 FQ	11.89 AW	20.61 TQ	FLBLS	10/01-12/01
Light or Delivery Service	Lakeland-Winter Haven MSA, FL	H	6.18 FQ	10.48 AW	16.35 TQ	FLBLS	10/01-12/01
Light or Delivery Service	Melbourne-Titusville-Palm Bay MSA, FL	H	6.16 FQ	10.14 AW	14.56 TQ	FLBLS	10/01-12/01
Light or Delivery Service	Miami PMSA, FL	H	7.07 FQ	10.63 AW	15.88 TQ	FLBLS	10/01-12/01
Light or Delivery Service	Naples MSA, FL	H	7.84 FQ	13.19 AW	23.83 TQ	FLBLS	10/01-12/01
Light or Delivery Service	Ocala MSA, FL	H	6.61 FQ	11.40 AW	16.93 TQ	FLBLS	10/01-12/01
Light or Delivery Service	Orlando MSA, FL	H	6.16 FQ	12.03 AW	19.98 TQ	FLBLS	10/01-12/01
Light or Delivery Service	Pensacola MSA, FL	H	6.00 FQ	9.77 AW	16.21 TQ	FLBLS	10/01-12/01
Light or Delivery Service	Sarasota-Bradenton MSA, FL	H	7.80 FQ	12.08 AW	16.75 TQ	FLBLS	10/01-12/01
Light or Delivery Service	Tallahassee MSA, FL	H	7.27 FQ	12.60 AW	23.42 TQ	FLBLS	10/01-12/01
Light or Delivery Service	Tampa-St. Petersburg-Clearwater MSA, FL	H	6.31 FQ	11.32 AW	18.53 TQ	FLBLS	10/01-12/01
Light or Delivery Service	West Palm Beach-Boca Raton MSA, FL	H	7.44 FQ	12.25 AW	18.20 TQ	FLBLS	10/01-12/01
Light or Delivery Service	Georgia	H	7.34 FQ	12.62 AW	20.27 TQ	GABLS	10/01-12/01
Light or Delivery Service	Atlanta MSA, GA	H	8.31 FQ	13.86 AW	21.42 TQ	GABLS	10/01-12/01
Light or Delivery Service	Augusta-Aiken MSA, GA-SC	H	7.16 FQ	11.67 AW	17.70 TQ	GABLS	10/01-12/01
Light or Delivery Service	Columbus MSA, GA-AL	H	6.68 FQ	10.53 AW	17.53 TQ	GABLS	10/01-12/01
Light or Delivery Service	Macon MSA, GA	H	6.50 FQ	11.22 AW	17.83 TQ	GABLS	10/01-12/01
Light or Delivery Service	Savannah MSA, GA	H	6.88 FQ	10.90 AW	16.51 TQ	GABLS	10/01-12/01
Light or Delivery Service	Hawaii	H	6.56 FQ	11.30 AW	17.45 TQ	HIBLS	10/01-12/01
Light or Delivery Service	Honolulu MSA, HI	H	6.58 FQ	11.29 AW	17.42 TQ	HIBLS	10/01-12/01
Light or Delivery Service	Idaho	H	5.98 FQ	10.44 AW	16.70 TQ	IDBLS	10/01-12/01
Light or Delivery Service	Boise City MSA, ID	H	6.14 FQ	11.08 AW	17.15 TQ	IDBLS	10/01-12/01
Light or Delivery Service	Illinois	H	7.83 FQ	14.30 AW	20.82 TQ	ILBLS	10/01-12/01
Light or Delivery Service	Champaign-Urbana MSA, IL	H	8.87 FQ	15.15 AW	20.58 TQ	ILBLS	10/01-12/01
Light or Delivery Service	Chicago PMSA, IL	H	8.70 FQ	14.99 AW	21.01 TQ	ILBLS	10/01-12/01
Light or Delivery Service	Peoria-Pekin MSA, IL	H	6.74 FQ	11.57 AW	18.26 TQ	ILBLS	10/01-12/01
Light or Delivery Service	Rockford MSA, IL	H	6.79 FQ	11.22 AW	16.44 TQ	ILBLS	10/01-12/01
Light or Delivery Service	Springfield MSA, IL	H	7.58 FQ	15.12 AW	30.01 TQ	ILBLS	10/01-12/01
Light or Delivery Service	Indiana	H	7.12 FQ	13.10 AW	23.04 TQ	INBLS	10/01-12/01
Light or Delivery Service	Elkhart-Goshen MSA, IN	H	7.63 FQ	11.33 AW	14.51 TQ	INBLS	10/01-12/01
Light or Delivery Service	Evansville-Henderson MSA, IN-KY	H	6.41 FQ	10.60 AW	16.22 TQ	INBLS	10/01-12/01
Light or Delivery Service	Fort Wayne MSA, IN	H	6.76 FQ	12.92 AW	21.72 TQ	INBLS	10/01-12/01
Light or Delivery Service	Gary PMSA, IN	H	7.37 FQ	14.22 AW	24.56 TQ	INBLS	10/01-12/01
Light or Delivery Service	Indianapolis MSA, IN	H	8.19 FQ	14.80 AW	24.85 TQ	INBLS	10/01-12/01
Light or Delivery Service	Lafayette MSA, IN	H	7.32 FQ	10.71 AW	15.57 TQ	INBLS	10/01-12/01
Light or Delivery Service	South Bend MSA, IN	H	7.56 FQ	12.90 AW	23.43 TQ	INBLS	10/01-12/01
Light or Delivery Service	Iowa	H	6.12 FQ	11.15 AW	17.49 TQ	IABLS	10/01-12/01
Light or Delivery Service	Cedar Rapids MSA, IA	H	7.05 FQ	12.22 AW	19.53 TQ	IABLS	10/01-12/01
Light or Delivery Service	Davenport-Moline-Rock Island MSA, IA-IL	H	6.10 FQ	12.29 AW	18.22 TQ	IABLS	10/01-12/01
Light or Delivery Service	Des Moines MSA, IA	H	7.94 FQ	11.96 AW	16.61 TQ	IABLS	10/01-12/01
Light or Delivery Service	Kansas	H	6.10 FQ	11.62 AW	20.10 TQ	KSBLS	10/01-12/01
Light or Delivery Service	Topeka MSA, KS	H	5.84 FQ	9.57 AW	17.84 TQ	KSBLS	10/01-12/01
Light or Delivery Service	Wichita MSA, KS	H	5.99 FQ	9.87 AW	18.35 TQ	KSBLS	10/01-12/01
Light or Delivery Service	Kentucky	H	6.33 FQ	10.67 AW	16.35 TQ	KYBLS	10/01-12/01

AAW Average annual wage **AE** Average entry wage **AEX** Average experienced wage **AO** Average offered **AOH** Average offered, high **AOL** Average offered, low **APH** Average pay, high range **APL** Average pay, low range **ASH** Average starting, high **ASL** Average starting, low **AW** Average wage paid **FQ** First quartile wage **H** Hourly **HI** Highest wage paid **HR** High end range **LR** Low end range **M** Monthly **MTC** Median total compensation **MW** Median wage paid **SQ** Second quartile wage **S** Special: hourly and annual **TQ** Third quartile wage **W** Weekly **Y** Yearly

Occupation/Type/Industry	Location	Per	Low	Mid	High	Source	Date
Truck Driver							
Light or Delivery Service	Lexington MSA, KY	H	7.72 FQ	11.89 AW	16.75 TQ	KYBLS	10/01-12/01
Light or Delivery Service	Louisville MSA, KY-IN	H	7.64 FQ	11.73 AW	17.32 TQ	KYBLS	10/01-12/01
Light or Delivery Service	Louisiana	H	6.35 FQ	11.79 AW	20.51 TQ	LABLS	10/01-12/01
Light or Delivery Service	Baton Rouge MSA, LA	H	7.03 FQ	13.23 AW	22.62 TQ	LABLS	10/01-12/01
Light or Delivery Service	Houma MSA, LA	H	6.32 FQ	11.05 AW	19.74 TQ	LABLS	10/01-12/01
Light or Delivery Service	Lafayette MSA, LA	H	5.93 FQ	11.00 AW	19.17 TQ	LABLS	10/01-12/01
Light or Delivery Service	Lake Charles MSA, LA	H	5.94 FQ	11.66 AW	22.83 TQ	LABLS	10/01-12/01
Light or Delivery Service	New Orleans MSA, LA	H	7.04 FQ	12.67 AW	20.93 TQ	LABLS	10/01-12/01
Light or Delivery Service	Shreveport-Bossier City MSA, LA	H	6.72 FQ	10.96 AW	17.38 TQ	LABLS	10/01-12/01
Light or Delivery Service	Maine	H	7.00 FQ	11.69 AW	19.74 TQ	MEBLS	10/01-12/01
Light or Delivery Service	Portland MSA, ME	H	7.58 FQ	11.94 AW	18.10 TQ	MEBLS	10/01-12/01
Light or Delivery Service	Maryland	H	7.28 FQ	13.78 AW	23.48 TQ	MDBLS	10/01-12/01
Light or Delivery Service	Baltimore PMSA, MD	H	7.57 FQ	13.42 AW	22.37 TQ	MDBLS	10/01-12/01
Light or Delivery Service	Massachusetts	H	8.26 FQ	14.42 AW	22.85 TQ	MABLS	10/01-12/01
Light or Delivery Service	Boston PMSA, MA-NH	H	9.02 FQ	14.58 AW	21.91 TQ	MABLS	10/01-12/01
Light or Delivery Service	Brockton PMSA, MA	H	8.78 FQ	15.06 AW	24.68 TQ	MABLS	10/01-12/01
Light or Delivery Service	Lawrence PMSA, MA-NH	H	7.31 FQ	11.39 AW	16.24 TQ	MABLS	10/01-12/01
Light or Delivery Service	New Bedford PMSA, MA	H	7.51 FQ	12.94 AW	20.98 TQ	MABLS	10/01-12/01
Light or Delivery Service	Springfield MSA, MA	H	7.48 FQ	11.78 AW	17.68 TQ	MABLS	10/01-12/01
Light or Delivery Service	Worcester PMSA, MA-CT	H	7.88 FQ	15.69 AW	24.59 TQ	MABLS	10/01-12/01
Light or Delivery Service	Michigan	H	7.69 FQ	13.10 AW	20.96 TQ	MIBLS	10/01-12/01
Light or Delivery Service	Ann Arbor PMSA, MI	H	6.21 FQ	11.53 AW	17.69 TQ	MIBLS	10/01-12/01
Light or Delivery Service	Detroit PMSA, MI	H	8.16 FQ	13.73 AW	23.19 TQ	MIBLS	10/01-12/01
Light or Delivery Service	Flint PMSA, MI	H	7.18 FQ	12.45 AW	19.97 TQ	MIBLS	10/01-12/01
Light or Delivery Service	Grand Rapids-Muskegon-Holland MSA, MI	H	8.54 FQ	13.13 AW	19.33 TQ	MIBLS	10/01-12/01
Light or Delivery Service	Kalamazoo-Battle Creek MSA, MI	H	7.46 FQ	13.48 AW	20.96 TQ	MIBLS	10/01-12/01
Light or Delivery Service	Lansing-East Lansing MSA, MI	H	7.81 FQ	13.79 AW	20.11 TQ	MIBLS	10/01-12/01
Light or Delivery Service	Saginaw-Bay City-Midland MSA, MI	H	6.69 FQ	11.30 AW	19.18 TQ	MIBLS	10/01-12/01
Light or Delivery Service	Minnesota	H	7.03 FQ	13.41 AW	21.87 TQ	MNBLS	10/01-12/01
Light or Delivery Service	Duluth-Superior MSA, MN-WI	H	5.84 FQ	11.02 AW	19.97 TQ	MNBLS	10/01-12/01
Light or Delivery Service	Minneapolis-St. Paul MSA, MN-WI	H	8.47 FQ	14.46 AW	22.57 TQ	MNBLS	10/01-12/01
Light or Delivery Service	St. Cloud MSA, MN	H	7.01 FQ	11.77 AW	19.55 TQ	MNBLS	10/01-12/01
Light or Delivery Service	Mississippi	H	6.19 FQ	12.98 AW	26.76 TQ	MSBLS	10/01-12/01
Light or Delivery Service	Biloxi-Gulfport-Pascagoula MSA, MS	H	6.26 FQ	10.50 AW	15.29 TQ	MSBLS	10/01-12/01
Light or Delivery Service	Jackson MSA, MS	H	5.75 FQ	10.14 AW	14.40 TQ	MSBLS	10/01-12/01
Light or Delivery Service	Missouri	H	6.90 FQ	12.73 AW	21.96 TQ	MOBLS	10/01-12/01
Light or Delivery Service	Kansas City MSA, MO-KS	H	7.79 FQ	13.04 AW	18.75 TQ	MOBLS	10/01-12/01
Light or Delivery Service	St. Louis MSA, MO-IL	H	7.53 FQ	13.99 AW	21.69 TQ	MOBLS	10/01-12/01
Light or Delivery Service	Springfield MSA, MO	H	6.92 FQ	13.90 AW	24.67 TQ	MOBLS	10/01-12/01
Light or Delivery Service	Montana	H	6.46 FQ	11.05 AW	17.64 TQ	MTBLS	10/01-12/01
Light or Delivery Service	Billings MSA, MT	H	6.43 FQ	10.62 AW	16.52 TQ	MTBLS	10/01-12/01
Light or Delivery Service	Nebraska	H	6.25 FQ	10.66 AW	17.06 TQ	NEBLS	10/01-12/01
Light or Delivery Service	Lincoln MSA, NE	H	6.95 FQ	11.84 AW	24.52 TQ	NEBLS	10/01-12/01
Light or Delivery Service	Omaha MSA, NE-IA	H	6.94 FQ	11.14 AW	16.83 TQ	NEBLS	10/01-12/01
Light or Delivery Service	Nevada	H	6.19 FQ	11.54 AW	18.98 TQ	NVBLS	10/01-12/01
Light or Delivery Service	Las Vegas MSA, NV-AZ	H	6.10 FQ	11.24 AW	19.55 TQ	NVBLS	10/01-12/01
Light or Delivery Service	Reno MSA, NV	H	7.54 FQ	12.51 AW	18.26 TQ	NVBLS	10/01-12/01
Light or Delivery Service	New Hampshire	H	7.24 FQ	12.80 AW	22.16 TQ	NHBLS	10/01-12/01
Light or Delivery Service	Manchester PMSA, NH	H	6.86 FQ	13.78 AW	23.53 TQ	NHBLS	10/01-12/01
Light or Delivery Service	Nashua PMSA, NH	H	6.91 FQ	12.20 AW	22.08 TQ	NHBLS	10/01-12/01
Light or Delivery Service	Portsmouth-Rochester PMSA, NH-ME	H	7.45 FQ	13.12 AW	22.83 TQ	NHBLS	10/01-12/01
Light or Delivery Service	New Jersey	H	7.28 FQ	13.55 AW	21.19 TQ	NJBLS	10/01-12/01
Light or Delivery Service	Atlantic-Cape May PMSA, NJ	H	6.05 FQ	10.53 AW	18.29 TQ	NJBLS	10/01-12/01
Light or Delivery Service	Bergen-Passaic PMSA, NJ	H	7.53 FQ	13.79 AW	21.11 TQ	NJBLS	10/01-12/01
Light or Delivery Service	Jersey City PMSA, NJ	H	7.67 FQ	15.69 AW	25.52 TQ	NJBLS	10/01-12/01
Light or Delivery Service	Middlesex-Somerset-Hunterdon PMSA, NJ	H	7.77 FQ	13.68 AW	20.58 TQ	NJBLS	10/01-12/01
Light or Delivery Service	Monmouth-Ocean PMSA, NJ	H	6.35 FQ	11.51 AW	18.01 TQ	NJBLS	10/01-12/01
Light or Delivery Service	Newark PMSA, NJ	H	7.65 FQ	13.38 AW	20.39 TQ	NJBLS	10/01-12/01
Light or Delivery Service	Trenton PMSA, NJ	H	7.27 FQ	12.89 AW	19.75 TQ	NJBLS	10/01-12/01
Light or Delivery Service	New Mexico	H	6.29 FQ	10.95 AW	19.16 TQ	NMBLS	10/01-12/01
Light or Delivery Service	Albuquerque MSA, NM	H	6.67 FQ	11.11 AW	20.89 TQ	NMBLS	10/01-12/01
Light or Delivery Service	Las Cruces MSA, NM	H	6.12 FQ	10.37 AW	15.31 TQ	NMBLS	10/01-12/01
Light or Delivery Service	New York	H	7.11 FQ	13.02 AW	20.11 TQ	NYBLS	10/01-12/01

AAW Average annual wage **AE** Average entry wage **AEX** Average experienced wage **AO** Average offered **AOH** Average offered, high **AOL** Average offered, low **APH** Average pay, high range **APL** Average pay, low range **ASH** Average starting, high **ASL** Average starting, low **AW** Average wage paid **FQ** First quartile wage **H** Hourly **HI** Highest wage paid **HR** High end range **LR** Low end range **M** Monthly **MTC** Median total compensation **MW** Median wage paid **SQ** Second quartile wage **S** Special: hourly and annual **TQ** Third quartile wage **W** Weekly **Y** Yearly

Occupation/Type/Industry	Location	Per	Low	Mid	High	Source	Date
Truck Driver							
Light or Delivery Service	Albany-Schenectady-Troy MSA, NY	H	7.14 FQ	13.17 AW	21.22 TQ	NYBLS	10/01-12/01
Light or Delivery Service	Binghamton MSA, NY	H	6.55 FQ	10.70 AW	17.35 TQ	NYBLS	10/01-12/01
Light or Delivery Service	Buffalo-Niagara Falls MSA, NY	H	7.15 FQ	12.08 AW	19.18 TQ	NYBLS	10/01-12/01
Light or Delivery Service	Dutchess County PMSA, NY	H	7.33 FQ	11.16 AW	16.14 TQ	NYBLS	10/01-12/01
Light or Delivery Service	Nassau-Suffolk PMSA, NY	H	7.78 FQ	14.09 AW	22.10 TQ	NYBLS	10/01-12/01
Light or Delivery Service	New York PMSA, NY	H	8.09 FQ	14.21 AW	20.28 TQ	NYBLS	10/01-12/01
Light or Delivery Service	Newburgh PMSA, NY-PA	H	8.02 FQ	13.78 AW	20.00 TQ	NYBLS	10/01-12/01
Light or Delivery Service	Rochester MSA, NY	H	6.10 FQ	10.60 AW	17.84 TQ	NYBLS	10/01-12/01
Light or Delivery Service	Syracuse MSA, NY	H	6.90 FQ	10.65 AW	16.62 TQ	NYBLS	10/01-12/01
Light or Delivery Service	Utica-Rome MSA, NY	H	6.15 FQ	10.62 AW	17.83 TQ	NYBLS	10/01-12/01
Light or Delivery Service	North Carolina	H	6.53 FQ	11.97 AW	18.94 TQ	NCBLS	10/01-12/01
Light or Delivery Service	Asheville MSA, NC	H	7.99 FQ	14.11 AW	21.12 TQ	NCBLS	10/01-12/01
Light or Delivery Service	Charlotte-Gastonia-Rock Hill MSA, NC-SC	H	8.15 FQ	13.18 AW	20.56 TQ	NCBLS	10/01-12/01
Light or Delivery Service	Fayetteville MSA, NC	H	7.09 FQ	13.26 AW	25.23 TQ	NCBLS	10/01-12/01
Light or Delivery Service	Greensboro-Winston-Salem-High Point MSA, NC	H	7.58 FQ	12.23 AW	19.31 TQ	NCBLS	10/01-12/01
Light or Delivery Service	Hickory-Morganton-Lenoir MSA, NC	H	7.80 FQ	12.99 AW	19.51 TQ	NCBLS	10/01-12/01
Light or Delivery Service	Raleigh-Durham-Chapel Hill MSA, NC	H	6.21 FQ	11.52 AW	16.88 TQ	NCBLS	10/01-12/01
Light or Delivery Service	Wilmington MSA, NC	H	5.47 FQ	9.29 AW	15.96 TQ	NCBLS	10/01-12/01
Light or Delivery Service	North Dakota	H	7.09 FQ	12.19 AW	21.88 TQ	NDBLS	10/01-12/01
Light or Delivery Service	Fargo-Moorhead MSA, ND-MN	H	6.76 FQ	10.62 AW	15.21 TQ	NDBLS	10/01-12/01
Light or Delivery Service	Ohio	H	6.69 FQ	12.38 AW	20.39 TQ	OHBLS	10/01-12/01
Light or Delivery Service	Akron PMSA, OH	H	7.96 FQ	14.20 AW	24.46 TQ	OHBLS	10/01-12/01
Light or Delivery Service	Canton-Massillon MSA, OH	H	7.04 FQ	12.13 AW	23.68 TQ	OHBLS	10/01-12/01
Light or Delivery Service	Cincinnati PMSA, OH-KY-IN	H	7.37 FQ	13.02 AW	20.99 TQ	OHBLS	10/01-12/01
Light or Delivery Service	Cleveland-Lorain-Elyria PMSA, OH	H	6.63 FQ	13.47 AW	21.24 TQ	OHBLS	10/01-12/01
Light or Delivery Service	Columbus MSA, OH	H	7.91 FQ	12.25 AW	18.01 TQ	OHBLS	10/01-12/01
Light or Delivery Service	Dayton-Springfield MSA, OH	H	6.08 FQ	11.13 AW	20.32 TQ	OHBLS	10/01-12/01
Light or Delivery Service	Hamilton-Middletown PMSA, OH	H	8.17 FQ	12.83 AW	19.75 TQ	OHBLS	10/01-12/01
Light or Delivery Service	Mansfield MSA, OH	H	7.11 FQ	11.35 AW	18.07 TQ	OHBLS	10/01-12/01
Light or Delivery Service	Toledo MSA, OH	H	7.04 FQ	11.32 AW	17.45 TQ	OHBLS	10/01-12/01
Light or Delivery Service	Youngstown-Warren MSA, OH	H	6.26 FQ	12.34 AW	22.85 TQ	OHBLS	10/01-12/01
Light or Delivery Service	Oklahoma	H	6.13 FQ	9.94 AW	15.42 TQ	OKBLS	10/01-12/01
Light or Delivery Service	Oklahoma City MSA, OK	H	6.31 FQ	10.16 AW	15.07 TQ	OKBLS	10/01-12/01
Light or Delivery Service	Tulsa MSA, OK	H	6.11 FQ	9.66 AW	15.10 TQ	OKBLS	10/01-12/01
Light or Delivery Service	Oregon	H	7.75 FQ	11.74 AW	16.73 TQ	ORBLS	10/01-12/01
Light or Delivery Service	Eugene-Springfield MSA, OR	H	7.35 FQ	10.92 AW	16.37 TQ	ORBLS	10/01-12/01
Light or Delivery Service	Medford-Ashland MSA, OR	H	7.29 FQ	11.89 AW	16.94 TQ	ORBLS	10/01-12/01
Light or Delivery Service	Portland-Vancouver PMSA, OR-WA	H	8.12 FQ	12.06 AW	17.17 TQ	ORBLS	10/01-12/01
Light or Delivery Service	Salem PMSA, OR	H	7.53 FQ	11.22 AW	16.16 TQ	ORBLS	10/01-12/01
Light or Delivery Service	Pennsylvania	H	6.24 FQ	11.80 AW	19.55 TQ	PABLS	10/01-12/01
Light or Delivery Service	Allentown-Bethlehem-Easton MSA, PA	H	6.47 FQ	12.50 AW	20.70 TQ	PABLS	10/01-12/01
Light or Delivery Service	Erie MSA, PA	H	5.84 FQ	10.48 AW	20.91 TQ	PABLS	10/01-12/01
Light or Delivery Service	Harrisburg-Lebanon-Carlisle MSA, PA	H	6.24 FQ	11.10 AW	18.35 TQ	PABLS	10/01-12/01
Light or Delivery Service	Johnstown MSA, PA	H	6.22 FQ	10.60 AW	17.05 TQ	PABLS	10/01-12/01
Light or Delivery Service	Lancaster MSA, PA	H	6.11 FQ	11.79 AW	18.23 TQ	PABLS	10/01-12/01
Light or Delivery Service	Philadelphia PMSA, PA-NJ	H	6.33 FQ	12.86 AW	20.95 TQ	PABLS	10/01-12/01
Light or Delivery Service	Pittsburgh MSA, PA	H	6.35 FQ	11.62 AW	18.16 TQ	PABLS	10/01-12/01
Light or Delivery Service	Reading MSA, PA	H	6.85 FQ	12.20 AW	19.57 TQ	PABLS	10/01-12/01
Light or Delivery Service	Scranton-Wilkes-Barre-Hazleton MSA, PA	H	6.43 FQ	11.54 AW	19.64 TQ	PABLS	10/01-12/01
Light or Delivery Service	York MSA, PA	H	6.83 FQ	11.09 AW	16.23 TQ	PABLS	10/01-12/01
Light or Delivery Service	Rhode Island	H	7.15 FQ	13.03 AW	21.59 TQ	RIBLS	10/01-12/01
Light or Delivery Service	Providence-Fall River-Warwick MSA, RI-MA	H	7.28 FQ	12.97 AW	21.31 TQ	RIBLS	10/01-12/01
Light or Delivery Service	South Carolina	H	6.88 FQ	11.42 AW	17.55 TQ	SCBLS	10/01-12/01
Light or Delivery Service	Charleston-North Charleston MSA, SC	H	6.80 FQ	11.44 AW	17.08 TQ	SCBLS	10/01-12/01
Light or Delivery Service	Columbia MSA, SC	H	6.34 FQ	11.72 AW	20.21 TQ	SCBLS	10/01-12/01

AAW	Average annual wage	**AOH**	Average offered, high	**ASH**	Average starting, high	**H**	Hourly	**M**	Monthly	**S**	Special: hourly and annual
AE	Average entry wage	**AOL**	Average offered, low	**ASL**	Average starting, low	**HI**	Highest wage paid	**MTC**	Median total compensation	**TQ**	Third quartile wage
AEX	Average experienced wage	**APH**	Average pay, high range	**AW**	Average wage paid	**HR**	High end range	**MW**	Median wage paid	**W**	Weekly
AO	Average offered	**APL**	Average pay, low range	**FQ**	First quartile wage	**LR**	Low end range	**SQ**	Second quartile wage	**Y**	Yearly

Occupation/Type/Industry	Location	Per	Low	Mid	High	Source	Date
Truck Driver							
Light or Delivery Service	Greenville-Spartanburg-Anderson MSA, SC	H	7.48 FQ	11.80 AW	17.14 TQ	SCBLS	10/01-12/01
Light or Delivery Service	Myrtle Beach MSA, SC	H	6.34 FQ	10.59 AW	17.03 TQ	SCBLS	10/01-12/01
Light or Delivery Service	South Dakota	H	6.77 FQ	11.20 AW	18.61 TQ	SDBLS	10/01-12/01
Light or Delivery Service	Sioux Falls MSA, SD	H	7.05 FQ	11.35 AW	16.47 TQ	SDBLS	10/01-12/01
Light or Delivery Service	Tennessee	H	6.69 FQ	12.11 AW	19.67 TQ	TNBLS	10/01-12/01
Light or Delivery Service	Chattanooga MSA, TN-GA	H	7.15 FQ	12.64 AW	21.39 TQ	TNBLS	10/01-12/01
Light or Delivery Service	Clarksville-Hopkinsville MSA, TN-KY	H	5.95 FQ	9.44 AW	14.04 TQ	TNBLS	10/01-12/01
Light or Delivery Service	Johnson City-Kingsport-Bristol MSA, TN-VA	H	6.13 FQ	11.80 AW	21.28 TQ	TNBLS	10/01-12/01
Light or Delivery Service	Knoxville MSA, TN	H	6.81 FQ	12.35 AW	23.16 TQ	TNBLS	10/01-12/01
Light or Delivery Service	Memphis MSA, TN-AR-MS	H	7.51 FQ	11.86 AW	17.13 TQ	TNBLS	10/01-12/01
Light or Delivery Service	Nashville MSA, TN	H	8.41 FQ	13.87 AW	23.99 TQ	TNBLS	10/01-12/01
Light or Delivery Service	Texas	H	6.69 FQ	11.87 AW	19.53 TQ	TXBLS	10/01-12/01
Light or Delivery Service	Amarillo MSA, TX	H	6.18 FQ	10.46 AW	15.71 TQ	TXBLS	10/01-12/01
Light or Delivery Service	Austin-San Marcos MSA, TX	H	7.58 FQ	13.00 AW	23.48 TQ	TXBLS	10/01-12/01
Light or Delivery Service	Beaumont-Port Arthur MSA, TX	H	6.42 FQ	11.63 AW	22.28 TQ	TXBLS	10/01-12/01
Light or Delivery Service	Brazoria PMSA, TX	H	6.75 FQ	12.10 AW	20.27 TQ	TXBLS	10/01-12/01
Light or Delivery Service	Brownsville-Harlingen-San Benito MSA, TX	H	5.96 FQ	10.16 AW	18.11 TQ	TXBLS	10/01-12/01
Light or Delivery Service	Corpus Christi MSA, TX	H	6.47 FQ	10.13 AW	15.70 TQ	TXBLS	10/01-12/01
Light or Delivery Service	Dallas PMSA, TX	H	7.61 FQ	13.08 AW	22.00 TQ	TXBLS	10/01-12/01
Light or Delivery Service	El Paso MSA, TX	H	5.98 FQ	10.89 AW	18.75 TQ	TXBLS	10/01-12/01
Light or Delivery Service	Fort Worth-Arlington PMSA, TX	H	7.92 FQ	13.71 AW	20.39 TQ	TXBLS	10/01-12/01
Light or Delivery Service	Galveston-Texas City PMSA, TX	H	6.66 FQ	10.30 AW	15.80 TQ	TXBLS	10/01-12/01
Light or Delivery Service	Houston PMSA, TX	H	6.48 FQ	10.98 AW	17.25 TQ	TXBLS	10/01-12/01
Light or Delivery Service	Killeen-Temple MSA, TX	H	6.87 FQ	11.26 AW	17.69 TQ	TXBLS	10/01-12/01
Light or Delivery Service	Laredo MSA, TX	H	6.07 FQ	10.35 AW	16.58 TQ	TXBLS	10/01-12/01
Light or Delivery Service	Longview-Marshall MSA, TX	H	6.84 FQ	13.07 AW	23.54 TQ	TXBLS	10/01-12/01
Light or Delivery Service	Lubbock MSA, TX	H	6.58 FQ	10.18 AW	16.42 TQ	TXBLS	10/01-12/01
Light or Delivery Service	McAllen-Edinburg-Mission MSA, TX	H	5.88 FQ	10.69 AW	17.04 TQ	TXBLS	10/01-12/01
Light or Delivery Service	Odessa-Midland MSA, TX	H	6.17 FQ	11.09 AW	17.77 TQ	TXBLS	10/01-12/01
Light or Delivery Service	San Antonio MSA, TX	H	6.93 FQ	11.23 AW	17.29 TQ	TXBLS	10/01-12/01
Light or Delivery Service	Tyler MSA, TX	H	6.35 FQ	13.40 AW	25.51 TQ	TXBLS	10/01-12/01
Light or Delivery Service	Waco MSA, TX	H	6.45 FQ	12.18 AW	21.33 TQ	TXBLS	10/01-12/01
Light or Delivery Service	Utah	H	7.40 FQ	11.98 AW	19.23 TQ	UTBLS	10/01-12/01
Light or Delivery Service	Provo-Orem MSA, UT	H	7.41 FQ	10.82 AW	15.82 TQ	UTBLS	10/01-12/01
Light or Delivery Service	Salt Lake City-Ogden MSA, UT	H	7.47 FQ	12.37 AW	20.51 TQ	UTBLS	10/01-12/01
Light or Delivery Service	Vermont	H	6.67 FQ	11.44 AW	19.49 TQ	VTBLS	10/01-12/01
Light or Delivery Service	Burlington MSA, VT	H	7.64 FQ	13.23 AW	22.58 TQ	VTBLS	10/01-12/01
Light or Delivery Service	Virginia	H	6.01 FQ	10.62 AW	16.46 TQ	VABLS	10/01-12/01
Light or Delivery Service	Lynchburg MSA, VA	H	6.68 FQ	11.34 AW	17.25 TQ	VABLS	10/01-12/01
Light or Delivery Service	Norfolk-Virginia Beach-Newport News MSA, VA-NC	H	6.50 FQ	10.09 AW	15.56 TQ	VABLS	10/01-12/01
Light or Delivery Service	Richmond-Petersburg MSA, VA	H	5.54 FQ	10.20 AW	17.60 TQ	VABLS	10/01-12/01
Light or Delivery Service	Roanoke MSA, VA	H	6.02 FQ	10.04 AW	16.27 TQ	VABLS	10/01-12/01
Light or Delivery Service	Washington	H	8.09 FQ	13.12 AW	19.99 TQ	WABLS	10/01-12/01
Light or Delivery Service	Bremerton PMSA, WA	H	7.83 FQ	12.71 AW	19.02 TQ	WABLS	10/01-12/01
Light or Delivery Service	Olympia PMSA, WA	H	7.93 FQ	11.82 AW	16.56 TQ	WABLS	10/01-12/01
Light or Delivery Service	Richland-Kennewick-Pasco MSA, WA	H	6.85 FQ	10.81 AW	21.93 TQ	WABLS	10/01-12/01
Light or Delivery Service	Seattle-Bellevue-Everett PMSA, WA	H	8.94 FQ	13.74 AW	20.20 TQ	WABLS	10/01-12/01
Light or Delivery Service	Spokane MSA, WA	H	6.96 FQ	10.64 AW	16.72 TQ	WABLS	10/01-12/01
Light or Delivery Service	Tacoma PMSA, WA	H	8.92 FQ	12.83 AW	17.52 TQ	WABLS	10/01-12/01
Light or Delivery Service	Yakima MSA, WA	H	8.11 FQ	11.80 AW	16.49 TQ	WABLS	10/01-12/01
Light or Delivery Service	West Virginia	H	6.00 FQ	10.44 AW	17.29 TQ	WVBLS	10/01-12/01
Light or Delivery Service	Charleston MSA, WV	H	5.90 FQ	9.58 AW	15.03 TQ	WVBLS	10/01-12/01
Light or Delivery Service	Huntington-Ashland MSA, WV-KY-OH	H	5.84 FQ	10.41 AW	21.48 TQ	WVBLS	10/01-12/01
Light or Delivery Service	Wisconsin	H	6.52 FQ	11.35 AW	17.39 TQ	WIBLS	10/01-12/01
Light or Delivery Service	Appleton-Oshkosh-Neenah MSA, WI	H	6.34 FQ	10.01 AW	13.97 TQ	WIBLS	10/01-12/01

AAW	Average annual wage	AOH	Average offered, high	ASH	Average starting, high	H	Hourly	M	Monthly	S	Special: hourly and annual
AE	Average entry wage	AOL	Average offered, low	ASL	Average starting, low	HI	Highest wage paid	MTC	Median total compensation	TQ	Third quartile wage
AEX	Average experienced wage	APH	Average pay, high range	AW	Average wage paid	HR	High end range	MW	Median wage paid	W	Weekly
AO	Average offered	APL	Average pay, low range	FQ	First quartile wage	LR	Low end range	SQ	Second quartile wage	Y	Yearly

Occupation/Type/Industry	Location	Per	Low	Mid	High	Source	Date
Truck Driver							
Light or Delivery Service	Green Bay MSA, WI	H	6.01 FQ	10.25 AW	16.45 TQ	WIBLS	10/01-12/01
Light or Delivery Service	Madison MSA, WI	H	5.93 FQ	10.90 AW	16.92 TQ	WIBLS	10/01-12/01
Light or Delivery Service	Milwaukee-Waukesha PMSA, WI	H	7.72 FQ	12.69 AW	19.80 TQ	WIBLS	10/01-12/01
Light or Delivery Service	Racine PMSA, WI	H	6.46 FQ	11.59 AW	20.09 TQ	WIBLS	10/01-12/01
Light or Delivery Service	Wyoming	H	6.12 FQ	11.83 AW	22.90 TQ	WYBLS	10/01-12/01
Light or Delivery Service	Cheyenne MSA, WY	H	6.10 FQ	14.16 AW	25.60 TQ	WYBLS	10/01-12/01
Light or Delivery Service	Puerto Rico	H	5.57 FQ	7.56 AW	10.26 TQ	PRBLS	10/01-12/01
Light or Delivery Service	Virgin Islands	H	7.19 FQ	9.45 AW	12.85 TQ	VIBLS	10/01-12/01
Light or Delivery Service	Guam	H	5.68 FQ	7.69 AW	10.56 TQ	GUBLS	10/01-12/01
Umpire, Referee, and Other Sports Official	California	Y	14790 FQ	27300 AW	36310 TQ	CABLS	10/01-12/01
	Oakland PMSA, CA	Y	17730 FQ	22850 AW	31850 TQ	CABLS	10/01-12/01
	Riverside-San Bernardino PMSA, CA	Y	13690 FQ	23830 AW	36790 TQ	CABLS	10/01-12/01
	Colorado	Y	16410 FQ	24130 AW	38270 TQ	COBLS	10/01-12/01
	Boulder-Longmont PMSA, CO	Y	16450 FQ	26460 AW	35840 TQ	COBLS	10/01-12/01
	Colorado Springs MSA, CO	Y	18560 FQ	23300 AW	36250 TQ	COBLS	10/01-12/01
	Denver PMSA, CO	Y	16260 FQ	24400 AW	34570 TQ	COBLS	10/01-12/01
	Connecticut	Y	14830 FQ	23700 AW	34670 TQ	CTBLS	10/01-12/01
	Delaware	Y	13360 FQ	27980 AW	45750 TQ	DEBLS	10/01-12/01
	Wilmington-Newark PMSA, DE-MD	Y	15060 FQ	31920 AW	47140 TQ	DEBLS	10/01-12/01
	Washington PMSA, DC-MD-VA-WV	Y	13470 FQ	25210 AW	37260 TQ	DCBLS	10/01-12/01
	Florida	Y	13550 FQ	22500 AW	36650 TQ	FLBLS	10/01-12/01
	Daytona Beach MSA, FL	Y	18470 FQ	28580 AW	52940 TQ	FLBLS	10/01-12/01
	Fort Lauderdale PMSA, FL	Y	14220 FQ	19710 AW	31930 TQ	FLBLS	10/01-12/01
	Miami PMSA, FL	Y	12660 FQ	24410 AW	41550 TQ	FLBLS	10/01-12/01
	Orlando MSA, FL	Y	14370 FQ	21950 AW	37380 TQ	FLBLS	10/01-12/01
	Georgia	Y	12060 FQ	22990 AW	41390 TQ	GABLS	10/01-12/01
	Atlanta MSA, GA	Y	12110 FQ	23020 AW	40750 TQ	GABLS	10/01-12/01
	Idaho	Y	12660 FQ	34950 AW	47280 TQ	IDBLS	10/01-12/01
	Indiana	Y	12480 FQ	19590 AW	30590 TQ	INBLS	10/01-12/01
	Indianapolis MSA, IN	Y	12560 FQ	19100 AW	31390 TQ	INBLS	10/01-12/01
	Iowa	Y	11620 FQ	12970 AW	14710 TQ	IABLS	10/01-12/01
	Kansas	Y	12360 FQ	19520 AW	28870 TQ	KSBLS	10/01-12/01
	Maryland	Y	13340 FQ	25680 AW	43510 TQ	MDBLS	10/01-12/01
	Baltimore PMSA, MD	Y	12620 FQ	21560 AW	35040 TQ	MDBLS	10/01-12/01
	Massachusetts	Y	14190 FQ	22570 AW	35190 TQ	MABLS	10/01-12/01
	Boston PMSA, MA-NH	Y	14100 FQ	22510 AW	38980 TQ	MABLS	10/01-12/01
	Michigan	Y	12470 FQ	27410 AW	36020 TQ	MIBLS	10/01-12/01
	Detroit PMSA, MI	Y	12840 FQ	29680 AW	36250 TQ	MIBLS	10/01-12/01
	Missouri	Y	14390 FQ	26830 AW	41170 TQ	MOBLS	10/01-12/01
	Kansas City MSA, MO-KS	Y	15340 FQ	22700 AW	32360 TQ	MOBLS	10/01-12/01
	St. Louis MSA, MO-IL	Y	12950 FQ	29350 AW	54930 TQ	MOBLS	10/01-12/01
	Nebraska	Y	12010 FQ	21690 AW	38750 TQ	NEBLS	10/01-12/01
	New Jersey	Y	17530 FQ	28830 AW	47390 TQ	NJBLS	10/01-12/01
	New Mexico	Y	15800 FQ	20180 AW	22270 TQ	NMBLS	10/01-12/01
	Albuquerque MSA, NM	Y	15770 FQ	19700 AW	22160 TQ	NMBLS	10/01-12/01
	Ohio	Y	14550 FQ	19240 AW	28870 TQ	OHBLS	10/01-12/01
	Oklahoma	Y	11760 FQ	16260 AW	26200 TQ	OKBLS	10/01-12/01
	Oregon	Y	13920 FQ	21740 AW	27990 TQ	ORBLS	10/01-12/01
	Pennsylvania	Y	13110 FQ	22730 AW	37570 TQ	PABLS	10/01-12/01
	Philadelphia PMSA, PA-NJ	Y	12620 FQ	21830 AW	30000 TQ	PABLS	10/01-12/01
	Tennessee	Y	12320 FQ	31550 AW	64150 TQ	TNBLS	10/01-12/01
	Texas	Y	11850 FQ	27150 AW	56480 TQ	TXBLS	10/01-12/01
	Houston PMSA, TX	Y	14080 FQ	44200 AW	89430 TQ	TXBLS	10/01-12/01
	Virginia	Y	12510 FQ	22690 AW	36370 TQ	VABLS	10/01-12/01
	Washington	Y	19250 FQ	29500 AW	35130 TQ	WABLS	10/01-12/01
	Seattle-Bellevue-Everett PMSA, WA	Y	28410 FQ	31330 AW	35140 TQ	WABLS	10/01-12/01
	Tacoma PMSA, WA	Y	18380 FQ	21240 AW	23150 TQ	WABLS	10/01-12/01
	West Virginia	Y	14040 FQ	29390 AW	41230 TQ	WVBLS	10/01-12/01
Upholsterer	Alabama	H	7.16 FQ	10.73 AW	13.35 TQ	ALBLS	10/01-12/01
	Birmingham MSA, AL	H	9.38 FQ	11.43 AW	13.32 TQ	ALBLS	10/01-12/01
	Montgomery MSA, AL	H	6.35 FQ	9.31 AW	12.82 TQ	ALBLS	10/01-12/01
	Alaska	H	9.82 FQ	14.09 AW	17.55 TQ	AKBLS	10/01-12/01
	Arizona	H	7.17 FQ	10.83 AW	14.65 TQ	AZBLS	10/01-12/01

AAW	Average annual wage	**AOH**	Average offered, high	**ASH**	Average starting, high	**H**	Hourly	**M**	Monthly	**S**	Special: hourly and annual
AE	Average entry wage	**AOL**	Average offered, low	**ASL**	Average starting, low	**HI**	Highest wage paid	**MTC**	Median total compensation	**TQ**	Third quartile wage
AEX	Average experienced wage	**APH**	Average pay, high range	**AW**	Average wage paid	**HR**	High end range	**MW**	Median wage paid	**W**	Weekly
AO	Average offered	**APL**	Average pay, low range	**FQ**	First quartile wage	**LR**	Low end range	**SQ**	Second quartile wage	**Y**	Yearly

Occupation/Type/Industry	Location	Per	Low	Mid	High	Source	Date
Upholsterer	Phoenix-Mesa MSA, AZ	H	6.99 FQ	11.16 AW	14.92 TQ	AZBLS	10/01-12/01
	Tucson MSA, AZ	H	7.50 FQ	10.48 AW	13.72 TQ	AZBLS	10/01-12/01
	Arkansas	H	7.40 FQ	10.77 AW	15.22 TQ	ARBLS	10/01-12/01
	Fort Smith MSA, AR-OK	H	8.75 FQ	10.52 AW	12.95 TQ	ARBLS	10/01-12/01
	California	H	6.87 FQ	11.63 AW	17.23 TQ	CABLS	10/01-12/01
	Los Angeles-Long Beach PMSA, CA	H	6.55 FQ	10.70 AW	15.44 TQ	CABLS	10/01-12/01
	Modesto MSA, CA	H	7.17 FQ	9.99 AW	13.97 TQ	CABLS	10/01-12/01
	Oakland PMSA, CA	H	9.58 FQ	14.42 AW	18.59 TQ	CABLS	10/01-12/01
	Orange County PMSA, CA	H	7.86 FQ	13.44 AW	20.03 TQ	CABLS	10/01-12/01
	Riverside-San Bernardino PMSA, CA	H	8.32 FQ	11.78 AW	18.07 TQ	CABLS	10/01-12/01
	Sacramento PMSA, CA	H	7.52 FQ	10.55 AW	16.55 TQ	CABLS	10/01-12/01
	San Diego MSA, CA	H	8.13 FQ	10.83 AW	13.87 TQ	CABLS	10/01-12/01
	San Francisco PMSA, CA	H	10.60 FQ	17.81 AW	22.95 TQ	CABLS	10/01-12/01
	San Jose PMSA, CA	H	8.45 FQ	12.61 AW	18.35 TQ	CABLS	10/01-12/01
	Santa Rosa PMSA, CA	H	8.89 FQ	16.92 AW	22.22 TQ	CABLS	10/01-12/01
	Stockton-Lodi MSA, CA	H	7.76 FQ	10.02 AW	12.95 TQ	CABLS	10/01-12/01
	Vallejo-Fairfield-Napa PMSA, CA	H	6.70 FQ	13.44 AW	17.15 TQ	CABLS	10/01-12/01
	Colorado	H	9.36 FQ	12.78 AW	17.37 TQ	COBLS	10/01-12/01
	Denver PMSA, CO	H	9.44 FQ	12.63 AW	16.97 TQ	COBLS	10/01-12/01
	Connecticut	H	7.89 FQ	14.18 AW	23.09 TQ	CTBLS	10/01-12/01
	Bridgeport PMSA, CT	H	8.47 FQ	16.49 AW	27.41 TQ	CTBLS	10/01-12/01
	Hartford MSA, CT	H	10.02 FQ	15.99 AW	25.55 TQ	CTBLS	10/01-12/01
	New Haven-Meriden PMSA, CT	H	6.96 FQ	12.37 AW	16.59 TQ	CTBLS	10/01-12/01
	Stamford-Norwalk PMSA, CT	H	7.79 FQ	13.09 AW	19.58 TQ	CTBLS	10/01-12/01
	Delaware	H	8.31 FQ	13.66 AW	20.80 TQ	DEBLS	10/01-12/01
	Washington PMSA, DC-MD-VA-WV	H	7.60 FQ	12.35 AW	19.36 TQ	DCBLS	10/01-12/01
	Florida	H	7.54 FQ	11.75 AW	16.92 TQ	FLBLS	10/01-12/01
	Fort Lauderdale PMSA, FL	H	7.11 FQ	10.51 AW	15.10 TQ	FLBLS	10/01-12/01
	Fort Myers-Cape Coral MSA, FL	H	6.51 FQ	10.31 AW	15.19 TQ	FLBLS	10/01-12/01
	Jacksonville MSA, FL	H	6.47 FQ	11.92 AW	17.46 TQ	FLBLS	10/01-12/01
	Lakeland-Winter Haven MSA, FL	H	9.00 FQ	12.10 AW	16.42 TQ	FLBLS	10/01-12/01
	Melbourne-Titusville-Palm Bay MSA, FL	H	9.60 FQ	13.48 AW	16.54 TQ	FLBLS	10/01-12/01
	Miami PMSA, FL	H	8.83 FQ	11.89 AW	17.35 TQ	FLBLS	10/01-12/01
	Orlando MSA, FL	H	7.23 FQ	11.51 AW	15.70 TQ	FLBLS	10/01-12/01
	Sarasota-Bradenton MSA, FL	H	9.64 FQ	13.99 AW	18.21 TQ	FLBLS	10/01-12/01
	Tampa-St. Petersburg-Clearwater MSA, FL	H	7.65 FQ	10.46 AW	15.07 TQ	FLBLS	10/01-12/01
	West Palm Beach-Boca Raton MSA, FL	H	9.49 FQ	15.71 AW	22.55 TQ	FLBLS	10/01-12/01
	Georgia	H	7.46 FQ	11.49 AW	17.49 TQ	GABLS	10/01-12/01
	Atlanta MSA, GA	H	8.61 FQ	12.55 AW	19.36 TQ	GABLS	10/01-12/01
	Augusta-Aiken MSA, GA-SC	H	7.63 FQ	10.67 AW	17.15 TQ	GABLS	10/01-12/01
	Columbus MSA, GA-AL	H	5.85 FQ	10.62 AW	16.96 TQ	GABLS	10/01-12/01
	Macon MSA, GA	H	6.28 FQ	10.10 AW	14.31 TQ	GABLS	10/01-12/01
	Hawaii	H	7.69 FQ	15.77 AW	25.81 TQ	HIBLS	10/01-12/01
	Idaho	H	7.85 FQ	12.22 AW	17.85 TQ	IDBLS	10/01-12/01
	Boise City MSA, ID	H	8.12 FQ	12.92 AW	19.09 TQ	IDBLS	10/01-12/01
	Illinois	H	7.90 FQ	12.80 AW	18.86 TQ	ILBLS	10/01-12/01
	Chicago PMSA, IL	H	8.06 FQ	12.94 AW	18.69 TQ	ILBLS	10/01-12/01
	Indiana	H	8.98 FQ	11.89 AW	16.43 TQ	INBLS	10/01-12/01
	Elkhart-Goshen MSA, IN	H	9.31 FQ	11.97 AW	16.06 TQ	INBLS	10/01-12/01
	Fort Wayne MSA, IN	H	9.00 FQ	12.24 AW	17.69 TQ	INBLS	10/01-12/01
	Indianapolis MSA, IN	H	9.83 FQ	13.63 AW	20.34 TQ	INBLS	10/01-12/01
	Iowa	H	8.79 FQ	13.26 AW	20.10 TQ	IABLS	10/01-12/01
	Kansas	H	7.07 FQ	11.32 AW	17.15 TQ	KSBLS	10/01-12/01
	Kentucky	H	7.64 FQ	11.70 AW	17.53 TQ	KYBLS	10/01-12/01
	Lexington MSA, KY	H	6.79 FQ	10.41 AW	14.94 TQ	KYBLS	10/01-12/01
	Louisville MSA, KY-IN	H	7.66 FQ	11.36 AW	16.05 TQ	KYBLS	10/01-12/01
	Louisiana	H	5.98 FQ	9.93 AW	13.89 TQ	LABLS	10/01-12/01
	Lafayette MSA, LA	H	5.76 FQ	8.97 AW	20.65 TQ	LABLS	10/01-12/01
	Maine	H	7.16 FQ	12.86 AW	17.11 TQ	MEBLS	10/01-12/01
	Maryland	H	7.44 FQ	12.56 AW	18.83 TQ	MDBLS	10/01-12/01
	Baltimore PMSA, MD	H	6.30 FQ	12.73 AW	21.41 TQ	MDBLS	10/01-12/01
	Massachusetts	H	7.78 FQ	12.58 AW	18.37 TQ	MABLS	10/01-12/01

AAW	Average annual wage	**AOH**	Average offered, high	**ASH**	Average starting, high	**H**	Hourly	**M**	Monthly	**S**	Special: hourly and annual
AE	Average entry wage	**AOL**	Average offered, low	**ASL**	Average starting, low	**HI**	Highest wage paid	**MTC**	Median total compensation	**TQ**	Third quartile wage
AEX	Average experienced wage	**APH**	Average pay, high range	**AW**	Average wage paid	**HR**	High end range	**MW**	Median wage paid	**W**	Weekly
AO	Average offered	**APL**	Average pay, low range	**FQ**	First quartile wage	**LR**	Low end range	**SQ**	Second quartile wage	**Y**	Yearly

Occupation/Type/Industry	Location	Per	Low	Mid	High	Source	Date
Upholsterer	Boston PMSA, MA-NH	H	7.98 FQ	12.21 AW	16.84 TQ	MABLS	10/01-12/01
	Springfield MSA, MA	H	6.95 FQ	12.69 AW	19.34 TQ	MABLS	10/01-12/01
	Worcester PMSA, MA-CT	H	7.86 FQ	13.30 AW	18.84 TQ	MABLS	10/01-12/01
	Michigan	H	9.21 FQ	12.57 AW	17.59 TQ	MIBLS	10/01-12/01
	Detroit PMSA, MI	H	10.07 FQ	14.07 AW	19.61 TQ	MIBLS	10/01-12/01
	Grand Rapids-Muskegon-Holland MSA, MI	H	9.55 FQ	12.05 AW	16.40 TQ	MIBLS	10/01-12/01
	Minnesota	H	8.69 FQ	13.99 AW	20.57 TQ	MNBLS	10/01-12/01
	Minneapolis-St. Paul MSA, MN-WI	H	9.43 FQ	14.88 AW	21.38 TQ	MNBLS	10/01-12/01
	Mississippi	H	8.42 FQ	12.43 AW	16.84 TQ	MSBLS	10/01-12/01
	Missouri	H	8.72 FQ	13.13 AW	17.62 TQ	MOBLS	10/01-12/01
	Kansas City MSA, MO-KS	H	8.67 FQ	11.09 AW	15.90 TQ	MOBLS	10/01-12/01
	St. Louis MSA, MO-IL	H	7.28 FQ	11.48 AW	17.16 TQ	MOBLS	10/01-12/01
	Springfield MSA, MO	H	9.12 FQ	11.31 AW	13.96 TQ	MOBLS	10/01-12/01
	Montana	H	7.52 FQ	11.14 AW	16.49 TQ	MTBLS	10/01-12/01
	Nebraska	H	6.43 FQ	13.60 AW	21.28 TQ	NEBLS	10/01-12/01
	Omaha MSA, NE-IA	H	6.10 FQ	11.60 AW	16.93 TQ	NEBLS	10/01-12/01
	Nevada	H	9.13 FQ	14.04 AW	21.00 TQ	NVBLS	10/01-12/01
	Las Vegas MSA, NV-AZ	H	9.81 FQ	14.50 AW	21.91 TQ	NVBLS	10/01-12/01
	Reno MSA, NV	H	8.37 FQ	12.93 AW	18.53 TQ	NVBLS	10/01-12/01
	New Hampshire	H	9.17 FQ	12.15 AW	18.92 TQ	NHBLS	10/01-12/01
	New Jersey	H	9.00 FQ	13.39 AW	17.92 TQ	NJBLS	10/01-12/01
	Bergen-Passaic PMSA, NJ	H	9.00 FQ	14.08 AW	20.13 TQ	NJBLS	10/01-12/01
	Middlesex-Somerset-Hunterdon PMSA, NJ	H	8.90 FQ	13.58 AW	20.29 TQ	NJBLS	10/01-12/01
	Newark PMSA, NJ	H	8.18 FQ	12.26 AW	17.34 TQ	NJBLS	10/01-12/01
	Trenton PMSA, NJ	H	11.71 FQ	13.18 AW	15.56 TQ	NJBLS	10/01-12/01
	New Mexico	H	7.90 FQ	11.15 AW	17.64 TQ	NMBLS	10/01-12/01
	New York	H	6.56 FQ	12.92 AW	21.51 TQ	NYBLS	10/01-12/01
	Albany-Schenectady-Troy MSA, NY	H	7.85 FQ	15.35 AW	20.81 TQ	NYBLS	10/01-12/01
	Buffalo-Niagara Falls MSA, NY	H	5.61 FQ	11.69 AW	18.55 TQ	NYBLS	10/01-12/01
	Nassau-Suffolk PMSA, NY	H	8.18 FQ	14.26 AW	21.50 TQ	NYBLS	10/01-12/01
	New York PMSA, NY	H	6.30 FQ	12.63 AW	22.84 TQ	NYBLS	10/01-12/01
	Rochester MSA, NY	H	8.18 FQ	12.71 AW	17.78 TQ	NYBLS	10/01-12/01
	North Carolina	H	9.41 FQ	15.50 AW	22.18 TQ	NCBLS	10/01-12/01
	Charlotte-Gastonia-Rock Hill MSA, NC-SC	H	7.88 FQ	12.24 AW	17.19 TQ	NCBLS	10/01-12/01
	Greensboro-Winston-Salem-High Point MSA, NC	H	9.36 FQ	14.63 AW	21.44 TQ	NCBLS	10/01-12/01
	Hickory-Morganton-Lenoir MSA, NC	H	11.13 FQ	17.36 AW	23.45 TQ	NCBLS	10/01-12/01
	Raleigh-Durham-Chapel Hill MSA, NC	H	9.42 FQ	12.05 AW	15.71 TQ	NCBLS	10/01-12/01
	Ohio	H	7.71 FQ	11.43 AW	16.31 TQ	OHBLS	10/01-12/01
	Akron PMSA, OH	H	8.94 FQ	11.43 AW	15.96 TQ	OHBLS	10/01-12/01
	Cincinnati PMSA, OH-KY-IN	H	6.95 FQ	9.98 AW	13.86 TQ	OHBLS	10/01-12/01
	Cleveland-Lorain-Elyria PMSA, OH	H	11.64 FQ	13.99 AW	17.30 TQ	OHBLS	10/01-12/01
	Columbus MSA, OH	H	9.94 FQ	13.26 AW	16.83 TQ	OHBLS	10/01-12/01
	Toledo MSA, OH	H	7.52 FQ	8.98 AW	11.52 TQ	OHBLS	10/01-12/01
	Youngstown-Warren MSA, OH	H	7.24 FQ	9.93 AW	13.71 TQ	OHBLS	10/01-12/01
	Oklahoma	H	5.94 FQ	9.35 AW	14.23 TQ	OKBLS	10/01-12/01
	Oklahoma City MSA, OK	H	5.84 FQ	8.35 AW	12.64 TQ	OKBLS	10/01-12/01
	Tulsa MSA, OK	H	7.43 FQ	11.34 AW	16.61 TQ	OKBLS	10/01-12/01
	Oregon	H	8.67 FQ	13.27 AW	20.32 TQ	ORBLS	10/01-12/01
	Eugene-Springfield MSA, OR	H	8.90 FQ	11.65 AW	15.41 TQ	ORBLS	10/01-12/01
	Portland-Vancouver PMSA, OR-WA	H	7.75 FQ	11.36 AW	15.86 TQ	ORBLS	10/01-12/01
	Pennsylvania	H	7.47 FQ	12.05 AW	17.50 TQ	PABLS	10/01-12/01
	Allentown-Bethlehem-Easton MSA, PA	H	8.66 FQ	13.22 AW	17.31 TQ	PABLS	10/01-12/01
	Johnstown MSA, PA	H	8.88 FQ	11.87 AW	17.20 TQ	PABLS	10/01-12/01
	Lancaster MSA, PA	H	9.92 FQ	13.75 AW	19.11 TQ	PABLS	10/01-12/01
	Philadelphia PMSA, PA-NJ	H	7.39 FQ	12.15 AW	17.28 TQ	PABLS	10/01-12/01
	Pittsburgh MSA, PA	H	7.38 FQ	11.66 AW	18.50 TQ	PABLS	10/01-12/01
	Scranton-Wilkes-Barre-Hazleton MSA, PA	H	7.57 FQ	10.78 AW	14.25 TQ	PABLS	10/01-12/01
	York MSA, PA	H	9.05 FQ	10.59 AW	13.87 TQ	PABLS	10/01-12/01
	Rhode Island	H	7.82 FQ	13.63 AW	19.01 TQ	RIBLS	10/01-12/01

AAW Average annual wage; AE Average entry wage; AEX Average experienced wage; AO Average offered; AOH Average offered, high; AOL Average offered, low; APH Average pay, high range; APL Average pay, low range; ASH Average starting, high; ASL Average starting, low; AW Average wage paid; FQ First quartile wage; H Hourly; HI Highest wage paid; HR High end range; LR Low end range; M Monthly; MTC Median total compensation; MW Median wage paid; SQ Second quartile wage; S Special: hourly and annual; TQ Third quartile wage; W Weekly; Y Yearly

Occupation/Type/Industry	Location	Per	Low	Mid	High	Source	Date
Upholsterer	Providence-Fall River-Warwick MSA, RI-MA	H	7.91 FQ	13.46 AW	18.89 TQ	RIBLS	10/01-12/01
	South Carolina	H	6.37 FQ	10.11 AW	15.05 TQ	SCBLS	10/01-12/01
	Tennessee	H	7.35 FQ	10.91 AW	16.90 TQ	TNBLS	10/01-12/01
	Knoxville MSA, TN	H	6.63 FQ	9.39 AW	12.84 TQ	TNBLS	10/01-12/01
	Memphis MSA, TN-AR-MS	H	8.52 FQ	12.37 AW	16.77 TQ	TNBLS	10/01-12/01
	Nashville MSA, TN	H	7.24 FQ	8.75 AW	11.38 TQ	TNBLS	10/01-12/01
	Texas	H	6.83 FQ	10.90 AW	16.21 TQ	TXBLS	10/01-12/01
	Austin-San Marcos MSA, TX	H	8.88 FQ	12.32 AW	16.28 TQ	TXBLS	10/01-12/01
	Corpus Christi MSA, TX	H	6.40 FQ	12.74 AW	20.51 TQ	TXBLS	10/01-12/01
	Dallas PMSA, TX	H	8.06 FQ	11.34 AW	14.41 TQ	TXBLS	10/01-12/01
	El Paso MSA, TX	H	5.92 FQ	9.62 AW	15.90 TQ	TXBLS	10/01-12/01
	Fort Worth-Arlington PMSA, TX	H	6.56 FQ	11.58 AW	22.51 TQ	TXBLS	10/01-12/01
	Houston PMSA, TX	H	6.71 FQ	10.87 AW	16.47 TQ	TXBLS	10/01-12/01
	San Antonio MSA, TX	H	7.19 FQ	10.29 AW	15.02 TQ	TXBLS	10/01-12/01
	Waco MSA, TX	H	6.07 FQ	10.09 AW	14.56 TQ	TXBLS	10/01-12/01
	Salt Lake City-Ogden MSA, UT	H	8.44 FQ	13.28 AW	21.34 TQ	UTBLS	10/01-12/01
	Virginia	H	7.53 FQ	10.55 AW	14.10 TQ	VABLS	10/01-12/01
	Norfolk-Virginia Beach-Newport News MSA, VA-NC	H	7.95 FQ	13.17 AW	20.25 TQ	VABLS	10/01-12/01
	Washington	H	7.15 FQ	14.37 AW	21.99 TQ	WABLS	10/01-12/01
	Seattle-Bellevue-Everett PMSA, WA	H	7.13 FQ	15.40 AW	22.93 TQ	WABLS	10/01-12/01
	Spokane MSA, WA	H	7.23 FQ	11.55 AW	17.16 TQ	WABLS	10/01-12/01
	West Virginia	H	7.06 FQ	9.13 AW	12.54 TQ	WVBLS	10/01-12/01
	Wisconsin	H	8.39 FQ	11.90 AW	16.04 TQ	WIBLS	10/01-12/01
	Appleton-Oshkosh-Neenah MSA, WI	H	8.66 FQ	13.64 AW	19.67 TQ	WIBLS	10/01-12/01
	Madison MSA, WI	H	9.27 FQ	12.13 AW	16.20 TQ	WIBLS	10/01-12/01
	Milwaukee-Waukesha PMSA, WI	H	7.35 FQ	11.36 AW	16.32 TQ	WIBLS	10/01-12/01
	Puerto Rico	H	5.54 FQ	6.67 AW	8.23 TQ	PRBLS	10/01-12/01
Urban and Regional Planner	Alabama	Y	23030 FQ	42010 AW	62430 TQ	ALBLS	10/01-12/01
	Montgomery MSA, AL	Y	30120 FQ	46240 AW	65150 TQ	ALBLS	10/01-12/01
	Alaska	Y	36410 FQ	53760 AW	73370 TQ	AKBLS	10/01-12/01
	Arizona	Y	32070 FQ	49860 AW	72500 TQ	AZBLS	10/01-12/01
	Phoenix-Mesa MSA, AZ	Y	36510 FQ	54880 AW	76500 TQ	AZBLS	10/01-12/01
	Tucson MSA, AZ	Y	29980 FQ	43010 AW	56340 TQ	AZBLS	10/01-12/01
	Arkansas	Y	18340 FQ	28260 AW	44470 TQ	ARBLS	10/01-12/01
	Fayetteville-Springdale-Rogers MSA, AR	Y	17880 FQ	20740 AW	22250 TQ	ARBLS	10/01-12/01
	Little Rock-North Little Rock MSA, AR	Y	24350 FQ	34340 AW	48040 TQ	ARBLS	10/01-12/01
	California	Y	36490 FQ	58430 AW	85670 TQ	CABLS	10/01-12/01
	Bakersfield MSA, CA	Y	40040 FQ	60900 AW	88030 TQ	CABLS	10/01-12/01
	Fresno MSA, CA	Y	17810 FQ	43400 AW	64820 TQ	CABLS	10/01-12/01
	Los Angeles-Long Beach PMSA, CA	Y	27540 FQ	51640 AW	70370 TQ	CABLS	10/01-12/01
	Oakland PMSA, CA	Y	49040 FQ	75110 AW	111540 TQ	CABLS	10/01-12/01
	Orange County PMSA, CA	Y	41980 FQ	63180 AW	88100 TQ	CABLS	10/01-12/01
	Redding MSA, CA	Y	38230 FQ	56460 AW	73580 TQ	CABLS	10/01-12/01
	Riverside-San Bernardino PMSA, CA	Y	40010 FQ	61130 AW	89510 TQ	CABLS	10/01-12/01
	Sacramento PMSA, CA	Y	45550 FQ	61990 AW	84600 TQ	CABLS	10/01-12/01
	Salinas MSA, CA	Y	31680 FQ	56600 AW	80730 TQ	CABLS	10/01-12/01
	San Diego MSA, CA	Y	33950 FQ	55500 AW	76850 TQ	CABLS	10/01-12/01
	San Francisco PMSA, CA	Y	45120 FQ	61560 AW	80880 TQ	CABLS	10/01-12/01
	San Jose PMSA, CA	Y	39380 FQ	61120 AW	86760 TQ	CABLS	10/01-12/01
	San Luis Obispo-Atascadero-Paso Robles MSA, CA	Y	27560 FQ	51230 AW	72670 TQ	CABLS	10/01-12/01
	Santa Barbara-Santa Maria-Lompoc MSA, CA	Y	35950 FQ	57120 AW	81560 TQ	CABLS	10/01-12/01
	Santa Rosa PMSA, CA	Y	27530 FQ	58090 AW	84280 TQ	CABLS	10/01-12/01
	Stockton-Lodi MSA, CA	Y	33600 FQ	48020 AW	71230 TQ	CABLS	10/01-12/01
	Vallejo-Fairfield-Napa PMSA, CA	Y	49760 FQ	65330 AW	85460 TQ	CABLS	10/01-12/01
	Ventura PMSA, CA	Y	44020 FQ	62070 AW	87030 TQ	CABLS	10/01-12/01
	Visalia-Tulare-Porterville MSA, CA	Y	39660 FQ	57070 AW	77840 TQ	CABLS	10/01-12/01

AAW	Average annual wage	**AOH**	Average offered, high	**ASH**	Average starting, high	**H**	Hourly	**M**	Monthly	**S**	Special: hourly and annual
AE	Average entry wage	**AOL**	Average offered, low	**ASL**	Average starting, low	**HI**	Highest wage paid	**MTC**	Median total compensation	**TQ**	Third quartile wage
AEX	Average experienced wage	**APH**	Average pay, high range	**AW**	Average wage paid	**HR**	High end range	**MW**	Median wage paid	**W**	Weekly
AO	Average offered	**APL**	Average pay, low range	**FQ**	First quartile wage	**LR**	Low end range	**SQ**	Second quartile wage	**Y**	Yearly

Occupation/Type/Industry	Location	Per	Low	Mid	High	Source	Date
Urban and Regional Planner	Colorado	Y	31090 FQ	48020 AW	69130 TQ	COBLS	10/01-12/01
	Boulder-Longmont PMSA, CO	Y	31110 FQ	50210 AW	69140 TQ	COBLS	10/01-12/01
	Colorado Springs MSA, CO	Y	36430 FQ	56280 AW	87510 TQ	COBLS	10/01-12/01
	Denver PMSA, CO	Y	30440 FQ	45900 AW	68580 TQ	COBLS	10/01-12/01
	Fort Collins-Loveland MSA, CO	Y	39260 FQ	53700 AW	70940 TQ	COBLS	10/01-12/01
	Connecticut	Y	37110 FQ	57900 AW	84220 TQ	CTBLS	10/01-12/01
	Hartford MSA, CT	Y	47500 FQ	66720 AW	87550 TQ	CTBLS	10/01-12/01
	New Haven-Meriden PMSA, CT	Y	37060 FQ	51960 AW	78350 TQ	CTBLS	10/01-12/01
	New London-Norwich MSA, CT-RI	Y	26880 FQ	42530 AW	56650 TQ	CTBLS	10/01-12/01
	Stamford-Norwalk PMSA, CT	Y	33390 FQ	54480 AW	76350 TQ	CTBLS	10/01-12/01
	Delaware	Y	32930 FQ	48330 AW	66040 TQ	DEBLS	10/01-12/01
	Wilmington-Newark PMSA, DE-MD	Y	33580 FQ	49470 AW	67790 TQ	DEBLS	10/01-12/01
	District of Columbia	Y	38750 FQ	68750 AW	93620 TQ	DCBLS	10/01-12/01
	Washington PMSA, DC-MD-VA-WV	Y	39460 FQ	60880 AW	86160 TQ	DCBLS	10/01-12/01
	Florida	Y	31660 FQ	49470 AW	73580 TQ	FLBLS	10/01-12/01
	Daytona Beach MSA, FL	Y	31760 FQ	43140 AW	58100 TQ	FLBLS	10/01-12/01
	Fort Lauderdale PMSA, FL	Y	37410 FQ	52080 AW	71350 TQ	FLBLS	10/01-12/01
	Fort Myers-Cape Coral MSA, FL	Y	31120 FQ	46280 AW	69720 TQ	FLBLS	10/01-12/01
	Fort Pierce-Port St. Lucie MSA, FL	Y	29370 FQ	44910 AW	67710 TQ	FLBLS	10/01-12/01
	Gainesville MSA, FL	Y	32110 FQ	53950 AW	82270 TQ	FLBLS	10/01-12/01
	Jacksonville MSA, FL	Y	30760 FQ	48310 AW	70840 TQ	FLBLS	10/01-12/01
	Miami PMSA, FL	Y	35570 FQ	56100 AW	85130 TQ	FLBLS	10/01-12/01
	Naples MSA, FL	Y	36710 FQ	73670 AW	96870 TQ	FLBLS	10/01-12/01
	Orlando MSA, FL	Y	31760 FQ	48010 AW	69000 TQ	FLBLS	10/01-12/01
	Pensacola MSA, FL	Y	25630 FQ	42940 AW	65470 TQ	FLBLS	10/01-12/01
	Tallahassee MSA, FL	Y	31620 FQ	56990 AW	82010 TQ	FLBLS	10/01-12/01
	Tampa-St. Petersburg-Clearwater MSA, FL	Y	33340 FQ	53300 AW	79990 TQ	FLBLS	10/01-12/01
	West Palm Beach-Boca Raton MSA, FL	Y	32980 FQ	46650 AW	66060 TQ	FLBLS	10/01-12/01
	Georgia	Y	29420 FQ	45990 AW	70370 TQ	GABLS	10/01-12/01
	Atlanta MSA, GA	Y	31130 FQ	49700 AW	77150 TQ	GABLS	10/01-12/01
	Savannah MSA, GA	Y	31760 FQ	39640 AW	49470 TQ	GABLS	10/01-12/01
	Hawaii	Y	36350 FQ	50290 AW	68570 TQ	HIBLS	10/01-12/01
	Honolulu MSA, HI	Y	36440 FQ	49970 AW	68390 TQ	HIBLS	10/01-12/01
	Idaho	Y	28660 FQ	41910 AW	56270 TQ	IDBLS	10/01-12/01
	Boise City MSA, ID	Y	31780 FQ	45610 AW	61640 TQ	IDBLS	10/01-12/01
	Illinois	Y	31690 FQ	49480 AW	73730 TQ	ILBLS	10/01-12/01
	Chicago PMSA, IL	Y	35620 FQ	52320 AW	76970 TQ	ILBLS	10/01-12/01
	Indiana	Y	11900 FQ	27940 AW	48340 TQ	INBLS	10/01-12/01
	Fort Wayne MSA, IN	Y	25380 FQ	41390 AW	54710 TQ	INBLS	10/01-12/01
	Gary PMSA, IN	Y	11470 FQ	13200 AW	14290 TQ	INBLS	10/01-12/01
	Indianapolis MSA, IN	Y	29240 FQ	40590 AW	55920 TQ	INBLS	10/01-12/01
	South Bend MSA, IN	Y	25870 FQ	33650 AW	44960 TQ	INBLS	10/01-12/01
	Iowa	Y	28100 FQ	41250 AW	59130 TQ	IABLS	10/01-12/01
	Cedar Rapids MSA, IA	Y	25880 FQ	35320 AW	46050 TQ	IABLS	10/01-12/01
	Davenport-Moline-Rock Island MSA, IA-IL	Y	21550 FQ	40310 AW	62520 TQ	IABLS	10/01-12/01
	Des Moines MSA, IA	Y	28590 FQ	43240 AW	65560 TQ	IABLS	10/01-12/01
	Kansas	Y	32100 FQ	48700 AW	70100 TQ	KSBLS	10/01-12/01
	Kentucky	Y	27870 FQ	45410 AW	67080 TQ	KYBLS	10/01-12/01
	Louisville MSA, KY-IN	Y	33530 FQ	47710 AW	67850 TQ	KYBLS	10/01-12/01
	Louisiana	Y	25070 FQ	39110 AW	63660 TQ	LABLS	10/01-12/01
	New Orleans MSA, LA	Y	25970 FQ	40150 AW	65070 TQ	LABLS	10/01-12/01
	Maine	Y	30910 FQ	43020 AW	58670 TQ	MEBLS	10/01-12/01
	Maryland	Y	33030 FQ	52290 AW	72000 TQ	MDBLS	10/01-12/01
	Baltimore PMSA, MD	Y	32410 FQ	49960 AW	69330 TQ	MDBLS	10/01-12/01
	Massachusetts	Y	33370 FQ	57160 AW	91610 TQ	MABLS	10/01-12/01
	Boston PMSA, MA-NH	Y	35450 FQ	60020 AW	98020 TQ	MABLS	10/01-12/01
	Michigan	Y	35440 FQ	53350 AW	78780 TQ	MIBLS	10/01-12/01
	Detroit PMSA, MI	Y	35310 FQ	54940 AW	85730 TQ	MIBLS	10/01-12/01
	Grand Rapids-Muskegon-Holland MSA, MI	Y	29610 FQ	48160 AW	68760 TQ	MIBLS	10/01-12/01
	Kalamazoo-Battle Creek MSA, MI	Y	33480 FQ	47230 AW	69070 TQ	MIBLS	10/01-12/01

AAW	Average annual wage	AOH	Average offered, high	ASH	Average starting, high	H	Hourly	M	Monthly	S	Special: hourly and annual
AE	Average entry wage	AOL	Average offered, low	ASL	Average starting, low	HI	Highest wage paid	MTC	Median total compensation	TQ	Third quartile wage
AEX	Average experienced wage	APH	Average pay, high range	AW	Average wage paid	HR	High end range	MW	Median wage paid	W	Weekly
AO	Average offered	APL	Average pay, low range	FQ	First quartile wage	LR	Low end range	SQ	Second quartile wage	Y	Yearly

Occupation/Type/Industry	Location	Per	Low	Mid	High	Source	Date
Urban and Regional Planner	Minnesota	Y	37330 FQ	52720 AW	69050 TQ	MNBLS	10/01-12/01
	Duluth-Superior MSA, MN-WI	Y	37810 FQ	48350 AW	66920 TQ	MNBLS	10/01-12/01
	Minneapolis-St. Paul MSA, MN-WI	Y	37320 FQ	51110 AW	68630 TQ	MNBLS	10/01-12/01
	Mississippi	Y	24700 FQ	40540 AW	62660 TQ	MSBLS	10/01-12/01
	Biloxi-Gulfport-Pascagoula MSA, MS	Y	23220 FQ	40920 AW	64990 TQ	MSBLS	10/01-12/01
	Jackson MSA, MS	Y	30130 FQ	42550 AW	63620 TQ	MSBLS	10/01-12/01
	Missouri	Y	31510 FQ	43430 AW	58700 TQ	MOBLS	10/01-12/01
	Kansas City MSA, MO-KS	Y	32660 FQ	50050 AW	72940 TQ	MOBLS	10/01-12/01
	St. Louis MSA, MO-IL	Y	31820 FQ	43710 AW	58940 TQ	MOBLS	10/01-12/01
	Springfield MSA, MO	Y	30480 FQ	40280 AW	54120 TQ	MOBLS	10/01-12/01
	Montana	Y	23820 FQ	37360 AW	56300 TQ	MTBLS	10/01-12/01
	Nebraska	Y	21220 FQ	40740 AW	59100 TQ	NEBLS	10/01-12/01
	Lincoln MSA, NE	Y	17080 FQ	38860 AW	58520 TQ	NEBLS	10/01-12/01
	Omaha MSA, NE-IA	Y	29570 FQ	42070 AW	59230 TQ	NEBLS	10/01-12/01
	Nevada	Y	40170 FQ	56880 AW	75410 TQ	NVBLS	10/01-12/01
	Las Vegas MSA, NV-AZ	Y	32800 FQ	54060 AW	74850 TQ	NVBLS	10/01-12/01
	Reno MSA, NV	Y	41700 FQ	57570 AW	74090 TQ	NVBLS	10/01-12/01
	New Hampshire	Y	30750 FQ	41510 AW	55810 TQ	NHBLS	10/01-12/01
	Portsmouth-Rochester PMSA, NH-ME	Y	32480 FQ	43140 AW	57310 TQ	NHBLS	10/01-12/01
	New Jersey	Y	35290 FQ	51350 AW	72450 TQ	NJBLS	10/01-12/01
	Atlantic-Cape May PMSA, NJ	Y	37180 FQ	51360 AW	69970 TQ	NJBLS	10/01-12/01
	Bergen-Passaic PMSA, NJ	Y	37160 FQ	50700 AW	70480 TQ	NJBLS	10/01-12/01
	Middlesex-Somerset-Hunterdon PMSA, NJ	Y	34250 FQ	47170 AW	68020 TQ	NJBLS	10/01-12/01
	Newark PMSA, NJ	Y	36290 FQ	52270 AW	74180 TQ	NJBLS	10/01-12/01
	New Mexico	Y	27830 FQ	40030 AW	54230 TQ	NMBLS	10/01-12/01
	Albuquerque MSA, NM	Y	30420 FQ	42870 AW	57590 TQ	NMBLS	10/01-12/01
	New York	Y	33440 FQ	52680 AW	72870 TQ	NYBLS	10/01-12/01
	Albany-Schenectady-Troy MSA, NY	Y	32800 FQ	49530 AW	66530 TQ	NYBLS	10/01-12/01
	Binghamton MSA, NY	Y	44010 FQ	48490 AW	55430 TQ	NYBLS	10/01-12/01
	Buffalo-Niagara Falls MSA, NY	Y	30730 FQ	46430 AW	74770 TQ	NYBLS	10/01-12/01
	Nassau-Suffolk PMSA, NY	Y	36950 FQ	55810 AW	82450 TQ	NYBLS	10/01-12/01
	Rochester MSA, NY	Y	30480 FQ	42820 AW	60380 TQ	NYBLS	10/01-12/01
	North Carolina	Y	30770 FQ	45350 AW	64130 TQ	NCBLS	10/01-12/01
	Charlotte-Gastonia-Rock Hill MSA, NC-SC	Y	33360 FQ	48150 AW	67310 TQ	NCBLS	10/01-12/01
	Greensboro-Winston-Salem-High Point MSA, NC	Y	33800 FQ	45410 AW	59520 TQ	NCBLS	10/01-12/01
	Raleigh-Durham-Chapel Hill MSA, NC	Y	30660 FQ	47020 AW	67650 TQ	NCBLS	10/01-12/01
	Wilmington MSA, NC	Y	37180 FQ	59920 AW	113200 TQ	NCBLS	10/01-12/01
	North Dakota	Y	27970 FQ	41400 AW	60430 TQ	NDBLS	10/01-12/01
	Ohio	Y	30350 FQ	46010 AW	68430 TQ	OHBLS	10/01-12/01
	Cincinnati PMSA, OH-KY-IN	Y	36090 FQ	53420 AW	81470 TQ	OHBLS	10/01-12/01
	Cleveland-Lorain-Elyria PMSA, OH	Y	13910 FQ	41180 AW	58830 TQ	OHBLS	10/01-12/01
	Dayton-Springfield MSA, OH	Y	31320 FQ	51750 AW	75620 TQ	OHBLS	10/01-12/01
	Oklahoma	Y	27790 FQ	47800 AW	73030 TQ	OKBLS	10/01-12/01
	Oregon	Y	35010 FQ	49770 AW	68100 TQ	ORBLS	10/01-12/01
	Eugene-Springfield MSA, OR	Y	31860 FQ	54080 AW	73710 TQ	ORBLS	10/01-12/01
	Portland-Vancouver PMSA, OR-WA	Y	37940 FQ	52770 AW	70330 TQ	ORBLS	10/01-12/01
	Salem PMSA, OR	Y	39630 FQ	51700 AW	66060 TQ	ORBLS	10/01-12/01
	Pennsylvania	Y	29540 FQ	44200 AW	67370 TQ	PABLS	10/01-12/01
	Allentown-Bethlehem-Easton MSA, PA	Y	27310 FQ	47290 AW	74800 TQ	PABLS	10/01-12/01
	Harrisburg-Lebanon-Carlisle MSA, PA	Y	31030 FQ	44820 AW	64390 TQ	PABLS	10/01-12/01
	Philadelphia PMSA, PA-NJ	Y	30500 FQ	46150 AW	69050 TQ	PABLS	10/01-12/01
	Pittsburgh MSA, PA	Y	28170 FQ	50190 AW	74690 TQ	PABLS	10/01-12/01
	Scranton-Wilkes-Barre-Hazleton MSA, PA	Y	13140 FQ	38670 AW	64470 TQ	PABLS	10/01-12/01
	Rhode Island	Y	39460 FQ	54490 AW	75230 TQ	RIBLS	10/01-12/01
	Providence-Fall River-Warwick MSA, RI-MA	Y	36200 FQ	52360 AW	72660 TQ	RIBLS	10/01-12/01
	South Carolina	Y	19950 FQ	41450 AW	71510 TQ	SCBLS	10/01-12/01

AAW	Average annual wage	AOH	Average offered, high	ASH	Average starting, high	H	Hourly	M	Monthly	S	Special: hourly and annual
AE	Average entry wage	AOL	Average offered, low	ASL	Average starting, low	HI	Highest wage paid	MTC	Median total compensation	TQ	Third quartile wage
AEX	Average experienced wage	APH	Average pay, high range	AW	Average wage paid	HR	High end range	MW	Median wage paid	W	Weekly
AO	Average offered	APL	Average pay, low range	FQ	First quartile wage	LR	Low end range	SQ	Second quartile wage	Y	Yearly

Occupation/Type/Industry	Location	Per	Low	Mid	High	Source	Date
Urban and Regional Planner	Charleston-North Charleston MSA, SC	Y	12280 FQ	38680 AW	82640 TQ	SCBLS	10/01-12/01
	Columbia MSA, SC	Y	30940 FQ	49820 AW	73620 TQ	SCBLS	10/01-12/01
	Greenville-Spartanburg-Anderson MSA, SC	Y	29180 FQ	39290 AW	56820 TQ	SCBLS	10/01-12/01
	South Dakota	Y	27490 FQ	39290 AW	52290 TQ	SDBLS	10/01-12/01
	Tennessee	Y	23910 FQ	40340 AW	58920 TQ	TNBLS	10/01-12/01
	Memphis MSA, TN-AR-MS	Y	24480 FQ	45190 AW	78360 TQ	TNBLS	10/01-12/01
	Nashville MSA, TN	Y	27390 FQ	41600 AW	58980 TQ	TNBLS	10/01-12/01
	Texas	Y	31130 FQ	48710 AW	75750 TQ	TXBLS	10/01-12/01
	Austin-San Marcos MSA, TX	Y	31270 FQ	42660 AW	58260 TQ	TXBLS	10/01-12/01
	Dallas PMSA, TX	Y	35840 FQ	56490 AW	89960 TQ	TXBLS	10/01-12/01
	El Paso MSA, TX	Y	31820 FQ	41060 AW	51450 TQ	TXBLS	10/01-12/01
	Fort Worth-Arlington PMSA, TX	Y	39720 FQ	56950 AW	87900 TQ	TXBLS	10/01-12/01
	Houston PMSA, TX	Y	35200 FQ	54850 AW	88680 TQ	TXBLS	10/01-12/01
	San Antonio MSA, TX	Y	31180 FQ	45020 AW	72500 TQ	TXBLS	10/01-12/01
	Utah	Y	28540 FQ	45830 AW	69770 TQ	UTBLS	10/01-12/01
	Provo-Orem MSA, UT	Y	27870 FQ	56830 AW	91620 TQ	UTBLS	10/01-12/01
	Salt Lake City-Ogden MSA, UT	Y	31850 FQ	45920 AW	63810 TQ	UTBLS	10/01-12/01
	Vermont	Y	14790 FQ	38090 AW	59650 TQ	VTBLS	10/01-12/01
	Virginia	Y	31800 FQ	51840 AW	76870 TQ	VABLS	10/01-12/01
	Norfolk-Virginia Beach-Newport News MSA, VA-NC	Y	31270 FQ	47960 AW	72790 TQ	VABLS	10/01-12/01
	Richmond-Petersburg MSA, VA	Y	29630 FQ	47560 AW	71740 TQ	VABLS	10/01-12/01
	Washington	Y	36640 FQ	57400 AW	84090 TQ	WABLS	10/01-12/01
	Bremerton PMSA, WA	Y	42350 FQ	59920 AW	83380 TQ	WABLS	10/01-12/01
	Olympia PMSA, WA	Y	36760 FQ	50210 AW	69880 TQ	WABLS	10/01-12/01
	Richland-Kennewick-Pasco MSA, WA	Y	38170 FQ	56120 AW	81310 TQ	WABLS	10/01-12/01
	Seattle-Bellevue-Everett PMSA, WA	Y	35900 FQ	60180 AW	88030 TQ	WABLS	10/01-12/01
	Spokane MSA, WA	Y	39320 FQ	60420 AW	91000 TQ	WABLS	10/01-12/01
	Tacoma PMSA, WA	Y	40340 FQ	53110 AW	70690 TQ	WABLS	10/01-12/01
	Yakima MSA, WA	Y	34050 FQ	52060 AW	76340 TQ	WABLS	10/01-12/01
	Wisconsin	Y	21910 FQ	46430 AW	70550 TQ	WIBLS	10/01-12/01
	Green Bay MSA, WI	Y	18850 FQ	40560 AW	58820 TQ	WIBLS	10/01-12/01
	Madison MSA, WI	Y	30830 FQ	54390 AW	84240 TQ	WIBLS	10/01-12/01
	Milwaukee-Waukesha PMSA, WI	Y	31530 FQ	51950 AW	76100 TQ	WIBLS	10/01-12/01
	Wyoming	Y	30820 FQ	41870 AW	58880 TQ	WYBLS	10/01-12/01
Usher, Lobby Attendant, and Ticket Taker	Alabama	H	5.46 FQ	6.18 AW	7.15 TQ	ALBLS	10/01-12/01
	Alaska	H	6.05 FQ	6.95 AW	7.86 TQ	AKBLS	10/01-12/01
	Arizona	H	5.54 FQ	6.80 AW	8.54 TQ	AZBLS	10/01-12/01
	Arkansas	H	5.58 FQ	7.08 AW	8.84 TQ	ARBLS	10/01-12/01
	California	H	6.40 FQ	8.45 AW	13.48 TQ	CABLS	10/01-12/01
	Colorado	H	5.69 FQ	7.12 AW	8.71 TQ	COBLS	10/01-12/01
	Connecticut	H	6.60 FQ	8.33 AW	10.65 TQ	CTBLS	10/01-12/01
	Delaware	H	6.47 FQ	7.66 AW	9.13 TQ	DEBLS	10/01-12/01
	District of Columbia	H	6.69 FQ	8.80 AW	14.68 TQ	DCBLS	10/01-12/01
	Florida	H	5.64 FQ	6.68 AW	8.48 TQ	FLBLS	10/01-12/01
	Georgia	H	5.67 FQ	6.70 AW	7.94 TQ	GABLS	10/01-12/01
	Hawaii	H	5.89 FQ	8.46 AW	12.47 TQ	HIBLS	10/01-12/01
	Idaho	H	5.49 FQ	6.27 AW	7.46 TQ	IDBLS	10/01-12/01
	Illinois	H	5.51 FQ	6.38 AW	6.99 TQ	ILBLS	10/01-12/01
	Indiana	H	5.51 FQ	6.54 AW	8.24 TQ	INBLS	10/01-12/01
	Iowa	H	5.44 FQ	6.28 AW	7.36 TQ	IABLS	10/01-12/01
	Kansas	H	5.59 FQ	6.45 AW	7.32 TQ	KSBLS	10/01-12/01
	Kentucky	H	5.67 FQ	7.00 AW	9.48 TQ	KYBLS	10/01-12/01
	Louisiana	H	5.46 FQ	6.32 AW	7.53 TQ	LABLS	10/01-12/01
	Maine	H	5.78 FQ	8.00 AW	10.61 TQ	MEBLS	10/01-12/01
	Maryland	H	5.54 FQ	6.77 AW	8.28 TQ	MDBLS	10/01-12/01
	Massachusetts	H	6.88 FQ	8.22 AW	10.27 TQ	MABLS	10/01-12/01
	Michigan	H	5.57 FQ	7.05 AW	8.88 TQ	MIBLS	10/01-12/01
	Minnesota	H	5.53 FQ	6.50 AW	8.20 TQ	MNBLS	10/01-12/01
	Mississippi	H	5.67 FQ	7.12 AW	9.29 TQ	MSBLS	10/01-12/01
	Missouri	H	5.64 FQ	7.04 AW	8.78 TQ	MOBLS	10/01-12/01

AAW	Average annual wage	**AOH**	Average offered, high	**ASH**	Average starting, high	**H**	Hourly	**M**	Monthly	**S**	Special: hourly and annual
AE	Average entry wage	**AOL**	Average offered, low	**ASL**	Average starting, low	**HI**	Highest wage paid	**MTC**	Median total compensation	**TQ**	Third quartile wage
AEX	Average experienced wage	**APH**	Average pay, high range	**AW**	Average wage paid	**HR**	High end range	**MW**	Median wage paid	**W**	Weekly
AO	Average offered	**APL**	Average pay, low range	**FQ**	First quartile wage	**LR**	Low end range	**SQ**	Second quartile wage	**Y**	Yearly

Occupation/Type/Industry	Location	Per	Low	Mid	High	Source	Date
Usher, Lobby Attendant, and Ticket Taker	Montana	H	5.61 FQ	7.10 AW	9.07 TQ	MTBLS	10/01-12/01
	Nebraska	H	5.58 FQ	6.52 AW	8.25 TQ	NEBLS	10/01-12/01
	Nevada	H	5.85 FQ	8.54 AW	12.51 TQ	NVBLS	10/01-12/01
	New Hampshire	H	5.68 FQ	7.42 AW	10.68 TQ	NHBLS	10/01-12/01
	New Jersey	H	5.51 FQ	7.15 AW	10.08 TQ	NJBLS	10/01-12/01
	New Mexico	H	5.47 FQ	6.14 AW	6.90 TQ	NMBLS	10/01-12/01
	New York	H	6.06 FQ	11.51 AW	16.92 TQ	NYBLS	10/01-12/01
	North Carolina	H	5.53 FQ	6.68 AW	8.37 TQ	NCBLS	10/01-12/01
	North Dakota	H	6.12 FQ	7.25 AW	8.29 TQ	NDBLS	10/01-12/01
	Ohio	H	5.57 FQ	6.88 AW	8.63 TQ	OHBLS	10/01-12/01
	Oklahoma	H	5.54 FQ	6.28 AW	7.27 TQ	OKBLS	10/01-12/01
	Oregon	H	6.69 FQ	7.47 AW	8.57 TQ	ORBLS	10/01-12/01
	Pennsylvania	H	5.57 FQ	7.23 AW	10.59 TQ	PABLS	10/01-12/01
	Rhode Island	H	6.53 FQ	8.14 AW	10.36 TQ	RIBLS	10/01-12/01
	South Carolina	H	5.61 FQ	6.54 AW	8.01 TQ	SCBLS	10/01-12/01
	South Dakota	H	5.54 FQ	6.61 AW	8.28 TQ	SDBLS	10/01-12/01
	Tennessee	H	5.53 FQ	7.18 AW	9.60 TQ	TNBLS	10/01-12/01
	Texas	H	5.58 FQ	6.89 AW	8.28 TQ	TXBLS	10/01-12/01
	Utah	H	5.59 FQ	6.50 AW	8.14 TQ	UTBLS	10/01-12/01
	Vermont	H	6.39 FQ	7.53 AW	9.25 TQ	VTBLS	10/01-12/01
	Virginia	H	5.59 FQ	6.94 AW	9.58 TQ	VABLS	10/01-12/01
	Washington	H	6.84 FQ	8.29 AW	10.54 TQ	WABLS	10/01-12/01
	West Virginia	H	5.74 FQ	7.18 AW	8.82 TQ	WVBLS	10/01-12/01
	Wisconsin	H	5.56 FQ	6.97 AW	9.62 TQ	WIBLS	10/01-12/01
	Wyoming	H	5.60 FQ	6.82 AW	9.30 TQ	WYBLS	10/01-12/01
	Puerto Rico	H	5.57 FQ	6.25 AW	7.21 TQ	PRBLS	10/01-12/01
Veterinarian	United States	Y		57100 AW		DOG	8/01-8/02
	Alabama	Y	38980 FQ	61840 AW	90320 TQ	ALBLS	10/01-12/01
	Birmingham MSA, AL	Y	46770 FQ	59390 AW	83270 TQ	ALBLS	10/01-12/01
	Huntsville MSA, AL	Y	34060 FQ	62820 AW	101360 TQ	ALBLS	10/01-12/01
	Mobile MSA, AL	Y	43860 FQ	67560 AW	94480 TQ	ALBLS	10/01-12/01
	Montgomery MSA, AL	Y	28200 FQ	58560 AW	129100 TQ	ALBLS	10/01-12/01
	Alaska	Y	37000 FQ	64500 AW	91060 TQ	AKBLS	10/01-12/01
	Anchorage MSA, AK	Y	35140 FQ	66060 AW	108040 TQ	AKBLS	10/01-12/01
	Arizona	Y	41630 FQ	61860 AW	98910 TQ	AZBLS	10/01-12/01
	Phoenix-Mesa MSA, AZ	Y	45670 FQ	59690 AW	77560 TQ	AZBLS	10/01-12/01
	Tucson MSA, AZ	Y	29350 FQ	66400 AW	112520 TQ	AZBLS	10/01-12/01
	Arkansas	Y	20900 FQ	47750 AW	72510 TQ	ARBLS	10/01-12/01
	Fayetteville-Springdale-Rogers MSA, AR	Y	12030 FQ	33140 AW	58170 TQ	ARBLS	10/01-12/01
	Little Rock-North Little Rock MSA, AR	Y	31170 FQ	48540 AW	58150 TQ	ARBLS	10/01-12/01
	California	Y	46790 FQ	80650 AW		CABLS	10/01-12/01
	Bakersfield MSA, CA	Y	50180 FQ	75800 AW	137810 TQ	CABLS	10/01-12/01
	Fresno MSA, CA	Y	48680 FQ	74070 AW	111740 TQ	CABLS	10/01-12/01
	Los Angeles-Long Beach PMSA, CA	Y	52860 FQ	93440 AW		CABLS	10/01-12/01
	Modesto MSA, CA	Y	49450 FQ	82540 AW		CABLS	10/01-12/01
	Oakland PMSA, CA	Y	49840 FQ	93450 AW		CABLS	10/01-12/01
	Orange County PMSA, CA	Y	48240 FQ	83940 AW	143090 TQ	CABLS	10/01-12/01
	Redding MSA, CA	Y	45830 FQ	51170 AW	56370 TQ	CABLS	10/01-12/01
	Riverside-San Bernardino PMSA, CA	Y	39810 FQ	76930 AW		CABLS	10/01-12/01
	Sacramento PMSA, CA	Y	47590 FQ	77340 AW	137730 TQ	CABLS	10/01-12/01
	Salinas MSA, CA	Y	46570 FQ	64640 AW	97020 TQ	CABLS	10/01-12/01
	San Diego MSA, CA	Y	46940 FQ	76380 AW	102210 TQ	CABLS	10/01-12/01
	San Francisco PMSA, CA	Y	44760 FQ	87480 AW		CABLS	10/01-12/01
	San Jose PMSA, CA	Y	42240 FQ	70350 AW	105840 TQ	CABLS	10/01-12/01
	San Luis Obispo-Atascadero-Paso Robles MSA, CA	Y	38120 FQ	67470 AW	110260 TQ	CABLS	10/01-12/01
	Santa Barbara-Santa Maria-Lompoc MSA, CA	Y	46810 FQ	72880 AW		CABLS	10/01-12/01
	Santa Cruz-Watsonville PMSA, CA	Y	35180 FQ	86540 AW		CABLS	10/01-12/01
	Santa Rosa PMSA, CA	Y	76680 FQ	90060 AW	112870 TQ	CABLS	10/01-12/01
	Vallejo-Fairfield-Napa PMSA, CA	Y	48820 FQ	69390 AW	107960 TQ	CABLS	10/01-12/01
	Ventura PMSA, CA	Y	58050 FQ	80510 AW	111160 TQ	CABLS	10/01-12/01
	Visalia-Tulare-Porterville MSA, CA	Y	50470 FQ	73220 AW	110600 TQ	CABLS	10/01-12/01

AAW	Average annual wage	AOH	Average offered, high	ASH	Average starting, high	H	Hourly	M	Monthly	S	Special: hourly and annual
AE	Average entry wage	AOL	Average offered, low	ASL	Average starting, low	HI	Highest wage paid	MTC	Median total compensation	TQ	Third quartile wage
AEX	Average experienced wage	APH	Average pay, high range	AW	Average wage paid	HR	High end range	MW	Median wage paid	W	Weekly
AO	Average offered	APL	Average pay, low range	FQ	First quartile wage	LR	Low end range	SQ	Second quartile wage	Y	Yearly

Occupation/Type/Industry	Location	Per	Low	Mid	High	Source	Date
Veterinarian	Colorado	Y	37160 FQ	59990 AW	111050 TQ	COBLS	10/01-12/01
	Boulder-Longmont PMSA, CO	Y	38750 FQ	50880 AW	72800 TQ	COBLS	10/01-12/01
	Colorado Springs MSA, CO	Y	40480 FQ	89770 AW	139860 TQ	COBLS	10/01-12/01
	Denver PMSA, CO	Y	37520 FQ	58760 AW	104440 TQ	COBLS	10/01-12/01
	Fort Collins-Loveland MSA, CO	Y	37230 FQ	56550 AW	85270 TQ	COBLS	10/01-12/01
	Greeley PMSA, CO	Y	56670 FQ	66410 AW	73510 TQ	COBLS	10/01-12/01
	Connecticut	Y	47090 FQ	72610 AW	126040 TQ	CTBLS	10/01-12/01
	Bridgeport PMSA, CT	Y	47960 FQ	73230 AW	117970 TQ	CTBLS	10/01-12/01
	Danbury PMSA, CT	Y	57540 FQ	77440 AW	127520 TQ	CTBLS	10/01-12/01
	Hartford MSA, CT	Y	50570 FQ	70770 AW	116410 TQ	CTBLS	10/01-12/01
	New Haven-Meriden PMSA, CT	Y	33170 FQ	67880 AW	107700 TQ	CTBLS	10/01-12/01
	New London-Norwich MSA, CT-RI	Y	39330 FQ	72630 AW	138420 TQ	CTBLS	10/01-12/01
	Stamford-Norwalk PMSA, CT	Y	48360 FQ	71830 AW	130440 TQ	CTBLS	10/01-12/01
	Delaware	Y	38330 FQ	64260 AW	102240 TQ	DEBLS	10/01-12/01
	Wilmington-Newark PMSA, DE-MD	Y	39030 FQ	63130 AW	95830 TQ	DEBLS	10/01-12/01
	District of Columbia	Y	44980 FQ	70800 AW	120690 TQ	DCBLS	10/01-12/01
	Washington PMSA, DC-MD-VA-WV	Y	49070 FQ	80430 AW	133970 TQ	DCBLS	10/01-12/01
	Florida	Y	40940 FQ	71750 AW	130730 TQ	FLBLS	10/01-12/01
	Daytona Beach MSA, FL	Y	48120 FQ	71140 AW		FLBLS	10/01-12/01
	Fort Lauderdale PMSA, FL	Y	45990 FQ	70370 AW	93030 TQ	FLBLS	10/01-12/01
	Fort Myers-Cape Coral MSA, FL	Y	44660 FQ	77160 AW	129640 TQ	FLBLS	10/01-12/01
	Fort Pierce-Port St. Lucie MSA, FL	Y	41840 FQ	63280 AW	88440 TQ	FLBLS	10/01-12/01
	Fort Walton Beach MSA, FL	Y	29980 FQ	40700 AW	55020 TQ	FLBLS	10/01-12/01
	Gainesville MSA, FL	Y	45340 FQ	64030 AW	101170 TQ	FLBLS	10/01-12/01
	Jacksonville MSA, FL	Y	42930 FQ	69330 AW	114720 TQ	FLBLS	10/01-12/01
	Lakeland-Winter Haven MSA, FL	Y	42540 FQ	77910 AW	114700 TQ	FLBLS	10/01-12/01
	Melbourne-Titusville-Palm Bay MSA, FL	Y	47140 FQ	78780 AW	113260 TQ	FLBLS	10/01-12/01
	Miami PMSA, FL	Y	42440 FQ	83240 AW		FLBLS	10/01-12/01
	Naples MSA, FL	Y	42860 FQ	71470 AW	93900 TQ	FLBLS	10/01-12/01
	Ocala MSA, FL	Y	27060 FQ	69170 AW		FLBLS	10/01-12/01
	Orlando MSA, FL	Y	45780 FQ	74080 AW	129910 TQ	FLBLS	10/01-12/01
	Pensacola MSA, FL	Y	38550 FQ	59690 AW	102290 TQ	FLBLS	10/01-12/01
	Sarasota-Bradenton MSA, FL	Y	48810 FQ	83080 AW		FLBLS	10/01-12/01
	Tallahassee MSA, FL	Y	45110 FQ	74940 AW		FLBLS	10/01-12/01
	Tampa-St. Petersburg-Clearwater MSA, FL	Y	46740 FQ	82270 AW		FLBLS	10/01-12/01
	West Palm Beach-Boca Raton MSA, FL	Y	32660 FQ	51280 AW	71290 TQ	FLBLS	10/01-12/01
	Georgia	Y	33480 FQ	69850 AW	129640 TQ	GABLS	10/01-12/01
	Atlanta MSA, GA	Y	47080 FQ	74380 AW	127820 TQ	GABLS	10/01-12/01
	Augusta-Aiken MSA, GA-SC	Y	52750 FQ	92330 AW		GABLS	10/01-12/01
	Savannah MSA, GA	Y	43150 FQ	88540 AW		GABLS	10/01-12/01
	Hawaii	Y	39120 FQ	69930 AW	116450 TQ	HIBLS	10/01-12/01
	Honolulu MSA, HI	Y	38350 FQ	69010 AW	116660 TQ	HIBLS	10/01-12/01
	Idaho	Y	25570 FQ	55040 AW	103760 TQ	IDBLS	10/01-12/01
	Boise City MSA, ID	Y	24220 FQ	46790 AW	71020 TQ	IDBLS	10/01-12/01
	Illinois	Y	31760 FQ	63270 AW	106530 TQ	ILBLS	10/01-12/01
	Chicago PMSA, IL	Y	31020 FQ	61340 AW	94710 TQ	ILBLS	10/01-12/01
	Peoria-Pekin MSA, IL	Y	34350 FQ	65160 AW	113260 TQ	ILBLS	10/01-12/01
	Rockford MSA, IL	Y	58700 FQ	78480 AW	111510 TQ	ILBLS	10/01-12/01
	Springfield MSA, IL	Y	40950 FQ	68900 AW	114680 TQ	ILBLS	10/01-12/01
	Indiana	Y	40800 FQ	68600 AW	111380 TQ	INBLS	10/01-12/01
	Elkhart-Goshen MSA, IN	Y	40050 FQ	59640 AW	123210 TQ	INBLS	10/01-12/01
	Evansville-Henderson MSA, IN-KY	Y	41830 FQ	69700 AW		INBLS	10/01-12/01
	Fort Wayne MSA, IN	Y	44010 FQ	67590 AW	126160 TQ	INBLS	10/01-12/01
	Gary PMSA, IN	Y	47460 FQ	81960 AW		INBLS	10/01-12/01
	Indianapolis MSA, IN	Y	44680 FQ	71500 AW	102560 TQ	INBLS	10/01-12/01
	Lafayette MSA, IN	Y	19190 FQ	43200 AW	80570 TQ	INBLS	10/01-12/01
	South Bend MSA, IN	Y	42020 FQ	66980 AW	93360 TQ	INBLS	10/01-12/01
	Iowa	Y	26910 FQ	80980 AW		IABLS	10/01-12/01
	Davenport-Moline-Rock Island MSA, IA-IL	Y	48000 FQ	71390 AW	107390 TQ	IABLS	10/01-12/01

AAW	Average annual wage	**AOH**	Average offered, high	**ASH**	Average starting, high	**H**	Hourly	**M**	Monthly	**S**	Special: hourly and annual
AE	Average entry wage	**AOL**	Average offered, low	**ASL**	Average starting, low	**HI**	Highest wage paid	**MTC**	Median total compensation	**TQ**	Third quartile wage
AEX	Average experienced wage	**APH**	Average pay, high range	**AW**	Average wage paid	**HR**	High end range	**MW**	Median wage paid	**W**	Weekly
AO	Average offered	**APL**	Average pay, low range	**FQ**	First quartile wage	**LR**	Low end range	**SQ**	Second quartile wage	**Y**	Yearly

Occupation/Type/Industry	Location	Per	Low	Mid	High	Source	Date
Veterinarian	Kansas	Y	37640 FQ	54810 AW	83430 TQ	KSBLS	10/01-12/01
	Topeka MSA, KS	Y	30160 FQ	43730 AW	58330 TQ	KSBLS	10/01-12/01
	Wichita MSA, KS	Y	47400 FQ	73440 AW		KSBLS	10/01-12/01
	Kentucky	Y	31870 FQ	70720 AW		KYBLS	10/01-12/01
	Lexington MSA, KY	Y	19790 FQ	86710 AW		KYBLS	10/01-12/01
	Louisville MSA, KY-IN	Y	40850 FQ	71890 AW	135380 TQ	KYBLS	10/01-12/01
	Louisiana	Y	34500 FQ	53220 AW	76190 TQ	LABLS	10/01-12/01
	Baton Rouge MSA, LA	Y	27970 FQ	54100 AW	95590 TQ	LABLS	10/01-12/01
	Lafayette MSA, LA	Y	25540 FQ	36450 AW	50860 TQ	LABLS	10/01-12/01
	Lake Charles MSA, LA	Y	39670 FQ	62050 AW	95340 TQ	LABLS	10/01-12/01
	New Orleans MSA, LA	Y	35580 FQ	48320 AW	66870 TQ	LABLS	10/01-12/01
	Shreveport-Bossier City MSA, LA	Y	40410 FQ	61840 AW	83930 TQ	LABLS	10/01-12/01
	Maine	Y	38060 FQ	57510 AW	89820 TQ	MEBLS	10/01-12/01
	Portland MSA, ME	Y	36880 FQ	57270 AW	91660 TQ	MEBLS	10/01-12/01
	Maryland	Y	47130 FQ	75540 AW	115730 TQ	MDBLS	10/01-12/01
	Baltimore PMSA, MD	Y	48110 FQ	70070 AW	106450 TQ	MDBLS	10/01-12/01
	Massachusetts	Y	41010 FQ	67430 AW	107790 TQ	MABLS	10/01-12/01
	Boston PMSA, MA-NH	Y	41630 FQ	66010 AW	103830 TQ	MABLS	10/01-12/01
	Brockton PMSA, MA	Y	37010 FQ	72160 AW		MABLS	10/01-12/01
	Lawrence PMSA, MA-NH	Y	48720 FQ	84660 AW	115690 TQ	MABLS	10/01-12/01
	Springfield MSA, MA	Y	37200 FQ	66900 AW	95880 TQ	MABLS	10/01-12/01
	Worcester PMSA, MA-CT	Y	45890 FQ	55370 AW	70220 TQ	MABLS	10/01-12/01
	Michigan	Y	38880 FQ	71890 AW	123080 TQ	MIBLS	10/01-12/01
	Ann Arbor PMSA, MI	Y	43210 FQ	69930 AW	108220 TQ	MIBLS	10/01-12/01
	Detroit PMSA, MI	Y	38380 FQ	72010 AW	113410 TQ	MIBLS	10/01-12/01
	Flint PMSA, MI	Y	25020 FQ	66040 AW		MIBLS	10/01-12/01
	Grand Rapids-Muskegon-Holland MSA, MI	Y	39280 FQ	64980 AW	102680 TQ	MIBLS	10/01-12/01
	Kalamazoo-Battle Creek MSA, MI	Y	43610 FQ	69660 AW	90670 TQ	MIBLS	10/01-12/01
	Lansing-East Lansing MSA, MI	Y	20660 FQ	59760 AW	92730 TQ	MIBLS	10/01-12/01
	Saginaw-Bay City-Midland MSA, MI	Y	48420 FQ	87640 AW	141470 TQ	MIBLS	10/01-12/01
	Minnesota	Y	44810 FQ	73830 AW	145030 TQ	MNBLS	10/01-12/01
	Duluth-Superior MSA, MN-WI	Y	27520 FQ	64540 AW	89260 TQ	MNBLS	10/01-12/01
	Minneapolis-St. Paul MSA, MN-WI	Y	40840 FQ	74970 AW		MNBLS	10/01-12/01
	St. Cloud MSA, MN	Y	38020 FQ	68110 AW	98180 TQ	MNBLS	10/01-12/01
	Mississippi	Y	28220 FQ	53950 AW	103930 TQ	MSBLS	10/01-12/01
	Biloxi-Gulfport-Pascagoula MSA, MS	Y	25780 FQ	37410 AW	44200 TQ	MSBLS	10/01-12/01
	Jackson MSA, MS	Y	30310 FQ	57830 AW		MSBLS	10/01-12/01
	Missouri	Y	32530 FQ	55450 AW	81380 TQ	MOBLS	10/01-12/01
	Kansas City MSA, MO-KS	Y	39210 FQ	59970 AW	90660 TQ	MOBLS	10/01-12/01
	St. Louis MSA, MO-IL	Y	37930 FQ	58580 AW	76510 TQ	MOBLS	10/01-12/01
	Springfield MSA, MO	Y	27000 FQ	45590 AW	58260 TQ	MOBLS	10/01-12/01
	Montana	Y	24470 FQ	39900 AW	66450 TQ	MTBLS	10/01-12/01
	Nebraska	Y	25400 FQ	54560 AW	85850 TQ	NEBLS	10/01-12/01
	Lincoln MSA, NE	Y	46560 FQ	67830 AW		NEBLS	10/01-12/01
	Omaha MSA, NE-IA	Y	49960 FQ	77090 AW		NEBLS	10/01-12/01
	Nevada	Y	36510 FQ	73350 AW	114980 TQ	NVBLS	10/01-12/01
	Las Vegas MSA, NV-AZ	Y	34750 FQ	74370 AW	115120 TQ	NVBLS	10/01-12/01
	Reno MSA, NV	Y	39160 FQ	62400 AW	82600 TQ	NVBLS	10/01-12/01
	New Hampshire	Y	37360 FQ	60840 AW	97870 TQ	NHBLS	10/01-12/01
	Manchester PMSA, NH	Y	38150 FQ	53390 AW	86570 TQ	NHBLS	10/01-12/01
	Portsmouth-Rochester PMSA, NH-ME	Y	31950 FQ	50130 AW	76140 TQ	NHBLS	10/01-12/01
	New Jersey	Y	50350 FQ	84970 AW	132980 TQ	NJBLS	10/01-12/01
	Atlantic-Cape May PMSA, NJ	Y	49670 FQ	74940 AW	112120 TQ	NJBLS	10/01-12/01
	Bergen-Passaic PMSA, NJ	Y	54310 FQ	88420 AW	118550 TQ	NJBLS	10/01-12/01
	Jersey City PMSA, NJ	Y	50810 FQ	73300 AW	110560 TQ	NJBLS	10/01-12/01
	Middlesex-Somerset-Hunterdon PMSA, NJ	Y	49980 FQ	82630 AW	129870 TQ	NJBLS	10/01-12/01
	Monmouth-Ocean PMSA, NJ	Y	52000 FQ	91950 AW		NJBLS	10/01-12/01
	Newark PMSA, NJ	Y	56770 FQ	90780 AW		NJBLS	10/01-12/01
	Trenton PMSA, NJ	Y	46910 FQ	78210 AW	145140 TQ	NJBLS	10/01-12/01
	New Mexico	Y	24110 FQ	55480 AW	88650 TQ	NMBLS	10/01-12/01
	Albuquerque MSA, NM	Y	21620 FQ	51410 AW	87830 TQ	NMBLS	10/01-12/01
	New York	Y	37390 FQ	77500 AW	138780 TQ	NYBLS	10/01-12/01
	Albany-Schenectady-Troy MSA, NY	Y	49380 FQ	69960 AW	105840 TQ	NYBLS	10/01-12/01

AAW	Average annual wage	AOH	Average offered, high	ASH	Average starting, high	H	Hourly	M	Monthly	S	Special: hourly and annual
AE	Average entry wage	AOL	Average offered, low	ASL	Average starting, low	HI	Highest wage paid	MTC	Median total compensation	TQ	Third quartile wage
AEX	Average experienced wage	APH	Average pay, high range	AW	Average wage paid	HR	High end range	MW	Median wage paid	W	Weekly
AO	Average offered	APL	Average pay, low range	FQ	First quartile wage	LR	Low end range	SQ	Second quartile wage	Y	Yearly

Occupation/Type/Industry	Location	Per	Low	Mid	High	Source	Date
Veterinarian	Buffalo-Niagara Falls MSA, NY	Y	49290 FQ	75140 AW	139400 TQ	NYBLS	10/01-12/01
	Dutchess County PMSA, NY	Y	47360 FQ	66140 AW	96410 TQ	NYBLS	10/01-12/01
	Nassau-Suffolk PMSA, NY	Y	59830 FQ	96240 AW		NYBLS	10/01-12/01
	New York PMSA, NY	Y	31250 FQ	78420 AW	137660 TQ	NYBLS	10/01-12/01
	Newburgh PMSA, NY-PA	Y	29630 FQ	59670 AW	109820 TQ	NYBLS	10/01-12/01
	Rochester MSA, NY	Y	49070 FQ	77020 AW	115040 TQ	NYBLS	10/01-12/01
	Syracuse MSA, NY	Y	42410 FQ	66510 AW	105800 TQ	NYBLS	10/01-12/01
	North Carolina	Y	30730 FQ	62980 AW	110650 TQ	NCBLS	10/01-12/01
	Asheville MSA, NC	Y	37980 FQ	56670 AW	77880 TQ	NCBLS	10/01-12/01
	Charlotte-Gastonia-Rock Hill MSA, NC-SC	Y	40520 FQ	65510 AW	111920 TQ	NCBLS	10/01-12/01
	Fayetteville MSA, NC	Y	36700 FQ	44630 AW	60220 TQ	NCBLS	10/01-12/01
	Greensboro-Winston-Salem-High Point MSA, NC	Y	39650 FQ	75780 AW		NCBLS	10/01-12/01
	Hickory-Morganton-Lenoir MSA, NC	Y	56150 FQ	88500 AW	116110 TQ	NCBLS	10/01-12/01
	Raleigh-Durham-Chapel Hill MSA, NC	Y	31330 FQ	62220 AW	106560 TQ	NCBLS	10/01-12/01
	Wilmington MSA, NC	Y	46110 FQ	75080 AW	130540 TQ	NCBLS	10/01-12/01
	North Dakota	Y	30740 FQ	53730 AW	86600 TQ	NDBLS	10/01-12/01
	Ohio	Y	42980 FQ	71330 AW	109760 TQ	OHBLS	10/01-12/01
	Akron PMSA, OH	Y	46630 FQ	69130 AW	88950 TQ	OHBLS	10/01-12/01
	Cincinnati PMSA, OH-KY-IN	Y	40960 FQ	62270 AW	92400 TQ	OHBLS	10/01-12/01
	Cleveland-Lorain-Elyria PMSA, OH	Y	47340 FQ	76930 AW	113360 TQ	OHBLS	10/01-12/01
	Columbus MSA, OH	Y	42210 FQ	78300 AW	110460 TQ	OHBLS	10/01-12/01
	Dayton-Springfield MSA, OH	Y	46670 FQ	80390 AW	139330 TQ	OHBLS	10/01-12/01
	Toledo MSA, OH	Y	41160 FQ	70560 AW	121210 TQ	OHBLS	10/01-12/01
	Youngstown-Warren MSA, OH	Y	45930 FQ	76550 AW	123520 TQ	OHBLS	10/01-12/01
	Oklahoma	Y	27700 FQ	58990 AW	103870 TQ	OKBLS	10/01-12/01
	Oklahoma City MSA, OK	Y	31180 FQ	53790 AW	87990 TQ	OKBLS	10/01-12/01
	Tulsa MSA, OK	Y	14480 FQ	57090 AW	120900 TQ	OKBLS	10/01-12/01
	Oregon	Y	38560 FQ	58990 AW	87630 TQ	ORBLS	10/01-12/01
	Eugene-Springfield MSA, OR	Y	26980 FQ	49590 AW	76500 TQ	ORBLS	10/01-12/01
	Medford-Ashland MSA, OR	Y	38310 FQ	55060 AW	71600 TQ	ORBLS	10/01-12/01
	Portland-Vancouver PMSA, OR-WA	Y	42840 FQ	60310 AW	85400 TQ	ORBLS	10/01-12/01
	Salem PMSA, OR	Y	39840 FQ	49210 AW	58810 TQ	ORBLS	10/01-12/01
	Pennsylvania	Y	39120 FQ	70780 AW	124000 TQ	PABLS	10/01-12/01
	Allentown-Bethlehem-Easton MSA, PA	Y	27590 FQ	55970 AW	95450 TQ	PABLS	10/01-12/01
	Erie MSA, PA	Y	26920 FQ	57770 AW	97400 TQ	PABLS	10/01-12/01
	Harrisburg-Lebanon-Carlisle MSA, PA	Y	43860 FQ	65710 AW	119380 TQ	PABLS	10/01-12/01
	Lancaster MSA, PA	Y	28080 FQ	74300 AW		PABLS	10/01-12/01
	Philadelphia PMSA, PA-NJ	Y	46920 FQ	78930 AW	140810 TQ	PABLS	10/01-12/01
	Pittsburgh MSA, PA	Y	39950 FQ	74910 AW	119780 TQ	PABLS	10/01-12/01
	Reading MSA, PA	Y	44350 FQ	64750 AW	87710 TQ	PABLS	10/01-12/01
	Scranton-Wilkes-Barre-Hazleton MSA, PA	Y	49840 FQ	67000 AW	127620 TQ	PABLS	10/01-12/01
	York MSA, PA	Y	31330 FQ	64550 AW	88770 TQ	PABLS	10/01-12/01
	Rhode Island	Y	53350 FQ	87410 AW	137500 TQ	RIBLS	10/01-12/01
	Providence-Fall River-Warwick MSA, RI-MA	Y	53730 FQ	86950 AW	136240 TQ	RIBLS	10/01-12/01
	South Carolina	Y	44600 FQ	73000 AW	133450 TQ	SCBLS	10/01-12/01
	Charleston-North Charleston MSA, SC	Y	43820 FQ	83740 AW		SCBLS	10/01-12/01
	Columbia MSA, SC	Y	39320 FQ	58330 AW	71340 TQ	SCBLS	10/01-12/01
	Greenville-Spartanburg-Anderson MSA, SC	Y	50490 FQ	72290 AW	103530 TQ	SCBLS	10/01-12/01
	South Dakota	Y	40750 FQ	57170 AW	73050 TQ	SDBLS	10/01-12/01
	Sioux Falls MSA, SD	Y	39630 FQ	45910 AW	54360 TQ	SDBLS	10/01-12/01
	Tennessee	Y	23790 FQ	61230 AW	111920 TQ	TNBLS	10/01-12/01
	Chattanooga MSA, TN-GA	Y	41290 FQ	84670 AW		TNBLS	10/01-12/01
	Johnson City-Kingsport-Bristol MSA, TN-VA	Y	39150 FQ	53720 AW	75440 TQ	TNBLS	10/01-12/01
	Knoxville MSA, TN	Y	16600 FQ	52190 AW	73180 TQ	TNBLS	10/01-12/01
	Memphis MSA, TN-AR-MS	Y	37560 FQ	73220 AW	142140 TQ	TNBLS	10/01-12/01
	Nashville MSA, TN	Y	13740 FQ	57470 AW	93760 TQ	TNBLS	10/01-12/01
	Texas	Y	41610 FQ	78520 AW		TXBLS	10/01-12/01
	Amarillo MSA, TX	Y	46660 FQ	56560 AW	72090 TQ	TXBLS	10/01-12/01

AAW	Average annual wage	AOH	Average offered, high	ASH	Average starting, high	H	Hourly	M	Monthly	S	Special: hourly and annual
AE	Average entry wage	AOL	Average offered, low	ASL	Average starting, low	HI	Highest wage paid	MTC	Median total compensation	TQ	Third quartile wage
AEX	Average experienced wage	APH	Average pay, high range	AW	Average wage paid	HR	High end range	MW	Median wage paid	W	Weekly
AO	Average offered	APL	Average pay, low range	FQ	First quartile wage	LR	Low end range	SQ	Second quartile wage	Y	Yearly

Occupation/Type/Industry	Location	Per	Low	Mid	High	Source	Date
Veterinarian	Austin-San Marcos MSA, TX	Y	39490 FQ	63270 AW	93800 TQ	TXBLS	10/01-12/01
	Beaumont-Port Arthur MSA, TX	Y	24770 FQ	73010 AW	119730 TQ	TXBLS	10/01-12/01
	Dallas PMSA, TX	Y	38750 FQ	70540 AW		TXBLS	10/01-12/01
	El Paso MSA, TX	Y	48010 FQ	66030 AW		TXBLS	10/01-12/01
	Fort Worth-Arlington PMSA, TX	Y	48030 FQ	85820 AW		TXBLS	10/01-12/01
	San Antonio MSA, TX	Y	48520 FQ	87650 AW	140410 TQ	TXBLS	10/01-12/01
	Utah	Y	21100 FQ	59350 AW	89340 TQ	UTBLS	10/01-12/01
	Salt Lake City-Ogden MSA, UT	Y	48490 FQ	71650 AW	92570 TQ	UTBLS	10/01-12/01
	Vermont	Y	40940 FQ	60540 AW	84010 TQ	VTBLS	10/01-12/01
	Burlington MSA, VT	Y	41140 FQ	69960 AW	134560 TQ	VTBLS	10/01-12/01
	Virginia	Y	40030 FQ	70420 AW	125530 TQ	VABLS	10/01-12/01
	Norfolk-Virginia Beach-Newport News MSA, VA-NC	Y	38740 FQ	62030 AW	100120 TQ	VABLS	10/01-12/01
	Richmond-Petersburg MSA, VA	Y	33970 FQ	62570 AW	91180 TQ	VABLS	10/01-12/01
	Roanoke MSA, VA	Y	42840 FQ	65240 AW	119460 TQ	VABLS	10/01-12/01
	Washington	Y	43820 FQ	62840 AW	88100 TQ	WABLS	10/01-12/01
	Olympia PMSA, WA	Y	40130 FQ	54030 AW	70440 TQ	WABLS	10/01-12/01
	Seattle-Bellevue-Everett PMSA, WA	Y	43410 FQ	62850 AW	85770 TQ	WABLS	10/01-12/01
	Spokane MSA, WA	Y	45290 FQ	56880 AW	84190 TQ	WABLS	10/01-12/01
	Tacoma PMSA, WA	Y	47230 FQ	75200 AW	143590 TQ	WABLS	10/01-12/01
	West Virginia	Y	44080 FQ	69570 AW	113880 TQ	WVBLS	10/01-12/01
	Charleston MSA, WV	Y	45370 FQ	71330 AW	117590 TQ	WVBLS	10/01-12/01
	Huntington-Ashland MSA, WV-KY-OH	Y	43020 FQ	73340 AW		WVBLS	10/01-12/01
	Wisconsin	Y	38330 FQ	63590 AW	104800 TQ	WIBLS	10/01-12/01
	Appleton-Oshkosh-Neenah MSA, WI	Y	37100 FQ	54650 AW	86350 TQ	WIBLS	10/01-12/01
	Green Bay MSA, WI	Y	48220 FQ	67620 AW	89370 TQ	WIBLS	10/01-12/01
	Madison MSA, WI	Y	37850 FQ	52260 AW	72700 TQ	WIBLS	10/01-12/01
	Milwaukee-Waukesha PMSA, WI	Y	41200 FQ	66650 AW	107690 TQ	WIBLS	10/01-12/01
	Wyoming	Y	22130 FQ	50900 AW	80490 TQ	WYBLS	10/01-12/01
	Puerto Rico	Y	31170 FQ	55410 AW	73060 TQ	PRBLS	10/01-12/01
Veterinary Assistant and Laboratory Animal Caretaker	United States	Y			18490 HI	FREEP1	1/00-1/00
	Alabama	H	5.72 FQ	7.42 AW	9.76 TQ	ALBLS	10/01-12/01
	Alaska	H	6.93 FQ	9.65 AW	14.54 TQ	AKBLS	10/01-12/01
	Arizona	H	6.10 FQ	8.85 AW	12.83 TQ	AZBLS	10/01-12/01
	Arkansas	H	5.65 FQ	7.88 AW	11.69 TQ	ARBLS	10/01-12/01
	California	H	6.60 FQ	9.37 AW	14.23 TQ	CABLS	10/01-12/01
	Colorado	H	6.40 FQ	10.21 AW	13.88 TQ	COBLS	10/01-12/01
	Connecticut	H	7.22 FQ	10.82 AW	17.70 TQ	CTBLS	10/01-12/01
	Delaware	H	6.94 FQ	9.45 AW	12.87 TQ	DEBLS	10/01-12/01
	District of Columbia	H	8.15 FQ	11.28 AW	15.67 TQ	DCBLS	10/01-12/01
	Florida	H	6.00 FQ	8.54 AW	11.09 TQ	FLBLS	10/01-12/01
	Georgia	H	6.00 FQ	9.17 AW	13.41 TQ	GABLS	10/01-12/01
	Hawaii	H	6.03 FQ	8.87 AW	13.36 TQ	HIBLS	10/01-12/01
	Idaho	H	5.97 FQ	7.75 AW	10.10 TQ	IDBLS	10/01-12/01
	Illinois	H	6.01 FQ	8.72 AW	14.36 TQ	ILBLS	10/01-12/01
	Indiana	H	5.86 FQ	8.06 AW	10.69 TQ	INBLS	10/01-12/01
	Iowa	H	6.54 FQ	8.99 AW	11.17 TQ	IABLS	10/01-12/01
	Kansas	H	5.78 FQ	8.31 AW	11.70 TQ	KSBLS	10/01-12/01
	Kentucky	H	5.84 FQ	8.57 AW	11.45 TQ	KYBLS	10/01-12/01
	Louisiana	H	5.67 FQ	7.52 AW	10.39 TQ	LABLS	10/01-12/01
	Maine	H	7.45 FQ	10.05 AW	13.79 TQ	MEBLS	10/01-12/01
	Maryland	H	6.61 FQ	10.04 AW	13.74 TQ	MDBLS	10/01-12/01
	Massachusetts	H	8.00 FQ	11.98 AW	16.53 TQ	MABLS	10/01-12/01
	Michigan	H	6.44 FQ	8.81 AW	11.55 TQ	MIBLS	10/01-12/01
	Minnesota	H	6.62 FQ	9.23 AW	12.30 TQ	MNBLS	10/01-12/01
	Mississippi	H	5.76 FQ	7.75 AW	11.33 TQ	MSBLS	10/01-12/01
	Missouri	H	6.29 FQ	8.54 AW	11.30 TQ	MOBLS	10/01-12/01
	Montana	H	6.41 FQ	7.93 AW	9.76 TQ	MTBLS	10/01-12/01
	Nebraska	H	6.01 FQ	8.57 AW	12.20 TQ	NEBLS	10/01-12/01
	Nevada	H	6.08 FQ	8.40 AW	10.61 TQ	NVBLS	10/01-12/01
	New Hampshire	H	5.97 FQ	8.50 AW	11.05 TQ	NHBLS	10/01-12/01

AAW	Average annual wage	**AOH**	Average offered, high	**ASH**	Average starting, high	**H**	Hourly	**M**	Monthly	**S**	Special: hourly and annual
AE	Average entry wage	**AOL**	Average offered, low	**ASL**	Average starting, low	**HI**	Highest wage paid	**MTC**	Median total compensation	**TQ**	Third quartile wage
AEX	Average experienced wage	**APH**	Average pay, high range	**AW**	Average wage paid	**HR**	High end range	**MW**	Median wage paid	**W**	Weekly
AO	Average offered	**APL**	Average pay, low range	**FQ**	First quartile wage	**LR**	Low end range	**SQ**	Second quartile wage	**Y**	Yearly

Occupation/Type/Industry	Location	Per	Low	Mid	High	Source	Date
Veterinary Assistant and Laboratory Animal Caretaker	New Jersey	H	6.64 FQ	9.78 AW	13.30 TQ	NJBLS	10/01-12/01
	New Mexico	H	6.06 FQ	8.11 AW	10.94 TQ	NMBLS	10/01-12/01
	New York	H	6.07 FQ	9.33 AW	13.20 TQ	NYBLS	10/01-12/01
	North Carolina	H	6.01 FQ	8.23 AW	10.97 TQ	NCBLS	10/01-12/01
	North Dakota	H	5.76 FQ	7.53 AW	9.75 TQ	NDBLS	10/01-12/01
	Ohio	H	5.97 FQ	8.60 AW	11.70 TQ	OHBLS	10/01-12/01
	Oklahoma	H	5.82 FQ	8.18 AW	11.63 TQ	OKBLS	10/01-12/01
	Oregon	H	6.93 FQ	8.85 AW	10.98 TQ	ORBLS	10/01-12/01
	Pennsylvania	H	6.28 FQ	8.86 AW	12.18 TQ	PABLS	10/01-12/01
	Rhode Island	H	6.91 FQ	9.98 AW	13.95 TQ	RIBLS	10/01-12/01
	South Carolina	H	6.00 FQ	8.75 AW	11.62 TQ	SCBLS	10/01-12/01
	South Dakota	H	5.74 FQ	7.41 AW	9.94 TQ	SDBLS	10/01-12/01
	Tennessee	H	5.93 FQ	8.23 AW	10.60 TQ	TNBLS	10/01-12/01
	Texas	H	6.20 FQ	8.70 AW	11.77 TQ	TXBLS	10/01-12/01
	Utah	H	5.92 FQ	8.39 AW	11.39 TQ	UTBLS	10/01-12/01
	Vermont	H	7.02 FQ	8.18 AW	10.04 TQ	VTBLS	10/01-12/01
	Virginia	H	5.99 FQ	8.40 AW	10.97 TQ	VABLS	10/01-12/01
	Washington	H	7.17 FQ	9.57 AW	12.43 TQ	WABLS	10/01-12/01
	West Virginia	H	5.68 FQ	7.10 AW	9.24 TQ	WVBLS	10/01-12/01
	Wisconsin	H	6.18 FQ	8.63 AW	10.84 TQ	WIBLS	10/01-12/01
	Wyoming	H	5.86 FQ	7.49 AW	8.81 TQ	WYBLS	10/01-12/01
	Puerto Rico	H	5.77 FQ	7.06 AW	8.87 TQ	PRBLS	10/01-12/01
Veterinary Technologist and Technician	United States	Y		18500-25760 AW		FREEP1	1/00-1/00
	Alabama	Y	14090 FQ	20500 AW	28200 TQ	ALBLS	10/01-12/01
	Alaska	Y	20320 FQ	30880 AW	43290 TQ	AKBLS	10/01-12/01
	Arizona	Y	16350 FQ	22760 AW	31830 TQ	AZBLS	10/01-12/01
	Arkansas	Y	12250 FQ	17210 AW	22410 TQ	ARBLS	10/01-12/01
	California	Y	17220 FQ	25250 AW	35090 TQ	CABLS	10/01-12/01
	Colorado	Y	18850 FQ	24340 AW	30690 TQ	COBLS	10/01-12/01
	Connecticut	Y	18520 FQ	27510 AW	37890 TQ	CTBLS	10/01-12/01
	Delaware	Y	18490 FQ	30500 AW	57510 TQ	DEBLS	10/01-12/01
	Florida	Y	15130 FQ	20930 AW	27820 TQ	FLBLS	10/01-12/01
	Georgia	Y	15740 FQ	22210 AW	30110 TQ	GABLS	10/01-12/01
	Hawaii	Y	14290 FQ	21570 AW	29020 TQ	HIBLS	10/01-12/01
	Idaho	Y	14870 FQ	19360 AW	23820 TQ	IDBLS	10/01-12/01
	Illinois	Y	16610 FQ	24640 AW	34940 TQ	ILBLS	10/01-12/01
	Indiana	Y	15990 FQ	23320 AW	33710 TQ	INBLS	10/01-12/01
	Iowa	Y	16820 FQ	23550 AW	30430 TQ	IABLS	10/01-12/01
	Kansas	Y	13580 FQ	22290 AW	28750 TQ	KSBLS	10/01-12/01
	Kentucky	Y	14030 FQ	21380 AW	29910 TQ	KYBLS	10/01-12/01
	Louisiana	Y	12290 FQ	16980 AW	22230 TQ	LABLS	10/01-12/01
	Maine	Y	17560 FQ	23090 AW	30880 TQ	MEBLS	10/01-12/01
	Maryland	Y	15370 FQ	22880 AW	30430 TQ	MDBLS	10/01-12/01
	Massachusetts	Y	18160 FQ	25220 AW	34110 TQ	MABLS	10/01-12/01
	Michigan	Y	16210 FQ	25040 AW	35260 TQ	MIBLS	10/01-12/01
	Minnesota	Y	19350 FQ	25430 AW	33970 TQ	MNBLS	10/01-12/01
	Mississippi	Y	16020 FQ	22170 AW	33960 TQ	MSBLS	10/01-12/01
	Missouri	Y	15450 FQ	24950 AW	33050 TQ	MOBLS	10/01-12/01
	Montana	Y	14780 FQ	20310 AW	24040 TQ	MTBLS	10/01-12/01
	Nebraska	Y	15260 FQ	20350 AW	25890 TQ	NEBLS	10/01-12/01
	Nevada	Y	15790 FQ	22690 AW	30250 TQ	NVBLS	10/01-12/01
	New Hampshire	Y	17050 FQ	23450 AW	31660 TQ	NHBLS	10/01-12/01
	New Jersey	Y	18330 FQ	27550 AW	37680 TQ	NJBLS	10/01-12/01
	New Mexico	Y	15850 FQ	21210 AW	26450 TQ	NMBLS	10/01-12/01
	New York	Y	16480 FQ	24930 AW	34920 TQ	NYBLS	10/01-12/01
	North Carolina	Y	15240 FQ	21950 AW	29050 TQ	NCBLS	10/01-12/01
	North Dakota	Y	16790 FQ	23180 AW	29750 TQ	NDBLS	10/01-12/01
	Ohio	Y	17190 FQ	23870 AW	31180 TQ	OHBLS	10/01-12/01
	Oklahoma	Y	14640 FQ	22230 AW	31820 TQ	OKBLS	10/01-12/01
	Oregon	Y	18170 FQ	23840 AW	30340 TQ	ORBLS	10/01-12/01
	Pennsylvania	Y	15910 FQ	23090 AW	32800 TQ	PABLS	10/01-12/01
	Rhode Island	Y	19060 FQ	25730 AW	33830 TQ	RIBLS	10/01-12/01
	South Carolina	Y	16020 FQ	20720 AW	25960 TQ	SCBLS	10/01-12/01
	South Dakota	Y	17600 FQ	21300 AW	26200 TQ	SDBLS	10/01-12/01
	Tennessee	Y	15110 FQ	21830 AW	29920 TQ	TNBLS	10/01-12/01
	Texas	Y	15490 FQ	23560 AW	33550 TQ	TXBLS	10/01-12/01
	Utah	Y	13510 FQ	19190 AW	25430 TQ	UTBLS	10/01-12/01
	Vermont	Y	17710 FQ	27420 AW	58550 TQ	VTBLS	10/01-12/01

AAW	Average annual wage	**AOH**	Average offered, high	**ASH**	Average starting, high	**H**	Hourly	**M**	Monthly	**S**	Special: hourly and annual
AE	Average entry wage	**AOL**	Average offered, low	**ASL**	Average starting, low	**HI**	Highest wage paid	**MTC**	Median total compensation	**TQ**	Third quartile wage
AEX	Average experienced wage	**APH**	Average pay, high range	**AW**	Average wage paid	**HR**	High end range	**MW**	Median wage paid	**W**	Weekly
AO	Average offered	**APL**	Average pay, low range	**FQ**	First quartile wage	**LR**	Low end range	**SQ**	Second quartile wage	**Y**	Yearly

Occupation/Type/Industry	Location	Per	Low	Mid	High	Source	Date
Veterinary Technologist and Technician	Virginia	Y	15550 FQ	24890 AW	36020 TQ	VABLS	10/01-12/01
	Washington	Y	18870 FQ	26080 AW	35310 TQ	WABLS	10/01-12/01
	West Virginia	Y	14080 FQ	18740 AW	23190 TQ	WVBLS	10/01-12/01
	Wisconsin	Y	16180 FQ	23020 AW	29940 TQ	WIBLS	10/01-12/01
	Wyoming	Y	16330 FQ	21760 AW	29010 TQ	WYBLS	10/01-12/01
	Puerto Rico	Y	15830 FQ	22580 AW	37000 TQ	PRBLS	10/01-12/01
Vice President							
E-Commerce	United States	Y		108100 AW		INFO4	1/01-1/02
E-Commerce	United States	Y		120000 AW		INFO	1/00-1/01
Information Systems	Baltimore, MD	Y		160328 AW		INFO5	1/00-1/01
Information Technology	United States	Y		125375 AW		INFO1	1/01-1/02
Quality Control	United States	Y			240000 HI	ASQ	1/00-1/01
Warehousing and Logistics and Distribution	United States	Y		60000-70000 AW		WARE	1/00-1/01
Vocational Education Teacher							
Middle School	Alabama	Y	34330 FQ	43310 AW	54820 TQ	ALBLS	10/01-12/01
Middle School	Birmingham MSA, AL	Y	36600 FQ	46000 AW	58400 TQ	ALBLS	10/01-12/01
Middle School	Alaska	Y	46590 FQ	53400 AW	66140 TQ	AKBLS	10/01-12/01
Middle School	Arizona	Y	23800 FQ	34740 AW	45150 TQ	AZBLS	10/01-12/01
Middle School	Phoenix-Mesa MSA, AZ	Y	25140 FQ	33620 AW	42820 TQ	AZBLS	10/01-12/01
Middle School	Arkansas	Y	28660 FQ	37360 AW	47360 TQ	ARBLS	10/01-12/01
Middle School	California	Y	23560 FQ	42560 AW	68750 TQ	CABLS	10/01-12/01
Middle School	Colorado	Y	31070 FQ	41490 AW	56530 TQ	COBLS	10/01-12/01
Middle School	Connecticut	Y	32080 FQ	53320 AW	72590 TQ	CTBLS	10/01-12/01
Middle School	Hartford MSA, CT	Y	27950 FQ	53540 AW	73860 TQ	CTBLS	10/01-12/01
Middle School	Wilmington-Newark PMSA, DE-MD	Y	31830 FQ	45510 AW	57420 TQ	DEBLS	10/01-12/01
Middle School	Washington PMSA, DC-MD-VA-WV	Y	29780 FQ	51600 AW	84560 TQ	DCBLS	10/01-12/01
Middle School	Florida	Y	30990 FQ	41720 AW	56190 TQ	FLBLS	10/01-12/01
Middle School	Orlando MSA, FL	Y	28040 FQ	44700 AW	60720 TQ	FLBLS	10/01-12/01
Middle School	Georgia	Y	33040 FQ	46210 AW	64760 TQ	GABLS	10/01-12/01
Middle School	Atlanta MSA, GA	Y	33720 FQ	44670 AW	59690 TQ	GABLS	10/01-12/01
Middle School	Illinois	Y	13900 FQ	38920 AW	58370 TQ	ILBLS	10/01-12/01
Middle School	Chicago PMSA, IL	Y	24400 FQ	43280 AW	65080 TQ	ILBLS	10/01-12/01
Middle School	Springfield MSA, IL	Y	12100 FQ	20060 AW	37570 TQ	ILBLS	10/01-12/01
Middle School	Indiana	Y	33050 FQ	46280 AW	57990 TQ	INBLS	10/01-12/01
Middle School	Indianapolis MSA, IN	Y	35230 FQ	49130 AW	60460 TQ	INBLS	10/01-12/01
Middle School	Kentucky	Y	29830 FQ	38490 AW	46940 TQ	KYBLS	10/01-12/01
Middle School	Maine	Y	24920 FQ	38450 AW	49880 TQ	MEBLS	10/01-12/01
Middle School	Maryland	Y	23390 FQ	42540 AW	60330 TQ	MDBLS	10/01-12/01
Middle School	Massachusetts	Y	29520 FQ	43150 AW	63590 TQ	MABLS	10/01-12/01
Middle School	Boston PMSA, MA-NH	Y	29060 FQ	42360 AW	61930 TQ	MABLS	10/01-12/01
Middle School	Michigan	Y	30970 FQ	51740 AW	69970 TQ	MIBLS	10/01-12/01
Middle School	Ann Arbor PMSA, MI	Y	51040 FQ	61020 AW	72810 TQ	MIBLS	10/01-12/01
Middle School	Grand Rapids-Muskegon-Holland MSA, MI	Y	25680 FQ	47050 AW	70210 TQ	MIBLS	10/01-12/01
Middle School	Minnesota	Y	30030 FQ	39180 AW	45810 TQ	MNBLS	10/01-12/01
Middle School	Minneapolis-St. Paul MSA, MN-WI	Y	29350 FQ	43300 AW	66240 TQ	MNBLS	10/01-12/01
Middle School	Mississippi	Y	26180 FQ	34760 AW	44950 TQ	MSBLS	10/01-12/01
Middle School	Biloxi-Gulfport-Pascagoula MSA, MS	Y	27620 FQ	38020 AW	52130 TQ	MSBLS	10/01-12/01
Middle School	Missouri	Y	14010 FQ	34790 AW	51830 TQ	MOBLS	10/01-12/01
Middle School	Kansas City MSA, MO-KS	Y	23510 FQ	35550 AW	53840 TQ	MOBLS	10/01-12/01
Middle School	St. Louis MSA, MO-IL	Y	30340 FQ	40510 AW	53850 TQ	MOBLS	10/01-12/01
Middle School	Montana	Y	24680 FQ	35890 AW	43760 TQ	MTBLS	10/01-12/01
Middle School	Nebraska	Y	20380 FQ	37730 AW	53610 TQ	NEBLS	10/01-12/01
Middle School	New Hampshire	Y	31210 FQ	35070 AW	37910 TQ	NHBLS	10/01-12/01
Middle School	New Jersey	Y	34710 FQ	52650 AW	71560 TQ	NJBLS	10/01-12/01
Middle School	Bergen-Passaic PMSA, NJ	Y	35500 FQ	53480 AW	81750 TQ	NJBLS	10/01-12/01
Middle School	New Mexico	Y	26730 FQ	39220 AW	56930 TQ	NMBLS	10/01-12/01
Middle School	New York	Y	32240 FQ	52180 AW	81800 TQ	NYBLS	10/01-12/01
Middle School	Albany-Schenectady-Troy MSA, NY	Y	31570 FQ	49890 AW	70360 TQ	NYBLS	10/01-12/01
Middle School	Buffalo-Niagara Falls MSA, NY	Y	35510 FQ	60300 AW	73310 TQ	NYBLS	10/01-12/01
Middle School	Nassau-Suffolk PMSA, NY	Y	39690 FQ	72820 AW	109000 TQ	NYBLS	10/01-12/01

AAW	Average annual wage	AOH	Average offered, high	ASH	Average starting, high	H	Hourly	M	Monthly	S	Special: hourly and annual
AE	Average entry wage	AOL	Average offered, low	ASL	Average starting, low	HI	Highest wage paid	MTC	Median total compensation	TQ	Third quartile wage
AEX	Average experienced wage	APH	Average pay, high range	AW	Average wage paid	HR	High end range	MW	Median wage paid	W	Weekly
AO	Average offered	APL	Average pay, low range	FQ	First quartile wage	LR	Low end range	SQ	Second quartile wage	Y	Yearly

Occupation/Type/Industry	Location	Per	Low	Mid	High	Source	Date
Vocational Education Teacher							
Middle School	Rochester MSA, NY	Y	39070 FQ	64720 AW	91020 TQ	NYBLS	10/01-12/01
Middle School	Syracuse MSA, NY	Y	28360 FQ	38730 AW	46260 TQ	NYBLS	10/01-12/01
Middle School	North Carolina	Y	24890 FQ	36610 AW	51790 TQ	NCBLS	10/01-12/01
Middle School	Charlotte-Gastonia-Rock Hill MSA, NC-SC	Y	31200 FQ	42340 AW	54230 TQ	NCBLS	10/01-12/01
Middle School	Fayetteville MSA, NC	Y	26940 FQ	34990 AW	44710 TQ	NCBLS	10/01-12/01
Middle School	Greensboro-Winston-Salem-High Point MSA, NC	Y	24970 FQ	32740 AW	43560 TQ	NCBLS	10/01-12/01
Middle School	Hickory-Morganton-Lenoir MSA, NC	Y	30210 FQ	35710 AW	45810 TQ	NCBLS	10/01-12/01
Middle School	Raleigh-Durham-Chapel Hill MSA, NC	Y	32210 FQ	46780 AW	61020 TQ	NCBLS	10/01-12/01
Middle School	Ohio	Y	28150 FQ	44610 AW	60100 TQ	OHBLS	10/01-12/01
Middle School	Akron PMSA, OH	Y	36610 FQ	48910 AW	63130 TQ	OHBLS	10/01-12/01
Middle School	Canton-Massillon MSA, OH	Y	33360 FQ	45770 AW	59310 TQ	OHBLS	10/01-12/01
Middle School	Cincinnati PMSA, OH-KY-IN	Y	34440 FQ	45740 AW	56650 TQ	OHBLS	10/01-12/01
Middle School	Cleveland-Lorain-Elyria PMSA, OH	Y	14190 FQ	48640 AW	70450 TQ	OHBLS	10/01-12/01
Middle School	Columbus MSA, OH	Y	26730 FQ	43500 AW	60020 TQ	OHBLS	10/01-12/01
Middle School	Dayton-Springfield MSA, OH	Y	35110 FQ	48250 AW	60060 TQ	OHBLS	10/01-12/01
Middle School	Toledo MSA, OH	Y	29960 FQ	47520 AW	65570 TQ	OHBLS	10/01-12/01
Middle School	Youngstown-Warren MSA, OH	Y	28250 FQ	43190 AW	57330 TQ	OHBLS	10/01-12/01
Middle School	Oklahoma	Y	29630 FQ	38910 AW	51260 TQ	OKBLS	10/01-12/01
Middle School	Oklahoma City MSA, OK	Y	31890 FQ	42290 AW	56370 TQ	OKBLS	10/01-12/01
Middle School	Tulsa MSA, OK	Y	29110 FQ	38470 AW	49120 TQ	OKBLS	10/01-12/01
Middle School	Oregon	Y	30800 FQ	43930 AW	58620 TQ	ORBLS	10/01-12/01
Middle School	Eugene-Springfield MSA, OR	Y	32550 FQ	42270 AW	54440 TQ	ORBLS	10/01-12/01
Middle School	Portland-Vancouver PMSA, OR-WA	Y	31920 FQ	47550 AW	65420 TQ	ORBLS	10/01-12/01
Middle School	Salem PMSA, OR	Y	30420 FQ	42550 AW	57400 TQ	ORBLS	10/01-12/01
Middle School	Pennsylvania	Y	33690 FQ	54220 AW	74060 TQ	PABLS	10/01-12/01
Middle School	Allentown-Bethlehem-Easton MSA, PA	Y	34460 FQ	63610 AW	104220 TQ	PABLS	10/01-12/01
Middle School	Philadelphia PMSA, PA-NJ	Y	34180 FQ	53030 AW	72430 TQ	PABLS	10/01-12/01
Middle School	Pittsburgh MSA, PA	Y	58040 FQ	74880 AW	105240 TQ	PABLS	10/01-12/01
Middle School	Reading MSA, PA	Y	32170 FQ	52730 AW	69340 TQ	PABLS	10/01-12/01
Middle School	Scranton-Wilkes-Barre-Hazleton MSA, PA	Y	28870 FQ	46470 AW	65270 TQ	PABLS	10/01-12/01
Middle School	South Carolina	Y	25830 FQ	39280 AW	53610 TQ	SCBLS	10/01-12/01
Middle School	South Dakota	Y	28990 FQ	32830 AW	37180 TQ	SDBLS	10/01-12/01
Middle School	Tennessee	Y	29250 FQ	35370 AW	44230 TQ	TNBLS	10/01-12/01
Middle School	Memphis MSA, TN-AR-MS	Y	28660 FQ	34250 AW	43250 TQ	TNBLS	10/01-12/01
Middle School	Texas	Y	30060 FQ	41610 AW	55130 TQ	TXBLS	10/01-12/01
Middle School	Austin-San Marcos MSA, TX	Y	26290 FQ	39950 AW	54600 TQ	TXBLS	10/01-12/01
Middle School	Dallas PMSA, TX	Y	31550 FQ	44210 AW	61270 TQ	TXBLS	10/01-12/01
Middle School	El Paso MSA, TX	Y	36310 FQ	40150 AW	44310 TQ	TXBLS	10/01-12/01
Middle School	Houston PMSA, TX	Y	32010 FQ	42860 AW	55330 TQ	TXBLS	10/01-12/01
Middle School	McAllen-Edinburg-Mission MSA, TX	Y	35960 FQ	44910 AW	55820 TQ	TXBLS	10/01-12/01
Middle School	San Antonio MSA, TX	Y	31500 FQ	41630 AW	55180 TQ	TXBLS	10/01-12/01
Middle School	Utah	Y	17840 FQ	33910 AW	51820 TQ	UTBLS	10/01-12/01
Middle School	Salt Lake City-Ogden MSA, UT	Y	21260 FQ	33490 AW	45860 TQ	UTBLS	10/01-12/01
Middle School	Vermont	Y	37640 FQ	41930 AW	46350 TQ	VTBLS	10/01-12/01
Middle School	Virginia	Y	30610 FQ	46860 AW	71060 TQ	VABLS	10/01-12/01
Middle School	Norfolk-Virginia Beach-Newport News MSA, VA-NC	Y	30720 FQ	40380 AW	53670 TQ	VABLS	10/01-12/01
Middle School	Richmond-Petersburg MSA, VA	Y	29970 FQ	38280 AW	50670 TQ	VABLS	10/01-12/01
Middle School	Washington	Y	28360 FQ	43260 AW	56810 TQ	WABLS	10/01-12/01
Middle School	Seattle-Bellevue-Everett PMSA, WA	Y	27470 FQ	42680 AW	57440 TQ	WABLS	10/01-12/01
Middle School	Wisconsin	Y	29640 FQ	46430 AW	63030 TQ	WIBLS	10/01-12/01
Middle School	Wyoming	Y	24740 FQ	33590 AW	45140 TQ	WYBLS	10/01-12/01
Middle School	Puerto Rico	Y	19520 FQ	21450 AW	23730 TQ	PRBLS	10/01-12/01
Postsecondary	Alabama	Y	18160 FQ	44650 AW	73330 TQ	ALBLS	10/01-12/01
Postsecondary	Birmingham MSA, AL	Y	27920 FQ	45510 AW	57080 TQ	ALBLS	10/01-12/01
Postsecondary	Huntsville MSA, AL	Y	23420 FQ	41450 AW	60210 TQ	ALBLS	10/01-12/01
Postsecondary	Mobile MSA, AL	Y	12970 FQ	31280 AW	50400 TQ	ALBLS	10/01-12/01
Postsecondary	Montgomery MSA, AL	Y	12470 FQ	25870 AW	44140 TQ	ALBLS	10/01-12/01

AAW	Average annual wage	AOH	Average offered, high	ASH	Average starting, high	H	Hourly	M	Monthly	S	Special: hourly and annual
AE	Average entry wage	AOL	Average offered, low	ASL	Average starting, low	HI	Highest wage paid	MTC	Median total compensation	TQ	Third quartile wage
AEX	Average experienced wage	APH	Average pay, high range	AW	Average wage paid	HR	High end range	MW	Median wage paid	W	Weekly
AO	Average offered	APL	Average pay, low range	FQ	First quartile wage	LR	Low end range	SQ	Second quartile wage	Y	Yearly

Occupation/Type/Industry	Location	Per	Low	Mid	High	Source	Date
Vocational Education Teacher							
Postsecondary	Alaska	Y	26800 FQ	50870 AW	74570 TQ	AKBLS	10/01-12/01
Postsecondary	Anchorage MSA, AK	Y	23650 FQ	47140 AW	65960 TQ	AKBLS	10/01-12/01
Postsecondary	Arizona	Y	17280 FQ	32550 AW	50320 TQ	AZBLS	10/01-12/01
Postsecondary	Phoenix-Mesa MSA, AZ	Y	17360 FQ	32970 AW	50780 TQ	AZBLS	10/01-12/01
Postsecondary	Arkansas	Y	20300 FQ	31960 AW	45040 TQ	ARBLS	10/01-12/01
Postsecondary	Fayetteville-Springdale-Rogers MSA, AR	Y	16580 FQ	28500 AW	42780 TQ	ARBLS	10/01-12/01
Postsecondary	Little Rock-North Little Rock MSA, AR	Y	21450 FQ	32520 AW	47250 TQ	ARBLS	10/01-12/01
Postsecondary	California	Y	26110 FQ	49040 AW	84160 TQ	CABLS	10/01-12/01
Postsecondary	Bakersfield MSA, CA	Y	29340 FQ	48520 AW	80570 TQ	CABLS	10/01-12/01
Postsecondary	Chico-Paradise MSA, CA	Y	32030 FQ	53960 AW	91850 TQ	CABLS	10/01-12/01
Postsecondary	Fresno MSA, CA	Y	22700 FQ	42970 AW	76970 TQ	CABLS	10/01-12/01
Postsecondary	Los Angeles-Long Beach PMSA, CA	Y	25860 FQ	43240 AW	72460 TQ	CABLS	10/01-12/01
Postsecondary	Modesto MSA, CA	Y	26940 FQ	51040 AW	86460 TQ	CABLS	10/01-12/01
Postsecondary	Oakland PMSA, CA	Y	27330 FQ	46020 AW	73310 TQ	CABLS	10/01-12/01
Postsecondary	Orange County PMSA, CA	Y	30300 FQ	55240 AW	87710 TQ	CABLS	10/01-12/01
Postsecondary	Riverside-San Bernardino PMSA, CA	Y	23560 FQ	41680 AW	65360 TQ	CABLS	10/01-12/01
Postsecondary	Sacramento PMSA, CA	Y	27170 FQ	48790 AW	80400 TQ	CABLS	10/01-12/01
Postsecondary	Salinas MSA, CA	Y	35240 FQ	64610 AW	100860 TQ	CABLS	10/01-12/01
Postsecondary	San Diego MSA, CA	Y	28740 FQ	50930 AW	84640 TQ	CABLS	10/01-12/01
Postsecondary	San Francisco PMSA, CA	Y	31970 FQ	58300 AW	104510 TQ	CABLS	10/01-12/01
Postsecondary	San Jose PMSA, CA	Y	31430 FQ	57300 AW	89660 TQ	CABLS	10/01-12/01
Postsecondary	San Luis Obispo-Atascadero-Paso Robles MSA, CA	Y	32550 FQ	60390 AW	90640 TQ	CABLS	10/01-12/01
Postsecondary	Santa Barbara-Santa Maria-Lompoc MSA, CA	Y	20850 FQ	50810 AW	90090 TQ	CABLS	10/01-12/01
Postsecondary	Santa Cruz-Watsonville PMSA, CA	Y	30420 FQ	63300 AW		CABLS	10/01-12/01
Postsecondary	Stockton-Lodi MSA, CA	Y	20440 FQ	33180 AW	46200 TQ	CABLS	10/01-12/01
Postsecondary	Vallejo-Fairfield-Napa PMSA, CA	Y	24240 FQ	42040 AW	68190 TQ	CABLS	10/01-12/01
Postsecondary	Ventura PMSA, CA	Y	27100 FQ	51920 AW	92670 TQ	CABLS	10/01-12/01
Postsecondary	Visalia-Tulare-Porterville MSA, CA	Y	18040 FQ	35380 AW	55910 TQ	CABLS	10/01-12/01
Postsecondary	Colorado	Y	26060 FQ	43970 AW	65270 TQ	COBLS	10/01-12/01
Postsecondary	Boulder-Longmont PMSA, CO	Y	28680 FQ	39100 AW	56610 TQ	COBLS	10/01-12/01
Postsecondary	Colorado Springs MSA, CO	Y	25270 FQ	44520 AW	69340 TQ	COBLS	10/01-12/01
Postsecondary	Denver PMSA, CO	Y	27350 FQ	44860 AW	70750 TQ	COBLS	10/01-12/01
Postsecondary	Fort Collins-Loveland MSA, CO	Y	23760 FQ	40000 AW	55760 TQ	COBLS	10/01-12/01
Postsecondary	Connecticut	Y	25390 FQ	44870 AW	68480 TQ	CTBLS	10/01-12/01
Postsecondary	Hartford MSA, CT	Y	24260 FQ	42690 AW	64060 TQ	CTBLS	10/01-12/01
Postsecondary	New Haven-Meriden PMSA, CT	Y	31760 FQ	49680 AW	59940 TQ	CTBLS	10/01-12/01
Postsecondary	New London-Norwich MSA, CT-RI	Y	23280 FQ	40320 AW	64400 TQ	CTBLS	10/01-12/01
Postsecondary	Stamford-Norwalk PMSA, CT	Y	22230 FQ	55920 AW	98650 TQ	CTBLS	10/01-12/01
Postsecondary	Delaware	Y	27160 FQ	45410 AW	66950 TQ	DEBLS	10/01-12/01
Postsecondary	Wilmington-Newark PMSA, DE-MD	Y	26370 FQ	44490 AW	66600 TQ	DEBLS	10/01-12/01
Postsecondary	District of Columbia	Y	25180 FQ	40640 AW	62000 TQ	DCBLS	10/01-12/01
Postsecondary	Washington PMSA, DC-MD-VA-WV	Y	27010 FQ	40800 AW	58020 TQ	DCBLS	10/01-12/01
Postsecondary	Florida	Y	22020 FQ	37760 AW	60790 TQ	FLBLS	10/01-12/01
Postsecondary	Daytona Beach MSA, FL	Y	22410 FQ	48110 AW	75560 TQ	FLBLS	10/01-12/01
Postsecondary	Fort Lauderdale PMSA, FL	Y	21120 FQ	40930 AW	68680 TQ	FLBLS	10/01-12/01
Postsecondary	Gainesville MSA, FL	Y	22860 FQ	46660 AW	74370 TQ	FLBLS	10/01-12/01
Postsecondary	Jacksonville MSA, FL	Y	22700 FQ	34260 AW	59480 TQ	FLBLS	10/01-12/01
Postsecondary	Lakeland-Winter Haven MSA, FL	Y	21860 FQ	32910 AW	46630 TQ	FLBLS	10/01-12/01
Postsecondary	Melbourne-Titusville-Palm Bay MSA, FL	Y	20240 FQ	32990 AW	50280 TQ	FLBLS	10/01-12/01
Postsecondary	Miami PMSA, FL	Y	18890 FQ	32840 AW	49700 TQ	FLBLS	10/01-12/01
Postsecondary	Orlando MSA, FL	Y	26430 FQ	37010 AW	54110 TQ	FLBLS	10/01-12/01
Postsecondary	Tallahassee MSA, FL	Y	21800 FQ	35820 AW	64460 TQ	FLBLS	10/01-12/01
Postsecondary	Tampa-St. Petersburg-Clearwater MSA, FL	Y	19690 FQ	36370 AW	62990 TQ	FLBLS	10/01-12/01

AAW	Average annual wage	AOH	Average offered, high	ASH	Average starting, high	H	Hourly	M	Monthly	S	Special: hourly and annual
AE	Average entry wage	AOL	Average offered, low	ASL	Average starting, low	HI	Highest wage paid	MTC	Median total compensation	TQ	Third quartile wage
AEX	Average experienced wage	APH	Average pay, high range	AW	Average wage paid	HR	High end range	MW	Median wage paid	W	Weekly
AO	Average offered	APL	Average pay, low range	FQ	First quartile wage	LR	Low end range	SQ	Second quartile wage	Y	Yearly

Occupation/Type/Industry	Location	Per	Low	Mid	High	Source	Date
Vocational Education Teacher							
Postsecondary	West Palm Beach-Boca Raton MSA, FL	Y	24900 FQ	36470 AW	48070 TQ	FLBLS	10/01-12/01
Postsecondary	Georgia	Y	21160 FQ	38710 AW	58400 TQ	GABLS	10/01-12/01
Postsecondary	Atlanta MSA, GA	Y	14640 FQ	37700 AW	58280 TQ	GABLS	10/01-12/01
Postsecondary	Augusta-Aiken MSA, GA-SC	Y	20600 FQ	47970 AW	88360 TQ	GABLS	10/01-12/01
Postsecondary	Macon MSA, GA	Y	28700 FQ	38660 AW	54090 TQ	GABLS	10/01-12/01
Postsecondary	Savannah MSA, GA	Y	30500 FQ	46240 AW	70620 TQ	GABLS	10/01-12/01
Postsecondary	Hawaii	Y	31490 FQ	49160 AW	73080 TQ	HIBLS	10/01-12/01
Postsecondary	Honolulu MSA, HI	Y	30030 FQ	48400 AW	75750 TQ	HIBLS	10/01-12/01
Postsecondary	Idaho	Y	26980 FQ	40940 AW	55510 TQ	IDBLS	10/01-12/01
Postsecondary	Boise City MSA, ID	Y	30910 FQ	40680 AW	51950 TQ	IDBLS	10/01-12/01
Postsecondary	Illinois	Y	17210 FQ	39980 AW	67570 TQ	ILBLS	10/01-12/01
Postsecondary	Chicago PMSA, IL	Y	22320 FQ	43430 AW	70360 TQ	ILBLS	10/01-12/01
Postsecondary	Indiana	Y	22510 FQ	38570 AW	53290 TQ	INBLS	10/01-12/01
Postsecondary	Evansville-Henderson MSA, IN-KY	Y	21070 FQ	38680 AW	57780 TQ	INBLS	10/01-12/01
Postsecondary	Gary PMSA, IN	Y	23720 FQ	46210 AW	69900 TQ	INBLS	10/01-12/01
Postsecondary	Indianapolis MSA, IN	Y	24590 FQ	38380 AW	51900 TQ	INBLS	10/01-12/01
Postsecondary	South Bend MSA, IN	Y	18530 FQ	31910 AW	54650 TQ	INBLS	10/01-12/01
Postsecondary	Iowa	Y	21430 FQ	40560 AW	62040 TQ	IABLS	10/01-12/01
Postsecondary	Cedar Rapids MSA, IA	Y	13140 FQ	31880 AW	46570 TQ	IABLS	10/01-12/01
Postsecondary	Davenport-Moline-Rock Island MSA, IA-IL	Y	20360 FQ	36880 AW	53150 TQ	IABLS	10/01-12/01
Postsecondary	Des Moines MSA, IA	Y	20550 FQ	44010 AW	66560 TQ	IABLS	10/01-12/01
Postsecondary	Kansas	Y	21640 FQ	36410 AW	52750 TQ	KSBLS	10/01-12/01
Postsecondary	Topeka MSA, KS	Y	22610 FQ	38130 AW	68120 TQ	KSBLS	10/01-12/01
Postsecondary	Wichita MSA, KS	Y	30480 FQ	40110 AW	51000 TQ	KSBLS	10/01-12/01
Postsecondary	Kentucky	Y	26880 FQ	40360 AW	55990 TQ	KYBLS	10/01-12/01
Postsecondary	Lexington MSA, KY	Y	31300 FQ	45120 AW	60390 TQ	KYBLS	10/01-12/01
Postsecondary	Louisville MSA, KY-IN	Y	30580 FQ	43200 AW	55710 TQ	KYBLS	10/01-12/01
Postsecondary	Louisiana	Y	20060 FQ	38810 AW	53860 TQ	LABLS	10/01-12/01
Postsecondary	Baton Rouge MSA, LA	Y	21370 FQ	35630 AW	47390 TQ	LABLS	10/01-12/01
Postsecondary	Houma MSA, LA	Y	26640 FQ	41350 AW	48270 TQ	LABLS	10/01-12/01
Postsecondary	Lafayette MSA, LA	Y	34140 FQ	42640 AW	53480 TQ	LABLS	10/01-12/01
Postsecondary	Lake Charles MSA, LA	Y	23460 FQ	37730 AW	51870 TQ	LABLS	10/01-12/01
Postsecondary	New Orleans MSA, LA	Y	18350 FQ	38830 AW	78090 TQ	LABLS	10/01-12/01
Postsecondary	Shreveport-Bossier City MSA, LA	Y	20430 FQ	37000 AW	48120 TQ	LABLS	10/01-12/01
Postsecondary	Maine	Y	23640 FQ	38460 AW	52840 TQ	MEBLS	10/01-12/01
Postsecondary	Portland MSA, ME	Y	22610 FQ	36420 AW	54510 TQ	MEBLS	10/01-12/01
Postsecondary	Maryland	Y	22400 FQ	40000 AW	62170 TQ	MDBLS	10/01-12/01
Postsecondary	Baltimore PMSA, MD	Y	21510 FQ	41380 AW	67480 TQ	MDBLS	10/01-12/01
Postsecondary	Massachusetts	Y	26700 FQ	46970 AW	72690 TQ	MABLS	10/01-12/01
Postsecondary	Boston PMSA, MA-NH	Y	28160 FQ	49120 AW	74380 TQ	MABLS	10/01-12/01
Postsecondary	Lowell PMSA, MA-NH	Y	25600 FQ	41900 AW	69550 TQ	MABLS	10/01-12/01
Postsecondary	Springfield MSA, MA	Y	29430 FQ	44180 AW	58390 TQ	MABLS	10/01-12/01
Postsecondary	Worcester PMSA, MA-CT	Y	19120 FQ	28460 AW	45730 TQ	MABLS	10/01-12/01
Postsecondary	Michigan	Y	19270 FQ	36290 AW	58410 TQ	MIBLS	10/01-12/01
Postsecondary	Ann Arbor PMSA, MI	Y	17810 FQ	32550 AW	53680 TQ	MIBLS	10/01-12/01
Postsecondary	Detroit PMSA, MI	Y	24750 FQ	37780 AW	58470 TQ	MIBLS	10/01-12/01
Postsecondary	Flint PMSA, MI	Y	15140 FQ	21870 AW	39260 TQ	MIBLS	10/01-12/01
Postsecondary	Grand Rapids-Muskegon-Holland MSA, MI	Y	25780 FQ	43410 AW	68820 TQ	MIBLS	10/01-12/01
Postsecondary	Kalamazoo-Battle Creek MSA, MI	Y	11950 FQ	28450 AW	50200 TQ	MIBLS	10/01-12/01
Postsecondary	Lansing-East Lansing MSA, MI	Y	15570 FQ	24300 AW	54700 TQ	MIBLS	10/01-12/01
Postsecondary	Minnesota	Y	28230 FQ	44350 AW	59980 TQ	MNBLS	10/01-12/01
Postsecondary	Duluth-Superior MSA, MN-WI	Y	37510 FQ	51480 AW	67560 TQ	MNBLS	10/01-12/01
Postsecondary	Minneapolis-St. Paul MSA, MN-WI	Y	30010 FQ	46770 AW	66090 TQ	MNBLS	10/01-12/01
Postsecondary	St. Cloud MSA, MN	Y	29180 FQ	44290 AW	61940 TQ	MNBLS	10/01-12/01
Postsecondary	Mississippi	Y	19830 FQ	37190 AW	55230 TQ	MSBLS	10/01-12/01
Postsecondary	Jackson MSA, MS	Y	15240 FQ	30080 AW	48800 TQ	MSBLS	10/01-12/01
Postsecondary	Missouri	Y	17930 FQ	36060 AW	56890 TQ	MOBLS	10/01-12/01
Postsecondary	Kansas City MSA, MO-KS	Y	22490 FQ	38440 AW	61310 TQ	MOBLS	10/01-12/01
Postsecondary	St. Louis MSA, MO-IL	Y	20550 FQ	41260 AW	74620 TQ	MOBLS	10/01-12/01
Postsecondary	Springfield MSA, MO	Y	24060 FQ	38090 AW	55250 TQ	MOBLS	10/01-12/01
Postsecondary	Montana	Y	16530 FQ	38000 AW	57210 TQ	MTBLS	10/01-12/01
Postsecondary	Billings MSA, MT	Y	25500 FQ	34990 AW	44220 TQ	MTBLS	10/01-12/01
Postsecondary	Nebraska	Y	30420 FQ	54640 AW	70790 TQ	NEBLS	10/01-12/01
Postsecondary	Omaha MSA, NE-IA	Y	20920 FQ	41520 AW	61580 TQ	NEBLS	10/01-12/01

AAW	Average annual wage	AOH	Average offered, high	ASH	Average starting, high	H	Hourly	M	Monthly	S	Special: hourly and annual
AE	Average entry wage	AOL	Average offered, low	ASL	Average starting, low	HI	Highest wage paid	MTC	Median total compensation	TQ	Third quartile wage
AEX	Average experienced wage	APH	Average pay, high range	AW	Average wage paid	HR	High end range	MW	Median wage paid	W	Weekly
AO	Average offered	APL	Average pay, low range	FQ	First quartile wage	LR	Low end range	SQ	Second quartile wage	Y	Yearly

Occupation/Type/Industry	Location	Per	Low	Mid	High	Source	Date
Vocational Education Teacher							
Postsecondary	Nevada	Y	24030 FQ	41500 AW	68170 TQ	NVBLS	10/01-12/01
Postsecondary	Las Vegas MSA, NV-AZ	Y	24800 FQ	43190 AW	69410 TQ	NVBLS	10/01-12/01
Postsecondary	Reno MSA, NV	Y	23630 FQ	37030 AW	64780 TQ	NVBLS	10/01-12/01
Postsecondary	New Hampshire	Y	31330 FQ	41570 AW	54460 TQ	NHBLS	10/01-12/01
Postsecondary	New Jersey	Y	24860 FQ	43980 AW	62650 TQ	NJBLS	10/01-12/01
Postsecondary	Atlantic-Cape May PMSA, NJ	Y	23980 FQ	28190 AW	34640 TQ	NJBLS	10/01-12/01
Postsecondary	Bergen-Passaic PMSA, NJ	Y	13540 FQ	48590 AW	138240 TQ	NJBLS	10/01-12/01
Postsecondary	Middlesex-Somerset-Hunterdon PMSA, NJ	Y	30460 FQ	45190 AW	63070 TQ	NJBLS	10/01-12/01
Postsecondary	Monmouth-Ocean PMSA, NJ	Y	24170 FQ	35740 AW	54880 TQ	NJBLS	10/01-12/01
Postsecondary	Newark PMSA, NJ	Y	29180 FQ	45250 AW	65260 TQ	NJBLS	10/01-12/01
Postsecondary	Trenton PMSA, NJ	Y	29240 FQ	44020 AW	56210 TQ	NJBLS	10/01-12/01
Postsecondary	New Mexico	Y	18830 FQ	32400 AW	46960 TQ	NMBLS	10/01-12/01
Postsecondary	Albuquerque MSA, NM	Y	12250 FQ	30900 AW	48040 TQ	NMBLS	10/01-12/01
Postsecondary	Las Cruces MSA, NM	Y	25950 FQ	35270 AW	49100 TQ	NMBLS	10/01-12/01
Postsecondary	New York	Y	22280 FQ	45160 AW	71940 TQ	NYBLS	10/01-12/01
Postsecondary	Albany-Schenectady-Troy MSA, NY	Y	21610 FQ	42280 AW	81890 TQ	NYBLS	10/01-12/01
Postsecondary	Buffalo-Niagara Falls MSA, NY	Y	20190 FQ	36350 AW	53420 TQ	NYBLS	10/01-12/01
Postsecondary	Dutchess County PMSA, NY	Y	34310 FQ	44310 AW	54890 TQ	NYBLS	10/01-12/01
Postsecondary	Nassau-Suffolk PMSA, NY	Y	32860 FQ	46650 AW	69160 TQ	NYBLS	10/01-12/01
Postsecondary	New York PMSA, NY	Y	21710 FQ	49600 AW	85960 TQ	NYBLS	10/01-12/01
Postsecondary	Newburgh PMSA, NY-PA	Y	12720 FQ	33520 AW	56630 TQ	NYBLS	10/01-12/01
Postsecondary	Rochester MSA, NY	Y	24520 FQ	40150 AW	55750 TQ	NYBLS	10/01-12/01
Postsecondary	Syracuse MSA, NY	Y	15880 FQ	35920 AW	52340 TQ	NYBLS	10/01-12/01
Postsecondary	Utica-Rome MSA, NY	Y	30240 FQ	42480 AW	54700 TQ	NYBLS	10/01-12/01
Postsecondary	North Carolina	Y	26320 FQ	39350 AW	53700 TQ	NCBLS	10/01-12/01
Postsecondary	Asheville MSA, NC	Y	25610 FQ	37110 AW	46570 TQ	NCBLS	10/01-12/01
Postsecondary	Charlotte-Gastonia-Rock Hill MSA, NC-SC	Y	28610 FQ	44280 AW	61430 TQ	NCBLS	10/01-12/01
Postsecondary	Fayetteville MSA, NC	Y	31940 FQ	48370 AW	57810 TQ	NCBLS	10/01-12/01
Postsecondary	Greensboro-Winston-Salem-High Point MSA, NC	Y	21420 FQ	37180 AW	54790 TQ	NCBLS	10/01-12/01
Postsecondary	Raleigh-Durham-Chapel Hill MSA, NC	Y	32190 FQ	41000 AW	50880 TQ	NCBLS	10/01-12/01
Postsecondary	Wilmington MSA, NC	Y	12990 FQ	35550 AW	55470 TQ	NCBLS	10/01-12/01
Postsecondary	North Dakota	Y	13010 FQ	29420 AW	49410 TQ	NDBLS	10/01-12/01
Postsecondary	Fargo-Moorhead MSA, ND-MN	Y	19690 FQ	41380 AW	55840 TQ	NDBLS	10/01-12/01
Postsecondary	Ohio	Y	19080 FQ	37260 AW	60410 TQ	OHBLS	10/01-12/01
Postsecondary	Akron PMSA, OH	Y	32810 FQ	49750 AW	66050 TQ	OHBLS	10/01-12/01
Postsecondary	Canton-Massillon MSA, OH	Y	19380 FQ	42080 AW	67960 TQ	OHBLS	10/01-12/01
Postsecondary	Cincinnati PMSA, OH-KY-IN	Y	15680 FQ	34390 AW	53660 TQ	OHBLS	10/01-12/01
Postsecondary	Cleveland-Lorain-Elyria PMSA, OH	Y	13300 FQ	29370 AW	44080 TQ	OHBLS	10/01-12/01
Postsecondary	Columbus MSA, OH	Y	20030 FQ	37800 AW	60450 TQ	OHBLS	10/01-12/01
Postsecondary	Dayton-Springfield MSA, OH	Y	18990 FQ	40020 AW	56250 TQ	OHBLS	10/01-12/01
Postsecondary	Hamilton-Middletown PMSA, OH	Y	21160 FQ	34370 AW	47290 TQ	OHBLS	10/01-12/01
Postsecondary	Toledo MSA, OH	Y	20250 FQ	47070 AW	72390 TQ	OHBLS	10/01-12/01
Postsecondary	Youngstown-Warren MSA, OH	Y	20400 FQ	31300 AW	43380 TQ	OHBLS	10/01-12/01
Postsecondary	Oklahoma	Y	23730 FQ	37380 AW	52740 TQ	OKBLS	10/01-12/01
Postsecondary	Oklahoma City MSA, OK	Y	25210 FQ	40170 AW	55740 TQ	OKBLS	10/01-12/01
Postsecondary	Tulsa MSA, OK	Y	21360 FQ	38300 AW	54820 TQ	OKBLS	10/01-12/01
Postsecondary	Oregon	Y	24700 FQ	54410 AW	91020 TQ	ORBLS	10/01-12/01
Postsecondary	Eugene-Springfield MSA, OR	Y	31050 FQ	57890 AW	83650 TQ	ORBLS	10/01-12/01
Postsecondary	Portland-Vancouver PMSA, OR-WA	Y	25210 FQ	54880 AW	93440 TQ	ORBLS	10/01-12/01
Postsecondary	Salem PMSA, OR	Y	18840 FQ	31170 AW	46030 TQ	ORBLS	10/01-12/01
Postsecondary	Pennsylvania	Y	22800 FQ	39770 AW	65600 TQ	PABLS	10/01-12/01
Postsecondary	Allentown-Bethlehem-Easton MSA, PA	Y	27220 FQ	42970 AW	56310 TQ	PABLS	10/01-12/01
Postsecondary	Erie MSA, PA	Y	21700 FQ	31590 AW	42250 TQ	PABLS	10/01-12/01
Postsecondary	Harrisburg-Lebanon-Carlisle MSA, PA	Y	25900 FQ	43110 AW	69270 TQ	PABLS	10/01-12/01
Postsecondary	Johnstown MSA, PA	Y	25200 FQ	36610 AW	48470 TQ	PABLS	10/01-12/01
Postsecondary	Lancaster MSA, PA	Y	26430 FQ	47650 AW	68540 TQ	PABLS	10/01-12/01
Postsecondary	Philadelphia PMSA, PA-NJ	Y	26650 FQ	48150 AW	76680 TQ	PABLS	10/01-12/01
Postsecondary	Pittsburgh MSA, PA	Y	20480 FQ	32300 AW	51000 TQ	PABLS	10/01-12/01

AAW	Average annual wage	**AOH**	Average offered, high	**ASH**	Average starting, high	**H**	Hourly	**M**	Monthly	**S**	Special: hourly and annual
AE	Average entry wage	**AOL**	Average offered, low	**ASL**	Average starting, low	**HI**	Highest wage paid	**MTC**	Median total compensation	**TQ**	Third quartile wage
AEX	Average experienced wage	**APH**	Average pay, high range	**AW**	Average wage paid	**HR**	High end range	**MW**	Median wage paid	**W**	Weekly
AO	Average offered	**APL**	Average pay, low range	**FQ**	First quartile wage	**LR**	Low end range	**SQ**	Second quartile wage	**Y**	Yearly

Occupation/Type/Industry	Location	Per	Low	Mid	High	Source	Date
Vocational Education Teacher							
Postsecondary	Scranton-Wilkes-Barre-Hazleton MSA, PA	Y	23450 FQ	36430 AW	55020 TQ	PABLS	10/01-12/01
Postsecondary	York MSA, PA	Y	27730 FQ	41740 AW	54640 TQ	PABLS	10/01-12/01
Postsecondary	Rhode Island	Y	25960 FQ	44650 AW	67570 TQ	RIBLS	10/01-12/01
Postsecondary	Providence-Fall River-Warwick MSA, RI-MA	Y	26050 FQ	43990 AW	67200 TQ	RIBLS	10/01-12/01
Postsecondary	South Carolina	Y	20540 FQ	45930 AW	82530 TQ	SCBLS	10/01-12/01
Postsecondary	Charleston-North Charleston MSA, SC	Y	20150 FQ	34190 AW	45170 TQ	SCBLS	10/01-12/01
Postsecondary	Columbia MSA, SC	Y	28300 FQ	49990 AW	71600 TQ	SCBLS	10/01-12/01
Postsecondary	Greenville-Spartanburg-Anderson MSA, SC	Y	24300 FQ	36990 AW	52730 TQ	SCBLS	10/01-12/01
Postsecondary	South Dakota	Y	23580 FQ	37300 AW	54420 TQ	SDBLS	10/01-12/01
Postsecondary	Sioux Falls MSA, SD	Y	27420 FQ	40920 AW	57920 TQ	SDBLS	10/01-12/01
Postsecondary	Tennessee	Y	20890 FQ	33690 AW	47190 TQ	TNBLS	10/01-12/01
Postsecondary	Chattanooga MSA, TN-GA	Y	19760 FQ	33040 AW	46800 TQ	TNBLS	10/01-12/01
Postsecondary	Clarksville-Hopkinsville MSA, TN-KY	Y	14470 FQ	25280 AW	43000 TQ	TNBLS	10/01-12/01
Postsecondary	Johnson City-Kingsport-Bristol MSA, TN-VA	Y	20900 FQ	33090 AW	46280 TQ	TNBLS	10/01-12/01
Postsecondary	Knoxville MSA, TN	Y	29580 FQ	46710 AW	68220 TQ	TNBLS	10/01-12/01
Postsecondary	Memphis MSA, TN-AR-MS	Y	19460 FQ	30170 AW	44020 TQ	TNBLS	10/01-12/01
Postsecondary	Nashville MSA, TN	Y	25180 FQ	34960 AW	48420 TQ	TNBLS	10/01-12/01
Postsecondary	Texas	Y	19350 FQ	39780 AW	67350 TQ	TXBLS	10/01-12/01
Postsecondary	Amarillo MSA, TX	Y	18530 FQ	42860 AW	65070 TQ	TXBLS	10/01-12/01
Postsecondary	Austin-San Marcos MSA, TX	Y	20610 FQ	38640 AW	64530 TQ	TXBLS	10/01-12/01
Postsecondary	Beaumont-Port Arthur MSA, TX	Y	28850 FQ	35300 AW	43770 TQ	TXBLS	10/01-12/01
Postsecondary	Corpus Christi MSA, TX	Y	20640 FQ	37480 AW	62630 TQ	TXBLS	10/01-12/01
Postsecondary	Dallas PMSA, TX	Y	29240 FQ	51830 AW	82430 TQ	TXBLS	10/01-12/01
Postsecondary	El Paso MSA, TX	Y	17450 FQ	25480 AW	33890 TQ	TXBLS	10/01-12/01
Postsecondary	Fort Worth-Arlington PMSA, TX	Y	24590 FQ	37840 AW	67290 TQ	TXBLS	10/01-12/01
Postsecondary	Galveston-Texas City PMSA, TX	Y	18890 FQ	37940 AW	62260 TQ	TXBLS	10/01-12/01
Postsecondary	Houston PMSA, TX	Y	23310 FQ	46950 AW	70600 TQ	TXBLS	10/01-12/01
Postsecondary	Killeen-Temple MSA, TX	Y	26850 FQ	36210 AW	44690 TQ	TXBLS	10/01-12/01
Postsecondary	Longview-Marshall MSA, TX	Y	13330 FQ	29370 AW	44530 TQ	TXBLS	10/01-12/01
Postsecondary	Lubbock MSA, TX	Y	20070 FQ	28100 AW	35800 TQ	TXBLS	10/01-12/01
Postsecondary	McAllen-Edinburg-Mission MSA, TX	Y	11460 FQ	19860 AW	34660 TQ	TXBLS	10/01-12/01
Postsecondary	Odessa-Midland MSA, TX	Y	16240 FQ	30240 AW	49980 TQ	TXBLS	10/01-12/01
Postsecondary	San Antonio MSA, TX	Y	19270 FQ	32060 AW	60790 TQ	TXBLS	10/01-12/01
Postsecondary	Tyler MSA, TX	Y	15500 FQ	31290 AW	56210 TQ	TXBLS	10/01-12/01
Postsecondary	Utah	Y	24200 FQ	40330 AW	57590 TQ	UTBLS	10/01-12/01
Postsecondary	Provo-Orem MSA, UT	Y	21250 FQ	38770 AW	58000 TQ	UTBLS	10/01-12/01
Postsecondary	Salt Lake City-Ogden MSA, UT	Y	26350 FQ	41870 AW	58730 TQ	UTBLS	10/01-12/01
Postsecondary	Vermont	Y	29500 FQ	42820 AW	60700 TQ	VTBLS	10/01-12/01
Postsecondary	Burlington MSA, VT	Y	30420 FQ	43770 AW	62220 TQ	VTBLS	10/01-12/01
Postsecondary	Virginia	Y	25290 FQ	37550 AW	51970 TQ	VABLS	10/01-12/01
Postsecondary	Lynchburg MSA, VA	Y	19770 FQ	32150 AW	47840 TQ	VABLS	10/01-12/01
Postsecondary	Norfolk-Virginia Beach-Newport News MSA, VA-NC	Y	26730 FQ	35840 AW	44620 TQ	VABLS	10/01-12/01
Postsecondary	Richmond-Petersburg MSA, VA	Y	22570 FQ	35090 AW	50430 TQ	VABLS	10/01-12/01
Postsecondary	Washington	Y	23400 FQ	43880 AW	79960 TQ	WABLS	10/01-12/01
Postsecondary	Bremerton PMSA, WA	Y	14350 FQ	36280 AW	58880 TQ	WABLS	10/01-12/01
Postsecondary	Olympia PMSA, WA	Y	23970 FQ	37050 AW	55060 TQ	WABLS	10/01-12/01
Postsecondary	Richland-Kennewick-Pasco MSA, WA	Y	22790 FQ	44990 AW	71330 TQ	WABLS	10/01-12/01
Postsecondary	Seattle-Bellevue-Everett PMSA, WA	Y	24510 FQ	48850 AW	87070 TQ	WABLS	10/01-12/01
Postsecondary	Spokane MSA, WA	Y	29290 FQ	42530 AW	56040 TQ	WABLS	10/01-12/01
Postsecondary	Tacoma PMSA, WA	Y	20790 FQ	34280 AW	60110 TQ	WABLS	10/01-12/01
Postsecondary	Yakima MSA, WA	Y	21450 FQ	43780 AW	64250 TQ	WABLS	10/01-12/01
Postsecondary	West Virginia	Y	12830 FQ	32210 AW	46410 TQ	WVBLS	10/01-12/01
Postsecondary	Charleston MSA, WV	Y	17420 FQ	34630 AW	47970 TQ	WVBLS	10/01-12/01
Postsecondary	Huntington-Ashland MSA, WV-KY-OH	Y	21410 FQ	37530 AW	53720 TQ	WVBLS	10/01-12/01

AAW	Average annual wage	**AOH**	Average offered, high	**ASH**	Average starting, high	**H**	Hourly	**M**	Monthly	**S**	Special: hourly and annual
AE	Average entry wage	**AOL**	Average offered, low	**ASL**	Average starting, low	**HI**	Highest wage paid	**MTC**	Median total compensation	**TQ**	Third quartile wage
AEX	Average experienced wage	**APH**	Average pay, high range	**AW**	Average wage paid	**HR**	High end range	**MW**	Median wage paid	**W**	Weekly
AO	Average offered	**APL**	Average pay, low range	**FQ**	First quartile wage	**LR**	Low end range	**SQ**	Second quartile wage	**Y**	Yearly

Occupation/Type/Industry	Location	Per	Low	Mid	High	Source	Date
Vocational Education Teacher							
Postsecondary	Wisconsin	Y	30680 FQ	52880 AW	73310 TQ	WIBLS	10/01-12/01
Postsecondary	Appleton-Oshkosh-Neenah MSA, WI	Y	28590 FQ	49460 AW	67740 TQ	WIBLS	10/01-12/01
Postsecondary	Madison MSA, WI	Y	29010 FQ	39470 AW	73540 TQ	WIBLS	10/01-12/01
Postsecondary	Milwaukee-Waukesha PMSA, WI	Y	34510 FQ	55020 AW	71530 TQ	WIBLS	10/01-12/01
Postsecondary	Wyoming	Y	26090 FQ	48060 AW	86340 TQ	WYBLS	10/01-12/01
Postsecondary	Puerto Rico	Y	12490 FQ	22000 AW	33490 TQ	PRBLS	10/01-12/01
Secondary School	Alabama	Y	33060 FQ	44020 AW	57110 TQ	ALBLS	10/01-12/01
Secondary School	Huntsville MSA, AL	Y	32790 FQ	42690 AW	54200 TQ	ALBLS	10/01-12/01
Secondary School	Montgomery MSA, AL	Y	32340 FQ	43260 AW	56490 TQ	ALBLS	10/01-12/01
Secondary School	Alaska	Y	38340 FQ	52600 AW	69730 TQ	AKBLS	10/01-12/01
Secondary School	Arizona	Y	19580 FQ	35840 AW	52240 TQ	AZBLS	10/01-12/01
Secondary School	Phoenix-Mesa MSA, AZ	Y	28590 FQ	40830 AW	57860 TQ	AZBLS	10/01-12/01
Secondary School	Tucson MSA, AZ	Y	16040 FQ	28880 AW	42170 TQ	AZBLS	10/01-12/01
Secondary School	Arkansas	Y	28540 FQ	38460 AW	50540 TQ	ARBLS	10/01-12/01
Secondary School	Fayetteville-Springdale-Rogers MSA, AR	Y	31760 FQ	41540 AW	54320 TQ	ARBLS	10/01-12/01
Secondary School	Fort Smith MSA, AR-OK	Y	30030 FQ	40450 AW	53580 TQ	ARBLS	10/01-12/01
Secondary School	Little Rock-North Little Rock MSA, AR	Y	27590 FQ	39180 AW	53250 TQ	ARBLS	10/01-12/01
Secondary School	California	Y	34510 FQ	55030 AW	75450 TQ	CABLS	10/01-12/01
Secondary School	Bakersfield MSA, CA	Y	35850 FQ	54060 AW	69590 TQ	CABLS	10/01-12/01
Secondary School	Chico-Paradise MSA, CA	Y	30550 FQ	45130 AW	59790 TQ	CABLS	10/01-12/01
Secondary School	Fresno MSA, CA	Y	32560 FQ	52320 AW	70780 TQ	CABLS	10/01-12/01
Secondary School	Los Angeles-Long Beach PMSA, CA	Y	40270 FQ	57800 AW	74230 TQ	CABLS	10/01-12/01
Secondary School	Merced MSA, CA	Y	36920 FQ	56040 AW	81680 TQ	CABLS	10/01-12/01
Secondary School	Modesto MSA, CA	Y	30540 FQ	49540 AW	71600 TQ	CABLS	10/01-12/01
Secondary School	Oakland PMSA, CA	Y	38820 FQ	53030 AW	71640 TQ	CABLS	10/01-12/01
Secondary School	Orange County PMSA, CA	Y	37310 FQ	55340 AW	74250 TQ	CABLS	10/01-12/01
Secondary School	Riverside-San Bernardino PMSA, CA	Y	33320 FQ	53790 AW	73410 TQ	CABLS	10/01-12/01
Secondary School	Sacramento PMSA, CA	Y	34900 FQ	52330 AW	70950 TQ	CABLS	10/01-12/01
Secondary School	Salinas MSA, CA	Y	47100 FQ	59350 AW	70350 TQ	CABLS	10/01-12/01
Secondary School	San Diego MSA, CA	Y	35650 FQ	54760 AW	73600 TQ	CABLS	10/01-12/01
Secondary School	San Francisco PMSA, CA	Y	22320 FQ	46740 AW	70820 TQ	CABLS	10/01-12/01
Secondary School	San Luis Obispo-Atascadero-Paso Robles MSA, CA	Y	24140 FQ	55460 AW	75470 TQ	CABLS	10/01-12/01
Secondary School	Santa Rosa PMSA, CA	Y	33780 FQ	52980 AW	73290 TQ	CABLS	10/01-12/01
Secondary School	Stockton-Lodi MSA, CA	Y	33670 FQ	53330 AW	70080 TQ	CABLS	10/01-12/01
Secondary School	Vallejo-Fairfield-Napa PMSA, CA	Y	37860 FQ	59940 AW	86420 TQ	CABLS	10/01-12/01
Secondary School	Ventura PMSA, CA	Y	37590 FQ	51560 AW	69630 TQ	CABLS	10/01-12/01
Secondary School	Colorado	Y	24730 FQ	40340 AW	58530 TQ	COBLS	10/01-12/01
Secondary School	Denver PMSA, CO	Y	31430 FQ	47670 AW	67290 TQ	COBLS	10/01-12/01
Secondary School	Connecticut	Y	23410 FQ	55040 AW	85450 TQ	CTBLS	10/01-12/01
Secondary School	Bridgeport PMSA, CT	Y	19450 FQ	45690 AW	71370 TQ	CTBLS	10/01-12/01
Secondary School	Danbury PMSA, CT	Y	37560 FQ	52780 AW	70110 TQ	CTBLS	10/01-12/01
Secondary School	Hartford MSA, CT	Y	31490 FQ	54120 AW	73880 TQ	CTBLS	10/01-12/01
Secondary School	New Haven-Meriden PMSA, CT	Y	36390 FQ	57090 AW	74060 TQ	CTBLS	10/01-12/01
Secondary School	New London-Norwich MSA, CT-RI	Y	36850 FQ	54810 AW	70870 TQ	CTBLS	10/01-12/01
Secondary School	Delaware	Y	38270 FQ	53850 AW	74100 TQ	DEBLS	10/01-12/01
Secondary School	Wilmington-Newark PMSA, DE-MD	Y	37670 FQ	53740 AW	75100 TQ	DEBLS	10/01-12/01
Secondary School	Washington PMSA, DC-MD-VA-WV	Y	31570 FQ	50830 AW	75750 TQ	DCBLS	10/01-12/01
Secondary School	Florida	Y	30400 FQ	45090 AW	65060 TQ	FLBLS	10/01-12/01
Secondary School	Orlando MSA, FL	Y	31550 FQ	43910 AW	58240 TQ	FLBLS	10/01-12/01
Secondary School	Pensacola MSA, FL	Y	33110 FQ	46460 AW	66130 TQ	FLBLS	10/01-12/01
Secondary School	Tampa-St. Petersburg-Clearwater MSA, FL	Y	33040 FQ	45900 AW	66450 TQ	FLBLS	10/01-12/01
Secondary School	Georgia	Y	32780 FQ	46150 AW	63230 TQ	GABLS	10/01-12/01
Secondary School	Atlanta MSA, GA	Y	32830 FQ	45610 AW	61870 TQ	GABLS	10/01-12/01
Secondary School	Augusta-Aiken MSA, GA-SC	Y	29880 FQ	39130 AW	52520 TQ	GABLS	10/01-12/01
Secondary School	Columbus MSA, GA-AL	Y	34700 FQ	45840 AW	58730 TQ	GABLS	10/01-12/01
Secondary School	Macon MSA, GA	Y	32420 FQ	44300 AW	57280 TQ	GABLS	10/01-12/01
Secondary School	Hawaii	Y	31660 FQ	46100 AW	65340 TQ	HIBLS	10/01-12/01
Secondary School	Honolulu MSA, HI	Y	32460 FQ	47370 AW	66550 TQ	HIBLS	10/01-12/01

AAW	Average annual wage	**AOH**	Average offered, high	**ASH**	Average starting, high	**H**	Hourly	**M**	Monthly	**S**	Special: hourly and annual
AE	Average entry wage	**AOL**	Average offered, low	**ASL**	Average starting, low	**HI**	Highest wage paid	**MTC**	Median total compensation	**TQ**	Third quartile wage
AEX	Average experienced wage	**APH**	Average pay, high range	**AW**	Average wage paid	**HR**	High end range	**MW**	Median wage paid	**W**	Weekly
AO	Average offered	**APL**	Average pay, low range	**FQ**	First quartile wage	**LR**	Low end range	**SQ**	Second quartile wage	**Y**	Yearly

Occupation/Type/Industry	Location	Per	Low	Mid	High	Source	Date
Vocational Education Teacher							
Secondary School	Illinois	Y	29310 FQ	52390 AW	85690 TQ	ILBLS	10/01-12/01
Secondary School	Champaign-Urbana MSA, IL	Y	27350 FQ	42600 AW	60740 TQ	ILBLS	10/01-12/01
Secondary School	Chicago PMSA, IL	Y	35160 FQ	63280 AW	91540 TQ	ILBLS	10/01-12/01
Secondary School	Peoria-Pekin MSA, IL	Y	30600 FQ	42260 AW	56600 TQ	ILBLS	10/01-12/01
Secondary School	Rockford MSA, IL	Y	29770 FQ	43770 AW	64360 TQ	ILBLS	10/01-12/01
Secondary School	Springfield MSA, IL	Y	26300 FQ	44920 AW	69210 TQ	ILBLS	10/01-12/01
Secondary School	Indiana	Y	31470 FQ	46360 AW	61900 TQ	INBLS	10/01-12/01
Secondary School	Elkhart-Goshen MSA, IN	Y	32700 FQ	45060 AW	57190 TQ	INBLS	10/01-12/01
Secondary School	Fort Wayne MSA, IN	Y	35040 FQ	46030 AW	57890 TQ	INBLS	10/01-12/01
Secondary School	Gary PMSA, IN	Y	33860 FQ	47980 AW	59940 TQ	INBLS	10/01-12/01
Secondary School	Indianapolis MSA, IN	Y	29210 FQ	48560 AW	70310 TQ	INBLS	10/01-12/01
Secondary School	Lafayette MSA, IN	Y	36150 FQ	52270 AW	68470 TQ	INBLS	10/01-12/01
Secondary School	Iowa	Y	26320 FQ	37220 AW	50750 TQ	IABLS	10/01-12/01
Secondary School	Cedar Rapids MSA, IA	Y	28990 FQ	37830 AW	48600 TQ	IABLS	10/01-12/01
Secondary School	Davenport-Moline-Rock Island MSA, IA-IL	Y	23820 FQ	40870 AW	64090 TQ	IABLS	10/01-12/01
Secondary School	Des Moines MSA, IA	Y	29830 FQ	41810 AW	55880 TQ	IABLS	10/01-12/01
Secondary School	Kansas	Y	29210 FQ	39180 AW	51780 TQ	KSBLS	10/01-12/01
Secondary School	Wichita MSA, KS	Y	29690 FQ	38930 AW	51360 TQ	KSBLS	10/01-12/01
Secondary School	Kentucky	Y	30810 FQ	44200 AW	56530 TQ	KYBLS	10/01-12/01
Secondary School	Louisiana	Y	26990 FQ	36900 AW	47000 TQ	LABLS	10/01-12/01
Secondary School	Lafayette MSA, LA	Y	30020 FQ	37780 AW	46550 TQ	LABLS	10/01-12/01
Secondary School	New Orleans MSA, LA	Y	28840 FQ	38850 AW	47400 TQ	LABLS	10/01-12/01
Secondary School	Shreveport-Bossier City MSA, LA	Y	27270 FQ	36340 AW	46690 TQ	LABLS	10/01-12/01
Secondary School	Maine	Y	30280 FQ	41460 AW	53220 TQ	MEBLS	10/01-12/01
Secondary School	Portland MSA, ME	Y	34370 FQ	43370 AW	54240 TQ	MEBLS	10/01-12/01
Secondary School	Maryland	Y	26760 FQ	46160 AW	71710 TQ	MDBLS	10/01-12/01
Secondary School	Baltimore PMSA, MD	Y	23330 FQ	47730 AW	88900 TQ	MDBLS	10/01-12/01
Secondary School	Massachusetts	Y	31500 FQ	48780 AW	67490 TQ	MABLS	10/01-12/01
Secondary School	Boston PMSA, MA-NH	Y	30540 FQ	47210 AW	66860 TQ	MABLS	10/01-12/01
Secondary School	Lawrence PMSA, MA-NH	Y	31680 FQ	49270 AW	68410 TQ	MABLS	10/01-12/01
Secondary School	Lowell PMSA, MA-NH	Y	42720 FQ	56910 AW	70710 TQ	MABLS	10/01-12/01
Secondary School	New Bedford PMSA, MA	Y	39270 FQ	50560 AW	60140 TQ	MABLS	10/01-12/01
Secondary School	Springfield MSA, MA	Y	32080 FQ	51320 AW	68960 TQ	MABLS	10/01-12/01
Secondary School	Michigan	Y	29610 FQ	48170 AW	68880 TQ	MIBLS	10/01-12/01
Secondary School	Ann Arbor PMSA, MI	Y	28230 FQ	56000 AW	73320 TQ	MIBLS	10/01-12/01
Secondary School	Detroit PMSA, MI	Y	29380 FQ	45000 AW	67670 TQ	MIBLS	10/01-12/01
Secondary School	Grand Rapids-Muskegon-Holland MSA, MI	Y	30630 FQ	53250 AW	71180 TQ	MIBLS	10/01-12/01
Secondary School	Lansing-East Lansing MSA, MI	Y	47740 FQ	59550 AW	70760 TQ	MIBLS	10/01-12/01
Secondary School	Saginaw-Bay City-Midland MSA, MI	Y	46990 FQ	55470 AW	70040 TQ	MIBLS	10/01-12/01
Secondary School	Minnesota	Y	29790 FQ	45170 AW	64010 TQ	MNBLS	10/01-12/01
Secondary School	Duluth-Superior MSA, MN-WI	Y	27870 FQ	41930 AW	57480 TQ	MNBLS	10/01-12/01
Secondary School	Minneapolis-St. Paul MSA, MN-WI	Y	31960 FQ	47970 AW	67100 TQ	MNBLS	10/01-12/01
Secondary School	St. Cloud MSA, MN	Y	34000 FQ	48480 AW	63590 TQ	MNBLS	10/01-12/01
Secondary School	Mississippi	Y	25700 FQ	34890 AW	45800 TQ	MSBLS	10/01-12/01
Secondary School	Biloxi-Gulfport-Pascagoula MSA, MS	Y	26580 FQ	36250 AW	47230 TQ	MSBLS	10/01-12/01
Secondary School	Jackson MSA, MS	Y	23250 FQ	32460 AW	44470 TQ	MSBLS	10/01-12/01
Secondary School	Missouri	Y	22860 FQ	37130 AW	56630 TQ	MOBLS	10/01-12/01
Secondary School	Kansas City MSA, MO-KS	Y	24590 FQ	38620 AW	54400 TQ	MOBLS	10/01-12/01
Secondary School	St. Louis MSA, MO-IL	Y	29380 FQ	47640 AW	69250 TQ	MOBLS	10/01-12/01
Secondary School	Springfield MSA, MO	Y	22500 FQ	35030 AW	49730 TQ	MOBLS	10/01-12/01
Secondary School	Montana	Y	20700 FQ	31980 AW	44370 TQ	MTBLS	10/01-12/01
Secondary School	Nebraska	Y	26930 FQ	38770 AW	51130 TQ	NEBLS	10/01-12/01
Secondary School	Omaha MSA, NE-IA	Y	27280 FQ	38840 AW	53950 TQ	NEBLS	10/01-12/01
Secondary School	Nevada	Y	21800 FQ	41620 AW	56580 TQ	NVBLS	10/01-12/01
Secondary School	New Hampshire	Y	21420 FQ	35690 AW	52180 TQ	NHBLS	10/01-12/01
Secondary School	New Jersey	Y	36750 FQ	53250 AW	72110 TQ	NJBLS	10/01-12/01
Secondary School	Middlesex-Somerset-Hunterdon PMSA, NJ	Y	37090 FQ	55450 AW	72790 TQ	NJBLS	10/01-12/01
Secondary School	Monmouth-Ocean PMSA, NJ	Y	39030 FQ	53310 AW	72500 TQ	NJBLS	10/01-12/01
Secondary School	Newark PMSA, NJ	Y	41330 FQ	58750 AW	74160 TQ	NJBLS	10/01-12/01
Secondary School	Trenton PMSA, NJ	Y	37270 FQ	52250 AW	70130 TQ	NJBLS	10/01-12/01
Secondary School	New Mexico	Y	26400 FQ	37520 AW	48890 TQ	NMBLS	10/01-12/01
Secondary School	Albuquerque MSA, NM	Y	31200 FQ	38460 AW	47300 TQ	NMBLS	10/01-12/01
Secondary School	New York	Y	31140 FQ	51140 AW	78400 TQ	NYBLS	10/01-12/01

AAW Average annual wage; **AE** Average entry wage; **AEX** Average experienced wage; **AO** Average offered; **AOH** Average offered, high; **AOL** Average offered, low; **APH** Average pay, high range; **APL** Average pay, low range; **ASH** Average starting, high; **ASL** Average starting, low; **AW** Average wage paid; **FQ** First quartile wage; **H** Hourly; **HI** Highest wage paid; **HR** High end range; **LR** Low end range; **M** Monthly; **MTC** Median total compensation; **MW** Median wage paid; **SQ** Second quartile wage; **S** Special: hourly and annual; **TQ** Third quartile wage; **W** Weekly; **Y** Yearly

Occupation/Type/Industry	Location	Per	Low	Mid	High	Source	Date
Vocational Education Teacher							
Secondary School	Albany-Schenectady-Troy MSA, NY	Y	30620 FQ	50360 AW	71170 TQ	NYBLS	10/01-12/01
Secondary School	Binghamton MSA, NY	Y	34740 FQ	50950 AW	67710 TQ	NYBLS	10/01-12/01
Secondary School	Buffalo-Niagara Falls MSA, NY	Y	29490 FQ	43300 AW	67950 TQ	NYBLS	10/01-12/01
Secondary School	Dutchess County PMSA, NY	Y	29980 FQ	51980 AW	85490 TQ	NYBLS	10/01-12/01
Secondary School	Nassau-Suffolk PMSA, NY	Y	39060 FQ	63310 AW	88200 TQ	NYBLS	10/01-12/01
Secondary School	New York PMSA, NY	Y	40760 FQ	66310 AW	94860 TQ	NYBLS	10/01-12/01
Secondary School	Rochester MSA, NY	Y	33000 FQ	52380 AW	77320 TQ	NYBLS	10/01-12/01
Secondary School	Syracuse MSA, NY	Y	31770 FQ	42560 AW	58420 TQ	NYBLS	10/01-12/01
Secondary School	Utica-Rome MSA, NY	Y	31550 FQ	55220 AW	89270 TQ	NYBLS	10/01-12/01
Secondary School	North Carolina	Y	28500 FQ	40810 AW	55320 TQ	NCBLS	10/01-12/01
Secondary School	Charlotte-Gastonia-Rock Hill MSA, NC-SC	Y	31280 FQ	43910 AW	56960 TQ	NCBLS	10/01-12/01
Secondary School	Fayetteville MSA, NC	Y	26490 FQ	38200 AW	51050 TQ	NCBLS	10/01-12/01
Secondary School	Greensboro-Winston-Salem-High Point MSA, NC	Y	26840 FQ	39040 AW	54930 TQ	NCBLS	10/01-12/01
Secondary School	Hickory-Morganton-Lenoir MSA, NC	Y	30680 FQ	38820 AW	46410 TQ	NCBLS	10/01-12/01
Secondary School	Raleigh-Durham-Chapel Hill MSA, NC	Y	32600 FQ	46290 AW	58600 TQ	NCBLS	10/01-12/01
Secondary School	Wilmington MSA, NC	Y	26390 FQ	39570 AW	53600 TQ	NCBLS	10/01-12/01
Secondary School	North Dakota	Y	21590 FQ	33350 AW	45470 TQ	NDBLS	10/01-12/01
Secondary School	Fargo-Moorhead MSA, ND-MN	Y	26710 FQ	38240 AW	51620 TQ	NDBLS	10/01-12/01
Secondary School	Ohio	Y	33130 FQ	47690 AW	62200 TQ	OHBLS	10/01-12/01
Secondary School	Akron PMSA, OH	Y	33610 FQ	46690 AW	59260 TQ	OHBLS	10/01-12/01
Secondary School	Canton-Massillon MSA, OH	Y	33990 FQ	48690 AW	63060 TQ	OHBLS	10/01-12/01
Secondary School	Cincinnati PMSA, OH-KY-IN	Y	35850 FQ	46720 AW	59320 TQ	OHBLS	10/01-12/01
Secondary School	Cleveland-Lorain-Elyria PMSA, OH	Y	35640 FQ	54230 AW	72470 TQ	OHBLS	10/01-12/01
Secondary School	Columbus MSA, OH	Y	36390 FQ	51570 AW	69000 TQ	OHBLS	10/01-12/01
Secondary School	Dayton-Springfield MSA, OH	Y	32260 FQ	46720 AW	59690 TQ	OHBLS	10/01-12/01
Secondary School	Mansfield MSA, OH	Y	34030 FQ	48710 AW	58440 TQ	OHBLS	10/01-12/01
Secondary School	Toledo MSA, OH	Y	39310 FQ	50910 AW	65170 TQ	OHBLS	10/01-12/01
Secondary School	Youngstown-Warren MSA, OH	Y	30210 FQ	42700 AW	55750 TQ	OHBLS	10/01-12/01
Secondary School	Oklahoma	Y	30280 FQ	39750 AW	52640 TQ	OKBLS	10/01-12/01
Secondary School	Oklahoma City MSA, OK	Y	29690 FQ	42660 AW	58380 TQ	OKBLS	10/01-12/01
Secondary School	Tulsa MSA, OK	Y	26280 FQ	37680 AW	49530 TQ	OKBLS	10/01-12/01
Secondary School	Oregon	Y	31190 FQ	45860 AW	58820 TQ	ORBLS	10/01-12/01
Secondary School	Eugene-Springfield MSA, OR	Y	29820 FQ	44310 AW	57380 TQ	ORBLS	10/01-12/01
Secondary School	Medford-Ashland MSA, OR	Y	31340 FQ	45080 AW	57790 TQ	ORBLS	10/01-12/01
Secondary School	Portland-Vancouver PMSA, OR-WA	Y	30500 FQ	46150 AW	60520 TQ	ORBLS	10/01-12/01
Secondary School	Salem PMSA, OR	Y	31570 FQ	46070 AW	58430 TQ	ORBLS	10/01-12/01
Secondary School	Pennsylvania	Y	29010 FQ	47810 AW	67590 TQ	PABLS	10/01-12/01
Secondary School	Allentown-Bethlehem-Easton MSA, PA	Y	25330 FQ	48200 AW	69970 TQ	PABLS	10/01-12/01
Secondary School	Erie MSA, PA	Y	40530 FQ	57070 AW	69660 TQ	PABLS	10/01-12/01
Secondary School	Harrisburg-Lebanon-Carlisle MSA, PA	Y	23260 FQ	44180 AW	62560 TQ	PABLS	10/01-12/01
Secondary School	Johnstown MSA, PA	Y	28870 FQ	41920 AW	55790 TQ	PABLS	10/01-12/01
Secondary School	Lancaster MSA, PA	Y	41210 FQ	48710 AW	55960 TQ	PABLS	10/01-12/01
Secondary School	Philadelphia PMSA, PA-NJ	Y	32510 FQ	48490 AW	66620 TQ	PABLS	10/01-12/01
Secondary School	Pittsburgh MSA, PA	Y	28320 FQ	49300 AW	70470 TQ	PABLS	10/01-12/01
Secondary School	Reading MSA, PA	Y	30930 FQ	47590 AW	67300 TQ	PABLS	10/01-12/01
Secondary School	Scranton-Wilkes-Barre-Hazleton MSA, PA	Y	26220 FQ	46030 AW	66970 TQ	PABLS	10/01-12/01
Secondary School	York MSA, PA	Y	32330 FQ	47740 AW	65890 TQ	PABLS	10/01-12/01
Secondary School	Rhode Island	Y	34860 FQ	52700 AW	68240 TQ	RIBLS	10/01-12/01
Secondary School	Providence-Fall River-Warwick MSA, RI-MA	Y	33280 FQ	50630 AW	67390 TQ	RIBLS	10/01-12/01
Secondary School	South Carolina	Y	29290 FQ	40490 AW	54750 TQ	SCBLS	10/01-12/01
Secondary School	Charleston-North Charleston MSA, SC	Y	30340 FQ	42920 AW	57500 TQ	SCBLS	10/01-12/01
Secondary School	Columbia MSA, SC	Y	27120 FQ	37440 AW	51240 TQ	SCBLS	10/01-12/01
Secondary School	Greenville-Spartanburg-Anderson MSA, SC	Y	31870 FQ	42800 AW	56270 TQ	SCBLS	10/01-12/01
Secondary School	South Dakota	Y	24640 FQ	31860 AW	41200 TQ	SDBLS	10/01-12/01
Secondary School	Sioux Falls MSA, SD	Y	23670 FQ	32140 AW	40380 TQ	SDBLS	10/01-12/01
Secondary School	Tennessee	Y	24450 FQ	36220 AW	51280 TQ	TNBLS	10/01-12/01

AAW	Average annual wage	**AOH**	Average offered, high	**ASH**	Average starting, high	**H**	Hourly	**M**	Monthly	**S**	Special: hourly and annual
AE	Average entry wage	**AOL**	Average offered, low	**ASL**	Average starting, low	**HI**	Highest wage paid	**MTC**	Median total compensation	**TQ**	Third quartile wage
AEX	Average experienced wage	**APH**	Average pay, high range	**AW**	Average wage paid	**HR**	High end range	**MW**	Median wage paid	**W**	Weekly
AO	Average offered	**APL**	Average pay, low range	**FQ**	First quartile wage	**LR**	Low end range	**SQ**	Second quartile wage	**Y**	Yearly

Occupation/Type/Industry	Location	Per	Low	Mid	High	Source	Date
Vocational Education Teacher							
Secondary School	Chattanooga MSA, TN-GA	Y	13990 FQ	38540 AW	56750 TQ	TNBLS	10/01-12/01
Secondary School	Johnson City-Kingsport-Bristol MSA, TN-VA	Y	28460 FQ	37490 AW	50000 TQ	TNBLS	10/01-12/01
Secondary School	Knoxville MSA, TN	Y	29920 FQ	41060 AW	55790 TQ	TNBLS	10/01-12/01
Secondary School	Memphis MSA, TN-AR-MS	Y	17750 FQ	38390 AW	54490 TQ	TNBLS	10/01-12/01
Secondary School	Nashville MSA, TN	Y	24780 FQ	34930 AW	46440 TQ	TNBLS	10/01-12/01
Secondary School	Texas	Y	30760 FQ	43720 AW	57620 TQ	TXBLS	10/01-12/01
Secondary School	Austin-San Marcos MSA, TX	Y	30830 FQ	41780 AW	56460 TQ	TXBLS	10/01-12/01
Secondary School	Beaumont-Port Arthur MSA, TX	Y	28850 FQ	39910 AW	53770 TQ	TXBLS	10/01-12/01
Secondary School	Brazoria PMSA, TX	Y	30830 FQ	39470 AW	47910 TQ	TXBLS	10/01-12/01
Secondary School	Brownsville-Harlingen-San Benito MSA, TX	Y	31520 FQ	42310 AW	54990 TQ	TXBLS	10/01-12/01
Secondary School	Corpus Christi MSA, TX	Y	33720 FQ	48690 AW	65120 TQ	TXBLS	10/01-12/01
Secondary School	Dallas PMSA, TX	Y	31470 FQ	44570 AW	61520 TQ	TXBLS	10/01-12/01
Secondary School	El Paso MSA, TX	Y	30780 FQ	40870 AW	53380 TQ	TXBLS	10/01-12/01
Secondary School	Fort Worth-Arlington PMSA, TX	Y	28500 FQ	47920 AW	73970 TQ	TXBLS	10/01-12/01
Secondary School	Galveston-Texas City PMSA, TX	Y	33190 FQ	44790 AW	57000 TQ	TXBLS	10/01-12/01
Secondary School	Houston PMSA, TX	Y	33290 FQ	45530 AW	58310 TQ	TXBLS	10/01-12/01
Secondary School	Killeen-Temple MSA, TX	Y	31850 FQ	46650 AW	75230 TQ	TXBLS	10/01-12/01
Secondary School	Longview-Marshall MSA, TX	Y	28760 FQ	39660 AW	52760 TQ	TXBLS	10/01-12/01
Secondary School	McAllen-Edinburg-Mission MSA, TX	Y	31750 FQ	44610 AW	56530 TQ	TXBLS	10/01-12/01
Secondary School	San Antonio MSA, TX	Y	32460 FQ	47340 AW	62620 TQ	TXBLS	10/01-12/01
Secondary School	Tyler MSA, TX	Y	26110 FQ	39120 AW	51500 TQ	TXBLS	10/01-12/01
Secondary School	Waco MSA, TX	Y	30300 FQ	40780 AW	54950 TQ	TXBLS	10/01-12/01
Secondary School	Utah	Y	27860 FQ	41610 AW	60140 TQ	UTBLS	10/01-12/01
Secondary School	Provo-Orem MSA, UT	Y	26870 FQ	38940 AW	49280 TQ	UTBLS	10/01-12/01
Secondary School	Salt Lake City-Ogden MSA, UT	Y	30420 FQ	44920 AW	65450 TQ	UTBLS	10/01-12/01
Secondary School	Vermont	Y	31320 FQ	43540 AW	56630 TQ	VTBLS	10/01-12/01
Secondary School	Burlington MSA, VT	Y	34930 FQ	47250 AW	58660 TQ	VTBLS	10/01-12/01
Secondary School	Virginia	Y	29490 FQ	42840 AW	58910 TQ	VABLS	10/01-12/01
Secondary School	Norfolk-Virginia Beach-Newport News MSA, VA-NC	Y	31750 FQ	42900 AW	56180 TQ	VABLS	10/01-12/01
Secondary School	Richmond-Petersburg MSA, VA	Y	34360 FQ	46280 AW	61480 TQ	VABLS	10/01-12/01
Secondary School	Washington	Y	28950 FQ	43530 AW	56980 TQ	WABLS	10/01-12/01
Secondary School	Bremerton PMSA, WA	Y	29750 FQ	42940 AW	55400 TQ	WABLS	10/01-12/01
Secondary School	Olympia PMSA, WA	Y	31010 FQ	44800 AW	57310 TQ	WABLS	10/01-12/01
Secondary School	Richland-Kennewick-Pasco MSA, WA	Y	28630 FQ	41990 AW	55790 TQ	WABLS	10/01-12/01
Secondary School	Seattle-Bellevue-Everett PMSA, WA	Y	27240 FQ	43480 AW	57780 TQ	WABLS	10/01-12/01
Secondary School	Spokane MSA, WA	Y	30910 FQ	45110 AW	58240 TQ	WABLS	10/01-12/01
Secondary School	Tacoma PMSA, WA	Y	29740 FQ	42060 AW	55880 TQ	WABLS	10/01-12/01
Secondary School	Yakima MSA, WA	Y	29990 FQ	43050 AW	55920 TQ	WABLS	10/01-12/01
Secondary School	West Virginia	Y	29720 FQ	38260 AW	46830 TQ	WVBLS	10/01-12/01
Secondary School	Huntington-Ashland MSA, WV-KY-OH	Y	27790 FQ	37260 AW	45880 TQ	WVBLS	10/01-12/01
Secondary School	Wisconsin	Y	29170 FQ	43600 AW	57620 TQ	WIBLS	10/01-12/01
Secondary School	Appleton-Oshkosh-Neenah MSA, WI	Y	26870 FQ	43090 AW	56870 TQ	WIBLS	10/01-12/01
Secondary School	Madison MSA, WI	Y	26080 FQ	39940 AW	55810 TQ	WIBLS	10/01-12/01
Secondary School	Milwaukee-Waukesha PMSA, WI	Y	32060 FQ	46920 AW	60960 TQ	WIBLS	10/01-12/01
Secondary School	Racine PMSA, WI	Y	45220 FQ	50900 AW	57790 TQ	WIBLS	10/01-12/01
Secondary School	Wyoming	Y	24610 FQ	36230 AW	46660 TQ	WYBLS	10/01-12/01
Secondary School	Puerto Rico	Y	18850 FQ	23190 AW	28810 TQ	PRBLS	10/01-12/01
Secondary School	Virgin Islands	Y	23650 FQ	35060 AW	53000 TQ	VIBLS	10/01-12/01
Waiter and Waitress	Alabama	H	5.49 FQ	6.34 AW	7.22 TQ	ALBLS	10/01-12/01
	Birmingham MSA, AL	H	5.52 FQ	6.33 AW	7.01 TQ	ALBLS	10/01-12/01
	Huntsville MSA, AL	H	5.43 FQ	6.48 AW	8.59 TQ	ALBLS	10/01-12/01
	Mobile MSA, AL	H	5.47 FQ	6.14 AW	6.95 TQ	ALBLS	10/01-12/01
	Montgomery MSA, AL	H	5.63 FQ	6.76 AW	8.25 TQ	ALBLS	10/01-12/01
	Alaska	H	5.89 FQ	7.04 AW	8.52 TQ	AKBLS	10/01-12/01
	Anchorage MSA, AK	H	5.87 FQ	7.04 AW	8.65 TQ	AKBLS	10/01-12/01
	Arizona	H	5.46 FQ	6.77 AW	8.48 TQ	AZBLS	10/01-12/01

AAW Average annual wage **AE** Average entry wage **AEX** Average experienced wage **AO** Average offered **AOH** Average offered, high **AOL** Average offered, low **APH** Average pay, high range **APL** Average pay, low range **ASH** Average starting, high **ASL** Average starting, low **AW** Average wage paid **FQ** First quartile wage **H** Hourly **HI** Highest wage paid **HR** High end range **LR** Low end range **M** Monthly **MTC** Median total compensation **MW** Median wage paid **SQ** Second quartile wage **S** Special: hourly and annual **TQ** Third quartile wage **W** Weekly **Y** Yearly

Occupation/Type/Industry	Location	Per	Low	Mid	High	Source	Date
Waiter and Waitress	Phoenix-Mesa MSA, AZ	H	5.46 FQ	6.98 AW	9.52 TQ	AZBLS	10/01-12/01
	Tucson MSA, AZ	H	5.40 FQ	6.40 AW	7.15 TQ	AZBLS	10/01-12/01
	Arkansas	H	5.54 FQ	6.65 AW	8.49 TQ	ARBLS	10/01-12/01
	Fayetteville-Springdale-Rogers MSA, AR	H	5.56 FQ	6.24 AW	7.01 TQ	ARBLS	10/01-12/01
	Fort Smith MSA, AR-OK	H	5.50 FQ	6.64 AW	9.04 TQ	ARBLS	10/01-12/01
	Little Rock-North Little Rock MSA, AR	H	5.61 FQ	6.71 AW	8.46 TQ	ARBLS	10/01-12/01
	California	H	6.38 FQ	7.91 AW	11.31 TQ	CABLS	10/01-12/01
	Bakersfield MSA, CA	H	6.42 FQ	7.52 AW	8.42 TQ	CABLS	10/01-12/01
	Chico-Paradise MSA, CA	H	6.43 FQ	7.93 AW	9.12 TQ	CABLS	10/01-12/01
	Fresno MSA, CA	H	6.33 FQ	7.15 AW	8.06 TQ	CABLS	10/01-12/01
	Los Angeles-Long Beach PMSA, CA	H	6.36 FQ	7.45 AW	8.96 TQ	CABLS	10/01-12/01
	Merced MSA, CA	H	6.34 FQ	7.48 AW	10.11 TQ	CABLS	10/01-12/01
	Modesto MSA, CA	H	6.38 FQ	7.57 AW	10.24 TQ	CABLS	10/01-12/01
	Oakland PMSA, CA	H	6.40 FQ	8.07 AW	11.29 TQ	CABLS	10/01-12/01
	Orange County PMSA, CA	H	6.37 FQ	7.64 AW	9.33 TQ	CABLS	10/01-12/01
	Redding MSA, CA	H	6.34 FQ	6.98 AW	8.11 TQ	CABLS	10/01-12/01
	Riverside-San Bernardino PMSA, CA	H	6.36 FQ	7.31 AW	8.47 TQ	CABLS	10/01-12/01
	Sacramento PMSA, CA	H	6.34 FQ	8.29 AW	10.37 TQ	CABLS	10/01-12/01
	Salinas MSA, CA	H	6.44 FQ	8.30 AW	12.69 TQ	CABLS	10/01-12/01
	San Diego MSA, CA	H	6.41 FQ	8.52 AW	14.27 TQ	CABLS	10/01-12/01
	San Francisco PMSA, CA	H	6.43 FQ	8.71 AW	15.17 TQ	CABLS	10/01-12/01
	San Jose PMSA, CA	H	6.42 FQ	8.00 AW	11.36 TQ	CABLS	10/01-12/01
	San Luis Obispo-Atascadero-Paso Robles MSA, CA	H	6.46 FQ	10.02 AW	14.20 TQ	CABLS	10/01-12/01
	Santa Barbara-Santa Maria-Lompoc MSA, CA	H	6.39 FQ	9.03 AW	15.54 TQ	CABLS	10/01-12/01
	Santa Cruz-Watsonville PMSA, CA	H	6.38 FQ	9.16 AW	16.67 TQ	CABLS	10/01-12/01
	Santa Rosa PMSA, CA	H	6.38 FQ	8.24 AW	12.95 TQ	CABLS	10/01-12/01
	Stockton-Lodi MSA, CA	H	6.33 FQ	6.99 AW	8.13 TQ	CABLS	10/01-12/01
	Vallejo-Fairfield-Napa PMSA, CA	H	6.39 FQ	8.90 AW	15.09 TQ	CABLS	10/01-12/01
	Ventura PMSA, CA	H	6.41 FQ	8.59 AW	14.11 TQ	CABLS	10/01-12/01
	Visalia-Tulare-Porterville MSA, CA	H	6.36 FQ	7.58 AW	8.73 TQ	CABLS	10/01-12/01
	Colorado	H	5.55 FQ	8.27 AW	10.75 TQ	COBLS	10/01-12/01
	Boulder-Longmont PMSA, CO	H	5.66 FQ	7.73 AW	10.84 TQ	COBLS	10/01-12/01
	Colorado Springs MSA, CO	H	5.63 FQ	8.78 AW	11.61 TQ	COBLS	10/01-12/01
	Denver PMSA, CO	H	5.51 FQ	8.61 AW	10.65 TQ	COBLS	10/01-12/01
	Fort Collins-Loveland MSA, CO	H	5.60 FQ	8.97 AW	10.81 TQ	COBLS	10/01-12/01
	Greeley PMSA, CO	H	5.63 FQ	6.70 AW	8.38 TQ	COBLS	10/01-12/01
	Connecticut	H	6.47 FQ	8.11 AW	11.76 TQ	CTBLS	10/01-12/01
	Bridgeport PMSA, CT	H	6.50 FQ	7.79 AW	9.80 TQ	CTBLS	10/01-12/01
	Danbury PMSA, CT	H	6.52 FQ	9.05 AW	13.56 TQ	CTBLS	10/01-12/01
	Hartford MSA, CT	H	6.46 FQ	7.74 AW	11.55 TQ	CTBLS	10/01-12/01
	New Haven-Meriden PMSA, CT	H	6.49 FQ	7.99 AW	10.99 TQ	CTBLS	10/01-12/01
	New London-Norwich MSA, CT-RI	H	6.46 FQ	7.46 AW	10.35 TQ	CTBLS	10/01-12/01
	Stamford-Norwalk PMSA, CT	H	6.46 FQ	9.31 AW	14.29 TQ	CTBLS	10/01-12/01
	Waterbury PMSA, CT	H	6.49 FQ	8.12 AW	12.33 TQ	CTBLS	10/01-12/01
	Delaware	H	6.34 FQ	7.30 AW	9.10 TQ	DEBLS	10/01-12/01
	Wilmington-Newark PMSA, DE-MD	H	6.22 FQ	7.30 AW	9.84 TQ	DEBLS	10/01-12/01
	District of Columbia	H	6.52 FQ	7.75 AW	9.94 TQ	DCBLS	10/01-12/01
	Washington PMSA, DC-MD-VA-WV	H	5.66 FQ	7.60 AW	10.77 TQ	DCBLS	10/01-12/01
	Florida	H	5.57 FQ	7.16 AW	10.20 TQ	FLBLS	10/01-12/01
	Daytona Beach MSA, FL	H	5.60 FQ	6.66 AW	8.51 TQ	FLBLS	10/01-12/01
	Fort Lauderdale PMSA, FL	H	5.65 FQ	7.43 AW	10.84 TQ	FLBLS	10/01-12/01
	Fort Myers-Cape Coral MSA, FL	H	5.53 FQ	7.26 AW	11.36 TQ	FLBLS	10/01-12/01
	Fort Pierce-Port St. Lucie MSA, FL	H	5.45 FQ	6.88 AW	9.76 TQ	FLBLS	10/01-12/01
	Fort Walton Beach MSA, FL	H	5.54 FQ	7.49 AW	11.33 TQ	FLBLS	10/01-12/01
	Gainesville MSA, FL	H	5.60 FQ	7.80 AW	11.81 TQ	FLBLS	10/01-12/01
	Jacksonville MSA, FL	H	5.54 FQ	7.17 AW	9.49 TQ	FLBLS	10/01-12/01

AAW	Average annual wage	AOH	Average offered, high	ASH	Average starting, high	H	Hourly	M	Monthly	S	Special: hourly and annual
AE	Average entry wage	AOL	Average offered, low	ASL	Average starting, low	HI	Highest wage paid	MTC	Median total compensation	TQ	Third quartile wage
AEX	Average experienced wage	APH	Average pay, high range	AW	Average wage paid	HR	High end range	MW	Median wage paid	W	Weekly
AO	Average offered	APL	Average pay, low range	FQ	First quartile wage	LR	Low end range	SQ	Second quartile wage	Y	Yearly

Occupation/Type/Industry	Location	Per	Low	Mid	High	Source	Date
Waiter and Waitress	Lakeland-Winter Haven MSA, FL	H	5.60 FQ	6.94 AW	9.78 TQ	FLBLS	10/01-12/01
	Melbourne-Titusville-Palm Bay MSA, FL	H	5.55 FQ	6.89 AW	9.46 TQ	FLBLS	10/01-12/01
	Miami PMSA, FL	H	5.56 FQ	7.00 AW	10.04 TQ	FLBLS	10/01-12/01
	Naples MSA, FL	H	5.73 FQ	9.50 AW	15.86 TQ	FLBLS	10/01-12/01
	Ocala MSA, FL	H	5.63 FQ	6.89 AW	8.17 TQ	FLBLS	10/01-12/01
	Orlando MSA, FL	H	5.54 FQ	6.54 AW	8.23 TQ	FLBLS	10/01-12/01
	Pensacola MSA, FL	H	5.59 FQ	6.81 AW	8.43 TQ	FLBLS	10/01-12/01
	Sarasota-Bradenton MSA, FL	H	5.58 FQ	7.33 AW	10.42 TQ	FLBLS	10/01-12/01
	Tallahassee MSA, FL	H	5.58 FQ	7.14 AW	10.68 TQ	FLBLS	10/01-12/01
	Tampa-St. Petersburg-Clearwater MSA, FL	H	5.60 FQ	7.23 AW	10.17 TQ	FLBLS	10/01-12/01
	West Palm Beach-Boca Raton MSA, FL	H	5.55 FQ	7.29 AW	12.14 TQ	FLBLS	10/01-12/01
	Georgia	H	5.49 FQ	7.10 AW	11.25 TQ	GABLS	10/01-12/01
	Atlanta MSA, GA	H	5.45 FQ	7.46 AW	12.17 TQ	GABLS	10/01-12/01
	Augusta-Aiken MSA, GA-SC	H	5.57 FQ	6.65 AW	8.48 TQ	GABLS	10/01-12/01
	Columbus MSA, GA-AL	H	5.45 FQ	6.13 AW	6.98 TQ	GABLS	10/01-12/01
	Macon MSA, GA	H	5.67 FQ	7.24 AW	9.97 TQ	GABLS	10/01-12/01
	Savannah MSA, GA	H	5.65 FQ	6.92 AW	9.54 TQ	GABLS	10/01-12/01
	Hawaii	H	5.85 FQ	9.52 AW	17.99 TQ	HIBLS	10/01-12/01
	Honolulu MSA, HI	H	5.87 FQ	9.44 AW	18.59 TQ	HIBLS	10/01-12/01
	Idaho	H	5.54 FQ	6.34 AW	7.17 TQ	IDBLS	10/01-12/01
	Boise City MSA, ID	H	5.58 FQ	6.15 AW	6.95 TQ	IDBLS	10/01-12/01
	Illinois	H	5.49 FQ	7.14 AW	10.97 TQ	ILBLS	10/01-12/01
	Champaign-Urbana MSA, IL	H	5.51 FQ	6.37 AW	7.56 TQ	ILBLS	10/01-12/01
	Chicago PMSA, IL	H	5.49 FQ	7.32 AW	11.62 TQ	ILBLS	10/01-12/01
	Peoria-Pekin MSA, IL	H	5.42 FQ	6.17 AW	7.02 TQ	ILBLS	10/01-12/01
	Rockford MSA, IL	H	5.64 FQ	7.08 AW	9.82 TQ	ILBLS	10/01-12/01
	Springfield MSA, IL	H	5.51 FQ	6.54 AW	8.41 TQ	ILBLS	10/01-12/01
	Indiana	H	5.55 FQ	6.92 AW	9.56 TQ	INBLS	10/01-12/01
	Elkhart-Goshen MSA, IN	H	5.57 FQ	7.85 AW	13.21 TQ	INBLS	10/01-12/01
	Evansville-Henderson MSA, IN-KY	H	5.45 FQ	6.86 AW	10.36 TQ	INBLS	10/01-12/01
	Fort Wayne MSA, IN	H	5.65 FQ	7.47 AW	11.16 TQ	INBLS	10/01-12/01
	Gary PMSA, IN	H	5.51 FQ	6.60 AW	8.51 TQ	INBLS	10/01-12/01
	Indianapolis MSA, IN	H	5.54 FQ	6.74 AW	8.42 TQ	INBLS	10/01-12/01
	Lafayette MSA, IN	H	5.57 FQ	6.47 AW	7.54 TQ	INBLS	10/01-12/01
	South Bend MSA, IN	H	5.48 FQ	6.92 AW	9.40 TQ	INBLS	10/01-12/01
	Iowa	H	5.48 FQ	6.51 AW	7.71 TQ	IABLS	10/01-12/01
	Cedar Rapids MSA, IA	H	5.57 FQ	6.46 AW	7.29 TQ	IABLS	10/01-12/01
	Davenport-Moline-Rock Island MSA, IA-IL	H	5.59 FQ	6.89 AW	9.29 TQ	IABLS	10/01-12/01
	Des Moines MSA, IA	H	5.58 FQ	6.37 AW	7.04 TQ	IABLS	10/01-12/01
	Kansas	H	5.56 FQ	6.71 AW	8.66 TQ	KSBLS	10/01-12/01
	Topeka MSA, KS	H	5.60 FQ	6.60 AW	8.82 TQ	KSBLS	10/01-12/01
	Wichita MSA, KS	H	5.58 FQ	6.60 AW	8.46 TQ	KSBLS	10/01-12/01
	Kentucky	H	5.59 FQ	6.84 AW	9.40 TQ	KYBLS	10/01-12/01
	Lexington MSA, KY	H	5.70 FQ	7.27 AW	11.43 TQ	KYBLS	10/01-12/01
	Louisville MSA, KY-IN	H	5.52 FQ	6.67 AW	8.62 TQ	KYBLS	10/01-12/01
	Louisiana	H	5.49 FQ	6.60 AW	8.37 TQ	LABLS	10/01-12/01
	Baton Rouge MSA, LA	H	5.48 FQ	6.11 AW	6.98 TQ	LABLS	10/01-12/01
	Houma MSA, LA	H	5.59 FQ	6.77 AW	8.69 TQ	LABLS	10/01-12/01
	Lafayette MSA, LA	H	5.56 FQ	6.66 AW	9.17 TQ	LABLS	10/01-12/01
	Lake Charles MSA, LA	H	5.59 FQ	6.45 AW	7.75 TQ	LABLS	10/01-12/01
	New Orleans MSA, LA	H	5.44 FQ	6.83 AW	10.64 TQ	LABLS	10/01-12/01
	Shreveport-Bossier City MSA, LA	H	5.56 FQ	6.71 AW	8.88 TQ	LABLS	10/01-12/01
	Maine	H	5.64 FQ	8.04 AW	12.50 TQ	MEBLS	10/01-12/01
	Portland MSA, ME	H	5.72 FQ	8.51 AW	13.37 TQ	MEBLS	10/01-12/01
	Maryland	H	5.50 FQ	6.88 AW	10.01 TQ	MDBLS	10/01-12/01
	Baltimore PMSA, MD	H	5.46 FQ	6.71 AW	9.27 TQ	MDBLS	10/01-12/01
	Massachusetts	H	6.86 FQ	9.83 AW	13.32 TQ	MABLS	10/01-12/01
	Boston PMSA, MA-NH	H	6.99 FQ	10.49 AW	13.60 TQ	MABLS	10/01-12/01
	Brockton PMSA, MA	H	6.75 FQ	8.35 AW	10.95 TQ	MABLS	10/01-12/01
	Lawrence PMSA, MA-NH	H	5.98 FQ	7.74 AW	10.98 TQ	MABLS	10/01-12/01
	Lowell PMSA, MA-NH	H	6.77 FQ	9.42 AW	13.23 TQ	MABLS	10/01-12/01
	New Bedford PMSA, MA	H	6.82 FQ	7.98 AW	10.14 TQ	MABLS	10/01-12/01
	Springfield MSA, MA	H	6.75 FQ	8.55 AW	10.95 TQ	MABLS	10/01-12/01
	Worcester PMSA, MA-CT	H	6.88 FQ	9.49 AW	12.82 TQ	MABLS	10/01-12/01
	Michigan	H	5.46 FQ	6.66 AW	8.67 TQ	MIBLS	10/01-12/01

AAW Average annual wage; **AE** Average entry wage; **AEX** Average experienced wage; **AO** Average offered; **AOH** Average offered, high; **AOL** Average offered, low; **APH** Average pay, high range; **APL** Average pay, low range; **ASH** Average starting, high; **ASL** Average starting, low; **AW** Average wage paid; **FQ** First quartile wage; **H** Hourly; **HI** Highest wage paid; **HR** High end range; **LR** Low end range; **M** Monthly; **MTC** Median total compensation; **MW** Median wage paid; **SQ** Second quartile wage; **S** Special: hourly and annual; **TQ** Third quartile wage; **W** Weekly; **Y** Yearly

Occupation/Type/Industry	Location	Per	Low	Mid	High	Source	Date
Waiter and Waitress	Ann Arbor PMSA, MI	H	5.50 FQ	7.08 AW	10.24 TQ	MIBLS	10/01-12/01
	Detroit PMSA, MI	H	5.44 FQ	6.63 AW	8.50 TQ	MIBLS	10/01-12/01
	Flint PMSA, MI	H	5.42 FQ	6.35 AW	7.81 TQ	MIBLS	10/01-12/01
	Grand Rapids-Muskegon-Holland MSA, MI	H	5.46 FQ	6.65 AW	8.78 TQ	MIBLS	10/01-12/01
	Kalamazoo-Battle Creek MSA, MI	H	5.48 FQ	6.35 AW	7.29 TQ	MIBLS	10/01-12/01
	Lansing-East Lansing MSA, MI	H	5.57 FQ	7.10 AW	10.45 TQ	MIBLS	10/01-12/01
	Saginaw-Bay City-Midland MSA, MI	H	5.50 FQ	6.48 AW	8.07 TQ	MIBLS	10/01-12/01
	Minnesota	H	5.51 FQ	6.97 AW	9.58 TQ	MNBLS	10/01-12/01
	Duluth-Superior MSA, MN-WI	H	5.59 FQ	7.11 AW	10.50 TQ	MNBLS	10/01-12/01
	Minneapolis-St. Paul MSA, MN-WI	H	5.50 FQ	7.07 AW	10.84 TQ	MNBLS	10/01-12/01
	St. Cloud MSA, MN	H	5.62 FQ	6.91 AW	7.14 TQ	MNBLS	10/01-12/01
	Mississippi	H	5.51 FQ	6.32 AW	7.24 TQ	MSBLS	10/01-12/01
	Biloxi-Gulfport-Pascagoula MSA, MS	H	5.54 FQ	6.37 AW	7.56 TQ	MSBLS	10/01-12/01
	Jackson MSA, MS	H	5.60 FQ	6.28 AW	7.09 TQ	MSBLS	10/01-12/01
	Missouri	H	5.57 FQ	7.21 AW	10.55 TQ	MOBLS	10/01-12/01
	Kansas City MSA, MO-KS	H	5.55 FQ	6.97 AW	10.03 TQ	MOBLS	10/01-12/01
	St. Louis MSA, MO-IL	H	5.57 FQ	7.51 AW	10.96 TQ	MOBLS	10/01-12/01
	Springfield MSA, MO	H	5.76 FQ	7.98 AW	11.03 TQ	MOBLS	10/01-12/01
	Montana	H	5.56 FQ	6.33 AW	7.12 TQ	MTBLS	10/01-12/01
	Billings MSA, MT	H	5.63 FQ	6.45 AW	7.30 TQ	MTBLS	10/01-12/01
	Nebraska	H	5.59 FQ	6.55 AW	8.16 TQ	NEBLS	10/01-12/01
	Lincoln MSA, NE	H	5.60 FQ	6.33 AW	7.20 TQ	NEBLS	10/01-12/01
	Omaha MSA, NE-IA	H	5.60 FQ	6.80 AW	9.47 TQ	NEBLS	10/01-12/01
	Nevada	H	5.66 FQ	7.74 AW	10.59 TQ	NVBLS	10/01-12/01
	Las Vegas MSA, NV-AZ	H	5.73 FQ	8.03 AW	10.67 TQ	NVBLS	10/01-12/01
	Reno MSA, NV	H	5.50 FQ	6.31 AW	7.27 TQ	NVBLS	10/01-12/01
	New Hampshire	H	5.67 FQ	7.21 AW	10.32 TQ	NHBLS	10/01 12/01
	Manchester PMSA, NH	H	5.96 FQ	8.41 AW	11.69 TQ	NHBLS	10/01-12/01
	Nashua PMSA, NH	H	5.78 FQ	7.75 AW	10.62 TQ	NHBLS	10/01-12/01
	Portsmouth-Rochester PMSA, NH-ME	H	5.61 FQ	7.59 AW	12.33 TQ	NHBLS	10/01-12/01
	New Jersey	H	5.68 FQ	8.42 AW	12.91 TQ	NJBLS	10/01-12/01
	Atlantic-Cape May PMSA, NJ	H	5.64 FQ	8.75 AW	13.64 TQ	NJBLS	10/01-12/01
	Bergen-Passaic PMSA, NJ	H	5.77 FQ	9.10 AW	13.58 TQ	NJBLS	10/01-12/01
	Jersey City PMSA, NJ	H	5.62 FQ	10.66 AW	24.60 TQ	NJBLS	10/01-12/01
	Middlesex-Somerset-Hunterdon PMSA, NJ	H	5.72 FQ	8.79 AW	12.95 TQ	NJBLS	10/01-12/01
	Monmouth-Ocean PMSA, NJ	H	5.58 FQ	7.35 AW	11.08 TQ	NJBLS	10/01-12/01
	Newark PMSA, NJ	H	5.81 FQ	8.91 AW	13.46 TQ	NJBLS	10/01-12/01
	Trenton PMSA, NJ	H	5.87 FQ	8.34 AW	11.03 TQ	NJBLS	10/01-12/01
	New Mexico	H	5.57 FQ	6.75 AW	8.43 TQ	NMBLS	10/01-12/01
	Albuquerque MSA, NM	H	5.74 FQ	7.22 AW	8.61 TQ	NMBLS	10/01-12/01
	Las Cruces MSA, NM	H	5.64 FQ	6.20 AW	7.10 TQ	NMBLS	10/01-12/01
	New York	H	5.56 FQ	8.75 AW	16.28 TQ	NYBLS	10/01-12/01
	Albany-Schenectady-Troy MSA, NY	H	5.51 FQ	8.33 AW	16.22 TQ	NYBLS	10/01-12/01
	Binghamton MSA, NY	H	5.54 FQ	6.41 AW	7.85 TQ	NYBLS	10/01-12/01
	Buffalo-Niagara Falls MSA, NY	H	5.48 FQ	6.60 AW	8.81 TQ	NYBLS	10/01-12/01
	Dutchess County PMSA, NY	H	5.49 FQ	7.64 AW	12.85 TQ	NYBLS	10/01-12/01
	Nassau-Suffolk PMSA, NY	H	5.60 FQ	7.76 AW	11.12 TQ	NYBLS	10/01-12/01
	New York PMSA, NY	H	5.67 FQ	10.97 AW	17.63 TQ	NYBLS	10/01-12/01
	Newburgh PMSA, NY-PA	H	5.69 FQ	8.22 AW	12.27 TQ	NYBLS	10/01-12/01
	Rochester MSA, NY	H	5.49 FQ	6.59 AW	8.03 TQ	NYBLS	10/01-12/01
	Syracuse MSA, NY	H	5.47 FQ	6.71 AW	8.92 TQ	NYBLS	10/01-12/01
	Utica-Rome MSA, NY	H	5.44 FQ	6.69 AW	8.98 TQ	NYBLS	10/01-12/01
	North Carolina	H	5.52 FQ	6.86 AW	9.83 TQ	NCBLS	10/01-12/01
	Asheville MSA, NC	H	5.69 FQ	8.20 AW	12.76 TQ	NCBLS	10/01-12/01
	Charlotte-Gastonia-Rock Hill MSA, NC-SC	H	5.61 FQ	6.82 AW	9.60 TQ	NCBLS	10/01-12/01
	Fayetteville MSA, NC	H	5.50 FQ	6.73 AW	9.85 TQ	NCBLS	10/01-12/01
	Greensboro-Winston-Salem-High Point MSA, NC	H	5.49 FQ	6.78 AW	9.13 TQ	NCBLS	10/01-12/01
	Hickory-Morganton-Lenoir MSA, NC	H	5.61 FQ	7.63 AW	11.16 TQ	NCBLS	10/01-12/01
	Raleigh-Durham-Chapel Hill MSA, NC	H	5.54 FQ	7.28 AW	10.89 TQ	NCBLS	10/01-12/01

AAW Average annual wage; AE Average entry wage; AEX Average experienced wage; AO Average offered; AOH Average offered, high; AOL Average offered, low; APH Average pay, high range; APL Average pay, low range; ASH Average starting, high; ASL Average starting, low; AW Average wage paid; FQ First quartile wage; H Hourly; HI Highest wage paid; HR High end range; LR Low end range; M Monthly; MTC Median total compensation; MW Median wage paid; SQ Second quartile wage; S Special: hourly and annual; TQ Third quartile wage; W Weekly; Y Yearly

Occupation/Type/Industry	Location	Per	Low	Mid	High	Source	Date
Waiter and Waitress	Wilmington MSA, NC	H	5.57 FQ	6.60 AW	8.27 TQ	NCBLS	10/01-12/01
	North Dakota	H	5.57 FQ	6.53 AW	8.12 TQ	NDBLS	10/01-12/01
	Fargo-Moorhead MSA, ND-MN	H	5.53 FQ	6.65 AW	9.26 TQ	NDBLS	10/01-12/01
	Ohio	H	5.50 FQ	6.83 AW	9.41 TQ	OHBLS	10/01-12/01
	Akron PMSA, OH	H	5.79 FQ	7.65 AW	10.23 TQ	OHBLS	10/01-12/01
	Canton-Massillon MSA, OH	H	5.53 FQ	6.42 AW	7.78 TQ	OHBLS	10/01-12/01
	Cincinnati PMSA, OH-KY-IN	H	5.58 FQ	6.95 AW	10.07 TQ	OHBLS	10/01-12/01
	Cleveland-Lorain-Elyria PMSA, OH	H	5.42 FQ	7.27 AW	11.85 TQ	OHBLS	10/01-12/01
	Columbus MSA, OH	H	5.56 FQ	6.72 AW	9.11 TQ	OHBLS	10/01-12/01
	Dayton-Springfield MSA, OH	H	5.49 FQ	6.69 AW	8.67 TQ	OHBLS	10/01-12/01
	Hamilton-Middletown PMSA, OH	H	5.59 FQ	6.47 AW	7.23 TQ	OHBLS	10/01-12/01
	Mansfield MSA, OH	H	5.57 FQ	6.48 AW	8.17 TQ	OHBLS	10/01-12/01
	Toledo MSA, OH	H	5.57 FQ	6.49 AW	8.14 TQ	OHBLS	10/01-12/01
	Youngstown-Warren MSA, OH	H	5.53 FQ	6.80 AW	10.12 TQ	OHBLS	10/01-12/01
	Oklahoma	H	5.55 FQ	6.59 AW	8.40 TQ	OKBLS	10/01-12/01
	Oklahoma City MSA, OK	H	5.66 FQ	7.05 AW	9.40 TQ	OKBLS	10/01-12/01
	Tulsa MSA, OK	H	5.58 FQ	6.49 AW	7.65 TQ	OKBLS	10/01-12/01
	Oregon	H	6.76 FQ	7.95 AW	9.95 TQ	ORBLS	10/01-12/01
	Eugene-Springfield MSA, OR	H	6.85 FQ	8.43 AW	11.31 TQ	ORBLS	10/01-12/01
	Medford-Ashland MSA, OR	H	6.85 FQ	7.82 AW	8.94 TQ	ORBLS	10/01-12/01
	Portland-Vancouver PMSA, OR-WA	H	6.77 FQ	7.81 AW	9.82 TQ	ORBLS	10/01-12/01
	Salem PMSA, OR	H	6.77 FQ	7.95 AW	9.89 TQ	ORBLS	10/01-12/01
	Pennsylvania	H	5.52 FQ	6.94 AW	9.76 TQ	PABLS	10/01-12/01
	Allentown-Bethlehem-Easton MSA, PA	H	5.58 FQ	6.90 AW	9.40 TQ	PABLS	10/01-12/01
	Erie MSA, PA	H	5.45 FQ	6.29 AW	7.09 TQ	PABLS	10/01-12/01
	Harrisburg-Lebanon-Carlisle MSA, PA	H	5.46 FQ	6.22 AW	7.07 TQ	PABLS	10/01-12/01
	Johnstown MSA, PA	H	5.59 FQ	6.57 AW	8.26 TQ	PABLS	10/01-12/01
	Lancaster MSA, PA	H	5.58 FQ	7.12 AW	10.08 TQ	PABLS	10/01-12/01
	Philadelphia PMSA, PA-NJ	H	5.57 FQ	7.50 AW	10.80 TQ	PABLS	10/01-12/01
	Pittsburgh MSA, PA	H	5.52 FQ	7.05 AW	10.38 TQ	PABLS	10/01-12/01
	Reading MSA, PA	H	5.63 FQ	7.18 AW	10.39 TQ	PABLS	10/01-12/01
	Scranton-Wilkes-Barre-Hazleton MSA, PA	H	5.51 FQ	6.44 AW	8.11 TQ	PABLS	10/01-12/01
	York MSA, PA	H	5.55 FQ	6.80 AW	9.51 TQ	PABLS	10/01-12/01
	Rhode Island	H	6.33 FQ	7.50 AW	10.19 TQ	RIBLS	10/01-12/01
	Providence-Fall River-Warwick MSA, RI-MA	H	6.35 FQ	7.64 AW	10.38 TQ	RIBLS	10/01-12/01
	South Carolina	H	5.57 FQ	6.68 AW	9.12 TQ	SCBLS	10/01-12/01
	Charleston-North Charleston MSA, SC	H	5.61 FQ	6.98 AW	10.05 TQ	SCBLS	10/01-12/01
	Columbia MSA, SC	H	5.58 FQ	6.70 AW	9.00 TQ	SCBLS	10/01-12/01
	Greenville-Spartanburg-Anderson MSA, SC	H	5.55 FQ	6.43 AW	7.22 TQ	SCBLS	10/01-12/01
	Myrtle Beach MSA, SC	H	5.62 FQ	6.99 AW	9.79 TQ	SCBLS	10/01-12/01
	South Dakota	H	5.42 FQ	6.10 AW	6.94 TQ	SDBLS	10/01-12/01
	Sioux Falls MSA, SD	H	5.59 FQ	6.21 AW	7.06 TQ	SDBLS	10/01-12/01
	Tennessee	H	5.52 FQ	6.79 AW	9.15 TQ	TNBLS	10/01-12/01
	Chattanooga MSA, TN-GA	H	5.58 FQ	7.66 AW	11.83 TQ	TNBLS	10/01-12/01
	Clarksville-Hopkinsville MSA, TN-KY	H	5.69 FQ	7.14 AW	10.11 TQ	TNBLS	10/01-12/01
	Johnson City-Kingsport-Bristol MSA, TN-VA	H	5.48 FQ	6.22 AW	7.14 TQ	TNBLS	10/01-12/01
	Knoxville MSA, TN	H	5.64 FQ	6.66 AW	8.63 TQ	TNBLS	10/01-12/01
	Memphis MSA, TN-AR-MS	H	5.61 FQ	7.57 AW	10.66 TQ	TNBLS	10/01-12/01
	Nashville MSA, TN	H	5.46 FQ	6.47 AW	8.25 TQ	TNBLS	10/01-12/01
	Texas	H	5.50 FQ	6.97 AW	10.34 TQ	TXBLS	10/01-12/01
	Amarillo MSA, TX	H	5.64 FQ	7.14 AW	10.30 TQ	TXBLS	10/01-12/01
	Austin-San Marcos MSA, TX	H	5.58 FQ	7.48 AW	10.72 TQ	TXBLS	10/01-12/01
	Beaumont-Port Arthur MSA, TX	H	5.53 FQ	6.94 AW	10.26 TQ	TXBLS	10/01-12/01
	Brazoria PMSA, TX	H	5.59 FQ	6.54 AW	8.27 TQ	TXBLS	10/01-12/01
	Brownsville-Harlingen-San Benito MSA, TX	H	5.60 FQ	6.49 AW	7.29 TQ	TXBLS	10/01-12/01
	Corpus Christi MSA, TX	H	5.56 FQ	6.31 AW	7.07 TQ	TXBLS	10/01-12/01
	Dallas PMSA, TX	H	5.49 FQ	6.94 AW	9.97 TQ	TXBLS	10/01-12/01
	El Paso MSA, TX	H	5.48 FQ	6.50 AW	9.07 TQ	TXBLS	10/01-12/01

AAW	Average annual wage	AOH	Average offered, high	ASH	Average starting, high	H	Hourly	M	Monthly	S	Special: hourly and annual
AE	Average entry wage	AOL	Average offered, low	ASL	Average starting, low	HI	Highest wage paid	MTC	Median total compensation	TQ	Third quartile wage
AEX	Average experienced wage	APH	Average pay, high range	AW	Average wage paid	HR	High end range	MW	Median wage paid	W	Weekly
AO	Average offered	APL	Average pay, low range	FQ	First quartile wage	LR	Low end range	SQ	Second quartile wage	Y	Yearly

Occupation/Type/Industry	Location	Per	Low	Mid	High	Source	Date
Waiter and Waitress	Fort Worth-Arlington PMSA, TX	H	5.66 FQ	8.13 AW	12.61 TQ	TXBLS	10/01-12/01
	Galveston-Texas City PMSA, TX	H	5.58 FQ	6.45 AW	7.15 TQ	TXBLS	10/01-12/01
	Houston PMSA, TX	H	5.45 FQ	7.11 AW	11.45 TQ	TXBLS	10/01-12/01
	Killeen-Temple MSA, TX	H	5.49 FQ	6.51 AW	8.44 TQ	TXBLS	10/01-12/01
	Laredo MSA, TX	H	5.48 FQ	6.54 AW	8.28 TQ	TXBLS	10/01-12/01
	Longview-Marshall MSA, TX	H	5.60 FQ	7.07 AW	10.85 TQ	TXBLS	10/01-12/01
	Lubbock MSA, TX	H	5.54 FQ	6.57 AW	8.17 TQ	TXBLS	10/01-12/01
	McAllen-Edinburg-Mission MSA, TX	H	5.40 FQ	6.16 AW	6.89 TQ	TXBLS	10/01-12/01
	Odessa-Midland MSA, TX	H	5.48 FQ	6.87 AW	10.04 TQ	TXBLS	10/01-12/01
	San Antonio MSA, TX	H	5.57 FQ	7.10 AW	10.69 TQ	TXBLS	10/01-12/01
	Tyler MSA, TX	H	5.47 FQ	6.59 AW	8.54 TQ	TXBLS	10/01-12/01
	Waco MSA, TX	H	5.57 FQ	6.84 AW	10.11 TQ	TXBLS	10/01-12/01
	Utah	H	5.61 FQ	7.63 AW	10.81 TQ	UTBLS	10/01-12/01
	Provo-Orem MSA, UT	H	5.63 FQ	7.89 AW	10.77 TQ	UTBLS	10/01-12/01
	Salt Lake City-Ogden MSA, UT	H	5.58 FQ	7.64 AW	10.74 TQ	UTBLS	10/01-12/01
	Vermont	H	6.40 FQ	8.95 AW	13.47 TQ	VTBLS	10/01-12/01
	Burlington MSA, VT	H	6.44 FQ	8.97 AW	13.03 TQ	VTBLS	10/01-12/01
	Virginia	H	5.60 FQ	7.22 AW	10.44 TQ	VABLS	10/01-12/01
	Lynchburg MSA, VA	H	5.62 FQ	6.71 AW	8.18 TQ	VABLS	10/01-12/01
	Norfolk-Virginia Beach-Newport News MSA, VA-NC	H	5.59 FQ	7.12 AW	9.96 TQ	VABLS	10/01-12/01
	Richmond-Petersburg MSA, VA	H	5.66 FQ	7.03 AW	10.26 TQ	VABLS	10/01-12/01
	Roanoke MSA, VA	H	5.69 FQ	7.63 AW	12.17 TQ	VABLS	10/01-12/01
	Washington	H	6.74 FQ	8.91 AW	14.91 TQ	WABLS	10/01-12/01
	Bremerton PMSA, WA	H	6.77 FQ	7.52 AW	8.68 TQ	WABLS	10/01-12/01
	Olympia PMSA, WA	H	6.75 FQ	8.15 AW	10.77 TQ	WABLS	10/01-12/01
	Richland-Kennewick-Pasco MSA, WA	H	6.74 FQ	7.51 AW	8.37 TQ	WABLS	10/01-12/01
	Seattle-Bellevue-Everett PMSA, WA	H	6.75 FQ	9.76 AW	17.15 TQ	WABLS	10/01-12/01
	Spokane MSA, WA	H	6.73 FQ	8.12 AW	12.44 TQ	WABLS	10/01-12/01
	Tacoma PMSA, WA	H	6.76 FQ	7.95 AW	8.83 TQ	WABLS	10/01-12/01
	Yakima MSA, WA	H	6.74 FQ	7.89 AW	11.79 TQ	WABLS	10/01-12/01
	West Virginia	H	5.57 FQ	6.41 AW	7.43 TQ	WVBLS	10/01-12/01
	Charleston MSA, WV	H	5.51 FQ	6.23 AW	7.10 TQ	WVBLS	10/01-12/01
	Huntington-Ashland MSA, WV-KY-OH	H	5.58 FQ	6.79 AW	8.78 TQ	WVBLS	10/01-12/01
	Wisconsin	H	5.53 FQ	6.84 AW	9.55 TQ	WIBLS	10/01-12/01
	Appleton-Oshkosh-Neenah MSA, WI	H	5.60 FQ	6.96 AW	9.72 TQ	WIBLS	10/01-12/01
	Green Bay MSA, WI	H	5.65 FQ	6.84 AW	9.25 TQ	WIBLS	10/01-12/01
	Madison MSA, WI	H	5.57 FQ	6.57 AW	7.92 TQ	WIBLS	10/01-12/01
	Milwaukee-Waukesha PMSA, WI	H	5.54 FQ	6.37 AW	7.17 TQ	WIBLS	10/01-12/01
	Racine PMSA, WI	H	5.51 FQ	6.33 AW	7.40 TQ	WIBLS	10/01-12/01
	Wyoming	H	5.60 FQ	7.57 AW	12.39 TQ	WYBLS	10/01-12/01
	Cheyenne MSA, WY	H	5.56 FQ	6.18 AW	7.01 TQ	WYBLS	10/01-12/01
	Puerto Rico	H	5.48 FQ	6.44 AW	7.20 TQ	PRBLS	10/01-12/01
	Virgin Islands	H	5.51 FQ	6.14 AW	6.95 TQ	VIBLS	10/01-12/01
	Guam	H	5.53 FQ	6.90 AW	9.26 TQ	GUBLS	10/01-12/01
Warehouse Manager	United States	Y		40000-50000 AW		WARE	1/00-1/01
Warehouse Professional	United States	Y		59000 AW		WARE	1/00-1/01
Watch Repairer	Alabama	H	5.77 FQ	11.75 AW	19.98 TQ	ALBLS	10/01-12/01
	Arizona	H	7.07 FQ	11.84 AW	17.61 TQ	AZBLS	10/01-12/01
	Phoenix-Mesa MSA, AZ	H	6.39 FQ	12.91 AW	18.73 TQ	AZBLS	10/01-12/01
	California	H	6.94 FQ	11.84 AW	17.68 TQ	CABLS	10/01-12/01
	Los Angeles-Long Beach PMSA, CA	H	9.20 FQ	14.20 AW	21.13 TQ	CABLS	10/01-12/01
	San Francisco PMSA, CA	H	7.46 FQ	11.02 AW	17.22 TQ	CABLS	10/01-12/01
	Connecticut	H	8.64 FQ	18.26 AW	32.43 TQ	CTBLS	10/01-12/01
	Florida	H	6.37 FQ	14.09 AW	25.24 TQ	FLBLS	10/01-12/01
	Fort Lauderdale PMSA, FL	H	7.38 FQ	13.85 AW	21.08 TQ	FLBLS	10/01-12/01
	Miami PMSA, FL	H	6.79 FQ	16.86 AW	27.04 TQ	FLBLS	10/01-12/01

AAW Average annual wage; AE Average entry wage; AEX Average experienced wage; AO Average offered; AOH Average offered, high; AOL Average offered, low; APH Average pay, high range; APL Average pay, low range; ASH Average starting, high; ASL Average starting, low; AW Average wage paid; FQ First quartile wage; H Hourly; HI Highest wage paid; HR High end range; LR Low end range; M Monthly; MTC Median total compensation; MW Median wage paid; SQ Second quartile wage; S Special: hourly and annual; TQ Third quartile wage; W Weekly; Y Yearly

Occupation/Type/Industry	Location	Per	Low	Mid	High	Source	Date
Watch Repairer	Orlando MSA, FL	H	5.88 FQ	8.62 AW	15.36 TQ	FLBLS	10/01-12/01
	Illinois	H	6.58 FQ	12.55 AW	17.57 TQ	ILBLS	10/01-12/01
	Chicago PMSA, IL	H	6.46 FQ	12.71 AW	17.55 TQ	ILBLS	10/01-12/01
	Indiana	H	9.18 FQ	11.61 AW	13.44 TQ	INBLS	10/01-12/01
	Maryland	H	7.29 FQ	9.82 AW	15.11 TQ	MDBLS	10/01-12/01
	Massachusetts	H	10.45 FQ	16.70 AW	25.51 TQ	MABLS	10/01-12/01
	Boston PMSA, MA-NH	H	11.14 FQ	16.99 AW	25.83 TQ	MABLS	10/01-12/01
	Michigan	H	9.07 FQ	15.93 AW	22.17 TQ	MIBLS	10/01-12/01
	Detroit PMSA, MI	H	9.37 FQ	13.45 AW	20.14 TQ	MIBLS	10/01-12/01
	Minnesota	H	6.42 FQ	10.89 AW	16.75 TQ	MNBLS	10/01-12/01
	Missouri	H	6.44 FQ	11.50 AW	18.70 TQ	MOBLS	10/01-12/01
	New Hampshire	H	6.23 FQ	10.91 AW	17.48 TQ	NHBLS	10/01-12/01
	New Jersey	H	9.21 FQ	14.06 AW	21.09 TQ	NJBLS	10/01-12/01
	Newark PMSA, NJ	H	8.91 FQ	12.53 AW	16.96 TQ	NJBLS	10/01-12/01
	New York	H	8.40 FQ	16.56 AW	27.17 TQ	NYBLS	10/01-12/01
	Nassau-Suffolk PMSA, NY	H	10.10 FQ	15.79 AW	18.82 TQ	NYBLS	10/01-12/01
	New York PMSA, NY	H	9.12 FQ	17.10 AW	28.40 TQ	NYBLS	10/01-12/01
	North Carolina	H	6.91 FQ	12.04 AW	17.82 TQ	NCBLS	10/01-12/01
	Ohio	H	5.77 FQ	10.89 AW	18.45 TQ	OHBLS	10/01-12/01
	Columbus MSA, OH	H	9.64 FQ	13.99 AW	20.43 TQ	OHBLS	10/01-12/01
	Dayton-Springfield MSA, OH	H	5.63 FQ	9.15 AW	18.12 TQ	OHBLS	10/01-12/01
	Oklahoma	H	5.98 FQ	10.92 AW	19.52 TQ	OKBLS	10/01-12/01
	Pennsylvania	H	7.49 FQ	16.88 AW	30.43 TQ	PABLS	10/01-12/01
	Texas	H	7.90 FQ	13.06 AW	19.82 TQ	TXBLS	10/01-12/01
	Dallas PMSA, TX	H	7.70 FQ	12.74 AW	18.42 TQ	TXBLS	10/01-12/01
	Houston PMSA, TX	H	9.57 FQ	14.63 AW	21.23 TQ	TXBLS	10/01-12/01
	Virginia	H	8.45 FQ	16.57 AW	27.66 TQ	VABLS	10/01-12/01
	Norfolk-Virginia Beach-Newport News MSA, VA-NC	H	9.08 FQ	17.11 AW	29.04 TQ	VABLS	10/01-12/01
	Washington	H	9.16 FQ	16.17 AW	21.63 TQ	WABLS	10/01-12/01
	Seattle-Bellevue-Everett PMSA, WA	H	8.92 FQ	13.52 AW	19.39 TQ	WABLS	10/01-12/01
Water and Liquid Waste Treatment Plant and System Operator	Alabama	H	7.18 FQ	12.59 AW	20.42 TQ	ALBLS	10/01-12/01
	Huntsville MSA, AL	H	9.79 FQ	15.92 AW	21.72 TQ	ALBLS	10/01-12/01
	Mobile MSA, AL	H	7.73 FQ	13.96 AW	21.23 TQ	ALBLS	10/01-12/01
	Alaska	H	11.66 FQ	20.96 AW	31.40 TQ	AKBLS	10/01-12/01
	Arizona	H	11.27 FQ	17.38 AW	25.62 TQ	AZBLS	10/01-12/01
	Phoenix-Mesa MSA, AZ	H	11.94 FQ	18.64 AW	27.11 TQ	AZBLS	10/01-12/01
	Tucson MSA, AZ	H	11.41 FQ	16.86 AW	22.34 TQ	AZBLS	10/01-12/01
	Arkansas	H	7.90 FQ	12.09 AW	17.95 TQ	ARBLS	10/01-12/01
	Fayetteville-Springdale-Rogers MSA, AR	H	9.34 FQ	11.87 AW	15.92 TQ	ARBLS	10/01-12/01
	Fort Smith MSA, AR-OK	H	6.73 FQ	12.11 AW	18.06 TQ	ARBLS	10/01-12/01
	Little Rock-North Little Rock MSA, AR	H	9.04 FQ	13.31 AW	18.52 TQ	ARBLS	10/01-12/01
	California	H	13.87 FQ	21.89 AW	31.02 TQ	CABLS	10/01-12/01
	Bakersfield MSA, CA	H	11.85 FQ	18.88 AW	27.83 TQ	CABLS	10/01-12/01
	Chico-Paradise MSA, CA	H	14.69 FQ	19.93 AW	28.17 TQ	CABLS	10/01-12/01
	Fresno MSA, CA	H	12.82 FQ	17.27 AW	23.55 TQ	CABLS	10/01-12/01
	Los Angeles-Long Beach PMSA, CA	H	15.18 FQ	23.47 AW	31.05 TQ	CABLS	10/01-12/01
	Merced MSA, CA	H	11.66 FQ	16.18 AW	21.13 TQ	CABLS	10/01-12/01
	Modesto MSA, CA	H	10.78 FQ	16.68 AW	22.75 TQ	CABLS	10/01-12/01
	Oakland PMSA, CA	H	21.67 FQ	27.82 AW	35.44 TQ	CABLS	10/01-12/01
	Orange County PMSA, CA	H	14.11 FQ	22.16 AW	29.33 TQ	CABLS	10/01-12/01
	Riverside-San Bernardino PMSA, CA	H	15.76 FQ	23.29 AW	32.15 TQ	CABLS	10/01-12/01
	Sacramento PMSA, CA	H	15.85 FQ	23.00 AW	31.92 TQ	CABLS	10/01-12/01
	Salinas MSA, CA	H	17.20 FQ	24.98 AW	34.80 TQ	CABLS	10/01-12/01
	San Diego MSA, CA	H	16.25 FQ	23.28 AW	28.42 TQ	CABLS	10/01-12/01
	San Francisco PMSA, CA	H	16.14 FQ	23.64 AW	32.17 TQ	CABLS	10/01-12/01
	San Jose PMSA, CA	H	14.97 FQ	22.18 AW	29.48 TQ	CABLS	10/01-12/01
	San Luis Obispo-Atascadero-Paso Robles MSA, CA	H	14.37 FQ	19.84 AW	27.10 TQ	CABLS	10/01-12/01
	Santa Barbara-Santa Maria-Lompoc MSA, CA	H	14.72 FQ	20.31 AW	26.82 TQ	CABLS	10/01-12/01
	Santa Cruz-Watsonville PMSA, CA	H	13.25 FQ	22.68 AW	29.12 TQ	CABLS	10/01-12/01

AAW	Average annual wage	**AOH**	Average offered, high	**ASH**	Average starting, high	**H**	Hourly	**M**	Monthly	**S**	Special: hourly and annual
AE	Average entry wage	**AOL**	Average offered, low	**ASL**	Average starting, low	**HI**	Highest wage paid	**MTC**	Median total compensation	**TQ**	Third quartile wage
AEX	Average experienced wage	**APH**	Average pay, high range	**AW**	Average wage paid	**HR**	High end range	**MW**	Median wage paid	**W**	Weekly
AO	Average offered	**APL**	Average pay, low range	**FQ**	First quartile wage	**LR**	Low end range	**SQ**	Second quartile wage	**Y**	Yearly

Occupation/Type/Industry	Location	Per	Low	Mid	High	Source	Date
Water and Liquid Waste Treatment Plant and System Operator	Santa Rosa PMSA, CA	H	15.01 FQ	22.10 AW	29.00 TQ	CABLS	10/01-12/01
	Stockton-Lodi MSA, CA	H	15.18 FQ	22.10 AW	28.21 TQ	CABLS	10/01-12/01
	Vallejo-Fairfield-Napa PMSA, CA	H	19.64 FQ	26.60 AW	34.73 TQ	CABLS	10/01-12/01
	Ventura PMSA, CA	H	12.59 FQ	17.57 AW	22.70 TQ	CABLS	10/01-12/01
	Visalia-Tulare-Porterville MSA, CA	H	10.86 FQ	14.82 AW	19.43 TQ	CABLS	10/01-12/01
	Colorado	H	11.72 FQ	17.94 AW	25.06 TQ	COBLS	10/01-12/01
	Boulder-Longmont PMSA, CO	H	13.03 FQ	18.98 AW	26.10 TQ	COBLS	10/01-12/01
	Colorado Springs MSA, CO	H	13.40 FQ	19.82 AW	27.40 TQ	COBLS	10/01-12/01
	Denver PMSA, CO	H	12.29 FQ	17.94 AW	24.50 TQ	COBLS	10/01-12/01
	Fort Collins-Loveland MSA, CO	H	14.97 FQ	20.37 AW	25.95 TQ	COBLS	10/01-12/01
	Greeley PMSA, CO	H	13.48 FQ	17.09 AW	23.71 TQ	COBLS	10/01-12/01
	Connecticut	H	12.20 FQ	18.95 AW	25.36 TQ	CTBLS	10/01-12/01
	Bridgeport PMSA, CT	H	18.82 FQ	22.66 AW	26.89 TQ	CTBLS	10/01-12/01
	Danbury PMSA, CT	H	12.92 FQ	19.02 AW	25.14 TQ	CTBLS	10/01-12/01
	Hartford MSA, CT	H	14.31 FQ	18.79 AW	23.64 TQ	CTBLS	10/01-12/01
	New Haven-Meriden PMSA, CT	H	13.65 FQ	19.11 AW	24.23 TQ	CTBLS	10/01-12/01
	New London-Norwich MSA, CT-RI	H	9.75 FQ	16.51 AW	22.75 TQ	CTBLS	10/01-12/01
	Stamford-Norwalk PMSA, CT	H	17.44 FQ	23.03 AW	27.42 TQ	CTBLS	10/01-12/01
	Waterbury PMSA, CT	H	14.59 FQ	19.38 AW	25.06 TQ	CTBLS	10/01-12/01
	Delaware	H	10.77 FQ	17.45 AW	24.54 TQ	DEBLS	10/01-12/01
	Wilmington-Newark PMSA, DE-MD	H	10.44 FQ	17.46 AW	24.96 TQ	DEBLS	10/01-12/01
	District of Columbia	H	17.66 FQ	22.41 AW	30.36 TQ	DCBLS	10/01-12/01
	Washington PMSA, DC-MD-VA-WV	H	11.90 FQ	19.52 AW	26.63 TQ	DCBLS	10/01-12/01
	Florida	H	10.68 FQ	15.72 AW	21.66 TQ	FLBLS	10/01-12/01
	Daytona Beach MSA, FL	H	11.15 FQ	15.31 AW	20.67 TQ	FLBLS	10/01-12/01
	Fort Lauderdale PMSA, FL	H	11.90 FQ	17.92 AW	24.96 TQ	FLBLS	10/01-12/01
	Fort Myers-Cape Coral MSA, FL	H	11.70 FQ	16.35 AW	22.78 TQ	FLBLS	10/01-12/01
	Fort Pierce-Port St. Lucie MSA, FL	H	10.91 FQ	15.51 AW	21.49 TQ	FLBLS	10/01-12/01
	Fort Walton Beach MSA, FL	H	8.88 FQ	13.85 AW	20.98 TQ	FLBLS	10/01-12/01
	Jacksonville MSA, FL	H	10.30 FQ	14.69 AW	20.48 TQ	FLBLS	10/01-12/01
	Lakeland-Winter Haven MSA, FL	H	9.89 FQ	14.04 AW	18.33 TQ	FLBLS	10/01-12/01
	Melbourne-Titusville-Palm Bay MSA, FL	H	10.72 FQ	14.76 AW	19.92 TQ	FLBLS	10/01-12/01
	Miami PMSA, FL	H	10.85 FQ	15.44 AW	20.98 TQ	FLBLS	10/01-12/01
	Naples MSA, FL	H	10.30 FQ	16.03 AW	22.09 TQ	FLBLS	10/01-12/01
	Ocala MSA, FL	H	11.17 FQ	15.31 AW	19.34 TQ	FLBLS	10/01-12/01
	Orlando MSA, FL	H	11.10 FQ	15.33 AW	20.98 TQ	FLBLS	10/01-12/01
	Pensacola MSA, FL	H	9.97 FQ	18.07 AW	38.46 TQ	FLBLS	10/01-12/01
	Sarasota-Bradenton MSA, FL	H	10.14 FQ	14.51 AW	18.78 TQ	FLBLS	10/01-12/01
	Tallahassee MSA, FL	H	9.64 FQ	15.28 AW	21.98 TQ	FLBLS	10/01-12/01
	Tampa-St. Petersburg-Clearwater MSA, FL	H	10.77 FQ	16.04 AW	22.12 TQ	FLBLS	10/01-12/01
	West Palm Beach-Boca Raton MSA, FL	H	13.23 FQ	18.15 AW	23.30 TQ	FLBLS	10/01-12/01
	Georgia	H	9.47 FQ	13.63 AW	18.25 TQ	GABLS	10/01-12/01
	Atlanta MSA, GA	H	10.23 FQ	14.15 AW	17.91 TQ	GABLS	10/01-12/01
	Augusta-Aiken MSA, GA-SC	H	9.27 FQ	16.28 AW	27.08 TQ	GABLS	10/01-12/01
	Columbus MSA, GA-AL	H	9.52 FQ	12.84 AW	17.23 TQ	GABLS	10/01-12/01
	Macon MSA, GA	H	9.74 FQ	14.18 AW	19.81 TQ	GABLS	10/01-12/01
	Savannah MSA, GA	H	10.27 FQ	14.73 AW	18.30 TQ	GABLS	10/01-12/01
	Hawaii	H	13.72 FQ	17.05 AW	23.47 TQ	HIBLS	10/01-12/01
	Honolulu MSA, HI	H	13.86 FQ	17.60 AW	24.84 TQ	HIBLS	10/01-12/01
	Idaho	H	9.98 FQ	14.58 AW	20.52 TQ	IDBLS	10/01-12/01
	Boise City MSA, ID	H	11.82 FQ	15.75 AW	21.32 TQ	IDBLS	10/01-12/01
	Illinois	H	6.72 FQ	17.22 AW	26.72 TQ	ILBLS	10/01-12/01
	Champaign-Urbana MSA, IL	H	7.66 FQ	12.91 AW	17.97 TQ	ILBLS	10/01-12/01
	Chicago PMSA, IL	H	6.13 FQ	19.07 AW	28.86 TQ	ILBLS	10/01-12/01
	Peoria-Pekin MSA, IL	H	6.37 FQ	16.74 AW	22.42 TQ	ILBLS	10/01-12/01
	Rockford MSA, IL	H	9.42 FQ	15.67 AW	23.76 TQ	ILBLS	10/01-12/01
	Springfield MSA, IL	H	10.41 FQ	15.77 AW	21.46 TQ	ILBLS	10/01-12/01

AAW Average annual wage **AOH** Average offered, high **ASH** Average starting, high **H** Hourly **M** Monthly **S** Special: hourly and annual
AE Average entry wage **AOL** Average offered, low **ASL** Average starting, low **HI** Highest wage paid **MTC** Median total compensation **TQ** Third quartile wage
AEX Average experienced wage **APH** Average pay, high range **AW** Average wage paid **HR** High end range **MW** Median wage paid **W** Weekly
AO Average offered **APL** Average pay, low range **FQ** First quartile wage **LR** Low end range **SQ** Second quartile wage **Y** Yearly

Occupation/Type/Industry	Location	Per	Low	Mid	High	Source	Date
Water and Liquid Waste Treatment Plant and System Operator	Indiana	H	8.64 FQ	14.12 AW	20.46 TQ	INBLS	10/01-12/01
	Elkhart-Goshen MSA, IN	H	12.71 FQ	16.31 AW	20.60 TQ	INBLS	10/01-12/01
	Evansville-Henderson MSA, IN-KY	H	10.98 FQ	13.49 AW	18.84 TQ	INBLS	10/01-12/01
	Fort Wayne MSA, IN	H	11.34 FQ	15.18 AW	21.29 TQ	INBLS	10/01-12/01
	Gary PMSA, IN	H	8.61 FQ	13.95 AW	19.22 TQ	INBLS	10/01-12/01
	Indianapolis MSA, IN	H	6.48 FQ	14.84 AW	21.38 TQ	INBLS	10/01-12/01
	Lafayette MSA, IN	H	13.01 FQ	16.89 AW	21.19 TQ	INBLS	10/01-12/01
	Iowa	H	11.58 FQ	15.76 AW	20.98 TQ	IABLS	10/01-12/01
	Cedar Rapids MSA, IA	H	10.68 FQ	15.52 AW	20.94 TQ	IABLS	10/01-12/01
	Davenport-Moline-Rock Island MSA, IA-IL	H	9.70 FQ	15.78 AW	21.02 TQ	IABLS	10/01-12/01
	Des Moines MSA, IA	H	12.94 FQ	17.02 AW	21.00 TQ	IABLS	10/01-12/01
	Kansas	H	9.18 FQ	13.32 AW	18.40 TQ	KSBLS	10/01-12/01
	Wichita MSA, KS	H	10.52 FQ	15.41 AW	22.84 TQ	KSBLS	10/01-12/01
	Kentucky	H	8.38 FQ	13.46 AW	19.74 TQ	KYBLS	10/01-12/01
	Lexington MSA, KY	H	11.55 FQ	15.43 AW	20.50 TQ	KYBLS	10/01-12/01
	Louisville MSA, KY-IN	H	11.42 FQ	16.97 AW	23.09 TQ	KYBLS	10/01-12/01
	Louisiana	H	7.53 FQ	12.79 AW	17.55 TQ	LABLS	10/01-12/01
	Baton Rouge MSA, LA	H	7.35 FQ	11.67 AW	17.41 TQ	LABLS	10/01-12/01
	Lafayette MSA, LA	H	7.19 FQ	12.15 AW	16.55 TQ	LABLS	10/01-12/01
	Lake Charles MSA, LA	H	7.69 FQ	12.35 AW	14.45 TQ	LABLS	10/01-12/01
	New Orleans MSA, LA	H	7.11 FQ	12.34 AW	20.09 TQ	LABLS	10/01-12/01
	Shreveport-Bossier City MSA, LA	H	6.24 FQ	11.26 AW	19.65 TQ	LABLS	10/01-12/01
	Maine	H	11.10 FQ	16.45 AW	21.52 TQ	MEBLS	10/01-12/01
	Portland MSA, ME	H	11.26 FQ	16.42 AW	21.30 TQ	MEBLS	10/01-12/01
	Maryland	H	10.85 FQ	16.70 AW	24.11 TQ	MDBLS	10/01-12/01
	Baltimore PMSA, MD	H	10.61 FQ	15.63 AW	21.61 TQ	MDBLS	10/01-12/01
	Massachusetts	H	12.85 FQ	18.28 AW	23.49 TQ	MABLS	10/01-12/01
	Boston PMSA, MA-NH	H	12.68 FQ	18.21 AW	23.66 TQ	MABLS	10/01-12/01
	Brockton PMSA, MA	H	14.96 FQ	19.39 AW	23.03 TQ	MABLS	10/01-12/01
	Lawrence PMSA, MA-NH	H	10.12 FQ	17.65 AW	23.02 TQ	MABLS	10/01-12/01
	Lowell PMSA, MA-NH	H	13.20 FQ	18.67 AW	22.52 TQ	MABLS	10/01-12/01
	Springfield MSA, MA	H	12.04 FQ	17.26 AW	22.82 TQ	MABLS	10/01-12/01
	Worcester PMSA, MA-CT	H	14.93 FQ	20.27 AW	26.61 TQ	MABLS	10/01-12/01
	Michigan	H	11.53 FQ	17.30 AW	23.87 TQ	MIBLS	10/01-12/01
	Ann Arbor PMSA, MI	H	13.54 FQ	18.16 AW	23.14 TQ	MIBLS	10/01-12/01
	Grand Rapids-Muskegon-Holland MSA, MI	H	14.21 FQ	17.71 AW	21.98 TQ	MIBLS	10/01-12/01
	Kalamazoo-Battle Creek MSA, MI	H	13.58 FQ	17.13 AW	25.11 TQ	MIBLS	10/01-12/01
	Lansing-East Lansing MSA, MI	H	15.51 FQ	19.39 AW	23.67 TQ	MIBLS	10/01-12/01
	Saginaw-Bay City-Midland MSA, MI	H	10.64 FQ	17.40 AW	23.57 TQ	MIBLS	10/01-12/01
	Minnesota	H	12.88 FQ	17.84 AW	22.26 TQ	MNBLS	10/01-12/01
	Duluth-Superior MSA, MN-WI	H	15.71 FQ	19.05 AW	22.04 TQ	MNBLS	10/01-12/01
	Minneapolis-St. Paul MSA, MN-WI	H	14.90 FQ	19.13 AW	22.99 TQ	MNBLS	10/01-12/01
	St. Cloud MSA, MN	H	12.60 FQ	17.41 AW	21.45 TQ	MNBLS	10/01-12/01
	Mississippi	H	7.78 FQ	13.25 AW	19.19 TQ	MSBLS	10/01-12/01
	Biloxi-Gulfport-Pascagoula MSA, MS	H	6.58 FQ	12.54 AW	17.59 TQ	MSBLS	10/01-12/01
	Jackson MSA, MS	H	10.23 FQ	14.11 AW	20.86 TQ	MSBLS	10/01-12/01
	Missouri	H	8.67 FQ	14.86 AW	25.94 TQ	MOBLS	10/01-12/01
	Kansas City MSA, MO-KS	H	8.89 FQ	15.27 AW	25.80 TQ	MOBLS	10/01-12/01
	St. Louis MSA, MO-IL	H	8.99 FQ	15.13 AW	24.30 TQ	MOBLS	10/01-12/01
	Springfield MSA, MO	H	11.39 FQ	21.63 AW	28.47 TQ	MOBLS	10/01-12/01
	Montana	H	8.28 FQ	12.86 AW	17.38 TQ	MTBLS	10/01-12/01
	Billings MSA, MT	H	9.26 FQ	13.51 AW	18.20 TQ	MTBLS	10/01-12/01
	Nebraska	H	9.39 FQ	14.85 AW	22.58 TQ	NEBLS	10/01-12/01
	Omaha MSA, NE-IA	H	12.52 FQ	19.38 AW	26.35 TQ	NEBLS	10/01-12/01
	Nevada	H	16.47 FQ	23.53 AW	31.76 TQ	NVBLS	10/01-12/01
	Las Vegas MSA, NV-AZ	H	16.48 FQ	23.53 AW	31.28 TQ	NVBLS	10/01-12/01
	Reno MSA, NV	H	17.52 FQ	21.94 AW	27.24 TQ	NVBLS	10/01-12/01
	New Hampshire	H	10.70 FQ	16.21 AW	21.62 TQ	NHBLS	10/01-12/01
	Nashua PMSA, NH	H	14.29 FQ	18.09 AW	21.88 TQ	NHBLS	10/01-12/01
	Portsmouth-Rochester PMSA, NH-ME	H	13.12 FQ	17.38 AW	21.92 TQ	NHBLS	10/01-12/01
	New Jersey	H	12.18 FQ	20.07 AW	30.47 TQ	NJBLS	10/01-12/01

AAW	Average annual wage	AOH	Average offered, high	ASH	Average starting, high	H	Hourly	M	Monthly	S	Special: hourly and annual
AE	Average entry wage	AOL	Average offered, low	ASL	Average starting, low	HI	Highest wage paid	MTC	Median total compensation	TQ	Third quartile wage
AEX	Average experienced wage	APH	Average pay, high range	AW	Average wage paid	HR	High end range	MW	Median wage paid	W	Weekly
AO	Average offered	APL	Average pay, low range	FQ	First quartile wage	LR	Low end range	SQ	Second quartile wage	Y	Yearly

Occupation/Type/Industry	Location	Per	Low	Mid	High	Source	Date
Water and Liquid Waste Treatment Plant and System Operator	Atlantic-Cape May PMSA, NJ	H	8.59 FQ	17.42 AW	24.72 TQ	NJBLS	10/01-12/01
	Bergen-Passaic PMSA, NJ	H	14.72 FQ	20.85 AW	30.34 TQ	NJBLS	10/01-12/01
	Jersey City PMSA, NJ	H	11.81 FQ	16.70 AW	24.80 TQ	NJBLS	10/01-12/01
	Middlesex-Somerset-Hunterdon PMSA, NJ	H	12.11 FQ	25.15 AW	36.82 TQ	NJBLS	10/01-12/01
	Monmouth-Ocean PMSA, NJ	H	8.39 FQ	18.00 AW	26.69 TQ	NJBLS	10/01-12/01
	Newark PMSA, NJ	H	6.35 FQ	17.98 AW	25.99 TQ	NJBLS	10/01-12/01
	Trenton PMSA, NJ	H	13.14 FQ	20.33 AW	28.40 TQ	NJBLS	10/01-12/01
	New Mexico	H	8.51 FQ	13.46 AW	20.36 TQ	NMBLS	10/01-12/01
	Albuquerque MSA, NM	H	9.52 FQ	13.37 AW	17.52 TQ	NMBLS	10/01-12/01
	Las Cruces MSA, NM	H	7.26 FQ	11.25 AW	15.82 TQ	NMBLS	10/01-12/01
	New York	H	12.12 FQ	17.74 AW	23.87 TQ	NYBLS	10/01-12/01
	Albany-Schenectady-Troy MSA, NY	H	12.23 FQ	16.76 AW	21.43 TQ	NYBLS	10/01-12/01
	Binghamton MSA, NY	H	12.44 FQ	16.27 AW	21.14 TQ	NYBLS	10/01-12/01
	Buffalo-Niagara Falls MSA, NY	H	14.06 FQ	17.53 AW	22.14 TQ	NYBLS	10/01-12/01
	Dutchess County PMSA, NY	H	14.14 FQ	20.08 AW	26.85 TQ	NYBLS	10/01-12/01
	Nassau-Suffolk PMSA, NY	H	11.94 FQ	18.55 AW	26.31 TQ	NYBLS	10/01-12/01
	Newburgh PMSA, NY-PA	H	12.84 FQ	16.79 AW	22.20 TQ	NYBLS	10/01-12/01
	Rochester MSA, NY	H	9.92 FQ	15.73 AW	21.25 TQ	NYBLS	10/01-12/01
	Syracuse MSA, NY	H	10.42 FQ	17.84 AW	26.99 TQ	NYBLS	10/01-12/01
	Utica-Rome MSA, NY	H	11.38 FQ	13.84 AW	17.30 TQ	NYBLS	10/01-12/01
	North Carolina	H	9.87 FQ	14.06 AW	19.46 TQ	NCBLS	10/01-12/01
	Charlotte-Gastonia-Rock Hill MSA, NC-SC	H	11.23 FQ	14.91 AW	20.09 TQ	NCBLS	10/01-12/01
	Fayetteville MSA, NC	H	10.83 FQ	14.98 AW	19.85 TQ	NCBLS	10/01-12/01
	Greensboro-Winston-Salem-High Point MSA, NC	H	11.28 FQ	14.91 AW	19.89 TQ	NCBLS	10/01-12/01
	Hickory-Morganton-Lenoir MSA, NC	H	9.98 FQ	13.75 AW	18.78 TQ	NCBLS	10/01-12/01
	Raleigh-Durham-Chapel Hill MSA, NC	H	10.15 FQ	14.28 AW	19.13 TQ	NCBLS	10/01-12/01
	Wilmington MSA, NC	H	11.56 FQ	15.63 AW	20.45 TQ	NCBLS	10/01-12/01
	North Dakota	H	8.57 FQ	13.76 AW	19.76 TQ	NDBLS	10/01-12/01
	Fargo-Moorhead MSA, ND-MN	H	9.44 FQ	15.75 AW	22.18 TQ	NDBLS	10/01-12/01
	Ohio	H	11.51 FQ	16.82 AW	22.09 TQ	OHBLS	10/01-12/01
	Akron PMSA, OH	H	13.73 FQ	18.97 AW	25.05 TQ	OHBLS	10/01-12/01
	Canton-Massillon MSA, OH	H	8.73 FQ	15.11 AW	20.39 TQ	OHBLS	10/01-12/01
	Cincinnati PMSA, OH-KY-IN	H	11.88 FQ	16.63 AW	21.45 TQ	OHBLS	10/01-12/01
	Cleveland-Lorain-Elyria PMSA, OH	H	13.01 FQ	18.04 AW	22.17 TQ	OHBLS	10/01-12/01
	Columbus MSA, OH	H	10.80 FQ	15.86 AW	20.41 TQ	OHBLS	10/01-12/01
	Dayton-Springfield MSA, OH	H	11.47 FQ	18.72 AW	29.39 TQ	OHBLS	10/01-12/01
	Hamilton-Middletown PMSA, OH	H	13.61 FQ	19.00 AW	23.19 TQ	OHBLS	10/01-12/01
	Mansfield MSA, OH	H	11.73 FQ	14.57 AW	17.84 TQ	OHBLS	10/01-12/01
	Toledo MSA, OH	H	12.91 FQ	17.28 AW	22.03 TQ	OHBLS	10/01-12/01
	Youngstown-Warren MSA, OH	H	13.65 FQ	17.28 AW	23.27 TQ	OHBLS	10/01-12/01
	Oklahoma	H	6.86 FQ	10.82 AW	16.05 TQ	OKBLS	10/01-12/01
	Oklahoma City MSA, OK	H	6.80 FQ	11.65 AW	17.03 TQ	OKBLS	10/01-12/01
	Tulsa MSA, OK	H	8.44 FQ	12.44 AW	17.12 TQ	OKBLS	10/01-12/01
	Oregon	H	11.52 FQ	17.38 AW	23.83 TQ	ORBLS	10/01-12/01
	Eugene-Springfield MSA, OR	H	13.64 FQ	20.99 AW	27.56 TQ	ORBLS	10/01-12/01
	Medford-Ashland MSA, OR	H	13.56 FQ	17.21 AW	21.41 TQ	ORBLS	10/01-12/01
	Portland-Vancouver PMSA, OR-WA	H	12.25 FQ	18.33 AW	25.07 TQ	ORBLS	10/01-12/01
	Salem PMSA, OR	H	11.24 FQ	18.00 AW	24.95 TQ	ORBLS	10/01-12/01
	Pennsylvania	H	11.35 FQ	16.96 AW	23.19 TQ	PABLS	10/01-12/01
	Allentown-Bethlehem-Easton MSA, PA	H	6.07 FQ	15.81 AW	22.31 TQ	PABLS	10/01-12/01
	Erie MSA, PA	H	14.26 FQ	17.27 AW	21.64 TQ	PABLS	10/01-12/01
	Harrisburg-Lebanon-Carlisle MSA, PA	H	13.85 FQ	18.56 AW	24.30 TQ	PABLS	10/01-12/01
	Johnstown MSA, PA	H	10.02 FQ	17.44 AW	26.89 TQ	PABLS	10/01-12/01
	Lancaster MSA, PA	H	11.29 FQ	15.75 AW	21.39 TQ	PABLS	10/01-12/01
	Philadelphia PMSA, PA-NJ	H	14.18 FQ	18.64 AW	24.31 TQ	PABLS	10/01-12/01
	Pittsburgh MSA, PA	H	12.00 FQ	18.68 AW	25.53 TQ	PABLS	10/01-12/01
	Reading MSA, PA	H	13.67 FQ	16.44 AW	20.83 TQ	PABLS	10/01-12/01

AAW	Average annual wage	**AOH**	Average offered, high	**ASH**	Average starting, high	**H**	Hourly	**M**	Monthly	**S**	Special: hourly and annual
AE	Average entry wage	**AOL**	Average offered, low	**ASL**	Average starting, low	**HI**	Highest wage paid	**MTC**	Median total compensation	**TQ**	Third quartile wage
AEX	Average experienced wage	**APH**	Average pay, high range	**AW**	Average wage paid	**HR**	High end range	**MW**	Median wage paid	**W**	Weekly
AO	Average offered	**APL**	Average pay, low range	**FQ**	First quartile wage	**LR**	Low end range	**SQ**	Second quartile wage	**Y**	Yearly

Occupation/Type/Industry	Location	Per	Low	Mid	High	Source	Date
Water and Liquid Waste Treatment Plant and System Operator	Scranton-Wilkes-Barre-Hazleton MSA, PA	H	9.01 FQ	14.85 AW	20.21 TQ	PABLS	10/01-12/01
	York MSA, PA	H	11.66 FQ	15.73 AW	20.26 TQ	PABLS	10/01-12/01
	Rhode Island	H	13.28 FQ	16.75 AW	20.86 TQ	RIBLS	10/01-12/01
	Providence-Fall River-Warwick MSA, RI-MA	H	13.21 FQ	16.92 AW	21.16 TQ	RIBLS	10/01-12/01
	South Carolina	H	9.41 FQ	15.89 AW	25.30 TQ	SCBLS	10/01-12/01
	Charleston-North Charleston MSA, SC	H	9.20 FQ	14.05 AW	21.39 TQ	SCBLS	10/01-12/01
	Columbia MSA, SC	H	9.59 FQ	19.96 AW	39.94 TQ	SCBLS	10/01-12/01
	Greenville-Spartanburg-Anderson MSA, SC	H	10.10 FQ	15.63 AW	21.70 TQ	SCBLS	10/01-12/01
	Myrtle Beach MSA, SC	H	9.76 FQ	13.38 AW	17.54 TQ	SCBLS	10/01-12/01
	South Dakota	H	9.26 FQ	13.35 AW	18.99 TQ	SDBLS	10/01-12/01
	Sioux Falls MSA, SD	H	9.73 FQ	14.68 AW	20.85 TQ	SDBLS	10/01-12/01
	Tennessee	H	8.75 FQ	14.44 AW	21.78 TQ	TNBLS	10/01-12/01
	Chattanooga MSA, TN-GA	H	9.29 FQ	14.41 AW	22.74 TQ	TNBLS	10/01-12/01
	Clarksville-Hopkinsville MSA, TN-KY	H	11.37 FQ	14.73 AW	20.07 TQ	TNBLS	10/01-12/01
	Johnson City-Kingsport-Bristol MSA, TN-VA	H	7.53 FQ	11.83 AW	17.81 TQ	TNBLS	10/01-12/01
	Knoxville MSA, TN	H	8.66 FQ	16.95 AW	25.12 TQ	TNBLS	10/01-12/01
	Memphis MSA, TN-AR-MS	H	8.88 FQ	14.74 AW	21.52 TQ	TNBLS	10/01-12/01
	Nashville MSA, TN	H	9.96 FQ	15.32 AW	21.37 TQ	TNBLS	10/01-12/01
	Texas	H	8.96 FQ	13.42 AW	19.41 TQ	TXBLS	10/01-12/01
	Austin-San Marcos MSA, TX	H	10.81 FQ	14.05 AW	18.43 TQ	TXBLS	10/01-12/01
	Beaumont-Port Arthur MSA, TX	H	8.65 FQ	14.03 AW	23.62 TQ	TXBLS	10/01-12/01
	Brazoria PMSA, TX	H	9.26 FQ	13.59 AW	21.26 TQ	TXBLS	10/01-12/01
	Brownsville-Harlingen-San Benito MSA, TX	H	7.10 FQ	10.22 AW	14.03 TQ	TXBLS	10/01-12/01
	Corpus Christi MSA, TX	H	8.96 FQ	12.30 AW	17.24 TQ	TXBLS	10/01-12/01
	Dallas PMSA, TX	H	9.98 FQ	15.01 AW	20.93 TQ	TXBLS	10/01-12/01
	El Paso MSA, TX	H	9.90 FQ	12.43 AW	14.58 TQ	TXBLS	10/01-12/01
	Fort Worth-Arlington PMSA, TX	H	9.36 FQ	13.30 AW	18.13 TQ	TXBLS	10/01-12/01
	Galveston-Texas City PMSA, TX	H	10.83 FQ	17.68 AW	23.30 TQ	TXBLS	10/01-12/01
	Houston PMSA, TX	H	10.11 FQ	15.64 AW	21.50 TQ	TXBLS	10/01-12/01
	Killeen-Temple MSA, TX	H	7.59 FQ	11.04 AW	16.00 TQ	TXBLS	10/01-12/01
	Laredo MSA, TX	H	7.12 FQ	10.56 AW	13.58 TQ	TXBLS	10/01-12/01
	Longview-Marshall MSA, TX	H	9.64 FQ	13.43 AW	17.68 TQ	TXBLS	10/01-12/01
	Lubbock MSA, TX	H	9.50 FQ	13.65 AW	17.80 TQ	TXBLS	10/01-12/01
	McAllen-Edinburg-Mission MSA, TX	H	5.88 FQ	9.02 AW	12.90 TQ	TXBLS	10/01-12/01
	San Antonio MSA, TX	H	9.34 FQ	14.49 AW	22.53 TQ	TXBLS	10/01-12/01
	Tyler MSA, TX	H	9.80 FQ	13.37 AW	18.00 TQ	TXBLS	10/01-12/01
	Waco MSA, TX	H	9.75 FQ	13.75 AW	18.15 TQ	TXBLS	10/01-12/01
	Utah	H	11.83 FQ	16.42 AW	21.43 TQ	UTBLS	10/01-12/01
	Provo-Orem MSA, UT	H	12.39 FQ	15.68 AW	20.47 TQ	UTBLS	10/01-12/01
	Salt Lake City-Ogden MSA, UT	H	12.69 FQ	17.13 AW	21.80 TQ	UTBLS	10/01-12/01
	Vermont	H	10.02 FQ	15.10 AW	20.73 TQ	VTBLS	10/01-12/01
	Burlington MSA, VT	H	11.27 FQ	16.56 AW	22.08 TQ	VTBLS	10/01-12/01
	Virginia	H	9.50 FQ	15.78 AW	22.17 TQ	VABLS	10/01-12/01
	Lynchburg MSA, VA	H	9.37 FQ	13.52 AW	18.54 TQ	VABLS	10/01-12/01
	Norfolk-Virginia Beach-Newport News MSA, VA-NC	H	10.25 FQ	17.60 AW	22.88 TQ	VABLS	10/01-12/01
	Richmond-Petersburg MSA, VA	H	9.65 FQ	15.09 AW	21.18 TQ	VABLS	10/01-12/01
	Roanoke MSA, VA	H	9.62 FQ	13.64 AW	18.53 TQ	VABLS	10/01-12/01
	Washington	H	15.21 FQ	21.06 AW	27.37 TQ	WABLS	10/01-12/01
	Bremerton PMSA, WA	H	12.83 FQ	19.41 AW	24.93 TQ	WABLS	10/01-12/01
	Richland-Kennewick-Pasco MSA, WA	H	14.12 FQ	21.27 AW	27.54 TQ	WABLS	10/01-12/01
	Seattle-Bellevue-Everett PMSA, WA	H	19.39 FQ	24.00 AW	28.24 TQ	WABLS	10/01-12/01
	Spokane MSA, WA	H	15.12 FQ	19.89 AW	27.13 TQ	WABLS	10/01-12/01
	Tacoma PMSA, WA	H	18.98 FQ	23.33 AW	27.59 TQ	WABLS	10/01-12/01

AAW Average annual wage; AE Average entry wage; AEX Average experienced wage; AO Average offered; AOH Average offered, high; AOL Average offered, low; APH Average pay, high range; APL Average pay, low range; ASH Average starting, high; ASL Average starting, low; AW Average wage paid; FQ First quartile wage; H Hourly; HI Highest wage paid; HR High end range; LR Low end range; M Monthly; MTC Median total compensation; MW Median wage paid; SQ Second quartile wage; S Special: hourly and annual; TQ Third quartile wage; W Weekly; Y Yearly

Occupation/Type/Industry	Location	Per	Low	Mid	High	Source	Date
Water and Liquid Waste Treatment Plant and System Operator	Yakima MSA, WA	H	14.39 FQ	18.72 AW	26.69 TQ	WABLS	10/01-12/01
	West Virginia	H	7.79 FQ	11.92 AW	16.32 TQ	WVBLS	10/01-12/01
	Charleston MSA, WV	H	8.85 FQ	12.95 AW	16.64 TQ	WVBLS	10/01-12/01
	Huntington-Ashland MSA, WV-KY-OH	H	9.33 FQ	13.11 AW	16.96 TQ	WVBLS	10/01-12/01
	Wisconsin	H	13.93 FQ	18.30 AW	23.03 TQ	WIBLS	10/01-12/01
	Appleton-Oshkosh-Neenah MSA, WI	H	14.20 FQ	17.99 AW	21.99 TQ	WIBLS	10/01-12/01
	Green Bay MSA, WI	H	15.89 FQ	21.53 AW	28.04 TQ	WIBLS	10/01-12/01
	Madison MSA, WI	H	14.51 FQ	18.62 AW	24.83 TQ	WIBLS	10/01-12/01
	Milwaukee-Waukesha PMSA, WI	H	15.31 FQ	19.62 AW	23.34 TQ	WIBLS	10/01-12/01
	Racine PMSA, WI	H	10.13 FQ	17.27 AW	21.75 TQ	WIBLS	10/01-12/01
	Wyoming	H	12.25 FQ	16.63 AW	21.28 TQ	WYBLS	10/01-12/01
	Puerto Rico	H	5.68 FQ	9.59 AW	13.99 TQ	PRBLS	10/01-12/01
	Guam	H	9.26 FQ	14.31 AW	19.62 TQ	GUBLS	10/01-12/01
Web Content Developer							
Information Technology	United States	Y	42000 AOL			IOMA5	1/01-1/02
Web Designer	United States	Y		59300 AW		INFO4	1/01-1/02
Web Designer and Developer							
Information Technology	United States	Y	46000 AOL			IOMA5	1/01-1/02
Web Developer	United States	Y		92833 AW		INFO3	1/00-1/01
	Phoenix, AZ	Y		50000 AW		TBJ	1/00-1/01
Webmaster							
Internet and E-Commerce	United States	Y		58000-82500 AW		IW	1/00-1/01
Webmaster and Internet Manager	United States	Y		60100 AW		INFO4	1/01-1/02
Weigher, Measurer, Checker, and Sampler, Recordkeeping	Alabama	H	7.17 FQ	10.99 AW	16.85 TQ	ALBLS	10/01-12/01
	Alaska	H	10.00 FQ	14.01 AW	17.45 TQ	AKBLS	10/01-12/01
	Arizona	H	7.62 FQ	11.28 AW	16.43 TQ	AZBLS	10/01-12/01
	Arkansas	H	7.46 FQ	10.65 AW	14.41 TQ	ARBLS	10/01-12/01
	California	H	7.50 FQ	13.67 AW	21.38 TQ	CABLS	10/01-12/01
	Colorado	H	8.81 FQ	13.27 AW	20.50 TQ	COBLS	10/01-12/01
	Connecticut	H	9.32 FQ	14.64 AW	21.99 TQ	CTBLS	10/01-12/01
	Delaware	H	8.74 FQ	17.94 AW	27.03 TQ	DEBLS	10/01-12/01
	Florida	H	7.06 FQ	12.20 AW	21.27 TQ	FLBLS	10/01-12/01
	Georgia	H	7.80 FQ	14.11 AW	25.01 TQ	GABLS	10/01-12/01
	Hawaii	H	8.16 FQ	14.95 AW	21.99 TQ	HIBLS	10/01-12/01
	Idaho	H	6.00 FQ	10.11 AW	14.37 TQ	IDBLS	10/01-12/01
	Illinois	H	7.92 FQ	13.00 AW	20.10 TQ	ILBLS	10/01-12/01
	Indiana	H	7.96 FQ	12.43 AW	18.11 TQ	INBLS	10/01-12/01
	Iowa	H	8.02 FQ	12.20 AW	16.91 TQ	IABLS	10/01-12/01
	Kansas	H	7.13 FQ	13.43 AW	23.37 TQ	KSBLS	10/01-12/01
	Kentucky	H	7.45 FQ	11.09 AW	16.14 TQ	KYBLS	10/01-12/01
	Louisiana	H	6.29 FQ	10.79 AW	16.82 TQ	LABLS	10/01-12/01
	Maine	H	8.67 FQ	12.36 AW	16.58 TQ	MEBLS	10/01-12/01
	Maryland	H	7.77 FQ	11.98 AW	16.89 TQ	MDBLS	10/01-12/01
	Massachusetts	H	8.40 FQ	15.06 AW	23.37 TQ	MABLS	10/01-12/01
	Michigan	H	8.88 FQ	16.47 AW	26.87 TQ	MIBLS	10/01-12/01
	Minnesota	H	7.53 FQ	11.85 AW	17.75 TQ	MNBLS	10/01-12/01
	Mississippi	H	6.01 FQ	8.88 AW	13.18 TQ	MSBLS	10/01-12/01
	Missouri	H	7.78 FQ	12.14 AW	18.68 TQ	MOBLS	10/01-12/01
	Montana	H	7.37 FQ	9.01 AW	10.88 TQ	MTBLS	10/01-12/01
	Nebraska	H	7.33 FQ	11.52 AW	16.30 TQ	NEBLS	10/01-12/01
	Nevada	H	6.91 FQ	10.64 AW	15.55 TQ	NVBLS	10/01-12/01
	New Hampshire	H	7.99 FQ	11.80 AW	16.74 TQ	NHBLS	10/01-12/01
	New Jersey	H	7.29 FQ	12.87 AW	19.42 TQ	NJBLS	10/01-12/01
	New Mexico	H	6.41 FQ	10.04 AW	14.60 TQ	NMBLS	10/01-12/01
	New York	H	8.25 FQ	13.70 AW	21.52 TQ	NYBLS	10/01-12/01
	North Carolina	H	7.52 FQ	11.56 AW	16.95 TQ	NCBLS	10/01-12/01
	North Dakota	H	6.80 FQ	8.16 AW	10.59 TQ	NDBLS	10/01-12/01
	Ohio	H	8.39 FQ	13.49 AW	19.91 TQ	OHBLS	10/01-12/01

AAW Average annual wage	**AOH** Average offered, high	**ASH** Average starting, high	**H** Hourly	**M** Monthly	**S** Special: hourly and annual
AE Average entry wage	**AOL** Average offered, low	**ASL** Average starting, low	**HI** Highest wage paid	**MTC** Median total compensation	**TQ** Third quartile wage
AEX Average experienced wage	**APH** Average pay, high range	**AW** Average wage paid	**HR** High end range	**MW** Median wage paid	**W** Weekly
AO Average offered	**APL** Average pay, low range	**FQ** First quartile wage	**LR** Low end range	**SQ** Second quartile wage	**Y** Yearly

Occupation/Type/Industry	Location	Per	Low	Mid	High	Source	Date
Weigher, Measurer, Checker, and Sampler, Recordkeeping	Oklahoma	H	7.58 FQ	11.57 AW	16.73 TQ	OKBLS	10/01-12/01
	Oregon	H	7.19 FQ	11.41 AW	18.94 TQ	ORBLS	10/01-12/01
	Pennsylvania	H	7.39 FQ	12.32 AW	17.96 TQ	PABLS	10/01-12/01
	Rhode Island	H	8.16 FQ	12.42 AW	17.53 TQ	RIBLS	10/01-12/01
	South Carolina	H	8.36 FQ	11.97 AW	14.56 TQ	SCBLS	10/01-12/01
	South Dakota	H	7.71 FQ	10.84 AW	13.46 TQ	SDBLS	10/01-12/01
	Tennessee	H	8.00 FQ	12.39 AW	18.11 TQ	TNBLS	10/01-12/01
	Texas	H	8.05 FQ	14.51 AW	22.27 TQ	TXBLS	10/01-12/01
	Utah	H	8.25 FQ	13.21 AW	21.27 TQ	UTBLS	10/01-12/01
	Vermont	H	8.64 FQ	12.05 AW	16.28 TQ	VTBLS	10/01-12/01
	Virginia	H	8.20 FQ	13.31 AW	20.61 TQ	VABLS	10/01-12/01
	Washington	H	8.56 FQ	14.70 AW	22.71 TQ	WABLS	10/01-12/01
	West Virginia	H	7.47 FQ	11.56 AW	17.38 TQ	WVBLS	10/01-12/01
	Wisconsin	H	8.03 FQ	14.87 AW	25.77 TQ	WIBLS	10/01-12/01
	Wyoming	H	7.06 FQ	10.80 AW	14.91 TQ	WYBLS	10/01-12/01
	Virgin Islands	H	7.66 FQ	10.97 AW	13.88 TQ	VIBLS	10/01-12/01
Welder, Cutter, Solderer, and Brazer	Alabama	H	8.85 FQ	13.27 AW	19.52 TQ	ALBLS	10/01-12/01
	Birmingham MSA, AL	H	9.11 FQ	13.89 AW	20.27 TQ	ALBLS	10/01-12/01
	Huntsville MSA, AL	H	9.17 FQ	15.77 AW	26.28 TQ	ALBLS	10/01-12/01
	Mobile MSA, AL	H	9.91 FQ	13.97 AW	19.42 TQ	ALBLS	10/01-12/01
	Montgomery MSA, AL	H	8.82 FQ	12.38 AW	16.95 TQ	ALBLS	10/01-12/01
	Alaska	H	15.41 FQ	22.18 AW	28.54 TQ	AKBLS	10/01-12/01
	Anchorage MSA, AK	H	14.17 FQ	21.67 AW	32.11 TQ	AKBLS	10/01-12/01
	Arizona	H	8.22 FQ	12.79 AW	19.32 TQ	AZBLS	10/01-12/01
	Phoenix-Mesa MSA, AZ	H	8.27 FQ	12.71 AW	18.79 TQ	AZBLS	10/01-12/01
	Tucson MSA, AZ	H	8.08 FQ	12.02 AW	17.66 TQ	AZBLS	10/01-12/01
	Arkansas	H	8.92 FQ	12.52 AW	17.68 TQ	ARBLS	10/01-12/01
	Fayetteville-Springdale-Rogers MSA, AR	H	9.07 FQ	11.00 AW	13.75 TQ	ARBLS	10/01-12/01
	Fort Smith MSA, AR-OK	H	9.27 FQ	13.10 AW	16.85 TQ	ARBLS	10/01-12/01
	Little Rock-North Little Rock MSA, AR	H	9.32 FQ	12.82 AW	17.37 TQ	ARBLS	10/01-12/01
	California	H	8.45 FQ	14.78 AW	23.30 TQ	CABLS	10/01-12/01
	Bakersfield MSA, CA	H	9.92 FQ	16.34 AW	25.76 TQ	CABLS	10/01-12/01
	Chico-Paradise MSA, CA	H	9.65 FQ	14.60 AW	21.06 TQ	CABLS	10/01-12/01
	Fresno MSA, CA	H	9.00 FQ	13.30 AW	17.03 TQ	CABLS	10/01-12/01
	Los Angeles-Long Beach PMSA, CA	H	7.56 FQ	13.37 AW	21.08 TQ	CABLS	10/01-12/01
	Merced MSA, CA	H	8.61 FQ	12.26 AW	15.99 TQ	CABLS	10/01-12/01
	Modesto MSA, CA	H	9.42 FQ	14.10 AW	19.81 TQ	CABLS	10/01-12/01
	Oakland PMSA, CA	H	12.40 FQ	20.48 AW	26.65 TQ	CABLS	10/01-12/01
	Orange County PMSA, CA	H	8.17 FQ	15.60 AW	26.78 TQ	CABLS	10/01-12/01
	Redding MSA, CA	H	8.89 FQ	13.34 AW	18.80 TQ	CABLS	10/01-12/01
	Riverside-San Bernardino PMSA, CA	H	8.31 FQ	12.97 AW	19.39 TQ	CABLS	10/01-12/01
	Sacramento PMSA, CA	H	9.17 FQ	13.37 AW	17.84 TQ	CABLS	10/01-12/01
	Salinas MSA, CA	H	9.32 FQ	14.24 AW	21.23 TQ	CABLS	10/01-12/01
	San Diego MSA, CA	H	8.81 FQ	14.27 AW	22.45 TQ	CABLS	10/01-12/01
	San Francisco PMSA, CA	H	9.10 FQ	16.63 AW	30.86 TQ	CABLS	10/01-12/01
	San Jose PMSA, CA	H	10.73 FQ	16.57 AW	23.95 TQ	CABLS	10/01-12/01
	San Luis Obispo-Atascadero-Paso Robles MSA, CA	H	9.22 FQ	14.30 AW	21.78 TQ	CABLS	10/01-12/01
	Santa Barbara-Santa Maria-Lompoc MSA, CA	H	9.80 FQ	15.39 AW	21.64 TQ	CABLS	10/01-12/01
	Santa Cruz-Watsonville PMSA, CA	H	9.49 FQ	13.61 AW	19.12 TQ	CABLS	10/01-12/01
	Santa Rosa PMSA, CA	H	11.19 FQ	16.60 AW	23.17 TQ	CABLS	10/01-12/01
	Stockton-Lodi MSA, CA	H	9.59 FQ	14.59 AW	20.78 TQ	CABLS	10/01-12/01
	Vallejo-Fairfield-Napa PMSA, CA	H	8.48 FQ	15.95 AW	21.90 TQ	CABLS	10/01-12/01
	Ventura PMSA, CA	H	8.41 FQ	13.96 AW	20.93 TQ	CABLS	10/01-12/01
	Visalia-Tulare-Porterville MSA, CA	H	9.13 FQ	13.89 AW	20.35 TQ	CABLS	10/01-12/01
	Colorado	H	9.31 FQ	14.56 AW	20.91 TQ	COBLS	10/01-12/01
	Boulder-Longmont PMSA, CO	H	9.94 FQ	15.56 AW	21.04 TQ	COBLS	10/01-12/01
	Colorado Springs MSA, CO	H	9.01 FQ	13.10 AW	18.23 TQ	COBLS	10/01-12/01
	Denver PMSA, CO	H	11.11 FQ	15.35 AW	20.82 TQ	COBLS	10/01-12/01
	Fort Collins-Loveland MSA, CO	H	9.33 FQ	13.13 AW	16.85 TQ	COBLS	10/01-12/01

AAW	Average annual wage	**AOH**	Average offered, high	**ASH**	Average starting, high	**H**	Hourly	**M**	Monthly	**S**	Special: hourly and annual
AE	Average entry wage	**AOL**	Average offered, low	**ASL**	Average starting, low	**HI**	Highest wage paid	**MTC**	Median total compensation	**TQ**	Third quartile wage
AEX	Average experienced wage	**APH**	Average pay, high range	**AW**	Average wage paid	**HR**	High end range	**MW**	Median wage paid	**W**	Weekly
AO	Average offered	**APL**	Average pay, low range	**FQ**	First quartile wage	**LR**	Low end range	**SQ**	Second quartile wage	**Y**	Yearly

Occupation/Type/Industry	Location	Per	Low	Mid	High	Source	Date
Welder, Cutter, Solderer, and Brazer	Greeley PMSA, CO	H	7.99 FQ	13.24 AW	20.48 TQ	COBLS	10/01-12/01
	Connecticut	H	8.88 FQ	15.25 AW	21.66 TQ	CTBLS	10/01-12/01
	Bridgeport PMSA, CT	H	12.32 FQ	17.27 AW	23.02 TQ	CTBLS	10/01-12/01
	Danbury PMSA, CT	H	11.88 FQ	17.13 AW	22.06 TQ	CTBLS	10/01-12/01
	Hartford MSA, CT	H	9.17 FQ	14.79 AW	21.93 TQ	CTBLS	10/01-12/01
	New Haven-Meriden PMSA, CT	H	7.95 FQ	13.27 AW	19.95 TQ	CTBLS	10/01-12/01
	New London-Norwich MSA, CT-RI	H	13.32 FQ	17.63 AW	21.19 TQ	CTBLS	10/01-12/01
	Stamford-Norwalk PMSA, CT	H	14.32 FQ	18.97 AW	26.07 TQ	CTBLS	10/01-12/01
	Waterbury PMSA, CT	H	6.69 FQ	13.14 AW	21.27 TQ	CTBLS	10/01-12/01
	Delaware	H	10.62 FQ	17.27 AW	26.14 TQ	DEBLS	10/01-12/01
	Wilmington-Newark PMSA, DE-MD	H	12.17 FQ	18.97 AW	29.98 TQ	DEBLS	10/01-12/01
	District of Columbia	H	12.22 FQ	20.48 AW	26.67 TQ	DCBLS	10/01-12/01
	Washington PMSA, DC-MD-VA-WV	H	10.01 FQ	15.60 AW	22.72 TQ	DCBLS	10/01-12/01
	Florida	H	8.39 FQ	13.22 AW	19.68 TQ	FLBLS	10/01-12/01
	Daytona Beach MSA, FL	H	9.47 FQ	12.89 AW	16.76 TQ	FLBLS	10/01-12/01
	Fort Lauderdale PMSA, FL	H	7.71 FQ	12.85 AW	19.06 TQ	FLBLS	10/01-12/01
	Fort Myers-Cape Coral MSA, FL	H	10.46 FQ	13.45 AW	16.90 TQ	FLBLS	10/01-12/01
	Fort Pierce-Port St. Lucie MSA, FL	H	8.78 FQ	13.37 AW	18.11 TQ	FLBLS	10/01-12/01
	Fort Walton Beach MSA, FL	H	9.16 FQ	12.99 AW	17.38 TQ	FLBLS	10/01-12/01
	Gainesville MSA, FL	H	9.06 FQ	12.14 AW	15.65 TQ	FLBLS	10/01-12/01
	Jacksonville MSA, FL	H	9.01 FQ	13.46 AW	19.01 TQ	FLBLS	10/01-12/01
	Lakeland-Winter Haven MSA, FL	H	8.04 FQ	11.49 AW	16.44 TQ	FLBLS	10/01-12/01
	Melbourne-Titusville-Palm Bay MSA, FL	H	9.49 FQ	14.72 AW	20.90 TQ	FLBLS	10/01 12/01
	Miami PMSA, FL	H	8.60 FQ	12.75 AW	19.39 TQ	FLBLS	10/01-12/01
	Naples MSA, FL	H	9.69 FQ	12.71 AW	16.55 TQ	FLBLS	10/01-12/01
	Ocala MSA, FL	H	8.66 FQ	12.13 AW	16.42 TQ	FLBLS	10/01-12/01
	Orlando MSA, FL	H	9.49 FQ	15.37 AW	21.22 TQ	FLBLS	10/01-12/01
	Pensacola MSA, FL	H	7.54 FQ	12.60 AW	22.31 TQ	FLBLS	10/01-12/01
	Sarasota-Bradenton MSA, FL	H	8.57 FQ	12.14 AW	16.09 TQ	FLBLS	10/01-12/01
	Tallahassee MSA, FL	H	7.39 FQ	11.11 AW	15.97 TQ	FLBLS	10/01-12/01
	Tampa-St. Petersburg-Clearwater MSA, FL	H	7.95 FQ	12.78 AW	19.10 TQ	FLBLS	10/01-12/01
	West Palm Beach-Boca Raton MSA, FL	H	9.57 FQ	14.34 AW	20.17 TQ	FLBLS	10/01-12/01
	Georgia	H	9.05 FQ	13.53 AW	18.14 TQ	GABLS	10/01-12/01
	Atlanta MSA, GA	H	8.73 FQ	13.69 AW	18.51 TQ	GABLS	10/01-12/01
	Augusta-Aiken MSA, GA-SC	H	10.14 FQ	14.94 AW	21.88 TQ	GABLS	10/01-12/01
	Columbus MSA, GA-AL	H	8.76 FQ	12.44 AW	16.82 TQ	GABLS	10/01-12/01
	Macon MSA, GA	H	9.64 FQ	14.06 AW	19.44 TQ	GABLS	10/01-12/01
	Savannah MSA, GA	H	9.73 FQ	15.38 AW	25.10 TQ	GABLS	10/01-12/01
	Hawaii	H	12.16 FQ	20.01 AW	28.18 TQ	HIBLS	10/01-12/01
	Honolulu MSA, HI	H	12.15 FQ	20.86 AW	28.90 TQ	HIBLS	10/01-12/01
	Idaho	H	9.50 FQ	13.88 AW	19.78 TQ	IDBLS	10/01-12/01
	Boise City MSA, ID	H	10.18 FQ	14.49 AW	20.25 TQ	IDBLS	10/01-12/01
	Illinois	H	9.39 FQ	14.87 AW	22.88 TQ	ILBLS	10/01-12/01
	Champaign-Urbana MSA, IL	H	9.47 FQ	14.17 AW	17.61 TQ	ILBLS	10/01-12/01
	Chicago PMSA, IL	H	9.59 FQ	15.69 AW	24.67 TQ	ILBLS	10/01-12/01
	Peoria-Pekin MSA, IL	H	10.11 FQ	14.38 AW	19.69 TQ	ILBLS	10/01-12/01
	Rockford MSA, IL	H	9.84 FQ	15.23 AW	22.74 TQ	ILBLS	10/01-12/01
	Springfield MSA, IL	H	9.72 FQ	15.32 AW	20.92 TQ	ILBLS	10/01-12/01
	Indiana	H	9.74 FQ	15.08 AW	22.45 TQ	INBLS	10/01-12/01
	Elkhart-Goshen MSA, IN	H	9.98 FQ	14.47 AW	20.41 TQ	INBLS	10/01-12/01
	Evansville-Henderson MSA, IN-KY	H	9.61 FQ	13.41 AW	17.87 TQ	INBLS	10/01-12/01
	Fort Wayne MSA, IN	H	10.60 FQ	15.56 AW	23.95 TQ	INBLS	10/01-12/01
	Gary PMSA, IN	H	7.60 FQ	16.60 AW	24.68 TQ	INBLS	10/01-12/01
	Indianapolis MSA, IN	H	9.75 FQ	15.29 AW	23.89 TQ	INBLS	10/01-12/01
	South Bend MSA, IN	H	8.59 FQ	11.84 AW	14.15 TQ	INBLS	10/01-12/01
	Iowa	H	9.33 FQ	13.62 AW	18.95 TQ	IABLS	10/01-12/01
	Cedar Rapids MSA, IA	H	10.17 FQ	15.63 AW	21.71 TQ	IABLS	10/01-12/01
	Davenport-Moline-Rock Island MSA, IA-IL	H	9.53 FQ	14.51 AW	22.35 TQ	IABLS	10/01-12/01
	Des Moines MSA, IA	H	10.08 FQ	15.72 AW	22.43 TQ	IABLS	10/01-12/01

AAW	Average annual wage	AOH	Average offered, high	ASH	Average starting, high	H	Hourly	M	Monthly	S	Special: hourly and annual
AE	Average entry wage	AOL	Average offered, low	ASL	Average starting, low	HI	Highest wage paid	MTC	Median total compensation	TQ	Third quartile wage
AEX	Average experienced wage	APH	Average pay, high range	AW	Average wage paid	HR	High end range	MW	Median wage paid	W	Weekly
AO	Average offered	APL	Average pay, low range	FQ	First quartile wage	LR	Low end range	SQ	Second quartile wage	Y	Yearly

Occupation/Type/Industry	Location	Per	Low	Mid	High	Source	Date
Welder, Cutter, Solderer, and Brazer	Kansas	H	8.73 FQ	13.26 AW	19.31 TQ	KSBLS	10/01-12/01
	Topeka MSA, KS	H	9.16 FQ	12.62 AW	16.77 TQ	KSBLS	10/01-12/01
	Wichita MSA, KS	H	9.23 FQ	15.23 AW	23.87 TQ	KSBLS	10/01-12/01
	Kentucky	H	8.87 FQ	13.36 AW	18.69 TQ	KYBLS	10/01-12/01
	Lexington MSA, KY	H	8.90 FQ	14.14 AW	19.25 TQ	KYBLS	10/01-12/01
	Louisville MSA, KY-IN	H	9.38 FQ	13.87 AW	17.91 TQ	KYBLS	10/01-12/01
	Louisiana	H	10.01 FQ	14.77 AW	19.68 TQ	LABLS	10/01-12/01
	Baton Rouge MSA, LA	H	10.55 FQ	15.14 AW	20.03 TQ	LABLS	10/01-12/01
	Houma MSA, LA	H	11.23 FQ	15.02 AW	19.35 TQ	LABLS	10/01-12/01
	Lafayette MSA, LA	H	8.93 FQ	15.09 AW	20.00 TQ	LABLS	10/01-12/01
	Lake Charles MSA, LA	H	11.79 FQ	16.23 AW	20.92 TQ	LABLS	10/01-12/01
	New Orleans MSA, LA	H	10.23 FQ	14.39 AW	18.49 TQ	LABLS	10/01-12/01
	Shreveport-Bossier City MSA, LA	H	9.80 FQ	15.15 AW	20.58 TQ	LABLS	10/01-12/01
	Maine	H	9.82 FQ	14.46 AW	18.81 TQ	MEBLS	10/01-12/01
	Portland MSA, ME	H	9.61 FQ	13.03 AW	17.52 TQ	MEBLS	10/01-12/01
	Maryland	H	10.17 FQ	14.86 AW	21.07 TQ	MDBLS	10/01-12/01
	Baltimore PMSA, MD	H	10.35 FQ	14.86 AW	21.15 TQ	MDBLS	10/01-12/01
	Massachusetts	H	10.37 FQ	16.62 AW	23.82 TQ	MABLS	10/01-12/01
	Boston PMSA, MA-NH	H	10.56 FQ	16.90 AW	24.21 TQ	MABLS	10/01-12/01
	Brockton PMSA, MA	H	11.14 FQ	16.62 AW	21.77 TQ	MABLS	10/01-12/01
	Lawrence PMSA, MA-NH	H	10.92 FQ	16.94 AW	24.32 TQ	MABLS	10/01-12/01
	Lowell PMSA, MA-NH	H	11.16 FQ	17.10 AW	24.49 TQ	MABLS	10/01-12/01
	New Bedford PMSA, MA	H	8.10 FQ	14.09 AW	19.69 TQ	MABLS	10/01-12/01
	Springfield MSA, MA	H	11.09 FQ	16.19 AW	22.13 TQ	MABLS	10/01-12/01
	Worcester PMSA, MA-CT	H	10.51 FQ	16.74 AW	24.55 TQ	MABLS	10/01-12/01
	Michigan	H	10.05 FQ	18.72 AW	28.50 TQ	MIBLS	10/01-12/01
	Ann Arbor PMSA, MI	H	10.07 FQ	19.06 AW	28.19 TQ	MIBLS	10/01-12/01
	Detroit PMSA, MI	H	10.71 FQ	21.41 AW	29.48 TQ	MIBLS	10/01-12/01
	Grand Rapids-Muskegon-Holland MSA, MI	H	10.02 FQ	15.06 AW	21.19 TQ	MIBLS	10/01-12/01
	Kalamazoo-Battle Creek MSA, MI	H	10.58 FQ	13.30 AW	16.87 TQ	MIBLS	10/01-12/01
	Lansing-East Lansing MSA, MI	H	9.30 FQ	18.68 AW	32.13 TQ	MIBLS	10/01-12/01
	Saginaw-Bay City-Midland MSA, MI	H	10.29 FQ	22.18 AW	34.13 TQ	MIBLS	10/01-12/01
	Minnesota	H	10.55 FQ	15.43 AW	21.47 TQ	MNBLS	10/01-12/01
	Duluth-Superior MSA, MN-WI	H	9.66 FQ	14.56 AW	20.45 TQ	MNBLS	10/01-12/01
	Minneapolis-St. Paul MSA, MN-WI	H	11.95 FQ	17.41 AW	24.22 TQ	MNBLS	10/01-12/01
	Mississippi	H	9.52 FQ	13.79 AW	19.16 TQ	MSBLS	10/01-12/01
	Biloxi-Gulfport-Pascagoula MSA, MS	H	12.38 FQ	16.33 AW	21.02 TQ	MSBLS	10/01-12/01
	Jackson MSA, MS	H	9.61 FQ	13.03 AW	16.90 TQ	MSBLS	10/01-12/01
	Missouri	H	8.79 FQ	14.12 AW	22.04 TQ	MOBLS	10/01-12/01
	Kansas City MSA, MO-KS	H	10.02 FQ	16.37 AW	26.25 TQ	MOBLS	10/01-12/01
	St. Louis MSA, MO-IL	H	9.73 FQ	14.82 AW	21.88 TQ	MOBLS	10/01-12/01
	Springfield MSA, MO	H	9.72 FQ	12.87 AW	16.82 TQ	MOBLS	10/01-12/01
	Montana	H	9.52 FQ	15.06 AW	21.12 TQ	MTBLS	10/01-12/01
	Billings MSA, MT	H	8.52 FQ	12.22 AW	16.73 TQ	MTBLS	10/01-12/01
	Nebraska	H	9.18 FQ	12.86 AW	17.41 TQ	NEBLS	10/01-12/01
	Lincoln MSA, NE	H	9.66 FQ	13.73 AW	17.42 TQ	NEBLS	10/01-12/01
	Omaha MSA, NE-IA	H	9.65 FQ	13.20 AW	17.15 TQ	NEBLS	10/01-12/01
	Nevada	H	8.74 FQ	15.31 AW	23.56 TQ	NVBLS	10/01-12/01
	Las Vegas MSA, NV-AZ	H	8.06 FQ	15.00 AW	23.94 TQ	NVBLS	10/01-12/01
	Reno MSA, NV	H	9.89 FQ	14.49 AW	20.08 TQ	NVBLS	10/01-12/01
	New Hampshire	H	10.80 FQ	16.05 AW	21.24 TQ	NHBLS	10/01-12/01
	Manchester PMSA, NH	H	10.75 FQ	16.93 AW	21.81 TQ	NHBLS	10/01-12/01
	Nashua PMSA, NH	H	10.65 FQ	15.05 AW	20.56 TQ	NHBLS	10/01-12/01
	Portsmouth-Rochester PMSA, NH-ME	H	13.58 FQ	18.15 AW	21.47 TQ	NHBLS	10/01-12/01
	New Jersey	H	10.36 FQ	16.77 AW	25.46 TQ	NJBLS	10/01-12/01
	Atlantic-Cape May PMSA, NJ	H	10.23 FQ	20.10 AW	32.98 TQ	NJBLS	10/01-12/01
	Bergen-Passaic PMSA, NJ	H	9.91 FQ	15.17 AW	21.46 TQ	NJBLS	10/01-12/01
	Jersey City PMSA, NJ	H	11.68 FQ	17.30 AW	24.73 TQ	NJBLS	10/01-12/01
	Middlesex-Somerset-Hunterdon PMSA, NJ	H	11.68 FQ	18.34 AW	27.53 TQ	NJBLS	10/01-12/01
	Monmouth-Ocean PMSA, NJ	H	10.51 FQ	16.69 AW	24.83 TQ	NJBLS	10/01-12/01
	Newark PMSA, NJ	H	9.25 FQ	16.53 AW	24.86 TQ	NJBLS	10/01-12/01
	Trenton PMSA, NJ	H	10.24 FQ	14.89 AW	21.00 TQ	NJBLS	10/01-12/01
	New Mexico	H	8.27 FQ	13.68 AW	22.15 TQ	NMBLS	10/01-12/01

AAW Average annual wage; AE Average entry wage; AEX Average experienced wage; AO Average offered; AOH Average offered, high; AOL Average offered, low; APH Average pay, high range; APL Average pay, low range; ASH Average starting, high; ASL Average starting, low; AW Average wage paid; FQ First quartile wage; H Hourly; HI Highest wage paid; HR High end range; LR Low end range; M Monthly; MTC Median total compensation; MW Median wage paid; SQ Second quartile wage; S Special: hourly and annual; TQ Third quartile wage; W Weekly; Y Yearly

Occupation/Type/Industry	Location	Per	Low	Mid	High	Source	Date
Welder, Cutter, Solderer, and Brazer	Albuquerque MSA, NM	H	9.15 FQ	12.81 AW	18.41 TQ	NMBLS	10/01-12/01
	Las Cruces MSA, NM	H	7.32 FQ	12.16 AW	18.00 TQ	NMBLS	10/01-12/01
	New York	H	8.96 FQ	15.02 AW	23.92 TQ	NYBLS	10/01-12/01
	Albany-Schenectady-Troy MSA, NY	H	10.49 FQ	15.52 AW	20.69 TQ	NYBLS	10/01-12/01
	Binghamton MSA, NY	H	7.39 FQ	10.58 AW	15.25 TQ	NYBLS	10/01-12/01
	Buffalo-Niagara Falls MSA, NY	H	10.25 FQ	18.49 AW	27.16 TQ	NYBLS	10/01-12/01
	Dutchess County PMSA, NY	H	9.77 FQ	13.10 AW	17.60 TQ	NYBLS	10/01-12/01
	Nassau-Suffolk PMSA, NY	H	8.39 FQ	14.23 AW	20.88 TQ	NYBLS	10/01-12/01
	New York PMSA, NY	H	8.83 FQ	15.82 AW	29.43 TQ	NYBLS	10/01-12/01
	Newburgh PMSA, NY-PA	H	7.87 FQ	14.58 AW	21.20 TQ	NYBLS	10/01-12/01
	Rochester MSA, NY	H	8.51 FQ	13.66 AW	19.77 TQ	NYBLS	10/01-12/01
	Syracuse MSA, NY	H	9.79 FQ	14.23 AW	17.57 TQ	NYBLS	10/01-12/01
	Utica-Rome MSA, NY	H	9.12 FQ	13.14 AW	17.73 TQ	NYBLS	10/01-12/01
	North Carolina	H	9.30 FQ	14.11 AW	19.33 TQ	NCBLS	10/01-12/01
	Asheville MSA, NC	H	9.02 FQ	13.51 AW	17.62 TQ	NCBLS	10/01-12/01
	Charlotte-Gastonia-Rock Hill MSA, NC-SC	H	8.25 FQ	13.58 AW	18.16 TQ	NCBLS	10/01-12/01
	Fayetteville MSA, NC	H	9.86 FQ	14.59 AW	19.80 TQ	NCBLS	10/01-12/01
	Greensboro-Winston-Salem-High Point MSA, NC	H	9.77 FQ	13.62 AW	17.56 TQ	NCBLS	10/01-12/01
	Hickory-Morganton-Lenoir MSA, NC	H	8.90 FQ	12.19 AW	16.46 TQ	NCBLS	10/01-12/01
	Raleigh-Durham-Chapel Hill MSA, NC	H	10.81 FQ	16.29 AW	20.73 TQ	NCBLS	10/01-12/01
	Wilmington MSA, NC	H	10.65 FQ	14.72 AW	20.98 TQ	NCBLS	10/01-12/01
	North Dakota	H	8.57 FQ	14.02 AW	21.43 TQ	NDBLS	10/01-12/01
	Fargo-Moorhead MSA, ND-MN	H	10.39 FQ	13.18 AW	16.67 TQ	NDBLS	10/01-12/01
	Ohio	H	9.94 FQ	15.47 AW	24.52 TQ	OHBLS	10/01-12/01
	Akron PMSA, OH	H	10.32 FQ	15.68 AW	24.89 TQ	OHBLS	10/01-12/01
	Canton-Massillon MSA, OH	H	9.74 FQ	13.19 AW	17.38 TQ	OHBLS	10/01-12/01
	Cincinnati PMSA, OH-KY-IN	H	10.65 FQ	15.02 AW	21.02 TQ	OHBLS	10/01-12/01
	Cleveland-Lorain-Elyria PMSA, OH	H	10.34 FQ	17.63 AW	26.51 TQ	OHBLS	10/01-12/01
	Columbus MSA, OH	H	10.84 FQ	14.16 AW	18.36 TQ	OHBLS	10/01-12/01
	Dayton-Springfield MSA, OH	H	10.19 FQ	17.11 AW	27.07 TQ	OHBLS	10/01-12/01
	Hamilton-Middletown PMSA, OH	H	9.34 FQ	15.05 AW	21.60 TQ	OHBLS	10/01-12/01
	Mansfield MSA, OH	H	9.65 FQ	14.93 AW	20.98 TQ	OHBLS	10/01-12/01
	Toledo MSA, OH	H	9.97 FQ	16.11 AW	25.85 TQ	OHBLS	10/01-12/01
	Youngstown-Warren MSA, OH	H	9.33 FQ	13.50 AW	19.03 TQ	OHBLS	10/01-12/01
	Oklahoma	H	8.88 FQ	13.33 AW	18.75 TQ	OKBLS	10/01-12/01
	Oklahoma City MSA, OK	H	9.07 FQ	13.66 AW	20.64 TQ	OKBLS	10/01-12/01
	Tulsa MSA, OK	H	9.49 FQ	14.49 AW	20.25 TQ	OKBLS	10/01-12/01
	Oregon	H	10.14 FQ	15.02 AW	20.59 TQ	ORBLS	10/01-12/01
	Eugene-Springfield MSA, OR	H	9.74 FQ	13.58 AW	17.56 TQ	ORBLS	10/01-12/01
	Medford-Ashland MSA, OR	H	9.17 FQ	12.93 AW	17.32 TQ	ORBLS	10/01-12/01
	Portland-Vancouver PMSA, OR-WA	H	11.32 FQ	15.95 AW	21.14 TQ	ORBLS	10/01-12/01
	Salem PMSA, OR	H	9.63 FQ	14.89 AW	18.76 TQ	ORBLS	10/01-12/01
	Pennsylvania	H	9.35 FQ	14.31 AW	19.84 TQ	PABLS	10/01-12/01
	Allentown-Bethlehem-Easton MSA, PA	H	11.35 FQ	15.12 AW	19.85 TQ	PABLS	10/01-12/01
	Erie MSA, PA	H	9.16 FQ	12.38 AW	16.01 TQ	PABLS	10/01-12/01
	Harrisburg-Lebanon-Carlisle MSA, PA	H	8.43 FQ	14.11 AW	19.91 TQ	PABLS	10/01-12/01
	Johnstown MSA, PA	H	7.69 FQ	11.28 AW	15.76 TQ	PABLS	10/01-12/01
	Lancaster MSA, PA	H	10.12 FQ	14.52 AW	19.32 TQ	PABLS	10/01-12/01
	Philadelphia PMSA, PA-NJ	H	10.05 FQ	15.88 AW	22.25 TQ	PABLS	10/01-12/01
	Pittsburgh MSA, PA	H	9.77 FQ	14.55 AW	20.39 TQ	PABLS	10/01-12/01
	Reading MSA, PA	H	11.20 FQ	14.91 AW	20.33 TQ	PABLS	10/01-12/01
	Scranton-Wilkes-Barre-Hazleton MSA, PA	H	9.13 FQ	14.58 AW	20.67 TQ	PABLS	10/01-12/01
	York MSA, PA	H	7.68 FQ	13.66 AW	20.41 TQ	PABLS	10/01-12/01
	Rhode Island	H	7.26 FQ	12.74 AW	17.90 TQ	RIBLS	10/01-12/01
	Providence-Fall River-Warwick MSA, RI-MA	H	7.36 FQ	12.71 AW	18.14 TQ	RIBLS	10/01-12/01
	South Carolina	H	9.58 FQ	14.18 AW	20.44 TQ	SCBLS	10/01-12/01

AAW	Average annual wage	**AOH**	Average offered, high	**ASH**	Average starting, high	**H**	Hourly	**M**	Monthly	**S**	Special: hourly and annual
AE	Average entry wage	**AOL**	Average offered, low	**ASL**	Average starting, low	**HI**	Highest wage paid	**MTC**	Median total compensation	**TQ**	Third quartile wage
AEX	Average experienced wage	**APH**	Average pay, high range	**AW**	Average wage paid	**HR**	High end range	**MW**	Median wage paid	**W**	Weekly
AO	Average offered	**APL**	Average pay, low range	**FQ**	First quartile wage	**LR**	Low end range	**SQ**	Second quartile wage	**Y**	Yearly

Occupation/Type/Industry	Location	Per	Low	Mid	High	Source	Date
Welder, Cutter, Solderer, and Brazer	Charleston-North Charleston MSA, SC	H	10.42 FQ	13.79 AW	17.25 TQ	SCBLS	10/01-12/01
	Columbia MSA, SC	H	8.46 FQ	12.18 AW	16.79 TQ	SCBLS	10/01-12/01
	Greenville-Spartanburg-Anderson MSA, SC	H	10.69 FQ	15.92 AW	22.12 TQ	SCBLS	10/01-12/01
	Myrtle Beach MSA, SC	H	8.32 FQ	11.84 AW	16.06 TQ	SCBLS	10/01-12/01
	South Dakota	H	9.05 FQ	11.63 AW	14.93 TQ	SDBLS	10/01-12/01
	Sioux Falls MSA, SD	H	9.50 FQ	12.43 AW	16.49 TQ	SDBLS	10/01-12/01
	Tennessee	H	9.27 FQ	13.06 AW	17.23 TQ	TNBLS	10/01-12/01
	Chattanooga MSA, TN-GA	H	9.70 FQ	12.97 AW	16.62 TQ	TNBLS	10/01-12/01
	Clarksville-Hopkinsville MSA, TN-KY	H	9.15 FQ	13.42 AW	20.23 TQ	TNBLS	10/01-12/01
	Johnson City-Kingsport-Bristol MSA, TN-VA	H	8.24 FQ	11.63 AW	15.81 TQ	TNBLS	10/01-12/01
	Knoxville MSA, TN	H	9.78 FQ	13.31 AW	17.91 TQ	TNBLS	10/01-12/01
	Memphis MSA, TN-AR-MS	H	10.16 FQ	14.56 AW	19.08 TQ	TNBLS	10/01-12/01
	Nashville MSA, TN	H	8.77 FQ	13.75 AW	20.09 TQ	TNBLS	10/01-12/01
	Texas	H	8.47 FQ	13.37 AW	19.17 TQ	TXBLS	10/01-12/01
	Amarillo MSA, TX	H	8.98 FQ	12.03 AW	18.91 TQ	TXBLS	10/01-12/01
	Austin-San Marcos MSA, TX	H	9.08 FQ	13.05 AW	17.93 TQ	TXBLS	10/01-12/01
	Beaumont-Port Arthur MSA, TX	H	10.39 FQ	14.70 AW	20.01 TQ	TXBLS	10/01-12/01
	Brazoria PMSA, TX	H	9.87 FQ	14.91 AW	21.02 TQ	TXBLS	10/01-12/01
	Brownsville-Harlingen-San Benito MSA, TX	H	7.27 FQ	9.99 AW	13.40 TQ	TXBLS	10/01-12/01
	Corpus Christi MSA, TX	H	9.31 FQ	13.92 AW	18.51 TQ	TXBLS	10/01-12/01
	Dallas PMSA, TX	H	7.60 FQ	13.71 AW	21.00 TQ	TXBLS	10/01-12/01
	El Paso MSA, TX	H	7.27 FQ	10.99 AW	16.21 TQ	TXBLS	10/01-12/01
	Fort Worth-Arlington PMSA, TX	H	9.20 FQ	13.29 AW	17.58 TQ	TXBLS	10/01-12/01
	Galveston-Texas City PMSA, TX	H	9.98 FQ	14.02 AW	17.36 TQ	TXBLS	10/01-12/01
	Houston PMSA, TX	H	9.25 FQ	14.18 AW	19.47 TQ	TXBLS	10/01-12/01
	Killeen-Temple MSA, TX	H	8.00 FQ	11.63 AW	17.11 TQ	TXBLS	10/01-12/01
	Laredo MSA, TX	H	7.13 FQ	11.57 AW	15.69 TQ	TXBLS	10/01-12/01
	Longview-Marshall MSA, TX	H	8.87 FQ	12.24 AW	16.17 TQ	TXBLS	10/01-12/01
	Lubbock MSA, TX	H	8.30 FQ	11.34 AW	13.95 TQ	TXBLS	10/01-12/01
	McAllen-Edinburg-Mission MSA, TX	H	6.11 FQ	9.84 AW	16.70 TQ	TXBLS	10/01-12/01
	Odessa-Midland MSA, TX	H	9.30 FQ	14.46 AW	20.45 TQ	TXBLS	10/01-12/01
	San Antonio MSA, TX	H	8.52 FQ	13.02 AW	18.47 TQ	TXBLS	10/01-12/01
	Tyler MSA, TX	H	7.63 FQ	12.35 AW	16.87 TQ	TXBLS	10/01-12/01
	Waco MSA, TX	H	8.88 FQ	11.24 AW	14.50 TQ	TXBLS	10/01-12/01
	Utah	H	9.38 FQ	13.74 AW	18.78 TQ	UTBLS	10/01-12/01
	Provo-Orem MSA, UT	H	8.35 FQ	13.71 AW	17.98 TQ	UTBLS	10/01-12/01
	Salt Lake City-Ogden MSA, UT	H	9.58 FQ	13.64 AW	17.86 TQ	UTBLS	10/01-12/01
	Vermont	H	8.78 FQ	12.82 AW	17.43 TQ	VTBLS	10/01-12/01
	Burlington MSA, VT	H	10.59 FQ	14.36 AW	18.49 TQ	VTBLS	10/01-12/01
	Virginia	H	10.19 FQ	15.09 AW	20.43 TQ	VABLS	10/01-12/01
	Lynchburg MSA, VA	H	10.40 FQ	13.84 AW	17.51 TQ	VABLS	10/01-12/01
	Norfolk-Virginia Beach-Newport News MSA, VA-NC	H	11.75 FQ	16.06 AW	20.03 TQ	VABLS	10/01-12/01
	Richmond-Petersburg MSA, VA	H	11.23 FQ	16.20 AW	23.74 TQ	VABLS	10/01-12/01
	Roanoke MSA, VA	H	10.12 FQ	14.09 AW	17.32 TQ	VABLS	10/01-12/01
	Washington	H	10.97 FQ	16.62 AW	23.72 TQ	WABLS	10/01-12/01
	Bremerton PMSA, WA	H	17.12 FQ	22.09 AW	26.50 TQ	WABLS	10/01-12/01
	Olympia PMSA, WA	H	6.91 FQ	12.04 AW	19.35 TQ	WABLS	10/01-12/01
	Richland-Kennewick-Pasco MSA, WA	H	10.77 FQ	16.63 AW	24.46 TQ	WABLS	10/01-12/01
	Seattle-Bellevue-Everett PMSA, WA	H	11.90 FQ	17.02 AW	22.12 TQ	WABLS	10/01-12/01
	Spokane MSA, WA	H	9.38 FQ	14.93 AW	22.88 TQ	WABLS	10/01-12/01
	Tacoma PMSA, WA	H	10.51 FQ	15.98 AW	21.43 TQ	WABLS	10/01-12/01
	Yakima MSA, WA	H	9.78 FQ	14.12 AW	19.00 TQ	WABLS	10/01-12/01
	West Virginia	H	8.56 FQ	14.68 AW	24.31 TQ	WVBLS	10/01-12/01
	Charleston MSA, WV	H	8.48 FQ	15.16 AW	25.21 TQ	WVBLS	10/01-12/01
	Huntington-Ashland MSA, WV-KY-OH	H	8.90 FQ	12.65 AW	17.33 TQ	WVBLS	10/01-12/01

AAW Average annual wage **AOH** Average offered, high **ASH** Average starting, high **H** Hourly **M** Monthly **S** Special: hourly and annual
AE Average entry wage **AOL** Average offered, low **ASL** Average starting, low **HI** Highest wage paid **MTC** Median total compensation **TQ** Third quartile wage
AEX Average experienced wage **APH** Average pay, high range **AW** Average wage paid **HR** High end range **MW** Median wage paid **W** Weekly
AO Average offered **APL** Average pay, low range **FQ** First quartile wage **LR** Low end range **SQ** Second quartile wage **Y** Yearly

Occupation/Type/Industry	Location	Per	Low	Mid	High	Source	Date
Welder, Cutter, Solderer, and Brazer	Wisconsin	H	10.87 FQ	14.96 AW	19.95 TQ	WIBLS	10/01-12/01
	Appleton-Oshkosh-Neenah MSA, WI	H	10.08 FQ	15.31 AW	21.19 TQ	WIBLS	10/01-12/01
	Green Bay MSA, WI	H	11.60 FQ	14.91 AW	19.08 TQ	WIBLS	10/01-12/01
	Madison MSA, WI	H	11.13 FQ	14.68 AW	19.39 TQ	WIBLS	10/01-12/01
	Milwaukee-Waukesha PMSA, WI	H	11.49 FQ	16.16 AW	21.43 TQ	WIBLS	10/01-12/01
	Racine PMSA, WI	H	10.57 FQ	15.33 AW	20.15 TQ	WIBLS	10/01-12/01
	Wyoming	H	9.24 FQ	14.58 AW	20.80 TQ	WYBLS	10/01-12/01
	Cheyenne MSA, WY	H	7.00 FQ	10.14 AW	14.79 TQ	WYBLS	10/01-12/01
	Puerto Rico	H	5.85 FQ	8.59 AW	12.65 TQ	PRBLS	10/01-12/01
	Virgin Islands	H	11.98 FQ	15.97 AW	20.78 TQ	VIBLS	10/01-12/01
	Guam	H	9.61 FQ	13.67 AW	18.02 TQ	GUBLS	10/01-12/01
Welding, Soldering, and Brazing Machine Setter, Operator, and Tender	Alabama	H	9.65 FQ	13.73 AW	18.61 TQ	ALBLS	10/01-12/01
	Arizona	H	8.79 FQ	13.37 AW	20.29 TQ	AZBLS	10/01-12/01
	Arkansas	H	9.53 FQ	12.69 AW	16.63 TQ	ARBLS	10/01-12/01
	California	H	7.85 FQ	13.82 AW	21.47 TQ	CABLS	10/01-12/01
	Colorado	H	10.20 FQ	14.16 AW	19.30 TQ	COBLS	10/01-12/01
	Connecticut	H	9.09 FQ	14.61 AW	20.83 TQ	CTBLS	10/01-12/01
	Delaware	H	11.85 FQ	14.84 AW	17.46 TQ	DEBLS	10/01-12/01
	Florida	H	7.60 FQ	11.72 AW	16.85 TQ	FLBLS	10/01-12/01
	Georgia	H	9.49 FQ	13.76 AW	17.92 TQ	GABLS	10/01-12/01
	Idaho	H	7.86 FQ	13.11 AW	17.48 TQ	IDBLS	10/01-12/01
	Illinois	H	8.77 FQ	14.07 AW	20.21 TQ	ILBLS	10/01-12/01
	Indiana	H	9.75 FQ	15.13 AW	25.12 TQ	INBLS	10/01-12/01
	Iowa	H	9.29 FQ	12.77 AW	16.78 TQ	IABLS	10/01-12/01
	Kansas	H	8.10 FQ	15.46 AW	26.49 TQ	KSBLS	10/01-12/01
	Kentucky	H	9.57 FQ	13.22 AW	17.81 TQ	KYBLS	10/01-12/01
	Louisiana	H	9.42 FQ	15.51 AW	23.80 TQ	LABLS	10/01-12/01
	Maine	H	11.30 FQ	15.28 AW	20.52 TQ	MEBLS	10/01-12/01
	Maryland	H	9.96 FQ	13.59 AW	17.45 TQ	MDBLS	10/01-12/01
	Massachusetts	H	9.93 FQ	15.46 AW	21.26 TQ	MABLS	10/01-12/01
	Michigan	H	9.92 FQ	20.04 AW	28.96 TQ	MIBLS	10/01-12/01
	Minnesota	H	9.80 FQ	15.12 AW	20.93 TQ	MNBLS	10/01-12/01
	Mississippi	H	8.00 FQ	12.19 AW	16.80 TQ	MSBLS	10/01-12/01
	Missouri	H	8.61 FQ	12.10 AW	16.83 TQ	MOBLS	10/01-12/01
	Nebraska	H	9.86 FQ	13.04 AW	16.60 TQ	NEBLS	10/01-12/01
	Nevada	H	10.35 FQ	15.98 AW	21.68 TQ	NVBLS	10/01-12/01
	New Hampshire	H	10.36 FQ	13.88 AW	18.23 TQ	NHBLS	10/01-12/01
	New Jersey	H	8.98 FQ	15.54 AW	21.87 TQ	NJBLS	10/01-12/01
	New York	H	8.79 FQ	14.81 AW	23.35 TQ	NYBLS	10/01-12/01
	North Carolina	H	9.35 FQ	12.89 AW	17.16 TQ	NCBLS	10/01-12/01
	Ohio	H	9.29 FQ	15.34 AW	25.37 TQ	OHBLS	10/01-12/01
	Oklahoma	H	8.16 FQ	12.76 AW	17.33 TQ	OKBLS	10/01-12/01
	Oregon	H	10.41 FQ	15.02 AW	19.77 TQ	ORBLS	10/01-12/01
	Pennsylvania	H	9.50 FQ	13.87 AW	18.14 TQ	PABLS	10/01-12/01
	Rhode Island	H	6.98 FQ	11.66 AW	16.76 TQ	RIBLS	10/01-12/01
	South Carolina	H	9.39 FQ	12.52 AW	16.83 TQ	SCBLS	10/01-12/01
	South Dakota	H	9.68 FQ	12.19 AW	14.74 TQ	SDBLS	10/01-12/01
	Tennessee	H	8.62 FQ	13.46 AW	19.70 TQ	TNBLS	10/01-12/01
	Texas	H	8.15 FQ	12.98 AW	19.08 TQ	TXBLS	10/01-12/01
	Utah	H	8.53 FQ	12.33 AW	16.96 TQ	UTBLS	10/01-12/01
	Vermont	H	6.58 FQ	9.98 AW	14.97 TQ	VTBLS	10/01-12/01
	Virginia	H	8.68 FQ	13.84 AW	18.05 TQ	VABLS	10/01-12/01
	Washington	H	11.11 FQ	15.67 AW	21.48 TQ	WABLS	10/01-12/01
	West Virginia	H	9.09 FQ	11.67 AW	15.63 TQ	WVBLS	10/01-12/01
	Wisconsin	H	9.59 FQ	13.90 AW	18.14 TQ	WIBLS	10/01-12/01
	Wyoming	H	9.69 FQ	19.84 AW	28.04 TQ	WYBLS	10/01-12/01
	Puerto Rico	H	6.04 FQ	7.87 AW	10.15 TQ	PRBLS	10/01-12/01
Wellhead Pumper	Arkansas	H	9.06 FQ	15.28 AW	26.54 TQ	ARBLS	10/01-12/01
	California	H	9.86 FQ	17.02 AW	23.95 TQ	CABLS	10/01-12/01
	Colorado	H	11.59 FQ	15.57 AW	20.73 TQ	COBLS	10/01-12/01
	Illinois	H	5.80 FQ	9.51 AW	14.68 TQ	ILBLS	10/01-12/01
	Kansas	H	11.26 FQ	12.74 AW	13.88 TQ	KSBLS	10/01-12/01
	Kentucky	H	7.27 FQ	11.79 AW	18.54 TQ	KYBLS	10/01-12/01
	Louisiana	H	12.07 FQ	17.65 AW	22.91 TQ	LABLS	10/01-12/01
	Michigan	H	10.43 FQ	16.68 AW	23.82 TQ	MIBLS	10/01-12/01

AAW	Average annual wage	**AOH**	Average offered, high	**ASH**	Average starting, high	**H**	Hourly	**M**	Monthly	**S**	Special: hourly and annual
AE	Average entry wage	**AOL**	Average offered, low	**ASL**	Average starting, low	**HI**	Highest wage paid	**MTC**	Median total compensation	**TQ**	Third quartile wage
AEX	Average experienced wage	**APH**	Average pay, high range	**AW**	Average wage paid	**HR**	High end range	**MW**	Median wage paid	**W**	Weekly
AO	Average offered	**APL**	Average pay, low range	**FQ**	First quartile wage	**LR**	Low end range	**SQ**	Second quartile wage	**Y**	Yearly

Occupation/Type/Industry	Location	Per	Low	Mid	High	Source	Date
Wellhead Pumper	Mississippi	H	12.96 FQ	19.07 AW	26.23 TQ	MSBLS	10/01-12/01
	Montana	H	12.67 FQ	17.07 AW	22.25 TQ	MTBLS	10/01-12/01
	Nebraska	H	6.96 FQ	11.08 AW	16.99 TQ	NEBLS	10/01-12/01
	New Mexico	H	9.92 FQ	16.22 AW	22.49 TQ	NMBLS	10/01-12/01
	New York	H	8.39 FQ	13.02 AW	17.29 TQ	NYBLS	10/01-12/01
	North Dakota	H	9.66 FQ	17.02 AW	28.91 TQ	NDBLS	10/01-12/01
	Ohio	H	9.00 FQ	15.14 AW	22.99 TQ	OHBLS	10/01-12/01
	Oklahoma	H	9.51 FQ	17.81 AW	26.30 TQ	OKBLS	10/01-12/01
	Texas	H	9.67 FQ	16.77 AW	22.67 TQ	TXBLS	10/01-12/01
	Utah	H	12.63 FQ	18.42 AW	26.76 TQ	UTBLS	10/01-12/01
	West Virginia	H	6.66 FQ	12.30 AW	18.36 TQ	WVBLS	10/01-12/01
	Wyoming	H	9.83 FQ	17.13 AW	27.03 TQ	WYBLS	10/01-12/01
Wholesale and Retail Buyer							
Except Farm Product	Alabama	Y	20400 FQ	36490 AW	60520 TQ	ALBLS	10/01-12/01
Except Farm Product	Birmingham MSA, AL	Y	23770 FQ	40140 AW	68080 TQ	ALBLS	10/01-12/01
Except Farm Product	Huntsville MSA, AL	Y	20020 FQ	40750 AW	68730 TQ	ALBLS	10/01-12/01
Except Farm Product	Mobile MSA, AL	Y	19660 FQ	30150 AW	40070 TQ	ALBLS	10/01-12/01
Except Farm Product	Montgomery MSA, AL	Y	21690 FQ	35530 AW	55390 TQ	ALBLS	10/01-12/01
Except Farm Product	Alaska	Y	21700 FQ	41300 AW	65540 TQ	AKBLS	10/01-12/01
Except Farm Product	Anchorage MSA, AK	Y	23020 FQ	43900 AW	68370 TQ	AKBLS	10/01-12/01
Except Farm Product	Arizona	Y	21990 FQ	39730 AW	61570 TQ	AZBLS	10/01-12/01
Except Farm Product	Phoenix-Mesa MSA, AZ	Y	25260 FQ	42990 AW	65960 TQ	AZBLS	10/01-12/01
Except Farm Product	Tucson MSA, AZ	Y	13550 FQ	28770 AW	45250 TQ	AZBLS	10/01-12/01
Except Farm Product	Arkansas	Y	17280 FQ	32400 AW	49800 TQ	ARBLS	10/01-12/01
Except Farm Product	Fort Smith MSA, AR-OK	Y	23310 FQ	33590 AW	50970 TQ	ARBLS	10/01-12/01
Except Farm Product	Little Rock-North Little Rock MSA, AR	Y	22140 FQ	37750 AW	54270 TQ	ARBLS	10/01-12/01
Except Farm Product	California	Y	24320 FQ	47450 AW	79300 TQ	CABLS	10/01-12/01
Except Farm Product	Bakersfield MSA, CA	Y	16800 FQ	29600 AW	42540 TQ	CABLS	10/01-12/01
Except Farm Product	Chico-Paradise MSA, CA	Y	19690 FQ	29280 AW	38510 TQ	CABLS	10/01-12/01
Except Farm Product	Fresno MSA, CA	Y	21180 FQ	37570 AW	57200 TQ	CABLS	10/01-12/01
Except Farm Product	Los Angeles-Long Beach PMSA, CA	Y	25960 FQ	53280 AW	97270 TQ	CABLS	10/01-12/01
Except Farm Product	Modesto MSA, CA	Y	19450 FQ	35690 AW	66600 TQ	CABLS	10/01-12/01
Except Farm Product	Oakland PMSA, CA	Y	27480 FQ	47580 AW	72500 TQ	CABLS	10/01-12/01
Except Farm Product	Orange County PMSA, CA	Y	25150 FQ	50650 AW	83060 TQ	CABLS	10/01-12/01
Except Farm Product	Redding MSA, CA	Y	17520 FQ	36190 AW	60450 TQ	CABLS	10/01-12/01
Except Farm Product	Riverside-San Bernardino PMSA, CA	Y	22260 FQ	45760 AW	75930 TQ	CABLS	10/01-12/01
Except Farm Product	Sacramento PMSA, CA	Y	19510 FQ	39660 AW	63140 TQ	CABLS	10/01-12/01
Except Farm Product	Salinas MSA, CA	Y	20950 FQ	47680 AW	85680 TQ	CABLS	10/01-12/01
Except Farm Product	San Diego MSA, CA	Y	24230 FQ	42290 AW	69280 TQ	CABLS	10/01-12/01
Except Farm Product	San Francisco PMSA, CA	Y	26440 FQ	50170 AW	81980 TQ	CABLS	10/01-12/01
Except Farm Product	San Jose PMSA, CA	Y	18860 FQ	44720 AW	71030 TQ	CABLS	10/01-12/01
Except Farm Product	San Luis Obispo-Atascadero-Paso Robles MSA, CA	Y	19140 FQ	33530 AW	48050 TQ	CABLS	10/01-12/01
Except Farm Product	Santa Barbara-Santa Maria-Lompoc MSA, CA	Y	23540 FQ	43240 AW	69930 TQ	CABLS	10/01-12/01
Except Farm Product	Santa Cruz-Watsonville PMSA, CA	Y	21560 FQ	34780 AW	53070 TQ	CABLS	10/01-12/01
Except Farm Product	Santa Rosa PMSA, CA	Y	22020 FQ	35720 AW	53410 TQ	CABLS	10/01-12/01
Except Farm Product	Stockton-Lodi MSA, CA	Y	22430 FQ	41920 AW	78650 TQ	CABLS	10/01-12/01
Except Farm Product	Vallejo-Fairfield-Napa PMSA, CA	Y	24880 FQ	46990 AW	83090 TQ	CABLS	10/01-12/01
Except Farm Product	Ventura PMSA, CA	Y	26620 FQ	41660 AW	59430 TQ	CABLS	10/01-12/01
Except Farm Product	Visalia-Tulare-Porterville MSA, CA	Y	23230 FQ	43610 AW	76230 TQ	CABLS	10/01-12/01
Except Farm Product	Colorado	Y	22100 FQ	40570 AW	65520 TQ	COBLS	10/01-12/01
Except Farm Product	Boulder-Longmont PMSA, CO	Y	23500 FQ	43820 AW	74130 TQ	COBLS	10/01-12/01
Except Farm Product	Colorado Springs MSA, CO	Y	17710 FQ	31000 AW	44670 TQ	COBLS	10/01-12/01
Except Farm Product	Denver PMSA, CO	Y	23450 FQ	43550 AW	69580 TQ	COBLS	10/01-12/01
Except Farm Product	Fort Collins-Loveland MSA, CO	Y	19770 FQ	32090 AW	53610 TQ	COBLS	10/01-12/01
Except Farm Product	Greeley PMSA, CO	Y	27110 FQ	35870 AW	44470 TQ	COBLS	10/01-12/01
Except Farm Product	Connecticut	Y	27140 FQ	49810 AW	77450 TQ	CTBLS	10/01-12/01
Except Farm Product	Bridgeport PMSA, CT	Y	27370 FQ	55480 AW	88210 TQ	CTBLS	10/01-12/01
Except Farm Product	Danbury PMSA, CT	Y	25700 FQ	48550 AW	79570 TQ	CTBLS	10/01-12/01
Except Farm Product	Hartford MSA, CT	Y	26530 FQ	48020 AW	73500 TQ	CTBLS	10/01-12/01
Except Farm Product	New Haven-Meriden PMSA, CT	Y	30840 FQ	49700 AW	66650 TQ	CTBLS	10/01-12/01
Except Farm Product	New London-Norwich MSA, CT-RI	Y	20880 FQ	39160 AW	65700 TQ	CTBLS	10/01-12/01

AAW Average annual wage; **AE** Average entry wage; **AEX** Average experienced wage; **AO** Average offered; **AOH** Average offered, high; **AOL** Average offered, low; **APH** Average pay, high range; **APL** Average pay, low range; **ASH** Average starting, high; **ASL** Average starting, low; **AW** Average wage paid; **FQ** First quartile wage; **H** Hourly; **HI** Highest wage paid; **HR** High end range; **LR** Low end range; **M** Monthly; **MTC** Median total compensation; **MW** Median wage paid; **SQ** Second quartile wage; **S** Special: hourly and annual; **TQ** Third quartile wage; **W** Weekly; **Y** Yearly

Occupation/Type/Industry	Location	Per	Low	Mid	High	Source	Date
Wholesale and Retail Buyer							
Except Farm Product	Stamford-Norwalk PMSA, CT	Y	32020 FQ	56840 AW	90470 TQ	CTBLS	10/01-12/01
Except Farm Product	Waterbury PMSA, CT	Y	22340 FQ	51230 AW	106420 TQ	CTBLS	10/01-12/01
Except Farm Product	Delaware	Y	22680 FQ	39950 AW	62770 TQ	DEBLS	10/01-12/01
Except Farm Product	Wilmington-Newark PMSA, DE-MD	Y	22530 FQ	42480 AW	65780 TQ	DEBLS	10/01-12/01
Except Farm Product	District of Columbia	Y	19320 FQ	36240 AW	59200 TQ	DCBLS	10/01-12/01
Except Farm Product	Washington PMSA, DC-MD-VA-WV	Y	22030 FQ	43360 AW	71590 TQ	DCBLS	10/01-12/01
Except Farm Product	Florida	Y	21420 FQ	43250 AW	78920 TQ	FLBLS	10/01-12/01
Except Farm Product	Daytona Beach MSA, FL	Y	19740 FQ	38000 AW	59660 TQ	FLBLS	10/01-12/01
Except Farm Product	Fort Lauderdale PMSA, FL	Y	24380 FQ	46720 AW	77560 TQ	FLBLS	10/01-12/01
Except Farm Product	Fort Myers-Cape Coral MSA, FL	Y	13500 FQ	35380 AW	55540 TQ	FLBLS	10/01-12/01
Except Farm Product	Fort Pierce-Port St. Lucie MSA, FL	Y	22610 FQ	46590 AW	71100 TQ	FLBLS	10/01-12/01
Except Farm Product	Fort Walton Beach MSA, FL	Y	21740 FQ	41160 AW	93040 TQ	FLBLS	10/01-12/01
Except Farm Product	Gainesville MSA, FL	Y	21620 FQ	40500 AW	70400 TQ	FLBLS	10/01-12/01
Except Farm Product	Jacksonville MSA, FL	Y	19680 FQ	41380 AW	69910 TQ	FLBLS	10/01-12/01
Except Farm Product	Lakeland-Winter Haven MSA, FL	Y	22880 FQ	62410 AW		FLBLS	10/01-12/01
Except Farm Product	Melbourne-Titusville-Palm Bay MSA, FL	Y	21320 FQ	41620 AW	71600 TQ	FLBLS	10/01-12/01
Except Farm Product	Miami PMSA, FL	Y	18330 FQ	38680 AW	74410 TQ	FLBLS	10/01-12/01
Except Farm Product	Naples MSA, FL	Y	23250 FQ	56960 AW		FLBLS	10/01-12/01
Except Farm Product	Ocala MSA, FL	Y	19010 FQ	30070 AW	48940 TQ	FLBLS	10/01-12/01
Except Farm Product	Orlando MSA, FL	Y	22390 FQ	40260 AW	70660 TQ	FLBLS	10/01-12/01
Except Farm Product	Pensacola MSA, FL	Y	18450 FQ	28830 AW	44280 TQ	FLBLS	10/01-12/01
Except Farm Product	Sarasota-Bradenton MSA, FL	Y	21660 FQ	33330 AW	52940 TQ	FLBLS	10/01-12/01
Except Farm Product	Tallahassee MSA, FL	Y	22720 FQ	31290 AW	53080 TQ	FLBLS	10/01-12/01
Except Farm Product	Tampa-St. Petersburg-Clearwater MSA, FL	Y	24540 FQ	48380 AW	89040 TQ	FLBLS	10/01-12/01
Except Farm Product	West Palm Beach-Boca Raton MSA, FL	Y	27140 FQ	52830 AW	85270 TQ	FLBLS	10/01-12/01
Except Farm Product	Georgia	Y	23510 FQ	41000 AW	66560 TQ	GABLS	10/01-12/01
Except Farm Product	Atlanta MSA, GA	Y	23900 FQ	41090 AW	64800 TQ	GABLS	10/01-12/01
Except Farm Product	Augusta-Aiken MSA, GA-SC	Y	24410 FQ	44500 AW	71480 TQ	GABLS	10/01-12/01
Except Farm Product	Columbus MSA, GA-AL	Y	24860 FQ	46930 AW	79340 TQ	GABLS	10/01-12/01
Except Farm Product	Macon MSA, GA	Y	19460 FQ	32070 AW	47740 TQ	GABLS	10/01-12/01
Except Farm Product	Savannah MSA, GA	Y	21890 FQ	47960 AW	72840 TQ	GABLS	10/01-12/01
Except Farm Product	Hawaii	Y	19480 FQ	37350 AW	57550 TQ	HIBLS	10/01-12/01
Except Farm Product	Honolulu MSA, HI	Y	20100 FQ	38500 AW	59230 TQ	HIBLS	10/01-12/01
Except Farm Product	Idaho	Y	19000 FQ	37130 AW	59420 TQ	IDBLS	10/01-12/01
Except Farm Product	Boise City MSA, ID	Y	24540 FQ	43550 AW	67540 TQ	IDBLS	10/01-12/01
Except Farm Product	Illinois	Y	23290 FQ	43770 AW	71330 TQ	ILBLS	10/01-12/01
Except Farm Product	Champaign-Urbana MSA, IL	Y	23860 FQ	44230 AW	58040 TQ	ILBLS	10/01-12/01
Except Farm Product	Chicago PMSA, IL	Y	24790 FQ	45450 AW	74060 TQ	ILBLS	10/01-12/01
Except Farm Product	Peoria-Pekin MSA, IL	Y	20450 FQ	35870 AW	63040 TQ	ILBLS	10/01-12/01
Except Farm Product	Rockford MSA, IL	Y	23050 FQ	41130 AW	61390 TQ	ILBLS	10/01-12/01
Except Farm Product	Springfield MSA, IL	Y	23420 FQ	43800 AW	96750 TQ	ILBLS	10/01-12/01
Except Farm Product	Indiana	Y	21090 FQ	39880 AW	65430 TQ	INBLS	10/01-12/01
Except Farm Product	Elkhart-Goshen MSA, IN	Y	20940 FQ	33090 AW	48730 TQ	INBLS	10/01-12/01
Except Farm Product	Evansville-Henderson MSA, IN-KY	Y	19570 FQ	36220 AW	56790 TQ	INBLS	10/01-12/01
Except Farm Product	Fort Wayne MSA, IN	Y	19750 FQ	40910 AW	69610 TQ	INBLS	10/01-12/01
Except Farm Product	Gary PMSA, IN	Y	16760 FQ	34430 AW	59400 TQ	INBLS	10/01-12/01
Except Farm Product	Indianapolis MSA, IN	Y	28030 FQ	47700 AW	79770 TQ	INBLS	10/01-12/01
Except Farm Product	Lafayette MSA, IN	Y	23080 FQ	39260 AW	58380 TQ	INBLS	10/01-12/01
Except Farm Product	South Bend MSA, IN	Y	19900 FQ	43700 AW	91560 TQ	INBLS	10/01-12/01
Except Farm Product	Iowa	Y	19850 FQ	41080 AW	71660 TQ	IABLS	10/01-12/01
Except Farm Product	Cedar Rapids MSA, IA	Y	21200 FQ	34570 AW	51570 TQ	IABLS	10/01-12/01
Except Farm Product	Davenport-Moline-Rock Island MSA, IA-IL	Y	25470 FQ	41060 AW	64970 TQ	IABLS	10/01-12/01
Except Farm Product	Des Moines MSA, IA	Y	25840 FQ	41340 AW	57990 TQ	IABLS	10/01-12/01
Except Farm Product	Kansas	Y	20970 FQ	41890 AW	66800 TQ	KSBLS	10/01-12/01
Except Farm Product	Topeka MSA, KS	Y	21290 FQ	42560 AW	64130 TQ	KSBLS	10/01-12/01
Except Farm Product	Kentucky	Y	18010 FQ	37350 AW	63940 TQ	KYBLS	10/01-12/01
Except Farm Product	Lexington MSA, KY	Y	12820 FQ	31270 AW	64440 TQ	KYBLS	10/01-12/01
Except Farm Product	Louisville MSA, KY-IN	Y	21750 FQ	43120 AW	76700 TQ	KYBLS	10/01-12/01
Except Farm Product	Louisiana	Y	20390 FQ	38720 AW	62230 TQ	LABLS	10/01-12/01
Except Farm Product	Baton Rouge MSA, LA	Y	16980 FQ	31350 AW	49550 TQ	LABLS	10/01-12/01
Except Farm Product	Houma MSA, LA	Y	23570 FQ	40460 AW	57700 TQ	LABLS	10/01-12/01

AAW	Average annual wage	**AOH**	Average offered, high	**ASH**	Average starting, high	**H**	Hourly	**M**	Monthly	**S**	Special: hourly and annual
AE	Average entry wage	**AOL**	Average offered, low	**ASL**	Average starting, low	**HI**	Highest wage paid	**MTC**	Median total compensation	**TQ**	Third quartile wage
AEX	Average experienced wage	**APH**	Average pay, high range	**AW**	Average wage paid	**HR**	High end range	**MW**	Median wage paid	**W**	Weekly
AO	Average offered	**APL**	Average pay, low range	**FQ**	First quartile wage	**LR**	Low end range	**SQ**	Second quartile wage	**Y**	Yearly

Occupation/Type/Industry	Location	Per	Low	Mid	High	Source	Date
Wholesale and Retail Buyer							
Except Farm Product	Lafayette MSA, LA	Y	20780 FQ	44020 AW	67120 TQ	LABLS	10/01-12/01
Except Farm Product	Lake Charles MSA, LA	Y	20620 FQ	32970 AW	49880 TQ	LABLS	10/01-12/01
Except Farm Product	New Orleans MSA, LA	Y	22470 FQ	40780 AW	65400 TQ	LABLS	10/01-12/01
Except Farm Product	Shreveport-Bossier City MSA, LA	Y	24540 FQ	38450 AW	59610 TQ	LABLS	10/01-12/01
Except Farm Product	Maine	Y	17450 FQ	32820 AW	52460 TQ	MEBLS	10/01-12/01
Except Farm Product	Portland MSA, ME	Y	23880 FQ	37780 AW	54250 TQ	MEBLS	10/01-12/01
Except Farm Product	Maryland	Y	22600 FQ	42820 AW	80000 TQ	MDBLS	10/01-12/01
Except Farm Product	Baltimore PMSA, MD	Y	23510 FQ	45280 AW	84380 TQ	MDBLS	10/01-12/01
Except Farm Product	Massachusetts	Y	24650 FQ	43520 AW	67890 TQ	MABLS	10/01-12/01
Except Farm Product	Boston PMSA, MA-NH	Y	25670 FQ	43860 AW	66990 TQ	MABLS	10/01-12/01
Except Farm Product	Lawrence PMSA, MA-NH	Y	26700 FQ	56210 AW	89770 TQ	MABLS	10/01-12/01
Except Farm Product	Lowell PMSA, MA-NH	Y	31780 FQ	54990 AW	76900 TQ	MABLS	10/01-12/01
Except Farm Product	New Bedford PMSA, MA	Y	25850 FQ	42900 AW	65950 TQ	MABLS	10/01-12/01
Except Farm Product	Springfield MSA, MA	Y	20010 FQ	32640 AW	46820 TQ	MABLS	10/01-12/01
Except Farm Product	Worcester PMSA, MA-CT	Y	23490 FQ	39620 AW	64190 TQ	MABLS	10/01-12/01
Except Farm Product	Michigan	Y	23970 FQ	50620 AW	87720 TQ	MIBLS	10/01-12/01
Except Farm Product	Ann Arbor PMSA, MI	Y	21880 FQ	48550 AW	112880 TQ	MIBLS	10/01-12/01
Except Farm Product	Detroit PMSA, MI	Y	27810 FQ	58290 AW	109040 TQ	MIBLS	10/01-12/01
Except Farm Product	Flint PMSA, MI	Y	23990 FQ	42760 AW	60130 TQ	MIBLS	10/01-12/01
Except Farm Product	Grand Rapids-Muskegon-Holland MSA, MI	Y	20250 FQ	40570 AW	60690 TQ	MIBLS	10/01-12/01
Except Farm Product	Kalamazoo-Battle Creek MSA, MI	Y	20490 FQ	40250 AW	67010 TQ	MIBLS	10/01-12/01
Except Farm Product	Lansing-East Lansing MSA, MI	Y	27050 FQ	50750 AW	88250 TQ	MIBLS	10/01-12/01
Except Farm Product	Saginaw-Bay City-Midland MSA, MI	Y	25530 FQ	62170 AW	87920 TQ	MIBLS	10/01-12/01
Except Farm Product	Minnesota	Y	26650 FQ	44680 AW	68180 TQ	MNBLS	10/01-12/01
Except Farm Product	Duluth-Superior MSA, MN-WI	Y	19530 FQ	35790 AW	58000 TQ	MNBLS	10/01-12/01
Except Farm Product	Minneapolis-St. Paul MSA, MN-WI	Y	29860 FQ	46630 AW	69960 TQ	MNBLS	10/01-12/01
Except Farm Product	St. Cloud MSA, MN	Y	27180 FQ	39500 AW	53340 TQ	MNBLS	10/01-12/01
Except Farm Product	Mississippi	Y	19550 FQ	42700 AW	70550 TQ	MSBLS	10/01-12/01
Except Farm Product	Jackson MSA, MS	Y	24100 FQ	41250 AW	61640 TQ	MSBLS	10/01-12/01
Except Farm Product	Missouri	Y	20180 FQ	39210 AW	62580 TQ	MOBLS	10/01-12/01
Except Farm Product	Kansas City MSA, MO-KS	Y	22870 FQ	42230 AW	61930 TQ	MOBLS	10/01-12/01
Except Farm Product	St. Louis MSA, MO-IL	Y	22490 FQ	41910 AW	68120 TQ	MOBLS	10/01-12/01
Except Farm Product	Springfield MSA, MO	Y	20030 FQ	30940 AW	44610 TQ	MOBLS	10/01-12/01
Except Farm Product	Montana	Y	16760 FQ	29200 AW	51410 TQ	MTBLS	10/01-12/01
Except Farm Product	Billings MSA, MT	Y	19150 FQ	27710 AW	42090 TQ	MTBLS	10/01-12/01
Except Farm Product	Nebraska	Y	21430 FQ	40190 AW	63040 TQ	NEBLS	10/01-12/01
Except Farm Product	Lincoln MSA, NE	Y	18540 FQ	35130 AW	55360 TQ	NEBLS	10/01-12/01
Except Farm Product	Omaha MSA, NE-IA	Y	25210 FQ	42880 AW	65190 TQ	NEBLS	10/01-12/01
Except Farm Product	Nevada	Y	25110 FQ	43120 AW	69440 TQ	NVBLS	10/01-12/01
Except Farm Product	Las Vegas MSA, NV-AZ	Y	25030 FQ	45470 AW	79800 TQ	NVBLS	10/01-12/01
Except Farm Product	Reno MSA, NV	Y	25050 FQ	39850 AW	63810 TQ	NVBLS	10/01-12/01
Except Farm Product	New Hampshire	Y	22970 FQ	45040 AW	72580 TQ	NHBLS	10/01-12/01
Except Farm Product	Manchester PMSA, NH	Y	25210 FQ	40140 AW	55550 TQ	NHBLS	10/01-12/01
Except Farm Product	Nashua PMSA, NH	Y	30730 FQ	52190 AW	72350 TQ	NHBLS	10/01-12/01
Except Farm Product	Portsmouth-Rochester PMSA, NH-ME	Y	20160 FQ	44090 AW	79010 TQ	NHBLS	10/01-12/01
Except Farm Product	New Jersey	Y	26310 FQ	54220 AW	93100 TQ	NJBLS	10/01-12/01
Except Farm Product	Atlantic-Cape May PMSA, NJ	Y	24210 FQ	44440 AW	70710 TQ	NJBLS	10/01-12/01
Except Farm Product	Bergen-Passaic PMSA, NJ	Y	32090 FQ	60260 AW	99630 TQ	NJBLS	10/01-12/01
Except Farm Product	Jersey City PMSA, NJ	Y	26810 FQ	52730 AW	89230 TQ	NJBLS	10/01-12/01
Except Farm Product	Middlesex-Somerset-Hunterdon PMSA, NJ	Y	30600 FQ	54330 AW	90810 TQ	NJBLS	10/01-12/01
Except Farm Product	Monmouth-Ocean PMSA, NJ	Y	17730 FQ	40740 AW	81030 TQ	NJBLS	10/01-12/01
Except Farm Product	Newark PMSA, NJ	Y	21470 FQ	55600 AW	113170 TQ	NJBLS	10/01-12/01
Except Farm Product	Trenton PMSA, NJ	Y	29590 FQ	41850 AW	65020 TQ	NJBLS	10/01-12/01
Except Farm Product	New Mexico	Y	19240 FQ	32510 AW	49670 TQ	NMBLS	10/01-12/01
Except Farm Product	Albuquerque MSA, NM	Y	19100 FQ	32260 AW	50610 TQ	NMBLS	10/01-12/01
Except Farm Product	New York	Y	24590 FQ	51950 AW	93730 TQ	NYBLS	10/01-12/01
Except Farm Product	Albany-Schenectady-Troy MSA, NY	Y	26560 FQ	45940 AW	71520 TQ	NYBLS	10/01-12/01
Except Farm Product	Binghamton MSA, NY	Y	24100 FQ	49720 AW	84190 TQ	NYBLS	10/01-12/01
Except Farm Product	Buffalo-Niagara Falls MSA, NY	Y	22470 FQ	43820 AW	69060 TQ	NYBLS	10/01-12/01
Except Farm Product	Dutchess County PMSA, NY	Y	26100 FQ	46370 AW	71970 TQ	NYBLS	10/01-12/01
Except Farm Product	Nassau-Suffolk PMSA, NY	Y	26680 FQ	54940 AW	101200 TQ	NYBLS	10/01-12/01
Except Farm Product	New York PMSA, NY	Y	24500 FQ	54520 AW	106150 TQ	NYBLS	10/01-12/01

AAW Average annual wage; AE Average entry wage; AEX Average experienced wage; AO Average offered; AOH Average offered, high; AOL Average offered, low; APH Average pay, high range; APL Average pay, low range; ASH Average starting, high; ASL Average starting, low; AW Average wage paid; FQ First quartile wage; H Hourly; HI Highest wage paid; HR High end range; LR Low end range; M Monthly; MTC Median total compensation; MW Median wage paid; SQ Second quartile wage; S Special: hourly and annual; TQ Third quartile wage; W Weekly; Y Yearly

Occupation/Type/Industry	Location	Per	Low	Mid	High	Source	Date
Wholesale and Retail Buyer							
Except Farm Product	Newburgh PMSA, NY-PA	Y	23690 FQ	49210 AW	85330 TQ	NYBLS	10/01-12/01
Except Farm Product	Rochester MSA, NY	Y	21660 FQ	45540 AW	75010 TQ	NYBLS	10/01-12/01
Except Farm Product	Syracuse MSA, NY	Y	24980 FQ	42490 AW	66780 TQ	NYBLS	10/01-12/01
Except Farm Product	Utica-Rome MSA, NY	Y	23740 FQ	38410 AW	59810 TQ	NYBLS	10/01-12/01
Except Farm Product	North Carolina	Y	21590 FQ	41100 AW	67850 TQ	NCBLS	10/01-12/01
Except Farm Product	Asheville MSA, NC	Y	24950 FQ	43800 AW	77190 TQ	NCBLS	10/01-12/01
Except Farm Product	Charlotte-Gastonia-Rock Hill MSA, NC-SC	Y	22830 FQ	46670 AW	83620 TQ	NCBLS	10/01-12/01
Except Farm Product	Fayetteville MSA, NC	Y	23560 FQ	51130 AW	114200 TQ	NCBLS	10/01-12/01
Except Farm Product	Greensboro-Winston-Salem-High Point MSA, NC	Y	17060 FQ	35590 AW	55740 TQ	NCBLS	10/01-12/01
Except Farm Product	Hickory-Morganton-Lenoir MSA, NC	Y	22890 FQ	45890 AW	70790 TQ	NCBLS	10/01-12/01
Except Farm Product	Raleigh-Durham-Chapel Hill MSA, NC	Y	21940 FQ	41810 AW	70890 TQ	NCBLS	10/01-12/01
Except Farm Product	Wilmington MSA, NC	Y	25020 FQ	47560 AW	83800 TQ	NCBLS	10/01-12/01
Except Farm Product	North Dakota	Y	19260 FQ	32490 AW	51990 TQ	NDBLS	10/01-12/01
Except Farm Product	Fargo-Moorhead MSA, ND-MN	Y	20850 FQ	38100 AW	64700 TQ	NDBLS	10/01-12/01
Except Farm Product	Ohio	Y	21870 FQ	41200 AW	67520 TQ	OHBLS	10/01-12/01
Except Farm Product	Akron PMSA, OH	Y	22030 FQ	42680 AW	69240 TQ	OHBLS	10/01-12/01
Except Farm Product	Canton-Massillon MSA, OH	Y	23560 FQ	37680 AW	58080 TQ	OHBLS	10/01-12/01
Except Farm Product	Cincinnati PMSA, OH-KY-IN	Y	22000 FQ	41160 AW	63470 TQ	OHBLS	10/01-12/01
Except Farm Product	Cleveland-Lorain-Elyria PMSA, OH	Y	24340 FQ	38740 AW	57600 TQ	OHBLS	10/01-12/01
Except Farm Product	Columbus MSA, OH	Y	22450 FQ	48740 AW	94720 TQ	OHBLS	10/01-12/01
Except Farm Product	Dayton-Springfield MSA, OH	Y	21680 FQ	43520 AW	71920 TQ	OHBLS	10/01-12/01
Except Farm Product	Hamilton-Middletown PMSA, OH	Y	24240 FQ	34590 AW	54290 TQ	OHBLS	10/01-12/01
Except Farm Product	Mansfield MSA, OH	Y	23170 FQ	33580 AW	46160 TQ	OHBLS	10/01-12/01
Except Farm Product	Toledo MSA, OH	Y	25050 FQ	45980 AW	73310 TQ	OHBLS	10/01-12/01
Except Farm Product	Youngstown-Warren MSA, OH	Y	19800 FQ	36680 AW	58100 TQ	OHBLS	10/01-12/01
Except Farm Product	Oklahoma	Y	17320 FQ	37300 AW	58670 TQ	OKBLS	10/01-12/01
Except Farm Product	Oklahoma City MSA, OK	Y	17260 FQ	38040 AW	57520 TQ	OKBLS	10/01-12/01
Except Farm Product	Tulsa MSA, OK	Y	21390 FQ	39890 AW	63210 TQ	OKBLS	10/01-12/01
Except Farm Product	Oregon	Y	23410 FQ	40990 AW	66120 TQ	ORBLS	10/01-12/01
Except Farm Product	Eugene-Springfield MSA, OR	Y	21170 FQ	37910 AW	58920 TQ	ORBLS	10/01-12/01
Except Farm Product	Medford-Ashland MSA, OR	Y	20140 FQ	37420 AW	54910 TQ	ORBLS	10/01-12/01
Except Farm Product	Portland-Vancouver PMSA, OR-WA	Y	25150 FQ	43710 AW	70020 TQ	ORBLS	10/01-12/01
Except Farm Product	Salem PMSA, OR	Y	16770 FQ	32350 AW	44910 TQ	ORBLS	10/01-12/01
Except Farm Product	Pennsylvania	Y	22210 FQ	41610 AW	66080 TQ	PABLS	10/01-12/01
Except Farm Product	Allentown-Bethlehem-Easton MSA, PA	Y	19030 FQ	44270 AW	86150 TQ	PABLS	10/01-12/01
Except Farm Product	Erie MSA, PA	Y	17530 FQ	34800 AW	52090 TQ	PABLS	10/01-12/01
Except Farm Product	Harrisburg-Lebanon-Carlisle MSA, PA	Y	22480 FQ	37540 AW	56910 TQ	PABLS	10/01-12/01
Except Farm Product	Johnstown MSA, PA	Y	20990 FQ	33580 AW	53150 TQ	PABLS	10/01-12/01
Except Farm Product	Lancaster MSA, PA	Y	23100 FQ	36240 AW	53920 TQ	PABLS	10/01-12/01
Except Farm Product	Philadelphia PMSA, PA-NJ	Y	25670 FQ	48220 AW	73090 TQ	PABLS	10/01-12/01
Except Farm Product	Pittsburgh MSA, PA	Y	21850 FQ	40260 AW	60880 TQ	PABLS	10/01-12/01
Except Farm Product	Reading MSA, PA	Y	24020 FQ	38250 AW	58770 TQ	PABLS	10/01-12/01
Except Farm Product	Scranton-Wilkes-Barre-Hazleton MSA, PA	Y	20390 FQ	33400 AW	51790 TQ	PABLS	10/01-12/01
Except Farm Product	York MSA, PA	Y	17500 FQ	32750 AW	46870 TQ	PABLS	10/01-12/01
Except Farm Product	Rhode Island	Y	27870 FQ	44940 AW	68990 TQ	RIBLS	10/01-12/01
Except Farm Product	Providence-Fall River-Warwick MSA, RI-MA	Y	26790 FQ	43550 AW	63520 TQ	RIBLS	10/01-12/01
Except Farm Product	South Carolina	Y	21040 FQ	43310 AW	70340 TQ	SCBLS	10/01-12/01
Except Farm Product	Charleston-North Charleston MSA, SC	Y	20990 FQ	37950 AW	66620 TQ	SCBLS	10/01-12/01
Except Farm Product	Columbia MSA, SC	Y	24520 FQ	56350 AW		SCBLS	10/01-12/01
Except Farm Product	Greenville-Spartanburg-Anderson MSA, SC	Y	24310 FQ	41240 AW	65520 TQ	SCBLS	10/01-12/01
Except Farm Product	Myrtle Beach MSA, SC	Y	19770 FQ	39040 AW	62160 TQ	SCBLS	10/01-12/01
Except Farm Product	South Dakota	Y	25100 FQ	34140 AW	45250 TQ	SDBLS	10/01-12/01
Except Farm Product	Sioux Falls MSA, SD	Y	25410 FQ	34790 AW	45650 TQ	SDBLS	10/01-12/01
Except Farm Product	Tennessee	Y	22770 FQ	41960 AW	69510 TQ	TNBLS	10/01-12/01
Except Farm Product	Chattanooga MSA, TN-GA	Y	24000 FQ	42900 AW	62010 TQ	TNBLS	10/01-12/01
Except Farm Product	Clarksville-Hopkinsville MSA, TN-KY	Y	18650 FQ	29790 AW	39560 TQ	TNBLS	10/01-12/01

AAW	Average annual wage	AOH	Average offered, high	ASH	Average starting, high	H	Hourly	M	Monthly	S	Special: hourly and annual
AE	Average entry wage	AOL	Average offered, low	ASL	Average starting, low	HI	Highest wage paid	MTC	Median total compensation	TQ	Third quartile wage
AEX	Average experienced wage	APH	Average pay, high range	AW	Average wage paid	HR	High end range	MW	Median wage paid	W	Weekly
AO	Average offered	APL	Average pay, low range	FQ	First quartile wage	LR	Low end range	SQ	Second quartile wage	Y	Yearly

Occupation/Type/Industry	Location	Per	Low	Mid	High	Source	Date
Wholesale and Retail Buyer							
Except Farm Product	Johnson City-Kingsport-Bristol MSA, TN-VA	Y	19000 FQ	36650 AW	61460 TQ	TNBLS	10/01-12/01
Except Farm Product	Knoxville MSA, TN	Y	22790 FQ	40210 AW	70270 TQ	TNBLS	10/01-12/01
Except Farm Product	Memphis MSA, TN-AR-MS	Y	26670 FQ	49290 AW	81720 TQ	TNBLS	10/01-12/01
Except Farm Product	Nashville MSA, TN	Y	17520 FQ	37260 AW	56060 TQ	TNBLS	10/01-12/01
Except Farm Product	Texas	Y	22540 FQ	46590 AW	76780 TQ	TXBLS	10/01-12/01
Except Farm Product	Amarillo MSA, TX	Y	16670 FQ	37400 AW	76510 TQ	TXBLS	10/01-12/01
Except Farm Product	Austin-San Marcos MSA, TX	Y	18670 FQ	36030 AW	55890 TQ	TXBLS	10/01-12/01
Except Farm Product	Beaumont-Port Arthur MSA, TX	Y	25900 FQ	42660 AW	77110 TQ	TXBLS	10/01-12/01
Except Farm Product	Brazoria PMSA, TX	Y	16590 FQ	37810 AW	67370 TQ	TXBLS	10/01-12/01
Except Farm Product	Brownsville-Harlingen-San Benito MSA, TX	Y	20280 FQ	44470 AW	78750 TQ	TXBLS	10/01-12/01
Except Farm Product	Corpus Christi MSA, TX	Y	21350 FQ	46740 AW	80870 TQ	TXBLS	10/01-12/01
Except Farm Product	Dallas PMSA, TX	Y	27850 FQ	56570 AW	92040 TQ	TXBLS	10/01-12/01
Except Farm Product	El Paso MSA, TX	Y	21110 FQ	39020 AW	56820 TQ	TXBLS	10/01-12/01
Except Farm Product	Fort Worth-Arlington PMSA, TX	Y	23970 FQ	48870 AW	70550 TQ	TXBLS	10/01-12/01
Except Farm Product	Houston PMSA, TX	Y	22820 FQ	41170 AW	69170 TQ	TXBLS	10/01-12/01
Except Farm Product	Laredo MSA, TX	Y	21250 FQ	48140 AW	122010 TQ	TXBLS	10/01-12/01
Except Farm Product	Lubbock MSA, TX	Y	24770 FQ	35470 AW	53090 TQ	TXBLS	10/01-12/01
Except Farm Product	McAllen-Edinburg-Mission MSA, TX	Y	20130 FQ	44210 AW	103560 TQ	TXBLS	10/01-12/01
Except Farm Product	Odessa-Midland MSA, TX	Y	18400 FQ	69520 AW		TXBLS	10/01-12/01
Except Farm Product	San Antonio MSA, TX	Y	18730 FQ	43540 AW	82100 TQ	TXBLS	10/01-12/01
Except Farm Product	Waco MSA, TX	Y	24960 FQ	47520 AW	71430 TQ	TXBLS	10/01-12/01
Except Farm Product	Utah	Y	16600 FQ	41700 AW	73570 TQ	UTBLS	10/01-12/01
Except Farm Product	Provo-Orem MSA, UT	Y	21750 FQ	36940 AW	55380 TQ	UTBLS	10/01-12/01
Except Farm Product	Salt Lake City-Ogden MSA, UT	Y	17120 FQ	44700 AW	76410 TQ	UTBLS	10/01-12/01
Except Farm Product	Vermont	Y	24280 FQ	45670 AW	94760 TQ	VTBLS	10/01-12/01
Except Farm Product	Burlington MSA, VT	Y	24900 FQ	42420 AW	65210 TQ	VTBLS	10/01-12/01
Except Farm Product	Virginia	Y	23600 FQ	42010 AW	65920 TQ	VABLS	10/01-12/01
Except Farm Product	Lynchburg MSA, VA	Y	20600 FQ	39070 AW	63660 TQ	VABLS	10/01-12/01
Except Farm Product	Norfolk-Virginia Beach-Newport News MSA, VA-NC	Y	23490 FQ	39230 AW	57150 TQ	VABLS	10/01-12/01
Except Farm Product	Richmond-Petersburg MSA, VA	Y	25260 FQ	43830 AW	73190 TQ	VABLS	10/01-12/01
Except Farm Product	Roanoke MSA, VA	Y	21820 FQ	37680 AW	57390 TQ	VABLS	10/01-12/01
Except Farm Product	Washington	Y	22420 FQ	43790 AW	71520 TQ	WABLS	10/01-12/01
Except Farm Product	Bremerton PMSA, WA	Y	17420 FQ	40910 AW	71420 TQ	WABLS	10/01-12/01
Except Farm Product	Olympia PMSA, WA	Y	20150 FQ	34770 AW	57830 TQ	WABLS	10/01-12/01
Except Farm Product	Richland-Kennewick-Pasco MSA, WA	Y	20060 FQ	34650 AW	55530 TQ	WABLS	10/01-12/01
Except Farm Product	Seattle-Bellevue-Everett PMSA, WA	Y	24810 FQ	46920 AW	73370 TQ	WABLS	10/01-12/01
Except Farm Product	Spokane MSA, WA	Y	21220 FQ	34560 AW	54630 TQ	WABLS	10/01-12/01
Except Farm Product	Tacoma PMSA, WA	Y	20640 FQ	39240 AW	62240 TQ	WABLS	10/01-12/01
Except Farm Product	Yakima MSA, WA	Y	21410 FQ	33520 AW	51660 TQ	WABLS	10/01-12/01
Except Farm Product	West Virginia	Y	18080 FQ	37790 AW	71420 TQ	WVBLS	10/01-12/01
Except Farm Product	Charleston MSA, WV	Y	17900 FQ	33360 AW	53660 TQ	WVBLS	10/01-12/01
Except Farm Product	Huntington-Ashland MSA, WV-KY-OH	Y	19810 FQ	38600 AW	59980 TQ	WVBLS	10/01-12/01
Except Farm Product	Wisconsin	Y	20930 FQ	39760 AW	63690 TQ	WIBLS	10/01-12/01
Except Farm Product	Appleton-Oshkosh-Neenah MSA, WI	Y	23620 FQ	35890 AW	47530 TQ	WIBLS	10/01-12/01
Except Farm Product	Madison MSA, WI	Y	24960 FQ	46830 AW	81520 TQ	WIBLS	10/01-12/01
Except Farm Product	Milwaukee-Waukesha PMSA, WI	Y	24400 FQ	43390 AW	68800 TQ	WIBLS	10/01-12/01
Except Farm Product	Racine PMSA, WI	Y	20270 FQ	37540 AW	61820 TQ	WIBLS	10/01-12/01
Except Farm Product	Wyoming	Y	18650 FQ	39200 AW	59510 TQ	WYBLS	10/01-12/01
Except Farm Product	Puerto Rico	Y	14140 FQ	27700 AW	44540 TQ	PRBLS	10/01-12/01
Except Farm Product	Virgin Islands	Y	23960 FQ	33070 AW	47670 TQ	VIBLS	10/01-12/01
Except Farm Product	Guam	Y	16950 FQ	30700 AW	58120 TQ	GUBLS	10/01-12/01
Woodworking Machine Setter, Operator, and Tender							
Except Sawing	Alabama	H	6.60 FQ	9.45 AW	12.84 TQ	ALBLS	10/01-12/01
Except Sawing	Birmingham MSA, AL	H	7.80 FQ	10.56 AW	15.15 TQ	ALBLS	10/01-12/01
Except Sawing	Mobile MSA, AL	H	5.80 FQ	9.75 AW	13.24 TQ	ALBLS	10/01-12/01

AAW	Average annual wage	**AOH**	Average offered, high	**ASH**	Average starting, high	**H**	Hourly	**M**	Monthly	**S**	Special: hourly and annual
AE	Average entry wage	**AOL**	Average offered, low	**ASL**	Average starting, low	**HI**	Highest wage paid	**MTC**	Median total compensation	**TQ**	Third quartile wage
AEX	Average experienced wage	**APH**	Average pay, high range	**AW**	Average wage paid	**HR**	High end range	**MW**	Median wage paid	**W**	Weekly
AO	Average offered	**APL**	Average pay, low range	**FQ**	First quartile wage	**LR**	Low end range	**SQ**	Second quartile wage	**Y**	Yearly

Occupation/Type/Industry	Location	Per	Low	Mid	High	Source	Date
Woodworking Machine Setter, Operator, and Tender							
Except Sawing	Montgomery MSA, AL	H	6.36 FQ	8.94 AW	11.76 TQ	ALBLS	10/01-12/01
Except Sawing	Alaska	H	8.42 FQ	13.61 AW	19.14 TQ	AKBLS	10/01-12/01
Except Sawing	Arizona	H	6.35 FQ	9.30 AW	13.30 TQ	AZBLS	10/01-12/01
Except Sawing	Phoenix-Mesa MSA, AZ	H	6.24 FQ	9.04 AW	12.92 TQ	AZBLS	10/01-12/01
Except Sawing	Tucson MSA, AZ	H	7.04 FQ	10.21 AW	14.53 TQ	AZBLS	10/01-12/01
Except Sawing	Arkansas	H	6.75 FQ	9.14 AW	12.59 TQ	ARBLS	10/01-12/01
Except Sawing	Fayetteville-Springdale-Rogers MSA, AR	H	7.51 FQ	9.35 AW	10.70 TQ	ARBLS	10/01-12/01
Except Sawing	Little Rock-North Little Rock MSA, AR	H	6.41 FQ	8.50 AW	10.63 TQ	ARBLS	10/01-12/01
Except Sawing	California	H	6.79 FQ	10.09 AW	15.35 TQ	CABLS	10/01-12/01
Except Sawing	Bakersfield MSA, CA	H	7.36 FQ	10.68 AW	16.67 TQ	CABLS	10/01-12/01
Except Sawing	Fresno MSA, CA	H	7.08 FQ	9.47 AW	13.67 TQ	CABLS	10/01-12/01
Except Sawing	Los Angeles-Long Beach PMSA, CA	H	6.68 FQ	9.33 AW	13.28 TQ	CABLS	10/01-12/01
Except Sawing	Modesto MSA, CA	H	7.94 FQ	9.83 AW	12.67 TQ	CABLS	10/01-12/01
Except Sawing	Oakland PMSA, CA	H	9.74 FQ	14.30 AW	21.42 TQ	CABLS	10/01-12/01
Except Sawing	Orange County PMSA, CA	H	6.50 FQ	8.92 AW	11.78 TQ	CABLS	10/01-12/01
Except Sawing	Redding MSA, CA	H	7.32 FQ	10.45 AW	15.01 TQ	CABLS	10/01-12/01
Except Sawing	Riverside-San Bernardino PMSA, CA	H	6.79 FQ	8.96 AW	12.73 TQ	CABLS	10/01-12/01
Except Sawing	Sacramento PMSA, CA	H	6.69 FQ	10.32 AW	15.48 TQ	CABLS	10/01-12/01
Except Sawing	San Diego MSA, CA	H	6.96 FQ	10.71 AW	15.84 TQ	CABLS	10/01-12/01
Except Sawing	San Francisco PMSA, CA	H	6.58 FQ	10.95 AW	16.40 TQ	CABLS	10/01-12/01
Except Sawing	San Jose PMSA, CA	H	7.87 FQ	12.93 AW	20.48 TQ	CABLS	10/01-12/01
Except Sawing	San Luis Obispo-Atascadero-Paso Robles MSA, CA	H	7.87 FQ	11.17 AW	16.08 TQ	CABLS	10/01-12/01
Except Sawing	Santa Cruz-Watsonville PMSA, CA	H	6.42 FQ	10.23 AW	17.87 TQ	CABLS	10/01-12/01
Except Sawing	Santa Rosa PMSA, CA	H	7.74 FQ	10.84 AW	15.59 TQ	CABLS	10/01-12/01
Except Sawing	Stockton-Lodi MSA, CA	H	6.96 FQ	9.62 AW	13.49 TQ	CABLS	10/01-12/01
Except Sawing	Vallejo-Fairfield-Napa PMSA, CA	H	9.65 FQ	14.54 AW	20.81 TQ	CABLS	10/01-12/01
Except Sawing	Ventura PMSA, CA	H	7.23 FQ	10.00 AW	13.30 TQ	CABLS	10/01-12/01
Except Sawing	Visalia-Tulare-Porterville MSA, CA	H	8.86 FQ	10.63 AW	12.96 TQ	CABLS	10/01-12/01
Except Sawing	Colorado	H	8.00 FQ	11.67 AW	16.69 TQ	COBLS	10/01-12/01
Except Sawing	Boulder-Longmont PMSA, CO	H	8.02 FQ	11.95 AW	18.24 TQ	COBLS	10/01-12/01
Except Sawing	Denver PMSA, CO	H	8.53 FQ	12.31 AW	17.82 TQ	COBLS	10/01-12/01
Except Sawing	Fort Collins-Loveland MSA, CO	H	8.88 FQ	11.28 AW	15.48 TQ	COBLS	10/01-12/01
Except Sawing	Connecticut	H	7.11 FQ	12.69 AW	17.92 TQ	CTBLS	10/01-12/01
Except Sawing	Bridgeport PMSA, CT	H	7.40 FQ	12.70 AW	17.29 TQ	CTBLS	10/01-12/01
Except Sawing	Hartford MSA, CT	H	6.93 FQ	12.41 AW	18.72 TQ	CTBLS	10/01-12/01
Except Sawing	New Haven-Meriden PMSA, CT	H	7.02 FQ	11.54 AW	14.91 TQ	CTBLS	10/01-12/01
Except Sawing	Washington PMSA, DC-MD-VA-WV	H	8.41 FQ	11.29 AW	15.43 TQ	DCBLS	10/01-12/01
Except Sawing	Florida	H	7.11 FQ	10.37 AW	14.11 TQ	FLBLS	10/01-12/01
Except Sawing	Fort Lauderdale PMSA, FL	H	7.86 FQ	11.52 AW	16.59 TQ	FLBLS	10/01-12/01
Except Sawing	Jacksonville MSA, FL	H	6.95 FQ	11.24 AW	15.66 TQ	FLBLS	10/01-12/01
Except Sawing	Lakeland-Winter Haven MSA, FL	H	7.27 FQ	10.83 AW	17.54 TQ	FLBLS	10/01-12/01
Except Sawing	Melbourne-Titusville-Palm Bay MSA, FL	H	7.68 FQ	10.52 AW	13.18 TQ	FLBLS	10/01-12/01
Except Sawing	Miami PMSA, FL	H	6.48 FQ	9.72 AW	13.53 TQ	FLBLS	10/01-12/01
Except Sawing	Ocala MSA, FL	H	8.09 FQ	10.18 AW	13.12 TQ	FLBLS	10/01-12/01
Except Sawing	Orlando MSA, FL	H	8.74 FQ	10.88 AW	13.35 TQ	FLBLS	10/01-12/01
Except Sawing	Sarasota-Bradenton MSA, FL	H	7.05 FQ	10.37 AW	14.70 TQ	FLBLS	10/01-12/01
Except Sawing	Tallahassee MSA, FL	H	5.63 FQ	7.87 AW	10.49 TQ	FLBLS	10/01-12/01
Except Sawing	Tampa-St. Petersburg-Clearwater MSA, FL	H	7.22 FQ	10.12 AW	13.90 TQ	FLBLS	10/01-12/01
Except Sawing	West Palm Beach-Boca Raton MSA, FL	H	9.02 FQ	13.11 AW	17.21 TQ	FLBLS	10/01-12/01
Except Sawing	Georgia	H	6.38 FQ	9.60 AW	13.30 TQ	GABLS	10/01-12/01
Except Sawing	Atlanta MSA, GA	H	6.12 FQ	9.94 AW	14.42 TQ	GABLS	10/01-12/01
Except Sawing	Augusta-Aiken MSA, GA-SC	H	7.19 FQ	11.15 AW	17.75 TQ	GABLS	10/01-12/01
Except Sawing	Savannah MSA, GA	H	8.60 FQ	10.74 AW	13.71 TQ	GABLS	10/01-12/01
Except Sawing	Hawaii	H	8.47 FQ	12.18 AW	16.93 TQ	HIBLS	10/01-12/01
Except Sawing	Idaho	H	7.67 FQ	11.76 AW	16.13 TQ	IDBLS	10/01-12/01

AAW	Average annual wage	**AOH**	Average offered, high	**ASH**	Average starting, high	**H**	Hourly	**M**	Monthly	**S**	Special: hourly and annual
AE	Average entry wage	**AOL**	Average offered, low	**ASL**	Average starting, low	**HI**	Highest wage paid	**MTC**	Median total compensation	**TQ**	Third quartile wage
AEX	Average experienced wage	**APH**	Average pay, high range	**AW**	Average wage paid	**HR**	High end range	**MW**	Median wage paid	**W**	Weekly
AO	Average offered	**APL**	Average pay, low range	**FQ**	First quartile wage	**LR**	Low end range	**SQ**	Second quartile wage	**Y**	Yearly

Occupation/Type/Industry	Location	Per	Low	Mid	High	Source	Date
Woodworking Machine Setter, Operator, and Tender							
Except Sawing	Boise City MSA, ID	H	7.43 FQ	10.07 AW	12.96 TQ	IDBLS	10/01-12/01
Except Sawing	Illinois	H	6.81 FQ	10.92 AW	15.64 TQ	ILBLS	10/01-12/01
Except Sawing	Champaign-Urbana MSA, IL	H	7.80 FQ	11.30 AW	13.98 TQ	ILBLS	10/01-12/01
Except Sawing	Chicago PMSA, IL	H	8.01 FQ	11.74 AW	16.32 TQ	ILBLS	10/01-12/01
Except Sawing	Rockford MSA, IL	H	8.65 FQ	12.98 AW	16.95 TQ	ILBLS	10/01-12/01
Except Sawing	Indiana	H	8.49 FQ	11.40 AW	15.13 TQ	INBLS	10/01-12/01
Except Sawing	Elkhart-Goshen MSA, IN	H	9.14 FQ	11.81 AW	14.83 TQ	INBLS	10/01-12/01
Except Sawing	Evansville-Henderson MSA, IN-KY	H	6.66 FQ	9.20 AW	11.95 TQ	INBLS	10/01-12/01
Except Sawing	Fort Wayne MSA, IN	H	8.04 FQ	11.29 AW	15.48 TQ	INBLS	10/01-12/01
Except Sawing	Gary PMSA, IN	H	8.82 FQ	10.94 AW	13.77 TQ	INBLS	10/01-12/01
Except Sawing	Indianapolis MSA, IN	H	9.38 FQ	12.03 AW	15.42 TQ	INBLS	10/01-12/01
Except Sawing	Lafayette MSA, IN	H	8.07 FQ	9.59 AW	10.90 TQ	INBLS	10/01-12/01
Except Sawing	South Bend MSA, IN	H	7.12 FQ	10.84 AW	16.12 TQ	INBLS	10/01-12/01
Except Sawing	Iowa	H	8.36 FQ	11.00 AW	14.45 TQ	IABLS	10/01-12/01
Except Sawing	Kansas	H	6.08 FQ	8.77 AW	11.87 TQ	KSBLS	10/01-12/01
Except Sawing	Wichita MSA, KS	H	6.69 FQ	8.71 AW	11.35 TQ	KSBLS	10/01-12/01
Except Sawing	Kentucky	H	7.31 FQ	10.20 AW	14.34 TQ	KYBLS	10/01-12/01
Except Sawing	Lexington MSA, KY	H	7.30 FQ	9.61 AW	13.16 TQ	KYBLS	10/01-12/01
Except Sawing	Louisville MSA, KY-IN	H	7.81 FQ	11.63 AW	16.21 TQ	KYBLS	10/01-12/01
Except Sawing	Louisiana	H	6.48 FQ	10.88 AW	15.34 TQ	LABLS	10/01-12/01
Except Sawing	Baton Rouge MSA, LA	H	9.68 FQ	13.17 AW	17.25 TQ	LABLS	10/01-12/01
Except Sawing	New Orleans MSA, LA	H	6.14 FQ	10.34 AW	13.89 TQ	LABLS	10/01-12/01
Except Sawing	Shreveport-Bossier City MSA, LA	H	7.58 FQ	12.62 AW	19.69 TQ	LABLS	10/01-12/01
Except Sawing	Maine	H	7.22 FQ	9.57 AW	12.98 TQ	MEBLS	10/01-12/01
Except Sawing	Portland MSA, ME	H	7.56 FQ	9.74 AW	12.53 TQ	MEBLS	10/01-12/01
Except Sawing	Maryland	H	7.58 FQ	11.58 AW	16.41 TQ	MDBLS	10/01-12/01
Except Sawing	Baltimore PMSA, MD	H	7.07 FQ	11.42 AW	16.55 TQ	MDBLS	10/01-12/01
Except Sawing	Massachusetts	H	8.24 FQ	11.61 AW	16.27 TQ	MABLS	10/01-12/01
Except Sawing	Boston PMSA, MA-NH	H	7.97 FQ	11.49 AW	16.12 TQ	MABLS	10/01-12/01
Except Sawing	Springfield MSA, MA	H	6.92 FQ	11.03 AW	15.32 TQ	MABLS	10/01-12/01
Except Sawing	Worcester PMSA, MA-CT	H	8.73 FQ	12.25 AW	16.86 TQ	MABLS	10/01-12/01
Except Sawing	Michigan	H	8.43 FQ	12.63 AW	17.14 TQ	MIBLS	10/01-12/01
Except Sawing	Detroit PMSA, MI	H	8.54 FQ	15.72 AW	26.03 TQ	MIBLS	10/01-12/01
Except Sawing	Grand Rapids-Muskegon-Holland MSA, MI	H	9.77 FQ	13.29 AW	16.97 TQ	MIBLS	10/01-12/01
Except Sawing	Kalamazoo-Battle Creek MSA, MI	H	8.28 FQ	12.52 AW	18.02 TQ	MIBLS	10/01-12/01
Except Sawing	Lansing-East Lansing MSA, MI	H	9.07 FQ	11.33 AW	14.00 TQ	MIBLS	10/01-12/01
Except Sawing	Saginaw-Bay City-Midland MSA, MI	H	7.21 FQ	10.46 AW	15.63 TQ	MIBLS	10/01-12/01
Except Sawing	Minnesota	H	8.64 FQ	12.57 AW	17.24 TQ	MNBLS	10/01-12/01
Except Sawing	Duluth-Superior MSA, MN-WI	H	8.02 FQ	13.47 AW	18.21 TQ	MNBLS	10/01-12/01
Except Sawing	Minneapolis-St. Paul MSA, MN-WI	H	9.46 FQ	12.96 AW	17.20 TQ	MNBLS	10/01-12/01
Except Sawing	Mississippi	H	6.44 FQ	9.84 AW	13.46 TQ	MSBLS	10/01-12/01
Except Sawing	Biloxi-Gulfport-Pascagoula MSA, MS	H	7.37 FQ	8.30 AW	9.81 TQ	MSBLS	10/01-12/01
Except Sawing	Jackson MSA, MS	H	7.36 FQ	9.64 AW	13.93 TQ	MSBLS	10/01-12/01
Except Sawing	Missouri	H	6.92 FQ	10.99 AW	17.45 TQ	MOBLS	10/01-12/01
Except Sawing	Kansas City MSA, MO-KS	H	6.33 FQ	14.81 AW	26.64 TQ	MOBLS	10/01-12/01
Except Sawing	St. Louis MSA, MO-IL	H	6.46 FQ	10.96 AW	16.14 TQ	MOBLS	10/01-12/01
Except Sawing	Springfield MSA, MO	H	5.98 FQ	8.46 AW	12.15 TQ	MOBLS	10/01-12/01
Except Sawing	Montana	H	7.48 FQ	10.51 AW	15.80 TQ	MTBLS	10/01-12/01
Except Sawing	Nebraska	H	7.46 FQ	11.43 AW	16.31 TQ	NEBLS	10/01-12/01
Except Sawing	Omaha MSA, NE-IA	H	9.09 FQ	13.45 AW	17.48 TQ	NEBLS	10/01-12/01
Except Sawing	Nevada	H	7.82 FQ	11.40 AW	16.10 TQ	NVBLS	10/01-12/01
Except Sawing	Las Vegas MSA, NV-AZ	H	7.39 FQ	10.15 AW	13.32 TQ	NVBLS	10/01-12/01
Except Sawing	New Hampshire	H	8.05 FQ	11.45 AW	16.23 TQ	NHBLS	10/01-12/01
Except Sawing	Portsmouth-Rochester PMSA, NH-ME	H	7.55 FQ	11.64 AW	17.19 TQ	NHBLS	10/01-12/01
Except Sawing	New Jersey	H	7.85 FQ	13.42 AW	21.02 TQ	NJBLS	10/01-12/01
Except Sawing	Atlantic-Cape May PMSA, NJ	H	7.68 FQ	9.86 AW	12.47 TQ	NJBLS	10/01-12/01
Except Sawing	Bergen-Passaic PMSA, NJ	H	8.01 FQ	15.12 AW	25.95 TQ	NJBLS	10/01-12/01
Except Sawing	Middlesex-Somerset-Hunterdon PMSA, NJ	H	10.40 FQ	17.90 AW	26.31 TQ	NJBLS	10/01-12/01
Except Sawing	Monmouth-Ocean PMSA, NJ	H	9.29 FQ	13.08 AW	18.67 TQ	NJBLS	10/01-12/01
Except Sawing	Newark PMSA, NJ	H	7.57 FQ	11.40 AW	17.79 TQ	NJBLS	10/01-12/01
Except Sawing	New Mexico	H	7.22 FQ	10.04 AW	13.12 TQ	NMBLS	10/01-12/01

AAW Average annual wage; **AE** Average entry wage; **AEX** Average experienced wage; **AO** Average offered; **AOH** Average offered, high; **AOL** Average offered, low; **APH** Average pay, high range; **APL** Average pay, low range; **ASH** Average starting, high; **ASL** Average starting, low; **AW** Average wage paid; **FQ** First quartile wage; **H** Hourly; **HI** Highest wage paid; **HR** High end range; **LR** Low end range; **M** Monthly; **MTC** Median total compensation; **MW** Median wage paid; **SQ** Second quartile wage; **S** Special: hourly and annual; **TQ** Third quartile wage; **W** Weekly; **Y** Yearly

Occupation/Type/Industry	Location	Per	Low	Mid	High	Source	Date
Woodworking Machine Setter, Operator, and Tender							
Except Sawing	Albuquerque MSA, NM	H	7.08 FQ	9.54 AW	12.08 TQ	NMBLS	10/01-12/01
Except Sawing	New York	H	7.40 FQ	11.45 AW	16.62 TQ	NYBLS	10/01-12/01
Except Sawing	Albany-Schenectady-Troy MSA, NY	H	8.13 FQ	12.87 AW	19.30 TQ	NYBLS	10/01-12/01
Except Sawing	Binghamton MSA, NY	H	7.59 FQ	10.33 AW	13.41 TQ	NYBLS	10/01-12/01
Except Sawing	Buffalo-Niagara Falls MSA, NY	H	8.96 FQ	13.86 AW	20.21 TQ	NYBLS	10/01-12/01
Except Sawing	Dutchess County PMSA, NY	H	7.49 FQ	10.65 AW	15.47 TQ	NYBLS	10/01-12/01
Except Sawing	Nassau-Suffolk PMSA, NY	H	6.96 FQ	12.05 AW	20.60 TQ	NYBLS	10/01-12/01
Except Sawing	New York PMSA, NY	H	8.35 FQ	12.63 AW	16.81 TQ	NYBLS	10/01-12/01
Except Sawing	Newburgh PMSA, NY-PA	H	6.68 FQ	11.77 AW	20.22 TQ	NYBLS	10/01-12/01
Except Sawing	Rochester MSA, NY	H	5.98 FQ	9.21 AW	12.92 TQ	NYBLS	10/01-12/01
Except Sawing	Syracuse MSA, NY	H	7.21 FQ	9.61 AW	13.34 TQ	NYBLS	10/01-12/01
Except Sawing	Utica-Rome MSA, NY	H	7.28 FQ	10.04 AW	13.17 TQ	NYBLS	10/01-12/01
Except Sawing	North Carolina	H	7.55 FQ	10.77 AW	13.79 TQ	NCBLS	10/01-12/01
Except Sawing	Charlotte-Gastonia-Rock Hill MSA, NC-SC	H	6.37 FQ	10.61 AW	16.34 TQ	NCBLS	10/01-12/01
Except Sawing	Greensboro-Winston-Salem-High Point MSA, NC	H	8.08 FQ	11.00 AW	13.79 TQ	NCBLS	10/01-12/01
Except Sawing	Hickory-Morganton-Lenoir MSA, NC	H	8.17 FQ	11.12 AW	13.95 TQ	NCBLS	10/01-12/01
Except Sawing	Raleigh-Durham-Chapel Hill MSA, NC	H	7.28 FQ	10.33 AW	13.23 TQ	NCBLS	10/01-12/01
Except Sawing	North Dakota	H	8.88 FQ	10.60 AW	13.31 TQ	NDBLS	10/01-12/01
Except Sawing	Fargo-Moorhead MSA, ND-MN	H	6.40 FQ	10.56 AW	13.97 TQ	NDBLS	10/01-12/01
Except Sawing	Ohio	H	7.50 FQ	11.26 AW	16.27 TQ	OHBLS	10/01-12/01
Except Sawing	Canton-Massillon MSA, OH	H	7.06 FQ	10.66 AW	16.44 TQ	OHBLS	10/01-12/01
Except Sawing	Cincinnati PMSA, OH-KY-IN	H	8.33 FQ	12.25 AW	17.47 TQ	OHBLS	10/01-12/01
Except Sawing	Cleveland-Lorain-Elyria PMSA, OH	H	7.72 FQ	12.67 AW	23.27 TQ	OHBLS	10/01-12/01
Except Sawing	Columbus MSA, OH	H	9.74 FQ	12.51 AW	16.25 TQ	OHBLS	10/01-12/01
Except Sawing	Dayton-Springfield MSA, OH	H	9.02 FQ	11.49 AW	14.16 TQ	OHBLS	10/01-12/01
Except Sawing	Hamilton-Middletown PMSA, OH	H	6.08 FQ	9.95 AW	14.00 TQ	OHBLS	10/01-12/01
Except Sawing	Mansfield MSA, OH	H	9.66 FQ	11.93 AW	14.18 TQ	OHBLS	10/01-12/01
Except Sawing	Toledo MSA, OH	H	9.07 FQ	11.02 AW	13.49 TQ	OHBLS	10/01-12/01
Except Sawing	Youngstown-Warren MSA, OH	H	7.34 FQ	11.76 AW	18.45 TQ	OHBLS	10/01-12/01
Except Sawing	Oklahoma	H	7.39 FQ	10.58 AW	13.77 TQ	OKBLS	10/01-12/01
Except Sawing	Oklahoma City MSA, OK	H	7.01 FQ	8.96 AW	11.28 TQ	OKBLS	10/01-12/01
Except Sawing	Tulsa MSA, OK	H	8.75 FQ	11.85 AW	16.71 TQ	OKBLS	10/01-12/01
Except Sawing	Oregon	H	9.04 FQ	13.08 AW	17.05 TQ	ORBLS	10/01-12/01
Except Sawing	Eugene-Springfield MSA, OR	H	9.05 FQ	12.27 AW	16.84 TQ	ORBLS	10/01-12/01
Except Sawing	Medford-Ashland MSA, OR	H	8.81 FQ	12.72 AW	16.64 TQ	ORBLS	10/01-12/01
Except Sawing	Portland-Vancouver PMSA, OR-WA	H	7.80 FQ	12.42 AW	17.06 TQ	ORBLS	10/01-12/01
Except Sawing	Salem PMSA, OR	H	9.23 FQ	12.82 AW	19.80 TQ	ORBLS	10/01-12/01
Except Sawing	Pennsylvania	H	7.27 FQ	10.86 AW	14.91 TQ	PABLS	10/01-12/01
Except Sawing	Allentown-Bethlehem-Easton MSA, PA	H	7.12 FQ	10.47 AW	14.44 TQ	PABLS	10/01-12/01
Except Sawing	Erie MSA, PA	H	7.03 FQ	11.30 AW	16.29 TQ	PABLS	10/01-12/01
Except Sawing	Harrisburg-Lebanon-Carlisle MSA, PA	H	7.48 FQ	11.10 AW	16.10 TQ	PABLS	10/01-12/01
Except Sawing	Johnstown MSA, PA	H	7.08 FQ	9.29 AW	12.41 TQ	PABLS	10/01-12/01
Except Sawing	Lancaster MSA, PA	H	8.63 FQ	12.30 AW	16.01 TQ	PABLS	10/01-12/01
Except Sawing	Philadelphia PMSA, PA-NJ	H	7.83 FQ	12.61 AW	19.53 TQ	PABLS	10/01-12/01
Except Sawing	Pittsburgh MSA, PA	H	9.24 FQ	12.18 AW	16.64 TQ	PABLS	10/01-12/01
Except Sawing	Reading MSA, PA	H	11.26 FQ	14.26 AW	16.82 TQ	PABLS	10/01-12/01
Except Sawing	Scranton-Wilkes-Barre-Hazleton MSA, PA	H	7.36 FQ	10.63 AW	13.89 TQ	PABLS	10/01-12/01
Except Sawing	York MSA, PA	H	7.77 FQ	10.76 AW	15.02 TQ	PABLS	10/01-12/01
Except Sawing	Rhode Island	H	7.53 FQ	11.59 AW	16.69 TQ	RIBLS	10/01-12/01
Except Sawing	Providence-Fall River-Warwick MSA, RI-MA	H	7.54 FQ	11.61 AW	16.53 TQ	RIBLS	10/01-12/01
Except Sawing	South Carolina	H	6.85 FQ	10.23 AW	14.67 TQ	SCBLS	10/01-12/01
Except Sawing	Charleston-North Charleston MSA, SC	H	7.02 FQ	10.76 AW	16.04 TQ	SCBLS	10/01-12/01
Except Sawing	Columbia MSA, SC	H	8.59 FQ	10.85 AW	13.59 TQ	SCBLS	10/01-12/01
Except Sawing	Greenville-Spartanburg-Anderson MSA, SC	H	8.51 FQ	11.09 AW	13.86 TQ	SCBLS	10/01-12/01

AAW	Average annual wage	AOH	Average offered, high	ASH	Average starting, high	H	Hourly	M	Monthly	S	Special: hourly and annual
AE	Average entry wage	AOL	Average offered, low	ASL	Average starting, low	HI	Highest wage paid	MTC	Median total compensation	TQ	Third quartile wage
AEX	Average experienced wage	APH	Average pay, high range	AW	Average wage paid	HR	High end range	MW	Median wage paid	W	Weekly
AO	Average offered	APL	Average pay, low range	FQ	First quartile wage	LR	Low end range	SQ	Second quartile wage	Y	Yearly

Occupation/Type/Industry	Location	Per	Low	Mid	High	Source	Date
Woodworking Machine Setter, Operator, and Tender							
Except Sawing	South Dakota	H	7.95 FQ	10.99 AW	14.74 TQ	SDBLS	10/01-12/01
Except Sawing	Sioux Falls MSA, SD	H	8.24 FQ	10.69 AW	13.61 TQ	SDBLS	10/01-12/01
Except Sawing	Tennessee	H	7.28 FQ	10.25 AW	13.82 TQ	TNBLS	10/01-12/01
Except Sawing	Chattanooga MSA, TN-GA	H	7.30 FQ	9.57 AW	12.80 TQ	TNBLS	10/01-12/01
Except Sawing	Johnson City-Kingsport-Bristol MSA, TN-VA	H	7.32 FQ	10.11 AW	14.31 TQ	TNBLS	10/01-12/01
Except Sawing	Knoxville MSA, TN	H	7.49 FQ	10.25 AW	13.87 TQ	TNBLS	10/01-12/01
Except Sawing	Nashville MSA, TN	H	9.36 FQ	12.96 AW	17.88 TQ	TNBLS	10/01-12/01
Except Sawing	Texas	H	6.34 FQ	9.24 AW	12.74 TQ	TXBLS	10/01-12/01
Except Sawing	Austin-San Marcos MSA, TX	H	6.70 FQ	9.88 AW	13.08 TQ	TXBLS	10/01-12/01
Except Sawing	Dallas PMSA, TX	H	7.10 FQ	9.97 AW	13.34 TQ	TXBLS	10/01-12/01
Except Sawing	El Paso MSA, TX	H	5.78 FQ	7.27 AW	8.66 TQ	TXBLS	10/01-12/01
Except Sawing	Fort Worth-Arlington PMSA, TX	H	7.67 FQ	10.10 AW	12.94 TQ	TXBLS	10/01-12/01
Except Sawing	Houston PMSA, TX	H	6.22 FQ	9.64 AW	14.03 TQ	TXBLS	10/01-12/01
Except Sawing	Longview-Marshall MSA, TX	H	5.78 FQ	7.94 AW	11.25 TQ	TXBLS	10/01-12/01
Except Sawing	Lubbock MSA, TX	H	5.97 FQ	8.84 AW	11.26 TQ	TXBLS	10/01-12/01
Except Sawing	San Antonio MSA, TX	H	5.93 FQ	8.10 AW	10.54 TQ	TXBLS	10/01-12/01
Except Sawing	Waco MSA, TX	H	6.12 FQ	9.73 AW	13.04 TQ	TXBLS	10/01-12/01
Except Sawing	Utah	H	6.60 FQ	10.96 AW	16.17 TQ	UTBLS	10/01-12/01
Except Sawing	Salt Lake City-Ogden MSA, UT	H	6.47 FQ	10.84 AW	16.17 TQ	UTBLS	10/01-12/01
Except Sawing	Vermont	H	7.62 FQ	10.68 AW	14.21 TQ	VTBLS	10/01-12/01
Except Sawing	Virginia	H	7.62 FQ	10.49 AW	13.43 TQ	VABLS	10/01-12/01
Except Sawing	Lynchburg MSA, VA	H	7.40 FQ	9.77 AW	13.45 TQ	VABLS	10/01-12/01
Except Sawing	Norfolk-Virginia Beach-Newport News MSA, VA-NC	H	7.64 FQ	10.19 AW	13.27 TQ	VABLS	10/01-12/01
Except Sawing	Richmond-Petersburg MSA, VA	H	7.51 FQ	10.13 AW	13.70 TQ	VABLS	10/01-12/01
Except Sawing	Roanoke MSA, VA	H	8.65 FQ	10.81 AW	13.91 TQ	VABLS	10/01-12/01
Except Sawing	Washington	H	8.63 FQ	12.06 AW	16.79 TQ	WABLS	10/01-12/01
Except Sawing	Olympia PMSA, WA	H	9.71 FQ	13.00 AW	16.50 TQ	WABLS	10/01-12/01
Except Sawing	Seattle-Bellevue-Everett PMSA, WA	H	8.04 FQ	11.26 AW	16.25 TQ	WABLS	10/01-12/01
Except Sawing	Spokane MSA, WA	H	9.07 FQ	10.34 AW	12.51 TQ	WABLS	10/01-12/01
Except Sawing	Tacoma PMSA, WA	H	9.33 FQ	13.00 AW	17.78 TQ	WABLS	10/01-12/01
Except Sawing	Yakima MSA, WA	H	9.12 FQ	11.97 AW	16.11 TQ	WABLS	10/01-12/01
Except Sawing	West Virginia	H	6.42 FQ	9.83 AW	14.43 TQ	WVBLS	10/01-12/01
Except Sawing	Wisconsin	H	7.94 FQ	11.44 AW	16.29 TQ	WIBLS	10/01-12/01
Except Sawing	Appleton-Oshkosh-Neenah MSA, WI	H	9.24 FQ	12.61 AW	16.85 TQ	WIBLS	10/01-12/01
Except Sawing	Green Bay MSA, WI	H	7.86 FQ	10.34 AW	13.16 TQ	WIBLS	10/01-12/01
Except Sawing	Madison MSA, WI	H	9.13 FQ	13.74 AW	19.06 TQ	WIBLS	10/01-12/01
Except Sawing	Milwaukee-Waukesha PMSA, WI	H	7.84 FQ	12.24 AW	18.04 TQ	WIBLS	10/01-12/01
Except Sawing	Racine PMSA, WI	H	7.26 FQ	12.50 AW	19.30 TQ	WIBLS	10/01-12/01
Except Sawing	Wyoming	H	7.25 FQ	9.12 AW	11.05 TQ	WYBLS	10/01-12/01
Except Sawing	Puerto Rico	H	5.51 FQ	6.26 AW	6.96 TQ	PRBLS	10/01-12/01
Word Processor and Typist	Alabama	H	7.36 FQ	10.68 AW	15.75 TQ	ALBLS	10/01-12/01
	Birmingham MSA, AL	H	7.30 FQ	11.30 AW	16.67 TQ	ALBLS	10/01-12/01
	Huntsville MSA, AL	H	7.52 FQ	12.18 AW	17.66 TQ	ALBLS	10/01-12/01
	Mobile MSA, AL	H	7.52 FQ	10.32 AW	13.92 TQ	ALBLS	10/01-12/01
	Montgomery MSA, AL	H	7.72 FQ	10.65 AW	14.55 TQ	ALBLS	10/01-12/01
	Alaska	H	10.66 FQ	14.10 AW	18.15 TQ	AKBLS	10/01-12/01
	Anchorage MSA, AK	H	10.81 FQ	14.41 AW	18.50 TQ	AKBLS	10/01-12/01
	Arizona	H	7.38 FQ	11.24 AW	16.43 TQ	AZBLS	10/01-12/01
	Phoenix-Mesa MSA, AZ	H	7.45 FQ	11.41 AW	16.52 TQ	AZBLS	10/01-12/01
	Tucson MSA, AZ	H	7.65 FQ	11.29 AW	17.25 TQ	AZBLS	10/01-12/01
	Arkansas	H	7.00 FQ	10.54 AW	15.49 TQ	ARBLS	10/01-12/01
	Fayetteville-Springdale-Rogers MSA, AR	H	6.57 FQ	9.61 AW	13.26 TQ	ARBLS	10/01-12/01
	Fort Smith MSA, AR-OK	H	8.04 FQ	11.21 AW	14.59 TQ	ARBLS	10/01-12/01
	Little Rock-North Little Rock MSA, AR	H	8.03 FQ	12.26 AW	17.25 TQ	ARBLS	10/01-12/01
	California	H	9.89 FQ	14.64 AW	21.42 TQ	CABLS	10/01-12/01
	Bakersfield MSA, CA	H	6.89 FQ	13.24 AW	20.93 TQ	CABLS	10/01-12/01
	Chico-Paradise MSA, CA	H	7.51 FQ	10.64 AW	15.79 TQ	CABLS	10/01-12/01
	Fresno MSA, CA	H	8.03 FQ	14.18 AW	23.43 TQ	CABLS	10/01-12/01

AAW Average annual wage; **AE** Average entry wage; **AEX** Average experienced wage; **AO** Average offered; **AOH** Average offered, high; **AOL** Average offered, low; **APH** Average pay, high range; **APL** Average pay, low range; **ASH** Average starting, high; **ASL** Average starting, low; **AW** Average wage paid; **FQ** First quartile wage; **H** Hourly; **HI** Highest wage paid; **HR** High end range; **LR** Low end range; **M** Monthly; **MTC** Median total compensation; **MW** Median wage paid; **SQ** Second quartile wage; **S** Special: hourly and annual; **TQ** Third quartile wage; **W** Weekly; **Y** Yearly

Occupation/Type/Industry	Location	Per	Low	Mid	High	Source	Date
Word Processor and Typist	Los Angeles-Long Beach PMSA, CA	H	10.64 FQ	14.30 AW	19.98 TQ	CABLS	10/01-12/01
	Merced MSA, CA	H	9.01 FQ	16.65 AW	26.16 TQ	CABLS	10/01-12/01
	Modesto MSA, CA	H	7.39 FQ	11.30 AW	14.71 TQ	CABLS	10/01-12/01
	Oakland PMSA, CA	H	11.78 FQ	16.77 AW	24.11 TQ	CABLS	10/01-12/01
	Orange County PMSA, CA	H	9.91 FQ	15.15 AW	22.15 TQ	CABLS	10/01-12/01
	Redding MSA, CA	H	9.85 FQ	15.81 AW	23.30 TQ	CABLS	10/01-12/01
	Riverside-San Bernardino PMSA, CA	H	10.51 FQ	14.09 AW	17.84 TQ	CABLS	10/01-12/01
	Sacramento PMSA, CA	H	7.90 FQ	14.07 AW	20.29 TQ	CABLS	10/01-12/01
	Salinas MSA, CA	H	9.51 FQ	15.79 AW	23.26 TQ	CABLS	10/01-12/01
	San Diego MSA, CA	H	10.03 FQ	13.92 AW	19.73 TQ	CABLS	10/01-12/01
	San Francisco PMSA, CA	H	12.80 FQ	19.84 AW	27.13 TQ	CABLS	10/01-12/01
	San Jose PMSA, CA	H	11.95 FQ	18.70 AW	27.13 TQ	CABLS	10/01-12/01
	San Luis Obispo-Atascadero-Paso Robles MSA, CA	H	11.77 FQ	15.25 AW	18.64 TQ	CABLS	10/01-12/01
	Santa Barbara-Santa Maria-Lompoc MSA, CA	H	10.78 FQ	13.60 AW	17.41 TQ	CABLS	10/01-12/01
	Santa Cruz-Watsonville PMSA, CA	H	11.59 FQ	13.85 AW	16.93 TQ	CABLS	10/01-12/01
	Santa Rosa PMSA, CA	H	9.93 FQ	14.55 AW	18.26 TQ	CABLS	10/01-12/01
	Stockton-Lodi MSA, CA	H	7.07 FQ	13.40 AW	21.77 TQ	CABLS	10/01-12/01
	Vallejo-Fairfield-Napa PMSA, CA	H	9.93 FQ	14.14 AW	19.68 TQ	CABLS	10/01-12/01
	Ventura PMSA, CA	H	6.49 FQ	11.42 AW	17.07 TQ	CABLS	10/01-12/01
	Visalia-Tulare-Porterville MSA, CA	H	8.01 FQ	13.36 AW	18.26 TQ	CABLS	10/01-12/01
	Colorado	H	9.36 FQ	13.30 AW	17.92 TQ	COBLS	10/01-12/01
	Boulder-Longmont PMSA, CO	H	9.64 FQ	14.27 AW	20.09 TQ	COBLS	10/01-12/01
	Colorado Springs MSA, CO	H	8.65 FQ	11.74 AW	16.76 TQ	COBLS	10/01-12/01
	Denver PMSA, CO	H	10.14 FQ	14.08 AW	18.30 TQ	COBLS	10/01-12/01
	Fort Collins-Loveland MSA, CO	H	9.37 FQ	12.56 AW	16.71 TQ	COBLS	10/01-12/01
	Greeley PMSA, CO	H	9.37 FQ	12.34 AW	15.90 TQ	COBLS	10/01-12/01
	Connecticut	H	9.77 FQ	13.62 AW	17.65 TQ	CTBLS	10/01-12/01
	Bridgeport PMSA, CT	H	10.26 FQ	13.70 AW	17.71 TQ	CTBLS	10/01-12/01
	Danbury PMSA, CT	H	10.65 FQ	14.14 AW	17.70 TQ	CTBLS	10/01-12/01
	Hartford MSA, CT	H	9.54 FQ	13.31 AW	16.95 TQ	CTBLS	10/01-12/01
	New Haven-Meriden PMSA, CT	H	10.69 FQ	14.06 AW	17.45 TQ	CTBLS	10/01-12/01
	New London-Norwich MSA, CT-RI	H	9.23 FQ	11.97 AW	16.11 TQ	CTBLS	10/01-12/01
	Stamford-Norwalk PMSA, CT	H	11.80 FQ	16.15 AW	20.72 TQ	CTBLS	10/01-12/01
	Waterbury PMSA, CT	H	8.75 FQ	11.60 AW	14.38 TQ	CTBLS	10/01-12/01
	Delaware	H	8.83 FQ	13.07 AW	18.91 TQ	DEBLS	10/01-12/01
	Wilmington-Newark PMSA, DE-MD	H	9.62 FQ	14.00 AW	20.27 TQ	DEBLS	10/01-12/01
	District of Columbia	H	9.77 FQ	13.28 AW	17.76 TQ	DCBLS	10/01-12/01
	Washington PMSA, DC-MD-VA-WV	H	9.64 FQ	13.83 AW	19.50 TQ	DCBLS	10/01-12/01
	Florida	H	8.02 FQ	11.48 AW	16.59 TQ	FLBLS	10/01-12/01
	Daytona Beach MSA, FL	H	7.76 FQ	12.04 AW	19.32 TQ	FLBLS	10/01-12/01
	Fort Lauderdale PMSA, FL	H	7.81 FQ	12.08 AW	17.32 TQ	FLBLS	10/01-12/01
	Fort Myers-Cape Coral MSA, FL	H	8.69 FQ	11.98 AW	18.52 TQ	FLBLS	10/01-12/01
	Fort Pierce-Port St. Lucie MSA, FL	H	8.58 FQ	10.96 AW	14.21 TQ	FLBLS	10/01-12/01
	Fort Walton Beach MSA, FL	H	7.19 FQ	9.87 AW	14.75 TQ	FLBLS	10/01-12/01
	Gainesville MSA, FL	H	7.39 FQ	10.90 AW	14.66 TQ	FLBLS	10/01-12/01
	Jacksonville MSA, FL	H	8.30 FQ	11.75 AW	17.07 TQ	FLBLS	10/01-12/01
	Lakeland-Winter Haven MSA, FL	H	7.63 FQ	10.82 AW	14.56 TQ	FLBLS	10/01-12/01
	Melbourne-Titusville-Palm Bay MSA, FL	H	8.11 FQ	13.04 AW	19.66 TQ	FLBLS	10/01-12/01
	Miami PMSA, FL	H	8.45 FQ	11.61 AW	16.52 TQ	FLBLS	10/01-12/01
	Naples MSA, FL	H	8.71 FQ	11.80 AW	14.67 TQ	FLBLS	10/01-12/01
	Ocala MSA, FL	H	6.07 FQ	10.29 AW	14.02 TQ	FLBLS	10/01-12/01
	Orlando MSA, FL	H	8.77 FQ	12.30 AW	18.87 TQ	FLBLS	10/01-12/01
	Pensacola MSA, FL	H	7.93 FQ	11.29 AW	16.80 TQ	FLBLS	10/01-12/01
	Sarasota-Bradenton MSA, FL	H	7.20 FQ	10.94 AW	15.21 TQ	FLBLS	10/01-12/01
	Tallahassee MSA, FL	H	8.77 FQ	14.77 AW	25.25 TQ	FLBLS	10/01-12/01

AAW	Average annual wage	**AOH**	Average offered, high	**ASH**	Average starting, high	**H**	Hourly	**M**	Monthly	**S**	Special: hourly and annual
AE	Average entry wage	**AOL**	Average offered, low	**ASL**	Average starting, low	**HI**	Highest wage paid	**MTC**	Median total compensation	**TQ**	Third quartile wage
AEX	Average experienced wage	**APH**	Average pay, high range	**AW**	Average wage paid	**HR**	High end range	**MW**	Median wage paid	**W**	Weekly
AO	Average offered	**APL**	Average pay, low range	**FQ**	First quartile wage	**LR**	Low end range	**SQ**	Second quartile wage	**Y**	Yearly

Occupation/Type/Industry	Location	Per	Low	Mid	High	Source	Date
Word Processor and Typist	Tampa-St. Petersburg-Clearwater MSA, FL	H	7.74 FQ	10.45 AW	13.59 TQ	FLBLS	10/01-12/01
	West Palm Beach-Boca Raton MSA, FL	H	8.94 FQ	11.36 AW	13.42 TQ	FLBLS	10/01-12/01
	Georgia	H	8.76 FQ	12.71 AW	17.21 TQ	GABLS	10/01-12/01
	Atlanta MSA, GA	H	10.04 FQ	13.22 AW	17.87 TQ	GABLS	10/01-12/01
	Columbus MSA, GA-AL	H	7.36 FQ	12.25 AW	16.68 TQ	GABLS	10/01-12/01
	Macon MSA, GA	H	7.66 FQ	12.14 AW	18.14 TQ	GABLS	10/01-12/01
	Savannah MSA, GA	H	9.57 FQ	13.42 AW	17.30 TQ	GABLS	10/01-12/01
	Hawaii	H	9.15 FQ	11.88 AW	15.72 TQ	HIBLS	10/01-12/01
	Honolulu MSA, HI	H	9.21 FQ	12.12 AW	16.31 TQ	HIBLS	10/01-12/01
	Idaho	H	9.06 FQ	12.79 AW	17.06 TQ	IDBLS	10/01-12/01
	Boise City MSA, ID	H	9.46 FQ	13.14 AW	17.10 TQ	IDBLS	10/01-12/01
	Illinois	H	7.63 FQ	12.51 AW	17.55 TQ	ILBLS	10/01-12/01
	Champaign-Urbana MSA, IL	H	6.56 FQ	10.20 AW	14.16 TQ	ILBLS	10/01-12/01
	Chicago PMSA, IL	H	9.21 FQ	13.20 AW	17.97 TQ	ILBLS	10/01-12/01
	Peoria-Pekin MSA, IL	H	7.76 FQ	11.33 AW	16.58 TQ	ILBLS	10/01-12/01
	Rockford MSA, IL	H	8.37 FQ	12.19 AW	17.29 TQ	ILBLS	10/01-12/01
	Springfield MSA, IL	H	7.25 FQ	10.49 AW	14.01 TQ	ILBLS	10/01-12/01
	Indiana	H	6.79 FQ	10.63 AW	14.86 TQ	INBLS	10/01-12/01
	Elkhart-Goshen MSA, IN	H	7.63 FQ	11.65 AW	17.86 TQ	INBLS	10/01-12/01
	Evansville-Henderson MSA, IN-KY	H	7.00 FQ	10.44 AW	14.33 TQ	INBLS	10/01-12/01
	Fort Wayne MSA, IN	H	8.19 FQ	11.12 AW	15.67 TQ	INBLS	10/01-12/01
	Gary PMSA, IN	H	7.91 FQ	10.90 AW	13.88 TQ	INBLS	10/01-12/01
	Indianapolis MSA, IN	H	6.46 FQ	10.83 AW	15.51 TQ	INBLS	10/01-12/01
	Lafayette MSA, IN	H	8.08 FQ	10.69 AW	13.61 TQ	INBLS	10/01-12/01
	South Bend MSA, IN	H	6.28 FQ	10.12 AW	13.75 TQ	INBLS	10/01-12/01
	Iowa	H	7.62 FQ	11.21 AW	14.92 TQ	IABLS	10/01-12/01
	Cedar Rapids MSA, IA	H	9.04 FQ	11.88 AW	13.91 TQ	IABLS	10/01-12/01
	Davenport-Moline-Rock Island MSA, IA-IL	H	5.84 FQ	10.63 AW	16.60 TQ	IABLS	10/01-12/01
	Des Moines MSA, IA	H	8.70 FQ	11.52 AW	14.62 TQ	IABLS	10/01-12/01
	Kansas	H	6.89 FQ	11.36 AW	16.92 TQ	KSBLS	10/01-12/01
	Topeka MSA, KS	H	9.32 FQ	13.79 AW	17.68 TQ	KSBLS	10/01-12/01
	Wichita MSA, KS	H	7.00 FQ	10.57 AW	14.62 TQ	KSBLS	10/01-12/01
	Kentucky	H	6.84 FQ	11.06 AW	16.50 TQ	KYBLS	10/01-12/01
	Lexington MSA, KY	H	7.72 FQ	11.50 AW	18.22 TQ	KYBLS	10/01-12/01
	Louisville MSA, KY-IN	H	6.30 FQ	11.20 AW	16.74 TQ	KYBLS	10/01-12/01
	Louisiana	H	6.25 FQ	9.51 AW	13.74 TQ	LABLS	10/01-12/01
	Baton Rouge MSA, LA	H	6.17 FQ	9.57 AW	14.18 TQ	LABLS	10/01-12/01
	Houma MSA, LA	H	5.95 FQ	9.21 AW	13.14 TQ	LABLS	10/01-12/01
	Lafayette MSA, LA	H	6.14 FQ	8.36 AW	10.99 TQ	LABLS	10/01-12/01
	Lake Charles MSA, LA	H	6.26 FQ	8.56 AW	10.71 TQ	LABLS	10/01-12/01
	New Orleans MSA, LA	H	6.66 FQ	10.25 AW	15.17 TQ	LABLS	10/01-12/01
	Shreveport-Bossier City MSA, LA	H	6.69 FQ	9.67 AW	13.33 TQ	LABLS	10/01-12/01
	Maine	H	8.65 FQ	10.87 AW	13.25 TQ	MEBLS	10/01-12/01
	Portland MSA, ME	H	9.32 FQ	11.21 AW	13.61 TQ	MEBLS	10/01-12/01
	Maryland	H	7.28 FQ	13.43 AW	19.57 TQ	MDBLS	10/01-12/01
	Baltimore PMSA, MD	H	6.69 FQ	13.24 AW	19.77 TQ	MDBLS	10/01-12/01
	Massachusetts	H	9.76 FQ	13.96 AW	19.19 TQ	MABLS	10/01-12/01
	Boston PMSA, MA-NH	H	10.01 FQ	14.25 AW	19.86 TQ	MABLS	10/01-12/01
	Brockton PMSA, MA	H	11.23 FQ	14.28 AW	18.57 TQ	MABLS	10/01-12/01
	Lawrence PMSA, MA-NH	H	9.65 FQ	13.69 AW	18.73 TQ	MABLS	10/01-12/01
	Lowell PMSA, MA-NH	H	9.82 FQ	13.89 AW	19.23 TQ	MABLS	10/01-12/01
	New Bedford PMSA, MA	H	9.42 FQ	12.73 AW	16.92 TQ	MABLS	10/01-12/01
	Springfield MSA, MA	H	8.84 FQ	12.75 AW	16.96 TQ	MABLS	10/01-12/01
	Worcester PMSA, MA-CT	H	9.29 FQ	13.23 AW	17.10 TQ	MABLS	10/01-12/01
	Michigan	H	8.94 FQ	13.18 AW	17.09 TQ	MIBLS	10/01-12/01
	Ann Arbor PMSA, MI	H	9.26 FQ	14.22 AW	18.40 TQ	MIBLS	10/01-12/01
	Detroit PMSA, MI	H	9.07 FQ	13.00 AW	16.90 TQ	MIBLS	10/01-12/01
	Flint PMSA, MI	H	6.75 FQ	13.38 AW	17.27 TQ	MIBLS	10/01-12/01
	Grand Rapids-Muskegon-Holland MSA, MI	H	8.19 FQ	12.91 AW	16.91 TQ	MIBLS	10/01-12/01
	Kalamazoo-Battle Creek MSA, MI	H	8.30 FQ	13.34 AW	17.10 TQ	MIBLS	10/01-12/01
	Lansing-East Lansing MSA, MI	H	10.25 FQ	14.31 AW	17.88 TQ	MIBLS	10/01-12/01
	Saginaw-Bay City-Midland MSA, MI	H	7.96 FQ	11.60 AW	16.12 TQ	MIBLS	10/01-12/01
	Minnesota	H	9.39 FQ	13.65 AW	18.36 TQ	MNBLS	10/01-12/01
	Duluth-Superior MSA, MN-WI	H	7.16 FQ	10.70 AW	15.69 TQ	MNBLS	10/01-12/01

AAW	Average annual wage	**AOH**	Average offered, high	**ASH**	Average starting, high	**H**	Hourly	**M**	Monthly	**S**	Special: hourly and annual
AE	Average entry wage	**AOL**	Average offered, low	**ASL**	Average starting, low	**HI**	Highest wage paid	**MTC**	Median total compensation	**TQ**	Third quartile wage
AEX	Average experienced wage	**APH**	Average pay, high range	**AW**	Average wage paid	**HR**	High end range	**MW**	Median wage paid	**W**	Weekly
AO	Average offered	**APL**	Average pay, low range	**FQ**	First quartile wage	**LR**	Low end range	**SQ**	Second quartile wage	**Y**	Yearly

Occupation/Type/Industry	Location	Per	Low	Mid	High	Source	Date
Word Processor and Typist	Minneapolis-St. Paul MSA, MN-WI	H	10.25 FQ	14.36 AW	19.21 TQ	MNBLS	10/01-12/01
	St. Cloud MSA, MN	H	9.23 FQ	12.89 AW	17.63 TQ	MNBLS	10/01-12/01
	Mississippi	H	7.12 FQ	9.90 AW	13.85 TQ	MSBLS	10/01-12/01
	Biloxi-Gulfport-Pascagoula MSA, MS	H	7.61 FQ	11.07 AW	15.14 TQ	MSBLS	10/01-12/01
	Jackson MSA, MS	H	7.19 FQ	10.06 AW	13.86 TQ	MSBLS	10/01-12/01
	Kansas City MSA, MO-KS	H	8.56 FQ	12.43 AW	17.63 TQ	MOBLS	10/01-12/01
	St. Louis MSA, MO-IL	H	7.00 FQ	11.12 AW	15.70 TQ	MOBLS	10/01-12/01
	Springfield MSA, MO	H	7.41 FQ	9.74 AW	14.57 TQ	MOBLS	10/01-12/01
	Montana	H	6.93 FQ	11.32 AW	16.97 TQ	MTBLS	10/01-12/01
	Lincoln MSA, NE	H	8.07 FQ	11.67 AW	16.24 TQ	NEBLS	10/01-12/01
	Nevada	H	8.90 FQ	12.81 AW	17.39 TQ	NVBLS	10/01-12/01
	Las Vegas MSA, NV-AZ	H	8.64 FQ	11.89 AW	16.28 TQ	NVBLS	10/01-12/01
	Reno MSA, NV	H	8.86 FQ	13.57 AW	17.53 TQ	NVBLS	10/01-12/01
	New Hampshire	H	8.88 FQ	12.02 AW	15.69 TQ	NHBLS	10/01-12/01
	Portsmouth-Rochester PMSA, NH-ME	H	10.79 FQ	13.19 AW	16.91 TQ	NHBLS	10/01-12/01
	New Jersey	H	8.96 FQ	13.92 AW	21.47 TQ	NJBLS	10/01-12/01
	Atlantic-Cape May PMSA, NJ	H	9.31 FQ	13.83 AW	20.00 TQ	NJBLS	10/01-12/01
	Bergen-Passaic PMSA, NJ	H	9.11 FQ	12.87 AW	17.55 TQ	NJBLS	10/01-12/01
	Jersey City PMSA, NJ	H	9.20 FQ	13.93 AW	20.23 TQ	NJBLS	10/01-12/01
	Middlesex-Somerset-Hunterdon PMSA, NJ	H	8.96 FQ	13.69 AW	18.71 TQ	NJBLS	10/01-12/01
	Monmouth-Ocean PMSA, NJ	H	8.22 FQ	12.34 AW	17.50 TQ	NJBLS	10/01-12/01
	Newark PMSA, NJ	H	9.49 FQ	16.62 AW	25.39 TQ	NJBLS	10/01-12/01
	New Mexico	H	7.42 FQ	11.88 AW	19.08 TQ	NMBLS	10/01-12/01
	Albuquerque MSA, NM	H	8.07 FQ	13.62 AW	22.29 TQ	NMBLS	10/01-12/01
	Las Cruces MSA, NM	H	7.47 FQ	9.93 AW	12.46 TQ	NMBLS	10/01-12/01
	New York	H	7.94 FQ	13.58 AW	19.92 TQ	NYBLS	10/01-12/01
	Albany-Schenectady-Troy MSA, NY	H	9.18 FQ	12.45 AW	16.32 TQ	NYBLS	10/01-12/01
	Binghamton MSA, NY	H	8.13 FQ	11.33 AW	15.42 TQ	NYBLS	10/01-12/01
	Buffalo-Niagara Falls MSA, NY	H	9.30 FQ	12.27 AW	15.53 TQ	NYBLS	10/01-12/01
	Dutchess County PMSA, NY	H	6.42 FQ	11.57 AW	16.00 TQ	NYBLS	10/01-12/01
	Nassau-Suffolk PMSA, NY	H	9.47 FQ	14.30 AW	20.03 TQ	NYBLS	10/01-12/01
	New York PMSA, NY	H	6.46 FQ	14.74 AW	21.83 TQ	NYBLS	10/01-12/01
	Newburgh PMSA, NY-PA	H	9.44 FQ	15.02 AW	22.15 TQ	NYBLS	10/01-12/01
	Rochester MSA, NY	H	9.29 FQ	12.74 AW	16.75 TQ	NYBLS	10/01-12/01
	Syracuse MSA, NY	H	7.98 FQ	11.90 AW	16.05 TQ	NYBLS	10/01-12/01
	Utica-Rome MSA, NY	H	8.91 FQ	12.02 AW	16.00 TQ	NYBLS	10/01-12/01
	North Carolina	H	7.81 FQ	12.63 AW	17.83 TQ	NCBLS	10/01-12/01
	Asheville MSA, NC	H	8.97 FQ	13.43 AW	18.82 TQ	NCBLS	10/01-12/01
	Charlotte-Gastonia-Rock Hill MSA, NC-SC	H	8.08 FQ	13.07 AW	18.62 TQ	NCBLS	10/01-12/01
	Fayetteville MSA, NC	H	6.16 FQ	10.55 AW	16.75 TQ	NCBLS	10/01-12/01
	Greensboro-Winston-Salem-High Point MSA, NC	H	8.55 FQ	12.76 AW	17.61 TQ	NCBLS	10/01-12/01
	Hickory-Morganton-Lenoir MSA, NC	H	8.05 FQ	10.83 AW	13.77 TQ	NCBLS	10/01-12/01
	Raleigh-Durham-Chapel Hill MSA, NC	H	9.89 FQ	13.87 AW	18.29 TQ	NCBLS	10/01-12/01
	Wilmington MSA, NC	H	6.18 FQ	8.91 AW	12.37 TQ	NCBLS	10/01-12/01
	North Dakota	H	8.36 FQ	10.78 AW	14.38 TQ	NDBLS	10/01-12/01
	Fargo-Moorhead MSA, ND-MN	H	8.55 FQ	10.76 AW	14.58 TQ	NDBLS	10/01-12/01
	Ohio	H	8.35 FQ	12.42 AW	16.80 TQ	OHBLS	10/01-12/01
	Akron PMSA, OH	H	9.14 FQ	12.67 AW	17.07 TQ	OHBLS	10/01-12/01
	Canton-Massillon MSA, OH	H	8.18 FQ	12.39 AW	15.97 TQ	OHBLS	10/01-12/01
	Cincinnati PMSA, OH-KY-IN	H	9.32 FQ	12.91 AW	16.83 TQ	OHBLS	10/01-12/01
	Cleveland-Lorain-Elyria PMSA, OH	H	7.33 FQ	11.83 AW	16.87 TQ	OHBLS	10/01-12/01
	Columbus MSA, OH	H	9.37 FQ	12.89 AW	17.00 TQ	OHBLS	10/01-12/01
	Dayton-Springfield MSA, OH	H	8.16 FQ	11.69 AW	15.91 TQ	OHBLS	10/01-12/01
	Hamilton-Middletown PMSA, OH	H	11.04 FQ	14.18 AW	17.85 TQ	OHBLS	10/01-12/01
	Mansfield MSA, OH	H	6.30 FQ	10.12 AW	15.62 TQ	OHBLS	10/01-12/01
	Toledo MSA, OH	H	9.67 FQ	12.71 AW	16.30 TQ	OHBLS	10/01-12/01
	Youngstown-Warren MSA, OH	H	8.06 FQ	11.88 AW	16.10 TQ	OHBLS	10/01-12/01
	Oklahoma	H	6.14 FQ	10.06 AW	15.76 TQ	OKBLS	10/01-12/01
	Oklahoma City MSA, OK	H	7.27 FQ	10.92 AW	16.45 TQ	OKBLS	10/01-12/01

AAW Average annual wage; **AE** Average entry wage; **AEX** Average experienced wage; **AO** Average offered; **AOH** Average offered, high; **AOL** Average offered, low; **APH** Average pay, high range; **APL** Average pay, low range; **ASH** Average starting, high; **ASL** Average starting, low; **AW** Average wage paid; **FQ** First quartile wage; **H** Hourly; **HI** Highest wage paid; **HR** High end range; **LR** Low end range; **M** Monthly; **MTC** Median total compensation; **MW** Median wage paid; **SQ** Second quartile wage; **S** Special: hourly and annual; **TQ** Third quartile wage; **W** Weekly; **Y** Yearly

Occupation/Type/Industry	Location	Per	Low	Mid	High	Source	Date
Word Processor and Typist	Tulsa MSA, OK	H	7.52 FQ	11.02 AW	16.22 TQ	OKBLS	10/01-12/01
	Oregon	H	9.14 FQ	13.23 AW	18.51 TQ	ORBLS	10/01-12/01
	Eugene-Springfield MSA, OR	H	9.02 FQ	14.99 AW	20.94 TQ	ORBLS	10/01-12/01
	Medford-Ashland MSA, OR	H	8.54 FQ	12.37 AW	17.00 TQ	ORBLS	10/01-12/01
	Portland-Vancouver PMSA, OR-WA	H	9.61 FQ	13.69 AW	18.93 TQ	ORBLS	10/01-12/01
	Salem PMSA, OR	H	9.51 FQ	12.56 AW	16.35 TQ	ORBLS	10/01-12/01
	Pennsylvania	H	8.63 FQ	12.93 AW	17.67 TQ	PABLS	10/01-12/01
	Allentown-Bethlehem-Easton MSA, PA	H	7.91 FQ	12.10 AW	16.53 TQ	PABLS	10/01-12/01
	Johnstown MSA, PA	H	6.30 FQ	11.35 AW	16.76 TQ	PABLS	10/01-12/01
	Lancaster MSA, PA	H	7.76 FQ	11.59 AW	16.06 TQ	PABLS	10/01-12/01
	Philadelphia PMSA, PA-NJ	H	9.45 FQ	13.12 AW	17.43 TQ	PABLS	10/01-12/01
	Pittsburgh MSA, PA	H	7.81 FQ	12.28 AW	17.24 TQ	PABLS	10/01-12/01
	Reading MSA, PA	H	8.02 FQ	12.65 AW	17.04 TQ	PABLS	10/01-12/01
	Scranton-Wilkes-Barre-Hazleton MSA, PA	H	8.38 FQ	12.72 AW	17.89 TQ	PABLS	10/01-12/01
	York MSA, PA	H	8.83 FQ	12.60 AW	17.77 TQ	PABLS	10/01-12/01
	Rhode Island	H	11.19 FQ	14.88 AW	17.71 TQ	RIBLS	10/01-12/01
	Providence-Fall River-Warwick MSA, RI-MA	H	11.00 FQ	14.78 AW	17.67 TQ	RIBLS	10/01-12/01
	South Carolina	H	7.08 FQ	11.67 AW	17.30 TQ	SCBLS	10/01-12/01
	Charleston-North Charleston MSA, SC	H	7.40 FQ	11.09 AW	17.29 TQ	SCBLS	10/01-12/01
	Columbia MSA, SC	H	6.88 FQ	10.15 AW	14.18 TQ	SCBLS	10/01-12/01
	Greenville-Spartanburg-Anderson MSA, SC	H	8.64 FQ	11.65 AW	14.57 TQ	SCBLS	10/01-12/01
	Tennessee	H	7.72 FQ	12.19 AW	17.43 TQ	TNBLS	10/01-12/01
	Chattanooga MSA, TN-GA	H	7.77 FQ	14.43 AW	24.16 TQ	TNBLS	10/01-12/01
	Clarksville-Hopkinsville MSA, TN-KY	H	6.81 FQ	10.02 AW	14.97 TQ	TNBLS	10/01-12/01
	Johnson City-Kingsport-Bristol MSA, TN-VA	H	7.30 FQ	10.18 AW	13.67 TQ	TNBLS	10/01-12/01
	Knoxville MSA, TN	H	7.60 FQ	11.38 AW	15.82 TQ	TNBLS	10/01-12/01
	Memphis MSA, TN-AR-MS	H	8.38 FQ	12.64 AW	17.80 TQ	TNBLS	10/01-12/01
	Nashville MSA, TN	H	8.00 FQ	12.74 AW	17.41 TQ	TNBLS	10/01-12/01
	Texas	H	8.27 FQ	13.21 AW	19.72 TQ	TXBLS	10/01-12/01
	Amarillo MSA, TX	H	6.20 FQ	11.80 AW	18.82 TQ	TXBLS	10/01-12/01
	Austin-San Marcos MSA, TX	H	9.32 FQ	13.22 AW	18.39 TQ	TXBLS	10/01-12/01
	Beaumont-Port Arthur MSA, TX	H	9.85 FQ	13.76 AW	22.01 TQ	TXBLS	10/01-12/01
	Brazoria PMSA, TX	H	9.28 FQ	11.46 AW	14.57 TQ	TXBLS	10/01-12/01
	Corpus Christi MSA, TX	H	5.99 FQ	9.54 AW	18.54 TQ	TXBLS	10/01-12/01
	Dallas PMSA, TX	H	9.73 FQ	14.58 AW	20.86 TQ	TXBLS	10/01-12/01
	El Paso MSA, TX	H	7.78 FQ	10.39 AW	12.89 TQ	TXBLS	10/01-12/01
	Fort Worth-Arlington PMSA, TX	H	7.35 FQ	11.79 AW	18.84 TQ	TXBLS	10/01-12/01
	Houston PMSA, TX	H	9.55 FQ	14.08 AW	20.83 TQ	TXBLS	10/01-12/01
	Killeen-Temple MSA, TX	H	6.91 FQ	11.14 AW	18.08 TQ	TXBLS	10/01-12/01
	Laredo MSA, TX	H	5.56 FQ	7.43 AW	10.34 TQ	TXBLS	10/01-12/01
	Longview-Marshall MSA, TX	H	7.51 FQ	17.45 AW	26.14 TQ	TXBLS	10/01-12/01
	Lubbock MSA, TX	H	8.21 FQ	11.60 AW	16.73 TQ	TXBLS	10/01-12/01
	McAllen-Edinburg-Mission MSA, TX	H	6.66 FQ	11.36 AW	16.66 TQ	TXBLS	10/01-12/01
	Odessa-Midland MSA, TX	H	9.00 FQ	10.72 AW	13.31 TQ	TXBLS	10/01-12/01
	San Antonio MSA, TX	H	7.69 FQ	11.43 AW	16.68 TQ	TXBLS	10/01-12/01
	Tyler MSA, TX	H	5.86 FQ	10.13 AW	14.57 TQ	TXBLS	10/01-12/01
	Waco MSA, TX	H	6.54 FQ	10.37 AW	15.10 TQ	TXBLS	10/01-12/01
	Utah	H	7.47 FQ	11.36 AW	16.95 TQ	UTBLS	10/01-12/01
	Provo-Orem MSA, UT	H	8.00 FQ	10.96 AW	15.08 TQ	UTBLS	10/01-12/01
	Salt Lake City-Ogden MSA, UT	H	7.48 FQ	11.53 AW	17.37 TQ	UTBLS	10/01-12/01
	Vermont	H	8.28 FQ	11.50 AW	15.50 TQ	VTBLS	10/01-12/01
	Burlington MSA, VT	H	9.06 FQ	11.98 AW	15.62 TQ	VTBLS	10/01-12/01
	Virginia	H	8.04 FQ	13.02 AW	19.29 TQ	VABLS	10/01-12/01
	Lynchburg MSA, VA	H	7.63 FQ	10.25 AW	13.85 TQ	VABLS	10/01-12/01
	Norfolk-Virginia Beach-Newport News MSA, VA-NC	H	7.17 FQ	11.58 AW	17.58 TQ	VABLS	10/01-12/01
	Richmond-Petersburg MSA, VA	H	7.15 FQ	12.33 AW	19.23 TQ	VABLS	10/01-12/01
	Roanoke MSA, VA	H	7.94 FQ	10.70 AW	14.06 TQ	VABLS	10/01-12/01

AAW	Average annual wage	**AOH**	Average offered, high	**ASH**	Average starting, high	**H**	Hourly	**M**	Monthly	**S**	Special: hourly and annual
AE	Average entry wage	**AOL**	Average offered, low	**ASL**	Average starting, low	**HI**	Highest wage paid	**MTC**	Median total compensation	**TQ**	Third quartile wage
AEX	Average experienced wage	**APH**	Average pay, high range	**AW**	Average wage paid	**HR**	High end range	**MW**	Median wage paid	**W**	Weekly
AO	Average offered	**APL**	Average pay, low range	**FQ**	First quartile wage	**LR**	Low end range	**SQ**	Second quartile wage	**Y**	Yearly

Occupation/Type/Industry	Location	Per	Low	Mid	High	Source	Date
Word Processor and Typist	Washington	H	9.82 FQ	14.62 AW	20.69 TQ	WABLS	10/01-12/01
	Bremerton PMSA, WA	H	10.11 FQ	13.98 AW	19.34 TQ	WABLS	10/01-12/01
	Olympia PMSA, WA	H	9.74 FQ	13.18 AW	16.31 TQ	WABLS	10/01-12/01
	Richland-Kennewick-Pasco MSA, WA	H	8.87 FQ	13.32 AW	19.34 TQ	WABLS	10/01-12/01
	Seattle-Bellevue-Everett PMSA, WA	H	10.40 FQ	15.75 AW	21.97 TQ	WABLS	10/01-12/01
	Spokane MSA, WA	H	9.40 FQ	12.51 AW	16.85 TQ	WABLS	10/01-12/01
	Tacoma PMSA, WA	H	10.35 FQ	14.40 AW	19.12 TQ	WABLS	10/01-12/01
	West Virginia	H	5.93 FQ	10.08 AW	17.29 TQ	WVBLS	10/01-12/01
	Charleston MSA, WV	H	5.79 FQ	7.68 AW	10.89 TQ	WVBLS	10/01-12/01
	Huntington-Ashland MSA, WV-KY-OH	H	6.49 FQ	9.68 AW	14.27 TQ	WVBLS	10/01-12/01
	Wisconsin	H	8.88 FQ	12.31 AW	16.33 TQ	WIBLS	10/01-12/01
	Appleton-Oshkosh-Neenah MSA, WI	H	8.57 FQ	11.56 AW	14.61 TQ	WIBLS	10/01-12/01
	Green Bay MSA, WI	H	8.25 FQ	11.84 AW	15.25 TQ	WIBLS	10/01-12/01
	Madison MSA, WI	H	9.90 FQ	13.64 AW	16.79 TQ	WIBLS	10/01-12/01
	Milwaukee-Waukesha PMSA, WI	H	9.25 FQ	12.56 AW	16.71 TQ	WIBLS	10/01-12/01
	Racine PMSA, WI	H	9.44 FQ	12.05 AW	15.20 TQ	WIBLS	10/01-12/01
	Wyoming	H	6.98 FQ	11.40 AW	16.87 TQ	WYBLS	10/01-12/01
	Puerto Rico	H	5.52 FQ	7.23 AW	9.96 TQ	PRBLS	10/01-12/01
	Virgin Islands	H	5.88 FQ	7.70 AW	9.80 TQ	VIBLS	10/01-12/01
	Guam	H	8.32 FQ	11.45 AW	14.59 TQ	GUBLS	10/01-12/01
Writer and Author	Alabama	Y	13750 FQ	35740 AW	61800 TQ	ALBLS	10/01-12/01
	Birmingham MSA, AL	Y	20440 FQ	38880 AW	71800 TQ	ALBLS	10/01-12/01
	Huntsville MSA, AL	Y	25690 FQ	46450 AW	67130 TQ	ALBLS	10/01-12/01
	Montgomery MSA, AL	Y	18160 FQ	32150 AW	51530 TQ	ALBLS	10/01-12/01
	Alaska	Y	25460 FQ	43100 AW	61610 TQ	AKBLS	10/01-12/01
	Anchorage MSA, AK	Y	29220 FQ	45520 AW	67170 TQ	AKBLS	10/01-12/01
	Arizona	Y	22450 FQ	49870 AW	95440 TQ	AZBLS	10/01-12/01
	Phoenix-Mesa MSA, AZ	Y	25150 FQ	54080 AW	115260 TQ	AZBLS	10/01-12/01
	Tucson MSA, AZ	Y	21190 FQ	45550 AW	101830 TQ	AZBLS	10/01-12/01
	Arkansas	Y	13870 FQ	28660 AW	52350 TQ	ARBLS	10/01-12/01
	Fayetteville-Springdale-Rogers MSA, AR	Y	13070 FQ	29220 AW	51550 TQ	ARBLS	10/01-12/01
	Little Rock-North Little Rock MSA, AR	Y	21320 FQ	36810 AW	58840 TQ	ARBLS	10/01-12/01
	California	Y	29560 FQ	65930 AW		CABLS	10/01-12/01
	Los Angeles-Long Beach PMSA, CA	Y	31910 FQ	68870 AW		CABLS	10/01-12/01
	Oakland PMSA, CA	Y	38350 FQ	69770 AW	126540 TQ	CABLS	10/01-12/01
	Orange County PMSA, CA	Y	27400 FQ	54590 AW	96110 TQ	CABLS	10/01-12/01
	Riverside-San Bernardino PMSA, CA	Y	20600 FQ	43230 AW	95800 TQ	CABLS	10/01-12/01
	Sacramento PMSA, CA	Y	25160 FQ	53710 AW	99810 TQ	CABLS	10/01-12/01
	San Diego MSA, CA	Y	19930 FQ	48600 AW	92250 TQ	CABLS	10/01-12/01
	San Francisco PMSA, CA	Y	37530 FQ	66680 AW		CABLS	10/01-12/01
	San Jose PMSA, CA	Y	32210 FQ	70410 AW	132470 TQ	CABLS	10/01-12/01
	Santa Barbara-Santa Maria-Lompoc MSA, CA	Y	23950 FQ	80870 AW		CABLS	10/01-12/01
	Ventura PMSA, CA	Y	28190 FQ	67200 AW		CABLS	10/01-12/01
	Colorado	Y	23600 FQ	42580 AW	67120 TQ	COBLS	10/01-12/01
	Boulder-Longmont PMSA, CO	Y	27930 FQ	46990 AW	72250 TQ	COBLS	10/01-12/01
	Colorado Springs MSA, CO	Y	20360 FQ	32780 AW	54210 TQ	COBLS	10/01-12/01
	Denver PMSA, CO	Y	26160 FQ	45310 AW	68560 TQ	COBLS	10/01-12/01
	Fort Collins-Loveland MSA, CO	Y	27480 FQ	41520 AW	61030 TQ	COBLS	10/01-12/01
	Connecticut	Y	30440 FQ	58680 AW	110860 TQ	CTBLS	10/01-12/01
	Bridgeport PMSA, CT	Y	25010 FQ	58020 AW	133420 TQ	CTBLS	10/01-12/01
	Danbury PMSA, CT	Y	28380 FQ	47770 AW	57730 TQ	CTBLS	10/01-12/01
	Hartford MSA, CT	Y	29620 FQ	51140 AW	80660 TQ	CTBLS	10/01-12/01
	New London-Norwich MSA, CT-RI	Y	25360 FQ	52890 AW		CTBLS	10/01-12/01
	Stamford-Norwalk PMSA, CT	Y	34450 FQ	63770 AW	132950 TQ	CTBLS	10/01-12/01
	Delaware	Y	22540 FQ	45430 AW	81600 TQ	DEBLS	10/01-12/01
	Wilmington-Newark PMSA, DE-MD	Y	24660 FQ	45700 AW	83520 TQ	DEBLS	10/01-12/01
	District of Columbia	Y	30550 FQ	51830 AW	78810 TQ	DCBLS	10/01-12/01
	Washington PMSA, DC-MD-VA-WV	Y	32230 FQ	53020 AW	78440 TQ	DCBLS	10/01-12/01

AAW	Average annual wage	**AOH**	Average offered, high	**ASH**	Average starting, high	**H**	Hourly	**M**	Monthly	**S**	Special: hourly and annual
AE	Average entry wage	**AOL**	Average offered, low	**ASL**	Average starting, low	**HI**	Highest wage paid	**MTC**	Median total compensation	**TQ**	Third quartile wage
AEX	Average experienced wage	**APH**	Average pay, high range	**AW**	Average wage paid	**HR**	High end range	**MW**	Median wage paid	**W**	Weekly
AO	Average offered	**APL**	Average pay, low range	**FQ**	First quartile wage	**LR**	Low end range	**SQ**	Second quartile wage	**Y**	Yearly

Occupation/Type/Industry	Location	Per	Low	Mid	High	Source	Date
Writer and Author	Florida	Y	14810 FQ	37330 AW	68390 TQ	FLBLS	10/01-12/01
	Fort Lauderdale PMSA, FL	Y	13110 FQ	43980 AW	93560 TQ	FLBLS	10/01-12/01
	Jacksonville MSA, FL	Y	25170 FQ	38560 AW	55060 TQ	FLBLS	10/01-12/01
	Miami PMSA, FL	Y	21220 FQ	45090 AW	84060 TQ	FLBLS	10/01-12/01
	Orlando MSA, FL	Y	18560 FQ	30210 AW	52150 TQ	FLBLS	10/01-12/01
	Pensacola MSA, FL	Y	13510 FQ	28280 AW	43520 TQ	FLBLS	10/01-12/01
	Tallahassee MSA, FL	Y	11620 FQ	19100 AW	35430 TQ	FLBLS	10/01-12/01
	Tampa-St. Petersburg-Clearwater MSA, FL	Y	18580 FQ	34140 AW	61230 TQ	FLBLS	10/01-12/01
	West Palm Beach-Boca Raton MSA, FL	Y	15120 FQ	42190 AW	70550 TQ	FLBLS	10/01-12/01
	Georgia	Y	25760 FQ	49030 AW	75280 TQ	GABLS	10/01-12/01
	Atlanta MSA, GA	Y	28750 FQ	52290 AW	79010 TQ	GABLS	10/01-12/01
	Columbus MSA, GA-AL	Y	23830 FQ	41290 AW	48260 TQ	GABLS	10/01-12/01
	Savannah MSA, GA	Y	29960 FQ	39630 AW	47300 TQ	GABLS	10/01-12/01
	Hawaii	Y	20970 FQ	40720 AW	65550 TQ	HIBLS	10/01-12/01
	Honolulu MSA, HI	Y	21840 FQ	42290 AW	68090 TQ	HIBLS	10/01-12/01
	Idaho	Y	22760 FQ	32360 AW	51760 TQ	IDBLS	10/01-12/01
	Boise City MSA, ID	Y	24740 FQ	35200 AW	58690 TQ	IDBLS	10/01-12/01
	Illinois	Y	17610 FQ	41960 AW	76770 TQ	ILBLS	10/01-12/01
	Chicago PMSA, IL	Y	28100 FQ	51940 AW	91570 TQ	ILBLS	10/01-12/01
	Indiana	Y	17960 FQ	37690 AW	63580 TQ	INBLS	10/01-12/01
	Indianapolis MSA, IN	Y	20830 FQ	40120 AW	67820 TQ	INBLS	10/01-12/01
	Iowa	Y	12800 FQ	25840 AW	40760 TQ	IABLS	10/01-12/01
	Davenport-Moline-Rock Island MSA, IA-IL	Y	23210 FQ	42030 AW	56650 TQ	IABLS	10/01-12/01
	Des Moines MSA, IA	Y	15640 FQ	32180 AW	54710 TQ	IABLS	10/01-12/01
	Kansas	Y	12500 FQ	27720 AW	50840 TQ	KSBLS	10/01-12/01
	Topeka MSA, KS	Y	21230 FQ	32460 AW	47800 TQ	KSBLS	10/01-12/01
	Kentucky	Y	19980 FQ	38110 AW	59680 TQ	KYBLS	10/01-12/01
	Lexington MSA, KY	Y	17620 FQ	33210 AW	48270 TQ	KYBLS	10/01-12/01
	Louisville MSA, KY-IN	Y	24400 FQ	42780 AW	73630 TQ	KYBLS	10/01-12/01
	Louisiana	Y	15860 FQ	30960 AW	49430 TQ	LABLS	10/01-12/01
	Baton Rouge MSA, LA	Y	20250 FQ	34790 AW	51240 TQ	LABLS	10/01-12/01
	New Orleans MSA, LA	Y	18760 FQ	34700 AW	54730 TQ	LABLS	10/01-12/01
	Maine	Y	20720 FQ	37230 AW	49900 TQ	MEBLS	10/01-12/01
	Portland MSA, ME	Y	20650 FQ	37080 AW	52850 TQ	MEBLS	10/01-12/01
	Maryland	Y	27650 FQ	55700 AW	97310 TQ	MDBLS	10/01-12/01
	Baltimore PMSA, MD	Y	24100 FQ	52530 AW	86950 TQ	MDBLS	10/01-12/01
	Massachusetts	Y	30240 FQ	52610 AW	75080 TQ	MABLS	10/01-12/01
	Boston PMSA, MA-NH	Y	32140 FQ	53920 AW	75280 TQ	MABLS	10/01-12/01
	Springfield MSA, MA	Y	30070 FQ	59650 AW		MABLS	10/01-12/01
	Worcester PMSA, MA-CT	Y	30720 FQ	42830 AW	71570 TQ	MABLS	10/01-12/01
	Michigan	Y	23200 FQ	44790 AW	76360 TQ	MIBLS	10/01-12/01
	Ann Arbor PMSA, MI	Y	25480 FQ	42990 AW	58120 TQ	MIBLS	10/01-12/01
	Detroit PMSA, MI	Y	27120 FQ	51740 AW	86650 TQ	MIBLS	10/01-12/01
	Grand Rapids-Muskegon-Holland MSA, MI	Y	23020 FQ	39680 AW	56390 TQ	MIBLS	10/01-12/01
	Lansing-East Lansing MSA, MI	Y	23360 FQ	32060 AW	45510 TQ	MIBLS	10/01-12/01
	Saginaw-Bay City-Midland MSA, MI	Y	24580 FQ	38720 AW	62910 TQ	MIBLS	10/01-12/01
	Minnesota	Y	24110 FQ	48470 AW	73610 TQ	MNBLS	10/01-12/01
	Duluth-Superior MSA, MN-WI	Y	19390 FQ	33760 AW	53810 TQ	MNBLS	10/01-12/01
	Minneapolis-St. Paul MSA, MN-WI	Y	30830 FQ	53680 AW	82540 TQ	MNBLS	10/01-12/01
	St. Cloud MSA, MN	Y	16430 FQ	39330 AW	59390 TQ	MNBLS	10/01-12/01
	Mississippi	Y	20380 FQ	33250 AW	51760 TQ	MSBLS	10/01-12/01
	Jackson MSA, MS	Y	23310 FQ	32860 AW	46430 TQ	MSBLS	10/01-12/01
	Missouri	Y	20820 FQ	42180 AW	72910 TQ	MOBLS	10/01-12/01
	Kansas City MSA, MO-KS	Y	15620 FQ	40070 AW	66570 TQ	MOBLS	10/01-12/01
	St. Louis MSA, MO-IL	Y	25570 FQ	48720 AW	88310 TQ	MOBLS	10/01-12/01
	Montana	Y	14790 FQ	26870 AW	43830 TQ	MTBLS	10/01-12/01
	Nebraska	Y	14090 FQ	34900 AW	55000 TQ	NEBLS	10/01-12/01
	Lincoln MSA, NE	Y	16940 FQ	41060 AW	58290 TQ	NEBLS	10/01-12/01
	Omaha MSA, NE-IA	Y	20250 FQ	35570 AW	55710 TQ	NEBLS	10/01-12/01
	Nevada	Y	18610 FQ	33440 AW	57580 TQ	NVBLS	10/01-12/01
	Las Vegas MSA, NV-AZ	Y	18440 FQ	31050 AW	53450 TQ	NVBLS	10/01-12/01
	Reno MSA, NV	Y	28220 FQ	43800 AW	79480 TQ	NVBLS	10/01-12/01
	New Hampshire	Y	13850 FQ	36670 AW	68350 TQ	NHBLS	10/01-12/01
	Manchester PMSA, NH	Y	20720 FQ	34840 AW	63750 TQ	NHBLS	10/01-12/01
	New Jersey	Y	29480 FQ	65070 AW		NJBLS	10/01-12/01
	Bergen-Passaic PMSA, NJ	Y	27950 FQ	53110 AW	89840 TQ	NJBLS	10/01-12/01

AAW Average annual wage **AE** Average entry wage **AEX** Average experienced wage **AO** Average offered **AOH** Average offered, high **AOL** Average offered, low **APH** Average pay, high range **APL** Average pay, low range **ASH** Average starting, high **ASL** Average starting, low **AW** Average wage paid **FQ** First quartile wage **H** Hourly **HI** Highest wage paid **HR** High end range **LR** Low end range **M** Monthly **MTC** Median total compensation **MW** Median wage paid **SQ** Second quartile wage **S** Special: hourly and annual **TQ** Third quartile wage **W** Weekly **Y** Yearly

Occupation/Type/Industry	Location	Per	Low	Mid	High	Source	Date
Writer and Author	Jersey City PMSA, NJ	Y	25930 FQ	46900 AW	80220 TQ	NJBLS	10/01-12/01
	Middlesex-Somerset-Hunterdon PMSA, NJ	Y	31680 FQ	58000 AW	92860 TQ	NJBLS	10/01-12/01
	Monmouth-Ocean PMSA, NJ	Y	21060 FQ	43360 AW	83190 TQ	NJBLS	10/01-12/01
	Trenton PMSA, NJ	Y	29330 FQ	45840 AW	71730 TQ	NJBLS	10/01-12/01
	New Mexico	Y	20760 FQ	38410 AW	61150 TQ	NMBLS	10/01-12/01
	Albuquerque MSA, NM	Y	20550 FQ	33970 AW	49100 TQ	NMBLS	10/01-12/01
	New York	Y	24350 FQ	52470 AW	90380 TQ	NYBLS	10/01-12/01
	Albany-Schenectady-Troy MSA, NY	Y	27350 FQ	52760 AW	94600 TQ	NYBLS	10/01-12/01
	Buffalo-Niagara Falls MSA, NY	Y	18400 FQ	49300 AW		NYBLS	10/01-12/01
	Dutchess County PMSA, NY	Y	16570 FQ	47740 AW	85510 TQ	NYBLS	10/01-12/01
	Nassau-Suffolk PMSA, NY	Y	26070 FQ	65650 AW	92640 TQ	NYBLS	10/01-12/01
	New York PMSA, NY	Y	24620 FQ	52210 AW	91110 TQ	NYBLS	10/01-12/01
	Rochester MSA, NY	Y	30630 FQ	49100 AW	77030 TQ	NYBLS	10/01-12/01
	Syracuse MSA, NY	Y	18190 FQ	41900 AW	61980 TQ	NYBLS	10/01-12/01
	Utica-Rome MSA, NY	Y	24440 FQ	49150 AW	71960 TQ	NYBLS	10/01-12/01
	North Carolina	Y	17260 FQ	39930 AW	73310 TQ	NCBLS	10/01-12/01
	Charlotte-Gastonia-Rock Hill MSA, NC-SC	Y	12460 FQ	39380 AW	71800 TQ	NCBLS	10/01-12/01
	Greensboro-Winston-Salem-High Point MSA, NC	Y	26180 FQ	44520 AW	81940 TQ	NCBLS	10/01-12/01
	Raleigh-Durham-Chapel Hill MSA, NC	Y	25210 FQ	51760 AW	91900 TQ	NCBLS	10/01-12/01
	North Dakota	Y	19550 FQ	32860 AW	47320 TQ	NDBLS	10/01-12/01
	Fargo-Moorhead MSA, ND-MN	Y	21200 FQ	41540 AW	70700 TQ	NDBLS	10/01-12/01
	Ohio	Y	19250 FQ	39990 AW	62060 TQ	OHBLS	10/01-12/01
	Akron PMSA, OH	Y	20340 FQ	34550 AW	59700 TQ	OHBLS	10/01-12/01
	Cincinnati PMSA, OH-KY-IN	Y	33100 FQ	44870 AW	67020 TQ	OHBLS	10/01-12/01
	Cleveland-Lorain-Elyria PMSA, OH	Y	17910 FQ	39450 AW	59710 TQ	OHBLS	10/01-12/01
	Columbus MSA, OH	Y	20940 FQ	35960 AW	49660 TQ	OHBLS	10/01-12/01
	Dayton-Springfield MSA, OH	Y	27730 FQ	47220 AW	68960 TQ	OHBLS	10/01-12/01
	Toledo MSA, OH	Y	15810 FQ	34620 AW	60400 TQ	OHBLS	10/01-12/01
	Oklahoma	Y	19010 FQ	35850 AW	53150 TQ	OKBLS	10/01-12/01
	Oklahoma City MSA, OK	Y	19160 FQ	38480 AW	58350 TQ	OKBLS	10/01-12/01
	Tulsa MSA, OK	Y	25440 FQ	36010 AW	45530 TQ	OKBLS	10/01-12/01
	Oregon	Y	14550 FQ	39080 AW	63800 TQ	ORBLS	10/01-12/01
	Portland-Vancouver PMSA, OR-WA	Y	26980 FQ	46110 AW	70310 TQ	ORBLS	10/01-12/01
	Pennsylvania	Y	16630 FQ	39380 AW	70490 TQ	PABLS	10/01-12/01
	Allentown-Bethlehem-Easton MSA, PA	Y	19110 FQ	42680 AW	58300 TQ	PABLS	10/01-12/01
	Harrisburg-Lebanon-Carlisle MSA, PA	Y	15010 FQ	36250 AW	64390 TQ	PABLS	10/01-12/01
	Lancaster MSA, PA	Y	14850 FQ	26230 AW	47360 TQ	PABLS	10/01-12/01
	Philadelphia PMSA, PA-NJ	Y	21130 FQ	48550 AW	83930 TQ	PABLS	10/01-12/01
	Pittsburgh MSA, PA	Y	20420 FQ	42550 AW	73550 TQ	PABLS	10/01-12/01
	Rhode Island	Y	26170 FQ	39140 AW	58220 TQ	RIBLS	10/01-12/01
	Providence-Fall River-Warwick MSA, RI-MA	Y	29410 FQ	40570 AW	56550 TQ	RIBLS	10/01-12/01
	South Carolina	Y	28560 FQ	47980 AW	61980 TQ	SCBLS	10/01-12/01
	South Dakota	Y	18170 FQ	29200 AW	42660 TQ	SDBLS	10/01-12/01
	Tennessee	Y	20560 FQ	40000 AW	70890 TQ	TNBLS	10/01-12/01
	Memphis MSA, TN-AR-MS	Y	26150 FQ	42590 AW	73080 TQ	TNBLS	10/01-12/01
	Nashville MSA, TN	Y	26440 FQ	46720 AW	74310 TQ	TNBLS	10/01-12/01
	Texas	Y	19660 FQ	42770 AW	75240 TQ	TXBLS	10/01-12/01
	Austin-San Marcos MSA, TX	Y	24520 FQ	45240 AW	77620 TQ	TXBLS	10/01-12/01
	Dallas PMSA, TX	Y	27120 FQ	51450 AW	89450 TQ	TXBLS	10/01-12/01
	Fort Worth-Arlington PMSA, TX	Y	16750 FQ	37060 AW	50460 TQ	TXBLS	10/01-12/01
	Houston PMSA, TX	Y	13940 FQ	38740 AW	66060 TQ	TXBLS	10/01-12/01
	Laredo MSA, TX	Y	19460 FQ	33750 AW	43850 TQ	TXBLS	10/01-12/01
	San Antonio MSA, TX	Y	26390 FQ	46510 AW	74250 TQ	TXBLS	10/01-12/01
	Utah	Y	15630 FQ	31000 AW	54380 TQ	UTBLS	10/01-12/01
	Provo-Orem MSA, UT	Y	14010 FQ	27410 AW	52370 TQ	UTBLS	10/01-12/01
	Salt Lake City-Ogden MSA, UT	Y	16780 FQ	32970 AW	55790 TQ	UTBLS	10/01-12/01
	Vermont	Y	23780 FQ	42390 AW	81850 TQ	VTBLS	10/01-12/01
	Burlington MSA, VT	Y	25700 FQ	45320 AW	83180 TQ	VTBLS	10/01-12/01

AAW Average annual wage; **AE** Average entry wage; **AEX** Average experienced wage; **AO** Average offered; **AOH** Average offered, high; **AOL** Average offered, low; **APH** Average pay, high range; **APL** Average pay, low range; **ASH** Average starting, high; **ASL** Average starting, low; **AW** Average wage paid; **FQ** First quartile wage; **H** Hourly; **HI** Highest wage paid; **HR** High end range; **LR** Low end range; **M** Monthly; **MTC** Median total compensation; **MW** Median wage paid; **SQ** Second quartile wage; **S** Special: hourly and annual; **TQ** Third quartile wage; **W** Weekly; **Y** Yearly

Occupation/Type/Industry	Location	Per	Low	Mid	High	Source	Date
Writer and Author	Virginia	Y	25370 FQ	46900 AW	69650 TQ	VABLS	10/01-12/01
	Norfolk-Virginia Beach-Newport News MSA, VA-NC	Y	20140 FQ	41870 AW	73230 TQ	VABLS	10/01-12/01
	Richmond-Petersburg MSA, VA	Y	22200 FQ	41750 AW	66170 TQ	VABLS	10/01-12/01
	Washington	Y	26190 FQ	43400 AW	64530 TQ	WABLS	10/01-12/01
	Olympia PMSA, WA	Y	28430 FQ	35700 AW	49100 TQ	WABLS	10/01-12/01
	Seattle-Bellevue-Everett PMSA, WA	Y	28230 FQ	45980 AW	67580 TQ	WABLS	10/01-12/01
	Spokane MSA, WA	Y	28440 FQ	38190 AW	53910 TQ	WABLS	10/01-12/01
	Tacoma PMSA, WA	Y	32180 FQ	47820 AW	62160 TQ	WABLS	10/01-12/01
	West Virginia	Y	18240 FQ	40980 AW	76200 TQ	WVBLS	10/01-12/01
	Charleston MSA, WV	Y	16980 FQ	39570 AW	82720 TQ	WVBLS	10/01-12/01
	Wisconsin	Y	14800 FQ	35390 AW	62930 TQ	WIBLS	10/01-12/01
	Green Bay MSA, WI	Y	18810 FQ	28090 AW	37090 TQ	WIBLS	10/01-12/01
	Madison MSA, WI	Y	23870 FQ	46560 AW	77810 TQ	WIBLS	10/01-12/01
	Milwaukee-Waukesha PMSA, WI	Y	14890 FQ	35890 AW	66250 TQ	WIBLS	10/01-12/01
	Puerto Rico	Y	18680 FQ	39960 AW	69290 TQ	PRBLS	10/01-12/01
Zoologist and Wildlife Biologist	Alaska	Y	28610 FQ	49600 AW	70510 TQ	AKBLS	10/01-12/01
	Arizona	Y	24240 FQ	42580 AW	64190 TQ	AZBLS	10/01-12/01
	Arkansas	Y	25830 FQ	41610 AW	55050 TQ	ARBLS	10/01-12/01
	California	Y	25050 FQ	40850 AW	65910 TQ	CABLS	10/01-12/01
	Colorado	Y	34330 FQ	49640 AW	63480 TQ	COBLS	10/01-12/01
	Connecticut	Y	34990 FQ	56120 AW	70960 TQ	CTBLS	10/01-12/01
	Florida	Y	27580 FQ	45530 AW	68440 TQ	FLBLS	10/01-12/01
	Georgia	Y	27390 FQ	43860 AW	64820 TQ	GABLS	10/01-12/01
	Hawaii	Y	37080 FQ	55270 AW	81600 TQ	HIBLS	10/01-12/01
	Idaho	Y	24910 FQ	43590 AW	65530 TQ	IDBLS	10/01-12/01
	Illinois	Y	31800 FQ	54830 AW	79770 TQ	ILBLS	10/01-12/01
	Iowa	Y	29380 FQ	48010 AW	66010 TQ	IABLS	10/01-12/01
	Kansas	Y	31900 FQ	44210 AW	59150 TQ	KSBLS	10/01-12/01
	Kentucky	Y	28870 FQ	40860 AW	55300 TQ	KYBLS	10/01-12/01
	Louisiana	Y	19100 FQ	38010 AW	66130 TQ	LABLS	10/01-12/01
	Maine	Y	28470 FQ	42200 AW	60550 TQ	MEBLS	10/01-12/01
	Maryland	Y	29290 FQ	63680 AW	100430 TQ	MDBLS	10/01-12/01
	Massachusetts	Y	27080 FQ	47030 AW	74220 TQ	MABLS	10/01-12/01
	Michigan	Y	38450 FQ	52190 AW	67760 TQ	MIBLS	10/01-12/01
	Minnesota	Y	33000 FQ	48480 AW	65240 TQ	MNBLS	10/01-12/01
	Mississippi	Y	26060 FQ	48140 AW	77760 TQ	MSBLS	10/01-12/01
	Montana	Y	36720 FQ	51950 AW	72490 TQ	MTBLS	10/01-12/01
	Nebraska	Y	30070 FQ	42960 AW	59510 TQ	NEBLS	10/01-12/01
	Nevada	Y	22350 FQ	40740 AW	55490 TQ	NVBLS	10/01-12/01
	New Hampshire	Y	34530 FQ	47480 AW	71380 TQ	NHBLS	10/01-12/01
	New Jersey	Y	28500 FQ	52220 AW	70180 TQ	NJBLS	10/01-12/01
	New Mexico	Y	35400 FQ	58710 AW	96170 TQ	NMBLS	10/01-12/01
	New York	Y	36380 FQ	51990 AW	68990 TQ	NYBLS	10/01-12/01
	North Carolina	Y	33430 FQ	48410 AW	70610 TQ	NCBLS	10/01-12/01
	North Dakota	Y	33020 FQ	47280 AW	66390 TQ	NDBLS	10/01-12/01
	Ohio	Y	28400 FQ	41320 AW	57500 TQ	OHBLS	10/01-12/01
	Oklahoma	Y	30100 FQ	45910 AW	69330 TQ	OKBLS	10/01-12/01
	Oregon	Y	32870 FQ	50830 AW	78520 TQ	ORBLS	10/01-12/01
	Pennsylvania	Y	36480 FQ	50400 AW	68500 TQ	PABLS	10/01-12/01
	Rhode Island	Y	38690 FQ	58160 AW	83520 TQ	RIBLS	10/01-12/01
	South Carolina	Y	31070 FQ	46370 AW	67830 TQ	SCBLS	10/01-12/01
	South Dakota	Y	29820 FQ	42510 AW	56110 TQ	SDBLS	10/01-12/01
	Tennessee	Y	23120 FQ	35740 AW	54070 TQ	TNBLS	10/01-12/01
	Texas	Y	29890 FQ	49440 AW	72340 TQ	TXBLS	10/01-12/01
	Utah	Y	30190 FQ	46200 AW	68320 TQ	UTBLS	10/01-12/01
	Vermont	Y	27770 FQ	42110 AW	55950 TQ	VTBLS	10/01-12/01
	Virginia	Y	27970 FQ	49820 AW	81050 TQ	VABLS	10/01-12/01
	Washington	Y	37110 FQ	51080 AW	67980 TQ	WABLS	10/01-12/01
	Wisconsin	Y	28800 FQ	41760 AW	62890 TQ	WIBLS	10/01-12/01
	Wyoming	Y	36980 FQ	50530 AW	67080 TQ	WYBLS	10/01-12/01

AAW	Average annual wage	**AOH**	Average offered, high	**ASH**	Average starting, high	**H**	Hourly	**M**	Monthly	**S**	Special: hourly and annual
AE	Average entry wage	**AOL**	Average offered, low	**ASL**	Average starting, low	**HI**	Highest wage paid	**MTC**	Median total compensation	**TQ**	Third quartile wage
AEX	Average experienced wage	**APH**	Average pay, high range	**AW**	Average wage paid	**HR**	High end range	**MW**	Median wage paid	**W**	Weekly
AO	Average offered	**APL**	Average pay, low range	**FQ**	First quartile wage	**LR**	Low end range	**SQ**	Second quartile wage	**Y**	Yearly

Appendix I

SOURCES

ABA

Terry Carter, "Justice Doesn't Pay: Low Salaries for Judges Draw ABA Panel's Scrutiny," *ABA Journal*, May 2002.

Survey Period: January 2001 - January 2002

ACC

Wendy Francis, "Where the Money Is," *American City & County*, October 2001, p. 44.

Survey Period: January 1999 - January 2000

ADAGE

"National Ad Agency Salary Survey 2001," *Advertising Age*, December 3, 2001, p. s2.

Survey Period: 2000 - 2001

AEAC

"Careers in Aviation - Pay Scales," *Airline Employment Assistance Corps & AV Jobs Worldwide*, January 25, 2001.

Survey Period: 2000

AKBLS

2001 Occupational Employment and Wage Estimates, 2001.

Alaska Department of Labor
Research and Analysis
1111 West 8th Street
Juneau, AK 99802-5501
Telephone: (907) 465-6035
Online: http://www.almis.labor.state.ak.us/
Survey Period: October 2001 - December 2001

Note: All data are provided by the State Employment Security Administration to the Occupational Employment Statistics (OES) survey conducted by the U.S. Department of Labor, Bureau of Labor Statistics.

ALBLS

2001 Occupational Employment and Wage Estimates, 2001.

Alabama Department of Industrial Relations
Labor Market Information
649 Monroe St., Room 427
Montgomery, AL 36130
Telephone: (334) 242-8859
Online: http://www.dir.state.al.us/lmi
Survey Period: October 2001 - December 2001

Note: All data are provided by the State Employment Security Administration to the Occupational Employment Statistics (OES) survey conducted by the U.S. Department of Labor, Bureau of Labor Statistics.

AM

Steven Williams, "Competitive Pay: A New Salary Study Sets Baselines for Mid-Level and Support Staff," *Association Management*, August 2002, p. 97.

Survey Period: January 2001 - January 2002

Note: Data are based on survey responses from 952 associations within the United States.

ARBLS

2001 Occupational Employment and Wage Estimates, 2001.

Arkansas Employment Security Department
Labor Market Information
P.O. Box 2981
Little Rock, AR 72203-2981
Telephone: (501) 682-319859
Online: http://www.state.ar.us/esd
Survey Period: October 2001 - December 2001

Note: All data are provided by the State Employment Security Administration to the Occupational Employment Statistics (OES) survey conducted by the U.S. Department of Labor, Bureau of Labor Statistics.

ASQ

"Quality Professionals Stand the Test," *Quality Progress*, December 2001.

Survey Period: January 2000 - January 2001

ASR

"Screener Pay Attractive to Many Workers," *Airport Security Report*, April 10, 2002.

Survey Period: January 2001 - January 2002

AVTODAY

Kathleen Kocks, "U.S. Aviation Maintenance Salary Survey," *Aviation Today*, December 19, 2002.

Survey Period: 2000

Note: Data are based on survey responses from 500+ aviation maintenance mechanics working in the United States.

AWST

"Corporate Pilots: More Than Merely Flying," *Aviation Week & Space Technology*, August 19, 2002, p. 50.

Survey Period: 2

Note: Data represent salaries of pilots employed by corporations with less than $100,000 in sales.

AWSTMS

"Aerospace Wages on Par With Comparable Industries," *Aviation Week & Space Technology Market Supplement*, March 19, 2001, p. S12.

Survey Period: 2000 - 200

Note: Data represent responses from aerospace engineers with at least 10 years' experience. The response rate to the magazine's survey was 53%.

AZBLS

2001 Occupational Employment and Wage Estimates, 2001.

Arizona Department of Economic Security
Research Administration
1789 West Jefferson Street, 733A
Phoenix, AZ 85007
Telephone: (602) 542-3871
Online: http://www.de.state.az.us/links/economic/webpage/page6.html
Survey Period: October 2001 - December 2001

Note: All data are provided by the State Employment Security Administration to the Occupational Employment Statistics (OES) survey conducted by the U.S. Department of Labor, Bureau of Labor Statistics.

BCAVIA

Shirley J. Mason, "Outlook: Salary," *Business & Commercial Aviation*, August 2002.

Survey Period: January 106 - 2,

BE

Winifred Desouza and Sonya A. Donaldson, "Where the Jobs Are," *Black Enterprise*, February 2002, p. 96.

Survey Period: January 2001 - January 2002

BEVA

"C-Store Salaries Up in 2001," *Beverage Aisle*, April 15, 2002, p. 8.

Survey Period: January 2001 - January 2002

BGLOBE

Mac Daniel, "Critics See No Savings in Boston Mayor's Proposed Towing Charges," *The Boston Globe*, April 25, 2002.

Survey Period: 2002

BND

Elizabeth Donald, "Collinsville, Ill., Teachers' Contract Increases School Deficit," *Belleville News-Democrat (Ill.)*, October 24, 2002.

Survey Period: January 2001 - January 2002

BOB

"$alary Survey Gauges Compensation for Sourcing Executives," *Bobbin*, November 2001, p. 44.

Survey Period: January 2000 - January 2001

BOB1

"Quality Should Be Job No. 1," *Bobbin*, August 20, 2.

Survey Period: January 2001 - January 2002

BSB

Georgina K. Carson, "2002 Industry Profile: Personnel," *BSB*, June 2002, p. 48.

Survey Period: January 2001 - January 2002

BTN

Erika S. Warcholak, "Tough Year Sees Fewer Buyers Get Bonuses As Salaries Soar," *Business Travel News*, July 12, 2002, p. 18.

Survey Period: January 2001 - January 2002

BUFNEWS

Sean Nealon, "Casino Delays Lead to Low Enrollment at Buffalo," *The Buffalo News*, July 30, 2002.

Survey Period: 2002

Note: Figure comes from the National Gaming Association.

BWIRE

"AuntMinnie.com Launches SalaryScan Compensation Research Tool for Radiology Professionals," *Business Wire*, June 10, 2002, p. 308.

Survey Period: January 2001 - January 2002

Note: Data are based on figures included in SalaryScan, created by AuntMinnie.com and CompHealth.

CABLS

2001 Occupational Employment and Wage Estimates, 2001.

California Employment Development Department
Labor Market Information Division
7000 Fralklin Boulevard Building 1100
Sacramento, CA 95823
Telephone: (916) 262-2160
Online: http://www.calmis.cahwnet.gov/
Survey Period: October 2001 - December 2001

Note: All data are provided by the State Employment Security Administration to the Occupational Employment Statistics (OES) survey conducted by the U.S. Department of Labor, Bureau of Labor Statistics.

CE

"IEEE Survey: Experienced Women in High-Tech Jobs Earn More Than Men," *Control Engineering*, February 1, 2002.

Survey Period: January 2001 - January 2002

CEN

Michael Heylin, "Salary Survey," *C&EN*, August 5, 2002, p. 37.

Survey Period: March 2001 - March 2002

CLTC

"In Brief: Onward & Upward," *Contemporary Long Term Care*, p. 9.

Survey Period: January 2000 - January 2001

CMI

"Do You Earn $60,714?," *Corporate Meetings & Incentives*.

Survey Period: 2002

Note: Meeting Professionals International received responses to their survey from 1,509 meeting planners.

COBLS

2001 Occupational Employment and Wage Estimates, 2001.

Colorado Department of Labor and Employment
Labor Market Information
1515 Arapahoe St., Tower 2, Suite 300
Denver, CO 80202-2117
Telephone: (303) 318-8898
Online: http://lmi.cdle.state.co.us
Survey Period: October 2001 - December 2001

Note: All data are provided by the State Employment Security Administration to the Occupational Employment Statistics (OES) survey conducted by the U.S. Department of Labor, Bureau of Labor Statistics.

CORPRO

Corrections Professional, April 5, 2002.

Survey Period: 2001 - 2002

COSGIRL

Lauren Smith, "Fashion Editor," *Cosmo Girl*, March 2002, p. 101.

Survey Period: January 2001 - January 2002

COSGIRL1

Lauren Smith, "Make It Happen," *Cosmo Girl*, May 2002, p. 112.

Survey Period: January 2001 - January 2002

COSGIRL2

Sara Glassman, "Make It Happen: The Retail Industry," *Cosmo Girl*, August 2002, p. 124.

Survey Period: January 2001 - January 2002

CP

"Safety Salaries," *Concrete Products*, March 2000, p. 56 .

Survey Period: 1997 - 1998

CR

"Controller Compensation," *The Controller's Report*, October 2000, p. 10.

Survey Period: January 2000 - January 2001

CRAINNY

Mary Sisson, "NY's Dentists Cleaning Up on Cosmetic Work; Boom for Procedures, as Well as Hygienists," *Crain's New York Business*, August 5, 2002, p. 4.

Survey Period: 2000 - 2002

CSE

"The Scoop on Salaries," *Consulting-Specifying Engineer*, March 1, 2002, p. 11.

Survey Period: January 101 - 2,

CTBLS

2001 Occupational Employment and Wage Estimates, 2001.

Connecticut Labor Department
Office of Research and Information
200 Folly Brook Blvd
Wethersfield, CT 06109-1114
Telephone: (860) 263-6255
Online: http://www.ctdol.state.ct.us/lmi/index.htm
Survey Period: October 2001 - December 2001

Note: All data are provided by the State Employment Security Administration to the Occupational Employment Statistics (OES) survey conducted by the U.S. Department of Labor, Bureau of Labor Statistics.

CTU

"Family Planning Providers Hold the Line on Salaries in 2002: Slight Increases Reported, Especially for Nurse Practitioners," *Contraceptive Technology Update*, December 2002, p. SSS.

Survey Period: January 2001 - January 2002

DCBLS

2001 Occupational Employment and Wage Estimates, 2001.

Department of Employment Services
Labor Market Information
77 P Street, N.E., Suite 3302
Washington, DC 20002
Telephone: (202) 671-1633
Online: http://www/does.dc.gov/info/labor_mkt.shtm
Survey Period: October 2001 - December 2001

Note: All data are provided by the State Employment Security Administration to the Occupational Employment Statistics (OES) survey conducted by the U.S. Department of Labor, Bureau of Labor Statistics.

DEATHBUS

"Study Claims the More Funeral Homes in an Area; the Higher the Pay; Study Says Funeral Industry Pay Linked to Number of Funeral Homes in aArea," *Death Care Business Advisor*, July 25, 1.

Survey Period: 2001

Note: Data are based on 1999 funeral service and crematory industries figures from the U.S. Department of Labor's Bureau of Labor Statistics and funeral home figures from the 2001 National Directory of Morticians and Buyers Guide.

DEBLS

2001 Occupational Employment and Wage Estimates, 2001.

Delaware Department of Labor
Labor Market Information
4425 N. Market St.-Fox Valley Annex
Wilmington, DE 19809
Telephone: (302) 761-8050
Online: http://www.oolmi.net
Survey Period: October 2001 - December 2001

Note: All data are provided by the State Employment Security Administration to the Occupational Employment Statistics (OES) survey conducted by the U.S. Department of Labor, Bureau of Labor Statistics.

DFMAR

"Firm Management," *Design Firm Management & Administration Report*, October 2002, p. 1.

Survey Period: January 2001 - January 2002

DIG

"Minimum and Average Teacher Salaries, by State: 1990-91, 1998-99, and 1999-2000," *Digest of Education Statistics 2001*, 2002, p. 88.

U.S. Department of Education
National Center for Education Statistics
555 New Jersey Ave. NW
Washington, DC 20208-5574
Online: http://www.ed.gov/NCES/
Survey Period: January 1999 - January 2000

Note: Average entry-level salary figures for teachers in Alabama, Arizona, Colorado, Delaware, Illinois, Massachusetts, Michigan, New Hampshire, New Jersey, New Mexico, Rhode Island, South Dakota, Vermont, and Virginia, were estimated by the American Federation of Teachers. Average salary figures for teachers in California, Colorado, Delaware, Illinois, Massachusetts, Minnesota, Nevada, Pennsylvania, and Rhode Island, were estimated by the American Federation of Teachers. Average entry-level salary figures for teachers in Georgia, and average salary figures for teachers in Arkansas, California, Georgia, Iowa, Kansas, Kentucky, Louisiana, Missouri, Montana, West Virginia, and Wisconsin, include pay for extra responsibilities. Average entry-level salary figures for teachers in Illinois and Nevada, and average salary figures for teachers in Illinois and Virginia, include pension and extra-duty pay where applicable. Average entry-level salary figure for teachers in Mississippi includes an estimated $1,000 in local supplements. Average entry-level and average salary figures for teachers in Oregon include employer pickup of employee pension contribution. Average salary figure for teachers in Kansas is estimated to include fringe benefits. Average salary figures for teachers in New Jersey and New York represent the average median salary.

DIYR

Peter Agostinelli, "Working 9 to 5-or 5 to 9," *Do-It-Yourself Retailing*, August 2002, p. 82.

Survey Period: January 2001 - January 2002

DMN

Victor Godinez , "Actuaries Rate Their Jobs Highly," *The Dallas Morning News*, May 26, 2002.

Survey Period: January 2001 - January 2002

DN

Bruce Wiebusch, "Tragedy or Comedy? The Results of the Latest Design News Salary Survey Are Decidedly Mixed," *Design News*, July 8, 2002, p. 56.

Survey Period: January 2001 - January 2002

DOG

Steve Dale, "Dollar$ and Dog$," *Dog World*, August 2002, p. 30.

Survey Period: August 2001 - August 2002

DTHSE

"Pharmacist Salaries At a Glance," *Drug Topics Health-System Edition*, May 20, 2002, p. HSE51.

Survey Period: January 2000 - January 2001

EBN

Robert Ristelbueber, "Salary & Opinion Survey," *EBN*, October 21, 2002, p. 31.

Survey Period: January 2001 - January 2002

Note: Data are from the *EBN* 2002 Salary Survey.

ELNEWS

Bernard Levine, "The Cutting Edge," *Electronic News*, June 3, 2002, p. 8.

Survey Period: January 1999 - January 2000

EXAM

Rose Mary Budge, "Your Best Friend's Keeper," *The San Francisco Examiner*, January 19, 2003.

Survey Period: January 2002 - January 2003

Note: Data are based on information from Pet Sitters International.

FLBLS

2001 Occupational Employment and Wage Estimates, 2001.

Department of Labor and Employment Security
Bureau of Labor Market and Performance Information
367 Marpan Lane Commerce Industrial Center
Tallahassee, FL 32311
Telephone: (850) 488-1048
Online: http://lmi.floridajobs.org/
Survey Period: October 2001 - December 2001

Note: All data are provided by the State Employment Security Administration to the Occupational Employment Statistics (OES) survey conducted by the U.S. Department of Labor, Bureau of Labor Statistics.

FLTU

Christopher Calnan, "'They're Like the Worker Bees of the River'; Tugboats Keep Docking Area's Annual $1.3 Billion Industry," *The Florida Times-Union*, October 14, 2000, pp. FB-12.

Survey Period: 100 - 2,

FREEP

"U.S. Symphony Orchestra Pay and Pension, 2000-2001," *Detroit Free Press*, August 10, 2001, p. 5H.

Survey Period: 2000 - 2002

Note: Figure cited for the Metropolitan Opera (NY) is low. According to the source, the orchestra is reputed to have among the highest-compensated musicians in the country. Rehearsal and radio pay have not been included. On average, Metropolitan Opera musicians earn about $92,000.

FREEP1

"The 30 Fastest-Growing U.S. Occupations," *Detroit Free Press*, December 30, 2002, p. 6A.

Survey Period: 2001 - 2002

GABLS

2001 Occupational Employment and Wage Estimates, 2001.

Georgia Department of Labor
Labor Market Information
148 International Boulevard NE
Atlanta, GA 30303-1751
Telephone: (404) 656-3177
Online: http://www.dol.state.ga.us/lmi
Survey Period: October 2001 - December 2001

Note: All data are provided by the State Employment Security Administration to the Occupational Employment Statistics (OES) survey conducted by the U.S. Department of Labor, Bureau of Labor Statistics.

GDHK

"Price Check: Baby-Sitters Club," *Good Housekeeping*, October 2002, p. 50.

Survey Period: 2002

GUBLS

2001 Occupational Employment and Wage Estimates, 2001.

Department of Labor
Guam Employment Services
125 Tun Jesus Crisostomo
Tamuning, Guam 96911
Telephone: (671) 647-7066
Online: http://gu.jobsearch.org
Survey Period: October 2001 - December 2001

Note: All data are provided by the State Employment Security Administration to the Occupational Employment Statistics (OES) survey conducted by the U.S. Department of Labor, Bureau of Labor Statistics.

HCM

"2002 Salary Survey," *Home Care Magazine*, September 1, 2002.

Survey Period: January 2001 - January 2002

HHN

Terese Hudson Thrall, "Physician Recruitment: The Value of Docs," *Hospitals & Health Networks*, May 2002, p. 32.

Survey Period: January 2001 - January 2002

HIBLS

2001 Occupational Employment and Wage Estimates, 2001.

Hawaii Department of Labor and Industrial Relations
Research and Statistics Office
830 Punchbowl St., Room 304
Honolulu, HI 96813
Telephone: (808) 586-8999
Online: http://www.state.hi.us/dlir/rs/loihi/
Survey Period: October 2001 - December 2001

Note: All data are provided by the State Employment Security Administration to the Occupational Employment Statistics (OES) survey conducted by the U.S. Department of Labor, Bureau of Labor Statistics.

HIBUS

"Call Centers: Emergence of a New Industry," *Hawaii Business*, January 2001, p. 26.

Survey Period: January 2000 - January 2002

HMA

"Hospice Administrator Salaries Are on the Rise," *Hospice Management Advisor*, November 1, 2000.

Survey Period: 1999 - 2000

HPN

"CS Salaries Enjoy Healthy Boost," *Healthcare Purchasing News*.

Survey Period: 2002

Note: Survey data are based on responses from 122 out of 574 workers, an 18% rate.

IABLS

2001 Occupational Employment and Wage Estimates, 2001.

Iowa Workforce Development
Research and Information Services
1000 East Grand Ave
Des Moines, IA 50319-0209
Telephone: (515) 281-0255
Online: http://www.state.ia.us/iwd
Survey Period: October 2001 - December 2001

Note: All data are provided by the State Employment Security Administration to the Occupational Employment Statistics (OES) survey conducted by the U.S. Department of Labor, Bureau of Labor Statistics.

IBJ

"Facility Managers Struggle to Find Reliable Cleaning Services," *Indianapolis Business Journal*, October 1, 2001, p. 10B.

Survey Period: January 2000 - January 2001

IDBLS

2001 Occupational Employment and Wage Estimates, 2001.

Idaho Department of Labor
Bureau of Research and Analysis
317 Main St
Boise, ID 83735-0670
Telephone: (208) 334-6170
Online: http://www.labor.state.id.us/lmi/id-lmi.htm
Survey Period: October 2001 - December 2001

Note: All data are provided by the State Employment Security Administration to the Occupational Employment Statistics (OES) survey conducted by the U.S. Department of Labor, Bureau of Labor Statistics.

ILBLS

2001 Occupational Employment and Wage Estimates, 2001.

Illinois Department of Employment Security
Economic Information and Analysis
401 South State St., Suite 215
Chicago, IL 60605
Telephone: (312) 793-2316
Online: http://lmi.ides.state.il.us
Survey Period: October 2001 - December 2001

Note: All data are provided by the State Employment Security Administration to the Occupational Employment Statistics (OES) survey conducted by the U.S. Department of Labor, Bureau of Labor Statistics.

INBLS

2001 Occupational Employment and Wage Estimates, 2001.

Indiana Department of Workforce Development
Labor Market Information
10 North Senate Ave
Indianapolis, IN 46204-2277
Telephone: (317) 232-7460
Online: http://www.dwd.state.in.us/
Survey Period: October 2001 - December 2001

Note: All data are provided by the State Employment Security Administration to the Occupational Employment Statistics (OES) survey conducted by the U.S. Department of Labor, Bureau of Labor Statistics.

INFO

Loretta W. Prencipe, "VP of E-Commerce," *Infoworld*, January 15, 2001, p. 61.

Survey Period: January 2000 - January 2001

INFO1

"CTO Compensation Survey," *Infoworld*, June 3, 2002, p. 45.

Survey Period: January 2000 - January 2001

INFO2

"Average Salaries by Industry," *Infoworld*, June 25, 2001, p. 46.

Survey Period: January 2000 - January 2001

INFO3

"Job Titles: WEB Developer," *Infoworld*, May 7, 2001, p. 79.

Survey Period: January 2000 - January 2001

INFO4

"Job Titles: IT Business Analyst," *Infoworld*, April 23, 2001, p. 83.

Survey Period: January 2000 - January 2001

INFO5

"State Snapshot: Maryland," *Infoworld*, January 2001, p. 63.

Survey Period: January 2000 - January 2001

INFO6

Loretta W. Prencipe, "Job Titles: Internet Manager," *Infoworld*, December 18, 2000, p. 73.

Survey Period: 1999 - 2000

IOMA

"Report on Salary Survey," *IOMA (Institute of Management and Administration)*, March 2002, p. 1 .

Survey Period: January 2001 - February 2002

Note: Data are derived from three reports: "Compensation in the Security/Loss Prevention Field," from Abbott, Langer & Associates; "Geographic Report on Middle Management Compensation," from Watson Wyatt Data Services; and "Middle Management Compensation," from Pricewaterhouse Coopers.

IOMA1

"Data Shows Pay Increases for Travel Pros Now Dropping," *IOMA (Institute of Management and Administration)*, March 2002, p. 2.

Survey Period: January 2001 - January 2002

IOMA2

"Report on Salary Surveys," *IOMA*, December 20, 1, p. 2.

Survey Period: January 2000 - January 2001

IOMA3

"New Survey Analyzes Pay Differences for Armed vs. Unarmed Guards," *IOMA (Institute of Management & Administration)*, September 2000, p. 3.

Survey Period: January 201 - 3,

Note: Data are based on the "2002/2003 ECS Geographic Report on Technician and Skilled Trades Personnel Compensation" from Watson Wyatt Data Services.

IOMA5

"IT Pay Takes a Hit and Falls 11% in One Year," *IOMA (Institute of Management and Administration*, June 2002, p. 3.

Survey Period: January 2001 - January 2002

IOMA6

"Online Salary Data for Controllers Reveals Wide City-by-City Variation," *IOMA (Institute of Management & Administration)*, June 2002.

Survey Period: January 2001 - January 2002

ITNA

"Seattle Technology Workers Earn Highest Average Salary Nationwide; $129,300 Average Wage Beats Out San Jose by $44,150," *ITAR/TASS News Agency*, December 5, 2000.

Survey Period: January 1999 - January 2000

IW

Internetweek, January 15, 2001.

Survey Period: January 2000 - January 2001

KRTNS

Lisa Heyamoto, "No Heyday for the Payday: Low Salaries Discourage Women from Going Into Coaching," *Knight Ridder/Tribune News Service*, June 20, 2002.

Survey Period: January 2001 - January 2002

KSBLS

2001 Occupational Employment and Wage Estimates, 2001.

Kansas Department of Human Resources
401 SW Topeka Blvd
Topeka, KS 66603-3182
Telephone: (785) 296-5058
Online: http://laborstats.hr.state.ks.us/
Survey Period: October 2001 - December 2001

Note: All data are provided by the State Employment Security Administration to the Occupational Employment Statistics (OES) survey conducted by the U.S. Department of Labor, Bureau of Labor Statistics.

KYBLS

2001 Occupational Employment and Wage Estimates, 2001.

Kentucky Department of Employment Services
Division of Administration/Financial Management
275 East Main St., Suite 2-C
Frankfort, KY 40621
Telephone: (502) 564-7976
Online: http://www.des.state.ky.us/agencies/wforce/des/lmi/lmi.htm
Survey Period: October 2001 - December 2001

Note: All data are provided by the State Employment Security Administration to the Occupational Employment Statistics (OES) survey conducted by the U.S. Department of Labor, Bureau of Labor Statistics.

LABLS

2001 Occupational Employment and Wage Estimates, 2001.

Louisiana Department of Labor
Research and Statistics Division
1001 North 23rd Street Baton Rouge, LA 70804-4094
Telephone: (225) 342-3140
Online: http://www.ldol.state.la.us/LMIQM.asp
Survey Period: October 2001 - December 2001

Note: All data are provided by the State Employment Security Administration to the Occupational Employment Statistics (OES) survey conducted by the U.S. Department of Labor, Bureau of Labor Statistics.

LIBN

Andrew J. Mitchell, "The Health Care Industry-Where the Jobs Are," *Long Island Business News*, July 26, 2.

Survey Period: January 2001 - January 2002

MABLS

2001 Occupational Employment and Wage Estimates, 2001.

Massachusetts Division of Employment and Training
Labor Market Information and Research
19 Staniford St., 5th Floor
Boston, MA 02114
Telephone: (617) 626-6556
Online: http://www.detma.org/lmiinfo.htm
Survey Period: October 2001 - December 2001

Note: All data are provided by the State Employment Security Administration to the Occupational Employment Statistics (OES) survey conducted by the U.S. Department of Labor, Bureau of Labor Statistics.

MC

"Weird Jobs That Pay," *Marie Claire (US)*, April 2002, p. 112.

Survey Period: 2001 - 2002

MDBLS

2001 Occupational Employment and Wage Estimates, 2001.

Maryland Department of Labor
Office of Labor Market Analysis and Information
1100 North Eutaw St., Room 316
Baltimore, MD 21201
Telephone: (410) 767-2250
Online: http://www.dllr.state.md.us/lmi/index.htm
Survey Period: October 2001 - December 2001

Note: All data are provided by the State Employment Security Administration to the Occupational Employment Statistics (OES) survey conducted by the U.S. Department of Labor, Bureau of Labor Statistics.

MEBLS

2001 Occupational Employment and Wage Estimates, 2001.

Maine Department of Labor
Labor Market Information Services
20 Union St
Augusta, ME 04330
Telephone: (207) 287-2271
Online: http://www.state.me.us/labor/lmis/index.html
Survey Period: October 2001 - December 2001

Note: All data are provided by the State Employment Security Administration to the Occupational Employment Statistics (OES) survey conducted by the U.S. Department of Labor, Bureau of Labor Statistics.

MIBLS

2001 Occupational Employment and Wage Estimates, 2001.

Michigan Jobs Commission, Employment Service Agency
Department of Career Development
3032 West Grand Blvd., 9th Floor
Detroit, MI 48202
Telephone: (313) 456-3090
Online: http://www.michlmi.org
Survey Period: October 2001 - December 2001

Note: All data are provided by the State Employment Security Administration to the Occupational Employment Statistics (OES) survey conducted by the U.S. Department of Labor, Bureau of Labor Statistics.

MINQ

"Company Touts Benefits of New Coal Mine to Muhlenberg County, Ky., Residents," *Messenger-Inquirer (Owensboro, Ky.)*.

Survey Period: 20, 1

MM&M

"2002MM&M Career & Salary Survey," *Medical Marketing & Media*, September 2002, p. 43.

Survey Period: January 2001 - January 2002

MNBLS

2001 Occupational Employment and Wage Estimates, 2001.

Minnesota Department of Economic Security
BLS Programs, Research and Statistical Office
390 North Robert St
St. Paul, MN 55101
Telephone: (612) 296-4087
Online: http://www.des.mnwfc.org/lmi.htm
Survey Period: October 2001 - December 2001

Note: All data are provided by the State Employment Security Administration to the Occupational Employment Statistics (OES) survey conducted by the U.S. Department of Labor, Bureau of Labor Statistics.

MOBLS

2001 Occupational Employment and Wage Estimates, 2001.

Missouri Department of Labor and Industrial Relations
Research and Analysis
301 West High Street
Jefferson City, MO 65101
Telephone: (573) 751-3637
Online: http://www.works.state.mo.us/lmi
Survey Period: October 2001 - December 2001

Note: All data are provided by the State Employment Security Administration to the Occupational Employment Statistics (OES) survey conducted by the U.S. Department of Labor, Bureau of Labor Statistics.

MSBLS

2001 Occupational Employment and Wage Estimates, 2001.

Mississippi Employment Security Commission
Labor Market Information
1520 West Capitol Street
Jackson, MS 39215-1699
Telephone: (601) 961-7424
Online: http://208.137.131.31/lmi/index.html
Survey Period: October 2001 - December 2001

Note: All data are provided by the State Employment Security Administration to the Occupational Employment Statistics (OES) survey conducted by the U.S. Department of Labor, Bureau of Labor Statistics.

MSW

Sherry Jones, "N.C. Community Colleges: Study Shows Staff, Faculty Salaries Low," *Morning Star (Wilmington, N.C.)*, November 26, 2000.

Survey Period: January 1999 - January 2000

MTBLS

2001 Occupational Employment and Wage Estimates, 2001.

Montana Department of Labor and Industry
Office of Research and Analysis
1327 Lockey & Roberts Street
Helena, MT 59601
Telephone: (406) 444-2430
Online: http://rad.dli.state.mt.us
Survey Period: October 2001 - December 2001

Note: All data are provided by the State Employment Security Administration to the Occupational Employment Statistics (OES) survey conducted by the U.S. Department of Labor, Bureau of Labor Statistics.

NCBLS

2001 Occupational Employment and Wage Estimates, 2001.

North Carolina Employment Security Commission
Labor Market Information
700 Wade Ave.
Raleigh, NC 27605
Telephone: (919) 733-2936
Online: http://www.ncesc.com
Survey Period: October 2001 - December 2001

Note: All data are provided by the State Employment Security Administration to the Occupational Employment Statistics (OES) survey conducted by the U.S. Department of Labor, Bureau of Labor Statistics.

NDBLS

2001 Occupational Employment and Wage Estimates, 2001.

North Dakota Job Service
Program Support
1000 East Divide Ave
Bismarck, ND 58501
Telephone: (701) 328-2868
Online: http://www.state.nd.us/jsnd/lmi.htm
Survey Period: October 2001 - December 2001

Note: All data are provided by the State Employment Security Administration to the Occupational Employment Statistics (OES) survey conducted by the U.S. Department of Labor, Bureau of Labor Statistics.

NEA

"Average Salaries of Public School Teachers, 1998-99," January 19, 2001.

National Education Association
1201 16th Street, NW
Washington, DC 20036
Telephone: (202) 833-4000
Online: http://www.nea.org
Survey Period: January 1998 - January 1999

Note: Figures for teacher salaries in Arizona, Arkansas, California, Colorado, District of Columbia, Massachusetts, Michigan, New Jersey, New York, Oklahoma, Utah, Virginia, and the United States are estimates.

NEBLS

2001 Occupational Employment and Wage Estimates, 2001.

Nebraska Department of Labor
Labor Market Information
550 South 17th St
Lincoln, NE 68509
Telephone: (402) 471-9964
Online: http://www.dol.state.ne.us/nelmi.htm
Survey Period: October 2001 - December 2001

Note: All data are provided by the State Employment Security Administration to the Occupational Employment Statistics (OES) survey conducted by the U.S. Department of Labor, Bureau of Labor Statistics.

NHBLS

2001 Occupational Employment and Wage Estimates, 2001.

New Hampshire Department of Employment Security
Economic and Labor Market Information Bureau
32 South Main St
Concord, NH 03301-4587
Telephone: (603) 228-4123
Online: http://www.nhworks.state.nh.us/lmipage.htm
Survey Period: October 2001 - December 2001

Note: All data are provided by the State Employment Security Administration to the Occupational Employment Statistics (OES) survey conducted by the U.S. Department of Labor, Bureau of Labor Statistics.

NJBLS

2001 Occupational Employment and Wage Estimates, 2001.

New Jersey Department of Labor
Labor Planning and Analysis
John Fitch Plaza
Trenton, NJ 08625
Telephone: (609) 292-0099
Online: http://www.state.nj.us/labor/lra/
Survey Period: October 2001 - December 2001

Note: All data are provided by the State Employment Security Administration to the Occupational Employment Statistics (OES) survey conducted by the U.S. Department of Labor, Bureau of Labor Statistics.

NMBLS

2001 Occupational Employment and Wage Estimates, 2001.

New Mexico Department of Labor
Economic Research and Analysis Bureau
501 Mountain Road
Albuquerque, NM 87102
Telephone: (505) 841-8645
Online: http://www3.state.nm.us/dol/dol_lmif.html
Survey Period: October 2001 - December 2001

Note: All data are provided by the State Employment Security Administration to the Occupational Employment Statistics (OES) survey conducted by the U.S. Department of Labor, Bureau of Labor Statistics.

NONPROF

Clint Carpenter, "Female Fundraisers Earn $24,000 Less. (General Ramblings)," *The Non-profit Times*, April 2, 2002, p. 12.

Survey Period: 2001

Note: Data are from the Association of Fundraising Professionals (AFP) 2001 salary survey of 3,560 of its more than 23,000 members. The Association received 1,216 responses.

NTT

David Quigg, "Pay, Benefits Climb Sharply for Tacoma, Wash., Sound Transit Employees," *The News Tribune (Tacoma, Wa.)*, September 20, 2002.

Survey Period: January 2001 - January 2002

NURSE

Cheryl L. Mee, RN, C, MSN and Katherine W. Carey, "Nursing 2001 Salary Survey," *Nursing*, March 2, 1, p. 44.

Survey Period: January 2000 - January 2001

Note: Figures are based on 1,965 usable responses from approximately 1400 replies.

NVBLS

2001 Occupational Employment and Wage Estimates, 2001.

Department of Employment and Training
Information Development and Processing Division
500 East Third St
Carson City, NV 89713-0020
Telephone: (775) 684-0387
Online: http://www.detr.state.nv.us/lmi/index.htm
Survey Period: October 2001 - December 2001

Note: All data are provided by the State Employment Security Administration to the Occupational Employment Statistics (OES) survey conducted by the U.S. Department of Labor, Bureau of Labor Statistics.

NYBLS

2001 Occupational Employment and Wage Estimates, 2001.

New York Department of Labor
Division of Research and Statistics
State Office Building Campus, Room 402
Albany, NY 12240
Telephone: (518) 457-6369
Online: http://www.labor.state.ny.us/
Survey Period: October 2001 - December 2001

Note: All data are provided by the State Employment Security Administration to the Occupational Employment Statistics (OES) survey conducted by the U.S. Department of Labor, Bureau of Labor Statistics.

NYT

"The Pay's the Thing," *The New York Times*, June 16, 1, p. B1.

Survey Period: 2001

Note: Figures for Pilots and Co-Pilots with major air carriers apply to those pilots with at least 12 years' experience and who fly 737s. Figures for Pilots and Co-Pilots with air carrier subsidiaries (American Eagle, Continental Express, Comair (Delta) apply to those pilots who fly 50-seat regional jets.

NYT1

Alan B. Krueger, "Economic Scene: A Small Dose of Common Sense Would Help Congress Break the Gridlock Over Airport Security," *The New York Times*, November 15, 2001, p. C2.

Survey Period: 2000 - 2001

NYT2

"Do You Speak Uzbek? Translators Are in Demand," *The New York Times*, October 21, 2001, p. 4.

Survey Period: 2001

Note: From data supplied by the American Translators Association.

OHBLS

2001 Occupational Employment and Wage Estimates, 2001.

Labor Market Information Division, 145 South Front St
Ohio Bureau of Employment Services
4300 Kimberly Parkway, 3rd Floor
Columbus, OH 43232
Telephone: (614) 752-9494
Online: http://lmi.state.oh.us/
Survey Period: October 2001 - December 2001

Note: All data are provided by the State Employment Security Administration to the Occupational Employment Statistics (OES) survey conducted by the U.S. Department of Labor, Bureau of Labor Statistics.

OKBLS

2001 Occupational Employment and Wage Estimates, 2001.

Oklahoma Employment Security Commission
Labor Market Information
2401 North Lincoln, Room 310
Oklahoma City, OK 73105
Telephone: (405) 557-7265
Online: http://www.oesc.state.ok.us/lmi/default.htm
Survey Period: October 2001 - December 2001

Note: All data are provided by the State Employment Security Administration to the Occupational Employment Statistics (OES) survey conducted by the U.S. Department of Labor, Bureau of Labor Statistics.

OOH

"Flight Attendants," *Occupational Outlook Handbook, 2002-2003*, February 2002.

Online: www.oohinfo@bls.gov
Survey Period: February 2002

OOH1

"Air Traffic Controllers," *Occupational Outlook Handbook, 2002-03*, February 2002.

Online: www.oohinfo@bls.gov
Survey Period: February 2002

OOH2

"Police and Detectives," *Occupational Outlook Handbook, 2002-03*, February 2002.

Online: www.oohinfo@bls.gov
Survey Period: February 2002

OOH3

"Emergency Medical Technicians and Paramedics," *Occupational Outlook Handbook, 2002-2003*, 2002 - 2003.

Online: www.oohinfo@bls.gov
Survey Period: 2002 - 2003

OOH4

"Cardiovascular Technologists & Technicians," *Occupational Outlook Handbook, 2002-2003*, February 2002.

Survey Period: February 2002

OOH5

"Securities, Commodities, and Financial Services Sales Agents," *Occupational Outlook Handbook, 2002-2003*, February 2002.

Survey Period: February 2002

OOH6

"Air Traffic Controllers," *Occupational Outlook Handbook*, 2002.

Survey Period: 2002

OOH7

Occupational Outlook Handbook, 2002-2003 "Judges, Magistrates, and Other Judicial Workers," 2002.

Survey Period: 2002

OOH8

"Roman Catholic Priests," *Occupational Outlook Handbook, 2002-2003*, 2002.

Survey Period: 2002

OOH9

Occupational Outlook Handbook, 2002-2003, 2002.

Survey Period: 1999 - 2000

OOH10

"Personal & Home Care Aides," *Occupational Outlook Handbook, 2002-2003*, 2002.

Survey Period: 1999 - 2000

OOH11

"Social and Human Service Assistants," *Occupational Outlook Handbook, 2002-2003*, 2002.

Survey Period: 1999 - 2000

OOH12

"Security Guards and Gaming Surveillance Officers," *Occupational Outlook Handbook, 2002-2003*, 2002.

Survey Period: 1999 - 2000

OPM

"2003 Special Salary Rate Table Number 999C," January 24, 2003.

U.S. Office of Personnel Management
Online: www.opm.gov
Survey Period: 2003

OPM1

"2003 Special Salary Rate Table Number 00029," January 24, 2003.

U.S. Office of Personnel Management
Online: www.opm.gov
Survey Period: 2003

OPM2

"2003 Special Salary Rate Table Number 983A," January 24, 2003.

U.S. Office of Personnel Management
Online: www.opm.gov
Survey Period: 2003

OPM3

"2003 Special Salary Rate Table Number 983B," January 24, 2003.

U.S. Office of Personnel Management
Online: www.opm.gov
Survey Period: 2003

OPM4

"2003 Special Salary Rate Table Number 983C," January 24, 2003.

U.S. Office of Personnel Management
Online: www.opm.gov
Survey Period: 2003

OPM5

"2003 Special Salary Rate Table Number 983D," January 24, 2003.

U.S. Office of Personnel Management
Online: www.opm.gov
Survey Period: 2003

OPM6

"2003 Special Salary Rate Table Number 983E," January 24, 2003.

U.S. Office of Personnel Management
Online: www.opm.gov
Survey Period: 2003

OPM7

"2003 Special Salary Rate Table Number 983F," January 24, 2003.

U.S. Office of Personnel Management
Online: www.opm.gov
Survey Period: 2003

OPM8

"2003 Special Salary Rate Table Number 999B" "2003 Special Salary Rate Table Number 999C," January 24, 2003.

U.S. Office of Personnel Management U.S. Office of Personnel Management
Online: www.opm.gov www.opm.gov
Survey Period: 2003 00002003

OPM10

"2003 Special Salary Rate Table Number 999D," January 24, 2003.

U.S. Office of Personnel Management
Online: www.opm.gov
Survey Period: 2003

OPM11

"2003 Special Salary Rate Table Number 999E," January 24, 2003.

U.S. Office of Personnel Management
Online: www.opm.gov
Survey Period: 2003

OPM12

"2003 Special Salary Rate Table Number 999F," January 24, 2003.

U.S. Office of Personnel Management
Online: www.opm.gov
Survey Period: 2003

OPM13

"Salary Table 2003-GS," January 24, 2003.

U.S. Office of Personnel Management
Online: www.opm.gov
Survey Period: 2003

ORBLS

2001 Occupational Employment and Wage Estimates, 2001.

Oregon Employment Department
Labor Market Information
875 Union St. NE, Room 220
Salem, OR 97311
Telephone: (503) 947-1212
Online: http://olmis.emp.state.or.us/
Survey Period: October 2001 - December 2001

Note: All data are provided by the State Employment Security Administration to the Occupational Employment Statistics (OES) survey conducted by the U.S. Department of Labor, Bureau of Labor Statistics.

PABLS

2001 Occupational Employment and Wage Estimates, 2001.

Pennsylvania Department of Labor and Industry
Bureau of Research and Statistics
7th and Forester Streets, Room 220
Harrisburg, PA 17120-0001
Telephone: (717) 787-3266
Online: http://www.lmi.state.pa.us/
Survey Period: October 2001 - December 2001

Note: All data are provided by the State Employment Security Administration to the Occupational Employment Statistics (OES) survey conducted by the U.S. Department of Labor, Bureau of Labor Statistics.

PR

"Salaries Spiral in 2000. Now What?," *PR Week*, March 26, 2001, p. 24.

Survey Period: January 2000 - January 2001

PRBLS

2001 Occupational Employment and Wage Estimates, 2001.

Puerto Rico Bureau of Employment Security
Research and Statistics Division
505 Munoz Rivera Ave., 17th Floor
Hato Rey, PR 00918
Telephone: (787) 754-5340
Survey Period: October 2001 - December 2001

Note: All data are provided by the State Employment Security Administration to the Occupational Employment Statistics (OES) survey conducted by the U.S. Department of Labor, Bureau of Labor Statistics.

PRW

"Salary Survey 2002," *PRWeek*, March 25, 2002, p. 17.

Survey Period: 2001 - 2002

PSBJ

Donna Sakson, "Technical Writers Can Overcome the Dot-Com Downturn," *Puget Sound Business Journal*, October 20, 2000.

Survey Period: January 1999 - January 2000

RIBLS

2001 Occupational Employment and Wage Estimates, 2001.

Rhode Island Department of Employment and Training
Labor Market Information
1511 Pontiac Ave.
Cranston, RI 02920
Telephone: (401) 462-8767
Online: http://www.det.state.ri.us/webdev/lmi/
Survey Period: October 2001 - December 2001

Note: All data are provided by the State Employment Security Administration to the Occupational Employment Statistics (OES) survey conducted by the U.S. Department of Labor, Bureau of Labor Statistics.

RTM

"NewsBriefs," *Research Technology Management*, October 2002, p. 10.

Survey Period: January 2001 - January 2002

SAEN

Melissa S. Monroe, "Computer Graphics Convention in San Antonio, Texas, Offers Latest Technology," *San Antonio Express-News*, July 24, 2002.

Survey Period: January 2001 - January 2002

SAFEDIR

"A Broad Look at Current Trends in Safety Salaries," *Safety Director's Report*, February 2001, p. 1.

Survey Period: 2000 - 2001

Note: Data are based on the National Safety Council's 2000 Salary Survey.

SAFEDIR1

"Good Pay News in a Tough Year for Security Directors," *Security Director's Report*, August 2002, p. 1.

Survey Period: January 2001 - January 2002

SCBLS

2001 Occupational Employment and Wage Estimates, 2001.

South Carolina Employment Security Commission
Labor Market Information
631 Hampton St
Columbia, SC 29201
Telephone: (803) 737-2660
Online: http://www.sces.org/lmi/index.htm
Survey Period: October 2001 - December 2001

Note: All data are provided by the State Employment Security Administration to the Occupational Employment Statistics (OES) survey conducted by the U.S. Department of Labor, Bureau of Labor Statistics.

SCJS

Kathleen Maguire and Ann L. Pastore, "Annual Salaries of Federal Judges," *Sourcebook of Criminal Justice Statistics Online*, 2002.

Online: http://www.albany.edu/sourcebook/
Survey Period: January 1, 2001

SDBJ

Mark Cafferty and Brandi Banks, "Survey Sniffs Out San Diego's Hottests Jobs: Diversity Keeps Region Growth Slow, But Steady," *San Diego Business Journal*, June 3, 2002.

Survey Period: January 2001 - January 2002

SDBJ1

Terri Bergman, *San Diego Business Journal*, September 30, 2002, p. B9.

Survey Period: January 1999 - January 2000

SDBLS

2001 Occupational Employment and Wage Estimates, 2001.

South Dakota Department of Labor
Labor Information Divison
420 S. Roosevelt Street
Aberdeen, SD 57401
Telephone: (605) 626-2314
Online: http://www.state.sd.us/dol/lmic/index.htm
Survey Period: October 2001 - December 2001

Note: All data are provided by the State Employment Security Administration to the Occupational Employment Statistics (OES) survey conducted by the U.S. Department of Labor, Bureau of Labor Statistics.

SDUT

Mark Arner, "Bus Drivers Call for Raise At Transit Board Meeting," *The San Diego Union Tribune*, February 11, 2000.

Survey Period: January 1999 - January 2000

SFLSS

Jenni Bergal, "Forensic Accountants Find Where Cash is Hidden," *South Florida Sun-Sentinel*, February 5, 2002, p. K1.

Survey Period: 2000 - 2001

Note: Data are from a 2001 survey by *Accounting Today*.

SLBJ

Gil Steunkel, "Good, New Public Courses Impact Club Memberships," *St. Louis Business Journal*, March 2, 2001, p. 30.

Survey Period: 2000 - 2001

SMM

"2002 Salary Survey: Our Exclusive Sales Compensation Survey Reveals the Impact of the Recession on Sales and Marketing Executives," *Sales & Marketing Management*, May 2002, p. 32.

Survey Period: January 2001 - January 2002

STLOUPD

Phillip O'Connor, "Studies Show Failure of Regulators' Efforts Against Nursing-Home Neglect," *St. Louis Post-Dispatch*.

Survey Period: January 2001 - January 2002

STLOUPD1

"Some Question Use of Consultants by Missouri Department of Transportation," *St. Louis Post-Dispatch*, September 22, 2002.

Survey Period: January 2001 - January 2002

TALL

Nancy Cook Lauer, "Study Urges Changes in Florida Government Hiring Practices," *Tallahassee Democrat (Fla.)*, December 19, 2000.

Survey Period: January 2001 - January 2002

TBJ

"Market Facts," *The Business Journal*, November 2, 2001.

Survey Period: 2000 - 2001

TIME

"Help Still Wanted: Panic Hiring Is Over, But There Are Still Lots of Jobs for the Class of '01," *Time*, May 7, 2001, p. 54.

Survey Period: January 2000 - January 2001

TNBLS

2001 Occupational Employment and Wage Estimates, 2001.

Tennessee Department of Employment Security
Research and Statistics Division
500 James Robertson Pkwy
Nashville, TN 37245-1000
Telephone: (615) 741-2284
Online: http://www.state.tn.us/labir-wfd/lmi.htm
Survey Period: October 2001 - December 2001

Note: All data are provided by the State Employment Security Administration to the Occupational Employment Statistics (OES) survey conducted by the U.S. Department of Labor, Bureau of Labor Statistics.

TPNO

Keith Darce and Jeffrey Meitrodt, "Masters of the River," *The Times-Picayune (New Orleans)*, November 4, 2001, p. 2.

Survey Period: 2000 - 2001

TRAIN

Joel Schettler, "Withering: 21st Annual Salary Survey; With Economic Conditions and Organizational Structures in Flux, Determining Your Value to the Corporation Remains An Arduous But Essential Responsibility," *Training*, November 2002, p. 3.

Survey Period: January 2001 - January 2002

TXBLS

2001 Occupational Employment and Wage Estimates, 2001.

Texas Workforce Commission
Labor Market Information
9001 North IH-35, Suite 103A
Austin, TX 75753
Telephone: (512) 491-4803
Online: http://www.twc.state.tx.us/lmi/lmi.html
Survey Period: October 2001 - December 2001

Note: All data are provided by the State Employment Security Administration to the Occupational Employment Statistics (OES) survey conducted by the U.S. Department of Labor, Bureau of Labor Statistics.

USATOD

Gary Stoller, "Feds Behind in Hiring Airport Screeners," *USA TODAY*, July 25, 2002.

Survey Period: January 2001 - January 2002

USATOD1

"What Mechanics Earn," *USA TODAY*, April 17, 2001, p. 3B.

Survey Period: 2000 - 2001

Note: Figures represent hourly wages for the top experienced mechanics under contract with each airline.

USATOD2

Lori Joseph, "Most Guard Commanders Receive Salaries in the Low Six-Figure Range," *USA TODAY*, December 18, 2001, p. 6A.

Survey Period: 2000

Note: Data are based on information from the National Conference of State Legislatures and the Council of State Governments.

USATOD3

Julie Appleby, "Nurse Anesthetists in Short Supply," *USA TODAY*, May 14, 2002, p. 3B.

Survey Period: January 2001 - January 2002

USATOD4

"Female Office Workers' Pay Trails Men's," *USA TODAY*, November 5, 2001, p. 1B.

Survey Period: January 2000 - January 2001

USWIRE

"HIMSS Salary Survey: Senior Management, Consulting Firm Staff Highest Paid in Healthcare IT," *US Newswire*, August 7, 2002.

Survey Period: January 2001 - January 2002

UTBLS

2001 Occupational Employment and Wage Estimates, 2001.

Utah Department of Workforce Services
Labor Market Information
140 East 300 South
Salt Lake City, UT 84111
Telephone: (801) 526-9401
Online: http://www.dws.state.ut.us/
Survey Period: October 2001 - December 2001

Note: All data are provided by the State Employment Security Administration to the Occupational Employment Statistics (OES) survey conducted by the U.S. Department of Labor, Bureau of Labor Statistics.

VABLS

2001 Occupational Employment and Wage Estimates, 2001.

Virginia Employment Commission
Economic Information and Services Division
703 East Main St
Richmond, VA 23219
Telephone: (804) 786-7496
Online: http://www.vec.state.va.us/
Survey Period: October 2001 - December 2001

Note: All data are provided by the State Employment Security Administration to the Occupational Employment Statistics (OES) survey conducted by the U.S. Department of Labor, Bureau of Labor Statistics.

VIBLS

2001 Occupational Employment and Wage Estimates, 2001.

Virgin Islands Department of Labor
Bureau of Labor Statistics
53A and 54B Kronprindsens Gade
Charlotte Amalie, St. Thomas, VI 00801
Telephone: (340) 776-3700
Online: http://www.vidol.org/
Survey Period: October 2001 - December 2001

Note: All data are provided by the State Employment Security Administration to the Occupational Employment Statistics (OES) survey conducted by the U.S. Department of Labor, Bureau of Labor Statistics.

VIRPIL

"Dockworker Dispute on West Coast Leaves Cargo Adrift," *The Virginian-Pilot (Norfolk, Va.)*, October 1, 2002.

Survey Period: 2001

VTBLS

2001 Occupational Employment and Wage Estimates, 2001.

Vermont Department of Employment and Training
Research and Analysis
5 Green Mountain Dr
Montpelier, VT 05602
Telephone: (802) 828-4153
Online: http://www.det.state.vt.us/
Survey Period: October 2001 - December 2001

Note: All data are provided by the State Employment Security Administration to the Occupational Employment Statistics (OES) survey conducted by the U.S. Department of Labor, Bureau of Labor Statistics.

WABLS

2001 Occupational Employment and Wage Estimates, 2001.

Employment Security Division
Labor Market and Economic Analysis
605 Woodland Square Loop
Lacey, WA 98506
Telephone: (360) 438-4804
Online: http://www.wa.gov/esd/lmea
Survey Period: October 2001 - December 2001

Note: All data are provided by the State Employment Security Administration to the Occupational Employment Statistics (OES) survey conducted by the U.S. Department of Labor, Bureau of Labor Statistics.

WARE

Jim Whalen, "A Forecast of Change: Despite A Stormy Year, Warehouse Executives Saw Moderate Salary Increases in 2001," *Warehousing Management*, August 1, 2002, p. 18.

Survey Period: January 2001 - January 2002

WATIMES

Brian E. Fallon, "WNBA Players Flirt With Strike for More Money," *The Washington Times*, July 15, 2002, p. C1.

Survey Period: 2002

WIBLS

2001 Occupational Employment and Wage Estimates, 2001.

Wisconsin Department of Workforce Development
LMI Data Development
201 East Washington Ave.
Madison, WI 53702
Telephone: (608) 267-9705
Online: http://www.dwd.state.wi.us/dwelmi
Survey Period: October 2001 - December 2001

Note: All data are provided by the State Employment Security Administration to the Occupational Employment Statistics (OES) survey conducted by the U.S. Department of Labor, Bureau of Labor Statistics.

WSJ

William M. Bulkeley, "Why Stenotypists Are Trying to Keep Paula O'Regan Quiet," *The Wall Street Journal*, June 3, 2002, p. A1.

Survey Period: 2001 - 2002

WSJ1

Kathy Chen, "Janitors' Union Plans East Coast Campaign," *Wall Street Journal*, April 1, p. A2.

Survey Period: January 2000 - January 2001

WT

"Lifestyles of the... Export Clerk," *World Trade*, July 2002, p. 47.

Survey Period: June 2001 - June 2002

WVBLS

2001 Occupational Employment and Wage Estimates, 2001.

West Virginia Bureau of Employment Programs
Research, Information and Analysis
112 California Ave, Room 107
Charleston, WV 25305-0112
Telephone: (304) 558-2660
Online: http://www.state.wv.us/bep/lmi/default.htm
Survey Period: October 2001 - December 2001

Note: All data are provided by the State Employment Security Administration to the Occupational Employment Statistics (OES) survey conducted by the U.S. Department of Labor, Bureau of Labor Statistics.

WW

"The 2001 Salary Survey," *Working Woman*, August 2001, p. 44.

Survey Period: 2000 - 2001

WYBLS

2001 Occupational Employment and Wage Estimates, 2001.

Wyoming Department of Employment
Research and Planning
246 South Cener Street, 2nd Floor
Casper, WY 82601
Telephone: (307) 473-3807
Online: http://wydoe.state.wy.us/
Survey Period: October 2001 - December 2001

Note: All data are provided by the State Employment Security Administration to the Occupational Employment Statistics (OES) survey conducted by the U.S. Department of Labor, Bureau of Labor Statistics.

Appendix II

SALARY CONVERSION TABLE

Hour	Week	Month	Year	Hour	Week	Month	Year	Hour	Week	Month	Year	Hour	Week	Month	Year
2.00	80	346	4,157	4.10	164	710	8,521	6.20	248	1,074	12,886	8.30	332	1,438	17,251
2.05	82	355	4,261	4.15	166	719	8,625	6.25	250	1,083	12,990	8.35	334	1,446	17,355
2.10	84	364	4,365	4.20	168	727	8,729	6.30	252	1,091	13,094	8.40	336	1,455	17,459
2.15	86	372	4,469	4.25	170	736	8,833	6.35	254	1,100	13,198	8.45	338	1,464	17,562
2.20	88	381	4,572	4.30	172	745	8,937	6.40	256	1,108	13,302	8.50	340	1,472	17,666
2.25	90	390	4,676	4.35	174	753	9,041	6.45	258	1,117	13,406	8.55	342	1,481	17,770
2.30	92	398	4,780	4.40	176	762	9,145	6.50	260	1,126	13,510	8.60	344	1,490	17,874
2.35	94	407	4,884	4.45	178	771	9,249	6.55	262	1,134	13,614	8.65	346	1,498	17,978
2.40	96	416	4,988	4.50	180	779	9,353	6.60	264	1,143	13,717	8.70	348	1,507	18,082
2.45	98	424	5,092	4.55	182	788	9,457	6.65	266	1,152	13,821	8.75	350	1,516	18,186
2.50	100	433	5,196	4.60	184	797	9,561	6.70	268	1,160	13,925	8.80	352	1,524	18,290
2.55	102	442	5,300	4.65	186	805	9,665	6.75	270	1,169	14,029	8.85	354	1,533	18,394
2.60	104	450	5,404	4.70	188	814	9,768	6.80	272	1,178	14,133	8.90	356	1,541	18,498
2.65	106	459	5,508	4.75	190	823	9,872	6.85	274	1,186	14,237	8.95	358	1,550	18,602
2.70	108	468	5,612	4.80	192	831	9,976	6.90	276	1,195	14,341	9.00	360	1,559	18,706
2.75	110	476	5,716	4.85	194	840	10,080	6.95	278	1,204	14,445	9.05	362	1,567	18,810
2.80	112	485	5,820	4.90	196	849	10,184	7.00	280	1,212	14,549	9.10	364	1,576	18,913
2.85	114	494	5,923	4.95	198	857	10,288	7.05	282	1,221	14,653	9.15	366	1,585	19,017
2.90	116	502	6,027	5.00	200	866	10,392	7.10	284	1,230	14,757	9.20	368	1,593	19,121
2.95	118	511	6,131	5.05	202	875	10,496	7.15	286	1,238	14,861	9.25	370	1,602	19,225
3.00	120	520	6,235	5.10	204	883	10,600	7.20	288	1,247	14,964	9.30	372	1,611	19,329
3.05	122	528	6,339	5.15	206	892	10,704	7.25	290	1,256	15,068	9.35	374	1,619	19,433
3.10	124	537	6,443	5.20	208	901	10,808	7.30	292	1,264	15,172	9.40	376	1,628	19,537
3.15	126	546	6,547	5.25	210	909	10,912	7.35	294	1,273	15,276	9.45	378	1,637	19,641
3.20	128	554	6,651	5.30	212	918	11,016	7.40	296	1,282	15,380	9.50	380	1,645	19,745
3.25	130	563	6,755	5.35	214	927	11,119	7.45	298	1,290	15,484	9.55	382	1,654	19,849
3.30	132	572	6,859	5.40	216	935	11,223	7.50	300	1,299	15,588	9.60	384	1,663	19,953
3.35	134	580	6,963	5.45	218	944	11,327	7.55	302	1,308	15,692	9.65	386	1,671	20,057
3.40	136	589	7,067	5.50	220	953	11,431	7.60	304	1,316	15,796	9.70	388	1,680	20,160
3.45	138	598	7,170	5.55	222	961	11,535	7.65	306	1,325	15,900	9.75	390	1,689	20,264
3.50	140	606	7,274	5.60	224	970	11,639	7.70	308	1,334	16,004	9.80	392	1,697	20,368
3.55	142	615	7,378	5.65	226	979	11,743	7.75	310	1,342	16,108	9.85	394	1,706	20,472
3.60	144	624	7,482	5.70	228	987	11,847	7.80	312	1,351	16,212	9.90	396	1,715	20,576
3.65	146	632	7,586	5.75	230	996	11,951	7.85	314	1,360	16,315	9.95	398	1,723	20,680
3.70	148	641	7,690	5.80	232	1,005	12,055	7.90	316	1,368	16,419	10.00	400	1,732	20,784
3.75	150	649	7,794	5.85	234	1,013	12,159	7.95	318	1,377	16,523	10.05	402	1,741	20,888
3.80	152	658	7,898	5.90	236	1,022	12,263	8.00	320	1,386	16,627	10.10	404	1,749	20,992
3.85	154	667	8,002	5.95	238	1,031	12,366	8.05	322	1,394	16,731	10.15	406	1,758	21,096
3.90	156	675	8,106	6.00	240	1,039	12,470	8.10	324	1,403	16,835	10.20	408	1,767	21,200
3.95	158	684	8,210	6.05	242	1,048	12,574	8.15	326	1,412	16,939	10.25	410	1,775	21,304
4.00	160	693	8,314	6.10	244	1,057	12,678	8.20	328	1,420	17,043	10.30	412	1,784	21,408
4.05	162	701	8,418	6.15	246	1,065	12,782	8.25	330	1,429	17,147	10.35	414	1,793	21,511

Hour	Week	Month	Year	Hour	Week	Month	Year	Hour	Week	Month	Year	Hour	Week	Month	Year
10.40	416	1,801	21,615	13.15	526	2,278	27,331	15.90	636	2,754	33,047	18.65	746	3,230	38,762
10.45	418	1,810	21,719	13.20	528	2,286	27,435	15.95	638	2,763	33,150	18.70	748	3,239	38,866
10.50	420	1,819	21,823	13.25	530	2,295	27,539	16.00	640	2,771	33,254	18.75	750	3,248	38,970
10.55	422	1,827	21,927	13.30	532	2,304	27,643	16.05	642	2,780	33,358	18.80	752	3,256	39,074
10.60	424	1,836	22,031	13.35	534	2,312	27,747	16.10	644	2,789	33,462	18.85	754	3,265	39,178
10.65	426	1,845	22,135	13.40	536	2,321	27,851	16.15	646	2,797	33,566	18.90	756	3,273	39,282
10.70	428	1,853	22,239	13.45	538	2,330	27,954	16.20	648	2,806	33,670	18.95	758	3,282	39,386
10.75	430	1,862	22,343	13.50	540	2,338	28,058	16.25	650	2,815	33,774	19.00	760	3,291	39,490
10.80	432	1,871	22,447	13.55	542	2,347	28,162	16.30	652	2,823	33,878	19.05	762	3,299	39,594
10.85	434	1,879	22,551	13.60	544	2,356	28,266	16.35	654	2,832	33,982	19.10	764	3,308	39,697
10.90	436	1,888	22,655	13.65	546	2,364	28,370	16.40	656	2,840	34,086	19.15	766	3,317	39,801
10.95	438	1,897	22,758	13.70	548	2,373	28,474	16.45	658	2,849	34,190	19.20	768	3,325	39,905
11.00	440	1,905	22,862	13.75	550	2,382	28,578	16.50	660	2,858	34,294	19.25	770	3,334	40,009
11.05	442	1,914	22,966	13.80	552	2,390	28,682	16.55	662	2,866	34,398	19.30	772	3,343	40,113
11.10	444	1,923	23,070	13.85	554	2,399	28,786	16.60	664	2,875	34,501	19.35	774	3,351	40,217
11.15	446	1,931	23,174	13.90	556	2,407	28,890	16.65	666	2,884	34,605	19.40	776	3,360	40,321
11.20	448	1,940	23,278	13.95	558	2,416	28,994	16.70	668	2,892	34,709	19.45	778	3,369	40,425
11.25	450	1,949	23,382	14.00	560	2,425	29,098	16.75	670	2,901	34,813	19.50	780	3,377	40,529
11.30	452	1,957	23,486	14.05	562	2,433	29,202	16.80	672	2,910	34,917	19.55	782	3,386	40,633
11.35	454	1,966	23,590	14.10	564	2,442	29,305	16.85	674	2,918	35,021	19.60	784	3,395	40,737
11.40	456	1,974	23,694	14.15	566	2,451	29,409	16.90	676	2,927	35,125	19.65	786	3,403	40,841
11.45	458	1,983	23,798	14.20	568	2,459	29,513	16.95	678	2,936	35,229	19.70	788	3,412	40,944
11.50	460	1,992	23,902	14.25	570	2,468	29,617	17.00	680	2,944	35,333	19.75	790	3,421	41,048
11.55	462	2,000	24,006	14.30	572	2,477	29,721	17.05	682	2,953	35,437	19.80	792	3,429	41,152
11.60	464	2,009	24,109	14.35	574	2,485	29,825	17.10	684	2,962	35,541	19.85	794	3,438	41,256
11.65	466	2,018	24,213	14.40	576	2,494	29,929	17.15	686	2,970	35,645	19.90	796	3,447	41,360
11.70	468	2,026	24,317	14.45	578	2,503	30,033	17.20	688	2,979	35,748	19.95	798	3,455	41,464
11.75	470	2,035	24,421	14.50	580	2,511	30,137	17.25	690	2,988	35,852	20.00	800	3,464	41,568
11.80	472	2,044	24,525	14.55	582	2,520	30,241	17.30	692	2,996	35,956	20.05	802	3,473	41,672
11.85	474	2,052	24,629	14.60	584	2,529	30,345	17.35	694	3,005	36,060	20.10	804	3,481	41,776
11.90	476	2,061	24,733	14.65	586	2,537	30,449	17.40	696	3,014	36,164	20.15	806	3,490	41,880
11.95	478	2,070	24,837	14.70	588	2,546	30,552	17.45	698	3,022	36,268	20.20	808	3,499	41,984
12.00	480	2,078	24,941	14.75	590	2,555	30,656	17.50	700	3,031	36,372	20.25	810	3,507	42,088
12.05	482	2,087	25,045	14.80	592	2,563	30,760	17.55	702	3,040	36,476	20.30	812	3,516	42,192
12.10	484	2,096	25,149	14.85	594	2,572	30,864	17.60	704	3,048	36,580	20.35	814	3,525	42,295
12.15	486	2,104	25,253	14.90	596	2,581	30,968	17.65	706	3,057	36,684	20.40	816	3,533	42,399
12.20	488	2,113	25,356	14.95	598	2,589	31,072	17.70	708	3,066	36,788	20.45	818	3,542	42,503
12.25	490	2,122	25,460	15.00	600	2,598	31,176	17.75	710	3,074	36,892	20.50	820	3,551	42,607
12.30	492	2,130	25,564	15.05	602	2,607	31,280	17.80	712	3,083	36,996	20.55	822	3,559	42,711
12.35	494	2,139	25,668	15.10	604	2,615	31,384	17.85	714	3,092	37,099	20.60	824	3,568	42,815
12.40	496	2,148	25,772	15.15	606	2,624	31,488	17.90	716	3,100	37,203	20.65	826	3,577	42,919
12.45	498	2,156	25,876	15.20	608	2,633	31,592	17.95	718	3,109	37,307	20.70	828	3,585	43,023
12.50	500	2,165	25,980	15.25	610	2,641	31,696	18.00	720	3,118	37,411	20.75	830	3,594	43,127
12.55	502	2,174	26,084	15.30	612	2,650	31,800	18.05	722	3,126	37,515	20.80	832	3,603	43,231
12.60	504	2,182	26,188	15.35	614	2,659	31,903	18.10	724	3,135	37,619	20.85	834	3,611	43,335
12.65	506	2,191	26,292	15.40	616	2,667	32,007	18.15	726	3,144	37,723	20.90	836	3,620	43,439
12.70	508	2,200	26,396	15.45	618	2,676	32,111	18.20	728	3,152	37,827	20.95	838	3,629	43,542
12.75	510	2,208	26,500	15.50	620	2,685	32,215	18.25	730	3,161	37,931	21.00	840	3,637	43,646
12.80	512	2,217	26,604	15.55	622	2,693	32,319	18.30	732	3,170	38,035	21.05	842	3,646	43,750
12.85	514	2,226	26,707	15.60	624	2,702	32,423	18.35	734	3,178	38,139	21.10	844	3,655	43,854
12.90	516	2,234	26,811	15.65	626	2,711	32,527	18.40	736	3,187	38,243	21.15	846	3,663	43,958
12.95	518	2,243	26,915	15.70	628	2,719	32,631	18.45	738	3,196	38,346	21.20	848	3,672	44,062
13.00	520	2,252	27,019	15.75	630	2,728	32,735	18.50	740	3,204	38,450	21.25	850	3,680	44,166
13.05	522	2,260	27,123	15.80	632	2,737	32,839	18.55	742	3,213	38,554	21.30	852	3,689	44,270
13.10	524	2,269	27,227	15.85	634	2,745	32,943	18.60	744	3,222	38,658	21.35	854	3,698	44,374

Hour	Week	Month	Year	Hour	Week	Month	Year	Hour	Week	Month	Year	Hour	Week	Month	Year
21.40	856	3,706	44,478	24.15	966	4,183	50,193	26.90	1,076	4,659	55,909	29.65	1,186	5,135	61,625
21.45	858	3,715	44,582	24.20	968	4,191	50,297	26.95	1,078	4,668	56,013	29.70	1,188	5,144	61,728
21.50	860	3,724	44,686	24.25	970	4,200	50,401	27.00	1,080	4,676	56,117	29.75	1,190	5,153	61,832
21.55	862	3,732	44,790	24.30	972	4,209	50,505	27.05	1,082	4,685	56,221	29.80	1,192	5,161	61,936
21.60	864	3,741	44,893	24.35	974	4,217	50,609	27.10	1,084	4,694	56,325	29.85	1,194	5,170	62,040
21.65	866	3,750	44,997	24.40	976	4,226	50,713	27.15	1,086	4,702	56,429	29.90	1,196	5,179	62,144
21.70	868	3,758	45,101	24.45	978	4,235	50,817	27.20	1,088	4,711	56,532	29.95	1,198	5,187	62,248
21.75	870	3,767	45,205	24.50	980	4,243	50,921	27.25	1,090	4,720	56,636	30.00	1,200	5,196	62,352
21.80	872	3,776	45,309	24.55	982	4,252	51,025	27.30	1,092	4,728	56,740	30.05	1,202	5,205	62,456
21.85	874	3,784	45,413	24.60	984	4,261	51,129	27.35	1,094	4,737	56,844	30.10	1,204	5,213	62,560
21.90	876	3,793	45,517	24.65	986	4,269	51,233	27.40	1,096	4,746	56,948	30.15	1,206	5,222	62,664
21.95	878	3,802	45,621	24.70	988	4,278	51,336	27.45	1,098	4,754	57,052	30.20	1,208	5,231	62,768
22.00	880	3,810	45,725	24.75	990	4,287	51,440	27.50	1,100	4,763	57,156	30.25	1,210	5,239	62,872
22.05	882	3,819	45,829	24.80	992	4,295	51,544	27.55	1,102	4,772	57,260	30.30	1,212	5,248	62,976
22.10	884	3,828	45,933	24.85	994	4,304	51,648	27.60	1,104	4,780	57,364	30.35	1,214	5,257	63,079
22.15	886	3,836	46,037	24.90	996	4,313	51,752	27.65	1,106	4,789	57,468	30.40	1,216	5,265	63,183
22.20	888	3,845	46,140	24.95	998	4,321	51,856	27.70	1,108	4,798	57,572	30.45	1,218	5,274	63,287
22.25	890	3,854	46,244	25.00	1,000	4,330	51,960	27.75	1,110	4,806	57,676	30.50	1,220	5,283	63,391
22.30	892	3,862	46,348	25.05	1,002	4,339	52,064	27.80	1,112	4,815	57,780	30.55	1,222	5,291	63,495
22.35	894	3,871	46,452	25.10	1,004	4,347	52,168	27.85	1,114	4,824	57,883	30.60	1,224	5,300	63,599
22.40	896	3,880	46,556	25.15	1,006	4,356	52,272	27.90	1,116	4,832	57,987	30.65	1,226	5,309	63,703
22.45	898	3,888	46,660	25.20	1,008	4,365	52,376	27.95	1,118	4,841	58,091	30.70	1,228	5,317	63,807
22.50	900	3,897	46,764	25.25	1,010	4,373	52,480	28.00	1,120	4,850	58,195	30.75	1,230	5,326	63,911
22.55	902	3,906	46,868	25.30	1,012	4,382	52,584	28.05	1,122	4,858	58,299	30.80	1,232	5,335	64,015
22.60	904	3,914	46,972	25.35	1,014	4,391	52,687	28.10	1,124	4,867	58,403	30.85	1,234	5,343	64,119
22.65	906	3,923	47,076	25.40	1,016	4,399	52,791	28.15	1,126	4,876	58,507	30.90	1,236	5,352	64,223
22.70	908	3,932	47,180	25.45	1,018	4,408	52,895	28.20	1,128	4,884	58,611	30.95	1,238	5,361	64,326
22.75	910	3,940	47,284	25.50	1,020	4,417	52,999	28.25	1,130	4,893	58,715	31.00	1,240	5,369	64,430
22.80	912	3,949	47,388	25.55	1,022	4,425	53,103	28.30	1,132	4,902	58,819	31.05	1,242	5,378	64,534
22.85	914	3,958	47,491	25.60	1,024	4,434	53,207	28.35	1,134	4,910	58,923	31.10	1,244	5,387	64,638
22.90	916	3,966	47,595	25.65	1,026	4,443	53,311	28.40	1,136	4,919	59,027	31.15	1,246	5,395	64,742
22.95	918	3,975	47,699	25.70	1,028	4,451	53,415	28.45	1,138	4,928	59,130	31.20	1,248	5,404	64,846
23.00	920	3,984	47,803	25.75	1,030	4,460	53,519	28.50	1,140	4,936	59,234	31.25	1,250	5,412	64,950
23.05	922	3,992	47,907	25.80	1,032	4,469	53,623	28.55	1,142	4,945	59,338	31.30	1,252	5,421	65,054
23.10	924	4,001	48,011	25.85	1,034	4,477	53,727	28.60	1,144	4,954	59,442	31.35	1,254	5,430	65,158
23.15	926	4,010	48,115	25.90	1,036	4,486	53,831	28.65	1,146	4,962	59,546	31.40	1,256	5,438	65,262
23.20	928	4,018	48,219	25.95	1,038	4,495	53,934	28.70	1,148	4,971	59,650	31.45	1,258	5,447	65,366
23.25	930	4,027	48,323	26.00	1,040	4,503	54,038	28.75	1,150	4,979	59,754	31.50	1,260	5,456	65,470
23.30	932	4,036	48,427	26.05	1,042	4,512	54,142	28.80	1,152	4,988	59,858	31.55	1,262	5,464	65,574
23.35	934	4,044	48,531	26.10	1,044	4,521	54,246	28.85	1,154	4,997	59,962	31.60	1,264	5,473	65,677
23.40	936	4,053	48,635	26.15	1,046	4,529	54,350	28.90	1,156	5,005	60,066	31.65	1,266	5,482	65,781
23.45	938	4,062	48,738	26.20	1,048	4,538	54,454	28.95	1,158	5,014	60,170	31.70	1,268	5,490	65,885
23.50	940	4,070	48,842	26.25	1,050	4,546	54,558	29.00	1,160	5,023	60,274	31.75	1,270	5,499	65,989
23.55	942	4,079	48,946	26.30	1,052	4,555	54,662	29.05	1,162	5,031	60,378	31.80	1,272	5,508	66,093
23.60	944	4,088	49,050	26.35	1,054	4,564	54,766	29.10	1,164	5,040	60,481	31.85	1,274	5,516	66,197
23.65	946	4,096	49,154	26.40	1,056	4,572	54,870	29.15	1,166	5,049	60,585	31.90	1,276	5,525	66,301
23.70	948	4,105	49,258	26.45	1,058	4,581	54,974	29.20	1,168	5,057	60,689	31.95	1,278	5,534	66,405
23.75	950	4,113	49,362	26.50	1,060	4,590	55,078	29.25	1,170	5,066	60,793	32.00	1,280	5,542	66,509
23.80	952	4,122	49,466	26.55	1,062	4,598	55,182	29.30	1,172	5,075	60,897	32.05	1,282	5,551	66,613
23.85	954	4,131	49,570	26.60	1,064	4,607	55,285	29.35	1,174	5,083	61,001	32.10	1,284	5,560	66,717
23.90	956	4,139	49,674	26.65	1,066	4,616	55,389	29.40	1,176	5,092	61,105	32.15	1,286	5,568	66,821
23.95	958	4,148	49,778	26.70	1,068	4,624	55,493	29.45	1,178	5,101	61,209	32.20	1,288	5,577	66,924
24.00	960	4,157	49,882	26.75	1,070	4,633	55,597	29.50	1,180	5,109	61,313	32.25	1,290	5,586	67,028
24.05	962	4,165	49,986	26.80	1,072	4,642	55,701	29.55	1,182	5,118	61,417	32.30	1,292	5,594	67,132
24.10	964	4,174	50,089	26.85	1,074	4,650	55,805	29.60	1,184	5,127	61,521	32.35	1,294	5,603	67,236

Hour	Week	Month	Year	Hour	Week	Month	Year	Hour	Week	Month	Year	Hour	Week	Month	Year
32.40	1,296	5,612	67,340	35.15	1,406	6,088	73,056	37.90	1,516	6,564	78,771	40.65	1,626	7,041	84,487
32.45	1,298	5,620	67,444	35.20	1,408	6,097	73,160	37.95	1,518	6,573	78,875	40.70	1,628	7,049	84,591
32.50	1,300	5,629	67,548	35.25	1,410	6,105	73,264	38.00	1,520	6,582	78,979	40.75	1,630	7,058	84,695
32.55	1,302	5,638	67,652	35.30	1,412	6,114	73,368	38.05	1,522	6,590	79,083	40.80	1,632	7,067	84,799
32.60	1,304	5,646	67,756	35.35	1,414	6,123	73,471	38.10	1,524	6,599	79,187	40.85	1,634	7,075	84,903
32.65	1,306	5,655	67,860	35.40	1,416	6,131	73,575	38.15	1,526	6,608	79,291	40.90	1,636	7,084	85,007
32.70	1,308	5,664	67,964	35.45	1,418	6,140	73,679	38.20	1,528	6,616	79,395	40.95	1,638	7,093	85,110
32.75	1,310	5,672	68,068	35.50	1,420	6,149	73,783	38.25	1,530	6,625	79,499	41.00	1,640	7,101	85,214
32.80	1,312	5,681	68,172	35.55	1,422	6,157	73,887	38.30	1,532	6,634	79,603	41.05	1,642	7,110	85,318
32.85	1,314	5,690	68,275	35.60	1,424	6,166	73,991	38.35	1,534	6,642	79,707	41.10	1,644	7,119	85,422
32.90	1,316	5,698	68,379	35.65	1,426	6,175	74,095	38.40	1,536	6,651	79,811	41.15	1,646	7,127	85,526
32.95	1,318	5,707	68,483	35.70	1,428	6,183	74,199	38.45	1,538	6,660	79,914	41.20	1,648	7,136	85,630
33.00	1,320	5,716	68,587	35.75	1,430	6,192	74,303	38.50	1,540	6,668	80,018	41.25	1,650	7,144	85,734
33.05	1,322	5,724	68,691	35.80	1,432	6,201	74,407	38.55	1,542	6,677	80,122	41.30	1,652	7,153	85,838
33.10	1,324	5,733	68,795	35.85	1,434	6,209	74,511	38.60	1,544	6,686	80,226	41.35	1,654	7,162	85,942
33.15	1,326	5,742	68,899	35.90	1,436	6,218	74,615	38.65	1,546	6,694	80,330	41.40	1,656	7,170	86,046
33.20	1,328	5,750	69,003	35.95	1,438	6,227	74,718	38.70	1,548	6,703	80,434	41.45	1,658	7,179	86,150
33.25	1,330	5,759	69,107	36.00	1,440	6,235	74,822	38.75	1,550	6,711	80,538	41.50	1,660	7,188	86,254
33.30	1,332	5,768	69,211	36.05	1,442	6,244	74,926	38.80	1,552	6,720	80,642	41.55	1,662	7,196	86,358
33.35	1,334	5,776	69,315	36.10	1,444	6,253	75,030	38.85	1,554	6,729	80,746	41.60	1,664	7,205	86,461
33.40	1,336	5,785	69,419	36.15	1,446	6,261	75,134	38.90	1,556	6,737	80,850	41.65	1,666	7,214	86,565
33.45	1,338	5,794	69,522	36.20	1,448	6,270	75,238	38.95	1,558	6,746	80,954	41.70	1,668	7,222	86,669
33.50	1,340	5,802	69,626	36.25	1,450	6,278	75,342	39.00	1,560	6,755	81,058	41.75	1,670	7,231	86,773
33.55	1,342	5,811	69,730	36.30	1,452	6,287	75,446	39.05	1,562	6,763	81,162	41.80	1,672	7,240	86,877
33.60	1,344	5,820	69,834	36.35	1,454	6,296	75,550	39.10	1,564	6,772	81,265	41.85	1,674	7,248	86,981
33.65	1,346	5,828	69,938	36.40	1,456	6,304	75,654	39.15	1,566	6,781	81,369	41.90	1,676	7,257	87,085
33.70	1,348	5,837	70,042	36.45	1,458	6,313	75,758	39.20	1,568	6,789	81,473	41.95	1,678	7,266	87,189
33.75	1,350	5,845	70,146	36.50	1,460	6,322	75,862	39.25	1,570	6,798	81,577	42.00	1,680	7,274	87,293
33.80	1,352	5,854	70,250	36.55	1,462	6,330	75,966	39.30	1,572	6,807	81,681	42.05	1,682	7,283	87,397
33.85	1,354	5,863	70,354	36.60	1,464	6,339	76,069	39.35	1,574	6,815	81,785	42.10	1,684	7,292	87,501
33.90	1,356	5,871	70,458	36.65	1,466	6,348	76,173	39.40	1,576	6,824	81,889	42.15	1,686	7,300	87,605
33.95	1,358	5,880	70,562	36.70	1,468	6,356	76,277	39.45	1,578	6,833	81,993	42.20	1,688	7,309	87,708
34.00	1,360	5,889	70,666	36.75	1,470	6,365	76,381	39.50	1,580	6,841	82,097	42.25	1,690	7,318	87,812
34.05	1,362	5,897	70,770	36.80	1,472	6,374	76,485	39.55	1,582	6,850	82,201	42.30	1,692	7,326	87,916
34.10	1,364	5,906	70,873	36.85	1,474	6,382	76,589	39.60	1,584	6,859	82,305	42.35	1,694	7,335	88,020
34.15	1,366	5,915	70,977	36.90	1,476	6,391	76,693	39.65	1,586	6,867	82,409	42.40	1,696	7,344	88,124
34.20	1,368	5,923	71,081	36.95	1,478	6,400	76,797	39.70	1,588	6,876	82,512	42.45	1,698	7,352	88,228
34.25	1,370	5,932	71,185	37.00	1,480	6,408	76,901	39.75	1,590	6,885	82,616	42.50	1,700	7,361	88,332
34.30	1,372	5,941	71,289	37.05	1,482	6,417	77,005	39.80	1,592	6,893	82,720	42.55	1,702	7,370	88,436
34.35	1,374	5,949	71,393	37.10	1,484	6,426	77,109	39.85	1,594	6,902	82,824	42.60	1,704	7,378	88,540
34.40	1,376	5,958	71,497	37.15	1,486	6,434	77,213	39.90	1,596	6,911	82,928	42.65	1,706	7,387	88,644
34.45	1,378	5,967	71,601	37.20	1,488	6,443	77,316	39.95	1,598	6,919	83,032	42.70	1,708	7,396	88,748
34.50	1,380	5,975	71,705	37.25	1,490	6,452	77,420	40.00	1,600	6,928	83,136	42.75	1,710	7,404	88,852
34.55	1,382	5,984	71,809	37.30	1,492	6,460	77,524	40.05	1,602	6,937	83,240	42.80	1,712	7,413	88,956
34.60	1,384	5,993	71,913	37.35	1,494	6,469	77,628	40.10	1,604	6,945	83,344	42.85	1,714	7,422	89,059
34.65	1,386	6,001	72,017	37.40	1,496	6,478	77,732	40.15	1,606	6,954	83,448	42.90	1,716	7,430	89,163
34.70	1,388	6,010	72,120	37.45	1,498	6,486	77,836	40.20	1,608	6,963	83,552	42.95	1,718	7,439	89,267
34.75	1,390	6,019	72,224	37.50	1,500	6,495	77,940	40.25	1,610	6,971	83,656	43.00	1,720	7,448	89,371
34.80	1,392	6,027	72,328	37.55	1,502	6,504	78,044	40.30	1,612	6,980	83,760	43.05	1,722	7,456	89,475
34.85	1,394	6,036	72,432	37.60	1,504	6,512	78,148	40.35	1,614	6,989	83,863	43.10	1,724	7,465	89,579
34.90	1,396	6,045	72,536	37.65	1,506	6,521	78,252	40.40	1,616	6,997	83,967	43.15	1,726	7,474	89,683
34.95	1,398	6,053	72,640	37.70	1,508	6,530	78,356	40.45	1,618	7,006	84,071	43.20	1,728	7,482	89,787
35.00	1,400	6,062	72,744	37.75	1,510	6,538	78,460	40.50	1,620	7,015	84,175	43.25	1,730	7,491	89,891
35.05	1,402	6,071	72,848	37.80	1,512	6,547	78,564	40.55	1,622	7,023	84,279	43.30	1,732	7,500	89,995
35.10	1,404	6,079	72,952	37.85	1,514	6,556	78,667	40.60	1,624	7,032	84,383	43.35	1,734	7,508	90,099

Hour	Week	Month	Year	Hour	Week	Month	Year	Hour	Week	Month	Year	Hour	Week	Month	Year
43.40	1,736	7,517	90,203	46.15	1,846	7,993	95,918	48.90	1,956	8,469	101,634	51.65	2,066	8,946	107,349
43.45	1,738	7,526	90,306	46.20	1,848	8,002	96,022	48.95	1,958	8,478	101,738	51.70	2,068	8,954	107,453
43.50	1,740	7,534	90,410	46.25	1,850	8,010	96,126	49.00	1,960	8,487	101,842	51.75	2,070	8,963	107,557
43.55	1,742	7,543	90,514	46.30	1,852	8,019	96,230	49.05	1,962	8,495	101,946	51.80	2,072	8,972	107,661
43.60	1,744	7,552	90,618	46.35	1,854	8,028	96,334	49.10	1,964	8,504	102,049	51.85	2,074	8,980	107,765
43.65	1,746	7,560	90,722	46.40	1,856	8,036	96,438	49.15	1,966	8,513	102,153	51.90	2,076	8,989	107,869
43.70	1,748	7,569	90,826	46.45	1,858	8,045	96,542	49.20	1,968	8,521	102,257	51.95	2,078	8,998	107,973
43.75	1,750	7,577	90,930	46.50	1,860	8,054	96,646	49.25	1,970	8,530	102,361	52.00	2,080	9,006	108,077
43.80	1,752	7,586	91,034	46.55	1,862	8,062	96,750	49.30	1,972	8,539	102,465	52.05	2,082	9,015	108,181
43.85	1,754	7,595	91,138	46.60	1,864	8,071	96,853	49.35	1,974	8,547	102,569	52.10	2,084	9,024	108,285
43.90	1,756	7,603	91,242	46.65	1,866	8,080	96,957	49.40	1,976	8,556	102,673	52.15	2,086	9,032	108,389
43.95	1,758	7,612	91,346	46.70	1,868	8,088	97,061	49.45	1,978	8,565	102,777	52.20	2,088	9,041	108,492
44.00	1,760	7,621	91,450	46.75	1,870	8,097	97,165	49.50	1,980	8,573	102,881	52.25	2,090	9,050	108,596
44.05	1,762	7,629	91,554	46.80	1,872	8,106	97,269	49.55	1,982	8,582	102,985	52.30	2,092	9,058	108,700
44.10	1,764	7,638	91,657	46.85	1,874	8,114	97,373	49.60	1,984	8,591	103,089	52.35	2,094	9,067	108,804
44.15	1,766	7,647	91,761	46.90	1,876	8,123	97,477	49.65	1,986	8,599	103,193	52.40	2,096	9,076	108,908
44.20	1,768	7,655	91,865	46.95	1,878	8,132	97,581	49.70	1,988	8,608	103,296	52.45	2,098	9,084	109,012
44.25	1,770	7,664	91,969	47.00	1,880	8,140	97,685	49.75	1,990	8,617	103,400	52.50	2,100	9,093	109,116
44.30	1,772	7,673	92,073	47.05	1,882	8,149	97,789	49.80	1,992	8,625	103,504	52.55	2,102	9,102	109,220
44.35	1,774	7,681	92,177	47.10	1,884	8,158	97,893	49.85	1,994	8,634	103,608	52.60	2,104	9,110	109,324
44.40	1,776	7,690	92,281	47.15	1,886	8,166	97,997	49.90	1,996	8,643	103,712	52.65	2,106	9,119	109,428
44.45	1,778	7,699	92,385	47.20	1,888	8,175	98,100	49.95	1,998	8,651	103,816	52.70	2,108	9,128	109,532
44.50	1,780	7,707	92,489	47.25	1,890	8,184	98,204	50.00	2,000	8,660	103,920	52.75	2,110	9,136	109,636
44.55	1,782	7,716	92,593	47.30	1,892	8,192	98,308	50.05	2,002	8,669	104,024	52.80	2,112	9,145	109,740
44.60	1,784	7,725	92,697	47.35	1,894	8,201	98,412	50.10	2,004	8,677	104,128	52.85	2,114	9,154	109,843
44.65	1,786	7,733	92,801	47.40	1,896	8,210	98,516	50.15	2,006	8,686	104,232	52.90	2,116	9,162	109,947
44.70	1,788	7,742	92,904	47.45	1,898	8,218	98,620	50.20	2,008	8,695	104,336	52.95	2,118	9,171	110,051
44.75	1,790	7,751	93,008	47.50	1,900	8,227	98,724	50.25	2,010	8,703	104,440	53.00	2,120	9,180	110,155
44.80	1,792	7,759	93,112	47.55	1,902	8,236	98,828	50.30	2,012	8,712	104,544	53.05	2,122	9,188	110,259
44.85	1,794	7,768	93,216	47.60	1,904	8,244	98,932	50.35	2,014	8,721	104,647	53.10	2,124	9,197	110,363
44.90	1,796	7,777	93,320	47.65	1,906	8,253	99,036	50.40	2,016	8,729	104,751	53.15	2,126	9,206	110,467
44.95	1,798	7,785	93,424	47.70	1,908	8,262	99,140	50.45	2,018	8,738	104,855	53.20	2,128	9,214	110,571
45.00	1,800	7,794	93,528	47.75	1,910	8,270	99,244	50.50	2,020	8,747	104,959	53.25	2,130	9,223	110,675
45.05	1,802	7,803	93,632	47.80	1,912	8,279	99,348	50.55	2,022	8,755	105,063	53.30	2,132	9,232	110,779
45.10	1,804	7,811	93,736	47.85	1,914	8,288	99,451	50.60	2,024	8,764	105,167	53.35	2,134	9,240	110,883
45.15	1,806	7,820	93,840	47.90	1,916	8,296	99,555	50.65	2,026	8,773	105,271	53.40	2,136	9,249	110,987
45.20	1,808	7,829	93,944	47.95	1,918	8,305	99,659	50.70	2,028	8,781	105,375	53.45	2,138	9,258	111,090
45.25	1,810	7,837	94,048	48.00	1,920	8,314	99,763	50.75	2,030	8,790	105,479	53.50	2,140	9,266	111,194
45.30	1,812	7,846	94,152	48.05	1,922	8,322	99,867	50.80	2,032	8,799	105,583	53.55	2,142	9,275	111,298
45.35	1,814	7,855	94,255	48.10	1,924	8,331	99,971	50.85	2,034	8,807	105,687	53.60	2,144	9,284	111,402
45.40	1,816	7,863	94,359	48.15	1,926	8,340	100,075	50.90	2,036	8,816	105,791	53.65	2,146	9,292	111,506
45.45	1,818	7,872	94,463	48.20	1,928	8,348	100,179	50.95	2,038	8,825	105,894	53.70	2,148	9,301	111,610
45.50	1,820	7,881	94,567	48.25	1,930	8,357	100,283	51.00	2,040	8,833	105,998	53.75	2,150	9,309	111,714
45.55	1,822	7,889	94,671	48.30	1,932	8,366	100,387	51.05	2,042	8,842	106,102	53.80	2,152	9,318	111,818
45.60	1,824	7,898	94,775	48.35	1,934	8,374	100,491	51.10	2,044	8,851	106,206	53.85	2,154	9,327	111,922
45.65	1,826	7,907	94,879	48.40	1,936	8,383	100,595	51.15	2,046	8,859	106,310	53.90	2,156	9,335	112,026
45.70	1,828	7,915	94,983	48.45	1,938	8,392	100,698	51.20	2,048	8,868	106,414	53.95	2,158	9,344	112,130
45.75	1,830	7,924	95,087	48.50	1,940	8,400	100,802	51.25	2,050	8,876	106,518	54.00	2,160	9,353	112,234
45.80	1,832	7,933	95,191	48.55	1,942	8,409	100,906	51.30	2,052	8,885	106,622	54.05	2,162	9,361	112,338
45.85	1,834	7,941	95,295	48.60	1,944	8,418	101,010	51.35	2,054	8,894	106,726	54.10	2,164	9,370	112,441
45.90	1,836	7,950	95,399	48.65	1,946	8,426	101,114	51.40	2,056	8,902	106,830	54.15	2,166	9,379	112,545
45.95	1,838	7,959	95,502	48.70	1,948	8,435	101,218	51.45	2,058	8,911	106,934	54.20	2,168	9,387	112,649
46.00	1,840	7,967	95,606	48.75	1,950	8,443	101,322	51.50	2,060	8,920	107,038	54.25	2,170	9,396	112,753
46.05	1,842	7,976	95,710	48.80	1,952	8,452	101,426	51.55	2,062	8,928	107,142	54.30	2,172	9,405	112,857
46.10	1,844	7,985	95,814	48.85	1,954	8,461	101,530	51.60	2,064	8,937	107,245	54.35	2,174	9,413	112,961

Appendix III

ABBREVIATIONS

Acronyms used to abbreviate data sources may be found in Appendix I.

AAW	Average annual wage
ABA	American Bar Association
AE	Average entry wage paid
AEX	Average experienced wage
AHW	Average hourly wage
AO	Avcragc offered
AOH	Average offered, high
AOL	Average offered, low
APH	Average pay, high range
APL	Average pay, low range
ASL	Average starting salary, low range
ASH	Average starting salary, high range
ASW	Average senior wage
AW	Average wage paid
AWO	Average wage offered
AWR	Average wage range
BLS	Bureau of Labor Statistics
BOR	Beginning of range
BR	Beginning range
CBT	Computer-based Training
CEO	Chief Executive Officer
D	Daily
EMT	Emergency Medical Technician
ENF	Experienced; new to firm
EOR	End of range
FBI	Federal Bureau of Investigation
FQ	First quartile wage
GED	General Educational Development
GS	Government Service (grade)
H	Hourly
HI	Highest wage paid
HIO	Highest wage offered
HR	High end of range
HTML	Hypertext Markup Language
IR	Intermediate range
LO	Lowest wage paid
LOO	Lowest wage offered
LR	Low end of range
M	Monthly
MDO	Median wage offered
MRI	Magnetic Resonance Imaging
MSN	Master of Science, Nursing
MW	Median wage paid
p	Publication date
RN	Registered Nurse
S	Special: hourly and annual
SQ	Second quartile wage
SR	Senior range
TMC	Total Median Compensation
TQ	Third quartile wage
W	Weekly
WEB	World-wide web
WWW	World-wide web
Y	Yearly

Appendix IV

EMPLOYMENT BY OCCUPATION - 2000 AND 2010

This appendix displays data from the *National Industry-Occupational Matrix* prepared by the Department of Labor (DOL) from time to time. The data show employment by occuption for 2000 with DOL projections to 2010. The appendix is divided into three parts. The first part shows the occupations in alphabetical order using occupation titles as defined by DOL. The only exceptions are cases where the DOL refers to "All other" followed by an occupation. These have been rendered by the name of the occupation, followed by the abbreviation 'nsk' to indicate 'not specified by kind.' The second arrangement shows occupations by 2000 employment, largest category first. The third sort is by rate of growth, 2000 to 2010, the fastest growing occupation shown first. Data were released in November 2001 and are referred to as *National OES Matrices*.

Alphabetical Order

Total Employment 2000	2010	% Change	Occupation
975,783	1,156,777	18.5	Accountants and auditors
99,181	125,665	26.7	Actors
14,271	15,044	5.4	Actuaries
14,261	14,413	1.1	Administrative law judges, adjudicators, and hearing officers
362,038	435,990	20.4	Administrative services managers
66,569	79,514	19.4	Adult literacy, remedial education, and GED teachers
100,475	134,906	34.3	Advertising and promotions managers
155,066	195,843	26.3	Advertising sales agents
21,062	22,241	5.6	Aerospace engineering and operations technicians
50,434	57,437	13.9	Aerospace engineers
17,461	22,339	27.9	Agents and business managers of artists, performers, athletes
17,604	20,281	15.2	Agricultural and food science technicians
17,461	19,005	8.8	Agricultural and food scientists
2,400	2,754	14.8	Agricultural engineers
14,964	15,958	6.6	Agricultural inspectors
26,645	28,566	7.2	Air traffic controllers
17,003	22,477	32.2	Air transportation workers, nsk
9,949	12,704	27.7	Aircraft cargo handling supervisors
157,884	184,176	16.7	Aircraft mechanics and service technicians
20,057	22,897	14.2	Aircraft structure, surfaces, rigging, and systems assemblers
4,815	6,118	27.1	Airfield operations specialists
98,080	104,391	6.4	Airline pilots, copilots, and flight engineers
549,010	618,980	12.7	All other production workers
34,543	38,208	10.6	All other woodworkers
15,249	20,384	33.7	Ambulance drivers and attendants, except emergency technicians
196,794	260,473	32.4	Amusement and recreation attendants
8,608	9,712	12.8	Animal control workers
14,579	17,256	18.4	Animal trainers
71,468	67,502	-5.5	Announcers
56,811	67,031	18.0	Appraisers and assessors of real estate
4,422	5,626	27.2	Arbitrators, mediators, and conciliators
102,403	121,320	18.5	Architects, except landscape and naval
6,252	8,037	28.5	Architects, surveyors, and cartographers, nsk
101,853	123,006	20.8	Architectural and civil drafters
21,494	24,053	11.9	Archivists, curators, and museum technicians
111,577	130,344	16.8	Art and design workers, nsk
46,517	56,346	21.1	Art directors
438,882	506,523	15.4	Assemblers and fabricators, nsk
10,063	11,121	10.5	Astronomers and physicists
17,735	21,724	22.5	Athletes and sports competitors
14,508	17,191	18.5	Athletic trainers
6,894	8,075	17.1	Atmospheric and space scientists
37,010	43,217	16.8	Audio and video equipment technicians
11,473	13,039	13.6	Audio-visual collections specialists
12,790	18,507	44.7	Audiologists
198,955	219,243	10.2	Automotive body and related repairers
21,955	24,262	10.5	Automotive glass installers and repairers
839,689	990,739	18.0	Automotive service technicians and mechanics
15,534	17,063	9.8	Avionics technicians
50,897	57,306	12.6	Baggage porters and bellhops
13,625	15,334	12.5	Bailiffs
159,912	186,706	16.8	Bakers
72,727	64,332	-11.5	Barbers
386,890	438,622	13.4	Bartenders
8,536	10,049	17.7	Bicycle repairers
400,233	501,615	25.3	Bill and account collectors
506,221	549,467	8.5	Billing and posting clerks and machine operators
105,476	113,226	7.3	Bindery workers
73,101	88,483	21.0	Biological scientists
41,465	52,424	26.4	Biological technicians
7,221	9,487	31.4	Biomedical engineers
26,960	27,523	2.1	Boilermakers
9,636	10,424	8.2	Bookbinders
1,990,762	2,030,069	2.0	Bookkeeping, accounting, and auditing clerks
144,380	162,426	12.5	Brickmasons and blockmasons
4,482	3,627	-19.1	Bridge and lock tenders
36,153	39,847	10.2	Broadcast technicians
69,537	68,552	-1.4	Brokerage clerks
70,019	80,238	14.6	Budget analysts
158,637	189,743	19.6	Building and grounds cleaning and maintenance workers, nsk
285,208	325,633	14.2	Bus and truck mechanics and diesel engine specialists
481,163	537,031	11.6	Bus drivers, school
184,547	216,627	17.4	Bus drivers, transit and intercity
826,925	959,852	16.1	Business operations specialists
141,071	128,500	-8.9	Butchers and meat cutters

Total Employment 2000	2010	% Change	Occupation
159,274	174,841	9.8	Cabinetmakers and bench carpenters
7,199	7,050	-2.1	Camera and photographic equipment repairers
26,526	33,364	25.8	Camera operators, television, video, and motion picture
38,663	52,174	34.9	Cardiovascular technologists and technicians
60,047	65,043	8.3	Cargo and freight agents
1,204,050	1,302,235	8.2	Carpenters
76,007	83,963	10.5	Carpet installers
6,995	8,292	18.5	Cartographers and photogrammetrists
3,324,980	3,798,735	14.2	Cashiers, except gaming
162,485	167,388	3.0	Cement masons and concrete finishers
35,614	38,016	6.7	Cementing and gluing machine operators and tenders
138,572	150,975	9.0	Chefs and head cooks
32,883	34,236	4.1	Chemical engineers
61,007	70,107	14.9	Chemical equipment operators and tenders
71,256	68,940	-3.3	Chemical plant and system operators
73,454	84,447	15.0	Chemical technicians
84,323	100,469	19.1	Chemists
547,042	640,925	17.2	Chief executives
1,192,578	1,319,338	10.6	Child care workers
281,306	356,975	26.9	Child, family, and school social workers
49,949	61,654	23.4	Chiropractors
10,808	12,418	14.9	Choreographers
93,503	104,607	11.9	Civil engineering technicians
232,046	255,826	10.2	Civil engineers
193,989	223,280	15.1	Claims adjusters, examiners, and investigators
321,580	381,897	18.8	Cleaners of vehicles and equipment
20,275	17,390	-14.2	Cleaning, washing, and metal pickling equipment workers
171,337	197,112	15.0	Clergy
99,391	116,854	17.6	Coaches and scouts
107,975	120,858	11.9	Coating, painting, and spraying machine workers
55,998	60,577	8.2	Coil winders, tapers, and finishers
36,803	43,594	18.5	Coin, vending, and amusement machine servicers and repairers
2,206,226	2,878,799	30.5	Combined food preparation and serving workers
50,036	61,924	23.8	Commercial and industrial designers
19,256	24,431	26.9	Commercial pilots
26,083	20,407	-21.8	Communications equipment operators, nsk
86,611	100,200	15.7	Compensation, benefits, and job analysis specialists
139,736	152,137	8.9	Compliance officers, exc. agriculture, construction, health
28,046	39,354	40.3	Computer and information scientists, research
312,953	462,923	47.9	Computer and information systems managers
59,964	74,909	24.9	Computer hardware engineers
194,438	161,171	-17.1	Computer operators
585,386	679,956	16.2	Computer programmers
379,969	760,059	100.0	Computer software engineers, applications
316,858	601,225	89.7	Computer software engineers, systems software
202,892	326,053	60.7	Computer specialists, nsk
505,616	995,915	97.0	Computer support specialists
431,428	689,183	59.7	Computer systems analysts
172,253	196,751	14.2	Computer, automated teller, and office machine repairers
161,979	193,850	19.7	Computer-controlled machine tool operators, metal and plastic
17,536	20,291	15.7	Concierges
16,192	17,536	8.3	Conservation scientists
74,590	85,772	15.0	Construction and building inspectors
123,010	155,869	26.7	Construction and related workers, nsk
791,324	925,980	17.0	Construction laborers
307,826	358,068	16.3	Construction managers
9,530	8,252	-13.4	Continuous mining machine operators
34,264	35,205	2.7	Control and valve installers, except mechanical door
63,006	71,400	13.3	Conveyor operators and tenders
521,560	517,855	-0.7	Cooks, fast food
464,756	499,968	7.6	Cooks, institution and cafeteria
5,250	4,307	-18.0	Cooks, private household
667,748	812,886	21.7	Cooks, restaurant
205,003	218,965	6.8	Cooks, short order
7,166	7,071	-1.3	Cooling and freezing equipment operators and tenders
413,781	547,921	32.4	Correctional officers and jailers
38,360	41,836	9.1	Correspondence clerks
210,920	245,815	16.5	Cost estimators
23,820	28,367	19.1	Costume, locker room and other attendants
244,421	290,389	18.8	Counselors, social, and religious workers, nsk
423,463	505,743	19.4	Counter and rental clerks
420,804	481,560	14.4	Counter attendants, cafeteria, food concession, and coffee shop
140,893	135,422	-3.9	Couriers and Messengers
18,385	21,360	16.2	Court reporters
104,709	117,276	12.0	Court, municipal, and license clerks
54,585	59,303	8.6	Crane and tower operators
60,035	69,625	16.0	Credit analysts
86,473	90,061	4.1	Credit authorizers, checkers, and clerks
74,079	80,510	8.7	Crossing guards
44,353	48,692	9.8	Crushing, grinding, and polishing machine workers
1,945,945	2,577,287	32.4	Customer service representatives
32,399	33,115	2.2	Cutters and trimmers, hand
82,725	84,131	1.7	Cutting and slicing machine workers
371,706	356,847	-4.0	Cutting, punching, and press machine workers, metal and plastic
15,243	17,884	17.3	Dancers
509,404	534,479	4.9	Data entry keyers
106,007	175,872	65.9	Database administrators
117,613	146,895	24.9	Demonstrators and product promoters
246,970	338,732	37.2	Dental assistants
146,629	201,033	37.1	Dental hygienists
43,017	45,730	6.3	Dental laboratory technicians
152,450	161,206	5.7	Dentists
16,109	16,122	0.1	Derrick operators, oil and gas
37,956	63,286	66.7	Desktop publishers
93,206	108,460	16.4	Detectives and criminal investigators
32,815	41,395	26.1	Diagnostic medical sonographers
25,648	32,736	27.6	Dietetic technicians
48,740	56,140	15.2	Dietitians and nutritionists
430,819	402,101	-6.7	Dining room and cafeteria attendants and bartender helpers
121,300	140,552	15.9	Directors, religious activities and education
524,549	482,620	-8.0	Dishwashers
168,294	205,624	22.2	Dispatchers, except police, fire, and ambulance
165,861	155,645	-6.2	Door-to-door sales workers, vendors, and related workers
155,727	191,922	23.2	Drafters, engineering, and mapping technicians, nsk
71,162	67,945	-4.5	Drilling and boring machine tool workers, metal and plastic
401,764	430,395	7.1	Driver/sales workers

Total Employment 2000	2010	% Change	Occupation
143,472	156,900	9.4	Drywall and ceiling tile installers
23,649	26,633	12.6	Earth drillers, except oil and gas
21,702	25,708	18.5	Economists
121,648	149,115	22.6	Editors
452,838	513,379	13.4	Education administrators
205,482	257,466	25.3	Educational, vocational, and school counselors
36,853	39,780	7.9	Electric motor, power tool, and related repairers
232,736	257,850	10.8	Electrical and electronic engineering technicians
378,772	354,979	-6.3	Electrical and electronic equipment assemblers
47,666	54,059	13.4	Electrical and electronic equipment mechanics, nsk
41,069	50,650	23.3	Electrical and electronics drafters
89,699	97,976	9.2	Electrical and electronics repairers, commercial/industrial
18,101	17,689	-2.3	Electrical and electronics repairers, power
13,594	15,444	13.6	Electrical and electronics repairers, transportation equipment
157,188	174,934	11.3	Electrical engineers
99,181	108,360	9.3	Electrical power-line installers and repairers
698,398	818,879	17.3	Electricians
43,451	49,740	14.5	Electro-mechanical technicians
72,976	76,231	4.5	Electromechanical equipment assemblers
12,809	14,805	15.6	Electronic equipment installers and repairers, motor vehicles
36,779	30,204	-17.9	Electronic home entertainment equipment installers and repairers
130,366	143,941	10.4	Electronics engineers, except computer
1,532,103	1,734,335	13.2	Elementary school teachers, except special education
23,076	27,045	17.2	Elevator installers and repairers
116,921	106,104	-9.3	Eligibility interviewers, government programs
7,180	7,140	-0.6	Embalmers
10,219	12,066	18.1	Emergency management specialists
172,110	225,996	31.3	Emergency medical technicians and paramedics
198,907	233,876	17.6	Employment, recruitment, and placement specialists
67,239	71,996	7.1	Engine and other machine assemblers
282,051	304,720	8.0	Engineering managers
252,988	254,022	0.4	Engineers, nsk
73,958	94,919	28.3	Entertainers and performers, sports and related workers, nsk
18,325	23,663	29.1	Environmental engineering technicians
52,421	66,034	26.0	Environmental engineers
27,133	33,778	24.5	Environmental science and protection technicians
63,723	77,954	22.3	Environmental scientists and specialists, including health
14,697	16,335	11.1	Etchers and engravers
76,455	87,786	14.8	Excavating and loading machine and dragline operators
1,445,097	1,611,832	11.5	Executive secretaries and administrative assistants
5,081	5,177	1.9	Explosives workers, ordnance handling experts, and blasters
18,851	16,840	-10.7	Extraction workers, nsk
125,987	142,944	13.5	Extruding and drawing machine workers, metal and plastic
41,356	43,716	5.7	Extruding and forming machine workers, synthetic/glass fibers
73,428	80,040	9.0	Extruding, forming, pressing, and compacting machine workers

Total Employment 2000	2010	% Change	Occupation
15,031	14,220	-5.4	Fabric and apparel patternmakers
13,415	12,251	-8.7	Fallers
10,682	11,333	6.1	Farm and home management advisors
41,172	41,528	0.9	Farm equipment mechanics
168,716	178,913	6.0	Farm, ranch, and other agricultural managers
1,293,664	965,479	-25.4	Farmers and ranchers
199,020	208,769	4.9	Farming, fishing, and forestry workers, nsk
908,779	938,799	3.3	Farmworkers
16,111	19,383	20.3	Fashion designers
28,957	30,297	4.6	Fence erectors
47,951	53,434	11.4	Fiberglass laminators and fabricators
287,725	313,993	9.1	File clerks
15,999	20,132	25.8	Film and video editors
144,730	181,689	25.5	Financial analysts
24,830	27,351	10.2	Financial examiners
657,944	779,821	18.5	Financial managers
169,127	216,466	28.0	Financial specialists, nsk
211,090	251,887	19.3	Financial, information, and record clerks, nsk
30,813	34,939	13.4	Fine artists, including painters, sculptors, and illustrators
257,568	280,432	8.9	Fire fighters
12,644	14,555	15.1	Fire inspectors
792,225	922,737	16.5	First-line supervisors of construction trades and mining workers
29,692	38,487	29.6	First-line supervisors of correctional officers
99,958	112,955	13.0	First-line supervisors of farming, fishing, forestry workers
61,664	66,075	7.2	First-line supervisors of fire fighting and prevention workers
648,944	731,468	12.7	First-line supervisors of food preparation and serving workers
153,121	182,020	18.9	First-line supervisors of helpers, laborers, and movers
218,904	249,957	14.2	First-line supervisors of housekeeping and janitorial workers
159,092	191,068	20.1	First-line supervisors of landscaping, lawn service workers
442,039	512,755	16.0	First-line supervisors of mechanics, installers, and repairers
432,285	457,224	5.8	First-line supervisors of non-retail sales workers
1,391,544	1,521,895	9.4	First-line supervisors of office workers
124,726	143,579	15.1	First-line supervisors of personal service workers
120,522	136,356	13.1	First-line supervisors of police and detectives
818,756	827,296	1.0	First-line supervisors of production and operating workers
61,116	77,689	27.1	First-line supervisors of protective service workers
2,071,641	2,240,113	8.1	First-line supervisors of retail sales workers
194,016	232,594	19.9	First-line supervisors of transportation workers and drivers
8,136	9,060	11.4	Fish and game wardens
52,737	46,312	-12.2	Fishers and fishing vessel operators
158,314	222,192	40.3	Fitness trainers and aerobics instructors
124,088	146,864	18.4	Flight attendants
23,236	26,897	15.8	Floor layers, except carpet, wood, and hard tiles
13,709	15,725	14.7	Floor sanders and finishers
102,447	117,735	14.9	Floral designers
18,236	16,589	-9.0	Food and tobacco roasting, drying machine operators and tenders

Total Employment 2000	2010	% Change	Occupation
65,800	66,736	1.4	Food batchmakers
37,120	37,344	0.6	Food cooking machine operators and tenders
143,444	136,787	-4.6	Food preparation and serving related workers, nsk
844,403	987,512	16.9	Food preparation workers
68,535	60,587	-11.6	Food processing workers, nsk
204,515	238,076	16.4	Food servers, nonrestaurant
465,172	534,882	15.0	Food service managers
6,399	7,230	13.0	Forensic science technicians
18,013	18,598	3.2	Forest and conservation technicians
21,334	22,162	3.9	Forest and conservation workers
12,440	13,314	7.0	Foresters
53,706	58,574	9.1	Forging machine workers, metal and plastic
59,308	58,575	-1.2	Foundry mold and coremakers
26,139	30,792	17.8	Funeral attendants
31,504	32,452	3.0	Funeral directors
32,559	33,591	3.2	Furnace, kiln, oven, drier, and kettle operators and tenders
45,403	49,229	8.4	Furniture finishers
12,154	14,776	21.6	Gaming and sports book writers and runners
21,837	27,339	25.2	Gaming cage workers
38,123	51,894	36.1	Gaming change persons and booth cashiers
87,648	116,064	32.4	Gaming dealers
4,160	5,410	30.0	Gaming managers
31,488	37,285	18.4	Gaming supervisors
10,989	12,836	16.8	Gaming surveillance officers and gaming investigators
6,682	7,001	4.8	Gas compressor and gas pumping station operators
12,087	11,321	-6.3	Gas plant operators
2,397,567	2,760,863	15.2	General and operations managers
10,105	10,757	6.5	Geological and petroleum technicians
25,497	30,103	18.1	Geoscientists, except hydrologists and geographers
48,670	55,855	14.8	Glaziers
63,257	69,002	9.1	Graders and sorters, agricultural products
189,911	240,705	26.7	Graphic designers
48,707	55,358	13.7	Grinding and polishing workers, hand
145,245	155,802	7.3	Grinding, lapping, polishing machine workers, metal and plastic
636,112	718,494	13.0	Hairdressers, hairstylists, and cosmetologists
20,878	24,777	18.7	Haming service workers, nsk
36,920	49,025	32.8	Hazardous materials removal workers
44,368	49,203	10.9	Health and safety engineers, except mining
57,062	71,196	24.8	Health diagnosing and treating practitioners, nsk
43,053	53,177	23.5	Health educators
211,533	253,194	19.7	Health practitioners and technical workers, nsk
181,119	219,387	21.1	Healthcare support workers, nsk
42,902	48,647	13.4	Heat treating equipment workers, metal and plastic
243,058	297,290	22.3	Heating, air conditioning, refrigeration mechanics
40,997	52,922	29.1	Helpers, construction trades, nsk
58,015	66,185	14.1	Helpers-Brickmasons, stonemasons, and tile and marble setters
100,919	107,601	6.6	Helpers-Carpenters
114,189	129,430	13.3	Helpers-Electricians
37,046	37,942	2.4	Helpers-Extraction workers
145,403	172,238	18.5	Helpers-Installation, maintenance, and repair workers
26,633	30,069	12.9	Helpers-Painters, paperhangers, plasterers, and stucco masons
86,128	96,039	11.5	Helpers-Pipelayers, plumbers, pipefitters, and steamfitters
524,513	586,810	11.9	Helpers-Production workers
23,442	27,957	19.3	Helpers-Roofers
151,167	158,998	5.2	Highway maintenance workers
8,892	9,633	8.3	Hoist and winch operators
42,999	45,676	6.2	Home appliance repairers
615,381	906,633	47.3	Home health aides
343,380	388,133	13.0	Hosts and hostesses, restaurant, lounge, and coffee shop
176,738	235,701	33.4	Hotel, motel, and resort desk clerks
177,187	211,407	19.3	Human resources assistants, except payroll and timekeeping
218,582	246,370	12.7	Human resources managers
7,837	9,854	25.7	Hydrologists
52,118	57,378	10.1	Industrial engineering technicians
153,636	160,550	4.5	Industrial engineers
198,276	204,992	3.4	Industrial machinery mechanics
255,418	271,128	6.2	Industrial production managers
634,899	706,914	11.3	Industrial truck and tractor operators
602,132	590,910	-1.9	Inspectors, testers, sorters, samplers, and weighers
227,925	254,202	11.5	Installation, maintenance, and repair workers, nsk
80,847	101,075	25.0	Instructional coordinators
52,893	60,102	13.6	Insulation workers
12,739	14,555	14.3	Insurance appraisers, auto damage
289,155	230,713	-20.2	Insurance claims and policy processing clerks
377,750	390,286	3.3	Insurance sales agents
106,547	108,650	2.0	Insurance underwriters
45,615	53,560	17.4	Interior designers
21,816	27,004	23.8	Interpreters and translators
153,888	205,347	33.4	Interviewers, except eligibility and loan
2,348,069	2,665,022	13.5	Janitors and cleaners, except maids and housekeeping cleaners
43,368	43,945	1.3	Jewelers and precious stone and metal workers
55,601	59,183	6.4	Job printers
24,008	24,269	1.1	Judges, magistrate judges, and magistrates
174,658	199,954	14.5	Kindergarten teachers, except special education
2,084,333	2,373,478	13.9	Laborers and freight, stock, and material movers
21,747	28,513	31.1	Landscape architects
894,187	1,153,717	29.0	Landscaping and groundskeeping workers
83,718	77,507	-7.4	Lathe and turning machine tool workers, metal and plastic
235,708	262,567	11.4	Laundry and dry-cleaning workers
31,290	35,431	13.2	Law clerks
680,794	803,355	18.0	Lawyers
18,378	17,271	-6.0	Lay-out workers, metal and plastic
108,947	130,953	20.2	Legal and related workers, nsk
279,164	335,892	20.3	Legal secretaries
54,336	61,242	12.7	Legislators
149,325	159,766	7.0	Librarians
98,348	117,738	19.7	Library assistants, clerical
108,904	130,098	19.5	Library technicians
87,131	99,309	14.0	Library, museum, training, and education workers, nsk
699,600	841,924	20.3	Licensed practical and licensed vocational nurses
28,233	32,724	15.9	Life scientists, nsk
132,630	161,355	21.7	Life, physical, and social science technicians, nsk
28,738	33,325	16.0	Loan counselors

Total Employment 2000	2010	% Change	Occupation
138,939	100,614	-27.6	Loan interviewers and clerks
235,952	247,552	4.9	Loan officers
23,324	25,343	8.7	Locksmiths and safe repairers
37,377	38,248	2.3	Locomotive engineers and firers
68,387	74,745	9.3	Lodging managers
7,996	7,677	-4.0	Log graders and scalers
47,117	46,183	-2.0	Logging equipment operators
181,833	159,433	-12.3	Machine feeders and offbearers
429,564	468,514	9.1	Machinists
1,633,057	1,716,345	5.1	Maids and housekeeping cleaners
187,948	206,642	9.9	Mail clerks and mail machine operators, except postal service
1,251,271	1,309,903	4.7	Maintenance and repair workers, general
113,805	120,352	5.8	Maintenance workers, machinery
500,910	645,767	28.9	Management analysts
980,934	1,074,394	9.5	Managers, nsk
40,232	50,908	26.5	Manicurists and pedicurists
17,001	20,250	19.1	Manufactured building and mobile home installers
5,117	5,223	2.1	Marine engineers and naval architects
90,021	111,982	24.4	Market research analysts
190,324	245,649	29.1	Marketing managers
21,107	27,417	29.9	Marriage and family therapists
34,400	44,858	30.4	Massage therapists
142,137	165,428	16.4	Material moving workers, nsk
62,790	72,506	15.5	Material recording, scheduling, and distributing workers, nsk
33,491	35,258	5.3	Materials engineers
7,710	9,233	19.8	Materials scientists
3,618	3,549	-1.9	Mathematicians
147,920	162,024	9.5	Meat, poultry, and fish cutters and trimmers
11,263	12,696	12.7	Mechanical door repairers
70,194	81,003	15.4	Mechanical drafters
58,108	66,163	13.9	Mechanical engineering technicians
221,443	250,523	13.1	Mechanical engineers
30,576	36,114	18.1	Media and communication equipment workers, nsk
90,429	110,371	22.1	Media and communication workers, nsk
146,793	174,733	19.0	Medical and clinical laboratory technicians
148,380	173,622	17.0	Medical and clinical laboratory technologists
249,515	330,069	32.3	Medical and health services managers
103,695	136,488	31.6	Medical and public health social workers
12,892	15,339	19.0	Medical appliance technicians
328,649	515,846	57.0	Medical assistants
33,267	39,332	18.2	Medical equipment preparers
28,482	32,735	14.9	Medical equipment repairers
135,733	202,206	49.0	Medical records and health information technicians
37,006	46,810	26.5	Medical scientists
313,902	373,435	19.0	Medical secretaries
101,864	132,260	29.8	Medical transcriptionists
33,882	41,793	23.3	Meeting and convention planners
83,125	115,654	39.1	Mental health and substance abuse social workers
67,195	81,789	21.7	Mental health counselors
75,787	87,873	15.9	Merchandise displayers and window trimmers
149,781	174,338	16.4	Metal workers and plastic workers, nsk
23,914	25,684	7.4	Metal-refining furnace operators and tenders
48,763	36,096	-26.0	Meter readers, utilities
570,009	624,759	9.6	Middle school teachers, except special and vocational education
34,259	31,977	-6.7	Milling and planing machine workers, metal and plastic
72,378	75,226	3.9	Millwrights
6,483	6,397	-1.3	Mining and geological engineers, including mine safety
4,839	4,967	2.7	Miscellaneous mathematical science occupations
12,389	10,837	-12.5	Miscellaneous mining machine operators
108,628	118,361	9.0	Mixing and blending machine workers
130,086	148,252	14.0	Mobile heavy equipment mechanics, except engines
10,238	11,877	16.0	Model makers and patternmakers, wood
10,616	10,275	-3.2	Model makers, metal and plastic
3,734	4,704	26.0	Models
42,282	45,431	7.4	Molders, shapers, and casters, except metal and plastic
176,092	193,393	9.8	Molding, coremaking, casting machine workers, metal and plastic
11,110	8,105	-27.0	Motion picture projectionists
111,856	132,205	18.2	Motor vehicle operators, nsk
25,016	27,262	9.0	Motorboat mechanics
14,461	15,706	8.6	Motorcycle mechanics
69,449	84,837	22.2	Multi-media artists and animators
105,068	120,564	14.7	Multiple machine tool workers, metal and plastic
49,685	56,185	13.1	Music directors and composers
7,068	7,732	9.4	Musical instrument repairers and tuners
190,533	228,854	20.1	Musicians and singers
41,741	44,913	7.6	Natural sciences managers
228,537	415,672	81.9	Network and computer systems administrators
118,684	210,636	77.5	Network systems and data communications analysts
86,589	88,917	2.7	New accounts clerks
77,875	80,063	2.8	News analysts, reporters and correspondents
130,612	158,765	21.6	Nonfarm animal caretakers
13,900	14,157	1.8	Nuclear engineers
18,219	22,305	22.4	Nuclear medicine technologists
3,763	3,636	-3.4	Nuclear power reactor operators
3,330	4,020	20.7	Nuclear technicians
23,774	27,727	16.6	Numerical tool and process control programmers
1,373,206	1,696,579	23.5	Nursing aides, orderlies, and attendants
34,929	40,161	15.0	Occupational health and safety specialists and technicians
8,508	12,352	45.2	Occupational therapist aides
16,537	23,098	39.7	Occupational therapist assistants
78,306	104,824	33.9	Occupational therapists
2,704,897	3,134,611	15.9	Office clerks, general
83,771	68,037	-18.8	Office machine operators, except computer
357,206	381,827	6.9	Operating engineers and other construction equipment operators
47,215	51,007	8.0	Operations research analysts
32,407	34,248	5.7	Ophthalmic laboratory technicians
67,803	80,686	19.0	Opticians, dispensing
31,417	37,288	18.7	Optometrists
348,231	277,291	-20.4	Order clerks
5,329	6,249	17.3	Orthotists and prosthetists
33,190	35,918	8.2	Outdoor power equipment and other small engine mechanics
378,652	433,109	14.4	Packaging and filling machine operators and tenders
1,090,520	1,300,470	19.3	Packers and packagers, hand
491,401	585,018	19.1	Painters, construction and maintenance
48,884	57,423	17.5	Painters, transportation equipment
38,065	44,870	17.9	Painting, coating, and decorating workers

Total Employment 2000	2010	% Change	Occupation
123,089	116,418	-5.4	Paper goods machine workers
26,820	32,245	20.2	Paperhangers
188,214	250,638	33.2	Paralegals and legal assistants
8,574	9,703	13.2	Parking enforcement workers
116,639	139,718	19.8	Parking lot attendants
259,866	248,322	-4.4	Parts salespersons
8,843	8,102	-8.4	Patternmakers, metal and plastic
54,528	62,982	15.5	Paving, surfacing, and tamping equipment operators
200,907	205,546	2.3	Payroll and timekeeping clerks
413,633	672,126	62.5	Personal and home care aides
162,852	198,190	21.7	Personal care and service workers, nsk
93,964	125,893	34.0	Personal financial advisors
57,817	70,574	22.1	Pest control workers
26,809	30,449	13.6	Pesticide handlers, sprayers, and applicators, vegetation
8,972	8,326	-7.2	Petroleum engineers
35,262	33,811	-4.1	Petroleum pump system operators, refinery operators, and gaugers
216,865	269,560	24.3	Pharmacists
56,797	67,846	19.5	Pharmacy aides
189,847	258,998	36.4	Pharmacy technicians
130,637	152,842	17.0	Photographers
26,273	24,117	-8.2	Photographic process workers
49,535	53,321	7.6	Photographic processing machine operators
33,020	36,109	9.4	Physical scientists, nsk
35,902	52,539	46.3	Physical therapist aides
43,937	63,622	44.8	Physical therapist assistants
131,822	175,682	33.3	Physical therapists
57,813	88,720	53.5	Physician assistants
597,852	704,956	17.9	Physicians and surgeons
4,423	5,041	14.0	Pile-driver operators
65,480	73,293	11.9	Pipelayers
48,590	54,133	11.4	Plant and system operators, nsk
54,096	60,506	11.9	Plasterers and stucco masons
65,356	71,996	10.2	Plating and coating machine workers, metal and plastic
502,616	553,792	10.2	Plumbers, pipefitters, and steamfitters
17,909	20,451	14.2	Podiatrists
606,800	747,632	23.2	Police and sheriff's patrol officers
85,979	98,429	14.5	Police, fire, and ambulance dispatchers
74,466	76,268	2.4	Postal service clerks
324,321	332,137	2.4	Postal service mail carriers
288,753	274,615	-4.9	Postal service mail sorters, processors
24,887	25,504	2.5	Postmasters and mail superintendents
1,343,982	1,659,342	23.5	Postsecondary teachers
16,475	17,619	6.9	Pourers and casters, metal
14,857	14,093	-5.1	Power distributors and dispatchers
36,242	36,894	1.8	Power plant operators
14,952	15,966	6.8	Precision instrument and equipment repairers, nsk
106,844	90,198	-15.6	Prepress technicians and workers
422,588	507,255	20.0	Preschool teachers, except special education
110,064	111,973	1.7	Pressers, textile, garment, and related materials
222,249	234,425	5.5	Printing machine operators
34,344	35,045	2.0	Printing workers, nsk
38,972	48,148	23.5	Private detectives and investigators
84,409	104,506	23.8	Probation officers and correctional treatment specialists
76,278	67,009	-12.2	Procurement clerks
58,489	74,342	27.1	Producers and directors
331,962	391,474	17.9	Production, planning, and expediting clerks
35,282	33,336	-5.5	Proofreaders and copy markers
270,116	331,413	22.7	Property, real estate, and community association managers
155,895	189,684	21.7	Protective service workers, nsk
64,705	73,258	13.2	Psychiatric aides
53,955	58,536	8.5	Psychiatric technicians
181,586	214,398	18.1	Psychologists
73,893	100,743	36.3	Public relations managers
136,687	186,076	36.1	Public relations specialists
13,899	14,572	4.8	Pump operators, except wellhead pumpers
19,600	22,902	16.8	Purchasing agents and buyers, farm products
236,919	265,982	12.3	Purchasing agents, except wholesale, retail, and farm products
131,805	124,561	-5.5	Purchasing managers
15,572	19,115	22.8	Radiation therapists
6,947	5,264	-24.2	Radio mechanics
2,934	3,116	6.2	Radio operators
167,413	206,052	23.1	Radiologic technologists and technicians
13,974	12,916	-7.6	Rail car repairers
7,169	6,878	-4.1	Rail transportation workers, nsk
3,831	3,658	-4.5	Rail yard engineers, dinkey operators, and hostlers
11,756	8,685	-26.1	Rail-track laying and maintenance equipment operators
21,863	8,565	-60.8	Railroad brake, signal, and switch operators
44,874	36,414	-18.9	Railroad conductors and yardmasters
92,751	101,665	9.6	Real estate brokers
339,058	371,106	9.5	Real estate sales agents
1,078,457	1,334,033	23.7	Receptionists and information clerks
268,801	322,928	20.1	Recreation workers
29,078	31,571	8.6	Recreational therapists
12,280	15,397	25.4	Recreational vehicle service technicians
124,117	144,775	16.6	Refuse and recyclable material collectors
2,194,224	2,755,325	25.6	Registered nurses
110,345	136,346	23.6	Rehabilitation counselors
27,455	32,264	17.5	Reinforcing iron and rebar workers
190,916	218,669	14.5	Reservation and transportation ticket agents and travel clerks
44,015	54,598	24.0	Residential advisors
83,010	111,902	34.8	Respiratory therapists
26,818	36,085	34.6	Respiratory therapy technicians
4,109,460	4,619,398	12.4	Retail salespersons
20,417	22,472	10.1	Riggers
49,162	49,865	1.4	Rolling machine workers, metal and plastic
157,776	188,355	19.4	Roofers
18,087	16,647	-8.0	Rotary drill operators, oil and gas
41,343	39,617	-4.2	Roustabouts, oil and gas
31,594	33,145	4.9	Sailors and marine oilers
621,206	757,749	22.0	Sales and related workers, nsk
85,164	100,196	17.7	Sales engineers
342,726	455,055	32.8	Sales managers
1,425,125	1,506,851	5.7	Sales representatives, wholesale and manufacturing
395,860	425,567	7.5	Sales representatives, wholesale and manufacturing, technical
57,318	64,037	11.7	Sawing machine setters, operators, and tenders, wood
1,003,679	1,190,434	18.6	Secondary school teachers, except special and vocational
645,407	639,461	-0.9	Secretaries, administrative assistants, and office workers, nsk
1,863,668	1,845,615	-1.0	Secretaries, except legal, medical, and executive
367,337	449,078	22.3	Securities, commodities, and financial services

Total Employment 2000	2010	% Change	Occupation
			sales agents
43,943	54,213	23.4	Security and fire alarm systems installers
1,105,530	1,496,564	35.4	Security guards
185,676	220,009	18.5	Self-enrichment education teachers
52,168	69,078	32.4	Semiconductor processors
38,967	39,808	2.2	Separating, filtering, clarifying, machine workers
15,349	17,879	16.5	Septic tank servicers and sewer pipe cleaners
112,355	110,456	-1.7	Service station attendants
10,963	10,831	-1.2	Service unit operators, oil, gas, and mining
11,935	15,151	27.0	Set and exhibit designers
42,576	39,781	-6.6	Sewers, hand
398,891	347,504	-12.9	Sewing machine operators
19,775	22,382	13.2	Shampooers
224,024	275,500	23.0	Sheet metal workers
25,352	26,213	3.4	Ship and boat captains and operators
8,576	9,070	5.8	Ship engineers
889,666	972,814	9.3	Shipping, receiving, and traffic clerks
18,867	14,834	-21.4	Shoe and leather workers and repairers
9,058	4,202	-53.6	Shoe machine operators and tenders
21,334	24,172	13.3	Skin care specialists
121,642	124,843	2.6	Slaughterers and meat packers
14,494	17,878	23.3	Slot key persons
128,030	159,779	24.8	Social and community service managers
270,849	417,683	54.2	Social and human service assistants
49,330	57,764	17.1	Social scientists and related workers, nsk
14,878	17,440	17.2	Social scientists, other
10,991	13,078	19.0	Sound engineering technicians
95,740	119,087	24.4	Special education teachers, middle school
233,986	320,096	36.8	Special education teachers, preschool, K-12
122,778	153,003	24.6	Special education teachers, secondary school
87,931	122,398	39.2	Speech-language pathologists
57,183	56,413	-1.3	Stationary engineers and boiler operators
21,160	21,604	2.1	Statistical assistants
19,482	19,936	2.3	Statisticians
1,678,730	1,820,934	8.5	Stock clerks and order fillers
13,710	16,560	20.8	Stonemasons
83,633	98,996	18.4	Structural iron and steel workers
100,655	120,332	19.5	Structural metal fabricators and fitters
60,947	82,261	35.0	Substance abuse and behavioral disorder counselors
71,185	95,884	34.7	Surgical technologists
22,581	30,369	34.5	Survey researchers
55,489	69,514	25.3	Surveying and mapping technicians
58,260	62,951	8.1	Surveyors
259,108	218,419	-15.7	Switchboard operators, including answering service
58,005	51,417	-11.4	Tailors, dressmakers, and custom sewers
18,575	21,083	13.5	Tank car, truck, and ship loaders
44,125	47,793	8.3	Tapers
79,428	86,036	8.3	Tax examiners, collectors, and revenue agents
68,557	80,517	17.4	Tax preparers
175,826	218,691	24.4	Taxi drivers and chauffeurs
1,261,531	1,562,432	23.9	Teacher assistants
648,331	776,064	19.7	Teachers, primary, secondary, and adult, nsk
1,458,353	1,544,998	5.9	Team assemblers
57,483	74,491	29.6	Technical writers
188,722	182,919	-3.1	Telecommunications equipment installers and repairers
163,719	208,864	27.6	Telecommunications line installers and repairers
571,820	698,580	22.2	Telemarketers
53,600	34,664	-35.3	Telephone operators
499,440	440,417	-11.8	Tellers
3,493	3,564	2.0	Terrazzo workers and finishers
36,573	40,505	10.8	Textile bleaching and dyeing machine operators and tenders
37,628	35,191	-6.5	Textile cutting machine setters, operators, and tenders
70,045	68,383	-2.4	Textile knitting and weaving machine workers
89,868	85,924	-4.4	Textile winding, twisting, and drawing out machine workers
94,929	111,972	18.0	Textile, apparel, and furnishings workers, nsk
53,990	62,412	15.6	Tile and marble setters
11,855	12,156	2.5	Timing device assemblers, adjusters, and calibrators
18,467	20,054	8.6	Tire builders
89,031	95,071	6.8	Tire repairers and changers
48,291	48,755	1.0	Title examiners, abstractors, and searchers
129,579	132,383	2.2	Tool and die makers
29,457	27,191	-7.7	Tool grinders, filers, and sharpeners
43,717	47,871	9.5	Tour and travel guides
4,434	5,057	14.1	Traffic technicians
204,442	244,146	19.4	Training and development specialists
5,756	6,708	16.5	Transit and railroad police
22,725	27,270	20.0	Transportation attendants, except flight and baggage
25,358	28,212	11.3	Transportation inspectors
46,045	54,286	17.9	Transportation workers, nsk
149,266	179,422	20.2	Transportation, storage, and distribution managers
134,666	139,015	3.2	Travel agents
52,149	60,629	16.3	Tree trimmers and pruners
1,749,270	2,094,973	19.8	Truck drivers, heavy and tractor-trailer
1,116,862	1,331,494	19.2	Truck drivers, light or delivery services
11,472	14,072	22.7	Umpires, referees, and other sports officials
58,480	52,932	-9.5	Upholsterers
29,822	34,722	16.4	Urban and regional planners
111,941	124,213	11.0	Ushers, lobby attendants, and ticket takers
59,830	71,570	19.6	Vehicle and mobile equipment mechanics, nsk
58,634	77,266	31.8	Veterinarians
55,219	77,180	39.8	Veterinary assistants and laboratory animal caretakers
49,408	68,821	39.3	Veterinary technologists and technicians
19,556	22,112	13.1	Vocational education teachers, middle school
108,876	123,477	13.4	Vocational education teachers, secondary school
1,982,964	2,346,536	18.3	Waiters and waitresses
5,242	5,564	6.2	Watch repairers
88,328	104,345	18.1	Water and liquid waste treatment plant and system operators
4,933	5,140	4.2	Water transportation workers, nsk
82,839	97,638	17.9	Weighers, measurers, checkers, and samplers, recordkeeping
446,482	532,475	19.3	Welders, cutters, solderers, and brazers
74,361	85,622	15.1	Welding, soldering, and brazing machine workers
11,708	10,708	-8.5	Wellhead pumpers
147,726	134,930	-8.7	Wholesale and retail buyers, except farm products
102,702	108,112	5.3	Woodworking machine workers, except sawing
296,730	239,995	-19.1	Word processors and typists
125,957	161,775	28.4	Writers and authors

Employment Order - 2000

Total Employment 2000	Total Employment 2010	% Change	Occupation
4,109,460	4,619,398	12.4	Retail salespersons
3,324,980	3,798,735	14.2	Cashiers, except gaming
2,704,897	3,134,611	15.9	Office clerks, general
2,397,567	2,760,863	15.2	General and operations managers
2,348,069	2,665,022	13.5	Janitors and cleaners, except maids and housekeeping cleaners
2,206,226	2,878,799	30.5	Combined food preparation and serving workers
2,194,224	2,755,325	25.6	Registered nurses
2,084,333	2,373,478	13.9	Laborers and freight, stock, and material movers
2,071,641	2,240,113	8.1	First-line supervisors of retail sales workers
1,990,762	2,030,069	2.0	Bookkeeping, accounting, and auditing clerks
1,982,964	2,346,536	18.3	Waiters and waitresses
1,945,945	2,577,287	32.4	Customer service representatives
1,863,668	1,845,615	-1.0	Secretaries, except legal, medical, and executive
1,749,270	2,094,973	19.8	Truck drivers, heavy and tractor-trailer
1,678,730	1,820,934	8.5	Stock clerks and order fillers
1,633,057	1,716,345	5.1	Maids and housekeeping cleaners
1,532,103	1,734,335	13.2	Elementary school teachers, except special education
1,458,353	1,544,998	5.9	Team assemblers
1,445,097	1,611,832	11.5	Executive secretaries and administrative assistants
1,425,125	1,506,851	5.7	Sales representatives, wholesale and manufacturing
1,391,544	1,521,895	9.4	First-line supervisors of office workers
1,373,206	1,696,579	23.5	Nursing aides, orderlies, and attendants
1,343,982	1,659,342	23.5	Postsecondary teachers
1,293,664	965,479	-25.4	Farmers and ranchers
1,261,531	1,562,432	23.9	Teacher assistants
1,251,271	1,309,903	4.7	Maintenance and repair workers, general
1,204,050	1,302,235	8.2	Carpenters
1,192,578	1,319,338	10.6	Child care workers
1,116,862	1,331,494	19.2	Truck drivers, light or delivery services
1,105,530	1,496,564	35.4	Security guards
1,090,520	1,300,470	19.3	Packers and packagers, hand
1,078,457	1,334,033	23.7	Receptionists and information clerks
1,003,679	1,190,434	18.6	Secondary school teachers, except special and vocational
980,934	1,074,394	9.5	Managers, nsk
975,783	1,156,777	18.5	Accountants and auditors
908,779	938,799	3.3	Farmworkers
894,187	1,153,717	29.0	Landscaping and groundskeeping workers
889,666	972,814	9.3	Shipping, receiving, and traffic clerks
844,403	987,512	16.9	Food preparation workers
839,689	990,739	18.0	Automotive service technicians and mechanics
826,925	959,852	16.1	Business operations specialists
818,756	827,296	1.0	First-line supervisors of production and operating workers
792,225	922,737	16.5	First-line supervisors of construction trades and mining workers
791,324	925,980	17.0	Construction laborers
699,600	841,924	20.3	Licensed practical and licensed vocational nurses
698,398	818,879	17.3	Electricians
680,794	803,355	18.0	Lawyers
667,748	812,886	21.7	Cooks, restaurant
657,944	779,821	18.5	Financial managers
648,944	731,468	12.7	First-line supervisors of food preparation and serving workers
648,331	776,064	19.7	Teachers, primary, secondary, and adult, nsk
645,407	639,461	-0.9	Secretaries, administrative assistants, and office workers, nsk
636,112	718,494	13.0	Hairdressers, hairstylists, and cosmetologists
634,899	706,914	11.3	Industrial truck and tractor operators
621,206	757,749	22.0	Sales and related workers, nsk
615,381	906,633	47.3	Home health aides
606,800	747,632	23.2	Police and sheriff's patrol officers
602,132	590,910	-1.9	Inspectors, testers, sorters, samplers, and weighers
597,852	704,956	17.9	Physicians and surgeons
585,386	679,956	16.2	Computer programmers
571,820	698,580	22.2	Telemarketers
570,009	624,759	9.6	Middle school teachers, except special and vocational education
549,010	618,980	12.7	All other production workers
547,042	640,925	17.2	Chief executives
524,549	482,620	-8.0	Dishwashers
524,513	586,810	11.9	Helpers-Production workers
521,560	517,855	-0.7	Cooks, fast food
509,404	534,479	4.9	Data entry keyers
506,221	549,467	8.5	Billing and posting clerks and machine operators
505,616	995,915	97.0	Computer support specialists
502,616	553,792	10.2	Plumbers, pipefitters, and steamfitters
500,910	645,767	28.9	Management analysts
499,440	440,417	-11.8	Tellers
491,401	585,018	19.1	Painters, construction and maintenance
481,163	537,031	11.6	Bus drivers, school
465,172	534,882	15.0	Food service managers
464,756	499,968	7.6	Cooks, institution and cafeteria
452,838	513,379	13.4	Education administrators
446,482	532,475	19.3	Welders, cutters, solderers, and brazers
442,039	512,755	16.0	First-line supervisors of mechanics, installers, and repairers
438,882	506,523	15.4	Assemblers and fabricators, nsk
432,285	457,224	5.8	First-line supervisors of non-retail sales workers
431,428	689,183	59.7	Computer systems analysts
430,819	402,101	-6.7	Dining room and cafeteria attendants and bartender helpers
429,564	468,514	9.1	Machinists
423,463	505,743	19.4	Counter and rental clerks
422,588	507,255	20.0	Preschool teachers, except special education
420,804	481,560	14.4	Counter attendants, cafeteria, food concession, and coffee shop
413,781	547,921	32.4	Correctional officers and jailers
413,633	672,126	62.5	Personal and home care aides
401,764	430,395	7.1	Driver/sales workers
400,233	501,615	25.3	Bill and account collectors
398,891	347,504	-12.9	Sewing machine operators
395,860	425,567	7.5	Sales representatives, wholesale and manufacturing, technical
386,890	438,622	13.4	Bartenders
379,969	760,059	100.0	Computer software engineers, applications
378,772	354,979	-6.3	Electrical and electronic equipment assemblers
378,652	433,109	14.4	Packaging and filling machine operators and tenders
377,750	390,286	3.3	Insurance sales agents
371,706	356,847	-4.0	Cutting, punching, and press machine workers,

Total Employment 2000	2010	% Change	Occupation
			metal and plastic
367,337	449,078	22.3	Securities, commodities, and financial services sales agents
362,038	435,990	20.4	Administrative services managers
357,206	381,827	6.9	Operating engineers and other construction equipment operators
348,231	277,291	-20.4	Order clerks
343,380	388,133	13.0	Hosts and hostesses, restaurant, lounge, and coffee shop
342,726	455,055	32.8	Sales managers
339,058	371,106	9.5	Real estate sales agents
331,962	391,474	17.9	Production, planning, and expediting clerks
328,649	515,846	57.0	Medical assistants
324,321	332,137	2.4	Postal service mail carriers
321,580	381,897	18.8	Cleaners of vehicles and equipment
316,858	601,225	89.7	Computer software engineers, systems software
313,902	373,435	19.0	Medical secretaries
312,953	462,923	47.9	Computer and information systems managers
307,826	358,068	16.3	Construction managers
296,730	239,995	-19.1	Word processors and typists
289,155	230,713	-20.2	Insurance claims and policy processing clerks
288,753	274,615	-4.9	Postal service mail sorters, processors
287,725	313,993	9.1	File clerks
285,208	325,633	14.2	Bus and truck mechanics and diesel engine specialists
282,051	304,720	8.0	Engineering managers
281,306	356,975	26.9	Child, family, and school social workers
279,164	335,892	20.3	Legal secretaries
270,849	417,683	54.2	Social and human service assistants
270,116	331,413	22.7	Property, real estate, and community association managers
268,801	322,928	20.1	Recreation workers
259,866	248,322	-4.4	Parts salespersons
259,108	218,419	-15.7	Switchboard operators, including answering service
257,568	280,432	8.9	Fire fighters
255,418	271,128	6.2	Industrial production managers
252,988	254,022	0.4	Engineers, nsk
249,515	330,069	32.3	Medical and health services managers
246,970	338,732	37.2	Dental assistants
244,421	290,389	18.8	Counselors, social, and religious workers, nsk
243,058	297,290	22.3	Heating, air conditioning, refrigeration mechanics
236,919	265,982	12.3	Purchasing agents, except wholesale, retail, and farm products
235,952	247,552	4.9	Loan officers
235,708	262,567	11.4	Laundry and dry-cleaning workers
233,986	320,096	36.8	Special education teachers, preschool, K-12
232,736	257,850	10.8	Electrical and electronic engineering technicians
232,046	255,826	10.2	Civil engineers
228,537	415,672	81.9	Network and computer systems administrators
227,925	254,202	11.5	Installation, maintenance, and repair workers, nsk
224,024	275,500	23.0	Sheet metal workers
222,249	234,425	5.5	Printing machine operators
221,443	250,523	13.1	Mechanical engineers
218,904	249,957	14.2	First-line supervisors of housekeeping and janitorial workers
218,582	246,370	12.7	Human resources managers
216,865	269,560	24.3	Pharmacists
211,533	253,194	19.7	Health practitioners and technical workers, nsk
211,090	251,887	19.3	Financial, information, and record clerks, nsk
210,920	245,815	16.5	Cost estimators
205,482	257,466	25.3	Educational, vocational, and school counselors
205,003	218,965	6.8	Cooks, short order
204,515	238,076	16.4	Food servers, nonrestaurant
204,442	244,146	19.4	Training and development specialists
202,892	326,053	60.7	Computer specialists, nsk
200,907	205,546	2.3	Payroll and timekeeping clerks
199,020	208,769	4.9	Farming, fishing, and forestry workers, nsk
198,955	219,243	10.2	Automotive body and related repairers
198,907	233,876	17.6	Employment, recruitment, and placement specialists
198,276	204,992	3.4	Industrial machinery mechanics
196,794	260,473	32.4	Amusement and recreation attendants
194,438	161,171	-17.1	Computer operators
194,016	232,594	19.9	First-line supervisors of transportation workers and drivers
193,989	223,280	15.1	Claims adjusters, examiners, and investigators
190,916	218,669	14.5	Reservation and transportation ticket agents and travel clerks
190,533	228,854	20.1	Musicians and singers
190,324	245,649	29.1	Marketing managers
189,911	240,705	26.7	Graphic designers
189,847	258,998	36.4	Pharmacy technicians
188,722	182,919	-3.1	Telecommunications equipment installers and repairers
188,214	250,638	33.2	Paralegals and legal assistants
187,948	206,642	9.9	Mail clerks and mail machine operators, except postal service
185,676	220,009	18.5	Self-enrichment education teachers
184,547	216,627	17.4	Bus drivers, transit and intercity
181,833	159,433	-12.3	Machine feeders and offbearers
181,586	214,398	18.1	Psychologists
181,119	219,387	21.1	Healthcare support workers, nsk
177,187	211,407	19.3	Human resources assistants, except payroll and timekeeping
176,738	235,701	33.4	Hotel, motel, and resort desk clerks
176,092	193,393	9.8	Molding, coremaking, casting machine workers, metal and plastic
175,826	218,691	24.4	Taxi drivers and chauffeurs
174,658	199,954	14.5	Kindergarten teachers, except special education
172,253	196,751	14.2	Computer, automated teller, and office machine repairers
172,110	225,996	31.3	Emergency medical technicians and paramedics
171,337	197,112	15.0	Clergy
169,127	216,466	28.0	Financial specialists, nsk
168,716	178,913	6.0	Farm, ranch, and other agricultural managers
168,294	205,624	22.2	Dispatchers, except police, fire, and ambulance
167,413	206,052	23.1	Radiologic technologists and technicians
165,861	155,645	-6.2	Door-to-door sales workers, vendors, and related workers
163,719	208,864	27.6	Telecommunications line installers and repairers
162,852	198,190	21.7	Personal care and service workers, nsk
162,485	167,388	3.0	Cement masons and concrete finishers
161,979	193,850	19.7	Computer-controlled machine tool operators, metal and plastic
159,912	186,706	16.8	Bakers
159,274	174,841	9.8	Cabinetmakers and bench carpenters
159,092	191,068	20.1	First-line supervisors of landscaping, lawn service workers
158,637	189,743	19.6	Building and grounds cleaning and

Total Employment 2000	2010	% Change	Occupation
			maintenance workers, nsk
158,314	222,192	40.3	Fitness trainers and aerobics instructors
157,884	184,176	16.7	Aircraft mechanics and service technicians
157,776	188,355	19.4	Roofers
157,188	174,934	11.3	Electrical engineers
155,895	189,684	21.7	Protective service workers, nsk
155,727	191,922	23.2	Drafters, engineering, and mapping technicians, nsk
155,066	195,843	26.3	Advertising sales agents
153,888	205,347	33.4	Interviewers, except eligibility and loan
153,636	160,550	4.5	Industrial engineers
153,121	182,020	18.9	First-line supervisors of helpers, laborers, and movers
152,450	161,206	5.7	Dentists
151,167	158,998	5.2	Highway maintenance workers
149,781	174,338	16.4	Metal workers and plastic workers, nsk
149,325	159,766	7.0	Librarians
149,266	179,422	20.2	Transportation, storage, and distribution managers
148,380	173,622	17.0	Medical and clinical laboratory technologists
147,920	162,024	9.5	Meat, poultry, and fish cutters and trimmers
147,726	134,930	-8.7	Wholesale and retail buyers, except farm products
146,793	174,733	19.0	Medical and clinical laboratory technicians
146,629	201,033	37.1	Dental hygienists
145,403	172,238	18.5	Helpers-Installation, maintenance, and repair workers
145,245	155,802	7.3	Grinding, lapping, polishing machine workers, metal and plastic
144,730	181,689	25.5	Financial analysts
144,380	162,426	12.5	Brickmasons and blockmasons
143,472	156,900	9.4	Drywall and ceiling tile installers
143,444	136,787	-4.6	Food preparation and serving related workers, nsk
142,137	165,428	16.4	Material moving workers, nsk
141,071	128,500	-8.9	Butchers and meat cutters
140,893	135,422	-3.9	Couriers and Messengers
139,736	152,137	8.9	Compliance officers, exc. agriculture, construction, health
138,939	100,614	-27.6	Loan interviewers and clerks
138,572	150,975	9.0	Chefs and head cooks
136,687	186,076	36.1	Public relations specialists
135,733	202,206	49.0	Medical records and health information technicians
134,666	139,015	3.2	Travel agents
132,630	161,355	21.7	Life, physical, and social science technicians, nsk
131,822	175,682	33.3	Physical therapists
131,805	124,561	-5.5	Purchasing managers
130,637	152,842	17.0	Photographers
130,612	158,765	21.6	Nonfarm animal caretakers
130,366	143,941	10.4	Electronics engineers, except computer
130,086	148,252	14.0	Mobile heavy equipment mechanics, except engines
129,579	132,383	2.2	Tool and die makers
128,030	159,779	24.8	Social and community service managers
125,987	142,944	13.5	Extruding and drawing machine workers, metal and plastic
125,957	161,775	28.4	Writers and authors
124,726	143,579	15.1	First-line supervisors of personal service workers
124,117	144,775	16.6	Refuse and recyclable material collectors
124,088	146,864	18.4	Flight attendants
123,089	116,418	-5.4	Paper goods machine workers
123,010	155,869	26.7	Construction and related workers, nsk
122,778	153,003	24.6	Special education teachers, secondary school
121,648	149,115	22.6	Editors
121,642	124,843	2.6	Slaughterers and meat packers
121,300	140,552	15.9	Directors, religious activities and education
120,522	136,356	13.1	First-line supervisors of police and detectives
118,684	210,636	77.5	Network systems and data communications analysts
117,613	146,895	24.9	Demonstrators and product promoters
116,921	106,104	-9.3	Eligibility interviewers, government programs
116,639	139,718	19.8	Parking lot attendants
114,189	129,430	13.3	Helpers-Electricians
113,805	120,352	5.8	Maintenance workers, machinery
112,355	110,456	-1.7	Service station attendants
111,941	124,213	11.0	Ushers, lobby attendants, and ticket takers
111,856	132,205	18.2	Motor vehicle operators, nsk
111,577	130,344	16.8	Art and design workers, nsk
110,345	136,346	23.6	Rehabilitation counselors
110,064	111,973	1.7	Pressers, textile, garment, and related materials
108,947	130,953	20.2	Legal and related workers, nsk
108,904	130,098	19.5	Library technicians
108,876	123,477	13.4	Vocational education teachers, secondary school
108,628	118,361	9.0	Mixing and blending machine workers
107,975	120,858	11.9	Coating, painting, and spraying machine workers
106,844	90,198	-15.6	Prepress technicians and workers
106,547	108,650	2.0	Insurance underwriters
106,007	175,872	65.9	Database administrators
105,476	113,226	7.3	Bindery workers
105,068	120,564	14.7	Multiple machine tool workers, metal and plastic
104,709	117,276	12.0	Court, municipal, and license clerks
103,695	136,488	31.6	Medical and public health social workers
102,702	108,112	5.3	Woodworking machine workers, except sawing
102,447	117,735	14.9	Floral designers
102,403	121,320	18.5	Architects, except landscape and naval
101,864	132,260	29.8	Medical transcriptionists
101,853	123,006	20.8	Architectural and civil drafters
100,919	107,601	6.6	Helpers-Carpenters
100,655	120,332	19.5	Structural metal fabricators and fitters
100,475	134,906	34.3	Advertising and promotions managers
99,958	112,955	13.0	First-line supervisors of farming, fishing, forestry workers
99,391	116,854	17.6	Coaches and scouts
99,181	125,665	26.7	Actors
99,181	108,360	9.3	Electrical power-line installers and repairers
98,348	117,738	19.7	Library assistants, clerical
98,080	104,391	6.4	Airline pilots, copilots, and flight engineers
95,740	119,087	24.4	Special education teachers, middle school
94,929	111,972	18.0	Textile, apparel, and furnishings workers, nsk
93,964	125,893	34.0	Personal financial advisors
93,503	104,607	11.9	Civil engineering technicians
93,206	108,460	16.4	Detectives and criminal investigators
92,751	101,665	9.6	Real estate brokers
90,429	110,371	22.1	Media and communication workers, nsk
90,021	111,982	24.4	Market research analysts
89,868	85,924	-4.4	Textile winding, twisting, and drawing out machine workers
89,699	97,976	9.2	Electrical and electronics repairers, commercial/industrial
89,031	95,071	6.8	Tire repairers and changers

Total Employment 2000	2010	% Change	Occupation
88,328	104,345	18.1	Water and liquid waste treatment plant and system operators
87,931	122,398	39.2	Speech-language pathologists
87,648	116,064	32.4	Gaming dealers
87,131	99,309	14.0	Library, museum, training, and education workers, nsk
86,611	100,200	15.7	Compensation, benefits, and job analysis specialists
86,589	88,917	2.7	New accounts clerks
86,473	90,061	4.1	Credit authorizers, checkers, and clerks
86,128	96,039	11.5	Helpers-Pipelayers, plumbers, pipefitters, and steamfitters
85,979	98,429	14.5	Police, fire, and ambulance dispatchers
85,164	100,196	17.7	Sales engineers
84,409	104,506	23.8	Probation officers and correctional treatment specialists
84,323	100,469	19.1	Chemists
83,771	68,037	-18.8	Office machine operators, except computer
83,718	77,507	-7.4	Lathe and turning machine tool workers, metal and plastic
83,633	98,996	18.4	Structural iron and steel workers
83,125	115,654	39.1	Mental health and substance abuse social workers
83,010	111,902	34.8	Respiratory therapists
82,839	97,638	17.9	Weighers, measurers, checkers, and samplers, recordkeeping
82,725	84,131	1.7	Cutting and slicing machine workers
80,847	101,075	25.0	Instructional coordinators
79,428	86,036	8.3	Tax examiners, collectors, and revenue agents
78,306	104,824	33.9	Occupational therapists
77,875	80,063	2.8	News analysts, reporters and correspondents
76,455	87,786	14.8	Excavating and loading machine and dragline operators
76,278	67,009	-12.2	Procurement clerks
76,007	83,963	10.5	Carpet installers
75,787	87,873	15.9	Merchandise displayers and window trimmers
74,590	85,772	15.0	Construction and building inspectors
74,466	76,268	2.4	Postal service clerks
74,361	85,622	15.1	Welding, soldering, and brazing machine workers
74,079	80,510	8.7	Crossing guards
73,958	94,919	28.3	Entertainers and performers, sports and related workers, nsk
73,893	100,743	36.3	Public relations managers
73,454	84,447	15.0	Chemical technicians
73,428	80,040	9.0	Extruding, forming, pressing, and compacting machine workers
73,101	88,483	21.0	Biological scientists
72,976	76,231	4.5	Electromechanical equipment assemblers
72,727	64,332	-11.5	Barbers
72,378	75,226	3.9	Millwrights
71,468	67,502	-5.5	Announcers
71,256	68,940	-3.3	Chemical plant and system operators
71,185	95,884	34.7	Surgical technologists
71,162	67,945	-4.5	Drilling and boring machine tool workers, metal and plastic
70,194	81,003	15.4	Mechanical drafters
70,045	68,383	-2.4	Textile knitting and weaving machine workers
70,019	80,238	14.6	Budget analysts
69,537	68,552	-1.4	Brokerage clerks
69,449	84,837	22.2	Multi-media artists and animators
68,557	80,517	17.4	Tax preparers
68,535	60,587	-11.6	Food processing workers, nsk

Total Employment 2000	2010	% Change	Occupation
68,387	74,745	9.3	Lodging managers
67,803	80,686	19.0	Opticians, dispensing
67,239	71,996	7.1	Engine and other machine assemblers
67,195	81,789	21.7	Mental health counselors
66,569	79,514	19.4	Adult literacy, remedial education, and GED teachers
65,800	66,736	1.4	Food batchmakers
65,480	73,293	11.9	Pipelayers
65,356	71,996	10.2	Plating and coating machine workers, metal and plastic
64,705	73,258	13.2	Psychiatric aides
63,723	77,954	22.3	Environmental scientists and specialists, including health
63,257	69,002	9.1	Graders and sorters, agricultural products
63,006	71,400	13.3	Conveyor operators and tenders
62,790	72,506	15.5	Material recording, scheduling, and distributing workers, nsk
61,664	66,075	7.2	First-line supervisors of fire fighting and prevention workers
61,116	77,689	27.1	First-line supervisors of protective service workers
61,007	70,107	14.9	Chemical equipment operators and tenders
60,947	82,261	35.0	Substance abuse and behavioral disorder counselors
60,047	65,043	8.3	Cargo and freight agents
60,035	69,625	16.0	Credit analysts
59,964	74,909	24.9	Computer hardware engineers
59,830	71,570	19.6	Vehicle and mobile equipment mechanics, nsk
59,308	58,575	-1.2	Foundry mold and coremakers
58,634	77,266	31.8	Veterinarians
58,489	74,342	27.1	Producers and directors
58,480	52,932	-9.5	Upholsterers
58,260	62,951	8.1	Surveyors
58,108	66,163	13.9	Mechanical engineering technicians
58,015	66,185	14.1	Helpers-Brickmasons, stonemasons, and tile and marble setters
58,005	51,417	-11.4	Tailors, dressmakers, and custom sewers
57,817	70,574	22.1	Pest control workers
57,813	88,720	53.5	Physician assistants
57,483	74,491	29.6	Technical writers
57,318	64,037	11.7	Sawing machine setters, operators, and tenders, wood
57,183	56,413	-1.3	Stationary engineers and boiler operators
57,062	71,196	24.8	Health diagnosing and treating practitioners, nsk
56,811	67,031	18.0	Appraisers and assessors of real estate
56,797	67,846	19.5	Pharmacy aides
55,998	60,577	8.2	Coil winders, tapers, and finishers
55,601	59,183	6.4	Job printers
55,489	69,514	25.3	Surveying and mapping technicians
55,219	77,180	39.8	Veterinary assistants and laboratory animal caretakers
54,585	59,303	8.6	Crane and tower operators
54,528	62,982	15.5	Paving, surfacing, and tamping equipment operators
54,336	61,242	12.7	Legislators
54,096	60,506	11.9	Plasterers and stucco masons
53,990	62,412	15.6	Tile and marble setters
53,955	58,536	8.5	Psychiatric technicians
53,706	58,574	9.1	Forging machine workers, metal and plastic
53,600	34,664	-35.3	Telephone operators
52,893	60,102	13.6	Insulation workers
52,737	46,312	-12.2	Fishers and fishing vessel operators

Total Employment 2000	2010	% Change	Occupation
52,421	66,034	26.0	Environmental engineers
52,168	69,078	32.4	Semiconductor processors
52,149	60,629	16.3	Tree trimmers and pruners
52,118	57,378	10.1	Industrial engineering technicians
50,897	57,306	12.6	Baggage porters and bellhops
50,434	57,437	13.9	Aerospace engineers
50,036	61,924	23.8	Commercial and industrial designers
49,949	61,654	23.4	Chiropractors
49,685	56,185	13.1	Music directors and composers
49,535	53,321	7.6	Photographic processing machine operators
49,408	68,821	39.3	Veterinary technologists and technicians
49,330	57,764	17.1	Social scientists and related workers, nsk
49,162	49,865	1.4	Rolling machine workers, metal and plastic
48,884	57,423	17.5	Painters, transportation equipment
48,763	36,096	-26.0	Meter readers, utilities
48,740	56,140	15.2	Dietitians and nutritionists
48,707	55,358	13.7	Grinding and polishing workers, hand
48,670	55,855	14.8	Glaziers
48,590	54,133	11.4	Plant and system operators, nsk
48,291	48,755	1.0	Title examiners, abstractors, and searchers
47,951	53,434	11.4	Fiberglass laminators and fabricators
47,666	54,059	13.4	Electrical and electronic equipment mechanics, nsk
47,215	51,007	8.0	Operations research analysts
47,117	46,183	-2.0	Logging equipment operators
46,517	56,346	21.1	Art directors
46,045	54,286	17.9	Transportation workers, nsk
45,615	53,560	17.4	Interior designers
45,403	49,229	8.4	Furniture finishers
44,874	36,414	-18.9	Railroad conductors and yardmasters
44,368	49,203	10.9	Health and safety engineers, except mining
44,353	48,692	9.8	Crushing, grinding, and polishing machine workers
44,125	47,793	8.3	Tapers
44,015	54,598	24.0	Residential advisors
43,943	54,213	23.4	Security and fire alarm systems installers
43,937	63,622	44.8	Physical therapist assistants
43,717	47,871	9.5	Tour and travel guides
43,451	49,740	14.5	Electro-mechanical technicians
43,368	43,945	1.3	Jewelers and precious stone and metal workers
43,053	53,177	23.5	Health educators
43,017	45,730	6.3	Dental laboratory technicians
42,999	45,676	6.2	Home appliance repairers
42,902	48,647	13.4	Heat treating equipment workers, metal and plastic
42,576	39,781	-6.6	Sewers, hand
42,282	45,431	7.4	Molders, shapers, and casters, except metal and plastic
41,741	44,913	7.6	Natural sciences managers
41,465	52,424	26.4	Biological technicians
41,356	43,716	5.7	Extruding and forming machine workers, synthetic/glass fibers
41,343	39,617	-4.2	Roustabouts, oil and gas
41,172	41,528	0.9	Farm equipment mechanics
41,069	50,650	23.3	Electrical and electronics drafters
40,997	52,922	29.1	Helpers, construction trades, nsk
40,232	50,908	26.5	Manicurists and pedicurists
38,972	48,148	23.5	Private detectives and investigators
38,967	39,808	2.2	Separating, filtering, clarifying, machine workers
38,663	52,174	34.9	Cardiovascular technologists and technicians
38,360	41,836	9.1	Correspondence clerks
38,123	51,894	36.1	Gaming change persons and booth cashiers
38,065	44,870	17.9	Painting, coating, and decorating workers
37,956	63,286	66.7	Desktop publishers
37,628	35,191	-6.5	Textile cutting machine setters, operators, and tenders
37,377	38,248	2.3	Locomotive engineers and firers
37,120	37,344	0.6	Food cooking machine operators and tenders
37,046	37,942	2.4	Helpers-Extraction workers
37,010	43,217	16.8	Audio and video equipment technicians
37,006	46,810	26.5	Medical scientists
36,920	49,025	32.8	Hazardous materials removal workers
36,853	39,780	7.9	Electric motor, power tool, and related repairers
36,803	43,594	18.5	Coin, vending, and amusement machine servicers and repairers
36,779	30,204	-17.9	Electronic home entertainment equipment installers and repairers
36,573	40,505	10.8	Textile bleaching and dyeing machine operators and tenders
36,242	36,894	1.8	Power plant operators
36,153	39,847	10.2	Broadcast technicians
35,902	52,539	46.3	Physical therapist aides
35,614	38,016	6.7	Cementing and gluing machine operators and tenders
35,282	33,336	-5.5	Proofreaders and copy markers
35,262	33,811	-4.1	Petroleum pump system operators, refinery operators, and gaugers
34,929	40,161	15.0	Occupational health and safety specialists and technicians
34,543	38,208	10.6	All other woodworkers
34,400	44,858	30.4	Massage therapists
34,344	35,045	2.0	Printing workers, nsk
34,264	35,205	2.7	Control and valve installers, except mechanical door
34,259	31,977	-6.7	Milling and planing machine workers, metal and plastic
33,882	41,793	23.3	Meeting and convention planners
33,491	35,258	5.3	Materials engineers
33,267	39,332	18.2	Medical equipment preparers
33,190	35,918	8.2	Outdoor power equipment and other small engine mechanics
33,020	36,109	9.4	Physical scientists, nsk
32,883	34,236	4.1	Chemical engineers
32,815	41,395	26.1	Diagnostic medical sonographers
32,559	33,591	3.2	Furnace, kiln, oven, drier, and kettle operators and tenders
32,407	34,248	5.7	Ophthalmic laboratory technicians
32,399	33,115	2.2	Cutters and trimmers, hand
31,594	33,145	4.9	Sailors and marine oilers
31,504	32,452	3.0	Funeral directors
31,488	37,285	18.4	Gaming supervisors
31,417	37,288	18.7	Optometrists
31,290	35,431	13.2	Law clerks
30,813	34,939	13.4	Fine artists, including painters, sculptors, and illustrators
30,576	36,114	18.1	Media and communication equipment workers, nsk
29,822	34,722	16.4	Urban and regional planners
29,692	38,487	29.6	First-line supervisors of correctional officers
29,457	27,191	-7.7	Tool grinders, filers, and sharpeners
29,078	31,571	8.6	Recreational therapists
28,957	30,297	4.6	Fence erectors
28,738	33,325	16.0	Loan counselors
28,482	32,735	14.9	Medical equipment repairers

Total Employment 2000	2010	% Change	Occupation
28,233	32,724	15.9	Life scientists, nsk
28,046	39,354	40.3	Computer and information scientists, research
27,455	32,264	17.5	Reinforcing iron and rebar workers
27,133	33,778	24.5	Environmental science and protection technicians
26,960	27,523	2.1	Boilermakers
26,820	32,245	20.2	Paperhangers
26,818	36,085	34.6	Respiratory therapy technicians
26,809	30,449	13.6	Pesticide handlers, sprayers, and applicators, vegetation
26,645	28,566	7.2	Air traffic controllers
26,633	30,069	12.9	Helpers-Painters, paperhangers, plasterers, and stucco masons
26,526	33,364	25.8	Camera operators, television, video, and motion picture
26,273	24,117	-8.2	Photographic process workers
26,139	30,792	17.8	Funeral attendants
26,083	20,407	-21.8	Communications equipment operators, nsk
25,648	32,736	27.6	Dietetic technicians
25,497	30,103	18.1	Geoscientists, except hydrologists and geographers
25,358	28,212	11.3	Transportation inspectors
25,352	26,213	3.4	Ship and boat captains and operators
25,016	27,262	9.0	Motorboat mechanics
24,887	25,504	2.5	Postmasters and mail superintendents
24,830	27,351	10.2	Financial examiners
24,008	24,269	1.1	Judges, magistrate judges, and magistrates
23,914	25,684	7.4	Metal-refining furnace operators and tenders
23,820	28,367	19.1	Costume, locker room and other attendants
23,774	27,727	16.6	Numerical tool and process control programmers
23,649	26,633	12.6	Earth drillers, except oil and gas
23,442	27,957	19.3	Helpers-Roofers
23,324	25,343	8.7	Locksmiths and safe repairers
23,236	26,897	15.8	Floor layers, except carpet, wood, and hard tiles
23,076	27,045	17.2	Elevator installers and repairers
22,725	27,270	20.0	Transportation attendants, except flight and baggage
22,581	30,369	34.5	Survey researchers
21,955	24,262	10.5	Automotive glass installers and repairers
21,863	8,565	-60.8	Railroad brake, signal, and switch operators
21,837	27,339	25.2	Gaming cage workers
21,816	27,004	23.8	Interpreters and translators
21,747	28,513	31.1	Landscape architects
21,702	25,708	18.5	Economists
21,494	24,053	11.9	Archivists, curators, and museum technicians
21,334	22,162	3.9	Forest and conservation workers
21,334	24,172	13.3	Skin care specialists
21,160	21,604	2.1	Statistical assistants
21,107	27,417	29.9	Marriage and family therapists
21,062	22,241	5.6	Aerospace engineering and operations technicians
20,878	24,777	18.7	Haming service workers, nsk
20,417	22,472	10.1	Riggers
20,275	17,390	-14.2	Cleaning, washing, and metal pickling equipment workers
20,057	22,897	14.2	Aircraft structure, surfaces, rigging, and systems assemblers
19,775	22,382	13.2	Shampooers
19,600	22,902	16.8	Purchasing agents and buyers, farm products
19,556	22,112	13.1	Vocational education teachers, middle school
19,482	19,936	2.3	Statisticians
19,256	24,431	26.9	Commercial pilots
18,867	14,834	-21.4	Shoe and leather workers and repairers
18,851	16,840	-10.7	Extraction workers, nsk
18,575	21,083	13.5	Tank car, truck, and ship loaders
18,467	20,054	8.6	Tire builders
18,385	21,360	16.2	Court reporters
18,378	17,271	-6.0	Lay-out workers, metal and plastic
18,325	23,663	29.1	Environmental engineering technicians
18,236	16,589	-9.0	Food and tobacco roasting, drying machine operators and tenders
18,219	22,305	22.4	Nuclear medicine technologists
18,101	17,689	-2.3	Electrical and electronics repairers, power
18,087	16,647	-8.0	Rotary drill operators, oil and gas
18,013	18,598	3.2	Forest and conservation technicians
17,909	20,451	14.2	Podiatrists
17,735	21,724	22.5	Athletes and sports competitors
17,604	20,281	15.2	Agricultural and food science technicians
17,536	20,291	15.7	Concierges
17,461	22,339	27.9	Agents and business managers of artists, performers, athletes
17,461	19,005	8.8	Agricultural and food scientists
17,003	22,477	32.2	Air transportation workers, nsk
17,001	20,250	19.1	Manufactured building and mobile home installers
16,537	23,098	39.7	Occupational therapist assistants
16,475	17,619	6.9	Pourers and casters, metal
16,192	17,536	8.3	Conservation scientists
16,111	19,383	20.3	Fashion designers
16,109	16,122	0.1	Derrick operators, oil and gas
15,999	20,132	25.8	Film and video editors
15,572	19,115	22.8	Radiation therapists
15,534	17,063	9.8	Avionics technicians
15,349	17,879	16.5	Septic tank servicers and sewer pipe cleaners
15,249	20,384	33.7	Ambulance drivers and attendants, except emergency technicians
15,243	17,884	17.3	Dancers
15,031	14,220	-5.4	Fabric and apparel patternmakers
14,964	15,958	6.6	Agricultural inspectors
14,952	15,966	6.8	Precision instrument and equipment repairers, nsk
14,878	17,440	17.2	Social scientists, other
14,857	14,093	-5.1	Power distributors and dispatchers
14,697	16,335	11.1	Etchers and engravers
14,579	17,256	18.4	Animal trainers
14,508	17,191	18.5	Athletic trainers
14,494	17,878	23.3	Slot key persons
14,461	15,706	8.6	Motorcycle mechanics
14,271	15,044	5.4	Actuaries
14,261	14,413	1.1	Administrative law judges, adjudicators, and hearing officers
13,974	12,916	-7.6	Rail car repairers
13,900	14,157	1.8	Nuclear engineers
13,899	14,572	4.8	Pump operators, except wellhead pumpers
13,710	16,560	20.8	Stonemasons
13,709	15,725	14.7	Floor sanders and finishers
13,625	15,334	12.5	Bailiffs
13,594	15,444	13.6	Electrical and electronics repairers, transportation equipment
13,415	12,251	-8.7	Fallers
12,892	15,339	19.0	Medical appliance technicians
12,809	14,805	15.6	Electronic equipment installers and repairers, motor vehicles
12,790	18,507	44.7	Audiologists

Total Employment 2000	2010	% Change	Occupation
12,739	14,555	14.3	Insurance appraisers, auto damage
12,644	14,555	15.1	Fire inspectors
12,440	13,314	7.0	Foresters
12,389	10,837	-12.5	Miscellaneous mining machine operators
12,280	15,397	25.4	Recreational vehicle service technicians
12,154	14,776	21.6	Gaming and sports book writers and runners
12,087	11,321	-6.3	Gas plant operators
11,935	15,151	27.0	Set and exhibit designers
11,855	12,156	2.5	Timing device assemblers, adjusters, and calibrators
11,756	8,685	-26.1	Rail-track laying and maintenance equipment operators
11,708	10,708	-8.5	Wellhead pumpers
11,473	13,039	13.6	Audio-visual collections specialists
11,472	14,072	22.7	Umpires, referees, and other sports officials
11,263	12,696	12.7	Mechanical door repairers
11,110	8,105	-27.0	Motion picture projectionists
10,991	13,078	19.0	Sound engineering technicians
10,989	12,836	16.8	Gaming surveillance officers and gaming investigators
10,963	10,831	-1.2	Service unit operators, oil, gas, and mining
10,808	12,418	14.9	Choreographers
10,682	11,333	6.1	Farm and home management advisors
10,616	10,275	-3.2	Model makers, metal and plastic
10,238	11,877	16.0	Model makers and patternmakers, wood
10,219	12,066	18.1	Emergency management specialists
10,105	10,757	6.5	Geological and petroleum technicians
10,063	11,121	10.5	Astronomers and physicists
9,949	12,704	27.7	Aircraft cargo handling supervisors
9,636	10,424	8.2	Bookbinders
9,530	8,252	-13.4	Continuous mining machine operators
9,058	4,202	-53.6	Shoe machine operators and tenders
8,972	8,326	-7.2	Petroleum engineers
8,892	9,633	8.3	Hoist and winch operators
8,843	8,102	-8.4	Patternmakers, metal and plastic
8,608	9,712	12.8	Animal control workers
8,576	9,070	5.8	Ship engineers
8,574	9,703	13.2	Parking enforcement workers
8,536	10,049	17.7	Bicycle repairers
8,508	12,352	45.2	Occupational therapist aides
8,136	9,060	11.4	Fish and game wardens
7,996	7,677	-4.0	Log graders and scalers
7,837	9,854	25.7	Hydrologists
7,710	9,233	19.8	Materials scientists
7,221	9,487	31.4	Biomedical engineers
7,199	7,050	-2.1	Camera and photographic equipment repairers
7,180	7,140	-0.6	Embalmers
7,169	6,878	-4.1	Rail transportation workers, nsk
7,166	7,071	-1.3	Cooling and freezing equipment operators and tenders
7,068	7,732	9.4	Musical instrument repairers and tuners
6,995	8,292	18.5	Cartographers and photogrammetrists
6,947	5,264	-24.2	Radio mechanics
6,894	8,075	17.1	Atmospheric and space scientists
6,682	7,001	4.8	Gas compressor and gas pumping station operators
6,483	6,397	-1.3	Mining and geological engineers, including mine safety
6,399	7,230	13.0	Forensic science technicians
6,252	8,037	28.5	Architects, surveyors, and cartographers, nsk
5,756	6,708	16.5	Transit and railroad police
5,329	6,249	17.3	Orthotists and prosthetists
5,250	4,307	-18.0	Cooks, private household
5,242	5,564	6.2	Watch repairers
5,117	5,223	2.1	Marine engineers and naval architects
5,081	5,177	1.9	Explosives workers, ordnance handling experts, and blasters
4,933	5,140	4.2	Water transportation workers, nsk
4,839	4,967	2.7	Miscellaneous mathematical science occupations
4,815	6,118	27.1	Airfield operations specialists
4,482	3,627	-19.1	Bridge and lock tenders
4,434	5,057	14.1	Traffic technicians
4,423	5,041	14.0	Pile-driver operators
4,422	5,626	27.2	Arbitrators, mediators, and conciliators
4,160	5,410	30.0	Gaming managers
3,831	3,658	-4.5	Rail yard engineers, dinkey operators, and hostlers
3,763	3,636	-3.4	Nuclear power reactor operators
3,734	4,704	26.0	Models
3,618	3,549	-1.9	Mathematicians
3,493	3,564	2.0	Terrazzo workers and finishers
3,330	4,020	20.7	Nuclear technicians
2,934	3,116	6.2	Radio operators
2,400	2,754	14.8	Agricultural engineers

Growth/Decline Order - 2000 to 2010

Total Employment 2000	2010	% Change	Occupation
379,969	760,059	100.0	Computer software engineers, applications
505,616	995,915	97.0	Computer support specialists
316,858	601,225	89.7	Computer software engineers, systems software
228,537	415,672	81.9	Network and computer systems administrators
118,684	210,636	77.5	Network systems and data communications analysts
37,956	63,286	66.7	Desktop publishers
106,007	175,872	65.9	Database administrators
413,633	672,126	62.5	Personal and home care aides
202,892	326,053	60.7	Computer specialists, nsk
431,428	689,183	59.7	Computer systems analysts
328,649	515,846	57.0	Medical assistants
270,849	417,683	54.2	Social and human service assistants
57,813	88,720	53.5	Physician assistants
135,733	202,206	49.0	Medical records and health information technicians
312,953	462,923	47.9	Computer and information systems managers
615,381	906,633	47.3	Home health aides
35,902	52,539	46.3	Physical therapist aides
8,508	12,352	45.2	Occupational therapist aides
43,937	63,622	44.8	Physical therapist assistants
12,790	18,507	44.7	Audiologists
28,046	39,354	40.3	Computer and information scientists, research
158,314	222,192	40.3	Fitness trainers and aerobics instructors
55,219	77,180	39.8	Veterinary assistants and laboratory animal caretakers
16,537	23,098	39.7	Occupational therapist assistants
49,408	68,821	39.3	Veterinary technologists and technicians
87,931	122,398	39.2	Speech-language pathologists
83,125	115,654	39.1	Mental health and substance abuse social workers
246,970	338,732	37.2	Dental assistants
146,629	201,033	37.1	Dental hygienists
233,986	320,096	36.8	Special education teachers, preschool, K-12
189,847	258,998	36.4	Pharmacy technicians
73,893	100,743	36.3	Public relations managers

Total Employment 2000	Total Employment 2010	% Change	Occupation
38,123	51,894	36.1	Gaming change persons and booth cashiers
136,687	186,076	36.1	Public relations specialists
1,105,530	1,496,564	35.4	Security guards
60,947	82,261	35.0	Substance abuse and behavioral disorder counselors
38,663	52,174	34.9	Cardiovascular technologists and technicians
83,010	111,902	34.8	Respiratory therapists
71,185	95,884	34.7	Surgical technologists
26,818	36,085	34.6	Respiratory therapy technicians
22,581	30,369	34.5	Survey researchers
100,475	134,906	34.3	Advertising and promotions managers
93,964	125,893	34.0	Personal financial advisors
78,306	104,824	33.9	Occupational therapists
15,249	20,384	33.7	Ambulance drivers and attendants, except emergency technicians
176,738	235,701	33.4	Hotel, motel, and resort desk clerks
153,888	205,347	33.4	Interviewers, except eligibility and loan
131,822	175,682	33.3	Physical therapists
188,214	250,638	33.2	Paralegals and legal assistants
36,920	49,025	32.8	Hazardous materials removal workers
342,726	455,055	32.8	Sales managers
196,794	260,473	32.4	Amusement and recreation attendants
413,781	547,921	32.4	Correctional officers and jailers
1,945,945	2,577,287	32.4	Customer service representatives
87,648	116,064	32.4	Gaming dealers
52,168	69,078	32.4	Semiconductor processors
249,515	330,069	32.3	Medical and health services managers
17,003	22,477	32.2	Air transportation workers, nsk
58,634	77,266	31.8	Veterinarians
103,695	136,488	31.6	Medical and public health social workers
7,221	9,487	31.4	Biomedical engineers
172,110	225,996	31.3	Emergency medical technicians and paramedics
21,747	28,513	31.1	Landscape architects
2,206,226	2,878,799	30.5	Combined food preparation and serving workers
34,400	44,858	30.4	Massage therapists
4,160	5,410	30.0	Gaming managers
21,107	27,417	29.9	Marriage and family therapists
101,864	132,260	29.8	Medical transcriptionists
29,692	38,487	29.6	First-line supervisors of correctional officers
57,483	74,491	29.6	Technical writers
18,325	23,663	29.1	Environmental engineering technicians
40,997	52,922	29.1	Helpers, construction trades, nsk
190,324	245,649	29.1	Marketing managers
894,187	1,153,717	29.0	Landscaping and groundskeeping workers
500,910	645,767	28.9	Management analysts
6,252	8,037	28.5	Architects, surveyors, and cartographers, nsk
125,957	161,775	28.4	Writers and authors
73,958	94,919	28.3	Entertainers and performers, sports and related workers, nsk
169,127	216,466	28.0	Financial specialists, nsk
17,461	22,339	27.9	Agents and business managers of artists, performers, athletes
9,949	12,704	27.7	Aircraft cargo handling supervisors
25,648	32,736	27.6	Dietetic technicians
163,719	208,864	27.6	Telecommunications line installers and repairers
4,422	5,626	27.2	Arbitrators, mediators, and conciliators
4,815	6,118	27.1	Airfield operations specialists
61,116	77,689	27.1	First-line supervisors of protective service workers
58,489	74,342	27.1	Producers and directors
11,935	15,151	27.0	Set and exhibit designers
281,306	356,975	26.9	Child, family, and school social workers
19,256	24,431	26.9	Commercial pilots
99,181	125,665	26.7	Actors
123,010	155,869	26.7	Construction and related workers, nsk
189,911	240,705	26.7	Graphic designers
40,232	50,908	26.5	Manicurists and pedicurists
37,006	46,810	26.5	Medical scientists
41,465	52,424	26.4	Biological technicians
155,066	195,843	26.3	Advertising sales agents
32,815	41,395	26.1	Diagnostic medical sonographers
52,421	66,034	26.0	Environmental engineers
3,734	4,704	26.0	Models
26,526	33,364	25.8	Camera operators, television, video, and motion picture
15,999	20,132	25.8	Film and video editors
7,837	9,854	25.7	Hydrologists
2,194,224	2,755,325	25.6	Registered nurses
144,730	181,689	25.5	Financial analysts
12,280	15,397	25.4	Recreational vehicle service technicians
400,233	501,615	25.3	Bill and account collectors
205,482	257,466	25.3	Educational, vocational, and school counselors
55,489	69,514	25.3	Surveying and mapping technicians
21,837	27,339	25.2	Gaming cage workers
80,847	101,075	25.0	Instructional coordinators
59,964	74,909	24.9	Computer hardware engineers
117,613	146,895	24.9	Demonstrators and product promoters
57,062	71,196	24.8	Health diagnosing and treating practitioners, nsk
128,030	159,779	24.8	Social and community service managers
122,778	153,003	24.6	Special education teachers, secondary school
27,133	33,778	24.5	Environmental science and protection technicians
90,021	111,982	24.4	Market research analysts
95,740	119,087	24.4	Special education teachers, middle school
175,826	218,691	24.4	Taxi drivers and chauffeurs
216,865	269,560	24.3	Pharmacists
44,015	54,598	24.0	Residential advisors
1,261,531	1,562,432	23.9	Teacher assistants
50,036	61,924	23.8	Commercial and industrial designers
21,816	27,004	23.8	Interpreters and translators
84,409	104,506	23.8	Probation officers and correctional treatment specialists
1,078,457	1,334,033	23.7	Receptionists and information clerks
110,345	136,346	23.6	Rehabilitation counselors
43,053	53,177	23.5	Health educators
1,373,206	1,696,579	23.5	Nursing aides, orderlies, and attendants
1,343,982	1,659,342	23.5	Postsecondary teachers
38,972	48,148	23.5	Private detectives and investigators
49,949	61,654	23.4	Chiropractors
43,943	54,213	23.4	Security and fire alarm systems installers
41,069	50,650	23.3	Electrical and electronics drafters
33,882	41,793	23.3	Meeting and convention planners
14,494	17,878	23.3	Slot key persons
155,727	191,922	23.2	Drafters, engineering, and mapping technicians, nsk
606,800	747,632	23.2	Police and sheriff's patrol officers
167,413	206,052	23.1	Radiologic technologists and technicians
224,024	275,500	23.0	Sheet metal workers
15,572	19,115	22.8	Radiation therapists
270,116	331,413	22.7	Property, real estate, and community association managers
11,472	14,072	22.7	Umpires, referees, and other sports officials

Total Employment 2000	2010	% Change	Occupation
121,648	149,115	22.6	Editors
17,735	21,724	22.5	Athletes and sports competitors
18,219	22,305	22.4	Nuclear medicine technologists
63,723	77,954	22.3	Environmental scientists and specialists, including health
243,058	297,290	22.3	Heating, air conditioning, refrigeration mechanics
367,337	449,078	22.3	Securities, commodities, and financial services sales agents
168,294	205,624	22.2	Dispatchers, except police, fire, and ambulance
69,449	84,837	22.2	Multi-media artists and animators
571,820	698,580	22.2	Telemarketers
90,429	110,371	22.1	Media and communication workers, nsk
57,817	70,574	22.1	Pest control workers
621,206	757,749	22.0	Sales and related workers, nsk
667,748	812,886	21.7	Cooks, restaurant
132,630	161,355	21.7	Life, physical, and social science technicians, nsk
67,195	81,789	21.7	Mental health counselors
162,852	198,190	21.7	Personal care and service workers, nsk
155,895	189,684	21.7	Protective service workers, nsk
12,154	14,776	21.6	Gaming and sports book writers and runners
130,612	158,765	21.6	Nonfarm animal caretakers
46,517	56,346	21.1	Art directors
181,119	219,387	21.1	Healthcare support workers, nsk
73,101	88,483	21.0	Biological scientists
101,853	123,006	20.8	Architectural and civil drafters
13,710	16,560	20.8	Stonemasons
3,330	4,020	20.7	Nuclear technicians
362,038	435,990	20.4	Administrative services managers
16,111	19,383	20.3	Fashion designers
279,164	335,892	20.3	Legal secretaries
699,600	841,924	20.3	Licensed practical and licensed vocational nurses
108,947	130,953	20.2	Legal and related workers, nsk
26,820	32,245	20.2	Paperhangers
149,266	179,422	20.2	Transportation, storage, and distribution managers
159,092	191,068	20.1	First-line supervisors of landscaping, lawn service workers
190,533	228,854	20.1	Musicians and singers
268,801	322,928	20.1	Recreation workers
422,588	507,255	20.0	Preschool teachers, except special education
22,725	27,270	20.0	Transportation attendants, except flight and baggage
194,016	232,594	19.9	First-line supervisors of transportation workers and drivers
7,710	9,233	19.8	Materials scientists
116,639	139,718	19.8	Parking lot attendants
1,749,270	2,094,973	19.8	Truck drivers, heavy and tractor-trailer
161,979	193,850	19.7	Computer-controlled machine tool operators, metal and plastic
211,533	253,194	19.7	Health practitioners and technical workers, nsk
98,348	117,738	19.7	Library assistants, clerical
648,331	776,064	19.7	Teachers, primary, secondary, and adult, nsk
158,637	189,743	19.6	Building and grounds cleaning and maintenance workers, nsk
59,830	71,570	19.6	Vehicle and mobile equipment mechanics, nsk
108,904	130,098	19.5	Library technicians
56,797	67,846	19.5	Pharmacy aides
100,655	120,332	19.5	Structural metal fabricators and fitters
66,569	79,514	19.4	Adult literacy, remedial education, and GED teachers
423,463	505,743	19.4	Counter and rental clerks
157,776	188,355	19.4	Roofers
204,442	244,146	19.4	Training and development specialists
211,090	251,887	19.3	Financial, information, and record clerks, nsk
23,442	27,957	19.3	Helpers-Roofers
177,187	211,407	19.3	Human resources assistants, except payroll and timekeeping
1,090,520	1,300,470	19.3	Packers and packagers, hand
446,482	532,475	19.3	Welders, cutters, solderers, and brazers
1,116,862	1,331,494	19.2	Truck drivers, light or delivery services
84,323	100,469	19.1	Chemists
23,820	28,367	19.1	Costume, locker room and other attendants
17,001	20,250	19.1	Manufactured building and mobile home installers
491,401	585,018	19.1	Painters, construction and maintenance
146,793	174,733	19.0	Medical and clinical laboratory technicians
12,892	15,339	19.0	Medical appliance technicians
313,902	373,435	19.0	Medical secretaries
67,803	80,686	19.0	Opticians, dispensing
10,991	13,078	19.0	Sound engineering technicians
153,121	182,020	18.9	First-line supervisors of helpers, laborers, and movers
321,580	381,897	18.8	Cleaners of vehicles and equipment
244,421	290,389	18.8	Counselors, social, and religious workers, nsk
20,878	24,777	18.7	Haming service workers, nsk
31,417	37,288	18.7	Optometrists
1,003,679	1,190,434	18.6	Secondary school teachers, except special and vocational
975,783	1,156,777	18.5	Accountants and auditors
102,403	121,320	18.5	Architects, except landscape and naval
14,508	17,191	18.5	Athletic trainers
6,995	8,292	18.5	Cartographers and photogrammetrists
36,803	43,594	18.5	Coin, vending, and amusement machine servicers and repairers
21,702	25,708	18.5	Economists
657,944	779,821	18.5	Financial managers
145,403	172,238	18.5	Helpers-Installation, maintenance, and repair workers
185,676	220,009	18.5	Self-enrichment education teachers
14,579	17,256	18.4	Animal trainers
124,088	146,864	18.4	Flight attendants
31,488	37,285	18.4	Gaming supervisors
83,633	98,996	18.4	Structural iron and steel workers
1,982,964	2,346,536	18.3	Waiters and waitresses
33,267	39,332	18.2	Medical equipment preparers
111,856	132,205	18.2	Motor vehicle operators, nsk
10,219	12,066	18.1	Emergency management specialists
25,497	30,103	18.1	Geoscientists, except hydrologists and geographers
30,576	36,114	18.1	Media and communication equipment workers, nsk
181,586	214,398	18.1	Psychologists
88,328	104,345	18.1	Water and liquid waste treatment plant and system operators
56,811	67,031	18.0	Appraisers and assessors of real estate
839,689	990,739	18.0	Automotive service technicians and mechanics
680,794	803,355	18.0	Lawyers
94,929	111,972	18.0	Textile, apparel, and furnishings workers, nsk
38,065	44,870	17.9	Painting, coating, and decorating workers
597,852	704,956	17.9	Physicians and surgeons
331,962	391,474	17.9	Production, planning, and expediting clerks
46,045	54,286	17.9	Transportation workers, nsk
82,839	97,638	17.9	Weighers, measurers, checkers, and samplers,

Total Employment 2000	2010	% Change	Occupation
			recordkeeping
26,139	30,792	17.8	Funeral attendants
8,536	10,049	17.7	Bicycle repairers
85,164	100,196	17.7	Sales engineers
99,391	116,854	17.6	Coaches and scouts
198,907	233,876	17.6	Employment, recruitment, and placement specialists
48,884	57,423	17.5	Painters, transportation equipment
27,455	32,264	17.5	Reinforcing iron and rebar workers
184,547	216,627	17.4	Bus drivers, transit and intercity
45,615	53,560	17.4	Interior designers
68,557	80,517	17.4	Tax preparers
15,243	17,884	17.3	Dancers
698,398	818,879	17.3	Electricians
5,329	6,249	17.3	Orthotists and prosthetists
547,042	640,925	17.2	Chief executives
23,076	27,045	17.2	Elevator installers and repairers
14,878	17,440	17.2	Social scientists, other
6,894	8,075	17.1	Atmospheric and space scientists
49,330	57,764	17.1	Social scientists and related workers, nsk
791,324	925,980	17.0	Construction laborers
148,380	173,622	17.0	Medical and clinical laboratory technologists
130,637	152,842	17.0	Photographers
844,403	987,512	16.9	Food preparation workers
111,577	130,344	16.8	Art and design workers, nsk
37,010	43,217	16.8	Audio and video equipment technicians
159,912	186,706	16.8	Bakers
10,989	12,836	16.8	Gaming surveillance officers and gaming investigators
19,600	22,902	16.8	Purchasing agents and buyers, farm products
157,884	184,176	16.7	Aircraft mechanics and service technicians
23,774	27,727	16.6	Numerical tool and process control programmers
124,117	144,775	16.6	Refuse and recyclable material collectors
210,920	245,815	16.5	Cost estimators
792,225	922,737	16.5	First-line supervisors of construction trades and mining workers
15,349	17,879	16.5	Septic tank servicers and sewer pipe cleaners
5,756	6,708	16.5	Transit and railroad police
93,206	108,460	16.4	Detectives and criminal investigators
204,515	238,076	16.4	Food servers, nonrestaurant
142,137	165,428	16.4	Material moving workers, nsk
149,781	174,338	16.4	Metal workers and plastic workers, nsk
29,822	34,722	16.4	Urban and regional planners
307,826	358,068	16.3	Construction managers
52,149	60,629	16.3	Tree trimmers and pruners
585,386	679,956	16.2	Computer programmers
18,385	21,360	16.2	Court reporters
826,925	959,852	16.1	Business operations specialists
60,035	69,625	16.0	Credit analysts
442,039	512,755	16.0	First-line supervisors of mechanics, installers, and repairers
28,738	33,325	16.0	Loan counselors
10,238	11,877	16.0	Model makers and patternmakers, wood
121,300	140,552	15.9	Directors, religious activities and education
28,233	32,724	15.9	Life scientists, nsk
75,787	87,873	15.9	Merchandise displayers and window trimmers
2,704,897	3,134,611	15.9	Office clerks, general
23,236	26,897	15.8	Floor layers, except carpet, wood, and hard tiles
86,611	100,200	15.7	Compensation, benefits, and job analysis specialists
17,536	20,291	15.7	Concierges

Total Employment 2000	2010	% Change	Occupation
12,809	14,805	15.6	Electronic equipment installers and repairers, motor vehicles
53,990	62,412	15.6	Tile and marble setters
62,790	72,506	15.5	Material recording, scheduling, and distributing workers, nsk
54,528	62,982	15.5	Paving, surfacing, and tamping equipment operators
438,882	506,523	15.4	Assemblers and fabricators, nsk
70,194	81,003	15.4	Mechanical drafters
17,604	20,281	15.2	Agricultural and food science technicians
48,740	56,140	15.2	Dietitians and nutritionists
2,397,567	2,760,863	15.2	General and operations managers
193,989	223,280	15.1	Claims adjusters, examiners, and investigators
12,644	14,555	15.1	Fire inspectors
124,726	143,579	15.1	First-line supervisors of personal service workers
74,361	85,622	15.1	Welding, soldering, and brazing machine workers
73,454	84,447	15.0	Chemical technicians
171,337	197,112	15.0	Clergy
74,590	85,772	15.0	Construction and building inspectors
465,172	534,882	15.0	Food service managers
34,929	40,161	15.0	Occupational health and safety specialists and technicians
61,007	70,107	14.9	Chemical equipment operators and tenders
10,808	12,418	14.9	Choreographers
102,447	117,735	14.9	Floral designers
28,482	32,735	14.9	Medical equipment repairers
2,400	2,754	14.8	Agricultural engineers
76,455	87,786	14.8	Excavating and loading machine and dragline operators
48,670	55,855	14.8	Glaziers
13,709	15,725	14.7	Floor sanders and finishers
105,068	120,564	14.7	Multiple machine tool workers, metal and plastic
70,019	80,238	14.6	Budget analysts
43,451	49,740	14.5	Electro-mechanical technicians
174,658	199,954	14.5	Kindergarten teachers, except special education
85,979	98,429	14.5	Police, fire, and ambulance dispatchers
190,916	218,669	14.5	Reservation and transportation ticket agents and travel clerks
420,804	481,560	14.4	Counter attendants, cafeteria, food concession, and coffee shop
378,652	433,109	14.4	Packaging and filling machine operators and tenders
12,739	14,555	14.3	Insurance appraisers, auto damage
20,057	22,897	14.2	Aircraft structure, surfaces, rigging, and systems assemblers
285,208	325,633	14.2	Bus and truck mechanics and diesel engine specialists
3,324,980	3,798,735	14.2	Cashiers, except gaming
172,253	196,751	14.2	Computer, automated teller, and office machine repairers
218,904	249,957	14.2	First-line supervisors of housekeeping and janitorial workers
17,909	20,451	14.2	Podiatrists
58,015	66,185	14.1	Helpers-Brickmasons, stonemasons, and tile and marble setters
4,434	5,057	14.1	Traffic technicians
87,131	99,309	14.0	Library, museum, training, and education workers, nsk
130,086	148,252	14.0	Mobile heavy equipment mechanics, except engines

Total Employment 2000	2010	% Change	Occupation
4,423	5,041	14.0	Pile-driver operators
50,434	57,437	13.9	Aerospace engineers
2,084,333	2,373,478	13.9	Laborers and freight, stock, and material movers
58,108	66,163	13.9	Mechanical engineering technicians
48,707	55,358	13.7	Grinding and polishing workers, hand
11,473	13,039	13.6	Audio-visual collections specialists
13,594	15,444	13.6	Electrical and electronics repairers, transportation equipment
52,893	60,102	13.6	Insulation workers
26,809	30,449	13.6	Pesticide handlers, sprayers, and applicators, vegetation
125,987	142,944	13.5	Extruding and drawing machine workers, metal and plastic
2,348,069	2,665,022	13.5	Janitors and cleaners, except maids and housekeeping cleaners
18,575	21,083	13.5	Tank car, truck, and ship loaders
386,890	438,622	13.4	Bartenders
452,838	513,379	13.4	Education administrators
47,666	54,059	13.4	Electrical and electronic equipment mechanics, nsk
30,813	34,939	13.4	Fine artists, including painters, sculptors, and illustrators
42,902	48,647	13.4	Heat treating equipment workers, metal and plastic
108,876	123,477	13.4	Vocational education teachers, secondary school
63,006	71,400	13.3	Conveyor operators and tenders
114,189	129,430	13.3	Helpers-Electricians
21,334	24,172	13.3	Skin care specialists
1,532,103	1,734,335	13.2	Elementary school teachers, except special education
31,290	35,431	13.2	Law clerks
8,574	9,703	13.2	Parking enforcement workers
64,705	73,258	13.2	Psychiatric aides
19,775	22,382	13.2	Shampooers
120,522	136,356	13.1	First-line supervisors of police and detectives
221,443	250,523	13.1	Mechanical engineers
49,685	56,185	13.1	Music directors and composers
19,556	22,112	13.1	Vocational education teachers, middle school
99,958	112,955	13.0	First-line supervisors of farming, fishing, forestry workers
6,399	7,230	13.0	Forensic science technicians
636,112	718,494	13.0	Hairdressers, hairstylists, and cosmetologists
343,380	388,133	13.0	Hosts and hostesses, restaurant, lounge, and coffee shop
26,633	30,069	12.9	Helpers-Painters, paperhangers, plasterers, and stucco masons
8,608	9,712	12.8	Animal control workers
549,010	618,980	12.7	All other production workers
648,944	731,468	12.7	First-line supervisors of food preparation and serving workers
218,582	246,370	12.7	Human resources managers
54,336	61,242	12.7	Legislators
11,263	12,696	12.7	Mechanical door repairers
50,897	57,306	12.6	Baggage porters and bellhops
23,649	26,633	12.6	Earth drillers, except oil and gas
13,625	15,334	12.5	Bailiffs
144,380	162,426	12.5	Brickmasons and blockmasons
4,109,460	4,619,398	12.4	Retail salespersons
236,919	265,982	12.3	Purchasing agents, except wholesale, retail, and farm products
104,709	117,276	12.0	Court, municipal, and license clerks

Total Employment 2000	2010	% Change	Occupation
21,494	24,053	11.9	Archivists, curators, and museum technicians
93,503	104,607	11.9	Civil engineering technicians
107,975	120,858	11.9	Coating, painting, and spraying machine workers
524,513	586,810	11.9	Helpers-Production workers
65,480	73,293	11.9	Pipelayers
54,096	60,506	11.9	Plasterers and stucco masons
57,318	64,037	11.7	Sawing machine setters, operators, and tenders, wood
481,163	537,031	11.6	Bus drivers, school
1,445,097	1,611,832	11.5	Executive secretaries and administrative assistants
86,128	96,039	11.5	Helpers-Pipelayers, plumbers, pipefitters, and steamfitters
227,925	254,202	11.5	Installation, maintenance, and repair workers, nsk
47,951	53,434	11.4	Fiberglass laminators and fabricators
8,136	9,060	11.4	Fish and game wardens
235,708	262,567	11.4	Laundry and dry-cleaning workers
48,590	54,133	11.4	Plant and system operators, nsk
157,188	174,934	11.3	Electrical engineers
634,899	706,914	11.3	Industrial truck and tractor operators
25,358	28,212	11.3	Transportation inspectors
14,697	16,335	11.1	Etchers and engravers
111,941	124,213	11.0	Ushers, lobby attendants, and ticket takers
44,368	49,203	10.9	Health and safety engineers, except mining
232,736	257,850	10.8	Electrical and electronic engineering technicians
36,573	40,505	10.8	Textile bleaching and dyeing machine operators and tenders
34,543	38,208	10.6	All other woodworkers
1,192,578	1,319,338	10.6	Child care workers
10,063	11,121	10.5	Astronomers and physicists
21,955	24,262	10.5	Automotive glass installers and repairers
76,007	83,963	10.5	Carpet installers
130,366	143,941	10.4	Electronics engineers, except computer
198,955	219,243	10.2	Automotive body and related repairers
36,153	39,847	10.2	Broadcast technicians
232,046	255,826	10.2	Civil engineers
24,830	27,351	10.2	Financial examiners
65,356	71,996	10.2	Plating and coating machine workers, metal and plastic
502,616	553,792	10.2	Plumbers, pipefitters, and steamfitters
52,118	57,378	10.1	Industrial engineering technicians
20,417	22,472	10.1	Riggers
187,948	206,642	9.9	Mail clerks and mail machine operators, except postal service
15,534	17,063	9.8	Avionics technicians
159,274	174,841	9.8	Cabinetmakers and bench carpenters
44,353	48,692	9.8	Crushing, grinding, and polishing machine workers
176,092	193,393	9.8	Molding, coremaking, casting machine workers, metal and plastic
570,009	624,759	9.6	Middle school teachers, except special and vocational education
92,751	101,665	9.6	Real estate brokers
980,934	1,074,394	9.5	Managers, nsk
147,920	162,024	9.5	Meat, poultry, and fish cutters and trimmers
339,058	371,106	9.5	Real estate sales agents
43,717	47,871	9.5	Tour and travel guides
143,472	156,900	9.4	Drywall and ceiling tile installers
1,391,544	1,521,895	9.4	First-line supervisors of office workers
7,068	7,732	9.4	Musical instrument repairers and tuners

Total Employment 2000	2010	% Change	Occupation
33,020	36,109	9.4	Physical scientists, nsk
99,181	108,360	9.3	Electrical power-line installers and repairers
68,387	74,745	9.3	Lodging managers
889,666	972,814	9.3	Shipping, receiving, and traffic clerks
89,699	97,976	9.2	Electrical and electronics repairers, commercial/industrial
38,360	41,836	9.1	Correspondence clerks
287,725	313,993	9.1	File clerks
53,706	58,574	9.1	Forging machine workers, metal and plastic
63,257	69,002	9.1	Graders and sorters, agricultural products
429,564	468,514	9.1	Machinists
138,572	150,975	9.0	Chefs and head cooks
73,428	80,040	9.0	Extruding, forming, pressing, and compacting machine workers
108,628	118,361	9.0	Mixing and blending machine workers
25,016	27,262	9.0	Motorboat mechanics
139,736	152,137	8.9	Compliance officers, exc. agriculture, construction, health
257,568	280,432	8.9	Fire fighters
17,461	19,005	8.8	Agricultural and food scientists
74,079	80,510	8.7	Crossing guards
23,324	25,343	8.7	Locksmiths and safe repairers
54,585	59,303	8.6	Crane and tower operators
14,461	15,706	8.6	Motorcycle mechanics
29,078	31,571	8.6	Recreational therapists
18,467	20,054	8.6	Tire builders
506,221	549,467	8.5	Billing and posting clerks and machine operators
53,955	58,536	8.5	Psychiatric technicians
1,678,730	1,820,934	8.5	Stock clerks and order fillers
45,403	49,229	8.4	Furniture finishers
60,047	65,043	8.3	Cargo and freight agents
16,192	17,536	8.3	Conservation scientists
8,892	9,633	8.3	Hoist and winch operators
44,125	47,793	8.3	Tapers
79,428	86,036	8.3	Tax examiners, collectors, and revenue agents
9,636	10,424	8.2	Bookbinders
1,204,050	1,302,235	8.2	Carpenters
55,998	60,577	8.2	Coil winders, tapers, and finishers
33,190	35,918	8.2	Outdoor power equipment and other small engine mechanics
2,071,641	2,240,113	8.1	First-line supervisors of retail sales workers
58,260	62,951	8.1	Surveyors
282,051	304,720	8.0	Engineering managers
47,215	51,007	8.0	Operations research analysts
36,853	39,780	7.9	Electric motor, power tool, and related repairers
464,756	499,968	7.6	Cooks, institution and cafeteria
41,741	44,913	7.6	Natural sciences managers
49,535	53,321	7.6	Photographic processing machine operators
395,860	425,567	7.5	Sales representatives, wholesale and manufacturing, technical
23,914	25,684	7.4	Metal-refining furnace operators and tenders
42,282	45,431	7.4	Molders, shapers, and casters, except metal and plastic
105,476	113,226	7.3	Bindery workers
145,245	155,802	7.3	Grinding, lapping, polishing machine workers, metal and plastic
26,645	28,566	7.2	Air traffic controllers
61,664	66,075	7.2	First-line supervisors of fire fighting and prevention workers
401,764	430,395	7.1	Driver/sales workers
67,239	71,996	7.1	Engine and other machine assemblers

Total Employment 2000	2010	% Change	Occupation
12,440	13,314	7.0	Foresters
149,325	159,766	7.0	Librarians
357,206	381,827	6.9	Operating engineers and other construction equipment operators
16,475	17,619	6.9	Pourers and casters, metal
205,003	218,965	6.8	Cooks, short order
14,952	15,966	6.8	Precision instrument and equipment repairers, nsk
89,031	95,071	6.8	Tire repairers and changers
35,614	38,016	6.7	Cementing and gluing machine operators and tenders
14,964	15,958	6.6	Agricultural inspectors
100,919	107,601	6.6	Helpers-Carpenters
10,105	10,757	6.5	Geological and petroleum technicians
98,080	104,391	6.4	Airline pilots, copilots, and flight engineers
55,601	59,183	6.4	Job printers
43,017	45,730	6.3	Dental laboratory technicians
42,999	45,676	6.2	Home appliance repairers
255,418	271,128	6.2	Industrial production managers
2,934	3,116	6.2	Radio operators
5,242	5,564	6.2	Watch repairers
10,682	11,333	6.1	Farm and home management advisors
168,716	178,913	6.0	Farm, ranch, and other agricultural managers
1,458,353	1,544,998	5.9	Team assemblers
432,285	457,224	5.8	First-line supervisors of non-retail sales workers
113,805	120,352	5.8	Maintenance workers, machinery
8,576	9,070	5.8	Ship engineers
152,450	161,206	5.7	Dentists
41,356	43,716	5.7	Extruding and forming machine workers, synthetic/glass fibers
32,407	34,248	5.7	Ophthalmic laboratory technicians
1,425,125	1,506,851	5.7	Sales representatives, wholesale and manufacturing
21,062	22,241	5.6	Aerospace engineering and operations technicians
222,249	234,425	5.5	Printing machine operators
14,271	15,044	5.4	Actuaries
33,491	35,258	5.3	Materials engineers
102,702	108,112	5.3	Woodworking machine workers, except sawing
151,167	158,998	5.2	Highway maintenance workers
1,633,057	1,716,345	5.1	Maids and housekeeping cleaners
509,404	534,479	4.9	Data entry keyers
199,020	208,769	4.9	Farming, fishing, and forestry workers, nsk
235,952	247,552	4.9	Loan officers
31,594	33,145	4.9	Sailors and marine oilers
6,682	7,001	4.8	Gas compressor and gas pumping station operators
13,899	14,572	4.8	Pump operators, except wellhead pumpers
1,251,271	1,309,903	4.7	Maintenance and repair workers, general
28,957	30,297	4.6	Fence erectors
72,976	76,231	4.5	Electromechanical equipment assemblers
153,636	160,550	4.5	Industrial engineers
4,933	5,140	4.2	Water transportation workers, nsk
32,883	34,236	4.1	Chemical engineers
86,473	90,061	4.1	Credit authorizers, checkers, and clerks
21,334	22,162	3.9	Forest and conservation workers
72,378	75,226	3.9	Millwrights
198,276	204,992	3.4	Industrial machinery mechanics
25,352	26,213	3.4	Ship and boat captains and operators
908,779	938,799	3.3	Farmworkers
377,750	390,286	3.3	Insurance sales agents
18,013	18,598	3.2	Forest and conservation technicians

Total Employment 2000	2010	% Change	Occupation
32,559	33,591	3.2	Furnace, kiln, oven, drier, and kettle operators and tenders
134,666	139,015	3.2	Travel agents
162,485	167,388	3.0	Cement masons and concrete finishers
31,504	32,452	3.0	Funeral directors
77,875	80,063	2.8	News analysts, reporters and correspondents
34,264	35,205	2.7	Control and valve installers, except mechanical door
4,839	4,967	2.7	Miscellaneous mathematical science occupations
86,589	88,917	2.7	New accounts clerks
121,642	124,843	2.6	Slaughterers and meat packers
24,887	25,504	2.5	Postmasters and mail superintendents
11,855	12,156	2.5	Timing device assemblers, adjusters, and calibrators
37,046	37,942	2.4	Helpers-Extraction workers
74,466	76,268	2.4	Postal service clerks
324,321	332,137	2.4	Postal service mail carriers
37,377	38,248	2.3	Locomotive engineers and firers
200,907	205,546	2.3	Payroll and timekeeping clerks
19,482	19,936	2.3	Statisticians
32,399	33,115	2.2	Cutters and trimmers, hand
38,967	39,808	2.2	Separating, filtering, clarifying, machine workers
129,579	132,383	2.2	Tool and die makers
26,960	27,523	2.1	Boilermakers
5,117	5,223	2.1	Marine engineers and naval architects
21,160	21,604	2.1	Statistical assistants
1,990,762	2,030,069	2.0	Bookkeeping, accounting, and auditing clerks
106,547	108,650	2.0	Insurance underwriters
34,344	35,045	2.0	Printing workers, nsk
3,493	3,564	2.0	Terrazzo workers and finishers
5,081	5,177	1.9	Explosives workers, ordnance handling experts, and blasters
13,900	14,157	1.8	Nuclear engineers
36,242	36,894	1.8	Power plant operators
82,725	84,131	1.7	Cutting and slicing machine workers
110,064	111,973	1.7	Pressers, textile, garment, and related materials
65,800	66,736	1.4	Food batchmakers
49,162	49,865	1.4	Rolling machine workers, metal and plastic
43,368	43,945	1.3	Jewelers and precious stone and metal workers
14,261	14,413	1.1	Administrative law judges, adjudicators, and hearing officers
24,008	24,269	1.1	Judges, magistrate judges, and magistrates
818,756	827,296	1.0	First-line supervisors of production and operating workers
48,291	48,755	1.0	Title examiners, abstractors, and searchers
41,172	41,528	0.9	Farm equipment mechanics
37,120	37,344	0.6	Food cooking machine operators and tenders
252,988	254,022	0.4	Engineers, nsk
16,109	16,122	0.1	Derrick operators, oil and gas
7,180	7,140	-0.6	Embalmers
521,560	517,855	-0.7	Cooks, fast food
645,407	639,461	-0.9	Secretaries, administrative assistants, and office workers, nsk
1,863,668	1,845,615	-1.0	Secretaries, except legal, medical, and executive
59,308	58,575	-1.2	Foundry mold and coremakers
10,963	10,831	-1.2	Service unit operators, oil, gas, and mining
7,166	7,071	-1.3	Cooling and freezing equipment operators and tenders
6,483	6,397	-1.3	Mining and geological engineers, including mine safety
57,183	56,413	-1.3	Stationary engineers and boiler operators
69,537	68,552	-1.4	Brokerage clerks
112,355	110,456	-1.7	Service station attendants
602,132	590,910	-1.9	Inspectors, testers, sorters, samplers, and weighers
3,618	3,549	-1.9	Mathematicians
47,117	46,183	-2.0	Logging equipment operators
7,199	7,050	-2.1	Camera and photographic equipment repairers
18,101	17,689	-2.3	Electrical and electronics repairers, power
70,045	68,383	-2.4	Textile knitting and weaving machine workers
188,722	182,919	-3.1	Telecommunications equipment installers and repairers
10,616	10,275	-3.2	Model makers, metal and plastic
71,256	68,940	-3.3	Chemical plant and system operators
3,763	3,636	-3.4	Nuclear power reactor operators
140,893	135,422	-3.9	Couriers and Messengers
371,706	356,847	-4.0	Cutting, punching, and press machine workers, metal and plastic
7,996	7,677	-4.0	Log graders and scalers
35,262	33,811	-4.1	Petroleum pump system operators, refinery operators, and gaugers
7,169	6,878	-4.1	Rail transportation workers, nsk
41,343	39,617	-4.2	Roustabouts, oil and gas
259,866	248,322	-4.4	Parts salespersons
89,868	85,924	-4.4	Textile winding, twisting, and drawing out machine workers
71,162	67,945	-4.5	Drilling and boring machine tool workers, metal and plastic
3,831	3,658	-4.5	Rail yard engineers, dinkey operators, and hostlers
143,444	136,787	-4.6	Food preparation and serving related workers, nsk
288,753	274,615	-4.9	Postal service mail sorters, processors
14,857	14,093	-5.1	Power distributors and dispatchers
15,031	14,220	-5.4	Fabric and apparel patternmakers
123,089	116,418	-5.4	Paper goods machine workers
71,468	67,502	-5.5	Announcers
35,282	33,336	-5.5	Proofreaders and copy markers
131,805	124,561	-5.5	Purchasing managers
18,378	17,271	-6.0	Lay-out workers, metal and plastic
165,861	155,645	-6.2	Door-to-door sales workers, vendors, and related workers
378,772	354,979	-6.3	Electrical and electronic equipment assemblers
12,087	11,321	-6.3	Gas plant operators
37,628	35,191	-6.5	Textile cutting machine setters, operators, and tenders
42,576	39,781	-6.6	Sewers, hand
430,819	402,101	-6.7	Dining room and cafeteria attendants and bartender helpers
34,259	31,977	-6.7	Milling and planing machine workers, metal and plastic
8,972	8,326	-7.2	Petroleum engineers
83,718	77,507	-7.4	Lathe and turning machine tool workers, metal and plastic
13,974	12,916	-7.6	Rail car repairers
29,457	27,191	-7.7	Tool grinders, filers, and sharpeners
524,549	482,620	-8.0	Dishwashers
18,087	16,647	-8.0	Rotary drill operators, oil and gas
26,273	24,117	-8.2	Photographic process workers
8,843	8,102	-8.4	Patternmakers, metal and plastic
11,708	10,708	-8.5	Wellhead pumpers
13,415	12,251	-8.7	Fallers
147,726	134,930	-8.7	Wholesale and retail buyers, except farm

Total Employment 2000	2010	% Change	Occupation
			products
141,071	128,500	-8.9	Butchers and meat cutters
18,236	16,589	-9.0	Food and tobacco roasting, drying machine operators and tenders
116,921	106,104	-9.3	Eligibility interviewers, government programs
58,480	52,932	-9.5	Upholsterers
18,851	16,840	-10.7	Extraction workers, nsk
58,005	51,417	-11.4	Tailors, dressmakers, and custom sewers
72,727	64,332	-11.5	Barbers
68,535	60,587	-11.6	Food processing workers, nsk
499,440	440,417	-11.8	Tellers
52,737	46,312	-12.2	Fishers and fishing vessel operators
76,278	67,009	-12.2	Procurement clerks
181,833	159,433	-12.3	Machine feeders and offbearers
12,389	10,837	-12.5	Miscellaneous mining machine operators
398,891	347,504	-12.9	Sewing machine operators
9,530	8,252	-13.4	Continuous mining machine operators
20,275	17,390	-14.2	Cleaning, washing, and metal pickling equipment workers
106,844	90,198	-15.6	Prepress technicians and workers
259,108	218,419	-15.7	Switchboard operators, including answering service
194,438	161,171	-17.1	Computer operators
36,779	30,204	-17.9	Electronic home entertainment equipment installers and repairers
5,250	4,307	-18.0	Cooks, private household
83,771	68,037	-18.8	Office machine operators, except computer
44,874	36,414	-18.9	Railroad conductors and yardmasters
4,482	3,627	-19.1	Bridge and lock tenders
296,730	239,995	-19.1	Word processors and typists
289,155	230,713	-20.2	Insurance claims and policy processing clerks
348,231	277,291	-20.4	Order clerks
18,867	14,834	-21.4	Shoe and leather workers and repairers
26,083	20,407	-21.8	Communications equipment operators, nsk
6,947	5,264	-24.2	Radio mechanics
1,293,664	965,479	-25.4	Farmers and ranchers
48,763	36,096	-26.0	Meter readers, utilities
11,756	8,685	-26.1	Rail-track laying and maintenance equipment operators
11,110	8,105	-27.0	Motion picture projectionists
138,939	100,614	-27.6	Loan interviewers and clerks
53,600	34,664	-35.3	Telephone operators
9,058	4,202	-53.6	Shoe machine operators and tenders
21,863	8,565	-60.8	Railroad brake, signal, and switch operators